RIA Federal Tax Regulations

RIA

"This publication is designed to provide accurate and authoritative information in regard to the subject matter covered. It is sold with the understanding that the publisher is not engaged in rendering legal, accounting or other professional service. If legal advice or other expert assistance is required, the services of a competent professional person should be sought." — from a Declaration of Principles jointly adopted by a Committee of The American Bar Association and a Committee of Publishers and Associations

RIA FEDERAL TAX REGULATIONS

Including Proposed Regulations
Current through January 15, 2010

VOLUME 6

---

§ 1.1361-0 Table of contents.

This section lists captions contained in §§ 1.1361-1, 1.1361-2, 1.1361-3, 1.1361-4, 1.1361-5, and 1.1361-6.

T.D. 8104, 9/25/86, amend T.D. 8419, 5/28/92, T.D. 8600, 7/20/95, T.D. 8869, 1/20/2000, T.D. 8994, 5/13/2002, T.D. 9422, 8/13/2008.

§ 1.1361-1 S Corporation defined.

Caution: The Treasury has not yet amended Reg § 1.1361-1 to reflect changes made by P.L. 108-357.

(a) In general. For purposes of this title, with respect to any taxable year—

(1) The term S corporation means a small business corporation (as defined in paragraph (b) of this section) for which an election under section 1362(a) is in effect for that taxable year.

(2) The term C corporation means a corporation that is not an S corporation for that taxable year.

(b) Small business corporation defined. *(1) In general.* For purposes of subchapter S, chapter 1 of the Code and the regulations thereunder, the term small business corporation means a domestic corporation that is not an ineligible corporation (as defined in section 1361(b)(2)) and that does not have—

(i) More than the number of shareholders provided in section 1361(b)(1)(A);

(ii) As a shareholder, a person (other than an estate, a trust described in section 1361(c)(2), or, for taxable years beginning after December 31, 1997, an organization described in section 1361(c)(6)) who is not an individual;

(iii) A nonresident alien as a shareholder; or

(iv) More than one class of stock.

(2) Estate in bankruptcy. The term estate, for purposes of this paragraph, includes the estate of an individual in a case under title 11 of the United States Code.

(3) Treatment of restricted stock. For purposes of subchapter S, stock that is issued in connection with the performance of services (within the meaning of § 1.83-3(f)) and that is substantially nonvested (within the meaning of § 1.83-3(b)) is not treated as outstanding stock of the corporation, and the holder of that stock is not treated as a shareholder solely by reason of holding the stock, unless the holder makes an election with respect to the stock under section 83(b). In the event of such an election, the stock is treated as outstanding stock of the corporation, and the holder of the stock is treated as a shareholder for purposes of subchapter S. See paragraphs (l)(1) and (3) of this section for rules for determining whether substantially nonvested stock with respect to which an election under section 83(b) has been made is treated as a second class of stock.

(4) Treatment of deferred compensation plans. For purposes of subchapter S, an instrument, obligation, or arrangement is not outstanding stock if it—

(i) Does not convey the right to vote;

(ii) Is an unfunded and unsecured promise to pay money or property in the future;

(iii) Is issued to an individual who is an employee in connection with the performance of services for the corporation or to an individual who is an independent contractor in connection with the performance of services for the corporation (and is not excessive by reference to the services performed); and

(iv) Is issued pursuant to a plan with respect to which the employee or independent contractor is not taxed currently on income.

A deferred compensation plan that has a current payment feature (e.g., payment of dividend equivalent amounts that are taxed currently as compensation) is not for that reason excluded from this paragraph (b)(4).

(5) Treatment of straight debt. For purposes of subchapter S, an instrument or obligation that satisfies the definition of straight debt in paragraph (l)(5) of this section is not treated as outstanding stock.

(6) Effective date provision. Section 1.1361-1(b) generally applies to taxable years of a corporation beginning on or after May 28, 1992. However, a corporation and its shareholders may apply this § 1.1361-1(b) to prior taxable years. In addition, substantially nonvested stock issued on or before May 28, 1992, that has been treated as outstanding by the corporation is treated as outstanding for purposes of subchapter S, and the fact that it is substantially nonvested and no section 83(b) election has been made with respect to it will not cause the stock to be treated as a second class of stock.

(c) Domestic corporation. For purposes of paragraph (b) of this section, the term *domestic corporation* means a domestic corporation as defined in § 301.7701-5 of this chapter, and the term corporation includes an entity that is classified as an association taxable as a corporation under § 301.7701-2 of this chapter.

(d) Ineligible corporation. *(1) General rule.* Except as otherwise provided in this paragraph (d), the term *ineligible corporation* means a corporation that is—

(i) For taxable years beginning on or after January 1, 1997, a financial institution that uses the reserve method of accounting for bad debts described in section 585 (for taxable years beginning prior to January 1, 1997, a financial institution to which section 585 applies (or would apply but for section 585(c)) or to which section 593 applies);

(ii) An insurance company subject to tax under subchapter L;

(iii) A corporation to which an election under section 936 applies; or

(iv) A DISC or former DISC.

(2) Exceptions. See the special rules and exceptions provided in sections 6(c)(2), (3) and (4) of Pub. L. 97-354 that are applicable for certain casualty insurance companies and qualified oil corporations.

(e) Number of shareholders. *(1) General rule.* A corporation does not qualify as a small business corporation if it has more than the number of shareholders provided in section 1361(b)(1)(A). Ordinarily, the person who would have to include in gross income dividends distributed with respect to the stock of the corporation (if the corporation were a C corporation) is considered to be the shareholder of the corporation. For example, if stock (owned other than by a husband and wife or members of a family described in section 1361(c)(1)) is owned by tenants in common or joint tenants, each tenant in common or joint tenant is generally considered to be a shareholder of the corporation. (For special rules relating to stock owned by husband and wife or members of a family, see paragraphs (e)(2) and (3) of this section, respectively; for special rules relating to restricted stock, see paragraphs (b)(3) and (6) of this section.) The person for whom stock of a corporation is held by a nominee, guardian, custodian, or an agent is considered to be the shareholder of the corporation for purposes of this paragraph (e) and paragraphs (f) and (g) of this section. For example, a partnership may be a nominee of S corporation stock for a person who qualifies as a shareholder of an S corporation. However, if the partnership is the beneficial owner of the stock, then the partnership is the shareholder, and the corporation does not qualify as a small business corporation. In addition, in the case of stock held for a minor under a uniform transfers to minors act or similar statute, the minor and not the custodian is the shareholder. Except as otherwise provided in paragraphs (h) and (j) of this section, and for purposes of this paragraph (e) and paragraphs (f) and (g) of this section, if stock is held by a decedent's estate or a trust described in section 1361(c)(2)(A)(ii) or (iii), the estate or trust (and not the beneficiaries of the estate or trust) is considered to be the shareholder; however, if stock is held by a subpart E trust (which includes a voting trust) or an electing QSST described in section 1361(d)(1), the deemed owner of the trust is considered to be the shareholder. If stock is held by an ESBT described in section 1361(c)(2)(A)(v), each potential current beneficiary of the trust shall be treated as a shareholder, except that the trust shall be treated as the shareholder during any period in which there is no potential current beneficiary of the trust. If stock is held by a trust described in section 1361(c)(2)(A)(vi), the individual for whose benefit the trust was created shall be treated as the shareholder. See paragraph (h) of this section for special rules relating to trusts.

(2) Special rules relating to stock owned by husband and wife. For purposes of paragraph (e)(1) of this section, stock owned by a husband and wife (or by either or both of their estates) is treated as if owned by one shareholder, regardless of the form in which they own the stock. For example, if husband and wife are owners of a subpart E trust, they will be treated as one individual. Both husband and wife must be U.S. citizens or residents, and a decedent spouse's estate must not be a foreign estate as defined in section 7701(a)(31). The treatment described in this paragraph (e)(2) will cease upon dissolution of the marriage for any reason other than death.

(3) Special rules relating to stock owned by members of a family. (i) In general. For purposes of paragraph (e)(1) of this section, stock owned by members of a family is treated as owned by one shareholder. Members of a family include a common ancestor, any lineal descendant of the common ancestor (without any generational limit), and any spouse (or former spouse) of the common ancestor or of any lineal descendants of the common ancestor. An individual shall not be considered to be a common ancestor if, on the applicable date, the individual is more than six generations removed from the youngest generation of shareholders who would be members of the family determined by deeming that individual as the common ancestor. For purposes of this six-generation test, a spouse (or former spouse) is treated as being of the same generation as the individual to whom the spouse is or was married. This test is applied on the latest of the date the election under section 1362(a) is made for the corporation, the earliest date that a member of the family (determined by deeming that individual as the common ancestor) holds stock in the corporation, or October 22, 2004. For this purpose, the date the election under section 1362(a) is made for the corporation is the effective date of the election, not the date it is signed or received by any person. The test is only applied as of the applicable date, and lineal descendants (and spouses) more than six generations removed from the common ancestor will be treated as members of the family even if they acquire stock in the corporation after that date. The members of a family are treated as one shareholder under this paragraph (e)(3) solely for purposes of section 1361(b)(1)(A), and not for any other purpose, whether under section 1361 or any other provision. Specifically, each member of the family who owns or is deemed to own stock must meet the requirements of sections 1361(b)(1)(B) and (C) (regarding permissible shareholders) and section 1362(a)(2) (regarding shareholder consents to an S corporation election). Although a person may be a member of more than one family under this paragraph (e)(3), each family (not all of whose members are also members of the other family) will be treated as one shareholder. For purposes of this paragraph (e)(3), any legally adopted child of an individual, any child who is lawfully placed with an individual for legal adoption by that individual, and any eligible foster child of an individual (within the meaning of section 152(f)(1)(C)), shall be treated as a child of such individual by blood.

(ii) Certain entities treated as members of a family. For purposes of this paragraph (e)(3), the estate or trust (described in section 1361(c)(2)(A)(ii) or (iii)) of a deceased member of the family will be considered to be a member of the family during the period in which the estate or such trust (if the trust is described in section 1361(c)(2)(A)(ii) or (iii)), holds stock in the S corporation. The members of the family also will include—

(A) In the case of an ESBT, each potential current beneficiary who is a member of the family;

(B) In the case of a QSST, the income beneficiary who makes the QSST election, if that income beneficiary is a member of the family;

(C) In the case of a trust created primarily to exercise the voting power of stock transferred to it, each beneficiary who is a member of the family;

(D) The individual for whose benefit a trust described in section 1361(c)(2)(A)(vi) was created, if that individual is a member of the family;

(E) The deemed owner of a trust described in section 1361(c)(2)(A)(i) if that deemed owner is a member of the family; and

(F) The owner of an entity disregarded as an entity separate from its owner under § 301.7701-3 of this chapter, if that owner is a member of the family.

(f) Shareholder must be an individual or estate. Except as otherwise provided in paragraph (e)(1) of this section (relating to nominees), paragraph (h) of this section (relating to certain trusts), and, for taxable years beginning after December 31, 1997, section 1361(c)(6) (relating to certain exempt organizations), a corporation in which any shareholder is a corporation, partnership, or trust does not qualify as a small business corporation.

(g) Nonresident alien shareholder. *(1) General rule.* (i) A corporation having a shareholder who is a nonresident alien as defined in section 7701(b)(1)(B) does not qualify as a small business corporation. If a U.S. shareholder's spouse is a nonresident alien who has a current ownership interest (as opposed, for example, to a survivorship interest) in the stock of the corporation by reason of any applicable law, such as a state community property law or a foreign country's law, the corporation does not qualify as a small business corporation from the time the nonresident alien spouse acquires the interest in the stock. If a corporation's S election is inadvertently terminated as a result of a nonresident alien spouse being considered a shareholder, the corporation may request relief under section 1362(f).

(ii) The following examples illustrate this paragraph (g)(1)(i):

Example (1). In 1990, W, a U.S. citizen, married H, a citizen of a foreign country. At all times H is a nonresident alien under section 7701(b)(1)(B). Under the foreign country's law, all property acquired by a husband and wife during the existence of the marriage is community property and owned jointly by the husband and wife. In 1996 while residing in the foreign country, W formed X, a U.S. corporation, and X simultaneously filed an election to be an S corporation. X issued all of its outstanding stock in W's name. Under the foreign country's law, X's stock became the community property of and jointly owned by H and W. Thus, X does not meet the definition of a small business corporation and therefore could not file a valid S election because H, a nonresident alien, has a current interest in the stock.

Example (2). Assume the same facts as Example 1, except that in 1991, W and H filed a section 6013(g) election allowing them to file a joint U.S. tax return and causing H to be treated as a U.S. resident for purposes of chapters 1, 5, and 24 of the Internal Revenue Code. The section 6013(g) election applies to the taxable year for which made and to all subsequent taxable years until terminated. Because H is treated as a U.S. resident under section 6013(g), X does meet the definition of a small business corporation. Thus, the election filed by X to be an S corporation is valid.

(2) Special rule for dual residents. [Reserved]

(h) Special rules relating to trusts. *(1) General rule.* In general, a trust is not a permitted small business corporation shareholder. However, except as provided in paragraph (h)(2) of this section, the following trusts are permitted shareholders:

(i) Qualified subpart E trust. A trust all of which is treated (under subpart E, part I, subchapter J, chapter 1) as owned by an individual (whether or not the grantor) who is a citizen or resident of the United States (a qualified subpart E trust). This requirement applies only during the period that the trust holds S corporation stock.

(ii) Subpart E trust ceasing to be a qualified subpart E trust after the death of deemed owner. A trust that was a qualified subpart E trust immediately before the death of the deemed owner and that continues in existence after the death of the deemed owner, but only for the 2-year period beginning on the day of the deemed owner's death. A trust is considered to continue in existence if the trust continues to hold the stock pursuant to the terms of the will or the trust agreement, or if the trust continues to hold the stock during a period reasonably necessary to wind up the affairs of the trust. See § 1.641(b)-3 for rules concerning the termination of trusts for federal income tax purposes.

(iii) Electing qualified subchapter S trusts. A qualified subchapter S trust (QSST) that has a section 1361(d)(2) election in effect (an electing QSST). See paragraph (j) of this section for rules concerning QSSTs including the manner for making the section 1361(d)(2) election.

(iv) Testamentary trusts. A trust (other than a qualified subpart E trust, an electing QSST, or an electing small business trust) to which S corporation stock is—

(A) Transferred pursuant to the terms of a will, but only for the 2-year period beginning on the day the stock is transferred to the trust except as otherwise provided in paragraph (h)(3)(i)(D) of this section; or

(B) Transferred pursuant to the terms of an electing trust as defined in § 1.645-1(b)(2) during the election period as defined in § 1.645-1(b)(6), or deemed to be distributed at the close of the last day of the election period pursuant to § 1.645-1(h)(1), but in each case only for the 2-year period beginning on the day the stock is transferred or deemed distributed to the trust except as otherwise provided in paragraph (h)(3)(i)(D) of this section.

(v) Qualified voting trusts. A trust created primarily to exercise the voting power of S corporation stock transferred to it. To qualify as a voting trust for purposes of this section (a qualified voting trust), the beneficial owners must be treated as the owners of their respective portions of the trust under subpart E and the trust must have been created pursuant to a written trust agreement entered into by the shareholders, that—

(A) Delegates to one or more trustees the right to vote;

(B) Requires all distributions with respect to the stock of the corporation held by the trust to be paid to, or on behalf of, the beneficial owners of that stock;

(C) Requires title and possession of that stock to be delivered to those beneficial owners upon termination of the trust; and

(D) Terminates, under its terms or by state law, on or before a specific date or event.

(vi) Electing small business trusts. An electing small business trust (ESBT) under section 1361(e). See paragraph (m) of this section for rules concerning ESBTs including the manner of making the election to be an ESBT under section 1361(e)(3).

(vii) Individual retirement accounts. In the case of a corporation which is a bank (as defined in section 581) or a depository institution holding company (as defined in section 3(w)(1) of the Federal Deposit Insurance Act (12 U.S.C. 1813(w)(1)), a trust which constitutes an individual retirement account under section 408(a), including one designated as a Roth IRA under section 408A, but only to the extent of the stock held by such trust in such bank or company as of October 22, 2004. Individual retirement accounts (including Roth IRAs) are not otherwise eligible S corporation shareholders.

(2) Foreign trust. For purposes of paragraph (h)(1) of this section, in any case where stock is held by a foreign trust as defined in section 7701(a)(31), the trust is considered to be the shareholder and is an ineligible shareholder. Thus, even

if a foreign trust qualifies as a subpart E trust (e.g., a qualified voting trust), any corporation in which the trust holds stock does not qualify as a small business corporation.

(3) Determination of shareholders. (i) General rule. For purposes of paragraph (b) of this section (qualification as a small business corporation), and, except as provided in paragraph (h)(3)(ii) of this section, for purposes of sections 1366 (relating to the pass-through of items of income, loss, deduction, or credit), 1367 (relating to adjustments to basis of shareholder's stock), and 1368 (relating to distributions), the shareholder of S corporation stock held by a trust that is a permitted shareholder under paragraph (h)(1) of this section is determined as follows:

(A) If stock is held by a qualified subpart E trust, the deemed owner of the trust is treated as the shareholder.

(B) If stock is held by a trust defined in paragraph (h)(1)(ii) of this section, the estate of the deemed owner is generally treated as the shareholder as of the day of the deemed owner's death. However, if stock is held by such a trust in a community property state, the decedent's estate is the shareholder only of the portion of the trust included in the decedent's gross estate (and the surviving spouse continues to be the shareholder of the portion of the trust owned by that spouse under the applicable state's community property law). The estate ordinarily will cease to be treated as the shareholder upon the earlier of the transfer of the stock by the trust or the expiration of the 2-year period beginning on the day of the deemed owner's death. If the trust qualifies and becomes an electing QSST, the beneficiary and not the estate is treated as the shareholder as of the effective date of the QSST election, and the rules provided in paragraph (j)(7) of this section apply. If the trust qualifies and becomes an ESBT, the shareholders are determined under paragraphs (h)(3)(i)(F) and (h)(3)(ii) of this section as of the effective date of the ESBT election, and the rules provided in paragraph (m) of this section apply.

(C) If stock is held by an electing QSST, see paragraph (j)(7) of this section for the rules on who is treated as the shareholder.

(D) If stock is transferred or deemed distributed to a testamentary trust described in paragraph (h)(1)(iv) of this section (other than a qualified subpart E trust, an electing QSST, or an ESBT), the estate of the testator is treated as the shareholder until the earlier of the transfer of that stock by the trust or the expiration of the 2-year period beginning on the day that the stock is transferred or deemed distributed to the trust. If the trust qualifies and becomes an electing QSST, the beneficiary and not the estate is treated as the shareholder as of the effective date of the QSST election, and the rules provided in paragraph (j)(7) of this section apply. If the trust qualifies and becomes an ESBT, the shareholders are determined under paragraphs (h)(3)(i)(F) and (h)(3)(ii) of this section as of the effective date of the ESBT election, and the rules provided in paragraph (m) of this section apply.

(E) If stock is held by a qualified voting trust, each beneficial owner of the stock, as determined under subpart E, is treated as a shareholder with respect to the owner's proportionate share of the stock held by the trust.

(F) If S corporation stock is held by an ESBT, each potential current beneficiary is treated as a shareholder. However, if for any period there is no potential current beneficiary of the ESBT, the ESBT is treated as the shareholder during such period. See paragraph (m)(4) of this section for the definition of potential current beneficiary.

(G) If stock in an S corporation bank or depository institution holding company is held by an individual retirement account (including a Roth IRA) described in paragraph (h)(1)(vii) of this section, the individual for whose benefit the trust was created shall be treated as the shareholder.

(ii) Exceptions. See § 1.641(c)-1 for the rules for the taxation of an ESBT. Solely for purposes of section 1366, 1367, and 1368 the shareholder of S corporation stock held by a trust is determined as follows—

(A) If stock is held by a trust as defined in paragraph (h)(1)(ii) of this section (other than an electing QSST or an ESBT), the trust is treated as the shareholder. If the trust continues to own the stock after the expiration of the 2-year period, the corporation's S election will terminate unless the trust is otherwise a permitted shareholder.

(B) If stock is transferred or deemed distributed to a testamentary trust described in paragraph (h)(1)(iv) of this section (other than a qualified subpart E trust, an electing QSST, or an ESBT), the trust is treated as the shareholder. If the trust continues to own the stock after the expiration of the 2-year period, the corporation's S election will terminate unless the trust otherwise qualifies as a permitted shareholder.

(i) [Reserved]

(j) Qualified subchapter S trust. *(1) Definition.* A qualified subchapter S trust (QSST) is a trust (whether intervivos or testamentary), other than a foreign trust described in section 7701(a)(31), that satisfies the following requirements:

(i) All of the income (within the meaning of § 1.643(b)-1) of the trust is distributed (or is required to be distributed) currently to one individual who is a citizen or resident of the United States. For purposes of the preceding sentence, unless otherwise provided under local law (including pertinent provisions of the governing instrument that are effective under local law), income of the trust includes distributions to the trust from the S corporation for the taxable year in question, but does not include the trust's pro rata share of the S corporation's items of income, loss, deduction, or credit determined under section 1366. See §§ 1.651(a)-2(a) and 1.663(b)-1(a) for rules relating to the determination of whether all of the income of a trust is distributed (or is required to be distributed) currently. If under the terms of the trust income is not required to be distributed currently, the trustee may elect under section 663(b) to consider a distribution made in the first 65 days of a taxable year as made on the last day of the preceding taxable year. See section 663(b) and § 1.663(b)-2 for rules on the time and manner for making the election. The income distribution requirement must be satisfied for the taxable year of the trust or for that part of the trust's taxable year during which it holds S corporation stock.

(ii) The terms of the trust must require that—

(A) During the life of the current income beneficiary, there will be only one income beneficiary of the trust;

(B) Any corpus distributed during the life of the current income beneficiary may be distributed only to that income beneficiary;

(C) The current income beneficiary's income interest in the trust will terminate on the earlier of that income beneficiary's death or the termination of the trust; and

(D) Upon termination of the trust during the life of the current income beneficiary, the trust will distribute all of its assets to that income beneficiary.

(iii) The terms of the trust must satisfy the requirements of paragraph (j)(1)(ii) of this section from the date the QSST election is made or from the effective date of the QSST election, whichever is earlier, throughout the entire period that the current income beneficiary and any successor income beneficiary is the income beneficiary of the trust. If the terms of the trust do not preclude the possibility that any of the requirements stated in paragraph (j)(1)(ii) of this section will not be met, the trust will not qualify as a QSST. For example, if the terms of the trust are silent with respect to corpus distributions, and distributions of corpus to a person other than the current income beneficiary are permitted under local law during the life of the current income beneficiary, then the terms of the trust do not preclude the possibility that corpus may be distributed to a person other than the current income beneficiary and, therefore, the trust is not a QSST.

(2) Special rules. (i) If a husband and wife are income beneficiaries of the same trust, the husband and wife file a joint return, and each is a U.S. citizen or resident, the husband and wife are treated as one beneficiary for purposes of paragraph (j) of this section. If a husband and wife are treated by the preceding sentence as one beneficiary, any action required by this section to be taken by an income beneficiary requires joinder of both of them. For example, each spouse must sign the QSST election, continue to be a U.S. citizen or resident, and continue to file joint returns for the entire period that the QSST election is in effect.

(ii) (A) Terms of the trust and applicable local law. The determination of whether the terms of a trust meet all of the requirements under paragraph (j)(1)(ii) of this section depends upon the terms of the trust instrument and the applicable local law. For example, a trust whose governing instrument provides that A is the sole income beneficiary of the trust is, nevertheless, considered to have two income beneficiaries if, under the applicable local law, A and B are considered to be the income beneficiaries of the trust.

(B) Legal obligation to support. If under local law a distribution to the income beneficiary is in satisfaction of the grantor's legal obligation of support to that income beneficiary, the trust will not qualify as a QSST as of the date of distribution because, under section 677(b), if income is distributed, the grantor will be treated as the owner of the ordinary income portion of the trust or, if trust corpus is distributed, the grantor will be treated as a beneficiary under section 662. See § 1.677(b)-1 for rules on the treatment of trusts for support and § 1.662(a)-4 for rules concerning amounts used in discharge of a legal obligation.

(C) Example. The following example illustrates the rules of paragraph (j)(2)(ii)(B) of this section:

Example. F creates a trust for the benefit of F's minor child, G. Under the terms of the trust, all income is payable to G until the trust terminates on the earlier of G's attaining age 35 or G's death. Upon the termination of the trust, all corpus must be distributed to G or G's estate. The trust includes all of the provisions prescribed by section 1361(d)(3)(A) and paragraph (j)(1)(ii) of this section, but does not preclude the trustee from making income distributions to G that will be in satisfaction of F's legal obligation to support G. Under the applicable local law, distributions of trust income to G will satisfy F's legal obligation to support G. If the trustee distributes income to G in satisfaction of F's legal obligation to support G, the trust will not qualify as a QSST because F will be treated as the owner of the ordinary income portion of the trust. Further, the trust will not be a qualified subpart E trust because the trust will be subject to tax on the income allocable to corpus.

(iii) If, under the terms of the trust, a person (including the income beneficiary) has a special power to appoint, during the life of the income beneficiary, trust income or corpus to any person other than the current income beneficiary, the trust will not qualify as a QSST. However, if the power of appointment results in the grantor being treated as the owner of the entire trust under the rules of subpart E, the trust may be a permitted shareholder under section 1361(c)(2)(A)(i) and paragraph (h)(1)(i) of this section.

(iv) If the terms of a trust or local law do not preclude the current income beneficiary from transferring the beneficiary's interest in the trust or do not preclude a person other than the current income beneficiary named in the trust instrument from being treated as a beneficiary of the trust under § 1.643(c)-1, the trust will still qualify as a QSST. However, if the income beneficiary transfers or assigns the income interest or a portion of the income interest to another, the trust may no longer qualify as a QSST, depending on the facts and circumstances, because any transferee of the current income beneficiary's income interest and any person treated as a beneficiary under § 1.643(c)-1 will be treated as a current income beneficiary for purposes of paragraph (j)(1)(ii) of this section and the trust may no longer meet the QSST requirements.

(v) If the terms of the trust do not preclude a person other than the current income beneficiary named in the trust instrument from being awarded an interest in the trust by the order of a court, the trust will qualify as a QSST assuming the trust meets the requirements of paragraphs (j)(1)(i) and (ii) of this section. However, if as a result of such court order, the trust no longer meets the QSST requirements, the trust no longer qualifies as a QSST and the corporation's S election will terminate.

(vi) A trust may qualify as a QSST even though a person other than the current income beneficiary is treated under subpart E as the owner of a part or all of that portion of a trust which does not consist of the S corporation stock, provided the entire trust meets the QSST requirements stated in paragraphs (j)(1)(i) and (ii) of this section.

(3) Separate and independent shares of a trust. For purposes of sections 1361(c) and (d), a substantially separate and independent share of a trust, within the meaning of section 663(c) and the regulations thereunder, is treated as a separate trust. For a separate share which holds S corporation stock to qualify as a QSST, the terms of the trust applicable to that separate share must meet the QSST requirements stated in paragraphs (j)(1)(i) and (ii) of this section.

(4) Qualified terminable interest property trust. If property, including S corporation stock, or stock of a corporation that intends to make an S election, is transferred to a trust and an election is made to treat all or a portion of the transferred property as qualified terminable interest property (QTIP) under section 2056(b)(7), the income beneficiary may make the QSST election if the trust meets the requirements set out in paragraphs (j)(1)(i) and (ii) of this section. However, if property is transferred to a QTIP trust under section 2523(f), the income beneficiary may not make a QSST election even if the trust meets the requirements set forth in paragraph (j)(1)(ii) of this section because the grantor would be treated as the owner of the income portion of the trust under section 677. In addition, if property is transferred to a QTIP trust under section 2523(f), the trust does not qualify as a permitted shareholder under section 1361(c)(2)(A)(i) and paragraph (h)(1)(i) of this section (a

qualified subpart E trust), unless under the terms of the QTIP trust, the grantor is treated as the owner of the entire trust under sections 671 to 677. If the grantor ceases to be the income beneficiary's spouse, the trust may qualify as a QSST if it otherwise satisfies the requirements under paragraphs (j)(1)(i) and (ii) of this section.

(5) Ceasing to meet the QSST requirements. If a QSST for which an election under section 1361(d)(2) has been made (as described in paragraph (j)(6) of this section) ceases to meet any of the requirements specified in paragraph (j)(1)(ii) of this section, the provisions of this paragraph (j) will cease to apply as of the first day on which that requirement ceases to be met. If such a trust ceases to meet the income distribution requirement specified in paragraph (j)(1)(i) of this section, but continues to meet all of the requirements in paragraph (j)(1)(ii) of this section, the provisions of this paragraph (j) will cease to apply as of the first day of the first taxable year beginning after the first taxable year for which the trust ceased to meet the income distribution requirement of paragraph (j)(1)(i) of this section. If a corporation's S election is inadvertently terminated as a result of a trust ceasing to meet the QSST requirements, the corporation may request relief under section 1362(f).

(6) Qualified subchapter S trust election. (i) In general. This paragraph (j)(6) applies to the election provided in section 1361(d)(2) (the QSST election) to treat a QSST (as defined in paragraph (j)(1) of this section) as a trust described in section 1361(c)(2)(A)(i), and thus a permitted shareholder. This election must be made separately with respect to each corporation whose stock is held by the trust. The QSST election does not itself constitute an election as to the status of the corporation; the corporation must make the election provided by section 1362(a) to be an S corporation. Until the effective date of a corporation's S election, the beneficiary is not treated as the owner of the stock of the corporation for purposes of section 678. Any action required by this paragraph (j) to be taken by a person who is under a legal disability by reason of age may be taken by that person's guardian or other legal representative, or if there be none, by that person's natural or adoptive parent.

(ii) Filing the QSST election. The current income beneficiary of the trust must make the election by signing and filing with the service center with which the corporation files its income tax return the applicable form or a statement that—

(A) Contains the name, address, and taxpayer identification number of the current income beneficiary, the trust, and the corporation;

(B) Identifies the election as an election made under section 1361(d)(2);

(C) Specifies the date on which the election is to become effective (not earlier than 15 days and two months before the date on which the election is filed);

(D) Specifies the date (or dates) on which the stock of the corporation was transferred to the trust; and

(E) Provides all information and representations necessary to show that:

(1) Under the terms of the trust and applicable local law—

(i) During the life of the current income beneficiary, there will be only one income beneficiary of the trust (if husband and wife are beneficiaries, that they will file joint returns and that both are U.S. residents or citizens);

(ii) Any corpus distributed during the life of the current income beneficiary may be distributed only to that beneficiary;

(iii) The current beneficiary's income interest in the trust will terminate on the earlier of the beneficiary's death or upon termination of the trust; and

(iv) Upon the termination of the trust during the life of such income beneficiary, the trust will distribute all its assets to such beneficiary.

(2) The trust is required to distribute all of its income currently, or that the trustee will distribute all of its income currently if not so required by the terms of the trust.

(3) No distribution of income or corpus by the trust will be in satisfaction of the grantor's legal obligation to support or maintain the income beneficiary.

(iii) When to file the QSST election. (A) If S corporation stock is transferred to a trust, the QSST election must be made within the 16-day-and-2-month period beginning on the day that the stock is transferred to the trust. If a C corporation has made an election under section 1362(a) to be an S corporation (S election) and, before that corporation's S election is in effect, stock of that corporation is transferred to a trust, the QSST election must be made within the 16-day-and-2-month period beginning on the day that the stock is transferred to the trust.

(B) If a trust holds C corporation stock and that C corporation makes an S election effective for the first day of the taxable year in which the S election is made, the QSST election must be made within the 16-day-and-2-month period beginning on the day that the S election is effective. If a trust holds C corporation stock and that C corporation makes an S election effective for the first day of the taxable year following the taxable year in which the S election is made, the QSST election must be made within the 16-day-and-2-month period beginning on the day that the S election is made. If a trust holds C corporation stock and that corporation makes an S election intending the S election to be effective for the first day of the taxable year in which the S election is made but, under § 1.1362-6(a)(2), such S election is subsequently treated as effective for the first day of the taxable year following the taxable year in which the S election is made, the fact that the QSST election states that the effective date of the QSST election is the first day of the taxable year in which the S election is made will not cause the QSST election to be ineffective for the first year in which the corporation's S election is effective.

(C) If a trust ceases to be a qualified subpart E trust, satisfies the requirements of a QSST, and intends to become a QSST, the QSST election must be filed within the 16-day-and-2-month period beginning on the date on which the trust ceases to be a qualified subpart E trust. If the estate of the deemed owner of the trust is treated as the shareholder under paragraph (h)(3)(i) of this section, the QSST election may be filed at any time, but no later than the end of the 16-day-and-2-month period beginning on the date on which the estate of the deemed owner ceases to be treated as a shareholder.

(D) If a testamentary trust is a permitted shareholder under paragraph (h)(1)(iv) of this section, satisfies the requirements of a QSST, and intends to become a QSST, the QSST election may be filed at any time, but no later than the end of the 16-day-and-2-month period beginning on the day after the end of the 2-year period.

(E) If a corporation's S election terminates because of a late QSST election, the corporation may request inadvertent termination relief under section 1362(f). See § 1.1362-4 for rules concerning inadvertent terminations.

(iv) Protective QSST election when a person is an owner under subpart E. If the grantor of a trust is treated as the owner under subpart E of all of the trust, or of a portion of the trust which consists of S corporation stock, and the current income beneficiary is not the grantor, the current income beneficiary may not make the QSST election, even if the trust meets the QSST requirements stated in paragraph (j)(1)(ii) of this section. See paragraph (j)(6)(iii)(C) of this section as to when the QSST election may be made. See also paragraph (j)(2)(vi) of this section. However, if the current income beneficiary (or beneficiaries who are husband and wife, if both spouses are U.S. citizens or residents and file a joint return) of a trust is treated under subpart E as owning all or a portion of the trust consisting of S corporation stock, the current income beneficiary (or beneficiaries who are husband and wife, if both spouses are U.S. citizens or residents and file a joint return) may make the QSST election. See Example 8 of paragraph (k)(1) of this section.

(7) Treatment as shareholder. (i) The income beneficiary who makes the QSST election and is treated (for purposes of section 678(a)) as the owner of that portion of the trust that consists of S corporation stock is treated as the shareholder for purposes of sections 1361(b)(1), 1366, 1367, and 1368.

(ii) If, upon the death of an income beneficiary, the trust continues in existence, continues to hold S corporation stock but no longer satisfies the QSST requirements, is not a qualified subpart E trust, and does not qualify as an ESBT, then, solely for purposes of section 1361(b)(1), as of the date of the income beneficiary's death, the estate of that income beneficiary is treated as the shareholder of the S corporation with respect to which the income beneficiary made the QSST election. The estate ordinarily will cease to be treated as the shareholder for purposes of section 1361(b)(1) upon the earlier of the transfer of that stock by the trust or the expiration of the 2-year period beginning on the day of the income beneficiary's death. During the period that the estate is treated as the shareholder for purposes of section 1361(b)(1), the trust is treated as the shareholder for purposes of sections 1366, 1367, and 1368. If, after the 2-year period, the trust continues to hold S corporation stock and does not otherwise qualify as a permitted shareholder, the corporation's S election terminates. If the termination is inadvertent, the corporation may request relief under section 1362(f).

(8) Coordination with grantor trust rules. If a valid QSST election is made, the income beneficiary is treated as the owner, for purposes of section 678(a), of that portion of the trust that consists of the stock of the S corporation for which the QSST election was made. However, solely for purposes of applying the preceding sentence to a QSST, an income beneficiary who is a deemed section 678 owner only by reason of section 1361(d)(1) will not be treated as the owner of the S corporation stock in determining and attributing the federal income tax consequences of a disposition of the stock by the QSST. For example, if the disposition is a sale, the QSST election terminates as to the stock sold and any gain or loss recognized on the sale will be that of the trust, not the income beneficiary. Similarly, if a QSST distributes its S corporation stock to the income beneficiary, the QSST election terminates as to the distributed stock and the consequences of the distribution are determined by reference to the status of the trust apart from the income beneficiary's terminating ownership status under sections 678 and 1361(d)(1). The portions of the trust other than the portion consisting of S corporation stock are subject to subparts A through D of subchapter J of chapter 1, except as otherwise required by subpart E of the Internal Revenue Code. However, solely for purposes of applying sections 465 and 469 to the income beneficiary, a disposition of S corporation stock by a QSST shall be treated as a disposition by the income beneficiary.

(9) Successive income beneficiary. (i) If the income beneficiary of a QSST who made a QSST election dies, each successive income beneficiary of that trust is treated as consenting to the election unless a successive income beneficiary affirmatively refuses to consent to the election. For this purpose, the term *successive income beneficiary* includes a beneficiary of a trust whose interest is a separate share within the meaning of section 663(c), but does not include any beneficiary of a trust that is created upon the death of the income beneficiary of the QSST and which is a new trust under local law.

(ii) The application of this paragraph (j)(9) is illustrated by the following examples:

Example (1). Shares of stock in Corporation X, an S corporation, are held by Trust A, a QSST for which a QSST election was made. B is the sole income beneficiary of Trust A. On B's death, under the terms of Trust A, J and K become the current income beneficiaries of Trust A. J and K each hold a separate and independent share of Trust A within the meaning of section 663(c). J and K are successive income beneficiaries of Trust A, and they are treated as consenting to B's QSST election.

Example (2). Assume the same facts as in Example 1, except that on B's death, under the terms of Trust A and local law, Trust A terminates and the principal is to be divided equally and held in newly created Trust B and Trust C. The sole income beneficiaries of Trust B and Trust C are J and K, respectively. Because Trust A terminated, J and K are not successive income beneficiaries of Trust A. J and K must make QSST elections for their respective trusts to qualify as QSSTs, if they qualify. The result is the same whether or not the trustee of Trusts B and C is the same as the trustee of trust A.

(10) Affirmative refusal to consent. (i) Required statement. A successive income beneficiary of a QSST must make an affirmative refusal to consent by signing and filing with the service center where the corporation files its income tax return a statement that—

(A) Contains the name, address, and taxpayer identification number of the successive income beneficiary, the trust, and the corporation for which the election was made;

(B) Identifies the refusal as an affirmative refusal to consent under section 1361(d)(2); and

(C) Sets forth the date on which the successive income beneficiary became the income beneficiary.

(ii) Filing date and effectiveness. The affirmative refusal to consent must be filed within 15 days and 2 months after the date on which the successive income beneficiary becomes the income beneficiary. The affirmative refusal to consent will be effective as of the date on which the successive income beneficiary becomes the current income beneficiary.

(11) Revocation of QSST election. A QSST election may be revoked only with the consent of the Commissioner. The Commissioner will not grant a revocation when one of its purposes is the avoidance of federal income taxes or when the taxable year is closed. The application for consent to revoke the election must be submitted to the Internal Revenue Service in the form of a letter ruling request under the ap-

propriate revenue procedure. The application must be signed by the current income beneficiary and must—

(i) Contain the name, address, and taxpayer identification number of the current income beneficiary, the trust, and the corporation with respect to which the QSST election was made;

(ii) Identify the election being revoked as an election made under section 1361(d)(2); and

(iii) Explain why the current income beneficiary seeks to revoke the QSST election and indicate that the beneficiary understands the consequences of the revocation.

(12) Converting a QSST to an ESBT. For a trust that seeks to convert from a QSST to an ESBT, the consent of the Commissioner is hereby granted to revoke the QSST election as of the effective date of the ESBT election, if all the following requirements are met:

(i) The trust meets all of the requirements to be an ESBT under paragraph (m)(1) of this section except for the requirement under paragraph (m)(1)(iv)(A) of this section that the trust not have a QSST election in effect.

(ii) The trustee and the current income beneficiary of the trust sign the ESBT election. The ESBT election must be filed with the service center where the S corporation files its income tax return. This ESBT election must state at the top of the document "ATTENTION ENTITY CONTROL—CONVERSION OF A QSST TO AN ESBT PURSUANT TO SECTION 1.1361-1(j)" and include all information otherwise required for an ESBT election under paragraph (m)(2) of this section. A separate election must be made with respect to the stock of each S corporation held by the trust.

(iii) The trust has not converted from an ESBT to a QSST within the 36-month period preceding the effective date of the new ESBT election.

(iv) The date on which the ESBT election is to be effective cannot be more than 15 days and two months prior to the date on which the election is filed and cannot be more than 12 months after the date on which the election is filed. If an election specifies an effective date more than 15 days and two months prior to the date on which the election is filed, it will be effective on the day that is 15 days and two months prior to the date on which it is filed. If an election specifies an effective date more than 12 months after the date on which the election is filed, it will be effective on the day that is 12 months after the date it is filed.

(k) *(1) Examples.* The provisions of paragraphs (h) and (j) of this section are illustrated by the following examples in which it is assumed that all noncorporate persons are citizens or residents of the United States:

Example (1). (i) Terms of the trust. In 1996, A and A's spouse, B, created an intervivos trust and each funded the trust with separately owned stock of an S corporation. Under the terms of the trust, A and B designated themselves as the income beneficiaries and each, individually, retained the power to amend or revoke the trust with respect to the trust assets attributable to their respective trust contributions. Upon A's death, the trust is to be divided into two separate parts; one part attributable to the assets A contributed to the trust and one part attributable to B's contributions. Before the trust is divided, and during the administration of A's estate, all trust income is payable to B. The part of the trust attributable to B's contributions is to continue in trust under the terms of which B is designated as the sole income beneficiary and retains the power to amend or revoke the trust. The part attributable to A's contributions is to be divided into two separate trusts both of which have B as the sole income beneficiary for life. One trust, the *Credit Shelter Trust,* is to be funded with an amount that can pass free of estate tax by reason of A's available estate tax unified credit. The terms of the Credit Shelter Trust meet the requirements of section 1361(d)(3) as a QSST. The balance of the property passes to a Marital Trust, the terms of which satisfy the requirements of section 1361(d)(3) as a QSST and section 2056(b)(7) as QTIP. The appropriate fiduciary under § 20.2056(b)-7(b)(3) is directed to make an election under section 2056(b)(7).

(ii) Results after deemed owner's death. On February 3, 1997, A dies and the portion of the trust assets attributable to A's contributions including the S stock contributed by A, is includible in A's gross estate under sections 2036 and 2038. During the administration of A's estate, the trust holds the S corporation stock. Under section 1361(c)(2)(B)(ii), A's estate is treated as the shareholder of the S corporation stock that was included in A's gross estate for purposes of section 1361(b)(1); however, for purposes of sections 1366, 1367, and 1368, the trust is treated as the shareholder. B's part of the trust continues to be a qualified subpart E trust of which B is the owner under sections 676 and 677. B, therefore, continues to be treated as the shareholder of the S corporation stock in that portion of the trust. On May 13, 1997, during the continuing administration of A's estate, the trust is divided into separate trusts in accordance with the terms of the trust instrument. The S corporation stock that was included in A's gross estate is distributed to the Marital Trust and to the Credit Shelter Trust. A's estate will cease to be treated as the shareholder of the S corporation under section 1361(c)(2)(B)(ii) on May 13, 1997 (the date on which the S corporation stock was transferred to the trusts). B, as the income beneficiary of the Marital Trust and the Credit Shelter Trust, must make the QSST election for each trust by July 28, 1997 (the end of the 16-day-and-2-month period beginning on the date the estate ceases to be treated as a shareholder) to have the trusts become permitted shareholders of the S corporation.

Example (2). (i) Qualified subpart E trust as shareholder. In 1997, A, an individual established a trust and transferred to the trust A's shares of stock of Corporation M, an S corporation. A has the power to revoke the entire trust. The terms of the trust require that all income be paid to B and otherwise meet the requirements of a QSST under section 1361(d)(3). The trust will continue in existence after A's death. The trust is a qualified subpart E trust described in section 1361(c)(2)(A)(i) during A's life, and A (not the trust) is treated as the shareholder for purposes of sections 1361(b)(1), 1366, 1367, and 1368.

(ii) Trust ceasing to be a qualified subpart E trust on deemed owner's death. Assume the same facts as paragraph (i) of this Example 2, except that A dies without having exercised A's power to revoke. Upon A's death, the trust ceases to be a qualified subpart E trust described in section 1361(c)(2)(A)(i). A's estate (and not the trust) is treated as the shareholder for purposes of section 1361(b)(1). A's estate will cease to be treated as the shareholder for purposes of section 1361(b)(1) upon the earlier of the transfer of the Corporation M stock by the trust (other than to A's estate), the expiration of the 2-year period beginning on the day of A's death, or the effective date of a QSST or ESBT election if the trust qualifies as a QSST or ESBT. However, until that time, because the trust continues in existence after A's death and will receive any distributions with respect to the stock it holds, the trust is treated as the shareholder for purposes of sections 1366, 1367, and 1368. If no QSST or ESBT election is made effective upon the expiration of the 2-year period, the corporation ceases to be an S corporation, but the trust continues as the shareholder of a C corporation.

(iii) Trust continuing to be a qualified subpart E trust on deemed owner's death. Assume the same facts as paragraph (ii) of this Example 2, except that the terms of the trust also provide that if A does not exercise the power to revoke before A's death, B will have the sole power to withdraw all trust property at any time after A's death. The trust continues to qualify as a qualified subpart E trust after A's death because, upon A's death, B is deemed to be the owner of the entire trust under section 678. Because the trust does not cease to be a qualified subpart E trust upon A's death, B (and not A's estate) is treated as the shareholder for purposes of sections 1361(b)(1), 1366, 1367, and 1368. Since the trust qualifies as a QSST, B may make a protective QSST election under paragraph (j)(6)(iv) of this section.

Example (3). (i) 2-year rule under section 1361(c)(2)(A)(ii) and (iii). F owns stock of Corporation P, an S corporation. In addition, F is the deemed owner of a qualified subpart E trust that holds stock in Corporation O, an S corporation. F dies on July 1, 2003. The trust continues in existence after F's death but is no longer a qualified subpart E trust. On August 1, 2003, F's shares of stock in Corporation P are transferred to the trust pursuant to the terms of F's will. Because the stock of Corporation P was not held by the trust when F died, section 1361(c)(2)(A)(ii) does not apply with respect to that stock. Under section 1361(c)(2)(A)(iii), the last day on which the trust could be treated as a permitted shareholder of Corporation P is July 31, 2005 (that is, the last day of the 2-year period that begins on the date of the transfer from the estate to the trust). With respect to the shares of stock in Corporation O held by the trust at the time of F's death, section 1361(c)(2)(A)(ii) applies and the last day on which the trust could be treated as a permitted shareholder of Corporation O is June 30, 2005 (that is, the last day of the 2-year period that begins on the date of F's death).

(ii) Section 645 electing trust and successor trust. Assume the same facts as in paragraph (i) of this Example 3, except that F's trust is a qualified revocable trust for which a valid section 645 election is made on October 1, 2003 (electing trust). Because under section 645 the electing trust is treated and taxed for purposes of subtitle A of the Code as part of F's estate, the trust may continue to hold the O stock pursuant to § 1361(b)(1)(B), without causing the termination of Corporation O's S election, for the duration of the section 645 election period. However, on January 1, 2004, during the election period, the shares of stock in Corporation O are transferred pursuant to the terms of the electing trust to a successor trust. Because the successor trust satisfies the definition of a testamentary trust under paragraph (h)(1)(iv) of this section, the successor trust is a permitted shareholder until the earlier of the expiration of the 2-year period beginning on January 1, 2004, or the effective date of a QSST or ESBT election for the successor trust.

Example (4). (i) QSST when terms do not require current distribution of income. Corporation Q, a calendar year corporation, makes an election to be an S corporation effective for calendar year 1996. On July 1, 1996, G, a shareholder of Corporation Q, transfers G's shares of Corporation Q stock to a trust with H as its current income beneficiary. The terms of the trust otherwise satisfy the QSST requirements, but authorize the trustee in its discretion to accumulate or distribute the trust income. However, the trust, which uses the calendar year as its taxable year, initially satisfies the income distribution requirement because the trustee is currently distributing all of the income. On August 1, 1996, H makes a QSST election with respect to Corporation Q that is effective as of July 1, 1996. Accordingly, as of July 1, 1996, the trust is a QSST and H is treated as the shareholder for purposes of sections 1361(b)(1), 1366, 1367, and 1368.

(ii) QSST when trust income is not distributed currently. Assume the same facts as in paragraph (i) of this Example 4, except that, for the taxable year ending on December 31, 1997, the trustee accumulates some trust income. The trust ceases to be a QSST on January 1, 1998, because the trust failed to distribute all of its income for the taxable year ending December 31, 1997. Thus, Corporation Q ceases to be an S corporation as of January 1, 1998, because the trust is not a permitted shareholder.

(iii) QSST when a person other than the current income beneficiary may receive trust corpus. Assume the same facts as in paragraph (i) of this Example 4, except that the events occur in 2003 and H dies on November 1, 2003, and the trust does not qualify as an ESBT. Under the terms of the trust, after H's death, L is the income beneficiary of the trust and the trustee is authorized to distribute trust corpus to L as well as to J. The trust ceases to be a QSST as of November 1, 2003, because corpus distributions may be made to someone other than L, the current (successive) income beneficiary. Under section 1361(c)(2)(B)(ii), H's estate (and not the trust) is considered to be the shareholder for purposes of section 1361(b)(1) for the 2-year period beginning on November 1, 2003. However, because the trust continues in existence after H's death and will receive any distributions from the corporation, the trust (and not H's estate) is treated as the shareholder for purposes of sections 1366, 1367, and 1368, during that 2-year period. After the 2-year period, the S election terminates and the trust continues as a shareholder of a C corporation. If the termination is inadvertent, Corporation Q may request relief under section 1362(f). However, the S election would not terminate if the trustee distributed all Corporation Q shares to L, J, or both on or before October 31, 2005, (the last day of the 2-year period) assuming that neither L nor J becomes the 76th shareholder of Corporation Q as a result of the distribution.

Example (5). QSST when current income beneficiary assigns the income interest to a person not named in the trust. On January 1, 1996, stock of Corporation R, a calendar year S corporation, is transferred to a trust that satisfies all of the requirements to be a QSST. Neither the terms of the trust nor local law preclude the current income beneficiary, K, from assigning K's income interest in the trust. K files a timely QSST election that is effective January 1, 1996. On July 1, 1996, K assigns the income interest in the trust to N. Under applicable state law, the trustee is bound as a result of the assignment to distribute the trust income to N. Thus, the QSST will cease to qualify as a QSST under section 1361(d)(3)(A)(iii) because N's interest will terminate on K's death (rather than on N's death). Accordingly, as of the date of the assignment, the trust ceases to be a QSST and Corporation R ceases to be an S corporation.

Example (6). QSST when terms fail to provide for distribution of trust assets upon termination during life of current income beneficiary. A contributes S corporation stock to a trust the terms of which provide for one income beneficiary, annual distributions of income, discretionary invasion of corpus only for the benefit of the income beneficiary, and termination of the trust only upon the death of the current income beneficiary. Since the trust can terminate only upon the death of the income beneficiary, the governing instrument fails to provide for any distribution of trust assets during the income beneficiary's life. The governing instrument's silence on this point does not disqualify the trust under section 1361(d)(3)(A)(ii) or (iv).

Example (7). QSST when settlor of trust retains a reversion in the trust. On January 10, 1996, M transfers to a trust shares of stock in corporation X, an S corporation. D, who is 13 years old and not a lineal descendant of M, is the sole income beneficiary of the trust. On termination of the trust, the principal (including the X shares) is to revert to M. The trust instrument provides that the trust will terminate upon the earlier of D's death or D's 21st birthday. The terms of the trust satisfy all of the requirements to be a QSST except those of section 1361(d)(3)(A)(ii) (that corpus may be distributed during the current income beneficiary's life only to that beneficiary) and (iv) (that, upon termination of the trust during the life of the current income beneficiary, the corpus, must be distributed to that beneficiary). On February 10, 1996, M makes a gift of M's reversionary interest to D. Until M assigns M's reversion in the trust to D, M is deemed to own the entire trust under section 673(a) and the trust is a qualified subpart E trust. For purposes of section 1361(b)(1), 1366, 1367, and 1368, M is the shareholder of X. The trust ceases to be a qualified subpart E trust on February 10, 1996. Assuming that, by virtue of the assignment to D of M's reversionary interest, D (upon his 21st birthday) or D's estate (in the case of D's death before reaching age 21) is entitled under local law to receive the trust principal, the trust will be deemed as of February 10, 1996, to have satisfied the conditions of section 1361(d)(3)(A)(ii) and (iv) even though the terms of the trust do not explicitly so provide. D must make a QSST election by no later than April 25, 1996 (the end of the 16-day-and-2-month period that begins on February 10, 1996, the date on which the X stock is deemed transferred to the trust by M). See example (5) of § 1.1001-2(c) of the regulations.

Example (8). QSST when the income beneficiary has the power to withdraw corpus. On January 1, 1996, F transfers stock of an S corporation to an irrevocable trust whose income beneficiary is F's son, C. Under the terms of the trust, C is given the noncumulative power to withdraw from the corpus of the trust the greater of $5,000 or 5 percent of the value of the corpus on a yearly basis. The terms of the trust meet the QSST requirements. Assuming the trust distributions are not in satisfaction of F's legal obligation to support C, the trust qualifies as a QSST. C (or if C is a minor, C's legal representative) must make the QSST election no later than March 16, 1996 (the end of the 16-day-and-2-month period that begins on the date the stock is transferred to the trust).

Example (9). (i) Filing the QSST election. On January 1, 1996, stock of Corporation T, a calendar year C corporation, is transferred to a trust that satisfies all of the requirements to be a QSST. On January 31, 1996, Corporation T files an election to be an S corporation that is to be effective for its taxable year beginning on January 1, 1996. In order for the S election to be effective for the 1996 taxable year, the QSST election must be effective January 1, 1996, and must be filed within the period beginning on January 1, 1996, and ending March 16, 1996 (the 16-day-and-2-month period beginning on the first day of the first taxable year for which the election to be an S corporation is intended to be effective).

(ii) QSST election when the S election is filed late. Assume the same facts as in paragraph (i) of this Example 9, except that Corporation T's election to be an S corporation is filed on April 1, 1996 (after the 15th day of the 3rd month of the first taxable year for which it is to be effective but before the end of that taxable year). Because the election to be an S corporation is not timely filed for the 1996 taxable year, under section 1362(b)(3), the S election is treated as made for the taxable year beginning on January 1, 1997. The QSST election must be filed within the 16-day-and-2-month period beginning on April 1, 1996, the date the S election was made, and ending on June 16, 1996.

Example (10). (i) Transfers to QTIP trust. On June 1, 1996, A transferred S corporation stock to a trust for the benefit of A's spouse B, the terms of which satisfy the requirements of section 2523(f)(2) as qualified terminable interest property. Under the terms of the trust, B is the sole income beneficiary for life. In addition, corpus may be distributed to B, at the trustee's discretion, during B's lifetime. However, under section 677(a), A is treated as the owner of the trust. Accordingly, the trust is a permitted shareholder of the S corporation under section 1361(c)(2)(A)(i), and A is treated as the shareholder for purposes of sections 1361(b)(1), 1366, 1367, and 1368.

(ii) Transfers to QTIP trust where husband and wife divorce. Assume the same facts as in paragraph (i) of this Example 10, except that A and B divorce on May 2, 1997. Under section 682, A ceases to be treated as the owner of the trust under section 677(a) because A and B are no longer husband and wife. Under section 682, after the divorce, B is the income beneficiary of the trust and corpus of the trust may only be distributed to B. Accordingly, assuming the trust otherwise meets the requirements of section 1361(d)(3), B must make the QSST election within 2 months and 15 days after the date of the divorce.

(iii) Transfers to QTIP trust where no corpus distribution is permitted. Assume the same facts as in paragraph (i) of this Example 10, except that the terms of the trust do not permit corpus to be distributed to B and require its retention by the trust for distribution to A and B's surviving children after the death of B. Under section 677, A is treated as the owner of the ordinary income portion of the trust, but the trust will be subject to tax on gross income allocable to corpus. Accordingly, the trust does not qualify as an eligible shareholder of the S corporation because it is neither a qualified subpart E trust nor a QSST.

(2) Effective date. (i) In general. Paragraph (a) of this section, and paragraphs (c) through (k) of this section (as contained in the 26 CFR edition revised April 1, 2003) apply to taxable years of a corporation beginning after July 21, 1995. For taxable years beginning on or before July 21, 1995, to which paragraph (a) of this section and paragraphs (c) through (k) of this section (as contained in the 26 CFR edition revised April 1, 2003) do not apply, see § 18.1361-1 of this chapter (as contained in the 26 CFR edition revised April 1, 1995). However, paragraphs (h)(1)(vi), (h)(3)(i)(F), (h)(3)(ii), and (j)(12) of this section (as contained in the 26 CFR edition revised April 1, 2003) are applicable for taxable years beginning on and after May 14, 2002. Otherwise, paragraphs (b)(1)(ii), (f), (h)(1)(ii), (h)(1)(iv), (h)(3)(i)(B), (h)(3)(i)(D), (h)(3)(ii)(A), (h)(3)(ii)(B), (j)(6)(iii)(C), (j)(6)(iii)(D), (j)(7)(ii), and (k)(1) Example 2(ii) fourth and last sentences, Example 3, and Example 4(iii) of this section apply on and after July 17, 2003. Paragraphs (b)(1)(i), (e)(1), (e)(3), (h)(1)(vii), (h)(3)(i)(G), and the fifth sentence of paragraph (j)(8) are effective on August 14, 2008.

(ii) Transition rules. Taxpayers may apply paragraph (h)(1)(iv)(B) of this section on and after December 24, 2002, and before July 17, 2003, to treat a trust as a testamentary trust, but not during any period for which a QSST or ESBT election was in effect for the trust. In addition, the Internal Revenue Service will not challenge the treatment of a trust described in paragraph (h)(1)(iv)(B) of this section as a permitted shareholder of an S corporation for periods after August 5, 1997, and before the earlier of July 17, 2003, or the effective date of any QSST or ESBT election for that trust.

(iii) Exception. If a QSST has sold or otherwise disposed of all or a portion of its S corporation stock in a tax year that is open for the QSST and the income beneficiary but on or before July 21, 1995, the QSST and the income beneficiary may both treat the transaction as if the beneficiary was the owner of the stock sold or disposed of, and thus recognize any gain or loss, or as if the QSST was the owner of the stock sold or disposed of as described in paragraph (j)(8) of this section. This exception applies only if the QSST and the income beneficiary take consistent reporting positions. The QSST and the income beneficiary must disclose by a statement on their respective returns (or amended returns), that they are taking consistent reporting positions.

(l) Classes of stock. *(1) General rule.* A corporation that has more than one class of stock does not qualify as a small business corporation. Except as provided in paragraph (l)(4) of this section (relating to instruments, obligations, or arrangements treated as a second class of stock), a corporation is treated as having only one class of stock if all outstanding shares of stock of the corporation confer identical rights to distribution and liquidation proceeds. Differences in voting rights among shares of stock of a corporation are disregarded in determining whether a corporation has more than one class of stock. Thus, if all shares of stock of an S corporation have identical rights to distribution and liquidation proceeds, the corporation may have voting and nonvoting common stock, a class of stock that may vote only on certain issues, irrevocable proxy agreements, or groups of shares that differ with respect to rights to elect members of the board of directors.

(2) Determination of whether stock confers identical rights to distribution and liquidation proceeds. (i) In general. The determination of whether all outstanding shares of stock confer identical rights to distribution and liquidation proceeds is made based on the corporate charter, articles of incorporation, bylaws, applicable state law, and binding agreements relating to distribution and liquidation proceeds (collectively, the governing provisions). A commercial contractual agreement, such as a lease, employment agreement, or loan agreement, is not a binding agreement relating to distribution and liquidation proceeds and thus is not a governing provision unless a principal purpose of the agreement is to circumvent the one class of stock requirement of section 1361(b)(1)(D) and this paragraph (l). Although a corporation is not treated as having more than one class of stock so long as the governing provisions provide for identical distribution and liquidation rights, any distributions (including actual, constructive, or deemed distributions) that differ in timing or amount are to be given appropriate tax effect in accordance with the facts and circumstances.

(ii) State law requirements for payment and withholding of income tax. State laws may require a corporation to pay or withhold state income taxes on behalf of some or all of the corporation's shareholders. Such laws are disregarded in determining whether all outstanding shares of stock of the corporation confer identical rights to distribution and liquidation proceeds, within the meaning of paragraph (l)(1) of this section, provided that, when the constructive distributions resulting from the payment or withholding of taxes by the corporation are taken into account, the outstanding shares confer identical rights to distribution and liquidation proceeds. A difference in timing between the constructive distributions and the actual distributions to the other shareholders does not cause the corporation to be treated as having more than one class of stock.

(iii) Buy-sell and redemption agreements. (A) In general. Buy-sell agreements among shareholders, agreements restricting the transferability of stock, and redemption agreements are disregarded in determining whether a corporation's outstanding shares of stock confer identical distribution and liquidation rights unless—

(1) A principal purpose of the agreement is to circumvent the one class of stock requirement of section 1361(b)(1)(D) and this paragraph (l), and

(2) The agreement establishes a purchase price that, at the time the agreement is entered into, is significantly in excess of or below the fair market value of the stock.

Agreements that provide for the purchase or redemption of stock at book value or at a price between fair market value and book value are not considered to establish a price that is significantly in excess of or below the fair market value of the stock and, thus, are disregarded in determining whether the outstanding shares of stock confer identical rights. For purposes of this paragraph (l)(2)(iii)(A), a good faith determination of fair market value will be respected unless it can be shown that the value was substantially in error and the determination of the value was not performed with reasonable diligence. Although an agreement may be disregarded in determining whether shares of stock confer identical distribution and liquidation rights, payments pursuant to the agreement may have income or transfer tax consequences.

(B) Exception for certain agreements. Bona fide agreements to redeem or purchase stock at the time of death, divorce, disability, or termination of employment are disregarded in determining whether a corporation's shares of stock confer identical rights. In addition, if stock that is substantially nonvested (within the meaning of § 1.83-3(b)) is treated as outstanding under these regulations, the forfeiture provisions that cause the stock to be substantially nonvested are disregarded. Furthermore, the Commissioner may provide by Revenue Ruling or other published guidance that other types of bona fide agreements to redeem or purchase stock are disregarded.

(C) Safe harbors for determinations of book value. A determination of book value will be respected if—

(1) The book value is determined in accordance with Generally Accepted Accounting Principles (including permitted optional adjustments); or

(2) The book value is used for any substantial nontax purpose.

(iv) Distributions that take into account varying interests in stock during a taxable year. A governing provision does not, within the meaning of paragraph (l)(2)(i) of this section, alter the rights to liquidation and distribution proceeds conferred by an S corporation's stock merely because the governing provision provides that, as a result of a change in stock ownership, distributions in a taxable year are to be made on the basis of the shareholders's varying interests in the S corporation's income in the current or immediately preceding taxable year. If distributions pursuant to the provision are not made within a reasonable time after the close of the taxable year in which the varying interests occur, the distributions may be recharacterized depending on the facts and circumstances, but will not result in a second class of stock.

(v) Special rule for section 338(h)(10) elections. If the shareholders of an S corporation sell their stock in a transaction for which an election is made under section 338(h)(10) and § 1.338(h)(10)-1, the receipt of varying amounts per share by the shareholders will not cause the S corporation to have more than one class of stock, provided that the varying amounts are determined in arm's length negotiations with the purchaser.

(vi) Examples. The application of paragraph (l)(2) of this section may be illustrated by the following examples. In each of the examples, the S corporation requirements of section 1361 are satisfied except as otherwise stated, the corporation has in effect an S election under section 1362, and the corporation has only the shareholders described.

Example (1). Determination of whether stock confers identical rights to distribution and liquidation proceeds.

(i) The law of State A requires that permission be obtained from the State Commissioner of Corporations before stock may be issued by a corporation. The Commissioner grants permission to S, a corporation, to issue its stock subject to the restriction that any person who is issued stock in exchange for property, and not cash, must waive all rights to receive distributions until the shareholders who contributed cash for stock have received distributions in the amount of their cash contributions.

(ii) The condition imposed by the Commissioner pursuant to state law alters the rights to distribution and liquidation proceeds conferred by the outstanding stock of S so that those rights are not identical. Accordingly, under paragraph (l)(2)(i) of this section, S is treated as having more than one class of stock and does not qualify as a small business corporation.

Example (2). Distributions that differ in timing.

(i) S, a corporation, has two equal shareholders, A and B. Under S's bylaws. A and B are entitled to equal distributions. S distributes $50,000 to A in the current year, but does not distribute $50,000 to B until one year later. The circumstances indicate that the difference in timing did not occur by reason of a binding agreement relating to distribution or liquidation proceeds.

(ii) Under paragraph (l)(2)(i) of this section, the difference in timing of the distributions to A and B does not cause S to be treated as having more than one class of stock. However, section 7872 or other recharacterization principles may apply to determine the appropriate tax consequences.

Example (3). Treatment of excessive compensation.

(i) S, a corporation, has two equal shareholders, C and D, who are each employed by S and have binding employment agreements with S. The compensation paid by S to C under C's employment agreement is reasonable. The compensation paid by S to D under D's employment agreement, however, is found to be excessive. The facts and circumstances do not reflect that a principal purpose to D's employment agreement is to circumvent the one class of stock requirement of section 1361(b)(1)(D) and this paragraph (l).

(ii) Under paragraph (l)(2)(i) of this section, the employment agreements are not governing provisions. Accordingly, S is not treated as having more than one class of stock by reason of the employment agreements, even though S is not allowed a deduction for the excessive compensation paid to D.

Example (4). Agreement to pay fringe benefits.

(i) S, a corporation, is required under binding agreements to pay accident and health insurance premiums on behalf of certain of its employees who are also shareholders. Different premium amounts are paid by S for each employee-shareholder. The facts and circumstances do not reflect that a principal purpose of the agreements is to circumvent the one class of stock requirement of section 1361(b)(1)(D) and this paragraph (l).

(ii) Under paragraph (l)(2)(i) of this section, the agreements are not governing provisions. Accordingly, S is not treated as having more than one class of stock by reason of the agreements. In addition, S is not treated as having more than one class of stock by reason of the payment of fringe benefits.

Example (5). Below-market corporation-shareholder loan.

(i) E is a shareholder of S, a corporation. S makes a below-market loan to E that is a corporation-shareholder loan to which section 7872 applies. Under section 7872, E is deemed to receive a distribution with respect to S stock by reason of the loan. The facts and circumstances do not reflect that a principal purpose of the loan is to circumvent the one class of stock requirement of section 1361(b)(1)(D) and this paragraph (l).

(ii) Under paragraph (l)(2)(i) of this section, the loan agreement is not a governing provision. Accordingly, S is not treated as having more than one class of stock by reason of the below-market loan to E.

Example (6). Agreement to adjust distributions for state tax burdens.

(i) S, a corporation, executes a binding agreement with its shareholders to modify its normal distribution policy by making upward adjustments of its distribution to those shareholders who bear heavier state tax burdens. The adjustments are based on a formula that will give the shareholders equal after-tax distributions.

(ii) The binding agreement relates to distribution or liquidation proceeds. The agreement is thus a governing provision that alters the rights conferred by the outstanding stock of S to distribution proceeds so that those rights are not identical. Therefore, under paragraph (l)(2)(i) of this section, S is treated as having more than one class of stock.

Example (7). State law requirements for payment and withholding of income tax.

(i) The law of State X requires corporations to pay state income taxes on behalf of nonresident shareholders. The law of State X does not require corporations to pay state income taxes on behalf of resident shareholders. S is incorporated in State X. S's resident shareholders have the right (for example, under the law of State X or pursuant to S's bylaws or a binding agreement) to distributions that take into account the payments S makes on behalf of its nonresident shareholders.

(ii) The payment by S of state income taxes on behalf of its nonresident shareholders are generally treated as constructive distributions to those shareholders. Because S's resident shareholders have the right to equal distributions, taking into account the constructive distributions to the nonresident shareholders, S's shares confer identical rights to distribution proceeds. Accordingly, under paragraph (l)(2)(ii) of this section, the state law requiring S to pay state income taxes on behalf of its nonresident shareholders is disregarded in determining whether S has more than one class of stock.

(iii) The same result would follow if the payments of state income taxes on behalf of nonresident shareholders are instead treated as advances to those shareholders and the governing provisions require the advances to be repaid or offset by reductions in distributions to those shareholders.

Example (8). Redemption agreements.

(i) F, G, and H are shareholders of S, a corporation. F is also an employee of S. By agreement, S is to redeem F's shares on the termination of F's employment.

(ii) On these facts, under paragraph (l)(2)(iii)(B) of this section, the agreement is disregarded in determining whether all outstanding shares of S's stock confer identical rights to distribution and liquidation proceeds.

Example (9). Analysis of redemption agreements.

(i) J, K, and L are shareholders of S, a corporation. L is also an employee of S. L's shares were not issued to L in connection with the performance of services. By agreement, S is to redeem L's shares for an amount significantly below their fair market value on the termination of L's employment or if S's sales fall below certain levels.

(ii) Under paragraph (l)(2)(iii)(B) of this section, the portion of the agreement providing for redemption of L's stock on termination of employment is disregarded. Under paragraph (l)(2)(iii)(A), the portion of the agreement providing for redemption of L's stock if S's sales fall below certain levels is disregarded unless a principal purpose of that portion of the agreement is to circumvent the one class of stock requirement of section 1361(b)(1)(D) and this paragraph (l).

(3) Stock taken into account. Except as provided in paragraphs (b)(3), (4), and (5) of this section (relating to restricted stock, deferred compensation plans, and straight debt), in determining whether all outstanding shares of stock confer identical rights to distribution and liquidation proceeds, all outstanding shares of stock of a corporation are taken into account. For example, substantially nonvested stock with respect to which an election under section 83(b) has been made is taken into account in determining whether a corporation has a second class of stock, and such stock is not treated as a second class of stock if the stock confers rights to distribution and liquidation proceeds that are identical, within the meaning of paragraph (l)(1) of this section, to the rights conferred by the other outstanding shares of stock.

(4) Other instruments, obligations, or arrangements treated as a second class of stock. (i) In general. Instruments, obligations, or arrangements are not treated as a second class of stock for purposes of this paragraph (l) unless they are described in paragraphs (l)(4)(ii) or (iii) of this section. However, in no event are instruments, obligations, or arrangements described in paragraph (b)(4) of this section (relating to deferred compensation plans), paragraphs (l)(4)(iii)(B) and (C) of this section (relating to the exceptions and safe harbor for options), paragraph (l)(4)(ii)(B) of this section (relating to the safe harbors for certain short-term unwritten advances and proportionally-held debt), or paragraph (l)(5) of this section (relating to the safe harbor for straight debt), treated as a second class of stock for purposes of this paragraph (l).

(ii) Instruments, obligations, or arrangements treated as equity under general principles. (A) In general. Except as provided in paragraph (l)(4)(i) of this section, any instrument, obligation, or arrangement issued by a corporation (other than outstanding shares of stock described in paragraph (l)(3) of this section), regardless of whether designated as debt, is treated as a second class of stock of the corporation—

(1) If the instrument, obligation, or arrangement constitutes equity or otherwise results in the holder being treated as the owner of stock under general principles of Federal tax law; and

(2) A principal purpose of issuing or entering into the instrument, obligation, or arrangement is to circumvent the rights to distribution or liquidation proceeds conferred by the outstanding shares of stock or to circumvent the limitation on eligible shareholders contained in paragraph (b)(1) of this section.

(B) Safe harbor for certain short-term unwritten advances and proportionately held obligations. (1) Short-term unwritten advances. Unwritten advances from a shareholder that do not exceed $10,000 in the aggregate at any time during the taxable year of the corporation, are treated as debt by the parties, and are expected to be repaid within a reasonable time are not treated as a second class of stock for that taxable year, even if the advances are considered equity under general principles of Federal tax law. The failure of an unwritten advance to meet this safe harbor will not result in a second class of stock unless the advance is considered equity under paragraph (l)(4)(ii)(A)(1) of this section and a principal purpose of the advance is to circumvent the rights of the outstanding shares of stock or the limitation on eligible shareholders under paragraph (l)(4)(ii)(A)(2) of this section.

(2) Proportionately-held obligations. Obligations of the same class that are considered equity under general principles of Federal tax law, but are owned solely by the owners of, and in the same proportion as, the outstanding stock of the corporation, are not treated as a second class of stock. Furthermore, an obligation or obligations owned by the sole shareholder of a corporation are always held proportionately to the corporation's outstanding stock. The obligations that are considered equity that do not meet this safe harbor will not result in a second class of stock unless a principal purpose of the obligations is to circumvent the rights of the outstanding shares of stock or the limitation on eligible shareholders under paragraph (l)(4)(ii)(A)(2) of this section.

(iii) Certain call options, warrants or similar instruments. (A) In general. Except as otherwise provided in this paragraph (l)(4)(iii), a call option, warrant, or similar instrument (collectively, call option) issued by a corporation is treated as a second class of stock of the corporation if, taking into account all the facts and circumstances, the call option is substantially certain to be exercised (by the holder or a potential transferee) and has a strike price substantially below the fair market value of the underlying stock on the date that the call option is issued, transferred by a person who is an eligible shareholder under paragraph (b)(1) of this section to a person who is not an eligible shareholder under paragraph (b)(1) of this section, or materially modified. For purposes of this paragraph (l)(4)(iii), if an option is issued in connection with a loan and the time period in which the option can be exercised is extended in connection with (and consistent with) a modification of the terms of the loan, the extension of the time period in which the option may be exercised is not considered a material modification. In addition, a call option does not have a strike price substantially below fair market value if the price at the time of exercise cannot, pursuant to the terms of the instrument, be substantially below the fair market value of the underlying stock at the time of exercise.

(B) Certain exceptions. (1) A call option is not treated as a second class of stock for purposes of this paragraph (l) if it is issued to a person that is actively and regularly engaged in the business of lending and issued in connection with a commercially reasonable loan to the corporation. This paragraph (l)(4)(iii)(B)(1) continues to apply if the call option is transferred with the loan (or if a portion of the call option is transferred with a corresponding portion of the loan). However, if the call option is transferred without a corresponding portion of the loan, this paragraph (l)(4)(iii)(B)(1) ceases to apply. Upon that transfer, the call option is tested under paragraph (l)(4)(iii)(A) (notwithstanding anything in that paragraph to the contrary) if, but for this paragraph, the call option would have been treated as a second class of stock on the date it was issued.

(2) A call option that is issued to an individual who is either an employee or an independent contractor in connection with the performance of services for the corporation or a related corporation (and that is not excessive by reference to the services performed) is not treated as a second class of stock for purposes of this paragraph (l) if—

(i) The call option is nontransferable within the meaning of § 1.83-3(d); and

(ii) The call option does not have a readily ascertainable fair market value as defined in § 1.83-7(b) at the time the option is issued.

If the call option becomes transferable, this paragraph (l)(4)(iii)(B)(2) ceases to apply. Solely for purposes of this paragraph (l)(4)(iii)(B)(2), a corporation is related to the issuing corporation if more than 50 percent of the total voting power and total value of its stock is owned by the issuing corporation.

(3) The Commissioner may provide other exceptions by Revenue Ruling or other published guidance.

(C) Safe harbor for certain options. A call option is not treated as a second class of stock if, on the date the call option is issued, transferred by a person who is an eligible shareholder under paragraph (b)(1) of this section to a person who is not an eligible shareholder under paragraph (b)(1) of this section, or materially modified, the strike price of the call option is at least 90 percent of the fair market value of the underlying stock on that date. For purposes of this paragraph (l)(4)(iii)(C), a good faith determination of fair market value by the corporation will be respected unless it can be shown that the value was substantially in error and the determination of the value was not performed with reasonable diligence to obtain a fair value. Failure of an option to meet this safe harbor will not necessarily result in the option being treated as a second class of stock.

(iv) Convertible debt. A convertible debt instrument is considered a second class of stock if—

(A) It would be treated as a second class of stock under paragraph (l)(4)(ii) of this section (relating to instruments, obligations, or arrangements treated as equity under general principles); or

(B) It embodies rights equivalent to those of a call option that would be treated as a second class of stock under paragraph (l)(4)(iii) of this section (relating to certain call options, warrants, and similar instruments).

(v) Examples. The application of this paragraph (l)(4) may be illustrated by the following examples. In each of the examples, the S corporation requirements of section 1361 are satisfied except as otherwise stated, the corporation has in effect an S election under section 1362, and the corporation has only the shareholders described.

Example (1). Transfer of call option by eligible shareholder to ineligible shareholder.

(i) S, a corporation, has 10 shareholders. S issues call options to A, B, and C, individuals who are U.S. residents. A, B, and C are not shareholders, employees, or independent contractors of S. The options have a strike price of $40 and are issued on a date when the fair market value of S stock is also $40. A year later, P, a partnership, purchases A's option. On the date of transfer, the fair market value of S stock is $80.

(ii) On the date the call option is issued, its strike price is not substantially below the fair market value of the S stock. Under paragraph (l)(4)(iii)(A) of this section, whether a call option is a second class of stock must be redetermined if the call option is transferred by a person who is an eligible shareholder under paragraph (b)(1) of this section to a person who is not an eligible shareholder under paragraph (b)(1) of this section. In this case, A is an eligible shareholder of S under paragraph (b)(1) of this section, but P is not. Accordingly, the option is retested on the date it is transferred to D.

(iii) Because on the date the call option is transferred to P its strike price is 50% of the fair market value, the strike price is substantially below the fair market value of the S stock. Accordingly, the call option is treated as a second class of stock as of the date it is transferred to P if, at that time, it is determined that the option is substantially certain to be exercised. The determination of whether the option is substantially certain to be exercised is made on the basis of all the facts and circumstances.

Example (2). Call option issued in connection with the performance of services.

(i) E is a bona fide employee of S, a corporation. S issues to E a call option in connection with E's performance of services. At the time the call option is issued, it is not transferable and does not have a readily ascertainable fair market value. However, the call option becomes transferable before it is exercised by E.

(ii) While the option is not transferable, under paragraph (l)(4)(iii)(B)(2) of this section, it is not treated as a second class of stock, regardless of its strike price. When the option becomes transferable, that paragraph ceases to apply, and the general rule of paragraph (l)(4)(iii)(A) of this section applies. Accordingly, if the option is materially modified or is transferred to a person who is not an eligible shareholder under paragraph (b)(1) of this section, and on the date of such modification or transfer, the option is substantially certain to be exercised and has a strike price substantially below the fair market value of the underlying stock, the option is treated as a second class of stock.

(iii) If E left S's employment before the option became transferable, the exception provided by paragraph (l)(4)(iii)(B)(2) would continue to apply until the option became transferable.

(5) Straight debt safe harbor. (i) In general. Notwithstanding paragraph (l)(4) of this section, straight debt is not treated as a second class of stock. For purposes of section 1361(c)(5) and this section, the term straight debt means a written unconditional obligation, regardless of whether embodied in a formal note, to pay a sum certain on demand, or on a specified due date, which—

(A) Does not provide for an interest rate or payment dates that are contingent on profits, the borrower's discretion, the payment of dividends with respect to common stock, or similar factors;

(B) Is not convertible (directly or indirectly) into stock or any other equity interest of the S corporation; and

(C) Is held by an individual (other than a nonresident alien), an estate, or a trust described in section 1361(c)(2).

(ii) Subordination. The fact that an obligation is subordinated to other debt of the corporation does not prevent the obligation from qualifying as straight debt.

(iii) Modification or transfer. An obligation that originally qualifies as straight debt ceases to so qualify if the obligation—

(A) Is materially modified so that it no longer satisfies the definition of straight debt; or

(B) Is transferred to a third party who is not an eligible shareholder under paragraph (b)(1) of this section.

(iv) Treatment of straight debt for other purposes. An obligation of an S corporation that satisfies the definition of straight debt in paragraph (l)(5)(i) of this section is not treated as a second class of stock even if it is considered equity under general principles of Federal tax law. Such an obligation is generally treated as debt and when so treated is subject to the applicable rules governing indebtedness for other purposes of the Code. Accordingly, interest paid or accrued with respect to a straight debt obligation is generally treated as interest by the corporation and the recipient and does not constitute a distribution to which section 1368 applies. However, if a straight debt obligation bears a rate of interest that is unreasonably high, an appropriate portion of the interest may be recharacterized and treated as a payment that is not interest. Such a recharacterization does not result in a second class of stock.

(v) Treatment of C corporation debt upon conversion to S status. If a C corporation has outstanding an obligation that satisfies the definition of straight debt in paragraph (l)(5)(i) of this section, but that is considered equity under general principles of Federal tax law, the obligation is not treated as a second class of stock for purposes of this section if the C corporation converts to S status. In addition, the conversion from C corporation status to S corporation status is not treated as an exchange of debt for stock with respect to such an instrument.

(6) Inadvertent terminations. See section 1362(f) and the regulations thereunder for rules relating to inadvertent terminations in cases where the one class of stock requirement has been inadvertently breached.

(7) Effective date. Section 1.1361-1(l) generally applies to taxable years of a corporation beginning on or after May 28, 1992. However, § 1.1361-1(l) does not apply to: an instrument, obligation, or arrangement issued or entered into before May 28, 1992, and not materially modified after that date; a buy-sell agreement, redemption agreement, or agreement restricting transferability entered into before May 28, 1992, and not materially modified after that date; or a call option or similar instrument issued before May 28, 1992, and not materially modified after that date. In addition, a corporation and its shareholders may apply this § 1.1361-1(l) to prior taxable years.

(m) Electing small business trust (ESBT). *(1) Definition.* (i) General rule. An electing small business trust (ESBT) means any trust if it meets the following requirements: the trust does not have as a beneficiary any person other than an individual, an estate, an organization described in section 170(c)(2) through (5), or an organization described in section 170(c)(1) that holds a contingent interest in such trust and is not a potential current beneficiary; no interest in the trust has been acquired by purchase; and the trustee of the trust makes a timely ESBT election for the trust.

(ii) Qualified beneficiaries. (A) In general. For purposes of this section, a beneficiary includes a person who has a present, remainder, or reversionary interest in the trust.

(B) Distributee trusts. A distributee trust is the beneficiary of the ESBT only if the distributee trust is an organization described in section 170(c)(2) or (3). In all other situations, any person who has a beneficial interest in a distributee trust is a beneficiary of the ESBT. A distributee trust is a trust that receives or may receive a distribution from an ESBT, whether the rights to receive the distribution are fixed or contingent, or immediate or deferred.

(C) Powers of appointment. A person in whose favor a power of appointment could be exercised is not a beneficiary of an ESBT until the holder of the power of appointment actually exercises the power in favor of such person.

(D) Nonresident aliens. A nonresident alien as defined in section 7701(b)(1)(B) is an eligible beneficiary of an ESBT. However, see paragraph (m)(4)(i) and (m)(5)(iii) of this section if the nonresident alien is a potential current beneficiary of the ESBT (which would result in an ineligible shareholder and termination of the S corporation election).

(iii) Interests acquired by purchase. A trust does not qualify as an ESBT if any interest in the trust has been acquired by purchase. Generally, if a person acquires an interest in the trust and thereby becomes a beneficiary of the trust as defined in paragraph (m)(1)(ii)(A), and any portion of the basis in the acquired interest in the trust is determined under section 1012, such interest has been acquired by purchase. This includes a net gift of a beneficial interest in the trust, in which the person acquiring the beneficial interest pays the gift tax. The trust itself may acquire S corporation stock or other property by purchase or in a part-gift, part-sale transaction.

(iv) Ineligible trusts. An ESBT does not include—

(A) Any qualified subchapter S trust (as defined in section 1361(d)(3)) if an election under section 1361(d)(2) applies with respect to any corporation the stock of which is held by the trust;

(B) Any trust exempt from tax or not subject to tax under subtitle A; or

(C) Any charitable remainder annuity trust or charitable remainder unitrust (as defined in section 664(d)).

(2) ESBT election. (i) In general. The trustee of the trust must make the ESBT election by signing and filing, with the service center where the S corporation files its income tax return, a statement that meets the requirements of paragraph (m)(2)(ii) of this section. If there is more than one trustee, the trustee or trustees with authority to legally bind the trust must sign the election statement. If any one of several trustees can legally bind the trust, only one trustee needs to sign the election statement. Generally, only one ESBT election is made for the trust, regardless of the number of S corporations whose stock is held by the ESBT. However, if the ESBT holds stock in multiple S corporations that file in different service centers, the ESBT election must be filed with all the relevant service centers where the corporations file their income tax returns. This requirement applies only at the time of the initial ESBT election; if the ESBT later acquires stock in an S corporation which files its income tax return at a different service center, a new ESBT election is not required.

(ii) Election statement. The election statement must include—

(A) The name, address, and taxpayer identification number of the trust, the potential current beneficiaries, and the S corporations in which the trust currently holds stock. If the trust includes a power described in paragraph (m)(4)(vi)(B) of this section, then the election statement must include a statement that such a power is included in the instrument, but does not need to include the name, address, or taxpayer identification number of any particular charity or any other information regarding the power.

(B) An identification of the election as an ESBT election made under section 1361(e)(3);

(C) The first date on which the trust owned stock in each S corporation;

(D) The date on which the election is to become effective (not earlier than 15 days and two months before the date on which the election is filed); and

(E) Representations signed by the trustee stating that—

(1) The trust meets the definitional requirements of section 1361(e)(1); and

(2) All potential current beneficiaries of the trust meet the shareholder requirements of section 1361(b)(1).

(iii) Due date for ESBT election. The ESBT election must be filed within the time requirements prescribed in paragraph (j)(6)(iii) of this section for filing a qualified subchapter S trust (QSST) election.

(iv) Election by a trust described in section 1361(c)(2)(A)(ii) or (iii). A trust that is a qualified S corporation shareholder under section 1361(c)(2)(A)(ii) or (iii) may elect ESBT treatment at any time during the 2-year period described in those sections or the 16-day-and-2-month period beginning on the date after the end of the 2-year period. If the trust makes an ineffective ESBT election, the trust will continue nevertheless to qualify as an eligible S corporation shareholder for the remainder of the period described in section 1361(c)(2)(A)(ii) or (iii).

(v) No protective election. A trust cannot make a conditional ESBT election that would be effective only in the event the trust fails to meet the requirements for an eligible trust described in section 1361(c)(2)(A)(i) through (iv). If a trust attempts to make such a conditional ESBT election and it fails to qualify as an eligible S corporation shareholder under section 1361(c)(2)(A)(i) through (iv), the S corporation election will be ineffective or will terminate because the corporation will have an ineligible shareholder. Relief may be available under section 1362(f) for an inadvertent ineffective S corporation election or an inadvertent S corporation election termination. In addition, a trust that qualifies as an ESBT may make an ESBT election notwithstanding that the trust is a wholly-owned grantor trust.

(3) Effect of ESBT election. (i) General rule. If a trust makes a valid ESBT election, the trust will be treated as an ESBT for purposes of chapter 1 of the Internal Revenue Code as of the effective date of the ESBT election.

(ii) Employer Identification Number. An ESBT has only one employer identification number (EIN). If an existing trust makes an ESBT election, the trust continues to use the EIN it currently uses.

(iii) Taxable year. If an ESBT election is effective on a day other than the first day of the trust's taxable year, the ESBT election does not cause the trust's taxable year to close. The termination of the ESBT election (including a termination caused by a conversion of the ESBT to a QSST) other than on the last day of the trust's taxable year also does not cause the trust's taxable year to close. In either case, the trust files one tax return for the taxable year.

(iv) Allocation of S corporation items. If, during the taxable year of an S corporation, a trust is an ESBT for part of the year and an eligible shareholder under section 1361(c)(2)(A)(i) through (iv) for the rest of the year, the S corporation items are allocated between the two types of trusts under section 1377(a). See § 1.1377-1(a)(2)(iii).

(v) Estimated taxes. If an ESBT election is effective on a day other than the first day of the trust's taxable year, the trust is considered one trust for purposes of estimated taxes under section 6654.

(4) Potential current beneficiaries. (i) In general. For purposes of determining whether a corporation is a small business corporation within the meaning of section 1361(b)(1), each potential current beneficiary of an ESBT generally is treated as a shareholder of the corporation. Subject to the provisions of this paragraph (m)(4), a potential current beneficiary generally is, with respect to any period, any person who at any time during such period is entitled to, or in the discretion of any person may receive, a distribution from the principal or income of the trust. A person is treated as a shareholder of the S corporation at any moment in time when that person is entitled to, or in the discretion of any person may, receive a distribution of principal or income of the trust. No person is treated as a potential current beneficiary solely because that person holds any future interest in the trust.

(ii) Grantor trusts. If all or a portion of an ESBT is treated as owned by a person under subpart E, part I, subchapter J, chapter 1 of the Internal Revenue Code, such owner is a potential current beneficiary in addition to persons described in paragraph (m)(4)(i) of this section.

(iii) Special rule for dispositions of stock. Notwithstanding the provisions of paragraph (m)(4)(i) of this section, if a trust disposes of all of the stock which it holds in an S corporation, then, with respect to that corporation, any person who first met the definition of a potential current beneficiary during the 1-year period ending on the date of such disposition is not a potential current beneficiary and thus is not a shareholder of that corporation.

(iv) Distributee trusts. (A) In general. This paragraph (m)(4)(iv) contains the rules for determining who are the potential current beneficiaries of an ESBT if a distributee trust becomes entitled to, or at the discretion of any person, may receive a distribution from principal or income of an ESBT. A distributee trust does not include a trust that is not currently in existence. For this purpose, a trust is not currently in existence if the trust has no assets and no items of income, loss, deduction, or credit. Thus, if a trust instrument provides for a trust to be funded at some future time, the future trust is not currently a distributee trust.

(B) If the distributee trust is not a trust described in section 1361(c)(2)(A), then the distributee trust is the potential current beneficiary of the ESBT and the corporation's S corporation election terminates.

(C) If the distributee trust is a trust described in section 1361(c)(2)(A), the persons who would be its potential current beneficiaries (as defined in paragraphs (m)(4)(i) and (ii) of this section) if the distributee trust were an ESBT are treated as the potential current beneficiaries of the ESBT. Notwithstanding the preceding sentence, however, if the distributee trust is a trust described in section 1361(c)(2)(A)(ii) or (iii), the estate described in section 1361(c)(2)(B) (ii) or (iii) is treated as the potential current beneficiary of the ESBT for the 2-year period during which such trust would be permitted as a shareholder.

(D) For the purposes of paragraph (m)(4)(iv)(C) of this section, a trust will be deemed to be described in section 1361(c)(2)(A) if such trust would qualify for a QSST election under section 1361(d) or an ESBT election under section 1361(e) if it owned S corporation stock.

(v) Contingent distributions. A person who is entitled to receive a distribution only after a specified time or upon the occurrence of a specified event (such as the death of the holder of a power of appointment) is not a potential current beneficiary until such time or the occurrence of such event.

(vi) Currently exercisable powers of appointment and other powers (A) Powers of appointment. A person to whom a distribution may be made during any period pursuant to a power of appointment (as described for transfer tax purposes in section 2041 and § 20.2041-1(b) of this chapter and section 2514 and § 25.2514-1(b) of this chapter) is not a potential current beneficiary unless the power is exercised in favor of that person during the period. It is immaterial for purposes of this paragraph (m)(4)(vi)(A) whether such power of appointment is a "general power of appointment" for transfer tax purposes as described in §§ 20.2041-1(c) and 25.2514-1(c) of this chapter. The mere existence of one or more powers of appointment during the lifetime of a power holder that would permit current distributions from the trust to be made to more than the number of persons described in section 1361(b)(1)(A) or to a person described in section 1361(b)(1)(B) or (C) will not cause the S corporation election to terminate unless one or more of such powers are exercised, collectively, in favor of an excessive number of persons or in favor of a person who is ineligible to be an S corporation shareholder. For purposes of this paragraph (m)(4)(vi)(A), a "power of appointment" includes a power, regardless of by whom held, to add a beneficiary or class of beneficiaries to the class of potential current beneficiaries, but generally does not include a power held by a fiduciary who is not also a beneficiary of the trust to spray or sprinkle trust distributions among beneficiaries. Nothing in this paragraph (m)(4)(vi)(A) alters the definition of "power of appointment" for purposes of any provision of the Internal Revenue Code or the regulations.

(B) Powers to distribute to certain organizations not pursuant to powers of appointment. If a trustee or other fiduciary has a power (that does not constitute a power of appointment for transfer tax purposes as described in §§ 20.2041-1(b) and 25.2514-1(b) of this chapter) to make distributions from the trust to one or more members of a class of organizations described in section 1361(c)(6), such organizations will be counted collectively as only one potential current beneficiary for purposes of this paragraph (m), except that each organization receiving a distribution also will be counted as a potential current beneficiary. This paragraph (m)(4)(vi)(B) shall not apply to a power to currently distribute to one or more particular charitable organizations described in section 1361(c)(6). Each of such organizations is a potential current beneficiary of the trust.

(vii) Number of shareholders. Each potential current beneficiary of the ESBT, as defined in paragraphs (m)(4)(i) through (vi) of this section, is counted as a shareholder of any S corporation whose stock is owned by the ESBT. During any period in which the ESBT has no potential current beneficiaries, the ESBT is counted as the shareholder. A person is counted as only one shareholder of an S corporation even though that person may be treated as a shareholder of the S corporation by direct ownership and through one or more eligible trusts described in section 1361(c)(2)(A). Thus, for example, if a person owns stock in an S corporation and is a potential current beneficiary of an ESBT that owns stock in the same S corporation, that person is counted as one shareholder of the S corporation. Similarly, if a husband owns stock in an S corporation and his wife is a potential current beneficiary of an ESBT that owns stock in the same S corporation, the husband and wife will be counted as one shareholder of the S corporation.

(viii) Miscellaneous. Payments made by an ESBT to a third party on behalf of a beneficiary are considered to be payments made directly to the beneficiary. The right of a beneficiary to assign the beneficiary's interest to a third party does not result in the third party being a potential current beneficiary until that interest is actually assigned.

(5) ESBT terminations. (i) Ceasing to meet ESBT requirements. A trust ceases to be an ESBT on the first day the trust fails to meet the definition of an ESBT under section 1361(e). The last day the trust is treated as an ESBT is the day before the date on which the trust fails to meet the definition of an ESBT.

(ii) Disposition of S stock. In general, a trust ceases to be an ESBT on the first day following the day the trust disposes of all S corporation stock. However, if the trust is using the installment method to report income from the sale or disposition of its stock in an S corporation, the trust ceases to be an ESBT on the day following the earlier of the day the last installment payment is received by the trust or the day the trust disposes of the installment obligation.

(iii) Potential current beneficiaries that are ineligible shareholders. If a potential current beneficiary of an ESBT is not an eligible shareholder of a small business corporation within the meaning of section 1361(b)(1), the S corporation election terminates. For example, the S corporation election will terminate if a nonresident alien becomes a potential current beneficiary of an ESBT. Such a potential current beneficiary is treated as an ineligible shareholder beginning on the day such person becomes a potential current beneficiary, and the S corporation election terminates on that date. However, see the special rule of paragraph (m)(4)(iii) of this section. If the S corporation election terminates, relief may be available under section 1362(f).

(6) Revocation of ESBT election. An ESBT election may be revoked only with the consent of the Commissioner. The application for consent to revoke the election must be submitted to the Internal Revenue Service in the form of a letter ruling request under the appropriate revenue procedure.

(7) Converting an ESBT to a QSST. For a trust that seeks to convert from an ESBT to a QSST, the consent of the Commissioner is hereby granted to revoke the ESBT election as of the effective date of the QSST election, if all the following requirements are met:

(i) The trust meets all of the requirements to be a QSST under section 1361(d).

(ii) The trustee and the current income beneficiary of the trust sign the QSST election. The QSST election must be filed with the service center where the S corporation files its income tax return. This QSST election must state at the top of the document "ATTENTION ENTITY CONTROL—CONVERSION OF AN ESBT TO A QSST PURSUANT TO SECTION 1.1361-1(m)" and include all information otherwise required for a QSST election under § 1.1361-1(j)(6). A separate QSST election must be made with respect to the stock of each S corporation held by the trust.

(iii) The trust has not converted from a QSST to an ESBT within the 36-month period preceding the effective date of the new QSST election.

(iv) The date on which the QSST election is to be effective cannot be more than 15 days and two months prior to the date on which the election is filed and cannot be more than 12 months after the date on which the election is filed. If an election specifies an effective date more than 15 days and two months prior to the date on which the election is filed, it will be effective on the day that is 15 days and two months prior to the date on which it is filed. If an election specifies an effective date more than 12 months after the date on which the election is filed, it will be effective on the day that is 12 months after the date it is filed.

(8) Examples. The provisions of this paragraph (m) are illustrated by the following examples in which it is assumed, unless otherwise specified, that all noncorporate persons are citizens or residents of the United States:

Example (1). (i) ESBT election with section 663(c) separate shares. On January 1, 2003, M contributes S corporation stock to Trust for the benefit of M's three children A, B, and C. Pursuant to section 663(c), each of Trust's separate shares for A, B, and C will be treated as separate trusts for purposes of determining the amount of distributable net income (DNI) in the application of sections 661 and 662. On January 15, 2003, the trustee of Trust files a valid ESBT election for Trust effective January 1, 2003. Trust will be treated as a single ESBT and will have a single S portion taxable under section 641(c).

(ii) ESBT acquires stock of an additional S corporation. On February 15, 2003, Trust acquires stock of an additional S corporation. Because Trust is already an ESBT, Trust does not need to make an additional ESBT election.

(iii) Section 663(c) shares of ESBT convert to separate QSSTs. Effective January 1, 2004, A, B, C, and Trust's trustee elect to convert each separate share of Trust into a separate QSST pursuant to paragraph (m)(7) of this section. For each separate share, they file a separate election for each S corporation whose stock is held by Trust. Each separate share will be treated as a separate QSST.

Example (2). (i) Invalid potential current beneficiary. Effective January 1, 2005, Trust makes a valid ESBT election. On January 1, 2006, A, a nonresident alien, becomes a potential current beneficiary of Trust. Trust does not dispose of all of its S corporation stock within one year after January 1, 2006. As of January 1, 2006, A is the potential current beneficiary of Trust and therefore is treated as a shareholder of the S corporation. Because A is not an eligible shareholder of an S corporation under section 1361(b)(1), the S corporation election of any corporation in which Trust holds stock terminates effective January 1, 2006. Relief may be available under section 1362(f).

(ii) Invalid potential current beneficiary and disposition of S stock. Assume the same facts as in Example 2 (i) except that within one year after January 1, 2006, trustee of Trust disposes of all Trust's S corporation stock. A is not considered a potential current beneficiary of Trust and therefore is not treated as a shareholder of any S corporation in which Trust previously held stock.

Example (3). Subpart E trust. M transfers stock in X, an S corporation, and other assets to Trust for the benefit of B and B's siblings. M retains no powers or interest in Trust. Under section 678(a), B is treated as the owner of a portion of Trust that includes a portion of the X stock. No beneficiary has acquired any portion of his or her interest in Trust by purchase, and Trust is not an ineligible trust under paragraph (m)(1)(iv) of this section. Trust is eligible to make an ESBT election.

Example (4). Subpart E trust continuing after grantor's death. On January 1, 2003, M transfers stock in X, an S corporation, and other assets to Trust. Under the terms of Trust, the trustee of Trust has complete discretion to distribute the income or principal to M during M's lifetime and to M's children upon M's death. During M's life, M is treated as the owner of Trust under section 677. The trustee of Trust makes a valid election to treat Trust as an ESBT effective January 1, 2003. On March 28, 2004, M dies. Under applicable local law, Trust does not terminate on M's death. Trust continues to be an ESBT after M's death, and no additional ESBT election needs to be filed for Trust after M's death.

Example (5). Potential current beneficiaries and distributee trust holding S corporation stock. Trust-1 has a valid ESBT election in effect. The trustee of Trust-1 has the power to make distributions to A directly or to any trust created for the benefit of A. On January 1, 2003, M creates Trust-2 for the benefit of A. Also on January 1, 2003, the trustee of Trust-1 distributes some S corporation stock to Trust-2. A, as the current income beneficiary of Trust-2, makes a timely and effective election to treat Trust-2 as a QSST. Because Trust-2 is a valid S corporation shareholder, the distribution to Trust-2 does not terminate the ESBT election of Trust-1. Trust-2 itself will not be counted toward the shareholder limit of section 1361(b)(1)(A). Additionally, because A is already counted as an S corporation shareholder because of A's status as a potential current income beneficiary of Trust-1, A is not counted again by reason of A's status as the deemed owner of Trust-2.

Example (6). Potential current beneficiaries and distributee trust not holding S corporation stock.

(i) Distributee trust that would itself qualify as an ESBT. Trust-1 holds stock in X, an S corporation, and has a valid ESBT election in effect. Under the terms of Trust-1, the trustee has discretion to make distributions to A, B, and Trust-2, a trust for the benefit of C, D, and E. Trust-2 would qualify to be an ESBT, but it owns no S corporation stock and has made no ESBT election. Under paragraph (m)(4)(iv) of this section, Trust-2's potential current beneficiaries are treated as the potential current beneficiaries of Trust-1 and are counted as shareholders for purposes of section 1361(b)(1). Thus, A, B, C, D, and E are potential current beneficiaries of Trust-1 and are counted as shareholders for purposes of section 1361(b)(1). Trust-2 itself will not be counted as a shareholder of Trust-1 for purposes of section 1361(b)(1).

(ii) Distributee trust that would not qualify as an ESBT or a QSST. Assume the same facts as in paragraph (i) of this Example 6 except that D is a nonresident alien. Trust-2 would not be eligible to make an ESBT or QSST election if it owned S corporation stock and therefore Trust-2 is a potential current beneficiary of Trust-1. Since Trust-2 is not an eligible shareholder, X's S corporation election terminates.

(iii) Distributee trust that is a section 1361(c)(2)(A)(ii) trust. Assume the same facts as in paragraph (i) of this Example 6 except that Trust-2 is a trust treated as owned by A under section 676 because A has the power to revoke Trust-2 at any time prior to A's death. On January 1, 2003, A dies. Because Trust-2 is a trust described in section 1361(c)(2)(A)(ii) during the 2-year period beginning on the day of A's death, under paragraph (m)(4)(iv)(C) of this section, Trust-2's only potential current beneficiary is the person listed in section 1361(c)(2)(B)(ii), A's estate. Thus, B and A's estate are potential current beneficiaries of Trust-1 and are counted as shareholders for purposes of section 1361(b)(1).

Example (7). Potential current beneficiaries and powers of appointment. M creates Trust from which A has a right to all net income and funds it with S corporation stock. A also has a currently exercisable power to appoint income or principal to anyone except A; A's creditors, A's estate, and the creditors of A's estate. The potential current beneficiaries of Trust for any period will be A and each person who receives a distribution from Trust pursuant to A's exercise of A's power of appointment during that period.

Example (8). Power to distribute to an unlimited class of charitable organizations not pursuant to a power of appointment. M creates Trust from which A has a right to all net income and funds it with S corporation stock. In addition, the trustee of Trust, who is not A or a descendant of M, has the power to make discretionary distributions of principal to the living descendants of M and to any organizations described in section 1361(c)(6). The potential current beneficiaries of Trust for any period will be A, each then-living descendant of M, and each exempt organization described in section 1361(c)(6) that receives a distribution during that period. In addition, the class of exempt organizations will be counted as one potential current beneficiary.

Example (9). Power to distribute to a class of named charitable organizations not pursuant to a power of appointment. M creates Trust from which A has a right to all net income and funds it with S corporation stock. In addition, the trustee of Trust, who is not A or a descendant of M, has the power to make discretionary distributions of principal to the living descendants of M and to X, Y, and Z, each of which is an organization described in section 1361(c)(6). The potential current beneficiaries of Trust for any period will be A, X, Y, Z, and each living descendant of M.

(9) Effective date. This paragraph (m) is applicable for taxable years of ESBTs beginning on and after May 14, 2002. Paragraphs (m)(2)(ii)(A), (m)(4)(iii) and (vi), and (m)(8), Example 2, Example 5, Example 7, Example 8, and Example 9 of this section are effective on August 14, 2008.

T.D. 8419, 5/28/92, amend T.D. 8600, 7/20/95, T.D. 8869, 1/20/2000, T.D. 8940, 2/12/2001, T.D. 8994, 5/13/2002, T.D. 9078, 7/16/2003, T.D. 9422, 8/13/2008.

§ 1.1361-2 Definitions relating to S corporation subsidiaries.

(a) In general. The term qualified subchapter S subsidiary (QSub) means any domestic corporation that is not an ineligible corporation (as defined in section 1361(b)(2) and the regulations thereunder), if—

(1) 100 percent of the stock of such corporation is held by an S corporation; and

(2) The S corporation properly elects to treat the subsidiary as a QSub under § 1.1361-3.

(b) Stock treated as held by S corporation. For purposes of satisfying the 100 percent stock ownership requirement in section 1361(b)(3)(B)(i) and paragraph (a)(1) of this section—

(1) Stock of a corporation is treated as held by an S corporation if the S corporation is the owner of that stock for Federal income tax purposes; and

(2) Any outstanding instruments, obligations, or arrangements of the corporation which would not be considered stock for purposes of section 1361(b)(1)(D) if the corporation were an S corporation are not treated as outstanding stock of the QSub.

(c) Straight debt safe harbor. Section 1.1361-1(l)(5)(iv) and (v) apply to an obligation of a corporation for which a QSub election is made if that obligation would satisfy the definition of straight debt in § 1.1361-1(l)(5) if issued by the S corporation.

(d) Examples. The following examples illustrate the application of this section:

Example (1). X, an S corporation, owns 100 percent of Y, a corporation for which a valid QSub election is in effect for the taxable year. Y owns 100 percent of Z, a corporation otherwise eligible for QSub status. X may elect to treat Z as a QSub under section 1361(b)(3)(B)(ii).

Example (2). Assume the same facts as in Example 1, except that Y is a business entity that is disregarded as an entity separate from its owner under § 301.7701-2(c)(2) of this chapter. X may elect to treat Z as a QSub.

Example (3). Assume the same facts as in Example 1, except that Y owns 50 percent of Z, and X owns the other 50 percent. X may elect to treat Z as a QSub.

Example (4). Assume the same facts as in Example 1, except that Y is a C corporation. Although Y is a domestic corporation that is otherwise eligible to be a QSub, no QSub election has been made for Y. Thus, X is not treated as holding the stock of Z. Consequently, X may not elect to treat Z as a QSub.

Example (5). Individuals A and B own 100 percent of the stock of corporation X, an S corporation, and, except for C's interest (described below), X owns 100 percent of corporation Y, a C corporation. Individual C holds an instrument issued by Y that is considered to be equity under general principles of tax law but would satisfy the definition of straight debt under § 1.1361-1(l)(5) if Y were an S corporation. In determining whether X owns 100 percent of Y for purposes of making the QSub election, the instrument held by C is not considered outstanding stock. In addition, under § 1.1361-1(l)(5)(v), the QSub election is not treated as an exchange of debt for stock with respect to such instrument, and § 1.1361-1(l)(5)(iv) applies to determine the tax treatment of payments on the instrument while Y's QSub election is in effect.

T.D. 8869, 1/20/2000.

§ 1.1361-3 QSub election.

(a) Time and manner of making election. *(1) In general.* The corporation for which the QSub election is made must meet all the requirements of section 1361(b)(3)(B) at the time the election is made and for all periods for which the election is to be effective.

(2) Manner of making election. Except as provided in section 1361(b)(3)(D) and § 1.1361-5(c) (five-year prohibition on re-election), an S corporation may elect to treat an eligible subsidiary as a QSub by filing a completed form to be prescribed by the IRS. The election form must be signed by a person authorized to sign the S corporation's return required to be filed under section 6037. Unless the election form provides otherwise, the election must be submitted to the service center where the subsidiary filed its most recent tax return (if applicable), and, if an S corporation forms a subsidiary and makes a valid QSub election (effective upon the date of the subsidiary's formation) for the subsidiary, the election should be submitted to the service center where the S corporation filed its most recent return.

(3) Time of making election. A QSub election may be made by the S corporation parent at any time during the taxable year.

(4) Effective date of election. A QSub election will be effective on the date specified on the election form or on the

date the election form is filed if no date is specified. The effective date specified on the form cannot be more than two months and 15 days prior to the date of filing and cannot be more than 12 months after the date of filing. For this purpose, the definition of the term month found in § 1.1362-6(a)(2)(ii)(C) applies. If an election form specifies an effective date more than two months and 15 days prior to the date on which the election form is filed, it will be effective two months and 15 days prior to the date it is filed. If an election form specifies an effective date more than 12 months after the date on which the election is filed, it will be effective 12 months after the date it is filed.

(5) Example. The following example illustrates the application of paragraph (a)(4) of this section:

Example. X has been a calendar year S corporation engaged in a trade or business for several years. X acquires the stock of Y, a calendar year C corporation, on April 1, 2002. On August 10, 2002, X makes an election to treat Y as a QSub. Unless otherwise specified on the election form, the election will be effective as of August 10, 2002. If specified on the election form, the election may be effective on some other date that is not more than two months and 15 days prior to August 10, 2002, and not more than 12 months after August 10, 2002.

(6) Extension of time for making a QSub election. An extension of time to make a QSub election may be available under the procedures applicable under §§ 301.9100-1 and 301.9100-3 of this chapter.

(b) Revocation of QSub election. *(1) Manner of revoking QSub election.* An S corporation may revoke a QSub election under section 1361 by filing a statement with the service center where the S corporation's most recent tax return was properly filed. The revocation statement must include the names, addresses, and taxpayer identification numbers of both the parent S corporation and the QSub, if any. The statement must be signed by a person authorized to sign the S corporation's return required to be filed under section 6037.

(2) Effective date of revocation. The revocation of a QSub election is effective on the date specified on the revocation statement or on the date the revocation statement is filed if no date is specified. The effective date specified on the revocation statement cannot be more than two months and 15 days prior to the date on which the revocation statement is filed and cannot be more than 12 months after the date on which the revocation statement is filed. If a revocation statement specifies an effective date more than two months and 15 days prior to the date on which the statement is filed, it will be effective two months and 15 days prior to the date it is filed. If a revocation statement specifies an effective date more than 12 months after the date on which the statement is filed, it will be effective 12 months after the date it is filed.

(3) Revocation after termination. A revocation may not be made after the occurrence of an event that renders the subsidiary ineligible for QSub status under section 1361(b)(3)(B).

(4) Revocation before QSub election effective. For purposes of Section 1361(b)(3)(D) and § 1.1361-5(c) (five-year prohibition on re-election), a revocation effective on the first day the QSub election was to be effective will not be treated as a termination of a QSub election.

T.D. 8869, 1/20/2000.

§ 1.1361-4 Effect of QSub election.

Caution: The Treasury has not yet amended Reg § 1.1361-4 to reflect changes made by P.L. 108-357.

(a) Separate existence ignored. *(1) In general.* Except as otherwise provided in paragraphs (a)(3), (a)(6), (a)(7), (a)(8), and (a)(9) of this section, for Federal tax purposes—

(i) A corporation that is a QSub shall not be treated as a separate corporation; and

(ii) All assets, liabilities, and items of income, deduction, and credit of a QSub shall be treated as assets, liabilities, and items of income, deduction, and credit of the S corporation.

(2) Liquidation of subsidiary. (i) In general. If an S corporation makes a valid QSub election with respect to a subsidiary, the subsidiary is deemed to have liquidated into the S corporation. Except as provided in paragraph (a)(5) of this section, the tax treatment of the liquidation or of a larger transaction that includes the liquidation will be determined under the Internal Revenue Code and general principles of tax law, including the step transaction doctrine. Thus, for example, if an S corporation forms a subsidiary and makes a valid QSub election (effective upon the date of the subsidiary's formation) for the subsidiary, the transfer of assets to the subsidiary and the deemed liquidation are disregarded, and the corporation will be deemed to be a QSub from its inception.

(ii) Examples. The following examples illustrate the application of this paragraph (a)(2)(i) of this section:

Example (1). Corporation X acquires all of the outstanding stock of solvent corporation Y from an unrelated individual for cash and short-term notes. Thereafter, as part of the same plan, X immediately makes an S election and a QSub election for Y. Because X acquired all of the stock of Y in a qualified stock purchase within the meaning of section 338(d)(3), the liquidation described in paragraph (a)(2) of this section is respected as an independent step separate from the stock acquisition, and the tax consequences of the liquidation are determined under sections 332 and 337.

Example (2). Corporation X, pursuant to a plan, acquires all of the outstanding stock of corporation Y from the shareholders of Y solely in exchange for 10 percent of the voting stock of X. Prior to the transaction, Y and its shareholders are unrelated to X. Thereafter, as part of the same plan, X immediately makes an S election and a QSub election for Y. The transaction is a reorganization described in section 368(a)(1)(C), assuming the other conditions for reorganization treatment (e.g., continuity of business enterprise) are satisfied.

Example (3). After the expiration of the transition period provided in paragraph (a)(5)(i) of this section, individual A, pursuant to a plan, contributes all of the outstanding stock of Y to his wholly owned S corporation, X, and immediately causes X to make a QSub election for Y. The transaction is a reorganization under section 368(a)(1)(D), assuming the other conditions for reorganization treatment (e.g., continuity of business enterprise) are satisfied. If the sum of the amount of liabilities of Y treated as assumed by X exceeds the total of the adjusted basis of the property of Y, then section 357(c) applies and such excess is considered as gain from the sale or exchange of a capital asset or of property which is not a capital asset, as the case may be.

(iii) Adoption of plan of liquidation. For purposes of satisfying the requirement of adoption of a plan of liquidation under section 332, unless a formal plan of liquidation that contemplates the QSub election is adopted on an earlier date, the making of the QSub election is considered to be the adoption of a plan of liquidation immediately before the deemed liquidation described in paragraph (a)(2)(i) of this section.

(iv) Example. The following example illustrates the application of paragraph (a)(2)(iii) of this section:

Example. Corporation X owns 75 percent of a solvent corporation Y, and individual A owns the remaining 25 percent of Y. As part of a plan to make a QSub election for Y, X causes Y to redeem A's 25 percent interest on June 1 for cash and makes a QSub election for Y effective on June 3. The making of the QSub election is considered to be the adoption of a plan of liquidation immediately before the deemed liquidation. The deemed liquidation satisfies the requirements of section 332.

(v) Stock ownership requirements of section 332. The deemed exercise of an option under § 1.1504-4 and any instruments, obligations, or arrangements that are not considered stock under § 1.1361-2(b)(2) are disregarded in determining if the stock ownership requirements of section 332(b) are met with respect to the deemed liquidation provided in paragraph (a)(2)(i) of this section.

(3) Treatment of banks. (i) In general. If an S corporation is a bank, or if an S corporation makes a valid QSub election for a subsidiary that is a bank, any special rules applicable to banks under the Internal Revenue Code continue to apply separately to the bank parent or bank subsidiary as if the deemed liquidation of any QSub under paragraph (a)(2) of this section had not occurred (except as other published guidance may apply section 265(b) and section 291(a)(3) and (e)(1)(B) not only to the bank parent or bank subsidiary but also to any QSub deemed to have liquidated under paragraph (a)(2) of this section). For any QSub that is a bank, however, all assets, liabilities, and items of income, deduction, and credit of the QSub, as determined in accordance with the special bank rules, are treated as assets, liabilities, and items of income, deduction, and credit of the S corporation. For purposes of this paragraph (a)(3)(i), the term bank has the same meaning as in section 581.

(ii) Examples. The following examples illustrate the application of this paragraph (a)(3):

Example (1). X, an S corporation, is a bank as defined in section 581. X owns 100 percent of Y and Z, corporations for which valid QSub elections are in effect. Y is a bank as defined in section 581, and Z is not a financial institution. Pursuant to paragraph (a)(3)(i) of this section, any special rules applicable to banks under the Internal Revenue Code continue to apply separately to X and Y and do not apply to Z. Thus, for example, section 265(b), which provides special rules for interest expense deductions of banks, applies separately to X and Y. That is, X and Y each must make a separate determination under section 265(b) of interest expense allocable to tax-exempt interest, and no deduction is allowed for that interest expense. Section 265(b) does not apply to Z except as published guidance may provide otherwise.

Example (2). X, an S corporation, is a bank holding company and thus is not a bank as defined in section 581. X owns 100 percent of Y, a corporation for which a valid QSub election is in effect. Y is a bank as defined in section 581. Pursuant to paragraph (a)(3)(i) of this section, any special rules applicable to banks under the Internal Revenue Code continue to apply to Y and do not apply to X. However, all of Y's assets, liabilities, and items of income, deduction, and credit, as determined in accordance with the special bank rules, are treated as those of X. Thus, for example, section 582(c), which provides special rules for sales and exchanges of debt by banks, applies only to sales and exchanges by Y. However, any gain or loss on such a transaction by Y that is considered ordinary income or ordinary loss pursuant to section 582(c) is treated as ordinary income or ordinary loss of X.

(iii) Effective date. This paragraph (a)(3) applies to taxable years beginning after December 31, 1996.

(4) Treatment of stock of QSub. Except for purposes of section 1361(b)(3)(B)(i) and § 1.1361-2(a)(1), the stock of a QSub shall be disregarded for all Federal tax purposes.

(5) Transitional relief. (i) General rule. If an S corporation and another corporation (the related corporation) are persons specified in section 267(b) prior to an acquisition by the S corporation of some or all of the stock of the related corporation followed by a QSub election for the related corporation, the step transaction doctrine will not apply to determine the tax consequences of the acquisition. This paragraph (a)(5) shall apply to QSub elections effective before January 1, 2001.

(ii) Examples. The following examples illustrate the application of this paragraph (a)(5):

Example (1). Individual A owns 100 percent of the stock of X, an S corporation. X owns 79 percent of the stock of Y, a solvent corporation, and A owns the remaining 21 percent. On May 4, 1998, A contributes its Y stock to X in exchange for X stock. X makes a QSub election with respect to Y effective immediately following the transfer. The liquidation described in paragraph (a)(2) of this section is respected as an independent step separate from the stock acquisition, and the tax consequences of the liquidation are determined under sections 332 and 337. The contribution by A of the Y stock qualifies under section 351, and no gain or loss is recognized by A, X, or Y.

Example (2). Individual A owns 100 percent of the stock of two solvent S corporations, X and Y. On May 4, 1998, A contributes the stock of Y to X. X makes a QSub election with respect to Y immediately following the transfer. The liquidation described in paragraph (a)(2) of this section is respected as an independent step separate from the stock acquisition, and the tax consequences of the liquidation are determined under sections 332 and 337. The contribution by A of the Y stock to X qualifies under section 351, and no gain or loss is recognized by A, X, or Y. Y is not treated as a C corporation for any period solely because of the transfer of its stock to X, an ineligible shareholder. Compare Example 3 of § 1.1361-4(a)(2)(ii).

(6) Treatment of certain QSubs. (i) In general. A QSub, even though it is generally not treated as a corporation separate from the S corporation, is treated as a separate corporation for purposes of:

(A) Federal tax liabilities of the QSub with respect to any taxable period for which the QSub was treated as a separate corporation.

(B) Federal tax liabilities of any other entity for which the QSub is liable.

(C) Refunds or credits of Federal tax.

(ii) Examples. The following examples illustrate the application of paragraph (a)(6)(i) of this section:

Example (1). X has owned all of the outstanding stock of Y, a domestic corporation that reports its taxes on a calendar year basis, since 2001. X and Y do not report their taxes on a consolidated basis. For 2003, X makes a timely S election and simultaneously makes a QSub election for Y. In 2004, the Internal Revenue Service (IRS) seeks to extend the period of limitations on assessment for Y's 2001 taxable year. Because Y was treated as a separate corporation for its 2001 taxable year, Y is the proper party to sign the consent to extend the period of limitations.

Example (2). The facts are the same as in Example 1, except that in 2004, the IRS determines that Y miscalculated and underreported its income tax liability for 2001. Because Y was treated as a separate corporation for its 2001 taxable year, the deficiency for Y's 2001 taxable year may be assessed against Y and, in the event that Y fails to pay the liability after notice and demand, a general tax lien will arise against all of Y's property and rights to property.

Example (3). X is a QSub of Y. In 2001, Z, a domestic corporation that reports its taxes on a calendar year basis, merges into X in a state law merger. Z was not a member of a consolidated group at any time during its taxable year ending in December 2000. Under the applicable state law, X is the successor to Z and is liable for all of Z's debts. In 2003, the IRS seeks to extend the period of limitations on assessment for Z's 2000 taxable year. Because X is the successor to Z and is liable for Z's 2000 taxes that remain unpaid, X is the proper party to execute the consent to extend the period of limitations on assessment.

(iii) Effective date. This paragraph (a)(6) applies on or after April 1, 2004.

(7) Treatment of QSubs for purposes of employment taxes. (i) In general. A QSub is treated as a separate corporation for purposes of Subtitle C—Employment Taxes and Collection of Income Tax (Chapters 21, 22, 23, 23A, 24, and 25 of the Internal Revenue Code).

(ii) Effective/applicability date. This paragraph (a)(7) applies with respect to wages paid on or after January 1, 2009.

(8) Treatment of QSubs for purposes of certain excise taxes. (i) In general. A QSub is treated as a separate corporation for purposes of—

(A) Federal tax liabilities imposed by Chapters 31, 32 (other than section 4181), 33, 34, 35, 36 (other than section 4461), and 38 of the Internal Revenue Code, or any floor stocks tax imposed on articles subject to any of these taxes;

(B) Collection of tax imposed by Chapter 33 of the Internal Revenue Code;

(C) Registration under sections 4101, 4222, and 4412; and

(D) Claims of a credit (other than a credit under section 34), refund, or payment related to a tax described in paragraph (a)(8)(i)(A) of this section or under section 6426 or 6427.

(ii) Effective/applicability date. This paragraph (a)(8) applies to liabilities imposed and actions first required or permitted in periods beginning on or after January 1, 2008.

(9) Information returns. (i) In general. Except to the extent provided by the Secretary or Commissioner in guidance (including forms or instructions), paragraph (a)(1) of this section shall not apply to part III of subchapter A of chapter 61, relating to information returns.

(ii) Effective/applicability date. This paragraph (a)(9) is effective on August 14, 2008.

(b) Timing of the liquidation. *(1) In general.* Except as otherwise provided in paragraph (b)(3) or (4) of this section, the liquidation described in paragraph (a)(2) of this section occurs at the close of the day before the QSub election is effective. Thus, for example, if a C corporation elects to be treated as an S corporation and makes a QSub election (effective the same date as the S election) with respect to a subsidiary, the liquidation occurs immediately before the S election becomes effective, while the S electing parent is still a C corporation.

(2) Application to elections in tiered situations. When QSub elections for a tiered group of subsidiaries are effective on the same date, the S corporation may specify the order of the liquidations. If no order is specified, the liquidations that are deemed to occur as a result of the QSub elections will be treated as occurring first for the lowest tier entity and proceed successively upward until all of the liquidations under paragraph (a)(2) of this section have occurred. For example, S, an S corporation, owns 100 percent of C, the common parent of an affiliated group of corporations that includes X and Y. C owns all of the stock of X and X owns all of the stock of Y. S elects under § 1.1361-3 to treat C, X and Y as QSubs effective on the same date. If no order is specified for the elections, the following liquidations are deemed to occur as a result of the elections, with each successive liquidation occuring on the same day immediately after the preceding liquidation: Y is treated as liquidating into X, then X is treated as liquidating into C, and finally C is treated as liquidating into S.

(3) Acquisitions. (i) In general. If an S corporation does not own 100 percent of the stock of the subsidiary on the day before the QSub election is effective, the liquidation described in paragraph (a)(2) of this section occurs immediately after the time at which the S corporation first owns 100 percent of the stock.

(ii) Special rules for acquired S corporations. Except as provided in paragraph (b)(4) of this section, if a corporation (Y) for which an election under section 1362(a) was in effect is acquired, and a QSub election is made effective on the day Y is acquired, Y is deemed to liquidate into the S corporation at the beginning of the day the termination of its S election is effective. As a result, if corporation X acquires Y, an S corporation, and makes an S election for itself and a QSub election for Y effective on the day of acquisition, Y liquidates into X at the beginning of the day when X's S election is effective, and there is no period between the termination of Y's S election and the deemed liquidation of Y during which Y is a C corporation. Y's taxable year ends for all Federal income tax purposes at the close of the preceding day. Furthermore, if Y owns Z, a corporation for which a QSub election was in effect prior to the acquisition of Y by X, and X makes QSub elections for Y and Z, effective on the day of acquisition, the transfer of assets to Z and the deemed liquidation of Z are disregarded. See §§ 1.1361-4(a)(2) and 1.1361-5(b)(1)(i).

(4) Coordination with section 338 election. An S corporation that makes a qualified stock purchase of a target may make an election under section 338 with respect to the acquisition if it meets the requirements for the election, and may make a QSub election with respect to the target. If an S corporation makes an election under section 338 with respect to a subsidiary acquired in a qualified stock purchase, a QSub election made with respect to that subsidiary is not effective before the day after the acquisition date (within the meaning of section 338(h)(2)). If the QSub election is effective on the day after the acquisition date, the liquidation under paragraph (a)(2) of this section occurs immediately after the deemed asset purchase by the new target corporation under section 338. If an S corporation makes an election under section 338 (without a section 338(h)(10) election) with respect to a target, the target must file a final return as a C corporation reflecting the deemed sale. See § 1.338-

10(a). If the target was an S corporation on the day before the acquisition date, the final return as a C corporation must reflect the activities of the target for the acquisition date, including the deemed sale. See § 1.338-10(a)(3).

(c) Carryover of disallowed losses and deductions. If an S corporation (S1) acquires the stock of another S corporation (S2), and S1 makes a QSub election with respect to S2 effective on the day of the acquisition, see § 1.1366-2(c)(1) for provisions relating to the carryover of losses and deductions with respect to a former shareholder of S2 that may be available to that shareholder as a shareholder of S1.

(d) Examples. The following examples illustrate the application of this section:

Example (1). X, an S corporation, owns 100 percent of the stock of Y, a C corporation. On June 2, 2002, X makes a valid QSub election for Y, effective June 2, 2002. Assume that, under general principles of tax law, including the step transaction doctrine, X's acquisition of the Y stock and the subsequent QSub election would not be treated as related. The liquidation described in paragraph (a)(2) of this section occurs at the close of the day on June 1, 2002, the day before the QSub election is effective, and the plan of liquidation is considered adopted on that date. Y's taxable year and separate existence for Federal tax purposes end at the close of June 1, 2002.

Example (2). X, a C corporation, owns 100 percent of the stock of Y, another C corporation. On December 31, 2002, X makes an election under section 1362 to be treated as an S corporation and a valid QSub election for Y, both effective January 1, 2003. Assume that, under general principles of tax law, including the step transaction doctrine, X's acquisition of the Y stock and the subsequent QSub election would not be treated as related. The liquidation described in paragraph (a)(2) of this section occurs at the close of December 31, 2002, the day before the QSub election is effective. The QSub election for Y is effective on the same day that X's S election is effective, and the deemed liquidation is treated as occurring before the S election is effective, when X is still a C corporation. Y's taxable year ends at the close of December 31, 2002. See § 1.381(b)-1.

Example (3). On June 1, 2002, X, an S corporation, acquires 100 percent of the stock of Y, an existing S corporation, for cash in a transaction meeting the requirements of a qualified stock purchase (QSP) under section 338. X immediately makes a QSub election for Y effective June 2, 2002, and also makes a joint election under section 338(h)(10) with the shareholder of Y. Under section 338(a) and § 1.338(h)(10)-1(d)(3), Y is treated as having sold all of its assets at the close of the acquisition date, June 1, 2002. Y is treated as a new corporation which purchased all of those assets as of the beginning of June 2, 2002, the day after the acquisition date. Section 338(a)(2). The QSub election is effective on June 2, 2002, and the liquidation under paragraph (a)(2) of this section occurs immediately after the deemed asset purchase by the new corporation.

Example (4). X, an S corporation, owns 100 percent of Y, a corporation for which a QSub election is in effect. On May 12, 2002, a date on which the QSub election is in effect, X issues Y a $10,000 note under state law that matures in ten years with a market rate of interest. Y is not treated as a separate corporation, and X's issuance of the note to Y on May 12, 2002, is disregarded for Federal tax purposes.

Example (5). X, an S corporation, owns 100 percent of the stock of Y, a C corporation. At a time when Y is indebted to X in an amount that exceeds the fair market value of Y's assets, X makes a QSub election effective on the date it is filed with respect to Y. The liquidation described in paragraph (a)(2) of this section does not qualify under sections 332 and 337 and, thus, Y recognizes gain or loss on the assets distributed, subject to the limitations of section 267.

T.D. 8869, 1/20/2000, amend T.D. 8940, 2/12/2001, T.D. 9183, 2/24/2005, T.D. 9356, 8/15/2007, T.D. 9422, 8/13/2008.

§ 1.1361-5 Termination of QSub election.

Caution: The Treasury has not yet amended Reg § 1.1361-5 to reflect changes made by P.L. 110-28.

(a) In general. *(1) Effective date.* The termination of a QSub election is effective—

(i) On the effective date contained in the revocation statement if a QSub election is revoked under § 1.1361-3(b);

(ii) At the close of the last day of the parent's last taxable year as an S corporation if the parent's S election terminates under § 1.1362-2; or

(iii) At the close of the day on which an event (other than an event described in paragraph (a)(1)(ii) of this section) occurs that renders the subsidiary ineligible for QSub status under section 1361(b)(3)(B).

(2) Information to be provided upon termination of QSub election by failure to qualify as a QSub. If a QSub election terminates because an event renders the subsidiary ineligible for QSub status, the S corporation must attach to its return for the taxable year in which the termination occurs a notification that a QSub election has terminated, the date of the termination, and the names, addresses, and employer identification numbers of both the parent corporation and the QSub.

(3) QSub joins a consolidated group. If a QSub election terminates because the S corporation becomes a member of a consolidated group (and no election under section 338(g) is made) the principles of § 1.1502-76(b)(1)(ii)(A)(2) (relating to a special rule for S corporations that join a consolidated group) apply to any QSub of the S corporation that also becomes a member of the consolidated group at the same time as the S corporation. See Example 4 of paragraph (a)(4) of this section.

(4) Examples. The following examples illustrate the application of this paragraph (a):

Example (1). Termination because parent's S election terminates. X, an S corporation, owns 100 percent of Y. A QSub election is in effect with respect to Y for 2001. Effective on January 1, 2002, X revokes its S election. Because X is no longer an S corporation, Y no longer qualifies as a QSub at the close of December 31, 2001.

Example (2). Termination due to transfer of QSub stock. X, an S corporation, owns 100 percent of Y. A QSub election is in effect with respect to Y. On December 10, 2002, X sells one share of Y stock to A, an individual. Because X no longer owns 100 percent of the stock of Y, Y no longer qualifies as a QSub. Accordingly, the QSub election made with respect to Y terminates at the close of December 10, 2002.

Example (3). No termination on stock transfer between QSub and parent. X, an S corporation, owns 100 percent of the stock of Y, and Y owns 100 percent of the stock of Z. QSub elections are in effect with respect to both Y and Z. Y transfers all of its Z stock to X. Because X is treated as owning the stock of Z both before and after the transfer of stock solely for purposes of determining whether the requirements of section 1361(b)(3)(B)(i) and § 1.1361-2(a)(1) have been satisfied, the transfer of Z stock does not terminate Z's QSub election. Because the stock of Z is disregarded for all other Federal tax purposes, no gain is recognized under section 311.

Example (4). Termination due to acquisition of S parent by a consolidated group. X, an S corporation, owns 100 percent of Y, a corporation for which a QSub election is in effect. Z, the common parent of a consolidated group of corporations, acquires 80 percent of the stock of X on June 1, 2002. Z does not make an election under section 338(g) with respect to the purchase of X stock. X's S election terminates as of the close of the preceding day, May 31, 2002. Y's QSub election also terminates at the close of May 31, 2002. Under § 1.1502-76(b)(1)(ii)(A)(2) and paragraph (a)(3) of this section, X and Y become members of Z's consolidated group of corporations as of the beginning of the day June 1, 2002.

Example (5). Termination due to acquisition of QSub by a consolidated group. The facts are the same as in Example 4, except that Z acquires 80 percent of the stock of Y (instead of X) on June 1, 2002. In this case; Y's QSub election terminates as of the close of June 1, 2002, and, under § 1.1502-76(b)(1)(ii)(A)(1), Y becomes a member of the consolidated group at that time.

(b) Effect of termination of QSub election. *(1) Formation of new corporation.* (i) In general. If a QSub election terminates under paragraph (a) of this section, the former QSub is treated as a new corporation acquiring all of its assets (and assuming all of its liabilities) immediately before the termination from the S corporation parent in exchange for stock of the new corporation. The tax treatment of this transaction or of a larger transaction that includes this transaction will be determined under the Internal Revenue Code and general principles of tax law, including the step transaction doctrine. For purposes of determining the application of section 351 with respect to this transaction, instruments, obligations, or other arrangements that are not treated as stock of the QSub under § 1.1361-2(b) are disregarded in determining control for purposes of section 368(c) even if they are equity under general principles of tax law.

(ii) Termination for tiered QSubs. If QSub elections terminate for tiered QSubs on the same day, the formation of any higher tier subsidiary precedes the formation of its lower tier subsidiary. See Example 6 in paragraph (b)(3) of this section.

(2) Carryover of disallowed losses and deductions. If a QSub terminates because the S corporation distributes the QSub stock to some or all of the S corporation's shareholders in a transaction to which section 368(a)(1)(D) applies by reason of section 355 (or so much of section 356 as relates to section 355), see § 1.1366-2(c)(2) for provisions relating to the carryover of disallowed losses and deductions that may be available.

(3) Examples. The following examples illustrate the application of this paragraph (b):

Example (1). X, an S corporation, owns 100 percent of the stock of Y, a corporation for which a QSub election is in effect. X sells 21 percent of the Y stock to Z, an unrelated corporation, for cash, thereby terminating the QSub election. Y is treated as a new corporation acquiring all of its assets (and assuming all of its liabilities) in exchange for Y stock immediately before the termination from the S corporation. The deemed exchange by X of assets for Y stock does not qualify under section 351 because X is not in control of Y within the meaning of section 368(c) immediately after the transfer as a result of the sale of stock to Z. Therefore, X must recognize gain, if any, on the assets transferred to Y in exchange for its stock. X's losses, if any, on the assets transferred are subject to the limitations of section 267.

Example (2). (i) X, an S corporation, owns 100 percent of the stock of Y, a corporation for which a QSub election is in effect. As part of a plan to sell a portion of Y, X causes Y to merge into T, a limited liability company wholly owned by X that is disregarded as an entity separate from its owner for Federal tax purposes. X then sells 21 percent of T to Z, an unrelated corporation, for cash. Following the sale, no entity classification election is made under § 301.7701-3(c) of this chapter to treat the limited liability company as an association for Federal tax purposes.

(ii) The merger of Y into T causes a termination of Y's QSub election. The new corporation (Newco) that is formed as a result of the termination is immediately merged into T, an entity that is disregarded for Federal tax purposes. Because, at the end of the series of transactions, the assets continue to be held by X for Federal tax purposes, under step transaction principles, the formation of Newco and the transfer of assets pursuant to the merger of Newco into T are disregarded. The sale of 21 percent of T is treated as a sale of a 21 percent undivided interest in each of T's assets. Immediately thereafter, X and Z are treated as contributing their respective interests in those assets to a partnership in exchange for ownership interests in the partnership.

(iii) Under section 1001, X recognizes gain or loss from the deemed sale of the 21 percent interest in each asset of the limited liability company to Z. Under section 721(a), no gain or loss is recognized by X and Z as a result of the deemed contribution of their respective interests in the assets to the partnership in exchange for ownership interests in the partnership.

Example (3). Assume the same facts as in Example 1, except that, instead of purchasing Y stock, Z contributes to Y an operating asset in exchange for 21 percent of the Y stock. Y is treated as a new corporation acquiring all of its assets (and assuming all of its liabilities) in exchange for Y stock immediately before the termination. Because X and Z are co-transferors that control the transferee immediately after the transfer, the transaction qualifies under section 351.

Example (4). X, an S corporation, owns 100 percent of the stock of Y, a corporation for which a QSub election is in effect. X distributes all of the Y stock pro rata to its shareholders, and the distribution terminates the QSub election. The transaction can qualify as a distribution to which sections 368(a)(1)(D) and 355 apply if the transaction otherwise satisfies the requirements of those sections.

Example (5). X, an S corporation, owns 100 percent of the stock of Y, a corporation for which a QSub election is in effect. X subsequently revokes the QSub election. Y is treated as a new corporation acquiring all of its assets (and assuming all of its liabilities) immediately before the revocation from its S corporation parent in a deemed exchange for Y stock. On a subsequent date, X sells 21 percent of the stock of Y to Z, an unrelated corporation, for cash. Assume that under general principles of tax law including the step transaction doctrine, the sale is not taken into account in determining whether X is in control of Y immediately after the deemed exchange of assets for stock. The deemed exchange by X of assets for Y stock and the deemed assumption by Y of its liabilities qualify under section 351 because, for purposes of that section, X is in control of Y within the meaning of section 368(c) immediately after the transfer.

Example (6). (i) X, an S corporation, owns 100 percent of the stock of Y, and Y owns 100 percent of the stock of Z. Y and Z are corporations for which QSub elections are in effect. X subsequently revokes the QSub elections and the effective date specified on each revocation statement is June 26, 2002, a date that is less than 12 months after the date on which the revocation statements are filed.

(ii) Immediately before the QSub elections terminate, Y is treated as a new corporation acquiring all of its assets (and assuming all of its liabilities) directly from X in exchange for the stock of Y. Z is treated as a new corporation acquiring all of its assets (and assuming all of its liabilities) directly from Y in exchange for the stock of Z.

Example (7). (i) The facts are the same as in Example 6, except that, prior to June 26, 2002 (the effective date of the revocations), Y distributes the Z stock to X under state law.

(ii) Immediately before the QSub elections terminate, Y is treated as a new corporation acquiring all of its assets (and assuming all of its liabilities) directly from X in exchange for the stock of Y. Z is also treated as a new corporation acquiring all of its assets (and assuming all of its liabilities) directly from X in exchange for the stock of Z.

Example (8). Merger of parent into QSub. X, an S corporation, owns 100 percent of the stock of Y, a corporation for which a QSub election is in effect. X merges into Y under state law, causing the QSub election for Y to terminate, and Y survives the merger. The formation of the new corporation, Y, and the merger of X into Y can qualify as a reorganization described in section 368(a)(1)(F) if the transaction otherwise satisfies the requirements of that section.

Example (9). Transfer of 100 percent of QSub. X, an S corporation, owns 100 percent of the stock of Y, a corporation for which a QSub election is in effect. Z, an unrelated C corporation, acquires 100 percent of the stock of Y. The deemed formation of Y by X (as a consequence of the termination of Y's QSub election) is disregarded for Federal income tax purposes. The transaction is treated as a transfer of the assets of Y to Z, followed by Z's transfer of these assets to the capital of Y in exchange for Y stock. Furthermore, if Z is an S corporation and makes a QSub election for Y effective as of the acquisition, Z's transfer of the assets of Y in exchange for Y stock, followed by the immediate liquidation of Y as a consequence of the QSub election are disregarded for Federal income tax purposes.

(c) Election after QSub termination. *(1) In general.* Absent the Commissioner's consent, and except as provided in paragraph (c)(2) of this section, a corporation whose QSub election has terminated under paragraph (a) of this section (or a successor corporation as defined in § 1.1362-5(b)) may not make an S election under section 1362 or have a QSub election under section 1361(b)(3)(B)(ii) made with respect to it for five taxable years (as described in section 1361(b)(3)(D)). The Commissioner may permit an S election by the corporation or a new QSub election with respect to the corporation before the five-year period expires. The corporation requesting consent to make the election has the burden of establishing that, under the relevant facts and circumstances, the Commissioner should consent to a new election.

(2) Exception. In the case of S and QSub elections effective after December 31, 1996, if a corporation's QSub election terminates, the corporation may, without requesting the Commissioner's consent, make an S election or have a QSub election made with respect to it before the expiration of the five-year period described in section 1361(b)(3)(D) and paragraph (c)(1) of this section, provided that—

(i) Immediately following the termination, the corporation (or its successor corporation) is otherwise eligible to make an S election or have a QSub election made for it; and

(ii) The relevant election is made effective immediately following the termination of the QSub election.

(3) Examples. The following examples illustrate the application of this paragraph (c):

Example (1). Termination upon distribution of QSub stock to shareholders of parent. X, an S corporation, owns Y, a QSub. X distributes all of its Y stock to X's shareholders. The distribution terminates the QSub election because Y no longer satisfies the requirements of a QSub. Assuming Y is otherwise eligible to be treated as an S corporation, Y's shareholders may elect to treat Y as an S corporation effective on the date of the stock distribution without requesting the Commissioner's consent.

Example (2). Sale of 100 percent of QSub stock. X, an S corporation, owns Y, a QSub. X sells 100 percent of the stock of Y to Z, an unrelated S corporation. Z may elect to treat Y as a QSub effective on the date of purchase without requesting the Commissioner's consent.

T.D. 8869, 1/20/2000.

§ 1.1361-6 Effective date.

Except as provided in §§ 1.1361-4(a)(3)(iii), 1.1361-4(a)(5)(i), 1.1361-4(a)(6)(iii), 1.1361-4(a)(7)(ii), 1.1361-4(a)(8)(ii), 1.1361-4(a)(9), and 1.1361-5(c)(2), the provisions of §§ 1.1361-2 through 1.1361-5 apply to taxable years beginning on or after January 20, 2000; however, taxpayers may elect to apply the regulations in whole, but not in part (aside from those sections with special dates of applicability), for taxable years beginning on or after January 1, 2000, provided all affected taxpayers apply the regulations in a consistent manner. To make this election, the corporation and all affected taxpayers must file a return or an amended return that is consistent with these rules for the taxable year for which the election is made. For purposes of this section, affected taxpayers means all taxpayers whose returns are affected by the election to apply the regulations.

T.D. 8869, 1/20/2000, T.D. 9356, 8/15/2007, T.D. 9422, 8/13/2008.

§ 1.1362-0 Table of contents.

This section lists the captions that appear in the regulations under section 1362.

(c) Termination by reason of excess passive investment income.

(1) In general.

(2) When effective.

(3) Subchapter C earnings and profits.

(4) Gross receipts.

(i) In general.

(ii) Special rules for sales of capital assets, stock and securities.

(A) Sales of capital assets.

(B) Sales of stock or securities.

(1) In general.

(2) Treatment of certain liquidations.

(3) Definition of stock or securities.

(4) General partner interests.

(i) In general.

(ii) Exception.

(iii) Other exclusions from gross receipts.

(5) Passive investment income.

(i) In general.

(ii) Definitions.

(A) Royalties.

(1) In general.

(2) Royalties derived in the ordinary course of a trade or business.

(3) Copyright, mineral, oil and gas, and active business computer software royalties.

(B) Rents.

(1) In general.

(2) Rents derived in the active trade or business of renting property.

(3) Produced film rents.

(4) Income from leasing self-produced tangible property.

(C) Dividends.

(D) Interest.

(1) In general.

(2) Interest on obligations acquired in the ordinary course of a trade or business.

(E) Annuities.

(F) Gross receipts from the sale of stock or securities.

(G) Identified income.

(iii) Special rules.

(A) Options or commodities dealers.

(B) Treatment of certain lending, financing and other businesses.

(1) In general.

(2) Directly derived.

(C) Payment to a patron of a cooperative.

(6) Examples.

§ 1.1362-3 Treatment of S termination year.

(a) In general.

(b) Allocations other than pro rata.

(1) Elections under section 1362(e)(3).

(2) Purchase of stock treated as an asset purchase.

(3) 50 percent change in ownership during S termination year.

(c) Special rules.

(1) S corporation that is a partner in a partnership.

(2) Tax for the C short year.

(3) Each short year treated as taxable year.

(4) Year for carryover purposes.

(5) Due date for S short year return.

(6) Year in which income from S short year is includible.

(d) Examples.

§ 1.1362-4 Inadvertent terminations and inadvertently invalid elections.

(a) In general.

(b) Inadvertent termination.

(c) Corporation's request for determination of an inadvertent termination.

(d) Adjustments.

(e) Corporation and shareholder consents.

(f) Status of corporation.

(g) Effective/applicability date.

§ 1.1362-5 Election after termination.

(a) In general.

(b) Successor corporation.

(c) Automatic consent after certain terminations.

§ 1.1362-6 Elections and consents.

(a) Time and manner of making elections.

(1) In general.

(2) Election to be an S corporation.

(i) Manner of making election.

(ii) Time of making election.

(A) In general.

(B) Elections made during the first 2½ months treated as made for the following taxable year.

(C) Definition of month and beginning of the taxable year.

(iii) Examples.

(3) Revocation of S election.

(i) Manner of revoking election.

(ii) Time of revoking election.

(iii) Examples.

(4) Rescission of a revocation.

(i) Manner of rescinding a revocation.

(ii) Time of rescinding a revocation.

(5) Election not to apply pro rata allocation.

(b) Shareholders' consents.

(1) Manner of consents in general.

(2) Persons required to consent.

(i) Community interest in stock.

(ii) Minor.

(iii) Estate.

(iv) Trust.

(3) Special rules for consent of shareholder to election to be an S corporation.

(i) In general.

(ii) Examples.

(iii) Extension of time for filing consents to an election.

(A) In general.

(B) Required consents.

§ 1.1362-7 Effective date.

(a) In general.

(b) Special effective date for passive investment income provisions.

§ 1.1362-8 Dividends received from affiliated subsidiaries.

(a) In general.

(b) Determination of active or passive earnings and profits.

(1) In general.

(2) Lower tier subsidiaries.

(3) De minimis exception.

(4) Special rules for earnings and profits accumulated by a C corporation prior to 80 percent acquisition.

(5) Gross receipts safe harbor.

(c) Allocating distributions to active or passive earnings and profits.

(1) Distributions from current earnings and profits.

(2) Distributions from accumulated earnings and profits.

(3) Adjustments to active earnings and profits.

(4) Special rules for consolidated groups.

(d) Examples.

(e) Effective date.

T.D. 8449, 11/24/92, amend T.D. 8869, 1/20/2000, T.D. 9422, 8/13/2008.

§ 1.1362-1 Election to be an S corporation.

(a) In general. Except as provided in § 1.1362-5, a small business corporation as defined in section 1361 may elect to be an S corporation under section 1362(a). An election may be made only with the consent of all of the shareholders of the corporation at the time of the election. See § 1.1362-6(a) for rules concerning the time and manner of making this election.

(b) Years for which election is effective. An election under section 1362(a) is effective for the entire taxable year of the corporation for which it is made and for all succeeding taxable years of the corporation, until the election is terminated.

T.D. 8449, 11/24/92.

§ 1.1362-2 Termination of election.

Caution: The Treasury has not yet amended Reg § 1.1362-2 to reflect changes made by P.L. 110-28, P.L. 108-357, P.L. 104-188.

(a) Termination by revocation. *(1) In general.* An election made under section 1362(a) is terminated if the corporation revokes the election for any taxable year of the corporation for which the election is effective, including the first taxable year. A revocation may be made only with the consent of shareholders who, at the time the revocation is made, hold more than one-half of the number of issued and outstanding shares of stock (including non-voting stock) of the corporation. See § 1.1362-6(a) for rules concerning the time and manner of revoking an election made under section 1362(a).

(2) When effective. (i) In general. Except as provided in paragraph (a)(2)(ii) of this section, a revocation made during the taxable year and before the 16th day of the third month of the taxable year is effective on the first day of the taxable year and a revocation made after the 15th day of the third month of the taxable year is effective for the following taxable year. If a corporation makes an election to be an S corporation that is to be effective beginning with the next taxable year and revokes its election on or before the first day of the next taxable year, the corporation is deemed to have revoked its election on the first day of the next taxable year.

(ii) Revocations specifying a prospective revocation date. If a corporation specifies a date for revocation and the date is expressed in terms of a stated day, month, and year that is on or after the date the revocation is filed, the revocation is effective on and after the date so specified.

(3) Effect on taxable year of corporation. In the case of a corporation that revokes its election to be an S corporation effective on the first day of the first taxable year for which its election is to be effective, any statement made with the election regarding a change in the corporation's taxable year has no effect.

(4) Rescission of a revocation. A corporation may rescind a revocation made under paragraph (a)(2) of this section at any time before the revocation becomes effective. A rescission may be made only with the consent of each person who consented to the revocation and by each person who became a shareholder of the corporation within the period beginning on the first day after the date the revocation was made and ending on the date on which the rescission is made. See § 1.1362-6(a) for rules concerning the time and manner of rescinding a revocation.

(b) Termination by reason of corporation ceasing to be a small business corporation. *(1) In general.* If a corporation ceases to be a small business corporation, as defined in section 1361(b), at any time on or after the first day of the first taxable year for which its election under section 1362(a) is effective, the election terminates. In the event of a termination under this paragraph (b)(1), the corporation should attach to its return for the taxable year in which the termination occurs a notification that a termination has occurred and the date of the termination.

(2) When effective. If an election terminates because of a specific event that causes the corporation to fail to meet the definition of a small business corporation, the termination is effective as of the date on which the event occurs. If a corporation makes an election to be an S corporation that is effective beginning with the following taxable year and is not a small business corporation on the first day of that following taxable year, the election is treated as having terminated on that first day. If a corporation is a small business corporation on the first day of the taxable year for which its election is effective, its election does not terminate even if the corporation was not a small business corporation during all or part of the period beginning after the date the election was made and ending before the first day of the taxable year for which the election is effective.

(3) Effect on taxable year of corporation. In the case of a corporation that fails to meet the definition of a small business corporation on the first day of the first taxable year for which its election to be an S corporation is to be effective, any statement made with the election regarding a change in the corporation's taxable year has no effect.

(c) Termination by reason of excess passive investment income. *(1) In general.* A corporation's election under section 1362(a) terminates if the corporation has subchapter C earnings and profits at the close of each of three consecutive taxable years and, for each of those taxable years, has passive investment income in excess of 25 percent of gross receipts. See section 1375 for the tax imposed on excess passive investment income.

(2) When effective. A termination under this paragraph (c) is effective on the first day of the first taxable year beginning after the third consecutive year in which the S corporation had excess passive investment income.

(3) Subchapter C earnings and profits. For purposes of this paragraph (c), subchapter C earnings and profits of a corporation are the earnings and profits of any corporation, including the S corporation or an acquired or predecessor corporation, for any period with respect to which an election under section 1362(a) (or under section 1372 of prior law) was not in effect. The subchapter C earnings and profits of an S corporation are modified as required by section 1371(c).

(4) Gross receipts. (i) In general. For purposes of this paragraph (c), gross receipts generally means the total amount received or accrued under the method of accounting used by the corporation in computing its taxable income and is not reduced by returns and allowances, cost of goods sold, or deductions.

(ii) Special rules for sales of capital assets, stock and securities. (A) Sales of capital assets. For purposes of this paragraph (c), gross receipts from the sales or exchanges of capital assets (as defined in section 1221), other than stock and securities, are taken into account only to the extent of capital gain net income (as defined in section 1222).

(B) Sales of stock or securities. (1) In general. For purposes of this paragraph (c), gross receipts from the sales or exchanges of stock or securities are taken into account only to the extent of gains therefrom. In addition, for purposes of computing gross receipts from sales or exchanges of stock or securities, losses do not offset gains.

(2) Treatment of certain liquidations. Gross receipts from the sales or exchanges of stock or securities do not include amounts described in section 1362(d)(3)(D)(iv), relating to the treatment of certain liquidations. For purposes of section 1362(d)(3)(D)(iv), stock of the liquidating corporation owned by an S corporation shareholder is not treated as owned by the S corporation.

(3) Definition of stock or securities. For purposes of this paragraph (c), stock or securities includes shares or certificates of stock, stock rights or warrants, or an interest in any corporation (including any joint stock company, insurance company, association, or other organization classified as a corporation under section 7701); an interest as a limited partner in a partnership; certificates of interest or participation in any profit-sharing agreement, or in any oil, gas, or other mineral property, or lease; collateral trust certificates; voting trust certificates; bonds; debentures; certificates of indebtedness; notes; car trust certificates; bills of exchange; or obligations issued by or on behalf of a State, Territory, or political subdivision thereof.

(4) General partner interests. (i) In general. Except as provided in paragraph (c)(4)(ii)(B)(4)(ii) of this section, if an S corporation disposes of a general partner interest, the gain on the disposition is treated as gain from the sale of stock or securities to the extent of the amount the S corporation would have received as a distributive share of gain from the sale of stock or securities held by the partnership if all of the stock and securities held by the partnership had been sold by the partnership at fair market value at the time the S corporation disposes of the general partner interest. In applying this rule, the S corporation's distributive share of gain from the sale of stock or securities held by the partnership is not reduced to reflect any loss that would be recognized from the sale of stock or securities held by the partnership. In the case of tiered partnerships, the rules of this section apply by looking through each tier.

(ii) Exception. An S corporation that disposes of a general partner interest may treat the disposition, for purposes of this paragraph (c), in the same manner as the disposition of an interest as a limited partner.

(iii) Other exclusions from gross receipts. For purposes of this paragraph (c), gross receipts do not include—

(A) Amounts received in nontaxable sales or exchanges except to the extent that gain is recognized by the corporation on the sale or exchange; or

(B) Amounts received as a loan, as a repayment of a loan, as a contribution to capital, or on the issuance by the corporation of its own stock.

(5) Passive investment income. (i) In general. In general, passive investment income means gross receipts (as defined in paragraph (c)(4) of this section) derived from royalties, rents, dividends, interest, annuities, and gains from the sales or exchanges of stock or securities.

(ii) Definitions. For purposes of this paragraph (c)(5), the following definitions apply:

(A) Royalties. (1) In general. Royalties means all royalties, including mineral, oil, and gas royalties, and amounts received for the privilege of using patents, copyrights, secret processes and formulas, good will, trademarks, tradebrands, franchises, and other like property. The gross amount of royalties is not reduced by any part of the cost of the rights under which the royalties are received or by any amount allowable as a deduction in computing taxable income.

(2) Royalties derived in the ordinary course of a trade or business. Royalties does not include royalties derived in the ordinary course of a trade or business of franchising or licensing property. Royalties received by a corporation are derived in the ordinary course of a trade or business of franchising or licensing property only if, based on all the facts and circumstances, the corporation—

(i) Created the property; or

(ii) Performed significant services or incurred substantial costs with respect to the development or marketing of the property.

(3) Copyright, mineral, oil and gas, and active business computer software royalties. Royalties does not include copyright royalties, nor mineral, oil and gas royalties if the income from those royalties would not be treated as personal holding company income under sections 543(a)(3) and (a)(4) if the corporation were a C corporation; amounts received upon disposal of timber, coal, or domestic iron ore with respect to which the special rules of sections 631(b) and (c) apply; and active business computer software royalties as defined under section 543(d) (without regard to paragraph (d)(5) of section 543).

(B) Rents. (1) In general. Rents means amounts received for the use of, or right to use, property (whether real or personal) of the corporation.

(2) Rents derived in the active trade or business of renting property. Rents does not include rents derived in the active trade or business of renting property. Rents received by a corporation are derived in an active trade or business of rent-

ing property only if, based on all the facts and circumstances, the corporation provides significant services or incurs substantial costs in the rental business. Generally, significant services are not rendered and substantial costs are not incurred in connection with net leases. Whether significant services are performed or substantial costs are incurred in the rental business is determined based upon all the facts and circumstances including, but not limited to, the number of persons employed to provide the services and the types and amounts of costs and expenses incurred (other than depreciation).

(3) Produced film rents. Rents does not include produced film rents as defined under section 543(a)(5).

(4) Income from leasing self-produced tangible property. Rents does not include compensation, however designated, for the use of, or right to use, any real or tangible personal property developed, manufactured, or produced by the taxpayer, if during the taxable year the taxpayer is engaged in substantial development, manufacturing, or production of real or tangible personal property of the same type.

(C) Dividends. Dividends includes dividends as defined in section 316, amounts to be included in gross income under section 551 (relating to foreign personal holding company income taxed to U.S. shareholders), and consent dividends as provided in section 565. See paragraphs (c)(5)(iii)(B) and (C) of this section for special rules for the treatment of certain dividends and certain payments to a patron of a cooperative. See § 1.1362-8 for special rules regarding the treatment of dividends received by an S corporation from a C corporation in which the S corporation holds stock meeting the requirements of section 1504(a)(2).

(D) Interest. (1) In general. Interest means any amount received for the use of money (including tax-exempt interest and amounts treated as interest under section 483, 1272, 1274, or 7872). See paragraph (c)(5)(iii)(B) of this section for a special rule for the treatment of interest derived in certain businesses.

(2) Interest on obligations acquired in the ordinary course of a trade or business. Interest does not include interest on any obligation acquired from the sale of property described in section 1221(1) [sic (a)(1)] or the performance of services in the ordinary course of a trade or business of selling the property or performing the services.

(E) Annuities. Annuities means the entire amount received as an annuity under an annuity, endowment, or life insurance contract, if any part of the amount would be includible in gross income under section 72.

(F) Gross receipts from the sale of stock or securities. Gross receipts from the sales or exchanges of stock or securities, as described in paragraph (c)(4)(ii)(B) of this section, are passive investment income to the extent of gains therefrom. See paragraph (c)(5)(iii)(B) of this section for a special rule for the treatment of gains derived in certain businesses.

(G) Identified income. Passive investment income does not include income identified by the Commissioner by regulations, revenue ruling, or revenue procedure as income derived in the ordinary course of a trade or business for purposes of this section.

(iii) Special rules. For purposes of this paragraph (c)(5), the following special rules apply:

(A) Options or commodities dealers. In the case of an options dealer or commodities dealer, passive investment income does not include any gain or loss (in the normal course of the taxpayer's activity of dealing in or trading section 1256 contracts) from any section 1256 contract or property related to the contract. Options dealer, commodities dealer, and section 1256 contract have the same meaning as in section 1362(d)(3)(E)(ii).

(B) Treatment of certain lending, financing and other businesses. (1) In general. Passive investment income does not include gross receipts that are directly derived in the ordinary course of a trade or business of—

(i) Lending or financing;

(ii) Dealing in property;

(iii) Purchasing or discounting accounts receivable, notes, or installment obligations; or

(iv) Servicing mortgages.

(2) Directly derived. For purposes of this paragraph (c)(5)(iii)(B), gross receipts directly derived in the ordinary course of business includes gain (as well as interest income) with respect to loans originated in a lending business, or interest income (as well as gain) from debt obligations of a dealer in such obligations. However, interest earned from the investment of idle funds in short-term securities does not constitute gross receipts directly derived in the ordinary course of business. Similarly, a dealer's income or gain from an item of property is not directly derived in the ordinary course of its trade or business if the dealer held the property for investment at any time before the income or gain is recognized.

(C) Payment to a patron of a cooperative. Passive investment income does not include amounts included in the gross income of a patron of a cooperative (within the meaning of section 1381(a), without regard to paragraph (2)(A) or (C) of section 1381(a)) by reason of any payment or allocation to the patron based on patronage occurring in the case of a trade or business of the patron.

(6) Examples. The principles of paragraphs (c)(4) and (c)(5) of this section are illustrated by the following examples. Unless otherwise provided in an example, S is an S corporation with subchapter C earnings and profits, and S's gross receipts from operations are gross receipts not derived from royalties, rents, dividends, interest, annuities, or gains from the sales or exchanges of stock or securities. S is a calendar year taxpayer and its first taxable year as an S corporation is 1993.

Example (1). Sales of capital assets, stock and securities.(i) S uses an accrual method of accounting and sells:

(1) a depreciable asset, held for more than 6 months, which is used in the corporation's business;

(2) a capital asset (other than stock or securities) for a gain;

(3) a capital asset (other than stock or securities) for a loss; and

(4) securities.

S receives payment for each asset partly in money and partly in the form of a note payable at a future time, and elects not to report the sales on the installment method.

(ii) The amount of money and the face amount (or issue price if different) of the note received for the business asset are considered gross receipts in the taxable year of sale and are not reduced by the adjusted basis of the property, costs of sale, or any other amount. With respect to the sales of the capital assets, gross receipts include the cash down payment and face amount (or issue price if different) of any notes, but only to the extent of S's capital gain net income. In the case of the sale of the securities, gross receipts include the cash down payment and face amount (or issue price if different) of the notes, but only to the extent of gain on the sale. In determining gross receipts from sales of securities, losses are not netted against gains.

Example (2). Long-term contract reported on percentage-of-completion method. S has a long-term contract as defined in § 1.460-1(b)(1) with respect to which it reports income according to the percentage-of-completion method as described in § 1.460-4(b). The portion of the gross contract price which corresponds to the percentage of the entire contract which has been completed during the taxable year is included in S's gross receipts for the year.

Example (3). Income reported on installment sale method. For its 1993 taxable year, S sells personal property on the installment plan and elects to report its taxable income from the sale of the property (other than property qualifying as a capital asset or stock or securities) on the installment method in accordance with section 453. The installment payment actually received in a given taxable year of S is included in gross receipts for the year.

Example (4). Partnership interests. In 1993, S and two of its shareholders contribute cash to form a general partnership, PRS. S receives a 50 percent interest in the capital and profits of PRS. S formed PRS to indirectly invest in marketable stocks and securities. The only assets of PRS are the stock and securities, and certain real and tangible personal property. In 1994, S needs cash in its business and sells its partnership interest at a gain rather than having PRS sell the marketable stock or securities that have appreciated. Under paragraph (c)(4)(ii)(B)(4) of this section, the gain on S's disposition of its interest in PRS is treated as gain from the sale or exchange of stock or securities to the extent of the amount the distributive share of gain S would have received from the sale of stock or securities held by PRS if PRS had sold all of its stock or securities at fair market value at the time S disposed of its interest in PRS.

Example (5). Royalties derived in ordinary course of trade or business.

(i) In 1993, S has gross receipts of $75,000. Of this amount, $5,000 is from royalty payments with respect to Trademark A, $8,000 is from royalty payments with respect to Trademark B, and $62,000 is gross receipts from operations. S created Trademark A, but S did not create Trademark B or perform significant services or incur substantial costs with respect to the development or marketing of Trademark B.

(ii) Because S created Trademark A, the royalty payments with respect to Trademark A are derived in the ordinary course of S's business and are not included within the definition of royalties for purposes of determining S's passive investment income. However, the royalty payments with respect to Trademark B are included within the definition of royalties for purposes of determining S's passive investment income. See paragraph (c)(5)(ii)(A) of this section. S's passive investment income for the year is $8,000, and S's passive investment income percentage for the taxable year is 10.67% ($8,000/$75,000). This does not exceed 25 percent of S's gross receipts and consequently the three-year period described in section 1362(d)(3) does not begin to run.

Example (6). Dividends; gain on sale of stock derived in the ordinary course of trade or business.

(i) In 1993, S receives dividends of $10,000 on stock of corporations P and O, recognizes a gain of $25,000 on sale of the P stock, and recognizes a loss of $12,000 on sale of the O stock. S held the P and O stock for investment, rather than for sale in the ordinary course of a trade or business. S has gross receipts from operations and from gain on the sale of stock in the ordinary course of its trade or business of $110,000.

(ii) S's gross receipts are calculated as follows:

$110,000	Gross receipts from operations and from gain on the sale of stock in the ordinary course of a trade or business
10,000	Gross dividend receipts
25,000	Gain on sale of P stock (Loss on O stock not taken into account)
$145,000	Total gross receipts

(iii) S's passive investment income is determined as follows:

$10,000	Gross dividend receipts
25,000	Gain on sale of P stock (Loss on O stock not taken into account)
$35,000	Total passive investment income

(iv) S's passive investment income percentage for its first year as an S corporation is 24.1% ($35,000/$145,000). This does not exceed 25 percent of S's gross receipts and consequently the three-year period described in section 1362(d)(3) does not begin to run.

Example (7). Interest on accounts receivable; netting of gain on sale of real property investments.

(i) In 1993, S receives $6,000 of interest on accounts receivable arising from S's sales of inventory property. S also receives dividends with respect to stock held for investment of $1,500. In addition, S sells two parcels of real property (Property J and Property K) that S had purchased and held for investment. S sells Property J, in which S has a basis of $5,000, for $10,000 (a gain of $5,000). S sells Property K, in which S has a basis of $12,000, for $9,000 (a loss of $3,000). S has gross receipts from operations of $90,000.

(ii) S's gross receipts are calculated as follows:

$90,000	Gross receipts from operations
6,000	Gross interest receipts
1,500	Gross dividend receipts
2,000	Net gain on sale of real property investments
$99,500	Total gross receipts

(iii) Under paragraph (c)(5)(ii)(D) of this section, S's gross interest receipts are not passive investment income. In addition, gain on the sale of real property ($2,000) is not passive investment income. S's passive investment income includes only the $1,500 of gross dividend receipts. Accordingly, S's passive investment income percentage for its first year as an S corporation is 1.51% ($1,500/$99,500). This does not exceed 25 percent of S's gross receipts and consequently the three-year period described in section 1362(d)(3) does not begin to run.

Example (8). Interest received in the ordinary course of a lending business.

(i) In 1993, S has gross receipts of $100,000 from loans and investments made in the ordinary course of S's mortgage banking business. This includes, for example, mortgage servicing fees, interest earned on mortgages prior to sale of the mortgages, and gain on sale of mortgages. In addition, S receives, from the investment of idle funds in short-term securities, $15,000 of gross interest income and $5,000 of gain.

(ii) S's gross receipts are calculated as follows:

$100,000	Gross receipts from operations
15,000	Gross interest receipts
5,000	Gain on sale of securities
$120,000	Total gross receipts

(iii) S's passive investment income is determined as follows:

$15,000	Gross interest receipts
5,000	Gain on sale of securities
$20,000	Total passive investment income

(iv) S's passive investment income percentage for its first year as an S corporation is 16.67% ($20,000/$120,000). This does not exceed 25 percent of S's gross receipts and consequently the three-year period described in section 1362(d)(3) does not begin to run.

T.D. 8449, 11/24/92, amend T.D. 8869, 1/20/2000, T.D. 8995, 5/14/2002.

§ 1.1362-3 Treatment of S termination year.

(a) In general. If an S election terminates under section 1362(d) on a date other than the first day of a taxable year of the corporation, the corporation's taxable year in which the termination occurs is an S termination year. The portion of the S termination year ending at the close of the day prior to the termination is treated as a short taxable year for which the corporation is an S corporation (the S short year). The portion of the S termination year beginning on the day the termination is effective is treated as a short taxable year for which the corporation is a C corporation (the C short year). Except as provided in paragraphs (b) and (c)(1) of this section, the corporation allocates income or loss for the entire year on a pro rata basis as described in section 1362(e)(2). To the extent that income or loss is not allocated on a pro rata basis under this section, items of income, gain, loss, deduction, and credit are assigned to each short taxable year on the basis of the corporation's normal method of accounting as determined under section 446. See, however, § 1.1502-76(b)(1)(ii)(A)(2) for special rules for an S election that terminates under section 1362(d) immediately before the S corporation becomes a member of a consolidated group (within the meaning of § 1.1502-1(h)). See § 1.460-4(k)(3)(iv)(D) for rules relating to the computation of the S corporation's income or loss from a contract accounted for under a long-term contract method of accounting in the S termination year.

(b) Allocations other than pro rata. *(1) Elections under section 1362(e)(3).* The pro rata allocation rules of section 1362(e)(2) do not apply if the corporation elects to allocate its S termination year income on the basis of its normal tax accounting method. This election may be made only with the consent of each person who is a shareholder in the corporation at any time during the S short year and of each person who is a shareholder in the corporation on the first day of the C short year. See § 1.1362-6(a) for rules concerning the time and manner of making this election.

(2) Purchase of stock treated as an asset purchase. The pro rata allocation rules of section 1362(e)(2) do not apply with respect to any item resulting from the application of section 338.

(3) 50 percent change in ownership during S termination year. The pro rata allocation rules of section 1362(e)(2) do not apply if at any time during the S termination year, as a result of sales or exchanges of stock in the corporation during that year, there is a change in ownership of 50 percent or more of the issued and outstanding shares of stock of the corporation. If stock has already been sold or exchanged during the S termination year, subsequent sales or exchanges of that stock are not taken into account for purposes of this paragraph (b)(3).

(c) Special rules. *(1) S corporation that is a partner in a partnership.* For purposes of section 706(c) only, the termination of the election of an S corporation that is a partner in a partnership during any portion of the S short year under § 1.1362-2(a) or (b), is treated as a sale or exchange of the corporation's entire interest in the partnership on the last day of the S short year, if—

(i) The pro rata allocation rules do not apply to the corporation; and

(ii) Any taxable year of the partnership ends with or within the C short year.

(2) Tax for the C short year. The taxable income for the C short year is determined on an annualized basis as described in section 1362(e)(5).

(3) Each short year treated as taxable year. Except as otherwise provided in paragraph (c)(4) of this section, the S and C short years are treated as two separate years for purposes of all provisions of the Internal Revenue Code.

(4) Year for carryover purposes. The S and C short years are treated as one year for purposes of determining the number of taxable years to which any item may be carried back or forward by the corporation.

(5) Due date for S short year return. The date by which the return for the S short year must be filed is the same as the date by which the return for the C short year must be filed (including extensions).

(6) Year in which income from S short year is includible. A shareholder must include in taxable income the shareholder's pro rata share of the items described in section 1366(a) for the S short year for the taxable year with or within which the S termination year ends.

(d) Examples. The provisions of this section are illustrated by the following examples:

Example (1). S termination year not created.

(i) On January 1, 1993, the first day of its taxable year, a subchapter C corporation had three eligible shareholders. During 1993, the corporation properly elected to be treated as an S corporation effective January 1, 1994, the first day of the succeeding taxable year. Subsequently, a transfer of some of the stock in the corporation was made to an ineligible shareholder. The ineligible shareholder still holds the stock on January 1, 1994.

(ii) The corporation fails to meet the definition of a small business corporation on January 1, 1994, and its election is treated as having terminated on that date. See § 1.1362-2(b)(2) for the termination rules. Because the corporation ceases to be a small business corporation on the first day of a taxable year, an S termination year is not created. In addition, if the corporation in the future meets the definition of a small business corporation and desires to elect to be treated as an S corporation, the corporation is automatically granted consent to reelect before the expiration of the 5-year waiting period. See § 1.1362-5 for special rules concerning automatic consent to reelect.

Example (2). More than 50 percent change in ownership during S short year. A, an individual, owns all 100 outstanding shares of stock of S, a calendar year S corporation. On January 31, 1993, A sells 60 shares of S stock to B, an individual. On June 1, 1993, A sells 5 shares of S stock to PRS, a partnership. S ceases to be a small business corporation on

June 1, 1993, and pursuant to section 1362(d)(2), its election terminates on that date. Because there was a more than 50 percent change in ownership of the issued and outstanding shares of S stock, S must assign the items of income, loss, deduction, or credit for the S termination year to the two short taxable years on the basis of S's normal method of accounting under the rules of paragraph (b)(3) of this section.

Example (3). More than 50 percent change in ownership during C short year. A, an individual, owns all 100 outstanding shares of stock of S, a calendar year S corporation. On June 1, 1993, A sells 5 shares of S stock to PRS, a partnership. S ceases to be a small business corporation on that date and pursuant to section 1362(d)(3), its election terminates on that date. On July 1, 1993, A sells 60 shares of S stock to B, an individual. Since there was a more than 50 percent change in ownership of the issued and outstanding shares of S stock during the S termination year, S must assign the items of income, loss, deduction, or credit for the S termination year to the two short taxable years on the basis of S's normal method of accounting under the rules of paragraph (b)(3) of this section.

Example (4). Stock acquired other than by sale or exchange. C and D are shareholders in S, a calendar year S corporation. Each owns 50 percent of the issued and outstanding shares of the corporation on December 31, 1993. On March 1, 1994, C makes a gift of his entire shareholder interest to T, a trust not permitted as a shareholder under section 1361(c)(2). S ceases to be a small business corporation on March 1, 1994, and pursuant to section 1362(d)(2), its S corporation election terminates effective on that date. As a result of the gift, T owns 50 percent of S's issued and outstanding stock. However, because T acquired the stock by gift from C rather than by sale or exchange, there has not been a more than 50 percent change in ownership by sale or exchange of S that would cause the rules of paragraph (b)(3) of this section to apply.

T.D. 8449, 11/24/92, amend T.D. 8842, 11/9/99, T.D. 9137, 7/15/2004.

§ 1.1362-4 Inadvertent terminations and inadvertently invalid elections.

Caution: The Treasury has not yet amended Reg § 1.1362-4 to reflect changes made by P.L. 108-357, P.L. 104-188.

(a) In general. A corporation is treated as continuing to be an S corporation or a QSub (or, an invalid election to be either an S corporation or a QSub is treated as valid) during the period specified by the Commissioner if—

(1) The corporation made a valid election under section 1362(a) or section 1361(b)(3) and the election terminated or the corporation made an election under section 1362(a) or section 1361(b)(3) that was invalid;

(2) The Commissioner determines that the termination or invalidity was inadvertent;

(3) Within a reasonable period of time after discovery of the terminating event or invalid election, steps were taken so that the corporation for which the election was made or the termination occurred is a small business corporation or a QSub, as the case may be, or to acquire the required shareholder consents; and

(4) The corporation and shareholders agree to adjustments that the Commissioner may require for the period.

(b) Inadvertent termination or inadvertently invalid election. For purposes of paragraph (a) of this section, the determination of whether a termination or invalid election was inadvertent is made by the Commissioner. The corporation has the burden of establishing that under the relevant facts and circumstances the Commissioner should determine that the termination or invalid election was inadvertent. The fact that the terminating event or invalidity of the election was not reasonably within the control of the corporation and, in the case of a termination, was not part of a plan to terminate the election, or the fact that the terminating event or circumstance took place without the knowledge of the corporation, notwithstanding its due diligence to safeguard itself against such an event or circumstance, tends to establish that the termination or invalidity of the election was inadvertent.

(c) Corporation's request for determination of an inadvertent termination or invalid election. A corporation that believes that the termination or invalidity of its election was inadvertent may request a determination from the Commissioner that the termination or invalidity of its election was inadvertent. The request is made in the form of a ruling request and should set forth all relevant facts pertaining to the event or circumstance including, but not limited to, the facts described in paragraph (b) of this section, the date of the corporation's election (or intended election) under section 1362(a) or 1361(b)(3), a detailed explanation of the event or circumstance causing the termination or invalidity, when and how the event or circumstance was discovered, and the steps taken under paragraph (a)(3) of this section.

(d) Adjustments. The Commissioner may require any adjustments that are appropriate. In general, the adjustments required should be consistent with the treatment of the corporation as an S corporation or QSub during the period specified by the Commissioner. In the case of stock held by an ineligible shareholder that causes an inadvertent termination or invalid election for an S corporation under section 1362(f), the Commissioner may require the ineligible shareholder to be treated as a shareholder of the S corporation during the period the ineligible shareholder actually held stock in the corporation. Moreover, the Commissioner may require protective adjustments that prevent the loss of any revenue due to the holding of stock by an ineligible shareholder (for example, a nonresident alien).

(e) Corporation and shareholder consents. The corporation and all persons who were shareholders of the corporation at any time during the period specified by the Commissioner must consent to any adjustments that the Commissioner may require. Each consent should be in the form of a statement agreeing to make the adjustments. The statement must be signed by the shareholder (in the case of shareholder consent) or a person authorized to sign the return required by section 6037 (in the case of corporate consent). See § 1.1362-6(b)(2) for persons required to sign consents. A shareholder's consent statement should include the name, address, and taxpayer identification numbers of the corporation and shareholder, the number of shares of stock owned by the shareholder, and the dates on which the shareholder owned any stock. The corporate consent statement should include the name, address, and taxpayer identification numbers of the corporation and each shareholder.

(f) Status of corporation. The status of the corporation after the terminating event or invalid election and before the determination of inadvertence is determined by the Commissioner. Inadvertent termination or inadvertent invalid election relief may be granted retroactively for all years for which the terminating event or circumstance giving rise to invalidity is effective, in which case the corporation is treated as if its election was valid or had not terminated. Alternatively, relief may be granted only for the period in which the corporation became eligible for subchapter S or QSub treatment, in which case the corporation is treated as a C corporation or, in the case of a QSub with an inadvertently terminated or invalid election, as a separate C corporation, during the period for which the corporation was not eligible for its intended status.

(g) Effective/applicability date. Paragraphs (a), (b), (c), (d), and (f) of this section are effective on August 14, 2008.

T.D. 8449, 11/24/92, amend T.D. 9422, 8/13/2008.

§ 1.1362-5 Election after termination.

Caution: The Treasury has not yet amended Reg § 1.1362-5 to reflect changes made by P.L. 104-188.

(a) In general. Absent the Commissioner's consent, an S corporation whose election has terminated (or a successor corporation) may not make a new election under section 1362(a) for five taxable years as described in section 1362(g). However, the Commissioner may permit the corporation to make a new election before the 5-year period expires. The corporation has the burden of establishing that under the relevant facts and circumstances, the Commissioner should consent to a new election. The fact that more than 50 percent of the stock in the corporation is owned by persons who did not own any stock in the corporation on the date of the termination tends to establish that consent should be granted. In the absence of this fact, consent ordinarily is denied unless the corporation shows that the event causing termination was not reasonably within the control of the corporation or shareholders having a substantial interest in the corporation and was not part of a plan on the part of the corporation or of such shareholders to terminate the election.

(b) Successor corporation. A corporation is a successor corporation to a corporation whose election under section 1362 has been terminated if—

(1) 50 percent or more of the stock of the corporation (the new corporation) is owned, directly or indirectly, by the same persons who, on the date of the termination, owned 50 percent or more of the stock of the corporation whose election terminated (the old corporation); and

(2) Either the new corporation acquires a substantial portion of the assets of the old corporation, or a substantial portion of the assets of the new corporation were assets of the old corporation.

(c) Automatic consent after certain terminations. A corporation may, without requesting the Commissioner's consent, make a new election under section 1362(a) before the 5-year period described in section 1362(g) expires if the termination occurred because the corporation—

(1) Revoked its election effective on the first day of the first taxable year for which its election was to be effective (see § 1.1362-2(a)(2)); or

(2) Failed to meet the definition of a small business corporation on the first day of the first taxable year for which its election was to be effective (see § 1.1362-2(b)(2)).

T.D. 8449, 11/24/92.

§ 1.1362-6 Elections and consents.

(a) Time and manner of making elections. *(1) In general.* An election statement made under this section must identify the election being made, set forth the name, address, and taxpayer identification number of the corporation, and be signed by a person authorized to sign the return required to be filed under section 6037.

(2) Election to be an S corporation. (i) Manner of making election. A small business corporation makes an election under section 1362(a) to be an S corporation by filing a completed Form 2553. The election form must be filed with the service center designated in the instructions applicable to Form 2553. The election is not valid unless all shareholders of the corporation at the time of the election consent to the election in the manner provided in paragraph (b) of this section. However, once a valid election is made, new shareholders need not consent to that election.

(ii) Time of making election (A) In general. The election described in paragraph (a)(2)(i) of this section may be made by a small business corporation at any time during the taxable year that immediately precedes the taxable year for which the election is to be effective, or during the taxable year for which the election is to be effective provided that the election is made before the 16th day of the third month of the year. If a corporation makes an election for a taxable year, and the election meets all the requirements of this section but is made during the period beginning after the 15th day of the third month of the taxable year, the election is treated as being made for the following taxable year provided that the corporation meets all the requirements of section 1361(b) at the time the election is made. For taxable years of 2½ months or less, an election made before the 16th day of the third month after the first day of the taxable year is treated as made during that year.

(B) Elections made during the first 2½ months treated as made for the following taxable year. A timely election made by a small business corporation during the taxable year for which it is intended to be effective is nonetheless treated as made for the following taxable year if—

(1) The corporation is not a small business corporation during the entire portion of the taxable year which occurs before the date the election is made; or

(2) Any person who held stock in the corporation at any time during the portion of the taxable year which occurs before the time the election is made, and who does not hold stock at the time the election is made, does not consent to the election.

(C) Definition of month and beginning of the taxable year. Month means a period commencing on the same numerical day of any calendar month as the day of the calendar month on which the taxable year began and ending with the close of the day preceding the numerically corresponding day of the succeeding calendar month or, if there is no corresponding day, with the close of the last day of the succeeding calendar month. In addition, the taxable year of a new corporation begins on the date that the corporation has shareholders, acquires assets, or begins doing business, whichever is the first to occur. The existence of incorporators does not necessarily begin the taxable year of a new corporation.

(iii) Examples. The provisions of this section are illustrated by the following examples:

Example (1). Effective election; no prior taxable year. A calendar year small business corporation begins its first taxable year on January 7, 1993. To be an S corporation beginning with its first taxable year, the corporation must make the election set forth in this section during the period that begins January 7, 1993, and ends before March 22, 1993. Because the corporation had no taxable year immediately preceding the taxable year for which the election is to be effective, an election made earlier than January 7, 1993, will not be valid.

Example (2). Effective election; taxable year less than 2½ months. A calendar year small business corporation begins its first taxable year on November 8, 1993. To be an S corporation beginning with its first taxable year, the corporation must make the election set forth in this section during the period that begins November 8, 1993, and ends before January 23, 1994.

Example (3). Election effective for the following taxable year; ineligible shareholder. On January 1, 1993, two individuals and a partnership own all of the stock of a calendar year subchapter C corporation. On January 31, 1993, the partnership dissolved and distributed its shares in the corporation to its five partners, all individuals. On February 28, 1993, the seven shareholders of the corporation consented to the corporation's election of subchapter S status. The corporation files a properly completed Form 2553 on March 2, 1993. The corporation is not eligible to be a subchapter S corporation for the 1993 taxable year because during the period of the taxable year prior to the election it had an ineligible shareholder. However, under paragraph (a)(2)(ii)(B) of this section, the election is treated as made for the corporation's 1994 taxable year.

(3) Revocation of S election. (i) Manner of revoking election. To revoke an election, the corporation files a statement that the corporation revokes the election made under section 1362(a). The statement must be filed with the service center where the election was properly filed. The revocation statement must include the number of shares of stock (including non-voting stock) issued and outstanding at the time the revocation is made. A revocation may be made only with the consent of shareholders who, at the time the revocation is made, hold more than one-half of the number of issued and outstanding shares of stock (including non-voting stock) of the corporation. Each shareholder who consents to the revocation must consent in the manner required under paragraph (b) of this section. In addition, each consent should indicate the number of issued and outstanding shares of stock (including non-voting stock) held by each shareholder at the time of the revocation.

(ii) Time of revoking election. For rules concerning when a revocation is effective, see § 1.1362-2(a)(2).

(iii) Examples. The principles of this paragraph (a)(3) are illustrated by the following examples:

Example (1). Revocation; consent of shareholders owning more than one-half of issued and outstanding shares. A calendar year S corporation has issued and outstanding 40,000 shares of class A voting common stock and 20,000 shares of class B non-voting common stock. The corporation wishes to revoke its election of subchapter S status. Shareholders owning 11,000 shares of class A stock sign revocation consents. Shareholders owning 20,000 shares of class B stock sign revocation consents. The corporation has obtained the required shareholder consent to revoke its subchapter S election because shareholders owning more than one-half of the total number of issued and outstanding shares of stock of the corporation consented to the revocation.

Example (2). Effective prospective revocation. In June 1993, a calendar year S corporation determines that it will revoke its subchapter S election effective August 1, 1993. To do so it must file its revocation statement with consents attached on or before August 1, 1993, and the statement must indicate that the revocation is intended to be effective August 1, 1993.

(4) Rescission of a revocation. (i) Manner of rescinding a revocation. To rescind a revocation, the corporation files a statement that the corporation rescinds the revocation made under section 1362(d)(1). The statement must be filed with the service center where the revocation was properly filed. A rescission may be made only with the consent (in the manner required under paragraph (b)(1) of this section) of each person who consented to the revocation and of each person who became a shareholder of the corporation within the period beginning on the first day after the date the revocation was made and ending on the date on which the rescission is made.

(ii) Time of rescinding a revocation. If the rescission statement is filed before the revocation becomes effective and is filed with proper service center, the rescission is effective on the date it is so filed.

(5) Election not to apply pro rata allocation. To elect not to apply the pro rata allocation rules to an S termination year, a corporation files a statement that it elects under section 1362(e)(3) not to apply the rules provided in section 1362(e)(2). In addition to meeting the requirements of paragraph (a)(1) of this section, the statement must set forth the cause of the termination and the date thereof. The statement must be filed with the corporation's return for the C short year. This election may be made only with the consent of all persons who are shareholders of the corporation at any time during the S short year and all persons who are shareholders of the corporation on the first day of the C short year (in the manner required under paragraph (b)(1) of this section).

(b) Shareholders' consents. *(1) Manner of consents in general.* A shareholder's consent required under paragraph (a) of this section must be in the form of a written statement that sets forth the name, address, and taxpayer identification number of the shareholder, the number of shares of stock owned by the shareholder, the date (or dates) on which the stock was acquired, the date on which the shareholder's taxable year ends, the name of the S corporation, the corporation's taxpayer identification number, and the election to which the shareholder consents. The statement must be signed by the shareholder under penalties of perjury. Except as provided in paragraph (b)(3)(iii) of this section, the election of the corporation is not valid if any required consent is not filed in accordance with the rules contained in this paragraph (b). The consent statement should be attached to the corporation's election statement.

(2) Persons required to consent. The following rules apply in determining persons required to consent:

(i) Community interest in stock. When stock of the corporation is owned by husband and wife as community property (or the income from the stock is community property), or is owned by tenants in common, joint tenants, or tenants by the entirety, each person having a community interest in the stock or income therefrom and each tenant in common, joint tenant and tenant by the entirety must consent to the election.

(ii) Minor. The consent of a minor must be made by the minor or by the legal representative of the minor (or by a natural or an adoptive parent of the minor if no legal representative has been appointed).

(iii) Estate. The consent of an estate must be made by an executor or administrator thereof, or by any other fiduciary appointed by testamentary instrument or appointed by the court having jurisdiction over the administration of the estate.

(iv) Trusts. In the case of a trust described in section 1361(c)(2)(A) (including a trust treated under section 1361(d)(1)(A) as a trust described in section 1361(c)(2)(A)(i) and excepting an electing small business trust described in section 1361(c)(2)(A)(v) (ESBT)), only the person treated as the shareholder for purposes of section 1361(b)(1) must consent to the election. When stock of the corporation is held by a trust, both husband and wife must consent to any election if the husband and wife have a community interest in the trust property. See paragraph (b)(2)(i) of this section for rules concerning community interests in S corporation stock. In the case of an ESBT, the trustee and the owner of any portion of the trust that consists of the stock in one or more S corporations under subpart E, part I, subchapter J, chapter 1 of the Internal Revenue Code must consent to the S corporation election. If there is more than one trustee, the trustee or trustees with authority to legally bind the trust must consent to the S corporation election.

(3) Special rules for consent of shareholder to election to be an S corporation. (i) In general. The consent of a shareholder to an election by a small business corporation under section 1362(a) may be made on Form 2553 or on a separate statement in the manner described in paragraph (b)(1) of this section. In addition, the separate statement must set forth the name, address, and taxpayer identification number of the corporation. A shareholder's consent is binding and may not be withdrawn after a valid election is made by the corporation. Each person who is a shareholder (including any person who is treated as a shareholder under section 1361(c)(2)(B)) at the time the election is made) must consent to the election. If the election is made before the 16th day of the third month of the taxable year and is intended to be effective for that year, each person who was a shareholder (including any person who was treated as a shareholder under section 1361(c)(2)(B)) at any time during the portion of that year which occurs before the time the election is made, and who is not a shareholder at the time the election is made, must also consent to the election. If the election is to be effective for the following taxable year, no consent need be filed by any shareholder who is not a shareholder on the date of the election. Any person who is considered to be a shareholder under applicable State law solely by virtue of his or her status as an incorporator is not treated as a shareholder for purposes of this paragraph (b)(3)(i).

(ii) Examples. The principles of this section are illustrated by the following examples:

Example (1). Effective election; shareholder consents. On January 1, 1993, the first day of its taxable year, a subchapter C corporation had 15 shareholders. On January 30, 1993, two of the C corporation's shareholders, A and B, both individuals, sold their shares in the corporation to P, Q, and R, all individuals. On March 1, 1993, the corporation filed its election to be an S corporation for the 1993 taxable year. The election will be effective (assuming the other requirements of section 1361(b) are met) provided that all of the shareholders as of March 1, 1993, as well as former shareholders A and B, consent to the election.

Example (2). Consent of new shareholder unnecessary. On January 1, 1993, three individuals own all of the stock of a calendar year subchapter C corporation. On April 15, 1993, the corporation, in accordance with paragraph (a)(2) of this section, files a properly completed Form 2553. The corporation anticipates that the election will be effective beginning January 1, 1994, the first day of the succeeding taxable year. On October 1, 1993, the three shareholders collectively sell 75% of their shares in the corporation to another individual. On January 1, 1994, the corporation's shareholders are the three original individuals and the new shareholder. Because the election was valid and binding when made, it is not necessary for the new shareholder to consent to the election. The corporation's subchapter S election is effective on January 1, 1994 (assuming the other requirements of section 1361(b) are met).

(iii) Extension of time for filing consents to an election (A) In general. An election that is timely filed for any taxable year and that would be valid except for the failure of any shareholder to file a timely consent is not invalid if consents are filed as required under paragraph (b)(3)(iii)(B) of this section and it is shown to the satisfaction of the district director or director of the service center with which the corporation files its income tax return that—

(1) There was reasonable cause for the failure to file the consent;

(2) The request for the extension of time to file a consent is made within a reasonable time under the circumstances; and

(3) The interests of the Government will not be jeopardized by treating the election as valid.

(B) Required consents. Consents must be filed within the extended period of time as may be granted by the Internal Revenue Service, by all persons who—

(1) Were shareholders of the corporation at any time during the period beginning as of the date of the invalid election and ending on the date on which an extension of time is granted in accordance with this paragraph (b)(3)(iii); and

(2) Have not previously consented to the election.

T.D. 8449, 11/24/92, amend T.D. 8994, 5/13/2002.

§ 1.1362-7 Effective dates.

(a) In general. The provisions of §§ 1.1362-1 through 1.1362-6 apply to taxable years of corporations beginning after December 31, 1992. For taxable years to which these regulations do not apply, corporations and shareholders subject to the provisions of section 1362 must take reasonable return positions taking into consideration the statute; its legislative history; the provisions of §§ 18.1362-1 through 18.1362-5 (see 26 CFR part 18 as contained in the CFR edition revised as of April 1, 1992). In addition, following these regulations is a reasonable return position. See Notice 92-56, 1992-49 I.R.B. (see § 601.601(d)(2)(ii)(b) of this chapter), for additional guidance regarding reasonable return positions for years to which §§ 1.1362-1 through 1.1362-6 do not apply. Section 1.1362-6(b)(2)(iv) is applicable for taxable years beginning on and after May 14, 2002.

(b) Special effective date for passive investment income provisions. For taxable years of an S corporation and all affected shareholders that are not closed, the S corporation and all affected shareholders may elect to apply the provisions of § 1.1362-2(c)(5). To make the election, the corporation and all affected shareholders must file a return or an amended return that is consistent with these rules for the taxable year for which the election is made and each subsequent taxable year. For purposes of this section, affected shareholders means all shareholders who received distributive shares of S corporation items in the taxable year for which the election is made and all shareholders of the S corporation for all subsequent taxable years. However, the Commissioner may, in appropriate circumstances, permit taxpayers to make this election even if all affected shareholders cannot file consistent returns.

T.D. 8449, 11/24/92, amend T.D. 8994, 5/13/2002.

§ 1.1362-8 Dividends received from affiliated subsidiaries.

(a) In general. For purposes of section 1362(d)(3), if an S corporation holds stock in a C corporation meeting the requirements of section 1504(a)(2), the term passive investment income does not include dividends from the C corporation to the extent those dividends are attributable to the earnings and profits of the C corporation derived from the active conduct of a trade or business (active earnings and profits). For purposes of applying section 1362(d)(3), earnings and profits of a C corporation are active earnings and profits to the extent that the earnings and profits are derived from activities that would not produce passive investment income (as defined in section 1362(d)(3)) if the C corporation were an S corporation.

(b) Determination of active or passive earnings and profits. *(1) In general.* An S corporation may use any reasonable method to determine the amount of dividends that are not treated as passive investment income under section 1362(d)(3)(E). Paragraph (b)(5) of this section describes a method of determining the amount of dividends that are not treated as passive investment income under section 1362(d)(3)(E) that is deemed to be reasonable under all circumstances.

(2) Lower tier subsidiaries. If a C corporation subsidiary (upper tier corporation) holds stock in another C corporation (lower tier subsidiary) meeting the requirements of section 1504(a)(2), the upper tier corporation's gross receipts attributable to a dividend from the lower tier subsidiary are considered to be derived from the active conduct of a trade or business to the extent the lower tier subsidiary's earnings and profits are attributable to the active conduct of a trade or business by the subsidiary under paragraph (b) (1), (3), (4), or (5) of this section. For purposes of this section, distributions by the lower tier subsidiary will be considered attributable to active earnings and profits according to the rule in paragraph (c) of this section. This paragraph (b)(2) does not apply to any member of a consolidated group (as defined in § 1.1502-1(h)).

(3) De minimis exception. If less than 10 percent of a C corporation's earnings and profits for a taxable year are derived from activities that would produce passive investment income if the C corporation were an S corporation, all earnings and profits produced by the corporation during that taxable year are considered active earnings and profits.

(4) Special rules for earnings and profits accumulated by a C corporation prior to 80 percent acquisition. A C corporation may treat all earnings and profits accumulated by the corporation in all taxable years ending before the S corporation held stock meeting the requirements of section 1504(a)(2) as active earnings and profits in the same proportion as the C corporation's active earnings and profits for the three taxable years ending prior to the time when the S corporation acquired 80 percent of the C corporation bears to the C corporation's total earnings and profits for those three taxable years.

(5) Gross receipts safe harbor. A corporation may treat its earnings and profits for a year as active earnings and profits in the same proportion as the corporation's gross receipts (as defined in § 1.1362-2(c)(4)) derived from activities that would not produce passive investment income (if the C corporation were an S corporation), including those that do not produce passive investment income under paragraphs (b)(2) through (b)(4) of this section, bear to the corporation's total gross receipts for the year in which the earnings and profits are produced.

(c) Allocating distributions to active or passive earnings and profits. *(1) Distributions from current earnings and profits.* Dividends distributed by a C corporation from current earnings and profits are attributable to active earnings and profits in the same proportion as current active earnings and profits bear to total current earnings and profits of the C corporation.

(2) Distributions from accumulated earnings and profits. Dividends distributed by a C corporation out of accumulated earnings and profits for a taxable year are attributable to active earnings and profits in the same proportion as accumulated active earnings and profits for that taxable year bear to total accumulated earnings and profits for that taxable year immediately prior to the distribution.

(3) Adjustments to active earnings and profits. For purposes of applying paragraph (c) (1) or (2) of this section to a distribution, the active earnings and profits of a corporation shall be reduced by the amount of any prior distribution properly treated as attributable to active earnings and profits from the same taxable year.

(4) Special rules for consolidated groups. For purposes of applying section 1362(d)(3) and this section to dividends received by an S corporation from the common parent of a consolidated group (as defined in § 1.1502-1(h)), the following rules apply—

(i) The current earnings and profits, accumulated earnings and profits, and active earnings and profits of the common parent shall be determined under the principles of § 1.1502-33 (relating to earnings and profits of any member of a consolidated group owning stock of another member); and

(ii) The gross receipts of the common parent shall be the sum of the gross receipts of each member of the consolidated group (including the common parent), adjusted to eliminate gross receipts from intercompany transactions (as defined in § 1.1502-13(b)(1)(i)).

(d) Examples. The following examples illustrate the principles of this section:

Example (1). (i) X, an S corporation, owns 85 percent of the one class of stock of Y. On December 31, 2002, Y declares a dividend of $100 ($85 to X), which is equal to Y's current earnings and profits. In 2002, Y has total gross receipts of $1,000, $200 of which would be passive investment income if Y were an S corporation.

(ii) One-fifth ($200/$1,000) of Y's gross receipts for 2002 is attributable to activities that would produce passive investment income. Accordingly, one-fifth of the $100 of earnings and profits is passive, and $17 (⅕ of $85) of the dividend from Y to X is passive investment income.

Example (2). (i) The facts are the same as in Example 1, except that Y owns 90 percent of the stock of Z. Y and Z do not join in the filing of a consolidated return. In 2002, Z has gross receipts of $15,000, $12,000 of which are derived from activities that would produce passive investment income. On December 31, 2002, Z declares a dividend of $1,000 ($900 to Y) from current earnings and profits.

(ii) Four-fifths ($12,000/$15,000) of the dividend from Z to Y are attributable to passive earnings and profits. Accordingly, $720 (⅘ of $900) of the dividend from Z to Y is considered gross receipts from an activity that would produce passive investment income. The $900 dividend to Y gives Y a total of $1,900 ($1,000 + $900) in gross receipts, $920

($200 + $720) of which is attributable to passive investment income-producing activities. Under these facts, $41 ($920/$1,900 of $85) of Y's distribution to X is passive investment income to X.

(e) Effective date. This section applies to dividends received in taxable years beginning on or after January 20, 2000; however, taxpayers may elect to apply the regulations in whole, but not in part, for taxable years beginning on or after January 1, 2000, provided all affected taxpayers apply the regulations in a consistent manner. To make this election, the corporation and all affected taxpayers must file a return or an amended return that is consistent with these rules for the taxable year for which the election is made. For purposes of this section, affected taxpayers means all taxpayers whose returns are affected by the election to apply the regulations.

T.D. 8869, 1/20/2000.

---

§ 1.1363-1 Effect of election on corporation.

(a) Exemption of corporation from income tax. *(1) In general.* Except as provided in this paragraph (a), a small business corporation that makes a valid election under section 1362(a) is exempt from the taxes imposed by chapter 1 of the Internal Revenue Code with respect to taxable years of the corporation for which the election is in effect.

(2) Corporate level taxes. An S corporation is not exempt from the tax imposed by section 1374 (relating to the tax imposed on certain built-in gains), or section 1375 (relating to the tax on excess passive investment income). See also section 1363(d) (relating to the recapture of LIFO benefits) for the rules regarding the payment by an S corporation of LIFO recapture amounts.

(b) Computation of corporate taxable income. The taxable income of an S corporation is computed as described in section 1363(b).

(c) Elections of the S corporation. *(1) In general.* Any elections (other than those described in paragraph (c)(2) of this section) affecting the computation of items derived from an S corporation are made by the corporation. For example, elections of methods of accounting, of computing depreciation, of treating soil and water conservation expenditures, and the option to deduct as expenses intangible drilling and development costs, are made by the corporation and not by the shareholders separately. All corporate elections are applicable to all shareholders.

(2) Exceptions. (i) Each shareholder's pro rata share of expenses described in section 617 paid or accrued by the S corporation is treated according to the shareholder's method of treating those expenses, notwithstanding the treatment of the expenses by the corporation.

(ii) Each shareholder may elect to amortize that shareholder's pro rata share of any qualified expenditure described in section 59(e) paid or accrued by the S corporation.

(iii) Each shareholder's pro rata share of taxes described in section 901 paid or accrued by the S corporation to foreign countries or possessions of the United States (according to its method of treating those taxes) is treated according to the shareholder's method of treating those taxes, and each shareholder may elect to use the total amount either as a credit against tax or as a deduction from income.

(d) Effective date. This section applies to taxable years of corporations beginning after December 31, 1992. For taxable years to which this section does not apply, corporations and shareholders subject to the provisions of section 1363 must take reasonable return positions taking into consideration the statute, its legislative history and these regulations. See Notice 92-56, 1992-49 I.R.B. (see § 601.601(d)(2)(ii)(b) of this chapter), for additional guidance regarding reasonable return positions for taxable years to which this section does not apply.

T.D. 8449, 11/24/92.

PAR. 2. Paragraph (b) of § 1.1363-1 is amended as follows:

1. Paragraph (b) is revised.

2. Paragraph (d) is amended by removing the language "This section applies" and adding the language "This section (except for paragraph (b)(2) of this section) applies" in its place.

3. The paragraph heading for (d) is revised.

4. A sentence is added at the end of paragraph (d).

The revision and additions read as follows:

Proposed § 1.1363-1 Effect of election on corporation. [*For Preamble, see ¶ 152,793*]

* * * * *

(b) Computation of corporate taxable income. *(1) In general.* The taxable income of an S corporation is computed as described in section 1363(b).

(2) Treatment of banks. Section 1363(b) (concerning computation of an S corporation's taxable income) does not affect an S corporation's status as a bank within the meaning of section 581, and it does not prevent the application to such an S corporation bank of any special rule applicable to banks under the Internal Revenue Code, such as sections 582(c) and 291(a)(3) and (e)(1)(B). See § 1.1361-4(a)(3) regarding application under subchapter S of the special rules applicable to banks. Further, section 1363(b)(4) causes section 291 to apply to an S corporation if the S corporation (or any predecessor) was a C corporation for any of the three immediately preceding taxable years, but section 1363(b)(4) does not prevent section 291 from applying to an S corporation to which section 291 otherwise applies.

(3) Example. The following example illustrates the application of this paragraph (b)(2):

Example. (i) Facts. X is described in section 581 and is an S corporation. Neither X nor any of X's predecessors was a C corporation for any of the three immediately preceding taxable years. During the current taxable year, X sold debt instrument DI at a loss. At the time of the sale, X's holding period in DI was more than one year and, but for section 582(c), the loss on the sale of DI would be capital. During the same taxable year, X held debt instrument QD, which it acquired after August 7, 1986. QD is a qualified tax-exempt obligation within the meaning of section 265(b)(3)(B).

(ii) X is described in section 581, and section 1363(b) does not affect X's status under section 581. Accordingly, X qualifies as a bank within the meaning of section 581. Also, section 1363(b) does not prevent any special rule applicable to banks under the Internal Revenue Code from applying to X. Thus, section 582(c), which is a special rule applicable to banks, imposes ordinary character on the loss that X recognized from the sale of debt instrument DI.

(iii) Because QD is a qualified tax-exempt obligation that was acquired after August 7, 1986, section 265(b)(3)(A) causes QD to be treated for purposes of section 291(e)(1)(B) as having been acquired on that date. For that reason, if section 291(e)(1)(B) applies to X, a portion of the interest expense that X incurs during the taxable year is interest on indebtedness incurred or continued to purchase or carry qualified tax-exempt obligations and thus is a financial institution preference item. Section 291(a)(3) and (e)(1)(B) is a special rule applicable to banks, and thus section 1363(b) does not prevent section 291(a)(3) and (e)(1)(B) from applying to X unless some other authority prevents that result.

(iv) Section 1363(b)(4) does not prevent section 291 from applying in situations in which section 291 otherwise applies. Therefore, section 1363(b)(4) does not prevent section 291(a)(3) and (e)(1)(B) from applying to X. It is irrelevant that neither X nor any predecessor of X was a C corporation for any of the three immediately preceding taxable years. X's status as a bank under section 581 causes section 291(a)(3) and (e)(1)(B) to apply.

* * * * *

(d) Effective dates. * * * Paragraph (b)(2) of this section applies to taxable years of corporations beginning on or after August 24, 2006.

§ 1.1363-2 Recapture of LIFO benefits.

(a) In general. A C corporation must include the LIFO recapture amount (as defined in section 1363(d)(3)) in its gross income—

(1) In its last taxable year as a C corporation if the corporation inventoried assets under the LIFO method for its last taxable year before its S corporation election becomes effective; or

(2) In the year of transfer by the C corporation to an S corporation of the LIFO inventory assets if paragraph (a)(1) of this section does not apply and the C corporation—

(i) Inventoried assets under the LIFO method during the taxable year of the transfer of those LIFO inventory assets; and

(ii) Transferred the LIFO inventory assets to the S corporation in a nonrecognition transaction (within the meaning of section 7701(a)(45)) in which the transferred assets constitute transferred basis property (within the meaning of section 7701(a)(43)).

(b) LIFO inventory held indirectly through partnership. A C corporation must include the lookthrough LIFO recapture amount (as defined in paragraph (c)(4) of this section) in its gross income—

(1) In its last taxable year as a C corporation if, on the last day of the corporation's last taxable year before its S corporation election becomes effective, the corporation held a lookthrough partnership interest (as defined in paragraph (c)(3) of this section); or

(2) In the year of transfer by the C corporation to an S corporation of a lookthrough partnership interest if the corporation transferred its lookthrough partnership interest to the S corporation in a nonrecognition transaction (within the meaning of section 7701(a)(45)) in which the transferred interest constitutes transferred basis property (within the meaning of section 7701(a)(43)).

(c) Definitions and special rules. *(1) Recapture date.* In the case of a transaction described in paragraph (a)(1) or (b)(1) of this section, the recapture date is the day before the effective date of the S corporation election. In the case of a transaction described in paragraph (a)(2) or (b)(2) of this section, the recapture date is the date of the transfer of the partnership interest to the S corporation.

(2) Determination of LIFO recapture amount. The LIFO recapture amount shall be determined as of the end of the recapture date for transactions described in paragraph (a)(1) of this section, and as of the moment before the transfer occurs for transactions described in paragraph (a)(2) of this section.

(3) Lookthrough partnership interest. A partnership interest is a lookthrough partnership interest if the partnership owns (directly or indirectly through one or more partnerships) assets accounted for under the last-in, first-out (LIFO) method (LIFO inventory).

(4) Lookthrough LIFO recapture amount. (i) In general. For purposes of this section, a corporation's lookthrough LIFO recapture amount is the amount of income that would be allocated to the corporation, taking into account section 704(c) and § 1.704-3, if the partnership sold all of its LIFO inventory for the inventory's FIFO value. For this purpose, the FIFO value of inventory is the inventory amount of the inventory assets under the first-in, first-out method of accounting authorized by section 471, determined in accordance with section 1363(d)(4)(C).

(ii) Determination of lookthrough LIFO recapture amount. Except as provided in paragraph (c)(4)(iii) of this section, the lookthrough LIFO recapture amount shall be determined as of the end of the recapture date for transactions described in paragraph (b)(1) of this section, and as of the moment before the transfer occurs for transactions described in paragraph (b)(2) of this section.

(iii) Alternative rule. If the partnership is not otherwise required to determine the inventory amount of the inventory using the LIFO method (the LIFO value) on the recapture date, the partnership may determine the lookthrough LIFO recapture amount as though the FIFO and LIFO values of the inventory on the recapture date equaled the FIFO and LIFO values of the opening inventory for the partnership's taxable year that includes the recapture date. For this purpose, the opening inventory includes inventory contributed by a partner to the partnership on or before the recapture date and excludes inventory distributed by the partnership to a partner on or before the recapture date. A partnership that applies the alternative method of this paragraph (c)(4)(iii) to calculate the lookthrough LIFO recapture amount must take into account any adjustments to the partnership's basis in its LIFO inventory that result from transactions occurring after the start of the partnership's taxable year and before the end of the recapture date. For example, the lookthrough LIFO recapture amount must be adjusted to take into account any adjustments to the basis of LIFO inventory during that period under sections 734(b), 737(c), or 751(b).

(d) Payment of tax. Any increase in tax caused by including the LIFO recapture amount or the lookthrough LIFO recapture amount in the gross income of the C corporation is payable in four equal installments. The C corporation must pay the first installment of this payment by the due date of its return, determined without regard to extensions, for the last taxable year it operated as a C corporation if paragraph (a)(1) or (b)(1) of this section applies, or for the taxable year of the transfer if paragraph (a)(2) or (b)(2) of this section applies. The three succeeding installments must be paid—

(1) For a transaction described in paragraph (a)(1) or (b)(1) of this section, by the corporation that made the election under section 1362(a) to be an S corporation, on or before the due date for the corporation's returns (determined without regard to extensions) for the succeeding three taxable years; and

(2) For a transaction described in paragraph (a)(2) or (b)(2) of this section, by the transferee S corporation on or before the due date for the transferee corporation's returns (determined without regard to extensions) for the succeeding three taxable years.

(e) Basis adjustments. *(1) General rule.* Appropriate adjustments to the basis of inventory are to be made to reflect any amount included in income under paragraph (a) of this section.

(2) LIFO inventory owned through a partnership. (i) Basis of corporation's partnership interest. Appropriate adjustments to the basis of the corporation's lookthrough partnership interest are to be made to reflect any amount included in income under paragraph (b) of this section.

(ii) Basis of partnership assets. A partnership directly holding LIFO inventory that is taken into account under paragraph (b) of this section may elect to adjust the basis of that LIFO inventory. In addition, a partnership that holds, through another partnership, LIFO inventory that is taken into account under paragraph (b) of this section may elect to adjust the basis of that partnership interest. Any adjustment under this paragraph (e)(2) to the basis of inventory held by the partnership is equal to the amount of LIFO recapture attributable to the inventory. Likewise, any adjustment under this paragraph (e)(2) to the basis of a lookthrough partnership interest held by the partnership is equal to the amount of LIFO recapture attributable to the interest. A basis adjustment under this paragraph (e)(2) is treated in the same manner and has the same effect as an adjustment to the basis of partnership property under section 743(b). See § 1.743-1(j).

(3) Election. A partnership elects to adjust the basis of its inventory and any lookthrough partnership interest that it owns by attaching a statement to its original or amended income tax return for the first taxable year ending on or after the date of the S corporation election or transfer described in paragraph (b) of this section. This statement shall state that the partnership is electing under this paragraph (e)(3) and must include the names, addresses, and taxpayer identification numbers of any corporate partner liable for tax under paragraph (d) of this section and of the partnership, as well as the amount of the adjustment and the portion of the adjustment that is attributable to each pool of inventory or lookthrough partnership interest that is held by the partnership.

(f) Examples. The following examples illustrate the rules of this section:

Example (1). (i) G is a C corporation with a taxable year ending on June 30. GH is a partnership with a calendar year taxable year. G has a 20 percent interest in GH. The remaining 80 percent interest is owned by an individual. On April 25, 2005, G contributed inventory that is LIFO inventory to GH, increasing G's interest in the partnership to 50 percent. GH holds no other LIFO inventory, and there are no other adjustments to the partnership's basis in its LIFO inventory between January 1, 2005 and the end of the recapture date. G elects to be an S corporation effective July 1, 2005. The recapture date is June 30, 2005 under paragraph (c)(1) of this section. GH elects to use the LIFO method for the inventory and determines that the FIFO and LIFO values of the opening inventory for GH's 2005 taxable year, including the inventory contributed by G, are $200 and $120, respectively.

(ii) Under paragraph (c)(4)(iii) of this section, GH is not required to determine the FIFO and LIFO values of the inventory on the recapture date. Instead, GH may determine the lookthrough LIFO recapture amount as though the FIFO and LIFO values of the inventory on the recapture date equaled the FIFO and LIFO values of the opening inventory for the partnership's taxable year (2005) that includes the recapture date. For this purpose, under paragraph (c)(4) of this section, the opening inventory includes the inventory contributed by G. The amount by which the FIFO value ($200) exceeds the LIFO value ($120) in GH's opening inventory is $80. Thus, if GH sold all of its LIFO inventory for $200, it would recognize $80 of income. G's lookthrough LIFO recapture amount is $80, the amount of income that would be allocated to G, taking into account section 704(c) and § 1.704-3, if GH sold all of its LIFO inventory for the FIFO value. Under paragraph (b)(1) of this section, G must include $80 in income in its taxable year ending on June 30, 2005. Under paragraph (e)(2) of this section, G must increase its basis in its interest in GH by $80. Under paragraphs (e)(2) and (3) of this section, and in accordance with section 743(b) principles, GH may elect to increase the basis (with respect to G only) of its LIFO inventory by $80.

Example (2). (i) J is a C corporation with a calendar year taxable year. JK is a partnership with a calendar year taxable year. J has a 30 percent interest in the partnership. JK owns LIFO inventory that is not section 704(c) property. J elects to be an S corporation effective January 1, 2005. The recapture date is December 31, 2004 under paragraph (c)(1) of this section. JK determines that the FIFO and LIFO values of the inventory on December 31, 2004 are $240 and $140, respectively.

(ii) The amount by which the FIFO value ($240) exceeds the LIFO value ($140) on the recapture date is $100. Thus, if JK sold all of its LIFO inventory for $240, it would recognize $100 of income. J's lookthrough LIFO recapture amount is $30, the amount of income that would be allocated to J if JK sold all of its LIFO inventory for the FIFO value (30 percent of $100). Under paragraph (b)(1) of this section, J must include $30 in income in its taxable year ending on December 31, 2004. Under paragraph (e)(2) of this section, J must increase its basis in its interest in JK by $30. Under paragraphs (e)(2) and (3) of this section, and in accordance with section 743(b) principles, JK may elect to increase the basis (with respect to J only) of its inventory by $30.

(g) Effective dates. *(1)* The provisions of paragraph (a)(1) of this section apply to S elections made after December 17, 1987. For an exception, see section 10227(b)(2) of the Revenue Act of 1987.

(2) The provisions of paragraph (a)(2) of this section apply to transfers made after August 18, 1993.

(3) The provisions of paragraphs (b), (c), (d), (e)(2), (e)(3), and (f) of this section apply to S elections and transfers made on or after August 13, 2004. The rules that apply to S elections and transfers made before August 13, 2004, are contained in § 1.1363-2 as in effect prior to August 13, 2004 (see 26 CFR part 1 revised as of April 1, 2005).

T.D. 8567, 10/6/94, amend T.D. 9210, 7/11/2005.

§ 1.1366-0 Table of contents.

The following table of contents is provided to facilitate the use of §§ 1.1366-1 through 1.1366-5:

T.D. 8852, 12/21/99, amend T.D. 9422, 8/13/2008.

---

§ 1.1366-1 Shareholder's share of items of an S corporation.

Caution: The Treasury has not yet amended Reg § 1.1366-1 to reflect changes made by P.L. 110-246.

(a) Determination of shareholder's tax liability. *(1) In general.* An S corporation must report, and a shareholder is required to take into account in the shareholder's return, the shareholder's pro rata share, whether or not distributed, of the S corporation's items of income, loss, deduction, or credit described in paragraphs (a)(2), (3), and (4) of this section. A shareholder's pro rata share is determined in accordance with the provisions of section 1377(a) and the regulations thereunder. The shareholder takes these items into account in determining the shareholder's taxable income and tax liability for the shareholder's taxable year with or within which the taxable year of the corporation ends. If the shareholder dies (or if the shareholder is an estate or trust and the estate or trust terminates) before the end of the taxable year of the corporation, the shareholder's pro rata share of these items is taken into account on the shareholder's final return. For the limitation on allowance of a shareholder's pro rata share of S corporation losses or deductions, see section 1366(d) and § 1.1366-2.

(2) Separately stated items of income, loss, deduction, or credit. Each shareholder must take into account separately the shareholder's pro rata share of any item of income (including tax-exempt income), loss, deduction, or credit of the S corporation that if separately taken into account by any shareholder could affect the shareholder's tax liability for that taxable year differently than if the shareholder did not take the item into account separately. The separately stated items of the S corporation include, but are not limited to, the following items—

(i) The corporation's combined net amount of gains and losses from sales or exchanges of capital assets grouped by applicable holding periods, by applicable rate of tax under section 1(h), and by any other classification that may be relevant in determining the shareholder's tax liability;

(ii) The corporation's combined net amount of gains and losses from sales or exchanges of property described in section 1231 (relating to property used in the trade or business and involuntary conversions), grouped by applicable holding periods, by applicable rate of tax under section 1(h), and by any other classification that may be relevant in determining the shareholder's tax liability;

(iii) Charitable contributions, grouped by the percentage limitations of section 170(b), paid by the corporation within the taxable year of the corporation;

(iv) The taxes described in section 901 that have been paid (or accrued) by the corporation to foreign countries or to possessions of the United States;

(v) Each of the corporation's separate items involved in the determination of credits against tax allowable under part IV of subchapter A (section 21 and following) of the Internal Revenue Code, except for any credit allowed under section 34 (relating to certain uses of gasoline and special fuels);

(vi) Each of the corporation's separate items of gains and losses from wagering transactions (section 165(d)); soil and water conservation expenditures (section 175); deduction under an election to expense certain depreciable business expenses (section 179); medical, dental, etc., expenses (section 213); the additional itemized deductions for individuals provided in part VII of subchapter B (section 212 and following) of the Internal Revenue Code; and any other itemized deductions for which the limitations on itemized deductions under sections 67 or 68 applies;

(vii) Any of the corporation's items of portfolio income or loss, and expenses related thereto, as defined in the regulations under section 469;

(viii) The corporation's tax-exempt income. For purposes of subchapter S, tax-exempt income is income that is permanently excludible from gross income in all circumstances in which the applicable provision of the Internal Revenue Code applies. For example, income that is excludible from gross income under section 101 (certain death benefits) or section 103 (interest on state and local bonds) is tax-exempt income, while income that is excludible from gross income under section 108 (income from discharge of indebtedness) or section 109 (improvements by lessee on lessor's property) is not tax-exempt income;

(ix) The corporation's adjustments described in sections 56 and 58, and items of tax preference described in section 57; and

(x) Any item identified in guidance (including forms and instructions) issued by the Commissioner as an item required to be separately stated under this paragraph (a)(2).

(3) Nonseparately computed income or loss. Each shareholder must take into account separately the shareholder's pro rata share of the nonseparately computed income or loss of the S corporation. For this purpose, nonseparately computed income or loss means the corporation's gross income less the deductions allowed to the corporation under chapter 1 of the Internal Revenue Code, determined by excluding any item requiring separate computation under paragraph (a)(2) of this section.

(4) Separate activities requirement. An S corporation must report, and each shareholder must take into account in the shareholder's return, the shareholder's pro rata share of an S corporation's items of income, loss, deduction, or credit described in paragraphs (a)(2) and (3) of this section for each of the corporation's activities as defined in section 469 and the regulations thereunder.

(5) Aggregation of deductions or exclusions for purposes of limitations. (i) In general. A shareholder aggregates the shareholder's separate deductions or exclusions with the shareholder's pro rata share of the S corporation's separately stated deductions or exclusions in determining the amount of any deduction or exclusion allowable to the shareholder under subtitle A of the Internal Revenue Code as to which a limitation is imposed.

(ii) Example. The provisions of paragraph (a)(5)(i) of this section are illustrated by the following example:

Example. In 1999, Corporation M, a calendar year S corporation, purchases and places in service section 179 property costing $10,000. Corporation M elects to expense the entire cost of the property. Shareholder A owns 50 percent of the stock of Corporation M. Shareholder A's pro rata share of this item after Corporation M applies the section 179(b) limitations is $5,000. Because the aggregate amount of Shareholder A's pro rata share and separately acquired section 179 expense may not exceed $19,000 (the aggregate maximum cost that may be taken into account under section 179(a) for the applicable taxable year), Shareholder A may elect to expense up to $14,000 of separately acquired section 179 property that is purchased and placed in service in 1999, subject to the limitations of section 179(b).

(b) Character of items constituting pro rata share. *(1) In general.* Except as provided in paragraph (b)(2) or (3) of this section, the character of any item of income, loss, deduction, or credit described in section 1366(a)(1)(A) or (B) and paragraph (a) of this section is determined for the S corporation and retains that character in the hands of the shareholder. For example, if an S corporation has capital gain on the sale or exchange of a capital asset, a shareholder's pro rata share of that gain will also be characterized as a capital gain regardless of whether the shareholder is otherwise a dealer in that type of property. Similarly, if an S corporation engages in an activity that is not for profit (as defined in section 183), a shareholder's pro rata share of the S corporation's deductions will be characterized as not for profit. Also, if an S corporation makes a charitable contribution to an organization qualifying under section 170(b)(1)(A), a shareholder's pro rata share of the S corporation's charitable contribution will be characterized as made to an organization qualifying under section 170(b)(1)(A).

(2) Exception for contribution of noncapital gain property. If an S corporation is formed or availed of by any shareholder or group of shareholders for a principal purpose of selling or exchanging contributed property that in the hands of the shareholder or shareholders would not have produced capital gain if sold or exchanged by the shareholder or shareholders, then the gain on the sale or exchange of the property recognized by the corporation is not treated as a capital gain.

(3) Exception for contribution of capital loss property. If an S corporation is formed or availed of by any shareholder or group of shareholders for a principal purpose of selling or exchanging contributed property that in the hands of the shareholder or shareholders would have produced capital loss if sold or exchanged by the shareholder or shareholders, then the loss on the sale or exchange of the property recognized by the corporation is treated as a capital loss to the extent that, immediately before the contribution, the adjusted basis of the property in the hands of the shareholder or shareholders exceeded the fair market value of the property.

(c) Gross income of a shareholder. *(1) In general.* Where it is necessary to determine the amount or character of the gross income of a shareholder, the shareholder's gross income includes the shareholder's pro rata share of the gross income of the S corporation. The shareholder's pro rata share of the gross income of the S corporation is the amount of gross income of the corporation used in deriving the shareholder's pro rata share of S corporation taxable income or loss (including items described in section 1366(a)(1)(A) or (B) and paragraph (a) of this section). For example, a shareholder is required to include the shareholder's pro rata share of S corporation gross income in computing the shareholder's gross income for the purposes of determining the necessity of filing a return (section 6012(a)) and the shareholder's gross income derived from farming (sections 175 and 6654(i)).

(2) Gross income for substantial omission of items. (i) In general. For purposes of determining the applicability of the 6-year period of limitation on assessment and collection provided in section 6501(e) (relating to omission of more than 25 percent of gross income), a shareholder's gross income includes the shareholder's pro rata share of S corporation

gross income (as described in section 6501(e)(1)(A)(i)). In this respect, the amount of S corporation gross income used in deriving the shareholder's pro rata share of any item of S corporation income, loss, deduction, or credit (as included or disclosed in the shareholder's return) is considered as an amount of gross income stated in the shareholder's return for purposes of section 6501(e).

(ii) Example. The following example illustrates the provisions of paragraph (c)(2)(i) of this section:

Example. Shareholder A, an individual, owns 25 percent of the stock of Corporation N, an S corporation that has $10,000 gross income and $2,000 taxable income. A reports only $300 as A's pro rata share of N's taxable income. A should have reported $500 as A's pro rata share of taxable income, derived from A's pro rata share, $2,500, of N's gross income. Because A's return included only $300 without a disclosure meeting the requirements of section 6501(e)(1)(A)(ii) describing the difference of $200, A is regarded as having reported on the return only $1,500 ($300/$500 of $2,500) as gross income from N.

(d) Shareholders holding stock subject to community property laws. If a shareholder holds S corporation stock that is community property, then the shareholder's pro rata share of any item or items listed in paragraphs (a)(2), (3), and (4) of this section with respect to that stock is reported by the husband and wife in accordance with community property rules.

(e) Net operating loss deduction of shareholder of S corporation. For purposes of determining a net operating loss deduction under section 172, a shareholder of an S corporation must take into account the shareholder's pro rata share of items of income, loss, deduction, or credit of the corporation. See section 1366(b) and paragraph (b) of this section for rules on determining the character of the items. In determining under section 172(d)(4) the nonbusiness deductions allowable to a shareholder of an S corporation (arising from both corporation sources and any other sources), the shareholder separately takes into account the shareholder's pro rata share of the deductions of the corporation that are not attributable to a trade or business and combines this amount with the shareholder's nonbusiness deductions from any other sources. The shareholder also separately takes into account the shareholder's pro rata share of the gross income of the corporation not derived from a trade or business and combines this amount with the shareholder's nonbusiness income from all other sources. See section 172 and the regulations thereunder.

(f) Cross-reference. For rules relating to the consistent tax treatment of subchapter S items, see section 6037(c).

T.D. 8852, 12/21/99.

§ 1.1366-2 Limitations on deduction of passthrough items of an S corporation to its shareholders.

Caution: The Treasury has not yet amended Reg § 1.1366-2 to reflect changes made by P.L. 108-357.

(a) In general. *(1) Limitation on losses and deductions.* The aggregate amount of losses and deductions taken into account by a shareholder under § 1.1366-1(a) (2), (3), and (4) for any taxable year of an S corporation cannot exceed the sum of—

(i) The adjusted basis of the shareholder's stock in the corporation (as determined under paragraph (a)(3)(i) of this section); and

(ii) The adjusted basis of any indebtedness of the corporation to the shareholder (as determined under paragraph (a)(3)(ii) of this section).

(2) Carryover of disallowance. A shareholder's aggregate amount of losses and deductions for a taxable year in excess of the sum of the adjusted basis of the shareholder's stock in an S corporation and of any indebtedness of the S corporation to the shareholder is not allowed for the taxable year. However, any disallowed loss or deduction retains its character and is treated as incurred by the corporation in the corporation's first succeeding taxable year, and subsequent taxable years, with respect to the shareholder. For rules on determining the adjusted bases of stock of an S corporation and indebtedness of the corporation to the shareholder, see paragraphs (a)(3) (i) and (ii) of this section.

(3) Basis limitation amount (i) Stock portion. A shareholder generally determines the adjusted basis of stock for purposes of paragraphs (a)(1)(i) and (2) of this section (limiting losses and deductions) by taking into account only increases in basis under section 1367(a)(1) for the taxable year and decreases in basis under section 1367(a)(2) (A), (D) and (E) (relating to distributions, noncapital, nondeductible expenses, and certain oil and gas depletion deductions) for the taxable year. In so determining this loss limitation amount, the shareholder disregards decreases in basis under section 1367(a)(2) (B) and (C) (for losses and deductions, including losses and deductions previously disallowed) for the taxable year. However, if the shareholder has in effect for the taxable year an election under § 1.1367-1(g) to decrease basis by items of loss and deduction prior to decreasing basis by noncapital, nondeductible expenses and certain oil and gas depletion deductions, the shareholder also disregards decreases in basis under section 1367(a)(2) (D) and (E). This basis limitation amount for stock is determined at the time prescribed under § 1.1367-1(d)(1) for adjustments to the basis of stock.

(iii) Indebtedness portion. A shareholder determines the shareholder's adjusted basis in indebtedness of the corporation for purposes of paragraphs (a)(1)(ii) and (2) of this section (limiting losses and deductions) without regard to any adjustment under section 1367(b)(2)(A) for the taxable year. This basis limitation amount for indebtedness is determined at the time prescribed under § 1.1367-2(d)(1) for adjustments to the basis of indebtedness.

(4) Limitation on losses and deductions allocated to each item. If a shareholder's pro rata share of the aggregate amount of losses and deductions specified in § 1.1366-1(a)(2), (3), and (4) exceeds the sum of the adjusted basis of the shareholder's stock in the corporation (determined in accordance with paragraph (a)(3)(i) of this section) and the adjusted basis of any indebtedness of the corporation to the shareholder (determined in accordance with paragraph (a)(3)(ii) of this section), then the limitation on losses and deductions under section 1366(d)(1) must be allocated among the shareholder's pro rata share of each loss or deduction. The amount of the limitation allocated to any loss or deduction is an amount that bears the same ratio to the amount of the limitation as the loss or deduction bears to the total of the losses and deductions. For this purpose, the total of losses and deductions for the taxable year is the sum of the shareholder's pro rata share of losses and deductions for the taxable year, and the losses and deductions disallowed and carried forward from prior years pursuant to section 1366(d)(2).

(5) Nontransferability of losses and deductions.

(i) In general. Except as provided in paragraph (a)(5)(ii) of this section, any loss or deduction disallowed under paragraph (a)(1) of this section is personal to the shareholder and cannot in any manner be transferred to another person. If a shareholder transfers some but not all of the shareholder's stock in the corporation, the amount of any disallowed loss or deduction under this section is not reduced and the transferee does not acquire any portion of the disallowed loss or deduction. If a shareholder transfers all of the shareholder's stock in the corporation, any disallowed loss or deduction is permanently disallowed.

(ii) Exceptions for transfers of stock under section 1041(a). If a shareholder transfers stock of an S corporation after December 31, 2004, in a transfer described in section 1041(a), any loss or deduction with respect to the transferred stock that is disallowed to the transferring shareholder under paragraph (a)(1) of this section shall be treated as incurred by the corporation in the following taxable year with respect to the transferee spouse or former spouse. The amount of any loss or deduction with respect to the stock transferred shall be determined by prorating any losses or deductions disallowed under paragraph (a)(1) of this section for the year of the transfer between the transferor and the spouse or former spouse based on the stock ownership at the beginning of the following taxable year. If a transferor claims a deduction for losses in the taxable year of transfer, then under paragraph (a)(4) of this section, if the transferor's pro rata share of the losses and deductions in the year of transfer exceeds the transferor's basis in stock and the indebtedness of the corporation to the transferor, then the limitation must be allocated among the transferor spouse's pro rata share of each loss or deduction, including disallowed losses and deductions carried over from the prior year.

(iii) Examples. The following examples illustrates the provisions of paragraph (a)(5)(ii) of this section:

Example (1). A owns all 100 shares in X, a calendar year S corporation. For X's taxable year ending December 31, 2006, A has zero basis in the shares and X does not have any indebtedness to A. For the 2006 taxable year, X had $100 in losses that A cannot use because of the basis limitation in section 1366(d)(1) and that are treated as incurred by the corporation with respect to A in the following taxable year. Halfway through the 2007 taxable year, A transfers 50 shares to B, A's former spouse in a transfer to which section 1041(a) applies. In the 2007 taxable year, X has $80 in losses. On A's 2007 individual income tax return, A may use the entire $100 carryover loss from 2006, as well as A's share of the $80 2007 loss determined under section 1377(a) ($60), assuming A acquires sufficient basis in the X stock. On B's 2007 individual income tax return, B may use B's share of the $80 2007 loss determined under section 1377(a) ($20), assuming B has sufficient basis in the X stock. If any disallowed 2006 loss is disallowed to A under section 1366(d)(1) in 2007, that loss is prorated between A and B based on their stock ownership at the beginning of 2008. On B's 2008 individual income tax return, B may use that loss, assuming B acquires sufficient basis in the X stock. If neither A nor B acquires any basis during the 2007 taxable year, then as of the beginning of 2008, the corporation will be treated as incurring $50 of loss with respect to A and $50 of loss with respect to B for the $100 of disallowed 2006 loss, and the corporation will be treated as incurring $60 of loss with respect to A and $20 with respect to B for the $80 of disallowed 2007 loss.

Example (2). Assume the same facts as Example 1, except that during the 2007 taxable year, A acquires $10 of basis in A's shares in X. For the 2007 taxable year, A may claim a $10 loss deduction, which represents $6.25 of the disallowed 2006 loss of $100 and $3.75 of A's 2007 loss of $60. The disallowed 2006 loss is reduced to $93.75. As of the beginning of 2008, the corporation will be treated as incurring half of the remaining $93.75 of loss with respect to A and half of that loss with respect to B for the remaining $93.75 of disallowed 2006 loss, and if B does not acquire any basis during 2007, the corporation will be treated as incurring $56.25 of loss with respect to A and $20 with respect to B for the remaining disallowed 2007 loss.

(6) Basis of stock acquired by gift. For purposes of section 1366(d)(1)(A) and paragraphs (a)(1)(i) and (2) of this section, the basis of stock in a corporation acquired by gift is the basis of the stock that is used for purposes of determining loss under section 1015(a).

(b) Special rules for carryover of disallowed losses and deductions to post-termination transition period described in section 1377(b). *(1) In general.* If, for the last taxable year of a corporation for which it was an S corporation, a loss or deduction was disallowed to a shareholder by reason of the limitation in paragraph (a) of this section, the loss or deduction is treated under section 1366(d)(3) as incurred by that shareholder on the last day of any post-termination transition period (within the meaning of section 1377(b)).

(2) Limitation on losses and deductions. The aggregate amount of losses and deductions taken into account by a shareholder under paragraph (b)(1) of this section cannot exceed the adjusted basis of the shareholder's stock in the corporation determined at the close of the last day of the post-termination transition period. For this purpose, the adjusted basis of a shareholder's stock in the corporation is determined at the close of the last day of the post-termination transition period without regard to any reduction required under paragraph (b)(4) of this section. If a shareholder disposes of a share of stock prior to the close of the last day of the post-termination transition period, the adjusted basis of that share is its basis as of the close of the day of disposition. Any losses and deductions in excess of a shareholder's adjusted stock basis are permanently disallowed. For purposes of section 1366(d)(3)(B) and this paragraph (b)(2), the basis of stock in a corporation acquired by gift is the basis of the stock that is used for purposes of determining loss under section 1015(a).

(3) Limitation on losses and deductions allocated to each item. If the aggregate amount of losses and deductions treated as incurred by the shareholder under paragraph (b)(1) of this section exceeds the adjusted basis of the shareholder's stock determined under paragraph (b)(2) of this section, the limitation on losses and deductions under section 1366(d)(3)(B) must be allocated among each loss or deduction. The amount of the limitation allocated to each loss or deduction is an amount that bears the same ratio to the amount of the limitation as the amount of each loss or deduction bears to the total of all the losses and deductions.

(4) Adjustment to the basis of stock. The shareholder's basis in the stock of the corporation is reduced by the amount allowed as a deduction by reason of this paragraph (b). For rules regarding adjustments to the basis of a shareholder's stock in an S corporation, see § 1.1367-1.

(c) Carryover of disallowed losses and deductions in the case of liquidations, reorganizations, and divisions. *(1) Liquidations and reorganizations.* If a corporation acquires the assets of an S corporation in a transaction to which section 381(a) applies, any loss or deduction disallowed under paragraph (a) of this section with respect to a shareholder of the distributor or transferor S corporation is available to that shareholder as a shareholder of the acquiring corporation. Thus, where the acquiring corporation is an S corporation, a loss or deduction of a shareholder of the distributor or transferor S corporation disallowed prior to or during the taxable year of the transaction is treated as incurred by the acquiring S corporation with respect to that shareholder if the shareholder is a shareholder of the acquiring S corporation after the transaction. Where the acquiring corporation is a C corporation, a post-termination transition period arises the day after the last day that an S corporation was in existence and the rules provided in paragraph (b) of this section apply with respect to any shareholder of the acquired S corporation that is also a shareholder of the acquiring C corporation after the transaction. See the special rules under section 1377 for the availability of the post-termination transition period if the acquiring corporation is a C corporation.

(2) Corporate separations to which section 368(a)(1)(D) applies. If an S corporation transfers a portion of its assets constituting an active trade or business to another corporation in a transaction to which section 368(a)(1)(D) applies, and immediately thereafter the stock and securities of the controlled corporation are distributed in a distribution or exchange to which section 355 (or so much of section 356 as relates to section 355) applies, any loss or deduction disallowed under paragraph (a) of this section with respect to a shareholder of the distributing S corporation immediately before the transaction is allocated between the distributing corporation and the controlled corporation with respect to the shareholder. Such allocation shall be made according to any reasonable method, including a method based on the relative fair market value of the shareholder's stock in the distributing and controlled corporations immediately after the distribution, a method based on the relative adjusted basis of the assets in the distributing and controlled corporations immediately after the distribution, or, in the case of losses and deductions clearly attributable to either the distributing or controlled corporation, any method that allocates such losses and deductions accordingly.

T.D. 8247, 4/4/89, amend T.D. 8852, 12/21/99, T.D. 9422, 8/13/2008.

§ 1.1366-3 Treatment of family groups.

Caution: The Treasury has not yet amended Reg § 1.1366-3 to reflect changes made by 110-172.

(a) In general. Under section 1366(e), if an individual, who is a member of the family of one or more shareholders of an S corporation, renders services for, or furnishes capital to, the corporation without receiving reasonable compensation, the Commissioner shall prescribe adjustments to those items taken into account by the individual and the shareholders as may be necessary to reflect the value of the services rendered or capital furnished. For these purposes, in determining the reasonable value for services rendered, or capital furnished, to the corporation, consideration will be given to all the facts and circumstances, including the amount that ordinarily would be paid in order to obtain comparable services or capital from a person (other than a member of the family) who is not a shareholder in the corporation. In addition, for purposes of section 1366(e), if a member of the family of one or more shareholders of the S corporation holds an interest in a passthrough entity (e.g., a partnership, S corporation, trust, or estate), that performs services for, or furnishes capital to, the S corporation without receiving reasonable compensation, the Commissioner shall prescribe adjustments to the passthrough entity and the corporation as may be necessary to reflect the value of the services rendered or capital furnished. For purposes of section 1366(e), the term family of any shareholder includes only the shareholder's spouse, ancestors, lineal descendants, and any trust for the primary benefit of any of these persons.

(b) Examples. The provisions of this section may be illustrated by the following examples:

Example (1). The stock of an S corporation is owned 50 percent by F and 50 percent by T, the minor son of F. For the taxable year, the corporation has items of taxable income equal to $70,000. Compensation of $10,000 is paid by the corporation to F for services rendered during the taxable year, and no compensation is paid to T, who rendered no services. Based on all the relevant facts and circumstances, reasonable compensation for the services rendered by F would be $30,000. In the discretion of the Internal Revenue Service, up to an additional $20,000 of the $70,000 of the corporation's taxable income, for tax purposes, may be allocated to F as compensation for services rendered. If the Internal Revenue Service allocates $20,000 of the corporation's taxable income to F as compensation for services, taxable income of the corporation would be reduced by $20,000 to $50,000, of which F and T each would be allocated $25,000. F would have $30,000 of total compensation paid by the corporation for services rendered.

Example (2). The stock of an S corporation is owned by A and B. For the taxable year, the corporation has paid compensation to a partnership that rendered services to the corporation during the taxable year. The spouse of A is a partner in that partnership. Consequently, if based on all the relevant facts and circumstances the partnership did not receive reasonable compensation for the services rendered to the corporation, the Internal Revenue Service, in its discretion, may make adjustments to those items taken into account by the partnership and the corporation as may be necessary to reflect the value of the services rendered.

T.D. 8852, 12/21/99.

§ 1.1366-4 Special rules limiting the passthrough of certain items of an S corporation to its shareholders.

(a) Passthrough inapplicable to section 34 credit. Section 1.1366-1(a) does not apply to any credit allowable under section 34 (relating to certain uses of gasoline and special fuels).

(b) Reduction in passthrough for tax imposed on built-in gains. For purposes of § 1.1366-1(a), if for any taxable year of the S corporation a tax is imposed on the corporation under section 1374, the amount of the tax imposed is treated as a loss sustained by the S corporation during the taxable year. The character of the deemed loss is determined by allocating the loss proportionately among the net recognized built-in gains giving rise to the tax and attributing the character of each net recognized built-in gain to the allocable portion of the loss.

(c) Reduction in passthrough for tax imposed on excess net passive income. For purposes of § 1.1366-1(a), if for any taxable year of the S corporation a tax is imposed on the corporation under section 1375, each item of passive investment income shall be reduced by an amount that bears the same ratio to the amount of the tax as the net amount of the item bears to the total net passive investment income for that taxable year.

T.D. 8852, 12/21/99.

§ 1.1366-5 Effective date.

Sections 1.1366-1 through 1.1366-4 apply to taxable years of an S corporation beginning on or after August 18, 1998. Sections 1.1366-2(a)(5)(i), (ii) and (iii) are effective on August 14, 2008.

T.D. 8852, 12/21/99, amend T.D. 9422, 8/13/2008.

§ 1.1367-0 Table of contents.

The following table of contents is provided to facilitate the use of §§ 1.1367-1 through 1.1367-3.

T.D. 8508, 12/30/93, amend T.D. 8852, 12/21/99.

§ 1.1367-1 Adjustments to basis of shareholder's stock in an S corporation.

Caution: The Treasury has not yet amended Reg § 1.1367-1 to reflect changes made by P.L. 104-188.

(a) In general. *(1) Adjustments under section 1367.* This section provides rules relating to adjustments required by section 1367 to the basis of a shareholder's stock in an S corporation. Paragraph (b) of this section provides rules concerning increases in the basis of a shareholder's stock, and paragraph (c) of this section provides rules concerning decreases in the basis of a shareholder's stock.

(2) Applicability of other Internal Revenue Code provisions. In addition to the adjustments required by section 1367 and this section, the basis of stock is determined or adjusted under other applicable provisions of the Internal Revenue Code.

(b) Increase in basis of stock. *(1) In general.* Except as provided in § 1.1367-2(c) (relating to restoration of basis of indebtedness to the shareholder), the basis of a shareholder's stock in an S corporation is increased by the sum of the items described in section 1367(a)(1). The increase in basis described in section 1367(a)(1)(C) for the excess of the deduction for depletion over the basis of the property subject to depletion does not include the depletion deduction attributable to oil or gas property. See section 613(A)(c)(11).

(2) Amount of increase in basis of individual shares. The basis of a shareholder's share of stock is increased by an amount equal to the shareholder's pro rata portion of the items described in section 1367(a)(1) that is attributable to that share, determined on a per share, per day basis in accordance with section 1377(a).

(c) Decrease in basis of stock. *(1) In general.* The basis of a shareholder's stock in an S corporation is decreased (but not below zero) by the sum of the items described in section 1367(a)(2).

(2) Noncapital, nondeductible expenses. For purposes of section 1367(a)(2)(D), expenses of the corporation not deductible in computing its taxable income and not properly chargeable to a capital account (noncapital, nondeductible expenses) are only those items for which no loss or deduction is allowable and do not include items the deduction for which is deferred to a later taxable year. Examples of noncapital, nondeductible expenses include (but are not limited to) the following: illegal bribes, kickbacks, and other payments not deductible under section 162(c); fines and penalties not deductible under section 162(f); expenses and interest relating to tax-exempt income under section 265; losses for which the deduction is disallowed under section 267(a)(1); the portion of meals and entertainment expenses disallowed under section 274; and the two-thirds portion of treble damages paid for violating antitrust laws not deductible under section 162.

(3) Amount of decrease in basis of individual shares. The basis of a shareholder's share of stock is decreased by an amount equal to the shareholder's pro rata portion of the passthrough items and distributions described in section 1367(a)(2) attributable to that share, determined on a per share, per day basis in accordance with section 1377(a). If the amount attributable to a share exceeds its basis, the ex-

cess is applied to reduce (but not below zero) the remaining bases of all other shares of stock in the corporation owned by the shareholder in proportion to the remaining basis of each of those shares.

(d) Time at which adjustments to basis of stock are effective. *(1) In general.* The adjustments described in section 1367(a) to the basis of a shareholder's stock are determined as of the close of the corporation's taxable year, and the adjustments generally are effective as of that date. However, if a shareholder disposes of stock during the corporation's taxable year, the adjustments with respect to that stock are effective immediately prior to the disposition.

(2) Adjustment for nontaxable item. An adjustment for a nontaxable item is determined for the taxable year in which the item would have been includible or deductible under the corporation's method of accounting for federal income tax purposes if the item had been subject to federal income taxation.

(3) Effect of election under section 1377(a)(2) or § 1.1368-1(g)(2). If an election under section 1377(a)(2) (to terminate the year in the case of the termination of a shareholder's interest) or under § 1.1368-1(g)(2) (to terminate the year in the case of a qualifying disposition) is made with respect to the taxable year of a corporation, this paragraph (d) applies as if the taxable year consisted of separate taxable years, the first of which ends at the close of the day on which either the shareholder's interest is terminated or a qualifying disposition occurs, whichever the case may be.

(e) Ordering rules for taxable years beginning before January 1, 1997. For any taxable year of a corporation beginning before January 1, 1997, except as provided in paragraph (g) of this section, the adjustments required by section 1367(a) are made in the following order—

(1) Any increase in basis attributable to the income items described in section 1367(a)(1)(A) and (B) and the excess of the deductions for depletion described in section 1367(a)(1)(C);

(2) Any decrease in basis attributable to noncapital, nondeductible expenses described in section 1367(a)(2)(D) and the oil and gas depletion deduction described in section 1367(a)(2)(E);

(3) Any decrease in basis attributable to items of loss or deduction described in section 1367(a)(2)(B) and (C); and

(4) Any decrease in basis attributable to a distribution by the corporation described in section 1367(a)(2)(A).

(f) Ordering rules for taxable years beginning on or after August 18, 1998. For any taxable year of a corporation beginning on or after August 18, 1998, except as provided in paragraph (g) of this section, the adjustments required by section 1367(a) are made in the following order—

(1) Any increase in basis attributable to the income items described in section 1367(a)(1)(A) and (B), and the excess of the deductions for depletion described in section 1367(a)(1)(C);

(2) Any decrease in basis attributable to a distribution by the corporation described in section 1367(a)(2)(A);

(3) Any decrease in basis attributable to noncapital, nondeductible expenses described in section 1367(a)(2)(D), and the oil and gas depletion deduction described in section 1367(a)(2)(E); and

(4) Any decrease in basis attributable to items of loss or deduction described in section 1367(a)(2)(B) and (C).

(g) Elective ordering rule. A shareholder may elect to decrease basis under paragraph (e)(3) or (f)(4) of this section, whichever applies, prior to decreasing basis under paragraph (e)(2) or (f)(3) of this section, whichever applies. If a shareholder makes this election, any amount described in paragraph (e)(2) or (f)(3) of this section, whichever applies, that is in excess of the shareholder's basis in stock and indebtedness is treated, solely for purposes of this section, as an amount described in paragraph (e)(2) or (f)(3) of this section, whichever applies, in the succeeding taxable year. A shareholder makes the election under this paragraph by attaching a statement to the shareholder's timely filed original or amended return that states that the shareholder agrees to the carryover rule of the preceding sentence. Once a shareholder makes an election under this paragraph with respect to an S corporation, the shareholder must continue to use the rules of this paragraph for that S corporation in future taxable years unless the shareholder receives the permission of the Commissioner.

(h) Examples. The following examples illustrate the principles of § 1.1367-1. In each example, the corporation is a calendar year S corporation:

Example (1). Adjustments to basis of stock for taxable years beginning before January 1, 1997.

(i) On December 31, 1994, A owns a block of 50 shares of stock with an adjusted basis per share of $6 in Corporation S. On December 31, 1994, A purchases for $400 an additional block of 50 shares of stock with an adjusted basis of $8 per share. Thus, A holds 100 shares of stock for each day of the 1995 taxable year. For S's 1995 taxable year, A's pro rata share of the amount of the items described in section 1367(a)(1)(A) (relating to increases in basis of stock) is $300, and A's pro rata share of the amount of the items described in section 1367(a)(2)(B) and (D) (relating to decreases in basis of stock) is $500. S makes a distribution to A in the amount of $100 during 1995.

(ii) Pursuant to the ordering rules of paragraph (e) of this section, A increases the basis of each share of stock by $3 ($300/100 shares) and decreases the basis of each share of stock by $5 ($500/100 shares). Then A reduces the basis of each share by $1 ($100/100 shares) for the distribution. Thus, on January 1, 1996, A has a basis of $3 per share in his original block of 50 shares ($6 + $3 − $5 − $1) and a basis of $5 per share in the second block of 50 shares ($8 + $3 − $5 − $1).

Example (2). Adjustments to basis of stock for taxable years beginning on or after August 18, 1998.

(i) On December 31, 2001, A owns a block of 50 shares of stock with an adjusted basis per share of $6 in Corporation S. On December 31, 2001, A purchases for $400 an additional block of 50 shares of stock with an adjusted basis of $8 per share. Thus, A holds 100 shares of stock for each day of the 2002 taxable year. For S's 2002 taxable year, A's pro rata share of the amount of items described in section 1367(a)(1)(A) (relating to increases in basis of stock) is $300, A's pro rata share of the amount of the items described in section 1367(a)(2)(B) (relating to decreases in basis of stock attributable to items of loss and deduction) is $300, and A's pro rata share of the amount of the items described in section 1367(a)(2)(D) (relating to decreases in basis of stock attributable to noncapital, nondeductible expenses) is $200. S makes a distribution to A in the amount of $100 during 2002.

(ii) Pursuant to the ordering rules of paragraph (f) of this section, A first increases the basis of each share of stock by $3 ($300/100 shares) and then decreases the basis of each share by $1 ($100/100 shares) for the distribution. A next decreases the basis of each share by $2 ($200/100 shares) for the noncapital, nondeductible expenses and then decreases the basis of each share by $3 ($300/100 shares) for the items of loss. Thus, on January 1, 2003, A has a basis of $3 per share in the original block of 50 shares ($6 + $3 - $1 - $2 - $3) and a basis of $5 per share in the second block of 100 shares ($8 + $3 - $1 - $2 - $3).

Example (3). Adjustments attributable to basis of individual shares of stock.

(i) On December 31, 1993, B owns one share of S corporation's 10 outstanding shares of stock. The basis of B's share is $30. On July 2, 1994, B purchases from another shareholder two shares for $25 each. During 1994, S corporation has no income or deductions but incurs a loss of $365. Under section 1377(a)(1)(A) and paragraph (c)(3) of this section, the amount of the loss assigned to each day of S's taxable year is $1.00 ($365/365 days). For each day, $.10 is allocated to each outstanding share ($1.00 amount of loss assigned to each day /10 shares).

(ii) B owned one share for 365 days and, therefore, reduces the basis of that share by the amount of loss attributable to it, i.e., $36.50 ($.10 × 365 days). B owned two shares for 182 days and, therefore, reduces the basis of each of those shares by the amount of the loss attributable to each, i.e., $18.20 ($.10 × 182 days).

(iii) The bases of the shares are decreased as follows:

Share	Original basis	Decrease	Adjusted basis	Excess basis reduction
No. 1	$30.00	$36.50	$ 0	$6.50
No. 2	25.00	18.20	6.80	0
No. 3	25.00	18.20	6.80	0
Total remaining basis			13.60	....

(iv) Because the decrease in basis attributable to share No. 1 exceeds the basis of share No. 1 by $6.50 ($36.50 – $30.00), the excess is applied to reduce the bases of shares No. 2 and No. 3 in proportion to their remaining bases. Therefore, the bases of share No. 2 and share No. 3 are each decreased by an additional $3.25 ($6.50 × $6.80/ $13.60). After this decrease, Share No. 1 has a basis of zero, Share No. 2 has a basis of $3.55, and Share No. 3 has a basis of $ 3.55.

Example (4). Effects of section 1377(a)(2) election and distribution on basis of stock for taxable years beginning before January 1, 1997.

(i) On January 1, 1994, individuals B and C each own 50 of the 100 shares of issued and outstanding stock of Corporation S. B's adjusted basis in each share of stock is $120, and C's is $80. On June 30, 1994, S distributes $6,000 to B and $6,000 to C. On June 30, 1994, B sells all of her S stock for $10,000 to D. S elects under section 1377(a)(2) to treat its 1994 taxable year as consisting of two taxable years, the first of which ends at the close of June 30, the date on which B terminates her interest in S.

(ii) For the period January 1, 1994, through June 30, 1994, S has nonseparately computed income of $6,000 and a separately stated deduction item of $4,000. Therefore, on June 30, 1994, B and C, pursuant to the ordering rules of paragraph (e) of this section, increase the basis of each share by $60 ($6,000/100 shares) and decrease the basis of each share by $40 ($4,000/100 shares). Then B and C reduce the basis of each share by $120 ($12,000/100 shares) for the distribution.

(iii) The basis of B's stock is reduced from $120 to $20 per share ($120 + $60 – $40 – $120). The basis of C's stock is reduced from $80 to $0 per share ($80 + $60 – $40 – $120). See section 1368 and § 1.1368-1(c) and (d) for rules relating to the tax treatment of the distributions.

(iv) Pursuant to paragraph (d)(3) of this section, the net reduction in the basis of B's shares of the S stock required by section 1367 and this section is effective immediately prior to B's sale of her stock. Thus, B's basis for determining gain or loss on the sale of the S stock is $20 per share, and B has a gain on the sale of $180 ($200 - $20) per share.

Example (5). Effects of section 1377(a)(2) election and distribution on basis of stock for taxable years beginning on or after August 18, 1998.

(i) The facts are the same as in Example 4, except that all of the events occur in 2001 rather than in 1994 and except as follows: On June 30, 2001, B sells 25 shares of her stock for $5,000 to D and 25 shares back to Corporation S for $5,000. Under section 1377(a)(2)(B) and § 1.1377-1(b)(2), B, C and D are affected shareholders because B has transferred shares to Corporation S and D. Pursuant to section 1377(a)(2)(A) and § 1.1377-1(b)(1), B, C and D, the affected shareholders, and Corporation S agree to treat the taxable year 2001 as if it consisted of two separate taxable years for all affected shareholders for the purposes set forth in § 1.1377-1(b)(3)(i).

(ii) On June 30, 2001, B and C, pursuant to the ordering rules of paragraph (f)(1) of this section, increase the basis of each share by $60 ($6,000/100 shares) for the nonseparately computed income. Then B and C reduce the basis of each share by $120 ($12,000/100 shares) for the distribution. Finally, B and C decrease the basis of each share by $40 ($4,000/100 shares) for the separately stated deduction item.

(iii) The basis of the stock of B is reduced from $120 to $20 per share ($120 + $60 - $120 - $40). Prior to accounting for the separately stated deduction item, the basis of the stock of C is reduced from $80 to $20 ($80 + $60 - $120). Finally, because the period from January 1 through June 30, 2001 is treated under § 1.1377-1(b)(3)(i) as a separate taxable year for purposes of making adjustments to the basis of stock, under section 1366(d) and § 1.1366-2(a)(2), C may deduct only $20 per share of the remaining $40 of the separately stated deduction item, and the basis of the stock of C is reduced from $20 per share to $0 per share. Under section 1366 and § 1.1366-2(a)(2), C's remaining separately stated deduction item of $20 per share is treated as having been incurred in the first succeeding taxable year of Corporation S, which, for this purpose, begins on July 1, 2001.

(i) [Reserved]

(j) Adjustments for items of income in respect of a decedent. The basis determined under section 1014 of any stock in an S corporation is reduced by the portion of the value of the stock that is attributable to items constituting income in respect of a decedent. For the determination of items realized by an S corporation constituting income in respect of a decedent, see sections 1367(b)(4)(A) and 691 and applicable regulations thereunder. For the determination of the allowance of a deduction for the amount of estate tax attributable to income in respect of a decedent, see section 691(c) and applicable regulations thereunder.

T.D. 8508, 12/30/93, amend T.D. 8852, 12/21/99.

PAR. 6. In § 1.1367-1, a new sentence is added at the end of paragraph (c)(2) to read as follows:

Proposed § 1.1367-1 Adjustments to basis of shareholder's stock in an S corporation. [*For Preamble, see ¶ 152,815*]

* * * * *

(c) * * *

(2) * * *For basis adjustments necessary to coordinate sections 1367 and 362(e)(2), see § 1.362-4(c)(7).

* * * * *

§ 1.1367-2 Adjustments to basis of indebtedness to shareholder.

(a) In general. *(1) Adjustments under section 1367.* This section provides rules relating to adjustments required by subchapter S to the basis of indebtedness (including open account debt as described in paragraph (a)(2) of this section) of an S corporation to a shareholder. The basis of indebtedness of the S corporation to a shareholder is reduced as provided in paragraph (b) of this section and restored as provided in paragraph (c) of this section in accordance with the timing rules in paragraph (d) of this section.

(2) Open Account Debt. (i) General rule. The term open account debt means shareholder advances not evidenced by separate written instruments and repayments on the advances, the aggregate outstanding principal of which does not exceed $25,000 of indebtedness of the S corporation to the shareholder at the close of the S corporation's taxable year. Advances and repayments on open account debt are treated as a single indebtedness.

(ii) Exception. If the shareholder advances not evidenced by a separate written instrument, net of repayments, exceeds an aggregate outstanding principal amount of $25,000 at the close of the S corporation's taxable year, for any subsequent taxable year the aggregate principal amount of that indebtedness is treated in the same manner as indebtedness evidenced by a separate written instrument for purposes of this section. For any subsequent taxable year, that indebtedness is not open account debt and is subject to all basis adjustment rules applicable to basis of indebtedness of an S corporation to a shareholder in this section.

(b) Reduction in basis of indebtedness. *(1) General rule.* If, after making the adjustments required by section 1367(a)(1) for any taxable year of the S corporation, the amounts specified in section 1367(a)(2)(B), (C), (D), and (E) (relating to losses, deductions, noncapital, nondeductible expenses, and certain oil and gas depletion deductions) exceed the basis of a shareholder's stock in the corporation, the excess is applied to reduce (but not below zero) the basis of any indebtedness of the S corporation to the shareholder held by the shareholder at the close of the corporation's taxable year. Any such indebtedness that has been satisfied by the corporation, or disposed of or forgiven by the shareholder, during the taxable year, is not held by the shareholder at the close of that year and is not subject to basis reduction.

(2) Termination of shareholder's interest in corporation during taxable year. If a shareholder terminates his or her interest in the corporation during the taxable year, the rules of this paragraph (b) are applied with respect to any indebtedness of the S corporation held by the shareholder immediately prior to the termination of the shareholder's interest in the corporation.

(3) Multiple indebtedness. If a shareholder holds more than one indebtedness at the close of the corporation's taxable year or, if applicable, immediately prior to the termination of the shareholder's interest in the corporation, the reduction in basis is applied to each indebtedness in the same proportion that the basis of each indebtedness bears to the aggregate bases of the indebtedness to the shareholder.

(c) Restoration of basis. *(1) General rule.* If, for any taxable year of an S corporation beginning after December 31, 1982, there has been a reduction in the basis of an indebtedness of the S corporation to a shareholder under section 1367(b)(2)(A), any net increase in any subsequent taxable year of the corporation is applied to restore that reduction. For purposes of this section, net increase with respect to a shareholder means the amount by which the shareholder's pro rata share of the items described in section 1367(a)(1) (relating to income items and excess deduction for depletion) exceed the items described in section 1367(a)(2) (relating to losses, deductions, noncapital, nondeductible expenses, certain oil and gas depletion deductions, and certain distributions) for the taxable year. These restoration rules apply only to indebtedness held by a shareholder as of the beginning of the taxable year in which the net increase arises. The reduction in basis of indebtedness must be restored before any net increase is applied to restore the basis of a shareholder's stock in an S corporation. In no event may the shareholder's basis of indebtedness be restored above the adjusted basis of the indebtedness under section 1016(a), excluding any adjustments under section 1016(a)(17) for prior taxable years, determined as of the beginning of the taxable year in which the net increase arises.

(2) Multiple indebtedness. If a shareholder holds more than one indebtedness (including any open account debt and any debt treated as a single indebtedness under paragraph (a)(2)(ii) of this section) as of the beginning of an S corporation's taxable year, any net increase is applied first to restore the reduction of basis in any indebtedness repaid (in whole or in part) in that taxable year to the extent necessary to offset any gain that would otherwise be realized on the repayment. Any remaining net increase is applied to restore each outstanding indebtedness (including any open account debt and any debt treated as a single indebtedness under paragraph (a)(2)(ii) of this section) in proportion to the amount that the basis of each outstanding indebtedness has been reduced under section 1367(b)(2)(A) and paragraph (b) of this section and not restored under section 1367(b)(2)(B) and this paragraph (c).

(d) Time at which adjustments to basis of indebtedness are effective. *(1) In general.* The amounts of the adjustments to basis of indebtedness (including open account debt) provided in section 1367(b)(2) and this section are determined as of the close of the S corporation's taxable year, and the adjustments are generally effective as of the close of the S corporation's taxable year. However, if the shareholder is not a shareholder in the S corporation at that time, these adjustments are effective immediately before the shareholder terminates his or her interest in the S corporation. Except as provided in paragraph (d)(2) of this section, if a debt is disposed of or repaid in whole or in part before the close of the taxable year, the basis of that indebtedness is restored under paragraph (c) of this section, effective immediately before the disposition or the first repayment on the debt during the taxable year. To the extent any indebtedness of the S corporation to the shareholder is disposed of or repaid (in whole or in part) during the taxable year and the shareholder's basis in that indebtedness has been reduced under paragraph (b) of this section and is not restored completely under paragraph (c) of this section, the disposition or repayment is a recognition event effective immediately before the indebtedness is disposed of or repaid (in whole or in part).

(2) Open account debt. (i) In general. All advances and repayments on open account debt (as described in paragraph (a)(2)(i) of this section) during the S corporation's taxable year are netted at the close of the S corporation's taxable year to determine the amount of any net advance or net repayment. The net advance or net repayment is combined with the outstanding aggregate principal balance of the existing open account debt and that amount is carried forward to the beginning of the subsequent taxable year as the outstanding aggregate principal amount of the open account debt (unless the aggregate principal amount meets the exception defined in paragraph (a)(2)(ii) of this section at the close of the taxable year). However, if the shareholder in the S corporation is not a shareholder of the S corporation at the close of the S corporation's taxable year, such advances and repayments on open account debt are netted, and the basis of that indebtedness is restored under paragraph (c) of this section, effective immediately before the shareholder terminates his or her interest in the S corporation. If any open account debt is disposed of before or upon the close of the taxable year, the disposition is effective at the close of the S corporation's taxable year, and all advances and repayments are netted immediately prior to the disposition and the basis of that indebtedness is restored under paragraph (c) of this section, effective at the close of the S corporation's taxable year.

(ii) Exception. Shareholder indebtedness that is open account debt at the beginning of the taxable year but meets the exception defined in paragraph (a)(2)(ii) of this section at the close of the taxable year, adjustments to the basis of the indebtedness for that taxable year follow the provisions for open account debt. The resulting aggregate principal amount of indebtedness is treated as the principal amount of a debt evidenced by a separate written instrument for any subsequent taxable year, and is no longer subject to the open account debt provisions of this section.

(3) Effect of election under section 1377(a)(2) or § 1.1368-1(g)(2). If an election is made under section 1377(a)(2) (to terminate the year in the case of the termination of a shareholder's interest) or under § 1.1368-1(g)(2) (to terminate the year in the case of a qualifying disposition), this paragraph (d) applies as if the taxable year consisted of separate taxable years, the first of which ends at the close of the day on which the shareholder either terminates his or her interest in the corporation or disposes of a substantial amount of stock, whichever the case may be.

(e) Examples. The following examples illustrate the principles of § 1.1367-2. In each example, the corporation is a calendar year S corporation. The lending transactions described in the examples do not result in foregone interest (within the meaning of section 7872(e)(2)), original issue discount (within the meaning of section 1273), or total unstated interest (within the meaning of section 483(b)).

Example (1). Reduction in basis of indebtedness.

(i) A has been the sole shareholder in Corporation S since 1992. In 1993, A loans S $1,000 (Debt No. 1), which is evidenced by a ten-year promissory note in the face amount of $1,000. In 1996, A loans S $5,000 (Debt No. 2), which is evidenced by a demand promissory note. On December 31, 1996, the basis of A's stock is zero; the basis of Debt No. 1 has been reduced under paragraph (b) of this section to $0; and the basis of Debt No. 2 has been reduced to $1,000. On January 1, 1997, A loans S $4,000 (Debt No. 3), which is evidenced by a demand promissory note. For S's 1997 taxable year, the sum of the amounts specified in section 1367(a)(1) (in this case, nonseparately computed income and the excess deduction for depletion) is $6,000, and the sum of the amounts specified in section 1367(a)(2)(B), (D) and (E) (in this case, items of separately stated deductions and losses, noncapital, nondeductible expenses, and certain oil and gas depletion deductions—there is no nonseparately computed loss) is $10,000. Corporation S makes no payments to A on any of the loans during 1997.

(ii) The $4,000 excess of loss and deduction items is applied to reduce the basis of each indebtedness in proportion to the basis of that indebtedness over the aggregate bases of the indebtedness to the shareholder (determined immediately before any adjustment under section 1367(b)(2)(A) and paragraph (b) of this section is effective for the taxable year). Thus, the basis of Debt No. 2 is reduced in an amount equal to $800 ($4,000 (excess) × $1,000 (basis of Debt No. 2) / $5,000 (total basis of all debt)). Similarly, the basis in Debt No. 3 is reduced in an amount equal to $3,200 ($4,000 × $4,000/$5,000). Accordingly, on December 31, 1997, A's basis in his stock is zero and his bases in the three debts are as follows:

Debt	1/1/96 basis	12/31/96 reduction	1/1/97 basis	12/31/97 reduction	1/1/98 basis
No. 1	$1,000	$1,000	$ 0	$ 0	$ 0
No. 2	5,000	4,000	1,000	800	200
No. 3			4,000	3,200	800

Example (2). Restoration of basis of indebtedness.

(i) The facts are the same as in Example 1. On July 1, 1998, S completely repays Debt No. 3, and, for S's 1998 taxable year, the net increase (within the meaning of paragraph (c) of this section) with respect to A equals $4,500.

(ii) The net increase is applied first to restore the bases in the debts held on January 1, 1998, before any of the net increase is applied to increase A's basis in his shares of S stock. The net increase is applied to restore first the reduction of basis in indebtedness repaid in 1998. Any remaining net increase is applied to restore the bases of the outstanding debts in proportion to the amount that each of these outstanding debts have been reduced previously under paragraph (b) of this section and have not been restored. As of December 31, 1998, the total reduction in A's debts held on January 1, 1998 equals $9,000. Thus, the basis of Debt No. 3 is restored by $3,200 (the amount of the previous reduction) to $4,000. A's basis in Debt No. 3 is treated as restored immediately before that debt is repaid. Accordingly, A does not realize any gain on the repayment. The remaining net increase of $1,300 ($4,500 − $3,200) is applied to restore the bases of Debt No. 1 and Debt No. 2. As of December 31, 1998, the total reduction in these outstanding debts is $5,800 ($9,000 − $3,200). The basis of Debt No. 1 is restored in an amount equal to $224 ($1,300 × $1,000/$5,800). Similarly, the basis in Debt No. 2 is restored in an amount equal to $1,076 ($1,300 × $4,800/$5,800). On December 31, 1998, A's basis in his S stock is zero and his bases in the two remaining debts are as follows:

Original basis	Amount reduced	1/1/98 basis	Amount restored	12/31/98 basis
$1,000	$1,000	$ 0	$ 224	$ 224
5,000	4,800	200	1,076	1,276

Example (3). Full restoration of basis in indebtedness when debt is repaid in part during the taxable year.

(i) C has been a shareholder in Corporation S since 1992. In 1997, C loans S $1,000. S issues its note to C in the amount of $1,000, of which $950 is payable on March 1, 1998, and $50 is payable on March 1, 1999. On December 31, 1997, C's basis in all her shares of S stock is zero and her basis in the note has been reduced under paragraph (b) of this section to $900. For 1998, the net increase (within the meaning of paragraph (c) of this section) with respect to C is $300.

(ii) Because C's basis of indebtedness was reduced in a prior taxable year under § 1.1367-2(b), the net increase for 1998 is applied to restore this reduction. The restored basis cannot exceed the adjusted basis of the debt as of the beginning of the first day of 1998, excluding prior adjustments under section 1367, or $1,000. Therefore, $100 of the $300 net increase is applied to restore the basis of the debt from $900 to $1,000 effective immediately before the repayment on March 1, 1998. The remaining net increase of $200 increases C's basis in her stock.

Example (4). Determination of net increase—Distribution in excess of increase in basis.

(i) D has been the sole shareholder in Corporation S since 1990. On January 1, 1996, D loans S $10,000 in return for a note from S in the amount of $10,000 of which $5,000 is payable on each of January 1, 2000, and January 1, 2001. On December 31, 1997, the basis of D's shares of S stock is zero, and his basis in the note has been reduced under paragraph (b) of this section to $8,000. During 1998, the sum of the items under section 1367(a)(1) (relating to increases in basis of stock) with respect to D equals $10,000 (in this case, nonseparately computed income), and the sum of the items under section 1367(a)(2)(B), (C), (D), and (E) (relating to decreases in basis of stock) with respect to D equals $0. During 1998, S also makes distributions to D totaling $11,000. This distribution is an item that reduces basis of stock under section 1367(a)(2)(A) and must be taken into account for purposes of determining whether there is a net increase for the taxable year. Thus, for 1998, there is no net increase with respect to D because the amount of the items provided in section 1367(a)(1) do not exceed the amount of the items provided in section 1367(a)(2).

(ii) Because there is no net increase with respect to D for 1998, none of the 1997 reduction in D's basis in the indebtedness is restored. The $10,000 increase in basis under section 1367(a)(1) is applied to increase D's basis in his S stock. Under section 1367(a)(2)(A), the $11,000 distribution with respect to D's stock reduces D's basis in his shares of S stock to $0. See section 1368 and § 1.1368-1(c) and (d) for the tax treatment of the $1,000 distribution in excess of D's basis.

Example (5). Distributions less than increase in basis.

(i) The facts are the same as in Example 4, except that in 1998 S makes distributions to D totaling $8,000. On these facts, for 1998, there is a net increase with respect to D of $2,000 (the amount by which the items provided in section 1367(a)(1) exceed the amount of the items provided in section 1367(a)(2)).

(ii) Because there is a net increase of $2,000 with respect to D for 1998, $2,000 of the $10,000 increase in basis under section 1367(a)(1) is first applied to restore D's basis in the indebtedness to $10,000 ($8,000 + $ 2,000). Accordingly, on December 31, 1998, D has a basis in his shares of S stock of $0 ($0 + $8,000 (increase in basis remaining after restoring basis in indebtedness) − $8,000 (distribution)) and a basis in the note of $10,000.

Example (6). The $25,000 aggregate principal amount applies to each shareholder. (i) A and B have been the two shareholders in Corporation S since 2000. As of the end of the 2008 taxable year, the bases of A's and B's stock are both zero. On June 1, 2009, A advances S $16,000, which is not evidenced by a written instrument. On August 1, 2009, B advances S $22,000, which is not evidenced by a written instrument. Both the $16,000 advance and the $22,000 advance are open account debt and remain outstanding at those amounts during 2009. There is no net increase under paragraph (c) of this section in year 2009.

(ii) At the close of the 2009 taxable year, A's open account debt does not exceed $25,000. A therefore carries forward to the beginning of the 2010 taxable year the $16,000 as open account debt.

(iii) At the close of the 2009 taxable year, B's open account debt does not exceed $25,000. B therefore carries forward to the beginning of the 2010 taxable year the $22,000 as open account debt.

Example (7). Treatment of open account debt.

(i) The facts are the same as in Example 6, in addition to which, on December 31, 2009, A's basis in the open account debt is reduced under paragraph (b) of this section to $8,000. On April 1, 2010, S repays A $4,000 of the open account indebtedness. On September 1, 2010, A advances S an additional $1,000, which is not evidenced by a written instrument. There is no net increase under paragraph (c) of this section in year 2010.

(ii) The $4,000 April repayment S makes to A and A's $1,000 September advance are netted to result in a net repayment of $3,000 for the taxable year on A's $16,000 open account debt carried forward from 2009. Because there is no net increase in 2010, no basis of indebtedness is restored for the 2010 taxable year, and A realizes $1,500 of income on the $3,000 net repayment at the close of the 2010 taxable year.

(iii) At close of the 2010 taxable year, A's open account debt does not exceed $25,000. The net repayment of $3,000 for the taxable year on A's $16,000 open account debt carried forward from 2009, leaves A with an open account debt of $13,000 to carry forward as open account debt to the beginning of the 2011 taxable year.

Example (8). Treatment of shareholder indebtedness not evidenced by a written instrument which exceeds $25,000.

(i) The facts are the same as in Example 7, in addition to which, on February 1, 2011, S repays $5,000 of the open account debt and on March 1, 2011, A advances S $20,000, which is not evidenced by a written instrument.

(ii) At the close of the 2010 taxable year, A has an open account debt of $13,000 to carry forward as open account debt to the beginning of the 2011 taxable year.

(iii) The 2011 advances and repayments are netted to result in a net advance of $15,000 on A's $13,000 open account debt carried forward from 2010, increasing A's open account debt to $28,000 as of the close of the 2011 taxable year. Because A's open account debt exceeds $25,000, for any subsequent taxable year the $28,000 indebtedness will be treated in the same manner as indebtedness evidenced by a separate written instrument for the purposes of this section. Because there is no net increase in 2011, no basis of indebtedness is restored for the 2011 taxable year.

T.D. 8508, 12/30/93, amend T.D. 9428, 10/17/2008.

§ 1.1367-3 Effective/Applicability date.

Section 1.1367-2(a), (c)(2), (d)(2), and (e) Example 6, Example 7, and Example 8 apply to any shareholder advances to the S corporation made on or after October 20, 2008 and repayments on those advances by the S corporation. The rules that apply with respect to shareholder advances to the S corporation made before October 20, 2008, are contained in § 1.1367-3 in effect prior to October 20, 2008. (See 26 CFR part 1 revised as of April 1, 2007.) Shareholders have the option to apply these rules to shareholder advances to the S corporation made before October 20, 2008, and repayments on those advances by the S corporation.

T.D. 8508, 12/30/93, amend T.D. 8852, 12/21/99, T.D. 9428, 10/17/2008.

§ 1.1368-0 Table of contents.

The following table of contents is provided to facilitate the use of §§ 1.1368-1 through 1.1368-4.

T.D. 8508, 12/30/93, amend T.D. 8696, 12/20/96, T.D. 8852, 12/21/99, T.D. 8869, 1/20/2000.

§ 1.1368-1 Distributions by S corporations.

Caution: The Treasury has not yet amended Reg § 1.1368-1 to reflect changes made by P.L. 104-188.

(a) In general. This section provides rules for distributions made by an S corporation with respect to its stock which, but for section 1368(a) and this section, would be subject to section 301(c) and other rules of the Internal Revenue Code that characterize a distribution as a dividend.

(b) Date distribution made. For purposes of section 1368, a distribution is taken into account on the date the corporation makes the distribution, regardless of when the distribution is treated as received by the shareholder.

(c) S corporation with no earnings and profits. A distribution made by an S corporation that has no accumulated earnings and profits as of the end of the taxable year of the S corporation in which the distribution is made is treated in the manner provided in section 1368(b).

(d) S corporation with earnings and profits. *(1) General treatment of distribution.* Except as provided in paragraph (d)(2) of this section, a distribution made with respect to its stock by an S corporation that has accumulated earnings and profits as of the end of the taxable year of the S corporation in which the distribution is made is treated in the manner provided in section 1368(c). See section 316 and § 1.316-2 for provisions relating to the allocation of earnings and profits among distributions.

(2) Previously taxed income. This paragraph (d)(2) applies to distributions by a corporation that has both accumulated earnings and profits and previously taxed income (within the meaning of section 1375(d)(2), as in effect prior to its amendment by the Subchapter S Revision Act of 1982, and the regulations thereunder) with respect to one or more shareholders. In the case of such a distribution, that portion remaining after the application of section 1368(c)(l) (relating to distributions from the accumulated adjustments account (AAA) as defined in § 1.1368-2(a)) is treated in the manner provided in section 1368(b) (relating to S corporations without earnings and profits) to the extent that portion is a distribution of money and does not exceed the shareholder's net share immediately before the distribution of the corporation's previously taxed income. The AAA and the earnings and profits of the corporation are not decreased by that portion of the distribution. Any distribution remaining after the application of this paragraph (d)(2) is treated in the manner provided in section 1368(c)(2) and (3).

(e) Certain adjustments taken into account. *(1) Taxable years beginning before January 1, 1997.* For any taxable year of the corporation beginning before January 1, 1997, paragraphs (c) and (d) of this section are applied only after taking into account—

(i) The adjustments to the basis of the shares of a shareholder's stock described in section 1367 (without regard to section 1367(a)(2)(A) (relating to decreases attributable to distributions not includible in income)) for the S corporation's taxable year; and

(ii) The adjustments to the AAA required by section 1368(e)(1)(A) (but without regard to the adjustments for distributions under § 1.1368-2(a)(3)(iii)) for the S corporation's taxable year.

(2) Taxable years beginning on or after August 18, 1998. For any taxable year of the corporation beginning on or after August 18, 1998, paragraphs (c) and (d) of this section are applied only after taking into account—

(i) The adjustments to the basis of the shares of a shareholder's stock described in section 1367(a)(1) (relating to increases in basis of stock) for the S corporation's taxable year; and

(ii) The adjustments to the AAA required by section 1368(e)(1)(A) (but without regard to the adjustments for distributions under § 1.1368-2(a)(3)(iii)) for the S corporation's taxable year. Any net negative adjustment (as defined in section 1368(e)(1)(C)(ii)) for the taxable year shall not be taken into account.

(f) Elections relating to source of distributions. *(1) In general.* An S corporation may modify the application of paragraphs (c) and (d) of this section by electing (pursuant to paragraph (f)(5) of this section)—

(i) To distribute earnings and profits first as described in paragraph (f)(2) of this section;

(ii) To make a deemed dividend as described in paragraph (f)(3) of this section; or

(iii) To forego previously taxed income as described in paragraph (f)(4) of this section.

(2) Election to distribute earnings and profits first. (i) In general. An S corporation with accumulated earnings and profits may elect under this paragraph (f)(2) for any taxable year to distribute earnings and profits first as provided in section 1368(e)(3). Except as provided in paragraph (f)(2)(ii) of this section, distributions made by an S corporation making this election are treated as made first from earnings and profits under section 1368(c)(2) and second from the AAA under section 1368(c)(1). Any remaining portion of the distribution is treated in the manner provided in section 1368(b). This election is effective for all distributions made during the year for which the election is made.

(ii) Previously taxed income. If a corporation to which paragraph (d)(2) of this section (relating to corporations with previously taxed income) applies makes the election provided in this paragraph (f)(2) for the taxable year, and does not make the election to forego previously taxed income under paragraph (f)(4) of this section, distributions by the S corporation during the taxable year are treated as made first, from previously taxed income under paragraph (d)(2) of this section; second, from earnings and profits under section 1368(c)(2); and third, from the AAA under section 1368(c)(1). Any portion of a distribution remaining after the previously taxed income, earnings and profits, and the AAA are exhausted is treated in the manner provided in section 1368(b).

(iii) Corporation with subchapter C and subchapter S earnings and profits. If an S corporation that makes the election provided in this paragraph (f)(2) has both subchapter C earnings and profits (as defined in section 1362(d)(3)(B)) and subchapter S earnings and profits in a taxable year of the corporation in which the distribution is made, the distribution is treated as made first from subchapter C earnings and profits, and second from subchapter S earnings and profits. *Subchapter S earnings and profits* are earnings and profits accumulated in a taxable year beginning before January 1, 1983 (or in the case of a qualified casualty insurance electing small business corporation or a qualified oil corporation, earnings and profits accumulated in any taxable year), for which an election under subchapter S of chapter 1 of the Internal Revenue Code was in effect.

(3) Election to make a deemed dividend. An S corporation may elect under this paragraph (f)(3) to distribute all or part of its subchapter C earnings and profits through a deemed dividend. If an S corporation makes the election provided in this paragraph (f)(3), the S corporation will be considered to have made the election provided in paragraph (f)(2) of this section (relating to the election to distribute earnings and profits first). The amount of the deemed dividend may not exceed the subchapter C earnings and profits of the corporation on the last day of the taxable year, reduced by any ac-

tual distributions of subchapter C earnings and profits made during the taxable year. The amount of the deemed dividend is considered, for all purposes of the Internal Revenue Code, as if it were distributed in money to the shareholders in proportion to their stock ownership, received by the shareholders, and immediately contributed by the shareholders to the corporation, all on the last day of the corporation's taxable year.

(4) Election to forego previously taxed income. An S corporation may elect to forego distributions of previously taxed income. If such an election is made, paragraph (d)(2) of this section (relating to corporations with previously taxed income) does not apply to any distribution made during the taxable year. Thus, distributions by a corporation that makes the election to forego previously taxed income for a taxable year under this paragraph (f)(4) and does not make the election to distribute earnings and profits first under paragraph (f)(2) of this section are treated in the manner provided in section 1368(c)(relating to distributions by corporations with earnings and profits). Distributions by a corporation that makes both the election to distribute earnings and profits first under paragraph (f)(2) of this section and the election to forego previously taxed income under this paragraph (f)(4), are treated in the manner provided in paragraph (f)(2)(i) of this section.

(5) Time and manner of making elections. (i) For earnings and profits. If an election is made under paragraph (f)(2) of this section to distribute earnings and profits first, see section 1368(e)(3) regarding the consent required by shareholders.

(ii) For previously taxed income and deemed dividends. If an election is made to forego previously taxed income under paragraph (f)(4) of this section or to make a deemed dividend under paragraph (f)(3) of this section, consent by each "affected shareholder," as defined in section 1368(e)(3)(B), is required.

(iii) Corporate statement regarding elections. A corporation makes an election for a taxable year under § 1.1368-1(f) by attaching a statement to a timely filed (including extensions) original or amended return required to be filed under section 6037 for that taxable year. In the statement, the corporation must identify the election it is making under § 1.1368-1(f) and must state that each shareholder consents to the election. In the case of elections for taxable years beginning before January 1, 2003, an officer of the corporation must sign under penalties of perjury the statement on behalf of the corporation. In the case of elections for taxable years beginning after December 31, 2002, the statement described in this paragraph (f)(5)(iii) shall be verified by signing the return. A statement of election to make a deemed dividend under § 1.1368-1(f) must include the amount of the deemed dividend that is distributed to each shareholder.

(iv) Irrevocable elections. The elections under this paragraph (f) are irrevocable and are effective only for the taxable year for which they are made. In applying the preceding sentence to elections under this paragraph (f), an election to terminate the taxable year under section 1377(a)(2) or § 1.1368-1(g)(2) is disregarded.

(g) Special rule. *(1) Election to terminate year under § 1.1368-1(g)(2).* If an election is made under paragraph (g)(2) of this section to terminate the year when there is a qualifying disposition, this section applies as if the taxable year consisted of separate taxable years, the first of which ends at the close of the day on which there is a qualifying disposition of stock.

(2) Election in case of a qualifying disposition. (i) In general. In the case of a qualifying disposition, a corporation may elect under this paragraph (g)(2)(i) to treat the year as if it consisted of separate taxable years, the first of which ends at the close of the day on which the qualifying disposition occurs. A *qualifying disposition* is—

(A) A disposition by a shareholder of 20 percent or more of the outstanding stock of the corporation in one or more transactions during any thirty-day period during the corporation's taxable year;

(B) A redemption treated as an exchange under section 302(a) or section 303(a) of 20 percent or more of the outstanding stock of the corporation from a shareholder in one or more transactions during any thirty-day period during the corporation's taxable year; or

(C) An issuance of an amount of stock equal to or greater than 25 percent of the previously outstanding stock to one or more new shareholders during any thirty-day period during the corporation's taxable year.

(ii) Effect of the election. A corporation making an election under paragraph (g)(2)(i) of this section must treat the taxable year as separate taxable years for purposes of allocating items of income and loss; making adjustments to the AAA, earnings and profits, and basis; and determining the tax effect of distributions under section 1368(b) and (c). An election made under paragraph (g)(2)(i) of this section may be made upon the occurrence of any qualifying disposition. Dispositions of stock that are taken into account as part of a qualifying disposition are not taken into account in determining whether a subsequent qualifying disposition has been made.

(iii) Corporate statement regarding elections. A corporation makes an election for a taxable year under § 1.1368-1(f) by attaching a statement to a timely filed (including extensions) original or amended return required to be filed under section 6037 for that taxable year. In the statement, the corporation must identify the election it is making under § 1.1368-1(f) and must state that each shareholder consents to the election. In the case of elections for taxable years beginning before January 1, 2003, an officer of the corporation must sign under penalties of perjury the statement on behalf of the corporation. In the case of elections for taxable years beginning after December 31, 2002, the statement described in this paragraph (f)(5)(iii) shall be verified by signing the return. A statement of election to make a deemed dividend under § 1.1368-1(f) must include the amount of the deemed dividend that is distributed to each shareholder.

(iv) Coordination with election under section 1377(a)(2). If the event resulting in a qualifying disposition also results in a termination of a shareholder's entire interest as described in § 1.1377-1(b)(4), the election under this paragraph (g)(2) cannot be made. Rather, the election under section 1377(a)(2) and § 1.1377-1(b) may be made. See § 1.1377-1(b) (concerning the election under section 1377(a)(2)).

T.D. 8508, 12/30/93, amend T.D. 8696, 12/20/96, T.D. 8852, 12/21/99, T.D. 9100, 12/18/2003, T.D. 9300, 12/7/2006.

§ 1.1368-2 Accumulated adjustments account (AAA).

Caution: The Treasury has not yet amended Reg § 1.1368-2 to reflect changes made by P.L. 104-188.

(a) Accumulated adjustments account. *(1) In general.* The accumulated adjustments account is an account of the S corporation and is not apportioned among shareholders. The

AAA is relevant for all taxable years beginning on or after January 1, 1983, for which the corporation is an S corporation. On the first day of the first year for which the corporation is an S corporation, the balance of the AAA is zero. The AAA is increased in the manner provided in paragraph (a)(2) of this section and is decreased in the manner provided in paragraph (a)(3) of this section. For the adjustments to the AAA in the case of redemptions, liquidations, reorganizations, and corporate separations, see paragraph (d) of this section.

(2) Increases to the AAA. The AAA is increased for the taxable year of the corporation by the sum of the following items with respect to the corporation for the taxable year:

(i) The items of income described in section 1366(a)(1)(A) other than income that is exempt from tax;

(ii) Any nonseparately computed income determined under section 1366 (a)(1)(B); and

(iii) The excess of the deductions for depletion over the basis of property subject to depletion unless the property is an oil or gas property the basis of which has been allocated to shareholders under section 613A(c)(11).

(3) Decreases to the AAA. (i) In general. The AAA is decreased for the taxable year of the corporation by the sum of the following items with respect to the corporation for the taxable year—

(A) The items of loss or deduction described in section 1366(a)(1)(A);

(B) Any nonseparately computed loss determined under section 1366(a)(1)(B);

(C) Any expense of the corporation not deductible in computing its taxable income and not properly chargeable to a capital account, other than—

(1) Federal taxes attributable to any taxable year in which the corporation was a C corporation; and

(2) Expenses related to income that is exempt from tax; and

(D) The sum of the shareholders' deductions for depletion for any oil or gas property held by the corporation described in section 1367(a)(2)(E).

(ii) Extent of allowable reduction. The AAA may be decreased under paragraph (a)(3)(i) of this section below zero. The AAA is decreased by noncapital, nondeductible expenses under paragraph (a)(3)(i)(C) of this section even though a portion of the noncapital, nondeductible expenses is not taken into account by a shareholder under § 1.1367-1(g) (relating to the elective ordering rule). The AAA is also decreased by the entire amount of any loss or deduction even though a portion of the loss or deduction is not taken into account by a shareholder under section 1366(d)(1) or is otherwise not currently deductible under the Internal Revenue Code. However, in any subsequent taxable year in which the loss, deduction, or noncapital, nondeductible expense is treated as incurred by the corporation with respect to the shareholder under section 1366(d)(2) or § 1.1367-1(g) (or in which the loss or deduction is otherwise allowed to the shareholder), no further adjustment is made to the AAA.

(iii) Decrease to the AAA for distributions. The AAA is decreased (but not below zero) by any portion of a distribution to which section 1368(b) or (c)(1) applies.

(4) Ordering rules for the AAA for taxable years beginning before January 1, 1997. For any taxable year beginning before January 1, 1997, the adjustments to the AAA are made in the following order—

(i) The AAA is increased under paragraph (a)(2) of this section before it is decreased under paragraph (a)(3) of this section for the taxable year;

(ii) The AAA is decreased under paragraph (a)(3)(i) of this section before it is decreased under paragraph (a)(3)(iii) of this section;

(iii) The AAA is decreased (but not below zero) by any portion of an ordinary distribution to which section 1368(b) or (c)(1) applies; and

(iv) The AAA is adjusted (whether negative or positive) for redemption distributions under paragraph (d)(1) of this section.

(5) Ordering rules for the AAA for taxable years beginning on or after August 18, 1998. For any taxable year of the S corporation beginning on or after August 18, 1998, the adjustments to the AAA are made in the following order—

(i) The AAA is increased under paragraph (a)(2) of this section before it is decreased under paragraph (a)(3)(i) of this section for the taxable year;

(ii) The AAA is decreased under paragraph (a)(3)(i) of this section (without taking into account any net negative adjustment (as defined in section 1368(e)(1)(C)(ii)) before it is decreased under paragraph (a)(3)(iii) of this section;

(iii) The AAA is decreased (but not below zero) by any portion of an ordinary distribution to which section 1368(b) or (c)(1) applies;

(iv) The AAA is decreased by any net negative adjustment (as defined in section 1368(e)(1)(C)(ii)); and

(v) The AAA is adjusted (whether negative or positive) for redemption distributions under paragraph (d)(1) of this section.

(b) Distributions in excess of the AAA. *(1) In general.* A portion of the AAA (determined under paragraph (b)(2) of this section) is allocated to each of the distributions made for the taxable year if—

(i) An S corporation makes more than one distribution of property with respect to its stock during the taxable year of the corporation (including an S short year as defined under section 1362(e)(1)(A));

(ii) The AAA has a positive balance at the close of the year; and

(iii) The sum of the distributions made during the corporation's taxable year exceeds the balance of the AAA at the close of the year.

(2) Amount of the AAA allocated to each distribution. The amount of the AAA allocated to each distribution is determined by multiplying the balance of the AAA at the close of the current taxable year by a fraction, the numerator of which is the amount of the distribution and the denominator of which is the amount of all distributions made during the taxable year. For purposes of this paragraph (b)(2), the term *all distributions made during the taxable year* does not include any distribution treated as from earnings and profits or previously taxed income pursuant to an election made under section 1368(e)(3) and § 1.1368-1(f)(2). See paragraph (d)(1) of this section for rules relating to the adjustments to the AAA for redemptions and distributions in the year of a redemption.

(c) Distribution of money and loss property. *(1) In general.* The amount of the AAA allocated to a distribution under this section must be further allocated (under paragraph (c)(2) of this section) if the distribution—

(i) Consists of property the adjusted basis of which exceeds its fair market value on the date of the distribution and money;

(ii) Is a distribution to which § 1.1368-1(d)(1) applies; and

(iii) Exceeds the amount of the corporation's AAA properly allocable to that distribution.

(2) Allocating the AAA to loss property. The amount of the AAA allocated to the property other than money is equal to the amount of the AAA allocated to the distribution multiplied by a fraction, the numerator of which is the fair market value of the property other than money on the date of distribution and the denominator of which is the amount of the distribution. The amount of the AAA allocated to the money is equal to the amount of the AAA allocated to the distribution reduced by the amount of the AAA allocated to the property other than money.

(d) Adjustment in the case of redemptions, liquidations, reorganizations, and divisions. *(1) Redemptions.* (i) General rule. In the case of a redemption distribution by an S corporation that is treated as an exchange under section 302(a) or section 303(a) (a *redemption distribution),* the AAA of the corporation is adjusted in an amount equal to the ratable share of the corporation's AAA (whether negative or positive) attributable to the redeemed stock as of the date of the redemption.

(ii) Special rule for years in which a corporation makes both ordinary and redemption distributions. In any year in which a corporation makes one or more distributions to which section 1368(a) applies (*ordinary distributions*) and makes one or more redemption distributions, the AAA of the corporation is adjusted first for any ordinary distributions and then for any redemption distributions.

(iii) Adjustments to earnings and profits. Earnings and profits are adjusted under section 312 independently of any adjustments made to the AAA.

(2) Liquidations or reorganizations. An S corporation acquiring the assets of another S corporation in a transaction to which section 381(a) applies will succeed to and merge its AAA (whether positive or negative) with the AAA (whether positive or negative) of the distributor or transferor S corporation as of the close of the date of distribution or transfer. Thus, the AAA of the acquiring corporation after the transaction is the sum of the AAAs of the corporations prior to the transaction.

(3) Corporate separations to which section 368(a)(1)(D) applies. If an S corporation with accumulated earnings and profits transfers a part of its assets constituting an active trade or business to another corporation in a transaction to which section 368(a)(1)(D) applies, and immediately thereafter the stock and securities of the controlled corporation are distributed in a distribution or exchange to which section 355 (or so much of section 356 as relates to section 355) applies, the AAA of the distributing corporation immediately before the transaction is allocated between the distributing corporation and the controlled corporation in a manner similar to the manner in which the earnings and profits of the distributing corporation are allocated under section 312(h). See § 1.312-10(a).

(e) Election to terminate year under section 1377(a)(2) or § 1.1368-1(g)(2). If an election is made under section 1377(a)(2) (to terminate the year in the case of termination of a shareholder's interest) or § 1.1368-1(g)(2) (to terminate the year in the case of a qualifying disposition), this section applies as if the taxable year consisted of separate taxable years, the first of which ends at the close of the day on which the shareholder terminated his or her interest in the corporation or makes a substantial disposition of stock, whichever the case may be.

T.D. 8508, 12/30/93, amend T.D. 8852, 12/21/99, T.D. 8869, 1/20/2000.

§ 1.1368-3 Examples.

Caution: The Treasury has not yet amended Reg § 1.1368-3 to reflect changes made by P.L. 104-188.

The principles of §§ 1.1368-1 and 1.1368-2 are illustrated by the examples below. In each example Corporation S is a calendar year corporation:

Example (1). Distributions by S corporations without C corporation earnings and profits for taxable years beginning before January 1, 1997.

(i) Corporation S, an S corporation, has no earnings and profits as of January 1, 1996, the first day of its 1996 taxable year. S's sole shareholder, A, holds 10 shares of S stock with a basis of $1 per share as of that date. On March 1, 1996, S makes a distribution of $38 to A. For S's 1996 taxable year, A's pro rata share of the amount of the items described in section 1367(a)(1) (relating to increases in basis of stock) is $50 and A's pro rata share of the amount of the items described in section 1367(a)(2)(B) through (D) (relating to decreases in basis of stock for items other than distributions) is $26.

(ii) Under section 1368(d)(1) and § 1.1368-1(e)(1), the adjustments to the bases of A's stock in S described in section 1367 are made before the distribution rules of section 1368 are applied. Thus, A's basis per share in the stock is $3.40 ($1 + [($50 − $26) / 10 shares]) before taking into account the distribution. Under section 1367(a)(2)(A), the basis of A's stock is decreased by distributions to A that are not includible in A's income. Under § 1.1367-1(c)(3), the amount of the distribution that is attributable to each share of A's stock is $3.80 ($38 distribution / 10 shares). However, A only has a basis of $3.40 in each share, and basis may not be reduced below zero. Therefore, the basis of each share of his stock is reduced by $3.40 to zero, and the remaining $4.00 of the distribution ([$3.80 − $3.40] × 10 shares) is treated as gain from the sale or exchange of property. As of January 1, 1997, A has a basis of $0 in his shares of S stock.

Example (2). Distributions by S corporations without earnings and profits for taxable years beginning on or after August 18, 1998.

(i) Corporation S, an S corporation, has no earnings and profits as of January 1, 2001, the first day of its 2001 taxable year. S's sole shareholder, A, holds 10 shares of S stock with a basis of $1 per share as of that date. On March 1, 2001, S makes a distribution of $38 to A. The balance in Corporation S's AAA is $100. For S's 2001 taxable year, A's pro rata share of the amount of the items described in section 1367(a)(1) (relating to increases in basis of stock) is $50. A's pro rata share of the amount of the items described in sections 1367(a)(2)(B) through (D) (relating to decreases in basis of stock for items other than distributions) is $26, $20 of which is attributable to items described in section 1367(a)(2)(B) and (C) and $6 of which is attributable to items described in section 1367(a)(2)(D) (relating to decreases in basis attributable to noncapital, nondeductible expenses).

(ii) Under section 1368(d)(1) and § 1.1368-1(e)(1) and (2), the adjustments to the basis of A's stock in S described in sections 1367(a)(1) are made before the distribution rules of section 1368 are applied. Thus, A's basis per share in the stock is $6.00 ($1 + [$50/10]) before taking into account the distribution. Under section 1367(a)(2)(A), the basis of A's stock is decreased by distributions to A that are not includible in A's income. Under § 1.1367-1(c)(3), the amount of the distribution that is attributable to each share of A's stock is $3.80 ($38 distribution/10 shares). Thus, A's basis per share in the stock is $2.20 ($6.00-$3.80), after taking into account the distribution. Under section 1367(a)(2)(D), the basis of each share of A's stock in S after taking into account the distribution, $2.20, is decreased by $.60 ($6 noncapital, nondeductible expenses/10). Thus, A's basis per share after taking into account the nondeductible, noncapital expenses is $1.60. Under section 1367(a)(2)(B) and (C), A's basis per share is further decreased by $2 ($20 items described in section 1367(a)(2)(B) and (C)/10 shares). However, basis may not be reduced below zero. Therefore, the basis of each share of A's stock is reduced to zero. As of January 1, 2002, A has a basis of $0 in his shares of S stock. Pursuant to section 1366(d)(2), the $.40 of loss in excess of A's basis in each of his shares of S stock is treated as incurred by the corporation in the succeeding taxable year with respect to A.

Example (3). Distributions by S corporations with C corporation earnings and profits for taxable years beginning before January 1, 1997.

(i) Corporation S properly elects to be an S corporation beginning January 1, 1997, and as of that date has accumulated earnings and profits of $30. B, an individual and sole shareholder of Corporation S, has 10 shares of S stock with a basis of $12 per share. In addition, B lends $30 to S evidenced by a demand note.

(ii) During 1997, S has a nonseparately computed loss of $150. S makes no distributions to B during 1997. Under section 1366(d)(1), B is allowed a loss equal to $150, the amount equal to the sum of B's bases in his shares of stock and his basis in the debt. Under section 1367, the loss reduces B's adjusted basis in his stock and debt to $0. Under § 1.1368-2(a)(3), S's AAA as of December 31, 1997, has a deficit of $150 as a result of S's loss for the year.

(iii) For 1998, S has $220 of separately stated income and distributes $110 to B. The balance in the AAA (negative $150 from 1997) is increased by $220 for S's income for the year and decreased to $0 for the portion of the distribution that is treated as being from the AAA ($70). Under § 1.1367-2(c), B's net increase is $150, determined by reducing the $220 of income by the $70 of the distribution not includible in income by B. Thus, B's basis in the debt is fully restored to $30, and B's basis in S stock (before accounting for the distribution) is increased from zero to $19 per share ([$220 − $30 applied to the debt] / 10). Thirty dollars of the distribution is considered a dividend to the extent of S's $30 of earnings and profits, and the remaining $10 of the distribution reduces B's basis in the S stock. Thus, B's basis in the S stock as of December 31, 1998, is $11 per share ($19 − [$70 AAA distribution / 10] − [10 distribution treated as a reduction in basis / 10]). The balance in the AAA is $0, S's earnings and profits are $0, and B's basis in the loan is $30.

Example (4). Distributions by S corporations with earnings and profits and no net negative adjustment for taxable years beginning on or after August 18, 1998.

(i) Corporation S, an S corporation, has accumulated earnings and profits of $1,000 and a balance in the AAA of $2,000 on January 1, 2001. S's sole shareholder B holds 100 shares of stock with a basis of $20 per share as of January 1, 2001. On April 1, 2001, S makes a distribution of $1,500 to B. B's pro rata share of the income earned by S during 2001 is $2,000 and B's pro rata share of S's losses is $1,500. For the taxable year ending December 31, 2001, S does not have a net negative adjustment as defined in section 1368(e)(1)(C). S does not make the election under section 1368(e)(3) and § 1.1368-1(f)(2) to distribute its earnings and profits before its AAA.

(ii) The AAA is increased from $2,000 to $4,000 for the $2,000 of income earned during the 2001 taxable year. The AAA is decreased from $4,000 to $2,500 for the $1,500 of losses. The AAA is decreased from $2,500 to $1,000 for the portion of the distribution ($1,500) to B that does not exceed the AAA.

(iii) As of December 31, 2001, B's basis in his stock is $10 ($20 + $20 ($2,000 income/100 shares)—$15 ($1,500 distribution/100 shares)—$15 ($1,500 loss/100 shares).

Example (5). Distributions by S corporations with earnings and profits and net negative adjustment for taxable years beginning on or after August 18, 1998.

(i) Corporation S, an S corporation, has accumulated earnings and profits of $1,000 and a balance in the AAA of $2,000 on January 1, 2001. S's sole shareholder B holds 100 shares of stock with a basis of $20 per share as of January 1, 2001. On April 1, 2001, S makes a distribution of $2,000 to B. B's pro rata share of the income earned by S during 2001 is $2,000 and B's pro rata share of S's losses is $3,500. For the taxable year ending December 31, 2001, S has a net negative adjustment as defined in section 1368(e)(1)(C). S does not make the election under section 1368(e)(3) and § 1.1368-1(f)(2) to distribute its earnings and profits before its AAA.

(ii) The AAA is increased from $2,000 to $4,000 for the $2,000 of income earned during the 2001 taxable year. Because under section 1368(e)(1)(C)(ii) and § 1.1368-2(a)(ii), the net negative adjustment is not taken into account, the AAA is decreased from $4,000 to $2,000 for the portion of the losses ($2,000) that does not exceed the income earned during the 2001 taxable year. The AAA is reduced from $2,000 to zero for the portion of the distribution to B ($2,000) that does not exceed the AAA. The AAA is decreased from zero to a negative $1,500 for the portion of the $3,500 of loss that exceeds the $2,000 of income earned during the 2001 taxable year.

(iii) Under § 1.1367-1(c)(1), the basis of a shareholder's share in an S corporation stock may not be reduced below zero. Accordingly, as of December 31, 2001, B's basis per share in his stock is zero ($20 + $20 income—$20 distribution—$35 loss). Pursuant to section 1366(d)(2), the $15 of loss in excess of B's basis in each of his shares of S stock is treated as incurred by the corporation in the succeeding taxable year with respect to B.

Example (6). Election in case of disposition of substantial amount of stock.

(i) Corporation S, an S corporation, has earnings and profits of $3,000 and a balance in the AAA of $1,000 on January 1, 1997. C, an individual and the sole shareholder of Corporation S, has 100 shares of S stock with a basis of $10 per share. On July 3, 1997, C sells 50 shares of his S stock to D, an individual, for $250. For 1997, S has taxable income of $1,000, of which $500 was earned on or before July

3, 1997, and $500 earned after July 3, 1997. During its 1997 taxable year, S distributes $1,000 to C on February 1 and $1,000 to each of C and D on August 1. S does not make the election under section 1368(e)(3) and § 1.1368-1(f)(2) to distribute its earnings and profits before its AAA. S makes the election under § 1.1368-1(g)(2) to treat its taxable year as if it consisted of separate taxable years, the first of which ends at the close of July 3, 1997, the date of the qualifying disposition.

(ii) Under § 1.1368-1(g)(2), for the period ending on July 3, 1997, S's AAA is $500 ($1,000 (AAA as of January 1, 1997) + $500 (income earned from January 1, 1997 through July 3, 1997) − $1,000 (distribution made on February 1, 1997)). C's bases in his shares of stock is decreased to $5 per share ($10 (original basis) + $5 (increase per share for income) − $10 (decrease per share for distribution)).

(iii) The AAA is adjusted at the end of the taxable year for the period July 4 through December 31, 1997. It is increased from $500 (AAA as of the close of July 3, 1997) to $1,000 for the income earned during this period and is decreased by $1,000, the portion of the distribution ($2,000 in total) made to C and D on August 1 that does not exceed the AAA. The $1,000 portion of the distribution that remains after the AAA is reduced to zero is attributable to earnings and profits. Therefore C and D each have a dividend of $500, which does not affect their basis or S's AAA. The earnings and profits account is reduced from $3,000 to $2,000.

(iv) As of December 31, 1997, C and D have bases in their shares of stock of zero ($5 (basis as of July 4) + $5 ($500 income / 100 shares) − $10 ($1,000 distribution / 100 shares)). C and D each will report $500 as dividend income, which does not affect their basis or S's AAA.

Example (7). Election to distribute earnings and profits first.

(i) Corporation S has been a calendar year C corporation since 1975. For 1982, S elects for the first time to be taxed under subchapter S, and during 1982 has $60 of earnings and profits. As of December 31, 1995, S has an AAA of $10 and earnings and profits of $160, consisting of $100 of subchapter C earnings and profits and $60 of subchapter S earnings and profits. For 1996, S has $200 of taxable income and the AAA is increased to $210 (before taking distributions into account). During 1996, S distributes $240 to its shareholders. With its 1996 tax return, S properly elects under section 1368(e)(3) and § 1.1368-1(f)(2) to distribute its earnings and profits before its AAA.

(ii) Because S elected to distribute its earnings and profits before its AAA, the first $100 of the distribution is characterized as a distribution from subchapter C earnings and profits; the next $60 of the distribution is characterized as a distribution from subchapter S earnings and profits. Because $160 of the distribution is from earnings and profits, the shareholders of S have a $160 dividend. The remaining $80 of the distribution is a distribution from S's AAA and is treated by the shareholders as a return of capital or gain from the sale or exchange of property, as appropriate, under § 1.1368-1(d)(1). S's AAA, as of December 31, 1996, equals $130 ($210 − $80).

Example (8). Distributions in excess of the AAA.

(i) On January 1, 1995, Corporation S has $40 of earnings and profits and a balance in the AAA of $100. S has two shareholders, E and F, each of whom own 50 shares of S's stock. For 1995, S has taxable income of $50, which increases the AAA to $150 as of December 31, 1995 (before taking into account distributions made during 1995). On February 1, 1995, S distributes $60 to each shareholder. On September 1, 1995, S distributes $30 to each shareholder. S does not make the election under section 1368(e)(3) and § 1.1368-1(f)(2) to distribute its earnings and profits before its AAA.

(ii) The sum of the distributions exceed S's AAA. Therefore, under § 1.1368-2(b), a portion of S's $150 balance in the AAA as of December 31, 1995, is allocated to each of the February 1 and September 1 distributions based on the respective sizes of the distributions. Accordingly, S must allocate $100 ($150 (AAA) × ($120 (February 1 distribution) / $180 (the sum of the distributions))) of the AAA to the February 1 distribution, and $50 ($150 × ($60 / $180)) to the September 1 distribution. The portions of the distributions to which the AAA is allocated are treated by the shareholder as a return of capital or gain from the sale or exchange of property, as appropriate. The remainder of the two distributions is treated as a dividend to the extent that it does not exceed S's earnings and profits. E and F must each report $10 of dividend income for the February 1 distribution. For the September 1 distribution, E and F must each report $5 of dividend income.

Example (9). Ordinary and redemption distributions in the same taxable year.

(i) On January 1, 1995, Corporation S, an S corporation, has $20 of earnings and profits and a balance in the AAA of $10. S has two shareholders, G and H, each of whom owns 50 shares of S's stock. For 1995, S has taxable income of $16, which increases the AAA to $26 as of December 31, 1995 (before taking into account distributions made during 1995). On February 1, 1995, S distributes $10 to each shareholder. On December 31, 1995, S redeems for $13 all of shareholder G's stock in a redemption that is treated as a sale or exchange under section 302(a).

(ii) The sum of the ordinary distributions does not exceed S's AAA. Therefore, S must reduce the $26 balance in the AAA by $20 for the February 1 ordinary distribution. The portions of the distribution by which the AAA is reduced are treated by the shareholders as a return of capital or gain from the sale or exchange of property. S must adjust the remaining AAA, $6, in an amount equal to the ratable share of the remaining AAA attributable to the redeemed stock, or $3 (50% × $6)

(iii) S also must adjust the earnings and profits of $20 in an amount equal to the ratable share of the earnings and profits attributable to the redeemed stock. Therefore, S adjusts the earnings and profits by $10 (50% × $20), the ratable share of the earnings and profits attributable to the redeemed stock.

T.D. 8508, 12/30/93, amend T.D. 8852, 12/21/99.

§ 1.1368-4 Effective date and transition rule.

Except for §§ 1.1368-1(e)(2), 1.1368-2(a)(5), and 1.1368-3 Example 2, Example 4, and Example 5, §§ 1.1368-1, 1.1368-2, and 1.1368-3 apply to taxable years of the corporation beginning on or after January 1, 1994. Section 1.1368-1(e)(2), § 1.1368-2(a)(5), and § 1.1368-3 Example 2, Example 4, and Example 5 apply only to taxable years of the corporation beginning on or after August 18, 1998. For taxable years beginning before January 1, 1994, and taxable years beginning on or after January 1, 1997, and before August 18, 1998, the treatment of distributions by an S corporation to its shareholders must be determined in a reasonable manner, taking into account the statute and legislative history. Except with regard to the deemed dividend rule under § 1.1368-1(f)(3), § 1.1368-1(e)(2), § 1.1368-2(a)(5), and § 1.1368-3 Example 2, Example 4, and Example 5, return positions consistent with §§ 1.1368-1, 1.1368-2, and 1.1368-3 are reasonable for taxable years beginning before January 1, 1994. Return positions consistent with §§ 1.1368-1(e)(2), 1.1368-2(a)(5), and 1.1368-3 Example 2, Example 4, and Example 5 are reasonable for taxable years beginning on or after January 1, 1997, and before August 18, 1998.

T.D. 8508, 12/30/93, amend T.D. 8852, 12/21/99.

---

§ 18.1371-1 Election to treat distributions as dividends during certain post-termination transition periods.

A corporation may make an election under section 1371(e) (as amended by section 721(o) of the Act) to treat all distributions of money made during the post-termination transition period described in section 1377(b)(1)(A) as coming out of the corporation's earnings and profits (after earnings and profits have been eliminated, the distributions are applied against and reduce the adjusted basis of the stock). The election may be made only with the consent of each shareholder to whom the corporation makes a distribution (whether or not it is a cash distribution) during such post-termination transition period. Any such election shall be made by the corporation by attaching to its income tax return for the C year in which such post-termination transition period ends a statement which clearly indicates that the corporation elects to have section 1371(e)(1) not apply to all distributions made during such post-termination transition period. The election shall not be effective unless such statement is signed by a person authorized to sign the return required to be filed under section 6012 and by each shareholder required to consent to the election.

T.D. 7976, 9/5/84.

---

§ 1.1374-0 Table of contents.

This section lists the major paragraph headings for §§ 1.1374-1 through 1.1374-10.

§ 1.1374-10 Effective date and additional rules.

(a) In general.

(b) Additional rules.

(1) Certain transfers to partnerships.

(2) Certain inventory dispositions.

(3) Certain contributions of built-in loss assets.

(4) Certain installment sales.

(i) In general.

(ii) Examples.

(c) Revocation and re-election of S corporation status.

(1) In general.

(2) Example.

T.D. 8579, 12/23/94, amend T.D. 9236, 12/20/2005.

§ 1.1374-1 General rules and definitions.

(a) Computation of tax. The tax imposed on the income of an S corporation by section 1374(a) for any taxable year during the recognition period is computed as follows—

(1) Step One: Determine the net recognized built-in gain of the corporation for the taxable year under section 1374(d)(2) and § 1.1374-2;

(2) Step Two: Reduce the net recognized built-in gain (but not below zero) by any net operating loss and capital loss carryforward allowed under section 1374(b)(2) and § 1.1374-5;

(3) Step Three: Compute a tentative tax by applying the rate of tax determined under section 1374(b)(1) for the taxable year to the amount determined under paragraph (a)(2) of this section;

(4) Step Four: Compute the final tax by reducing the tentative tax (but not below zero) by any credit allowed under section 1374(b)(3) and § 1.1374-6.

(b) Anti-trafficking rules. If section 382, 383, or 384 would have applied to limit the use of a corporation's recognized built-in loss or section 1374 attributes at the beginning of the first day of the recognition period if the corporation had remained a C corporation, these sections apply to limit their use in determining the S corporation's pre-limitation amount, taxable income limitation, net unrealized built-in gain limitation, deductions against net recognized built-in gain, and credits against the section 1374 tax.

(c) Section 1374 attributes. Section 1374 attributes are the loss carryforwards allowed under section 1374(b)(2) as a deduction against net recognized built-in gain and the credit and credit carryforwards allowed under section 1374(b)(3) as a credit against the section 1374 tax.

(d) Recognition period. The recognition period is the 10-year (120-month) period beginning on the first day the corporation is an S corporation or the day an S corporation acquires assets in a section 1374(d)(8) transaction. For example, if the first day of the recognition period is July 14, 1996, the last day of the recognition period is July 13, 2006. If the recognition period for certain assets ends during an S corporation's taxable year (for example, because the corporation was on a fiscal year as a C corporation and changed to a calendar year as an S corporation or because an S corporation acquired assets in a section 1374(d)(8) transaction during a taxable year), the S corporation must determine its pre-limitation amount (as defined in § 1.1374-2(a)(1)) for the year as if the corporation's books were closed at the end of the recognition period.

(e) Predecessor corporation. For purposes of section 1374(c)(1), if the basis of an asset of the S corporation is determined (in whole or in part) by reference to the basis of the asset (or any other property) in the hands of another corporation, the other corporation is a predecessor corporation of the S corporation.

T.D. 8579, 12/23/94.

§ 1.1374-1A Tax imposed on certain capital gains.

Caution: The Treasury has not yet amended Reg § 1.1374-1A to reflect changes made by P.L. 110-246.

(a) General rule. Except as otherwise provided in paragraph (c) of this section, if for a taxable year beginning after 1982 of an S corporation—

(1) The net capital gain of such corporation exceeds $25,000, and

(2) The net capital gain of such corporation exceeds 50 percent of its taxable income (as defined in paragraph (d) of this section) for such year, and

(3) The taxable income of such corporation (as defined in paragraph (d) of this section) for such year exceeds $25,000,

section 1374 imposes a tax (computed under paragraph (b) of this section) on the income of such corporation. The tax is imposed on the S corporation and not on the shareholders.

(b) Amount of tax. The amount of tax shall be the lower of—

(1) An amount equal to the tax, determined as provided in section 1201(a)(2), on the amount by which the net capital gain of the corporation for the taxable year exceeds $25,000, or

(2) An amount equal to the tax which would be imposed by section 11 on the taxable income of the corporation (as defined in paragraph (d) of this section) for the taxable year were it not an S corporation.

No credit shall be allowable under Part IV of Subchapter A of Chapter 1 of the Internal Revenue Code of 1954 (other than under section 34) against the tax imposed by section 1374(a) and this section, See section 1375(c)(2) and § 1.1375-1(c)(2) for a special rule that reduces the amount of the net capital gain of the corporation for purposes of this paragraph (b) in cases where a net capital gain is taxed as excess net passive income under section 1375. See section 1374(c)(3) and paragraph (c)(1)(ii) of this section for a special rule that limits the amount of tax on property with a substituted basis in certain cases.

(c) Exceptions to taxation. *(1) New corporations and corporations with election in effect for 3 immediately preceding years.* (i) In general. If an S corporation would be subject to the tax imposed by section 1374 for a taxable year pursuant to paragraph (a) of this section, the corporation shall, nevertheless, not be subject to such tax for such year, if:

(A) The election under section 1362(a) which is in effect with respect to such corporation for such year has been in effect for the corporation's three immediately preceding taxable years, or

(B) An election under section 1362(a) has been in effect with respect to such corporation for each of its taxable years for which it has been in existence, unless there is a net capital gain for the taxable year which is attributable to property with a substituted basis within the meaning of paragraph (c)(1)(iii) of this section.

(ii) Amount of tax on net capital gain attributable to property with a substituted basis. If for a taxable year of an S corporation either paragraph (c)(1)(i)(A) or (B) of this section is satisfied, but the S corporation has a net capital gain for such taxable year which is attributable to property with a substituted basis (within the meaning of paragraph (c)(1)(iii) of this section), then paragraph (a) of this section shall apply for the taxable year, but the amount of tax determined under paragraph (b) of this section shall not exceed a tax, determined as provided in section 1201(a), on the net capital gain attributable to property with a substituted basis.

(iii) Property with substituted basis. For purposes of this section, the term "property with a substituted basis" means:

(A) Property acquired by a corporation ("the acquiring corporation") during the period beginning 36 months before the first day of the acquiring corporation's taxable year and ending on the last day of such year;

(B) The basis of such property in the hands of the acquiring corporation is determined in whole or in part by reference to the basis of any property in the hands of another corporation; and

(C) Such other corporation was not an S corporation throughout the period beginning the later of:

(1) 36 months before the first day of the acquiring corporation's taxable year, or

(2) The time such other corporation came into existence, and ending on the date such other corporation transferred the property, the basis of which is used to determine, in whole or in part, the basis of the property in the hands of the acquiring corporation. An S corporation and any predecessor corporation shall not be treated as one corporation for purposes of this paragraph (c)(1).

(iv) Existence of a corporation. For purposes of this section, a corporation shall not be considered to be in existence for any month which precedes the first month in which such corporation has shareholders or acquires assets or begins business, whichever is first to occur.

(v) References to prior law included. For purposes of this paragraph (c), the term "S corporation" shall include an electing small business corporation under prior Subchapter S law, and the term "election under section 1362(a)" shall include an election under section 1372 of prior Subchapter S law.

(vi) Examples. The provisions of this paragraph may be illustrated by the following examples:

Example (1). M Corporation was organized and began business in 1977. M subsequently made an election under section 1362(a) which was effective for its 1984 taxable year. If such election does not terminate under section 1362 for its taxable years 1984, 1985, and 1986, M is not subject to the tax imposed by section 1374 for its taxable year 1987, or for any subsequent year for which such election remains in effect, unless it has, for any such year, an excess of net long-term capital gain over net short-term capital loss attributable to property with a substituted basis. If there is such an excess for any such year, and the requirements of paragraph (a) of this section are met, M will be subject to the tax for such year. If there is no such excess for any year after 1986, M will not be subject to the tax for any such year even though the requirements of paragraph (a) of this section are met.

Example (2). N corporation was organized in 1983, and was an S corporation for its first taxable year, N is not subject to the tax imposed by section 1374 for 1983, or for any subsequent year for which its original election under section 1362(a) has not terminated under section 1362(d), unless, for any such year, it has an excess of net long-term capital gain over net short-term capital loss attributable to property with a substituted basis and the requirements of paragraph (a) of this section are met.

(2) Treatment of certain gains of options and commodities dealers. (i) Exclusion of certain capital gains. For purposes of this section, the net capital gain of any options dealer or commodities dealer shall be determined by not taking into account any gain or loss (in the normal course of the taxpayer's activity of dealing in or trading section 1256 contracts) from any section 1256 contract or property related to such a contract.

(ii) Definitions. For purposes of this paragraph (c)(2)—

(A) Options dealer. The term "options dealer" has the meaning given to such term by section 1256(g)(8).

(B) Commodities dealer. The term "commodities dealer" means a person who is actively engaged in trading section 1256 contracts and is registered with a domestic board of trade which is designated as a contract market by the Commodities Futures Trading Commission.

(C) Section 1256 contracts. The term "section 1256 contracts" has the meaning given to such term by section 1256(b).

(iii) Effective dates. (A) In general. Except as otherwise provided in this paragraph (c)(2)(iii), this paragraph (c)(2) shall apply to positions established after July 18, 1984, in taxable years ending after such date.

(B) Special rule for options on regulated futures contracts. In the case of any option with respect to a regulated futures contract (within the meaning of section 1256), this paragraph (c)(2) shall apply to positions established after October 31, 1983, in taxable years ending after such date.

(C) Elections with respect to property held on or before July 18, 1984. See §§ 1.1256(h)-1T and 1.1256(h)-2T for rules concerning an election to have this paragraph (c)(2) apply to certain property held on or before July 18, 1984.

(d) Determination of taxable income. *(1) General rule.* For purposes of this section, taxable income of the corporation shall be determined under section 63(a) as if the corporation were a C corporation rather than an S corporation, except that the following deductions shall not apply in the computation—

(i) The deduction allowed by section 172 (relating to net operating loss deduction), and

(ii) The deductions allowed by Part VIII of Subchapter B (other than the deduction allowed by section 248, relating to organization expenditures).

For any taxable year in which a tax under this section is imposed on an S corporation, the S corporation shall attach a Form 1120 completed in accordance with this paragraph (d) and the instructions to Form 1120S to its tax return filed for such taxable year

(2) Special rule for net capital gains taxed as excess net passive income under section 1375. See section 1375(c)(2) and § 1.1375-1(c)(2) for a special rule that reduces the taxable income of the corporation for purposes of section 1374(b)(2) and § 1.1374-1(b)(2) in cases where a net capital gain is taxed as excess net passive income under section 1375.

(e) Reduction in pass-thru for tax imposed on capital gain. See section 1366(f)(2) for a special rule reducing the S corporation's long-term capital gains and the corporation's gain from sales or exchanges of property described in section 1231 for purposes of section 1366(a) by an amount of tax imposed under section 1374 and this section.

(f) Examples. The following examples illustrate the principles of this section and assume that a tax will not be imposed under section 1375:

Example (1). Corporation M is an S corporation for its taxable year beginning January 1, 1983. For 1983, M has an excess of net long-term capital gain over net short-term capital loss in the amount of $30,000. However, its taxable income for the year is only $20,000 as a result of other deductions in excess of other income. Thus, although the excess of the net long-term capital gain over the net short-term capital loss exceeds $25,000 and also exceeds 50 percent of taxable income, M is not subject to the tax imposed by section 1374 for 1983 because its taxable income does not exceed $25,000.

Example (2). Corporation N is an S Corporation for its 1983 taxable year. For 1983, N has an excess of net long-term capital gain over net short-term capital loss in the amount of $30,000, and taxable income of $65,000. Thus, although N's net capital gain ($30,000) exceeds $25,000, it does not exceed 50 percent of the corporation's taxable income for the year (50 percent of $65,000, or $32,500), and therefore N is not subject to the tax imposed by section 1374 for such year.

Example (3). Assume that Corporation O, an S corporation, is subject to the tax imposed by section 1374 for its taxable year 1983. For 1983, O has an excess of net long-term capital gain over net short-term capital loss in the amount of $73,000, and taxable income within the meaning of section 1374, which includes capital gains and losses, of $100,000. The amount of tax computed under paragraph (b)(1) of this section is 28 percent of $48.00 ($73,000 − $25,000), or $13,440. Since this is lower than the amount computed under paragraph (b)(2) of this section, which is $25,750 ($3,750 + $4,500 of tax imposed by section 1374.

Example (4). Assume that in example (3) the taxable income of O for 1983 is $35,000. This results from an excess of deductions over income with respect to items which were not included in determining the excess of the net long-term capital gain over the net short-term capital loss. In such case, the amount of tax, computed under paragraph (b)(2) of this section, is $5,550. Since this is lower than the amount computed under paragraph (b)(1) of this section, $5,550 is the amount of tax imposed by section 1374.

Example (5). Corporation P, an S corporation, for its taxable year 1983 has an excess of net long-term capital gain over net short-term capital loss in the amount of $65,000 and has taxable income of $80,000. P's election under section 1362 has been in effect for its three immediately preceding taxable years, but P, nevertheless, is subject to the tax imposed by section 1374 for 1983 since it has an excess of net long-term capital gain over net short-term capital loss (in the amount of $20,000) attributable to property with a substituted basis. The tax computed under paragraph (b)(1) of this section, $11,200 (28 percent of $40,000 ($65,000 − $25,000)), is less than the tax computed under paragraph (b)(2) of this section, $17,750. However, under the limitation provided in paragraph (c) of this section which is applicable in this factual situation, the tax imposed by section 1374 for 1983 may not exceed $5,600 (28 percent of $20,000, the excess of net long-term capital gain over net short-term capital loss attributable to property with a substituted basis).

T.D. 8104, 9/25/86, amend T.D. 8419, 5/28/92, T.D. 8579, 12/23/94.

§ 1.1374-2 Net recognized built-in gain.

(a) In general. An S corporation's net recognized built-in gain for any taxable year is the least of—

(1) Its taxable income determined by using all rules applying to C corporations and considering only its recognized built-in gain, recognized built-in loss, and recognized built-in gain carryover (pre-limitation amount);

(2) Its taxable income determined by using all rules applying to C corporations as modified by section 1375(b)(1)(B) (taxable income limitation); and

(3) The amount by which its net unrealized built-in gain exceeds its net recognized built-in gain for all prior taxable years (net unrealized built-in gain limitation).

(b) Allocation rule. If an S corporation's pre-limitation amount for any taxable year exceeds its net recognized built-in gain for that year, the S corporation's net recognized built-in gain consists of a ratable portion of each item of income, gain, loss, and deduction included in the pre-limitation amount.

(c) Recognized built-in gain carryover. If an S corporation's net recognized built-in gain for any taxable year is equal to its taxable income limitation, the amount by which its pre-limitation amount exceeds its taxable income limitation is a recognized built-in gain carryover included in its pre-limitation amount for the succeeding taxable year. The recognized built-in gain carryover consists of that portion of each item of income, gain, loss, and deduction not included in the S corporation's net recognized built-in gain for the year the carryover arose, as determined under paragraph (b) of this section.

(d) Accounting methods. In determining its taxable income for pre-limitation amount and taxable income limitation purposes, a corporation must use the accounting method(s) it uses for tax purposes as an S corporation.

(e) Example. The rules of this section are illustrated by the following example.

Example. Net recognized built-in gain. X is a calendar year C corporation that elects to become an S corporation on January 1, 1996. X has a net unrealized built-in gain of $50,000 and no net operating loss or capital loss carryforwards. In 1996, X has a pre-limitation amount of $20,000, consisting of ordinary income of $15,000 and capital gain of $5,000, a taxable income limitation of $9,600, and a net unrealized built-in gain limitation of $50,000. Therefore, X's net recognized built-in gain for 1996 is $9,600, because that is the least of the three amounts described in paragraph (a) of this section. Under paragraph (b) of this section, X's net recognized built-in gain consists of recognized built-in ordinary income of $7,200 [$15,000 × ($9,600/$20,000) = $7,200] and recognized built-in capital gain of $2,400 [$5,000 × ($9,600/$20,000) = $2,400]. Under paragraph (c) of this section, X has a recognized built-in gain carryover to 1997 of $10,400 ($20,000 − $9,600 = $10,400), consisting of $7,800 ($15,000 − $7,200 = $7,800) of recognized built-in ordinary income and $2,600 ($5,000 − $2,400 = $2,600) of recognized built-in capital gain.

T.D. 8579, 12/23/94.

§ 1.1374-3 Net unrealized built-in gain.

(a) In general. An S corporation's net unrealized built-in gain is the total of the following—

(1) The amount that would be the amount realized if, at the beginning of the first day of the recognition period, the corporation had remained a C corporation and had sold all its assets at fair market value to an unrelated party that assumed all its liabilities; decreased by

(2) Any liability of the corporation that would be included in the amount realized on the sale referred to in paragraph (a)(1) of this section, but only if the corporation would be allowed a deduction on payment of the liability; decreased by

(3) The aggregate adjusted bases of the corporation's assets at the time of the sale referred to in paragraph (a)(1) of this section; increased or decreased by

(4) The corporation's section 481 adjustments that would be taken into account on the sale referred to in paragraph (a)(1) of this section; and increased by

(5) Any recognized built-in loss that would not be allowed as a deduction under section 382, 383, or 384 on the sale referred to in paragraph (a)(1) of this section.

(b) Adjustment to net unrealized built-in gain. *(1) In general.* If section 1374(d)(8) applies to an S corporation's acquisition of assets, some or all of the stock of the corporation from which such assets were acquired was taken into account in the computation of the net unrealized built-in gain for a pool of assets of the S corporation, and some or all of such stock is redeemed or canceled in such transaction, then, subject to the limitations of paragraph (b)(2) of this section, such net unrealized built-in gain is adjusted to eliminate any effect that any built-in gain or built-in loss in the redeemed or canceled stock (other than stock with respect to which a loss under section 165 is claimed) had on the initial computation of net unrealized built-in gain for that pool of assets. For purposes of this paragraph, stock described in section 1374(d)(6) shall be treated as taken into account in the computation of the net unrealized built-in gain for a pool of assets of the S corporation.

(2) Limitations on adjustment. (i) Recognized built-in gain or loss. Net unrealized built-in gain for a pool of assets of the S corporation is only adjusted under paragraph (b)(1) of this section to reflect built-in gain or built-in loss in the redeemed or canceled stock that has not resulted in recognized built-in gain or recognized built-in loss during the recognition period.

(ii) Anti-duplication rule. Paragraph (b)(1) of this section shall not be applied to duplicate an adjustment to the net unrealized built-in gain for a pool of assets made pursuant to paragraph (b)(1) of this section.

(3) Effect of adjustment. Any adjustment to the net unrealized built-in gain made pursuant to this paragraph (b) only affects computations of the amount subject to tax under section 1374 for taxable years that end on or after the date of the acquisition to which section 1374(d)(8) applies.

(4) Pool of assets. For purposes of this section, a pool of assets means—

(i) The assets held by the corporation on the first day it became an S corporation, if the corporation was previously a C corporation; or

(ii) The assets the S corporation acquired from a C corporation in a section 1374(d)(8) transaction.

(c) Examples. The following examples illustrate the rules of this section:

Example (1). Computation of net unrealized built-in gain. (i) (A) X, a calendar year C corporation using the cash method, elects to become an S corporation on January 1, 1996. On December 31, 1995, X has assets and liabilities as follows:

Assets	FMV	Basis
Factory	$ 500,000	$900,000
Accounts Receivable	300,000	0
Goodwill	250,000	0
Total	$1,050,000	$900,000
Liabilities	Amount	
Mortgage	$ 200,000	
Accounts Payable	100,000	
Total	$ 300,000	

(B) Further, X must include a total of $60,000 in taxable income in 1996, 1997, and 1998 under section 481(a).

(ii) If, on December 31, 1995, X sold all its assets to a third party that assumed all its liabilities, X's amount realized would be $1,050,000 ($750,000 cash received + $300,000 liabilities assumed = $1,050,000). Thus, X's net unrealized built-in gain is determined as follows:

Amount realized	$1,050,000
Deduction allowed	(100,000)
Basis of X's assets	(900,000)
Section 481 adjustments	60,000
Net unrealized built-in gain	$ 110,000.

Example (2). Adjustment to net unrealized built-in gain for built-in gain in eliminated C corporation stock. (i) X, a calendar year C corporation, elects to become an S corporation effective January 1, 2005. On that date, X's assets (the first pool of assets) have a net unrealized built-in gain of $15,000. Among the assets in the first pool of assets is all of the outstanding stock of Y, a C corporation, with a fair market value of $33,000 and an adjusted basis of $18,000. On March 1, 2009, X sells an asset that it owned on January 1, 2005, and as a result has $10,000 of recognized built-in gain. X has had no other recognized built-in gain or built-in loss. X's taxable income limitation for 2009 is $50,000. Effective June 1, 2009, X elects under section 1361 to treat Y as a qualified subchapter S subsidiary (QSub). The election is treated as a transfer of Y's assets to X in a liquidation to which sections 332 and 337(a) apply.

(ii) Under paragraph (b) of this section, the net unrealized built in-gain of the first pool of assets is adjusted to account for the elimination of the Y stock in the liquidation. The net unrealized built-in gain of the first pool of assets, therefore, is decreased by $15,000, the amount by which the fair market value of the Y stock exceeded its adjusted basis as of January 1, 2005. Accordingly, for taxable years ending after June 1, 2009, the net unrealized built-in gain of the first pool of assets is $0.

(iii) Under § 1.1374-2(a), X's net recognized built-in gain for any taxable year equals the least of X's pre-limitation amount, taxable income limitation, and net unrealized built-in gain limitation. In 2009, X's pre-limitation amount is $10,000, X's taxable income limitation is $50,000, and X's net unrealized built-in gain limitation is $0. Because the net unrealized built-in gain of the first pool of assets has been adjusted to $0, despite the $10,000 of recognized built-in gain in 2009, X has $0 net recognized built-in gain for the taxable year ending on December 31, 2009.

Example (3). Adjustment to net unrealized built-in gain for built-in loss in eliminated C corporation stock. (i) X, a calendar year C corporation, elects to become an S corporation effective January 1, 2005. On that date, X's assets (the first pool of assets) have a net unrealized built-in gain of negative $5,000. Among the assets in the first pool of assets is 10 percent of the outstanding stock of Y, a C corporation, with a fair market value of $18,000 and an adjusted basis of $33,000. On March 1, 2009, X sells an asset that it owned on January 1, 2005, resulting in $8,000 of recognized built-in gain. X has had no other recognized built-in gains or built-in losses. X's taxable income limitation for 2009 is $50,000. On June 1, 2009, Y transfers its assets to X in a reorganization under section 368(a)(1)(C).

(ii) Under paragraph (b) of this section, the net unrealized built in-gain of the first pool of assets is adjusted to account for the elimination of the Y stock in the reorganization. The net unrealized built-in gain of the first pool of assets, therefore, is increased by $15,000, the amount by which the adjusted basis of the Y stock exceeded its fair market value as of January 1, 2005. Accordingly, for taxable years ending after June 1, 2009, the net unrealized built-in gain of the first pool of assets is $10,000.

(iii) Under § 1.1374-2(a), X's net recognized built-in gain for any taxable year equals the least of X's pre-limitation amount, taxable income limitation, and net unrealized built-in gain limitation. In 2009, X's pre-limitation amount is $8,000 and X's taxable income limitation is $50,000. The net unrealized built-in gain of the first pool of assets has been adjusted to $10,000, so X's net unrealized built-in gain limitation is $10,000. X, therefore, has $8,000 net recognized built-in gain for the taxable year ending on December 31, 2009. X's net unrealized built-in gain limitation for 2010 is $2,000.

Example (4). Adjustment to net unrealized built-in gain in case of prior gain recognition. (i) X, a calendar year C corporation, elects to become an S corporation effective January 1, 2005. On that date, X's assets (the first pool of assets) have a net unrealized built-in gain of $30,000. Among the assets in the first pool of assets is all of the outstanding stock of Y, a C corporation, with a fair market value of $45,000 and an adjusted basis of $10,000. Y has no current or accumulated earnings and profits. On April 1, 2007, Y distributes $18,000 to X, $8,000 of which is treated as gain to X from the sale or exchange of property under section 301(c)(3). That $8,000 is recognized built-in gain to X under section 1374(d)(3), and results in $8,000 of net recognized built-in gain to X for 2007. X's net unrealized built-in gain limitation for 2008 is $22,000. On June 1, 2009, Y transfers its assets to X in a liquidation to which sections 332 and 337(a) apply.

(ii) Under paragraph (b) of this section, the net unrealized built in-gain of the first pool of assets is adjusted to account for the elimination of the Y stock in the liquidation. The net unrealized built-in gain of that pool of assets, however, can only be adjusted to reflect the amount of built-in gain that was inherent in the Y stock on January 1, 2005 that has not resulted in recognized built-in gain during the recognition period. In this case, therefore, the net unrealized built-in gain of the first pool of assets cannot be reduced by more than $27,000 ($35,000, the amount by which the fair market value of the Y stock exceeded its adjusted basis as of January 1, 2005, minus $8,000, the recognized built-in gain with respect to the stock during the recognition period). Accordingly, for taxable years ending after June 1, 2009, the net unrealized built-in gain of the first pool of assets is $3,000. The net unrealized built-in gain limitation for 2009 is $0.

T.D. 8579, 12/23/94, amend T.D. 9180, 2/22/2005.

§ 1.1374-4 Recognized built-in gain or loss.

(a) Sales and exchanges. *(1) In general.* Section 1374(d)(3) or 1374(d)(4) applies to any gain or loss recognized during the recognition period in a transaction treated as a sale or exchange for federal income tax purposes.

(2) Oil and gas property. For purposes of paragraph (a)(1) of this section, an S corporation's adjusted basis in oil and gas property equals the sum of the shareholders' adjusted bases in the property as determined in section 613A(c)(11)(B).

(3) Examples. The rules of this paragraph (a) are illustrated by the following examples.

Example (1). Production and sale of oil. X is a C corporation that purchased a working interest in an oil and gas property for $100,000 on July 1, 1993. X elects to become an S corporation effective January 1, 1996. On that date, the working interest has a fair market value of $250,000 and an adjusted basis of $50,000, but no oil has as yet been extracted. In 1996, X begins production of the working interest, sells oil that it has produced to a refinery for $75,000, and includes that amount in gross income. Under paragraph (a)(1) of this section, the $75,000 is not recognized built-in gain because as of the beginning of the recognition period X held only a working interest in the oil and gas property (since the oil had not yet been extracted from the ground), and not the oil itself.

Example (2). Sale of oil and gas property. Y is a C corporation that elects to become an S corporation effective January 1, 1996. Y has two shareholders, A and B. A and B each own 50 percent of Y's stock. In addition, Y owns a royalty interest in an oil and gas property with a fair market value of $300,000 and an adjusted basis of $200,000. Under section 613A(c)(11)(B), Y's $200,000 adjusted basis in the royalty interest is allocated $100,000 to A and $100,000 to B. During 1996, A and B take depletion deductions with respect to the royalty interest of $10,000 and $15,000, respectively. As of January 1, 1997, A and B have a basis in the royalty interest of $90,000 and $85,000, respectively. On January 1, 1997, Y sells the royalty interest for $250,000. Under paragraph (a)(1) of this section, Y has gain recognized and recognized built-in gain of $75,000 ($250,000 − ($90,000 + $85,000) = $75,000) on the sale.

(b) Accrual method rule. *(1) Income items.* Except as otherwise provided in this section, any item of income properly taken into account during the recognition period is recognized built-in gain if the item would have been properly included in gross income before the beginning of the recognition period by an accrual method taxpayer (disregarding any method of accounting for which an election by the taxpayer must be made unless the taxpayer actually used the method when it was a C corporation).

(2) Deduction items. Except as otherwise provided in this section, any item of deduction properly taken into account during the recognition period is recognized built-in loss if the item would have been properly allowed as a deduction against gross income before the beginning of the recognition period to an accrual method taxpayer (disregarding any method of accounting for which an election by the taxpayer must be made unless the taxpayer actually used the method when it was a C corporation). In determining whether an

item would have been properly allowed as a deduction against gross income by an accrual method taxpayer for purposes of this paragraph, section 461(h)(2)(C) and § 1.461-4(g) (relating to liabilities for tort, worker's compensation, breach of contract, violation of law, rebates, refunds, awards, prizes, jackpots, insurance contracts, warranty contracts, service contracts, taxes, and other liabilities) do not apply.

(3) Examples. The rules of this paragraph (b) are illustrated by the following examples.

Example (1). Accounts receivable. X is a C corporation using the cash method that elects to become an S corporation effective January 1, 1996. On January 1, 1996, X has $50,000 of accounts receivable for services rendered before that date. On that date, the accounts receivable have a fair market value of $40,000 and an adjusted basis of $0. In 1996, X collects $50,000 on the accounts receivable and includes that amount in gross income. Under paragraph (b)(1) of this section, the $50,000 included in gross income in 1996 is recognized built-in gain because it would have been included in gross income before the beginning of the recognition period if X had been an accrual method taxpayer. However, if X instead disposes of the accounts receivable for $45,000 on July 1, 1996, in a transaction treated as a sale or exchange for federal income tax purposes, X would have recognized built-in gain of $40,000 on the disposition.

Example (2). Contingent liability. Y is a C corporation using the cash method that elects to become an S corporation effective January 1, 1996. In 1995, a lawsuit was filed against Y claiming $1,000,000 in damages. In 1996, Y loses the lawsuit, pays a $500,000 judgment, and properly claims a deduction for that amount. Under paragraph (b)(2) of this section, the $500,000 deduction allowed in 1996 is not recognized built-in loss because it would not have been allowed as a deduction against gross income before the beginning of the recognition period if Y had been an accrual method taxpayer (even disregarding section 461(h)(2)(C) and § 1.461-4(g)).

Example (3). Deferred payment liabilities. X is a C corporation using the cash method that elects to become an S corporation on January 1, 1996. In 1995, X lost a lawsuit and became obligated to pay $150,000 in damages. Under section 461(h)(2)(C), this amount is not allowed as a deduction until X makes payment. In 1996, X makes payment and properly claims a deduction for the amount of the payment. Under paragraph (b)(2) of this section, the $150,000 deduction allowed in 1996 is recognized built-in loss because it would have been allowed as a deduction against gross income before the beginning of the recognition period if X had been an accrual method taxpayer (disregarding section 461(h)(2)(C) and § 1.461-4(g)).

Example (4). Deferred prepayment income. Y is a C corporation using an accrual method that elects to become an S corporation effective January 1, 1996. In 1995, Y received $2,500 for services to be rendered in 1996, and properly elected to include the $2,500 in gross income in 1996 under Rev. Proc. 71-21, 1971-2 C.B. 549 (see § 601.601(d)(2)(ii)(b) of this chapter). Under paragraph (b)(1) of this section, the $2,500 included in gross income in 1996 is not recognized built-in gain because it would not have been included in gross income before the beginning of the recognition period by an accrual method taxpayer using the method that Y actually used before the beginning of the recognition period.

Example (5). Change in method. X is a C corporation using an accrual method that elects to become an S corporation effective January 1, 1996. In 1995, X received $5,000 for services to be rendered in 1996, and properly included the $5,000 in gross income. In 1996, X properly elects to include the $5,000 in gross income in 1996 under Rev. Proc. 71-21, 1971-2 C.B. 549 (see § 601.601(d)(2)(ii)(b) of this chapter). As a result of the change in method of accounting, X has a $5,000 negative section 481(a) adjustment. Under paragraph (b)(1) of this section, the $5,000 included in gross income in 1996 is recognized built-in gain because it would have been included in gross income before the beginning of the recognition period by an accrual method taxpayer using the method that X actually used before the beginning of the recognition period. In addition, the $5,000 negative section 481(a) adjustment is recognized built-in loss because it relates to an item (the $5,000 X received for services in 1995) attributable to periods before the beginning of the recognition period under the principles for determining recognized built-in gain or loss in this section. See paragraph (d) of this section for rules regarding section 481(a) adjustments.

(c) Section 267(a)(2) and 404(a)(5) deductions. *(1) Section 267(a)(2).* Notwithstanding paragraph (b)(2) of this section, any amount properly deducted in the recognition period under section 267(a)(2), relating to payments to related parties, is recognized built-in loss to the extent—

(i) All events have occurred that establish the fact of the liability to pay the amount, and the exact amount of the liability can be determined, as of the beginning of the recognition period; and

(ii) The amount is paid—

(A) In the first two and one-half months of the recognition period; or

(B) To a related party owning, under the attribution rules of section 267, less than 5 percent, by voting power and value, of the corporation's stock, both as of the beginning of the recognition period and when the amount is paid.

(2) Section 404(a)(5). Notwithstanding paragraph (b)(2) of this section, any amount properly deducted in the recognition period under section 404(a)(5), relating to payments for deferred compensation, is recognized built-in loss to the extent—

(i) All events have occurred that establish the fact of the liability to pay the amount, and the exact amount of the liability can be determined, as of the beginning of the recognition period; and

(ii) The amount is not paid to a related party to which section 267(a)(2) applies.

(3) Examples. The rules of this paragraph (c) are illustrated by the following examples.

Example (1). Fixed annuity. X is a C corporation that elects to become an S corporation effective January 1, 1996. On December 31, 1995, A is age 60, has provided services to X as an employee for 20 years, and is a vested participant in X's unfunded nonqualified retirement plan. Under the plan, A receives $1,000 per month upon retirement until death. The plan provides no additional benefits. A retires on December 31, 1997, after working for X for 22 years. A at no time is a shareholder of X. X's deductions under section 404(a)(5) in the recognition period on paying A the $1,000 per month are recognized built-in loss because all events have occurred that establish the fact of the liability to pay the amount, and the exact amount of the liability can be determined, as of the beginning of the recognition period.

Example (2). Increase in annuity for working beyond 20 years. The facts are the same as Example 1, except that under the plan A receives $1,000 per month, plus $100 per month for each year A works for X beyond 20 years, upon retirement until death. X's deductions on paying A the $1,000 per month are recognized built-in loss. However, X's deductions on paying A the $200 per month for the two years A worked for X beyond 20 years are not recognized built-in loss because all events have not occurred that establish the fact of the liability to pay the amount, and the exact amount of the liability cannot be determined, as of the beginning of the recognition period.

Example (3). Cost of living adjustment. The facts are the same as Example 1, except that under the plan A receives $1,000 per month, plus annual cost of living adjustments, upon retirement until death. X's deductions under section 404(a)(5) on paying A the $1,000 per month are recognized built-in loss. However, X's deductions under section 404(a)(5) on paying A the annual cost of living adjustment are not recognized built-in loss because all events have not occurred that establish the fact of the liability to pay the amount, and the exact amount of the liability cannot be determined, as of the beginning of the recognition period.

(d) Section 481(a) adjustments. *(1) In general.* Any section 481(a) adjustment taken into account in the recognition period is recognized built-in gain or loss to the extent the adjustment relates to items attributable to periods before the beginning of the recognition period under the principles for determining recognized built-in gain or loss in this section. The principles for determining recognized built-in gain or loss in this section include, for example, the accrual method rule under paragraph (b) of this section.

(2) Examples. The rules of this paragraph (d) are illustrated by the following examples.

Example (1). Omitted item attributable to pre-recognition period. X is a C corporation that elects to become an S corporation effective January 1, 1996. X improperly capitalizes repair costs and recovers the costs through depreciation of the related assets. In 1999, X properly changes to deducting repair costs as they are incurred. Under section 481(a), the basis of the related assets are reduced by an amount equal to the excess of the repair costs incurred before the year of change over the repair costs recovered through depreciation before the year of change. In addition, X has a negative section 481(a) adjustment equal to the basis reduction. Under paragraph (d)(1) of this section, the portion of X's negative section 481(a) adjustment relating to the repair costs incurred before the recognition period is recognized built-in loss because those repair costs are items attributable to periods before the beginning of the recognition period under the principles for determining recognized built-in gain or loss in this section.

Example (2). Duplicated item attributable to pre-recognition period. Y is a C corporation that elects to become an S corporation effective January 1, 1996. Y improperly uses an accrual method without regard to the economic performance rules of section 461(h) to account for worker's compensation claims. As a result, Y takes deductions when claims are filed. In 1999, Y properly changes to an accrual method with regard to the economic performance rules under section 461(h)(2)(C) for worker's compensation claims. As a result, Y takes deductions when claims are paid. The positive section 481(a) adjustment resulting from the change is equal to the amount of claims filed, but unpaid, before the year of change. Under paragraph (b)(2) of this section, the deduction allowed in the recognition period for claims filed, but unpaid, before the recognition period is recognized built-in loss because a deduction was allowed for those claims before the recognition period under an accrual method without regard to section 461(h)(2)(C). Under paragraph (d)(1) of this section, the portion of Y's positive section 481(a) adjustment relating to claims filed, but unpaid, before the recognition period is recognized built-in gain because those claims are items attributable to periods before the beginning of the recognition period under the principles for determining recognized built-in gain or loss in this section.

(e) Section 995(b)(2) deemed distributions. Any item of income properly taken into account during the recognition period under section 995(b)(2) is recognized built-in gain if the item results from a DISC termination or disqualification occurring before the beginning of the recognition period.

(f) Discharge of indebtedness and bad debts. Any item of income or deduction properly taken into account during the first year of the recognition period as discharge of indebtedness income under section 61(a)(12) or as a bad debt deduction under section 166 is recognized built-in gain or loss if the item arises from a debt owed by or to an S corporation at the beginning of the recognition period.

(g) Completion of contract. Any item of income properly taken into account during the recognition period under the completed contract method (as described in § 1.460-4(d)) where the corporation began performance of the contract before the beginning of the recognition period is recognized built-in gain if the item would have been included in gross income before the beginning of the recognition period under the percentage of completion method (as described in § 1.460-4(b)). Any similar item of deduction is recognized built-in loss if the item would have been allowed as a deduction against gross income before the beginning of the recognition period under the percentage of completion method.

(h) Installment method. *(1) In general.* If a corporation sells an asset before or during the recognition period and reports the income from the sale using the installment method under section 453 during or after the recognition period, that income is subject to tax under section 1374.

(2) Limitation on amount subject to tax. For purposes of paragraph (h)(1) of this section, the taxable income limitation under § 1.1374-2(a)(2) is equal to the amount by which the S corporation's net recognized built-in gain would have been increased from the year of the sale to the earlier of the year the income is reported under the installment method or the last year of the recognition period, assuming all income from the sale had been reported in the year of the sale and all provisions of section 1374 applied. For purposes of the preceding sentence, if the corporation sells the asset before the recognition period, the income from the sale that is not reported before the recognition period is treated as having been reported in the first year of the recognition period.

(3) Rollover rule. If the limitation in paragraph (h)(2) of this section applies, the excess of the amount reported under the installment method over the amount subject to tax under the limitation is treated as if it were reported in the succeeding taxable year(s), but only for succeeding taxable year(s) in the recognition period. The amount reported in the succeeding taxable year(s) under the preceding sentence is reduced to the extent that the amount not subject to tax under the limitation in paragraph (h)(2) of this section was not subject to tax because the S corporation had an excess of recognized built-in loss over recognized built-in gain in the taxable year of the sale and succeeding taxable year(s) in the recognition period.

(4) Use of losses and section 1374 attributes. If income is reported under the installment method by an S corporation for a taxable year after the recognition period and the in-

come is subject to tax under paragraph (h)(1) of this section, the S corporation's section 1374 attributes may be used to the extent their use is allowed under all applicable provisions of the Code in determining the section 1374 tax. However, the S corporation's loss recognized for a taxable year after the recognition period that would have been recognized built-in loss if it had been recognized in the recognition period may not be used in determining the section 1374 tax.

(5) Examples. The rules of this paragraph (h) are illustrated by the following examples.

Example (1). Rollover rule. X is a C corporation that elects to become an S corporation effective January 1, 1996. On that date, X sells Blackacre with a basis of $0 and a value of $100,000 in exchange for a $100,000 note bearing a market rate of interest payable on January 1, 2001. X does not make the election under section 453(d) and, therefore, reports the $100,000 gain using the installment method under section 453. In the year 2001, X has income of $100,000 on collecting the note, unexpired C year attributes of $0, recognized built-in loss of $0, current losses of $100,000, and taxable income of $0. If X had reported the $100,000 gain in 1996, X's net recognized built-in gain from 1996 through 2001 would have been $75,000 greater than otherwise. Under paragraph (h) of this section, X has $75,000 net recognized built-in gain subject to tax under section 1374. X also must treat the $25,000 excess of the amount reported, $100,000, over the amount subject to tax, $75,000, as income reported under the installment method in the succeeding taxable year(s) in the recognition period, except to the extent X establishes that the $25,000 was not subject to tax under section 1374 in the year 2001 because X had an excess of recognized built-in loss over recognized built-in gain in the taxable year of the sale and succeeding taxable year(s) in the recognition period.

Example (2). Use of losses. Y is a C corporation that elects to become an S corporation effective January 1, 1996. On that date, Y sells Whiteacre with a basis of $0 and a value of $250,000 in exchange for a $250,000 note bearing a market rate of interest payable on January 1, 2006. Y does not make the election under section 453(d) and, therefore, reports the $250,000 gain using the installment method under section 453. In the year 2006, Y has income of $250,000 on collecting the note, unexpired C year attributes of $0, loss of $100,000 that would have been recognized built-in loss if it had been recognized in the recognition period, current losses of $150,000, and taxable income of $0. If Y had reported the $250,000 gain in 1996, X's net recognized built-in gain from 1996 through 2005 (that is, during the recognition period) would have been $225,000 greater than otherwise. Under paragraph (h) of this section, X has $225,000 net recognized built-in gain subject to tax under section 1374.

Example (3). Use of section 1374 attribute. Z is a C corporation that elects to become an S corporation effective January 1, 1996. On that date, Z sells Greenacre with a basis of $0 and a value of $500,000 in exchange for a $500,000 note bearing a market rate of interest payable on January 1, 2011. Z does not make the election under section 453(d) and, therefore, reports the $500,000 gain using the installment method under section 453. In the year 2011, Z has income of $500,000 on collecting the note, loss of $0 that would have been recognized built-in loss if it had been recognized in the recognition period, current losses of $0, taxable income of $500,000, and a minimum tax credit of $60,000 arising in 1995. None of Z's minimum tax credit is limited under sections 53(c) or 383. If Z had reported the $500,000 gain in 1996, Z's net recognized built-in gain from 1996 through 2005 (that is, during the recognition period) would have been $350,000 greater than otherwise. Under paragraph (h) of this section, Z has $350,000 net recognized built-in gain subject to tax under section 1374, a tentative section 1374 tax of $122,500 ($350,000 × .35 = $122,500), and a section 1374 tax after using its minimum tax credit arising in 1995 of $62,250 ($122,500 – $60,000 = $62,250).

(i) Partnership interests. *(1) In general.* If an S corporation owns a partnership interest at the beginning of the recognition period or transfers property to a partnership in a transaction to which section 1374(d)(6) applies during the recognition period, the S corporation determines the effect on net recognized built-in gain from its distributive share of partnership items as follows—

(i) Step One: Apply the rules of section 1374(d) to the S corporation's distributive share of partnership items of income, gain, loss, or deduction included in income or allowed as a deduction under the rules of subchapter K to determine the extent to which it would have been treated as recognized built-in gain or loss if the partnership items had originated in and been taken into account directly by the S corporation (partnership 1374 items);

(ii) Step Two: Determine the S corporation's net recognized built-in gain without partnership 1374 items;

(iii) Step Three: Determine the S corporation's net recognized built-in gain with partnership 1374 items; and

(iv) Step Four: If the amount computed under Step Three (paragraph (i)(1)(iii) of this section) exceeds the amount computed under Step Two (paragraph (i)(1)(ii) of this section), the excess (as limited by paragraph (i)(2)(i) of this section) is the S corporation's partnership RBIG, and the S corporation's net recognized built-in gain is the sum of the amount computed under Step Two (paragraph (i)(1)(ii) of this section) plus the partnership RBIG. If the amount computed under Step Two (paragraph (i)(1)(ii) of this section) exceeds the amount computed under Step Three (paragraph (i)(1)(iii) of this section), the excess (as limited by paragraph (i)(2)(ii) of this section) is the S corporation's partnership RBIL, and the S corporation's net recognized built-in gain is the remainder of the amount computed under Step Two (paragraph (i)(1)(ii) of this section) after subtracting the partnership RBIL.

(2) Limitations. (i) Partnership RBIG. An S corporation's partnership RBIG for any taxable year may not exceed the excess (if any) of the S corporation's RBIG limitation over its partnership RBIG for prior taxable years. The preceding sentence does not apply if a corporation forms or avails of a partnership with a principal purpose of avoiding the tax imposed under section 1374.

(ii) Partnership RBIL. An S corporation's partnership RBIL for any taxable year may not exceed the excess (if any) of the S corporation's RBIL limitation over its partnership RBIL for prior taxable years.

(3) Disposition of partnership interest. If an S corporation disposes of its partnership interest, the amount that may be treated as recognized built-in gain may not exceed the excess (if any) of the S corporation's RBIG limitation over its partnership RBIG during the recognition period. Similarly, the amount that may be treated as recognized built-in loss may not exceed the excess (if any) of the S corporation's RBIL limitation over its partnership RBIL during the recognition period.

(4) RBIG and RBIL limitations. (i) Sale of partnership interest. An S corporation's RBIG or RBIL limitation is the total of the following—

(A) The amount that would be the amount realized if, at the beginning of the first day of the recognition period, the corporation had remained a C corporation and had sold its partnership interest (and any assets the corporation contributed to the partnership during the recognition period) at fair market value to an unrelated party; decreased by

(B) The corporation's adjusted basis in the partnership interest (and any assets the corporation contributed to the partnership during the recognition period) at the time of the sale referred to in paragraph (i)(4)(i)(A) of this section; and increased or decreased by

(C) The corporation's allocable share of the partnership's section 481(a) adjustments at the time of the sale referred to in paragraph (i)(4)(i)(A) of this section.

(ii) Amounts of limitations. If the result in paragraph (i)(4)(i) of this section is a positive amount, the S corporation has a RBIG limitation equal to that amount and a RBIL limitation of $0, but if the result in paragraph (i)(4)(i) of this section is a negative amount, the S corporation has a RBIL limitation equal to that amount and a RBIG limitation of $0.

(5) Small interest exception. (i) In general. Paragraph (i)(1) of this section does not apply to a taxable year in the recognition period if the S corporation's partnership interest represents less than 10 percent of the partnership's capital and profits at all times during the taxable year and prior taxable years in the recognition period, and the fair market value of the S corporation's partnership interest as of the beginning of the recognition period is less than $100,000.

(ii) Contributed assets. For purposes of paragraph (i)(5)(i) of this section, if the S corporation contributes any assets to the partnership during the recognition period and the S corporation held the assets as of the beginning of the recognition period, the fair market value of the S corporation's partnership interest as of the beginning of the recognition period is determined as if the assets were contributed to the partnership before the beginning of the recognition period (using the fair market value of each contributed asset as of the beginning of the recognition period). The contribution does not affect whether paragraph (i)(5)(i) of this section applies for taxable years in the recognition period before the taxable year in which the contribution was made.

(iii) Anti-abuse rule. Paragraph (i)(5)(i) of this section does not apply if a corporation forms or avails of a partnership with a principal purpose of avoiding the tax imposed under section 1374.

(6) Section 704(c) gain or loss. Solely for purposes of section 1374, an S corporation's section 704(c) gain or loss amount with respect to any asset is not reduced during the recognition period, except for amounts treated as recognized built-in gain or loss with respect to that asset under this paragraph.

(7) Disposition of distributed partnership asset. If on the first day of the recognition period an S corporation holds an interest in a partnership that holds an asset and during the recognition period the partnership distributes the asset to the S corporation that thereafter disposes of the asset, the asset is treated as having been held by the S corporation on the first day of the recognition period and as having the fair market value and adjusted basis in the hands of the S corporation that it had in the hands of the partnership on that day.

(8) Examples. The rules of this paragraph (i) are illustrated by the following examples.

Example (1). Pre-conversion partnership interest. X is a C corporation that elects to become an S corporation on January 1, 1996. On that date, X owns a 50 percent interest in partnership P and P owns (among other assets) Blackacre with a basis of $25,000 and a value of $45,000. In 1996, P buys Whiteacre for $50,000. In 1999, P sells Blackacre for $55,000 and recognizes a gain of $30,000 of which $15,000 is included in X's distributive share. P also sells Whiteacre in 1999 for $42,000 and recognizes a loss of $8,000 of which $4,000 is included in X's distributive share. Under this paragraph and section 1374(d)(3), X's $15,000 gain is presumed to be recognized built-in gain and thus treated as a partnership 1374 item, but this presumption is rebutted if X establishes that P's gain would have been only $20,000 ($45,000 − $25,000 = $20,000) if Blackacre had been sold on the first day of the recognition period. In such a case, only X's distributive share of the $20,000 built-in gain, $10,000, would be treated as a partnership 1374 item. Under this paragraph and section 1374(d)(4), X's $4,000 loss is not treated as a partnership 1374 item because P did not hold Whiteacre on the first day of the recognition period.

Example (2). Post-conversion contribution. Y is a C corporation that elects to become an S corporation on January 1, 1996. On that date, Y owns (among other assets) Blackacre with a basis of $100,000 and a value of $200,000. On January 1, 1998, when Blackacre has a basis of $100,000 and a value of $200,000, Y contributes Blackacre to partnership P for a 50 percent interest in P. On January 1, 2000, P sells Blackacre for $300,000 and recognizes a gain of $200,000 on the sale ($300,000 − $100,000 = $200,000). P is allocated $100,000 of the gain under section 704(c), and another $50,000 of the gain for its fifty percent share of the remainder, for a total of $150,000. Under this paragraph and section 1374(d)(3), if Y establishes that P's gain would have been only $100,000 ($200,000 − $100,000 = $100,000) if Blackacre had been sold on the first day of the recognition period, Y would treat only $100,000 as a partnership 1374 item.

Example (3). RBIG limitation of $100,000 or $50,000. X is a C corporation that elects to become an S corporation on January 1, 1996. On that date, X owns a 50 percent interest in partnership P with a RBIG limitation of $100,000 and a RBIL limitation of $0. P owns (among other assets) Blackacre with a basis of $50,000 and a value of $200,000. In 1996, P sells Blackacre for $200,000 and recognizes a gain of $150,000 of which $75,000 is included in X's distributive share and treated as a partnership 1374 item. X's net recognized built-in gain for 1996 computed without partnership 1374 items is $35,000 and with partnership 1374 items is $110,000. Thus, X has a partnership RBIG of $75,000 except as limited under paragraph (i)(2)(i) of this section. Because X's RBIG limitation is $100,000, X's partnership RBIG of $75,000 is not limited and X's net recognized built-in gain for the year is $110,000 ($35,000 + $75,000 = $110,000). However, if X had a RBIG limitation of $50,000 instead of $100,000, X's partnership RBIG would be limited to $50,000 under paragraph (i)(2)(i) of this section and X's net recognized built-in gain would be $85,000 ($35,000 + $50,000 = $85,000).

Example (4). RBIL Limitation of $60,000 or $40,000. Y is a C corporation that elects to become an S corporation on January 1, 1996. On that date, Y owns a 50 percent interest in partnership P with a RBIG limitation of $0 and a RBIL limitation of $60,000. P owns (among other assets) Blackacre with a basis of $225,000 and a value of $125,000. In 1996, P sells Blackacre for $125,000 and recognizes a loss of $100,000 of which $50,000 is included in Y's distributive share and treated as a partnership 1374 item. Y's net recognized built-in gain for 1996 computed without partnership 1374 items is $75,000 and with partnership 1374 items is $25,000. Thus, Y has a partnership RBIL of $50,000 for the year except as limited under paragraph (i)(2)(ii) of this section. Because Y's RBIL limitation is $60,000, Y's partnership RBIL for the year is not limited and Y's net recognized built-in gain for the year is $25,000 ($75,000 − $50,000 = $25,000). However, if Y had a RBIL limitation of $40,000 instead of $60,000, Y's partnership RBIL would be limited to $40,000 under paragraph (i)(2)(ii) of this section and Y's net recognized built-in gain for the year would be $35,000 ($75,000 − $40,000 = $35,000).

Example (5). RBIG limitation of $0. (i) X is a C corporation that elects to become an S corporation on January 1, 1996. X owns a 50 percent interest in partnership P with a RBIG limitation of $0 and a RBIL limitation of $25,000.

(a) In 1996, P's partnership 1374 items are—

(1) Ordinary income of $25,000; and

(2) Capital gain of $75,000.

(b) X itself has—

(1) Recognized built-in ordinary income of $40,000; and

(2) Recognized built-in capital loss of $90,000.

(ii) X's net recognized built-in gain for 1996 computed without partnership 1374 items is $40,000 and with partnership 1374 items is $65,000 ($40,000 + $25,000 = $65,000). Thus, X's partnership RBIG is $25,000 for the year except as limited under paragraph (i)(2)(i) of this section. Because X's RBIG limitation is $0, X's partnership RBIG of $25,000 is limited to $0 and X's net recognized built-in gain for the year is $40,000.

Example (6). RBIL limitation of $0. (i) Y is a C corporation that elects to become an S corporation on January 1, 1996. Y owns a 50 percent interest in partnership P with a RBIG limitation of $60,000 and a RBIL limitation of $0.

(a) In 1996, P's partnership 1374 items are—

(1) Ordinary income of $25,000; and

(2) Capital loss of $90,000.

(b) Y itself has—

(1) recognized built-in ordinary income of $40,000; and

(2) recognized built-in capital gain of $75,000.

(ii) Y's net recognized built-in gain for 1996 computed without partnership 1374 items is $115,000 ($40,000 + $75,000 = $115,000) and with partnership 1374 items is $65,000 ($40,000 + $25,000 = $65,000). Thus, Y's partnership RBIL is $50,000 for the year except as limited under paragraph (i)(2)(ii) of this section. Because Y's RBIL limitation is $0, Y's partnership RBIL of $50,000 is limited to $0 and Y's net recognized built-in gain is $115,000.

Example (7). Disposition of partnership interest. X is a C corporation that elects to become an S corporation on January 1, 1996. On that date, X owns a 50 percent interest in partnership P with a RBIG limitation of $200,000 and a RBIL limitation of $0. P owns (among other assets) Blackacre with a basis of $20,000 and a value of $140,000. In 1996, P sells Blackacre for $140,000 and recognizes a gain of $120,000 of which $60,000 is included in X's distributive share and treated as a partnership 1374 item. X's net recognized built-in gain for 1996 computed without partnership 1374 items is $95,000 and with partnership 1374 items is $155,000. Thus, X has a partnership RBIG of $60,000. In 1999, X sells its entire interest in P for $350,000 and recognizes a gain of $250,000. Under paragraph (i)(3) of this section, X's recognized built-in gain on the sale is limited by its RBIG limitation to $140,000 ($200,000 − $60,000 = $140,000).

Example (8). Section 704(c) case. Y is a C corporation that elects to become an S corporation on January 1, 1996. On that date, Y contributes Asset 1, 5-year property with a value of $40,000 and a basis of $0, and an unrelated party contributes $40,000 in cash, each for a 50 percent interest in partnership P. The partnership adopts the traditional method under § 1.704-3(b). If P sold Asset 1 for $40,000 immediately after it was contributed by Y, P's $40,000 gain would be allocated to Y under section 704(c). Instead, Asset 1 is sold by P in 1999 for $36,000 and P recognizes gain of $36,000 ($36,000 − $0 = $36,000) on the sale. However, because book depreciation of $8,000 per year has been taken on Asset 1 in 1996, 1997, and 1998, Y is allocated only $16,000 of P's $36,000 gain ($40,000 − (3 × $8,000) = ($16,000 − $0) = $16,000) under section 704(c). The remaining $20,000 of P's $36,000 gain ($36,000 − $16,000 = $20,000) is allocated 50 percent to each partner under section 704(b). Thus, a total of $26,000 ($16,000 + $10,000 = $26,000) of P's $36,000 gain is allocated to Y. However, under paragraph (i)(6) of this section, Y treats $36,000 as a partnership 1374 item on P's sale of Asset 1.

Example (9). Disposition of distributed partnership asset. X is a C corporation that elects to become an S corporation on January 1, 1996. On that date, X owns a fifty percent interest in partnership P and P owns (among other assets) Blackacre with a basis of $20,000 and a value of $40,000. On January 1, 1998, P distributes Blackacre to X, when Blackacre has a basis of $20,000 and a value of $50,000. Under section 732(a)(1), X has a transferred basis of $20,000 in Blackacre. On January 1, 1999, X sells Blackacre for $60,000 and recognizes a gain of $40,000. Under paragraph (i)(7) of this section and section 1374(d)(3), X has recognized built-in gain from the sale of $20,000, the amount of built-in gain in Blackacre on the first day of the recognition period.

T.D. 8579, 12/23/94, amend T.D. 8995, 5/14/2002.

§ 1.1374-5 Loss carryforwards.

(a) In general. The loss carryforwards allowed as deductions against net recognized built-in gain under section 1374(b)(2) are allowed only to the extent their use is allowed under the rules applying to C corporations. Any other loss carryforwards, such as charitable contribution carryforwards under section 170(d)(2), are not allowed as deductions against net recognized built-in gain.

(b) Example. The rules of this section are illustrated by the following example.

Example. Section 382 limitation. X is a C corporation that has an ownership change under section 382(g)(1) on January 1, 1994. On that date, X has a fair market value of $500,000, NOL carryforwards of $400,000, and a net unrealized built-in gain under section 382(h)(3)(A) of $0. Assume X's section 382 limitation under section 382(b)(1) is $40,000. X elects to become an S corporation on January 1, 1998. On that date, X has NOL carryforwards of $240,000 (having used $160,000 of its pre-change net operating losses in its 4 preceding taxable years) and a section 1374 net unrealized built-in gain of $250,000. In 1998, X has net recognized built-in gain of $100,000. X may use $40,000 of its NOL carryforwards as a deduction against its $100,000 net recognized built-in gain, because X's section 382 limitation is $40,000.

T.D. 8579, 12/23/94.

§ 1.1374-6 Credits and credit carryforwards.

(a) In general. The credits and credit carryforwards allowed as credits against the section 1374 tax under section 1374(b)(3) are allowed only to the extent their use is allowed under the rules applying to C corporations. Any other credits or credit carryforwards, such as foreign tax credits under section 901, are not allowed as credits against the section 1374 tax.

(b) Limitations. The amount of business credit carryforwards and minimum tax credit allowed against the section 1374 tax are subject to the limitations described in section 38(c) and section 53(c), respectively, as modified by this paragraph. The tentative tax determined under paragraph (a)(3) of § 1.1374-1 is treated as the regular tax liability described in sections 38(c)(1) and 53(c)(1), and as the net income tax and net regular tax liability described in section 38(c)(1). The tentative minimum tax described in section 55(b) is determined using the rate of tax applicable to corporations and without regard to any alternative minimum tax foreign tax credit described in that section and by treating the net recognized built-in gain determined under § 1.1374-2, modified to take into account the adjustments of sections 56 and 58 applicable to corporations and the preferences of section 57, as the alternative minimum taxable income described in section 55(b)(2).

(c) Examples. The rules of this section are illustrated by the following examples.

Example (1). Business credit carryforward. X is a C corporation that elects to become an S corporation effective January 1, 1996. On that date, X has a $500,000 business credit carryforward from a C year and Asset #1 with a fair market value of $400,000, a basis for regular tax purposes of $95,000, and a basis for alternative minimum tax purposes of $150,000. In 1996, X has net recognized built-in gain of $305,000 from selling Asset #1 for $400,000. Thus, X's tentative tax under paragraph (a)(3) of section 1.1374-1 and regular tax liability under paragraph (b) of this section is $106,750 ($400,000 − $95,000 = $305,000 × .35 = $106,750, assuming a 35 percent tax rate). Also, X's tentative minimum tax determined under paragraph (b) of this section is $47,000 [$400,000 − $150,000 = $250,000 − $15,000 ($40,000 corporate exemption amount − $25,000 phase-out = $15,000) = $235,000 × .20 = $47,000, assuming a 20 percent tax rate]. Thus, the business credit limitation under section 38(c) is $59,750 [$106,750 − $47,000 (the greater of $47,000 or $20,438 (.25 × $81,750 ($106,750 − $25,000 = $81,750))) = $59,750]. As a result, X's section 1374 tax is $47,000 ($106,750 − $59,750 = $47,000) for 1996 and X has $440,250 ($500,000 − $59,750 = $440,250) of business credit carryforwards for succeeding taxable years.

Example (2). Minimum tax credit. Y is a C corporation that elects to become an S corporation effective January 1, 1996. On that date, Asset #1 has a fair market value of $5,000,000, a basis for regular tax purposes of $4,000,000, and a basis for alternative minimum tax purposes of $4,750,000. Y also has a minimum tax credit of $310,000 from 1995. Y has no other assets, no net operating or capital loss carryforwards, and no business credit carryforwards. In 1996, Y's only transaction is the sale of Asset #1 for $5,000,000. Therefore, Y has net recognized built-in gain in 1996 of $1,000,000 ($5,000,000 − $4,000,000 = $1,000,000) and a tentative tax under paragraph (a)(3) of § 1.1374-1 of $350,000 ($1,000,000 × .35 = $350,000, assuming a 35 percent tax rate). Also, Y's tentative minimum tax determined under paragraph (b) of this section is $47,000 [$5,000,000 − $4,750,000 = $250,000 − $15,000 ($40,000 corporate exemption amount − $25,000 phase-out = $15,000) = $235,000 × .20 = $47,000, assuming a 20 percent tax rate]. Thus, Y may use its minimum tax credit in the amount of $303,000 ($350,000 − $47,000 = $303,000) to offset its section 1374 tentative tax. As a result, Y's section 1374 tax is $47,000 ($350,000 − $303,000 = $47,000) in 1996 and Y has a minimum tax credit attributable to years for which Y was a C corporation of $7,000 ($310,000 − $303,000 = $7,000).

T.D. 8579, 12/23/94.

§ 1.1374-7 Inventory.

(a) Valuation. The fair market value of the inventory of an S corporation on the first day of the recognition period equals the amount that a willing buyer would pay a willing seller for the inventory in a purchase of all the S corporation's assets by a buyer that expects to continue to operate the S corporation's business. For purposes of the preceding sentence, the buyer and seller are presumed not to be under any compulsion to buy or sell and to have reasonable knowledge of all relevant facts.

(b) Identity of dispositions. The inventory method used by an S corporation for tax purposes must be used to identify whether the inventory it disposes of during the recognition period is inventory it held on the first day of that period. Thus, a corporation using the LIFO method does not dispose of inventory it held on the first day of the recognition period unless the carrying value of its inventory for a taxable year during that period is less than the carrying value of its inventory on the first day of the recognition period (determined using the LIFO method as described in section 472). However, if a corporation changes its method of accounting for inventory (for example, from the FIFO method to the LIFO method or from the LIFO method to the FIFO method) with a principal purpose of avoiding the tax imposed under section 1374, it must use its former method to identify its dispositions of inventory.

T.D. 8579, 12/23/94.

§ 1.1374-8 Section 1374(d)(8) transactions.

(a) In general. If any S corporation acquires any asset in a transaction in which the S corporation's basis in the asset is determined (in whole or in part) by reference to a C corporation's basis in the assets (or any other property) (a section 1374(d)(8) transaction), section 1374 applies to the net recognized built-in gain attributable to the assets acquired in any section 1374(d)(8) transaction.

(b) Effective date of section 1374(d)(8). Section 1374(d)(8) applies to any section 1374(d)(8) transaction, as defined in paragraph (a)(1) of this section, that occurs on or after December 27, 1994, without regard to the date of the corporation's election to be an S corporation under section 1362.

(c) Separate determination of tax. For purposes of the tax imposed under section 1374(d)(8), a separate determination of tax is made with respect to the assets the S corporation acquires in one section 1374(d)(8) transaction from the assets the S corporation acquires in another section 1374(d)(8) transaction and from the assets the corporation held when it became an S corporation. Thus, an S corporation's section 1374 attributes when it became an S corporation may only be used to reduce the section 1374 tax imposed on dispositions of assets the S corporation held at that time. Similarly, an S corporation's section 1374 attributes acquired in a section 1374(d)(8) transaction may only be used to reduce a section 1374 tax imposed on dispositions of assets the S corporation acquired in the same transaction. If an S corporation makes QSub elections under section 1361(b)(3) for a tiered group of subsidiaries effective on the same day, see § 1.1361-4(b)(2).

(d) Taxable income limitation. For purposes of paragraph (a) of this section, an S corporation's taxable income limitation under § 1.1374-2(a)(2) for any taxable year is allocated between or among each of the S corporation's separate determinations of net recognized built-in gain for that year (determined without regard to the taxable income limitation) based on the ratio of each of those determinations to the sum of all of those determinations.

(e) Examples. The rules of this section are illustrated by the following examples.

Example (1). Separate determination of tax. (i) X is a C corporation that elected to become an S corporation effective January 1, 1986 (before section 1374 was amended in the Tax Reform Act of 1986). X has a net operating loss carryforward of $20,000 arising in 1985 when X was a C corporation. On January 1, 1996, Y (an unrelated C corporation) merges into X in a transaction to which section 368(a)(1)(A) applies. Y has no loss carryforwards, credits, or credit carryforwards. The assets X acquired from Y are subject to tax under section 1374 and have a net unrealized built-in gain of $150,000.

(ii) In 1996, X has a pre-limitation amount of $50,000 on dispositions of assets acquired from Y and a taxable income limitation of $100,000 (because only one group of assets is subject to section 1374, there is no allocation of the taxable income limitation). As a result, X has a net recognized built-in gain on those assets of $50,000. X's $20,000 net operating loss carryforward may not be used as a deduction against its $50,000 net recognized built-in gain on the assets X acquired from Y. Therefore, X has a section 1374 tax of $17,500 ($50,000 × .35 = $17,500, assuming a 35 percent tax rate) for its 1996 taxable year.

Example (2). Allocation of taxable income limitation. (i) Y is a C corporation that elects to become an S corporation effective January 1, 1996. The assets Y holds when it becomes an S corporation have a net unrealized built-in gain of $5,000. Y has no loss carryforwards, credits, or credit carryforwards. On January 1, 1997, Z (an unrelated C corporation) merges into Y in a transaction to which section 368(a)(1)(A) applies. Z has no loss carryforwards, credits, or credit carryforwards. The assets Y acquired from Z are subject to tax under section 1374 and have a net unrealized built-in gain of $80,000.

(ii) In 1997, Y has a pre-limitation amount on the assets it held when it became an S corporation of $15,000, a pre-limitation amount on the assets Y acquired from Z of $15,000, and a taxable income limitation of $10,000. However, because the assets Y held on becoming an S corporation have a net unrealized built-in gain of $5,000, its net recognized built-in gain on those assets is limited to $5,000 before taking into account the taxable income limitation. Y's taxable income limitation of $10,000 is allocated between the assets Y held on becoming an S corporation and the assets Y acquired from Z for purposes of determining the net recognized built-in gain from each pool of assets. Thus, Y's net recognized built-in gain on the assets Y held on becoming an S corporation is $2,500 [$10,000 × ($5,000/$20,000) = $2,500]. Y's net recognized built-in gain on the assets Y acquired from Z is $7,500 [$10,000 × ($15,000/$20,000) = $7,500]. Therefore, Y has a section 1374 tax of $3,500 [($2,500 + $7,500) × .35 = $3,500, assuming a 35 percent tax rate] for its 1997 taxable year.

T.D. 8579, 12/23/94, amend T.D. 8869, 1/20/2000, T.D. 9170, 12/21/2004, T.D. 9236, 12/20/2005.

§ 1.1374-9 Anti-stuffing rule.

If a corporation acquires an asset before or during the recognition period with a principal purpose of avoiding the tax imposed under section 1374, the asset and any loss, deduction, loss carryforward, credit, or credit carryforward attributable to the asset is disregarded in determining the S corporation's pre-limitation amount, taxable income limitation, net unrealized built-in gain limitation, deductions against net recognized built-in gain, and credits against the section 1374 tax.

T.D. 8579, 12/23/94.

§ 1.1374-10 Effective date and additional rules.

(a) In general. Sections 1.1374-1 through 1.1374-9, other than § 1.1374-3(b) and (c) Examples 2 through 4, apply for taxable years ending on or after December 27, 1994, but only in cases where the S corporation's return for the taxable year is filed pursuant to an S election or a section 1374(d)(8) transaction occurring on or after December 27, 1994. Section 1.1374-3(b) and (c) Examples 2 through 4 apply to section 1374(d)(8) transactions that occur in taxable years beginning after February 23, 2005. In addition, an S corporation may apply § 1.1374-3(b) and (c) Examples 2 through 4 to section 1374(d)(8) transactions that occur in taxable years beginning on or before February 23, 2005, if the S corporation (and any predecessors or successors) and all affected shareholders file original or amended returns that are consistent with these provisions for taxable years of the S corporation during the recognition period of the pool of assets the net unrealized built-in gain of which would be adjusted pursuant to those provisions that are not closed as of the first date after February 23, 2005, that the S corporation files an original or amended return. For purposes of this section, affected shareholders means all shareholders who received distributive shares of S corporation items in such taxable years. However, the Commissioner may, in appropriate circumstances, permit taxpayers to apply these provisions even if all affected shareholders cannot file consistent returns. In addition, for this purpose, a predecessor of an S corporation is a corporation that transfers its assets to the S corporation in a transaction to which section 381 applies. A successor of an S corporation is a corporation to which the S corporation transfers its assets in a transaction to which section 381 applies.

(b) Additional rules. This paragraph (b) provides rules applicable to certain S corporations, assets, or transactions to which §§ 1.1374-1 through 1.1374-9 do not apply.

(1) Certain transfers to partnerships. If a corporation transfers an asset to a partnership in a transaction to which section 721(a) applies and the transfer is made in contemplation of an S election or during the recognition period, section 1374 applies on a disposition of the asset by the partnership as if the S corporation had disposed of the asset itself. This paragraph (b)(1) applies as of the effective date of section 1374, unless the recognition period with respect to the con-

tributed asset is pursuant to an S election or a section 1374(d)(8) transaction occurring on or after December 27, 1994.

(2) Certain inventory dispositions. For purposes of section 1374(d)(2)(A), the inventory method used by the taxpayer for tax purposes (FIFO, LIFO, etc.) must be used to identify whether goods disposed of following conversion to S corporation status were held by the corporation at the time of conversion. Thus, for example, a corporation using the LIFO inventory method will not be subject to the built-in gain tax with respect to sales of inventory except to the extent that a LIFO layer existing prior to the beginning of the first taxable year as an S corporation is invaded after the beginning of that year. This paragraph (b)(2) applies as of the effective date of section 1374, unless the recognition period with respect to the inventory is pursuant to an S election or a section 1374(d)(8) transaction occurring on or after December 27, 1994.

(3) Certain contributions of built-in loss assets. If a built-in loss asset (that is, an asset with an adjusted tax basis in excess of its fair market value) is contributed to a corporation within 2 years before the earlier of the beginning of its first taxable year as an S corporation, or the filing of its S election, the loss inherent in the asset will not reduce net unrealized built-in gain, as defined in section 1374(d)(1), unless the taxpayer demonstrates a clear and substantial relationship between the contributed property and the conduct of the corporation's current or future business enterprises. This paragraph (b)(3) applies as of the effective date of section 1374, unless the recognition period with respect to the contributed asset is pursuant to an S election or a section 1374(d)(8) transaction occurring on or after December 27, 1994.

(4) Certain installment sales. (i) In general. If a taxpayer sells an asset either prior to or during the recognition period and recognizes income either during or after the recognition period from the sale under the installment method, the income will, when recognized, be taxed under section 1374 to the extent it would have been so taxed in prior taxable years if the selling corporation had made the election under section 453(d) not to report the income under the installment method. For purposes of determining the extent to which the income would have been subject to tax if the section 453(d) election had not been made, the taxable income limitation of section 1374(d)(2)(A)(ii) and the built-in gain carryover rule of section 1374(d)(2)(B) will be taken into account. This paragraph (b)(4) applies for installment sales occurring on or after March 26, 1990, and before December 27, 1994.

(ii) Examples. The rules of this paragraph (b)(4) are illustrated by the following examples.

Example (1). In year 1 of the recognition period under section 1374, a corporation realizes a gain of $100,000 on the sale of an asset with built-in gain. The corporation is to receive full payment for the asset in year 11. Because the corporation does not make an election under section 453(d), all $100,000 of the gain from the sale is reported under the installment method in year 11. If the corporation had made an election under section 453(d) with respect to the sale, the gain would have been recognized in year 1 and, taking into account the corporation's income and gains from other sources, application of the taxable income limitation of section 1374(d)(2)(A)(ii) and the built-in gain carryover rule of section 1374(d)(2)(B) would have resulted in $40,000 of the gain being subject to tax during the recognition period under section 1374. Therefore, $40,000 of the gain recognized in year 11 is subject to tax under section 1374.

Example (2). In year 1 of the recognition period under section 1374, a corporation realizes a gain of $100,000 on the sale of an asset with built-in gain. The corporation is to receive full payment for the asset in year 6. Because the corporation does not make an election under section 453(d), all $100,000 of the gain from the sale is reported under the installment method in year 6. If the corporation had made an election under section 453(d) with respect to the sale, the gain would have been recognized in year 1 and, taking into account the corporation's income and gains from other sources, application of the taxable income limitation of section 1374(d)(2)(A)(ii) and the built-in gain carryover rule of section 1374(d)(2)(B) would have resulted in all of the gain being subjected to tax under section 1374 in years 1 through 5. Therefore, notwithstanding that the taxable income limitation of section 1374(d)(2)(A)(ii) might otherwise limit the taxation of the gain recognized in year 6, the entire $100,000 of gain will be subject to tax under section 1374 when it is recognized in year 6.

(c) Termination and re-election of S corporation status. *(1) In general.* For purposes of section 633(d)(8) of the Tax Reform Act of 1986, as amended, any reference to an election to be an S corporation under section 1362 shall be treated as a reference to the corporation's most recent election to be an S corporation under section 1362. This paragraph (c) applies for taxable years beginning after December 22, 2004, without regard to the date of the corporation's most recent election to be an S corporation under section 1362.

(2) Example. The following example illustrates the rules of this paragraph (c):

Example. (i) Effective January 1, 1988, X, a C corporation that is a qualified corporation under section 633(d) of the Tax Reform Act of 1986, as amended, elects to be an S corporation under section 1362. Effective January 1, 1990, X revokes its S status and becomes a C corporation. On January 1, 2004, X again elects to be an S corporation under section 1362. X disposes of assets in 2006, 2007, and 2008, recognizing gain.

(ii) X is not eligible for treatment under the transition rule of section 633(d)(8) of the Tax Reform Act of 1986, as amended, with respect to these assets. Accordingly, X is subject to section 1374, as amended by the Tax Reform Act of 1986 and the Technical and Miscellaneous Revenue Act of 1988, and the 10-year recognition period begins on January 1, 2004.

(iii) To the extent the gain that X recognizes on the asset sales in 2006, 2007, and 2008 reflects built-in gain inherent in such assets in X's hands on January 1, 2004, such gain is subject to tax under section 1374 as amended by the Tax Reform Act of 1986 and the Technical and Miscellaneous Revenue Act of 1988.

T.D. 8579, 12/23/94, amend T.D. 9170, 12/21/2004, T.D. 9180, 2/22/2005, T.D. 9236, 12/20/2005.

PAR. 20. Section 1.1374-10, the first sentence of paragraph (a) is revised to read as follows:

Proposed § 1.1374-10 Effective date and additional rules. [*For Preamble, see ¶ 153,091*]

(a) In general. For transactions to which § 1.302-5 applies [Reserved]. Sections 1.1374-1 through 1.1374-9, other than § 1.1374-3(b) and (c) Examples 2 through 4, apply for taxable years ending on or after December 27, 1994, but only in cases where the S corporation's return for the taxable year is filed pursuant to an S election or a section 1374(d)(8) transaction occurring on or after December 27, 1994. * * *

* * * * *

§ 1.1375-1 Tax imposed when passive investment income of corporation having Subchapter C earnings and profits exceed 25 percent of gross receipts.

Caution: The Treasury has not yet amended Reg § 1.1375-1 to reflect changes made by P.L. 104-188.

(a) General rule. For taxable years beginning after 1981, section 1375(a) imposes a tax on the income of certain S corporations that have passive investment income. In the case of a taxable year beginning during 1982, an electing small business corporation may elect to have the rules under this section not apply. See the regulations under section 1362 for rules on the election. For purposes of this section, the term "S corporation" shall include an electing small business corporation under prior law. This tax shall apply to an S corporation for a taxable year if the S corporation has—

(1) Subchapter C earnings and profits at the close of such taxable year, and

(2) Gross receipts more than 25 percent of which are passive investment income.

If the S corporation has no Subchapter C earnings and profits at the close of the taxable year (because, for example, such earnings and profits were distributed in accordance with section 1368), the tax shall not be imposed even though the S corporation has passive investment income for the taxable year. If the tax is imposed, the tax shall be computed by multiplying the excess net passive income (as defined in paragraph (b) of this section) by the highest rate of tax specified in section 11(b).

(b) Definitions. *(1) Excess net passive income.* (i) In general. The term "excess net passive income" is defined in section 1375(b)(1), and can be expressed by the following formula:

$$\text{ENPI} = \text{NPI} \times \frac{\text{PII} - (.25 \times \text{GR})}{\text{PII}}$$

Where:

ENPI = excess net passive income
NPI = net passive income
PII = passive investment income
GR = total gross receipts

(ii) Limitation. The amount of the excess net passive income for any taxable year shall not exceed the corporation's taxable income for the taxable year (determined in accordance with section 1374(d) and § 1.1374-1(d)).

(2) Net passive income. The term "net passive income" means—

(i) Passive investment income, reduced by

(ii) The deductions allowable under Chapter 1 of the Internal Revenue Code of 1954 which are directly connected (within the meaning of paragraph (b)(3) of this section) with the production of such income (other than deductions allowable under section 172 and Part VIII of Subchapter B).

(3) Directly connected. (i) In general. For purposes of paragraph (b)(2)(ii) of this section to be directly connected with the production of income, an item of deduction must have proximate and primary relationship to the income. Expenses, depreciation, and similar items attributable solely to such income qualify for deduction.

(ii) Allocation of deduction. If an item of deduction is attributable (within the meaning of paragraph (b)(3)(i) of this section) in part to passive investment income and in part to income other than passive investment income, the deduction shall be allocated between the two types of items on a reasonable basis. The portion of any deduction so allocated to passive investment income shall be treated as proximately and primarily related to such income.

(4) Other definitions. The terms "subchapter C earnings and profits," "passive investment income," and "gross receipts" shall have the same meaning given these terms in section 1362(d)(3) and the regulations thereunder.

(c) Special rules. *(1) Disallowance of credits.* No credit is allowed under Part IV of Subchapter A of Chapter 1 of the Code (other than section 34) against the tax imposed by section 1375(a) and this section.

(2) Coordination with section 1374. If any gain—

(i) is taken into account in determining passive income for purposes of this section, and

(ii) is taken into account under section 1374.

the amount of such gain taken into account under section 1374(b) and § 1.1374-1(b)(1) and (2) in determining the amount of tax shall be reduced by the portion of the excess net passive income for the taxable year which is attributable (on a pro rata basis) to such gain. For purposes of the preceding sentence, the portion of excess net passive income for the taxable year which is attributable to such capital gain is equal to the amount determined by multiplying the excess net passive income by the following fraction:

$$\frac{\text{NCG} - \text{E}}{\text{NPI}}$$

Where:

NCG = net capital gain
NPI = net passive income.
E = Expense attributable to net capital gain.

(d) Waiver of tax in certain cases. *(1) In general.* If an S corporation establishes to the satisfaction of the Commissioner that—

(i) It determined in good faith that it had no Subchapter C earnings and profits at the close of the taxable year, and

(ii) During a reasonable period of time after it was determined that it did have Subchapter C earnings and profits at the close of such taxable year such earnings and profits were distributed,

the Commissioner may waive the tax imposed by section 1375 for such taxable year. The S corporation has the burden of establishing that under the relevant facts and circumstances the Commissioner should waive the tax.

For example, if an S corporation establishes that in good faith and using due diligence it determined that it had no Subchapter C earnings and profits at the close of a taxable year, but it was later determined on audit that it did have Subchapter C earnings and profits at the close of such taxable year, and if the corporation establishes that it distributed such earnings and profits within a reasonable time after the audit, it may be appropriate for the Commissioner to waive the tax on passive income for such taxable year.

(2) Corporation's request for a waiver. A request for waiver of the tax imposed by section 1375 shall be made in writing to the district director and shall contain all relevant facts to establish that the requirements of paragraph (d)(1) of this section are met. Such request shall contain a description of how and on what date the S corporation in good faith and using due diligence determined that it had no Subchapter C

earnings and profits at the close of the taxable year, a description of how and on what date it was determined that the S corporation had Subchapter C earnings and profits at the close of the year and a description (including dates) of any steps taken to distribute such earnings and profits. If the earnings and profits have not yet been distributed, the request shall contain a timetable for distribution and an explanation of why such timetable is reasonable. On the date the waiver is to become effective, all Subchapter C earnings and profits must have been distributed.

(e) Reduction in pass-thru for tax imposed on excess net passive income. See section 1366(f)(3) for a special rule reducing each item of the corporation's passive investment income for purposes of section 1366(a) if a tax is imposed on the corporation under section 1375.

(f) Examples. The following example illustrates the principles of this section:

Example (1). Assume Corporation M, an S corporation, has for its taxable year total gross receipts of $200,000, passive investment income of $100,000, $60,000 of which is interest income, and expenses directly connected with the production of such interest income in the amount of $10,000. Assume also that at the end of the taxable year Corporation M has Subchapter C earnings and profits. Since more than 25 percent of the Corporation M's total gross receipts are passive investment income, and since Corporation M has Subchapter C earnings and profits at the end of the taxable year, Corporation M will be subject to the tax imposed by section 1375. The amount of excess net passive investment income is $45,000 ($90,000 × (50,000/100,000)). Assume that the other $40,000 of passive investment income is attributable to net capital gain and that there are no expenses directly connected with such gain. Under these facts, $20,000 of the excess net passive income is attributable to the net capital gain ($45,000 × ($40,000/$90,000)). Accordingly, the amount of gain taken into account under section 1374(b)(1) and the taxable income of Corporation M under section 1374(b)(2) shall be reduced by $20,000.

Example (2). Assume an S corporation with subchapter C earnings and profits has tax-exempt income of $400, its only passive income, gross receipts of $1,000 and taxable income of $250 and there are no expenses associated with the tax-exempt income. The corporation's excess net income for the taxable year would total $150 (400 × ((400 − 250/400)). This amount is subject to the tax imposed by section 1375, notwithstanding that such amount is otherwise tax-exempt income.

T.D. 8104, 9/25/86, amend T.D. 8419, 5/28/92.

§ 1.1377-0 Table of contents.

The following table of contents is provided to facilitate the use of §§ 1.1377-1 through 1.1377-3:

T.D. 8696, 12/20/96, amend T.D. 8994, 5/13/2002.

§ 1.1377-1 Pro rata share.

(a) Computation of pro rata shares. *(1) In general.* For purposes of subchapter S of chapter 1 of the Internal Revenue Code and this section, each shareholder's pro rata share of any S corporation item described in section 1366(a) for any taxable year is the sum of the amounts determined with respect to the shareholder by assigning an equal portion of the item to each day of the S corporation's taxable year, and then dividing that portion pro rata among the shares outstanding on that day. See paragraph (b) of this section for rules pertaining to the computation of each shareholder's pro rata share when an election is made under section 1377(a)(2) to treat the taxable year of an S corporation as if it consisted of two taxable years in the case of a termination of a shareholder's entire interest in the corporation. See § 1.460-4(k)(3)(iv)(D) for rules relating to the computation of the shareholders' pro rata share of S corporation's income or loss from a contract accounted for under a long-term contract method of accounting.

(2) Special rules. (i) Days on which stock has not been issued. Solely for purposes of determining a shareholder's pro rata share of an item for a taxable year under section 1377(a) and this section, the beneficial owners of the corporation are treated as the shareholders of the corporation for any day on which the corporation has not issued any stock.

(ii) Determining shareholder for day of stock disposition. A shareholder who disposes of stock in an S corporation is treated as the shareholder for the day of the disposition. A shareholder who dies is treated as the shareholder for the day of the shareholder's death.

(iii) Shareholder trust conversions. If, during the taxable year of an S corporation, a trust that is an eligible shareholder of the S corporation converts from a trust described in section 1361(c)(2)(A)(i), (ii), (iii), or (v) for the first part of the year to a trust described in a different subpart of section 1361(c)(2)(A)(i), (ii), or (v) for the remainder of the year, the trust's share of the S corporation items is allocated between the two types of trusts. The first day that a qualified subchapter S trust (QSST) or an electing small business trust (ESBT) is treated as an S corporation shareholder is the effective date of the QSST or ESBT election. Upon the conversion, the trust is not treated as terminating its entire interest in the S corporation for purposes of paragraph (b) of this section, unless the trust was a trust described in section 1361(c)(2)(A)(ii) or (iii) before the conversion.

(b) Election to terminate year. *(1) In general.* If a shareholder's entire interest in an S corporation is terminated during the S corporation's taxable year and the corporation and all affected shareholders agree, the S corporation may elect under section 1377(a)(2) and this paragraph (b) (terminating election) to apply paragraph (a) of this section to the affected shareholders as if the corporation's taxable year consisted of two separate taxable years, the first of which ends at the close of the day on which the shareholder's entire interest in the S corporation is terminated. If the event resulting in the termination of the shareholder's entire interest also constitutes a qualifying disposition as described in § 1.1368-1(g)(2)(i), the election under § 1.1368-1(g)(2) cannot be made. An S corporation may not make a terminating election if the cessation of a shareholder's interest occurs in a transaction that results in a termination under section 1362(d)(2) of the corporation's election to be an S corporation. (See section 1362(e)(3) for an election to have items assigned to each short taxable year under normal tax accounting rules in the case of a termination of a corporation's election to be an S corporation.) A terminating election is irrevocable and is effective only for the terminating event for which it is made.

(2) Affected shareholders. For purposes of the terminating election under section 1377(a)(2) and paragraph (b) of this section, the term affected shareholders means the shareholder whose interest is terminated and all shareholders to whom such shareholder has transferred shares during the taxable year. If such shareholder has transferred shares to the corporation, the term affected shareholders includes all persons who are shareholders during the taxable year.

(3) Effect of the terminating election. (i) In general. An S corporation that makes a terminating election for a taxable year must treat the taxable year as separate taxable years for all affected shareholders for purposes of allocating items of income (including tax-exempt income), loss, deduction, and credit; making adjustments to the accumulated adjustments account, earnings and profits, and basis; and determining the tax effect of a distribution. An S corporation that makes a terminating election must assign items of income (including tax-exempt income), loss, deduction, and credit to each deemed separate taxable year using its normal method of accounting as determined under section 446(a).

(ii) Due date of S corporation return. A terminating election does not affect the due date of the S corporation's return required to be filed under section 6037(a) for a taxable year (determined without regard to a terminating election).

(iii) Taxable year of inclusion by shareholder. A terminating election does not affect the taxable year in which an affected shareholder must take into account the affected shareholder's pro rata share of the S corporation's items of income, loss, deduction, and credit.

(iv) S corporation that is a partner in a partnership. A terminating election by an S corporation that is a partner in a partnership is treated as a sale or exchange of the corporation's entire interest in the partnership for purposes of section 706(c) (relating to closing the partnership taxable year), if the taxable year of the partnership ends after the shareholder's interest is terminated and within the taxable year of the S corporation (determined without regard to any terminating election) for which the terminating election is made.

(4) Determination of whether an S shareholder's entire interest has terminated. For purposes of the terminating election under section 1377(a)(2) and paragraph (b) of this section, a shareholder's entire interest in an S corporation is terminated on the occurrence of any event through which a shareholder's entire stock ownership in the S corporation ceases, including a sale, exchange, or other disposition of all of the stock held by the shareholder; a gift under section 102(a) of all the shareholder's stock; a spousal transfer under section 1041(a) of all the shareholder's stock; a redemption, as defined in section 317(b), of all the shareholder's stock, regardless of the tax treatment of the redemption under section 302; and the death of the shareholder. A shareholder's entire interest in an S corporation is not terminated if the shareholder retains ownership of any stock (including an interest treated as stock under § 1.1361-1(l)) that would result in the shareholder continuing to be considered a shareholder of the corporation for purposes of section 1362(a)(2). Thus, in determining whether a shareholder's entire interest in an S corporation has been terminated, any interest held by the shareholder as a creditor, employee, director, or in any other non-shareholder capacity is disregarded.

(5) Time and manner of making a terminating election. (i) In general. An S corporation makes a terminating election by attaching a statement to its timely filed original or amended return required to be filed under section 6037(a) (that is, a Form 1120S) for the taxable year during which a shareholder's entire interest is terminated. A single election statement may be filed by the S corporation for all terminating elections for the taxable year. The election statement must include—

(A) A declaration by the S corporation that it is electing under section 1377(a)(2) and this paragraph (b) to treat the taxable year as if it consisted of two separate taxable years;

(B) Information setting forth when and how the shareholder's entire interest was terminated (for example, a sale or gift);

(C) The signature on behalf of the S corporation of an authorized officer of the corporation under penalties of perjury, except that for taxable years beginning after December 31, 2002, the election statement described in § 1.1377-1(b)(5)(i) of this section shall be verified, and the requirement of this paragraph (b)(5)(i)(C) is satisfied, by the signature on the Form 1120S filed by the S corporation.

(D) A statement by the corporation that the corporation and each affected shareholder consent to the S corporation making the terminating election.

(ii) Affected shareholders required to consent. For purposes of paragraph (b)(5)(i)(D) of this section, a shareholder of the S corporation for the taxable year is a shareholder as described in section 1362(a)(2). For example, the person who under § 1.1362-6(b)(2) must consent to a corporation's S election in certain special cases is the person who must consent to the terminating election. In addition, an executor or administrator of the estate of a deceased affected shareholder may consent to the terminating election on behalf of the deceased affected shareholder.

(iii) More than one terminating election. A shareholder whose entire interest in an S corporation is terminated in an event for which a terminating election was made is not required to consent to a terminating election made with respect to a subsequent termination within the same taxable year unless the shareholder is an affected shareholder with respect to the subsequent termination.

(c) Examples. The following examples illustrate the provisions of this section:

Example (1). Shareholder's pro rata share in the case of a partial disposition of stock. (i) On January 6, 1997, X incorporates as a calendar year corporation, issues 100 shares of common stock to each of A and B, and files an election to be an S corporation for its 1997 taxable year. On July 24, 1997, B sells 50 shares of X stock to C. Thus, in 1997, A owned 50 percent of the outstanding shares of X on each day of X's 1997 taxable year, B owned 50 percent on each day from January 6, 1997, to July 24, 1997 (200 days), and 25 percent from July 25, 1997, to December 31, 1997 (160 days), and C owned 25 percent from July 25, 1997, to December 31, 1997 (160 days).

(ii) Because B's entire interest in X is not terminated when B sells 50 shares to C on July 24, 1997, X cannot make a terminating election under section 1377(a)(2) and paragraph (b) of this section for B's sale of 50 shares to C. Although B's sale of 50 shares to C is a qualifying disposition under § 1.1368-1(g)(2)(i), X does not make an election to terminate its taxable year under § 1.1368-1(g)(2). During its 1997 taxable year, X has nonseparately computed income of $720,000.

(iii) For each day in X's 1997 taxable year, A's daily pro rata share of X's nonseparately computed income is $1,000 ($720,000/360 days × 50%). Thus, A's pro rata share of X's nonseparately computed income for 1997 is $360,000 ($1,000 × 360 days). B's daily pro rata share of X's nonseparately computed income is $1,000 ($720,000/360 × 50%) for the first 200 days of X's 1997 taxable year, and $500 ($720,000/360 × 25%) for the following 160 days in 1997. Thus, B's pro rata share of X's nonseparately computed income for 1997 is $280,000 (($1,000 × 200 days) + ($500 × 160 days)). C's daily pro rata share of X's nonseparately computed income is $500 ($720,000/360 × 25%) for 160 days in 1997. Thus, C's pro rata share of X's nonseparately computed income for 1997 is $80,000 ($500 × 160 days).

Example (2). Shareholder's pro rata share when an S Corporation makes a terminating election under section 1377(a)(2). (i) On January 6, 1997, X incorporates as a calendar year corporation, issues 100 shares of common stock to each of A and B, and files an election to be an S corporation for its 1997 taxable year. On July 24, 1997, B sells B's entire 100 shares of X stock to C. With the consent of B and C, X makes an election under section 1377(a)(2) and paragraph (b) of this section for the termination of B's entire interest arising from B's sale of 100 shares to C. As a result of the election, the pro rata shares of B and C are determined as if X's taxable year consisted of two separate taxable years, the first of which ends on July 24, 1997, the date B's entire interest in X terminates. Because A is not an affected shareholder as defined by section 1377(a)(2)(B) and paragraph (b)(2) of this section, the treatment as separate taxable years does not apply to A.

(ii) During its 1997 taxable year, X has nonseparately computed income of $720,000. Under X's normal method of accounting, $200,000 of the $720,000 of nonseparately computed income is allocable to the period of January 6, 1997, through July 24, 1997 (the first deemed taxable year), and the remaining $520,000 is allocable to the period of July 25, 1997, through December 31, 1997 (the second deemed taxable year).

(iii) B's pro rata share of the $200,000 of nonseparately computed income for the first deemed taxable year is determined by assigning the $200,000 of nonseparately computed income to each day of the first deemed taxable year ($200,000/200 days = $1,000 per day). Because B held 50% of X's authorized and issued shares on each day of the first deemed taxable year, B's daily pro rata share for each day of the first deemed taxable year is $500 ($1,000 per day × 50%). Thus, B's pro rata share of the $200,000 of nonseparately computed income for the first deemed taxable year is $100,000 ($500 per day × 200 days). B must report this amount for B's taxable year with or within which X's full taxable year ends (December 31, 1997).

(iv) C's pro rata share of the $520,000 of nonseparately computed income for the second deemed taxable year is determined by assigning the $520,000 of nonseparately computed income to each day of the second deemed taxable year ($520,000/160 days = $3,250 per day). Because C held 50% of X's authorized and issued shares on each day of the second deemed taxable year, C's daily pro rata shares for each day of the second deemed taxable year is $1,625 ($3,250 per day × 50%). Therefore, C's pro rata share of the $520,000 of nonseparately computed income is $260,000 ($1,625 per day × 160 days). C must report this amount for C's taxable year with or within which X's full taxable year ends (December 31, 1997).

Example (3). Effect of conversion of a qualified subchapter S trust (QSST) to an electing small business trust (ESBT). (i) On January 1, 2003, Trust receives stock of S corporation. Trust's current income beneficiary makes a timely QSST election under section 1361(d)(2), effective January 1, 2003. Subsequently, the trustee and current income beneficiary of Trust elect, pursuant to § 1.1361-1(j)(12), to terminate the QSST election and convert to an ESBT, effective July 1, 2004. The taxable year of S corporation is the calendar year. In 2004, Trust's pro rata share of S corporation's nonseparately computed income is $100,000.

(ii) For purposes of computing the income allocable to the QSST and to the ESBT, Trust is treated as a QSST through June 30, 2004, and Trust is treated as an ESBT beginning July 1, 2004. Pursuant to section 1377(a)(1), the pro rata share of S corporation income allocated to the QSST is $49,727 ($100,000 x 182 days/366 days), and the pro rata share of S corporation income allocated to the ESBT is $50,273 ($100,000 x 184 days/366 days).

T.D. 8696, 12/20/96, amend T.D. 8994, 5/13/2002, T.D. 9100, 12/18/2003, T.D. 9137, 7/15/2004, T.D. 9300, 12/7/2006.

§ 1.1377-2 Post-termination transition period.

Caution: The Treasury has not yet amended Reg § 1.1377-2 to reflect changes made by P.L. 108-311.

(a) In general. For purposes of subchapter S of chapter 1 of the Internal Revenue Code (Code) and this section, the term post-termination transition period means—

(1) The period beginning on the day after the last day of the corporation's last taxable year as an S corporation and ending on the later of—

(i) The day which is 1 year after such last day; or

(ii) The due date for filing the return for the last taxable year as an S corporation (including extensions);

(2) The 120-day period beginning on the date of any determination pursuant to an audit of the taxpayer which follows the termination of the corporation's election and which

adjusts a subchapter S item of income, loss, or deduction of the corporation arising during the S period (as defined in section 1368(e)(2)); and

(3) The 120-day period beginning on the date of a determination that the corporation's election under section 1362(a) had terminated for a previous taxable year.

(b) Special rules for post-termination transition period. Pursuant to section 1377(b)(1) and paragraph (a)(1) of this section, a post-termination transition period arises the day after the last day that an S corporation was in existence if a C corporation acquires the assets of the S corporation in a transaction to which section 381(a)(2) applies. However, if an S corporation acquires the assets of another S corporation in a transaction to which section 381(a)(2) applies, a post-termination transition period does not arise. (See § 1.1368-2(d)(2) for the treatment of the acquisition of the assets of an S corporation by another S corporation in a transaction to which section 381(a)(2) applies.) The special treatment under section 1371(e)(1) of distributions of money by a corporation with respect to its stock during the post-termination transition period is available only to those shareholders who were shareholders in the S corporation at the time of the termination.

(c) Determination defined. For purposes of section 1377(b)(1) and paragraph (a) of this section, the term determination means—

(1) A determination as defined in section 1313(a);

(2) A written agreement between the corporation and the Commissioner (including a statement acknowledging that the corporation's election to be an S corporation terminated under section 1362(d)) that the corporation failed to qualify as an S corporation;

(3) For a corporation subject to the audit and assessment provisions of subchapter C of chapter 63 of subtitle A of the Code, the expiration of the period specified in section 6226 for filing a petition for readjustment of a final S corporation administrative adjustment finding that the corporation failed to qualify as an S corporation, provided that no petition was timely filed before the expiration of the period; and

(4) For a corporation not subject to the audit and assessment provisions of subchapter C of chapter 63 of subtitle A of the Code, the expiration of the period for filing a petition under section 6213 for the shareholder's taxable year for which the Commissioner has made a finding that the corporation failed to qualify as an S corporation, provided that no petition was timely filed before the expiration of the period.

(d) Date a determination becomes effective. *(1) Determination under section 1313(a).* A determination under paragraph (c)(1) of this section becomes effective on the date prescribed in section 1313 and the regulations thereunder.

(2) Written agreement. A determination under paragraph (c)(2) of this section becomes effective when it is signed by the district director having jurisdiction over the corporation (or by another Service official to whom authority to sign the agreement is delegated) and by an officer of the corporation authorized to sign on its behalf. Neither the request for a written agreement nor the terms of the written agreement suspend the running of any statute of limitations.

(3) Implied agreement. A determination under paragraph (c)(3) or (4) of this section becomes effective on the day after the date of expiration of the period specified under section 6226 or 6213, respectively.

T.D. 8696, 12/20/96.

§ 1.1377-3 Effective dates.

Section 1.1377-1 and 1.1377-2 apply to taxable years of an S corporation beginning after December 31, 1996, except that § 1.1377-1(a)(2)(iii), and (c) Example 3 are applicable for taxable years beginning on and after May 14, 2002.

T.D. 8696, 12/20/96, amend T.D. 8994, 5/13/2002.

§ 1.1378-1 Taxable year of S corporation.

(a) In general. The taxable year of an S corporation must be a permitted year. A permitted year is the required taxable year (i.e., a taxable year ending on December 31), a taxable year elected under section 444, a 52-53-week taxable year ending with reference to the required taxable year or a taxable year elected under section 444, or any other taxable year for which the corporation establishes a business purpose to the satisfaction of the Commissioner under section 442.

(b) Adoption of taxable year. An electing S corporation may adopt, in accordance with § 1.441-1(c), its required taxable year, a taxable year elected under section 444, or a 52-53-week taxable year ending with reference to its required taxable year or a taxable year elected under section 444 without the approval of the Commissioner. See § 1.441-1. An electing S corporation that wants to adopt any other taxable year, must establish a business purpose and obtain the approval of the Commissioner under section 442.

(c) Change in taxable year. *(1) Approval required.* An S corporation or electing S corporation that wants to change its taxable year must obtain the approval of the Commissioner under section 442 or make an election under section 444. However, an S corporation or electing S corporation may obtain automatic approval for certain changes, including a change to its required taxable year, pursuant to administrative procedures published by the Commissioner.

(2) Short period tax return. An S corporation or electing S corporation that changes its taxable year must make its return for a short period in accordance with section 443, but must not annualize the corporation's taxable income.

(d) Retention of taxable year. In certain cases, an S corporation or electing S corporation will be required to change its taxable year unless it obtains the approval of the Commissioner under section 442, or makes an election under section 444, to retain its current taxable year. For example, a corporation using a June 30 fiscal year that elects to be an S corporation and, as a result, is required to use the calendar year must obtain the approval of the Commissioner to retain its current fiscal year.

(e) Procedures for obtaining approval or making a section 444 election. *(1) In general.* See § 1.442-1(b) for procedures to obtain the approval of the Commissioner (automatically or otherwise) to adopt, change, or retain a taxable year. See §§ 1.444-1T and 1.444-2T for qualifications, and 1.444-3T for procedures, for making an election under section 444.

(2) Special rules for electing S corporations. An electing S corporation that wants to adopt, change to, or retain a taxable year other than its required taxable year must request approval of the Commissioner on Form 2553, "Election by a Small Business Corporation," when the election to be an S corporation is filed pursuant to section 1362(b) and § 1.1362-6. See § 1.1362-6(a)(2)(i) for the manner of making an election to be an S corporation. If such corporation receives permission to adopt, change to, or retain a taxable year other than its required taxable year, the election to be an S corporation will be effective. Denial of the request renders the election ineffective unless the corporation agrees

that, in the event the request to adopt, change to, or retain a taxable year other than its required taxable year is denied, it will adopt, change to, or retain its required taxable year or, if applicable, make an election under section 444.

(f) Effective date. The rules of this section are applicable for taxable years ending on or after May 17, 2002.

T.D. 8996, 5/16/2002.

§ 18.1379-1 Transitional rules on enactment.

(a) Prior elections. Any election that was made under section 1372(a) (as in effect before the enactment of the Subchapter S Revision Act of 1982), and that is still in effect as of the first day of a taxable year beginning in 1983, shall be treated as being an election made under section 1362(a). In addition, any election that was made under section 1371(g)(2) (as in effect before the enactment of that Act), and that is still in effect as of the first day of a taxable year beginning in 1983, shall be treated as being an election made under section 1362(d)(2).

(b) Prior terminations. For purposes of section 1362(g), any termination under section 1372(e) (as in effect before the enactment of the Subchapter S Revision Act of 1982) shall not be taken into account.

(c) Time and manner of making an election under section 6(c)(3)(B) of the Subchapter S Revision Act of 1982. In the case of a qualified oil corporation (as defined in section 6(c)(3)(B) of the Subchapter S Revision Act of 1982), the corporation may elect under that section of the Act to have the amendments made by the Act not apply and to have subchapter S (as in effect on July 1, 1982), chapter 1 of the Internal Revenue Code of 1954 apply. The election shall be made by the corporation by filing a statement that—

(1) Contains the name, address, and taxpayer identification number of the corporation and of each shareholder,

(2) Identifies the election as an election under section 6(c)(3)(B) of the Subchapter S Revision Act of 1982, and

(3) Provides all information necessary in the judgment of the district director to show that the corporation meets the requirements (other than the requirement of making this election) of a qualified oil corporation.

The statement shall be signed by any person authorized to sign the return required to be filed under section 6037 and by each person who is or was a shareholder in the corporation at any time during the taxable year beginning in 1983 and shall be filed with the return for that taxable year.

T.D. 7872, 1/21/83.

§ 18.1379-2 Special rules for all elections, consents, and refusals.

(a) Additional information required. If later regulations issued under the section of the Code or of the Subchapter S Revision Act of 1982 under which the election, consent, or refusal was made require the furnishing of information in addition to that which was furnished with the statement of election, consent, or refusal as provided by Part 18 of this Title, and if an office of the Internal Revenue Service requests the taxpayer to provide the additional information, the taxpayer shall furnish the additional information in a statement filed with that office of the Internal Revenue Service within 60 days after the date on which the request is made. This statement shall also—

(1) Contain the name, address, and taxpayer identification number of each party identified in connection with the election, consent, or refusal,

(2) Identify the election, consent, or refusal by reference to the section of the Code or Act under which the election, consent, or refusal was made, and

(3) Specify the scope of the election, consent, or refusal.

If the additional information is not provided within 60 days after the date on which the request is made, the election, consent, or refusal may, at the discretion of the Commissioner, be held invalid.

(b) State law incorporator. For purposes of any election, consent, or refusal provided in Part 18 of this Title, any person who is considered to be a shareholder for state law purposes solely by virtue of his or her status as an incorporator shall not be treated as a shareholder.

T.D. 7872, 1/21/83.

§ 1.1381-1 Organizations to which part applies.

(a) In general. Except as provided in paragraph (b) of this section, part I, subchapter T, chapter 1 of the Code, applies to any corporation operating on a cooperative basis and allocating amounts to patrons on the basis of the business done with or for such patrons.

(b) Exceptions. Part I of such subchapter T does not apply to—

(1) Any organization which is exempt from income taxes under chapter 1 of the Code (other than an exempt farmers' cooperative described in section 521);

(2) Any organization which is subject to the provisions of part II (section 591 and following), subchapter H, chapter 1 of the Code (relating to mutual savings banks, etc.);

(3) Any organization which is subject to the provisions of subchapter L (section 801 and following), chapter 1 of the Code (relating to insurance companies); or

(4) Any organization which is engaged in generating, transmitting, or otherwise furnishing electric energy, or which provides telephone service, to persons in rural areas. The terms "rural areas" and "telephone service" shall have the meaning assigned to them in section 5 of the Rural Electrification Act of 1936, as amended (7 U.S.C. 924).

T.D. 6643, 4/1/63.

§ 1.1381-2 Tax on certain farmers' cooperatives.

(a) In general. *(1)* For taxable years beginning after December 31, 1962, farmers, fruit growers, or like associations, organized and operated in compliance with the requirements of section 521 and § 1.521-1, shall be subject to the taxes imposed by section 11 or section 1201. Although such associations are subject to both normal tax and surtax, as in the case of corporations generally, certain special deductions are provided for them in section 1382(c) and § 1.1382-3. For the purpose of any law which refers to organizations exempt from income taxes such an association shall, however, be considered as an organization exempt under section 501. Thus, the provisions of section 243, providing a credit for dividends received from a domestic corporation subject to taxation, are not applicable to dividends received from a cooperative association organized and operated in compliance with the requirements of section 521 and § 1.521-1. The provisions of section 1501, relating to consolidated returns, are likewise not applicable.

(2) Rules governing the manner in which amounts paid as patronage dividends are allowable as deductions in computing the taxable income of such an association are set forth in section 1382(b) and § 1.1382-2. For the tax treatment, as to patrons, of amounts received during the taxable year as patronage dividends, see section 1385 and the regulations thereunder.

(b) Cross references. For tax treatment of exempt cooperative associations for taxable years beginning before January 1, 1963, or for taxable years beginning after December 31, 1962, with respect to payments attributable to patronage occurring during taxable years beginning before January 1, 1963, see section 522 and the regulations thereunder. For requirements of annual returns by such associations, see sections 6012 and 6072(d) and paragraph (f) of § 1.6012-2.

T.D. 6643, 4/1/63.

§ 1.1382-1 Taxable income of cooperatives; gross income.

Caution: The Treasury has not yet amended Reg § 1.1382-1 to reflect changes made by P.L. 95-345, P.L. 94-455, P.L. 91-172.

(a) Introduction. Section 1382(b) provides that the amount of certain patronage dividends (and amounts paid in redemption of nonqualified written notices of allocation) shall not be taken into account by a cooperative organization in determining its taxable income. Such section also provides that, for purposes of the Internal Revenue Code, an amount not taken into account is to be treated in the same manner as an item of gross income and as a deduction therefrom. Therefore, such an amount is treated as a deduction for purposes of applying the Internal Revenue Code and the regulations thereunder and, for simplicity, is referred to as a deduction in the regulations under such Code. However, this should not be regarded as a determination of the character of the amount for other purposes.

(b) Computation of gross income. Any cooperative organization to which part I, subchapter T, chapter 1 of the Code, applies shall not, for any purpose under the Code, exclude from its gross income (as a reduction in gross receipts, an increase in cost of goods sold, or otherwise) the amount of any allocation or distribution to a patron out of the net earnings of such organization with respect to patronage occurring during a taxable year beginning after December 31, 1962. See, however, section 1382(b) and § 1.1382-2 for deductions for certain amounts paid to patrons out of net earnings.

T.D. 6643, 4/1/63.

§ 1.1382-2 Taxable income of cooperatives; treatment of patronage dividends.

Caution: The Treasury has not yet amended Reg § 1.1382-2 to reflect changes made by P.L. 89-809.

(a) In general. *(1)* In determining the taxable income of any cooperative organization to which part I, subchapter T, chapter 1 of the Code, applies, there shall be allowed as deductions from gross income, in addition to the other deductions allowable under chapter 1 of the Code, the deductions with respect to patronage dividends provided in section 1382(b) and paragraphs (b) and (c) of this section.

(2) For the definition of terms used in this section see section 1388 and § 1.1388-1; to determine the payment period for a taxable year, see section 1382(d) and § 1.1382-4.

(b) Deduction for patronage dividends. *(1) In general.* In the case of a taxable year beginning after December 31, 1962, there is allowed as a deduction from the gross income of any cooperative organization to which part I of subchapter T applies, amounts paid to patrons during the payment period for the taxable year as patronage dividends with respect to patronage occurring during such taxable year, but only to the extent that such amounts are paid in money, qualified written notices of allocation, or other property (other than nonqualified written notices of allocation). See section 1382(e) and (f) and §§ 1.1382-5 and 1.1382-6 for special rules relating to the time when patronage is deemed to occur where products are marketed under a pooling arrangement or where earnings are includible in the gross income of the cooperative organization for a taxable year after the year in which the patronage occurred. For purposes of this paragraph, a written notice of allocation is considered paid when it is issued to the patron. A patronage dividend shall be treated as paid in money during the payment period for the taxable year to the extent it is paid by a qualified check which is issued during the payment period for such taxable year and endorsed and cashed on or before the ninetieth day after the close of such payment period. In determining the amount paid which is allowable as a deduction under this paragraph, property (other than written notices of allocation) shall be taken into account at its fair market value when paid, and a qualified written notice of allocation shall be taken into account at its stated dollar amount.

(2) Special rule for certain taxable years. No deduction is allowed under this section for amounts paid during taxable years beginning before January 1, 1963, or for amounts paid during taxable years beginning after December 31, 1962, with respect to patronage occurring during taxable years beginning before January 1, 1963. With respect to such amounts, the Internal Revenue Code of 1954 (including section 522 and the regulations thereunder) shall be applicable without regard to subchapter T.

(c) Deduction for amounts paid in redemption of certain nonqualified written notices of allocation. In the case of a taxable year beginning after December 31, 1962, there is allowed as a deduction from the gross income of a cooperative organization to which part I of subchapter T applies, amounts paid by such organization during the payment period for such taxable year in redemption of a nonqualified written notice of allocation which was previously paid as a patronage dividend during the payment period for the taxable year during which the patronage occurred, but only to the extent such amounts (1) are paid in money or other property (other than written notices of allocation) and (2) do not exceed the stated dollar amount of such written notice of allocation. No deduction shall be allowed under this paragraph, however, for amounts paid in redemption of nonqualified written notices of allocation which were paid with respect to patronage occurring during a taxable year beginning before January 1, 1963. For purposes of this paragraph, if an amount is paid within the payment period for two or more taxable years, it will be allowable as a deduction only for the earliest of such taxable years. Thus, if a cooperative which reports its income on a calendar year basis pays an amount in redemption of a nonqualified written notice of allocation on January 15, 1966, it will be allowed a deduction for such amount only for its 1965 taxable year. In determining the amount paid which is allowable as a deduction under this paragraph, property (other than written notices of allocation) shall be taken into account at its fair market value when paid. Amounts paid in redemption of a nonqualified written notice of allocation in excess of its stated dollar amount shall be treated under the applicable provisions of the Code. For example, if such excess is in the nature of interest, its deductibility will be governed by section 163 and the regulations thereunder.

T.D. 6643, 4/1/63.

§ 1.1382-3 Taxable income of cooperatives; special deductions for exempt farmers' cooperatives.

Caution: The Treasury has not yet amended Reg § 1.1382-3 to reflect changes made by P.L. 95-345, P.L. 94-455, P.L. 91-172, P.L. 89-809.

(a) In general. *(1)* Section 1382(c) provides that in determining the taxable income of a farmers fruit growers or like association, described in section 1381(a)(1) and organized and operated in compliance with the requirements of section 521 and § 1.521-1, there shall be allowed as deductions from the gross income of such organization, in addition to the other deductions allowable under chapter 1 of the Code (including the deductions allowed by section 1382(b)) the special deductions provided in section 1382(c) and paragraphs (b), (c), and (d) of this section.

(2) For the definition of terms used in this section, see section 1388 and § 1.1388-1; to determine the payment period for a taxable year, see section 1382(d) and § 1.1382-4.

(b) Deduction for dividends paid on capital stock. In the case of a taxable year beginning after December 31, 1962, there is allowed as a deduction from the gross income of a cooperative association operated in compliance with the requirements of section 521 and § 1.521-1, amounts paid as dividends during the taxable year on the capital stock of such cooperative association. For the purpose of the preceding sentence, the term "capital stock" includes common stock (whether voting or nonvoting), preferred stock, or any other form of capital represented by capital retain certificates, revolving fund certificates, letters of advice, or other evidence of a proprietary interest in a cooperative association. Such deduction is applicable only to the taxable year in which the dividends are actually or constructively paid to the holder of capital stock or other proprietary interest in the cooperative association. If a dividend is paid by check and the check bearing a date within the taxable year is deposited in the mail, in a cover properly stamped and addressed to the shareholder at his last known address, at such time that in the ordinary handling of the mails the check would be received by such holder within the taxable year, a presumption arises that the dividend was paid to such holder in such year. The determination of whether a dividend has been paid to such holder by the corporation during its taxable year is in no way dependent upon the method of accounting regularly employed by the corporation in keeping its books. For further rules as to the determination of the right to a deduction for dividends paid, under certain specific circumstances, see section 561 and the regulations thereunder.

(c) Deduction for amounts allocated from income not derived from patronage. *(1) In general.* In the case of a taxable year beginning after December 31, 1962, there is allowed as a deduction from the gross income of a cooperative association operated in compliance with the requirements of section 521 and § 1.521-1, amounts paid to patrons, during the payment period for the taxable year, on a patronage basis with respect to its income derived during such taxable year either from business done with or for the United States or any of its agencies or from sources other than patronage, but only to the extent such amounts are paid in money, qualified written notices of allocation, or other property (other than nonqualified written notices of allocation). For purposes of this subparagraph a written notice of allocation is considered paid when it is issued to the patron. An amount shall be treated as paid in money during the payment period for the taxable year to the extent it is paid by a qualified check which is issued during the payment period for such taxable year and endorsed and cashed on or before the ninetieth day after the close of such payment period. In determining the amount paid which is allowable as a deduction under this paragraph, property (other than written notices of allocation) shall be taken into account at its fair market value when paid, and a qualified written notice of allocation shall be taken into account at its stated dollar amount.

(2) Definition. As used in this paragraph, the term "income derived from sources other than patronage" means incidental income derived from sources not directly related to the marketing, purchasing, or service activities of the cooperative association. For example, income derived from the lease of premises, from investment in securities, or from the sale or exchange of capital assets, constitutes income derived from sources other than patronage.

(3) Basis of distribution. In order that the deduction for amounts paid with respect to income derived from business done with or for the United States or any of its agencies or from sources other than patronage may be applicable, it is necessary that the amount sought to be deducted be paid on a patronage basis in proportion, insofar as is practicable, to the amount of business done by or for patrons during the period to which such income is attributable. For example, if capital gains are realized from the sale or exchange of capital assets acquired and disposed of during the taxable year, income realized from such gains must be paid to patrons of such year in proportion to the amount of business done by such patrons during the taxable year. Similarly, if capital gains are realized by the association from the sale or exchange of capital assets held for a period extending into more than one taxable year income realized from such gains must be paid, insofar as is practicable, to the persons who were patrons during the taxable years in which the asset was owned by the association in proportion to the amount of business done by such patrons during such taxable years.

(4) Special rules for certain taxable years. No deduction is allowable under this paragraph for amounts paid during taxable years beginning before January 1, 1963, or for amounts paid during taxable years beginning after December 31, 1962, with respect to income derived during taxable years beginning before January 1, 1963. With respect to such amounts, the Internal Revenue Code of 1954 (including section 522 and the regulations thereunder) shall be applicable without regard to subchapter T.

(d) Deduction for amounts paid in redemption of certain nonqualified written notices of allocation. In the case of a taxable year beginning after December 31, 1962, there is allowed as a deduction from the gross income of a cooperative association operated in compliance with the requirements of section 521 and § 1.521-1, amounts paid by such association during the payment period for such taxable year in redemption of certain nonqualified written notices of allocation, but only to the extent such amounts (1) are paid in money or other property (other than written notices of allocation) and (2) do not exceed the stated dollar amount of such nonqualified written notices of allocation. The nonqualified written notices of allocation referred to in the preceding sentence are those which were previously paid to patrons on a patronage basis with respect to earnings derived either from business done with or for the United States or any of its agencies or from sources other than patronage, provided that such nonqualified written notices of allocation were paid during the payment period for the taxable year during which such earnings were derived. No deduction shall be allowed under this paragraph, however, for amounts paid in redemption of nonqualified written notices of allocation which were paid with respect to earnings derived during a taxable year beginning before January 1, 1963. For purposes of this paragraph, if an amount is paid within the payment period for two or more taxable years, it will be allowable as a deduction only for the earliest of such taxable years. In determining the amount paid which is allowable as a deduction under this paragraph, property (other than written notices of allocation) shall be taken into account at its fair market value when paid. Amounts paid in redemption of a nonqualified written notice of allocation in excess of its stated dollar amount shall be treated under the applicable provisions of the Code.

T.D. 6643, 4/1/63.

§ 1.1382-4 Taxable income of cooperatives; payment period for each taxable year.

Caution: The Treasury has not yet amended Reg § 1.1382-4 to reflect changes made by P.L. 95-345, P.L. 94-455, P.L. 91-172, P.L. 89-809.

The payment period for a taxable year is the period beginning with the first day of such taxable year and ending with the fifteenth day of the ninth month following the close of such year.

T.D. 6643, 4/1/63.

§ 1.1382-5 Taxable income of cooperatives; products marketed under pooling arrangements.

Caution: The Treasury has not yet amended Reg § 1.1382-5 to reflect changes made by P.L. 95-345, P.L. 94-455, P.L. 91-172, P.L. 89-809.

For purposes of section 1382(b) and § 1.1382-2, in the case of a pooling arrangement for the marketing of products the patronage under such pool shall be treated as occurring during the taxable year in which the pool closes. The determination of when a pool is closed will be made on the basis of the facts and circumstances in each case, but generally the practices and operations of the cooperative organization shall control. This section may be illustrated by the following example:

Example. Farmer A delivers to the X Cooperative 100 bushels of wheat on August 15, 1963, at which time he receives a "per bushel" advance. (Both farmer A and the X Cooperative file returns on a calendar year basis.) On October 15, 1963 farmer A receives an additional "per bushel" payment. The pool sells some of its wheat in 1963 and the remainder in January of 1964. The pool is closed on February 15, 1964. For purposes of section 1382(b), A's patronage is considered as occurring in 1964.

T.D. 6643, 4/1/63.

§ 1.1382-6 Taxable income of cooperatives; treatment of earnings received after patronage occurred.

Caution: The Treasury has not yet amended Reg § 1.1382-6 to reflect changes made by P.L. 95-345, P.L. 94-455, P.L. 91-172, P.L. 89-809.

If earnings derived from business done with or for patrons are includible in the gross income of the cooperative organization for a taxable year after the taxable year during which the patronage occurred, then, for purposes of determining whether the cooperative is allowed a deduction under section 1382(b) and § 1.1382-2, the patronage to which these earnings relate shall be considered to have occurred during the taxable year for which such earnings are includible in the cooperative's gross income. Thus, if the cooperative organization pays these earnings out as patronage dividends during the payment period for the taxable year for which the earnings are includible in its gross income, it will be allowed a deduction for such payments under section 1382(b)(1) and paragraph (b) of § 1.1382-2, to the extent they are paid in money, qualified written notices of allocation, or other property (other than written notices of allocation).

T.D. 6643, 4/1/63.

§ 1.1382-7 Special rules applicable to cooperative associations exempt from tax before January 1, 1952.

(a) Basis of property. The adjustments to the cost or other basis provided in sections 1011 and 1016 and the regulations thereunder, are applicable for the entire period since the acquisition of the property. Thus, proper adjustment to basis must be made under section 1016 for depreciation, obsolescence, amortization, and depletion for all taxable years beginning prior to January 1, 1952, although the cooperative association was exempt from tax under section 521 or corresponding provisions of prior law for such years. However, no adjustment for percentage or discovery depletion is to be made for any year during which the association was exempt from tax. If a cooperative association has made a proper election in accordance with section 1020 and the regulations prescribed thereunder with respect to a taxable year beginning before 1952 in which the association was not exempt from tax, the adjustment to basis for depreciation for such years shall be limited in accordance with the provisions of section 1016(a)(2).

(b) Amortization of bond premium. In the case of tax exempt and partially taxable bonds purchased at a premium and subject to amortization under section 171, proper adjustment to basis must be made to reflect amortization with respect to such premium from the date of acquisition of the bond. (For principles governing the method of computation, see the example in paragraph (b) of § 1.1016-9, relating to mutual savings banks, building and loan associations, and cooperative banks.) The basis of a fully taxable bond purchased at a premium shall be adjusted from the date of the election to amortize such premium in accordance with the provisions of section 171 except that no adjustment shall be allowable for such portion of the premium attributable to the period prior to the election.

(c) Amortization of mortgage premium. In the case of a mortgage acquired at a premium where the principal of such mortgage is payable in installments, adjustments to the basis for the premium must be made for all taxable years (whether or not the association was exempt from tax under section 521 during such years) in which installment payments are received. Such adjustments may be made on an individual mortgage basis or on a composite basis by reference to the average period of payments of the mortgage loans of such association. For the purpose of this adjustment, the term "premium" includes the excess of the acquisition value of the mortgage over its maturity value. The acquisition value of the mortgage is the cost including buying commissions, attorneys' fees, or brokerage fees, but such value does not include amounts paid for accrued interest.

T.D. 6643, 4/1/63.

§ 1.1383-1 Computation of tax where cooperative redeems nonqualified written notices of allocation.

Caution: The Treasury has not yet amended Reg § 1.1383-1 to reflect changes made by P.L. 89-809.

(a) General rule. *(1)* If, during the taxable year, a cooperative organization is entitled to a deduction under section 1382(b)(2) or (c)(2)(B) for amounts paid in redemption of nonqualified written notices of allocation, the tax imposed for the taxable year by chapter 1 of the Code shall be the lesser of—

(i) The tax for the taxable year computed under section 1383(a)(1), that is, with such deduction taken into account, or

(ii) The tax for the taxable year computed under section 1383(a)(2), that is, without taking such deduction into account, minus the decrease in tax (under chapter 1 of the Code) for any prior taxable year (or years) which would result solely from treating all such nonqualified written notices of allocation redeemed during the taxable year as qualified written notices of allocation when paid. For the purpose of this subdivision, the amount of the decrease in tax is not limited to the amount of the tax for the taxable year. See paragraph (c) of this section for rules relating to a refund of tax where the decrease in tax for the prior taxable year (or years) exceeds the tax for the taxable year.

(2) If the cooperative organization computes its tax for the taxable year under the provisions of section 1383(a)(2) and subparagraph (1)(ii) of this paragraph, then no deduction under section 1382(b)(2) or (c)(2)(B) shall be taken into account in computing taxable income or loss for the taxable year, including the computation of any net operating loss carryback or carryover. However, the amount of the deduction shall be taken into account in adjusting earnings and profits for the taxable year.

(3) If the tax determined under subparagraph (1)(i) of this paragraph is the same as the tax determined under subparagraph (1)(ii) of this paragraph, the tax imposed for the taxable year under chapter 1 of the Code shall be the tax determined under subparagraph (1)(i) of this paragraph, and section 1383 and this section shall not otherwise apply. The tax imposed for the taxable year shall be the tax determined under subparagraph (1)(ii) of this paragraph in any case when a credit or refund would be allowable for the taxable year under section 1383(b)(1).

(b) Determination of decrease in tax for prior taxable years. *(1) Prior taxable years.* The prior taxable year (or years) referred to in paragraph (a) of this section is the year (or years) within the payment period for which the nonqualified written notices of allocation were paid and, in addition, any other prior taxable year (or years) which is affected by the adjustment to income by reason of treating such nonqualified written notices of allocation as qualified written notices of allocation when paid.

(2) Adjustment to income in prior taxable years. The deduction for the prior taxable year (or years) in determining the decrease in tax under section 1383(a)(2)(B) and paragraph (a)(1)(ii) of this section shall be the amount paid in redemption of the nonqualified written notices of allocation which, without regard to section 1383, is allowable as a deduction under section 1382(b)(2) or (c)(2)(B) for the current taxable year.

(3) Computation of decrease in tax for prior taxable years. In computing the amount of decrease in tax for a prior taxable year (or years) resulting under this section, there must first be ascertained the amount of tax previously determined for the taxpayer for such prior taxable year (or years). The tax previously determined shall be the sum of the amounts shown as such tax by the taxpayer on his return or returns, plus any amounts which have been previously assessed (or collected without assessment) as deficiencies, reduced by the amount of any rebates which have previously been made. The amount shown as the tax by the taxpayer on his return and the amount of any rebates or deficiencies shall be determined in accordance with the provisions of section 6211 and the regulations thereunder. After the tax previously determined has been ascertained, a recomputation must then be made to determine the decrease in tax, if any, resulting under this section. In determining the decrease in tax for the prior taxable year (or years), appropriate adjustment shall be made to any item which is dependent upon the amount of gross income or taxable income (such as charitable contributions, net operating losses, the foreign tax credit, and the dividends received credit).

(c) Refunds. If the decrease in tax for the prior taxable year (or years) determined under section 1383(a)(2)(B) and paragraph (a)(1)(ii) of this section exceeds the tax imposed by chapter 1 of the Code for the taxable year computed without the deduction under section 1382(b) or (c)(2)(B), the excess shall be considered to be a payment of tax for the taxable year of the deduction. Such payment is deemed to have been made on the last day prescribed by law for the payment of tax for the taxable year and shall be refunded or credited in the same manner as if it were an overpayment of tax for such taxable year. See section 6151 and the regulations thereunder, for rules relating to time and place for paying tax shown on returns.

(d) Example. The application of section 1383 may be illustrated by the following example:

Example. The X Cooperative (which reports its income on a calendar year basis) pays patronage dividends of $100,000 in nonqualified written notices of allocation on February 1, 1964, with respect to patronage occurring in 1963. Since the patronage dividends of $100,000 were paid in nonqualified written notices of allocation the X Cooperative is not allowed a deduction for that amount for 1963. On December 1, 1966, the X Cooperative redeems these nonqualified written notices of allocation for $50,000. Under section 1382(b)(2), a deduction of $50,000 is allowable in computing its taxable income for 1966. However, the X Cooperative has a loss for 1966 determined without regard to this deduction. The X Cooperative, therefore, makes the computation under the alternative method provided in section 1383(a)(2). Under this alternative method, it will claim a credit or refund (as an overpayment of tax for 1966) of the decrease in tax for 1963 and for such other years prior to 1966 as are affected which results from recomputing its tax for 1963 (and such other years affected) as if patronage dividends of $50,000 had been paid on February 1, 1964, in qualified written notices of allocation. In addition, under this alternative method the X Cooperative cannot use the $50,000 as a deduction for 1966 so as to increase its net operating loss for such year for purposes of computing a net operating loss carryback or carryover. If the X Cooperative also redeems on December 1, 1966, nonqualified written notices of allocation which were paid as patronage dividends on February 1,

1965, with respect to patronage occurring in 1964, it will claim a credit or refund (as an overpayment of tax for 1966) of the decrease in tax for 1964 and for such other years prior to 1966 as are affected. It shall not, however, apply one method for computing the tax with respect to the redemptions in 1966 of the nonqualified written notices of allocation paid in 1964 and the other method with respect to the redemption in 1966 of the nonqualified written notices of allocation paid in 1965.

T.D. 6643, 4/1/63.

§ 1.1385-1 Amounts includible in patron's gross income.

(a) General rules. Section 1385(a) requires every person to include in gross income the following amounts received by him during the taxable year, to the extent paid by the organization in money, a qualified written notice of allocation, or other property (other than a nonqualified written notice of allocation):

(1) The amount of any patronage dividend received from an organization subject to the provisions of part I, subchapter T, chapter 1 of the Code, unless such amount is excludable from gross income under the provisions of section 1385(b) and paragraph (c) of this section, and

(2) The amount of any distribution received from a farmers fruit growers or like association, organized and operated in compliance with the requirements of section 521 and § 1.521-1, which is paid on a patronage basis with respect to earnings derived by such association either from business done with or for the United States or any of its agencies or from sources other than patronage.

The amounts described in subparagraphs (1) and (2) of this paragraph are includible in gross income for the taxable year in which they are received even though the cooperative organization was allowed a deduction for such amounts for its preceding taxable year because they were paid during the payment period for such preceding taxable year. Similarly, such amounts are includible in gross income even though the cooperative organization is not permitted any deduction for such amounts under the provisions of section 1382 because such amounts were not paid within the time prescribed by such section.

(b) Treatment of certain nonqualified written notices of allocation. *(1)* Except as provided in paragraph (c) of this section, any gain on the redemption, sale, or other disposition of a nonqualified written notice of allocation described in subparagraph (2) of this paragraph shall, to the extent that the stated dollar amount of such written notice of allocation exceeds its basis, be considered as gain from the sale or exchange of property which is not a capital asset, whether such gain is realized by the patron who received the nonqualified written notice of allocation initially or by any subsequent holder. Any amount realized on the redemption, sale, or other disposition of such a nonqualified written notice of allocation in excess of its stated dollar amount will be treated under the applicable provisions of the Code. For example, amounts received in redemption of a nonqualified written notice of allocation which are in excess of the stated dollar amount of such written notice of allocation and which, in effect, constitute interest shall be treated by the recipient as interest.

(2) The nonqualified written notices of allocation to which subparagraph (1) of this paragraph applies are the following:

(i) A nonqualified written notice of allocation which was paid as a patronage dividend (within the meaning of section 1388(a) and paragraph (a) of § 1.1388-1), by a cooperative organization subject to the provisions of part I of subchapter T, and

(ii) A nonqualified written notice of allocation which was paid by a farmers fruit growers or like association, organized and operated in compliance with the requirements of section 521 and § 1.521-1, to patrons on a patronage basis with respect to earnings derived either from business done with or for the United States or any of its agencies or from sources other than patronage.

(3) The basis of any nonqualified written notice of allocation described in subparagraph (2) of this paragraph, in the hands of the patron to whom such written notice of allocation was initially paid shall be zero, and the basis of such a written notice of allocation which was acquired from a decedent shall be its basis in the hands of the decedent.

(4) The application of this paragraph may be illustrated by the following example:

Example. A, a farmer, receives a patronage dividend from the X Cooperative, in the form of a nonqualified written notice of allocation, which is attributable to the sale of his crop to that cooperative organization. The stated dollar amount of the nonqualified written notice of allocation is $100. The basis of the written notice of allocation in the hands of A is zero and he must report any amount up to $100 received by him on its redemption, sale, or other disposition, as ordinary income. If A gives the written notice of allocation to his son B, B takes A's (the donor's) basis which is zero, and any gain up to $100 which B later realizes on its redemption, sale, or other disposition is ordinary income. Similarly, if A dies before realizing any gain on the nonqualified written notice of allocation, B, his legatee, has a zero basis for such written notice of allocation and any gain up to $100 which he then realizes on its redemption, sale, or other disposition is also ordinary income. Such gain is income in respect of a decedent within the meaning of section 691(a) and § 1.691(a)-1.

(c) Treatment of patronage dividends received with respect to certain property. *(1) Exclusions from gross income.* Except as provided in subparagraph (2) of this paragraph, gross income shall not include—

(i) Any amount of a patronage dividend described in paragraph (a)(1) of this section which is received with respect to the purchase of supplies, equipment, or services, which were not used in the trade or business and the cost of which was not deductible under section 212, or which is received with respect to the marketing or purchasing of a capital asset (as defined in section 1221) or property used in the trade or business of a character which is subject to the allowance for depreciation provided in section 167; and

(ii) Any amount (to the extent treated as ordinary income under paragraph (b) of this section) received on the redemption, sale, or other disposition of a nonqualified written notice of allocation which was received as a patronage dividend with respect to the purchase of supplies, equipment, or services, which were not used in the trade or business and the cost of which was not deductible under section 212, or which was received as a patronage dividend with respect to the marketing or purchasing of a capital asset (as defined in section 1221) or property used in the trade or business of a character which is subject to the allowance for depreciation provided in section 167.

(2) Special rules. (i) If an amount described in subparagraph (1) of this paragraph relates to the purchase of a capital asset (as defined in section 1221), or property used in the

trade or business of a character which is subject to the allowance for depreciation provided in section 167, and the person receiving such amount owned such asset or property at any time during the taxable year in which such amount is received, then such amount shall be taken into account as an adjustment to the basis of such property or asset as of the first day of the taxable year in which such amount is received. To the extent that such amount exceeds the adjusted basis of such property it shall be taken into account as ordinary income.

(ii) If an amount described in subparagraph (1) of this paragraph relates to the marketing or purchasing of a capital asset (as defined in section 1221), or property used in the trade or business of a character which is subject to the allowance for depreciation provided in section 167, and the person receiving such amount did not own the asset or property at any time during the taxable year in which such amount is received, then such amount shall be included in gross income as ordinary income except that—

(a) If such amount relates to a capital asset (as defined in section 1221) which was held by the recipient for more than six months and with respect to which a loss was or would have been deductible under section 165, such amount shall be taken into account as gain from the sale or exchange of a capital asset held for more than 1 year (6 months for taxable years beginning before 1977; 9 months for taxable years beginning in 1977);

(b) If such amount relates to a capital asset (as defined in section 1221) with respect to which a loss was not or would not have been deductible under section 165, such amount shall not be taken into account.

(iii) If an amount described in subparagraph (1) of this paragraph relates to the marketing of a capital asset (as defined in section 1221) or property used in the trade or business of a character which is subject to the allowance for depreciation provided in section 167, and such amount is received by the patron in the same taxable year during which he marketed the asset to which it relates, such amount shall be treated as an additional amount received on the sale or other disposition of such asset.

(iv) If a person receiving a patronage dividend or an amount on the redemption, sale, or other disposition of a nonqualified written notice of allocation which was received as a patronage dividend is unable to determine the item to which it relates, he shall include such patronage dividend or such amount in gross income as ordinary income in the manner and to the extent provided in paragraph (a) or (b) of this section, whichever is applicable.

(3) The application of this paragraph may be illustrated by the following examples:

Example (1). On July 1, 1964, P, a patron of a cooperative association, purchases an implement for use in his farming business from such association for $2,900. The implement has an estimated useful life of three years and has an estimated salvage value of $200 which P chooses to take into account in the computation of depreciation. P files his income tax returns on a calendar year basis. For 1964 P claims depreciation of $450 with respect to the implement pursuant to his use of the straight-line method at the rate of $900 per year. On July 1, 1965, the cooperative association pays a patronage dividend to P of $300 in cash with respect to his purchase of the farm implement. P will adjust the basis of the implement and will compute his depreciation deduction for 1965 (and subsequent taxable years) as follows:

Cost of farm implement, July 1, 1964	$2,900
Less:	
Salvage value	200
Depreciation for 1964 (6 mos.)	450
Adjustment as of Jan. 1, 1965 for cash patronage dividend	300
Total	950
Basis for depreciation for the remaining 2½ years of estimated life	1,950
Depreciation deduction for 1965 ($1,950 divided by the 2½ years of remaining life)	780

Example (2). Assume the same facts as in example (1), except that on July 1, 1965, the cooperative association paid a patronage dividend to P with respect to his purchase of the implement in the form of a nonqualified written notice of allocation having a stated dollar amount of $300. Since such written notice of allocation was not qualified, no amount of the patronage dividend was taken into account by P as an adjustment to the basis of the implement, or in computing his depreciation deduction, for the year 1965. In 1968, P receives $300 cash from the association in full redemption of the written notice of allocation. Prior to 1968, he had recovered through depreciation $2,700 of the cost of the implement, leaving an adjusted basis of $200 (the salvage value). For the year 1968, the redemption proceeds of $300 are applied against the adjusted basis of $200, reducing the basis of the implement to zero, and the balance of the redemption proceeds, $100, is includable as ordinary income in P's gross income for the calendar year 1968. If the patronage dividend paid to P on July 1, 1965, had been in the form of $60 cash (20 percent of $300) and a qualified written notice of allocation with a stated dollar amount of $240, then the tax treatment of such patronage dividend would be that illustrated in example (1).

Example (3). Assume the same facts as in example (2), except that the nonqualified written notice of allocation is redeemed in cash on July 1, 1966. The full $300 received on redemption will reduce the adjusted basis of the implement as of January 1, 1966, and the depreciation allowances for 1966 and 1967 are computed as follows:

Cost of farm implement, July 1, 1964	$2,900
Less:	
Salvage value	200
Depreciation for 1964 (6 mos.)	450
Depreciation for 1965	900
Adjustment as of Jan. 1, 1966 for proceeds of the redemption	300
Total	1,850
Basis for depreciation on Jan. 1, 1966	1,050
If P uses the implement in his business until fully depreciated, he would be entitled to the following depreciation allowances with respect to such implement:	
For 1966	700
For 1967	350
Total	1,050
Balance to be depreciated	0

Example (4). Assume the same facts as in example (3), except that P sells the implement in 1965. The entire $300 received in 1966 in redemption of the nonqualified written notice of allocation is includible as ordinary income in P's gross income for the year 1966.

(d) Determination of amount received. In determining the amount received for purposes of this section—

(1) Property (other than written notices of allocation) shall be taken into account at its fair market value when received;

(2) A qualified written notice of allocation shall be taken into account at its stated dollar amount; and

(3) The amount of a qualified check shall be considered an amount received in money during the taxable year in which such check is received if the check is endorsed and cashed on or before the ninetieth day after the close of the payment period for the taxable year of the cooperative organization in which the patronage to which such amount relates occurred.

(e) Effective date. This section shall not apply to any distribution or allocation received from a cooperative organization, or to any gain or loss on the redemption, sale, or other disposition of any allocation received from such an organization, if such distribution or allocation was received with respect to patronage occurring in a taxable year of the organization beginning before January 1, 1963. See § 1.61-5 for the tax treatment by patrons of such distributions or allocations.

T.D. 6643, 4/1/63, amend T.D. 7728, 10/31/80.

§ 1.1388-1 Definitions and special rules.

Caution: The Treasury has not yet amended Reg § 1.1388-1 to reflect changes made by P.L. 108-357, P.L. 94-455, P.L. 91-172, P.L. 89-809.

(a) Patronage dividend. *(1) In general.* The term "patronage dividend" means an amount paid to a patron by a cooperative organization subject to the provisions of part I, subchapter T, chapter 1 of the Code, which is paid—

(i) On the basis of quantity or value of business done with or for such patron,

(ii) Under a valid enforceable written obligation of such organization to the patron to pay such amount, which obligation existed before the cooperative organization received the amount so paid, and

(iii) Which is determined by reference to the net earnings of the cooperative organization from business done with or for its patrons.

For the purpose of subdivision (ii) of this subparagraph, amounts paid by a cooperative organization are paid under a valid enforceable written obligation if such payments are required by State law or are paid pursuant to provisions of the bylaws, articles of incorporation, or other written contract, whereby the organization is obligated to make such payment. The term "net earnings" , for purposes of subdivision (iii) of this subparagraph, includes the excess of amounts retained (or assessed) by the organization to cover expenses or other items over the amount of such expenses or other items. For purposes of such subdivision (iii), net earnings shall not be reduced by any taxes imposed by subtitle A of the Code, but shall be reduced by dividends paid on capital stock or other proprietary capital interests.

(2) Exceptions. The term "patronage dividend" does not include the following:

(i) An amount paid to a patron by a cooperative organization to the extent that such amount is paid out of earnings not derived from business done with or for patrons.

(ii) An amount paid to a patron by a cooperative organization to the extent that such amount is paid out of earnings from business done with or for other patrons to whom no amounts are paid, or to whom smaller amounts are paid, with respect to substantially identical transactions. Thus, if a cooperative organization does not pay any patronage dividends to nonmembers, any portion of the amounts paid to members which is out of net earnings from patronage with nonmembers, and which would have been paid to the nonmembers if all patrons were treated alike, is not a patronage dividend.

(iii) An amount paid to a patron by a cooperative organization to the extent that such amount is paid in redemption of capital stock, or in redemption or satisfaction of certificates of indebtedness, revolving fund certificates, retain certificates, letters of advice, or other similar documents, even if such documents were originally paid as patronage dividends.

(iv) An amount paid to a patron by a cooperative organization to the extent that such amount is fixed without reference to the net earnings of the cooperative organization from business done with or for its patrons.

(3) Examples. The application of subparagraphs (1) and (2) of this paragraph may be illustrated by the following examples:

Example (1). (i) Cooperative A, a marketing association operating on a pooling basis, receives the products of patron W on January 5, 1964. On the same day cooperative A advances to W 45 cents per unit for the products so delivered and allocates to him a "retain certificate" having a face value calculated at the rate of 5 cents per unit. During the operation of the pool, and before substantially all the products in the pool are disposed of, cooperative A advances to W an additional 40 cents per unit, the amount being determined by reference to the market price of the products sold and the anticipated price of the unsold products. At the close of the pool on November 10, 1964, cooperative A determines the excess of its receipts over the sum of its expenses and its previous advances to patrons, and allocates to W an additional 3 cents per unit and shares of the capital stock of A having an aggregate stated dollar amount calculated at the rate of 2 cents per unit. Under the provisions of section 1382(e), W's patronage is deemed to occur in 1964, the year in which the pool is closed.

(ii) The patronage dividend paid to W during 1964 amounts to 5 cents per unit, consisting of the aggregate of the following per-unit allocations: The amount of the cash distribution (3 cents), and the stated dollar amount of the capital stock of A (2 cents), which are fixed with reference to the net earnings of A. The amount of the two distributions in cash (85 cents) and the face amount of the "retain certificate" (5 cents), which are fixed without reference to the net earnings of A, do not constitute patronage dividends.

Example (2). Cooperative B, a marketing association operating on a pooling basis, receives the products of patron X on March 5, 1964. On the same day cooperative B pays to X $1.00 per unit for such products, this amount being determined by reference to the market price of the product when received, and issues to him a participation certificate having no face value but which entitles X on the close of the pool to the proceeds derived from the sale of his products less the previous payment of $1.00 and the expenses and other charges attributable to such products. On March 5, 1967, cooperative B, having sold the products in the pool, having deducted the previous payments for such products, and having determined the expenses and other charges of the pool pays to X, in cash, 10 cents per unit pursuant to the participation certificate. Under the provisions of section 1382(e), X's patronage is deemed to occur in 1967, the year in which the pool is closed. The payment made to X during 1967, amounting to 10 cents per unit, is a patronage dividend. Neither the payment to X in 1964 of $1.00 nor the issuance to him of the participation certificate in that year constitutes a patronage dividend.

Example (3). Cooperative C, a purchasing association, obtains supplies for patron Y on May 1, 1964, and receives in return therefor $100. On February 1, 1965, cooperative C, having determined the excess of its receipts over its costs and expenses, pays to Y a cash distribution of $1.00 and a revolving fund certificate with a stated dollar amount of $1.00. The amount of patronage dividend paid to Y in 1965 is $2.00, the aggregate of the cash distribution ($1.00) and the stated dollar amount of the revolving fund certificate ($1.00).

Example (4). Cooperative D, a service association, sells the products of members on a fee basis. It receives the products of patron Z under an agreement not to pool his products with those of other members, to sell his products, and to deliver to him the proceeds of the sale. Patron Z makes payments to cooperative D during 1964 aggregating $75 for service rendered him by cooperative D during the year. On May 15, 1965, cooperative D, having determined the excess of its receipts over its costs and expenses, pays to Z a cash distribution of $2.00. Such amount is a patronage dividend paid by cooperative D during 1965.

(b) Written notice of allocation. The term "written notice of allocation" means any capital stock, revolving fund certificate, retain certificate, certificate of indebtedness, letter of advice, or other written notice, which discloses to the patron the stated dollar amount allocated to him on the books of the cooperative organization, and the portion thereof, if any, which constitutes a patronage dividend. Thus, a mere credit to the account of a patron on the books of the organization without disclosure to the patron, is not a written notice of allocation. A written notice of allocation may disclose to the patron the amount of the allocation which constitutes a patronage dividend either as a dollar amount or as a percentage of the stated dollar amount of the written notice of allocation.

(c) Qualified written notice of allocation. *(1) In general.* The term "qualified written notice of allocation" means a written notice of allocation—

(i) Which meets the requirements of subparagraph (2) or (3) of this paragraph, and

(ii) Which is paid as part of a patronage dividend, or as part of a payment by a cooperative association organized and operated in compliance with the provisions of section 521 and § 1.521-1 to patrons on a patronage basis with respect to earnings derived from business done with or for the United States or any of its agencies or from sources other than patronage, that also includes a payment in money or by qualified check equal to at least 20 percent of such patronage dividend or such payment.

In determining, for purposes of subdivision (ii) of this subparagraph, whether 20 percent of a patronage dividend or a payment with respect to non-patronage earnings is paid in money or by qualified check, any portion of such dividend or payment which is paid in nonqualified written notices of allocation may be disregarded. Thus, if a cooperative pays a patronage dividend of $100 in the form of a nonqualified written notice of allocation with a stated dollar amount of $50, a written notice of allocation with a stated dollar amount of $40, and money in the amount of $10, the written notice of allocation with a stated dollar amount of $40 will constitute a qualified written notice of allocation if it meets the requirements of subparagraph (2) or (3) of this paragraph. A "payment in money", as that term is used in subdivision (ii) of this subparagraph, includes a payment by a check drawn on a bank but does not include a credit against amounts owed by the patron to the cooperative organization, a credit against the purchase price of a share of stock or of a membership in such organization, nor does it include a payment by means of a document redeemable by such organization for money.

(2) Written notice of allocation redeemable in cash. The term "qualified written notice of allocation" includes a written notice of allocation which meets the requirement of subparagraph (1)(ii) of this paragraph and which may be redeemed in cash at its stated dollar amount at any time within a period beginning on the date such written notice of allocation is paid and ending not earlier than 90 days from such date, but only if the distributee receives written notice of the right of redemption at the time he receives such written notice of allocation. The written notice of the right of redemption referred to in the preceding sentence shall be given separately to each patron. Thus, a written notice of the right of redemption which is published in a newspaper or posted at the cooperative's place of business would not be sufficient to qualify a written notice of allocation which is otherwise described in this subparagraph.

(3) Consent of patron. The term "qualified written notice of allocation" also includes a written notice of allocation which meets the requirement of subparagraph (1)(ii) of this paragraph and which the distributee has consented, in a manner provided in this subparagraph, to take into account at its stated dollar amount as provided in section 1385 and § 1.1385-1.

(i) Consent in writing. A distributee may consent to take the stated dollar amount of written notices of allocation into account under section 1385 by signing and furnishing a written consent to the cooperative organization. No special form is required for the written consent so long as the document on which it is made clearly discloses the terms of the consent. Thus, the written consent may be made on a signed invoice, sales slip, delivery ticket, marketing agreement, or other document, on which appears the appropriate consent. Unless the written consent specifically provides to the contrary, it shall be effective with respect to all patronage occurring during the taxable year of the cooperative organization in which such consent is received by such organization and, unless revoked under section 1388(c)(3)(B), for all subsequent taxable years. Section 1388(c)(3)(B)(i) provides that a written consent may be revoked by the patron at any time. Thus, any written consent which is, by its terms, irrevocable is not a consent that would qualify a written notice of allocation. A revocation, to be effective, must be in writing, signed by the patron, and furnished to the cooperative organization. Such a revocation shall be effective only with respect to patronage occurring after the close of the taxable year of the cooperative organization during which the revocation is filed with it. In the case of a pooling arrangement described in section 1382(e) and § 1.1382-5, a written consent which is made at any time before the close of the taxable year of the cooperative organization during which the pool closes shall be effective with respect to all patronage under that pool. In addition, any subsequent revocation of such consent by the patron will not be effective for that pool or any other pool with respect to which he has been a patron before such revocation.

(ii) Consent by membership. (a) A distributee may consent to take the stated dollar amount of written notices of allocation into account under section 1385 by obtaining or retaining membership in the cooperative organization after such organization has adopted a valid bylaw providing that membership in such cooperative organization constitutes such consent, but such consent shall take effect only after the distributee has received a written notification of the adoption of the bylaw provision and a copy of such bylaw. The bylaw must have been adopted by the cooperative organization after October 16, 1962, and must contain a clear statement that membership in the cooperative organization constitutes the prescribed consent. The written notification from the cooperative organization must inform the patron that this bylaw has been adopted and of its significance. The notification and copy of the bylaw shall be given separately to each member (or prospective member); thus, a written notice and copy of the bylaw which are published in a newspaper or posted at the cooperative's place of business are not sufficient to qualify a written notice of allocation under this subdivision. A member (or prospective member) is presumed to have received the notification and copy of the bylaw if they were sent to his last known address by ordinary mail. A prospective member must receive the notification and copy of the bylaw before he becomes a member of the organization in order to have his membership in the organization constitute consent. A consent made in the manner described in this subdivision shall be effective only with respect to patronage occurring after the patron has received a copy of the bylaw and the prerequisite notice and while he is a member of the organization. Thus, any such consent shall not be effective with respect to any patronage occurring after the patron ceases to be a member of the cooperative organization or after the bylaw provision is repealed by such organization. In the case of a pooling arrangement described in section 1382(e) and § 1.1382-5, a consent made under this subdivision will be effective only with respect to the patron's actual patronage occurring after he receives the notification and copy of the bylaw and while he is a member of the cooperative organization. Thus such a consent shall not be effective with respect to any patronage under a pool after the patron ceases to be a member of the cooperative organization or after the bylaw provision is repealed by the organization.

(b) The following is an example of a bylaw provision which would meet the requirements prescribed in (a) of this subdivision.

Example. Each person who hereafter applies for and is accepted to membership in this cooperative and each member of this cooperative on the effective date of this bylaw who continues as a member after such date shall, by such act alone, consent that the amount of any distributions with respect to his patronage occurring after __, which are made in written notices of allocation (as defined in 26 USC 1388) and which are received by him from the cooperative, will be taken into account by him at their stated dollar amounts in the manner provided in 26 USC 1385(a) in the taxable year in which such written notices of allocation are received by him.

(c) For purposes of this subdivision the term "member" means a person who is entitled to participate in the management of the cooperative organization.

(iii) Consent by qualified check. (a) A distributee may consent to take the stated dollar amount of a written notice of allocation into account under section 1385 by endorsing and cashing a qualified check which is paid as a part of the same patronage dividend or payment described in subparagraph (1)(ii) of this paragraph of which the written notice of allocation is also a part. In order to constitute an effective consent under this subdivision, however, the qualified check must be endorsed and cashed by the payee on or before the ninetieth day after the close of the payment period for the taxable year of the cooperative organization with respect to which the patronage dividend or payment is paid (or on or before such earlier day as may be prescribed by the cooperative organization). The endorsing and cashing of a qualified check shall be considered a consent only with respect to written notices of allocation which are part of the same patronage dividend or payment as the qualified check and for which a consent under subdivision (i) or (ii) of this subparagraph is not in effect. A qualified check is presumed to be endorsed and cashed within the 90-day period if the earliest bank endorsement which appears thereon bears a date no later than 3 days after the end of such 90-day period (excluding Saturdays, Sundays, and legal holidays).

(b) The term "qualified check" means a check, or other instrument redeemable in money, which is paid as a part of a patronage dividend or payment described in subparagraph (1)(ii) of this paragraph, on which there is clearly imprinted a statement that the endorsement and cashing of the check or other instrument constitutes the consent of the payee to take into account, as provided in the Federal income tax laws, the stated dollar amount of any written notices of allocation which are paid as a part of the patronage dividend or payment of which such check or other instrument is also a part. A qualified check need not be in the form of an ordinary check which is payable through the banking system. It may, for example, be in the form of an instrument which is redeemable in money by the cooperative organization. The term "qualified check" does not include a check or other instrument paid as part of a patronage dividend or payment with respect to which a consent under subdivision (i) or (ii) of this subparagraph is in effect. In addition, the term "qualified check" does not include a check or other instrument which is paid as part of a patronage dividend or payment, if such patronage dividend or payment does not also include a written notice of allocation (other than a written notice of allocation that may be redeemed in cash at its stated dollar amount which meets the requirements of section 1388(c)(1)(A) and subparagraph (2) of this paragraph). Thus, a check which is paid as part of a patronage dividend is not a qualified check (even though it has the required statement imprinted on it) if the remaining portion of such patronage dividend is paid in cash or if the only written notices of allocation included in the payment are qualified under section 1388(c)(1)(A) and subparagraph (2) of this paragraph (relating to certain written notices of allocation which are redeemable by the patron within a period of at least 90 days).

(c) The provisions of this subdivision may be illustrated by the following example:

Example. (1) The A Cooperative is a cooperative organization filing its income tax returns on a calendar year basis. None of its patrons have consented in the manner prescribed in section 1388(c)(2)(A) or (B). On August 1, 1964, the A Cooperative pays patronage dividends to its patrons with respect to their 1963 patronage, and the payment to each such patron is partly by a qualified check and partly in the form of a written notice of allocation which is not redeemable for cash. Each patron who endorses and cashes his qualified check on or before December 14, 1964 (the ninetieth day following the close of the 1963 payment period) shall be considered to have consented with respect to the accompanying written notice of allocation and the amount of such check is treated as a patronage dividend paid in money on August 1, 1964.

(2) As to any patron who has not endorsed and cashed his qualified check by December 14, 1964, there is no consent and both the written notice of allocation and the qualified check constitute nonqualified written notices of allocation within the meaning of section 1388(d) and paragraph (d) of this section. If such a patron then cashes his check on January 2, 1965, he shall treat the amount received as an amount received on January 2, 1965, in redemption of a nonqualified written notice of allocation. Likewise, the cooperative shall treat the amount of the check as an amount paid on January 2, 1965, in redemption of a nonqualified written notice of allocation.

(d) Nonqualified written notice of allocation. The term "nonqualified written notice of allocation" means a written notice of allocation which is not a qualified written notice of allocation described in section 1388(c) and paragraph (c) of this section, or a qualified check which is not cashed on or before the ninetieth day after the close of the payment period for the taxable year of the cooperative organization for which the payment of which it is a part is paid.

(e) Patron. The term "patron" includes any person with whom or for whom the cooperative association does business on a cooperative basis, whether a member or a nonmember of the cooperative association, and whether an individual, a trust, estate, partnership, company, corporation, or cooperative association.

T.D. 6643, 4/1/63.

§ 1.1394-0 Table of contents.

Caution: The Treasury has not yet amended Reg § 1.1394-0 to reflect changes made by P.L. 105-34.

This section lists the major paragraph headings contained in § 1.1394-1.

T.D. 8673, 5/30/96.

§ 1.1394-1 Enterprise zone facility bonds.

Caution: The Treasury has not yet amended Reg § 1.1394-1 to reflect changes made by P.L. 105-34.

(a) Scope. This section contains rules relating to tax-exempt bonds under section 1394 (enterprise zone facility bonds) to provide enterprise zone facilities in both empowerment zones and enterprise communities (zones). See sections 1394, 1397B, and 1397C for other rules and definitions.

(b) Period of compliance. *(1) In general.* Except as provided in paragraphs (b)(2) and (c) of this section, the requirements under sections 1394(a) and (b) applicable to enterprise zone facility bonds must be complied with throughout the greater of the following—

(i) The remainder of the period during which the zone designation is in effect under section 1391 (zone designation period); and

(ii) The period that ends on the weighted average maturity date of the enterprise zone facility bonds.

(2) Compliance after an issue is retired. Except as provided in paragraph (c)(3) of this section, the requirements applicable to enterprise zone facility bonds do not apply to an issue after the date on which no enterprise zone facility bonds of the issue are outstanding.

(3) Deemed compliance. (i) General rule. An issue is deemed to comply with the requirements of sections 1394 (a) and (b) if—

(A) The issuer and the principal user in good faith attempt to meet the requirements of sections 1394(a) and (b) throughout the period of compliance required under this section; and

(B) Any failure to meet these requirements is corrected within a one-year period after the failure is first discovered.

(ii) Exception. The provisions of paragraph (b)(3)(i) of this section do not apply to the requirements of section 1397B(d)(5)(A) (relating to certain prohibited business activities).

(iii) Good faith. In order to satisfy the good faith requirement of paragraph (b)(3)(i)(A) of this section, the principal user must at least annually demonstrate to the issuer the principal user's monitoring of compliance with the requirements of sections 1394(a) and (b).

(c) Special rules for requirements of sections 1397B and 1397C. *(1) Start of compliance period.* Except as provided in paragraph (c)(2) of this section, the requirements of sections 1397B (relating to qualification as an enterprise zone business) and 1397C (relating to satisfaction of the rules for qualified zone property) do not apply prior to the initial testing date (as defined in paragraph (c)(4) of this section) if—

(i) The issuer and the principal user reasonably expect on the issue date of the enterprise zone facility bonds that those requirements will be met by the principal user on or before the initial testing date; and

(ii) The issuer and the principal user exercise due diligence to meet those requirements prior to the initial testing date.

(2) Compliance period for certain prohibited activities. The requirements of section 1397B (d)(5)(A) (relating to certain prohibited business activities) must be complied with throughout the term of the enterprise zone facility bonds.

(3) Minimum compliance period. The requirements of sections 1397B(b) or (c) and 1397C must be satisfied for a continuous period of at least three years after the initial testing date, notwithstanding that—

(i) The period of compliance required under paragraph (b)(1) of this section expires before the end of the three-year period; or

(ii) The enterprise zone facility bonds are retired before the end of the three-year period.

(4) Initial testing date. (i) In general. Except as otherwise provided in paragraph (c)(4)(ii) of this section, the initial testing date is the date that is 18 months after the later of the issue date of the enterprise zone facility bonds or the date on which the financed property is placed in service; provided, however, it is not later than—

(A) Three years after the issue date; or

(B) Five years after the issue date, if the issue finances a construction project for which both the issuer and a licensed architect or engineer certify on or before the issue date of the enterprise zone facility bonds that more than three years after the issue date is necessary to complete construction of the project.

(ii) Alternative initial testing date. If the issuer identifies as the initial testing date a date after the issue date of the enterprise zone facility bonds and prior to the initial testing date that would have been determined under paragraph (c)(4)(i) of this section, that earlier date is treated as the initial testing date.

(d) Testing on an average basis. Compliance with each of the requirements of section 1397B(b) or (c) is tested each taxable year. Compliance with any of the requirements may be tested on an average basis, taking into account up to four immediately preceding taxable years plus the current taxable year. The earliest taxable year that may be taken into account for purposes of the preceding sentence is the taxable year that includes the initial testing date. A taxable year is disregarded if the part of the taxable year that falls in a required compliance period does not exceed 90 days.

(e) Resident employee requirements. *(1) Determination of employee status.* For purposes of the requirement of section 1397B(b)(6) or (c)(5) that at least 35 percent of the employees are residents of the zone, the issuer and the principal user may rely on a certification, signed under penalties of perjury by the employee, provided—

(i) The certification provides to the principal user the address of the employee's principal residence;

(ii) The employee is required by the certification to notify the principal user of a change of the employee's principal residence; and

(iii) Neither the issuer nor the principal user has actual knowledge that the principal residence set forth in the certification is not the employee's principal residence.

(2) Employee treated as zone resident. If an issue fails to comply with the requirement of section 1397B(b)(6) or (c)(5) because an employee who initially resided in the zone moves out of the zone, that employee is treated as still residing in the zone if—

(i) That employee was a bona fide resident of the zone at the time of the certification described in paragraph (e)(1) of this section;

(ii) That employee continues to perform services for the principal user in an enterprise zone business and substantially all of those services are performed in the zone; and

(iii) A resident of the zone meeting the requirements of section 1397B(b)(5) or (c)(4) is hired by the principal user for the next available comparable (or lesser) position.

(3) Resident employee percentage. For purposes of meeting the requirement of section 1397B (b)(6) or (c)(5) that at least 35 percent of the employees of an enterprise zone business are residents of a zone, paragraphs (e)(3)(i) and (ii) of this section apply.

(i) The term *employee* includes a self-employed individual within the meaning of section 401(c)(1).

(ii) The resident employee percentage is determined on any reasonable basis consistently applied throughout the period of compliance required under this section. The per-employee fraction (as defined in paragraph (e)(3)(ii)(A) of this section) or the employee actual work hour fraction (as defined in paragraph (e)(3)(ii)(B) of this section) are both reasonable methods.

(A) The term *per-employee fraction* means the fraction, the numerator of which is, during the taxable year, the number of employees who work at least 15 hours a week for the principal user, who reside in the zone, and who are employed for at least 90 days, and the denominator of which is, during the same taxable year, the aggregate number of all employees who work at least 15 hours a week for the principal user and who are employed for at least 90 days.

(B) The term *employee actual work hour fraction* means the fraction, the numerator of which is the aggregate total actual hours of work for the principal user of employees who reside in the zone during a taxable year, and the denominator of which is the aggregate total actual hours of work for the principal user of all employees during the same taxable year.

(f) Application to pooled financing bond and loan recycling programs. In the case of a pooled financing bond program described in paragraph (g)(2) of this section or a loan recycling program described in paragraph (m)(2)(ii) of this section, the requirements of paragraphs (b) through (e) of this section apply on a loan-by-loan basis. See also paragraphs (g)(2) (relating to limitation on amount of bonds), (m)(2) (relating to maturity limitations), (m)(3) (relating to volume cap), and (m)(4) (relating to remedial actions) of this section.

(g) Limitation on amount of bonds. *(1) Determination of outstanding amount.* Whether an issue satisfies the requirements of section 1394(c) (relating to the $3 million and $20 million aggregate limitations on the amount of outstanding enterprise zone facility bonds) is determined as of the issue date of that issue, based on the issue price of that issue and the adjusted issue price of outstanding enterprise zone facility bonds. Amounts of outstanding enterprise zone facility bonds allocable to any entity are determined under rules contained in section 144(a)(10)(C) and the underlying regulations. Thus, the definition of *principal user* for purposes of section 1394(c) is different from the definition of *principal user* for purposes of paragraph (j) of this section.

(2) Pooled financing bond programs. (i) In general. The limitations of section 1394(c) for an issue for a pooled financing bond program are determined with regard to the amount of the actual loans to enterprise zone businesses rather than the amount lent to *intermediary lenders* as defined in paragraph (g)(2)(ii) of this section. This paragraph (g)(2) applies only to the extent the proceeds of those enterprise zone facility bonds are loaned to one or more enterprise zone businesses within 42 months of the issue date of the enterprise zone facility bonds or are used to redeem enterprise zone facility bonds of the issue within that 42-month period.

(ii) Pooled financing bond program defined. For purposes of this section, a *pooled financing bond program* is a program in which the issuer of enterprise zone facility bonds, in order to provide loans to enterprise zone businesses, lends the proceeds of the enterprise zone facility bonds to a bank or similar intermediary (intermediary lender) which must then relend the proceeds to two or more enterprise zone businesses.

(h) Original use requirement for purposes of qualified zone property. In general, for purposes of section 1397C(a)(1)(B), the term *original use* means the first use to which the property is put within the zone. For purposes of section 1394, if property is vacant for at least a one-year period including the date of zone designation, use prior to that period is disregarded for purposes of determining original use. For this purpose, de minimis incidental uses of property, such as renting the side of a building for a billboard, are disregarded.

(i) Land. The determination of whether land is functionally related and subordinate to qualified zone property is made in a manner consistent with the rules for exempt facilities under section 142.

(j) Principal user. *(1) In general.* Except as provided in paragraph (j)(2) of this section, the term *principal user* means the owner of financed property.

(2) Rental of real property. (i) A lessee as the principal user. If an owner of real property financed with enterprise zone facility bonds is not an enterprise zone business within the meaning of section 1397B, but the rental of the property is a qualified business within the meaning of section 1397B (d)(2), the term *principal user* for purposes of sections 1394(b) and (e) means the lessee or lessees.

(ii) Allocation of enterprise zone facility bonds. If a lessee is the principal user of real property under paragraph (j)(2)(i) of this section, then proceeds of enterprise zone facility bonds may be allocated to expenditures for real property only to the extent of the property allocable to the lessee's leased space, including expenditures for common areas.

(3) Pooled financing bond program. An intermediary lender in a pooled financing bond program described in paragraph (g)(2) of this section is not treated as the principal user.

(k) Treatment as separately incorporated business. For purposes of section 1394(b)(3)(B), a trade or business may be treated as separately incorporated if allocations of income and activities attributable to the business conducted within the zone are made using a reasonable allocation method and if that trade or business has evidence of those allocations sufficient to establish compliance with the requirements of paragraphs (b) through (f) of this section. Whether an allocation method is reasonable will depend upon the facts and circumstances. An allocation method will not be considered to be reasonable unless the allocation method is applied consistently by the trade or business and is consistent with the purposes of section 1394.

(l) Substantially all. For purposes of sections 1397B and 1397C(a), the term *substantially all* means 85 percent.

(m) Application of sections 142 and 146 through 150. *(1) In general.* Except as provided in this paragraph (m), enterprise zone facility bonds are treated as exempt facility bonds that are described in section 142(a), and all regulations generally applicable to exempt facility bonds apply to enterprise zone facility bonds. For this purpose, enterprise zone businesses are treated as meeting the public use requirement. Sections 147(c)(1)(A) (relating to limitations on financing the acquisition of land), 147(d) (relating to financing the acquisition of existing property), and 142(b)(2) (relating to limitations on financing office space) do not apply to enterprise zone facility bonds. See also paragraph (n)(4) of this section.

(2) Maturity limitation. (i) Requirements. An issue of enterprise zone facility bonds, the proceeds of which are to be used as part of a loan recycling program, satisfies the requirements of section 147(b) if—

(A) Each loan satisfies the requirements of section 147(b) (determined by treating each separate loan as a separate issue); and

(B) The term of the issue does not exceed 30 years.

(ii) Loan recycling program defined. A *loan recycling program* is a program in which—

(A) The issuer reasonably expects as of the issue date of the enterprise zone facility bonds that loan repayments from principal users will be used to make additional loans during the zone designation period;

(B) Repayments of principal on loans (including prepayments) received during the zone designation period are used within six months of the date of receipt either to make new loans to enterprise zone businesses or to redeem enterprise zone facility bonds that are part of the issue; and

(C) Repayments of principal on loans (including prepayments) received after the zone designation period are used to redeem enterprise zone facility bonds that are part of the issue within six months of the date of receipt.

(3) Volume cap. For purposes of applying section 146(f)(5)(A) (relating to elective carryforward of unused volume limitation), issuing enterprise zone facility bonds is a carryforward purpose.

(4) Remedial actions. In the case of a pooled financing bond program described in paragraph (g)(2) of this section or a loan recycling program described in paragraph (m)(2)(ii) of this section, if a loan fails to meet the requirements of paragraphs (b) through (f) of this section, within six months of noncompliance (after taking into account the deemed compliance provisions of paragraph (b)(3) of this section, if applicable), an amount equal to the outstanding loan principal must be prepaid and the issuer must—

(i) Reloan the amount of the prepayment; or

(ii) Use the prepayment to redeem an amount of outstanding enterprise zone facility bonds equal to the outstanding principal amount of the loan that no longer meets those requirements.

(n) Continuing compliance and change of use penalties. *(1) In general.* The penalty provisions of section 1394(e) apply throughout the period of compliance required under paragraph (b)(1) of this section.

(2) Coordination with deemed compliance provisions. Section 1394(e)(2) does not apply during any period during which the issue is deemed to comply with the requirements of section 1394 under the deemed compliance provisions of paragraph (b)(3) of this section.

(3) Application to pooled financing bond and loan recycling programs. In the case of a pooled financing bond program described in paragraph (g)(2) of this section or a loan recycling program described in paragraph (m)(2)(ii) of this section, section 1394(e) applies on a loan-by-loan basis.

(4) Section 150(b)(4) inapplicable. Section 150(b)(4) does not apply to enterprise zone facility bonds.

(o) Refunding bonds. *(1) In general.* An issue of bonds issued after the zone designation period to refund enterprise zone facility bonds (other than in an advance refunding) are treated as enterprise zone facility bonds if the refunding issue and the prior issue, if treated as a single combined issue, would meet all of the requirements for enterprise zone facility bonds, except the requirements in section 1394(c). For example, the compliance period described in paragraph (b)(1) of this section is calculated taking into account any extension of the weighted average maturity of the refunding issue compared to the remaining weighted average maturity of the prior issue. The proceeds of the refunding issue are allocated to the same expenditures and purpose investments as the prior issue.

(2) Maturity limitation. The maturity limitation of section 147(b) is applied to a refunding issue by taking into account the issuer's reasonable expectations about the economic life of the financed property as of the issue date of the prior issue and the actual weighted average maturity of the combined refunding issue and prior issue.

(p) Examples. The following examples illustrate paragraphs (a) through (o) of this section:

Example (1). Averaging of enterprise zone business requirements. City C issues enterprise zone facility bonds, the proceeds of which are loaned by C to Corporation B to finance the acquisition of equipment for its existing business located in a zone. On the issue date of the enterprise zone facility bonds, B meets all of the requirements of section 1397B(b), except that only 25% of B's employees reside in the zone. C and B reasonably expect on the issue date to meet all requirements of section 1397B(b) by the date that is 18 months after the equipment is placed in service (the initial testing date). In each of the first, second, and third taxable years after the initial testing date, 35%, 40% and 45%, respectively, of B's employees are zone residents. In the fourth year after the testing date, only 25% of B's employees are zone residents. B continues to meet the 35% resident employee requirement, because the average of zone resident employees for those four taxable years is approximately 36%. The percentage of zone residents employed by B before the initial testing date is not included in determining whether B continues to comply with the 35% resident employee requirement.

Example (2). Measurement of resident employee percentage. Authority D issues enterprise zone facility bonds, the proceeds of which are loaned to Sole Proprietor F to establish an accounting business in a zone. In the first year after the initial testing date, the staff working for F includes F, who works 40 hours per week and does not live in the zone, one employee who resides in the zone and works 40 hours per week, one employee who does not reside in the zone and works 20 hours per week, and one employee who does not reside in the zone and works 10 hours per week. F meets the 35% resident employee test by calculating the percentage on the basis of employee actual work hours as described in paragraph (e)(3)(ii)(B) of this section. If F uses the per-employee basis as described in paragraph (e)(3)(ii)(A) of this section to determine if the resident employee test is met, the percentage of employees who are zone residents on a per-employee basis is only 33% because F must exclude from the numerator and the denominator the employee who works only 10 hours per week. If F calculates the resident employee test as a percentage of employee actual work hours as described in paragraph (e)(3)(ii)(B) of this section in the first year, F must calculate the resident employee test as a percentage of employee actual work hours each year.

Example (3). Active conduct of business within the zone. State G issues enterprise zone facility bonds and loans the proceeds to Corporation H to finance the acquisition of equipment for H's mail order clothing business, which is located in a zone. H purchases the supplies for its clothing business from suppliers located both within and outside of the zone and expects that orders will be received both from customers who will reside or work within the zone and from others outside the zone. All orders are received and filled at, and are shipped from, H's clothing business located in the zone. H meets the requirement that at least 80% of its gross income is derived from the active conduct of business within the zone.

Example (4). Enterprise zone business definition. City J issues enterprise zone facility bonds, the proceeds of which are loaned to Partnership K to finance the acquisition of equipment for its printing operation located in the zone. All orders are taken and completed, and all billing and accounting activities are performed, at the print shop located in the zone. K, on occasion, uses its equipment (including its trucks) and employees to deliver large print jobs to customers who reside outside of the zone. So long as K is able to establish that its trucks are used in the zone at least 85% of the time and its employees perform at least 85% of services for K in the zone, K meets the requirements of sections 1397B(b)(3) and (5).

Example (5). Treatment as a separately incorporated business. The facts are the same as in Example 4 except that six years after the issue date of the enterprise zone facility bonds, K determines to expand its operations to a second location outside of the boundaries of the zone. Although the expansion would result in the failure of K to meet the tests of 1397B(b), K, using a reasonable allocation method, allocates income and activities to its operations within the zone and has evidence of these allocations sufficient to establish compliance with the requirements of paragraphs (b) through (f) of this section. The bonds will not fail to be enterprise zone facility bonds merely because of the expansion.

Example (6). Treatment of pooled financing bond programs. Authority L issues bonds in the aggregate principal amount of $5,000,000 and loans the proceeds to Bank M pursuant to a loans-to-lenders program. M does not meet the definition of enterprise zone business contained in section 1397B. Prior to the issue date of the bonds, L held a public hearing regarding issuance of the bonds for the loans-to-lenders program, describing the projects of identified borrowers to be financed initially with $4,000,000 of the proceeds of the bonds. The applicable elected representative of L approved issuance of the bonds subsequent to the public hearing. The loan agreement between L and M provides that the other proceeds of the bonds will be held by M and loaned to borrowers that qualify as enterprise zone businesses, following a public hearing and approval by the applicable elected representative of L of each loan by M to an enterprise zone business. None of the loans will be in principal amounts in excess of $3,000,000. The loans by M will otherwise meet the requirements of section 1394. The bonds will be enterprise zone facility bonds.

Example (7). Original use requirement for purposes of qualified zone property. City N issues enterprise zone facility bonds, the proceeds of which are loaned to Corporation P to finance the acquisition of equipment. P uses the proceeds after the zone designation date to purchase used equipment located outside of the zone and places the equipment in service at its location in the zone. Substantially all of the use of the equipment is in the zone and is in the active conduct of a qualified business by P. The equipment is treated as qualified enterprise zone property under section 1397C because P makes the first use of the property within the zone after the zone designation date.

Example (8). Principal user. State R issues enterprise zone facility bonds and loans the proceeds to Partnership S to finance the construction of a small shopping center to be located in a zone. S is in the business of commercial real estate. S is not an enterprise zone business, but has secured one anchor lessee, Corporation T, for the shopping center. T would qualify as an enterprise zone business. S will derive 60% of its gross rental income of the shopping center from T. S does not anticipate that the remaining rental income will come from enterprise zone businesses. T will occupy 60% of the total rentable space in the shopping center. S can use enterprise zone facility bond proceeds to finance the portion of the costs of the shopping center allocable to T (60%) because T is treated as the principal user of the enterprise zone facility bond proceeds.

Example (9). Remedial actions. State W issues pooled financing enterprise zone facility bonds, the proceeds of which will be loaned to several enterprise zone businesses in the two enterprise communities and one empowerment zone in W. Proceeds of the pooled financing bonds are loaned to Corporation X, an enterprise zone business, for a term of 10 years. Six years after the date of the loan, X expands its operations beyond the empowerment zone and is no longer able to meet the requirements of section 1394. X does not reasonably expect to be able to cure the noncompliance. The loan documents provide that X must prepay its loan in the event of noncompliance. W does not expect to be able to reloan the prepayment by X within six months of noncompliance. X's noncompliance will not affect the qualification of the pooled financing bonds as enterprise zone facility bonds if W uses the proceeds from the loan prepayment to redeem outstanding enterprise zone facility bonds within six months of noncompliance in an amount comparable to the outstanding amount of the loan immediately prior to prepayment. X will be denied an interest expense deduction for the interest accruing from the first day of the taxable year in which the noncompliance began.

(q) Effective dates. *(1) In general.* Except as otherwise provided in this section, the provisions of this section apply to all issues issued after July 30, 1996, and subject to section 1394.

(2) Elective retroactive application in whole. An issuer may apply the provisions of this section in whole, but not in part, to any issue that is outstanding on July 30, 1996, and is subject to section 1394.

T.D. 8673, 5/30/96.

§ 1.1396-1 Qualified zone employees.

(a) In general. A qualified zone employee of an employer is an employee who satisfies the location-of-services requirement and the abode requirement with respect to the same empowerment zone and is not otherwise excluded by section 1396(d).

(1) Location-of-services requirement. The location-of-services requirement is satisfied if substantially all of the services performed by the employee for the employer are performed in the empowerment zone in a trade or business of the employer.

(2) Abode requirement. The abode requirement is satisfied if the employee's principal place of abode while performing those services is in the empowerment zone.

(b) Period for applying location-of-services requirement. In applying the location-of-services requirement, an employer may use either the pay period method described in paragraph (b)(1) of this section or the calendar year method described in paragraph (b)(2) of this section. For each taxable year of an employer, the employer must either use the pay period method with respect to all of its employees or use the calendar year method with respect to all of its employees. The employer may change the method applied to all of its employees from one taxable year to the next.

(1) Pay period method. (i) Relevant period. Under the pay period method, the relevant period for applying the location-of-services requirement is each pay period in which an employee provides services to the employer during the calendar year with respect to which the credit is being claimed (i.e., the calendar year that ends with or within the relevant taxable year). If an employer has one pay period for certain employees and a different pay period for other employees (e.g., a weekly pay period for hourly wage employees and a bi-weekly pay period for salaried employees), the pay period actually applicable to a particular employee is the relevant pay period for that employee under this method.

(ii) Application of method. Under this method, an employee does not satisfy the location-of-services requirement during a pay period unless substantially all of the services performed by the employee for the employer during that pay period are performed within the empowerment zone in a trade or business of the employer.

(2) Calendar year method. (i) Relevant period. Under the calendar year method, the relevant period for an employee is the entire calendar year with respect to which the credit is being claimed. However, for any employee who is employed by the employer for less than the entire calendar year, the relevant period is the portion of that calendar year during which the employee is employed by the employer.

(ii) Application of method. Under this method, an employee does not satisfy the location-of-services requirement during any part of a calendar year unless substantially all of the services performed by the employee for the employer during that calendar year (or, if the employee is employed by the employer for less than the entire calendar year, the portion of that calendar year during which the employee is employed by the employer) are performed within the empowerment zone in a trade or business of the employer.

(3) Examples. This paragraph (b) may be illustrated by the following examples. In each example, the following assumptions apply. The employees satisfy the abode requirement at all relevant times and all services performed by the employees for their employer are performed in a trade or business of the employer. The employees are not precluded from being qualified zone employees by section 1396(d)(2) (certain employees ineligible). No portion of the employees' wages is precluded from being qualified zone wages by section 1396(c)(2) (only first $15,000 of wages taken into account) or section 1396(c)(3) (coordination with targeted jobs credit and work opportunity credit). The examples are as follows:

Example (1). (i) Employer X has a weekly pay period for all its employees. Employee A works for X throughout 1997. During each of the first 20 weekly pay periods in 1997, substantially all of A's work for X is performed within the empowerment zone in which A resides. A also works in the zone at various times during the rest of the year, but there is no other pay period in which substantially all of A's work for X is performed within the empowerment zone. Employer X uses the pay period method.

(ii) For each of the first 20 pay periods of 1997, A is a qualified zone employee, all of A's wages from X are qualified zone wages, and X may claim the empowerment zone employment credit with respect to those wages. X cannot claim the credit with respect to any of A's wages for the rest of 1997.

Example (2). (i) Employer Y has a weekly pay period for its factory workers and a bi-weekly pay period for its office workers. Employee B works for Y in various factories and Employee C works for Y in various offices. Employer Y uses the pay period method.

(ii) Y must use B's weekly pay periods to determine the periods (if any) in which B is a qualified zone employee. Y may claim the empowerment zone employment credit with respect to B's wages only for the weekly pay periods for which B is a qualified zone employee, because those are B's only wages that are qualified zone wages. Y must use C's bi-weekly pay periods to determine the periods (if any) in which C is a qualified zone employee. Y may claim the credit with respect to C's wages only for the bi-weekly pay periods for which C is a qualified zone employee, because those are C's only wages that are qualified zone wages.

Example (3). (i) Employees D and E work for Employer Z throughout 1997. Although some of D's work for Z in 1997 is performed outside the empowerment zone in which D resides, substantially all of it is performed within that empowerment zone. E's work for Z is performed within the empowerment zone in which E resides for several weeks of 1997 but outside the zone for the rest of the year so that, viewed on an annual basis, E's work is not substantially all performed within the empowerment zone. Employer Z uses the calendar year method.

(ii) D is a qualified zone employee for the entire year, all of D's 1997 wages from Z are qualified zone wages, and Z may claim the empowerment zone employment credit with respect to all of those wages, including the portion attributable to work outside the zone. Under the calendar year method, E is not a qualified zone employee for any part of 1997, none of E's 1997 wages are qualified zone wages, and Z cannot claim any empowerment zone employment credit with respect to E's wages for 1997. Z cannot use the calendar year method for D and the pay period method for E because Z must use the same method for all employees. For 1998, however, Z can switch to the pay period method for E if Z also switches to the pay period method for D and all of Z's other employees.

(c) Effective date. This section applies with respect to wages paid or incurred on or after December 21, 1994.

T.D. 8747, 12/29/97.

§ 1.1397E-1 Qualified zone academy bonds.

Caution: The Treasury has not yet amended Reg § 1.1397E-1 to reflect changes made by P.L. 110-343.

(a) Overview. In general, a qualified zone academy bond is a taxable bond issued by a state or local government the proceeds of which are used to improve certain eligible public schools. An eligible taxpayer that holds a qualified zone academy bond generally is allowed annual federal income tax credits in lieu of periodic interest payments. These credits compensate the eligible taxpayer for lending money to the issuer and function as payments of interest on the bond. Accordingly, this section generally treats the allowance of a credit as if it were a payment of interest on the bond. In addition, this section provides rules to determine the credit rate, the present value of qualified contributions from private entities, and the maximum term of a qualified zone academy bond.

(b) Credit rate. The Secretary shall determine monthly (or more often as deemed necessary by the Secretary) the credit rate the Secretary estimates will generally permit the issuance of a qualified zone academy bond without discount and without interest cost to the issuer. The manner for ascertaining the credit rate for a qualified zone academy bond as determined by the Secretary shall be set forth in procedures, notices, forms, or instructions prescribed by the Commissioner.

(c) Private business contribution requirement. *(1) Reasonable discount rate.* To determine the present value (as of the issue date) of qualified contributions from private entities under section 1397E(d)(2), the issuer must use a reasonable discount rate. The credit rate determined under paragraph (b) of this section is a reasonable discount rate.

(2) Definition of private entities. For purposes of section 1397E(d)(2)(A), the term private entities includes any person (as defined in section 7701(a)) other than the United States, a State or local government, or any agency or instrumentality thereof or related party with respect thereto. To determine whether a person is related to the United States or a State or local government under this paragraph (c)(2), rules similar to those for determining whether a person is a related

party under § 1.150-1(b) shall apply (treating the United States as a governmental unit for purposes of § 1.150-1(b)).

(3) Qualified contribution. For purposes of section 1397E(d)(2)(A), the term qualified contribution means any contribution (of a type and quality acceptable to the eligible local education agency) of any property or service described in section 1397E(d)(2)(B)(i), (ii), (iii), (iv) or (v). In addition, cash received with respect to a qualified zone academy from a private entity (other than cash received indirectly from a person that is not a private entity as part of a plan to avoid the requirements of section 1397E) constitutes a qualified contribution if it is to be used to purchase any property or service described in section 1397E(d)(2)(B)(i), (ii), (iii), (iv) or (v). Services of employees of the eligible local education agency do not constitute qualified contributions.

(d) Maximum term. The maximum term for a qualified zone academy bond is determined under section 1397E(d)(3) by using a discount rate equal to 110 percent of the long-term adjusted AFR, compounded semi-annually, for the month in which the bond is issued. The Internal Revenue Service publishes this figure each month in a revenue ruling that is published in the Internal Revenue Bulletin. See § 601.601(d)(2)(ii)(b) of this Chapter.

(e) Tax credit. *(1) Eligible taxpayer.* An eligible taxpayer (within the meaning of section 1397E(d)(6)) that holds a qualified zone academy bond on a credit allowance date is allowed a tax credit against the federal income tax imposed on the taxpayer for the taxable year that includes the credit allowance date. The amount of the credit is equal to the product of the credit rate and the outstanding principal amount of the bond on the credit allowance date. The credit is subject to a limitation based on the eligible taxpayer's income tax liability. See section 1397E(c).

(2) Ineligible taxpayer. A taxpayer that is not an eligible taxpayer is not allowed a credit.

(f) Treatment of the allowance of the credit as a payment of interest. *(1) General rule.* The holder of a qualified zone academy bond must treat the bond as if it pays qualified stated interest (within the meaning of § 1.1273-1(c)) on each credit allowance date. The amount of the deemed payment of interest on each credit allowance date is equal to the product of the credit rate and the outstanding principal amount of the bond on that date. Thus, for example, if the holder uses an accrual method of accounting, the holder must accrue as interest income the amount of the credit over the one-year accrual period that ends on the credit allowance date.

(2) Adjustment if the holder cannot use the credit to offset a tax liability. If a holder holds a qualified zone academy bond on the credit allowance date but cannot use all or a portion of the credit to reduce its income tax liability (for example, because the holder is not an eligible taxpayer or because the limitation in section 1397E(c) applies), the holder is allowed a deduction for the taxable year that includes the credit allowance date (or, at the option of the holder, the next succeeding taxable year). The amount of the deduction is equal to the amount of the unused credit deemed paid on the credit allowance date.

(g) Not a tax-exempt obligation. A qualified zone academy bond is not an obligation the interest on which is excluded from gross income under section 103(a).

(h) Reimbursement. An expenditure for a qualified purpose may be reimbursed with proceeds of a qualified zone academy bond. For this purpose, rules similar to those in § 1.150-2 shall apply.

(i) and (j) [Reserved]. For further guidance, see § 1.1397E-1T(i) and (j).

(k) State or local government. *(1) In general.* For purposes of section 1397E(d)(1)(B), the term State or local government means a State or political subdivision as defined for purposes of section 103(c).

(2) On behalf of issuer. A qualified zone academy bond may be issued on behalf of a State or local government under rules similar to those for determining whether a bond issued on behalf of a State or political subdivision constitutes an obligation of that State or political subdivision for purposes of section 103.

(l) Cross-references. See section 171 and the regulations thereunder for rules relating to amortizable bond premium. See § 1.61-7(d) for the seller's treatment of a bond sold between interest payment dates (credit allowance dates) and § 1.61-7(c) for the buyer's treatment of a bond purchased between interest payment dates (credit allowance dates).

(m) Effective/applicability dates. Except as provided in this paragraph (m), this section applies to bonds sold on or after September 26, 2000. Each of paragraphs (c) and (k) of this section may be applied by issuers to bonds that are sold before September 26, 2000.

T.D. 8755, 1/6/98, amend T.D. 8826, 6/30/99, T.D. 8903, 9/25/2000, T.D. 9339, 7/13/2007.

PAR. 2. Section 1.1397E-1 is amended by revising paragraphs (a), (d), (h), (i), (j), (k), (l), and (m) to read as follows:

Proposed § 1.1397E-1 Qualified zone academy bonds.
[*For Preamble, see ¶ 152,883*]

(a) [The text of the proposed amendment to § 1.1397E-1(a) is the same as the text of § 1.1397E-1T(a) published elsewhere in this issue of the Federal Register]. [*See T.D. 9339, 07/16/2007, 72 Fed. Reg. 135.*]

* * * * *

(d) [The text of the proposed amendment to § 1.1397E-1(d) is the same as the text of § 1.1397E-1T(d) published elsewhere in this issue of the Federal Register]. [*See T.D. 9339, 07/16/2007, 72 Fed. Reg. 135.*]

* * * * *

(h) [The text of the proposed amendment to § 1.1397E-1(h) is the same as the text of § 1.1397E-1T(h) published elsewhere in this issue of the Federal Register]. [*See T.D. 9339, 07/16/2007, 72 Fed. Reg. 135.*]

(i) [The text of the proposed amendment to § 1.1397E-1(i) is the same as the text of § 1.1397E-1T(i) published elsewhere in this issue of the Federal Register]. [*See T.D. 9339, 07/16/2007, 72 Fed. Reg. 135.*]

(j) [The text of the proposed amendment to § 1.1397E-1(j) is the same as the text of § 1.1397E-1T(j) published elsewhere in this issue of the Federal Register]. [*See T.D. 9339, 07/16/2007, 72 Fed. Reg. 135.*]

(k) [The text of the proposed amendment to § 1.1397E-1(k) is the same as the text of § 1.1397E-1T(k) published elsewhere in this issue of the Federal Register]. [*See T.D. 9339, 07/16/2007, 72 Fed. Reg. 135.*]

(l) [The text of the proposed amendment to § 1.1397E-1(l) is the same as the text of § 1.1397E-1T(l) published elsewhere in this issue of the Federal Register]. [See T.D. 9339, 07/16/2007].

(m) [The text of the proposed amendment to § 1.1397E-1(m) is the same as the text of § 1.1397E-1T(m)(1) and (m)(2) published elsewhere in this issue of the Federal Register]. [*See T.D. 9339, 07/16/2007, 72 Fed. Reg. 135.*]

* * * * *

PAR. 2. Section 1.1397E-1 as proposed to be added at 63 FR 708 is amended by:

1. Revising paragraphs (b) and (j);
2. Redesignating paragraph (h) as paragraph (i);
3. Adding new paragraph (h).

The revisions and addition read as follows:

Proposed § 1.1397E-1 Qualified zone academy bonds.

[*For Preamble, see ¶ 151,983*]

[The text of proposed paragraphs (b), (h) and (j) is the same as the text of § 1.1397E-1T(b), (h), and (j) published elsewhere in this issue of the Federal Register.] [*See T.D. 8826, 6/30/99, 64 Fed. Reg. 126.*]

§ 1.1397E-1T Qualified zone academy bonds (temporary).

Caution: The Treasury has not yet amended Reg § 1.1397E-1T to reflect changes made by P.L. 110-343.

(a) In general. *(1) Overview.* In general, a qualified zone academy bond (QZAB or QZABs) is a taxable bond issued by a state or local government the proceeds of which are used to improve certain eligible public schools. An eligible taxpayer that holds a QZAB generally is allowed annual Federal income tax credits in lieu of periodic interest payments. These credits compensate the eligible taxpayer for lending money to the issuer and function as payments of interest on the bond. Accordingly, this section generally treats the allowance of a credit as if it were a payment of interest on the bond. This section also provides other rules for QZABs, including rules governing the credit rate, the private business contribution requirement, the maximum term, use and expenditure of proceeds, remedial actions, eligible issuers, arbitrage investment restrictions, and information reporting.

(2) Certain definitions. (i) In general. For purposes of this section, except as otherwise provided in this section, the following definitions apply: the definitions set forth in this section; the definitions used for general tax-exempt bond purposes in § 1.150-1; and the definitions used for purposes of the arbitrage investment restrictions on tax-exempt bonds in § 1.148-1(b).

(ii) Applicable definition of proceeds. (A) Use and expenditure provisions. Except as provided in paragraphs (a)(2)(ii)(B) and (a)(2)(ii)(C) of this section, for purposes of all applicable requirements regarding use and expenditure of proceeds of QZABs under section 1397E and this section, proceeds means "sale proceeds," as defined in § 1.148-1(b), plus "investment proceeds," as defined in § 1.148-1(b).

(B) Private business contribution requirement. For purposes of the private business contribution requirement of section 1397E(d)(2), proceeds means "sale proceeds," as defined in § 1.148-1(b).

(C) Arbitrage investment restrictions. For purposes of the scope of application of the arbitrage investment restrictions under section 1397E(g) and paragraph (i) of this section, proceeds generally means gross proceeds, as defined in § 1.148-1(b). In addition, in applying the arbitrage investment restrictions under paragraph (i) of this section and section 148, the various applicable definitions of the various types of proceeds of tax-exempt bonds under § 1.148-1(b) shall apply.

(b) and (c) [Reserved]. For further guidance, see § 1.1397E-1(b) and (c).

(d) Maximum term. The maximum term for a QZAB is determined under section 1397E(d)(3) by using a discount rate equal to 110 percent of the long-term adjusted applicable Federal rate (AFR), compounded semi-annually, for the month in which the bond is sold. The Internal Revenue Service publishes this figure each month in a revenue ruling that is published in the Internal Revenue Bulletin. See § 601.601(d)(2)(ii)(b) of this chapter. A bond is sold on the sale date, as defined in § 1.150-1(c)(6), which is the first day on which there is a binding contract in writing for the sale or exchange of the bond.

(e) through (g) [Reserved]. For further guidance, see § 1.1397E-1(e) through (g).

(h) Use of proceeds. *(1) In general.* Section 1397E(d)(1) provides that a bond issued as part of an issue is a QZAB only if, among other requirements, at least 95 percent of the proceeds of the issue are to be used for a qualified purpose with respect to a qualified zone academy established by an eligible local education agency (as defined in section 1397E(d)(4)(B)), and the issue meets the requirements of section 1397E(f) and (g). Section 1397E(d)(5) defines qualified purpose, with respect to any qualified zone academy, as rehabilitating or repairing the public school facility in which such academy is established, providing equipment for use at such academy, developing course materials for education to be provided at such academy, and training teachers and other school personnel in such academy. Section 1397E(d)(4)(A) defines qualified zone academy as any public school (or academic program within a public school) that is established by and operated under the supervision of an eligible local education agency to provide education or training below the postsecondary level and that meets the requirements of section 1397E(d)(4)(A)(i), (ii), (iii) and (iv).

(2) Use of proceeds requirements. An issue meets the requirements of sections 1397E(d)(1)(A) and (f) only if—

(i) The issuer reasonably expects, as of the issue date of the issue, that—

(A) At least 95 percent of the proceeds from the sale of the issue are to be spent for 1 or more qualified purposes with respect to qualified zone academies within the 5-year period beginning on the issue date of the QZAB;

(B) A binding commitment with a third party to spend at least 10 percent of the proceeds from the sale of the issue will be incurred within the 6-month period beginning on the issue date of the QZAB;

(C) At least 95 percent of the proceeds from the sale of the issue will be spent for a qualified purpose with respect to a qualified zone academy with due diligence (with due diligence measured by the reasonableness standard under § 1.148-1(b); and

(D) At least 95 percent of the proceeds of the issue will be used for a qualified purpose with respect to a qualified zone academy for the entire term of the issue (without regard to any redemption provision); and

(ii) Except as otherwise provided in paragraph (h)(7) of this section, at least 95 percent of the proceeds of the issue are actually used for a qualified purpose with respect to a qualified academy for the entire term of the issue (without regard to any redemption provision).

(iii) Extension of 5-year period. The Commissioner may extend the period described in paragraph (h)(2)(i)(A) of this section if the issuer, prior to the end of such period, submits a private ruling request, and establishes to the satisfaction of the Commissioner that—

(A) The failure to satisfy the 5-year spending requirement is due to reasonable cause; and

(B) The expenditure of at least 95 percent of the proceeds from the sale of the issue for a qualified purpose with respect to a qualified zone academy will continue to proceed with due diligence.

(3) Unspent proceeds. For purposes of paragraphs (h)(2)(i)(D) and (h)(2)(ii) of this section, during the period described in paragraph (h)(2)(i)(A) of this section, including any extension under paragraph (h)(2)(iii) of this section, unspent proceeds are treated as used for a qualified purpose with respect to a qualified zone academy if the issuer reasonably expects to proceed with due diligence to spend those proceeds for a qualified purpose with respect to a qualified zone academy during that period.

(4) Proceeds spent for rehabilitation, repair or equipment. (i) In general. Under section 1397E(d)(5)(A) the term qualified purpose with respect to any qualified zone academy includes rehabilitating or repairing the public school facility in which such academy is established. For this purpose, in determining whether proceeds are spent for rehabilitation, rules similar to those under section 47(c) (other than sections 47(c)(1)(B) and 47(c)(2)(B)(iv)) shall apply. Under section 1397E(d)(5)(B) the term qualified purpose also includes providing equipment for use at such academy. If proceeds of an issue are spent for a purpose described in section 1397E(d)(5)(A) or (B) with respect to a qualified zone academy, then those proceeds are treated as used for a qualified purpose with respect to the academy during any period after such expenditure that—

(A) The property financed with those proceeds is used for the purposes of the academy; and

(B) The academy maintains its status as a qualified zone academy under section 1397E(d)(4).

(ii) Retirement from service. The retirement from service of financed property due to normal wear or obsolescence does not cause the property to fail to be used for a qualified purpose with respect to a qualified zone academy.

(5) Proceeds spent to develop course materials or train teachers. Section 1397E(d)(5)(C) and (D) provides that the term qualified purpose with respect to any qualified zone academy includes developing course materials for education to be provided at such academy, and training teachers and other school personnel in such academy. If proceeds of an issue are spent for a purpose described in section 1397E(d)(5)(C) or (D) with respect to a qualified zone academy, then those proceeds are treated as used for a qualified purpose with respect to the academy during any period after such expenditure.

(6) Special rule for determining status as qualified zone academy. Section 1397E(d)(4)(A)(iv) provides that a public school (or academic program within a public school) is a qualified zone academy only if, among other requirements, the public school is located in an empowerment zone or enterprise community (as defined in section 1393), or there is a reasonable expectation (as of the issue date of the issue) that at least 35 percent of the students attending the school or participating in the program (as the case may be) will be eligible for free or reduced-cost lunches under the school lunch program established under the Richard B. Russell National School Lunch Act. For purposes of determining whether an issue complies with section 1397E(d)(4)(A)(iv)—

(i) A public school is treated as located in an empowerment zone or enterprise community for the entire term of the issue if the public school is located in an empowerment zone or enterprise community on the issue date of the issue; and

(ii) The determination of whether there is a reasonable expectation (as of the issue date of the issue) that at least 35 percent of the students attending the school or participating in the program (as the case may be) will be eligible for free or reduced-cost lunches under the school lunch program established under the Richard B. Russell National School Lunch Act is based on expectations regarding the one-year period following the issue date.

(7) Remedial actions. (i) General rule. If less than 95 percent of the proceeds of an issue are properly used (as determined under paragraph (h)(7)(ii)(D) of this section), the issue will be treated as meeting the requirements of section 1397E(d)(1)(A) if the issue met the requirements of paragraph (h)(2)(i) of this section and a remedial action is taken under paragraph (h)(7)(ii) or (iii) of this section.

(ii) Redemption or defeasance. (A) In general. A remedial action is taken under this paragraph (h)(7)(ii) if the requirements of paragraphs (h)(7)(ii)(B) and (C) of this section are met.

(B) Retirement of nonqualified bonds. (1) In general. The requirements of this paragraph (h)(7)(ii)(B) are met if—

(i) All of the nonqualified bonds of the issue (determined by applying the principles of § 1.142-2(e)) are redeemed within 90 days after the date on which the failure to properly use proceeds occurs; or

(ii) To the extent of proceeds of the issue that have been actually spent for a qualified purpose with respect to a qualified zone academy, if any nonqualified bonds of the issue are not redeemed within 90 days after the date on which the failure to properly use such proceeds occurs (the unredeemed nonqualified bonds), a defeasance escrow is established for the unredeemed nonqualified bonds within 90 days after the date on which the failure to properly use proceeds occurs.

(2) Special rule for dispositions for cash. If the failure to properly use proceeds is a disposition of financed property described in section 1397E(d)(5)(A) or (B) and the consideration for the disposition is exclusively cash, the requirements of this paragraph (h)(7)(ii)(B) are met if all of the disposition proceeds (as defined in paragraph (h)(7)(iv) of this section) are used within 90 days after the date of the disposition to redeem, or establish a defeasance escrow for, a pro rata portion of the nonqualified bonds of the issue.

(3) Definition of defeasance escrow. For purposes of this section, a defeasance escrow is an irrevocable escrow established to retire nonqualified bonds on the earliest call date after the date on which the failure to properly use proceeds occurs in an amount that is sufficient to retire nonqualified bonds on that call date. At least 90 percent of the weighted average amount in a defeasance escrow must be invested in investments (as defined in § 1.148-1(b)), except that no amount in a defeasance escrow may be invested in any investment the obligor (or any person that is a related party with respect to the obligor within the meaning of § 1.150-1(b)) of which is a user of proceeds of the bonds. All purchases or sales of an investment in a defeasance escrow must be made at the fair market value of the investment within the meaning of § 1.148-5(d)(6).

(C) Additional rules. (1) Limitation on source of funding. Proceeds of an issue of QZABs (other than unspent proceeds of the issue for which the failure to properly use proceeds occurs) must not be used to redeem or defease nonqualified bonds under paragraph (h)(7)(ii)(B) of this section.

(2) Rebate requirement. The issuer must pay to the United States, at the same time and in the same manner as rebate amounts are required to be paid under § 1.148-3 (or at such other time or in such other manner as the Commissioner may prescribe), any investment earnings on amounts in a defeasance escrow established under paragraph (h)(7)(ii)(B) of this section that are in excess of the yield on the issue of QZABs with respect to which the defeasance escrow was established. For this purpose, the first computation period begins on the date on which the defeasance escrow is established.

(3) Notice of defeasance. The issuer must provide written notice to the Commissioner, at the place designated in § 1.150-5(a), of the establishment of the defeasance escrow within 90 days of the date the defeasance escrow is established.

(D) When a failure to properly use proceeds occurs. (1) Unspent proceeds. For unspent proceeds, a failure to properly use proceeds occurs on the earlier of—

(i) The first date on which the public school (or academic program within the public school) fails to constitute a qualified zone academy;

(ii) The first date on which the issuer fails to have a reasonable expectation to proceed with due diligence to spend at least 95 percent of the proceeds of the issue for a qualified purpose with respect to a qualified zone academy; or

(iii) The last day of the period described in paragraph (h)(2)(i)(A) of this section, including any extension, if less than 95 percent of the proceeds of the issue are actually spent for a qualified purpose with respect to a qualified zone academy.

(2) Proceeds spent for rehabilitation, repair or equipment. For proceeds that have been spent for a purpose described in section 1397E(d)(5)(A) or (B) with respect to a qualified zone academy, a failure to properly use proceeds occurs on the earlier of—

(i) The first date on which the public school (or academic program within the public school) fails to constitute a qualified zone academy; and

(ii) The first date on which an action is taken that causes the issuer to fail actually to use at least 95 percent of the proceeds of the issue for a qualified purpose with respect to a qualified zone academy.

(3) Proceeds spent for course materials or training. If proceeds have been spent for a purpose described in section 1397E(d)(5)(C) or (D) with respect to a qualified zone academy, no event subsequent to such expenditure shall constitute a failure to properly use such proceeds.

(iii) Alternative use of disposition proceeds. A remedial action is taken under this paragraph (h)(7)(iii) if all of the requirements of paragraphs (h)(7)(iii)(A) through (D) of this section are met—

(A) The failure to properly use proceeds (as determined under paragraph (h)(7)(ii)(D) of this section) is a disposition of financed property described in section 1397E(d)(5)(A) or (B) and the consideration for the disposition is exclusively cash;

(B) The issuer reasonably expects as of the date of the disposition that—

(1) All of the disposition proceeds will be spent within the two-year period beginning with the date of the disposition for a qualified purpose with respect to a qualified zone academy; or

(2) To the extent not expected to be so spent, the disposition proceeds will be used within 90 days after the date of the disposition to redeem or defease bonds in a manner that meets the requirements of paragraph (h)(7)(ii) of this section;

(C) The disposition proceeds are treated as proceeds for purposes of section 1397E; and

(D) If all of the disposition proceeds are not actually used in the manner described in paragraph (h)(7)(iii)(B) of this section, the remainder of such amounts are used within 90 days after the end of the period described in paragraph (h)(7)(iii)(B)(1) of this section for a remedial action that meets the requirements of paragraph (h)(7)(ii) of this section.

(iv) Definition of disposition proceeds and allocation among multiple funding sources. For purposes of this paragraph (h)(7), disposition proceeds means disposition proceeds, as defined in § 1.141-12(c)(1), plus amounts derived from investing disposition proceeds. If property has been financed with an issue of QZABs and one or more other funding sources, any disposition proceeds from that property are allocated to the issue under the principles of § 1.141-12(c)(3).

(8) Payment of principal, interest or redemption price. (i) In general. Except as provided in paragraphs (h)(8)(ii) and (h)(8)(iii) of this section, the use of proceeds of a bond to pay principal, interest, or redemption price of the bond or another bond is not a qualified purpose within the meaning of section 1397E(d)(5).

(ii) Exception for certain eligible reimbursements of interim refinancings. The use of proceeds of a bond (the refinancing bond) to pay principal, interest or redemption price of another bond (the prior bond) is a qualified purpose within the meaning of section 1397E(d)(5) to the extent that—

(A) The prior bond was not a QZAB (and, in the case of a series of refinancings, no earlier bond in the series was a QZAB);

(B) The proceeds of the prior bond (or the original bond in the case of a series of refinancings, as applicable) were spent for a qualified purpose under section 1397E(d)(5) (the original expenditure); and

(C) The issuer makes a valid reimbursement allocation to allocate the proceeds of the refinancing bond to the payment of the original expenditure (the reimbursement allocation), which allocation satisfies the requirements for reimbursements under paragraph (h)(9) of this section. For purposes of applying the rules for reimbursement, a refinancing bond which otherwise meets the requirements of this paragraph (h)(8)(ii) is eligible for reimbursement and is not treated as a disqualified refunding under § 1.150-2(g).

(iii) Reissuance of a QZAB. For purposes of determining whether the establishing of a defeasance escrow under paragraph (h)(7)(ii)(B)(1)(ii) of this section results in an exchange under § 1.1001-1(a), the QZAB is treated as a tax-exempt bond under § 1.1001-3(e)(5)(ii)(B)(1).

(9) Reimbursement. An expenditure for a qualified purpose may be reimbursed with proceeds of a QZAB. For this purpose, rules similar to those on reimbursement of expenditures in § 1.142-4(b) and § 1.150-2 shall apply. In applying these reimbursement rules, expenditures eligible for reimbursement under § 1.150-2(d)(3) shall be deemed to mean

any expenditure for a qualified purpose under section 1397E(d)(5).

(i) Arbitrage investment restrictions. *(1) In general.* Under section 1397E(g) and this paragraph (i), and except as otherwise provided in this paragraph (i), the arbitrage investment restrictions and rebate requirements under section 148 and § 1.148-1 to § 1.148-11, inclusive, and the exceptions to those restrictions, apply broadly to gross proceeds of QZABs issued under section 1397E to the same extent and in the same manner as they apply to gross proceeds of tax-exempt state or local governmental bonds. For this purpose, references in those sections to tax-exempt bonds generally shall be deemed to refer to QZABs and, to the extent that any particular arbitrage restriction depends on whether bonds are private activity bonds under section 141, the determination of whether QZABs are private activity bonds shall be based on the general definition of private activity bonds under section 141. In applying section 148 and the regulations under that section to QZABs, the modifications set forth in paragraphs (i)(2) through (6) of this section shall apply.

(2) 5-year temporary period exception to arbitrage yield restriction. If an issue of QZABs meets the requirements of section 1397E(f)(1) and paragraph (h)(2)(i) of this section, then the proceeds of the issue of QZABs are treated as qualifying for a 5-year temporary period exception to arbitrage yield restriction under § 1.148-2(e)(2) beginning on issue date of the issue.

(3) Disregard QZAB credit in QZAB yield for arbitrage purposes. In determining the yield on an issue of QZABs for arbitrage purposes under § 1.148-4, the QZAB credit allowed under section 1397E(a) is disregarded.

(4) Non-AMT tax-exempt bond investment exception inapplicable. The exception to arbitrage yield restriction for investments of gross proceeds of tax-exempt bonds in specified tax-exempt bond investments not subject to section 148(b)(3)(B) (relating to an exception to the definition of "investment property" for specified tax-exempt bonds) and § 1.148-2(d)(2)(v) (relating to a corresponding exception to arbitrage yield limitations) is inapplicable.

(5) Application of small issuer exception to the arbitrage rebate requirement. Except as otherwise provided in paragraph (i)(6) of this section, for purposes of the small issuer exception to the arbitrage rebate requirement under section 148(f)(4)(D) and § 1.148-8, both QZABs and tax-exempt bonds (other than private activity bonds) that are actually issued or reasonably expected to be issued by the QZAB issuer (and applicable entities aggregated under section 148(f)(4)(D)) within a calendar year are taken into account in measuring the applicable size limitation.

(6) Certain defeasance escrow earnings. With respect to a defeasance escrow established in a remedial action for an issue of QZABs that meets the special rebate requirement under paragraph (h)(7)(ii)(C)(2) of this section, the QZAB issuer is treated as ineligible for the small issuer exception to arbitrage rebate under section 148(f)(4)(D) and paragraph (i)(5) of this section and compliance with that special rebate requirement is treated as satisfying applicable arbitrage investment restrictions under section 148 for that defeasance escrow.

(j) Information reporting requirement. Under section 1397E(h) and this paragraph (j), issuers of QZABs are required to submit information reporting returns to the IRS similar to the information reporting returns required to be submitted to the IRS under section 149(e) for tax-exempt state or local governmental bonds at the same time and in the same manner as those reports are required to be submitted to the IRS on such forms as shall be prescribed by the Commissioner for such purpose.

(k) and (l) [Reserved]. For further guidance, see § 1.1397E-1(k) and (l).

(m) Effective/applicability dates. *(1) In general.* Except as otherwise provided in this paragraph (m), this section applies to bonds sold on or after September 14, 2007.

(2) Special effective dates. (i) Effective dates for paragraphs (h)(2), (i), and (j) of this section in general. Paragraphs (h)(2), (i), and (j) of this section apply to bonds issued pursuant to allocations of the national qualified zone academy bond volume cap authority for calendar years after 2005 and sold on or after September 14, 2007.

(ii) Permissive retroactive application.

(A) In general. Except as otherwise provided in this paragraph (m), issuers and taxpayers may apply this section in whole, but not in part, to bonds sold before September 14, 2007.

(B) Special rule for certain provisions. For purposes of the permissive retroactive application rule in paragraph (m)(2)(ii)(A) of this section, paragraphs (h)(2), (i), and (j) of this section need not be applied to any bonds to which those provisions do not otherwise apply under the general effective date provisions for those provisions in paragraph (m)(2)(i) of this section.

(C) Definition of proceeds. Issuers and taxpayers may apply paragraphs (d) and (h) of this section, without regard to the definition of proceeds in paragraph (a)(2)(ii) of this section, to bonds sold before September 14, 2007.

(D) Bonds issued before July 1, 1999. Paragraphs (d) and (h)(9) of this section may not be applied to bonds issued before July 1, 1999.

(3) Expiration date. The applicability of this section expires on or before July 13, 2010.

T.D. 9339, 7/13/2007.

§ 1.1398-1 Treatment of passive activity losses and passive activity credits in individuals' title 11 cases.

(a) Scope. This section applies to cases under chapter 7 or chapter 11 of title 11 of the United States Code, but only if the debtor is an individual.

(b) Definitions and rules of general application. For purposes of this section—

(1) Passive activity and former passive activity have the meanings given in section 469(c) and (f)(3);

(2) The unused passive activity loss (determined as of the first day of a taxable year) is the passive activity loss (as defined in section 469(d)(1)) that is disallowed under section 469 for the previous taxable year; and

(3) The unused passive activity credit (determined as of the first day of a taxable year) is the passive activity credit (as defined in section 469(d)(2)) that is disallowed under section 469 for the previous taxable year.

(c) Estate succeeds to losses and credits upon commencement of case. The bankruptcy estate (estate) succeeds to and takes into account, beginning with its first taxable year, the debtor's unused passive activity loss and unused passive activity credit (determined as of the first day of the debtor's taxable year in which the case commences).

(d) Transfers from estate to debtor. *(1) Transfer not treated as taxable event.* If, before the termination of the estate, the estate transfers an interest in a passive activity or former passive activity to the debtor (other than by sale or exchange), the transfer is not treated as a disposition for purposes of any provision of the Internal Revenue Code assigning tax consequences to a disposition. The transfers to which this rule applies include transfers from the estate to the debtor of property that is exempt under section 522 of title 11 of the United States Code and abandonments of estate property to the debtor under section 554(a) of such title.

(2) Treatment of passive activity loss and credit. If, before the termination of the estate, the estate transfers an interest in a passive activity or former passive activity to the debtor (other than by sale or exchange)—

(i) The estate must allocate to the transferred interest, in accordance with § 1.469-1(f)(4), part or all of the estate's unused passive activity loss and unused passive activity credit (determined as of the first day of the estate's taxable year in which the transfer occurs); and

(ii) The debtor succeeds to and takes into account, beginning with the debtor's taxable year in which the transfer occurs, the unused passive activity loss and unused passive activity credit (or part thereof) allocated to the transferred interest.

(e) Debtor succeeds to loss and credit of the estate upon its termination. Upon termination of the estate, the debtor succeeds to and takes into account, beginning with the debtor's taxable year in which the termination occurs, the passive activity loss and passive activity credit disallowed under section 469 for the estate's last taxable year.

(f) Effective date. *(1) Cases commencing on or after November 9, 1992.* This section applies to cases commencing on or after November 9, 1992.

(2) Cases commencing before November 9, 1992 (i) Election required.

This section applies to a case commencing before November 9, 1992, and terminating on or after that date if the debtor and the estate jointly elect its application in the manner prescribed in paragraph (f)(2)(v) of this section (the election). The caption "ELECTION PURSUANT TO § 1.1398-1" must be placed prominently on the first page of each of the debtor's returns that is affected by the election (other than returns for taxable years that begin after the termination of the estate) and on the first page of each of the estate's returns that is affected by the election. In the case of returns that are amended under paragraph (f)(2)(iii) of this section, this requirement is satisfied by placing the caption on the amended return.

(ii) Scope of election. This election applies to the passive and former passive activities and unused passive activity losses and passive activity credits of the taxpayers making the election.

(iii) Amendment of previously filed returns. The debtor and the estate making the election must amend all returns (except to the extent they are for a year that is a closed year within the meaning of paragraph (f)(2)(iv)(D) of this section) they filed before the date of the election to the extent necessary to provide that no claim of a deduction or credit is inconsistent with the succession under this section to unused losses and credits. The Commissioner may revoke or limit the effect of the election if either the debtor or the estate fails to satisfy the requirement of this paragraph (f)(2)(iii).

(iv) Rules relating to closed years. (A) Estate succeeds to debtor's passive activity loss and credit as of the commencement date. If, by reason of an election under this paragraph (f), this section applies to a case that was commenced in a closed year, the estate, nevertheless, succeeds to and takes into account the unused passive activity loss and unused passive activity credit of the debtor (determined as of the first day of the debtor's taxable year in which the case commenced).

(B) No reduction of unused passive activity loss and credit for passive activity loss and credit not claimed for a closed year. In determining a taxpayer's carryover of a passive activity loss or credit to its taxable year following a closed year, a deduction or credit that the taxpayer failed to claim in the closed year, if attributable to an unused passive activity loss or credit to which the taxpayer succeeded under this section, is treated as a deduction or credit that was disallowed under section 469.

(C) Passive activity loss and credit to which taxpayer succeeds reflects deductions of prior holder in a closed year. A loss or credit to which a taxpayer would otherwise succeed under this section is reduced to the extent the loss or credit was allowed to its prior holder for a closed year.

(D) Closed year. For purposes of this paragraph (f)(2)(iv), a taxable year is closed to the extent the assessment of a deficiency or refund of an overpayment is prevented, on the date of the election and at all times thereafter, by any law or rule of law.

(v) Manner of making election. (A) Chapter 7 cases. In a case under chapter 7 of title 11 of the United States Code, the election is made by obtaining the written consent of the bankruptcy trustee and filing a copy of the written consent with the returns (or amended returns) of the debtor and the estate for their first taxable years ending after November 9, 1992.

(B) Chapter 11 cases. In a case under chapter 11 of title 11 of the United States Code, the election is made by incorporating the election into a bankruptcy plan that is confirmed by the bankruptcy court or into an order of such court and filing the pertinent portion of the plan or order with the returns (or amended returns) of the debtor and the estate for their first taxable years ending after November 9, 1992.

(vi) Election is binding and irrevocable. Except as provided in paragraph (f)(2)(iii) of this section, the election, once made, is binding on both the debtor and the estate and is irrevocable.

T.D. 8537, 5/12/94.

§ 1.1398-2 Treatment of section 465 losses in individuals' title 11 cases.

(a) Scope. This section applies to cases under chapter 7 or chapter 11 of title 11 of the United States Code, but only if the debtor is an individual.

(b) Definition and rules of general application. For purposes of this section—

(1) Section 465 activity means an activity to which section 465 applies; and

(2) For each section 465 activity, the unused section 465 loss from the activity (determined as of the first day of a taxable year) is the loss (as defined in section 465(d)) that is not allowed under section 465(a)(1) for the previous taxable year.

(c) Estate succeeds to losses upon commencement of case. The bankruptcy estate (the estate) succeeds to and takes into account, beginning with its first taxable year, the debtor's unused section 465 losses (determined as of the first day of the debtor's taxable year in which the case commences).

(d) Transfers from estate to debtor. *(1) Transfer not treated as taxable event.* If, before the termination of the estate, the estate transfers an interest in a section 465 activity to the debtor (other than by sale or exchange), the transfer is not treated as a disposition for purposes of any provision of the Internal Revenue Code assigning tax consequences to a disposition. The transfers to which this rule applies include transfers from the estate to the debtor of property that is exempt under section 522 of title 11 of the United States Code and abandonments of estate property to the debtor under section 554(a) of such title.

(2) Treatment of section 465 losses. If, before the termination of the estate, the estate transfers an interest in a section 465 activity to the debtor (other than by sale or exchange) the debtor succeeds to and takes into account, beginning with the debtor's taxable year in which the transfer occurs, the transferred interest's share of the estate's unused section 465 loss from the activity (determined as of the first day of the estate's taxable year in which the transfer occurs). For this purpose, the transferred interest's share of such loss is the amount, if any, by which such loss would be reduced if the transfer had occurred as of the close of the preceding taxable year of the estate and been treated as a disposition on which gain or loss is recognized.

(e) Debtor succeeds to losses of the estate upon its termination. Upon termination of the estate, the debtor succeeds to and takes into account, beginning with the debtor's taxable year in which the termination occurs, the losses not allowed under section 465 for the estate's last taxable year.

(f) Effective date. *(1) Cases commencing on or after November 9, 1992.* This section applies to cases commencing on or after November 9, 1992.

(2) Cases commencing before November 9, 1992. (i) Election required. This section applies to a case commencing before November 9, 1992, and terminating on or after that date if the debtor and the estate jointly elect its application in the manner prescribed in paragraph (f)(2)(v) of this section (the election). The caption "ELECTION PURSUANT TO § 1.1398-2" must be placed prominently on the first page of each of the debtor's returns that is affected by the election (other than returns for taxable years that begin after the termination of the estate) and on the first page of each of the estate's returns that is affected by the election. In the case of returns that are amended under paragraph (f)(2)(iii) of this section, this requirement is satisfied by placing the caption on the amended return.

(ii) Scope of election. This election applies to the section 465 activities and unused losses from section 465 activities of the taxpayers making the election.

(iii) Amendment of previously filed returns. The debtor and the estate making the election must amend all returns (except to the extent they are for a year that is a closed year within the meaning of paragraph (f)(2)(iv)(D) of this section) they filed before the date of the election to the extent necessary to provide that no claim of a deduction is inconsistent with the succession under this section to unused losses from section 465 activities. The Commissioner may revoke or limit the effect of the election if either the debtor or the estate fails to satisfy the requirement of this paragraph (f)(2)(iii).

(iv) Rules relating to closed years. (A) Estate succeeds to debtor's section 465 loss as of the commencement date. If, by reason of an election under this paragraph (f), this section applies to a case that was commenced in a closed year, the estate, nevertheless, succeeds to and takes into account the section 465 losses of the debtor (determined as of the first day of the debtor's taxable year in which the case commenced).

(B) No reduction of unused section 465 loss for loss not claimed for a closed year. In determining a taxpayer's carryover of an unused section 465 loss to its taxable year following a closed year, a deduction that the taxpayer failed to claim in the closed year, if attributable to an unused section 465 loss to which the taxpayer succeeds under this section, is treated as a deduction that was not allowed under section 465.

(C) Loss to which taxpayer succeeds reflects deductions of prior holder in a closed year. A loss to which a taxpayer would otherwise succeed under this section is reduced to the extent the loss was allowed to its prior holder for a closed year.

(D) Closed year. For purposes of this paragraph (f)(2)(iv), a taxable year is closed to the extent the assessment of a deficiency or refund of an overpayment is prevented, on the date of the election and at all times thereafter, by any law or rule of law.

(v) Manner of making election. (A) Chapter 7 cases. In a case under chapter 7 of title 11 of the United States Code, the election is made by obtaining the written consent of the bankruptcy trustee and filing a copy of the written consent with the returns (or amended returns) of the debtor and the estate for their first taxable years ending after November 9, 1992.

(B) Chapter 11 cases. In a case under chapter 11 of title 11 of the United States Code, the election is made by incorporating the election into a bankruptcy plan that is confirmed by the bankruptcy court or into an order of such court and filing the pertinent portion of the plan or order with the returns (or amended returns) of the debtor and the estate for their first taxable years ending after November 9, 1992.

(vi) Election is binding and irrevocable. Except as provided in paragraph (f)(2)(iii) of this section, the election, once made, is binding on both the debtor and the estate and is irrevocable.

T.D. 8537, 5/12/94.

§ 1.1398-3 Treatment of section 121 exclusion in individuals' title 11 cases.

(a) Scope. This section applies to cases under chapter 7 or chapter 11 of title 11 of the United States Code, but only if the debtor is an individual.

(b) Definition and rules of general application. For purposes of this section, section 121 exclusion means the exclusion of gain from the sale or exchange of a debtor's principal residence available under section 121.

(c) Estate succeeds to exclusion upon commencement of case. The bankruptcy estate succeeds to and takes into account the section 121 exclusion with respect to the property transferred into the estate.

(d) Effective date. This section is applicable for sales or exchanges on or after December 24, 2002.

T.D. 9030, 12/23/2002.

§ 301.9100-14T Individual's election to terminate taxable year when case commences (temporary).

(a) Scope. The regulations prescribed in this section provide rules for making the election under section 1398(d)(2) to terminate the taxable year of an individual taxpayer.

(b) Availability of election. This election is available to an individual taxpayer in a case commenced after March 24, 1981, under chapter 7 (relating to liquidations) or chapter 11 (relating to reorganizations) of title 11 of the United States Code. If the case is dismissed, the taxpayer cannot make the election, and an election previously made will be void. For purposes of this section, a partnership is not treated as an individual. If the taxpayer making the election is married (within the meaning of section 143), the election is available to the taxpayer's spouse, but only if the spouse is eligible to file, and does file, a joint return with the taxpayer for the taxable year ended as a result of the election.

(c) Effect of election. The election terminates the taxable year of the taxpayer (and of a spouse who joins in the election) on the day before the commencement date of the case. A new taxable year begins on the commencement date and (unless terminated earlier) ends on the date on which the taxpayer's taxable year in which the case commenced would have ended if the election had not been made.

(d) Time and manner. A taxpayer to whom the election is available makes the election by filing a return for the short taxable year ending the day before commencement of the case (the "first short taxable year") on or before the 15th day of the fourth full month following the end of that first short taxable year. The spouse of such a taxpayer makes the election by making a joint return with the taxpayer for that first short taxable year within the time prescribed in the preceding sentence. To facilitate processing, the taxpayer should write "Section 1398 Election" at the top of the return. A taxpayer may also make the election by attaching a statement of election to an application for extension of time for filing a return that satisfies the requirements under section 6081 for the first short taxable year. The application for extension must be submitted under section 6081 on or before the due date of the return for the first short taxable year. The statement must state that the taxpayer elects under section 1398(d)(2) to close his or her taxable year as of the day before commencement of the case. If the taxpayer's spouse elects to close his or her taxable year, the spouse must join in the application for extension and in the statement of election. If a joint return is not filed for the first short taxable year, the election of the spouse made with the application is void.

(e) Irrevocability of election. The election is irrevocable.

(f) Subsequent bankruptcy case of debtor's spouse. If a case under chapter 7 or chapter 11 of title 11 of the United States Code commences with respect to the spouse of a debtor to whom an election under this section was available, the spouse can make an election under this section even if the spouse's case commences in the same taxable year in which the debtor's case commences. The spouse can make the election whether or not the spouse previously joined in the debtor's election. If the spouse joined in the debtor's election, or if the debtor did not make the election, the debtor may join in the spouse's election, assuming the debtor is otherwise eligible to file a joint return with the spouse.

(g) Examples. *(1)* Assume that husband and wife are calendar-year taxpayers, that a bankruptcy case involving only the husband commences on March 1, 1982, and that a bankruptcy case involving only the wife commences on October 10, 1982.

(2) If the husband does not make an election, his taxable year would not be affected; i.e., it does not terminate on February 28. If the husband does make an election, his first short taxable year would be January 1 through February 28; his second short taxable year would begin March 1. The tax return for his first short taxable year would be due on June 15. The wife could join in the husband's election, but only if they file a joint return for the taxable year January 1 through February 28.

(3) The wife could elect to terminate her taxable year on October 9. If she did, and if the husband had not made an election or if the wife had not joined in the husband's election, she would have two taxable years in 1982—the first from January 1 through October 9, and the second from October 10 through December 31. The tax return for her first short taxable year would be due on February 15, 1983. If the husband had not made an election to terminate his taxable year on February 28, the husband could join in an election by his wife, but only if they file a joint return for the taxable year January 1 through October 9. If the husband had made an election but the wife had not joined in the husband's election, the husband could not join in an election by the wife to terminate her taxable year on October 9, since they could not file a joint return for such year.

(4) If the wife makes the election relating to her own bankruptcy case, and had joined the husband in making an election relating to his case, she would have two additional taxable years with respect to her 1982 income and deductions—the second short taxable year would be March 1 through October 9, and the third short taxable year would be October 10 through December 31. The husband could join in the wife's election if they file a joint return for the second short taxable year. If the husband joins in the wife's election, they could file joint returns for the short taxable year ending December 31, but would not be required to do so.

T.D. 7775, 5/1/81, amend T.D. 8435, 9/18/92.

§ 1.1400L(b)-1 Additional first year depreciation deduction for qualified New York Liberty Zone property.

(a) Scope. This section provides the rules for determining the 30-percent additional first year depreciation deduction allowable under section 1400L(b) for qualified New York Liberty Zone property.

(b) Definitions. For purposes of section 1400L(b) and this section, the definitions of the terms in § 1.168(k)-1(a)(2) apply and the following definitions also apply:

(1) Building and structural components have the same meanings as those terms are defined in § 1.48-1(e).

(2) New York Liberty Zone is the area located on or south of Canal Street, East Broadway (east of its intersection with Canal Street), or Grand Street (east of its intersection with East Broadway) in the Borough of Manhattan in the City of New York, New York.

(3) Nonresidential real property and residential rental property have the same meanings as those terms are defined in section 168(e)(2).

(4) Real property is a building or its structural components, or other tangible real property.

(c) Qualified New York Liberty Zone property. *(1) In general.* Qualified New York Liberty Zone property is depreciable property that meets all the following requirements in the first taxable year in which the property is subject to depreciation by the taxpayer whether or not depreciation deductions for the property are allowable—

(i) The requirements in § 1.1400L(b)-1(c)(2) (description of property);

(ii) The requirements in § 1.1400L(b)-1(c)(3) (substantial use);

(iii) The requirements in § 1.1400L(b)-1(c)(4) (original use);

(iv) The requirements in § 1.1400L(b)-1(c)(5) (acquisition of property by purchase); and

(v) The requirements in § 1.1400L(b)-1(c)(6) (placed-in-service date).

(2) Description of qualified New York Liberty Zone property. (i) In general. Depreciable property will meet the requirements of this paragraph (c)(2) if the property is—

(A) Described in § 1.168(k)-1(b)(2)(i); or

(B) Nonresidential real property or residential rental property depreciated under section 168, but only to the extent it rehabilitates real property damaged, or replaces real property destroyed or condemned, as a result of the terrorist attacks of September 11, 2001. Property is treated as replacing destroyed or condemned property if, as part of an integrated plan, the property replaces real property that is included in a continuous area that includes real property destroyed or condemned. For purposes of this section, real property is considered as destroyed or condemned only if an entire building or structure was destroyed or condemned as a result of the terrorist attacks of September 11, 2001. Otherwise, the real property is considered damaged real property. For example, if certain structural components (for example, walls, floors, and plumbing fixtures) of a building are damaged or destroyed as a result of the terrorist attacks of September 11, 2001, but the building is not destroyed or condemned, then only costs related to replacing the damaged or destroyed structural components qualify under this paragraph (c)(2)(i)(B).

(ii) Property not eligible for additional first year depreciation deduction. Depreciable property will not meet the requirements of this paragraph (c)(2) if—

(A) Section 168(k) or § 1.168(k)-1 applies to the property;

(B) The property is described in section 168(f);

(C) The property is required to be depreciated under the alternative depreciation system of section 168(g) pursuant to section 168(g)(1)(A) through (D) or other provisions of the Internal Revenue Code (for example, property described in section 263A(e)(2)(A) if the taxpayer (or any related person) has made an election under section 263A(d)(3), or property described in section 280F(b)(1));

(D) The property is included in any class of property for which the taxpayer elects not to deduct the additional first year depreciation under paragraph (e) of this section; or

(E) The property is qualified New York Liberty Zone leasehold improvement property as described in section 1400L(c)(2).

(3) Substantial use. Depreciable property will meet the requirements of this paragraph (c)(3) if substantially all of the use of the property is in the New York Liberty Zone and is in the active conduct of a trade or business by the taxpayer in New York Liberty Zone. For purposes of this paragraph (c)(3), "substantially all" means 80 percent or more.

(4) Original use. Depreciable property will meet the requirements of this paragraph (c)(4) if the original use of the property commences with the taxpayer in the New York Liberty Zone after September 10, 2001. The original use rules in § 1.168(k)-1(b)(3) apply for purposes of this paragraph (c)(4). In addition, used property will satisfy the original use requirement in this paragraph (c)(4) so long as the property has not been previously used within the New York Liberty Zone.

(5) Acquisition of property by purchase. (i) In general. Depreciable property will meet the requirements of this paragraph (c)(5) if the property is acquired by the taxpayer by purchase (as defined in section 179(d) and § 1.179-4(c)) after September 10, 2001, but only if no written binding contract for the acquisition of the property was in effect before September 11, 2001. For purposes of this paragraph (c)(5), the rules in § 1.168(k)-1(b)(4)(ii) (binding contract), the rules in § 1.168(k)-1(b)(4)(iii) (self-constructed property), and the rules in § 1.168(k)-1(b)(4)(iv) (disqualified transactions) apply. For purposes of the preceding sentence, the rules in § 1.168(k)-1(b)(4)(iii) shall be applied without regard to "and before January 1, 2005."

(ii) Exception for certain transactions. For purposes of this section, the new partnership of a transaction described in § 1.168(k)-1(f)(1)(ii) (technical termination of a partnership) or the transferee of a transaction described in § 1.168(k)-1(f)(1)(iii) (section 168(i)(7) transactions) is deemed to acquire the depreciable property by purchase.

(6) Placed-in-service date. Depreciable property will meet the requirements of this paragraph (c)(6) if the property is placed in service by the taxpayer on or before December 31, 2006. However, nonresidential real property and residential rental property described in paragraph (c)(2)(i)(B) of this section must be placed in service by the taxpayer on or before December 31, 2009. The rules in § 1.168(k)-1(b)(5)(ii) (relating to sale-leaseback and syndication transactions), the rules in § 1.168(k)-1(b)(5)(iii) (relating to a technical termination of a partnership under section 708(b)(1)(B)), and the rules in § 1.168(k)-1(b)(5)(iv) (relating to section 168(i)(7) transactions) apply for purposes of this paragraph (c)(6).

(d) Computation of depreciation deduction for qualified New York Liberty Zone property. The computation of the allowable additional first year depreciation deduction and the otherwise allowable depreciation deduction for qualified New York Liberty Zone property is made in accordance with the rules for qualified property in § 1.168(k)-1(d)(1)(i) and (2).

(e) Election not to deduct additional first year depreciation. *(1) In general.* A taxpayer may make an election not to deduct the 30-percent additional first year depreciation for any class of property that is qualified New York Liberty Zone property placed in service during the taxable year. If a taxpayer makes an election under this paragraph (e), the election applies to all qualified New York Liberty Zone property that is in the same class of property and placed in service in the same taxable year, and no additional first year depreciation deduction is allowable for the class of property.

(2) Definition of class of property. For purposes of this paragraph (e), the term class of property means—

(i) Except for the property described in paragraphs (e)(2)(ii), (iv), and (v) of this section, each class of property described in section 168(e) (for example, 5-year property);

(ii) Water utility property as defined in section 168(e)(5) and depreciated under section 168;

(iii) Computer software as defined in, and depreciated under, section 167(f)(1) and the regulations thereunder;

(iv) Nonresidential real property as defined in paragraph (b)(3) of this section and as described in paragraph (c)(2)(B) of this section; or

(v) Residential rental property as defined in paragraph (b)(3) of this section and as described in paragraph (c)(2)(B) of this section

(3) Time and manner for making election. (i) Time for making election. Except as provided in paragraph (e)(4) of this section, the election specified in paragraph (e)(1) of this section must be made by the due date (including extensions) of the Federal tax return for the taxable year in which the qualified New York Liberty Zone property is placed in service by the taxpayer.

(ii) Manner of making election. Except as provided in paragraph (e)(4) of this section, the election specified in paragraph (e)(1) of this section must be made in the manner prescribed on Form 4562, "Depreciation and Amortization," and its instructions. The election is made separately by each person owning qualified New York Liberty Zone property (for example, for each member of a consolidated group by the common parent of the group, by the partnership, or by the S corporation). If Form 4562 is revised or renumbered, any reference in this section to that form shall be treated as a reference to the revised or renumbered form.

(4) Special rules for 2000 or 2001 returns. For the election specified in paragraph (e)(1) of this section for qualified New York Liberty Zone property placed in service by the taxpayer during the taxable year that included September 11, 2001, the taxpayer should refer to the guidance provided by the Internal Revenue Service for the time and manner of making this election on the 2000 or 2001 Federal tax return for the taxable year that included September 11, 2001 (for further guidance, see sections 3.03(3) and 4 of Rev. Proc. 2002-33 (2002-1 C.B. 963), Rev. Proc. 2003-50 (2003-29 I.R.B. 119), and § 601.601(d)(2)(ii)(b) of this chapter).

(5) Failure to make election. If a taxpayer does not make the election specified in paragraph (e)(1) of this section within the time and in the manner prescribed in paragraph (e)(3) or (e)(4) of this section, the amount of depreciation allowable for that property under section 167(f)(1) or under section 168, as applicable, must be determined for the placed-in-service year and for all subsequent taxable years by taking into account the additional first year depreciation deduction. Thus, the election specified in paragraph (e)(1) of this section shall not be made by the taxpayer in any other manner (for example, the election cannot be made through a request under section 446(e) to change the taxpayer's method of accounting).

(6) Alternative minimum tax. If a taxpayer makes an election under this paragraph (e) for a class of property, the depreciation adjustments under section 56 and the regulations under section 56 apply to the property to which the election applies for purposes of computing the taxpayer's alternative minimum taxable income.

(7) Revocation of election. (i) In general. Except as provided in paragraph (e)(7)(ii) of this section, an election under this paragraph (e), once made, may be revoked only with the written consent of the Commissioner of Internal Revenue. To seek the Commissioner's consent, the taxpayer must submit a request for a letter ruling.

(ii) Automatic 6-month extension. If a taxpayer made an election under this paragraph (e) for a class of property, an automatic extension of 6 months from the due date of the taxpayer's Federal tax return (excluding extensions) for the placed-in-service year of the class of property is granted to revoke that election, provided the taxpayer timely filed the taxpayer's Federal tax return for the placed-in-service year of the class of property and, within this 6-month extension period, the taxpayer (and all taxpayers whose tax liability would be affected by the election) files an amended Federal tax return for the placed-in-service year of the class of property in a manner that is consistent with the revocation of the election.

(f) Special rules. *(1) Property placed in service and disposed of in the same taxable year.* Rules similar to those provided in § 1.168(k)-T(f)(1) apply for purposes of this paragraph (f)(1).

(2) Redetermination of basis. If the unadjusted depreciable basis (as defined in § 1.168(k)-1(a)(2)(iii)) of qualified New York Liberty Zone property is redetermined (for example, due to contingent purchase price or discharge of indebtedness) on or before December 31, 2006 (or on or before December 31, 2009, for nonresidential real property and residential rental property described in paragraph (c)(2)(i)(B) of this section), the additional first year depreciation deduction allowable for the qualified New York Liberty Zone property is redetermined in accordance with the rules provided in § 1.168(k)-1(f)(2).

(3) Section 1245 and 1250 depreciation recapture. The rules provided in § 1.168(k)-1(f)(3) apply for purposes of this paragraph (f)(3).

(4) Coordination with section 169. Rules similar to those provided in § 1.168(k)-1(f)(4) apply for purposes of this paragraph (f)(4).

(5) Like-kind exchanges and involuntary conversions. This paragraph (f)(5) applies to acquired MACRS property (as defined in § 1.168(k)-1(f)(5)(ii)(A)) or acquired computer software (as defined in § 1.168(k)-1(f)(5)(ii)(C)) that is eligible for the additional first year depreciation deduction under section 1400L(b) at the time of replacement provided the time of replacement is after September 10, 2001, and on or before December 31, 2006, or in the case of acquired MACRS property or acquired computer software that is qualified New York Liberty Zone property described in paragraph (c)(2)(i)(B) of this section, the time of replacement is after September 10, 2001, and on or before December 31, 2009. The rules and definitions similar to those provided in § 1.168(k)-1(f)(5) apply for purposes of this paragraph (f)(5).

(6) Change in use. Rules similar to those provided in § 1.168(k)-1(f)(6) apply for purposes of this paragraph (f)(6).

(7) Earnings and profits. The rule provided in § 1.168(k)-1(f)(7) applies for purposes of this paragraph (f)(7).

(8) Section 754 election. Rules similar to those provided in § 1.168(k)-1(f)(9) apply for purposes of this paragraph (f)(8).

(9) Coordination with section 47. Rules similar to those provided in § 1.168(k)-1(f)(10) apply for purposes of this paragraph (f)(9).

(10) Coordination with section 514(a)(3). Rules similar to those provided in § 1.168(k)-1(f)(11) apply for purposes of this paragraph (f)(10).

(g) Effective date. *(1) In general.* Except as provided in paragraphs (g)(2), (3), and (5) of this section, this section applies to qualified New York Liberty Zone property acquired by a taxpayer after September 10, 2001.

(2) Technical termination of a partnership or section 168(i)(7) transactions. If qualified New York Liberty Zone property is transferred in a technical termination of a partnership under section 708(b)(1)(B) or in a transaction de-

scribed in section 168(i)(7) for a taxable year ending on or before September 8, 2003, and the additional first year depreciation deduction allowable for the property was not determined in accordance with paragraph (f)(1) of this section, the Internal Revenue Service will allow any reasonable method of determining the additional first year depreciation deduction allowable for the property in the year of the transaction that is consistently applied to the property by all parties to the transaction.

(3) Like-kind exchanges and involuntary conversions. If a taxpayer did not claim on a federal tax return for a taxable year ending on or before September 8, 2003, the additional first year depreciation deduction for the remaining carryover basis of qualified New York Liberty Zone property acquired in a transaction described in section 1031(a), (b), or (c), or in a transaction to which section 1033 applies and the taxpayer did not make an election not to deduct the additional first year depreciation deduction for the class of property applicable to the remaining carryover basis, the Internal Revenue Service will treat the taxpayer's method of not claiming the additional first year depreciation deduction for the remaining carryover basis as a permissible method of accounting and will treat the amount of the additional first year depreciation deduction allowable for the remaining carryover basis as being equal to zero, provided the taxpayer does not claim the additional first year depreciation deduction for the remaining carryover basis in accordance with paragraph (g)(4)(ii) of this section.

(4) Change in method of accounting. (i) Special rules for 2000 or 2001 returns. If a taxpayer did not claim on the federal tax return for the taxable year that included September 11, 2001, any additional first year depreciation deduction for a class of property that is qualified New York Liberty Zone property and did not make an election not to deduct the additional first year depreciation deduction for that class of property, the taxpayer should refer to the guidance provided by the Internal Revenue Service for the time and manner of claiming the additional first year depreciation deduction for the class of property (for further guidance, see section 4 of Rev. Proc. 2002-33 (2002-1 C.B. 963), Rev. Proc. 2003-50 (2003-29 I.R.B. 119), and § 601.601(d)(2)(ii)(b) of this chapter).

(ii) Like-kind exchanges and involuntary conversions. If a taxpayer did not claim on a federal tax return for any taxable year ending on or before September 8, 2003, the additional first year depreciation deduction allowable for the remaining carryover basis of qualified New York Liberty Zone property acquired in a transaction described in section 1031(a), (b), or (c), or in a transaction to which section 1033 applies and the taxpayer did not make an election not to deduct the additional first year depreciation deduction for the class of property applicable to the remaining carryover basis, the taxpayer may claim the additional first year depreciation deduction allowable for the remaining carryover basis in accordance with paragraph (f)(5) of this section either—

(A) By filing an amended return (or a qualified amended return, if applicable (for further guidance, see Rev. Proc. 94-69 (1994-2 C.B. 804) and § 601.601(d)(2)(ii)(b) of this chapter)) on or before December 31, 2003, for the year of replacement and any affected subsequent taxable year; or,

(B) By following the applicable administrative procedures issued under § 1.446-1(e)(3)(ii) for obtaining the Commissioner's automatic consent to a change in method of accounting (for further guidance, see Rev. Proc. 2002-9 (2002-1 C.B. 327) and § 601.601(d)(2)(ii)(b) of this chapter).

(iii) Revisions made in paragraphs (b)(4) and (c)(2)(ii) of this section. If a taxpayer did not claim on a Federal tax return for a taxable year ending on or after September 11, 2001, and on or before September 1, 2006, any additional first year depreciation deduction for qualified New York Liberty Zone property because of the application of § 1.1400L(b)-1T(b)(4) or because the taxpayer made an election under § 1.168(k)-1T(e)(1) for a class of property that included such qualified New York Liberty Zone property, the taxpayer may claim the additional first year depreciation deduction for such qualified New York Liberty Zone property under this section in accordance with the applicable administrative procedures issued under § 1.446-1(e)(3)(ii) for obtaining the Commissioner's consent to a change in method of accounting. Section 481(a) applies to a request to claim the additional first year depreciation deduction for such qualified New York Liberty Zone property under this paragraph (g)(4)(iii).

(5) Revision to paragraphs (b)(4) and (b)(6). The addition of "(or, in the case of multiple units of property subject to the same lease, within three months after the date the final unit is placed in service, so long as the period between the time the first unit is placed in service and the time the last unit is placed in service does not exceed 12 months)" to § 1.168(k)-1(b)(3)(iii)(B) and § 1.168(k)-1(b)(5)(ii)(B) applies to property sold after June 4, 2004, for purposes of paragraphs (b)(4) and (b)(6) of this section.

(6) Rehabilitation credit. If a taxpayer did not claim on a Federal tax return for a taxable year ending on or before September 1, 2006, the rehabilitation credit provided by section 47(a) with respect to the portion of the basis of a qualified rehabilitated building that is attributable to qualified rehabilitation expenditures and the qualified rehabilitation expenditures are qualified New York Liberty Zone property, and the taxpayer did not make the election specified in paragraph (e)(1) of this section for the class of property that includes the qualified rehabilitation expenditures, the taxpayer may claim the rehabilitation credit for the remaining rehabilitated basis (as defined in § 1.168(k)-1(f)(10)(i)(B)) of the qualified rehabilitated building that is attributable to the qualified rehabilitation expenditures (assuming all the requirements of section 47 are met) in accordance with paragraph (f)(9) of this section by filing an amended Federal tax return for the taxable year for which the rehabilitation credit is to be claimed. The amended Federal tax return must include the adjustment to the tax liability for the rehabilitation credit and any collateral adjustments to taxable income or to the tax liability (for example, the amount of depreciation allowed or allowable in that taxable year for the qualified rehabilitated building). Such adjustments must also be made on amended Federal tax returns for any affected succeeding taxable years.

T.D. 9091, 9/5/2003, amend T.D. 9283, 8/28/2006.

§ 1.1401-1 Tax on self-employment income.

(a) There is imposed, in addition to other taxes, a tax upon the self-employment income of every individual at the rates prescribed in section 1401(a) (old age, survivors, and disability insurance) and (b) (hospital insurance). (See subparagraphs (1) and (2) of paragraph (b) of this section.) This tax shall be levied, assessed, and collected as part of the income tax imposed by subtitle A of the Code and, except as otherwise expressly provided, will be included with the tax imposed by section 1 or 3 in computing any deficiency or overpayment and in computing the interest and additions to any deficiency, overpayment, or tax. Since the tax on self-employment income is part of the income tax, it is subject to the jurisdiction of the Tax Court of the United States to the same extent and in the same manner as the other taxes under subtitle A of the Code. Furthermore, with respect to taxable years beginning after December 31, 1966, this tax must be taken into account in computing any estimate of the taxes required to be declared under section 6015.

(b) The rates of tax on self-employment income are as follows:

(1) For old-age, survivors, and disability insurance:

Taxable Year	Percent
Beginning before January 1, 1957	3
Beginning after December 31, 1956 and before January 1, 1959	3.375
Beginning after December 31, 1958 and before January 1, 1960	3.75
Beginning after December 31, 1959 and before January 1, 1962	4.5
Beginning after December 31, 1961 and before January 1, 1963	4.7
Beginning after December 31, 1962 and before January 1, 1966	5.4
Beginning after December 31, 1965 and before January 1, 1967	5.8
Beginning after December 31, 1966 and before January 1, 1968	5.9
Beginning after December 31, 1967 and before January 1, 1969	5.8
Beginning after December 31, 1968 and before January 1, 1971	6.3
Beginning after December 31, 1970 and before January 1, 1973	6.9
Beginning after December 31, 1972	7.0

(2) For hospital insurance:

Taxable Year	Percent
Beginning after December 31, 1965 and before January 1, 1967	0.35
Beginning after December 31, 1966 and before January 1, 1968	.50
Beginning after December 31, 1967 and before January 1, 1973	.60
Beginning after December 31, 1972 and before January 1, 1974	1.0
Beginning after December 31, 1973 and before January 1, 1978	.90
Beginning after December 31, 1977 and before January 1, 1981	1.10
Beginning after December 31, 1980 and before January 1, 1986	1.35
Beginning after December 31, 1985	1.50

(c) In general, self-employment income consists of the net earnings derived by an individual (other than a nonresident alien) from a trade or business carried on by him as sole proprietor or by a partnership of which he is a member, including the net earnings of certain employees as set forth in § 1.1402(c)-3, and of crew leaders, as defined in section 3121(o) (see such section and the regulations thereunder in Part 31 of this chapter (Employment Tax Regulations)). See, however, the exclusions, exceptions, and limitations set forth in §§ 1.1402(a)-1 through 1.1402(h)-1.

T.D. 6196, 8/13/56, amend T.D. 6691, 12/2/63, T.D. 6993, 1/17/69, T.D. 7333, 12/19/74.

§ 1.1402(a)-1 Definition of net earnings from self-employment.

Caution: The Treasury has not yet amended Reg § 1.1402(a)-1 to reflect changes made by P.L. 108-357, P.L. 101-508, P.L. 95-216.

(a) Subject to the special rules set forth in §§ 1.1402(a)-3 to 1.1402(a)-17, inclusive, and to the exclusions set forth in §§ 1.1402(c)-2 to 1.1402(c)-7, inclusive, the term "net earnings from self-employment" means—

(1) The gross income derived by an individual from any trade or business carried on by such individual, less the deductions allowed by chapter 1 of the Code which are attributable to such trade or business, plus

(2) His distributive share (whether or not distributed), as determined under section 704, of the income (or minus the loss), described in section 702(a)(9) and as computed under section 703, from any trade or business carried on by any partnership of which he is a member.

(b) Gross income derived by an individual from a trade or business includes payments received by him from a partnership of which he is a member for services rendered to the partnership or for the use of capital by the partnership, to the extent the payments are determined without regard to the income of the partnership. However, such payments received from a partnership not engaged in a trade or business within the meaning of section 1402(c) and § 1.1402(c)-1 do not constitute gross income derived by an individual from a trade or business. See section 707(c) and the regulations thereunder, relating to guaranteed payments to a member of a partnership for services or the use of capital. See also section 706(a) and the regulations thereunder, relating to the taxable year of the partner in which such guaranteed payments are to be included in computing taxable income.

(c) Gross income derived by an individual from a trade or business includes gross income received (in the case of an individual reporting income on the cash receipts and disbursements method) or accrued (in the case of an individual reporting income on the accrual method) in the taxable year from a trade or business even though such income may be attributable in whole or in part to services rendered or other acts performed in a prior taxable year as to which the individual was not subject to the tax on self-employment income.

T.D. 6196, 8/13/56, amend T.D. 6691, 12/2/63, T.D. 7333, 12/19/74.

§ 1.1402(a)-2 Computation of net earnings from self-employment.

Caution: The Treasury has not yet amended Reg § 1.1402(a)-2 to reflect changes made by P.L. 98-21.

(a) General rule. In general, the gross income and deductions of an individual attributable to a trade or business (including a trade or business conducted by an employee referred to in paragraphs (b), (c), (d), or (e) of § 1.1402(c)-3), for the purpose of ascertaining his net earnings from self-employment, are to be determined by reference to the provisions of law and regulations applicable with respect to the taxes imposed by sections 1 and 3. Thus, if an individual uses the accrual method of accounting in computing taxable income from a trade or business for the purpose of the tax imposed by section 1 or 3, he must use the same method in determining net earnings from self-employment. Likewise, if a taxpayer engaged in a trade or business of selling property on the installment plan elects, under the provisions of section 453, to use the installment method in computing income for purposes of the tax under section 1 or 3, he must use the same method in determining net earnings from self-employment. Income which is excludable from gross income under any provision of subtitle A of the Internal Revenue Code is not taken into account in determining net earnings from self-employment except as otherwise provided in § 1.1402(a)-9, relating to certain residents of Puerto Rico, in § 1.1402(a)-11, relating to ministers or members of religious orders, and in § 1.1402(a)-12, relating to the term "possession of the United States" as used for purposes of the tax on self-employment income. Thus, in the case of a citizen of the United States conducting, in a foreign country, a trade or business in which both personal services and capital are material income-producing factors, any part of the income as earned income therefrom which is excluded from gross income as earned income under the provisions of section 911 and the regulations thereunder is not taken into account in determining net earnings from self-employment.

(b) Trade or business carried on. The trade or business must be carried on by the individual, either personally or through agents or employees. Accordingly, income derived from a trade or business carried on by an estate or trust is not included in determining the net earnings from self-employment of the individual beneficiaries of such estate or trust.

(c) Aggregate net earnings. Where an individual is engaged in more than one trade or business within the meaning of section 1402(c) and § 1.1402(c)-1, his net earnings from self-employment consist of the aggregate of the net income and losses (computed subject to the special rules provided in §§ 1.1402(a)-1 to 1.1402(a)-17, inclusive) of all such trades or businesses carried on by him. Thus, a loss sustained in one trade or business carried on by an individual will operate to offset the income derived by him from another trade or business.

(d) Partnerships. The net earnings from self-employment of an individual include, in addition to the earnings from a trade or business carried on by him, his distributive share of the income or loss, described in section 702(a)(9), from any trade or business carried on by each partnership of which he is a member. An individual's distributive share of such income or loss of a partnership shall be determined as provided in section 704, subject to the special rules set forth in section 1402(a) and in §§ 1.1402(a)-1 to 1.1402(a)-17, inclusive, and to the exclusions provided in section 1402(c) and §§ 1.1402(c)-2 to 1.1402(c)-7, inclusive. For provisions relating to the computation of the taxable income of a partnership, see section 703.

(e) Different taxable years. If the taxable year of a partner differs from that of the partnership, the partner shall include, in computing net earnings from self-employment, his distributive share of the income or loss, described in section 702(a)(9), of the partnership for its taxable year ending with or within the taxable year of the partner. For the special rule in case of the termination of a partner's taxable year as result of death, see §§ 1.1402(f) and 1.1402(f)-1.

(f) Meaning of partnerships. For the purpose of determining net earnings from self-employment, a partnership is one which is recognized as such for income tax purposes. For income tax purposes, the term "partnership" includes not only a partnership as known at common law, but, also a syndicate, group, pool, joint venture, or other unincorporated organization which carries on any trade or business, financial operation, or venture, and which is not, within the meaning of the Code, a trust, estate, or a corporation. An organization described in the preceding sentence shall be treated as a partnership for purposes of the tax on self-employment income even though such organization has elected, pursuant to section 1361 and the regulations thereunder, to be taxed as a domestic corporation.

(g) Nature of partnership interest. The net earnings from self-employment of a partner include his distributive share of the income or loss, described in section 702(a)(9), of the partnership of which he is a member, irrespective of the nature of his membership. Thus, in determining his net earnings from self-employment, a limited or inactive partner includes his distributive share of such partnership income or loss. In the case of a partner who is a member of a partnership with respect to which an election has been made pursuant to section 1361 and the regulations thereunder to be taxed as a domestic corporation, net earnings from self-employment include his distributive share of the income or loss, described in section 702(a)(9), from the trade or business carried on by the partnership computed without regard to the fact that the partnership has elected to be taxed as a domestic corporation.

(h) Proprietorship taxed as domestic corporation. A proprietor of an unincorporated business enterprise with respect to which an election has been made pursuant to section 1361 and the regulations thereunder to be taxed as a domestic corporation shall compute his net earnings from self-employment without regard to the fact that such election has been made.

T.D. 6691, 12/2/63, amend T.D. 7333, 12/19/74.

PAR. 2. Section 1.1402(a)-2 is amended by:

1. Revising the first sentence of paragraph (d).

2. Removing the reference "section 702(a)(9)" in the first sentence of paragraph (e) and adding "section 702(a)(8)" in its place.

3. Revising the last sentence of paragraph (f).

4. Revising paragraphs (g) and (h).

5. Adding new paragraphs (i) and (j).

The revisions and additions read as follows:

Proposed § 1.1402(a)-2 Computation of net earnings from self-employment. [*For Preamble, see ¶ 151,791*]

Caution: The Treasury has not yet amended Reg § 1.1402(a)-2 to reflect changes made by P.L. 105-34.

* * * * *

(d) * * * Except as otherwise provided in section 1402(a) and paragraph (g) of this section, an individual's net earnings from self-employment include the individual's distributive share (whether or not distributed) of income or loss described in section 702(a)(8) from any trade or business carried on by each partnership of which the individual is a partner. * * *

* * * * *

(f) * * * For rules governing the classification of an organization as a partnership or otherwise, see §§ 301.7701-1, 301.7701-2, and 301.7701-3 of this chapter.

(g) Distributive share of limited partner. An individual's net earnings from self-employment do not include the individual's distributive share of income or loss as a limited partner described in paragraph (h) of this section. However, guaranteed payments described in section 707(c) made to the individual for services actually rendered to or on behalf of the partnership engaged in a trade or business are included in the individual's net earnings from self-employment.

(h) Definition of limited partner. *(1) In general.* Solely for purposes of section 1402(a)(13) and paragraph (g) of this section, an individual is considered to be a limited partner to the extent provided in paragraphs (h)(2), (h)(3), (h)(4), and (h)(5) of this section.

(2) Limited partner. An individual is treated as a limited partner under this paragraph (h)(2) unless the individual—

(i) Has personal liability (as defined in § 301.7701-3(b)(2)(ii) of this chapter for the debts of or claims against the partnership by reason of being a partner;

(ii) Has authority (under the law of the jurisdiction in which the partnership is formed) to contract on behalf of the partnership; or

(iii) Participates in the partnership's trade or business for more than 500 hours during the partnership's taxable year.

(3) Exception for holders of more than one class of interest. An individual holding more than one class of interest in the partnership who is not treated as a limited partner under paragraph (h)(2) of this section is treated as a limited partner under this paragraph (h)(3) with respect to a specific class of partnership interest held by such individual if, immediately after the individual acquires that class of interest—

(i) Limited partners within the meaning of paragraph (h)(2) of this section own a substantial, continuing interest in that specific class of partnership interest; and,

(ii) The individual's rights and obligations with respect to that specific class of interest are identical to the rights and obligations of that specific class of partnership interest held by the limited partners described in paragraph (h)(3)(i) of this section.

(4) Exception for holders of only one class of interest. An individual who is not treated as a limited partner under paragraph (h)(2) of this section solely because that individual participates in the partnership's trade or business for more than 500 hours during the partnership's taxable year is treated as a limited partner under this paragraph (h)(4) with respect to the individual's partnership interest if, immediately after the individual acquires that interest—

(i) Limited partners within the meaning of paragraph (h)(2) of this section own a substantial, continuing interest in that specific class of partnership interest; and

(ii) The individual's rights and obligations with respect to the specific class of interest are identical to the rights and obligations of the specific class of partnership interest held by the limited partners described in paragraph (h)(4)(i) of this section.

(5) Exception for service partners in service partnerships. An individual who is a service partner in a service partnership may not be a limited partner under paragraphs (h)(2), (h)(3), or (h)(4) of this section.

(6) Additional definitions. Solely for purposes of this paragraph (h)—

(i) A *class of interest* is an interest that grants the holder specific rights and obligations. If a holder's rights and obligations from an interest are different from another holder's rights and obligations, each holder's interest belongs to a separate class of interest. An individual may hold more than one class of interest in the same partnership provided that each class grants the individual different rights or obligations. The existence of a guaranteed payment described in section 707(c) made to an individual for services rendered to or on behalf of a partnership, however, is not a factor in determining the rights and obligations of a class of interest.

(ii) A *service partner* is a partner who provides services to or on behalf of the service partnership's trade or business. A partner is not considered to be a service partner if that partner only provides a de minimis amount of services to or on behalf of the partnership.

(iii) A *service partnership* is a partnership substantially all the activities of which involve the performance of services in the fields of health, law, engineering, architecture, accounting, actuarial science, or consulting.

(iv) A *substantial interest in a class of interest* is determined based on all of the relevant facts and circumstances. In all cases, however, ownership of 20 percent or more of a specific class of interest is considered substantial.

(i) Example. The following example illustrates the principles of paragraphs (g) and (h) of this section:

Example. (i) A, B, and C form LLC, a limited liability company, under the laws of State to engage in a business that is not a service partnership described in paragraph (h)(6)(iii) of this section. LLC, classified as a partnership for federal tax purposes, allocates all items of income, deduction, and credit of LLC to A, B, and C in proportion to their ownership of LLC. A and C each contribute $1xfor one LLC unit. B contributes $2x for two LLC units. Each LLC unit entitles its holder to receive 25 percent of LLC's tax items, including profits. A does not perform services for LLC; however, each year B receives a guaranteed payment of $6xfor 600 hours of services rendered to LLC and C receives a guaranteed payment of $10x for 1000 hours of services rendered to LLC. C also is elected LLC's manager. Under State's law, C has the authority to contract on behalf of LLC.

(ii) Application of general rule of paragraph (h)(2) of this section. A is treated as a limited partner in LLC under paragraph (h)(2) of this section because A is not liable personally for debts of or claims against LLC, A does not have authority to contract for LLC under State's law, and A does not participate in LLC's trade or business for more than 500 hours during the taxable year. Therefore, A's distributive share attributable to A's LLC unit is excluded from A's net earnings from self-employment under section 1402(a)(13).

(iii) Distributive share not included in net earnings from self-employment under paragraph (h)(4) of this section. B's guaranteed payment of $6xis included in B's net earnings from self-employment under section 1402(a)(13). B is not treated as a limited partner under paragraph (h)(2) of this section because, although B is not liable for debts of or claims against LLC and B does not have authority to contract for LLC under State's law, B does participates in LLC's trade or business for more than 500 hours during the taxable year. Further, B is not treated as a limited partner under paragraph (h)(3) of this section because B does not hold more than one class of interest in LLC. However, B is treated as a limited partner under paragraph (h)(4) of this section because B is not treated as a limited partner under paragraph (h)(2) of this section solely because B participated in LLC's business for more than 500 hours and because A is a limited partner under paragraph (h)(2) of this section who owns a substantial interest with rights and obligations that are identical to B's rights and obligations. In this example, B's distributive share is deemed to be a return on B's investment in LLC and not remuneration for B's service to LLC. Thus, B's distributive share attributable to B's two LLC units is not net earnings from self-employment under section 1402(a)(13).

(iv) Distributive share included in net earnings from self-employment. C's guaranteed payment of $10xis included in C's net earnings from self-employment under section 1402(a). In addition, C's distributive share attributable to C's LLC unit also is net earnings from self-employment under section 1402(a) because C is not a limited partner under paragraphs (h)(2), (h)(3), or (h)(4) of this section. C is not treated as a limited partner under paragraph (h)(2) of this section because C has the authority under State's law to enter into a binding contract on behalf of LLC and because C participates in LLC's trade or business for more than 500 hours during the taxable year. Further, C is not treated as a limited partner under paragraph (h)(3) of this section because C does not hold more than one class of interest in LLC. Finally, C is not treated as a limited partner under paragraph (h)(4) of this section because C has the power to bind LLC. Thus, C's guaranteed payment and distributive share both are included in C's net earnings from self-employment under section 1402(a).

(j) Effective date. Paragraphs (d), (e), (f), (g), (h), and (i) are applicable beginning with the individual's first taxable year beginning on or after the date this section is published as a final regulation in the Federal Register.

§ 1.1402(a)-3 Special rules for computing net earnings from self-employment.

For the purpose of computing net earnings from self-employment, the gross income derived by an individual from a trade or business carried on by him, the allowable deductions attributable to such trade or business, and the individual's distributive share of the income or loss, described in section 702(a)(9), from any trade or business carried on by a partnership of which he is a member shall be computed in accordance with the special rules set forth in §§ 1.1402(a)-4 to 1.1402(a)-17, inclusive.

T.D. 6691, 12/2/63, amend T.D. 7333, 12/19/74.

§ 1.1402(a)-4 Rentals from real estate.

(a) In general. Rentals from real estate and from personal property leased with the real estate (including such rentals paid in crop shares) and the deductions attributable thereto, unless such rentals are received by an individual in the course of a trade or business as a real-estate dealer, are excluded, whether or not an individual is engaged in the trade or business of a real-estate dealer is determined by the application of the principles followed in respect of the taxes imposed by sections 1 and 3. In general, an individual who is engaged in the business of selling real estate to customers with a view to the gains and profits that may be derived from such sales is a real-estate dealer. On the other hand, an individual who merely holds real estate for investment or speculation and receives rentals therefrom is not considered a real-estate dealer. Where a real-estate dealer holds real estate for investment or speculation in addition to real estate held for sale to customers in the ordinary course of his trade or business as a real-estate dealer, only the rentals from the real estate held for sale to customers in the ordinary course of his trade or business as a real-estate dealer, and the deductions attributable thereto, are included in determining net earnings from self-employment; the rentals from the real estate held for investment or speculation, and the deductions attributable thereto, are excluded. Rentals paid in crop shares include income derived by an owner or lessee of land under an agreement entered into with another person pursuant to which such other person undertakes to produce a crop or livestock on such land and pursuant to which (1) the crop or livestock, or the proceeds thereof, are to be divided between such owner or lessee and such other person, and (2) the share of the owner or lessee depends on the amount of the crop or livestock produced. See, however, paragraph (b) of this section.

(b) Special rule for "includible farm rental income". *(1) In general.* Notwithstanding the rules set forth in paragraph (a) of this section, there shall be included in determining net earnings from self-employment for taxable years ending after 1955 any income derived by an owner or tenant of land, if the following requirements are met with respect to such income:

(i) The income is derived under an arrangement between the owner or tenant of land and another person which provides that such other person shall produce agricultural or horticultural commodities on such land, and that there shall be material participation by the owner or tenant in the production or the management of the production of such agricultural or horticultural commodities; and

(ii) There is material participation by the owner or tenant with respect to any such agricultural or horticultural commodity.

Income so derived shall be referred to in this section as "includible farm rental income".

(2) Requirement that income be derived under an arrangement. In order for rental income received by an owner or tenant of land to be treated as includible farm rental income, such income must be derived pursuant to a share-farming or other rental arrangement which contemplates material participation by the owner or tenant in the production or management of production of agricultural or horticultural commodities.

(3) Nature of arrangement. (i) The arrangement between the owner or tenant and the person referred to in subparagraph (1) of this paragraph may be either oral or written. The arrangement must impose upon such other person the obligation to produce one or more agricultural or horticultural commodities (including livestock, bees, poultry, and fur-bearing animals and wildlife) on the land of the owner or tenant. In addition, it must be within the contemplation of the parties that the owner or tenant will participate in the production or the management of the production of the agricultural or horticultural commodities required to be produced by the other person under such arrangement to an extent which is material with respect either to the production or to the management of production of such commodities or is material with respect to the production and management of production when the total required participation in connection with both is considered.

(ii) The term "production", wherever used in this paragraph, refers to the physical work performed and the expenses incurred in producing a commodity. It includes such activities as the actual work of planting, cultivating, and harvesting crops, and the furnishing of machinery, implements, seed, and livestock. An arrangement will be treated as contemplating that the owner or tenant will materially participate in the "production" of the commodities required to be produced by the other person under the arrangement if under the arrangement it is understood that the owner or tenant is to engage to a material degree in the physical work related to the production of such commodities. The mere undertaking to furnish machinery, implements, and livestock and to incur expenses is not, in and of itself, sufficient. Such factors may be significant, however, in cases where the degree of physical work intended of the owner or tenant is not material. For example, if under the arrangement it is understood that the owner or tenant is to engage periodically in physical work to a degree which is not material in and of itself and, in addition, to furnish a substantial portion of the machinery, implements, and livestock to be used in the production of the commodities or to furnish or advance funds or assume financial responsibility for a substantial part of the expense involved in the production of the commodities, the arrangement will be treated as contemplating material participation of the owner or tenant in the production of such commodities.

(iii) The term "management of the production", wherever used in this paragraph, refers to services performed in making managerial decisions relating to the production, such as when to plant, cultivate, dust, spray, or harvest the crop, and includes advising and consulting, making inspections, and making decisions as to matters such as rotation of crops, the type of crops to be grown, the type of livestock to be raised, and the type of machinery and implements to be furnished. An arrangement will be treated as contemplating that the owner or tenant is to participate materially in the "management of the production" of the commodities required to be produced by the other person under the arrangement if the owner or tenant is to engage to a material degree in the management decisions related to the production of such commodities. The services which are considered of particular importance in making such management decisions are those services performed in making inspections of the production activities and in advising and consulting with such person as to the production of the commodities. Thus, if under the arrangement it is understood that the owner or tenant is to advise or consult periodically with the other person as to the production of the commodities required to be produced by such person under the arrangement and to inspect periodically the production activities on the land, a strong inference will be drawn that the arrangement contemplates participation by the owner or tenant in the management of the production of such commodities. The mere undertaking to select the crops or livestock to be produced or the type of machinery and implements to be furnished or to make decisions as to the rotation of crops generally is not, in and of itself, sufficient. Such factors may be significant, however, in making the overall determination of whether the arrangement contemplates that the owner or tenant is to participate materially in the management of the production of the commodities. Thus, if in addition to the understanding that the owner or tenant is to advise or consult periodically with the other person as to the production of the commodities and to inspect periodically the production activities on the land, it is also understood that the owner is to select the type of crops and livestock to be produced and the type of machinery and implements to be furnished and to make decisions as to the rotation of crops, the arrangement will be treated as contemplating material participation of the owner or tenant in the management of production of such commodities.

(4) Actual participation. In order for the rental income received by the owner or tenant of land to be treated as includible farm rental income, not only must it be derived pursuant to the arrangement described in subparagraph (1) of this paragraph, but also the owner or tenant must actually participate to a material degree in the production or in the management of the production of any of the commodities required to be produced under the arrangement, or he must actually participate in both the production and the management of the production to an extent that his participation in the one when combined with his participation in the other will be considered participation to a material degree. If the owner or tenant shows that he periodically advises or consults with the other person, who under the arrangement produces the agricultural or horticultural commodities, as to the production of any of these commodities and also shows that he periodically inspects the production activities on the land, he will have presented strong evidence of the existence of the degree of participation contemplated by section 1402(a)(1). If, in addition to the foregoing, the owner or tenant shows that he furnishes a substantial portion of the machinery, implements, and livestock used in the production of the commodities or that he furnishes or advances funds, or assumes financial responsibility, for a substantial part of the expense involved in the production of the commodities, he will have established the existence of the degree of participation contemplated by section 1402(a)(1) and this paragraph.

(5) Employees or agents. An agreement entered into by an employee or agent of an owner or tenant and another person is considered to be an arrangement entered into by the owner or tenant for purposes of satisfying the requirement set forth in paragraph (b)(2) that the income must be derived under an arrangement between the owner or tenant and another person. For purposes of determining whether the arrangement satisfies the requirement set forth in paragraph (b)(3) that the parties contemplate that the owner or tenant will materially participate in the production or management of production of a commodity, services which will be performed by an employee or agent of the owner or tenant are not considered to be services which the arrangement contemplates will be performed by the owner or tenant. Services actually performed by such employee or agent are not considered services performed by the owner or tenant in determining the extent to which the owner or tenant has participated in the production or management of production of a commodity. For taxable years beginning before January 1, 1974, contemplated or actual services of an agent or an employee of the owner or tenant are deemed to be contemplated or actual services of the owner or tenant under paragraphs (b)(3) and (b)(4) of this section.

(6) Examples. Application of the rules prescribed in this paragraph may be illustrated by the following examples:

Example (1). After the death of her husband, Mrs. A rents her farm, together with its machinery and equipment, to B for one-half of the proceeds from the commodities produced on such farm by B. It is agreed that B will live in the tenant house on the farm and be responsible for the over-all operation of the farm, such as planting, cultivating, and harvesting the field crops, caring for the orchard and harvesting the fruit and caring for the livestock and poultry. It also is agreed that Mrs. A will continue to live in the farm residence and help B operate the farm. Under the agreement it is contemplated that Mrs. A will regularly operate and clean the cream separator and feed the poultry flock and collect the eggs. When possible she will assist B in such work as spraying the fruit trees, penning livestock, culling the poultry, and controlling weeds. She will also assist in preparing the meals when B engages seasonal workers. The agreement between Mrs. A and B clearly provides that she will materially participate in the over-all production operations to be conducted on her farm by B. In actual practice, Mrs. A performs such regular and intermittent services. The regularly performed services are material to the production of an agricultural commodity, and the intermittent services performed are material to the production operations to which they relate. The furnishing of a substantial portion of the farm machinery and equipment also adds support to a conclusion that Mrs. A has materially participated. Accordingly, the rental income Mrs. A receives from her farm should be included in net earnings from self-employment.

Example (2). D agrees to produce a crop on C's cotton farm under an arrangement providing that C and D will each receive one-half of the proceeds from such production. C agrees to furnish all the necessary equipment, and it is understood that he is to advise D when to plant the cotton and when it needs to be chopped, plowed, sprayed, and picked. It is also understood that during the growing season C is to inspect the crop every few days to determine whether D is properly taking care of the crop. Under the arrangement, D is required to furnish all labor needed to grow and harvest the crop. C, in fact, renders such advice, makes such inspections, and furnishes such equipment. C's contemplated participation in management decisions is considered material with respect to the management of the cotton production operation. C's actual participation pursuant to the arrangement is also considered to be material with respect to the management of the production of cotton. Accordingly, the income C receives from his cotton farm is to be included in computing his net earnings from self-employment.

Example (3). E owns a grain farm and turns its operation over to his son, F. By the oral rental arrangement between E and F, the latter agrees to produce crops of grain on the farm, and E agrees that he will be available for consultation and advice and will inspect and help to harvest the crops. E furnishes most of the equipment, including a tractor, a combine, plows, wagons, drills, and harrows; he continues to live on the farm and does some of the work such as repairing barns and farm machinery, going to town for supplies, cutting weeds, etc.; he regularly inspects the crops during the growing season; and he helps F to harvest the crops. Although the final decisions are made by F, he frequently consults with his father regarding the production of the crops. An evaluation of all of E's actual activities indicates that they are sufficiently substantial and regular to support a conclusion that he is materially participating in the crop production operations and the management thereof. If it can be shown that the degree of E's actual participation was contemplated by the arrangement, E's income from the grain farm will be included in computing net earnings from self-employment.

Example (4). G owns a fully-equipped farm which he rents to H under an arrangement which contemplates that G shall materially participate in the management of the production of crops raised on the farm pursuant to the arrangement. G lives in town about 5 miles from the farm. About twice a month he visits the farm and looks over the buildings and equipment. G may occasionally, in an emergency, discuss with H some phase of a crop production activity. In effect, H has complete charge of the management of farming operations regardless of the understanding between him and G. Although G pays one-half of the cost of the seed and fertilizer and is charged for the cost of materials purchased by H to make all necessary repairs, G's activities do not constitute material participation in the crop production activities. Accordingly, G's income from the crops is not included in computing net earnings from self-employment.

Example (5). I owned a farm several miles from the town in which he lived. He rented the farm to J under an arrangement which contemplated I's material participation in the management of production of wheat. I furnished one-half of the seed and fertilizer and all the farm equipment and livestock. He employed K to perform all the services in advising, consulting, and inspecting contemplated by the arrangement. I is not materially participating in the management of production of wheat by J. The work done by I's employee, K, is not attributable to I in determining the extent of I's participation. I's rental income from the arrangement is, therefore, not to be included in computing his net earnings from self-employment. For taxable years beginning before January 1, 1974, however, I's rental income would be includible in those earnings.

Example (6). L, a calendar-year taxpayer, appointed M as his agent to rent his fully equipped farm for 1974. M entered into a rental arrangement with N under which M was to direct the planting of crops, inspect them weekly during the growing season, and consult with N on any problems that might arise in connection with irrigation, etc., while N furnished all the labor needed to grow and harvest the crops. M did in fact fulfill its responsibilities under the arrangement. Although the arrangement entered into by M and N is considered to have been made by L, M's services are not attributable to L, and L's furnishing of a fully equipped farm is insufficient by itself to constitute material participation in the production of the crops. Accordingly, L's rental income from the arrangement is not included in his net earnings from self-employment for that year. For taxable years beginning before January 1, 1974, however, L's rental income would be includible in those earnings.

(c) Rentals from living quarters. *(1) No services rendered for occupants.* Payments for the use or occupancy of entire private residences or living quarters in duplex or multiple-housing units are generally rentals from real estate. Except in the case of real-estate dealers, such payments are excluded in determining net earnings from self-employment even though such payments are in part attributable to personal property furnished under the lease.

(2) Services rendered for occupants. Payments for the use or occupancy of rooms or other space where services are also rendered to the occupant, such as for the use or occupancy of rooms or other quarters in hotels, boarding houses, or apartment houses furnishing hotel services, or in tourist camps or tourist homes, or payments for the use or occupancy of space in parking lots, warehouses, or storage garages, do not constitute rentals from real estate; consequently, such payments are included in determining net earnings from self-employment. Generally, services are considered rendered to the occupant if they are primarily for his convenience and are other than those usually or customarily rendered in connection with the rental of rooms or other space for occupancy only. The supplying of maid service, for example, constitutes such service; whereas the furnishing of heat and light, the cleaning of public entrances, exits, stairways and lobbies, the collection of trash, and so forth, are not considered as services rendered to the occupant.

(3) Example. The application of this paragraph may be illustrated by the following example:

Example. A, an individual, owns a building containing four apartments. During the taxable year, he receives $1,400 from apartments numbered 1 and 2, which are rented without services rendered to the occupants, and $3,600 from apartments numbered 3 and 4, which are rented with services rendered to the occupants. His fixed expenses for the four apartments aggregate $1,200 during the taxable year. In addition, he has $500 of expenses attributable to the services rendered to the occupants of apartments 3 and 4. In determining his net earnings from self-employment, A includes the $3,600 received from apartments 3 and 4, and the expenses of $1,100 ($500 plus one-half of $1,200) attributable thereto. The rentals and expenses attributable to apartments 1 and 2 are excluded. Therefore, A has $2,500 of net earnings from self-employment for the taxable year from the building.

(d) Treatment of business income which includes rentals from real estate. Except in the case of a real-estate dealer, where an individual or a partnership is engaged in a trade or business the income of which is classifiable in part as rentals from real estate, only that portion of such income which is not classifiable as rentals from real estate, and the expenses attributable to such portion, are included in determining net earnings from self-employment.

T.D. 6691, 12/2/63, amend T.D. 7710, 7/28/80.

§ 1.1402(a)-5 Dividends and interest.

(a) All dividends on shares of stock are excluded unless they are received by an individual in the course of his trade or business as a dealer in stocks or securities.

(b) Interest on any bond, debenture, note, or certificate, or other evidence of indebtedness, issued with interest coupons or in registered form by any corporation (including one issued by a government or political subdivision thereof) is excluded unless such interest is received in the course of a trade or business as a dealer in stocks or securities. However, interest with respect to which a credit against tax is allowable as provided in section 35, that is, interest on certain obligations of the United States and its instrumentalities, is not included in net earnings from self-employment even though received in the course of a trade or business as a dealer in stocks or securities. Only interest on bonds, debentures, notes, or certificates, or other evidence of indebtedness, issued with interest coupons or in registered form by a corporation, is excluded in the case of all persons other than dealers in stocks or securities; other interest received in the course of any trade or business (such as interest received by a pawnbroker on his loans or interest received by a merchant on his accounts or notes receivable) is not excluded.

(c) Dividends and interest of the character excludable under paragraphs (a) and (b) of this section received by an individual on stocks or securities held for speculation or investment are excluded whether or not the individual is a dealer in stocks or securities.

(d) A dealer in stocks or securities is a merchant of stocks or securities with an established place of business, regularly engaged in the business of purchasing stocks or securities and reselling them to customers; that is, he is one who as a merchant buys stocks or securities and sells them to customers with a view to the gains and profits that may be derived therefrom. Persons who buy and sell or hold stocks or securities for investment or speculation, irrespective of whether such buying or selling constitutes the carrying on of a trade or business, are not dealers in stocks or securities.

T.D. 6691, 12/2/63.

§ 1.1402(a)-6 Gain or loss from disposition of property.

Caution: The Treasury has not yet amended Reg § 1.1402(a)-6 to reflect changes made by P.L. 98-369.

(a) There is excluded any gain or loss: (1) Which is considered as gain or loss from the sale or exchange of a capital asset; (2) from the cutting of timber or the disposal of timber, coal, or iron ore, even though held primarily for sale to customers, if section 631 is applicable to such gain or loss; and (3) from the sale, exchange, involuntary conversion, or other disposition of property if such property is neither (i) stock in trade or other property of a kind which would properly be includible in inventory if on hand at the close of the taxable year, nor (ii) property held primarily for sale to customers in the ordinary course of a trade or business. For the purpose of the special rule in subparagraph (3) of this paragraph, it is immaterial whether a gain or loss is treated as a capital gain or loss or as an ordinary gain or loss for purposes other than determining net earnings from self-employment. For instance, where the character of a loss is governed by the provisions of section 1231, such loss is excluded in determining net earnings from self-employment even though such loss is treated under section 1231 as an ordinary loss. For the purposes of this special rule, the term "involuntary conversion" means a compulsory or involuntary conversion of property into other property or money as a result of its destruction in whole or in part, theft or seizure, or an exercise of the power of requisition or condemnation or the threat or imminence thereof; and the term "other disposition" includes the destruction or loss, in whole or in part, of property by fire, storm, shipwreck, or other casualty, or by theft, even though there is no conversion of such property into other property or money.

(b) The application of this section may be illustrated by the following example:

Example. During the taxable year 1954, A, who owns a grocery store, realized a net profit of $1,500 from the sale of groceries and a gain of $350 from the sale of a refrigerator case. During the same year, he sustained a loss of $2,000 as a result of damage by fire to the store building. In computing taxable income, all of these items are taken into account. In determining net earnings from self-employment, however, only the $1,500 of profit derived from the sale of groceries is included. The $350 gain and the $2,000 loss are excluded.

T.D. 6691, 12/2/63, amend T.D. 6841, 7/26/65.

§ 1.1402(a)-7 Net operating loss deduction.

The deduction provided by section 172, relating to net operating losses sustained in years other than the taxable year, is excluded.

T.D. 6691, 12/2/63.

§ 1.1402(a)-8 Community income.

Caution: The Treasury has not yet amended Reg § 1.1402(a)-8 to reflect changes made by P.L. 94-455.

(a) In case of an individual. If any of the income derived by an individual from a trade or business (other than a trade or business carried on by a partnership) is community income under community property laws applicable to such income, all of the gross income, shall be treated as the gross income and deductions of the husband unless the wife exercises substantially all of the management and control of such trade or business, in which case all of such gross income and deductions shall be treated as the gross income and deductions of the wife. For the purpose of this special rule, the term "management and control" means management and control in fact, not the management and control imputed to the husband under the community property laws. For example, a wife who operates a beauty parlor without any appreciable collaboration on the part of her husband will be considered as having substantially all of the management and control of such business despite the provision of any community property law vesting in the husband the right of management and control of community property; and the income and deductions attributable to the operation of such beauty parlor will be considered the income and deductions of the wife.

(b) In case of a partnership. Even though a portion of a partner's distributive share of the income or loss, described in section 702(a)(9), from a trade or business carried on by a partnership is community income or loss under the community property laws applicable to such share, all of such distributive share shall be included in computing the net earnings from self-employment of such partner; no part of such share shall be taken into account in computing the net earnings from self-employment of the spouse of such partner. In any case in which both spouses are members of the same partnership, the distributive share of the income or loss of each spouse is included in computing the net earnings from self-employment of that spouse.

T.D. 6691, 12/2/63.

§ 1.1402(a)-9 Puerto Rico.

(a) Residents. A resident of Puerto Rico, whether or not a bona fide resident thereof during the entire taxable year, and whether or not an alien, a citizen of the United States, or a citizen of Puerto Rico, shall compute his net earnings from self-employment in the same manner as would a citizen of the United States residing in the United States. See paragraph (d) of § 1.1402(b)-1 for regulations relating to nonresident aliens. For the purpose of the tax on self-employment income, the gross income of such a resident of Puerto Rico also includes income from Puerto Rican sources. Thus, under this special rule, income from Puerto Rican sources will be included in determining net earnings from self-employment of a resident of Puerto Rico engaged in the active conduct of a trade or business in Puerto Rico despite the fact that, under section 933, such income may not be taken into account for purposes of the tax under section 1 or 3.

(b) Nonresidents. A citizen of Puerto Rico who is also a citizen of the United States and who is not a resident of Puerto Rico will compute his net earnings from self-employment in the same manner and subject to the same provisions of law and regulations as other citizens of the United States.

T.D. 6691, 12/2/63.

§ 1.1402(a)-10 Personal exemption deduction.

The deduction provided by section 151, relating to personal exemptions, is excluded.

T.D. 6691, 12/2/63.

§ 1.1402(a)-11 Ministers and members of religious orders.

Caution: The Treasury has not yet amended Reg § 1.1402(a)-11 to reflect changes made by P.L. 95-615.

(a) In general. For each taxable year ending after 1954 in which a minister or member of a religious order is engaged in a trade or business, within the meaning of section 1402(c) and § 1.1402(c)-5, with respect to service performed in the exercise of his ministry or in the exercise of duties required by such order, net earnings from self-employment from such trade or business include the gross income derived during the taxable year from any such service, less the deductions attributable to such gross income. For each taxable year ending on or after December 31, 1957, such minister or member of a religious order shall compute his net earnings from self-employment derived from the performance of such service without regard to the exclusions from gross income provided by section 107 (relating to rental value of parsonages) and section 119 (relating to meals and lodging furnished for the convenience of the employer). Thus, a minister who is subject to self-employment tax with respect to his services as a minister will include in the computation of his net earnings from self-employment for a taxable year ending on or after December 31, 1957, the rental value of a home furnished to him as remuneration for services performed in the exercise of his ministry or the rental allowance paid to him as remuneration for such services irrespective of whether such rental value or rental allowance is excluded from gross income by section 107. Similarly, the value of any meals or lodging furnished to a minister or to a member of a religious order in connection with service performed in the exercise of his ministry or as a member of such order will be included in the computation of his net earnings from self-employment for a taxable year ending on or after December 31, 1957, notwithstanding the exclusion of such value from gross income by section 119.

(b) In employ of American employer. If a minister or member of a religious order engaged in a trade or business described in section 1402(c) and § 1.1402(c)-5 is a citizen of the United States and performs service, in his capacity as a minister or member of a religious order, as an employee of an American employer, as defined in section 3121(h) and the regulations thereunder in part 31 of this chapter (Employment Tax Regulations), his net earnings from self-employment derived from such service shall be computed as provided in paragraph (a) of this section but without regard to the exclusions from gross income provided in section 911, relating to earned income from sources without the United States, and section 931, relating to income from sources within certain possessions of the United States. Thus, even though all the income of the minister or member for service of the character to which this paragraph is applicable was derived from sources without the United States, or from sources within certain possessions of the United States, and therefore may be excluded from gross income, such income is included in computing net earnings from self-employment.

(c) Minister in a foreign country whose congregation is composed predominantly of citizens of the United States. *(1) Taxable years ending after 1956.* For any taxable year ending after 1956, a minister of a church, who is engaged in a trade or business within the meaning of section 1402(c) and § 1.1402(c)-5, is a citizen of the United States, is performing service in the exercise of his ministry in a foreign country, and has a congregation composed predominantly of United States citizens, shall compute his net earnings from self-employment derived from his services as a minister for such taxable year without regard to the exclusion from gross income provided in section 911, relating to earned income from sources without the United States. For taxable years ending on or after December 31, 1957, such minister shall also disregard sections 107 and 119 in the computation of his net earnings from self-employment. (See paragraph (a) of this section.) For purposes of section 1402(a)(8) and this paragraph a "congregation composed predominantly of citizens of the United States" means a congregation the majority of which throughout the greater portion of its minister's taxable year were United States citizens.

(2) Election for taxable years ending after 1954 and before 1957. (i) A minister described in subparagraph (1) of this paragraph who, for a taxable year ending after 1954 and before 1957, had income from service described in such subparagraph which would have been included in computing net earnings from self-employment if such income had been derived in a taxable year ending after 1956 by an individual who had filed a waiver certificate under section 1402(e), may elect to have section 1402(a)(8) and subparagraph (1) of this paragraph apply to his income from such service for his taxable years ending after 1954 and before 1957. If such minister filed a waiver certificate prior to August 1, 1956, in accordance with § 1.1402(e)(1)-1, or he files such a waiver certificate on or before the due date of his return (including any extensions thereof) for his last taxable year ending before 1957, he must make such election on or before the due date of his return (including any extensions thereof) for such taxable year or before April 16, 1957, whichever is the later. If the waiver certificate is not so filed, the minister must make his election on or before the due date of the return (including any extensions thereof) for his first taxable year ending after 1956. Notwithstanding the expiration of the period prescribed by section 1402(e)(2) for filing such waiver, the minister may file a waiver certificate at the time he makes the election. In no event shall an election be valid unless the minister files prior to or at the time of the election a waiver certificate in accordance with § 1.1402(e)(1)-1.

(ii) The election shall be made by filing with the district director of internal revenue with whom the waiver certificate, Form 2031, is filed a written statement indicating that, by reason of the Social Security Amendments of 1956, the minister desires to have the Federal old-age, survivors, and disability insurance system established by title II of the Social Security Act extended to his services performed in a foreign country as a minister of a congregation composed predominantly of United States citizens beginning with the first taxable year ending after 1954 and prior to 1957 for which he had income from such services. The statement shall be dated and signed by the minister and shall clearly state that it is an election for retroactive self-employment tax coverage under the Self-Employment Contributions Act of 1954. In addition, the statement shall include the following information:

(a) The name and address of the minister.

(b) His social security account number, if he has one.

(c) That he is a duly ordained, commissioned, or licensed minister of a church.

(d) That he is a citizen of the United States.

(e) That he is performing services in the exercise of his ministry in a foreign country.

(f) That his congregation is composed predominantly of citizens of the United States.

(g) (1) That he has filed a waiver certificate and, if so, where and under what circumstances the certificate was filed and the taxable year for which it is effective; or (2) That he is filing a waiver certificate with his election for retroactive coverage and, if so, the taxable year for which it is effective.

(h) That he has or has not filed income tax returns for his taxable years ending after 1954 and before 1957. If he has filed such returns, he shall state the years for which they were filed and indicate the district director of internal revenue with whom they were filed.

(iii) Notwithstanding section 1402(e)(3), a waiver certificate filed pursuant to § 1.1402(e)(1)-1 by a minister making an election under this paragraph shall be effective (regardless of when such certificate is filed) for such minister's first taxable year ending after 1954 in which he had income from service described in subparagraph (1) of this paragraph or for the taxable year of the minister prescribed by section 1402(e)(3), if such taxable year is earlier, and for all succeeding taxable years.

(iv) No interest or penalty shall be assessed or collected for failure to file a return within the time prescribed by law if such failure arises solely by reason of an election made by a minister pursuant to this paragraph or for any underpayment of self-employment income tax arising solely by reason of such election, for the period ending with the date such minister makes an election pursuant to this paragraph.

(d) Treatment of certain remuneration paid in 1955 and 1956 as wages. For treatment of remuneration paid to an individual for service described in section 3121(b)(8)(A) which was erroneously treated by the organization employing him as employment within the meaning of chapter 21 of the Internal Revenue Code, see § 1.1402(e)(4)-1.

T.D. 6691, 12/2/63, amend T.D. 9194, 4/6/2005.

§ 1.1402(a)-12 Continental shelf and certain possessions of the United States.

(a) Certain possessions. For purposes of the tax on self-employment income, the exclusion from gross income provided by section 931 (relating to bona fide residents of certain possessions of the United States) will not apply. Net earnings from self-employment are subject to the tax on self-employment income even if such amounts are excluded from gross income under section 931.

(b) Continental shelf. For the definition of the term "United States" and for other geographical definitions relating to the continental shelf, see section 638 and § 1.638-1.

(c) Effective/applicability date. This section applies to taxable years ending after April 9, 2008.

T.D. 6691, 12/2/63, amend T.D. 7277, 5/14/73, T.D. 9194, 4/6/2005, T.D. 9391, 4/4/2008.

§ 1.1402(a)-13 Income from agricultural activity.

(a) Agricultural trade or business. *(1)* An agricultural trade or business is one in which, if the trade or business were carried on exclusively by employees, the major portion of the services would constitute agricultural labor as defined in section 3121(g) and the regulations thereunder in Part 31 of this chapter (Employment Tax Regulations). In case the services are in part agricultural and in part nonagricultural, the time devoted to the performance of each type of service is the test to be used to determine whether the major portion of the services would constitute agricultural labor. If more than half of the time spent in performing all the services is spent in performing services which would constitute agricultural labor under section 3121(g), the trade or business is agricultural. If only half, or less, of the time spent in performing all the services is spent in performing services which would constitute agricultural labor under section 3121(g), the trade or business is not agricultural. In every case the time spent in performing the services will be computed by adding the time spent in the trade or business during the taxable year by every individual (including the individual carrying on such trade or business and the members of his family) in performing such services. The operation of this special rule is not affected by section 3121(c), relating to the included-excluded rule for determining employment.

(2) The rules prescribed in subparagraph (1) of this paragraph have no application where the nonagricultural services are performed in connection with an enterprise which constitutes a trade or business separate and distinct from the trade or business conducted as an agricultural enterprise. Thus, the operation of a roadside automobile service station on farm premises constitutes a trade or business separate and distinct from the agricultural enterprise, and the gross income derived from such service station, less the deductions attributable thereto, is to be taken into account in determining net earnings from self-employment.

(b) Farm operator's income for taxable years ending before 1955. Income derived in a taxable year ending before 1955 from any agricultural trade or business (see paragraph (a) of this section), and all deductions attributable to such income, are excluded in computing net earnings from self-employment.

(c) Farm operator's income for taxable years ending after 1954. Income derived in a taxable year ending after 1954 from an agricultural trade or business (see paragraph (a) of this section) is includible in computing net earnings from self-employment. Income derived from an agricultural trade or business includes income derived by an individual under an agreement entered into by such individual with another person pursuant to which such individual undertakes to produce agricultural or horticultural commodities (including livestock, bees, poultry, and fur-bearing animals and wildlife) on land owned or leased by such other person and pursuant to which the agricultural or horticultural commodities produced by such individual, or the proceeds therefrom, are to be divided between such individual and such other person, and the amount of such individual's share depends on the amount of the agricultural or horticultural commodities produced. However, except as provided in paragraph (d) of this section, relating to arrangements involving material participation, the income derived under such an agreement by the owner or lessee of the land is not includible in computing net earnings from self-employment. See § 1.1402(a)-4. For options relating to the computation of net earnings from self-employment, see §§ 1.1402(a)-14 and 1.1402(a)-15.

(d) Includible farm rental income for taxable years ending after 1955. For taxable years ending after 1955, income derived from an agricultural trade or business (see paragraph (a) of this section) includes also income derived by the owner or tenant of land under an arrangement between such owner or tenant and another person, if such arrangement provides that such other person shall produce agricultural or horticultural commodities (including livestock, bees, poultry, and fur-bearing animals and wildlife) on such land, and that there shall be material participation by the owner or tenant in the production or the management of the production of such agricultural or horticultural commodities, and if there is material participation by the owner or tenant with respect to any such agricultural or horticultural commodity. See paragraph (b) of § 1.1402(a)-4. For options relating to the computation of net earnings from self-employment, see §§ 1.1402(a)-14 and 1.1402(a)-15.

(e) Income from service performed after 1956 as a crew leader. Income derived by a crew leader (see section 3121(o) and the regulations thereunder in Part 31 of this chapter (Employment Tax Regulations)) from service performed after 1956 in furnishing individuals to perform agricultural labor for another person and from service performed after 1956 in agricultural labor as a member of the crew is considered to be income derived from a trade or business for purposes of § 1.1402(c)-1. Whether such trade or business is an agricultural trade or business shall be determined by applying the rules set forth in this section.

T.D. 6691, 12/2/63.

§ 1.1402(a)-14 Options available to farmers in computing net earnings from self-employment for taxable years ending after 1954 and before December 31, 1956.

(a) Computation of net earnings. In the case of any trade or business which is carried on by an individual who reports his income on the cash receipts and disbursements method, and in which, if it were carried on exclusively by employees, the major portion of the services would constitute agricultural labor as defined in section 3121(g) (see paragraph (a) of § 1.1402(a)-13), net earnings from self-employment may, for a taxable year ending after 1954, at the option of the taxpayer, be computed as follows:

(1) Gross income $1,800 or less. If the gross income, computed as provided in paragraph (b) of this section, from such trade or business is $1,800 or less, the taxpayer may, at his option, treat as net earnings from self-employment from such trade or business an amount equal to 50 percent of such gross income. If the taxpayer so elects, the amount equal to 50 percent of such gross income shall be used in computing his self-employment income in lieu of his actual net earnings from such trade or business, if any.

(2) Gross income in excess of $1,800. If the gross income, computed as provided in paragraph (b) of this section, from such trade or business is more than $1,800, and the actual net earnings from self-employment from such trade or business are less than $900, the taxpayer may, at his option, treat $900 as net earnings from self-employment. If the taxpayer so elects, $900 shall be used in computing his self-employment income in lieu of his actual net earnings from such trade or business, if any. However, if the taxpayer's actual net earnings from such trade or business, as computed in accordance with §§ 1.1402(a)-1 through 1.1402(a)-3 are $900 or more, such actual net earnings shall be used in computing his self-employment income.

(b) Computation of gross income. For purposes of paragraph (a) of this section, gross income shall consist of the gross receipts from such trade or business reduced by the cost or other basis of property which was purchased and sold in carrying on such trade or business, adjusted (after such reduction) in accordance with the provisions of § 1-1402(a)-3, relating to income and deductions not included in computing net earnings from self-employment.

(c) Two or more agricultural activities. If an individual is engaged in more than one agricultural trade or business within the meaning of paragraph (a) of § 1.1402(a)-13 (for example, the business of ordinary farming and the business of cotton ginning), the gross income derived from each agricultural trade or business shall be aggregated for purposes of the optional method provided in paragraph (a) of this section for computing net earnings from self-employment.

(d) Examples. Application of the regulations prescribed in paragraphs (a) and (b) of this section may be illustrated by the following examples:

Example (1). F, a farmer, uses the cash receipts and disbursements method of accounting in making his income tax returns. F's books and records show that during the calendar year 1955 he received $1,200 from the sale of produce raised on the farm, $200 from the sale of livestock raised on the farm and not held for breeding or dairy purposes, and $600 from the sale of a tractor. The income from the sale of the tractor is of a type which is excluded from net earnings from self-employment by section 1402(a). F's actual net earnings from self-employment, computed in accordance with the provisions of §§ 1.1402(a)-1 through 1.1402(a)-3, are $450. F may report $450 as his net earnings from self-employment or he may elect to report $700 (one-half of $1,400).

Example (2). C, a cattleman, uses the cash receipts and disbursements method of accounting in making his income tax returns. C had actual net earnings from self-employment, computed in accordance with the provisions of §§ 1.1402(a)-1 through 1.1402(a)-3, of $725. His gross receipts were $1,000 from the sale of produce raised on the farm and $1,200 from the sale of feeder cattle, which C bought for $500. The income from the sale of the feeder cattle is of a type which is included in computing net earnings from self-employment. Therefore, C may report $725 as his net earnings from self-employment or he may elect to report $850, one-half of $1,700 ($2,200 minus $500).

Example (3). R, a rancher, has gross income of $3,000 from the operation of his ranch, computed as provided in paragraph (b) of this section. His actual net earnings from self-employment from farming activities are less than $900. R, nevertheless, may elect to report $900 as net earnings from self-employment from such trade or business. If R had actual net earnings from self-employment from his farming activities in the amount of $900 or more, he would be required to report such amount in computing his self-employment income.

(e) Members of farm partnerships. The optional method provided by paragraph (a) of this section for computing net earnings from self-employment is not available to a member of a partnership with respect to his distributive share of the income or loss from any trade or business carried on by any partnership of which he is a member.

T.D. 6691, 12/2/63.

§ 1.1402(a)-15 Options available to farmers in computing net earnings from self-employment for taxable years ending on or after December 31, 1956.

Caution: The Treasury has not yet amended Reg § 1.1402(a)-15 to reflect changes made by P.L. 110-246, P.L. 94-455.

(a) Computation of net earnings. In the case of any trade or business which is carried on by an individual or by a partnership and in which, if such trade or business were carried on exclusively by employees, the major portion of the services would constitute agricultural labor as defined in section 3121(g) (see paragraph (a) of § 1.1402(a)-13), net earnings from self-employment may, for a taxable year ending on or after December 31, 1956, at the option of the taxpayer, be computed as follows:

(1) In case of an individual. (i) Gross income of less than specified amount. If the gross income, computed as provided in paragraph (b) of this section, from such trade or business is $2,400 or less ($1,800 or less for a taxable year ending on or after Dec. 31, 1956, and beginning before Jan. 1, 1966), the taxpayer may, at his option, treat as net earnings from self-employment from such trade or business an amount equal to 66⅔ percent of such gross income. If the taxpayer so elects, the amount equal to 66⅔ percent of such gross income shall be used in computing his self-employment income in lieu of his actual net earnings from such trade or business, if any.

(ii) Gross income in excess of specified amount. If the gross income, computed as provided in paragraph (b) of this section, from such trade or business is more than $2,400 ($1,800 for a taxable year ending on or after Dec. 31, 1956, and beginning before Jan. 1, 1966), and the net earnings from self-employment from such trade or business (computed without regard to this section) are less than $1,600 ($1,200 for a taxable year ending on or after Dec. 31, 1956, and beginning before Jan. 1, 1966), the taxpayer may, at his option, treat $1,600 ($1,200 for a taxable year ending on or after Dec. 31, 1956, and beginning before Jan. 1, 1966) as net earnings from self-employment. If the taxpayer so elects, $1,600 ($1,200 for a taxable year ending on or after Dec. 31, 1956, and beginning before Jan. 1, 1966) shall be used in computing his self-employment income in lieu of his actual net earnings from such trade or business, if any. However, if the taxpayer's actual net earnings from such trade or business, as computed in accordance with the applicable provisions of §§ 1.1402(a)-1 to 1.1402(a)-13, inclusive, are $1,600 or more ($1,200 or more for a taxable year ending on or after Dec. 31, 1956, and beginning before Jan. 1, 1966) such actual net earnings shall be used in computing his self-employment income.

(2) In case of a member of a partnership. (i) Distributive share of gross income of less than specified amount. If a taxpayer's distributive share of the gross income of a partnership (as such gross income is computed under the provisions of paragraph (b) of this section) derived from such trade or business (after such gross income has been reduced by the sum of all payments to which section 707(c) applies) is $2,400 or less ($1,800 or less for a taxable year ending on or after Dec. 31, 1956, and beginning before Jan. 1, 1966), the taxpayer may, at his option, treat as his distributive share of income described in section 702(a)(9) derived from such trade or business an amount equal to 66⅔ percent of his distributive share of such gross income (after such gross income has been reduced by the sum of all payments to which section 707(c) applies). If the taxpayer so elects, the amount equal to 66⅔ percent of his distributive share of such gross income shall be used by him in the computation of his net earnings from self-employment in lieu of the actual amount of his distributive share of income described in section 702(a)(9) from such trade or business, if any.

(ii) Distributive share of gross income in excess of specified amount. If a taxpayer's distributive share of the gross income of the partnership (as such gross income is computed under the provisions of paragraph (b) of this section) derived from such trade or business (after such gross income has been reduced by the sum of all payments to which section 707(c) applies) is more than $2,400 ($1,800 for a taxable year ending on or after Dec. 31, 1956, and beginning before Jan. 1, 1966) and the actual amount of his distributive share (whether or not distributed) of income described in section 702(a)(9) derived from such trade or business (computed without regard to this section) is less than $1,600 ($1,200 for a taxable year ending on or after Dec. 31, 1956, and beginning before Jan. 1, 1966), the taxpayer may, at his option, treat $1,600 ($1,200 for a taxable year ending on or after Dec. 31, 1956, and beginning before Jan. 1, 1966) as his distributive share of income described in section 702(a)(9) derived from such trade or business. If the taxpayer so elects, $1,600 ($1,200 for a taxable year ending on or after Dec. 31,

1956, and beginning before Jan. 1, 1966) shall be used by him in the computation of his net earnings from self-employment in lieu of the actual amount of his distributive share of income described in section 702(a)(9) from such trade or business, if any. However, if the actual amount of the taxpayer's distributive share of income described in section 702(a)(9) from such trade or business, as computed in accordance with the applicable provisions of §§ 1.1402(a)-1 to 1.1402(a)-13, inclusive, is $1,600 or more ($1,200 or more for a taxable year ending on or after Dec. 31, 1956, and beginning before Jan. 1, 1966), such actual amount of the taxpayer's distributive share shall be used in computing his net earnings from self-employment.

(iii) Cross reference. For a special rule in the case of certain deceased partners, see paragraph (c) of § 1.1402(f)-1.

(b) Computation of gross income. For purposes of this section gross income has the following meanings:

(1) In the case of any such trade or business in which the income is computed under a cash receipts and disbursements method, the gross receipts from such trade or business reduced by the cost or other basis of property which was purchased and sold in carrying on such trade or business (see paragraphs (a) and (c), other than paragraph (a)(5), of § 1.61-4), adjusted (after such reduction) in accordance with the applicable provisions of §§ 1.1402(a)-3 to 1.1402(a)-13, inclusive.

(2) In the case of any such trade or business in which the income is computed under an accrual method (see paragraphs (b) and (c), other than paragraph (b)(5), of § 1.61-4), the gross income from such trade or business, adjusted in accordance with the applicable provisions of §§ 1.1402(a)-3 to 1.1402(a)-13, inclusive.

(c) Two or more agricultural activities. If an individual (including a member of a partnership) derives gross income (as defined in paragraph (b) of this section) from more than one agricultural trade or business, such gross income (including his distributive share of the gross income of any partnership derived from any such trade or business) shall be deemed to have been derived from one trade or business. Thus, such an individual shall aggregate his gross income derived from each agricultural trade or business carried on by him (which includes, under paragraph (b) of § 1.1402(a)-1, any guaranteed payment, within the meaning of section 707(c), received by him from a farm partnership of which he is a member) and his distributive share of partnership gross income (after such gross income has been reduced by any guaranteed payment within the meaning of section 707(c)) derived from each farm partnership of which he is a member. Such gross income is the amount to be considered for purposes of the optional method provided in this section for computing net earnings from self-employment. If the aggregate gross income of an individual includes income derived from an agricultural trade or business carried on by him and a distributive share of partnership income derived from an agricultural trade or business carried on by a partnership of which he is a member, such aggregate gross income shall be treated as income derived from a single trade or business carried on by him, and such individual shall apply the optional method applicable to individuals set forth in paragraph (a)(1) of this section for purposes of computing his net earnings from self-employment.

(d) Examples. The application of this section may be illustrated by the following examples:

Example (1). F is engaged in the business of farming and computes his income under the cash receipts and disbursements method. He files his income tax returns on the basis of the calendar year. During the year 1966. F's gross income from the business of farming (computed in accordance with paragraph (b)(1) of this section) is $2,325. His actual net earnings from self-employment derived from such business are $1,250. As his net earnings from self-employment, F may report $1,250 or, by the optional computation method, he may report $1,550 (66⅔ percent of $2,325).

Example (2). G is engaged in the business of farming and computes his income under the accrual method. His income tax returns are filed on the calendar year basis. For the year 1966 G's gross income from the operation of his farm (computed in accordance with paragraph (b)(2) of this section) is $2,800. He has actual net earnings from self-employment derived from such farm in the amount of $1,250. As his net earnings from self-employment derived from his farm, G may report his actual net earnings of $1,250, or by the optional method he may report $1,600. If G's actual net earnings from self-employment from his farming activities for 1966 were in an amount of $1,600 or more, he would be required to report such amount in computing his self-employment income.

Example (3). M, who files his income tax returns on a calendar year basis, is one of the three partners of the XYZ Company, a partnership, engaged in the business of farming. The taxable year of the partnership is the calendar year, and its income is computed under the cash receipts and disbursements method. For M's services in connection with the planting, cultivating, and harvesting of the crops during the year 1966, the partnership agrees to pay him $500, the full amount of which is determined without regard to the income of the partnership and constitutes a guaranteed payment within the meaning of section 707(c). This guaranteed payment to M is the only such payment made during such year. The gross income derived from the business for the year 1966, computed in accordance with paragraph (b)(1) of this section and after being reduced by the guaranteed payment of $500 made to M, is $3,000. One-third of the $3,000 ($1,000), is M's distributive share of such gross income. Under paragraph (c) of this section, the guaranteed payment ($500) received by M and his distributive share of the partnership gross income ($1,000) are deemed to have been derived from one trade or business, and such amounts must be aggregated for purposes of the optional method of computing net earnings from self-employment. Since M's combined gross income from his two agricultural businesses ($1,000 and $500) is not more than $2,400 and since such income is deemed to be derived from one trade or business, M's net earnings from self-employment derived from such farming business may, at his option, be deemed to be $1,000 (66⅔ percent of $1,500).

Example (4). A is one of the two partners of the AB partnership which is engaged in the business of farming. The taxable year of the partnership is the calendar year and its income is computed under the accrual method. A files his income tax returns on the calendar year basis. The partnership agreement provides for an equal sharing in the profits and losses of the partnership by the two partners. A is an experienced farmer and for his services as manager of the partnership's farm activities during the year 1966, he receives $6,000 which amount constitutes a guaranteed payment within the meaning of section 707(c). The gross income of the partnership derived from such business for the year 1966, computed in accordance with paragraph (b)(2) of this section and after being reduced by the guaranteed payment made to A, is $9,600. A's distributive share of such gross income is $4,800, and his distributive share of income described in section 702(a)(9) derived from the partnership's business is $1,900. Under paragraph (c) of this section, the guaranteed payment received by A and his distributive share of the partnership gross income are deemed to have been derived from one trade or business, and such amounts must be aggregated for purposes of the optional method of computing his net earnings from self-employment. Since the aggregate of A's guaranteed payment ($6,000) and his distributive share of partnership gross income ($4,800) is more than $2,400 and since the aggregate of A's guaranteed payment ($6,000) and his distributive share ($1,900) of partnership income described in section 702(a)(9) is not less than $1,600, the optional method of computing net earnings from self-employment is not available to A.

Example (5). F is a member of the EFG partnership which is engaged in the business of farming. F files his income tax returns on the calendar year basis. The taxable year of the partnership is the calendar year, and its income is computed under a cash receipts and disbursements method. Under the partnership agreement the partners are to share equally the profits or losses of the business. The gross income derived from the partnership business for the year 1966, computed in accordance with paragraph (b)(1) of this section is $7,500. F's share of such gross income is $2,500. Due to drought and an epidemic among the livestock, the partnership sustains a net loss of $7,800 for the year 1966 of which loss F's share is $2,600. Since F's distributive share of gross income derived from such business is in excess of $2,400 and since F does not receive income described in section 702(a)(9) of $1,600 or more from such business, he may, at his option, be deemed to have received $1,600 as his distributive share of income described in section 702(a)(9) from such business.

T.D. 6691, 12/2/63, amend T.D. 6993, 1/17/69.

§ 1.1402(a)-16 Exercise of option.

A taxpayer shall, for each taxable year with respect to which he is eligible to use the optional method described in § 1.1402(a)-14 or § 1.1402(a)-15, make a determination as to whether his net earnings from self-employment are to be computed in accordance with such method. If the taxpayer elects the optional method for a taxable year, he shall signify such election by computing net earnings from self-employment under the optional method as set forth in Schedule F (Form 1040) of the income tax return filed by the taxpayer for such taxable year. If the optional method is not elected at the time of the filing of the return for a taxable year with respect to which the taxpayer is eligible to elect such optional method, such method may be elected on an amended return (or on such other form as may be prescribed for such use) filed within the period prescribed by section 6501 and the regulations thereunder for the assessment of the tax for such taxable year. If the taxpayer is deceased or unable to make an election, the person designated in section 6012(b) and the regulations thereunder may, within the period prescribed in this section elect the optional method for any taxable year with respect to which the taxpayer is eligible to use the optional method and revoke an election previously made by or for the taxpayer.

T.D. 6691, 12/2/63.

§ 1.1402(a)-17 Retirement payments to retired partners.

(a) In general. There shall be excluded, in computing net earnings from self-employment for taxable years ending on or after December 31, 1967, certain payments made on a periodic basis by a partnership, pursuant to a written plan of the partnership, to a retired partner on account of his retirement. The exclusion applies only if the payments are made pursuant to a plan which meets the requirements prescribed in paragraph (b) of this section, and, in addition, the conditions set forth in paragraph (c) of this section are met.

(b) Retirement plan of partnership. *(1)* To meet the requirements of section 1402(a)(10), the written plan of the partnership must set forth the terms and conditions of the program or system established by the partnership for the purpose of making payments to retired partners on account of their retirement. To qualify as payments on account of retirement, the payments must constitute bona fide retirement income. Thus, payments of benefits not customarily included in a pension or retirement plan such as layoff benefits are not payments on account of retirement. Eligibility for retirement generally is established on the basis of age, physical condition, or a combination of age or physical condition and years of service. Generally, retirement benefits are measured by, and based on, such factors as years of service and compensation received. In determining whether the plan of the partnership provides for payments on account of retirement, factors, formulas, etc., reflected in public, and in broad based private, pension or retirement plans in prescribing eligibility requirements and in computing benefits may be taken into account.

(2) The plan of the partnership must provide for payments on account of retirement—

(i) To partners generally or to a class or classes of partners,

(ii) On a periodic basis, and

(iii) Which continue at least until the partner's death.

For purposes of subdivision (i) of this subparagraph, a class of partners may, in an appropriate case, contain only one member. Payments are made on a periodic basis if made at regularly recurring intervals (usually monthly) not exceeding one year.

(c) Conditions relating to exclusion. *(1) In general.* A payment made pursuant to a written plan of a partnership which meets the requirements of paragraph (b) of this section shall be excluded, in computing net earnings from self-employment, only if—

(i) The retired partner to whom the payment is made rendered no service with respect to any trade or business carried on by the partnership (or its successors) during the taxable year of the partnership (or its successors), which ends within or with the taxable year of the retired partner and in which the payment was received by him;

(ii) No obligation (whether certain in amount or contingent on a subsequent event) exists (as of the close of the partnership's taxable year referred to in subdivision (i) of this subparagraph) from the other partners to the retired partner except with respect to retirement payments under the plan or rights such as benefits payable on account of sickness, accident, hospitalization, medical expenses, or death; and

(iii) The retired partner's share (if any) of the capital of the partnership has been paid to him in full before the close of the partnership's taxable year referred to in subdivision (i) of this subparagraph.

By application of the conditions set forth in this subparagraph, either all payments on account of retirement received by a retired partner during the taxable year of the partnership ending within or with his taxable year are excluded or none of the payments are excluded. Subdivision (ii) of this subparagraph has application only to obligations from other partners in their capacity as partners as distinguished from an obligation which arose and exists from a transaction unrelated to the partnership or to a trade or business carried on by the partnership. The effect of the conditions set forth in subdivisions (ii) and (iii) of this subparagraph is that the exclusion may apply with respect to payments received by a retired partner during the taxable year of the partnership ending within or with his taxable year only if at the close of the partnership's taxable year the retired partner had no financial interest in the partnership except for the right to retirement payments.

(2) Examples. The application of subparagraph (1) of this paragraph may be illustrated by the following examples. Each example assumes that the partnership plan pursuant to which the payments are made meets the requirements of paragraph (b) of this section.

Example (1). A, who files his income tax returns on a calendar year basis, is a partner in the ABC partnership. The taxable year of the partnership is the period July 1 to June 30, inclusive. A retired from the partnership on January 1, 1973, and receives monthly payments on account of his retirement. As of June 30, 1973, no obligation existed from the other partners to A (except with respect to retirement payments under the plan) and A's share of the capital of the partnership had been paid to him in full. The monthly retirement payments received by A from the partnership in his taxable year ending on December 31, 1973, are not excluded from net earnings from self-employment since A rendered service to the partnership during a portion of the partnership's taxable year (July 1, 1972, through June 30, 1973) which ends within A's taxable year ending on December 31, 1973.

Example (2). D, a partner in the DEF partnership, retired from the partnership as of the close of December 31, 1972. The taxable year of both D and the partnership is the calendar year. During the partnership's taxable year ending December 31, 1973, D rendered no service with respect to any trade or business carried on by the partnership. On or before December 31, 1973, all obligations (other than with respect to retirement payments under the plan) from the other partners to D have been liquidated, and D's share of the capital of the partnership has been paid to him. Retirement payments received by D pursuant to the partnership's plan in his taxable year ending December 31, 1973, are excluded in determining his net earnings from self-employment (if any) for that taxable year.

Example (3). Assume the same facts as in example (2) except that as of the close of December 31, 1973, D has a right to a fixed percentage of any amounts collected by the partnership after that date which are attributable to services rendered by him prior to his retirement for clients of the partnership. The monthly payments received by D in his taxable year ending December 31, 1973, are not excluded from net earnings from self-employment since as of the close of the partnership's taxable year which ends with D's taxable year, an obligation (other than an obligation with respect to retirement payments) exists from the other partners to D.

T.D. 7333, 12/19/74.

§ 1.1402(a)-18 Split-dollar life insurance arrangements.

See §§ 1.61-22 and 1.7872-15 for rules relating to the treatment of split-dollar life insurance arrangements.

T.D. 9092, 9/11/2003.

§ 1.1402(b)-1 Self-employment income.

Caution: The Treasury has not yet amended Reg § 1.1402(b)-1 to reflect changes made by P.L. 101-508, P.L. 99-514, P.L. 99-509, P.L. 99-272, P.L. 98-21, P.L. 97-248, P.L. 94-455, P.L. 94-92.

(a) In general. Except for the exclusions in paragraphs (b) and (c) of this section and the exception in paragraph (d) of this section, the term "self-employment income" means the net earnings from self-employment derived by an individual during a taxable year.

(b) Maximum self-employment income. *(1) General rule.* Subject to the special rules described in subparagraph (2) of this paragraph, the maximum self-employment income of an individual for a taxable year (whether a period of 12 months or less) is—

(i) For any taxable year beginning in a calendar year after 1974, an amount equal to the contribution and benefit base (as determined under section 230 of the Social Security Act) which is effective for such calendar year; and

(ii) For any taxable year—

Ending before 1955	$ 3,600
Ending after 1954 and before 1959	4,200
Ending after 1958 and before 1966	4,800
Ending after 1965 and before 1968	6,600
Ending after 1967 and beginning before 1972	7,800
Beginning after 1971 and before 1973	9,000
Beginning after 1972 and before 1974	10,800
Beginning after 1973 and before 1975	13,200

(2) Special rules. (i) If an individual is paid wages as defined in subparagraph (3) of this paragraph in a taxable year, the maximum self-employment income for such taxable year is computed as provided in subdivision (ii) or (iii) of this subparagraph.

(ii) If an individual is paid wages as defined in subparagraph (3)(i) or (ii) of this paragraph in a taxable year, the maximum self-employment income of such individual for such taxable year is the excess of the amounts indicated in subparagraph (1) of this paragraph over the amount of the wages, as defined in subparagraph (3)(i) and (ii) of this paragraph, paid to him during the taxable year. For example, if for his taxable year beginning in 1974, an individual has $15,000 of net earnings from self-employment and during such taxable year is paid $1,000 of wages as defined in section 3121(a) (see subparagraph (3)(i) of this paragraph), he has $12,200 ($13,200 – $1,000) of self-employment income for the taxable year.

(iii) For taxable years ending on or after December 31, 1968, wages, as defined in subparagraph (3)(iii) of this paragraph, are taken into account in determining the maximum self-employment income of an individual for purposes of the tax imposed under section 1401(b) (hospital insurance), but not for purposes of the tax imposed under section 1401(a) (old-age, survivors, and disability insurance). If an individual is paid wages as defined in subparagraph (3)(iii) of this paragraph in a taxable year, his maximum self-employment income for such taxable year for purposes of the tax imposed under section 1401(a) is computed under subparagraph (1) of this paragraph or subdivision (ii) of this subparagraph (whichever is applicable), and his maximum self-employment income for such taxable year for purposes of the tax imposed under section 1401(b) is the excess of his section 1401(a) maximum self-employment income over the amount of wages, as defined in subparagraph (3)(iii) of this paragraph, paid to him during the taxable year. For purposes of this subdivision, wages as defined in subparagraph (3)(iii) of this paragraph are deemed paid to an individual in the period with respect to which the payment is made, that is, the period in which the compensation was earned or deemed earned within the meaning of section 3231(e). For an explanation of the term "compensation" and for provisions relating to when compensation is earned, see the regulations under section 3231(e) in Part 31 of this chapter (Employment Tax Regulations). The application of the rules set forth in this subdivision may be illustrated by the following example:

Example. M, a calendar-year taxpayer, has $15,000 of net earnings from self-employment for 1974 and during the taxable year is paid $1,000 of wages as defined in section 3121(a) (see subparagraph (3)(i) of this paragraph) and $1,600 of compensation subject to tax under section 3201 (see subparagraph (3)(iii) of this paragraph). Of the $1,600 of taxable compensation, $1,200 represents compensation for services rendered in 1974 and the balance ($400) represents compensation which pursuant to the provisions of section 3231(e) is earned or deemed earned in 1973. M's maximum self-employment income for 1974 for purposes of the tax imposed under section 1401(a), computed as provided in subdivision (ii) of this subparagraph, is $12,200 ($13,200 − $1,000), and for purposes of the tax imposed under section 1401(b) is $11,000 ($12,200 − $1,200). However, M may recompute his maximum self-employment income for 1973 for purposes of the tax imposed under section 1401(b) by taking into account the $400 of compensation which is deemed paid in 1973.

(3) Meaning of term "wages". For the purpose of the computation described in subparagraph (2) of this paragraph, the term "wages" includes:

(i) Wages as defined in section 3121(a);

(ii) Such remuneration paid to an employee for services covered by—

(a) An agreement entered into pursuant to section 218 of the Social Security Act (42 U.S.C. 418), which section provides for extension of the Federal old-age, survivors and disability insurance system to State and local government employees under voluntary agreements between the States and the Secretary of Health, Education, and Welfare (Federal Security Administrator before April 11, 1953), or

(b) An agreement entered into pursuant to the provisions of section 3121(l), relating to coverage of citizens of the United States who are employees of foreign subsidiaries of domestic corporations,

as would be wages under section 3121(a) if such services constituted employment under section 3121(b). For an explanation of the term "wages", see the regulations under section 3121(a) in Part 31 of this chapter (Employment Tax Regulations); and

(iii) Compensation, as defined in section 3231(e), which is subject to the employee tax imposed by section 3201 or the employee representative tax imposed by section 3211.

(c) Minimum net earnings from self-employment. Self-employment income does not include the net earnings from self-employment of an individual when the amount of such earnings for the taxable year is less than $400. Thus, an individual having only $300 of net earnings from self-employment for the taxable year would not have any self-employment income. However, an individual having net earnings from self-employment of $400 or more for the taxable year may, by application of paragraph (b)(2) of this section, have less than $400 of self-employment income for purposes of the tax imposed under section 1401(a) and the tax imposed under section 1401(b) or may have self-employment income of $400 or more for purposes of the tax imposed under section 1401(a) and of less than $400 for purposes of the tax imposed under section 1401(b). This could occur in a case in which the amount of the individual's net earnings from self-employment is $400 or more for a taxable year and the amount of such net earnings from self-employment plus the amount of wages, as defined in paragraph (b)(3) of this section, paid to him during the taxable year exceed the maximum self-employment income, as set forth in paragraph (b)(1) of this section, for the taxable year. However, the result occurs only if such maximum self-employment income exceeds the amount of such wages. The application of this paragraph may be illustrated by the following example:

Example. For 1974 M, a calendar-year taxpayer, has net earnings from self-employment of $2,000 and wages (as defined in paragraph (b)(3)(i) and (ii) of this section) of $12,500. Since M's net earnings from self-employment plus his wages exceed the maximum self-employment income for 1974 ($13,200), his self-employment income for 1974 is $700 ($13,200 − $12,500). If M also had wages, as defined in paragraph (b)(3)(iii) of this section, of $200, his self-employment income would be $700 for purposes of the tax imposed under section 1401(a) and $500 ($13,200 − $12,700 ($12,500 + $200)) for purposes of the tax imposed under section 1401(b).

For provisions relating to when wages as defined in paragraph (b)(3)(iii) of this section are treated as paid, see paragraph (b)(2)(iii) of this section.

(d) Nonresident aliens. A nonresident alien individual never has self-employment income. While a nonresident alien individual who derives income from a trade or business carried on within the United States, Puerto Rico, the Virgin Islands, Guam, or American Samoa (whether by agents or employees, or by a partnership of which he is a member) may be subject to the applicable income tax provisions on such income, such nonresident alien individual will not be subject to the tax on self-employment income, since any net earnings which he may have from self-employment do not constitute self-employment income. For the purpose of the tax on self-employment income, an individual who is not a citizen of the United States but who is a resident of the Commonwealth of Puerto Rico, the Virgin Islands, or, for taxable years beginning after 1960, of Guam or American Samoa is not considered to be a nonresident alien individual.

T.D. 6196, 8/13/56, amend T.D. 6691, 12/2/63, T.D. 6993, 1/17/69, T.D. 7333, 12/19/74.

§ 1.1402(c)-1 Trade or business.

In order for an individual to have net earnings from self-employment, he must carry on a trade or business, either as an individual or as a member of a partnership. Except for the exclusions discussed in §§ 1.1402(c)-2 to 1.1402(c)-7, inclusive, the term "trade or business", for the purpose of the tax on self-employment income, shall have the same meaning as when used in section 162. An individual engaged in one of the excluded activities specified in such sections of the regulations may also be engaged in carrying on activities which constitute a trade or business for purposes of the tax on self-employment income. Whether or not he is also engaged in carrying on a trade or business will be dependent upon all of the facts and circumstances in the particular case. An individual who is a crew leader, as defined in section 3121(o) (see such section and the regulations thereunder in Part 31 of this chapter (Employment Tax Regulations)), is considered to be engaged in carrying on a trade or business with respect to services performed by him after 1956 in furnishing individuals to perform agricultural labor for another person or services performed by him after 1956 as a member of the crew.

T.D. 6196, 8/13/56, amend T.D. 6691, 12/2/63, T.D. 6978, 10/29/68.

§ 1.1402(c)-2 Public office.

(a) In general. *(1) General rule.* Except as otherwise provided in subparagraph (2) of this paragraph, the performance of the functions of a public office does not constitute a trade or business.

(2) Fee basis public officials. (i) In general. If an individual receives fees after 1967 for the performance of the functions of a public office of a State or a political subdivision thereof for which he is compensated solely on a fee basis, and if the service performed in such office is eligible for (but is not made the subject of) an agreement between the State and the Secretary of Health, Education, and Welfare pursuant to section 218 of the Social Security Act to extend social security coverage thereto, the service for which such fees are received constitutes a trade or business within the meaning of section 1402(c) and § 1.1402(c)-1. If an individual performs service for a State or a political subdivision thereof in any period in more than one position, each position is treated separately for purposes of the preceding sentence. See also paragraph (f) of § 1.1402(c)-3 relating to the performance of service by an individual as an employee of a State or a political subdivision thereof in a position compensated solely on a fee basis.

(ii) Election with respect to fees received in 1968. (A) Any individual who in 1968 receives fees for service performed by him with respect to the functions of a public office of a State or a political subdivision thereof in any period in which the functions are performed in a position compensated solely on a fee basis may elect, if the performance of the service for which such fees are received constitutes a trade or business pursuant to the provisions of subdivision (i) of this subparagraph, to have such performance of service treated as excluded from the term "trade or business" for the purpose of the tax on self-employment income, pursuant to the provisions of section 122(c)(2) of the Social Security Amendments of 1967 (as quoted in § 1.1402(c)). Such election shall not be limited to service to which the fees received in 1968 are attributable but must also be applicable to service (if any in subsequent years which, except for the election, would constitute a trade or business pursuant to the provisions of subdivision (i) of this subparagraph. An election made pursuant to the provisions of this subparagraph is irrevocable.

(B) The election referred to in subdivision (ii)(A) of this subparagraph shall be made by filing a certificate of election of exemption (Form 4415) on or before the due date of the income tax return (see section 6072), including any extension thereof (see section 6081), for the taxable year of the individual making the election which begins in 1968. The certificate of election of exemption shall be filed with an internal revenue office in accordance with the instructions on the certificate.

(b) Meaning of public office. The term "public office" includes any elective or appointive office of the United States or any possession thereof, of the District of Columbia, of a State or its political subdivisions, or a wholly-owned instrumentality of any one or more of the foregoing. For example, the President, the Vice President, a governor, a mayor, the Secretary of State, a member of Congress, a State representative, a county commissioner, a judge, a justice of the peace, a county or city attorney, a marshal, a sheriff, a constable, a registrar of deeds, or a notary public performs the functions of a public office. (However, the service of a notary public could not be made the subject of a section 218 agreement under the Social Security Act because notaries are not "employees" within the meaning of that section. Accordingly, such service does not constitute a trade or business.)

T.D. 6691, 12/2/63, amend T.D. 7333, 12/19/74, T.D. 7372, 7/23/75.

§ 1.1402(c)-3 Employees.

Caution: The Treasury has not yet amended Reg § 1.1402(c)-3 to reflect changes made by P.L. 98-369.

(a) General rule. Generally, the performance of service by an individual as an employee, as defined in the Federal Insurance Contributions Act (chapter 21 of the Internal Revenue Code) does not constitute a trade or business within the meaning of section 1402(c) and § 1.1402(c)-1. However, in six cases set forth in paragraphs (b) to (g), inclusive, of this section, the performance of service by an individual is considered to constitute a trade or business within the meaning of section 1402(c) and § 1.1402(c)-1. (As to when an individual is an employee, see section 3121(d) and (o) and section 3506 and the regulations under those sections in Part 31 of this chapter (Employment Tax Regulations).)

(b) Newspaper vendors. Service performed by an individual who has attained the age of 18 constitutes a trade or business for purposes of the tax on self-employment income within the meaning of section 1402(c) and § 1.1402(c)-1 if performed in, and at the time of, the sale of newspapers or magazines to ultimate consumers, under an arrangement under which the newspapers or magazines are to be sold by him at a fixed price, his compensation being based on the retention of the excess of such price over the amount at which the newspapers or magazines are charged to him, whether or not he is guaranteed a minimum amount of compensation for such service, or is entitled to be credited with the unsold newspapers or magazines turned back.

(c) Sharecroppers. Service performed by an individual under an arrangement with the owner or tenant of land pursuant to which—

(1) Such individual undertakes to produce agricultural or horticultural commodities (including livestock, bees, poultry, and fur-bearing animals and wild life) on such land,

(2) The agricultural or horticultural commodities produced by such individual, or the proceeds therefrom, are to be divided between such individual and such owner or tenant, and

(3) The amount of such individual's share depends on the amount of the agricultural or horticultural commodities produced,

constitutes a trade or business within the meaning of section 1402(c) and § 1.1402(c)-1.

(d) Employees of foreign government, instrumentality wholly owned by foreign government, or international organization. Service performed in the United States, as defined in section 3121(e)(2) (see such section and the regulations thereunder in Part 31 of this chapter (Employment Tax Regulations)), by an individual who is a citizen of the United States constitutes a trade or business within the meaning of section 1402(c) and § 1.1402(c)-1 if such service is excepted from employment, for purposes of the Federal Insurance Contributions Act (chapter 21 of the Code), by—

(1) Section 3121(b)(11), relating to service in the employ of a foreign government (for regulations under section 3121(b)(11), see § 31.3121(b)(11)-1 of this chapter);

(2) Section 3121(b)(12), relating to service in the employ of an instrumentality wholly owned by a foreign government (for regulations under section 3121(b)(12), see § 31.3121(b)(12)-1 of this chapter); or

(3) Section 3121(b)(15), relating to service in the employ of an international organization (for regulations under section 3121(b)(15), see § 31.3121(b)(15)-1 of this chapter). This paragraph is applicable to service performed in any taxable year ending on or after December 31, 1960, except that it does not apply to service performed before 1961 in Guam or American Samoa.

(e) Ministers and members of religious orders. *(1) Taxable years ending before 1968.* Service described in section 1402(c)(4) performed by an individual during taxable years ending before 1968 for which a certificate filed pursuant to section 1402(e) is in effect constitutes a trade or business within the meaning of section 1402(c) and § 1.1402(c)-1. See also § 1.1402(c)-5.

(2) Taxable years ending after 1967. Service described in section 1402(c)(4) performed by an individual during taxable years ending after 1967 constitutes a trade or business within the meaning of section 1402(c) and § 1.1402(c)-1 unless an exemption under section 1402(e) (see §§ 1.1402(e)-1A through 1.1402(e)-4A) is effective with respect to such individual for the taxable year during which the service is performed. See also § 1.1402(c)-5.

(f) State and local government employees compensated on fee basis. *(1) In general.* (i) Section 1402(c)(2)(E) and this paragraph are applicable only with respect to fees received by an individual after 1967 for service performed by him as an employee of a State or a political subdivision thereof in a position compensated solely on a fee basis. If an individual performs service for a State or a political subdivision thereof in more than one position, each position is treated separately for purposes of determining whether the service performed in such position is performed by an employee and whether compensation for service performed in the position is solely on a fee basis.

(ii) If an individual receives fees after 1967 for service performed by him as an employee of a State or a political subdivision thereof in a position compensated solely on a fee basis, the service for which such fees are received constitutes a trade or business within the meaning of section 1402(c) and § 1.1402(c)-1 except that if service performed in such position is covered under an agreement entered into by the State and the Secretary of Health, Education, and Welfare pursuant to section 218 of the Social Security Act at the time a fee is received, the service to which such fee relates does not constitute a trade or business. See also paragraph (a) of § 1.1402(c)-2, relating, in part, to the performance of the functions of a public office of a State or a political subdivision thereof by an individual.

(2) Election with respect to fees received in 1968. (i) Any individual who in 1968 receives fees for service as an employee of a State or a political subdivision thereof in a position compensated solely on a fee basis may elect, if the performance of the service for which such fees are received constitutes a trade or business pursuant to the provisions of subparagraph (1) of this paragraph, to have such performance of service treated as excluded from the term "trade or business" for the purpose of the tax on self-employment income, pursuant to the provisions of section 122(c)(2) of the Social Security Amendments of 1967 (as quoted in § 1.1402(c)). Such election shall not be limited to service to which the fees received in 1968 are attributable but must also be applicable to service (if any) in subsequent years which, except for the election, would constitute a trade or business pursuant to the provisions of subparagraph (1) of this paragraph. An election made pursuant to the provisions of this subparagraph is irrevocable.

(ii) The election referred to in subdivision (i) of this subparagraph shall be made by filing a certificate of election of exemption (Form 4415) on or before the due date of the income tax return (see section 6072), including any extension thereof (see section 6081), for the taxable year of the individual making the election which begins in 1968. The certificate of election of exemption shall be filed with an internal revenue office in accordance with the instructions on the certificate.

(g) Individuals engaged in fishing. For taxable years ending after December 31, 1954, service performed by an individual on a boat engaged in catching fish or other forms of aquatic animal life (hereinafter "fish") constitutes a trade or business within the meaning of section 1402(c) and § 1.1402(c)-1 if the service is excepted from the definition of employment by section 3121(b)(20) and § 31.3121(b)(20)-1(a). However, the preceding sentence does not apply to services performed after December 31, 1954, and before October 4, 1976, on a boat engaged in catching fish if the owner or operator of the boat treated the individual as an employee in the manner described in § 31.3121(b)(20)-1(b).

T.D. 6691, 12/2/63, amend T.D. 6978, 10/29/68, T.D. 7333, 12/19/74, T.D. 7691, 4/8/80, T.D. 7716, 8/26/80.

§ 1.1402(c)-4 Individuals under Railroad Retirement System.

The performance of service by an individual as an employee or employee representative as defined in section 3231(b) and (c), respectively (see §§ 31.3231(b)-1 and 31.3231(c)-1 of Part 31 of this chapter (Employment Tax Regulations)), that is, an individual covered under the railroad retirement system, does not constitute a trade or business.

T.D. 6691, 12/2/63.

§ 1.1402(c)-5 Ministers and members of religious orders.

(a) In general. *(1) Taxable years ending before 1968.* For taxable years ending before 1955, a duly ordained, commissioned, or licensed minister of a church or a member of a religious order is not engaged in carrying on a trade or business with respect to service performed by him in the exercise of his ministry or in the exercise of duties required by such order. However, for taxable years ending after 1954 and before 1968, any individual who is a duly ordained, commissioned, or licensed minister of a church or a member of a religious order (other than a member of a religious order who has taken a vow of poverty as a member of such order) may elect, as provided in § 1.1402(e)(1)-1, to have the Federal old-age, survivors, and disability insurance system established by title II of the Social Security Act extended to service performed by him in his capacity as such a minister or member. If such a minister or a member of a religious order makes an election pursuant to § 1.1402(e)(1)-1 he is, with respect to service performed by him in such capacity, engaged in carrying on a trade or business for each taxable year to which the election is effective. An election by a minister or member of a religious order has no application to service performed by such minister or member which is not in the exercise of his ministry or in the exercise of duties required by such order.

(2) Taxable years ending after 1967. For any taxable year ending after 1967, a duly ordained, commissioned, or licensed minister of a church or a member of a religious order (other than a member of a religious order who has taken a vow of poverty as a member of such order) is engaged in carrying on a trade or business with respect to service performed by him in the exercise of his ministry or in the exercise of duties required by such order unless an exemption under section 1402(e) (see §§ 1.1402(e)-1A through 1.1402(e)-4A) is effective with respect to such individual for the taxable year during which the service is performed. An exemption which is effective with respect to a minister or a member of a religious order has no application to service performed by such minister or member which is not in the exercise of his ministry or in the exercise of duties required by such order.

(b) Service by a minister in the exercise of his ministry. *(1)* (i) A certificate of election filed by a duly ordained, commissioned, or licensed minister of a church under the provisions of § 1.1402(e)(1)-1 has application only to service performed by him in the exercise of his ministry.

(ii) An exemption under section 1402(e) (see §§ 1.1402(e)-1A through 1.1402(e)-4A) which is effective with respect to a duly ordained, commissioned, or licensed minister of a church has application only to service performed by him in the exercise of his ministry.

(2) Except as provided in paragraph (c)(3) of this section, service performed by a minister in the exercise of his ministry includes the ministration of sacerdotal functions and the conduct of religious worship, and the control, conduct, and maintenance of religious organizations (including the religious boards, societies, and other integral agencies of such organizations), under the authority of a religious body constituting a church or church denomination. The following rules are applicable in determining whether services performed by a minister are performed in the exercise of his ministry:

(i) Whether service performed by a minister constitutes the conduct of religious worship or the ministration of sacerdotal functions depends on the tenets and practices of the particular religious body constituting his church or church denomination.

(ii) Service performed by a minister in the control, conduct, and maintenance of a religious organization relates to directing, managing, or promoting the activities of such organization. Any religious organization is deemed to be under the authority of a religious body constituting a church or church denomination if it is organized and dedicated to carrying out the tenets and principles of a faith in accordance with either the requirements or sanctions governing the creation of institutions of the faith. The term "religious organization" has the same meaning and application as is given to the term for income tax purposes.

(iii) If a minister is performing service in the conduct of religious worship or the ministration of sacerdotal functions, such service is in the exercise of his ministry whether or not it is performed for a religious organization. The application of this rule may be illustrated by the following example:

Example. M, a duly ordained minister, is engaged to perform service a chaplain at N University. M devotes his entire time to performing his duties as chaplain which include the conduct of religious worship, offering spiritual counsel to the university students, and teaching a class in religion. M is performing service in the exercise of his ministry.

(iv) If a minister is performing service for an organization which is operated as an integral agency of a religious organization under the authority of a religious body constituting a church or church denomination, all service performed by the minister in the conduct of religious worship, in the ministration of sacerdotal functions, or in the control, conduct, and maintenance of such organization (see subparagraph (2)(ii) of this paragraph) is in the exercise of his ministry. The application of this rule may be illustrated by the following example:

Example. M, a duly ordained minister, is engaged by the N Religious Board to serve as director of one of its departments. He performs no other service. The N Religious Board is an integral agency of O, a religious organization operating under the authority of a religious body constituting a church denomination. M is performing service in the exercise of his ministry.

(v) If a minister, pursuant to an assignment or designation by a religious body constituting his church, performs service for an organization which is neither a religious organization nor operated as an integral agency of a religious organization, all service performed by him, even though such service may not involve the conduct of religious worship or the ministration of sacerdotal functions, is in the exercise of his ministry. The application of this rule may be illustrated by the following example:

Example. M, a duly ordained minister, is assigned by X, the religious body constituting his church, to perform advisory service to Y Company in connection with the publication of a book dealing with the history of M's church denomination. Y is neither a religious organization nor operated as an integral agency of a religious organization. M performs no other service for X or Y. M is performing service in the exercise of his ministry.

(c) Service by a minister not in the exercise of his ministry. *(1)* (i) A certificate filed by a duly ordained, commissioned, or licensed minister of a church under the provisions of § 1.1402(e)(1)-1 has no application to service performed by him which is not in the exercise of his ministry.

(ii) An exemption under section 1402(e) (see §§ 1.1402(e)-1A through 1.1402(e)-4A) which is effective with respect to a duly ordained, commissioned, or licensed minister of a church has no application to service performed by him which is not in the exercise of his ministry.

(2) If a minister is performing service for an organization which is neither a religious organization nor operated as an integral agency of a religious organization and the service is not performed pursuant to an assignment or designation by his ecclesiastical superiors, then only the service performed by him in the conduct of religious worship or the ministration of sacerdotal functions is in the exercise of his ministry. See, however, subparagraph (3) of this paragraph. The application of the rule in this subparagraph may be illustrated by the following example:

Example. M, a duly ordained minister, is engaged by N University to teach history and mathematics. He performs no other service for N although from time to time he performs marriages and conducts funerals for relatives and friends. N University is neither a religious organization nor operated as an integral agency of a religious organization. M is not performing the service for N pursuant to an assignment or designation by his ecclesiastical superiors. The service performed by M for N University is not in the exercise of his ministry. However, service performed by M in performing marriages and conducting funerals is in the exercise of his ministry.

(3) Service performed by a duly ordained, commissioned, or licensed minister of a church as an employee of the United States, or a State, Territory, or possession of the United States, or the District of Columbia, or a foreign government, or a political subdivision of any of the foregoing, is not considered to be in the exercise of his ministry for purposes of the tax on self-employment income, even though such service may involve the ministration of sacerdotal functions or the conduct of religious worship. Thus, for example, service performed by an individual as a chaplain in the Armed Forces of the United States is considered to be performed by a commissioned officer in his capacity as such, and not by a minister in the exercise of his ministry. Similarly, service performed by an employee of a State as a chaplain in a State prison is considered to be performed by a civil servant of the State and not by a minister in the exercise of his ministry.

(d) Service in the exercise of duties required by a religious order. *(1) Certificate of election.* A certificate of election filed by a member of a religious order (other than a member of a religious order who has taken a vow of poverty as a member of such order) under the provisions of § 1.1402(e)(1)-1 has application to all duties required of him by such order.

(2) Exemption. An exemption under section 1402(e) (see §§ 1.1402(e)-1A through 1.1402(e)-4A) which is effective with respect to a member of a religious order (other than a member of a religious order who has taken a vow of poverty as a member of such order) has application only to the duties required of him by such order.

(3) Service. For purposes of subparagraphs (1) and (2) of this paragraph, the nature or extent of the duties required of the member by the order is immaterial so long as it is a service which he is directed or required to perform by his ecclesiastical superiors.

T.D. 6691, 12/2/63, amend T.D. 6978, 10/29/68.

§ 1.1402(c)-6 Members of certain professions.

(a) Periods of exclusion. *(1) Taxable years ending before 1955.* For taxable years ending before 1955, an individual is not engaged in carrying on a trade or business with respect to the performance of service in the exercise of his profession as a physician, lawyer, dentist, osteopath, veterinarian, chiropractor, naturopath, optometrist, Christian Science practitioner, architect, certified public accountant, accountant registered or licensed as an accountant under State or municipal law, full-time practicing public accountant, funeral director, or professional engineer.

(2) Taxable years ending in 1955. Except as provided in paragraph (b) of this section, for a taxable year ending in 1955 an individual is not engaged in carrying on a trade or business with respect to the performance of service in the exercise of his profession as a physician, lawyer, dentist, osteopath, veterinarian, chiropractor, naturopath, optometrist, or Christian Science practitioner.

(3) Taxable years ending after 1955. (i) Doctors of medicine. For taxable years ending after 1955 and before December 31, 1965, an individual is not engaged in carrying on a trade or business with respect to the performance of service in the exercise of his profession as a doctor of medicine. For taxable years ending after December 30, 1965, an individual is engaged in carrying on a trade or business with respect to the performance of service in the exercise of his profession as a doctor of medicine.

(ii) Christian Science practitioners. Except as provided in paragraph (b)(1) of this section, for taxable years ending after 1955 and before 1968, an individual is not engaged in carrying on a trade or business with respect to the performance of service in the exercise of his profession as a Christian Science practitioner. For provisions relating to the performance of service in taxable years ending after 1967 by an individual in the exercise of his profession as a Christian Science practitioner, see paragraph (b)(2) of this section.

(b) Christian Science practitioner. *(1) Certain taxable years ending before 1968; election.* For taxable years ending after 1954 and before 1968, a Christian Science practitioner may elect, as provided in § 1.1402(e)(1)-1, to have the Federal old-age, survivors, and disability insurance system established by title II of the Social Security Act extended to service performed by him in the exercise of his profession as a Christian Science practitioner. If an election is made pursuant to § 1.1402(e)(1)-1, the Christian Science practitioner is, with respect to the performance of service in the exercise of such profession, engaged in carrying on a trade or business for each taxable year for which the election is effective. An election by a Christian Science practitioner has no application to service performed by him which is not in the exercise of his profession as a Christian Science practitioner.

(2) Taxable years ending after 1967; exemption. For a taxable year ending after 1967, a Christian Science practitioner is, with respect to the performance of service in the exercise of his profession as a Christian Science practitioner, engaged in carrying on a trade or business unless an exemption under section 1402(e) (see §§ 1.1402(e)-1A through 1.1402(e)-4A) is effective with respect to him for the taxable year during which the service is performed. An exemption which is effective with respect to a Christian Science practitioner has no application to service performed by him which is not in the exercise of his profession as a Christian Science practitioner.

(c) Meaning of terms. The designations in this section are to be given their commonly accepted meanings. For taxable years ending after 1955, an individual who is a doctor of osteopathy, and who is not a doctor of medicine within the commonly accepted meaning of that term, is deemed, for purposes of this section, not to be engaged in carrying on a trade or business in the exercise of the profession of doctor of medicine.

(d) Legal requirements. The exclusions specified in paragraph (a) of this section apply only if the individuals meet the legal requirements, if any, for practicing their professions in the place where they perform the service.

(e) Partnerships. In the case of a partnership engaged in the practice of any of the designated excluded professions, the partnership shall not be considered as carrying on a trade or business for the purpose of the tax on self-employment income, and none of the distributive shares of the income or loss, described in section 702(a)(9), of such partnership shall be included in computing net earnings from self-employment of any member of the partnership. On the other hand, where a partnership is engaged in a trade or business not within any of the designated excluded professions, each partner must include his distributive share of the income or loss, described in section 702(a)(9), of such partnership in computing his net earnings from self-employment, irrespective of whether such partner is engaged in the practice of one or more of such professions and contributes his professional services to the partnership.

T.D. 6691, 12/2/63, amend T.D. 6978, 10/29/68.

§ 1.1402(c)-7 Members of religious groups opposed to insurance.

The performance of service by an individual—

(a) Who is a member of a recognized religious sect or division thereof, and

(b) Who is an adherent of established tenets or teachings of such sect or division by reason of which he is conscientiously opposed to acceptance of the benefits of any private or public insurance which makes payments in the event of death, disability, old age, or retirement or makes payments toward the cost of, or provides services for, medical care (including the benefits of any insurance system established by the Social Security Act),

during any taxable year for which he is granted a tax exemption, pursuant to section 1402(h), does not constitute a trade or business within the meaning of section 1402(c) and § 1.1402(c)-1. See also §§ 1.1402(h) and 1.1402(h)-1.

T.D. 6978, 10/29/68, amend T.D. 6993, 1/17/69.

§ 1.1402(d)-1 Employee and wages.

For the purpose of the tax on self-employment income, the term "employee" and the term "wages" shall have the same meaning as when used in the Federal Insurance Contributions Act. For an explanation of these terms, see Subpart B of Part 31 of this chapter (Employment Tax Regulations).

T.D. 6196, 8/13/56, amend T.D. 6691, 12/2/63.

§ 1.1402(e)-1A Application of regulations under section 1402(e).

The regulations in §§ 1.1402(e)-2A through 1.1402(e)-4A relate to section 1402(e) as amended by section 115(b)(2) of the Social Security Amendments of 1967 (81 Stat. 839) and apply to taxable years ending after 1968. Section 1.1402(e)-5A reflects changes made by section 1704(a) of the Tax Reform Act of 1986 (100 Stat. 2085, 2779) and applies to applications for exemption under section 1402(e) filed after December 31, 1986. For regulations under section 1402(e) (as in effect prior to amendment by the Social Security Amendments of 1967) applicable to taxable years ending before 1968, see §§ 1.1402(e)(1)-1 through 1.1402(e)(6)-1.

T.D. 6978, 10/29/68, amend T.D. 8221, 8/30/88.

§ 1.1402(e)-2A Ministers, members of religious orders and Christian Science practitioners; application for exemption from self-employment tax.

(a) In general. *(1)* Subject to the limitations set forth in subparagraphs (2) and (3) of this paragraph, any individual who is (i) a duly ordained, commissioned, or licensed minister of a church or a member of a religious order (other than a member of a religious order who has taken a vow of poverty as a member of such order) or (ii) a Christian Science practitioner may request an exemption from the tax on self-employment income (see §§ 1.1401 and 1.1401-1) with respect to services performed by him in his capacity as a minister or member, or as a Christian Science practitioner, as the case may be. Such a request shall be made by filing an application for exemption on Form 4361 in the manner provided in paragraph (b) of this section and within the time specified in § 1.1402(e)-3A. For provisions relating to the taxable year or years for which an exemption from the tax on self-employment income with respect to service performed by a minister or member or a Christian Science practitioner in his capacity as such is effective, see § 1.1402(e)-4A. For additional provisions applicable to services performed by individuals referred to in this subparagraph, see paragraph (e) of § 1.1402(c)-3 and § 1.1402(c)-5 relating to ministers and members of religious orders, and paragraphs (a)(3)(ii) and (b) of § 1.1402(c)-6 relating to Christian Science practitioners.

(2) The application for exemption shall contain, or there shall be filed with such application, a statement to the effect that the individual making application for exemption is conscientiously opposed to, or because of religious principles is opposed to, the acceptance (with respect to services performed by him in his capacity as a minister, member, or Christian Science practitioner) of any public insurance which makes payments in the event of death, disability, old age, or retirement or makes payments toward the cost of, or provides services for, medical care (including the benefits of any insurance system established by the Social Security Act). Thus, ministers, members of religious orders, and Christian Science Practitioners requesting exemption from social security coverage must meet either of two alternative tests: (1) A religious principles test which refers to the institutional principles and discipline of the particular religious denomination to which he belongs, or (2) a conscientious opposition test which refers to the opposition because of religious considerations of individual ministers, members of religious orders, and Christian Science Practitioners (rather than opposition based upon the general conscience of any such individual or individuals). The term "public insurance", as used in section 1402(e) and this paragraph, refers to governmental, as distinguished from private, insurance and does not include insurance carried with a commercial insurance carrier. To be eligible to file an application for exemption on Form 4361, a minister, member, or Christian Science practitioners need not be opposed to the acceptance of all public insurance making payments of this specified type; he must, however, be opposed on religious grounds to the acceptance of any such payment which, in whole or in part, is based on, or measured by earnings from, services performed by him in his capacity as a minister or member (see § 1.1402(c)-5) or in his capacity as a Christian Science practitioner (see paragraph (b)(2) of § 1.1402(c)-6). For example, a minister performing service in the exercise of his ministry may be eligible to file an application for exemption on Form 4361 even though he is not opposed to the acceptance of benefits under the Social Security Act with respect to service performed by him which is not in the exercise of his ministry.

(3) An exemption from the tax imposed on self-employment income with respect to service performed by a minister, member, or Christian Science practitioner in his capacity as such may not be granted to a minister, member, or practitioner who (in accordance with the provisions of section 1402(e) as in effect prior to amendment by section 115(b)(2) of the Social Security Amendments of 1967 (81 Stat. 839))

filed a valid waiver certificate on Form 2031 electing to have the Federal old-age, survivors, and disability insurance system establish by title II of the Social Security Act extended to service performed by him in the exercise of his ministry or in the exercise of duties required by the order of which he is a member, or in the exercise of his profession as a Christian Science practitioner. For provisions relating to waiver certificates on Form 2031, see §§ 1.1402(e)(1)-1 through 1.1402(e)(6)-1.

(b) Application for exemption. An application for exemption on Form 4361 shall be filed in triplicate with the internal revenue officer or the internal revenue office, as the case may be, designated in the instructions relating to the application for exemption. The application for exemption must be filed within the time prescribed in § 1.1402(e)-3A. If the last original Federal income tax return of an individual to whom paragraph (a) of this section applies which was filed before the expiration of such time limitation for filing an application for exemption shows no liability for tax on self-employment income, such return will be treated as an application for exemption, provided that before February 28, 1975 such individual also files a properly executed Form 4361.

(c) Approval of application for exemption. The filing of an application for exemption on Form 4361 by a minister, a member of a religious order, or a Christian Science practitioner does not constitute an exemption from the tax on self-employment income with respect to services performed by him in his capacity as a minister, member, or practitioner. The exemption is granted only if the application is approved by an appropriate internal revenue officer. See § 1.1402(e)-4A relating to the period for which an exemption is effective.

T.D. 7333, 12/19/74.

§ 1.1402(e)-3A Time limitation for filing application for exemption.

(a) General rule. *(1)* Any individual referred to in paragraph (a) of § 1.1402(e)-2A who desires an exemption from the tax on self-employment income with respect to service performed by him in his capacity as a minister or member of a religious order or as a Christian Science practitioner must file the application for exemption (Form 4361) prescribed by § 1.1402(e)-2A on or before whichever of the following dates is later:

(i) The due date of the income tax return (see section 6072), including any extension thereof (see section 6081), for his second taxable year ending after 1967, or

(ii) The due date of the income tax return, including any extension thereof, for his second taxable year beginning after 1953 for which he has net earnings from self-employment of $400 or more, any part of which—

(a) In the case of a duly ordained, commissioned, or licensed minister of a church, consists of remuneration for service performed in the exercise of his ministry,

(b) In the case of a member of a religious order who has not taken a vow of poverty as a member of such order, consists of remuneration for service performed in the exercise of duties required by such order, or

(c) In the case of a Christian Science practitioner, consists of remuneration for service performed in the exercise of his profession as a Christian Science practitioner.

See paragraph (c) of this section for provisions relating to the computation of net earnings from self-employment.

(2) If a minister, a member of a religious order, or a Christian Science practitioner derives gross income in a taxable year both from service performed in such capacity and from the conduct of another trade or business, and the deductions allowed by chapter 1 of the Internal Revenue Code which are attributable to the gross income derived from service performed in such capacity equal or exceed the gross income derived from service performed in such capacity, no part of the net earnings from self-employment (computed as prescribed in paragraph (c) of this section) for the taxable year shall be considered as derived from service performed in such capacity.

(3) The application of the rules set forth in subparagraphs (1) and (2) of this paragraph may be illustrated by the following examples:

Example (1). M, who makes his income tax returns on a calendar year basis, was ordained as a minister in January 1960. During each of two or more taxable years ending before 1968 M has net earnings from self-employment in excess of $400 some part of which is from service performed in the exercise of his ministry. M has not filed an effective waiver certificate on Form 2031 (see paragraph (a)(3) of § 1.1402(e)-2A). If M desires an exemption from the tax on self-employment income with respect to service performed in the exercise of his ministry, he must file an application for exemption on or before the due date of his income tax return for 1969 (his second taxable year ending after 1967), or any extension thereof.

Example (2). M, who makes his income tax returns on a calendar year basis, was ordained as a minister in January 1966. M has net earnings of $350 for the taxable year 1966 and has net earnings in excess of $400 for each of his taxable years 1967 and 1968 (some part or all of which is derived from service performed in the exercise of his ministry). M has not filed an effective waiver certificate on Form 2031 (see paragraph (a)(3) of § 1.1402(e)-2A. If M desires an exemption from the tax on self-employment income with respect to service performed in the exercise of his ministry, he must file an application for exemption on or before the due date of his income tax return for 1969 (his second taxable year ending after 1967), or any extension thereof.

Example (3). Assume the same facts as in example (2) except that M has net earnings in excess of $400 for each of his taxable years 1967 and 1969 (but less than $400 in 1968). The application for exemption must be filed on or before the due date of his income tax return for 1969, or any extension thereof.

Example (4). M was ordained as a minister in May 1973. During each of the taxable years 1973 and 1975, M, who makes his income tax returns on a calendar year basis, derives net earnings in excess of $400 from his activities as a minister. M has net earnings of $350 for the taxable year 1974, $200 of which is derived from service performed by him in the exercise of his ministry. If M desires an exemption from the tax on self-employment income with respect to service performed in the exercise of his ministry, he must file an application for exemption on or before the due date of his income tax return for 1975, or any extension thereof.

Example (5). M, who was ordained a minister in January 1973, is employed as a toolmaker by the XYZ Corporation for the taxable years 1973 and 1974 and also engages in activities as a minister on weekends. M makes his income tax returns on the basis of a calendar year. During each of the taxable years 1973 and 1974 M receives wages of $14,000 from the XYZ Corporation and derives net earnings of $400 from his activities as a minister. If M desires an exemption from the tax on self-employment income with respect to service performed in the exercise of his ministry, he must file an application for exemption on or before the due date of his income tax return for 1974, or any extension thereof. It should be noted that although by reason of section 1402(b)(1)(G) and (H) no part of the $400 represents "self-employment income", nevertheless the entire $400 constitutes "net earnings from self-employment" for purposes of fulfilling the requirements of section 1402(e)(2).

Example (6). M, who files his income tax returns on a calendar year basis, was ordained as a minister in March 1973. During 1973 he receives $410 for service performed in the exercise of his ministry. In addition to his ministerial services, M is engaged during the year 1973 in a mercantile venture from which he derives net earnings from self-employment in the amount of $4,000. The expenses incurred by him in connection with his ministerial services during 1973 and which are allowable deductions under chapter 1 of the Internal Revenue Code amount to $410. During 1974 and 1975, M has net earnings from self-employment in amounts of $4,600 and $4,800, respectively, and some part of each of these amounts is from the exercise of his ministry. The deductions allowed in each of the years 1974 and 1975 by chapter 1 which are attributable to the gross income derived by M from the exercise of his ministry in each of such years, respectively, do not equal or exceed such gross income in such year. If M desires an exemption from the tax on self-employment income with respect to service performed in the exercise of his ministry, he must file an application for exemption on or before the due date of his income tax return for 1975, or an extension thereof.

(b) Effect of death. The right of an individual to file an application for exemption shall cease upon his death. Thus, the surviving spouse, administrator, or executor of a decedent shall not be permitted to file an application for exemption for such decedent.

(c) Computation of net earnings. *(1) Taxable years ending before 1968.* For purposes of this section net earnings from self-employment for taxable years ending before 1968 shall be determined without regard to the fact that, without an election under section 1402(e) (as in effect prior to amendment by section 115(b)(2) of the Social Security Amendments of 1967, see § 1.1402(e)-1A), the performance of services by a duly ordained, commissioned, or licensed minister of a church in the exercise of his ministry, or by a member of a religious order in the exercise of duties required by such order, or the performance of service by an individual in the exercise of his profession as a Christian Science practitioner, does not constitute a trade or business for purposes of the tax on self-employment income.

(2) Taxable years ending after 1967. For purposes of this section and § 1.1402(e)-4A net earnings from self-employment for taxable years ending after 1967 shall be determined without regard to section 1402(c)(4) and (5). See § 1.1402(c)-3(e)(2) and § 1.1402(c)-5 relating to ministers and members of religious orders, and paragraphs (a)(3)(ii) and (b) of § 1.1402(c)-6 relating to Christian Science practitioners.

T.D. 7333, 12/19/74.

§ 1.1402(e)-4A Period for which exemption is effective.

Caution: The Treasury has not yet amended Reg § 1.1402(e)-4A to reflect changes made by P.L. 106-170.

(a) In general. If an application for exemption on Form 4361—

(1) Is filed by a minister, a member of a religious order, or a Christian Science practitioner eligible to file such an application (see particularly paragraph (a)(2) and (3) of § 1.1402(e)-2A), and

(2) Is approved (see paragraph (c) of § 1.1402(e)-2A),

the exemption from the tax on self-employment income shall be effective for the first taxable year ending after 1967 for which such minister, member, or practitioner has net earnings from self-employment of $400 or more any part of which was derived from the performance of service in his capacity as a minister, member, or practitioner, and for all succeeding taxable years. See, however, paragraphs (b)(1)(ii) and (d)(2) of § 1.1402(c)-6 relating to Christian Science practitioners.

(b) Exemption irrevocable. An exemption granted to a minister, a member of a religious order, or a Christian Science practitioner pursuant to the provisions of section 1402(e) is irrevocable.

T.D. 7333, 12/19/74.

§ 1.1402(e)-5A Applications for exemption from self-employment taxes filed after December 31, 1986, by ministers, certain members of religious orders, and Christian Science practitioners.

(a) In general. *(1)* Except as provided in paragraph (a)(2) of this section, this section applies to any individual who is a duly ordained, commissioned, or licensed minister of a church, member of a religious order (other than a member of a religious order who has taken a vow of poverty as a member of such order), or a Christian Science practitioner who files an application after December 31, 1986, for exemption from the tax on self-employment income (see section 1401 and 1.1401-1) with respect to services performed by him or her in his or her capacity as a minister, member, or practitioner pursuant to §§ 1.1402(e)-2A through 1.1402(e)-4A. This section does not apply to applications for exemption under section 1402(e) that are filed before January 1, 1987.

(2) Application of this section to Christian Science practitioners. Paragraph (b) of this section does not apply to Christian Science practitioners. Thus, Christian Science practitioners filing applications for exemption from self-employment taxes under section 1402(e) should follow the procedures set forth in §§ 1.1402(e)-2A through 1.1402(e)-4A, and are not required to include the statement described in paragraph (b)(1)(ii) of this section. However, see paragraph (c) of this section for verification procedures with respect to applications for exemption from self-employment taxes filed after December 31, 1986, by Christian Science practitioners.

(b) Church or order must be informed. *(1) In general.* Any individual, other than a Christian Science practitioner, who files an application for exemption from the tax on self-employment income under section 1402(e) after December 31, 1986:

(i) Shall file such application in accordance with the procedures set forth in §§ 1.1402(e)-2A through 1.1402(e)-4A, and

(ii) Shall include with such application a statement to the effect that the individual making application for exemption has informed the ordaining, commissioning, or licensing body of the church or order that he or she is opposed to the acceptance (for services performed as a minister or member of a religious order not under a vow of poverty) of any public insurance that makes payments in the event of death, disability, old age, or retirement, or that makes payments toward the cost of, or provides services for, medical care (including the benefits of any insurance system established by the Social Security Act).

(2) Statement to be filed with Form. If the form provided by the Service for applying for exemption under 1402(e) does not contain the statement set forth in paragraph (b)(1)(ii) of this section, any individual required to include this statement with his or her application under this paragraph (b) shall file such statement with the individual's application at the time and place prescribed for filing such application under §§ 1.1402(e)-2A and 1.1402(e)-3A. The statement shall contain the information set forth in paragraph (b)(1)(ii) of this section and shall be signed by such individual under penalties of perjury.

(c) Verification of application. *(1) In general.* The Service will approve an application for an exemption filed by an individual to whom this section applies only after verifying that the individual applying for the exemption is aware of the grounds on which the individual may receive an exemption under section 1402(e) (See § 1.1402(e)-2A) and that the individual seeks exemption on such grounds in accordance with the procedures set forth in paragraph (c)(2) of this section.

(2) Verification procedure. Upon receipt of an application for exemption from self-employment taxes under section 1402(e) and this section, the Service will mail to the applicant a statement that describes the grounds on which an individual may receive an exemption under section 1402(e). The individual filing the application shall certify that he or she has read the statement and that he or she seeks exemption from self-employment taxes on the grounds listed in the statement. The certification shall be made by signing a copy of the statement under penalties of perjury and mailing the signed copy to the Service Center from which the statement was issued not later than 90 days after the date on which the statement was mailed to the individual. If the signed copy of the statement is not mailed to the Service Center within 90 days of the date on which the statement was mailed to the individual, that individual's exemption will not be effective until the date that the signed copy of the statement is received at the Service Center.

T.D. 8136, 4/14/87, amend T.D. 8221, 8/30/88.

§ 1.1402(f)-1 Computation of partner's net earnings from self-employment for taxable year which ends as result of his death.

Caution: The Treasury has not yet amended Reg § 1.1402(f)-1 to reflect changes made by P.L. 95-216.

(a) Taxable years ending after August 28, 1958. *(1) In general.* The rules for the computation of a partner's net earnings from self-employment are set forth in paragraphs (d) to (g), inclusive, of § 1.1402(a)-2. In addition to the net earnings from self-employment computed under such rules for the last taxable year of a deceased partner, if a partner's taxable year ends after August 28, 1958, solely because of death, and on a day other than the last day of the partnership's taxable year, the deceased partner's net earnings from self-employment for such year shall also include so much of the deceased partner's distributive share of partnership ordinary income or loss (see subparagraph (3) of this paragraph) for the taxable year of the partnership in which his death occurs as is attributable to an interest in the partnership prior to the month following the month of his death.

(2) Computation. (i) The deceased partner's distributive share of partnership ordinary income or loss for the partnership taxable year in which he died shall be determined by applying the rules contained in paragraphs (d) to (g), inclusive, of § 1.1402(a)-2, except that paragraph (e) shall not apply.

(ii) The portion of such distributive share to be included under this section in the deceased partner's net earnings from self-employment for his last taxable year shall be determined by treating the ordinary income or loss constituting such distributive share as having been realized or sustained ratably over the period of the partnership taxable year during which the deceased partner had an interest in the partnership and during which his estate, or any other person succeeding by reason of his death to rights with respect to his partnership interest, held such interest in the partnership or held a right with respect to such interest. The amount to be included under this section in the deceased partner's net earnings from self-employment for his last taxable year will, therefore, be determined by multiplying the deceased partner's distributive share of partnership ordinary income or loss for the partnership taxable year in which he died, as determined under subdivision (i) of this subparagraph, by a fraction, the denominator of which is the number of calendar months in the partnership taxable year over which the ordinary income or loss constituting the deceased partner's distributive share of partnership income or loss for such year is treated as having been realized or sustained under the preceding sentence and the numerator of which is the number of calendar months in such partnership taxable year that precede the month following the month of his death.

(3) Definition of "deceased partner's distributive share". For the purpose of this section, the term "deceased partner's distributive share" includes the distributive share of his estate or of any other person succeeding, by reason of his death, to rights with respect to his partnership interest. It does not include any share attributable to a partnership interest which was not held by the deceased partner at the time of his death. Thus, if a deceased partner's estate should acquire an interest in a partnership additional to the interest to which it succeeded upon the death of the deceased partner, the amount of the distributive share attributable to such additional interest acquired by the estate would not be included in computing the "deceased partner's distributive share" of the partnership's ordinary income or loss for the partnership taxable year.

(4) Examples. The application of this paragraph may be illustrated by the following examples:

Example (1). B, an individual who files his income tax returns on the calendar year basis, is a member of the ABC partnership, the taxable year of which ends on June 30. B dies on October 17, 1958, and his estate succeeds to his partnership interest and continues as a partner in its own right under local law until June 30, 1959. B's distributive share of the partnership's ordinary income, as determined under paragraphs (d) to (g), inclusive, of § 1.1402(a)-2, for the taxable year of the partnership ended June 30, 1958 is $2,400. His distributive share, including the share of his estate, of such partnership's ordinary income, as determined under paragraphs (d) to (g), inclusive, of § 1.1402(a)-2 (with the exception of paragraph (e)), for the taxable year of the partnership ended June 30, 1959 is $4,500. The portion of such $4,500 attributable to an interest in the partnership prior to the month following the month in which he died is

$4,500 × 4/12 (4 being the number of months in the partnership taxable year in which B died which precede the month following the month of his death and 12 being the number of months in such partnership taxable year in which B and his estate had an interest in the partnership) or $1,500. The amount to be included in the deceased partner's net earnings from self-employment for his last taxable year is $3,900 ($2,400 plus $1,500).

Example (2). If in the preceding example B's estate is entitled to only $1,000, the amount of B's distributive share of partnership ordinary income for the period July 1, 1958 through October 17, 1958, such $1,000 is considered to have been realized ratably over the period preceding B's death and will be included in B's net earnings from self-employment for his last taxable year.

Example (3). X, who reports his income on a calendar year basis, is a member of a partnership which also reports its income on a calendar year basis. X dies on June 30, 1959, and his estate succeeds to his partnership interest and continues as a partner in its own right under local law. On September 15, 1959, X's estate sells the partnership interest to which it succeeded on the death of X. X's distributive share of partnership income for 1959 is $5,500. $600 of such amount is X's share of the gain from the sale of a capital asset which occurs on May 1, 1959, and $400 of such amount is the estate's share of the gain from the sale of a capital asset which occurs on July 15, 1959. The remainder of such amount is income from services rendered. X's distributive share of partnership ordinary income for 1959, as determined under paragraphs (d) to (g), inclusive, of § 1.1402(a)-2 (with the exception of paragraph (e)), is $4,500 ($5,500 minus $1,000). The portion of such share attributable to an interest in the partnership prior to the month following the month of his death is $4,500 × 6/8.5 (6 being the number of months in the partnership taxable year in which X died as precede the month following the month of his death and 8.5 being the number of months in such partnership taxable year in which X and his estate had an interest in the partnership) or $3,176.47.

(b) Options available to farmers. *(1) Special rule.* In determining whether the optional method available to a member of a farm partnership in computing his net earnings from self-employment may be applied, and in applying such method, it is necessary to determine the partner's distributive share of partnership gross income and the partner's distributive share of income described in section 702(a)(9). See section 1402(a) and § 1.1402(a)-15. If section 1402(f) and this section apply, or may be made applicable under section 403(b)(2) of the Social Security Amendments of 1958 and paragraph (c) of this section, for the last taxable year of a deceased partner, such partner's distributive share of income described in section 702(a)(9) for his last taxable year shall be determined by including therein any amount which is included under section 1402(f) and this section in his net earnings from self-employment for such taxable year. Such a partner's distributive share of partnership gross income for his last taxable year shall be determined by including therein so much of the deceased partner's distributive share (see paragraph (a)(3) of this section) of partnership gross income, as defined in section 1402(a) and paragraph (b) of § 1.1402(a)-15, for the partnership taxable year in which he died as is attributable to an interest in the partnership prior to the month following the month of his death. Such allocation shall be made in the same manner as is prescribed in paragraph (a)(2) of this section for determining the portion of a deceased partner's distributive share of partnership ordinary income or loss to be included under section 1402(f) and this section in his net earnings from self-employment for his last taxable year.

(2) Examples. The principles set forth in this paragraph may be illustrated by the following examples:

Example (1). X, an individual who files his income tax returns on a calendar year basis, is a member of the XYZ farm partnership, the taxable year of which ends on March 31. X dies on May 31, 1967, and his estate succeeds to his partnership interest and continues as a partner in its own right under local law until March 31, 1968. X's distributive share of the partnership's ordinary income, determined under paragraphs (d) to (g), inclusive, of § 1.1402(a)-2, for the taxable year of the partnership ended March 31, 1967, is $1,600. His distributive share, including the share of his estate, of such partnership's ordinary loss as determined under paragraphs (d) to (g), inclusive, of § 1.1402(a)-2 (with the exception of paragraph (e)), for the taxable year of the partnership ended March 31, 1968, is $1,200. The portion of such $1,200 attributable to an interest in the partnership prior to the month following the month in which he died is $1,200 × 2/12 (2 being the number of months in the partnership taxable year in which X died which precede the month following the month of his death and 12 being the number of months in such partnership taxable year in which X and his estate had an interest in the partnership) or $200. X is also a member of the ABX farm partnership, the taxable year of which ends on May 31. His distributive share of the partnership loss described in section 702(a)(9) for the partnership taxable year ending May 31, 1967, is $300. Section 1402(f) and this section do not apply with respect to such $300 since X's last taxable year ends, as a result of his death, with the taxable year of the ABX partnership. Under this paragraph the $200 loss must be included in determining X's distributive share of XYZ partnership income described in section 702(a)(9) for the purpose of applying the optional method available to farmers for computing net earnings from self-employment. Further, the resulting $1,400 of income must be aggregated, pursuant to paragraph (c) of § 1.1402(a)-15, with the $300 loss, X's distributive share of ABX partnership loss described in section 702(a)(9), for purposes of applying such option. The representative of X's estate may exercise the option described in paragraph (a)(2)(ii) of § 1.1402(a)-15, provided the portion of X's distributive share of XYZ partnership gross income for the taxable year ended March 31, 1968, attributable to an interest in the partnership prior to the month following the month in which he died (the allocation being made in the manner prescribed for allocating his $1,200 distributive share of XYZ partnership loss for such year), when aggregated with his distributive share of XYZ partnership gross income for the partnership taxable year ended March 31, 1967, and with his distributive share of ABX partnership gross income for the partnership taxable year ended May 31, 1967, results in X having more than $2,400 of gross income from the trade or business of farming. If such aggregate amount of gross income is not more than $2,400, the option described in paragraph (a)(2)(i) of § 1.1402(a)-15, is available.

Example (2). A, a sole proprietor engaged in the business of farming, files his income tax returns on a calendar year basis. A is also a member of a partnership engaged in an agricultural activity. The partnership files its returns on the basis of a fiscal year ending March 31. A dies June 29, 1967. A's gross income from farming as a sole proprietor for the 6-month period comprising his taxable year which ends because of death is $1,600 and his actual net earnings from self-employment based thereon are $400. As of March 31, 1967, A's distributive share of the gross income of the farm partnership is $2,200 and his distributive share of income described in section 702(a)(9) based thereon is $1,000. The amount of A's distributive share of the partnership's ordinary income for its taxable year ended March 31, 1968, which may be included in his net earnings from self-employment under section 1402(f) and paragraph (a) of this section is $300. The amount of the deceased partner's distributive share of partnership gross income attributable to an interest in the partnership prior to the month following the month of his death as is determined, pursuant to subparagraph (1) of this paragraph, under paragraph (a) of this section is $2,000. An aggregation of the above figures produces a gross income from farming of $5,800 and actual net earnings from self-employment of $1,700. Under these circumstances none of the options provided by section 1402(a) may be used. If the actual net earnings from self-employment had been less than $1,600, the option described in paragraph (a)(2)(ii) of § 1.1402(a)-15 would have been available.

(c) Taxable years ending after 1955 and on or before August 28, 1958. *(1) Requirement of election.* If a partner's taxable year ended, as a result of his death, after 1955 and on or before August 28, 1958, the rules set forth in paragraph (a) of this section may be made applicable in computing the deceased partner's net earnings from self-employment for his last taxable year provided that—

(i) Before January 1, 1960, there is filed, by the person designated in section 6012(b)(1) and paragraph (b)(1) of § 1.6012-3, a return (or amended return) of the tax imposed by chapter 2 for the taxable year ending as a result of death, and

(ii) Such return, if filed solely for the purpose of reporting net earnings from self-employment resulting from the enactment of section 1402(f), is accompanied by the amount of tax attributable to such net earnings.

(2) Administrative rule of special application. Notwithstanding the provisions of sections 6601, 6651, and 6653 (see such sections and the regulations thereunder) no interest or penalty shall be assessed or collected on the amount of any self-employment tax due solely by reason of the operation of section 1402(f) in the case of an individual who died after 1955 and before August 29, 1958.

T.D. 6691, 12/2/63, amend T.D. 6993, 1/17/69.

§ 1.1402(g)-1 Treatment of certain remuneration erroneously reported as net earnings from self-employment.

Caution: The Treasury has not yet amended Reg § 1.1402(g)-1 to reflect changes made by P.L. 94-455.

(a) General rule. If an amount is erroneously paid as self-employment tax, for any taxable year ending after 1954 and before 1962, with respect to remuneration for service (other than service described in section 3121(b)(8)(A)) performed in the employ of an organization described in section 501(c)(3) and exempt from income tax under section 501(a), and if such remuneration is reported as self-employment income on a return filed on or before the due date prescribed for filing such return (including any extension thereof), the individual who paid such amount (or a fiduciary acting for such individual or his estate, or his survivor (within the meaning of section 205(c)(1)(C) of the Social Security Act)), may request that such remuneration be deemed to constitute net earnings from self-employment. If such request is filed during the period September 14, 1960, to April 16, 1962, inclusive, and on or after the date on which the organization which paid such remuneration to such individual for services performed in its employ has filed, pursuant to section 3121(k), a certificate waiving exemption from taxes under the Federal Insurance Contributions Act, and if no credit or refund of any portion of the amount erroneously paid for such taxable year as self-employment tax (other than a credit or refund which would be allowable if such tax were applicable with respect to such remuneration) has been obtained before the date on which such request is filed or, if obtained, the amount credited or refunded (including any interest under section 6611) is repaid on or before such date, then, for purposes of the Self-Employment Contributions Act of 1954 and the Federal Insurance Contributions Act, any amount of such remuneration which is paid to such individual before the calendar quarter in which such request is filed (or before the succeeding quarter if such certificate first becomes effective with respect to services performed by such individual in such succeeding quarter) and with respect to which no tax (other than an amount erroneously paid as tax) has been paid under the Federal Insurance Contributions Act, shall be deemed to constitute net earnings from self-employment and not remuneration for employment. If the certificate filed by such organization pursuant to section 3121(k) is not effective with respect to services performed by such individual on or before the first day of the calendar quarter in which the request is filed, then, for purposes of section 3121(b)(8)(B)(ii) and (iii), such individual shall be deemed to have become an employee of such organization (or to have become a member of a group, described in section 3121(k)(1)(E), of employees of such organization) on the first day of the succeeding quarter.

(b) Request for validation. *(1)* No particular form is prescribed for making a request under paragraph (a) of this section. The request should be in writing, should be signed and dated by the person making the request, and should indicate clearly that it is a request that, pursuant to section 1402(g) of the Code, remuneration for service described in section 3121(b)(8) (other than service described in section 3121(b)(8)(A)) erroneously reported as self-employment income for one or more specified years be deemed to constitute net earnings from self-employment and not remuneration for employment. In addition, the following information shall be shown in connection with the request:

(i) The name, address, and social security account number of the individual with respect to whose remuneration the request is made.

(ii) The taxable year or years (ending after 1954 and before 1962) to which the request relates.

(iii) A statement that the remuneration was erroneously reported as self-employment income on the individual's return for each year specified and that the return was filed on or before its due date (including any extension thereof).

(iv) Location of the office of the district director with whom each return was filed.

(v) A statement that no portion of the amount erroneously paid by the individual as self-employment tax with respect to the remuneration has been credited or refunded (other than a credit or refund which would have been allowable if the tax had been applicable with respect to the remuneration); or, if a credit or refund of any portion of such amount has been obtained, a statement identifying the credit or refund and showing how and when the amount credited or refunded, together with any interest received in connection therewith, was repaid.

(vi) The name and address of the organization which paid the remuneration to the individual.

(vii) The date on which the organization filed a waiver certificate on Form SS-15, and the location of the office of the district director with whom it was filed.

(viii) The date on which the certificate became effective with respect to services performed by the individual.

(ix) If the request is made by a person other than the individual to whom the remuneration was paid, the name and address of that person and evidence which shows the authority of such person to make the request.

(2) The request should be filed with the district director of internal revenue with whom the latest of the returns specified in the request pursuant to subparagraph (1)(iii) of this paragraph was filed.

(c) Cross references. For regulations relating to section 3121(b)(8) and (k), see §§ 31.3121(b)(8)-2 and 31.3121(k)-1 of Subpart B of Part 31 of this chapter (Employment Tax Regulations). For regulations relating to exemption from income tax of an organization described in section 501(c)(3), see § 1.501(c)(3)-1.

T.D. 6691, 12/2/63.

§ 1.1402(h)-1 Members of certain religious groups opposed to insurance.

Caution: The Treasury has not yet amended Reg § 1.1402(h)-1 to reflect changes made by P.L. 100-647, P.L. 94-455.

(a) In general. An individual—

(1) Who is a member of a recognized religious sect or division thereof and

(2) Who is an adherent of established tenets or teachings of such sect or division and by reason thereof is conscientiously opposed to acceptance of the benefits of any private or public insurance which makes payments in the event of death, disability, old age, or retirement or makes payments toward the cost of, or provides services for, medical care (including the benefits of any insurance system established by the Social Security Act),

may file an application for exemption from the tax under section 1401. The form of insurance to which section 1402(h) and this section refer does not include liability insurance of a kind that provides only for the protection of other persons, or property of other persons, who may be injured or damaged by or on property belonging to, or by an action of, an individual who otherwise meets the requirements of this section. An application for exemption under section 1402(h) and this section shall be made in the manner provided in paragraph (b) of this section and within the time specified in paragraph (c) of this section. For provisions relating to the filing of an application for exemption by a fiduciary or survivor, see paragraph (d) of this section.

(b) Application for exemption. The application for exemption shall be filed on Form 4029 in duplicate with the internal revenue official or office designated on the form. The filing of a return by a member of a religious group opposed to insurance showing no self-employment income or self-employment tax shall not be construed as an application for exemption referred to in paragraph (a) of this section.

(c) Time limitation for filing application for exemption. *(1) Taxable years ending before December 31, 1967.* A member of a religious group opposed to insurance within the meaning of paragraph (a) of this section—

(i) Who has self-employment income (determined without regard to subsections (c)(6) and (h) of section 1402 and this section) for one or more taxable years ending before December 31, 1967, and

(ii) Who desires to be exempt from the payment of the self-employment tax under section 1401,

must file the application for exemption on or before December 31, 1968.

(2) Taxable year ending on or after December 31, 1967. (i) General rule. Except as provided in subdivision (ii) of this subparagraph, a member of a religious group opposed to insurance within the meaning of paragraph (a) of this section—

(a) Who has no self-employment income (determined without regard to subsections (c)(6) and (h) of section 1402 and this section) for any taxable year ending before December 31, 1967, and

(b) Who desires to be exempt from the payment of the self-employment tax under section 1401 for any taxable year ending on or after December 31, 1967,

must file the application for exemption on or before the due date of the income tax return (see section 6072), including any extension thereof (see section 6081), for the first taxable year ending on or after December 31, 1967, for which he has self-employment income (determined without regard to subsections (c)(6) and (h) of section 1402 and this section.

(ii) Exception to general rule. If an individual to whom subdivision (i) of this subparagraph applies—

(a) Is notified in writing by a district director of internal revenue or the Director of International Operations that he has not filed the application for exemption on or before the date specified in such subdivision (i), and

(b) Files the application for exemption on or before the last day of the third calendar month following the calendar month in which he is so notified,

such application shall be considered a timely filed application for exemption.

(d) Application by fiduciary or survivor. If an individual who was a member of a religious group opposed to insurance dies before the expiration of the time prescribed in section 1402(h)(2) and paragraph (c) of this section during which an application could have been filed by him, an application for exemption with respect to such deceased individual may be filed by a fiduciary acting for such individual's estate or by such individual's survivor within the meaning of section 205(c)(1)(C) of the Social Security Act. An application for exemption with respect to a deceased individual executed by a fiduciary or survivor may be approved only if it could have been approved if the individual were not deceased and had filed the application on the date the application was filed by the fiduciary or executor.

(e) Approval of application for exemption. *(1) In general.* The filing of an application for exemption on Form 4029 by a member of a religious group opposed to insurance does not constitute an exemption from the payment of the tax on self-employment income. An individual who files such an application is exempt from the payment of the tax only if the application is approved by the official with whom the application is required to be filed (see paragraph (b) of this section).

(2) Conditions relating to approval or disapproval of application. An application for exemption on Form 4029 will not be approved unless the Secretary of Health, Education, and Welfare finds with respect to the religious sect or divi-

sion thereof of which the individual filing the application is a member—

(i) That the sect or division thereof has the established tenets or teachings by reason of which the individual applicant is conscientiously opposed to the benefits of insurance of the type referred to in section 1402(h) (see paragraph (a) of this section),

(ii) That it is the practice, and has been for a period of time which the Secretary of Health, Education, and Welfare deems to be substantial, for members of such sect or division thereof to make provisions for their dependent members which, in the judgment of such Secretary, is reasonable in view of the general level of living of the members of the sect or division thereof; and

(iii) That the sect or division thereof has been in existence continuously since December 31, 1950. In addition, an application for exemption on Form 4029 will not be approved if any benefit or other payment under title II of title XVIII of the Social Security Act became payable (or, but for section 203, relating to reduction of insurance benefits, or 222(b), relating to reduction of insurance benefits on account of refusal to accept rehabilitation services, of the Social Security Act would have been payable) at or before the time of the filing of the application for exemption. Any determination required to be made pursuant to the preceding sentence will be made by the Secretary of Health, Education, and Welfare.

(f) Period for which exemption is effective. *(1) General rule.* An application for exemption shall be in effect (if approved as provided in paragraph (e) of this section) for all taxable years beginning after December 31, 1950, except as otherwise provided in subparagraph (2) of this paragraph.

(2) Exceptions. An application for exemption referred to in subparagraph (1) of this paragraph shall not be effective for any taxable year which—

(i) Begins (a) before the taxable year in which the individual filing the application first met the requirements of subparagraphs (1) and (2) of paragraph (a) of this section, or (b) before the time as of which the Secretary of Health, Education, and Welfare finds that the sect or division thereof of which the individual is a member met the requirements of subparagraphs (C) and (D) of section 1402(h)(1) (see subdivisions (i) and (ii) of paragraph (e)(2) of this section), or

(ii) Ends (a) after the time at which the individual filing the application ceases to meet the requirements of subparagraphs (1) and (2) of paragraph (a) of this section, or (b) after the time as of which the Secretary of Health, Education, and Welfare finds that the sect or division thereof of which the individual is a member ceases to meet the requirements of subparagraphs (C) and (D) of section 1402(h)(1) (see subdivisions (i) and (ii) of paragraph (e)(2) of this section).

(g) Refund or credit. An application for exemption on Form 4029 filed on or before December 31, 1968 (if approved as provided in paragraph (e) of this section), shall constitute a claim for refund or credit of any tax on self-employment income under section 1401 (or under section 480 of the Internal Revenue Code of 1939) paid or incurred in respect of any taxable year beginning after December 31, 1950, and ending before December 31, 1967, for which an exemption is granted. Refund or credit of any tax referred to in the preceding sentence may be made, pursuant to the provisions of section 501(c) of the Social Security Amendments of 1967 (81 Stat. 933), notwithstanding that the refund or credit would otherwise be prevented by operation of any law or rule of law. No interest shall be allowed or paid in respect of any refund or credit made or allowed in connection with a claim for refund or credit made on Form 4029.

T.D. 6993, 1/17/69.

§ 1.1403-1 Cross references.

Caution: The Treasury has not yet amended Reg § 1.1403-1 to reflect changes made by P.L. 98-369.

For provisions relating to the requirement for filing returns with respect to net earnings from self-employment, see § 1.6017-1. For provisions relating to declarations of estimated tax on self-employment income, see §§ 1.6015(a) to 1.6015(j)-1, inclusive. For other administrative provisions relating to the tax on self-employment income, see the applicable sections of the regulations in this part (§ 1.6001-1 *et seq.*) and the applicable sections of the regulations in Part 301 of this chapter (Regulations on Procedure and Administration).

T.D. 6196, 8/13/56, amend T.D. 6691, 12/2/63, T.D. 7427, 8/9/76.

§ 1.1441-0 Outline of regulation provisions for section 1441.

This section lists captions contained in §§ 1.1441-1 through 1.1441-9.

§ 1.1441-1 Requirement for the deduction and withholding of tax on payments to foreign persons.

(a) Purpose and scope.

(b) General rules of withholding.

(1) Requirement to withhold on payments to foreign persons.

(2) Determination of payee and payee's status.

(i) In general.

(ii) Payments to a U.S. agent of a foreign person.

(iii) Payments to wholly-owned entities.

(A) Foreign-owned domestic entity.

(B) Foreign entity.

(iv) Payments to a U.S. branch of certain foreign banks or foreign insurance companies

(A) U.S. branch treated as a U.S. person in certain cases.

(B) Consequences to the withholding agent.

(C) Consequences to the U.S. branch.

(D) Definition of payment to a U.S. branch.

(E) Payments to other U.S. branches.

(v) Payments to a foreign intermediary.

(A) Payments treated as made to persons for whom the intermediary collects the payment.

(B) Payments treated as made to foreign intermediary.

(vi) Other payees.

(vii) Rules for reliably associating a payment with a withholding certificate or other appropriate documentation.

(A) Generally.

(B) Special rules applicable to a withholding certificate from a nonqualified intermediary or flow-through entity.

(C) Special rules applicable to a withholding certificate provided by a qualified intermediary that does not assume primary withholding responsibility.

(D) Special rules applicable to a withholding certificate provided by a qualified intermediary that assumes primary withholding responsibility under chapter 3 of the Internal Revenue Code.

(E) Special rules applicable to a withholding certificate provided by a qualified intermediary that assumes primary Form 1099 reporting and backup withholding responsibility but not primary withholding under chapter 3.

(F) Special rules applicable to a withholding certificate provided by a qualified intermediary that assumes primary withholding responsibility under chapter 3 and primary Form 1099 reporting and backup withholding responsibility and a withholding certificate provided by a withholding foreign partnership.

(3) Presumptions regarding payee's status in the absence of documentation.

(i) General rules.

(ii) Presumptions of classification as individual, corporation, partnership, etc.

(A) In general.

(B) No documentation provided.

(C) Documentary evidence furnished for offshore account.

(iii) Presumption of U.S. or foreign status.

(A) Payments to exempt recipients.

(B) Scholarships and grants.

(C) Pensions, annuities, etc.

(D) Certain payments to offshore accounts.

(iv) Grace period.

(v) Special rules applicable to payments to foreign intermediaries.

(A) Reliance on claim of status as foreign intermediary.

(B) Beneficial owner documentation or allocation information is lacking or unreliable.

(C) Information regarding allocation of payment is lacking or unreliable.

(D) Certification that the foreign intermediary has furnished documentation for all of the persons to whom the intermediary certificate relates is lacking or unreliable.

(vi) U.S. branches.

(vii) Joint payees.

(A) In general.

(B) Special rule for offshore accounts.

(viii) Rebuttal of presumptions.

(ix) Effect of reliance on presumptions and of actual knowledge or reason to know otherwise.

(A) General rule.

(B) Actual knowledge or reason to know that amount of withholding is greater than is required under the presumptions or that reporting of the payment is required.

(x) Examples.

(4) List of exemptions from, or reduced rates of, withholding under chapter 3 of the Code.

(5) Establishing foreign status under applicable provisions of chapter 61 of the Code.

(6) Rules of withholding for payments by a foreign intermediary or certain U.S. branches.

(i) In general.

(ii) Example.

(7) Liability for failure to obtain documentation timely or to act in accordance with applicable presumptions.

(i) General rule.

(ii) Proof that tax liability has been satisfied.

(iii) Liability for interest and penalties.

(iv) Special effective date.

(v) Examples.

(8) Adjustments, refunds, or credits of overwithheld amounts.

(9) Payments to joint owners.

(c) Definitions.

(1) Withholding.

(2) Foreign and U.S. person.

(3) Individual.

(i) Alien individual.

(ii) Nonresident alien individual.

(4) Certain foreign corporations.

(5) Financial institution and foreign financial institution.

(6) Beneficial owner.

(i) General rule.

(ii) Special rules.

(A) General rule.

(B) Foreign partnership.

(C) Foreign simple trusts and foreign grantor trusts.

(D) Other foreign trusts and foreign estates.

(7) Withholding agent.

(8) Person

(9) Source of income.

(10) Chapter 3 of the Code.

(11) Reduced rate.

(12) Payee.

(13) Intermediary.

(14) Nonqualified intermediary.

(15) Qualified intermediary.

(16) Withholding certificate.

(17) Documentary evidence; other appropriate documentation.

(18) Documentation.

(19) Payor.

(20) Exempt recipient.

(21) Non-exempt recipient.

(22) Reportable amounts.

(23) Flow-through entity.

(24) Foreign simple trust.

(25) Foreign complex trust.

(26) Foreign grantor trust.

(27) Partnership.

(28) Nonwithholding foreign partnership.

(29) Withholding foreign partnership.

(d) Beneficial owner's or payee's claim of U.S. status.

(1) In general.

(2) Payments for which a Form W-9 is otherwise required.

(3) Payments for which a Form W-9 is not otherwise required.

(4) When a payment to an intermediary or flow-through entity may be treated as made to a U.S. payee.

(e) Beneficial owner's claim of foreign status.

(4) Liability of U.S. withholding agent.

(5) Filing of returns.

(d) United States obligations.

(e) Assumed obligations.

(f) Conduit financing arrangements.

(g) Effective date.

§ 1.1441-8 Exemption from withholding for payments to foreign governments, international organizations, foreign central banks of issue, and the Bank for International Settlements.

(a) Foreign governments.

(b) Reliance on claim of exemption by foreign government.

(c) Income of a foreign central bank of issue or the Bank for International Settlements.

(1) Certain interest income.

(2) Bankers' acceptances.

(d) Exemption for payments to international organizations.

(e) Failure to receive withholding certificate timely and other applicable procedures.

(f) Effective date.

(1) In general.

(2) Transition rules.

§ 1.1441-9 Exemption from withholding on exempt income of a foreign tax-exempt organization, including foreign private foundations.

(a) Exemption from withholding for exempt income.

(b) Reliance on foreign organization's claim of exemption from withholding.

(1) General rule.

(2) Withholding certificate.

(3) Presumptions in the absence of documentation.

(4) Reason to know.

(c) Failure to receive withholding certificate timely and other applicable procedures.

(d) Effective date.

(1) In general.

(2) Transition rules.

T.D. 8734, 10/6/97, amend T.D. 8804, 12/30/98, T.D. 8881, 5/15/2000, T.D. 9023, 11/22/2002, T.D. 9272, 7/31/2006, T.D. 9415, 7/11/2008.

---

§ 1.1441-1 Requirement for the deduction and withholding of tax on payments to foreign persons.

(a) Purpose and scope. This section, §§ 1.1441-2 through 1.1441-9, and 1.1443-1 provide rules for withholding under sections 1441, 1442, and 1443 when a payment is made to a foreign person. This section provides definitions of terms used in chapter 3 of the Internal Revenue Code (Code) and regulations thereunder. It prescribes procedures to determine whether an amount must be withheld under chapter 3 of the Code and documentation that a withholding agent may rely upon to determine the status of a payee or a beneficial owner as a U.S. person or as a foreign person and other relevant characteristics of the payee that may affect a withholding agent's obligation to withhold under chapter 3 of the Code and the regulations thereunder. Special procedures regarding payments to foreign persons that act as intermediaries are also provided. Section 1.1441-2 defines the income subject to withholding under section 1441, 1442, and 1443 and the regulations under these sections. Section 1.1441-3 provides rules regarding the amount subject to withholding. Section 1.1441-4 provides exemptions from withholding for, among other things, certain income effectively connected with the conduct of a trade or business in the United States, including certain compensation for the personal services of an individual. Section 1.1441-5 provides rules for withholding on payments made to flow-through entities and other similar arrangements. Section 1.1441-6 provides rules for claiming a reduced rate of withholding under an income tax treaty. Section 1.1441-7 defines the term withholding agent and provides due diligence rules governing a withholding agent's obligation to withhold. Section 1.1441-8 provides rules for relying on claims of exemption from withholding for payments to a foreign government, an international organization, a foreign central bank of issue, or the Bank for International Settlements. Sections 1.1441-9 and 1.1443-1 provide rules for relying on claims of exemption from withholding for payments to foreign tax exempt organizations and foreign private foundations.

(b) General rules of withholding. *(1) Requirement to withhold on payments to foreign persons.* A withholding agent must withhold 30-percent of any payment of an amount subject to withholding made to a payee that is a foreign person unless it can reliably associate the payment with documentation upon which it can rely to treat the payment as made to a beneficial owner that is a U.S. person or as made to a beneficial owner that is a foreign person entitled to a reduced rate of withholding. However, a withholding agent making a payment to a foreign person need not withhold where the foreign person assumes responsibility for withholding on the payment under chapter 3 of the Code and the regulations thereunder as a qualified intermediary (see paragraph (e)(5) of this section), as a U.S. branch of a foreign person (see paragraph (b)(2)(iv) of this section), as a withholding foreign partnership (see § 1.1441-5(c)(2)(i)), or as an authorized foreign agent (see § 1.1441-7(c)(1)). This section (dealing with general rules of withholding and claims of foreign or U.S. status by a payee or a beneficial owner), and §§ 1.1441-4, 1.1441-5, 1.1441-6, 1.1441-8, 1.1441-9, and 1.1443-1 provide rules for determining whether documentation is required as a condition for reducing the rate of withholding on a payment to a foreign beneficial owner or to a U.S. payee and if so, the nature of the documentation upon which a withholding agent may rely in order to reduce such rate. Paragraph (b)(2) of this section prescribes the rules for determining who the payee is, the extent to which a payment is treated as made to a foreign payee, and reliable association of a payment with documentation. Paragraph (b)(3) of this section describes the applicable presumptions for determining the payee's status as U.S. or foreign and the payee's other characteristics (i.e., as an owner or intermediary, as an individual, partnership, corporation, etc.). Paragraph (b)(4) of this section lists the types of payments for which the 30-percent withholding rate may be reduced. Because the treatment of a payee as a U.S. or a foreign person also has consequences for purposes of making an information return under the provisions of chapter 61 of the Code and for withholding under other provisions of the Code, such as sections 3402, 3405 or 3406, paragraph (b)(5) of this section lists applicable provisions outside chapter 3 of the Code that require certain payees to establish their foreign status (e.g., in order to be exempt from information reporting). Paragraph (b)(6) of this section describes the withholding obligations of a foreign person making a payment that it has received in its capacity as an intermediary. Paragraph (b)(7) of this section describes the liability of a withholding agent that fails to withhold at the required 30-percent rate in the absence of documentation. Paragraph (b)(8) of this section deals with adjustments and refunds in the case of overwithholding. Paragraph (b)(9) of this section deals with determining the status of the payee when the payment is jointly owned. See paragraph (c)(6) of this section for a definition of beneficial owner. See § 1.1441-7(a) for a definition of withholding agent. See § 1.1441-2(a) for the determination of an amount subject to withholding. See § 1.1441-2(e) for the definition of a payment and when it is considered made. Except as otherwise provided, the provisions of this section apply only for purposes of determining a withholding agent's obligation to withhold under chapter 3 of the Code and the regulations thereunder.

(2) Determination of payee and payee's status. (i) In general. Except as otherwise provided in this paragraph (b)(2) and § 1.1441-5(c)(1) and (e)(3), a payee is the person to whom a payment is made, regardless of whether such person is the beneficial owner of the amount (as defined in paragraph (c)(6) of this section). A foreign payee is a payee who is a foreign person. A U.S. payee is a payee who is a U.S. person. Generally, the determination by a withholding agent of the U.S. or foreign status of a payee and of its other relevant characteristics (e.g., as a beneficial owner or intermediary, or as an individual, corporation, or flow-through entity) is made on the basis of a withholding certificate that is a Form W-8 or a Form 8233 (indicating foreign status of the payee or beneficial owner) or a Form W-9 (indicating U.S. status of the payee). The provisions of this paragraph (b)(2), paragraph (b)(3) of this section, and § 1.1441-5 (c), (d), and (e) dealing with determinations of payee and applicable presumptions in the absence of documentation, apply only to payments of amounts subject to withholding under chapter 3 of the Code (within the meaning of § 1.1441-2(a)). Similar payee and presumption provisions are set forth under § 1.6049-5(d) for payments of amounts that are not subject to withholding under chapter 3 of the Code (or the regulations thereunder) but that may be reportable under provisions of chapter 61 of the Code (and the regulations thereunder). See paragraph (d) of this section for documentation upon which the withholding agent may rely in order to treat the payee or beneficial owner as a U.S. person. See paragraph (e) of this section for documentation upon which the withholding agent may rely in order to treat the payee or beneficial owner as a foreign person. For applicable presumptions of status in the absence of documentation, see paragraph (b)(3) of this section and § 1.1441-5(d). For definitions of a foreign person and U.S. person, see paragraph (c)(2) of this section.

(ii) Payments to a U.S. agent of a foreign person. A withholding agent making a payment to a U.S. person (other than to a U.S. branch that is treated as a U.S. person pursuant to paragraph (b)(2)(iv) of this section) and who has actual knowledge that the U.S. person receives the payment as an agent of a foreign person must treat the payment as made to the foreign person. However, the withholding agent may treat the payment as made to the U.S. person if the U.S. person is a financial institution and the withholding agent has no reason to believe that the financial institution will not comply with its obligation to withhold. See paragraph (c)(5) of this section for the definition of a financial institution.

(iii) Payments to wholly-owned entities. (A) Foreign-owned domestic entity. A payment to a wholly-owned domestic entity that is disregarded for federal tax purposes under § 301.7701-2(c)(2) of this chapter as an entity separate from its owner and whose single owner is a foreign person shall be treated as a payment to the owner of the entity, subject to the provisions of paragraph (b)(2)(iv) of this section. For purposes of this paragraph (b)(2)(iii)(A), a domestic entity means a person that would be treated as a U.S. person if it had an election in effect under § 301.7701-3(c)(1)(i) of this chapter to be treated as a corporation. For example, a limited liability company, A, organized under the laws of the State of Delaware, opens an account at a U.S. bank. Upon opening of the account, the bank requests A to furnish a Form W-9 as required under section 6049(a) and the regulations under that section. A does not have an election in effect under § 301.7701-3(c)(1)(i) of this chapter and, therefore, is not treated as an organization taxable as a corporation, including for purposes of the exempt recipient provisions in § 1.6049-4(c)(1). If A has a single owner and the owner is a foreign person (as defined in paragraph (c)(2) of this section), then A may not furnish a Form W-9 because it may not represent that it is a U.S. person for purposes of the provisions of chapters 3 and 61 of the Code, and section 3406. Therefore, A must furnish a Form W-8 with the name, address, and taxpayer identifying number (TIN) (if required) of the foreign person who is the single owner in the same manner as if the account were opened directly by the foreign single owner. See §§ 1.894-1T(d) and 1.1441-6(b)(4) for special rules where the entity's owner is claiming a reduced rate of withholding under an income tax treaty.

(B) Foreign entity. A payment to a wholly-owned foreign entity that is disregarded under § 301.7701-2(c)(2) of this chapter as an entity separate from its owner shall be treated as a payment to the single owner of the entity, subject to the provisions of paragraph (b)(2)(iv) of this section if the foreign entity has a U.S. branch in the United States. For purposes of this paragraph (b)(2)(iii)(B), a foreign entity means a person that would be treated as a foreign person if it had an election in effect under § 301.7701-3(c)(1)(i) of this chapter to be treated as a corporation. See §§ 1.894-1T(d) and 1.1441-6(b)(4) for special rules where the foreign entity or its owner is claiming a reduced rate of withholding under an income tax treaty. Thus, for example, if the foreign entity's single owner is a U.S. person, the payment shall be treated as a payment to a U.S. person. Therefore, based on the savings clause in U.S. income tax treaties, such an entity may not claim benefits under an income tax treaty even if the entity is organized in a country with which the United States has an income tax treaty in effect and treats the entity as a non-fiscally transparent entity. See § 1.894-1T(d)(6), Example 10. Unless it has actual knowledge or reason to know that the foreign entity to whom the payment is made is disregarded under § 301.7701-2(c)(2) of this chapter, a withholding agent may treat a foreign entity as an entity separate from its owner unless it can reliably associate the payment with a withholding certificate from the entity's owner.

(iv) Payments to a U.S. branch of certain foreign banks or foreign insurance companies. (A) U.S. branch treated as a U.S. person in certain cases. A payment to a U.S. branch of a foreign person is a payment to a foreign person. However, a U.S. branch described in this paragraph (b)(2)(iv)(A) and a withholding agent (including another U.S. branch described in this paragraph (b)(2)(iv)(A)) may agree to treat the branch as a U.S. person for purposes of withholding on specified payments to the U.S. branch. Notwithstanding the preceding sentence, a withholding agent making a payment to a U.S. branch treated as a U.S. person under this paragraph (b)(2)(iv)(A) shall not treat the branch as a U.S. person for purposes of reporting the payment made to the branch.

Therefore, a payment to such U.S. branch shall be reported on Form 1042-S under § 1.1461-1(c). Further, a U.S. branch that is treated as a U.S. person under this paragraph (b)(2)(iv)(A) shall not be treated as a U.S. person for purposes of the withholding certificate it may provide to a withholding agent. Therefore, the U.S. branch must furnish a U.S. branch withholding certificate on Form W-8 as provided in paragraph (e)(3)(v) of this section and not a Form W-9. An agreement to treat a U.S. branch as a U.S. person must be evidenced by a U.S. branch withholding certificate described in paragraph (e)(3)(v) of this section furnished by the U.S. branch to the withholding agent. A U.S. branch described in this paragraph (b)(2)(iv)(A) is any U.S. branch of a foreign bank subject to regulatory supervision by the Federal Reserve Board or a U.S. branch of a foreign insurance company required to file an annual statement on a form approved by the National Association of Insurance Commissioners with the Insurance Department of a State, a Territory, or the District of Columbia. In addition, a financial institution organized in a possession of the United States will be treated as a U.S. branch for purposes of this paragraph (b)(2)(iv)(A). The Internal Revenue Service (IRS) may approve a list of U.S. branches that may qualify for treatment as a U.S. person under this paragraph (b)(2)(iv)(A) (see § 601.601(d)(2) of this chapter). See § 1.6049-5(c)(5)(vi) for the treatment of U.S. branches as U.S. payors if they make a payment that is subject to reporting under chapter 61 of the Internal Revenue Code. Also see § 1.6049-5(d)(1)(ii) for the treatment of U.S. branches as foreign payees under chapter 61 of the Internal Revenue Code.

(B) Consequences to the withholding agent. Any person that is otherwise a withholding agent regarding a payment to a U.S. branch described in paragraph (b)(2)(iv)(A) of this section shall treat the payment in one of the following ways—

(1) As a payment to a U.S. person, in which case the withholding agent is not responsible for withholding on such payment to the extent it can reliably associate the payment with a withholding certificate described in paragraph (e)(3)(v) of this section that has been furnished by the U.S. branch under its agreement with the withholding agent to be treated as a U.S. person;

(2) As a payment directly to the persons whose names are on withholding certificates or other appropriate documentation forwarded by the U.S. branch to the withholding agent when no agreement is in effect to treat the U.S. branch as a U.S. person for such payment, to the extent the withholding agent can reliably associate the payment with such certificates or documentation; or

(3) As a payment to a foreign person of income that is effectively connected with the conduct of a trade or business in the United States if the withholding agent cannot reliably associate the payment with a withholding certificate from the U.S. branch or any other certificate or other appropriate documentation from another person. See § 1.1441-4(a)(2)(ii).

(C) Consequences to the U.S. branch. A U.S. branch that is treated as a U.S. person under paragraph (b)(2)(iv)(A) of this section shall be treated as a separate person solely for purposes of section 1441(a) and all other provisions of chapter 3 of the Internal Revenue Code and the regulations thereunder (other than for purposes of reporting the payment to the U.S. branch under § 1.1461-1(c) or for purposes of the documentation such a branch must furnish under paragraph (e)(3)(v) of this section) for any payment that it receives as such. Thus, the U.S. branch shall be responsible for withholding on the payment in accordance with the provisions under chapter 3 of the Internal Revenue Code and the regulations thereunder and other applicable withholding provisions of the Internal Revenue Code. For this purpose, it shall obtain and retain documentation from payees or beneficial owners of the payments that it receives as a U.S. person in the same manner as if it were a separate entity. For example, if a U.S. branch receives a payment on behalf of its home office and the home office is a qualified intermediary, the U.S. branch must obtain a qualified intermediary withholding certificate described in paragraph (e)(3)(ii) of this section from its home office. In addition, a U.S. branch that has not provided documentation to the withholding agent for a payment that is, in fact, not effectively connected income is a withholding agent with respect to that payment. See paragraph (b)(6) of this section and § 1.1441-4(a)(2)(ii).

(D) Definition of payment to a U.S. branch. A payment is treated as a payment to a U.S. branch of a foreign bank or foreign insurance company if the payment is credited to an account maintained in the United States in the name of a U.S. branch of the foreign person, or the payment is made to an address in the United States where the U.S. branch is located and the name of the U.S. branch appears on documents (in written or electronic form) associated with the payment (e.g., the check mailed or a letter addressed to the branch).

(E) Payments to other U.S. branches. Similar withholding procedures may apply to payments to U.S. branches that are not described in paragraph (b)(2)(iv)(A) of this section to the extent permitted by the district director or the Assistant Commissioner (International). Any such branch must establish that its situation is analogous to that of a U.S. branch described in paragraph (b)(2)(iv)(A) of this section regarding its registration with, and regulation by, a U.S. governmental institution, the type and amounts of assets it is required to, or actually maintain in the United States, and the personnel who carry out the activities of the branch in the United States. In the alternative, the branch must establish that the withholding and reporting requirements under chapter 3 of the Code and the regulations thereunder impose an undue administrative burden and that the collection of the tax imposed by section 871(a) or 881(a) on the foreign person (or its members in the case of a foreign partnership) will not be jeopardized by the exemption from withholding. Generally, an undue administrative burden will be found to exist in a case where the person entitled to the income, such as a foreign insurance company, receives from the withholding agent income on securities issued by a single corporation, some of which is, and some of which is not, effectively connected with conduct of a trade or business within the United States and the criteria for determining the effective connection are unduly difficult to apply because of the circumstances under which such securities are held. No exemption from withholding shall be granted under this paragraph (b)(2)(iv)(E) unless the person entitled to the income complies with such other requirements as may be imposed by the district director or the Assistant Commissioner (International) and unless the district director or the Assistant Commissioner (International) is satisfied that the collection of the tax on the income involved will not be jeopardized by the exemption from withholding. The IRS may prescribe such procedures as are necessary to make these determinations (see § 601.601(d)(2) of this chapter).

(v) Payments to a foreign intermediary. (A) Payments treated as made to persons for whom the intermediary collects the payment. Except as otherwise provided in paragraph (b)(2)(v)(B) of this section, the payee of a payment to a person that the withholding agent may treat as a foreign intermediary in accordance with the provisions of paragraph (b)(3)(ii)(C) or (b)(3)(v)(A) of this section is the person or persons for whom the intermediary collects the payment. Thus, for example, the payee of a payment that the withholding agent can reliably associate with a withholding certificate from a qualified intermediary (defined in paragraph (e)(5)(ii) of this section) that does not assume primary withholding responsibility or a payment to a nonqualified intermediary are the persons for whom the qualified intermediary or nonqualified intermediary acts and not to the intermediary itself. See paragraph (b)(3)(v) of this section for presumptions that apply if the payment cannot be reliably associated with valid documentation. For similar rules for payments to flow-through entities, see § 1.1441-5(c)(1) and (e)(3).

(B) Payments treated as made to foreign intermediary. The payee of a payment to a person that the withholding agent may treat as a qualified intermediary is the qualified intermediary to the extent that the qualified intermediary assumes primary withholding responsibility under paragraph (e)(5)(iv) of this section for the payment. For example if a qualified intermediary assumes primary withholding responsibility under chapter 3 of the Internal Revenue Code but does not assume primary reporting or withholding responsibility under chapter 61 or section 3406 of the Internal Revenue Code and therefore provides Forms W-9 for U.S. non-exempt recipients, the qualified intermediary is the payee except to the extent the payment is reliably associated with a Form W-9 from a U.S. non-exempt recipient.

(vi) Other payees. A payment to a person described in § 1.6049-4(c)(1)(ii) that the withholding agent would treat as a payment to a foreign person without obtaining documentation for purposes of information reporting under section 6049 (if the payment were interest) is treated as a payment to a foreign payee for purposes of chapter 3 of the Code and the regulations thereunder (or to a foreign beneficial owner to the extent provided in paragraph (e)(1)(ii)(A) (6) or (7) of this section). Further, payments that the withholding agent can reliably associate with documentary evidence described in § 1.6049-5(c)(4) relating to the payee is treated as a payment to a foreign payee. A payment that the withholding agent may treat as a payment to an authorized foreign agent (as defined in § 1.1441-7(c)(2)) is treated as a payment to the agent and not to the persons for whom the agent collects the payment. See § 1.1441-5 (b)(1) and (c)(1) for payee determinations for payments to partnerships. See § 1.1441-5(e) for payee determinations for payments to foreign trusts or foreign estates.

(vii) Rules for reliably associating a payment with a withholding certificate or other appropriate documentation. (A) Generally. The presumption rules of paragraph (b)(3) of this section and §§ 1.1441-5(d) and (e)(6) and 1.6049-5(d) apply to any payment, or portion of a payment, that a withholding agent cannot reliably associate with valid documentation. Generally, a withholding agent can reliably associate a payment with valid documentation if, prior to the payment, it holds valid documentation (either directly or through an agent), it can reliably determine how much of the payment relates to the valid documentation, and it has no actual knowledge or reason to know that any of the information, certifications, or statements in, or associated with, the documentation are incorrect. Special rules apply for payments made to intermediaries, flow-through entities, and certain U.S. branches. See paragraph (b)(2)(vii)(B) through (F) of this section. The documentation referred to in this paragraph (b)(2)(vii) is documentation described in paragraphs (c)(16) and (17) of this section upon which a withholding agent may rely to treat the payment as a payment made to a payee or beneficial owner, and to ascertain the characteristics of the payee or beneficial owner that are relevant to withholding or reporting under chapter 3 of the Internal Revenue Code and the regulations thereunder. For purposes of this paragraph (b)(2)(vii), documentation also includes the agreement that the withholding agent has in effect with an authorized foreign agent in accordance with § 1.1441-7(c)(2)(i). A withholding agent that is not required to obtain documentation with respect to a payment is considered to lack documentation for purposes of this paragraph (b)(2)(vii). For example, a withholding agent paying U.S. source interest to a person that is an exempt recipient, as defined in § 1.6049-4(c)(1)(ii), is not required to obtain documentation from that person in order to determine whether an amount paid to that person is reportable under an applicable information reporting provision under chapter 61 of the Internal Revenue Code. The withholding agent must, however, treat the payment as made to an undocumented person for purposes of chapter 3 of the Internal Revenue Code. Therefore, the presumption rules of paragraph (b)(3)(iii) of this section apply to determine whether the person is presumed to be a U.S. person (in which case, no withholding is required under this section), or whether the person is presumed to be a foreign person (in which case 30-percent withholding is required under this section). See paragraph (b)(3)(v) of this section for special reliance rules in the case of a payment to a foreign intermediary and § 1.1441-5(d) and (e)(6) for special reliance rules in the case of a payment to a flow-through entity.

(B) Special rules applicable to a withholding certificate from a nonqualified intermediary or flow-through entity. (1) In the case of a payment made to a nonqualified intermediary, a flow-through entity (as defined in paragraph (c)(23) of this section), and a U.S. branch described in paragraph (b)(2)(iv) of this section (other than a branch that is treated as a U.S. person), a withholding agent can reliably associate the payment with valid documentation only to the extent that, prior to the payment, the withholding agent can allocate the payment to a valid nonqualified intermediary, flow-through, or U.S. branch withholding certificate; the withholding agent can reliably determine how much of the payment relates to valid documentation provided by a payee as determined under paragraph (c)(12) of this section (i.e., a person that is not itself an intermediary, flow-through entity, or U.S. branch); and the withholding agent has sufficient information to report the payment on Form 1042-S or Form 1099, if reporting is required. See paragraph (e)(3)(iii) of this section for the requirements of a nonqualified intermediary withholding certificate, paragraph (e)(3)(v) of this section for the requirements of a U.S. branch certificate, and §§ 1.1441-5(c)(3)(iii) and (e)(5)(iii) for the requirements of a flow-through withholding certificate. Thus, a payment cannot be reliably associated with valid documentation provided by a payee to the extent such documentation is lacking or unreliable, or to the extent that information required to allocate and report all or a portion of the payment to each payee is lacking or unreliable. If a withholding certificate attached to an intermediary, U.S. branch, or flow-through withholding certificate is another intermediary, U.S. branch, or flow-through withholding certificate, the rules of this paragraph (b)(2)(vii)(B) apply by treating the share of the payment allocable to the other intermediary, U.S. branch, or flow-through entity as if the payment were made directly to such other entity. See paragraph (e)(3)(iv)(D) of this section for rules permitting information allocating a payment to documentation to be received after the payment is made.

(2) The rules of paragraph (b)(2)(vii)(B)(1) of this section are illustrated by the following examples:

Example (1). WH, a withholding agent, makes a payment of U.S. source interest to NQI, an intermediary that is a nonqualified intermediary. NQI provides a valid intermediary withholding certificate under paragraph (e)(3)(iii) of this section. NQI does not, however, provide valid documentation from the persons on whose behalf it receives the interest payment, and, therefore, the interest payment cannot be reliably associated with valid documentation provided by a payee. WH must apply the presumption rules of paragraph (b)(3)(v) of this section to the payment.

Example (2). The facts are the same as in Example 1, except that NQI does attach valid beneficial owner withholding certificates (as defined in paragraph (e)(2)(i) of this section) from A, B, C, and D establishing their status as foreign persons. NQI does not, however, provide WH with any information allocating the payment among A, B, C, and D and, therefore, WH cannot determine the portion of the payment that relates to each beneficial owner withholding certificate. The interest payment cannot be reliably associated with valid documentation from a payee and WH must apply the presumption rules of paragraph (b)(3)(v) of this section to the payment. See, however, paragraph (e)(3)(iv)(D) of this section providing special rules permitting allocation information to be received after a payment is made.

Example (3). The facts are the same as in Example 2, except that NQI does provide allocation information associated with its intermediary withholding certificate indicating that 25 percent of the interest payment is allocable to A and 25 percent to B. NQI does not provide any allocation information regarding the remaining 50 percent of the payment. WH may treat 25 percent of the payment as made to A and 25 percent as made to B. The remaining 50 percent of the payment cannot be reliably associated with valid documentation from a payee, however, since NQI did not provide information allocating the payment. Thus, the remaining 50 percent of the payment is subject to the presumption rules of paragraph (b)(3)(v) of this section.

Example (4). WH makes a payment of U.S. source interest to NQI1, an intermediary that is not a qualified intermediary. NQI1 provides WH with a valid nonqualified intermediary withholding certificate as well a valid beneficial owner withholding certificates from A and B and a valid nonqualified intermediary withholding certificate from NQI2. NQI2 has provided valid beneficial owner documentation from C sufficient to establish C's status as a foreign person. Based on information provided by NQI1, WH can allocate 20 percent of the interest payment to A, and 20 percent to B. Based on information that NQI2 provided NQI1 and that NQI1 provides to WH, WH can allocate 60 percent of the payment to NQI 2, but can only allocate one half of that payment (30 percent) to C. Therefore, WH cannot reliably associate 30 percent of the payment made to NQI2 with valid documentation and must apply the presumption rules of paragraph (b)(3)(v) of this section to that portion of the payment.

(C) Special rules applicable to a withholding certificate provided by a qualified intermediary that does not assume primary withholding responsibility. (1) If a payment is made to a qualified intermediary that does not assume primary withholding responsibility under chapter 3 of the Internal Revenue Code or primary Form 1099 reporting and backup withholding responsibility under chapter 61 and section 3406 of the Internal Revenue Code for the payment, a withholding agent can reliably associate the payment with valid documentation only to the extent that, prior to the payment, the withholding agent has received a valid qualified intermediary withholding certificate and the withholding agent can reliably determine the portion of the payment that relates to a withholding rate pool, as defined in paragraph (e)(5)(v)(C) of this section. In the case of a withholding rate pool attributable to a U.S. non-exempt recipient, a payment cannot be reliably associated with valid documentation unless, prior to the payment, the qualified intermediary has provided the U.S. person's Form W-9 (or, in the absence of the form, the name, address, and TIN, if available, of the U.S. person) and sufficient information for the withholding agent to report the payment on Form 1099. See paragraph (e)(5)(v)(C)(2) of this section for special rules regarding allocation of payments among U.S. non-exempt recipients.

(2) The rules of this paragraph (b)(2)(vii)(C) are illustrated by the following examples:

Example (1). WH, a withholding agent, makes a payment of U.S. source dividends to QI. QI provides WH with a valid qualified intermediary withholding certificate on which it indicates that it does not assume primary withholding responsibility under chapter 3 of the Internal Revenue Code or primary Form 1099 reporting and backup withholding responsibility under chapter 61 and section 3406 of the Internal Revenue Code. QI does not provide any information allocating the dividend to withholding rate pools. WH cannot reliably associate the payment with valid payee documentation and therefore must apply the presumption rules of paragraph (b)(3)(v) of this section.

Example (2). WH makes a payment of U.S. source dividends to QI. QI has 5 customers: A, B, C, D, and E. QI has obtained documentation from A and B establishing their entitlement to a 15 percent rate of tax on U.S. source dividends under an income tax treaty. C is a U.S. person that is an exempt recipient as defined in paragraph (c)(20) of this section. D and E are U.S. non-exempt recipients who have provided Forms W-9 to QI. A, B, C, D, and E are each entitled to 20 percent of the dividend payment. QI provides WH with a valid qualified intermediary withholding certificate as described in paragraph (e)(2)(ii) of this section with which it associates the Forms W-9 from D and E. QI associates the following allocation information with its qualified intermediary withholding certificate: 40 percent of the payment is allocable to the 15 percent withholding rate pool, and 20 percent is allocable to each of D and E. QI does not provide any allocation information regarding the remaining 20 percent of the payment. WH cannot reliably associate 20 percent of the payment with valid documentation and, therefore, must apply the presumption rules of paragraph (b)(3)(v) of this section to that portion of the payment. The 20 percent of the payment allocable to the 15 percent withholding rate pool, and the portion of the payments allocable to D and E are payments that can be reliably associated with documentation.

(D) Special rules applicable to a withholding certificate provided by a qualified intermediary that assumes primary withholding responsibility under chapter 3 of the Internal Revenue Code. (1) In the case of a payment made to a qualified intermediary that assumes primary withholding responsibility under chapter 3 of the Internal Revenue Code with respect to that payment (but does not assume primary Form 1099 reporting and backup withholding responsibility under chapter 61 and section 3406 of the Internal Revenue Code), a withholding agent can reliably associate the payment with valid documentation only to the extent that, prior to the payment, the withholding agent has received a valid qualified intermediary withholding certificate and the withholding agent can reliably determine the portion of the payment that relates to the withholding rate pool for which the qualified intermediary assumes primary withholding responsibility under chapter 3 of the Internal Revenue Code and the portion of the payment attributable to withholding rate pools for each U.S. non-exempt recipient for whom the qualified intermediary has provided a Form W-9 (or, in absence of the form, the name, address, and TIN, if available, of the U.S. non-exempt recipient). See paragraph (e)(5)(v)(C)(2) of this section for alternative allocation procedures for payments made to U.S. persons that are not exempt recipients.

(2) Examples. The following examples illustrate the rules of paragraph (b)(2)(vii)(D)(1) of this section:

Example (1). WH makes a payment of U.S. source interest to QI, a qualified intermediary. QI provides WH with a withholding certificate that indicates that QI will assume primary withholding responsibility under chapter 3 of the Internal Revenue Code with respect to the payment. In addition, QI attaches a Form W-9 from A, a U.S. non-exempt recipient, as defined in paragraph (c)(21) of this section, and provides the name, address, and TIN of B, a U.S. person that is also a non-exempt recipient but who has not provided a Form W-9. QI associates a withholding statement with its qualified intermediary withholding certificate indicating that 10 percent of the payment is attributable to A, and 10 percent to B, and that QI will assume primary withholding responsibility with respect to the remaining 80 percent of the payment. WH can reliably associate the entire payment with valid documentation. Although under the presumption rule of paragraph (b)(3)(v) of this section, an undocumented person receiving U.S. source interest is generally presumed to be a foreign person, WH has actual knowledge that B is a U.S. non-exempt recipient and therefore must report the payment on Form 1099 and backup withhold on the interest payment under section 3406.

Example (2). The facts are the same as in Example 1, except that no Forms W-9 or other information have been provided for the 20 percent of the payment that is allocable to A and B. Thus, QI has accepted withholding responsibility for 80 percent of the payment, but has provided no information for the remaining 20 percent. In this case, 20 percent of the payment cannot be reliably associated with valid documentation, and WH must apply the presumption rule of paragraph (b)(3)(v) of this section.

(E) Special rules applicable to a withholding certificate provided by a qualified intermediary that assumes primary Form 1099 reporting and backup withholding responsibility but not primary withholding under chapter 3. (1) If a payment is made to a qualified intermediary that assumes primary Form 1099 reporting and backup withholding responsibility for the payment (but does not assume primary withholding responsibility under chapter 3 of the Internal Revenue Code), a withholding agent can reliably associate the payment with valid documentation only to the extent that, prior to the payment, the withholding agent has received a valid qualified intermediary withholding certificate and the withholding agent can reliably determine the portion of the payment that relates to a withholding rate pool or pools provided as part of the qualified intermediary's withholding statement and the portion of the payment for which the qualified intermediary assumes primary Form 1099 reporting and backup withholding responsibility.

(2) The following example illustrates the rules of paragraph (b)(2)((vii)(D)(1) of this section:

Example. WH makes a payment of U.S. source dividends to QI, a qualified intermediary. QI has provided WH with a valid qualified intermediary withholding certificate. QI states on its withholding statement accompanying the certificate that it assumes primary Form 1099 reporting and backup withholding responsibility but does not assume primary withholding responsibility under chapter 3 of the Internal Revenue Code. QI represents that 15 percent of the dividend is subject to a 30 percent rate of withholding, 75 percent of the dividend is subject to a 15 percent rate of withholding, and that QI assumed primary Form 1099 reporting and backup withholding for the remaining 10 percent of the payment. The entire payment can be reliably associated with valid documentation.

(F) Special rules applicable to a withholding certificate provided by a qualified intermediary that assumes primary withholding responsibility under chapter 3 and primary Form 1099 reporting and backup withholding responsibility and a withholding certificate provided by a withholding foreign partnership. If a payment is made to a qualified intermediary that assumes both primary withholding responsibility under chapter 3 of the Internal Revenue Code and primary Form 1099 reporting and backup withholding responsibility under chapter 61 and section 3406 of the Internal Revenue Code for the payment, a withholding agent can reliably associate a payment with valid documentation provided that it receives a valid qualified intermediary withholding certificate as described in paragraph (e)(3)(ii) of this section. In the case of a payment made to a withholding foreign partnership, the withholding agent can reliably associate the payment with valid documentation to the extent it can associate the payment with a valid withholding certificate described in § 1.1441-5(c)(2)(iv).

(3) Presumptions regarding payee's status in the absence of documentation. (i) General rules. A withholding agent that cannot, prior to the payment, reliably associate (within the meaning of paragraph (b)(2)(vii) of this section) a payment of an amount subject to withholding (as described in § 1.1441-2(a)) with valid documentation may rely on the presumptions of this paragraph (b)(3) to determine the status of the payee as a U.S. or a foreign person and the payee's other relevant characteristics (e.g., as an owner or intermediary, as an individual, trust, partnership, or corporation). The determination of withholding and reporting requirements applicable to payments to a person presumed to be a foreign person is governed only by the provisions of chapter 3 of the Code and the regulations thereunder. For the determination of withholding and reporting requirements applicable to payments to a person presumed to be a U.S. person, see chapter 61 of the Code, section 3402, 3405, or 3406, and the regulations under these provisions. A presumption that a payee is a foreign payee is not a presumption that the payee is a foreign beneficial owner. Therefore, the provisions of this paragraph (b)(3) have no effect for purposes of reducing the withholding rate if associating the payment with documentation of foreign beneficial ownership is required as a condition for such rate reduction. See paragraph (b)(3)(ix) of this section for consequences to a withholding agent that fails to withhold in accordance with the presumptions set forth in this paragraph (b)(3) or if the withholding agent has actual knowledge or reason to know of facts that are contrary to the presumptions set forth in this paragraph (b)(3). See paragraph (b)(2)(vii) of this section for rules regarding the extent which a withholding agent can reliably associate a payment with documentation.

(ii) Presumptions of classification as individual, corporation, partnership, etc. (A) In general. A withholding agent that cannot reliably associate a payment with a valid withholding certificate or that has received valid documentary evidence under §§ 1.1441-1(e)(1)(ii)(2) and 1.6049-5(c)(1) or (4) but cannot determine a payee's classification from the documentary evidence must apply the rules of this paragraph (b)(3)(ii) to determine the payee's classification as an individual, trust, estate, corporation, or partnership. The fact that a payee is presumed to have a certain status under the provisions of this paragraph (b)(3)(ii) does not mean that it is excused from furnishing documentation if documentation is otherwise required to obtain a reduced rate of withholding under this section. For example, if, for purposes of this paragraph (b)(3)(ii), a payee is presumed to be a tax-exempt organization based on § 1.6049-4(c)(1)(ii)(B), the withholding agent cannot rely on this presumption to reduce the rate of withholding on payments to such person (if such person is also presumed to be a foreign person under paragraph (b)(3)(iii)(A) of this section) because a reduction in the rate of withholding for payments to a foreign tax-exempt organization generally requires that a valid Form W-8 described in § 1.1441-9(b)(2) be furnished to the withholding agent.

(B) No documentation provided. If the withholding agent cannot reliably associate a payment with a valid withholding certificate or valid documentary evidence, it must presume that the payee is an individual, a trust, or an estate, if the payee appears to be such person (e.g., based on the payee's name or other indications). In the absence of reliable indications that the payee is an individual, trust, or an estate, the withholding agent must presume that the payee is a corporation or one of the persons enumerated under § 1.6049-4(c)(1)(ii)(B) through (Q) if it can be so treated under § 1.6049-4(c)(1)(ii)(A)(1) or any one of the paragraphs under § 1.6049-4(c)(1)(ii)(B) through (Q) without the need to furnish documentation. If the withholding agent cannot treat a payee as a person described in § 1.6049-4(c)(1)(ii)(A)(1) through (Q), then the payee shall be presumed to be a partnership. If such a partnership is presumed to be foreign, it is not the beneficial owner of the income paid to it. See paragraph (c)(6) of this section. If such a partnership is presumed to be domestic, it is a U.S. non-exempt recipient for purposes of chapter 61 of the Internal Revenue Code.

(C) Documentary evidence furnished for offshore account. If the withholding agent receives valid documentary evidence, as described in § 1.6049-5(c)(1) or (4), with respect to an offshore account from an entity but the documentary evidence does not establish the entity's classification as a corporation, trust, estate, or partnership, the withholding agent may presume (in the absence of actual knowledge otherwise) that the entity is the type of person enumerated under § 1.6049-4(c)(1)(ii)(B) through (Q) if it can be so treated under any one of those paragraphs without the need to furnish documentation. If the withholding agent cannot treat a payee as a person described in § 1.6049-4(c)(1)(ii)(B) through (Q), then the payee shall be presumed to be a corporation unless the withholding agent knows, or has reason to know, that the entity is not classified as a corporation for U.S. tax purposes, the withholding agent is required to presume the payee is a U.S. person under paragraph (b)(3)(iii) of this section, or there are indicia of U.S. status. If the withholding agent must presume the payee is a U.S. person, or there are indicia of U.S. status, the withholding agent shall treat the entity as a partnership, and therefore as a U.S. non-exempt recipient for purposes of chapter 61 of the Internal Revenue Code; however backup withholding under section 3406 shall not apply if backup withholding is not required under § 31.3406(g)-1(e) of this chapter. Indicia of U.S. status exists if payments are regularly made to a payee in the United States, the payee has an account with the same withholding agent in the United States, or the payee has a U.S. address. If a payee is, or is presumed to be, a corporation under this paragraph (b)(3)(ii)(C) and a foreign person under paragraph (b)(3)(iii) of this section, a withholding agent shall not treat the payee as the beneficial owner of income if the withholding agent knows, or has reason to know, that the payee is not the beneficial owner of the income. For this purpose, a withholding agent shall have reason to know that the payee is not a beneficial owner if the documentary evidence indicates that the payee is a bank, broker, intermediary, custodian, or other agent, or is treated under § 1.6049-4(c)(1)(ii)(B) through (Q) as such a person. A withholding agent may, however, treat such a person as a beneficial owner if the foreign person provides a statement, in writing and signed by a person with authority to sign the statement, that is attached to the documentary evidence stating it is the beneficial owner of the income.

(iii) Presumption of U.S. or foreign status. A payment that the withholding agent cannot reliably associate with documentation is presumed to be made to a U.S. person, except as otherwise provided in this paragraph (b)(3)(iii), in paragraphs (b)(3) (iv) and (v) of this section, or in § 1.1441-5 (d) or (e).

(A) Payments to exempt recipients. If a withholding agent cannot reliably associate a payment with documentation from the payee and the payee is an exempt recipient (as determined under the provisions of § 1.6049-4(c)(1)(ii) in the case of interest, or under similar provisions under chapter 61 of the Code applicable to the type of payment involved, but not including a payee that the withholding agent may treat as a foreign intermediary in accordance with paragraph (b)(3)(v) of this section), the payee is presumed to be a foreign person and not a U.S. person—

(1) If the withholding agent has actual knowledge of the payee's employer identification number and that number begins with the two digits "98";

(2) If the withholding agent's communications with the payee are mailed to an address in a foreign country;

(3) If the name of the payee indicates that the entity is the type of entity that is on the per se list of foreign corporations contained in § 301.7701-2(b)(8)(i) of this chapter; or

(4) If the payment is made outside the United States (as defined in § 1.6049-5(e)).

(B) Scholarships and grants. A payment representing taxable scholarship or fellowship grant income that does not represent compensation for services (but is not excluded from tax under section 117) and that a withholding agent that cannot reliably associate with documentation is presumed to be made to a foreign person if the withholding agent has a record that the payee has a U.S. visa that is not an immigrant visa. See section 871(c) and § 1.1441-4(c) for applicable tax rate and withholding rules.

(C) Pensions, annuities, etc. A payment from a trust described in section 401(a), an annuity plan described in section 403(a), a payment with respect to any annuity, custodial account, or retirement income account described in section 403(b), or a payment from an individual retirement account or individual retirement annuity described in section 408 that a withholding agent cannot reliably associate with documentation is presumed to be made to a U.S. person only if the withholding agent has a record of a Social Security number for the payee and relies on a mailing address described in the following sentence. A mailing address is an address used for purposes of information reporting or otherwise communicating with the payee that is an address in the United States or in a foreign country with which the United States has an income tax treaty in effect and the treaty provides that the payee, if an individual resident in that country, would be entitled to an exemption from U.S. tax on amounts described in this paragraph (b)(3)(iii)(C). Any payment described in this paragraph (b)(3)(iii)(C) that is not presumed to be made to a U.S. person is presumed to be made to a foreign person. A withholding agent making a payment to a person presumed to be a foreign person may not reduce the 30-percent amount of withholding required on such payment unless it receives a withholding certificate described in paragraph (e)(2)(i) of this section furnished by the beneficial owner. For reduction in the 30-percent rate, see §§ 1.1441-4(e) or 1.1441-6(b).

(D) Certain payments to offshore accounts. A payment is presumed made to a foreign payee if the payment is made outside the United States (as defined in § 1.6049-5(e)) to an offshore account (as defined in § 1.6049-5(c)(1)) and the withholding agent does not have actual knowledge that the payee is a U.S. person. See § 1.6049-5(d)(2) and (3) for exceptions to this rule.

(E) Certain payments for services. A payment for services is presumed to be made to a foreign person if--

(1) The payee is an individual;

(2) The withholding agent does not know, or have reason to know, that the payee is a U.S. citizen or resident;

(3) The withholding agent does not know, or have reason to know, that the income is (or may be) effectively connected with the conduct of a trade or business within the United States; and

(4) All of the services for which the payment is made were performed by the payee outside of the United States.

(iv) Grace period. A withholding agent may choose to apply the provisions of § 1.6049-5(d)(2)(ii) regarding a 90-day grace period for purposes of this paragraph (b)(3) (by applying the term withholding agent instead of the term payor) to amounts described in § 1.1441-6(c)(2) and to amounts covered by a Form 8233 described in § 1.1441-4(b)(2)(ii). Thus, for these amounts, a withholding agent may choose to treat an account holder as a foreign person and withhold under chapter 3 of the Internal Revenue Code (and the regulations thereunder) while awaiting documentation. For purposes of determining the rate of withholding under this section, the withholding agent must withhold at the unreduced 30-percent rate at the time that the amounts are credited to an account. However, a withholding agent who can reliably associate the payment with a withholding certificate that is otherwise valid within the meaning of the applicable provisions except for the fact that it is transmitted by facsimile may rely on that facsimile form for purposes of withholding at the claimed reduced rate. For reporting of amounts credited both before and after the grace period, see § 1.1461-1(c)(4)(i)(A). The following adjustments shall be made at the expiration of the grace period:

(A) If, at the end of the grace period, the documentation is not furnished in the manner required under this section and the account holder is presumed to be a U.S. non-exempt recipient, then backup withholding applies to amounts credited to the account after the expiration of the grace period only. Amounts credited to the account during the grace period shall be treated as owned by a foreign payee and adjustments must be made to correct any underwithholding on such amounts in the manner described in § 1.1461-2.

(B) If, at the end of the grace period, the documentation is not furnished in the manner required under this section, or if documentation is furnished that does not support the claimed rate reduction, and the account holder is presumed to be a foreign person then adjustments must be made to correct any underwithholding on amounts credited to the account during the grace period, based on the adjustment procedures described in § 1.1461-2.

(v) Special rules applicable to payments to foreign intermediaries. (A) Reliance on claim of status as foreign intermediary. The presumption rules of paragraph (b)(3)(v)(B) of this section apply to a payment made to an intermediary (whether the intermediary is a qualified or nonqualified intermediary) that has provided a valid withholding certificate under paragraph (e)(3)(ii) or (iii) of this section (or has provided documentary evidence described in paragraph (b)(3)(ii)(C) of this section that indicates it is a bank, broker, custodian, intermediary, or other agent) to the extent the withholding agent cannot treat the payment as being reliably associated with valid documentation under the rules of paragraph (b)(2)(vii) of this section. For this purpose, a U.S. person's foreign branch that is a qualified intermediary defined in paragraph (e)(5)(ii) of this section shall be treated as a foreign intermediary. A payee that the withholding agent may not reliably treat as a foreign intermediary under this paragraph (b)(3)(v)(A) is presumed to be a payee other than an intermediary whose classification as an individual, corporation, partnership, etc., must be determined in accordance with paragraph (b)(3)(ii) of this section to the extent relevant. In addition, such payee is presumed to be a U.S. or a foreign payee based upon the presumptions described in paragraph (b)(3)(iii) of this section. The provisions of paragraph (b)(3)(v)(B) of this section are not relevant to a withholding agent that can reliably associate a payment with a withholding certificate from a person representing to be a qualified intermediary to the extent the qualified intermediary has assumed primary withholding responsibility in accordance with paragraph (e)(5)(iv) of this section.

(B) Beneficial owner documentation or allocation information is lacking or unreliable. Any portion of a payment that the withholding agent may treat as made to a foreign intermediary (whether a nonqualified or a qualified intermediary) but that the withholding agent cannot treat as reliably associated with valid documentation under the rules of paragraph (b)(2)(vii) of this section is presumed made to an unknown, undocumented foreign payee. As a result, a withholding agent must deduct and withhold 30 percent from any payment of an amount subject to withholding. If a withholding certificate attached to an intermediary certificate is another intermediary withholding certificate or a flow-through withholding certificate, the rules of this paragraph (b)(3)(v)(B) (or § 1.1441-5(d)(3) or (e)(6)(iii)) apply by treating the share of the payment allocable to the other intermediary or flow-through entity as if it were made directly to the other intermediary or flow-through entity. Any payment of an amount subject to withholding that is presumed made to an undocumented foreign person must be reported on Form 1042-S. See § 1.1461-1(c). See § 1.6049-5(d) for payments that are not subject to withholding.

(vi) U.S. branches. The rules of paragraph (b)(3)(v)(B) of this section shall apply to payments to a U.S. branch described in paragraph (b)(2)(iv)(A) of this section that has not agreed to be treated as a U.S. person.

(vii) Joint payees. (A) In general. Except as provided in paragraph (b)(3)(vii)(B) of this section, if a withholding agent makes a payment to joint payees and cannot reliably associate a payment with valid documentation from all payees, the payment is presumed made to an unidentified U.S. person. However, if one of the joint payees provides a Form W-9 furnished in accordance with the procedures described in §§ 31.3406(d)-1 through 31.3406(d)-5 of this chapter, the payment shall be treated as made to that payee. See § 31.3406(h)-2 of this chapter for rules to determine the relevant payee if more than one Form W-9 is provided. For purposes of applying this paragraph (b)(3), the grace period rules in paragraph (b)(3)(iv) of this section shall apply only if each payee meets the conditions described in paragraph (b)(3)(iv) of this section.

(B) Special rule for offshore accounts. If a withholding agent makes a payment to joint payees and cannot reliably associate a payment with valid documentation from all payees, the payment is presumed made to an unknown foreign payee if the payment is made outside the United States (as defined in § 1.6059-5(e)) to an offshore account (as defined in § 1.6049-5(c)(1)).

(viii) Rebuttal of presumptions. A payee or beneficial owner may rebut the presumptions described in this paragraph (b)(3) by providing reliable documentation to the withholding agent or, if applicable, to the IRS.

(ix) Effect of reliance on presumptions and of actual knowledge or reason to know otherwise. (A) General rule. Except as otherwise provided in paragraph (b)(3)(ix)(B) of this section, a withholding agent that withholds on a payment under section 3402, 3405 or 3406 in accordance with the presumptions set forth in this paragraph (b)(3) shall not be liable for withholding under this section even it is later established that the beneficial owner of the payment is, in fact, a foreign person. Similarly, a withholding agent that withholds on a payment under this section in accordance with the presumptions set forth in this paragraph (b)(3) shall not be liable for withholding under section 3402 or 3405 or for backup withholding under section 3406 even if it is later established that the payee or beneficial owner is, in fact, a U.S. person. A withholding agent that, instead of relying on the presumptions described in this paragraph (b)(3), relies on its own actual knowledge to withhold a lesser amount, not withhold, or not report a payment, even though reporting of the payment or withholding a greater amount would be required if the withholding agent relied on the presumptions described in this paragraph (b)(3) shall be liable for tax, interest, and penalties to the extent provided under section 1461 and the regulations under that section. See paragraph (b)(7) of this section for provisions regarding such liability if the withholding agent fails to withhold in accordance with the presumptions described in this paragraph (b)(3).

(B) Actual knowledge or reason to know that amount of withholding is greater than is required under the presumptions or that reporting of the payment is required. Notwithstanding the provisions of paragraph (b)(3)(ix)(A) of this section, a withholding agent may not rely on the presumptions described in this paragraph (b)(3) to the extent it has actual knowledge or reason to know that the status or characteristics of the payee or of the beneficial owner are other than what is presumed under this paragraph (b)(3) and, if based on such knowledge or reason to know, it should withhold (under this section or another withholding provision of the Code) an amount greater than would be the case if it relied on the presumptions described in this paragraph (b)(3) or it should report (under this section or under another provision of the Code) an amount that would not otherwise be reportable if it relied on the presumptions described in this paragraph (b)(3). In such a case, the withholding agent must rely on its actual knowledge or reason to know rather than on the presumptions set forth in this paragraph (b)(3). Failure to do so and, as a result, failure to withhold the higher amount or to report the payment, shall result in liability for tax, interest, and penalties to the extent provided under sections 1461 and 1463 and the regulations under those sections.

(x) Examples. The provisions of this paragraph (b)(3) are illustrated by the following examples:

Example (1). A withholding agent, W, makes a payment of U.S. source dividends to person X, Inc. at an address outside the United States. W cannot reliably associate the payment to X with documentation. Under §§ 1.6042-3(b)(1)(vii) and 1.6049-4(c)(1)(ii)(A)(1), W may treat X as a corporation. Thus, under the presumptions described in paragraph (b)(3)(iii) of this section, W must presume that X is a foreign person (because the payment is made outside the United States). However, W knows that X is a U.S. person who is an exempt recipient. W may not rely on its actual knowledge to not withhold under this section. If W s knowledge is, in fact, incorrect, W would be liable for tax, interest, and, if applicable, penalties, under section 1461. W would be permitted to reduce or eliminate its liability for the tax by establishing, in accordance with paragraph (b)(7) of this section, that the tax is not due or has been satisfied. If W s actual knowledge is, in fact, correct, W may nevertheless be liable for tax, interest, or penalties under section 1461 for the amount that W should have withheld based upon the presumptions. W would be permitted to reduce or eliminate its liability for the tax by establishing, in accordance with paragraph (b)(7) of this section, that its actual knowledge was, in fact, correct and that no tax or a lesser amount of tax was due.

Example (2). A withholding agent, W, makes a payment of U.S. source dividends to Y who does not qualify as an exempt recipient under §§ 1.6042-3(b)(1)(vii) and 1.6049-4(c)(1)(ii). W cannot reliably associate the payment to Y with documentation. Under the presumptions described in paragraph (b)(3)(iii) of this section, W must presume that Y is a U.S. person who is not an exempt recipient for purposes of section 6042. However, W knows that Y is a foreign person. W may not rely on its actual knowledge to withhold under this section rather than backup withhold under section 3406. If W s knowledge is, in fact, incorrect, W would be liable for tax, interest, and, if applicable, penalties, under section 3403. If W s actual knowledge is, in fact, correct, W may nevertheless be liable for tax, interest, or penalties under section 3403 for the amount that W should have withheld based upon the presumptions. Paragraph (b)(7) of this section does not apply to provide relief from liability under section 3403.

Example (3). A withholding agent, W, makes a payment of U.S. source dividends to X, Inc. W cannot reliably associate the payment to X, Inc. with documentation. X, nc. presents none of the indicia of foreign status described in paragraph (b)(3)(iii)(A) of this section, but W has actual knowledge that X, Inc. is a foreign corporation. W may treat X, Inc. as an exempt recipient under § 1.6042-3(b)(1)(vii). Because there are no indicia of foreign status, W would, absent actual knowledge or reason to know otherwise, be permitted to treat X, Inc. as a domestic corporation in accordance with the presumptions of paragraph (b)(3)(iii) of this section. However, under paragraph (b)(3)(ix)(B) of this section, W may not rely on the presumption of U.S. status since reliance on its actual knowledge requires that it withhold an amount greater than would be the case under the presumptions.

Example (4). A withholding agent, W, is a plan administrator who makes pension payments to person X with a mailing address in a foreign country with which the United States has an income tax treaty in effect. Under that treaty, the type of pension income paid to X is taxable solely in the country of residence. The plan administrator has a record of X's U.S. social security number. W has no actual knowledge or reason to know that X is a foreign person. W may rely on the presumption of paragraph (b)(3)(iii)(C) of this section in order to treat X as a U.S. person. Therefore, any withholding and reporting requirements for the payment are governed by the provisions of section 3405 and the regulations under that section.

(4) List of exemptions from, or reduced rates of, withholding under chapter 3 of the Code. A withholding agent that has determined that the payee is a foreign person for purposes of paragraph (b)(1) of this section must determine whether the payee is entitled to a reduced rate of withholding under section 1441, 1442, or 1443. This paragraph (b)(4) identifies items for which a reduction in the rate of withholding may apply and whether the rate reduction is conditioned upon documentation being furnished to the withholding agent. Documentation required under this paragraph (b)(4) is documentation that a withholding agent must be able to associate with a payment upon which it can rely to treat the payment as made to a foreign person that is the beneficial owner of the payment in accordance with paragraph (e)(1)(ii) of this section. This paragraph (b)(4) also cross-references other sections of the Code and applicable regulations in which some of these exceptions, exemptions, or reductions are further explained. See, for example, paragraph (b)(4)(viii) of this section, dealing with effectively connected income, that cross-references § 1.1441-4(a); see paragraph (b)(4)(xv) of this section, dealing with exemptions from, or reductions of, withholding under an income tax treaty, that cross-references § 1.1441-6. This paragraph (b)(4) is not an exclusive list of items to which a reduction of the rate of withholding may apply and, thus, does not preclude an exemption from, or reduction in, the rate of withholding that may otherwise be allowed under the regulations under the provisions of chapter 3 of the Code for a particular item of income identified in this paragraph (b)(4).

(i) Portfolio interest described in section 871(h) or 881(c) and substitute interest payments described in § 1.871-7(b)(2)(i) or 1.881-2(b)(2) are exempt from withholding under section 1441(a). See § 1.871-14 for regulations regarding portfolio interest and section 1441(c)(9) for exemption from withholding. Documentation establishing foreign status is required for interest on an obligation in registered form to qualify as portfolio interest. See section 871(h)(2)(B)(ii) and § 1.871-14(c)(1)(ii)(C). For special documentation rules regarding foreign-targeted registered obligations described in § 1.871-14(e)(2), see § 1.871-14(e) (3) and (4) and, in particular, § 1.871-14(e)(4)(i)(A) and (ii)(A) regarding the time when the withholding agent must receive the documentation. The documentation furnished for purposes of qualifying interest as portfolio interest serves as the basis for the withholding exemption for purposes of this section and for purposes of establishing foreign status for purposes of section 6049. See § 1.6049-5(b)(8). Documentation establishing foreign status is not required for qualifying interest on an obligation in bearer form described in § 1.871-14(b)(1) as portfolio interest. However, in certain cases, documentation for portfolio interest on a bearer obligation may have to be furnished in order to establish foreign status for purposes of the information reporting provisions of section 6049 and backup withholding under section 3406. See § 1.6049-5(b)(7).

(ii) Bank deposit interest and similar types of deposit interest (including original issue discount) described in section 871(i)(2)(A) or 881(d) that are from sources within the United States are exempt from withholding under section 1441(a). See section 1441(c)(10). Documentation establishing foreign status is not required for purposes of this withholding exemption but may have to be furnished for purposes of the information reporting provisions of section 6049 and backup withholding under section 3406. See § 1.6049-5(d)(3)(iii) for exceptions to the foreign payee and exempt recipient rules regarding this type of income. See also § 1.6049-5(b)(11) for applicable documentation exemptions for certain bank deposit interest paid on obligations in bearer form.

(iii) Bank deposit interest (including original issue discount) described in section 861(a)(1)(B) is exempt from withholding under sections 1441(a) as income that is not from U.S. sources. Documentation establishing foreign status is not required for purposes of this withholding exemption but may have to be furnished for purposes of the information reporting provisions of section 6049 and backup withholding under section 3406. Reporting requirements for payments of such interest are governed by section 6049 and the regulations under that section. See § 1.6049-5(b)(12) and alternative documentation rules under § 1.6049-5(c)(4).

(iv) Interest or original issue discount from sources within the United States on certain short-term obligations described in section 871(g)(1)(B) or 881(a)(3) is exempt from withholding under sections 1441(a). Documentation establishing foreign status is not required for purposes of this withholding exemption but may have to be furnished for purposes of the information reporting provisions of section 6049 and backup withholding under section 3406. See § 1.6049-5(b)(12) for applicable documentation for establishing foreign status and § 1.6049-5(d)(3)(iii) for exceptions to the foreign payee and exempt recipient rules regarding this type of income. See also § 1.6049-5(b)(10) for applicable documentation exemptions for certain obligations in bearer form.

(v) Income from sources without the United States is exempt from withholding under sections 1441(a). Documentation establishing foreign status is not required for purposes of this withholding exemption but may have to be furnished for purposes of the information reporting provisions of section 6049 or other applicable provisions of chapter 61 of the Code and backup withholding under section 3406. See, for example, § 1.6049-5(b) (6) and (12) and alternative documentation rules under § 1.6049-5(c)(4). See also paragraph (b)(5) of this section for cross references to other applicable provisions of the regulations under chapter 61 of the Code.

(vi) Distributions from certain domestic corporations described in section 871(i)(2)(B) or 881(d) are exempt from withholding under section 1441(a). See section 1441(c)(10). Documentation establishing foreign status is not required for purposes of this withholding exemption but may have to be furnished for purposes of the information reporting provisions of section 6042 and backup withholding under section 3406. See § 1.6042-3(b)(1) (iii) through (vi).

(vii) Dividends paid by certain foreign corporations that are treated as income from sources within the United States by reason of section 861(a)(2)(B) are exempt from withholding under section 884(e)(3) to the extent that the distributions are paid out of earnings and profits in any taxable year that the corporation was subject to branch profits tax for that year. Documentation establishing foreign status is not required for purposes of this withholding exemption but may have to be furnished for purposes of the information reporting provisions of section 6042 and backup withholding under section 3406. See § 1.6042-3(b)(1) (iii) through (vii).

(viii) Certain income that is effectively connected with the conduct of a U.S. trade or business is exempt from withholding under section 1441(a). See section 1441(c)(1). Documentation establishing foreign status and status of the income as effectively connected must be furnished for purposes of this withholding exemption to the extent required under the provisions of § 1.1441-4(a). Documentation furnished for this purpose also serves as documentation establishing foreign status for purposes of applicable information reporting provisions under chapter 61 of the Code and for backup withholding under section 3406. See, for example, § 1.6041-4(a)(1).

(ix) Certain income with respect to compensation for personal services of an individual that are performed in the United States is exempt from withholding under section 1441(a). See section 1441(c)(4) and § 1.1441-4(b). However, such income may be subject to withholding as wages under section 3402. Documentation establishing foreign status must be furnished for purposes of any withholding exemption or reduction to the extent required under § 1.1441-4(b) or 31.3401(a)(6)-1 (e) and (f) of this chapter. Documentation furnished for this purpose also serves as documentation establishing foreign status for purposes of information reporting under section 6041. See § 1.6041-4(a)(1).

(x) Amounts described in section 871(f) that are received as annuities from certain qualified plans are exempt from withholding under section 1441(a). See section 1441(c)(7). Documentation establishing foreign status must be furnished for purposes of the withholding exemption as required under § 1.1441-4(d). Documentation furnished for this purpose also serves as documentation establishing foreign status for purposes of information reporting under section 6041. See § 1.6041-4(a)(1).

(xi) Payments to a foreign government (including a foreign central bank of issue) that are excludable from gross income under section 892(a) are exempt from withholding under section 1442. See § 1.1441-8(b). Documentation establishing status as a foreign government is required for purposes of this withholding exemption. Payments to a foreign government are exempt from information reporting under chapter 61 of the Code (see § 1.6049-4(c)(1)(ii)(F)).

(xii) Payments of certain interest income to a foreign central bank of issue or the Bank for International Settlements that are exempt from tax under section 895 are exempt from withholding under section 1442. Documentation establishing eligibility for such exemption is required to the extent provided in § 1.1441-8(c)(1). Payments to a foreign central bank of issue or to the Bank for International Settlements are exempt from information reporting under chapter 61 of the Code (see § 1.6049-4(c)(1)(ii) (H) and (M)).

(xiii) Amounts derived by a foreign central bank of issue from bankers' acceptances described in section 871(i)(2)(C) or 881(d) are exempt from tax and, therefore, from withholding. See section 1441(c)(10). Documentation establishing foreign status is not required for purposes of this withholding exemption if the name of the payee and other facts surrounding the payment reasonably indicate that the beneficial owner of the payment is a foreign central bank of issue as defined in § 1.861-2(b)(4). See § 1.1441-8(c)(2) for withholding procedures. See also §§ 1.6049-4(c)(1)(ii)(H) and 1.6041-3(q)(8) for a similar exemption from information reporting.

(xiv) Payments to an international organization from investments in the United States of stocks, bonds, or other domestic securities or from interest on deposits in banks in the United States of funds belonging to such international organization are exempt from tax under section 892(b) and, thus, from withholding. Documentation establishing status as an international organization is not required if the name of the payee and other facts surrounding the payment reasonably indicate that the beneficial owner of the payment is an international organization within the meaning of section 7701(a)(18). See § 1.1441-8(d). Payments to an international organization are exempt from information reporting under chapter 61 of the Code (see § 1.6049-4(c)(1)(ii)(G)).

(xv) Amounts may be exempt from, or subject to a reduced rate of, withholding under an income tax treaty. Documentation establishing eligibility for benefits under an income tax treaty is required for this purpose as provided under §§ 1.1441-6. Documentation furnished for this purpose also serves as documentation establishing foreign status for purposes of applicable information reporting provisions under chapter 61 of the Code and for backup withholding under section 3406. See, for example, § 1.6041-4(a)(1).

(xvi) Amounts of scholarships and grants paid to certain exchange or training program participants that do not represent compensation for services but are not excluded from tax under section 117 are subject to a reduced rate of withholding of 14-percent under section 1441(b). Documentation establishing foreign status is required for purposes of this reduction in rate as provided under § 1.1441-4(c). This income is not subject to information reporting under chapter 61 of the Code nor to backup withholding under section 3406. The compensatory portion of a scholarship or grant is reportable as wage income. See § 1.6041-3(o).

(xvii) Amounts paid to a foreign organization described in section 501(c) are exempt from withholding under section 1441 to the extent that the amounts are not income includible under section 512 in computing the organization's unrelated business taxable income and are not subject to the tax imposed by section 4948(a). Documentation establishing status as a tax-exempt organization is required for purposes of this exemption to the extent provided in § 1.1441-9. Amounts includible under section 512 in computing the organization's unrelated business taxable income are subject to withholding to the extent provided in section 1443(a) and § 1.1443-1(a). Gross investment income (as defined in section 4940(c)(2)) of a private foundation is subject to withholding at a 4-percent rate to the extent provided in section 1443(b) and § 1.1443-1(b). Payments to a tax-exempt organization are exempt from information reporting under chapter 61 of the Code and the regulations thereunder (see § 1.6049-4(c)(1)(ii)(B)(1)).

(xviii) Per diem amounts for subsistence paid by the U.S. government to a nonresident alien individual who is engaged in any program of training in the United States under the Mutual Security Act of 1954 are exempt from withholding under section 1441(a). See section 1441(c)(6). Documentation of foreign status is required under § 1.1441-4(e) for purposes of establishing eligibility for this exemption. See § 1.6041-3(p).

(xix) Interest with respect to tax-free covenant bonds issued prior to 1934 is subject to special withholding procedures set forth in § 1.1461-1 in effect prior to January 1, 1999 (see § 1.1461-1 as contained in 26 CFR part 1, revised April 1, 1997).

(xx) Income from certain gambling winnings of a nonresident alien individual is exempt from tax under section 871(j) and from withholding under section 1441(a). See section 1441(c)(11). Documentation establishing foreign status is not required for purposes of this exemption but may have to be furnished for purposes of the information reporting provisions of section 6041 and backup withholding under section 3406. See §§ 1.6041-1 and 1.6041-4(a)(1).

(xxi) Any payments not otherwise mentioned in this paragraph (b)(4) shall be subject to withholding at the rate of 30-percent if it is an amount subject to withholding (as defined in § 1.1441-2(a)) unless and to the extent the IRS may otherwise prescribe in published guidance (see § 601.601(d)(2) of this chapter) or unless otherwise provided in regulations under chapter 3 of the Code.

(5) Establishing foreign status under applicable provisions of chapter 61 of the Code. This paragraph (b)(5) identifies relevant provisions of the regulations under chapter 61 of the Code that exempt payments from information reporting, and therefore, from backup withholding under section 3406, based on the payee's status as a foreign person. Many of these exemptions require that the payee's foreign status be established in order for the exemption to apply. The regulations under applicable provisions of chapter 61 of the Code generally provide that the documentation described in this section may be relied upon for purposes of determining foreign status.

(i) Payments to a foreign person that are governed by section 6041 (dealing with certain trade or business income) are exempt from information reporting under § 1.6041-4(a).

(ii) Payments to a foreign person that are governed by section 6041A (dealing with remuneration for services and certain sales) are exempt from information reporting under § 1.6041A-1(d)(3).

(iii) Payments to a foreign person that are governed by section 6042 (dealing with dividends) are exempt from information reporting under § 1.6042-3(b)(1) (iii) through (vi).

(iv) Payments to a foreign person that are governed by section 6044 (dealing with patronage dividends) are exempt from information reporting under § 1.6044-3(c)(1).

(v) Payments to a foreign person that are governed by section 6045 (dealing with broker proceeds) are exempt from information reporting under § 1.6045-1(g).

(vi) Payments to a foreign person that are governed by section 6049 (dealing with interest) to a foreign person are exempt from information reporting under § 1.6049-5(b) (6) through (15).

(vii) Payments to a foreign person that are governed by section 6050N (dealing with royalties) are exempt from information reporting under § 1.6050N-1(c).

(viii) Payments to a foreign person that are governed by section 6050P (dealing with income from cancellation of debt) are exempt from information reporting under section 6050P or the regulations under that section except to the extent provided in Notice 96-61 (I.R.B. 1996-49); see also § 601.601(b)(2) of this chapter.

(6) Rules of withholding for payments by a foreign intermediary or certain U.S. branches. (i) In general. A foreign intermediary described in paragraph (e)(3)(i) of this section or a U.S. branch described in paragraph (b)(2)(iv) of this section that receives an amount subject to withholding (as defined in § 1.1441-2(a)) shall be required to withhold (if another withholding agent has not withheld the full amount required) and report such payment under chapter 3 of the Internal Revenue Code and the regulations thereunder except as otherwise provided in this paragraph (b)(6). A nonqualified intermediary or U.S. branch described in paragraph (b)(2)(iv) of this section (other than a branch that is treated as a U.S. person) shall not be required to withhold or report if it has provided a valid nonqualified intermediary withholding certificate or a U.S. branch withholding certificate, it has provided all of the information required by paragraph (e)(3)(iv) of this section (withholding statement), and it does not know, and has no reason to know, that another withholding agent failed to withhold the correct amount or failed to report the payment correctly under § 1.1461-1(c). A qualified intermediary's obligations to withhold and report shall be determined in accordance with its qualified intermediary withholding agreement.

(ii) Examples. The following examples illustrate the rules of paragraph (b)(6)(i) of this section:

Example (1). FB, a foreign bank, acts as intermediary for five different persons, A, B, C, D, and E, each of whom owns U.S. securities that generate U.S. source dividends. The dividends are paid by USWA, a U.S. withholding agent. FB furnished USWA with a nonqualified intermediary withholding certificate, described in paragraph (e)(3)(iii) of this section, to which it attached the withholding certificates of each of A, B, C, D, and E. The withholding certificates from A and B claim a 15 percent reduced rate of withholding under an income tax treaty. C, D, and E claim no reduced rate of withholding. FB provides a withholding statement that meets all of the requirements of paragraph (e)(3)(iv) of this section, including information allocating 20 percent of each dividend payment to each of A, B, C, D, and E. FB does not have actual knowledge or reason to know that USWA did not withhold the correct amounts or report the dividends on Forms 1042-S to each of A, B, C, D, and E. FB is not required to withhold or to report the dividends to A, B, C, D, and E.

Example (2). The facts are the same as in Example 1, except that FB did not provide any information for USWA to determine how much of the dividend payments were made to A, B, C, D, and E. Because USWA could not reliably associate the dividend payments with documentation under paragraph (b)(2)(vii) of this section, USWA applied the presumption rules of paragraph (b)(3)(v) of this section and withheld 30 percent from all dividend payments. In addition, USWA filed a single Form 1042-S reporting the payment to an unknown foreign payee. FB is deemed to know that USWA did not report the payment to A, B, C, D, and E because it did not provide all of the information required on a withholding statement under paragraph (e)(3)(iv) of this section (i.e., allocation information). Although FB is not required to withhold on the payment because the full 30 percent withholding was imposed by USWA, it is required to report the payments on Forms 1042-S to A, B, C, D, and E. FB's intentional failure to do so will subject it to intentional disregard penalties under sections 6721 and 6722.

(7) Liability for failure to obtain documentation timely or to act in accordance with applicable presumptions. (i) General rule. A withholding agent that cannot reliably associate a payment with documentation on the date of payment and that does not withhold under this section, or withholds at less than the 30-percent rate prescribed under section 1441(a) and paragraph (b)(1) of this section, is liable under section 1461 for the tax required to be withheld under chapter 3 of the Code and the regulations thereunder, without the benefit of a reduced rate unless—

(A) The withholding agent has appropriately relied on the presumptions described in paragraph (b)(3) of this section (including the grace period described in paragraph (b)(3)(iv) of this section) in order to treat the payee as a U.S. person or, if applicable, on the presumptions described in § 1.1441-4(a) (2)(i) or (3) to treat the payment as effectively connected income; or

(B) The withholding agent can demonstrate to the satisfaction of the district director or the Assistant Commissioner (International) that the proper amount of tax, if any, was in fact paid to the IRS; or

(C) No documentation is required under section 1441 or this section in order for a reduced rate of withholding to apply.

(D) The withholding agent has complied with the provisions of § 1.1441-6(c) or (g).

(ii) Proof that tax liability has been satisfied. Proof of payment of tax may be established for purposes of paragraph (b)(7)(i)(B) of this section on the basis of a Form 4669 (or such other form as the IRS may prescribe in published guidance (see § 601.601(d)(2) of this chapter)), establishing the amount of tax, if any, actually paid by or for the beneficial owner on the income. Proof that a reduced rate of withholding was, in fact, appropriate under the provisions of chapter 3 of the Code and the regulations thereunder may also be established after the date of payment by the withholding agent on the basis of a valid withholding certificate or other appropriate documentation furnished after that date. However, in the case of a withholding certificate or other appropriate documentation received after the date of payment (or after the grace period specified in paragraph (b)(3)(iv) of this section), the district director or the Assistant Commissioner (International) may require additional proof if it is determined that the delays in obtaining the withholding certificate affect its reliability.

(iii) Liability for interest and penalties. For payments made after December 31, 2000, if a withholding agent fails to deduct and withhold any tax imposed under sections 1441 or 1442, and the tax against which such tax may be credited under section 1462 is paid, then the amount of tax required to be deducted and withheld shall not be collected from the withholding agent. However, the withholding agent is not relieved from liability for interest or any penalties or additions to the tax otherwise applicable in respect of the failure to deduct and withhold. See section 1463. Further, in the event that a tax liability is assessed against the beneficial owner under section 871, 881, or 882 and interest under section 6601(a) is assessed against, and collected from, the beneficial owner, the interest charge imposed on the withholding agent shall be abated to that extent so as to avoid the imposition of a double interest charge.

(iv) Special effective date. See paragraph (f)(2)(ii) of this section for the special effective date applicable to this paragraph (b)(7).

(8) Adjustments, refunds, or credits of overwithheld amounts. If the amount withheld under section 1441, 1442, or 1443 is greater than the tax due by the withholding agent or the taxpayer, adjustments may be made in accordance with the procedures described in § 1.1461-2(a). Alternatively, refunds or credits may be claimed in accordance with the procedures described in § 1.1464-1, relating to refunds or credits claimed by the beneficial owner, or § 1.6414-1, relating to refunds or credits claimed by the withholding agent. If an amount was withheld under section 3406 or is subsequently determined to have been paid to a foreign person, see paragraph (b)(3)(vii) of this section and § 31.6413(a)-3(a)(1) of this chapter.

(9) Payments to joint owners. A payment to joint owners that requires documentation in order to reduce the rate of withholding under chapter 3 of the Code and the regulations thereunder does not qualify for such reduced rate unless the withholding agent can reliably associate the payment with documentation from each owner. Notwithstanding the preceding sentence, a payment to joint owners qualifies as a payment exempt from withholding under this section if any one of the owners provides a certificate of U.S. status on a Form W-9 in accordance with paragraph (d) (2) or (3) of this section or the withholding agent can associate the payment with a withholding certificate upon which it can rely to treat the payment as made to a U.S. beneficial owner under paragraph (d)(4) of this section. See § 31.3406(h)-2(a)(3)(i)(B) of this chapter.

(c) Definitions. *(1) Withholding.* The term withholding means the deduction and withholding of tax at the applicable rate from the payment.

(2) Foreign and U.S. person. The term foreign person means a nonresident alien individual, a foreign corporation, a foreign partnership, a foreign trust, a foreign estate, and any other person that is not a U.S. person described in the next sentence. Solely for purposes of the regulations under chapter 3 of the Internal Revenue Code, the term foreign person also means, with respect to a payment by a withholding agent, a foreign branch of a U.S. person that furnishes an intermediary withholding certificate described in paragraph (e)(3)(ii) of this section. Such a branch continues to be a U.S. payor for purposes of chapter 61 of the Internal Revenue Code. See § 1.6049-5(c)(4). A U.S. person is a person described in section 7701(a)(30), the U.S. government (including an agency or instrumentality thereof), a State (including an agency or instrumentality thereof), or the District of Columbia (including an agency or instrumentality thereof).

(3) Individual. (i) Alien individual. The term alien individual means an individual who is not a citizen or a national of the United States. See § 1.1-1(c).

(ii) Nonresident alien individual. The term nonresident alien individual means a person described in section 7701(b)(1)(B), an alien individual who is a resident of a foreign country under the residence article of an income tax treaty and § 301.7701(b)-7(a)(1) of this chapter, or an alien individual who is a resident of Puerto Rico, Guam, the Commonwealth of Northern Mariana Islands, the U.S. Virgin Islands, or American Samoa as determined under § 301.7701(b)-1(d) of this chapter. An alien individual who has made an election under section 6013 (g) or (h) to be treated as a resident of the United States is nevertheless treated as a nonresident alien individual for purposes of withholding under chapter 3 of the Code and the regulations thereunder.

(4) Certain foreign corporations. For purposes of this section, a corporation created or organized in Guam, the Commonwealth of Northern Mariana Islands, the U.S. Virgin Islands, and American Samoa, is not treated as a foreign corporation if the requirements of sections 881(b)(1) (A), (B), and (C) are met for such corporation. Further, a payment made to a foreign government or an international organization shall be treated as a payment made to a foreign corporation for purposes of withholding under chapter 3 of the Code and the regulations thereunder.

(5) Financial institution and foreign financial institution. For purposes of the regulations under chapter 3 of the Code, the term financial institution means a person described in § 1.165-12(c)(1)(iv) (not including a person providing pension or other similar benefits or a regulated investment company or other mutual fund, unless otherwise indicated) and the term foreign financial institution means a financial institution that is a foreign person, as defined in paragraph (c)(2) of this section.

(6) Beneficial owner. (i) General rule. This paragraph (c)(6) defines the term beneficial owner for payments of income other than a payment for which a reduced rate of withholding is claimed under an income tax treaty. The term beneficial owner means the person who is the owner of the income for tax purposes and who beneficially owns that income. A person shall be treated as the owner of the income to the extent that it is required under U.S. tax principles to include the amount paid in gross income under section 61 (determined without regard to an exclusion or exemption from gross income under the Internal Revenue Code). Beneficial ownership of income is determined under the provisions of section 7701(l) and the regulations under that section and any other applicable general U.S. tax principles, including principles governing the determination of whether a transaction is a conduit transaction. Thus, a person receiving income in a capacity as a nominee, agent, or custodian for another person is not the beneficial owner of the income. In the case of a scholarship, the student receiving the scholarship is the beneficial owner of that scholarship. In the case of a payment of an amount that is not income, the beneficial owner determination shall be made under this paragraph (c)(6) as if the amount were income.

(ii) Special rules. (A) General rule. The beneficial owners of income paid to an entity described in this paragraph (c)(6)(ii) are those persons described in paragraphs (c)(6)(ii)(B) through (D) of this section.

(B) Foreign partnerships. The beneficial owners of income paid to a foreign partnership (whether a nonwithholding or a withholding foreign partnership) are the partners in the partnership, unless they themselves are not the beneficial owners of the income under this paragraph (c)(6). For example, a partnership (first tier) that is a partner in another partnership (second tier) is not the beneficial owner of income paid to the second tier partnership since the first tier partnership is not the owner of the income under U.S. tax principles. Rather, the partners of the first tier partnership are the beneficial owners (to the extent they are not themselves persons that are not beneficial owners under this paragraph (c)(6)). See § 1.1441-5(b) for applicable withholding procedures for payments to a domestic partnership. See also § 1.1441-5(c)(3)(ii) for applicable withholding procedures for payments to a foreign partnership where one of the partners (at any level in the chain of tiers) is a domestic partnership.

(C) Foreign simple trusts and foreign grantor trusts. The beneficial owners of income paid to a foreign simple trust, as described in paragraph (c)(23) of this section, are the beneficiaries of the trust, unless they themselves are not the beneficial owners of the income under this paragraph (c)(6). The beneficial owners of income paid to a foreign grantor trust, as described in paragraph (c)(26) of this section, are the persons treated as the owners of the trust, unless they themselves are not the beneficial owners of the income under this paragraph (c)(6).

(D) Other foreign trusts and foreign estates. The beneficial owner of income paid to a foreign complex trust as defined in paragraph (c)(25) of this section or to a foreign estate is the foreign complex trust or estate itself.

(7) Withholding agent. For a definition of the term withholding agent and applicable rules, see § 1.1441-7.

(8) Person. For purposes of the regulations under chapter 3 of the Code, the term person shall mean a person described in section 7701(a)(1) and the regulations under that section and a U.S. branch to the extent treated as a U.S. person under paragraph (b)(2)(iv) of this section. For purposes of the regulations under chapter 3 of the Code, the term person does not include a wholly-owned entity that is disregarded for federal tax purposes under § 301.7701-2(c)(2) of this chapter as an entity separate from its owner. See paragraph (b)(2)(iii) of this section for procedures applicable to payments to such entities.

(9) Source of income. The source of income is determined under the provisions of part I (section 861 and following) , subchapter N, chapter 1 of the Code and the regulations under those provisions.

(10) Chapter 3 of the Code. For purposes of the regulations under sections 1441, 1442, and 1443, any reference to chapter 3 of the Code shall not include references to sections 1445 and 1446, unless the context indicates otherwise.

(11) Reduced rate. For purposes of regulations under chapter 3 of the Code, and other withholding provisions of the Code, the term reduced rate, when used in regulations under chapter 3 of the Code, shall include an exemption from tax.

(12) Payee. For purposes of chapter 3 of the Internal Revenue Code, the term payee of a payment is determined under paragraph (b)(2) of this section, § 1.1441-5(c)(1) (relating to partnerships), and § 1.1441-5(e)(2) and (3) (relating to trusts and estates) and includes foreign persons, U.S. exempt recipients, and U.S. non-exempt recipients. A nonqualified intermediary and a qualified intermediary (to the extent it does not assume primary withholding responsibility) are not payees if they are acting as intermediaries and not the beneficial owner of income. In addition, a flow-through entity is not a payee unless the income is (or is deemed to be) effectively connected with the conduct of a trade or business in the United States. See § 1.6049-5(d)(1) for rules to determine the payee for purposes of chapter 61 of the Internal Revenue Code. See §§ 1.1441-1(b)(3), 1.1441-5(d), and (e)(6) and 1.6049-5(d)(3) for presumption rules that apply if a payee's identity cannot be determined on the basis of valid documentation.

(13) Intermediary. An intermediary means, with respect to a payment that it receives, a person that, for that payment, acts as a custodian, broker, nominee, or otherwise as an agent for another person, regardless of whether such other person is the beneficial owner of the amount paid, a flow-through entity, or another intermediary.

(14) Nonqualified intermediary. A nonqualified intermediary means any intermediary that is not a qualified intermediary, as defined in paragraph (e)(5)(ii) of this section, or a qualified intermediary that is not acting in its capacity as a qualified intermediary with respect to a payment. For example, to the extent an entity that is a qualified intermediary provides another withholding agent with a foreign beneficial owner withholding certificate as defined in paragraph (e)(2)(i) of this section, the entity is not acting in its capacity as a qualified intermediary. Notwithstanding the preceding sentence, a qualified intermediary is acting as a qualified intermediary to the extent it provides another withholding agent with Forms W-9, or other information regarding U.S.

non-exempt recipients pursuant to its qualified intermediary agreement with the IRS.

(15) Qualified intermediary. The term qualified intermediary is defined in paragraph (e)(5)(ii) of this section.

(16) Withholding certificate. The term withholding certificate means a Form W-8 described in paragraph (e)(2)(i) of this section (relating to foreign beneficial owners), paragraph (e)(3)(i) of this section (relating to foreign intermediaries), § 1.1441-5(c)(2)(iv), (c)(3)(iii), and (e)(3)(iv) (relating to flow-through entities), a Form 8233 described in § 1.1441-4(b)(2), a Form W-9 as described in paragraph (d) of this section, a statement described in § 1.871-14(c)(2)(v) (relating to portfolio interest), or any other certificates that under the Internal Revenue Code or regulations certifies or establishes the status of a payee or beneficial owner as a U.S. or a foreign person.

(17) Documentary evidence; other appropriate documentation. The terms documentary evidence or other appropriate documentation refer to documents other than a withholding certificate that may be provided for payments made outside the United States to offshore accounts or any other evidence that under the Internal Revenue Code or regulations certifies or establishes the status of a payee or beneficial owner as a U.S. or foreign person. See §§ 1.1441-6(b)(2), (c)(3) and (4) (relating to treaty benefits), and 1.6049-5(c)(1) and (4) (relating to chapter 61 reporting). Also see § 1.1441-4(a)(3)(ii) regarding documentary evidence for notional principal contracts.

(18) Documentation. The term documentation refers to both withholding certificates, as defined in paragraph (c)(16) of this section, and documentary evidence or other appropriate documentation, as defined in paragraph (c)(17) of this section.

(19) Payor. The term payor is defined in § 31.3406(a)-2 of this chapter and § 1.6049-4(a)(2) and generally includes a withholding agent, as defined in § 1.1441-7(a). The term also includes any person that makes a payment to an intermediary, flow-through entity, or U.S. branch that is not treated as a U.S. person to the extent the intermediary, flow-through, or U.S. branch provides a Form W-9 or other appropriate information relating to a payee so that the payment can be reported under chapter 61 of the Internal Revenue Code and, if required, subject to backup withholding under section 3406. This latter rule does not preclude the intermediary, flow-through entity, or U.S. branch from also being a payor.

(20) Exempt recipient. The term exempt recipient means a person that is exempt from reporting under chapter 61 of the Internal Revenue Code and backup withholding under section 3406 and that is described in §§ 1.6041-3(q), 1.6045-2(b)(2)(i), and 1.6049-4(c)(1)(ii), and § 5f.6045-1(c)(3)(i)(B) of this chapter. Exempt recipients are not exempt from withholding under chapter 3 of the Internal Revenue Code unless they are U.S. persons or foreign persons entitled to an exemption from withholding under chapter 3.

(21) Non-exempt recipient. A non-exempt recipient is any person that is not an exempt recipient under paragraph (c)(20) of this section.

(22) Reportable amounts. Reportable amounts are defined in paragraph (e)(3)(vi) of this section.

(23) Flow-through entity. A flow-through entity means any entity that is described in this paragraph (c)(23) and that may provide documentation on behalf of others to a withholding agent. The entities described in this paragraph are a foreign partnership (other than a withholding foreign partnership), a foreign simple trust (other than a withholding foreign trust) that is described in paragraph (c)(24) of this section, a foreign grantor trust (other than a withholding foreign trust) that is described in paragraph (c)(25) of this section, or, for any payments for which a reduced rate of withholding under an income tax treaty is claimed, any entity to the extent the entity is considered to be fiscally transparent under section 894 with respect to the payment by an interest holder's jurisdiction.

(24) Foreign simple trust. A foreign simple trust is a foreign trust that is described in section 651(a).

(25) Foreign complex trust. A foreign complex trust is a foreign trust other than a trust described in section 651(a) or sections 671 through 679.

(26) Foreign grantor trust. A foreign grantor trust is a foreign trust but only to the extent all or a portion of the income of the trust is treated as owned by the grantor or another person under sections 671 through 679.

(27) Partnership. The term partnership means any entity treated as a partnership under § 301.7701-2 or -3 of this chapter.

(28) Nonwithholding foreign partnership. A nonwithholding foreign partnership is a foreign partnership that is not a withholding foreign partnership, as defined in § 1.1441-5(c)(2)(i).

(29) Withholding foreign partnership. A withholding foreign partnership is defined in § 1.1441-5(c)(2)(i).

(30) Possessions of the United States. For purposes of the regulations under chapters 3 and 61 of the Internal Revenue Code, possessions of the United States means Guam, American Samoa, the Northern Mariana Islands, Puerto Rico, and the Virgin Islands.

(d) Beneficial owner's or payee's claim of U.S. status. *(1) In general.* Under paragraph (b)(1) of this section, a withholding agent is not required to withhold under chapter 3 of the Code on payments to a U.S. payee, to a person presumed to be a U.S. payee in accordance with the provisions of paragraph (b)(3) of this section, or to a person that the withholding agent may treat as a U.S. beneficial owner of the payment. Absent actual knowledge or reason to know otherwise, a withholding agent may rely on the provisions of this paragraph (d) in order to determine whether to treat a payee or beneficial owner as a U.S. person.

(2) Payments for which a Form W-9 is otherwise required. A withholding agent may treat as a U.S. payee any person who is required to furnish a Form W-9 and who furnishes it in accordance with the procedures described in §§ 31.3406(d)-1 through 31.3406(d)-5 of this chapter (including the requirement that the payee furnish its taxpayer identifying number (TIN)) if the withholding agent meets all the requirements described in § 31.3406(h)-3(e) of this chapter regarding reliance by a payor on a Form W-9. Providing a Form W-9 or valid substitute form shall serve as a statement that the person whose name is on the form is a U.S. person. Therefore, a foreign person, including a U.S. branch treated as a U.S. person under paragraph (b)(2)(iv) of this section, shall not provide a Form W-9. A U.S. branch of a foreign person may establish its status as a foreign person exempt from reporting under chapter 61 and backup withholding under section 3406 by providing a withholding certificate on Form W-8.

(3) Payments for which a Form W-9 is not otherwise required. In the case of a payee who is not required to furnish a Form W-9 under section 3406 (e.g., a person exempt from reporting under chapter 61 of the Internal Revenue Code),

the withholding agent may treat the payee as a U.S. payee if the payee provides the withholding agent with a Form W-9 or a substitute form described in § 31.3406(h)-3(c)(2) of this chapter (relating to forms for exempt recipients) that contains the payee's name, address, and TIN. The form must be signed under penalties of perjury by the payee if so required by the form or by § 31.3406(h)-3 of this chapter. Providing a Form W-9 or valid substitute form shall serve as a statement that the person whose name is on the certificate is a U.S. person. A Form W-9 or valid substitute form shall not be provided by a foreign person, including any U.S. branch of a foreign person whether or not the branch is treated as a U.S. person under paragraph (b)(2)(iv) of this section. See paragraph (e)(3)(v) of this section for withholding certificates provided by U.S. branches described in paragraph (b)(2)(iv) of this section. The procedures described in § 31.3406(h)-2(a) of this chapter shall apply to payments to joint payees. A withholding agent that receives a Form W-9 to satisfy this paragraph (d)(3) must retain the form in accordance with the provisions of § 31.3406(h)-3(g) of this chapter, if applicable, or of paragraph (e)(4)(iii) of this section (relating to the retention of withholding certificates) if § 31.3406(h)-3(g) of this chapter does not apply. The rules of this paragraph (d)(3) are only intended to provide a method by which a withholding agent may determine that a payee is a U.S. person and do not otherwise impose a requirement that documentation be furnished by a person who is otherwise treated as an exempt recipient for purposes of the applicable information reporting provisions under chapter 61 of the Internal Revenue Code (e.g., § 1.6049-4(c)(1)(ii) for payments of interest).

(4) When a payment to an intermediary or flow-through entity may be treated as made to a U.S. payee. A withholding agent that makes a payment to an intermediary (whether a qualified intermediary or nonqualified intermediary), a flow-through entity, or a U.S. branch described in paragraph (b)(2)(iv) of this section may treat the payment as made to a U.S. payee to the extent that, prior to the payment, the withholding agent can reliably associate the payment with a Form W-9 described in paragraph (d)(2) or (3) of this section attached to a valid intermediary, flow-through, or U.S. branch withholding certificate described in paragraph (e)(3)(i) of this section or to the extent the withholding agent can reliably associate the payment with a Form W-8 described in paragraph (e)(3)(v) of this section that evidences an agreement to treat a U.S. branch described in paragraph (b)(2)(iv) of this section as a U.S. person. In addition, a withholding agent may treat the payment as made to a U.S. payee only if it complies with the electronic confirmation procedures described in paragraph (e)(4)(v) of this section, if required, and it has not been notified by the IRS that any of the information on the withholding certificate or other documentation is incorrect or unreliable. In the case of a Form W-9 that is required to be furnished for a reportable payment that may be subject to backup withholding, the withholding agent may be notified in accordance with section 3406(a)(1)(B) and the regulations under that section. See applicable procedures under section 3406(a)(1)(B) and the regulations under that section for payors who have been notified with regard to such a Form W-9. Withholding agents who have been notified in relation to other Forms W-9, including under section 6724(b) pursuant to section 6721, may rely on the withholding certificate or other documentation only to the extent provided under procedures as prescribed by the IRS (see § 601.601(d)(2) of this chapter).

(e) Beneficial owner's claim of foreign status. *(1) Withholding agent's reliance.* (i) In general. Absent actual knowledge or reason to know otherwise, a withholding agent may treat a payment as made to a foreign beneficial owner in accordance with the provisions of paragraph (e)(1)(ii) of this section. See paragraph (e)(4)(viii) of this section for applicable reliance rules. See paragraph (b)(4) of this section for a description of payments for which a claim of foreign status is relevant for purposes of claiming a reduced rate of withholding for purposes of section 1441, 1442, or 1443. See paragraph (b)(5) of this section for a list of payments for which a claim of foreign status is relevant for other purposes, such as claiming an exemption from information reporting under chapter 61 of the Code.

(ii) Payments that a withholding agent may treat as made to a foreign person that is a beneficial owner. (A) General rule. The withholding agent may treat a payment as made to a foreign person that is a beneficial owner if it complies with the requirements described in paragraph (e)(1)(ii)(B) of this section and, then, only to the extent—

(1) That the withholding agent can reliably associate the payment with a beneficial owner withholding certificate described in paragraph (e)(2) of this section furnished by the person whose name is on the certificate or attached to a valid foreign intermediary, flow-through, or U.S. branch withholding certificate;

(2) That the payment is made outside the United States (within the meaning of § 1.6049-5(e)) with respect to an offshore account (within the meaning of § 1.6049-5(c)(1)) and the withholding agent can reliably associate the payment with documentary evidence described in §§ 1.1441-6(c)(3) or (4), or 1.6049-5(c)(1) relating to the beneficial owner;

(3) That the withholding agent can reliably associate the payment with a valid qualified intermediary withholding certificate, as described in paragraph (e)(3)(ii) of this section, and the qualified intermediary has provided sufficient information for the withholding agent to allocate the payment to a withholding rate pool other than a withholding rate pool or pools established for U.S. non-exempt recipients;

(4) That the withholding agent can reliably associate the payment with a withholding certificate described in § 1.1441-5(c)(3)(iii) or (e)(5)(iii) from a flow-through entity claiming the income is effectively connected income;

(5) That the withholding agent identifies the payee as a U.S. branch described in paragraph (b)(2)(iv) of this section, the payment to which it treats as effectively connected income in accordance with § 1.1441-4(a) (2)(ii) or (3);

(6) That the withholding agent identifies the payee as an international organization (or any wholly-owned agency or instrumentality thereof) as defined in section 7701(a)(18) that has been designated as such by executive order (pursuant to 22 U.S.C. 288 through 288(f)); or

(7) That the withholding agent pays interest from bankers' acceptances and identifies the payee as a foreign central bank of issue (as defined in § 1.861-2(b)(4)).

(B) Additional requirements. In order for a payment described in paragraph (e)(1)(ii)(A) of this section to be treated as made to a foreign beneficial owner, the withholding agent must hold the documentation (if required) prior to the payment, comply with the electronic confirmation procedures described in paragraph (e)(4)(v) of this section (if required), and must not have been notified by the IRS that any of the information on the withholding certificate or other documentation is incorrect or unreliable. If the withholding agent has been so notified, it may rely on the withholding certificate or other documentation only to the extent provided under procedures prescribed by the IRS (see § 601.601(d)(2) of this chapter). See paragraph (b)(2)(vii) of this section for rules regarding reliable association of a payment with a withholding certificate or other appropriate documentation.

(2) Beneficial owner withholding certificate. (i) In general. A beneficial owner withholding certificate is a statement by which the beneficial owner of the payment represents that it is a foreign person and, if applicable, claims a reduced rate of withholding under section 1441. A separate withholding certificate must be submitted to each withholding agent. If the beneficial owner receives more than one type of payment from a single withholding agent, the beneficial owner may have to submit more than one withholding certificate to the single withholding agent for the different types of payments as may be required by the applicable forms and instructions, or as the withholding agent may require (such as to facilitate the withholding agent's compliance with its obligations to determine withholding under this section or the reporting of the amounts under § 1.1461-1 (b) and (c)). For example, if a beneficial owner claims that some but not all of the income it receives is effectively connected with the conduct of a trade or business in the United States, it may be required to submit two separate withholding certificates, one for income that is not effectively connected and one for income that is so connected. See § 1.1441-6(b)(4)(ii) for special rules for determining who must furnish a beneficial owner withholding certificate when a benefit is claimed under an income tax treaty. See paragraph (e)(4)(ix) of this section for reliance rules in the case of certificates held by another person or at a different branch location of the same person.

(ii) Requirements for validity of certificate. A beneficial owner withholding certificate is valid only if it is provided on a Form W-8, or a Form 8233 in the case of personal services income described in § 1.1441-4(b) or certain scholarship or grant amounts described in § 1.1441-4(c) (or a substitute form described in paragraph (e)(4)(vi) of this section, or such other form as the IRS may prescribe). A Form W-8 is valid only if its validity period has not expired, it is signed under penalties of perjury by the beneficial owner, and it contains all of the information required on the form. The required information is the beneficial owner's name, permanent residence address, and TIN (if required), the country under the laws of which the beneficial owner is created, incorporated, or governed (if a person other than an individual), the classification of the entity, and such other information as may be required by the regulations under section 1441 or by the form or accompanying instructions in addition to, or in lieu of, the information described in this paragraph (e)(2)(ii). A person's permanent residence address is an address in the country where the person claims to be a resident for purposes of that country's income tax. In the case of a certificate furnished in order to claim a reduced rate of withholding under an income tax treaty, the residence must be determined in the manner prescribed under the applicable treaty. See § 1.1441-6(b)(4)(i). The address of a financial institution with which the beneficial owner maintains an account, a post office box, or an address used solely for mailing purposes is not a residence address for this purpose. If the beneficial owner is an individual who does not have a tax residence in any country, the permanent residence address is the place at which the beneficial owner normally resides. If the beneficial owner is not an individual and does not have a tax residence in any country, then the permanent residence address is the place at which the person maintains its principal office. See paragraph (e)(4)(vii) of this section for circumstances in which a TIN is required on a beneficial owner withholding certificate. See paragraph (f)(2)(i) of this section for continued validity of certificates during a transition period.

(3) Intermediary, flow-through, or U.S. branch withholding certificate. (i) In general. An intermediary withholding certificate is a Form W-8 by which a payee represents that it is a foreign person and that it is an intermediary (whether a qualified or nonqualified intermediary) with respect to a payment and not the beneficial owner. See paragraphs (e)(3)(ii) and (iii) of this section. A flow-through withholding certificate is a Form W-8 used by a flow-through entity as defined in paragraph (c)(23) of this section. See § 1.1441-5(c)(3)(iii) (a nonwithholding foreign partnership), § 1.1441-5(e)(5)(iii) (a foreign simple trust or foreign grantor trust) or § 1.1441-6(b)(2) (foreign entity presenting claims on behalf of its interest holders for a reduced rate of withholding under an income tax treaty). A U.S. branch certificate is a Form W-8 furnished under paragraph (e)(3)(v) of this section by a U.S. branch described in paragraph (b)(2)(iv) of this section. See paragraph (e)(4)(viii) of this section for applicable reliance rules.

(ii) Intermediary withholding certificate from a qualified intermediary. A qualified intermediary shall provide a qualified intermediary withholding certificate for reportable amounts received by the qualified intermediary. See paragraph (e)(3)(vi) of this section for the definition of reportable amount. A qualified intermediary withholding certificate is valid only if it is furnished on a Form W-8, an acceptable substitute form, or such other form as the IRS may prescribe, it is signed under penalties of perjury by a person with authority to sign for the qualified intermediary, its validity has not expired, and it contains the following information, statement, and certifications—

(A) The name, permanent residence address (as described in paragraph (e)(2)(ii) of this section), qualified intermediary employer identification number (QI-EIN), and the country under the laws of which the intermediary is created, incorporated, or governed. A qualified intermediary that does not act in its capacity as a qualified intermediary must not use its QI-EIN. Rather the intermediary should provide a nonqualified intermediary withholding certificate, if it is acting as an intermediary, and should use the taxpayer identification number, if any, that it uses for all other purposes;

(B) A certification that, with respect to accounts it identifies on its withholding statement (as described in paragraph (e)(5)(v) of this section), the qualified intermediary is not acting for its own account but is acting as a qualified intermediary;

(C) A certification that the qualified intermediary has provided, or will provide, a withholding statement as required by paragraph (e)(5)(v) of this section; and

(D) Any other information, certifications, or statements as may be required by the form or accompanying instructions in addition to, or in lieu of, the information and certifications described in this paragraph (e)(3)(ii) or paragraph (e)(3)(v) of this section. See paragraph (e)(5)(v) of this section for the requirements of a withholding statement associated with the qualified intermediary withholding certificate.

(iii) Intermediary withholding certificate from a nonqualified intermediary. A nonqualified intermediary shall provide a nonqualified intermediary withholding certificate for reportable amounts received by the nonqualified intermediary. See paragraph (e)(3)(vi) of this section for the definition of reportable amount. A nonqualified intermediary withholding certificate is valid only to the extent it is furnished on a Form W-8, an acceptable substitute form, or such other form as the IRS may prescribe, it is signed under penalties of perjury by a person authorized to sign for the nonqualified intermediary, it contains the information, statements, and certifications described in this paragraph (e)(3)(iii) and paragraph (e)(3)(iv) of this section, its validity has not expired, and the withholding certificates and other appropriate documentation for all persons to whom the certificate relates are associated with the certificate. Withholding certificates and other appropriate documentation consist of beneficial owner withholding certificates described in paragraph (e)(2)(i) of this section, intermediary and flow-through withholding certificates described in paragraph (e)(3)(i) of this section, withholding foreign partnership certificates described in § 1.1441-5(c)(2)(iv), documentary evidence described in §§ 1.1441-6(c)(3) or (4) and 1.6049-5(c)(1), and any other documentation or certificates applicable under other provisions of the Internal Revenue Code or regulations that certify or establish the status of the payee or beneficial owner as a U.S. or a foreign person. If a nonqualified intermediary is acting on behalf of another nonqualified intermediary or a flow-through entity, then the nonqualified intermediary must associate with its own withholding certificate the other nonqualified intermediary withholding certificate or the flow-through withholding certificate and separately identify all of the withholding certificates and other appropriate documentation that are associated with the withholding certificate of the other nonqualified intermediary or flow-through entity. Nothing in this paragraph (e)(3)(iii) shall require an intermediary to furnish original documentation. Copies of certificates or documentary evidence may be transmitted to the U.S. withholding agent, in which case the nonqualified intermediary must retain the original documentation for the same time period that the copy is required to be retained by the withholding agent under paragraph (e)(4)(iii) of this section and must provide it to the withholding agent upon request. For purposes of this paragraph (e)(3)(iii), a valid intermediary withholding certificate also includes a statement described in § 1.871-14(c)(2)(v) furnished for interest to qualify as portfolio interest for purposes of sections 871(h) and 881(c). The information and certifications required on a Form W-8 described in this paragraph (e)(3)(iii) are as follows—

(A) The name and permanent resident address (as described in paragraph (e)(2)(ii) of this section) of the nonqualified intermediary, and the country under the laws of which the nonqualified intermediary is created, incorporated, or governed;

(B) A certification that the nonqualified intermediary is not acting for its own account;

(C) If the nonqualified intermediary withholding certificate is used to transmit withholding certificates or other appropriate documentation for more than one person on whose behalf the nonqualified intermediary is acting, a withholding statement associated with the Form W-8 that provides all the information required by paragraph (e)(3)(iv) of this section; and

(D) Any other information, certifications, or statements as may be required by the form or accompanying instructions in addition to, or in lieu of, the information, certifications, and statements described in this paragraph (e)(3)(iii) or paragraph (e)(3)(iv) of this section.

(iv) Withholding statement provided by nonqualified intermediary. (A) In general. A nonqualified intermediary shall provide a withholding statement required by this paragraph (e)(3)(iv) to the extent the nonqualified intermediary is required to furnish, or does furnish, documentation for payees on whose behalf it receives reportable amounts (as defined in paragraph (e)(3)(vi) of this section) or to the extent it otherwise provides the documentation of such payees to a withholding agent. A nonqualified intermediary is not required to disclose information regarding persons for whom it collects reportable amounts unless it has actual knowledge that any such person is a U.S. non-exempt recipient as defined in paragraph (c)(21) of this section. Information regarding U.S. non-exempt recipients required under this paragraph (e)(3)(iv) must be provided irrespective of any requirement under foreign law that prohibits the disclosure of the identity of an account holder of a nonqualified intermediary or financial information relating to such account holder. Although a nonqualified intermediary is not required to provide documentation and other information required by this paragraph (e)(3)(iv) for persons other than U.S. non-exempt recipients, a withholding agent that does not receive documentation and such information must apply the presumption rules of paragraph (b) of this section, §§ 1.1441-5(d) and (e)(6) and 1.6049-5(d) or the withholding agent shall be liable for tax, interest, and penalties. A withholding agent must apply the presumption rules even if it is not required under chapter 61 of the Internal Revenue Code to obtain documentation to treat a payee as an exempt recipient and even though it has actual knowledge that the payee is a U.S. person. For example, if a nonqualified intermediary fails to provide a withholding agent with a Form W-9 for an account holder that is a U.S. exempt recipient, the withholding agent must presume (even if it has actual knowledge that the account holder is a U.S. exempt recipient), that the account holder is an undocumented foreign person with respect to amounts subject to withholding. See paragraph (b)(3)(v) of this section for applicable presumptions. Therefore, the withholding agent must withhold 30 percent from the payment even though if a Form W-9 had been provided, no withholding or reporting on the payment attributable to a U.S. exempt recipient would apply. Further, a nonqualified intermediary that fails to provide the documentation and the information under this paragraph (e)(3)(iv) for another withholding agent to report the payments on Forms 1042-S and Forms 1099 is not relieved of its responsibility to file information returns. See paragraph (b)(6) of this section. Therefore, unless the nonqualified intermediary itself files such returns and provides copies to the payees, it shall be liable for penalties under sections 6721 (failure to file information returns), and 6722 (failure to furnish payee statements), including the penalties under those sections for intentional failure to file information returns. In addition, failure to provide either the documentation or the information required by this paragraph (e)(3)(iv) results in a payment not being reliably associated with valid documentation. Therefore, the beneficial owners of the payment are not entitled to reduced rates of withholding and if the full amount required to be held under the presumption rules is not withheld by the withholding agent, the nonqualified intermediary must withhold the difference between the amount withheld by the withholding agent and the amount required to be withheld. Failure to withhold shall result in the nonqualified intermediary being liable for tax under section 1461, interest, and penalties, including penalties under section 6656 (failure to deposit) and section 6672 (failure to collect and pay over tax).

(B) General requirements. A withholding statement must be provided prior to the payment of a reportable amount and must contain the information specified in paragraph (e)(3)(iv)(C) of this section. The statement must be updated as often as required to keep the information in the withholding statement correct prior to each subsequent payment. The withholding statement forms an integral part of the withholding certificate provided under paragraph (e)(3)(iii) of this section, and the penalties of perjury statement provided on the withholding certificate shall apply to the withholding statement. The withholding statement may be provided in any manner the nonqualified intermediary and the withholding agent mutually agree, including electronically. If the withholding statement is provided electronically, there must be sufficient safeguards to ensure that the information received by the withholding agent is the information sent by the nonqualified intermediary and all occasions of user access that result in the submission or modification of the withholding statement information must be recorded. In addition, an electronic system must be capable of providing a hard copy of all withholding statements provided by the nonqualified intermediary. A withholding agent will be liable for tax, interest, and penalties in accordance with paragraph (b)(7) of this section to the extent it does not follow the presumption rules of paragraph (b)(3) of this section or §§ 1.1441-5(d) and (e)(6), and 1.6049-5(d) for any payment of a reportable amount, or portion thereof, for which it does not have a valid withholding statement prior to making a payment.

(C) Content of withholding statement. The withholding statement provided by a nonqualified intermediary must contain the information required by this paragraph (e)(3)(iv)(C).

(1) The withholding statement must contain the name, address, TIN (if any) and the type of documentation (documentary evidence, Form W-9, or type of Form W-8) for every person from whom documentation has been received by the nonqualified intermediary to the withholding agent and whether that person is a U.S. exempt recipient, a U.S. non-exempt recipient, or a foreign person. See paragraphs (c)(2), (20), and (21) of this section for the definitions of foreign person, U.S. exempt recipient, and U.S. non-exempt recipient. In the case of a foreign person, the statement must indicate whether the foreign person is a beneficial owner or an intermediary, flow-through entity, or U.S. branch described in paragraph (b)(2)(iv) of this section and include the type of recipient, based on recipient codes used for filing Forms 1042-S, if the foreign person is a recipient as defined in § 1.1461-1(c)(1)(ii).

(2) The withholding statement must allocate each payment, by income type, to every payee (including U.S. exempt recipients) for whom documentation has been provided. Any payment that cannot be reliably associated with valid documentation from a payee shall be treated as made to an unknown payee in accordance with the presumption rules of paragraph (b) of this section and §§ 1.1441-5(d) and (e)(6) and 1.6049-5(d). For this purpose, a type of income is determined by the types of income required to be reported on Forms 1042-S or 1099, as appropriate. Notwithstanding the preceding sentence, deposit interest (including original issue discount) described in section 871(i)(2)(A) or 881(d) and interest or original issue discount on short-term obligations as described in section 871(g)(1)(B) or 881(e) is only required to be allocated to the extent it is required to be reported on Form 1099 or Form 1042-S. See § 1.6049-8 (regarding reporting of bank deposit interest to certain foreign persons). If a payee receives income through another nonqualified intermediary, flow-through entity, or U.S. branch described in paragraph (e)(2)(iv) of this section (other than a U.S. branch treated as a U.S. person), the withholding certificate must also state, with respect to the payee, the name, address, and TIN, if known, of the other nonqualified intermediary or U.S. branch from which the payee directly receives the payment or the flow-through entity in which the payee has a direct ownership interest. If another nonqualified intermediary, flow-through entity, or U.S. branch fails to allocate a payment, the name of the nonqualified intermediary, flow-through entity, or U.S. branch that failed to allocate the payment shall be provided with respect to such payment.

(3) If a payee is identified as a foreign person, the nonqualified intermediary must specify the rate of withholding to which the payee is subject, the payee's country of residence and, if a reduced rate of withholding is claimed, the basis for that reduced rate (e.g., treaty benefit, portfolio interest, exempt under section 501(c)(3), 892, or 895). The allocation statement must also include the taxpayer identification numbers of those foreign persons for whom such a number is required under paragraph (e)(4)(vii) of this section or § 1.1441-6(b)(1) (regarding claims for treaty benefits). In the case of a claim of treaty benefits, the nonqualified intermediary's withholding statement must also state whether the limitation on benefits and section 894 statements required by § 1.1441-6(c)(5) have been provided, if required, in the beneficial owner's Form W-8 or associated with such owner's documentary evidence.

(4) The withholding statement must also contain any other information the withholding agent reasonably requests in order to fulfill its obligations under chapter 3, chapter 61 of the Internal Revenue Code, and section 3406.

(D) Alternative procedures. (1) In general. Under the alternative procedures of this paragraph (e)(3)(iv)(D), a nonqualified intermediary may provide information allocating a payment of a reportable amount to each payee (including U.S. exempt recipients) otherwise required under paragraph (e)(3)(iv)(B)(2) of this section after a payment is made. To use the alternative procedure of this paragraph (e)(3)(iv)(D), the nonqualified intermediary must inform the withholding agent on a statement associated with its nonqualified intermediary withholding certificate that it is using the procedure under this paragraph (e)(3)(iv)(D) and the withholding agent must agree to the procedure. If the requirements of the alternative procedure are met, a withholding agent, including the nonqualified intermediary using the procedures, can treat the payment as reliably associated with documentation and, therefore, the presumption rules of paragraph (b)(3) of this section and §§ 1.1441-5(d) and (e)(6) and 1.6049-5(d) do not apply even though information allocating the payment to each payee has not been received prior to the payment. See paragraph (e)(3)(iv)(D)(7) of this section, however, for a nonqualified intermediary's liability for tax and penalties if the requirements of this paragraph (e)(3)(iv)(D) are not met. These alternative procedures shall not be used for payments that are allocable to U.S. non-exempt recipients. Therefore, a nonqualified intermediary is required to provide a withholding agent with information allocating payments of reportable amounts to U.S. non-exempt recipients prior to the payment being made by the withholding agent.

(2) Withholding rate pools. In place of the information required in paragraph (e)(3)(iv)(B)(2) of this section allocating payments to each payee, the nonqualified intermediary must provide a withholding agent with withholding rate pool information prior to the payment of a reportable amount. The withholding statement must contain all other information required by paragraph (e)(3)(iv)(B) of this section. Further, each payee listed in the withholding statement must be assigned to an identified withholding rate pool. To the extent a nonqualified intermediary is required to, or does provide, documentation, the alternative procedures do not relieve the

nonqualified intermediary from the requirement to provide documentation prior to the payment being made. Therefore, withholding certificates or other appropriate documentation and all information required by paragraph (e)(3)(iv)(B) of this section (other than allocation information) must be provided to a withholding agent before any new payee receives a reportable amount. In addition, the withholding statement must be updated by assigning a new payee to a withholding rate pool prior to the payment of a reportable amount. A withholding rate pool is a payment of a single type of income, determined in accordance with the categories of income used to file Form 1042-S, that is subject to a single rate of withholding. A withholding rate pool may be established by any reasonable method to which the nonqualified intermediary and a withholding agent agree (e.g., by establishing a separate account for a single withholding rate pool, or by dividing a payment made to a single account into portions allocable to each withholding rate pool). The nonqualified intermediary shall determine withholding rate pools based on valid documentation or, to the extent a payment cannot be reliably associated with valid documentation, the presumption rules of paragraph (b)(3) of this section and §§ 1.1441-5(d) and (e)(6) and 1.6049-5(d).

(3) Allocation information. The nonqualified intermediary must provide the withholding agent with sufficient information to allocate the income in each withholding rate pool to each payee (including U.S. non-exempt recipients) within the pool no later than January 31 of the year following the year of payment. Any payments that are not allocated to payees for whom documentation has been provided shall be allocated to an undocumented payee in accordance with the presumption rules of paragraph (b)(3) of this section and §§ 1.1441-5(d) and (e)(6) and 1.6049-5(d). Notwithstanding the preceding sentence, deposit interest (including original issue discount) described in section 871(i)(2)(A) or 881(d) and interest or original issue discount on short-term obligations as described in section 871(g)(1)(B) or 881(e) is not required to be allocated to a U.S. exempt recipient or a foreign payee, except as required under § 1.6049-8 (regarding reporting of deposit interest paid to certain foreign persons).

(4) Failure to provide allocation information. If a nonqualified intermediary fails to provide allocation information, if required, by January 31 for any withholding rate pool, a withholding agent shall not apply the alternative procedures of this paragraph (e)(3)(iv)(D) to any payments of reportable amounts paid after January 31 in the taxable year following the calendar year for which allocation information was not given and any subsequent taxable year. Further, the alternative procedures shall be unavailable for any other withholding rate pool even though allocation information was given for that other pool. Therefore, the withholding agent must withhold on a payment of a reportable amount in accordance with the presumption rules of paragraph (b)(3) of this section, and §§ 1.1441-5(d) and (e)(6) and 1.6049-5(d), unless the nonqualified intermediary provides all of the information, including information sufficient to allocate the payment to each specific payee, required by paragraph (e)(3)(iv)(A) through (C) of this section prior to the payment. A nonqualified intermediary must allocate at least 90 percent of the income required to be allocated for each withholding rate pool or the nonqualified intermediary will be treated as having failed to provide allocation information for purposes of this paragraph (e)(3)(iv)(D). See paragraph (e)(3)(iv)(D)(7) of this section for liability for tax and penalties if a nonqualified intermediary fails to provide allocation information in whole or in part.

(5) Cure provision. A nonqualified intermediary may cure any failure to provide allocation information by providing the required allocation information to the withholding agent no later than February 14 following the calendar year of payment. If the withholding agent receives the allocation information by that date, it may apply the adjustment procedures of § 1.1461-2 to any excess withholding for payments made on or after February 1 and on or before February 14. Any nonqualified intermediary that fails to cure by February 14, may request the ability to use the alternative procedures of this paragraph (e)(3)(iv)(D) by submitting a request, in writing, to the Assistant Commissioner (International). The request must state the reason that the nonqualified intermediary did not comply with the alternative procedures of this paragraph (e)(3)(iv)(D) and steps that the nonqualified intermediary has taken, or will take, to ensure that no failures occur in the future. If the Assistant Commissioner (International) determines that the alternative procedures of this paragraph (e)(3)(iv)(D) may apply, a determination to that effect will be issued by the IRS to the nonqualified intermediary.

(6) Form 1042-S reporting in case of allocation failure. If a nonqualified intermediary fails to provide allocation information by February 14 following the year of payment for a withholding rate pool, the withholding agent must file Forms 1042-S for payments made to each payee in that pool (other than U.S. exempt recipients) in the prior calendar year by pro rating the payment to each payee (including U.S. exempt recipients) listed in the withholding statement for that withholding rate pool. If the nonqualified intermediary fails to allocate10 percent or less of an amount required to be allocated for a withholding rate pool, a withholding agent shall report the unallocated amount as paid to a single unknown payee in accordance with the presumption rules of paragraph (b) of this section and §§ 1.1441-5(d) and (e)(6) and 1.6049-5(d). The portion of the payment that can be allocated to specific recipients, as defined in § 1.1461-1(c)(1)(ii), shall be reported to each recipient in accordance with the rules of § 1.1461-1(c).

(7) Liability for tax, interest, and penalties. If a nonqualified intermediary fails to provide allocation information by February 14 following the year of payment for all or a portion of the payments made to any withholding rate pool, the withholding agent from whom the nonqualified intermediary received payments of reportable amounts shall not be liable for any tax, interest, or penalties, due solely to the errors or omissions of the nonqualified intermediary. See § 1.1441-7(b)(2) through (10) for the due diligence requirements of a withholding agent. Because failure by the nonqualified intermediary to provide allocation information results in a payment not being reliably associated with valid documentation, the beneficial owners for whom the nonqualified intermediary acts are not entitled to a reduced rate of withholding. Therefore, the nonqualified intermediary, as a withholding agent, shall be liable for any tax not withheld by the withholding agent in accordance with the presumption rules, interest on the under withheld tax if the nonqualified intermediary fails to pay the tax timely, and any applicable penalties, including the penalties under sections 6656 (failure to deposit), 6721 (failure to file information returns) and 6722 (failure to file payee statements). Failure to provide allocation information for more than 10 percent of the payments made to a particular withholding rate pool will be presumed to be an intentional failure within the meaning of sections 6721(e) and 6722(c). The nonqualified intermediary may rebut the presumption.

(8) Applicability to flow-through entities and certain U.S. branches. See paragraph (e)(3)(v) of this section and § 1.1441-5(c)(3)(iv) and (e)(5)(iv) for the applicability of this paragraph (e)(3)(iv) to U.S. branches described in paragraph (b)(2)(iv) of this section (other than U.S. branches treated as U.S. persons) and flow-through entities.

(E) Notice procedures. The IRS may notify a withholding agent that the alternative procedures of paragraph (e)(3)(iv)(D) of this section are not applicable to a specified nonqualified intermediary, a U.S. branch described in paragraph (b)(2)(iv) of this section, or a flow-through entity. If a withholding agent receives such a notice, it must commence withholding in accordance with the presumption rules of paragraph (b)(3) of this section and §§ 1.1441-5(d) and (e)(6) and 1.6049-5(d) unless the nonqualified intermediary, U.S. branch, or flow-through entity complies with the procedures in paragraphs (e)(3)(iv)(A) through (C) of this section. In addition, the IRS may notify a withholding agent, in appropriate circumstances, that it must apply the presumption rules of paragraph (b)(3) of this section and §§ 1.1441-5(d) and (e)(6) and 1.6049-5(d) to payments made to a nonqualified intermediary, a U.S. branch, or a flow-through entity even if the nonqualified intermediary, U.S. branch or flow-through entity provides allocation information prior to the payment. A withholding agent that receives a notice under this paragraph (e)(3)(iv)(E) must commence withholding in accordance with the presumption rules within 30 days of the date of the notice. The IRS may withdraw its prohibition against using the alternative procedures of paragraph (e)(3)(iv)(D) of this section, or its requirement to follow the presumption rules, if the nonqualified intermediary, U.S. branch, or flow-through entity can demonstrate to the satisfaction of the Assistant Commissioner (International) or his delegate that it is capable of complying with the rules under chapter 3 of the Internal Revenue Code and any other conditions required by the Assistant Commissioner (International).

(v) Withholding certificate from certain U.S. branches. A U.S. branch certificate is a withholding certificate provided by a U.S. branch described in paragraph (b)(2)(iv) of this section that is not the beneficial owner of the income. The withholding certificate is provided with respect to reportable amounts and must state that such amounts are not effectively connected with the conduct of a trade or business in the United States. The withholding certificate must either transmit the appropriate documentation for the persons for whom the branch receives the payment (i.e., as an intermediary) or be provided as evidence of its agreement with the withholding agent to be treated as a U.S. person with respect to any payment associated with the certificate. A U.S. branch withholding certificate is valid only if it is furnished on a Form W-8, an acceptable substitute form, or such other form as the IRS may prescribe, it is signed under penalties of perjury by a person authorized to sign for the branch, its validity has not expired, and it contains the information, statements, and certifications described in this paragraph (e)(3)(v). If the certificate is furnished to transmit withholding certificates and other documentation, it must contain the information, certifications, and statements described in paragraphs (e)(3)(v)(A) through (C) of this section and in paragraphs (e)(3)(iii) and (iv) (alternative procedures) of this section, applying the term U.S. branch instead of the term nonqualified intermediary. If the certificate is furnished pursuant to an agreement to treat the U.S. branch as a U.S. person, the information and certifications required on the withholding certificate are limited to the following—

(A) The name of the person of which the branch is a part and the address of the branch in the United States;

(B) A certification that the payments associated with the certificate are not effectively connected with the conduct of its trade or business in the United States; and

(C) Any other information, certifications, or statements as may be required by the form or accompanying instructions in addition to, or in lieu of, the information and certification described in this paragraph (e)(3)(v).

(vi) Reportable amounts. For purposes of chapter 3 of the Internal Revenue Code, a nonqualified intermediary, qualified intermediary, flow-through entity, and U.S. branch described in paragraph (b)(2)(iv) of this section (other than a U.S. branch that agrees to be treated as a U.S. person) must provide a withholding certificate and associated documentation and other information with respect to reportable amounts. For purposes of the regulations under chapter 3 of the Internal Revenue Code, the term reportable amount means an amount subject to withholding within the meaning of § 1.1441-2(a), bank deposit interest (including original issue discount) and similar types of deposit interest described in section 871(i)(2)(A) or 881(d) that are from sources within the United States, and any amount of interest or original issue discount from sources within the United States on the redemption of certain short-term obligations described in section 871(g)(1)(B) or 881(e). Reportable amounts shall not include amounts received on the sale or exchange (other than a redemption) of an obligation described in section 871(g)(1)(B) or 881(e) that is effected at an office outside the United States. See § 1.6045-1(g)(3) to determine whether a sale is effected at an office outside the United States. Reportable amounts also do not include payments with respect to deposits with banks and other financial institutions that remain on deposit for a period of two weeks or less, to amounts of original issue discount arising from a sale and repurchase transaction that is completed within a period of two weeks or less, or to amounts described in § 1.6049-5(b)(7), (10) or (11) (relating to certain obligations issued in bearer form). While short-term OID and bank deposit interest are not subject to withholding under chapter 3 of the Internal Revenue Code, such amounts may be subject to information reporting under section 6049 if paid to a U.S. person who is not an exempt recipient described in § 1.6049-4(c)(1)(ii) and to backup withholding under section 3406 in the absence of documentation. See § 1.6049-5(d)(3)(iii) for applicable procedures when such amounts are paid to a foreign intermediary.

(4) Applicable rules. The provisions in this paragraph (e)(4) describe procedures applicable to withholding certificates on Form W-8 or Form 8233 (or a substitute form) or documentary evidence furnished to establish foreign status. These provisions do not apply to Forms W-9 (or their substitutes). For corresponding provisions regrading Form W-9 (or a substitute form), see section 3406 and the regulations under that section.

(i) Who may sign the certificate. A withholding certificate (or other acceptable substitute) may be signed by any person authorized to sign a declaration under penalties of perjury on behalf of the person whose name is on the certificate as provided in section 6061 and the regulations under that section (relating to who may sign generally for an individual, estate, or trust, which includes certain agents who may sign returns and other documents), section 6062 and the regulations under that section (relating to who may sign corporate returns), and section 6063 and the regulations under that section (relating to who may sign partnership returns).

(ii) Period of validity. (A) Three-year period. A withholding certificate described in paragraph (e)(2)(i) of this section, or a certificate described in § 1.871-14(c)(2)(v) (furnished to qualify interest as portfolio interest for purposes of sections 871(h) and 881(c)), shall remain valid until the earlier of the last day of the third calendar year following the year in which the withholding certificate is signed or the day that a change in circumstances occurs that makes any information on the certificate incorrect. For example, a withholding certificate signed on September 30, 2001, remains valid through December 31, 2004, unless circumstances change that make the information on the form no longer correct. Documentary evidence described in §§ 1.1441-6(c)(3) or (4) or 1.6049-5(c)(1) shall remain valid until the earlier of the last day of the third calendar year following the year in which the documentary evidence is provided to the withholding agent or the day that a change in circumstances occurs that makes any information on the documentary evidence incorrect.

(B) Indefinite validity period. Notwithstanding paragraph (e)(4)(ii)(A) of this section, the following certificates or parts of certificates shall remain valid until the status of the person whose name is on the certificate is changed in a way relevant to the certificate or circumstances change that make the information on the certificate no longer correct:

(1) A withholding certificate described in paragraph (e)(2)(ii) of this section that is furnished with a TIN, provided that the withholding agent reports at least one payment annually to the beneficial owner under § 1.1461-1(c) or the TIN furnished on the certificate is reported to the IRS under the procedures described in § 1.1461-1(d). For example, assume a withholding agent receives a Form W-8 in 2001 from a beneficial owner with respect to an account that contains bonds, the interest on which must be reported on Form 1042-S under § 1.1461-1(c). The Form W-8 contains a valid TIN and the withholding agent reports on Forms 1042-S interest to the beneficial owner for 2001 through 2005. In 2005, the beneficial owner sells some of the bonds. For purposes of the exemption from Form 1099 reporting under § 1.6045-1(g), the withholding agent may consider the Form W-8 as valid, even though the payment of the sales proceeds is not reportable on Form 1042-S under § 1.1461-1(c) and even though the Form W-8 was provided more than three years previously.

(2) A certificate described in paragraph (e)(3)(ii) of this section (a qualified intermediary withholding certificate) but not including the withholding certificates, documentary evidence, statements or other information associated with the certificate.

(3) A certificate described in paragraph (e)(3)(iii) of this section (a nonqualified intermediary certificate), but not including the withholding certificates, documentary evidence, statements or other information associated with the certificate.

(4) A certificate described in paragraph (e)(3)(v) of this section (a U.S. branch withholding certificate), but not including the withholding certificates, documentary evidence, statements or other information associated with the certificate.

(5) A certificate described in § 1.1441-5(c)(2)(iv) (dealing with a certificate from a person representing to be a withholding foreign partnership).

(6) A certificate described in § 1.1441-5(c)(3)(iii) (a withholding certificate from a nonwithholding foreign partnership) but not including the withholding certificates, documentary evidence, statements or other information required to be associated with the certificate.

(7) A certificate furnished by a person representing to be an integral part of a foreign government (within the meaning of § 1.892-2T(a)(2)) in accordance with § 1.1441-8(b), or by a person representing to be a foreign central bank of issue (within the meaning of § 1.861-2(b)(4)) or the Bank for International Settlements in accordance with § 1.1441-8(c)(1).

(8) A withholding certificate described in § 1.1441-5(e)(5)(iii) provided by a foreign simple trust or a foreign grantor trust to transmit documentation of beneficiaries or owners, but not including the withholding certificates, documentary evidence, statements or other information associated with the certificate.

(C) Withholding certificate for effectively connected income. Notwithstanding paragraph (e)(4)(ii)(B)(1) of this section, the period of validity of a withholding certificate furnished to a withholding agent to claim a reduced rate of withholding for income that is effectively connected with the conduct of a trade or business within the United States shall be limited to the three-year period described in paragraph (e)(4)(ii)(A) of this section.

(D) Change in circumstances. If a change in circumstances makes any information on a certificate or other documentation incorrect, then the person whose name is on the certificate or other documentation must inform the withholding agent within 30 days of the change and furnish a new certificate or new documentation. A certificate or documentation becomes invalid from the date that the withholding agent holding the certificate or documentation knows or has reason to know that circumstances affecting the correctness of the certificate or documentation have changed. However, a withholding agent may choose to apply the provisions of paragraph (b)(3)(iv) of this section regarding the 90-day grace period as of that date while awaiting a new certificate or documentation or while seeking information regarding changes, or suspected changes, in the person's circumstances. If an intermediary (including a U.S. branch described in paragraph (b)(2)(iv)(A) of this section that passes through certificates to a withholding agent) or a flow-through entity becomes aware that a certificate or other appropriate documentation it has furnished to the person from whom it collects the payment is no longer valid because of a change in the circumstances of the person who issued the certificate or furnished the other appropriate documentation, then the intermediary or flow-through entity must notify the person from whom it collects the payment of the change of circumstances. It must also obtain a new withholding certificate or new appropriate documentation to replace the existing certificate or documentation whose validity has expired due to the change in circumstances. If a beneficial owner withholding certificate is used to claim foreign status only (and not, also, residence in a particular foreign country for purposes of an income tax treaty), a change of address is a change in circumstances for purposes of this paragraph (e)(4)(ii)(D) only if it changes to an address in the United States. Further, a change of address within the same foreign country is not a change in circumstances for purposes of this paragraph (e)(4)(ii)(D). A change in the circumstances affecting the withholding information provided to the withholding agent in accordance with the provisions in paragraph (e) (3)(iv) or (5)(v) of this section or in § 1.1441-5(c)(3)(iv) shall terminate the validity of the withholding certificate with respect to the information that is no longer reliable unless the information is updated. A withholding agent may rely on a certificate without having to inquire into possible changes of circumstances that may affect the validity of the statement, unless it knows or has reason to know that circumstances have changed. A withholding agent may require a new certificate at any time prior to a payment, even though the withholding agent has no actual knowledge or reason to know that any information stated on the certificate has changed.

(iii) Retention of withholding certificate. A withholding agent must retain each withholding certificate and other documentation for as long as it may be relevant to the determination of the withholding agent's tax liability under section 1461 and § 1.1461-1.

(iv) Electronic transmission of information. (A) In general. A withholding agent may establish a system for a beneficial owner or payee to electronically furnish a Form W-8, an acceptable substitute Form W-8, or such other form as the Internal Revenue Service may prescribe. The system must meet the requirements described in paragraph (e)(4)(iv)(B) of this section. A withholding agent may accept Forms W-8 that are furnished electronically on or after January 1, 2000, provided the requirements of paragraph (e)(4)(iv)(B) of this section are met.

(B) Requirements. (1) In general. The electronic system must ensure that the information received is the information sent, and must document all occasions of user access that result in the submission renewal, or modification of a Form W-8. In addition, the design and operation of the electronic system, including access procedures, must make it reasonably certain that the person accessing the system and furnishing Form W-8 is the person named in the Form.

(2) Same information as paper Form W-8. The electronic transmission must provide the withholding agent or payor with exactly the same information as the paper Form W-8.

(3) Perjury statement and signature requirements. The electronic transmission must contain an electronic signature by the person whose name is on the Form W-8 and the signature must be under penalties of perjury in the manner described in this paragraph (e)(4)(iv)(B)(3).

(i) Perjury statement. The perjury statement must contain the language that appears on the paper Form W-8. The electronic system must inform the person whose name is on the Form W-8 that the person must make the declaration contained in the perjury statement and that the declaration is made by signing the Form W-8. The instructions and the language of the perjury statement must immediately follow the person's certifying statements and immediately precede the person's electronic signature.

(ii) Electronic signature. The act of the electronic signature must be effected by the person whose name is on the electronic Form W-8. The signature must also authenticate and verify the submission. For this purpose, the terms authenticate and verify have the same meanings as they do when applied to a written signature on a paper Form W-8. An electronic signature can be in any form that satisfies the foregoing requirements. The electronic signature must be the final entry in the person's Form W-8 submission.

(4) Requests for electronic Form W-8 data. Upon request by the Internal Revenue Service during an examination, the withholding agent must supply a hard copy of the electronic Form W-8 and a statement that, to the best of the withholding agent's knowledge, the electronic Form W-8 was filed by the person whose name is on the form. The hard copy of the electronic Form W-8 must provide exactly the same information as, but need not be identical to, the paper Form W-8.

(C) Special requirements for transmission of Forms W-8 by an intermediary. [Reserved]

(v) Electronic confirmation of taxpayer identifying number on withholding certificate. The Commissioner may prescribe procedures in a revenue procedure (see § 601.601(d)(2) of this chapter) or other appropriate guidance to require a withholding agent to confirm electronically with the IRS information concerning any TIN stated on a withholding certificate.

(vi) Acceptable substitute form. A withholding agent may substitute its own form instead of an official Form W-8 or 8233 (or such other official form as the IRS may prescribe). Such a substitute for an official form will be acceptable if it contains provisions that are substantially similar to those of the official form, it contains the same certifications relevant to the transactions as are contained on the official form and these certifications are clearly set forth, and the substitute form includes a signature-under-penalties-of-perjury statement identical to the one stated on the official form. The substitute form is acceptable even if it does not contain all of the provisions contained on the official form, so long as it contains those provisions that are relevant to the transaction for which it is furnished. For example, a withholding agent that pays no income for which treaty benefits are claimed may develop a substitute form that is identical to the official form, except that it does not include information regarding claim of benefits under an income tax treaty. A withholding agent who uses a substitute form must furnish instructions relevant to the substitute form only to the extent and in the manner specified in the instructions to the official form. A withholding agent may refuse to accept a certificate from a payee or beneficial owner (including the official Form W-8 or 8233) if the certificate is not provided the acceptable substitute form provided by the withholding agent. However, a withholding agent may refuse to accept a certificate provided by a payee or beneficial owner only if the withholding agent furnishes the payee or beneficial owner with an acceptable substitute form immediately upon receipt of an unacceptable form or within 5 business days of receipt of an unacceptable form from the payee or beneficial owner. In that case, the substitute form is acceptable only if it contains a notice that the withholding agent has refused to accept the form submitted by the payee or beneficial owner and that the payee or beneficial owner must submit the acceptable form provided by the withholding agent in order for the payee or beneficial owner to be treated as having furnished the required withholding certificate.

(vii) Requirement of taxpayer identifying number. A TIN must be stated on a withholding certificate when required by this paragraph (e)(4)(vii). A TIN is required to be stated on—

(A) A withholding certificate on which a beneficial owner is claiming the benefit of a reduced rate under an income tax treaty (other than for amounts described in § 1.1441-6(c)(2);

(B) A withholding certificate on which a beneficial owner is claiming exemption from withholding because income is effectively connected with a U.S. trade or business;

(C) A withholding certificate on which a beneficial owner is claiming exemption from withholding under section 871(f) for certain annuities received under qualified plans;

(D) A withholding certificate on which a beneficial owner is claiming an exemption based solely on a foreign organization's claim of tax exempt status under section 501(c) or private foundation status (however, a TIN is not required from a foreign private foundation that is subject to the 4-percent tax under section 4948(a) on income if that income would be exempt from withholding but for section 4948(a) (e.g., portfolio interest));

(E) A withholding certificate from a person representing to be a qualified intermediary described in paragraph (e)(5)(ii) of this section;

(F) A withholding certificate from a person representing to be a withholding foreign partnership described in § 1.1441-5(c)(2)(i));

(G) A withholding certificate provided by a foreign organization that is described in section 501(c);

(H) A withholding certificate from a person representing to be a U.S. branch described in paragraph (b)(2)(iv) of this section.

(viii) Reliance rules. A withholding agent may rely on the information and certifications stated on withholding certificates or other documentation without having to inquire into the truthfulness of this information or certification, unless it has actual knowledge or reason to know that the same is untrue. In the case of amounts described in § 1.1441-6(b)(2)(ii), a withholding agent described in § 1.1441-7(b)(2)(ii) has reason to know that the information or certifications on a certificate are untrue only to the extent provided in § 1.1441-7(b)(2)(ii). See § 1.1441-6(b)(4)(ii) for reliance on representations regarding eligibility for a reduced rate under an income tax treaty. Paragraphs (e)(4)(viii) (A) and (B) of this section provide examples of such reliance.

(A) Classification. A withholding agent may rely on the claim of entity classification indicated on the withholding certificate that it receives from or for the beneficial owner, unless it has actual knowledge or reason to know that the classification claimed is incorrect. A withholding agent may not rely on a person's claim of classification other than as a corporation if the name of the corporation indicates that the person is a per se corporation described in § 301.7701-2(b)(8)(i) of this chapter unless the certificate contains a statement that the person is a grandfathered per se corporation described in § 301.7701-2(b)(8) of this chapter and that its grandfathered status has not been terminated. In the absence of reliable representation or information regarding the classification of the payee or beneficial owner, see § 1.1441-1(b)(3)(ii) for applicable presumptions.

(B) Status of payee as an intermediary or as a person acting for its own account. A withholding agent may rely on the type of certificate furnished as indicative of the payee's status as an intermediary or as an owner, unless the withholding agent has actual knowledge or reason to know otherwise. For example, a withholding agent that receives a beneficial owner withholding certificate from a foreign financial institution may treat the institution as the beneficial owner, unless it has information in its records that would indicate otherwise or the certificate contains information that is not consistent with beneficial owner status (e.g., sub-account numbers or names). If the financial institution also acts as an intermediary, the withholding agent may request that the institution furnish two certificates, i.e., a beneficial owner certificate described in paragraph (e)(2)(i) of this section for the amounts that it receives as a beneficial owner, and an intermediary withholding certificate described in paragraph (e)(3)(i) of this section for the amounts that it receives as an intermediary. In the absence of reliable representation or information regarding the status of the payee as an owner or as an intermediary, see paragraph (b)(3)(v)(A) for applicable presumptions.

(ix) Certificates to be furnished for each account unless exception applies. Unless otherwise provided in this paragraph (e)(4)(ix), a withholding agent that is a financial institution with which a customer may open an account shall obtain withholding certificates or other appropriate documentation on an account-by-account basis.

(A) Coordinated account information system in effect. A withholding agent may rely on the withholding certificate or other appropriate documentation furnished by a customer for a pre-existing account under any one or more of the circumstances described in this paragraph (e)(4)(ix)(A).

(1) A withholding agent may rely on documentation furnished by a customer for another account if all such accounts are held at the same branch location.

(2) A withholding agent may rely on documentation furnished by a customer for an account held at another branch location of the same withholding agent or at a branch location of a person related to the withholding agent if the withholding agent and the related person are part of a universal account system that uses a customer identifier that can be used to retrieve systematically all other accounts of the customer. See § 31.3406(c)1(c)(3)(ii) and (iii)(C) of this chapter for an identical procedure for purposes of backup withholding. For purposes of this paragraph (e)(4)(ix)(A), a withholding agent is related to another person if it is related within the meaning of section 267(b) or 707(b).

(3) A withholding agent may rely on documentation furnished by a customer for an account held at another branch location of the same withholding agent or at a branch location of a person related to the withholding agent if the withholding agent and the related person are part of an information system other than a universal account system and the information system is described in this paragraph (e)(4)(ix)(A)(3). The system must allow the withholding agent to easily access data regarding the nature of the documentation, the information contained in the documentation, and its validity status, and must allow the withholding agent to easily transmit data into the system regarding any facts of which it becomes aware that may affect the reliability of the documentation. The withholding agent must be able to establish how and when it has accessed the data regarding the documentation and, if applicable, how and when it has transmitted data regarding any facts of which it became aware that may affect the reliability of the documentation. In addition, the withholding agent or the related party must be able to establish that any data it has transmitted to the information system has been processed and appropriate due diligence has been exercised regarding the validity of the documentation.

(4) A withholding agent may rely on documentation furnished by a beneficial owner or payee to an agent of the withholding agent. The agent may retain the documentation as part of an information system maintained for a single or multiple withholding agents provided that the system permits any withholding agent that uses the system to easily access data regarding the nature of the documentation, the information contained in the documentation, and its validity, and must allow the withholding agent to easily transmit data into the system regarding any facts of which it becomes aware that may affect the reliability of the documentation. The withholding agent must be able to establish how and when it has accessed the data regarding the documentation and, if applicable, how and when it has transmitted data regarding any facts of which it became aware that may affect the reliability of the documentation. In addition, the withholding agent must be able to establish that any data it has transmit-

ted to the information system has been processed and appropriate due diligence has been exercised regarding the validity of the documentation.

(B) Family of mutual funds. An interest in a mutual fund that has a common investment advisor or common principal underwriter with other mutual funds (within the same family of funds) may, in the discretion of the mutual fund, be represented by one single withholding certificate where shares are acquired or owned in any of the funds. See § 31.3406(h)-3(a)(2) of this chapter for an identical procedures for purposes of backup withholding.

(C) Special rule for brokers. (1) In general. A withholding agent may rely on the certification of a broker that the broker holds a valid beneficial owner withholding certificate described in paragraph (e)(2)(i) of this section or other appropriate documentation for that beneficial owner with respect to any readily tradable instrument, as defined in § 31.3406(h)-1(d) of this chapter, if the broker is a United States person (including a U.S. branch treated as a U.S. person under paragraph (b)(2)(iv) of this section) that is acting as the agent of a beneficial owner and the U.S. broker has been provided a valid Form W-8 or other appropriate documentation. The certification must be in writing or in electronic form and contain all of the information required of a nonqualified intermediary under paragraphs (e)(3)(iv)(B) and (C) of this section. If a U.S. broker chooses to use this paragraph (e)(4)(ix)(C), that U.S. broker will be solely responsible for applying the rules of § 1.1441-7(b) to the withholding certificates or other appropriate documentation. For purposes of this paragraph (c)(4)(ix)(C), the term broker means a person treated as a broker under § 1.6045-1(a).

(2) The following example illustrates the rules of this paragraph (e)(4)(ix)(C):

Example. SCO is a U.S. securities clearing organization that provides clearing services for correspondent broker, CB, a U.S. corporation. Pursuant to a fully disclosed clearing agreement, CB fully discloses the identity of each of its customers to SCO. Part of SCO's clearing duties include the crediting of income and gross proceeds of readily tradeable instruments (as defined in § 31.3406(h)-1(d)) to each customer's account. For each disclosed customer that is a foreign beneficial owner, CB provides SCO with information required under paragraphs (e)(3)(iv)(B) and (C) of this section that is necessary to apply the correct rate of withholding and to file Forms 1042-S. SCO may use the representations and beneficial owner information provided by CB to determine the proper amount of withholding and to file Forms 1042-S. CB is responsible for determining the validity of the withholding certificates or other appropriate documentation under § 1.1441-1(b).

(5) Qualified intermediaries. (i) General rule. A qualified intermediary, as defined in paragraph (e)(5)(ii) of this section, may furnish a qualified intermediary withholding certificate to a withholding agent. The withholding certificate provides certifications on behalf of other persons for the purpose of claiming and verifying reduced rates of withholding under section 1441 or 1442 and for the purpose of reporting and withholding under other provisions of the Internal Revenue Code, such as the provisions under chapter 61 and section 3406 (and the regulations under those provisions). Furnishing such a certificate is in lieu of transmitting to a withholding agent withholding certificates or other appropriate documentation for the persons for whom the qualified intermediary receives the payment, including interest holders in a qualified intermediary that is fiscally transparent under the regulations under section 894. Although the qualified intermediary is required to obtain withholding certificates or other appropriate documentation from beneficial owners, payees, or interest holders pursuant to its agreement with the IRS, it is generally not required to attach such documentation to the intermediary withholding certificate. Notwithstanding the preceding sentence a qualified intermediary must provide a withholding agent with the Forms W-9, or disclose the names, addresses, and taxpayer identifying numbers, if known, of those U.S. non-exempt recipients for whom the qualified intermediary receives reportable amounts (within the meaning of paragraph (e)(3)(vi) of this section) to the extent required in the qualified intermediary's agreement with the IRS. A person may claim qualified intermediary status before an agreement is executed with the IRS if it has applied for such status and the IRS authorizes such status on an interim basis under such procedures as the IRS may prescribe.

(ii) Definition of qualified intermediary. With respect to a payment to a foreign person, the term qualified intermediary means a person that is a party to a withholding agreement with the IRS and such person is—

(A) A foreign financial institution or a foreign clearing organization (as defined in § 1.163-5(c)(2)(i)(D)(8), without regard to the requirement that the organization hold obligations for members), other than a U.S. branch or U.S. office of such institution or organization;

(B) A foreign branch or office of a U.S. financial institution or a foreign branch or office of a U.S. clearing organization (as defined in § 1.163-5(c)(2)(i)(D)(8), without regard to the requirement that the organization hold obligations for members);

(C) A foreign corporation for purposes of presenting claims of benefits under an income tax treaty on behalf of its shareholders; or

(D) Any other person acceptable to the IRS.

(iii) Withholding agreement. (A) In general. The IRS may, upon request, enter into a withholding agreement with a foreign person described in paragraph (e)(5)(ii) of this section pursuant to such procedures as the IRS may prescribe in published guidance (see § 601.601(d)(2) of this chapter). Under the withholding agreement, a qualified intermediary shall generally be subject to the applicable withholding and reporting provisions applicable to withholding agents and payors under chapters 3 and 61 of the Internal Revenue Code, section 3406, the regulations under those provisions, and other withholding provisions of the Internal Revenue Code, except to the extent provided under the agreement.

(B) Terms of the withholding agreement. Generally, the agreement shall specify the type of certifications and documentation upon which the qualified intermediary may rely to ascertain the classification (e.g., corporation or partnership) and status (i.e., U.S. or foreign) of beneficial owners and payees who receive payments collected by the qualified intermediary and, if necessary, entitlement to the benefits of a reduced rate under an income tax treaty. The agreement shall specify if, and to what extent, the qualified intermediary may assume primary withholding responsibility in accordance with paragraph (e)(5)(iv) of this section. It shall also specify the extent to which applicable return filing and information reporting requirements are modified so that, in appropriate cases, the qualified intermediary may report payments to the IRS on an aggregated basis, without having to disclose the identity of beneficial owners and payees. However, the qualified intermediary may be required to provide to the IRS the name and address of those foreign customers who benefit from a reduced rate under an income tax treaty pursuant to the qualified intermediary arrangement for purposes of verifying entitlement to such benefits, particularly under an applicable limitation on benefits provision. Under the agreement, a qualified intermediary may agree to act as an acceptance agent to perform the duties described in § 301.6109-1(d)(3)(iv)(A) of this chapter. The agreement may specify the manner in which applicable procedures for adjustments for underwithholding and overwithholding, including refund procedures, apply in the context of a qualified intermediary arrangement and the extent to which applicable procedures may be modified. In particular, a withholding agreement may allow a qualified intermediary to claim refunds of overwithheld amounts. If relevant, the agreement shall specify the manner in which the qualified intermediary may deal with payments to other intermediaries and flow-through entities. In addition, the agreement shall specify the manner in which the IRS will verify compliance with the agreement. In appropriate cases, the IRS may agree to rely on audits performed by an intermediary's approved auditor. In such a case, the IRS's audit may be limited to the audit of the auditor's records (including work papers of the auditor and reports prepared by the auditor indicating the methodology employed to verify the entity's compliance with the agreement). For this purpose, the agreement shall specify the auditor or class of auditors that are approved. Generally, an auditor will not be approved if the auditor is not subject to laws, regulations, or rules that impose sanctions for failure to exercise its independence and to perform the audit competently. The agreement may include provisions for the assessment and collection of tax in the event that failure to comply with the terms of the agreement results in the failure by the withholding agent or the qualified intermediary to withhold and deposit the required amount of tax. Further, the agreement may specify the procedures by which deposits of amounts withheld are to be deposited, if different from the deposit procedures under the Internal Revenue Code and applicable regulations. To determine whether to enter a qualified intermediary withholding agreement and the terms of any particular withholding agreement, the IRS will consider appropriate factors including whether or not the foreign person agrees to assume primary withholding responsibility, the type of local know-your-customer laws and practices to which it is subject, the extent and nature of supervisory and regulatory control exercised under the laws of the foreign country over the foreign person, the volume of investments in U.S. securities (determined in dollar amounts and number of account holders), the financial condition of the foreign person, and whether the qualified intermediary is a resident of a country with which the United States has an income tax treaty.

(iv) Assignment of primary withholding responsibility. Any person who meets the definition of a withholding agent under § 1.1441-7(a) (whether a U.S. person or a foreign person) is required to withhold and deposit any amount withheld under § 1.1461-1(a) and to make the returns prescribed by § 1.1461-1(b) and (c). If permitted by its qualified intermediary agreement, a qualified intermediary agreement may, however, inform a withholding agent from which it receives a payment that it will assume the primary obligation to withhold, deposit, and report amounts under chapter 3 of the Internal Revenue Code and/or under chapter 61 of the Internal Revenue Code and section 3406. If a withholding agent makes a payment of an amount subject to withholding, as defined in § 1.1441-2(a), or a reportable payment, as defined in section 3406(b), to a qualified intermediary that represents to the withholding agent that it has assumed primary withholding responsibility for the payment, the withholding agent is not required to withhold on the payment. The withholding agent is not required to determine that the qualified intermediary agreement actually permits the qualified intermediary to assume primary withholding responsibility. A qualified intermediary that assumes primary withholding responsibility under chapter 3 of the Internal Revenue Code or primary reporting and backup withholding responsibility under chapter 61 and section 3406 is not required to assume primary withholding responsibility for all accounts it has with a withholding agent but must assume primary withholding responsibility for all payments made to any one account that it has with the withholding agent. A qualified intermediary may agree with the withholding agent to assume primary withholding responsibility under chapter 3 and section 3406, only if expressly permitted to do so under its agreement with the IRS.

(v) Withholding statement. (A) In general. A qualified intermediary must provide each withholding agent from which it receives reportable amounts, as defined in paragraph (e)(3)(vi) of this section, as a qualified intermediary with a written statement (the withholding statement) containing the information specified in paragraph (e)(5)(v)(B) of this section. A withholding statement is not required, however, if all of the information a withholding agent needs to fulfill its withholding and reporting requirements is contained in the withholding certificate. The qualified intermediary agreement may require, in appropriate circumstances, the qualified intermediary to include information in its withholding statement relating to payments other than payments of reportable amounts. The withholding statement forms an integral part of the qualified intermediary's qualified intermediary withholding certificate and the penalties of perjury statement provided on the withholding certificate shall apply to the withholding statement as well. The withholding statement may be provided in any manner, and in any form, to which qualified intermediary and the withholding agent mutually agree, including electronically. If the withholding statement is provided electronically, there must be sufficient safeguards to ensure that the information received by the withholding agent is the information sent by qualified intermediary and must also document all occasions of user access that result in the submission or modification of withholding statement information. In addition, the electronic system must be capable of providing a hard copy of all withholding statements provided by the qualified intermediary. The withholding statement shall be updated as often as necessary for the withholding agent to meet its reporting and withholding obligations under chapters 3 and 61 of the Internal Revenue Code and section 3406. A withholding agent will be liable for tax, interest, and penalties in accordance with paragraph (b)(7) of this section to the extent it does not follow the presumption rules of paragraph (b)(3) of this section, §§ 1.1441-5(d) and (e)(6), and 1.6049-5(d) for any payment, or portion thereof, for which it does not have a valid withholding statement prior to making a payment.

(B) Content of withholding statement. The withholding statement must contain sufficient information for a withholding agent to apply the correct rate of withholding on payments from the accounts identified on the statement and to properly report such payments on Forms 1042-S and Forms 1099, as applicable. The withholding statement must—

(1) Designate those accounts for which the qualified intermediary acts as a qualified intermediary;

(2) Designate those accounts for which qualified intermediary assumes primary withholding responsibility under chapter 3 of the Internal Revenue Code and/or primary re-

porting and backup withholding responsibility under chapter 61 and section 3406; and

(3) Provide information regarding withholding rate pools, as described in paragraph (e)(5)(v)(C) of this section.

(C) Withholding rate pools. (1) In general. Except to the extent it has assumed both primary withholding responsibility under chapter 3 of the Internal Revenue Code and primary reporting and backup withholding responsibility under chapter 61 and section 3406 with respect to a payment, a qualified intermediary shall provide as part of its withholding statement the withholding rate pool information that is required for the withholding agent to meet its withholding and reporting obligations under chapters 3 and 61 of the Internal Revenue Code and section 3406. A withholding rate pool is a payment of a single type of income, determined in accordance with the categories of income reported on Form 1042-S or Form 1099, as applicable, that is subject to a single rate of withholding. A withholding rate pool may be established by any reasonable method on which the qualified intermediary and a withholding agent agree (e.g., by establishing a separate account for a single withholding rate pool, or by dividing a payment made to a single account into portions allocable to each withholding rate pool). To the extent a qualified intermediary does not assume primary reporting and backup withholding responsibility under chapter 61 and section 3406, a qualified intermediary's withholding statement must establish a separate withholding rate pool for each U.S. non-exempt recipient account holder that the qualified intermediary has disclosed to the withholding agent unless the qualified intermediary uses the alternative procedures in paragraph (e)(5)(v)(C)(2) of this section. A qualified intermediary shall determine withholding rate pools based on valid documentation that it obtains under its withholding agreement with the IRS, or if a payment cannot be reliably associated with valid documentation, under the applicable presumption rules. If a qualified intermediary has an account holder that is another intermediary (whether a qualified intermediary or a nonqualified intermediary) or a flow-through entity, the qualified intermediary may combine the account holder information provided by the intermediary or flow-through entity with the qualified intermediary's direct account holder information to determine the qualified intermediary's withholding rate pools.

(2) Alternative procedure for U.S. non-exempt recipients. If permitted under its agreement with the IRS, a qualified intermediary may, by mutual agreement with a withholding agent, establish a single withholding rate pool (not subject to backup withholding) for all U.S. non-exempt recipient account holders for whom the qualified intermediary has provided Forms W-9 prior to the withholding agent paying any reportable payments, as defined in section 3406(b), and a separate withholding rate pool (subject to 31-percent withholding) for all U.S. non-exempt recipient account holders for whom a qualified intermediary has not provided Forms W-9 prior to the withholding agent paying any reportable payments. If a qualified intermediary chooses the alternative procedure of this paragraph (e)(5)(v)(C)(2), the qualified intermediary must provide sufficient information to the withholding agent no later than January 15 of the year following the year in which the reportable payments are paid that allocates the reportable payments to each U.S. non-exempt recipient account holder. Failure to provide such information will result in the application of penalties to the qualified intermediary under sections 6721 and 6722, as well as any other applicable penalties, and may result in the termination of the qualified intermediary's withholding agreement with the IRS. A withholding agent shall not be liable for tax, interest, or penalties for failure to backup withhold or report information under chapter 61 of the Internal Revenue Code due solely to the errors or omissions of the qualified intermediary. If a qualified intermediary fails to provide the allocation information required by this paragraph (e)(5)(v)(C)(2), the withholding agent shall report the entire amount paid from the withholding rate pool to an unknown recipient, or otherwise in accordance with the appropriate Form 1099 and the instructions accompanying the form.

(f) Effective date. *(1) In general.* This section applies to payments made after December 31, 2000.

(2) Transition rules. (i) Special rules for existing documentation. For purposes of paragraphs (d)(3) and (e)(2)(i) of this section, the validity of a withholding certificate (namely, Form W-8, 8233, 1001, 4224, or 1078 , or a statement described in § 1.1441-5 in effect prior to January 1, 2001 (see § 1.1441-5 as contained in 26 CFR part 1, revised April 1, 1999)) that was valid on January 1, 1998 under the regulations in effect prior to January 1, 2001 (see 26 CFR parts 1 and 35a, revised April 1, 1999) and expired, or will expire, at any time during 1998, is extended until December 31, 1998. The validity of a withholding certificate that is valid on or after January 1, 1999, remains valid until its validity expires under the regulations in effect prior to January 1, 2001 (see 26 CFR parts 1 and 35a, revised April 1, 1999) but in no event will such withholding certificate remain valid after December 31, 2001. The rule in this paragraph (f)(2)(i), however, does not apply to extend the validity period of a withholding certificate that expires solely by reason of changes in the circumstances of the person whose name is on the certificate. Notwithstanding the first three sentences of this paragraph (f)(2)(i), a withholding agent may choose to not take advantage of the transition rule in this paragraph (f)(2)(i) with respect to one or more withholding certificates valid under the regulations in effect prior to January 1, 2001 (see 26 CFR parts 1 and 35a, revised April 1, 1999) and, therefore, to require withholding certificates conforming to the requirements described in this section (new withholding certificates). For purposes of this section, a new withholding certificate is deemed to satisfy the documentation requirement under the regulations in effect prior to January 1, 2001 (see 26 CFR parts 1 and 35a, revised April 1, 1999). Further, a new withholding certificate remains valid for the period specified in paragraph (e)(4)(ii) of this section, regardless of when the certificate is obtained.

(ii) Lack of documentation for past years. A taxpayer may elect to apply the provisions of paragraphs (b)(7)(i)(B), (ii), and (iii) of this section, dealing with liability for failure to obtain documentation timely, to all of its open tax years, including tax years that are currently under examination by the IRS. The election is made by simply taking action under those provisions in the same manner as the taxpayer would take action for payments made after December 31, 2000.

T.D. 6187, 7/5/56, amend T.D. 6592, 2/27/62, T.D. 6908, 12/30/66, T.D. 7157, 12/29/71, T.D. 7385, 10/28/75, T.D. 7670, 1/30/80, T.D. 8734, 10/6/97, T.D. 8804, 12/30/98, T.D. 8856, 12/29/99, T.D. 8881, 5/15/2000, T.D. 9023, 11/22/2002, T.D. 9253, 03/13/2006, T.D. 9323, 04/11/2007.

§ 1.1441-2 Amounts subject to withholding.

Caution: The Treasury has not yet amended Reg § 1.1441-2 to reflect changes made by P.L. 102-318.

(a) In general. For purposes of the regulations under chapter 3 of the Internal Revenue Code, the term amounts subject to withholding means amounts from sources within the United States that constitute either fixed or determinable annual or periodical income described in paragraph (b) of this section or other amounts subject to withholding described in paragraph (c) of this section. For purposes of this paragraph (a), an amount shall be treated as being from sources within the United States if the source of the amount cannot be determined at the time of payment. See § 1.1441-3(d)(1) for determining the amount to be withheld from a payment in the absence of information at the time of payment regarding the source of the amount. Amounts subject to withholding include amounts that are not fixed or determinable annual or periodical income and upon which withholding is specifically required under a provision of this section or another section of the regulations under chapter 3 of the Internal Revenue Code (such as corporate distributions upon which withholding is required under § 1.1441-3(c)(1) that do not constitute dividend income). Amounts subject to withholding do not include—

(1) Amounts described in § 1.1441-1(b)(4)(i) to the extent they involve interest on obligations in bearer form or on foreign-targeted registered obligations (but, in the case of a foreign-targeted registered obligation, only to the extent of those amounts paid to a registered owner that is a financial institution within the meaning of section 871(h)(5)(B) or a member of a clearing organization which member is the beneficial owner of the obligation);

(2) Amounts described in § 1.1441-1(b)(4)(ii) (dealing with bank deposit interest and similar types of interest (including original issue discount) described in section 871(i)(2)(A) or 881(d));

(3) Amounts described in § 1.1441-1(b)(4)(iv) (dealing with interest or original issue discount on certain short-term obligations described in section 871(g)(1)(B) or 881(e));

(4) Amounts described in § 1.1441-1(b)(4)(xx) (dealing with income from certain gambling winnings exempt from tax under section 871(j));

(5) Amounts paid as part of the purchase price of an obligation sold or exchanged between interest payment dates, unless the sale or exchange is part of a plan the principal purpose of which is to avoid tax and the withholding agent has actual knowledge or reason to know of such plan;

(6) Original issue discount paid as part of the purchase price of an obligation sold or exchanged in a transaction other than a redemption of such obligation, unless the purchase is part of a plan the principal purpose of which is to avoid tax and the withholding agent has actual knowledge or reason to know of such plan; and

(7) Insurance premiums paid with respect to a contract that is subject to the section 4371 excise tax.

(b) Fixed or determinable annual or periodical income. *(1) In general.* (i) Definition . For purposes of chapter 3 of the Internal Revenue Code and the regulations thereunder, fixed or determinable annual or periodical income includes all income included in gross income under section 61 (including original issue discount) except for the items specified in paragraph (b)(2) of this section. Items of income that are excluded from gross income under a provision of law without regard to the U.S. or foreign status of the owner of the income, such as interest excluded from gross income under section 103(a) or qualified scholarship income under section 117, shall not be treated as fixed or determinable annual or periodical income under chapter 3 of the Internal Revenue Code. Income excluded from gross income under section 892 (income of foreign governments) or section 115 (income of a U.S. possession) is fixed or determinable annual or periodical income since the exclusion from gross income under those sections is dependent on the foreign status of the owner of the income. See § 1.306-3(h) for treating income from the disposition of section 306 stock as fixed or determinable annual or periodical income.

(ii) Manner of payment. The term *fixed or determinable annual or periodical* is merely descriptive of the character of a class of income. If an item of income falls within the class of income contemplated in the statute and described in paragraph (a) of this section, it is immaterial whether payment of that item is made in a series of payments or in a single lump sum. Further, the income need not be paid annually if it is paid periodically; that is to say, from time to time, whether or not at regular intervals. The fact that a payment is not made annually or periodically does not, however, prevent it from being fixed or determinable annual or periodical income (e.g., a lump sum payment). In addition, the fact that the length of time during which the payments are to be made may be increased or diminished in accordance with someone s will or with the happening of an event does not disqualify the payment as determinable or periodical. For this purpose, the share of the fixed or determinable annual or periodical income of an estate or trust from sources within the United States which is required to be distributed currently, or which has been paid or credited during the taxable year, to a nonresident alien beneficiary of such estate or trust constitutes fixed or determinable annual or periodical income.

(iii) Determinability of amount. An item of income is fixed when it is to be paid in amounts definitely pre-determined. An item of income is determinable if the amount to be paid is not known but there is a basis of calculation by which the amount may be ascertained at a later time. For example, interest is determinable even if it is contingent in that its amount cannot be determined at the time of payment of an amount with respect to a loan because the calculation of the interest portion of the payment is contingent upon factors that are not fixed at the time of the payment. For purposes of this section, an amount of income does not have to be determined at the time that the payment is made in order to be determinable. An amount of income described in paragraph (a) of this section which the withholding agent knows is part of a payment it makes but which it cannot calculate exactly at the time of payment, is nevertheless determinable if the determination of the exact amount depends upon events expected to occur at a future date. In contrast, a payment which may be income in the future based upon events that are not anticipated at the time the payment is made is not determinable. For example, loan proceeds may become income to the borrower when and to the extent the loan is canceled without repayment. While the cancellation of the debt is income to the borrower when it occurs, it is not determinable at the time the loan proceeds are disbursed to the borrower if the lack of repayment leading to the cancellation of part or all of the debt was not anticipated at the time of disbursement. The fact that the source of an item of income cannot be determined at the time that the payment is made does not render a payment not determinable. See § 1.1441-3(d)(1) for determining the amount to be withheld from a payment in the absence of information at the time of payment regarding the source of the amount.

(2) Exceptions. For purposes of chapter 3 of the Code and the regulations thereunder, the items of income described in this paragraph (b)(2) are not fixed or determinable annual or periodical income—

(i) Gains derived from the sale of property (including market discount and option premiums), except for gains described in paragraph (b)(3) or (c) of this section; and

(ii) Any other income that the Internal Revenue Service (IRS) may determine, in published guidance (see § 601.601(d)(2) of this chapter), is not fixed or determinable annual or periodical income.

(3) Original issue discount. (i) Amount subject to tax. An amount representing original issue discount is fixed or determinable annual or periodical income that is subject to tax under sections 871(a)(1)(C) and 881(a)(3) to the extent provided in those sections and this paragraph (b)(3) if not otherwise excluded under paragraph (a) of this section. An amount of original issue discount is subject to tax with respect to a foreign beneficial owner of an obligation carrying original issue discount upon a sale or exchange of the obligation or when a payment is made on such obligation. The amount taxable is the amount of original issue discount that accrued while the foreign person held the obligation up to the time that the obligation is sold or exchanged or that a payment is made on the obligation, reduced by any amount of original issue discount that was taken into account prior to that time (due to a payment made on the obligation). In the case of a payment made on the obligation, the tax due on the amount of original issue discount may not exceed the amount of the payment reduced by the tax imposed on any portion of the payment that is qualified stated interest.

(ii) Amounts subject to withholding. A withholding agent must withhold on the taxable amount of original issue discount paid on the redemption of an original issue discount obligation unless an exception to withholding applies (e.g., portfolio interest or treaty exception). In addition, withholding is required on the taxable amount of original issue discount upon the sale or exchange of an original issue discount obligation, other than in a redemption, to the extent the withholding agent has actual knowledge or reason to know that the sale or exchange is part of a plan the principal purpose of which is to avoid tax. If a withholding agent cannot determine the taxable amount of original issue discount on the redemption of an original issue discount obligation (or on the sale or exchange of such an obligation if the principal purpose of the sale is to avoid tax), then it must withhold on the entire amount of original issue discount accrued from the date of issue until the date of redemption (or the date the obligation is sold or exchanged) determined on the basis of the most recently published "List of Original Issue Discount Instruments" (IRS Publication 1212, available from the IRS Forms Distribution Center) or similar list published by the IRS as if the beneficial owner of the obligation had held the obligation since its original issue.

(iii) Exceptions to withholding. To the extent that this paragraph (b)(3) applies to require withholding by a person other than an issuer of an original issue discount obligation, or the issuer's agent, it shall apply only to obligations issued after December 31, 2000.

(4) Securities lending transactions and equivalent transactions. See §§ 1.871-7(b)(2) and 1.881-2(b)(2) regarding the character of substitute payments as fixed and determinable annual or periodical income. Such amounts constitute income subject to withholding to the extent they are from sources within the United States, as determined under §§ 1.861-2(a)(7) and 1.861-3(a)(6). See §§ 1.6042-3(a)(2) and 1.6049-5(a)(5) for reporting requirements applicable to substitute dividend and interest payments, respectively.

(5) REMIC residual interests. Amounts subject to withholding include an excess inclusion described in § 1.860G-3(b)(2) and the portion of an amount described in § 1.860G-3(b)(1) that is an excess inclusion.

(c) Other income subject to withholding. Withholding is also required on the following items of income—

(1) Gains described in section 631(b) or (c), relating to treatment of gain on disposal of timber, coal, or domestic iron ore with a retained economic interest; and

(2) Gains subject to the 30-percent tax under section 871(a)(1)(D) or 881(a)(4), relating to contingent payments received from the sale or exchange of patents, copyrights, and similar intangible property.

(d) Exceptions to withholding where no money or property is paid or lack of knowledge. *(1) General rule.* A withholding agent who is not related to the recipient or beneficial owner has an obligation to withhold under section 1441 only to the extent that, at any time between the date that the obligation to withhold would arise (but for the provisions of this paragraph (d)) and the due date for the filing of return on Form 1042 (including extensions) for the year in which the payment occurs, it has control over, or custody of money or property owned by the recipient or beneficial owner from which to withhold an amount and has knowledge of the facts that give rise to the payment. The exemption from the obligation to withhold under this paragraph (d) shall not apply, however, to distributions with respect to stock or if the lack of control or custody of money or property from which to withhold is part of a pre-arranged plan known to the withholding agent to avoid withholding under section 1441, 1442, or 1443. For purposes of this paragraph (d), a withholding agent is related to the recipient or beneficial owner if it is related within the meaning of section 482. Any exemption from withholding pursuant to this paragraph (d) applies without a requirement that documentation be furnished to the withholding agent. However, documentation may have to be furnished for purposes of the information reporting provisions under chapter 61 of the Code and backup withholding under section 3406. The exemption from withholding under this paragraph (d) is not a determination that the amounts are not fixed or determinable annual or periodical income, nor does it constitute an exemption from reporting the amount under § 1.1461-1(b) and (c).

(2) Cancellation of debt. A lender of funds who forgives any portion of the loan is deemed to have made a payment of income to the borrower under § 1.61-12 at the time the event of forgiveness occurs. However, based on the rules of paragraph (d)(1) of this section, the lender shall have no obligation to withhold on such amount to the extent that it does not have custody or control over money or property of the borrower at any time between the time that the loan is forgiven and the due date (including extensions) of the Form 1042 for the year in which the payment is deemed to occur. A payment received by the lender from the borrower in partial settlement of the debt obligation does not, for this purpose, constitute an amount of money or property belonging to the borrower from which the withholding tax liability can be satisfied.

(3) Satisfaction of liability following underwithholding by withholding agent. A withholding agent who, after failing to withhold the proper amount from a payment, satisfies the underwithheld amount out of its own funds may cause the beneficial owner to realize income to the extent of such satisfaction or may be considered to have advanced funds to the beneficial owner. Such determination depends upon the contractual arrangements governing the satisfaction of such tax liability (e.g., arrangements in which the withholding agent agrees to pay the amount due under section 1441 for

the beneficial owner) or applicable laws governing the transaction. If the satisfaction of the tax liability is considered to constitute an advance of funds by the withholding agent to the beneficial owner and the withholding agent fails to collect the amount from the beneficial owner, a cancellation of indebtedness may result, giving rise to income to the beneficial owner under § 1.61-12. While such income is annual or periodical fixed or determinable, the withholding agent shall have no liability to withhold on such income to the extent the conditions set forth in paragraphs (d)(1) and (2) of this section are satisfied with respect to this income. Contrast the rules of this paragraph (d)(3) with the rules in § 1.1441-3(f)(1) dealing with a situation in which the satisfaction of the beneficial owner's tax liability itself constitutes additional income to the beneficial owner. See, also, § 1.1441-3(c)(2)(ii)(B) for a special rule regarding underwithholding on corporate distributions due to underestimating an amount of earnings and profits.

(4) Withholding exemption inapplicable. The exemption in § 1.1441-2(d) from the obligation to withhold shall not apply to amounts described in § 1.860G-3(b)(1) (regarding certain partnership allocations of REMIC net income with respect to a REMIC residual interest).

(e) Payment. *(1) General rule.* A payment is considered made to a person if that person realizes income whether or not such income results from an actual transfer of cash or other property. For example, realization of income from cancellation of debt results in a deemed payment. A payment is considered made when the amount would be includible in the income of the beneficial owner under the U.S. tax principles governing the cash basis method of accounting. A payment is considered made whether it is made directly to the beneficial owner or to another person for the benefit of the beneficial owner (e.g., to the agent of the beneficial owner). Thus, a payment of income is considered made to a beneficial owner if it is paid in complete or partial satisfaction of the beneficial owner's debt to a creditor. In the event of a conflict between the rules of this paragraph (e)(1) governing whether a payment has occurred and its timing and the rules of § 31.3406(a)-4 of this chapter, the rules in § 31.3406(a)-4 of this chapter shall apply to the extent that the application of section 3406 is relevant to the transaction at issue.

(2) Income allocated under section 482. A payment is considered made to the extent income subject to withholding is allocated under section 482. Further, income arising as a result of a secondary adjustment made in conjunction with a reallocation of income under section 482 from a foreign person to a related U.S. person is considered paid to a foreign person unless the taxpayer to whom the income is reallocated has entered into a repatriation agreement with the IRS and the agreement eliminates the liability for withholding under this section. For purposes of determining the liability for withholding, the payment of income is deemed to have occurred on the last day of the taxable year in which the transactions that give rise to the allocation of income and the secondary adjustments, if any, took place.

(3) Blocked income. Income is not considered paid if it is blocked under executive authority, such as the President's exercise of emergency power under the Trading with the Enemy Act (50 U.S.C. App. 5), or the International Emergency Economic Powers Act (50 U.S.C. 1701 *et seq.*). However, on the date that the blocking restrictions are removed, the income that was blocked is considered constructively received by the beneficial owner (and therefore paid for purposes of this section) and subject to withholding under § 1.1441-1. Any exemption from withholding pursuant to this paragraph (e)(3) applies without a requirement that documentation be furnished to the withholding agent. However, documentation may have to be furnished for purposes of the information reporting provisions under chapter 61 of the Code and backup withholding under section 3406. The exemption from withholding granted by this paragraph (e)(3) is not a determination that the amounts are not fixed or determinable annual or periodical income.

(4) Special rules for dividends. For purposes of sections 1441 and 6042, in the case of stock for which the record date is earlier than the payment date, dividends are considered paid on the payment date. In the case of a corporate reorganization, if a beneficial owner is required to exchange stock held in a former corporation for stock in a new corporation before dividends that are to be paid with respect to the stock in the new corporation will be paid on such stock, the dividend is considered paid on the date that the payee or beneficial owner actually exchanges the stock and receives the dividend. See § 31.3406(a)-4(a)(2) of this chapter.

(5) Certain interest accrued by a foreign corporation. For purposes of sections 1441 and 6049, a foreign corporation shall be treated as having made a payment of interest as of the last day of the taxable year if it has made an election under § 1.884-4(c)(1) to treat accrued interest as if it were paid in that taxable year.

(6) Payments other than in U.S. dollars. For purposes of section 1441, a payment includes amounts paid in a medium other than U.S. dollars. See § 1.1441-3(e) for rules regarding the amount subject to withholding in the case of such payments.

(f) Effective/applicability date. This section applies to payments made after December 31, 2000. Paragraphs (b)(5) and (d)(4) of this section apply to payments made after August 1, 2006.

T.D. 6187, 7/5/56, amend T.D. 6464, 5/11/60, T.D. 6592, 2/27/62, T.D. 6841, 7/26/65, T.D. 6873, 1/24/66, T.D. 6908, 12/30/66, T.D. 7977, 9/19/84, T.D. 8734, 10/6/97, T.D. 8804, 12/30/98, T.D. 8856, 12/29/99, T.D. 8881, 5/15/2000, T.D. 9272, 7/31/2006, T.D. 9415, 7/11/2008.

---

§ 1.1441-3 Determination of amounts to be withheld.

Caution: The Treasury has not yet amended Reg § 1.1441-3 to reflect changes made by P.L. 103-66, P.L. 102-318, P.L. 100-647.

(a) Withholding on gross amount. Except as otherwise provided in regulations under section 1441, the amount subject to withholding under § 1.1441-1 is the gross amount of income subject to withholding that is paid to a foreign person. The gross amount of income subject to withholding may not be reduced by any deductions, except to the extent that one or more personal exemptions are allowed as provided under § 1.1441-4(b)(6).

(b) Withholding on payments on certain obligations. *(1) Withholding at time of payment of interest.* When making a payment on an interest-bearing obligation, a withholding agent must withhold under § 1.1441-1 upon the gross amount of stated interest payable on the interest payment date, regardless of whether the payment constitutes a return of capital or the payment of income within the meaning of section 61. To the extent an amount was withheld on an amount of capital rather than interest, see the rules for adjustments, refunds, or credits under § 1.1441-1(b)(8).

(2) No withholding between interest payment dates. (i) In general . A withholding agent is not required to withhold under § 1.1441-1 upon interest accrued on the date of a sale

or exchange of a debt obligation when that sale occurs between two interest payment dates (even though the amount is treated as interest under § 1.61-7(c) or (d) and is subject to tax under section 871 or 881). See § 1.6045-1(c) for reporting requirements by brokers with respect to sale proceeds. See § 1.61-7(c) regarding the character of payments received by the acquirer of an obligation subsequent to such acquisition (that is, as a return of capital or interest accrued after the acquisition). Any exemption from withholding pursuant to this paragraph (b)(2)(i) applies without a requirement that documentation be furnished to the withholding agent. However, documentation may have to be furnished for purposes of the information reporting provisions under section 6045 or 6049 and backup withholding under section 3406. The exemption from withholding granted by this paragraph (b)(2) is not a determination that the accrued interest is not fixed or determinable annual or periodical income under section 871(a) or 881(a).

(ii) Anti-abuse rule. The exemption in paragraph (b)(2)(i) of this section does not apply if the sale of securities is part of a plan the principal purpose of which is to avoid tax by selling and repurchasing securities and the withholding agent has actual knowledge or reason to know of such plan.

(c) Corporate distributions. *(1) General rule.* General rule. A corporation making a distribution with respect to its stock or any intermediary (described in § 1.1441-1(c)(13)) making a payment of such a distribution is required to withhold under section 1441, 1442, or 1443 on the entire amount of the distribution, unless it elects to reduce the amount of withholding under the provisions of this paragraph (c). Any exceptions from withholding provided by this paragraph (c) apply without any requirement to furnish documentation to the withholding agent. However, documentation may have to be furnished for purposes of the information reporting provisions under section 6042 or 6045 and backup withholding under section 3406. See § 1.1461-1(c) to determine whether amounts excepted from withholding under this section are considered amounts that are subject to reporting.

(2) Exception to withholding on distributions. (i) In general. An election described in paragraph (c)(1) of this section is made by actually reducing the amount of withholding at the time that the payment is made. An intermediary that makes a payment of a distribution is not required to reduce the withholding based on the distributing corporation's estimates under this paragraph (c)(2), even if the distributing corporation itself elects to reduce the withholding on payments of distributions that it itself makes to foreign persons. Conversely, an intermediary may elect to reduce the amount of withholding with respect to the payment of a distribution even if the distributing corporation does not so elect for the payments of distributions that it itself makes of distributions to foreign persons. The amounts with respect to which a distributing corporation or intermediary may elect to reduce the withholding are as follows:

(A) A distributing corporation or intermediary may elect to not withhold on a distribution to the extent it represents a nontaxable distribution payable in stock or stock rights.

(B) A distributing corporation or intermediary may elect to not withhold on a distribution to the extent it represents a distribution in part or full payment in exchange for stock.

(C) A distributing corporation or intermediary may elect to not withhold on a distribution (actual or deemed) to the extent it is not paid out of accumulated earnings and profits or current earnings and profits, based on a reasonable estimate determined under paragraph (c)(2)(ii) of this section.

(D) A regulated investment company or intermediary may elect to not withhold on a distribution representing a capital gain dividend (as defined in section 852(b)(3)(C)) or an exempt interest dividend (as defined in section 852(b)(5)(A)) based on the applicable procedures described under paragraph (c)(3) of this section.

(E) A U.S. Real Property Holding Corporation (defined in section 897(c)(2)) or a real estate investment trust (defined in section 856) or intermediary may elect to not withhold on a distribution to the extent it is subject to withholding under section 1445 and the regulations under that section. See paragraph (c)(4) of this section for applicable procedures.

(ii) Reasonable estimate of accumulated and current earnings and profits on the date of payment. (A) General rule. A reasonable estimate for purposes of paragraph (c)(2)(i)(C) of this section is a determination made by the distributing corporation at a time reasonably close to the date of payment of the extent to which the distribution will constitute a dividend, as defined in section 316. The determination is based upon the anticipated amount of accumulated earnings and profits and current earnings and profits for the taxable year in which the distribution is made, the distributions made prior to the distribution for which the estimate is made and all other relevant facts and circumstances. A reasonable estimate may be made based on the procedures described in § 31.3406(b)(2)-4(c)(2) of this chapter.

(B) Procedures in case of underwithholding. A distributing corporation or intermediary that is a withholding agent with respect to a distribution and that determines at the end of the taxable year in which the distribution is made that it underwithheld under section 1441 on the distribution shall be liable for the amount underwithheld as a withholding agent under section 1461. However, for purposes of this section and § 1.1461-1, any amount underwithheld paid by a distributing corporation, its paying agent, or an intermediary shall not be treated as income subject to additional withholding even if that amount is treated as additional income to the shareholders unless the additional amount is income to the shareholder as a result of a contractual arrangement between the parties regarding the satisfaction of the shareholder's tax liabilities. In addition, no penalties shall be imposed for failure to withhold and deposit the tax if—

(1) The distributing corporation made a reasonable estimate as provided in paragraph (c)(2)(ii)(A) of this section; and

(2) Either—

The corporation or intermediary pays over the underwithheld amount on or before the due date for filing a Form 1042 for the calendar year in which the distribution is made, pursuant to § 1.1461-2(b); or

The corporation or intermediary is not a calendar year taxpayer and it files an amended return on Form 1042X (or such other form as the Commissioner may prescribe) for the calendar year in which the distribution is made and pays the underwithheld amount and interest within 60 days after the close of the taxable year in which the distribution is made.

(C) Reliance by intermediary on reasonable estimate. For purposes of determining whether the payment of a corporate distribution is a dividend, a withholding agent that is not the distributing corporation may, absent actual knowledge or reason to know otherwise, rely on representations made by the distributing corporation regarding the reasonable estimate of the anticipated accumulated and current earnings and profits made in accordance with paragraph (c)(2)(ii)(A) of this section. Failure by the withholding agent to withhold the required amount due to a failure by the distributing corporation to reasonably estimate the portion of the distribution treated as a dividend or to properly communicate the information to the withholding agent shall be imputed to the distributing corporation. In such a case, the Internal Revenue Service (IRS) may collect from the distributing corporation any underwithheld amount and subject the distributing corporation to applicable interest and penalties as a withholding agent.

(D) Example. The rules of this paragraph (c)(2) are illustrated by the following example:

Example (i). Facts. Corporation X, a publicly traded corporation with both U.S. and foreign shareholders and a calendar year taxpayer, has an accumulated deficit in earnings and profits at the close of 2000. In 2001, Corporation X generates $1 million of current earnings and profits each month and makes an $18 million distribution, resulting in a $12 million dividend. Corporation X plans to make an additional $18 million distribution on October 1, 2002. Approximately one month before that date, Corporation X s management receives an internal report from its legal and accounting department concerning Corporation X s estimated current earnings and profits. The report states that Corporation X should generate only $5.1 million of current earnings and profits by the close of the third quarter due to costs relating to substantial organizational and product changes, but these changes will enable Corporation X to generate $1.3 million of earnings and profits monthly for the last quarter of the 2002 fiscal year. Thus, the total amount of current and earnings and profits for 2002 is estimated to be $9 million.

Example (ii). Analysis. Based on the facts in paragraph (i) of this Example, including the fact that earnings and profits estimate was made within a reasonable time before the distribution, Corporation X can rely on the estimate under paragraph (c)(2)(ii)(A) of this section. Therefore, Corporation X may treat $9 million of the $18 million of the October 1, 2002, distribution to foreign shareholders as a non-dividend distribution.

(3) Special rules in the case of distributions from a regulated investment company. (i) General rule. If the amount of any distributions designated as being subject to section 852(b)(3)(C) or 5(A), or 871(k)(1)(C) or (2)(C), exceeds the amount that may be designated under those sections for the taxable year, then no penalties will be asserted for any resulting underwithholding if the designations were based on a reasonable estimate (made pursuant to the same procedures as described in paragraph (c)(2)(ii)(A) of this section) and the adjustments to the amount withheld are made within the time period described in paragraph (c)(2)(ii)(B) of this section. Any adjustment to the amount of tax due and paid to the IRS by the withholding agent as a result of underwithholding shall not be treated as a distribution for purposes of section 562(c) and the regulations thereunder. Any amount of U.S. tax that a foreign shareholder is treated as having paid on the undistributed capital gain of a regulated investment company under section 852(b)(3)(D) may be claimed by the foreign shareholder as a credit or refund under § 1.1464-1.

(ii) Reliance by intermediary on reasonable estimate. For purposes of determining whether a payment is a distribution designated as subject to section 852(b)(3)(C) or (5)(A), or 871(k)(1)(C) or (2)(C), a withholding agent that is not the distributing regulated investment company may, absent actual knowledge or reason to know otherwise, rely on the designations that the distributing company represents have been made in accordance with paragraph (c)(3)(i) of this section. Failure by the withholding agent to withhold the required amount due to a failure by the regulated investment company to reasonably estimate the required amounts or to properly communicate the relevant information to the withholding agent shall be imputed to the distributing company. In such a case, the IRS may collect from the distributing company any underwithheld amount and subject the company to applicable interest and penalties as a withholding agent.

(4) Coordination with withholding under section 1445. (i) In general. A distribution from a U.S. Real Property Holding Corporation (USRPHC) (or from a corporation that was a USRPHC at any time during the five-year period ending on the date of distribution) with respect to stock that is a U.S. real property interest under section 897(c) or from a Real Estate Investment Trust (REIT) with respect to its stock is subject to the withholding provisions under section 1441 (or section 1442 or 1443) and section 1445. A USRPHC making a distribution shall be treated as satisfying its withholding obligations under both sections if it withholds in accordance with one of the procedures described in either paragraph (c)(4)(i)(A) or (B) of this section. A USRPHC must apply the same withholding procedure to all the distributions made during the taxable year. However, the USRPHC may change the applicable withholding procedure from year to year. For rules regarding distributions by REITs, see paragraph (c)(4)(i)(C) of this section.

(A) Withholding under section 1441. The USRPHC may choose to withhold on a distribution only under section 1441 (or 1442 or 1443) and not under section 1445. In such a case, the USRPHC must withhold under section 1441 (or 1442 or 1443) on the full amount of the distribution, whether or not any portion of the distribution represents a return of basis or capital gain. If a reduced tax rate under an income tax treaty applies to the distribution by the USRPHC, then the applicable rate of withholding on the distribution shall be no less than 10-percent, unless the applicable treaty specifies an applicable lower rate for distributions from a USRPHC, in which case the lower rate may apply.

(B) Withholding under both §§ 1441 and 1445. As an alternative to the procedure described in paragraph (c)(4)(i)(A) of this section, a USRPHC may choose to withhold under both §§ 1441 (or 1442 or 1443) and 1445 under the procedures set forth in this paragraph (c)(4)(i)(B). The USRPHC must make a reasonable estimate of the portion of the distribution that is a dividend under paragraph (c)(2)(ii)(A) of this section, and must—

(1) Withhold under section 1441 (or 1442 or 1443) on the portion of the distribution that is estimated to be a dividend under paragraph (c)(2)(ii)(A) of this section; and

(2) Withhold under section 1445(e)(3) and § 1.1445-5(e) on the remainder of the distribution or on such smaller portion based on a withholding certificate obtained in accordance with § 1.1445-5(e)(2)(iv).

(C) Coordination with REIT withholding. Withholding is required under section 1441 (or 1442 or 1443) on the portion of a distribution from a REIT that is not designated as a capital gain dividend, a return of basis, or a distribution in excess of a shareholder's adjusted basis in the stock of the REIT that is treated as a capital gain under section 301(c)(3). A distribution in excess of a shareholder's adjusted basis in the stock of the REIT is, however, subject to withholding under section 1445, unless the interest in the REIT is not a U.S. real property interest (e.g., an interest in a domestically controlled REIT under section 897(h)(2)). In addition, withholding is required under section 1445 on the portion of the distribution designated by a REIT as a capital gain dividend. See § 1.1445-8.

(ii) Intermediary reliance rule. A withholding agent that is not the distributing USRPHC must withhold under paragraph (c)(4)(i) of this section, but may, absent actual knowledge or reason to know otherwise, rely on representations made by the USRPHC regarding the determinations required under paragraph (c)(4)(i) of this section. Failure by the withholding agent to withhold the required amount due to a failure by the distributing USRPHC to make these determinations in a reasonable manner or to properly communicate the determinations to the withholding agent shall be imputed to the distributing USRPHC. In such a case, the IRS may collect from the distributing USRPHC any underwithheld amount and subject the distributing USRPHC to applicable interest and penalties as a withholding agent.

(d) Withholding on payments that include an undetermined amount of income. *(1) In general.* Where the withholding agent makes a payment and does not know at the time of payment the amount that is subject to withholding because the determination of the source of the income or the calculation of the amount of income subject to tax depends upon facts that are not known at the time of payment, then the withholding agent must withhold an amount under § 1.1441-1 based on the entire amount paid that is necessary to assure that the tax withheld is not less than 30 percent (or other applicable percentage) of the amount that will subsequently be determined to be from sources within the United States or to be income subject to tax. The amount so withheld shall not exceed 30 percent of the amount paid. In the alternative, the withholding agent may make a reasonable estimate of the amount from U.S. sources or of the taxable amount and set aside a corresponding portion of the amount due under the transaction and hold such portion in escrow until the amount from U.S. sources or the taxable amount can be determined, at which point withholding becomes due under § 1.1441-1. See § 1.1441-1(b)(8) regarding adjustments in the case of overwithholding. The provisions of this paragraph (d)(1) shall not apply to the extent that other provisions of the regulations under chapter 3 of the Internal Revenue Code (Code) specify the amount to be withheld, if any, when the withholding agent lacks knowledge at the time of payment (e.g., lack of reliable knowledge regarding the status of the payee or beneficial owner, addressed in § 1.1441-1(b)(3), or lack of knowledge regarding the amount of original issue discount under § 1.1441-2(b)(3)).

(2) Withholding on certain gains. Absent actual knowledge or reason to know otherwise, a withholding agent may rely on a claim regarding the amount of gain described in § 1.1441-2(c) if the beneficial owner withholding certificate, or other appropriate withholding certificate, states the beneficial owner's basis in the property giving rise to the gain. In the absence of a reliable representation on a withholding certificate, the withholding agent must withhold an amount under § 1.1441-1 that is necessary to assure that the tax withheld is not less than 30 percent (or other applicable percentage) of the recognized gain. For this purpose, the recognized gain is determined without regard to any deduction allowed by the Code from the gains. The amount so withheld shall not exceed 30 percent of the amount payable by reason of the transaction giving rise to the recognized gain. See § 1.1441-1(b)(8) regarding adjustments in the case of overwithholding.

(e) Payments other than in U.S. dollars. *(1) In general.* The amount of a payment made in a medium other than U.S. dollars is measured by the fair market value of the property or services provided in lieu of U.S. dollars. The withholding agent may liquidate the property prior to payment in order to withhold the required amount of tax under section 1441 or obtain payment of the tax from an alternative source. However, the obligation to withhold under section 1441 is not deferred even if no alternative source can be located. Thus, for purposes of withholding under chapter 3 of the Code, the provisions of § 31.3406(h)-2(b)(2)(ii) of this chapter (relating to backup withholding from another source) shall not apply. If the withholding agent satisfies the tax liability related to such payments, the rules of paragraph (f) of this section apply.

(2) Payments in foreign currency. If the amount subject to withholding tax is paid in a currency other than the U.S. dollar, the amount of withholding under section 1441 shall be determined by applying the applicable rate of withholding to the foreign currency amount and converting the amount withheld into U.S. dollars on the date of payment at the spot rate (as defined in § 1.988-1(d)(1)) in effect on that date. A withholding agent making regular or frequent payments in foreign currency may use a month-end spot rate or a monthly average spot rate. In addition, such a withholding agent may use the spot rate on the date the amount of tax is deposited (within the meaning of § 1.6302-2(a)), provided that such deposit is made within seven days of the date of the payment giving rise to the obligation to withhold. A spot rate convention must be used consistently for all non-dollar amounts withheld and from year to year. Such convention cannot be changed without the consent of the Commissioner. The U.S. dollar amount so determined shall be treated by the beneficial owner as the amount of tax paid on the income for purposes of determining the final U.S. tax liability and, if applicable, claiming a refund or credit of tax.

(f) Tax liability of beneficial owner satisfied by withholding agent. *(1) General rule.* In the event that the satisfaction of a tax liability of a beneficial owner by a withholding agent constitutes income to the beneficial owner and such income is of a type that is subject to withholding, the amount of the payment deemed made by the withholding agent for purposes of this paragraph (f) shall be determined under the gross-up formula provided in this paragraph (f)(1). Whether the payment of the tax by the withholding agent constitutes a satisfaction of the beneficial owner's tax liability and whether, as such, it constitutes additional income to the beneficial owner, must be determined under all the facts and circumstances surrounding the transaction, including any agreements between the parties and applicable law. The formula described in this paragraph (f)(1) is as follows:

(2) Example. The following example illustrates the provisions of this paragraph (f):

Example. College X awards a qualified scholarship within the meaning of section 117(b) to foreign student, FS, who is in the United States on an F visa. FS is a resident of a country that does not have an income tax treaty with the United States. The scholarship is $20,000 to be applied to tuition, mandatory fees and books, plus benefits in kind consisting of room and board and roundtrip air transportation. College X agrees to pay any U.S. income tax owed by FS with respect to the scholarship. The fair market value of the room and board measured by the amount College X charges nonscholarship students is $6,000. The cost of the roundtrip air transportation is $2,600. Therefore, the total fair market value of the scholarship received by FS is $28,600. However, the amount taxable is limited to the fair market value of the benefits in kind ($8,600) because the portion of the scholarship amount for tuition, fees, and books is not included in gross income under section 117. The applicable rate of withholding is 14 percent under section 1441(b). Therefore, under the gross-up formula, College X is deemed to make a payment of $10,000 ($8,600 divided by (1-.14). The U.S. tax that must be deducted and withheld from the payment under section 1441(b) is $1,400 (.14 x $10,000). College X reports scholarship income of $30,000 and $1,400 of U.S. tax withheld on Forms 1042 and 1042-S.

(g) Conduit financing arrangements. *(1) Duty to withhold.* A financed entity or other person required to withhold tax under section 1441 with respect to a financing arrangement that is a conduit financing arrangement within the meaning of § 1.881-3(a)(2)(iv) shall be required to withhold under section 1441 as if the district director had determined, pursuant to § 1.881-3(a)(3), that all conduit entities that are parties to the conduit financing arrangement should be disregarded. The amount of tax required to be withheld shall be determined under § 1.881-3(d). The withholding agent may withhold tax at a reduced rate if the financing entity establishes that it is entitled to the benefit of a treaty that provides a reduced rate of tax on a payment of the type deemed to have been paid to the financing entity. Section 1.881-3(a)(3)(ii)(E) shall not apply for purposes of determining whether any person is required to deduct and withhold tax pursuant to this paragraph (g), or whether any party to a financing arrangement is liable for failure to withhold or entitled to a refund of tax under section 1441 or 1461 to 1464 (except to the extent the amount withheld exceeds the tax liability determined under § 1.881-3(d)). See § 1.1441-7(d) relating to withholding tax liability of the withholding agent in conduit financing arrangements subject to § 1.881-3.

(2) Effective date. This paragraph (g) is effective for payments made by financed entities on or after September 11, 1995. This paragraph shall not apply to interest payments covered by section 127(g)(3) of the Tax Reform Act of 1984, and to interest payments with respect to ether debt obligations issued prior to October 15, 1984 (whether or not such debt was issued by a Netherlands Antilles corporation).

(h) Effective date. Except as otherwise provided in paragraph (g) of this section, this section applies to payments made after December 31, 2000.

T.D. 6187, 7/5/56, amend T.D. 6592, 2/27/62, T.D. 6636, 2/25/63, T.D. 6669, 8/26/63, T.D. 6777, 12/15/64, T.D. 6908, 12/30/66, T.D. 7378, 9/29/75, T.D. 7977, 9/19/84, T.D. 8611, 8/10/95, T.D. 8734, 10/6/97, T.D. 8804, 12/30/98, T.D. 8856, 12/29/99, T.D. 8881, 5/15/2000, T.D. 9253, 3/13/2006.

PAR. 2. In section 1.1441-3, paragraph (b) is revised to read as follows:

Proposed § 1.1441-3 Determination of amount to be withheld. [*For Preamble, see ¶ 151,817*]

* * * * *

(b) Withholding on payments on certain obligations. *(1) Withholding at time of payment of interest.* When making a payment on an interest-bearing obligation, a withholding agent must withhold under section 1.1441-1 upon the gross amount of stated interest payable on the interest payment date, regardless of whether the payment constitutes a return of capital or the payment of income within the meaning of section 61, unless the withholding agent has knowledge of the actual amount of interest paid. For this purpose, the withholding agent may rely on information provided by the issuer (or its paying agent), on a representation from the beneficial owner, or on information that the withholding agent has in its records. To the extent an amount was withheld on an amount of capital rather than interest, see rules for adjustments, refunds, or credits under section 1.1441-1(b)(8).

(2) No withholding between interest payment dates. (i) General rule. A withholding agent is not required to withhold under section 1.1441-1 upon interest accrued on the date of a sale of debt obligations when that sale occurs between two interest payment dates (even though the amount is treated as interest under section 1.61-7(c) or (d) and is subject to tax under section 871(a) or 881(a)), unless the withholding agent has knowledge of the amount paid as interest. For purposes of this paragraph (b)(2)(i), a withholding agent is treated as having knowledge in the same manner as a withholding agent has knowledge for purposes of section 1.1441-2(b)(3)(ii), dealing with withholding on original issue discount. In addition, notwithstanding lack of knowledge (within the meaning of section 1.1441-2(b)(3)(ii)), withholding is required on the entire amount of stated interest paid with respect to the obligation as determined as of the date of original issue if the withholding agent, pursuant to the provisions in section 1.1441-1(b)(3), treats the payment as made to a foreign payee because it cannot associate the payment with required documentation and the amount would qualify as portfolio interest. See section 1.1441-1(b)(8) for adjustments to any amount that has been overwithheld as a result of this provision.

(ii) Applicable rules. Any exemption from withholding pursuant to paragraph (b)(2)(i) of this section applies without a requirement that documentation be furnished to the withholding agent. However, documentation may have to be furnished for purposes of the information reporting provisions under section 6049 and backup withholding under section 3406. See section 1.6045-1(c) for reporting requirements by brokers with respect to sale proceeds. Any exemption from withholding under paragraph (b)(2)(i) of this section is not a determination that the accrued interest is not fixed or determinable annual or periodical income. See section 1.61-7(c) regarding the character of payments received by the acquirer of an obligation subsequent to such acquisition (that is, as a return of capital or interest accrued after the acquisition).

* * * * *

PAR. 2. Section 1.1441-3 is amended as follows:

1. A sentence is added at the end of paragraph (c)(2)(i)(B).

2. Paragraph (c)(5) is added.

3. A sentence is added at the end of paragraph (d)(1).

The additions read as follows.

Proposed § 1.1441-3 Determination of amounts to be withheld. [*For Preamble, see ¶ 152,919*]

* * * * *

(c) * * *

(2) * * *

(i) * * *

(B) * * * The preceding sentence shall not apply to a public section 302 distribution to which paragraph (c)(5) applies.

* * * * *

(5) Special rules for certain distributions to which section 302 applies. (i) Withholding responsibility. (A) General rule. A corporation that makes a public section 302 distribution, or any intermediary (described in § 1.1441-1(c)(13))

making a payment of such a distribution, is required to withhold under section 1441, 1442 or 1443 on the entire amount of the distribution unless the provisions of paragraph (c)(5)(iii) of this section have been applied. The provisions of paragraph (c)(2)(i)(B) or (d)(1) of this section do not apply to a public section 302 distribution.

(B) Effective/applicability date. The rules of this paragraph (c)(5) apply to public section 302 distributions made after December 31, 2008.

(ii) Definitions. Solely for purposes of this paragraph (c)(5), the following definitions shall apply:

(A) Public section 302 distribution means a distribution by a corporation in redemption of its stock for which there is an established financial market within the meaning of § 1.1092(d)-1.

(B) Section 302 payment means payment of a public section 302 distribution.

(C) Distributing corporation means a corporation making or treated as making a public section 302 distribution.

(iii) Escrow procedure. (A) Application. (1) In general. The escrow procedure in this paragraph (c)(5)(iii) may be applied only by an intermediary (described in § 1.1441-1(c)(13)) that is a U.S. financial institution. A U.S. financial institution making a section 302 payment to a foreign account holder, and applying this escrow procedure, is not required to withhold on the entire amount of a section 302 payment under the general rule of paragraph (c)(5)(i).

(B) Escrow account. (1) In general. A U.S. financial institution shall set aside in an escrow account on the date it receives a section 302 payment from a distributing corporation with respect to stock of a foreign account holder 30 percent (or the applicable dividend rate provided by a tax treaty for a qualifying foreign account holder) of the amount and shall credit the foreign account holder's account with the balance of the section 302 payment.

(2) Qualified intermediaries. The amount set aside, under paragraph (c)(5)(iii)(B)(1) of this section shall include 30 percent (or the applicable dividend rate provided by a treaty) of the amount paid to any qualified intermediary (QI) (whether or not the QI has assumed primary withholding responsibility) and to any withholding foreign partnership or withholding foreign trust (WP/WT).

(C) Request for section 302 payment certification. On or before the date it receives the section 302 payment, the U.S. financial institution shall provide the following information and instructions, in writing, to the foreign beneficial owner—

(1) The total number of distributing corporation's shares outstanding before and after the public section 302 distribution;

(2) An explanation of the conditions under which the section 302 payment will be treated as a dividend or a payment in exchange for stock for Federal income tax purposes (including an explanation of any applicable constructive ownership rules); and

(3) A request that the beneficial owner of the account provide a certification (section 302 payment certification), within 60 days of the section 302 payment, stating whether the section 302 payment is either a dividend or a payment in exchange for stock under the Internal Revenue Code.

(D) Content of section 302 payment certification. The section 302 payment certification must include the following information:

(1) The beneficial owner's name and account number.

(2) The distributing corporation's name.

(3) The total shares of the distributing corporation outstanding immediately before and immediately after the public section 302 distribution.

(4) A certification from the beneficial owner that either—

(i) The section 302 payment is a payment in exchange for stock because the beneficial owner's proportionate interest has been reduced but not completely terminated;

(ii) The section 302 payment is a payment in exchange for stock because the beneficial owner's interest in the distributing corporation is completely terminated; or

(iii) The section 302 payment is a dividend.

(5) With respect to the certifications in paragraph (c)(5)(iii)(D)(4)(i) and (ii) of this section, the number of shares actually and constructively owned by the beneficial owner before and after the distribution and the beneficial owner's percentage ownership before and after the distribution.

(6) A penalties of perjury statement.

(7) The signature of the beneficial owner and date of signature.

(E) Receipt of section 302 payment certification. (1) Payment in exchange for stock. If, within the 60-day period described in paragraph (c)(5)(iii)(C)(3), the U.S. financial institution receives from the foreign beneficial owner a section 302 payment certification stating that the section 302 payment is a payment in exchange for stock, and if the U.S. financial institution does not know or have reason to know that the information in the section 302 payment certification is unreliable or incorrect, the U.S. financial institution shall credit the account with the amount set aside with respect to the beneficial owner who provides the certification. The entire amount paid (including the amount initially set aside) shall be reported as capital gains on Form 1042-S Foreign Person's U.S. Source Income Subject to Withholding.

(2) Unreliable or incorrect exchange certification. If the U.S. financial institution knows or has reason to know that the information in the section 302 payment certification is unreliable or incorrect, the U.S. financial institution shall treat the payment as a payment for which no section 302 payment certification has been received and shall follow the withholding and reporting procedures in paragraph (c)(5)(iii)(E)(4) of this section.

(3) Dividend. If, within the 60-day period, the U.S. financial institution receives a section 302 payment certification from the foreign beneficial owner stating that the section 302 payment is a dividend, the U.S. financial institution shall treat the amount set aside as tax withheld as of the time it receives the section 302 payment certification, and shall deposit that amount pursuant to the applicable regulations. The entire amount paid shall be reported on Form 1042-S as dividends.

(4) No timely certification received. If, within the 60-day period, the U.S. financial institution does not receive a section 302 payment certification, or is treated under paragraph (c)(5)(iii)(E)(2) of this section as not receiving a section 302 payment certification, the U.S. financial institution shall treat the amount set aside as tax withheld as of the 61st day, and shall deposit that amount pursuant to the applicable regulations. The entire amount paid shall be reported on Form 1042-S as dividends.

(5) Late certification. If, after the 60-day period has expired, the U.S. financial institution receives a section 302 payment certification from a foreign beneficial owner that

the section 302 payment is a payment in exchange for stock and the conditions stated in § 1.1461-2(a) are satisfied, the U.S. financial institution may apply the refund or offset procedures of that paragraph.

(6) Determination of incorrect treatment. If, after the 60-day period has expired, the U.S. financial institution determines that the section 302 payment was incorrectly treated as a distribution in exchange for stock, the procedures set forth regarding underwithholding in § 1.1461-2(b) are applicable.

(7) Undocumented beneficial owners. The U.S. financial institution shall withhold at 30 percent on the entire amount paid to a beneficial owner that is not properly documented under §§ 1.1441-1, 1.1441-5, etc. and that is presumed to be a foreign person, whether or not the U.S. financial institution has received a section 302 payment certification from such beneficial owner. The U.S. financial institution shall report the entire amount paid on Form 1042-S as dividends.

(F) Amounts in excess of section 302 payment. If the amount the U.S. financial institution credits to the account of the foreign beneficial owner from the escrow account includes an amount in excess of the section 302 payment, such as interest accrued on the escrowed funds, the U.S. financial institution shall report and withhold on such excess amount in accordance with the rules under Chapter 3 of the Internal Revenue Code.

(G) U.S. non-exempt recipients. The U.S. financial institution shall treat beneficial owners that are U.S. non-exempt recipients, and that hold stock in the distributing corporation through QIs, WPs/WTs, NQIs and flow-throughs, in accordance with the section 302 payment certifications obtained from those U.S. non-exempt recipients and shall instruct foreign intermediaries and foreign flow-through entities to do the same.

(H) Notice to distributing corporation. The U.S. financial institution shall notify the distributing corporation, in writing, by the filing date of Form 1042-S, of the aggregate amount of the section 302 payment that the U.S. financial institution has reported on Forms 1042-S as capital gains, and the aggregate amount of the section 302 payment that it has reported on Forms 1042-S as dividends.

(I) Application of Escrow Procedure to Qualified Intermediaries. As provided in paragraph (c)(5)(iii)(A) of this section, only the U.S. financial institution may establish an escrow account and the amounts set aside in the escrow account shall include 30 percent (or the applicable treaty rate applicable to dividends) on payments made to a direct account holder that is a QI (including a QI that has assumed primary withholding responsibility). Under the procedure described in paragraph (c)(5)(iii)(I)(3), a QI shall provide the U.S. financial institution with a withholding statement as required in the QI Agreement. If there is a chain of QIs, each QI in the chain shall apply the procedure. The procedures described in this paragraph (I) shall be applied to withholding foreign partnerships and withholding foreign trusts within the meaning of §§ 1.1441-5(c)(2) and (e)(5)(v), respectively, in the same manner as the procedures apply to a QI.

(1) Request for section 302 payment certification. The U.S. financial institution shall provide the information and instructions described in paragraph (c)(5)(iii)(C) of this section to the QI, and the QI shall provide the same information and instructions to its account holders including account holders that are U.S. non-exempt recipients.

(2) Content of section 302 payment certification. The content of the section 302 payment certification shall include the information described in paragraph (c)(5)(iii)(D) of this section.

(3) Receipt of section 302 payment certification. (i) Payment in exchange for stock. If, within the 60-day period described in paragraph (c)(5)(iii)(C), the QI receives from the beneficial owner a section 302 payment certification stating that the section 302 payment is a payment in exchange for stock and if the QI does not know or have reason to know that the information in the section 302 payment certification is unreliable or incorrect, the QI shall reflect such treatment in its withholding statement provided to the U.S. financial institution, and, based upon the withholding statement, the U.S. financial institution shall release payment from its escrow and the QI shall credit the beneficial owner's account with the amount set aside by the U.S. financial institution with respect to the beneficial owner who provided the certification. The entire amount paid (including the amount initially set aside) shall be reported on the QI's pooled basis Form 1042-S as capital gains.

(ii) Unreliable or incorrect exchange certification. If the QI knows or has reason to know that the information in the section 302 payment certification is unreliable or incorrect, the QI shall treat the payment as a payment for which no section 302 payment certification has been received and shall follow the withholding and reporting procedures in paragraph (c)(5)(iii)(I)(3)(iv) of this section.

(iii) Dividend. If, within the 60-day period, QI receives a section 302 payment certification stating that the section 302 payment is a dividend, the QI shall reflect such treatment in its withholding statement and shall treat the payment as a dividend for purposes of its reporting and withholding responsibilities under the QI agreement. The entire amount paid shall be reported on its pooled basis Form 1042-S as dividends.

(iv) No timely certification received. If, within the 60-day period, the QI does not receive a section 302 payment certification, or is treated under paragraph (c)(5)(iii)(I)(3)(ii) of this section as not receiving a section 302 payment certification, the QI shall reflect such treatment in its withholding statement provided to the U.S. financial institution and shall treat the payment as a dividend for purposes of its reporting and withholding responsibilities under the QI agreement. The entire amount paid shall be reported on its pooled basis Form 1042-S as dividends.

(v) Late certification. If, after the 60-day period has expired, the QI receives a section 302 payment certification from a beneficial owner that the section 302 payment is a payment in exchange for stock and the conditions stated in the QI agreement regarding the refund and offset procedures are satisfied, the QI may apply such refund or offset procedures.

(vi) Determination of incorrect treatment. If, after the 60-day period has expired, the QI determines that the section 302 payment was incorrectly treated as a distribution in exchange for stock, the procedures set forth regarding adjustments for underwithholding in the QI agreement are applicable.

(vii) Undocumented beneficial owners. The QI shall withhold at 30 percent on the entire amount paid to a beneficial owner that is not properly documented and that is presumed to be a foreign person, whether or not the QI has received a section 302 payment certification from such beneficial owner. The QI shall report the entire amount paid on its pooled basis Form 1042-S as dividends.

(4) U.S. non-exempt recipients. The QI shall treat direct account holders that are U.S. non-exempt recipients, and that hold stock in the distributing corporation, in accordance with the section 302 payment certifications obtained from those U.S. non-exempt recipients and shall instruct foreign intermediaries and foreign flow-through entities to do the same.

(J) Intermediaries that are not qualified intermediaries. If the U.S. financial institution has an account holder that is an intermediary that is not a QI ("NQI"), the U.S. financial institution shall apply the rules of paragraph (c)(5)(iii)(J)(1) through (4) of this section. Where the provisions of this paragraph (J) refer only to the U.S. financial institution, they shall apply in the same manner to a QI or WP/WT and where they refer to an NQI, they shall apply in the same manner to a flow-through that is not a WP or WT.

(1) The U.S. financial institution shall provide the information and instructions described in paragraph (c)(5)(iii)(C) of this section to the NQI and the NQI shall provide the same information and instructions to its account holders.

(2) The content of the section 302 payment certification shall include the information described in paragraph (c)(5)(iii)(D) of this section.

(3) The NQI shall provide the section 302 payment certification to the U.S. financial institution together with the otherwise required documentation and a withholding statement made in accordance with the section 302 payment certification.

(4) The U.S. financial institution shall treat the section 302 payment as a dividend or a payment in exchange for stock based on the information and documentation provided to it under paragraph (c)(5)(iii)(J)(3) of this section. The U.S. financial institution shall withhold and report on a specific payee basis in accordance with this information.

(d) * * * *(1)* * * * This paragraph does not apply to a public section 302 distribution to which paragraph (c)(5) applies.

* * * * *

§ 1.1441-4 Exemptions from withholding for certain effectively connected income and other amounts.

(a) Certain income connected with a U.S. trade or business. *(1) In general.* No withholding is required under section 1441 on income otherwise subject to withholding if the income is (or is deemed to be) effectively connected with the conduct of a trade or business within the United States and is includible in the beneficial owner's gross income for the taxable year. For purposes of this paragraph (a), an amount is not deemed to be includible in gross income if the amount is (or is deemed to be) effectively connected with the conduct of a trade or business within the United States and the beneficial owner claims an exemption from tax under an income tax treaty because the income is not attributable to a permanent establishment in the United States. To claim a reduced rate of withholding because the income is not attributable to a permanent establishment, see § 1.1441-6(b)(1). This paragraph (a) does not apply to income of a foreign corporation to which section 543(a)(7) applies for the taxable year or to compensation for personal services performed by an individual. See paragraph (b) of this section for compensation for personal services performed by an individual.

(2) Withholding agent's reliance on a claim of effectively connected income. (i) In general. Absent actual knowledge or reason to know otherwise, a withholding agent may rely on a claim of exemption based upon paragraph (a)(1) of this section if, prior to the payment to the foreign person, the withholding agent can reliably associate the payment with a Form W-8 upon which it can rely to treat the payment as made to a foreign beneficial owner in accordance with § 1.1441-1(e)(1)(ii). For purposes of this paragraph (a), a withholding certificate is valid only if, in addition to other applicable requirements, it includes the taxpayer identifying number of the person whose name is on the Form W-8 and represents, under penalties of perjury, that the amounts for which the certificate is furnished are effectively connected with the conduct of a trade or business in the United States and is includable in the beneficial owner's gross income for the taxable year. In the absence of a reliable claim that the income is effectively connected with the conduct of a trade or business in the United States, the income is presumed not to be effectively connected, except as otherwise provided in paragraph (a)(2)(ii) or (3) of this section. See § 1.1441-1(e)(4)(ii)(C) for the period of validity applicable to a certificate provided under this section and § 1.1441-1(e)(4)(ii)(D) for changes in circumstances arising during the taxable year indicating that the income to which the certificate relates is not, or is no longer expected to be, effectively connected with the conduct of a trade or business within the United States. A withholding certificate shall be effective only for the item or items of income specified therein. The provisions of § 1.1441-1(b)(3)(iv) dealing with a 90-day grace period shall apply for purposes of this section.

(ii) Special rules for U.S. branches of foreign persons. (A) U.S. branches of certain foreign banks or foreign insurance companies. A payment to a U.S. branch described in § 1.1441-1(b)(2)(iv)(A) is presumed to be effectively connected with the conduct of a trade or business in the United States without the need to furnish a certificate, unless the U.S. branch provides a U.S. branch withholding certificate described in § 1.1441-1(e)(3)(v) that represents otherwise. If no certificate is furnished but the income is not, in fact, effectively connected income, then the branch must withhold whether the payment is collected on behalf of other persons or on behalf of another branch of the same entity. See § 1.1441-1(b)(2)(iv) and (6) for general rules applicable to payments to U.S. branches of foreign persons.

(B) Other U.S. branches. See § 1.1441-1(b)(2)(iv)(E) for similar procedures for other U.S. branches to the extent provided in a determination letter from the district director or the Assistant Commissioner (International).

(3) Income on notional principal contracts. (i) General rule. A withholding agent that pays amounts attributable to a notional principal contract described in § 1.863-7(a) or 1.988-2(e) shall have no obligation to withhold on the amounts paid under the terms of the notional principal contract regardless of whether a withholding certificate is provided. However, a withholding agent must file returns under § 1.1461-1(b) and (c) reporting the income that it must treat as effectively connected with the conduct of a trade or business in the United States under the provisions of this paragraph (a)(3). Except as otherwise provided in paragraph (a)(3)(ii) of this section, a withholding agent must treat the income as effectively connected with the conduct of a U.S. trade or business if the income is paid to, or to the account of, a qualified business unit of a foreign person located in the United States or, if the payment is paid to, or to the account of, a qualified business unit of a foreign person lo-

cated outside the United States, the withholding agent knows, or has reason to know, the payment is effectively connected with the conduct of a trade or business within the United States. Income on a notional principal contract does not include the amount characterized as interest under the provisions of § 1.446-3(g)(4).

(ii) Exception for certain payments. A payment shall not be treated as effectively connected with the conduct of a trade or business within the United States for purposes of paragraph (a)(3)(i) of this section even if no withholding certificate is furnished if the payee provides a representation in a master agreement that governs the transactions in notional principal contracts between the parties (for example an International Swaps and Derivatives Association (ISDA) Agreement, including the Schedule thereto) or in the confirmation on the particular notional principal contract transaction that the payee is a U.S. person or a non-U.S. branch of a foreign person.

(b) Compensation for personal services of an individual. *(1) Exemption from withholding.* Withholding is not required under § 1.1441-1 from salaries, wages, remuneration, or any other compensation for personal services of a nonresident alien individual if such compensation is effectively connected with the conduct of a trade or business within the United States and—

(i) Such compensation is subject to withholding under section 3402 (relating to withholding on wages) and the regulations under that section;

(ii) Such compensation would be subject to withholding under section 3402 but for the provisions of section 3401(a) (not including section 3401(a)(6)) and the regulations under that section. This paragraph (b)(1)(ii) does not apply to payments to a nonresident alien individual from any trust described in section 401(a), any annuity plan described in section 403(a), any annuity, custodial account, or retirement income account described in section 403(b), or an individual retirement account or individual retirement annuity described in section 408. Instead, these payments are subject to withholding under this section to the extent they are exempted from the definition of wages under section 3401(a)(12) or to the extent they are from an annuity, custodial account, or retirement income account described in section 403(b), or an individual retirement account or individual retirement annuity described in section 408. Thus, for example, payments to a nonresident alien individual from a trust described in section 401(a) are subject to withholding under section 1441 and not under section 3405 or section 3406.

(iii) Such compensation is for services performed by a nonresident alien individual who is a resident of Canada or Mexico and who enters and leaves the United States at frequent intervals;

(iv) Such compensation is, or will be, exempt from the income tax imposed by chapter 1 of the Code by reason of a provision of the Internal Revenue Code or a tax treaty to which the United States is a party;

(v) Such compensation is paid after January 3, 1979 as a commission or rebate paid by a ship supplier to a nonresident alien individual, who is employed by a nonresident alien individual, foreign partnership, or foreign corporation in the operation of a ship or ships of foreign registry, for placing orders for supplies to be used in the operation of such ship or ships with the supplier. See section 162(c) and the regulations thereunder for denial of deductions for illegal bribes, kickbacks, and other payments; or

(vi) Compensation that is exempt from withholding under section 3402 by reason of section 3402(e), provided that the employee and his employer enter into an agreement under section 3402(p) to provide for the withholding of income tax upon payments of amounts described in § 31.3401(a)-3(b)(1) of this chapter. An employee who desires to enter into such an agreement should furnish his employer with Form W-4 (withholding exemption certificate) (or such other form as the Internal Revenue Service (IRS) may prescribe). See section 3402(f) and the regulations thereunder and § 31.3402(p)-1 of this chapter.

(2) Manner of obtaining withholding exemption under tax treaty. (i) In general. In order to obtain the exemption from withholding by reason of a tax treaty, provided by paragraph (b)(1)(iv) of this section, a nonresident alien individual must submit a withholding certificate (described in paragraph (b)(2)(ii) of this section) to each withholding agent from whom amounts are to be received. A separate withholding certificate must be filed for each taxable year of the alien individual. If the withholding agent is satisfied that an exemption from withholding is warranted (see paragraph (b)(2)(iii) of this section), the withholding certificate shall be accepted in the manner set forth in paragraph (b)(2)(iv) of this section. The exemption from withholding becomes effective for payments made at least ten days after a copy of the accepted withholding certificate is forwarded to the Assistant Commissioner (International). The withholding agent may rely on an accepted withholding certificate only if the IRS has not objected to the certificate. For purposes of this paragraph (b)(2)(i), the IRS will be considered to have not objected to the certificate if it has not notified the withholding agent within a 10-day period beginning from the date that the withholding certificate is forwarded to the IRS pursuant to paragraph (b)(2)(v) of this section. After expiration of the 10-day period, the withholding agent may rely on the withholding certificate retroactive to the date of the first payment covered by the certificate. The fact that the IRS does not object to the withholding certificate within the 10-day period provided in this paragraph (b)(2)(i) shall not preclude the IRS from examining the withholding agent at a later date in light of facts that the withholding agent knew or had reason to know regarding the payment and eligibility for a reduced rate and that were not disclosed to the IRS as part of the 10-day review process.

(ii) Withholding certificate claiming withholding exemption. The statement claiming an exemption from withholding shall be made on Form 8233 (or an acceptable substitute or such other form as the IRS may prescribe). Form 8233 shall be dated, signed by the beneficial owner under penalties of perjury, and contain the following information—

(A) The individual's name, permanent residence address, taxpayer identifying number (or a copy of a completed Form W-7 or SS-5 showing that a number has been applied for), and the U.S. visa number, if any;

(B) The individual's current immigration status and visa type;

(C) The individual's original date of entry into the United States;

(D) The country that issued the individual's passport and the number of such passport, or the individual's permanent address if a citizen of Canada or Mexico;

(E) The taxable year for which the statement is to apply, the compensation to which it relates, and the amount (or estimated amount if exact amount not known) of such compensation;

(F) A statement that the individual is not a citizen or resident of the United States;

(G) The number of personal exemptions claimed by the individual;

(H) A statement as to whether the compensation to be paid to him or her during the taxable year is or will be exempt from income tax and the reason why the compensation is exempt;

(I) If the compensation is exempt from withholding by reason of an income tax treaty to which the United States is a party, the tax treaty and provision under which the exemption from withholding is claimed and the country of which the individual is a resident;

(J) Sufficient facts to justify the claim in exemption from withholding; and

(K) Any other information as may be required by the form or accompanying instructions in addition to, or in lieu of, the information described in this paragraph (b)(2)(ii).

(iii) Review by withholding agent. The exemption from withholding provided by paragraph (b)(1)(iv) of this section shall not apply unless the withholding agent accepts (in the manner provided in paragraph (b)(2)(iv) of this section) the statement on Form 8233 supplied by the nonresident alien individual. Before accepting the statement the withholding agent must examine the statement. If the withholding agent knows or has reason to know that any of the facts or assertions on Form 8233 may be false or that the eligibility of the individual's compensation for the exemption cannot be readily determined, the withholding agent may not accept the statement on Form 8233 and is required to withhold under this section. If the withholding agent accepts the statement and subsequently finds that any of the facts or assertions contained on Form 8233 may be false or that the eligibility of the individual's compensation for the exemption can no longer be readily determined, then the withholding agent shall promptly so notify the Assistant Commissioner (International) by letter, and the withholding agent is not relieved of liability to withhold on any amounts still to be paid. If the withholding agent is notified by the Foreign Operations District that the eligibility of the individual's compensation for the exemption is in doubt or that such compensation is not eligible for the exemption, the withholding agent is required to withhold under this section. The rules of this paragraph are illustrated by the following examples.

Example (1). C, a nonresident alien individual, submits Form 8233 to W, a withholding agent. The statement on Form 8233 does not include all the information required by paragraph (b)(2)(ii) of this section. Therefore, W has reason to know that he or she cannot readily determine whether C's compensation for personal services is eligible for an exemption from withholding and, therefore, W must withhold.

Example (2). D, a nonresident alien, is performing services for W, a withholding agent. W has accepted a statement on Form 8233 submitted by D, according to the provisions of this section. W receives notice from the Internal Revenue Service that the eligibility of D's compensation for a withholding exemption is in doubt. Therefore, W has reason to know that the eligibility of the compensation for a withholding exemption cannot be readily determined, as of the date W receives the notification, and W must withhold tax under section 1441 on amounts paid after receipt of the notification.

Example (3). E, a nonresident alien individual, submits Form 8233 to W, a withholding agent for whom E is to perform personal services. The statement contains all the information requested on Form 8233. E claims an exemption from withholding based on a personal exemption amount computed on the number of days E will perform personal services for W in the United States. If W does not know or have reason to know that any statement on the Form 8233 is false or that the eligibility of E's compensation for the withholding exemption cannot be readily determined, W can accept the statement on Form 8233 and exempt from withholding the appropriate amount of E's income.

(iv) Acceptance by withholding agent. If after the review described in paragraph (b)(2)(iii) of this section the withholding agent is satisfied that an exemption from withholding is warranted, the withholding agent may accept the statement by making a certification, verified by a declaration that it is made under the penalties of perjury, on Form 8233. The certification shall be—

(A) That the withholding agent has examined the statement,

(B) That the withholding agent is satisfied that an exemption from withholding is warranted, and

(C) That the withholding agent does not know or have reason to know that the individual's compensation is not entitled to the exemption or that the eligibility of the individual's compensation for the exemption cannot be readily determined.

(v) Copies of Form 8233. The withholding agent shall forward one copy of each Form 8233 that is accepted under paragraph (b)(2)(iv) of this section to the Assistant Commissioner (International), within five days of such acceptance. The withholding agent shall retain a copy of Form 8233.

(3) Withholding agreements. Compensation for personal services of a nonresident alien individual who is engaged during the taxable year in the conduct of a trade or business within the United States may be wholly or partially exempted from the withholding required by § 1.1441-1 if an agreement is reached between the Assistant Commissioner (International) and the alien individual with respect to the amount of withholding required. Such agreement shall be available in the circumstances and in the manner set forth by the Internal Revenue Service, and shall be effective for payments covered by the agreement that are made after the agreement is executed by all parties. The alien individual must agree to timely file an income tax return for the current taxable year.

(4) Final payment exemption. (i) General rule. Compensation for independent personal services of a nonresident alien individual who is engaged during the taxable year in the conduct of a trade or business within the United States may be wholly or partially exempted from the withholding required by § 1.1441-1 from the final payment of compensation for independent personal services. This exemption does not apply to wages. This exemption from withholding is available only once during an alien individual's taxable year and is obtained by the alien individual presenting to the withholding agent a letter in duplicate from a district director stating the amount of compensation subject to the exemption and the amount that would otherwise be withheld from such final payment under section 1441 that shall be paid to the alien individual due to the exemption. The alien individual shall attach a copy of the letter to his or her income tax return for the taxable year for which the exemption is effective.

(ii) Final payment of compensation for personal services. For purposes of this paragraph, final payment of compensation for personal services means the last payment of compensation, other than wages, for personal services rendered within the United States that the individual expects to receive from any withholding agent during the taxable year.

(iii) Manner of applying for final payment exemption. In order to obtain the final payment exemption provided by paragraph (b)(4)(i) of this section, the nonresident alien individual (or his or her agent) must file the forms and provide the information required by the district director. Ordinary and necessary business expenses may be taken into account if substantiated to the satisfaction of the district director. The alien individual must submit a statement, signed by him or her and verified by a declaration that it is made under the penalties of perjury, that all the information provided is true and that to his or her knowledge no relevant information has been omitted. The information required to be submitted includes, but is not limited to—

(A) A statement by each withholding agent from whom amounts of gross income effectively connected with the conduct of a trade or business within the United States have been received by the alien individual during the taxable year, of the amount of such income paid and the amount of tax withheld, signed and verified by a declaration that it is made under penalties of perjury;

(B) A statement by the withholding agent from whom the final payment of compensation for personal services will be received, of the amount of such final payment and the amount which would be withheld under § 1.1441-1 if a final payment exemption under paragraph (b)(4)(i) of this section is not granted, signed and verified by a declaration that it is made under penalties of perjury;

(C) A statement by the individual that he or she does not intend to receive any other amounts of gross income effectively connected with the conduct of a trade or business within the United States during the current taxable year;

(D) The amount of tax which has been withheld (or paid) under any other provision of the Code or regulations with respect to any income effectively connected with the conduct of a trade or business within the United States during the current taxable year;

(E) The amount of any outstanding tax liabilities (and interest and penalties relating thereto) from the current taxable year or prior taxable periods; and

(F) The provision of any income tax treaty under which a partial or complete exemption from withholding may be claimed, the country of the individual's residence, and a statement of sufficient facts to justify an exemption pursuant to such treaty.

(iv) Letter to withholding agent. If the district director is satisfied that the information provided under paragraph (b)(4)(iii) of this section is sufficient, the district director will, after coordination with the Director of the Foreign Operations District, ascertain the amount of the alien individual's tentative income tax for the taxable year with respect to gross income that is effectively connected with the conduct of a trade or business within the United States. After the tentative tax has been ascertained, the district director will provide the alien individual with a letter to the withholding agent stating the amount of the final payment of compensation for personal services that is exempt from withholding, and the amount that would otherwise be withheld under section 1441 that shall be paid to the alien individual due to the exemption. The amount of compensation for personal services exempt from withholding under this paragraph (b)(4) shall not exceed $5,000.

Example (1). On July 15, 1983, B, a nonresident alien individual, appears before a district director with the information required by paragraph (b)(4)(iii) of this section. B has received personal service income in 1983 from which $3,000 has been withheld under section 1441. On August 1, 1983, B will receive $5,000 in personal service income from W. B does not intend to receive any other income subject to U.S. tax during 1983. Taking into account B's substantiated deductible business expenses, the district director computes the tentative tax liability on B's income effectively connected with the conduct of a trade or business in the United States during 1983 (including the $5,000 payment to be made on August 1, 1983) to be $3,300. B does not owe U.S. tax for any other taxable periods. The amount of B's final payment exemption is determined as follows:

(1) The amount of total withholding is $4,500 ($3,000 previously withheld plus $1,500, 30% of the $5,000 final payment);

(2) The amount of tentative excess withholding is $1,200 (total withholding of $4,500 minus B's tentative tax liability of $3,300); and

(3) To allow B to receive $1,200 of the amount which would otherwise have been withheld from the final payment, the district director allows a withholding exemption for $4,000 of B's final payment. W must withhold $300 from the final payment.

Example (2). The facts are the same as in Example 1 except B will receive a final payment of compensation on August 1, 1983, in the amount of $10,000 and B's tentative tax liability is $3,900. The amount of B's final payment exemption is determined as follows:

(1) The amount of total withholding is $6,000 ($3,000 previously withheld plus $3,000, 30% of the $10,000 final payment);

(2) The amount of tentative excess withholding is $2,100 (total withholding of $6,000 minus B's tentative tax liability of $3,900); and

(3) To allow B to receive $2,100 of the amount which would otherwise be withheld from the final payment, $7,000 of the final payment would have to be exempt from withholding; however, as no more than $5,000 of the final payment can be exempt from withholding under this paragraph (b)(4), the district director allows a withholding exemption for $5,000 of B's final payment. B must file a claim for refund at the end of the taxable year to obtain a refund of $600. W must withhold $1,500 from the final payment.

(5) Requirement of return. The tentative tax determined by the district director under paragraph (b)(4)(iv) of this section or by the Director of the Foreign Operations District under the withholding agreement procedure of paragraph (b)(3) of this section shall not constitute a final determination of the income tax liability of the nonresident alien individual, nor shall such determination constitute a tax return of the nonresident alien individual for any taxable period. An alien individual who applies for or obtains an exemption from withholding under the procedures of paragraphs (b)(2), (3), or (4) of this section is not relieved of the obligation to file a return of income under section 6012.

(6) Personal exemption. (i) In general. To determine the tax to be withheld at source under § 1.1441-1 from remuneration paid for personal services performed within the United States by a nonresident alien individual and from scholarship and fellowship income described in paragraph (c) of this section, a withholding agent may take into account one personal exemption pursuant to sections 873(b)(3) and 151 regardless

of whether the income is effectively connected. For purposes of withholding under section 1441 on remuneration for personal services, the exemption must be prorated upon a daily basis for the period during which the personal services are performed within the United States by the nonresident alien individual by dividing by 365 the number of days in the period during which the individual is present in the United States for the purpose of performing the services and multiplying the result by the amount of the personal exemption in effect for the taxable year. See § 31.3402(f)(6)-1 of this chapter.

(ii) Multiple exemptions. More than one personal exemption may be claimed in the case of a resident of a contiguous country or a national of the United States under section 873(b)(3). In addition, residents of a country with which the United States has an income tax treaty in effect may be eligible to claim more than one personal exemption if the treaty so provides. Claims for more than one personal exemption shall be made on the withholding certificate furnished to the withholding agent. The exemption must be prorated on a daily basis in the same manner as described in paragraph (b)(6)(i) of this section.

(iii) Special rule where both certain scholarship and compensation income are received. The fact that both non-compensatory scholarship income and compensation income (including compensatory scholarship income) are received during the taxable year does not entitle the taxpayer to claim more than one personal exemption amount (or more than the additional amounts permitted under paragraph (b)(6)(ii) of this section). Thus, if a nonresident alien student receives non-compensatory taxable scholarship income from one withholding agent and compensation income from another withholding agent, no more than the total personal exemption amount permitted under the Internal Revenue Code or under an income tax treaty may be taken into account by both withholding agents. For this purpose, the withholding agent may rely on a representation from the beneficial owner that the exemption amount claimed does not exceed the amount permissible under this section.

(c) Special rules for scholarship and fellowship income. *(1) In general.* Under section 871(c), certain amounts paid as a scholarship or fellowship for study, training, or research in the United States to a nonresident alien individual temporarily present in the United States as a nonimmigrant under section 101(a)(15)(F), (J), (M), or (Q) of the Immigration and Nationality Act are treated as income effectively connected with the conduct of a trade or business within the United States. The amounts described in the preceding sentence are those amounts that do not represent compensation for services. Such amounts (as described in the second sentence of section 1441(b)) are subject to withholding under section 1441, but at the lower rate of 14 percent. That rate may be reduced under the provisions of an income tax treaty. Claims of a reduced rate under an income tax treaty shall be made under the procedures described in § 1.1441-6(b)(1). Therefore, claims for reduction in withholding under an income tax treaty on amounts described in this paragraph (c)(1) may not be made on a Form 8233. However, if the payee is receiving both compensation for personal services (including compensatory scholarship income) and non-compensatory scholarship income described in this paragraph (c)(1) from the same withholding agent, claims for reduction of withholding on both types of income may be made on Form 8233.

(2) Alternate withholding election. A withholding agent may elect to withhold on the amounts described in paragraph (c)(1) of this section at the rates applicable under section 3402, as if the income were wages. Such election shall be made by obtaining a Form W-4 (or an acceptable substitute or such other form as the IRS may prescribe) from the beneficial owner. The fact that the withholding agent asks the beneficial owner to furnish a Form W-4 for such fellowship or scholarship income or to take such income into account in preparing such Form W-4 shall serve as notice to the beneficial owner that the income is being treated as wages for purposes of withholding tax under section 1441.

(d) Annuities received under qualified plans. Withholding is not required under § 1.1441-1 in the case of any amount received as an annuity if the amount is exempt from tax under section 871(f) and the regulations under that section. The withholding agent may exempt the payment from withholding if, prior to payment, it can reliably associate the payment with documentation upon which it can rely to treat the payment as made to a beneficial owner in accordance with § 1.1441-1(e)(1)(ii). A beneficial owner withholding certificate furnished for purposes of claiming the benefits of the exemption under this paragraph (d) is valid only if, in addition to other applicable requirements, it contains a taxpayer identifying number.

(e) Per diem of certain alien trainees. Withholding is not required under section 1441(a) and § 1.1441-1 on per diem amounts paid for subsistence by the United States Government (directly or by contract) to any nonresident alien individual who is engaged in any program of training in the United States under the Mutual Security Act of 1954, as amended (22 U.S.C. chapter 24). This rule shall apply even though such amounts are subject to tax under section 871. Any exemption from withholding pursuant to this paragraph (e) applies without a requirement that documentation be furnished to the withholding agent. However, documentation may have to be furnished for purposes of the information reporting provisions under section 6041 and backup withholding under section 3406. The exemption from withholding granted by this paragraph (e) is not a determination that the amounts are not fixed or determinable annual or periodical income.

(f) Failure to receive withholding certificates timely or to act in accordance with applicable presumptions. See applicable procedures described in § 1.1441-1(b)(7) in the event the withholding agent does not hold an appropriate withholding certificate or other appropriate documentation at the time of payment or does not act in accordance with applicable presumptions described in paragraph (a)(2)(i), (2)(ii), or (3) of this section.

(g) Effective date. *(1) General rule.* This section applies to payments made after December 31, 2000.

(2) Transition rules. The validity of a Form 4224 or 8233 that was valid on January 1, 1998, under the regulations in effect prior to January 1, 2001 (see 26 CFR part 1, revised April 1, 1999) and expired, or will expire, at any time during 1998, is extended until December 31, 1998. The validity of a Form 4224 or 8233 that is valid on or after January 1, 1999, remains valid until its validity expires under the regulations in effect prior to January 1, 2001 (see 26 CFR part 1, revised April 1, 1999) but in no event will such form remain valid after December 31, 2000. The rule in this paragraph (g)(2), however, does not apply to extend the validity period of a Form 4224 or 8223 that expires solely by reason of changes in the circumstances of the person whose name is on the certificate. Notwithstanding the first three sentences of this paragraph (g)(2), a withholding agent may choose to not take advantage of the transition rule in this paragraph

(g)(2) with respect to one or more withholding certificates valid under the regulations in effect prior to January 1, 2001 (see 26 CFR part 1, revised April 1, 1999) and, therefore, to require withholding certificates conforming to the requirements described in this section (new withholding certificates). For purposes of this section, a new withholding certificate is deemed to satisfy the documentation requirement under the regulations in effect prior to January 1, 2001 (see 26 CFR part 1, revised April 1, 1999). Further, a new withholding certificate remains valid for the period specified in § 1.1441-1(e)(4)(ii), regardless of when the certificate is obtained.

T.D. 6187, 7/5/56, amend T.D. 6229, 4/22/57, T.D. 6592, 2/27/62, T.D. 6908, 12/30/66, T.D. 6922, 6/16/67, T.D. 7378, 9/29/75, T.D. 7582, 1/2/79, T.D. 7777, 5/18/81, T.D. 7842, 11/2/82, T.D. 7977, 9/19/84, T.D. 8015, 3/25/85, T.D. 8288, 2/2/90, T.D. 8734, 10/6/97, T.D. 8804, 12/30/98, T.D. 8856, 12/29/99, T.D. 8881, 5/15/2000.

§ 1.1441-5 Withholding on payments to partnerships, trusts, and estates.

(a) In general. This section describes the rules that apply to payments made to partnerships, trusts, and estates. Paragraph (b) of this section prescribes the rules that apply to a withholding agent making a payment to a U.S. partnership, trust, or estate. It also prescribes the obligations of a U.S. partnership, trust, or estate that makes a payment to a foreign partner, beneficiary, or owner. Paragraph (c) of this section prescribes rules that apply to a withholding agent that makes a payment to a foreign partnership. Paragraph (d) of this section provides presumption rules that apply to payments made to foreign partnerships. Paragraph (e) of this section prescribes rules, including presumption rules, that apply to a withholding agent that makes a payment to a foreign trust or foreign estate.

(b) Rules applicable to U.S. partnerships, trusts, and estates. *(1) Payments to U.S. partnerships, trusts, and estates.* No withholding is required under section 1.1441-1(b)(1) on a payment of an amount subject to withholding (as defined in § 1.1441-2(a)) that a withholding agent may treat as made to a U.S. payee. Therefore, if a withholding agent can reliably associate (within the meaning of § 1.1441-2(b)(vii)) a Form W-9 provided in accordance with § 1.1441-1(d)(2) or (4) by a U.S. partnership, U.S. trust, or a U.S. estate the withholding agent may treat the payment as made to a U.S. payee and the payment is not subject to withholding under section 1441 even though the partnership, trust, or estate may have foreign partners, beneficiaries, or owners. A withholding agent is also not required to withhold under section 1441 on a payment it makes to an entity presumed to be a U.S. payee under paragraphs (d)(2) and (e)(6)(ii) of this section.

(2) Withholding by U.S. payees. (i) U.S. partnerships. (A) In general. A U.S. partnership is required to withhold under § 1.1441-1 as a withholding agent on an amount subject to withholding (as defined in § 1.1441-2(a)) that is includible in the gross income of a partner that is a foreign person. Subject to paragraph (b)(2)(v) of this section, a U.S. partnership shall withhold when any distributions that include amounts subject to withholding (including guaranteed payments made by a U.S. partnership) are made. To the extent a foreign partner's distributive share of income subject to withholding has not actually been distributed to the foreign partner, the U.S. partnership must withhold on the foreign partner's distributive share of the income on the earlier of the date that the statement required under section 6031(b) is mailed or otherwise provided to the partner or the due date for furnishing the statement.

(B) Effectively connected income of partners. Withholding on items of income that are effectively connected income in the hands of the partners who are foreign persons is governed by section 1446 and not by this section. In such a case, partners in a domestic partnership are not required to furnish a withholding certificate in order to claim an exemption from withholding under section 1441(c)(1) and § 1.1441-4.

(ii) U.S. simple trusts. A U.S. trust that is described in section 651(a) (a U.S. simple trust) is required to withhold under chapter 3 of the Internal Revenue Code as a withholding agent on the distributable net income includible in the gross income of a foreign beneficiary to the extent the distributable net income is an amount subject to withholding (as defined in § 1.1441-2(a)). A U.S. simple trust shall withhold when a distribution is made to a foreign beneficiary. The U.S. trust may make a reasonable estimate of the portion of the distribution that constitutes distributable net income consisting of an amount subject to withholding and apply the appropriate rate of withholding to the estimated amount. If, at the end of the taxable year in which the distribution is made, the U.S. simple trust determines that it underwithheld under section 1441 or 1442, the trust shall be liable as a withholding agent for the amount under withheld under section 1461. No penalties shall be imposed for failure to withhold and deposit the tax if the U.S. simple trust's estimate was reasonable and the trust pays the underwithheld amount on or before the due date of Form 1042 under section 1461. Any payment of underwithheld amounts by the U.S. simple trust shall not be treated as income subject to additional withholding even if that amount is treated as additional income to the foreign beneficiary, unless the additional amount is income to the foreign beneficiary as a result of a contractual arrangement between the parties regarding the satisfaction of the foreign beneficiary's tax liability. To the extent a U.S. simple trust is required to, but does not, distribute such income to a foreign beneficiary, the U.S. trust must withhold on the foreign beneficiary's allocable share at the time the income is required (without extension) to be reported on Form 1042-S under § 1.1461-1(c).

(iii) U.S. complex trusts and U.S. estates. A U.S. trust that is not a trust described in section 651(a) (a U.S. complex trust) is required to withhold under chapter 3 of the Internal Revenue Code as a withholding agent on the distributable net income includible in the gross income of a foreign beneficiary to the extent the distributable net income consists of an amount subject to withholding (as defined in § 1.1441-2(a)) that is, or is required to be, distributed currently. The U.S. complex trust shall withhold when a distribution is made to a foreign beneficiary. The trust may use the same procedures regarding an estimate of the amount subject to withholding as a U.S. simple trust under paragraph (b)(2)(ii) of this section. To the extent an amount subject to withholding is required to be, but is not actually distributed, the U.S. complex trust must withhold on the foreign beneficiary's allocable share at the time the income is required to be reported on Form 1042-S under § 1.1461-1(c), without extension. A U.S. estate is required to withhold under chapter 3 of the Internal Revenue Code on the distributable net income includible in the gross income of a foreign beneficiary to the extent the distributable net income consists of an amount subject to withholding (as defined in § 1.1441-2(a)) that is actually distributed. A U.S. estate may also use the reasonable estimate procedures of paragraph (b)(2)(ii) of this section. However, those procedures apply to an estate that has a taxable year other than a calendar year only if the estate files an amended return on Form 1042 for the calendar year in which the distribution was made and pays the underwithheld tax and interest within 60 days after the close of the taxable year in which the distribution was made.

(iv) U.S. grantor trusts. A U.S. trust that is described in section 671 through 679 (a U.S. grantor trust) must withhold on any income includible in the gross income of a foreign person that is treated as an owner of the grantor trust to the extent the amount includible consists of an amount that is subject to withholding (as described in § 1.1441-2(a)). The withholding must occur at the time the income is received by, or credited to, the trust.

(v) Subsequent distribution. If a U.S. partnership or U.S. trust withholds on a foreign partner, beneficiary, or owner's share of an amount subject to withholding before the amount is actually distributed to the partner, beneficiary, or owner, withholding is not required when the amount is subsequently distributed.

(c) Foreign partnerships. *(1) Determination of payee.* (i) Payments treated as made to partners. Except as otherwise provided in paragraph (c)(1)(ii) of this section, the payees of a payment to a person that the withholding agent may treat as a nonwithholding foreign partnership under paragraph (c)(3)(i) or (d)(2) of this section are the partners (looking through partners that are foreign intermediaries or flow-through entities) as follows—

(A) If the withholding agent can reliably associate a partner's distributive share of the payment with a valid Form W-9 provided under § 1.1441-1(d), the partner is a U.S. payee;

(B) If the withholding agent can reliably associate a partner's distributive share of the payment with a valid Form W-8, or other appropriate documentation, provided under § 1.1441-1(e)(1)(ii), the partner is a payee that is a foreign beneficial owner;

(C) If the withholding agent can reliably associate a partner's distributive share of the payment with a qualified intermediary withholding certificate under § 1.1441-1(e)(3)(ii), a nonqualified intermediary withholding certificate under § 1.1441-1(e)(3)(iii), or a U.S. branch certificate under § 1.1441-1(e)(3)(v), then the rules of § 1.1441-1(b)(2)(v) shall apply to determine who the payee is in the same manner as if the partner's distributive share of the payment had been paid directly to such intermediary or U.S. branch;

(D) If the withholding agent can reliably associate the partner's distributive share with a withholding foreign partnership certificate under paragraph (c)(2)(iv) of this section or a nonwithholding foreign partnership certificate under paragraph (c)(3)(iii) of this section, then the rules of this paragraph (c)(1)(i) or paragraph (c)(1)(ii) of this section shall apply to determine whether the payment is treated as made to the partners of the higher-tier partnership under this paragraph (c)(1)(i) or to the higher-tier partnership itself (under the rules of paragraph (c)(1)(ii) of this section) in the same manner as if the partner's distributive share of the payment had been paid directly to the higher-tier foreign partnership;

(E) If the withholding agent can reliably associate the partner's distributive share with a withholding certificate described in paragraph (e) of this section regarding a foreign trust or estate, then the rules of paragraph (e) of this section shall apply to determine who the payees are; and

(F) If the withholding agent cannot reliably associate the partner's distributive share with a withholding certificate or other appropriate documentation, the partners are considered to be the payees and the presumptions described in paragraph (d)(3) of this section shall apply to determine their classification and status.

(ii) Payments treated as made to the partnership. A payment to a person that the withholding agent may treat as a foreign partnership is treated as a payment to the foreign partnership and not to its partners only if—

(A) The withholding agent can reliably associate the payment with a withholding certificate described in paragraph (c)(2)(iv) of this section (withholding certificate of a withholding foreign partnership);

(B) The withholding agent can reliably associate the payment with a withholding certificate described in paragraph (c)(3)(iii) of this section (nonwithholding foreign partnership) certifying that the payment is income that is effectively connected with the conduct of a trade or business in the United States; or

(C) The withholding agent can treat the income as effectively connected income under the presumption rules of § 1.1441-4(a)(2)(ii) or (3)(i).

(iii) Rules for reliably associating a payment with documentation . For rules regarding the reliable association of a payment with documentation, see § 1.1441-1(b)(2)(vii). In the absence of documentation, see §§ 1.1441-1(b)(3) and 1.6049-5(d) and paragraphs (d) and (e)(6) of this section for applicable presumptions.

(iv) Examples.The rules of paragraphs (c)(1)(i) and (ii) of this section are illustrated by the following examples:

Example (1). FP is a nonwithholding foreign partnership organized in Country X. FP has two partners, FC, a foreign corporation, and USP, a U.S. partnership. USWH, a U.S. withholding agent, makes a payment of U.S. source interest to FP. FP has provided USWH with a valid nonwithholding foreign partnership certificate, as described in paragraph (c)(3)(iii) of this section, with which it associates a beneficial owner withholding certificate from FC and a Form W-9 from USP together with the withholding statement required by paragraph (c)(3)(iv) of this section. USWH can reliably associate the payment of interest with the withholding certificates from FC and USP. Under paragraph (c)(1)(i) of this section, the payees of the interest payment are FC and USP.

Example (2). The facts are the same as in Example 1, except that FP1, a nonwithholding foreign partnership, is a partner in FP rather than USP. FP1 has two partners, A and B, both foreign persons. FP provides USWH with a valid nonwithholding foreign partnership certificate, as described in paragraph (c)(3)(iii) of this section, with which it associates a beneficial owner withholding certificate from FC and a nonwithholding foreign partnership certificate from FP1. In addition, foreign beneficial owner withholding certificates from A and B are associated with the nonwithholding foreign partnership withholding certificate from FP1. FP also provides the withholding statement required by paragraph (c)(3)(iv) of this section. USWH can reliably associate the interest payment with the withholding certificates provided by FC, A, and B. Therefore, under paragraph (c)(1)(i) of this section, the payees of the interest payment are FC, A, and B.

Example (3). USWH makes a payment of U.S. source dividends to WFP, a withholding foreign partnership. WFP has two partners, FC1 and FC2, both foreign corporations. USWH can reliably associate the payment with a valid withholding foreign partnership withholding certificate from WFP. Therefore, under paragraph (c)(1)(ii)(A) of this section, WFP is the payee of the dividends.

Example (4). USWH makes a payment of U.S. source royalties to FP, a foreign partnership. USWH can reliably associate the royalties with a valid withholding certificate from FP on which FP certifies that the income is effectively connected with the conduct of a trade or business in the United States. Therefore, under paragraph (c)(1)(ii)(B) of this section, FP is the payee of the royalties.

(2) Withholding foreign partnerships. (i) Reliance on claim of withholding foreign partnership status . A withholding foreign partnership is a foreign partnership that has entered into an agreement with the Internal Revenue Service (IRS), as described in paragraph (c)(2)(ii) of this section, with respect to distributions and guaranteed payments it makes to its partners. A withholding agent that can reliably associate a payment with a certificate described in paragraph (c)(2)(iv) of this section may treat the person to whom it makes the payment as a withholding foreign partnership for purposes of withholding under chapter 3 of the Internal Revenue Code, information reporting under chapter 61 of the Internal Revenue Code, backup withholding under section 3406, and withholding under other provisions of the Internal Revenue Code. Furnishing such a certificate is in lieu of transmitting to a withholding agent withholding certificates or other appropriate documentation for its partners. Although the withholding foreign partnership generally will be required to obtain withholding certificates or other appropriate documentation from its partners pursuant to its agreement with the IRS, it will generally not be required to attach such documentation to its withholding foreign partnership withholding certificate. A foreign partnership may act as a qualified intermediary under § 1.1441-1(e)(5) with respect to payments it makes to persons other than its partners. In addition, the IRS may permit a foreign partnership to act as a qualified intermediary under § 1.1441-1(e)(5)(ii)(D) with respect to its partners in appropriate circumstances.

(ii) Withholding agreement. The IRS may, upon request, enter into a withholding agreement with a foreign partnership pursuant to such procedures as the IRS may prescribe in published guidance (see § 601.601(d)(2) of this chapter). Under the withholding agreement, a foreign partnership shall generally be subject to the applicable withholding and reporting provisions applicable to withholding agents and payors under chapters 3 and 61 of the Internal Revenue Code, section 3406, the regulations under those provisions, and other withholding provisions of the Internal Revenue Code, except to the extent provided under the agreement. Under the agreement, a foreign partnership may agree to act as an acceptance agent to perform the duties described in § 301.6109-1(d)(3)(iv)(A) of this chapter. The agreement may specify the manner in which applicable procedures for adjustments for underwithholding and overwithholding, including refund procedures, apply to the withholding foreign partnership and its partners and the extent to which applicable procedures may be modified. In particular, a withholding agreement may allow a withholding foreign partnership to claim refunds of overwithheld amounts on behalf of its customers. In addition, the agreement must specify the manner in which the IRS will audit the foreign partnership's books and records in order to verify the partnership's compliance with its agreement. A withholding foreign partnership must file a return on Form 1042 and information returns on Form 1042-S. The withholding foreign partnership agreement may also require a withholding foreign partnership to file a partnership return under section 6031(a) and partner statements under 6031(b).

(iii) Withholding responsibility. A withholding foreign partnership must assume primary withholding responsibility under chapter 3 of the Internal Revenue Code. It is not required to provide information to the withholding agent regarding each partner's distributive share of the payment. The withholding foreign partnership will be responsible for reporting the payments under § 1.1461-1(c) and chapter 61 of the Internal Revenue Code. A withholding agent making a payment to a withholding foreign partnership is not required to withhold any amount under chapter 3 of the Internal Revenue Code on a payment to the withholding foreign partnership, unless it has actual knowledge or reason to know that the foreign partnership is not a withholding foreign partnership. The withholding foreign partnership shall withhold the payments under the same procedures and at the same time as prescribed for withholding by a U.S. partnership under paragraph (b)(2) of this section, except that, for purposes of determining the partner's status, the provisions of paragraph (d)(4) of this section shall apply.

(iv) Withholding certificate from a withholding foreign partnership. The rules of § 1.1441-1(e)(4) shall apply to withholding certificates described in this paragraph (c)(2)(iv). A withholding certificate furnished by a withholding foreign partnership is valid with regard to any partner on whose behalf the certificate is furnished only if it is furnished on a Form W-8, an acceptable substitute form, or such other form as the IRS may prescribe, it is signed under penalties of perjury by a partner with authority to sign for the partnership, its validity has not expired, and it contains the information, statement, and certifications described in this paragraph (c)(2)(iv) as follows—

(A) The name, permanent residence address (as described in § 1.1441-1(e)(2)(ii)), and the employer identification number of the partnership, and the country under the laws of which the partnership is created or governed;

(B) A certification that the partnership is a withholding foreign partnership within the meaning of paragraph (c)(2)(i) of this section; and

(C) Any other information, certifications or statements as may be required by the withholding foreign partnership agreement with the IRS or the form or accompanying instructions in addition to, or in lieu of, the information, statements, and certifications described in this paragraph (c)(2)(iv).

(3) Nonwithholding foreign partnerships. (i) Reliance on claim of foreign partnership status. A withholding agent may treat a person as a nonwithholding foreign partnership if it receives from that person a nonwithholding foreign partnership withholding certificate as described in paragraph (c)(3)(iii) of this section. A withholding agent that does not receive a nonwithholding foreign partnership withholding certificate, or does not receive a valid withholding certificate, from an entity it knows, or has reason to know, is a foreign partnership, must apply the presumption rules of §§ 1.1441-1(b)(3) and 1.6049-5(d) and paragraphs (d) and (e)(6) of this section. In addition, to the extent a withholding agent cannot, prior to a payment, reliably associate the payment with valid documentation from a payee that is associated with the nonwithholding foreign partnership withholding certificate or has insufficient information to report the payment on Form 1042-S or Form 1099, to the extent reporting is required, must also apply the presumption rules. See § 1.1441-1(b)(2)(vii)(A) and (B) for rules regarding reliable association. See paragraph (c)(3)(iv) of this section and § 1.1441-1(e)(3)(iv) for alternative procedures permitting allocation information to be received after a payment is made.

(ii) Reliance on claim of reduced withholding by a partnership for its partners. This paragraph (c)(3)(ii) describes the manner in which a withholding agent may rely on a claim of reduced withholding when making a payment to a nonwithholding foreign partnership. To the extent that a withholding agent treats a payment to a nonwithholding foreign partnership as a payment to the nonwithholding foreign partnership's partners (whether direct or indirect) in accordance with paragraph (c)(1)(i) of this section, it may rely on a claim for reduced withholding by the partner if, prior to the payment, the withholding agent can reliably associate the payment (within the meaning of § 1.1441-1(b)(2)(vii)) with a valid withholding certificate or other appropriate documentation from the partner that establishes entitlement to a reduced rate of withholding. A withholding certificate or other appropriate documentation that establishes entitlement to a reduced rate of withholding is a beneficial owner withholding certificate described in § 1.1441-1(e)(2)(i), documentary evidence described in § 1.1441-6(c)(3) or (4) or 1.6049-5(c)(1) (for a partner claiming to be a foreign person and a beneficial owner, determined under the provisions of § 1.1441-1(c)(6)), a Form W-9 described in § 1.1441-1(d) (for a partner claiming to be a U.S. payee), or a withholding foreign partnership withholding certificate described in paragraph (c)(2)(iv) of this section. Unless a nonwithholding foreign partnership withholding certificate is provided for income claimed to be effectively connected with the conduct of a trade or business in the United States, a claim must be presented for each portion of the payment that represents an item of income includible in the distributive share of a partner as required under paragraph (c)(3)(iii)(C) of this section. When making a claim for several partners, the partnership may present a single nonwithholding foreign partnership withholding certificate to which the partners' certificates or other appropriate documentation are associated. Where the nonwithholding foreign partnership withholding certificate is provided for income claimed to be effectively connected with the conduct of a trade or business in the United States under paragraph (c)(3)(iii)(D) of this section, the claim may be presented without having to identify any partner's distributive share of the payment.

(iii) Withholding certificate from a nonwithholding foreign partnership. A nonwithholding foreign partnership shall provide a nonwithholding foreign partnership withholding certificate with respect to reportable amounts received by the nonwithholding foreign partnership. A nonwithholding foreign partnership withholding certificate is valid only to the extent it is furnished on a Form W-8 (or an acceptable substitute form or such other form as the IRS may prescribe), it is signed under penalties of perjury by a partner with authority to sign for the partnership, its validity has not expired, and it contains the information, statements, and certifications described in this paragraph (c)(3)(iii) and paragraph (c)(3)(iv) of this section, and the withholding certificates and other appropriate documentation for all the persons to whom the certificate relates are associated with the certificate. The rules of § 1.1441-1(e)(4) shall apply to withholding certificates described in this paragraph (c)(3)(iii). No withholding certificates or other appropriate documentation from persons who derive income through a partnership (whether or not U.S. exempt recipients) are required to be associated with the nonwithholding foreign partnership withholding certificate if the certificate is furnished solely for income claimed to be effectively connected with the conduct of a trade or business in the United States. Withholding certificates and other appropriate documentation that may be associated with the nonwithholding foreign partnership withholding certificate consist of beneficial owner withholding certificates under § 1.1441-1(e)(2)(i), intermediary withholding certificates under § 1.1441-1(e)(3)(i), withholding foreign partnership withholding certificates under paragraph (c)(2)(iv) of this section, nonwithholding foreign partnership withholding certificates under this paragraph (c)(3)(iii), withholding certificates from foreign trusts or estates under paragraph (e) of this section, documentary evidence described in § 1.1441-6(c)(3) or (4) or documentary evidence described in § 1.6049-5(c)(1), and any other documentation or certificates applicable under other provisions of the Internal Revenue Code or regulations that certify or establish the status of the payee or beneficial owner as a U.S. or a foreign person. Nothing in this paragraph (c)(3)(iii) shall require a nonwithholding foreign partnership to furnish original documentation. Copies of certificates or documentary evidence may be transmitted to the U.S. withholding agent, in which case the nonwithholding foreign partnership must retain the original documentation for the same time period that the copy is required to be retained by the withholding agent under § 1.1441-1(e)(4)(iii) and must provide it to the withholding agent upon request. The information, statement, and certifications required on the withholding certificate are as follows—

(A) The name, permanent residence address (as described in § 1.1441-1(e)(2)(ii)), and the employer identification number of the partnership, if any, and the country under the laws of which the partnership is created or governed;

(B) A certification that the person whose name is on the certificate is a foreign partnership;

(C) A withholding statement associated with the nonwithholding foreign partnership withholding certificate that provides all of the information required by paragraph (c)(3)(iv) of this section and § 1.1441-1(e)(3)(iv). No withholding statement is required, however, for a nonwithholding foreign partnership withholding certificate furnished for income claimed to be effectively connected with the conduct of a trade or business in the United States;

(D) A certification that the income is effectively connected with the conduct of a trade or business in the United States, if applicable; and

(E) Any other information, certifications, or statements required by the form or accompanying instructions in addition to, or in lieu of, the information and certifications described in this paragraph (c)(3)(iii).

(iv) Withholding statement provided by nonwithholding foreign partnership. The provisions of § 1.1441-1(e)(3)(iv) (regarding a withholding statement) shall apply to a nonwithholding foreign partnership by substituting the term nonwithholding foreign partnership for the term nonqualified intermediary.

(v) Withholding and reporting by a foreign partnership. A nonwithholding foreign partnership described in this paragraph (c)(3) that receives an amount subject to withholding (as defined in § 1.1441-2(a)) shall be required to withhold and report such payment under chapter 3 of the Internal Revenue Code and the regulations thereunder except as otherwise provided in this paragraph (c)(3)(v). A nonwithholding foreign partnership shall not be required to withhold and report if it has provided a valid nonwithholding foreign partnership withholding certificate, it has provided all of the information required by paragraph (c)(3)(iv) of this section (withholding statement), and it does not know, and has no reason to know, that another withholding agent failed to withhold the correct amount or failed to report the payment correctly under § 1.1461-1(c). A withholding foreign partnership's obligations to withhold and report shall be determined in accordance with its withholding foreign partnership agreement.

(d) Presumption rules. *(1) In general.* This paragraph (d) contains the applicable presumptions for a withholding agent (including a partnership) to determine the classification and status of a partnership and its partners in the absence of documentation. The provisions of § 1.1441-1(b)(3)(iv) (regarding the 90-day grace period) and § 1.1441-1(b)(3)(vii) through (ix) shall apply for purposes of this paragraph (d).

(2) Determination of partnership status as U.S. or foreign in the absence of documentation. In the absence of a valid representation of U.S. partnership status in accordance with paragraph (b)(1) of this section or of foreign partnership status in accordance with paragraph (c)(2)(i) or (3)(i) of this section, the withholding agent shall determine the classification of the payee under the presumptions set forth in § 1.1441-1(b)(3)(ii). If the withholding agent treats the payee as a partnership under § 1.1441-1(b)(3)(ii), the withholding agent shall presume the partnership to be a U.S. partnership unless there are indicia of foreign status. If there are indicia of foreign status, the withholding agent may presume the partnership to be foreign. Indicia of foreign status exist only if the withholding agent has actual knowledge of the payee's employer identification number and that number begins with the two digits "98," the withholding agent's communications with the payee are mailed to an address in a foreign country, or the payment is made outside the United States (as defined in § 1.6049-5(e)). For rules regarding reliable association with a withholding certificate from a domestic or a foreign partnership, see § 1.1441-1(b)(2)(vii).

(3) Determination of partners' status in the absence of certain documentation. If a nonwithholding foreign partnership has provided a nonwithholding foreign partnership withholding certificate under paragraph (c)(3)(iii) of this section that would be valid except that the withholding agent cannot reliably associate all or a portion of the payment with valid documentation from a partner of the partnership, then the withholding agent may apply the presumption rule of this paragraph (d)(3) with respect to all or a portion of the payment for which documentation has not been received. See § 1.1441-1(b)(2)(vii)(A) and (B) for rules regarding reliable association. The presumption rule of this paragraph (d)(3) also applies to a person that is presumed to be a foreign partnership under the rule of paragraph (d)(2) of this section. Any portion of a payment that the withholding agent cannot treat as reliably associated with valid documentation from a partner may be presumed made to a foreign payee. As a result, any payment of an amount subject to withholding is subject to withholding at a rate of 30 percent. Any payment that is presumed to be made to an undocumented foreign payee must be reported on Form 1042-S. See § 1.1461-1(c).

(4) Determination by a withholding foreign partnership of the status of its partners. A withholding foreign partnership shall determine whether the partners or some other persons are the payees of the partners' distributive shares of any payment made by a withholding foreign partnership by applying the rules of § 1.1441-1(b)(2), paragraph (c)(1) of this section (in the case of a partner that is a foreign partnership), and paragraph (e)(3) of this section (in the case of a partner that is a foreign estate or a foreign trust). Further, the provisions of paragraph (d)(3) of this section shall apply to determine the status of partners and the applicable withholding rates to the extent that, at the time the foreign partnership is required to withhold on a payment, it cannot reliably associate the amount with documentation for any one or more of its partners.

(e) Foreign trusts and estates. *(1) In general.* This paragraph (e) provides rules applicable to payments of amounts subject to withholding (as defined in § 1.1441-2(a)) that a withholding agent may treat as made to any foreign trust or a foreign estate. For rules relating to payments to a U.S. trust or a U.S. estate, see paragraph (b) of this section. For the definitions of foreign simple trust, foreign complex trust, and foreign grantor trust, see § 1.1441-1(c)(24), (25), and (26).

(2) Payments to foreign complex trusts and foreign estates. Under § 1.1441-1(c)(6)(ii)(D), a foreign complex trust or foreign estate is generally considered to be the beneficial owner of income paid to the foreign complex trust or foreign estate. See paragraph (e)(4) of this section for rules describing when a withholding agent may treat a payment as made to a foreign complex trust or a foreign estate.

(3) Payees of payments to foreign simple trusts and foreign grantor trusts. (i) Payments for which beneficiaries and owners are payees. For purposes of the regulations under chapters 3 and 61 of the Internal Revenue Code and section 3406, a foreign simple trust is not a beneficial owner or a payee of a payment. Also, a foreign grantor trust (or a portion of a trust that is a foreign grantor trust) is not considered a beneficial owner or a payee of a payment. Except as otherwise provided in paragraph (e)(3)(ii) of this section, the payees of a payment made to a person that the withholding agent may treat as a foreign simple trust or a foreign grantor trust (or a portion of a trust that is a foreign grantor trust) are determined under the rules of this paragraph (e)(3)(i). The payees shall be treated as the beneficial owners if they may be so treated under § 1.1441-1(c)(6)(ii)(C) and they provide documentation supporting their status as the beneficial owners. The payees of a payment to a foreign simple trust or foreign grantor trust are determined as follows—

(A) If the withholding agent can reliably associate a payment with a valid Form W-9 provided under § 1.1441-1(d) from a beneficiary or owner of the foreign trust, then the beneficiary or owner is a U.S. payee;

(B) If the withholding agent can reliably associate a payment with a valid Form W-8, or other appropriate documentation, provided under § 1.1441-1(e)(1)(ii) from a beneficiary or owner of the foreign trust, then the beneficiary or owner is a payee that is a foreign beneficial owner;

(C) If the withholding agent can reliably associate a payment with a qualified intermediary withholding certificate under § 1.1441-1(e)(3)(ii), a nonqualified intermediary withholding certificate under § 1.1441-1(e)(3)(ii), or a U.S. branch withholding certificate under § 1.1441-1(e)(3)(v), then the rules of § 1.1441-1(b)(2)(v) shall apply to determine the payee in the same manner as if the payment had been paid directly to such intermediary or U.S. branch;

(D) If the withholding agent can reliably associate a payment with a withholding foreign partnership withholding certificate under paragraph (c)(2)(iv) of this section or a nonwithholding foreign partnership withholding certificate under paragraph (c)(3)(iii) of this section, then the rules of paragraph (c)(1)(i) or (ii) of this section shall apply to determine the payee;

(E) If the withholding agent can reliably associate the payment with a foreign simple trust withholding certificate or a foreign grantor trust withholding certificate (both described in paragraph (e)(5)(iii) of this section) from a second or higher-tier foreign simple trust or foreign grantor trust, then the rules of this paragraph (e)(3)(i) or paragraph (e)(3)(ii) of this section shall apply to determine whether the payment is treated as made to a beneficiary or owner of the higher-tier trust or to the trust itself in the same manner as if the payment had been made directly to the higher-tier trust; and

(F) If the withholding agent cannot reliably associate a payment with a withholding certificate or other appropriate documentation, the payees shall be determined by applying the presumptions described in paragraph (e)(6) of this section.

(ii) Payments for which trust is payee. A payment to a person that the withholding agent may treat as made to a foreign trust under paragraph (e)(5)(iii) of this section is treated as a payment to the trust, and not to a beneficiary of the trust, only if—

(A) The withholding agent can reliably associate the payment with a foreign complex trust withholding certificate under paragraph (e)(4) of this section;

(B) The withholding agent can reliably associate the payment with a foreign simple trust withholding certificate under paragraph (e)(5)(iii) of this section certifying that the payment is income that is treated as effectively connected with the conduct of a trade or business in the United States; or

(C) The withholding agent can treat the income as effectively connected income under the presumption rules of § 1.1441-4(a)(3)(i).

(4) Reliance on claim of foreign complex trust or foreign estate status. A withholding agent may treat a payment as made to a foreign complex trust or a foreign estate if the withholding agent can reliably associate the payment with a beneficial owner withholding certificate described in § 1.1441-1(e)(2)(i) or other documentary evidence under § 1.1441-6(c)(3) or (4) (regarding a claim for treaty benefits) or § 1.6049-5(c)(1) (regarding documentary evidence to establish foreign status for purposes of chapter 61 of the Internal Revenue Code) that establishes the foreign complex trust or foreign estate's status as a beneficial owner. See paragraph (e)(6) of this section for presumption rules if documentation is lacking.

(5) Foreign simple trust and foreign grantor trust. (i) Reliance on claim of foreign simple trust or foreign grantor trust status. A withholding agent may treat a person as a foreign simple trust or foreign grantor trust if it receives from that person a foreign simple trust or foreign grantor trust withholding certificate as described in paragraph (e)(5)(iii) of this section. A withholding agent must apply the presumption rules of §§ 1.1441-1(b)(3) and 1.6049-5(d) and paragraphs (d) and (e)(6) of this section to the extent it cannot, prior to the payment, reliably associate a payment (within the meaning of § 1.1441-1(b)(2)(vii)) with a valid foreign simple trust or foreign grantor trust withholding certificate, it cannot reliably determine how much of the payment relates to valid documentation provided by a payee (e.g., a person that is not itself a nonqualified intermediary, flow-through entity, or U.S. branch) associated with the foreign simple trust or foreign grantor trust withholding certificate, or it does not have sufficient information to report the payment on Form 1042-S or Form 1099, if reporting is required. See § 1.1441-1(b)(2)(vii)(A) and (B).

(ii) Reliance on claim of reduced withholding by a foreign simple trust or foreign grantor trust for its beneficiaries or owners. This paragraph (e)(5)(ii) describes the manner in which a withholding agent may rely on a claim of reduced withholding when making a payment to a foreign simple trust or foreign grantor trust. To the extent that a withholding agent treats a payment to a foreign simple trust or foreign grantor trust as a payment to payees other than the trust in accordance with paragraph (e)(3)(i) of this section, it may rely on a claim for reduced withholding by a beneficiary or owner if, prior to the payment, the withholding agent can reliably associate the payment (within the meaning of § 1.1441-1(b)(2)(vii)) with a valid withholding certificate or other appropriate documentation from a payee or beneficial owner that establishes entitlement to a reduced rate of withholding. A withholding certificate or other appropriate documentation that establishes entitlement to a reduced rate of withholding is a beneficial owner withholding certificate described in § 1.1441-1(e)(2)(i) or documentary evidence described in § 1.1441-6(c)(3) or(4) or in § 1.6049-5(c)(1) (for a beneficiary or owner claiming to be a foreign person and a beneficial owner, determined under the provisions of § 1.1441-1(c)(6)), a Form W-9 described in § 1.1441-1(d) (for a beneficiary or owner claiming to be a U.S. payee), or a withholding foreign partnership withholding certificate described in paragraph (c)(2)(iv) of this section. Unless a foreign simple trust or foreign grantor trust withholding certificate is provided for income treated as income effectively connected with the conduct of a trade or business in the United States, a claim must be presented for each payee's portion of the payment. When making a claim for several payees, the trust may present a single foreign simple trust or foreign grantor trust withholding certificate with which the payees' certificates or other appropriate documentation are associated. Where the foreign simple trust or foreign grantor trust withholding certificate is provided for income that is treated as effectively connected with the conduct of a trade or business in the United States under paragraph (e)(5)(iii)(D) of this section, the claim may be presented without having to identify any beneficiary's or grantor's distributive share of the payment.

(iii) Withholding certificate from foreign simple trust or foreign grantor trust. A withholding certificate furnished by a foreign simple trust or a foreign grantor trust that is not a withholding foreign trust (within the meaning of paragraph (e)(5)(v) of this section) is valid only if it is furnished on a Form W-8, an acceptable substitute form, or such other form as the IRS may prescribe, it is signed under penalties of perjury by a trustee, its validity has not expired, it contains the information, statements, and certifications required by this paragraph (e)(5)(iii) and § 1.1441-1(e)(3)(iv), and the withholding certificates or other appropriate documentation for all of the payees (as determined under paragraph (e)(3)(i) of this section) to whom the certificate relates are associated with the foreign simple trust or foreign grantor trust withholding certificate. The rules of § 1.1441-1(e)(4) shall apply to withholding certificates described in this paragraph (e)(5)(iii). No withholding certificates or other appropriate documentation from persons who derive income through a foreign simple trust or a foreign grantor trust (whether or not U.S. exempt recipients) are required to be associated with the foreign simple trust or foreign grantor trust withholding certificate if the certificate is furnished solely for income that is treated as effectively connected with the conduct of a trade or business in the United States. Withholding certificates and other appropriate documentation (as determined under paragraph (e)(3)(i) of this section) that may be associated with a foreign simple trust or foreign grantor trust withholding certificate consist of beneficial owner withholding certificates under § 1.1441-1(e)(2)(i), intermediary withholding certificates under § 1.1441-1(e)(3)(i), withholding foreign partnership withholding certificates under paragraph (c)(2)(iv) of this section, nonwithholding foreign partnership withholding certificates under paragraph (c)(3)(iii) of this section, withholding certificates from foreign trusts or estates under paragraph (e)(4) or (5)(iii) of this section, documentary evidence described in §§ 1.1441-6(c)(3) or (4), or 1.6049-5(c)(1), and any other documentation or certificates applicable under other provisions of the Internal Revenue Code or regulations that certify or establish the status of the payee or beneficial owner as a U.S. or a foreign person. Nothing in this paragraph (e)(5)(iii) shall require a foreign simple trust or foreign grantor trust to provide original documentation. Copies of certificates or documentary evidence may be passed up to the U.S. withholding agent, in which case the foreign simple trust or foreign grantor trust must retain the original documentation for the same time period that the copy is required to be retained by the withholding agent under § 1.1441-1(e)(4)(iii) and must provide it to the withholding agent upon request. The information, statement, and certifications required on a foreign simple trust or foreign grantor trust withholding certificate are as follows—

(A) The name, permanent residence address (as described in § 1.1441-1(e)(2)(ii)), and the employer identification number, if required, of the trust and the country under the laws of which the trust is created;

(B) A certification that the person whose name is on the certificate is a foreign simple trust or a foreign grantor trust;

(C) A withholding statement associated with the foreign simple trust or foreign grantor trust withholding certificate that provides all of the information required by paragraph (e)(5)(iv) of this section. No withholding statement is required, however, for a foreign simple trust withholding certificate furnished for income that is treated as effectively connected with the conduct of a trade or business in the United States;

(D) A certification on a foreign simple trust withholding certificate that the income is treated as effectively connected with the conduct of a trade or business in the United States, if applicable; and

(E) Any other information, certifications, or statements required by the form or accompanying instructions in addition to, or in lieu of, the information, certifications, and statements described in this paragraph (e)(5)(iii);

(iv) Withholding statement provided by a foreign simple trust or foreign grantor trust. The provisions of § 1.1441-1(e)(3)(iv) (regarding a withholding statement) shall apply to a foreign simple trust or foreign grantor trust by substituting the term foreign simple trust or foreign grantor trust for the term nonqualified intermediary.

(v) Withholding foreign trusts. The IRS may enter an agreement with a foreign trust to treat the trust or estate as a withholding foreign trust. Such an agreement shall generally follow the same principles as an agreement with a withholding foreign partnership under paragraph (c)(2)(ii) of this section. A withholding agent may treat a payment to a withholding foreign trust in the same manner the withholding agent would treat a payment to a withholding foreign partnership. The IRS may also enter an agreement to treat a trust as a qualified intermediary in appropriate circumstances. See § 1.1441-1(e)(5)(ii)(D).

(6) Presumption rules. (i) In general. This paragraph (e)(6) contains the applicable presumptions for a withholding agent (including a trust or estate) to determine the classification and status of a trust or estate and its beneficiaries or owners in the absence of valid documentation. The provisions of § 1.1441-1(b)(3)(iv) (regarding the 90-day grace period) and § 1.1441-1(b)(3)(vii) through (ix) shall apply for purposes of this paragraph (e)(6).

(ii) Determination of status as U.S. or foreign trust or estate in the absence of documentation. In the absence of valid documentation that establishes the U.S. status of a trust or estate under paragraph (b)(1) of this section and of documentation that establishes the foreign status of a trust or estate under paragraph (e)(4) or (5)(iii) of this section, the withholding agent shall determine the classification of the payee based upon the presumptions set forth in § 1.1441-1(b)(3)(ii). If, based upon those presumptions, the withholding agent classifies the payee as a trust or estate, the trust or estate shall be presumed to be a U.S. trust or U.S. estate unless there are indicia of foreign status, in which case the trust or estate shall be presumed to be foreign. Indicia of foreign status exists if the withholding agent has actual knowledge of the payee's employer identification number and that number begins with the two digits "98," the withholding agent's communications with the payee are mailed to an address in a foreign country, or the payment is made outside the United States (as defined in § 1.6049-5(e)). If an undocumented payee is presumed to be a foreign trust it shall be presumed to be a foreign complex trust. If a withholding agent has documentary evidence that establishes that an entity is a foreign trust, but the withholding agent cannot determine whether the foreign trust is a complex trust, a simple trust, or foreign grantor trust, the withholding agent may presume that the trust is a foreign complex trust.

(iii) Determination of beneficiary or owner's status in the absence of certain documentation. If a foreign simple trust or foreign grantor trust has provided a foreign simple trust or foreign grantor trust withholding certificate under paragraph (e)(5)(iii) of this section but the payment to such trust cannot be reliably associated with valid documentation from a specific beneficiary or owner of the trust, then any portion of a payment that a withholding agent cannot treat as reliably associated with valid documentation from a beneficiary or owner may be presumed made to a foreign payee. As a result, any payment of an amount subject to withholding is subject to withholding at a rate of 30 percent. Any such payment that is presumed to be made to an undocumented foreign person must be reported on Form 1042-S. See § 1.1461-1(c).

(f) Failure to receive withholding certificate timely or to act in accordance with applicable presumptions. See applicable procedures described in § 1.1441-1(b)(7) in the event the withholding agent does not hold an appropriate withholding certificate or other appropriate documentation at the time of payment or fails to rely on the presumptions set forth in § 1.1441-1(b)(3) or in paragraph (d) or (e) of this section.

(g) Effective date. *(1) General rule.* This section applies to payments made after December 31, 2000.

(2) Transition rules. The validity of a withholding certificate that was valid on January 1, 1998, under the regulations in effect prior to January 1, 2001 (see 26 CFR parts 1 and 35a, revised April 1, 1999) and expired, or will expire, at any time during 1998, is extended until December 31, 1998. The validity of a withholding certificate that is valid on or after January 1, 1999, remains valid until its validity expires under the regulations in effect prior to January 1, 2001 (see 26 CFR parts 1 and 35a, revised April 1, 1999) but in no event will such a withholding certificate remain valid after December 31, 2000. The rule in this paragraph (g)(2), however, does not apply to extend the validity period of a withholding certificate that expires solely by reason of changes

in the circumstances of the person whose name is on the certificate. Notwithstanding the first three sentences of this paragraph (g)(2), a withholding agent may choose to not take advantage of the transition rule in this paragraph (g)(2) with respect to one or more withholding certificates valid under the regulations in effect prior to January 1, 2001 (see 26 CFR parts 1 and 35a, revised April 1, 1999) and, therefore, to require withholding certificates conforming to the requirements described in this section (new withholding certificates). For purposes of this section, a new withholding certificate is deemed to satisfy the documentation requirement under the regulations in effect prior to January 1, 2001 (see 26 CFR parts 1 and 35a, revised April 1, 1999). Further, a new withholding certificate remains valid for the period specified in § 1.1441-1(e)(4)(ii), regardless of when the certificate is obtained.

T.D. 6187, 7/5/56, amend T.D. 6238, 6/10/57, T.D. 6908, 12/30/66, T.D. 7277, 5/14/73, T.D. 7842, 11/2/82, T.D. 7977, 9/19/84, T.D. 8160, 9/8/87, T.D. 8411, 4/24/92, T.D. 8734, 10/6/97, T.D. 8804, 12/30/98, T.D. 8856, 12/29/99, T.D. 8881, 5/15/2000.

§ 1.1441-6 Claim of reduced withholding under an income tax treaty.

(a) In general. The rate of withholding on a payment of income subject to withholding may be reduced to the extent provided under an income tax treaty in effect between the United States and a foreign country. Most benefits under income tax treaties are to foreign persons who reside in the treaty country. In some cases, benefits are available under an income tax treaty to U.S. citizens or U.S. residents or to residents of a third country.

See paragraph (b)(5) of this section for claims of benefits by U.S. persons. If the requirements of this section are met, the amount withheld from the payment may be reduced at source to account for the treaty benefit. See also § 1.1441-4(b)(2) for rules regarding claims of reduced rate of withholding under an income tax treaty in the case of compensation from personal services.

(b) Reliance on claim of reduced withholding under an income tax treaty. *(1) In general.* The withholding imposed under section 1441, 1442, or 1443 on any payment to a foreign person is eligible for reduction under the terms of an income tax treaty only to the extent that such payment is treated as derived by a resident of an applicable treaty jurisdiction, such resident is a beneficial owner, and all other requirements for benefits under the treaty are satisfied. See section 894 and the regulations thereunder to determine whether a resident of a treaty country derives the income. Absent actual knowledge or reason to know otherwise, a withholding agent may rely on a claim that a beneficial owner is entitled to a reduced rate of withholding based upon an income tax treaty if, prior to the payment, the withholding agent can reliably associate the payment with a beneficial owner withholding certificate, as described in § 1.1441-1(e)(2), that contains the information necessary to support the claim, or, in the case of a payment of income described in paragraph (c)(2) of this section made outside the United States with respect to an offshore account, documentary evidence described in paragraphs (c)(3), (4), and (5) of this section. See § 1.6049-5(e) for the definition of payments made outside the United States and § 1.6049-5(c)(1) for the definition of offshore account. For purposes of this paragraph (b)(1), a beneficial owner withholding certificate described in § 1.1441-1(e)(2)(i) contains information necessary to support the claim for a treaty benefit only if it includes the beneficial owner's taxpayer identifying number (except as otherwise provided in paragraph (c)(1) of this section and § 1.1441-6(g)) and the representations that the beneficial owner derives the income under section 894 and the regulations thereunder, if required, and meets the limitation on benefits provisions of the treaty, if any. The withholding certificate must also contain any other representations required by this section and any other information, certifications, or statements as may be required by the form or accompanying instructions in addition to, or in place of, the information and certifications described in this section. Absent actual knowledge or reason to know that the claims are incorrect (and subject to the standards of knowledge in § 1.1441-7(b)), a withholding agent may rely on the claims made on a withholding certificate or on documentary evidence. A withholding agent may also rely on the information contained in a withholding statement provided under § 1.1441-1(e)(3)(iv) and 1.1441-5(c)(3)(iv) and (e)(5)(iv) to determine whether the appropriate statements regarding section 894 and limitation on benefits have been provided in connection with documentary evidence. The Internal Revenue Service (IRS) may apply the provisions of § 1.1441-1(e)(1)(ii)(B) to notify the withholding agent that the certificate cannot be relied upon to grant benefits under an income tax treaty. See § 1.1441-1(e)(4)(viii) regarding reliance on a withholding certificate by a withholding agent. The provisions of § 1.1441-1(b)(3)(iv) dealing with a 90-day grace period shall apply for purposes of this section.

(2) Payment to fiscally transparent entity. (i) In general. If the person claiming a reduced rate of withholding under an income tax treaty is the interest holder of an entity that is considered to be fiscally transparent (as defined in the regulations under section 894) by the interest holder's jurisdiction with respect to an item of income, then, with respect to such income derived by that person through the entity, the entity shall be treated as a flow-through entity and may provide a flow-through withholding certificate with which the withholding certificate or other documentary evidence of the interest holder that supports the claim for treaty benefits is associated. For purposes of the preceding sentence, interest holders do not include any direct or indirect interest holders that are themselves treated as fiscally transparent entities with respect to that income by the interest holder's jurisdiction. See § 1.1441-1(c)(23) and (e)(3)(i) for the definition of flow-through entity and flow-through withholding certificate. The entity may provide a beneficial owner withholding certificate, or beneficial owner documentation, with respect to any remaining portion of the income to the extent the entity is receiving income and is not treated as fiscally transparent by its own jurisdiction. Further, the entity may claim a reduced rate of withholding with respect to the portion of a payment for which it is not treated as fiscally transparent if it meets all the requirements to make such a claim and, in the case of treaty benefits, it provides the documentation required by paragraph (b)(1) of this section. If dual claims, as described in paragraph (b)(2)(iii) of this section, are made, multiple withholding certificates may have to be furnished. Multiple withholding certificates may also have to be furnished if the entity receives income for which a reduction of withholding is claimed under a provision of the Internal Revenue Code (e.g., portfolio interest) and income for which a reduction of withholding is claimed under an income tax treaty.

(ii) Certification by qualified intermediary. Notwithstanding paragraph (b)(2)(i) of this section, a foreign entity that is fiscally transparent, as defined in the regulations under section 894, that is also a qualified intermediary for purposes of claiming a reduced rate of withholding under an income tax treaty for its interest holders (who are deriving the income paid to the entity as residents of an applicable treaty jurisdiction) may furnish a single qualified intermediary withholding certificate, as described in § 1.1441-1(e)(3)(ii), for amounts for which it claims a reduced rate of withholding under an income tax treaty on behalf of its interest holders.

(iii) Dual treatment. Under paragraph (b)(2)(i) of this section, a withholding agent may make a payment to a foreign entity that is simultaneously claiming to be the beneficial owner of a portion of the income (whether or not it is also claiming a reduced rate of tax on its own behalf) and a reduced rate on behalf of persons in their capacity as interest holders in the entity with respect to the same, or a different, portion of the income. If the same portion of a payment may be reliably associated with both the entity's claim and an interest holder's claim, the withholding agent may choose to reject both claims and request new documentation and information allocating the payment among the beneficial owners of the payment or the withholding agent may choose which claim to apply. If the entity and the interest holder's claims are reliably associated with separate portions of the payment, the withholding agent may, at its option, accept such dual claims based on withholding certificates or other appropriate documentation furnished by the entity and its interest holders with respect to their respective shares of the payment even though this will result in the withholding agent treating the entity differently with respect to different portions of the same payment. Alternatively, the withholding agent may choose to apply only the claim made by the entity, provided the entity may be treated as a beneficial owner of the income. If the withholding agent does not accept claims for a reduced rate of withholding presented by any one or more of the interest holders, or by the entity, any interest holder or the entity may subsequently claim a refund or credit of any amount so withheld to the extent the interest holder's or entity's share of such withholding exceeds the amount of tax due.

(iv) Examples. The following examples illustrate the rules of this paragraph (b)(2):

Example (1). (i) Facts. Entity E is a business organization formed under the laws of country Y. Country Y has an income tax treaty with the United States. The treaty contains a limitation on benefits provision. E receives U.S. source royalties from withholding agent W and claims a reduced rate of withholding under the U.S.-Y tax treaty on its own behalf (rather than on behalf of its interest holders). E furnishes a beneficial owner withholding certificate described in paragraph (b)(1) of this section that represents that E is a resident of country Y (within the meaning of the U.S.-Y tax treaty), is the beneficial owner of the income, derives the income under section 894 and the regulations thereunder, and is not precluded from claiming benefits by the treaty's limitation on benefits provision.

(ii) Analysis. Absent actual knowledge or reason to know otherwise, W may rely on the representations made by E to apply a reduced rate of withholding.

Example (1). (i) Facts. The facts are the same as under Example 1, except that one of E's interest holders, H, is an entity organized in country Z. The U.S.-Z tax treaty reduces the rate on royalties to zero whereas the rate on royalties under the U.S.-Y tax treaty applicable to E is 5 percent. H is not fiscally transparent under country Z's tax law with respect to such income. H furnishes a beneficial owner withholding certificate to E that represents that H derives, within the meaning of section 894 and the regulations thereunder, its share of the royalty income paid to E as a resident of country Z, is the beneficial owner of the royalty income, and is not precluded from claiming treaty benefits by virtue of the limitation on benefits provision in the U.S.-Z treaty. E furnishes to W a flow-through withholding certificate described in § 1.1441-1(e)(3)(i) to which it attaches H's beneficial owner withholding certificate and a withholding statement for the portion of the payment that H claims as its distributive share of the royalty income. E also furnishes to W a beneficial owner withholding certificate for itself for the portion of the payment that H does not claim as its distributive share.

(ii) Analysis. Absent actual knowledge or reason to know otherwise, W may rely on the documentation furnished by E to treat the royalty payment to a single foreign entity (E) as derived by different residents of tax treaty countries as a result of the claims presented under different treaties. W may, at its option, grant dual treatment, that is, a reduced rate of zero percent under the U.S.-Z treaty on the portion of the royalty payment that H claims to derive as a resident of country Z and a reduced rate of 5 percent under the U.S.-Y treaty for the balance. However, under paragraph (b)(2)(iii) of this section, W may, at its option, treat E as the only relevant person deriving the royalty and grant benefits under the U.S.-Y treaty only.

Example (3). (i) Facts. E is a business organization formed under the laws of country X. Country X has an income tax treaty with the United States. E has two interest holders, H1, organized in country Y, and H2, organized in country Z. E receives from W, a U.S. withholding agent, U.S. source royalties and interest that is eligible for the portfolio interest exception under sections 871(h) and 881(c), provided W receives the appropriate beneficial owner statement required under section 871(h)(5). E is classified as a corporation under U.S. tax law principles. Country X, E's country of organization, treats E as an entity that is not fiscally transparent with respect to items of income under the regulations under section 894. Under the U.S.-X income tax treaty, royalties are subject to 5 percent rate of withholding. Country Y, H1's country of organization, treats E as fiscally transparent with respect to items of income under section 894 and H1 as not fiscally transparent with respect to items of income. Under the country Y-U.S. income tax treaty, royalties are exempt from U.S. tax. Country Z, H2's country of organization, treats E as not fiscally transparent under section 894 with respect to items of income. E provides W with a flow-through beneficial owner withholding certificate with which it associates a beneficial owner withholding certificate from H1. H1's withholding certificate states that H1 is a resident of country Y, derives the royalty income under section 894, meets the applicable limitations on benefits provisions of the U.S.-Y treaty, and is the beneficial owner of the income. The withholding statement attached to E's flow-through withholding certificate allocates one-half of the royalty payment to H1. E also provides W with a beneficial owner withholding certificate for the interest income and the remaining one-half of the royalty income. The withholding certificate states that E is a resident of country X, derives the royalty income under section 894, meets the limitation on benefits provisions of the U.S.-X treaty, and is the beneficial owner of the income.

(ii) Analysis. Absent actual knowledge or reason to know that the claims are incorrect, W may treat one-half of the royalty derived by E as subject to a 5 percent withholding rate and one-half of the royalty as derived by H1 and subject to no withholding. Further, it may treat all of the interest as being paid to E and as qualifying for the portfolio interest exception. W can, at its option, treat the entire royalty as paid to E and subject it to withholding at a 5 percent rate of withholding. In that case, H1 would be entitled to claim a refund with respect to its one-half of the royalty.

(3) Certified TIN. The IRS may issue guidance requiring a foreign person claiming treaty benefits and for whom a TIN is required to establish with the IRS, at the time the TIN is requested or after the TIN is issued, that the person is a resident in a treaty country and meets other conditions (such as limitation on benefits provisions) of the treaty. See § 601.601(d)(2) of this chapter.

(4) Claim of benefits under an income tax treaty by a U.S. person. In certain cases, a U.S. person may claim the benefit of an income tax treaty. For example, under certain treaties, a U.S. citizen residing in the treaty country may claim a reduced rate of U.S. tax on certain amounts representing a pension or an annuity from U.S. sources. Claims of treaty benefits by a U.S. person may be made by furnishing a Form W-9 to the withholding agent or such other form as the IRS may prescribe in published guidance (see § 601.601(d)(2) of this chapter).

(c) Exemption from requirement to furnish a taxpayer identifying number and special documentary evidence rules for certain income. *(1) General rule.* In the case of income described in paragraph (c)(2) of this section, a withholding agent may rely on a beneficial owner withholding certificate described in paragraph (b)(1) of this section without regard to the requirement that the withholding certificate include the beneficial owner's taxpayer identifying number. In the case of payments of income described in paragraph (c)(2) of this section made outside the United States (as defined in § 1.6049-5(e)) with respect to an offshore account (as defined in § 1.6049-5(c)(1)), a withholding agent may, as an alternative to a withholding certificate described in paragraph (b)(1) of this section, rely on a certificate of residence described in paragraph (c)(3) of this section or documentary evidence described in paragraph (c)(4) of this section, relating to the beneficial owner, that the withholding agent has reviewed and maintains in its records in accordance with § 1.1441-1(e)(4)(iii). In the case of a payment to a person other than an individual, the certificate of residence or documentary evidence must be accompanied by the statements described in paragraphs (c)(5)(i) and (ii) of this section regarding limitation on benefits and whether the amount paid is derived by such person or by one of its interest holders. The withholding agent maintains the reviewed documents by retaining either the documents viewed or a photocopy thereof and noting in its records the date on which, and by whom, the documents were received and reviewed. This paragraph (c)(1) shall not apply to amounts that are exempt from withholding based on a claim that the income is effectively connected with the conduct of a trade or business in the United States.

(2) Income to which special rules apply. The income to which paragraph (c)(1) of this section applies is dividends and interest from stocks and debt obligations that are actively traded, dividends from any redeemable security issued by an investment company registered under the Investment Company Act of 1940 (15 U.S.C. 80a-1), dividends, interest, or royalties from units of beneficial interest in a unit investment trust that are (or were upon issuance) publicly offered and are registered with the Securities and Exchange Commission under the Securities Act of 1933 (15 U.S.C. 77a) and amounts paid with respect to loans of securities described in this paragraph (c)(2). For purposes of this paragraph (c)(2), a stock or debt obligation is actively traded if it is actively traded within the meaning of section 1092(d) and § 1.1092(d)-1 when documentation is provided.

(3) Certificate of residence. A certificate of residence referred to in paragraph (c)(1) of this section is a certification issued by an appropriate tax official of the treaty country of which the taxpayer claims to be a resident that the taxpayer has filed its most recent income tax return as a resident of that country (within the meaning of the applicable tax treaty). The certificate of residence must have been issued by such official within three years prior to its being presented to the withholding agent, or such other period as the IRS may prescribe in published guidance (see § 601.601(d)(2) of this chapter). See § 1.1441-1(e)(4)(ii)(A) for the period during which a withholding agent may rely on a certificate of residence. The competent authorities may agree to a different procedure for certifying residence, in which case such procedure shall govern for payments made to a person claiming to be a resident of the country with which such an agreement is in effect.

(4) Documentary evidence establishing residence in the treaty country. (i) Individuals. For an individual, the documentary evidence referred to in paragraph (c)(1) of this section is any documentation that includes the individuals name, address, and photograph, is an official document issued by an authorized governmental body (i.e., a government or agency thereof, or a municipality), and has been issued no more than three years prior to presentation to the withholding agent. A document older than three years may be relied upon as proof of residence only if it is accompanied by additional evidence of the person's residence in the treaty country (e.g., a bank statement, utility bills, or medical bills). Documentary evidence must be in the form of original documents or certified copies thereof.

(ii) Persons other than individuals. For a person other than an individual, the documentary evidence referred to in paragraph (c)(1) of this section is any documentation that includes the name of the entity and the address of its principal office in the treaty country, and is an official document issued by an authorized governmental body (e.g., a government or agency thereof, or a municipality).

(5) Statements regarding entitlement to treaty benefits. (i) Statement regarding conditions under a limitation on benefits provision. In addition to the documentary evidence described in (c)(4)(ii) of this section, a taxpayer that is not an individual must provide a statement that it meets one or more of the conditions set forth in the limitation on benefits article (if any, or in a similar provision) contained in the applicable tax treaty.

(ii) Statement regarding whether the taxpayer derives the income . A taxpayer that is not an individual must also provide, in addition to the documentary evidence and the statement described in paragraph (c)(5)(i) of this section, a statement that any income for which it intends to claim benefits under an applicable income tax treaty is income that will properly be treated as derived by itself as a resident of the applicable treaty jurisdiction within the meaning of section 894 and the regulations thereunder. This requirement does not apply if the taxpayer furnishes a certificate of residence that certifies that fact.

(d) Joint owners. In the case of a payment to joint owners, each owner must furnish a withholding certificate or, if applicable, documentary evidence or a certificate of residence. The applicable rate of withholding tax on a payment of income to joint owners shall be the highest applicable rate.

(e) Competent authority. The procedures described in this section may be modified to the extent the U.S. competent authority may agree with the competent authority of a country with which the United States has an income tax treaty in effect.

(f) Failure to receive withholding certificate timely. See applicable procedures described in § 1.1441-1(b)(7) in the event the withholding agent does not hold an appropriate withholding certificate or other appropriate documentation at the time of payment.

(g) Special taxpayer identifying number rule for certain foreign individuals claiming treaty benefits. *(1) General rule.* Except as provided in paragraph (c) or (g)(2) of this section, for purposes of paragraph (b)(1) of this section, a withholding agent may not rely on a beneficial owner withholding certificate, described in paragraph (b)(1) of this section, that does not include the beneficial owner's taxpayer identifying number (TIN).

(2) Special rule. For purposes of satisfying the TIN requirement of paragraph (b)(1) of this section, a withholding agent may rely on a beneficial owner withholding certificate, described in such paragraph, without regard to the requirement that the withholding certificate include the beneficial owner's TIN, if—

(i) A withholding agent, who is also an acceptance agent, as defined in § 301.6109-1(d)(3)(iv) of this chapter (the payor), has entered into an acceptance agreement that permits the acceptance agent to request an individual taxpayer identification number (ITIN) on an expedited basis because of the circumstances of payment or unexpected nature of payments required to be made by the payor;

(ii) The payor was required to make an unexpected payment to the beneficial owner who is a foreign individual;

(iii) An ITIN for the beneficial owner cannot be received by the payor from the Internal Revenue Service (IRS) because the IRS is not issuing ITINs at the time of payment or any time prior to the time of payment when the payor has knowledge of the unexpected payment;

(iv) The unexpected payment to the beneficial owner could not be reasonably delayed to permit the payor to obtain an ITIN for the beneficial owner on an expedited basis; and

(v) The payor satisfies the provisions of paragraph (g)(3) of this section.

(3) Requirement that an ITIN be requested during the first business day following payment. The payor must submit a beneficial owner payee application for an ITIN (Form W-7 "Application for IRS Individual Taxpayer Identification Number") that complies with the requirements of § 301.6109-1(d)(3)(ii) of this chapter, and also the certification described in § 301.6109-1(d)(3)(iv)(A)(4) of this chapter, to the IRS during the first business day after payment is made

(4) Definition of unexpected payment. For purposes of this section, an unexpected payment is a payment that, because of the nature of the payment or the circumstances in which it is made, could not reasonably have been anticipated by the payor or beneficial owner during a time when the payor or beneficial owner could obtain an ITIN from the IRS. For purposes of this paragraph (g)(4), a payor or beneficial owner will not lack the requisite knowledge of the forthcoming payment solely because the amount of the payment is not fixed.

(5) Examples. The rules of this paragraph (g) are illustrated by the following examples:

Example (1). G, a citizen and resident of Country Y, a country with which the United States has an income tax treaty that exempts U.S. source gambling winnings from U.S. tax, is visiting the United States for the first time. During his visit, G visits Casino B, a casino that has entered into a special acceptance agent agreement with the IRS that permits Casino B to request an ITIN on an expedited basis. During that visit, on a Sunday, G wins $5000 in slot machine play at Casino B and requests immediate payment from Casino B. ITINs are not available from the IRS on Sunday and would not again be available until Monday. G, who does not have an individual taxpayer identification number, furnishes a beneficial owner withholding certificate, described in § 1.1441-1(e)(2), to the Casino upon winning at the slot machine. The beneficial owner withholding certificate represents that G is a resident of Country Y (within the meaning of the U.S.—Y tax treaty) and meets all applicable requirements for claiming benefits under the U.S.—Y tax treaty. The beneficial owner withholding certificate does not, however, contain an ITIN for G. On the following Monday, Casino B faxes a completed Form W-7, including the required certification, for G, to the IRS for an expedited ITIN. Pursuant to paragraph (b) and (g)(2) of this section, absent actual knowledge or reason to know otherwise, Casino B, may rely on the documentation furnished by G at the time of payment and pay the $5000 to G without withholding U.S. tax based on the treaty exemption.

Example (2). The facts are the same as Example 1, except G visits Casino B on Monday. G requests payment Monday afternoon. In order to pay the winnings to G without withholding the 30 percent tax, Casino B must apply for and obtain an ITIN for G because an expedited ITIN is available from the IRS at the time of the $5000 payment to G.

Example (3). The facts are the same as Example 1, except G requests payment fifteen minutes before the time when the IRS begins issuing ITINs. Under these facts, it would be reasonable for Casino B to delay payment to G. Therefore, Casino B must apply for and obtain an ITIN for G if G wishes to claim an exemption from U.S. withholding tax under the U.S.—Y tax treaty at the time of payment.

Example (4). P, a citizen and resident of Country Z, is a lawyer and a well-known expert on real estate transactions. P is scheduled to attend a three-day seminar on complex real estate transactions, as a participant, at University U, a U.S. university, beginning on a Saturday and ending on the following Monday, which is a holiday. University U has entered into a special acceptance agent agreement with the IRS that permits University U to request an ITIN on an expedited basis. Country Z is a country with which the United States has an income tax treaty that exempts certain income earned from the performance of independent personal services from U.S. tax. It is P's first visit to the United States. On Saturday, prior to the start of the seminar, Professor Q, one of the lecturers at the seminar, cancels his lecture. That same day the Dean of University U offers P $5000, to replace Professor Q at the seminar, payable at the conclusion of the seminar on Monday. P agrees. P gives her lecture Sunday afternoon. ITINs are not available from the IRS on that Saturday, Sunday, or Monday. After the seminar ends on Monday, P, who does not have an ITIN, requests payment for her teaching. P furnishes a beneficial owner withholding certificate, described in § 1.1441-1(e)(2), to University U that represents that P is a resident of Country Z (within the meaning of the U.S.—Z tax treaty) and meets all applicable requirements for claiming benefits under the U.S.—Z tax treaty. The beneficial owner withholding certificate does not, however, contain an ITIN for P. On Tuesday, University U faxes a completed Form W-7, including the required certification, for P, to the IRS for an expedited ITIN. Pursuant to paragraph (b) and (g)(2) of this section, absent actual knowledge or reason to know otherwise, University U may rely on the documentation furnished by P and pay $5000 to P without withholding U.S. tax based on the treaty exemption.

(h) Effective dates. *(1) General rule.* This section applies to payments made after December 31, 2000, except for paragraph (g) of this section which applies to payments made after December 31, 2001.

(2) Transition rules. For purposes of this section, the validity of a Form 1001 or 8233 that was valid on January 1, 1998, under the regulations in effect prior to January 1, 2001 (see 26 CFR parts 1 and 35a, revised April 1, 1999) and expired, or will expire, at any time during 1998, is extended until December 31, 1998. The validity of a Form 1001 or 8233 that is valid on or after January 1, 1999, remains valid until its validity expires under the regulations in effect prior to January 1, 2001 (see 26 CFR parts 1 and 35a, revised April 1, 1999) but in no event will such a form remain valid after December 31, 2000. The rule in this paragraph (h)(2), however, does not apply to extend the validity period of a Form 1001 or 8233 that expires solely by reason of changes in the circumstances of the person whose name is on the certificate or in interpretation of the law under the regulations under § 1.894-1T(d). Notwithstanding the first three sentences of this paragraph (h)(2), a withholding agent may choose to not take advantage of the transition rule in this paragraph (h)(2) with respect to one or more withholding certificates valid under the regulations in effect prior to January 1, 2001 (see 26 CFR parts 1 and 35a, revised April 1, 1999) and, therefore, to require withholding certificates conforming to the requirements described in this section (new withholding certificates). For purposes of this section, a new withholding certificate is deemed to satisfy the documentation requirement under the regulations in effect prior to January 1, 2001 (see 26 CFR parts 1 and 35a, revised April 1, 1999). Further, a new withholding certificate remains valid for the period specified in § 1.1441-1(e)(4)(ii), regardless of when the certificate is obtained.

T.D. 7157, 12/29/71, amend T.D. 7842, 11/2/82, T.D. 7977, 9/19/84, T.D. 8734, 10/6/97, T.D. 8804, 12/30/98, T.D. 8856, 12/29/99, T.D. 8881, 5/15/2000, T.D. 8977, 1/16/2002, T.D. 9023, 11/22/2002, T.D. 9253, 3/13/2006.

§ 1.1441-7 General provisions relating to withholding agents.

Caution: The Treasury has not yet amended Reg § 1.1441-7 to reflect changes made by P.L. 98-369.

(a) Withholding agent defined. *(1) In general.* For purposes of chapter 3 of the Internal Revenue Code and the regulations under such chapter, the term withholding agent means any person, U.S. or foreign, that has the control, receipt, custody, disposal, or payment of an item of income of a foreign person subject to withholding, including (but not limited to) a foreign intermediary described in § 1.1441-1(e)(3)(i), a foreign partnership, or a U.S. branch described in § 1.1441-1(b)(2)(iv)(A) or (E). See § 1.1441-1(b)(2) and (3) and 1.1441-5(c), (d), and (e), for rules to determine whether a payment is considered made to a foreign person. Any person who meets the definition of a withholding agent is required to deposit any tax withheld under § 1.1461-1(a) and to make the returns prescribed by § 1.1461-1(b) and (c), except as otherwise may be required by a qualified intermediary withholding agreement, a withholding foreign partnership agreement, or a withholding foreign trust agreement. When several persons qualify as withholding agents with respect to a single payment, only one tax is required to be withheld and deposited. See § 1.1461-1. A person who, as a nominee described in § 1.6031(c)-1T, has furnished to a partnership all of the information required to be furnished under § 1.6031(c)-1T(a) shall not be treated as a withholding agent if it has notified the partnership that it is treating the provision of information to the partnership as a discharge of its obligations as a withholding agent.

(2) Examples. The following examples illustrate the rules of paragraph (a)(1) of this section:

Example (1). USB is a broker organized in the United States. USB pays U.S. source dividends and interest, which are amounts subject to withholding under § 1.1441-2(a), to FC, a foreign corporation that has an investment account with USB. USB is a withholding agent as defined in paragraph (a)(1) of this section.

Example (2). USB is a bank organized in the United States. FB is a bank organized in country X. X has an omnibus account with USB through which FB invests in debt and equity instruments that pay amounts subject to withholding as defined in § 1.1441-2(a). FB is a nonqualified intermediary, as defined in § 1.1441-1(c)(14). Both USB and FB are withholding agents as defined in paragraph (a)(1) of this section.

Example (3). The facts are the same as in Example 2, except that FB is a qualified intermediary. Both USB and FB are withholding agents as defined in paragraph (a)(1) of this section.

Example (4). FB is a bank organized in country X. FB has a branch in the United States. FB's branch has customers that are foreign persons who receive amounts subject to withholding, as defined in § 1.1441-2(a). FB is a withholding agent under paragraph (a)(1) of this section and is required to withhold and report payments of amounts subject to withholding in accordance with chapter 3 of the Internal Revenue Code.

Example (5). X is a foreign corporation. X pays dividends to shareholders who are foreign persons. Under section 861(a)(2)(B), a portion of the dividends are from sources within the United States and constitute amounts subject to withholding within the meaning of § 1.1441-2(a). The dividends are not subject to tax under section 884(a). See 884(e)(3). X is a withholding agent under paragraph (a)(1) of this section.

(b) Standards of knowledge. *(1) In general.* A withholding agent must withhold at the full 30-percent rate under section 1441, 1442, or 1443(a) or at the full 4-percent rate under section 1443(b) if it has actual knowledge or reason to know that a claim of U.S. status or of a reduced rate of withholding under section 1441, 1442, or 1443 is unreliable or incorrect. A withholding agent shall be liable for tax, interest, and penalties to the extent provided under sections 1461 and 1463 and the regulations under those sections if it fails to withhold the correct amount despite its actual knowledge or reason to know the amount required to be withheld. For purposes of the regulations under sections 1441, 1442, and 1443, a withholding agent may rely on information or certifications contained in, or associated with, a withholding certificate or other documentation furnished by or for a beneficial owner or payee unless the withholding agent has actual knowledge or reason to know that the information or certifications are incorrect or unreliable and, if based on such knowledge or reason to know, it should withhold (under chapter 3 of the Code or another withholding provision of the Code) an amount greater than would be the case if it relied on the information or certifications, or it should report (under chapter 3 of the Code or under another provision of the Code) an amount that would not otherwise be reportable if it relied on the information or certifications. See § 1.1441-1(e)(4)(viii) for applicable reliance rules. A withholding agent that has received notification by the Internal Revenue Service (IRS) that a claim of U.S. status or of a reduced rate is incorrect has actual knowledge beginning on the date that is 30 calendar days after the date the notice is received. A withholding agent that fails to act in accordance with the presumptions set forth in §§ 1.1441-1(b)(3), 1.1441-4(a), 1.1441-5(d) and (e), or 1.1441-9(b)(3) may also be liable for tax, interest, and penalties. See § 1.1441-1(b)(3)(ix) and (7).

(2) Reason to know. A withholding agent shall be considered to have reason to know if its knowledge of relevant facts or of statements contained in the withholding certificates or other documentation is such that a reasonably prudent person in the position of the withholding agent would question the claims made.

(3) Financial institutions—limits on reason to know. For purposes of this paragraph (b)(3) and paragraphs (b)(4) through (b)(10) of this section, the terms withholding certificate, documentary evidence, and documentation are defined in § 1.1441-1(c)(16), (17) and (18). Except as otherwise provided in paragraphs (b)(4) through (b)(9) of this section, a withholding agent that is a financial institution (including a regulated investment company) that has a direct account relationship with a beneficial owner (a direct account holder) has a reason to know, with respect to amounts described in § 1.1441-6(c)(2), that documentation provided by the direct account holder is unreliable or incorrect only if one or more of the circumstances described in paragraphs (b)(4) through (b)(9) of this section exist. If a direct account holder has provided documentation that is unreliable or incorrect under the rules of paragraph (b)(4) through (b)(9) of this section, the withholding agent may require new documentation. Alternatively, the withholding agent may rely on the documentation originally provided if the rules of paragraphs (b)(4) through (b)(9) of this section permit such reliance based on additional statements and documentation. Paragraph (b)(10) of this section provides limits on reason to know for financial institutions that receive beneficial owner documentation from persons (indirect account holders) that have an account relationship with, or an ownership interest in, a direct account holder. For rules regarding reliance on Form W-9, see § 31.3406(g)-3(e)(2) of this chapter.

(4) Rules applicable to withholding certificates. (i) In general. A withholding agent has reason to know that a beneficial owner withholding certificate provided by a direct account holder in connection with a payment of an amount described in § 1.1441-6(c)(2) is unreliable or incorrect if the withholding certificate is incomplete with respect to any item on the certificate that is relevant to the claims made by the direct account holder, the withholding certificate contains any information that is inconsistent with the direct account holder's claim, the withholding agent has other account information that is inconsistent with the direct account holder's claim, or the withholding certificate lacks information necessary to establish entitlement to a reduced rate of withholding. For purposes of establishing a direct account holder's status as a foreign person or resident of a treaty country a withholding certificate shall be considered unreliable or inconsistent with an account holder's claims only if it is not reliable under the rules of paragraphs (b)(5) and (6) of this section. A withholding agent that relies on an agent to review and maintain a withholding certificate is considered to know or have reason to know the facts within the knowledge of the agent.

(ii) Examples. The rules of paragraph (b)(4) of this section are illustrated by the following examples:

Example (1). F, a foreign person that has a direct account relationship with USB, a bank that is a U.S. person, provides USB with a beneficial owner withholding certificate for the purpose of claiming a reduced rate of withholding on U.S. source dividends. F resides in a treaty country that has a limitation on benefits provision in its income tax treaty with the United States. The withholding certificate, however, does not contain a statement regarding limitations on benefits or deriving the income under section 894 as required by § 1.1441-6(b)(1). USB cannot rely on the withholding certificate to grant a reduced rate of withholding because it is incomplete with respect to the claim made by F.

Example (2). F, a foreign person that has a direct account relationship with USB, a broker that is a U.S. person, provides USB with a withholding certificate for the purpose of claiming the portfolio interest exception under section 881(c), which applies to foreign corporations. F indicates on its withholding certificate, however, that it is a partnership. USB may not treat F as a beneficial owner of the interest for purposes of the portfolio interest exception because F has indicated on its withholding certificate that it is a foreign partnership, and therefore under § 1.1441-1(c)(6)(ii) it is not the beneficial owner of the interest payment.

(5) Withholding certificate—establishment of foreign status. A withholding agent has reason to know that a beneficial owner withholding certificate (as defined in § 1.1441-1(e)(2)) provided by a direct account holder in connection with a payment of an amount described in § 1.1441-6(c)(2) is unreliable or incorrect for purposes of establishing the account holder's status as a foreign person if the certificate is described in paragraph (b)(5)(i) or (ii) of this section.

(i) A withholding certificate is unreliable or incorrect if the withholding certificate has a permanent residence address (as defined in § 1.1441-1(e)(2)(ii)) in the United States, the withholding certificate has a mailing address in the United States, the withholding agent has a residence or mailing address as part of its account information that is an address in the United States, or the direct account holder notifies the withholding agent of a new residence or mailing address in the United States (whether or not provided on a withholding certificate). A withholding agent may, however, rely on the beneficial owner withholding certificate as establishing the account holder's foreign status if it may do so under the provisions of paragraph (b)(5)(i)(A) or (B) of this section.

(A) A withholding agent may treat a direct account holder as a foreign person if the beneficial owner withholding certificate has been provided by an individual and—

(1) The withholding agent has in its possession or obtains documentary evidence (which does not contain a U.S. address) that has been provided within the last three years, was validat the time it was provided, the documentary evidence supports the claim of foreign status, and the direct account holder provides the withholding agent with a reasonable explanation, in writing, supporting the account holder's foreign status; or

(2) The account is maintained at an office of the withholding agent outside the United States and the withholding agent is required to report annually a payment to the direct account holder on a tax information statement that is filed with the tax authority of the country in which the office is located and that country has an income tax treaty in effect with the United States.

(B) A withholding agent may treat an account holder as a foreign person if the beneficial owner withholding certificate has been provided by an entity that the withholding agent does not know, or does not have reason to know, is a flow-through entity and—

(1) The withholding agent has in its possession, or obtains, documentation that substantiates that the entity is actually organized or created under the laws of a foreign country; or

(2) The account is maintained at an office of the withholding agent outside the United States and the withholding agent is required to report annually a payment to the direct account holder on a tax information statement that is filed with the tax authority of the country in which the office is located and that country has an income tax treaty in effect with the United States.

(ii) A beneficial owner withholding certificate is unreliable or incorrect if it is provided with respect to an offshore account (as defined in § 1.6049-5(c)(1)) and the direct account holder has standing instructions directing the withholding agent to pay amounts from its account to an address or an account maintained in the United States. The withholding agent may treat the direct account holder as a foreign person, however, if the direct account holder provides a reasonable explanation in writing that supports its foreign status.

(6) Withholding certificate—claim of reduced rate of withholding under treaty. A withholding agent has reason to know that a withholding certificate (other than Form W-9) provided by a direct account holder in connection with a payment of an amount described in § 1.1441-6(c)(2) is unreliable or incorrect for purposes of establishing that the direct account holder is a resident of a country with which the United States has an income tax treaty if it is described in paragraphs (b)(6)(i) through (iii) of this section.

(i) A beneficial owner withholding certificate is unreliable or incorrect if the permanent residence address on the beneficial owner withholding certificate is not in the country whose treaty is invoked, or the direct account holder notifies the withholding agent of a new permanent residence address that is not in the treaty country. A withholding agent may, however, treat a direct account holder as entitled to a reduced rate of withholding under an income tax treaty if the direct account holder provides a reasonable explanation for the permanent residence address outside the treaty country (e.g., the address is the address of a branch of the beneficial owner located outside the treaty country in which the entity is a resident) or the withholding agent has in its possession, or obtains, documentary evidence that establishes residency in a treaty country.

(ii) A beneficial owner withholding certificate is unreliable or incorrect if the permanent residence address on the withholding certificate is in the applicable treaty country but the withholding certificate contains a mailing address outside the treaty country or the withholding agent has a mailing address as part of its account information that is outside the treaty country. A mailing address that is a P.O. Box, in-care-of address, or address at a financial institution (if the financial institution is not a beneficial owner) shall not preclude a withholding agent from treating the direct account holder as a resident of a treaty country if such address is in the treaty country. If a withholding agent has a mailing address (whether or not contained on the withholding certificate) outside the applicable treaty country, the withholding agent may nevertheless treat a direct account holder as a resident of an applicable treaty country if—

(A) The withholding agent has in its possession, or obtains, additional documentation supporting the direct account holder's claim of residence in the applicable treaty country (and the additional documentation does not contain an address outside the treaty country);

(B) The withholding agent has in its possession, or obtains, documentation that establishes that the direct account holder is an entity organized in a treaty country (or an entity managed and controlled in a treaty country, if the applicable treaty so requires);

(C) The withholding agent knows that the address outside the applicable treaty country (other than a P.O. box, or in-care-of address) is a branch of a bank or insurance company that is a resident of the applicable treaty country; or

(D) The withholding agent obtains a written statement from the direct account holder that reasonably establishes entitlement to treaty benefits.

(iii) A beneficial owner withholding certificate is unreliable or incorrect to establish entitlement to a reduced rate of withholding under an income tax treaty if the direct account holder has standing instructions for the withholding agent to pay amounts from its account to an address or an account outside the treaty country unless the direct account holder provides a reasonable explanation, in writing, establishing the direct account holder's residence in the applicable treaty country.

(7) Documentary evidence. A withholding agent shall not treat documentary evidence provided by a direct account holder as valid if the documentary evidence does not reasonably establish the identity of the person presenting the documentary evidence. For example, documentary evidence is not valid if it is provided in person by a direct account holder that is a natural person and the photograph or signature on the documentary evidence, if any, does not match the appearance or signature of the person presenting the document. A withholding agent shall not rely on documentary evidence to reduce the rate of withholding that would otherwise apply under the presumption rules of §§ 1.1441-1(b)(3), 1.1441-5(d) and (e)(6), and 1.6049-5(d) if the documentary evidence contains information that is inconsistent with the direct account holder's claim of a reduced rate of withholding, the withholding agent has other account information that is inconsistent with the direct account holder's claim, or the documentary evidence lacks information necessary to establish entitlement to a reduced rate of withholding. For example, if a direct account holder provides documentary evidence to claim treaty benefits and the documentary evidence establishes the direct account holder's status as a foreign person and a resident of a treaty country, but the account holder fails to provide the treaty statements required by § 1.1441-6(c)(5), the documentary evidence does not establish the direct account holder's entitlement to a reduced rate of withholding. For purposes of establishing a direct account holder's status as a foreign person or resident of a country with which the United States has an income tax treaty with respect to income described in § 1.1441-6(c)(2), documentary evidence shall be considered unreliable or incorrect only

if it is not reliable under the rules of paragraph (b)(8) and (9) of this section.

(8) Documentary evidence—establishment of foreign status. A withholding agent has reason to know that documentary evidence provided in connection with a payment of an amount described in § 1.1441-6(c)(2) is unreliable or incorrect for purposes of establishing the direct account holder's status as a foreign person if the documentary evidence is described in paragraphs (b)(8)(i), (ii), (iii) or (iv) of this section.

(i) A withholding agent shall not treat documentary evidence provided by an account holder after December 31, 2000, as valid for purposes of establishing the direct account holder's foreign status if the only mailing or residence address that is available to the withholding agent is an address at a financial institution (unless the financial institution is a beneficial owner of the income), an in-care-of address, or a P.O. box. In this case, the withholding agent must obtain additional documentation that is sufficient to establish the direct account holder's status as a foreign person. A withholding agent shall not treat documentary evidence provided by an account holder before January 1, 2001, as valid for purposes of establishing a direct account holder's status as a foreign person if it has actual knowledge that the direct account holder is a U.S. person or if it has a mailing or residence address for the direct account holder in the United States. If a withholding agent has an address for the direct account holder in the United States, the withholding agent may nevertheless treat the direct account holder as a foreign person if it can so treat the direct account holder under the rules of paragraph (b)(8)(ii) of this section.

(ii) Documentary evidence is unreliable or incorrect to establish a direct account holder's status as a foreign person if the withholding agent has a mailing or residence address (whether or not on the documentation) for the direct account holder in the United States or if the direct account holder notifies the withholding agent of a new address in the United States. A withholding agent may, however, rely on documentary evidence as establishing the direct account holder's foreign status if it may do so under the provisions of paragraph (b)(8)(ii)(A) or (B) of this section.

(A) A withholding agent may treat a direct account holder that is an individual as a foreign person even if it has a mailing or residence address for the direct account holder in the United States if the withholding agent—

(1) Has in its possession or obtains additional documentary evidence (which does not contain a U.S. address) supporting the claim of foreign status and a reasonable explanation in writing supporting the account holder's foreign status;

(2) Has in its possession or obtains a valid beneficial owner withholding certificate on Form W-8 and the Form W-8 contains a permanent residence address outside the United States and a mailing address outside the United States (or if a mailing address is inside the United States the direct account holder provides a reasonable explanation in writing supporting the direct account holder's foreign status); or

(3) The account is maintained at an office of the withholding agent outside the United States and the withholding agent is required to report annually a payment to the direct account holder on a tax information statement that is filed with the tax authority of the country in which the office is located and that country has an income tax treaty in effect with the United States.

(B) A withholding agent may treat a direct account holder that is an entity (other than a flow-through entity) as a foreign person even if it has a mailing or residence address for the direct account holder in the United States if the withholding agent—

(1) Has in its possession, or obtains, documentation that substantiates that the entity is actually organized or created under the laws of a foreign country;

(2) Obtains a valid beneficial owner withholding certificate on Form W-8 and the Form W-8 contains a permanent residence address outside the United States and a mailing address outside the United States (or if a mailing address is inside the United States the direct account holder provides additional documentary evidence sufficient to establish the direct account holder's foreign status); or

(3) The account is maintained at an office of the withholding agent outside the United States and the withholding agent is required to report annually a payment to the direct account holder on a tax information statement that is filed with the tax authority of the country in which the office is located and that country has an income tax treaty in effect with the United States.

(iii) Documentary evidence is unreliable or incorrect if the direct account holder has standing instructions directing the withholding agent to pay amounts from its account to an address or an account maintained in the United States. The withholding agent may treat the direct account holder as a foreign person, however, if the account holder provides a reasonable explanation in writing that supports its foreign status.

(9) Documentary evidence—claim of reduced rate of withholding under treaty. A withholding agent has reason to know that documentary evidence provided in connection with a payment of an amount described in § 1.1441-6(c)(2) is unreliable or incorrect for purposes of establishing that a direct account holder is a resident of a country with which the United States has an income tax treaty if it is described in paragraph (b)(9)(i) or (ii) of this section.

(i) Documentary evidence is unreliable or incorrect if the withholding agent has a mailing or residence address for the direct account holder (whether or not on the documentary evidence) that is outside the applicable treaty country, or the only address that the withholding agent has (whether in or outside of the applicable treaty country) is a P.O. box, an in-care-of address, or the address of a financial institution (if the financial institution is not the beneficial owner). If a withholding agent has a mailing or residence address for the direct account holder outside the applicable treaty country, the withholding agent may nevertheless treat a direct account holder as a resident of an applicable treaty country if the withholding agent—

(A) Has in its possession, or obtains, additional documentary evidence supporting the direct account holder's claim of residence in the applicable treaty country (and the documentary evidence does not contain an address outside the applicable treaty country, a P.O. box, an in-care-of address, or the address of a financial institution);

(B) Has in its possession, or obtains, documentary evidence that establishes the direct account holder is an entity organized in a treaty country (or an entity managed and controlled in a treaty country, if the applicable treaty so requires); or

(C) Obtains a valid beneficial owner withholding certificate on Form W-8 that contains a permanent residence address and a mailing address in the applicable treaty country.

(ii) Documentary evidence is unreliable or incorrect if the direct account holder has standing instructions directing the withholding agent to pay amounts from its account to an address or an account maintained outside the treaty country unless the direct account holder provides a reasonable explanation, in writing, establishing the direct account holder's residence in the applicable treaty country.

(10) Limits on reason to know—indirect account holders. A financial institution that receives documentation from a payee through a nonqualified intermediary, a flow-through entity, or a U.S. branch described in § 1.1441-1(b)(2)(iv) (other than a U.S. branch that is treated as a U.S. person) with respect to a payment of an amount described in § 1.1441-6(c)(2) has reason to know that the documentation is unreliable or incorrect if a reasonably prudent person in the position of a withholding agent would question the claims made. This standard requires, but is not limited to, a withholding agent's compliance with the rules of paragraphs (b)(10)(i) through (iii).

(i) The withholding agent must review the withholding statement described in § 1.1441-1(e)(3)(iv) and may not rely on information in the statement to the extent the information does not support the claims made for any payee. For this purpose, a withholding agent may not treat a payee as a foreign person if an address in the United States is provided for such payee and may not treat a person as a resident of a country with which the United States has an income tax treaty if the address for that person is outside the applicable treaty country. Notwithstanding a U.S. address or an address outside a treaty country, the withholding agent may treat a payee as a foreign person or a foreign person as a resident of a treaty country if a reasonable explanation is provided, in writing, by the nonqualified intermediary, flow-through entity, or U.S. branch supporting the payee's foreign status or the foreign person's residency in a treaty country.

(ii) The withholding agent must review each withholding certificate in accordance with the requirements of paragraphs (b)(5) and (6) of this section and verify that the information on the withholding certificate is consistent with the information on the withholding statement required under § 1.1441-1(e)(3)(iv). If there is a discrepancy between the withholding certificate and the withholding statement, the withholding agent may choose to rely on the withholding certificate, if valid, and instruct the nonqualified intermediary, flow-through entity, or U.S. branch to correct the withholding statement or apply the presumption rules of §§ 1.1441-1(b), 1.1441-5(d) and (e)(6), and 1.6049-5(d) to the payment allocable to the payee who provided the withholding certificate. A withholding agent that receives a withholding certificate before December 31, 2001, is not required to review the information on withholding certificates or determine if it is consistent with the information on the withholding statement until December 31, 2001. A withholding agent may withhold and report in accordance with a withholding statement until December 31, 2001, unless it has actually performed the verification procedures required by this paragraph (b)(10)(ii) and determined that the withholding statement is inaccurate with respect to a particular payee.

(iii) The withholding agent must review the documentary evidence provided by the nonqualified intermediary, flow-through entity, or U.S. branch to determine that there is no obvious indication that the payee is a U.S. non-exempt recipient or that the documentary evidence does not establish the identity of the person who provided the documentation (e.g., the documentary evidence does not appear to be an identification document).

(11) Additional guidance. The IRS may prescribe other circumstances for which a withholding certificate or documentary evidence is unreliable or incorrect in addition to the circumstances described in paragraph (b) of this section to establish an account holder's status as a foreign person or a beneficial owner entitled to a reduced rate of withholding in published guidance (see § 601.601(d)(2) of this chapter).

(c) Authorized agent. *(1) In general.* The acts of an agent of a withholding agent (including the receipt of withholding certificates, the payment of amounts of income subject to withholding, and the deposit of tax withheld) are imputed to the withholding agent on whose behalf it is acting. However, if the agent is a foreign person, a withholding agent that is a U.S. person may treat the acts of the foreign agent as its own for purposes of determining whether it has complied with the provisions of this section, but only if the agent is an authorized foreign agent, as defined in paragraph (c)(2) of this section. An authorized foreign agent cannot apply the provisions of this paragraph (c) to appoint another person its authorized foreign agent with respect to the payments it receives from the withholding agent.

(2) Authorized foreign agent. An agent is an authorized foreign agent only if—

(i) There is a written agreement between the withholding agent and the foreign person acting as agent;

(ii) The notification procedures described in paragraph (c)(3) of this section have been complied with;

(iii) Books and records and relevant personnel of the foreign agent are available (on a continuous basis, including after termination of the relationship) for examination by the IRS in order to evaluate the withholding agent's compliance with the provisions of chapters 3 and 61 of the Code, section 3406, and the regulations under those provisions; and

(iv) The U.S. withholding agent remains fully liable for the acts of its agent and does not assert any of the defenses that may otherwise be available, including under common law principles of agency in order to avoid tax liability under the Internal Revenue Code.

(3) Notification. A withholding agent that appoints an authorized agent to act on its behalf for purposes of § 1.871-14(c)(2), the withholding provisions of chapter 3 of the Code, section 3406 or other withholding provisions of the Internal Revenue Code, or the reporting provisions of chapter 61 of the Code, is required to file notice of such appointment with the Office of the Assistant Commissioner (International). Such notice shall be filed before the first payment for which the authorized agent acts as such. Such notice shall acknowledge the withholding agent liability as provided in paragraph (c)(2)(iv) of this section.

(4) Liability of U.S. withholding agent. An authorized foreign agent is subject to the same withholding and reporting obligations that apply to any withholding agent under the provisions of chapter 3 of the Code and the regulations thereunder. In particular, an authorized foreign agent does not benefit from the special procedures or exceptions that may apply to a qualified intermediary. A withholding agent acting through an authorized foreign agent is liable for any failure of the agent, such as failure to withhold an amount or make payment of tax, in the same manner and to the same extent as if the agent's failure had been the failure of the U.S. withholding agent. For this purpose, the foreign agent's actual knowledge or reason to know shall be imputed to the U.S. withholding agent. The U.S. withholding agent's liability shall exist irrespective of the fact that the authorized foreign agent is also a withholding agent and is itself separately

liable for failure to comply with the provisions of the regulations under section 1441, 1442, or 1443. However, the same tax, interest, or penalties shall not be collected more than once.

(5) Filing of returns. See § 1.1461-1(b)(2)(iii) and (c)(4)(iii) regarding returns required to be made where a U.S. withholding agent acts through an authorized foreign agent.

(d) United States obligations. If the United States is a withholding agent for an item of interest, including original issue discount, on obligations of the United States or of any agency or instrumentality thereof, the withholding obligation of the United States is assumed and discharged by—

(1) The Commissioner of the Public Debt, for interest paid by checks issued through the Bureau of the Public Debt;

(2) The Treasurer of the United States, for interest paid by him or her, whether by check or otherwise;

(3) Each Federal Reserve Bank, for interest paid by it, whether by check or otherwise; or

(4) Such other person as may be designated by the IRS.

(e) Assumed obligations. If, in connection with the sale of a corporation's property, payment on the bonds or other obligations of the corporation is assumed by a person, then that person shall be a withholding agent to the extent amounts subject to withholding are paid to a foreign person. Thus, the person shall withhold such amounts under § 1.1441-1 as would be required to be withheld by the seller or corporation had no such sale or assumption been made.

(f) Conduit financing arrangements. *(1) Liability of withholding agent.* Subject to paragraph (f)(2) of this section, any person that is required to deduct and withhold tax under § 1.1441-3(g) is made liable for that tax by section 1461. A person that is required to deduct and withhold tax but fails to do so is liable for the payment of the tax and any applicable penalties and interest.

(2) Exception for withholding agents that do not know of conduit financing arrangement (i) In general. A withholding agent will not be liable under paragraph (f)(1) of this section for failing to deduct and withhold with respect to a conduit financing arrangement unless the person knows or has reason to know that the financing arrangement is a conduit financing arrangement. This standard shall be satisfied if the withholding agent knows or has reason to know of facts sufficient to establish that the financing arrangement is a conduit financing arrangement, including facts sufficient to establish that the participation of the intermediate entity in the financing arrangement is pursuant to a tax avoidance plan. A withholding agent that knows only of the financing transactions that comprise the financing arrangement will not be considered to know or have reason to know of facts sufficient to establish that the financing arrangement is a conduit financing arrangement.

(ii) Examples. The following examples illustrate the operation of paragraph (d)(2) of this section.

Example (1). (i) DS is a U.S. subsidiary of FP, a corporation organized in Country N, a country that does not have an income tax treaty with the United States. FS is a special purpose subsidiary of FP that is incorporated in Country T, a country that has an income tax treaty with the United States that prohibits the imposition of withholding tax on payments of interest. FS is capitalized with $10,000,000 in debt from EK, a Country N bank, and $1,000,000 in capital from FS.

(ii) On May 1, 1995, C, a U.S. person, purchases an automobile from DS in return for an installment note. On July 1, 1995, DS sells a number of installment notes, including C's, to FS in exchange for $10,000,000. DS continues to service the installment notes for FS and C is not notified of the sale of its obligation and continues to make payments to DS. But for the withholding tax on payments of interest by DS to BK, DS would have borrowed directly from BK, pledging the installment notes as collateral.

(iii) The C installment note is a financing transaction, whether held by DS or by FS, and the FS note held by BK also is a financing transaction. After FS purchases the installment note, and during the time the installment note is held by FS, the transactions constitute a financing arrangement, within the meaning of § 1.881-3(a)(2)(i). BK is the financing entity, FS is the intermediate entity, and C is the financed entity. Because the participation of FS in the financing arrangement reduces the tax imposed by section 881 and because there was a tax avoidance plan, FS is a conduit entity.

(iv) Because C does not know or have reason to know of the tax avoidance plan (and by extension that the financing arrangement is a conduit financing arrangement), C is not required to withhold tax under section 1441. However, DS, who knows that FS's participation in the financing arrangement is pursuant to a tax avoidance plan and is a withholding agent for purposes of section 1441, is not relieved of its withholding responsibilities.

Example (2). Assume the same facts as in Example 1, except that C receives a new payment booklet on which DS is described as "agent". Although C may deduce that its installment note has been sold, without more C has no reason to know of the existence of a financing arrangement. Accordingly, C is not liable for failure to withhold, although DS still is not relieved of its withholding responsibilities.

Example (3). (i) DC is a U.S. corporation that is in the process of negotiating a loan of $10,000,000 from BK1, a bank located in Country N, a country that does not have an income tax treaty with the United States. Before the loan agreement is signed, DC's tax lawyers point out that interest on the loan would not be subject to withholding tax if the loan were made by BK2, a subsidiary of BK1 that is incorporated in Country T, a country that has an income tax treaty with the United States that prohibits the imposition of withholding tax on payments of interest. BK1 makes a loan to BK2 to enable BK2 to make the loan to DC. Without the loan from BK1 to BK2, BK2 would not have been able to make the loan to DC.

(ii) The loan from BK1 to BK2 and the loan from BK2 to DC are both financing transactions and together constitute a financing arrangement within the meaning of § 1.881-3(a)(2)(i). BK1 is the financing entity, BK2 is the intermediate entity, and DC is the financed entity. Because the participation of BK2 in the financing arrangement reduces the tax imposed by section 881 and because there is a tax avoidance plan, BK2 is a conduit entity.

(iii) Because DC is a party to the tax avoidance plan (and accordingly knows of its existence), DC must withhold tax under section 1441. If DC does not withhold tax on its payment of interest, BK2, a party to the plan and a withholding agent for purposes of section 1441, must withhold tax as required by section 1441.

Example (4). (i) DC is a U.S. corporation that has a longstanding banking relationship with BK2, a U.S. subsidiary of BK1, a bank incorporated in Country N, a country that does not have an income tax treaty with the United States. DC has borrowed amounts of as much as $75,000,000 from BK2 in the past. On January 1, 1995, DC asks to borrow $50,000,000 from BK2. BK2 does not have the funds available to make a loan of that size. BK2 considers asking BK1 to enter into a loan with DC but rejects this possibility because of the additional withholding tax that would be incurred. Accordingly, BK2 borrows the necessary amount from BK1 with the intention of on-lending to DC. BK1 does not make the loan directly to DC because of the withholding tax that would apply to payments of interest from DC to BK1. DC does not negotiate with BK1 and has no reason to know that BK1 was the source of the loan.

(ii) The loan from BK2 to DC and the loan from BK1 to BK2 are both financing transactions and together constitute a financing arrangement within the meaning of § 1.881-3(a)(2)(i). BK1 is the financing entity, BK2 is the intermediate entity, and DC is the financed entity. The participation of BK2 in the financing arrangement reduces the tax imposed by section 881. Because the participation of BK2 in the financing arrangement reduces the tax imposed by section 881 and because there was a tax avoidance plan, BK2 is a conduit entity.

(iii) Because DC does not know or have reason to know of the tax avoidance plan (and by extension that the financing arrangement is a conduit financing arrangement), DC is not required to withhold tax under section 1441. However, BK2, who is also a withholding agent under section 1441 and who knows that the financing arrangement is a conduit financing arrangement, is not relieved of its withholding responsibilities.

(3) Effective date. This paragraph (f) is effective for payments made by financed entities on or after September 11, 1995. This paragraph shall not apply to interest payments covered by section 127(g)(3) of the Tax Reform Act of 1984, and to interest payments with respect to other debt obligations issued prior to October 15, 1984 (whether or not such debt was issued by a Netherlands Antilles corporation).

(g) Effective date. Except as otherwise provided in paragraph (f)(3) of this section, this section applies to payments made after December 31, 2000.

T.D. 7977, 9/19/84, amend T.D. 8611, 8/10/95, T.D. 8734, 10/6/97, T.D. 8804, 12/30/98, T.D. 8856, 12/29/99, T.D. 8881, 5/15/2000.

§ 1.1441-8 Exemption from withholding for payments to foreign governments, international organizations, foreign central banks of issue, and the Bank for International Settlements. [Generally effective after 12/31/2000.]

(a) Foreign governments. Under section 892, certain specific types of income received by foreign governments are excluded from gross income and are exempt from taxation, unless derived from the conduct of a commercial activity or received from or by a controlled commercial entity. Accordingly, withholding is not required under § 1441.1 with regard to any item of income which is exempt from taxation under section 892.

(b) Reliance on claim of exemption by foreign government. Absent actual knowledge or reason to know otherwise, the withholding agent may rely upon a claim of exemption made by the foreign government if, prior to the payment, the withholding agent can reliably associate the payment with documentation upon which it can rely to treat the payment as made to a beneficial owner in accordance with § 1.1441-1(e)(1)(ii). A Form W-8 furnished by a foreign government for purposes of claiming an exemption under this paragraph (b) is valid only if, in addition to other applicable requirements, it certifies that the income is, or will be, exempt from taxation under section 892 and the regulations under that section and whether the person whose name is on the certificate is an integral part of a foreign government (as defined in § 1.892-2T(a)(2)) or a controlled entity (as defined in § 1.892-2T(a)(3)).

(c) Income of a foreign central bank of issue or the Bank for International Settlements. *(1) Certain interest income.* Section 895 provides for the exclusion from gross income of certain income derived by a foreign central bank of issue, or by the Bank for International Settlements, from obligations of the United States or of any agency or instrumentality thereof or from interest on deposits with persons carrying on the banking business if the bank is the owner of the obligations or deposits and does not hold the obligations or deposits for, or use them in connection with, the conduct of a commercial banking function or other commercial activity by such bank. See § 1.895-1. Absent actual knowledge or reason to know that a foreign central bank of issue, or the Bank for International Settlements, is operating outside the scope of the exclusion granted by section 895 and the regulations under that section, the withholding agent may rely on a claim of exemption if, prior to the payment, the withholding agent can reliably associate the payment with documentation upon which it can rely to treat the foreign central bank of issue or the Bank for International Settlements as the beneficial owner of the payment in accordance with § 1.1441-1(e)(1)(ii). A Form W-8 furnished by a foreign central bank of issue or the Bank for International Settlements for purposes of claiming an exemption under this paragraph (c)(1) is valid only if, in addition to other applicable requirements, it certifies that the person whose name is on the certificate is a foreign central bank of issue, or the Bank for International Settlements, and that the bank does not, and will not, hold the obligations or the bank deposits covered by the Form W-8 for, or use them in connection with, the conduct of a commercial banking function or other commercial activity.

(2) Bankers' acceptances. Interest derived by a foreign central bank of issue from bankers' acceptances is exempt from tax under sections 871(i)(2)(C) and 881(d) and § 1.861-2(b)(4). With respect to bankers' acceptances, a withholding agent may treat a payee as a foreign central bank of issue without requiring a withholding certificate if the name of the payee and other facts surrounding the payment reasonably indicate that the payee or beneficial owner is a foreign central bank of issue, as defined in § 1.861-2(b)(4).

(d) Exemption for payments to international organizations. A payment to an international organization (within the meaning of section 7701(a)(18)) is exempt from withholding on any payment. A withholding agent may treat a payee as an international organization without requiring a withholding certificate if the name of the payee is one that is designated as an international organization by executive order (pursuant to 22 U.S.C. 288 through 288(f)) and other facts surrounding the transaction reasonably indicate that the international organization is the beneficial owner of the payment.

(e) Failure to receive withholding certificate timely and other applicable procedures. See applicable procedures described in § 1.1441-1(b)(7) in the event the withholding agent does not hold a valid withholding certificate described in paragraph (b) or (c)(1) of this section or other appropriate documentation at the time of payment. Further, the provisions of § 1.1441-1(e)(4) shall apply to withholding certificates and other documents related thereto furnished under the provisions of this section.

(f) Effective date. *(1) In general.* This section applies to payments made after December 31, 2000.

(2) Transition rules. For purposes of this section, the validity of a Form 8709 that was valid on January 1, 1998, under the regulations in effect prior to January 1, 2001 (see 26 CFR part 1, revised April 1, 1999) and expired, or will expire, at any time during 1998, is extended until December 31, 1998. The validity of a Form 8709 that is valid on or after January 1, 1999, remains valid until its validity expires under the regulations in effect prior to January 1, 2001 (see 26 CFR part 1, revised April 1, 1999) but in no event shall such a form remain valid after December 31, 2000. The rule in this paragraph (f)(2), however, does not apply to extend the validity period of a Form 8709 that expires solely by reason of changes in the circumstances of the person whose name is on the certificate. Notwithstanding the first three sentences of this paragraph (f)(2), a withholding agent may choose to not take advantage of the transition rule in this paragraph (f)(2) with respect to one or more withholding certificates valid under the regulations in effect prior to January 1, 2001 (see 26 CFR part 1, revised April 1, 1999) and, therefore, to require withholding certificates conforming to the requirements described in this section (new withholding certificates). For purposes of this section, a new withholding certificate is deemed to satisfy the documentation requirement under the regulations in effect prior to January 1, 2001 (see 26 CFR part 1, revised April 1, 1999). Further, a new withholding certificate remains valid for the period specified in § 1.1441-1(e)(4)(ii), regardless of when the certificate is obtained.

T.D. 8211, 6/24/88, amend T.D. 8734, 10/6/97, T.D. 8804, 12/30/98, T.D. 8856, 12/29/99.

§ 1.1441-9 Exemption from withholding on exempt income of a foreign tax-exempt organization, including foreign private foundations.

(a) Exemption from withholding for exempt income. No withholding is required under section 1441(a) or 1442, and the regulations under those sections, on amounts paid to a foreign organization that is described in section 501(c) to the extent that the amounts are not income includible under section 512 in computing the organization's unrelated business taxable income. See, however, § 1.1443-1 for withholding on payments of unrelated business income to foreign tax-exempt organizations and on payments subject to tax under section 4948. For a foreign organization to claim an exemption from withholding under section 1441(a) or 1442 based on its status as an organization described in section 501(c), it must furnish the withholding agent with a withholding certificate described in paragraph (b)(2) of this section. A foreign organization described in section 501(c) may choose to claim a reduced rate of withholding under the procedures described in other sections of the regulations under section 1441 and not under this section. In particular, if an organization chooses to claim benefits under an income tax treaty, the withholding procedures applicable to claims of such a reduced rate are governed solely by the provisions of § 1.1441-6 and not of this section.

(b) Reliance on foreign organization's claim of exemption from withholding. *(1) General rule.* A withholding agent may rely on a claim of exemption under this section only if, prior to the payment, the withholding agent can reliably associate the payment with a valid withholding certificate described in paragraph (b)(2) of this section.

(2) Withholding certificate. A withholding certificate under this paragraph (b)(2) is valid only if it is a Form W-8 and if, in addition to other applicable requirements, the Form W-8 includes the taxpayer identifying number of the organization whose name is on the certificate, and it certifies that the Internal Revenue Service (IRS) has issued a favorable determination letter (and the date thereof) that is currently in effect, what portion, if any, of the amounts paid constitute income includible under section 512 in computing the organization's unrelated business taxable income, and, if the organization is described in section 501(c)(3), whether it is a private foundation described in section 509. Notwithstanding the preceding sentence, if the organization cannot certify that it has been issued a favorable determination letter that is still in effect, its withholding certificate is nevertheless valid under this paragraph (b)(2) if the organization attaches to the withholding certificate an opinion that is acceptable to the withholding agent from a U.S. counsel (or any other person as the IRS may prescribe in published guidance (see § 601.601(d)(2) of this chapter)) concluding that the organization is described in section 501(c). If the determination letter or opinion of counsel to which the withholding certificate refers concludes that the organization is described in section 501(c)(3), and the certificate further certifies that the organization is not a private foundation described in section 509, an affidavit of the organization setting forth sufficient facts concerning the operations and support of the organization for the Internal Revenue Service (IRS) to determine that such organization would be likely to qualify as an organization described in section 509(a)(1), (2), (3), or (4) must be attached to the withholding certificate. An organization that provides an opinion of U.S. counsel or an affidavit may provide the same opinion or affidavit to more than one withholding agent provided that the opinion is acceptable to each withholding agent who receives it in conjunction with a withholding certificate. Any such opinion of counsel or affidavit must be renewed whenever there is a change in facts or circumstances that are relevant to determine the organization's status under section 501(c) or, if relevant, that the organization is or is not a private foundation described in section 509.

(3) Presumptions in the absence of documentation. Notwithstanding paragraph (b)(1) of this section, if the organization's certification with respect to whether amounts paid constitute income includible under section 512 in computing the organization's unrelated business taxable income is not reliable or is lacking but all other certifications are reliable, the withholding agent may rely on the certificate but the amounts paid are presumed to be income includible under section 512 in computing the organization's unrelated business taxable income. If the certification regarding private foundation status is not reliable, the withholding agent may rely on the certificate but the amounts paid are presumed to be paid to a foreign beneficial owner that is a private foundation.

(4) Reason to know. Reliance by a withholding agent on the information and certifications stated on a withholding certificate is subject to the agent's actual knowledge or reason to know that such information or certification is incorrect as provided in § 1.1441-7(b). For example, a withholding agent must cease to treat a foreign organization's claim for exemption from withholding based on the organization's tax-exempt status as valid beginning on the earlier of the date on which such agent knows that the IRS has given notice to such foreign organization that it is not an organization described in section 501(c) or the date on which the IRS

gives notice to the public that such foreign organization is not an organization described in section 501(c). Similarly, a withholding agent may no longer rely on a certification that an amount is not subject to tax under section 4948 beginning on the earlier of the date on which such agent knows that the IRS has given notice to such foreign organization that it is subject to tax under section 4948 or the date on which the IRS gives notice that such foreign organization is a private foundation within the meaning of section 509(a).

(c) Failure to receive withholding certificate timely and other applicable procedures. See applicable procedures described in § 1.1441-1(b)(7) in the event the withholding agent does not hold a valid withholding certificate or other appropriate documentation at the time of payment. Further, the provisions of § 1.1441-1(e)(4) shall apply to withholding certificates and other documents related thereto furnished under the provisions of this section.

(d) Effective date. *(1) In general.* This section applies to payments made after December 31, 2000.

(2) Transition rules. For purposes of this section, the validity of a Form W-8, 1001, or 4224 or a statement that was valid on January 1, 1998, under the regulations in effect prior to January 1, 2001 (see 26 CFR parts 1 and 35a, revised April 1, 1999) and expired, or will expire, at any time during 1998, is extended until December 31, 1998. The validity of a Form W-8, 1001, or 4224 or a statement that is valid on or after January 1, 1999 remains valid until its validity expires under the regulations in effect prior to January 1, 2001 (see 26 CFR parts 1 and 35a, revised April 1, 1999) but in no event shall such form or statement remain valid after December 31, 2000. The rule in this paragraph (d)(2), however, does not apply to extend the validity period of a Form W-8, 1001, or 4224 or a statement that expires solely by reason of changes in the circumstances of the person whose name is on the certificate. Notwithstanding the first three sentences of this paragraph (d)(2), a withholding agent may choose to not take advantage of the transition rule in this paragraph (d)(2) with respect to one or more withholding certificates valid under the regulations in effect prior to January 1, 2001 (see 26 CFR parts 1 and 35a, revised April 1, 1999) and, therefore, to require withholding certificates conforming to the requirements described in this section (new withholding certificates). For purposes of this section, a new withholding certificate is deemed to satisfy the documentation requirement under the regulations in effect prior to January 1, 2001 (see 26 CFR parts 1 and 35a, revised April 1, 1999). Further, a new withholding certificate remains valid for the period specified in § 1.1441-1(e)(4)(ii), regardless of when the certificate is obtained.

T.D. 8734, 10/6/97, amend T.D. 8804, 12/30/98, T.D. 8856, 12/29/99, T.D. 8881, 5/15/2000.

§ 1.1441-10 Withholding agents with respect to fast-pay arrangements.

(a) In general. A corporation that issues fast-pay stock in a fast-pay arrangement described in § 1.7701(l)-3(b)(1) is a withholding agent with respect to payments made on the fast-pay stock and payments deemed made under the recharacterization rules of § 1.7701(l)-3. Except as provided in this paragraph (a) or in paragraph (b) of this section, the withholding tax rules under section 1441 and section 1442 apply with respect to a fast-pay arrangement described in § 1.7701(l)-3(c)(1)(i) in accordance with the recharacterization rules provided in § 1.7701(l)-3(c). In all cases, notwithstanding paragraph (b) of this section, if at any time the withholding agent knows or has reason to know that the Commissioner has exercised the discretion under either § 1.7701(l)-3(c)(1)(ii) to apply the recharacterization rules of § 1.7701(l)-3(c), or § 1.7701(l)-3(d) to depart from the recharacterization rules of § 1.7701(l)-3(c) for a taxpayer, the withholding agent must withhold on payments made (or deemed made) to that taxpayer in accordance with the characterization of the fast-pay arrangement imposed by the Commissioner under § 1.7701(l)-3.

(b) Exception. If at any time the withholding agent knows or has reason to know that any taxpayer entered into a fast-pay arrangement with a principal purpose of applying the recharacterization rules of § 1.7701(l)-3(c) to avoid tax under section 871(a) or section 881, then for each payment made or deemed made to such taxpayer under the arrangement, the withholding agent must withhold, under section 1441 or section 1442, the higher of—

(1) The amount of withholding that would apply to such payment determined under the form of the arrangement; or

(2) The amount of withholding that would apply to deemed payments determined under the recharacterization rules of § 1.7701(l)-3(c).

(c) Liability. Any person required to deduct and withhold tax under this section is made liable for that tax by section 1461, and is also liable for applicable penalties and interest for failing to comply with section 1461.

(d) Examples. The following examples illustrate the rules of this section:

Example (1). REIT W issues shares of fast-pay stock to foreign individual A, a resident of Country C. United States source dividends paid to residents of C are subject to a 30 percent withholding tax. W issues all shares of benefited stock to foreign individuals who are residents of Country D. D's income tax convention with the United States reduces the United States withholding tax on dividends to 15 percent. Under § 1.7701(l). 3(c), the dividends paid by W to A are deemed to be paid by W to the benefited shareholders. W has reason to know that A entered into the fast-pay arrangement with a principal purpose of using the recharacterization rules of § 1.7701(l)-3(c) to reduce United States withholding tax. W must withhold at the 30 percent rate because the amount of withholding that applies to the payments determined under the form of the arrangement is higher than the amount of withholding that applies to the payments determined under § 1.7701(l)-3(c).

Example (2). The facts are the same as in Example 1 of this paragraph (d) except that W does not know, or have reason to know, that A entered into the arrangement with a principal purpose of using the recharacterization rules of § 1.7701(l)-3(c) to reduce United States withholding tax. Further, the Commissioner has not exercised the discretion under § 1.7701(l)-3(d) to depart from the recharacterization rules of § 1.7701(l)-3(c). Accordingly, W must withhold tax at a 15 percent rate on the dividends deemed paid to the benefited shareholders.

(e) Effective date. This section applies to payments made (or deemed made) on or after January 6, 1999.

T.D. 8853, 1/7/2000.

§ 1.1442-1 Withholding of tax on foreign corporations.

For regulations concerning the withholding of tax at source under section 1442 in the case of foreign corporations, foreign governments, international organizations, foreign tax-exempt corporations, or foreign private foundations, see §§ 1.1441-1 through 1.1441-9.

T.D. 6187, 7/5/56, amend T.D. 6908, 12/30/66, T.D. 8734, 10/6/97.

§ 1.1442-2 Exemption under a tax treaty.

For regulations providing for a claim of reduced withholding tax under section 1442 by certain foreign corporations pursuant to the provisions of an income tax treaty, see § 1.1441-6.

T.D. 6908, 12/30/66, amend T.D. 8734, 10/6/97.

§ 1.1442-3 Tax exempt income of a foreign tax-exempt corporations.

For regulations providing for a claim of exemption for income exempt from tax under section 501(a) of a foreign tax-exempt corporation, see § 1.1441-9. See § 1.1443-1 for withholding rules applicable to foreign private foundations and to the unrelated business income of foreign tax-exempt organizations.

T.D. 8734, 10/6/97, amend T.D. 8804, 12/30/98.

§ 1.1443-1 Foreign tax-exempt organizations.

(a) Income includible in computing unrelated business taxable income. In the case of a foreign organization that is described in section 501(c), amounts paid or effectively connected taxable income allocable to the organization that are includible under section 512 and section 513 in computing the organization's unrelated business taxable income are subject to withholding under §§ 1.1441-1, 1.1441-4, 1.1441-6, and 1.1446-1 through 1.1446-6, in the same manner as payments or allocations of effectively connected taxable income of the same amounts made to any foreign person that is not a tax-exempt organization. Therefore, a foreign organization receiving amounts includible under section 512 and section 513 in computing the organization's unrelated business taxable income may claim an exemption from withholding or a reduced rate of withholding with respect to that income in the same manner as a foreign person that is not a tax-exempt organization. See § 1.1441-9(b)(3) for a presumption that amounts are includible under section 512 and section 513 in computing the organization's unrelated business taxable income in the absence of reliable certification. See also § 1.1446-3(c)(3), applying this presumption in the context of section 1446.

(b) Income subject to tax under section 4948. *(1) In general.* The gross investment income (as defined in section 4940(c)(2)) of a foreign private foundation is subject to withholding under section 1443(b) at the rate of 4 percent to the extent that the income is from sources within the United States and is subject to the tax imposed by section 4948(a) and the regulations under that section. Withholding under this paragraph (b) is required irrespective of the fact that the income may be effectively connected with the conduct of a trade or business in the United States by the foreign organization. See § 1.1441-9(b)(3) for applicable presumptions that amounts are subject to tax under section 4948. The withholding imposed under this paragraph (b)(1) does not obviate a private foundation's obligation to file any return required by law with respect to such organization, such as the form that the foundation is required to file under section 6033 for the taxable year.

(2) Reliance on a foreign organization's claim of foreign private foundation status. For reliance by a withholding agent on a foreign organization's claim of foreign private foundation status, see § 1.1441-9(b) and (c).

(3) Applicable procedures. A withholding agent withholding the 4-percent amount pursuant to paragraph (b)(1) of this section shall treat such withholding as withholding under section 1441(a) or 1442(a) for all purposes, including reporting of the payment on a Form 1042 and a Form 1042-S pursuant to § 1.1461-1(b) and (c). Similarly, the foreign private foundation shall treat the 4-percent withholding as withholding under section 1441(a) or 1442(a), including for purposes of claims for refunds and credits.

(4) Claim of benefits under an income tax treaty. The withholding procedures applicable to claims of a reduced rate under an income tax treaty are governed solely by the provisions of § 1.1441-6 and not by this section.

(c) Effective date. *(1) In general.* This section applies to payments made after December 31, 2000, except that the references in paragraph (a) of this section to effectively connected taxable income and withholding under section 1446 shall apply to partnership taxable years beginning after May 18, 2005, or such earlier time as the regulations under §§ 1.1446-1 through 1.1446-5 apply by reason of an election under § 1.1446-7.

(2) Transition rules. For purposes of this section, the validity of an affidavit or opinion of counsel described in § 1.1443-1(b)(4)(i) in effect prior to January 1, 2001 (see § 1.1443-1(b)(4)(i) as contained in 26 CFR part 1, revised April 1, 1999) is extended until December 31, 2000. However, a withholding agent may choose to not take advantage of the transition rule in this paragraph (c)(2) with respect to one or more withholding certificates valid under the regulations in effect prior to January 1, 2001 (see 26 CFR part 1, revised April 1, 1999) and, therefore, to require withholding certificates conforming to the requirements described in this section (new withholding certificates). For purposes of this section, a new withholding certificate is deemed to satisfy the documentation requirement under the regulations in effect prior to January 1, 2001 (see 26 CFR part 1, revised April 1, 1999). Further, a new withholding certificate remains valid for the period specified in § 1.1441-1(e)(4)(ii), regardless of when the certificate is obtained.

T.D. 6187, 7/5/56, amend T.D. 6908, 12/30/66, T.D. 7229, 12/20/72, T.D. 7247, 12/29/72, T.D. 8734, 10/6/97, T.D. 8804, 12/30/98, T.D. 8856, 12/29/99, T.D. 9200, 5/13/2005, T.D. 9394, 4/28/2008.

§ 1.1445-1 Withholding on dispositions of U.S. real property interests by foreign persons: In general.

(a) Purpose and scope of regulations. These regulations set forth rules relating to the withholding requirements of section 1445. In general, section 1445(a) provides that any person who acquires a U.S. real property interest from a foreign person must withhold a tax of 10 percent from the amount realized by the transferor foreign person (or a lesser amount established by agreement with the Internal Revenue Service). Section 1445(e) provides special rules requiring withholding on distributions and certain other transactions by corporations, partnerships, trusts, and estates. This § 1.1445-1 provides general rules concerning the withholding requirement of sections 1445(a), as well as definitions applicable under both section 1445(a) and 1445(e). Section 1.1445-2 provides for various situations in which withholding is not required under section 1445(a). Section 1.1445-3 provides for adjustments to the amount required to be withheld by transferees under section 1445(a). Section 1.1445-4 prescribes the duties of agents in transactions subject to withholding under either section 1445(a) or 1445(e). Section 1.1445-5 provides rules concerning the withholding required under section 1445(e), while § 1.1445-6 provides for adjustments to the amount required to be withheld under section 1445(e). Finally, § 1.1445-7 provides rules concerning the treatment of a foreign corporation that has made an election under section 897(i) to be treated as a domestic corporation.

(b) Duty to withhold. *(1) In general.* Transferees of U.S. real property interests are required to deduct and withhold a tax equal to 10 percent of the amount realized by the transferor, if the transferor is a foreign person and the disposition takes place on or after January 1, 1985. Neither the transferee's duty to withhold nor the amount required to be withheld is affected by the amount of cash to be paid by the transferee. Amounts withheld must be reported and paid over in accordance with the requirements of paragraph (c) of this section. Failures to withhold and pay over are subject to the liabilities set forth in paragraph (e) of this section. If two or more persons are joint transferees of a U.S. real property interest, each such person is subject to the obligation to withhold. That obligation is fulfilled with respect to each such person if any one of them withholds and pays over the required amount in accordance with the rules of this section. If the amount realized (as defined in paragraph (g)(5) of this section) by the transferor is zero, then no withholding is required. For example, if a real property interest is transferred as a gift (i.e, the recipient does not assume any liabilities or furnish any other consideration to the transferor) then no withholding is required. Withholding is not required with respect to dispositions that takes place before January 1, 1985, even if the first payment of consideration is made after December 31, 1984.

(2) U.S. real property interest owned jointly by foreign and non-foreign transferors. The amount subject to withholding under paragraph (b)(1) of this section with respect to the transfer of a U.S. real property interest owned by one or more foreign persons (as defined in § 1.897-1(k)) and one or more nonforeign persons shall be determined by allocating the amount realized from the transfer between (or among) such transferors based upon the capital contribution of each transferor with respect to the property and by aggregating the amounts allocated to any foreign person (or persons). For this purpose, a husband and wife will each be deemed to have contributed 50 percent of the aggregate capital contributed by such husband and wife. See § 1.1445-1(f)(3)(iv) with respect to the crediting of the amount withheld between or among joint foreign transferors.

(3) Options to acquire a U.S. real property interest. (i) No withholding on grant of option. No withholding is required under section 1445 with respect to any amount realized by the grantor on the grant of an option to acquire a U.S. real property interest.

(ii) No withholding upon lapse of option. No withholding is required under section 1445 with respect to any amount realized by the grantor upon the lapse of an option to acquire a U.S. real property interest.

(iii) Withholding required upon the sale or exchange of option. A transferee of an option to acquire a U.S. real property interest must deduct and withhold a tax equal to 10 percent of the amount realized by the transferor upon the disposition. This § 1.1445-1(b)(3)(iii) does not apply to require withholding upon the initial grant of an option.

(iv) Withholding required on exercise of option. If the holder exercises an option to purchase a U.S. real property interest, the amount paid for the option shall be considered an amount realized by the grantor/transferor upon the transfer of the property with respect to which the option was granted, and shall thus be subject to withholding on the day that such underlying property is transferred. The preceding sentence applies regardless of whether or not the terms of the option specifically provide that the option price is applied to the purchase price.

(4) Exceptions and modifications. The duty to withhold under section 1445(a) is subject to the exceptions and modifications contained in §§ 1.1445-2 and 1.1445-3. Generally, § 1.1445-2 provides rules for determining that withholding is not required because either the transfer is not a foreign person or the interest transferred is not a U.S. real property interest. In addition, § 1.1445-2 provides exceptions to the withholding requirement, including a rule that exempts from withholding any person who acquires a U.S. real property interest for use as a residence for a contract price of $300,000 or less. If withholding is required under section 1445(a), § 1.1445-3 allows the amount withheld to be modified pursuant to a withholding certificate issued by the Internal Revenue Service. If a transferee cannot withhold the full amount required because the first payment of consideration for the transfer does not involve sufficient cash (or other liquid assets convertible into cash, such as foreign currency), then a withholding certificate must be obtained pursuant to § 1.1445-3.

(c) Reporting and paying over of withheld amounts. *(1) In general.* A transferee must report and pay over any tax withheld by the 20th day after the date of the transfer. Forms 8288 and 8288-A are used for this purpose, and must be filed at the location as provided in the instructions to Forms 8288 and 8288-A. Pursuant to section 7502 and regulations thereunder, the timely mailing of Forms 8288 and 8228-A will be treated as their timely filing. Form 8288-A will be stamped by the IRS to show receipt, and a stamped copy will be mailed by the IRS to the transferor (at the address reported on the form) for the transferor's use. See §§ 1.1445-1(f) and 1.1445-3(f). Forms 8288 and 8288-A are required to include the identifying numbers of both the transferor and the transferee, as provided in paragraph (d) of this section. If any identifying number as required by such forms is not provided, the transferee must still report and pay over any tax withheld on Form 8288, although the transferor cannot obtain a credit or refund of tax on the basis of a Form 8288-A that does not include the transferor's identifying number (see paragraph (f)(2) of this section).

(2) Pending application for withholding certificate. (i) In general. (A) Delayed reporting and payment with respect to application submitted by transferee. If an application for a withholding certificate with respect to a transfer of a U.S. real property interest is submitted to the Internal Revenue Service by the transferee on the day of or at any time prior to the transfer, the transferee must withhold 10 percent of the amount realized as required by paragraph (b) of this section. However, the amount withheld, or a lesser amount as determined by the Service, need not be reported and paid over to the Service until the 20th day following the Service's final determination with respect to the application for a withholding certificate. For this purpose, the Service's final determination occurs on the day when the withholding certificate is mailed to the transferee by the Service or when a notification denying the request for a withholding certificate is mailed to the transferee by the Service. An application is submitted to the Service on the day it is actually received by the Service at the address provided in § 1.1445-1(g)(10) or, under the rules of section 7502, on the day it is mailed to the Service at the address provided in § 1.1445-1(g)(10).

(B) Delayed reporting and payment with respect to application submitted by transferor. If an application for a withholding certificate with respect to a transfer of a U.S. real property interest is submitted to the Internal Revenue Service by the Transferor on the day of or any time prior to the transfer, such transferor must provide notice to the transferee prior to the transfer. No particular form is required but the notice must set forth the name, address, and taxpayer identification number of the transferor, a brief description of the property which is the subject of the application, and the date the application was submitted to the Service. The transferee must withhold 10 percent of the amount realized as required in paragraph (b) of this section but need not report or pay over to the Service such amount (or a lesser amount as determined by the Service) until the 20th day following the Service's final determination with respect to the application.

The Service will send a copy of the withholding certificate or copy of the notification denying the request for a withholding certificate to the transferee. For this purpose, the Service's final determination will be deemed to occur on the day when the copy of the withholding certificate or the copy of the notification denying the request for a withholding certificate is mailed by the Service to the transferee (or transferees). An application is submitted to the Service on the day it is actually received by the Service at the address provided in § 1.1445-1(g)(10) or, under the rules of § 7502, on the day it is mailed to the Service at the address provided in § 1.1445-1(g)(10).

(ii) Anti-abuse rule. (A) In general. A transferee that in reliance upon the rules of this paragraph (c)(2) fails to report and pay over amounts withheld by the 20th day following the date of the transfer, shall be subject to the payment of interest and penalties if the relevant application for a withholding certificate (or an amendment to the application for a withholding certificate) was submitted for a principal purpose of delaying the transferee's payment to the IRS of the amount withheld. Interest and penalties shall be assessed on the amount that is ultimately paid over (or collected pursuant to the agreement) with respect to the period between the 20th day after the date of the transfer and the date on which payment is made (or collected).

(B) Presumption. A principal purpose of delaying payment of the amount withheld shall be presumed if—

(1) The transferee applies for a withholding certificate pursuant to § 1.1445-3(c) based on a determination of the transferor's maximum tax liability, and

(2) Such liability is ultimately determined to be equal to 90 percent or more of the amount that was otherwise required to be withheld and paid over. However, the presumption created by the previous sentence may be rebutted by evidence establishing that delaying payment of the amount withheld was not a principal purpose of the transaction.

(d) Contents of Forms 8288 and 8288-A. *(1) Transactions subject to section 1445(a).* Any person that is required to file Forms 8288 and 8288-A pursuant to section 1445(a) and the rules of this section must set forth thereon the following information:

(i) The name, identifying number, and home address (in the case of an individual) or office address (in the case of any entity) of the transferee(s) filing the return;

(ii) The name, identifying number, and home address (in the case of an individual) or office address (in the case of any entity) of the transferor(s);

(iii) A brief description of the U.S. real property interest transferred, including its location and the nature of any substantial improvements in the case of real property, and the class or type and amount of interests transferred in the case of interests in a corporation that constitute U.S. real property interests;

(iv) The date of the transfer;

(v) The amount realized by the transferor, as defined in paragraph (g)(5) of this section;

(vi) The amount withheld by the transferee and whether withholding is at the statutory or reduced rate; and

(vii) Such other information as the Commissioner may require.

For purposes of paragraph (d)(1)(i) and (ii), mailing addresses may be provided in addition to, but not in lieu of, home addresses or office addresses.

(2) Transactions subject to section 1445(e). Any person that is required to file Forms 8288 and 8288-A pursuant to the rules of § 1.1445-5 must set forth thereon the following information:

(i) The name, identifying number, and office address of the entity or fiduciary filing the return;

(ii) The amount withheld by the entity or fiduciary;

(iii) The date of the transfer;

(iv) In the case of a transaction subject to withholding pursuant to section 1445(e)(1) and § 1.1445-5(c):

(A) A brief description of the U.S. real property interest transferred, as described in paragraph (d)(1)(iii) of this section;

(B) The name, identifying number, and home address (in the case of an individual) or office address (in the case of an entity) of each holder of an interest in the entity that is a foreign person; and

(C) Each such interest-holder's pro rata share of the amount withheld;

(v) In the case of a distribution subject to withholding pursuant to section 1445(e)(2) and § 1.1445-5(d):

(A) A brief description of the U.S. real property interest transferred, as described in paragraph (d)(1)(iii) of this section; and

(B) The amount of gain recognized upon the distribution by the corporation.

(vi) In the case of a distribution subject to withholding pursuant to section 1445(e)(3) and § 1.1445-5(e):

(A) A brief description of the property distributed by the corporation;

(B) The name, identifying number, and home address (in case of an individual) or office address (in the case of an entity) of each holder of an interest in the entity that is a foreign person;

(C) The amount realized upon the distribution by each such foreign interest holder; and

(D) Each foreign interest-holder's pro rata share of the amount withheld; and

(vii) Such other information as the Commissioner may require.

(e) Liability of transferee upon failure to withhold. *(1) In general.* Every person required to deduct and withhold tax under section 1445 is made liable for that tax by section 1461. Therefore, a person that is required to deduct and withhold tax but fails to do so may be held liable for the payment of the tax and any applicable penalties and interest.

(2) Transferor's liability not otherwise satisfied. (i) Tax and penalties. Except as provided in paragraph (e)(3) of this section, if a transferee is required to deduct and withhold tax under section 1445 but fails to do so, then the tax shall be assessed against and collected from that transferee. Such person may also be subject to any of the civil and criminal penalties that apply. Corporate officers or other responsible persons may be subject to a civil penalty under section 6672 equal to the amount that should have been withheld and paid over.

(ii) Interest. If a transferee is required to deduct and withhold tax under section 1445 but fails to do so, then such transferee shall be liable for the payment of interest pursuant to section 6601 and the regulations thereunder. Interest shall be payable with respect to the period between—

(A) The last date on which the tax imposed under section 1445 was required to be paid over by the transferee, and

(B) The date on which such tax is actually paid. Interest shall be payable with respect to the entire amount that is required to be deducted and withheld. However, if the Service issues a withholding certificate providing for withholding of a reduced amount, then, for the period after the issuance of the certificate, interest shall be payable with respect to that reduced amount.

(3) Transferor's liability otherwise satisfied. (i) Tax and penalties. If a transferee is required to deduct and withhold tax under section 1445 but fails to do so, and the transferor's tax liability with respect to the transfer was satisfied (or was established to be zero) by—

(A) The transferor's filing of an income tax return (and payment of any tax due) with respect to the transfer, or

(B) The issuance of a withholding certificate by the Internal Revenue Service establishing that the transferor's maximum tax liability is zero.

then the tax required to be withheld under section 1445 shall not be collected from the transferee. Such transferee's liability for tax, and the requirement that such person file Forms 8288 and 8288-A, shall be deemed to have been satisfied as of the date on which the transferor's income tax return was filed or the withholding certificate was issued. No penalty shall be imposed on or collected from such person for failure to return or pay the tax, unless such failure was fraudulent and for the purpose of evading payment. A transferee that seeks to avoid liability for tax and penalties pursuant to the rule of paragraph (e)(3)(i) must provide sufficient information for the Service to determine whether the transferor's tax liability was satisfied (or was established to be zero).

(ii) Interest. If a transferee is required to deduct and withhold tax under section 1445 but fails to do so, then such person shall be liable for the payment of interest under section 6601 and regulations thereunder. Such transferee's liability for the payment of interest shall not be excused by reason of the deemed satisfaction, pursuant to subdivision (i) of this paragraph (e)(3), of the transferee's liability under section 1445, because the deemed satisfaction of that liability is the equivalent of the late payment of a liability, on which interest must be paid. Interest shall be payable with respect to the period between—

(A) The last date on which the tax imposed under section 1445 was required to be paid over, and

(B) The date (established from information supplied to the Service by the transferee) on which any tax due is paid with respect to the transferor's relevant income tax return, or the date the withholding certificate is issued establishing that the transferor's maximum tax liability is zero. Interest shall be payable with respect to the entire amount that is required to be deducted and withheld. However, if the Service issues a withholding certificate providing for withholding of a reduced amount, then for the period after the issuance of the certificate interest shall be payable with respect to that reduced amount.

(4) Coordination with entity with holding rules. For purposes of section 1445(e) and §§ 1.1445-5, 1.1445-6, 1.1445-7, and 1.1445-8T, the rules of this paragraph (e) shall be applied by—

(i) Substituting the words "person required to withhold" for the word "transferee" each place it appears in this paragraph (e), and

(ii) Substituting the words "person subject to withholding" for the word "transferor" each place it appears in this paragraph (e).

(f) Effect of withholding on transferor. *(1) In general.* The withholding of tax under section 1445(a) does not excuse a foreign person that disposes of a U.S. real property interest from filing a U.S. tax return with respect to the income arising from the disposition. Form 1040NR, 1041, or 1120F, as appropriate, must be filed, and any tax due must be paid, by the filing deadline generally applicable to such person. (The return may be filed by such later date as is provided in an extension granted by the Internal Revenue Service.) Any tax withheld under section 1445(a) shall be credited against the amount of income tax as computed in such return.

(2) Manner of obtaining credit or refund. A stamped copy of Form 8288-A will be provided to the transferor by the Service (under paragraph (c) of this section) if the Form 8288-A is complete, including the transferor's identifying number. Except as provided in paragraph (f)(3) of this section, a stamped copy of Form 8288-A must be attached to the transferor's return to establish the amount withheld that is available as a credit. If to establish the amount with that is available as a credit. If the amount withheld under section 1445(a) constitutes less than the full amount of the transferor's U.S. tax liability for that taxable year, then a payment of estimated tax may be required to be made pursuant to section 6154 or 6654 prior to the filing of the income tax return for that year. Alternatively, if the amount withheld under section 1445(a) exceeds the transferor's maximum tax liability with respect to the disposition (as determined by the IRS), then the transferor may seek an early refund of the excess pursuant to § 1.1445-3(g), or a normal refund upon the filing of a tax return.

(3) Special rules. (i) Failure to receive Form 8288-A. If a stamped copy of Form 8288-A has not been provided to the transferor by the Service, the transferor may establish the amount of tax withheld by the transferee by attaching to its return substantial evidence (e.g., closing documents) of such amount. Such a transferor must attach to its return a statement which supplies all of the information required by § 1.1445-1(d), including the transferor's identifying number.

(ii) U.S. persons subjected to withholding. If a transferee withholds tax under section 1445(a) with respect to a person who is not a foreign person, such person may credit the amount of any tax withheld against his income tax liability in accordance with the provisions of this § 1.1145-1(f) or apply for an early refund under § 1.1445-3(g).

(iii) Refund in case of installment sale. A transferor that takes gain into account in accordance with the provisions of section 453 shall not be entitled to a refund of the amount withheld, unless a withholding certificate providing for such a refund is obtained from the Internal Revenue Service pursuant to the provisions of § 1.1445-3.

(iv) Joint foreign transferors. If two or more foreign persons jointly transfer a U.S. real property interest, each transferor shall be credited with such portion of the amount withheld as such transferors mutually agree. Such transferors must request that the transferee reflect the agreed-upon crediting of the amount withheld on the Forms 8288-A filed by the transferee. If the foreign transferors fail to request that the transferee reflect the agreed-upon crediting of the amount withheld by the 10th day after the date of transfer, the transferee must credit the amount withheld equally between (or among) the foreign transferors. In such case, the transferee is indemnified pursuant to section 1461 against any claim by a transferor objecting to the resulting division of credits. For rules regarding the amount realized allocated to joint foreign and non-foreign transferors, see § 1.1445-1(b)(2).

(g) Definitions. *(1) In general.* Unless otherwise specified, the definitions of terms provided in § 1.897-1 shall apply for purposes of this section and §§ 1.1445-2 through 1.1445-7. For purposes of section 1445 and the regulations thereunder, definitions of other relevant terms are provided in this paragraph (g). In addition, the term "residence" is defined in § 1.1445-2(d)(1), the terms "transferor's agent" and "transferee's agent" are defined in § 1.1445-4(f), and the term "relevant taxpayer" is defined in § 1.1445-6(a)(2).

(2) Transfer. The term "transfer" means any transaction that would constitute a disposition for any purpose, of the Internal Revenue Code and regulations thereunder. For purposes of §§ 1.1445-5 and 1.1445-6, the term includes distribution to shareholders of a corporation, partners of a partnership and beneficiaries of a trust or estate.

(3) Transferor. The term "transferor" means any person, foreign or domestic, that disposes of a U.S. real property interest by sale, exchange, gift, or any other transfer. The term "U.S. real property interest" is defined in § 1.897-1(c).

(4) Transferee. The term "transferee" means any person, foreign or domestic, that acquires a U.S. real property interest by purchase, exchange, gift, or any other transfer.

(5) Amount realized. The amount realized by the transferor for the transfer of a U.S. real property interest is the sum of.

(i) The cash paid, or to be paid.

(ii) The fair market value of other property transferred, or to be transferred, and

(iii) The outstanding amount of any liability assumed by the transferee or to which the U.S. real property interest is subject immediately before and after the transfer.

The term "cash paid or to be paid" does not include stated or unstated interest or original issue discount (as determined under the rules of sections 1271 through 1275).

(6) Contract price. The contract price of a U.S. real property interest is the sum that is agreed to by the transferee and transferor as the total amount of consideration to be paid for the property. That amount will generally be equal to the amount realized by the transferor, as defined in paragraph (b)(5) of this section.

(7) Fair market value. The fair market value of property means the price at which the property would change hands between an unrelated willing buyer and willing seller, neither being under any compulsion to buy or to sell and both having reasonable knowledge of all relevant facts.

(8) Date of transfer. The date of transfer of a U.S. real property interest is the first date on which consideration is paid (or a liability assumed) by the transferee. However, for purposes of section 1445(e)(2), (3), and (4) and §§ 1.1445-5(c)(1)(iii) and 1.1445-5(c)(3) only, the date of transfer is the date of the distribution that gives rise to the obligation to withhold. For purposes of this paragraph (g)(8), the payment of consideration does not include the payment, prior to the passage of legal or equitable title (other than pursuant to an initial contract for purchase), of earnest money, a good-faith deposit, or any similar sum that is primarily intended to bind the transferee or transferor to the entering or performance of a contract. Such a payment will not constitute a payment of consideration solely because it may ultimately be applied against the amount owed to the transferor by the transferee. Such a payment is presumed to be earnest money, a good faith deposit, or a similar sum if it is subject to forfeiture in the event of a failure to enter into a contract or a breach of contract. However, a payment that is not forfeitable may nevertheless be found to constitute earnest money, a good faith deposit, or a similar sum.

(9) Identifying number. Pursuant to § 1.897-1(p), an individual's identifying number is the social security number or the identification number assigned by the Internal Revenue Service (see § 301.6109-1 of this chapter). The identifying number of any other person is its United States employer identification number.

(10) Address of the Director, Philadelphia Service Center. Any written communication directed to the Director, Philadelphia Service Center is to be addressed as follows: P.O. Box 21086, Drop Point 8731, FIRPTA Unit, Philadelphia, PA 19114-0586.

(h) Effective date for taxpayer identification numbers. The requirement in paragraphs (c)(2)(i)(B), (d)(1)(i) and (ii), (d)(2)(i), (d)(2)(iv)(B), and (d)(2)(vi)(B) of this section that taxpayer identification numbers be provided (in all cases) is applicable for dispositions of U.S. real property interests occurring after November 3, 2003.

T.D. 8113, 12/18/86, amend T.D. 8647, 12/20/95, T.D. 9082, 8/4/2003.

§ 1.1445-2 Situations in which withholding is not required under section 1445(a).

(a) Purpose and scope of section. This section provides rules concerning various situations in which withhold is not required under section 1445(a). In general, a transferee has a duty to withhold under section 1445(a) only if both of the following are true:

(1) The transferor is a foreign person: and

(2) The transferee is acquiring a U.S. real property interest.

Thus, paragraphs (b) and (c) of this section provide rules under which a transferee of property can ascertain that he has no duty to withhold because one or the other of the two key elements is missing. Under paragraph (b), a transferee may determine that no withholding is required because the transferor is not a foreign person. Under paragraph (c), a transferee may determine that no withholding is required because the property acquired is not a U.S. real property interest. Finally, paragraph (d) of this section provides rules concerning exceptions to the withholding requirement.

(b) Transferor not a foreign person. *(1) In general.* No withholding is required under section 1445 if the transferor of a U.S. real property interest is not a foreign person. Therefore, paragraph (b)(2) of this section provides rules pursuant to which the transferor can provide a certification of nonforeign status to inform the transferee that withholding is not required. A transferee that obtains such a certification must retain that document for five years, as provided in paragraph (b)(3) of this section. Except to the extent provided in paragraph (b)(4) of this section, the obtaining of this certification excuses the transferee from any liability otherwise imposed by section 1445 and § 1.1445-1(e). However, section 1445 and the rules of this section do not impose any obligation upon a transferee to obtain a certification from the transferor, thus, a transferee may instead rely upon other means to ascertain the non-foreign status of the transferor. If, however, the transferee relies upon other means and the transferor was, in fact, a foreign person, then the transferee is subject to the liability imposed by section 1445 and § 1.1445-1(e).

A transferee is in no event required to rely upon other means to ascertain the non-foreign status of the transferor and may demand a certification of non-foreign status. If the certification is not provided, the transferee may withhold tax under section 1445 and will be considered, for purposes of sections 1461 through 1463, to have been required to withhold such tax.

(2) Transferor's certification of non-foreign status. (i) In general. A transferee of a U.S. real property interest is not required to withhold under section 1445(a) if, prior to or at the time of the transfer, the transferor furnishes to the transferee a certification that—

(A) States that the transferor is not a foreign person.

(B) Sets forth the transferor's name, identifying number and home address (in the case of an individual) or office address (in the case of an entity), and

(C) Is signed under penalties of perjury.

In general, a foreign person is a nonresident alien individual, foreign corporation, foreign partnership, foreign trust, or foreign estate, but not a resident alien individual. In this regard, see § 1.897-1(k). However, a foreign corporation that has made a valid election under section 897(i) is generally not treated as a foreign person for purposes of section 1445. In this regard, see § 1.1445-7. Pursuant to § 1.897-1(p), an individual's identifying number is the individual's Social Security number and any other person's identifying number is its U.S. employer identification number. A certification pursuant to this paragraph (b) must be verified as true and signed under penalties of perjury by a responsible officer in the case of a corporation, by a general partner in the case of a partnership, and by a trustee, executor, or equivalent fiduciary in the case of a trust or estate. No particular form is needed for a certification pursuant to this paragraph (b), nor is any particular language required, so long as the document meets the requirements of this paragraph (b)(2)(i). Samples of acceptable certifications are provided in paragraph (b)(2)(iii) of this section.

(ii) Foreign corporation that "has made election under section 897(i). A foreign corporation that has made a valid election under section 897(i) to be treated as a domestic corporation for purposes of section 897 may provide a certification of non-foreign status pursuant to this paragraph (b)(2). However, an electing foreign corporation must attach to such certification a copy of the acknowledgment of the election provided to the corporation by the Internal Revenue Service pursuant to § 1.897-3(d)(4).

An acknowledgment is valid for this purpose only if it states that the information required by § 1.897-3 has been determined to be complete.

(iii) Disregarded entities. A disregarded entity may not certify that it is the transferor of a U.S. real property interest, as the disregarded entity is not the transferor for U.S. tax purposes, including sections 897 and 1445. Rather, the owner of the disregarded entity is treated as the transferor of property and must provide a certificate of non-foreign status to avoid withholding under section 1445. A disregarded entity for these purposes means an entity that is disregarded as an entity separate from its owner under § 301.7701-3 of this chapter, a qualified REIT subsidiary as defined in section 856(i), or a qualified subchapter S subsidiary under section 1361(b)(3)(B). Any domestic entity must include in its certification of non-foreign status with respect to the transfer a certification that it is not a disregarded entity. This paragraph (b)(2)(iii) and the sample certification provided in paragraph (b)(2)(iv)(B) of this section (to the extent it addresses disregarded entities) is applicable for dispositions occurring [after] September 4, 2003.

(iv) Sample certifications. (A) Individual transferor. "Section 1445 of the Internal Revenue Code provides that a transferee (buyer) of a U.S. real property interest must withhold tax if the transferor (seller) is a foreign person. To inform the transferee (buyer) that withholding of tax is not required upon my disposition of a U.S. real property interest, I, *[name of transferor]*, hereby certify the following:

1. I am not a nonresident alien for purposes of U.S. income taxation;
2. My U.S. taxpayer identifying number [Social Security number] is ________; and
3. My home address is:

____

____

I understand that this certification may be disclosed to the Internal Revenue Service by the transferee and that any false statement I have made here could be punished by fine, imprisonment, or both.

Under penalties of perjury I declare that I have examined this certification and to the best of my knowledge and belief it is true, correct, and complete. [Signature and Date]"

(B) Entity transferor. "Section 1445 of the Internal Revenue Code provides that a transferee of a U.S. real property interest must withhold tax if the transferor is a foreign person. For U.S. tax purposes (including section 1445), the owner of a disregarded entity (which has legal title to a U.S. real property interest under local law) will be the transferor of the property and not the disregarded entity. To inform the transferee that withholding of tax is not required upon the disposition of a U.S. real property interest by [name of transferor] , the undersigned hereby certifies the following on behalf of [name of the transferor]:

1. [Name of transferor] is not a foreign corporation, foreign partnership, foreign trust, or foreign estate (as those terms are defined in the Internal Revenue Code and Income Tax Regulations);

2. [Name of transferor] is not a disregarded entity as defined in § 1.1445-2(b)(2)(iii);

3. [Name of transferor]'s U.S. employer identification number is;

____ and

4. [Name of transferor]'s office address is

____

[Name of transferor] understands that this certification may be disclosed to the Internal Revenue Service by transferee and that any false statement contained herein could be punished by fine, imprisonment, or both.

Under penalties of perjury I declare that I have examined this certification and to the best of my knowledge and belief it is true, correct, and complete, and I further declare that I have authority to sign this document on behalf of [name of transferor].

[Signature(s) and date] [Title(s)] _________'

(3) Transferee must retain certification. If a transferee obtains a transferor's certification pursuant to the rules of this paragraph (b), then the transferee must retain that certification until the end of the fifth taxable year following the taxable year in which the transfer takes place. The transferee must retain the certification, and make it available to the Internal Revenue Service when requested in accordance with the requirements of section 6001 and regulations thereunder.

(4) Reliance upon certification not permitted. (i) In general. A transferee may not rely upon a transferor's certification pursuant to this paragraph (b) under the circumstances set forth in either subdivision (ii) or (iii) of this paragraph (b)(4). In either of those circumstances, a transferee's withholding obligation shall apply as if a certification had never been obtained, and the transferee is fully liable pursuant to section 1445 and § 1.1445-1(e) for any failure to withhold.

(ii) Failure to attach IRS acknowledgment of election. A transferee that knows that the transferor is a foreign corporation may not rely upon a certification of non-foreign status provided by the corporation on the basis of election under section 897(i), unless there is attached to the certification a copy of the acknowledgment by the Internal Revenue Service of the corporation's election, as required by paragraph (b)(2)(ii) of this section.

(iii) Knowledge of falsity. A transferee is not entitled to rely upon a transferor's certification if prior to or at the time of the transfer the transferee either—

(A) Has actual knowledge that the transferor's certification is false; or

(B) Receives a notice that the certification is false from a transferor's or transferee's agent, pursuant to § 1.1445-4.

(iv) Belated notice of false certification. If after the date of the transfer a transferee receives a notice that a certification is false, then that transferee is entitled to rely upon the certification only with respect to consideration that was paid prior to receipt for the notice. Such a transferee is required to withhold a full 10 percent of the amount realized from the consideration that remains to be paid to the transferor if possible. Thus, if 10 percent or more of the amount realized remains to be paid to the transferor then the transferee is required to withhold and pay over the full 10 percent. The transferee must do so by withholding and paying over the entire amount of each successive payment of consideration to the transferor until the full 10 percent of the amount realized has been withheld and paid over. Amounts so withheld must be reported and paid over by the 20th day following the date on which each such payment of consideration is made. A transferee that is subject to the rules of this paragraph (b)(4)(iv) may not obtain a withholding certificate pursuant to § 1.1445-3, but must instead withhold and pay over the amounts required by this paragraph.

(c) Transferred property not a U.S. real property interest. *(1) In general.* No withholding is required under section 1445 if the transferee acquires only property that is not a U.S. real property interest. As defined in section 897(c) and § 1.897-1(c), a U.S. real property interest includes certain interests in U.S. corporations, as well as direct interests in real property and certain associated personal property. This paragraph (c) provides rules pursuant to which a person acquiring an interest in a U.S. corporation may determine that withholding is not required because that interest is not a U.S. real property interest. To determine whether an interest in tangible property constitutes a U.S. real property interest the acquisition of which would be subject to withholding, see § 1.897-1(b) and (c).

(2) Interests in publicly traded entities. No withholding is required under section 1445(a) upon the acquisition of an interest in a domestic corporation if any class of stock of the corporation is regularly traded on an established securities market.

This exemption shall apply if the disposition is incident to an initial public offering of stock pursuant to a registration statement filed with the Securities and Exchange Commission. Similarly, no withholding is required under section 1445(a) upon the acquisition of an interest in a publicly traded partnership or trust. However, the rule of this paragraph (c)(2) shall not apply to the acquisition, from a single transferor (in a single or related transferors (as defined in § 1.897-1(i)) transaction (or related transactions), of an interest described in § 1.897-1(c)(2)(iii)(B) (relating to substantial amounts of non-publicly traded interests in publicly traded corporations) or to similar interests in publicly traded partnerships or trusts. The person making an acquisition described in the preceding sentence must otherwise determine whether withholding is required, pursuant to section 1445 and the regulations thereunder. Transactions shall be deemed to be related if they are undertaken within 90 days of one another or if it can otherwise be shown that they were undertaken in pursuance of a prearranged plan.

(3) Transferee receives statement that interest in corporation is not a U.S. real property interest. (i) In general. No withholding is required under section 1445(a) upon the acquisition of an interest in a domestic corporation, if the transferor provides the transferee with a copy of a statement, issued by the corporation pursuant to § 1.897-2(h), certifying that the interest is not a U.S. real property interest. In general, a corporation may issue such a statement only if the corporation was not a U.S. real property holding corporation at any time during the previous five years (or the period in which the interest was held by its present holder, if shorter) or if interests in the corporation ceased to be United States real property interests under section 897(c)(1)(B). (A corporation may not provide such a statement based on its determination that the interest in question is an interest solely as a creditor). See § 1.897-2(f) and (h). The corporation may provide such a statement directly to the transferee at the transferor's request. The transferor must request such a statement prior to the transfer, and shall, to the extent possible, specify the anticipated date of the transfer. A corporation's statement may be relied upon for purposes of this paragraph (c)(3) only if the statement is dated not more than 30 days prior to the date of the transfer. A transferee may also rely upon a corporation's statement that is voluntarily provided by the corporation in response to a request from the transferee, if that statement otherwise complies with the requirements of this paragraph (c)(3) and § 1.897-2(h).

(ii) Reliance on statement not permitted. A transferee is not entitled to rely upon a statement that a corporation is not a U.S. real property holding corporation if, prior to or at the time of the transfer, the transferee either—

(A) Has actual knowledge that the statement is false, or

(B) Receives a notice that the statement is false from a transferor's or transferee's agent, pursuant to § 1.1445-4.

Such a transferee's withholding obligations shall apply as if a statement had never been given, and such a transferee may be held fully liable pursuant to § 1.1445-1(e) for any failure to withhold.

(iii) Belated notice of false statement. If after the date of the transfer, a transferee receives notice that a statement provided under § 1.1445-2(c)(3)(i) (that an interest in a corporation is not a U.S. real property interest) is false, then such transferee may rely on the statement only with respect to consideration that was paid prior to the receipt of the notice.

Such a transferee is required to withhold a full 10 percent of the amount realized from the consideration that remains to be paid to the transferor, if possible. Thus, if 10 percent or more of the amount realized remains to be paid to the transferor, then the transferee is required to withhold and pay over the full 10 percent. The transferee must do so by withholding and paying over the entire amount of each successive payment of consideration to the transferor, until the full 10 percent of the amount realized has been withheld and paid over. Amounts so withheld must be reported and paid over by the 20th day following the date on which each such payment of consideration is made. A transferee that is subject to the rules of this § 1.1445-2(c)(3)(iii) may not obtain a withholding certificate pursuant to § 1.1445-3, but must instead withhold and pay over the amounts required by this paragraph.

(d) Exceptions to requirement of withholding. *(1) Purchase of residence for $300,000 or less.* No withholding is required under section 1445(a) if one or more individual transferees acquire a U.S. real property interest for use as a residence and the amount realized on the transaction is $300,000 or less. For purposes of this section, a U.S. real property interest is acquired for use as a residence if on the date of the transfer the transferee (or transferees) has definite plans to reside at the property for at least 50 percent of the number of days that the property is used by any person during each of the first two 12-month periods following the date of the transfer. The number of days that the property will be vacant is not taken into account in determining the number of days such property is used by any person. A transferee shall be considered to reside at a property on any day on which a member of the transferee's family, as defined in section 267(c)(4), resides at the property. No form or other document need be filed with the Internal Revenue Service to establish a transferee's entitlement to rely upon the exception provided by this paragraph (d)(1). A transferee who fails to withhold in reliance upon this exception, but who does not in fact reside at the property for the minimum number of days set forth above, shall be liable for the failure to withhold (if the transferor was a foreign person and did not pay the full U.S. tax due on any gain recognized upon the transfer). However, if the transferee establishes that the failure to reside the minimum number of days was caused by a change in circumstances that could not reasonably have been anticipated at the time of the transfer, then the transferee shall not be liable for the failure to withhold.

The exception provided by paragraph (d)(1) does not apply in any case where the transferee is other than an individual even if the property is acquired for or on behalf of an individual who will use the property as a residence. However, this exception applies regardless of the organizational structure of the transferor (i.e., regardless of whether the transferor is an individual, partnership, trust, corporation, etc.).

(2) Coordination with nonrecognition provisions. (i) In general. A transferee shall not be required to withhold under section 1445(a) with respect to the transfer of a U.S. real property interest if—

(A) The transferor notifies the transferee, in the manner described in paragraph (d)(2)(iii) of this section, that by reason of the operation of a nonrecognition provision of the Internal Revenue Code or the provisions of any United States treaty the transferor is not required to recognize any gain or loss with respect to the transfer, and

(B) By the 20th day after the date of the transfer the transferee provides a copy of the transferor's notice to the Director, Philadelphia Service Center, at the address provided in § 1.1445-1(g)(10), together with a cover letter setting forth the name, identifying number, and home address (in the case of an individual) or office address (in the case of an entity) of the transferee providing the notice to the Service. The rule of this paragraph (d)(2)(i) is subject to the exceptions set forth in paragraph (d)(2)(ii). For purposes of this paragraph (d)(2) a nonrecognition provision is any provision of the Internal Revenue Code for not recognizing gain or loss.

(ii) Exceptions. A transferee may not rely upon the rule of paragraph (d)(2)(i) of this section, and must therefore withhold under section 1445(a) with respect to the transfer of a U.S. real property interest, if either:

(A) The transferor qualifies for nonrecognition treatment with respect to part, but not all, of the gain realized by the transferor upon the transfer, or

(B) The transferee knows or has reason to know that the transferor is not entitled to the nonrecognition treatment claimed by the transferor.

In either of the above circumstances the transferee or transferor may request a withholding certificate from the Internal Revenue Service pursuant to the rules of § 1.1445-3.

(iii) Contents of the notice. No particular form is required for a transferor's notice to a transferee that the transferor is not required to recognize gain or loss with respect to a transfer. The notice must be verified as true and signed under penalties of perjury by the transferor, by a responsible officer in the case of a corporation, by a general partner in the case of a partnership, and by a trustee or equivalent fiduciary in the case of a trust or estate. The following information must be set forth in paragraphs labeled to correspond with the designation set forth as follows—

(A) A statement that the document submitted constitutes a notice of a nonrecognition transaction or a treaty provision pursuant to the requirements of § 1.1445-2(d)(2);

(B) The name, identifying number, and home address (in the case of an individual) or office address (in the case of an entity) of the transferor submitting the notice;

(C) A statement that the transferor is not required to recognize any gain or loss with respect to the transfer;

(D) A brief description of the transfer; and

(E) A brief summary of the law and facts supporting the claim that recognition of gain or loss is not required with respect to the transfer.

(iv) No notice allowed. The provisions of this paragraph (d)(2) do not apply to exclusions from income under section 121, to simultaneous like-kind exchanges under section 1031 that do not qualify for nonrecognition treatment in their entirety (see paragraph (d)(2)(ii)(A) of this section), and to non-simultaneous like-kind exchanges under section 1031 where the transferee cannot determine that the exchange has been completed and all the conditions for nonrecognition have been satisfied at the time it is otherwise required to pay the section 1445 withholding tax and file the withholding tax return (Form 8288, "U.S. Withholding Tax Return for Dispositions by Foreign Persons of U.S. Real Property Interests"). In these cases, the transferee is excused from withholding only upon the timely application for and receipt of a withholding certificate under § 1.1445-3 (see § 1.1445-3(b)(5) and (6) for specific rules applicable to transactions under sections 121 and 1031). This paragraph (d)(2)(iv) is applicable for dispositions and exchanges occurring [after] September 4, 2003.

(3) Special procedural rules applicable to foreclosures. (i) Amount to be withheld. (A) Foreclosures. A transferee that acquires a U.S. real property interest pursuant to a repossession or foreclosure on such property under a mortgage, security agreement, deed of trust or other instrument securing a debt must withhold tax under section 1445(a) equal to 10 percent of the amount realized on such sale. Such amount must be reported and paid over to the Service under the general rules of § 1.1445-1. However, if the transferee complies with the notice requirements of § 1.1445-2(d)(3)(ii) and (iii), such transferee may report and pay over to the Service on or before the 20th day following the final determination by a court or trustee with jurisdiction over the foreclosure action, the lesser of:

(1) The amount otherwise required to be withheld under section 1445(a), or

(2) The "alternative amount" as defined in the succeeding sentence.

The alternative amount is the entire amount, if any, determined by a court or trustee with jurisdiction over the matter, that accrues to the debtor/transferor out of the amount realized from the foreclosure sale. The amount of any mortgage, lien, or other security agreement secured by the property, that is terminated, assumed by another person, or otherwise extinguished (as to the debtor/transferor) shall not be treated as an amount that accrues to the debtor/transferor for purposes of this § 1.1445-2(d)(3)(i)(A). If the alternative amount is zero, no withholding is required. Any difference between the amount withheld at the time of the foreclosure sale and the amount to be reported and paid over to the Service must be transferred to the court or trustee with jurisdiction over the foreclosure action. Amounts withheld, if any, are to be reported and paid to the Service by using Forms 8288 and 8288-A in conformity with § 1.1445-1(d).

(B) Deeds in lieu of foreclosures. A transferee of a U.S. real property interest pursuant to a deed in lieu of foreclosure must withhold tax equal to 10 percent of the amount realized by the debtor/transferor on the transfer. However, no withholding is required if:

(1) The transferee is the only person with a security interest in the property,

(2) No cash or other property (other than incidental fees incurred with respect to the transfer) is paid, directly or indirectly, to any person with respect to the transfer, and

(3) The notice requirement of § 1.1445-2(d)(3) are satisfied.

The amount withheld, if any, must be reported and paid over to the Service not later than the 20th day following the date of transfer. In a case where withholding would otherwise be required, a withholding certificate may be requested in accordance with § 1.1445-3.

(ii) Notice to the court or trustee in a foreclosure action. (A) Notice on day of purchase. A transferee in a foreclosure sale that chooses to use the special rules applicable to foreclosures must provide notice to the court or trustee with jurisdiction over the foreclosure action on the day the property is transferred with respect to such transferee's withholding obligation. No particular form is necessary but the notice must set forth the transferee's name, home address in the case of an individual, office address in the case of an entity, a brief description of the property, the date of the transfer, the amount realized on the sale of the foreclosed property and the amount withheld under section 1445(a).

(B) Notice whether amount withheld or alternative amount is reported and paid over to the Service. A purchaser/transferee in a foreclosure that chooses to use the special rules applicable to foreclosures must provide notice to the court or trustee with jurisdiction over the foreclosure action regarding whether the amount withheld or the alternative amount will be (or has been) reported and paid over to the Service. The notice should set forth all the information required by the preceding paragraph (d)(3)(ii)(A), the amount withheld or alternative amount that will be (or has been) reported and paid over to the Service, and the amount that will be (or has been) paid over to the court or trustee.

(iii) Notice to the Service. (A) General rule. A transferee that in reliance upon the rules of this paragraph (d)(3) withholds an alternative amount (or does not withhold because the alternative amount is zero) must, on or before the 20th day following the final determination by a court or trustee in a foreclosure action or on or before the 20th day following the date of the transfer with respect to a transfer pursuant to a deed in lieu of foreclosure, provide notice thereof to the Assistant Commissioner (International) at the address provided in § 1.1445-1(g)(10). (The filing of such a notice shall not relieve a creditor of any obligation it may have to file a notice pursuant to section 6050J and the regulations thereunder.) No particular form is required but the following information must be set forth in paragraphs labelled to correspond with the numbers set forth below.

(1) A statement that the notice constitutes a notice of foreclosure action or transfer pursuant to a deed in lieu of foreclosure under § 1.1445-2(d)(3).

(2) The name, identifying number and home address (in the case of an individual) or office address (in the case of an entity) of the purchaser/transferee.

(3) The name, identifying number, and home address (in the case of an individual) or office address (in the case of an entity) of the debtor/transferor.

(4) In a foreclosure action, the date of the final determination by a court or trustee regarding the distribution of the amount realized from the foreclosure sale. In a transfer pursuant to a deed in lieu of foreclosure, the date the property is transferred to the purchaser/transferee.

(5) A brief description of the property.

(6) The amount realized from the foreclosure sale or with respect to the transfer pursuant to a deed in lieu of foreclosure.

(7) The alternative amount.

(B) Special rule for lenders required to file Form 1099-A where the alternative amount is zero. A person required under section 6050J to file Form 1099-A does not have to comply with the notice requirement of § 1.1445-2(d)(3)(iii)(A) if the alternative amount is zero. In such case, the filing of the Form 1099-A will be deemed to satisfy the notice requirements of § 1.1445-2(d)(3)(iii)(A).

(iv) Requirements not applicable. A transferee is not required to withhold tax or provide notice pursuant to the rules of this paragraph (d)(3) if no substantive withholding liability applies to the transfer of the property by the debtor/transferor. For example, if the debtor/transferor provides the transferee with a certification of nonforeign status pursuant to paragraph (b) of this section, then no substantive withholding liability would exist with respect to the acquisition of the property from the debtor transferor. In such a case, no withholding of tax or notice to the Internal Revenue Service is required of the transferee with respect to the repossession or foreclosure.

(v) Anti-abuse rule. If a U.S. real property interest is transferred in foreclosure or pursuant to a deed in lieu of foreclosure for a principal purpose of avoiding the requirements of section 1445(a), then the provisions of this paragraph (d)(3) shall not apply to the transfer and the transferee shall be fully liable for any failure to withhold with respect to the transfer. A principal purpose to avoid section 1445(a) will be presumed (subject to rebuttal on the basis of all relevant facts and circumstances) if:

(A) The transferee acquires property in which it, or a related party, has a security interest;

(B) The security interest did not arise in connection with the debtor/transferor's or a related party's or predecessor in interest's acquisition, improvement, or maintenance of the property; and

(C) The total amount of all debts secured by the property exceeds 90 percent of the fair market value of the property.

(4) Installment payments. A transferee of a U.S. real property interest is not required to withhold under section 1445 when making installment payments on an obligation arising out of a dispositions that took place before January 1, 1985. With respect to disposition that take place after December 31, 1984, the transferee shall be required to satisfy its entire withholding obligation within the time specified in § 1.1445-1(c) regardless of the amount actually paid by the transferee. Thereafter, no withholding is required upon further installment payments on an obligation arising out of the transfer. A transferee that is unable to satisfy its entire withholding obligation within the time specified in § 1.1445-1(c) may request a withholding certificate pursuant to § 1.1445-3.

(5) Acquisitions by governmental bodies. No withholding of tax is required under section 1445 with respect to any acquisition of property by the United States, a state or possession of the United States, a political subdivision thereof, or the District of Columbia.

(6) [Reserved]

(7) Withholding certificate obtained by transferee or transferor. No withholding is required under section 1445(a) if the transferee is provided with a withholding certificate that so specifies. Either the transferor or the transferee may seek a withholding certificate from the Internal Revenue Service, pursuant to the provisions of § 1.1445-3.

(8) Amount realized by transferor is zero. If the amount realized by transferor on a transfer of a U.S. real property interest is zero, no withholding is required.

(e) Effective date for taxpayer identification numbers. The requirement in paragraphs (d)(2)(i)(B), (d)(2)(iii)(B), and (d)(3)(iii)(A)(2) and (3) of this section that taxpayer identification numbers be provided (in all cases) is applicable for dispositions of U.S. real property interests occurring after November 3, 2003.

T.D. 8113, 12/18/86, amend T.D. 8198, 5/4/88, T.D. 9082, 8/4/2003.

---

§ 1.1445-3 Adjustments to amount required to be withheld pursuant to withholding certificate.

Caution: The Treasury has not yet amended Reg § 1.1445-3 to reflect changes made by P.L. 108-27.

(a) In general. Withholding under section 1445(a) may be reduced or eliminated pursuant to a withholding certificate issued by the Internal Revenue Service in accordance with the rules of this section. A withholding certificate may be issued by the Service in cases where reduced withholding is appropriate (see paragraph (c) of this section), where the transferor is exempt from U.S. tax (see paragraph (d) of this section), or where an agreement for the payment of tax is entered into with the Service (see paragraph (e) of this section). A withholding certificate that is obtained prior to a transfer notifies the transferee that no withholding is required. A withholding certificate that is obtained after a transfer has been made may authorize a normal refund or an early refund pursuant to paragraph (g) of this section. Either a transferee or transferor may apply for a withholding certificate. The Internal Revenue Service will act upon an application for a withholding certificate not later than the 90th day after it is received. Solely for this purpose (i.e., determining the day upon which the 90-day period commences), an application is received by the Service on the date that all information necessary for the Service to make a determination is provided by the applicant. In no event, however, will a withholding certificate be issued without the transferor's identifying number. (For rules regarding whether an application for a withholding certificate has been timely submitted, see § 1.445-1(c)(2).) The Service may deny a request for a withholding certificate where, after due notice, an applicant fails to provide information necessary for the Service to make a determination. The Service will act upon an application for an early refund not later than the 90th day after it is received. An application for an early refund must either (1) include a copy of a withholding certificate issued by the Service with respect to the transaction or, (2) be combined with an application for a withholding certificate. Where an application for an early refund is combined with an application for a withholding certificate, the Service will act upon both applications not later than the 90th day after receipt. In the case of an application for a certificate based on non-conforming security under paragraph (e)(3)(v) of this section, and in unusually complicated cases, the Service may be unable to provide a final withholding certificate by the 90th day. In such a case the Service will notify the applicant, by the 45th day after receipt of the application, that additional processing time will be necessary. The Service's notice may request additional information or explanation concerning particular aspects of the application, and will provide a target date for final action (contingent upon the application's timely submission of any requested information). A withholding certificate issued pursuant to the provisions of this section serves to fulfill the requirements of section 1445(b)(4) concerning qualifying statements, section 1445(c)(1) concerning the transferor's maximum tax liability, or section 1445(c)(2) concerning the Secretary's authority to prescribe reduced withholding.

(b) Applications for withholding certificates. *(1) In general.* An application for a withholding certificate must be submitted to the Director, Philadelphia Service Center, at the address provided in § 1.1445-1(g)(10). An application for a withholding certificate must be signed by a responsible officer in the case of a corporation, by a general partner in the case of a partnership, by a trustee, executor, or equivalent fiduciary in the case of a trust or estate, and in the case of an individual by the individual himself. A duly authorized agent may sign the application but the application must contain a valid power of attorney authorizing the agent to sign the application on behalf of the applicant. The person signing the application must verify under penalties of perjury that all representations made in connection with the application are true, correct, and complete to his knowledge and belief. No particular form is required for an application, but the application must set forth the information described in paragraphs (b), (2), (3), and (4), and to the extent applicable, paragraph (b)(5) or (6) of this section.

(2) Parties to the transaction. The application must set forth the name, address, and identifying number of the person submitting the application (specifying whether that person is the transferee or transferor), and the name, address, and identifying number of other parties to the transaction (specifying whether each such party is a transferee or transferor). The Service will deny the application if complete information, including the identifying numbers of all the parties, is not provided. Thus, for example, the applicant should determine if an identifying number exists for each party, and, if none exists for a particular party, the applicant should notify the particular party of the obligation to get an identifying number before the application can be submitted to the Service. The address provided in the case of an individual must be that individual's home address, and the address provided in the case of an entity must be that entity's office address. A mailing address may be provided in addition to, but not in lieu of, a home address or office address.

(3) Real property interest to be transferred. The application must set forth information concerning the U.S. real property interest with respect to which the withholding certificate is sought, including the type of interest, the contract price, and, in the case of an interest in real property, its location and general description, or in the case of an interest in a U.S. real property holding corporation, the class or type and amount of the interest.

(4) Basis for certificate. (i) Reduced withholding. If a withholding certificate is sought on the basis of a claim that reduced withholding in appropriate, the application must include:

(A) A calculation of the maximum tax that may be imposed on the disposition in accordance with paragraph (c)(2) of this section. Such calculation must be accompanied by a copy of the relevant contract and depreciation schedules or other evidence that confirms the contract price and adjusted basis of the property. If no depreciation schedules are provided, the application must state the nature of the use of the property and why depreciation was not allowable. Evidence that supports any claimed adjustment to the maximum tax on the disposition must also be provided;

(B) A calculation of the transferor's unsatisfied withholding liability, or evidence supporting the claim that no such liability exists, in accordance with paragraph (c)(3) of this section; and

(C) In the case of a request for a special reduction of withholding pursuant to paragraph (c)(4) of this section, a statement of law and facts in support of the request.

(ii) Exemption. If a withholding certificate is sought on the basis of the transferor's exemption from U.S. tax, the application must set forth a brief statement of the law and facts that support the claimed exemption. In this regard, see paragraph (d) of this section.

(iii) Agreement. If a withholding certificate is sought on the basis of an agreement for the payment of tax, the application must include a signed copy of the agreement proposed by the applicant and a copy of the security instrument (if any) proposed by the applicant. In this regard, see paragraph (e) of this section.

(5) Special rule for exclusions from income under section 121. A withholding certificate may be sought on the basis of a section 121 exclusion as a reduction in the amount of tax due under paragraph (c)(2)(v) of this section. The application must include information establishing that the transferor, who is a nonresident alien individual at the time of the sale (and is therefore subject to sections 897 and 1445) is entitled to claim the benefits of section 121. For example, a claim for reduced withholding as a result of section 121 must include information that the transferor occupied the U.S. real property interest as his or her personal residence for the required period of time.

(6) Special rule for like-kind exchanges under Section 1031. A withholding certificate may be requested with respect to a like-kind exchange under section 1031 as a transaction subject to a nonrecognition provision under paragraph (c)(2)(ii) of this section. The application must include information substantiating the requirements of section 1031. The IRS may require additional information during the course of the application process to determine that the requirements of section 1031 are satisfied. In the case of a deferred like-kind exchange, the withholding agent is excused from reporting and paying the withholding tax to the IRS within 20 days after the transfer only if an application for a withholding certificate is submitted prior to or on the date of transfer. See § 1.1445-1(c)(2) for rules concerning delayed reporting and payment where an application for a withholding certificate has been submitted to the IRS prior to or on the date of transfer.

(c) Adjustment of amount required to be withheld. *(1) In general.* The Internal Revenue Service may issue a withholding certificate that excuses withholding or that permits the transferee to withhold an adjusted amount reflecting the transferor's maximum tax liability. The transferor's maximum tax liability is the sum of—

(i) The maximum amount which could be imposed as tax under section 871 or 882 upon the transferor's disposition of the subject real property interest, as determined under paragraph (c)(2) of this section, and

(ii) The transferor's unsatisfied withholding liability with respect to the subject real property interest, as determined under paragraph (c)(3) of this section.

In addition, the Internal Revenue Service may issue a withholding certificate that permits the transferee to withhold a reduced amount if the Service determines pursuant to paragraph (c)(4) of this section that reduced withholding will not jeopardize the collection of tax.

(2) Maximum tax imposed on disposition. The first element of the transferor's maximum tax liability is the maximum amount which the transferor could be required to pay as tax upon the disposition of the subject real property interest. In the case of an individual transferor that amount will generally be the contract price of the property minus its adjusted basis, multiplied by the maximum individual income tax rate applicable to long term capital gain. In the case of a corporate transferor, that amount will generally be the contract price of the property minus its adjusted basis, multi-

plied by the maximum corporate income tax rate applicable to long term capital gain. However, that amount must be adjusted to take into account the following:

(i) Any reduction of tax to which the transferor is entitled under the provisions of a U.S. income tax treaty;

(ii) The effect of any nonrecognition provision that is applicable to the transaction;

(iii) Any losses realized and recognized upon the previous disposition of U.S. real property interests during the taxable year;

(iv) Any amount that is required to be treated as ordinary income; and

(v) Any other factor that may increase or reduce the tax upon the disposition.

(3) Transferor's unsatisfied withholding liability. (i) In general. The second element of the transferor's maximum tax liability is the transferor's unsatisfied withholding liability. That liability is the amount of any tax that the transferor was required to but did not withhold and pay over under section 1445 upon the acquisition of the subject U.S. real property interest or a predecessor interest. The transferor's unsatisfied withholding liability is included in the calculation of maximum tax liability so that such prior withholding liability can be satisfied by the transferee's withholding upon the current transfer. Alternatively, the transferor's unsatisfied withholding liability may be disregarded for purposes of calculating the maximum tax liability, if either—

(A) Such prior withholding liability is fully satisfied by a payment that is made with the application submitted pursuant to this section; or

(B) An agreement is entered into for the payment of that liability pursuant to the rules of paragraph (e) of this section. Because section 1445 only requires withholding after December 31, 1984, no transferor's unsatisfied withholding liability can exist unless the transferor acquired the subject or predecessor real property interest after that date. For purposes of this paragraph (c), a predecessor interest is one that was exchanged for the subject U.S. real property interest in a transaction in which the transferor was not required to recognize the full amount of the gain or loss realized upon the transfer.

(ii) Evidence that no unsatisfied withholding liability exists. For purposes of paragraph (b)(4)(i)(B) of this section (concerning information that must be submitted with an application for a withholding certificate), evidence that the transferor has no unsatisfied withholding liability includes any one of the following documents:

(A) Evidence that the transferor acquired the subject or predecessor real property interest prior to January 1, 1985;

(B) A copy of the Form 8288 that was filed by the transferor, and proof of payment of the amount shown due thereon, with respect to the transferor's acquisition of the subject or predecessor real property interest;

(C) A copy of a withholding certificate with respect to the transferor's acquisition of the subject or predecessor real property interest, plus a copy of Form 8288 and proof of payment with respect to any withholding required under that certificate;

(D) A copy of the non-foreign certification furnished by the person from whom the subject or predecessor U.S. real property interest was acquired, executed at the time of that acquisition;

(E) Evidence that the transferor purchased the subject or predecessor real property for $300,000 or less, and a statement signed by the transferor under penalties of perjury, that the transferor purchased the property for use as a residence within the meaning of § 1.1445-2(d)(1);

(F) Evidence that the person from whom the transferor acquired the subject or predecessor U.S. real property interest fully paid any tax imposed on that transaction pursuant to section 897.

(G) A copy of a notice of nonrecognition treatment provided to the transferor pursuant to § 1.1445-2(d)(2) by person from whom the transferor acquired the subject or predecessor U.S. real property interest; and

(H) A statement, signed by the transferor under penalties of perjury, setting forth the facts and circumstances that supported the transferor's conclusion that no withholding was required under section 1445(a) with respect to the transferor's acquisition of the subject or predecessor real property interest.

(4) Special reduction of amount required to be withheld. The Internal Revenue Service may, in its discretion, issue a withholding certificate that permits the transferee to withhold a reduced amount based upon a determination that reduced withholding will not jeopardize the collection of tax. A transferor that requests a withholding certificate pursuant to this paragraph (c)(4) is required pursuant to paragraph (b)(4)(i)(C) of this section to submit a statement of law and facts in support of the request. That statement must explain why the transferor is unable to enter into an agreement for the payment of tax pursuant to paragraph (e) of this section.

(d) Transferor's exemption from U.S. tax. *(1) In general.* The Internal Revenue Service will issue a withholding certificate that excuses all withholding by a transferee if it is established that:

(i) The transferor's gain from the disposition of the subject U.S. real property interest will be exempt from U.S. tax, and

(ii) The transferor has no unsatisfied withholding liability.

For the available exemptions, see paragraph (d)(2) of this section. The transferor's unsatisfied withholding liability shall be determined in accordance with the provisions of paragraph (c)(3) of this section. A transferor that is entitled to a reduction of (rather than an exemption from) U.S. tax may obtain a withholding certificate to that effect pursuant to the provisions of paragraph (c) of this section.

(2) Available exemptions. A transferor's gain from the disposition of a U.S. real property interest may be exempt from U.S. tax because either:

(i) The transferor is an integral part or controlled entity of a foreign government and the disposition of the subject property is not a commercial activity, as determined pursuant to section 892 and the regulations thereunder; or

(ii) The transferor is entitled to the benefits of an income tax treaty that provides for such an exemption (subject to the limitations imposed by section 1125(c) of Pub. L. 96-499, which, in general, overrides such benefits as of January 1, 1985).

(e) Agreement for the payment of tax. *(1) In general.* The Internal Revenue Service will issue a withholding certificate that excuses withholding or that permits a transferee to withhold a reduced amount, if either the transferee or the transferor enters into an agreement for the payment of tax pursuant to the provisions of this paragraph (e). An agreement for the payment of tax is a contract between the Service and any other person that consists of two necessary elements. Those elements are—

(i) A contract between the Service and the other person, setting forth in detail the rights and obligations of each; and

(ii) A security instrument or other form of security acceptable to the Director, Foreign Operations District.

(2) Contents of agreement. (i) In general. An agreement for the payment of tax must cover an amount described in subdivision (ii) or (iii) of this paragraph (e)(2). The agreement may either provide adequate security for the payment of the chosen amount in accordance with paragraph (e)(3) of this section, or provide for the payment of that amount through a combination of security and withholding of tax by the transferee.

(ii) Tax that would otherwise be withheld. An agreement for the payment of tax may cover the amount of tax that would otherwise be required to be withheld pursuant to section 1445(a). In addition to the amount computed pursuant to section 1445(a), the applicant must agree to pay interest upon that amount, at the rate established under section 6621, with respect to the period between the date on which the tax imposed by section 1445(a) would otherwise be due (i.e., the 20th day after the date of transfer) and the date on which the transferor's payment of tax with respect to the disposition will be due under the agreement. The amount of interest agreed upon must be paid by the applicant regardless of whether or not the Service is required to draw upon any security provided pursuant to the agreement. The interest may be paid either with the return or by the Service drawing upon the security.

(iii) Maximum tax liability. An agreement for the payment of tax may cover the transferor's maximum tax liability, determined in accordance with paragraph (c) of this section. The agreement must also provide for the payment of an additional amount equal to 25 percent of the amount determined under paragraph (c) of this section. This additional amount secures the interest and penalties that would accrue between the date of a failure to file a return and pay tax with respect to the disposition, and the date on which the Service collects upon that liability pursuant to the agreement. Such additional amount will only be collected if the Service finds it necessary to draw upon any security provided due to the transferor's failure to file a return and pay tax with respect to the relevant disposition.

(3) Major types of security. (i) In general. The following are the major types of security acceptable to the Service. Further details with respect to the terms and conditions of each type may be specified by Revenue Procedure.

(ii) Bond with surety or guarantor. The Service may accept as security with respect to a transferor's tax liability a bond that is executed with a satisfactory surety or guarantor. Only the following persons may act as surety or guarantor for this purpose

(A) A surety company holding a certificate of authority from the Secretary as an acceptable surety on Federal bonds, as listed in Treasury Department Circular No. 570, published annually in the FEDERAL REGISTER on the first working day of July;

(B) A person that is engaged within or without the United States in the conduct of a banking, financing, or similar business under the principles of § 1.864-4(c)(5), and that is subject to U.S. or foreign local or national regulation of such business, if that person is otherwise acceptable to the Service; and

(C) A person that is engaged within or without the United States in the conduct of an insurance business that is subject to U.S. or foreign local or national regulation, if that person is otherwise acceptable to the Service.

(iii) Bond with collateral. The Service may accept as security with respect to a transferor's tax liability a bond that is secured by acceptable collateral. All collateral must be deposited with a responsible financial institution acting as escrow agent, or, in the Service's discretion, with the Service. Only the following types of collateral are acceptable:

(A) Bonds, notes, or other public debt obligations of the United States, in accordance with the rules of 31 CFR Part 225; and

(B) A certified, cashier's, or treasurer's check, drawn on an entity acceptable to the Service that is engaged within or without the United States in the conduct of a banking, financing, or similar business under the principles of § 1.864-4(c)(5) and that is subject to U.S. or foreign local or national regulation of such business.

(iv) Letter of credit. The Service may accept as security with respect to a transferor's tax liability an irrevocable letter of credit. The Service may accept a letter of credit issued by an entity acceptable to the Service that is engaged within or without the United States in the conduct of a banking, financing, or similar business under the principles of § 1.864-4(c)(5) and that is subject to U.S. or foreign local or national regulation of such business. However, the Director will accept a letter of credit from an entity that is not engaged in trade or business in the United States only if such letter may be drawn on an advising bank within the United States.

(v) Guarantees and other nonconforming security (A) Guarantee. The Service may in its discretion accept as security with respect to a transferor's tax liability the applicant's guarantee that it will pay such liability. The Service will in general accept such a guarantee only from a corporation, foreign or domestic, any class of stock of which is regularly traded on an established securities market on the date of the transfer.

(B) Other forms of security. The Service may in unusual circumstances and at its discretion accept any form of security that it finds to be adequate. An application for a withholding certificate that proposes a form of security that does not conform with any of the preferred types set forth in paragraph (e)(3)(ii) through (iv) of this section or any relevant Revenue Procedure must include:

(1) A detailed statement of the facts and circumstances supporting the use of the proposed form of security, and

(2) A memorandum of law concerning the validity and enforceability of the proposed form of security.

(4) Terms of security instrument. Any security instrument that is furnished pursuant to this section must provide that—

(i) The amount of each deposit of estimated tax that will be required with respect to the gain realized on the subject disposition may be collected by levy upon the security as of the date following the date on which each such deposit is due (unless such deposit is timely made);

(ii) The entire amount of the liability may be collected by levy upon the security at any time during the nine months following the date on which the payment of tax with respect to the subject disposition is due, subject to release of the security upon the full payment of the tax and any interest and penalties due. If the transferor requests an extension of time to file a return with respect to the disposition, then the Director may require that the term of the security instrument be extended until the date that is nine months after the filing deadline as extended.

(f) Amendments to application for withholding certificate. *(1) In general.* An applicant for a withholding certificate may amend an otherwise complete application by submitting an amending statement to the Director, Philadelphia Service Center, at the address provided in § 1.1445-1(g)(10). The amending statement shall provide the information required by § 1.1445-3(f)(3) and must be signed and accompanied by a penalties of perjury statement in accordance with § 1.1445-3(b)(1).

(2) Extension of time for the Service to process requests for withholding certificates. (i) In general. If an amending statement is submitted, the time in which the Internal Revenue Service must act upon the amended application shall be extended by 30 days.

(ii) Substantial amendments. If an amending statement is submitted and the Service finds that the statement substantially amends the facts of the underlying application or substantially alters the terms of the withholding certificate as requested in the initial application, the time within which the Service must act upon the amended application shall be extended by 60 days. The applicant shall be so notified.

(iii) Amending statement received after the requested withholding certificate has been signed by the Director, Philadelphia Service Center. If an amending statement is received after the withholding certificate, drafted in response to the underlying application, has been signed by the Director, Philadelphia Service Center or his delegate and prior to the day such certificate is mailed to the applicant, the time in which the Service must act upon the amended application shall be extended by 90 days. The applicant will be so notified.

(3) Information required to be submitted. No particular form is required for an amending statement but the statement must provide the following information:

(i) Identification of applicant. The amending statement must set forth the name, address and identifying number of the person submitting the amending statement (specifying whether that person is the transferee or transferor).

(ii) Date of underlying application. The amending statement must set forth the date of the underlying) application for a withholding certificate.

(iii) Real property interest to be (or that has been) transferred. The amending statement must set forth a brief description of the real property interest with respect to which the underlying application for a withholding certificate was submitted.

(iv) Amending information. The amending statement must fully set forth the basis for the amendment including any modification of the facts supporting the application for a withholding certificate and any change sought in the terms of the withholding certificate.

(g) Early refund of overwithheld amounts. If a transferor receives a withholding certificate pursuant to this section, and an amount greater than that specified in the certificate was withheld by the transferee, then pursuant to the rules of this paragraph (g) the transferor may apply for a refund (without interest) of the excess amount prior to the date on which the transferor's tax return is due (without extensions). (Any interest payable on refunds issued after the filing of a tax return shall be determined in accordance with the provisions of section 6611 and regulations thereunder.) An application for an early refund must be addressed to Director, Philadelphia Service Center, at the address provided in § 1.1445-1(g)(10). No particular form is required for the application, but the following information must be set forth in separate paragraphs numbered to correspond with the number given below:

(1) Name, address, and identifying number of the transferor seeking the refund;

(2) Amount required to be withheld pursuant to withholding certificate issued by Internal Revenue Service;

(3) Amount withheld by transferee (attach a copy of Form 8288-A stamped by IRS pursuant to § 1.1445-1(c))

(4) Amount to be refunded to transferor. An application for an early refund cannot be processed unless the required copy of Form 8288-A (or substantial evidence of the amount withheld in the case of a failure to receive Form 8288-A as provided in § 1.1445-1(f)(3)) is attached to the application. If an application for a withholding certificate based upon the transferor's maximum tax liability is submitted after the transfer takes place, then that application may be combined with an application for an early refund. The Service will act upon a claim for refund within the time limits set forth in paragraph (a) of this section.

(h) Effective date for taxpayer identification numbers. The requirement in paragraphs (b)(2), (f)(3)(i), and (g)(1) of this section that taxpayer identification numbers be provided (in all cases) is applicable for dispositions of U.S. real property interests occurring after November 3, 2003.

T.D. 8113, 12/18/86, amend T.D. 9082, 8/4/2003.

§ 1.1445-4 Liability of agents.

(a) Duty to provide notice of false certification or statement to transferee. A transferee's or transferor's agent must provide notice to the transferee if either—

(1) The transferee is furnished with a non-U.S. real property interest statement pursuant to § 1.1445-2(c)(3) and the agent knows that the statement is false; or

(2) The transferee is furnished with a non-foreign certification pursuant to § 1.1445-2(b)(2) and either (i) the agent knows that the certification is false, or (ii) the agent represents a transferor that is a foreign corporation. An agent that represents a transferor that is a foreign corporation is not required to provide notice to the transferee if the foreign corporation provided a non-foreign certification to the transferee prior to such agent's employment and the agent does not know that the corporation did so.

(b) Duty to provide notice of false certification or statement to entity or fiduciary. A transferee's or transferor's agent must provide notice to an entity or fiduciary that plans to carry out a transaction described in section 1445(e)(1), (2), (3), or (4) if either—

(1) The entity or fiduciary is furnished with a non-U.S. real property interest statement pursuant to § 1.1445-5(b)(4)(iii) and the agent knows that such statement is false; or

(2) The entity or fiduciary is furnished with a non-foreign certification pursuant to § 1.1445-5(b)(3)(ii) and either (i) the agent knows that such certification is false, or (ii) the agent represents a foreign corporation that made such a certification.

(c) Procedural requirements. *(1) Notice to transferee, entity, or fiduciary.* An agent who is required by this section to provide notice must do so in writing as soon as possible after learning of the false certification or statement, but not later than the date of the transfer (prior to the transferee's payment of consideration). If an agent first learns of a false certification or statement after the date of the transfer, notice must be given by the third day following that discovery. The notice must state that the certification or statement is false and may not be relied upon. The notice must also explain the possible consequences to the recipient of a failure to withhold. The notice need not disclose the information on which the agent's statement is based. The following is an example of an acceptable notice. "This is to notify you that you may be required to withhold tax in connection with (describe transaction). You have been provided with a certification of non-foreign status (or a non-U.S. real property interest statement) in connection with that transaction. I have learned that that document is false. Therefore, you may not rely upon it as a basis for failing to withhold under section 1445 of the Internal Revenue Code. Section 1445 provides that any person who acquires a U.S. real property interest from a foreign person must withhold a tax equal to 10 percent of the total purchase price. (The term U.S. real property interest includes real property, stock in U.S. corporations whose assets are primarily real property, and some personal property associated with realty.) Any person who is required to withhold but fails to do so can be held liable for the tax. Thus, if you do not withhold the 10 percent tax from the total that you pay on this transaction you could be required to pay the tax yourself, if what you are acquiring is a U.S. real property interest and the transferor is a foreign person. Tax that is withheld must be promptly paid over to the IRS using Form 8288. For further information see sections 897 and 1445 of the Internal Revenue Code and the related regulations."

(2) Notice to be filed with IRS. An agent who is required by paragraph (a) or (b) of this section to provide notice to a transferee, entity, or fiduciary must furnish a copy of that notice to the Internal Revenue Service by the date on which the notice is required to be given to the transferee, entity, or fiduciary. The copy of the notice must be delivered to the Director, Philadelphia Service Center at the address provided in § 1.1445-1(g)(10) and must be accompanied by a cover letter stating that the copy is being filed pursuant to the requirements of this § 1.1445-4(c)(2).

(d) Effect on recipient. A transferee, entity, or fiduciary that receives a notice pursuant to this section prior to the date of the transfer from any agent of the transferor or transferee may not rely upon the subject certification or statement for purposes of excusing withholding pursuant to § 1.1445-2 or § 1.1445-5. Therefore, the recipient of a notice may be held liable for any failure to deduct and withhold tax under section 1445 as if such certification or statement had never been given. For special rules concerning the effect of the receipt of a notice after the date of the transfer, see §§ 1.1445-2(b)(4)(iv) and 1.1445-5(c), (d) and (e).

(e) Failure to provide notice. Any agent who is required to provide notice but who fails to do so in the manner required by paragraph (a) or (b) of this section shall be held liable for the tax that the recipient of the notice would have been required to withhold under section 1445 if such notice had been given. However, an agent's liability under this paragraph (e) is limited to the amount of compensation that that agent derives from the transaction. In addition, an agent who assists in the preparation of, or fails to disclose knowledge of, a false certification or statement may be liable for civil or criminal penalties.

(f) Definition of transferor's or transferee's agent. *(1) In general.* For purposes of this section, the terms "transferor's agent" and "transferee's agent" means any person who represents the transferor or transferee (respectively)—

(i) In any negotiation with another person (or another person's agent) relating to the transaction; or

(ii) In settling the transaction.

(2) Transactions subject to section 1445(e). In the case of transactions subject section 1445(e), the following definitions apply.

(i) The term "transferor's agent" means any person that represents or advises an entity or fiduciary with respect to the planning, arrangement, or consummation by the entity of a transaction described in section 1445(e)(1), (2), (3), or (4).

(ii) The term "transferee's agent" means any person that represents or advises the holder of an interest in an entity with respect to the planning, arrangement or consummation by the entity of a transaction described in section 1445(e)(1), (2), (3), or (4).

(3) Exclusion of settlement officers and clerical personnel. For purposes of this section, a person shall not be treated as a transferor's agent or transferee's agent with respect to any transaction solely because such person performs one or more of the following activities.

(i) The receipt and disbursement of any portion of the consideration for the transaction;

(ii) The recording of any document in connection with the transaction;

(iii) Typing, copying, and other clerical tasks;

(iv) The obtaining of title insurance reports and reports concerning the condition of the real property that is the subject of the transaction; or

(v) The transmission or delivery of documents between the parties.

(4) Exclusion for governing body of a condominium association and the board of directors of a cooperative housing corporation. The members of a board, committee or other governing body of a condominium association and the board of directors and officers of a cooperative housing corporation will not be deemed agents of the transferor or transferee if such individuals function exclusively in their capacity as representatives of such association or corporation with respect to the transaction. In addition, the managing agent of a cooperative housing corporation or condominium association will not be deemed to be an agent of the transferee or transferor if such person functions exclusively in its capacity as a managing agent. If a person's activities include advising the transferee or transferor with respect to the transfer, this exclusion shall not apply.

T.D. 8113, 12/18/86, amend T.D. 9082, 8/4/2003.

§ 1.1445-5 Special rules concerning distributions and other transactions by corporations, partnerships, trusts, and estates.

Caution: The Treasury has not yet amended Reg § 1.1445-5 to reflect changes made by P.L. 104-188.

(a) Purpose and scope. This section provides special rules concerning the withholding that is required under section 1445(e) upon distributions and other transactions involving domestic or foreign corporations, partnerships, trusts, and estates. Paragraph (b) of this section provides rules that apply generally to the various withholding requirements set forth in this section. Under section 1445(e)(1) and paragraph (c) of this section, a domestic partnership or the fiduciary of a domestic trust or estate is required to withhold tax upon the entity's disposition of a U.S. real property interest if any foreign persons are partners or beneficiaries of the entity. Paragraph (d) provides rules concerning the requirement of section 1445(e)(2) that a foreign corporation withhold tax upon its distribution of a U.S. real property interest to its interest-holders. Finally, under section 1445(e)(3) and paragraph (e) of this section a domestic U.S. real property holding corporation is required to withhold tax upon certain distributions to interest-holders that are foreign persons. Paragraphs (f) and (g) of this section are reserved to provide rules concerning transactions involving interests in partnerships, trusts, and estates that will be subject to withholding pursuant to sections 1445(e)(4) and (5).

(b) Rules of general application. *(1) Double withholding not required.* If tax is required to be withheld with respect to a transfer of property in accordance with the rules of this section, then no additional tax is required to be withheld by the transferee of the property with respect to that transfer pursuant to the general rules of section 1445(a) and § 1.1445-1. For rules coordinating the withholding under section 1441 (or section 1442 or 1443) and under section 1445 on distributions from a corporation, see § 1.1441-3(b)(4). If a transfer of a U.S. real property interest described in section 1445(e) is exempt from withholding under the rules of this section, then no withholding is required under the general rules of section 1445(a) and § 1.1445-1.

(2) Coordination with nonrecognition provisions. (i) In general. Withholding shall not be required under the rules of this section with respect to a transfer described in section 1445(e) of a U.S. real property interest if—

(A) By reason of the operation of a nonrecognition provision of the Internal Revenue Code or the provisions of any treaty of the United States no gain or loss is required to be recognized by the foreign person with respect to which withholding would otherwise be required; and

(B) The entity or fiduciary that is otherwise required to withhold complies with the notice requirements of paragraph (b)(2)(ii) of this section. The entity or fiduciary must determine whether gain or loss is required to be recognized pursuant to the rules of section 897 and the applicable nonrecognition provisions of the Internal Revenue Code. An entity or fiduciary may obtain a withholding certificate from the Internal Revenue Service that confirms the applicability of a nonrecognition provision, but is not required to do so. For purposes of this paragraph (b)(2), a nonrecognition provision is any provision of the Internal Revenue Code for not recognizing gain or loss. If nonrecognition treatment is available only with respect to part of the gain realized on a transfer, the exemption from withholding provided by this paragraph (b)(2) shall not apply. In such cases a withholding certificate may be sought pursuant to the provisions of § 1.1445-6.

(ii) Notice of nonrecognition transfer. An entity or fiduciary that fails to withhold tax with respect to a transfer in reliance upon the rules of this paragraph (b)(2) must be by the 20th day after the date of the transfer deliver a notice thereof to the Director, Philadelphia Service Center, at the address provided in § 1.1445-1(g)(10). No particular form is required for a notice of transfer, but the following information must be set forth in paragraphs labelled to correspond with the letter set forth below:

(A) A statement that the document submitted constitutes a notice of a nonrecognition transfer pursuant to the requirements of § 1.1445-5(b)(2)(ii);

(B) The name, office address, and identifying number of the entity of fiduciary submitting the notice;

(C) The name, identifying number, and home address (in the case of an individual) or office address (in the case of an entity) of each foreign person with respect to which withholding would otherwise be required;

(D) A brief description of the transfer; and

(E) A brief statement of the law and facts supporting the claim that recognition of gain or loss is not required with respect to the transfer.

(3) Interest-holder not a foreign person. (i) In general. Pursuant to the provisions of paragraphs (c) and (e) of this section, an entity or fiduciary is required to withhold with respect to certain transfers of property if a holder of an interest in the entity is a foreign person. For purposes of determining whether a holder of an interest is a foreign person, and entity or fiduciary may rely upon a certification of nonforeign status provided by that person in accordance with paragraph (b)(3)(ii) of this section. Except to the extent provided in paragraph (b)(3)(iii) of this section, such a certification excuses the entity or fiduciary from any liability otherwise imposed pursuant to section 1445(e) and regulations thereunder. However, no obligation is imposed upon an entity or fiduciary to obtain certifications from interest-holders; an entity or fiduciary may instead rely upon other means to ascertain the nonforeign status of an interest-holder. If the entity or fiduciary does rely upon other means but the interest-holder proves, in fact, to be a foreign person, then the entity or fiduciary is subject to any liability imposed pursuant to section 1445 and regulations thereunder.

An entity or fiduciary is not required to rely upon other means to ascertain the non-foreign status of an interest-holder and may demand a certification of non-foreign status. If the certification is not provided, the entity or fiduciary may withhold tax under section 1445 and will be considered, for purposes of sections 1461 through 1463, to have been required to withhold such tax.

(ii) Interest-holder's certification of non-foreign status. (A) In general. For purposes of this section, an entity or fiduciary may treat any holder of an interest in the entity as a U.S. person if that interest-holder furnishes to the entity or fiduciary a certification stating that the interest-holder is not a foreign person, in accordance with the provisions of paragraph (b)(3)(ii)(B) of this section. In general, a foreign person is a nonresident alien individual, foreign corporation, foreign partnership, foreign trust, or foreign estate, but not a resident alien individual. In this regard, see § 1.897-1(k).

(B) Procedural rules. An interest-holder's certification of non-foreign status must—

(1) State that the interest-holder is not a foreign person;

(2) Set forth the interest-holder's name, identifying number, home address (in the case of an individual), or office address (in the case of an entity), and place of incorporation (in the case of a corporation); and

(3) Be signed under penalties of perjury.

Pursuant to § 1.897-1(p), an individual's identifying number is the individual's Social Security number and any other person's identifying number is its U.S. employer identification number. The certification must be signed by a responsible officer in the case of a corporation, by a general partner in the case of a partnership, and by a trustee, executor, or equivalent fiduciary in the case of a trust or estate. No particular form is needed for a certification pursuant to this paragraph (b)(3)(ii)(B), nor is any particular language required, so long as the document meets the requirements of this paragraph. Samples of acceptable certifications are provided in paragraph (b)(3)(ii)(D) of this section. An entity may rely upon a certification pursuant to this paragraph (b)(3)(ii)(B) for a period of two calendar years following the close of the calendar year in which the certification was given.

If an interest holder becomes a foreign person within the period described in the preceding sentence, the interest-holder must notify the entity prior to any further dispositions or distributions and upon receipt of such notice (or any other notification of the foreign status of the interest-holder) the entity may no longer rely upon the prior certification. An entity that obtains and relies upon a certification must retain that certification with its books and records for a period of three calendar years following the close of the last calendar year in which the entity relied upon the certification.

(C) Foreign corporation that has made an election under section 897(i). A foreign corporation that has made a valid election under section 897(i) to be treated as a domestic corporation for purposes of section 897 may provide a certification of non-foreign status pursuant to this paragraph (b)(3)(ii). However, an electing foreign corporation must attach to such certification a copy of the acknowledgment of the election provided to the corporation by the Internal Revenue Service pursuant to § 1.897-3(d)(4).

An acknowledgment is valid for this purpose only if it states that the information required by § 1.897-3 has been determined to be complete.

(D) Sample certifications. (1) Individual interest-holder.

"Under section 1445(e) of the Internal Revenue Code, a corporation, partnership, trust or estate must withhold tax with respect to certain transfers of property if a holder of an interest in the entity is a foreign person. To inform (name of entity) that no withholding is required with respect to my interest in it, I, (name of interest-holder), hereby certify the following:

1. I am not a nonresident alien for purposes of U.S. income taxation;

2. My U.S. taxpayer identifying number (Social Security number) is ________; and

3. My home address is ______________________________.

I agree to inform [name of entity] promptly if I become a nonresident alien at any time during the three years immediately following the date of this notice.

I understand that this certification may be disclosed to the Internal Revenue Service by [name of entity] and that any false statement I have made here could be punished by fine, imprisonment, or both.

Under penalties of perjury I declare that I have examined this certification and to the best of my knowledge and belief it is true, correct, and complete.

[Signature and date]'

(2) Entity interest-holder.

"Under section 1445(e) of the Internal Revenue Code, a corporation, partnership, trust, or estate must withhold tax with respect to certain transfers of property if a holder of an interest in the entity is a foreign person. To inform [name of entity] that no withholding is required with respect to [name of interest-holder]'s interest in it, the undersigned hereby certifies the following on behalf of [name of interest-holder]:

1. [Name of interest-holder] is not a foreign corporation, foreign partnership, foreign trust, or foreign estate (as those terms are defined in the Internal Revenue Code and Income Tax Regulations);

2. [Name of interest-holder]'s U.S. employer identification number is ______; and

3. [Name of interest-holder]'s office address is ________ ________________________________

and place of incorporation (if applicable) is ________ ________________________________

[Name of interest holder] agrees to inform [name of entity] if it becomes a foreign person at any time during the three year period immediately following the date of this notice.

[Name of interest-holder] understands that this certification may be disclosed to the Internal Revenue Service by [name of entity] and that any false statement contained herein could be punished by fine, imprisonment, or both.

Under penalties of perjury I declare that I have examined this certification and to the best of my knowledge and belief it is true, correct, and complete, and I further declare that I have authority to sign this document on behalf of

[name of interest-holder].

[Signature and date]

[Title]'

(iii) Reliance upon certification not permitted. An entity or fiduciary may not rely upon an interest-holder's certification of non-foreign status if, prior to or at the time of the transfer with respect to which withholding would be required, the entity or fiduciary either—

(A) Has actual knowledge that the certification is false;

(B) Has received a notice that the certification is false from a transferor's or transferee's agent, pursuant to § 1.1445-4; or

(C) Has received from a corporation that it knows to be a foreign corporation a certification that does not have attached to it a copy of the IRS acknowledgment of the corporation's election under section 897(i), as required by paragraph (b)(3)(ii)(C) of this section. Such an entity's or fiduciary's withholding obligations shall apply as if a statement had never been given, and such an entity or fiduciary may be held fully liable pursuant to § 1.1445-1(e) for any failure to withhold. For special rules concerning an entity's belated receipt of a notice concerning a false certification, see paragraphs (c)(2)(ii) and (e)(2)(iii) of this section.

(4) Property transferred not a U.S. real property interest. (i) In general. Pursuant to the provisions of paragraphs (c) and (d) of this section, an entity or fiduciary is required to withhold with respect to certain transfers of property, if the property transferred is a U.S. real property interest. (In addition, taxable distributions of U.S. real property interests by domestic or foreign partnerships, trusts, and estates will be subject to withholding pursuant to section 1445(e)(4) and paragraph (f) of this section after publication of a Treasury decision under sections 897(e)(2) and (g). As defined in section 897(c) and § 1.897-1(c), a U.S. real property interest includes certain interests in U.S. corporations, as well as direct interests in real property and certain associated personal property. This paragraph (b)(4) provides rules pursuant to which an entity (or fiduciary thereof) that transfers an interest in a U.S. corporation may determine that withholding is not required because the interest transferred is not a U.S. real property interest. To determine whether an interest in tangible property constitutes a U.S. real property interest the transfer of which would be subject to withholding, see § 1.897-1(b) and (c).

(ii) Interests in publicly traded entities. Withholding is not required under paragraph (c) or (d) of this section upon an entity's transfer of an interest in a domestic corporation if any class of stock of the corporation is regularly traded on an established securities market. This exemption shall apply to a disposition incident to an initial public offering of stock pursuant to a registration statement filed with the Securities and Exchange Commission.

Similarly, no withholding is required under paragraph (c) or (d) of this section upon an entity's transfer of an interest in a publicly traded partnership or trust. However, the rule of this paragraph (b)(4)(ii) shall not apply to the transfer, to a single transferee (or related transferees as defined in § 1.897-1(i)) in a single transaction (or related transactions), of an interest described in § 1.897-1(c)(2)(iii)(B) (relating to substantial amounts of non-publicly traded interests in publicly traded corporations) or of similar interests in publicly traded partnerships or trusts. The entity making a transfer described in the preceding sentence must otherwise determine whether withholding is required, pursuant to section 1445(e) and the regulations thereunder. Transactions shall be deemed to be related if they are undertaken within 90 days of one another or if it can otherwise be shown that they were undertaken in pursuance of a prearranged plan.

(iii) Corporation's statement that interest is not a U.S. real property interest. (A) In general. No withholding is required under paragraph (c) or (d) of this section upon an entity's transfer of an interest in a domestic corporation if, prior to the transfer, the entity or fiduciary obtains a statement, issued by the corporation pursuant to § 1.897-2(h), certifying that the interest is not a U.S. real property interest. In general, a corporation may issue such a statement only if the corporation was not a U.S. real property holding corporation at any time during the previous five years (or the period in which the interest was held by its present holder, if shorter) or if interests in the corporation ceased to be United States real property interests under section 897(c)(1)(B). (A corporation may not provide such a statement based on its determination that the interest in question is an interest solely as a creditor.) See § 1.897-2(f) and (h). A corporation's statement may be relied upon for purposes of this paragraph (b)(4)(iii) only if the statement is dated not more than 30 days prior to the date of the transfer.

(B) Reliance on statement not permitted. An entity or fiduciary is not entitled to rely upon a statement that an interest in a corporation is not a U.S. real property interest, if, prior to or at the time of the transfer, the entity or fiduciary either—

(1) Has actual knowledge that the statement is false, or

(2) Receives a notice that the statement is false from a transferor's or transferee's agent, pursuant to § 1.1445-4.

Such an entity's or fiduciary's withholding obligations shall apply as if a statement had never been given, and such an entity or fiduciary may be held fully liable pursuant to § 1.1445-1(e) for any failure to withhold. For special rules concerning an entity's belated receipt of a notice concerning a false statement, see paragraphs (c)(2)(iii) and (d)(2)(i) of this section.

(5) Reporting and paying over of withheld amounts. (i) In General. An entity or fiduciary must report and pay over to the Internal Revenue Service any tax withheld pursuant to section 1445(e) and this section by the 20th day after the date of the transfer (as defined in § 1.1445-1(g)(8). Forms 8288 and 8288-A are used for this purpose and must be filed at the location as provided in the instructions to Forms 8288 and 8288-A. The contents of Forms 8288 and 8288-A are described in § 1.1445-1(d). Pursuant to section 7502 and regulations thereunder, the timely mailing of Forms 8288 and 8288-A by U.S. mail will be treated as their timely filing. Form 8288-A will be stamped by the Internal Revenue Service to show receipt, and a stamped copy will be mailed by the Service to the interest holder if the Form 8288 is complete, including the transferor's identifying number, at the address shown on the form, for the interest-holder's use. See paragraph (b)(7) of this section. If an application for a withholding certificate with respect to a transfer of a U.S. real property interest was submitted to the Internal Revenue Service on the day of or at any time prior to the transfer, the entity or fiduciary must withhold the amount required under section 1445(e) and the rules of this section. However, the amount withheld, or a lesser amount as determined by the Service, need not be reported and paid over to the Service until the 20th day following the Service's final determination. For this purpose, the Service's final determination occurs on the day when the withholding certificate is mailed to the applicant by the Service or when a notification denying the request for a withholding certificate is mailed to the applicant by the Service. An application is submitted to the Service on the day it is actually received by the Service at the address provided in § 1.1445-1(g)(10) or, under the rules of section 7502, on the day it is mailed to the Service at the address provided in § 1.1445-1(g)(10). For rules concerning the issuance of withholding certificates, see § 1.1445-6.

(ii) Anti-abuse rule. An entity or fiduciary that in reliance upon the rules of this paragraph (b)(5)(ii) fails to report and pay over amounts withheld by the 20th day following the date of the transfer, shall be subject to the payment of interest and penalties if the relevant application for a withholding certificate (or an amendment of the application for a withholding certificate) was submitted for a principle purpose of delaying the payment to the IRS of the amount withheld. Interest and penalties shall be assessed on the amount that is ultimately paid over, with respect to the period between the 20th day after the date of the transfer and the date on which payment is made.

(6) Liability upon failure to withhold. For rules regarding liability upon failure to withhold under section 1445(e) and this § 1.1445-5, see § 1.1445-1(e).

(7) Effect of withholding by entity or fiduciary upon interest holder. The withholding of tax under section 1445(e) does not excuse a foreign person that is subject to U.S. tax by reason of the operation of section 897 from filing a U.S. tax return. Thus, Form 1040NR, 1041, or 1120F, as appropriate must be filed and any tax due must be paid, by the filing date otherwise applicable to such person (or any extension thereof). The tax withheld with respect to the foreign person under section 1445(e) (as shown on Form 8288-A) shall be credited against the amount of income tax as computed in such return, but only if the stamped copy of Form 8288-A provided to the entity or fiduciary (under paragraph (b)(5) of this section) is attached to the return or substantial evidence of the amount of tax withheld is attached to the return in accordance with the succeeding sentence. If a stamped copy of Form 8288-A has not been provided to the interest-holder by the Service, the interest-holder may establish the amount of tax withheld by the entity or fiduciary by attaching to its return substantial evidence of such amount. Such an interest-holder must attach to its return a statement which supplies all of the information required by § 1.1445-1(d)(2). If the amount withheld under section 1445(e) constitutes less than the full amount of the foreign person's U.S. tax liability for that taxable year, then a payment of estimated tax may be required to be made pursuant to section 6154 or 6654 prior to the filing of the income tax return for the year. Alternatively, if the amount withheld under section

1445(e) exceeds the foreign person's maximum tax liability with respect to the transaction (as reflected in a withholding certificate issued by the Internal Revenue Service pursuant to § 1.1445-6) then the foreign person may seek an early refund of the excess pursuant to § 1.1445-6(g). A foreign person that takes gain into account in accordance with the provisions of section 453 shall not be entitled to a refund to the amount withheld, unless a withholding certificate providing for such a refund is obtained pursuant to § 1.1445-6. If an entity or fiduciary withholds tax under section 1445(e) with respect to a beneficial owner of an interest who is not a foreign person, such beneficial owner may credit the amount of any tax withheld against his income tax liability in accordance with the provisions of this § 1.1445-5(b)(7) or apply for an early refund under § 1.1445-6(g).

(8) Effective dates. (i) Partnership, trust, and estate dispositions of U.S. real property interests. The provisions of section 1445(e)(1) and paragraph (c) of this section, requiring withholding upon certain dispositions of U.S. real property interests by domestic partnerships, trusts, and estates, shall apply to any disposition on or after January 1, 1985.

(ii) Certain distributions by foreign corporations. The provisions of section 1445(e)(2) and paragraph (d) of this section, requiring withholding upon distributions of U.S. real property interests by foreign corporations shall apply to distributions made on or after January 1, 1985.

(iii) Distributions by certain domestic corporations to foreign shareholders. The provisions of section 1445(e)(3) and paragraph (e)(1) of this section, requiring withholding upon distributions in redemption of stock under section 302(a) or liquidating distributions under Part II of subchapter C of the Internal Revenue Code by U.S. real property holding corporations to foreign shareholders, shall apply to distributions made on or after January 1, 1985. The provisions of section 1445(e)(3) and paragraph (e)(1) of this section requiring withholding on distributions under section 301 by U.S. real property holding corporations to foreign shareholders shall apply to distributions made after August 20, 1996. The provisions of paragraph (e) of this section providing for the coordination of withholding between sections 1445 and 1441 (or 1442 or 1443) for distributions under section 301 by U.S. real property holding corporations to foreign shareholders apply to distributions after December 31, 2000 (see §§ 1.1441-3(c)(4) and (h)).

(iv) Taxable distributions by domestic or foreign partnerships, trusts, and estates. The provisions of section 1445(e)(4), requiring withholding upon certain taxable distributions by domestic or foreign partnerships, trusts, and estates, shall apply to distributions made on or after the effective date of a Treasury decision under section 897(e)(2)(B)(ii) and (g).

(v) [Reserved]

(vi) Tiered partnerships. No withholding is required upon the disposition of a U.S. real property interest by a partnership which is directly owned, in whole or in part, by another domestic partnership (but only to the extent that the amount realized is attributable to the partnership interest of that other partnership) until the effective date of a Treasury Decision published under section 1445(e) providing rules governing this matter.

(c) Dispositions of U.S. real property interests by domestic partnerships, trusts, and estates. *(1) Withholding required.* (i) In general. If a domestic partnership, trust, or estate disposes of a U.S. real property interest and any partner, beneficiary, or owner of the entity is a foreign person, then the partnership or the trustee, executor, or equivalent fiduciary of the trust or estate must withhold tax with respect to each such foreign person in accordance with the provisions of subdivision (ii) or (iii), or (iv) of this paragraph (c)(1) (as applicable). The withholding obligation imposed by this paragraph (c) applies to the fiduciary of a trust even if the grantor of the trust or another person is treated as the owner of the trust or any portion thereof for purposes of the Internal Revenue Code. Thus, the withholding obligation imposed by this paragraph (c) applies to the trustee of a land trust or similar arrangement, even if such a trustee is not ordinarily treated under the applicable provisions of local law as a true fiduciary.

(ii) Disposition by partnership. A partnership must withhold a tax equal to 35 percent (or the highest rate specified in section 1445(e)(1)) of each foreign partner's distributive share of the gain realized by the partnership upon the disposition of each U.S. real property interest. Such distributive share of the gain must be determined pursuant to the principles of section 704 and the regulations thereunder. For the rules applicable to partnerships, interests in which are regularly traded on an established securities market, see § 1.1445-8.

(iii) Disposition by trust or estate. (A) In general. A trustee, fiduciary, executor or equivalent fiduciary (hereafter collectively referred to as the fiduciary) of a trust or estate having one or more foreign beneficiaries must withhold tax in accordance with the rules of this § 1.1445-5(c)(1)(iii). Such a fiduciary must establish a U.S. real property interest account and must enter in such account all gains and losses realized during the taxable year of the trust or estate from dispositions of U.S. real property interests. The fiduciary must withhold 35 percent (or the highest rate specified in section 1445(e)(1)) of any distribution to a foreign beneficiary that is attributable to the balance in the U.S. real property interest account on the day of the distribution. A distribution from a trust or estate to a beneficiary (domestic or foreign) shall, solely for purposes of section 1445(e)(1), be deemed to be attributable first to any balance in the U.S. real property interest account and then to other amounts. However, a distribution that occurs prior to the transfer of a U.S. real property interest in a taxable year or at any other time when the amount contained in the U.S. real property interest account is zero, is not subject to withholding under this § 1.1445-5(c)(1)(iii). The U.S. real property interest account is reduced by the amount distributed to all beneficiaries (domestic and foreign) attributable to such account during the taxable year of the trust or estate. Any ending balance of the U.S. real property interest account not distributed by the close of the taxable year of the trust or estate is cancelled and is not carried over (or carried back) to any other year. Thus, the beginning balance of such account in any taxable year of the trust or estate is always zero. For rules applicable to grantor trusts see § 1.1445-5(c)(1)(iv). For rules applicable to trusts, interests in which are regularly traded on an established securities market and real estate investment trusts, see § 1.1445-8.

(B) Example. The following example illustrates the rules of paragraph (c)(1)(iii)(A) of this section.

On January 1, 1994, A establishes a domestic trust (which has as its taxable year, the calendar year) for the benefit of B, a nonresident alien, and C, a U.S. citizen. The trust is not a trust subject to sections 671 through 679. Under the terms of the trust, the trustee, T, is given discretion to distribute income and corpus of the trust to provide for the reasonable needs of B and C. During the trust's 1994 tax year, T disposes of three parcels of vacant land located in the United States. The following chart illustrates the computation of the amount subject to withholding under section 1445 with respect to distributions made by T to B and C during 1994.

Date	Parcel sold	Gains or (loss) realized	Distributions to C	Distributions to B (before withholding)	Section 1445 withholding 35% rate	U.S. real property interest account
1/01/94	-0-	-0-	-0-	-0-	-0-	-0-
3/01/94	Parcel 1	140,000	-0-	-0-	-0-	140,000
3/05/94	-0-	-0-	5,000	10,000	3,500	125,000
3/15/94	-0-	-0-	10,000	5,000	1,750	110,000
5/01/94	Parcel 2	300,000	-0-	-0-	-0-	410,000
5/15/94	Parcel 3	(50,000)	-0-	-0-	-0-	360,000
12/01/94	-0-	-0-	170,000	170,000	59,500	20,000
1/01/95	-0-	-0-	-0-	-0-	—	-0-

(iv) Disposition by grantor trust. The trustee or equivalent fiduciary of a trust that is subject to the provisions of subpart E of part I of subchapter J (sections 671 through 679) must withhold a tax equal to 35 percent (or the highest rate specified in section 1445(e)(1)) of the gain realized from each disposition of a U.S. real property interest to the extent such gain is allocable to a portion of the trust treated as owned by a foreign person under subpart E of part I of subchapter J.

(2) Withholding not required under paragraph (c). (i) [Reserved]

(ii) Interest-holder not a foreign person. (A) In general. A domestic partnership, trust, or estate that disposes of a U.S. real property interest shall not be required to withhold with respect to any partner or beneficiary that it determines, pursuant to the rules of paragraph (b)(3) of this section, not to be a foreign person.

(B) Belated notice of false certification. If after the date of the transfer a partnership or fiduciary learns that a partner's or beneficiary's certification of non-foreign status is false, then that partnership or fiduciary shall be required to withhold, with respect to the foreign partner or beneficiary that gave the false certification, the lessor of—

(1) The amount otherwise required to be withheld under the rules of this paragraph (c), or

(2) An amount equal to that partner's or beneficiary's remaining interests in the income or assets of the partnership, trust, or estate. Amounts so withheld must be reported and paid over by the 60th day following the date on which the partnership or fiduciary learns that the certification is false. For rules concerning the notifications of false certifications that may be required to be given to partnerships and fiduciaries, see § 1.1445-4(b).

(iii) Property disposed of not a U.S. real property interest. (A) In general. No withholding is required under this paragraph (c) if a domestic partnership, trust, or estate that disposes of property determines pursuant to the rules of paragraph (b)(4) of this section that the property disposed of is not a U.S. real property interest.

(B) Belated notice of false statement. If after the date of the transfer a partnership or fiduciary learns that a corporation's statement (that an interest in the corporation is not a U.S. real property interest) is false, then that partnership or fiduciary shall be required to withhold, with respect to each foreign partner or beneficiary, the lesser of—

(1) The amount otherwise required to be withheld under the rules of this paragraph (c), or

(2) An amount equal to that partner's or beneficiary's remaining interests in the income or assets of the partnership, trust, or estate.

Amounts so withheld must be reported and paid over by the 60th day following the date on which the partnership or fiduciary learns that the statement is false. For rules concerning the notifications of false statements that may be required to be given to partnerships or fiduciaries, see § 1.1445-4(b).

(iv) Withholding certificate. No withholding is required under this paragraph (c) with respect to the transfer of a U.S. real property interest if the Internal Revenue Service issues a withholding certificate that so provides. For rules concerning the issuance of withholding certificates, see § 1.1445-6.

(v) Nonrecognition transactions. For special rules concerning transactions entitled to nonrecognition of gain or loss, see paragraph (b)(2) of this section.

(3) Large partnerships or trusts. (i) In general. If a partnership or trust has more than 100 partners or beneficiaries, then the partnership or fiduciary of the trust may elect to withhold in accordance with the provisions of this § 1.1445-5(c)(3) in lieu of withholding in the manner required by § 1.1445-5(c)(1). However, the rules of this § 1.1445-5(c)(3) shall not apply to any partnership or trust interests in which are regularly traded on an established securities market except as described in § 1.1445-8(c)(1). The rules of this § 1.1445-5(c)(3) shall not apply to any real estate investment trust. See § 1.1445-8.

(ii) Amount to be withheld. A partnership or trust electing to withhold under this § 1.1445-5(c)(3) shall withhold from each distribution to a foreign person an amount equal to 35 percent (or the highest rate specified in section 1445(e)(1)) of the amount attributable to section 1445(e)(1) transfers.

(iii) Amounts attributable to section 1445(e)(1) transfers. A distribution is attributable to section 1445(e)(1) transfers to the extent of the partner's or beneficiary's proportionate share of the current balance of the entity's section 1445(e)(1) account. A distribution from a partnership or trust that has made an election under this § 1.1445-5(c)(3) shall be deemed first to be attributable to a section 1445(e)(1) transfer to the extent of the balance in the section 1445(e)(1) account. An entity's section 1445(e)(1) account shall be equal to—

(A) The total amount of net gain realized by the entity upon all transfers of U.S. real property interests carried out by the entity after the date of its election under this § 1.1445-5(c)(3); minus

(B) The total amount of all distributions by the entity to domestic and foreign distributees from such account.

(iv) Special rules for entities that make recurring sales of growing crops and timber. An entity that makes an election under § 1.1445-5(c)(3) and that makes recurring sales of growing crops and timber may further elect to determine the amount subject to withholding under the rules of this § 1.1445-5(c)(3)(iv). Such an entity must withhold from each distribution to a foreign partner or beneficiary an amount equal to 10 percent of such partner's or beneficiary's proportionate share of the current balance of the entity's gross section 1445(e)(1) account. An entity's gross section 1445(e)(1) account equals—

(A) The total amount realized by the entity upon all transfers of U.S. real property interest carried out by the entity after the date of its election under this § 1.1445-5(c)(3)(iv); minus

(B) The total amount of all distributions to domestic and foreign distributees from such account.

An entity that elects to compute the amount subject to withholding under this § 1.1445-5(c)(3)(iv), shall make such election in accordance with § 1.1445-5(c)(3)(vi) and shall be subject to the provisions otherwise applicable under § 1.1445-5(c)(3).

(v) Procedural rules. An election under paragraph (c)(3) may be made by filing a notice thereof with the Director, Philadelphia Service Center, at the address provided in § 1.1445-1(g)(10). The notice must be submitted by a general partner (in the case of a partnership) or the trustee or equivalent fiduciary (in the case of a trust). The notice must set forth the name, office address, and identifying number of the partnership or fiduciary making the election, and, in the case of a partnership, must include the name, office address, and identifying number of the general partner submitting the election. An election under this paragraph (c)(3) may be revoked only with the consent of the Internal Revenue Service. Consent of the Service may be requested by filing an application to revoke the election with the Director, Philadelphia Service Center at the address stated above. This application must include all information provided to the Service with the election notice and must provide an explanation of the reasons for revoking the election. The application to revoke an election must also specify the amount remaining to be distributed in the section 1445(e)(1) account or the gross section 1445(e)(1) account.

An entity that ceases to qualify under section 1.1445-5(c)(3) because such entity does not have more than 100 partners or beneficiaries may revoke its election only with the consent of the Internal Revenue Service.

(d) Distributions of U.S. real property interests by foreign corporations. *(1) In general.* A foreign corporation that distributes a U.S. real property interest must deduct and withhold a tax equal to 35 percent (or the rate specified in section 1445(e)(2)) of the amount of gain recognized by the corporation on the distribution. The amount of gain required to be recognized by the corporation must be determined pursuant to the rules of section 897 and any other applicable section. For special rules concerning the applicability of a nonrecognition provision to a distribution, see paragraph (b)(2) of this section. The withholding liability imposed by this paragraph (d) applies to the same taxpayer that owes the related substantive income tax liability pursuant to the operation of section 897. Only one such liability will be assessed and collected from a foreign corporation, but separate penalties for failures to comply with the two requirements will be asserted.

(2) Withholding not required. (i) Property distributed not a U.S. real property interest. (A) In general. No withholding is required under this paragraph (d) if a foreign corporation that distributes property determines pursuant to the rules of paragraph (b)(3) of this section that the property distributed is not a U.S. real property interest.

(B) Belated notice of false statement. If after the date of a distribution described in paragraph (d)(1) of this section a foreign corporation learns that another corporation's statement (that an interest in that other corporation is not a U.S. real property interest) is false, then the foreign corporation may not rely upon that statement for any purpose. Such a foreign corporation's withholding obligations under this paragraph (d) shall apply if a statement had never been given, and such a corporation may be held fully liable pursuant to § 1.1445-5(b)(5) for any failure to withhold. Amounts withheld pursuant to the rule of this paragraph (d)(2)(i)(B) must be reported and paid over by the 60th day following the date on which the foreign corporation learns that the statement is false. No penalties or interest will be assessed for failures to withhold prior to that date. For rules concerning the notifications of false statements that may be required to be given to foreign corporations, see § 1.1445-4(b).

(ii) Withholding certificate. No withholding is required under this paragraph (d) with respect to a foreign corporation's distribution of a U.S. real property interest if the distributing corporation obtains a withholding certificate from the Internal Revenue Service that so provides. For rules concerning the issuance of withholding certificates, see § 1.1445-6.

(e) Distributions to foreign persons by U.S. real property holding corporations. *(1) In general.* A domestic corporation that distributes any property to a foreign person that holds an interest in the corporation must deduct and withhold a tax equal to 10 percent of the fair market value of the property distributed to the foreign person, if—

(i) The foreign person's interest in the corporation constitutes a U.S. real property interest under the provisions of section 897 and regulations thereunder; and

(ii) There is a distribution of property in redemption of stock treated as an exchange under section 302(a), in liquidation of the corporation pursuant to the provisions of Part II of subchapter C of the Internal Revenue Code (sections 331 through section 346), or with respect to stock under section 301 that is not made out of earnings and profits of the corporation.

(2) Coordination rules for Section 301 distributions. If a domestic corporation makes a distribution of property under section 301 to a foreign person whose interest in such corporation constitutes a U.S. real property interest under the provisions of section 897 and the regulations thereunder, then see § 1.1441-3(c)(4) for rules coordinating withholding obligations under sections 1445 and 1441 (or 1442 or 1443)).

(3) Withholding not required. (i) Foreign person's interest not a U.S. real property interest. Withholding is required under this paragraph (e) only with respect to distributions to foreign persons holding interests in the corporation that constitute U.S. real property interests. In general, a foreign person's interest in a domestic corporation constitutes a U.S. real property interest if the corporation was a U.S. real property holding corporation at any time during the shorter of (A) the period in which the foreign person held the interest or (B) the previous five years (but not earlier than June 19, 1980). See section 897(c) and §§ 1.897-1(c) and 1.897-2(b) and (h). However, an interest in such a corporation ceases to

be a U.S. real property interest after all of the U.S. real property interests held by the corporation itself are disposed of in transactions on which gain or loss is recognized. See section 897(c)(1)(B) and § 1.897-2(f)(2). Thus, if a U.S. real property holding corporation in the process of liquidation does not elect section 337 nonrecognition treatment upon its sale of all U.S. real property interests held by the corporation, and recognizes gain or loss upon such sales, interests in that corporation cease to be U.S. real property interests. Therefore, no withholding would be required with respect to that corporation's subsequent liquidating distribution to a foreign shareholder of property other than a U.S. real property interest.

(ii) Nonrecognition transactions. For special rules concerning the applicability of a nonrecognition provision to a distribution described in paragraph (e)(1) of this section, see paragraph (b)(2) of this section.

(iii) Interest-holder not a foreign person. (A) In general. A domestic corporation shall not be required to withhold under this paragraph (e) with respect to a distribution of property to any distributee that it determines, pursuant to the rules of paragraph (b)(3) of this section, not to be a foreign person.

(B) Belated notice of false certification. If after the date of a distribution described in paragraph (e)(1) of this section a domestic corporation learns that an interest-holder's certification of non-foreign status is false, then the corporation may rely upon that certification only if the person providing the false certification holds (or held) less than 10 percent of the value of the outstanding stock of the corporation. With respect to less than 10 percent interest-holders, no withholding is required under this paragraph (e) upon receipt of a belated notice of false certification. With respect to 10 percent or greater interest-holders, the corporation's withholding obligations under this paragraph (e) shall apply as if a certification had never been given, and such a corporation may be held fully liable pursuant to § 1.1445-5(b)(6) for any failure to withhold as of the date specified in this § 1.1445-5(e)(3)(iii)(B). Amounts withheld pursuant to the rule of this paragraph (e)(3)(iii)(B) must be reported and paid over by the 60th day following the date on which the corporation learns that the certification is false. No penalties or interest for failures to withhold will be assessed prior to that date. For rules concerning the notifications of false certifications that may be required to be given to U.S. real property holding corporations, see § 1.1445-4(b).

(iv) Withholding certificate. No withholding, or reduced withholding, is required under this paragraph (e) with respect to a domestic corporation's distribution of property if the distributing corporation obtains a withholding certificate from the Internal Revenue Service that so provides. For rules concerning the issuance of withholding certificates, see § 1.1445-6.

(f) Taxable distributions by domestic or foreign partnerships, trusts, or estates. [Reserved]

(g) Dispositions of interests in partnerships, trusts, and estates. [Reserved]

(h) Effective date for taxpayer identification numbers. The requirement in paragraphs (b)(2)(ii)(B) and (C) of this section that taxpayer identification numbers be provided (in all cases) is applicable for dispositions of U.S. real property interests occurring after November 3, 2003.

T.D. 8113, 12/18/86, amend T.D. 8198, 5/4/88, T.D. 8321, 12/6/90, T.D. 8647, 12/20/95, T.D. 8734, 10/6/97, T.D. 9082, 8/4/2003.

§ 1.1445-6 Adjustments pursuant to withholding certificate of amount required to be withheld under section 1445(e).

(a) Withholding certificate for purposes of section 1445(e). *(1) In general.* Pursuant to the provisions of § 1.1445-5(c)(2)(iv), (d)(2)(ii), and (e)(2)(iv), withholding under section 1445(e) may be reduced or eliminated pursuant to a withholding certificate issued by the Internal Revenue Service in accordance with the rules of this § 1.1445-6. A withholding certificate may be issued in cases where adjusted withholding is appropriate (e.g., because of the applicability of a nonrecognition provision—see paragraph (c) of this section), where the relevant taxpayers are exempt from U.S. tax (see paragraph (d) of this section), or where an agreement for the payment of tax is entered into with the Service (see paragraph (e) of this section). A withholding certificate that is obtained prior to a transfer allows the entity or fiduciary to withhold a reduced amount or excuses withholding entirely. A withholding certificate that is obtained after a transfer has been made may authorize a normal refund or an early refund pursuant to paragraph (g) of this section. The Internal Revenue Service will act upon an application for a withholding certificate not later than the 90th day after it is received. (The Service may deny a request for a withholding certificate where, after due notice, an applicant fails to provide the information necessary to make a determination.) Solely for this purpose (i.e., determining the day upon which the 90 day period commences), an application is received by the Service on the date when all information necessary for the Service to make a determination is provided by the applicant. In no event, however, will a withholding certificate be issued without the transferor's identifying number. (For rules regarding whether an application has been timely submitted, see § 1.1445-5(b)(5)). The Internal Revenue Service will act upon an application for an early refund not later than the 90th day after it is received. An application for an early refund must either (i) include a copy of a withholding certificate issued by the Service with respect to the transaction, or (ii) be combined with an application for a withholding certificate. Where an application for an early refund is combined with an application for a withholding certificate, the Service will act upon both applications not later than the 90th day after receipt. Either an entity, a fiduciary, or a relevant taxpayer (as defined in paragraph (a)(2) of this section) may apply for a withholding certificate. An entity or fiduciary may apply for a withholding certificate with respect to all or less than all relevant taxpayers. For special rules concerning the issuance of a withholding certificate to a foreign corporation that has made an election under section 897(i), see § 1.1445-7(d).

(2) Relevant taxpayer. For purposes of this section, the term "relevant taxpayer" means any foreign person that will bear substantive income tax liability by reason of the operation of section 897 with respect to a transaction upon which withholding is required under section 1445(e).

(b) Applications for withholding certificates. *(1) In general.* An application for a withholding certificate pursuant to this § 1.1445-6 must be submitted in the manner provided in § 1.1445-3(b). However, in lieu of the information required to be submitted pursuant to § 1.1445-3(b)(4), the applicant must provide the information required by paragraph (b)(2) of this section. In addition, the information required by paragraph (b)(3) of this section must be submitted with the application.

(2) Basis for certificate. (i) Adjusted withholding. If a withholding certificate is sought on the basis of a claim that adjusted withholding is appropriate, the application must include a calculation, in accordance with paragraph (c) of this section, of the maximum tax that may be imposed on each relevant taxpayer with respect to which adjusted withholding is sought. The application must also include all evidence necessary to substantiate the claimed calculation, such as records of adjustments to basis or appraisals of fair market value.

(ii) Exemption. If a withholding certificate is sought on the basis of a relevant taxpayer's exemption from U.S. tax, the application must set forth a brief statement of the law and facts that support the claimed exemption. See paragraph (d) of this section.

(iii) Agreement. If a withholding certificate is sought on the basis of an agreement for the payment of tax, the application must include a copy of the agreement proposed by the applicant and a copy of the security instrument (if any) proposed by the applicant. In this regard, see paragraph (e) of this section.

(3) Relevant taxpayers. An application for withholding certificate pursuant to this section must include all of the following information: the name, identifying number, and home address (in the case of an individual) or office address (in the case of an entity) of each relevant taxpayer with respect to which adjusted withholding is sought.

(c) Adjustment of amount required to be withheld. The Internal Revenue Service may issue a withhold certificate that excuses withholding or that permits an entity or fiduciary to withhold an adjusted amount reflecting the relevant taxpayers' maximum tax liability. A relevant taxpayer's maximum tax liability is the maximum amount which that taxpayer could be required to pay as tax by reason of the transaction upon which withholding is required. In the case of an individual taxpayer that amount will generally be the gain realized by the individual, multiplied by the maximum individual income tax rate applicable to long term capital gain. In the case of a corporate taxpayer, that amount will generally be the gain realized by the corporation, multiplied by the maximum corporate income tax rate applicable to long term capital gain. However, that amount must be adjusted to take into account the following:

(1) Any reduction of tax to which the relevant taxpayer is entitled under the provisions of a U.S. income tax treaty;

(2) The effect of any nonrecognition provision that is applicable to the transaction;

(3) Any losses previously realized and recognized by the relevant taxpayer during the taxable year by reason of the operation of section 897;

(4) Any amount realized upon the subject transfer by the relevant taxpayer that is required to be treated as ordinary income under any provision of the Code; and

(5) Any other factor that may increase or reduce the tax upon the transaction.

(d) Relevant taxpayer's exemption from U.S. tax. *(1) In general.* The Internal Revenue Service will issue a withholding certificate that excuses withholding by an entity or fiduciary if it is established that a relevant taxpayer's income from the transaction will be exempt from U.S. tax. For the available exemptions, see paragraph (d)(2) of this section. If a relevant taxpayer is entitled to a reduction of (rather than an exemption from) U.S. tax, then the entity or fiduciary may obtain a withholding certificate to that effect pursuant to the provisions of paragraph (c) of this section.

(2) Available exemptions. A relevant taxpayer's income from a transaction with respect to which withholding is required under section 1445(e) may be exempt from U.S. tax because either:

(i) The relevant taxpayer is an integral part or controlled entity of a foreign government and the subject income is exempt from U.S. tax pursuant to section 892 and the regulations thereunder; or

(ii) The relevant taxpayer is entitled to the benefits of an income tax treaty that provides for such an exemption (subject to the limitations imposed by section 1125(c) of Pub. L. 96-499, which, in general overrides such benefits as of January 1, 1985).

(e) Agreement for the payment of tax. *(1) In general.* The Internal Revenue Service will issue a withholding certificate that excuses withholding or that permits an entity or fiduciary to withhold a reduced amount, if the entity, fiduciary, or a relevant taxpayer enters into an agreement for the payment of tax pursuant to the provisions of this paragraph (e). An agreement for the payment of tax is a contract between the Service and the entity, fiduciary, or relevant taxpayer that consists of two necessary elements. Those elements are—

(i) A contract between the Service and the other person, setting forth in detail the rights and obligations of each; and

(ii) A security instrument or other form of security acceptable to the Assistant Commissioner (International).

(2) Contents of agreement. (i) In general. An agreement for the payment of tax must cover an amount described in subdivision (ii) or (iii) of this paragraph (e)(2). The agreement may either provide adequate security for the payment of the chosen amount with respect to the relevant taxpayer in accordance with paragraph (e)(3) of this section or provide for the payment of that amount through a combination of security and withholding of tax by the entity or fiduciary.

(ii) Tax that would otherwise be withheld. An agreement for the payment of tax may cover the amount of tax that would otherwise be required to be withheld with respect to the relevant taxpayer pursuant to section 1445(e). In addition to the amount computed pursuant to section 1445(e), the applicant must agree to pay interest upon that amount, at the rate established under section 6621, with respect to the period between the date on which withholding tax under section 1445(e) would otherwise be due and the date on which the relevant taxpayer's payment of tax with respect to the disposition will be due. The amount of interest agreed upon must be paid by the applicant regardless of whether or not the Service is required to draw upon any security provided pursuant to the agreement. The interest may be paid either with the return or by the Service drawing upon the security.

(iii) Maximum tax liability. An agreement for the payment of tax may cover the relevant taxpayer's maximum tax liability, determined in accordance with paragraph (c) of this section. The agreement must also provide for the payment of an additional amount equal to 25 percent of the amount determined under paragraph (c) of this section. This additional amount secures the interest and penalties that would accrue between the date of the relevant taxpayer's failure to file a return and pay tax with respect to the disposition, and the date of which the Service collects upon that liability pursuant to the agreement.

(iv) Allocation of payment. An agreement for the payment of tax pursuant to this section must set forth an allocation of the payment provided for by the agreement among the relevant taxpayers with respect to which the withholding certificate is sought. In the case of an agreement that covers an amount described in subdivision (ii) of this paragraph (e)(2), such allocation must be based upon the amount that would otherwise be required to be withheld with respect to each relevant taxpayer. In the case of an agreement that covers an amount described in subdivision (iii) of this paragraph (e)(2), such allocation must be based upon each relevant taxpayer's maximum tax liability.

(3) Major types of security. The major types of security that are acceptable to the Internal Revenue Service for purposes of this section are described in § 1.1445-3(e)(3).

(4) Terms of security instrument. Any security instrument that is furnished pursuant to this section must contain the terms described in § 1.1445-3(e)(4).

(f) Amendments to application for withholding certificates. *(1) In general.* An applicant for a withholding certificate may amend an otherwise complete application by submitting an amending statement to the Director, Philadelphia Service Center at the address provided in § 1.1445-1(g)(10). The amending statement shall provide the information required by § 1.1445-6(f)(3) and must be signed and accompanied by a penalties of perjury statement in accordance with § 1.1445-6(b).

(2) Extension of time for the Service to process requests for withholding certificates. (i) In general. If an amending statement is submitted, the time in which the Internal Revenue Service must act upon the amended application shall be extended by 30 days.

(ii) Substantial amendments. If an amending statement is submitted and the Service finds that the statement substantially amends to the facts of the underlying application or substantially alters the terms of the withholding certificate as requested in the initial application, the time within which the Service must act upon the amended application shall be extended by 60 days. The applicant shall be so notified.

(iii) Amending statement received after the requested withholding certificate has been signed by the Director, Philadelphia Service Center. If an amending statement is received after the withholding certificate, drafted in response to the underlying application, has been signed by the Director, Philadelphia Service Center or his delegate and prior to the day such certificate is mailed to the applicant, the time in which the Service must act upon the amended application shall be extended by 90 days.

(3) Information required to be submitted. No particular form is required for an amending statement but the statement must provide the following information:

(i) Identification of applicant. The amending statement must set forth the name, address, and identifying number of the person submitting the amending statement.

(ii) Date of application. The amending statement must set forth the date of the underlying application for a withholding certificate.

(iii) Real property interest to be (or that has been) transferred. The amending statement must set forth a brief description of the real property interest with respect to which the underlying application for a withholding certificate was submitted.

(iv) Amending information. The amending statement must fully set forth the basis for the amendment including any modification of the facts supporting the application for a withholding certificate and any change sought in the terms of the withholding certificate.

(g) Early refund of overwithheld amounts. If the Internal Revenue Service issues a withholding certificate pursuant to this section, and an amount greater than that specified in the certificate was withheld by the entity or fiduciary, then pursuant to the rules of this paragraph (g) a relevant taxpayer may apply for an early refund of a proportionate share of the excess amount (without interest) prior to the date on which the relevant taxpayer's return is due (without extensions). An application for an early refund must be addressed to the Director, Philadelphia Service Center, at the address provided in § 1.1445-1(g)(10). No particular form is required for the application, but the following information must be set forth in separate paragraphs numbered to correspond with the numbers given below:

(1) Name, address, and identifying number of the relevant taxpayer seeking the refund;

(2) Amount required to be withheld pursuant to withholding certificate;

(3) Amount withheld by entity or fiduciary (attach a copy of Form 8288-A stamped by IRS pursuant to § 1.1445-5(b)(4) or provide substantial evidence of the amount withheld in the case of a failure to receive Form 8288-A, as provided in § 1.1445-5(b)(7)); and

(4) Amount to be refunded to the relevant taxpayer.

An application for an early refund cannot be processed unless the required copy of Form 8288-A or substantial evidence of the amount withheld in the case of a failure to receive Form 8288-A (as provided in § 1.1445-5(b)(7)) is attached to the application. If an application for a withholding certificate is submitted after the transfer takes place, then that application may be combined with an application for an early refund. The Service will act upon a claim for refund within the time limits set forth in § 1.1445-6(a)(1).

(h) Effective date for taxpayer identification numbers. The requirement in paragraphs (b)(3), (f)(3)(i), and (g)(1) of this section that taxpayer identification numbers be provided (in all cases) is applicable for dispositions of U.S. real property interests occurring after November 3, 2003.

T.D. 8113, 12/18/86, amend T.D. 9082, 8/4/2003.

§ 1.1445-7 Treatment of foreign corporation that has made an election under section 897(i) to be treated as a domestic corporation.

(a) In general. Pursuant to section 897(i) a foreign corporation may elect to be treated as a domestic corporation for purposes of sections 897 and 6039C. A foreign corporation that has made such an election shall also be treated as a domestic corporation for purposes of the withholding required under section 1445, in accordance with the provisions of this section.

(b) Withholding under section 1445(a). *(1) Dispositions by corporation.* A foreign corporation that has made an election under section 897(i) may provide a transferee with a certification of non-foreign status in connection with the corporation's disposition of a U.S. real property interest. However, in accordance with the provisions of §§ 1.1445-2(b)(2)(ii) and 1.1445-5(b)(3)(ii)(C), such an electing foreign corporation must attach to such certification a copy of the acknowledgment of the election provided to the corporation by the Internal Revenue Service pursuant to § 1.897-3(d)(4) which states that the information required by § 1.897-3 has been determined to be complete.

(2) Dispositions of interests in corporation. Dispositions of interests in electing foreign corporations shall be subject to the withholding requirements of section 1445(a) and the rules of §§ 1.1445-1 through 1.1445-4. Therefore, if a foreign person disposes of an interest in such a corporation, and that interest is a U.S. real property interest under the provisions of section 897 and regulations thereunder, then the transferee is required to withhold under section 1445(a).

(c) Withholding under section 1445(e). Because a foreign corporation that has made an election under section 897(i) is treated as a domestic corporation for purposes of determining withholding obligations under section 1445, such a corporation is not subject to the requirement of section 1445(e)(2) that a foreign corporation withhold at the corporate capital gain rate from the gain recognized upon the distribution of a U.S. real property interest. Such a corporation is subject to the provisions of section 1445(e)(3). Thus, if interests in an electing corporation constitute U.S. real property interests, then the corporation is required to withhold with respect to the non-dividend distribution of any property to an interest-holder that is a foreign person. See § 1.1445-5(e). Dividend distributions (distributions that are described in section 301) shall be treated as provided in sections 897(f), 1441 and 1442. In addition, if interests in an electing foreign corporation do not constitute U.S. real property interests, then distributions by such corporation shall be treated as provided in sections 897(f) (if applicable), 1441 and 1442. (Approved by the Office of Management and Budget under control number 545-0902.)

T.D. 8113, 12/18/86.

§ 1.1445-8 Special rules regarding publicly traded partnerships, publicly traded trusts and real estate investment trusts (REITs).

Caution: The Treasury has not yet amended Reg § 1.1445-8 to reflect changes made by P.L. 109-222.

(a) Entities to which this section applies. The rules of this section apply to—

(1) Any partnership or trust, interests in which are regularly traded on an established securities market (regardless of the number of its partners or beneficiaries), and

(2) Any REIT (regardless of the form of its organization).

For purposes of paragraph (a)(1) of this section, the rules of section 1445(e)(1) and this section shall not apply to a publicly traded partnership (as defined in section 7704) which is treated as a corporation under section 7704(a), or to those entities that are classified as "associations" and taxed as corporations. See § 301.7701-2.

(b) Obligation to withhold. *(1) In general.* An entity described in paragraph (a) of this section is not required to withhold under the provisions of § 1.1445-5(c), which states the withholding requirements of domestic partnerships, trusts and estates upon the disposition of U.S. real property interests. Except as otherwise provided in this paragraph (b), an entity described in paragraph (a) of this section shall be liable to withhold tax upon the distribution of any amount attributable to the disposition of a U.S. real property interest, with respect to each holder of an interest in the entity that is a foreign person. The amount to be withheld is described in paragraph (c) of this section.

(2) Publicly traded partnerships. Publicly traded partnerships which comply with the withholding procedures under section 1446 will be deemed to have satisfied their withholding obligations under this paragraph (b).

(3) Special rule for certain distributions to nominees. In the case of a person that—

(i) Is a nominee (as defined in paragraph (d) of this section),

(ii) Receives a distribution attributable to the disposition of a U.S. real property interest directly from an entity described in paragraph (a) of this section or indirectly from such entity through a nominee,

(iii) Receives the distribution for payment to any foreign person, or the account of any foreign person, and

(iv) Receives a qualified notice pursuant to paragraph (f) of this section, then the obligation to withhold in accordance with the general rules of section 1445(e)(1) and this paragraph (b) shall be imposed solely on that person to the extent of the amount specified by the qualified notice. A person obligated to withhold by reason of this paragraph (b)(3) is referred to as a withholding agent.

(4) Person designated to act for withholding agent. The rules stated in § 1.1441-7(b)(1) and (2) regarding a person designated to act for a withholding agent shall apply for purposes of this section.

(5) Effect of withholding exemption granted under § 1.1441-4(f). A letter issued by a district director under the provisions of § 1.1441-4(f), which exempts a person from withholding under section 1441 or section 1442, shall also exempt that person from withholding under this paragraph (b), if—

(i) The letter identifies another person as the withholding agent for purposes of section 1441 or 1442, and

(ii) Such other person enters into a written agreement, with the district director who issued the letter, to be the withholding agent for purposes of this paragraph (b).

The exemption granted, and the corresponding withholding obligation imposed, by this paragraph (b)(5) shall apply with respect to the first distribution made after execution of the agreement described in the preceding sentence and shall continue to apply to all distributions made during the period in which the exemption granted under § 1.1441-4(f) is in effect.

(6) Payment other than in money. The rule stated in § 1.1441-7(c) regarding payment other than in money shall apply for purposes of this section.

(c) Amount to be withheld. *(1) Distribution from a publicly traded partnership or publicly traded trust.* The amount to be withheld under this section with respect to a distribution by a publicly traded partnership or publicly traded trust shall be computed in the manner described in § 1.1445-5(c)(3)(ii) and (iii), subject to the rules of this section.

(2) REITs. (i) In general. The amount to be withheld with respect to a distribution by a REIT, under this section shall be equal to 35 percent (or the highest rate specified in section 1445(e)(1)) of the amount described in paragraph (c)(2)(ii) of this section.

(ii) Amount subject to withholding. (A) In general. Except as otherwise provided in paragraph (c)(2)(ii)(C) of this section, the amount subject to withholding is the amount of any distribution, determined with respect to each share or certificate of beneficial interest, designated by a REIT as a capital gain dividend, multiplied by the number of shares or certificates of beneficial interest owned by the foreign person. Solely for purposes of this paragraph, the largest amount of any distribution occurring after March 7, 1991 that could be designated as a capital gain dividend under section 857(b)(3)(C) shall be deemed to have been designated by a REIT as a capital gain dividend regardless of the amount actually designated.

(B) Distribution attributable to net short-term capital gain from the disposition of a U.S. real property interest. [Reserved]

(C) Designation of prior distribution as capital gain dividend. If a REIT makes an actual designation of a prior distribution, in whole or in part, as a capital gain dividend, such prior distribution shall not be subject to withholding under this section. Rather, a REIT must characterize and treat as a capital gain dividend distribution (solely for purposes of section 1445(e)(1)) each distribution, determined with respect to each share or certificate of beneficial interest, made on the day of, or any time subsequent to, such designation as a capital gain dividend until such characterized amounts equal the amount of the prior distribution designated as a capital gain dividend. The provisions of this paragraph shall not be applicable in any taxable year in which the REIT adopts a formal or informal resolution or plan of complete liquidation.

(iii) Example. The following example illustrates the rules of paragraph (c)(2)(ii)(C) of this section.

In the first quarter of 1988, XYZ REIT makes a dividend distribution of $2X. In the second quarter of 1988, XYZ sells real property, recognizing a long term capital gain of $15X, and makes a dividend distribution of $5X. In the third quarter of 1988, XYZ makes a distribution of $3X. In the fourth quarter of 1988, XYZ sells real property recognizing a long term capital loss of $2X. Within 30 days after the close of the taxable year, XYZ designates a capital gain dividend for the year of $13X. It subsequently makes a fourth quarter distribution of $7X. Since XYZ has made an actual designation of prior distributions during the taxable year as capital gain dividends, withholding on those prior distributions will not be required. However, the REIT must characterize, solely for purposes of section 1445(e)(1), a total amount of $13X of dividend distributions as capital gain dividends. Therefore, the fourth quarter dividend distribution of $7X must be characterized as a capital gain dividend subject to withholding under this section. In addition, XYZ will be required to characterize an additional $6X of subsequent dividend distributions as capital gain dividends.

(d) Definition of nominee. For purposes of this section, the term "nominee" means a domestic person that holds an interest in an entity described in paragraph (a) of this section on behalf of another domestic or foreign person.

(e) Determination of non-foreign status by withholding agent. A withholding agent may rely on a certificate of non-foreign status pursuant to § 1.1445-2(b) or on the statements and address provided to it on Form W-9 or a form that is substantially similar to such form, to determine whether an interest holder is a domestic person. Reliance on these documents will excuse the withholding agent from liability imposed under section 1445(e)(1) in the absence of actual knowledge that the interest holder is a foreign person. A withholding agent may also employ other means to determine the status of an interest holder, but, if the agent relies on such other means and the interest holder proves, in fact, to be a foreign person, then the withholding agent is subject to any liability imposed pursuant to section 1445 and the regulations thereunder for failure to withhold.

(f) Qualified notice. A qualified notice for purposes of paragraph (b)(3)(iv) of this section is a notice given by a partnership, trust or REIT regarding a distribution that is attributable to the disposition of a U.S. real property interest in accordance with the notice requirements with respect to dividends described in 17 CFR 240.10b-17(b)(1) or (3) issued pursuant to the Securities Exchange Act of 1934, 15 U.S.C. 78a *et seq.* In the case of a REIT, a qualified notice is only a notice of a distribution, all or any portion of which the REIT actually designates, or characterizes in accordance with paragraph (c)(2)(ii)(C) of this section, as a capital gain dividend in accordance with 17 CFR 240.10b-17(b)(1) or (3), with respect to each share or certificate of beneficial interest. A deemed designation under paragraph (c)(2)(ii)(A) of this section may not be the subject of a qualified notice under this paragraph (f). A person described in paragraph (b)(3) of this section shall be treated as receiving a qualified notice at the time such notice is published in accordance with 17 CFR 240.10b-17(b)(1) or (3).

(g) Reporting and paying over withheld amounts. With respect to an amount withheld under this section, a withholding agent is not required to conform to the requirements of § 1.1445-5(b)(5) but is required to report and pay over to the Internal Revenue Service any amount required to be withheld pursuant to the rules and procedures of section 1461, the regulations thereunder and § 1.6302-2. Forms 1042 and 1042S are to be used for this purpose.

(h) Early refund procedure not available. The early refund procedure set forth in § 1.1445-6(g) shall not apply to amounts withheld under the rules of this section. For adjustment of over-withheld amounts, see § 1.1461-4.

(i) Liability upon failure to withhold. For rules regarding liability upon failure to withhold under section 1445(e) and this section, see § 1.1445-1(e).

T.D. 8321, 12/6/90, amend T.D. 8647, 12/20/95.

§ 1.1445-10T Special rule for foreign governments (temporary).

(a) This section provides a temporary regulation that, if and when adopted as a final regulation will add a new paragraph (d)(6) to § 1.1445-2. Paragraph (b) of this section would then appear as paragraph (d)(6) of § 1.1445-2.

(b) Foreign government. *(1) As transferor.* A foreign government is subject to U.S. taxation under section 897 on the disposition of a U.S. real property interest except to the extent specifically otherwise provided in the regulations issued under section 892. A foreign government that disposes of a U.S. real property interest that is not subject to taxation as specifically provided by the regulations under section 892 may present a notice of nonrecognition treatment pursuant to paragraph (d)(2) of this section that specifically cites the provision of such regulation, and thereby avoids withholding by the transferee of the property. A foreign government that disposes of a U.S. real property interest or the transferee of the property may obtain a withholding certificate from the Internal Revenue Service that confirms the applicability of section 892, but neither is required to do so. Rules concerning the issuance of withholding certificates are provided in § 1.1445-3.

(2) As transferee. A foreign government or international organization that acquires a U.S. real property interest is fully subject to section 1445 and the regulations thereunder. Therefore, such an entity is required to withhold tax upon

the acquisition of a U.S. real property interest from a foreign person.

(c) Effective date. The rules of this section shall be effective for transfers, exchanges, distributions and other dispositions occurring on or after June 6, 1988.

T.D. 8198, 5/4/88.

§ 1.1445-11T Special rules requiring withholding under § 1.1445-5 (temporary).

(a) Purpose and scope. This section provides temporary regulations that, if and when adopted as a final regulation will add certain new paragraphs within § 1.1445-5(b) and (c). The paragraphs of this section would then appear as set forth below. Paragraph (b) of this section would then appear as paragraph (b)(8)(v) of § 1.1445-5. Paragraph (c) of this section would then appear as paragraph (c)(2)(i) of § 1.1445-5. Paragraph (d) of this section would then appear as paragraph (g) of § 1.1445-5.

(b) Dispositions of interests in partnerships, trusts, and estates. The provisions of section 1445(e)(5), requiring withholding upon certain dispositions of interests in partnerships, trusts, and estates, that own directly or indirectly a U.S. real property interest shall apply to dispositions on or after the effective date of a later Treasury decision under section 897(g) of the Code except in the case of dispositions of interests in partnerships in which fifty percent of the value of the gross assets consist of U.S. real property interests and ninety percent or more of the value of the gross assets consist of U.S. real property interests plus any cash or cash equivalents. The provisions of section 1445(e)(5), shall apply, however, to dispositions after June 6, 1988, of interests in partnerships in which fifty percent or more of the value of the gross assets consist of U.S. real property interests, and ninety percent or more of the value of the gross assets consist of U.S. real property interests plus any cash or cash equivalents. See paragraph (d) of this section.

(c) Transactions covered elsewhere. No withholding is required under this paragraph (c) with respect to the distribution of a U.S. real property interests by a partnership, trust, or estate. Such distributions shall be subject to withholding under section 1445(e)(4) and paragraph (f) of this § 1.1445-5 on the effective date of a later Treasury decision published under section 897(g) of the Code. No withholding is required at this time for distributions described in the preceding sentence. See paragraph (b)(8)(iv) of this § 1.1445-5. No withholding is required under this paragraph with respect to the disposition of an interest in a trust, estate, or partnership except in the case of a partnership in which fifty percent or more of the value of the gross assets consist of U.S. real property interests, and ninety percent or more of the value of the gross assets consist of U.S. real property interests plus any cash or cash equivalents. See paragraph (b)(8)(v) of § 1.1445-5. Withholding shall be required as provided in section 1445(e)(5) and paragraph (g) of this section with respect to the disposition after June 6, 1988, of an interest in a partnership in which fifty percent or more of the value of the gross assets consist of U.S. real property interests, and ninety percent or more of the value of the gross assets consist of U.S. real property interests plus any cash or cash equivalents.

(d) Dispositions of interests in partnerships, trusts or estates. *(1) Withholding required on disposition of certain partnership interests.* Withholding is required under section 1445(e)(5) and this paragraph with respect to the disposition by a foreign partner of an interest in a domestic or foreign partnership in which fifty percent or more of the value of the gross assets consist of U.S. real property interests, and ninety percent or more of the value of the gross assets consist of U.S. real property interests plus any cash or cash equivalents. For purposes of this paragraph cash equivalents mean any asset readily convertible into cash (whether or not denominated in U.S. dollars), including, but not limited to, bank accounts, certificates of deposit, money market accounts, commercial paper, U.S. and foreign treasury obligations and bonds, corporate obligations and bonds, precious metals or commodities, and publicly traded instruments. The taxpayer on filing an income tax return for the year of the disposition may demonstrate the extent to which the gain on the disposition of the interest is not attributable to U.S. real property interests. A taxpayer is also permitted by § 1.1445-3 to apply for a withholding certificate in instances where reduced withholding is appropriate.

(2) Withholding not required. (i) Transferee receives statement that interest in partnership is not described in paragraph (d)(1). No withholding is required under paragraph (d)(1) of this section upon the disposition of a partnership interest otherwise described in that paragraph if the transferee is provided a statement, issued by the partnership and signed by a general partner under penalties of perjury no earlier than 30 days before the transfer, certifying that fifty percent or more of the value of the gross assets does not consist of U.S. real property interests, or that ninety percent or more of the value of the gross assets of the partnership does not consist of U.S. real property interests plus cash or cash equivalents.

(ii) Reliance on statement not permitted. A transferee is not entitled to rely upon a statement described in paragraph (d)(2)(i) of this section if, prior to or at the time of the transfer, the transferee either—

(A) Has actual knowledge that the statement is false, or

(B) Receives a notice, pursuant to § 1.1445-4.

Such a transferee's withholding obligations shall apply as if the statement had never been given, and such a transferee may be held fully liable pursuant to § 1.1445-1(e) for any failure to withhold.

(iii) Belated notice of false statement. If, after the date of the transfer, a transferee receives notice that a statement provided under paragraph (d)(2)(i) of this section is false, then such transferee may rely on the statement only with respect to consideration that was paid prior to the receipt of the notice. Such a transferee is required to withhold a full 10 percent of the amount realized from the consideration that remains to be paid to the transferor. Thus, if 10 percent or more of the amount realized remains to be paid to the transferor, then the transferee is required to withhold and pay over the full 10 percent. The transferee must do so by withholding and paying over the entire amount of each successive payment of consideration to the transferor, until the full 10 percent of the amount realized has been withheld and paid over. Amounts so withheld must be reported and paid over by the 20th day following the date on which each such payment of consideration is made. A transferee that is subject to the rules of this § 1.1445-10T(d)(2)(iii) may not obtain a withholding certificate pursuant to § 1.1445-3, but must instead withhold and pay over the amounts required by this paragraph.

(e) Effective date. The rules of this section are effective for transactions after June 6, 1988.

T.D. 8198, 5/4/88.

§ 1.1446-0 Table of contents.

This section lists the captions contained in §§ 1.1446-1 through 1.1446-7.

(7) Partner's certificate valid only for partnership taxable year for which submitted.

(d) Effect of certificate of deductions and losses on partner and partnership.

(1) Effect on partner.

(i) No effect on liability for income tax of foreign partner.

(ii) No effect on partner's estimated tax obligations.

(iii) No effect on partner's obligation to file U.S. income tax return.

(2) Effect on partnership.

(i) Reasonable reliance to relieve partnership from addition to tax under section 6665.

(ii) Continuing liability for withholding tax under section 1461 and for applicable interest and penalties.

(A) In general.

(B) Certificate defective because of amount or character of deductions and losses.

(3) Partnership level rules and requirements.

(i) Fling requirement.

(ii) Reasonable cause for failure to timely file a valid certificate and computation.

(A) Determining reasonable cause.

(B) Notification.

(e) Examples.

(f) Effective/Applicability date.

(g) Transition rule.

§ 1.1446-7 Effective/Applicability date.

T.D. 9200, 5/13/2005, amend T.D. 9394, 4/28/2008.

§ 1.1446-1 Withholding tax on foreign partners' share of effectively connected taxable income.

(a) In general. If a domestic or foreign partnership has effectively connected taxable income (ECTI) as computed under § 1.1446-2 for any partnership tax year, and any portion of such taxable income is allocable under section 704 to a foreign partner, then the partnership must pay a withholding tax under section 1446 (1446 tax) at the time and in the manner prescribed in this section, and §§ 1.1446-2 through 1.1446-6.

(b) Steps in determining 1446 tax obligation. In general, a partnership determines its 1446 tax as follows. The partnership determines whether it has any foreign partners in accordance with paragraph (c) of this section. If the partnership does not have any foreign partners (including any person presumed to be foreign under paragraph (c) of this section and any domestic trust treated as foreign under § 1.1446-3(d)) during its taxable year, it generally will not have a 1446 tax obligation. If the partnership has one or more foreign partners, it then determines under § 1.1446-2 whether it has ECTI any portion of which is allocable under section 704 to one or more of the foreign partners. If the partnership has ECTI allocable under section 704 to one or more of its foreign partners, the partnership computes its 1446 tax, pays over 1446 tax, and reports the amount paid in accordance with the rules in § 1.1446-3. For special rules applicable to publicly traded partnerships, see § 1.1446-4. For special rules applicable to tiered partnership structures, see § 1.1446-5. For special rules that may apply in determining the amount of 1446 tax due with respect to a partner, see § 1.1446-6.

(c) Determining whether a partnership has a foreign partner. *(1) In general.* Except as otherwise provided in this section, § 1.1446-3, and § 1.1446-5, only a partnership that has at least one foreign partner during the partnership's taxable year can have a 1446 tax liability. Generally, the term foreign partner means any partner of the partnership that is not a U.S. person within the meaning of section 7701(a)(30). Thus, a partner of the partnership is generally a foreign partner if the partner is a nonresident alien, foreign partnership (see § 1.1446-5 for rules that allow a lower-tier partnership to look through an upper-tier foreign partnership to the partners of such partnership for purposes of computing its 1446 tax), foreign corporation (which includes a foreign government pursuant to section 892(a)(3)), foreign estate or trust (see paragraph (c)(2) of this section for rules that instruct a partnership to consider the grantor or other owner of a trust under subpart E of subchapter J as the partner for purposes of computing the partnership's 1446 tax), as those terms are defined under section 7701 and the regulations thereunder, or a foreign organization described in section 501(c), or other foreign person. A person also is a foreign partner if the person is presumed to be a foreign person under paragraph (c)(3) of this section. For purposes of this section, a partner that is treated as a U.S. person for all income tax purposes (by election or otherwise, see e.g., sections 953(d) and 1504(d)) will not be a foreign partner, provided the partner has provided the partnership a valid Form W-9, "Request for Taxpayer Identification Number and Certification," or the partnership uses other means to determine that the partner is not a foreign partner (see paragraph (c)(3) of this section). A partner that is treated as a U.S. person only for certain specified purposes is considered a foreign partner for purposes of section 1446, and a partnership must pay 1446 tax on the portion of ECTI allocable to that partner. For example, a partnership must generally pay 1446 tax on ECTI allocable to a foreign corporate partner that has made an election under section 897(i).

(2) Submission of Forms W-8BEN, W-8IMY, W-8ECI, W-8EXP, and W-9. (i) In general. Except as otherwise provided in this paragraph (c)(2) or paragraph (c)(3) of this section, a partnership must generally determine whether a partner is a foreign partner, and the partner's tax classification (e.g., corporate or non-corporate), by obtaining a withholding certificate from the partner that is a Form W-8BEN, "Certificate of Foreign Status of Beneficial Owner for United States Tax Withholding," Form W-8IMY, "Certificate of Foreign Intermediary, Flow-Through Entity, or Certain U.S. Branches for United States Tax Withholding," Form W-8ECI, "Certificate of Foreign Person's Claim for Exemption from Withholding on Income Effectively Connected With the Conduct of a Trade or Business in the United States," Form W-8EXP, "Certificate of Foreign Government or other Foreign Organization for United States Tax Withholding," or a Form W-9, as applicable, or an acceptable substitute form permitted under paragraph (c)(5) of this section. Generally, a foreign partner that is a nonresident alien, a foreign estate or trust (other than a grantor trust described in this paragraph (c)(2)), a foreign corporation, or a foreign government should provide a valid Form W-8BEN.

(ii) Withholding certificate applicable to each type of partner. A partner that submits a valid Form W-8 (e.g., Form W-8BEN) for purposes of section 1441 or 1442 will generally satisfy the documentation requirements of this section provided that the submission of such form is not inconsistent with the rules of this paragraph (c)(2) or paragraph (c)(3) of this section. The following rules shall apply for purposes of this section.

(A) U.S. person. A partner that is a U.S. person (other than a grantor trust described in this paragraph (c)(2)), including a domestic partnership and domestic simple or complex trust (including an estate), shall provide a valid Form W-9.

(B) Nonresident alien. A Form W-8 (e.g., Form W-8BEN) submitted by a nonresident alien for purposes of withholding under section 1441 will generally be accepted for purposes of section 1446. If no such form is submitted for purposes of section 1441, such nonresident alien shall submit Form W-8BEN for purposes of section 1446.

(C) Foreign partnership. A partner that is a foreign partnership generally shall provide a valid Form W-8IMY for purposes of section 1446. See § 1.1446-5 (permitting a lower-tier partnership to look through an upper-tier foreign partnership in certain circumstances when computing 1446 tax).

(D) Disregarded entities. An entity that is disregarded as an entity separate from its owner under § 301.7701-3 of this chapter (whether domestic or foreign) shall not submit a Form W-8 (e.g., Form W-8BEN) or Form W-9. Instead, the owner of such entity for Federal tax purposes shall submit appropriate documentation to comply with this section. See §§ 301.7701-1 through 301.7701-3 of this chapter for determining the U.S. Federal tax classification of a partner.

(E) Domestic and foreign grantor trusts. To the extent that a grantor or other person is treated as the owner of any portion of a trust under subpart E of subchapter J of the Internal Revenue Code, such trust shall provide documentation under this paragraph (c)(2) to identify the trust as a grantor trust and provide documentation on behalf of the grantor or other person treated as the owner of all or a portion of such trust as required by this paragraph (c)(2). If such trust is a foreign trust, the trust shall submit Form W-8IMY to the partnership identifying itself as a foreign grantor trust and shall provide such documentation (e.g., Forms W-8BEN, W-8IMY, W-8ECI, W-8EXP, or W-9) and information pertaining to its grantor or other owner to the partnership that permits the partnership to reliably associate (within the meaning of § 1.1441-1(b)(2)(vii)) such portion of the trust's allocable share of partnership ECTI with the grantor or other person that is the owner of such portion of the trust. If such trust is a domestic trust, the trust shall furnish the partnership a statement under penalty of perjury that the trust is, in whole or in part, a domestic grantor trust and such statement shall identify that portion of the trust that is treated as owned by a grantor or another person under subpart E of subchapter J of the Internal Revenue Code. The trust shall also provide such documentation and information (e.g., Forms W-8BEN, W-8IMY, W-8ECI, W-8EXP, or W-9) pertaining to its grantor or other owner(s) to the partnership that permits the partnership to reliably associate (within the meaning of § 1.1441-1(b)(2)(vii)) such portion of the trust's allocable share of partnership ECTI with the grantor or other person that is the owner of such portion of the trust.

(F) Nominees. Where a nominee holds an interest in a partnership on behalf of another person, the beneficial owner of the partnership interest, not the nominee, shall submit a Form W-8 (e.g., Form W-8BEN) or Form W-9 to the partnership or nominee that is the withholding agent.

(G) Foreign governments, foreign tax-exempt organizations and other foreign persons. A Form W-8 (e.g., Form W-8EXP) submitted by a partner that is a foreign government, foreign tax-exempt organization, or other foreign person for purposes of withholding under §§ 1441 through 1443 will also operate to establish the foreign status of such partner under this section. However, except as set forth in § 1.1446-3(c)(3) (regarding certain tax-exempt organizations described in section 501(c)), the submission of Form W-8EXP will have no effect on whether there is a 1446 tax due with respect to such partner's allocable share of partnership ECTI. For example, a partnership must still pay 1446 tax with respect to a foreign government partner's allocable share of ECTI because such partner is treated as a foreign corporation under section 892(a)(3). If no Form W-8 is submitted for purposes of withholding under sections 1441 through 1443, then such government, tax-exempt organization, or person must generally submit Form W-8BEN.

(H) Foreign corporations, certain foreign trusts, and foreign estates. Consistent with the rules of this paragraph (c)(2) and paragraph (c)(3) of this section, a foreign corporation, a foreign trust (other than a foreign grantor trust described in paragraph (c)(2)(ii)(E) of this section), or a foreign estate may generally submit any appropriate Form W-8 (e.g., Form W-8BEN) to the partnership to establish its foreign status for purposes of section 1446.

(iii) Effect of Forms W-8BEN, W-8IMY, W-8ECI, W-8EXP, W-9, and statement. (A) Partnership reliance on withholding certificate. In general, for purposes of this section, a partnership may rely on a valid Form W-8 (e.g., Form W-8BEN) or Form W-9, or statement described in this paragraph (c)(2) from a partner, beneficial owner, or grantor trust to determine whether that person, beneficial owner, or the owner of a grantor trust, is a non-foreign or foreign partner for purposes of computing 1446 tax, and if such person is a foreign partner, to determine whether or not such person is a corporation for U.S. tax purposes. The rules of paragraph (c)(3) of this section shall apply to a partnership that receives a Form W-8IMY from a foreign grantor trust or a statement described in this paragraph (c)(2) from a domestic grantor trust, but does not receive a Form W-8 (e.g., Form W-8BEN) or Form W-9 identifying such grantor or other person. Further, a partnership may not rely on a Form W-8 or Form W-9, or statement described in this paragraph (c)(2), and such form or statement is therefore not valid for any installment period or Form 8804 filing date during which the partnership has actual knowledge or has reason to know that any information on the withholding certificate or statement is incorrect or unreliable and, if based on such knowledge or reason to know, the partnership should pay 1446 tax in an amount greater than would be the case if it relied on the certificate or statement.

(B) Reason to know. A partnership has reason to know that information on a withholding certificate or statement is incorrect or unreliable if its knowledge of relevant facts or statements contained on the form or other documentation is such that a reasonably prudent person in the position of the withholding agent would question the claims made. See §§ 1.1441-1(e)(4)(viii) and 1.1441-7(b)(1) and (2).

(C) Subsequent knowledge and impact on penalties. If the partnership does not have actual knowledge or reason to know that a Form W-8BEN, Form W-8IMY, Form W-8ECI, Form W-8EXP, Form W-9, or statement received from a partner, beneficial owner, or grantor trust contains incorrect or unreliable information, but it subsequently determines that the certificate or statement contains incorrect or unreliable information, and, based on such knowledge the partnership should pay 1446 tax in an amount greater than would be the case if it relied on the certificate or statement, then the partnership will not be subject to penalties for its failure to pay the 1446 tax in reliance on such certificate or statement for any installment payment date prior to the date that the determination is made. See §§ 1.1446-1(c)(4) and 1.1446-3 concerning penalties for failure to pay the withholding tax when a partnership knows or has reason to know that a withholding certificate or statement is incorrect or unreliable.

(iv) Requirements for certificates to be valid. Except as otherwise provided in this paragraph (c), for purposes of this section, the validity of a Form W-9 shall be determined under section 3406 and § 31.3406(h)-3(e) of this chapter which establish when such form may be reasonably relied upon. A Form W-8BEN, Form W-8IMY, Form W-8ECI, or Form W-8EXP is only valid for purposes of this section if its validity period has not expired, the partner submitting the form has signed it under penalties of perjury, and it contains all the required information.

(A) When period of validity expires. For purposes of this section, a Form W-8BEN, Form W-8IMY, Form W-8ECI, or Form W-8EXP submitted by a partner shall be valid until the end of the period of validity determined for such form under § 1.1441-1(e). With respect to a foreign partnership submitting Form W-8IMY, the period of validity of such form shall be determined under § 1.1441-1(e) as if such foreign partnership submitted the form required of a nonwithholding foreign partnership. See § 1.1441-1(e)(4)(ii).

(B) Required information for Forms W-8BEN, W-8IMY, W-8ECI, and W-8EXP. Forms W-8BEN, W-8IMY, W-8ECI, and W-8EXP submitted under this section must contain the partner's name, permanent address and Taxpayer Identification Number (TIN), the country under the laws of which the partner is formed, incorporated or governed (if the person is not an individual), the classification of the partner for U.S. Federal tax purposes (e.g., partnership, corporation), and any other information required to be submitted by the forms or instructions for such form, as applicable.

(v) Partner must provide new withholding certificate when there is a change in circumstances. The principles of § 1.1441-1(e)(4)(ii)(D) shall apply when a change in circumstances has occurred (including situations where the status of a U.S. person changes) that requires a partner to provide a new withholding certificate.

(vi) Partnership must retain withholding certificates. A partnership or nominee who has responsibility for paying 1446 tax under this section or § 1.1446-4 must retain each withholding certificate, statement, and other information received from its direct and indirect partners for as long as it may be relevant to the determination of the withholding agent's 1446 tax liability under section 1461 and the regulations thereunder.

(3) Presumptions in the absence of valid Form W-8BEN, Form W-8IMY, Form W-8ECI, Form W-8EXP, Form W-9, or statement. Except as otherwise provided in this paragraph (c)(3), a partnership that does not receive a valid Form W-8BEN, Form W-8IMY, Form W-8ECI, Form W-8EXP, Form W-9, or statement required by paragraph (c)(2) of this section from a partner, beneficial owner, or grantor trust, or a partnership that receives a withholding certificate or statement but has actual knowledge or reason to know that the information on the certificate or statement is incorrect or unreliable, must presume that the partner is a foreign person. Except as provided in § 1.1446-3(a)(2) and § 1.1446-5(c)(2), a partnership that knows that a partner is an individual shall treat the partner as a nonresident alien. Except as provided in § 1.1446-3(a)(2) and § 1.1446-5(c)(2), a partnership that knows that a partner is an entity shall treat the partner as a corporation if the entity is a corporation as defined in § 301.7701-2(b)(8) of this chapter. See § 1.1446-3(a)(2) which prohibits a partnership in certain circumstances from considering preferential tax rates in computing its 1446 tax when the presumption and rules of this paragraph (c)(3) apply. In all other cases, the partnership shall treat the partner as either a nonresident alien or a foreign corporation, whichever classification results in a higher 1446 tax being due, and shall pay the 1446 tax in accordance with this presumption. Except as provided in § 1.1446-5(c)(2), the presumption set forth in this paragraph (c)(3) that a partner is a foreign person shall not apply to the extent that the partnership relies on other means to ascertain the non-foreign status of a partner and the partnership is correct in its determination that such partner is a U.S. person. A partnership is in no event required to rely upon other means to determine the non-foreign status of a partner and may demand that a partner furnish an acceptable certificate under this section. If a certificate is not provided in such circumstances, the partnership may presume that the partner is a foreign partner, and for purposes of sections 1461 through 1463, will be considered to have been required to pay 1446 tax on such partner's allocable share of partnership ECTI.

(4) Consequences when partnership knows or has reason to know that Form W-8BEN, Form W-8IMY, Form W-8ECI, Form W-8EXP, or Form W-9 is incorrect or unreliable and does not withhold. If a partnership has actual knowledge or has reason to know that a Form W-8BEN, Form W-8IMY, Form W-8ECI, Form W-8EXP, Form W-9, or statement required by paragraph (c)(2) of this section submitted by a partner, beneficial owner, or grantor trust contains incorrect or unreliable information (either because the certificate or statement when given to the partnership contained incorrect information or because there has been a change in facts that makes information on the certificate or statement incorrect), and the partnership pays less than the full amount of 1446 tax due on ECTI allocable to that partner, the partnership shall be fully liable under section 1461 and § 1.1461-3 (§ 1.1461-1 for publicly traded partnerships subject to § 1.1446-4) and § 1.1446-3, and for all applicable penalties and interest, for any failure to pay the 1446 tax for the period during which the partnership has such knowledge or reason to know that the certificate contained incorrect or unreliable information and for all subsequent installment periods. If a partner, beneficial owner, or grantor trust submits a new valid Form W-8BEN, Form W-8IMY, Form W-8ECI, Form W-8EXP, Form W-9, or statement, as applicable, the partnership may rely on that documentation when paying 1446 tax (or any installment of such tax) for any payment date that has not passed at the time such form is received.

(5) Acceptable substitute form. A partnership or withholding agent responsible for paying 1446 tax (or any installment of such tax) may substitute its own form for the official version of Form W-8 (e.g., Form W-8BEN) that is recognized under this section to ascertain the identity of its partners, provided such form is consistent with § 1.1441-1(e)(4)(vi). All references under this section or §§ 1.1446-2 through 1.1446-6 to a Form W-8 (e.g., Form W-8BEN, Form W-8IMY, Form W-8ECI, Form W-8EXP) shall include the acceptable substitute form recognized under this paragraph (c)(5).

T.D. 9200, 5/13/2005, amend T.D. 9394, 4/28/2008.

§ 1.1446-2 Determining a partnership's effectively connected taxable income allocable to foreign partners under section 704.

(a) In general. A partnership's effectively connected taxable income (ECTI) is generally the partnership's taxable income as computed under section 703, with adjustments as provided in section 1446(c) and this section, and computed with consideration of only those partnership items which are effectively connected (or treated as effectively connected) with the conduct of a trade or business in the United States. For purposes of determining the section 1446 withholding tax (1446 tax) or any installment of such tax under § 1.1446-3, partnership ECTI allocable under section 704 to foreign partners is the sum of the allocable shares of ECTI of each of the partnership's foreign partners as determined under paragraph (b) of this section. See § 1.1446-6 (special rules permitting the partnership to consider partner-level deductions and losses to reduce the partnership's 1446 tax). The calculation of partnership ECTI allocable to foreign partners as set forth in paragraph (b) of this section and the partnership's withholding tax obligation are partnership-level computations solely for purposes of determining the 1446 tax. Therefore, any deduction that is not taken into account in calculating a partner's allocable share of partnership ECTI (e.g., percentage depletion), but which is a deduction that under U.S. tax law the foreign partner is otherwise entitled to claim, can still be claimed by the foreign partner when computing its U.S. tax liability and filing its U.S. income tax return, subject to any restriction or limitation that otherwise may apply.

(b) Computation. *(1) In general.* A foreign partner's allocable share of partnership ECTI for the partnership's taxable year that is allocable under section 704 to a particular foreign partner is equal to that foreign partner's distributive share of partnership gross income and gain for the partnership's taxable year that is effectively connected and properly allocable to the partner under section 704 and the regulations thereunder, reduced by the foreign partner's distributive share of partnership deductions for the partnership taxable year that are connected with such income under section 873(a) or 882(c) and properly allocable to the partner under section 704 and the regulations thereunder, in each case, after application of the rules of this section. See § 1.1446-6 (special rules permitting the partnership to consider partner-level deductions and losses to reduce the partnership's 1446 tax). For these purposes, a foreign partner's distributive share of effectively connected gross income and gain and the deductions connected with such income shall be computed by considering allocations that are respected under the rules of section 704 and § 1.704-1(b)(1), including special allocations in the partnership agreement (as defined in § 1.704-1(b)(2)(ii)(h)), and adjustments to the basis of partnership property described in section 743 pursuant to an election by the partnership under section 754 (see § 1.743-1(j)). The character of effectively connected partnership items (capital versus ordinary) shall be separately considered only to the extent set forth in paragraph (b)(3)(v) of this section and, when applicable, sections 1.1446-3(a)(2)(consideration of preferential rates when computing 1446 tax) and section 1.1446-6 (special rules permitting the partnership to consider partner-level deductions and losses to reduce the partnership's 1446 tax).

(2) Income and gain rules. For purposes of computing a foreign partner's allocable share of partnership ECTI under this paragraph (b), the following rules shall apply with respect to partnership income and gain.

(i) Application of the principles of section 864. The determination of whether a partnership's items of gross income are effectively connected shall be made by applying the principles of section 864 and the regulations thereunder.

(ii) Income treated as effectively connected. A partnership's items of gross income that are effectively connected include any income that is treated as effectively connected income, including partnership income subject to a partner's election under section 871(d) or section 882(d), any partnership income treated as effectively connected with the conduct of a U.S. trade or business pursuant to section 897, and any other items of partnership income treated as effectively connected under another provision of the Internal Revenue Code, without regard to whether those amounts are taxable to the partner. A partner that makes the election under section 871(d) or section 882(d) shall furnish to the partnership a statement that indicates that such election has been made. See § 1.871-10(d)(3). If a partnership receives a valid Form W-8ECI from a partner, the partner is deemed, for purposes of section 1446, to have effectively connected income subject to withholding under section 1446 to the extent of the items identified on the form.

(iii) Exempt income. A foreign partner's allocable share of partnership ECTI does not include income or gain exempt from U.S. tax by reason of a provision of the Internal Revenue Code. A foreign partner's allocable share of partnership ECTI also does not include income or gain exempt from U.S. tax by operation of any U.S. income tax treaty or reciprocal agreement. In the case of income excluded by reason of a treaty provision, such income must be derived by a resident of an applicable treaty jurisdiction, the resident must be the beneficial owner of the item, and all other requirements for benefits under the treaty must be satisfied. The partnership must have received from the partner a valid withholding certificate, that is, Form W-8BEN (see § 1.1446-1(c)(2)(iii) regarding when a Form W-8BEN is valid for purposes of this section), containing the information necessary to support the claim for treaty benefits required in the forms and instructions. In addition, for purposes of this section, the withholding certificate must contain the beneficial owner's taxpayer identification number.

(3) Deductions and losses. For purposes of computing a foreign partner's allocable share of partnership ECTI under this paragraph (b), the following rules shall apply with respect to deductions and losses.

(i) Oil and gas interests. The deduction for depletion with respect to oil and gas wells shall be allowed, but the amount of such deduction shall be determined without regard to sections 613 and 613A.

(ii) Charitable contributions. The deduction for charitable contributions provided in section 170 shall not be allowed.

(iii) Net operating losses and other suspended or carried losses. Except as provided in § 1.1446-6, the net operating loss deduction of any foreign partner provided in section 172 shall not be taken into account. Further, except as provided in § 1.1446-6, the partnership shall not take into account any suspended losses (e.g., losses in excess of a partner's basis in the partnership, see section 704(d)) or any capital loss carrybacks or carryovers available to a foreign partner.

(iv) Interest deductions. The rules of this paragraph (b)(3)(iv) shall apply for purposes of determining the amount of interest expense that is allocable to income which is (or is treated as) effectively connected with the conduct of a trade or business for purposes of calculating a foreign partner's allocable share of partnership ECTI. In the case of a non-corporate foreign partner, the rules of § 1.861-9T(e)(7) shall apply. In the case of a corporate foreign partner, the rules of § 1.882-5 shall apply by treating the partnership as a foreign corporation and using the partner's pro-rata share of the partnership's assets and liabilities for these purposes. For these purposes, the rules governing elections under § 1.882-5(a)(7) shall be made at the partnership level.

(v) Limitation on capital losses. Losses from the sale or exchange of capital assets allocable under section 704 to a partner shall be allowed only to the extent of gains from the sale or exchange of capital assets allocable under section 704 to such partner.

(vi) Other deductions. No deduction shall be allowed for personal exemptions provided in section 151 or the additional itemized deductions for individuals provided in part VII of subchapter B of the Internal Revenue Code (section 211 and following).

(vii) Limitations on deductions. Except as provided in § 1.1446-6 and this paragraph (b)(3), any limitations on losses or deductions that apply at the partner level when determining ECTI allocable to a foreign partner shall not be taken into account.

(4) Other rules. (i) Exclusion of items allocated to U.S. partners. Except as provided in § 1.1446-5(e), in computing partnership ECTI, the partnership shall not take into account any item of income, gain, loss, or deduction to the extent allocable to any partner that is not a foreign partner, as that term is defined in § 1.1446-1(c).

(ii) Partnership credits. See § 1.1446-3(a) providing that the 1446 tax is computed without regard to a partner's distributive share of the partnership's tax credits.

(5) Examples. The following examples illustrate the application of this section. In considering the examples, disregard the potential application of § 1.1446-3(b)(2)(v)(F) (relating to the de minimis exception to paying 1446 tax). The examples are as follows:

Example (1). Limitation on capital losses. PRS partnership has two equal partners, A and B. A is a nonresident alien and B is a U.S. citizen. A provides PRS with a valid Form W-8BEN, and B provides PRS with a valid Form W-9. PRS has the following annualized tax items for the relevant installment period, all of which are effectively connected with its U.S. trade or business and are allocated equally between A and B: $100 of long-term capital gain, $400 of long-term capital loss, $300 of ordinary income, and $100 of ordinary deductions. Assume that these allocations are respected under section 704(b) and the regulations thereunder. Accordingly, A's allocable share of PRS's effectively connected items includes $50 of long-term capital gain, $200 of long-term capital loss, $150 of ordinary income, and $50 of ordinary deductions. In determining A's allocable share of partnership ECTI, the amount of the long-term capital loss that may be taken into account pursuant to paragraph (b)(3)(v) of this section is limited to A's allocable share of gain from the sale or exchange of capital assets. Accordingly, A's share of partnership ECTI allocable under section 704 pursuant to § 1.1446-2 is $100 ($150 of ordinary income less $50 of ordinary deductions, plus $50 of capital gain less $50 of capital loss).

Example (2). Limitation on capital losses—special allocations. PRS partnership has two equal partners, A and B. A and B are both nonresident aliens. A and B each provide PRS with a valid Form W-8BEN. PRS has the following annualized tax items for the relevant installment period, all of which are effectively connected with its U.S. trade or business: $200 of long-term capital gain, $200 of long-term capital loss, and $400 of ordinary income. A and B have equal shares in the ordinary income, however, pursuant to the partnership agreement, capital gains and losses are subject to special allocations. The long-term capital gain is allocable to A, and the long-term capital loss is allocable to B. Assume that these allocations are respected under section 704(b) and the regulations thereunder. Pursuant to paragraph (b)(3)(v) of this section, A's allocable share of partnership ECTI under § 1.1446-2 is $400 (consisting of $200 of ordinary income and $200 of long-term capital gain), and B's allocable share of partnership ECTI is $200 (consisting of $200 of ordinary income).

Example (3). Withholding tax obligation where partner has net operating losses. PRS partnership has two equal partners, FC, a foreign corporation, and DC, a domestic corporation. FC and DC provide a valid Form W-8BEN and Form W-9, respectively, to PRS. Both FC and PRS are on a calendar taxable year. PRS is engaged in the conduct of a trade or business in the United States and for its first installment period during its taxable year has $100 of annualized ECTI that is allocable to FC. As of the beginning of the taxable year, FC had an unused effectively connected net operating loss carryover in the amount of $300. FC's net operating loss carryover is not taken into account in determining FC's allocable share of partnership ECTI under § 1.1446-2 and, absent the application of § 1.1446-6 (permitting a foreign partner to certify deductions and losses reasonably expected to be available to reduce the partner's U.S. income tax liability on the effectively connected income or gain allocable from the partnership), is not considered in computing the 1446 tax installment payment due on behalf of FC. Accordingly, PRS must pay 1446 tax with respect to the $100 of ECTI allocable to FC.

T.D. 9200, 5/13/2005, amend T.D. 9394, 4/28/2008.

§ 1.1446-3 Time and manner of calculating and paying over the 1446 tax.

(a) In general. *(1) Calculating 1446 tax.* This section provides rules for calculating, reporting, and paying over the section 1446 withholding tax (1446 tax). A partnership's 1446 tax equals the amount determined under this section and shall be paid in installments during the partnership's taxable year (see paragraph (d)(1) of this section for installment payment due dates), with any remaining tax due paid with the partnership's annual return required to be filed pursuant to paragraph (d) of this section. For these purposes, a partnership shall not take into account either a partner's liability for any other tax imposed under any other provision of the Internal Revenue Code (e.g., section 55 or 884) or a partner's distributive share of the partnership's tax credits when determining the amount of the partnership's 1446 tax.

(2) Applicable percentage. (i) In general. Except as provided in this paragraph (a)(2), in the case of a foreign partner that is a corporation for U.S. tax purposes, the applicable percentage is the highest rate of tax specified in section 11(b)(1) for such taxable year. Except as provided in this paragraph (a)(2) and § 1.1446-5, in the case of a foreign partner that is not a corporation for U.S. tax purposes (e.g., a partnership, individual, trust or estate), the applicable percentage is the highest rate of tax specified in section 1.

(ii) Special types of income or gain. Except as otherwise provided, a partnership is permitted to consider as the applicable percentage under this paragraph (a)(2) the highest rate of tax applicable to a particular type of income or gain allocable to a partner (e.g., long-term capital gain allocable to a non-corporate partner, unrecaptured section 1250 gain, collectibles gain under section 1(h)), to the extent of a partner's allocable share of such income or gain. Consideration of the highest rate of tax applicable to a particular type of income or gain under the previous sentence shall be made without regard to the amount of such partner's income. A partnership is not permitted to consider the highest rate of tax applicable to a particular type of income or gain under this paragraph (a)(2)(ii) if the application of the preferential rate depends upon the corporate or non-corporate status of the person reporting the income or gain and, either no documentation has been provided to the partnership under § 1.1446-1 to establish the corporate or non-corporate status of the partner required to pay tax on the income or gain, or the partnership is otherwise required to compute and pay 1446 tax on such portion of the income or gain using the highest applicable percentage under section 1446(b). See e.g., §§ 1.1446-1(c)(3) (presumption of foreign status in the absence of documentation) and 1.1446-5(c)(2) (requirement to pay 1446 tax at higher of rates in section 1446(b) where a lower-tier partnership cannot reliably associate income with a partner of the upper-tier partnership).

(b) Installment payments. *(1) In general.* Except as provided in § 1.1446-4 for certain publicly traded partnerships, a partnership must pay its 1446 tax by making installment payments of the 1446 tax based on the amount of partnership effectively connected taxable income (ECTI) allocable under section 704 to its foreign partners, without regard to whether the partnership makes any distributions to its partners during the partnership's taxable year. The amount of the installment payments is determined in accordance with this paragraph (b), and the tax must be paid at the times set forth in paragraph (d) of this section. Subject to paragraphs (b)(2)(v) and (b)(3)(ii) of this section, in computing its first installment of 1446 tax for a taxable year, a partnership must decide whether it will pay its 1446 tax for the entire taxable year by using the safe harbor set forth in paragraph (b)(3)(i) of this section, or by using one of several annualization methods available under paragraph (b)(2)(ii) of this section for computing partnership ECTI allocable to foreign partners. In the case of a partnership's underpayment of an installment of 1446 tax, the partnership shall be subject to an addition to the tax equal to the amount determined under section 6655, as modified by this section, as if such partnership were a corporation, as well as any other applicable interest and penalties. See § 1.1446-3(f). Section 6425 (permitting an adjustment for an overpayment of estimated tax by a corporation) shall not apply to a partnership's payment of its 1446 tax.

(2) Calculation. (i) Application of the principles of section 6655. (A) In general. Installment payments of 1446 tax required during the partnership's taxable year are based upon partnership ECTI for the portion of the partnership taxable year to which the payments relate, and, except as set forth in this paragraph (b)(2) or paragraph (b)(3) of this section, shall be calculated using the principles of section 6655. The principles of section 6655, except as otherwise provided in § 1.6655-2, are applied to annualize the partnership's items of effectively connected income, gain, loss, and deduction to determine each foreign partner's allocable share of partnership ECTI. Each foreign partner's allocable share of partnership ECTI is then multiplied by the relevant applicable percentage for the type of income allocable to the foreign partner under paragraph (a)(2) of this section. The respective 1446 tax amounts are then added for each foreign partner to yield an annualized 1446 tax with respect to such partner. The installment of 1446 tax due with respect to a foreign partner equals the excess of the section 6655(e)(2)(B)(ii) percentage of the annualized 1446 tax for that partner (or, if applicable, the adjusted seasonal amount) for the relevant installment period, over the aggregate amount of 1446 tax installment payments previously paid with respect to that partner during the partnership's taxable year. The partnership's total 1446 tax installment payment equals the sum of the installment payments due for such period on behalf of all the partnership's foreign partners.

(B) Calculation rules when certificates are submitted under § 1.1446-6. (1) To the extent applicable, in computing the 1446 tax due with respect to a foreign partner, a partnership may consider a certificate received from such partner under § 1.1446-6(c)(1)(i) or (ii) and the amount of state and local taxes permitted to be considered under § 1.1446-6(c)(1)(iii). For this purpose, a partnership shall first annualize the partner's allocable share of the partnership's items of effectively connected income, gain, deduction, and loss before—

(i) Considering under § 1.1446-6(c)(1)(i) the partner's certified deductions and losses;

(ii) Determining under § 1.1446-6(c)(1)(ii) whether the 1446 tax otherwise due with respect to that partner is less than $1,000 (determined with regard to any certified deductions or losses); or

(iii) Considering under § 1.1446-6 (c)(1)(iii) the amount of state and local taxes withheld and remitted on behalf of the partner.

(2) The amount of the limitation provided in § 1.1446-6(c)(1)(i)(C) shall be based on the partner's allocable share of these annualized amounts. For any installment period in which the partnership considers a partner's certificate, the partnership must also consider the following events to the extent they occur prior to the due date for paying the 1446 tax for such installment period—

(i) The receipt of an updated certificate or status update from the partner under § 1.1446-6(c)(2)(ii)(B) certifying an amount of deductions or losses that is less than the amount reflected on the superseded certificate (see § 1.1446-6(e)(2) Example 4);

(ii) The failure to receive an updated certificate or status update from the partner that should have been provided under § 1.1446-6(c)(2)(ii)(B); and

(iii) The receipt of a notification from the IRS under § 1.1446-6(c)(3) or (c)(5) (see § 1.1446-6(e)(2) Example 5).

(ii) Annualization methods. A partnership that decides to annualize its income for the taxable year shall use one of the annualization methods set forth in section 6655(e) and the regulations thereunder, and as described in the forms and instructions for Form 8804, "Annual Return for Partnership Withholding Tax (Section 1446)," Form 8805, "Foreign Partner's Information Statement of Section 1446 Withholding Tax," and Form 8813, "Partnership Withholding Tax Payment Voucher."

(iii) Partner's estimated tax payments. In computing its installment payments of 1446 tax, a partnership may not take into account a partner's estimated tax payments.

(iv) Partner whose interest terminates during the partnership's taxable year. If a partner's interest in the partnership terminates prior to the end of the partnership's taxable year, the partnership shall take into account the income that is allocable to the partner for the portion of the partnership taxable year that the person was a partner.

(v) Exceptions and modifications to the application of the principles under section 6655. To the extent not otherwise modified in §§ 1.1446-1 through 1.1446-7 or inconsistent with those rules, the principles of section 6655 apply to the calculation of the installment payments of 1446 tax made by a partnership as set forth in this paragraph (b)(2)(v).

(A) Inapplicability of special rules for large corporations. The principles of section 6655(d)(2), concerning large corporations (as defined in section 6655(g)(2)), shall not apply.

(B) Inapplicability of special rules regarding early refunds. The principles of section 6655(h), applicable to amounts excessively credited or refunded under section 6425, shall not apply. See paragraph (b)(1) of this section providing that section 6425 shall not apply for purposes of the 1446 tax. This paragraph (b)(2)(v)(B) shall apply to 1446 tax paid by a partnership or nominee, as well as to amounts that a partner is deemed to have paid for estimated tax purposes by reason of the partnership's or nominee's 1446 tax payments under § 1.1446-3(d)(1)(i).

(C) Period of underpayment. The period of the underpayment set forth in section 6655(b)(2) shall end on the earlier of the 15th day of the 4th month following the close of the partnership's taxable year (or, in the case of a partnership described in § 1.6081-5(a)(1) of this chapter, the 15th day of the 6th month following the close of the partnership's taxable year), or with respect to any portion of the underpayment, the date on which such portion is paid.

(D) Other taxes. Section 6655 shall be applied without regard to any references to alternative minimum taxable income and modified alternative minimum taxable income.

(E) 1446 tax treated as tax under section 11. The principles of section 6655(g)(1) shall be applied to treat the 1446 tax as a tax imposed by section 11, and any partnership required to pay such tax shall be treated as a corporation.

(F) Application of section 6655(f). A partnership subject to section 1446 shall apply section 6655(f) after aggregating the 1446 tax due (or any installment of such tax) for all its foreign partners. See § 1.1446-6 for an exception to this rule when a nonresident alien partner certifies to the partnership that the partnership investment is the nonresident alien partner's only activity giving rise to effectively connected items.

(G) Application of section 6655(i). If a partnership has a taxable year of less than 12 months, the partnership is required to pay 1446 tax (including installments of such tax) in accordance with this section § 1.1446-3, if the partnership has ECTI allocable under section 704 to foreign partners. In such a case, the partnership shall adjust its installment payments of 1446 tax in a reasonable manner (e.g., the annualized amounts of ECTI estimated to be allocable to a foreign partner, and the section 6655(e)(2)(B)(ii) percentage to be applied to each installment) to account for the short-taxable year. However, if the partnership's taxable year is a period of less than 4 months, the partnership shall not be required to make installment payments of 1446 tax, but will only be required to file Forms 8804 and 8805 in accordance with this section § 1.1446-3, and report and pay the appropriate 1446 tax for the short-taxable year.

(H) Current year tax safe harbor. The safe harbor set forth in section 6655(d)(1)(B)(i) shall apply to a partnership subject to section 1446.

(I) Prior year tax safe harbor. The safe harbor set forth in section 6655(d)(1)(B)(ii) shall not apply and instead the safe harbor set forth in paragraph (b)(3) of this section applies.

(3) 1446 tax safe harbor. (i) In general. The addition to tax under section 6655 shall not apply to a partnership with respect to a current installment of 1446 tax if—

(A) The average of the amount of the current installment and prior installments during the taxable year is at least 25 percent of the total 1446 tax (without regard to § 1.1446-6) for the prior taxable year;

(B) The prior taxable year consisted of twelve months;

(C) The partnership timely files (including extensions) an information return under section 6031 for the prior year; and

(D) The amount of ECTI for the prior taxable year is not less than 50 percent of the ECTI shown on the annual return of section 1446 withholding tax that is (or will be) timely filed for the current year.

(ii) Permission to change to standard annualization method. Except as otherwise provided in this paragraph (b)(3)(ii), if a partnership decides to pay its 1446 tax for the first installment period based upon the safe harbor method set forth in paragraph (b)(3)(i), the partnership must use the safe harbor method for each installment payment made during the partnership's taxable year. Notwithstanding the previous sentence, if a partnership paying over 1446 tax during the taxable year pursuant to this paragraph (b)(3) determines during an installment period (based upon the standard option annualization method set forth in section 6655(e) and the regulations thereunder, as modified by the forms and instructions to Forms 8804, 8805, and 8813) that it will not qualify for the safe harbor in this paragraph (b)(3) because the prior year's ECTI will not meet the 50-percent threshold in paragraph (b)(3)(i)(D) of this section, then the partnership is permitted, without being subject to the addition to the tax under section 6655 (as applied through this section), to pay over its 1446 tax for the period in which such determination is made, and all subsequent installment periods during the taxable year, using the standard option annualization method. A change pursuant to this paragraph shall be disclosed in a statement attached to the Form 8804 the partnership files for the taxable year and shall include information to allow the IRS to determine whether the change was appropriate.

(c) Coordination with other withholding rules. *(1) Fixed or determinable, annual or periodical income.* Fixed or determinable, annual or periodical income subject to tax under section 871(a) or section 881 is not subject to withholding under section 1446, and such income is subject to the withholding requirements of sections 1441 and 1442 and the regulations thereunder.

(2) Real property gains. (i) Domestic partnerships. Except as otherwise provided in this paragraph (c)(2), a domestic partnership that is otherwise subject to the withholding requirements of sections 1445 and 1446 will be subject to the payment and reporting requirements of section 1446 only and not section 1445(e)(1) and the regulations thereunder, with respect to partnership gain from the disposition of a U.S. real property interest (as defined in section 897(c)). A partnership that has complied with the requirements of section 1446 will be deemed to satisfy the withholding requirements of section 1445 and the regulations thereunder. However, a domestic partnership that would otherwise be exempt from section 1445 withholding by operation of a nonrecognition provision must continue to comply with the requirements of § 1.1445-5(b)(2). In the event that amounts are withheld under section 1445(e) at the time of the disposition

of a U.S. real property interest, such amounts may be credited against the partnership's 1446 tax. A partnership that fails to comply fully with the requirements of section 1446 pursuant to this paragraph (c)(2) shall be liable for any unpaid 1446 tax and subject to any applicable addition to the tax, interest, and penalties under section 1446. See § 1.1446-4(f)(4) for rules coordinating the withholding liability of publicly traded partnerships under sections 1445 and 1446.

(ii) Foreign partnerships. A foreign partnership that is subject to withholding under section 1445(a) during its taxable year may credit the amount withheld under section 1445(a) against its section 1446 tax liability for that taxable year only to the extent such amount is allocable to foreign partners.

(3) Coordination with section 1443. A partnership that has ECTI allocable under section 704 to a foreign organization described in section 501(c) shall be required to pay 1446 tax on such ECTI only to the extent such ECTI is includible under section 512 and section 513 in computing the organization's unrelated business taxable income. The certificate procedure available under § 1.1441-9(b)(1) by which a partner may set forth the amounts it believes will and will not be includible in its computation of unrelated business taxable income under section 512 and section 513 shall also apply to a partner in a partnership subject to section 1446. Such certificate shall be made by a partner in the same manner as under § 1.1441-9(b)(2). A partnership that determines that the partner's certificate as to certain partnership items is unreliable or lacking must presume, consistent with § 1.1441-9(b)(3) (regarding amounts includible under section 512 in computing the organization's unrelated business taxable income), that such partnership items would be includible in computing the partner's UBTI.

(d) Reporting and crediting the 1446 tax. *(1) Reporting 1446 tax.* This paragraph (d) sets forth the rules for reporting and crediting the 1446 tax paid by a partnership. To the extent that 1446 tax is paid on ECTI allocable to a domestic trust (including a grantor or other person treated as an owner of a portion of such trust) or a grantor or other person treated as the owner of a portion of a foreign trust, the rules of this paragraph (d) applicable to a foreign trust or its beneficiaries shall be applied to such domestic or foreign trust and its beneficiaries or owners, as applicable, so that appropriate credit for the 1446 tax may be claimed by the trust, beneficiary, grantor, or other person.

(i) Reporting of installment tax payments and notification to partners of installment tax payments. Each partnership required to make an installment payment of 1446 tax must file Form 8813, "Partnership Withholding Tax Payment Voucher (Section 1446)," in accordance with the instructions to that form. Form 8813 is generally used to transmit an installment payment of 1446 tax to the IRS with respect to partnership ECTI estimated to be allocated to foreign partners. However, see § 1.1446-6 (relating to circumstances where a partnership must file Form 8813 when no payment is required under section 1446). Except as provided in this section, a partnership must notify each foreign partner of the 1446 tax paid on the partner's behalf when the partnership makes an installment payment of 1446 tax. The notice required to be given to a foreign partner under the previous sentence must be provided within 10 days of the installment payment due date, or, if paid later, the date such installment payment is made. A foreign partner generally may credit an installment of 1446 tax paid by the partnership on the partner's behalf against the partner's estimated tax that the partner must pay during the partner's own taxable year. See § 1.1446-5(b) (relating to tiered partnership structures). However, a foreign partner may not obtain an early refund of such amounts under the estimated tax rules. See § 1.1446-3(b)(2)(v)(B). See paragraph (d)(2) of this section for the amount of 1446 tax a partner may credit against its U.S. income tax liability. No particular form is required for a partnership's notification to a foreign partner, but each notification must include the partnership's name, the partnership's Taxpayer Identification Number (TIN), the partnership's address, the partner's name, the partner's TIN, the partner's address, the annualized ECTI estimated to be allocated to the foreign partner (or prior year's safe harbor amount, if applicable), and the amount of tax paid on behalf of the partner for both the current and any prior installment periods during the partnership's taxable year. Notwithstanding any other provision of this paragraph (d), a withholding agent is not required to notify a partner of an installment of 1446 tax paid on the partner's behalf, unless requested by the partner, if—

(A) The partnership's agent responsible for providing notice pursuant to this paragraph is the same person that acts as an agent of the foreign partner for purposes of filing the partner's U.S. Federal income tax return for the partner's taxable year that includes the installment payment date; or

(B) The partnership has at least 500 foreign partners and the total 1446 tax that the partnership determines will be required to be paid for the partnership taxable year on behalf of such partner (based on paragraph (b)(2)(ii) or (3) of this section) with respect to the partner's allocable share of ECTI is less than $1,000.

(ii) Payment due dates. The 1446 tax is calculated based on partnership ECTI allocable under section 704 to foreign partners during the partnership's taxable year, as determined under section 706. Installment payments of the 1446 tax generally must be made during the partnership's taxable year in which such income is derived. A partnership must pay to the Internal Revenue Service a portion of its estimated annual 1446 tax in installments on or before the 15th day of the fourth, sixth, ninth, and twelfth months of the partnership's taxable year as provided in section 6655. Any additional amount determined to be due is to be paid with the filing of the annual return of tax required under paragraph (d)(1)(iii) of this section and clearly designated as for the prior taxable year. Form 8813 should not be submitted for a payment made under the preceding sentence.

(iii) Annual return and notification to partners. Every partnership (except a publicly traded partnership subject to § 1.1446-4) that has effectively connected gross income for the partnership's taxable year allocable under section 704 to one or more of its foreign partners (or is treated as having paid 1446 tax under § 1.1446-5(b)), must file Form 8804, "Annual Return for Partnership Withholding Tax (Section 1446)." Additionally, every partnership that is required to file Form 8804 also must file Form 8805, "Foreign Partner's Information Statement of Section 1446 Withholding Tax," for each of its foreign partners on whose behalf it paid 1446 tax, and furnish Form 8804 and the Forms 8805 to the Internal Revenue Service and the respective Form 8805 to each of its partners. Notwithstanding the previous sentence, a partnership that considers a foreign partner's certificate under § 1.1446-6 when computing its 1446 tax on Form 8804 is required to furnish such partner and the Internal Revenue Service a Form 8805, even if the form submitted to the partner shows no payment of 1446 tax on behalf of the partner. Forms 8804 and 8805 are separate from Form 1065, "U.S. Return of Partnership Income," and the attachments thereto, and are not to be filed as part of the partnership's

Form 1065. A partnership must generally file Forms 8804 and 8805 on or before the due date for filing the partnership's Form 1065. See § 1.6031(a)-1(c) for rules concerning the due date of a partnership's Form 1065. However, with respect to partnerships described in § 1.6081-5(a)(1), Forms 8804 and 8805 are not due until the 15th day of the sixth month following the close of the partnership's taxable year.

(iv) Information provided to beneficiaries of foreign trusts and estates. A foreign trust or estate that is a partner in a partnership subject to withholding under section 1446 shall be provided Form 8805 by the partnership. The foreign trust or estate must provide to each of its beneficiaries a copy of the Form 8805 furnished by the partnership. In addition, the foreign trust or estate must provide a statement for each of its beneficiaries to inform each beneficiary of the amount of the credit that may be claimed under section 33 (as determined under this section) for the 1446 tax paid by the partnership. Until an official Internal Revenue Service form is available, the statement from a foreign trust or estate that is described in this paragraph (d)(1)(iv) shall contain the following information—

(A) Name, address, and TIN of the foreign trust or estate;

(B) Name, address, and TIN of the partnership;

(C) The amount of the partnership's ECTI allocated to the foreign trust or estate for the partnership taxable year (as shown on the Form 8805 provided to the trust or estate);

(D) The amount of 1446 tax paid by the partnership on behalf of the foreign trust or estate (as shown on Form 8805 to the trust or estate);

(E) Name, address, and TIN of the beneficiary of the foreign trust or estate;

(F) The amount of the partnership's ECTI allocated to the trust or estate for purposes of section 1446 that is to be included in the beneficiary's gross income; and

(G) The amount of 1446 tax paid by the partnership on behalf of the foreign trust or estate that the beneficiary is entitled to claim on its return as a credit under section 33.

(v) Attachments required of foreign trusts and estates. The statement furnished to each foreign beneficiary under this paragraph (d)(1) must also be attached to the foreign trust or estate's U.S. Federal income tax return filed for the taxable year that includes the installment periods to which the statement relates.

(vi) Attachments required of beneficiaries of foreign trusts and estates. The beneficiary of the foreign trust or estate must attach the statement provided by the trust or estate pursuant to paragraph (d)(1)(iv) of this section, along with a copy of the Form 8805 furnished by the partnership to such trust or estate, to its U.S. income tax return for the year in which it claims a credit for the 1446 tax. See § 1.1446-3(d)(2)(ii) for additional rules regarding a partner or beneficial owner claiming a credit for the 1446 tax.

(vii) Information provided to beneficiaries of foreign trusts and estates that are partners in certain publicly traded partnerships. A statement similar to the statement required by paragraph (d)(1)(iv) of this section shall be provided by trusts or estates that hold interests in publicly traded partnerships subject to § 1.1446-4.

(2) Crediting 1446 tax against a partner's U.S. tax liability. (i) In general. A partnership's payment of 1446 tax on the portion of ECTI allocable to a foreign partner generally relates to the partner's U.S. income tax liability for the partner's taxable year in which the partner is subject to U.S. tax on that income. Subject to paragraphs (d)(2)(ii) and (iii) of this section, a partner may claim as a credit under section 33 the 1446 tax paid by the partnership with respect to ECTI allocable to that partner. The partner may not claim an early refund of these amounts under the estimated tax rules. See paragraph (d)(1)(i) of this section regarding a partner's ability to credit an installment of 1446 tax paid on the partner's behalf against the partner's estimated tax payments due for the taxable year. See also § 1.1446-5(b) (relating to tiered partnership structures).

(ii) Substantiation for purposes of claiming the credit under section 33. A partner may credit the amount paid under section 1446 with respect to such partner against its U.S. income tax liability only if it attaches proof of payment to its U.S. income tax return for the partner's taxable year in which the items comprising such partner's allocable share of partnership ECTI are included in the partner's income. Except as provided in the next sentence, proof of payment consists of a copy of the Form 8805 the partnership provides to the partner (or in the case of a beneficiary of a foreign trust or estate, the statement required under paragraph (d)(1)(iv) or (vii) of this section to be provided by such trust or estate and a copy of the related Form 8805 furnished to such trust or estate), but only if the name and TIN on the Form 8805 (or the statement provided by a foreign trust or estate) match the name and TIN on the partner's U.S. tax return, and such form (or statement) identifies the partner (or beneficiary) as the person entitled to the credit under section 33. In the case of a partner of a publicly traded partnership that is subject to withholding on distributions under § 1.1446-4, proof of payment consists of a copy of the Form 1042-S, "Foreign Person's U.S. Source Income Subject to Withholding," provided to the partner by the partnership.

(iii) Special rules for apportioning the tax credit under section 33. (A) Foreign trusts and estates. Section 1446 tax paid on the portion of ECTI allocable under section 704 to a foreign trust or estate that the foreign trust or estate may claim as a credit under section 33 shall bear the same ratio to the total 1446 tax paid on behalf of the trust or estate as the total ECTI allocable to such trust or estate and not distributed (or treated as distributed) to the beneficiaries of such trust or estate, and, accordingly not deducted under section 651 or section 661 in calculating the trust or estate's taxable income, bears to the total ECTI allocable to such trust or estate. The 1446 tax that a foreign trust or estate is not entitled to claim as a credit under this paragraph (d)(2) may be claimed as a credit by the beneficiary of such trust or estate that includes the partnership ECTI allocated to the trust or estate in gross income under section 652 or section 662 (whether distributed or deemed to be distributed and with the same character as effectively connected income as in the hands of the trust or estate). In the case of a foreign trust or estate with multiple beneficiaries, each beneficiary may claim a portion of the 1446 tax that may be claimed by all beneficiaries under the previous sentence as a credit in the same proportion as the amount of ECTI included in such beneficiary's gross income bears to the total amount of ECTI included by all beneficiaries. The trust or estate must provide each beneficiary with a copy of the Form 8805 provided to it by the partnership and prepare the statement required by paragraph (d)(1)(iv) of this section.

(B) Use of domestic trusts to circumvent section 1446. This paragraph (d)(2)(iii)(B) shall apply if a partnership knows or has reason to know that a foreign person holds its interest in the partnership through a domestic trust, and such domestic trust was formed or availed of with a principal purpose of avoiding the 1446 tax. The use of a domestic trust may have a principal purpose of avoiding the 1446 tax even though the tax avoidance purpose is outweighed by other purposes when taken together. In such case, a partnership is required to pay 1446 tax under this paragraph as if the domestic trust was a foreign trust for purposes of section 1446 and the regulations thereunder. Accordingly, all applicable additions to the tax, interest, and penalties shall apply to the partnership for its failure to pay 1446 tax under this paragraph (d)(2)(iii)(B), commencing with the installment period during which the partnership knows or has reason to know that this paragraph (d)(2)(iii)(B) applies. A publicly traded partnership within the meaning of § 1.1446-4 (or a nominee required to pay 1446 tax under § 1.1446-4) will not be considered to know or have reason to know a domestic trust is being used to avoid the 1446 tax under this paragraph (d)(2)(iii)(B), provided the interest held in such entity by the domestic trust is publicly traded.

(iv) Refunds to withholding agent. A withholding agent (i.e., the partnership) may obtain a refund of the 1446 tax paid (or deemed paid under § 1.1446-5(b)) to the extent of the excess of the amount paid to the Internal Revenue Service by the partnership, over the partnership's section 1446 tax liability as determined by the sum of the total tax creditable to each partner indicated on all Forms 8805 for the taxable year. If a partnership issues Form 8805 to a partner, then the partnership may not claim a refund for any amount of tax shown on that form as paid on behalf of the partner. If a partnership incorrectly withholds upon a United States person under section 1446 of the Internal Revenue Code and issues a Form 8805 to that person, the partnership may not file for a refund of the amount incorrectly withheld. Instead, the United States person may file for a refund of that amount on its annual return. For rules concerning refunds to withholding agents who pay 1446 tax on distributions of effectively connected income or gain under § 1.1446-4 (i.e., publicly traded partnerships or nominees), see § 1.1464-1.

(v) 1446 tax treated as cash distribution to partners. Except as otherwise provided in this paragraph (d)(2)(v), a partnership's payment of 1446 tax on behalf of a foreign partner is treated under section 1446(d) and this section as a deemed distribution of money to the partner on the earliest of the day on which the partnership paid the tax, the last day of the partnership's taxable year for which the amount was paid, or the last day on which the partner owned an interest in the partnership during the taxable year for which the tax was paid. However, a deemed distribution of money under section 1446(d) resulting from a partnership's installment payment of 1446 tax on behalf of a partner is treated as an advance or drawing of money under § 1.731-1(a)(1)(ii) to the extent of the partner's distributive share of income for the partnership taxable year. The rule treating a deemed distribution as an advance or drawing of money under this paragraph (d)(2)(v) applies only for purposes of determining the tax results of the deemed distribution to the partner under sections 705, 731, and 733, and does not affect the date that the partnership is considered to have paid any installment of 1446 tax for purposes of section 6655 (as applied through this section) or the date a foreign partner is deemed to have paid estimated tax by reason of such installment payment. See paragraph (d)(1)(i) of this section (permitting a partner to credit 1446 tax paid on the partner's behalf against the partner's estimated tax obligation). An amount treated as an advance or drawing of money is taken into account at the end of the partnership taxable year or the last day during the partnership's taxable year on which the partner owned an interest in the partnership. Any 1446 tax paid after the close of the partnership's taxable year, including amounts paid with the filing of Form 8804, that are on account of partnership ECTI allocated to partners for the prior taxable year shall be treated under section 1446(d) and this section as a distribution from the partnership on the earlier of the last day of the partnership's prior taxable year for which the tax is paid, or the last day in such prior taxable year on which such foreign partner held an interest in the partnership.

(vi) Examples. The following examples illustrate the application of this section. In considering the examples, disregard the potential application of paragraph (b)(2)(v)(F) of this section (relating to the de minimis exception to paying 1446 tax). The examples are as follows:

Example (1). Simple trust that reports entire amount of ECTI. PRS is a partnership that has two partners, FT, a foreign trust, and A, a U.S. person. FT is a simple trust under section 651. FT and A each provide PRS with a valid Form W-8BEN and Form W-9, respectively. FT has one beneficiary, NRA, a nonresident alien. PRS and FT each maintain a calendar taxable year. PRS estimated for each installment period during the partnership's taxable year that FT would be allocated $100 of ECTI for the taxable year, and that all such ECTI would be ordinary in character. Assume that the allocation of the $100 would be respected under section 704(b) and the regulations thereunder. PRS pays installments of 1446 tax based upon its estimates and timely pays a total of $35 of 1446 tax over the course of the partnership's taxable year ($100 ECTI x .35). Assume that PRS' estimates of ECTI allocable to FT during the taxable year equal the actual amount of ECTI allocable to FT for the taxable year. Assume also that FT's only income for the taxable year is the $100 of income from PRS, and that, pursuant to the terms of the trust's governing instrument and local law, the $100 of ECTI is not included in FT's fiduciary accounting income and the deemed distribution of the $35 withholding tax paid under paragraph (d)(2)(v) of this section is not included in FT's fiduciary accounting income. Accordingly, the $100 of ECTI is not income required to be distributed by FT, and FT may not claim a deduction under section 651 for this amount. FT must report the $100 of ECTI in its gross income and may claim a credit under section 33 as determined under paragraph (d)(2)(iii) of this section of $35 for the 1446 tax paid by PRS. NRA is not required to include any of the ECTI in gross income and accordingly may not claim a credit for any amount of the $35 of 1446 tax PRS paid.

Example (2). Simple trust that distributes a portion of ECTI to the beneficiary. Assume the same facts as in Example 1, except that PRS distributes $60 to FT, which FT includes in its fiduciary accounting income under local law. FT will report the $100 of ECTI in its gross income and may claim a deduction for the $60 required to be distributed under section 651(a) to NRA. Pursuant to paragraph (d)(2)(iii) of this section, FT may claim a $14 credit under section 33 for the 1446 tax PRS paid ($40/$100 multiplied by $35). NRA is required to include the $60 of the ECTI in gross income under section 652 (as ECTI) and may claim a $21 credit under section 33 for the 1446 tax PRS paid ($35 less $14 or $60/$100 multiplied by $35).

Example (3). Complex trust that distributes entire ECTI to the beneficiary. Assume the same facts as in Example 1, except that FT is a complex trust under section 661. PRS distributes $60 to FT, which FT includes in its fiduciary accounting income. FT distributes the $60 of fiduciary accounting income to NRA and also properly distributes an additional $40 to NRA from FT's principal. FT will report the $100 of ECTI in its gross income and may deduct the $60 required to be distributed to NRA under section 661(a)(1) and may deduct the $40 distributed to NRA under section 661(a)(2). Pursuant to paragraph (d)(2)(iii) of this section, FT may not claim a credit under section 33 for any of the $35 of 1446 tax paid by PRS. NRA is required to include $100 of the ECTI in gross income under section 662 (as ECTI) and may claim a $35 credit under section 33 for the 1446 tax paid by PRS ($35 less $0).

(e) Liability of partnership for failure to withhold. *(1) In general.* Every partnership required to pay 1446 tax is made liable for that tax by section 1461. Therefore, a partnership that is required to pay 1446 tax but fails to do so, or pays less than the amount required under this section, is liable under section 1461 for the payment of the tax required to be withheld under chapter 3 of the Internal Revenue Code and the regulations thereunder unless, and to the extent, the partnership can demonstrate pursuant to paragraph (e)(2) of this section, to the satisfaction of the Commissioner or his delegate, that a foreign partner has paid the full amount of tax required to be paid by such partner to the Internal Revenue Service. See paragraph (e)(3) of this section and section 1463 regarding a partnership's liability for penalties and interest even though a foreign partner has satisfied the underlying tax liability. See also § 1.1461-3 for applicable penalties when a partnership fails to pay 1446 tax. See paragraph (b) of this section for an addition to the tax under section 6655 when there is an underpayment of 1446 tax.

(2) Proof that tax liability has been satisfied and deemed payment of 1446 tax. Proof of payment of tax may be established for purposes of paragraph (e)(1) of this section consistent with § 1.1445-1(e)(3). Under that standard, a partnership must provide sufficient information to the IRS to determine that the partner's tax liability was satisfied or established to be zero in accordance with the rules of this section. Under this section, a partnership's liability for 1446 tax shall be deemed to have been satisfied (deemed payment), to the extent of the 1446 tax due with respect to the ECTI allocable to a foreign partner, on the later of the date that such partner is considered to have paid all tax that is required to be shown on such partner's U.S. income tax return under section 6513(a) and (b)(2) (prescribing the date tax is considered paid for purposes of sections 6511(b)(2), (c), and 6512), or the last date for payment of the 1446 tax without extensions (the unextended due date for Form 8804). The deemed payment rule of this paragraph (e)(2) shall apply for purposes sections of 1446, 1461, and 1463, and any additions to the tax, interest, or penalties potentially applicable to such partnership under section 1446, including sections 6601, 6651, and 6655. Any deemed payment of 1446 tax under this paragraph (e)(2) shall not be treated as a deemed distribution under section 1446(d) and this section.

(3) Liability for interest, penalties, and additions to the tax. (i) Partnership. Notwithstanding paragraph (e)(2) of this section, a partnership that fails to pay 1446 tax is not relieved from liability under section 6655 (as applied through this section) or for interest under section 6601, when applicable. See § 1.1463-1. Such liability may exist even if there is no underlying tax liability due from a foreign partner on its allocable share of partnership ECTI. The addition to the tax under section 6655 or the interest charge under section 6601 that is required by those sections shall be imposed as set forth in those sections, as modified by this section. The section 6601 interest charge shall accrue beginning on the last date prescribed for payment of the 1446 tax due under section 1461 (which is the due date, without extensions, for filing Form 8804). The section 6601 interest charge shall stop accruing on the 1446 tax liability on the date, and to the extent, that the unpaid tax liability under section 1446 is satisfied (or is deemed satisfied under this paragraph (e)). Further, a partnership's liability under section 6655 (as applied through this section) for any underpaid installment payment shall accrue beginning on the relevant installment payment date, and shall stop accruing on the earlier of the date (and to the extent) that the 1446 tax liability is actually satisfied or the date prescribed in paragraph (b)(2)(v)(C) of this section. See paragraph (e)(4) of this section for examples illustrating that a partner's payment of estimated tax has no effect on the partnership's calculation of its addition to the tax under section 6655 and this section. See § 1.1461-3 for a list of the additions to tax, interest, and penalties that may apply to a partnership that fails to comply with section 1446. See § 1.1446-6 for exceptions to the application of the addition to the tax under section 6655 (as applied through this section) when a partnership reasonably relies on a foreign partner's certificate to reduce 1446 tax.

(ii) Foreign partner. A foreign partner is permitted to reduce any addition to the tax under section 6654 or section 6655 by the amount of any section 6655 addition to the tax paid by the partnership with respect to the partnership's failure to pay adequate installment payments of the 1446 tax on ECTI allocable to the foreign partner.

(4) Examples. The following examples illustrate the application of this section. In considering the examples, disregard the potential application of paragraph (b)(2)(v)(F) of this section (relating to the de minimis exception to paying 1446 tax). Further, in each of the examples where a partnership is deemed to have paid 1446 tax with respect to ECTI allocable to a partner, it is assumed that the partnership has presented to the IRS the appropriate information under paragraph (e)(2) of this section for the IRS to conclude that the deemed payment is appropriate. The examples are as follows:

Example (1). Foreign partnership fails to pay 1446 tax and sole foreign partner fails to pay all tax required to be shown on partner's U.S. income tax return.

(i) PRS is a foreign partnership engaged in a trade or business in the United States and has two equal partners, A, a U.S. person, and B, a nonresident alien. PRS is described in § 1.6081-5(a) (PRS keeps its books and records outside the United States and Puerto Rico) and, therefore, is required to file Form 8804 by the 15th day of the 6th month following the close of its taxable year. Both partners and PRS are calendar year taxpayers. PRS has received a valid Form W-9 and W-8BEN from A and B, respectively, but has not received any other documents or certificates. B is engaged in multiple trades or businesses (including the PRS partnership) that give rise to effectively connected income. PRS will use an acceptable annualization method under this section for computing its 1446 tax.

(ii) In PRS's first year of operations (Year 1), PRS estimates for each installment period described in § 1.1446-3 that B will be allocated $100 of ordinary ECTI for the taxable year. Therefore, for each installment period PRS is required to pay one fourth of the tax on the annualized ECTI allocable to B, or $8.75 (.25 x ($100 x .35)). PRS fails to make any installment payments. PRS's operations actually result in $100 of ECTI allocated to B. Therefore, PRS was required to have paid 1446 tax of $35 on or before the due date, without extensions, for filing its Form 8804 which is June 15, Year 2 (the last date prescribed for payment of the 1446 tax). PRS does not file Forms 8804 or 8805.

(iii) B pays estimated taxes and makes the following payments on the following dates: June 15, Year 1—$20, September 15, Year 1— $15, and January 15, Year 2—$10. B's total estimated tax payments equal $45. B files its U.S. Federal income tax return timely on June 15, Year 2, and reports all effectively connected income required to be shown on its return. Assume that B's total correct tax liability as shown on the return is $50. B does not make a payment with its return and so B still owes $5 to the Internal Revenue Service (excluding any interest, penalties, and additions to the tax that may apply). Assume that B is not subject to an addition to the tax under section 6654.

(iv) Under the rules of paragraph (e)(2) of this section, for purposes of sections 1446, 1461, and 1463, PRS is not considered to have paid any 1446 tax because B has not paid all of B's U.S. income tax liability.

(v) Further, under the principles of section 6655 and the rules of § 1.1446-3(e), a partner's estimated tax payments will not affect the calculation of a partnership's addition to the tax. Accordingly, PRS will be liable under the principles of section 6655 and § 1.1446-3 for failing to withhold for each installment payment. The addition to the tax will accrue beginning with the due date of each installment payment on the $8.75 underpayment for each respective installment period and will continue to accrue until June 15, Year 2 (the date prescribed in paragraph (b)(2)(v)(C) of this section).

(vi) Further, beginning on June 15, Year 2 (the last date prescribed for payment of 1446 tax without extensions), PRS will be liable for interest under section 6601 with respect to the unpaid 1446 tax, $35. This interest will stop accruing on the earlier of the date that the 1446 tax is paid by PRS or is deemed paid under paragraph (e)(2) of this section by reason of B's payment of its full tax liability.

(vii) Further, beginning on June 15, Year 2 (the due date for filing Form 8804), PRS will be liable for the addition to the tax under section 6651(a)(1) for failing to file Form 8804. This addition to the tax accrues on the amount required to be shown as the 1446 tax liability on Form 8804, $35. This addition to the tax will accrue at the rate of 5 percent per month until the date that PRS files Form 8804 for Year 1, or the maximum accrual of the penalty (25 percent of the tax required to be shown on the return) under that section has been reached.

(viii) PRS may be liable for other penalties and additions to the tax for its failure to withhold or to furnish statements to its foreign partner B. See § 1.1461-3 for a list of the penalties that may apply.

Example (2). Foreign partnership fails to pay 1446 tax but sole foreign partner pays all tax required to be shown on the partner's U.S. income tax return. The facts are the same as Example 1, except that B pays $5 with the filing of B's return and has therefore paid all tax required to be shown on B's return within the meaning of paragraph (e)(2) of this section.

(i) For purposes of sections 1446, 1461, and 1463, PRS is deemed to have paid its 1446 tax liability under paragraph (e)(2) of this section as of the later of the date that B is considered to have paid its tax under section 6513(a) and (b)(2) (June 15, Year 2) and the last date for PRS to pay its 1446 tax without extensions (also June 15, Year 2). Therefore, PRS is deemed to have paid all of its 1446 tax liability as of June 15, Year 2. PRS has no continuing liability for 1446 tax under section 1461, however, additions to the tax, interest, and penalties may apply.

(ii) For purposes of section 6655 and § 1.1446-3, under paragraph (e)(2) PRS is deemed to have paid its 1446 tax on June 15, Year 2. Even if B had fully paid its tax liability as of March 15, Year 2, the rule in paragraph (e)(2) of this section would not deem PRS to have paid its 1446 tax until June 15, Year 2. As a result, B's estimated tax payments will have no effect on PRS's calculation of its addition to the tax. The addition to the tax under 6655 and § 1.1446-3 shall begin to accrue on each installment date with respect to the underpaid installment ($8.75), and will stop accruing on June 15, Year 2, the date prescribed in paragraph (b)(2)(v)(C) of this section.

(iii) Because PRS is deemed to have paid its full 1446 tax liability as of June 15, Year 2 (the last date prescribed for payment of 1446 tax without extensions), PRS is not subject to an interest charge under section 6601, or a failure to file penalty under section 6651 (see section 6651(b)(1)).

(iv) PRS may be liable for other penalties and additions to the tax for its failure to withhold or to furnish statements to its foreign partner B. See § 1.1461-3 for a list of the penalties that may apply.

(v) If PRS had several foreign partners, PRS would conduct the same analysis as set forth above with respect to each partner. That is, under paragraph (e) of this section, PRS may be deemed to have paid 1446 tax with respect to the ECTI allocable to some but not all of its foreign partners.

Example (3). Domestic partnership fails to pay 1446 tax but sole foreign partner fully pays all tax required to be shown on partner's U.S. income tax return. The facts are the same as Example 2, except that PRS is a domestic partnership whose last date prescribed for paying 1446 tax without extensions (i.e., generally the unextended due date for Form 8804) is April 15, Year 2.

(i) For purposes of sections 1446, 1461, and 1463, PRS is deemed to have paid its 1446 tax liability on the later of the date that B is considered to have paid tax under section 6513(a) and (b)(2) (June 15, Year 2) and the last date for paying 1446 tax without extensions (i.e., the unextended due date for Form 8804, April 15, Year 2). Accordingly, PRS is not considered to have fully paid its 1446 tax liability until June 15, Year 2. PRS has no continuing liability for 1446 tax under section 1461, however, additions to the tax, interest, and penalties may apply.

(ii) For purposes of section 6655 and § 1.1446-3, PRS is subject to an underpayment addition to the tax that accrues on the same amount as in Example 1 and Example 2 because PRS is not deemed to have paid 1446 tax under paragraph (e)(2) of this section until June 15, Year 2. The addition to the tax will stop accruing on the date prescribed in paragraph (b)(2)(v)(C) of this section (i.e., April 15, Year 2, the due date, without extensions, for filing Form 8804).

(iii) For purposes of section 6601, as of the last date prescribed for paying 1446 tax without extensions (April 15, Year 2), PRS has not paid or been deemed to have paid any 1446 tax. Accordingly, the interest charge under section 6601 shall begin to accrue on April 15, Year 2, and shall accrue until the 1446 liability is paid or deemed to have been paid. In this case, the interest charge will accrue until June 15, Year 2, the date that PRS is deemed to have paid its 1446 tax under paragraph (e)(2) of this section.

(iv) For purposes of section 6651(a)(1), as of April 15, Year 2, PRS's amount required to be shown as tax on its Form 8804 is $35. This amount cannot be reduced under section 6651(b)(1) because PRS is not deemed to have paid

1446 tax under paragraph (e)(2) of this section until June 15, Year 2, a date falling after the last date for PRS to pay its 1446 tax, April 15, Year 2. Accordingly, the failure to file penalty will begin to accrue on April 15, Year 2 (filing due date for Form 8804), and shall stop accruing on the earlier of the date that PRS files Form 8804 or the maximum accrual of the penalty (25 percent of the amount required to be shown as tax on the return) is reached.

(v) PRS may be liable for other penalties and additions to the tax for its failure to withhold or to furnish statements to its foreign partner B. See § 1.1461-3 for a list of the penalties that may apply.

(f) Effect of withholding on partner. The payment of the 1446 tax by a partnership does not excuse a foreign partner to which a portion of ECTI is allocable from filing a U.S. tax or informational return, as appropriate, with respect to that income. Information concerning installment payments of 1446 tax paid during the partnership's taxable year on behalf of a foreign partner shall be provided to such foreign partner in accordance with paragraph (d) of this section and such information may be taken into account by the foreign partner when computing the partner's estimated tax liability during the taxable year. Form 1040NR, "U.S. Nonresident Alien Income Tax Return," Form 1065, "U.S. Return of Partnership Income," Form 1120F, "U.S. Income Tax Return of a Foreign Corporation," or such other return as appropriate, must be filed by the partner, and any tax due must be paid, by the filing deadline (including extensions) generally applicable to such person. Pursuant to paragraph (d) of this section, a partner may generally claim a credit under section 33 for its share of any 1446 tax paid by the partnership against the amount of income tax (or 1446 tax in the case of tiers of partnerships) as computed in such partner's return. See § 1.1446-3(e)(3)(ii) for rules permitting a partner to reduce its addition to tax under section 6654 or section 6655.

T.D. 9200, 5/13/2005, amend T.D. 9394, 4/28/2008.

§ 1.1446-4 Publicly traded partnerships.

(a) In general. This section sets forth rules for applying the section 1446 withholding tax (1446 tax) to publicly traded partnerships. A publicly traded partnership (as defined in paragraph (b) of this section) that has effectively connected gross income, gain or loss must pay 1446 tax by withholding from distributions to a foreign partner. Publicly traded partnerships that withhold on distributions must pay over and report any 1446 tax as provided in paragraph (c) of this section, and generally are not to pay over and report the 1446 tax under the rules in § 1.1446-3. The amount of the withholding tax on distributions, other than distributions excluded under paragraph (f) of this section, that are made during any partnership taxable year, equals the applicable percentage (defined in paragraph (b)(2) of this section) of such distributions. For penalties and additions to the tax for failure to comply with this section, see §§ 1.1461-1 and 1.1461-3.

(b) Definitions. *(1) Publicly traded partnership.* For purposes of this section, the term publicly traded partnership has the same meaning as in section 7704 (including the regulations thereunder), but does not include a publicly traded partnership treated as a corporation under that section.

(2) Applicable percentage. For purposes of this section, applicable percentage shall have the meaning as set forth in § 1.1446-3(a)(2), except that the partnership or nominee required to pay 1446 tax may not consider a preferential rate in computing the 1446 tax due with respect to a partner.

(3) Nominee. For purposes of this section, the term nominee means a domestic person that holds an interest in a publicly traded partnership on behalf of a foreign person.

(4) Qualified notice. For purposes of this section, a qualified notice is a notice given by a publicly traded partnership regarding a distribution that is attributable to effectively connected income, gain or loss of the partnership, and in accordance with the notice requirements with respect to dividends described in 17 CFR 240.10b-17(b)(1) or (3) issued pursuant to the Securities Exchange Act of 1934 (15 U.S.C. 78a). See paragraph (d) of this section regarding when a nominee is considered to have received a qualified notice.

(c) Paying and reporting 1446 tax. The withholding tax required under this section is to be paid pursuant to the rules and procedures of section 1461, §§ 1.1461-1, 1.1461-2, and 1.6302-2, as supplemented by the rules of this section. However, the reimbursement and set-off procedures set forth in § 1.1461-2 shall not apply. A withholding agent under this section must use Form 1042, "Annual Withholding Tax Return for U.S. Source Income of Foreign Persons," and Form 1042-S, "Foreign Person's U.S. Source Income Subject to Withholding," to report withholding from distributions under this section. See § 1.1461-1(b). Further, a withholding agent under this section may obtain a refund for 1446 tax paid in accordance with section 1464 and the regulations thereunder. See § 1.1446-3(d)(1)(iv) and (vii) (relating to a foreign trust or estate that holds an interest in a publicly traded partnership) and § 1.1446-5(d) (relating to a publicly traded partnership that is part of a tiered partnership structure) for additional guidance.

(d) Rules for designation of nominees to withhold tax under section 1446. A nominee that receives a distribution from a publicly traded partnership subject to withholding under this section, and which is to be paid to (or for the account of) any foreign person, may be treated as a withholding agent under this section. A nominee is treated as a withholding agent under this section only to the extent of the amount specified in the qualified notice (as defined in paragraph (b)(4) of this section) received by the nominee. A nominee is treated as receiving a qualified notice at the time such notice is published in accordance with 17 CFR 240.10b-17(b)(1) or (3). Where a nominee is designated as a withholding agent with respect to a foreign partner of the partnership, the obligation to withhold on distributions to such foreign partner in accordance with the rules of this section shall be imposed solely on the nominee. A nominee responsible for withholding under the rules of this section shall be subject to liability under sections 1461 and 6655, as well as all applicable penalties and interest, as if such nominee was a partnership responsible for withholding under this section.

(e) Determining foreign status of partners. The rules of § 1.1446-1 shall apply in determining whether a partner of a publicly traded partnership is a foreign partner for purposes of the 1446 tax. A partnership or nominee obligated to withhold under this section shall be entitled to rely on any of the forms acceptable under § 1.1446-1 received from persons on whose behalf it holds interests in the partnership to the same extent a partnership is entitled to rely on such forms under those rules.

(f) Distributions subject to withholding. *(1) In general.* Except as provided in this paragraph (f)(1), a publicly traded partnership must withhold at the applicable percentage with respect to any actual distribution made to a foreign partner. The amount of a distribution subject to 1446 tax includes the amount of any 1446 tax required to be withheld on the distribution. In the case of a partnership (upper-tier partnership) that receives a partnership distribution from another partnership in which it is a partner (lower-tier partnership) (i.e., a tiered structure described in § 1.1446-5), any 1446 tax that was paid by the lower-tier partnership may be credited by the upper-tier partnership and shall be treated as a distribution under section 1446. For example, a foreign publicly traded partnership, UTP, owns an interest in domestic publicly traded partnership, LTP. LTP makes a distribution subject to section 1446 of $100 to UTP during its taxable year beginning January 1, 2005, and withholds 35 percent (the highest rate in section 1)($35) of that distribution under section 1446. UTP receives a net distribution of $65 which it immediately redistributes to its partners. UTP has a liability to pay 35 percent of the total actual and deemed distribution it makes to its foreign partners as a section 1446 withholding tax. UTP may credit the $35 withheld by LTP against this liability as if it were paid by UTP. See § 1.1462-1(b) and § 1.1446-5(b)(1). When UTP distributes the $65 it actually receives from LTP to its partners, UTP is treated for purposes of section 1446 as if it made a distribution of $100 to its partners ($65 actual distribution and $35 deemed distribution). UTP's partners (U.S. and foreign) may claim a credit against their U.S. income tax liability for their allocable share of the $35 of 1446 tax paid on their behalf.

(2) In-kind distributions. If a publicly traded partnership distributes property other than money, the partnership shall not release the property until it has funds sufficient to enable the partnership to pay over in money the required 1446 tax.

(3) Ordering rule relating to distributions. Distributions from publicly traded partnerships are deemed to be paid out of the following types of income in the order indicated—

(i) Amounts attributable to income described in section 1441 or 1442 that are not effectively connected, without regard to whether such amounts are subject to withholding because of a treaty or statutory exemption;

(ii) Amounts effectively connected with a U.S. trade or business, but not subject to withholding under section 1446 (e.g., amounts exempt by treaty);

(iii) Amounts subject to withholding under section 1446; and

(iv) Amounts not listed in paragraphs (f)(3)(i) through (iii) of this section.

(4) Coordination with section 1445(e)(1). Except as otherwise provided in this section, a publicly traded partnership that complies with the requirements of withholding under section 1446 and this section will be deemed to have satisfied the requirements of section 1445(e)(1) and the regulations thereunder. Notwithstanding the excluded amounts set forth in paragraph (f)(3) of this section, distributions subject to withholding at the applicable percentage shall include the following—

(i) Amounts subject to withholding under section 1445(e)(1) upon distribution pursuant to an election under § 1.1445-5(c)(3) of the regulations; and

(ii) Amounts not subject to withholding under section 1445 because the distributee is a partnership or is a foreign corporation that has made an election under section 897(i).

T.D. 9200, 5/13/2005.

---

§ 1.1446-5 Tiered partnership structures.

(a) In general. The rules of this section shall apply in cases where a partnership (lower-tier partnership) that has effectively connected taxable income (ECTI), has a partner that is a partnership (upper-tier partnership). Except as provided in paragraph (e) of this section, if an upper-tier domestic partnership directly owns an interest in a lower-tier partnership, the lower-tier partnership is not required to pay the section 1446 withholding tax (1446 tax) with respect to the upper-tier partnership's allocable share of net income, regardless of whether the upper-tier domestic partnership's partners are foreign. Paragraph (b) of this section prescribes the reporting requirements for upper-tier and lower-tier partnerships subject to section 1446. Paragraph (c) of this section prescribes rules requiring a lower-tier partnership to look through an upper-tier foreign partnership to a partner of such upper-tier partnership to the extent it has sufficient documentation to determine the status of such partner and determine such partner's indirect share of the lower-tier partnership's effectively connected taxable income (ECTI). Paragraph (d) of this section prescribes rules applicable to a publicly traded partnership in a tiered partnership structure. Paragraph (e) of this section prescribes rules permitting a domestic upper-tier partnership to elect to apply the look through rules of paragraph (c) of this section. Paragraph (f) of this section sets forth examples illustrating the rules of this section.

(b) Reporting requirements. *(1) In general.* Notwithstanding paragraph (c) of this section, to the extent that an upper-tier partnership that is a foreign partnership is a partner in a lower-tier partnership, and the lower-tier partnership has paid 1446 tax (including installment payments of such tax) with respect to ECTI allocable to the upper-tier partnership, the lower-tier partnership shall comply with §§ 1.1446-1 through 1.1446-3 and provide the upper-tier partnership notice of such payments and a copy of the statements and forms filed with respect to the upper-tier partnership's interest in the lower-tier partnership (e.g., Form 8805, "Foreign Partner's Information Statement of Section 1446 Withholding Tax"). The upper-tier partnership may treat the 1446 tax (or any installment of such tax) paid by the lower-tier partnership on its behalf as a credit against its liability to pay 1446 tax (or any installment of such tax), as if the upper-tier partnership actually paid over the amounts at the time that the amounts were paid by the lower-tier partnership. See § 1.1462-1(b) and § 1.1446-3(d). To the extent required in § 1.1446-3(d)(1)(iii), the upper-tier partnership will file Form 8804, "Annual Return for Partnership Withholding Tax (Section 1446)," and Form 8805, "Foreign Partner's Information Statement of Section 1446 Withholding Tax," for each of its foreign partners with respect to its 1446 tax obligation. To the extent the upper-tier partnership does not claim a refund of the 1446 tax it paid (or is considered to have paid), the upper-tier partnership will pass the credit for the 1446 tax paid to its partners on the Forms 8805 it issues. See § 1.1446-3(d). The rules of this paragraph (b) shall apply to an upper-tier and lower-tier partnership to the extent that an election has been made and consented to under paragraph (e) of this section.

(2) Publicly traded partnerships. In the case of an upper-tier foreign partnership that is a publicly traded partnership, the rules of § 1.1446-4(c) shall apply. See also paragraph (d) of this section.

(c) Look through rules for foreign upper-tier partnerships. For purposes of computing the 1446 tax obligation of a lower-tier partnership, if an upper-tier foreign partnership owns an interest in the lower-tier partnership, the upper-tier partnership's allocable share of ECTI from the lower-tier partnership shall be treated as allocable to a partner of the upper-tier partnership, to the extent of such partner's indirect share of such ECTI (as if such partner were a direct partner in the lower-tier partnership), if—

(1) The upper-tier foreign partnership furnishes the lower-tier partnership a valid Form W-8IMY, "Certificate of Foreign Intermediary, Flow Through Entity, or Certain U.S. Branches for United States Tax Withholding," indicating that it is a look-through foreign partnership for purposes of section 1446; and

(2) The lower-tier partnership can reliably associate (within the meaning of § 1.1441-1(b)(2)(vii)) effectively connected partnership items allocable to the upper-tier partnership (and indirectly to such partner) with a Form W-8 (e.g., Form W-8BEN), Form W-9, "Request for Taxpayer Identification Number and Certification," or other form acceptable under § 1.1446-1, establishing the status of such partner provided by the upper-tier partnership. The lower-tier partnership required to pay 1446 tax must be able to provide the information necessary for the IRS to determine the chain of ownership, allocation of effectively connected items at each partnership level, as well as to the ultimate beneficial owner of the effectively connected items, and whether the amount of 1446 tax paid was appropriate. This information should permit each partnership in the tiered structure and the IRS to reliably associate any effectively connected items allocable to such upper-tier partnership, as well as to the ultimate beneficial owner of the effectively connected items. The principles of § 1.1441-1(b)(2)(vii) shall apply to determine whether a lower-tier partnership can reliably associate effectively connected partnership items allocable to the upper-tier partnership with a partner of the upper-tier partnership. To the extent the lower-tier partnership receives a valid Form W-8IMY from the upper-tier partnership but cannot reliably associate a portion of the upper-tier partnership's allocable share of effectively connected partnership items with a partner of such upper-tier partnership, then the lower-tier partnership shall pay 1446 tax on such portion at the higher of the applicable percentages in section 1446(b). See § 1.1446-3(a)(2) for the treatment of any income or gain potentially subject to a preferential rate. If a lower-tier partnership has not received a valid Form W-8IMY from the upper-tier partnership, the lower-tier partnership shall withhold on the upper-tier partnership's entire allocable share of ECTI at the higher of the applicable percentages in section 1446(b). The look through regime set forth in this paragraph (c) is for purposes of computing the lower-tier partnership's 1446 tax obligation only and does not alter the persons considered to be partners in the lower-tier partnership for partnership reporting purposes (e.g., issuing Form 8805, Schedule K-1).

(d) Publicly traded partnerships. *(1) Upper-tier publicly traded partnership.* The rules set forth in paragraph (c) shall not apply to look through an upper-tier partnership whose interests are publicly traded (as defined in § 1.1446-4(b)(1)).

(2) Lower-tier publicly traded partnership. The look through rules of paragraph (c) of this section shall apply, if the requirements of that paragraph are met, to a lower-tier partnership that is a publicly traded partnership within the meaning of § 1.1446-4(b)(1) only if the upper-tier partnership is not described in paragraph (d)(1) of this section. For example, a lower-tier publicly traded partnership (or nominee) shall look through an upper-tier foreign partnership (or domestic partnership to the extent an election is made and consented to under paragraph (e) of this section) when computing its 1446 tax liability, provided the upper-tier partnership is not a publicly traded partnership and the appropriate documentation needed to satisfy the standards set forth in § 1.1441-1(b)(2)(vii) and paragraph (c) of this section have been furnished.

(e) Election by a domestic upper-tier partnership to apply look through rules. *(1) In general.* Subject to the rules of this paragraph (e), a domestic partnership that is a partner in a lower-tier partnership may elect to apply the rules of this section 1.1446-5 and have the lower-tier partnership look through such upper-tier partnership to the partners of such domestic partnership for purposes of computing the lower-tier partnership's 1446 tax liability. A domestic partnership shall make this election by attaching to the Form W-9 submitted to the lower-tier partnership, a written statement and information (described in paragraph (e)(2) of this section) that identifies the upper-tier partnership as a domestic partnership and that states that such partnership is making the election under this paragraph (e). This paragraph (e)(1) shall not apply to a publicly traded partnership described in § 1.1446-4(b)(1). See paragraph (d)(1) of this section.

(2) Information required for valid election statement. In addition to the requirements of paragraphs (e)(1) and (3) of this section, the election statement submitted under this paragraph (e)(2) is not valid and cannot be accepted by the lower-tier partnership pursuant to paragraph (e)(3) of this section unless the upper-tier partnership attaches valid documentation pursuant to § 1.1446-1 (e.g., Form W-8BEN) with respect to one or more of its foreign partners. The information and documentation submitted with the election must comply with the rules of this section to permit the lower-tier partnership to reliably associate (within the meaning of § 1.1441-1(b)(2)(vii)) at least a portion of the upper-tier partnership's allocable share of ECTI with one or more foreign partners of the upper-tier partnership. The election statement must identify the upper-tier partnership by name, address, and TIN, and specify the percentage interest the domestic partnership holds in the lower-tier partnership. The statement may also include such information the upper-tier partnership deems necessary to enable the lower-tier partnership to apply the provisions of this section. If at any time the upper-tier partnership determines that the information or documentation previously provided to the lower-tier partnership is no longer correct, the upper-tier partnership shall update such information and documentation. Except as provided in paragraph (e)(3) of this section, an election that is effective under this paragraph (e) shall apply for subsequent taxable years until such upper-tier partnership revokes the election in writing. A revocation under this section shall be effective for any installment due date arising more than 15 days subsequent to the date that the lower-tier partnership receives such revocation.

(3) Consent of lower-tier partnership. An election made under this paragraph (e) is not effective until the lower-tier partnership consents in writing to the upper-tier partnership that it agrees to apply the provisions of this section. A lower-tier partnership may not consent to an election submitted under this paragraph (e) for any installment date or Form 8804 filing date arising within 15 days of the lower-tier partnership's receipt of such election. The lower-tier partnership's written consent must specify the extent to which it will look through the upper-tier partnership in computing its 1446 tax (or any installment of such tax). To the extent that the lower-tier partnership does not consent to an election to apply the look through provisions of paragraph (c) of this section, the lower-tier partnership shall consider such portion

of the upper-tier partnership's allocable share of ECTI as allocable to a domestic person for purposes of computing its 1446 tax obligation. A lower-tier partnership that has consented to an election under this paragraph (e) may revoke or modify its consent, in writing, at any time.

(f) Examples. The following examples illustrate the provisions of this section. In considering the examples, disregard the potential application of § 1.1446-3(b)(2)(v)(F) (relating to the de minimis exception to paying 1446 tax). The examples are as follows:

Example (1). Sufficient documentation—tiered partnership structure. (i) Nonresident alien (NRA) and foreign corporation (FC) are partners in PRS, a foreign partnership, and share profits and losses in PRS 70 and 30 percent, respectively. All of PRS's partnership items are allocated based upon each partner's respective ownership interest and it is assumed that these allocations are respected under section 704(b) and the regulations thereunder. NRA and FC each furnish PRS with a valid Form W-8BEN establishing themselves as a foreign individual and foreign corporation, respectively. PRS holds a 40 percent interest in the profits, losses and capital of LTP, a lower-tier partnership. NRA holds the remaining 60 percent interest in profits, losses and capital of LTP. All of LTP's partnership items are allocated based upon each partner's respective ownership interest and it is assumed that these allocations are respected under section 704(b) and the regulations thereunder. LTP has $100 of annualized ECTI for the relevant installment period. All of this income is ordinary income and there is no potential application of a preferential rate applicable percentage under § 1.1446-3(a)(2). Further, § 1.1446-6 does not apply. PRS has no income other than the income allocated from LTP. PRS provides LTP with a valid Form W-8IMY indicating that it is a foreign partnership and attaches the valid Form W-8BENs executed by NRA and FC, as well as a statement describing the allocation of PRS's effectively connected items among its partners. The information that PRS submits to LTP is sufficient to permit LTP to reliably associate (within the meaning of § 1.1441-1(b)(2)(vii)) PRS's allocable share of effectively connected items with NRA and FC pursuant to this section. Further, NRA provides a valid Form W-8BEN to LTP.

(ii) LTP must pay 1446 tax on the $60 allocable to its direct partner NRA using the applicable percentage for noncorporate partners (the highest rate in section 1).

(iii) With respect to the effectively connected partnership items that LTP can reliably associate with NRA through PRS (70 percent of PRS's 40 percent allocable share ($40), or $28), LTP will pay 1446 tax on NRA's allocable share of LTP's ECTI (as determined by looking through PRS) using the applicable percentage for non-corporate partners (the highest rate in section 1).

(iv) With respect to the effectively connected partnership items that LTP can reliably associate with FC through PRS (30 percent of PRS's 40 percent allocable share ($40), or $12), LTP will pay 1446 tax on FC's allocable share of LTP's ECTI (as determined by looking through PRS) using the applicable percentage for corporate partners (the highest rate in section 11).

(v) LTP's payment of the 1446 tax is treated as a distribution to NRA and PRS, its direct partners, that those partners may credit against their respective tax obligations. PRS will report its 1446 tax obligation with respect to its direct foreign partners, NRA and FC, on the Form 8804 and Forms 8805 that it files with the Internal Revenue Service pursuant to paragraph (b) of this section and will credit the amount withheld by LTP on its Form 8804. This credit will satisfy PRS's 1446 tax liability as reported on the Form 8804 it files because PRS's only income is from LTP, and LTP paid 1446 tax with respect to all of PRS's allocable share in LTP by looking through to PRS's partners NRA and FC. Further, PRS will pass along the credit for the 1446 tax withheld by LTP to its partners, NRA and FC on the Form 8805 issued to each partner. The credit passed to each partner on Form 8805 will be treated as a distribution to the respective partners under section 1446(d).

Example (2). Insufficient documentation—tiered partnership structure. (i) LTP is a domestic partnership that has two equal partners A and PRS. A is a nonresident alien and PRS is a foreign partnership that has two equal foreign partners, C and D. Neither A nor PRS provides LTP with a valid Form W-8 or Form W-9. Neither C nor D provides PRS with a valid Form W-8 or Form W-9. Pursuant to § 1.1446-1(c)(3), LTP must presume that PRS is a foreign person subject to withholding under section 1446 at the higher of the highest rate under section 1 or section 11(b)(1). LTP has also not received any documentation with respect to A. LTP must presume that A is a foreign person, and, if LTP knows that A is an individual, compute and pay 1446 tax, subject to § 1.1446-3(a)(2), based on that knowledge.

(ii) Assume a change of facts where C provides a form W-8 (e.g., Form W-8BEN) to PRS, and PRS in turn, furnishes that form to LTP along with its Form W-8IMY, and information regarding how effectively connected items are allocated to C and D. Based upon the additional facts, LTP can reliably associate one-half of PRS's allocable share of ECTI with documentation related with C. Therefore, under paragraph (c)(2) of this section, LTP will look through PRS to C when computing its 1446 tax to the extent of C's indirect share and will not look through with respect to the remainder of PRS's allocable share (D's indirect share).

T.D. 9200, 5/13/2005, amend T.D. 9394, 4/28/2008.

§ 1.1446-6 Special rules to reduce a partnership's 1446 tax with respect to a foreign partner's allocable share of effectively connected taxable income.

(a) In general. *(1) Purpose and scope.* This section provides rules regarding when a partnership required to pay withholding tax under section 1446 (1446 tax), or an installment of 1446 tax, may consider certain partner-level deductions and losses in computing its 1446 tax obligation under § 1.1446-3, or otherwise not pay a de minimis amount of 1446 tax due with respect to a nonresident alien individual partner. A partnership determines the applicability of the rules of this section on a partner-by-partner basis for each installment period and when completing its Form 8804, "Annual Return for Partnership Withholding Tax (Section 1446)," and paying 1446 tax for the partnership taxable year. Except with respect to certain state and local taxes paid by the partnership on behalf of the partner, to apply the rules of this section with respect to a foreign partner, the partnership must receive a certificate from such partner for each partnership taxable year. Paragraph (b) of this section identifies the foreign partners to which this section applies. Paragraph (c) of this section identifies the deductions and losses that a foreign partner may certify to the partnership as well as the state and local taxes paid by the partnership on behalf of the foreign partner that can be taken into account without a certification, and establishes an exception that permits a partnership to not pay a de minimis amount of 1446 tax with respect to a nonresident alien partner. Paragraph (c) of this section also sets forth the requirements for a valid certificate. Paragraphs (a)(2) and (d) of this section establish when a partnership may rely on and consider a foreign partner's certificate in computing its 1446 tax, and the effects of relying on such a certificate. Paragraph (d) of this section also describes the effects of a partnership relying on a certificate (including an updated certificate) and the reporting requirements of a partnership with respect to a certificate. Paragraph (e) of this section sets forth examples that illustrate the rules of this section. Paragraph (f) of this section provides the Effective/Applicability date. Paragraph (g) of this section provides a transition rule.

(2) Reasonable reliance on a certificate. Subject to § 1.1446-2 and the rules of this section, a partnership receiving a certificate (including an updated certificate or status update under paragraph (c)(2)(ii)(B) of this section) of deductions and losses from a partner provided in accordance with the provisions of this section may reasonably rely on such certificate (to the extent of the certified deductions and losses or other representations set forth in the certificate) until such time that it has actual knowledge or reason to know that the certificate is defective or that the time for receiving an updated certificate or status update from the partner under paragraph (c)(2)(ii)(B) of this section has expired. For this purpose, a partnership shall be considered to have actual knowledge or reason to know that a certificate is defective upon receipt of written notification from the IRS under paragraph (c)(3) or (c)(5) of this section.

(b) Foreign partner to whom this section applies. *(1) In general.* Except as otherwise provided in paragraph (b)(3) of this section, a foreign partner to whom this section applies is a foreign partner that meets the requirements of this paragraph (b)(1).

(i) The partner has provided valid documentation to the partnership to which a certificate is submitted under this section in accordance with § 1.1446-1.

(ii) If the partner's current taxable year is the first taxable year in which the partner submits a certificate to any partnership, the partner has filed (or will file) a qualifying U.S. income tax return for each of its three taxable years ending before the end of the partnership's taxable year for which the partner is submitting a certificate (regardless of whether it was a partner in that partnership during each of these years). A qualifying U.S. income tax return for a taxable year that is prior to the first taxable year the partner submits a certificate to any partnership is a U.S. income tax return filed within the time specified in paragraph (b)(2)(iii) of this section.

(iii) If the current taxable year of the partner is not the first taxable year in which the partner submits a certificate to any partnership, the partner met the requirements in paragraph (b)(1)(ii) of this section for the first taxable year in which it submitted a certificate to any partnership and has filed (or will file) a qualifying U.S. income tax return for its first taxable year in which it submitted a certificate to any partnership and each subsequent taxable year ending before the beginning of the current taxable year (regardless of whether it was a partner in any partnership during each of those years). A qualifying U.S. income tax return for a taxable year that is prior to the taxable year the partner submits a certificate to any partnership is a U.S. income tax return filed within the time specified in paragraph (b)(2)(iii) of this section.

(iv) The partner files a qualifying U.S. income tax return (within the meaning of paragraph (b)(2)(iii) of this section) for its taxable year in which a certificate is provided to any partnership.

(2) Definitions. (i) U.S. income tax return. A U.S. income tax return means a Form 1040NR, "U.S. Nonresident Alien Income Tax Return," in the case of a nonresident alien individual and a Form 1120F, "U.S. Income Tax Return of a Foreign Corporation," in the case of a foreign corporation.

(ii) Timely-filed. Only for purposes of this section, a U.S. income tax return shall be considered timely-filed if the return is filed on or before the due date set forth in section 6072(c), plus any extension of time to file such return granted under section 6081.

(iii) Qualifying U.S. income tax return. A U.S. income tax return shall constitute a qualifying U.S. income tax return if the return reports income or gain that is effectively connected with a U.S. trade or business or deductions or losses properly allocated and apportioned to such activities and if the return is described in paragraph (b)(2)(iii)(A), (B), or (C) of this section. A protective return described in § 1.874-1(b)(6) or § 1.882-4(a)(3)(vi) is not a qualifying U.S. income tax return for purposes of this section.

(A) A U.S. income tax return for a partner's preceding taxable year in which it did not submit a certificate to any partnership (but not including a taxable year following the first taxable year in which the partner submitted a certificate to any partnership), with a due date as set forth in section 6072(c), not including any extensions of time to file, which falls before the beginning of the current partnership taxable year for which the certificate is provided is described in this paragraph (b)(2)(iii)(A) if the return is filed and all amounts due with respect to such return (including interest, penalties, and additions to tax, if any) are paid on or before the earlier of—

(1) The date that is one year after the due date set forth in section 6072(c) for such return, not including any extensions of time to file; or

(2) The date on which the certificate for the current partnership taxable year is submitted to the partnership.

(B) A U.S. income tax return for a partner's preceding taxable year in which it did not submit a certificate to any partnership (but not including a taxable year following the first taxable year in which the partner submitted a certificate to any partnership), with a due date as set forth in section 6072(c), not including any extensions of time to file, which falls within the current partnership taxable year for which the certificate is provided is described in this paragraph (b)(2)(iii)(B) if the return is timely-filed and all amounts due with respect to such return are timely paid.

(C) A U.S. income tax return for a taxable year in which the partner submits a certificate to any partnership and for a taxable year following the first taxable year in which the partner submits a certificate to any partnership is described in this paragraph (b)(2)(iii)(C) if the return is timely-filed and all amounts due with such return are timely paid with respect to such return.

(3) Special rules. (i) In the case of a partnership (upper-tier partnership) that is a partner in another partnership (lower-tier partnership)—

(A) The rules of this section may apply to reduce or eliminate the 1446 tax (or any installment of such tax) of the lower-tier partnership with respect to a foreign partner of the upper-tier partnership only to the extent the provisions of

§ 1.1446-5 apply to look through the upper-tier partnership to the foreign partner of such upper-tier partnership and the certificate described in paragraph (c) of this section is provided by such foreign partner to the upper-tier partnership and, in turn, provided to the lower-tier partnership with other appropriate documentation (see § 1.1446-5(c) and (e));

(B) An upper-tier partnership that submits a certificate of deductions and losses or a de minimis certificate to a lower-tier partnership may not submit that certificate to another lower-tier partnership;

(C) An upper-tier partnership that relies on a certificate submitted to it by a foreign partner under this section for computing its 1446 tax due on effectively connected taxable income (ECTI) allocable to that partner (other than ECTI allocable to it from a lower-tier partnership) may not submit that certificate to any lower-tier partnership; and

(D) In addition to any other information required by this section, a lower-tier partnership must submit with a Form 8813, "Partnership Withholding Tax Payment Voucher (Section 1446)," and Form 8805, "Foreign Partner's Information Statement of Section 1446 Withholding Tax," for which it relies on a certificate from an upper-tier partnership to reduce the 1446 tax due with respect to a foreign partner of the upper-tier partnership, sufficient information so that the IRS may reliably associate the ECTI and the certificate of deductions and losses with the partner in the upper-tier partnership submitting the certificate, including the name, taxpayer identification number (TIN) and allocation of effectively connected items at each partnership tier, as well as to the ultimate upper-tier partner submitting the certificate.

(ii) This section shall not apply to a partner that is a foreign estate or its beneficiaries.

(iii) This section shall not apply to a partner that is a trust or to its beneficiaries, except to the extent that such trust is owned by a grantor or other person under subpart E of subchapter J of the Internal Revenue Code, the documentation requirements of § 1.1446-1 have been met by the grantor or other owner of such trust, and the certificate described in paragraph (c) of this section is provided by the grantor or other owner of such trust to the partnership.

(iv) This section shall not apply to a partner in a publicly-traded partnership subject to § 1.1446-4.

(c) Reduction of 1446 tax with respect to a foreign partner. *(1) General rules.* Under paragraph (c)(1)(i) of this section a foreign partner to whom this section applies may certify to a partnership for a partnership taxable year that it has certain deductions (other than charitable deductions) and losses properly allocated and apportioned to gross income that is effectively connected (or treated as effectively connected) with the conduct of the partner's trade or business in the United States, and that the partner reasonably expects those deductions and losses to be available and claimed on the partner's U.S. income tax return to be filed for that taxable year. Under paragraph (c)(1)(ii) of this section, a nonresident alien individual partner to whom this section applies may also certify to a partnership for a partnership taxable year that its only investment or activity giving rise to effectively connected items for the partnership's taxable year that ends with or within the partner's taxable year is (and will be) the partner's investment in the partnership. A certificate submitted by a foreign partner to a partnership under this section must be in accordance with the form and requirements set forth in paragraph (c)(2)(ii) of this section. Under paragraph (c)(1)(iii) of this section, a partnership may take into account certain state and local taxes withheld by the partnership on behalf of the partner.

(i) Certified deductions and losses. (A) Deductions and losses from the partnership. Under this paragraph (c)(1)(i)(A), a partner may certify to a partnership for a partnership taxable year deductions (other than charitable deductions) and losses properly allocated and apportioned to gross income which is effectively connected (or treated as effectively connected) with the conduct of the partner's trade or business in the United States, that are reported on a Form 1065 (Schedule K-1), "Partner's Share of Income, Credits, Deductions, etc.," issued (or to be issued) to the partner by the partnership for a prior partnership taxable year, that are (or will be) reported on a qualifying U.S. income tax return for a partner's taxable year that ends before the installment due date or the close of the partnership taxable year for which the partner is certifying such deductions and losses, and that the partner reasonably expects to be available and claimed on a qualifying U.S. income tax return for the partner's taxable year ending with or after the close of the partnership taxable year. A partner that has a loss reported on a Form 1065 (Schedule K-1) issued (or to be issued) to the partner by the partnership for a prior partnership taxable year, but that is not (and will not be) reported on a qualifying U.S. income tax return for a prior taxable year of the partner because the loss is suspended under section 704(d) may also certify such suspended loss to the partnership under this paragraph (c)(1)(i)(A).

(B) Deductions and losses from other sources. Under this paragraph (c)(1)(i)(B), a foreign partner may certify to a partnership for a partnership taxable year deductions (other than charitable deductions) and losses properly allocated and apportioned to gross income that is effectively connected (or treated as effectively connected) with the conduct of the partner's trade or business in the United States and that are from sources other than the partnership to whom the certificate is submitted if the deductions and losses are (or will be) reported on a qualifying U.S. income tax return of the partner for a taxable year that ends before the installment due date or the close of the partnership taxable year for which the partner is certifying the deductions and losses and the partner reasonably expects the deductions and losses to be available and claimed on the qualifying U.S. income tax return filed for its taxable year ending with or after the close of the partnership taxable year. Any deductions and losses certified under this paragraph (c)(1)(i)(B) that are allocated to the partner from another partnership must be reported on a Form 1065 (Schedule K-1) issued (or to be issued) to the partner by such other partnership. However, the partner may not certify any deduction or loss allocated to it from another partnership that is suspended under section 704(d).

(C) Limit on the consideration of a partner's net operating loss deduction. A partnership may not consider a net operating loss deduction (as determined under section 172) certified by the partner under this paragraph (c)(1)(i) in an amount greater than the percentage limitation, if any, provided in section 56(a)(4) and (d) multiplied by the partner's allocable share of ECTI from the partnership reduced by all other certified deductions and losses whether or not taken into account by the partnership, as well as deductions considered under paragraph (c)(1)(iii) of this section.

(D) Limitation on losses subject to certain partner level limitations. Pursuant to paragraph (c)(2)(i) of this section, a partner must identify any certified losses or deductions that are subject to special limitations at the partner level (for example, sections 465 and 469) and provide information to the partnership that will allow the partnership to take the special limitations into account. For example, where a partner certifies a loss to the partnership that is a passive activity loss under section 469, the partner shall identify the activities the partnership conducts that the partner expects will be passive activities. The partnership shall then ensure that these limitations are taken into account when determining the 1446 tax due with respect to the partner.

(E) Certification of deductions and losses to other partnerships. Deductions and losses certified to a partnership for a taxable year of the partnership may not be certified for the taxable year of another partnership that begins or ends with or within the taxable year of the partnership to which the deductions and losses were certified.

(F) Partner level use of deductions and losses certified to a partnership. Any deductions and losses certified to a partnership for a taxable year of the partner and considered by the partnership in computing its section 1446 tax due may not be considered by that partner for the same taxable year in computing the amount of its required installments under section 6654(d) or 6655(d) on income unrelated to the partnership to which the partner has submitted the certificate.

(ii) De minimis certificate for nonresident alien individual partners. (A) In general. Under this paragraph (c)(1)(ii), a nonresident alien individual partner to whom this section applies and that satisfies the requirements of paragraph (c)(1)(ii)(B) of this section may certify to a partnership that its only activity giving rise to effectively connected income, gain, deduction, or loss for the partnership's taxable year that ends with or within the partner's taxable year is (and will be) the partner's investment in the partnership. A partnership that receives a certificate from a nonresident alien partner under this paragraph (c)(1)(ii) and that may reasonably rely on such certificate is not required to pay 1446 tax (or any installment of such tax) with respect to such partner if the partnership estimates that the annualized (or, in the case of a partnership completing its Form 8804, the actual) 1446 tax otherwise due with respect to such partner is less than $1,000, without taking into account any deductions or losses certified by the partner to the partnership under paragraph (c)(1)(i) of this section or any amounts under paragraph (c)(1)(iii) of this section.

(B) Requirements for exception. The requirements of this paragraph (c)(1)(ii)(B) are met if the nonresident individual alien partner's only activity giving rise to effectively connected income, gain, deduction, or loss for the partnership taxable year that ends with or within the partner's taxable year is (and will be) the partner's investment in the partnership. For this purpose, if the partner has (or has reason to expect to have) income or gain described in section 864(c)(6), such income or gain shall be considered derived from a separate investment activity. A certificate submitted by a nonresident alien individual partner under this paragraph (c)(1)(ii) is valid even if such certificate does not certify deductions and losses to partnership under this section. A nonresident alien individual partner that submits a certificate to a partnership under this paragraph (c)(1)(ii) must notify the partnership in writing and revoke such certificate within 10 days of the date that the partner invests or otherwise engages in another activity that may give rise to effectively connected income, gain, deduction, or loss for the partner's taxable year. For example, while an investment in a U.S. real property interest (as defined in section 897(c)) would not give rise to an activity requiring a notification (unless an election is in effect under section 871(d)), the disposition of the U.S. real property interest would give rise to an activity requiring a notification.

(iii) Consideration of certain current year state and local taxes. In addition to any deductions and losses certified by a foreign partner to a partnership under paragraph (c)(1)(i) of this section, the partnership may consider as a deduction of such partner 90-percent of any state and local income taxes withheld and remitted by the partnership on behalf of such partner with respect to the partner's allocable share of partnership ECTI. The partnership may consider the amount of state and local taxes of the foreign partner determined under this paragraph (c)(1)(iii) regardless of whether the foreign partner submits a certificate to the partnership under paragraph (c)(1)(i) or (ii) of this section.

(2) Form and time of certification. (i) Form of certification. A partner's certification to a partnership under paragraph (c)(1)(i) or (iii) of this section shall be made using Form 8804-C, "Certificate Of Partner-Level Items to Reduce Section 1446 Withholding" in accordance with the instructions of the form and the rules of this section.

(ii) Time for certification provided to partnership.

(A) First certificate submitted for a partnership's taxable year. Provided the other requirements of this section are met, a partnership may only rely on the first certificate received from a foreign partner for any 1446 tax installment due or Form 8804 filing due (without regard to extensions) on or after the date on which the certificate is received. See § 1.1446-3 for 1446 tax installment due dates. See also paragraph (e) of this section for examples illustrating the rules of this paragraph (c)(2).

(B) Updated certificates and status updates. (1) Preceding year tax returns not yet filed. If a foreign partner's U.S. income tax return for a preceding taxable year has not been filed as of the time the partner submits to the partnership its first certificate under this paragraph (c), the certificate shall specify this fact and set forth the filing due date for such return set forth in section 6072(c), plus any extension of time to file such return granted under section 6081 and the regulations under section 6081. The partner shall also submit an updated certificate to the partnership in accordance with this paragraph (c) within 10 days of the date the partner files its U.S. income tax return for any such taxable year. In addition, prior to the partnership's final 1446 tax installment due date the partner shall provide to the partnership, under penalties of perjury, a status update regarding any U.S. income tax return for the prior taxable year that has not (or will not) be filed as of the final installment due date. The status update must identify the due date, set forth in section 6072(c), plus any extension of time to file such return granted under section 6081 and the regulations under section 6081, for any un-filed return identified in the first certificate and state whether the first certificate submitted may continue to be considered by the partnership. If the partnership does not receive an updated certificate or a status update from the partner prior to the partnership's final installment due date, the partnership shall disregard the partner's certificate when computing the 1446 tax due with respect to that partner for the final installment period and when completing its Form 8804 for the taxable year. In addition, the foreign partner shall not be permitted to submit an additional or substitute certificate for the disregarded certificate. See § 1.1446-3(b)(2)(i) for computation requirements for installment payments of 1446 tax when a partnership receives, or fails to receive, an updated certificate or status update. See also paragraph (e)(2) Examples 4 and 8 of this section. Notwithstanding this paragraph (c)(2)(ii)(B)(1), a partner that can meet the requirements of this section for a subsequent partnership taxable year may submit a certificate to the partnership under this section for such taxable year.

(2) Other circumstances requiring an updated certificate. If at any time during the partnership taxable year the partner determines that its most recent certificate furnished to the partnership for such taxable year is incorrect, then the partner shall submit to the partnership an updated certificate in accordance with this paragraph (c) within 10 days of such determination. For example, if the partner determines that the amount or character of the certified deductions or losses is incorrect, the partner shall submit an updated certificate to the partnership. See § 1.1446-3(b)(2)(i) for computation requirements for installment payments of 1446 tax when a partnership receives an updated certificate.

(3) Form and content of updated certificate. The updated certificate required by this paragraph (c)(2)(ii) must be provided using the form and instructions identified in paragraph (c)(2)(i) of this section. The updated certificate must indicate that it is an updated certificate filed in accordance with this paragraph (c)(2)(ii). The partner is not required to attach to the updated certificate a copy of the certificate that is being updated (superseded certificate).

(4) Partnership consideration of an updated certificate. A partnership may consider an updated certificate, that meets the requirements of this paragraph (c), that is received prior to an installment due date in the same partnership taxable year for which the superseded certificate was provided, or prior to the due date of its Form 8804 (without regard to extensions) to be filed for the year the superseded certificate was provided. A partnership must consider an updated certificate that meets all the requirements of this paragraph (c) if it would increase the amount of 1446 tax the partnership would pay by the next installment due date, if any, or the due date of its Form 8804. An updated certificate considered by the partnership under this paragraph (c)(2)(ii)(B)(4) supersedes all prior certificates submitted by the foreign partner for the same partnership taxable year, beginning with the installment period or Form 8804 filing date for which the partnership considers the updated certificate. See paragraph (e)(2) Example 4 of this section.

(3) Notification to partnership when a partner's certificate cannot be relied upon. If the IRS determines, in its discretion based on all the facts and circumstances, that a foreign partner's certificate is defective (or that it lacks information sufficient to make this determination after providing written request for such information to the partnership), the IRS shall notify the partnership of such determination in writing. Upon receipt of such written notification, the partnership shall not rely on any certificate submitted by that foreign partner for the partnership taxable year to which the defective certificate relates (or any subsequent partnership taxable year), until the IRS provides written notification to the partnership revoking or modifying the original written notification. For purposes of this section, a foreign partner's certificate of deductions and losses shall be defective if—

(i) The partner is not described in paragraph (b) of this section;

(ii) Any deductions or losses set forth in such certificate are not described in paragraph (c)(1)(i) of this section;

(iii) The timing requirements under paragraph (c)(2) of this section for submitting an original certificate, an updated certificate or a status update to the partnership are not met;

(iv) The certificate does not include all of the information required by paragraph (c)(2)(i) of this section;

(v) Any representation made on the certificate is incorrect;

(vi) The actual amount of deductions and losses available to the partner is less than the amount of deductions and losses certified to the partnership for the partnership taxable year and considered by the partnership in determining its 1446 tax due; or

(vii) There is a failure to comply with any other provision of this section.

(4) Partner to receive copy of notice. If the IRS notifies a partnership under paragraph (c)(3) of this section that a certificate of a foreign partner is defective, the IRS shall send a copy of such notice to the partner's address as shown on the certificate. The partnership shall also promptly furnish a copy of the IRS notice to such partner.

(5) Notification to partnership when no foreign partner's certificate can be relied upon. If the IRS determines, in its discretion based on all the facts and circumstances, that there would be a substantial reduction in section 1446 tax as a result of the submission of one or more defective certificates or that a substantial portion of all certificates being submitted by partners to the partnership and by the partnership to the IRS are defective (or lack information sufficient to make this determination), then the IRS shall notify the partnership of such determination in writing. Upon receipt of such written notification, the partnership shall not rely on any certificate submitted by any partner for the partnership taxable year to which the notice relates or any subsequent partnership taxable year, until the IRS provides written notification to the partnership revoking or modifying the original notice.

(6) Partnership notification to partner regarding use of deductions and losses. Unless § 1.1446-3(d)(1)(i)(A) or (B) applies (relating to waiver of notice of tax paid during the partnership taxable year), a partnership must notify each foreign partner of the amount of such partner's certified deductions and losses and state and local taxes, if any, taken into account under this paragraph (c) in determining the 1446 tax due with respect to such partner for each installment period or Form 8804 filing date, as applicable.

(7) Partner's certificate valid only for partnership taxable year for which submitted. A partnership that receives a certificate from a partnership under this paragraph (c) shall consider such certificate only for the partnership taxable year for which the certificate is submitted, as set forth on the certificate.

(d) Effect of certificate of deductions and losses on partners and partnership. *(1) Effect on partner.* (i) No effect on liability for income tax of foreign partner. A foreign partner that certifies deductions and losses to a partnership under this section is not relieved of liability for income tax on its allocable share of ECTI from the partnership. Further, the submission of a certificate under this section does not constitute an acceptance by the IRS of the amount or character of the deductions or losses certified therein.

(ii) No effect on partner's estimated tax obligations. A foreign partner that certifies deductions and losses to a partnership under this section is not relieved of any estimated tax obligation otherwise applicable to such partner with respect to income or gain allocated to such partner from the partnership.

(iii) No effect on partner's obligation to file U.S. income tax return. The submission of a certificate under paragraph (c) of this section does not relieve the foreign partner from its obligation to file a U.S. income tax return even if as a result of the partnership considering the certificate the partner would have no additional tax due with such return. See also § 1.1446-3(f).

(2) Effect on partnership. (i) Reasonable reliance to relieve partnership from addition to tax under section 6655. A partnership that has reasonably relied on a certificate received from a foreign partner and complied with the filing requirements of paragraph (d)(3)(i) of this section, shall not be liable for any addition to tax under section 6655 (as applied through § 1.1446-3) for any period during which the partnership reasonably relied on such certificate, even if such certificate is later determined to be defective or the partner submits an updated certificate under paragraph (c)(2) of this section that increases the 1446 tax due with respect to such partner.

(ii) Continuing liability for withholding tax under section 1461 and for applicable interest and penalties. (A) In general. Except as otherwise provided in this section, a partnership that has reasonably relied on a certificate received from a foreign partner and complied with the filing requirements of paragraph (d)(3)(i) of this section, is not relieved from liability for the 1446 tax (or any installment of such tax) under section 1461, any additions to the tax, interest or penalties. However, the partnership may be relieved of additions to the tax or penalties in certain circumstances. See §§ 301.6651-1(c) and 301.6724-1 of this chapter. Further, see § 1.1446-3(e) which deems a partnership to have paid 1446 tax with respect to ECTI allocable to a partner in certain circumstances. See also paragraph (e)(2) Example 5 of this section.

(B) Certificate defective because of amount or character of deductions and losses. If a certificate is determined to be defective because the actual amount of deductions and losses available to the partner is less than the amount reflected on the certificate (other than when it is determined that the partner certified the same deduction or loss to more than one partnership), or because the character of the certified deductions and losses is erroneous, the partnership shall be liable for 1446 tax under section 1461 (or any installment of such tax) with respect to such partner to the extent the partnership considered an amount of certified deductions and losses greater than the amount actually available to the partner and permitted to be used under §§ 1.1446-1 through 1.1446-5 and this section, or to the extent that the proper character of the certified deductions and losses results in a greater amount of 1446 tax due with respect to such partner. See paragraph (e)(2) Example 6 of this section.

(3) Partnership level rules and requirements. (i) Filing requirement. A partnership that relies in whole or in part on a certificate received from a partner under this section in computing its 1446 tax due with respect to such partner must still file Form 8813 or Form 8804 and 8805, whichever is applicable, for the period for which the certificate is considered, even if as a result of relying on the certificate no 1446 tax (or an installment of such tax) is due with respect to such foreign partner. See generally § 1.1446-3(d)(1). Except as otherwise provided in this paragraph (d)(3)(i), the partnership must attach a copy of the foreign partner's certificate, and the computation of the 1446 tax due with respect to such partner, to both the Form 8813 and Form 8805 filed with the IRS for any installment period or year for which such certificate is considered in computing the partnership's 1446 tax. See § 1.1446-3(d)(1)(iii) requiring the partnership to furnish Form 8805 to the IRS and such foreign partner even if no 1446 tax is paid on behalf of the partner. The partnership must include in that computation the amount of state and local taxes described in paragraph (c)(1)(iii) of this section taken into account in computing the 1446 tax due with respect to that partner. The partnership must also attach a computation of the 1446 tax due with respect to a partner for whom only state and local taxes described in paragraph (c)(1)(iii) are taken into account. For an installment period other than the first installment period for which the partnership considers a foreign partner's certificate or updated certificate, the partnership may, instead of attaching any partner's certificate, attach to Form 8813 a list containing the name, TIN, the amount of certified deductions and losses, and the amount of state and local taxes the partnership may consider under paragraph (c)(1)(iii) of this section for each foreign partner whose certificate was relied upon. For purposes of the preceding sentence, if the partnership is relying on a certificate received under paragraph (c)(1)(ii) of this section, instead of providing the amounts described in the prior sentence, it should attach a statement to Form 8813 which provides that, relying on that certificate, no 1446 tax is due with respect to that partner.

(ii) Reasonable cause for failure to timely file a valid certificate and computation. This paragraph (d)(3)(ii) provides the sole source of relief for a partnership that fails to timely file a valid certificate or attach a computation of 1446 tax as required under paragraph (d)(3)(i) of this section. To permit the partnership to reasonably rely on such certificate, the partnership shall be considered to have satisfied the requirements of paragraph (d)(3)(i) of this section if the partnership demonstrates that such failure was due to reasonable cause and not willful neglect and if once the partnership becomes aware of the failure, the partnership attaches the certificate and computation, as well as a written statement setting forth the reasons for the failure to comply with the requirements of paragraph (d)(3)(i) of this section, to an amended Form 8813 or amended Forms 8804 and 8805 for the relevant period. All such submissions should be sent to the address provided in the instructions to Form 8804-C.

(A) Determining reasonable cause. In determining whether the partnership has reasonable cause, the Director shall consider whether the partnership acted reasonably and in good faith considering all the facts and circumstances.

(B) Notification. If the IRS has notified, as provided in paragraph (c)(3) of this section, the partnership that the certificate is defective or that no foreign partner's certificate may be relied upon, as provided in paragraph (c)(5) of this section, the partnership will be deemed not to have acted reasonably and in good faith. Otherwise, the Director shall notify the partnership in writing within 120 days of the amended filing if it is determined that the failure to comply was not due to reasonable cause, or if additional time will be needed to make such determination. If the Director fails to notify the partnership within 120 days of the amended filing, the partnership shall be considered to have demonstrated to the Director that such failure was due to reasonable cause and not willful neglect.

(e) Examples. *(1)* The rules of this section are illustrated by the examples in paragraph (e)(2) of this section. Except as otherwise provided, in each example assume:

(i) Section 1.1446-3(b)(2)(v)(F) (relating to the de minimis exception to paying 1446 tax) does not apply;

(ii) Paragraph (c)(1)(ii) of this section (relating to a nonresident alien individual partner whose sole investment generating effectively connected income or gain is the partnership) does not apply;

(iii) All income and losses are ordinary;

(iv) For purposes of applying paragraph (c)(1)(i)(C) of this section, the percentage limitation under section 56(a)(4) and (d) is 90 percent;

(v) Any loss is not a passive activity loss within the meaning of section 469;

(vi) The partnership uses an acceptable annualization method under § 1.1446-3;

(vii) NRA is a nonresident alien individual who maintains a calendar taxable year for U.S. tax purpose;

(viii) B and C are U.S. individuals who maintain a calendar taxable year; and

(ix) Any partnership maintains a calendar taxable year.

(2) The examples are as follows:

Example (1). Qualifying U.S. income tax return. (i) NRA and B form a partnership (PRS) in year 4 to conduct a trade or business in the United States. NRA and B provide PRS appropriate documentation under § 1.1446-1 to establish their status for purposes of section 1446. NRA submits a certificate to PRS (using Form 8804-C) on March 20, year 4, to be considered by PRS in determining its 1446 tax due with respect to NRA for the first installment period in the year 4. The Form 8804-C states that NRA reasonably expects to have an effectively connected net operating loss of $5,000 available to offset its allocable share of ECTI from PRS in year 4. Prior to year 4, NRA had not submitted a certificate to a partnership under this section. NRA filed (or will file) its year 1 U.S. income tax return on March 11, year 3; its year 2 U.S. income tax return on February 12, year 4; its year 3 U.S. income tax return on April 13, year 4; and its year 4 U.S. income tax return on May 14, year 5. NRA paid or (will pay) all amounts due with respect to the returns (including interest, penalties, and additions to tax, if any) by the date they are filed. NRA's years 1 though 3 U.S. income tax returns report income or gain effectively connected with a U.S. trade or business or deductions or losses properly allocated and apportioned to such activities.

(ii) To be eligible to submit a certificate of deductions and losses to PRS under this section, NRA must satisfy the requirements of paragraph (b)(1) of this section. In accordance with § 1.1446-1, NRA provided valid documentation to PRS to establish its status for purposes of section 1446. NRA's year 1 U.S. income tax return is a qualifying U.S. income tax return because it reported income or gain effectively connected with a U.S. trade or business or deductions or losses properly allocated and apportioned to such activities and is described under paragraph (b)(2)(iii)(A) of this section. Although NRA filed its year 1 return after the due date of the return (determined under section 6072(c) without regard to any extension of time to file) the return was filed on March 11, year 3, which was on or before the earlier of June 15, year 3, the date one year after its section 6072(c) due date without regard to any extension of time to file, and March 20, year 4, the date on which NRA submitted the certificate to PRS. NRA's year 2 U.S. income tax return is a qualifying U.S. income tax return because it reported income or gain effectively connected with a U.S. trade or business or deductions or losses properly allocated and apportioned to such activities and is described under paragraph (b)(2)(iii)(A) of this section. Although NRA filed its year 2 return after the due date of the return (determined under section 6072(c) without regard to any extension of time to file) the return was filed on February 12, year 4, which was on or before the earlier of June 15, year 4, the date one year after its section 6072(c) due date without regard to any extension of time to file, and March 20, year 4, the date on which NRA submitted the certificate to PRS. NRA's year 3 U.S. income tax return is a qualifying U.S. income tax return because it reported income or gain effectively connected with a U.S. trade or business or deductions or losses properly allocated and apportioned to such activities and is described under paragraph (b)(2)(iii)(B) of this section. Because NRA filed its year 3 U.S. income tax return on April 13, year 4, the return will be considered timely-filed under paragraph (b)(2)(ii) of this section, as the due date under section 6072(c) was June 15, year 4. NRA's year 4 U.S. income tax return is a qualifying U.S. income tax return because it reported income or gain effectively connected with a U.S. trade or business or deductions or losses properly allocated and apportioned to such activities and is described under paragraph (b)(2)(iii)(C) of this section. Because NRA filed its year 4 U.S. income tax return on May 14, year 5, the return will be considered timely-filed under paragraph (b)(2)(ii) of this section. Accordingly, NRA meets the conditions of paragraph (b)(1) of this section and is eligible to provide a certificate of deductions and losses to PRS for year 4.

Example (2). Subsequent year qualifying U.S. income tax return. (i) Assume the same facts as in Example 1. Further, NRA and C form a second partnership (XYZ) in year 7 to conduct a trade or business in the United States. NRA and C provide XYZ appropriate documentation under § 1.1446-1 to establish their status for purposes of section 1446. NRA did not submit a certificate under this section to any partnership for years 5 and 6. NRA submits a certificate to XYZ (using Form 8804-C) on April 10, year 7, to be considered by XYZ in determining its 1446 tax due with respect to NRA for its first installment period in year 7. The certificate states that NRA reasonably expects to have an effectively connected net operating loss of $8,000 available to offset its allocable share of ECTI from XYZ in year 7. Further, the certificate contains all of the necessary representations required under this section. NRA will file its U.S. income tax return for year 5 on March 25, year 7, (after its section 6072(c) due date and any extension of time to file that could have been granted under section 6081), its U.S. income tax return for year 6 on April 26, year 7; and its U.S. income tax return for year 7 on May 27, year 8. NRA will pay all amounts due with the returns (including interest, penalties, and additions to tax, if any) by the dates they are filed. NRA's years 5, 6, and 7 U.S. income tax returns will report income or gain that is effectively connected with a U.S. trade or business or deductions or losses properly allocated and apportioned to such activities.

(ii) To be eligible to submit a certificate of deductions and losses to XYZ under this section, NRA must satisfy the requirements of paragraph (b)(1) of this section. NRA provided valid documentation to XYZ in accordance with § 1.1446-1. As described in Example 1, NRA's year 4 U.S. income tax return is a qualifying U.S. income tax return because it will report income or gain effectively connected with a U.S. trade or business and is described under paragraph (b)(2)(iii)(C) of this section. Although NRA's year 5 U.S. income tax return reports income or gain effectively connected with a U.S. trade or business or deductions or losses properly allocated and apportioned to such activities it is not a qualifying U.S. income tax return under paragraph (b)(2)(iii) of this section. Because NRA submitted a certificate to PRS in year 4, to constitute a qualifying U.S. income tax return the year 5 U.S. income tax return must be timely-filed and all amounts due with such return must be timely paid. See paragraph (b)(2)(iii)(C) of this section. However, NRA will not file its U.S. income tax return for year 5 until

March 25, year 7, (after its section 6072(c) due date and any extension of time to file that could have been granted under section 6081). Because the year 5 tax return is not a qualifying U.S. income tax return under paragraph (b)(2)(iii) of this section, NRA does not satisfy the requirements of paragraph (b)(1)(ii) of this section and, therefore, may not submit a certificate of deductions and losses to XYZ under this section in year 7.

Example (3). General application of the rules of this section. NRA and B form a partnership (PRS) to conduct a trade or business in the United States. NRA and B are equal partners under the partnership agreement. NRA and B provide PRS appropriate documentation under § 1.1446-1 to establish their status for purposes of section 1446. Prior to the formation of PRS, NRA had not invested in or engaged in the conduct of a U.S. trade or business. PRS incurs a $1,500 effectively connected net operating loss in years 1 and 2. The loss incurred in each is allocated equally between NRA and B. NRA has filed a qualifying U.S. income tax return (within the meaning of paragraph (b)(2)(iii) of this section) for years 1 and 2 that report its allocable share of effective connected net operating loss allocated to it from PRS, as reported on the Form 1065 (Schedule K-1) issued to NRA for each year.

(i) In year 3, NRA may not submit a certificate to PRS under paragraph (c) because it will not have filed qualifying U.S. income tax returns for the preceding three years. In year 3, PRS has ECTI of $1,000 that is allocated equally between NRA and B. PRS satisfies its 1446 tax obligation with respect to NRA for year 3.

(ii) In year 4, PRS estimates that it will have ECTI of $4,000, which will be allocated equally between NRA and B. On or before April 15th of year 4 (the first installment due date), NRA submits a certificate to PRS under this section (using Form 8804-C) certifying that it reasonably expects to have an effectively connected net operating loss of $1,000 ($750 loss in both years 1 and 2, less $500 of income in year 3) available to offset its allocable share of ECTI from PRS in year 4. As of the date the certificate is submitted, NRA has received the Form 1065 (Schedule K-1) from PRS for year 3 but has not yet filed its U.S. income tax return for year 3.

(iii) With respect to year 4, and based upon paragraph (b)(1) of this section, NRA can include year 3 (NRA's preceding taxable year) as one of the preceding three years that it has filed or will file qualifying U.S. income tax returns (within the meaning of paragraph (b)(2)(iii) of this section). Therefore, provided PRS has, in accordance with paragraph (a)(2) of this section, no actual knowledge or reason to know the certificate is defective, PRS may reasonably rely on NRA's certificate. Accordingly, PRS may consider NRA's certificate to reduce the 1446 tax that would otherwise be required to be paid on NRA's behalf. Specifically, subject to paragraph (c)(1)(i)(C) of this section, the $1,000 of net losses that have been reported on Forms 1065 (Schedule K-1) issued to NRA that are available to reduce NRA's U.S. income tax on NRA's allocable share of effectively connected income or gain allocable from PRS may be used to reduce the $2,000 of ECTI estimated to be allocable to NRA. As a result, PRS must pay 1446 tax on only $1,100 of NRA's allocable share of partnership ECTI for the first installment period in year 5 ($2,000-($1,000 x .90)). PRS must pay 1446 tax of $96.25 for its first installment period with respect to the ECTI allocable to NRA ($1,100 (net ECTI after considering certified losses) x .35 (withholding tax rate) x .25 (section 6655(e)(2)(B) percentage for the first installment period)). See § 1.1446-3(b)(2). Pursuant to paragraph (d)(3) of this section, PRS must attach NRA's certificate and PRS's computation of its 1446 tax obligation with respect to NRA to its Form 8813, "Partnership Withholding Tax Payment Voucher (Section 1446)," filed for the first installment period. Under paragraph (c)(2)(ii)(B) of this section, NRA is required to provide an updated certificate on or before the 10th day after NRA files its U.S. income tax return for year 3, even if the updated certificate results in no change to the amount of deductions and losses reported on the superseded certificate.

(iv) The results are the same if NRA had not yet received a Form 1065 (Schedule K-1) from PRS for year 3. See paragraph (c)(1)(i)(A) of this section.

Example (4). Updated certificate submitted for losses. On January 1, year 8, NRA and B form a partnership (PRS) to conduct a trade or business in the United States. NRA and B are equal partners in PRS. NRA and B provide PRS appropriate documentation under § 1.1446-1 to establish their status for purposes of section 1446. During years 1 through 7 NRA held an interest in another partnership (XYZ) that conducted a trade or business in the United States. NRA timely-filed (within the meaning of paragraph (b)(2) of this section) U.S. income tax returns for years 1 through 6 reporting its allocable share of ECTI (or loss) from XYZ (and timely paid all tax shown on such returns). NRA files its U.S. income tax return for year 7 on June 9, year 8 (and timely pays all tax due with such return). Therefore, NRA has filed qualifying U.S. income tax returns (within the meaning of paragraph (b)(2)(iii) of this section) for years 1 through 7. During years 1 through 7, NRA's only investment generating effectively connected items was its interest in XYZ. The XYZ partnership liquidated and ceased doing business on December 31, year 7.

(i) On or before April 15, year 8, PRS receives from NRA a valid certificate under this section using Form 8804-C in which NRA certifies that it reasonably expects to have available effectively connected net operating losses in the amount of $5,000. Among other statements made in accordance with paragraph (c) of this section, NRA represents that it has not yet filed its year 7 U.S. income tax return, but will timely file such return (and timely pay all tax due with such return). For its first installment period in year 8, PRS estimates that it will earn taxable income of $10,000 for the year which will be allocated equally to NRA and B (NRA's allocable share of PRS's ECTI is $5,000).

(ii) Provided PRS has, in accordance with paragraph (a)(2) of this section, no actual knowledge or reason to know the certificate is defective, PRS may reasonably rely on NRA's certificate when computing its 1446 tax obligation for the first installment period. PRS is limited under paragraph (c)(1)(i)(C) of this section and PRS may only consider $4,500 ($5,000 x .90) of the certified net operating loss. After consideration of the certified loss, PRS owes 1446 tax in the amount of $43.75 for the first installment period ($5,000 estimated allocable ECTI less $4,500 (certified loss as limited under paragraph (c)(1)(i)(C)) x .35 (1446 tax applicable percentage) x .25 (section 6655(e)(2)(B) percentage for the first installment period)). See § 1.1446-3(b)(2). Pursuant to paragraph (d)(3) of this section, PRS must attach a copy of NRA's certificate and the computation of 1446 tax due with respect to NRA to the Form 8813 filed with respect to NRA.

(iii) PRS's estimate of ECTI allocable to NRA for the second installment period remains unchanged from the first installment period. On June 10, year 8, NRA provides PRS an updated certificate reporting that NRA now reasonably expects to have an effectively connected net operating loss of $4,000 available to offset its allocable share of ECTI from PRS in year 4. NRA provided the updated certificate within 10 days of filing its U.S. income tax return for the year 7 taxable year, as required by paragraph (c)(2)(ii)(B) of this section. Provided the updated certificate is otherwise valid, PRS may rely on the updated certificate for the second installment period (due date June 15, year 8). Even if the updated certificate were not valid, PRS could no longer rely on the original certificate.

(iv) Under paragraph (d) of this section, PRS is not relieved from liability for the 1446 tax due with respect to NRA under section 1461 if it relies on a certificate determined to be defective, or if it receives an updated certificate reporting an amount of deductions and losses less than the amount reported on the superseded certificate. Under the principles of section 6655 (as applied through § 1.1446-3), PRS is required to have paid 50-percent of the annualized 1446 tax due with respect to NRA on or before the due date of the second installment period (section 6655(e)(2)(B) percentage for the second installment period). Under paragraph (c)(2)(ii)(B) of this section, because NRA's updated certificate is valid for the second installment period, if PRS considers a certificate for that period it must consider the updated certificate. Under paragraph (c)(1)(i)(C) of this section, PRS can only consider $3,600 ($4,000 x .90) of NRA's updated effectively connected net operating loss. Assuming PRS considers NRA's updated certificate for the second installment period, PRS must have paid a total of $245 of 1446 tax with respect to the ECTI estimated to be allocable to NRA as of the second installment due date ($1,400 ($5,000 ECTI less $3,600 net operating loss deduction) x .35 (withholding tax rate) x .50 (section 6655(e)(2)(B) percentage for the second installment period)). After considering PRS's payment of 1446 tax for the first installment period, PRS is required to pay $201.25 for the second installment period ($245 less previous payment of $43.75). See § 1.1446-3(b)(2). Further, if PRS considers NRA's updated certificate for the second installment period, when PRS files Form 8813 it must attach the updated certificate along with PRS's computation of 1446 tax due with respect to NRA.

(v) Under paragraph (d) of this section, PRS is not liable for the addition to the tax under section 6655 (as applied through § 1.1446-3) for the first installment period because PRS reasonably relied on NRA's certificate of losses for that period.

(vi) Assume that PRS's estimate of its ECTI allocable to NRA for the third and fourth installment periods is the same as for the first and second installment periods. Assume PRS may reasonably rely on NRA's updated certificate in calculating its payment of 1446 tax for the third and fourth installment periods. The third installment of 1446 tax would be $122.50 (($5,000 - $3,600) x .35 x .75 = $367.50 - $245 (total previous payments)). The fourth installment of 1446 tax would be $122.50 (($5,000 - $3,600) x .35 x 1.00 = $490 - $367.50 (total previous payments)). See § 1.1446-3(b)(2). PRS must attach to each Form 8813 a computation of the 1446 tax due with respect to NRA that takes into account the amount of effectively connected net operating loss reported on NRA's updated certificate.

(vii) Because NRA's certified net operating loss has not changed for the third and fourth installments, in lieu of attaching NRA's certificate, PRS may attach a statement containing NRA's name, TIN, and the certified net operating loss amount. However, PRS must attach NRA's certificate and a computation of the 1446 tax due with respect to NRA that takes into account NRA's certified net operating loss to the Form 8805 filed with respect to NRA. See paragraph (d)(3) of this section.

Example (5). IRS determines in subsequent taxable year that partner's certificate is defective because partner failed to timely file a U.S. income tax return. NRA and B form a partnership (PRS) in year 1 to conduct a trade or business in the United States. NRA and B provide PRS appropriate documentation under § 1.1446-1 to establish their status for purposes of section 1446. In year 4, NRA timely submits a certificate under this section (using Form 8804-C) to be considered by PRS for its first installment period. The certificate reports that NRA reasonably expects to have an effectively connected net operating loss of $5,000 available to offset its allocable share of ECTI from PRS in year 4. Further, the certificate contains all of the necessary representations required under this section. PRS estimates for each installment period that NRA's allocable share of ECTI will be $5,000 for the taxable year. PRS's actual operating results for the year result in $5,000 of ECTI allocable to NRA.

(i) PRS reasonably relies on (within the meaning of paragraph (a)(2) of this section) NRA's certificate when computing each installment payment during year 4 and the 1446 tax due on Form 8804 and appropriately considers the limitation in paragraph (c)(1)(i)(C) of this section. As a result, PRS paid $175 of 1446 tax on behalf of NRA for the taxable year ($5,000 of ECTI less $4,500 net operating loss deduction x .35 applicable percentage). As required under paragraph (d) of this section, PRS attached the certificate to the Form 8813 for the first installment period and the Form 8805 for year 4. Because NRA did not submit an updated certificate to PRS in year 4, PRS attached to the Forms 8813 for the second, third and fourth installment periods a statement containing NRA's name, TIN, and the certified net operating loss as well as the computation of 1446 tax due with respect to NRA reflecting the amount of net operating loss considered.

(ii) In year 5, NRA timely submits to PRS a certificate under this section to be considered for the first installment period. The certificate represents that NRA reasonably expects to have an effectively connected net operating loss of $5,000 available to offset its allocable share of ECTI from PRS in year 5. For the first installment period, PRS estimates that NRA's allocable share of partnership ECTI is $5,000. PRS reasonably relies on the certificate for the first installment period and determines that it is required to make a 1446 tax installment payment of $43.75 ($5,000 allocable ECTI less $4,500 (certified net operating loss as limited under paragraph (c)(1)(i)(C) of this section) x .35 (1446 tax applicable percentage) x .25 (section 6655(e)(2)(B) percentage for the first installment period)). See § 1.1446-3(b)(2). PRS makes the installment payment with the Form 8813 filed for the first installment period, and complies with paragraph (d)(3) of this section by attaching NRA's certificate and the computation of 1446 tax due with respect to NRA to the Form 8813.

(iii) The IRS provides written notification to PRS on June 1, year 5, (pursuant to paragraph (c)(3) of this section) that the certificate received from NRA in year 4 is defective because NRA failed to file a qualifying U.S. income tax return (within the meaning of paragraph (b)(2)(iii) of this section) for one of the preceding taxable years as required under paragraph (b)(1) of this section. The notice further states that PRS is not to rely on any certificate received from NRA in year 5.

(iv) Under paragraph (d)(2)(ii) of this section, because the certificate submitted by NRA in year was determined to be defective for a reason other than the amount or character of the certified deductions and losses, under section 1461 PRS is fully liable for the 1446 tax due with respect to NRA's allocable share of ECTI year 4 without regard to the certificate. The total 1446 tax due for year 4 without regard to the certificate is $1,750 ($5,000 ECTI x .35) and PRS paid $175 of 1446 tax in year 4. Therefore, PRS owes $1,575 of 1446 tax. However, PRS may be deemed to have paid the outstanding 1446 tax due if NRA paid all of its U.S. tax due in year 4. See § 1.1446-3(e).

(v) However, because PRS did not have actual knowledge or reason to know that the certificate NRA submitted in year 4 was defective, PRS reasonably relied on the certificate for purposes of paragraph (d)(2) of this section. Therefore, PRS is not liable for an addition to the tax with respect to its underpayment of 1446 tax under the principles of section 6655 (as applied through § 1.1446-3) for any installment period in year 4.

(vi) However, PRS is generally liable for interest under section 6601 and for the failure to pay addition to tax under section 6651(a)(2) on the $1,575 of 1446 tax due for year 4 for the period from April 15, year 5 (last date prescribed for payment of 1446 tax) to the date PRS pays the 1446 tax or is deemed to have paid the 1446 tax under § 1.1446-3(e).

(vii) With respect to the year 5, PRS reasonably relied on NRA's certificate when computing its first installment payment (due on April 15, year 5). Therefore, in accordance with paragraph (d)(2)(i) of this section, PRS will not be liable for an addition to the tax under the principles of section 6655 (as applied through § 1.1446-3) for the first installment period. However, because the IRS provided written notification to PRS on June 1, year 5, to disregard any certificate received from NRA for year 5, PRS may not rely on any certificate received from NRA certificate (or any new certificate provided by NRA) when it computes its second installment payment in year 5. PRS is not permitted to consider any certificate submitted by NRA until the IRS provides written notification to PRS revoking or modifying the original notice. PRS's second installment payment in year 5 must include the additional amount of 1446 tax it would have paid for the first installment period without regard to the certificate received from NRA.

Example (6). IRS determines in subsequent taxable year that partner's certificate is defective because partner's actual losses are less than amount certified and considered by the partnership. Assume the same facts as in Example 5, except that the IRS determines that NRA's certificate submitted in year 4 is defective because the actual effectively connected net operating loss available to NRA for year 4 was $1,000 rather than the $5,000 certified.

(i) Under paragraph (d)(2)(ii) of this section, PRS is not relieved from its liability for 1446 tax under section 1461 when it relies on a certificate of losses from a foreign partner that is later determined to be defective. However, when the IRS determines that a partner's certificate is defective because of the amount of the certified deductions and losses, the partnership is liable for the 1446 tax, interest, additions to tax, and penalties to the extent the amount of certified deductions and losses taken into account when computing 1446 tax (or, unless there was reasonable reliance on the certificate, any installment of such tax) is greater than the actual amount of available deductions and losses. Here, PRS considered the certified deductions and losses in the amount of $4,500. The IRS subsequently determined that NRA only had $1,000 of actual losses, only $900 of which were permitted to be considered under paragraph (c)(1)(i)(C) of this section. Accordingly, PRS is liable for the 1446 tax due with respect to the portion of the overstated losses that it considered when computing its 1446 tax. The remaining 1446 tax due for year 4 is $1,260 ($3,600 ($4,500 less $900) of excess losses considered x .35). However, PRS may be deemed to have paid the $1,260 of 1446 tax under § 1.1446-3(e) if NRA has paid all of NRA's U.S. income tax.

(ii) If PRS had considered only $900 (or a lesser amount) of NRA's certified net operating loss when computing and paying its 1446 tax during year 4 then, under paragraph (d)(2)(iii) of this section, PRS would not be liable for 1446 tax because it did not consider a net operating loss greater than the amount actually available to NRA.

Example (7). Partner with different taxable year than partnership. PRS partnership has two equal partners, FC, a foreign corporation, and DC, a domestic corporation. PRS conducts a trade or business in the United States and generates effectively connected income. FC maintains a June 30 fiscal taxable year end, while DC and PRS maintain a calendar taxable year end. FC and DC provide a valid Form W-8BEN and Form W-9, respectively, to PRS. FC and DC are the only persons that have ever been partners in PRS. For its year 1 through year 3 taxable years, PRS issued Forms 1065 (Schedule K-1) reporting in the aggregate $100 of net loss to each partner. For its year 4 taxable year, PRS issued Forms 1065 (Schedule K-1) to its partners reporting $150 of loss to each partner. All of the losses reported on the Forms 1065 (Schedule K-1) are effectively connected to PRS's and FC's trade or business in the United States.

(i) Assume that FC submits a valid certificate under this section certifying losses to the partnership for the partnership's year 5 taxable year. Further, assume that FC's only source of effectively connected income, gain, deduction, or loss is the activity of PRS.

(ii) For PRS's first installment period in year 5, FC may only certify deductions and losses under this section in the amount of $100 (the losses as reported on the Forms 1065 (Schedule K-1) issued for PRS's year 1 through 3 taxable years). Under section 706, the taxable income of a partner shall include the income, gain, loss, deduction, or credit of the partnership for the partnership taxable year ending within or with the taxable year of the partner. PRS's year 4 calendar taxable year ends during FC's fiscal taxable year ending June 30, year 5. Therefore, under paragraph (c)(1) of this section, as of April 15, year 5 (the last date FC may submit its first certificate under paragraph (c) of this section to have it considered for PRS's first installment due date of April 15, year 5), FC's allocable share of the PRS losses for years 1 through 3 are the only losses that FC can represent have been or will be reported on an FC U.S. income tax return filed for a taxable year ending prior to such installment due date.

(iii) The result in paragraph (ii) of this Example 7 is the same for the year 5 second installment period, the due date of which is June 15, year 5.

(iv) FC may submit an updated certificate under this section after June 30, year 5, which includes the $150 loss for year 4. PRS may consider such an updated certificate for its third installment period (due date September 15, year 5), provided the updated certificate is received by the due date for such installment in accordance with paragraph (c) of this section.

Example (8). Failure to provide status update with respect to prior year unfiled returns. FC, a foreign corporation, and DC, a domestic corporation, form a partnership (PRS) to conduct a trade or business in the United States. FC and DC provide PRS appropriate documentation under § 1.1446-1 to establish their status for purposes of section 1446. FC and DC are equal partners in PRS, and all partnership items are allocated equally between FC and DC.

(i) In the current taxable year FC submits a certificate under this section using Form 8804-C prior to PRS's first installment due date. FC represents that it has filed or will file a qualifying U.S. income tax return (within the meaning of paragraph (b)(2)(iii) of this section) in each of the preceding three taxable years. FC specifies that it has not filed its U.S. income tax return for the immediately preceding taxable year. FC also represents that it will timely file its U.S. income tax return for the partnership taxable year during which the certificate is considered (and will timely pay all tax due with such return). Assume all other requirements under paragraph (c) of this section are met for FC's certificate to be valid.

(ii) Provided that PRS does not possess actual knowledge or reason to know that FC's certificate is defective under paragraph (a)(2) of this section, PRS may reasonably rely on FC's certificate for its first, second, and third installment payments.

(iii) If FC does not submit to PRS either an updated certificate or a status update as required by paragraph (c)(2)(ii)(B)(1) of this section by December 15th (PRS's final installment due date), PRS must disregard FC's certificate when computing its fourth installment payment of 1446 tax and when completing its Form 8804 for the taxable year. PRS's payment of 1446 tax for its fourth installment period must include the additional amount of 1446 tax it would have paid in the first, second and third installment periods had it not considered FC's certificate. Further, even if the status update is provided by December 15th, PRS may only rely on the certificate if the status update does not contradict the original certificate and such update indicates that the immediately preceding year's return will be timely filed. Finally, even if the status update is provided by December 15th, FC must also submit an updated certificate to the partnership in accordance with paragraph (c) of this section within 10 days of the date FC timely files its U.S. income tax return for the preceding taxable year.

Example (9). Partnership consideration of certified deductions and losses or de minimis certificate. For purposes of this example assume paragraph (c)(1)(ii) of this section may apply. On January 1, year 4, NRA and B form a partnership (PRS) to conduct a trade or business in the United States. NRA and B are equal partners in PRS and all partnership items are shared equally. NRA and B provide PRS appropriate documentation under § 1.1446-1 to establish their status for purposes of section 1446. During years 1 through 3, NRA's only activity generating effectively connected items was an interest in partnership XYZ. XYZ allocated NRA a loss for all three years. NRA filed qualifying U.S. income tax returns (within the meaning of paragraph (b)(2)(iii) of this section) reporting its allocable share of losses from XYZ in years 1 through 3. The XYZ partnership dissolved on December 31, year 3.

(i) In year 4, NRA's only activity giving rise to effectively connected income, gain, deduction, or loss is its interest in PRS. NRA submits to PRS a valid certificate (using Form 8804-C) certifying under paragraph (c)(1)(i) its effectively connected net operating losses from years 1 through 3 and under (c)(1)(ii) of this section that its only activity giving rise to effectively connected income, gain, deduction, or loss for the PRS taxable year that ends with or within its taxable year is (and will be) its investment in PRS.

(ii) During year 4, PRS allocates ECTI to NRA. If the 1446 tax otherwise due on the annualized amount allocated to NRA is less than $1,000, determined without regard to any deductions and losses certified by NRA under paragraph (c)(1)(i) of this section, PRS may consider the certificate received from NRA under paragraph (c)(1)(ii) of this section and not pay 1446 tax (or any installment of such tax) with respect to NRA. Alternatively, PRS may consider the deductions and losses certified by NRA under paragraph (c)(1)(i) of this section.

(iii) Regardless of whether PRS considers NRA's certification under paragraph (c)(1)(i) or (c)(1)(ii) of this section in computing its 1446 tax due with respect to NRA, PRS must file Form 8813 for all installment periods as well as a Form 8805 for NRA with its Form 8804. If PRS considers NRA's certification under paragraph (c)(1)(i) or (c)(1)(ii) of this section, PRS must attach to each Form 8813, as well as to the Form 8805, a computation of the 1446 tax with respect to NRA that takes into account its consideration of NRA's certificate. In addition, PRS must attach NRA's certificate to the Form 8813 for the first installment period it considers the certificate, as well as to the Form 8805. For all subsequent installment periods, PRS may attach a statement containing NRA's name, and TIN. If PRS is relying on NRA's certified losses under paragraph (c)(1)(i) of this section, the statement must indicate the amount of losses and deductions NRA certified. If PRS is relying on NRA's certification under paragraph (c)(ii) of this section, the statement must indicate that it is relying on NRA meeting the requirements under paragraph (c)(1)(ii) of this section and the 1446 tax on the annualized amount allocated to NRA is less than $1,000. See paragraph (d)(3)(i) of this section.

Example (10). Application of transition rule. NRA and B form a partnership (PRS) on January 1, 2004, to conduct a trade or business in the United States. NRA and B are equal partners in PRS and all partnership items are shared equally. NRA and B provide PRS appropriate documentation under § 1.1446-1 to establish their status for purposes of section 1446. For its 2004 through 2007 tax years, PRS issued Forms 1065 (Schedule K-1) to NRA and B reporting a $1,000 net loss from its U.S. trade or business to each partner for each year (for an aggregate loss of $4,000 per partner). During the 2004 through 2007 tax years, NRA's only activity generating effectively connected items was its investment in PRS.

(i) On February 10, 2008, NRA submitted a certificate to PRS, reporting its aggregate $4,000 effectively connected loss to PRS, that met the requirements of § 1.1446-6T(c) (See 26 CFR Part 1, revised as of April 1, 2007), as in effect before January 1, 2008. The certificate stated that NRA had timely filed its U.S. income tax returns for the 2004, 2005 and 2006 tax years, and that it would timely file a U.S. income tax return for its 2007 tax year. For the first and second installments period in 2008, PRS estimates that it will earn ECTI of $10,000.

(ii) Because the certificate submitted by NRA to PRS on February 10, 2008, met the requirements of § 1.1446-6T (See 26 CFR Part 1, revised as of April 1, 2007), as in effect before January 1, 2008, PRS may consider such certificate when computing its 1446 tax due for the first and second installment period even if the certificate does not meet all the requirements of paragraph (c) of this section.

(iii) NRA timely files its U.S. income tax return for the 2007 tax year on July 24, 2008. In accordance with paragraph (c)(2)(ii)(B)(1) of this section, within 10 days of filing such return NRA prepares an updated certificate to be submitted to PRS certifying that it reasonably expects to have only $3,500 of losses available to reduce its allocable share of ECTI from PRS. Because the updated certificate will be submitted after July 28, 2008, to be valid the updated certificate must meet the requirements of paragraph (c) this section.

(f) Effective/Applicability date. Except as otherwise provided in this paragraph (f), the rules of this section are applicable for partnership taxable years beginning after December 31, 2007. The rules of paragraphs (b)(3)(i)(B) through (D) shall apply to partnership taxable years beginning after July 28, 2008.

(g) Transition rule. A certificate that met the requirements of § 1.1446-6T(c) (See 26 CFR Part 1, revised as of April 1, 2007), as in effect before January 1, 2008, submitted on or before July 28, 2008 by a partner that met the requirements of § 1.1446-6T(b) (See 26 CFR Part 1, revised as of April 1, 2007), as in effect before January 1, 2008, shall not be considered defective because it does not meet the requirements of this section. However, any certificate (including any updated certificates and status updates) submitted, or required to be submitted, under paragraph (c) of this section after July 28, 2008, must meet the requirements of this section. See paragraph (e)(2) Example 10 of this section.

T.D. 9394, 4/28/2008.

§ 1.1446-7 Effective/Applicability date.

Sections 1.1446-1 through 1.1446-5 shall apply to partnership taxable years beginning after May 18, 2005. However, a partnership may elect to apply all of the provisions of §§ 1.1446-1 through 1.1446-5 to partnership taxable years beginning after December 31, 2004. A partnership shall make the election under this section by complying with the provisions of §§ 1.1446-1 through § 1.1446-5 and attaching a statement to the Form 8804 or Form 1042 annual return, filed for the taxable year in which the regulation provisions first apply, that indicates that the partnership is making the election under this section. The revisions to §§ 1.1446-3(b)(2), 1.1446-3(b)(3)(i)(A) and 1.1446-5(c)(2) contained in the final regulations published in 2008 apply to partnership taxable years beginning after December 31, 2007. See § 1.1446-6(f) and (g) for the Effective/ Applicability date and Transition rule for § 1.1446-6.

T.D. 9200, 5/13/2005, amend T.D. 9394, 4/28/2008.

§ 1.1451-1 Tax-free covenant bonds issued before January 1, 1934.

Caution: The Treasury has not yet amended Reg § 1.1451-1 to reflect changes made by P.L. 98-369.

(a) Rates of withholding. *(1) Rate of 2 percent.* Withholding of a tax equal to 2 percent is required in the case of interest upon bonds or other corporate obligations containing a tax-free covenant and issued before January 1, 1934, paid to an individual, a fiduciary, or a partnership, whether resident or nonresident, or to a nonresident foreign corporation, regardless of whether the liability assumed by the obligor is less than, equal to, or greater than 2 percent.

(2) Rate of 30 percent. Notwithstanding subparagraph (1) of this paragraph, if the liability assumed by the obligor does not exceed 2 percent of the interest, withholding is required at the rate of 30 percent in the case of payments to a nonresident alien individual, a nonresident partnership composed in whole or in part of nonresident aliens, a nonresident foreign corporation, or an owner who is unknown to the withholding agent.

(3) Obligations of resident payers. The rates of withholding specified in subparagraphs (1) and (2) of this paragraph are applicable to interest on such tax-free covenant bonds issued by a domestic corporation or by a resident foreign corporation.

(4) Obligations of nonresident payers. A nonresident foreign corporation having a fiscal or paying agent in the United States is required to withhold a tax of 2 percent in the case of interest upon its tax-free covenant bonds issued before January 1, 1934, which is paid to an individual or fiduciary who is a citizen or resident of the United States, to a partnership any member of which is a citizen or resident, or to an unknown owner.

(5) Interest from sources without the United States. Withholding is not required under section 1451 in the case of interest upon bonds or other corporate obligations issued before January 1, 1934, and containing a tax-free covenant if the interest is not to be treated as income from sources within the United States and the payments are made to a nonresident alien, a partnership composed wholly of nonresident aliens, or a nonresident foreign corporation.

(6) Tax treaties. The rates of tax to be withheld in accordance with this paragraph shall be reduced as may be provided by treaty with any country. See section 894 and § 1.1441-6 relating to income subject to a reduced rate of, or an exemption from, income tax pursuant to an income tax convention.

(b) Date of issue. The withholding provisions of section 1451 are applicable only to bonds, mortgages, or deeds of trust, or other similar obligations of a corporation which were issued before January 1, 1934, and which contain a tax-free covenant. For the purpose of section 1451, bonds, mortgages, or deeds of trust, or other similar obligations of a corporation, are issued when delivered. If a broker or other person acts as selling agent of the obligor, the obligation is issued when delivered by the agent to the purchaser. If a broker or other person purchases the obligation outright for the purpose of holding or reselling it, the obligation is issued when delivered to such broker or other person.

(c) Extended maturity date. In cases where on or after January 1, 1934, the maturity date of bonds or other obligations of a corporation is extended, the bonds or other obligations shall be considered to have been issued on or after January 1, 1934. The interest on such obligations is not subject to the withholding provisions of section 1451 but falls within the class of interest described in section 1441. See paragraph (c)(5)(iii) of § 1.1441-3.

(d) Covenant in trust deed. Bonds issued under a trust deed containing a tax-free covenant are treated as if they contain such a covenant. If neither the bonds nor the trust deeds given by the obligor to secure them contained a tax-free covenant, but the original trust deeds were modified before January 1, 1934, by supplemental agreements containing a tax-free covenant executed by the obligor corporation and the trustee, the bonds issued before January 1, 1934, are subject to the provisions of section 1451, provided appropriate authority existed for the modification of the trust deeds in this manner. The authority must have been contained in the original trust deeds or actually secured from the bondholders.

(e) Notation showing date of issue. In order that the date of issue of bonds, mortgages, deeds of trust, or other similar corporate obligations containing a tax-free covenant may be readily determined by the owner for the purpose of preparing the ownership certificates required by § 1.1461-1, the issuing or debtor corporation shall indicate the date of issue by an appropriate notation, or use the phrase "issued on or after January 1, 1934," on each such obligation or in a statement accompanying the delivery of the obligation.

(f) Effect of withholding on income taxes of bondholder and issuing corporation. *(1) Federal tax.* In the case of corporate bonds or other corporate obligations issued before January 1, 1934, and containing a tax-free covenant, the corporation paying a Federal tax, or any part of it, for someone else pursuant to its agreement is not entitled to deduct such payment from its gross income on any ground; nor shall the tax so paid be included in the gross income of the bondholder. The amount of the tax so paid may, nevertheless, be claimed by the bondholder in accordance with paragraph (a) of § 1.1462-1 as a credit against the total amount of income tax due. See also section 32. The tax so paid by the corporation upon tax-free covenant bond interest payable to a domestic or resident fiduciary and allocable to any nonresident alien beneficiary under section 652 or 662 is allowable, pro rata, as a credit against—

(i) The tax required to be withheld by the fiduciary in accordance with paragraph (f) of § 1.1441-3 from the income of the beneficiary, and

(ii) The total income tax computed in the return of the beneficiary, as indicated in paragraph (a) of § 1.1462-1.

(2) State taxes. In the case of corporate bonds or other obligations containing an appropriate tax-free covenant, the corporation paying for someone else, pursuant to its agreement, a State tax or any tax other than a Federal tax may deduct such payment as interest paid on indebtedness.

(g) Alien resident of Puerto Rico. For purposes of this section the term "nonresident alien individual" includes an alien resident of Puerto Rico.

(h) Other rules for withholding of tax under section 1451. The rules for withholding stated in paragraphs (c)(2) and (3), (f), and (g) of § 1.1441-3 shall also apply for purposes of withholding the tax under this section.

T.D. 6187, 7/5/56, amend T.D. 7157, 12/29/71.

§ 1.1451-2 Exemptions from withholding under section 1451.

Caution: The Treasury has not yet amended Reg § 1.1451-2 to reflect changes made by P.L. 98-369.

(a) Claiming personal exemptions. Withholding under § 1.1451-1 from interest on bonds or other obligations of corporations issued before January 1, 1934, and containing a tax-free covenant shall not be required if there is filed with the withholding agent when presenting coupons for payment, or not later than February 1 of the following year, an ownership certificate on Form 1000 stating—

(1) In the case of a citizen or resident of the United States, that his taxable income does not exceed his deductions for personal exemptions allowed under section 151; or

(2) In the case of an estate or trust the fiduciary of which is a citizen or resident of the United States, that its taxable income does not exceed the deduction for the personal exemption allowed under section 642(b).

(b) Claiming residence in United States. To claim residence in the United States for purposes of section 1451, see § 1.1441-5.

(c) Other exemptions. The exemptions allowed by paragraphs (d) and (h) of § 1.1441-4 shall also apply for purposes of section 1451.

T.D. 6187, 7/5/56, amend T.D. 6908, 12/30/66.

§ 1.1461-1 Payment and returns of tax withheld.

(a) Payment of withheld tax. *(1) Deposits of tax.* Every withholding agent who withholds tax pursuant to chapter 3 of the Internal Revenue Code (Code) and the regulations under such chapter shall deposit such amount of tax with an authorized financial institution as provided in § 1.6302-2(a). If for any reason the total amount of tax required to be returned for any calendar year pursuant to paragraph (b) of this section has not been deposited pursuant to § 1.6302-2, the withholding agent shall pay the balance of tax due for such year at such place as the Internal Revenue Service (IRS) shall specify. The tax shall be paid when filing the return required under paragraph (b)(1) of this section for such year, unless the IRS specifies otherwise. With respect to withholding under section 1446, this section shall only apply to publicly traded partnerships. See § 1.1461-3 for penalties applicable to partnerships that fail to withhold under section 1446 on effectively connected taxable income allocable to foreign partners. The previous two sentences shall apply to partnership taxable years beginning after May 18, 2005, or such earlier time as the regulations under §§ 1.1446-1 through 1.1446-5 apply by reason of an election under § 1.1446-7.

(2) Penalties for failure to pay tax. For penalties and additions to the tax for failure to timely pay the tax required to be withheld under chapter 3 of the Code, see sections 6656, 6672, and 7202 and the regulations under those sections.

(b) Income tax return. *(1) General rule.* A withholding agent shall make an income tax return on Form 1042 (or such other form as the IRS may prescribe) for income paid during the preceding calendar year that the withholding agent is required to report on an information return on Form 1042-S (or such other form as the IRS may prescribe) under paragraph (c)(1) of this section. See section 6011 and § 1.6011-1(c). The withholding agent must file the return on or before March 15 of the calendar year following the year in which the income was paid. The return must show the aggregate amount of income paid and tax withheld required to be reported on all the Forms 1042-S for the preceding calendar year by the withholding agent, in addition to such information as is required by the form and accompanying instructions. Withholding certificates or other statements or information provided to a withholding agent are not required to be attached to the return. A return must be filed under this paragraph (b)(1) even though no tax was required to be withheld during the preceding calendar year. The withholding agent must retain a copy of Form 1042 for the applicable statute of limitations on assessments and collection with respect to the amounts required to be reported on the Form 1042. See section 6501 and the regulations thereunder for the applicable statute of limitations. Adjustments to the total amount of tax withheld, as described in § 1.1461-2, shall be stated on the return as prescribed by the form and accompanying instructions.

(2) Amended returns. An amended return may be filed on a Form 1042 or such other form as the IRS may prescribe. An amended return must include such information as the form or accompanying instructions shall require, including, with respect to any information that has changed from the time of the filing of the return, the information that was shown on the original return and the corrected information.

(c) **Information returns.** *(1) Filing requirement.* (i) In general. A withholding agent (other than an individual who is not acting in the course of a trade or business with respect to a payment) must make an information return on Form 1042-S (or such other form as the IRS may prescribe) to report the amounts subject to reporting, as defined in paragraph (c)(2) of this section, that were paid during the preceding calendar year. Notwithstanding the preceding sentence, any person that withholds or is required to withhold an amount under sections 1441, 1442, 1443, or § 1.1446-4(a) (applicable to publicly traded partnerships required to pay tax under section 1446 on distributions) must file a Form 1042-S, "Foreign Person's U.S. Source Income Subject to Withholding," for the payment withheld upon whether or not that person is engaged in a trade or business and whether or not the payment is an amount subject to reporting. The reference in the previous sentence to withholding under § 1.1446-4 shall apply to partnership taxable years beginning after May 18, 2005, or such earlier time as the regulations under §§ 1.1446-1 through 1.1446-5 apply by reason of an election under § 1.1446-7. A Form 1042-S shall be prepared for each recipient of an amount subject to reporting. The Form 1042-S shall be prepared in such manner as the form and accompanying instructions prescribe. One copy of the Form 1042-S shall be filed with the IRS on or before March 15 of the calendar year following the year in which the amount subject to reporting was paid. It shall be filed with a transmittal form as provided in the instructions to the Form 1042-S and to the transmittal form. Withholding certificates, documentary evidence, or other statements or documentation provided to a withholding agent are not required to be attached to the form. Another copy of the Form 1042-S must be furnished to the recipient for whom the form is prepared (or any other person, as required under this paragraph (c) or the instructions to the form) on or before March 15 of the calendar year following the year in which the amount subject to reporting was paid. The withholding agent must retain a copy of each Form 1042-S for the statute of limitations on assessment and collection applicable to the Form 1042 to which the Form 1042-S relates.

(ii) Recipient. (A) Defined. For purposes of this section, the term recipient means—

(1) A beneficial owner as defined in § 1.1441-1 (c)(6), including a foreign estate or a foreign complex trust, as defined in § 1.1441-1(c)(25);

(2) A qualified intermediary as defined in § 1.1441-1(e)(5)(ii);

(3) A withholding foreign partnership as defined in § 1.1441-5(c)(2) or a withholding foreign trust under § 1.1441-5(e)(5)(v);

(4) An authorized foreign agent as defined in § 1.1441-7(c);

(5) A U.S. branch that is treated as a U.S. person under § 1.1441-1(b)(2)(iv)(A);

(6) A nonwithholding foreign partnership or a foreign simple trust as defined in § 1.1441-1(c)(24), but only to the extent the income is (or is treated as) effectively connected with the conduct of a trade or business in the United States by such entity;

(7) A payee, as defined in § 1.1441-1(b)(2) that is presumed to be a foreign person under the presumption rules of § 1.1441-1(b)(3); 1.1441-5(d) or (e)(6), or 1.6049-5(d); and

(8) A partner receiving a distribution from a publicly traded partnership subject to withholding under section 1446 and § 1.1446-4 on distributions of effectively connected income. This paragraph (c)(1)(ii)(A)(8) shall apply to partnership taxable years beginning after May 18, 2005, or such earlier time as the regulations under §§ 1.1446-1 through 1.1446-5 apply by reason of an election under § 1.1446-7.

(9) Any other person as required on Form 1042-S or the instructions to the form.

(B) Persons that are not recipients. A recipient does not include—

(1) A nonqualified intermediary;

(2) A payment to a wholly-owned entity that is disregarded under § 301.7701-2(c)(2) of this chapter as an entity separate from its owner;

(3) A flow-through entity, as defined in § 1.1441-1(c)(23) (to the extent it is receiving amounts subject to reporting other than income effectively connected with the conduct of a trade or business in the United States); and

(4) A U.S. branch described in § 1.1441-1(b)(2)(iv) that is not treated as a U.S. person under that section.

(2) Amounts subject to reporting. (i) In general. Subject to the exceptions described in paragraph (c)(2)(ii) of this section, amounts subject to reporting on Form 1042-S are amounts paid to a foreign payee or partner (including persons presumed to be foreign) that are amounts subject to withholding as defined in § 1.1441-2(a) or § 1.1446-4(a) (addressing publicly traded partnerships required to pay withholding tax under section 1446 on distributions of effectively connected income). The reference in the previous sentence to withholding under § 1.1446-4 shall apply to partnership taxable years beginning after May 18, 2005, or such earlier time as the regulations under §§ 1.1446-1 through 1.1446-5 apply by reason of an election under § 1.1446-7. Amounts subject to reporting include amounts subject to withholding even if no amount is deducted and withheld from the payment because of a treaty or Internal Revenue Code exception to taxation or because an amount withheld was reimbursed to the payee under the adjustment procedures of § 1.1461-2. In addition, amounts subject to reporting include any amounts paid to a foreign payee on which a withholding agent withheld an amount (either under chapter 3 of the Internal Revenue Code or section 3406) whether or not the amount is subject to withholding. Amounts subject to reporting include, but are not limited to, the following items—

(A) The entire amount of a corporate distribution (whether actual or deemed) irrespective of any estimate of the portion of the distribution that represents a taxable dividend;

(B) Interest, including the portion of a notional principal contract payment that is characterized as interest. Interest shall also be reported on Form 1042-S if it is bank deposit interest paid to nonresident alien individuals as required under § 1.6049-8;

(C) Rents;

(D) Royalties;

(E) Compensation for dependent and independent personal services performed in the United States;

(F) Annuities;

(G) Pension distributions and other deferred income;

(H) Gambling winnings that are not exempt from tax under section 871(j);

(I) Income from the cancellation of indebtedness unless the withholding agent is unrelated to the debtor and does not have knowledge of the facts that give rise to the payment (see § 1.1441-2(d));

(J) Amounts that are (or are presumed to be) effectively connected with the conduct of a trade or business in the United States (including deposit interest as defined in sections 871(i)(2)(A) and 881(d)) even if no withholding certificate is required to be furnished by the payee or beneficial owner. In the case of amounts paid on a notional principal contract described in § 1.1441-4(a)(3) that are presumed to be effectively connected with the conduct of a trade or business in the United States, the amount required to be reported is limited to the amount of cash paid from the notional principal contract;

(K) Scholarship, fellowship, or grant income and compensation for personal services that is not excludible from gross income under section 117 (whether or not the taxable scholarship, fellowship, grant income, or compensation for personal services is exempt from tax under an income tax treaty) paid to foreign students, trainees, teachers, or researchers;

(L) Amounts paid to foreign governments, international organizations, or the Bank for International Settlements, whether or not documentation must be provided; and

(M) Original issue discount paid on the redemption of an OID obligation. The amount to be reported is the amount of OID includible in the gross income of the holder of the obligation, if known, or, if not known, the total amount of original issue discount determined as if the holder held the obligation from its original issuance. A withholding agent may determine the total amount of OID by using the most recently published "List of Original Issue Discount Instruments," (Publication 1212, available from the IRS Forms Distribution Centers).

(ii) Exceptions to reporting. The amounts listed in this paragraph (c)(2)(ii) are not required to be reported on Form 1042-S—

(A) Interest (including original issue discount) that is deposit interest under sections 871(i)(2)(A) and 881(d) and that is not effectively connected with the conduct of a trade or business in the United States, unless reporting is required under § 1.6049-8 (regarding payments to certain foreign residents) or is interest that is effectively connected with the conduct of a trade or business in the United States;

(B) Interest or original issue discount on certain short-term obligations, described in section 871(g)(1)(B) or 881(a)(3);

(C) Interest paid on obligations sold between interest payment dates and the portion of the purchase price of an OID obligation that is sold or exchanged in a transaction other than a redemption, unless the sale or exchange is part of a plan, the principal purpose of which is to avoid tax and the withholding agent has actual knowledge or reason to know of such plan (see § 1.1441-2(a)(5) and (6));

(D) Any item required to be reported on a Form W-2, including an item required to be shown on Form W-2 solely by reason of § 1.6041-2 (relating to return of information for payments to employees) or § 1.6052-1 (relating to information regarding payment of wages in the form of group-term life insurance);

(E) Any item required to be reported on Form 1099, and such other forms as are prescribed pursuant to the information reporting provisions of sections 6041 through 6050P and the regulations under those sections;

(F) Amounts paid on a notional principal contract described in § 1.1441-4(a)(3)(i) that are not effectively connected with the conduct of a trade or business in the United States (or not treated as effectively connected pursuant to § 1.1441-4(a)(3)(ii));

(G) Amounts required to be reported on Form 8288 (U.S. Withholding Tax Return for Dispositions by Foreign Persons of U.S. Real Property Interests) or Form 8804 (Annual Return for Partnership Withholding Tax (section 1446)). A withholding agent that must report a distribution partly on a Form 8288 or 8804 and partly on a Form 1042-S may elect to report the entire amount on a Form 8288 or 8804;

(H) Interest (including original issue discount) paid with respect to foreign-targeted registered obligations described in § 1.871-14(e)(2) to the extent the documentation requirements described in § 1.871-14(e)(3) and (4) are required to be satisfied (taking into account the provisions of § 1.871-14(e)(4)(ii), if applicable;

(I) Interest on a foreign targeted bearer obligation (see § 1.1441-1(b)(4)(i) and 1.1441-2(a));

(J) Gain described in section 301(c)(3); and

(K) Amounts described in § 1.1441-1(b)(4)(xviii) (dealing with certain amounts paid by the U.S. government).

(3) Required information. The information required to be furnished under this paragraph (c)(3) shall be based upon the information provided by or on behalf of the recipient of an amount subject to reporting (as corrected and supplemented based on the withholding agent's actual knowledge) or the presumption rules of §§ 1.1441-1(b)(3), 1.1441-4(a), 1.1441-5(d) and (e), 1.1441-9(b)(3), 1.1446-1(c)(3) (as applied to publicly traded partnerships required to pay tax under section 1446 on distributions of effectively connected income) or 1.6049-5(d). The reference in the previous sentence to presumption rules applicable to withholding under section 1446 shall apply to partnership taxable years beginning after May 18, 2005, or such earlier time as the regulations under §§ 1.1446-1 through 1.1446-5 apply by reason of an election under § 1.1446-7. The Form 1042-S must include the following information, if applicable—

(i) The name, address, and taxpayer identifying number of the withholding agent;

(ii) A description of each category of income paid based on the income codes provided on the form (e.g., interest, dividends, royalties, etc.) and the aggregate amount in each category expressed in U.S. dollars;

(iii) The rate of withholding applied or the basis for exempting the payment from withholding (based on exemption codes provided on the form);

(iv) The name and address of the recipient;

(v) The name and address of any nonqualified intermediary, flow-through entity, or U.S. branch as described in § 1.1441-1(b)(2)(iv) (other than a branch that is treated as a U.S. person) to which the payment was made;

(vi) The taxpayer identifying number of the recipient if required under § 1.1441-1(e)(4)(vii) or if actually known to the withholding agent making the return;

(vii) The taxpayer identifying number of a nonqualified intermediary or flow-through entity (to the extent it is not a recipient) or other flow-through entity to the extent it is known to the withholding agent;

(viii) The country (based on the country codes provided on the form) of the recipient and of any nonqualified intermediary or flow-through entity the name of which appears on the form; and

(ix) Such information as the form or the instructions may require in addition to, or in lieu of, information required under this paragraph (c)(3).

(4) Method of reporting. (i) Payments by U.S. withholding agents to recipients. A withholding agent that is a U.S. person (other than a foreign branch of a U.S. person that is a qualified intermediary as defined in § 1.1441-1(e)(5)(ii)) and that makes payments of amounts subject to reporting on Form 1042-S must file a separate Form 1042-S for each recipient who receives such amount. For purposes of this paragraph (c)(4), a U.S. person includes a U.S. branch described in § 1.1441-1(e)(2)(iv)(A) or (E) that agrees to be treated as a U.S. person. Except as may otherwise be required on Form 1042-S or the instructions to the form, only payments for which the income code, exemption code, withholding rate and recipient code are the same may be reported on a single Form 1042-S. See paragraph (c)(4)(ii) of this section for reporting of payments made to a person that is not a recipient.

(A) Payments to beneficial owners. If a U.S. withholding agent makes a payment directly to a beneficial owner it must complete Form 1042-S treating the beneficial owner as the recipient. Under the grace period rule of § 1.1441-1(b)(3)(iv), a U.S. withholding agent may, under certain circumstances, treat a payee as a foreign person while the withholding agent awaits a valid withholding certificate. A U.S. withholding agent who relies on the grace period rule to treat a payee as a foreign person must file a Form 1042-S to report all payments on Form 1042-S during the period that person was presumed to be foreign even if that person is later determined to be a U.S. person based on appropriate documentation or is presumed to be a U.S. person after the grace period ends. In the case of joint owners, a withholding agent may provide a single Form 1042-S made out to the owner whose status the U.S. withholding agent relied upon to determine the applicable rate of withholding. If, however, any one of the owners requests its own Form 1042-S, the withholding agent must furnish a Form 1042-S to the person who requests it. If more than one Form 1042-S is issued for a single payment, the aggregate amount paid and tax withheld that is reported on all Forms 1042-S cannot exceed the total amounts paid to joint owners and the tax withheld thereon.

(B) Payments to a qualified intermediary, a withholding foreign partnership, or a withholding foreign trust. A U.S. withholding agent that makes payments to a qualified intermediary (whether or not the qualified intermediary assumes primary withholding responsibility), a withholding foreign partnership, or a withholding foreign trust shall complete Forms 1042-S treating the qualified intermediary or withholding foreign partnership as the recipient. The U.S. withholding agent must complete a separate Form 1042-S for each withholding rate pool. A withholding rate pool is a payment of a single type of income (determined by the income codes on Form 1042-S) that is subject to a single rate of withholding. A qualified intermediary that does not assume primary withholding responsibility on all payments it receives provides information regarding the proportions of income subject to a particular withholding rate to the withholding agent on a withholding statement associated with a qualified intermediary withholding certificate. A qualified intermediary may provide a U.S. withholding agent with information regarding withholding rate pools for U.S. non-exempt recipients (as defined under § 1.1441-1(c)(21)). Amounts paid with respect to such withholding rate pools must be reported on Form 1099 completed for each U.S. non-exempt recipient to the extent they are subject to Form 1099 reporting. These amounts must not be reported on Form 1042-S. In addition, the qualified intermediary may provide the U.S. withholding agent information regarding withholding rate pools for U.S. persons that are exempt recipients as defined under § 1.1441-1(c)(20). If such information is provided, a U.S. withholding agent should not report such withholding rate pools on Form 1042-S.

(C) Amounts paid to U.S. branches treated as U.S. persons. A U.S. withholding agent making a payment to a U.S. branch of a foreign person described in § 1.1441-1(b)(2)(iv) shall complete Form 1042-S as follows—

(1) If the branch has provided the U.S. withholding agent with a withholding certificate that evidences its agreement with the withholding agent to be treated as a U.S. person, the U.S. withholding agent files Forms 1042-S treating the U.S. branch as the recipient;

(2) If the branch has provided the U.S. withholding agent with a withholding certificate that transmits information regarding beneficial owners, qualified intermediaries, withholding foreign partnerships, or other recipients, the U.S. withholding agent must complete a separate Form 1042-S for each recipient whose documentation is associated with the U.S. branch's withholding certificate; or

(3) If the U.S. withholding agent cannot reliably associate a payment with a valid withholding certificate from the U.S. branch, it shall treat the U.S. branch as the recipient and report the income as effectively connected with the conduct of a trade or business in the United States.

(D) Amounts paid to an authorized foreign agent. If a U.S. withholding agent makes a payment to an authorized foreign agent, the withholding agent files Forms 1042-S treating the authorized foreign agent as the recipient, provided that the authorized foreign agent reports the payments on Forms 1042-S to each recipient to which it makes payments. If the authorized foreign agent fails to report the amounts paid on Forms 1042-S for each recipient to which the payment is made, the U.S. withholding agent remains responsible for such reporting.

(E) Dual Claims. A U.S. withholding agent may make a payment to a foreign entity that is simultaneously claiming a reduced rate of tax on its own behalf for a portion of the payment and a reduced rate on behalf of persons in their capacity as interest holders in that entity on the remaining portion. See § 1.1441-6(b)(2)(iii). If the claims are consistent and the withholding agent accepts the multiple claims, the withholding agent must file a separate Form 1042-S for those payments for which the entity is treated as the beneficial owner and Forms 1042-S for each of the interest holder in the entity for which the interest holder is treated as the recipient. For those payments for which the interest holder in an entity is treated as the recipient, the U.S. withholding agent shall prepare the Form 1042-S in the same manner as a payment made to a nonqualified intermediary or flow-through entity as set forth in paragraph (c)(4)(ii) of this section. If the claims are consistent but the withholding agent has not chosen to accept the multiple claims, or if the claims are inconsistent, the withholding agent must file a separate Form 1042-S for the person or persons it has chosen to treat as the recipients.

(ii) Payments made by U.S. withholding agents to persons that are not recipients.

(A) Amounts paid to a nonqualified intermediary, a flow-through entity, and certain U.S. branches. If a U.S. withholding agent makes a payment to a nonqualified intermediary, a flow-through entity, or a U.S. branch described in § 1.1441-1(b)(2)(iv) (other than a branch that agrees to be treated as a U.S. person), it must complete a separate Form 1042-S for each recipient to the extent the withholding agent can reliably associate a payment with valid documentation (within the meaning of § 1.1441-1(b)(2)(vii)) from the recipient which is associated with the withholding certificate provided by the nonqualified intermediary, flow-through entity, or U.S. branch. If a payment is made through tiers of nonqualified intermediaries or flow-through entities, the withholding agent must nevertheless complete Form 1042-S for the recipients to the extent it can reliably associate the payment with documentation from the recipients. A withholding agent that is completing a Form 1042-S for a recipient that receives a payment through a nonqualified intermediary, a flow-through entity, or a U.S. branch must include on the Form 1042-S the name of the nonqualified intermediary or flow-through entity from which the recipient directly receives the payment. If a U.S. withholding agent cannot reliably associate the payment, or any portion of the payment, with valid documentation from a recipient either because no such documentation has been provided or because the nonqualified intermediary, flow-through entity, or U.S. branch has failed to provide sufficient allocation information so that the withholding agent can associate the payment, or any portion thereof, with valid documentation, then the withholding agent must report the payments as made to an unknown recipient in accordance with the appropriate presumption rules for that payment. Thus, if under the presumption rules the payment is presumed to be made to a foreign person, the withholding agent must generally withhold 30 percent of the payment and report the payment on Form 1042-S made out to an unknown recipient and shall also include the name of the nonqualified intermediary or flow-through entity that received the payment on behalf of the unknown recipient. If, however, the recipient is presumed to be a U.S. non-exempt recipient (as defined in § 1.1441-1(c)(21)), the withholding agent must withhold on the payment as required under section 3406 and report the payment as made to an unknown recipient on the appropriate Form 1099 as required under chapter 61 of the Internal Revenue Code.

(B) Disregarded entities. If a U.S. withholding agent makes a payment to a disregarded entity but receives a valid withholding certificate or other documentary evidence from a foreign person that is the single owner of a disregarded entity, the withholding agent must file a Form 1042-S treating the foreign single owner as the recipient. The taxpayer identifying number on the Form 1042-S, if required, must be the foreign single owner's TIN.

(iii) Reporting by qualified intermediaries, withholding foreign partnerships, and withholding foreign trusts. A qualified intermediary, a withholding foreign partnership, and a withholding foreign trust shall report payments on Form 1042-S as provided in their agreements with the IRS and the instructions to the form.

(iv) Reporting by a nonqualified intermediary, flow-through entity, and certain U.S. branches. A nonqualified intermediary, flow-through entity, or U.S. branch described in § 1.1441-1(e)(2)(iv) (other than a U.S. branch that is treated as a U.S. person) is a withholding agent and must file Forms 1042-S for amounts paid to recipients in the same manner as a U.S. withholding agent. A Form 1042-S will not be required, however, if another withholding agent has reported the same amount to the same recipient for which the nonqualified intermediary, flow-through entity, or U.S. branch would be required to file a return and the entire amount that should be withheld from such payment has been withheld. A nonqualified intermediary, flow-through entity, or U.S. branch must report payments made to recipients to the extent it has failed to provide the appropriate documentation to another withholding agent together with the information required for that withholding agent to reliably associate the payment with the recipient documentation or to the extent it knows, or has reason to know, that less than the required amount has been withheld. A nonqualified intermediary or flow-through entity that is required to report a payment on Form 1042-S must follow the same rules as apply to a U.S. withholding agent under paragraph (c)(4)(i) and (ii) of this section.

(v) Pro rata reporting for allocation failures. If a nonqualified intermediary, flow-through entity, or U.S. branch described in § 1.1441-1(b)(2)(iv) (other than a branch treated as a U.S. person) that uses the alternative procedures of § 1.1441-1(e)(3)(iv)(D) fails to provide information sufficient to allocate the amount subject to reporting paid to a withholding rate pool to the payees identified for that pool, then the withholding agent shall report the payment in accordance with the rule provided in § 1.1441-1(e)(3)(iv)(D)(6).

(vi) Other withholding agents. Any person that is a withholding agent not described in paragraph (c)(4)(i), (iii), or (iv) of this section (e.g., a foreign person that is not a qualified intermediary, flow-through entity, or U.S. branch) shall file Form 1042-S in the same manner as a U.S. withholding agent and in accordance with the instructions to the form.

(5) Magnetic media reporting. A withholding agent that makes 250 or more Form 1042-S information returns for a taxable year must file Form 1042-S returns on magnetic media. See § 301.6011-2 of this chapter for requirements applicable to a withholding agent that files Forms 1042-S with the IRS on magnetic media and publications of the IRS relating to magnetic media filing.

(d) Report of taxpayer identifying numbers. When so required under procedures that the IRS may prescribe in published guidance (see § 601.601(d)(2) of this chapter), a withholding agent must attach to the Form 1042 a list of all the taxpayer identifying numbers (and corresponding names) that have been furnished to the withholding agent and upon which the withholding agent has relied to grant a reduced rate of withholding and that are not otherwise required to be reported on a Form 1042-S under the provisions of this section.

(e) Indemnification of withholding agent. A withholding agent is indemnified against the claims and demands of any person for the amount of any tax it deducts and withholds in accordance with the provisions of chapter 3 of the Code and the regulations under that chapter. A withholding agent that withholds based on a reasonable belief that such withholding is required under chapter 3 of the Code and the regulations under that chapter is treated for purposes of section 1461 and this paragraph (e) as having withheld tax in accordance with the provisions of chapter 3 of the Code and the regulations under that chapter. In addition, a withholding agent is indemnified against the claims and demands of any person for the amount of any payments made in accordance with the grace period provisions set forth in § 1.1441-1(b)(3)(iv). This paragraph (e) does not apply to relieve a withholding agent from tax liability under chapter 3 of the Code or the regulations under that chapter.

(f) Amounts paid not constituting gross income. Any amount withheld in accordance with § 1.1441-3 shall be reported and paid in accordance with this section, even though the amount paid to the beneficial owner may not constitute gross income in whole or in part. For this purpose, a reference in this section and § 1.1461-2 to an amount shall, where appropriate, be deemed to refer to the amount subject to withholding under § 1.1441-3.

(g) Extensions of time to file Forms 1042 and 1042-S. The IRS may grant an extension of time in which to file a Form 1042 or a Form 1042-S. Form 2758, Application for Extension of Time to File Certain Excise, Income, Information, and Other Returns (or such other form as the IRS may prescribe), must be used to request an extension of time for a Form 1042. Form 8809, Request for Extension of Time to File Information Returns (or such other form as the IRS may prescribe) must be used to request an extension of time for a Form 1042-S. The request must contain a statement of the reasons for requesting the extension and such other information as the forms or instructions may require. It must be mailed or delivered not later than March 15 of the year following the end of the calendar year for which the return will be filed.

(h) Penalties. For penalties and additions to the tax for failure to file returns or furnish statements in accordance with this section, see sections 6651, 6662, 6663, 6721, 6722, 6723, 6724(c), 7201, 7203, and the regulations under those sections.

(i) Effective date. Unless otherwise provided in this section, this section shall apply to returns required for payments made after December 31, 2000.

T.D. 6187, 7/5/56, amend T.D. 6213, 11/20/56, T.D. 6908, 12/30/66, T.D. 7157, 12/29/71, T.D. 7977, 9/19/84, T.D. 8734, 10/6/97, T.D. 8804, 12/30/98, T.D. 8856, 12/29/99, T.D. 8881, 5/15/2000, T.D. 8952, 6/25/2001, T.D. 9200, 5/13/2005.

§ 1.1461-2 Adjustments for overwithholding or underwithholding of tax.

(a) Adjustments of overwithheld tax. *(1) In general.* Except for partnerships or nominees required to withhold under section 1446, a withholding agent that has overwithheld under chapter 3 of the Internal Revenue Code, and made a deposit of the tax as provided in § 1.6302-2(a) may adjust the overwithheld amount either pursuant to the reimbursement procedure described in paragraph (a)(2) of this section or pursuant to the set-off procedure described in paragraph (a)(3) of this section. References in the previous sentence excepting from this section certain partnerships withholding under section 1446 shall apply to partnership taxable years beginning after May 18, 2005, or such earlier time as the regulations under §§ 1.1446-1 through 1.1446-5 apply by reason of an election under § 1.1446-7. Adjustments under this paragraph (a) may only be made within the time prescribed under paragraph (a)(2) or (3) of this section. After such time, a refund of the amount overwithheld can only be claimed by the beneficial owner with the Internal Revenue Service (IRS) pursuant to the procedures described in chapter 65 of the Code. For purposes of this section, the term overwithholding means any amount actually withheld (determined before application of the adjustment procedures under this section) from an item of income pursuant to chapter 3 of the Code or the regulations thereunder in excess of the actual tax liability due, regardless of whether such overwithholding was in error or appeared correct at the time it occurred.

(2) Reimbursement of tax. (i) General rule. Under the reimbursement procedure, the withholding agent repays the beneficial owner or payee for the amount overwithheld. In such a case, the withholding agent may reimburse itself by reducing, by the amount of tax actually repaid to the beneficial owner or payee, the amount of any deposit of tax made by the withholding agent under § 1.6302-2(a)(1)(iii) for any subsequent payment period occurring before the end of the calendar year following the calendar year of overwithholding. Any such reduction that occurs for a payment period in the calendar year following the calendar year of overwithholding shall be allowed only if—

(A) The withholding agent states, on a timely filed (not including extensions) Form 1042-S for the calendar year of overwithholding, the amount of tax withheld and the amount of any actual repayment; and

(B) The withholding agent states on a timely filed (not including extensions) Form 1042 for the calendar year of overwithholding, that the filing of the Form 1042 constitutes a claim for credit in accordance with § 1.6414-1.

(ii) Record maintenance. If the beneficial owner is repaid an amount of withholding tax under the provisions of this paragraph (a)(2), the withholding agent shall keep as part of its records a receipt showing the date and amount of repayment and the withholding agent must provide a copy of such receipt to the beneficial owner. For this purpose, a canceled check or an entry in a statement is sufficient provided that the check or statement contains a specific notation that it is a refund of tax overwithheld.

(3) Set-offs. Under the set-off procedure, the withholding agent may repay the beneficial owner or payee by applying the amount overwithheld against any amount which otherwise would be required under chapter 3 of the Code or the regulations thereunder to be withheld from income paid by the withholding agent to such person before the earlier of the due date (without regard to extensions) for filing the Form 1042-S for the calendar year of overwithholding or the date that the Form 1042-S is actually filed with the IRS. For purposes of making a return on Form 1042 or 1042-S (or an amended form) for the calendar year of overwithholding and for purposes of making a deposit of the amount withheld, the reduced amount shall be considered the amount required to be withheld from such income under chapter 3 of the Code and the regulations thereunder.

(4) Examples. The principles of this paragraph (a) are illustrated by the following examples:

Example (1). (i) N is a nonresident alien individual who is a resident of the United Kingdom. In December 2001, a domestic corporation C pays a dividend of $100 to N, at which time C withholds $30 and remits the balance of $70 to N. On February 10, 2002, prior to the time that C files its Form 1042, N furnishes a valid Form W-8 described in § 1.1441-1(e)(2)(i) upon which C may rely to reduce the rate of withholding to 15 percent under the provisions of the U.S.-U.K. tax treaty. Consequently, N advises C that its tax liability is only $15 and not $30 and requests reimbursement of $15. Although C has already deposited the $30 that was withheld, as required by § 1.6302-2(a)(1)(iv), C repays N in the amount of $15.

(ii) During 2001, C makes no other payments upon which tax is required to be withheld under chapter 3 of the Code; accordingly, its return on Form 1042 for such year, which is filed on March 15, 2002, shows total tax withheld of $30, an adjusted total tax withheld of $15, and $30 previously paid for such year. Pursuant to § 1.6414-1(b), C claims a credit for the overpayment of $15 shown on the Form 1042 for 2002. Accordingly, it is permitted to reduce by $15 any deposit required by § 1.6302-2 to be made of tax withheld during the calendar year 2001. The Form 1042-S required to be filed by C with respect to the dividend of $100 paid to N in 2001 is required to show tax withheld of $30 and tax released of $15.

Example (2). The facts are the same as in Example 1. In addition, during 2002, C makes payments to N upon which it is required to withhold $200 under chapter 3 of the Code, all of which is withheld in June 2002. Pursuant to § 1.6302-2(a)(1)(iii), C deposits the amount of $185 on July 15, 2002 ($200 less the $15 for which credit is claimed on the Form 1042 for 2001). On March 15, 2003, C Corporation files its return on Form 1042 for calendar year 2002, which shows total tax withheld of $200, $185 previously deposited by C, and $15 allowable credit.

Example (3). The facts are the same as in *Example 1.* Under § 1.6032-2(a)(1)(ii)), C is required to deposit on a quarter-monthly basis the tax withheld under chapter 3 of the Code. C withholds tax of $100 between February 8 and February 15, 2000, and deposits $75 [($100 × 90 percent) less $15] of the withheld tax within 3 banking days after February 15, 2002, and by depositing $10 [($100 – $15) less $75] within 3 banking days after March 15, 2002.

(b) Withholding of additional tax when underwithholding occurs. A withholding agent may withhold from future payments (or distributions of effectively connected income under section 1446) made to a beneficial owner the tax that should have been withheld from previous payments (or distributions subject to section 1446) to such beneficial owner under chapter 3 of the Internal Revenue Code. In the alternative, the withholding agent may satisfy the tax from property that it holds in custody for the beneficial owner or property over which it has control. Such additional withholding or satisfaction of the tax owed may only be made before the date that the Form 1042 is required to be filed (not including extensions) for the calendar year in which the underwithholding occurred. See § 1.6302-2 for making deposits of tax or § 1.1461-1(a) for making payment of the balance due for a calendar year. See also §§ 1.1461-1, 1.1461-3, and 1.1446-1 through 1.1446-7 for rules relating to withholding under section 1446. References in this paragraph (b) to withholding under section 1446 shall apply to partnership taxable years beginning after May 18, 2005, or such earlier time as the regulations under §§ 1.1446-1 through 1.1446-5 apply by reason of an election under § 1.1446-7.

(c) Definition. For purposes of this section, the term *payment period* means the period for which the withholding agent is required by § 1.6302-2(a)(1) to make a deposit of tax withheld under chapter 3 of the Code.

(d) Effective date. Unless otherwise provided in this section, this section applies to payments made after December 31, 2000.

T.D. 6213, 11/20/56, amend T.D. 6922, 6/16/67, T.D. 7157, 12/29/71, T.D. 7284, 8/2/73, T.D. 7977, 9/19/84, T.D. 8734, 10/6/97, T.D. 8804, 12/30/98, T.D. 8856, 12/29/99, T.D. 9200, 5/13/2005.

§ 1.1461-3 Withholding under section 1446.

For rules relating to the withholding tax liability of a partnership or nominee under section 1446, see §§ 1.1446-1 through 1.1446-7. For interest, penalties, and additions to the tax for failure to timely pay the tax required to be paid under section 1446, see sections 6601, 6651, 6655 (in the case of publicly traded partnerships, see section 6656), 6672, and 7202 and the regulations under those sections. For additional penalties and additions to the tax for failure to comply with the regulations under section 1446, see sections 6651, 6662, 6663, 6721, 6722, 6723, 6724(c), 7201, 7203, and the regulations under those sections. This section shall apply to partnership taxable years beginning after May 18, 2005, or such earlier time as the regulations under §§ 1.1446-1 through 1.1446-5 apply by reason of an election under § 1.1446-7.

T.D. 9200, 5/13/2005.

§ 1.1462-1 Withheld tax as credit to recipient of income.

(a) Creditable tax. The entire amount of the income from which the tax is required to be withheld (including amounts calculated under the gross-up formula in § 1.1441-3(f)(1)) shall be included in gross income in the return required to be made by the beneficial owner of the income, without deduction for the amount required to be or actually withheld, but the amount of tax actually withheld shall be allowed as a credit against the total income tax computed in the beneficial owner's return.

(b) Amounts paid to persons who are not the beneficial owner. Amounts withheld at source under chapter 3 of the Internal Revenue Code on payments to (or effectively connected taxable income allocable to) a fiduciary, partnership, or intermediary are deemed to have been paid by the taxpayer ultimately liable for the tax upon such income. Thus, for example, if a beneficiary of a trust is subject to the taxes imposed by section 1, 2, 3, or 11 upon any portion of the income received from a foreign trust, the part of any amount withheld at source which is properly allocable to the income so taxed to such beneficiary shall be credited against the amount of the income tax computed upon the beneficiary's return, and any excess shall be refunded. See § 1.1446-3 for examples applying this rule in the context of a partnership interest held by a foreign trust or estate. Further, if a partnership withholds an amount under chapter 3 of the Internal Revenue Code with respect to the allocable share of a partner that is a partnership (upper-tier partnership) or with respect to the allocable share of partners in an upper-tier partnership, such amount is deemed to have been withheld by the upper-tier partnership. See § 1.1446-5 for rules applicable to tiered partnership structures. References in this paragraph (b) to withholding under section 1446 shall apply to partnership taxable years beginning after May 18, 2005, or such earlier time as the regulations under §§ 1.1446-1 through 1.1446-5 apply by reason of an election under § 1.1446-7.

(c) Effective date. Unless otherwise provided in this section, this section applies to payments made after December 31, 2000.

T.D. 6187, 7/5/56, amend T.D. 7977, 9/19/84, T.D. 8734, 10/6/97, T.D. 8804, 12/30/98, T.D. 8856, 12/29/99, T.D. 9200, 5/13/2005.

§ 1.1463-1 Tax paid by recipient of income.

Caution: The Treasury has not yet amended Reg § 1.1463-1 to reflect changes made by P.L. 101-239.

(a) Tax paid. If the tax required to be withheld under chapter 3 of the Internal Revenue Code is paid by the beneficial owner of the income or by the withholding agent, it shall not be re-collected from the other, regardless of the original liability therefor. However, this section does not relieve the person that did not withhold tax from liability for interest or any penalties or additions to tax otherwise applicable. See § 1.1441-7(b) for additional applicable rules. See § 1.1446-3(e) and (f) for application of the rule of this paragraph (a), and for additional rules, where the withholding tax was required to be paid under section 1446. The previous sentence shall apply to partnership taxable years beginning after May 18, 2005, or such earlier time as the regulations under §§ 1.1446-1 through 1.1446-5 apply by reason of an election under § 1.1446-7.

(b) Effective date. Unless otherwise provided in this section, this section applies to failures to withhold occurring after December 31, 2000.

T.D. 6187, 7/5/56, amend T.D. 8734, 10/6/97, T.D. 8804, 12/30/98, T.D. 8856, 12/29/99, T.D. 9200, 5/13/2005.

§ 1.1464-1 Refunds and credits.

(a) In general. The refund or credit under chapter 65 of the Code of an overpayment of tax which has actually been withheld at the source under chapter 3 of the Code shall be made to the taxpayer from whose income the amount of such tax was in fact withheld. To the extent that the overpayment under chapter 3 was not in fact withheld at the source, but was paid, by the withholding agent the refund or credit under chapter 65 of the overpayment shall be made to the withholding agent. Thus, where a debtor corporation assumes liability pursuant to its tax-free covenant for the tax required to be withheld under chapter 3 upon interest and pays the tax in behalf of its bondholder, and it can be shown that the bondholder is not in fact liable for any tax, the overpayment of tax shall be credited or refunded to the withholding agent in accordance with chapter 65 since the tax was not actually deducted and withheld from the interest paid to the bondholder. In further illustration, where a withholding agent who is required by chapter 3 to withhold $300 tax from rents paid to a nonresident alien individual mistakenly withholds $320 and mistakenly pays $350 as internal revenue tax, the amount of $30 shall be credited or refunded to the withholding agent in accordance with chapter 65 and the amount of $20 shall be credited or refunded in accordance with such chapter to the person from whose income such amount has been withheld. With respect to section 1446, this section shall only apply to a publicly traded partnership described in § 1.1446-4.

(b) Tax repaid to payee. For purposes of this section and § 1.6414-1, any amount of tax withheld under chapter 3 of the Code, which, pursuant to paragraph (a)(1) of § 1.1461-2, is repaid by the withholding agent to the person from whose income such amount was erroneously withheld shall be considered as tax which, within the meaning of sections 1464 and 6414, was not actually withheld by the withholding agent.

(c) Effective/Applicability date. The last sentence in paragraph (a) of this section shall apply to partnership taxable years beginning after April 29, 2008.

T.D. 6187, 7/5/56, amend T.D. 6922, 6/16/67, T.D. 8804, 12/30/98, T.D. 9394, 4/28/2008.

§ 1.1491-1 Imposition of tax.

> ***Caution:*** The Treasury has not yet amended Reg § 1.1491-1 to reflect changes made by P.L. 105-34, P.L. 104-188, P.L. 95-600, P.L. 94-455.

Section 1491 imposes an excise tax upon transfers of stock or securities by a citizen or resident of the United States, or by a domestic corporation or partnership, or by a trust which is not a foreign trust, to a foreign corporation as paid-in surplus or as a contribution to capital, or to a foreign trust, or to a foreign partnership. The tax is in an amount equal to 27½ percent of the excess of (a) the value of the stock or securities so transferred over (b) its adjusted basis, as provided in section 1011, for determining gain in the hands of the transferor.

T.D. 6127, 3/17/55.

§ 1.1492-1 Nontaxable transfers.

> ***Caution:*** The Treasury has not yet amended Reg § 1.1492-1 to reflect changes made by P.L. 105-34, P.L. 98-369, P.L. 95-600, P.L. 94-455, P.L. 91-681.

(a) The tax imposed by section 1491 does not apply:

(1) If the transferee is an organization (other than an organization described in section 401(a)) exempt from income tax under the provisions of sections 501 to 504, inclusive; or

(2) If before the transfer it has been established to the satisfaction of the Commissioner that the transfer is not in pursuance of a plan having as one of its principal purposes the avoidance of Federal income taxes.

(b) Whether a transfer of stock or securities is in pursuance of a plan having as one of its principal purposes the avoidance of Federal income taxes is a question to be determined from the facts and circumstances of each particular case. In any such case where a transferor desires to establish that the transfer is not in pursuance of such a plan, a statement of the facts relating to the plan under which the transfer is to be made or was made, together with a copy of the plan if in writing, shall be forwarded to the Commissioner of Internal Revenue, Washington 25, D.C., for a ruling. This statement shall contain, or be verified by, a written declaration that it is made under the penalties of perjury. A letter notifying the transferor of the Commissioner's determination will be mailed to the transferor.

T.D. 6127, 3/17/55.

§ 1.1493-1 Definition of foreign trust.

> ***Caution:*** The Treasury has not yet amended Reg § 1.1493-1 to reflect changes made by P.L. 89-809.

For taxable years beginning before January 1, 1967, a trust is to be considered a "foreign trust" within the meaning of chapter 5 of the Code, if, assuming a subsequent sale by the trustee, outside the United States and for cash, of the property transferred to the trust, the profit, if any, from such sale (being income from sources without the United States under the provisions of part I (section 861 and following), subchapter N, chapter 1 of the Code), would not be included in the gross income of the trust under subtitle A of the Code. For taxable years beginning after December 31, 1966, the term "foreign trust," as used in chapter 5 of the Code, shall have the meaning prescribed by section 7701(a)(31).

T.D. 6127, 3/17/55, amend T.D. 7332, 12/20/74.

§ 1.1494-1 Returns; payment and collection of tax.

Caution: The Treasury has not yet amended Reg § 1.1494-1 to reflect changes made by P.L. 105-34, P.L. 104-188.

(a) Returns and payment. Every person making a transfer described in section 1491 shall make a return to the district director on the day on which the transfer is made and, unless the transfer is nontaxable under section 1492, pay the tax due on such transfer. This return, which shall contain or be verified by, a written declaration that it is made under the penalties of perjury, shall be made on Form 926 and shall be filed with the district director to whom the transferor's return of income is required to be made. The return shall set forth in detail the following information:

(1) Name and address of the transferor, and place of organization or creation, if a corporation, partnership, or trust.

(2) Name and address of transferee, and place of organization or creation, and whether the transferee is a foreign corporation, a foreign trust, or a foreign partnership. If the transferee is a foreign trust or a foreign partnership, the name and address of the fiduciary and each beneficiary, in the case of a trust, or of each partner, in the case of a partnership, must be shown.

(3) Description and amount of stock or securities transferred, the date of transfer, and a complete statement showing all the facts relating to the transfer, accompanied by a copy of the plan under which the transfer was made.

(4) The fair market value of the stock or securities transferred as of the date of transfer, and the adjusted basis provided in section 1011 for determining gain in the hands of the transferor.

(5) Whether the transfer was made in pursuance of a plan submitted to and approved by the Commissioner as not having as one of its principal purposes the avoidance of Federal income taxes. If the plan has been so approved, a copy of the Commissioner's letter approving the plan shall accompany the return.

(6) Such other information as may be required by the return form.

(b) Certificate. *(1)* If the transferee of the stock or securities, the transfer of which is reported in the return, is a foreign organization meeting the tests of exemption from income tax provided in part I (section 501 and following), subchapter F, chapter 1 of the Code, and the transferor on that account claims that no liability for tax is imposed by section 1491, such transferor must file with Form 926 a certificate establishing the exemption of the transferee under such part I. This certificate, which shall contain, or be verified by, a written declaration that it is made under the penalties of perjury, shall contain complete information showing the character of the transferee, the purpose for which it was organized, its actual activities, the source of its income and the disposition of such income, whether or not any of its income is credited to surplus or may inure to the benefit of any private shareholder or individual, and in general all facts relating to its operations which affect its right to exemption. To such certificate shall be attached a copy of the charter or articles of incorporation, the by-laws of the organization, and the latest financial statement showing the assets, liabilities, receipts, and disbursements of the organization.

(2) If the transferee is a foreign organization which has been held to be exempt from income tax under such part I (or corresponding provisions of prior law), a copy of the Commissioner's letter so holding shall be filed with Form 926 in lieu of the above certificate and attachments.

(c) Assessment and collection. The determination, assessment, and collection of the tax and the examination of returns and claims filed pursuant to chapter 5 of the Code will be made under such procedure as may be prescribed from time to time by the Commissioner.

T.D. 6127, 3/17/55.

§ 1.1494-2 Effective date.

Caution: The Treasury has not yet amended Reg § 1.1494-2 to reflect changes made by P.L. 105-34, P.L. 104-188.

Chapter 5 (section 1491 and following) of the Internal Revenue Code of 1954 and the regulations prescribed thereunder apply with respect to transfers occurring after December 31, 1954. (See section 7851(a)(1)(B).) Chapter 7 (section 1250 and following) of the Internal Revenue Code of 1939 and the regulations applicable thereto apply with respect to transfers occurring prior to January 1, 1955.

T.D. 6127, 3/17/55.

§ 1.1502-0 Effective dates.

(a) The regulations under section 1502 are applicable to taxable years beginning after December 31, 1965, except as otherwise provided therein.

(b) The provisions of § 1.1502-0A through 1.1502-3A, 1.1502-10A through 1.1502-19A, and 1.1502-30A through 1.1502-51A (as contained in the 26 CFR part 1 edition revised April 1, 1996) are applicable to taxable years beginning before January 1, 1966.

T.D. 6894, 9/7/66, amend T.D. 8677, 6/26/96.

§ 1.1502-1 Definitions.

(a) Group. The term "group" means an affiliated group of corporations as defined in section 1504. See § 1.1502-75(d) as to when a group remains in existence. Except as the context otherwise requires, references to a group are references to a consolidated group (as defined in paragraph (h) of this section).

(b) Member. The term *member* means a corporation (including the common parent) that is included in the group, or as the contest may require, a corporation that is included in a subgroup.

(c) Subsidiary. The term "subsidiary" means a corporation other than the common parent which is a member of such group.

(d) Consolidated return year. The term "consolidated return year" means a taxable year for which a consolidated return is filed or required to be filed by such group.

(e) Separate return year. The term "separate return year" means a taxable year of a corporation for which it files a separate return or for which it joins in the filing of a consolidated return by another group.

(f) Separate return limitation year. *(1) In general.* Except as provided in paragraphs (f)(2) and (3) of this section, the term *separate return limitation year* (or *SRLY*) means any separate return year of a member or of a predecessor of a member.

(2) Exceptions. The term *separate return limitation year* (or *SRLY*) does not include:

(i) A separate return year of the corporation which is the common parent for the consolidated return year to which the tax attribute is to be carried (except as provided in § 1.1502-75(d)(2)(ii) and subparagraph (3) of this paragraph),

(ii) A separate return year of any corporation which was a member of the group for each day of such year, or

(iii) A separate return year of a predecessor of any member if such predecessor was a member of the group for each day of such year,

provided that an election under section 1562(a) (relating to the privilege of elect multiple surtax exemptions) was never effective (or is no longer effective as a result of a termination of such election) for such year. An election under section 1562(a) which is effective for a taxable year beginning in 1963 and ending in 1964 shall be disregarded.

(3) Reverse acquisitions. In the event of an acquisition to which § 1.1502-75(d)(3) applies, all taxable years of the first corporation and of each of its subsidiaries ending on or before the date of the acquisition shall be treated as separate return limitation years, and the separate return years (if any) of the second corporation and each of its subsidiaries shall not be treated as separate return limitation years (unless they were so treated immediately before the acquisition). For example, if corporation P merges into corporation T, and the persons who were stockholders of P immediately before the merger, as a result of owning the stock of P, own more than 50 percent of the fair market value of the outstanding stock of T, then a loss incurred before the merger by T (even though it is the common parent), or by a subsidiary of T, is treated as having been incurred in a separate return limitation year. Conversely, a loss incurred before the merger by P, or by a subsidiary of P in a separate return year during all of which such subsidiary was a member of the group of which P was the common parent and for which section 1562 was not effective, is treated as having been incurred in a year which is not a separate return limitation year.

(4) Predecessor and successors. The term *predecessor* means a transferor or distributor of assets to a member (the successor) in a transaction—

(i) To which section 381(a) applies; or

(ii) That occurs on or after January 1, 1997, in which the successor's basis for the assets is determined, directly or indirectly, in whole or in part, by reference to the basis of the assets of the transferor or distributor, but in the case of a transaction that occurs before June 25, 1999, only if the amount by which basis differs from value, in the aggregate, is material. For a transaction that occurs before June 25, 1999, only one member may be considered a predecessor to or a successor of one other member.

(g) Consolidated return change of ownership. *(1) In general.* A consolidated return change of ownership occurs during any taxable year (referred to in this subparagraph as, the "year of change") of the corporation which is the common parent for the taxable year to which the tax attribute is to be carried, if, at the end of the year of change—

(i) Any one or more of the persons described in section 382(a)(2) own a percentage of the fair market value of the outstanding stock of such corporation which is more than 50 percentage points greater than such person or persons owned at—

(a) The beginning of such taxable year or,

(b) The beginning of the preceding taxable year and

(ii) The increase in percentage points at the end of such year is attributable to—

(a) A purchase (within the meaning of section 382(a)(4)) by such person or persons of such stock, the stock of another corporation owning stock in such corporation, or an interest in a partnership or trust owning stock in such corporation, or

(b) A decrease in the amount of such stock outstanding or the amount of stock outstanding of another corporation owning stock in such corporation, except a decrease resulting from a redemption to pay death taxes to which section 303 applies.

For purposes of subdivision (i)(a) and (b) of this subparagraph, the beginning of the taxable years specified therein shall be the beginning of such taxable years or October 1, 1965, whichever occurs later.

(2) Operating rules. For purposes of this paragraph—

(i) The term "stock" means all shares except nonvoting stock which is limited and preferred as to dividends, and

(ii) Section 318 (relating to constructive ownership of stock) shall apply in determining the ownership of stock, except that section 318(a)(2)(C) and (3)(C) shall be applied without regard to the 50-percent limitation contained therein.

(3) Old members. The term "old members" of a group means—

(i) Those corporations which were members of such group immediately preceding the first day of the taxable year in which the consolidated return change of ownership occurs, or

(ii) If the group was not in existence prior to the taxable year in which the consolidated return change of ownership occurs, the corporation which is the common parent for the taxable year to which the tax attribute is to be carried.

(4) Reverse acquisitions. If there has been a consolidated return change of ownership of a corporation under subparagraph (1) of this paragraph and the stock or assets of such corporation are subsequently acquired by another corporation in an acquisition to which § 1.1502-75(d)(3) applies so that the group of which the former corporation is the common parent is treated as continuing in existence, then the "old members", as defined in subparagraph (3) of this paragraph, of such group immediately before the acquisition shall continue to be treated as "old members" immediately after the acquisition. For example, assume that corporations P and S comprise group PS, and PS undergoes a consolidated return change of ownership. Subsequently, the stock of P, the common parent, is acquired by corporation T, the common parent of group TU, in an acquisition to which section 368(a)(1)(B) and § 1.1502-75(d)(3) apply. The PS group is treated as continuing in existence with T as the common parent. P and S continue to be treated as old members, as defined in subparagraph (3) of this paragraph.

(h) Consolidated group. The term "consolidated group" means a group filing (or required to file) consolidated returns for the tax year.

(i) [Reserved]

(j) Affiliated. Corporations are affiliated if they are members of a group with each other.

T.D. 6894, 9/7/66, amend T.D. 7246, 12/29/72, T.D. 8294, 3/9/90, T.D. 8319, 11/19/90, T.D. 8560, 8/12/94, T.D. 8677, 6/26/96, T.D. 8823, 6/25/99.

PAR. 3. Section 1.1502-1 is amended by reserving paragraph (i) and adding paragraph (j) to read as follows:

Proposed § 1.1502-1 Definitions. [*For Preamble, see ¶ 151,475*]

* * * * *

* * * * *

(i) [Reserved]

(j) Tax liability. Except as provided otherwise, references relating to the "tax liability" of a consolidated group are to the consolidated tax liability determined in accordance with § 1.1502-2. However, references in § 1.1552-1(a) through (f) (relating to the computation of earnings and profits) to the tax liability of a consolidated group are to the regular tax liability of the group, determined in accordance with section 26(b), reduced by the credits allowable under part IV of subchapter A of the Internal Revenue Code (other than the consolidated minimum tax credit under § 1.1502-55(h)). Similarly, references to a member's tax liability determined as if it had filed separate returns under § 1.1502-33(d), or the separate return tax liability of a member under § 1.1552-1(a)(3)(ii)(b), are to the regular tax liability of the member under section 26(b), reduced by the above-referenced credits.

§ 1.1502-2 Computation of tax liability.

The tax liability of a group for a consolidated return year shall be determined by adding together—

(a) The tax imposed by section 11 on the consolidated taxable income for such year (see § 1.1502-11 for the computation of consolidated taxable income);

(b) The tax imposed by section 541 on the consolidated undistributed personal holding company income;

(c) If paragraph (b) of this section does not apply, the aggregate of the taxes imposed by section 541 on the separate undistributed personal holding company income of the members which are personal holding companies;

(d) If paragraph (b) of this section does not apply, the tax imposed by section 531 on the consolidated accumulated taxable income (see § 1.1502-43);

(e) The tax imposed by section 594(a) in lieu of the taxes imposed by section 11 or 1201 on the taxable income of a life insurance department of the common parent of a group which is a mutual savings bank;

(f) The tax imposed by section 802(a) on consolidated life insurance company taxable income;

(g) The tax imposed by section 831(a) on the consolidated insurance company taxable income of the members which are subject to such tax;

(h) The tax imposed by section 1201, instead of the taxes computed under paragraphs (a) and (g) of this section, computed by reference to the net capital gain of the group (see § 1.1502-22) (or, for consolidated return years to which § 1.1502-22 does not apply, computed by reference to the excess of the consolidated net long-term capital gain over the consolidated net short-term capital loss (see § 1.1502-41A for the determination of the consolidated net long-term capital gain and the consolidated net short-term capital loss));

(i) [Reserved]

(j) The tax imposed by section 1333 on war loss recoveries; and

by allowing as a credit against such taxes the investment credit under section 38 (see § 1.1502-3), and the foreign tax credit under section 33 (see § 1.1502-4). For purposes of this section, the surtax exemption of the group for a consolidated return year is $25,000, or if a lesser amount is allowed under section 1561, such lesser amount. See § 1.1561-2(a)(2). For increase in tax due to the application of section 47, see § 1.1502-3(f). For amount of tax surcharge, see section 51 and § 1.1502-7.

T.D. 6894, 9/7/66, amend T.D. 7093, 3/12/71, T.D. 7937, 1/26/84, T.D. 8677, 6/26/96, T.D. 8823, 6/25/99.

PAR. 4. Section 1.1502-2 is revised to read as follows:

Proposed § 1.1502-2 Computation of consolidated tax liability. [*For Preamble, see ¶ 151,475*]

(a) Consolidated tax liability. The "consolidated tax liability" of a group is the excess of—

(1) The sum of—

(i) The consolidated regular tax liability of the group, computed in accordance with section 26(b);

(ii) The consolidated AMT, computed in accordance with § 1.1502-55;

(iii) The consolidated environmental tax, as defined in § 1.1552-1(h)(2); and

(iv) The consolidated additional taxes, as defined in paragraph (b) of this section; over

(2) The credits allowable under part IV of subchapter A of chapter 1 of the Internal Revenue Code.

(b) Consolidated additional taxes. For purposes of this section, the consolidated additional taxes of a group are the sum of—

(1) Any tax imposed by section 541 on the group or the members of the group;

(2) Any tax imposed by section 531 on the group or the members of the group (see § 1.1502-43); and

(3) The aggregate of the taxes specified in section 26(b)(2) imposed on members, other than the taxes imposed under section 55 (alternative minimum tax), section 59A (environmental tax), section 531 (accumulated earnings tax), and section 541 (personal holding company tax).

(c) Effective date. This section applies to any consolidated return year for which the due date of the income tax return (without regard to extensions) is on or after [the date that is sixty days after final regulations are filed with the FEDERAL REGISTER]. For prior years, see § 1.1502-2 (as contained in the 26 CFR edition revised as of April 1, 1992).

§ 1.1502-3 Consolidated tax credits.

> ***Caution:*** The Treasury has not yet amended Reg § 1.1502-3 to reflect changes made by P.L. 104-188, P.L. 96-613.

(a) Determination of amount of consolidated credit. *(1) In general.* The credit allowed by section 38 for a consolidated return year of a group shall be equal to the consolidated credit earned. The consolidated credit earned is equal to the aggregate of the credit earned (as determined under subparagraph (2) of this paragraph) by all members of the group for the consolidated return year.

(2) Determination of credit earned. The credit earned of a member is an amount equal to 7 percent of such member's qualified investment (determined under section 46(c)). For purposes of computing a member's qualified investment, the basis of property shall not include any gain or loss realized with respect to such property by another member in an intercompany transaction (as defined in § 1.1502-13(b)), whether or not such gain or loss is deferred. Thus, if section 38 property acquired in an intercompany transaction has a basis of $100 to the purchasing member, and if the selling

member has a $20 gain with respect to such property, the basis of such property for purposes of computing the purchaser's qualified investment is only $80. Such $80 basis shall also be used for purposes of applying section 47 to such property. See paragraph (f) of this section.

(3) Consolidated limitation based on amount of tax. (i) Notwithstanding the amount of the consolidated credit earned for the taxable year, the consolidated credit allowed by section 38 to the group for the consolidated return year is limited to—

(a) So much of the consolidated liability for tax as does not exceed $25,000, plus

(b) for taxable years ending on or before March 9, 1967, 25 percent of the consolidated liability for tax in excess of $25,000, or

(c) For taxable years ending after March 9, 1967, 50 percent of the consolidated liability for tax in excess of $25,000.

The $25,000 amount referred to in the preceding sentence shall be reduced by any part of such $25,000 amount apportioned under § 1.46-1 to component members of the controlled group (as defined in section 46(a)(5)) which do not join in the filing of the consolidated return. For further rules for computing the limitation based on amount of tax with respect to the suspension period (as defined in section 48(j)), see section 46(a)(2). The amount determined under this subparagraph is referred to in this section as the "consolidated limitation based on amount of tax."

(ii) If an organization to which section 593 applies or a cooperative organization described in section 1381(a) joins in the filing of the consolidated return, the $25,000 amount referred to in subdivision (i) of this subparagraph (reduced as provided in such subdivision) shall be apportioned equally amoung the members of the group filing the consolidated return. The amount so apportioned equally to any such organization shall then be decreased in accordance with the provisions of section 46(d). Finally, the sum of all such equal portions (as decreased under section 46(d)) of each member of the group shall be substituted for the $25,000 amount referred to in subdivision (i) of this subparagraph.

(4) Consolidated liability for tax. For purposes of subparagraph (3) of this paragraph, the consolidated liability for tax shall be the income tax imposed for the taxable year upon the group by chapter 1 of the Code, reduced by the consolidated foreign tax credit allowable under § 1.1502-4. The tax imposed by section 56 (relating to minimum tax for tax preferences), section 531 (relating to accumulated earnings tax), section 541 (relating to personal holding company tax), and any additional tax imposed by section 1351(d)(1) (relating to recoveries of foreign expropriation losses) shall not be considered tax imposed by chapter 1 of the Code. In addition, any increase in tax resulting from the application of section 47 (relating to certain dispositions, etc., of section 38 property) shall not be treated as tax imposed by chapter 1 for purposes of computing the consolidated liability for tax.

(b) Carryback and carryover of unused credits. *(1) Allowance of unused credit as consolidated carryback or carryover.* A group shall be allowed to add to the amount allowable as a credit under paragraph (a)(1) of this section for any consolidated return year an amount equal to the aggregate of the consolidated investment credit carryovers and carrybacks to such year. The consolidated investment credit carryovers and carrybacks to the taxable year shall consist of any consolidated unused credits of the group, plus any unused credits of members of the group arising in separate return years of such members, which may be carried over or back to the taxable year under the principles of section 46(b). However, such consolidated carryovers and carrybacks shall not include any consolidated unused credits apportioned to a corporation for a separate return year pursuant to paragraph (c) of § 1.1502-79 and shall be subject to the limitations contained in paragraphs (c) and (e) of this section. A consolidated unused credit for any consolidated return year is the excess of the consolidated credit earned over the consolidated limitation based on amount of tax for such year.

(2) Absorption rules. For purposes of determining the amount, if any, of an unused credit (whether consolidated or separate) which can be carried to a taxable year (consolidated or separate), the amount of such unused credit which is absorbed in a prior consolidated return year under section 46(b) shall be determined by—

(i) Applying all unused credits which can be carried to such prior year in the order of the taxable years in which such unused credits arose, beginning with the taxable year which ends earliest, and

(ii) Applying all such unused credits which can be carried to such prior year from taxable years ending on the same date on a pro rata basis.

(3) Example. The provisions of paragraphs (a) and (b) of this section may be illustrated by the following example:

Example. (i) Corporation P is incorporated on January 1, 1966. On that same day P incorporates corporation S, a wholly owned subsidiary. P and S file consolidated returns for calendar years 1966 and 1967. P's and S's credit earned, the consolidated credit earned, and the consolidated limitation based on amount of tax for 1966 and 1967 are as follows:

	Credit earned	Consolidated credit earned	Consolidated limitation based on amount of tax
1966:			
P	$60,000		
S	30,000	$90,000	$100,000
1967:			
P	40,000		
S	25,000	65,000	50,000

(ii) P's and S's credit earned for 1966 are aggregated, and the group's consolidated credit earned, $90,000, is allowable in full to the group as a credit under section 38 for 1966 since such amount is less than the consolidated limitation based on amount of tax for 1966, $100,000.

(iii) Since the consolidated limitation based on amount of tax for 1967 is $50,000, only $50,000 of the $65,000 consolidated credit earned for such year is allowable to the group under section 38 as a credit for 1967. The consolidated unused credit for 1967 of $15,000 ($65,000 less $50,000) is a consolidated investment credit carryback and carryover to the years prescribed in section 46(b). In this case the consolidated unused credit is a consolidated investment credit carryback to 1966 (since P and S were not in existence in 1964 and 1965) and a consolidated investment credit carryover to 1968 and subsequent years. The portion of the consolidated unused credit for 1967 which is allowable as a credit for 1966 is $10,000. This amount shall be added to the amount allowable as a credit to the group for 1966. The balance of the consolidated unused credit for 1967 to be carried to 1968 is $5,000. These amounts are computed as follows:

Consolidated carryback to 1966	....	....	$15,000
1966 consolidated limitation based on tax	....	$100,000	....
Less: Consolidated credit earned for 1966	$90,000		
Consolidated unused credits attributable to years preceding 1967	0	90,000	....
Limit on amount of 1967 consolidated unused credit which may be added as a credit for 1966	....	....	10,000
Balance of 1967 consolidated unused credit to be carried to 1968	....	....	5,000

(c) Limitation on investment credit carryovers and carrybacks from separate return limitation years applicable for consolidated return years for which the due date of the return is on or before March 13, 1998. *(1) General rule.* In the case of an unused credit of a member of the group arising in a separate return limitation year (as defined in § 1.1502-1(f)) of such member (and in a separate return limitation year of any predecessor of such member), the amount which may be included under paragraph (b) of this section (computed without regard to the limitation contained in paragraph (e) of this section) shall not exceed the amount determined under paragraph (c)(2) of this section.

(2) Computation of limitation. The amount referred to in paragraph (c)(1) of this section with respect to a member of the group is the excess, if any, of—

(i) The limitation based on amount of tax of the group, minus such limitation recomputed by excluding the items of income, deduction, and foreign tax credit of such member; over

(ii) The sum of the investment credit earned by such member for such consolidated return year, and the unused credits attributable to such member which may be carried to such consolidated return year arising in unused credit years ending prior to the particular separate return limitation year.

(3) Special effective date. The paragraph (c) applies to consolidated return years for which the due date of the income tax return (without extensions) is on or before March 13, 1998. See paragraph (d) of this section for the rule that limits the group's use of a section 38 credit carryover or carryback from a SRLY for a consolidated return year for which the due date of the income tax return (without extensions) is after March 13, 1998. See also paragraph (d)(4) of this section for an optional effective date rule (generally making the rules of this paragraph (c) inapplicable to a consolidated return year beginning after December 31, 1996, if the due date of the income tax return (without extensions) for such year is on or before March 13, 1998).

(4) Examples. The provisions of this paragraph (c) may be illustrated by the following examples:

Example (1). (i) Assume the same facts as in the example contained in paragraph (b)(3) of this section, except that all the stock of corporation T, also a calendar year taxpayer, is acquired by P on January 1, 1968, and that P, S, and T file a consolidated return for 1968. In 1966, T had an unused credit of $10,000 which has not been absorbed and is available as an investment credit carryover to 1968. Such carryover is from a separate return limitation year. P's and S's credit earned for 1968 is $10,000 each, and T's credit earned is $8,000; the consolidated credit earned is therefore $28,000. The group's consolidated limitation based on amount of tax for 1968 is $50,000. Such limitation recomputed by excluding the items of income, deduction, and foreign tax credit of T is $30,000. Thus, the amount determined under paragraph (c)(2)(i) of this section is $20,000 ($50,000 minus $30,000). Accordingly, the limitation on the carryover of T's unused credit is $12,000, the excess of $20,000 over $8,000 (the sum of T's credit earned for the taxable year and any carryovers from prior unused credit years (none in this case)). Therefore T's $10,000 unused credit from 1966 may be carried over to the consolidated return year without limitation.

(ii) The group's consolidated credit earned for 1968, $28,000, is allowable in full as a credit under section 38 since such amount is less than the consolidated limitation based on amount of tax, $50,000.

(iii) The group's consolidated investment credit carryover to 1968 is $15,000, consisting of the consolidated unused credits of the group ($5,000) plus T's separate return year unused credit ($10,000). The entire $15,000 consolidated carryover shall be added to the amount allowable to the group as a credit under section 38 for 1968, since such amount is less than $22,000 (the excess of the consolidated limitation based on tax, $50,000, over the sum of the consolidated credit earned for 1968, $28,000, and unused credits arising in prior unused credit years, zero).

Example (2). Assume the same facts as in Example 1, except that the amount determined under paragraph (c)(2)(i) of this section is $12,000. Therefore, the limitation on the carryover of T's unused credit is $4,000. Accordingly, the consolidated investment credit carryover is only $9,000 since the amount of T's separate return year unused credit which may be added to the group's $ 5,000 consolidated unused credit is $4,000. These amounts are computed as follows:

T's carryover to 1968	....	....	$10,000
Consolidated limitation based on amount of tax minus recomputed limitation	....	$12,000	....
Less: T's credit earned for 1968	$8,000	....	....
Unused credits attributable to T arising in unused credit years preceding 1966	0	$8,000	....
Limit on amount of 1966 unused credit of T which may be added to consolidated investment credit carryover	....	....	4,000
Balance of 1966 unused credit of T to be carried to 1969 (subject to the limitation contained in paragraph (c) of this section)	....	....	6,000

(d) Limitation on tax credit carryovers and carrybacks from separate return limitation years applicable for consolidated return years for which the due date of the return is after March 13, 1998. *(1) General rule.* The aggregate of a member's unused section 38 credits arising in SRLYs that are included in the consolidated section 38 credits for all consolidated return years of the group may not exceed—

(i) The aggregate for all consolidated return years of the member's contributions to the consolidated section 38(c) limitation for each consolidated return year; reduced by

(ii) The aggregate of the member's section 38 credits arising and absorbed in all consolidated return years (whether or not absorbed by the member).

(2) Computational rules. (i) Member's contribution to the consolidated section 38(c) limitation. If the consolidated section 38(c) limitation for a consolidated return year is determined by reference to the consolidated tentative minimum tax (see section 38(c)(1)(A)), then a member's contribution to the consolidated section 38(c) limitation for such year equals the member's share of the consolidated net income tax minus the member's share of the consolidated tentative minimum tax. If the consolidated section 38(c) limitation for a consolidated return year is determined by reference to the consolidated net regular tax liability (see section 38(c)(1)(B)), then a member's contribution to the consolidated section 38(c) limitation for such year equals the member's share of the consolidated net income tax minus 25 percent of the quantity which is equal to so much of the member's share of the consolidated net regular tax liability less its portion of the $25,000 amount specified in section 38(c)(1)(B). The group computes the member's shares by applying to the respective consolidated amounts the principles of section 1552 and the percentage method under § 1.1502-33(d)(3), assuming a 100% allocation of any decreased tax liability. The group must make proper adjustments so that taxes and credits not taken into account in computing the limitation under section 38(c) are not taken into account in computing the member's share of the consolidated net income tax, etc. (See, for example, the taxes described in section 26(b) that are disregarded in computing regular tax liability.) Also, the group may apportion all or a part of the $25,000 amount (or lesser amount if reduced by section 38(c)(3)) for any year to one or more members.

(ii) Years included in computation. For purposes of computing the limitation under this paragraph (d), the consolidated return years of the group include only those years, including the year to which a credit is carried, that the member has been continuously included in the group's consolidated return, but exclude—

(A) For carryovers, any years ending after the year to which the credit is carried; and

(B) For carrybacks, any years ending after the year in which the credit arose.

(iii) Subgroups and successors. The SRLY subgroup principles under § 1.1502-21(c)(2) apply for purposes of this paragraph (d). The predecessor and successor principles under § 1.1502-21(f) also apply for purposes of this paragraph (d).

(iv) Overlap with section 383. The principles under § 1.1502-21(g) apply for purposes of this paragraph (d). For example, an overlap of paragraph (d) of this section and the application of section 383 with respect to a credit carryover occurs if a corporation becomes a member of a consolidated group (the SRLY event) within six months of the change date of an ownership change giving rise to a section 383 credit limitation with respect to that carryover (the section 383 event), with the result that the limitation of this paragraph (d) does not apply. See §§ 1.1502-21(g)(2)(ii)(A) and 1.383-1; see also § 1.1502-21(g)(4) (subgroup rules).

(3) Effective date. (i) In general. This paragraph (d) generally applies to consolidated return years for which the due date of the income tax return (without extensions) is after March 13, 1998.

(A) Contribution years. Except as provided in paragraph (d)(4)(ii) of this section, a group does not take into account a consolidated taxable year for which the due date of the income tax return (without extensions) is on or before March 13, 1998, in determining a member's (or subgroup's) contributions to the consolidated section 38(c) limitation under this paragraph (d).

(B) Special subgroup rule. In the event that the principles of § 1.1502-21(g)(1) do not apply to a particular credit carryover in the current group, then solely for purposes of applying paragraph (d) of this section to determine the limitation with respect to that carryover and with respect to which the SRLY register (the aggregate of the member's or subgroup's contribution to consolidated section 38(c) limitation reduced by the aggregate of the member's or subgroup's section 38 credits arising and absorbed in all consolidated return years) began in a taxable year for which the due date of the return is on or before May 25, 2000, the principles of § 1.1502-21(c)(2) shall be applied without regard to the phrase "or for a carryover that was subject to the overlap rule described in paragraph (g) of this section or § 1.1502-15(g) with respect to another group (the former group)."

(ii) Overlap rule. Paragraph (d)(2)(iv) of this section (relating to overlap with section 383) applies to taxable years for which the due date (without extensions) of the consolidated return is after May 25, 2000. For purposes of paragraph (d)(2)(iv) of this section, only an ownership change to which section 383, as amended by the Tax Reform Act of 1986 (100 Stat. 2085), applies and which results in a section 383 credit limitation shall constitute a section 383 event.

(4) Optional effective date of January 1, 1997. (i) For consolidated taxable years beginning on or after January 1, 1997, for which the due date of the income tax return (without extensions) is on or before March 13, 1998, in lieu of paragraphs (c) and (e)(3) of this section (relating to the gen-

eral business credit), § 1.1502-4(f)(3) and (g)(3) (relating to the foreign tax credit), the next to last sentence of § 1.1502-9A(a)(2), § 1.1502-9A(b)(1)(v) (relating to overall foreign losses), and § 1.1502-55(h)(4)(iii) (relating to the alternative minimum tax credit), a consolidated group may apply the corresponding provisions as they appear in 1998-1 C.B. 655 through 661 (see § 601.601(d)(2) of this chapter) (treating references in such corresponding provisions to §§ 1.1502-9(b)(1)(ii), (iii), and (iv) as references to §§ 1.1502-9A(b)(1)(ii), (iii), and (iv)). Also, in the case of a consolidated return change of ownership that occurs on or after January 1, 1997, in a taxable year for which the due date of the income tax return (without extensions) is on or before March 13, 1998, a consolidated group may choose not to apply paragraph (e) of this section and § 1.1502-4(g) to taxable years ending after December 31, 1996. A consolidated group making the choices described in the two preceding sentences generally must apply all such corresponding provisions (including not applying paragraph (e) of this section and § 1.1502-4(g)) for all relevant years. However, a consolidated group making the election provided in § 1.1502-9A(b)(1)(vi) (electing not to apply § 1.1502-9A(b)(1)(v) to years beginning before January 1, 1998) may nevertheless choose to apply all such corresponding provisions referred to in this paragraph (d)(4)(i) other than the provision corresponding to § 1.1502-9A(b)(1)(v) for all relevant years.

(ii) If a consolidated group chooses to apply the corresponding provisions referred to in paragraph (d)(4)(i) of this section, the consolidated group shall not take into account a consolidated taxable year beginning before January 1, 1997, in determining a member's (or subgroup's) contributions to the consolidated section 38(c) limitation under this paragraph (d).

(5) Example. The following example illustrates the provisions of this paragraph (d):

Example. (i) Individual A owns all of the stock of P and T. P is the common parent of the P group. P acquires all the stock of T at the beginning of Year 2. T carries over an unused section 38 general business credit from Year 1 of $100,000. The table in paragraph (i) of this Example shows the group's net consolidated income tax, consolidated tentative minimum tax, and consolidated net regular tax liabilities, and T's share of such taxes computed under the principles of section 1552 and the percentage method under § 1.1502-33(d)(3), assuming a 100% allocation of any decreased tax liability, for Year 2. (The effects of the lower section 11 brackets are ignored, there are no other tax credits affecting a group amount or member's share, and $1,000s are omitted.)

Year 2	Group	P's share of col. 1	T's share of col. 1
1. consolidated taxable income	$2,000	$1,200	$800
2. consolidated net regular tax	$ 700	$ 420	$280
3. consolidated alternative minimum taxable income	$4,000	$3,200	$800
4. consolidated tentative minimum tax	$ 800	$ 640	$160
5. consolidated net income tax	$ 800	$ 520	$280
6. greater of line 4 or 25% of (line 2 minus $25,000 for the group)	$ 800		
7. consolidated § 38(c) limitation (line 5 minus line 6)	$ 0		

(ii) T's Year 1 is a SRLY with respect to the P group. See § 1.1502-1(f)(2)(ii). T did not undergo an ownership change giving rise to a section 383 credit limitation within 6 months of joining the P group. Thus, T's $100,000 general business credit arising in Year 1 is subject to a SRLY limitation in the P group. The amount of T's unused section 38 credits from Year 1 that are included in the consolidated section 38 credits for Year 2 may not exceed T's contribution to the consolidated section 38(c) limitation. For Year 2, the group determines the consolidated section 38(c) limitation by reference to consolidated tentative minimum tax for Year 2. Therefore, T's contribution to the consolidated section 38(c) limitation for Year 2 equals its share of consolidated net income tax minus its share of consolidated tentative minimum tax. T's contribution is $280,000 minus $160,000, or $120,000. However, because the group has a consolidated section 38 limitation of zero, it may not include any of T's unused section 38 credits in the consolidated section 38 credits for Year 2.

(iii) The following table shows similar information for the group for Year 3:

Year 3	Group	P's share of col. 1	T's share of col. 1
1. consolidated taxable income	$1,200	$1,500	$(300)
2. consolidated net regular tax	$ 420	$ 525	$(105)
3. consolidated alternative minimum taxable income	$1,500	$1,700	$(200)
4. consolidated tentative minimum tax	$ 300	$ 340	$ (40)
5. consolidated net income tax	$ 420	$ 525	$(105)
6. greater of line 4 or 25% of (line 2 minus $25,000 for the group)	$ 300		

7. consolidated § 38(c) limitation (line 5 minus line 6)	$ 120

(iv) The amount of T's unused section 38 credits from Year 1 that are included in the consolidated section 38 credits for Year 3 may not exceed T's aggregate contribution to the consolidated section 38(c) limitation for Years 2 and 3. For Year 3, the group determines the consolidated section 38(c) limitation by reference to the consolidated tentative minimum tax for Year 3. Therefore, T's contribution to the consolidated section 38(c) limitation for Year 3 equals its share of consolidated net income tax minus its share of consolidated tentative minimum tax. Applying the principles of section 1552 and § 1.1502-33(d) (taking into account, for example, that T's positive earnings and profits adjustment under § 1.1502-33(d) reflects its losses actually absorbed by the group), T's contribution is $(105,000) minus $(40,000), or $(65,000). T's aggregate contribution to the consolidated section 38(c) limitation for Years 2 and 3 is $120,000 + $(65,000), or $55,000. The group may include $55,000 of T's Year 1 unused section 38 credits in its consolidated section 38 tax credit in Year 3.

(e) Limitation on investment credit carryovers where there has been a consolidated return change of ownership. *(1) General rule.* If a consolidated return change of ownership (as defined in paragraph (g) of § 1.1502-1) occurs during the taxable year or an earlier taxable year, the amount which may be included under paragraph (b) of this section in the consolidated investment credit carryovers to the taxable year with respect to the aggregate unused credits attributable to old members of the group (as defined in paragraph (g)(3) of § 1.1502-1) arising in taxable years (consolidated or separate) ending on the same day and before the taxable year in which the consolidated return change of ownership occurred shall not exceed the amount determined under subparagraph (2) of this paragraph.

(2) Computation of limitation. The amount referred to in subparagraph (1) of this paragraph shall be the excess of the consolidated limitation based on the amount of tax for the taxable year, recomputed by including only the items of income, deduction, and foreign tax credit of the old members, over the sum of—

(i) The aggregate investment credits earned by the old members for the taxable year, and

(ii) The aggregate unused investment credits attributable to the old members which may be carried to the taxable year arising in unused credit years ending prior to the particular unused credit year or years.

(3) Special effective date. This paragraph (e) applies only to a consolidated return change of ownership that occurred during a consolidated return year for which the due date of the income tax return (without extensions) is on or before March 13, 1998. See paragraph (d)(4) of this section for an optional effective date rule (generally making the rules of this paragraph (e) also inapplicable if the consolidated return change of ownership occurred on or after January 1, 1997, and during a consolidated return year for which the due date of the income tax return (without extensions) is on or before March 13, 1998).

(f) Early dispositions, etc., of section 38 property. *(1) Dispositions of section 38 property during and after consolidated return year.* If property is subject to section 47(a)(1) or (2) with respect to a member during a consolidated return year, any increase in tax shall be added to the tax liability of the group under § 1.1502-2 (regardless of whether the property was placed in service in a consolidated or separate return year). Also, if property is subject to section 47(a)(1) or (2) with respect to a corporation during a taxable year for which such corporation files on a separate return basis, any increase in tax shall be added to the tax liability of such corporation (regardless of whether such property was placed in service in a consolidated or separate return year).

(2) Exception for transfer to another member. (i) Except as provided in subdivisions (ii) and (iii) of this subparagraph, a transfer of section 38 property from one member of the group to another member of such group during a consolidated return year shall not be treated as a disposition or cessation within the meaning of section 47(a)(1). If such section 38 property is disposed of, or otherwise ceases to be section 38 property or becomes public utility property with respect to the transferee, before the close of the estimated useful life which was taken into account in computing qualified investment, then section 47(a)(1) or (2) shall apply to the transferee with respect to such property (determined by taking into account the period of use, qualified investment, other dispositions, etc., of the transferor). Any increase in tax due to the application of section 47(a)(1) or (2) shall be added to the tax liability of such transferee (or the tax liability of a group, if the transferee joins in the filing of a consolidated return).

(ii) Except as provided in subdivision (iii) of this subparagraph, if section 38 property is disposed of during a consolidated return year by one member of the group to another member of such group which is an organization to which section 593 applies or a cooperative organization described in section 1381(a), the tax under chapter 1 of the Code for such consolidated return year shall be increased by an amount equal to the aggregate decrease in the credits allowed under section 38 for all prior taxable years which would result solely from treating such property, for purposes of determining qualified investment, as placed in service by such organization to which section 593 applies or such cooperative organization described in section 1381(a), as the case may be, but with due regard to the use of the property before such transfer.

(iii) Section 47(a)(1) shall apply to a transfer of section 38 property by a corporation during a consolidated return year if such corporation is liquidated in a transaction to which section 334(b)(2) applies.

(3) Examples. The provisions of this paragraph may be illustrated by the following examples:

Example (1). P, S, and T file a consolidated return for calendar year 1967. In such year S places in service section 38 property having an estimated useful life of more than 8 years. In 1968, P, S, and T file a consolidated return, and in such year S sells such property to T. Such sale will not cause section 47(a)(1) to apply.

Example (2). Assume the same facts as in example (1), except that P, S, and T filed separate returns for 1967. The sale from S to T will not cause section 47(a)(1) to apply.

Example (3). Assume the same facts as in example (1), except that P, S, and T continue to file a consolidated return through 1971 and in such year T disposes of the property to individual A. Section 47(a)(1) will apply to the group and any increase in tax shall be added to the tax liability of the group. For the purposes of determining the actual period of use by T, such period shall include S's period of use.

Example (4). Assume the same facts as in example (3), except that T files a separate return in 1971. Again, the actual periods of use by S and T will be combined in applying section 47. If the disposition results in an increase in tax under section 47(a)(1), such additional tax shall be added to the separate tax liability of T.

Example (5). Assume the same facts as in example (1), except that in 1969, P sells all the stock of T to a third party. Such sale will not cause section 47(a)(1) to apply.

T.D. 6894, 9/7/66, amend T.D. 7246, 12/29/72, T.D. 8597, 7/12/95, T.D. 8751, 1/9/98, T.D. 8766, 3/13/98, T.D. 8884, 5/24/2000.

§ 1.1502-4 Consolidated foreign tax credit.

(a) In general. The credit under section 901 for taxes paid or accrued to any foreign country or possession of the United States shall be allowed to the group only if the common parent corporation chooses to use such credit in the computation of the tax liability of the group for the consolidated return year. If this choice is made, no deduction may be taken on the consolidated return for such taxes paid or accrued by any member of the group. See section 275(a)(4).

(b) Limitation effective under section 904(a) for the group. *(1) Common parent's limitation effective for group.* The determination of whether the overall limitation or the per-country limitation applies for a consolidated return year shall be made by reference to the limitation effective with respect to the common parent corporation for such year. If the limitation effective with respect to a member for its immediately preceding separate return year differs from the limitation effective with respect to the common parent corporation for the consolidated return year, then such member shall, if the overall limitation is effective with respect to the common parent, be deemed to have made an election to use such overall limitation, or, if the per-country limitation is effective with respect to the common parent, be deemed to have revoked its election to use the overall limitation. Consent of the Secretary or his delegate (if otherwise required) is hereby given to such member for such election or revocation. Any such election or revocation shall apply only prospectively beginning with such consolidated return year.

(2) Limitation effective for subsequent years. The limitation effective with respect to a member for the last year for which it joins in the filing of a consolidated return with a group shall remain in effect for a subsequent separate return year and may be changed by such corporation for such subsequent year only in accordance with the provisions of section 904(b) (and this paragraph if it joins in the filing of a consolidated return with another group). Any retroactive change in the limitation by the common parent corporation for such member's last consolidated return year shall change the election effective with respect to such member for such last period. Thus, if the common parent (P) elects the overall limitation with respect to calendar year 1966, such election would be effective with respect to its subsidiary S for 1966. If S leaves the group at the beginning of calendar year 1967, such election shall be effective for 1967 with respect to S (unless S revokes such election for 1967 or a subsequent year in accordance with section 904(b), or this paragraph if it joins in the filing of a consolidated return with another group). However, if P retroactively changes back to the per-country limitation with respect to 1966, such limitation would be effective with respect to S for 1966 and subsequent years (unless S elects the overall limitation for any such subsequent year).

(c) Computation of consolidated foreign tax credit. The foreign tax credit for the consolidated return year shall be determined on a consolidated basis under the principles of sections 901 through 905 and section 960. For example, if the per-country limitation applies to the consolidated return year, taxes paid or accrued for such year (including those deemed paid or accrued under sections 902 and 960(a) and paragraph (e) of this section) to each foreign country or possession by the members of the group shall be aggregated. If the overall limitation applies, taxes paid or accrued for such year (including those deemed paid or accrued) to all foreign countries and possessions by members of the group shall be aggregated. If the overall limitation applies and a member of the group qualifies as a Western Hemisphere trade corporation, see section 1503(b).

(d) Computation of limitation on credit. For purposes of computing the group's applicable limitation under section 904(a), the following rules shall apply:

(1) Computation of taxable income from foreign sources. The numerator of the applicable limiting fraction under section 904(a) shall be an amount (not in excess of the amount determined under subparagraph (2) of this paragraph) equal to the aggregate of the separate taxable incomes of the members from sources within each foreign country or possession of the United States (if the per-country limitation is applicable), or from sources without the United States (if the overall limitation is applicable), determined under § 1.1502-12, adjusted for the following items taken into account in the computation of consolidated taxable income:

(i) The portion of the consolidated net operating loss deduction, the consolidated charitable contributions deduction, the consolidated dividends received deduction, and the consolidated section 922 deduction, attributable to such foreign source income;

(ii) Any such foreign source capital gain net income (net capital gain for taxable years beginning before January 1, 1977) (determined without regard to any net capital loss carryover or carryback);

(iii) Any such foreign source net capital loss and section 1231 net loss, reduced by the portion of the consolidated net capital loss attributable to such foreign source loss; and

(iv) The portion of any consolidated net capital loss carryover or carryback attributable to such foreign source income which is absorbed in the taxable year.

(2) Computation of entire taxable income. The denominator of the applicable limiting fraction under section 904(a) (that is, the entire taxable income of the group) shall be the consolidated taxable income of the group computed in accordance with § 1.1502-11.

(3) Computation of tax against which credit is taken. The tax against which the limiting fraction under section 904(a) is applied shall be the consolidated tax liability of the group determined under § 1.1502-2, but without regard to paragraphs (b), (c), (d), and (j) thereof, and without regard to any credit against such liability.

(e) Carryover and carryback of unused foreign tax. *(1) Allowance of unused foreign tax as consolidated carryover or carryback.* The aggregate of the consolidated unused foreign tax carryovers and carrybacks to the taxable year, to the extent absorbed for such year under the principles of section 904(d), shall be deemed to be paid or accrued to a foreign country or possession for such year. The consolidated unused foreign tax carryovers and carrybacks to the taxable year shall consist of any consolidated unused foreign tax, plus any unused foreign tax of members for separate return years of such members, which may be carried over or back to the taxable year under the principles of section 904(d) and (e). However, such consolidated carryovers and carrybacks shall not include any consolidated unused foreign taxes apportioned to a corporation for a separate return year pursuant to § 1.1502-79(d) and shall be subject to the limitations contained in paragraphs (f) and (g) of this section. A consolidated unused foreign tax is the excess of the foreign taxes paid or accrued by the group (or deemed paid or accrued by the group, other than by reason of section 904(d)) over the applicable limitation for the consolidated return year.

(2) Absorption rules. For purposes of determining the amount, if any, of an unused foreign tax (consolidated or separate) which can be carried to a taxable year (consolidated or separate), the amount of such unused tax which is absorbed in a prior consolidated return year under section 904(d) shall be determined by—

(i) Applying all unused foreign taxes which can be carried to such prior year in the order of the taxable years in which such unused taxes arose, beginning with the taxable year which ends earliest, and

(ii) Applying all such unused taxes which can be carried to such prior year from taxable years ending on the same date on a pro rata basis.

(f) Limitation on unused foreign tax carryover or carryback from separate return limitation years. *(1) General rule.* In the case of an unused foreign tax of a member of the group arising in a separate return limitation year (as defined in paragraph (f) of § 1.1502-1) of such member, the amount which may be included under paragraph (e) of this section (computed without regard to the limitation contained in paragraph (g) of this section) shall not exceed the amount determined under subparagraph (2) of this paragraph.

(2) Computation of limitation. The amount referred to in subparagraph (1) of this paragraph with respect to a member of the group is the excess, if any, of—

(i) The section 904(a) limitation of the group, minus such limitation recomputed by excluding the items of income and deduction of such member, over

(ii) The sum of (a) the foreign taxes paid (or deemed paid, other than by reason of section 904(d)) by such member for the consolidated return year, and (b) the unused foreign tax attributable to such member which may be carried to such consolidated return year arising in taxable years ending prior to the particular separate return limitation year.

(3) Limitation on unused foreign tax credit carryover or carryback from separate return limitation years. Paragraphs (f)(1) and (2) of this section do not apply for consolidated return years for which the due date of the income tax return (without extensions) is after March 13, 1998. For consolidated return years for which the due date of the income tax return (without extensions) is after March 13, 1998, a group shall include an unused foreign tax of a member arising in a SRLY without regard to the contribution of the member to consolidated tax liability for the consolidated return year. See also § 1.1502-3(d)(4) for an optional effective date rule (generally making the rules of paragraphs (f)(1) and (2) of this section also inapplicable to a consolidated return year beginning on or after January 1, 1997, if the due date of the income tax return (without extensions) for such year is on or before March 13, 1998).

(g) Limitation on unused foreign tax carryover where there has been a consolidated return change of ownership. *(1) General rule.* If a consolidated return change of ownership (as defined in paragraph (g) of § 1.1502-1) occurs during the taxable year or an earlier taxable year, the amount which may be included under paragraph (e) of this section in the consolidated unused foreign tax carryovers to the taxable year with respect to the aggregate unused credits attributable to the old members of the group (as defined in paragraph (g)(3) of § 1.1502-1) arising in taxable years (consolidated or separate) ending on the same day and before the taxable year in which the consolidated return change of ownership occurred shall not exceed the amount determined under subparagraph (2) of this paragraph.

(2) Computation of limitation. The amount referred to in subparagraph (1) of this paragraph shall be the excess of the section 904(a) limitation of the group for the taxable year, recomputed by including only the items of income and deduction of the old members of the group, over the sum of—

(i) The aggregate foreign taxes paid (or deemed paid, other than by reason of section 904(d)) by the old members for the taxable year, and

(ii) The aggregate unused foreign tax attributable to the old members which can be carried to the taxable year arising in taxable years ending prior to the particular unused foreign tax year or years.

(3) Special effective date for CRCO limitation. Paragraphs (g)(1) and (2) of this section apply only to a consolidated return change of ownership that occurred during a consolidated return year for which the due date of the income tax return (without extensions) is on or before March 13, 1998. See also § 1.1502-3(d)(4) for an optional effective date rule (generally making the rules of paragraph (g)(1) and (2) of this section also inapplicable if the consolidated return change of ownership occurred on or after January 1, 1997, and during a consolidated return year for which the due date of the income tax return (without extensions) is on or before March 13, 1998).

(h) Amount of credit with respect to interest income. If any member of the group has interest income described in section 904(f)(2) (for a year for which it filed on a consolidated or separate basis), the group's foreign tax credit with respect to such interest shall be computed separately in accordance with the principles of section 904(f) and this section.

(i) [Reserved]

(j) Examples. The provisions of this section may be illustrated by the following examples:

Example (1). Domestic corporation P is incorporated on January 1, 1966. On that same day it also incorporates domestic corporations S and T, wholly owned subsidiaries. P, S, and T file consolidated returns for 1966 and 1967 on the basis of a calendar year. T engages in business solely in country A. S transacts business solely in countries A and B. P does business solely in the United States. During 1966 T sold an item of inventory to P at a profit of $2,000. Under § 1.1502-13 (as contained in the 26 CFR part 1 edition revised as of April 1, 1995) such profit is deferred and none of the circumstances of restoration contained in paragraph (d), (e), or (f) of § 1.1502-13 have occurred as of the close of 1966. The taxable income for 1966 from foreign and United States sources, and the foreign taxes paid on such foreign income are as follows:

Corporation	U.S. taxable income	Country A Taxable income	Country A Foreign tax paid	Country B Taxable income	Country B Foreign tax paid	Total taxable income
P	$40,000					$40,000
T		$20,000	$12,000			20,000
S		10,000	6,000	$10,000	$3,000	20,000
						80,000

Such taxable income was computed by taking into account the rules provided in § 1.1502-12. Thus, the $2,000 deferred profit is not included in T's taxable income for 1966 (but will be included for the taxable year for which one of the events specified in paragraph (d), (e), or (f) of § 1.1502-13 occurs). The consolidated taxable income of the group (computed in accordance with § 1.1502-11) is $80,000. The consolidated tax liability against which the credit may be taken (computed in accordance with paragraph (d)(3) of this section) is $31,900.

(i) Assuming P chooses to use the foreign taxes paid as a credit and the group is subject to the per-country limitation, the group may take as a credit against the consolidated tax liability $11,962.50 of the amount paid to country A, plus the $3,000 paid to country B. Such amounts are computed as follows: The aggregate taxes paid to country A of $18,000 is limited to $11,962.50 ($31,900 times $30,000/$80,000). The unused foreign tax with respect to country A is $6,037.50 ($18,000 less $11,962.50), and is a consolidated unused foreign tax which shall be carried to the years prescribed by section 904(d). A credit of $3,000 is available with respect to the taxes paid to country B since such amount is less than the limitation of $3,987.50 ($31,900 times $10,000/$30,000).

(ii) Assuming the overall limitation is in effect for the taxable year, the group may take $15,950 as a credit, computed as follows: The aggregate taxes paid to all foreign countries of $21,000 is limited to $15,950 ($31,900 times $40,000/$80,000). The unused foreign tax is $5,050 ($21,000 less $15,950), and is a consolidated unused foreign tax which shall be carried to the years prescribed by section 904(d).

Example (2). Assume the same facts as in example (1), except that T has a $10,000 long-term capital gain (derived from a sale to a nonmember in country A) and P has a $10,000 long-term capital loss (derived from a sale to a nonmember in the United States). Notwithstanding that the consolidated net capital gain (capital gain net income for taxable years beginning after December 31, 1976) of the group is zero, T's capital gain shall be reflected in full in the computation of taxable income from foreign sources.

Example (3). Assume the same facts as in example (1), except that the group had a consolidated section 172 deduction of $8,000 which is attributable to a net operating loss sustained by T. The $8,000 consolidated net operating loss deduction is offset against T's income from country A, thus reducing T's taxable income from country A to $12,000.

T.D. 6894, 9/7/66, amend T.D. 7637, 8/6/79, T.D. 7728, 10/31/80, T.D. 8597, 7/12/95, T.D. 8751, 1/9/98, T.D. 8766, 3/13/98, T.D. 8884, 5/24/2000.

§ 1.1502-5 Estimated tax.

(a) General rule. *(1) Consolidated estimated tax.* If a group files a consolidated return for two consecutive taxable years, it must make payments of estimated tax on a consolidated basis for each subsequent taxable year, until such time as separate returns are properly filed. Until such time, the group is treated as a single corporation for purposes of section 6154 (relating to payment of estimated tax by corporations). If separate returns are filed by the members for a taxable year, the amount of any estimated tax payments made with respect to a consolidated payment of estimated tax for such year shall be credited against the separate tax liabilities of the members in any manner designated by the common parent which is satisfactory to the Commissioner. The consolidated payments of estimated tax shall be deposited with the authorized financial institution with which the common parent deposits its estimated tax payments. A statement should be attached to the payment setting forth the name, address, employer identification number, and internal revenue service center of each member.

(2) First two consolidated return years. For the first 2 years for which a group files a consolidated return, it may make payments of estimated tax on either a consolidated or separate basis. If a consolidated return is filed for such year, the amount of any estimated tax payments made for such year by any member shall be credited against the tax liability of the group.

(3) Effective date. This section applies to taxable years for which the due date (without extensions) for filing returns is after August 6, 1979. For prior taxable years see 26 CFR 1.1502-5 (Revised as of April 1, 1978).

(b) Addition to tax for failure to pay estimated tax under section 6655. *(1) Consolidated return filed.* For the first two taxable years for which a group files a consolidated return, the group may compute the amount of the penalty (if any) under section 6655 on a consolidated basis or separate member basis, regardless of the method of payment. Thereafter, for a taxable year for which the group files a consolidated return, the group must compute the penalty on a consolidated basis.

(2) Computation of penalty on consolidated basis. (i) This paragraph (b)(2) gives the rules for computing the penalty under section 6655 on a consolidated basis.

(ii) The tax and facts shown on the return for the preceding taxable year referred to in section 6655(d)(1) and (2) are, if a consolidated return was filed for that preceding year, such items shown on the consolidated return for that preceding year or, if one was not filed for that preceding year, the aggregate taxes and the facts shown on the separate returns of the common parent and any other corporation that was a member of the same affiliated group as the common parent for that preceding year.

(iii) If estimated tax was not paid on a consolidated basis, then the amount of the group's payments of estimated tax for the taxable year is the aggregate of the payments made by all members for the year.

(iv) Section 6655(d)(1) applies only if the common parent's consolidated return, or each member's separate return, for the preceding taxable year (as the case may be) was a taxable year of 12 months.

(3) Computation of penalty on separate member basis. To compute any penalty under section 6655 on a separate member basis, for purposes of section 6655(b)(1), the "tax shown on the return for the taxable year" is the portion of the tax shown on the consolidated return allocable to the member under paragraph (b)(5) of this section. If the member was included in the consolidated return filed by the group for the preceding taxable year then—

(i) For purposes of section 6655(d)(1), the "tax shown on the return" for any member shall be the portion of the tax shown on the consolidated return for the preceding year allocable to the member under paragraph (b)(5) of this section.

(ii) For purposes of section 6655(d)(2), the "facts shown on the return" shall be the facts shown on the consolidated return for the preceding year and the tax computed under that section shall be allocated under the rules of paragraph (b)(5) of this section.

(4) Consolidated payments if separate returns filed. If the group does not file a consolidated return for the taxable year, but makes payments of estimated tax on a consolidated basis, for purposes of section 6655(b)(2), the "amount, if any of the installment paid" by any member is an amount apportioned to the member in a manner designated by the common parent that is satisfactory to the Commissioner. If the member was included in the consolidated return filed by the group for the preceding taxable year, the amount of a member's penalty under section 6655 is computed on the separate member basis described in paragraph (b)(3)(i) and (ii) of this section.

(5) Rules for allocation of consolidated tax liability. For purposes of subparagraphs (1) and (2) of this paragraph, the tax shown on a consolidated return shall be allocated to the members of the group under the method which the group has elected pursuant to section 1552 and § 1.1502-33(d)(2).

(c) Examples. The provisions of this section may be illustrated by the following examples:

Example (1). Corporations P and S-1 file a consolidated return for the first time for calendar year 1978. P and S-1 also file consolidated returns for 1979 and 1980. For 1978 and 1979, P and S-1 may make payments of estimated tax on either a separate or consolidated basis. For 1980, however, the group must pay its estimated tax on a consolidated basis. In determining whether P and S-1 come within the exception provided in section 6655(d)(1) for 1980, the "tax shown on the return" is the tax shown on the consolidated return for 1979.

Example (2). Assume the same facts as in example (1). Assume further that corporation S-2 is a member of the group during 1979, and joins in the filing of the consolidated return for such year but ceases to be a member of the group on September 15, 1980. In determining whether the group (which no longer includes S-2) comes within the exception provided in section 6655(d)(1) for 1980, the "tax shown on the return" is the tax shown on the consolidated return for 1979.

Example (3). Assume the same facts as in example (1). Assume further that corporation S-2 becomes a member of the group on July 1, 1980, and joins in the filing of the consolidated return for 1980. In determining whether the group (which now includes S-2) comes within the exception provided in section 6655(d)(1) for 1980, the "tax shown on the return" is the tax shown on the consolidated return for 1979. Any tax of S-2 for any separate return year is not included as a part of the "tax shown on the return" for purposes of applying section 6655(d)(1).

Example (4). Corporations X and Y filed consolidated returns for the calendar years 1977 and 1978 and separate returns for 1979. In determining whether X or Y comes within the exception provided in section 6655(d)(1) for 1979, the "tax shown on the return" is the amount of tax shown on the consolidated return for 1978 allocable to X and to Y in accordance with paragraph (b)(5) of this section.

(d) Cross reference. For provisions relating to quick refunds of corporate estimated tax payments, see § 1.1502-78, and §§ 1.6425-1 through 1.6425-3.

T.D. 6894, 9/7/66, amend T.D. 7059, 9/16/70, T.D. 7637, 8/6/79, T.D. 8952, 6/25/2001.

PAR. 5. Section 1.1502-5 is revised to read as follows:

Proposed § 1.1502-5 Estimated tax. [*For Preamble, see ¶ 151,475*]

(a) General rule. *(1) Consolidated estimated tax.* If a group files a consolidated return for two consecutive taxable years, it must make payments of estimated tax on a consolidated basis for each subsequent taxable year, until separate returns are filed. When filing on a consolidated basis, the group is generally treated as a single corporation for purposes of section 6655 (relating to payment of estimated tax by corporations). If separate returns are filed by the members for a taxable year, the amount of any estimated tax payments made with respect to a consolidated estimated tax for the year is credited against the separate tax liabilities of the members in any reasonable manner designated by the common parent. Consolidated payments of estimated tax must be deposited with the authorized commercial depositary or Federal Reserve Bank with which the common parent deposits its estimated tax payments. A statement must be attached to the payment setting forth the name, address, employer identification number, and Internal Revenue Service Center of each member.

(2) First two consolidated return years. For its first two consolidated return years, a group may make payments of estimated tax on either a consolidated or a separate member basis, and the amount of any separate estimated tax payments is credited against the consolidated tax liability of the group.

(b) Addition to tax for failure to pay estimated tax under section 6655. *(1) Consolidated return filed.* For its first two consolidated return years, a group may compute the amount of the penalty (if any) under section 6655 on a consolidated basis or a separate member basis, regardless of the method of payment. Thereafter, the group must compute the penalty for any consolidated return year on a consolidated basis.

(2) Computation of penalty on consolidated basis. (i) This paragraph (b)(2) provides rules for computing the penalty under section 6655 on a consolidated basis.

(ii) The tax shown on the return for the preceding taxable year referred to in section 6655(d)(1)(B)(ii) is, if a consolidated return was filed for that preceding year, the tax shown on the consolidated return for that preceding year or, if a consolidated return was not filed for that preceding year, the aggregate of the taxes shown on the separate returns of the common parent and any other corporation that was a member of the same affiliated group as the common parent for that preceding year.

(iii) If estimated tax was not paid on a consolidated basis, the amount of the group's payments of estimated tax for the taxable year is the aggregate of the payments made by all members for the year.

(iv) If the common parent is otherwise eligible to use the section 6655(d)(1)(B)(ii) required annual payment rule, that rule applies only if the group's consolidated return, or each member's separate return if the group did not file a consolidated return, for the preceding taxable year was a taxable year of 12 months.

(3) Computation of penalty on separate member basis. To compute any penalty under section 6655 on a separate member basis, for purposes of section 6655(d)(1)(B)(i), the "tax

shown on the return" for the taxable year is the portion of the tax shown on the consolidated return allocable to the member under paragraph (b)(6) of this section. If the member was included in the consolidated return filed by the group for the preceding taxable year, for purposes of section 6655(d)(1)(B)(ii), the "tax shown on the return" for the preceding taxable year for any member is the portion of the tax shown on the consolidated return for the preceding year allocable to the member under paragraph (b)(6) of this section.

(4) Consolidated payments if separate returns filed. If the group does not file a consolidated return for the taxable year but makes payments of estimated tax on a consolidated basis, for purposes of section 6655(b)(1)(B), the "amount (if any) of the installment paid" by any member is an amount apportioned to the member in any reasonable manner designated by the common parent. If a member was included in the consolidated return filed by the group for the preceding taxable year, the amount of the member's penalty under section 6655 is computed on the separate member basis described in paragraph (b)(3) of this section.

(5) Tax defined. For purposes of this section, "tax" means the excess of—

(i) The sum of—

(A) The consolidated tax imposed by section 11, section 1201(a)1 or subchapter L of chapter 1, whichever applies;

(B) The consolidated AMT determined under § 1.1502-55; and

(C) The consolidated environmental tax defined under § 1.1552-1(h)(2); over

(ii) The credits allowable under part IV of subchapter A of chapter 1 of the Internal Revenue Code against the consolidated taxes in paragraphs (b)(5)(i)(A), (B), and (C) of this section.

(6) Rules for allocation of consolidated tax liability. For purposes of this section, the tax shown on a consolidated return shall be allocated to the members of the group by allocating—

(i) Any tax described in paragraph (b)(5)(i)(A) of this section, net of allowable credits under paragraph (b)(5)(ii) (other than the allowable consolidated MTC defined in § 1.1502-55(h)), under the method that the group has elected pursuant to section 1552 and § 1.1502-33(d);

(ii) Any allowable consolidated MTC (as defined in § 1.1502-55(h)) in accordance with the requirements of § 1.1552- 1(g);

(iii) Any consolidated AMT described in paragraph (b)(5)(i)(B) of this section in accordance with the requirements of § 1.1552-1(g); and

(iv) Any consolidated environmental tax described in paragraph (b)(5)(i)(C) of this section in accordance with the requirements of § 1.1552-1(h).

(c) Examples. The provisions of this section are illustrated by the following examples.

Example (1). Corporations P and S1 file a consolidated return for the first time for calendar year 1992. P and S1 also file consolidated returns for 1993 and 1994. Under paragraph (a)(2) of this section, for 1992 and 1993 P and S1 may pay estimated tax on either a separate or consolidated basis. Under paragraph (a)(1) of this section, for 1994 the group must pay its estimated tax on a consolidated basis. In determining whether P and S1 come within the exception provided in section 6655(d)(1)(B)(ii) for 1994, the "tax shown on the return" is the tax shown on the consolidated return for 1993.

Example (2). Corporations P, S1, and S2 file a consolidated return for the first time for calendar year 1992 and file their second consolidated return in 1993. S2 ceases to be a member of the group on September 15, 1994. Under paragraph (b)(2) of this section, in determining whether the group (which no longer includes S2) comes within the exception provided in section 6655(d)(1)(B)(ii) for 1994, the "tax shown on the return" is the tax shown on the consolidated return for 1993.

Example (3). Corporations P and S1 file a consolidated return for the first time for calendar year 1992 and file their second consolidated return in 1993. Corporation S2 becomes a member of the group on July 1, 1994, and joins in the filing of the consolidated return for 1994. Under paragraph (b)(2) of this section, in determining whether the group (which now includes S2) comes within the exception provided in section 6655(d)(1)(B)(ii) for 1994, the "tax shown on the return" is the tax shown on the consolidated return for 1993. Any tax of S2 for any separate return year is not included as a part of the "tax shown on the return" for purposes of applying section 6655(d)(1)(B)(ii).

Example (4). Corporations X and Y file consolidated returns for the calendar years 1992 and 1993 and separate returns for 1994. Under paragraph (b)(3) of this section, in determining whether X or Y comes within the exception provided in section 6655(d)(1)(B)(ii) for 1994, the "tax shown on the return" is the amount of tax shown on the consolidated return for 1993 allocable to X and to Y in accordance with paragraph (b)(6) of this section.

(d) Cross reference. For provisions relating to quick refunds of corporate estimated tax payments, see § 1.1502-78 and §§ 1.6425-1 through 1.6425-3.

(e) Effective date. This section applies to any taxable year for which the due date of the income tax return (without regard to extensions) is on or after [the date that is sixty days after final regulations are filed with the FEDERAL REGISTER]. For prior years, see § 1.1502-5 (as contained in the 26 CFR edition revised as of April 1, 1992).

§ 1.1502-6 Liability for tax.

(a) Several liability of members of group. Except as provided in paragraph (b) of this section, the common parent corporation and each subsidiary which was a member of the group during any part of the consolidated return year shall be severally liable for the tax for such year computed in accordance with the regulations under section 1502 prescribed on or before the due date (not including extensions of time) for the filing of the consolidated return for such year.

(b) Liability of subsidiary after withdrawal. If a subsidiary has ceased to be a member of the group and if such cessation resulted from a bona fide sale or exchange of its stock for fair value and occurred prior to the date upon which any deficiency is assessed, the Commissioner may, if he believes that the assessment or collection of the balance of the deficiency will not be jeopardized, make assessment and collection of such deficiency from such former subsidiary in an amount not exceeding the portion of such deficiency which the Commissioner may determine to be allocable to it. If the Commissioner makes assessment and collection of any part of a deficiency from such former subsidiary, then for the purposes of any credit or refund of the amount collected from such former subsidiary the agency of the common parent under the provisions of § 1.1502-77 shall not apply.

(c) Effect of intercompany agreements. No agreement entered into by one or more members of the group with any other member of such group or with any other person shall in any case have the effect of reducing the liability prescribed under this section.

T.D. 6894, 9/7/66, amend T.D. 9002, 6/27/2002.

§ 1.1502-9 Consolidated overall foreign losses, separate limitation losses, and overall domestic losses.

[Reserved]. For further guidance, see § 1.1502-9T.

T.D. 8833, 8/10/99, amend T.D. 9371, 12/20/2007.

PAR. 8.

Section 1.1502-9 is revised to read as follows:

Proposed § 1.1502-9 Consolidated overall foreign losses and separate limitation losses. [*For Preamble, see ¶ 152,941*]

[The text of proposed § 1.1502-9 is the same as the text of § 1.1502-9T(a) through (e) published elsewhere in this issue of the Federal Register.] [*See T.D. 9371, 12/21/2007, 72 Fed. Reg. 245.*]

§ 1.1502-9A Application of overall foreign loss recapture rules to corporations filing consolidated returns due on or before August 11, 1999.

(a) Scope. *(1) Effective date.* This section applies only to consolidated return years for which the due date of the income tax return (without extensions) is on or before August 11, 1999.

(2) In general. An affiliated group of corporations filing a consolidated return sustains an overall foreign loss (a consolidated overall foreign loss) in any taxable year in which its gross income from sources without the United States subject to a separate limitation (as defined in § 1.904(f)-1(c)(2)) is exceeded by the sum of the deductions properly allocated and apportioned thereto. However, for taxable years prior to 1983, affiliated groups may have determined their overall foreign losses for income subject to the passive interest limitation, DISC dividend limitation, and general limitation on a combined basis in accordance with the rules in § 1.904(f)-1(c)(1). The rules contained in §§ 1.904(f)-1 through 1.904(f)-6 are applicable to affiliated groups filing consolidated returns. This section provides special rules for applying those sections to such groups. Paragraph (b) provides rules for additions and subtractions of a portion of overall foreign losses to and from consolidated overall foreign loss accounts. Paragraph (c) requires that separate notional overall foreign loss accounts be kept for each member of the group that contributes to a consolidated overall foreign loss account and provides for allocation of a portion of the group's overall foreign loss account to a member when the member leaves the group prior to recapture of the entire amount of the loss account. These rules are similar to the rules provided in § 1.1502-21(b)(2) (or § 1.1502-79A, as appropriate) concerning the apportionment of consolidated net operating losses to a member who leaves the group. However, the rules differ somewhat because the absorption rule of § 1.1502-21(b)(1) or § 1.1502-79A, as appropriate) is applied year-by-year, consistently with the sequence rules of section 172(b), and recapture of overall foreign losses is based on overall foreign loss accounts that may consist of losses in more than one year. Paragraph (d) provides rules for recapture of amounts in consolidated overall foreign loss accounts. Paragraph (e) provides special rules pertaining to section 904(f)(3) dispositions between members of a group. Paragraphs (b), (c), and (e) also contain special rules that apply to overall foreign losses that arise in separate return limitation years; the principles therein also apply to overall foreign losses when there has been a consolidated return change of ownership (as defined in § 1.1502-1(g)). See § 1.1502-9T(b)(1)(v) for the rule that ends the separate return limitation year limitation for consolidated return years for which the due date of the income tax return (without extensions) is after March 13, 1998, and § 1.1502-9T(b)(1)(vi) for an election to continue the separate return limitation year limitation for consolidated return years beginning before January 1, 1998. See also § 1.1502-3(d)(4) for an optional effective date rule (generally making the rules of paragraphs (b)(1)(iii) and (iv) of this section inapplicable for a consolidated return year beginning after December 31, 1996, if the due date of the income tax return (without extensions) for such year is on or before March 13, 1998).

(b) Consolidated overall foreign loss accounts. Any group that sustains an overall foreign loss (or acquires a member with a balance in an overall foreign loss account) must establish a consolidated overall foreign loss account for such loss, and amounts shall be added to and subtracted from such account as provided in §§ 1.904(f)-1 through 1.904(f)-6 and this section.

(1) Additions to the consolidated overall foreign loss accounts. (i) Consolidated overall foreign losses. Any consolidated overall foreign loss shall be added to the applicable consolidated overall foreign loss account for such separate limitation, to the extent that the overall foreign loss has reduced United States source income, in accordance with the rules of §§ 1.904(f)-1 and 1.904(f)-3.

(ii) Overall foreign losses from separate return years. If a corporation joins in the filing of a consolidated return in a taxable year in which such corporation has a balance in an overall foreign loss account from a prior separate return year that is not a separate return limitation year, such balance shall be added to the applicable consolidated overall foreign loss account in such year and treated as a consolidated overall foreign loss incurred in the previous year (and shall therefore be subject to recapture, in accordance with paragraph (d) of this section, beginning in the same year in which it is added to the consolidated overall foreign loss account).

(iii) Overall foreign losses from separate return limitation years. If a corporation joins in the filing of a consolidated return in a taxable year in which such corporation has a balance in an overall foreign loss account from a prior separate return limitation year, such balance shall be added to the applicable consolidated overall foreign loss account in such consolidated return year to the extent of the lesser of the balance in the overall foreign loss account from the separate return limitation year or 50 percent (or such larger percentage as the taxpayer may elect) of the difference between the consolidated foreign source taxable income subject to the same separate limitation (computed in accordance with §§ 1.904(f)-2(b) and 1.1502-4(d)(1)) minus such consolidated foreign source taxable income recomputed by excluding the items of income and deduction of such corporation (but not less than zero). The amount added to a consolidated overall foreign loss account in any taxable year under this paragraph (b)(1)(iii) shall be treated as a consolidated overall foreign loss in the previous year (and shall therefore be subject to recapture, in accordance with paragraph (d) of this section, beginning in the same year in which it is added to the consolidated overall foreign loss account).

(iv) Overall foreign losses that are part of a net operating loss or net capital loss carried over from a separate return limitation year. Overall foreign losses that are part of a net operating loss or net capital loss carryover from a separate return limitation year of a member that is absorbed in a consolidated return year shall be treated as though they were added to an overall foreign loss account in a separate return limitation year of such member and will be subject to the limitation on recapture of SRLY losses contained in paragraph (b)(1)(iii) of this section. See paragraph (c)(2) of this section for rules regarding the addition of such losses to the applicable overall foreign loss account of such member.

(v) Special effective date for SRLY limitation. Except as provided in paragraph (b)(1)(vi) of this section, paragraphs (b)(1)(iii) and (iv) of this section apply only to consolidated return years for which the due date of the income tax return (without extensions) is on or before March 13, 1998. For consolidated return years for which the due date of the income tax return (without extensions) is after March 13, 1998, the rules of paragraph (b)(1)(ii) of this section shall apply to overall foreign losses from separate return years that are separate return limitation years. For purposes of applying paragraph (b)(1)(ii) of this section in such years, the group treats a member with a balance in an overall foreign loss account from a separate return limitation year on the first day of the first consolidated return year for which the due date of the income tax return (without extensions) is after March 13, 1998, as a corporation joining the group on such first day. An overall foreign loss that is part of a net operating loss or net capital loss carryover from a separate return limitation year of a member that is absorbed in a consolidated return year for which the due date of the income tax return (without extensions) is after March 13, 1998, shall be added to the appropriate consolidated overall foreign loss account in the year that it is absorbed. For consolidated return years for which the due date of the income tax return (without extensions) is after March 13, 1998, similar principles apply to overall foreign losses when there has been a consolidated return change of ownership (regardless of when the change of ownership occurred). See also § 1.1502-3(d)(4) for an optional effective date rule (generally making this paragraph (b)(1)(v) applicable to a consolidated return year beginning after December 31, 1996, if the due date of the income tax return (without extensions) for such year is on or before March 13, 1998).

(vi) Election to defer application of special effective date. A consolidated group may elect not to apply paragraph (b)(1)(v) of this section to consolidated return years beginning before January 1, 1998. To make this election, a consolidated group must write "Election Pursuant to Notice 98-40" across the top of page 1 of an original or amended tax return for each consolidated return year subject to the election. For the first consolidated return year to which the overall foreign loss provisions of paragraph (b)(1)(v) of this section apply (i.e., the first year beginning on or after January 1, 1998), such consolidated group must write "Notice 98-40 Election in Effect in Prior Years" across the top of page 1 of the consolidated tax return for that year. For purposes of applying paragraph (b)(1)(ii) of this section with respect to such year, any member with a balance in an overall foreign loss account from a separate return limitation year on the first day of such year shall be treated as joining the group on such first day.

(2) Reductions of the consolidated overall foreign loss accounts. (i) Amounts allocated to members leaving the group. When a member leaves the group, each applicable consolidated overall foreign loss account shall be reduced by the amount allocated from such account to such member in accordance with paragraph (c)(3)(i) of this section.

(ii) Amounts recaptured. A consolidated overall foreign loss account shall be reduced by the amount of any overall foreign loss under the same separate limitation that is recaptured from consolidated income in accordance with § 1.904(f)-2.

(c) Allocation of overall foreign losses among members of an affiliated group. *(1) Notional overall foreign loss accounts.* Separate notional overall foreign loss accounts shall be established for each member of a group that contributes to a consolidated overall foreign loss account. Additions to and reductions of such notional accounts shall be made when additions or reductions are made to consolidated overall foreign loss accounts in accordance with paragraph (b) of this section and § 1.904(f)-1.

(i) Additions to notional accounts. (A) Consolidated overall foreign losses. When a consolidated overall foreign loss is added to a consolidated overall foreign loss account, each member shall add its pro rata share of the amount of such loss to the member's notional overall foreign loss account. A member's pro rata share of a consolidated overall foreign loss for any taxable year is determined by multiplying the consolidated loss by a fraction. The numerator of this fraction is the amount by which the member's separate gross income for the taxable year from sources without the United States subject to the applicable separate limitation is exceeded by the sum of the deductions properly allocated and apportioned thereto (including such member's share of any consolidated net operating loss deduction and consolidated net capital loss carryovers and carrybacks to the taxable year), for each member with such deductions in excess of such income. The denominator of this fraction is the sum of the numerators of this fraction for all such members of the group.

(B) Overall foreign losses from separate return years and separate return limitation years. When an amount from a member's overall foreign loss account from a separate return year or separate return limitation year is added to a consolidated overall foreign loss account in accordance with paragraph (b)(1)(ii) or (iii) of this section, such amount shall also be added to that member's notional overall foreign loss account for such separate limitation.

(ii) Reductions of notional accounts. When a consolidated overall foreign loss account is reduced by recapture, in accordance with paragraph (b)(2)(ii) of this section, each member of the group shall reduce its notional overall foreign loss account for that separate limitation by its pro rata share of the amount by which the consolidated overall foreign loss account is reduced. A member's pro rata share of the amount by which a consolidated overall foreign loss account is reduced and determined by multiplying the amount recaptured by a fraction, the numerator of which is the amount in such member's notional account under such separate limitation, and the denominator of which is the amount in the consolidated overall foreign loss account under such separate limitation before reduction for the amount recaptured for that taxable year.

(2) Overall foreign losses that are part of a net operating loss or net capital loss from a separate return limitation year. An overall foreign loss that is part of a net operating loss or net capital loss carryover from a separate return limitation year of a member that is absorbed in a consolidated return year shall be treated as an overall foreign loss of such mem-

ber (rather than the group) and shall be added to such member's separate overall foreign loss account to the extent it reduces United States source income, in accordance with § 1.904(f)-1(d)(5). Such overall foreign losses shall be added to the appropriate consolidated overall foreign loss account in later years in accordance with paragraph (b)(1)(iii) of this section.

(3) Allocation of a portion of overall foreign loss accounts to a member leaving the group. (i) Consolidated overall foreign losses. When a corporation ceases to be a member of an affiliated group filing consolidated returns, a portion of the balance in each applicable consolidated overall foreign loss account shall be allocated to such corporation. The amount allocated to such corporation shall be equal to the amount, if any, in such member's notional overall foreign loss account under the same separate limitation.

(ii) Overall foreign losses from separate return limitation years. When a corporation ceases to be a member of an affiliated group filing consolidated returns, it shall take with it the remaining portion of each separate overall foreign loss account for overall foreign losses from separate return limitation years (including amounts added to such accounts under paragraph (c)(2) of this section).

(d) Recapture of consolidated overall foreign losses. The amount in any consolidated overall foreign loss account shall be recaptured under §§ 1.904(f)-1 through 1.904(f)-6 by recharacterizing consolidated foreign source taxable income subject to the separate limitation under which the loss arose as United States source taxable income. For purposes of recapture, consolidated foreign source taxable income subject to the separate limitation under which the loss arose shall be determined in accordance with §§ 1.904(f)-2 and 1.1502-4. Amounts in a member's excess loss account that are included in income under § 1.1502-19 shall be subject to recapture to the extent that they are included in consolidated foreign source taxable income subject to the separate limitation under which the loss arose.

(e) Dispositions of property between members of the same affiliated group during a consolidated return year. *(1) In general.* Except as provided in paragraph (2) with respect to overall foreign losses of a selling member from a separate return limitation year, the rules of § 1.1502-13 with respect to intercompany transactions will apply to dispositions of property to which section 904(f)(3)(A) applies.

(2) Recapture of overall foreign loss from a separate return limitation year. Paragraph (1) will not apply and gain will be recognized to the extent that the selling member has a balance in its overall foreign loss account from a separate return limitation year unless the selling member adds the entire amount of its overall foreign loss account from separate return limitation years to the applicable consolidated overall foreign loss account and treats such amount as an overall foreign loss incurred in the previous year. Such loss shall be subject to recapture, in accordance with paragraph (d) of § 1.1502-9, beginning in the same year in which it is added to the consolidated overall foreign loss account.

(f) Illustrations. The provisions of this section are illustrated by the following examples. All foreign source income or loss in these examples is subject to the general limitation.

Example (1). A, B, and C are the members of an affiliated group of corporations (as defined in section 1504), and all use the calendar year as their taxable year. For 1983, A, B, and C file a consolidated return. ABC has United States source income of $1,000 and foreign source losses (overall foreign loss) of $400. In accordance with paragraph (b)(1)(i) of this section, ABC adds $400 to its consolidated overall foreign loss account at the end of 1983. For 1983, the separate foreign source taxable income (or loss) of A is $400, of B is ($200), and of C is ($600). Under paragraph (c)(1) of this section, B and C must establish separate notional overall foreign loss accounts. Under paragraph (c)(1)(i)(A) of this section, the amount added to each notional account is the pro rata share of the consolidated overall foreign loss of each member contributing to such loss. The pro rata share is determined by multiplying the consolidated loss by the member's proportionate share of the total foreign source losses of all members having such losses. B's foreign source loss if $200 and C's foreign source loss is $600, totaling $800. B must add $400 × 200/800, or $100, to its notional overall foreign loss account. C must add $400 × 600/800, or $300, to its notional overall foreign loss account.

Example (2). The facts are the same as in example (1). In 1984, ABC has consolidated foreign source taxable income of $200. Under paragraph (d) of this section and § 1.904(f)-2, ABC is required to recapture $100 of the amount in its consolidated overall foreign loss account, which reduces that account by $100 under paragraph (b)(2)(ii) of this section. In accordance with paragraph (c)(1)(ii) of this section, B reduces its notional account by $100 × 100/400, or $25, and C reduces it notional account by $100 × 300/400, or $75. At the end of 1984 ABC has $300 in its consolidated overall foreign loss account, B has $75 in its notional account, and C has $225 in its notional account.

Example (3). D and E are members of an affiliated group and file separate returns using the calendar year as their taxable year for 1980. In 1980, D has an overall foreign loss of $200, which it adds to its overall foreign loss account, and E has no overall foreign losses. For 1981, D and E file a consolidated return, and DE must establish a consolidated overall foreign loss account, to which D's overall foreign loss from 1980 is added under paragraph (b)(1)(ii) of this section. D also adds the same amount $200 to its notional account under paragraph (c)(1)(i)(B) of this section. In 1981, DE has consolidated foreign source taxable income of $300. Since the amount added to the consolidated overall foreign loss account in 1981 is treated as a consolidated overall foreign loss from 1980, DE must recapture $150 in 1981 under paragraph (d) of this section and § 1.904(f)-2. DE's consolidated overall foreign loss account is reduced by $150 under paragraph (b)(2)(ii) of this section, and D's notional account is reduced by $150 under paragraph (c)(1)(ii) of this section, leaving balances of $50 in each of those accounts at the end of 1981.

Example (4). F and G are not members of an affiliated group in 1980, and G has an overall foreign loss of $200, which it adds to its overall foreign loss account. F has no overall foreign loss. On January 1, 1981, F acquires G, and FG files a consolidated return for the calendar year 1981. In 1981, F has no foreign source taxable income or loss, and G has $100 of foreign source taxable income. FG's consolidated foreign source taxable income, $100, minus such income without G's items of income and deduction, $0, is $100. Therefore 50% of that amount, $50, of G's overall foreign loss from its 1980 separate return limitation year is added to FG's consolidated overall foreign loss account under paragraph (b)(1)(iii) of this section, and the same amount is added to G's notional account under paragraph (c)(1)(i)(B) of this section. In accordance with paragraph (d) of this section and § 1.904(f)-2, FG must recapture the $50 balance in its consolidated overall foreign loss account in 1981 because the amount added from G's separate return limitation year is treated as a 1980 consolidated overall foreign loss. At the end of 1981, FG has a balance of $0 in its consolidated overall foreign loss account, G has $0 in its notional account, and G also has $150 remaining from its 1980 overall foreign loss that has not yet been added to the consolidated overall foreign loss account.

On January 1, 1982, F sells G and G leaves the affiliated group. Under paragraph (c)(3)(i) of this section, G takes with it the balance in its overall foreign loss account from 1980 (its prior separate return limitation year) that has not been added to the consolidated account. G has $150 of overall foreign loss in its overall foreign loss account. Because the amount in the consolidated overall foreign loss account is zero, no amount from that account is allocated to G.

Example (5). (i) In 1982 corporation H has United States source income of $300 and foreign source losses to $500, resulting in a net operating loss of $200 and a balance in H's overall foreign loss account at the end of 1982 of $300.

(ii) On January 1, 1983, H is acquired by J, and for the calendar year 1983 JH files a consolidated return. JH has consolidated taxable income of $700 in 1983, including a consolidated net operating loss deduction of $100. This net operating loss deduction is $100 of H's $200 net operating loss from 1982 (a separate return limitation year), which is limited by § 1.1502-21A(c). For 1983, H has separate taxable income of $100, comprised of $100 of United States source taxable income and zero foreign source taxable income, and J has separate taxable income of $700, comprised of $700 of United States source taxable income and zero foreign source taxable income. Under paragraph (c)(2) of this section, H adds $100 to its separate overall foreign loss account, since that amount of its net operating loss has reduced United States source income. H has $400 in its separate overall foreign loss account at the end of 1983, none of which has been added to a consolidated overall foreign loss account.

(iii) In 1984, H has separate taxable income of $400, comprised of $100 of United States source taxable income and $300 of foreign source taxable income. J has separate taxable income of $900, comprised of $700 of United States source taxable income and $200 of foreign source taxable income. JH has consolidated taxable income of $1200, which includes $100 of consolidated net operating loss deduction from H's 1982 net operating loss, since this net operating loss deduction is allocated to foreign source income, it does not reduce United States source income and will not be added to an overall foreign loss account. Under paragraph (b)(1)(iii) of this section, $100, from H's overall foreign loss is added to the consolidated overall foreign loss account computed as follows:

Consolidated foreign source taxable income	$400
Consolidated foreign source taxable income recomputed by excluding H's foreign source income and deduction	– 200
$200	
× 50%	$100
Amount from H's separate return limitation year overall foreign loss account added to the consolidated overall foreign loss account	$100

This amount is subject to recapture beginning in the same taxable year, as it is treated as a consolidated overall foreign loss incurred in a previous year. Therefore, under paragraph (d) of this section and § 1.904(f)-2 JH also recaptures this $100, reducing the consolidated overall foreign loss account to $0. H has $300 remaining in its separate overall foreign loss account at the end of 1984.

(iv) In 1985, H has separate taxable income of $400, comprised of $100 of United States source taxable income and $300 of foreign source taxable income. J has separate taxable income of $300 comprised of $600 of United States source taxable income and $300 of foreign source losses. JH has consolidated taxable income of $700, all of which is United States source. Under paragraph (b)(1)(iii) of this section an additional $150 from H's separate overall foreign loss is added to the consolidated overall foreign loss account, computed as follows:

Consolidated foreign source taxable income	$0
Consolidated foreign source taxable income recomputed by excluding H's foreign source income and deductions	– (300)
300	
× 50%	$150
Amount from H's separate return limitation year overall foreign loss account added to the consolidated overall foreign loss account	$150

Thus, an additional $150 of H's separate overall foreign loss is added to the consolidated overall foreign loss account, and, under paragraph (c)(1)(i)(B) of this section, the same amount is added to J's notional account. While this amount is subject to recapture beginning in the same taxable year, JH has no consolidated foreign source taxable income on 1985, so no overall foreign loss is recaptured. H has a remaining balance of $150 in its separate return limitation year overall foreign loss account and HJ has $150 in its consolidated overall foreign loss account.

Example (6). A, B, and C are members of an affiliated group of corporations (as defined in section 1504), and all use the calendar year as their taxable year. For 1986, A, B, and C file a consolidated return. A has an overall foreign loss account which arose in a separate return limitation year. The amount in the overall foreign loss account is $2,000. A makes a disposition of all its assets to B on January 1, 1986. The gain on the transfer is $1,500, all of which would be recognized under section 904(f)(3). However, if A adds the total amount of its overall foreign loss from separate return limitation years to ABC's consolidated overall foreign loss account, no gain will be recognized on the transfer until the intercompany gain is taken into account under § 1.1502-13. In the interim, any foreign source gain of the purchasing member (or any other member of the consolidated group) may be used to recapture on a consolidated basis the amount in ABC's consolidated overall foreign loss account.

T.D. 8153, 8/21/87, amend T.D. 8597, 7/12/95, T.D. 8677, 6/26/96, T.D. 8751, 1/9/98, T.D. 8766, 3/13/98, T.D. 8800, 12/28/98, T.D. 8823, 6/25/99, T.D. 8833, 8/10/99, T.D. 8884, 5/24/2000.

§ 1.1502-9T Consolidated overall foreign losses, separate limitation losses, and overall domestic losses (temporary).

(a) In general. This section provides rules for applying section 904(f) and (g) (including its definitions and nomenclature) to a group and its members. Generally, section 904(f) concerns rules relating to overall foreign losses (OFLs) and separate limitation losses (SLLs) and the consequences of such losses. Under section 904(f)(5), losses are computed separately in each category of income described in section 904(d)(1) or § 1.904-4(m) (separate category). Section 904(g) concerns rules relating to overall domestic losses (ODLs) and the consequences of such losses. Paragraph (b) of this section defines terms and provides computational and accounting rules, including rules regarding recapture. Paragraph (c) of this section provides rules that apply to OFLs, SLLs, and ODLs when a member becomes or ceases to be a member of a group. Paragraph (d) of this section provides a predecessor and successor rule. Paragraph (e) of this section provides effective dates.

(b) Consolidated application of section 904(f) and (g). A group applies section 904(f) and (g) for a consolidated return year in accordance with that section, subject to the following rules:

(1) Computation of CSLI or CSLL and consolidated U.S.-source taxable income or CDL. The group computes its consolidated separate limitation income (CSLI) or consolidated separate limitation loss (CSLL) for each separate category under the principles of § 1.1502-11 by aggregating each member's foreign-source taxable income or loss in such separate category computed under the principles of § 1.1502-12, and taking into account the foreign portion of the consolidated items described in § 1.1502-11(a)(2) through (8) for such separate category. The group computes its consolidated U.S.-source taxable income or consolidated domestic loss (CDL) under similar principles.

(2) Netting CSLLs, CSLIs, and consolidated U.S.-source taxable income. The group applies section 904(f)(5) to determine the extent to which a CSLL for a separate category reduces CSLI for another separate category or consolidated U.S.-source taxable income.

(3) Netting CDL and CSLI. The group applies section 904(g)(2) to determine the extent to which a CDL reduces CSLI.

(4) CSLL, COFL, and CODL accounts. To the extent provided in section 904(f), the amount by which a CSLL for a separate category (the loss category) reduces CSLI for another separate category (the income category) shall result in the creation of (or addition to) a CSLL account for the loss category with respect to the income category. Likewise, the amount by which a CSLL for a loss category reduces consolidated U.S.-source taxable income will create (or add to) a consolidated overall foreign loss account (a COFL account). To the extent provided in section 904(g), the amount by which a CDL reduces CSLI shall result in the creation of (or addition to) a consolidated overall domestic loss (CODL) account for the income category reduced by the CDL.

(5) Recapture of COFL, CSLL, and CODL accounts. In the case of a COFL account for a loss category, section 904(f)(1) and (3) recharacterizes some or all of the foreign-source income in the loss category as U.S.-source income. In the case of a CSLL account for a loss category with respect to an income category, section 904(f)(5)(C) and (F) recharacterizes some or all of the foreign-source income in the loss category as foreign-source income in the income category. In the case of a CODL account, section 904(g)(3) recharacterizes some of the U.S.-source income as foreign-source income in the separate category that was offset by the CDL. The COFL account, CSLL account, or CODL account is reduced to the extent income is recharacterized with respect to such account.

(6) Intercompany transactions. (i) Nonapplication of section 904(f) disposition rules. Neither section 904(f)(3) (in the case of a COFL account) nor section 904(f)(5)(F) (in the case of a CSLL account) applies at the time of a disposition that is an intercompany transaction to which § 1.1502-13 applies. Instead, section 904(f)(3) and (5)(F) applies only at such time and only to the extent that the group is required under § 1.1502-13 (without regard to section 904(f)(3) and (5)(F)) to take into account any intercompany items resulting from the disposition, based on the COFL or CSLL account existing at the end of the consolidated return year during which the group takes the intercompany items into account.

(ii) Examples. Paragraph (b)(6)(i) of this section is illustrated by the following examples. The identity of the parties and the basic assumptions set forth in § 1.1502-13(c)(7)(i) apply to the examples. Except as otherwise stated, assume further that the consolidated group recognizes no foreign-source income other than as a result of the transactions described. The examples are as follows:

Example (1). (i) On June 10, year 1, S transfers nondepreciable property with a basis of $100 and a fair market value of $250 to B in a transaction to which section 351 applies. The property was predominantly used without the United States in a trade or business, within the meaning of section 904(f)(3). B continues to use the property without the United States. The group has a COFL account in the relevant loss category of $120 as of December 31, year 1.

(ii) Because the contribution from S to B is an intercompany transaction, section 904(f)(3) does not apply to result in any gain recognition in year 1. See paragraph (b)(5)(i) of this section.

(iii) On January 10, year 4, B ceases to be a member of the group. Because S did not recognize gain in year 1 under section 351, no gain is taken into account in year 4 under § 1.1502-13. Thus, no portion of the group's COFL account is recaptured in year 4. For rules requiring apportionment of a portion of the COFL account to B, see paragraph (c)(2) of this section.

Example (2). (i) The facts are the same as in paragraph (i) of Example 1. On January 10, year 4, B sells the property to X for $300. As of December 31, year 4, the group's COFL account is $40. (The COFL account was reduced between year 1 and year 4 due to unrelated foreign-source income taken into account by the group.)

(ii) B takes into account gain of $200 in year 4. The $40 COFL account in year 4 recharacterizes $40 of the gain as U.S. source. See section 904(f)(3).

Example (3). (i) On June 10, year 1, S sells nondepreciable property with a basis of $100 and a fair market value of $250 to B for $250 cash. The property was predominantly used without the United States in a trade or business, within the meaning of section 904(f)(3). The group has a COFL account in the relevant loss category of $120 as of December 31, year 1. B predominantly uses the property in a trade or business without the United States.

(ii) Because the sale is an intercompany transaction, section 904(f)(3) does not require the group to take into account any gain in year 1. Thus, under paragraph (b)(5)(i) of this section, the COFL account is not reduced in year 1.

(iii) On January 10, year 4, B sells the property to X for $300. As of December 31, year 4, the group's COFL account is $60. (The COFL account was reduced between year 1 and year 4 due to unrelated foreign-source income taken into account by the group.)

(iv) In year 4, S's $150 intercompany gain and B's $50 corresponding gain are taken into account to produce the same effect on consolidated taxable income as if S and B were divisions of a single corporation. See § 1.1502-13(c). All of B's $50 corresponding gain is recharacterized under section 904(f)(3). If S and B were divisions of a single corporation and the intercompany sale were a transfer between the divisions, B would succeed to S's $100 basis in the property and would have $200 of gain ($60 of which would be recharacterized under section 904(f)(3)), instead of a $50 gain. Consequently, S's $150 intercompany gain and B's $50 corresponding gain are taken into account, and $10 of S's gain is recharacterized under section 904(f)(3) as U.S. source income to reflect the $10 difference between B's $50 recharacterized gain and the $60 recomputed gain that would have been recharacterized.

(c) Becoming or ceasing to be a member of a group. *(1) Adding separate accounts on becoming a member.* At the time that a corporation becomes a member of a group (a new member), the group adds to the balance of its COFL, CSLL or CODL account the balance of the new member's corresponding OFL account, SLL account or ODL account. A new member's OFL account corresponds to a COFL account if the account is for the same loss category. A new member's SLL account corresponds to a CSLL account if the account is for the same loss category and with respect to the same income category. A new member's ODL account corresponds to a CODL account if the account is with respect to the same income category. If the group does not have a COFL, CSLL or CODL account corresponding to the new member's account, it creates a COFL, CSLL or CODL account with a balance equal to the balance of the member's account.

(2) Apportionment of consolidated account to departing member. (i) In general. A group apportions to a member that ceases to be a member (a departing member) a portion of each COFL, CSLL and CODL account as of the end of the year during which the member ceases to be a member and after the group makes the additions or reductions to such account required under paragraphs (b)(4), (b)(5) and (c)(1) of this section (other than an addition under paragraph (c)(1) of this section attributable to a member becoming a member after the departing member ceases to be a member). The group computes such portion under paragraph (c)(2)(ii) of this section, as limited by paragraph (c)(2)(iii) of this section. The departing member carries such portion to its first separate return year after it ceases to be a member. Also, the group reduces each account by such portion and carries such reduced amount to its first consolidated return year beginning after the year in which the member ceases to be a member. If two or more members cease to be members in the same year, the group computes the portion allocable to each such member (and reduces its accounts by such portion) in the order that the members cease to be members.

(ii) Departing member's portion of group's account. A departing member's portion of a group's COFL, CSLL or CODL account for a loss category is computed based upon the member's share of the group's assets that generate income subject to recapture at the time that the member ceases to be a member. Under the characterization principles of §§ 1.861-9T(g)(3) and 1.861-12T, the group identifies the assets of the departing member and the remaining members that generate U.S.-source income (domestic assets) and foreign-source income (foreign assets) in each separate category. The assets are characterized based upon the income that the assets are reasonably expected to generate after the member ceases to be a member. The member's portion of a group's COFL or CSLL account for a loss category is the group's COFL or CSLL account, respectively, multiplied by a fraction, the numerator of which is the value of the member's foreign assets for the loss category and the denominator of which is the value of the foreign assets of the group (including the departing member) for the loss category. The member's portion of a group's CODL account for each income category is the group's CODL account multiplied by a fraction, the numerator of which is the value of the member's domestic assets and the denominator of which is the value of the domestic assets of the group (including the departing member). The value of the domestic and foreign assets is determined under the asset valuation rules of § 1.861-9T(g)(1) and (2) using either tax book value or fair market value under the method chosen by the group for purposes of interest apportionment as provided in § 1.861-9T(g)(1)(ii). For purposes of this paragraph (c)(2)(ii), § 1.861-9T(g)(2)(iv) (assets in intercompany transactions) shall apply, but § 1.861-9T(g)(2)(iii) (adjustments for directly allocated interest) shall not apply. If the group uses the tax book value method, the member's portions of COFL, CSLL, and CODL accounts are limited by paragraph (c)(2)(iii) of this section. In addition, for purposes of this paragraph (c)(2)(ii), the tax book value of assets transferred in intercompany transactions shall be determined without regard to previously deferred gain or loss that is taken into account by the group as a result of the transaction in which the member ceases to be a member. The assets should be valued at the time the member ceases to be a member, but values on other dates may be used unless this creates substantial distortions. For example, if a member ceases to be a member in the middle of the group's consolidated return year, an average of the values of assets at the beginning and end of the year (as provided in § 1.861-9T(g)(2)) may be used or, if a member ceases to be a member in the early part of the group's consolidated return year, values at the beginning of the year may be used, unless this creates substantial distortions.

(iii) Limitation on member's portion for groups using tax book value method. If a group uses the tax book value method of valuing assets for purposes of paragraph (c)(2)(ii) of this section and the aggregate of a member's portions of COFL and CSLL accounts for a loss category (with respect to one or more income categories) determined under paragraph (c)(2)(ii) of this section exceeds 150 percent of the actual fair market value of the member's foreign assets in the loss category, the member's portion of the COFL or CSLL accounts for the loss category shall be reduced (proportionately, in the case of multiple accounts) by such excess. In addition, if the aggregate of a member's portions of CODL accounts (with respect to one or more income categories) determined under paragraph (c)(2)(ii) of this section exceeds 150 percent of the actual fair market value of the member's domestic assets, the member's portion of the CODL accounts shall be reduced (proportionately, in the case of multiple accounts) by such excess. This rule does not apply in the case of COFL or CSLL accounts if the departing member and all other members that cease to be members as part of the same transaction own all (or substantially all) the foreign assets in the loss category. In the case of CODL accounts, this rule does not apply if the departing member and all other members that cease to be members as part of the same transaction own all (or substantially all) the domestic assets.

(iv) Determination of values of domestic and foreign assets binding on departing member. The group's determination of the value of the member's and the group's domestic and foreign assets for a loss category is binding on the member, unless the Commissioner concludes that the determination is not appropriate. The common parent of the group must attach a statement to the return for the taxable year that the departing member ceases to be a member of the group that sets forth the name and taxpayer identification number of the departing member, the amount of each COFL and

CSLL for each loss category and each CODL that is apportioned to the departing member under this paragraph (c)(2), the method used to determine the value of the member's and the group's domestic and foreign assets in each such loss category, and the value of the member's and the group's domestic and foreign assets in each such loss category. The common parent must also furnish a copy of the statement to the departing member.

(v) Anti-abuse rule. If a corporation becomes a member and ceases to be a member, and a principal purpose of the corporation becoming and ceasing to be a member is to transfer the corporation's OFL account, SLL account or ODL account to the group or to transfer the group's COFL, CSLL or CODL account to the corporation, appropriate adjustments will be made to eliminate the benefit of such a transfer of accounts. Similarly, if any member acquires assets or disposes of assets (including a transfer of assets between members of the group and the departing member) with a principal purpose of affecting the apportionment of accounts under paragraph (c)(2)(i) of this section, appropriate adjustments will be made to eliminate the benefit of such acquisition or disposition.

(vi) Examples. The following examples illustrate the rules of this paragraph (c):

Example (1). (i) On November 6, year 1, S, a member of the P group, a consolidated group with a calendar consolidated return year, ceases to be a member of the group. On December 31, year 1, the P group has a $40 COFL account for the general category, a $20 CSLL account for the general category (that is, the loss category) with respect to the passive category (that is, the income category), and a $10 CODL account with respect to the passive category (that is, the income category). No member of the group has foreign-source income or loss in year 1. The group apportions its interest expense according to the tax book value method.

(ii) On November 6, year 1, the group identifies S's assets and the group's assets (including S's assets) expected to produce foreign-source general category income. Use of end-of-the-year values will not create substantial distortions in determining the relative values of S's and the group's relevant assets on November 6, year 1. The group determines that S's relevant assets have a tax book value of $2,000 and a fair market value of $2,200. Also, the group's relevant assets (including S's assets) have a tax book value of $8,000. On November 6, year 1, S has no assets expected to produce U.S. source income.

(iii) Under paragraph (c)(2)(ii) of this section, S takes a $10 COFL account for the general category ($40 x $2000/$8000) and a $5 CSLL account for the general category with respect to the passive category ($20 x $2000/$8000). S does not take any portion of the CODL account. The limitation described in paragraph (c)(2)(iii) of this section does not apply because the aggregate of the COFL and CSLL accounts for the general category that are apportioned to S ($15) is less than 150 percent of the actual fair market value of S's general category foreign assets ($2,200 x 150%).

Example (2). (i) Assume the same facts as in Example 1, except that the fair market value of S's general category foreign assets is $4 as of November 6, year 1.

(ii) Under paragraph (c)(2)(iii) of this section, S's COFL and CSLL accounts for the general category must be reduced by $9, which is the excess of $15 (the aggregate amount of the accounts apportioned under paragraph (c)(2)(ii) of this section) over $6 (150 percent of the $4 actual fair market value of S's general category foreign assets). S thus takes a $4 COFL account for the general category ($10-($9 x $10/$15)) and a $2 CSLL account for the general category with respect to the passive category ($5-($9 x $5/$15)).

Example (3). (i) Assume the same facts as in Example 1, except that S also has assets that are expected to produce U.S. source income.

(ii) On November 6, year 1, the group identifies S's assets and the group's assets (including S's assets) expected to produce U.S. source income. Use of end-of-the-year values will not create substantial distortions in determining the relative values of S's and the group's relevant assets on November 6, year 1. The group determines that S's relevant assets have a tax book value of $3,000 and a fair market value of $2,500. Also, the group's relevant assets (including S's assets) have a tax book value of $6,000.

(iii) Under paragraph (c)(2)(ii) of this section, S takes a $5 CODL account ($10 x $3,000/$6,000), in addition to the COFL and CSLL accounts determined in Example 1. The limitation described in paragraph (c)(2)(iii) of this section does not apply because the CODL account that is apportioned to S ($5) is less than 150 percent of the actual fair market value of S's U.S. assets ($2,500 x 150%).

(d) Predecessor and successor. A reference to a member includes, as the context may require, a reference to a predecessor or successor of the member. See § 1.1502-1(f).

(e) Effective/applicability date. This section applies to consolidated return years beginning after December 21, 2007. Taxpayers may choose to apply the provisions of this section relating to overall domestic losses to other consolidated return years beginning after December 31, 2006, as well. For rules relating to overall foreign losses and separate limitation losses in consolidated return years beginning on or before December 21, 2007 see 26 CFR 1.1502-9 (revised as of April 1, 2007).

(f) Expiration date. The applicability of this section expires on December 20, 2010.

T.D. 9371, 12/20/2007.

§ 1.1502-11 Consolidated taxable income.

(a) In general. The consolidated taxable income for a consolidated return year shall be determined by taking into account—

(1) The separate taxable income of each member of the group (see § 1.1502-12 for the computation of separate taxable income);

(2) Any consolidated net operating loss deduction (see § 1.1502-21 (or § 1.1502-21A, as appropriate) for the computation of the consolidated net operating loss deduction);

(3) Any consolidated capital gain net income (net capital gain for taxable years beginning before January 1, 1977) (see § 1.1502-22 (or § 1.1502-22A, as appropriate) for the computation of the consolidated capital gain net income (net capital gain for taxable years beginning before January 1, 1977);

(4) Any consolidated section 1231 net loss (see § 1.1502-23 (or § 1.1502-23A, as appropriate) for the computation of the consolidated section 1231 net loss);

(5) Any consolidated charitable contributions deduction (see § 1.1502-24 for the computation of the consolidated charitable contributions deduction);

(6) Any consolidated section 922 deduction (see § 1.1502-25 for the computation of the consolidated section 922 deduction);

(7) Any consolidated dividends received deduction (see § 1.1502-26 for the computation of the consolidated dividends received deduction); and

(8) Any consolidated section 247 deduction (see § 1.1502-27 for the computation of the consolidated section 247 deduction).

(b) Elimination of circular stock basis adjustments when there is no excluded COD income. *(1) In general.* If one member (P) disposes of the stock of another member (S), this paragraph (b) limits the use of S's deductions and losses in the year of disposition and the carryback of items to prior years. The purpose of the limitation is to prevent P's income or gain from the disposition of S's stock from increasing the absorption of S's deductions and losses, because the increased absorption would reduce P's basis (or increase its excess loss account) in S's stock under § 1.1502-32 and, in turn, increase P's income or gain. See paragraph (b)(3) of this section for the application of these principles to P's deduction or loss from the disposition of S's stock, and paragraph (b)(4) of this section for the application of these principles to multiple stock dispositions. This paragraph (b) applies only when no member realizes discharge of indebtedness income that is excluded from gross income under section 108(a) (excluded COD income) during the taxable year of the disposition. See paragraph (c) of this section for rules that apply when a member realizes excluded COD income during the taxable year of the disposition. See § 1.1502-19(c) for the definition of disposition.

(2) Limitation on deductions and losses. (i) Determination of amount of limitation. If P disposes of one or more shares of S's stock, the extent to which S's deductions and losses for the tax year of the disposition (and its deductions and losses carried over from prior years) may offset income and gain is subject to limitation. The amount of S's deductions and losses that may offset income and gain is determined by tentatively computing taxable income (or loss) for the year of disposition (and any prior years to which the deductions or losses may be carried) without taking into account P's income and gain from the disposition.

(ii) Application of limitation. S's deductions and losses offset income and gain only to the extent of the amount determined under paragraph (b)(2)(i) of this section. To the extent S's deductions and losses in the year of disposition cannot offset income or gain because of the limitation under this paragraph (b), the items are carried to other years under the applicable provisions of the Internal Revenue Code and regulations as if they were the only items incurred by S in the year of disposition. For example, to the extent S incurs an operating loss in the year of disposition that is limited, the loss is treated as a separate net operating loss attributable to S arising in that year. The tentative computation does not affect the manner in which S's unlimited deductions and losses are absorbed or the manner in which deductions and losses of other members are absorbed. (If the amount of S's unlimited deductions and losses actually absorbed is less than the amount absorbed in the tentative computation, P's stock basis adjustments under § 1.1502-32 reflect only the amounts actually absorbed.)

(iii) Examples. For purposes of the examples in this paragraph (b), unless otherwise stated, P owns all of the only class of S's stock for the entire year, S owns no stock of lower-tier members, the tax year of all persons is the calendar year, all persons use the accrual method of accounting, the facts set forth the only corporate activity, all transactions are between unrelated persons, and tax liabilities are disregarded. The principles of this paragraph (b)(2) are illustrated by the following examples.

Example (1). Limitation on losses with respect to stock gain.

(a) P has a $500 basis in S's stock. For Year 1, P has ordinary income of $30 (determined without taking P's gain or loss from the disposition of S's stock into account) and S has an $80 ordinary loss. P sells S's stock for $520 at the close of Year 1.

(b) To determine the amount of the limitation on S's loss under paragraph (b)(2)(i) of this section, and the effect under § 1.1502-32(b) of the absorption of S's loss on P's basis in S's stock, P's gain or loss from the disposition of S's stock is not taken into account. The group is tentatively treated as having a consolidated net operating loss of $50 (P's $30 of income minus S's $80 loss). Thus, $50 of S's loss is limited under this paragraph (b).

(c) Because $30 of S's loss is absorbed in the determination of consolidated taxable income under paragraph (b)(2)(ii) of this section, P's basis in S's stock is reduced under § 1.1502-32(b) from $500 to $470 immediately before the disposition. Consequently, P recognizes a $50 gain from the sale of S's stock and the group has consolidated taxable income of $50 for Year 1 (P's $30 of ordinary income and $50 gain from the sale of S's stock, less the $30 of S's loss). In addition, S's limited loss of $50 is treated as a separate net operating loss attributable to S and, because S ceases to be a member, the loss is apportioned to S under § 1.1502-21 (or § 1.1502-79A, as appropriate) and carried to its first separate return year.

Example (2). Carrybacks and carryovers.

(a) For Year 1, the P group has consolidated taxable income of $30, and a consolidated net capital loss of $100 ($50 attributable to P and $50 to S). At the beginning of Year 2, P has a $300 basis in S's stock. For Year 2, P has ordinary income of $30, and a $20 capital gain (determined without taking the $100 consolidated net capital loss carryover or P's gain or loss from the disposition of S's stock into account), and S has a $100 ordinary loss. P sells S's stock for $280 at the close of Year 2.

(b) To determine the amount of the limitation under paragraph (b)(2)(i) of this section on S's losses, and the effect of the absorption of S's losses on P's basis in S's stock under § 1.1502-32(b), P's gain or loss from the disposition of S's stock is not taken into account. For Year 2, the P group is tentatively treated as having a $70 consolidated net operating loss (S's $100 ordinary loss, less P's $30 of ordinary income). The P group is also treated as having no consolidated net capital gain in Year 2, because P's $20 capital gain is reduced by $20 of the consolidated net capital loss carryover from Year 1 under section 1212(a) (the absorption of which is attributed equally to P and S). In addition, of the $70 consolidated net operating loss, $30 is carried back to Year 1 and offsets P's ordinary income in that year, and $40 is carried forward. Consequently, $40 of S's operating loss from Year 2, and $40 of the consolidated net capital loss carryover from Year 1 attributable to S, are limited under this paragraph (b).

(c) Under paragraph (b)(2)(ii) of this section, the limitation under this paragraph (b) does not affect the absorption of any deductions and losses attributable to P, $60 of S's operating loss from Year 2, and $10 of the consolidated net capital loss from Year 1 attributable to S. Consequently, P's basis in S's stock is reduced under § 1.1502-32(b) by $70, from $300 to $230, and P recognizes a $50 gain from the sale of S's stock in Year 2. Thus, the P group is treated as having a $20 unlimited net operating loss that is carried back to Year 1:

Ordinary income:	
P	$ 30
S (excluding the $40 limited loss)	(60)
Sub Total	($ 30)
Consolidated net capital gain:	
P ($20 + $50 from S stock − $50 (from Year 1))	$ 20
S (− $10 from Year 1)	(10)
Sub Total	$ 10
Consolidated taxable income	($ 20)

(d) Under paragraph (b)(2)(ii) of this section, S's $40 ordinary loss from Year 2 that is limited under this paragraph (b) is treated as a separate net operating loss arising in Year 2. Similarly, $40 of the consolidated net capital loss from Year 1 attributable to S is treated as a separate net capital loss carried over from Year 1. Because S ceases to be a member, the $40 net operating loss from Year 2 and the $40 consolidated net capital loss from Year 1 are allocated to S under §§ 1.1502-21 and 1.1502-22 respectively (or § 1.1502-79A, as appropriate) and are carried to S's first separate return year.

Example (3). Allocation of basis adjustments.

(a) For Year 1, the P group has consolidated taxable income of $100. At the beginning of Year 2, P has a $40 basis in each of the 10 shares of S's stock. For Year 2, P has an $80 ordinary loss (determined without taking into account P's gain or loss from the disposition of S's stock) and S has an $80 ordinary loss. P sells 2 shares of S's stock for $85 each at the close of Year 2.

(b) Under paragraph (b)(2)(i) of this section, the amount of the limitation on S's loss is determined by tentatively treating the P group as having a $160 consolidated net operating loss for Year 2. Of this amount, $100 is carried back under section 172 and absorbed in Year 1 ($50 attributable to S and $50 attributable to P). Consequently, $30 of S's loss is limited under this paragraph (b).

(c) Under paragraph (b)(2)(ii) of this section, the limitation under this paragraph (b) does not affect the absorption of P's $80 ordinary loss or $50 of S's ordinary loss. Consequently, P's basis in each share of S's stock is reduced from $40 to $35 under § 1.1502-32(b), and P recognizes a $100 gain from the sale of the 2 shares. Thus, the P group is treated as having a $30 unlimited net operating loss:

Ordinary loss:	
P	($ 80)
S (excluding the $30 limited loss)	(50)
Sub Total	($130)
Consolidated net capital gain:	
P	$100
S	0
Sub Total	$100
Unlimited consolidated net operating loss	($ 30)

(d) A portion of the $130 of unlimited operating losses for Year 2 is fully absorbed in that year, and a portion is carried back to Year 1. Thus, $61.50 of P's $80 loss ($100 multiplied by $80/$130) and $38.50 of S's $50 unlimited loss ($100 multiplied by $50/$130) are absorbed in Year 2. P's remaining $18.50 of loss and S's remaining $11.50 of loss are not subject to limitation and are carried back and absorbed in Year 1.

(e) Under paragraph (b)(2)(ii) of this section, S's $30 of loss limited under this paragraph (b) is treated as a separate net operating loss.

(3) Loss dispositions. (i) General rule. The principles of paragraph (b)(2) of this section apply to the extent necessary to carry out the purposes of paragraph (b)(1) of this section if P recognizes a deduction or loss from the disposition of S's stock.

(ii) Example. The principles of this paragraph (b)(3) are illustrated by the following example.

Example. (a) P has a $400 basis in S's stock. For Year 1, P has a capital gain of $100 (determined without taking P's gain or loss from the disposition of S's stock into account) and S has both a $60 capital loss and a $200 ordinary loss. P sells S's stock for $140 at the close of Year 1.

(b) Under paragraph (b)(3) of this section, the amount of S's ordinary and capital losses that may offset income and gain is determined by tentatively computing the group's consolidated net operating loss and consolidated net capital loss without taking into account P's loss from the disposition of S's stock. The limitation is necessary to prevent P's loss from the disposition of S's stock from affecting the absorption of S's losses and thereby the adjustments to P's basis in S's stock under § 1.1502-32(b) (which would, in turn, affect P's loss).

(c) Under the principles of paragraph (b)(2)(i) of this section, the amount of the limitation on S's loss is determined by tentatively treating the P group as having a $40 consolidated net capital gain and a $200 ordinary loss, which results in a $160 consolidated net operating loss for Year 1, all of which is attributable to S. Thus, $160 of S's ordinary loss is limited under this paragraph (b). See also §§ 1.337(d)-2, 1.1502-35, and 1.1502-36 for rules relating to basis adjustments and allowance of stock loss on dispositions of stock of a subsidiary member.

(4) Multiple dispositions. (i) Stock of a member. To the extent income, gain, deduction, or loss from a prior disposition of S's stock is deferred under any rule of law, the limitation under paragraph (b)(2) of this section is determined by treating the year the deferred amount is taken into account as the year of the disposition.

(ii) Stock of different members. If S is a higher-tier corporation with respect to another member (T), and all of T's items of income, gain, deduction, and loss (including the absorption of T's deduction or loss) would be fully reflected in P's basis in S's stock under § 1.1502-32, the limitation under paragraph (b)(2)(i) of this section with respect to T's deductions and losses is determined without taking into account any income, gain, deduction, or loss from the disposition of the stock of S or T (or of the stock of members owned in the chain connecting S and T). However, this paragraph (b) does not otherwise limit the absorption of one member's deduction or loss with respect to the disposition of another member's stock.

(iii) Examples. The principles of this paragraph (b)(4) are illustrated by the following examples.

Example (1). Chain of subsidiaries.

(a) P owns all of S's stock with a $500 basis, and S owns all of T's stock with a $500 basis. For Year 1, P has ordinary income of $30, S has no income or loss, and T has an $80 ordinary loss. P sells S's stock for $520 at the close of Year 1.

(b) Under paragraph (b)(4) of this section, to determine the amount of the limitation under paragraph (b) of this section on T's loss, and the effect of the absorption of T's loss on P's basis in S's stock under section 1.1502-32(b), P's gain or loss from the disposition of S's stock is not taken into account. The group is tentatively treated as having a consolidated net operating loss of $50 (P's $30 of income minus T's $80 loss). Because only $30 of T's loss offsets income or gain, P's basis in S's stock is reduced under § 1.1502-32(b) from $500 to $470 immediately before the disposition of S's stock. Thus, P takes into account a $50 gain from the sale of S's stock.

(c) The facts are the same as in paragraph (a) of this Example 1, except that S has a $10 excess loss account in T's stock (rather than a $500 basis). Under paragraph (b)(4) of this section, neither P's gain or loss from the disposition of S's stock nor S's gain or loss from the disposition of T's stock (under § 1.1502-19) are taken into account for purposes of the tentative computations and the effect of any absorption under § 1.1502-32(b) on P's basis in S's stock and S's excess loss account in T's stock. The group is tentatively treated as having a consolidated net operating loss of $50 (P's $30 of income minus T's $80 loss), and only $30 of T's loss may offset the group's income or gain. Under § 1.1502-32(b), the absorption of $30 of T's loss increases S's excess loss account in T's stock to $40 and, under § 1.1502-19, the excess loss account is taken into account. Moreover, under § 1.1502-32(b), P's basis in S's stock is increased immediately before the sale by $10 (S's $40 gain under § 1.1502-19(b) minus T's $30 loss absorbed and tiered up under § 1.1502-32(b)), from $500 to $510. Thus, P takes into account a $10 gain from the sale of S's stock, and S takes into account a $40 gain from its excess loss account in T's stock.

Example (2). Brother-sister subsidiaries.

(a) P owns all of the stock of S1 and S2, each with a $50 basis. For Year 1, the group has a $100 consolidated net operating loss ($50 of which is attributable to S1, and $50 to S2) determined without taking gain or loss from the disposition of member stock into account. At the close of Year 1, P sells the stock of S1 and S2 for $100 each.

(b) Paragraph (b)(4) of this section does not limit the loss of S1 or S2 with respect to the disposition of stock of the other. Consequently, each subsidiary's loss may offset P's gain from the disposition of the stock of the other subsidiary. Because this absorption results in a $50 reduction in P's basis in the stock of each subsidiary under § 1.1502-32(b), P's aggregate gain from the stock dispositions is increased from $100 to $200, $100 of which is offset by the losses of the subsidiaries.

(5) Effective date. This paragraph (b) applies to stock dispositions occurring in consolidated return years beginning on or after January 1, 1995. For prior years, see § 1.1502-11(b) as contained in the 26 CFR part 1 edition revised as of April 1, 1994.

(c) Elimination of circular stock basis adjustments when there is excluded COD income. *(1) In general.* If one member (P) disposes of the stock of another member (S) in a year during which any member realizes excluded COD income, this paragraph (c) limits the use of S's deductions and losses in the year of disposition and the carryback of items to prior years, the amount of the attributes of certain members that can be reduced in respect of excluded COD income of certain other members, and the attributes that can be used to offset an excess loss account taken into account by reason of the application of § 1.1502-19(c)(1)(iii)(B). In addition to the purpose set forth in paragraph (b)(1) of this section, the purpose of these limitations is to prevent the reduction of tax attributes in respect of excluded COD income from affecting P's income, gain, or loss on the disposition of S stock (including a disposition of S stock that results from the application of § 1.1502-19(c)(1)(iii)(B)) and, in turn, affecting the attributes available for reduction pursuant to sections 108 and 1017 and § 1.1502-28. See § 1.1502-19(c) for the definition of disposition.

(2) Computation of tax liability, reduction of attributes, and computation of limits on absorption and reduction of attributes. If a member realizes excluded COD income in the taxable year during which P disposes of S stock, the steps used to compute tax liability, to effect the reduction of attributes, and to compute the limitations on the absorption and reduction of attributes are as follows. These steps also apply to determine whether and to what extent an excess loss account must be taken into account as a result of the application of § 1.1502-19(b)(1) and (c)(1)(iii)(B).

(i) Limitation on deductions and losses to offset income or gain. First, the determination of the extent to which S's deductions and losses for the tax year of the disposition (and its deductions and losses carried over from prior years) may offset income and gain is made pursuant to paragraphs (b)(2) and (3) of this section.

(ii) Tentative adjustment of stock basis. Second, § 1.1502-32 is tentatively applied to adjust the basis of the S stock to reflect the amount of S's income and gain included, and unlimited deductions and losses that are absorbed, in the tentative computation of taxable income or loss for the year of the disposition (and any prior years) that is made pursuant to paragraph (b)(2) of this section, but not to reflect the realization of excluded COD income and the reduction of attributes in respect thereof.

(iii) Tentative computation of stock gain or loss. Third, in the case of a disposition of S stock that does not result from the application of § 1.1502-19(c)(1)(iii)(B), P's income, gain, or loss from the disposition of S stock is computed. For this purpose, the result of the computation pursuant to paragraph (c)(2)(ii) of this section is treated as the basis of such stock.

(iv) Tentative computation of tax imposed. Fourth, the tax imposed by chapter 1 of the Internal Revenue Code for the year of disposition (and any prior years) is tentatively computed. For this purpose, in the case of a disposition of S stock that does not result from the application of § 1.1502-19(c)(1)(iii)(B), the tentative computation of tax imposed takes into account P's income, gain, or loss from the disposition of S stock computed pursuant to paragraph (c)(2)(iii) of this section. The tentative computation of tax imposed is made without regard to whether all or a portion of an excess loss account in a share of S stock is required to be taken into account pursuant to § 1.1502-19(b)(1) and (c)(1)(iii)(B).

(v) Tentative reduction of attributes. Fifth, the rules of sections 108 and 1017 and § 1.1502-28 are tentatively applied to reduce the attributes remaining after the tentative computation of tax imposed pursuant to paragraph (c)(2)(iv) of this section.

(vi) Actual adjustment of stock basis. Sixth, § 1.1502-32 is applied to reflect the amount of S's income and gain included, and unlimited deductions and losses that are absorbed, in the tentative computation of tax imposed for the year of the disposition (and any prior years) made pursuant to paragraph (c)(2)(iv) of this section, and the excluded COD income applied to reduce attributes and the attributes tentatively reduced in respect of the excluded COD income pursuant to paragraph (c)(2)(v) of this section.

(vii) Actual computation of stock gain or loss. Seventh, the group's actual gain or loss on the disposition of S stock (including a disposition that results from the application of § 1.1502-19(c)(1)(iii)(B)) is computed. The result of the computation pursuant to paragraph (c)(2)(vi) of this section is treated as the basis of such stock.

(viii) Actual computation of tax imposed. Eighth, the tax imposed by chapter 1 of the Internal Revenue Code for the year of the disposition (and any prior years) is computed. The actual tax imposed on the group for the year of the disposition is computed by applying the limitation computed pursuant to paragraph (c)(2)(i) of this section, and by including the gain or loss recognized on the disposition of S stock computed pursuant to paragraph (c)(2)(vii) of this section. However, attributes that were tentatively used in the computation of tax imposed pursuant to paragraph (c)(2)(iv) of this section and attributes that were tentatively reduced pursuant to paragraph (c)(2)(v) of this section cannot offset any excess loss account taken into account as a result of the application of § 1.1502-19(b)(1) and (c)(1)(iii)(B).

(ix) Actual reduction of attributes. Ninth, the rules of sections 108 and 1017 and § 1.1502-28 are actually applied to reduce the attributes remaining after the actual computation of tax imposed pursuant to paragraph (c)(2)(viii) of this section.

(A) S or a lower-tier corporation realizes excluded COD income. If S or a lower-tier corporation of S realizes excluded COD income, the aggregate amount of excluded COD income that is applied to reduce attributes attributable to members other than S and any lower-tier corporation of S pursuant to this paragraph (c)(2)(ix) shall not exceed the aggregate amount of excluded COD income that was tentatively applied to reduce attributes attributable to members other than S and any lower-tier corporation of S pursuant to paragraph (c)(2)(v) of this section. The amount of the actual reduction of attributes attributable to S and any lower-tier corporation of S that may be reduced in respect of the excluded COD income of S or a lower-tier corporation of S shall not be so limited.

(B) A member other than S or a lower-tier corporation realizes excluded COD income. If a member other than S or a lower-tier corporation of S realizes excluded COD income, the aggregate amount of excluded COD income that is applied to reduce attributes (other than credits) attributable to S and any lower-tier corporation of S pursuant to this paragraph (c)(2)(ix) shall not exceed the aggregate amount of excluded COD income that was tentatively applied to reduce attributes (other than credits) attributable to S and any lower-tier corporation of S pursuant to paragraph (c)(2)(v) of this section. The amount of the actual reduction of attributes attributable to any member other than S and any lower-tier corporation of S that may be reduced in respect of the excluded COD income of S or a lower-tier corporation of S shall not be so limited.

(3) Special rules. (i) If the reduction of attributes attributable to a member is prevented as a result of a limitation described in paragraph (c)(2)(ix)(B) of this section, the excluded COD income that would have otherwise been applied to reduce such attributes is applied to reduce the remaining attributes of the same type that are available for reduction under § 1.1502-28(a)(4), on a pro rata basis, prior to reducing attributes of a different type. The reduction of such remaining attributes, however, is subject to any applicable limitation described in paragraph (c)(2)(ix)(B) of this section.

(ii) To the extent S's deductions and losses in the year of disposition (or those of a lower-tier corporation of S) cannot offset income or gain because of the limitation under paragraph (b) of this section or this paragraph (c) and are not reduced pursuant to sections 108 and 1017 and § 1.1502-28, such items are carried to other years under the applicable provisions of the Internal Revenue Code and regulations as if they were the only items incurred by S (or a lower-tier corporation of S) in the year of disposition. For example, to the extent S incurs an operating loss in the year of disposition that is limited and is not reduced pursuant to section 108 and § 1.1502-28, the loss is treated as a separate net operating loss attributable to S arising in that year.

(4) Definition of lower-tier corporation. A corporation is a lower-tier corporation of S if all of its items of income, gain, deduction, and loss (including the absorption of deduction or loss and the reduction of attributes other than credits) would be fully reflected in P's basis in S's stock under § 1.1502-32.

(5) Examples. For purposes of the examples in this paragraph (c), unless otherwise stated, the tax year of all persons is the calendar year, all persons use the accrual method of accounting, the facts set forth the only corporate activity, all transactions are between unrelated persons, tax liabilities are disregarded, and no election under section 108(b)(5) is made. The principles of this paragraph (c) are illustrated by the following examples:

Example (1). Departing member realizes excluded COD income. (i) Facts. P owns all of S's stock with a $90 basis. For Year 1, P has ordinary income of $30, and S has an $80 ordinary loss and $100 of excluded COD income from the discharge of non-intercompany indebtedness. P sells the S stock for $20 at the close of Year 1. As of the beginning of Year 2, S has Asset A with a basis of $0 and a fair market value of $20.

(ii) Analysis. The steps used to compute the tax imposed on the group, to effect the reduction of attributes, and to compute the limitations on the use and reduction of attributes are as follows:

(A) Computation of limitation on deductions and losses to offset income or gain. To determine the amount of the limitation under paragraph (c)(2)(i) of this section on S's loss and the effect of the absorption of S's loss on P's basis in S's stock under § 1.1502-32(b), P's gain or loss from the disposition of S's stock is not taken into account. The group is tentatively treated as having a consolidated net operating loss of $50 (P's $30 of income minus S's $80 loss). Thus, $30 of S's loss is unlimited and $50 of S's loss is limited under paragraph (c)(2)(i) of this section. Under the principles of § 1.1502-21(b)(2)(iv), all of the consolidated net operating loss is attributable to S.

(B) Tentative adjustment of stock basis. Then, pursuant to paragraph (c)(2)(ii) of this section, § 1.1502-32 is tentatively applied to adjust the basis of S stock. For this purpose, however, adjustments attributable to the excluded COD income and the reduction of attributes in respect thereof are not taken into account. Under § 1.1502-32(b), the absorption of $30 of S's loss decreases P's basis in S's stock by $30 to $60.

(C) Tentative computation of stock gain or loss. Then, P's income, gain, or loss from the sale of S stock is computed pursuant to paragraph (c)(2)(iii) of this section using the basis computed in the previous step. Thus, P is treated as recognizing a $40 loss from the sale of S stock.

(D) Tentative computation of tax imposed. Pursuant to paragraph (c)(2)(iv) of this section, the tax imposed for the year of disposition is then tentatively computed, taking into account P's $40 loss on the sale of the S stock computed pursuant to paragraph (c)(2)(iii) of this section. The group has a $50 consolidated net operating loss for Year 1 that, under the principles of § 1.1502-21(b)(2)(iv), is wholly attributable to S and a consolidated capital loss of $40 that, under the principles of § 1.1502-21(b)(2)(iv), is wholly attributable to P.

(E) Tentative reduction of attributes. Next, pursuant to paragraph (c)(2)(v) of this section, the rules of sections 108 and 1017 and § 1.1502-28 are tentatively applied to reduce attributes remaining after the tentative computation of the tax imposed. Pursuant to § 1.1502-28(a)(2), the tax attributes attributable to S would first be reduced to take into account its $100 of excluded COD income. Accordingly, the consolidated net operating loss for Year 1 would be reduced by $50, the portion of that consolidated net operating loss attributable to S under the principles of § 1.1502-21(b)(2)(iv), to $0. Then, pursuant to § 1.1502-28(a)(4), S's remaining $50 of excluded COD income would reduce the consolidated capital loss attributable to P of $40 by $40 to $0. The remaining $10 of excluded COD income would have no effect.

(F) Actual adjustment of stock basis. Pursuant to paragraph (c)(2)(vi) of this section, § 1.1502-32 is applied to reflect the amount of S's income and gain included, and unlimited deductions and losses that are absorbed, in the tentative computation of the tax imposed for the year of the disposition and the excluded COD income tentatively applied to reduce attributes and the attributes reduced in respect of the excluded COD income pursuant to the previous step. Under § 1.1502-32(b), the absorption of $30 of S's loss, the application of $90 of S's excluded COD income to reduce attributes of P and S, and the reduction of the $50 loss attributable to S in respect of the excluded COD income results in a positive adjustment of $10 to P's basis in the S stock. P's basis in the S stock, therefore, is $100.

(G) Actual computation of stock gain or loss. Pursuant to paragraph (c)(2)(vii) of this section, P's actual gain or loss on the sale of the S stock is computed using the basis computed in the previous step. Accordingly, P recognizes an $80 loss on the disposition of the S stock.

(H) Actual computation of tax imposed. Pursuant to paragraph (c)(2)(viii) of this section, the tax imposed is computed by taking into account P's $80 loss from the sale of S stock. Before the application of § 1.1502-28, therefore, the group has a consolidated net operating loss of $50 that is wholly attributable to S under the principles of § 1.1502-21(b)(2)(iv), and a consolidated capital loss of $80 that is wholly attributable to P under the principles of § 1.1502-21(b)(2)(iv).

(I) Actual reduction of attributes. Pursuant to paragraph (c)(2)(ix) of this section, sections 108 and 1017 and § 1.1502-28 are then actually applied to reduce attributes remaining after the actual computation of the tax imposed. Pursuant to § 1.1502-28(a)(2), the tax attributes attributable to S must first be reduced to take into account its $100 of excluded COD income. Accordingly, the consolidated net operating loss for Year 1 is reduced by $50, the portion of that consolidated net operating loss attributable to S under the principles of § 1.1502-21(b)(2)(iv), to $0. Then, pursuant to § 1.1502-28(a)(4), S's remaining $50 of excluded COD income reduces consolidated tax attributes. In particular, without regard to the limitation imposed by paragraph (c)(2)(ix)(A) of this section, the $80 consolidated capital loss, which under the principles of § 1.1502-21(b)(2)(iv) is attributable to P, would be reduced by $50 from $80 to $30. However, the limitation imposed by paragraph (c)(2)(ix)(A) of this section prevents the reduction of the consolidated capital loss attributable to P by more than $40. Therefore, the consolidated capital loss attributable to P is reduced by only $40 in respect of S's excluded COD income. The remaining $10 of excluded COD income has no effect.

Example (2). Member other than departing member realizes excluded COD income. (i) Facts. P owns all of S1's and S2's stock. P's basis in S2's stock is $600. For Year 1, P has ordinary income of $30, S1 has a $100 ordinary loss and $100 of excluded COD income from the discharge of nonintercompany indebtedness, and S2 has $200 of ordinary loss. P sells the S2 stock for $600 at the close of Year 1. As of the beginning of Year 2, S1 has Asset A with a basis of $0 and a fair market value of $10.

(ii) Analysis. The steps used to compute the tax imposed on the group, to effect the reduction of attributes, and to compute the limitations on the use and reduction of attributes are as follows:

(A) Computation of limitation on deductions and losses to offset income or gain. To determine the amount of the limitation under paragraph (c)(2)(i) of this section on S2's loss and the effect of the absorption of S2's loss on P's basis in S2's stock under § 1.1502-32(b), P's gain or loss from the sale of S2's stock is not taken into account. The group is tentatively treated as having a consolidated net operating loss of $270 (P's $30 of income minus S1's $100 loss and S2's $200 loss). Consequently, $20 of S2's loss from Year 1 is unlimited and $180 of S2's loss from Year 1 is limited under paragraph (c)(2)(i) of this section. Under the principles of § 1.1502-21(b)(2)(iv), $90 of the consolidated net operating loss is attributable to S1 and $180 of the consolidated net operating loss is attributable to S2.

(B) Tentative adjustment of stock basis. Then, pursuant to paragraph (c)(2)(ii) of this section, § 1.1502-32 is tentatively applied to adjust the basis of S2's stock. For this purpose, however, adjustments to the basis of S2's stock attributable to the reduction of attributes in respect of S1's excluded COD income are not taken into account. Under § 1.1502-32(b), the absorption of $20 of S2's loss decreases P's basis in S2's stock by $20 to $580.

(C) Tentative computation of stock gain or loss. Then, P's income, gain, or loss from the disposition of S2 stock is computed pursuant to paragraph (c)(2)(iii) of this section using the basis computed in the previous step. Thus, P is treated as recognizing a $20 gain from the sale of the S2 stock.

(D) Tentative computation of tax imposed. Pursuant to paragraph (c)(2)(iv) of this section, the tax imposed for the year of disposition is then tentatively computed, taking into account P's $20 gain from the sale of S2 stock computed pursuant to paragraph (c)(2)(iii) of this section. Although S2's limited loss cannot be used to offset P's $20 gain from the sale of S2's stock under the rules of this section, S1's loss will offset that gain. Therefore, the group is tentatively treated as having a consolidated net operating loss of $250, $70 of which is attributable to S1 and $180 of which is attributable to S2 under the principles of § 1.1502-21(b)(2)(iv).

(E) Tentative reduction of attributes. Next, pursuant to paragraph (c)(2)(v) of this section, the rules of sections 108 and 1017 and § 1.1502-28 are tentatively applied to reduce attributes remaining after the tentative computation of the tax imposed. Pursuant to § 1.1502-28(a)(2), the tax attributes attributable to S1 would first be reduced to take into account its $100 of excluded COD income. Accordingly, the consolidated net operating loss for Year 1 would be reduced by

$70, the portion of that consolidated net operating loss attributable to S1 under the principles of § 1.1502-21(b)(2)(iv), to $0. Then, pursuant to § 1.1502-28(a)(4), S1's remaining $30 of excluded COD income would reduce the consolidated net operating loss for Year 1 attributable to S2 of $180 by $30 to $150.

(F) Actual adjustment of stock basis. Pursuant to paragraph (c)(2)(vi) of this section, § 1.1502-32 is applied to reflect the amount of S2's income and gain included, and unlimited deductions and losses that are absorbed, in the tentative computation of the tax imposed for the year of the disposition and the excluded COD income tentatively applied to reduce attributes and the attributes reduced in respect of the excluded COD income pursuant to the previous step. Under § 1.1502-32(b), the absorption of $20 of S2's loss to offset a portion of P's income and the application of $30 of S1's excluded COD income to reduce attributes attributable to S2 results in a negative adjustment of $50 to P's basis in the S2 stock. P's basis in the S2 stock, therefore, is $550.

(G) Actual computation of stock gain or loss. Pursuant to paragraph (c)(2)(vii) of this section, P's actual gain or loss on the sale of the S2 stock is computed using the basis computed in the previous step. Therefore, P recognizes a $50 gain on the disposition of the S2 stock.

(H) Actual computation of tax imposed. Pursuant to paragraph (c)(2)(viii) of this section, the tax imposed is computed by taking into account P's $50 gain from the disposition of the S2 stock. Before the application of § 1.1502-28, therefore, the group has a consolidated net operating loss of $220, $40 of which is attributable to S1 and $180 of which is attributable to S2 under the principles of § 1.1502-21(b)(2)(iv).

(I) Actual reduction of attributes. Pursuant to paragraph (c)(2)(ix) of this section, sections 108 and 1017 and § 1.1502-28 are then actually applied to reduce attributes remaining after the actual computation of the tax imposed. Pursuant to § 1.1502-28(a)(2), the tax attributes attributable to S1 must first be reduced to take into account its $100 of excluded COD income. Accordingly, the consolidated net operating loss for Year 1 is reduced by $40, the portion of that consolidated net operating loss attributable to S1 under the principles of § 1.1502-21(b)(2)(iv), to $0. Then, pursuant to § 1.1502-28(a)(4), without regard to the limitation imposed by paragraph (c)(2)(ix)(B) of this section, S1's remaining $60 of excluded COD income would reduce S2's net operating loss of $180 to $120. However, the limitation imposed by paragraph (c)(2)(ix)(B) of this section prevents the reduction of S2's loss by more than $30. Therefore, S2's loss of $180 is reduced by $30 to $150 in respect of S1's excluded COD income. The remaining $30 of excluded COD income has no effect.

Example (3). Lower-tier corporation of departing member realizes excluded COD income. (i) Facts. P owns all of S1's stock, S2's stock, and S3's stock. S1 owns all of S4's stock. P's basis in S1's stock is $50 and S1's basis in S4's stock is $50. For Year 1, P has $50 of ordinary loss, S1 has $100 of ordinary loss, S2 has $150 of ordinary loss, S3 has $50 of ordinary loss, and S4 has $50 of ordinary loss and $80 of excluded COD income from the discharge of non-intercompany indebtedness. P sells the S1 stock for $100 at the close of Year 1. As of the beginning of Year 2, S4 has Asset A with a fair market value of $10. After the computation of tax imposed for Year 1 and before the application of sections 108 and 1017 and § 1.1502-28, Asset A has a basis of $0.

(ii) Analysis. The steps used to compute the tax imposed on the group, to effect the reduction of attributes, and to compute the limitations on the use and reduction of attributes are as follows:

(A) Computation of limitation on deductions and losses to offset income or gain. To determine the amount of the limitation under paragraph (c)(2)(i) of this section on S1's and S4's losses and the effect of the absorption of S1's and S4's losses on P's basis in S1's stock under § 1.1502-32(b), P's gain or loss from the sale of S1's stock is not taken into account. The group is tentatively treated as having a consolidated net operating loss of $400. Consequently, $100 of S1's loss and $50 of S4's loss is limited under paragraph (c)(2)(i) of this section.

(B) Tentative adjustment of stock basis. Then, pursuant to paragraph (c)(2)(ii) of this section, § 1.1502-32 is tentatively applied to adjust the basis of S1's stock. For this purpose, adjustments to the basis of S1's stock attributable to S4's realization of excluded COD income and the reduction of attributes in respect of such excluded COD income are not taken into account. There is no adjustment under § 1.1502-32 to the basis of the S1 stock. Therefore, P's basis in the S1 stock for this purpose is $50.

(C) Tentative computation of stock gain or loss. Then, P's income, gain, or loss from the sale of S1 stock is computed pursuant to paragraph (c)(2)(iii) of this section using the basis computed in the previous step. Thus, P is treated as recognizing a $50 gain from the sale of the S1 stock.

(D) Tentative computation of tax imposed. Pursuant to paragraph (c)(2)(iv) of this section, the tax imposed for the year of disposition is then tentatively computed, taking into account P's $50 gain from the sale of the S1 stock computed pursuant to paragraph (c)(2)(iii) of this section. Although S1's and S4's limited losses cannot be used to offset P's $50 gain from the sale of S1's stock under the rules of this section, $10 of P's loss, $30 of S2's loss, and $10 of S3's loss will offset that gain. Therefore, the group is tentatively treated as having a consolidated net operating loss of $350, $40 of which is attributable to P, $100 of which is attributable to S1, $120 of which is attributable to S2, $40 of which is attributable to S3, and $50 of which is attributable to S4 under the principles of § 1.1502-21(b)(2)(iv).

(E) Tentative reduction of attributes. Next, pursuant to paragraph (c)(2)(v) of this section, the rules of sections 108 and 1017 and § 1.1502-28 are tentatively applied to reduce attributes remaining after the tentative computation of the tax imposed. Pursuant to § 1.1502-28(a)(2), the tax attributes attributable to S4 would first be reduced to take into account its $80 of excluded COD income. Accordingly, the consolidated net operating loss for Year 1 would be reduced by $50, the portion of the consolidated net operating loss attributable to S4 under the principles of § 1.1502-21(b)(2)(iv), to $300. Then, pursuant to § 1.1502-28(a)(4), S4's remaining $30 of excluded COD income would reduce the consolidated net operating loss for Year 1 that is attributable to other members. Therefore, the consolidated net operating loss for Year 1 would be reduced by $30. Of that amount, $4 is attributable to P, $10 is attributable to S1, $12 is attributable to S2, and $4 is attributable to S3.

(F) Actual adjustment of stock basis. Pursuant to paragraph (c)(2)(vi) of this section, § 1.1502-32 is applied to reflect the amount of S1's and S4's income and gain included, and unlimited deductions and losses that are absorbed, in the tentative computation of tax imposed for the year of the disposition and the excluded COD income tentatively applied to reduce attributes and the attributes reduced in respect of the excluded COD income pursuant to the previous step. Under § 1.1502-32(b), the application of $80 of S4's excluded COD income to reduce attributes, and the reduction of S4's loss in the amount of $50 and S1's loss in the amount of $10 in respect of the excluded COD income results in a positive adjustment of $20 to P's basis in the S1 stock. Accordingly, P's basis in S1 stock is $70.

(G) Actual computation of stock gain or loss. Pursuant to paragraph (c)(2)(vii) of this section, P's actual gain or loss on the sale of the S1 stock is computed using the basis computed in the previous step. Accordingly, P recognizes a $30 gain on the disposition of the S1 stock.

(H) Actual computation of tax imposed. Pursuant to paragraph (c)(2)(viii) of this section, the tax imposed is computed by taking into account P's $30 gain from the sale of S1 stock. Before the application of § 1.1502-28, therefore, the group has a consolidated net operating loss of $370, $44 of which is attributable to P, $100 of which is attributable to S1, $132 of which is attributable to S2, $44 of which is attributable to S3, and $50 of which is attributable to S4.

(I) Actual reduction of attributes. Pursuant to paragraph (c)(2)(ix) of this section, sections 108 and 1017 and § 1.1502-28 are then actually applied to reduce attributes remaining after the actual computation of the tax imposed. Pursuant to § 1.1502-28(a)(2), the tax attributes attributable to S4 must first be reduced to take into account its $80 of excluded COD income. Accordingly, the consolidated net operating loss for Year 1 is reduced by $50, the portion of that consolidated net operating loss attributable to S4 under the principles of § 1.1502-21(b)(2)(iv), to $320. Then, pursuant to § 1.1502-28(a)(4), without regard to the limitation imposed by paragraph (c)(2)(ix)(A) of this section, S4's remaining $30 of excluded COD income would reduce the consolidated net operating loss for Year 1 by $30 ($4.12 of the consolidated net operating loss attributable to P, $9.38 of the consolidated net operating loss attributable to S1, $12.38 of the consolidated net operating loss attributable to S2, and $4.12 of the consolidated net operating loss attributable to S3) to $290. However, the limitation imposed by paragraph (c)(2)(ix)(A) of this section prevents the reduction of the consolidated net operating loss attributable to P, S2, and S3 by more than $4, $12, and $4 respectively. The $.62 of excluded COD income that would have otherwise reduced the consolidated net operating loss attributable to P, S2, and S3 is applied to reduce the consolidated net operating loss attributable to S1. Therefore, S1 carries forward $90 of loss.

Example (4). Excess loss account taken into account. (i) Facts. P is the common parent of a consolidated group. On Day 1 of Year 2, P acquired all of the stock of S1. As of the beginning of Year 2, S1 had a $30 net operating loss carryover from Year 1, a separate return limitation year. A limitation under § 1.1502-21(c) applies to the use of that loss by the P group. For Years 1 and 2, the P group had no consolidated taxable income or loss. On Day 1 of Year 3, S1 acquired all of the stock of S2 for $10. In Year 3, P had ordinary income of $10, S1 had ordinary income of $25, and S2 had an ordinary loss of $50. In addition, in Year 3, S2 realized $20 of excluded COD income from the discharge of non-intercompany indebtedness. After the discharge of this indebtedness, S2 had no liabilities. As of the beginning of Year 4, S2 had Asset A with a fair market value of $10. After the computation of tax imposed for Year 3 and before the application of sections 108 and 1017 and § 1.1502-28, Asset A has a basis of $0. S2 had no taxable income (or loss) for Year 1 and Year 2.

(ii) Analysis. The steps used to compute the tax imposed on the group, to effect the reduction of attributes, and to compute the limitations on the use and reduction of attributes are as follows:

(A) Computation of limitation on deductions and losses to offset income or gain, tentative basis adjustments, tentative computation of stock gain or loss. Because it is not initially apparent that there has been a disposition of stock, paragraph (c)(2)(i) of this section does not limit the use of deductions to offset income or gain, no adjustments to the basis are required pursuant to paragraph (c)(2)(ii) of this section, and no stock gain or loss is computed pursuant to paragraph (c)(2)(iii) of this section or taken into account in the tentative computation of tax imposed pursuant to paragraph (c)(2)(iv) of this section.

(B) Tentative computation of tax imposed. Pursuant to paragraph (c)(2)(iv) of this section, the tax imposed for Year 3 is tentatively computed. For Year 3, the P group has a consolidated taxable loss of $15, all of which is attributable to S2 under the principles of § 1.1502-21(b)(2)(iv).

(C) Tentative reduction of attributes. Next, pursuant to paragraph (c)(2)(v) of this section, the rules of sections 108 and 1017 and § 1.1502-28 are tentatively applied to reduce attributes remaining after the tentative computation of tax imposed. Pursuant to § 1.1502-28(a)(2), the tax attributes attributable to S2 would first be reduced to take into account its $20 of excluded COD income. Accordingly, the consolidated net operating loss for Year 3 is reduced by $15, the portion of that consolidated net operating loss attributable to S2 under the principles of § 1.1502-21(b)(2)(iv), to $0. The remaining $5 of excluded COD income is not applied to reduce attributes as there are no remaining attributes that are subject to reduction.

(D) Actual adjustment of stock basis. Pursuant to paragraph (c)(2)(vi) of this section, § 1.1502-32 is applied to reflect the amount of S2's income and gain included, and unlimited deductions and losses that are absorbed, in the tentative computation of tax imposed for the year of the disposition and the excluded COD income tentatively applied to reduce attributes and the attributes reduced in respect of the excluded COD income pursuant to the previous step. Under § 1.1502-32, the absorption of $35 of S2's loss, the application of $15 in respect of S2's excluded COD income to reduce attributes, and the reduction of $15 in respect of the loss attributable to S2 reduced in respect of the excluded COD income results in a negative adjustment of $35 to the basis of the S2 stock. Therefore, S1 has an excess loss account of $25 in the S2 stock.

(E) Actual computation of stock gain or loss. Pursuant to paragraph (c)(2)(vii) of this section, S1's actual gain or loss, if any, on the S2 stock is computed. Because S2 realized $5 of excluded COD income that was not applied to reduce attributes, pursuant to § 1.1502-19(b)(1) and (c)(1)(iii)(B), S1 is required to take into account $5 of its excess loss account in the S2 stock.

(F) Actual computation of tax imposed. Pursuant to paragraph (c)(2)(viii) of this section, the tax imposed is computed by taking into account the $5 of the excess loss account in the S2 stock required to be taken into account. See § 1.1502-28(b)(6) (requiring an excess loss account that is required to be taken into account as a result of the application of § 1.1502-19(c)(1)(iii)(B) to be included in the group's tax return for the year that includes the date of the debt discharge). However, pursuant to paragraph (c)(2)(viii) of this section, such amount may not be offset by any of the consolidated net operating loss attributable to S2. It may, however, subject to applicable limitations, be offset by the separate net operating loss of S1 from Year 1.

(G) Actual reduction of attributes. Pursuant to paragraph (c)(2)(ix) of this section, sections 108 and 1017 and § 1.1502-28 are then actually applied to reduce attributes remaining after the actual computation of the tax imposed. Attributes will be actually reduced in the same way that they were tentatively reduced.

(6) Additional rules for multiple dispositions. [Reserved]

(7) Effective date. This paragraph (c) applies to dispositions of subsidiary stock that occur after March 22, 2005. Taxpayers may apply § 1.1502-11(c) of REG-167265-03 (2004-15 IRB 730) (see § 601.601(d)(2) of this chapter) in whole, but not in part, to any disposition of subsidiary stock that occurs on or before March 22, 2005, if a member of the group realized excluded COD income after August 29, 2003, in the taxable year that includes the date of the disposition of such subsidiary stock.

(d) Disallowance of loss attributable to pre-1966 distributions. No loss shall be allowed upon the sale or other disposition of stock, bonds, or other obligations of a member or former member to the extent that such loss is attributable to a distribution made in an affiliated year beginning before January 1, 1966, out of earnings and profits accumulated before the distributing corporation became a member.

T.D. 6894, 9/7/66, amend T.D. 7246, 12/29/72, T.D. 7728, 10/31/80, T.D. 8560, 8/12/94, T.D. 8677, 6/24/96, T.D. 8823, 6/25/99, T.D. 9048, 3/11/2003, T.D. 9187, 3/2/2005, T.D. 9192, 3/21/2005, T.D. 9254, 3/09/2006, T.D. 9424, 9/10/2008.

§ 1.1502-12 Separate taxable income.

Caution: The Treasury has not yet amended Reg § 1.1502-12 to reflect changes made by P.L. 104-188.

The separate taxable income of a member (including a case in which deductions exceed gross income) is computed in accordance with the provisions of the Code covering the determination of taxable income of separate corporations, subject to the following modifications:

(a) Transactions between members and transactions with respect to stock, bonds, or other obligations of members shall be reflected according to the provisions of § 1.1502-13;

(b) Any deduction which is disallowed under §§ 1.1502-15A or § 1.1502-15 shall be taken into account as provided in those sections;

(c) The limitation on deductions provided in section 615(c) or section 617(h) shall be taken into account as provided in § 1.1502-16;

(d) The method of accounting under which such computation is made and the adjustments to be made because of any change in method of accounting shall be determined under § 1.1501-17;

(e) Inventory adjustments shall be made as provided in § 1.1502-18;

(f) Any amount included in income under § 1.1502-19 shall be taken into account;

(g) In the computation of the deduction under section 167, property shall not lose its character as new property as a result of a transfer from one member to another member during a consolidated return year if—

(1) The transfer occurs on or before January 4, 1973, or

(2) The transfer occurs after January 4, 1973, and the transfer is an intercompany transaction as defined in § 1.1502-13 or the basis of the property in the hands of the transferee is determined (in whole or in part) by reference to its basis in the hands of the transferor:

(h) No net operating loss deduction shall be taken into account;

(i) [Reserved]

(j) No capital gains or losses shall be taken into account;

(k) No gains and losses subject to section 1231 shall be taken into account;

(l) No deduction under section 170 with respect to charitable contributions shall be taken into account;

(m) No deduction under section 922 (relating to the deduction for Western Hemisphere trade corporations) shall be taken into account;

(n) No deductions under section 243 (a)(1), 244(a), 245, or 247 (relating to deductions with respect to dividends received and dividends paid) shall be taken into account;

(o) Basis shall be determined under §§ 1.1502-31 and 1.1502-32, and earnings and profits shall be determined under § 1.1502-33; and

(p) The limitation on deductions provided in section 613A shall be taken into account for each member's oil and gas properties as provided in § 1.1502-44.

(q) A thrift institution's deduction under section 593(b)(2) (relating to the addition to the reserve for bad debts of a thrift institution under the percentage of taxable income method) shall be determined under § 1.1502-42.

(r) See §§ 1.337(d)-2, 1.1502-35, and 1.1502-36 for rules relating to basis adjustments and allowance of stock loss on dispositions or transfers of subsidiary stock.

T.D. 6894, 9/7/66, amend T.D. 7192, 6/29/72, T.D. 7246, 12/29/72, T.D. 7725, 9/30/80, T.D. 7876, 3/14/83, T.D. 8294, 3/9/90, T.D. 8319, 11/19/90, T.D. 8364, 9/13/91, T.D. 8597, 7/12/95, T.D. 8677, 6/26/96, T.D. 8823, 6/25/99, T.D. 9048, 3/11/2003, T.D. 9187, 3/2/2005, T.D. 9254, 3/9/2006, T.D. 9424, 9/10/2008.

PAR. 10. Section 1.1502-12 as amended by adding paragraph (s) to read as follows:

Proposed § 1.1502-12 Separate taxable income. [*For Preamble, see ¶ 152,795*]

* * * * *

(s) The exclusion from gross income of previously taxed earnings and profits shall be determined by the rules of § 1.959-3(g).

§ 1.1502-13 Intercompany transactions.

Caution: The Treasury has not yet amended Reg § 1.1502-13 to reflect changes made by P.L. 108-27, P.L. 104-188.

(a) In general. *(1) Purpose.* This section provides rules for taking into account items of income, gain, deduction, and loss of members from intercompany transactions. The purpose of this section is to provide rules to clearly reflect the taxable income (and tax liability) of the group as a whole by preventing intercompany transactions from creating, accelerating, avoiding, or deferring consolidated taxable income (or consolidated tax liability).

(2) Separate entity and single entity treatment. Under this section, the selling member (S) and the buying member (B) are treated as separate entities for some purposes but as divisions of a single corporation for other purposes. The *amount* and *location* of S's intercompany items and B's corresponding items are determined on a separate entity basis (separate

entity treatment). For example, S determines its gain or loss from a sale of property to B on a separate entity basis, and B has a cost basis in the property. The *timing*, and the *character, source,* and other *attributes* of the intercompany items and corresponding items, although initially determined on a separate entity basis, are redetermined under this section to produce the effect of transactions between divisions of a single corporation (single entity treatment). For example, if S sells land to B at a gain and B sells the land to a nonmember, S does not take its gain into account until B's sale to the nonmember.

(3) Timing rules as a method of accounting. (i) In general. The timing rules of this section are a method of accounting for intercompany transactions, to be applied by each member in addition to the member's other methods of accounting. See § 1.1502-17 and, with regard to consolidated return years beginning on or after November 7, 2001, § 1.446-1(c)(2)(iii). To the extent the timing rules of this section are inconsistent with a member's otherwise applicable methods of accounting, the timing rules of this section control. For example, if S sells property to B in exchange for B's note, the timing rules of this section apply instead of the installment sale rules of section 453. S's or B's application of the timing rules of this section to an intercompany transaction clearly reflects income only if the effect of that transaction as a whole (including, for example, related costs and expenses) on consolidated taxable income is clearly reflected.

(ii) Automatic consent for joining and departing members. (A) Consent granted. Section 446(e) consent is granted under this section to the extent a change in method of accounting is necessary solely by reason of the timing rules of this section—

(1) For each member, with respect to its intercompany transactions, in the first consolidated return year which follows a separate return year and in which the member engages in an intercompany transaction; and

(2) For each former member, with respect to its transactions with members that would otherwise be intercompany transactions if the former member were still a member, in the first separate return year in which the former member engages in such a transaction.

(B) Cut-off basis. Any change in method of accounting described in paragraph (a)(3)(ii)(A) of this section is to be effected on a cut-off basis for transactions entered into on or after the first day of the year for which consent is granted under paragraph (a)(3)(ii)(A) of this section.

(4) Application of other rules of law. See § 1.1502-80(a) regarding the general applicability of other rules of law and a limitation on duplicative adjustments. The rules of this section apply in addition to other applicable law (including nonstatutory authorities). For example, this section applies in addition to sections 267(f) (additional rules for certain losses), 269 (acquisitions to evade or avoid income tax), and 482 (allocations among commonly controlled taxpayers). Thus, an item taken into account under this section can be deferred, disallowed, or eliminated under other applicable law, for example, section 1091 (losses from wash sales).

(5) References. References in other sections to this section include, as appropriate, references to prior law. For effective dates and prior law see paragraph (l) of this section.

(6) Overview. (i) In general. The principal rules of this section that implement single entity treatment are the matching rule and the acceleration rule of paragraphs (c) and (d) of this section. Under the matching rule, S and B are generally treated as divisions of a single corporation for purposes of taking into account their items from intercompany transactions. The acceleration rule provides additional rules for taking the items into account if the effect of treating S and B as divisions cannot be achieved (for example, if S or B becomes a nonmember). Paragraph (b) of this section provides definitions. Paragraph (e) of this section provides simplifying rules for certain transactions. Paragraphs (f) and (g) of this section provide additional rules for stock and obligations of members. Paragraphs (h) and (j) of this section provide anti-avoidance rules and miscellaneous operating rules.

(ii) Table of examples. Set forth below is a table of the examples contained in this section.

Matching rule. (§ 1.1502-13(c)(7)(ii))

Example 1. Intercompany sale of land.

Example 2. Dealer activities.

Example 3. Intercompany section 351 transfer.

Example 4. Depreciable property.

Example 5. Intercompany sale followed by installment sale.

Example 6. Intercompany sale of installment obligation.

Example 7. Performance of services.

Example 8. Rental of property.

Example 9. Intercompany sale of a partnership interest.

Example 10. Net operating losses subject to section 382 or the SRLY rules.

Example 11. Section 475.

Example 12. Section 1092.

Example 13. [Reserved].

Example 14. Source of income under section 863.

Example 15. Section 1248.

Acceleration rule. (§ 1.1502-13(d)(3))

Example 1. Becoming a nonmember—timing.

Example 2. Becoming a nonmember—attributes.

Example 3. Selling member's disposition of installment note.

Example 4. Cancellation of debt and attribute reduction under section 108(b).

Example 5. Section 481.

Simplifying rules—inventory. (§ 1.1502-13(e)(1)(v))

Example 1. Increment averaging method.

Example 2. Increment valuation method.

Example 3. Other reasonable inventory methods.

Stock of members. (§ 1.1502-13(f)(7))

Example 1. Dividend exclusion and property distribution.

Example 2. Excess loss accounts.

Example 3. Intercompany reorganizations.

Example 4. All cash intercompany reorganization under section 368(a)(1)(D).

Example 5. Stock redemptions and distributions.

Example 6. Intercompany stock sale followed by section 332 liquidation.

Example 7. Intercompany stock sale followed by section 355 distribution.

Obligations of members. (§ 1.1502-13(g)(7)(ii))

Example 1. Interest on intercompany obligation.

Example 2. Intercompany obligation becomes nonintercompany obligation.

(b) Definitions. For purposes of this section. *(1) Intercompany transactions.* (i) In general. An intercompany transaction is a transaction between corporations that are members of the same consolidated group immediately after the transaction. S is the member transferring property or providing services, and B is the member receiving the property or services. Intercompany transactions include—

(A) S's sale of property (or other transfer, such as an exchange or contribution) to B, whether or not gain or loss is recognized;

(B) S's performance of services for B, and B's payment or accrual of its expenditure for S's performance;

(C) S's licensing of technology, rental of property, or loan of money to B, and B's payment or accrual of its expenditure; and

(D) S's distribution to B with respect to S stock.

(ii) Time of transaction. If a transaction occurs in part while S and B are members and in part while they are not members, the transaction is treated as occurring when performance by either S or B takes place, or when payment for performance would be taken into account under the rules of this section if it were an intercompany transaction, whichever is earliest. Appropriate adjustments must be made in such cases by, for example, dividing the transaction into two separate transactions reflecting the extent to which S or B has performed.

(iii) Separate transactions. Except as otherwise provided in this section, each transaction is analyzed separately. For example, if S simultaneously sells two properties to B, one at a gain and the other at a loss, each property is treated as sold in a separate transaction. Thus, the gain and loss cannot be offset or netted against each other for purposes of this section. Similarly, each payment or accrual of interest on a loan is a separate transaction. In addition, an accrual of premium is treated as a separate transaction, or as an offset to interest that is not a separate transaction, to the extent required under separate entity treatment. If two members exchange property, each member is S with respect to the property it transfers and B with respect to the property it receives. If two members enter into a notional principal contract, each payment under the contract is a separate transaction and the member making the payment is B with respect to that payment and the member receiving the payment is S. See paragraph (j)(4) of this section for rules aggregating certain transactions.

(2) Intercompany items. (i) In general. S's income, gain, deduction, and loss from an intercompany transaction are its intercompany items. For example, S's gain from the sale of property to B is intercompany gain. An item is an intercompany item whether it is directly or indirectly from an intercompany transaction.

(ii) Related costs or expenses. S's costs or expenses related to an intercompany transaction are included in determining its intercompany items. For example, if S sells inventory to B, S's direct and indirect costs properly includible under section 263A are included in determining its intercompany income. Similarly, related costs or expenses that are not capitalized under S's separate entity method of accounting are included in determining its intercompany items. For example, deductions for employee wages, in addition to other related costs, are included in determining S's intercompany items from performing services for B, and depreciation deductions are included in determining S's intercompany items from renting property to B.

(iii) Amounts not yet recognized or incurred. S's intercompany items include amounts from an intercompany transaction that are not yet taken into account under its separate entity method of accounting. For example, if S is a cash method taxpayer, S's intercompany income might be taken into account under this section even if the cash is not yet received. Similarly, an amount reflected in basis (or an amount equivalent to basis) under S's separate entity method of accounting that is a substitute for income, gain, deduction or loss from an intercompany transaction is an intercompany item.

(3) Corresponding items. (i) In general. B's income, gain, deduction, and loss from an intercompany transaction, or from property acquired in an intercompany transaction, are its corresponding items. For example, if B pays rent to S, B's deduction for the rent is a corresponding deduction. If B buys property from S and sells it to a nonmember, B's gain or loss from the sale to the nonmember is a corresponding gain or loss; alternatively, if B recovers the cost of the property through depreciation, B's depreciation deductions are corresponding deductions. An item is a corresponding item whether it is directly or indirectly from an intercompany transaction (or from property acquired in an intercompany transaction).

(ii) Disallowed or eliminated amounts. B's corresponding items include amounts that are permanently disallowed or permanently eliminated, whether directly or indirectly. Thus, corresponding items include amounts disallowed under section 265 (expenses relating to tax-exempt income), and amounts not recognized under section 311(a) (nonrecognition of loss on distributions), section 332 (nonrecognition on liquidating distributions), or section 355(c) (certain distributions of stock of a subsidiary). On the other hand, an amount is not permanently disallowed or permanently eliminated (and therefore is not a corresponding item) to the extent it is not recognized in a transaction in which B receives a successor asset within the meaning of paragraph (j)(1) of this section. For example, B's corresponding items do not include amounts not recognized from a transaction with a nonmember to which section 1031 applies or from another transaction in which B receives exchanged basis property.

(4) Recomputed corresponding items. The recomputed corresponding item is the corresponding item that B would take into account if S and B were divisions of a single corporation and the intercompany transaction were between those divisions. For example, if S sells property with a $70 basis to B for $100, and B later sells the property to a nonmember for $90, B's corresponding item is its $10 loss, and the recomputed corresponding item is $20 of gain (determined by comparing the $90 sales price, with the $70 basis the property would have if S and B were divisions of a single corporation). Although neither S nor B actually takes the recomputed corresponding item into account, it is computed as if B did take it into account (based on reasonable and consistently applied assumptions, including any provision of the Internal Revenue Code or regulations that would affect its timing or attributes).

(5) Treatment as a separate entity. Treatment as a separate entity means treatment without application of the rules of this section, but with the application of the other consolidated return regulations. For example, if S sells the stock of another member to B, S's gain or loss on a separate entity basis is determined with the application of § 1.1502-80(b) (non-applicability of section 304), but without redetermination under paragraph (c) or (d) of this section.

(6) Attributes. The attributes of an intercompany item or corresponding item are all of the item's characteristics, except *amount, location,* and *timing,* necessary to determine the item's effect on taxable income (and tax liability). For example, attributes include character, source, treatment as excluded from gross income or as a noncapital, nondeductible amount, and treatment as built-in gain or loss under section 382(h) or 384. In contrast, the characteristics of property, such as a member's holding period, or the fact that property is included in inventory, are not attributes of an item, but these characteristics might affect the determination of the attributes of items from the property.

(c) Matching rule. For each consolidated return year, B's corresponding items and S's intercompany items are taken into account under the following rules:

(1) Attributes and holding periods. (i) Attributes. The separate entity attributes of S's intercompany items and B's corresponding items are redetermined to the extent necessary to produce the same effect on consolidated taxable income (and consolidated tax liability) as if S and B were divisions of a single corporation, and the intercompany transaction were a transaction between divisions. Thus, the activities of both S and B might affect the attributes of both intercompany items and corresponding items. For example, if S holds property for sale to unrelated customers in the ordinary course of its trade or business, S sells the property to B at a gain and B sells the property to an unrelated person at a further gain, S's intercompany gain and B's corresponding gain might be ordinary because of S's activities with respect to the property. Similar principles apply if S performs services, rents property, or engages in any other intercompany transaction.

(ii) Holding periods. The holding period of property transferred in an intercompany transaction is the aggregate of the holding periods of S and B. However, if the basis of the property is determined by reference to the basis of other property, the property's holding period is determined by reference to the holding period of the other property. For example, if S distributes stock to B in a transaction to which section 355 applies, B's holding period in the distributed stock is determined by reference to B's holding period in the stock of S.

(2) Timing. (i) B's items. B takes its corresponding items into account under its accounting method, but the redetermination of the attributes of a corresponding item might affect its timing. For example, if B's sale of property acquired from S is treated as a dealer disposition because of S's activities, section 453(b) prevents any corresponding income of B from being taken into account under the installment method.

(ii) S's items. S takes its intercompany item into account to reflect the difference for the year between B's corresponding item taken into account and the recomputed corresponding item.

(3) Divisions of a single corporation. As divisions of a single corporation, S and B are treated as engaging in their actual transaction and owning any actual property involved in the transaction (rather than treating the transaction as not occurring). For example, S's sale of land held for investment to B for cash is not disregarded, but is treated as an exchange of land for cash between divisions (and B therefore succeeds to S's basis in the property). Similarly, S's issuance of its own stock to B in exchange for property is not disregarded, B is treated as owning the stock it receives in the exchange, and section 1032 does not apply to B on its subsequent sale of the S stock. Although treated as divisions, S and B nevertheless are treated as:

(i) Operating separate trades or businesses. See, e.g., § 1.446-1(d) (accounting methods for a taxpayer engaged in more than one business).

(ii) Having any special status that they have under the Internal Revenue Code or regulations. For example, a bank defined in section 581, a domestic building and loan association defined in section 7701(a)(19), and an insurance company to which section 801 or 831 applies are treated as divisions having separate special status. On the other hand, the fact that a member holds property for sale to customers in the ordinary course of its trade or business is not a special status.

(4) Conflict or allocation of attributes. This paragraph (c)(4) provides special rules for redetermining and allocating attributes under paragraph (c)(1)(i) of this section.

(i) Offsetting amounts. (A) In general. To the extent B's corresponding item offsets S's intercompany item in amount, the attributes of B's corresponding item, determined based on both S's and B's activities, control the attributes of S's offsetting intercompany item. For example, if S sells depreciable property to B at a gain and B depreciates the property, the attributes of B's depreciation deduction (ordinary deduction) control the attributes of S's offsetting intercompany gain. Accordingly, S's gain is ordinary.

(B) B controls unreasonable. To the extent the results under paragraph (c)(4)(i)(A) are inconsistent with treating S and B as divisions of a single corporation, the attributes of the offsetting items must be redetermined in a manner consistent with treating S and B as divisions of a single corporation. To the extent, however, that B's corresponding item on a separate entity basis is excluded from gross income, is a noncapital, nondeductible amount, or is otherwise permanently disallowed or eliminated, the attributes of B's corresponding item always control the attributes of S's offsetting intercompany item.

(ii) Allocation. To the extent S's intercompany item and B's corresponding item do not offset in amount, the attributes redetermined under paragraph (c)(1)(i) of this section must be allocated to S's intercompany item and B's corresponding item by using a method that is reasonable in light of all the facts and circumstances, including the purposes of this section and any other rule affected by the attributes of S's intercompany item and B's corresponding item. A method of allocation or redetermination is unreasonable if it is not used consistently by all members of the group from year to year.

(5) Special status. Notwithstanding the general rule of paragraph (c)(1)(i) of this section, to the extent an item's attributes determined under this section are permitted or not permitted to a member under the Internal Revenue Code or regulations by reason of the member's special status, the attributes required under the Internal Revenue Code or regulations apply to that member's items (but not the other member). For example, if S is a bank to which section 582(c) applies, and sells debt securities at a gain to B, a nonbank, the character of S's intercompany gain is ordinary as required under section 582(c), but the character of B's corresponding item as capital or ordinary is determined under paragraph (c)(1)(i) of this section without the application of section 582(c). For other special status issues, see, for example, sections 595(b) (foreclosure on property securing loans), 818(b) (life insurance company treatment of capital gains and losses), and 1503(c) (limitation on absorption of certain losses).

(6) Treatment of intercompany items if corresponding items are excluded or nondeductible. (i) In general. Under paragraph (c)(1)(i) of this section, S's intercompany item might be redetermined to be excluded from gross income or treated as a noncapital, nondeductible amount. For example, S's intercompany loss from the sale of property to B is treated as a noncapital, nondeductible amount if B distributes the property to a nonmember shareholder at no further gain or loss (because, if S and B were divisions of a single corporation, the loss would not have been recognized under section 311(a)). Paragraph (c)(6)(ii) of this section, however, provides limitations on the application of this rule to intercompany income or gain. See also §§ 1.1502-32 and 1.1502-33 (adjustments to S's stock basis and earnings and profits to reflect amounts so treated).

(ii) Limitation on treatment of intercompany items as excluded from gross income. Notwithstanding the general rule of paragraph (c)(1)(i) of this section, S's intercompany income or gain is redetermined to be excluded from gross income only to the extent one of the following applies:

(A) Disallowed amounts. B's corresponding item is a deduction or loss and, in the taxable year the item is taken into account under this section, it is permanently and explicitly disallowed under another provision of the Internal Revenue Code or regulations. For example, deductions that are disallowed under section 265 are permanently and explicitly disallowed. An amount is not permanently and explicitly disallowed, for example, to the extent that—

(1) The Internal Revenue Code or regulations provide that the amount is not recognized (for example, a loss that is realized but not recognized under section 332 or section 355(c) is not permanently and explicitly disallowed, notwithstanding that it is a corresponding item within the meaning of paragraph (b)(3)(ii) of this section (certain disallowed or eliminated amounts));

(2) A related amount might be taken into account by B with respect to successor property, such as under section 280B (demolition costs recoverable as capitalized amounts);

(3) A related amount might be taken into account by another taxpayer, such as under section 267(d) (disallowed loss under section 267(a) might result in nonrecognition of gain for a related person);

(4) A related amount might be taken into account as a deduction or loss, including as a carryforward to a later year, under any provision of the Internal Revenue Code or regulations (whether or not the carryforward expires in a later year); or

(5) The amount is reflected in the computation of any credit against (or other reduction of) Federal income tax (whether allowed for the taxable year or carried forward to a later year).

(B) Section 311.* The corresponding item is a loss that is realized, but not recognized under section 311(a) on a distribution to a nonmember (even though the loss is not a permanently and explicitly disallowed amount within the meaning of paragraph (c)(6)(ii)(A) of this section).

(C) [Reserved]. For further guidance, see § 1.1502-13T(c)(6)(ii)(C).

(D) Other amounts. The Commissioner determines that treating S's intercompany item as excluded from gross income is consistent with the purposes of this section and other applicable provisions of the Internal Revenue Code and regulations.

(7) Examples. (i) In general. For purposes of the examples in this section, unless otherwise stated, P is the common parent of the P consolidated group, P owns all of the only class of stock of subsidiaries S and B, X is a person unrelated to any member of the P group, the taxable year of all persons is the calendar year, all persons use the accrual method of accounting, tax liabilities are disregarded, the facts set forth the only corporate activity, no member has any special status, and the transaction is not otherwise subject to recharacterization. If a member acts as both a selling member and a buying member (e.g., with respect to different aspects of a single transaction, or with respect to related transactions), the member is referred to as M, M1, or M2 (rather than as S or B).

(ii) Matching rule. The matching rule of this paragraph (c) is illustrated by the following examples.

Example (1). Intercompany sale of land followed by sale to a nonmember.

(a) Facts. S holds land for investment with a basis of $70. S has held the land for more than one year. On January 1 of Year 1, S sells the land to B for $100. B also holds the land for investment. On July 1 of Year 3, B sells the land to X for $110.

(b) Definitions. Under paragraph (b)(1) of this section, S's sale of the land to B is an intercompany transaction, S is the selling member, and B is the buying member. Under paragraphs (b)(2) and (3) of this section, S's $30 gain from the sale to B is its intercompany item, and B's $10 gain from the sale to X is its corresponding item.

(c) Attributes. Under the matching rule of paragraph (c) of this section, S's $30 intercompany gain and B's $10 corresponding gain are taken into account to produce the same effect on consolidated taxable income (and consolidated tax liability) as if S and B were divisions of a single corporation. In addition, the holding periods of S and B for the land are aggregated. Thus, the group's entire $40 of gain is long-term capital gain. Because both S's intercompany item and B's corresponding item on a separate entity basis are long-term capital gain, the attributes are not redetermined under paragraph (c)(1)(i) of this section.

(d) Timing. For each consolidated return year, S takes its intercompany item into account under the matching rule to reflect the difference for the year between B's corresponding item taken into account and the recomputed corresponding item. If S and B were divisions of a single corporation and the intercompany sale were a transfer between the divisions, B would succeed to S's $70 basis in the land and would have a $40 gain from the sale to X in Year 3, instead of a $10 gain. Consequently, S takes no gain into account in Years 1 and 2, and takes the entire $30 gain into account in Year 3, to reflect the $30 difference in that year between the $10 gain B takes into account and the $40 recomputed gain (the recomputed corresponding item). Under §§ 1.1502-32 and 1.1502-33, P's basis in its S stock and the earnings and profits of S and P do not reflect S's $30 gain until the gain is taken into account in Year 3. (Under paragraph (a)(3) of this section, the results would be the same if S sold the land to B in an installment sale to which section 453 would otherwise apply, because S must take its intercompany gain into account under this section.)

(e) Intercompany loss followed by sale to a nonmember at a gain. The facts are the same as in paragraph (a) of this Example 1, except that S's basis in the land is $130 (rather than $70). The attributes and timing of S's intercompany loss and B's corresponding gain are determined under the matching rule in the manner provided in paragraphs (c) and (d) of this Example 1. If S and B were divisions of a single corporation and the intercompany sale were a transfer between the divisions, B would succeed to S's $130 basis in the land and would have a $20 loss from the sale to X instead of a $10 gain. Thus, S takes its entire $30 loss into account in Year 3 to reflect the $30 difference between B's $10 gain taken into account and the $20 recomputed loss. (The results are the same under section 267(f).) S's $30 loss is long-term capital loss, and B's $10 gain is long-term capital gain.

(f) Intercompany gain followed by sale to a nonmember at a loss. The facts are the same as in paragraph (a) of this Example 1, except that B sells the land to X for $90 (rather than $110). The attributes and timing of S's intercompany gain and B's corresponding loss are determined under the matching rule. If S and B were divisions of a single corporation and the intercompany sale were a transfer between the divisions, B would succeed to S's $70 basis in the land and would have a $20 gain from the sale to X instead of a $10 loss. Thus, S takes its entire $30 gain into account in Year 3 to reflect the $30 difference between B's $10 loss taken into account and the $20 recomputed gain. S's $30 gain is long-term capital gain, and B's $10 loss is long-term capital loss.

(g) Intercompany gain followed by distribution to a nonmember at a loss. The facts are the same as in paragraph (a) of this Example 1, except that B distributes the land to X, a minority shareholder of B, and at the time of the distribution the land has a fair market value of $90. The attributes and timing of S's intercompany gain and B's corresponding loss are determined under the matching rule. Under section 311(a), B does not recognize its $10 loss on the distribution to X. If S and B were divisions of a single corporation and the intercompany sale were a transfer between divisions, B would succeed to S's $70 basis in the land and would have a $20 gain from the distribution to X instead of an unrecognized $10 loss. Under paragraph (b)(3)(ii) of this section, B's loss that is not recognized under section 311(a) is a corresponding item. Thus, S takes its $30 gain into account under the matching rule in Year 3 to reflect the difference between B's $10 corresponding unrecognized loss and the $20 recomputed gain. B's $10 corresponding loss offsets $10 of S's intercompany gain and, under paragraph (c)(4)(i) of this section, the attributes of B's corresponding item control the attributes of S's intercompany item. Paragraph (c)(6) of this section does not prevent the redetermination of S's intercompany item as excluded from gross income. (See paragraph (c)(6)(ii)(B) of this section). Thus, $10 of S's $30 gain is redetermined to be excluded from gross income.

(h) Intercompany sale followed by section 1031 exchange with nonmember. The facts are the same as in paragraph (a) of this Example 1, except that, instead of selling the land to X, B exchanges the land for land owned by X in a transaction to which section 1031 applies. There is no difference in Year 3 between B's $0 corresponding item taken into account and the $0 recomputed corresponding item. Thus, none of S's intercompany gain is taken into account under the matching rule as a result of the section 1031 exchange. Instead, B's gain is preserved in the land received from X and, under the successor asset rule of paragraph (j)(1) of this section, S's intercompany gain is taken into account by reference to the replacement property. (If B takes gain into account as a result of boot received in the exchange, S's intercompany gain is taken into account under the matching rule to the extent the boot causes a difference between B's gain taken into account and the recomputed gain.)

(j) Intercompany sale followed by section 351 transfer to nonmember. The facts are the same as in paragraph (a) of this Example 1, except that, instead of selling the land to X, B transfers the land to X in a transaction to which section 351(a) applies and X remains a nonmember. There is no difference in Year 3 between B's $0 corresponding item taken into account and the $0 recomputed corresponding item. Thus, none of S's intercompany gain is taken into account under the matching rule as a result of the section 351(a) transfer. However, S's entire gain is taken into account in Year 3 under the acceleration rule of paragraph (d) of this section (because X, a nonmember, reflects B's $100 cost basis in the land under section 362).

Example (2). Dealer activities.

(a) Facts. S holds land for investment with a basis of $70. On January 1 of Year 1, S sells the land to B for $100. B develops the land as residential real estate, and sells developed lots to customers during Year 3 for an aggregate amount of $110.

(b) Attributes. S and B are treated under the matching rule as divisions of a single corporation for purposes of determining the attributes of S's intercompany item and B's corresponding item. Thus, although S held the land for investment, whether the gain is treated as from the sale of property described in section 1221(1) is based on the activities of both S and B. If, based on both S's and B's activities, the land is described in section 1221(1), both S's gain and B's gain are ordinary income.

Example (3). Intercompany section 351 transfer.

(a) Facts. S holds land with a $70 basis and a $100 fair market value for sale to customers in the ordinary course of business. On January 1 of Year 1, S transfers the land to B in exchange for all of the stock of B in a transaction to which section 351 applies. S has no gain or loss under section 351(a), and its basis in the B stock is $70 under section 358. Under section 362, B's basis in the land is $70. B holds the land for investment. On July 1 of Year 3, B sells the land to X for $100. Assume that if S and B were divisions of a single corporation, B's gain from the sale would be ordinary income because of S's activities.

(b) Timing and attributes. Under paragraph (b)(1) of this section, S's transfer to B is an intercompany transaction. Under paragraph (c)(3) of this section, S is treated as transferring the land in exchange for B's stock even though, as divisions, S could not own stock of B. S has no intercompany item, but B's $30 gain from its sale of the land to X is a corresponding item because the land was acquired in an intercompany transaction. B's $30 gain is ordinary income that is taken into account under B's method of accounting.

(c) Intercompany section 351 transfer with boot. The facts are the same as in paragraph (a) of this Example 3, except that S receives $10 cash in addition to the B stock in the transfer. S recognizes $10 of gain under section 351(b), and its basis in the B stock is $70 under section 358. Under section 362, B's basis in the land is $80. S takes its $10 intercompany gain into account in Year 3 to reflect the $10 difference between B's $20 corresponding gain taken into account and the $30 recomputed gain. Both S's $10 gain and B's $20 gain are ordinary income.

(d) Partial disposition. The facts are the same as in paragraph (c) of this Example 3, except B sells a only a one-half, undivided interest in the land to X for $50. The timing and attributes are determined in the manner provided in paragraph (b) of this Example 3, except that S takes only $5 of its gain into account in Year 3 to reflect the $5 difference between B's $10 gain taken into account and the $15 recomputed gain.

Example (4). Depreciable property.

(a) Facts. On January 1 of Year 1, S buys 10-year recovery property for $100 and depreciates it under the straight-line method. On January 1 of Year 3, S sells the property to B for $130. Under section 168(i)(7), B is treated as S for purposes of section 168 to the extent B's $130 basis does not exceed S's adjusted basis at the time of the sale. B's additional basis is treated as new 10-year recovery property for which B elects the straight-line method of recovery. (To simplify the example, the half-year convention is disregarded.)

(b) Depreciation through year 3; intercompany gain. S claims $10 of depreciation for each of Years 1 and 2 and has an $80 basis at the time of the sale to B. Thus, S has a $50 intercompany gain from its sale to B. For Year 3, B has $10 of depreciation with respect to $80 of its basis (the portion of its $130 basis not exceeding S's adjusted basis). In addition, B has $5 of depreciation with respect to the $50 of its additional basis that exceeds S's adjusted basis.

(c) Timing. S's $50 gain is taken into account to reflect the difference for each consolidated return year between B's depreciation taken into account with respect to the property and the recomputed depreciation. For Year 3, B takes $15 of depreciation into account. If the intercompany transaction were a transfer between divisions of a single corporation, B would succeed to S's adjusted basis in the property and take into account only $10 of depreciation for Year 3. Thus, S takes $5 of gain into account in Year 3. In each subsequent year that B takes into account $15 of depreciation with respect to the property, S takes into account $5 of gain.

(d) Attributes. Under paragraph (c)(1)(i) of this section, the attributes of S's gain and B's depreciation must be redetermined to the extent necessary to produce the same effect on consolidated taxable income as if the intercompany transaction were between divisions of a single corporation (the group must have a net depreciation deduction of $10). In each year, $5 of B's corresponding depreciation deduction offsets S's $5 intercompany gain taken into account and, under paragraph (c)(4)(i) of this section, the attributes of B's corresponding item control the attributes of S's intercompany item. Accordingly, S's intercompany gain that is taken into account as a result of B's depreciation deduction is ordinary income.

(e) Sale of property to a nonmember. The facts are the same as in paragraph (a) of this Example 4, except that B sells the property to X on January 1 of Year 5 for $110. As set forth in paragraphs (c) and (d) of this Example 4, B has $15 of depreciation with respect to the property in each of Years 3 and 4, causing S to take $5 of intercompany gain into account in each year as ordinary income. The $40 balance of S's intercompany gain is taken into account in Year 5 as a result of B's sale to X, to reflect the $40 difference between B's $10 gain taken into account and the $50 of recomputed gain ($110 of sale proceeds minus the $60 basis B would have if the intercompany sale were a transfer between divisions of a single corporation). Treating S and B as divisions of a single corporation, $40 of the gain is section 1245 gain and $10 is section 1231 gain. On a separate entity basis, S would have more than $10 treated as section 1231 gain, and B would have no amount treated as section 1231 gain. Under paragraph (c)(4)(ii) of this section, all $10 of the section 1231 gain is allocated to S. S's remaining $30 of gain, and all of B's $10 gain, is treated as section 1245 gain.

Example (5). Intercompany sale followed by installment sale.

(a) Facts. S holds land for investment with a basis of $70x. On January 1 of Year 1, S sells the land to B for $100x. B also holds the land for investment. On July 1 of Year 3, B sells the land to X in exchange for X's $110x note. The note bears a market rate of interest in excess of the applicable Federal rate, and provides for principal payments of $55x in Year 4 and $55x in Year 5. The interest charge under section 453A(c) applies to X's note.

(b) Timing and attributes. S takes its $30x gain into account to reflect the difference in each consolidated return year between B's gain taken into account for the year and the recomputed gain. Under section 453, B takes into account $5x of gain in Year 4 and $5x of gain in Year 5. Thus, S takes into account $15x of gain in Year 4 and $15x of gain in Year 5 to reflect the $15x difference in each of those years between B's $5x gain taken into account and the $20x recomputed gain. Both S's $30x gain and B's $10x gain are subject to the section 453A(c) interest charge beginning in Year 3.

(c) Election out under section 453(d). If, under the facts in paragraph (a) of this Example 5, the P group wishes to elect not to apply section 453 with respect to S's gain, an election under section 453(d) must be made for Year 3 with respect to B's gain. This election will cause B's $10x gain to be taken into account in Year 3. Under the matching rule, this will result in S's $30x gain being taken into account in Year 3. (An election by the P group solely with respect to S's gain has no effect because the gain from S's sale to B is taken into account under the matching rule, and therefore must reflect the difference between B's gain taken into account and the recomputed gain.)

(d) Sale to a nonmember at a loss, but overall gain. The facts are the same as in paragraph (a) of this Example 5, except that B sells the land to X in exchange for X's $90x note (rather than $110x note). If S and B were divisions of a single corporation, B would succeed to S's basis in the land, and the sale to X would be eligible for installment reporting under section 453, because it resulted in an overall gain. However, because only gains may be reported on the installment method, B's $10x corresponding loss is taken into account in Year 3. Under paragraph (b)(4) of this section the recomputed corresponding item is $20x gain that would be taken into account under the installment method, $0 in Year 3 and $10x in each of Years 4 and 5. Thus, in Year 3, S takes $10x of gain into account to reflect the difference between B's $10x loss taken into account and the $0 recomputed gain for Year 3. Under paragraph (c)(4)(i) of this section, B's $10x corresponding loss offsets $10x of S's intercompany gain, and B's attributes control. S takes $10x of gain into account in each of Years 4 and 5 to reflect the difference in those years between B's $0 gain taken into account and the $10x recomputed gain that would be taken into account under the installment method. Only the $20x of S's gain taken into account in Years 4 and 5 is subject to the interest charge under section 453A(c) beginning in Year 3. (If P elects under section 453(d) for Year 3 not to apply section 453 with respect to the gain, all of S's $30x gain will be taken into account in Year 3 to reflect the difference between B's $10x loss taken into account and the $20x recomputed gain.)

(e) Intercompany loss, installment gain. The facts are the same as in paragraph (a) of this Example 5, except that S has a $130x (rather than $70x) basis in the land. Under paragraph (c)(1)(i) of this section, the separate entity attributes of S's and B's items from the intercompany transaction must be redetermined to produce the same effect on consolidated taxable income (and tax liability) as if the transaction had been a transfer between divisions. If S and B were divisions of a single corporation, B would succeed to S's basis in the land and the group would have $20x loss from the sale to X, installment reporting would be unavailable, and the interest charge under section 453A(c) would not apply. Accordingly, B's gain from the transaction is not eligible for installment treatment under section 453. B takes its $10x gain into account in Year 3, and S takes its $30x of loss into account in Year 3 to reflect the difference between B's $10x gain and the $20x recomputed loss.

(f) Recapture income. The facts are the same as in paragraph (a) of this Example 5, except that S bought depreciable property (rather than land) for $100x, claimed depreciation deductions, and reduced the property's basis to $70x before Year 1. (To simplify the example, B's depreciation is disregarded.) If the intercompany sale of property had been a transfer between divisions of a single corporation, $30x of the $40x gain from the sale to X would be section 1245 gain (which is ineligible for installment reporting) and $10x would be section 1231 gain (which is eligible for installment reporting). On a separate entity basis, S would have $30x of section 1245 gain and B would have $10x of section 1231 gain. Accordingly, the attributes are not redetermined under paragraph (c)(1)(i) of this section. All of B's $10x gain is eligible for installment reporting and is taken into account $5x each in Years 4 and 5 (and is subject to the interest charge under section 453A(c)). S's $30x gain is taken into account in Year 3 to reflect the difference between B's $0 gain taken into account and the $30x of recomputed gain. (If S had bought the depreciable property for $110x and its recomputed basis under section 1245 had been $110x (rather than $100x), B's $10x gain and S's $30x gain would both be recapture income ineligible for installment reporting.)

Example (6). Intercompany sale of installment obligation.

(a) Facts. S holds land for investment with a basis of $70x. On January 1 of Year 1, S sells the land to X in exchange for X's $100x note, and S reports its gain on the installment method under section 453. X's note bears interest at a market rate of interest in excess of the applicable Federal rate, and provides for principal payments of $50x in Year 5 and $50x in Year 6. Section 453A applies to X's note. On July 1 of Year 3, S sells X's note to B for $100x, resulting in $30x gain from S's prior sale of the land to X under section 453B(a).

(b) Timing and attributes. S's sale of X's note to B is an intercompany transaction, and S's $30x gain is intercompany gain. S takes $15x of the gain into account in each of Years 5 and 6 to reflect the $15x difference in each year between B's $0 gain taken into account and the $15x recomputed gain. S's gain continues to be treated as its gain from the sale to X, and the deferred tax liability remains subject to the interest charge under section 453A(c).

(c) Worthlessness. The facts are the same as in paragraph (a) of this Example 6, except that X's note becomes worthless on December 1 of Year 3 and B has a $100x short-term capital loss under section 165(g) on a separate entity basis. Under paragraph (c)(1)(ii) of this section, B's holding period for X's note is aggregated with S's holding period. Thus, B's loss is a long-term capital loss. S takes its $30x gain into account in Year 3 to reflect the $30x difference between B's $100x loss taken into account and the $70x recomputed loss. Under paragraph (c)(1)(i) of this section, S's gain is long-term capital gain.

(d) Pledge. The facts are the same as in paragraph (a) of this Example 6, except that, on December 1 of Year 3, B borrows $100x from an unrelated bank and secures the indebtedness with X's note. X's note remains subject to section 453A(d) following the sale to B. Under section 453A(d), B's $100x of proceeds from the secured indebtedness is treated as an amount received on December 1 of Year 3 by B on X's note. Thus, S takes its entire $30x gain into account in Year 3.

Example (7). Performance of services.

(a) Facts. S is a driller of water wells. B operates a ranch in a remote location, and B's taxable income from the ranch is not subject to section 447. B's ranch requires water to maintain its cattle. During Year 1, S drills an artesian well on B's ranch in exchange for $100 from B, and S incurs $80 of expenses (e.g., for employees and equipment). B capitalizes its $100 cost for the well under section 263, and takes into account $10 of cost recovery deductions in each of Years 2 through 11. Under its separate entity method of accounting, S would take its income and expenses into account in Year 1. If S and B were divisions of a single corporation, the costs incurred in drilling the well would be capitalized.

(b) Definitions. Under paragraph (b)(1) of this section, the service transaction is an intercompany transaction, S is the selling member, and B is the buying member. Under paragraph (b)(2)(ii) of this section, S's $100 of income and $80 of related expenses are both included in determining its intercompany income of $20.

(c) Timing and attributes. S's $20 of intercompany income is taken into account under the matching rule to reflect the $20 difference between B's corresponding items taken into account (based on its $100 cost basis in the well) and the recomputed corresponding items (based on the $80 basis that B would have if S and B were divisions of a single corporation and B's basis were determined by reference to S's $80 of expenses). In Year 1, S takes into account $80 of its income and the $80 of expenses. In each of Years 2 through 11, S takes $2 of its $20 intercompany income into account to reflect the annual $2 difference between B's $10 of cost recovery deductions taken into account and the $8 of recomputed cost recovery deductions. S's $100 income and $80 expenses, and B's cost recovery deductions, are ordinary items (because S's and B's items would be ordinary on a separate entity basis, the attributes are not redetermined under paragraph (c)(1)(i) of this section). If S's offsetting $80 of income and expense would not be taken into account in the same year under its separate entity method of accounting, they nevertheless must be taken into account under this section in a manner that clearly reflects consolidated taxable income. See paragraph (a)(3)(i) of this section.

(d) Sale of capitalized services. The facts are the same as in paragraph (a) of this Example 7, except that B sells the ranch before Year 11 and recognizes gain attributable to the well. To the extent of S's income taken into account as a result of B's cost recovery deductions, as well as S's offsetting $80 of income and expense, the timing and attributes are determined in the manner provided in paragraph (c) of this Example 7. The attributes of the remainder of S's $20 of income and B's gain from the sale are redetermined to produce the same effect on consolidated taxable income as if S and B were divisions of a single corporation. Accordingly, S's remaining intercompany income is treated as recapture income or section 1231 gain, even though it is from S's performance of services.

Example (8). Rental of property. B operates a ranch that requires grazing land for its cattle. S owns undeveloped land adjoining B's ranch. on January 1 of Year 1, S leases grazing rights to B for Year 1. B's $100 rent expense is deductible for Year 1 under its separate entity accounting method. Under paragraph (b)(1) of this section, the rental transaction is an intercompany transaction, S is the selling member, and B is the buying member. S takes its $100 of income into account in Year 1 to reflect the $100 difference between B's rental deduction taken into account and the $0 recomputed rental deduction. S's income and B's deduction are ordinary items (because S's intercompany item and B's corresponding item would both be ordinary on a separate entity basis, the attributes are not redetermined under paragraph (c)(1)(i) of this section).

Example (9). Intercompany sale of a partnership interest.

(a) Facts. S owns a 20% interest in the capital and profits of a general partnership. The partnership holds land for investment with a basis equal to its value, and operates depreciable assets which have value in excess of basis. S's basis in its partnership interest equals its share of the adjusted basis of the partnership's land and depreciable assets. The partnership has an election under section 754 in effect. On January 1 of Year 1, S sells its partnership interest to B at a gain. During Years 1 through 10, the partnership depreciates the operating assets, and B's depreciation deductions from the partnership reflect the increase in the basis of the depreciable assets under section 743(b).

(b) Timing and attributes. S's gain is taken into account during Years 1 though 10 to reflect the difference in each year between B's depreciation deductions from the partnership taken into account and the recomputed depreciation deductions from the partnership. Under paragraphs (c)(1)(i) and (c)(4)(i) of this section, S's gain taken into account is ordinary income. (The acceleration rule does not apply to S's gain as a result of the section 743(b) adjustment, because the adjustment is solely with respect to B and therefore no nonmember reflects any part of the intercompany transaction.)

(c) Partnership sale of assets. The facts are the same as in paragraph (a) of this Example 9, and the partnership sells some of its depreciable assets to X at a gain on December 31 of Year 4. In addition to the intercompany gain taken into account as a result of the partnership's depreciation, S takes intercompany gain into account in Year 4 to reflect the difference between B's partnership items taken into account from the sale (which reflect the basis increase under section 743(b)) and the recomputed partnership items. The attributes of S's additional gain are redetermined to produce the same effect on consolidated taxable income as if S and B were divisions of a single corporation (recapture income or section 1231 gain).

(d) B's sale of partnership interest. The facts are the same as in paragraph (a) of this Example 9, and on December 31 of Year 4, B sells its partnership interest to X at no gain or loss. In addition to the intercompany gain taken into account as a result of the partnership's depreciation, the remaining balance of S's intercompany gain is taken into account in Year 4 to reflect the difference between B's $0 gain taken into account from the sale of the partnership interest and the recomputed gain. The character of S's remaining intercompany item and B's corresponding item are determined on a separate entity basis under section 751, and then redetermined to the extent necessary to produce the same effect as treating the intercompany transaction as occurring between divisions of a single corporation.

(e) No section 754 election. The facts are the same as in paragraph (d) of this Example 9, except that the partnership does not have a section 754 election in effect, and B recognizes a capital loss from its sale of the partnership interest to X on December 31 of Year 4. Because there is no difference between B's depreciation deductions from the partnership taken into account and the recomputed depreciation deductions, S does not take any of its gain into account during Years 1 through 4 as a result of B's partnership's items. Instead, S's entire intercompany gain is taken into account in Year 4 to reflect the difference between B's loss taken into account from the sale to X and the recomputed gain or loss.

Example (10). Net operating losses subject to section 382 or the SRLY rules.

(a) Facts. On January 1 of Year 1, P buys all of S's stock. S has net operating loss carryovers from prior years. P's acquisition results in an ownership change under section 382 with respect to S's loss carryovers, and S has a net unrealized built-in gain (within the meaning of section 382(h)(3)). S owns nondepreciable property with a $70 basis and $100 value. On July 1 of Year 3, S sells the property to B for $100, and its $30 gain is recognized built-in gain (within the meaning of section 382(h)(2)) on a separate entity basis. on December 1 of Year 5, B sells the property to X for $90.

(b) Timing and attributes. S's $30 gain is taken into account in Year 5 to reflect the $30 difference between B's $10 loss taken into account and the recomputed $20 gain. S and B are treated as divisions of a single corporation for purposes of applying section 382 in connection with the intercompany transaction. Under a single entity analysis, the single corporation has losses subject to limitation under section 382, and this limitation may be increased under section 382(h) if the single corporation has recognized built-in gain with respect to those losses. B's $10 corresponding loss offsets $10 of S's intercompany gain, and thus, under paragraph (c)(4)(i) of this section, $10 of S's intercompany gain is redetermined not to be recognized built-in gain. S's remaining $20 intercompany gain continues to be treated as recognized built-in gain.

(c) B's recognized built-in gain. The facts are the same as in paragraph (a) of this Example 10, except that the property declines in value after S becomes a member of the P group, S sells the property to B for its $70 basis, and B sells the property to X for $90 during Year 5. Treating S and B as divisions of a single corporation, S's sale to B does not cause the property to cease to be built-in gain property. Thus, B's $20 gain from its sale to X is recognized built-in gain that increases the section 382 limitation applicable to S's losses.

(d) SRLY limitation. The facts are the same as in paragraph (a) of this Example 10, except that P's acquisition of S is not subject to the overlap rule of § 1.1502-21(g), and S's net operating loss carryovers are subject to the separate return limitation year (SRLY) rules. See § 1.1502-21(c). The application of the SRLY rules depends on S's status as a separate corporation having losses from separate return limitation years. Under paragraph (c)(5), the attribute of S's intercompany item as it relates to S's SRLY limitation is not redetermined, because the SRLY limitation depends on S's special status. Accordingly, S's $30 intercompany gain is included in determining its SRLY limitation for Year 5.

Example (11). Section 475.

(a) Facts. S, a dealer in securities within the meaning of section 475(c), owns a security with a basis of $70. The security is held for sale to customers and is not identified under section 475(b) as within an exception to marking to market. On July 1 of Year 1, S sells the security to B for $100. B is not a dealer and holds the security for investment. On December 31 of Year 1, the fair market value of the security is $100. on July 1 of Year 2, B sells the security to X for $110.

(b) Attributes. Under section 475, a dealer in securities can treat a security as within an exception to marking to market under section 475(b) only if it timely identifies the security as so described. Under the matching rule, attributes must be redetermined by treating S and B as divisions of a single corporation. As a result of S's activities, the single corporation is treated as a dealer with respect to securities, and B must continue to mark to market the security acquired from S. Thus, B's corresponding items and the recomputed corresponding items are determined by continuing to treat the security as not within an exception to marking to market. Under section 475(d)(3), it is possible for the character of S's intercompany items to differ from the character of B's corresponding items.

(c) Timing and character. S has a $30 gain when it disposes of the security by selling it to B. This gain is intercompany gain that is taken into account in Year 1 to reflect the $30 difference between B's $0 gain taken into account from marking the security to market under section 475 and the recomputed $30 gain that would be taken into account. The character of S's gain and B's gain are redetermined as if the security were transferred between divisions. Accordingly, S's gain is ordinary income under section 475(d)(3)(A)(i), but under section 475(d)(3)(B)(ii) B's $10 gain from its sale to X is capital gain that is taken into account in Year 2.

(d) Nondealer to dealer. The facts are the same as in paragraph(a) of this Example 11, except that S is not a dealer and holds the security for investment with a $70 basis, B is a dealer to which section 475 applies and, immediately after acquiring the security from S for $100, B holds the security for sale to customers in the ordinary course of its trade or business. Because S is not a dealer and held the security for investment, the security is treated as properly identified as held for investment under section 475(b)(1) until it is sold to B. Under section 475(b)(3), the security thereafter ceases to be described in section 475(b)(1) because B holds the security for sale to customers. The mark-to-market requirement applies only to changes in the value of the security after B's acquisition. B's mark-to-market gain taken into account and the recomputed mark-to-market gain are both determined based on changes from the $100 value of the security at the time of B's acquisition. There is no difference between B's $0 mark-to-market gain taken into account in Year 1 and the $0 recomputed mark-to-market gain. Therefore, none of S's gain is taken into account in Year 1 as a result of B's marking the security to market in Year 1. In Year 2, B has a $10 gain when it disposes of the security by selling it to X, but would have had a $40 gain if S and B were divisions of a single corporation. Thus, S takes its $30 gain into account in Year 2 under the matching rule. Under section 475(d)(3), S's gain is capital gain even though B's subsequent gain or loss from marking to market or disposing of the security is ordinary gain or loss. If B disposes of the security at a $10 loss in Year 2, S's gain taken into account in Year 2 is still capital because on a single entity basis section 475(d)(3) would provide for $30 of capital gain and $10 of ordinary loss. Because the attributes are not redetermined under paragraph (c)(1)(i) of this section, paragraph (c)(4)(i) of this section does not apply. Furthermore, if B held the security for investment, and so identified the security under section 475(b)(1), the security would continue to be excepted from marking to market.

Example (12). Section 1092.

(a) Facts. On July 1 of Year 1, S enters into offsetting long and short positions with respect to actively traded personal property. The positions are not section 1256 contracts, and they are the only positions taken into account for purposes of applying section 1092. On August 1 of Year 1, S sells the long position to B at an $11 loss, and there is $11 of unrealized gain in the offsetting short position. on December 1 of Year 1, B sells the long position to X at no gain or loss. On December 31 of Year 1, there is still $11 of unrealized gain in the short position. On February 1 of Year 2, S closes the short position at an $11 gain.

(b) Timing and attributes. If the sale from S to B were a transfer between divisions of a single corporation, the $11 loss on the sale to X would have been deferred under section 1092(a)(1)(A). Accordingly, there is no difference in Year 1 between B's corresponding item of $0 and the recomputed corresponding item of $0. S takes its $11 loss into account in Year 2 to reflect the difference between B's corresponding item of $0 taken into account in Year 2 and the recomputed loss of $11 that would have been taken into account in Year 2 under section 1092(a)(1)(B) if S and B had been divisions of a single corporation. (The results are the same under section 267(f).)

Example (13). [Reserved.]

Example (14). Source of income under section 863.

(a) Intercompany sale with no independent factory price. S manufactures inventory in the United States, and recognizes $75 of income on sales to B in Year 1. B distributes the inventory in Country Y and recognizes $25 of income on sales to X, also in Year 1. Title passes from S to B, and from B to X, in Country Y. There is no independent factory price (as defined in regulations under section 863) for the sale from S to B. Under the matching rule, S's $75 intercompany income and B's $25 corresponding income are taken into account in Year 1. In determining the source of income, S and B are treated as divisions of a single corporation, and section 863 applies as if $100 of income were recognized from producing in the United States and selling in Country Y. Assume that applying the section 863 regulations on a single entity basis, $50 is treated as foreign source income and $50 as U.S. source income. Assume further that on a separate entity basis, S would have $37.50 of foreign source income and $37.50 of U.S. source income, and that all of B's $25 of income would be foreign source income. Thus, on a separate entity basis, S and B would have $62.50 of combined foreign source income and $37.50 of U.S. source income. Accordingly, under single entity treatment, $12.50 that would be treated as foreign source income on a separate entity basis is redetermined to be U.S. source income. Under paragraph (c)(1)(i) of this section, attributes are redetermined only to the extent of the $12.50 necessary to achieve the same effect as a single entity determination. Under paragraph (c)(4)(ii) of this section, the redetermined attribute must be allocated between S and B using a reasonable method. For example, it may be reasonable to recharacterize only S's foreign source income as U.S. source income because only S would have any U.S. source income on a separate entity basis. However, it may also be reasonable to allocate the redetermined attribute between S and B in proportion to their separate entity amounts of foreign source income (in a 3:2 ratio, so that $7.50 of S's foreign source income is redetermined to be U.S. source and $5 of B's foreign source income is redetermined to be U.S. source), provided the same method is applied to all similar transactions within the group.

(b) Intercompany sale with independent factory price. The facts are the same as in paragraph (a) of this Example 14, except that an independent factory price exists for the sale by S to B such that $70 of S's $75 of income is attributable to the production function. Assume that on a single entity basis, $70 is treated as U.S. source income (because of the existence of the independent factory price) and $30 is treated as foreign source income. Assume that on a separate entity basis, $70 of S's income would be treated as U.S. source, $5 of S's income would be treated as foreign source income, and all of B's $25 income would be treated as foreign source income. Because the results are the same on a single entity basis and a separate entity basis, the attributes are not redetermined under paragraph (c)(1)(i) of this section.

(c) Sale of property reflecting intercompany services or intangibles. S earns $10 of income performing services in the United States for B. B capitalizes S's fees into the basis of property that it manufactures in the United States and sells to an unrelated person in Year 1 at a $90 profit, with title passing in Country Y. Under the matching rule, S's $10 income and B's $90 income are taken into account in Year 1. In determining the source of income, S and B are treated as divisions of a single corporation, and section 863 applies as if $100 were earned from manufacturing in the United States and selling in Country Y. Assume that on a single entity basis $50 is treated as foreign source income and $50 is treated as U.S. source income. Assume that on a separate entity basis, S would have $10 of U.S. source income, and B would have $45 of foreign source income and $45 of U.S. source income. Accordingly, under single entity treatment, $5 of income that would be treated as U.S. source income on a separate entity basis is redetermined to be foreign source income. Under paragraph (c)(1)(i) of this section, attributes are redetermined only to the extent of the $5 necessary to achieve the same effect as a single entity determination. Under paragraph (c)(4)(ii) of this section, the redetermined attribute must be allocated between S and B using a reasonable method. (If instead of performing services, S licensed an intangible to B and earned $10 that would be treated as U.S. source income on a separate entity basis, the results would be the same.)

Example (15). Section 1248.

(a) Facts. On January 1 of Year 1, S forms FT, a wholly owned foreign subsidiary, with a $10 contribution. During Years 1 through 3, FT has earnings and profits of $40. None of the earnings and profits is taxed as subpart F income under section 951, and FT distributes no dividends to S during this period. On January 1 of Year 4, S sells its FT stock to B for $50. While B owns FT, FT has a deficit in earnings and profits of $10. On July 1 of Year 6, B sells its FT stock for $70 to X, an unrelated foreign corporation.

(b) Timing. S's $40 of intercompany gain is taken into account in Year 6 to reflect the difference between B's $20 of gain taken into account and the $60 recomputed gain.

(c) Attributes. Under the matching rule, the attributes of S's intercompany gain and B's corresponding gain are redetermined to have the same effect on consolidated taxable income (and consolidated tax liability) as if S and B were divisions of a single corporation. On a single entity basis, there is $60 of gain and the portion which is characterized as a dividend under section 1248 is determined on the basis of FT's $30 of earnings and profits at the time of the sale of FT to X (the sum of FT's $40 of earnings and profits while held by S and FT's $10 deficit in earnings and profits while held by B). Therefore, $30 of the $60 gain is treated as a dividend under section 1248. The remaining $30 is treated as capital gain. On a separate entity basis, all of S's $40 gain would be treated as a dividend under section 1248 and all of B's $20 gain would be treated as capital gain. Thus, as a result of the single entity determination, $10 that would be treated as a dividend under section 1248 on a separate entity basis is redetermined to be capital gain. Under paragraph (c)(4)(ii) of this section, this redetermined attribute must be allocated between S's intercompany item and B's corresponding item by using a reasonable method. On a separate entity basis, only S would have any amount treated as a dividend under section 1248 available for redetermination. Accordingly, $10 of S's income is redetermined to be not subject to section 1248, with the result that $30 of S's intercompany gain is treated as a dividend and the remaining $10 is treated as capital gain. All of B's corresponding gain is treated as capital gain, as it would be on a separate entity basis.

(d) B has loss. The facts are the same as in paragraph (a) of this Example 15, except that FT has no earnings and profits or deficit in earnings and profits while B owns FT, and B sells the FT stock to X for $40. On a single entity basis, there is $30 of gain, and section 1248 is applied on the basis of FT's $40 earnings and profits at the time of the sale of FT to X. Under section 1248, the amount treated as a dividend is limited to $30 (the amount of the gain). On a separate entity basis, S's entire $40 gain would be treated as a dividend under section 1248, and B's $10 loss would be a capital loss. B's $10 corresponding loss offsets $10 of S's intercompany gain and, under paragraph (c)(4)(i) of this section, the attributes of B's corresponding item control. Accordingly, $10 of S's gain must be redetermined to be capital gain. B's $10 loss remains a capital loss. (If, however, S sold FT to B at a loss and B sold FT to X at a gain, it may be unreasonable for the attributes of B's corresponding gain to control S's offsetting intercompany loss. If B's attributes were to control, for example, the group could possibly claim a larger foreign tax credit than would be available if S and B were divisions of a single corporation.)

(d) Acceleration rule. S's intercompany items and B's corresponding items are taken into account under this paragraph (d) to the extent they cannot be taken into account to produce the effect of treating S and B as divisions of a single corporation. For this purpose, the following rules apply:

(1) S's items. (i) Timing. S takes its intercompany items into account to the extent they cannot be taken into account to produce the effect of treating S and B as divisions of a single corporation. The items are taken into account immediately before it first becomes impossible to achieve this effect. For this purpose, the effect cannot be achieved—

(A) To the extent an intercompany item or corresponding item will not be taken into account in determining the group's consolidated taxable income (or consolidated tax liability) under the matching rule (for example, if S or B becomes a nonmember, or if S's intercompany item is no longer reflected in the difference between B's basis (or an amount equivalent to basis) in property and the basis (or equivalent amount) the property would have if S and B were divisions of a single corporation); or

(B) To the extent a nonmember reflects, directly or indirectly, any aspect of the intercompany transaction (e.g., if B's cost basis in property purchased from S is reflected by a nonmember under section 362 following a section 351 transaction).

(ii) Attributes. The attributes of S's intercompany items taken into account under this paragraph (d)(1) are determined as follows:

(A) Sale, exchange, or distribution. If the item is from an intercompany sale, exchange, or distribution of property, its attributes are determined under the principles of the matching rule as if B sold the property, at the time the item is taken into account under paragraph (d)(1)(i) of this section, for a cash payment equal to B's adjusted basis in the property (i.e., at no net gain or loss), to the following person:

(1) Property leaves the group. If the property is owned by a nonmember immediately after S's item is taken into account, B is treated as selling the property to that nonmember. If the nonmember is related for purposes of any provision of the Internal Revenue Code or regulations to any party to the intercompany transaction (or any related transaction) or to the common parent, the nonmember is treated as related to B for purposes of that provision. For example, if the nonmember is related to P within the meaning of section 1239(b), the deemed sale is treated as being described in section 1239(a). See paragraph (j)(6) of this section, under which property is not treated as being owned by a nonmember if it is owned by the common parent after the common parent becomes the only remaining member.

(2) Property does not leave the group. If the property is not owned by a nonmember immediately after S's item is taken into account, B is treated as selling the property to an affiliated corporation that is not a member of the group.

(B) Other transactions. If the item is from an intercompany transaction other than a sale, exchange, or distribution of property (e.g., income from S's services capitalized by B), its attributes are determined on a separate entity basis.

(2) B's items. (i) Attributes. The attributes of B's corresponding items continue to be redetermined under the principles of the matching rule, with the following adjustments:

(A) If S and B continue to join with each other in the filing of consolidated returns, the attributes of B's corresponding items (and any applicable holding periods) are determined by continuing to treat S and B as divisions of a single corporation.

(B) Once S and B no longer join with each other in the filing of consolidated returns, the attributes of B's corresponding items are determined as if the S division (but not the B division) were transferred by the single corporation to an unrelated person. Thus, S's activities (and any applicable holding period) before the intercompany transaction continue to affect the attributes of the corresponding items (and any applicable holding period).

(ii) Timing. If paragraph (d)(1) of this section applies to S, B nevertheless continues to take its corresponding items into account under its accounting method. However, the redetermination of the attributes of a corresponding item under this paragraph (d)(2) might affect its timing.

(3) Examples. The acceleration rule of this paragraph (d) is illustrated by the following examples.

Example (1). Becoming a nonmember—timing.

(a) Facts. S owns land with a basis of $70. On January 1 of Year 1, S sells the land to B for $100. On July 1 of Year 3, P sells 60% of S's stock to X for $60 and, as a result, S becomes a nonmember.

(b) Matching rule. Under the matching rule, none of S's $30 gain is taken into account in Years 1 through 3 because there is no difference between B's $0 gain or loss taken into account and the recomputed gain or loss.

(c) Acceleration of S's intercompany items. Under the acceleration rule of paragraph (d) of this section, S's $30 gain is taken into account in computing consolidated taxable income (and consolidated tax liability) immediately before the effect of treating S and B as divisions of a single corporation cannot be produced. Because the effect cannot be produced once S becomes a nonmember, S takes its $30 gain into account in Year 3 immediately before becoming a nonmember. S's gain is reflected under § 1.1502-32 in P's basis in the S stock immediately before P's sale of the stock. Under § 1.1502-32, P's basis in the S stock is increased by $30, and therefore P's gain is reduced (or loss is increased) by $18 (60% of $30). See also §§ 1.1502-33 and 1.1502-76(b). (The results would be the same if S sold the land to B in an installment sale to which section 453 would otherwise apply, because S must take its intercompany gain into account under this section.)

(d) B's corresponding items. Notwithstanding the acceleration of S's gain, B continues to take its corresponding items into account under its accounting method. Thus, B's items from the land are taken into account based on subsequent events (e.g., its sale of the land).

(e) Sale of B's stock. The facts are the same as in paragraph (a) of this Example 1, except that P sells 60% of B's stock (rather than S stock) to X for $60 and, as a result, B becomes a nonmember. Because the effect of treating S and B as divisions of a single corporation cannot be produced once B becomes a nonmember, S takes its $30 gain into account under the acceleration rule immediately before B becomes a nonmember. (The results would be the same if S sold the land to B in an installment sale to which section 453 would otherwise apply, because S must take its intercompany gain into account under this section.)

(f) Discontinue filing consolidated returns. The facts are the same as in paragraph (a) of this Example 1, except that the P group receives permission under § 1.1502-75(c) to discontinue filing consolidated returns beginning in Year 3. Under the acceleration rule, S takes its $30 gain into account on December 31 of Year 2.

(g) No subgroups. The facts are the same as in paragraph (a) of this Example 1, except that P simultaneously sells all of the stock of both S and B to X (rather than 60% of S's stock), and S and B become members of the X consolidated group. Because the effect of treating S and B as divisions of a single corporation in the P group cannot be produced once S and B become nonmembers, S takes its $30 gain into account under the acceleration rule immediately before S and B become nonmembers. (Paragraph (j)(5) of this section does not apply to treat the X consolidated group as succeeding to the P group because the X group acquired only the stock of S and B.) However, so long as S and B continue to join with each other in the filing of consolidated returns, B continues to treat S and B as divisions of a single corporation for purposes of determining the attributes of B's corresponding items from the land.

Example (2). Becoming a nonmember—attributes.

(a) Facts. S holds land for investment with a basis of $70. On January 1 of Year 1, S sells the land to B for $100. B holds the land for sale to customers in the ordinary course of business, and expends substantial resources over a two-year period subdividing, developing, and marketing the land. On July 1 of Year 3, before B has sold any of the land, P sells 60% of S's stock to X for $60 and, as a result, S becomes a nonmember.

(b) Attributes. Under the acceleration rule, the attributes of S's gain are redetermined under the principles of the matching rule as if B sold the land to an affiliated corporation that is not a member of the group for a cash payment equal to B's adjusted basis in the land (because the land continues to be held within the group). Thus, whether S's gain is capital gain or ordinary income depends on the activities of both S and B. Because S and B no longer join with each other in the filing of consolidated returns, the attributes of B's corresponding items (e.g., from its subsequent sale of the land) are redetermined under the principles of the matching rule as if the S division (but not the B division) were transferred by the single corporation to an unrelated person at the time of P's sale of the S stock. Thus, B continues to take into account the activities of S with respect to the land before the intercompany transaction.

(c) Depreciable property. The facts are the same as in paragraph (a) of this Example 2, except that the property sold by S to B is depreciable property. Section 1239 applies to treat all of S's gain as ordinary income because it is taken into account as a result of B's deemed sale of the property to a affiliated corporation that is not a member of the group (a related person within the meaning of section 1239(b)).

Example (3). Selling member's disposition of installment note.

(a) Facts. S owns land with a basis of $70. On January 1 of Year 1, S sells the land to B in exchange for B's $110 note. The note bears a market rate of interest in excess of the applicable Federal rate, and provides for principal payments of $55 in Year 4 and $55 in Year 5. On July 1 of Year 3, S sells B's note to X for $110.

(b) Timing. S's intercompany gain is taken into account under this section, and not under the rules of section 453. Consequently, S's sale of B's note does not result in its intercompany gain from the land being taken into account (e.g., under section 453B). The sale does not prevent S's intercompany items and B's corresponding items from being taken into account in determining the group's consolidated taxable income under the matching rule, and X does not reflect any aspect of the intercompany transaction (X has its own cost basis in the note). S will take the intercompany gain into account under the matching rule or acceleration rule based on subsequent events (e.g., B's sale of the land). See also paragraph (g) of this section for additional rules applicable to B's note as an intercompany obligation.

Example (4). Cancellation of debt and attribute reduction under section 108(b).

(a) Facts. S holds land for investment with a basis of $0. On January 1 of Year 1, S sells the land to B for $100. B also holds the land for investment. During Year 3, B is insolvent and B's nonmember creditors discharge $60 of B's indebtedness. Because of insolvency, B's $60 discharge is excluded from B's gross income under section 108(a), and B reduces the basis of the land by $60 under sections 108(b) and 1017.

(b) Acceleration rule. As a result of B's basis reduction under section 1017, $60 of S's intercompany gain will not be taken into account under the matching rule (because there is only a $40 difference between B's $40 basis in the land and the $0 basis the land would have if S and B were divisions of a single corporation). Accordingly, S takes $60 of its gain into account under the acceleration rule in Year 3. S's gain is long-term capital gain, determined under paragraph (d)(1)(ii) of this section as if B sold the land to an affiliated corporation that is not a member of the group for $100 immediately before the basis reduction.

(c) Purchase price adjustment. Assume instead that S sells the land to B in exchange for B's $100 purchase money note, B remains solvent, and S subsequently agrees to discharge $60 of the note as a purchase price adjustment to which section 108(e)(5) applies. Under applicable principles of tax law, $60 of S's gain and $60 of B's basis in the land are eliminated and never taken into account. Similarly, the note is not treated as satisfied and reissued under paragraph (g) of this section.

Example (5). Section 481.

(a) Facts. S operates several trades or businesses, including a manufacturing business. S receives permission to change its method of accounting for valuing inventory for its manufacturing business. S increases the basis of its ending inventory by $100, and the related $100 positive section 481(a) adjustment is to be taken into account ratably over six taxable years, beginning in Year 1. During Year 3, S sells all of the assets used in its manufacturing business to B at a gain. Immediately after the transfer, B does not use the same inventory valuation method as S. On a separate entity basis, S's sale results in an acceleration of the balance of the section 481(a) adjustment to Year 3.

(b) Timing and attributes. Under paragraph (b)(2) of this section, the balance of S's section 481(a) adjustment accelerated to Year 3 is intercompany income. However, S's $100 basis increase before the intercompany transaction eliminates the related difference for this amount between B's corresponding items taken into account and the recomputed corresponding items in subsequent periods. Because the accelerated section 481(a) adjustment will not be taken into account in determining the group's consolidated taxable income (and consolidated tax liability) under the matching rule, the balance of S's section 481 adjustment is taken into account under the acceleration rule as ordinary income at the time of the intercompany transaction. (If S's sale had not resulted in accelerating S's section 481(a) adjustment on a separate entity basis, S would have no intercompany income to be taken into account under this section.)

(e) Simplifying rules. *(1) Dollar-value LIFO inventory methods.* (i) In general. This paragraph (e)(1) applies if either S or B uses a dollar-value LIFO inventory method to account for intercompany transactions. Rather than applying the matching rule separately to each intercompany inventory transaction, this paragraph (e)(1) provides methods to apply an aggregate approach that is based on dollar-value LIFO inventory accounting. Any method selected under this paragraph (e)(1) must be applied consistently.

(ii) B uses dollar-value LIFO. (A) In general. If B uses a dollar-value LIFO inventory method to account for its intercompany inventory purchases, and includes all of its inventory costs incurred for a year in its cost of goods sold for the year (that is, B has no inventory increment for the year), S takes into account all of its intercompany inventory items for the year. If B does not include all of its inventory costs incurred for the year in its cost of goods sold for the year (that is, B has an inventory increment for the year), S does not take all of its intercompany inventory income or loss into account. The amount not taken into account is determined under either the increment averaging method of paragraph (e)(1)(ii)(B) of this section or the increment valuation method of paragraph (e)(1)(ii)(C) of this section. Separate computations are made for each pool of B that receives intercompany purchases from S, and S's amount not taken into account is layered based on B's LIFO inventory layers.

(B) Increment averaging method. Under this paragraph (e)(1)(ii)(B), the amount not taken into account is the amount of S's intercompany inventory income or loss multiplied by the ratio of the LIFO value of B's current-year costs of its layer of increment to B's total inventory costs incurred for the year under its LIFO inventory method. If B includes more than its inventory costs incurred during any subsequent year in its cost of goods sold (a decrement), S takes into account the intercompany inventory income or loss layers in the same manner and proportion as B takes into account its inventory decrements.

(C) Increment valuation method. Under this paragraph (e)(1)(ii)(C), the amount not taken into account is the amount of S's intercompany inventory income or loss for the appropriate period multiplied by the ratio of the LIFO value of B's current-year costs of its layer of increment to B's total inventory costs incurred in the appropriate period under its LIFO inventory method. The principles of paragraph (e)(1)(ii)(B) of this section otherwise apply. The appropriate period is the period of B's year used to determine its current-year costs.

(iii) S uses dollar-value LIFO. If S uses a dollar-value LIFO inventory method to account for its intercompany inventory sales, S may use any reasonable method of allocating its LIFO inventory costs to intercompany transactions. LIFO inventory costs include costs of prior layers if a decrement occurs. For example, a reasonable allocation of the most recent costs incurred during the consolidated return year can be used to compute S's intercompany inventory income or loss for the year if S has an inventory increment and uses the earliest acquisitions costs method, but S must apportion costs from the most recent appropriate layers of increment if an inventory decrement occurs for the year.

(iv) Other reasonable methods. S or B may use a method not specifically provided in this paragraph (e)(1) that is expected to reasonably take into account intercompany items and corresponding items from intercompany inventory transactions. However, if the method used results, for any year, in a cumulative amount of intercompany inventory items not taken into account by S that significantly exceeds the cumulative amount that would not be taken into account under paragraph (e)(1)(ii) or (iii) of this section, S must take into account for that year the amount necessary to eliminate the excess. The method is thereafter applied with appropriate adjustments to reflect the amount taken into account.

(v) Examples. The inventory rules of this paragraph (e)(1) are illustrated by the following examples.

Example (1). Increment averaging method.

(a) Facts. Both S and B use a double-extension, dollar-value LIFO inventory method, and both value inventory increments using the earliest acquisitions cost valuation method. During Year 2, S sells 25 units of product Q to B on January 15 at $10/unit. S sells another 25 units on April 15, on July 15, and on September 15, at $12/unit. S's earliest cost of product Q is $7.50/unit and S's most recent cost of product Q is $8.00/unit. Both S and B have an inventory increment for the year. B's total inventory costs incurred during Year 2 are $6,000 and the LIFO value of B's Year 2 layer of increment is $600.

(b) Intercompany inventory income. Under paragraph (e)(1)(iii) of this section, S must use a reasonable method of allocating its LIFO inventory costs to intercompany transactions. Because S has an inventory increment for Year 2 and uses the earliest acquisitions cost method, a reasonable method of determining its intercompany cost of goods sold for product Q is to use its most recent costs. Thus, its intercompany cost of goods sold is $800 ($8.00 most recent cost, multiplied by 100 units sold to B), and its intercompany inventory income is $350 ($1,150 sales proceeds from B minus $800 cost).

(c) Timing.

(i) Under the increment averaging method of paragraph (e)(1)(ii)(B) of this section, $35 of S's $350 of intercompany inventory income is not taken into account in Year 2, computed as follows:

$$\frac{\text{LIFO value of B's Year 2 layer of increment}}{\text{B's total inventory costs for Year 2}} = \frac{\$\ 600}{\$6{,}000} = 10\%$$

10% × S's $350 intercompany inventory income = $35

(ii) Thus, $315 of S's intercompany inventory income is taken into account in Year 2 ($350 of total intercompany inventory income minus $35 not taken into account).

(d) S incurs a decrement. The facts are the same as in paragraph (a) of this Example 1, except that in Year 2, S incurs a decrement equal to 50% of its Year 1 layer. Under paragraph (e)(1)(iii) of this section, S must reasonably allocate the LIFO cost of the decrement to the cost of goods sold to B to determine S's intercompany inventory income.

(e) B incurs a decrement. The facts are the same as in paragraph (a) of this Example 1, except that B incurs a decrement in Year 2. S must take into account the entire $350 of Year 2 intercompany inventory income because all 100 units of product Q are deemed sold by B in Year 2.

Example (2). Increment valuation method.

(a) The facts are the same as in Example 1. In addition, B's use of the earliest acquisition's cost method of valuing its increments results in B valuing its year-end inventory using costs incurred from January through March. B's costs incurred during the year are: $1,428 in the period January through March; $1,498 in the period April through June; $1,524 in the period July through September; and $1,550 in the period October through December. S's intercompany inventory income for these periods is: $50 in the period January through March ((25 × $10) − (25 × $8)); $100 in the period April through June ((25 × $12) − (25 × $8)); $100 in the period July through September ((25 × $12) − (25 × $8)); and $100 in the period October through December ((25 × $12) − (25 × $8)).

(b) Timing.

(i) Under the increment valuation method of paragraph (e)(1)(ii)(C) of this section, $21 of S's $350 of intercompany inventory income is not taken into account in Year 2, computed as follows:

$$\frac{\text{LIFO value of B's Year 2 layer of increment}}{\text{B's total inventory costs from January through March of Year 2}} = \frac{\$\ 600}{\$1{,}428} = 42\%$$

42% × S's $50 intercompany inventory income for the period from January through March = $21

(ii) Thus, $329 of S's intercompany inventory income is taken into account in Year 2 ($350 of total intercompany inventory income minus $21 not taken into account).

(c) B incurs a subsequent decrement. The facts are the same as in paragraph (a) of this Example 2. In addition, assume that in Year 3, B experiences a decrement in its pool that receives intercompany purchases from S. B's decrement equals 20% of the base-year costs for its Year 2 layer. The fact that B has incurred a decrement means that all of its inventory costs incurred for Year 3 are included in cost of goods sold. As a result, S takes into account its entire amount of intercompany inventory income from its Year 3 sales. In addition, S takes into account $4.20 of its Year 2 layer of intercompany inventory income not already taken into account (20% of $21).

Example (3). Other reasonable inventory methods.

(a) Facts. Both S and B use a dollar-value LIFO inventory method for their inventory transactions. During Year 1, S sells inventory to B and to X. Under paragraph (e)(1)(iv) of this section, to compute its intercompany inventory income and the amount of this income not taken into account, S computes its intercompany inventory income using the transfer price of the inventory items less a FIFO cost for the goods, takes into account these items based on a FIFO cost flow assumption for B's corresponding items, and the LIFO methods used by S and B are ignored for these computations. These computations are comparable to the methods used by S and B for financial reporting purposes, and the book methods and results are used for tax purposes. S adjusts the amount of intercompany inventory items not taken into account as required by section 263A.

(b) Reasonable method. The method used by S is a reasonable method under paragraph (e)(1)(iv) of this section if the cumulative amount of intercompany inventory items not taken into account by S is not significantly greater than the cumulative amount that would not be taken into account under the methods specifically described in paragraph (e)(1) of this section. If, for any year, the method results in a cumulative amount of intercompany inventory items not taken into account by S that significantly exceeds the cumulative amount that would not be taken into account under the methods specifically provided, S must take into account for that year the amount necessary to eliminate the excess. The method is thereafter applied with appropriate adjustments to reflect the amount taken into account (e.g., to prevent the amount from being taken into account more than once).

(2) Reserve accounting. (i) Banks and thrifts. Except as provided in paragraph (g)(4)(v) of this section (deferral of items from an intercompany obligation), a member's addition to, or reduction of, a reserve for bad debts that is maintained under section 585 is taken into account on a separate entity basis. For example, if S makes a loan to a nonmember and subsequently sells the loan to B, any deduction for an addition to a bad debt reserve under section 585 and any recapture income (or reduced bad debt deductions) are taken into account on a separate entity basis rather than as intercompany items or corresponding items taken into account under this section. Any gain or loss of S from its sale of the loan to B is taken into account under this section, however, to the extent it is not attributable to recapture of the reserve.

(ii) Insurance companies. (A) Direct insurance. If a member provides insurance to another member in an intercompany transaction, the transaction is taken into account by both members on a separate entity basis. For example, if one member provides life insurance coverage for another member with respect to its employees, the premiums, reserve increases and decreases, and death benefit payments are determined and taken into account by both members on a separate entity basis rather than taken into account under this section as intercompany items and corresponding items.

(B) Reinsurance. (1) In general. Paragraph (e)(2)(ii)(A) of this section does not apply to a reinsurance transaction that is an intercompany transaction. For example, if a member assumes all or a portion of the risk on an insurance contract written by another member, the amounts transferred as reinsurance premiums, expense allowances, benefit reimbursements, reimbursed policyholder dividends, experience rating adjustments, and other similar items are taken into account under the matching rule and the acceleration rule. For purposes of this section, the assuming company is treated as B and the ceding company is treated as S.

(2) Reserves determined on a separate entity basis. For purposes of determining the amount of a member's increase or decrease in reserves, the amount of any reserve item listed in section 807(c) or 832(b)(5) resulting from a reinsurance transaction that is an intercompany transaction is determined on a separate entity basis. But see section 845, under which the Commissioner may allocate between or among the members any items, recharacterize any such items, or make any other adjustments necessary to reflect the proper source and character of the separate taxable income of a member.

(3) Consent to treat intercompany transactions on a separate entity basis. (i) General rule. The common parent may request consent to take into account on a separate entity basis items from intercompany transactions other than intercompany transactions with respect to stock or obligations of members. Consent may be granted for all items, or for items from a class or classes of transactions. The consent is effective only if granted in writing by the Internal Revenue Service. Unless revoked with the written consent of the Internal Revenue Service, the separate entity treatment applies to all affected intercompany transactions in the consolidated return year for which consent is granted and in all subsequent consolidated return years. Consent under this paragraph (e)(3) does not apply for purposes of taking into account losses and deductions deferred under section 267(f).

(ii) Time and manner for requesting consent. The request for consent described in paragraph (e)(3)(i) of this section must be made in the form of a ruling request. The request must be signed by the common parent, include any information required by the Internal Revenue Service, and be filed on or before the due date of the consolidated return (not including extensions of time) for the first consolidated return year to which the consent is to apply. The Internal Revenue

Service may impose terms and conditions for granting consent. A copy of the consent must be attached to the group's consolidated returns (or amended returns) as required by the terms of the consent.

(iii) Effect of consent on methods of accounting. A consent for separate entity accounting under this paragraph (e)(3), and a revocation of that consent, may require changes in members' methods of accounting for intercompany transactions. Because the consent, or a revocation of the consent, is effective for all intercompany transactions occurring in the consolidated return year for which the consent or revocation is first effective, any change in method is effected on a cutoff basis. Section 446(e) consent is granted for any changes in methods of accounting for intercompany transactions that are necessary solely to conform a member's methods to a binding consent with respect to the group under this paragraph (e)(3) or the revocation of that consent, provided the changes are made in the first consolidated return year for which the consent or revocation under this paragraph (e)(3) is effective. Therefore, section 446(e) consent must be separately requested under applicable administrative procedures if a member has failed to conform its practices to the separate entity accounting provided under this paragraph (e)(3) or the revocation of that treatment in the first consolidated return year for which the consent to use separate entity accounting or revocation of that consent is effective.

(iv) Consent to treat intercompany transactions on a separate entity basis under prior law. A group that has received consent that is in effect as of the first day of the first consolidated return year beginning on or after July 12, 1995 to treat certain intercompany transactions as provided in § 1.1502-13(c)(3) of the regulations (as contained in the 26 CFR part 1 edition revised as of April 1, 1995) will be considered to have obtained the consent of the Commissioner to take items from intercompany transactions into account on a separate entity basis as provided in paragraph (e)(3)(i) of this section. This treatment is applicable only to the items, class or classes of transactions for which consent was granted under prior law.

(f) Stock of members. *(1) In general.* In addition to the general rules of this section, the rules of this paragraph (f) apply to stock of members.

(2) Intercompany distributions to which section 301 applies. (i) In general. This paragraph (f)(2) provides rules for intercompany transactions to which section 301 applies (intercompany distributions). For purposes of determining whether a distribution is an intercompany distribution, it is treated as occurring under the principles of the entitlement rule of paragraph (f)(2)(iv) of this section. A distribution is not an intercompany distribution to the extent it is deducted by the distributing member. See, for example, section 1382(c)(1).

(ii) Distributee member. An intercompany distribution is not included in the gross income of the distributee member (B). However, this exclusion applies to a distribution only to the extent there is a corresponding negative adjustment reflected under § 1.1502-32 in B's basis in the stock of the distributing member (S). For example, no amount is included in B's gross income under section 301(c)(3) from a distribution in excess of the basis of the stock of a subsidiary that results in an excess loss account under § 1.1502-32(a) which is treated as negative basis under § 1.1502-19. B's dividend received deduction under section 243(a)(3) is determined without regard to any intercompany distributions under this paragraph (f)(2) to the extent they are not included in gross income. See § 1.1502-26(b) (applicability of the dividends received deduction to distributions not excluded from gross income, such as a distribution from the common parent to a subsidiary owning stock of the common parent).

(iii) Distributing member. The principles of section 311(b) apply to S's loss, as well as gain, from an intercompany distribution of property. Thus, S's loss is taken into account under the matching rule if the property is subsequently sold to a nonmember. However, section 311(a) continues to apply to distributions to nonmembers (for example, loss is not recognized).

(iv) Entitlement rule. (A) In general. For all Federal income tax purposes, an intercompany distribution is treated as taken into account when the shareholding member becomes entitled to it (generally on the record date). For example, if B becomes entitled to a cash distribution before it is made, the distribution is treated as made when B becomes entitled to it. For this purpose, B is treated as entitled to a distribution no later than the time the distribution is taken into account under the Internal Revenue Code (e.g., under section 305(c)). To the extent a distribution is not made, appropriate adjustments must be made as of the date it was taken into account.

(B) Nonmember shareholders. If nonmembers own stock of the distributing corporation at the time the distribution is treated as occurring under this paragraph (f)(2)(iv), appropriate adjustments must be made to prevent the acceleration of the distribution to members from affecting distributions to nonmembers.

(3) Boot in an intercompany reorganization. (i) Scope. This paragraph (f)(3) provides additional rules for an intercompany transaction in which the receipt of money or other property (nonqualifying property) results in the application of section 356. For example, the distribution of stock of a lower-tier member to a higher-tier member in an intercompany transaction to which section 355 would apply but for the receipt of nonqualifying property is a transaction to which this paragraph (f)(3) applies. This paragraph (f)(3) does not apply if a party to the transaction becomes a member or nonmember as part of the same plan or arrangement. For example, if S merges into a nonmember in a transaction described in section 368(a)(1)(A), this paragraph (f)(3) does not apply.

(ii) Treatment. Nonqualifying property received as part of a transaction described in this paragraph (f)(3) is treated as received by the member shareholder in a separate transaction. See, for example, sections 302 and 311 (rather than sections 356 and 361). The nonqualifying property is treated as taken into account immediately after the transaction if section 354 would apply but for the fact that nonqualifying property is received. It is treated as taken into account immediately before the transaction if section 355 would apply but for the fact that nonqualifying property is received. The treatment under this paragraph (f)(3)(ii) applies for all Federal income tax purposes.

(4) Acquisition by issuer of its own stock. If a member acquires its own stock, or an option to buy or sell its own stock, in an intercompany transaction, the member's basis in that stock or option is treated as eliminated for all purposes. Accordingly, S's intercompany items from the stock or options of B are taken into account under this section if B acquires the stock or options in an intercompany transaction (unless, for example, B acquires the stock in exchange for successor property within the meaning of paragraph (j)(1) of this section in a nonrecognition transaction). For example, if B redeems its stock from S in a transaction to which section

302(a) applies, S's gain from the transaction is taken into account immediately under the acceleration rule.

(5) Certain liquidations and distributions. (i) Netting allowed. S's intercompany item from a transfer to B of the stock of another corporation (T) is taken into account under this section in certain circumstances even though the T stock is never held by a nonmember after the intercompany transaction. For example, if S sells all of T's stock to B at a gain, and T subsequently liquidates into B in a separate transaction to which section 332 applies, S's gain is taken into account under the matching rule. Under paragraph (c)(6)(ii) of this section, S's intercompany gain taken into account as a result of a liquidation under section 332 or a comparable nonrecognition transaction is not redetermined to be excluded from gross income. Under this paragraph (f)(5)(i), if S has both intercompany income or gain and intercompany deduction or loss attributable to stock of the same corporation having the same material terms, only the income or gain in excess of the deduction or loss is subject to paragraph (c)(6)(ii) of this section. This paragraph (f)(5)(i) applies only to a transaction in which B's basis in its T stock is permanently eliminated in a liquidation under section 332 or any comparable nonrecognition transaction, including—

(A) A merger of B into T under section 368(a);

(B) A distribution by B of its T stock in a transaction described in section 355; or

(C) A deemed liquidation of T resulting from an election under section 338(h)(10).

(ii) Elective relief. (A) In general. If an election is made pursuant to this paragraph (f)(5)(ii), certain transactions are recharacterized to prevent S's items from being taken into account or to provide offsets to those items. This paragraph (f)(5)(ii) applies only if T is a member throughout the period beginning with S's transfer and ending with the completion of the nonrecognition transaction.

(B) Section 332. (1) [Reserved]. For further guidance, see § 1.1502-13T(f)(5)(ii)(B)(1).

(2) [Reserved]. For further guidance, see § 1.1502-13T(f)(5)(ii)(B)(2).

(3) Downstream merger, etc. The principles of this paragraph (f)(5)(ii)(B) apply, with appropriate adjustments, if B's basis in the T stock is eliminated in a transaction similar to a section 332 liquidation, such as a transaction described in section 368 in which B merges into T. For example, if S and B are subsidiaries, and S sells all of T's stock to B at a gain followed by B's merger into T in a separate transaction described in section 368(a), S's gain is not taken into account solely as a result of the merger if T (as successor to B) forms new T with substantially all of T's former assets.

(C) Section 338(h)(10). (1) In general. This paragraph (f)(5)(ii)(C) applies to a deemed liquidation of T under section 332 as the result of an election under section 338(h)(10). This paragraph (f)(5)(ii)(C) does not apply if paragraph (f)(5)(ii)(B) of this section is applied to the deemed liquidation. Under this paragraph, B is treated with respect to each share of its T stock as recognizing as a corresponding item any loss or deduction it would recognize (determined after adjusting stock basis under § 1.1502-32) if section 331 applied to the deemed liquidation. For all other Federal income tax purposes, the deemed liquidation remains subject to section 332.

(2) Limitation on amount of loss. The amount of B's loss or deduction under this paragraph (f)(5)(ii)(C) is limited as follows—

(i) The aggregate amount of loss recognized with respect to T stock cannot exceed the amount of S's intercompany income or gain that is in excess of S's intercompany deduction or loss with respect to shares of T stock having the same material terms as the shares giving rise to S's intercompany income or gain; and

(ii) The aggregate amount of loss recognized under this paragraph (f)(5)(ii)(C) from T's deemed liquidation cannot exceed the net amount of deduction or loss (if any) that would be taken into account from the deemed liquidation if section 331 applied with respect to all T shares.

(3) Asset sale, etc. The principles of this paragraph (f)(5)(ii)(C) apply, with appropriate adjustments, if T transfers all of its assets to a nonmember and completely liquidates in a transaction comparable to the section 338(h)(10) transaction described in paragraph (f)(5)(ii)(C)(1) of this section. For example, if S sells all of T's stock to B at a gain followed by T's merger into a nonmember in exchange for a cash payment to B in a transaction treated for Federal income tax purposes as T's sale of its assets to the nonmember and complete liquidation, the merger is ordinarily treated as a comparable transaction.

(D) Section 355. If B distributes the T stock in an intercompany transaction to which section 355 applies (including an intercompany transaction to which 355 applies because of the application of paragraph (f)(3) of this section), the redetermination of the basis of the T stock under section 358 could cause S's gain or loss to be taken into account under this section. This paragraph (f)(5)(ii)(D) applies to treat B's distribution as subject to section 301 and 311 (as modified by this paragraph (f)), rather than section 355. The election will prevent S's gain or loss from being taken into account immediately to the extent matching remains possible, but B's gain or loss from the distribution will also be taken into account under this section.

(E) Election. An election to apply paragraph (f)(5)(ii) of this section is made in a separate statement entitled, "[INSERT NAME AND EMPLOYER IDENTIFICATION NUMBER OF COMMON PARENT] HEREBY ELECTS THE APPLICATION OF § 1.1502-13(f)(5)(ii) FOR AN INTERCOMPANY TRANSACTION INVOLVING [INSERT NAME AND EMPLOYER IDENTIFICATION NUMBER OF S] AND [INSERT NAME AND EMPLOYER IDENTIFICATION NUMBER OF T]." A separate election must be made for each such application. The election must be filed by including the statement on or with the consolidated group's income tax return for the year of T's liquidation (or other transaction). The Commissioner may impose reasonable terms and conditions to the application of paragraph (f)(5)(ii) of this section that are consistent with the purposes of such section. The statement must—

(1) Identify S's intercompany transaction and T's liquidation (or other transaction); and

(2) Specify which provision of paragraph (f)(5)(ii) of this section applies and how it alters the otherwise applicable results under this section (including, for example, the amount of S's intercompany items and the amount deferred or offset as a result of paragraph (f)(5)(ii) of this section).

(6) Stock of common parent. In addition to the general rules of this section, this paragraph (f)(6) applies to parent stock (P stock) and positions in P stock held or entered into by another member. For this purpose, P stock is any stock of the common parent held (directly or indirectly) by another member or any stock of a member (the issuer) that was the

common parent if the stock was held (directly or indirectly) by another member while the issuer was the common parent.

(i) Loss stock. (A) Recognized loss. Any loss recognized, directly or indirectly, by a member with respect to P stock is permanently disallowed and does not reduce earnings and profits. See § 1.1502-32(b)(3)(iii)(A) for a corresponding reduction in the basis of the member's stock.

(B) Other cases. If a member, M, owns P stock, the stock is subsequently owned by a nonmember, and, immediately before the stock is owned by the nonmember, M's basis in the share exceeds its fair market value, then, to the extent paragraph (f)(6)(i)(A) of this section does not apply, M's basis in the share is reduced to the share's fair market value immediately before the share is held by the nonmember. For example, if M owns shares of P stock with a $100x basis and M becomes a nonmember at a time when the P shares have a value of $60x, M's basis in the P shares is reduced to $60x immediately before M becomes a nonmember. Similarly, if M contributes the P stock to a nonmember in a transaction subject to section 351, M's basis in the shares is reduced to $60x immediately before the contribution. See § 1.1502-32(b)(3)(iii)(B) for a corresponding reduction in the basis of M's stock.

(C) Waiver of built-in loss on P stock. (1) In general. If a nonmember that owns P stock with a basis in excess of its fair market value becomes a member of the P consolidated group in a qualifying cost basis transaction, the group may make an irrevocable election to reduce the basis of the P stock to its fair market value immediately before the nonmember becomes a member of the P group. If the nonmember was a member of another consolidated group immediately before becoming a member of the P group, the reduction in basis is treated as occurring immediately after it ceases to be a member of the prior group. A qualifying cost basis transaction is the purchase (i.e., a transaction in which basis is determined under section 1012) by members of the P consolidated group (while they are members) in a 12-month period of an amount of the nonmember's stock satisfying the requirements of section 1504(a)(2).

(2) Election. The election described in paragraph (f)(6)(i)(C)(1) of this section must be made in a separate statement entitled, "ELECTION TO REDUCE BASIS OF P STOCK UNDER § 1.1502-13(f)(6) HELD BY [INSERT NAME AND EMPLOYER IDENTIFICATION NUMBER OF MEMBER WHOSE BASIS IN P STOCK IS REDUCED]." The election must be filed by including the statement on or with the consolidated group's income tax return for the year in which the nonmember becomes a member. The statement must identify the member's basis in the P stock (taking into account the effect of this election) and the number of shares of P stock held by the member.

(ii) Gain stock. For dispositions of P stock occurring before May 16, 2000, see § 1.1502-13(f)(6)(ii) as contained in 26 CFR part 1 in effect on April 1, 2000. For dispositions of P stock occurring on or after May 16, 2000, see § 1.1032-3.

(iii) Mark-to-market of P stock. Paragraphs (f)(6)(i) and (ii) of this section shall not apply to any gain or loss from a share of P stock held by a member, M, if—

(A) M regularly trades in P stock (of the same class) with customers in the ordinary course of its business as a dealer;

(B) The gain or loss on the share is taken into account by M pursuant to section 475(a);

(C) M's basis in the share is not adjusted by reference to the basis of any other property or by reference to income, gain, deduction, or loss from other property; and

(D) Neither M nor any other member of the group has structured or engaged in any transaction while a member (or in anticipation of becoming a member), during the taxable year or in any year within the preceding five taxable years that is open for assessment under section 6501, with a principal purpose of avoiding gain or creating loss on P stock subject to section 475(a).

(iv) Options, warrants, and other positions. (A) In general. This paragraph (f)(6) applies with appropriate adjustments to positions in P stock to the extent that P's gain or loss from an equivalent position would not be recognized under section 1032. Thus, if M purchases an option to buy or sell P stock and sells the option at a loss, the loss is permanently disallowed under paragraph (f)(6)(i)(A) of this section. Similarly, if M is the grantor of such an option and becomes a nonmember, then the principles of paragraph (f)(6)(i)(B) of this section apply to the extent that M would recognize loss from cash settlement of the option at its fair market value immediately before M becomes a nonmember, and proper adjustments must be made in the amount of any gain or loss subsequently realized from the position by M. If P grants M an option to acquire P stock in a transaction meeting the requirements of § 1.1032-3, M is treated as having purchased the option from P for fair market value with cash contributed to M by P.

(B) Mark-to-market of positions in P stock. For purposes of paragraph (f)(6)(iii) of this section, gain or loss with respect to a position taken into account under section 1256(a) is treated as taken into account under section 475(a) to the extent that the gain or loss would be taken into account under the principles of section 475.

(v) Effective date. This paragraph (f)(6) applies to gain or loss taken into account on or after July 12, 1995, and to transactions occurring on or after July 12, 1995. For example, if S sells P stock to B at a loss prior to July 12, 1995, and B sells the P stock to a nonmember after July 12, 1995, S's loss is disallowed because it is taken into account after July 12, 1995. If a taxpayer takes a gain or loss into account or engages in a transaction on or after July 12, 1995, during a tax year ending prior to December 31, 1995, the taxpayer may treat the gain or loss or the transaction under the rules of § 1.1502-13T(f)(6) (published in 1995-32 I.R.B. 47), instead of under the rules of this paragraph (f)(6).

(7) Examples.

(i) In general. The application of this section to intercompany transactions with respect to stock of members is illustrated by the following examples.

Example (1). Dividend exclusion and property distribution.

(a) Facts. S owns land with a $70 basis and $100 value. On January 1 of Year 1, P's basis in S's stock is $100. During Year 1, S declares and makes a dividend distribution of the land to P. Under section 311(b), S has a $30 gain. Under section 301(d), P's basis in the land is $100. On July 1 of Year 3, P sells the land to X for $110.

(b) Dividend elimination and stock basis adjustments. Under paragraph (b)(1) of this section, S's distribution to P is an intercompany distribution. Under paragraph (f)(2)(ii) of this section, P's $100 of dividend income is not included in gross income. Under § 1.1502-32, P's basis in S's stock is reduced from $100 to $0 in Year 1.

(c) Matching rule and stock basis adjustments. Under the matching rule (treating P as the buying member and S as the selling member), S takes its $30 gain into account in Year 3 to reflect the $30 difference between P's $10 gain taken into account and the $40 recomputed gain. Under § 1.1502-32, P's basis in S's stock is increased from $0 to $30 in Year 3.

(d) Loss property. The facts are the same as in paragraph (a) of this Example 1, except that S has a $130 (rather than $70) basis in the land. Under paragraph (f)(2)(iii) of this section, the principles of section 311(b) apply to S's loss from the intercompany distribution. Thus, S has a $30 loss that is taken into account under the matching rule in Year 3 to reflect the $30 difference between P's $10 gain taken into account and the $20 recomputed loss. (The results are the same under section 267(f).) Under § 1.1502-32, P's basis in S's stock is reduced from $100 to $0 in Year 1, and from $0 to a $30 excess loss account in Year 3. (If P had distributed the land to its shareholders, rather than selling the land to X, P would take its $10 gain under section 311(b) into account, and S would take its $30 loss into account under the matching rule with $10 offset by P's gain and $20 recharacterized as a noncapital, nondeductible amount.)

(e) Entitlement rule. The facts are the same as in paragraph (a) of this Example 1, except that, after P becomes entitled to the distribution but before the distribution is made, S issues additional stock to the public and becomes a nonmember. Under paragraph (f)(2)(i) of this section, the determination of whether a distribution is an intercompany distribution is made under the entitlement rule of paragraph (f)(2)(iv) of this section. Treating S's distribution as made when P becomes entitled to it results in the distribution being an intercompany distribution. Under paragraph (f)(2)(ii) of this section, the distribution is not included in P's gross income. S's $30 gain from the distribution is intercompany gain that is taken into account under the acceleration rule immediately before S becomes a nonmember. Thus, there is a net $70 decrease in P's basis in its S stock under § 1.1502-32 ($100 decrease for the distribution and a $30 increase for S's $30 gain). Under paragraph (f)(2)(iv) of this section, P does not take the distribution into account again under separate return rules when received, and P is not entitled to a dividends received deduction.

Example (2). Excess loss accounts.

(a) Facts. S owns all of T's only class of stock with a $10 basis and $100 value. S has substantial earnings and profits, and T has $10 of earnings and profits. On January 1 of Year 1, S declares and distributes a dividend of all of the T stock to P. Under section 311(b), S has a $90 gain. Under section 301(d), P's basis in the T stock is $100. During Year 3, T borrows $90 and declares and makes a $90 distribution to P to which section 301 applies, and P's basis in the T stock is reduced under § 1.1502-32 from $100 to $10. During Year 6, T has $5 of earnings that increase P's basis in the T stock under § 1.1502-32 from $10 to $15. On December 1 of Year 9, T issues additional stock to X and, as a result, T becomes a nonmember.

(b) Dividend exclusion. Under paragraph (f)(2)(ii) of this section, P's $100 of dividend income from S's distribution of the T stock, and its $10 of dividend income from T's $90 distribution, are not included in gross income.

(c) Matching and acceleration rules. Under § 1.1502-19(b)(1), when T becomes a nonmember P must include in income the amount of its excess loss account (if any) in T stock. P has no excess loss account in the T stock. Therefore P's corresponding item from the deconsolidation of T is $0. Treating S and P as divisions of a single corporation, the T stock would continue to have a $10 basis after the distribution, and the adjustments under § 1.1502-32 for T's $90 distribution and $5 of earnings would result in a $75 excess loss account. Thus, the recomputed corresponding item from the deconsolidation is $75. Under the matching rule, S takes $75 of its $90 gain into account in Year 9 as a result of T becoming a nonmember, to reflect the difference between P's $0 gain taken into account and the $75 recomputed gain. S's remaining $15 of gain is taken into account under the matching and acceleration rules based on subsequent events (for example, under the matching rule if P subsequently sells its T stock, or under the acceleration rule if S becomes a nonmember).

(d) Reverse sequence. The facts are the same as in paragraph (a) of this Example 2, except that T borrows $90 and makes its $90 distribution to S before S distributes T's stock to P. Under paragraph (f)(2)(ii) of this section, T's $90 distribution to S ($10 of which is a dividend) is not included in S's gross income. The corresponding negative adjustment under § 1.1502-32 reduces S's basis in the T stock from $10 to an $80 excess loss account. Under section 311(b), S has a $90 gain from the distribution of T stock to P. Under section 301(d) P's initial basis in the T stock is $10 (the stock's fair market value), and the basis increases to $15 under § 1.1502-32 as a result of T's earnings in Year 6. The timing and attributes of S's gain are determined in the manner provided in paragraph (c) of this Example 2. Thus, $75 of S's gain is taken into account under the matching rule in Year 9 as a result of T becoming a nonmember, and the remaining $15 is taken into account under the matching and acceleration rules based on subsequent events.

(e) Partial stock sale. The facts are the same as in paragraph (a) of this Example 2, except that P sells 10% of T's stock to X on December 1 of Year 9 for $1.50 (rather than T's issuing additional stock and becoming a nonmember). Under the matching rule, S takes $9 of its gain into account to reflect the difference between P's $0 gain taken into account ($1.50 sale proceeds minus $1.50 basis) and the $9 recomputed gain ($1.50 sale proceeds plus $7.50 excess loss account).

(f) Loss, rather than cash distribution. The facts are the same as in paragraph (a) of this Example 2, except that T retains the loan proceeds and incurs a $90 loss in Year 3 that is absorbed by the group. The timing and attributes of S's gain are determined in the same manner provided in paragraph (c) of this Example 2. Under § 1.1502-32, the loss in Year 3 reduces P's basis in the T stock from $100 to $10, and T's $5 of earnings in Year 6 increase the basis to $15. Thus, $75 of S's gain is taken into account under the matching rule in Year 9 as a result of T becoming a nonmember, and the remaining $15 is taken into account under the matching and acceleration rules based on subsequent events. (The timing and attributes of S's gain would be determined in the same manner provided in paragraph (d) of this Example 2 if T incurred the $90 loss before S's distribution of the T stock to P.)

(g) Stock sale, rather than stock distribution. The facts are the same as in paragraph (a) of this Example 2, except that S sells the T stock to P for $100 (rather than distributing the stock). The timing and attributes of S's gain are determined in the same manner provided in paragraph (c) of this Example 2. Thus, $75 of S's gain is taken into account under the matching rule in Year 9 as a result of T becoming a nonmember, and the remaining $15 is taken into account under the matching and acceleration rules based on subsequent events.

Example (3). Intercompany reorganization.

(a) Facts. P forms S and B by contributing $200 to the capital of each. During Years 1 through 4, S and B each earn $50, and under § 1.1502-32 P adjusts its basis in the stock of each to $250. (See § 1.1502-33 for adjustments to earnings and profits.) On January 1 of Year 5, the fair market value of S's assets and its stock is $500, and S merges into B in a tax-free reorganization. Pursuant to the plan of reorganization, P receives B stock with a fair market value of $350 and $150 of cash.

(b) Treatment as a section 301 distribution. The merger of S into B is a transaction to which paragraph (f)(3) of this section applies. P is treated as receiving additional B stock with a fair market value of $500 and, under section 358, a basis of $250. Immediately after the merger, $150 of the stock received is treated as redeemed, and the redemption is treated under section 302(d) as a distribution to which section 301 applies. Because the $150 distribution is treated as not received as part of the merger, section 356 does not apply and no basis adjustments are required under section 358(a)(1)(A) and (B). Because B is treated under section 381(c)(2) as receiving S's earnings and profits and the redemption is treated as occurring after the merger, $100 of the distribution is treated as a dividend under section 301 and P's basis in the B stock is reduced correspondingly under § 1.1502-32. The remaining $50 of the distribution reduces P's basis in the B stock. Section 301(c)(2) and § 1.1502-32. Under paragraph (f)(2)(ii) of this section, P's $100 of dividend income is not included in gross income. Under § 1.302-2(c), proper adjustments are made to P's basis in its B stock to reflect its basis in the B stock redeemed, with the result that P's basis in the B stock is reduced by the entire $150 distribution.

(c) Depreciated property. The facts are the same as in paragraph (a) of this Example 3, except that property of S with a $200 basis and $150 fair market value is distributed to P (rather than cash of B). As in paragraph (b) of this Example 3, P is treated as receiving additional B stock in the merger and a $150 distribution to which section 301 applies immediately after the merger. Under paragraph (f)(2)(iii) of this section, the principles of section 311(b) apply to B's $50 loss and the loss is taken into account under the matching and acceleration rules based on subsequent events (e.g., under the matching rule if P subsequently sells the property, or under the acceleration rule if B becomes a nonmember). The results are the same under section 267(f).

(d) Divisive transaction. Assume instead that, pursuant to a plan, S distributes the stock of a lower-tier subsidiary in a spin-off transaction to which section 355 applies together with $150 of cash. The distribution of stock is a transaction to which paragraph (f)(3) of this section applies. P is treated as receiving the $150 of cash immediately before the section 355 distribution, as a distribution to which section 301 applies. Section 356(b) does not apply and no basis adjustments are required under section 358(a)(1)(A) and (B). Because the $150 distribution is treated as made before the section 355 distribution, the distribution reduces P's basis in the S stock under § 1.1502-32, and the basis allocated under section 358(c) between the S stock and the lower-tier subsidiary stock received reflects this basis reduction.

Example (4). All cash intercompany reorganization under section 368(a)(1)(D). (a) Facts. P owns all of the stock of M and B. M owns all of the stock of S with a basis of $25. On January 1 of Year 2, the fair market value of S's assets and its stock is $100, and S sells all of its assets to B for $100 cash and liquidates. The transaction qualifies as a reorganization described in section 368(a)(1)(D). Pursuant to § 1.368-2(l), B will be deemed to issue a nominal share of B stock to S in addition to the $100 of cash actually exchanged for the S assets, and S will be deemed to distribute all of the consideration to M. M will be deemed to distribute the nominal share of B stock to P.

(b) Treatment as a section 301 distribution. The sale of S's assets to B is a transaction to which paragraph (f)(3) of this section applies. In addition to the nominal share issued by B to S under § 1.368-2(l), S is treated as receiving additional B stock with a fair market value of $100 (in lieu of the $100) and, under section 358, a basis of $25 which S distributes to M in liquidation. Immediately after the sale, the B stock (with the exception of the nominal share which is still held by M) received by M is treated as redeemed for $100, and the redemption is treated under section 302(d) as a distribution to which section 301 applies. M's basis of $25 in the B stock is reduced under § 1.1502-32(b)(3)(v), resulting in an excess loss account of $75 in the nominal share. (See § 1.302-2(c)). M's deemed distribution of the nominal share of B stock to P under § 1.368-2(l) will result in M generating an intercompany gain under section 311(b) of $75, to be subsequently taken into account under the matching and acceleration rules.

Example (5). Stock redemptions and distributions.

(a) Facts. Before becoming a member of the P group, S owns P stock with a $30 basis. On January 1 of Year 1, P buys all of S's stock. On July 1 of Year 3, P redeems the P stock held by S for $100 in a transaction to which section 302(a) applies.

(b) Gain under section 302. Under paragraph (f)(4) of this section, P's basis in the P stock acquired from S is treated as eliminated. As a result of this elimination, S's intercompany item will never be taken into account under the matching rule because P's basis in the stock does not reflect S's intercompany item. Therefore, S's $70 gain is taken into account under the acceleration rule in Year 3. The attributes of S's item are determined under paragraph (d)(1)(ii) of this section by applying the matching rule as if P had sold the stock to an affiliated corporation that is not a member of the group at no gain or loss. Although P's corresponding item from a sale of its stock would have been excluded from gross income under section 1032, paragraph (c)(6)(ii) of this section prevents S's gain from being treated as excluded from gross income; instead S's gain is capital gain.

(c) Gain under section 311. The facts are the same as in paragraph (a) of this Example 4, except that S distributes the P stock to P in a transaction to which section 301 applies (rather than the stock being redeemed), and S has a $70 gain under section 311(b). The timing and attributes of S's gain are determined in the manner provided in paragraph (b) of this Example 4.

(d) Loss stock. The facts are the same as in paragraph (a) of this Example 4, except that S has a $130 (rather than $30) basis in the P stock and has a $30 loss under section 302(a). The limitation under paragraph (c)(6)(ii) of this section does not apply to intercompany losses. Thus, S's loss is taken into account in Year 3 as a noncapital, nondeductible amount.

Example (6). Intercompany stock sale followed by section 332 liquidation.

(a) Facts. S owns all of the stock of T, with a $70 basis and $100 value, and T's assets have a $10 basis and $100 value. On January 1 of Year 1, S sells all of T's stock to B for $100. On July 1 of Year 3, when T's assets are still worth $100, T distributes all of its assets to B in an unrelated complete liquidation to which section 332 applies.

(b) Timing and attributes. Under paragraph (b)(3)(ii) of this section, B's unrecognized gain or loss under section 332 is a corresponding item for purposes of applying the matching rule. In Year 3 when T liquidates, B has $0 of unrecognized gain or loss under section 332 because B has a $100 basis in the T stock and receives a $100 distribution with respect to its T stock. Treating S and B as divisions of a single corporation, the recomputed corresponding item would have been $30 of unrecognized gain under section 332 because B would have succeeded to S's $70 basis in the T stock. Thus, under the matching rule, S's $30 intercompany gain is taken into account in Year 3 as a result of T's liquidation. Under paragraph (c)(1)(i) of this section, the attributes of S's gain and B's corresponding item are redetermined as if S and B were divisions of a single corporation. Although S's gain ordinarily would be redetermined to be treated as excluded from gross income to reflect the nonrecognition of B's gain under section 332, S's gain remains capital gain because B's unrecognized gain under section 332 is not permanently and explicitly disallowed under the Code. See paragraph (c)(6)(ii) of this section. However, relief may be elected under paragraph (f)(5)(ii) of this section.

(c) Intercompany sale at a loss. The facts are the same as in paragraph (a) of this Example 5, except that S has a $130 (rather than $70) basis in the T stock. The limitation under paragraph (c)(6)(ii) of this section does not apply to intercompany losses. Thus, S's intercompany loss is taken into account in Year 3 as a noncapital, nondeductible amount. However, relief may be elected under paragraph (f)(5)(ii) of this section.

Example (7). Intercompany stock sale followed by section 355 distribution.

(a) Facts. S owns all of the stock of T with a $70 basis and a $100 value. On January 1 of Year 1, S sells all of T's stock to M for $100. On June 1 of Year 6, M distributes all of its T stock to its nonmember shareholders in a transaction to which section 355 applies. At the time of the distribution, M has a basis in T stock of $100 and T has a value of $150.

(b) Timing and attributes. Under paragraph (b)(3)(ii) of this section, M's $50 gain not recognized on the distribution under section 355 is a corresponding item. Treating S and M as divisions of a single corporation, the recomputed corresponding item would be $80 of unrecognized gain under section 355 because M would have succeeded to S's $70 basis in the T stock. Thus, under the matching rule, S's $30 intercompany gain is taken into account in Year 6 as a result of the distribution. Under paragraph (c)(1)(i) of this section, the attributes of S's intercompany item and M's corresponding item are redetermined to produce the same effect on consolidated taxable income as if S and M were divisions of a single corporation. Although S's gain ordinarily would be redetermined to be treated as excluded from gross income to reflect the nonrecognition of M's gain under section 355(c), S's gain remains capital gain because M's unrecognized gain under section 355(c) is not permanently and explicitly disallowed under the Code. See paragraph (c)(6)(ii) of this section. Because M's distribution of the T stock is not an intercompany transaction, relief is not available under paragraph (f)(5)(ii) of this section.

(c) Section 355 distribution within the group. The facts are the same as under paragraph (a) of this Example 6, except that M distributes the T stock to B (another member of the group), and B takes a $75 basis in the T stock under section 358. Under paragraph (j)(2) of this section, B is a successor to M for purposes of taking S's intercompany gain into account, and therefore both M and B might have corresponding items with respect to S's intercompany gain. To the extent it is possible, matching with respect to B's corresponding items produces the result most consistent with treating S, M, and B as divisions of a single corporation. See paragraphs (j)(3) and (j)(4) of this section. However, because there is only $5 difference between B's $75 basis in the T stock and the $70 basis the stock would have if S, M, and B were divisions of a single corporation, only $5 can be taken into account under the matching rule with respect to B's corresponding items. (This $5 is taken into account with respect to B's corresponding items based on subsequent events.) The remaining $25 of S's $30 intercompany gain is taken into account in Year 6 under the matching rule with respect to M's corresponding item from its distribution of the T stock. The attributes of S's remaining $25 of gain are determined in the same manner as in paragraph (b) of this Example 6.

(d) Relief elected. The facts are the same as in paragraph (c) of this Example 6 except that P elects relief pursuant to paragraph (f)(5)(ii)(D) of this section. As a result of the election, M's distribution of the T stock is treated as subject to sections 301 and 311 instead of section 355. Accordingly, M recognizes $50 of intercompany gain from the distribution, B takes a basis in the stock equal to its fair market value of $150, and S and M take their intercompany gains into account with respect to B's corresponding items based on subsequent events. (None of S's gain is taken into account in Year 6 as a result of M's distribution of the T stock.)

Example (8). Reserved]. For further guidance, see § 1.1502-13T(f)(7)(i) Example 7.

Example (9). [Reserved]. For further guidance, see § 1.1502-13T(f)(7)(i) Example 8.

(ii) [Reserved]. For further guidance, see § 1.1502-13T(f)(7)(ii).

(g) Obligations of members.

(1) In general. In addition to the general rules of this section, the rules of this paragraph (g) apply to intercompany obligations.

(2) Definitions. For purposes of this section, the following definitions apply—

(i) Obligation of a member is a debt or security of a member.

(A) Debt of a member is any obligation of the member constituting indebtedness under general principles of Federal income tax law (for example, under nonstatutory authorities, or under section 108, section 163, or § 1.1275-1(d)), but not an executory obligation to purchase or provide goods or services.

(B) Security of a member is any security of the member described in section 475(c)(2)(D) or (E), and any commodity of the member described in section 475(e)(2)(A), (B), or (C), but not if the security or commodity is a position with respect to the member's stock. See paragraphs (f)(4) and (f)(6) of this section for special rules applicable to positions with respect to a member's stock.

(ii) Intercompany obligation is an obligation between members, but only for the period during which both parties are members.

(iii) Intercompany obligation subgroup is comprised of two or more members that include the creditor and debtor on an intercompany obligation if the creditor and debtor bear the relationship described in section 1504(a)(1) to each other through an intercompany obligation subgroup parent.

(iv) Intercompany obligation subgroup parent is the corporation (including either the creditor or debtor) that bears the same relationship to the other members of the intercompany obligation subgroup as a common parent bears to the members of a consolidated group. Any reference to an intercompany obligation subgroup parent includes, as the context may require, a reference to a predecessor or successor. For this purpose, a predecessor is a transferor of assets to a transferee (the successor) in a transaction to which section 381(a) applies.

(v) Tax benefit is the benefit of, for Federal tax purposes, a net reduction in income or gain, or a net increase in loss, deduction, credit, or allowance. A tax benefit includes, but is not limited to, the use of a built-in item or items from an intercompany obligation to reduce gain or increase loss on the sale of member stock, or to create or absorb a tax attribute of a member or subgroup.

(vi) Eighty-percent chain is a chain of two or more corporations in which stock meeting the requirements of section 1504(a)(2) of each lower-tier member is held directly by a higher-tier member of such chain.

(3) Deemed satisfaction and reissuance of intercompany obligations in triggering transactions— (i) Scope— (A) Triggering transactions. For purposes of this paragraph (g)(3), a triggering transaction includes the following:

(1) Assignment and extinguishment transactions. Any intercompany transaction in which a member realizes an amount, directly or indirectly, from the assignment or extinguishment of all or part of its remaining rights or obligations under an intercompany obligation or any comparable transaction in which a member realizes any such amount, directly or indirectly, from an intercompany obligation (for example, a mark to fair market value of an obligation or a bad debt deduction). However, a reduction of the basis of an intercompany obligation pursuant to § 1.1502-36(d) (attribute reduction to prevent duplication of loss), or pursuant to sections 108 and 1017 and § 1.1502-28 (basis reductions upon the exclusion from gross income of discharge of indebtedness) or any other provision that adjusts the basis of an intercompany obligation as a substitute for income, gain, deduction, or loss, is not a comparable transaction.

(2) Outbound transactions. Any transaction in which an intercompany obligation becomes an obligation that is not an intercompany obligation.

(B) Exceptions. Except as provided in paragraph (g)(3)(i)(C) of this section, a transaction is not a triggering transaction as described in paragraph (g)(3)(i)(A) of this section if any of the exceptions in this paragraph (g)(3)(i)(B) apply. In making this determination, if a creditor or debtor realizes an amount in a transaction in which a creditor assigns all or part of its rights under an intercompany obligation to the debtor, or a debtor assigns all or part of its obligations under an intercompany obligation to the creditor, the transaction will be treated as an extinguishment and will be excepted from the definition of "triggering transaction" only if either of the exceptions in paragraphs (g)(3)(i)(B)(5) or (6) of this section apply. The exceptions are as follows.

(1) Intercompany section 361, 332, or 351 exchange. The transaction is an intercompany exchange to which section 361(a), sections 332 and 337(a), or (except as provided in the following sentence) section 351 applies in which no amount of income, gain, deduction or loss is recognized by the creditor or debtor. The assignment of an intercompany obligation by a creditor member in an intercompany exchange to which section 351 applies is a triggering transaction, notwithstanding the preceding sentence, if a member of the group is described in, or engages in a transaction that is described in, any of the following paragraphs.

(i) The transferor or transferee member has a loss subject to a limitation (for example, a loss from a separate return limitation year that is subject to limitation under § 1.1502-21(c), or a dual consolidated loss that is subject to limitation under § 1.1503(d)-4), but only if the other member is not subject to a comparable limitation;

(ii) The transferor or transferee member has a special status within the meaning of § 1.1502-13(c)(5) (for example, a bank defined in section 581, or a life insurance company subject to tax under section 801) that the other member does not also possess;

(iii) A member of the group realizes discharge of indebtedness income that is excluded from gross income under section 108(a) within the same taxable year as that of the exchange, and the tax attributes attributable to either the transferor or the transferee member are reduced under sections 108, 1017, and § 1.1502-28 (except if the attribute reduction results solely from the application of § 1.1502-28(a)(4) (reduction of certain tax attributes attributable to other members));

(iv) The transferee member has a nonmember shareholder;

(v) The transferee member issues preferred stock to the transferor member in exchange for the assignment of the intercompany obligation; or

(vi) The stock of the transferee member (or a higher-tier member other than a higher-tier member of an 80-percent chain that includes the transferor and transferee) is disposed of within 12 months from the assignment of the intercompany obligation, unless at the time of the assignment, the transferor member, transferee member (or in the case of successive section 351 exchanges, each transferor and transferee member) and the debtor member are all in the same 80-percent chain; and all of the stock of the transferee (or in the case of successive section 351 exchanges, the lowest-tier transferee) held by members of the group is disposed of as part of the same plan or arrangement, either directly or indirectly, to persons that are notmembers of the group.

(2) Intercompany assumption transaction. All of the debtor's obligations under an intercompany obligation are assumed in connection with the debtor's sale or other disposition of property (other than solely money) in an intercompany transaction in which gain or loss is recognized under section 1001.

(3) Exception to the application of section 108(e)(4). The obligation became an intercompany obligation by reason of an event described in § 1.108-2(e)(2) (exception to the application of section 108(e)(4) in the case of acquisitions by securities dealers).

(4) Reserve accounting. The amount realized is from reserve accounting under section 585 (see paragraph (g)(4)(v) of this section for special rules).

(5) Intercompany extinguishment transaction. All or part of the rights and obligations under the intercompany obligation are extinguished in an intercompany transaction (other than an exchange or deemed exchange of an intercompany obligation for a newly issued intercompany obligation), the adjusted issue price of the obligation is equal to the creditor's basis in the obligation, and the debtor's corresponding item and the creditor's intercompany item (after taking into

account the special rules of paragraph (g)(4)(i)(C) of this section) with respect to the obligation offset in amount.

(6) Routine modification of intercompany obligation. All of the rights and obligations under the intercompany obligation are extinguished in an intercompany transaction that is an exchange (or deemed exchange) for a newly issued intercompany obligation, and the issue price of the newly issued obligation equals both the adjusted issue price of the extinguished obligation and the creditor's basis in the extinguished obligation. Solely for purposes of the preceding sentence, a newly issued intercompany obligation includes an obligation that is issued (or deemed issued) by a member other than the original debtor if such other member assumes the original debtor's obligations under the original obligation in a transaction that is described in either paragraph (g)(3)(i)(B)(1) or (g)(3)(i)(B)(2) of this section and the assumption results in a significant modification of the original obligation under § 1.1001-3(e)(4) and a deemed exchange under § 1.1001-3(b).

(7) Outbound distribution of newly issued intercompany obligation. The intercompany obligation becomes an obligation that is not an intercompany obligation in a transaction in which a member that is a party to the reorganization exchanges property in pursuance of the plan of reorganization for a newly issued intercompany obligation of another member that is a party to the reorganization and distributes such intercompany obligation to a nonmember shareholder or nonmember creditor in a transaction to which section 361(c) applies.

(8) Outbound subgroup exception. The intercompany obligation becomes an obligation that is not an intercompany obligation in a transaction in which the members of an intercompany obligation subgroup cease to be members of a consolidated group, neither the creditor nor the debtor recognize any income, gain, deduction, or loss with respect to the intercompany obligation, and such members constitute an intercompany obligation subgroup of another consolidated group immediately after the transaction.

(C) Tax benefit rule. If an assignment or extinguishment of an intercompany obligation in an intercompany transaction is otherwise excepted from the definition of triggering transaction under paragraph (g)(3)(i)(B)(1), (2), (5), or (6) of this section (and not also under paragraph (g)(3)(i)(B)(3) or (4) of this section), and the assignment or extinguishment is engaged in with a view to shift items of built-in gain, loss, income, or deduction from the obligation from one member to another member in order to secure a tax benefit (as defined in paragraph (g)(2)(v) of this section) that the group or its members would not otherwise enjoy in a consolidated or separate return year, then the assignment or extinguishment will be a triggering transaction to which paragraph (g)(3)(ii) of this section applies.

(ii) Application of deemed satisfaction and reissuance. This paragraph (g)(3)(ii) applies if a triggering transaction occurs.

(A) General rule. If the intercompany obligation is debt of a member, then (except as provided in the following sentence) the debt is treated for all Federal income tax purposes as having been satisfied by the debtor for cash in an amount equal to its fair market value, and then as having been reissued as a new obligation (with a new holding period but otherwise identical terms) for the same amount of cash, immediately before the triggering transaction. However, if the creditor realizes an amount with respect to the debt in the triggering transaction that differs from the debt's fair market value, and the triggering transaction is not an exchange (or deemed exchange) of debt of a member for newly issued debt of a member, then the debt is treated for all Federal income tax purposes as having been satisfied by the debtor for cash in an amount equal to such amount realized, and reissued as a new obligation (with a new holding period but otherwise identical terms) for the same amount of cash, immediately before the triggering transaction. If the triggering transaction is a mark to fair market value under section 475, then the intercompany obligation will be deemed satisfied and reissued for its fair market value (as determined under section 475 and applicable regulations) and section 475 will not otherwise apply with respect to that triggering transaction. If the intercompany obligation is a security of a member, similar principles apply (with appropriate adjustments) to treat the security as having been satisfied and reissued immediately before the triggering transaction.

(B) Treatment as separate transaction. The deemed satisfaction and deemed reissuance are treated as transactions separate and apart from the triggering transaction. The deemed satisfaction and reissuance of a member's debt will not cause the debt to be recharacterized as other than debt for Federal income tax purposes.

(4) Special rules— (i) Timing and attributes. For purposes of applying the matching rule and the acceleration rule to a transaction involving an intercompany obligation (other than a transaction to which paragraph (g)(5) of this section applies)—

(A) Paragraph (c)(6)(i) of this section (treatment of intercompany items if corresponding items are excluded or nondeductible) will not apply to exclude any amount of income or gain attributable to a reduction of the basis of the intercompany obligation pursuant to § 1.1502-36(d), or pursuant to sections 108 and 1017 and § 1.1502-28 or any other provision that adjusts the basis of an intercompany obligation as a substitute for income or gain;

(B) Paragraph (c)(6)(ii) of this section (limitation on treatment of intercompany income or gain as excluded from gross income) does not apply to prevent any intercompany income or gain from the intercompany obligation from being excluded from gross income;

(C) Any income, gain, deduction, or loss from the intercompany obligation is not subject to section 108(a), section 354, section 355(a)(1), section 1091, or, in the case of an extinguishment of an intercompany obligation in a transaction in which the creditor transfers the obligation to the debtor in exchange for stock in such debtor, section 351(a); and

(D) Section 108(e)(7) does not apply upon the extinguishment of an intercompany obligation.

(ii) Newly issued obligation in intercompany exchange. If an intercompany obligation is exchanged (or is deemed exchanged) for a newly issued intercompany obligation and the exchange (or deemed exchange) is not a routine modification of an intercompany obligation (as described in paragraph (g)(3)(i)(B)(6) of this section), then the newly issued obligation will be treated for all Federal income tax purposes as having an issue price equal to its fair market value.

(iii) Off-market issuance. If an intercompany obligation is issued at a rate of interest that is materially off-market (off-market obligation) with a view to shift items of built-in gain, loss, income, or deduction from the obligation from one member to another member in order to secure a tax benefit (as defined in paragraph (g)(2)(v) of this section), then the intercompany obligation will be treated, for all Federal income tax purposes, as originally issued for its fair market value, and any difference between the amount loaned and the fair market value of the obligation will be treated as transferred between the creditor and the debtor at the time the obligation is issued. For example, if S lends $100 to B in return for an off-market B note valued at $130, and the note is issued with a view to shift items from the note to secure a tax benefit, then the B note will be treated as issued for $130. The $30 difference will be treated as a distribution or capital contribution between S and B (as appropriate) at the time of issuance, and this amount will be reflected in future payments on the note as bond issuance premium. An adjustment to an off-market obligation under this paragraph (g)(4)(iii) will be made without regard to the application of, and in lieu of any adjustment under, section 467 (certain payments for the use of property or services), 482 (allocations among commonly controlled taxpayers), 483 (interest on certain deferred payments), 1274 (determination of issue price for certain debt instruments issued for property), or 7872 (treatment of loans with below-market interest rates).

(iv) Deferral of loss or deduction with respect to nonmember indebtedness acquired in certain debt exchanges. If a creditor transfers an intercompany obligation to a nonmember (former intercompany obligation) in exchange for newly issued debt of a nonmember (nonmember debt), and the issue price of the nonmember debt is not determined by reference to its fair market value (for example, the issue price is determined under section 1273(b)(4) or 1274(a) or any other provision of applicable law), then any loss of the creditor otherwise allowable on the subsequent disposition of the nonmember debt, or any comparable tax benefit that would otherwise be available in any other transaction that directly or indirectly results from the disposition of the nonmember debt, is deferred until the date the debtor retires the former intercompany obligation.

(v) Bad debt reserve. A member's deduction under section 585 for an addition to its reserve for bad debts with respect to an intercompany obligation is not taken into account, and is not treated as realized for purposes of paragraph (g)(3)(i)(A)(1) of this section, until the intercompany obligation is extinguished or becomes an obligation that is not an intercompany obligation.

(5) Deemed satisfaction and reissuance of obligations becoming intercompany obligations— (i) Application of deemed satisfaction and reissuance— (A) In general. This paragraph (g)(5) applies if an obligation that is not an intercompany obligation becomes an intercompany obligation.

(B) Exceptions. This paragraph (g)(5) does not apply to an intercompany obligation if either of the following exceptions apply.

(1) Exception to the application of section 108(e)(4). The obligation becomes an intercompany obligation by reason of an event described in § 1.108-2(e)(2) (exception to the application of section 108(e)(4) in the case of acquisitions by securities dealers); or

(2) Inbound subgroup exception. The obligation becomes an intercompany obligation in a transaction in which the members of an intercompany obligation subgroup cease to be members of a consolidated group, neither the creditor nor the debtor recognize any income, gain, deduction, or loss with respect to the intercompany obligation, and such members constitute an intercompany obligation subgroup of another consolidated group immediately after the transaction.

(ii) Deemed satisfaction and reissuance— (A) General rule. If the intercompany obligation is debt of a member, then the debt is treated for all Federal income tax purposes, immediately after it becomes an intercompany obligation, as having been satisfied by the debtor for cash in an amount determined under the principles of § 1.108-2(f), and then as having been reissued as a new obligation (with a new holding period but otherwise identical terms) for the same amount of cash. If the intercompany obligation is a security of a member, similar principles apply (with appropriate adjustments) to treat the security, immediately after it becomes an intercompany obligation, as satisfied and reissued by the debtor for cash in an amount equal to its fair market value.

(B) Treatment as separate transaction. The deemed satisfaction and deemed reissuance are treated as transactions separate and apart from the transaction in which the debt becomes an intercompany obligation, and the tax consequences of the transaction in which the debt becomes an intercompany obligation must be determined before the deemed satisfaction and reissuance occurs. (For example, if the debt becomes an intercompany obligation in a transaction to which section 351 applies, any limitation imposed by section 362(e) on the basis of the intercompany obligation in the hands of the transferee member is determined before the deemed satisfaction and reissuance.) The deemed satisfaction and reissuance of a member's debt will not cause the debt to be recharacterized as other than debt for Federal income tax purposes.

(6) Special rules— (i) Timing and attributes. If paragraph (g)(5) of this section applies to an intercompany obligation—

(A) Section 108(e)(4) does not apply;

(B) The attributes of all items taken into account from the satisfaction of the intercompany obligation are determined on a separate entity basis, rather than by treating S and B as divisions of a single corporation; and

(C) Any intercompany gain or loss realized by the creditor is not subject to section 354 or section 1091.

(ii) Waiver of loss carryovers from separate return limitation years. Solely for purposes of § 1.1502-32(b)(4) and the effect of any election under that provision, any loss taken into account under paragraph (g)(5) of this section by a corporation that becomes a member as a result of the transaction in which the obligation becomes an intercompany obligation is treated as a loss carryover from a separate return limitation year.

(iii) Deduction of repurchase premium in certain debt exchanges. If an obligation to which paragraph (g)(5) of this section applies is acquired in exchange for the issuance of an obligation to a nonmember and the issue price of this newly issued obligation is not determined by reference to its fair market value (for example, the issue price is determined under section 1273(b)(4) or 1274(a) or any other provision of applicable law), then, under the principles of § 1.163-7(c), any repurchase premium from the deemed satisfaction of the intercompany obligation under paragraph (g)(5)(ii) of this section will be amortized by the debtor over the term of the obligation issued to the nonmember in the same manner as if it were original issue discount and the obligation to the nonmember had been issued directly by the debtor.

(7) Examples— (i) In general. For purposes of the examples in this paragraph (g), unless otherwise stated, interest is qualified stated interest under § 1.1273-1(c), and the intercompany obligations are capital assets and are not subject to section 475.

(ii) The application of this section to obligations of members is illustrated by the following examples:

Example (1). Interest on intercompany obligation. (i) Facts. On January 1 of year 1, B borrows $100 from S in return for B's note providing for $10 of interest annually at the end of each year, and repayment of $100 at the end of year 5. B fully performs its obligations. Under their separate entity methods of accounting, B accrues a $10 interest deduction annually under section 163, and S accrues $10 of interest income annually under section 61(a)(4) and § 1.446-2.

(ii) Matching rule. Under paragraph (b)(1) of this section, the accrual of interest on B's note is an intercompany transaction. Under the matching rule, S takes its $10 of income into account in each of years 1 through 5 to reflect the $10 difference between B's $10 of interest expense taken into account and the $0 recomputed expense. S's income and B's deduction are ordinary items. (Because S's intercompany item and B's corresponding item would both be ordinary on a separate entity basis, the attributes are not redetermined under paragraph (c)(1)(i) of this section.)

(ii) Original issue discount. The facts are the same as in paragraph (i) of this Example 1, except that B borrows $90 (rather than $100) from S in return for B's note providing for $10 of interest annually and repayment of $100 at the end of year 5. The principles described in paragraph (ii) of this Example 1 for stated interest also apply to the $10 of original issue discount. Thus, as B takes into account its corresponding expense under section 163(e), S takes into account its intercompany income under section 1272. S's income and B's deduction are ordinary items.

(iv) Tax-exempt income. The facts are the same as in paragraph (i) of this Example 1, except that B's borrowing from S is allocable under section 265 to B's purchase of state and local bonds to which section 103 applies. The timing of S's income is the same as in paragraph (ii) of this Example 1. Under paragraph (c)(4)(i) of this section, the attributes of B's corresponding item of disallowed interest expense control the attributes of S's offsetting intercompany interest income. Paragraph (c)(6) of this section does not prevent the redetermination of S's intercompany item as excluded from gross income because section 265(a)(2) permanently and explicitly disallows B's corresponding deduction and because, under paragraph (g)(4)(i)(B) of this section, paragraph (c)(6)(ii) of this section does not apply to prevent any intercompany income from the B note from being excluded from gross income. Accordingly, S's intercompany income is treated as excluded from gross income.

Example (2). Intercompany obligation becomes nonintercompany obligation. (i) Facts. On January 1 of year 1, B borrows $100 from S in return for B's note providing for $10 of interest annually at the end of each year, and repayment of $100 at the end of year 5. As of January 1 of year 3, B has paid the interest accruing under the note and S sells B's note to X for $70, reflecting an increase in prevailing market interest rates. B is never insolvent within the meaning of section 108(d)(3).

(ii) Deemed satisfaction and reissuance. Because the B note becomes an obligation that is not an intercompany obligation, the transaction is a triggering transaction under paragraph (g)(3)(i)(A)(2) of this section. Under paragraph (g)(3)(ii) of this section, B's note is treated as satisfied and reissued for its fair market value of $70 immediately before S's sale to X. As a result of the deemed satisfaction of the note for less than its adjusted issue price, B takes into account $30 of discharge of indebtedness income under § 1.61-12. On a separate entity basis, S's $30 loss would be a capital loss under section 1271(a)(1). Under the matching rule, however, the attributes of S's intercompany item and B's corresponding item must be redetermined to produce the same effect as if the transaction had occurred between divisions of a single corporation. Under paragraph (c)(4)(i) of this section, the attributes of B's $30 of discharge of indebtedness income control the attributes of S's loss. Thus, S's loss is treated as ordinary loss. B is also treated as reissuing, immediately after the satisfaction, a new note to S with a $70 issue price, a $100 stated redemption price at maturity, and a $70 basis in the hands of S. S is then treated as selling the new note to X for the $70 received by S in the actual transaction. Because S has a basis of $70 in the new note, S recognizes no gain or loss from the sale to X. After the sale, the new note held by X is not an intercompany obligation, it has a $70 issue price, a $100 stated redemption price at maturity, and a $70 basis. The $30 of original issue discount will be taken into account by B and X under sections 163(e) and 1272.

(iii) Creditor deconsolidation. The facts are the same as in paragraph (i) of this Example 2, except that P sells S's stock to X (rather than S selling B's note to X). Because the B note becomes an obligation that is not an intercompany obligation, the transaction is a triggering transaction under paragraph (g)(3)(i)(A)(2) of this section. Under paragraph (g)(3)(ii) of this section, B's note is treated as satisfied and reissued for its $70 fair market value immediately before S becomes a nonmember. The treatment of S's $30 of loss and B's $30 of discharge of indebtedness income is the same as in paragraph (ii) of this Example 2. The new note held by S upon deconsolidation is not an intercompany obligation, it has a $70 issue price, a $100 stated redemption price at maturity, and a $70 basis. The $30 of original issue discount will be taken into account by B and S under sections 163(e) and 1272.

(iv) Debtor deconsolidation. The facts are the same as in paragraph (i) of this Example 2, except that P sells B's stock to X (rather than S selling B's note to X). The results to S and B are the same as in paragraph (iii) of this Example 2.

(v) Subgroup exception. The facts are the same as in paragraph (i) of this Example 2, except that P owns all of the stock of S, S owns all of the stock of B, and P sells all of the S stock to X, the parent of another consolidated group. Because B and S, members of an intercompany obligation subgroup, cease to be members of the P group in a transaction that does not cause either member to recognize an item with respect to the B note, and such members constitute an intercompany obligation subgroup in the X group, P's sale of S stock is not a triggering transaction under paragraph (g)(3)(i)(B)(8) of this section, and the note is not treated as satisfied and reissued under paragraph (g)(3)(ii) of this section. After the sale, the note held by S has a $100 issue price, a $100 stated redemption price at maturity, and a $100 basis. The results are the same if the S stock is sold to an individual and the S-B affiliated group elects to file a consolidated return for the period beginning on the day after S and B cease to be members of the P group.

(vi) Section 338 election. The facts are the same as paragraph (i) of this Example 2, except that P sells S's stock to X and a section 338 election is made with respect to the stock sale. Under section 338, S is treated as selling all of its assets to new S, including the B note, at the close of the acquisition date. The aggregate deemed sales price (within the meaning of § 1.338-4) allocated to the B note is $70. Because the B note becomes an obligation that is not an intercompany obligation, the transaction is a triggering transaction under paragraph (g)(3)(i)(A)(2) of this section. Under paragraph (g)(3)(ii) of this section, B's note is treated as satisfied and reissued immediately before S's deemed sale to new S for $70, the amount realized with respect to the note (the aggregate deemed sales price allocated to the note under § 1.338-6). The results to S and B are the same as in paragraph (ii) of this Example 2.

(vii) Appreciated note. The facts are the same as in paragraph (i) of this Example 2, except that S sells B's note to X for $130 (rather than $70), reflecting a decline in prevailing market interest rates. Because the B note becomes an obligation that is not an intercompany obligation, the transaction is a triggering transaction under paragraph (g)(3)(i)(A)(2) of this section. Under paragraph (g)(3)(ii) of this section, B's note is treated as satisfied and reissued for its fair market value of $130 immediately before S's sale to X. As a result of the deemed satisfaction of the note for more than its adjusted issue price, B takes into account $30 of repurchase premium under § 1.163-7(c). On a separate entity basis, S's $30 gain would be a capital gain under section 1271(a)(1). Under the matching rule, however, the attributes of S's intercompany item and B's corresponding item must be redetermined to produce the same effect as if the transaction had occurred between divisions of a single corporation. Under paragraph (c)(4)(i) of this section, the attributes of B's premium deduction control the attributes of S's gain. Accordingly, S's gain is treated as ordinary income. B is also treated as reissuing, immediately after the satisfaction, a new note to S with a $130 issue price, $100 stated redemption price at maturity, and $130 basis in the hands of S. S is then treated as selling the new note to X for the $130 received by S in the actual transaction. Because S has a basis of $130 in the new note, S recognizes no gain or loss from the sale to X. After the sale, the new note held by X is not an intercompany obligation, it has a $130 issue price, a $100 stated redemption price at maturity, and a $130 basis. The treatment of B's $30 of bond issuance premium under the new note is determined under § 1.163-13.

(viii) Deferral of loss or deduction with respect to nonmember indebtedness acquired in debt exchange. The facts are the same as in paragraph (i) of this Example 2, except that S sells B's note to X for a non-publicly traded X note with an issue price and face amount of $100 and a fair market value of $70, and that, subsequently, S sells the X note for $70. Because the B note becomes an obligation that is not an intercompany obligation, the transaction is a triggering transaction under paragraph (g)(3)(i)(A)(2) of this section. Under paragraph (g)(3)(ii) of this section, B's note is treated as satisfied and reissued immediately before S's sale to X for $100, the amount realized with respect to the note (determined under section 1274). As a result of the deemed satisfaction, neither S nor B take into account any items of income, gain, deduction, or loss. S is then treated as selling the new B note to X for the X note received by S in the actual transaction. Because S has a basis of $100 in the new note, S recognizes no gain or loss from the sale to X. After the sale, the new B note held by X is not an intercompany obligation, it has a $100 issue price, a $100 stated redemption price at maturity, and a $100 basis. S also holds an X note with a basis of $100 but a fair market value of $70. When S disposes of the X note, S's loss on the disposition is deferred under paragraph (g)(4)(iv) of this section, until B retires its note (the former intercompany obligation in the hands of X).

Example (3). Loss or bad debt deduction with respect to intercompany obligation. (i) Facts. On January 1 of year 1, B borrows $100 from S in return for B's note providing for $10 of interest annually at the end of each year, and repayment of $100 at the end of year 5. On January 1 of year 3, the fair market value of the B note has declined to $60 and S sells the B note to P for property with a fair market value of $60. B is never insolvent within the meaning of section 108(d)(3). The B note is not a security within the meaning of section 165(g)(2).

(ii) Deemed satisfaction and reissuance. Because S realizes an amount of loss from the assignment of the B note, the transaction is a triggering transaction under paragraph (g)(3)(i)(A)(1) of this section. Under paragraph (g)(3)(ii) of this section, B's note is treated as satisfied and reissued for its fair market value of $60 immediately before S's sale to P. As a result of the deemed satisfaction of the note for less than its adjusted issue price ($100), B takes into account $40 of discharge of indebtedness income under § 1.61-12. On a separate entity basis, S's $40 loss would be a capital loss under section 1271(a)(1). Under the matching rule, however, the attributes of S's intercompany item and B's corresponding item must be redetermined to produce the same effect as if the transaction had occurred between divisions of a single corporation. Under paragraph (c)(4)(i) of this section, the attributes of B's $40 of discharge of indebtedness income control the attributes of S's loss. Thus, S's loss is treated as ordinary loss. B is also treated as reissuing, immediately after the satisfaction, a new note to S with a $60 issue price, $100 stated redemption price at maturity, and $60 basis in the hands of S. S is then treated as selling the new note to P for the $60 of property received by S in the actual transaction. Because S has a basis of $60 in the new note, S recognizes no gain or loss from the sale to P. After the sale, the note is an intercompany obligation, it has a $60 issue price and a $100 stated redemption price at maturity, and the $40 of original issue discount will be taken into account by B and P under sections 163(e) and 1272.

(iii) Partial bad debt deduction. The facts are the same as in paragraph (i) of this Example 3, except that S claims a $40 partial bad debt deduction under section 166(a)(2) (rather than selling the note to P). Because S realizes a deduction from a transaction comparable to an assignment of the B note, the transaction is a triggering transaction under paragraph (g)(3)(i)(A)(1) of this section. Under paragraph (g)(3)(ii) of this section, B's note is treated as satisfied and reissued for its fair market value of $60 immediately before section 166(a)(2) applies. The treatment of S's $40 loss and B's $40 of discharge of indebtedness income are the same as in paragraph (ii) of this Example 3. After the reissuance, S has a basis of $60 in the new note. Accordingly, the application of section 166(a)(2) does not result in any additional deduction for S. The $40 of original issue discount on the new note will be taken into account by B and S under sections 163(e) and 1272.

(iv) Insolvent debtor. The facts are the same as in paragraph (i) of this Example 3, except that B is insolvent within the meaning of section 108(d)(3) at the time that S sells the note to P. As explained in paragraph (ii) of this Example 3, the transaction is a triggering transaction and the B note is treated as satisfied and reissued for its fair market value of $60 immediately before S's sale to P. On a separate entity basis, S's $40 loss would be capital, B's $40 income would be excluded from gross income under section 108(a), and B would reduce attributes under section 108(b) or section 1017 (see also § 1.1502-28). However, under paragraph (g)(4)(i)(C) of this section, section 108(a) does not apply to characterize B's income as excluded from gross income. Accordingly, the attributes of S's loss and B's income are redetermined in the same manner as in paragraph (ii) of this Example 3.

Example (4). Intercompany nonrecognition transactions. (i) Facts. On January 1 of year 1, B borrows $100 from S in return for B's note providing for $10 of interest annually at the end of each year, and repayment of $100 at the end of year 5. As of January 1 of year 3, B has fully performed its obligations, but the note's fair market value is $130, reflecting a decline in prevailing market interest rates. On January 1 of year 3, S transfers the note and other assets to a newly formed corporation, Newco, for all of Newco's common stock in an exchange to which section 351 applies.

(ii) No deemed satisfaction and reissuance. Because the assignment of the B note is an exchange to which section 351 applies and neither S nor B recognize gain or loss, the transaction is not a triggering transaction under paragraph (g)(3)(i)(B)(1) of this section, and the note is not treated as satisfied and reissued under paragraph (g)(3)(ii) of this section.

(iii) Receipt of other property. The facts are the same as in paragraph (i) of this Example 4, except that the other assets transferred to Newco have a basis of $100 and a fair market value of $260, and S receives, in addition to Newco common stock, $15 of cash. Because S would recognize $15 of gain under section 351(b), the assignment of the B note is a triggering transaction under paragraph (g)(3)(i)(A)(1) of this section. Under paragraph (g)(3)(ii) of this section, B's note is treated as satisfied and reissued for its fair market value of $130 immediately before the transfer to Newco. As a result of the deemed satisfaction of the note for more than its adjusted issue price, B takes into account $30 of repurchase premium under § 1.163-7(c). On a separate entity basis, S's $30 gain would be a capital gain under section 1271(a)(1). Under the matching rule, however, the attributes of S's intercompany item and B's corresponding item must be redetermined to produce the same effect as if the transaction had occurred between divisions of a single corporation. Under paragraph (c)(4)(i) of this section, the attributes of B's premium deduction control the attributes of S's gain. Accordingly, S's gain is treated as ordinary income. B is also treated as reissuing, immediately after the satisfaction, a new note to S with a $130 issue price, $100 stated redemption price at maturity, and $130 basis in the hands of S. S is then treated as transferring the new note to Newco for the Newco stock and cash received by S in the actual transaction. Because S has a basis of $130 in the new B note, S recognizes no gain or loss with respect to the transfer of the note in the section 351 exchange, and S recognizes $10 of gain with respect to the transfer of the other assets under section 351(b). After the transfer, the note has a $130 issue price and a $100 stated redemption price at maturity. The treatment of B's $30 of bond issuance premium under the new note is determined under § 1.163-13.

(iv) Transferee loss subject to limitation. The facts are the same as in paragraph (i) of this Example 4, except that T is a member with a loss from a separate return limitation year that is subject to limitation under § 1.1502-21(c) (a SRLY loss), and on January 1 of year 3, S transfers the assets and the B note to T in an exchange to which section 351 applies. Because the transferee, T, has a loss that is subject to a limitation, the assignment of the B note is a triggering transaction under paragraph (g)(3)(i)(A)(1) of this section (the exception in paragraph (g)(3)(i)(B)(1) of this section does not apply). Under paragraph (g)(3)(ii) of this section, B's note is treated as satisfied and reissued for its fair market value, immediately before S's transfer to T. As a result of the deemed satisfaction of the note for more than its adjusted issue price, B takes into account $30 of repurchase premium under § 1.163-7(c). On a separate entity basis, S's $30 gain would be a capital gain under section 1271(a)(1). Under the matching rule, however, the attributes of S's intercompany item and B's corresponding item must be redetermined to produce the same effect as if the transaction had occurred between divisions of a single corporation. Under paragraph (c)(4)(i) of this section, the attributes of B's premium deduction control the attributes of S's gain. Accordingly, S's gain is treated as ordinary income. B is also treated as reissuing, immediately after the satisfaction, a new note to S with a $130 issue price, $100 stated redemption price at maturity, and $130 basis in the hands of S. The treatment of B's $30 of bond issuance premium under the new note is determined under § 1.163-13. S is then treated as transferring the new note to T as part of the section 351 exchange. Because T will have a fair market value basis in the reissued B note immediately after the exchange, T's intercompany item from the subsequent retirement of the B note will not reflect any of S's built-in gain (and the amount of T's SRLY loss that may be absorbed by such item will be limited to any appreciation in the B note accruing after the exchange).

(v) Intercompany obligation transferred in section 332 transaction. The facts are the same as in paragraph (i) of this Example 4, except that S transfers the B note to P in complete liquidation under section 332. Because the transaction is an exchange to which section 332 and section 337(a) applies, and neither S nor B recognize gain or loss, the transaction is not a triggering transaction under paragraph (g)(3)(i)(B)(1) of this section, and the note is not treated as satisfied and reissued under paragraph (g)(3)(ii) of this section.

Example (5). Assumption of intercompany obligation. (i) Facts. On January 1 of year 1, B borrows $100 from S in return for B's note providing for $10 of interest annually at the end of each year, and repayment of $100 at the end of year 5. The note is fully recourse and is incurred for use in Business Z. As of January 1 of year 3, B has fully performed its obligations, but the note's fair market value is $110 reflecting a decline in prevailing market interest rates. Business Z has a fair market value of $95. On January 1 of year 3, B transfers all of the assets of Business Z and $15 of cash (substantially all of B's assets) to member T in exchange for the assumption by T of all of B's obligations under the note in a transaction in which gain or loss is recognized under section 1001. The terms and conditions of the note are not modified in connection with the sales transaction, the transaction does not result in a change in payment expectations, and no amount of income, gain, deduction, or loss is recognized by S, B, or T with respect to the note.

(ii) No deemed satisfaction and reissuance. Because all of B's obligations under the B note are assumed by T in connection with the sale of the Business Z assets, the assignment of B's obligations under the note is not a triggering transaction under paragraph (g)(3)(i)(B)(2) of this section, and the note is not treated as satisfied and reissued under paragraph (g)(3)(ii) of this section.

Example (6). Extinguishment of intercompany obligation. (i) Facts. On January 1 of year 1, B borrows $100 from S in return for B's note providing for $10 of interest annually at the end of each year, and repayment of $100 at the end of year 20. The note is a security within the meaning of section 351(d)(2). As of January 1 of year 3, B has fully performed its obligations, but the fair market value of the B note is $130, reflecting a decline in prevailing market interest rates, and S transfers the note to B in exchange for $130 of B stock in a transaction to which both section 351 and section 354 applies.

(ii) No deemed satisfaction and reissuance. As a result of the satisfaction of the note for more than its adjusted issue price, B takes into account $30 of repurchase premium under § 1.163-7(c). Although the transfer of the B note is a transaction to which both section 351 and section 354 applies, under paragraph (g)(4)(i)(C) of this section, any gain or loss from the intercompany obligation is not subject to either section 351(a) or section 354, and therefore, S has a $30 gain under section 1001. Because the note is extinguished in a transaction in which the adjusted issue price of the note is equal to the creditor's basis in the note, and the debtor's and creditor's items offset in amount, the transaction is not a triggering transaction under paragraph (g)(3)(i)(B)(5) of this section, and the note is not treated as satisfied and reissued under paragraph (g)(3)(ii) of this section. On a separate entity basis, S's $30 gain would be a capital gain under section 1271(a)(1). Under the matching rule, however, the attributes of S's intercompany item and B's corresponding item must be redetermined to produce the same effect as if the transaction had occurred between divisions of a single corporation. Under paragraph (c)(4)(i) of this section, the attributes of B's premium deduction control the attributes of S's gain. Accordingly, S's gain is treated as ordinary income. Under paragraph (g)(4)(i)(D) of this section, section 108(e)(7) does not apply upon the extinguishment of the B note, and therefore, the B stock received by S in the exchange will not be treated as section 1245 property.

Example (7). Exchange of intercompany obligations. (i) Facts. On January 1 of year 1, B borrows $100 from S in return for B's note providing for $10 of interest annually at the end of each year, and repayment of $100 at the end of year 20. As of January 1 of year 3, B has fully performed its obligations and, pursuant to a recapitalization to which section 368(a)(1)(E) applies, B issues a new note to S in exchange for the original B note. The new B note has an issue price, stated redemption price at maturity, and stated principal amount of $100, but contains terms that differ sufficiently from the terms of the original B note to cause a realization event under § 1.1001-3. The original B note and the new B note are both securities (within the meaning of section 354(a)(1)).

(ii) No deemed satisfaction and reissuance. Because the original B note is extinguished in exchange for a newly issued B note and the issue price of the new B note is equal to both the adjusted issue price of the original B note and S's basis in the original B note, the transaction is not a triggering transaction under paragraph (g)(3)(i)(B)(6) of this section, and the note is not treated as satisfied and reissued under paragraph (g)(3)(ii) of this section. B has neither income from discharge of indebtedness under section 108(e)(10) nor a deduction for repurchase premium under § 1.163-7(c). Although the exchange of the original B note for the new B note is a transaction to which section 354 applies, under paragraph (g)(4)(i)(C) of this section, any gain or loss from the intercompany obligation is not subject to section 354. Under section 1001, S has no gain or loss from the exchange of notes.

Example (8). Tax benefit rule. (i) Facts. On January 1 of year 1, B borrows $100 from S in return for B's note providing for $10 of interest annually at the end of each year, and repayment of $100 at the end of year 5. As of January 1 of year 3, B has fully performed its obligations, but the note's fair market value has depreciated, reflecting an increase in prevailing market interest rates. On that date, S transfers the B note to member T as part of an exchange for T common stock which is intended to qualify for nonrecognition treatment under section 351 but with a view to sell the T stock at a reduced gain. On February 1 of year 4, all of the stock of T is sold at a reduced gain.

(ii) Deemed satisfaction and reissuance. Because the assignment of the B note does not occur within 12 months of the sale of T stock, paragraph (g)(3)(i)(B)(1)(vi) of this section does not apply to treat the assignment as a triggering transaction. However, because the assignment of the B note was engaged in with a view to shift built-in loss from the obligation in order to secure a tax benefit that the group or its members would not otherwise enjoy, under paragraph (g)(3)(i)(C) of this section, the assignment of the B note is a triggering transaction to which paragraph (g)(3)(ii) of this section applies. Under paragraph (g)(3)(ii) of this section, B's note is treated as satisfied and reissued for its fair market value, immediately before S's transfer to T. As a result of the deemed satisfaction of the note for less than its adjusted issue price, B takes into account discharge of indebtedness income and S has a corresponding loss which is treated as ordinary loss. B is also treated as reissuing, immediately after the deemed satisfaction, a new note to S with an issue price and basis equal to its fair market value. S is then treated as transferring the new note to T as part of the section 351 exchange. Because S's basis in the T stock received with respect to the transferred B note is equal to its fair market value, S's gain with respect to the T stock will not reflect any of the built-in loss attributable to the B note. (This example does not address common law doctrines or other authorities that might apply to recharacterize the transaction or to otherwise affect the tax treatment of the transaction.)

Example (9). Issuance at off-market rate of interest. (ii) Facts. T is a member with a SRLY loss. T's sole shareholder, P, borrows an amount of cash from T in return for a P note that provides for a materially above market rate of interest. The P note is issued with a view to generate additional interest income to T over the term of the note to facilitate the absorption of T's SRLY loss.

(ii) With a view. Because the P note is issued with a view to shift interest income from the off-market obligation in order to secure a tax benefit that the group or its members would not otherwise enjoy, under paragraph (g)(4)(iii) of this section, the intercompany obligation is treated, for all Federal income tax purposes, as originally issued for its fair market value so T is treated as purchasing the note at a premium. The difference between the amount loaned and the fair market value of the obligation is treated as transferred from P to T as a capital contribution at the time the note is issued. Throughout the term of the note, T takes into account interest income and bond premium and P takes into account interest deduction and bond issuance premium under generally applicable Internal Revenue Code sections. The adjustment under paragraph (g)(4)(iii) of this section is made without regard to the application of, and in lieu of any adjustment under, section 482 or 1274.

Example (10). Nonintercompany obligation becomes intercompany obligation. (i) Facts. On January 1 of year 1, B borrows $100 from X in return for B's note providing for $10 of interest annually at the end of each year, and repayment of $100 at the end of year 5. As of January 1 of year 3, B has fully performed its obligations, but the note's fair market value is $70, reflecting an increase in prevailing market interest rates. On January 1 of year 3, P buys all of X's stock. B is solvent within the meaning of section 108(d)(3).

(ii) Deemed satisfaction and reissuance. Under paragraph (g)(5)(ii) of this section, B's note is treated as satisfied for $70 (determined under the principles of § 1.108-2(f)(2)) immediately after it becomes an intercompany obligation. Both X's $30 capital loss (under section 1271(a)(1)) and B's $30 of discharge of indebtedness income (under § 1.61-12) are taken into account in determining consolidated taxable income for year 3. Under paragraph (g)(6)(i)(B) of this section, the attributes of items resulting from the satisfaction are determined on a separate entity basis. But see section 382 and § 1.1502-15 (as appropriate). B is also treated as reissuing a new note to X. The new note is an intercompany obligation, it has a $70 issue price and $100 stated redemption price at maturity, and the $30 of original issue discount will be taken into account by B and X in the same manner as provided in paragraph (iii) of Example 1 of this paragraph (g)(7).

(iii) Amortization of repurchase premium. The facts are the same as in paragraph (i) of this Example 10, except that on January 1 of year 3, the B note has a fair market value of $130 and rather than P purchasing the X stock, P purchases the B note from X by issuing its own note. The P note has an issue price, stated redemption price at maturity, stated principal amount, and fair market value of $130. Under paragraph (g)(5)(ii) of this section, B's note is treated as satisfied for $130 (determined under the principles of § 1.108-2(f)(1)) immediately after it becomes an intercompany obligation. As a result of the deemed satisfaction of the note, P has no gain or loss and B has $30 of repurchase premium. Under paragraph (g)(6)(iii) of this section, B's $30 of repurchase premium from the deemed satisfaction is amortized by B over the term of the newly issued P note in the same manner as if it were original issue discount and the newly issued P note had been issued directly by B. B is also treated as reissuing a new note to P. The new note is an intercompany obligation, it has a $130 issue price and $100 stated redemption price at maturity, and the treatment of B's $30 of bond issuance premium under the new B note is determined under § 1.163-13.

(iv) Election to file consolidated returns. Assume instead that B borrows $100 from S during year 1, but the P group does not file consolidated returns until year 3. Under paragraph (g)(5)(ii) of this section, B's note is treated as satisfied and reissued as a new note immediately after the note becomes an intercompany obligation. The satisfaction and reissuance are deemed to occur on January 1 of year 3, for the fair market value of the obligation (determined under the principles of § 1.108-2(f)(2)) at that time.

Example (11). Notional principal contracts. (i) Facts. On April 1 of year 1, M1 enters into a contract with counterparty M2 under which, for a term of five years, M1 is obligated to make a payment to M2 each April 1, beginning in year 2, in an amount equal to the London Interbank Offered Rate (LIBOR), as determined by reference to LIBOR on the day each payment is due, multiplied by a $1,000 notional principal amount. M2 is obligated to make a payment to M1 each April 1, beginning in year 2, in an amount equal to 8 percent multiplied by the same notional principal amount. LIBOR is 7.80 percent on April 1 of year 2, and therefore, M2 owes $2 to M1.

(ii) Matching rule. Under § 1.446-3(d), the net income (or net deduction) from a notional principal contract for a taxable year is included in (or deducted from) gross income. Under § 1.446-3(e), the ratable daily portion of M2's obligation to M1 as of December 31 of year 1 is $1.50 ($2 multiplied by 275/365). Under the matching rule, M1's net income for year 1 of $1.50 is taken into account to reflect the difference between M2's net deduction of $1.50 taken into account and the $0 recomputed net deduction. Similarly, the $.50 balance of the $2 of net periodic payments made on April 1 of year 2 is taken into account for year 2 in M1's and M2's net income and net deduction from the contract. In addition, the attributes of M1's intercompany income and M2's corresponding deduction are redetermined to produce the same effect as if the transaction had occurred between divisions of a single corporation. Under paragraph (c)(4)(i) of this section, the attributes of M2's corresponding deduction control the attributes of M1's intercompany income. (Although M1 is the selling member with respect to the payment on April 1 of year 2, it might be the buying member in a subsequent period if it owes the net payment.)

(iii) Dealer. The facts are the same as in paragraph (i) of this Example 11, except that M2 is a dealer in securities, and the contract with M1 is not inventory in the hands of M2. Under section 475, M2 must mark its securities to fair market value at year-end. Assume that under section 475, M2's loss from marking to fair market value the contract with M1 is $10. Because M2 realizes an amount of loss from the mark to fair market value of the contract, the transaction is a triggering transaction under paragraph (g)(3)(i)(A)(1) of this section. Under paragraph (g)(3)(ii) of this section, M2 is treated as making a $10 payment to M1 to terminate the contract immediately before a new contract is treated as reissued with an up-front payment by M1 to M2 of $10. M1's $10 of income from the termination payment is taken into account under the matching rule to reflect M2's deduction under § 1.446-3(h). The attributes of M1's intercompany income and M2's corresponding deduction are redetermined to produce the same effect as if the transaction had occurred between divisions of a single corporation. Under paragraph (c)(4)(i) of this section, the attributes of M2's corresponding deduction control the attributes of M1's intercompany income. Accordingly, M1's income is treated as ordinary income. Under § 1.446-3(f), the deemed $10 up-front payment by M1 to M2 in connection with the issuance of a new contract is taken into account over the term of the new contract in a manner reflecting the economic substance of the contract (for example, allocating the payment in accordance with the forward rates of a series of cash-settled forward contracts that reflect the specified index and the $1,000 notional principal amount). (The timing of taking items into account is the same if M1, rather than M2, is the dealer subject to the mark-to-market requirement of section 475 at year-end. However in this case, because the attributes of the corresponding deduction control the attributes of the intercompany income, M1's income from the deemed termination payment from M2 might be ordinary or capital). Under paragraph (g)(3)(ii)(A) of this section, section 475 does not apply to mark the notional principal contract to fair market value after its deemed satisfaction and reissuance.

(8) Effective/applicability date. The rules of this paragraph (g) apply to transactions involving intercompany obligations occurring in consolidated return years beginning on or after December 24, 2008.

(h) Anti-avoidance rules. *(1) In general.* If a transaction is engaged in or structured with a principal purpose to avoid the purposes of this section (including, for example, by avoiding treatment as an intercompany transaction), adjustments must be made to carry out the purposes of this section.

(2) Examples. The anti-avoidance rules of this paragraph (h) are illustrated by the following examples. The examples set forth below do not address common law doctrines or other authorities that might apply to recast a transaction or to otherwise affect the tax treatment of a transaction. Thus, in addition to adjustments under this paragraph (h), the Commissioner can, for example, apply the rules of section 269 or § 1.701-2 to disallow a deduction or to recast a transaction.

Example (1). Sale of a partnership interest.

(a) Facts. S owns land with a $10 basis and $100 value. B has net operating losses from separate return limitation years (SRLYs) subject to limitation under § 1.1502-21(c). Pursuant to a plan to absorb the losses without limitation by the SRLY rules, S transfers the land to an unrelated, calendar-year partnership in exchange for a 10% interest in the capital and profits of the partnership in a transaction to which section 721 applies. The partnership does not have a section 754 election in effect. S later sells its partnership interest to B for $100. In the following year, the partnership sells the land to X for $100. Because the partnership does not have a section 754 election in effect, its $10 basis in the land does not reflect B's $100 basis in the partnership interest. Under section 704(c), the partnership's $90 built-in gain is allocated to B, and B's basis in the partnership interest increases to $190 under section 705. In a later year, B sells the partnership interest to a nonmember for $100.

(b) Adjustments. Under § 1.1502-21(c), the partnership's $90 built-in gain allocated to B ordinarily increases the amount of B's SRLY limitation, and B's $90 loss from its sale of the partnership interest ordinarily is not subject to limitation under the SRLY rules. Because the contribution of property to the partnership and the sale of the partnership interest were part of a plan a principal purpose of which was to achieve a reduction in consolidated tax liability by creating offsetting gain and loss for B while deferring S's intercompany gain, B's allocable share of the partnership's gain from its sale of the land is treated under paragraph (h)(1) of this section as not increasing the amount of B's SRLY limitation.

Example (2). Transitory status as an intercompany obligation.

(a) Facts. P historically has owned 70% of X's stock and the remaining 30% is owned by unrelated shareholders. On January 1 of Year 1, S borrows $100 from X in return for S's note requiring $10 of interest annually at the end of each year, and repayment of $100 at the end of Year 20. As of January 1 of Year 3, the P group has substantial net operating loss carryovers, and the fair market value of S's note falls to $70 due to an increase in prevailing market interest rates. X is not permitted under section 166(a)(2) to take into account a $30 loss with respect to the note. Pursuant to a plan to permit X to take into account its $30 loss without disposing of the note, P acquires an additional 10% of X's stock, causing X to become a member, and P subsequently resells the 10% interest. X's $30 loss with respect to the note is a net unrealized built-in loss within the meaning of § 1.1502-15.

(b) Adjustments. Under paragraph (g)(4) of this section, X ordinarily would take into account its $30 loss as a result of the note becoming an intercompany obligation, and S would take into account $30 of discharge of indebtedness income. Under § 1.1502-22(c), X's loss is not combined with items of the other members and the loss would be carried to X's separate return years as a result of X becoming a nonmember. However, the transitory status of S's indebtedness to X as an intercompany obligation is structured with a principal purpose to accelerate the recognition of X's loss. Thus, S's note is treated under paragraph (h)(1) of this section as not becoming an intercompany obligation.

Example (3). Corporate mixing bowl.

(a) Facts. M1 and M2 are subsidiaries of P. M1 operates a manufacturing business on land it leases from M2. The land is the only asset held by M2. P intends to dispose of the M1 business, including the land owned by M2; P's basis in the M1 stock is equal to the stock's fair market value. M2's land has a value of $20 and a basis of $0 and P has a $0 basis in the stock of M2. In Year 1, with a principal purpose of avoiding gain from the sale of the land (by transferring the land to M1 with a carry-over basis without affecting P's basis in the stock of M1 or M2), M1 and M2 form corporation T; M1 contributes cash in exchange for 80% of the T stock and M2 contributes the land in exchange for 20% of the stock. In Year 3, T liquidates, distributing $20 cash to M2 and the land (plus $60 cash) to M1. Under § 1.1502-34, section 332 applies to both M1 and M2. Under section 337, T recognizes no gain or loss from its liquidating distribution of the land to M1. T has neither gain nor loss on its distribution of cash to M2. In Year 4, P sells all of the stock of M1 to X and liquidates M2.

(b) Adjustments. A principal purpose for the formation and liquidation of T was to avoid gain from the sale of M2's land. Thus, under paragraph (h)(1) of this section, M2 must take $20 of gain into account when the stock of M1 is sold to X.

Example (4). Partnership mixing bowl.

(a) Facts. M1 owns a self-created intangible asset with a $0 basis and a fair market value of $100. M2 owns land with a basis of $100 and a fair market value of $100. In Year 1, with a principal purpose of creating basis in the intangible asset (which would be eligible for amortization under section 197), M1 and M2 form partnership PRS; M1 contributes the intangible asset and M2 contributes the land. X, an unrelated person, contributes cash to PRS in exchange for a substantial interest in the partnership. PRS uses the contributed assets in legitimate business activities. Five years and six months later, PRS liquidates, distributing the land to M1, the intangible to M2, and cash to X. The group reports no gain under sections 707(a)(2)(B) and 737(a) and claims that M2's basis in the intangible asset is $100 under section 732 and that the asset is eligible for amortization under section 197.

(b) Adjustments. A principal purpose of the formation and liquidation of PRS was to create additional amortization without an offsetting increase in consolidated taxable income by avoiding treatment as an intercompany transaction. Thus, under paragraph (h)(1) of this section, appropriate adjustments must be made.

Example (5). Sale and leaseback.

(a) Facts. S operates a factory with a $70 basis and $100 value, and has loss carryovers from SRLYs. Pursuant to a plan to take into account the $30 unrealized gain while continuing to operate the factory, S sells the factory to X for $100 and leases it back on a long-term basis. In the transaction, a substantial interest in the factory is transferred to X. The sale and leaseback are not recharacterized under general principles of Federal income tax law. As a result of S's sale to X, the $30 gain is taken into account and increases S's SRLY limitation.

(b) No adjustments. Although S's sale was pursuant to a plan to accelerate the $30 gain, it is not subject to adjustment under paragraph (h)(1) of this section. The sale is not treated as engaged in or structured with a principal purpose to avoid the purposes of this section.

(i) [Reserved]

(j) Miscellaneous operating rules. For purposes of this section—

(1) Successor assets. Any reference to an asset includes, as the context may require, a reference to any other asset the basis of which is determined, directly or indirectly, in whole or in part, by reference to the basis of the first asset.

(2) Successor persons. (i) In general. Any reference to a person includes, as the context may require, a reference to a predecessor or successor. For this purpose, a predecessor is a transferor of assets to a transferee (the successor) in a transaction—

(A) To which section 381(a) applies;

(B) In which substantially all of the assets of the transferor are transferred to members in a complete liquidation;

(C) In which the successor's basis in assets is determined (directly or indirectly, in whole or in part) by reference to the basis of the transferor, but the transferee is a successor only with respect to the assets the basis of which is so determined; or

(D) Which is an intercompany transaction, but only with respect to assets that are being accounted for by the transferor in a prior intercompany transaction.

(ii) Intercompany items. If the assets of a predecessor are acquired by a successor member, the successor succeeds to, and takes into account (under the rules of this section), the predecessor's intercompany items. If two or more successor members acquire assets of the predecessor, the successors take into account the predecessor's intercompany items in a manner that is consistently applied and reasonably carries out the purposes of this section and applicable provisions of law.

(3) Multiple triggers. If more than one corresponding item can cause an intercompany item to be taken into account under the matching rule, the intercompany item is taken into account in connection with the corresponding item most consistent with the treatment of members as divisions of a single corporation. For example, if S sells a truck to B, its intercompany gain from the sale is not taken into account by reference to B's depreciation if the depreciation is capitalized under section 263A as part of B's cost for a building; instead, S's gain relating to the capitalized depreciation is taken into account when the building is sold or as it is depreciated. Similarly, if B purchases appreciated land from S and transfers the land to a lower-tier member in exchange for stock, thereby duplicating the basis of the land in the basis of the stock, items with respect to both the stock and the land can cause S's intercompany gain to be taken into account; if the lower-tier member becomes a nonmember as a result of the sale of its stock, the attributes of S's intercompany gain are determined with respect to the land rather than the stock.

(4) Multiple or successive intercompany transactions. If a member's intercompany item or corresponding item affects the accounting for more than one intercompany transaction, appropriate adjustments are made to treat all of the intercompany transactions as transactions between divisions of a single corporation. For example, if S sells property to M, and M sells the property to B, then S, M, and B are treated as divisions of a single corporation for purposes of applying the rules of this section. Similar principles apply with respect to intercompany transactions that are part of the same plan or arrangement. For example, if S sells separate properties to different members as part of the same plan or arrangement, all of the participating members are treated as divisions of a single corporation for purposes of determining the attributes (which might also affect timing) of the intercompany items and corresponding items from each of the properties.

(5) Acquisition of group. (i) Scope. This paragraph (j)(5) applies only if a consolidated group (the terminating group) ceases to exist as a result of—

(A) The acquisition of either the assets of the common parent of the terminating group in a reorganization described in section 381(a)(2), or the stock of the common parent of the terminating group; or

(B) The application of the principles of § 1.1502-75(d)(2) or (d)(3).

(ii) Application. If the terminating group ceases to exist under circumstances described in paragraph (j)(5)(i) of this section, the surviving group is treated as the terminating group for purposes of applying this section to the intercompany transactions of the terminating group. For example, intercompany items and corresponding items from intercompany transactions between members of the terminating group are taken into account under the rules of this section by the surviving group. This treatment does not apply, however, to members of the terminating group that are not members of the surviving group immediately after the terminating group ceases to exist (for example, under section 1504(a)(3) relating to reconsolidation, or section 1504(c) relating to includible insurance companies).

(6) Former common parent treated as continuation of group. If a group terminates because the common parent is the only remaining member, the common parent succeeds to the treatment of the terminating group for purposes of applying this section so long as it neither becomes a member of an affiliated group filing separate returns nor becomes a corporation described in section 1504(b). For example, if the only subsidiary of the group liquidates into the common parent in a complete liquidation to which section 332 applies, or the common parent merges into the subsidiary and the subsidiary is treated as the common parent's successor under paragraph (j)(2)(i) of this section, the taxable income of the surviving corporation is treated as the group's consolidated taxable income in which the intercompany and corresponding items must be included. See § 1.267(f)-1 for additional rules applicable to intercompany losses or deductions.

(7) Becoming a nonmember. For purposes of this section, a member is treated as becoming a nonmember if it has a separate return year (including another group's consolidated return year). A member is not treated as having a separate return year if its items are treated as taken into account in computing the group's consolidated taxable income under paragraph (j)(5) or (6) of this section.

(8) Recordkeeping. Intercompany and corresponding items must be reflected on permanent records (including work papers). See also section 6001, requiring records to be maintained. The group must be able to identify from these permanent records the amount, location, timing, and attributes of the items, so as to permit the application of the rules of this section for each year.

(9) Examples. The operating rules of this paragraph (j) are illustrated generally throughout this section, and by the following examples.

Example (1). Intercompany sale followed by section 351 transfer to member.

(a) Facts. S holds land for investment with a basis of $70. On January 1 of Year 1, S sells the land to M for $100. M also holds the land for investment. On July 1 of Year 3, M transfers the land to B in exchange for all of B's stock in a transaction to which section 351 applies. Under section 358, M's basis in the B stock is $100. B holds the land for sale to customers in the ordinary course of business and, under section 362(b), B's basis in the land is $100. On December 1 of Year 5, M sells 20% of the B stock to X for $22. In an unrelated transaction on July 1 of Year 8, B sells 20% of the land for $22.

(b) Definitions. Under paragraph (b)(1) of this section, S's sale of the land to M and M's transfer of the land to B are both intercompany transactions. S is the selling member and M is the buying member in the first intercompany transaction, and M is the selling member and B is the buying member in the second intercompany transaction. M has no intercompany items under paragraph (b)(2) of this section. Because B acquired the land in an intercompany transaction, B's items from the land are corresponding items to be taken into account under this section. Under the successor asset rule of paragraph (j)(1) of this section, references to the land include references to M's B stock. Under the successor person rule of paragraph (j)(2) of this section, references to M include references to B with respect to the land.

(c) Timing and attributes resulting from the stock sale. Under paragraph (c)(3) of this section, M is treated as owning and selling B's stock for purposes of the matching rule even though, as divisions, M could not own and sell stock in B. Under paragraph (j)(3) of this section, both M's B stock and B's land can cause S's intercompany gain to be taken into account under the matching rule. Thus, S takes $6 of its gain into account in Year 5 to reflect the $6 difference between M's $2 gain taken into account from its sale of B stock and the $8 recomputed gain. Under paragraph (j)(4) of this section, the attributes of this gain are determined by treating S, M, and B as divisions of a single corporation. Under paragraph (c)(1) of this section, S's $6 gain and M's $2 gain are treated as long-term capital gain. The gain would be capital on a separate entity basis (assuming that section 341 does not apply), and this treatment is not inconsistent with treating S, M, and B as divisions of a single corporation because the stock sale and subsequent land sale are unrelated transactions and B remains a member following the sale.

(d) Timing and attributes resulting from the land sale. Under paragraph (j)(3) of this section, S takes $6 of its gain into account in Year 8 under the matching rule to reflect the $6 difference between B's $2 gain taken into account from its sale of an interest in the land and the $8 recomputed gain. Under paragraph (j)(4) of this section, the attributes of this gain are determined by treating S, M, and B as divisions of a single corporation and taking into account the activities of S, M, and B with respect to the land. Thus, both S's gain and B's gain might be ordinary income as a result of B's activities. (If B subsequently sells the balance of the land, S's gain taken into account is limited to its remaining $18 of intercompany gain.)

(e) Sale of successor stock resulting in deconsolidation. The facts are the same as in paragraph (a) of this Example 1, except that M sells 60% of the B stock to X for $66 on December 1 of Year 5 and B becomes a nonmember. Under the matching rule, M's sale of B stock results in $18 of S's gain being taken into account (to reflect the difference between M's $6 gain taken into account and the $24 recomputed gain). Under the acceleration rule, however, the entire $30 gain is taken into account (to reflect B becoming a nonmember, because its basis in the land reflects M's $100 cost basis from the prior intercompany transaction). Under paragraph (j)(4) of this section, the attributes of S's gain are determined by treating S, M, and B as divisions of a single corporation. Because M's cost basis in the land will be reflected by B as a nonmember, all of S's gain is treated as from the land (rather than a portion being from B's stock), and B's activities with respect to the land might therefore result in S's gain being ordinary income.

Example (2). Intercompany sale of member stock followed by recapitalization.

(a) Facts. Before becoming a member of the P group, S owns P stock with a basis of $70. On January 1 of Year 1, P buys all of S's stock. On July 1 of Year 3, S sells the P stock to M for $100. On December 1 of Year 5, P acquires M's original P stock in exchange for new P stock in a recapitalization described in section 368(a)(1)(E).

(b) Timing and attributes. Although P's basis in the stock acquired from M is eliminated under paragraph (f)(4) of this section, the new P stock received by M is exchanged basis property (within the meaning of section 7701(a)(44)) having a basis under section 358 equal to M's basis in the original P stock. Under the successor asset rule of paragraph (j)(1) of this section, references to M's original P stock include references to M's new P stock. Because it is still possible to take S's intercompany item into account under the matching rule with respect to the successor asset, S's gain is not taken into account under the acceleration rule as a result of the basis elimination under paragraph (f)(4) of this section. Instead, the gain is taken into account based on subsequent events with respect to M's new P stock (for example, a subsequent distribution or redemption of the new stock).

Example (3). Back-to-back intercompany transactions—matching.

(a) Facts. S holds land for investment with a basis of $70. On January 1 of Year 1, S sells the land to M for $90. M also holds the land for investment. On July 1 of Year 3, M sells the land for $100 to B, and B holds the land for sale to customers in the ordinary course of business. During Year 5, B sells all of the land to customers for $105.

(b) Timing. Under paragraph (b)(1) of this section, S's sale of the land to M and M's sale of the land to B are both intercompany transactions. S is the selling member and M is the buying member in the first intercompany transaction, and M is the selling member and B is the buying member in the second intercompany transaction. Under paragraph (j)(4) of this section, S, M and B are treated as divisions of a single corporation for purposes of determining the timing of their items from the intercompany transactions. See also paragraph (j)(2) of this section (B is treated as a successor to M for purposes of taking S's intercompany gain into account). Thus, S's $20 gain and M's $10 gain are both taken into account in Year 5 to reflect the difference between B's $5 gain taken into account with respect to the land and the $35 recomputed gain (the gain that B would have taken into account if the intercompany sales had been transfers between divisions of a single corporation, and B succeeded to S's $70 basis).

(c) Attributes. Under paragraphs (j)(4) of this section, the attributes of the intercompany items and corresponding items of S, M, and B are also determined by treating S, M, and B as divisions of a single corporation. For example, the attributes of S's and M's intercompany items are determined by taking B's activities into account.

Example (4). Back-to-back intercompany transactions—acceleration.

(a) Facts. During Year 1, S performs services for M in exchange for $10 from M. S incurs $8 of employee expenses. M capitalizes the $10 cost of S's services under section 263 as part of M's cost to acquire real property from X. Under its separate entity method of accounting, S would take its income and expenses into account in Year 1. M holds the real property for investment and, on July 1 of Year 5, M sells it to B at a gain. B also holds the real property for investment. On December 1 of Year 8, while B still owns the real property, P sells all of M's stock to X and M becomes a nonmember.

(b) M's items. M takes its gain into account immediately before it becomes a nonmember. Because the real property stays in the group, the acceleration rule redetermines the attributes of M's gain under the principles of the matching rule as if B sold the real property to an affiliated corporation that is not a member of the group for a cash payment equal to B's adjusted basis in the real property, and S, M, and B were divisions of a single corporation. Thus, M's gain is capital gain.

(c) S's items. Under paragraph (b)(2)(ii) of this section, S includes the $8 of expenses in determining its $2 intercompany income. In Year 1, S takes into account $8 of income and $8 of expenses. Under paragraph (j)(4) of this section, appropriate adjustments must be made to treat both S's performance of services for M and M's sale to B as occurring between divisions of a single corporation. Thus, S's $2 of intercompany income is not taken into account as a result of M becoming a nonmember, but instead will be taken into account based on subsequent events (e.g., under the matching rule based on B's sale of the real property to a nonmember, or under the acceleration rule based on P's sale of the stock of S or B to a nonmember). See the successor person rules of paragraph (j)(2) of this section (B is treated as a successor to M for purposes of taking S's intercompany income into account).

(d) Sale of S's stock. The facts are the same as in paragraph (a) of this Example 4, except that P sells all of S's stock (rather than M's stock) and S becomes a nonmember on July 1 of Year 5. S's remaining $2 of intercompany income is taken into account immediately before S becomes a nonmember. Because S's intercompany income is not from an intercompany sale, exchange, or distribution of property, the attributes of the intercompany income are determined on a separate entity basis. Thus, S's $2 of intercompany income is ordinary income. M does not take any of its intercompany gain into account as a result of S becoming a nonmember.

(e) Intercompany income followed by intercompany loss. The facts are the same as in paragraph (a) of this Example 4, except that M sells the real property to B at a $1 loss (rather than a gain). M takes its $1 loss into account under the acceleration rule immediately before M becomes a nonmember. But see § 1.267(f)-1 (which might further defer M's loss if M and B remain in a controlled group relationship after M becomes a nonmember). Under paragraph (j)(4) of this section appropriate adjustments must be made to treat the group as if both intercompany transactions occurred between divisions of a single corporation. Accordingly, P's sale of M stock also results in S taking into account $1 of intercompany income as capital gain to offset M's $1 of corresponding capital loss. The remaining $1 of S's intercompany income is taken into account based on subsequent events.

Example (5). Successor group.

(a) Facts. On January 1 of Year 1, B borrows $100 from S in return for B's note providing for $10 of interest annually at the end of each year, and repayment of $100 at the end of Year 20. As of January 1 of Year 3, B has paid the interest accruing under the note. On that date, X acquires all of P's stock and the former P group members become members of the X consolidated group.

(b) Successor. Under paragraph (j)(5) of this section, although B's note ceases to be an intercompany obligation of the P group, the note is not treated as satisfied and reissued under paragraph (g) of this section as a result of X's acquisition of P stock. Instead, the X consolidated group succeeds to the treatment of the P group for purposes of paragraph (g) of this section, and B's note is treated as an intercompany obligation of the X consolidated group.

Example (6). Liquidation—80% distributee.

(a) Facts. X has had preferred stock described in section 1504(a)(4) outstanding for several years. On January 1 of Year 1, S buys all of X's common stock for $60, and B buys all of X's preferred stock for $40. X's assets have a $0 basis and $100 value. On July 1 of Year 3, X distributes all of its assets to S and B in a complete liquidation. Under § 1.1502-34, section 332 applies to both S and B. Under section 337, X has no gain or loss from its liquidating distribution to S. Under sections 336 and 337(c), X has a $40 gain from its liquidating distribution to B. B has a $40 basis under section 334(a) in the assets received from X, and S has a $0 basis under section 334(b) in the assets received from X.

(b) Intercompany items from the liquidation. Under the matching rule, X's $40 gain from its liquidating distribution to B is not taken into account under this section as a result of the liquidation (and therefore is not yet reflected under §§ 1.1502-32 and 1.1502-33). Under the successor person rule of paragraph (j)(2)(i) of this section, S and B are both successors to X. Under section 337(c), X recognizes gain or loss only with respect to the assets distributed to B. Under paragraph (j)(2)(ii) of this section, to be consistent with the purposes of this section, S succeeds to X's $40 intercompany gain. The gain will be taken into account by S under the matching and acceleration rules of this section based on subsequent events. (The allocation of the intercompany gain to S does not govern the allocation of any other attributes.)

Example (7). Liquidation—no 80% distributee.

(a) Facts. X has only common stock outstanding. On January 1 of Year 1, S buys 60% of X's stock for $60, and B buys 40% of X's stock for $40. X's assets have a $0 basis and $100 value. On July 1 of Year 3, X distributes all of its assets to S and B in a complete liquidation. Under § 1.1502-34, section 332 applies to both S and B. Under sections 336 and 337(c), X has a $100 gain from its liquidating distributions to S and B. Under section 334(b), S has a $60 basis in the assets received from X and B has a $40 basis in the assets received from X.

(b) Intercompany items from the liquidation. Under the matching rule, X's $100 intercompany gain from its liquidating distributions to S and B is not taken into account under this section as a result of the liquidation (and therefore is not yet reflected under §§ 1.1502-32 and 1.1502-33). Under the successor person rule of paragraph (j)(2)(i) of this section, S and B are both successors to X. Under paragraph (j)(2)(ii) of this section, to be consistent with the purposes of this section, S succeeds to X's $40 intercompany gain with respect to the assets distributed to B, and B succeeds to X's $60 intercompany gain with respect to the assets distributed to S.

The gain will be taken into account by S and B under the matching and acceleration rules of this section based on subsequent events. (The allocation of the intercompany gain does not govern the allocation of any other attributes.)

(k) Cross references. *(1) Section 108.* See § 1.108-3 for the treatment of intercompany deductions and losses as subject to attribute reduction under section 108(b).

(2) Section 263A(f). See section 263A(f) and § 1.263A-9(g)(5) for special rules regarding interest from intercompany transactions.

(3) Section 267(f). See section 267(f) and § 1.267(f)-1 for special rules applicable to certain losses and deductions from transactions between members of a controlled group.

(4) Section 460. See § 1.460-4(j) for special rules regarding the application of section 460 to intercompany transactions.

(5) Section 469. See § 1.469-1(h) for special rules regarding the application of section 469 to intercompany transactions.

(6) Section 1.1502-80. See § 1.1502-80 for the non-application of certain Internal Revenue Code rules.

(l) Effective/applicability dates. *(1) In general.* This section applies with respect to transactions occurring in years beginning on or after July 12, 1995. If both this section and prior law apply to a transaction, or neither applies, with the result that items may be duplicated, omitted, or eliminated in determining taxable income (or tax liability), or items may be treated inconsistently, prior law (and not this section) applies to the transaction. For example, S's and B's items from S's sale of property to B which occurs in a consolidated return year beginning before July 12, 1995, are taken into account under prior law, even though B may dispose of the property in a consolidated return year beginning on or after July 12, 1995. Similarly, an intercompany distribution to which a shareholder becomes entitled in a consolidated return year beginning before July 12, 1995, but which is distributed in a consolidated return year beginning on or after that date is taken into account under prior law (generally when distributed), because this section generally takes dividends into account when the shareholder becomes entitled to them but this section does not apply at that time. If application of prior law to S's deferred gain or loss from a deferred intercompany transaction (as defined under prior law) occurring in a consolidated return year beginning prior to July 12, 1995, would be affected by an intercompany transaction (as defined under this section) occurring in a consolidated return year beginning on or after July 12, 1995, S's deferred gain or loss continues to be taken into account as provided under prior law, and the items from the subsequent intercompany transaction are taken into account under this section. Appropriate adjustments must be made to prevent items from being duplicated, omitted, or eliminated in determining taxable income as a result of the application of both this section and prior law to the successive transactions, and to ensure the proper application of prior law. Paragraphs (a)(4), (f)(6)(ii), (f)(6)(iv)(A), (g)(3)(ii)(B)(2), and (j)(5)(i)(A) of this section apply with respect to transactions occurring on or after September 17, 2008. However, taxpayers may apply paragraph (j)(5)(i)(A) of this section to transactions that occurred prior to September 17, 2008.

(2) Avoidance transactions. This paragraph (l)(2) applies if a transaction is engaged in or structured on or after April 8, 1994, with a principal purpose to avoid the rules of this section (and instead to apply prior law). If this paragraph (l)(2) applies, appropriate adjustments must be made in years beginning on or after July 12, 1995, to prevent the avoidance, duplication, omission, or elimination of any item (or tax liability), or any other inconsistency with the rules of this section. For example, if S is a dealer in real property and sells land to B on March 16, 1995 with a principal purpose of converting any future appreciation in the land to capital gain, B's gain from the sale of the land on May 11, 1997 might be characterized as ordinary income under this paragraph (l)(2).

(3) Election for certain stock elimination transactions. (i) In general. A group may elect pursuant to this paragraph (l)(3) to apply this section (including the elections available under paragraph (f)(5)(ii) of this section) to stock elimination transactions to which prior law would otherwise apply. If an election is made, this section, and not prior law, applies to determine the timing and attributes of S's and B's gain or loss from stock with respect to all stock elimination transactions.

(ii) Stock elimination transactions. For purposes of this paragraph (l)(3), a stock elimination transaction is a transaction in which stock transferred from S to B—

(A) Is cancelled or redeemed on or after July 12, 1995;

(B) Is treated as cancelled in a liquidation pursuant to an election under section 338(h)(10) with respect to a qualified stock purchase with an acquisition date on or after July 12, 1995;

(C) Is distributed on or after July 12, 1995; or

(D) Is exchanged on or after July 12, 1995 for stock of a member (determined immediately after the exchange) in a transaction that would cause S's gain or loss from the transfer to be taken into account under prior law.

(iii) Time and manner of making election. An election under this paragraph (l)(3) is made by attaching to a timely filed original return (including extensions) for the consolidated return year including July 12, 1995 a statement entitled "[Insert Name and Employer Identification Number of Common Parent] HEREBY ELECTS THE APPLICATION OF § 1.1502-13(l)(3)." See paragraph (f)(5)(ii)(E) of this section for the manner of electing the relief provisions of paragraph (f)(5)(ii) of this section.

(4) Prior law. For transactions occurring in S's years beginning before July 12, 1995, see the applicable regulations issued under section 1502. See §§ 1.1502-13, 1.1502-13T, 1.1502-14, 1.1502-14T, 1.1502-31, and 1.1502-32 (as contained in the 26 CFR part 1 edition revised as of April 1, 1995).

(5) Consent to adopt method of accounting. For intercompany transactions occurring in a consolidated group's first taxable year beginning on or after July 12, 1995, the Commissioner's consent under section 446(e) is hereby granted for any changes in methods of accounting that are necessary solely by reason of the timing rules of this section. Changes in method of accounting for these transactions are to be effected on a cut-off basis.

(m) Effective/applicability date. Paragraphs (f)(5)(ii)(E) and (f)(6)(i)(C)(2) of this section apply to any original consolidated Federal income tax return due (without extensions) after June 14, 2007. For original consolidated Federal income tax returns due (without extensions) after May 30, 2006, and on or before June 14, 2007, see § 1.1502-13T as contained in 26 CFR part 1 in effect on April 1, 2007. For original consolidated Federal income tax returns due (without extensions) on or before May 30, 2006, see § 1.1502-13 as contained in 26 CFR part 1 in effect on April 1, 2006.

T.D. 6894, 9/7/66, amend T.D. 7246, 12/29/72, T.D. 8131, 3/24/87, T.D. 8196, 4/14/88, T.D. 8295, 3/9/90, T.D. 8478, 3/9/93, T.D. 8482, 8/6/93, T.D. 8560, 8/12/94, T.D. 8584, 12/28/94, T.D. 8597, 7/12/95, T.D. 8660, 3/13/96, T.D. 8677, 6/26/96, T.D. 8823, 6/25/99, T.D. 9025, 12/13/2002, T.D. 9048, 3/11/2003, T.D. 9117, 3/12/2004, T.D. 9192, 3/21/2005, T.D. 9261, 5/5/2006, T.D. 9264, 5/26/2006, T.D. 9329, 6/13/2007, T.D. 9383, 3/6/2008, T.D. 9424, 9/10/2008, T.D. 9442, 12/24/2008, T.D. 9458, 9/3/2009, T.D. 9475, 12/17/2009.

PAR. 2. Section 1.1502-13 is amended by revising paragraphs (f)(5)(ii)(B) and adding paragraph (f)(5)(ii)(F) to read as follows:

Proposed § 1.1502-13 Intercompany transactions. [*For Preamble, see ¶ 153,119*]

* * * * *

(f) * * *

(5) * * *

(ii) * * *

(B) (1) [The text of the proposed amendments to § 1.1502-13(f)(5)(ii)(B)(1) is the same as the text of § 1.1502-13T(f)(5)(ii)(B)(1) published elsewhere in this issue of the Federal Register.

(2) [The text of the proposed amendments to § 1.1502-13(f)(5)(ii)(B)(2) is the same as the text of § 1.1502-13T(f)(5)(ii)(B)(2) published elsewhere in this issue of the Federal Register.

* * * * *

(F) [The text of the proposed amendments to § 1.1502-13(f)(5)(ii)(F) is the same as the text of § 1.1502-13T(f)(5)(ii)(F) published elsewhere in this issue of the Federal Register.

* * * * *

PAR. 2. Section 1.1502-13 is amended by revising paragraphs (c)(6)(ii)(C), (f)(7)(i) and (f)(7)(ii)(A) to read as follows:

Proposed § 1.1502-13 Intercompany transactions. [*For Preamble, see ¶ 152,969*]

(c) * * *

(6) * * *

(ii) * * *

(C) [The text of proposed § 1.1502-13(c)(6)(ii)(C) is the same as the text of § 1.1502-13T(c)(6)(ii)(C) published elsewhere in this issue of the Federal Register]. [*See T.D. 9383, 03/07/2008, 73 Fed. Reg. 46.*]

(1) [The text of proposed § 1.1502-13(c)(6)(ii)(C)(1) is the same as the text of § 1.1502-13T(c)(6)(ii)(C)(1) published elsewhere in this issue of the Federal Register.] [*See T.D. 9383, 03/07/2008, 73 Fed. Reg. 46.*]

(2) [The text of proposed § 1.1502-13(c)(6)(ii)(C)(2) is the same as the text of § 1.1502-13T(c)(6)(ii)(C)(2) published elsewhere in this issue of the Federal Register.] [*See T.D. 9383, 03/07/2008, 73 Fed. Reg. 46.*]

(i) [The text of proposed § 1.1502-13(c)(6)(ii)(C)(2)(i) is the same as the text of § 1.1502-13T(c)(6)(ii)(C)(2)(i) published elsewhere in this issue of the Federal Register]. [*See T.D. 9383, 03/07/2008, 73 Fed. Reg. 46.*]

* * * * *

(f) * * *

(7) [The text of proposed § 1.1502-13(f)(7) is the same as the text of § 1.1502-13T(f)(7) published elsewhere in this issue of the Federal Register]. [*See T.D. 9383, 03/07/2008, 73 Fed. Reg. 46.*]

(i) [The text of proposed § 1.1502-13(f)(7)(i) is the same as the text of § 1.1502-13T(f)(7)(i) published elsewhere in this issue of the Federal Register]. [*See T.D. 9383, 03/07/2008, 73 Fed. Reg. 46.*]

(ii) [The text of proposed § 1.1502-13(f)(7)(ii) is the same as the text of § 1.1502-13T(f)(7)(ii) published elsewhere in this issue of the Federal Register]. [*See T.D. 9383, 03/07/2008, 73 Fed. Reg. 46.*]

(A) [The text of proposed § 1.1502-13(f)(7)(ii)(A) is the same as the text of § 1.1502-13T(f)(7)(ii)(A) published elsewhere in this issue of the Federal Register]. [*See T.D. 9383, 03/07/2008, 73 Fed. Reg. 46.*]

* * * * *

PAR. 2. Section 1.1502-13 is amended by:

1. Adding a sentence at the end of paragraph (j)(2)(ii).
2. Adding paragraph (j)(2)(iii).
3. Redesignating paragraph (j)(9) introductory text as paragraph (j)(9)(i).
4. Revising Example 6 and Example 7 of newly designated paragraph (j)(9)(i).
5. Adding paragraph (j)(9)(ii).

The revisions and additions read as follows:

Proposed § 1.1502-13 Intercompany transactions. [*For Preamble, see ¶ 152,629*]

• ***Caution:*** This Notice of Proposed Rulemaking was partially finalized by TD 9376, 01/14/2008. Reg. § 1.1502-13 remains proposed.

* * * * *

(j) * * *

(2) * * *

(ii) Intercompany items. * * * For example, if the assets of a predecessor are acquired by more than one successor in a transaction to which section 381(a)(1) applies, each successor succeeds to, and takes into account (under the rules of this section), each of the predecessor's intercompany items (whether resulting from distributions in liquidation or otherwise) to the extent that such items would have been reflected in investment basis adjustments to the stock of the predecessor owned by that successor under the principles of § 1.1502-32(c) if, immediately prior to the liquidation, any stock of the predecessor owned by nonmembers had been redeemed in exchange for the money or property distributed to that nonmember in the transaction to which section 381(a)(1) applies, and then such items had been taken into account under § 1.1502-13(d).

(iii) Effective date. The third sentence of paragraph (j)(2)(ii) of this section applies to transactions occurring after the date these regulations are published as final regulations in the Federal Register.

* * * * *

(9) Examples. (i) The operating rules of this paragraph (j) are illustrated generally throughout this section, and by the following examples:

* * * * *

Example (6). Liquidation—80% distributee. (i) Facts. B1, B2, and S are members of the same consolidated group. S has only common stock outstanding. B1 owns 80% of S's stock, and B2 owns the remaining 20%. On January 1 of Year 2, S sells two assets to another member of the group. S recognizes $100 of gain with respect to the first asset and $100 of loss with respect to the second asset. On July 1 of Year 3, S distributes all of its remaining assets to B1 and B2 in a complete liquidation. At the time of the liquidation, S's assets have an aggregate basis of $0 and an aggregate value of $100, and neither the gain nor the loss from the prior two asset sales has been taken into account under this section. Under § 1.1502-34, section 332 applies to both B1 and B2. Under section 337, S has no gain or loss from its liquidating distribution to B1. Under sections 336 and 337(c), S has a $20 gain from its liquidating distribution to B2. On January 1 of Year 4, B2 ceases to be a member of the group.

(ii) Succession to intercompany items. Under the matching rule, S's $20 gain from its liquidating distribution to B2 is not taken into account under this section as a result of the liquidation (and, therefore, is not yet reflected under Sec. § 1.1502-32 and 1.1502-33). Under the successor person rule of paragraph (j)(2)(i) of this section, B1 and B2 are both successors to S. Under paragraph (j)(2)(ii) of this section, B1 and B2 each succeeds to S's intercompany items to the extent that such items would have been reflected in investment basis adjustments to its stock of S under the principles of § 1.1502-32(c) if, immediately prior to the liquidation, such items had been taken into account under § 1.1502-13(d). Therefore, B1 succeeds to 80% of the $20 of intercompany gain from the assets distributed to B2 in the liquidation, and 80% of the $100 of intercompany gain and 80% of the $100 of intercompany loss from the assets that S sold prior to the liquidation. In addition, B2 succeeds to 20% of the $20 of intercompany gain from the assets distributed to B2 in the liquidation and 20% of the $100 of intercompany gain and 20% of the $100 of intercompany loss from the assets that S sold prior to the liquidation.

(iii) Taking into account intercompany items. S's gain from its liquidating distribution to B2 and S's gain and loss from the sale of the two assets prior to the liquidation will be taken into account by B1 and B2 under the matching and acceleration rules of this section based on subsequent events. Therefore, in connection with B2 ceasing to be a member of the group, B1 will take into account $16 of the intercompany gain from the assets distributed to B2 in the liquidation. In addition, B2 will take into account $4 of the intercompany gain from the assets distributed to B2 in the liquidation and $20 of the intercompany gain and $20 of the intercompany loss from the two assets that S sold prior to the liquidation.

Example (7). Liquidation—no 80% distributee.

(i) Facts. B1, B2, and S are members of the same consolidated group. S has only common stock outstanding. B1 and B2 each owns 40% of S's stock, and A, a nonmember, owns the remaining 20% of S's stock. On January 1 of Year 2, S sells two assets to another member of the group. S recognizes $100 of gain with respect to the first asset and $100 of loss with respect to the second asset. On July 1 of Year 3, S distributes all of its remaining assets to B1, B2, and A in complete liquidation. At the time of the liquidation, S's assets have an aggregate basis of $0 and an aggregate value of $100, and neither the gain nor the loss from the prior two asset sales has been taken into account under this section. Under § 1.1502-34, section 332 applies to both B1 and B2. Under sections 336 and 337(c), S has a $100 gain from its liquidating distributions to B1, B2, and A.

(ii) Succession to intercompany items. Under the matching rule, S's $80 gain from its liquidating distributions to B1 and B2 is not taken into account under this section as a result of the liquidation (and, therefore, is not yet reflected under Sec. § 1.1502-32 and 1.1502-33). Under the successor person rule of paragraph (j)(2)(i) of this section, B1 and B2 are successors to S. Under paragraph (j)(2)(ii) of this section, B1 and B2 each succeeds to S's intercompany items to the extent that such items would have been reflected in investment basis adjustments to its stock of S under the principles of § 1.1502-32(c) if, immediately prior to the liquidation, the stock of S owned by A had been redeemed in exchange for the money or property distributed to A in the liquidation, and then such items had been taken into account under § 1.1502-13(d). If A had been redeemed, then S's items would have produced investment basis adjustments in the stock of S owned by each of B1 and B2 equally. Therefore, each of B1 and B2 succeeds to 50% of the $80 of intercompany gain from the assets distributed to B1 and B2 in the liquidation and 50% of the $100 of intercompany gain and 50% of the $100 of intercompany loss from the assets that S sold prior to the liquidation. S's $20 gain with respect to the assets that are distributed to A in the liquidation is taken into account immediately.

(iii) Taking into account intercompany items. S's gain from its liquidating distributions to B1 and B2 and S's gain and loss from the sale of the two assets prior to the liquidation will be taken into account by B1 and B2 under the matching and acceleration rules of this section based on subsequent events.

(ii) Effective dates. Paragraph (j)(9)(i) Examples 6 and 7 apply to transactions occurring after the date these regulations are published as final regulations in the Federal Register.

* * * * *

PAR. 3. Section 1.1502-13 is amended by:

1. Adding a sentence after the second sentence of paragraph (c)(6)(ii)(A).

2. Adding paragraph (c)(6)(iii).

3. Revising the first sentence of Example 1(d) of paragraph (g)(5).

The revisions and additions read as follows:

Proposed § 1.1502-13 Intercompany transactions. [*For Preamble, see ¶ 152,525*]

* * * * *

(c) * * *

(6) * * *

(ii) * * *

(A) * * * However, see § 1.265-2(c) for special rules related to the application of paragraph (c)(6)(i) of this section to interest income with respect to certain intercompany obligations the interest deduction on which is disallowed under section 265(a)(2). * * *

* * * * *

(iii) Effective date. The third sentence of paragraph (c)(6)(ii)(A) of this section shall apply to taxable years beginning on or after the date these regulations are published as final regulations in the Federal Register.

* * * * *

(g) * * *

(5) * * *

Example (1). * * *

* * * * *

(d) Tax-exempt income. The facts are the same as in paragraph (a) of this Example 1, except that B's borrowing from S is allocable under section 265 to B's purchase of state and local bonds to which section 103 applies and § 1.265-2(c) does not apply. * * *

* * * * *

§ 1.1502-13T Intercompany transactions (temporary).

(a) through (c)(6)(ii)(B) [Reserved]. For further guidance, see § 1.1502-13(a) through (c)(6)(ii)(B).

(c) *(6)* (ii) (C) Certain intercompany gains on member stock. (1) In general. Notwithstanding paragraph (c)(6)(ii)(A)(1), intercompany gain with respect to member stock is redetermined to be excluded from gross income to the extent that—

(i) The gain is the common parent's (P) intercompany item;

(ii) Immediately before the intercompany gain is taken into account, P holds the member stock with respect to which the intercompany gain was realized;

(iii) P's basis in such member stock that reflects the intercompany gain that is taken into account is eliminated without the recognition of gain or loss (and such eliminated basis is not further reflected in the basis of any successor asset);

(iv) The group has not and will not derive any Federal income tax benefit from the intercompany transaction that gave rise to such intercompany gain or the redetermination of the intercompany gain (including any adjustment to basis in member stock under § 1.1502-32); and

(v) The effects of the intercompany transaction have not previously been reflected, directly or indirectly, on the group's consolidated return. For this purpose, the redetermination of the intercompany gain is not in and of itself considered a Federal income tax benefit.

(2) Effective/applicability date. (i) In general. This paragraph (c)(6)(ii)(C) applies with respect to items taken into account on or after March 7, 2008.

(ii) Expiration date. The applicability of this paragraph (c)(6)(ii)(C) will expire on March 7, 2011.

(D) through (f)(5)(ii)(A) [Reserved]. For further guidance, see § 1.1502-13(c)(6)(ii)(D) through (f)(5)(ii)(A).

(f) *(5)* (ii) (B) Section 332. (1) In general. If section 332 would otherwise apply to T's (old T's) liquidation into B, and B transfers substantially all of old T's assets to a new member (new T), and if a direct transfer of substantially all of old T's assets to new T would qualify as a reorganization described in section 368(a), then, for all Federal income tax purposes, T's liquidation into B and B's transfer of substantially all of old T's assets to new T will be disregarded and instead, the transaction will be treated as if old T transferred substantially all of its assets to new T in exchange for new T stock and the assumption of T's liabilities in a reorganization described in section 368(a). (Under § 1.1502-13(j)(1), B's stock in new T would be a successor asset to B's stock in old T, and S's gain would be taken into account based on the new T stock.)

(2) Time limitation and adjustments. The transfer of old T's assets to new T qualifies under paragraph (f)(5)(ii)(B)(1) of this section only if B has entered into a written plan, on or before the due date of the group's consolidated income tax return (including extensions), to transfer the T assets to new T, and the statement described in paragraph (f)(5)(ii)(E) of this section is included on or with a timely filed consolidated tax return for the tax year that includes the date of the liquidation (including extensions). However, see paragraph (f)(5)(ii)(F) of this section for certain situations in which the plan may be entered into after the due date of the return and the statement described in paragraph (f)(5)(ii)(E) of this section may be included on either an original tax return or an amended tax return filed after the due date of the return. In either case, the transfer of substantially all of T's assets to new T must be completed within 12 months of the filing of the return. Appropriate adjustments are made to reflect any events occurring before the formation of new T and to reflect any assets not transferred to new T, or liabilities not assumed by new T. For example, if B retains an asset of old T, the asset is treated under § 1.1502-13(f)(3) as acquired by new T but distributed to B immediately after the reorganization.

(3) through (f)(5)(ii)(E) [Reserved]. For further guidance, see § 1.1502-13(f)(5)(ii)(B)(3) through (f)(5)(ii)(E).

(F) Effective/Applicability date. (1) General rule. Paragraphs (f)(5)(ii)(B)(1) and (2) of this section apply to transactions in which old T's liquidation into B occurs on or after October 25, 2007.

(2) Prior periods. For transactions in which old T's liquidation into B occurs before October 25, 2007, see § 1.1502-13(f)(5)(ii)(B)(1) and (2) in effect prior to October 25, 2007 as contained in 26 CFR part 1, revised April 1, 2009.

(3) Special rule for tax returns filed before November 3, 2009 In the case of a liquidation on or after October 25, 2007, by a taxpayer whose original tax return for the year of liquidation was filed on or before November 3, 2009 then, notwithstanding paragraph (f)(5)(ii)(B)(2) of this section and § 1.1502-13(f)(5)(ii)(E), the election to apply paragraph (f)(5)(ii)(B) of this section may be made by entering into the written plan described in paragraph (f)(5)(ii)(B) of this section on or before November 3, 2009, including the statement described in § 1.1502-13(f)(5)(ii)(E) on or with an original tax return or an amended tax return for the tax year that includes the liquidation filed on or before November 3, 2009, and transferring substantially all of T's assets to new T within 12 months of the filing of such original or amended return.

(G) Expiration date. Paragraphs (f)(5)(ii)(B), (B)(1), (B)(2) and (F)(1), (2), and (3) of this section will expire on September 3, 2012.

(6) through (f)(7)(i) Example 6 [Reserved]. For further guidance, see § 1.1502-13(f)(6) through (f)(7)(i) Example 6.

(7) (i)

Example (7). Intercompany stock sale followed by section 332 liquidation into common parent. (i) Facts. P owns all of the stock of S, S owns all the stock of T, and T owns all of the stock of T1. On January 1 of Year 1, S distributes all of the T stock to P in a distribution to which section 301 applies. At the time of this distribution, the value of the T stock is $100 and S has a $40 basis in the T stock. Under section 311(b), S recognizes a $60 gain. Under section 301(d), P's basis in the T stock is $100. S will take its $60 gain into account under the matching rule in paragraph (c) of this section. On January 1 of Year 4, in an independent transaction, S distributes all of its assets to P in a complete liquidation to which section 332 applies, and, under paragraph (j)(2) of this section, P succeeds to S's $60 gain. On January 1 of Year 7, T distributes all of its T1 stock to P in a transaction to which section 355 applies. At the time of this distribution, P has a basis in the T stock of $100, the value of the T stock (without regard to T1) is $75, and the value of the T1 stock is $25. Under section 358, P allocates $25 of its $100 basis in the T stock to the T1 stock, and, under paragraph (j)(1) of this section, the T1 stock becomes a successor asset to the T stock. On January 1 of Year 9, in an independent transaction, when T's assets have a value of $75, T distributes all of its assets to P in a complete liquidation to which section 332 applies.

(ii) Analysis. Under paragraphs (b)(1) and (f)(2) of this section, S's distribution of the T stock to P is an intercompany transaction, S is the selling member, and P is the buying member. In Year 9 when T liquidates, P has $0 of unrecognized gain or loss under section 332 because P has a $75 basis in the stock of T and receives a $75 distribution with respect to its T stock. Under paragraph (b)(3)(ii) of this section, P's $0 of unrecognized gain or loss with respect to the T stock under section 332 is a corresponding item. P takes $45 of its intercompany gain into account under the matching rule in Year 9 to reflect the difference between P's $0 of unrecognized gain and P's $45 of recomputed unrecognized gain. (If P and S were divisions of a single corporation, P would have had a $40 basis in the T stock, and, after the Year 7 distribution of the T1 stock, would have held the T stock with a $30 basis.) Paragraph (c)(6) of this section does not prevent the redetermination of P's intercompany gain as excluded from gross income to the extent that the gain is P's intercompany item, P holds the T stock with respect to which this portion of the intercompany gain was realized, P's basis in the T stock that reflects the $45 intercompany gain taken into account is eliminated without the recognition of gain or loss (and this eliminated basis is not further reflected in the basis of any successor asset), the group has not derived any Federal income tax benefit from the basis in the T stock and will not derive any Federal income tax benefit from a redetermination of this portion of the gain, and the effects of the intercompany transaction have not previously been reflected, directly or indirectly, on the P group's consolidated return. (See paragraph (c)(6)(ii)(C) of this section). Accordingly, under paragraph (c)(6)(ii)(C) of this section, the $45 intercompany gain that P takes into account is redetermined to be excluded from gross income.

Example (8). Intercompany stock sale followed by section 355 distribution by the common parent. (i) Facts. The facts are the same as Example 7, except that T does not distribute the stock of T1, instead, in Year 7, T makes a distribution of $50 to P in a transaction to which section 301 applies. Under § 1.1502-32, P's basis in its T stock is reduced by $50 and, under paragraph (f)(2)(ii) of this section, the intercompany distribution is excluded from P's gross income. Further, in Year 9, instead of liquidating T, P distributes the T stock to its shareholders in a transaction to which section 355 applies.

(ii) Analysis. On the distribution of the T stock, P has $0 of unrecognized gain under section 355(c) because P has a $50 basis in the stock of T which has a value of $50. Under paragraph (b)(3)(ii) of this section, P's $0 of unrecognized gain or loss with respect to the T stock under section 355(c) is a corresponding item. P takes its $60 intercompany gain into account under the matching rule in Year 9 to reflect the difference between P's $0 of unrecognized gain and P's $60 of recomputed gain ($50 unrecognized gain and $10 recognized gain). (If P and S were divisions of a single corporation, P would have had a $40 basis in the T stock, and, after the Year 7 distribution, would have held the T stock with a $10 excess loss account.) Paragraph (c)(6) of this section does not prevent the redetermination of P's intercompany gain as excluded from gross income to the extent that the gain is P's intercompany gain, P holds the T stock with respect to which this portion of the intercompany gain was realized, P's basis in the T stock that reflects the $60 intercompany gain taken into account is eliminated without the recognition of gain or loss (and this eliminated basis is not further reflected in any successor asset), the group has not derived any Federal income tax benefit from the basis in the T stock and will not derive any Federal income tax benefit from a redetermination of this portion of the gain, and the effects of the intercompany transaction have not previously been reflected, directly or indirectly, on the P group's consolidated return. (See paragraph (c)(6)(ii)(C) of this section). The intercompany transaction with respect to the T stock resulted in an increase in the basis of the T stock, and this increase in the basis of the T stock prevented P from holding the T stock with a $10 excess loss account (as a result of the Year 7 distribution) at the time of the section 355 distribution. Accordingly, the group derived a Federal income tax benefit from the intercompany transaction to the extent of $10. As such, under paragraph (c)(6)(ii)(C) of this section, only $50 of the $60 intercompany gain that P takes into account is redetermined to be excluded from gross income.

(iii) Application of section 355(e). If it was determined that section 355(e) applied to P's distribution of the T stock, P would recognize $0 of gain and derive a Federal income tax benefit to the extent of the full $60 increase in the basis of the T stock. Therefore, no portion of P's intercompany gain would be redetermined to be excluded from gross income under paragraph (c)(6)(ii)(C) of this section.

(ii) Effective/applicability date. (A) In general. Paragraph (f)(7)(i) Examples 7 and 8 of this section apply with respect to items taken into account on or after March 7, 2008.

(B) Expiration date. The applicability of paragraph (f)(7)(i) Examples 7 and 8 of this section will expire on March 7, 2011.

(g) through (m) [Reserved]. For further guidance, see § 1.1502-13(g) through (m).

T.D. 9383, 3/6/2008, amend T.D. 9458, 9/3/2009.

---

§ 1.1502-15 SRLY limitation on built-in losses.

(a) SRLY limitation. Except as provided in paragraph (f) of this section (relating to built-in losses of the common parent) and paragraph (g) of this section (relating to an overlap with section 382), built-in losses are subject to the SRLY limitation under §§ 1.1502-21(c) and 1.1502-22(c) (including applicable subgroup principles). Built-in losses are treated as deductions or losses in the year recognized, except for the purpose of determining the amount of, and the extent to which the built-in loss is limited by, the SRLY limitation for the year in which it is recognized. Solely for such purpose, a built-in loss is treated as a hypothetical net operating loss carryover or net capital loss carryover arising in a SRLY, instead of as a deduction or loss in the year recognized. To the extent that a built-in loss is allowed as a deduction under this section in the year it is recognized, it offsets any consolidated taxable income for the year before any loss carryovers or carrybacks are allowed as a deduction. To the extent not so allowed, it is treated as a separate net operating loss or net capital loss carryover or carryback arising in the year of recognition and, under §§ 1.1502-21(c) or 1.1502-22(c), the year of recognition is treated as a SRLY.

(b) Built-in losses. *(1) Defined.* If a corporation has a net unrealized built-in loss under section 382(h)(3) (as modified by this section) on the day it becomes a member of the group (whether or not the group is a consolidated group), its deductions and losses are built-in losses under this section to the extent they are treated as recognized built-in losses under section 382(h)(2)(B) (as modified by this section). This paragraph (b) generally applies separately with respect to each member, but see paragraph (c) of this section for circumstances in which it is applied on a subgroup basis.

(2) Operating rules. Solely for purposes of applying paragraph (b)(1) of this section, the principles of § 1.1502-94(c) apply with appropriate adjustments, including the following:

(i) Stock acquisition. A corporation is treated as having an ownership change under section 382(g) on the day the corporation becomes a member of a group, and no other events (e.g., a subsequent ownership change under section 382(g) while it is a member) are treated as causing an ownership change.

(ii) Asset acquisition. In the case of an asset acquisition by a group, the assets and liabilities acquired directly from the same transferor (whether corporate or non-corporate, foreign or domestic) pursuant to the same plan are treated as the assets and liabilities of a corporation that becomes a member of the group (and has an ownership change) on the date of the acquisition.

(iii) Recognized built-in gain or loss. A loss that is included in the determination of net unrealized built-in gain or loss and that is recognized but disallowed or deferred (e.g., under § 1.337(d)-2, § 1,1502-35, § 1.1502-36, or section 267) is not treated as a built-in loss unless and until the loss would be allowed during the recognition period without regard to the application of this section. Section 382(h)(1)(B)(ii) does not apply to the extent it limits the amount of recognized built-in loss that may be treated as a pre-change loss to the amount of the net unrealized built-in loss.

(c) Built-in losses of subgroups. *(1) In general.* In the case of a subgroup, the principles of paragraph (b) of this section apply to the subgroup, and not separately to its members. Thus, the net unrealized built-in loss and recognized built-in loss for purposes of paragraph (b) of this section are based on the aggregate amounts for each member of the subgroup.

(2) Members of subgroups. A subgroup is composed of those members that have been continuously affiliated with each other for the 60 consecutive month period ending immediately before they become members of the group in which the loss is recognized. A member remains a member of the subgroup until it ceases to be affiliated with the loss member. For this purpose, the principles of § 1.1502-21(c)(2)(iv) through (vi) apply with appropriate adjustments.

(3) Coordination of 60 month affiliation requirement with the overlap rule. If one or more corporations become members of a group and are included in the determination of a net unrealized built-in loss that is subject to the overlap rule described in paragraph (g)(1) of this section, then for purposes of paragraph (c)(2) of this section, such corporations that become members of the group are treated as having been affiliated for 60 consecutive months with the common parent of the group and are also treated as having been affiliated with any other members who have been affiliated or are treated as having been affiliated with the common parent at such time. The corporations are treated as having been affiliated with such other members for the same period of time that those members have been affiliated or are treated as having been affiliated with the common parent. If two or more corporations become members of the group at the same time, but this paragraph (c)(3) does not apply to every such corporation, then immediately after the corporations become members of the group, and solely for purposes of paragraph (c)(2) of this section, the corporations to which this paragraph (c)(3) applies are treated as having not been previously affiliated with the corporations to which this paragraph (c)(3) does not apply. If the common parent has become the common parent of an existing group within the previous five year period in a transaction described in § 1.1502-75(d)(2)(ii) or (3), the principles of §§ 1.1502-91(g)(6) and 1.1502-96(a)(2)(iii) shall apply.

(4) Built-in amounts. Solely for purposes of determining whether the subgroup has a net unrealized built-in loss or whether it has a recognized built-in loss, the principles of § 1.1502-91(g) and (h) apply with appropriate adjustments.

(d) Examples. For purposes of the examples in this section, unless otherwise stated, all groups file consolidated returns, all corporations have calendar taxable years, the facts set forth the only corporate activity, value means fair market value and the adjusted basis of each asset equals its value, all transactions are with unrelated persons, and the application of any limitation or threshold under section 382 is disregarded. The principles of this section are illustrated by the following examples:

Example (1). Determination of recognized built-in loss.

(i) Individual A owns all of the stock of P and T. T has two depreciable assets. Asset 1 has an unrealized loss of $55 (basis $75, value $20), and asset 2 has an unrealized gain of $20 (basis $30, value $50). P acquires all the stock of T from Individual A during Year 1, and T becomes a member of the P group. P's acquisition of T is not an ownership change as defined by section 382(g). Paragraph (g) of this section does not apply because there is not an overlap of the application of the rules contained in paragraph (a) of this section and section 382.

(ii) Under paragraph (b)(2)(i) of this section, and solely for purposes of applying paragraph (b)(1) of this section, T is treated as having an ownership change under section 382(g) on becoming a member of the P group. Under paragraph (b)(1) of this section, none of T's $55 of unrealized loss is treated as a built-in loss unless T has a net unrealized built-in loss under section 382(h)(3) on becoming a member of the P group.

(iii) Under section 382(h)(3)(A), T has a $35 net unrealized built-in loss on becoming a member of the P group (($55) + $20 = ($35)). Assume that this amount exceeds the threshold requirement in section 382(h)(3)(B). Under section 382(h)(2)(B), the entire amount of T's $55 unrealized loss is treated as a built-in loss to the extent it is recognized during the 5-year recognition period described in section 382(h)(7). Under paragraph (b)(2)(iii) of this section, the restriction under section 382(h)(1)(B)(ii), which limits the amount of recognized built-in loss that is treated as pre-change loss to the amount of the net unrealized built-in loss, is inapplicable for this purpose. Consequently, the entire $55 of unrealized loss (not just the $35 net unrealized loss) is treated under paragraph (b)(1) of this section as a built-in loss to the extent it is recognized within 5 years of T's becoming a member of the P group. Under paragraph (a) of this section, a built-in loss is subject to the SRLY limitation under § 1.1502-21(c)(1).

(iv) Under paragraph (b)(2)(ii) of this section, the built-in loss would similarly be subject to a SRLY limitation under § 1.1502-21(c)(1) if T transferred all of its assets and liabilities to a subsidiary of the P group in a single transaction described in section 351. To the extent the built-in loss is recognized within 5 years of T's transfer, all of the items contributed by the acquiring subsidiary to consolidated taxable income (and not just the items attributable to the assets and liabilities transferred by T) are included for purposes of determining the SRLY limitation under § 1.1502-21(c)(1).

Example (2). Actual application of section 382 not relevant.

(i) Individual A owns all of the stock of P, and Individual B owns all of the stock of T. T has two depreciable assets. Asset 1 has an unrealized loss of $25 (basis $75, value $50), and asset 2 has an unrealized gain of $20 (basis $30, value $50). P buys 55 percent of the stock of T in January of Year 1, resulting in an ownership change of T under section 382(g). During March of Year 2, P buys the 45 percent balance of the T stock, and T becomes a member of the P group.

(ii) Although T has an ownership change for purposes of section 382 in Year 1 and not Year 2, T's joining the P group in Year 2 is treated as an ownership change under section 382(g) solely for purposes of this section. Consequently, for purposes of this section, whether T has a net unrealized built-in loss under section 382(h)(3) is determined as if the day T joined the P group were a change date.

Example (3). Determination of a recognized built-in loss of a subgroup.

(i) Individual A owns all of the stock of P, S, and M. P and M are each the common parent of a consolidated group. During Year 1, P acquires all of the stock of S from Individual A, and S becomes a member of the P group. P's acquisition of S is not an ownership change as defined by section 382(g). At the beginning of Year 7, M acquires all of the stock of P from Individual A, and P and S become members of the M group. M's acquisitions of P and S are also not ownership changes as defined by section 382(g). At the time of M's acquisition of the P stock, P has (disregarding the stock of S) a $10 net unrealized built-in gain (two depreciable assets, asset 1 with a basis of $35 and a value of $55, and asset 2 with a basis of $55 and a value of $45), and S has a $75 net unrealized built-in loss (two depreciable assets, asset 3 with a basis of $95 and a value of $10, and asset 4 with a basis of $10 and a value of $20).

(ii) Under paragraph (c) of this section, P and S compose a subgroup on becoming members of the M group because P and S were continuously affiliated for the 60 month period ending immediately before they became members of the M group. Consequently, paragraph (b) of this section does not apply to P and S separately. Instead, their separately computed unrealized gains and losses are aggregated for purposes of determining whether, and the extent to which, any unrealized loss is treated as built-in loss under this section and is subject to the SRLY limitation under § 1.1502-21(c).

(iii) Under paragraph (c) of this section, the P subgroup has a net unrealized built-in loss on the day P and S become members of the M group, determined by treating the day they become members as a change date. The net unrealized built-in loss is the aggregate of P's net unrealized built-in gain of $10 and S's net unrealized built-in loss of $75, or an aggregate net unrealized built-in loss of $65. (The stock of S owned by P is disregarded for purposes of determining the net unrealized built-in loss. However, any loss allowed on the sale of the stock within the recognition period is taken into account in determining recognized loss.) Assume that the $65 net unrealized built-in loss exceeds the threshold requirement under section 382(h)(3)(B).

(iv) Under paragraphs (b)(1), (b)(2)(iii), and (c) of this section, a loss recognized during the 5-year recognition period on an asset of P or S held on the day that P and S became members of the M group is a built-in loss except to the extent the group establishes that such loss exceeds the amount by which the adjusted basis of such asset on the day the member became a member exceeded the fair market value of such asset on that same day. If P sells asset 2 for $45 in Year 7 and recognizes a $10 loss, the entire $10 loss is treated as a built-in loss under paragraphs (b)(2)(iii) and (c) of this section. If S sells asset 3 for $10 in Year 7 and recognizes an $85 loss, the entire $85 loss is treated as a built-in loss under paragraphs (b)(2)(iii) and (c) of this section (not just the $55 balance of the P subgroup's $65 net unrealized built-in loss).

(v) The determination of whether P and S constitute a SRLY subgroup for purposes of loss carryovers and carrybacks, and the extent to which built-in losses are not allowed under the SRLY limitation, is made under § 1.1502-21(c).

Example (4). Computation of SRLY limitation.

(i) Individual A owns all of the stock of P, the common parent of a consolidated group. During Year 1, Individual A forms T by contributing $300 and T sustains a $100 net operating loss. During Year 2, T's assets decline in value to $100. At the beginning of Year 3, P acquires all the stock of T from Individual A, and T becomes a member of the P group with a net unrealized built-in loss of $100. P's acquisition of T is not an ownership change as defined by section 382(g). Assume that $100 exceeds the threshold requirements of section 382(h)(3)(B). During Year 3, T recognizes its unrealized built-in loss as a $100 ordinary loss. The members of the P group contribute the following net income to the consolidated taxable income of the P group (disregarding T's recognized built-in loss and any consolidated net operating loss deduction under § 1.1502-21) for Years 3 and 4:

	Year 3	Year 4	Total
P group (without T)	$100	$100	$ 200
T	60	40	100
CTI	$160	$140	$300.

(ii) Under paragraph (b) of this section, T's $100 ordinary loss in Year 3 (not taken into account in the consolidated taxable income computations above) is a built-in loss. Under paragraph (a) of this section, the built-in loss is treated as a net operating loss carryover for purposes of determining the SRLY limitation under § 1.1502-21(c).

(iii) For Year 3, § 1.1502-21(c) limits T's $100 built-in loss and $100 net operating loss carryover from Year 1 to the aggregate of the P group's consolidated taxable income through Year 3, determined by reference to only T's items. For this purpose, consolidated taxable income is determined without regard to any consolidated net operating loss deductions under § 1.1502-21(a).

(iv) The P group's consolidated taxable income through Year 3 is $60 when determined by reference to only T's items. Under § 1.1502-21(c), the SRLY limitation for Year 3 is therefore $60.

(v) Under paragraph (a) of this section, the $100 built-in loss is treated as a current deduction for all purposes other than determination of the SRLY limitation under § 1.1502-21(c). Consequently, a deduction for the built-in loss is allowed in Year 3 before T's loss carryover from Year 1 is allowed, but only to the extent of the $60 SRLY limitation. None of T's Year 1 loss carryover is allowed because the built-in loss ($100) exceeds the SRLY limitation for Year 3.

(vi) The $40 balance of the built-in loss that is not allowed in Year 3 because of the SRLY limitation is treated as a $40 net operating loss arising in Year 3 that is carried to other years in accordance with the rules of § 1.1502-21(b). The $40 net operating loss is treated under paragraph (a) of this section and § 1.1502-21(c)(1)(ii) as a loss carryover or carryback from Year 3 that arises in a SRLY, and is subject to the rules of § 1.1502-21 (including § 1.1502-21(c)) rather than this section. See also § 1.1502-21(c)(1)(iii) Example 4.

(vii) The facts are the same as in paragraphs (i) through (vi) of this Example 4, except that T has an additional built-in loss when it joins the P group which is recognized in Year 4. For purposes of determining the SRLY limitation for this additional loss in Year 4 (or any subsequent year), the $60 of built-in loss allowed as a deduction in Year 3 is treated under paragraph (a) of this section as a deduction in Year 3 that reduces the P group's consolidated taxable income when determined by reference to only T's items.

Example (5). Built-in loss exceeding consolidated taxable income in the year recognized.

(i) Individual A owns all of the stock of P and T. During Year 1, P acquires all the stock of T from Individual A, and T becomes a member of the P group. P's acquisition of T was not an ownership change as defined by section 382(g). At the time of acquisition, T has a noncapital asset with an unrealized loss of $45 (basis $100, value $55), which exceeds the threshold requirements of section 382(h)(3)(B). During Year 2, T sells its asset for $55 and recognizes the unrealized built-in loss. The P group has $10 of consolidated taxable income in Year 2, computed by disregarding T's recognition of the $45 built-in loss and the consolidated net operating loss deduction, while the consolidated taxable income would be $25 if determined by reference to only T's items (other than the $45 loss).

(ii) T's $45 loss is recognized in Year 2 and, under paragraph (b) of this section, constitutes a built-in loss. Under paragraph (a) of this section and § 1.1502-21(c)(1)(ii), the loss is treated as a net operating loss carryover to Year 2 for purposes of applying the SRLY limitation under § 1.1502-21(c).

(iii) For Year 2, T's SRLY limitation is the aggregate of the P group's consolidated taxable income through Year 2 determined by reference to only T's items. For this purpose, consolidated taxable income is determined by disregarding any built-in loss that is treated as a net operating loss carryover, and any consolidated net operating loss deductions under § 1.1502-21(a). Consolidated taxable income so determined is $25.

(iv) Under § 1.1502-21(c), $25 of the $45 built-in loss could be deducted in Year 2. Because the P group has only $10 of consolidated taxable income (determined without regard to the $45), the $25 loss creates a consolidated net operating loss of $15. This loss is carried back or forward under the rules of § 1.1502-21(b) and absorbed under the rules of § 1.1502-21(a). This loss is not treated as arising in a SRLY (see § 1.1502-21(c)(1)(ii)) and therefore is not subject to the SRLY limitation under § 1.1502-21(c) in any consolidated return year of the group to which it is carried. The remaining $20 is treated as a loss carryover arising in a SRLY and is subject to the limitation of § 1.1502-21(c) in the year to which it is carried.

(e) Predecessors and successors. For purposes of this section, any reference to a corporation or member includes, as the context may require, a reference to a successor or predecessor, as defined in § 1.1502-1(f)(4).

(f) Built-in losses recognized by common parent of group. *(1) General rule.* Paragraph (a) of this section does not apply to any loss recognized by the group on an asset held by the common parent on the date the group is formed. Following an acquisition described in § 1.1502-75(d)(2) or (3), references to the common parent are to the corporation that was the common parent immediately before the acquisition.

(2) Anti-avoidance rule. If a corporation that becomes a common parent of a group acquires assets with a net unrealized built-in loss in excess of the threshold requirement of section 382(h)(3)(B) (and thereby increases its net unrealized built-in loss or decreases its net unrealized built-in gain) prior to, and in anticipation of, the formation of the group, paragraph (f)(1) of this section does not apply.

(g) Overlap with section 382. *(1) General rule.* The limitations provided in §§ 1.1502-21(c) and 1.1502-22(c) do not apply to recognized built-in losses or to loss carryovers or carrybacks attributable to recognized built-in losses when the application of paragraph (a) of this section results in an overlap with the application of section 382.

(2) Definitions. (i) Generally. For purposes of this paragraph (g), the definitions and nomenclature contained in section 382, the regulations thereunder, and §§ 1.1502-90 through 1.1502-99 apply.

(ii) Overlap. (A) An overlap of the application of paragraph (a) of this section and the application of section 382 with respect to built-in losses occurs if a corporation becomes a member of a consolidated group (the SRLY event) within six months of the change date of an ownership change giving rise to a section 382(a) limitation that would apply with respect to the corporation's recognized built-in losses (the section 382 event). Except as provided in paragraph (g)(3) of this section, application of the overlap rule does not require that the size and composition of the corporation's net unrealized built-in loss is the same on the date of the section 382 event and the SRLY event.

(B) For special rules in the event that there is a SRLY subgroup and/or a loss subgroup as defined in § 1.1502-91(d)(2) with respect to built-in losses, see paragraph (g)(4) of this section.

(3) Operating rules. (i) Section 382 event before SRLY event. If a SRLY event occurs on the same date as a section 382 event or within the six month period beginning on the date of the section 382 event, paragraph (g)(1) of this section applies beginning with the tax year that includes the SRLY event. Paragraph (g)(1) of this section does not apply, however, if a corporation that would otherwise be subject to the overlap rule acquires assets from a person other than a member of the group with a net unrealized built-in loss in excess of the threshold requirement of section 382(h)(3)(B) (and thereby increases its net unrealized built-in loss) after the section 382 event, and before the SRLY event.

(ii) SRLY event before section 382 event. If a section 382 event occurs within the period beginning the day after the SRLY event and ending six months after the SRLY event, paragraph (g)(1) of this section applies starting with the first tax year that begins after the section 382 event. However, paragraph (g)(1) of this section does not apply at any time if a corporation that otherwise would be subject to paragraph (g)(1) of this section transfers assets with an unrealized built-in loss to another member of the group after the SRLY event, but before the section 382 event, unless the corporation recognizes the built-in loss upon the transfer.

(4) Subgroup rules. In general, in the case of built-in losses for which there is a SRLY subgroup and the corporations joining the group at the time of the SRLY event also constitute a loss subgroup (as defined in § 1.1502-91(d)(2)), the principles of this paragraph (g) apply to the SRLY subgroup, and not separately to its members. However, paragraph (g)(1) of this section applies with respect to built-in losses only if—

(i) All members of the SRLY subgroup with respect to those built-in losses are also included in a loss subgroup (as defined in § 1.1502-91(d)(2)); and

(ii) All members of a loss subgroup (as defined in § 1.1502-91(d)(2)) are also members of a SRLY subgroup with respect to those built-in losses.

(5) Asset acquisitions. Notwithstanding the application of this paragraph (g), paragraph (a) of this section applies to asset acquisitions by the corporation that occurs after the latter of the SRLY event and the section 382 event. See, paragraph (b)(2)(ii) of this section.

(6) Examples. The principles of this paragraph (g) are illustrated by the following examples:

Example (1). Determination of subgroup.

(i) Individual A owns all of the stock of P, P1, and S. In Year 1, P acquires all of the stock of P1, and they file a consolidated return. In Year 3, P acquires all of the stock of S, and S joins the P group. Individual B, unrelated to Individual A, owns all of the stock of M and K, each the common parent of a consolidated group. Individual C, unrelated to either Individual A or Individual B, owns all of the stock of T.

(ii) At the beginning of Year 7, M acquires all of the stock of P from Individual A, and, as a result, P, P1, and S become members of the M group. At the time of M's acquisition of the P stock, P has a $15 net unrealized built-in loss (disregarding the stock of P1), P1 has a net unrealized built-in gain of $10, and S has a net unrealized built-in gain of $5.

(iii) During Year 8, M acquires all of the stock of T, and T joins the M group. At the time of M's acquisition of the T stock, T had an unrealized built-in loss of $15. At the beginning of Year 9, K acquires all of the stock of M from Individual B, and the members of the M consolidated group including P, P1, S, and T become members of the K group. At the time of K's acquisition of the M stock, M has (disregarding the stock of P and T) a $15 net unrealized built-in loss, P has a $20 net unrealized built-in loss (disregarding the stock of P1), P1 has a net unrealized built-in gain of $5, S has a net unrealized built-in loss of $35, and T has a $15 net unrealized built-in loss.

(iv) M's acquisition of P in Year 7 results in P, P1, and S becoming members of the M group (the SRLY event). Under paragraph (c) of this section, P and P1 compose a SRLY built-in loss subgroup because they have been affiliated for the 60 consecutive month period immediately preceding joining the M group. S is not a member of the subgroup because on becoming a member of the M group it had not been continuously affiliated with P and P1 for the 60 month period ending immediately before it became a member of the M group. Consequently, § 1.1502-15 applies to S separately from the P and P1 subgroup.

(v) Assuming that the $5 net unrealized built-in loss of the P/P1 subgroup exceeds the threshold requirement under section 382(h)(3)(B), M's acquisition of P resulted in an ownership change of P and P1 within the meaning of section 382(g) that subjects P and P1 to a limitation under section 382(a) (the section 382 event). Because, with respect to P and P1, the SRLY event and the change date of the section 382 event occur on the same date and because the loss subgroup and SRLY subgroup are coextensive, there is an overlap of the application of the SRLY rules and the application of section 382.

(vi) S was not a loss corporation because it did not have a net operating loss carryover, or a net unrealized built-in loss, and therefore, M's acquisition of P did not result in an ownership change of S within the meaning of section 382(g). S, therefore is not subject to the overlap rule of paragraph (g) of this section.

(vii) M's acquisition of T resulted in T becoming a member of the M group (the SRLY event). Assuming that T's $15 net unrealized built-in loss exceeds the threshold requirement under section 382(h)(3)(B), M's acquisition of T also resulted in an ownership change of T within the meaning of section 382(g) that subjects T to a limitation under section 382(a) (the section 382 event). Because, with respect to T, the SRLY event and the change date of the section 382 event occur on the same date, there is an overlap of the application of the SRLY rules and the application of section 382 within the meaning of paragraph (g) of this section.

(viii) K's acquisition of M results in the members of the M consolidated group, including T, P, P1, and S, becoming members of the K group (the SRLY event). Because T, P, and P1 were each included in the determination of a net unrealized built-in loss that was subject to the overlap rule described in paragraph (g)(1) of this section when they each became members of the M group, they are deemed under paragraph (c)(3) of this section to have been continuously affiliated with M for the 60 month period ending immediately before becoming a member of the M group, notwithstanding their actual affiliation history. As a result, M, T, P, and P1 compose a SRLY built-in loss subgroup under paragraph (c)(2) of this section. K's acquisition of M is not subject to paragraph (g) of this section because it does not result in a section 382 event.

(ix) S, however, is not a member of the subgroup under paragraph (c)(2) of this section. Because S was not included in the determination of a net unrealized built-in loss that was subject to the overlap rule described in paragraph (g)(1) of this section when it joined the M group, S is treated as becoming an affiliate of M on the date it joined the M group. Furthermore, under paragraph (c)(3) of this section, S is deemed to have begun its affiliation with P and P1 on the date it joined the M group. Consequently, § 1.1502-15 applies to S separately to the extent its built-in loss is recognized within the recognition period.

Example (2). Post-overlap acquisition of assets.

(i) Individual A owns all of the stock of P, the common parent of a consolidated group. B, an individual unrelated to Individual A, owns all of the stock of T. T has two depreciable assets. Asset 1 has an unrealized built-in loss of $25 (basis $75, value $50), and asset 2 has an unrealized built-in gain of $20 (basis $30, value $50). During Year 3, P buys all of the stock of T from Individual B. On January 1, Year 4, P contributes $80 cash and Individual A contributes asset

3, a depreciable asset, with a net unrealized built-in loss of $45 (basis $65, value $20), in exchange for T stock in a transaction that is described in section 351.

(ii) P's acquisition of T results in T becoming a member of the P group (the SRLY event) and also results in an ownership change of T, within the meaning of section 382(g), that gives rise to a limitation under section 382(a) (the section 382 event).

(iii) Because the SRLY event and the change date of the section 382 event occur on the same date, there is an overlap of the application of the SRLY rules and the application of section 382. Consequently, under paragraph (g) of this section, the limitation under paragraph (a) of this section does not apply to T's net unrealized built-in loss when it joined the P group.

(iv) Individual A's Year 4 contribution of a depreciable asset occurred after T was a member of the P group. Assuming that the amount of the net unrealized built-in loss exceeds the threshold requirement of section 382(h)(3)(B), the sale of asset 3 within the recognition period is subject to the SRLY limitation of paragraphs (a) and (b)(2)(ii) of this section.

Example (3). Overlap rule.

(i) Individual A owns all of the stock of P, the common parent of a consolidated group. B, an individual unrelated to Individual A, owns all of the stock of T. T has two depreciable assets. Asset 1 has an unrealized loss of $55 (basis $75, value $20), and asset 2 has an unrealized gain of $30 (basis $30, value $60). On February 28 of Year 2, P purchases 55% of T from Individual B. On June 30, of Year 2, P purchases an additional 35% of T from Individual B.

(ii) The February 28 purchase of 55% of T is a section 382 event because it results in an ownership change of T that gives rise to a section 382(a) limitation. The June 30 purchase of 35% of T results in T becoming a member of the P group and is therefore a SRLY event.

(iii) Because the SRLY event occurred within six months of the change date of the section 382 event, there is an overlap of the application of the SRLY rules and the application of section 382, and paragraph (a) of this section does not apply. Therefore, the SRLY limitation does not apply to any of the $55 loss in asset 1 recognized by T after T joined the P group. See § 1.1502-94 for rules relating to the application of section 382 with respect to T's $25 unrealized built-in loss.

Example (4). Overlap rule-Fluctuation in value.

(i) The facts are the same as in Example 3, except that by June 30, of Year 2, asset 1 had declined in value by a further $10. Thus asset 1 had an unrealized loss of $65 (basis $75, value $10), and asset 2 had an unrealized gain of $30 (basis $30, value $60).

(ii) Because paragraph (a) of this section does not apply, the further decrease in asset 1's value is disregarded. Consequently, the results are the same as in Example 3.

(h) Effective date. *(1) In general.* This section generally applies to built-in losses recognized in taxable years for which the due date (without extensions) of the consolidated return is after June 25, 1999. However—

(i) In the event that paragraphs (f)(1) and (g)(1) of this section do not apply to a particular built-in loss in the current group, then solely for purposes of applying paragraph (a) of this section to determine a limitation with respect to that built-in loss and with respect to which the SRLY register (consolidated taxable income determined by reference to only the member's (or subgroup's) items of income, gain, deduction or loss) began in a taxable year for which the due date of the return was on or before June 25, 1999), paragraph (c)(3) of this section shall not apply; and

(ii) For purposes of paragraph (g) of this section, only an ownership change to which section 382(a) as amended by the Tax Reform Act of 1986 applies shall constitute a section 382 event.

(2) Prior periods. For certain taxable years ending on or before June 25, 1999, see § 1.1502-15T in effect prior to June 25, 1999, as contained in 26 CFR part 1 revised April 1, 1999, as applicable.

T.D. 8823, 6/25/99, amend T.D. 9048, 3/11/2003, T.D. 9187, 3/2/2005, T.D. 9254, 3/9/2006, T.D. 9424, 9/10/2008.

§ 1.1502-15A Limitations on the allowance of built-in deductions for consolidated return years beginning before January 1, 1997.

(a) Limitation on built-in deductions. *(1) General rule.* Built-in deductions (as defined in subparagraph (2) of this paragraph) for a taxable year shall be subject to the limitation of § 1.1502-21A(c) (determined without regard to such deductions and without regard to net operating loss carryovers to such year) and the limitation of § 1.1502-22A(c) (determined without regard to such deductions and without regard to capital loss carryovers to such year). If as a result of applying such limitations, built-in deductions are not allowable in such consolidated return year, such deductions shall be treated as a net operating loss or net capital loss (as the case may be) sustained in such year and shall be carried to those taxable years (consolidated or separate) to which a consolidated net operating loss or a consolidated net capital loss could be carried under §§ 1.1502-21A, 1.1502-22A, and 1.1502-79A (or §§ 1.1502-21T and 1.1502-22T, as appropriate), except that such losses shall be treated as losses subject to the limitations contained in §§ 1.1502-21T(c) or § 1.1502-22T(c) (or §§ 1.1502-21A(c) and 1.1502-22A(c), as appropriate) as the case may be. Thus, for example, if member X sells a capital asset during a consolidated return year at a $1,000 loss and such loss is treated as a built-in deduction, then such loss shall be subject to the limitation contained in § 1.1502-22(c), which, in general, would allow such loss to be offset only against X's own capital gain net income (net capital gain for taxable years beginning before January 1, 1977). Assuming X had no capital gain net income (net capital gain for taxable years beginning before January 1, 1977) reflected in such year (after taking into account its capital losses, other than capital loss carryovers and the built-in deduction), such $1,000 loss shall be treated as a net capital loss and shall be carried over for 5 years under § 1.1502-22, subject to the limitation contained in § 1.1502-22(c) for consolidated return years.

(2) Built-in deductions. (i) For purposes of this paragraph, the term "built-in deductions" for a consolidated return year means those deductions or losses of a corporation which are recognized in such year, or which are recognized in a separate return year and carried over in the form of a net operating or net capital loss to such year, but which are economically accrued in a separate return limitation year (as defined in § 1.1502-1(f)). Such term does not include deductions or losses incurred in rehabilitating such corporation. Thus, for example, assume P is the common parent of a group filing consolidated returns on the basis of a calendar year and that P purchases all of the stock of S on December 31, 1966. Assume further that on December 31, 1966, S owns a capital

asset with an adjusted basis of $100 and a fair market value of $50. If the group files a consolidated return for 1967, and S sells the asset for $30, $50 of the $70 loss is treated as a built-in deduction, since it was economically accrued in a separate return limitation year. If S sells the asset for $80 instead of $30, the $20 loss is treated as a built-in deduction. On the other hand, if such asset is a depreciable asset and is not sold by S, depreciation deductions attributable to the $50 difference between basis and fair market value are treated as built-in deductions.

(ii) In determining, for purposes of subdivision (i) of this subparagraph, whether a deduction or loss with respect to any asset is economically accrued in a separate return limitation year, the term "predecessor" as used in § 1.1502-1(f)(1) shall include any transferor of such asset if the basis of the asset in the hands of the transferee is determined (in whole or in part) by reference to its basis in the hands of such transferor.

(3) Transitional rule. If the assets which produced the built-in deductions were acquired (either directly or by acquiring a new member) by the group on or before January 4, 1973, and the separate return limitation year in which such deductions were economically accrued ended before such date, then at the option of the taxpayer, the provisions of this paragraph before amendment by T.D. 7246 shall apply, and, in addition, if such assets were acquired on or before April 17, 1968, and the separate return limitation year in which the built-in deductions were economically accrued ended on or before such date, then at the option of the taxpayer, the provisions of § 1.1502-31A(b)(9) (as contained in the 26 C.F.R. edition revised as of April 1, 1996) shall apply in lieu of this paragraph.

(4) Exceptions. (i) Subparagraphs (1), (2), and (3) of this paragraph shall not limit built-in deductions in a taxable year with respect to assets acquired (either directly or by acquiring a new member) by the group if—

(a) The group acquired the assets more than 10 years before the first day of such taxable year, or

(b) Immediately before the group acquired the assets, the aggregate of the adjusted basis of all assets (other than cash, marketable securities, and goodwill) acquired from the transferor or owned by the new member did not exceed the fair market value of all such assets by more than 15 percent.

(ii) For purposes of subdivision (i)(b) of this subparagraph, a security is not a marketable security if immediately before the group acquired the assets—

(a) The fair market value of the security is less than 95 percent of its adjusted basis, or

(b) The transferor or new member has held the security for at least 24 months, or

(c) The security is stock in a corporation at least 50 percent of the fair market value of the outstanding stock of which is owned by the transferor or new member.

(b) Effective date. This section applies to any consolidated return years to which § 1.1502-21T does not apply. See § 1.1502-21T(g) for effective dates of that section.

T.D. 6894, 9/7/66, amend T.D. 6909, 12/29/66, T.D. 7246, 12/29/72, T.D. 7728, 10/31/80, T.D. 8677, 6/26/96.

§ 1.1502-16 Mine exploration expenditures.

(a) Section 617. *(1) In general.* If the aggregate amount of the expenditures to which section 617(a) applies, paid or incurred with respect to mines or deposits located outside the United States (as defined in section 638 and the regulations thereunder), does not exceed—

(i) $400,000 minus

(ii) All amounts deducted or deferred during the taxable year and all preceding taxable years under section 617 or section 615 of the Internal Revenue Code of 1954 and section 23(ff) of the Internal Revenue Code of 1939 by corporations which are members of the group during the taxable year (and individuals or corporations which have transferred any mineral property to any such member within the meaning of section 617(g)(2)(B)) for taxable years ending after December 31, 1950 and prior to the taxable year, then the deduction under section 617 with respect to such foreign expenditures and paragraph (c) of § 1.1502-12 for each member shall be no greater than an allocable portion of such amount hereinafter referred to as the "consolidated foreign exploration limitation." Such allocable portion shall be determined under subparagraph (2) of this paragraph. If the amount of such expenditures exceeds the consolidated foreign exploration limitation, no deduction shall be allowed with respect to such excess.

(2) Allocable portion of limitation. A member's allocable portion of the consolidated foreign exploration limitation for a consolidated return year shall be—

(i) The amount allocated by the common parent pursuant to an allocation plan adopted by the consolidated group, but in no event shall a member be allocated more than the amount it could have deducted had it filed a separate return. Such allocation plan must include a statement which also contains the total foreign exploration expenditures of each member which could have been deducted under section 617 if the member had filed a separate return. Such plan must be attached to a consolidated return filed on or before the due date of such return (including extensions of time), and may not be changed after such date, or

(ii) If no plan is filed in accordance with subdivision (i) of this subparagraph, then the portion of the consolidated foreign exploration limitation allocable to each member incurring such expenditures is an amount equal to such limitation multiplied by a fraction, the numerator of which is the amount of foreign exploration expenditures which could have been deducted under section 617 by such member had it filed a separate return and the denominator of which is the aggregate of such amounts for all members of the group.

(b) Section 615. *(1) In general.* If the aggregate amount of the expenditures, to which section 615(a) applies, which are paid or incurred by the members of the group during any consolidated return year exceeds the lesser of—

(i) $100,000, or

(ii) $400,000 minus all such expenditures deducted (or deferred) by corporations which are members of the group during the taxable year (and individuals or corporations which have transferred any mineral property to any such member within the meaning of section 615(c)(2)(B)) for taxable years ending after December 31, 1950, and prior to the taxable year, then the deduction (or amount deferrable) under section 615 and paragraph (c) of § 1.1502-12 for each member shall be no greater than an allocable portion of such lesser amount, hereinafter referred to as the "consolidated exploration limitation." Such allocable portion shall be determined under subparagraph (2) of this paragraph.

(2) Allocable portion of limitation. A member's allocable portion of the consolidated exploration limitation for a consolidated return year shall be—

(i) The amount allocated by the common parent pursuant to an allocation plan adopted by the consolidated group, but in no event shall a member be allocated more than the amount it could have deducted (or deferred) had it filed a separate return. Such allocation plan must include a statement which also contains the total exploration expenditures of each member for the taxable year, and the expenditures of each member which could have been deducted (or deferred) under section 615 if the member had filed a separate return. Such plan must be attached to a consolidated return filed on or before the due date of such return (including extensions of time), and may not be changed after such date, or

(ii) If no plan is filed in accordance with subdivision (i) of this subparagraph, then the portion of the consolidated limitation allocable to each member incurring such expenditures is an amount equal to such limitation multiplied by a fraction, the numerator of which is the amount which could have been deducted (or deferred) under section 615 by such member had it filed a separate return and the denominator of which is the aggregate of such amounts for all members of the group.

(c) Examples. The provisions of this section may be illustrated by the following examples:

Example (1). Corporation X and its wholly owned subsidiaries, corporations Y and Z, file a consolidated return for the calendar year 1971. None of the corporations have incurred exploration expenditures described in section 617 in previous years. During 1971, X incurred foreign exploration expenditures of $30,000, Y of $20,000, and Z of $40,000. The amount of foreign exploration expenditures deductible under section 617 for purposes of computing separate taxable income under § 1.1502-12 will be the amount actually expended by each corporation.

Example (2). Assume the same facts as in example (1) except that prior to 1971, X, Y, and Z had deducted (or deferred) under section 615 and 617 a total of $300,000 of exploration expenditures. During 1971, with respect to deposits located outside the United States X incurred exploration expenditures of $25,000, Y of $75,000, and Z of $125,000. The consolidated exploration limitation under paragraph (a) of this section with respect to the foreign deposits (there is no limitation with respect to the domestic expenditures) is $100,000. X may allocate the $100,000 in any manner among the three members, except that X may not be allocated more than $25,000 nor Y more than $75,000, the amount actually expended by X and Y and which they could have deducted had they each filed a separate return. If the allocation is not made in accordance with paragraph (a)(2)(i) of this section, the $100,000 limitation will be allocated under paragraph (a)(2)(ii) of this section as follows:

Corporation	Expenditure	Fraction	Limitation	Allocable Portion
X	$ 25,000	$\frac{25,000}{200,000}$	× $100,000	= $12,500
Y	$ 75,000	$\frac{75,000}{200,000}$	× $100,000	= $37,500
Z	$125,000	$\frac{100,000}{200,000}$	× $100,000	= $50,000

The denominator of $200,000 was calculated as follows:

X = $25,000
Y = $75,000
Z = $100,000 (maximum amount allowed if filed separately)

Total $200,000.

Example (3). Assume the same facts as in example (2) and that on January 1, 1971, X acquired all of the stock of corporation T which prior to its taxable year beginning January 1, 1971, had previously deducted (or deferred) $310,000 of exploration expenditures. Assume further that in 1971 X incurred $25,000 of foreign exploration expenditures, Y $50,000, T $50,000, and Z none. A consolidated return is filed for 1971. None of the expenditures may be deducted under section 617 since the consolidated exploration limitation is zero. The limitation is zero since the aggregate amount of previously deducted (or deferred) exploration expenditures by the members of the group exceeds $400,000. (The total of such expenditures is $410,000, of which $310,000 is attributable to T and, assuming the allocation of the limitation in example (2) is made under paragraph (a)(2)(ii) of this section, $12,500 is attributable to X, $37,500 to Y, and $50,000 to Z.

Example (4). Assume the same facts as in example (3) except that on December 31, 1971, X sold all of the stock in Z to an unrelated party. The consolidated exploration limitation for 1972 will be $40,000, computed by subtracting from $400,000, the aggregate amount of previously deducted (or deferred) exploration expenditures incurred by the members of the group prior to 1972. (The total of such expenditures is $360,000, of which $12,500 is attributable to X, $37,500 to Y and $310,000 to T.) Amounts previously deducted (or deferred) by Z are not taken into account since it was not a member of the group at any time during 1972. Amounts previously deducted (or deferred) by Z shall be taken into account by it for subsequent separate return years.

T.D. 6894, 9/7/66, amend T.D. 7192, 6/29/72.

§ 1.1502-17 Methods of accounting.

(a) General rule. The method of accounting to be used by each member of the group shall be determined in accordance with the provisions of section 446 as if such member filed a separate return. For treatment of depreciable property after a transfer within the group, see paragraph (g) of § 1.1502-12.

(b) Adjustments required if method of accounting changes. *(1) General rule.* If a member of a group changes its method of accounting for a consolidated return year, the terms and conditions prescribed by the Commissioner under section 446(e), including section 481(a) where applicable, shall apply to the member. If the requirements of section 481(b) are met because applicable adjustments under section 481(a) are substantial, the increase in tax for any prior year shall be computed upon the basis of a consolidated return or a separate return, whichever was filed for such prior year.

(2) Changes in method of accounting for intercompany transactions. If a member changes its method of accounting for intercompany transactions for a consolidated return year, the change in method generally will be effected on a cut-off basis.

(c) Anti-avoidance rules. *(1) General rule.* If one member (B) directly or indirectly acquires an activity of another member (S), or undertakes S's activity, with the principal purpose to avail the group of an accounting method that would be unavailable (or would be unavailable without securing consent from the Commissioner) if S and B were treated as divisions of a single corporation, B must use the accounting method for the acquired or undertaken activity determined under paragraph (c)(2) of this section or must secure consent from the Commissioner under applicable administrative procedures to use a different method.

(2) Treatment as divisions of a single corporation. B must use the method of accounting that would be required if B acquired the activity from S in a transaction to which section 381 applied. Thus, the principles of section 381(c)(4) and (c)(5) apply to resolve any conflicts between the accounting methods of S and B, and the acquired or undertaken activity is treated as having the accounting method used by S. Appropriate adjustments are made to treat all acquisitions or undertakings that are part of the same plan or arrangement as a single acquisition or undertaking.

(d) Examples. The provisions of this section are illustrated by the following examples:

Example (1). Separate return treatment generally. X and its wholly-owned subsidiary Y filed separate returns for their calendar years ending December 31, 1965. During calendar year 1965, X employed an accrual method of accounting, established a reserve for bad debts, and elected under section 171 to amortize bond premiums with respect to its fully taxable bonds. During calendar year 1965, Y employed the cash receipts and disbursements method, used the specific charge-off method with respect to its bad debts, and did not elect to amortize bond premiums under section 171 with respect to its bonds. X and Y filed a consolidated return for 1966. For 1966 X and Y must continue to compute income under their respective methods of accounting (unless a change in method under section 446 is made).

Example (2). Adopting methods. Corporation P is a member of a consolidated group. P provides consulting services to customers under various agreements. For one type of customer, P's agreements require payment only when the contract is completed (payment-on-completion contracts). P uses an overall accrual method of accounting. Accordingly, P takes its income from consulting contracts into account when earned, received, or due, whichever is earlier. With the principal purpose to avoid seeking the consent of the Commissioner to change its method of accounting for the payment-on-completion contracts to the cash method, P forms corporation S, and S begins to render services to those customers subject to the payment-on-completion contracts. P continues to render services to those customers not subject to these contracts.

(b) Under paragraph (c) of this section, S must account for the consulting income under the payment-on-completion contracts on an accrual method rather than adopting the cash method contemplated by P.

Example (3). Changing inventory sub-method.

(a) Corporation P is a member of a consolidated group. P operates a manufacturing business that uses dollar-value LIFO, and has built up a substantial LIFO reserve. P has historically manufactured all its inventory and has used one natural business unit pool. P begins purchasing goods identical to its own finished goods from a foreign supplier, and is concerned that it must establish a separate resale pool under § 1.472-8(c). P anticipates that it will begin to purchase, rather than manufacture, a substantial portion of its inventory, resulting in a recapture of most of its LIFO reserve because of decrements in its manufacturing pool. With the principal purpose to avoid the decrements, P forms corporation S in Year 1. S operates as a distributor to nonmembers, and P sells all of its existing inventories to S. S adopts LIFO, and elects dollar-value LIFO with one resale pool. Thereafter, P continues to manufacture and purchase inventory, and to sell it to S for resale to nonmembers. P's intercompany gain from sales to S is taken into account under § 1.1502-13. S maintains its Year 1 base dollar value of inventory so that P will not be required to take its intercompany items (which include the effects of the LIFO reserve recapture) into account.

(b) Under paragraph (c) of this section, S must maintain two pools (manufacturing and resale) to the same extent that P would be required to maintain those pools under § 1.472-8 if it had not formed S.

(e) Effective dates. Paragraph (b) of this section applies to changes in method of accounting effective for years beginning on or after July 12, 1995. For changes in method of accounting effective for years beginning before that date, see § 1.1502-17 (as contained in the 26 CFR part 1 edition revised as of April 1, 1995). Paragraphs (c) and (d) apply with respect to acquisitions occurring or activities undertaken in years beginning on or after July 12, 1995.

T.D. 6894, 9/7/66, amend T.D. 8597, 7/12/95.

§ 1.1502-18 Inventory adjustment.

(a) Definition of intercompany profit amount. For purposes of this section, the term "intercompany profit amount" for a taxable year means an amount equal to the profits of a corporation (other than those profits which such corporation has elected not to defer pursuant to § 1.1502-13(c)(3) or which have been taken into account pursuant to § 1.1502-13(f)(1)(viii)) arising in transactions with other members of the group with respect to goods which are, at the close of such corporation's taxable year, included in the inventories of any member of the group. See § 1.1502-13(c)(2) with respect to the determination of profits. See the last sentence of § 1.1502-13(f)(1)(i) for rules for determining which goods are considered to be disposed of outside the group and therefore not included in inventories of members.

(b) Addition of initial inventory amount to taxable income. If a corporation—

(1) Is a member of a group filing a consolidated return for the taxable year,

(2) Was a member of such group for its immediately preceding taxable year, and

(3) Filed a separate return for such preceding year,

then the intercompany profit amount of such corporation for such separate return year (hereinafter referred to as the "initial inventory amount") shall be added to the income of such corporation for the consolidated return year (or years) in which the goods to which the initial inventory amount is attributable are disposed of outside the group or such corporation becomes a nonmember. Such amount shall be treated as gain from the sale or exchange of property which is neither a capital asset nor property described in section 1231.

(c) Recovery of initial inventory amount. *(1) Unrecovered inventory amount.* The term "unrecovered inventory amount" for any consolidated return year means the lesser of—

(i) The intercompany profit amount for such year, or

(ii) The initial inventory amount.

However, if a corporation ceases to be a member of the group during a consolidated return year, its unrecovered inventory amount for such year shall be considered to be zero.

(2) Recovery during consolidated return years. (i) To the extent that the unrecovered inventory amount of a corpora-

tion for a consolidated return year is less than such amount for its immediately preceding year, such decrease shall be treated for such year by such corporation as a loss from the sale or exchange of property which is neither a capital asset nor property described in section 1231.

(ii) To the extent that the unrecovered inventory amount for a consolidated return year exceeds such amount for the preceding year, such increase shall be treated as gain from the sale or exchange of property which is neither a capital asset nor property described in section 1231.

(3) Recovery during first separate return year. For the first separate return year of a member following a consolidated return year, the unrecovered inventory amount for such consolidated return year (minus any part of the initial inventory amount which has not been added to income pursuant to paragraph (b) of this section) shall be treated as a loss from the sale or exchange of property which is neither a capital asset nor property described in section 1231.

(4) Acquisition of group. For purposes of this section, a member of a group shall not become a nonmember or be considered as filing a separate return solely because of a termination of the group (hereinafter referred to as the "terminating group") resulting from—

(i) The acquisition by a nonmember corporation of (a) the assets of the common parent in a reorganization described in subparagraph (A), (C), or (D) (but only if the requirements of subparagraphs (A) and (B) of section 354(b)(1) are met) of section 368(a)(1), or (b) stock of the common parent, or

(ii) The acquisition (in a transaction to which § 1.1502-75(d)(3) applies) by a member of (a) the assets of a nonmember corporation in a reorganization referred to in subdivision (i) of this subparagraph, or (b) stock of a nonmember corporation,

if all the members of the terminating group (other than such common parent if its assets are acquired) immediately before the acquisition are members immediately after the acquisition of another group (hereinafter referred to as the "succeeding group") which files a consolidated return for the first taxable year ending after the date of acquisition. The members of the succeeding group shall succeed to any initial inventory amount and to any unrecovered inventory amount of members of the terminating group. This subparagraph shall not apply with respect to acquisitions occurring before August 25, 1971.

(d) Examples. The provisions of paragraphs (a), (b), and (c) of this section may be illustrated by the following examples:

Example (1). Corporations P, S, and T report income on the basis of a calendar year. Such corporations file separate returns for 1965. P manufactures widgets which it sells to both S and T, who act as distributors. The inventories of S and T at the close of 1965 are comprised of widgets which they purchased from P and with respect to which P derived profits of $5,000 and $8,000, respectively. P, S, and T file a consolidated return for 1966. During 1966, P sells widgets to S and T with respect to which it derives profits of $7,000 and $10,000, respectively. The inventories of S and T as of December 31, 1966, are comprised of widgets on which P derived net profits of $4,000 and $8,000, respectively. P's initial inventory amount is $13,000, P's intercompany profit amount for 1965 (such $13,000 amount is the profits of P with respect to goods sold to S and T and included in their inventories at the close of 1965). Assuming that S and T identify their goods on a first-in, first-out basis, the entire opening inventory amount of $13,000 is added to P's income for 1966 as gain from the sale or exchange of property which is neither a capital asset nor properly described in section 1231, since the goods to which the initial inventory amount is attributable were disposed of in 1966 outside the group. However, since P's unrecovered inventory amount for 1966, $12,000 (the intercompany profit amount for the year, which is less than the initial inventory amount), is less than the unrecovered inventory amount for 1965, $13,000, this decrease of $1,000 is treated by P for 1966 as a loss from the sale or exchange of property which is neither a capital asset nor property described in section 1231.

Example (2). Assume the same facts as in example (1) and that at the close of 1967, a consolidated return year, the inventories of S and T are comprised of widgets on which P derived profits of $5,000 and $3,000, respectively. Since P's unrecovered inventory amount for 1967, $8,000, is less than $12,000, the unrecovered inventory amount for 1966, this decrease of $4,000 is treated by P for 1967 as a loss from the sale or exchange of property which is neither a capital asset nor property described in section 1231.

Example (3). Assume the same facts as in examples (1) and (2) and that in 1968, a consolidated return year, P's intercompany profit amount is $11,000. P will report $3,000 (the excess of $11,000, P's unrecovered inventory amount for 1968, over $8,000, P's unrecovered inventory amount for 1967) for 1968 as a gain from the sale or exchange of property which is neither a capital asset nor property described in section 1231.

Example (4). Assume the same facts as in examples (1), (2), and (3) and that in 1969 P, S, and T file separate returns. P will report $11,000 (its unrecovered inventory amount for 1968, $11,000, minus the portion of the initial inventory amount which has not been added to income during 1966, 1967, and 1968, zero) as a loss from the sale or exchange of property which is neither a capital asset nor property described in section 1231.

Example (5). Corporations P and S file a consolidated return for the first time for the calendar year 1966. P manufacturers machines and sells them to S, which sells them to users throughout the country. At the close of 1965, S has on hand 20 machines which it purchased from P and with respect to which P derived profits of $3,500. During 1966, P sells 6 machines to S on which it derives profits of $1,300, and S sells 5 machines which it had on hand at the beginning of the year (S specifically identifies the machines which it sells) and on which P had derived profits of $900. P's initial inventory amount is $3,500, of which $900 is added to P's income in 1966 as gain from the sale or exchange of property which is neither a capital asset nor property described in section 1231, since such $900 amount is attributable to goods disposed of in 1966 outside the group, which goods were included in S's inventory at the close of 1965. If P and S continue to file consolidated returns, the remaining $2,600 of the initial inventory amount will be added to P's income as the machines on which such profits were derived are disposed of outside the group.

Example (6). Assume that in example (5) S had elected to inventory its goods under section 472 (relating to last-in, first-out inventories). None of P's initial inventory amount of $3,500 would be added to P's income in 1966, since none of the goods to which such amount is attributable would be considered to be disposed of during such year under the last-in, first-out method of identifying inventories.

(e) Section 381 transfer. If a member of the group is a transferor or distributor of assets to another member of the group within the meaning of section 381(a), then the acquiring corporation shall be treated as succeeding to the initial inventory amount of the transferor or distributor corporation to the extent that as of the date of distribution or transfer such amount has not yet been added to income. Such amount shall then be added to the acquiring corporation's income under the provisions of paragraph (b) of this section. For purposes of applying paragraph (c) of this section—

(1) The initial inventory amount of the transferor or distributor corporation shall be added to such amount of the acquiring corporation as of the close of the acquiring corporation's taxable year in which the date of distribution or transfer occurs, and

(2) The unrecovered inventory amount of the transferor or distributor corporation for its taxable year preceding the taxable year of the group in which the date of distribution or transfer occurs shall be added to such amount of the acquiring corporation.

(f) Transitional rules for years before 1966. *(1) In general.* If—

(i) A group filed a consolidated return for the taxable year immediately preceding the first taxable year to which this section applies,

(ii) Any member of such group made an opening adjustment to its inventory pursuant to paragraph (b) of § 1.1502-39A, (as contained in the 26 C.F.R. edition revised as of April 1, 1996) and

(iii) Paragraph (c) of § 1.1502-39A (as contained in the 26 C.F.R. edition revised as of April 1, 1996) has not been applicable for any taxable year subsequent to the taxable year for which such adjustment was made,

then subparagraphs (2) and (3) of this paragraph shall apply.

(2) Closing adjustment to inventory. (i) For the first consolidated return year to which this section applies, the increase in inventory prescribed in paragraph (c) of § 1.1502-39A (as contained in the 26 C.F.R. edition revised as of April 1, 1996) shall be made as if such year were a separate return year.

(ii) For the first separate return year of a member to which this section applies the adjustment to inventory (whether an increase or a decrease) prescribed in paragraph (c) of § 1.1502-39A, (as contained in the 26 C.F.R. edition revised as of April 1, 1996) minus any adjustment already made pursuant to subdivision (i) of this subparagraph, shall be made to the inventory of such member.

(3) Addition and recovery of initial inventory amount. Each selling member shall treat as an initial inventory amount its share of the net amount by which the inventories of all members are increased pursuant to subparagraph (2)(i) of this paragraph for the first taxable year to which this section applies. A member's share shall be such net amount multiplied by a fraction, the numerator of which is its initial inventory amount (computed under paragraph (b) as if such taxable year were its first consolidated return year), and the denominator of which is the sum of such initial inventory amounts of all members. Such initial inventory amount shall be added to the income of such selling member and shall be recovered at the time and in the manner prescribed in paragraphs (b) and (c) of this section.

(4) Example. The provisions of this paragraph may be illustrated by the following example:

Example. (i) Corporations P, S, and T file consolidated returns for calendar 1966, having filed consolidated returns continuously since 1962. P is a wholesale distributor of groceries selling to chains of supermarkets, including those owned by S and T. The opening inventories of S and T for 1962 were reduced by $40,000 and $80,000, respectively, pursuant to paragraph (b) of § 1.1502-39A (as contained in the 26 C.F.R. edition revised as of April 1, 1996). At the close of 1965, S and T have on hand in their inventories goods on which P derived profits of $80,000 and $90,000, respectively. The inventories of S and T at the close of 1966 include goods which they purchased from P during the year on which P derived profits of $85,000 and $105,000, respectively.

(ii) The opening inventories of S and T for 1966, the first year to which this section applies, are increased by $40,000 and $80,000, respectively, pursuant to the provisions of subparagraph (2)(i) of this paragraph. P will take into account (as provided in paragraphs (b) and (c) of this section) an initial inventory amount of $120,000 as of the beginning of 1966, the net amount by which the inventories of S and T were increased in such year. Since the increases in the inventories of S and T are the maximum allowable under paragraph (c) of § 1.1502-39A (as contained in the 26 C.F.R. edition revised as of April 1, 1996) (i.e., the amount by which such inventories were originally decreased), no further adjustments will be made pursuant to subparagraph (2)(ii) of this paragraph to such inventories in the event that separate returns are subsequently filed.

(5) Election not to eliminate. If a group filed a consolidated return for the taxable year immediately preceding the first taxable year to which this section applies, and for such preceding year the members of the group did not eliminate gain or loss on intercompany inventory transactions pursuant to the adoption under § 1.1502-31A(b)(1) (as contained in the 26 C.F.R. edition revised as of April 1, 1996) of a consistent accounting practice taking into account such gain or loss, then for purposes of this section each member shall be treated as if it had filed a separate return for such immediately preceding year.

(g) Transitional rules for years beginning on or after July 12, 1995. Paragraphs (a) through (f) of this section do not apply for taxable years beginning on or after July 12, 1995. Any remaining unrecovered inventory amount of a member under paragraph (c) of this section is recovered in the first taxable year beginning on or after July 12, 1995, under the principles of paragraph (c)(3) of this section by treating the first taxable year as the first separate return year of the member. The unrecovered inventory amount can be recovered only to the extent it was previously included in taxable income. The principles of this section apply, with appropriate adjustments, to comparable amounts under paragraph (f) of this section.

T.D. 6894, 9/7/66, amend T.D. 7246, 12/29/72, T.D. 8597, 7/12/95, T.D. 8677, 6/26/96.

§ 1.1502-19 Excess loss accounts.

Caution: The Treasury has not yet amended Reg § 1.1502-19 to reflect changes made by P.L. 105-34, M.L. 104-7.

(a) In general. *(1) Purpose.* This section provides rules for a member (M) to include in income its excess loss account in the stock of another member (S). The purpose of the excess loss account is to recapture in consolidated taxable income M's negative adjustments with respect to S's stock (e.g., under § 1.1502-32 from S's deductions, losses, and distributions), to the extent the negative adjustments exceed M's basis in the stock. This section also provides rules for eliminating losses and other attributes attributable to S in certain cases in which S stock becomes worthless or S ceases to be a member and does not have a separate return year.

(2) Excess loss accounts. (i) In general. M's basis in S's stock is adjusted under the consolidated return regulations and other rules of law. Negative adjustments may exceed M's basis in S's stock. The resulting negative amount is M's excess loss account in S's stock. For example:

(A) Once M's negative adjustments under § 1.1502-32 exceed its basis in S's stock, the excess is M's excess loss account in the S stock. If M has further adjustments, they first increase or decrease the excess loss account.

(B) If M forms S by transferring property subject to liabilities in excess of basis, § 1.1502-80 (d) provides for the nonapplicability of section 357(c) and the resulting negative basis under section 358 is M's excess loss account in the S stock.

(ii) Treatment as negative basis. M's excess loss account is treated for all Federal income tax purposes as basis that is a negative amount, and a reference to M's basis in S's stock includes a reference to M's excess loss account.

(3) Application of other rules of law, duplicative recapture. See § 1.1502-80(a) regarding the general applicability of other rules of law and a limitation on duplicative adjustments and recapture.

(b) Excess loss account taken into account as income or gain. *(1) Operating rules.* (i) General rule. Except as provided in paragraph (b)(1)(ii) of this section, if M is treated under this section as disposing of a share of S's stock, M takes into account its excess loss account in the share as income or gain from the disposition.

(ii) Special limitation on amount taken into account. Notwithstanding paragraph (b)(1)(i) of this section, if M is treated as disposing of a share of S's stock as a result of the application of paragraph (c)(1)(iii)(B) of this section, the aggregate amount of its excess loss account in the shares of S's stock that M takes into account as income or gain from the disposition shall not exceed the amount of S's indebtedness that is discharged that is neither included in gross income nor treated as tax-exempt income under § 1.1502-32(b)(3)(ii)(C)(1). If more than one share of S's stock has an excess loss account, such excess loss accounts shall be taken into account pursuant to the preceding sentence, to the extent possible, in a manner that equalizes the excess loss accounts in S's shares that have an excess loss account.

(iii) Treatment of disposition. Except as provided in paragraph (b)(4) of this section, the disposition is treated as a sale or exchange for purposes of determining the character of the income or gain.

(iv) Reduction of attributes in the case of certain dispositions by worthlessness or where S ceases to be a member and does not become a nonmember. If this paragraph (b)(1)(iv) applies, any net operating or capital loss carryover that is attributable to S, including any losses that would be apportioned to S under the principles of § 1.1502-21(b)(2) if S had a separate return year, any deferred deductions attributable to S, including S's portion of such consolidated tax attributes (for example, consolidated excess charitable contributions that would be apportioned to S under the principles of § 1.1502-79(e) if S had a separate return year), and any credit carryover attributable to S, including any consolidated credits that would be apportioned to S under the principles of § 1.1502-79 if S had a separate return year, are eliminated. Attributes other than consolidated tax attributes (determined as of the disposition) are eliminated under this paragraph (b)(1)(iv) immediately before the disposition resulting in the application of this paragraph (b)(1)(iv). The elimination of attributes under this paragraph (b)(1)(iv) is not a noncapital, nondeductible expense described in § 1.1502-32(b)(2)(iii). This paragraph (b)(1)(iv) applies if--

(A) A share of S stock becomes worthless under section 165, the requirements of paragraph (c)(1)(iii) of this section are satisfied, M does not recognize a net deduction or loss on the S stock, and S is a member of the group on the day following the last day of the group's taxable year during which the share becomes worthless; or

(B) M recognizes any amount that is not a net deduction or loss on the stock of S in a transaction in which S ceases to be a member and does not become a nonmember.

(2) Nonrecognition or deferral. (i) In general. M's income or gain under paragraph (b)(1) of this section is subject to any nonrecognition or deferral rules applicable to the disposition. For example, if S liquidates and the exchange of M's stock in S is subject to section 332, or M transfers all of its assets (including S's stock) to S in a reorganization to which section 361(a) applies, M's income or gain from the excess loss account is not recognized under these rules.

(ii) Nonrecognition or deferral inapplicable. If M's income or gain under paragraph (b)(1) of this section is from a disposition described in paragraph (c)(1)(ii) or (iii) of this section (relating to deconsolidations and worthlessness), the income or gain is taken into account notwithstanding any nonrecognition or deferral rules (even if the disposition is also described in paragraph (c)(1)(i) of this section). For example, if M transfers S's stock to a nonmember in a transaction to which section 351 applies, M's income or gain from the excess loss account is taken into account.

(3) Tiering up in chains. If the stock of more than one subsidiary is disposed of in the same transaction, the income or gain under this section is taken into account in the order of the tiers, from the lowest to the highest.

(4) Insolvency. (i) In general. Gain under this section is treated as ordinary income to the extent of the amount by which S is insolvent (within the meaning of section 108 (d)(3)) immediately before the disposition. For this purpose S's liabilities include any amount to which preferred stock would be entitled if S were liquidated immediately before the disposition, and any former liabilities that were discharged to the extent the discharge was treated as tax-exempt income under § 1.1502-32(b)(3)(ii)(C) (special rule for discharges).

(ii) Reduction for amount of distributions. The amount treated as ordinary income under this paragraph (b)(4) is reduced to the extent it exceeds the amount of M's excess loss account redetermined without taking into account S's distributions to M to which § 1.1502-32(b)(2)(iv) applies.

(c) Disposition of stock. For purposes of this section:

(1) In general. M is treated as disposing of a share of S's stock:

(i) Transfer, cancellation, etc. At the time—

(A) M transfers or otherwise ceases to own the share for Federal income tax purposes, even if no gain or loss is taken into account; or

(B) M takes into account gain or loss (in whole or in part) with respect to the share.

(ii) Deconsolidation. At the time—

(A) M becomes a nonmember, or a nonmember determines its basis in the share (or any other asset) by reference to M's basis in the share, directly or indirectly, in whole or in part (e.g., under section 362); or

(B) S becomes a nonmember, or M's basis in the share is reflected, directly or indirectly, in whole or in part, in the basis of any asset other than member stock (e.g., under section 1071).

(iii) Worthlessness. At the time—

(A) All of S's assets (other than its corporate charter and those assets, if any, necessary to satisfy state law minimum capital requirements to maintain corporate existence) are treated as disposed of, abandoned, or destroyed for Federal income tax purposes (for example, under section 165(a) or § 1.1502-80(c), or, if S's asset is stock of a lower-tier member, the stock is treated as disposed of under this paragraph (c)). An asset of S is not considered to be disposed of or abandoned to the extent the disposition is in complete liquidation of S under section 332 or is in exchange for consideration (other than relief from indebtedness);

(B) An indebtedness of S is discharged, if any part of the amount discharged is not included in gross income and is not treated as tax-exempt income under § 1.1502-32 (b)(3)(ii)(C); or

(C) A member takes into account a deduction or loss for the uncollectibility of an indebtedness of S, and the deduction or loss is not matched in the same tax year by S's taking into account a corresponding amount of income or gain from the indebtedness in determining consolidated taxable income.

(2) Becoming a nonmember. A member is treated as becoming a nonmember if it has a separate return year (including another group's consolidated return year). For example, S may become a nonmember if it issues additional stock to nonmembers, but S does not become a nonmember as a result of its complete liquidation. A disposition under paragraph (c)(1)(ii) of this section must be taken into account in the consolidated return of the group. For example, if a group ceases under § 1.1502-75 (c) to file a consolidated return as of the close of its consolidated return year, the disposition under paragraph (c)(1)(ii) of this section is treated as occurring immediately before the close of the year. If S becomes a nonmember because M sells S's stock to a nonmember, M's sale is a disposition under both paragraphs (c)(1)(i) and (ii) of this section. If a group terminates under § 1.1502-75(d) because the common parent is the only remaining member, the common parent is not treated as having a deconsolidation event under paragraph (c)(1)(ii) of this section.

(3) Exception for acquisition of group. (i) Application. This paragraph (c)(3) applies only if a consolidated group (the terminating group) ceases to exist as a result of—

(A) The acquisition of either the assets of the common parent of the terminating group in a reorganization described in section 381(a)(2), or the stock of the common parent of the terminating group; or

(B) The application of the principles of § 1.1502-75(d)(2) or (d)(3).

(ii) General rule. Paragraph (c)(1)(ii) of this section does not apply solely by reason of the termination of a group in a transaction to which this paragraph (c)(3) applies, if there is a surviving group that is, immediately thereafter, a consolidated group. Instead, the surviving group is treated as the terminating group for purposes of applying this section to the terminating group. This treatment does not apply, however, to members of the terminating group that are not members of the surviving group immediately after the terminating group ceases to exist (e.g., under section 1504(a)(3) relating to reconsolidation, or section 1504(c) relating to includible insurance companies).

(d) Special allocation of basis in connection with an adjustment or determination. *(1) Excess loss account in original shares.* If a member has an excess loss account in shares of a class of S's stock at the time of a basis adjustment or determination under the Internal Revenue Code with respect to shares of the same class of S's stock owned by the member, the adjustment or determination is allocated first to equalize and eliminate that member's excess loss account. See § 1.1502-32(c) for similar allocations of investment adjustments to prevent or eliminate excess loss accounts.

(2) Excess loss account in new S shares. If a member would otherwise determine shares of a class of S's stock (new shares) to have an excess loss account and such member owns one or more other shares of the same class of S's stock, the basis of such other shares is allocated to eliminate and equalize any excess loss account that would otherwise be in the new shares.

(e) Anti-avoidance rule. If any person acts with a principal purpose contrary to the purposes of this section, to avoid the effect of the rules of this section or apply the rules of this section to avoid the effect of any other provision of the consolidated return regulations, adjustments must be made as necessary to carry out the purposes of this section.

(f) Predecessors and successors. For purposes of this section, any reference to a corporation (or to a share of the corporation's stock) includes a reference to a successor or predecessor (or to a share of stock of a predecessor or successor), as the context may require.

(g) Examples. For purposes of the examples in this section, unless otherwise stated, M owns all 100 shares of the only class of S's stock and S owns all 100 shares of the only class of T's stock, the stock is owned for the entire year, T owns no stock of lower-tier members, the tax year of all persons is the calendar year, all persons use the accrual method of accounting, the facts set forth the only corporate activity, all transactions are between unrelated persons, and tax liabilities are disregarded. The principles of this section are illustrated by the following examples.

Example (1). Taxable disposition of stock.

(a) Facts. M has a $150 basis in S's stock, and S has a $100 basis in T's stock. For Year 1, M has $500 of ordinary income, S has no income or loss, and T has a $200 ordinary loss. S sells T's stock to a nonmember for $60 at the close of Year 1.

(b) Analysis. Under paragraph (c) of this section, the sale is a disposition of T's stock at the close of Year 1 (the day of the sale). Under § 1.1502-32(b), T's loss results in S having a $100 excess loss account in T's stock immediately before the sale. Under paragraph (b)(1) of this section, S takes into account the $100 excess loss account as an additional $100 of gain from the sale. Consequently, S takes into account a $160 gain from the sale in determining the group's consolidated taxable income. Under § 1.1502-32(b), T's $200 loss and S's $160 gain result in a net $40 decrease in M's basis in S's stock as of the close of Year 1, from $150 to $110.

(c) Intercompany sale followed by sale to nonmember. The facts are the same as in paragraph (a) of this Example 1, except that S sells T's stock to M for $60 at the close of

Year 1, and M sells T's stock to a nonmember at a gain at the beginning of Year 5. Under paragraph (c) of this section, S's sale is treated as a disposition of T's stock at the close of Year 1 (the day of the sale). Under § 1.1502-13 and paragraph (b)(2) of this section, S's $160 gain from the sale is deferred and taken into account in Year 5 as a result of M's sale of the T stock. Under § 1.1502-32 (b), the absorption of T's $200 loss in Year 1 results in M having a $50 excess loss account in S's stock at the close of Year 1. In Year 5, S's $160 gain taken into account eliminates M's excess loss account in S's stock and increases M's basis in the stock to $110.

(d) Intercompany distribution followed by sale to a nonmember. The facts are the same as in paragraph (a) of this Example 1, except that the value of the T stock is $60 and S declares and distributes a dividend of all of the T stock to M at the close of Year 1, and M sells the T stock to a nonmember at a gain at the beginning of Year 5. Under paragraph (c) of this section, S's distribution is treated as a disposition of T's stock at the close of Year 1 (the day of the distribution). S's $100 excess loss account in T's stock is treated as additional gain under section 311(b) from the distribution. Under § 301(d), M's basis in the T stock is $60. Under § 1.1502-13, and paragraph (b)(2) of this section, S's $160 gain from the distribution is deferred and taken into account in Year 5 as a result of M's sale of the T stock. Under § 1.1502-32 (b), T's $200 loss and S's $60 distribution result in M having a $110 excess loss account in S's stock at the close of Year 1. In Year 5, S's $160 gain taken into account eliminates M's excess loss account in S's stock and increases M's basis in the stock to $50.

Example (2). Basis determinations under the Internal Revenue Code in intercompany reorganizations—transfer of shares without an excess loss account. (i) Facts. M owns all of the sole class of stock of each of S and T. M has 150 shares of S stock that it acquired on Date 1. Each S share has a $1 basis and a fair market value of $1. M has 100 shares of T stock that it acquired on Date 2. Each T share has a $1.20 excess loss account and a fair market value of $1. M transfers S's stock to T without receiving additional T stock. The transfer is an exchange described in both section 351 and section 354.

(ii) Analysis. Under sections 351 and 354, M does not recognize gain in connection with the transfer. Under § 1.358-2(a)(2)(iii), M is deemed to receive 150 shares of T stock of the same class. Without regard to the application of paragraph (d) of this section, under section 358 and § 1.358-2(a)(2)(i), M would have a $1 basis in each such share.

However, because the basis of the additional shares of T stock will be determined when M has an excess loss account in its original shares of T stock, under paragraph (d)(1) of this section, the basis that M would otherwise have in such additional shares will eliminate the excess loss account in M's original shares of T stock such that each original share of T stock will have a basis of $0 and each share of T stock deemed received will have a basis of $0.20. Then, under § 1.358-2(a)(2)(iii), the T stock is deemed to be recapitalized in a reorganization under section 368(a)(1)(E) in which M receives 100 shares of T stock (those shares M actually owns immediately after the transfer) in exchange for those 100 shares of T stock that M held immediately prior to the transfer and those 150 shares of T stock M is deemed to receive in the transfer. Under § 1.358-2(a)(2)(i), immediately after the transfer, M holds 100 shares of T stock, 60 of which take a basis of $0.50 each and 40 of which take a basis of $0 each. In addition, T takes a $1 basis in each share of S stock under section 362. (If M had actually received an additional 150 shares of T stock of the same class, paragraph (d)(1) of this section would apply to shift basis from such additional T shares to M's original T shares because the basis of the additional T stock would be determined when M had an excess loss account in its original T shares. M would have a basis of $0 in each of the original T shares and a basis of $0.20 in each of the additional T shares.)

(iii) Transfer of shares with an excess loss account. The facts are the same as in paragraph (i) of this Example 2, except that M transfers T's stock to S without receiving additional S stock. The transfer is an exchange described in both section 351 and section 354. Under paragraph (c) of this section, M's transfer is treated as a disposition of T's stock. Under sections 351 and 354 and paragraph (b)(2) of this section, M does not recognize gain from the disposition. Under § 1.358-2(a)(2)(iii), M is deemed to have received 100 shares of S stock of the same class. Without regard to the application of paragraph (d) of this section, M would have a $1.20 excess loss account in each such share. However, because M will have an excess loss account in such shares and M owns other shares of S stock of the same class, under paragraph (d)(2) of this section, the excess loss account that M would otherwise have in such shares will decrease M's basis in its original shares of S's stock such that each such original share will have a basis of $0.20 and each share deemed received will have a basis of $0. Then, under § 1.358-2(a)(2)(iii), the S stock is deemed to be recapitalized in a reorganization under section 368(a)(1)(E) in which M receives 150 shares of S stock (those shares M actually owns immediately after the transfer) in exchange for those 150 shares of S stock that M held immediately prior to the transfer and those 100 shares of S stock that M is deemed to receive in connection with the transfer. Under § 1.358-2(a)(2)(i), immediately after the transfer, M holds 150 shares of S stock, 90 of which take a basis of $0.33 each and 60 of which take a basis of $0 each. In addition, S takes an excess loss account of $1.20 in each share of T stock under section 362. (If M had actually received 100 additional shares of S stock of the same class, paragraph (d)(2) of this section would apply to shift basis from M's original S stock because M would have otherwise had an excess loss account in such additional shares and M owned other shares of S stock of the same class. The excess loss account that M would have otherwise had in such additional shares would have decreased M's basis in its original shares of S's stock. M would have had a basis of $0.20 in each of the original shares and a basis of $0 in each of the additional shares.)

(iv) Intercompany merger—shares with excess loss account retained. The facts are the same as in paragraph (i) of this Example 2, except that S merges into T in a reorganization described in section 368(a)(1)(A) (and in section 368(a)(1)(D)), and M receives 150 additional shares of T stock of the same class in the reorganization. Under section 354, M does not recognize gain. Without regard to the application of paragraph (d) of this section, under section 358 and § 1.358-2(a)(2)(i), M would have a $1 basis in each such share. However, because the basis of the additional shares of T stock will be determined when M has an excess loss account in its original shares of T stock, under paragraph (d)(1) of this section, the basis that M would otherwise have in such additional shares eliminates the excess loss account in M's original shares of T stock such that each original share of T stock has a basis of $0 and each additional share of T stock has a basis of $0.20.

(v) Intercompany merger—shares with excess loss account surrendered. The facts are the same as in paragraph (i) of this Example 2, except that T merges into S in a reorganization described in section 368(a)(1)(A) (and in section 368(a)(1)(D)), and M receives 100 additional shares of S stock of the same class in the reorganization. Under section 354 and paragraph (b)(2) of this section, M does not recognize gain from the disposition. Without regard to the application of paragraph (d) of this section, under section 358 and § 1.358-2(a)(2)(i), M would have a $1.20 excess loss account in each additional share of S stock received. However, because M would have an excess loss account in such shares and M owns other shares of S stock of the same class, under paragraph (d)(2) of this section, the excess loss account that M would otherwise have in such shares decreases M's basis in its original shares of S's stock such that each original share of S stock has a basis of $0.20 and each additional share of S stock has a basis of $0.

Example (3). Section 355 distribution of stock with an excess loss account.

(a) Facts. M has a $30 excess loss account in S's stock, and S has a $90 excess loss account in T's stock. S distributes the T stock to M in a transaction to which section 355 applies, and neither M nor S recognizes any gain or loss. At the time of the distribution, the T stock represents 33% of the value of the S stock. Following the distribution, M's basis in the S stock is allocated under § 1.358-2 in proportion to the fair market values of the S stock and the T stock.

(b) Analysis. Under paragraph (c) of this section, S's distribution of the T stock is treated as a disposition. Under section 355 (c) and paragraph (b)(2) of this section, S does not recognize any gain from the distribution. Under section 358, S's excess loss account in the T stock is eliminated, and M's $30 excess loss account in the S stock is treated as basis allocated between the S stock and the T stock based on their relative values. Consequently, M has a $20 excess loss account in the S stock and a $10 excess loss account in the T stock. (If M had a $30 basis rather than a $30 excess loss account in the S stock, S would not recognize gain, its excess loss account in the T stock would be eliminated, and M's basis in the stock of S and T would be $20 and $10, respectively.)

(c) Section 355 distribution to nonmember. The facts are the same as in paragraph (a) of this Example 3, except that M also distributes the T stock to its shareholders in a transaction to which section 355 applies. Under paragraph (c) of this section, M's distribution is treated as a disposition of T's stock. Under paragraph (b)(2) of this section, because M's disposition is described in paragraph (c)(1)(ii) of this section, M's $10 excess loss account in the T stock must be taken into account at the time of the distribution, notwithstanding the nonrecognition rules of section 355(c).

Example (4). Deconsolidation of a member.

(a) Facts. M has a $50 excess loss account in S's stock, and S has a $100 excess loss account in T's stock. T issues additional stock to a nonmember and, as a consequence, T becomes a nonmember.

(b) Analysis. Under paragraph (c)(2) of this section, S is treated as disposing of each of its shares of T's stock immediately before T becomes a nonmember. Under paragraph (b)(1) of this section, S takes into account its $100 excess loss account as gain from the sale or exchange of T's stock. Under § 1.1502-32 (b) of this section, S's $100 gain eliminates M's excess loss account in S's stock and increases M's basis in S's stock to $50.

(c) Deconsolidation of a higher-tier member. The facts are the same as in paragraph (a) of this Example 4, except that S (rather than T) issues the stock and, as a consequence, both S and T become nonmembers. Under paragraph (c)(2) of this section, M is treated as disposing of S's stock and S is treated as disposing of T's stock immediately before S and T become nonmembers. Under § 1.1502-32(b) and paragraph (b)(3) of this section, because S and T become nonmembers in the same transaction and T is the lower-tier member, S is first treated under paragraph (b)(1) of this section as taking into account its $100 excess loss account as gain from the sale or exchange of T's stock. Under § 1.1502-32(b), S's $100 gain eliminates M's excess loss account in S's stock and increases M's basis in S's stock to $50 immediately before S becomes a nonmember. Thus, only S's $100 gain is taken into account in the determination of the group's consolidated taxable income.

(d) Intercompany gain and deconsolidation. The facts are the same as in paragraph (c) of this Example 4, except that T has $30 of gain that is deferred under § 1.1502-13 and taken into account in determining consolidated taxable income immediately before T becomes a nonmember. Under § 1.1502-32(b), T's $30 gain decreases S's excess loss account in T's stock from $100 to $70 immediately before S is treated as disposing of T's stock. Under paragraph (b)(1) of this section, S is treated as taking into account its $70 excess loss account as gain from the disposition of T's stock. Under § 1.1502-32(b), S's $70 gain from the excess loss account and T's $30 deferred gain that is taken into account eliminate M's $50 excess loss account in S's stock and increase M's basis in S's stock to $50 immediately before S becomes a nonmember.

Example (5). Worthlessness.

(a) Facts. M forms S with a $150 contribution, and S borrows $150. For Year 1, S has a $50 ordinary loss that is carried over as part of the group's consolidated net operating loss. For Year 2, M has $160 of ordinary income, and S has a $160 ordinary loss. Under § 1.1502-32(b), S's loss results in M having a $10 excess loss account in S's stock. During Year 3, the value of S's assets (without taking S's liabilities into account) continues to decline and S's stock becomes worthless within the meaning of section 165(g) (without taking into account § 1.1502-80(c)). For Year 4, S has $10 of ordinary income.

(b) Analysis. Under paragraph (c)(1)(iii)(A) of this section, M is not treated as disposing of S's stock in Year 3 solely because S's stock becomes worthless within the meaning of section 165(g) (taking S's liabilities into account). In addition, because S's stock is not treated as worthless, section 382(g)(4)(D) does not prevent the Year 1 consolidated net operating loss carryover from offsetting S's $10 of income in Year 4.

(c) Discharge of indebtedness. The facts are the same as in paragraph (a) of this Example 5, except that, instead of S's stock becoming worthless within the meaning of section 165(g), S's creditor discharges $40 of S's indebtedness during Year 3, S is insolvent by more than $40 before the discharge, the discharge is excluded from the M group's gross income under section 108(a), and $40 of the $50 consolidated net operating loss carryover attributable to S is eliminated under section 108(b). Under § 1.1502-32(b)(3)(ii)(C), S's $40 of discharge income is treated as tax-exempt income because there is a corresponding decrease under § 1.1502-32(b)(3)(iii) for elimination of the loss carryover. Under paragraph (c)(1)(iii)(B) of this section, M is treated as disposing of S's stock if the amount discharged is not included in gross income and is not treated as tax-exempt income under § 1.1502-32(b)(3)(ii)(C). Because the discharge is treated as tax-exempt income, M is not treated as disposing of S's stock by reason of the discharge.

Example (6). Avoiding worthlessness.

(a) Facts. M forms S with a $100 contribution and S borrows $150. For Years 1 through 5, S has a $210 ordinary loss that is absorbed by the group. Under § 1.1502-32(b), S's loss results in M having a $110 excess loss account in S's stock. S defaults on the indebtedness, but the creditor does not discharge the debt (or initiate collection procedures). At the beginning of Year 6, S ceases any substantial operations with respect to the assets, but maintains their ownership with a principal purpose to avoid M's taking into account its excess loss account in S's stock.

(b) Analysis. Under paragraph (c)(1)(iii)(A) of this section, M's excess loss account on each of its shares of S's stock ordinarily is taken into account at the time substantially all of S's assets are treated as disposed of, abandoned, or destroyed for Federal income tax purposes. Under paragraph (e) of this section, however, S's assets are not taken into account at the beginning of Year 6 for purposes of applying paragraph (c)(1)(iii)(A) of this section. Consequently, S is treated as worthless at the beginning of Year 6, and M's $110 excess loss account is taken into account.

(h) Effective/applicability dates. *(1) Application.* This section applies with respect to determinations of the basis of (including an excess loss account in) the stock of a member in consolidated return years beginning on or after January 1, 1995. If this section applies, basis (and excess loss accounts) must be determined or redetermined as if this section were in effect for all years (including, for example, the consolidated return years of another consolidated group to the extent adjustments during those consolidated return years are still reflected). However, taxpayers may apply paragraph (c)(3)(i)(A) of this section to transactions that occurred prior to September 17, 2008. Paragraphs (a)(3), (c)(1)(iii)(A), and (c)(3)(i)(A) of this section apply with respect to determinations and transactions occurring on or after September 17, 2008. However, taxpayers may elect to apply paragraph (c)(3)(i)(A) of this section to transactions that occurred prior to September 17, 2008. The last sentence of paragraph (a)(1) and paragraph (b)(1)(iv) of this section applies with respect to dispositions on or after December 16, 2008.

(2) Dispositions of stock. (i) Dispositions of stock before effective date. If M was treated as disposing of stock of S in a tax year beginning before January 1, 1995 (including, for example, a deemed disposition because S was worthless) under the rules of this section then in effect, the amount of M's income, gain, deduction, or loss, and the stock basis reflected in that amount, are not redetermined under paragraph (h)(1) of this section. See paragraph (h)(3) of this section for the applicable rules.

(ii) Application of special limitation. If M was treated as disposing of stock of S because S was treated as worthless as a result of the application of paragraph (c)(1)(iii)(B) of this section after August 29, 2003, the amount of M's income, gain, deduction, or loss, and the stock basis reflected in that amount, are determined or redetermined with regard to paragraph (b)(1)(ii) of this section. If M was treated as disposing of stock of S because S was treated as worthless as a result of the application of paragraph (c)(1)(iii)(B) of this section on or before August 29, 2003, the group may determine or redetermine the amount of M's income, gain, deduction, or loss, and the stock basis reflected in that amount with regard to paragraph (b)(1)(ii) of this section.

(iii) Intercompany amounts. For purposes of this paragraph (h)(2), a disposition does not include a transaction to which § 1.1502-13, § 1.1502-13T, § 1.1502-14, or § 1.1502-14T applies. Instead, the transaction is deemed to occur as the income, gain, deduction, or loss (if any) is taken into account.

(iv) Intercompany reorganizations. Paragraphs (d) and (g) Example 2 of this section apply to transactions occurring on or after July 18, 2007. For transactions occurring on or after January 23, 2006, and before July 18, 2007, see § 1.1502-19T as contained in 26 CFR part 1 in effect April 1, 2007. For transactions occurring before January 23, 2006, see § 1.1502-19 as contained in 26 CFR part 1 in effect April 1, 2005.

(3) Prior law. For prior determinations, see prior regulations under section 1502 as in effect with respect to the determination. See, e.g., § 1.1502-19 as contained in the 26 CFR part 1 edition revised as of April 1, 1994. For guidance regarding determinations of the basis of the stock of a subsidiary acquired in an intercompany reorganization before January 23, 2006, see paragraph (d) and (g) Example 2 of § 1.1502-19 as contained in the 26 CFR part 1 edition revised as of April 1, 2005.

T.D. 6909, 12/29/66, amend T.D. 7246, 12/29/72, T.D. 8364, 9/13/91, T.D. 8560, 8/12/94, T.D. 9089, 8/29/2003, T.D. 9192, 3/21/2005, T.D. 9244, 1/23/2006, T.D. 9341, 7/17/2007, T.D. 9424, 9/10/2008.

PAR. 3. In § 1.1502-20, paragraph (i) is added to read as follows:

Proposed § 1.1502-20 Disposition or deconsolidation of subsidiary stock. [*For Preamble, see ¶ 152,251*]

[The text of this proposed section is the same as the text of § 1.1502-20T(i) published elsewhere in this issue of the Federal Register].

PAR. 3. Section 1.1502-20 is amended by revising paragraphs (i)(3)(v) and (i)(4) to read as follows:

Proposed § 1.1502-20 Disposition or deconsolidation of subsidiary stock. [*For Preamble, see ¶ 152,283*]

[The text of this proposed section is the same as the text of § 1.1502-20T published elsewhere in this issue of the Federal Register].

PAR. 2. Section 1.1502-20 is amended by redesignating paragraph (i)(5) as (i)(6) and by adding paragraphs (i)(3)(viii) and (i)(5) to read as follows:

Proposed § 1.1502-20 Disposition or deconsolidation of subsidiary stock. [*For Preamble, see ¶ 152,381*]

[The text of this proposed section is the same as the text of § 1.1502-20T(i)(3)(viii) and (i)(5) published elsewhere in this issue of the Federal Register.]

PAR. 2. Section 1.1502-20 is amended by:

1. Revising the first sentence of paragraph (i)(4).
2. Redesignating paragraph (i)(6) as (i)(7).
3. Adding new paragraph (i)(6).

The revisions and addition read as follows:

Proposed § 1.1502-20 Disposition or deconsolidation of subsidiary stock. [*For Preamble, see ¶ 152,591*]

* * * * *

(i) * * *

(4) [The text of proposed § 1.1502-20(i)(4) is the same as the text of § 1.1502-20T(i)(4) published elsewhere in this issue of the Federal Register.]

* * * * *

(6) [The text of proposed § 1.1502-20(i)(6) is the same as the text of § 1.1502-20T(i)(6) published elsewhere in this issue of the Federal Register.]

§ 1.1502-21 Net operating losses.

(a) Consolidated net operating loss deduction. The consolidated net operating loss deduction (or CNOL deduction) for any consolidated return year is the aggregate of the net operating loss carryovers and carrybacks to the year. The net operating loss carryovers and carrybacks consist of—

(1) Any CNOLs (as defined in paragraph (e) of this section) of the consolidated group; and

(2) Any net operating losses of the members arising in separate return years.

(b) Net operating loss carryovers and carrybacks to consolidated return and separate return years. Net operating losses of members arising during a consolidated return year are taken into account in determining the group's CNOL under paragraph (e) of this section for that year. Losses taken into account in determining the CNOL may be carried to other taxable years (whether consolidated or separate) only under this paragraph (b).

(1) Carryovers and carrybacks generally. The net operating loss carryovers and carrybacks to a taxable year are determined under the principles of section 172 and this section. Thus, losses permitted to be absorbed in a consolidated return year generally are absorbed in the order of the taxable years in which they arose, and losses carried from taxable years ending on the same date, and which are available to offset consolidated taxable income for the year, generally are absorbed on a pro rata basis. In addition, the amount of any CNOL absorbed by the group in any year is apportioned among members based on the percentage of the CNOL attributable to each member as of the beginning of the year. The percentage of the CNOL attributable to a member is determined pursuant to paragraph (b)(2)(iv)(B) of this section. Additional rules provided under the Internal Revenue Code or regulations also apply. See, e.g., section 382(l)(2)(B) (if losses are carried from the same taxable year, losses subject to limitation under section 382 are absorbed before losses that are not subject to limitation under section 382). See paragraph (c)(1)(iii) of this section, Example 2, for an illustration of pro rata absorption of losses subject to a SRLY limitation.

(2) Carryovers and carrybacks of CNOLs to separate return years. (i) In general. If any CNOL that is attributable to a member may be carried to a separate return year of the member, the amount of the CNOL that is attributable to the member is apportioned to the member (apportioned loss) and carried to the separate return year. If carried back to a separate return year, the apportioned loss may not be carried back to an equivalent, or earlier, consolidated return year of the group; if carried over to a separate return year, the apportioned loss may not be carried over to an equivalent, or later, consolidated return year of the group.

(ii) Special rules. (A) Year of departure from group. If a corporation ceases to be a member during a consolidated return year, net operating loss carryovers attributable to the corporation are first carried to the consolidated return year, then are subject to reduction under section 108 and § 1.1502-28 (regarding discharge of indebtedness income that is excluded from gross income under section 108(a)), and then are subject to reduction under § 1.1502-36 (regarding transfers of loss shares of subsidiary stock). Only the amount that is neither absorbed by the group in that year nor reduced under section 108 and § 1.1502-28 or under § 1.1502-36 may be carried to the corporation's first separate return year. For rules concerning a member departing a subgroup, see paragraph (c)(2)(vii) of this section.

(B) Offspring rule. In the case of a member that has been a member continuously since its organization (determined without regard to whether the member is a successor to any other corporation), the CNOL attributable to the member is included in the carrybacks to consolidated return years before the member's existence. If the group did not file a consolidated return for a carryback year, the loss may be carried back to a separate return year of the common parent under paragraph (b)(2)(i) of this section, but only if the common parent was not a member of a different consolidated group or of an affiliated group filing separate returns for the year to which the loss is carried or any subsequent year in the carryback period. Following an acquisition described in § 1.1502-75(d)(2) or (3), references to the common parent are to the corporation that was the common parent immediately before the acquisition.

(iii) Equivalent years. Taxable years are equivalent if they bear the same numerical relationship to the consolidated return year in which a CNOL arises, counting forward or backward from the year of the loss. For example, in the case of a member's third taxable year (which was a separate return year) that preceded the consolidated return year in which the loss arose, the equivalent year is the third consolidated return year preceding the consolidated return year in which the loss arose. See paragraph (b)(3)(iii) of this section for certain short taxable years that are disregarded in making this determination.

(iv) Operating rules. (A) Amount of CNOL attributable to a member. The amount of a CNOL that is attributable to a member shall equal the product of the CNOL and the percentage of the CNOL attributable to such member.

(B) Percentage of CNOL attributable to a member. (1) In general. Except as provided in paragraph (b)(2)(iv)(B)(2) of this section, the percentage of the CNOL attributable to a member shall equal the separate net operating loss of the member for the year of the loss divided by the sum of the separate net operating losses for that year of all members having such losses. For this purpose, the separate net operating loss of a member is determined by computing the CNOL by reference to only the member's items of income, gain, deduction, and loss, including the member's losses and deductions actually absorbed by the group in the taxable year (whether or not absorbed by the member).

(2) Special rules. (i) Carryback to a separate return year. If a portion of the CNOL attributable to a member for a taxable year is carried back to a separate return year, the percentage of the CNOL attributable to each member as of immediately after such portion of the CNOL is carried back shall be recomputed pursuant to paragraph (b)(2)(iv)(B)(2)(v) of this section.

(ii) Excluded discharge of indebtedness income. If during a taxable year a member realizes discharge of indebtedness income that is excluded from gross income under section 108(a) and such amount reduces any portion of the CNOL attributable to any member pursuant to section 108 and § 1.1502-28, the percentage of the CNOL attributable to each member as of immediately after the reduction of attributes pursuant to sections 108 and 1017 and § 1.1502-28 shall be recomputed pursuant to paragraph (b)(2)(iv)(B)(2)(v) of this section.

(iii) Departing member. If during a taxable year a member that had a separate net operating loss for the year of the CNOL ceases to be a member, the percentage of the CNOL attributable to each member as of the first day of the following consolidated return year shall be recomputed pursuant to paragraph (b)(2)(iv)(B)(2)(v) of this section.

(iv) Reduction of attributes for stock loss. If during a taxable year a member does not cease to be a member of the group and any portion of the CNOL attributable to any member is reduced under § 1.1502-36, the percentage of the CNOL attributable to each member as of immediately after the reduction of attributes under § 1.1502-36 shall be recomputed pursuant to paragraph (b)(2)(iv)(B)(2)(v) of this section.

(v) Recomputed percentage. The recomputed percentage of the CNOL attributable to each member shall equal the unabsorbed CNOL attributable to the member at the time of the recomputation divided by the sum of the unabsorbed CNOL attributable to all of the members at the time of the recomputation. For purposes of the preceding sentence, a CNOL that is reduced under section 108 and § 1.1502-28, or under § 1.1502-36, or that is otherwise permanently disallowed or eliminated, shall be treated as absorbed.

(v) Examples. For purposes of the examples in this section, unless otherwise stated, all groups file consolidated returns, all corporations have calendar taxable years, the facts set forth the only corporate activity, value means fair market value and the adjusted basis of each asset equals its value, all transactions are with unrelated persons, and the application of any limitation or threshold under section 382 is disregarded. The principles of this paragraph (b)(2) are illustrated by the following examples:

Example (1). Offspring rule.

(i) During Year 1, Individual A forms P and T, and they each file a separate return. P forms S on March 15 of Year 2, and P and S file a consolidated return. P acquires all the stock of T from Individual A at the beginning of Year 3, and T becomes a member of the P group. P's acquisition of T is not an ownership change within the meaning of section 382. P, S, and T sustain a $1,100 CNOL in Year 3 and, under paragraph (b)(2)(iv) of this section, the loss is attributable $200 to P, $300 to S, and $600 to T.

(ii) Of the $1,100 CNOL in Year 3, the $500 amount of the CNOL that is attributable to P and S ($200 + $300) may be carried to P's separate return in Year 1. Even though S was not in existence in Year 1, the $300 amount of the CNOL attributable to S may be carried back to P's separate return in Year 1 because S (unlike T) has been a member of the P group since its organization and P is a qualified parent under paragraph (b)(2)(ii)(B) of this section. To the extent not absorbed in that year, the loss may then be carried to the P group's return in Year 2. The $600 amount of the CNOL attributable to T is a net operating loss carryback to T's separate return in Year 1, and if not absorbed in Year 1, then to Year 2.

Example (2). Departing members.

(i) The facts are the same as in Example 1. In addition, on June 15 of Year 4, P sells all the stock of T. The P group's consolidated return for Year 4 includes the income of T through June 15. T files a separate return for the period from June 16 through December 31.

(ii) $600 of the Year 3 CNOL attributable to T is apportioned to T and is carried back to its separate return in Year 1. To the extent the $600 is not absorbed in T's separate return in Year 1 or Year 2, it is carried to the consolidated return in Year 4 before being carried to T's separate return in Year 4. Any portion of the loss not absorbed in T's Year 1 or Year 2 or in the P group's Year 4 is then carried to T's separate return in Year 4.

Example (3). Offspring rule following acquisition.

(i) Individual A owns all of the stock of P, the common parent of a consolidated group. In Year 1, B, an individual unrelated to Individual A, forms T. P acquires all of the stock of T at the beginning of Year 3, and T becomes a member of the P group. The P group has $200 of consolidated taxable income in Year 2, and $300 of consolidated taxable income in Year 3 (computed without regard to the CNOL deduction). At the beginning of Year 4, T forms a subsidiary, Y, in a transaction described in section 351. The P group has a $300 consolidated net operating loss in Year 4, and under paragraph (b)(2)(iv) of this section, the loss is attributable entirely to Y.

(ii) Even though Y was not in existence in Year 2, $300, the amount of the consolidated net operating loss attributable to Y, may be carried back to the P group's Year 2 consolidated return under paragraph (b)(2)(ii)(B) of this section because Y has been a member of the P group since its organization. To the extent not absorbed in that year, the loss may then be carried to the P group's consolidated return in Year 3.

(3) Special rules. (i) Election to relinquish carryback. A group may make an irrevocable election under section 172(b)(3) to relinquish the entire carryback period with respect to a CNOL for any consolidated return year. Except as provided in § 1.1502-21(b)(3)(ii)(B), the election may not be made separately for any member (whether or not it remains a member), and must be made in a separate statement entitled "THIS IS AN ELECTION UNDER § 1.1502-21(b)(3)(i) TO WAIVE THE ENTIRE CARRYBACK PERIOD PURSUANT TO SECTION 172(b)(3) FOR THE [insert consolidated return year] CNOLs OF THE CONSOLIDATED GROUP OF WHICH [insert name and employer identification number of common parent] IS THE COMMON PARENT." The statement must be filed with the group's income tax return for the consolidated return year in which the loss arises. If the consolidated return year in which the loss arises begins before January 1, 2003, the statement making the election must be signed by the common parent. If the consolidated return year in which the loss arises begins after December 31, 2002, the election may be made in an unsigned statement.

(ii) Special elections. (A) Groups that include insolvent financial institutions. For rules applicable to relinquishing the entire carryback period with respect to losses attributable to insolvent financial institutions, see § 301.6402-7 of this chapter.

(B) Acquisition of member from another consolidated group. If one or more members of a consolidated group becomes a member of another consolidated group, the acquiring group may make an irrevocable election to relinquish, with respect to all consolidated net operating losses attributable to the member, the portion of the carryback period for which the corporation was a member of another group, provided that any other corporation joining the acquiring group that was affiliated with the member immediately before it joined the acquiring group is also included in the waiver.

This election is not a yearly election and applies to all losses that would otherwise be subject to a carryback to a former group under section 172. The election must be made in a separate statement entitled "THIS IS AN ELECTION UNDER § 1.1502-21(b)(3)(ii)(B)(2) TO WAIVE THE PRE-[insert first taxable year for which the member (or members) was not a member of another group] CARRYBACK PERIOD FOR THE CNOLs attributable to [insert names and employer identification number of members]." The statement must be filed with the acquiring consolidated group's original income tax return for the year the corporation (or corporations) became a member. If the year in which the corporation (or corporations) became a member begins before January 1, 2003, the statement must be signed by the common parent and each of the members to which it applies. If the year in which the corporation (or corporations) became a member begins after December 31, 2002, the election may be made in an unsigned statement.

(C) [Reserved]. For further guidance, see § 1.1502-21T(b)(3)(ii)(C).

(iii) Short years in connection with transactions to which section 381(a) applies. If a member distributes or transfers assets to a corporation that is a member immediately after the distribution or transfer in a transaction to which section 381(a) applies, the transaction does not cause the distributor or transferor to have a short year within the consolidated return year of the group in which the transaction occurred that is counted as a separate year for purposes of determining the years to which a net operating loss may be carried.

(iv) Special status losses. [Reserved]

(c) Limitations on net operating loss carryovers and carrybacks from separate return limitation years. *(1) SRLY limitation.* (i) General rule. Except as provided in paragraph (g) of this section (relating to an overlap with section 382), the aggregate of the net operating loss carryovers and carrybacks of a member arising (or treated as arising) in SRLYs that are included in the CNOL deductions for all consolidated return years of the group under paragraph (a) of this section may not exceed the aggregate consolidated taxable income for all consolidated return years of the group determined by reference to only the member's items of income, gain, deduction, and loss. For this purpose—

(A) Consolidated taxable income is computed without regard to CNOL deductions;

(B) Consolidated taxable income takes into account the member's losses and deductions (including capital losses) actually absorbed by the group in consolidated return years (whether or not absorbed by the member);

(C) In computing consolidated taxable income, the consolidated return years of the group include only those years, including the year to which the loss is carried, that the member has been continuously included in the group's consolidated return, but exclude—

(1) For carryovers, any years ending after the year to which the loss is carried; and

(2) For carrybacks, any years ending after the year in which the loss arose; and

(D) The treatment under § 1.1502-15 of a built-in loss as a hypothetical net operating loss carryover in the year recognized is solely for purposes of determining the limitation under this paragraph (c) with respect to the loss in that year and not for any other purpose. Thus, for purposes of determining consolidated taxable income for any other losses, a built-in loss allowed under this section in the year it arises is taken into account.

(ii) Losses treated as arising in SRLYs. If a net operating loss carryover or carryback did not arise in a SRLY but is attributable to a built-in loss (as defined under § 1.1502-15), the carryover or carryback is treated for purposes of this paragraph (c) as arising in a SRLY if the built-in loss was not allowed, after application of the SRLY limitation, in the year it arose. For an illustration, see § 1.1502-15(d), Example 5. But see § 1.1502-15(g)(1).

(iii) Examples. The principles of this paragraph (c)(1) are illustrated by the following examples:

Example (1). Determination of SRLY limitation.

(i) Individual A owns P. In Year 1, Individual A forms T, and T sustains a $100 net operating loss that is carried forward. P acquires all the stock of T at the beginning of Year 2, and T becomes a member of the P group. The P group has $300 of consolidated taxable income in Year 2 (computed without regard to the CNOL deduction). Such consolidated taxable income would be $70 if determined by reference to only T's items.

(ii) T's $100 net operating loss carryover from Year 1 arose in a SRLY. See § 1.1502-1(f)(2)(iii). P's acquisition of T was not an ownership change as defined by section 382(g). Thus, the $100 net operating loss carryover is subject to the SRLY limitation in paragraph (c)(1) of this section. The SRLY limitation for Year 2 is consolidated taxable income determined by reference to only T's items, or $70. Thus, $70 of the loss is included under paragraph (a) of this section in the P group's CNOL deduction for Year 2.

(iii) The facts are the same as in paragraph (i) of this Example 1, except that such consolidated taxable income (computed without regard to the CNOL deduction and by reference to only T's items) for Year 2 is a loss (a CNOL) of $370. Because the SRLY limitation may not exceed the consolidated taxable income determined by reference to only T's items, and such items aggregate to a CNOL, T's $ 100 net operating loss carryover from Year 1 is not allowed under the SRLY limitation in Year 2. Moreover, if consolidated taxable income (computed without regard to the CNOL deduction and by reference to only T's items) did not exceed $370 in Year 3, the carryover would still be restricted under paragraph (c) of this section in Year 3, because the aggregate consolidated taxable income for all consolidated return years of the group computed by reference to only T's items would not be a positive amount.

Example (2). Net operating loss carryovers.

(i) In Year 1, Individual A forms P, and P sustains a $40 net operating loss that is carried forward. P has no income in Year 2. Individual A also owns T which sustains a net operating loss of $50 in Year 2 that is carried forward. P acquires the stock of T from Individual A during Year 3, but T is not a member of the P group for each day of the year. P and T file separate returns and sustain net operating losses of $120 and $60, respectively, for Year 3. The P group files consolidated returns beginning in Year 4. During Year 4, the P group has $160 of consolidated taxable income (computed without regard to the CNOL deduction). Such consolidated taxable income would be $70 if determined by reference to only T's items. These results are summarized as follows:

	Separate year 1	Separate year 2	Separate affiliated year 3	Consolidated year 4
P	$(40)	$0	$(120)	$ 90
T	0	(50)	(60)	70
CTI				$160

(ii) P's Year 1, Year 2, and Year 3 are not SRLYs with respect to the P group. See § 1.1502-1(f)(2)(i). Thus, P's $ 40 net operating loss arising in Year 1 and $120 net operating loss arising in Year 3 are not subject to the SRLY limitation under paragraph (c) of this section. Under the principles of section 172, paragraph (b) of this section requires that the loss arising in Year 1 be the first loss absorbed by the P group in Year 4. Absorption of this loss leaves $120 of the group's consolidated taxable income available for offset by other loss carryovers.

(iii) T's Year 2 and Year 3 are SRLYs with respect to the P group. See § 1.1502-1(f)(2)(ii). P's acquisition of T was not an ownership change as defined by section 382(g). Thus, T's $50 net operating loss arising in Year 2 and $60 net operating loss arising in Year 3 are subject to the SRLY limitation. Under paragraph (c)(1) of this section, the SRLY limitation for Year 4 is $70, and under paragraph (b) of this section, T's $50 loss from Year 2 must be included under paragraph (a) of this section in the P group's CNOL deduction for Year 4. The absorption of this loss leaves $70 of the group's consolidated taxable income available for offset by other loss carryovers.

(iv) P and T each carry over net operating losses to Year 4 from a taxable year ending on the same date (Year 3). The losses carried over from Year 3 total $180. Under paragraph (b) of this section, the losses carried over from Year 3 are absorbed on a pro rata basis, even though one arises in a SRLY and the other does not. However, the group cannot absorb more than $20 of T's $60 net operating loss arising in Year 3 because its $70 SRLY limitation for Year 4 is reduced by T's $50 Year 2 SRLY loss already included in the CNOL deduction for Year 4. Thus, the absorption of Year 3 losses is as follows:

Amount of P's Year 3 losses absorbed = $120/($120 + $20) × $70 = $60

Amount of T's Year 3 losses absorbed = $20/($120 + $20) × $70 = $10.

(v) The absorption of $10 of T's Year 3 loss further reduces T's SRLY limitation to $10 ($70 of initial SRLY limitation, reduced by the $60 net operating loss already included in the CNOL deductions for Year 4 under paragraph (a) of this section).

(vi) P carries its remaining $60 Year 3 net operating loss and T carries its remaining $50 Year 3 net operating loss over to Year 5. Assume that, in Year 5, the P group has $90 of consolidated taxable income (computed without regard to the CNOL deduction). The group's CTI determined by reference to only T's items is a CNOL of $4. For Year 5, the CNOL deduction is $66, which includes $60 of P's Year 3 loss and $6 of T's Year 3 loss (the aggregate consolidated taxable income for Years 4 and 5 determined by reference to T's items, or $66, reduced by T's SRLY losses actually absorbed by the group in Year 4, or $60).

Example (3). Net operating loss carrybacks.

(i) P owns all of the stock of S and T. The members of the P group contribute the following to the consolidated taxable income of the P group for Years 1, 2, and 3:

	Year 1	Year 2	Year 3	Total
P	$100	$60	$ 80	$ 240
S	20	20	30	70
T	30	10	(50)	(10)
CTI	$150	$90	$ 60	$ 300

(ii) P sells all of the stock of T to Individual A at the beginning of Year 4. For its Year 4 separate return year, T has a net operating loss of $30.

(iii) T's Year 4 is a SRLY with respect to the P group. See § 1.1502-1(f)(1). T's $30 net operating loss carryback to the P group from Year 4 is not allowed under paragraph (c) of this section to be included in the CNOL deduction under paragraph (a) of this section for Year 1, 2, or 3, because the P group's consolidated taxable income would not be a positive amount if determined by reference to only T's items for all consolidated return years through Year 4 (without regard to the $30 net operating loss). The $30 loss is carried forward to T's Year 5 and succeeding taxable years as provided under the Internal Revenue Code.

Example (4). Computation of SRLY limitation for built-in losses treated as net operating loss carryovers.

(i) Individual A owns P. In Year 1, Individual A forms T by contributing $300 and T sustains a $100 net operating loss. During Year 2, T's assets decline in value by $100. At the beginning of Year 3, P acquires all the stock of T from Individual A, and T becomes a member of the P group in a transaction that does not result in an ownership change under section 382(g). At the time of the acquisition, T has a $100 net unrealized built-in loss, which exceeds the threshold requirements of section 382(h)(3)(B). During Year 3, T recognizes its unrealized loss as a $100 ordinary loss. The members of the P group contribute the following to the consolidated taxable income of the P group for Years 3 and 4 (computed without regard to T's recognition of its unrealized loss and any CNOL deduction under this section):

	Year 3	Year 4	Total
P group (without T)	$100	$100	$200
T	60	40	100
CTI	$160	$140	$300

(ii) Under § 1.1502-15(a), T's $100 of ordinary loss in Year 3 constitutes a built-in loss that is subject to the SRLY limitation under paragraph (c) of this section. The amount of the limitation is determined by treating the deduction as a net operating loss carryover from a SRLY. The built-in loss is therefore subject to a $60 SRLY limitation for Year 3. The built-in loss is treated as a net operating loss carryover solely for purposes of determining the extent to which the loss is not allowed by reason of the SRLY limitation, and for all other purposes the loss remains a loss arising in Year

3. Consequently, under paragraph (b) of this section, the $60 allowed under the SRLY limitation is absorbed by the P group before T's $100 net operating loss carryover from Year 1 is allowed.

(iii) Under § 1.1502-15(a), the $40 balance of the built-in loss that is not allowed in Year 3 because of the SRLY limitation is treated as a $40 net operating loss arising in Year 3 that is subject to the SRLY limitation because, under paragraph (c)(1)(ii) of this section, Year 3 is treated as a SRLY, and is carried to other years in accordance with the rules of paragraph (b) of this section. The SRLY limitation for Year 4 is the P group's consolidated taxable income for Year 3 and Year 4 determined by reference to only T's items and without regard to the group's CNOL deductions ($60 + $40), reduced by T's loss actually absorbed by the group in Year 3 ($60). The SRLY limitation for Year 4 is $40.

(iv) Under paragraph (c) of this section and the principles of section 172(b), $40 of T's $100 net operating loss carryover from Year 1 is included in the CNOL deduction under paragraph (a) of this section in Year 4.

Example (5). Dual SRLY registers and accounting for SRLY losses actually absorbed.

(i) In Year 1, T sustains a $ 100 net operating loss and a $50 net capital loss. At the beginning of Year 2, T becomes a member of the P group in a transaction that does not result in an ownership change under section 382(g). Both of T's carryovers from Year 1 are subject to SRLY limits under this paragraph (c) and § 1.1502-22(c). The members of the P group contribute the following to the consolidated taxable income for Years 2 and 3 (computed without regard to T's CNOL deduction under this section or net capital loss carryover under § 1.1502-22):

		P	T
Year 1 (SRLY)	Ordinary		(100)
	Capital		(50)
Year 2	Ordinary	30	60
	Capital	0	(20)
Year 3	Ordinary	10	40
	Capital	0	30

(ii) For Year 2, the group computes separate SRLY limits for each of T's SRLY carryovers from Year 1. The group determines its ability to use its capital loss carryover before it determines its ability to use its ordinary loss carryover. Under section 1212, because the group has no Year 2 capital gain, it cannot absorb any capital losses in Year 2. T's Year 1 net capital loss and the group's Year 2 consolidated net capital loss (all of which is attributable to T) are carried over to Year 3.

(iii) Under this section, the aggregate amount of T's $100 net operating loss carryover from Year 1 that may be included in the CNOL deduction of the group for Year 2 may not exceed $60—the amount of the consolidated taxable income computed by reference only to T's items, including losses and deductions to the extent actually absorbed (i.e., $60 of T's ordinary income for Year 2). Thus, the group may include $60 of T's ordinary loss carryover from Year 1 in its Year 2 CNOL deduction. T carries over its remaining $40 of its Year 1 loss to Year 3.

(iv) For Year 3, the group again computes separate SRLY limits for each of T's SRLY carryovers from Year 1. The group has consolidated net capital gain (without taking into account a net capital loss carryover deduction) of $30. Under § 1.1502-22(c), the aggregate amount of T's $50 capital loss carryover from Year 1 that may be included in computing the group's consolidated net capital gain for all years of the group (here Years 2 and 3) may not exceed $30 (the aggregate consolidated net capital gain computed by reference only to T's items, including losses and deductions actually absorbed (i.e., $30 of capital gain in Year 3)). Thus, the group may include $30 of T's Year 1 capital loss carryover in its computation of consolidated net capital gain for Year 3, which offsets the group's capital gains for Year 3. T carries over its remaining $20 of its Year 1 loss to Year 4. The group carries over the Year 2 consolidated net capital loss to Year 4.

(v) Under this section, the aggregate amount of T's net operating loss carryover from Year 1 that may be included in the CNOL deduction of the group for Years 2 and 3 may not exceed $100, which is the amount of the aggregate consolidated taxable income for Years 2 and 3 determined by reference only to T's items, including losses and deductions actually absorbed (i.e., $60 of ordinary income in Year 2 plus $40 of ordinary income, $30 of capital gain, and $30 of SRLY capital losses actually absorbed in Year 3). The group included $60 of T's ordinary loss carryover in its Year 2 CNOL deduction. It may include the remaining $40 of the carryover in its Year 3 CNOL deduction.

(2) SRLY subgroup limitation. In the case of a net operating loss carryover or carryback for which there is a SRLY subgroup, the principles of paragraph (c)(1) of this section apply to the SRLY subgroup, and not separately to its members. Thus, the contribution to consolidated taxable income and the net operating loss carryovers and carrybacks arising (or treated as arising) in SRLYs that are included in the CNOL deductions for all consolidated return years of the group under paragraph (a) of this section are based on the aggregate amounts of income, gain, deduction, and loss of the members of the SRLY subgroup for the relevant consolidated return years (as provided in paragraph (c)(1)(i)(C) of this section). For an illustration of aggregate amounts during the relevant consolidated return years following the year in which a member of a SRLY subgroup ceases to be a member of the group, see paragraph (c)(2)(viii) Example 4 of this section. A SRLY subgroup may exist only for a carryover or carryback arising in a year that is not a SRLY (and is not treated as a SRLY under paragraph (c)(1)(ii) of this section) with respect to another group (the former group), whether or not the group is a consolidated group, or for a carryover that was subject to the overlap rule described in paragraph (g) of this section or § 1.1502-15(g) with respect to another group (the former group). A separate SRLY subgroup is determined for each such carryover or carryback. A consolidated group may include more than one SRLY subgroup and a member may be a member of more than one SRLY subgroup. Solely for purposes of determining the members of a SRLY subgroup with respect to a loss:

(i) Carryovers. In the case of a carryover, the SRLY subgroup is composed of the member carrying over the loss (the loss member) and each other member that was a member of the former group that becomes a member of the group at the same time as the loss member. A member remains a member of the SRLY subgroup until it ceases to be affiliated with the loss member. The aggregate determination described in paragraph (c)(1) of this section and this paragraph (c)(2) includes the amounts of income, gain, deduction, and loss of each member of the SRLY subgroup for the consolidated return years during which it remains a member of the SRLY subgroup. For an illustration of the aggregate determination of a SRLY subgroup, see paragraph (c)(2)(viii) Example 2 of this section.

(ii) Carrybacks. In the case of a carryback, the SRLY subgroup is composed of the member carrying back the loss (the loss member) and each other member of the group from which the loss is carried back that has been continuously affiliated with the loss member from the year to which the loss is carried through the year in which the loss arises.

(iii) Built-in losses. In the case of a built-in loss, the SRLY subgroup is composed of the member recognizing the loss (the loss member) and each other member that was part of the subgroup with respect to the loss determined under § 1.1502-15(c)(2) immediately before the members became members of the group. The principles of paragraphs (c)(2)(i) and (ii) of this section apply to determine the SRLY subgroup for the built-in loss that is, under paragraph (c)(1)(ii) of this section, treated as arising in a SRLY with respect to the group in which the loss is recognized. For this purpose and as the context requires, a reference in paragraphs (c)(2)(i) and (ii) of this section to a group or former group is a reference to the subgroup determined under § 1.1502-15(c)(2).

(iv) Principal purpose of avoiding or increasing a SRLY limitation. The members composing a SRLY subgroup are not treated as a SRLY subgroup if any of them is formed, acquired, or availed of with a principal purpose of avoiding the application of, or increasing any limitation under, this paragraph (c). Any member excluded from a SRLY subgroup, if excluded with a principal purpose of so avoiding or increasing any SRLY limitation, is treated as included in the SRLY subgroup.

(v) Coordination with other limitations. This paragraph (c)(2) does not allow a net operating loss to offset income to the extent inconsistent with other limitations or restrictions on the use of losses, such as a limitation based on the nature or activities of members. For example, any dual consolidated loss may not reduce the taxable income to an extent greater than that allowed under section 1503(d) and §§ 1.1503(d)-1 through 1.1503(d)-8. See also § 1.1502-47(q) (relating to preemption of rules for life-nonlife groups).

(vi) Anti-duplication. If the same item of income or deduction could be taken into account more than once in determining a limitation under this paragraph (c), or in a manner inconsistent with any other provision of the Internal Revenue Code or regulations incorporating this paragraph (c), the item of income or deduction is taken into account only once and in such manner that losses are absorbed in accordance with the ordering rules in paragraph (b) of this section and the underlying purposes of this section.

(vii) Corporations that leave a SRLY subgroup. If a loss member ceases to be affiliated with a SRLY subgroup, the amount of the member's remaining SRLY loss from a specific year is determined pursuant to the principles of paragraphs (b)(2)(ii)(A) and (b)(2)(iv) of this section.

(viii) Examples. The principles of this paragraph (c)(2) are illustrated by the following examples:

Example (1). Members of SRLY subgroups.

(i) Individual A owns all of the stock of P, S, T and M. P and M are each the common parent of a consolidated group. During Year 1, P sustains a $50 net operating loss. At the beginning of Year 2, P acquires all the stock of S at a time when the aggregate basis of S's assets exceeds their aggregate value by $70 and S becomes a member of the P group. At the beginning of Year 3, P acquires all the stock of T, T has a $60 net operating loss carryover at the time of the acquisition, and T becomes a member of the P group. During Year 4, S forms S1 and T forms T1, each by contributing assets with built-in gains which are, in the aggregate, material. S1 and T1 become members of the P group. During Year 7, M acquires all of the stock of P, and the members of the P group become members of the M group for the balance of Year 7. The $50 and $60 loss carryovers of P and T are carried to Year 7 of the M group, and the value and basis of S's assets did not change after it became a member of the former P group. None of the transactions described above resulted in an ownership change under section 382(g).

(ii) Under paragraph (c)(2) of this section, a separate SRLY subgroup is determined for each loss carryover and built-in loss. In the P group, P's $50 loss carryover is not treated as arising in a SRLY. See § 1.1502-1(f). Consequently, the carryover is not subject to limitation under paragraph (c) of this section in the P group.

(iii) In the M group, P's $50 loss carryover is treated as arising in a SRLY and is subject to the limitation under paragraph (c) of this section. A SRLY subgroup with respect to that loss is composed of members which were members of the P group, the group as to which the loss was not a SRLY. The SRLY subgroup is composed of P, the member carrying over the loss, and each other member of the P group that became a member of the M group at the same time as P. A member of the SRLY subgroup remains a member until it ceases to be affiliated with P. For Year 7, the SRLY subgroup is composed of P, S, T, S1, and T1.

(iv) In the P group, S's $70 unrealized loss, if recognized within the 5-year recognition period after S becomes a member of the P group, is subject to limitation under paragraph (c) of this section. See § 1.1502-15 and paragraph (c)(1)(ii) of this section. Because S was not continuously affiliated with P, T, or T1 for 60 consecutive months prior to joining the P group, these corporations cannot be included in a SRLY subgroup with respect to S's unrealized loss in the P group. See paragraph (c)(2)(iii) of this section. As a successor to S, S1 is included in a subgroup with S in the P group, and because 100 percent of S1's stock is owned directly by corporations that were members of the SRLY subgroup when the members of the SRLY subgroup became members of the P group, its net positive income is not excluded from the consolidated taxable income of the P group that may be offset by the built-in loss. See paragraph (f) of this section.

(v) In the M group, S's $70 unrealized loss, if recognized within the 5-year recognition period after S becomes a member of the M group, is subject to limitation under paragraph (c) of this section. Prior to becoming a member of the M group, S had been continuously affiliated with P (but not T or T1) for 60 consecutive months and S1 is a successor that has remained continuously affiliated with S. Those members had a net unrealized built-in loss immediately before they became members of the group under § 1.1502-15(c). Consequently, in Year 7, S, S1, and P compose a subgroup in the M group with respect to S's unrealized loss. Because S1 was a member of the SRLY subgroup when it became a member of the M group and also because 100 percent of S1's stock is owned directly by corporations that were members of the SRLY subgroup when the members of the SRLY subgroup became members of the M group its net positive income is not excluded from the consolidated taxable income of the M group that may be offset by the recognized built-in loss. See paragraph (f) of this section.

(vi) In the P group, T's $60 loss carryover arose in a SRLY and is subject to limitation under paragraph (c) of this section. P, S, and S1 were not members of the group in which T's loss arose and T's loss carryover was not subject to the overlap rule described in paragraph (g) of this section with respect to the P group (the former group). Thus, P, S, and S1 are not members of a SRLY subgroup with respect to the T carryover in the P group. See paragraph (c)(2)(i) of this section. As a successor to T, T1 is included in a SRLY subgroup with T in the P group; and, because 100 percent of T1's stock is owned directly by corporations that were members of the SRLY subgroup when the members of the SRLY subgroup became members of the P group, its net positive income is not excluded from the consolidated taxable income of the P group that may be offset by the carryover. See paragraph (f) of this section.

(vii) In the M group, T's $60 loss carryover arose in a SRLY and is subject to limitation under paragraph (c) of this section. T and T1 remain the only members of a SRLY subgroup with respect to the carryover. Because T1 was a member of the SRLY subgroup when it became a member of the M group and also because 100 percent of T1's stock is owned directly by corporations that were members of the SRLY subgroup when the members of the SRLY subgroup became members of the M group, its net positive income is not excluded from the consolidated taxable income of the M group that may be offset by the carryover. See paragraph (f) of this section.

Example (2). Computation of SRLY subgroup limitation.

(i) Individual A owns all of the stock of S, T, P and M. P and M are each the common parent of a consolidated group. In Year 2, P acquires all the stock of S and T from Individual A, and S and T become members of the P group. For Year 3, the P group has a $45 CNOL, which is attributable to P, and which P carries forward. M is the common parent of another group. At the beginning of Year 4, M acquires all of the stock of P and the former members of the P group become members of the M group. None of the transactions described above resulted in an ownership change under section 382(g).

(ii) P's year to which the loss is attributable, Year 3, is a SRLY with respect to the M group. See § 1.1502-1(f)(1). However, P, S, and T compose a SRLY subgroup with respect to the Year 3 loss under paragraph (c)(2)(i) of this section because Year 3 is not a SRLY (and is not treated as a SRLY) with respect to the P group. P's loss is carried over to the M group's Year 4 and is therefore subject to the SRLY subgroup limitation in paragraph (c)(2) of this section.

(iii) In Year 4, the M group has $10 of consolidated taxable income (computed without regard to the CNOL deduction for Year 4). Such consolidated taxable income would be $45 if determined by reference to only the items of P, S, and T, the members included in the SRLY subgroup with respect to P's loss carryover. Therefore, the SRLY subgroup limitation under paragraph (c)(2) of this section for P's net operating loss carryover from Year 3 is $45. Because the M group has only $10 of consolidated taxable income in Year 4, however, only $10 of P's net operating loss carryover is included in the CNOL deduction under paragraph (a) of this section in Year 4.

(iv) In Year 5, the M group has $100 of consolidated taxable income (computed without regard to the CNOL deduction for Year 5). Neither P, S, nor T has any items of income, gain, deduction, or loss in Year 5. Although the members of the SRLY subgroup do not contribute to the $100 of consolidated taxable income in Year 5, the SRLY subgroup limitation for Year 5 is $35 (the sum of SRLY subgroup consolidated taxable income of $45 in Year 4 and $0 in Year 5, less the $10 net operating loss carryover actually absorbed by the M group in Year 4). Therefore, $35 of P's net operating loss carryover is included in the CNOL deduction under paragraph (a) of this section in Year 5.

Example (3). Inclusion in more than one SRLY subgroup.

(i) Individual A owns all of the stock of S, T, P and M. S, P and M are each the common parent of a consolidated group. At the beginning of Year 1, S acquires all the stock of T from Individual A, and T becomes a member of the S group. For Year 1, the S group has a CNOL of $10, all of which is attributable to S and is carried over to Year 2. At the beginning of Year 2, P acquires all the stock of S, and S and T become members of the P group. For Year 2, the P group has a CNOL of $35, all of which is attributable to P and is carried over to Year 3. At the beginning of Year 3, M acquires all of the stock of P and the former members of the P group become members of the M group. None of the transactions described above resulted in an ownership change under section 382(g).

(ii) P's and S's net operating losses arising in SRLYs with respect to the M group are subject to limitation under paragraph (c) of this section. P, S, and T compose a SRLY subgroup for purposes of determining the limitation for P's $35 net operating loss carryover arising in Year 2 because, under paragraph (c)(2)(i) of this section, Year 2 is not a SRLY with respect to the P group. Similarly, S and T compose a SRLY subgroup for purposes of determining the limitation for S's $10 net operating loss carryover arising in Year 1 because Year 1 is not a SRLY with respect to the S group.

(iii) S and T are members of both the SRLY subgroup with respect to P's losses and the SRLY subgroup with respect to S's losses. Under paragraph (c)(2) of this section, S's and T's items cannot be included in the determination of the SRLY subgroup limitation for both SRLY subgroups for the same consolidated return year; paragraph (c)(2)(vi) of this section requires the M group to consider the items of S and T only once so that the losses are absorbed in the order of the taxable years in which they were sustained. Because S's loss was incurred in Year 1, while P's loss was incurred in Year 2, the items will be added in the determination of the consolidated taxable income of the S and T SRLY subgroup to enable S's loss to be absorbed first. The taxable income of the P, S, and T SRLY subgroup is then computed by including the consolidated taxable income for the S and T SRLY subgroup less the amount of any net operating loss carryover of S that is absorbed after applying this section to the S subgroup for the year.

Example (4). Corporation ceases to be affiliated with a SRLY subgroup.

(i) Individual A owns all of the stock of P and M. P and S are members of the P group and the P group has a CNOL of $30 in Year 1, all of which is attributable to P and carried over to Year 2. At the beginning of Year 2, M acquires all of the stock of P, and P and S become members of the M group. P and S compose a SRLY subgroup with respect to P's net operating loss carryover. For Year 2, consolidated taxable income of the M group determined by reference to only the items of P (and without regard to the CNOL deduction for Year 2) is $40. However, such consolidated taxable income of the M group determined by reference to the items of both P and S is a loss of $20. Thus, the SRLY subgroup limitation under paragraph (c)(2) of this section prevents the M group from including any of P's net operating loss carryover in the CNOL deduction under paragraph (a) of this section in Year 2, and P carries the Year 1 loss to Year 3.

(ii) At the end of Year 2, P sells all of the S stock and S ceases to be a member of the M group and the P subgroup. For Year 3, consolidated taxable income of the M group is $50 (determined without regard to the CNOL deduction for Year 3), and such consolidated taxable income would be $10 if determined by reference to only items of P. However, the limitation under paragraph (c) of this section for Year 3 for P's net operating loss carryover still prevents the M group from including any of P's loss in the CNOL deduction under paragraph (a) of this section. The limitation results from the inclusion of S's items for Year 2 in the determination of the SRLY subgroup limitation for Year 3 even though S ceased to be a member of the M group (and the P subgroup) at the end of Year 2. Thus, the M group's consolidated taxable income determined by reference to only the SRLY subgroup members' items for all consolidated return years of the group through Year 3 (determined without regard to the CNOL deduction) is not a positive amount.

(ix) Application to other than loss carryovers. Paragraph (g) of this section and the phrase "or for a carryover that was subject to the overlap rule described in paragraph (g) of this section or § 1.1502-15(g) with respect to another group (the former group)" in this paragraph (c)(2) apply only to carryovers of net operating losses, net capital losses, and for taxable years for which the due date (without extensions) of the consolidated return is after May 25, 2000, to carryovers of credits described in section 383(a)(2). Accordingly, as the context may require, if another regulation references this section and such other regulation does not concern a carryover of net operating losses, net capital losses, or for taxable years for which the due date (without extensions) of the consolidated return is after May 25, 2000, carryovers of credits described in section 383(a)(2), then such reference does not include a reference to such paragraph or phrase.

(d) Coordination with consolidated return change of ownership limitation and transactions subject to old section 382. *(1) Consolidated return changes of ownership.* If a consolidated return change of ownership occurred before January 1, 1997, the principles of § 1.1502-21A(d) apply to determine the amount of the aggregate of the net operating losses attributable to old members of the group that may be included in the consolidated net operating loss deduction under paragraph (a) of this section. For this purpose, § 1.1502-1(g) is applied by treating that date as the end of the year of change.

(2) Old section 382. The principles of § 1.1502-21A(e) apply to disallow or reduce the amount of a net operating loss carryover of a member as a result of a transaction subject to old section 382.

(e) Consolidated net operating loss. Any excess of deductions over gross income, as determined under § 1.1502-11(a) (without regard to any consolidated net operating loss deduction), is also referred to as the consolidated net operating loss (or CNOL).

(f) Predecessors and successors. *(1) In general.* For purposes of this section, any reference to a corporation, member, common parent, or subsidiary, includes, as the context may require, a reference to a successor or predecessor, as defined in § 1.1502-1(f)(4).

(2) Limitation on SRLY subgroups. (i) General rule. Except as provided in paragraph (f)(2)(ii) of this section, if a successor's items of income and gain exceed the successor's items of deduction and loss (net positive income), then the net positive income attributable to the successor is excluded from the computation of the consolidated taxable income of a SRLY subgroup.

(ii) Exceptions. A successor's net positive income is not excluded from the consolidated taxable income of a SRLY subgroup if—

(A) The successor acquires substantially all the assets and liabilities of its predecessor and the predecessor ceases to exist;

(B) The successor was a member of the SRLY subgroup when the SRLY subgroup members became members of the group;

(C) 100 percent of the stock of the successor is owned directly by corporations that were members of the SRLY subgroup when the SRLY subgroup members became members of the group; or

(D) The Commissioner so determines.

(g) Overlap with section 382. *(1) General rule.* The limitation provided in paragraph (c) of this section does not apply to net operating loss carryovers (other than a hypothetical carryover described in paragraph (c)(1)(i)(D) of this section and a carryover described in paragraph (c)(1)(ii) of this section) when the application of paragraph (c) of this section results in an overlap with the application of section 382. For a similar rule applying in the case of net operating loss carryovers described in paragraphs (c)(1)(i)(D) and (c)(1)(ii) of this section, see § 1.1502-15(g).

(2) Definitions. (i) Generally. For purposes of this paragraph (g), the definitions and nomenclature contained in section 382, the regulations thereunder, and §§ 1.1502-90 through 1.1502-99 apply.

(ii) Overlap. (A) An overlap of the application of paragraph (c) of this section and the application of section 382 with respect to a net operating loss carryover occurs if a corporation becomes a member of a consolidated group (the SRLY event) within six months of the change date of an ownership change giving rise to a section 382(a) limitation with respect to that carryover (the section 382 event).

(B) If an overlap described in paragraph (g)(2)(ii)(A) of this section occurs with respect to net operating loss carryovers of a corporation whose SRLY event occurs within the six month period beginning on the date of a section 382 event, then an overlap is treated as also occurring with respect to that corporation's net operating loss carryover that arises within the period beginning with the section 382 event and ending with the SRLY event.

(C) For special rules in the event that there is a SRLY subgroup and/or a loss subgroup as defined in § 1.1502-91(d)(1) with respect to a carryover, see paragraph (g)(4) of this section.

(3) Operating rules. (i) Section 382 event before SRLY event. If a SRLY event occurs on the same date as a section 382 event or within the six month period beginning on the date of the section 382 event, paragraph (g)(1) of this section applies beginning with the tax year that includes the SRLY event.

(ii) SRLY event before section 382 event. If a section 382 event occurs within the period beginning the day after the SRLY event and ending six months after the SRLY event, paragraph (g)(1) of this section applies starting with the first tax year that begins after the section 382 event.

(4) Subgroup rules. In general, in the case of a net operating loss carryover for which there is a SRLY subgroup and a loss subgroup (as defined in § 1.1502-91(d)(1)), the princi-

ples of this paragraph (g) apply to the SRLY subgroup, and not separately to its members. However, paragraph (g)(1) of this section applies—

(i) With respect to a carryover described in paragraph (g)(2)(ii)(A) of this section only if—

(A) All members of the SRLY subgroup with respect to that carryover are also included in a loss subgroup with respect to that carryover; and

(B) All members of a loss subgroup with respect to that carryover are also members of a SRLY subgroup with respect to that carryover; and

(ii) With respect to a carryover described in paragraph (g)(2)(ii)(B) of this section only if all members of the SRLY subgroup for that carryover are also members of a SRLY subgroup that has net operating loss carryovers described in paragraph (g)(2)(ii)(A) of this section that are subject to the overlap rule of paragraph (g)(1) of this section.

(5) Examples. The principles of this paragraph (g) are illustrated by the following examples:

Example (1). Overlap—Simultaneous Acquisition.

(i) Individual A owns all of the stock of P, which in turn owns all of the stock of S. P and S file a consolidated return. In Year 2, B, an individual unrelated to Individual A, forms T which incurs a $100 net operating loss for that year. At the beginning of Year 3, S acquires T.

(ii) S's acquisition of T results in T becoming a member of the P group (the SRLY event) and also results in an ownership change of T, within the meaning of section 382(g), that gives rise to a limitation under section 382(a) (the section 382 event) with respect to the T carryover.

(iii) Because the SRLY event and the change date of the section 382 event occur on the same date, there is an overlap of the application of the SRLY rules and the application of section 382.

(iv) Consequently, under this paragraph (g), in Year 3 the SRLY limitation does not apply to the Year 2 $100 net operating loss.

Example (2). Overlap—Section 382 event before SRLY event.

(i) Individual A owns all of the stock of P, which in turn owns all of the stock of S. P and S file a consolidated return. In Year 1, B, an individual unrelated to Individual A, forms T which incurs a $100 net operating loss for that year. On February 28 of Year 2, S purchases 55% of T from Individual B. On June 30, of Year 2, S purchases an additional 35% of T from Individual B.

(ii) The February 28 purchase of 55% of T is a section 382 event because it results in an ownership change of T, under section 382(g), that gives rise to a section 382(a) limitation with respect to the T carryover. The June 30 purchase of 35% of T results in T becoming a member of the P group and is therefore a SRLY event.

(iii) Because the SRLY event occurred within six months of the change date of the section 382 event, there is an overlap of the application of the SRLY rules and the application of section 382.

(iv) Consequently, under paragraph (g) of this section, in Year 2 the SRLY limitation does not apply to the Year 1 $100 net operating loss.

Example (3). No overlap--Section 382 event before SRLY event.

(i) The facts are the same as in Example 2 except that Individual B does not sell the additional 35% of T to S until September 30, Year 2.

(ii) The February 28 purchase of 55% of T is a section 382 event because it results in an ownership change of T, under section 382(g), that gives rise to a section 382(a) limitation with respect to the T carryover. The September 30 purchase of 35% of T results in T becoming a member of the P group and is therefore a SRLY event.

(iii) Because the SRLY event did not occur within six months of the change date of the section 382 event, there is no overlap of the application of the SRLY rules and the application of section 382. Consequently, the Year 1 net operating loss is subject to a SRLY limitation and a section 382 limitation.

Example (4). Overlap—SRLY event before section 382 event.

(i) P and S file a consolidated return. S has owned 40% of T for 6 years. For Year 6, T has a net operating loss of $500 that is carried forward. On March 31, Year 7, S acquires an additional 40% of T, and on August 31, Year 7, S acquires the remaining 20% of T.

(ii) The March 31 purchase of 40% of T results in T becoming a member of the P group and is therefore a SRLY event. The August 31 purchase of 20% of T is a section 382 event because it results in an ownership change of T, under section 382(g), that gives rise to a section 382(a) limitation with respect to the T carryover.

(iii) Because the SRLY event occurred within six months of the change date of the section 382 event, there is an overlap of the application of the SRLY rules and the application of section 382 within the meaning of this paragraph (g).

(iv) Under this paragraph (g), the SRLY rules of paragraph (c) of this section will apply to the Year 7 tax year. Beginning in Year 8 (the year after the section 382 event), any unabsorbed portion of the Year 6 net operating loss will not be subject to a SRLY limitation.

Example (5). Overlap—Coextensive subgroups.

(i) Individual A owns all of the stock of S, which in turn owns all of the stock of T. S and T file a consolidated return beginning in Year 1. B, an individual unrelated to Individual A, owns all of the stock of P, the common parent of a consolidated group. In Year 2, the S group has a $200 consolidated net operating loss which is carried forward, of which $100 is attributable to S, and $100 is attributable to T. At the beginning of Year 3, the P group acquires all of the stock of S from Individual A.

(ii) P's acquisition of S results in S and T becoming members of the P group (the SRLY event). With respect to the Year 2 net operating loss carryover, S and T compose a SRLY subgroup under paragraph (c)(2) of this section.

(iii) S and T also compose a loss subgroup under § 1.1502-91(d)(1) with respect to the Year 2 net operating loss carryover. P's acquisition also results in an ownership change of S, the subgroup parent, within the meaning of section 382(g), that gives rise to a limitation under section 382(a) (the section 382 event) with respect to the Year 2 carryover.

(iv) Because the SRLY event and the change date of the section 382 event occur on the same date, there is an overlap of the application of the SRLY rules and the application of section 382 within the meaning of paragraph (g) of this section. Because the SRLY subgroup and the loss subgroup are coextensive, under paragraph (g) of this section, the SRLY limitation does not apply to the Year 2 $200 net operating loss.

Example (6). No Overlap—Different subgroups.

(i) Individual B owns all of the stock of P, the common parent of a consolidated group. P owns all of the stock of S and all of the stock of T. Individual A owns all of the stock of X, the common parent of another consolidated group. In Year 1, the P group has a $200 consolidated net operating loss, of which $100 is attributable to S and $100 is attributable to T. At the beginning of Year 3, the X group acquires all of the stock of S and T from P and does not make an election under § 1.1502-91(d)(4) (concerning an election to treat the loss subgroup parent requirement as having been satisfied).

(ii) X's acquisition of S and T results in S and T becoming members of the X group (the SRLY event). With respect to the Year 1 net operating loss, S and T compose a SRLY subgroup under paragraph (c)(2) of this section.

(iii) S and T do not bear (and are not treated as bearing) a section 1504(a)(1) relationship. Therefore S and T do not qualify as a loss subgroup under § 1.1502-91(d)(1). X's acquisition of S and T results in separate ownership changes of S and T, that give rise to separate limitations under section 382(a) (the section 382 events) with respect to each of S and T's Year 1 net operating loss carryovers. See § 1.1502-94.

(iv) The SRLY event and the change dates of the section 382 events occur on the same date. However, paragraph (g)(1) of this section does not apply because the SRLY subgroup (composed of S and T) is not coextensive with a loss subgroup with respect to the Year 1 carryovers. Consequently, the Year 1 net operating loss is subject to both a SRLY subgroup limitation and also separate section 382 limitations for each of S and T.

Example (7). No Overlap—Different subgroups.

(i) Individual A owns all of the stock of T and all of the stock of S, the common parent of a consolidated group. B, an individual unrelated to Individual A, owns all of the stock of P, the common parent of another consolidated group. In Year 1, T has a net operating loss of $100 that is carried forward. At the end of Year 2, S acquires all of the stock of T from Individual A. In Year 3, the S group sustains a $200 consolidated net operating loss that is carried forward. In Year 8, the P group acquires all of the stock of S from Individual A.

(ii) S's acquisition of T in Year 1 results in T becoming a member of the S group. The acquisition, however, did not result in an ownership change under section 382(g). As a result, T's Year 1 net operating loss is subject to SRLY within the S group. At the end of Year 7, § 1.1502-96(a) treats T's Year 1 net operating loss as not having arisen in a SRLY with respect to the S group. Section 1.1502-96(a), however, applies only for purposes of §§ 1.1502-91 through 1.1502-96 and § 1.1502-98 but not for purposes of this section. See § 1.1502-96(a)(5).

(iii) P's acquisition of S in Year 8 results in S and T becoming members of the P group (the SRLY event). With respect to the Year 1 net operating loss, S and T do not compose a SRLY subgroup under paragraph (c)(2) of this section.

(iv) S and T compose a loss subgroup under § 1.1502-91(d)(1) with respect to the Year 1 net operating loss carryover. P's acquisition of S results in an ownership change of the loss subgroup, within the meaning of section 382(g), that gives rise to a subgroup limitation under section 382(a) (the section 382 event) with respect to that carryover.

(v) The SRLY event and the change date of the section 382 event occur on the same date. However, under paragraph (g)(4) of this section, because the SRLY subgroup and the loss subgroup are not coextensive, T's Year 1 net operating loss carryover is subject to a SRLY limitation.

(vi) With respect to the Year 3 net operating loss carryover, S and T compose both a SRLY subgroup and a loss subgroup under § 1.1502-91(d)(1). Thus, paragraph (g)(1) of this section applies and the S group's Year 3 net operating loss carryover is not subject to a SRLY limitation.

Example (8). SRLY after overlap.

(i) Individual A owns all of the stock of R and M, each the common parent of a consolidated group. B, an individual unrelated to Individual A, owns all of the stock of D. In Year 1, D incurs a $100 net operating loss that is carried forward. At the beginning of Year 3, R acquires all of the stock of D. In Year 5, M acquires all of the stock of R in a transaction that did not result in an ownership change of R.

(ii) R's Year 3 acquisition of D results in D becoming a member of the R group (the SRLY event) and also results in an ownership change of D, that gives rise to a limitation under section 382(a) (the section 382 event) with respect to D's net operating loss carryover.

(iii) Because the SRLY event and the change date of the section 382 event occur on the same date, there is an overlap of the application of paragraph (c) of this section and section 382 with respect to D's net operating loss. Consequently, under this paragraph (g), D's Year 1 $100 net operating loss is not subject to a SRLY limitation in the R group.

(iv) M's Year 5 acquisition of R results in R and D becoming members of the M group (the SRLY event), but does not result in an ownership change of R or D that gives rise to a limitation under section 382(a). Because there is no section 382 event, the application of the SRLY rules and section 382 do not overlap. Consequently, D's Year 1 $100 net operating loss is subject to a SRLY limitation in the M group.

(v) Because D's Year 1 net operating loss carryover was subject to the overlap rule of paragraph (g) of this section when it joined the R group, under § 1.1502-21(c)(2) the SRLY subgroup with respect to that carryover includes all of the members of the R group that joined the M group at the same time as D.

Example (9). Overlap—Interim losses.

(i) Individual A owns all of the stock of P and S, each the common parent of a consolidated group. S owns all of the stock of T, its only subsidiary. B, an individual unrelated to Individual A, owns all of the stock of M, the common parent of a consolidated group. In Year 1, the S group has a $100 consolidated net operating loss. On January 1 of Year 2, P acquires all of the stock of S from Individual A. On December 31 of Year 2, M acquires 51% of the stock of P from Individual A. On May 31 of Year 3, M acquires the remaining 49% of the stock of P from Individual A. The P group, for the Year 3 period prior to June 1 had a $50 consolidated net operating loss, and under paragraph (b)(2)(iv) of this section, the loss is attributable entirely to S. Other than the losses described above, the P group does not have any other consolidated net operating losses.

(ii) In the P group, S's $100 loss carryover is treated as arising in a SRLY and is subject to the limitation under paragraph (c) of this section. A SRLY subgroup with respect to that loss is composed of S and T, the members which were members of the S group as to which the loss was not a SRLY.

(iii) M's December 31 purchase of 51% of P is a section 382 event because it results in an ownership change of the S loss subgroup that gives rise to a section 382(a) limitation (the section 382 event) with respect to the Year 1 net operating loss carryover. The purchase, however, does not result in an ownership change of P because it is not a loss corporation under section 382(k)(1). M's May 31 purchase of 49% of P results in P, S, and T becoming members of the M group and is therefore a SRLY event.

(iv) With respect to the Year 1 net operating loss, S and T compose a SRLY subgroup under paragraph (c)(2) of this section and a loss subgroup under § 1.1502-91(d)(1). The loss subgroup does not include P because the only loss at the time of the section 382 event was subject to SRLY with respect to the P group. See § 1.1502-91(d)(1).

(v) Because the SRLY event occured within six months of the change date of the section 382 event and the SRLY subgroup and loss subgroup are coextensive with respect to the Year 1 net operating loss carryover, there is an overlap of the application of the SRLY rules and the application of section 382 within the meaning of paragraph (g) of this section. Thus, the SRLY limitation does not apply to that carryover.

(vi) The Year 3 net operating loss, which arose between the section 382 event and the SRLY event, is a net operating loss described in paragraph (g)(2)(ii)(B) of this section because it is the net operating loss of a corporation whose SRLY event occurs within the six month period beginning on the date of a section 382 event.

(vii) With respect to the Year 3 net operating loss, P, S, and T compose a SRLY subgroup under paragraph (c)(2) of this section. Because P, a member of the SRLY subgroup for the Year 3 carryover, is not also a member of a SRLY subgroup that has net operating loss carryovers described in paragraph (g)(2)(ii)(A) of this section (the Year 1 net operating loss), the Year 3 carryover is subject to a SRLY limitation in the M group. See paragraph (g)(4)(ii) of this section.

(h) Effective/applicability dates. *(1) In general.* This section generally applies to taxable years for which the due date (without extensions) of the consolidated return is after June 25, 1999. However—

(i) In the event that paragraph (g)(1) of this section does not apply to a particular net operating loss carryover in the current group, then solely for purposes of applying paragraph (c) of this section to determine a limitation with respect to that carryover and with respect to which the SRLY register (consolidated taxable income determined by reference to only the member's or subgroup's items of income, gain, deduction or loss) began in a taxable year for which the due date of the return was on or before June 25, 1999), paragraph (c)(2) of this section shall be applied without regard to the phrase "or for a carryover that was subject to the overlap rule described in paragraph (g) of this section or § 1.1502-15(g) with respect to another group (the former group)"; and

(ii) For purposes of paragraph (g) of this section, only an ownership change to which section 382(a), as amended by the Tax Reform Act of 1986, applies shall constitute a section 382 event.

(iii) Paragraphs (b)(2)(ii)(A) and (b)(2)(iv)(B)(2) of this section apply to taxable years for which the due date of the original return (without regard to extensions) is on or after September 17, 2008.

(2) SRLY limitation. Except in the case of those members (including members of a SRLY subgroup) described in paragraph (h)(3) of this section, a group does not take into account a consolidated taxable year beginning before January 1, 1997, in determining the aggregate of the consolidated taxable income under paragraph (c)(1) of this section (including for purposes of § 1.1502-15 and § 1.1502-22(c)) for the members (or SRLY subgroups).

(3) Prior retroactive election. A consolidated group that applied the rules of § 1.1502-21T(g)(3) in effect prior to June 25, 1999, as contained in 26 CFR part 1 revised April 1, 1999, to all consolidated return years ending on or after January 29, 1991, and beginning before January 1, 1997, does not take into account a consolidated taxable year beginning before January 29, 1991, in determining the aggregate of the consolidated taxable income under paragraph (c)(1) of this section (including for purposes of § 1.1502-15 and § 1.1502-22(c)) for the members (or SRLY subgroups).

(4) Offspring rule. Paragraph (b)(2)(ii)(B) of this section applies to net operating losses arising in taxable years ending on or after June 25, 1999.

(5) Waiver of carrybacks. Paragraph (b)(3)(ii)(B) of this section (relating to the waiver of carrybacks for acquired members) applies to acquisitions occurring after June 25, 1999.

(6) Certain prior periods. Paragraphs (b)(1), (b)(2)(iv)(A), (b)(2)(iv)(B)(1), and (c)(2)(vii) of this section apply to taxable years for which the due date of the original return (without regard to extensions) is after March 21, 2005. Paragraphs (b)(2)(ii)(A) and (b)(2)(iv)(B)(2) (as contained in 26 CFR part 1 revised as of April 1, 2008) apply to taxable years for which the due date of the original return (without regard to extensions) is on or after March 21, 2005, and before September 17, 2008. Paragraph (b)(2)(ii)(A) of this section and § 1.1502-21T(b)(1), (b)(2)(iv), and (c)(2)(vii), as contained in 26 CFR part 1 revised as of April 1, 2004, apply to taxable years for which the due date of the original return (without regard to extensions) is after August 29, 2003, and on or before March 21, 2005. For taxable years for which the due date of the original return (without regard to extensions) is on or before August 29, 2003, see paragraphs (b)(1), (b)(2)(ii)(A), (b)(2)(iv), and (c)(2)(vii) of this section and § 1.1502-21T(b)(1) as contained in 26 CFR part 1 revised as of April 1, 2003.

(7) Prior periods. For certain taxable years ending on or before June 25, 1999, see § 1.1502-21T in effect prior to June 25, 1999, as contained in 26 CFR part 1 revised April 1, 1999, as applicable.

(8) Losses treated as expired under § 1.1502-35(f)(1). Paragraph (b)(3)(v) of this section is effective for losses treated as expired under § 1.1502-35(f) on and after March 10, 2006. Losses treated as expired under § 1.1502-35(f)(1). For rules regarding losses treated as expired under § 1.1502-35(f) on or after March 10, 2006, see § 1.1502-21(b)(3)(v) as contained in 26 CFR part 1 in effect on April 1, 2006.

T.D. 8823, 6/25/99, amend T.D. 8884, 5/24/2000, T.D. 8997, 5/30/2002, T.D. 9048, 3/11/2003, T.D. 9089, 8/29/2003, T.D. 9100, 12/18/2003, T.D. 9192, 3/21/2005, T.D. 9254, 3/9/2006, T.D. 9300, 12/7/2006, T.D. 9315, 3/16/2007, T.D. 9424, 9/10/2008.

PAR. 2. Section 1.1502-21 is amended by adding paragraph (b)(3)(ii)(C) to read as follows:

Proposed § 1.1502-21 Net operating losses. [*For Preamble, see ¶ 152,281*]

[The text of proposed § 1.1502-21(b)(3)(ii)(c) is the same as the text of § 1.1502-21T(b)(3)(ii)(c) published elsewhere in this issue of the Federal Register]. [*See T.D. 8997, 5/30/2002, 67 Fed. Reg. 105.*]

PAR. 2. Section 1.1502-21 is amended by:

1. Revising paragraph (b)(1).

2. Adding paragraph (b)(3)(v) and (h)(7).

The revision and addition read as follows:

Proposed § 1.1502-21 Net operating losses. [*For Preamble, see ¶ 152,369*]

* * * * *

(b) * * *

(1) [The text of the proposed amendment to § 1.1502-21(b)(1) is the same as the text of § 1.1502-21T(b)(1) published elsewhere in this issue of the Federal Register].

* * * * *

(3) * * *

(v) [The text of the proposed amendment to § 1.1502-21(b)(3)(v) is the same as the text of § 1.1502-21T(b)(3)(v) published elsewhere in this issue of the Federal Register].

* * * * *

(h) * * *

(7) [The text of the proposed amendment to § 1.1502-21(h)(7) is the same as the text of § 1.1502-21T(h)(7) published elsewhere in this issue of the Federal Register].

§ 1.1502-21A Consolidated net operating loss deduction generally applicable for consolidated return years beginning before January 1, 1997.

(a) In general. The consolidated net operating loss deduction shall be an amount equal to the aggregate of the consolidated net operating loss carryovers and carrybacks to the taxable year (as determined under paragraph (b) of this section).

(b) Consolidated net operating loss carryovers and carrybacks. *(1) In general.* The consolidated net operating loss carryovers and carrybacks to the taxable year shall consist of any consolidated net operating losses (as determined under paragraph (f) of this section) of the group, plus any net operating losses sustained by members of the group in separate return years, which may be carried over or back to the taxable year under the principles of section 172(b). However, such consolidated carryovers and carrybacks shall not include any consolidated net operating loss apportioned to a corporation for a separate return year pursuant to § 1.1502-79A(a), and shall be subject to the limitations contained in paragraphs (c), (d), and (e) of this section and to the limitation contained in § 1.1502-15A (or § 1.1502-11(c), as appropriate).

(2) Rules for applying section 172(b)(1). (i) Regulated transportation corporations. For purposes of applying section 172(b)(1)(C) (relating to net operating losses sustained by regulated transportation corporations), in the case of a consolidated net operating loss sustained in a taxable year for which a member of the group was a regulated transportation corporation (as defined in section 172(j)(1)), the portion, if any, of such consolidated net operating loss which is attributable to such corporation (as determined under this paragraph) shall be a carryover to the sixth taxable year following the loss year only if such corporation is a regulated transportation corporation for such sixth year, and shall be a carryover to the seventh taxable year following the loss year only if such corporation is a regulated transportation corporation for both such sixth and seventh years.

(ii) Trade expansion losses. In the case of a carryback of a consolidated net operating loss from a taxable year for which a member of the group has been issued a certification under section 317 of the Trade Expansion Act of 1962 and with respect to which the requirements of section 172(b)(3)(A) have been met, section 172(b)(1)(A)(ii) shall apply only to the portion of such consolidated net operating loss attributable to such member.

(iii) Foreign expropriation losses. An election under section 172(b)(3)(C) (relating to 10-year carryover of portion of net operating loss attributable to a foreign expropriation loss) may be made for a consolidated return year only if the sum of the foreign expropriation losses (as defined in section 172(k)) of the members of the group for such year equals or exceeds 50 percent of the consolidated net operating loss for such year. If such election is made, the amount which may be carried over under section 172(b)(1)(D) is the smaller of (a) the sum of such foreign expropriation losses, or (b) the consolidated net operating loss.

(3) Absorption rules. For purposes of determining the amount, if any, of a net operating loss (whether consolidated or separate) which can be carried to a taxable year (consolidated or separate), the amount of such net operating loss which is absorbed in a prior consolidated return year under section 172(b)(2) shall be determined by—

(i) Applying all net operating losses which can be carried to such prior year in the order of the taxable years in which such losses were sustained, beginning with the taxable year which ends earliest, and

(ii) Applying all such losses which can be carried to such prior year from taxable years ending on the same date on a pro rata basis, except that any portion of a net operating loss attributable to a foreign expropriation loss to which section 172(b)(1)(D) applies shall be applied last.

(c) Limitation on net operating loss carryovers and carrybacks from separate return limitation years. *(1) General rule.* In the case of a net operating loss of a member of the group arising in a separate return limitation year (as defined in paragraph (f) of § 1.1502-1) of such member (and in a separate return limitation year of any predecessor of such member), the amount which may be included under paragraph (b) of this section (computed without regard to the limitation contained in paragraph (d) of this section) in the consolidated net operating loss carryovers and carrybacks to a consolidated return year of the group shall not exceed the amount determined under subparagraph (2) of this paragraph.

(2) Computation of limitation. The amount referred to in subparagraph (1) of this paragraph with respect to a member of the group is the excess, if any, of—

(i) Consolidated taxable income (computed without regard to the consolidated net operating loss deduction), minus such consolidated taxable income recomputed by excluding the items of income and deduction of such member, over

(ii) The net operating losses attributable to such member which may be carried to the consolidated return year arising in taxable years ending prior to the particular separate return limitation year.

(3) Examples. The provisions of this paragraph and paragraphs (a) and (b) of this section may be illustrated by the following examples:

Example (1). (i) Corporation P formed corporations S and T on January 1, 1965. P, S, and T filed separate returns for the calendar year 1965, a year for which an election under section 1562 was effective. T's return for that year reflected a net operating loss of $10,000. The group filed a consolidated return for 1966 reflecting consolidated taxable income of $30,000 (computed without regard to the consolidated net operating loss deduction). Among the transactions occurring during 1966 were the following:

(a) P sold goods to T deriving deferred profits of $7,000 on such sales, $2,000 of which was restored to consolidated taxable income on the sale of such goods to outsiders;

(b) T sold a machine to S deriving a deferred profit of $5,000, $1,000 of which was restored to consolidated taxable income as a result of S's depreciation deductions;

(c) T distributed $3,000 dividend to P; and

(d) In addition to the transactions described above, T had other taxable income of $6,000.

(ii) The carryover of T's 1965 net operating loss to 1966 is subject to the limitation contained in this paragraph, since 1965 was a separate return limitation year (an election under section 1562 was effective for such year). Thus, only $7,000 of T's $10,000 net operating loss is a consolidated net operating loss carryover to 1966, since such carryover is limited to consolidated taxable income (computed without regard to the consolidated net operating loss deduction), $30,000, minus such consolidated taxable income recomputed by excluding the items of income and deduction of T, $23,000 (i.e., consolidated taxable income computed without regard to the $1,000 restoration of T's deferred gain and T's $6,000 of other income). In making such recomputation, no change is made in the effect on consolidated taxable income of P's sale to T, or of the dividend from T to P.

Example (2). (i) Corporation P was formed on January 1, 1966. P filed separate returns for the calendar years 1966 and 1967 reflecting net operating losses of $4,000 and $12,000, respectively. P purchased corporation S on March 15, 1967. S was formed on February 1, 1966, and filed a separate return for the taxable year ending January 31, 1967. S also filed a short period return for the period from February 1 to December 31, 1967, and joined with P in filing a consolidated return for 1968. S sustained net operating losses of $5,000 and $6,000 for its taxable years ending January 31, 1967, and December 31, 1967, respectively. An election under section 1562 was not effective for P and S during the period involved. Consolidated taxable income for 1968 (computed without regard to the consolidated net operating loss deduction) was $16,000; such consolidated taxable income recomputed by disregarding the items of income and deduction of S was $9,000.

(ii) In order of time, the following losses are absorbed in 1968:

(a) P's $4,000 net operating loss for the calendar year 1966 (such loss is not subject to the limitation contained in this paragraph since P is the common parent corporation for 1968);

(b) S's $5,000 net operating loss for the year ended January 31, 1967. Such loss is subject to the limitation contained in this paragraph, since S was not a member of the group on each day of such year. However, such loss can be carried over and absorbed in full since such limitation is $7,000 (consolidated taxable income computed without regard to the consolidated net operating loss deduction, $16,000, minus such consolidated taxable income recomputed, $9,000); and

(c) $6,000 of P's net operating loss and $1,000 of S's net operating loss for the taxable years ending December 31, 1967. This is determined by applying the losses from such year which can be carried to 1968 (P's $12,000 loss and $2,000 of S's $6,000 loss, since such $6,000 loss is limited under this paragraph) on a pro rata basis against the amount of such losses which can be absorbed in that year, $7,000 (consolidated taxable income of $16,000 less the $9,000 of losses absorbed from prior years). The carryover of S's loss to 1968 is subject to the limitation contained in that paragraph, since S was not a member of the group on each day of its taxable year ending December 31, 1967. Such loss is limited to $2,000, the excess of $7,000 (as determined under (ii)(b)) over $5,000 (S's carryover from the year ended January 31, 1967). If a consolidated return is filed in 1969, the consolidated net operating loss carryovers will consist of P's unabsorbed loss of $6,000 ($12,000 minus $6,000) from 1967 and, subject to the limitation contained in this paragraph, S's unabsorbed loss of $5,000 ($6,000 minus $1,000) from its year ended December 31, 1967.

(d) Limitation on carryovers where there has been a consolidated return change of ownership. *(1) General rule.* If a consolidated return change of ownership (as defined in paragraph (g) of § 1.1502-1) occurs during the taxable year or an earlier taxable year, the amount which may be included under paragraph (b) of this section in the consolidated net operating loss carryovers to the taxable year with respect to the aggregate of the net operating losses attributable to old members of the group (as defined in paragraph (g)(3) of § 1.1502-1) arising in taxable years (consolidated or separate) ending on the same day and before the taxable year in which the consolidated return change of ownership occurred shall not exceed the amount determined under subparagraph (2) of this paragraph.

(2) Computation of limitation. The amount referred to in subparagraph (1) of this paragraph shall be the excess of—

(i) The consolidated taxable income for the taxable year (determined without regard to the consolidated net operating loss deduction) recomputed by including only the items of income and deduction of the old members of the group, over

(ii) The sum of the net operating losses attributable to the old members of the group which may be carried to the taxable year arising in taxable years ending prior to the particular loss year or years.

(3) Example. The provisions of this paragraph may be illustrated by the following example:

Example. (i) Corporation P is formed on January 1, 1967, and on the same day it forms corporation S. P and S file a consolidated return for the calendar year 1967, reflecting a consolidated net operating loss of $500,000. On January 1, 1968, individual X purchases all of the outstanding stock of P. X subsequently contributes $1,000,000 to P and P purchases the stock of corporation T. P, S, and T file a consolidated return for 1968 reflecting consolidated taxable income of $600,000 (computed without regard to the consolidated net operating loss deduction). Such consolidated taxable income recomputed by including only the items of income and deduction of P and S is $350,000.

(ii) Since a consolidated return change of ownership took place in 1968 (there was more than a 50 percent change of ownership of P), the amount of the consolidated net operating loss from 1967 which can be carried over to 1968 is limited to $350,000, the excess of $350,000 (consolidated taxable income recomputed by including only the items of income and deduction of the old members of the group, P and S) over zero (the amount of the consolidated net operating loss carryovers attributable to the old members of the group arising in taxable years ending before 1967).

(4) Cross-reference. See § 1.1502-21T(d)(1) for the rule that applies the principles of this paragraph (d) in consolidated return years beginning on or after January 1, 1997, with respect to a consolidated return change of ownership occurring before January 1, 1997.

(e) Limitations on net operating loss carryovers under section 382. *(1) Section 382(a).* (i) If at the end of a taxable year (consolidated or separate) there has been an increase in ownership of the stock of the common parent of a group (within the meaning of section 382(a)(1)(A) and (B)), and any member of the group has not continued to carry on a trade or business substantially the same as that conducted before any such increase (within the meaning of section 382(a)(1)(C)), then the portion of any consolidated net operating loss sustained in prior taxable years attributable to such member (as determined under this paragraph) shall not be allowed as a carryover to such taxable year or to any subsequent taxable year.

(ii) If the provisions of section 382(a) disallow the deduction of a net operating loss carryover from a separate return year of a member of the group to a subsequent taxable year, no amount shall be included under paragraph (b) of this section as a consolidated net operating loss carryover to such a subsequent consolidated return year with respect to such separate return year of such member.

(iii) The provisions of this subparagraph may be illustrated by the following example:

Example. P, S, and T file a consolidated return for the calendar year 1969, reflecting a consolidated net operating loss attributable in part to each member. P owns 80 percent of S's stock and S owns 80 percent of T's stock. On January 1, 1970, A purchases 50 percent of P's stock. During 1970 T's business is discontinued. Since there has been a 50 percentage point increase in ownership of P, the common parent of the group, and since T has not continued to carry on the same trade or business after such increase, the portion of the 1969 consolidated net operating loss attributable to T shall not be included in any net operating loss deduction for 1970 or for any subsequent taxable years, whether consolidated or separate.

(2) Section 382(b). If a net operating loss carryover from a separate return year of a predecessor of a member of the group to the taxable year is reduced under the provisions of section 382(b), the amount included under paragraph (b) of this section with respect to such predecessor shall be so reduced.

(3) Effective date. This paragraph (e) disallows or reduces the net operating loss carryovers of a member as a result of a transaction to which old section 382 (as defined in § 1.382-2T(f)(21)) applies. See § 1.1502-21T(d)(2) for the rule that applies the principles of this paragraph (e) in consolidated return years beginning on or after January 1, 1997, with respect to such a transaction.

(f) Consolidated net operating loss. The consolidated net operating loss shall be determined by taking into account the following:

(1) The separate taxable income (as determined under § 1.1502-12) of each member of the group, computed without regard to any deduction under section 242;

(2) Any consolidated capital gain net income (net capital gain for taxable years beginning before January 1, 1977)

(3) Any consolidated section 1231 net loss;

(4) Any consolidated charitable contributions deduction;

(5) Any consolidated dividends received deduction (determined under § 1.1502-26 without regard to paragraph (a)(2) of that section); and

(6) Any consolidated section 247 deduction (determined under § 1.1502-27 without regard to paragraph (a)(1)(ii) of that section).

(g) Groups that include insolvent financial institutions. For rules applicable to relinquishing the entire carryback period with respect to losses attributable to insolvent financial institutions, see § 301.6402-7 of this chapter.

(h) Effective date. Except as provided in § 1.1502-21T(d)(1), (d)(2), and (g)(3), this section applies to consolidated return years beginning before January 1, 1997.

T.D. 6894, 9/7/66, amend T.D. 7728, 10/31/80, T.D. 8387, 12/30/91, T.D. 8446, 11/5/92, T.D. 8677, 6/26/96.

§ 1.1502-21T Net operating losses (temporary).

• ***Caution:*** Under Code § 7805, temporary regulations expire within three years of the date of issuance. This temporary regulation was issued on 5/30/2002.

(a) through (b)(3)(ii)(B) [Reserved]. For further guidance, see § 1.1502-21(a) through (b)(3)(ii)(B).

(b) *(3)* (ii) (C) Partial waiver of carryback period for 2001 and 2002 losses. (1) Application. The acquiring group may make the elections described in paragraphs (b)(3)(ii)(C)(2) and (3) of this section with respect to an acquired member or members only if it did not file a valid election described in § 1.1502-21(b)(3)(ii)(B) with respect to such acquired member or members on or before May 31, 2002.

(2) Partial waiver of entire pre-acquisition carryback period. If one or more members of a consolidated group become members of another consolidated group after June 25, 1999, then, with respect to all consolidated net operating losses attributable to the member for the taxable year ending during either 2001 or 2002, or both, the acquiring group may make an irrevocable election to relinquish the portion of the carryback period for such losses for which the corporation was a member of another group, provided that any other corporation joining the acquiring group that was affiliated with the member immediately before it joined the acquiring group is also included in the waiver and that the conditions of this paragraph are satisfied. The acquiring group cannot make the election described in this paragraph with respect to any consolidated net operating losses arising in a particular taxable year if any carryback is claimed, as provided in paragraph (b)(3)(ii)(C)(4) of this section, with respect to any such losses on a return or other filing by a group of which the acquired member was previously a member and such claim is filed on or before the date the election described in this paragraph is filed. The election must be made in a separate statement entitled "THIS IS AN ELECTION UNDER SECTION 1.1502-21T(b)(3)(ii)(C)(2) TO WAIVE THE PRE-[insert first day of the first taxable year for which the member (or members) was a member of the acquiring group] CARRYBACK PERIOD FOR THE CNOLS ATTRIBUTABLE TO THE [insert taxable year of losses] TAXABLE YEAR(S) OF [insert names and employer identification

numbers of members]." Such statement must be filed as provided in paragraph (b)(3)(ii)(C)(5) of this section.

(3) Partial waiver of pre-acquisition extended carryback period. If one or more members of a consolidated group become members of another consolidated group, then, with respect to all consolidated net operating losses attributable to the member for the taxable year ending during either 2001 or 2002, or both, the acquiring group may make an irrevocable election to relinquish the portion of the carryback period for such losses for which the corporation was a member of another group to the extent that such carryback period includes one or more taxable years that are prior to the taxable year that is 2 taxable years preceding the taxable year of the loss, provided that any other corporation joining the acquiring group that was affiliated with the member immediately before it joined the acquiring group is also included in the waiver and that the conditions of this paragraph are satisfied. The acquiring group cannot make the election described in this paragraph with respect to any consolidated net operating losses arising in a particular taxable year if a carryback to one or more taxable years that are prior to the taxable year that is 2 taxable years preceding the taxable year of the loss is claimed, as provided in paragraph (b)(3)(ii)(C)(4) of this section, with respect to any such losses on a return or other filing by a group of which the acquired member was previously a member and such claim is filed on or before the date the election described in this paragraph is filed. The election must be made in a separate statement entitled "THIS IS AN ELECTION UNDER SECTION 1.1502-21T(b)(3)(ii)(C)(3) TO WAIVE THE PRE-[insert first day of the first taxable year for which the member (or members) was a member of the acquiring group] EXTENDED CARRYBACK PERIOD FOR THE CNOLS ATTRIBUTABLE TO THE [insert taxable year of losses] TAXABLE YEAR(S) OF [insert names and employer identification numbers of members]." Such statement must be filed as provided in paragraph (b)(3)(ii)(C)(5) of this section.

(4) Claim for a carryback. For purposes of paragraphs (b)(3)(ii)(C)(2) and (3) of this section, a carryback is claimed with respect to a consolidated net operating loss if there is a claim for refund, an amended return, an application for a tentative carryback adjustment, or any other filing that claims the benefit of the net operating loss in a taxable year prior to the taxable year of the loss, whether or not subsequently revoked in favor of a claim based on 5-year carryback period.

(5) Time and manner for filing statement. A statement described in paragraph (b)(3)(ii)(C)(2) or (3) of this section that relates to consolidated net operating losses attributable to a taxable year ending during 2001 must be filed with the acquiring consolidated group's timely filed (including extensions) original or amended return for the taxable year ending during 2001, provided that such original or amended return is filed on or before October 31, 2002. A statement described in paragraph (b)(3)(ii)(C)(2) or (3) of this section that relates to consolidated net operating losses attributable to a taxable year ending during 2002 must be filed with the acquiring consolidated group's timely filed (including extensions) original or amended return for the taxable year ending during 2001 or 2002, provided that such original or amended return is filed on or before September 15, 2003.

(iii) and (b)(3)(iv) [Reserved]. For further guidance, see § 1.1502-21(b)(3)(iii) and (b)(3)(iv).

(c) *(1)* through (h)(7) [Reserved]. For further guidance, see § 1.1502-21(c)(1) through (h)(7).

T.D. 8997, 5/30/2002, amend T.D. 9048, 3/11/2003, T.D. 9089, 8/29/2003, T.D. 9100, 12/18/2003, T.D. 9192, 3/21/2005, T.D. 9254, 3/9/2006, T.D. 9300, 12/7/2006.

§ 1.1502-22 Consolidated capital gain and loss.

(a) Capital gain. The determinations under section 1222, including capital gain net income, net long-term capital gain, and net capital gain, with respect to members during consolidated return years are not made separately. Instead, consolidated amounts are determined for the group as a whole. The consolidated capital gain net income for any consolidated return year is determined by reference to—

(1) The aggregate gains and losses of members from sales or exchanges of capital assets for the year (other than gains and losses to which section 1231 applies);

(2) The consolidated net section 1231 gain for the year (determined under § 1.1502-23); and

(3) The net capital loss carryovers or carrybacks to the year.

(b) Net capital loss carryovers and carrybacks. *(1) In general.* The determinations under section 1222, including net capital loss and net short-term capital loss, with respect to members during consolidated return years are not made separately. Instead, consolidated amounts are determined for the group as a whole. Losses included in the consolidated net capital loss may be carried to consolidated return years, and, after apportionment, may be carried to separate return years. The net capital loss carryovers and carrybacks consist of—

(i) Any consolidated net capital losses of the group; and

(ii) Any net capital losses of the members arising in separate return years.

(2) Carryovers and carrybacks generally. The net capital loss carryovers and carrybacks to a taxable year are determined under the principles of section 1212 and this section. Thus, losses permitted to be absorbed in a consolidated return year generally are absorbed in the order of the taxable years in which they were sustained, and losses carried from taxable years ending on the same date, and which are available to offset consolidated capital gain net income, generally are absorbed on a pro rata basis. Additional rules provided under the Internal Revenue Code or regulations also apply, as well as the SRLY limitation under paragraph (c) of this section. See, e.g., section 382(l)(2)(B).

(3) Carryovers and carrybacks of consolidated net capital losses to separate return years. If any consolidated net capital loss that is attributable to a member may be carried to a separate return year under the principles of § 1.1502-21(b)(2), the amount of the consolidated net capital loss that is attributable to the member is apportioned and carried to the separate return year (apportioned loss).

(4) Special rules. (i) Short years in connection with transactions to which section 381(a) applies. If a member distributes or transfers assets to a corporation that is a member immediately after the distribution or transfer in a transaction to which section 381(a) applies, the transaction does not cause the distributor or transferor to have a short year within the consolidated return year of the group in which the transaction occurred that is counted as a separate year for purposes of determining the years to which a net capital loss may be carried.

(ii) Special status losses. [Reserved]

(c) Limitations on net capital loss carryovers and carrybacks from separate return limitation years. The aggregate of the net capital losses of a member arising (or treated as arising) in SRLYs that are included in the determination of consolidated capital gain net income for all consolidated return years of the group under paragraph (a) of this section may not exceed the aggregate of the consolidated capital gain net income for all consolidated return years of the group determined by reference to only the member's items of gain and loss from capital assets as defined in section 1221 and trade or business assets defined in section 1231(b), including the member's losses actually absorbed by the group in the taxable year (whether or not absorbed by the member). The principles of § 1.1502-21(c)(including the SRLY subgroup principles under § 1.1502-21(c)(2)) apply with appropriate adjustments for purposes of applying this paragraph (c).

(d) Coordination with respect to consolidated return change of ownership limitation occurring in consolidated return years beginning before January 1, 1997. If a consolidated return change of ownership occurred before January 1, 1997, the principles of § 1.1502-22A(d) apply to determine the amount of the aggregate of the net capital loss attributable to old members of the group (as those terms are defined in § 1.1502-1(g)), that may be included in the net capital loss carryover under paragraph (b) of this section. For this purpose, § 1.1502-1(g) is applied by treating that date as the end of the year of change.

(e) Consolidated net capital loss. Any excess of losses over gains, as determined under paragraph (a) of this section (without regard to any carryovers or carrybacks), is also referred to as the consolidated net capital loss.

(f) Predecessors and successors. For purposes of this section, the principles of § 1.1502-21(f) apply with appropriate adjustments.

(g) Overlap with section 383. *(1) General rule.* The limitation provided in paragraph (c) of this section does not apply to net capital loss carryovers ((other than a hypothetical carryover like those described in § 1.1502-21(c)(1)(i)(D) and a carryover like those described in § 1.1502-21(c)(1)(ii)) when the application of paragraph (c) of this section results in an overlap with the application of section 383. For a similar rule applying in the case of net capital loss carryovers like those described in § 1.1502-21(c)(1)(i)(D) and (c)(1)(ii), see § 1.1502-15(g).

(2) Definitions. (i) Generally. For purposes of this paragraph (g), the definitions and nomenclature contained in sections 382 and 383, the regulations thereunder, and § 1.1502-90 through 1.1502-99 apply.

(ii) Overlap. (A) An overlap of the application of paragraph (c) of this section and the application of section 383 with respect to a net capital loss carryover occurs if a corporation becomes a member of the consolidated group (the SRLY event) within six months of the change date of an ownership change giving rise to a section 382 limitation with respect to that carryover (the section 383 event).

(B) If an overlap described in paragraph (g)(2)(ii)(A) of this section occurs with respect to net capital loss carryovers of a corporation whose SRLY event occurs within the six month period beginning on the date of a section 383 event, then an overlap is treated as also occurring with respect to that corporation's net capital loss carryover that arises within the period beginning with the section 383 event and ending with the SRLY event.

(C) For special rules in the event that there is a SRLY subgroup and/or a loss subgroup as defined in § 1.1502-91(d)(1) with respect to a carryover, see paragraph (g)(4) of this section.

(3) Operating rules. (i) Section 383 event before SRLY event. If a SRLY event occurs on the same date as a section 383 event or within the six month period beginning on the date of the section 383 event, paragraph (g)(1) of this section applies beginning with the tax year that includes the SRLY event.

(ii) SRLY event before section 383 event. If a section 383 event occurs within the period beginning the day after the SRLY event and ending six months after the SRLY event, paragraph (g)(1) of this section applies starting with the first tax year that begins after the section 383 event.

(4) Subgroup rules. In general, in the case of a net capital loss carryover for which there is a SRLY subgroup and a loss subgroup (as defined in § 1.1502-91(d)(1)), the principles of this paragraph (g) apply to the SRLY subgroup, and not separately to its members. However, paragraph (g)(1) of this section applies—

(i) With respect to a carryover described in paragraph (g)(2)(ii)(A) of this section only if—

(A) All members of the SRLY subgroup with respect to that carryover are also included in a loss subgroup with respect to that carryover; and

(B) All members of a loss subgroup with respect to that carryover are also members of a SRLY subgroup with respect to that carryover; and

(ii) With respect to a carryover described in paragraph (g)(2)(ii)(B) of this section only if all members of the SRLY subgroup for that carryover are also members of a SRLY subgroup that has net capital loss carryovers described in paragraph (g)(2)(ii)(A) of this section that are subject to the overlap rule of paragraph (g)(1) of this section.

(h) Effective date. *(1) In general.* This section generally applies to taxable years for which the due date (without extensions) of the consolidated return is after June 25, 1999. However—

(i) In the event that paragraph (g)(1) of this section does not apply to a particular net capital loss carryover in the current group, then solely for purposes of applying paragraph (c) of this section to determine a limitation with respect to that carryover and with respect to which the SRLY register (consolidated taxable income determined by reference to only the member's or subgroup's items of income, gain, deduction or loss) began in a taxable year for which the due date of the return was on or before June 25, 1999), the principles of § 1.1502-21(c)(2) shall be applied without regard to the phrase Aor for a carryover that was subject to the overlap rule described in paragraph (g) of this section or § 1.1502-15(g) with respect to another group (the former group)@; and

(ii) For purposes of paragraph (g) of this section, only an ownership change to which section 383, as amended by the Tax Reform Act of 1986, applies and which results in a section 382 limitation shall constitute a section 383 event.

(2) Prior periods. For certain taxable years ending on or before June 25, 1999, see § 1.1502-22T in effect prior to June 25, 1999, as contained in 26 CFR part 1 revised April 1, 1999, as applicable.

T.D. 8823, 6/25/99.

§ 1.1502-22A Consolidated capital gain net income or loss generally applicable for consolidated return years beginning before January 1, 1997.

(a) Computation. *(1) Consolidated capital gain net income.* The consolidated capital gain net income (net capital gain for taxable years beginning before January 1, 1977) for the taxable year shall be determined by taking into account—

(i) The aggregate of the capital gains and losses (determined without regard to gains or losses to which section 1231 applies or net capital loss carryovers or carrybacks) of the members of the group for the consolidated return year,

(ii) The consolidated section 1231 net gain for such year (computed in accordance with §§ 1.1502-23A or 1.1502-23T), and

(iii) The consolidated net capital loss carryovers or carrybacks to such year (as determined under paragraph (b) of this section).

(2) Consolidated net capital loss. The consolidated net capital loss shall be determined under subparagraph (1) of this paragraph but without regard to subdivision (iii) thereof.

(3) Special rules. For purposes of this section, capital gains and losses on intercompany transactions and transactions with respect to stock, bonds, and other obligations of a member of the group shall be reflected as provided in §§ 1.1502-13 and 1.1502-19, and capital losses shall be limited as provided in §§ 1.1502-15A and 1.1502-11(c).

(4) [Reserved]

(5) Example. The provisions of this paragraph may be illustrated by the following example:

Example. (i) Corporations P, S, and T file consolidated returns on a calendar year basis for 1966 and 1967. The members had the following transactions involving capital assets during 1967: P sold an asset with a $10,000 basis to S for $17,000 and none of the circumstances of restoration described in § 1.1502-13 occurred by the end of the consolidated return year; S sold an asset to individual A for $7,000 which S had purchased during 1966 from P for $10,000, and with respect to which P had deferred a gain of $2,000; T sold an asset with a basis of $10,000 to individual B for $25,000. The group has a consolidated net capital loss carryover to the taxable year of $10,000.

(ii) The consolidated net capital gain of the group is $4,000, determined as follows: P's net capital gain of $2,000, representing the deferred gain on the sale to S during the taxable year 1966, restored into income during taxable year 1967 (the $7,000 gain on P's deferred intercompany transaction is not taken into account for the current year), plus T's net capital gain of $15,000, minus S's net capital loss of $3,000 and the consolidated net capital loss carryover of $10,000.

(b) Consolidated net capital loss carryovers. *(1) In general.* The consolidated net capital loss carryovers and carrybacks to the taxable year shall consist of any consolidated net capital losses of the group, plus any net capital losses of members of the group arising in separate return years of such members, which may be carried over or back to the taxable year under the principles of section 1212(a). However, such consolidated carryovers and carrybacks shall not include any consolidated net capital loss apportioned to a corporation for a separate return year pursuant to § 1.1502-79A(b) (or § 1,1502-22T(b), as appropriate) and shall be subject to the limitations contained in paragraphs (c) and (d) of this section. For purposes of section 1212(a)(1), the portion of any consolidated net capital loss for any taxable year attributable to a foreign expropriation capital loss is the amount of the foreign expropriation capital losses of all the members for such year (but not in excess of the consolidated net capital loss for such year).

(2) Absorption rules. For purposes of determining the amount, if any, of a net capital loss (whether consolidated or separate) which can be carried to a taxable year (consolidated or separate), the amount of such net capital loss which is absorbed in a prior consolidated return year under section 1212(a)(1) shall be determined by—

(i) Applying all net capital losses which can be carried to such prior year in the order of the taxable years in which such losses were sustained, beginning with the taxable year which ends earliest, and

(ii) Applying all such losses which can be carried to such prior year from taxable years ending on the same date on a pro-rata basis, except that any portion of a net capital loss attributable to a foreign expropriation capital loss to which section 1212(a)(1)(B) applies shall be applied last.

(c) Limitation on net capital loss carryovers and carrybacks from separate return limitation years. *(1) General rule.* In the case of a net capital loss of a member of the group arising in a separate return limitation year (as defined in paragraph (f) of § 1.502-1) of such member (and in a separate return limitation year of any predecessor of such member), the amount that may be included under paragraph (b) of this section (computed without regard to the limitation contained in paragraph (d) of this section) shall not exceed the amount determined under subparagraph (2) of this paragraph.

(2) Computation of limitation. The amount referred to in subparagraph (1) of this paragraph with respect to a member of the group is the excess, if any, of—

(i) The consolidated capital-gain net income (net capital gain for taxable years beginning before January 1, 1977) for the taxable year (computed without regard to any net capital loss carryovers or carrybacks), minus such consolidated capital gain net income (net capital gain for taxable years beginning before January 1, 1977) for the taxable year recomputed by excluding the capital gains and losses and the gains and losses to which section 1231 applies of such member, over

(ii) The net capital losses attributable to such member which can be carried to the taxable year arising in taxable years ending prior to the particular separate return limitation year.

(d) Limitation on capital loss carryovers where there has been a consolidated return change of ownership. *(1) General rule.* If a consolidated return change of ownership (as defined in paragraph (g) of § 1.1502-1) occurs during the taxable year or an earlier taxable year, the amount which may be included under paragraph (b) of this section in the consolidated net capital loss carryovers to the taxable year with respect to the aggregate of the net capital losses attributable to old members of the group (as defined in paragraph (g)(3) of § 1.1502-1) arising in taxable years (consolidated or separate) ending on the same day and before the taxable year in which the consolidated return change of ownership occurred shall not exceed the amount determined under subparagraph (2) of this paragraph.

(2) Computation of limitation. The amount referred to in subparagraph (1) of this paragraph shall be the excess of—

(i) The consolidated capital gain net income (net capital gain for taxable years beginning before January 1, 1977) (determined without regard to any net capital loss carryovers for the taxable year) recomputed by including only capital gains and losses and gains and losses to which section 1231 applies of the old members of the group, over

(ii) The aggregate net capital losses attributable to the old members of the group which may be carried to the taxable year arising in taxable years ending prior to the particular loss year or years.

(3) Cross-reference. See § 1.1502-22T(d) for the rule that applies the principles of this paragraph (d) in consolidated return years beginning on or after January 1, 1997, with respect to a consolidated return change of ownership occurring before January 1, 1997.

(e) Effective date. This section applies to any consolidated return years to which § 1.1502-21T(g) does not apply. See § 1.1502-21T(g) for effective dates of that section.

T.D. 6894, 9/7/66, amend T.D. 7637, 8/6/79, T.D. 7728, 10/31/80, T.D. 8597, 7/12/95, T.D. 8677, 6/26/96.

§ 1.1502-23 Consolidated net section 1231 gain or loss.

(a) In general. Net section 1231 gains and losses of members arising during consolidated return years are not determined separately. Instead, the consolidated net section 1231 gain or loss is determined under this section for the group as a whole.

(b) Example. The following example illustrates the provisions of this section:

Example. Use of SRLY registers with net gains and net losses under section 1231.

(i) In Year 1, T sustains a $20 net capital loss. At the beginning of Year 2, T becomes a member of the P group. T's capital loss carryover from Year 1 is subject to SRLY limits under § 1.1502-22(c). The members of the P group contribute the following to the consolidated taxable income for Year 2 (computed without regard to T's net capital loss carryover under § 1.1502-22):

		P	T
Year 1 (SRLY)	Ordinary		
	Capital		(20)
Year 2	Ordinary	10	20
	Capital	70	0
	§ 1231	(60)	30

(ii) Under section 1231, if the section 1231 losses for any taxable year exceed the section 1231 gains for such taxable year, such gains and losses are treated as ordinary gains or losses. Because the P group's section 1231 losses, $(60), exceed the section 1231 gains, $30, the P group's net loss is treated as an ordinary loss. T's net section 1231 gain has the same character as the P group's consolidated net section 1231 loss, so T's $30 of section 1231 income is treated as ordinary income for purposes of applying § 1.1502-22(c). Under § 1.1502-22(c), the group's consolidated net capital gain determined by reference only to T's items is $0. None of T's capital loss carryover from Year 1 may be taken into account in Year 2.

(c) Recapture of ordinary loss. [Reserved]

(d) Effective date. *(1) In general.* This section applies to gains and losses arising in the determination of consolidated net section 1231 gain or loss for taxable years for which the due date (without extensions) of the consolidated return is after June 25, 1999.

(2) Application to prior periods. See § 1.1502-21(h)(3) for rules applicable to groups that applied the rules of this section to consolidated return years ending on or after January 29, 1991, and beginning before January 1, 1997.

T.D. 8823, 6/25/99.

§ 1.1502-23A Consolidated net section 1231 gain or loss generally applicable for consolidated return years beginning before January 1, 1997.

(a) The consolidated section 1231 net gain or loss for the taxable year shall be determined by taking into account the aggregate of the gains and losses to which section 1231 applies of the members of the group for the consolidated return year. Section 1231 gains and losses on intercompany transactions shall be reflected as provided in § 1.1502-13. Section 1213 losses that are "built-in deductions" shall be subject to the limitations of §§ 1.1502-21A(c) and 1.1502-22A(c), as provided in § 1.1502-15A(a) (or § 1.1502-21T(c) in effect prior to June 25, 1999, as contained in 26 CFR part 1 revised April 1, 1999 and § 1.1502-22T(c) in effect prior to June 25, 1999, as contained in 26 CFR part 1 revised April 1, 1999, as provided in § 1.1502-15T(a) in effect prior to June 25, 1999, as contained in 26 CFR part 1 revised April 1, 1999) or §§ 1.1502-21(c) and 1.1502-22(c), as provided in § 1.1502-15(a), as applicable)), as appropriate).

(b) Effective date. This section applies to any consolidated return years to which § 1.1502-21(h) or § 1.1502-21T(g) in effect prior to June 25, 1999, as contained in 26 CFR part 1 revised April 1, 1999, as applicable does not apply. See § 1.1502-21(h) or 1.1502-21T(g) in effect prior to June 25, 1999, as contained in 26 CFR part 1 revised April 1, 1999, as applicable for effective dates of these sections.

T.D. 6894, 9/7/66, amend T.D. 7246, 12/29/72, T.D. 8677, 6/26/96, T.D. 8823, 6/25/99.

§ 1.1502-24 Consolidated charitable contributions deduction.

(a) Determination of amount of consolidated charitable contributions deduction. The deduction allowed by section 170 for the taxable year shall be the lesser of—

(1) The aggregate deductions of the members of the group allowable under section 170 (determined without regard to section 170(b)(2), plus the consolidated charitable contribution carryovers to such year, or

(2) Five percent of the adjusted consolidated taxable income as determined under paragraph (c) of this section.

(b) Carryover of excess charitable contributions. The consolidated charitable contribution carryovers to any consolidated return year shall consist of any excess consolidated charitable contributions of the group, plus any excess charitable contributions of members of the group arising in separate return years of such members, which may be carried over to the taxable year under the principles of section 170(b)(2) and (3). However, such consolidated carryovers shall not include any excess charitable contributions apportioned to a corporation for a separate return year pursuant to paragraph (e) of § 1.1502-79.

(c) Adjusted consolidated taxable income. For purposes of this section, the adjusted consolidated taxable income of the group for any consolidated return year shall be the consolidated taxable income computed without regard to this section, section 242, section 243(a)(2) and (3), § 1.1502-25, § 1.1502-26, and § 1.1502-27, and without regard to any consolidated net operating or net capital loss carrybacks to such year.

T.D. 6894, 9/7/66, amend T.D. 7637, 8/6/79.

§ 1.1502-26 Consolidated dividends received deduction.

Caution: The Treasury has not yet amended Reg § 1.1502-26 to reflect changes made by P.L. 104-188.

(a) In general. *(1)* The consolidated dividends received deduction for the taxable year shall be the lesser of—

(i) The aggregate of the deduction of the members of the group allowable under sections 243(a)(1), 244(a) and 245 (computed without regard to the limitations provided in section 246(b)), or

(ii) 85 percent of the consolidated taxable income computed without regard to the consolidated net operating loss deduction, consolidated section 247 deduction, the consolidated dividends received deduction, and any consolidated net capital loss carryback to the taxable year.

Subdivision (ii) of this subparagraph shall not apply for any consolidated return year for which there is a consolidated net operating loss. (See §§ 1.1502-21(e) or 1.1502-21A(f), as appropriate, for the definition of a consolidated net operating loss.)

(2) If any member computes a deduction under section 593(b)(2) for a taxable year beginning after July 11, 1969, and ending before August 30, 1975, the deduction otherwise computed under this section shall be reduced by an amount determined by multiplying the deduction (determined without regard to this sentence and without regard to dividends received by the common parent if such parent does not use the percentage of income method provided by section 593(b)(2)) by the applicable percentage of the member with the highest applicable percentage (determined under subparagraphs (A) and (B) of section 593(b)(2)).

(3) For taxable years ending on or after August 30, 1975, the deduction otherwise computed under this section shall be reduced by the sum of the amounts determined under paragraph (a)(4) of this section for each member that is a thrift institution that computes a deduction under section 593(b)(2).

(4) For each thrift institution, the amount determined under this subparagraph is the product of—

(i) The portion of the deduction determined with regard to the sum of the dividends received by (A) the thrift institution, and (B) any member in which that thrift institution owns, directly and with the application of paragraph (a)(5) of this section, 5 percent or more of the stock on any day during the consolidated return year, and

(ii) The thrift institution's applicable percentage determined under subparagraphs (A) and (B) of section 593(b)(2).

For purposes of this subparagraph, dividends allocated to a thrift institution under § 1.596-1(c) shall be considered received by the thrift institution.

(5) For purposes of paragraph (a)(4)(i) of this section, a member owning stock of another member (the "second member") shall be considered as owning its proportionate share of any stock of a member owned by the second member. Stock considered as being owned by reason of the preceding sentence shall, for purposes of applying that sentence, be treated as actually owned. The proportionate share of stock in a member owned by another member is the proportion which the value of the stock so owned bears to the value of all the outstanding stock in the member. For purposes of this paragraph the term "stock" includes nonvoting stock which is limited and preferred as to dividends.

(6) For purposes of paragraph (a)(4)(i) of this section, if two or more thrift institutions that are both members of the group each owns 5 percent or more of the same member's stock, the member's stock will be considered to be owned only by the thrift institution with the highest applicable percentage.

(b) Intercompany dividends. The deduction determined under paragraph (a) of this section is determined without taking into account intercompany dividends to the extent that, under § 1.1502-13(f)(2), they are not included in gross income. See § 1.1502-13 for additional rules relating to intercompany dividends.

(c) Examples. The provisions of this section may be illustrated by the following examples:

Example (1). Corporations P, S, and S-1 filed a consolidated return for the calendar year 1966 showing consolidated taxable income of $100,000 (determined without regard to the consolidated net operating loss deduction, consolidated dividends received deduction, and the consolidated section 247 deduction). Such corporations received dividends during such year from nonmember domestic corporations as follows:

Corporation:	Dividends
P	$ 6,000
S	10,000
S-1	34,000
Total	50,000

The dividends received deduction allowable to each member under section 243(a)(1) (computed without regard to the limitation in section 246(b)) is as follows: P has $5,100 (85 percent of $6,000), S has $8,500 (85 percent of $10,000), and S-1 has $28,900 (85 percent of $34,000), or a total of $42,500. Since $42,500 is less than $85,000 (85 percent of $100,000), the consolidated dividends received deduction is $42,500.

Example (2). Assume the same facts as in example (1) except that consolidated taxable income (computed without regard to the consolidated net operating loss deduction, consolidated dividends received deduction, and the consolidated section 247 deduction) was $40,000. The aggregate of the dividends received deductions, $42,500, computed without regard to section 246(b), results in a consolidated net operating loss of $2,500. See section 172(d)(6). Therefore, paragraph (a)(2) of this section does not apply and the consolidated dividends received deduction is $42,500.

T.D. 6894, 9/7/66, amend T.D. 7246, 12/29/72, T.D. 7631, 7/10/79, T.D. 8597, 7/12/95, T.D. 8677, 6/26/96, T.D. 8823, 6/25/99.

§ 1.1502-27 Consolidated section 247 deduction.

(a) Amount of deduction. The consolidated section 247 deduction for the taxable year shall be an amount computed as follows:

(1) First, determine the amount which is the lesser of—

(i) The aggregate of the dividends paid (within the meaning of section 247(a) during such year by members of the group which are public utilities (within the meaning of section 247(b)(1)) on preferred stock (within the meaning of section 247(b)(2)), other than dividends paid to other members of the group, or

(ii) The aggregate of the taxable income (or loss) (as determined under paragraph (b) of this section) of each such member which is a public utility.

(2) Then, multiply the amount determined under subparagraph (1) of this paragraph by the fraction specified in section 247(a)(2).

(b) Computation of taxable income. For purposes of paragraph (a)(1)(ii) of this section, the taxable income (or loss) of a member of the group described in paragraph (a)(1)(i) shall be determined under § 1.1502-12, adjusted for the following items taken into account in the computation of consolidated taxable income:

(1) The portion of the consolidated net operating loss deduction, the consolidated charitable contributions deduction, and the consolidated dividends received deduction, attributable to such member;

(2) Such member's capital gain net income (net capital gain for taxable years beginning before January 1, 1977) (determined without regard to any net capital loss carryover or carryback attributable to such member);

(3) Such member's net capital loss and section 1231 net loss, reduced by the portion of the consolidated net capital loss attributable to such member; and

(4) The portion of any consolidated net capital loss carryover or carryback attributable to such member which is absorbed in the taxable year.

T.D. 6894, 9/7/66, amend T.D. 7637, 8/6/79, T.D. 7728, 10/31/80.

§ 1.1502-28 Consolidated section 108.

(a) In general. This section sets forth rules for the application of section 108(a) and the reduction of tax attributes pursuant to section 108(b) when a member of the group realizes discharge of indebtedness income that is excluded from gross income under section 108(a) (excluded COD income).

(1) Application of section 108(a). Section 108(a)(1)(A) and (B) is applied separately to each member that realizes excluded COD income. Therefore, the limitation of section 108(a)(3) on the amount of discharge of indebtedness income that is treated as excluded COD income is determined based on the assets (including stock and securities of other members) and liabilities (including liabilities to other members) of only the member that realizes excluded COD income.

(2) Reduction of tax attributes attributable to the debtor. (i) In general. With respect to a member that realizes excluded COD income in a taxable year, the tax attributes attributable to that member (and its direct and indirect subsidiaries to the extent required by section 1017(b)(3)(D) and paragraph (a)(3) of this section), including basis of assets and losses and credits arising in separate return limitation years, shall be reduced as provided in sections 108 and 1017 and this section. Basis of subsidiary stock, however, shall not be reduced below zero pursuant to paragraph (a)(2) of this section (including when subsidiary stock is treated as depreciable property under section 1017(b)(3)(D) when there is an election under section 108(b)(5)).

(ii) Consolidated tax attributes attributable to a member. For purposes of this section, the amount of a consolidated tax attribute (e.g., a consolidated net operating loss) that is attributable to a member shall be determined pursuant to the principles of § 1.1502-21(b)(2)(iv). In addition, if the member is a member of a separate return limitation year subgroup, the amount of a tax attribute that arose in a separate return limitation year that is attributable to that member shall also be determined pursuant to the principles of § 1.1502-21(b)(2)(iv).

(3) Look-through rules. (i) Priority of section 1017(b)(3)(D). If a member treats stock of a subsidiary as depreciable property pursuant to section 1017(b)(3)(D), the basis of the depreciable property of such subsidiary shall be reduced pursuant to section 1017(b)(3)(D) prior to the application of paragraph (a)(3)(ii) of this section.

(ii) Application of additional look-through rule. If the basis of stock of a corporation (the lower-tier member) that is owned by another corporation (the higher-tier member) is reduced pursuant to sections 108 and 1017 and paragraph (a)(2) of this section (but not as a result of treating subsidiary stock as depreciable property pursuant to section 1017(b)(3)(D)), and both of such corporations are members of the same consolidated group on the last day of the higher-tier member's taxable year that includes the date on which the excluded COD income is realized or the first day of the higher-tier member's taxable year that follows the taxable year that includes the date on which the excluded COD income is realized, solely for purposes of sections 108 and 1017 and this section other than paragraphs (a)(4) and (b)(1) of this section, the lower-tier member shall be treated as realizing excluded COD income on the last day of the taxable year of the higher-tier member that includes the date on which the higher-tier member realized the excluded COD income. The amount of such excluded COD income shall be the amount of such basis reduction. Accordingly, the tax attributes attributable to such lower-tier member shall be reduced as provided in sections 108 and 1017 and this section. To the extent that the excluded COD income realized by the lower-tier member pursuant to this paragraph (a)(3) does not reduce a tax attribute attributable to the lower-tier member, such excluded COD income shall not be applied to reduce tax attributes attributable to any member under paragraph (a)(4) of this section and shall not cause an excess loss account to be taken into account under § 1.1502-19(b)(1) and (c)(1)(iii)(B).

(4) Reduction of certain tax attributes attributable to other members. To the extent that, pursuant to paragraph (a)(2) of this section, the excluded COD income is not applied to reduce the tax attributes attributable to the member that realizes the excluded COD income, after the application of paragraph (a)(3) of this section, such amount shall be applied to reduce the remaining consolidated tax attributes of the group, other than consolidated tax attributes to which a SRLY limitation applies, as provided in section 108 and this section. Such amount also shall be applied to reduce the tax attributes attributable to members that arose (or are treated as arising) in a separate return limitation year to the extent that the member that realizes excluded COD income is a member of the separate return limitation year subgroup with respect to such attribute if a SRLY limitation applies to the use of such attribute. In addition, such amount shall be applied to reduce the tax attributes attributable to members that arose in a separate return year or that arose (or are treated as arising) in a separate return limitation year if no SRLY limitation applies to the use of such attribute. The reduction of each tax attribute pursuant to the three preceding sentences shall be made in the order prescribed in section 108(b)(2) and pursuant to the principles of § 1.1502-21(b)(1). Except as otherwise provided in this paragraph (a)(4), a tax attribute that arose in a separate return year or that arose (or is treated

as arising) in a separate return limitation year is not subject to reduction pursuant to this paragraph (a)(4). Basis in assets is not subject to reduction pursuant to this paragraph (a)(4). Finally, to the extent that the realization of excluded COD income by a member pursuant to paragraph (a)(3) does not reduce a tax attribute attributable to such lower-tier member, such excess shall not be applied to reduce tax attributes attributable to any member pursuant to this paragraph (a)(4).

(b) Special rules. *(1) Multiple debtor members.* (i) Reduction of tax attributes attributable to debtor members prior to reduction of consolidated tax attributes. If in a single taxable year multiple members realize excluded COD income, paragraphs (a)(2) and (3) of this section shall apply with respect to the excluded COD income of each such member before the application of paragraph (a)(4) of this section.

(ii) Reduction of higher-tier debtor's tax attributes. If in a single taxable year multiple members realize excluded COD income and one such member is a higher-tier member of another such member, paragraphs (a)(2) and (3) of this section shall be applied with respect to the excluded COD income of the higher-tier member before such paragraphs are applied to the excluded COD income of the other such member. In applying the rules of paragraph (a)(2) and (3) of this section with respect to the excluded COD income of the higher-tier member, the liabilities that give rise to the excluded COD income of the other such member shall not be treated as discharged for purposes of computing the limitation on basis reduction under section 1017(b)(2). A member (the first member) is a higher-tier member of another member (the second member) if the first member is the common parent or investment adjustments under § 1.1502-32 with respect to the stock of the second member would affect investment adjustments with respect to the stock of the first member.

(iii) Reduction of additional tax attributes. If more than one member realizes excluded COD income that has not been applied to reduce a tax attribute attributable to such member (the remaining COD amount) and the remaining tax attributes available for reduction under paragraph (a)(4) of this section are less than the aggregate of the remaining COD amounts, after the application of paragraph (a)(2) of this section, each such member's remaining COD amount shall be applied on a pro rata basis (based on the relative remaining COD amounts), pursuant to paragraph (a)(4) of this section, to reduce such remaining available tax attributes.

(iv) Ownership of lower-tier member by multiple higher-tier members. If stock of a corporation is held by more than one higher-tier member of the group and more than one such higher-tier member reduces its basis in such stock, then under paragraph (a)(3) of this section the excluded COD income resulting from the stock basis reductions shall be applied on a pro rata basis (based on the amount of excluded COD income caused by each basis reduction) to reduce the attributes of the corporation.

(v) Ownership of lower-tier member by multiple higher-tier members in multiple groups. If a corporation is a member of one group (the first group) on the last day of the first group's higher-tier member's taxable year that includes the date on which that higher-tier member realizes excluded COD income and is a member of another group (the second group) on the following day and the first group's higher-tier member and the second group's higher-tier member both reduce their basis in the stock of such corporation pursuant to sections 108 and 1017 and this section, paragraph (a)(3) of this section shall first be applied in respect of the excluded COD income that results from the reduction of the basis of the corporation's stock owned by the first group's higher-tier member and then shall be applied in respect of the excluded COD income that results from the reduction of the basis of the corporation's stock owned by the second group's higher-tier member.

(2) Election under section 108(b)(5). (i) Availability of election. The group may make the election described in section 108(b)(5) for any member that realizes excluded COD income. The election is made separately for each member. Therefore, an election may be made for one member that realizes excluded COD income (either actually or pursuant to paragraph (a)(3) of this section) while another election, or no election, may be made for another member that realizes excluded COD income (either actually or pursuant to paragraph (a)(3) of this section). See § 1.108-4 for rules relating to the procedure for making an election under section 108(b)(5).

(ii) Treatment of shares with an excess loss account. For purposes of applying section 108(b)(5)(B), the basis of stock of a subsidiary that has an excess loss account shall be treated as zero.

(3) Application of section 1017. (i) Timing of basis reduction. Basis of property shall be subject to reduction pursuant to the rules of sections 108 and 1017 and this section after the determination of the tax imposed by chapter 1 of the Internal Revenue Code for the taxable year during which the member realizes excluded COD income and any prior years and coincident with the reduction of other attributes pursuant to section 108 and this section. However, only the basis of property held as of the beginning of the taxable year following the taxable year during which the excluded COD income is realized is subject to reduction pursuant to sections 108 and 1017 and this section.

(ii) Limitation of section 1017(b)(2). The limitation of section 1017(b)(2) on the reduction in basis of property shall be applied by reference to the aggregate of the basis of the property held by the member that realizes excluded COD income, not the aggregate of the basis of the property held by all of the members of the group, and the liabilities of such member, not the aggregate liabilities of all of the members of the group.

(iii) Treatment of shares with an excess loss account. For purposes of applying section 1017(b)(2) and § 1.1017-1, the basis of stock of a subsidiary that has an excess loss account shall be treated as zero.

(4) Application of section 1245. Notwithstanding section 1017(d)(1)(B), a reduction of the basis of subsidiary stock is treated as a deduction allowed for depreciation only to the extent that the amount by which the basis of the subsidiary stock is reduced exceeds the total amount of the attributes attributable to such subsidiary that are reduced pursuant to the subsidiary's consent under section 1017(b)(3)(D) or as a result of the application of paragraph (a)(3)(ii) of this section.

(5) Reduction of basis of intercompany obligations and former intercompany obligations. (i) Intercompany obligations that cease to be intercompany obligations. If excluded COD income is realized in a consolidated return year in which an intercompany obligation becomes an obligation that is not an intercompany obligation because the debtor or creditor becomes a nonmember, or because the assets of the debtor or the creditor are acquired by a nonmember in a transaction to which section 381 applies, then the basis of such intercompany obligation (or new obligation if the intercompany obligation is deemed reissued under § 1.1502-13(g)(3)) is available for reduction in respect of such ex-

cluded COD income pursuant to sections 108 and 1017 and this section.

(ii) Intercompany obligations. The reduction of the basis of an intercompany obligation pursuant to sections 108 and 1017 and this section shall not result in the satisfaction and reissuance of the obligation under § 1.1502-13(g). Therefore, any income or gain (or reduction of loss or deduction) attributable to a reduction of the basis of an intercompany obligation will be taken into account when § 1.1502-13(g)(3) applies to such obligation. Furthermore, § 1.1502-13(c)(6)(i) (regarding the treatment of intercompany items if corresponding items are excluded or nondeductible) will not apply to exclude any amount of income or gain attributable to a reduction of the basis of an intercompany obligation pursuant to sections 108 and 1017 and this section. See § 1.1502-13(g)(3)(i)(A)(1) and (g)(4)(i)(A).

(6) Taking into account excess loss account. (i) Determination of inclusion. The determination of whether any portion of an excess loss account in a share of stock of a subsidiary that realizes excluded COD income is required to be taken into account as a result of the application of § 1.1502-19(c)(1)(iii)(B) is made after the determination of the tax imposed by chapter 1 of the Internal Revenue Code for the year during which the member realizes excluded COD income (without regard to whether any portion of an excess loss account in a share of stock of the subsidiary is required to be taken into account) and any prior years, after the reduction of tax attributes pursuant to sections 108 and 1017 and this section, and after the adjustment of the basis of the share of stock of the subsidiary pursuant to § 1.1502-32 to reflect the amount of the subsidiary's deductions and losses that are absorbed in the computation of taxable income (or loss) for the year of the disposition and any prior years, and the excluded COD income applied to reduce attributes and the attributes reduced in respect thereof. See § 1.1502-11(c) for special rules related to the computation of tax that apply when an excess loss account is required to be taken into account.

(ii) Timing of inclusion. To the extent an excess loss account in a share of stock of a subsidiary that realizes excluded COD income is required to be taken into account as a result of the application of § 1.1502-19(c)(1)(iii)(B), such amount shall be included on the group's tax return for the taxable year that includes the date on which the subsidiary realizes such excluded COD income.

(7) Dispositions of stock. See § 1.1502-11(c) for limitations on the reduction of tax attributes when a member disposes of stock of another member (including dispositions that result from the application of § 1.1502-19(c)(1)(iii)(B)) during a taxable year in which any member realizes excluded COD income.

(8) Departure of member. If the taxable year of a member (the departing member) during which such member realizes excluded COD income ends on or prior to the last day of the consolidated return year and, on the first day of the taxable year of such member that follows the taxable year during which such member realizes excluded COD income, such member is not a member of the group and does not have a successor member (within the meaning of paragraph (b)(10) of this section), all tax attributes listed in section 108(b)(2) that remain after the determination of the tax imposed that belong to members of the group (including the departing member and subsidiaries of the departing member) shall be subject to reduction as provided in section 108 and the regulations promulgated thereunder (including § 1.108-7(c), if applicable) and this section.

(9) Intragroup reorganization. (i) In general. If the taxable year of a member during which such member realizes excluded COD income ends prior to the last day of the consolidated return year and, on the first day that follows the taxable year of such member during which such member realizes excluded COD income, such member has a successor member, for purposes of applying the rules of sections 108 and 1017 and this section, notwithstanding § 1.108-7, the successor member shall be treated as the member that realized the excluded COD income. Thus, all attributes attributable to the successor member listed in section 108(b)(2) (including attributes that were attributable to the successor member prior to the date such member became a successor member) are available for reduction under paragraph (a)(2) of this section.

(ii) Group structure change. If a member that realizes excluded COD income acquires the assets of the common parent of the consolidated group in a transaction to which section 381(a) applies and succeeds such common parent under the principles of § 1.1502-75(d)(2) as the common parent of the consolidated group, the member's attributes that remain after the determination of tax for the group for the consolidated return year during which the excluded COD income is realized (and any prior years) (including attributes that were attributable to the former common parent prior to the date of the transaction to which section 381(a) applies) shall be available for reduction under paragraph (a)(2) of this section.

(10) Definition of successor member. A successor member means a person to which the member that realizes excluded COD income (or a successor member) transfers its assets in a transaction to which section 381(a) applies if such transferee is a member of the group immediately after the transaction.

(11) Non-application of next day rule. For purposes of applying the rules of sections 108 and 1017 and this section, the next day rule of § 1.1502-76(b)(1)(ii)(B) shall not apply to treat a member's excluded COD income as realized at the beginning of the day following the day on which such member's status as a member changes.

(c) Examples. The principles of paragraphs (a) and (b) of this section are illustrated by the following examples. Unless otherwise indicated, no election under section 108(b)(5) has been made and the taxable year of all consolidated groups is the calendar year. The examples are as follows:

Example (1). (i) Facts. P is the common parent of a consolidated group that includes subsidiary S1. P owns 80 percent of the stock of S1. In Year 1, the P group sustained a $250 consolidated net operating loss. Under the principles of § 1.1502-21(b)(2)(iv), of that amount, $125 was attributable to P and $125 was attributable to S1. On Day 1 of Year 2, P acquired 100 percent of the stock of S2, and S2 joined the P group. As of the beginning of Year 2, S2 had a $50 net operating loss carryover from Year 1, a separate return limitation year. In Year 2, the P group sustained a $200 consolidated net operating loss. Under the principles of § 1.1502-21(b)(2)(iv), of that amount, $90 was attributable to P, $70 was attributable to S1, and $40 was attributable to S2. In Year 3, S2 realized $200 of excluded COD income from the discharge of non-intercompany indebtedness. In that same year, the P group sustained a $50 consolidated net operating loss, of which $40 was attributable to S1 and $10 was attributable to S2 under the principles of § 1.1502-21(b)(2)(iv). As of the beginning of Year 4, S2 had Asset A with a fair market value of $10. After the computation of tax imposed for Year 3 and before the application of sections 108 and 1017 and this section, Asset A had a basis of $40 and S2 had no liabilities.

(ii) Analysis. (A) Reduction of tax attributes attributable to debtor. Pursuant to paragraph (a)(2) of this section, the tax attributes attributable to S2 must first be reduced to take into account its excluded COD income in the amount of $200.

(1) Reduction of net operating losses. Pursuant to section 108(b)(2)(A) and paragraph (a) of this section, the net operating loss and the net operating loss carryovers attributable to S2 under the principles of § 1.1502-21(b)(2)(iv) are reduced in the order prescribed by section 108(b)(4)(B). Accordingly, the consolidated net operating loss for Year 3 is reduced by $10, the portion of the consolidated net operating loss attributable to S2, to $40. Then, again pursuant to section 108(b)(4)(B), S2's net operating loss carryover of $50 from its separate return limitation year is reduced to $0. Finally, the consolidated net operating loss carryover from Year 2 is reduced by $40, the portion of that consolidated net operating loss carryover attributable to S2, to $160.

(2) Reduction of basis. Following the reduction of the net operating loss and the net operating loss carryovers attributable to S2, S2 reduces its basis in its assets pursuant to section 1017 and § 1.1017-1. Accordingly, S2 reduces its basis in Asset A by $40, from $40 to $0.

(B) Reduction of remaining consolidated tax attributes. The remaining $60 of excluded COD income then reduces consolidated tax attributes pursuant to paragraph (a)(4) of this section. In particular, the remaining $40 consolidated net operating loss for Year 3 is reduced to $0. Then, the consolidated net operating loss carryover from Year 1 is reduced by $20 from $250 to $230. Pursuant to paragraph (a)(4) of this section, a pro rata amount of the consolidated net operating loss carryover from Year 1 that is attributable to each of P and S1 is treated as reduced. Therefore, $10 of the consolidated net operating loss carryover from Year 1 that is attributable to each of P and S1 is treated as reduced.

Example (2). (i) Facts. P is the common parent of a consolidated group that includes subsidiaries S1 and S2. P owns 100 percent of the stock of S1 and S1 owns 100 percent of the stock of S2. None of P, S1, or S2 has a separate return limitation year. In Year 1, the P group sustained a $50 consolidated net operating loss. Under the principles of § 1.1502-21(b)(2)(iv), of that amount, $10 was attributable to P, $20 was attributable to S1, and $20 was attributable to S2. In Year 2, the P group sustained a $70 consolidated net operating loss. Under the principles of § 1.1502-21(b)(2)(iv), of that amount, $30 was attributable to P, $30 was attributable to S1, and $10 was attributable to S2. In Year 3, S1 realized $170 of excluded COD income from the discharge of non-intercompany indebtedness. In that same year, the P group sustained a $50 consolidated net operating loss, of which $10 was attributable to S1 and $40 was attributable to S2 under the principles of § 1.1502-21(b)(2)(iv). As of the beginning of Year 4, S1's sole asset was the stock of S2, and S2 had Asset A with a $10 value. After the computation of tax imposed for Year 3 and before the application of sections 108 and 1017 and this section, S1 had an $80 basis in the S2 stock, Asset A had a basis of $0, and neither S1 nor S2 had any liabilities.

(ii) Analysis. (A) Reduction of tax attributes attributable to debtor. Pursuant to paragraph (a)(2) of this section, the tax attributes attributable to S1 must first be reduced to take into account its excluded COD income in the amount of $170.

(1) Reduction of net operating losses. Pursuant to section 108(b)(2)(A) and paragraph (a) of this section, the net operating loss and the net operating loss carryovers attributable to S1 under the principles of § 1.1502-21(b)(2)(iv) are reduced in the order prescribed by section 108(b)(4)(B). Accordingly, the consolidated net operating loss for Year 3 is reduced by $10, the portion of the consolidated net operating loss for Year 3 attributable to S1, to $40. Then, the consolidated net operating loss carryover from Year 1 is reduced by $20, the portion of that consolidated net operating loss carryover attributable to S1, to $30, and the consolidated net operating loss carryover from Year 2 is reduced by $30, the portion of that consolidated net operating loss carryover attributable to S1, to $40.

(2) Reduction of basis. Following the reduction of the net operating loss and the net operating loss carryovers attributable to S1, S1 reduces its basis in its assets pursuant to section 1017 and § 1.1017-1. Accordingly, S1 reduces its basis in the stock of S2 by $80, from $80 to $0.

(3) Tiering down of stock basis reduction. Pursuant to paragraph (a)(3) of this section, for purposes of sections 108 and 1017 and this section, S2 is treated as realizing $80 of excluded COD income. Pursuant to section 108(b)(2)(A) and paragraph (a) of this section, therefore, the net operating loss and net operating loss carryovers attributable to S2 under the principles of § 1.1502-21(b)(2)(iv) are reduced in the order prescribed by section 108(b)(4)(B). Accordingly, the consolidated net operating loss for Year 3 is reduced by an additional $40, the portion of the consolidated net operating loss for Year 3 attributable to S2, to $0. Then, the consolidated net operating loss carryover from Year 1 is reduced by $20, the portion of that consolidated net operating loss carryover attributable to S2, to $10. Then, the consolidated net operating loss carryover from Year 2 is reduced by $10, the portion of that consolidated net operating loss carryover attributable to S2, to $30. S2's remaining $10 of excluded COD income does not reduce consolidated tax attributes attributable to P or S1 under paragraph (a)(4) of this section.

(B) Reduction of remaining consolidated tax attributes. Finally, pursuant to paragraph (a)(4) of this section, S1's remaining $30 of excluded COD income reduces the remaining consolidated tax attributes. In particular, the remaining $10 consolidated net operating loss carryover from Year 1 is reduced by $10 to $0, and the remaining $30 consolidated net operating loss carryover from Year 2 is reduced by $20 to $10.

Example (3). (i) Facts. P is the common parent of a consolidated group that includes subsidiaries S1, S2, and S3. P owns 100 percent of the stock of S1, S1 owns 100 percent of the stock of S2, and S2 owns 100 percent of the stock of S3. None of P, S1, S2, or S3 had a separate return limitation year prior to Year 1. In Year 1, the P group sustained a $150 consolidated net operating loss. Under the principles of § 1.1502-21(b)(2)(iv), of that amount, $50 was attributable to S2, and $100 was attributable to S3. In Year 2, the P group sustained a $50 consolidated net operating loss. Under the principles of § 1.1502-21(b)(2)(iv), of that amount, $40 was attributable to S1 and $10 was attributable to S2. In Year 3, S1 realized $170 of excluded COD income from the discharge of non-intercompany indebtedness. In that same year, the P group sustained a $50 consolidated net operating loss, of which $10 was attributable to S1, $20 was attributable to S2, and $20 was attributable to S3 under the principles of § 1.1502-21(b)(2)(iv). At the beginning of Year 4, S1's only asset was the stock of S2, and S2's only asset was the stock of S3 with a value of $10. After the computation of tax imposed for Year 3 and before the application of sections 108 and 1017 and this section, S1's stock of S2 had a basis of

$120 and S2's stock of S3 had a basis of $180. In addition, none of S1, S2, and S3 had any liabilities.

(ii) Analysis. (A) Reduction of tax attributes attributable to debtor. Pursuant to paragraph (a)(2) of this section, the tax attributes attributable to S1 must first be reduced to take into account its excluded COD income in the amount of $170.

(1) Reduction of net operating losses. Pursuant to section 108(b)(2)(A) and paragraph (a) of this section, the net operating loss and the net operating loss carryovers attributable to S1 under the principles of § 1.1502-21(b)(2)(iv) are reduced in the order prescribed by section 108(b)(4)(B). Accordingly, the consolidated net operating loss for Year 3 is reduced by $10, the portion of the consolidated net operating loss attributable to S1, to $40. Then, the consolidated net operating loss carryover from Year 2 is reduced by $40, the portion of that consolidated net operating loss carryover attributable to S1, to $10.

(2) Reduction of basis. Following the reduction of the net operating loss and the net operating loss carryovers attributable to S1, S1 reduces its basis in its assets pursuant to section 1017 and § 1.1017-1. Accordingly, S1 reduces its basis in the stock of S2 by $120, from $120 to $0.

(B) Tiering down of stock basis reduction to S2. Pursuant to paragraph (a)(3) of this section, for purposes of sections 108 and 1017 and this section, S2 is treated as realizing $120 of excluded COD income. Pursuant to section 108(b)(2)(A) and paragraph (a) of this section, therefore, the net operating loss and net operating loss carryovers attributable to S2 under the principles of § 1.1502-21(b)(2)(iv) are reduced in the order prescribed by section 108(b)(4)(B). Accordingly, the consolidated net operating loss for Year 3 is further reduced by $20, the portion of the consolidated net operating loss attributable to S2, to $20. Then, the consolidated net operating loss carryover from Year 1 is reduced by $50, the portion of that consolidated net operating loss carryover attributable to S2, to $100. Then, the consolidated net operating loss carryover from Year 2 is further reduced by $10, the portion of that consolidated net operating loss carryover attributable to S2, to $0. Following the reduction of the net operating loss and the net operating loss carryovers attributable to S2, S2 reduces its basis in its assets pursuant to section 1017 and § 1.1017-1. Accordingly, S2 reduces its basis in its S3 stock by $40 to $140.

(C) Tiering down of stock basis reduction to S3. Pursuant to paragraph (a)(3) of this section, for purposes of sections 108 and 1017 and this section, S3 is treated as realizing $40 of excluded COD income. Pursuant to section 108(b)(2)(A) and paragraph (a) of this section, therefore, the net operating loss and the net operating loss carryovers attributable to S3 under the principles of § 1.1502-21(b)(2)(iv) are reduced in the order prescribed by section 108(b)(4)(B). Accordingly, the consolidated net operating loss for Year 3 is further reduced by $20, the portion of the consolidated net operating loss attributable to S3, to $0. Then, the consolidated net operating loss carryover from Year 1 is reduced by $20, the lesser of the portion of that consolidated net operating loss carryover attributable to S3 and the remaining excluded COD income, to $80.

Example (4). (i) Facts. P is the common parent of a consolidated group that includes subsidiaries S1, S2, and S3. P owns 100 percent of the stock of each of S1 and S2. Each of S1 and S2 owns stock of S3 that represents 50 percent of the value of the stock of S3. None of P, S1, S2, or S3 had a separate return limitation year prior to Year 1. In Year 1, the P group sustained a $160 consolidated net operating loss. Under the principles of § 1.1502-21(b)(2)(iv), of that amount, $10 was attributable to P, $50 was attributable to S2, and $100 was attributable to S3. In Year 2, the P group sustained a $110 consolidated net operating loss. Under the principles of § 1.1502-21(b)(2)(iv), of that amount, $40 was attributable to S1 and $70 was attributable to S2. In Year 3, S1 realized $200 of excluded COD income from the discharge of non-intercompany indebtedness, and S2 realized $270 of excluded COD income from the discharge of non-intercompany indebtedness. In that same year, the P group sustained a $50 consolidated net operating loss, of which $10 was attributable to S1, $20 was attributable to S2, and $20 was attributable to S3 under the principles of § 1.1502-21(b)(2)(iv). At the beginning of Year 4, S3 had one asset with a value of $10. After the computation of tax imposed for Year 3 and before the application of sections 108 and 1017 and this section, S1's basis in its S3 stock was $60, S2's basis in its S3 stock was $120, and S3's asset had a basis of $200. In addition, none of S1, S2, and S3 had any liabilities.

(ii) Analysis. (A) Reduction of tax attributes attributable to debtors. Pursuant to paragraph (b)(1)(i) of this section, the tax attributes attributable to each of S1 and S2 are reduced pursuant to paragraph (a)(2) of this section. Then, pursuant to paragraph (a)(3) of this section, the tax attributes attributable to S3 are reduced so as to reflect a reduction of S1's and S2's basis in the stock of S3. Then, paragraph (a)(4) is applied to reduce additional tax attributes.

(1) Reduction of net operating losses generally. Pursuant to section 108(b)(2)(A) and paragraph (a) of this section, the net operating losses and the net operating loss carryovers attributable to S1 and S2 under the principles of § 1.1502-21(b)(2)(iv) are reduced in the order prescribed by section 108(b)(4)(B).

(2) Reduction of net operating losses attributable to S1. The consolidated net operating loss for Year 3 is reduced by $10, the portion of the consolidated net operating loss attributable to S1, to $40. Then, the consolidated net operating loss carryover from Year 2 is reduced by $40, the portion of that consolidated net operating loss carryover attributable to S1, to $70.

(3) Reduction of net operating losses attributable to S2. The consolidated net operating loss for Year 3 is also reduced by $20, the portion of the consolidated net operating loss attributable to S2, to $20. Then, the consolidated net operating loss carryover from Year 1 is reduced by $50, the portion of that consolidated net operating loss carryover attributable to S2, to $110. Then, the consolidated net operating loss carryover from Year 2 is reduced by $70, the portion of that consolidated net operating loss carryover attributable to S2, to $0.

(4) Reduction of basis. Following the reduction of the net operating losses and the net operating loss carryovers attributable to S1 and S2, S1 and S2 must reduce their basis in their assets pursuant to section 1017 and § 1.1017-1. Accordingly, S1 reduces its basis in the stock of S3 by $60, from $60 to $0, and S2 reduces its basis in the stock of S3 by $120, from $120 to $0.

(B) Tiering down of basis reduction. Pursuant to paragraph (a)(3) of this section, for purposes of sections 108 and 1017 and this section, S3 is treated as realizing $180 of excluded COD income. Pursuant to section 108(b)(2)(A) and paragraph (a) of this section, therefore, the net operating loss and the net operating loss carryovers attributable to S3 under the principles of § 1.1502-21(b)(2)(iv) are reduced in the order prescribed by section 108(b)(4)(B). Accordingly, the consolidated net operating loss for Year 3 is further reduced by $20, the portion of the consolidated net operating loss attributable to S3, to $0. Then, the consolidated net operating loss carryover from Year 1 is reduced by $100, the portion of that consolidated net operating loss carryover attributable to S3, to $10. Following the reduction of the net operating loss and the net operating loss carryover attributable to S3, S3 reduces its basis in its asset pursuant to section 1017 and § 1.1017-1. Accordingly, S3 reduces its basis in its asset by $60, from $200 to $140.

(C) Reduction of remaining consolidated tax attributes. Finally, pursuant to paragraph (a)(4) of this section, the remaining $90 of S1's excluded COD income and the remaining $10 of S2's excluded COD income reduce the remaining consolidated tax attributes. In particular, the remaining $10 consolidated net operating loss carryover from Year 1 is reduced by $10 to $0. Because that amount is less than the aggregate amount of remaining excluded COD income, such income is applied on a pro rata basis to reduce the remaining consolidated tax attributes. Accordingly, $9 of S1's remaining excluded COD income and $1 of S2's remaining excluded COD income is applied to reduce the remaining consolidated net operating loss carryover from Year 1. Consequently, of S1's excluded COD income of $200, only $119 is applied to reduce tax attributes, and, of S2's excluded COD income of $270, only $261 is applied to reduce tax attributes.

Example (5). (i) Facts. P is the common parent of a consolidated group that includes subsidiaries S1, S2, and S3. P owns 100 percent of the stock of S1 and S2, and S1 owns 100 percent of the stock of S3. None of P, S1, S2, or S3 has a separate return limitation year prior to Year 1. In Year 1, the P group sustained a $90 consolidated net operating loss. Under the principles of § 1.1502-21(b)(2)(iv), of that amount, $10 was attributable to P, $15 was attributable to S1, $20 was attributable to S2, and $45 was attributable to S3. On January 1 of Year 2, P realized $140 of excluded COD income from the discharge of non-intercompany indebtedness. On December 31 of Year 2, S1 issued stock representing 50 percent of the vote and value of its outstanding stock to a person that was not a member of the group. As a result of the issuance of stock, S1 and S3 ceased to be members of the P group. For the consolidated return year of Year 2, the P group sustained a $60 consolidated net operating loss, of which $5 was attributable to S1, $40 was attributable to S2, and $15 was attributable to S3 under the principles of § 1.1502-21(b)(2)(iv). As of the beginning of Year 3, P's only assets were the stock of S1 and S2, S1's sole asset was the stock of S3, S2 had Asset A with a value of $10, and S3 had Asset B with a value of $10. After the computation of tax imposed for Year 2 and before the application of sections 108 and 1017 and this section, P had a $80 basis in the S1 stock and a $50 basis in the S2 stock, S1 had a $80 basis in the S3 stock, and Asset A and B each had a basis of $10. In addition, none of P, S1, S2, and S3 had any liabilities.

(ii) Analysis. Pursuant to paragraph (a)(2) of this section, the tax attributes attributable to P must first be reduced to take into account its excluded COD income in the amount of $140.

(A) Reduction of net operating losses. Pursuant to section 108(b)(2)(A) and paragraph (a) of this section, the net operating loss and the net operating loss carryover attributable to P under the principles of § 1.1502-21(b)(2)(iv) are reduced in the order prescribed by section 108(b)(4)(B). Accordingly, the consolidated net operating loss carryover from Year 1 is reduced by $10, the portion of that consolidated net operating loss carryover attributable to P, to $80.

(B) Reduction of basis. Following the reduction of the net operating loss and the net operating loss carryover attributable to P, P reduces its basis in its assets pursuant to section 1017 and § 1.1017-1. Accordingly, P reduces its basis in the stock of S1 by $80, from $80 to $0, and its basis in the stock of S2 by $50, from $50 to $0.

(C) Tiering down of stock basis reduction to S1. Pursuant to paragraph (a)(3) of this section, for purposes of sections 108 and 1017 and this section, S1 is treated as realizing $80 of excluded COD income, despite the fact that it ceases to be a member of the group at the end of the day on December 31 of Year 2. Pursuant to section 108(b)(2)(A) and paragraph (a) of this section, therefore, the net operating loss and net operating loss carryovers attributable to S1 under the principles of § 1.1502-21(b)(2)(iv) are reduced in the order prescribed by section 108(b)(4)(B). Accordingly, the consolidated net operating loss for Year 2 is reduced by $5, the portion of the consolidated net operating loss for Year 2 attributable to S1, to $55. Then, the consolidated net operating loss carryover from Year 1 is reduced by an additional $15, the portion of that consolidated net operating loss carryover attributable to S1, to $65. Following the reduction of the net operating loss and the net operating loss carryover attributable to S1, S1 reduces its basis in its assets pursuant to section 1017 and § 1.1017-1. Accordingly, S1 reduces its basis in the stock of S3 by $60, from $80 to $20.

(D) Tiering down of stock basis reduction to S2. Pursuant to paragraph (a)(3) of this section, for purposes of sections 108 and 1017 and this section, S2 is treated as realizing $50 of excluded COD income. Pursuant to section 108(b)(2)(A) and paragraph (a) of this section, therefore, the net operating loss and net operating loss carryovers attributable to S2 under the principles of § 1.1502-21(b)(2)(iv) are reduced in the order prescribed by section 108(b)(4)(B). Accordingly, the consolidated net operating loss for Year 2 is reduced by an additional $40, the portion of the consolidated net operating loss for Year 2 attributable to S2, to $15. Then, the consolidated net operating loss carryover from Year 1 is reduced by an additional $10, a portion of the consolidated net operating loss carryover attributable to S2, to $55.

(E) Tiering down of stock basis reduction to S3. Pursuant to paragraph (a)(3) of this section, for purposes of sections 108 and 1017 and this section, S3 is treated as realizing $60 of excluded COD income (by reason of S1's reduction in its basis of its S3 stock). Pursuant to section 108(b)(2)(A) and paragraph (a) of this section, therefore, the net operating loss and net operating loss carryovers attributable to S3 under the principles of § 1.1502-21(b)(2)(iv) are reduced in the order prescribed by section 108(b)(4)(B). Accordingly, the consolidated net operating loss for Year 2 is reduced by an additional $15, the portion of the consolidated net operating loss for Year 2 attributable to S3, to $0. Then, the consolidated net operating loss carryover from Year 1 is reduced by an additional $45, the portion of that consolidated net operating loss carryover attributable to S3, to $10.

Example (6). (i) Facts. P1 is the common parent of a consolidated group that includes subsidiaries S1, S2, and S3. P1 owns 100 percent of the stock of S1 and S2. S1 owns 100 percent of the stock of S3. None of P1, S1, S2, or S3 has a separate return limitation year prior to Year 1. In Year 1, the P1 group sustained a $120 consolidated net operating loss. Under the principles of § 1.1502-21(b)(2)(iv), of that amount, $40 was attributable to P1, $35 was attributable to

S1, $30 was attributable to S2, and $15 was attributable to S3. On January 1 of Year 2, S3 realized $65 of excluded COD income from the discharge of non-intercompany indebtedness. On June 30 of Year 2, S3 issued stock representing 80 percent of the vote and value of its outstanding stock to P2, the common parent of another group. As a result of the issuance of stock, S3 ceased to be a member of the P1 group and became a member of the P2 group. For the consolidated return year of Year 2, the P1 group sustained a $50 consolidated net operating loss, of which $5 was attributable to S1, $40 was attributable to S2, and $5 was attributable to S3 under the principles of § 1.1502-21(b)(2)(iv). As of the beginning of its taxable year beginning on July 1 of Year 2, S3's sole asset was Asset A with a $10 value. After the computation of tax imposed for Year 2 on the P1 group and before the application of sections 108 and 1017 and this section and the computation of tax imposed for Year 2 on the P2 group, Asset A had a basis of $0. In addition, S3 had no liabilities. On January 1 of Year 3, P1 sold all of its stock of S1.

(ii) Analysis. (A) Reduction of tax attributes attributable to debtor. Pursuant to paragraph (a)(2) of this section, the tax attributes attributable to S3 must first be reduced to take into account its excluded COD income in the amount of $65. Pursuant to section 108(b)(2)(A) and paragraph (a) of this section, the net operating loss and the net operating loss carryover attributable to S3 under the principles of § 1.1502-21(b)(2)(iv) are reduced in the order prescribed by section 108(b)(4)(B). Accordingly, the consolidated net operating loss for Year 2 is reduced by $5, the portion of the consolidated net operating loss for Year 2 attributable to S3, to $45. Then, the consolidated net operating loss carryover from Year 1 is reduced by $15, the portion of that consolidated net operating loss carryover attributable to S3, to $105.

(B) Reduction of remaining consolidated tax attributes. Pursuant to paragraphs (a)(4) and (b)(8) of this section, S3's remaining $45 of excluded COD income reduces the remaining consolidated tax attributes in the P1 group. In particular, the remaining $45 consolidated net operating loss for Year 2 is reduced by an additional $45 to $0.

(C) Basis Adjustments. For purposes of computing P1's gain or loss on the sale of the S1 stock in Year 3, P1's basis in its S1 stock will reflect a net positive adjustment of $40, which is the excess of the amount of S3's excluded COD income that is applied to reduce attributes ($65) over the reduction of S1's and S3's attributes in respect of such excluded COD income ($25).

Example (7). (i) Facts. P is the common parent of a consolidated group that includes subsidiaries S1 and S2. P owns 100 percent of the stock of S1, and S1 owns 100 percent of the stock of S2. None of P, S1, or S2 has a separate return limitation year prior to Year 1. In Year 1, the P group sustained a $50 consolidated net operating loss. Under the principles of § 1.1502-21(b)(2)(iv), of that amount, $10 was attributable to P, $20 was attributable to S1, and $20 was attributable to S2. On January 1 of Year 2, S1 realized $55 of excluded COD income from the discharge of non-intercompany indebtedness. On June 30 of Year 2, P transferred all of its assets to S1 in a transaction to which section 381(a) applied. As a result of that transaction, pursuant to § 1.1502-75(d)(2)(ii), S1 succeeded P as the common parent of the group. Pursuant to § 1.1502-75(d)(2)(iii), S1's taxable year closed on the date of the acquisition. However, P's taxable year did not close. On the consolidated return for Year 2, the group sustained a $50 consolidated net operating loss. Under the principles of § 1.1502-21(b)(2)(iv), of that amount, $10 was attributable to S1 for its taxable year that ended on June 30, $15 was attributable to S1 as the successor of P, and $25 was attributable to S2.

(ii) Analysis. Pursuant to paragraph (a)(2) of this section, the tax attributes attributable to S1 must first be reduced to take into account its excluded COD income in the amount of $55. For this purpose, S1's attributes that remain after the determination of tax for the group for Year 2 are subject to reduction. Pursuant to section 108(b)(2)(A) and paragraph (a) of this section, the net operating loss and the net operating loss carryover attributable to S1 under the principles of § 1.1502-21(b)(2)(iv) are reduced. Accordingly, the consolidated net operating loss for Year 2 is reduced by $25, the portion of the consolidated net operating loss for Year 2 attributable to S1, to $25. Then, the consolidated net operating loss carryover from Year 1 is reduced by $30, the portion of that consolidated net operating loss carryover attributable to S1 (which includes the portion attributable to P), to $20.

(d) Effective dates. This section applies to discharges of indebtedness that occur after March 21, 2005. Groups, however, may apply this section in whole, but not in part, to discharges of indebtedness that occur on or before March 21, 2005, and after August 29, 2003. For discharges of indebtedness occurring on or before March 21, 2005, and after August 29, 2003, with respect to which a group chooses not to apply this section, see § 1.1502-28T as contained in 26 CFR part 1 revised as of April 1, 2004. Furthermore, groups may apply paragraph (b)(4) of this section to discharges of indebtedness that occur on or before August 29, 2003, in cases in which section 1017(b)(3)(D) was applied. Paragraph (b)(5)(i) of this section and the last sentence of paragraph (b)(5)(ii) of this section applies to transactions occurring in consolidated return years beginning on or after December 24, 2008.

T.D. 9192, 3/21/2005, amend T.D. 9442, 12/24/2008.

§ 1.1502-30 Stock basis after certain triangular reorganizations.

(a) Scope. This section provides rules for determining the basis of the stock of an acquiring corporation as a result of a triangular reorganization. The definitions and nomenclature contained in § 1.358-6 apply to this section.

(b) General rules. *(1) Forward triangular merger, triangular C reorganization, or triangular B reorganization.* P adjusts its basis in the stock of S as a result of a forward-triangular merger, triangular C reorganization, or triangular B reorganization under § 1.358-6(c) and (d), except that § 1.358-6(c)(1)(ii) and (d)(2) do not apply. Instead, P adjusts such basis by taking into account the full amount of—

(i) T liabilities assumed by S or the amount of liabilities to which the T assets acquired by S are subject, and

(ii) The fair market value of any consideration not provided by P pursuant to the plan of reorganization.

(2) Reverse triangular merger. If P adjusts its basis in the T stock acquired as a result of a reverse triangular merger under § 1.358-6(c)(2)(i) and (d), § 1.358-6(c)(1)(ii) and (d)(2) do not apply. Instead, P adjusts such basis by taking into account the full amount of—

(i) T liabilities deemed assumed by S or the amount of liabilities to which the T assets deemed acquired by S are subject, and

(ii) The fair market value of any consideration not provided by P pursuant to the plan of reorganization.

(3) Excess loss accounts. Negative adjustments under this section may exceed P's basis in its S or T stock. The resulting negative amount is P's excess loss account in its S or T stock. See § 1.1502-19 for rules treating excess loss accounts as negative basis, and treating references to stock basis as including references to excess loss accounts.

(4) Application of other rules of law. If a transaction otherwise subject to this section is also a group structure change subject to § 1.1502-31, the provisions of § 1.1502-31 and not this section apply to determine stock basis. See § 1.1502-80(a) regarding the general applicability of other rules of law and a limitation on duplicative adjustments. See § 1.1502-80(d) for the non-application of section 357(c) to P.

(5) Examples. The rules of this paragraph (b) are illustrated by the following examples. For purposes of these examples, P, S, and T are domestic corporations, P and S file consolidated returns, P owns all of the only class of S stock, the P stock exchanged in the transaction satisfies the requirements of the applicable triangular reorganization provisions, the facts set forth the only corporate activity, and tax liabilities are disregarded.

Example (1). Liabilities.

(a) Facts. T has assets with an aggregate basis of $60 and fair market value of $100. T's assets are subject to $70 of liabilities. Pursuant to a plan, P forms S with $5 of cash (which S retains), and T merges into S. In the merger, the T shareholders receive P stock worth $30 in exchange for their T stock. The transaction is a reorganization to which sections 368(a)(1)(A) and (a)(2)(D) apply.

(b) Basis adjustment. Under § 1.358-6, P adjusts its $5 basis in the S stock as if P had acquired the T assets with a carryover basis under section 362 and transferred these assets to S in a transaction in which P determines its basis in the S stock under section 358. Under the rules of this section, the limitation described in § 1.358-6(c)(1)(ii) does not apply. Thus, P adjusts its basis in the S stock by -$10 (the aggregate adjusted basis of T's assets decreased by the amount of liabilities to which the T assets are subject). Consequently, as a result of the reorganization, P has an excess loss account of $5 in its S stock.

Example (2). Consideration not provided by p.

(a) Facts. T has assets with an aggregate basis of $10 and fair market value of $100 and no liabilities. S is an operating company with substantial assets that has been in existence for several years. P has a $5 basis in its S stock. Pursuant to a plan, T merges into S and the T shareholders receive $70 of P stock provided by P pursuant to the plan of reorganization and $30 of cash provided by S in exchange for their T stock. The transaction is a reorganization to which sections 368(a)(1)(A) and (a)(2)(D) apply.

(b) Basis adjustment. Under § 1.358-6, P adjusts its $5 basis in the S stock as if P had acquired the T assets with a carryover basis under section 362 and transferred these assets to S in a transaction in which P determines its basis in the S stock under section 358. Under the rules of this section, the limitation described in § 1.358-6(d)(2) does not apply. Thus, P adjusts its basis in the S stock by -$20 (the aggregate adjusted basis of T's assets decreased by the fair market value of the consideration provided by S). As a result of the reorganization, P has an excess loss account of $15 in its S stock.

(c) Appreciated asset. The facts are the same as in paragraph (a) of this Example 2, except that in the reorganization S provides an asset with a $20 adjusted basis and $30 fair market value instead of $30 cash. The basis is adjusted in the same manner as in paragraph (b) of this Example 2. In addition, because S recognizes a $10 gain from the asset under section 1001, P's basis in its S stock is increased under § 1.1502-32(b) by S's $10 gain. Consequently, as a result of the reorganization, P has an excess loss account of $5 in its S stock. (The results would be the same if the appreciated asset provided by S was P stock with respect to which S recognized gain. See § 1.1032-2(c)).

Example (3). Reverse triangular merger.

(a) Facts. T has assets with an aggregate basis of $60 and fair market value of $100. T's assets are subject to $70 of liabilities. P owns all of the only class of S stock. P has a $5 basis in its S stock. Pursuant to a plan, S merges into T with T surviving. In the merger, the T shareholders exchange their T stock for $2 cash from P and $28 worth of P stock provided by P pursuant to the plan. The transaction is a reorganization to which sections 368(a)(1)(A) and (a)(2)(E) apply.

(b) Basis adjustment. Under section 1.358-6, P's basis in the T stock acquired equals its $5 basis in its S stock immediately before the transaction adjusted by the $60 basis in the T assets deemed transferred, and the $70 of liabilities to which the T assets are subject. Under the rules of this section, the limitation described in § 1.358-6(c)(1)(ii) does not apply. Consequently, P has an excess loss account of $5 in its T stock as a result of the transaction.

(c) Effective/applicability date. This section applies to reorganizations occurring on or after December 21, 1995. However, paragraph (b)(4) of this section applies to reorganizations occurring on or after September 17, 2008.

T.D. 8648, 12/20/95, amend T.D. 9424, 9/10/2008.

§ 1.1502-31 Stock basis after a group structure change.

(a) In general. *(1) Overview.* If one corporation (P) succeeds another corporation (T) under the principles of § 1.1502-75(d)(2) or (3) as the common parent of a consolidated group in a group structure change, the basis of members in the stock of the former common parent (or the stock of a successor) is adjusted or determined under this section. See § 1.1502-33(f)(1) for the definition of group structure change. For example, if P owns all of the stock of another corporation (S), and T merges into S in a group structure change that is a reorganization described in section 368(a)(2)(D) in which P becomes the common parent of the T group, P's basis in S's stock must be adjusted to reflect the change in S's assets and liabilities. The rules of this section coordinate with the earnings and profits adjustments required under § 1.1502-33(f)(1), generally conforming the results of transactions in which the T group continues under § 1.1502-75 with P as the common parent. By preserving in P the relationship between T's earnings and profits and asset basis, these adjustments limit possible distortions under section 1502 (e.g., in the deconsolidation rules for earnings and profits under § 1.1502-33(e), and the continued filing requirements under § 1.1502-75(a)). This section applies whether or not T continues to exist after the group structure change.

(2) Application of other rules of law. If a transaction subject to this section is also a triangular reorganization otherwise subject to § 1.1502-30, the provisions of this section and not those of § 1.1502-30 apply to determine stock basis. See § 1.1502-80(a) regarding the general applicability of other rules of law and a limitation on duplicative adjustments.

(b) General rules. Except as otherwise provided in this section—

(1) Asset acquisitions. If a corporation acquires the former common parent's assets (and any liabilities assumed or to which the assets are subject) in a group structure change, the basis of members in the stock of the acquiring corporation is adjusted immediately after the group structure change to reflect the acquiring corporation's allocable share of the former common parent's net asset basis as determined under paragraph (c) of this section. For example, if S acquires all of T's assets in a group structure change that is a reorganization described in section 368(a)(2)(D), P's basis in S's stock is adjusted to reflect T's net asset basis. If P owned some of T's stock before the group structure change, the results would be the same because P's basis in the T stock is not taken into account in determining P's basis in S's stock. If T's net asset basis is a negative amount, it reduces P's basis in S's stock and, if the reduction exceeds P's basis in S's stock, the excess is P's excess loss account in S's stock. See § 1.1502-19 for rules treating P's excess loss account as negative basis, and treating a reference to P's basis in S's stock as including an excess loss account.

(2) Stock acquisitions. If a corporation acquires stock of the former common parent in a group structure change, the basis of the members in the former common parent's stock immediately after the group structure change (including any stock of the former common parent owned before the group structure change) that is, or would otherwise be, transferred basis property is redetermined in accordance with the results for an asset acquisition described in paragraph (b)(1) of this section. For example, if all of T's stock is contributed to P in a group structure change to which section 351 applies, P's basis in T's stock is T's net asset basis, rather than the amount determined under section 362. Similarly, if S merges into T in a group structure change described in section 368(a)(2)(E) and P acquires all of the T stock, P's basis in T's stock is the basis that P would have in S's stock under paragraph (b)(1) of this section if T had merged into S in a group structure change described in section 368(a)(2)(D).

(c) Net asset basis. The former common parent's net asset basis is the basis it would have in the stock of a newly formed subsidiary, if—

(1) The former common parent transferred its assets (and any liabilities assumed or to which the assets are subject) to the subsidiary in a transaction to which section 351 applies;

(2) The former common parent and the subsidiary were members of the same consolidated group (see § 1.1502-80(d) for the non-application of section 357(c) to the transfer); and

(3) The asset basis taken into account is each asset's basis immediately after the group structure change (e.g., taking into account any income or gain recognized in the group structure change and reflected in the asset's basis).

(d) Additional adjustments. In addition to the adjustments in paragraph (b) of this section, the following adjustments are made:

(1) Consideration not provided by P. The basis is reduced to reflect the fair market value of any consideration not provided by the member. For example, if S acquires T's assets in a group structure change described in section 368(a)(2)(D), and S provides an appreciated asset (e.g., stock of P) as partial consideration in the transaction, P's basis in S's stock is reduced by the fair market value of the asset.

(2) Allocable share. (i) Asset acquisitions. If a corporation receives less than all of the former common parent's assets and liabilities in the group structure change, the former common parent's net asset basis taken into account under paragraph (b)(1) of this section is adjusted accordingly.

(ii) Stock acquisitions. If less than all of the former common parent's stock is subject to the redetermination described in paragraph (b)(2) of this section, the percentage of the former common parent's net asset basis taken into account in the redetermination equals the percentage (by fair market value) of the former common parent's stock subject to the redetermination. For example, if P owns less than all of the former common parent's stock immediately after the group structure change and such stock would otherwise be transferred basis property, only an allocable part of the basis determined under this section is reflected in the shares owned by P (and the amount allocable to shares owned by nonmembers has no effect on the basis of their shares). Alternatively, if P acquired 10 percent of the former common parent's stock in a transaction in which the stock basis was determined by P's cost, and P later acquires the remaining 90 percent of the former common parent's stock in a separate transaction that is described in paragraph (b)(2) of this section, P retains its cost basis in its original stock and the basis of P's newly acquired shares reflects only an allocable part of the former common parent's net asset basis.

(3) Allocation among shares of stock. The basis determined under this section is allocated among shares under the principles of section 358. For example, if P owns multiple classes of the former common parent's stock immediately after the group structure change, only an allocable part of the basis determined under this section is reflected in the basis of each share. See § 1.1502-19(d), for special allocations with respect to excess loss accounts.

(4) Higher-tier members. To the extent that the former common parent is owned by members other than the new common parent, the basis of members in the stock of all subsidiaries owning, directly or indirectly, in whole or in part, an interest in the former common parent's assets or liabilities is adjusted in accordance with the principles of this section. The adjustments are applied in the order of the tiers, from the lowest to the highest.

(e) Waiver of loss carryovers of former common parent. *(1) General rule.* An irrevocable election may be made to treat all or any portion of a loss carryover attributable to the common parent as expiring for all Federal income tax purposes immediately before the group structure change. Thus, if the loss carryover is treated as expiring under the election, it will not result in a negative adjustment to the basis of P's stock under § 1.1502-32(b).

(2) Election. The election described in paragraph (e)(1) of this section must be made in a separate statement entitled, "ELECTION TO TREAT LOSS CARRYOVER AS EXPIRING UNDER § 1.1502-31(e)." The election must be filed by including the statement on or with the consolidated group's income tax return for the year that includes the group structure change. The statement must identify the amount of each loss carryover deemed to expire (or the amount of each loss carryover deemed not to expire, with any balance of any loss carryovers being deemed to expire).

(f) Predecessors and successors. For purposes of this section, any reference to a corporation includes a reference to a successor or predecessor as the context may require. See § 1.1502-32(f) for definitions of predecessor and successor.

(g) Examples. For purposes of the examples in this section, unless otherwise stated, all corporations have only one class of stock outstanding, the tax year of all persons is the calendar year, all persons use the accrual method of accounting, the facts set forth the only corporate activity, all transactions are between unrelated persons, and tax liabilities are disregarded. The principles of this section are illustrated by the following examples:

Example (1). Forward triangular merger.

(i) Facts. P is the common parent of one group and T is the common parent of another. T has assets with an aggregate basis of $60 and fair market value of $100 and no liabilities. T's shareholders have an aggregate basis of $50 in T's stock. In Year 1, pursuant to a plan, P forms S and T merges into S with the T shareholders receiving $100 of P stock in exchange for their T stock. The transaction is a reorganization described in section 368(a)(2)(D). The transaction is also a reverse acquisition under § 1.1502-75(d)(3) because the T shareholders, as a result of owning T's stock, own more than 50% of the value of P's stock immediately after the transaction. Thus, the transaction is a group structure change under § 1.1502-33(f)(1), and P's earnings and profits are adjusted to reflect T's earnings and profits immediately before T ceases to be the common parent of the T group.

(ii) Analysis. Under paragraph (b)(1) of this section, P's basis in S's stock is adjusted to reflect T's net asset basis. Under paragraph (c) of this section, T's net asset basis is $60, the basis T would have in the stock of a subsidiary under section 358 if T had transferred all of its assets and liabilities to the subsidiary in a transaction to which section 351 applies. Thus, P has a $60 basis in S's stock.

(iii) Pre-existing S. The facts are the same as in paragraph (i) of this Example 1, except that P has owned the stock of S for several years and P has a $50 basis in the S stock before the merger with T. Under paragraph (b)(1) of this section, P's $50 basis in S's stock is adjusted to reflect T's net asset basis. Thus, P's basis in S's stock is $110 ($50 plus $60).

(iv) Excess loss account included in former common parent's net asset basis. The facts are the same as in paragraph (i) of this Example 1, except that T has two assets, an operating asset with an $80 basis and $90 fair market value, and stock of a subsidiary with a $20 excess loss account and $10 fair market value. Under paragraph (c) of this section, T's net asset basis is $60 ($80 minus $20). See sections 351 and 358, and § 1.1502-19. Consequently, P has a $60 basis in S's stock. Under section 362 and § 1.1502-19, S has an $80 basis in the operating asset and a $20 excess loss account in the stock of the subsidiary.

(v) Liabilities in excess of basis. The facts are the same as in paragraph (i) of this Example 1, except that T's assets have a fair market value of $170 (and $60 basis) and are subject to $70 of liabilities. Under paragraph (c) of this section, T's net asset basis is negative $10 ($60 minus $70). See sections 351 and 358, and §§ 1.1502-19 and 1.1502-80(d). Thus, P has a $10 excess loss account in S's stock. Under section 362, S has a $60 basis in its assets (which are subject to $70 of liabilities). (Under paragraph (a)(2) of this section, because the liabilities are taken into account in determining net asset basis under paragraph (c) of this section, the liabilities are not also taken into account as consideration not provided by P under paragraph (d)(1) of this section.)

(vi) Consideration provided by S. The facts are the same as in paragraph (i) of this Example 1, except that P forms S with a $100 contribution at the beginning of Year 1, and during Year 6, pursuant to a plan, S purchases $100 of P stock and T merges into S with the T shareholders receiving P stock in exchange for their T stock. Under paragraph (b)(1) of this section, P's $100 basis in S's stock is increased by $60 to reflect T's net asset basis. Under paragraph (d)(1) of this section, P's basis in S's stock is decreased by $100 (the fair market value of the P stock) because the P stock purchased by S and used in the transaction is consideration not provided by P.

(vii) Appreciated asset provided by S. The facts are the same as in paragraph (i) of this Example 1, except that P has owned the stock of S for several years, and the shareholders of T receive $60 of P stock and an asset of S with a $30 adjusted basis and $40 fair market value. S recognizes a $10 gain from the asset under section 1001. Under paragraph (b)(1) of this section, P's basis in S's stock is increased by $60 to reflect T's net asset basis. Under paragraph (d)(1) of this section, P's basis in S's stock is decreased by $40 (the fair market value of the asset provided by S). In addition, P's basis in S's stock is increased under § 1.1502-32(b) by S's $10 gain.

(viii) Depreciated asset provided by S. The facts are the same as in paragraph (i) of this Example 1, except that P has owned the stock of S for several years, and the shareholders of T receive $60 of P stock and an asset of S with a $50 adjusted basis and $40 fair market value. S recognizes a $10 loss from the asset under section 1001. Under paragraph (b)(1) of this section, P's basis in S's stock is increased by $60 to reflect T's net asset basis. Under paragraph (d)(1) of this section, P's basis in S's stock is decreased by $40 (the fair market value of the asset provided by S). In addition, S's $10 loss is taken into account under § 1.1502-32(b) in determining P's basis adjustments under that section.

Example (2). Stock acquisition.

(i) Facts. P is the common parent of one group and T is the common parent of another. T has assets with an aggregate basis of $60 and fair market value of $100 and no liabilities. T's shareholders have an aggregate basis of $50 in T's stock. Pursuant to a plan, P forms S and S acquires all of T's stock in exchange for P stock in a transaction described in section 368(a)(1)(B). The transaction is also a reverse acquisition under § 1.1502-75(d)(3). Thus, the transaction is a group structure change under § 1.1502-33(f)(1), and the earnings and profits of P and S are adjusted to reflect T's earnings and profits immediately before T ceases to be the common parent of the T group.

(ii) Analysis. Under paragraph (d)(4) of this section, although S is not the new common parent of the T group, adjustments must be made to S's basis in T's stock in accordance with the principles of this section. Although S's basis in T's stock would ordinarily be determined under section 362 by reference to the basis of T's shareholders in T's stock immediately before the group structure change, under the principles of paragraph (b)(2) of this section, S's basis in T's stock is determined by reference to T's net asset basis. Thus, S's basis in T's stock is $60.

(iii) Higher-tier adjustments. Under paragraph (d)(4) of this section, P's basis in S's stock is increased by $60 (to be consistent with the adjustment to S's basis in T's stock).

(iv) Cross ownership. 1 The facts are the same as in paragraph (i) of this Example 2, except S purchased 10% of T's stock from an unrelated person for cash. In an unrelated transaction, S acquires the remaining 90% of T's stock in exchange for P stock. S's basis in the initial 10% of T's stock is not redetermined under this section. However, S's basis in the additional 90% of T's stock is redetermined under this section. S's basis in that stock is adjusted to $54 (90% of T's net asset basis).

(v) Allocable share. The facts are the same as in paragraph (i) of this Example 2, except that P owns only 90% of S's stock immediately after the group structure change. S's basis in T's stock is the same as in paragraph (ii) of this Example 2. Under paragraph (d)(2) of this section, P's basis in its S stock is increased by $54 (90% of S's $60 adjustment).

Example (3). Taxable stock acquisition.

(i) Facts. P is the common parent of one group and T is the common parent of another. T has assets with an aggregate basis of $60 and fair market value of $100 and no liabilities. T's shareholders have an aggregate basis of $50 in T's stock. Pursuant to a plan, P acquires all of T's stock in exchange for $70 of P's stock and $30 in a transaction that is a group structure change under § 1.1502-33(f)(1). P's acquired T stock is not transferred basis property. (Because of P's use of cash, the acquisition is not a transaction described in section 368(a)(1)(B).)

(ii) Analysis. The rules of this section do not apply to determine P's basis in T's stock. Therefore, P's basis in T's stock is $100.

(h) Effective/applicability dates. *(1) General rule.* This section applies to group structure changes that occur after April 26, 2004. However, a group may apply this section to group structure changes that occurred on or before April 26, 2004, and in consolidated return years beginning on or after January 1, 1995. In addition, paragraph (a)(2) of this section applies to group structure changes that occurred on or after September 17, 2008. Paragraph (e)(2) of this section applies to any original consolidated Federal income tax return due (without extensions) after June 14, 2007. For original consolidated Federal income tax returns due (without extensions) after May 30, 2006, and on or before June 14, 2007, see § 1.1502-31T as contained in 26 CFR part 1 in effect on April 1, 2007. For original consolidated Federal income tax returns due (without extensions) on or before May 30, 2006, see § 1.1502-31 as contained in 26 CFR part 1 in effect on April 1, 2006.

(2) Prior law. For group structure changes that occur on or before April 26, 2004, and in consolidated return years beginning on or after January 1, 1995, with respect to which the group does not elect to apply the provisions of this section, see § 1.1502-31 as contained in the 26 CFR part 1 edition revised as of April 1, 2003. For group structure changes that occur in consolidated return years beginning before January 1, 1995, see § 1.1502-31T as contained in the 26 CFR part 1 edition revised as of April 1, 1994.

T.D. 6909, 12/29/66, amend T.D. 7246, 12/29/72, T.D. 8226, 9/7/88, T.D. 8560, 8/12/94, T.D. 9122, 4/23/2004, T.D. 9264, 5/26/2006, T.D. 9329, 6/13/2007, T.D. 9424, 9/10/2008.

§ 1.1502-32 Investment adjustments.

(a) In general. *(1) Purpose.* This section provides rules for adjusting the basis of the stock of a subsidiary (S) owned by another member (M). These rules modify the determination of M's basis in S's stock under applicable rules of law by adjusting M's basis to reflect S's distributions and S's items of income, gain, deduction, and loss taken into account for the period that S is a member of the consolidated group. The purpose of the adjustments is to treat M and S as a single entity so that consolidated taxable income reflects the group's income. For example, if M forms S with a $100 contribution, and S takes into account $10 of income, M's $100 basis in S's stock under section 358 is increased by $10 under this section to prevent S's income from being taken into account a second time on M's disposition of S's stock. Comparable adjustments are made for tax-exempt income and noncapital, nondeductible expenses that S takes into account, to preserve their treatment under the Internal Revenue Code.

(2) Application of other rules of law, duplicative adjustments. See § 1.1502-80(a) regarding the general applicability of other rules of law and a limitation on duplicative adjustments. See, e.g., section 358 (basis determinations for distributees), section 1016 (adjustments to basis), § 1.1502-11(b) (limitations on the use of losses), § 1.1502-19 (treatment of excess loss accounts), § 1.1502-31 (basis after a group structure change), and § 1.1502-35 (additional rules relating to stock loss, including losses attributable to worthlessness and certain dispositions not followed by a separate return year). M's basis in S's stock must not be adjusted under this section and other rules of law in a manner that has the effect of duplicating an adjustment.

(3) Overview. (i) In general. The amount of the stock basis adjustments and their timing are determined under paragraph (b) of this section. Under paragraph (c) of this section, the amount of the adjustment is allocated among the shares of S's stock. Paragraphs (d) through (g) of this section provide definitions, an anti-avoidance rule, successor rules, and recordkeeping requirements.

(ii) Excess loss account. Negative adjustments under this section may exceed M's basis in S's stock. The resulting negative amount is M's excess loss account in S's stock. See § 1.1502-19 for rules treating excess loss accounts as negative basis, and treating references to stock basis as including references to excess loss accounts.

(iii) Tiering up of adjustments. The adjustments to S's stock under this section are taken into account in determining adjustments to higher-tier stock. The adjustments are applied in the order of the tiers, from the lowest to the highest. For example, if M is also a subsidiary, M's adjustment to S's stock is taken into account in determining the adjustments to stock of M owned by other members.

(b) Stock basis adjustments. *(1) Timing of adjustments.* (i) In general. Adjustments under this section are made as of the close of each consolidated return year, and as of any other time (an interim adjustment) if a determination at that time is necessary to determine a tax liability of any person. For example, adjustments are made as of M's sale of S's stock in order to measure M's gain or loss from the sale, and if M's interest in S's stock is not uniform throughout the year (e.g., because M disposes of a portion of its S stock, or S issues additional shares to another person), the adjustments under this section are made by taking into account the varying interests. An interim adjustment may be necessary even if tax liability is not affected until a later time. For example, if M sells only 50% of S's stock and S becomes a nonmember, adjustments must be made for the retained stock as of the disposition (whether or not M has an excess loss account in that stock). Similarly, if S liquidates during a consolidated return year, adjustments must be made as of the liquidation (even if the liquidation is tax free under section 332).

(ii) Special rule for discharge of indebtedness income. Adjustments under this section resulting from the realization of discharge of indebtedness income of a member that is excluded from gross income under section 108(a) (excluded COD income) and from the reduction of attributes in respect thereof pursuant to sections 108 and 1017 and § 1.1502-28 (including reductions in the basis of property) when a member (the departing member) ceases to be a member of the group on or prior to the last day of the consolidated return year that includes the date the excluded COD income is realized are made immediately after the determination of tax for the group for the taxable year during which the excluded COD income is realized (and any prior years) and are effective immediately before the beginning of the taxable year of the departing member following the taxable year during which the excluded COD income is realized. Such adjustments when a corporation (the new member) is not a member of the group on the last day of the consolidated return year that includes the date the excluded COD income is realized but is a member of the group at the beginning of the following consolidated return year are also made immediately after the determination of tax for the group for the taxable year during which the excluded COD income is realized (and any prior years) and are effective immediately before the beginning of the taxable year of the new member following the taxable year during which the excluded COD income is realized. If the new member was a member of another group immediately before it became a member of the group, such adjustments are treated as occurring immediately after it ceases to be a member of the prior group.

(iii) Allocation of items. If § 1.1502-76(b) applies to S for purposes of an adjustment before the close of the group's consolidated return year, the amount of the adjustment is determined under that section. If § 1.1502-76(b) does not apply to the interim adjustment, the adjustment is determined under the principles of § 1.1502-76(b), consistently applied, and ratable allocation under the principles of § 1.1502-76(b)(2)(ii) or (iii) may be used without filing an election under § 1.1502-76(b)(2). The principles would apply, for example, if M becomes a nonmember but S remains a member.

(2) Amount of adjustments. M's basis in S's stock is increased by positive adjustments and decreased by negative adjustments under this paragraph (b)(2). The amount of the adjustment, determined as of the time of the adjustment, is the net amount of S's—

(i) Taxable income or loss;

(ii) Tax-exempt income;

(iii) Noncapital, nondeductible expenses; and

(iv) Distributions with respect to S's stock.

(3) Operating rules. For purposes of determining M's adjustments to the basis of S's stock under paragraph (b)(2) of this section—

(i) Taxable income or loss. S's taxable income or loss is consolidated taxable income (or loss) determined by including only S's items of income, gain, deduction, and loss taken into account in determining consolidated taxable income (or loss), treating S's deductions and losses as taken into account to the extent they are absorbed by S or any other member. For this purpose:

(A) To the extent that S's deduction or loss is absorbed in the year it arises or is carried forward and absorbed in a subsequent year (e.g., under section 172, 465, or 1212), the deduction or loss is taken into account under paragraph (b)(2) of this section in the year in which it is absorbed.

(B) To the extent that S's deduction or loss is carried back and absorbed in a prior year (whether consolidated or separate), the deduction or loss is taken into account under paragraph (b)(2) of this section in the year in which it arises and not in the year in which it is absorbed.

(ii) Tax-exempt income. (A) In general. S's tax-exempt income is its income and gain which is taken into account but permanently excluded from its gross income under applicable law, and which increases, directly or indirectly, the basis of its assets (or an equivalent amount). For example, S's dividend income to which § 1.1502-13(f)(2)(ii) applies, and its interest excluded from gross income under section 103, are treated as tax-exempt income. However, S's income not recognized under section 1031 is not treated as tax-exempt income because the corresponding basis adjustments under section 1031(d) prevent S's nonrecognition from being permanent. Similarly, S's tax-exempt income does not include gain not recognized under section 332 from the liquidation of a lower-tier subsidiary, or not recognized under section 118 or section 351 from a transfer of assets to S.

(B) Equivalent deductions. To the extent that S's taxable income or gain is permanently offset by a deduction or loss that does not reduce, directly or indirectly, the basis of S's assets (or an equivalent amount), the income or gain is treated as tax-exempt income and is taken into account under paragraph (b)(3)(ii)(A) of this section. In addition, the income and the offsetting item are taken into account under paragraph (b)(3)(i) of this section. For example, if S receives a $100 dividend with respect to which a $70 dividends received deduction is allowed under section 243, $70 of the dividend is treated as tax-exempt income. Accordingly, M's basis in S's stock increases by $100 because the $100 dividend and $70 deduction are taken into account under paragraph (b)(3)(i) of this section (resulting in $30 of the increase), and $70 of the dividend is also taken into account under paragraph (b)(3)(ii)(A) of this section as tax-exempt income (resulting in $70 of the increase). (See paragraph (b)(3)(iii) of this section if there is a corresponding negative adjustment under section 1059.) Similarly, income from mineral properties is treated as tax-exempt income to the extent it is offset by deductions for depletion in excess of the basis of the property.

(C) Discharge of indebtedness income. (1) In general. Excluded COD income is treated as tax-exempt income only to the extent the discharge is applied to reduce tax attributes attributable to any member of the group under section 108, section 1017 or § 1.1502-28. However, if S is treated as realizing excluded COD income pursuant to § 1.1502-28(a)(3), S shall not be treated as realizing excluded COD income for purposes of the preceding sentence.

(2) Expired loss carryovers. If the amount of the discharge exceeds the amount of the attribute reduction under sections 108 and 1017, and § 1.1502-28, the excess nevertheless is treated as applied to reduce tax attributes to the extent a loss carryover attributable to S expired without tax benefit, the expiration was taken into account as a noncapital, nondeductible expense under paragraph (b)(3)(iii) of this section, and the loss carryover would have been reduced had it not expired.

(D) Basis shifts. An increase in the basis of S's assets (or an equivalent as described in paragraph (b)(3)(iv)(B) of this section) is treated as tax-exempt income to the extent that the increase is not otherwise taken into account in determining stock basis, it corresponds to a negative adjustment that is taken into account by the group under this paragraph (b) (or incurred by the common parent), and it has the effect (viewing the group in the aggregate) of a permanent recovery of the reduction. For example, S's basis increase under section 50(c)(2) is treated as tax-exempt income to the extent the preceding basis reduction under section 50(c)(1) is reflected in the basis of a member's stock. On the other hand, if S increases the basis of an asset as the result of an accounting method change, and the related positive section 481(a) adjustment is taken into account over time, the basis increase is not treated as tax-exempt income.

(iii) Noncapital, nondeductible expenses. (A) In general. S's noncapital, nondeductible expenses are its deductions and losses that are taken into account but permanently disallowed or eliminated under applicable law in determining its taxable income or loss, and that decrease, directly or indirectly, the basis of its assets (or an equivalent amount). For example, S's Federal taxes described in section 275 and loss not recognized under section 311(a) are noncapital, nondeductible expenses. Similarly, if a loss carryover (e.g., under section 172 or 1212) attributable to S expires or is reduced under section 108(b) and § 1.1502-28, it becomes a noncapital, nondeductible expense at the close of the last tax year to which it may be carried. However, when a tax attribute attributable to S is reduced as required pursuant to § 1.1502-28(a)(3), the reduction of the tax attribute is not treated as a noncapital, nondeductible expense of S. Finally, if S sells and repurchases a security subject to section 1091, the disallowed loss is not a noncapital, nondeductible expense because the corresponding basis adjustments under section 1091(d) prevent the disallowance from being permanent.

(B) Nondeductible basis recovery. Any other decrease in the basis of S's assets (or an equivalent as described in paragraph (b)(3)(iv)(B) of this section) may be a noncapital, nondeductible expense to the extent that the decrease is not otherwise taken into account in determining stock basis and is permanently eliminated for purposes of determining S's taxable income or loss. Whether a decrease is so treated is determined by taking into account both the purposes of the Code or regulatory provision resulting in the decrease and the purposes of this section. For example, S's noncapital, nondeductible expenses include any basis reduction under section 50(c)(1), section 1017, section 1059, § 1.1502-35(b) or (f)(2). Also included as a noncapital, nondeductible expense is the amount of any gross-up for taxes paid by another taxpayer that S is treated as having paid (e.g., income included under section 78, or the portion of an undistributed capital gain dividend that is treated as tax deemed to have been paid by a shareholder under section 852(b)(3)(D)(ii), whether or not any corresponding amount is claimed as a tax credit). In contrast, a decrease generally is not a noncapital, nondeductible expense if it results because S redeems stock in a transaction to which section 302(a) applies, S receives assets in a liquidation to which section 332 applies and its basis in the assets is less than its basis in the stock canceled, or S distributes the stock of a subsidiary in a distribution to which section 355 applies.

(iv) Special rules for tax-exempt income and noncapital, nondeductible expenses. For purposes of paragraphs (b)(3)(ii) and (iii) of this section:

(A) Treatment as permanent. An amount is permanently excluded from gross income, or permanently disallowed or eliminated, if it is so treated by S even though another person may take a corresponding amount into account. For example, if S sells property to a nonmember at a loss that is disallowed under section 267(a), S's loss is a noncapital, nondeductible expense even though under section 267(d) the nonmember may treat a corresponding amount of gain as not recognized. (If the nonmember is a subsidiary in another consolidated group, its gain not recognized under section 267(d) is tax-exempt income under paragraph (b)(3)(ii)(A) of this section.)

(B) Amounts equivalent to basis and adjustments to basis. Amounts equivalent to basis include the amount of money, the amount of a loss carryover, and the amount of an adjustment to gain or loss under section 475(a) for securities described in section 475(a)(2). An equivalent to a basis increase includes a decrease in an excess loss account, and an equivalent to a basis decrease includes the denial of basis for taxable income.

(C) Timing. An amount is taken into account in the year in which it would be taken into account under paragraph (b)(3)(i) of this section if it were subject to Federal income taxation.

(D) Tax sharing agreements. Taxes are taken into account by applying the principles of section 1552 and the percentage method under § 1.1502-33(d)(3) (and by assuming a 100% allocation of any decreased tax liability). The treatment of amounts allocated under this paragraph (b)(3)(iv)(D) is analogous to the treatment of allocations under § 1.1552-1(b)(2). For example, if one member owes a payment to a second member, the first member is treated as indebted to the second member. The right to receive payment is treated as a positive adjustment under paragraph (b)(3)(ii) of this section, and the obligation to make payment is treated as a negative adjustment under paragraph (b)(3)(iii) of this section. If the obligation is not paid, the amount not paid generally is treated as a distribution, contribution, or both, depending on the relationship between the members.

(v) Distributions. Distributions taken into account under paragraph (b)(2) of this section are distributions with respect to S's stock to which section 301 applies and all other distributions treated as dividends (e.g., under section 356(a)(2)). See § 1.1502-13(f)(2)(iv) for taking into account distributions to which section 301 applies (but not other distributions treated as dividends) under the entitlement rule.

(4) Waiver of loss carryovers from separate return limitation years. (i) General rule. If S has a loss carryover from a separate return limitation year when it becomes a member of a consolidated group, the group may make an irrevocable election to treat all or any portion of the loss carryover as expiring for all Federal income tax purposes immediately before S becomes a member of the consolidated group (deemed expiration). If S was a member of another group immediately before it became a member of the consolidated group, the expiration is also treated as occurring immediately after it ceases to be a member of the prior group.

(ii) Stock basis adjustments from a waiver. (A) Qualifying transactions. If S becomes a member of the consolidated group in a qualifying cost basis transaction and an election under this paragraph (b)(4) is made, the noncapital, nondeductible expense resulting from the deemed expiration does not result in a corresponding stock basis adjustment for any member under this section. A qualifying cost basis transaction is the purchase (i.e., a transaction in which basis is determined under section 1012) by members of the acquiring consolidated group (while they are members) in a 12-month period of an amount of S's stock satisfying the requirements of section 1504(a)(2).

(B) Nonqualifying transactions. If S becomes a member of the consolidated group other than in a qualifying cost basis transaction and an election under this paragraph (b)(4) is made, the basis of its stock that is owned by members immediately after it becomes a member is subject to reduction under the principles of this section to reflect the deemed expiration. The reduction occurs immediately before S becomes a member, but after it ceases to be a member of any prior group, and it therefore does not result in a corresponding stock basis adjustment for any higher-tier member of the transferring or acquiring consolidated group. Any basis reduction under this paragraph (b)(4)(ii)(B) is taken into account in making determinations of basis under the Code with respect to S's stock (e.g., a determination under section 362 because the stock is acquired in a transaction described in section 368(a)(1)(B)), but it does not result in corresponding stock basis adjustments under this section for any higher-tier member. If the basis reduction exceeds the basis of S's stock, the excess is treated as an excess loss account to which the members owning S's stock succeed.

(C) Higher-tier corporations. If S becomes a member of the consolidated group as a result, in whole or in part, of a higher-tier corporation becoming a member (whether or not in a qualifying cost basis transaction), additional adjustments are required. The highest-tier corporation (T) whose becoming a member resulted in S becoming a member, and T's chain of lower-tier corporations that includes S, are subject to the adjustment. The deemed expiration of S's loss carryover that results in a negative adjustment for the first higher-tier corporation is treated as an expiring loss carryover of that higher-tier corporation for purposes of applying paragraph (b)(4)(ii)(B) of this section to that corporation. For example, if M purchases all of the stock of T, T owns all of the stock of T1, T1 owns all of the stock of S, S becomes a member as a result of T becoming a member, and the election under this paragraph (b)(4) is made, the basis of the S stock is reduced and the reduction tiers up to T1, T1 treats the negative adjustment to its basis in S's stock as an expiring loss carryover of T1, and T then adjusts its basis in T1's stock. In addition, if T becomes a member of the acquiring group in a transaction other than a qualifying cost basis transaction, the amount that tiers up to T also reduces the basis of its stock under paragraph (b)(4)(ii)(B) of this section (but the amount does not tier up to higher-tier members).

(iii) Net asset basis limitation. Basis reduced under this paragraph (b)(4) is restored before S becomes a member (and before the basis of S's stock is taken into account in determining basis under the Code) to the extent necessary to conform a share's basis to its allocable portion of net asset basis. In the case of higher-tier corporations under paragraph (b)(4)(ii)(C) of this section, the restoration does not tier up but is instead applied separately to each higher-tier corporation. For purposes of determining each corporation's net asset basis (including the basis of stock in lower-tier corporations), the restoration is applied in the order of tiers, from the lowest to the highest. For purposes of the restoration:

(A) A member's net asset basis is the positive or negative difference between the adjusted basis of its assets (and the amount of any of its loss carryovers that are not deemed to expire) and its liabilities. Appropriate adjustments must be made, for example, to disregard liabilities that subsequently will give rise to deductions (e.g., liabilities to which section 461(h) applies).

(B) Within a class of stock, each share has the same allocable portion of net asset basis. If there is more than one class of common stock, the net asset basis is allocated to each class by taking into account the terms of each class and all other facts and circumstances relating to the overall economic arrangement.

(iv) Election. The election described in paragraph (b)(4) of this section must be made in a separate statement entitled, "ELECTION TO TREAT LOSS CARRYOVER OF [INSERT NAME AND EMPLOYER IDENTIFICATION NUMBER OF S] AS EXPIRING UNDER § 1.1502-32(b)(4)." The election must be filed by including a statement on or with the consolidated group's income tax return for the year S becomes a member. A separate statement must be made for each member whose loss carryover is deemed to expire. The statement must identify the amount of each loss carryover deemed to expire (or the amount of each loss carryover deemed not to expire, with any balance of any loss carryovers being deemed to expire) and the basis of any stock reduced as a result of the deemed expiration.

(v) Special rule for loss carryovers of a subsidiary acquired in a transaction for which an election under § 1.1502-20(i)(2) is made— (A) Expired losses. Notwithstanding paragraph (b)(4)(iv) of this section, unless a group otherwise chooses, to the extent that S's loss carryovers are increased by reason of an election under § 1.1502-20(i)(2) and such loss carryovers expire or would have been properly used to offset income in a taxable year for which the refund of an overpayment is prevented by any law or rule of law as of the date the group files its original return for the taxable year in which S receives the notification described in § 1.1502-20(i)(3)(iv) and at all times thereafter, the group will be deemed to have made an election under paragraph (b)(4) of this section to treat all of such loss carryovers as expiring for all Federal income tax purposes immediately before S became a member of the consolidated group. A group may choose not to apply the rule of the previous sentence to all of such loss carryovers of S by taking a position on an original or amended tax return for each relevant taxable year that is consistent with having made such choice.

(B) Available losses. Notwithstanding paragraph (b)(4)(iv) of this section, to the extent that S's loss carryovers are increased by reason of an election under § 1.1502-20(i)(2) and such loss carryovers have not expired and would not have been properly used to offset income in a taxable year for which the refund of an overpayment is prevented by any law or rule of law as of the date the group files its original return for the taxable year in which S receives the notification described in § 1.1502-20(i)(3)(iv) and at all times thereafter, the group may make an election under paragraph (b)(4) of this section to treat all or a portion of such loss carryovers as expiring for all Federal income tax purposes immediately before S became a member of the consolidated group. Such election must be filed with the group's original return for the taxable year in which S receives the notification described in § 1.1502-20(i)(3)(iv).

(C) Effective dates. Paragraph (b)(4)(v) of this section is applicable on and after March 3, 2005. For prior periods, see § 1.1502-32T(b)(4)(v) as contained in the 26 CFR part 1 in effect on March 2, 2005.

(vi) Special rules in the case of certain transactions subject to § 1.1502-35. If a member of a consolidated group transfers stock of a subsidiary and such stock has a basis that exceeds its value immediately before such transfer or a subsidiary is deconsolidated and any stock of such subsidiary owned by members of the group immediately before such deconsolidation has a basis that exceeds its value, all members of the group are subject to the provisions of § 1.1502-35(b), which generally require a redetermination of members' basis in all shares of subsidiary stock.

(vii) Special rules for amending waiver of loss carryovers from separate return limitation year. (A) Waivers that increased allowable loss or reduced basis reduction required. If, in connection with the acquisition of S, the group made an election pursuant to paragraph (b)(4) of this section to treat all or any portion of S's loss carryovers as expiring, and the prior group elected to determine the amount of the allowable loss or the basis reduction required with respect to the stock of S or a higher-tier corporation of S by applying the provisions described in § 1.1502-20(i)(2)(i) or (ii), then the group may reduce the amount of any loss carryover deemed to expire (or increase the amount of any loss carryover deemed not to expire) as a result of the election made pursuant to paragraph (b)(4) of this section. The aggregate amount of loss carryovers that may be treated as not expiring as a result of amendments made pursuant to this paragraph (b)(4)(vii)(A) with respect to S and any higher- and lower-tier corporation of S may not exceed the amount described in § 1.1502-20(c)(1)(iii) with respect to the acquired stock (computed without regard to the effect of the group's election or elections pursuant to paragraph (b)(4) of this section, but with regard to the effect of the prior group's election pursuant to § 1.1502-20(g), if any, prior to the application of § 1.1502-20(i)(3)). For purposes of determining the aggregate amount of loss carryovers that may be treated as not expiring as a result of amendments made pursuant to this paragraph (b)(4)(vii)(A) with respect to S and any higher- and lower-tier corporation of S, the group may rely on a written notification provided by the prior group. Nothing in this paragraph shall be construed as permitting a group to increase the amount of any loss carryover deemed to expire (or reduce the amount of any loss carryover deemed not to expire) as a result of the election made pursuant to paragraph (b)(4) of this section.

(B) Inadvertent waivers of loss carryovers previously subject to an election described in § 1.1502-20(g). If, in connection with the acquisition of S, the group made an election pursuant to paragraph (b)(4) of this section to waive loss carryovers of S by identifying the amount of each loss carryover deemed not to expire, the prior group elected to determine the amount of the allowable loss or the basis reduction required with respect to the stock of S or a higher-tier corporation of S by applying the provisions described in § 1.1502-20(i)(2)(i) or (ii), and the amount of S's loss carryovers treated as reattributed to the prior group pursuant to the election described in § 1.1502-20(g) is reduced pursuant to § 1.1502-20(i)(3), then the group may amend its election made pursuant to paragraph (b)(4) of this section to provide that all or a portion of the loss carryovers of S that are treated as loss carryovers of S as a result of the prior group's election to apply the provisions described in § 1.1502-20(i)(2)(i) or (ii) are deemed not to expire. This paragraph (b)(4)(vii)(B), however, does not permit a group to reduce the amount of any loss carryover deemed not to expire as a result of the election made pursuant to paragraph (b)(4) of this section.

(C) Time and manner of amending an election under § 1.1502-32(b)(4). The amendment of an election made pursuant to paragraph (b)(4) of this section must be made in a statement entitled Amendment of Election to Treat Loss Carryover as Expiring Under § 1.1502-32(b)(4) Pursuant to § 1.1502-32(b)(4)(vii). The statement must be filed with or as part of any timely filed (including extensions) original return for the taxable year that includes August 26, 2004, or with or as part of an amended return filed before the date the original return for the taxable year that includes August 26, 2004, is due (with regard to extensions). A separate statement shall be filed for each election made pursuant to paragraph (b)(4) of this section that is being amended pursuant to this paragraph (b)(4)(vii). For purposes of making this statement, the group may rely on the statements set forth in a written notification provided by the prior group. The statement filed under this paragraph must include the following—

(1) The name and employer identification number (E.I.N.) of S;

(2) In the case of an amendment made pursuant to paragraph (b)(4)(vii)(A), a statement that the group has received a written notification from the prior group confirming that the group's prior election or elections pursuant to paragraph (b)(4) of this section had the effect of either increasing the prior group's allowable loss on the disposition of subsidiary stock or reducing the prior group's amount of basis reduction required;

(3) The amount of each loss carryover of S deemed to expire (or the amount of loss carryover deemed not to expire) as set forth in the election made pursuant to paragraph (b)(4) of this section;

(4) The amended amount of each loss carryover of S deemed to expire (or the amended amount of loss carryover deemed not to expire); and

(5) In the case of an amendment made pursuant to paragraph (b)(4)(vii)(A) of this section, a statement that the aggregate amount of loss carryovers of S and any higher- and lower-tier corporation of S that will be treated as not expiring as a result of amendments made pursuant to paragraph (b)(4)(vii)(A) of this section will not exceed the amount described in § 1.1502-20(c)(1)(iii) with respect to the acquired stock (computed without regard to the effect of the group's election or elections pursuant to paragraph (b)(4) of this section, but with regard to the effect of the prior group's election pursuant to § 1.1502-20(g), if any, prior to the application of § 1.1502-20(i)(3)).

(D) Items taken into account in open years. An amendment to an election made pursuant to paragraph (b)(4) of this section affects the group's items of income, gain, deduction, or loss only to the extent that the amendment gives rise, directly or indirectly, to items or amounts that would properly be taken into account in a year for which an assessment of deficiency or a refund for overpayment, as the case may be, is not prevented by any law or rule of law. Under this paragraph, if the year to which a loss previously deemed to expire as a result of an election made pursuant to paragraph (b)(4) of this section is deemed not to expire as a result of an election made pursuant to this paragraph would have been carried back or carried forward is a year for which a refund of overpayment is prevented by law, then to the extent that the absorption of such loss in such year would have affected the tax treatment of another item (e.g., another loss that was absorbed in such year) that has an effect in a year for which a refund of overpayment is not prevented by any law or rule of law, the amendment to the election made pursuant to paragraph (b)(4) of this section will affect the treatment of such other item. Therefore, if the absorption of such loss (the first loss) in a year for which a refund of overpayment is prevented by law would have prevented the absorption of another loss (the second loss) in such year and such second loss would have been carried to and used in a year for which a refund of overpayment is not prevented by any law or rule of law (the other year), the amendment of the election makes the second loss available for use in the other year.

(E) Higher- and lower-tier corporations of S. A higher-tier corporation of S is a corporation that was a member of the prior group and, as a result of such higher-tier corporation becoming a member of the group, S became a member of the group. A lower-tier corporation of S is a corporation that was a member of the prior group and became a member of the group as a result of S becoming a member of the group.

(F) Effective date. This paragraph (b)(4)(vii) is applicable on and after March 3, 2005. For prior periods, see § 1.1502-32T(b)(4)(vii) as contained in the 26 CFR part 1 in effect on March 2, 2005.

(5) Examples. (i) In general. For purposes of the examples in this section, unless otherwise stated, M owns all of the only class of S's stock, the stock is owned for the entire year, S owns no stock of lower-tier members, the tax year of all persons is the calendar year, all persons use the accrual method of accounting, the facts set forth the only corporate activity, preferred stock is described in section 1504(a)(4), all transactions are between unrelated persons, and tax liabilities are disregarded.

(ii) Stock basis adjustments. The principles of this paragraph (b) are illustrated by the following examples.

Example (1). Taxable income.

(a) Current taxable income. For Year 1, the M group has $100 of taxable income when determined by including only S's items of income, gain, deduction, and loss taken into account. Under paragraph (b)(1) of this section, M's basis in S's stock is adjusted under this section as of the close of Year 1. Under paragraph (b)(2) of this section, M's basis in S's stock is increased by the amount of the M group's taxable income determined by including only S's items taken into account. Thus, M's basis in S's stock is increased by $100 as of the close of Year 1.

(b) Intercompany gain that is not taken into account. The facts are the same as in paragraph (a) of this Example 1, except that S also sells property to another member at a $25 gain in Year 1, the gain is deferred under § 1.1502-13 and taken into account in Year 3, and M sells 10% of S's stock to nonmembers in Year 2. Under paragraph (b)(3)(i) of this section, S's deferred gain is not additional taxable income for Year 1 or 2 because it is not taken into account in determining the M group's consolidated taxable income for either of those years. The deferred gain is not tax-exempt income under paragraph (b)(3)(ii) of this section because it is not permanently excluded from S's gross income. The deferred gain does not result in a basis adjustment until Year 3, when it is taken into account in determining the M group's consolidated taxable income. Consequently, M's basis in the S shares sold is not increased to reflect S's gain from the intercompany sale of the property. In Year 3, the deferred gain is taken into account, but the amount allocable to the shares sold by M does not increase their basis because these shares are held by nonmembers.

(c) Intercompany gain taken into account. The facts are the same as in paragraph (b) of this Example 1, except that M sells all of S's stock in Year 2 (rather than only 10%). Under § 1.1502-13, S takes the $25 gain into account immediately before S becomes a nonmember. Thus, M's basis in S's stock is increased to reflect S's gain from the intercompany sale of the property.

Example (2). Tax loss.

(a) Current absorption. For Year 2, the M group has a $50 consolidated net operating loss when determined by taking into account only S's items of income, gain, deduction, and loss. S's loss is absorbed by the M group in Year 2, offsetting M's income for that year. Under paragraph (b)(3)(i)(A) of this section, because S's loss is absorbed in the year it arises, M has a $50 negative adjustment with respect to S's stock. Under paragraph (b)(2) of this section, M reduces its basis in S's stock by $50. Under paragraph (a)(3)(ii) of this section, if the decrease exceeds M's basis in S's stock, the excess is M's excess loss account in S's stock.

(b) Interim determination from stock sale. The facts are the same as in paragraph (a) of this Example 2, except that S's Year 2 loss arises in the first half of the calendar year, M sells 50% of S's stock on July 1 of Year 2, and M's income for Year 2 does not arise until after the sale of S's stock. M's income for Year 2 (exclusive of the sale of S's stock) is offset by S's loss, even though the income arises after the stock sale, and no loss remains to be apportioned to S. See §§ 1.1502-11 and 1.1502-21(b). Under paragraph (b)(3)(i)(A) of this section, because S's $50 loss is absorbed in the year it arises, it reduces M's basis in the S shares sold by $25 immediately before the stock sale. Because S becomes a nonmember, the loss also reduces M's basis in the retained S shares by $25 immediately before S becomes a nonmember.

(c) Loss carryback. The facts are the same as in paragraph (a) of this Example 2, except that M has no income or loss for Year 2, S's $50 loss is carried back and absorbed by the M group in Year 1 (offsetting the income of M or S), and the M group receives a $17 tax refund in Year 2 that is paid to S. Under paragraph (b)(3)(i)(B) of this section, because the $50 loss is carried back and absorbed in Year 1, it is treated as a tax loss for Year 2 (the year in which it arises). Under paragraph (b)(3)(ii) of this section, the refund is treated as tax-exempt income of S. Under paragraph (b)(3)(iv)(C) of this section, the tax-exempt income is taken into account in Year 2 because that is the year it would be taken into account under S's method of accounting if it were subject to Federal income taxation. Thus, under paragraph (b)(2) of this section, M reduces its basis in S's stock by $33 as of the close of Year 2 (the $50 tax loss, less the $17 tax refund).

(d) Loss carryforward. The facts are the same as in paragraph (a) of this Example 2, except that M has no income or loss for Year 2, and S's loss is carried forward and absorbed by the M group in Year 3 (offsetting the income of M or S). Under paragraph (b)(3)(i)(A) of this section, the loss is not treated as a tax loss under paragraph (b)(2) of this section until Year 3.

Example (3). Tax-exempt income and noncapital, nondeductible expenses.

(a) Facts. For Year 1, the M group has $500 of consolidated taxable income. However, the M group has a $100 consolidated net operating loss when determined by including only S's items of income, gain, deduction, and loss taken into account. Also for Year 1, S has $80 of interest income that is permanently excluded from gross income under section 103, and S incurs $60 of related expense for which a deduction is permanently disallowed under section 265.

(b) Analysis. Under paragraph (b)(3)(i)(A) of this section, S has a $100 tax loss for Year 1. Under paragraph (b)(3)(ii)(A) of this section, S has $80 of tax-exempt income. Under paragraph (b)(3)(iii)(A) of this section, S has $60 of noncapital, nondeductible expense. Under paragraph (b)(3)(iv)(C) of this section, the tax-exempt income and noncapital, nondeductible expense are taken into account in Year 1 because that is the year they would be taken into account under S's method of accounting if they were subject to Federal income taxation. Thus, under paragraph (b) of this section, M reduces its basis in S's stock as of the close of Year 1 by an $80 net amount (the $100 tax loss, less $80 of tax-exempt income, plus $60 of noncapital, nondeductible expenses).

Example (4). Discharge of indebtedness. (a) Facts. M forms S on January 1 of Year 1 and S borrows $200. During Year 1, S's assets decline in value and the M group has a $100 consolidated net operating loss. Of that amount, $10 is attributable to M and $90 is attributable to S under the principles of § 1.1502-21(b)(2)(iv). None of the loss is absorbed by the group in Year 1, and S is discharged from $100 of indebtedness at the close of Year 1. M has a $0 basis in the S stock. M and S have no attributes other than the consolidated net operating loss. Under section 108(a), S's $100 of discharge of indebtedness income is excluded from gross income because of insolvency. Under section 108(b) and § 1.1502-28, the consolidated net operating loss is reduced to $0.

(b) Analysis. Under paragraph (b)(3)(iii)(A) of this section, the reduction of $90 of the consolidated net operating loss attributable to S is treated as a noncapital, nondeductible expense in Year 1 because that loss is permanently disallowed by section 108(b) and § 1.1502-28. Under paragraph (b)(3)(ii)(C)(1) of this section, all $100 of S's discharge of indebtedness income is treated as tax-exempt income in Year 1 because the discharge results in a $100 reduction to the consolidated net operating loss. Consequently, the loss and the cancellation of the indebtedness result in a net positive $10 adjustment to M's basis in its S stock.

(c) Insufficient attributes. The facts are the same as in paragraph (a) of this Example 4, except that S is discharged from $120 of indebtedness at the close of Year 1. Under section 108(a), S's $120 of discharge of indebtedness income is excluded from gross income because of insolvency. Under section 108(b) and § 1.1502-28, the consolidated net operating loss is reduced by $100 to $0 after the determination of tax for Year 1. Under paragraph (b)(3)(iii)(A) of this section, the reduction of $90 of the consolidated net operating loss attributable to S is treated as a noncapital, nondeductible expense. Under paragraph (b)(3)(ii)(C)(1) of this section, only $100 of the discharge is treated as tax-exempt income because only that amount is applied to reduce tax attributes. The remaining $20 of discharge of indebtedness income excluded from gross income under section 108(a) has no effect on M's basis in S's stock.

(d) Purchase price adjustment. Assume instead that S buys land in Year 1 in exchange for S's $100 purchase money note (bearing interest at a market rate of interest in excess of the applicable Federal rate, and providing for a principal payment at the end of Year 10), and the seller agrees with S in Year 4 to discharge $60 of the note as a purchase price adjustment to which section 108(e)(5) applies. S has no discharge of indebtedness income that is treated as tax-exempt income under paragraph (b)(3)(ii) of this section. In addition, the $60 purchase price adjustment is not a noncapital, nondeductible expense under paragraph (b)(3)(iii) of this section. A purchase price adjustment is not equivalent to a discharge of indebtedness that is offset by a deduction or loss. Consequently, the purchase price adjustment results in no net adjustment to M's basis in S's stock under paragraph (b) of this section.

Example (5). Distributions.

(a) Amounts declared and distributed. For Year 1, the M group has $120 of consolidated taxable income when determined by including only S's items of income, gain, deduction, and loss taken into account. S declares and makes a $10 dividend distribution to M at the close of Year 1. Under paragraph (b) of this section, M increases its basis in S's stock as of the close of Year 1 by a $110 net amount ($120 of taxable income, less a $10 distribution).

(b) Distributions in later years. The facts are the same as in paragraph (a) of this Example 5, except that S does not declare and distribute the $10 until Year 2. Under paragraph (b) of this section, M increases its basis in S's stock by $120 as of the close of Year 1, and decreases its basis by $10 as of the close of Year 2. (If M were also a subsidiary, the basis of its stock would also be increased in Year 1 to reflect M's $120 adjustment to basis of S's stock; the basis of M's stock would not be changed as a result of S's distribution in Year 2, because M's $10 of tax-exempt dividend income under paragraph (b)(3)(ii) of this section would be offset by the $10 negative adjustment to M's basis in S's stock for the distribution.)

(c) Amounts declared but not distributed. The facts are the same as in paragraph (a) of this Example 5, except that, during December of Year 1, S declares (and M becomes entitled to) another $70 dividend distribution with respect to its stock, but M does not receive the distribution until after it sells all of S's stock at the close of Year 1. Under § 1.1502-13(f)(2)(iv), S is treated as making a $70 distribution to M at the time M becomes entitled to the distribution. (If S is distributing an appreciated asset, its gain under section 311 is also taken into account under paragraph (b)(3)(i) of this section at the time M becomes entitled to the distribution.) Consequently, under paragraph (b) of this section, M increases its basis in S's stock as of the close of Year 1 by only a $40 net amount ($120 of taxable income, less two distributions totalling $80). Any further adjustments after S ceases to be a member and the $70 distribution is made would be duplicative, because the stock basis has already been adjusted for the distribution. Accordingly, the distribution will not result in further adjustments or gain, even if the distribution is a payment to which section 301(c)(2) or (3) applies.

Example (6). Reorganization with boot. (i) Facts. M owns all the stock of S and T. M owns ten shares of the same class of common stock of S and ten shares of the same class of common stock of T. The fair market value of each share of S stock is $10 and the fair market value of each share of T stock is $10. On January 1 of Year 1, M has a $5 basis in each of its ten shares of S stock and a $10 basis in each of its ten shares of T stock. S and T have no items of income, gain, deduction, or loss for Year 1. S and T each have substantial earnings and profits. At the close of Year 1, T merges into S in a reorganization described in section 368(a)(1)(A) (and in section 368(a)(1)(D)). M receives no additional S stock, but does receive $10 which is treated as a dividend under section 356(a)(2).

(ii) Analysis. The merger of T into S is a transaction to which § 1.1502-13(f)(3) applies. Under § 1.1502-13(f)(3) and § 1.358-2(a)(2)(iii), M is deemed to receive ten additional shares of S stock with a total fair market value of $100 (the fair market value of the T stock surrendered by M). Under § 1.358-2(a)(2)(i), M will have a basis of $10 in each share of S stock deemed received in the reorganization. Under § 1.358-2(a)(2)(iii), M is deemed to surrender all twenty shares of its S stock in a recapitalization under section 368(a)(1)(E) in exchange for the ten shares of S stock, the number of shares of S stock held by M immediately after the transaction. Thus, under § 1.358-2(a)(2)(i), M has five shares of S stock each with a basis of $10 and five shares of S stock each with a basis of $20. The $10 M received is treated as a dividend distribution under section 301 and, under paragraph (b)(3)(v) of this section, the $10 is a distribution to which paragraph (b)(2)(iv) of this section applies. Accordingly, M's total basis in the S stock is decreased by the $10 distribution.

Example (7). Tiering up of basis adjustments. M owns all of S's stock, and S owns all of T's stock. For Year 1, the M group has $100 of consolidated taxable income when determined by including only T's items of income, gain, deduction, and loss taken into account, and $50 of consolidated taxable income when determined by including only S's items taken into account. S increases its basis in T's stock by $100 under paragraph (b) of this section. Under paragraph (a)(3) of this section, this $100 basis adjustment is taken into account in determining M's adjustments to its basis in S's stock. Thus, M increases its basis in S's stock by $150 under paragraph (b) of this section.

Example (8). Allocation of items.

(a) Acquisition in mid-year. M is the common parent of a consolidated group, and S is an unaffiliated corporation filing separate returns on a calendar-year basis. M acquires all of S's stock and S becomes a member of the M group on July 1 of Year 1. For the entire calendar Year 1, S has $100 of ordinary income and under § 1.1502-76(b) $60 is allocated to the period from January 1 to June 30 and $40 to the period from July 1 to December 31. Under paragraph (b) of this section, M increases its basis in S's stock by $40.

(b) Sale in mid-year. The facts are the same as in paragraph (a) of this Example 8, except that S is a member of the M group at the beginning of Year 1 but ceases to be a member on June 30 as a result of M's sale of S's stock. Under paragraph (b) of this section, M increases its basis in S's stock by $60 immediately before the stock sale. (P's basis increase would be the same if S became a nonmember because S issued additional shares to nonmembers.)

(c) Absorption of loss carryovers. Assume instead that S is a member of the M group at the beginning of Year 1 but ceases to be a member on June 30 as a result of M's sale of S's stock, and a $100 consolidated net operating loss attributable to S is carried over by the M group to Year 1. The consolidated net operating loss may be apportioned to S for its first separate return year only to the extent not absorbed by the M group during Year 1. Under paragraph (b)(3)(i) of this section, if the loss is absorbed by the M group in Year 1, whether the offsetting income arises before or after M's sale of S's stock, the absorption of the loss carryover is included in the determination of S's taxable income or loss for Year 1. Thus, M's basis in S's stock is adjusted under paragraph (b) of this section to reflect any absorption of the loss by the M group.

Example (9). Gross-ups.

(a) Facts. M owns all of the stock of S, and S owns all of the stock of T, a newly formed controlled foreign corporation that is not a passive foreign investment company. In Year 1, T has $100 of subpart F income and pays $34 of foreign income tax, leaving T with $66 of earnings and profits. The M group has $100 of consolidated taxable income when determined by taking into account only S's items (the inclusion under section 951(a), taking into account the section 78 gross-up). As a result of the section 951(a) inclusion, S increases its basis in T's stock by $66 under section 961(a).

(b) Analysis. Under paragraph (b)(3)(i) of this section, S has $100 of taxable income. Under paragraph (b)(3)(iii)(B) of this section, the $34 gross-up for taxes paid by T that S is treated as having paid is a noncapital, nondeductible expense (whether or not any corresponding amount is claimed by the M group as a tax credit). Thus, M increases it basis in S's stock under paragraph (b) of this section by the net adjustment of $66.

(c) Subsequent distribution. The facts are the same as in paragraph (a) of this Example 9, except that T distributes its $66 of earnings and profits in Year 2. The $66 distribution received by S is excluded from S's income under section 959(a) because the distribution represents earnings and profits attributable to amounts that were included in S's income under section 951(a) for Year 1. In addition, S's basis in T's stock is decreased by $66 under section 961(b). The excluded distribution is not tax-exempt income under paragraph (b)(3)(ii) of this section because of the corresponding reduction to S's basis in T's stock. Consequently, M's basis in S's stock is not adjusted under paragraph (b) of this section for Year 2.

Example (10). Recapture of tax-exempt items.

(a) Facts. S is a life insurance company. For Year 1, the M group has $200 of consolidated taxable income, determined by including only S's items of income, gain, deduction, and loss taken into account (including a $300 small company deduction under section 806). In addition, S has $100 of tax-exempt interest income, $60 of which is S's company share. The remaining $40 of tax-exempt income is the policyholders' share that reduces S's deduction for increase in reserves.

(b) Tax-exempt items generally. Under paragraph (b)(3)(i) of this section, S has $200 of taxable income for Year 1. Also for Year 1, S has $100 of tax-exempt income under paragraph (b)(3)(ii)(A) of this section, and another $300 is treated as tax-exempt income under paragraph (b)(3)(ii)(B) of this section because of the deduction under section 806. Under paragraph (b)(3)(iii) of this section, S has $40 of noncapital, nondeductible expenses for Year 1 because S's deduction under section 807 for its increase in reserves has been permanently reduced by the $40 policyholders' share of the tax-exempt interest income. Thus, M increases its basis in S's stock by $560 under paragraph (b) of this section.

(c) Recapture. Assume instead that S is a property and casualty company and, for Year 1, S accrues $100 of estimated salvage recoverable under section 832. Of this amount, $87 (87% of $100) is excluded from gross income because of the "fresh start" provisions of § 11305(c) of M.L. 101-508 (the Omnibus Budget Reconciliation Act of 1990). Thus, S has $87 of tax-exempt income under paragraph (b)(3)(ii)(A) of this section that increases M's basis in S's stock for Year 1. (S also has $13 of taxable income over the period of inclusion under section 481.) In Year 5, S determines that the $100 salvage recoverable was overestimated by $30 and deducts $30 for the reduction of the salvage recoverable. However, S has $26.10 (87% of $30) of taxable income in Year 5 due to the partial recapture of its fresh start. Because S has no basis corresponding to this income, S is treated under paragraph (b)(3)(iii)(B) of this section as having a $26.10 noncapital, nondeductible expense in Year 5. This treatment is necessary to reflect the elimination of the erroneous fresh start in S's stock basis and causes a decrease in M's basis in S's stock by $30 for Year 5 (a $3.90 taxable loss and a $26.10 special adjustment).

(c) Allocation of adjustments among shares of stock. *(1) In general.* (i) Distributions. The adjustment that is described in paragraph (b)(2)(iv) of this section (negative adjustments for distributions) is allocated to the shares of S stock to which the distribution relates.

(ii) Special rules applicable in the case of certain loss transfers of subsidiary stock. (A) Losses reattributed pursuant to an election under § 1.1502-36(d)(6). (1) General rule. If a member transfers loss shares of S stock and the common parent elects under § 1.1502-36(d)(6) to reattribute all or a portion of S's attributes, S's resulting noncapital, nondeductible expense is allocated to all loss shares of S stock transferred by members in the transaction. The expense is allocated among those S shares in proportion to the loss in the shares. The tier-up of that expense is included in the remaining adjustment (see paragraph (c)(1)(iii) of this section).

(2) Reattribution of attributes of a subsidiary that is lower-tier to S. If a member transfers loss shares of S stock and the common parent elects under § 1.1502-36(d)(6) to reattribute attributes of a subsidiary (S2) that is lower-tier to S, S2's resulting noncapital, nondeductible expense is allocated among S2 shares held by members as of the transaction, other than those transferred in the transaction and with respect to which gain or loss was recognized (recognition transfer), in a manner that permits the full amount of the expense to tier up and be applied to the bases of the loss shares of S stock transferred by members in the transaction. The expense is allocated among those S2 shares with positive basis in a manner that, first, reduces the bases of S2's preferred shares to equalize and then eliminate loss and, second, reduces the bases of S2's common shares in a manner that reduces disparity among the bases of those common shares to the greatest extent possible. The noncapital, nondeductible expense applied to the S2 shares tiers up and is applied to the stock of any subsidiaries that are lower-tier to S (middle-tier subsidiaries) in a manner that will permit the full amount of this expense to be applied to reduce the bases of the loss shares of S stock transferred by members in the transaction. Similar to the allocation among the S2 shares, the tier-up of this expense is allocated among the middle-tier subsidiary shares held by members as of the transaction, other than those transferred in a recognition transfer, in a manner that permits the full amount of the expense to tier up and be applied to the bases of the loss shares of S stock transferred by members in the transaction. The tier-up of this expense is allocated among those middle-tier subsidiary shares with positive basis in a manner that, first, reduces the bases of the middle-tier subsidiary's preferred shares to equalize and then eliminate loss and, second, reduces the bases of the middle-tier subsidiary's common shares in a manner that reduces disparity among the bases of those common shares to the greatest extent possible. The tier-up of this expense is allocated to the loss shares of S stock transferred by members in the transaction in the same manner as provided in paragraph (c)(1)(ii)(A)(1) of this section, and thereafter the tier-up of that expense is included in the remaining adjustment (see paragraph (c)(1)(iii) of this section).

(3) Example. The following example illustrates the rules of this paragraph (c)(1)(ii)(A).

Example. Assume P owns M1, P and M1 own M2, M2 owns S, M1 and S own S1, and M1 and S1 own S2. If S sells a portion of the S1 shares at a gain and M2 sells all of the S stock at a net loss (after adjusting the basis for the gain recognized by S on the sale of the S1 shares), and P elects under § 1.1502-36(d)(6) to reattribute attributes of S2, the resulting noncapital, nondeductible expense is allocated entirely to the S2 shares held by S1 with positive basis in a manner that reduces the disparity in those bases to the greatest extent possible. The tier-up of this amount is allocated entirely to the S1 shares held by S (excluding the S1 shares sold) with positive basis in a manner that reduces the disparity in those bases to the greatest extent possible. The tier-up of this amount is allocated to the loss shares of S stock sold by M2 in proportion to the loss in those shares. The tier-up of this amount is then included in the remaining adjustment and tiers up from M2 to M1 and P, and from M1 to P under the general rules of this section.

(B) Tier-up of reallocated investment adjustments subject to prior use limitation. If the reallocation of an investment adjustment under § 1.1502-36(b)(2) is subject to the prior use limitation in § 1.1502-36(b)(2)(iii)(B)(2), no amount of the tier-up of such reallocated investment adjustment shall be allocated to any share whose prior use resulted in the application of the limitation. Thereafter, the tier-up of this amount is included in the remaining adjustment (see paragraph (c)(1)(iii) of this section).

(iii) Remaining adjustment. The remaining adjustment is the adjustment that consists of the items described in paragraphs (b)(2)(i) through (b)(2)(iii) of this section (adjustments for taxable income or loss, tax-exempt income, and noncapital, nondeductible expenses), including adjustments to lower-tier stock basis that tier up under paragraph (a)(3)(iii) of this section, but only to the extent not specially allocated under paragraph (c)(1)(ii) of this section. The remaining adjustment is allocated among the shares of S stock as provided in paragraphs (c)(2) through (c)(4) of this section. If the remaining adjustment is positive, it is allocated first to any preferred stock as provided in paragraph (c)(3) of this section, and then to the common stock as provided in paragraph (c)(2) of this section. If the remaining adjustment is negative, it is allocated only to common stock as provided in paragraph (c)(2) of this section.

(iv) Nonmember shares. No adjustment under this section that is allocated to a share for the period it is owned by a nonmember affects the basis of the share.

(v) Cross-references. See paragraph (c)(4) of this section for the reallocation of adjustments, and paragraph (d) of this section for definitions. See § 1.1502-19(d) for special allocations of basis determined or adjusted under the Internal Revenue Code (Code) with respect to excess loss accounts.

(2) Common stock. (i) Allocation within a class. The remaining adjustment described in paragraph (c)(1)(iii) of this section that is allocable to a class of common stock is generally allocated equally to each share within the class. However, if a member has an excess loss account in a share of a class of common stock at the time a positive remaining adjustment is to be allocated, the portion of the positive remaining adjustment allocable to the member with respect to the class is allocated first to equalize and then eliminate that member's excess loss accounts. It is then allocated equally among the members' shares in that class. Similarly, the portion of any negative remaining adjustment allocable to the member with respect to the class is allocated equally to the member's shares with positive bases, eliminating all positive basis in shares of the class before creating or increasing any excess loss accounts. After positive basis is eliminated, any remaining portion of the negative remaining adjustment is allocated to equalize the member's excess loss accounts in the shares of that class to the greatest extent possible. Distributions and any adjustments or determinations under the Internal Revenue Code (for example, under section 358, including any modifications under § 1.1502-19(d)) are taken into account before the allocation is made under this paragraph (c)(2)(i).

(ii) Allocation among classes. (A) General rule. If S has more than one class of common stock, the extent to which the remaining adjustment described in paragraph (c)(1)(iii) of this section is allocated to each class is determined, based on consistently applied assumptions, by taking into account the terms of each class and all other facts and circumstances relating to the overall economic arrangement. The allocation generally must reflect the manner in which the classes participate in the economic benefit or burden (if any) corresponding to the items of income, gain, deduction, or loss allocated. In determining participation, any differences in voting rights are not taken into account, and the following factors are among those to be considered—

(1) The interest of each share in economic profits and losses (if different from the interest in taxable income);

(2) The interest of each share in cash flow and other nonliquidating distributions; and

(3) The interest of each share in distributions in liquidation.

(B) Distributions and code adjustments. Distributions and any adjustments or determinations under the Internal Revenue Code are taken into account before the allocation is made under this paragraph (c)(2)(ii).

(3) Preferred stock. If the remaining adjustment described in paragraph (c)(1)(iii) of this section is positive, it is allocated to preferred stock to the extent required (when aggregated with prior allocations to the preferred stock during the period that S is a member of the consolidated group) to reflect distributions described in section 301 (and all other distributions treated as dividends) to which the preferred stock becomes entitled, and arrearages arising, during the period that S is a member of the consolidated group. For this purpose, the preferred stock is treated as entitled to a distribution no later than the time the distribution is taken into account under the Internal Revenue Code (e.g., under section 305). If the amount of distributions and arrearages exceeds the positive amount (when aggregated with prior allocations), the positive amount is first allocated among classes of preferred stock to reflect their relative priorities, and the amount allocated to each class is then allocated pro rata within the class. An allocation to a share with respect to arrearages and distributions for the period the share is owned by a nonmember is not reflected in the basis of the share under paragraph (b) of this section. However, if M and S cease to be members of one consolidated group and remain affiliated as members of another consolidated group, M's ownership of S's stock during consolidated return years of the prior group is treated for this purpose as ownership by a member to the extent that the adjustments during the prior consolidated return years are still reflected in the basis of the preferred stock.

(4) Cumulative redetermination. (i) General rule. A member's basis in each share of S preferred and common stock must be redetermined whenever necessary to determine the tax liability of any person. See paragraph (b)(1) of this section. The redetermination is made by reallocating S's adjustments described in paragraphs (c)(1)(ii)(B) (specially allocated adjustments for tier-up of reallocated investment adjustments subject to prior use limitation) and (c)(1)(iii) (remaining adjustments) of this section for each consolidated return year (or other applicable period) of the group by taking into account all of the facts and circumstances affecting allocations under this paragraph (c) as of the redetermination date with respect to all of the S shares. For this purpose:

(A) Amounts may be reallocated from one class of S's stock to another class, but not from one share of a class to another share of the same class.

(B) If there is a change in the equity structure of S (e.g., as the result of S's issuance, redemption, or recapitalization of shares), a cumulative redetermination is made for the period before the change. If a reallocation is required by another redetermination after a change, amounts arising after the change are reallocated before amounts arising before the change.

(C) If S becomes a nonmember as a result of a change in its equity structure, any reallocation is made only among the shares of S's stock immediately before the change. For example, if S issues stock to a nonmember creditor in exchange for its debt, and the exchange results in S becoming a nonmember, any reallocation is only among the shares of S's stock immediately before the exchange.

(D) Any reallocation is treated for all purposes after it is made (including subsequent redeterminations) as the original allocation of an amount under this paragraph (c), but the reallocation does not affect any prior period.

(ii) Prior use of allocations. An amount may not be reallocated under paragraph (c)(4)(i) of this section to the extent that the amount has been used before the reallocation. For this purpose, an amount has been used to the extent it has been taken into account, directly or indirectly, by any member in determining income, gain, deduction, or loss, or in determining the basis of any property that is not subject to this section (e.g., stock of a corporation that has become a nonmember). For example, if M sells a share of S stock, an amount previously allocated to the share cannot be reallocated to another share of S stock, but an amount allocated to another share of S stock can still be reallocated to the sold share because the reallocated amount has not been taken into account; however, any adjustment reallocated to the sold share may effectively be eliminated, because the reallocation was not in effect when the share was previously sold and M's gain or loss from the sale is not redetermined. If, however, M sells the share of S stock to another member, the amount is not used until M's gain or loss is taken into account under § 1.1502-13.

(5) Examples. The principles of this paragraph (c) are illustrated by the following examples.

Example (1). Ownership of less than all the stock.

(a) Facts. M owns 80% of S's only class of stock with an $800 basis. For Year 1, S has $100 of taxable income.

(b) Analysis. Under paragraph (c)(1) of this section, the $100 positive adjustment under paragraph (b) of this section for S's taxable income is allocated among the shares of S's stock, including shares owned by nonmembers. Under paragraph (c)(2)(i) of this section, the adjustment is allocated equally to each share of S's stock. Thus, M increases its basis in S's stock under paragraph (b) of this section as of the close of Year 1 by $80. (The basis of the 20% of S's stock owned by nonmembers is not adjusted under this section.)

(c) Varying interest. The facts are the same as in paragraph (a) of this Example 1, except that M buys the remaining 20% of S's stock at the close of business on June 30 of Year 1 for $208. Under paragraph (b)(1) of this section and the principles of § 1.1502-76(b), S's $100 of taxable income is allocable $40 to the period from January 1 to June 30 and $60 to the period from July 1 to December 31. Thus, for the period ending June 30, M is treated as having a $32 adjustment with respect to the S stock that M has owned since January 1 (80% of $40) and, under paragraph (c)(2)(i) of this section, the adjustment is allocated equally among those shares. For the period ending December 31, M is treated as having a $60 adjustment (100% of $60) that is also allocated equally among M's shares of S's stock owned after June 30. M's basis in the shares owned as of the beginning of the year therefore increases by $80 (the sum of 80% of $40 and 80% of $60), from $800 to $880, and M's basis in the shares purchased on June 30 increases by $12 (20% of $60), from $208 to $220. Thus, M's aggregate basis in S's stock as of the end of Year 1 is $1,100.

(d) Tax liability. The facts are the same as in paragraph (a) of this Example 1, except that M pays S's $34 share of the group's consolidated tax liability resulting from S's taxable income, and S does not reimburse M. S's $100 of taxable income results in a positive adjustment under paragraph (b)(3)(i) of this section, and S's $34 of tax liability results in a negative adjustment under paragraph (b)(3)(iv)(D) of this section and the principles of section 1552. Because S does not make any payment in recognition of the additional tax liability, by analogy to the treatment under § 1.1552-1(b)(2), S is treated as having made a $34 payment that is described in paragraph (b)(3)(iii) of this section (noncapital, nondeductible expenses) and as having received an equal amount from M as a capital contribution. Thus, M increases its basis in its S stock by $52.80 (80% of the $100 of taxable income, less 80% of the $34 tax payment). In addition, M increases its basis in S's stock by $34 under the Internal Revenue Code and paragraph (a)(2) of this section to reflect the capital contribution. In the aggregate, M increases its basis in S's stock by $86.80. (If, as in paragraph (c) of this Example 1, M buys the remaining 20% of S's stock at the close of business on June 30, M increases its basis in S's stock by another $7.90 for the additional 20% interest in S's income after June 30 ($60 multiplied by 20%, less 20% of the $20.40 tax payment on $60); the $34 capital contribution by M is reflected in all of its S shares (not just the original 80%), and M's aggregate basis adjustment under this section is $94.70 ($86.80 plus $7.90).

Example (2). Preferred stock.

(a) Facts. M owns all of S's common stock with an $800 basis, and nonmembers own all of S's preferred stock. The preferred stock was issued for $200, has a $20 annual, cumulative preference as to dividends, and has an initial liquidation preference of $200. For Year 1, S has 50 of taxable income and no distributions are declared or made.

(b) Analysis of arrearages. Under paragraphs (c)(1) and (3) of this section, $20 of the $50 positive adjustment under paragraph (b) of this section is allocated first to the preferred stock to reflect the dividend arrearage arising in Year 1. The remaining $30 of the positive adjustment is allocated to the common stock, increasing M's basis from $800 to $830 as of the close of Year 1. (The basis of the preferred stock owned by nonmembers is not adjusted under this section.)

(c) Current distribution. The facts are the same as in paragraph (a) of this Example 2, except that S declares and makes a $20 distribution with respect to the preferred stock during Year 1 in satisfaction of its preference. The results are the same as in paragraph (b) of this Example 2.

(d) Varying interest. The facts are the same as in paragraph (a) of this Example 2, except that S has no income or loss for Years 1 and 2, M purchases all of S's preferred stock at the beginning of Year 3 for $240, and S has $70 of taxable income for Year 3. Under paragraph (c)(3) of this section, $60 of the $70 positive adjustment under paragraph (b) of this section is allocated to the preferred stock to reflect the dividends arrearages for Years 1 through 3, but only the $20 for Year 3 is reflected in the basis of the preferred stock under paragraph (b) of this section. (The remaining $40 is not reflected because the preferred stock was owned by nonmembers during Years 1 and 2.) Thus, M increases its basis in S's preferred stock from $240 to $260, and its basis in S's common stock from $800 to $810, as of the close of Year 3. (If M had acquired all of S's preferred stock in a transaction to which section 351 applies, and M's initial basis in S's preferred stock was $200 under section 362, M's basis in S's preferred stock would increase from $200 to $220.)

(e) Varying interest with current distributions. The facts are the same as in paragraph (d) of this Example 2, except that S declares and makes a $20 distribution with respect to the preferred stock in each of Years 1 and 2 in satisfaction of its preference, and M purchases all of S's preferred stock at the beginning of Year 3 for $200. Under paragraph (c)(3) of this section, $40 of the $70 positive adjustment under paragraph (b) of this section is allocated to the preferred stock to reflect the distributions in Years 1 and 2, and $20 of the $70 is allocated to the preferred stock to reflect the arrearage for Year 3. However, as in paragraph (d) of this Example 2, only the $20 attributable to Year 3 is reflected in the basis of the preferred stock under paragraph (b) of this section. Thus, M increases its basis in S's preferred stock from $200 to $220, and M increases its basis in S's common stock from $800 to $810.

Example (3). Cumulative redetermination.

(a) Facts. M owns all of S's common and preferred stock. The preferred stock has a $100 annual, cumulative preference as to dividends. For Year 1, S has $200 of taxable income, the first $100 of which is allocated to the preferred stock and the remaining $100 of which is allocated to the common stock. For Year 2, S has no adjustment under paragraph (b) of this section, and M sells all of S's common stock at the close of Year 2.

(b) Analysis. Under paragraph (c)(4) of this section, M's basis in S's common stock must be redetermined as of the sale of the stock. The redetermination is made by reallocating the $200 positive adjustment under paragraph (b) of this section for Year 1 by taking into account all of the facts and circumstances affecting allocations as of the sale. Thus, the $200 positive adjustment for Year 1 is reallocated entirely to the preferred stock to reflect the dividend arrearages for Years 1 and 2. The reallocation away from the common stock reflects the fact that, because of the additional amount of arrearage in Year 2, the common stock is not entitled to any part of the $200 of taxable income from Year 1. Thus, the common stock has no positive or negative adjustment, and the preferred stock has a $200 positive adjustment. These reallocations are treated as the original allocations for Years 1 and 2. (The results for the common stock would be the same if the common and preferred stock were not owned by the same member, or the preferred stock were owned by nonmembers.)

(c) Preferred stock issued after adjustment arises. The facts are the same as in paragraph (a) of this Example 3, except that S does not issue its preferred stock until the beginning of Year 2, S has no further adjustment under paragraph (b) of this section for Years 2 and 3, and M sells S's common stock at the close of Year 3. Under paragraphs (c)(1) and (2) of this section, the $200 positive adjustment for Year 1 is initially allocated entirely to the common stock. Under paragraph (c)(4) of this section, the $200 adjustment is reallocated to the preferred stock to reflect the arrearages for Years 2 and 3. Thus, the common stock has no positive or negative adjustment.

(d) Common stock issued after adjustment arises. The facts are the same as in paragraph (a) of this Example 3, except that S has no preferred stock, S issues additional common stock of the same class at the beginning of Year 2, S has no further adjustment under paragraph (b) of this section in Years 2 and 3, and M sells its S common stock at the close of Year 3. Under paragraphs (c)(1) and (2) of this section, the $200 positive adjustment for Year 1 is initially allocated entirely to the original common stock. Under paragraph (c)(4)(i)(A) of this section, the $200 adjustment is not reallocated among the original common stock and the additional stock. Unlike the preferred stock in paragraph (c) of this Example 3, the additional common stock is of the same class as the original stock, and there is no reallocation between shares of the same class.

(e) Positive and negative adjustments. The facts are the same as in paragraph (a) of this Example 3, except that S has a $200 loss for Year 2 that results in a negative adjustment to the common stock before any redetermination. For purposes of the basis redetermination under paragraph (c)(4) of this section, the Year 1 and 2 adjustments under paragraph (b) of this section are not netted. Thus, as in paragraph (b) of this Example 3, the redetermination is made by reallocating the $200 positive adjustment for Year 1 entirely to the preferred stock. The $200 negative adjustment for Year 2 is allocated entirely to the common stock. Consequently, the preferred stock has a $200 positive cumulative adjustment, and the common stock has a $200 negative cumulative adjustment. (The results would be the same if there were no other adjustments described in paragraph (b) of this section, M sells S's common stock at the close of Year 3 rather than Year 2, and an additional $100 arrearage arises in Year 3; only adjustments under paragraph (b) of this section may be reallocated, and there is no additional adjustment for Year 3.)

(f) Current distributions. The facts are the same as in paragraph (a) of this Example 3, except that, during Year 1, S declares and makes a distribution to M of $100 as a dividend on the preferred stock and $100 as a dividend on the common stock. The taxable income and distributions result in no Year 1 adjustment under paragraph (b) of this section for either the common or preferred stock. However, as in paragraph (b) of this Example 3, the redetermination under paragraph (c)(4) of this section is made by reallocating a $200 positive adjustment for Year 1 (S's net adjustment described in paragraph (b) of this section, determined without taking distributions into account) to the preferred stock. Consequently, the preferred stock has a $100 positive cumulative adjustment ($200 of taxable income, less a $100 distribution with respect to the preferred stock) and the common stock has a $100 negative cumulative adjustment (for the distribution).

(g) Convertible preferred stock. The facts are the same as in paragraph (a) of this Example 3, except that the preferred stock is convertible into common stock that is identical to the common stock already outstanding, the holders of the preferred stock convert the stock at the close of Year 2, and no stock is sold until the close of Year 5. Under paragraph (c)(4) of this section, the $200 positive adjustment for Year 1 is reallocated entirely to the preferred stock immediately before the conversion. The newly issued common stock is treated as a second class of S common stock, and adjustments under paragraph (b) of this section are allocated between the original and the new common stock under paragraph (c)(2)(ii) of this section. Although the preferred stock is converted to common stock, the $200 adjustment to the preferred stock is not subsequently reallocated between the original and the new common stock. Because the original and the new stock are equivalent, adjustments under paragraph (b) of this section for subsequent periods are allocated equally to each share.

(h) Prior use of allocations. The facts are the same as in paragraph (a) of this Example 3, except that M sells 10% of S's common stock at the close of Year 1, and the remaining 90% at the close of Year 2. M's basis in the common stock sold in Year 1 reflects $10 of the adjustment allocated to the common stock for Year 1. Under paragraph (c)(4)(ii) of this section, because $10 of the Year 1 adjustment was used in determining M's gain or loss, only $90 is reallocated to the preferred stock, and $10 remains allocated to the common stock sold.

(i) Lower-tier members. The facts are the same as in paragraph (a) of this Example 3, except that M owns only S's common stock, and M is also a subsidiary. If there is a redetermination under paragraph (c)(4) of this section by a member owning M's stock, a redetermination with respect to S's stock must be made first, and the effect of that redetermination on M's adjustments is taken into account under paragraph (b) of this section. However, as in paragraph (h) of this Example 3, to the extent an amount of the initial adjustments with respect to S's common stock have already been tiered up and used by a member owning M's stock, that amount remains with S's common stock (and the higher-tier member using the adjustment with respect to M's stock), and may not be reallocated to S's preferred stock.

Example (4). Allocation to preferred stock between groups.

(a) Facts. M owns all of S's only class of stock, and S owns all of T's common and preferred stock. The preferred stock has a $100 annual, cumulative preference as to dividends. For Year 1, T has $200 of taxable income, the first $100 of which is allocated to the preferred stock and the remaining $100 of which is allocated to the common stock, and S has no adjustments other than the amounts tiered up from T. S and T have no adjustments under paragraph (b) of this section for Years 2 and 3. X, the common parent of another consolidated group, purchases all of S's stock at the close of Year 3, and S and T become members of the X group. For Year 4, T has $200 of taxable income, and S has no adjustments other than the amounts tiered up from T.

(b) Analysis for Years 1 through 3. Under paragraph (c)(4) of this section, the allocation of S's adjustments under paragraph (b) of this section (determined without taking distributions into account) must be redetermined as of the time M sells S's stock. As a result of this redetermination, T's common stock has no positive or negative adjustment and the preferred stock has a $200 positive adjustment.

(c) Analysis for Year 4. Under paragraph (c)(3) of this section, the allocation of T's $200 positive adjustment in Year 4 to T's preferred stock with respect to arrearages is made by taking into account the consolidated return years of both the M group and the X group. Thus, the allocation of the $200 positive adjustment for Year 4 to T's preferred stock is not treated as an allocation for a period for which the preferred stock is owned by a nonmember. Thus, the $200 adjustment is reflected in S's basis in T's preferred stock under paragraph (b) of this section.

(d) Definitions. For purposes of this section—

(1) Class. The shares of a member having the same material terms (without taking into account voting rights) are treated as a single class of stock.

(2) Preferred stock. Preferred stock is stock that is limited and preferred as to dividends and has a liquidation preference. A class of stock that is not described in section 1504(a)(4), however, is not treated as preferred stock for purposes of paragraph (c) of this section if members own less than 80% of each class of common stock (determined without taking this paragraph (d)(2) into account).

(3) Common stock. Common stock is stock that is not preferred stock.

(4) Becoming a nonmember. A member is treated as becoming a nonmember if it has a separate return year (including another group's consolidated return year). For example, S may become a nonmember if it issues additional stock to nonmembers, but S does not become a nonmember as a result of its complete liquidation.

(e) Anti-avoidance rule. *(1) General rule.* If any person acts with a principal purpose contrary to the purposes of this section, to avoid the effect of the rules of this section or apply the rules of this section to avoid the effect of any other provision of the consolidated return regulations, adjustments must be made as necessary to carry out the purposes of this section.

(2) Examples. The principles of this paragraph (e) are illustrated by the following examples.

Example (1). Preferred stock treated as common stock.

(a) Facts. S has 100 shares of common stock and 100 shares of preferred stock described in section 1504(a)(4). M owns 80 shares of S's common stock and all of S's preferred stock. The shareholders expect that S will have negative adjustments under paragraph (b) of this section for Years 1 and 2 (all of which will be allocable to S's common stock), the negative adjustments will have no significant effect on the value of S's stock, and S will have offsetting positive adjustments thereafter. When the preferred stock was issued, M intended to cause S to recapitalize the preferred stock into additional common stock at the end of Year 2 in a transaction described in section 368(a)(1)(E). M's temporary ownership of the preferred stock is with a principal purpose to limit M's basis reductions under paragraph (b) of this section to 80% of the anticipated negative adjustments. The recapitalization is intended to cause significantly more than 80% of the anticipated positive adjustments to increase M's basis in S's stock because of M's increased ownership of S's common stock immediately after the recapitalization.

(b) Analysis. S has established a transitory capital structure with a principal purpose to enhance M's basis in S's stock under this section. Under paragraph (e)(1) of this section, all of S's common and preferred stock is treated as a single class of common stock in Years 1 and 2 for purposes of this section. Thus, S's items are allocated under the principles of paragraph (c)(2)(ii) of this section, and M decreases its basis in both the common and preferred stock accordingly.

Example (2). Contribution of appreciated property.

(a) Facts. M owns all of the stock of S and T, and S and T each own 50% of the stock of U. M's S stock has a $150 basis and $200 value, and M's T stock has a $200 basis and $200 value. With a principal purpose to eliminate M's gain from an anticipated sale of S's stock, T contributes to U an asset with a $100 value and $0 basis, and S contributes $100 cash. U sells T's asset and recognizes a $100 gain that results in a $100 positive adjustment under paragraph (b) of this section.

(b) Analysis. Under paragraph (c)(2) of this section, U's adjustment ordinarily would be allocated equally to each share of U's stock. If so allocated, M's basis in S's stock would increase from $150 to $200 and M would recognize no gain from the sale of S's stock for $200. Under paragraph (e)(1) of this section, however, because T transferred an appreciated asset to U with a principal purpose to shift a portion of the stock basis increase from M's stock in T to M's stock in S, the allocation of the $100 positive adjustment under paragraph (c) of this section between the shares of U's stock must take into account the contribution. Consequently, all $100 of the positive adjustment is allocated to the U stock owned by T, rather than $50 to the U stock owned by S and $50 to the U stock owned by T. M's basis in S's stock remains $150, and its basis in T's stock increases to $300. Thus, M recognizes a $50 gain from its sale of S's stock for $200.

Example (3). Reorganizations.

(a) Facts. M forms S with an $800 contribution, $200 of which is in exchange for S's preferred stock described in section 1504(a)(4) and the balance of which is for S's common stock. For Years 1 through 3, S has a total of $160 of ordinary income, $60 of which is distributed with respect to the preferred stock in satisfaction of its $20 annual preference as to dividends. Under this section, M's basis in S's preferred stock is unchanged, and its basis in S's common stock is increased from $600 to $700. To reduce its gain from an anticipated sale of S's preferred stock, M forms T at the close of Year 3 with a contribution of all of S's stock in exchange for corresponding common and preferred stock of T in a transaction to which section 351 applies. At the time of the contribution, the fair market value of the common stock is $700 and the fair market value of the preferred stock is $300 (due to a decrease in prevailing market interest rates). M subsequently sells T's preferred stock for $300.

(b) Analysis. Under section 358(b), M ordinarily has a $630 basis in T's common stock (70% of the $900 aggregate stock basis) and a $270 basis in T's preferred stock (30% of the $900 aggregate stock basis). However, because M transferred S's stock to T with a principal purpose to shift the allocation of basis adjustments under this section, adjustments are made under paragraph (e)(1) of this section to preserve the allocation under this section. Thus, M has a $700 basis in T's common stock and a $200 basis in T's preferred stock. Consequently, M recognizes a $100 gain from the sale of T's preferred stock.

Example (4). Post-deconsolidation basis adjustments.

(a) Facts. For Year 1, the M group has $40 of taxable income when determined by including only S's items of income, gain, deduction, and loss taken into account, and M increases its basis in S's stock by $40 under paragraph (b) of this section. M anticipates that S will have a $40 ordinary loss for Year 2 that will be carried back and offset S's income in Year 1 and result in a $40 reduction to M's basis in S's stock for Year 2 under paragraph (b) of this section. With a principal purpose to avoid the reduction, M causes S to issue voting preferred stock that results in S becoming a nonmember at the beginning of Year 2. As anticipated, S has a $40 loss for Year 2, which is carried back to Year 1 and offsets S's income from Year 1.

(b) Analysis. Under paragraph (e)(1) of this section, because M caused S to become a nonmember with a principal purpose to absorb S's loss but avoid the corresponding negative adjustment under this section, and M bears a substantial portion of the loss because of its continued ownership of S common stock, the basis of M's common stock in S is decreased by $40 for Year 2. (If M has less than a $40 basis in the retained S stock, M must recognize income for Year 2 to the extent of the excess.) Section 1504(a)(3) limits the ability of S to subsequently rejoin the M group's consolidated return.

(c) Carryback to pre-consolidation year. The facts are the same as in paragraph (a) of this Example 4, except that M anticipates that S's loss will be carried back and absorbed in a separate return year of S before Year 1 (rather than to the M group's consolidated return for Year 1). Although M causes S to become a nonmember with a principal purpose to avoid the negative adjustment under this section, and M bears a substantial portion of the loss because of its continued ownership of S common stock, both S's income and loss are taken into account under the separate return rules. Consequently, no one has acted with a principal purpose contrary to the purposes of this section, and no adjustments are necessary to carry out the purposes of this section.

Example (5). Pre-consolidation basis adjustments.

(a) Facts. M forms S with a $100 contribution, and S becomes a member of the M affiliated group which does not file consolidated returns. For Years 1 through 3, S earns $300. M anticipates that it will elect under section 1501 for the M group to begin filing consolidated returns in Year 5. In anticipation of filing consolidated returns, and to avoid the negative stock basis adjustment that would result under paragraph (b) of this section from distributing S's earnings after Year 5, M causes S to distribute $300 during Year 4 as a qualifying dividend within the meaning of section 243(b). There is no plan or intention to recontribute the funds to S after the distribution.

(b) Analysis. Although S's distribution of $300 is with a principal purpose to avoid a corresponding negative adjustment under this section, the $300 was both earned and distributed entirely under the separate return rules. Consequently, M and S have not acted with a principal purpose contrary to the purposes of this section, and no adjustments are necessary to carry out the purposes of this section.

(f) Predecessors and successors. For purposes of this section, any reference to a corporation or to a share of stock includes a reference to a successor or predecessor as the context may require. A corporation is a successor if the basis of its assets is determined, directly or indirectly, in whole or in part, by reference to the basis of another corporation (the predecessor). For example, if T merges into S, S is treated, as the context may require, as a successor to T and as becoming a member of the group. A share is a successor if its basis is determined, directly or indirectly, in whole or in part, by reference to the basis of another share (the predecessor).

(g) Recordkeeping. Adjustments under this section must be reflected annually on permanent records (including work papers). See also section 6001, requiring records to be maintained. The group must be able to identify from these permanent records the amount and allocation of adjustments, including the nature of any tax-exempt income and noncapital, nondeductible expenses, so as to permit the application of the rules of this section for each year.

(h) Effective/applicability date. *(1) General rule.* Except as provided in paragraph (h)(8) of this section, this section applies with respect to determinations of the basis of the stock of a subsidiary (e.g., for determining gain or loss from a disposition of stock), in consolidated return years beginning on or after January 1, 1995. If this section applies, basis must be determined or redetermined as if this section were in effect for all years (including, for example, the consolidated return years of another consolidated group to the extent adjustments from those years are still reflected). For example, if the portion of a consolidated net operating loss carryover attributable to S expired in 1990 and is treated as a noncapital, nondeductible expense under paragraph (b) of this section, it is taken into account in tax years beginning on or after January 1, 1995 as a negative adjustment for 1990. Any such determination or redetermination does not, however, affect any prior period. Thus, the negative adjustment for S's noncapital, nondeductible expense is not taken into account for tax years beginning before January 1, 1995.

(2) Dispositions of stock before effective date. (i) In general. If M disposes of stock of S in a consolidated return year beginning before January 1, 1995, the amount of M's income, gain, deduction, or loss, and the basis reflected in that amount, are not redetermined under this section. See § 1.1502-19 as contained in the 26 CFR part 1 edition revised as of April 1, 1994 for the definition of disposition, and paragraph (h)(5) of this section for the rules applicable to such dispositions.

(ii) Lower-tier members. Although M disposes of S's stock in a tax year beginning before January 1, 1995, S's determinations or adjustments with respect to the stock of a lower-tier member with which it continues to file a consolidated return are redetermined in accordance with the rules of this section (even if they were previously taken into account by M and reflected in income, gain, deduction, or loss from the disposition of S's stock). For example, assume that M owns all of S's stock, S owns all of T's stock, and T owns all of U's stock. If S sells 80% of T's stock in a tax year beginning before January 1, 1995 (the effective date), the amount of S's income, gain, deduction, or loss from the sale, and the stock basis adjustments reflected in that amount, are not redetermined if M sells S's stock after the effective date. If S sells the remaining 20% of T's stock after the effective date, S's stock basis adjustments with respect to that T stock are also not redetermined because T became a nonmember before the effective date. However, if T and U continue to file a consolidated return with each other and T sells U's stock after the effective date, T's stock basis adjustments with respect to U's stock are redetermined (even though some of those adjustments may have been taken into account by S in its prior sale of T's stock before the effective date).

(iii) Deferred amounts. For purposes of this paragraph (h)(2), a disposition does not include a transaction to which § 1.1502-13, § 1.1502-13T, § 1.1502-14, or § 1.1502-14T applies. Instead, the transaction is deemed to occur as the income, gain, deduction, or loss (if any) is taken into account.

(3) Distributions. (i) Deemed dividend elections. If there is a deemed distribution and recontribution pursuant to § 1.1502-32(f)(2) as contained in the 26 CFR part 1 edition revised as of April 1, 1994 in a consolidated return year beginning before January 1, 1995, the deemed distribution and recontribution under the election are treated as an actual distribution by S and recontribution by M as provided under the election.

(ii) Affiliated earnings and profits. This section does not apply to reduce the basis in S's stock as a result of a distribution of earnings and profits accumulated in separate return years, if the distribution is made in a consolidated return year beginning before January 1, 1995, and the distribution does not cause a negative adjustment under the investment adjustment rules in effect at the time of the distribution. See paragraph (h)(5) of this section for the rules in effect with respect to the distribution.

(4) Expiring loss carryovers. If S became a member of a consolidated group in a consolidated return year beginning before January 1, 1995, and S had a loss carryover from a separate return limitation year at that time, the group does not treat any expiration of the loss carryover (even if in a tax year beginning on or after January 1, 1995) as a noncapital, nondeductible expense resulting in a negative adjustment under this section. If S becomes a member of a consolidated group in a consolidated return year beginning on or

after January 1, 1995, and S has a loss carryover from a separate return limitation year at that time, adjustments with respect to the expiration are determined under this section.

(5) Prior law. (i) In general. For prior determinations, see prior regulations under section 1502 as in effect with respect to the determination. See, e.g., §§ 1.1502-32 and 1.1502-32T as contained in the 26 CFR part 1 edition revised as of April 1, 1994.

(ii) Continuing basis reductions for certain deconsolidated subsidiaries. If a subsidiary ceases to be a member of a group in a consolidated return year beginning before January 1, 1995, and its basis was subject to reduction under § 1.1502-32T or § 1.1502-32(g) as contained in the 26 CFR part 1 edition revised as of April 1, 1994, its basis remains subject to reduction under those principles. For example, if S ceased to be a member in 1990, and M's basis in any retained S stock was subject to a basis reduction account, the basis remains subject to reduction. Similarly, if an election could be made to apply § 1.1502-32T instead of § 1.1502-32(g), the election remains available. However, §§ 1.1502-32T and 1.1502-32(g) do not apply as a result of a subsidiary ceasing to be a member in tax years beginning on or after January 1, 1995.

(6) Loss suspended under § 1.1502-35(c) or disallowed under § 1.1502-35(g)(3)(iii). Paragraphs (a)(2), (b)(3)(iii)(C), (b)(3)(iii)(D) and (b)(4)(vi) of this section are applicable on and after March 10, 2006. For rules applicable before March 10, 2006, see § 1.1502-32T(h)(6) as contained in 26 CFR part 1 in effect on January 1, 2006.

(7) Rules related to discharge of indebtedness income excluded from gross income. Paragraphs (b)(1)(ii), (b)(3)(ii)(C)(1), (b)(3)(iii)(A), and (b)(5)(ii), Example 4, paragraphs (a), (b), and (c) of this section apply with respect to determinations of the basis of the stock of a subsidiary in consolidated return years the original return for which is due (without regard to extensions) after March 21, 2005. However, groups may apply those provisions with respect to determinations of the basis of the stock of a subsidiary in consolidated return years the original return for which is due (without regard to extensions) on or before March 21, 2005, and after August 29, 2003.

For determinations of the basis of the stock of a subsidiary in consolidated return years the original return for which is due (without regard to extensions) on or before March 21, 2005, and after August 29, 2003, with respect to which a group chooses not to apply paragraphs (b)(1)(ii), (b)(3)(ii)(C)(1), (b)(3)(iii)(A), and (b)(5)(ii), Example 4, paragraphs (a), (b), and (c) of this section, see § 1.1502-32T(b)(3)(ii)(C)(1), (b)(3)(iii)(A), and (b)(5)(ii), Example 4, paragraphs (a), (b), and (c) as contained in 26 CFR part 1 revised as of April 1, 2004.

(8) Determination of stock basis in reorganization with boot. Paragraph (b)(5)(ii) Example 6 of this section applies only with respect to determinations of the basis of the stock of a subsidiary on or after January 23, 2006. For determinations of the basis of the stock of a subsidiary before January 23, 2006, see § 1.1502-32(b)(5)(ii) Example 6 as contained in the 26 CFR part 1 edition revised as of April 1, 2005.

(9) Allocations of investment adjustments, including adjustments attributable to certain loss transfers; certain conforming amendments. Paragraphs (a)(2), (b)(3)(ii)(C)(2), (c)(1), (c)(2)(i), (c)(2)(ii)(A), (c)(3), and (c)(4)(i) of this section are applicable for determinations of the basis of stock of a subsidiary on or after September 17, 2008.

(i) [Reserved]. For further guidance, see § 1.1502-32T(i).

(j) Effective/applicability date. Paragraph (b)(4)(iv) of this section applies to any original consolidated Federal income tax return due (without extensions) after June 14, 2007. For original consolidated Federal income tax returns due (without extensions) after May 30, 2006, and on or before June 14, 2007, see § 1.1502-32T as contained in 26 CFR part 1 in effect on April 1, 2007. For original consolidated Federal income tax returns due (without extensions) on or before May 30, 2006, see § 1.1502-32 as contained in 26 CFR part 1 in effect on April 1, 2006.

(k) [Reserved]. For further guidance, see § 1.1502-32T(k).

T.D. 6909, 12/29/66, amend T.D. 7246, 12/29/72, T.D. 7655, 11/28/79, T.D. 7637, 8/6/79, T.D. 7947, 3/5/84, T.D. 8188, 3/14/88, T.D. 8245, 3/14/89, T.D. 8294, 3/9/90, T.D. 8319, 11/19/90, T.D. 8364, 9/13/91, T.D. 8401, 3/13/92, T.D. 8560, 8/12/94, T.D. 8677, 6/26/96, T.D. 8823, 6/25/99, T.D. 8984, 3/7/2002, T.D. 9048, 3/11/2003, T.D. 9089, 8/29/2003, T.D. 9187, 3/2/2005, T.D. 9192, 3/21/2005, T.D. 9244, 1/23/2006, T.D. 9254, 3/9/2006, T.D. 9264, 5/26/2006, T.D. 9322, 4/9/2007, T.D. 9329, 6/13/2007, T.D. 9424, 9/10/2008.

PAR. 2. Section 1.1502-32 is amended by revising paragraph (b)(3)(iii)(D) and adding paragraph (k) to read as follows:

Proposed § 1.1502-32 Investment adjustments. [*For Preamble, see ¶ 152,847*]

* * * * *

(b) * * *

(3) * * *

(iii) * * *

(D) [The text of the proposed amendment to § 1.1502-32(b)(3)(iii)(D) is the same as the text of § 1.1502-32T(b)(3)(iii)(D) published elsewhere in this issue of the Federal Register]. [See T.D. 9322, 04/10/2007, 72 Fed. Reg. 68.]

* * * * *

(k) [The text of the proposed amendment to § 1.1502-32(k) is the same as the text of § 1.1502-32T(k) published elsewhere in this issue of the Federal Register]. [See T.D. 9322, 04/10/2007, 72 Fed. Reg. 68.]

PAR. 11. In § 1.1502-32, add a sentence after the second sentence in paragraph (b)(3)(ii)(D), add a sentence after the fourth sentence in paragraph (b)(3)(iii)(B), and add Example 11 in paragraph (b)(5)(ii) to read as follows:

Proposed § 1.1502-32 Investment adjustments. [*For Preamble, see ¶ 152,795*]

* * * * *

(b) * * *

(3) * * *

(ii) * * *

(D) * * * Further, an increase to a member's previously taxed earnings and profits account under § 1.959-3(g)(1)(i)(B) that pursuant to section 961(a) and § 1.961-1(b) results in an increase to a member's basis in the stock in a CFC shall be treated as the receipt of tax exempt income. * * *

(iii) * * *

(B) * * * Also included as a noncapital, nondeductible expense is a decrease to a member's previously taxed earnings and profits account under § 1.959-3(g)(1)(i)(A) that results in a decrease to a member's basis in the stock in a CFC pursuant to section 961(b) and § 1.961-2(a). * * *

* * * * *

(5) * * *

(ii) * * *

Example (11). (a) Facts. P owns all of the stock of S and S1. S, a United States shareholder, owns 50 percent of the stock in FC, a CFC that uses the U.S. dollar as its functional currency. S1, a United States shareholder owns the remaining 50 percent of the stock in FC. Entering year 1, S has a previously taxed earnings and profits account with respect to its stock in FC consisting of $50x of section 959(c)(2) earnings and profits and S1 has a previously taxed earnings and profits account with respect to its stock in FC consisting of $200x of section 959(c)(2) earnings and profits. Entering year 1, FC has section 959(c)(2) earnings and profits of $250x and non-previously taxed earnings and profits of $100x. In year 1, FC generates no earnings and profits and makes a $100x distribution of earnings and profits on FC stock held by S and a $100x distribution of earnings and profits on the FC stock held by S1.

(b) Analysis. First, pursuant to § 1.959-3(e)(2)(ii), the section 959(c)(2) earnings and profits in S's previously taxed earnings and profits account with respect to its FC stock are decreased from $50x to $0 and the section 959(c)(2) earnings and profits in S1's previously taxed earnings and profits account with respect to its FC stock are decreased from $200x to $100x. Then, pursuant to § 1.959-2(e)(2)(v) and (g)(1)(i)(A), the section 959(c)(2) earnings and profits in S1's previously taxed earnings and profits account with respect to its FC stock are decreased from $100x to $50x and, pursuant to § 1.959-3(e)(2)(ii)(B) and (g)(1)(i)(B), the section 959(c)(2) earnings and profits in S's previously taxed earnings and profits account with respect to its FC stock are increased from $0 to $50x and then decreased from $50x to $0. Pursuant to § 1.959-1(c) of this section, the entire $100x distribution to S and $100x distribution to S1 are excluded from S's and S1's gross incomes. Pursuant to paragraph (b)(3)(ii)(D) of this section, the $50x increase to the section 959(c)(2) earnings and profits in S's previously taxed earnings and profits account with respect to its FC stock pursuant to § 1.959-3(g)(1)(i)(B) is treated as the receipt of $50x of tax-exempt income by S. Pursuant to paragraph (b)(2)(ii) of this section, P's basis in S's stock is increased by $50x. Pursuant to paragraph (b)(3)(iii)(B) of this section, the $50x decrease to the section 959(c)(2) earnings and profits in S1's previously taxed earnings and profits account with respect to its FC stock pursuant to § 1.959-3(g)(1)(i)(A) is treated as a noncapital nondeductible expense to S1. Pursuant to paragraph (b)(2)(iii) of this section, P's basis in S1's stock is decreased by $50x.

* * * * *

PAR. 3. Section 1.1502-32(b)(4)(vii)(C) is amended by removing the language "May 7, 2003" and adding the language "August 25, 2004" each time it appears.

Proposed § 1.1502-32 [*For Preamble, see ¶ 152,591*]

PAR. 2. Section 1.1502-32 is amended by revising paragraph (b)(4)(v)(A) and (C).

Proposed § 1.1502-32 Investment adjustments. [*For Preamble, see ¶ 152,581*]

* * * * *

(b) * * *

(4) * * *

(v) [The text of this proposed paragraph is the same as the text of § 1.1502-32T(b)(4)(v)(A) and (C) published elsewhere in this issue of the Federal Register].

* * * * *

PAR. 3. Section 1.1502-32 is amended by adding paragraph (b)(4)(vii) to read as follows:

Proposed § 1.1502-32 Investment adjustments. [*For Preamble, see ¶ 152,381*]

[The text of this proposed section is the same as the text of § 1.1502-32T(b)(4)(vii) published elsewhere in this issue of the Federal Register].

* * * * *

PAR. 3. Section 1.1502-32 is amended by:

1. Revising paragraphs (a)(2) and (h).

2. Adding paragraphs (b)(3)(iii)(C), (b)(3)(iii)(D), (b)(3)(vi) and (h)(6).

The revision and additions read as follows:

Proposed § 1.1502-32 Investment adjustments. [*For Preamble, see ¶ 152,369*]

* * * * *

(a) *(2)* [The proposed amendment to § 1.1502-32(a)(2) is the same as § 1.1502-32T(a)(2) published elsewhere in this issue of the Federal Register].

* * * * *

(b) * * * *(1)* * * *

(3) * * *

(iii) * * *

(C) and (D) [The proposed amendment to § 1.1502-32(b)(3)(iii)(C) and (b)(3)(iii)(D) are the same as § 1.1502-32T(b)(3)(iii)(C) and (b)(3)(iii)(D) published elsewhere in this issue of the Federal Register].

* * * * *

(4) (i) * * *

(vi) [The proposed amendment to § 1.1502-32(b)(4)(vi) is the same as § 1.1502-32T(b)(4)(vi) published elsewhere in this issue of the Federal Register].

* * * * *

(h) *(6)* [The proposed amendment to § 1.1502-32(h)(6) is the same as § 1.1502-32T(h)(6) published elsewhere in this issue of the Federal Register].

PAR. 4. In § 1.1502-32, paragraph (b)(4)(v) is added to read as follows:

Proposed § 1.1502-32 Investment adjustments. [*For Preamble, see ¶ 152,251*]

[The text of this proposed section is the same as the text of § 1.1502-32T(b)(4)(v) published elsewhere in this issue of the Federal Register].

§ 1.1502-33 Earnings and profits.

Caution: The Treasury has not yet amended Reg § 1.1502-33 to reflect changes made by P.L. 104-188.

(a) In general. *(1) Purpose.* This section provides rules for adjusting the earnings and profits of a subsidiary (S) and any member (P) owning S's stock. These rules modify the determination of P's earnings and profits under applicable rules of law, including section 312, by adjusting P's earnings and profits to reflect S's earnings and profits for the period that S is a member of the consolidated group. The purpose for modifying the determination of earnings and profits is to treat P and S as a single entity by reflecting the earnings and profits of lower-tier members in the earnings and profits of higher-tier members and consolidating the group's earnings and profits in the common parent. References in this section to earnings and profits include deficits in earnings and profits.

(2) Application of other rules of law, duplicative adjustments. See Sec. 1.1502-80(a) regarding the general applicability of other rules of law and a limitation on duplicative adjustments. For example, the allowance for depreciation is determined in accordance with section 312(k). P's earnings and profits must not be adjusted under this section and other rules of law in a manner that has the effect of duplicating an adjustment. For example, if S's earnings and profits are reflected in P's earnings and profits under paragraph (b) of this section, and S transfers its assets to P in a liquidation to which section 332 applies, S's earnings and profits that P succeeds to under section 381 must be adjusted to prevent duplication.

(b) Tiering up earnings and profits. *(1) General rule.* P's earnings and profits are adjusted under this section to reflect changes in S's earnings and profits in accordance with the applicable principles of § 1.1502-32, consistently applied, and an adjustment to P's earnings and profits for a tax year under this paragraph (b)(1) is treated as earnings and profits of P for the tax year in which the adjustment arises. Under these principles, for example, the adjustments are made as of the close of each consolidated return year, and as of any other time if a determination at that time is necessary to determine the earnings and profits of any person. Similarly, S's earnings and profits are allocated under the principles of § 1.1502-32(c), and the adjustments are applied in the order of the tiers, from the lowest to the highest. However, modifications to the principles include:

(i) The amount of P's adjustment is determined by reference to S's earnings and profits, rather than S's taxable and tax-exempt items (and therefore, for example, the deferral of a negative adjustment for S's unabsorbed losses does not apply).

(ii) The tax sharing rules under paragraph (d) of this section apply rather than those of § 1.1502-32(b)(3)(iv)(D).

(2) Affiliated earnings and profits. The reduction in S's earnings and profits under section 312 from a distribution of earnings and profits accumulated in separate return years of S that are not separate return limitation years does not tier up to P's earnings and profits. Thus, the increase in P's earnings and profits under section 312 from receipt of the distribution is not offset by a corresponding reduction.

(3) Examples. (i) In general. For purposes of the examples in this section, unless otherwise stated, P owns all of the only class of S's stock, the stock is owned for the entire year, S owns no stock of lower-tier members, the tax year of all persons is the calendar year, all persons use the accrual method of accounting, the facts set forth the only corporate activity, preferred stock is described in section 1504(a)(4), all transactions are between unrelated persons, and tax liabilities are disregarded.

(ii) Tiering up earnings and profits. The principles of this paragraph (b) are illustrated by the following examples.

Example (1). Tier-up and distribution of earnings and profits.

(a) Facts. P forms S in Year 1 with a $100 contribution. S has $100 of earnings and profits for Year 1 and no earnings and profits for Year 2. During Year 2, S declares and distributes a $50 dividend to P.

(b) Analysis. Under paragraph (b)(1) of this section, S's $100 of earnings and profits for Year 1 increases P's earnings and profits for Year 1. P has no additional earnings and profits for Year 2 as a result of the $50 distribution in Year 2, because there is a $50 increase in P's earnings and profits as a result of the receipt of the dividend and a corresponding $50 decrease in S's earnings and profits under section 312(a) that is reflected in P's earnings and profits under paragraph (b)(1) of this section.

(c) Distribution of current earnings and profits. The facts are the same as in paragraph (a) of this Example 1, except that S distributes the $50 dividend at the end of Year 1 rather than during Year 2. Under paragraph (b)(1) of this section, P's earnings and profits are increased by $100 (S's $50 of undistributed earnings and profits, plus P's receipt of the $50 distribution). Thus, S's earnings and profits increase by $50 and P's earnings and profits increase by $100.

(d) Affiliated earnings and profits. The facts are the same as in paragraph (a) of this Example 1, except that P and S do not begin filing consolidated returns until Year 2. Because P and S file separate returns for Year 1, P's basis in S's stock remains $100 under § 1.1502-32 and this section, S has $100 of earnings and profits, and none of S's earnings and profits is reflected in P's earnings and profits under paragraph (b) of this section. S's distribution in Year 2 ordinarily would reduce S's earnings and profits but not increase P's earnings and profits. (P's $50 of earnings and profits from the dividend would be offset by S's $50 reduction in earnings and profits that tiers up under paragraph (b) of this section.) However, under paragraph (b)(2) of this section, the negative adjustment for S's distribution to P does not apply. Thus, S's distribution reduces its earnings and profits by $50 but increases P's earnings and profits by $50. (If S's earnings and profits had been accumulated in a separate return limitation year, paragraph (b)(2) of this section would not apply and the distribution would reduce S's earnings and profits but not increase P's earnings and profits.)

(e) Earnings and profits deficit. Assume instead that after P forms S in Year 1 with a $100 contribution, S borrows additional funds and has a $150 deficit in earnings and profits for Year 1. The corresponding loss for tax purposes is not absorbed in Year 1, and is included in the group's consolidated net operating loss carried forward to Year 2. Under paragraph (b)(1) of this section, however, S's $150 deficit in earnings and profits decreases P's earnings and profits for Year 1 by $150. (Absorption of the loss in a later tax year has no effect on the earnings and profits of P and S.)

Example (2). Section 355 distribution.

(a) Facts. P owns all of S's stock and S owns all of T's stock. For Year 1, T has $100 of earnings and profits. Under paragraph (b)(1) of this section, the earnings and profits of T tier up to S and to P. S and P have no other earnings and profits for Year 1. S distributes T's stock to P at the end of Year 1 in a distribution to which section 355 applies.

(b) Analysis. Because S's distribution of T's stock is a distribution to which section 355 applies, the applicable principles of § 1.1502-32(b)(2)(iv) do not require P's earnings and profits to be adjusted by reason of the distribution. In addition, although S's earnings and profits may be reduced under section 312(h) as a result of the distribution, the applicable principles of § 1.1502-32(b)(3)(iii) do not require P's earnings and profits to be adjusted to reflect this reduction in S's earnings and profits.

Example (3). Allocating earnings and profits among shares. P owns 80% of S's stock throughout Year 1. For Year 1, S has $100 of earnings and profits. Under paragraph (b)(1) of this section, $80 of S's earnings and profits is allocated to P based on P's ownership of S's stock. Accordingly, $80 of S's earnings and profits for Year 1 is reflected in P's earnings and profits for Year 1.

(c) Special rules. For purposes of this section—

(1) Stock of members. For purposes of determining P's earnings and profits from the disposition of S's stock, P's basis in S's stock is adjusted to reflect S's earnings and profits determined under paragraph (b) of this section, rather than under § 1.1502-32. For example, P's basis in S's stock is increased by positive earnings and profits and decreased by deficits in earnings and profits. Similarly, P's basis in S's stock is not reduced for distributions to which paragraph (b)(2) of this section applies (affiliated earnings and profits). P may have an excess loss account in S's stock for earnings and profits purposes (whether or not there is an excess loss account under § 1.1502-32), and the excess loss account is determined, adjusted, and taken into account in accordance with the principles of § 1.1502-19 and 1.1502-32.

(2) Intercompany transactions. Intercompany items and corresponding items are not reflected in earnings and profits before they are taken into account under § 1.1502-13. See § 1.1502-13 for the applicable rules and definitions.

(3) Example. The principles of this paragraph (c) are illustrated by the following example.

Example. Adjustments to stock basis.

(a) Facts. P forms S in Year 1 with a $100 contribution. For Year 1, S has $75 of taxable income and $100 of earnings and profits. For Year 2, S has no taxable income or earnings and profits, and S declares and distributes a $50 dividend to P. P sells all of S's stock for $150 at the end of Year 2.

(b) Analysis. Under paragraph (c)(1) of this section, P's basis in S's stock for earnings and profits purposes immediately before the sale is $150 (the $100 initial basis, plus S's $100 of earnings and profits for Year 1, minus the $50 distribution of earnings and profits in Year 2). Thus, P recognizes no gain or loss from the sale of S's stock for earnings and profits purposes.

(c) Earnings and profits deficit. Assume instead that S has a $100 tax loss and earnings and profits deficit for Year 1. The tax loss is not absorbed in Year 1 and is included in the group's consolidated net operating loss carried forward to Year 2. Under paragraph (b) of this section, S's $100 deficit in earnings and profits decreases P's earnings and profits for Year 1. Under paragraph (c) of this section, P decreases its basis in S's stock for purposes of determining earnings and profits from $100 to $0. (If S had borrowed an additional $50 that it also lost in Year 1, P would have decreased its earnings and profits for Year 1 by the additional $50, and P would have had a $50 excess loss account in S's stock for earnings and profits purposes, which would be taken into account in determining P's earnings and profits from its sale of S's stock.)

(d) Affiliated earnings and profits. Assume instead that P and S do not begin filing consolidated returns until Year 2. Under paragraph (b) of this section, the negative adjustment under § 1.1502-32(b) for distributions does not apply to S's distribution of earnings and profits accumulated in a separate return year that is a not separate return limitation year. Thus, P's basis in S's stock for earnings and profits purposes remains $100, and P has $50 of earnings and profits from the sale of S's stock.

(d) Federal income tax liability. *(1) In general.* (i) Extension of tax allocations. Section 1552 allocates the tax liability of a consolidated group among its members for purposes of determining the amounts by which their earnings and profits are reduced for taxes. Section 1552 does not reflect the absorption by one member of another member's tax attributes (e.g., losses, deductions and credits). For example, if P's $100 of income is offset by S's $100 of deductions, consolidated tax liability is $0 and no amount is allocated under section 1552. However, the group may elect under this paragraph (d) to allocate additional amounts to reflect the absorption by one member of the tax attributes of another member. Permissible methods are set forth in paragraphs (d)(2) through (4) of this section, and election procedures are provided in paragraph (d)(5) of this section. Allocations under this paragraph (d) must be reflected annually on permanent records (including work papers). Any computations of separate return tax liability are subject to the principles of section 1561.

(ii) Effect of extended tax allocations. The amounts allocated under this paragraph (d) are treated as allocations of tax liability for purposes of § 1.1552-1(b)(2). For example, if P's taxable income is offset by S's loss, and tax liability is allocated under the percentage method of paragraph (d)(3) of this section, P's earnings and profits are reduced as if its income were subject to tax, P is treated as liable to S for the amount of the tax, and corresponding adjustments are made to S's earnings and profits. If the liability of one member to another is not paid, the amount not paid generally is treated as a distribution, contribution, or both, depending on the relationship between the members.

(2) Wait-and-see method. The wait-and-see method under this paragraph (d)(2) is derived from Securities and Exchange Commission procedures. In the year that a member's tax attribute is absorbed, the group's consolidated tax liability is allocated in accordance with the group's method under section 1552. When, in effect, the member with the tax attribute could have absorbed the attribute on a separate return basis in a later year, a portion of the group's consolidated tax liability for the later year that is otherwise allocated to members under section 1552 is reallocated. The reallocation takes into account all consolidated return years to which this paragraph (d) applies (the computation period), and is determined by comparing the tax allocated to a member during the computation period with the member's tax liability determined as if it had filed separate returns during the computation period.

(i) Cap on allocation under section 1552. A member's allocation under section 1552 for a tax year may not exceed the excess, if any, of—

(A) The total of the tax liabilities of the member for the computation period (including the current year), determined as if the member had filed separate returns; over

(B) The total amount allocated to the member under section 1552 and this paragraph (d) for the computation period (except the current year).

(ii) Reallocation of capped amounts. To the extent that the amount allocated to a member under section 1552 exceeds the limitation under paragraph (d)(2)(i) of this section, the excess is allocated among the remaining members in proportion to (but not to exceed the amount of) each member's excess, if any, of—

(A) The total of the tax liabilities of the member for the computation period (including the current year), determined as if the member had filed separate returns; over

(B) The total amount allocated to the member under section 1552 and this paragraph (d) for the computation period (including for the current year only the amount allocated under section 1552).

(iii) Reallocation of excess capped amounts. If the reductions under paragraph (d)(2)(i) of this section exceed the amounts allocable under paragraph (d)(2)(ii) of this section, the excess is allocated among the members in accordance with the group's method under section 1552 without taking this paragraph (d)(2) into account.

(3) Percentage method. The percentage method under this paragraph (d)(3) allocates tax liability based on the absorption of tax attributes, without taking into account the ability of any member to subsequently absorb its own tax attributes. The allocation under this method is in addition to the allocation under section 1552.

(i) Decreased earnings and profits. A member's allocation under section 1552 for any year is increased, thereby decreasing its earnings and profits, by a fixed percentage (not to exceed 100%) of the excess, if any, of—

(A) The member's separate return tax liability for the consolidated return year as determined under § 1.1552-1(a)(2)(ii); over

(B) The amount allocated to the member under section 1552.

(ii) Increased earnings and profits. An amount equal to the total decrease in earnings and profits under paragraph (d)(3)(i) of this section (including amounts allocated as a result of a carryback) increases the earnings and profits of the members whose attributes are absorbed, and is allocated among them in a manner that reasonably reflects the absorption of the tax attributes.

(4) Additional methods. The absorption by one member of the tax attributes of another member may be reflected under any other method approved in writing by the Commissioner.

(5) Election of allocation method. (i) In general. Tax liability may be allocated under this paragraph (d) only if an election is filed with the group's first return. The election must—

(A) Be made in a separate statement entitled "ELECTION TO ALLOCATE TAX LIABILITY UNDER § 1.1502-33(d)";

(B) State the allocation method elected under § 1.1502-33(d) and under section 1552;

(C) If the percentage method is elected, state the percentage (not to exceed 100%) to be used; and

(D) If a method is permitted under paragraph (d)(4) of this section, provide the date and control number of the private letter ruling issued by the Internal Revenue Service approving such method.

(ii) Consent. (A) Electing or changing methods. An election for a later year, or an election to change methods, may be made only with the written consent of the Commissioner.

(B) Prior law elections. An election in effect for the last tax year beginning before January 1, 1995, remains in effect under this section. However, a group may elect to conform its earnings and profits computations to the method described in § 1.1502-32(b)(3)(iv)(D) (the percentage method, using a 100% allocation), whether or not it has previously made an election for earnings and profits purposes. If a conforming election is made, the group must make all adjustments necessary to prevent amounts from being duplicated or omitted. The conforming election is made by attaching a statement entitled "ELECTION TO CONFORM TAX ALLOCATIONS UNDER §§ 1.1502-32 and 1.1502-33(d)" to the consolidated group's return for its first tax year beginning on or after January 1, 1995. The statement must be signed by the common parent, and must specify whether the method is conformed only for years beginning on or after January 1, 1995 or as if the method were in effect for all prior years. The statement must also describe the adjustments made by reason of the change (e.g., to reflect prior use of earnings and profits).

(6) Examples. The principles of this paragraph (d) are illustrated by the following examples.

Example (1). Wait-and-see method.

(a) Facts. P owns all of the stock of S1 and S2. The P group uses the wait-and-see method of allocation under paragraph (d)(2) of this section in conjunction with § 1.1552-1(a)(1). For Year 1, each member's taxable income, both for purposes of § 1.1552-1(a)(1) and redetermined as if the member had filed separate returns, is as follows: P $0, S1 $2,000, and S2 ($1,000). Thus, the P group's consolidated tax liability for Year 1 is $340 (assuming a 34% tax rate).

(b) Analysis. Under § 1.1552-1(a)(1)(i), the tax liability of the P group is allocated among the members in accordance with the portion of the consolidated taxable income attributable to each member having taxable income. Thus, all of the P group's $340 consolidated tax liability is allocated to S1. As a result, S1 decreases its earnings and profits under section 1552 by $340 (even if S1 does not pay the tax liability). No further allocations are made under paragraph (d)(2) of this section because S2 cannot yet absorb its loss on a separate return basis.

(c) Payment of tax liability. If S1 pays the $340 tax liability, there is no further effect on the income, earnings and profits, or stock basis of any member. If P pays the $340 tax liability (and the payment is not a loan from P to S1), P is treated as making a $340 contribution to the capital of S1; if S2 pays the $340 tax liability (and the payment is not a loan from S2 to S1), S2 is treated as making a $340 distribution to P with respect to its stock, and P is treated as making a $340 contribution to the capital of S1. See § 1.1552-1(b)(2).

(d) Year 2. For Year 2, each member's taxable income, under § 1.1552-1(a)(1)(ii) and redetermined as if the member had filed separate returns, without taking into account any carryover from Year 1, is as follows: P $0, S1 $1,000, and S2 $3,000. Thus, the P group's consolidated tax liability for Year 2 is $1,360 (assuming a 34% tax rate). Of this amount, section 1552 would allocate $340 to S1 and $1,020 to S2. However, under paragraph (d)(2)(i) of this section, no more than $680 may be allocated to S2. This is because S2 would have had an aggregate tax liability of $680 if it had filed separate returns for Years 1 and 2 (a $0 tax liability for Year 1, and a $680 tax liability for Year 2, taking into account a $1,000 net operating loss carryover from Year 1). Under paragraph (d)(2)(ii) of this section, the entire excess of $340 which would otherwise be allocated to S2 under § 1.1552-1(a)(1) is allocated to S1. This is because S1 would have had an additional $340 of aggregate tax liability if it had filed separate returns for Years 1 and 2 (a $680 tax liability for Year 1, and a $340 tax liability for Year 2, not taking into account S2's $1,000 net operating loss for Year 1). The effect of the allocation of $680 to S1 and $680 to S2 is determined under § 1.1552-1(b)(2).

Example (2). Percentage method.

(a) Facts. The facts are the same as in Example 1, but the P group uses the percentage method of allocation under paragraph (d)(3) of this section, with a percentage of 100%. In addition, the taxable incomes and losses of the members are the same if computed as provided in § 1.1552-1(a)(2)(ii).

(b) Analysis. Under § 1.1552-1(a)(2)(ii), $340 of tax liability is allocated to S1 for Year 1. Under paragraph (d)(3)(i) of this section, S1 is allocated another $340 of tax liability because S1 would have had a $680 tax liability if it had filed separate returns but only $340 is allocated to S1 under section 1552. Thus, S1's earnings and profits are decreased by the $680 total. Under paragraph (d)(3)(ii) of this section, S2's earnings and profits are increased by $340 because the additional $340 allocated to S1 under paragraph (d)(3)(i) of this section is attributable to the absorption of S2's losses.

(c) Payment of tax liability. If S1 pays the $340 tax liability of the P group and pays $340 to S2, the Year 1 tax liability results in no further adjustments to the income, earnings and profits, or basis of any member's stock. If S1 pays the $340 tax liability of the P group and pays the other $340 to P instead of S2 because, for example, of an agreement among the members, S2 is treated as distributing $340 to P with respect to its stock in the year that S1 makes the payment to P. See § 1.1552-1(b)(2).

(d) Year 2. For Year 2, $340 is allocated to S1 and $1,020 is allocated to S2 under section 1552. No additional amounts are allocated under paragraph (d)(3) of this section.

(e) Deconsolidations. *(1) In general.* Immediately before it becomes a nonmember, S's earnings and profits are eliminated to the extent they were taken into account by any member under this section. If S's earnings and profits are eliminated under this paragraph (e)(1), no corresponding adjustment is made to the earnings and profits of P (or any other member) under paragraph (b) of this section or to any basis in a member's stock under paragraph (c) of this section. For this purpose, S is treated as becoming a nonmember on the first day of its first separate return year (including another group's consolidated return year).

(2) Acquisition of group. (i) Application. This paragraph (e)(2) applies only if a consolidated group (the terminating group) ceases to exist as a result of—

(A) The acquisition of either the assets of the common parent of the terminating group in a reorganization described in section 381(a)(2), or the stock of the common parent of the terminating group; or

(B) The application of the principles of § 1.1502-75(d)(2) or (d)(3).

(ii) General rule. Paragraph (e)(1) of this section does not apply solely by reason of the termination of a group because it is acquired, if there is a surviving group that is, immediately thereafter, a consolidated group. Instead, the surviving group is treated as the terminating group for purposes of applying this paragraph (e) to the terminating group. This treatment does not apply, however, to members of the terminating group that are not members of the surviving consolidated group immediately after the terminating group ceases to exist (e.g., under section 1504(a)(3) relating to reconsolidation, or section 1504(c) relating to includible insurance companies).

(3) Certain corporate separations and reorganizations. The adjustments under paragraph (e)(1) of this section must be modified to the extent necessary to effectuate the principles of section 312(h). Thus, P's earnings and profits rather than S's earnings and profits may be eliminated immediately before S becomes a nonmember. P's earnings and profits are eliminated to the extent that its earnings and profits reflect S's earnings and profits after applying section 312(h) immediately after S becomes a nonmember (determined without taking this paragraph (e) into account).

(4) Special uses of earnings and profits. Paragraph (e)(1) of this section does not apply for purposes of determining—

(i) The extent to which a distribution is charged to reserve accounts under section 593(e);

(ii) The extent to which a distribution is taxable to the recipient under sections 805(a)(4) and 832; and

(iii) Any other special use identified in guidance published in the Internal Revenue Bulletin.

(5) Example. The principles of this paragraph (e) are illustrated by the following example.

Example. (a) Facts. Individuals A and B own all of P's stock, and P owns all of the stock of S and T, each with a $500 basis. For Year 1, S has $100 of earnings and profits and T has $50 of earnings and profits. Under paragraph (b)(1) of this section, the earnings and profits of S and T tier up to P, and P has $150 of earnings and profits for Year 1. P sells all of S's stock for $600 at the close of Year 1.

(b) Analysis. Under paragraph (e)(1) of this section, S's $100 of earnings and profits is eliminated immediately before S becomes a nonmember because the earnings and profits are taken into account under paragraph (b) of this section in P's earnings and profits. However, no corresponding adjustment is made to P's earnings and profits or to P's basis in S's stock for purposes of earnings and profits. P's earnings and profits for Year 1 remain $150 following the sale of S's stock.

(c) Forward merger. The facts are the same as in paragraph (a) of this Example, except that, rather than P selling S's stock, S merges into a nonmember in a transaction described in section 368(a)(2)(D). Under paragraph (h) of this section, the nonmember is treated as a successor to S. Thus, as in paragraph (b) of this Example, S's $100 of earnings and profits is eliminated immediately before S ceases to be a member.

(d) Acquisition of entire group. The facts are the same as in paragraph (a) of this Example, except that X, the common parent of another consolidated group, purchases all of P's stock at the close of Year 1, and P sells S's stock during Year 3. Under paragraph (e)(2) of this section, the earnings and profits of S and T are not eliminated as a result of X purchasing P's stock. However, S's earnings and profits from consolidated return years of both the P group and the X group are eliminated immediately before S becomes a nonmember of the X group.

(e) Earnings and profits deficit. The facts are the same as in paragraph (d) of this Example, except that S has a $550 deficit in earnings and profits for Year 1. The effect of paragraph (e)(1) of this section is the same. Under paragraph (c)(1) of this section, P would have an excess loss account in S's stock for earnings and profits purposes under the principles of §§ 1.1502-19 and 1.1502-32, and, under the principles of § 1.1502-19(c)(2), the excess loss account is not taken into account as a result of X's purchase of P's stock. Under paragraph (e)(2) of this section, S's deficit is not eliminated under paragraph (e)(1) of this section immediately before X's purchase of P's stock. However, S's earnings and profits (or deficit) is eliminated immediately before S becomes a nonmember of the X group.

(f) Section 355 distribution. The facts are the same as in paragraph (a) of this Example, except that, rather than selling S's stock, P distributes S's stock to A at the close of Year 1 in a distribution to which section 355 applies. Under paragraph (e)(3) of this section, P's earnings and profits may be reduced under section 312(h) as a result of the distribution. To the extent that P's earnings and profits are reduced, S's earnings and profits are not eliminated under paragraph (e)(1) of this section.

(f) Changes in the structure of the group. *(1) Changes in the common parent.* (i) General rule. If P succeeds another corporation under the principles of § 1.1502-75(d)(2) or (3) as the common parent of a consolidated group (a group structure change), the earnings and profits of P are adjusted immediately after P becomes the new common parent to reflect the earnings and profits of the former common parent immediately before the former common parent ceases to be the common parent. The adjustment is made as if P succeeds to the earnings and profits of the former common parent in a transaction described in section 381(a). See § 1.1502-31 for the basis of the stock of members following a group structure change.

(ii) Minority shareholders. If the former common parent's stock is not wholly owned by members of the consolidated group immediately after the former common parent ceases to be the common parent, appropriate adjustments must be made to reflect in the new common parent only an allocable part of the former common parent's earnings and profits.

(iii) Higher-tier members. To the extent that earnings and profits are adjusted under this paragraph (f)(1), and the former common parent is owned by members other than P, the earnings and profits of the intermediate subsidiaries must be adjusted in accordance with the principles of this section.

(iv) Example. The principles of this paragraph (f)(1) are illustrated by the following example.

Example. (a) Facts. X is the common parent of a consolidated group with $100 of earnings and profits, and P is the common parent of another consolidated group with $20 of earnings and profits. P acquires all of X's stock at the close of Year 1 in exchange for 70% of P's stock. The exchange is a reverse acquisition under § 1.1502-75(d)(3), and the X group is treated as remaining in existence with P as its new common parent.

(b) Adjustments for X group earnings and profits. Under paragraph (f)(1) of this section, P's earnings and profits are adjusted immediately after P becomes the new common parent, to reflect X's $100 of earnings and profits immediately before X ceases to be the common parent. The adjustment is made as if P succeeds to X's earnings and profits in a transaction described in section 381(a). Thus, immediately after the acquisition, P has $120 of accumulated earnings and profits and X continues to have $100 of accumulated earnings and profits.

(c) Adjustments for P group earnings and profits. Although the P group terminates on P's acquisition of X's stock, under paragraph (e)(2) of this section, no adjustments are made to the earnings and profits of any subsidiaries in the terminating P group.

(d) Acquisition of separate return corporation. The facts are the same as in paragraph (a) of this Example, except that, immediately before the acquisition of its stock by P, X is not affiliated with any other corporation. The exchange is a reverse acquisition under § 1.1502-75(d)(3), and P is treated as the common parent of the X group. Consequently, the results are the same as in paragraphs (b) and (c) of this Example.

(2) Change in the location of subsidiaries. If the location of a member within a group changes, appropriate adjustments must be made to the earnings and profits of the members to prevent the earnings and profits from being eliminated. For example, if P transfers all of S's stock to another member in a transaction to which section 351 and § 1.1502-13 apply, the transferee's earnings and profits are adjusted immediately after the transfer to reflect S's earnings and profits immediately before the transfer from consolidated return years. On the other hand, if the transferee purchases S's stock from P, the transferee's earnings and profits are not adjusted.

(g) Anti-avoidance rule. If any person acts with a principal purpose contrary to the purposes of this section, to avoid the effect of the rules of this section or apply the rules of this section to avoid the effect of any other provision of the consolidated return regulations, adjustments must be made as necessary to carry out the purposes of this section.

(h) Predecessors and successors. For purposes of this section, any reference to a corporation or to a share includes a reference to a successor or predecessor as the context may require. A corporation is a successor if its earnings and profits are determined, directly or indirectly, in whole or in part, by reference to the earnings and profits of another corporation (the predecessor). A share is a successor if its basis is determined, directly or indirectly, in whole or in part, by reference to the basis of another share (the predecessor).

(i) [Reserved]

(j) Effective/applicability date. *(1) General rule.* This section applies with respect to determinations of the earnings and profits of a member (e.g., for purposes of a characterizing a distribution to which section 301 applies) in consolidated return years beginning on or after January 1, 1995. If this section applies, earnings and profits must be determined or redetermined as if this section were in effect for all years (including, for example, the consolidated return years of another consolidated group to the extent the earnings and profits from those years are still reflected). For example, if a distribution by P to a nonmember shareholder in 1990 was a dividend because of an unabsorbed loss carryover attributable to S, P's earnings and profits in tax years beginning after January 1, 1995 are redetermined by taking into account a negative adjustment in the tax year S's loss arose and in 1990 for P's distribution, and any subsequent absorption of the loss has no effect on earnings and profits. Any such determination or redetermination does not, however, affect any prior period. Thus, the shareholder's treatment in 1990 of the distribution as a dividend (and the effect of the distribution on stock basis) is not redetermined under this section. Paragraphs (a)(2) and (e)(2)(i)(A) of this section apply with respect to determinations of the earnings and profits of a member in consolidated return years beginning on or after September 17, 2008. However, taxpayers may apply paragraph (e)(2)(i)(A) of this section with respect to determinations of the earnings and profits of a member in consolidated return years beginning prior to September 17, 2008.

(2) Dispositions of stock before effective date. (i) In general. If P disposes of stock of S in a consolidated return year beginning before January 1, 1995, the amount of P's earnings and profits with respect to S are not redetermined under paragraph (j)(1) of this section. See § 1.1502-19 as contained in the 26 CFR part 1 edition revised as of April 1, 1994 for

the definition of disposition, and paragraph (j)(5) of this section for the rules applicable to such dispositions.

(ii) Lower-tier members. Although P disposes of S's stock in a tax year beginning before January 1, 1995, S's determinations or adjustments with respect to lower-tier members with which it continues to file a consolidated return are redetermined in accordance with the rules of this section (even if S's earnings and profits were previously taken into account by P). For example, assume that P owns all of S's stock, S owns all of T's stock, and T owns all of U's stock. If S sells 80% of T's stock in a tax year beginning before January 1, 1995 (the effective date), the amount of S's earnings and profits from the sale, and the adjustments to stock basis for earnings and profits purposes that are reflected in that amount, are not redetermined if P sells S's stock after the effective date. If S sells the remaining 20% of T's stock after the effective date, S's stock basis adjustments with respect to that T stock are also not redetermined because T became a nonmember before the effective date. However, if T and U continue to file a consolidated return with each other, paragraph (e)(1) of this section did not apply, and T sells U's stock after the effective date, T's earnings and profits with respect to U are redetermined (even though some of the earnings and profits may have been taken into account by S in its prior sale of T's stock before the effective date).

(iii) Deferred amounts. For purposes of this paragraph (j)(2), a disposition does not include a transaction to which § 1.1502-13, § 1.1502-13T, § 1.1502-14, or § 1.1502-14T applies. Instead, the transaction is deemed to occur as the earnings and profits (if any) are taken into account.

(3) Deconsolidations and group structure changes. (i) In general. Paragraphs (e) and (f) of this section apply with respect to deconsolidations and group structure changes occurring in consolidated return years beginning on or after January 1, 1995.

(ii) Prior period group structure changes. If there was a group structure change in a consolidated return year beginning before January 1, 1995, and earnings and profits were not determined under § 1.1502-33T(a) as contained in the 26 CFR part 1 edition revised as of April 1, 1994, a distribution in a tax year ending after September 7, 1988, of earnings and profits that are not reflected in the earnings and profits of the distributee member, but would have been so reflected if § 1.1502-33T(a) as contained in the 26 CFR part 1 edition revised as of April 1, 1994 had applied, the negative adjustment under paragraph (b) of this section for distributions does not apply (and there is therefore no offset to the increase in the earnings and profits of the distributee).

(4) Deemed dividend elections. If there is a deemed distribution and recontribution pursuant to § 1.1502-32(f)(2) as contained in the 26 CFR part 1 edition revised as of April 1, 1994 in a consolidated return year beginning before January 1, 1995, the deemed distribution and recontribution under the election are treated as an actual distribution by S and recontribution by P as provided under the election.

(5) Prior law. For prior determinations, see prior regulations under section 1502 as in effect with respect to the determination. See, e.g., §§ 1.1502-33 and 1.1502-33T as contained in the 26 CFR part 1 edition revised as of April 1, 1994.

(k) Effective/applicability date. Paragraph (d)(5)(i)(D) of this section applies to any original consolidated Federal income tax return due (without extensions) after June 14, 2007. For original consolidated Federal income tax returns due (without extensions) after May 30, 2006, and on or before June 14, 2007, see § 1.1502-33T as contained in 26 CFR part 1 in effect on April 1, 2007. For original consolidated Federal income tax returns due (without extensions) on or before May 30, 2006, see § 1.1502-33 as contained in 26 CFR part 1 in effect on April 1, 2006.

T.D. 6909, 12/29/66, amend T.D. 6943, 1/15/68, T.D. 6962, 7/2/68, T.D. 7246, 12/29/72, T.D. 8226, 9/7/88, T.D. 8294, 3/9/90, T.D. 8319, 11/19/90, T.D. 8364, 9/13/91, T.D. 8560, 8/12/94, T.D. 8597, 7/12/95, T.D. 9264, 5/26/2006, T.D. 9329, 6/13/2007, T.D. 9424, 9/10/2008.

PAR. 6. Proposed § 1.1502-33, published in the FEDERAL REGISTER on November 12, 1992 (57 FR 53634), is amended by adding the following sentence at the end of paragraph (d)(1)(i) to read as follows:

Proposed § 1.1502-33 Earnings and profits. [*For Preamble, see ¶ 151,475*]

* * * * *

(d) * * *

(1) * * *

(i) * * * See paragraphs (g), (h), and (j) of § 1.1552-1 for rules relating to the allocation of the consolidated AMT (as computed under § 1.1502-55), the consolidated environmental tax (defined in § 1.1552-1(h)), and the consolidated additional taxes (defined in § 1.1502-2(b)) among members of the group.

* * * * *

§ 1.1502-34 Special aggregate stock ownership rules.

Caution: The Treasury has not yet amended Reg § 1.1502-34 to reflect changes made by P.L. 106-554.

For purposes of §§ 1.1502-1 through 1.1502-80, in determining the stock ownership of a member of the group in another corporation (the "issuing corporation") for purposes of determining the application of section 165(g)(3)(A), 332(b)(1), 333(b), 351(a), 732(f), or 904(f), in a consolidated return year, there shall be included stock owned by all other members of the group in the issuing corporation. Thus, assume that members A, B, and C each own 33⅓ percent of the stock issued by D. In such case, A, B, and C shall each be treated as meeting the 80-percent stock ownership requirement for purposes of section 332, and no member can elect to have section 333 apply. Furthermore, the special rule for minority shareholders in section 337(d) cannot apply with respect to amounts received by A, B, or C in liquidation of D.

T.D. 6894, 9/7/66, amend T.D. 8949, 6/18/2001.

---

§ 1.1502-35 Transfers of subsidiary stock and deconsolidations of subsidiaries.

(a) In general. *(1) Purpose.* The purpose of this section is to prevent a group from obtaining more than one tax benefit from a single economic loss. The provisions of this section shall be construed in a manner that is consistent with that purpose and in a manner that reasonably carries out that purpose.

(2) Dates of applicability. This section applies if--

(i) On or after March 7, 2002, a member recognizes a loss on the disposition of a share of stock of a subsidiary (or, on or after April 10, 2007, a share of stock of a former subsidiary) or a carryover basis asset (subject to paragraph (c)(6) of this section),

(ii) The member's loss on the share of subsidiary stock or the carryover basis asset is allowed on or before the date that is ten years after the disposition of the share or carryover basis asset, and

(iii) If the disposition is of a share of subsidiary stock, it is not a transfer to which § 1.1502-36 applies.

(b) Redetermination of basis on certain nondeconsolidating transfers of subsidiary stock and on certain deconsolidations of subsidiaries. *(1) Redetermination of basis on certain nondeconsolidating transfers of subsidiary stock.* Except as provided in paragraph (b)(3)(i) of this section, if, immediately after a transfer of stock of a subsidiary that has a basis that exceeds its value, the subsidiary remains a member of the group, then the basis in each share of subsidiary stock owned by each member of the group shall be redetermined in accordance with the provisions of this paragraph (b)(1) immediately before such transfer. All of the members' bases in the shares of subsidiary stock immediately before such transfer shall be aggregated. Such aggregated basis shall be allocated first to the shares of the subsidiary's preferred stock that are owned by the members of the group immediately before such transfer, in proportion to, but not in excess of, the value of those shares at such time. After allocation of the aggregated basis to all shares of the preferred stock of the subsidiary pursuant to the preceding sentence, any remaining basis shall be allocated among all common shares of subsidiary stock held by members of the group immediately before the transfer, in proportion to the value of such shares at such time.

(2) Redetermination of basis on certain deconsolidations of subsidiaries. (i) Allocation of reallocable basis amount. Except as provided in paragraph (b)(3)(ii) of this section, if, immediately before a deconsolidation of a subsidiary, any share of stock of such subsidiary owned by a member of the group has a basis that exceeds its value, then the basis in each share of the subsidiary's stock owned by each member of the group shall be redetermined in accordance with the provisions of this paragraph (b)(2) immediately before such deconsolidation. The basis in each share of the subsidiary's stock held by members of the group immediately before the deconsolidation that has a basis in excess of value at such time shall be reduced, but not below such share's value, in a manner that, to the greatest extent possible, causes the ratio of the basis to the value of each such share to be the same; provided, however, that the aggregate amount of such reduction shall not exceed the reallocable basis amount (as computed pursuant to paragraph (b)(2)(ii) of this section). Then, to the extent of the reallocable basis amount, the basis of each share of the preferred stock of the subsidiary that are held by members of the group immediately before the deconsolidation shall be increased, but not above such share's value, in a manner that, to the greatest extent possible, causes the ratio of the basis to the value of each such share to be the same. Then, to the extent that the reallocable basis amount does not increase the basis of shares of preferred stock of the subsidiary pursuant to the third sentence of this paragraph (b)(2)(i), such amount shall increase the basis of all common shares of the subsidiary's stock held by members of the group immediately before the deconsolidation in a manner that, to the greatest extent possible, causes the ratio of the basis to the value of each such share to be the same.

(ii) Calculation of reallocable basis amount. The reallocable basis amount shall equal the lesser of—

(A) The aggregate of all amounts by which, immediately before the deconsolidation, the basis exceeds the value of a share of subsidiary stock owned by any member of the group at such time; and

(B) The total of the subsidiary's (and any predecessor's) items of deduction and loss, and the subsidiary's (and any predecessor's) allocable share of items of deduction and loss of all lower-tier subsidiaries, that were taken into account in computing the adjustment under § 1.1502-32 to the bases of shares of stock of the subsidiary (and any predecessor) held by members of the group immediately before the deconsolidation, other than shares that have bases in excess of value immediately before the deconsolidation.

(3) Exceptions to application of redetermination rules. (i) Paragraph (b)(1) of this section shall not apply to a transfer of subsidiary stock if—

(A) During the taxable year of such transfer, in one or more fully taxable transactions, the members of the group dispose of all of the shares of the subsidiary stock that they own immediately before the transfer, other than the shares the transfer of which would otherwise trigger the application of paragraph (b)(1) of this section, to a person or persons that are not members of the group;

(B) During the taxable year of such transfer, the members of the group are allowed a worthless stock loss under section 165(g) (taking into account the provisions of § 1.1502-80(c)) with respect to all of the shares of subsidiary stock that they own immediately before the transfer, other than the shares the transfer of which would otherwise trigger the application of paragraph (b)(1) of this section; or

(C) Such transfer is to a member of the group and section 332 (provided the stock is transferred to an 80-percent distributee), section 351, section 354, or section 361 applies to such transfer.

(ii) Paragraph (b)(2) of this section shall not apply to a deconsolidation of a subsidiary if—

(A) During the taxable year of such deconsolidation, in one or more fully taxable transactions, the members of the group dispose of all of the shares of the subsidiary stock that they own immediately before the deconsolidation to a person or persons that are not members of the group;

(B) Such deconsolidation results from a fully taxable disposition, to a person or persons that are not members of the group, of some of the shares of the subsidiary, and, during the taxable year of such deconsolidation, the members of the group are allowed a worthless stock loss under section 165(g) with respect to all of the shares of the subsidiary stock that they own immediately after the deconsolidation;

(C) The members of the group are allowed a worthless stock loss under section 165(g) with respect to all of the shares of the subsidiary stock that they own immediately before the deconsolidation;

(D) The deconsolidation of the subsidiary results from the deconsolidation of a higher-tier subsidiary and, immediately after the deconsolidation of the subsidiary, none of the stock of the subsidiary is owned by a group member; or

(E) The deconsolidation of the subsidiary results from a termination of the group.

(4) Special rule for lower-tier subsidiaries. If, immediately after a transfer of subsidiary stock or a deconsolidation of a subsidiary, a lower-tier subsidiary some of the stock of which is owned by the subsidiary is a member of the group, then, for purposes of applying this paragraph (b), the subsidiary shall be treated as having transferred its stock of the lower-tier subsidiary. This principle shall apply to stock of subsidiaries that are owned by such lower-tier subsidiary.

(5) Stock basis adjustments for higher-tier stock. The basis adjustments required under this paragraph (b) result in basis adjustments to higher-tier member stock. The adjustments are applied in the order of the tiers, from the lowest to highest. For example, if a common parent owns stock of a subsidiary that owns stock of a lower-tier subsidiary and the subsidiary recognizes a loss on the disposition of a portion of its shares of the lower-tier subsidiary stock, the common parent must adjust its basis in its subsidiary stock under the principles of § 1.1502-32 to reflect the adjustments that the subsidiary must make to its basis in its stock of the lower-tier subsidiary.

(6) Ordering rules. (i) The rules of this paragraph (b) apply after the rules of § 1.1502-32 are applied.

(ii) The rules of this paragraph (b) apply before the rules of § 1.337(d)-2 and paragraphs (c) and (f) of this section are applied.

(iii) This paragraph (b) (and any resulting basis adjustments to higher-tier member stock made pursuant to paragraph (b)(5) of this section) applies to redetermine the basis of stock of a lower-tier subsidiary before this paragraph (b) applies to a higher-tier member of such lower-tier subsidiary.

(c) Loss suspension. *(1) General rule.* Any loss recognized by a member of a consolidated group with respect to the disposition of a share of subsidiary stock shall be suspended to the extent of the duplicated loss with respect to such share of stock if, immediately after the disposition, the subsidiary is a member of the consolidated group of which it was a member immediately prior to the disposition (or any successor group).

(2) Special rule for lower-tier subsidiaries. This paragraph (c)(2) applies if neither paragraph (c)(1) nor (f) of this section applies to a member's disposition of a share of stock of a subsidiary (the departing member), a loss is recognized on the disposition of such share, and the departing member owns stock of one or more other subsidiaries (a remaining member) that is a member of such group immediately after the disposition. In that case, such loss shall be suspended to the extent the duplicated loss with respect to the departing member stock disposed of is attributable to the remaining member or members.

(3) Treatment of suspended loss. (i) General rule. For purposes of the rules of § 1.1502-32, any loss suspended pursuant to paragraph (c)(1) or (c)(2) of this section is treated as a noncapital, nondeductible expense of the member that disposes of subsidiary stock, incurred during the taxable year that includes the date of the disposition of stock to which paragraph (c)(1) or (c)(2) of this section applies. See § 1.1502-32(b)(3)(iii)(C). Consequently, the basis of a higher-tier member's stock of the member that disposes of subsidiary stock is reduced by the suspended loss in the year it is suspended.

(ii) Location of suspended loss following deconsolidation of selling member. If a member recognizes a loss that is suspended under this paragraph (c) but that member ceases to be a member of the group before the loss is allowable, the common parent is treated as succeeding to the loss in a transaction to which section 381(a) applies.

(4) Reduction of suspended loss. (i) General rule. The amount of any loss suspended pursuant to paragraph (c)(1) or (c)(2) of § 1.1502-35 shall be reduced, but not below zero, by the subsidiary's (and any successor's) items of deduction and loss, and the subsidiary's (and any successor's) allocable share of items of deduction and loss of all lower-tier subsidiaries, that are allocable to the period beginning on the date of the disposition that gave rise to the suspended loss and ending on the day before the first date on which the subsidiary (and any successor) is not a member of the group of which it was a member immediately prior to the disposition (or any successor group), and that are taken into account in determining consolidated taxable income (or loss) of such group for any taxable year that includes any date on or after the date of the disposition and before the first date on which the subsidiary (and any successor) is not a member of such group; provided, however, that such reduction shall not exceed the excess of the amount of such items over the amount of such items that are taken into account in determining the basis adjustments made under § 1.1502-32 to stock of the subsidiary (or any successor) owned by members of the group. The preceding sentence shall not apply to items of deduction and loss to the extent that the group can establish that all or a portion of such items was not reflected in the computation of the duplicated loss with respect to the subsidiary on the date of the disposition of stock that gave rise to the suspended loss.

(ii) Operating rules. (A) Year in which deduction or loss is taken into account. For purposes of paragraph (c)(4)(i) of this section, a subsidiary's (or any successor's) deductions and losses are treated as taken into account when and to the extent they are absorbed by the subsidiary (or any successor) or any other member. To the extent that the subsidiary's (or any successor's) deduction or loss is absorbed in the year it arises or is carried forward and absorbed in a subsequent year (e.g., under section 172, 465, or 1212), the deduction is treated as taken into account in the year in which it is absorbed. To the extent that a subsidiary's (or any successor's) deduction or loss is carried back and absorbed in a prior year (whether consolidated or separate), the deduction or loss is treated as taken into account in the year in which it arises and not in the year in which it is absorbed.

(B) Determination of items that are allocable to the post-disposition, pre-deconsolidation period. For purposes of paragraph (c)(4)(i) of this section, the determination of whether a subsidiary's (or any successor's) items of deduction and loss and allocable share of items of deduction and loss of all lower-tier subsidiaries are allocable to the period beginning on the date of the disposition of subsidiary stock that gave rise to the suspended loss and ending on the day before the first date on which the subsidiary (or any successor) is not a member of the consolidated group of which it was a member immediately prior to the disposition (or any successor group) is determined pursuant to the rules of § 1.1502-76(b)(2), without regard to § 1.1502-76(b)(2)(ii)(D), as if the subsidiary ceased to be a member of the group at the end of the day before the disposition and filed separate returns for the period beginning on the date of the disposition and ending on the day before the first date on which it is not a member of such group.

(5) Allowable loss. (i) General rule. To the extent not reduced under paragraph (c)(4) of this section, any loss suspended pursuant to paragraph (c)(1) or (c)(2) of this section shall be allowed, to the extent otherwise allowable under applicable provisions of the Internal Revenue Code and regulations, on a return filed by the group of which the subsidiary was a member on the date of the disposition of subsidiary stock that gave rise to the suspended loss (or any successor group) for the taxable year that includes the earlier of--

(A) The day before the first date on which the subsidiary (and any successor) is not a member of such group or the date the group is allowed a worthless stock loss under section 165 (taking into account the provisions of § 1.1502-

80(c)) with respect to all of the subsidiary stock owned by members and;

(B) The date that is ten years after the date of the disposition of subsidiary stock that gave rise to the suspended loss.

(ii) No tiering up of certain adjustments. No adjustments shall be made to a member's basis of stock of a subsidiary (or any successor) for a suspended loss that is taken into account under paragraph (c)(5)(i) of this section. See § 1.1502-32(a)(2).

(iii) Statement of allowed loss. Paragraph (c)(5)(i) of this section applies only if the separate statement required under this paragraph (c)(5)(iii) is filed with, or as part of, the taxpayer's return for the year in which the loss is allowable. The statement must be entitled "ALLOWED LOSS UNDER § 1.1502-35(c)(5)" and must contain the name and employer identification number of the subsidiary the stock of which gave rise to the loss.

(6) Special rule for dispositions of certain carryover basis assets. If—

(i) A member of a group recognizes a loss on the disposition of an asset other than stock of a subsidiary;

(ii) Such member's basis in the asset disposed of was determined, directly or indirectly, in whole or in part, by reference to the basis of stock of a subsidiary and, at the time of the determination of the member's basis in the asset disposed of, there was a duplicated loss with respect to such stock of the subsidiary; and

(iii) Immediately after the disposition, the subsidiary is a member of such group, then such loss shall be suspended pursuant to the principles of paragraphs (c)(1) and (c)(2) of this section to the extent of the duplicated loss with respect to such stock at the time of the determination of basis of the asset disposed of. Principles similar to those set forth in paragraphs (c)(3), (c)(4), and (c)(5) of this section shall apply to a loss suspended pursuant to this paragraph (c)(6).

(7) Coordination with loss deferral, loss disallowance, and other rules. (i) In general. Loss recognized on the disposition of subsidiary stock or another asset is subject to redetermination, deferral, or disallowance under other applicable provisions of the Internal Revenue Code and regulations thereunder, including sections 267(f) and 482. Paragraphs (c)(1), (c)(2), and (c)(6) of this section do not apply to a loss that is disallowed under any other provision. If loss is deferred under any other provision, paragraphs (c)(1), (c)(2), and (c)(6) of this section apply when the loss would otherwise be taken into account under such other provision. However, if an overriding event described in paragraph (c)(7)(ii) of this section occurs before the deferred loss is taken into account, paragraphs (c)(1), (c)(2), and (c)(6) of this section apply to the loss immediately before the event occurs, even though the loss may not be taken into account until a later time.

(ii) Overriding events. For purposes of paragraph (c)(7)(i) of this section, the following are overriding events—

(A) The stock ceases to be owned by a member of the consolidated group;

(B) The stock is canceled or redeemed (regardless of whether it is retired or held as treasury stock); or

(C) The stock is treated as disposed of under § 1.1502-19(c)(1)(ii)(B) or (c)(1)(iii).

(8) No elimination of economic loss. This paragraph (c) shall not be applied in a manner that permanently disallows a deduction for an economic loss, provided that such deduction is otherwise allowable. If the application of any provision of this paragraph (c) results in such a disallowance, proper adjustment may be made to prevent such a disallowance. Whether a provision of this paragraph (c) has resulted in such a disallowance is determined on the date on which the subsidiary (or any successor) the disposition of the stock of which gave rise to a suspended stock loss is not a member of the group or the date the group is allowed a worthless stock loss under section 165(g) (taking into account the provisions of § 1.1502-80(c)) with respect to all of such subsidiary stock owned by members. Proper adjustment in such cases shall be made by restoring the suspended stock loss immediately before the subsidiary ceases to be a member of the group or the group is allowed a worthless stock loss under section 165(g) (taking into account the provisions of § 1.1502-80(c)) with respect to all of such subsidiary stock owned by members, to the extent that its reduction pursuant to paragraph (c)(4) of this section had the result of permanently disallowing a deduction for an economic loss.

(9) Ordering rule. The rules of this paragraph (c) apply after the rules of paragraph (b) of this section and § 1.337(d)-2 are applied.

(d) Definitions. *(1)* Disposition means any event in which gain or loss is recognized, in whole or in part.

(2) Deconsolidation means any event that causes a subsidiary to no longer be a member of the consolidated group.

(3) Value means fair market value.

(4) Duplicated loss. (i) In general. Duplicated loss is determined immediately after a disposition and equals the excess, if any, of—

(A) The sum of—

(1) The aggregate adjusted basis of the subsidiary's assets other than any stock that subsidiary owns in another subsidiary;

(2) Any losses attributable to the subsidiary and carried to the subsidiary's first taxable year following the disposition; and

(3) Any deductions of the subsidiary that have been recognized but are deferred under a provision of the Internal Revenue Code (such as deductions deferred under section 469); over

(B) The sum of—

(1) The value of the subsidiary's stock; and

(2) Any liabilities of the subsidiary that have been taken into account for tax purposes.

(ii) Special rules.

(A) The amounts determined under paragraph (d)(4)(i) (other than amounts described in paragraph (d)(4)(i)(B)(1)) of this section with respect to a subsidiary include its allocable share of corresponding amounts with respect to all lower-tier subsidiaries. If 80 percent or more in value of the stock of a subsidiary is acquired by purchase in a single transaction (or in a series of related transactions during any 12-month period), the value of the subsidiary's stock may not exceed the purchase price of the stock divided by the percentage of the stock (by value) so purchased. For this purpose, stock is acquired by purchase if the transferee is not related to the transferor within the meaning of sections 267(b) and 707(b)(1), using the language "10 percent" instead of "50 percent" each place that it appears, and the transferee's basis in the stock is determined wholly by reference to the consideration paid for such stock.

(B) The amounts determined under paragraph (d)(4)(i) of this section are not applied more than once to suspend a loss under this section.

(5) Predecessor and successor. A predecessor is a transferor of assets to a transferee (the successor) in a transaction—

(i) To which section 381(a) applies;

(ii) In which substantially all of the assets of the transferor are transferred to members in a complete liquidation;

(iii) In which the successor's basis in assets is determined (directly or indirectly, in whole or in part) by reference to the transferor's basis in such assets, but the transferee is a successor only with respect to the assets the basis of which is so determined; or

(iv) Which is an intercompany transaction, but only with respect to assets that are being accounted for by the transferor in a prior intercompany transaction.

(6) Successor group. A surviving group is treated as a successor group of a consolidated group (the terminating group) that ceases to exist as a result of—

(i) The acquisition by a member of another consolidated group of either the assets of the common parent of the terminating group in a reorganization described in section 381(a)(2), or the stock of the common parent of the terminating group; or

(ii) The application of the principles of § 1.1502-75(d)(2) or (3).

(7) Preferred stock, common stock. Preferred stock and common stock shall have the meanings set forth in § 1.1502-32(d)(2) and (3), respectively.

(8) Higher-tier. A subsidiary is higher-tier with respect to a member if or to the extent investment adjustments under § 1.1502-32 with respect to the stock of the latter member would affect investment adjustments with respect to the stock of the former member.

(9) Lower-tier. A subsidiary is lower-tier with respect to a member if or to the extent investment basis adjustments under § 1.1502-32 with respect to the stock of the former member would affect investment adjustments with respect to the stock of the latter member.

(e) Examples. For purposes of the examples in this section, unless otherwise stated, all groups file consolidated returns on a calendar-year basis, the facts set forth the only corporate activity, all transactions are between unrelated persons, and tax liabilities are disregarded. In addition, all transactions described in section 362(a) are completed before October 22, 2004, and therefore are not subject to section 362(e)(2). The principles of paragraphs (a) through (d) of this section are illustrated by the following examples:

Example (1). Nondeconsolidating sale of preferred stock of lower-tier subsidiary. (i) Facts. P owns 100 percent of the common stock of each of S1 and S2. S1 and S2 each have only one class of stock outstanding. P's basis in the stock of S1 is $100 and the value of such stock is $130. P's basis in the stock of S2 is $120 and the value of such stock is $90. P, S1, and S2 are all members of the P group. S1 and S2 form S3. In Year 1, in transfers to which section 351 applies, S1 contributes $100 to S3 in exchange for all of the common stock of S3 and S2 contributes an asset with a basis of $50 and a value of $20 to S3 in exchange for all of the preferred stock of S3. S3 becomes a member of the P group. In Year 3, in a transaction that is not part of the plan that includes the contributions to S3, S2 sells the preferred stock of S3 for $20. Immediately after the sale, S3 is a member of the P group.

(ii) Application of basis redetermination rule. Because S2's basis in the preferred stock of S3 exceeds its value immediately prior to the sale and S3 is a member of the P group immediately after the sale, all of the P group members' bases in the stock of S3 is redetermined pursuant to paragraph (b)(1) of this section. Of the group members' total basis of $150 in the S3 stock, $20 is allocated to the preferred stock, the fair market value of the preferred stock on the date of the sale, and $130 is allocated to the common stock. S2's sale of the preferred stock results in the recognition of $0 of gain/loss. Pursuant to paragraph (b)(5) of this section, the redetermination of S1's and S2's bases in the stock of S3 results in adjustments to P's basis in the stock of S1 and S2. In particular, P's basis in the stock of S1 is increased by $30 to $130 and its basis in the stock of S2 is decreased by $30 to $90.

Example (2). Deconsolidating sale of common stock. (i) Facts. In Year 1, in a transfer to which section 351 applies, P contributes Asset A with a basis of $900 and a value of $200 to S in exchange for one share of S common stock (CS1). In Years 2 and 3, in successive but unrelated transfers to which section 351 applies, P transfers $200 to S in exchange for one share of S common stock (CS2), Asset B with a basis of $300 and a value of $200 in exchange for one share of S common stock (CS3), and Asset C with a basis of $1000 and a value of $200 in exchange for one share of S common stock (CS4). In Year 4, S sells Asset A for $200, recognizing $700 of loss that is used to offset income of P recognized during Year 4. As a result of the sale of Asset A, the basis of each of P's four shares of S common stock is reduced by $175. Therefore, the basis of CS1 is $725. The basis of CS2 is $25. The basis of CS3 is $125, and the basis of CS4 is $825. In Year 5 in a transaction that is not part of a plan that includes the Year 1 contribution, P sells CS4 for $200. Immediately after the sale of CS4, S is not a member of the P group.

(ii) Application of basis redetermination rule. Because P's basis in each of CS1 and CS4 exceeds its value immediately prior to the deconsolidation of S, P's basis in its shares of S common stock is redetermined pursuant to paragraph (b)(2) of this section. Pursuant to paragraph (b)(2)(ii) of this section, the reallocable basis amount is $350 (the lesser of $1150, the gross loss inherent in the stock of S owned by P immediately before the sale, and $350, the aggregate amount of S's items of deduction and loss that were previously taken into account in the computation of the adjustment to the basis of the stock of S that P did not hold at a loss immediately before the deconsolidation). Pursuant to paragraph (b)(2)(i) of this section, first, P's basis in CS1 is reduced from $725 to $600 and P's basis in CS4 is reduced from $825 to $600. Then, the reallocable basis amount increases P's basis in CS2 from $25 to $250 and P's basis in CS3 from $125 to $250. P recognizes $400 of loss on the sale of CS4. The loss suspension rule does not apply because S is no longer a member of the P group. Thus, the loss is allowable at that time.

Example (3). Nondeconsolidating sale of common stock. (i) Facts. In Year 1, P forms S with a contribution of $80 in exchange for 80 shares of the common stock of S, which at that time represents all of the outstanding stock of S. S becomes a member of the P group. In Year 2, P contributes Asset A with a basis of $50 and a value of $20 in exchange for 20 shares of the common stock of S in a transfer to which section 351 applies. In Year 4, in a transaction that is not part of the plan that includes the Year 2 contribution, P sells the 20 shares of the common stock of S that it acquired in Year 2 for $20. Immediately after the Year 4 stock sale, S is a member of the P group. At the time of the Year 4 stock sale, S has $80 and Asset A. In Year 5, S sells Asset A, the basis and value of which have not changed since its contribution to S. On the sale of Asset A for $20, S recognizes a $30 loss. The P group cannot establish that all or a portion of the $30 loss was not reflected in the calculation of the duplicated loss of S on the date of the Year 4 stock sale. The $30 loss is used on the P group return to offset income of P. In Year 6, P sells its remaining S common stock for $80.

(ii) Application of basis redetermination and loss suspension rules. Because P's basis in the common stock sold exceeds its value immediately prior to the sale and S is a member of the P group immediately after the sale, P's basis in all of the stock of S is redetermined pursuant to paragraph (b)(1) of this section. Of P's total basis of $130 in the S common stock, a proportionate amount is allocated to each of the 100 shares of S common stock. Accordingly, $26 is allocated to the common stock of S that is sold and $104 is allocated to the common stock of S that is retained. On P's sale of the 20 shares of the common stock of S for $20, P recognizes a loss of $6. Because the sale of the 20 shares of common stock of S does not result in the deconsolidation of S, under paragraph (c)(1) of this section, that loss is suspended to the extent of the duplicated loss with respect to the shares sold. The duplicated loss with respect to the shares sold is $6. Therefore, the entire $6 loss is suspended.

(iii) Effect of subsequent asset sale on stock basis. Of the $30 loss recognized on the sale of Asset A, $24 is taken into account in determining the basis adjustments made under § 1.1502-32 to the stock of S owned by P. Accordingly, P's basis in its S stock is reduced by $24 from $104 to $80.

(iv) Effect of subsequent asset sale on suspended loss. Because P cannot establish that all or a portion of the loss recognized on the sale of Asset A was not reflected in the calculation of the duplicated loss of S on the date of the Year 4 stock sale and such loss is allocable to the period beginning on the date of the Year 4 disposition of the S stock and ending on the day before the first date on which S is not a member of the P group and is taken into account in determining consolidated taxable income (or loss) of the P group for a taxable year that includes a date on or after the date of the Year 4 disposition and before the first date on which S is not a member of the P group, such asset loss reduces the suspended loss pursuant to paragraph (c)(4) of this section. The amount of such reduction, however, cannot exceed $6, the excess of the amount of such loss, $30, over the amount of such loss that is taken into account in determining the basis adjustment made to the stock of S owned by P, $24. Therefore, the suspended loss is reduced to zero.

(v) Effect of subsequent stock sale. P recognizes $0 gain/loss on the Year 6 sale of its remaining S common stock. No amount of suspended loss remains to be allowed under paragraph (c)(5) of this section.

Example (4). Nondeconsolidating sale of common stock of lower-tier subsidiary. (i) Facts. In Year 1, P forms S1 with a contribution of $200 in exchange for all of the common stock of S1, which represents all of the outstanding stock of S1. In the same year, S1 forms S2 with a contribution of $80 in exchange for 80 shares of the common stock of S2, which at that time represents all of the outstanding stock of S2. S1 and S2 become members of the P group. In the same year, S2 purchases Asset A for $80. In Year 2, S1 contributes Asset B with a basis of $50 and a value of $20 in exchange for 20 shares of the common stock of S2 in a transfer to which section 351 applies. In Year 4, S1 sells the 20 shares of the common stock of S2 that it acquired in Year 2 for $20. Immediately after the Year 4 stock sale, S2 is a member of the P group. At the time of the Year 4 stock sale, the bases and values of Asset A and Asset B are unchanged. In Year 5, S2 sells Asset B for $45, recognizing a $5 loss. The P group cannot establish that all or a portion of the $5 loss was not reflected in the calculation of the duplicated loss of S2 on the date of the Year 4 stock sale. The $5 loss is used on the P group return to offset income of P. In Year 6, S1 sells its remaining S2 common stock for $100.

(ii) Application of basis redetermination and loss suspension rules. Because S1's basis in the S2 common stock sold exceeds its value immediately prior to the sale and S2 is a member of the P group immediately after the sale, S1's basis in all of the stock of S2 is redetermined pursuant to paragraph (b)(1) of this section. Of S1's total basis of $130 in the S2 common stock, a proportionate amount is allocated to each of the 100 shares of S2 common stock. Accordingly, a total of $26 is allocated to the common stock of S2 that is sold and $104 is allocated to the common stock of S2 that is retained. On S1's sale of the 20 shares of the common stock of S2 for $20, S1 recognizes a loss of $6. Because the sale of the 20 shares of common stock of S2 does not result in the deconsolidation of S2, under paragraph (c)(1) of this section, that loss is suspended to the extent of the duplicated loss with respect to the shares sold. The duplicated loss with respect to the shares sold is $6. Therefore, the entire $6 loss is suspended. Pursuant to paragraph (c)(3) of this section and § 1.1502-32(b)(3)(iii)(C), the suspended loss is treated as a noncapital, nondeductible expense incurred by S1 during the tax year that includes the date of the disposition of stock to which paragraph (c)(1) of this section applies. Accordingly, P's basis in its S1 stock is reduced from $200 to $194.

(iii) Effect of subsequent asset sale on stock basis. Of the $5 loss recognized on the sale of Asset B, $4 is taken into account in determining the basis adjustments made under § 1.1502-32 to the stock of S2 owned by S1. Accordingly, S1's basis in its S2 stock is reduced by $4 from $104 to $100 and P's basis in its S1 stock is reduced by $4 from $194 to $190.

(iv) Effect of subsequent asset sale on suspended loss. Because P cannot establish that all or a portion of the loss recognized on the sale of Asset B was not reflected in the calculation of the duplicated loss of S2 on the date of the Year 4 stock sale and such loss is allocable to the period beginning on the date of the Year 4 disposition of the S2 stock and ending on the day before the first date on which S2 is not a member of the P group and is taken into account in determining consolidated taxable income (or loss) of the P group for a taxable year that includes a date on or after the date of the Year 4 disposition and before the first date on which S2 is not a member of the P group, such asset loss reduces the suspended loss pursuant to paragraph (c)(4) of this section. The amount of such reduction, however, cannot exceed $1, the excess of the amount of such loss, $5, over the amount of such loss that is taken into account in determining the basis adjustment made to the stock of S2 owned by members of the P group, $4. Therefore, the suspended loss is reduced to $5.

(v) Effect of subsequent stock sale. In year 6, when S1 sells its remaining S2 stock for $100, it recognizes $0 gain/loss. Pursuant to paragraph (c)(5) of this section, the remaining $5 of the suspended loss is allowed on the P group's return for Year 6 when S1 sells its remaining S2 stock.

Example (5). Deconsolidating sale of subsidiary owning stock of another subsidiary that remains in group. (i) Facts. In Year 1, P forms S1 with a contribution of Asset A with a basis of $50 and a value of $20 in exchange for 100 shares of common stock of S1 in a transfer to which section 351 applies. Also in Year 1, P and S1 form S2. P contributes $80 to S2 in exchange for 80 shares of common stock of S2. S1 contributes Asset A to S2 in exchange for 20 shares of common stock of S2 in a transfer to which section 351 applies. In Year 3, in a transaction that is not part of a plan that includes the Year 1 contributions, P sells its 100 shares of S1 common stock for $20. Immediately after the Year 3 stock sale, S2 is a member of the P group. At the time of the Year 3 stock sale, S1 owns 20 shares of common stock of S2, and S2 has $80 and Asset A. In Year 4, S2 sells Asset A, the basis and value of which have not changed since its contribution to S2. On the sale of Asset A for $20, S2 recognizes a $30 loss. That $30 loss is used on the P group return to offset income of P. In Year 5, P sells its S2 common stock for $80.

(ii) Application of basis redetermination and loss suspension rules. Pursuant to paragraph (b)(4) of this section, because immediately before P's transfer of S1 stock S1 owns stock of S2 (another subsidiary of the same group) that has a basis that exceeds its value, paragraph (b) of this section applies as if S1 had transferred its stock of S2. Because S2 is a member of the group immediately after the transfer of the S1 stock, the group member's basis in the S2 stock is redetermined pursuant to paragraph (b)(1) of this section immediately prior to the sale of the S1 stock. Of the group members' total basis of $130 in the S2 stock, $26 is allocated to S1's 20 shares of S2 common stock and $104 is allocated to P's 80 shares of S2 common stock. Pursuant to paragraph (b)(5) of this section, the redetermination of S1's basis in the stock of S2 results in an adjustment to P's basis in the stock of S1. In particular, P's basis in the stock of S1 is decreased by $24 to $26. On P's sale of its 100 shares of S1 common stock for $20, P recognizes a loss of $6. Because S1 is not a member of the P group immediately after P's sale of the S1 stock, paragraph (c)(1) of this section does not apply to suspend such loss. However, because P recognizes a loss with respect to the disposition of the S1 stock and S1 owns stock of S2 (which is a member of the P group immediately after the disposition), paragraph (c)(2) of this section does apply to suspend up to $6 of that loss, an amount equal to the amount by which the duplicated loss with respect to the stock of S1 sold is attributable to S2's adjusted basis in its assets, loss carryforwards, and deferred deductions.

(iii) Effect of subsequent asset sale on stock basis. Of the $30 loss recognized on the sale of Asset A, $24 is taken into account in determining the basis adjustments made under § 1.1502-32 to the stock of S2 owned by P. Accordingly, P's basis in its S2 stock is reduced by $24 from $104 to $80.

(iv) Effect of subsequent asset sale on suspended loss. Because P cannot establish that all or a portion of the loss recognized on the sale of Asset A was not reflected in the calculation of the duplicated loss of S2 on the date of the Year 3 stock sale and such loss is allocable to the period beginning on the date of the Year 3 deemed disposition of the S2 stock and ending on the day before the first date on which S2 is not a member of the P group and is taken into account in determining consolidated taxable income (or loss) of the P group for a taxable year that includes a date on or after the date of the Year 3 deemed disposition and before the first date on which S2 is not a member of the P group, such asset loss reduces the suspended loss pursuant to paragraph (c)(4) of this section. The amount of such reduction, however, cannot exceed $6, the excess of the amount of such loss, $30, over the amount of such loss that is taken into account in determining the basis adjustment made to the stock of S2 owned by P, $24. Therefore, the suspended loss is reduced to zero.

(v) Effect of subsequent stock sale. P recognizes $0 gain/loss on the Year 5 sale of its remaining S2 common stock. No amount of suspended loss remains to be allowed under paragraph (c)(5) of this section.

Example (6). Loss recognized on asset with basis determined by reference to stock basis of subsidiary. (i) In Year 1, P forms S with a contribution of $80 in exchange for 80 shares of common stock of S which at that time represents all of the outstanding stock of S. S becomes a member of the P group. In Year 2, P contributes Asset A with a basis of $50 and a value of $20 in exchange for 20 shares of common stock of S in a transfer to which section 351 applies. In Year 4, in a transaction that is not part of a plan that includes the Year 1 and Year 2 contributions, P contributes the 20 shares of S common stock it acquired in Year 2 to PS, a partnership, in exchange for a 20 percent capital and profits interest in a transaction described in section 721. Immediately after the contribution to PS, S is a member of the P group. In Year 5, P sells its interest in PS for $20.

(ii) Application of basis redetermination rule upon nonrecognition transfer. Because P's basis in the S common stock contributed to PS exceeds its value immediately prior to the transfer and S is a member of the P group immediately after the transfer, P's basis in all of the S stock is redetermined pursuant to paragraph (b)(1) of this section. Of P's total basis of $130 in the common stock of S, a proportionate amount is allocated to each share of S common stock. Accordingly, $26 is allocated to the S common stock that is contributed to PS and, under section 722, P's basis in its interest in PS is $26.

(iii) Application of loss suspension rule on disposition of asset with basis determined by reference to stock basis of subsidiary. P recognizes a $6 loss on its disposition of its interest in PS. Because P's basis in its interest in PS was determined by reference to the basis of S stock and at the time of the determination of P's basis in its interest in PS such S stock had a duplicated loss of $6, and, immediately after the disposition, S is a member of the P group, such loss is suspended to the extent of such duplicated loss. Principles similar to those of paragraphs (c)(3), (c)(4), and (c)(5) of this section shall apply to such suspended loss.

(f) Worthlessness not followed by separate return years. Notwithstanding any other provision in the regulations under section 1502, if a member of a group (the claiming group) treats stock of a subsidiary as worthless under section 165 (taking into account the provisions of § 1.1502-80(c)) and, on the day following the last day of the claiming group's taxable year in which the worthless stock deduction is claimed, the subsidiary (or its successor, determined without regard to paragraphs (d)(5)(iii) and (iv) of this section) is a member of a group that includes any corporation that, during that taxable year, was a member of the claiming group (other than a lower-tier subsidiary of the subsidiary) or is a successor (determined without regard to paragraphs (d)(5)(iii) and (iv) of this section) of such a member, then all losses treated as attributable to the subsidiary under the principles of § 1.1502-21(b)(2)(iv) shall be treated as expired as of the beginning of the day following the last day of the claiming group's taxable year in which the worthless stock deduction is claimed. In addition, notwithstanding any other provision in the regulations under section 1502, if a member recognizes a loss with respect to subsidiary stock and on the following day the subsidiary is not a member of the group and does not have a separate return year, then all losses treated as attributable to the subsidiary under the principles of § 1.1502-21(b)(2)(iv) shall be treated as expired as of the beginning of the day following the last day of the group's taxable year in which the stock loss is claimed. For purposes of this paragraph (f), the determination of the losses attributable to the subsidiary shall be made after computing the taxable income of the group for the taxable year in which the group treats the stock of the subsidiary as worthless or the subsidiary liquidates and after computing the taxable income for any taxable year to which such losses may be carried back. The loss treated as expired under this paragraph (f) shall not be treated as a noncapital, nondeductible expense under § 1.1502-32(b)(2)(iii). This paragraph (f) applies to worthlessness determinations and liquidations that occur on or after March 10, 2006. For rules applicable to worthless determinations and liquidations before March 10, 2006, see § 1.1502-35T(f)(1) and (2) as contained in 26 CFR part 1 in effect on January 1, 2006.

(g) Anti-avoidance rules. *(1) Transfer of share without a loss in avoidance.* If a share of subsidiary stock has a basis that does not exceed its value and the share is transferred with a view to avoiding application of the rules of paragraph (b) of this section prior to the transfer of a share of subsidiary stock that has a basis that does exceed its value or a deconsolidation of a subsidiary, the rules of paragraph (b) of this section shall apply immediately prior to the transfer of stock that has a basis that does not exceed its value.

(2) Transfers of loss property in avoidance. If a member of a consolidated group contributes an asset with a basis that exceeds its value to a partnership in a transaction described in section 721 or a corporation that is not a member of such group in a transfer described in section 351, such partnership or corporation contributes such asset to a subsidiary in a transfer described in section 351, and such contributions are undertaken with a view to avoiding the rules of paragraph (b) or (c) of this section, adjustments must be made to carry out the purposes of this section.

(3) Anti-loss reimportation rule. (i) Conditions for application. This paragraph (g)(3) applies when--

(A) A member of a group (selling group) recognized and was allowed a loss with respect to a share of stock of S, a subsidiary or former subsidiary of the selling group;

(B) That stock loss was duplicated (in whole or in part) in S's attributes (duplicating items) at the earlier of the time that the loss was recognized or that S ceased to be a member; and

(C) Within ten years of the date that S ceased to be a member, there is a reimportation event. For this purpose, a reimportation event is any event after which a duplicating item is a reimported item. A reimported item is any duplicating item that is reflected in the attributes of any member of the selling group, including S, or, if not reflected in the attributes, would be properly taken into account by any member of the selling group (for example as the result of a carryback).

(ii) Effect of application. Immediately before the time that a reimported item (or any portion of a reimported item) would be properly taken into account (but for the application of this paragraph (g)(3)), such item (or such portion of the item) is reduced to zero and no deduction or loss is allowed, directly or indirectly, with respect to that item.

(iii) Operating rules. For purposes of this paragraph (g)(3)--

(A) The terms member, subsidiary, and group include their predecessors and successors to the extent necessary to effectuate the purposes of this section; and

(B) The reduction of a reimported item (other than duplicating items that are carried back to a consolidated return year of the selling group) is a noncapital, nondeductible expense within the meaning of § 1.1502-32(b)(3)(iii).

(4) Avoidance of recognition of gain. (i) If a transaction is structured with a view to, and has the effect of, deferring or avoiding the recognition of gain on a disposition of stock by invoking the application of paragraph (b)(1) of this section to redetermine the basis of stock of a subsidiary, and the stock loss that gives rise to the application of paragraph (b)(1) of this section is not significant, paragraphs (b) and (c) of this section shall not apply.

(ii) If a transaction is structured with a view to, and has the effect of, deferring or avoiding the recognition of gain on a disposition of stock by invoking the application of paragraph (b)(2) of this section to redetermine the basis of stock of a subsidiary, and the duplicated loss of the subsidiary that is reflected in stock of the subsidiary owned by members of the group immediately before the deconsolidation is not significant, paragraphs (b) and (c) of this section shall not apply.

(5) Examples. For purposes of the examples in this section, all transactions described in section 362(a) are completed before October 22, 2004, and therefore are not subject to section 362(e)(2). The principles of this paragraph (g) are illustrated by the following examples:

Example (1). Transfers of property in avoidance of basis redetermination rule. (i) Facts. In Year 1, P forms S with a contribution of $100 in exchange for 100 shares of common stock of S which at that time represents all of the outstanding stock of S. S becomes a member of the P group. In Year 2, P contributes 20 shares of common stock of S to PS, a partnership, in exchange for a 20 percent capital and profits interest in a transaction described in section 721. In Year 3, P contributes Asset A with a basis of $50 and a value of $20 to PS in exchange for an additional capital and profits interest in PS in a transaction described in section 721. Also in Year 3, PS contributes Asset A to S and P contributes an additional $80 to S in transfers to which section 351 applies. In Year 4, S sells Asset A for $20, recognizing a loss of $30. The P group uses that loss to offset income of P. In Year 5, P sells its entire interest in PS for $40.
(ii) Analysis. Pursuant to paragraph (g)(2) of this section, if P's contributions of S stock and Asset A to PS were undertaken with a view to avoiding the application of the basis redetermination or the loss suspension rule, adjustments must be made such that the group does not obtain more than one tax benefit from the $30 loss inherent in Asset A.

Example (2). Transfers effecting a reimportation of loss. (i) Facts. In Year 1, P forms S with a contribution of Asset A with a value of $100 and a basis of $120, Asset B with a value of $50 and a basis of $70, and Asset C with a value of $90 and a basis of $100 in exchange for all of the common stock of S and S becomes a member of the P group. In Year 2, in a transaction that is not part of a plan that includes the contribution, P sells the stock of S for $240, recognizing a loss of $50. At such time, the bases and values of Assets A, B, and C have not changed since their contribution to S. In Year 3, S sells Asset A, recognizing a $20 loss. In Year 3, S merges into M in a reorganization described in section 368(a)(1)(A). In Year 8, P purchases all of the stock of M for $300. At that time, M has a $10 net operating loss. In addition, M owns Asset D, which was acquired in an exchange described in section 1031 in connection with the surrender of Asset B. Asset C has a value of $80 and a basis of $100. Asset D has a value of $60 and a basis of $70. In Year 9, P has operating income of $100 and M recognizes $20 of loss on the sale of Asset C. In Year 10, P has operating income of $50 and M recognizes $50 of loss on the sale of Asset D.

(ii) Analysis. P's $50 loss on the sale of S stock is entirely attributable to duplicated loss. Therefore, pursuant to paragraph (g)(3) of this section, assuming the P group cannot establish otherwise, M's $10 net operating loss is treated as attributable to assets that were owned by S on the date of the disposition and that had bases in excess of value on such date. Without regard to any other limitations on the group's use of M's net operating loss, the P group cannot use M's $10 net operating loss pursuant to paragraph (g)(3)(iii)(D) of this section. Pursuant to paragraph (g)(3)(iv) of this section and § 1.1502-32(b)(3)(iii)(D), such loss is treated as a noncapital, nondeductible expense of M incurred during the taxable year that it would otherwise be absorbed, namely in Year 9. In addition, the P group is denied the use of $10 of the loss recognized on the sale of Asset C. Finally, the P group is denied the use of $10 of the loss recognized on the sale of Asset D. Pursuant to paragraph (g)(3)(iv) of this section and § 1.1502-32(b)(3)(iii)(D), each such disallowed loss is treated as a noncapital, nondeductible expense of M incurred during the taxable year that includes the date of the disposition of the asset with respect to which such loss was recognized.

Example (3). Transfers to avoid recognition of gain.

(i) Facts. P owns all of the stock of S1 and S2. The S2 stock has a basis of $400 and a value of $500. S1 owns 50% of the S3 common stock with a basis of $150. S2 owns the remaining 50% of the S3 common stock with a basis of $100 and a value of $200 and one share of S3 preferred stock with a basis of $10 and a value of $9. P intends to sell all of its S2 stock to an unrelated buyer. P, therefore, engages in the following steps to dispose of S2 without recognizing a substantial portion of the built-in gain in S2. First, P causes a recapitalization of S3 in which S2's S3 common stock is exchanged for new S3 preferred shares. P then sells all of its S2 stock. Immediately after the sale of the S2 stock, S3 is a member of the P group.

(ii) Analysis. Pursuant to paragraph (b)(4) of this section, because S2 owns stock of S3 (another subsidiary of the same group) and, immediately after the sale of the S2 stock, S3 is a member of the group, then for purposes of applying paragraph (b) of this section, S2 is deemed to have transferred its S3 stock. Because S3 is a member of the group immediately after the transfer of the S2 stock and the S3 stock deemed transferred has a basis in excess of value, the group in the S3 stock is redetermined pursuant to paragraph (b)(1) of this section immediately prior to the sale of the S2 stock. Accordingly, P would recognize only $1 of gain on the sale of its S2 stock. However, because the recapitalization of the S3 was structured with a view to, and has the effect of, avoiding the recognition of gain on a disposition of stock by invoking the application of paragraph (b) of this section, paragraph (g)(4)(i) of this section applies. Accordingly, paragraph (b) of this section does not apply upon P's disposition of the S2 stock and P recognizes $100 gain on the disposition of the S2 stock.

(6) General anti-avoidance rule. If a taxpayer acts with a view to avoid the purposes of this section, appropriate adjustments will be made to carry out the purposes of this section.

(h) Application of other rules of law. See § 1.1502-80(a) regarding the general applicability of other rules of law.

(i) [Reserved].

(j) Effective/applicability dates. This section applies with respect to stock transfers, deconsolidations of subsidiaries, determinations of worthlessness, and stock dispositions on or after September 17, 2008. For prior law, see §§ 1.1502-35 and 1.1502-35T as contained in 26 CFR part 1 in effect on April 1, 2008.

T.D. 9254, 3/9/2006, amend T.D. 9264, 5/26/2006, T.D. 9322, 4/9/2007, T.D. 9342, 7/19/2007, T.D. 9424, 9/10/2008.

PAR. 3. Section 1.1502-35 is amended by:

1. Revising paragraphs (g)(3) and (h).
2. Adding new paragraph (g)(6).
3. Revising paragraph (j).

The revisions and additions read as follows:

Proposed § 1.1502-35 Transfers of subsidiary stock and deconsolidations of subsidiaries. [*For Preamble, see ¶ 152,847*]

* * * * *

(g) * * *

(3) [The text of the proposed amendment to § 1.1502-35(g)(3) is the same as the text of § 1.1502-35T(g)(3) published elsewhere in this issue of the Federal Register]. [See T.D. 9322, 04/10/2007, 72 Fed. Reg. 68.]

* * * * *

(6) [The text of the proposed amendment to § 1.1502-35(g)(6) is the same as the text of § 1.1502-35T(g)(6) published elsewhere in this issue of the Federal Register]. [See T.D. 9322, 04/10/2007, 72 Fed. Reg. 68.]

(h) [The text of the proposed amendment to § 1.1502-35(h) is the same as the text of § 1.1502-35T(h) published elsewhere in this issue of the Federal Register]. [See T.D. 9322, 04/10/2007, 72 Fed. Reg. 68.]

* * * * *

(j) [The text of the proposed amendment to § 1.1502-35(j) is the same as the text of § 1.1502-35T(j) published elsewhere in this issue of the Federal Register]. [See T.D. 9322, 04/10/2007, 72 Fed. Reg. 68.]

* * * * *

Proposed § 1.1502-35 Transfers and issuances of subsidiary member stock. [*For Preamble, see ¶ 152,369*]

[The text of proposed § 1.1502-35 is the same as the text of § 1.1502-35T published elsewhere in this issue of the Federal Register].

* * * * *

PAR. 3. Section 1.1502-35(f)(1) is added to read as follows:

Proposed § 1.1502-35 Transfers of subsidiary member stock and deconsolidations of subsidiary members. [*For Preamble, see ¶ 152,509*]

[The text of this proposed section is the same as the text of § 1.1502-35T published elsewhere in this issue of the Federal Register].

§ 1.1502-36 Unified loss rule.

(a) In general.

(1) Scope. This section provides rules for adjusting members' bases in stock of a subsidiary (S) and for reducing S's attributes when a member (M) transfers a loss share of S stock. See paragraph (f) of this section for definitions of the terms used in this section, including transfer and value.

(2) Purpose. The rules in this section have two principal purposes. The first is to prevent the consolidated return provisions from reducing a group's consolidated taxable income through the creation and recognition of noneconomic loss on S stock. The second is to prevent members (including former members) of the group from collectively obtaining more than one tax benefit from a single economic loss. Additional purposes are set forth in other paragraphs of this section. The rules of this section must be interpreted and applied in a manner that is consistent with and reasonably carries out the purposes of this section.

(3) Overview. (i) General application of section. This section applies when M transfers a share of S stock and, after taking into account the effects of all applicable rules of law (even if the adjustments required by such provisions are not deemed effective until after the transfer, such as certain adjustments required under sections 108 and 1017 and § 1.1502-28), the share is a loss share. When this section applies, paragraph (b) of this section applies first and may redetermine members' bases in their shares of S stock. If the transferred share is a loss share after any basis redetermination under paragraph (b) of this section, paragraph (c) of this section applies and may reduce M's basis in the transferred loss share. If the transferred share is a loss share after any basis reduction required by paragraph (c) of this section, paragraph (d) of this section applies and may reduce attributes of S and subsidiaries that are lower-tier to S. Although the determination of whether there is a transfer of a loss share is made as of the transfer, this section applies, and any adjustments it requires are given effect, immediately before the transfer. Paragraphs (e), (f), and (g) of this section provide general operating rules (including rules for transfers of S stock between members), definitions, and an anti-abuse rule, respectively.

(ii) Stock of multiple subsidiaries transferred in the transaction— (A) Initial application of section to transferred shares in lowest tier. If shares of stock of more than one subsidiary are transferred in a transaction, the application of this section begins at the lowest tier. If no transferred shares of stock of the lowest-tier subsidiary (S2) are loss shares, any gain recognized with respect to the S2 shares immediately tiers up and adjusts members' bases in subsidiary stock under § 1.1502-32. However, if any of the transferred S2 shares are loss shares, paragraph (b) of this section applies with respect to those shares. If, after the application of paragraph (b) of this section, any transferred S2 shares are still loss shares, paragraph (c) of this section applies with respect to those shares. If, after the application of paragraph (c) of this section, any transferred S2 shares are still loss shares and P makes an election under paragraph (d)(6) of this section with respect to those S2 shares, then paragraph (d) of this section applies with respect to those shares, but only to the extent necessary to give effect to the election. After taking into account the effects of any adjustments required by this initial application of this section, recognized gain or loss is computed on all transferred S2 shares. Any adjustments under paragraph (b) or (c) of this section, the effect of any election under paragraph (d)(6) of this section, any gain or loss recognized on the transferred S2 shares (whether allowed or disallowed), and any other related or resulting adjustments then tier-up and apply to adjust members' bases in subsidiary stock under § 1.1502-32.

(B) Initial application of section to transferred shares in higher tiers. After taking into account the effects of any adjustments described in paragraph (a)(3)(ii)(A) of this section, transferred shares in the next higher tier, and then in each next higher tier successively, other than the transferred loss shares at the highest tier, are treated in the manner described in paragraph (a)(3)(ii)(A) of this section.

(C) Application of section to transferred shares in highest tier. After paragraphs (b) and (c) of this section, and, to the extent necessary to give effect to any election under paragraph (d)(6) of this section, paragraph (d) of this section, have been applied to or with respect to all lower-tier transferred loss shares, and after all lower-tier adjustments have been taken into account (whether resulting from the application of paragraph (b) or (c) of this section, an election under paragraph (d)(6) of this section, the recognition of gain or loss on a transfer, or otherwise), paragraphs (b), then (c), and then (d) of this section apply with respect to the highest-tier shares that are transferred loss shares.

(D) Final application of section to transferred shares in lower tiers. After paragraph (d) of this section has been applied with respect to transferred loss shares in the highest tier, it is applied with respect to transferred shares in each next lower tier, successively, to the extent such shares are loss shares after the application of paragraph (d) of this section.

(4) Other rules of law and coordination with deferral and disallowance provisions. In general, this section applies and has effect immediately upon the transfer of a loss share even if the loss is deferred, disallowed, or otherwise not taken into account under any other applicable rules of law. However, see paragraph (e)(3) of this section for special rules applicable to shares of S stock transferred in an intercompany transaction. See section § 1.1502-80(a) for the general applicability of other rules of law and a limitation on duplicative adjustments.

(5) Nomenclature, factual assumptions adopted in this section. Unless otherwise stated, for purposes of this section, the following nomenclature and assumptions are adopted. P is the common parent of a consolidated group of which S, M, and M1 are members. X is not a member of the P group. If a corporation has preferred stock outstanding, it is stock described in section 1504(a)(4). The examples set forth the only facts, elections, and activities relevant to the example. All transactions are between unrelated persons and are independent of each other. Tax liabilities and their effect, and the application of any other loss disallowance or deferral provisions of the Internal Revenue Code (Code) or regulations, including but not limited to section 267, are disregarded. All persons report on a calendar year basis and use the accrual method of accounting. All parties comply with filing and other requirements of this section and all other provisions of the Code and regulations.

(b) Basis redetermination to reduce disparity. *(1) In general.* (i) Purpose and scope. The rules of this paragraph (b) reduce the extent to which there is disparity in members' bases in shares of S stock. These rules supplement the operation of the investment adjustment system; their purpose is to prevent the realization of noneconomic loss and facilitate the elimination of duplicated loss when members hold S shares with disparate bases. The rules of this paragraph (b) only reallocate investment adjustments previously applied to members' bases in shares of S stock, thus they do not alter the aggregate amount of basis in shares of S stock held by members or the aggregate amount of investment adjustments applied to shares of S stock.

(ii) Special rules for applicability of redetermination rule. Notwithstanding the general rule in paragraph (b)(2) of this section, members' bases in shares of S stock are not redetermined under this paragraph (b) if—

(A) There is no disparity among members' bases in shares of S common stock and no member owns a share of S preferred stock with respect to which there is unrecognized gain or loss; or

(B) All the shares of S stock held by members are transferred to one or more nonmembers, become worthless under section 165 (taking into account the provisions of § 1.1502-80(c)), or a combination thereof, in one fully taxable transaction. However, in such a case, P may elect to redetermine such bases under this paragraph (b). Such an election is made in the manner provided in paragraph (e)(5) of this section. If stock of more than one subsidiary is transferred in the transaction, the election may be made with respect to one or more of such subsidiaries.

(iii) Investment adjustment. For purposes of this paragraph (b), the term investment adjustment includes adjustments specially allocated under § 1.1502-32(c)(1)(ii)(B) and remaining adjustments described in § 1.1502-32(c)(1)(iii). In applying any provision of this section, the term includes all such adjustments reflected in the basis of the share as of the application of the provision, whether originally allocated under § 1.1502-32 or otherwise. The term therefore includes adjustments previously reallocated to the share, and it does not include adjustments previously reallocated from the share, whether pursuant to this section or any other provision of law. It also includes the proportionate amount of adjustments reflected in the exchanged basis of a share, such as the basis determined under section 358 in connection with a reorganization or a transaction qualifying under section 355.

(2) Basis redetermination rule. If M transfers a loss share of S stock, all members' bases in all their shares of S stock are subject to redetermination under this paragraph (b). The determination of whether a share is a loss share is made as of the transfer, taking into account the effects of all applicable rules of law. The redeterminations are made immediately before applying paragraph (c) of this section and in accordance with the following:

(i) Decreasing the bases of transferred loss shares—

(A) Removing positive investment adjustments from transferred loss shares of common stock. M's basis in each of its transferred loss shares of S common stock is first reduced, but not below value, by removing positive investment adjustments previously applied to the basis of the share. The positive investment adjustments removed from transferred loss shares of S common stock are reallocated under paragraph (b)(2)(ii) of this section after negative investment adjustments are reallocated under paragraph (b)(2)(i)(B) of this section.

(B) Reallocating negative investment adjustments from shares of S common stock. If a transferred share is still a loss share after applying paragraph (b)(2)(i)(A) of this section, M's basis in the share is reduced, but not below value, by reallocating negative investment adjustments to the transferred loss share (whether common or preferred stock) from members' shares of S common stock that are not transferred loss shares. The adjustments reallocated under this paragraph (b)(2)(i)(B) are reallocated and applied first to M's bases in transferred loss shares of S preferred stock and then to M's bases in transferred loss shares of S common stock. Reallocations under this paragraph (b)(2)(i)(B) are made in a manner that, to the greatest extent possible, reduces the disparity among members' bases in all transferred loss shares of S preferred stock, and reduces the disparity among members' bases in all shares of S common stock.

(ii) Increasing the bases of gain preferred and all common shares— (A) Preferred stock. After the application of paragraph (b)(2)(i) of this section, the positive investment adjustments removed from transferred loss shares of S common stock under paragraph (b)(2)(i)(A) of this section are reallocated and applied to increase, but not above value, members' bases in shares of S preferred stock (without regard to whether such shares are transferred in the transaction). Reallocations under this paragraph (b)(2)(ii)(A) are made in a manner that, to the greatest extent possible, reduces the disparity among members' bases in all shares of S preferred stock.

(B) Common stock. Any positive investment adjustments removed from transferred loss shares of S common stock under paragraph (b)(2)(i)(A) of this section and not reallocated and applied to S preferred shares are reallocated and applied to increase members' bases in shares of S common stock. Reallocations are made to shares of S common stock without regard to whether a particular share is a loss share or a transferred share, and without regard to the share's value. Reallocations under this paragraph (b)(2)(ii)(B) are made in a manner that, to the greatest extent possible, reduces the disparity among members' bases in all shares of S common stock.

(iii) Operating rules— (A) Method. In general, reallocations should be made first with respect to the earliest available adjustments. However, the overall application of this paragraph (b) to a transaction must be made in a manner that, to the greatest extent possible, reduces basis disparity (as provided in paragraphs (b)(2)(i)(B) and (b)(2)(ii) of this section). The specific reallocation of an investment adjustment under this paragraph (b) may be made using any reasonable method or formula that is consistent with the provisions of this paragraph (b)(2) and furthers the purposes of this section.

(B) Limits on reallocation— (1) Restriction to members' outstanding shares. Investment adjustments can only be reallocated to shares that were held by members at the time the adjustment was originally applied.

(2) Limitation by prior use— (i) In general. In order to prevent the reallocation of investment adjustments from either increasing or decreasing members' aggregate bases in subsidiary stock, no investment adjustment (positive or negative) may be reallocated under this paragraph (b)(2) to the extent that it was (or would have been) used prior to the time that it would otherwise be reallocated under this paragraph (b)(2). For this purpose, an investment adjustment was used (or would have been used) to the extent that it was reflected in (or would have been reflected in) the basis of a share of subsidiary stock and the basis of that share has already been taken into account, directly or indirectly, in determining income, gain, deduction, or loss (including by affecting the application of this section to a prior transfer of subsidiary stock) or in determining the basis of any property that is not subject to § 1.1502-32. However, if the prior use was in an intercompany transaction, an investment adjustment may be reallocated to the extent that § 1.1502-13 has prevented the gain or loss on the transaction from being taken into account. (In that case, appropriate adjustments

must be made to the intercompany item from the prior intercompany transaction that has not yet been taken into account.) Further, if an investment adjustment was reflected in (or would have been reflected in) the basis of a share that has been taken into account, the limitation on reallocation under this paragraph (b)(2)(iii)(B)(2) does not apply to the extent the basis of that share would not change as a result of the reallocation (for example, because the reallocation is between shares that are both lower-tier to the share with the previously used basis). See § 1.1502-32(c)(1)(ii)(B) regarding special allocations applicable to the tier-up of the reallocated investment adjustment if the reallocation is limited under this paragraph (b)(2)(iii)(B)(2) due to prior use at a higher tier.

(ii) Example. The application of this paragraph (b)(2)(iii)(B)(2) is illustrated by the following example:

Example. (i) Facts. P owns all 20 shares of M stock, and 10 shares of S stock. M owns the remaining 10 shares of S stock. In year 1, S recognizes $200 of income that results in a $10 positive investment adjustment being allocated to each share of S stock. The group does not recognize any other items. The $100 positive adjustment to M's basis in the S stock tiers up, and results in a $5 positive adjustment to each share of M stock. In year 2, P sells one share of M stock and recognizes a gain. In year 3, M sells one loss share of S stock, and this paragraph (b) applies and requires a reallocation of the year 1 positive investment adjustment applied to the basis of the transferred S share.

(ii) Application of limitation by prior use. M's basis in the transferred loss share of S stock reflects a $10 positive investment adjustment attributable to S's year 1 income. Under the general rule of this paragraph (b), that $10 would be subject to reallocation to reduce basis disparity. However, that $10 adjustment had originally tiered up to adjust P's basis in its M shares and, as a result, $.50 of that adjustment was reflected in P's basis in each share of M stock. When P sold the share of M stock, the basis of that share (which included the tiered-up $.50) was used in determining the gain on the sale. Thus, $.50 of the $10 investment adjustment originally allocated to the transferred S share that tiered-up to the sold M share was previously used and, as such, cannot be reallocated in a manner that would (if it were the original allocation) affect the basis of the sold M share. Accordingly, no more than $9.50 of the adjustment to M's transferred S share could be reallocated to P's shares of S stock. If so, under the special allocation rule in § 1.1502-32(c)(1)(ii)(B), the tier-up of this $9.50 would only be allocated among P's remaining 19 shares of M stock. Alternatively, all $10 of the investment adjustment could be reallocated to M's other S shares (because the tier-up to P's M shares would have been the same regardless which of M's shares of S stock were adjusted).

(iii) Application of limitation where adjustment would have been used. The facts are the same as in paragraph (i) of this Example except that M does not sell any shares of S stock and, in year 3, P sells a loss share of S stock. As in paragraph (i) of this Example, when P sold the share of M stock, the basis of that share was used in determining the gain on the share. When P sells the loss share of S stock, the $10 positive investment adjustment from S's year 1 income cannot be reallocated in a manner that would (if it were the original adjustment) affect the basis of the sold M share. If this $10 positive investment adjustment had originally been allocated to the S shares held by M, $.50 of the $10 investment adjustment would have tiered up to the M share that P sold, would have been reflected in P's basis in that M share, and would have been used in determining P's gain or loss on the sale. Accordingly, up to $9.50 of the $10 investment adjustment applied to the basis of P's transferred S share could be reallocated to M's shares of S stock. If so, under the special allocation rule in § 1.1502-32(c)(1)(ii)(B), the tier-up of this $9.50 would only be allocated among P's remaining 19 shares of M stock. Alternatively, all $10 of the investment adjustment could be reallocated to P's other S shares.

(3) Examples. The general application of this paragraph (b) is illustrated by the following examples:

Example (1). Transfer of stock received in section 351 exchange.

(i) Redetermination to prevent noneconomic loss. (A) Facts. For many years, M has owned two assets, Asset 1 and Asset 2. On January 1, year 1, M receives the only four outstanding shares of S common stock (Block 1 shares) in exchange for Asset 1, which has a basis and value of $80. Section 351 applies to the exchange and, therefore, under section 358, M's aggregate basis in the Block 1 shares is $80 ($20 per share). On July 1, year 2, M receives another share of S common stock (Block 2 share) in exchange for Asset 2, which has a basis of $0 and value of $20. Section 351 applies to this exchange and, under section 358, M's basis in the Block 2 share is $0. On October 1, year 3, S sells Asset 2 for $20, recognizing a $20 gain. On December 31, year 3, M sells one of its Block 1 shares to X for $20. After taking into account the effects of all applicable rules of law, M's basis in each Block 1 share is $24 (M's original $20 basis increased under § 1.1502-32 by $4, the share's allocable portion of the $20 gain recognized on the sale of Asset 2). In addition, M's basis in its Block 2 share is $4 (M's original $0 basis increased under § 1.1502-32 by $4 (the share's allocable portion of the $20 gain recognized on the sale of Asset 2)). M's sale of the Block 1 share is a transfer of a loss share and therefore subject to this section.

(B) Basis redetermination under this paragraph (b). Under this paragraph (b), M's bases in all its shares of S stock are subject to redetermination. First, paragraph (b)(2)(i)(A) of this section applies to reduce M's basis in the transferred loss share, but not below value, by removing positive investment adjustments applied to the basis of the share. Accordingly, M's basis in the transferred Block 1 share is reduced by $4 (the amount of the positive investment adjustment applied to the share), from $24 to $20. Even if there were negative investment adjustments applied to adjust the bases of nontransferred common shares, no further reduction to the basis of the share would be required under this paragraph (b) because the basis of the transferred share is then equal to the share's value. Under paragraph (b)(2)(ii)(B) of this section, the positive investment adjustment removed from the transferred loss share is reallocated and applied to increase M's bases in its S common shares in a manner that reduces disparity in M's bases in all the S common shares, to the greatest extent possible. Accordingly, the $4 positive investment adjustment removed from the Block 1 share is reallocated and applied to the basis of the Block 2 share, increasing it from $4 to $8.

(C) Application of paragraphs (c) and (d) of this section. Because M's sale of the Block 1 share is not a transfer of a loss share after the application of this paragraph (b), neither paragraph (c) of this section nor paragraph (d) of this section applies to the transfer.

(ii) Redetermination to eliminate duplicated loss. (A) Facts. The facts are the same as in paragraph (i)(A) of this Example 1, except that, at the time of the second contribution, the value of Asset 1 had declined to $20 and so, instead of contributing Asset 2, M contributed Asset 3 to S in exchange for the Block 2 share. At the time of that exchange, Asset 3 had a basis and value of $5. On October 1, year 3, S sells Asset 1 for $20, recognizing a $60 loss that is absorbed by the group. On December 31, year 3, M sells one of its Block 1 shares to X for $5. After taking into account the effects of all applicable rules of law, M's basis in each Block 1 share is $8 (M's original $20 basis decreased under § 1.1502-32 by $12 (the share's allocable portion of the $60 loss recognized on the sale of Asset 1)). M's basis in its Block 2 share is an excess loss account of $7 (M's original basis of $5 reduced under § 1.1502-32 by $12, the share's allocable portion of the loss recognized on the sale of Asset 1). M's sale of the Block 1 share is a transfer of a loss share and therefore subject to this section.

(B) Basis redetermination under this paragraph (b). Under this paragraph (b), M's bases in all its shares of S stock are subject to redetermination. There are no positive investment adjustments and so there is no adjustment under paragraph (b)(2)(i)(A) of this section. However, under paragraph (b)(2)(i)(B) of this section, M's basis in the transferred Block 1 share is reduced, but not below value, by reallocating negative investment adjustments from common shares that are not transferred loss shares. In total, there were $48 of negative investment adjustments applied to common shares that are not transferred loss shares. Accordingly, M's basis in the Block 1 share is reduced by $3, from $8 to its value of $5. Under paragraph (b)(2)(i)(B) of this section, the negative investment adjustments applied to the transferred share are reallocated from (and therefore cause an increase in the basis of) S common shares that are not transferred loss shares in a manner that reduces disparity among members' bases in all S common shares to the greatest extent possible. Accordingly, the $3 negative investment adjustment reallocated and applied to the transferred Block 1 share is reallocated entirely from the Block 2 share, increasing the basis in the Block 2 share from an excess loss account of $7 to an excess loss account of $4.

(C) Application of paragraphs (c) and (d) of this section. Because M's sale of the Block 1 share is not a transfer of a loss share after the application of this paragraph (b), neither paragraph (c) of this section nor paragraph (d) of this section applies to the transfer.

(iii) Nonapplicability of redetermination rule to sale of entire interest. The facts are the same as in paragraph (ii)(A) of this Example 1, except that, on December 31, year 3, M sells all its shares of S stock to X for $25. M's sale of the S stock to X is a transfer of all of the shares of S stock held by members to one or more nonmembers in one fully taxable transaction and, therefore, basis is not redetermined under this paragraph (b). Accordingly, the sale of the Block 1 shares remains a transfer of loss shares and, as such, subject to paragraphs (c) and (d) of this section. However, paragraphs (c)(7) and (d)(3)(i)(A) of this section apply netting principles to prevent adjustments under either paragraph (c) or paragraph (d) of this section, respectively. Alternatively, the group could elect to apply this paragraph (b). In that case, the $12 negative adjustment applied to the Block 2 shares would be reallocated to the Block 1 shares with the result that there would be no loss (or gain) on any of the transferred shares following the application of this paragraph (b). In that case, there would be no further application of this section to the transfer.

(iv) Transfer of entire interest, partially taxable. The facts are the same as in paragraph (iii) of this Example 1, except that, instead of selling the Block 2 share to X, M contributes the share to a nonmember in a section 351 exchange that is part of the same transaction. Although all the S shares held by members are transferred in the transaction, not all the shares are transferred to one or more nonmembers in one fully taxable transaction. Therefore, paragraph (b)(1)(ii)(B) of this section does not apply and M must redetermine its bases in its shares of S stock under this paragraph (b). In total, there were $12 of negative investment adjustments applied to common shares that are not transferred loss shares (the Block 2 share, a gain share). Accordingly, M's basis in each of the Block 1 shares is reduced by $3, from $8 to its value of $5. Under paragraph (b)(2)(i)(B) of this section, the negative investment adjustments applied to the transferred shares are reallocated from (and therefore cause an increase in the basis of) S shares that are not transferred loss shares in a manner that reduces disparity among members' bases in all S common shares to the greatest extent possible. Accordingly, the $12 negative investment adjustment reallocated and applied to the transferred Block 1 shares is reallocated entirely from the Block 2 share, increasing the basis in the Block 2 share from an excess loss account of $7 to a basis of $5. Because M's transfer is not a transfer of loss shares after the application of this paragraph (b), neither paragraph (c) of this section nor paragraph (d) of this section applies to the transfer.

Example (2). Redetermination increases basis of transferred loss share.

(i) Facts. On January 1, year 1, M owns all 10 outstanding shares of S common stock. Five of the shares have a basis of $20 per share (Block 1 shares) and five of the shares have a basis of $10 per share (Block 2 shares). S's only asset, Asset 1, has a basis of $50. S has no other attributes. On October 1, year 1, S sells Asset 1 for $100, recognizing a $50 gain. On December 31, year 2, M sells one Block 1 share and one Block 2 share to X for $10 per share. After taking into account the effects of all applicable rules of law, M's basis in each Block 1 share is $25 (M's original $20 basis increased under Sec. 1.1502-32 by $5, the share's allocable portion of the $50 gain recognized on the sale of Asset 1), and M's basis in each Block 2 share is $15 (M's original $10 basis increased under Sec. 1.1502-32 by $5, the share's allocable portion of the $50 gain recognized on the sale of Asset 1). M's sale of the Block 1 and Block 2 shares is a transfer of loss shares and therefore subject to this section.

(ii) Basis redetermination under this paragraph (b). Under this paragraph (b), M's bases in all its shares of S stock are subject to redetermination. First, paragraph (b)(2)(i)(A) of this section applies to reduce M's basis in the transferred Block 1 and Block 2 shares, but not below value, by removing the positive investment adjustments applied to the bases of the transferred loss shares. Accordingly, the basis of the transferred Block 1 share is reduced by $5, from $25 to $20. The basis of the transferred Block 2 share is also reduced by $5, from $15 to $10. (Although the transferred Block 1 share is still a loss share, there is no reduction to its basis under paragraph (b)(2)(i)(B) of this section because there were no negative investment adjustments applied to the bases of the S common shares that are not transferred loss shares.) Next, paragraph (b)(2)(ii)(B) of this section applies to reallocate and apply the $10 of positive investment adjustments removed from the transferred loss shares to increase M's bases in its S common shares in a manner that reduces the disparity in its bases in all S common shares to the greatest extent possible. Accordingly, of the $10 of positive investment adjustments to be reallocated, $6 is reallocated and applied to the basis of the transferred Block 2 share (increasing it from

$10 to $16) and $4 is reallocated and applied equally to the basis of each of the four retained Block 2 shares (increasing the basis of each from $15 to $16). After giving effect to the reallocations under this paragraph (b), M's basis in each retained Block 1 share is $25, M's basis in the transferred Block 1 share is $20, and M's basis in each Block 2 share is $16.

(iii) Application of paragraph (c) of this section. After the application of this paragraph (b), M's sale of the Block 1 and Block 2 shares is still a transfer of loss shares and, accordingly, subject to paragraph (c) of this section. No adjustment is required to the basis of the transferred Block 1 share under paragraph (c) of this section because, after its basis is redetermined under this paragraph (b), the net positive adjustment to the basis of the share is $0. See paragraph (c)(3) of this section. However, under paragraph (c) of this section M's basis in the transferred Block 2 share is reduced by $6 (the lesser of its net positive adjustment, $6, and its disconformity amount, $6), from $16 to $10, its value. See paragraph (c)(2) of this section.

(iv) Application of paragraph (d) of this section. After the application of paragraph (c) of this section, M's sale of the Block 1 share is still a transfer of a loss share and, accordingly, subject to paragraph (d) of this section. No adjustment is required under paragraph (d) of this section because there is no aggregate inside loss. See paragraph (d)(3)(iii) of this section. Because M's sale of the Block 2 share is no longer a transfer of a loss share after the application of paragraph (c) of this section, paragraph (d) of this section does not apply to the transfer of the Block 2 share.

Example (3). Tiered subsidiaries.

(i) Transfer of all shares of common stock. (A) Facts. P owns the sole outstanding share of S stock with a basis of $100, and the sole outstanding share of M stock with a basis of $300. M has $200 and owns an asset with a basis of $0. S owns one asset, Asset 1, with a basis of $100. At a time when Asset 1 has a value of $200, S issues a second share of common stock to M in exchange for $200. Later S sells Asset 1 for $200, recognizing a $100 gain. After taking into account the effects of all applicable rules of law, P's basis in its S stock is $150 (P's original $100 basis increased under § 1.1502-32 by $50, the share's allocable portion of the $100 gain recognized on the sale of Asset 1), M's basis in its S stock is $250 (M's original $200 basis increased under § 1.1502-32 by $50, the share's allocable portion of the $100 gain recognized on the sale of Asset 1), and P's basis in its M stock is $350 (P's original $300 basis increased under § 1.1502-32 by $50, the tier-up of M's increase in its basis in its S stock). P then sells its M share and its S share to X for $300 and $200, respectively. M and S are not members of the same consolidated group immediately after the sale. Therefore, the M share and both of the S shares are transferred in the transaction. Regarding P's sale of its share of S stock and its share of M stock, see paragraph (f)(10)(i)(A) of this section (ceasing to own a share in a taxable transaction) and paragraph (f)(10)(i)(C) of this section (nonmember acquires share); regarding M's share of S stock, see paragraph (f)(10)(i)(B) of this section (ceasing to be members of the same group). The application of this section begins with respect to the stock of S, the subsidiary at the lowest tier in which there is a transfer of subsidiary stock. See paragraph (a)(3)(ii) of this section. Although both P and M transfer their S shares, only M's S share is a loss share. Thus, only M's transfer is a transfer of a loss share of S stock and only M's transfer is subject to this section.

(B) Application of section to transferred S shares. Although only M's transfer is subject to this section, all members' bases in their shares of S stock are subject to redetermination under this paragraph (b). First, paragraph (b)(2)(i)(A) of this section applies to reduce M's basis in its transferred S share, but not below value, by removing the positive investment adjustment applied to that share. Accordingly, the basis of M's S share is reduced by $50, from $250 to $200 (under § 1.1502-32, that redetermination adjustment tiers up to reduce P's basis in its M stock by $50, from $350 to $300). Because there are no negative adjustments to reallocate under paragraph (b)(2)(i)(B) of this section, paragraph (b)(2)(ii)(B) of this section then applies to reallocate and apply the $50 positive investment adjustment removed from the transferred loss S share to increase P's basis in its S share in a manner that reduces disparity among members' bases in all S common shares to the greatest extent possible. Accordingly, all $50 of the positive investment adjustment is reallocated and applied to P's basis in its S share (increasing the basis from $150 to $200). Because M's transfer of its S share is not a transfer of a loss share after the application of this paragraph (b), neither paragraph (c) of this section nor paragraph (d) of this section applies to that transfer.

(C) Application of section to transfers at next higher tier. After the adjustments to M's share of S stock are given effect, P's transfer of its share of M stock is not a transfer of a loss share and so this section does not apply to that transfer.

(D) Result of application of section. After the application of this section, P recognizes no gain or loss on its sale of either the S share or the M share. In addition, the unrecognized (noneconomic) loss in M's basis in its S share is eliminated. The results would be the same if, in addition to the facts in paragraph (i)(A) of this Example 3, M transferred its S share to X in a fully taxable transaction and, as permitted under paragraph (b)(1)(ii)(B) of this section, P elected to redetermine basis under this paragraph (b).

(ii) Transfer of less than all lower-tier shares of stock. (A) Facts. The facts are the same as in paragraph (i)(A) of this Example 1, except that M and S are members of the same consolidated group immediately after the sale. Therefore, in this case, M's S share is not transferred and so this section has no application with respect to M's S share. P's transfer of its S share is not a transfer of a loss share and so is also not subject to this section. However, P's sale of its share of M stock is a transfer of a loss share and is subject to this section.

(B) Basis redetermination under this paragraph (b). Although P's transfer of its share of M stock is subject to this section, this paragraph (b) does not apply to the transfer because there is only one share of M stock outstanding (and so there can be no disparity among members' bases in common shares and there are no outstanding preferred shares with respect to which there can be unrecognized gain or loss). Accordingly, after the application of this paragraph (b), P's sale of its M share is still a transfer of a loss share and therefore subject to paragraph (c) of this section.

(C) Application of paragraphs (c) and (d) of this section. Under paragraph (c) of this section, P must reduce its basis in its M share by $50, the lesser of its net positive adjustment ($50, see paragraph (c)(3) of this section) and its disconformity amount ($150, see paragraphs (c)(4), (c)(5), and (c)(6) of this section). As a result, the share is no longer a loss share and the transfer is not subject to paragraph (d) of this section.

(D) Result of application of section. After the application of this section, P recognizes a $50 gain on its sale of the S share and no loss on its sale of the M share. Although there is unrecognized loss preserved in M's basis in its S share, if M later transfers the share when it is a loss share, that transfer will be subject to this section.

Example (4). Application to outstanding common and preferred shares.

(i) Facts. P owns all the stock of M and all eight outstanding shares of S common stock. S also has two shares of non-voting preferred stock outstanding; the preferred shares each have a $100 annual, cumulative preference as to dividends. M owns one of the preferred shares (PS1) and P owns the other (PS2). On January 1, year 1, the bases and values of the outstanding S shares are:

	Preferred		Common							
	PS1 (M)	PS2 (P)	CS1 (P)	CS2 (P)	CS3 (P)	CS4 (P)	CS5 (P)	CS6 (P)	CS7 (P)	CS8 (P)
Basis	1250	990	1025	710	550	400	375	250	215	100
Value	1000	1000	375	375	375	375	375	375	375	375

(A) As of January 1, year 1, there are no arrearages on the preferred stock. In year 1, S has a $1100 capital loss and $100 of ordinary income. The group absorbs the loss and the negative remaining adjustment of $1000 is allocable entirely to the common stock, equally to each common share ($125 per share). See § 1.1502-32(c)(1)(iii) and (c)(2).

(B) In year 2, S has $700 of ordinary income and a $100 ordinary loss. Also, on October 1, year 2, S declares and makes a $200 dividend distribution with respect to the preferred stock ($100 per share). Under § 1.1502-32(c)(1)(i), a negative adjustment of $100 is first allocated to each of the preferred shares to reflect the declaration of the dividend. The $600 positive remaining adjustment determined under § 1.1502-32(c)(1)(iii) (reflecting S's net income reduced by the distribution) is then allocated to each of the preferred shares to the extent of its entitlement to dividends accruing in year 1 and year 2 ($200 per share). See § 1.1502-32(c)(1)(iii) and (c)(3). The $200 of the positive remaining adjustment not allocated to the preferred shares is then allocated to the common stock, equally to each common share ($25 per share). See § 1.1502-32(c)(1)(iii) and (c)(2). After taking into account the effects of all applicable rules of law, the adjusted bases and the values of the shares as of January 1, year 3, are:

	Preferred		Common							
	PS1 (M)	PS2 (P)	CS1 (P)	CS2 (P)	CS3 (P)	CS4 (P)	CS5 (P)	CS6 (P)	CS7 (P)	CS8 (P)
Basis	1250	990	1025	710	550	400	375	250	215	100
Year 1§ 1.1502-32 adjustments	N/A	N/A	-125	-125	-125	-125	-125	-125	-125	-125
Year 2§ 1.1502-32 adjustments	-100	-100	+25	+25	+25	+25	+25	+25	+25	+25
	+200	+200								
	+100	+100								
Adjusted basis	1350	1090	925	610	450	300	275	150	115	0
Value	1100	1100	275	275	275	275	275	275	275	275
Unrecognized gain/(loss)	(250)	10	(650)	(335)	(175)	(25)	0	125	160	275

(C) On January 1, year 3, M sells PS1 for $1100 and P sells CS2 for $275. The sales of PS1 and CS2 are transfers of loss shares and therefore subject to this section.

(ii) Basis redetermination under this paragraph (b). Under this paragraph (b), all members' bases in shares of S stock are subject to redetermination in accordance with the following:

(A) Removing positive investment adjustments from transferred loss common shares. First, paragraph (b)(2)(i)(A) of this section applies to reduce P's basis in CS2, but not below value, by removing the positive investment adjustment applied to the basis of the share. Accordingly, P's basis in CS2 is reduced by $25, from $610 to $585.

(B) Reallocating negative investment adjustments from common shares that are not transferred loss shares. Because the transferred shares remain loss shares after the removal of positive investment adjustments, their bases are further reduced under paragraph (b)(2)(i)(B) of this section, but not below value, by reallocating negative investment adjustments applied to common shares that are not transferred loss shares. Reallocations are made first to preferred shares and then to the common shares, in a manner that reduces disparity among members' bases in transferred loss preferred shares, and reduces disparity among members' bases in all common shares, to the greatest extent possible. The loss on PS1 is $250, the remaining loss on CS2 is $310, and the total amount of negative investment adjustments applied to shares that are not transferred loss shares is $875 (the sum of the negative adjustments applied to all common shares other than CS2). Thus, $250 of negative investment adjustments are reallocated and applied to the basis of PS1, reducing it to the share's value, $1100. The negative investment adjustments are reallocated from the common shares that are not transferred loss shares in a manner that reduces disparity among members' bases in all common shares to the greatest extent possible. The negative investment adjustments may be reallocated to PS1 from the common shares that are not transferred loss shares as follows: $125 from each of CS7 and CS8. Such reallocations increase the basis of CS7 by $125, from $115 to $240, and increase the basis of CS8 by $125, from $0 to $125. Negative investment adjustments are then reallocated to CS2 from the common shares that are not transferred loss shares in a manner that reduces disparity among members' bases in all common shares to the greatest extent possible. The negative investment adjustments may be reallocated to CS2 from the other common shares as follows: $80 from CS4, $105 from CS5, and $125 from CS6. Such reallocations reduce the basis of CS2 by $310, from $585 to $275, increase the basis of CS4 by $80, from $300 to $380, increase the basis of CS5 by $105, from $275 to $380, and increase the basis of CS6 by $125, from $150 to $275. However, there may be other reasonable reallocations.

(C) Increasing basis by reallocated positive investment adjustments. Under paragraph (b)(2)(ii)(A) of this section, the $25 positive investment adjustment removed from CS2 (the transferred loss common share) is then reallocated and applied to increase the basis of preferred shares, but not above value. Accordingly, $10 of that amount is reallocated to PS2, increasing its basis from $1090 to $1100, its value. Under paragraph (b)(2)(ii)(B) of this section, the remaining $15 is reallocated and applied to the common shares in a manner that reduces disparity among members' bases in all common shares to the greatest extent possible. The $15 positive investment adjustment that is reallocated to common shares may be reallocated entirely to CS8, increasing its basis from $125 to $140. However, there may be other reasonable reallocations.

(D) Summary of the reallocation of adjustments. The adjustments made under this paragraph (b) are:

	Preferred		Common							
	PS1 (M)	PS2 (P)	CS1 (P)	CS2 (P)	CS3 (P)	CS4 (P)	CS5 (P)	CS6 (P)	CS7 (P)	CS8 (P)
Adjusted basis before redetermination	1350	1090	925	610	450	300	275	150	115	0
Removing positive adjustments from transferred loss shares	......	.....	.....	-25						
Reallocating negative adjustments	-250	.....	.....	-310	.....	+80	+105	+125	+125	+125
Applying positive adjustments removed from transferred loss shares	......	+10	.....	......	.....	......	......	.....	......	+15
Basis after redetermination	1100	1100	925	275	450	380	380	275	240	140
Value	1100	1100	275	275	275	275	275	275	275	275
Gain/(loss)	0	0	(650)	0	(175)	(105)	(105)	0	35	135

(iii) Application of paragraphs (c) and (d) of this section. Because M's sale of PS1 and P's sale of CS2 are not transfers of loss shares after the application of this paragraph (b), paragraphs (c) and (d) of this section do not apply.

(iv) Higher-tier effects. The $250 reduction in the basis of PS1 under this paragraph (b) is a noncapital, nondeductible expense under § 1.1502-32(b)(3)(iii)(B) that will be included in the year 3 investment adjustment to be applied to P's basis in its M stock.

(c) Stock basis reduction to prevent noneconomic loss. *(1) In general.* The rules of this paragraph (c) reduce M's basis in a transferred share of S stock to prevent noneconomic stock loss and thus promote the clear reflection of the group's income. These rules limit the reduction to M's basis in the S share to the amount of net unrealized appreciation reflected in the share's basis as of the transfer (the disconformity amount). These rules also limit the reduction to M's basis in the S share to the portion of the share's basis that is attributable to investment adjustments made pursuant to the consolidated return regulations.

(2) Basis reduction rule. This paragraph (c) applies if M transfers a share of S stock and, after taking into account the effects of all applicable rules of law, including any adjustments under paragraph (b) of this section, the share is a loss share. Under this paragraph (c), M's basis in the share is reduced, but not below value, by the lesser of—

(i) The share's net positive adjustment (as defined in paragraph (c)(3) of this section); and

(ii) The share's disconformity amount (as defined in paragraph (c)(4) of this section).

(3) Net positive adjustment. A share's net positive adjustment is the greater of—

(i) Zero; and

(ii) The sum of all investment adjustments reflected in the basis of the share. The term investment adjustment has the same meaning as in paragraph (b)(1)(iii) of this section, except that it includes all adjustments specially allocated under § 1.1502-32(c)(1)(ii).

(4) Disconformity amount. A share's disconformity amount is the excess, if any, of—

(i) M's basis in the share; over

(ii) The share's allocable portion of S's net inside attribute amount (as defined in paragraph (c)(5) of this section).

(5) Net inside attribute amount. S's net inside attribute amount is determined as of the transfer, taking into account all applicable rules of law (even if the adjustments required by such rules are not deemed effective until after the transfer, such as certain adjustments required under sections 108 and 1017 and § 1.1502-28). S's net inside attribute amount is the sum of S's net operating and capital loss carryovers, deferred deductions, money, and basis in assets other than money, reduced by the amount of S's liabilities. For this purpose, S's basis in any share of lower-tier subsidiary stock is generally S's basis in that share, adjusted to reflect any gain or loss recognized in the transaction with respect to the share and any other related or resulting adjustments to the basis of the share. However, see paragraph (c)(6) of this section for special rules regarding the computation of S's net inside attribute amount for purposes of this paragraph (c) if S holds stock of a subsidiary that is not transferred in the transaction. See paragraph (f) of this section for definitions of "allocable portion," "deferred deduction," "liability," "loss carryover," and other relevant terms.

(6) Determination of S's net inside attribute amount if S owns stock of a lower-tier subsidiary. (i) Overview. If a loss share of S stock is transferred when S holds a share of stock of another subsidiary (S1) and the S1 share is not transferred in the same transaction, S's net inside attribute amount is de-

termined by treating S's basis in its S1 share as tentatively reduced under this paragraph (c)(6). The purpose of this rule is to reduce the extent to which S1's investment adjustments increase noneconomic loss on S stock (as a result of S1's recognition of items that are indirectly reflected in a member's basis in a share of S stock).

(ii) General rule for nontransferred shares of lower-tier subsidiary stock. For purposes of determining the disconformity amount of a share of S stock, S's basis in a nontransferred share of S1 stock is treated as reduced by the share's tentative reduction amount. The tentative reduction amount is the lesser of the S1 share's net positive adjustment and the S1 share's disconformity amount.

(iii) Multiple tiers of nontransferred shares. If S directly or indirectly owns nontransferred shares of stock of subsidiaries in multiple tiers, then, subject to the limitations in paragraph (c)(6)(iv) of this section (regarding nontransferred shares that are lower-tier to transferred shares), the rules of this paragraph (c)(6) first apply to determine the tentatively reduced basis of stock of the subsidiary at the lowest tier. These rules then apply to determine the tentatively reduced basis of nontransferred shares of stock of subsidiaries successively at each next higher tier that is lower-tier to S. The tentative reductions at each tier are treated as noncapital, nondeductible expenses that tier up under the principles of Sec. 1.1502-32, and, as such, result in a tentative reduction of basis and any net positive adjustment of subsidiary shares that are lower-tier to S.

(iv) Nonapplicability of tentative basis reduction rule to transferred shares. The tentative basis reduction rule in this paragraph (c)(6) does not apply to any share of stock of a lower-tier subsidiary (S1) that is transferred in the same transaction in which the S share is transferred. Further, for purposes of determining the S share's disconformity amount, the tentative basis reduction rule in this paragraph (c)(6) only applies with respect to stock of a lower-tier subsidiary if such stock is lower-tier to a nontransferred S1 share. The purpose of this rule is to prevent tentative adjustments to the bases of lower-tier shares if this paragraph (c) has already applied with respect to the shares, without regard to whether such application resulted in the reduction of the basis of any share.

(v) Example. The rules of this paragraph (c)(6) are illustrated by the following example:

Example.

(0) Facts. M owns the sole outstanding share of S stock, S owns the sole outstanding share of S1 stock, S1 owns all five outstanding shares of S2 stock (the bases of which are equal), and S2 owns the sole outstanding share of S3 stock. The basis of each of the shares reflects its allocable portion of a $5 positive investment adjustment attributable to income recognized by S3. The basis of the S share exceeds its value by $10 and the basis of the S1 share exceeds its value by $5. The basis of each S2 share is $1 less than its value. In one transaction, M sells its S share to X, S1 issues new shares in an amount that prevents S and S1 from being members of the same group, and S1 sells one of its S2 shares to an unrelated individual. S1, S2, and S3 elect to file a consolidated return following the transaction.

(ii) General applicability of section. As a result of the transaction, there is a transfer of the S share and the S2 share that was sold (because both shares were sold to nonmembers) and of the S1 share (because S and S1 cease to be members of the same group as a result of the stock issuance). The transfer of the S2 share is not a transfer of a loss share, and so this section does not apply to that transfer. The transfers of the S and S1 shares are transfers of loss shares, and so this section applies to those transfers. The S3 share and the four retained S2 shares are not transferred in the transaction. Under paragraph (a)(3)(ii)(A) of this section, this section applies first to the transfer of the S1 share because it is the lowest-tier transferred loss share.

(iii) Application of paragraph (b) of this section and this paragraph (c) to transfer of S1 stock. First, the $1 gain recognized on the transfer of the S2 share tiers up to adjust the basis of each upper-tier share. The transferred S1 share is still a loss share (by $4) and is therefore subject to this section. Although the transfer is subject to paragraph (b) of this section, there is no basis redetermination under paragraph (b) of this section because there is only one share of S1 stock outstanding (and so there can be no disparity among members' bases in common shares and there are no outstanding preferred shares with respect to which there can be unrecognized gain or loss). See paragraph (b)(1)(ii)(A) of this section. Therefore, after the application of paragraph (b) of this section, the S1 share is still a loss share and, as such, subject to this paragraph (c). In determining the amount of any basis reduction under this paragraph (c), the disconformity amount of the S1 share is computed by comparing S's basis in its S1 share to S1's net inside attribute amount (because there is only one S1 share outstanding, the entire amount is allocable to that share). In determining S1's net inside attribute amount, the tentative reduction rule in this paragraph (c)(6) applies to nontransferred lower-tier shares (provided they are lower-tier to nontransferred shares). Thus, the rule applies to S1's four retained shares of S2 stock and to S2's share of S3 stock. The tentative reduction begins at the lowest level (S2's share of S3 stock) and any tentative reduction amount tiers up as a noncapital, nondeductible expense under the principles of § 1.1502-32, tentatively reducing the bases of any upper tier nontransferred shares that are lower-tier to the transferred loss share (the S1 share). Accordingly, each of S1's nontransferred share of S2 stock is tentatively reduced by its portion of the tentative reduction to S2's share of S3 stock. S1 then applies the tentative reduction rule to its four nontransferred S2 shares. S1's net inside attribute amount is the sum of its basis in each of its nontransferred S2 shares, as tentatively reduced under this paragraph (c)(6) and S1's actual basis in the transferred S2 share, increased to reflect the gain recognized on the sale of that share. After the application of this paragraph (c) to the transfer of the S1 share, paragraph (b) of this section applies to M's transfer of the S share.

(iv) Application of section to transfer of S stock. Because the S share is still a loss share after applying paragraph (b) of this section and this paragraph (c) to the transfer of the S1 stock, this section applies to M's transfer of the S share. Although paragraph (b) of this section applies to the transfer, there is no basis redetermination under paragraph (b) of this section because there is only one share of S stock outstanding (and so there can be no disparity among members' bases in common shares and there are no outstanding preferred shares with respect to which there can be unrecognized gain or loss). See paragraph (b)(1)(ii)(A) of this section. Therefore, after the application of paragraph (b) of this section, the share is still a loss share and, as such, subject to this paragraph (c). In determining the disconformity amount of the S share, S's net inside attribute amount is determined using S's actual basis in the transferred S1 stock (after any reduction under this paragraph (c)), because the tentative reduction rule in this paragraph (c)(6) does not apply to shares that are transferred in the transaction. All other shares are lower-tier to the transferred S1 share and are therefore also not subject to tentative reduction for purposes of determining the disconformity amount of the S share. After the application of this paragraph (c) to the transfer of the S share, paragraph (d) of this section applies with respect to M's transfer of the S share. After the application of paragraph (d) of this section with respect to the transfer of the S share, if the S1 share is still a loss share, paragraph (d) of this section applies with respect to S's transfer of the S1 share.

(7) Netting of gains and losses taken into account. (i) General rule. Solely for purposes of computing the basis reduction required under this paragraph (c), the basis of each transferred loss share of S stock is treated as reduced proportionately (as to loss) by the amount of income or gain taken into account by members with respect to transferred shares of S stock, provided that—

(A) The shares are transferred in one transaction; and

(B) The gain is taken into account as of the transaction.

(ii) Example. The netting rule of this paragraph (c)(7) is illustrated by the following example:

Example. Disposition of gain and loss shares.

(i) Facts. M owns the only three outstanding shares of S stock. Share A has a basis of $54, Share B has a basis of $100, and Share C has a basis of $80. In the same transaction, M sells all three S shares to X for $60 each. M realizes a gain of $6 on Share A, a loss of $40 on Share B, and a loss of $20 on Share C. M's sales of Share B and Share C are transfers of loss shares and therefore subject to this section. M's sale is a transfer of all of the shares of S stock held by members to one or more nonmembers in one fully taxable transaction and, therefore, basis is not redetermined under paragraph (b) of this section. See paragraph (b)(1)(ii)(B) of this section. The transfer is then subject to this paragraph (c). However, for this purpose, M treats its bases in Share B and Share C as reduced by the $6 gain taken into account on Share A. The gain is allocated to Share B and Share C proportionately based on the amount of loss in each share. Thus, $4 of gain ($40/$60 x $6) is treated as allocated to Share B and $2 of gain ($20/$60 x $6) is treated as allocated to Share C. Accordingly, M computes the basis reduction required under this paragraph (c) by treating its basis in Share B as $96 ($100 less $4) and its basis in Share C as $78 ($80 less $2). If, after the application of this paragraph (c), the sales of Share B and Share C are still transfers of loss shares, then the transfers are subject to paragraph (d) of this section. (Although the bases of Share B and Share C are not actually reduced by any portion of the gain, paragraph (d)(3)(i)(A) of this section applies netting principles to limit adjustments under paragraph (d) of this section.)

(ii) Disposition of stock with deferred gain. The facts are the same as in paragraph (i) of this Example, except that M sells the gain share to another member. Under Sec. 1.1502-13, M's gain recognized on Share A is not taken into account in the taxable year of the transfer and therefore cannot be treated as reducing M's loss recognized on Share B and Share C for purposes of this paragraph (c). The applicability of this section to the transfer of Share A is determined as of the time that the intercompany item (the gain on M's sale to the other member) is taken into account; see paragraph (e)(3) of this section. However, if Share B (instead of Share A) were sold to a member, the entire gain on Share A would be treated as reducing the loss on Share C for purposes of applying this paragraph (c); see paragraph (e)(3) of this section.

(8) Examples. The application of this paragraph (c) is illustrated by the following examples.

Example (1). Appreciation reflected in stock basis at acquisition. (i) Appreciation recognized as gain.

(A) Facts. On January 1, year 1, M purchases the sole outstanding share of S stock for $100. At that time, S owns two assets, Asset 1 with a basis of $0 and a value of $40, and Asset 2 with a basis and value of $60. In year 1, S sells Asset 1 for $40, recognizing a $40 gain. On December 31, year 1, M sells its S share for $100. After taking into account the effects of all applicable rules of law, M's basis in the S share is $140 (M's original $100 basis increased under Sec. 1.1502-32 by $40, the share's allocable portion of the gain recognized on the sale of Asset 1). M's sale of the S share is a transfer of a loss share and therefore subject to this section.

(B) Application of paragraph (b) of this section. Although the transfer is subject to this section, there is no basis redetermination under paragraph (b) of this section because there is only one share of S stock outstanding (and so there can be no disparity among members' bases in common shares and there are no outstanding preferred shares with respect to which there can be unrecognized gain or loss). See paragraph (b)(1)(ii)(A) of this section. Therefore, after the application of paragraph (b) of this section, the share is still a loss share and, as such, subject to this paragraph (c).

(C) Basis reduction under this paragraph (c). Under this paragraph (c), M's basis in the S share, $140, is reduced, but not below value, $100, by the lesser of the share's net positive adjustment and disconformity amount. The share's net positive adjustment is the greater of zero and the sum of all investment adjustments (as defined in paragraph (b)(1)(iii) of this section) applied to the basis of the share. The only investment adjustment applied to the basis of the share is the $40 adjustment attributable to the gain recognized on the sale of Asset 1. Thus, the share's net positive adjustment is $40. The share's disconformity amount is the excess, if any, of its basis, $140, over its allocable portion of S's net inside attribute amount. S's net inside attribute amount is the sum of S's money ($40 from the sale of Asset 1) and S's basis in Asset 2, $60, or $100. The share is the only outstanding S share and so its allocable portion of the $100 net inside attribute amount is the entire $100. Thus, the share's disconformity amount is $40, the excess of $140 over $100. The lesser of the net positive adjustment, $40, and the share's disconformity amount, $40, is $40. Accordingly, immediately before the application of paragraph (d) of this section, M's basis in the share is reduced by $40, from $140 to $100.

(D) Application of paragraph (d) of this section. Because M's sale of the S share is not a transfer of a loss share after the application of this paragraph (c), paragraph (d) of this section does not apply to the transfer.

(ii) Appreciation recognized as income earned in the consumption of built-in gain. The facts are the same as in paragraph (i)(A) of this Example 1, except that, instead of selling Asset 1, the value of Asset 1 is consumed in the production of $40 of income in year 1 (reducing the value of Asset 1 to $0). Because the net positive adjustment includes items of income as well as items of gain, the results are the same as those described in paragraph (i) of this Example 1.

(iii) Post-acquisition appreciation eliminates stock loss. The facts are the same as in paragraph (i)(A) of this Example 1 except that, in addition, the value of Asset 2 increases to $100 before the stock is sold. As a result, M sells the S share for $140. Because M's sale of the S share is not a transfer of a loss share, this section does not apply to the transfer, notwithstanding that P's basis in the S share was increased by the gain recognized on Asset 1.

(iv) Distributions. (A) Facts. The facts are the same as in paragraph (i)(A) of this Example 1 except that, in addition, S declares and makes a $10 dividend distribution before the end of year 1. As a result, the value of the share decreases and M sells the share for $90. After taking into account the effects of all applicable rules of law, M's basis in the S share is $130 (M's original $100 basis increased under § 1.1502-32 by $30, the $10 distribution on the share reduced by the share's allocable portion of the $40 gain recognized on the sale of Asset 1). M's sale of the S share is a transfer of a loss share and therefore subject to this section.

(B) Application of paragraph (b) of this section. Although the transfer is subject to this section, there is no basis redetermination under paragraph (b) of this section for the reasons set forth in paragraph (i)(B) of this Example 1. Therefore, after the application of paragraph (b) of this section, the share is still a loss share and, as such, subject to this paragraph (c).

(C) Basis reduction under this paragraph (c). Under this paragraph (c), M's basis in the S share, $130, is reduced, but not below value, $90, by the lesser of the share's net positive adjustment and disconformity amount. The share's net positive adjustment is $40 (the sum of all investment adjustments (as defined in paragraph (b)(1)(iii) of this section) applied to the basis of the share). The share's disconformity amount is the excess of its basis, $130, over its allocable portion of S's net inside attribute amount. S's net inside attribute amount is $90, the sum of S's money ($30, the $40 sale proceeds less the $10 distribution) and S's basis in Asset 2, $60. The share is the only outstanding S share and so its allocable portion of the $90 net inside attribute amount is the entire $90. The lesser of the share's net positive adjustment, $40, and its disconformity amount, $40, is $40. Accordingly, immediately before the application of paragraph (d) of this section, the basis in the share is reduced by $40, from $130 to $90.

(D) Application of paragraph (d) of this section. Because M's sale of the S share is not a transfer of a loss share after the application of this paragraph (c), paragraph (d) of this section does not apply to the transfer.

Example (2). Loss of appreciation reflected in basis. (i) Facts. On January 1, year 1, M purchases the sole outstanding share of S stock for $100. At that time, S owns two assets, Asset 1 with a basis of $0 and a value of $40, and Asset 2 with a basis and value of $60. The value of Asset 1 declines to $0 and M sells its S share for $60. After taking into account the effects of all applicable rules of law, M's basis in the S share is $100. M's sale of the S share is a transfer of a loss share and therefore subject to this section.

(ii) Application of paragraph (b) of this section. Although the transfer is subject to this section, there is no basis redetermination under paragraph (b) of this section because there is only one share of S stock outstanding (and so there can be no disparity among members' bases in common shares and there are no outstanding preferred shares with respect to which there can be unrecognized gain or loss). See paragraph (b)(1)(ii)(A) of this section. Therefore, after the application of paragraph (b) of this section, the share is still a loss share and, as such, subject to this paragraph (c).

(iii) Basis reduction under this paragraph (c). Under this paragraph (c), M's $100 basis in the S share is reduced, but not below its $60 value by the lesser of the share's net positive adjustment and disconformity amount. There were no investment adjustments applied to M's basis in the share and so the share's net positive adjustment is $0. Thus, although the share's disconformity amount is $40 (the excess of M's $100 basis in the share over the share's $60 allocable portion of S's net inside attribute amount), no basis reduction is required under this paragraph (c).

(iv) Application of paragraph (d) of this section. After the application of this paragraph (c), M's sale of the S share is still a transfer of a loss share, and, accordingly, subject to paragraph (d) of this section. No adjustment is required under paragraph (d) of this section because there is no aggregate inside loss. See paragraph (d)(3)(iii) of this section.

Example (3). Items accruing after S becomes a member. (i) Recognition of loss accruing after S becomes a member. (A) Facts. On January 1, year 1, M purchases the sole outstanding share of S stock for $100. At that time, S owns two assets, Asset 1, with a basis of $0 and a value of $40, and Asset 2, with a basis and value of $60. In year 1, S sells Asset 1 for $40, recognizing a $40 gain. Also in year 1, the value of Asset 2 declines and S sells Asset 2 for $20, recognizing a $40 loss that is absorbed by the group. On December 31, year 1, M sells its S share for $60. After taking into account the effects of all applicable rules of law, M's basis in the S share is $100 (M's original $100 basis, unadjusted under Sec. 1.1502-32 because the $40 gain recognized on the sale of Asset 1 and the $40 loss on the sale of Asset 2 net, resulting in an adjustment of $0). M's sale of the S share is a transfer of a loss share and therefore subject to this section.

(B) Application of paragraph (b) of this section. Although the transfer is subject to this section, there is no basis redetermination under paragraph (b) of this section because there is only one share of S stock outstanding (and so there can be no disparity among members' bases in common shares and there are no outstanding preferred shares with respect to which there can be unrecognized gain or loss). See paragraph (b)(1)(ii)(A) of this section. Therefore, after the application of paragraph (b) of this section, the share is still a loss share and, as such, subject to this paragraph (c).

(C) Basis reduction under this paragraph (c). Under this paragraph (c), M's basis in the S share is reduced, but not below the share's $60 value, by the lesser of the share's net positive adjustment and disconformity amount. The share's net positive adjustment is $0. Thus, although the share has a disconformity amount of $40 (the excess of M's basis in the share, $100, over the share's allocable portion of S's net inside attribute amount, $60), no basis reduction is required under this paragraph (c).

(D) Application of paragraph (d) of this section. After the application of this paragraph (c), M's sale of the S share is still a transfer of a loss share, and, accordingly, subject to paragraph (d) of this section. No adjustment is required under paragraph (d) of this section because there is no aggregate inside loss. See paragraph (d)(3)(iii) of this section.

(ii) Recognition of gain accruing after S becomes a member. (A) Facts. The facts are the same as in paragraph (i)(A) of this Example 3, except that M does not sell the S share and S does not sell either asset in year 1. In addition, in year 2, the value of Asset 1 declines to $0, the value of Asset 2 returns to $60, and S creates Asset 3 (with a basis of $0). In year 3, S sells Asset 3 for $40, recognizing a $40 gain. On

December 31, year 3, M sells its S share for $100. After taking into account the effects of all applicable rules of law, M's basis in the S share is $140 (M's original $100 basis increased under § 1.1502-32 by $40 (the share's allocable portion of the gain recognized on the sale of Asset 3 in year 3)). M's sale of the S share is a transfer of a loss share and therefore subject to this section.

(B) Application of paragraph (b) of this section. Although the transfer is subject to this section, there is no basis redetermination under paragraph (b) of this section for the reasons set forth in paragraph (i)(B) of this Example 3. Therefore, after the application of paragraph (b) of this section, the share is still a loss share and, as such, subject to this paragraph (c).

(C) Basis reduction under this paragraph (c). Under this paragraph (c), M's basis in the S share, $140, is reduced, but not below value, $100, by the lesser of the share's net positive adjustment and disconformity amount. The share's net positive adjustment is $40 (the year 3 investment adjustment). The share's disconformity amount is the excess of its basis, $140, over its allocable portion of S's net inside attribute amount. S's net inside attribute amount is $100, the sum of S's money ($40 from the sale of Asset 3) and its basis in its assets ($60 (the sum of Asset 1's basis of $0 and Asset 2's basis of $60)). S's $100 net inside attribute amount is allocable entirely to the sole outstanding S share. Thus, the share's disconformity amount is the excess of $140 over $100, or $40. The lesser of the share's net positive adjustment, $40, and its disconformity amount, $40, is $40. Accordingly, the basis in the share is reduced by $40, from $140 to $100.

(D) Application of paragraph (d) of this section. Because M's sale of the S share is not a transfer of a loss share after the application of this paragraph (c), paragraph (d) of this section does not apply to the transfer.

(iii) Recognition of income earned after S becomes a member. The facts are the same as in paragraph (ii)(A) of this Example 3, except that instead of creating Asset 3, S earns $40 of income from services provided in year 3. Because the net positive adjustment includes items of income as well as items of gain, the results are the same as those described in paragraph (ii) of this Example 3.

Example (4). Computing the disconformity amount. (i) Unrecognized loss reflected in stock basis. (A) Facts. M owns the sole outstanding share of S stock with a basis of $100. S owns two assets, Asset 1 with a basis of $20 and a value of $60, and Asset 2 with a basis of $60 and a value of $40. In year 1, S sells Asset 1 for $60, recognizing a $40 gain. On December 31, year 1, M sells the S share for $100. After taking into account the effects of all applicable rules of law, M's basis in the S share is $140 (M's original $100 basis increased under Sec. 1.1502-32 by $40, the share's allocable portion of the gain recognized on the sale of Asset 1). M's sale of the S share is a transfer of a loss share and therefore subject to this section.

(B) Application of paragraph (b) of this section. Although the transfer is subject to this section, there is no basis redetermination under paragraph (b) of this section because there is only one share of S stock outstanding (and so there can be no disparity among members' bases in common shares and there are no outstanding preferred shares with respect to which there can be unrecognized gain or loss). See paragraph (b)(1)(ii)(A) of this section. Therefore, after the application of paragraph (b) of this section, the share is still a loss share and, as such, subject to this paragraph (c).

(C) Basis reduction under this paragraph (c). Under this paragraph (c), M's basis in the S share, $140, is reduced, but not below the share's $100 value, by the lesser of the share's net positive adjustment and disconformity amount. The share's net positive adjustment is $40 (the year 1 investment adjustment). The share's disconformity amount is the excess of its basis, $140, over its allocable portion of S's net inside attribute amount. S's net inside attribute amount is $120, the sum of S's money ($60 from the sale of Asset 1) and S's basis in Asset 2, $60. S's net inside attribute amount is allocable entirely to the sole outstanding S share. Thus, the share's disconformity amount is $20, the excess of $140 over $120. The lesser of the share's net positive adjustment, $40, and its disconformity amount, $20, is $20. Accordingly, the basis in the share is reduced by $20, from $140 to $120.

(D) Application of paragraph (d) of this section. After the application of this paragraph (c), M's sale of the S share is still a transfer of a loss share, and, accordingly, S's attributes (to the extent of the $20 duplicated loss) are subject to reduction under paragraph (d) of this section.

(ii) Loss carryover. The facts are the same as in paragraph (i)(A) of this Example 4, except that Asset 2 has a basis of $0 (rather than $60) and S has a $60 loss carryover (as defined in paragraph (f)(6) of this section). The analysis is the same as paragraph (i) of this Example 4. Furthermore, the analysis of the application of this paragraph (c) would be the same if the $60 loss carryover were subject to a section 382 limitation from a prior ownership change, or if, instead, the $60 loss carryover were subject to the limitation in § 1.1502-21(c) on losses carried from separate return limitation years.

(iii) Liabilities. The facts are the same as in paragraph (i)(A) of this Example 4, except that S borrows $100 before M sells the S share. S's net inside attribute amount remains $120, computed as the sum of S's money ($160, $60 from the sale of Asset 1 plus the $100 borrowed) and S's basis in Asset 2, $60, less its liabilities, $100. Thus, the S share's disconformity amount remains the excess of $140 over $120, or $20. The results are the same as in paragraph (i) of this Example 4.

Example (5). Computing the allocable portion of the net inside attribute amount. (i) Facts. On January 1, year 1, M owns all five outstanding shares of S stock with a basis of $20 per share. S owns Asset with a basis of $0. In year 1, S sells Asset for $100, recognizing a $100 gain. On December 31, year 1, M sells one of the S shares, Share 1, for $20. After taking into account the effects of all applicable rules of law, M's basis in Share 1 is $40 (M's original $20 basis increased under Sec. 1.1502-32 by $20 (the share's allocable portion of the gain recognized on the sale of Asset)). M's sale of Share 1 is a transfer of a loss share and therefore subject to this section.

(ii) Application of paragraph (b) of this section. Although the transfer is subject to this section, basis is not redetermined under paragraph (b) of this section because there is no disparity among M's bases in shares of S common stock and there are no shares of S preferred stock outstanding (so there can be no unrecognized gain or loss with respect to preferred shares). See paragraph (b)(1)(ii)(A) of this section. After the application of paragraph (b) of this section, M's sale of Share 1 is still a transfer of a loss share and therefore subject to this paragraph (c).

(iii) Basis reduction under this paragraph (c). Under this paragraph (c), M's $40 basis in Share 1 is reduced, but not below its $20 value by the lesser of the share's net positive adjustment and disconformity amount. Share 1's net positive adjustment is $20 (the year 1 investment adjustment). Share 1's disconformity amount is the excess of its $40 basis over its allocable portion of S's net inside attribute amount. S's net inside attribute amount is equal to the amount of S's money ($100 from the sale of the asset). Share 1's allocable portion of S's $100 net inside attribute amount is $20 (1/ 5 x $100). Thus, Share 1's disconformity amount is the excess of $40 over $20, or $20. The lesser of the share's $20 net positive adjustment and its $20 disconformity amount is $20. Accordingly, the basis in the share is reduced by $20, from $40 to $20.

(iv) Application of paragraph (d) of this section. Because M's sale of Share 1 is not a transfer of a loss share after the application of this paragraph (c), paragraph (d) of this section does not apply to the transfer.

Example (6). Liabilities. (i) In general. (A) Facts. On January 1, year 1, M purchases the sole outstanding share of S stock for $100. At that time, S owns Asset, with a basis of $0 and value of $100, and $100 cash. S also has a $100 liability. In year 1, S declares and makes a $60 dividend distribution to M and recognizes $20 of income. The value of Asset declines to $60 and, on December 31, year 1, M sells the S share for $20. After taking into account the effects of all applicable rules of law, M's basis in the S share is $60 (M's original $100 basis decreased under Sec. 1.1502-32 by $40 (the net of the $60 distribution and the $20 income recognized)). M's sale of the S share is a transfer of a loss share and therefore subject to this section.

(B) Application of paragraph (b) of this section. Although the transfer is subject to this section, there is no basis redetermination under paragraph (b) of this section because there is only one share of S stock outstanding (and so there can be no disparity among members' bases in common shares and there are no outstanding preferred shares with respect to which there can be unrecognized gain or loss). See paragraph (b)(1)(ii)(A) of this section. Therefore, after the application of paragraph (b) of this section, the share is still a loss share and, as such, subject to this paragraph (c).

(C) Basis reduction under this paragraph (c). Under this paragraph (c), M's basis in the S share, $60, is reduced, but not below value, $20, by the lesser of the share's net positive adjustment and disconformity amount. The share's net positive adjustment is $20 (the year 1 investment adjustment, as defined in paragraph (b)(1)(iii) of this section). The share's disconformity amount is the excess of its basis, $60, over its allocable portion of S's net inside attribute amount. S's net inside attribute amount is negative $40, computed as the sum of S's money ($60 ($100 less the $60 distribution plus the $20 income recognized)) and S's basis in Asset, $0, less S's liability, $100. S's net inside attribute amount is allocable entirely to the sole outstanding S share. Thus, the share's disconformity amount is the excess of $60 over negative $40, or $100. The lesser of the share's net positive adjustment, $20, and its disconformity amount, $100, is $20. Accordingly, the basis in the share is reduced by $20, from $60 to $40.

(D) Application of paragraph (d) of this section. After the application of this paragraph (c), the S share is still a loss share and, accordingly, S's attributes are subject to reduction under paragraph (d) of this section. No adjustment is required under paragraph (d) of this section, however, because there is no aggregate inside loss. See paragraph (d)(3)(iii) of this section.

(ii) Excluded cancellation of indebtedness income—insufficient attributes available for reduction under sections 108 and 1017, and § 1.1502-28. (A) Facts. The facts are the same as in paragraph (i)(A) of this Example 6, except that M does not sell the S share. Instead, in year 4, Asset is destroyed in a fire and S spends its $60 on deductible expenses that are not absorbed by the group. S's loss becomes part of the consolidated net operating loss (CNOL). In year 5, S becomes insolvent and S's debt is discharged. Because of S's insolvency, S's discharge of indebtedness income is excluded under section 108 and, as a result, S's attributes are subject to reduction under sections 108 and 1017, and § 1.1502-28. S's only attribute is the portion of the CNOL attributable to S, $60, and it is reduced to $0. There are no other consolidated attributes. In year 5, the S stock (which is treated as a capital asset) becomes worthless under section 165, taking into account § 1.1502-80(c). After taking into account the effects of all applicable rules of law, M's basis in the S share is $60 (M's original $100 basis decreased under § 1.1502-32 by the year 1 investment adjustment of $40 (the net of the $60 distribution and the $20 income recognized). The investment adjustment for year 5 is $0 (the net of the $60 tax exempt income from the excluded COD applied to reduce attributes and the $60 noncapital, nondeductible expense from the reduction of S's portion of the CNOL). Under paragraph (f)(10)(i)(D) of this section, a share is transferred on the last day of the taxable year during which it becomes worthless under section 165 if the share is treated as a capital asset, or the date the share becomes worthless if the share is not treated as a capital asset, taking into account § 1.1502-80(c). Accordingly, M transfers the loss share of S stock on December 31, year 5, and the transfer is therefore subject to this section.

(B) Application of paragraph (b) of this section. Although the transfer is subject to this section, there is no basis redetermination under paragraph (b) of this section for the reasons set forth in paragraph (i)(B) of this Example 6. Therefore, after the application of paragraph (b) of this section, the share is still a loss share and, as such, subject to this paragraph (c).

(C) Basis reduction under this paragraph (c). Under this paragraph (c), M's basis in its S share, $60, is reduced, but not below value, $0, by the lesser of the share's net positive adjustment and disconformity amount. The share's net positive adjustment is $20 (the year 1 investment adjustment, as defined in paragraph (b)(1)(iii) of this section). The share's disconformity amount is the excess of its basis, $60, over its allocable portion of S's net inside attribute amount. S's net inside attribute amount is $0. (The effects of the attribute reduction required under sections 108 and 1017 and § 1.1502-28 are taken into account in applying this section; therefore, for purposes of this section, S's portion of the CNOL is treated as eliminated under section 108 and § 1.1502-28.) S's net inside attribute amount is allocable entirely to the sole outstanding S share. Thus, the share's disconformity amount is the excess of $60 over $0, or $60. The lesser of the share's net positive adjustment, $20, and its disconformity amount, $60, is $20. Accordingly, the basis in the share is reduced by $20, from $60 to $40, immediately before the transfer.

(D) Application of paragraph (d) of this section. After the application of this paragraph (c), the S share is still a loss share, and, accordingly, S's attributes are subject to reduction under paragraph (d) of this section. No adjustment is required under paragraph (d) of this section, however, because there is no aggregate inside loss. See paragraph (d)(3)(iii) of this section.

(iii) Excluded cancellation of indebtedness income—full attribute reduction under sections 108 and 1017, and § 1.1502-28 (using attributes attributable to another member). (A) Facts. The facts are the same as in paragraph (ii)(A) of this Example 6 except that M loses the $60 distributed in year 1 and the group does not absorb the loss. Thus, as of December 31, year 5, the CNOL is $120, attributable $60 to S and $60 to P. As a result, under § 1.1502-28(a)(4), after the portion of the CNOL attributable to S is reduced to $0, the remaining $40 of excluded COD applies to the portion of the CNOL attributable to P, reducing it from $60 to $20. After taking into account the effects of all applicable rules of law, M's basis in the S share at the end of year 5 is $100 (M's original $100 basis decreased under Sec. 1.1502-32 by $40 at the end of the year 1 and then increased under Sec. 1.1502-32 by $40 at end of the year 5 (the net of the $100 tax exempt income from the excluded COD applied to reduce attributes and the $60 noncapital, nondeductible expense from the reduction of S's portion of the CNOL)). Under paragraph (f)(10)(i)(D) of this section, a share is transferred on the last day of the taxable year during which it becomes worthless under section 165 if the share is treated as a capital asset, or the date the share becomes worthless if the share is not treated as a capital asset, taking into account § 1.1502-80(c). Accordingly, M transfers the loss share of S stock on December 31, year 5, and the transfer is therefore subject to this section.

(B) Application of paragraph (b) of this section. Although the transfer is subject to this section, there is no basis redetermination under paragraph (b) of this section for the reasons set forth in paragraph (i)(B) of this Example 6. Therefore, after the application of paragraph (b) of this section, the share is still a loss share and, as such, subject to this paragraph (c).

(C) Basis reduction under this paragraph (c). Under this paragraph (c), M's basis in the S share, $100, is reduced, but not below value, $0, by the lesser of the share's net positive adjustment and disconformity amount. The share's net positive adjustment is $60 (the sum of the year 1 investment adjustment, as defined in paragraph (b)(1)(iii) of this section, $20, and the year 5 investment adjustment, $40). The share's disconformity amount is the excess of its basis, $100, over its allocable portion of S's net inside attribute amount. S's net inside attribute amount is $0 (taking into account the effects of the attribute reduction required under sections 108 and 1017 and § 1.1502-28). S's net inside attribute amount is allocable entirely to the sole outstanding S share. The share's disconformity amount is therefore $100. The lesser of the share's net positive adjustment, $60, and its disconformity amount, $100, is $60. Accordingly, M's basis in the share is reduced by $60, from $100 to $40, immediately before the transfer.

(D) Application of paragraph (d) of this section. After the application of this paragraph (c), the S share is still a loss share, and, accordingly, S's attributes are subject to reduction under paragraph (d) of this section. No adjustment is required under paragraph (d) of this section, however, because there is no aggregate inside loss. See paragraph (d)(3)(iii) of this section.

Example (7). Lower-tier subsidiary (no transfer of lower-tier stock). (i) Facts. M owns the sole outstanding share of S stock with a basis of $160. S owns two assets, Asset 1 with a basis and value of $100, and the sole outstanding share of S1 stock with a basis of $60. S1 owns one asset, Asset 2, with a basis of $20 and value of $60. In year 1, S1 sells Asset 2 to X for $60, recognizing a $40 gain. On December 31, year 1, M sells its S share to Y, a member of another consolidated group, for $160. After taking into account the effects of all applicable rules of law, M's basis in the S share is $200 (M's original $160 basis increased under § 1.1502-32 by $40 (to reflect the tier-up of the adjustment to S's basis in the S1 stock for the gain recognized on S1's sale of Asset 2)). M's sale of the S share is a transfer of a loss share and therefore subject to this section. (S does not transfer the S1 share because S and S1 are members of the same group following the transfer. See paragraph (f)(10) of this section.)

(ii) Application of paragraph (b) of this section. Although the transfer is subject to this section, there is no basis redetermination under paragraph (b) of this section because there is only one share of S stock outstanding (and so there can be no disparity among members' bases in common shares and there are no outstanding preferred shares with respect to which there can be unrecognized gain or loss). See paragraph (b)(1)(ii)(A) of this section. Therefore, after the application of paragraph (b) of this section, the share is still a loss share and, as such, subject to this paragraph (c).

(iii) Basis reduction under this paragraph (c). (A) In general. Under this paragraph (c), M's basis in the S share, $200, is reduced, but not below value, $160, by the lesser of the share's net positive adjustment and disconformity amount. The S share's net positive adjustment is $40. The share's disconformity amount is the excess of its basis, $200, over the share's allocable portion of S's net inside attribute amount. S's net inside attribute amount is the sum of S's basis in Asset 1, $100, and S's basis in the S1 share.

(B) S's basis in the S1 share. Although S's actual basis in the S1 share is $100 (S's original $60 basis increased under § 1.1502-32 by $40 (the share's allocable portion of the gain recognized on the sale of Asset 2)), for purposes of computing the S share's disconformity amount, S's net inside attribute amount is determined by treating S's basis in the S1 share as tentatively reduced by the lesser of the S1 share's net positive adjustment and the S1 share's disconformity amount. The S1 share's net positive adjustment is $40 (the year 1 investment adjustment). The S1 share's disconformity amount is the excess of its basis, $100, over the share's allocable portion of S1's net inside attribute amount. S1's net inside attribute amount is equal to the amount of S1's money ($60 from the sale of Asset 2), and is allocable entirely to the sole outstanding S1 share. Thus, the S1 share's disconformity amount is the excess of $100 over $60, or $40. The lesser of the S1 share's net positive adjustment, $40, and its disconformity amount, $40, is $40. Accordingly, for purposes of computing the disconformity amount of the S share, S's net inside attribute amount is determined by treating S's basis in its S1 share as tentatively reduced by $40, from $100 to $60.

(C) The disconformity amount of M's S share. S's net inside attribute amount is treated as the sum of its basis in Asset 1, $100, and its tentatively reduced basis in the S1 share, $60, or $160. S's net inside attribute amount is allocable entirely to the sole outstanding S share. Thus, the S share's disconformity amount is the excess of $200 over $160, or $40.

(D) Amount of reduction. M's basis in its S share is reduced by the lesser of the S share's net positive adjustment, $40, and disconformity amount, $40, or $40. Accordingly, M's basis in the S share is reduced by $40, from $200 to $160.

(E) Effect on S's basis in its S1 share. The tentative reduction under this paragraph (c) has no effect on S's actual basis in the S1 share. Thus, after the application of this paragraph (c), S owns the S1 share with a basis of $100 (S's original $60 basis increased under § 1.1502-32 by $40 (the share's allocable portion of the gain recognized on the sale of Asset 2)).

(iv) Application of paragraph (d) of this section. Because M's sale of the S share is not a transfer of a loss share after the application of this paragraph (c), paragraph (d) of this section does not apply to the transfer.

(d) Attribute reduction to prevent duplication of loss. *(1) In general.* The rules of this paragraph (d) reduce attributes of S and its lower-tier subsidiaries to the extent they duplicate a net loss on shares of S stock transferred by members in one transaction. This rule furthers single-entity principles by preventing S (or its lower-tier subsidiaries) from using deductions and losses to the extent that the group or its members (including former members) have either used, or preserved for later use, a corresponding loss in S shares.

(2) Attribute reduction rule. (i) General rule. If a transferred share is a loss share after taking into account the effects of all applicable rules of law, including any adjustments under paragraph (b), (c), or (d)(5)(iii) of this section, S's attributes are reduced by S's attribute reduction amount immediately before the transfer. S's attribute reduction amount is determined under paragraph (d)(3) of this section and applied in accordance with the provisions of paragraphs (d)(4), (d)(5), and (d)(6) of this section. In addition, paragraph (d)(7) of this section provides for additional attribute reduction in the case of certain transfers due to worthlessness and certain transfers not followed by a separate return year.

(ii) Attribute reduction amount less than five percent of value. This paragraph (d) generally does not apply to a transaction if the aggregate attribute reduction amount in the transaction is less than five percent of the aggregate value of the shares transferred by members in the transaction. However, in such a case, P may elect to apply this paragraph (d) to the transaction. If such an election is made, this paragraph (d) will apply with respect to the entire aggregate attribute reduction amount determined in the transaction. Such an election is made in the manner provided in paragraph (e)(5) of this section.

(3) Attribute reduction amount. (i) In general. S's attribute reduction amount is the lesser of—

(A) The net stock loss (as defined in paragraph (d)(3)(ii) of this section); and

(B) S's aggregate inside loss (as defined in paragraph (d)(3)(iii) of this section).

(ii) Net stock loss. The net stock loss is the excess, if any, of—

(A) The aggregate basis of all shares of S stock transferred by members in the transaction; over

(B) The aggregate value of those shares.

(iii) Aggregate inside loss. (A) In general. S's aggregate inside loss is the excess, if any, of—

(1) S's net inside attribute amount; over

(2) The value of all outstanding shares of S stock.

(B) Net inside attribute amount. S's net inside attribute amount generally has the same meaning as in paragraph (c)(5) of this section. However, if S holds stock of a lower-tier subsidiary, the provisions of paragraph (d)(5) of this section (and not the provisions of paragraph (c)(6) of this section) modify the computation of S's net inside attribute amount for purposes of this paragraph (d).

(iv) Lower-tier subsidiaries. See paragraph (d)(5) of this section for special rules relating to the application of this paragraph (d) if S owns shares of stock of a subsidiary.

(4) Application of attribute reduction amount. (i) Attributes available for reduction. S's attributes available for reduction under this paragraph (d) are—

(A) Category A. Capital loss carryovers;

(B) Category B. Net operating loss carryovers;

(C) Category C. Deferred deductions; and

(D) Category D. Basis of assets other than assets identified as Class I assets in § 1.338-6(b)(1).

(ii) Rules of application. (A) Category A, Category B, and Category C attributes. S's attribute reduction amount is first allocated and applied to reduce the attributes in Category A, Category B, and Category C.

(1) Attribute reduction amount less than total attributes in Category A, Category B, and Category C. If S's attribute reduction amount is less than S's total attributes in Category A, Category B, and Category C, all of S's attribute reduction amount will be applied to reduce such attributes. However, P may specify the allocation of S's attribute reduction amount among such attributes. An election to specify the allocation of S's attribute reduction amount is made in the manner provided in paragraph (e)(5) of this section. To the extent that P does not specify an allocation of S's attribute reduction amount, S's attribute reduction amount will be applied to reduce any Category A attributes not reduced as a result of the specific allocation of S's attribute reduction amount, from oldest to newest, until they are eliminated. Then, any remaining attribute reduction amount will be applied to reduce any Category B attributes not reduced as a result of the specific allocation of S's attribute reduction amount, from oldest to newest, until they are eliminated. Finally, any remaining attribute reduction amount will be applied to reduce any Category C attributes not reduced as a result of the specific allocation of S's attribute reduction amount, proportionately.

(2) Attribute reduction amount not less than the total attributes in Category A, Category B, and Category C. If S's attribute reduction amount equals or exceeds S's total attributes in Category A, Category B, and Category C, all such attributes are eliminated and any remaining attribute reduction amount is allocated and applied as provided in paragraphs (d)(4)(ii)(B) and (d)(4)(ii)(C) of this section.

(B) Category D attributes. Any attribute reduction amount not applied to reduce S's Category A, Category B, and Category C attributes is allocated and applied as provided in this paragraph (d)(4)(ii)(B) and, to the extent applicable, paragraph (d)(5) of this section.

(1) Allocation if S holds stock of another subsidiary. If S holds shares of stock of another subsidiary, the attribute reduction amount not applied to reduce S's Category A, Category B, and Category C attributes is first allocated between S's shares of lower-tier subsidiary stock and S's other Category D assets in the manner provided in paragraph (d)(5)(ii) of this section. S's attribute reduction amount allocated to shares of lower-tier subsidiary stock is applied to reduce S's bases in those shares, becomes an attribute reduction amount of the lower-tier subsidiary, and, subject to certain limitations, reduces the lower-tier subsidiary's attributes. See paragraphs (d)(5)(iii) through (d)(5)(vi) of this section.

(2) Allocation and application of attribute reduction amount not applied to lower-tier subsidiary stock. Any portion of S's attribute reduction amount not applied to reduce S's Category A, Category B, and Category C attributes and not allocated to lower-tier subsidiary stock is allocated to S's Category D assets other than lower-tier subsidiary stock in the manner provided in this paragraph (d)(4)(ii)(B)(2). Such amount is first allocated to S's bases (if any) in its assets identified as Class VII assets in § 1.338-6(b)(2)(vii). If the attribute reduction amount allocated to Class VII assets is less than S's aggregate basis in those assets, it is applied proportionately (by basis) to reduce the bases of such assets. If the attribute reduction amount allocated to Class VII assets equals or exceeds S's aggregate basis in those assets, it is applied to reduce the bases of such assets to zero. Any remaining attribute reduction amount is then allocated and applied in the same manner to reduce S's bases (if any) in assets identified as Class VI assets in § 1.338-6(b)(2)(vi), and then to reduce S's bases (if any) in its assets identified in § 1.338-6(b)(2) as Class V, Class IV, Class III, and Class II, successively.

(C) Attribute reduction amount exceeding attributes available for reduction. If the amount to be allocated and applied to attributes in Category D other than lower-tier subsidiary stock exceeds the amount of attributes in that category, then—

(1) To the extent of any liabilities of S that are not taken into account for tax purposes before the transfer, such excess amount is suspended. The suspended amount is applied proportionately to reduce any amounts attributable to S that would be deductible or capitalizable as a result of such liabilities being taken into account by S or any other person. Solely for purposes of this paragraph (d)(4)(ii)(C)(1) and paragraph (d)(5)(ii)(B) of this section, the term liability means any liability or obligation the satisfaction of which would be required to be capitalized as an assumed liability by a person that purchased all of S's assets and assumed all of S's liabilities in a single transaction.

(2) To the extent such excess amount is greater than any amount suspended under paragraph (d)(4)(ii)(C)(1) of this section, it is disregarded and has no further effect.

(iii) Time and effect of attribute reduction. In general, the reduction of attributes is effective immediately before the transfer of a loss share of S stock. If the reduction to a member's basis in a share of lower-tier subsidiary stock exceeds the basis of that share, to the extent the excess is not restored under paragraph (d)(5)(vi) of this section it is an excess loss account in that share (and such excess loss account is not taken into account under § 1.1502-19 or otherwise as a result of the transaction). The reductions to attributes required under this paragraph (d)(4), including by reason of paragraph (d)(5)(v) of this section (tier down of attribute reduction amounts to lower-tier subsidiaries), are not noncapital, nondeductible expenses described in § 1.1502-32(b)(2)(iii).

(5) Special rules applicable if S holds stock of another subsidiary. If S holds shares of stock of any other subsidiary (S1) as of a transfer of loss shares of S stock, the rules of this paragraph (d)(5) apply with respect to each such subsidiary.

(i) Treatment of lower-tier subsidiary stock for computation of S's attribute reduction amount. For purposes of determining S's net inside attribute amount and attribute reduction amount under paragraph (d)(3) of this section—

(A) Single share. All of S's shares of S1 stock held as of the transfer of S stock (whether or not transferred in, or held by S immediately after, the transaction) are treated as a single share of stock (generally referred to as the S1 stock); and

(B) Deemed basis. S's basis in its S1 stock is treated as its deemed basis in the stock, which is equal to the greater of—

(1) The sum of S's basis in each share of S1 stock (adjusted to reflect any gain or loss recognized on the transfer of any S1 shares in the transaction, whether allowed or disallowed); and

(2) The portion of S1's net inside attribute amount allocable to S's shares of S1 stock.

(C) Multiple tiers. For purposes of computing deemed basis under paragraph (d)(5)(i)(B) of this section, a subsidiary's basis in stock of a lower-tier subsidiary is the deemed basis in that lower-tier subsidiary stock. Thus, if stock is held in multiple tiers, the computation of deemed basis begins at the lowest tier, so that the computation of deemed basis at each tier takes into account the deemed basis of all lower-tier shares.

(ii) Allocation of S's attribute reduction amount between lower-tier subsidiary stock and other Category D assets. The portion of S's attribute reduction amount that is not applied to reduce S's Category A, Category B, and Category C attributes must be allocated between each of S's deemed single shares of S1 stock and all of S's other Category D assets. For this purpose, S's Category D assets other than lower-tier subsidiary stock are treated as one asset with a basis equal to the aggregate bases of all Category D assets other than lower-tier subsidiary stock (non-stock Category D asset). S's attribute reduction amount is allocated proportionately (by basis) between (among) the non-stock Category D asset and S's deemed single share(s) of subsidiary stock. (See paragraphs (d)(4)(ii)(B)(2) and (d)(4)(ii)(C) of this section regarding the portion of S's attribute reduction amount allocated to the Category D assets other than lower-tier subsidiary stock.) For allocation purposes, S's basis in each deemed single share of S1 stock is its deemed basis (determined under paragraphs (d)(5)(i)(B) and (d)(5)(i)(C) of this section), reduced by—

(A) The value of S's transferred shares of S1 stock; and

(B) The nontransferred S1 shares' allocable portion of the excess of S1's non-loss assets over S1's liabilities (including liabilities described in paragraph (d)(4)(ii)(C)(1) of this section). For this purpose, S1's non-loss assets are—

(1) S1's assets identified as Class I assets in § 1.338-6(b)(1),

(2) The value of S1's transferred shares of lower-tier subsidiary stock, and

(3) The nontransferred lower-tier subsidiary shares' allocable portions of lower-tier non-loss assets (net of liabilities, including liabilities described in paragraph (d)(4)(ii)(C)(1) of this section) of all lower-tier subsidiaries.

(iii) Application of attribute reduction amount to S's S1 stock. The portion of S's attribute reduction amount allocated under paragraph (d)(5)(ii) of this section to each deemed single share of S1 stock (allocated attribute reduction amount) is apportioned among, and applied to reduce S's bases in, individual S1 shares in accordance with the following—

(A) No portion of the allocated attribute reduction amount is apportioned to an individual share of transferred S1 stock if gain or loss is recognized on its transfer (recognition transfer);

(B) The allocated attribute reduction amount is apportioned among all of S's other shares of S1 stock in a manner that, first reduces the loss in and disparity among S's bases in loss shares of S1 preferred stock to the greatest extent possible, and then reduces the disparity among S's bases in the shares of S1 common stock (other than those transferred in a recognition transfer) to the greatest extent possible;

(C) The allocated attribute reduction amount apportioned to an individual S1 share is applied to reduce the basis of that share to, but not below, value if the share is either a preferred share or a common share that is transferred other than in a recognition transfer; and

(D) The allocated attribute reduction amount apportioned to an individual S1 share is applied to reduce the basis of that share without regard to value if the share is a common share that is not transferred in the transaction.

(iv) Unapplied allocated attribute reduction amount. Any portion of the allocated attribute reduction amount that is not applied to reduce S's basis in a share of S1 stock has no effect on any other attributes of S, it is not a noncapital, nondeductible expense of S, and it does not cause S to recognize income or gain. However, such amounts continue to be part of the allocated attribute reduction amount for purposes of the tier down rule in paragraph (d)(5)(v) of this section.

(v) Tier down of attribute reduction amount. (A) General rule. The allocated attribute reduction amount of each deemed single share of S1 stock is an attribute reduction amount of S1 (tier-down attribute reduction amount). Accordingly, the tier-down attribute reduction amount, in combination with any attribute reduction amount computed with respect to the transferred S1 shares (if any) (direct S1 attribute reduction amount), applies to reduce S1's attributes under the provisions of this paragraph (d). The tier-down attribute reduction amount is an attribute reduction amount of S1 that must be allocated to S1's assets, and may become an allocated attribute reduction amount of lower-tier subsidiary stock (and thus a tier-down attribute reduction amount of a lower-tier subsidiary), even if its application to S1's attributes is limited under paragraph (d)(5)(v)(B) of this section.

(B) Conforming limitation on reduction of lower-tier subsidiary's attributes. Notwithstanding the general rule in paragraph (d)(5)(v)(A) of this section, and unless P elects otherwise in the manner provided in paragraph (e)(5) of this section, the application of S1's tier-down attribute reduction amount to S1's attributes is limited to an amount equal to the excess of the portion of S1's net inside attribute amount that is allocable to all S1 shares held by members as of the transaction (whether or not transferred in the transaction) over the sum of—

(1) Any direct S1 attribute reduction amount;

(2) The aggregate value of all S1 shares transferred by members in the transaction with respect to which gain or loss was recognized (recognition transfer);

(3) The sum of all members' bases (after any reduction under this section, including this paragraph (d)) in any shares of S1 stock transferred by members in the transaction (other than in a recognition transfer), reduced by any direct S1 attribute reduction amount computed with respect to the transfer of such S1 shares; and

(4) The sum of all members' bases (after any reduction under this section, including this paragraph (d)) in any nontransferred shares of S1 stock held as of the transaction.

(vi) Stock basis restoration. (A) In general. After paragraph (d)(5)(v) of this section has applied with respect to all shares of subsidiary stock transferred in the transaction, lower-tier subsidiary stock basis is restored under this paragraph (d)(5)(vi). Under this paragraph (d)(5)(vi), the reductions to members' bases in shares of lower-tier subsidiary stock under paragraph (d)(5)(iii) of this section are reversed to the extent necessary to restore such bases to an amount that conforms the basis of each such share to its allocable portion of the subsidiary's net inside attribute amount, taking into account any reductions under this paragraph (d). Restoration adjustments are first made at the lowest tier and then at each next higher tier successively. Restoration adjustments do not tier up to affect the bases of higher-tier shares. Rather, restoration is computed and applied separately at each tier. For purposes of this rule, when computing a subsidiary's net inside attribute amount—

(1) The subsidiary's basis in stock of a lower-tier subsidiary is the actual basis of the stock after application of this paragraph (d); and

(2) Any attribute reduction amount allocated to the subsidiary's Category D assets other than lower-tier subsidiary stock that is suspended under paragraph (d)(4)(ii)(C)(1) of this section is treated as reducing the subsidiary's net inside attribute amount.

(B) Election not to restore basis. Notwithstanding paragraph (d)(5)(vi)(A) of this section, P may elect not to restore basis in stock of a lower-tier subsidiary that was reduced under paragraph (d)(5)(iii) of this section. An election not to restore lower-tier subsidiary stock basis is made in the manner provided in paragraph (e)(5) of this section.

(6) Elections to reduce the potential for loss duplication. (i) In general. Notwithstanding the general operation of this paragraph (d), P may elect to reduce the potential for loss duplication, and thereby reduce or avoid attribute reduction. To the extent of S's attribute reduction amount tentatively computed without regard to any election under this paragraph (d)(6), P may elect—

(A) To reduce all or any portion (including any portion in excess of a specified amount) of members' bases in transferred loss shares of S stock;

(B) To reattribute all or any portion (including any portion in excess of a specified amount) of S's Category A, Category B, and Category C attributes (including such attributes of lower-tier subsidiaries), to the extent they would otherwise be subject to reduction under this paragraph (d); or

(C) Any combination thereof.

(ii) Manner and effect of election. An election to reduce loss duplication under this paragraph (d)(6) is made in the manner provided in paragraph (e)(5) of this section. Although such elections are irrevocable, they have no effect—

(A) If there is no attribute reduction amount; or

(B) To the extent S's attribute reduction amount is less than the amount specified in the election.

(iii) Order of application. (A) Stock of one subsidiary transferred in the transaction. If shares of stock of only one subsidiary are transferred in the transaction, any stock basis reduction and reattribution of attributes (including from lower-tier subsidiaries) is deemed to occur immediately before the application of this paragraph (d). If a transferred share is still a loss share after giving effect to this election, the other provisions of this paragraph (d) then apply with respect to that share.

(B) Stock of multiple subsidiaries transferred in the transaction. If shares of stock of more than one subsidiary are transferred in the transaction and elections under this paragraph (d)(6) are made with respect to transfers of stock of subsidiaries in multiple tiers, effect is given to the elections from the lowest tier to the highest tier in the manner provided in this paragraph (d)(6)(iii)(B). The amount of the election for the transfer at the lowest tier is determined by applying this paragraph (d) with respect to the transferred loss shares of this lowest-tier subsidiary immediately after applying paragraphs (b) and (c) of this section to the stock of such subsidiary. The effect of any stock basis reduction or reattribution of losses immediately tiers up under § 1.1502-32 to adjust members' bases in higher-tier shares. Elections and adjustments are then made with respect to transfers at each next higher tier successively.

(iv) Special rules for reattribution elections. (A) In general. Because the reattribution election is intended to provide the group a means to retain certain S attributes, and not to change the location of attributes where S continues to be a member of the same group as P, the election to reattribute attributes may only be made if S becomes a nonmember (within the meaning of § 1.1502-19(c)(2)) as a result of the transaction and S does not become a member of any group that includes P. The election to reattribute S's attributes can only be made for attributes in Category A, Category B, and Category C. The attributes that would otherwise be reduced under paragraph (d)(4) of this section may be reattributed to P. Accordingly, P may specify the attributes in Category A, Category B, and Category C to be reattributed. Such an election is made in the manner provided in paragraph (e)(5) of this section. To the extent that P elects to reattribute attributes but does not specify the attributes to be reattributed, any attributes not specifically reattributed will be reattributed in the default amount, order, and category described in paragraph (d)(4)(ii)(A)(1) of this section. P succeeds to reattributed attributes as if such attributes were succeeded to in a transaction to which section 381(a) applies. Any owner shift of the subsidiary (including any deemed owner shift resulting from section 382(g)(4)(D) or section 382(l)(3)) in connection with the transaction is not taken into account under section 382 with respect to the reattributed attributes. (See § 1.1502-96(d) for rules relating to section 382 and the reattribution of losses under this paragraph (d)(6).) The reattribution of S's attributes is a noncapital, nondeductible expense described in § 1.1502-32(b)(2)(iii). See § 1.1502-32(c)(1)(ii)(A) regarding special allocations applicable to such noncapital, nondeductible expense. If P elects to reattribute S attributes (including attributes of a lower-tier subsidiary) and reduce S stock basis, the reattribution is given effect before the stock basis reduction.

(B) Insolvency limitation. If S, or any higher-tier subsidiary, is insolvent within the meaning of section 108(d)(3) at the time of the transfer, S's losses may be reattributed only to the extent they exceed the sum of the separate insolvencies of any subsidiaries (taking into account only S and its higher-tier subsidiaries) that are insolvent. For purposes of determining insolvency, liabilities owed to higher-tier members are not taken into account, and stock of a subsidiary that is limited and preferred as to dividends and that is not owned by higher-tier members is treated as a liability to the extent of the amount of preferred distributions to which the stock would be entitled if the subsidiary were liquidated on the date of the transfer.

(C) Limitation on reattribution from lower-tier subsidiaries. P's ability to reattribute attributes of lower-tier subsidiaries is limited under this paragraph (d)(6)(iv)(C) in order to prevent circular computations of the attribute reduction amount. Accordingly, attributes that would otherwise be reduced as a result of tier-down attribute reduction under paragraph (d)(5)(v) of this section may only be reattributed to the extent that the reduction in the basis of any lower-tier subsidiary stock resulting from the noncapital, nondeductible expense (as allocated under § 1.1502-32(c)(1)(ii)(A)(2)) will not create an excess loss account in any such stock.

(v) Special rules for stock basis reduction elections. (A) In general. An election to reduce basis in S stock is made with respect to all members' bases in loss shares of S stock that are transferred in the transaction. The reduction is allocated among all such shares in proportion to the amount of loss on each share. This reduction in S stock basis is a noncapital, nondeductible expense described in § 1.1502-32(b)(2)(iii) of the transferring member.

(B) Adjustment to the attribute reduction amount. The attribute reduction amount (determined under paragraph (d)(3)(i) of this section) is treated as reduced by the amount of any elective reduction in the basis of the S stock under this paragraph (d)(6). Accordingly, the election to reduce stock basis under this paragraph (d)(6) is treated as reducing or eliminating the duplication even if the shares of S stock are loss shares after giving effect to the election.

(C) Deemed stock basis reduction election in the case of certain disallowed stock losses. If there is a net stock loss in transferred shares after taking into account any actual elections under this paragraph (d)(6), and the stock loss would otherwise be permanently disallowed (for example, under section 311(a)), P will be deemed to have made a stock basis reduction election equal to such net stock loss.

(7) Additional attribute reduction in the case of certain transfers due to worthlessness and certain transfers not followed by a separate return year. (i) In general. Notwithstanding any other provision of this paragraph (d), if a transfer is subject to this paragraph (d)(7) any of S's Category A, Category B, and Category C attributes not otherwise reduced or reattributed under this paragraph (d), and any credit carryover attributable to S, including any consolidated credits that would be apportioned to S under the principles of § 1.1502-79 if S had a separate return year, are eliminated. Attributes other than consolidated tax attributes are eliminated under this paragraph (d)(7)(i) immediately before the transfer subject to this paragraph (d)(7)(i). The elimination of attributes under this paragraph (d)(7)(i) is not a noncapital, nondeductible expense described in § 1.1502-32(b)(2)(iii).

(ii) Transfers subject to this paragraph (d)(7). A transfer is subject to this paragraph (d)(7) if—

(A) M transfers a share of S stock solely by reason of a transfer defined in paragraph (f)(10)(i)(D) of this section (worthlessness where the provisions of § 1.1502-80(c) are satisfied), M recognizes a net deduction or loss on the share, and S is a member of the group on the day following the last day of the group's taxable year during which the share becomes worthless under section 165 (taking into account the provisions of § 1.1502-80(c)), or

(B) M recognizes a net deduction or loss on the stock of S in a transaction in which S ceases to be a member and does not become a nonmember within the meaning of § 1.1502-19(c)(2).

(iii) Example. The application of this paragraph (d) to transfers due to worthlessness and to loss transfers not followed by separate return years is illustrated by the following example.

Example. (i) Worthlessness where S continues as a member. M owns the sole share of S stock. The share is worthless under section 165. In addition, S has disposed of all its assets within the meaning of § 1.1502-19(c)(1)(iii)(A) and therefore satisfies the provisions of § 1.1502-80(c). M claims a worthless securities deduction with respect to the share. The worthlessness is a transfer of the S share, a loss share, and therefore subject to this section. After the application of paragraphs (b) and (c) of this section, M's basis in the share (and therefore M's net stock loss) is $75. The portion of the consolidated net operating loss attributable to S is $100. Under the general rules of this paragraph (d), S's attribute reduction amount is $75 (the lesser of M's $75 net stock loss and S's $100 aggregate inside loss ($100 net inside attribute amount over $0 value of S share)). S's attributes are reduced by $75, from $100 to $25. In addition, if S remains a member of the P group, this paragraph (d)(7) applies to eliminate the remaining $25 of the consolidated net operating loss attributable to S because the S share is worthless, and M recognizes a deduction (taking into account § 1.1502-80(c)) with respect to the share. Accordingly, after the application of this section, M recognizes a $75 worthless securities deduction, S has $0 net inside attributes, and the consolidated net operating loss is reduced by a total of $100.

(ii) Dissolution of insolvent subsidiary. The facts are the same as in paragraph (i) of this Example, except that S is insolvent, does not dispose of all its assets within the meaning of § 1.1502-19(c)(1)(iii)(A), M causes S to be legally dissolved, and the S share held by M is cancelled without consideration. Under paragraph (d)(7)(ii)(B) of this section, the dissolution of S is subject to this paragraph (d)(7) and the result is the same as in paragraph (i) of this Example. The result would also be the same if instead of being legally dissolved, S was converted into an entity that is disregarded as separate from M.

(iii) Stock cancelled in connection with a section 381(a) transaction with another member. M owns the sole share of S common stock with a basis of $75. M1 owns the sole share of S preferred stock. The value of S's assets (net of liabilities) is less than the liquidation preference on the S preferred stock. In a reorganization described in section 368(a)(1)(D), S transfers all of its assets to M2 in exchange for M2 common stock and M2's assumption of S's liabilities, S distributes all of the M2 common stock received in the exchange to M1 in exchange for M1's S preferred stock, the S common stock held by M is cancelled without consideration, and S ceases to exist. Notwithstanding that M is not entitled to treat its common share of S stock as worthless until § 1.1502-80(c) is satisfied, M's share is transferred within the meaning of paragraph (f)(10)(i)(A) of this section because M ceases to own the share in a transaction in which, but for this section (and notwithstanding the deferral of any amount recognized on the transfer, other than by reason of § 1.1502-13), M would recognize a loss or deduction with respect to the share. Accordingly, there is a transfer of the S common share and this section applies to the transfer. There are no adjustments under paragraphs (b) or (c) of this section because no investment adjustments have been applied to the bases of the shares. The transfer of the S common stock is subject to the general rules of this paragraph (d), but is not subject to the additional attribute reduction under this paragraph (d)(7) because the transfer was not solely by reason of worthlessness where § 1.1502-80(c) is satisfied, and S did not cease to be a member because M2 is a successor to S.

(iv) Stock cancelled in connection with a section 381(a) transaction with a nonmember. The facts are the same as in paragraph (iii) of this Example, except that the S preferred share is held by X, instead of M2 acquiring S's assets, S merges into Y in a reorganization described in section 368(a)(1)(A), M1 receives all of the Y stock issued in the merger in exchange for M1's S preferred stock, and Y does not become a member as a result of the transaction. M treats the cancelled S common stock as worthless, and § 1.1502-80(c) is satisfied because S ceases to be a member. In this case, there is a transfer of M's S common share because it becomes worthless (taking into account § 1.1502-80(c)); because M ceases to own the share in a transaction in which, but for this section (and notwithstanding the deferral of any amount recognized on the transfer, other than by reason of § 1.1502-13), M would recognize a loss or deduction with respect to the share; and because M and S cease to be members of the same group. The transfer of the S common stock is subject to the general rules of this paragraph (d), but is not subject to the additional attribute reduction under this paragraph (d)(7) because the transfer was not solely by reason of worthlessness where § 1.1502-80(c) is satisfied and, although S did cease to be a member, S became a nonmember within the meaning of § 1.1502-19(c)(2) because Y is a successor to S.

(8) Examples. The application of this paragraph (d) is illustrated by the following examples:

Example (1). Computation of attribute reduction amount. (i) Transfer of all S shares. (A) Facts. M owns all 100 of the outstanding shares of S stock with a basis of $2 per share. S owns land with a basis of $100, has a $120 loss carryover, and has no liabilities. Each share has a value of $1. M sells 30 of the S shares to X for $30. As a result of the sale, M and S cease to be members of the same group. Accordingly, all 100 of the S shares are transferred. See paragraphs (f)(10)(i)(A), (f)(10)(i)(B), and (f)(10)(i)(C) (with respect to the 30 S shares sold to X) of this section. M's transfer of the S shares is a transfer of loss shares and therefore subject to this section.

(B) Application of paragraphs (b) and (c) of this section. Although the transfer is subject to this section, there is no basis redetermination under paragraph (b) of this section because there is no disparity among M's bases in shares of S common stock and there are no shares of S preferred stock outstanding (so there can be no unrecognized gain or loss on preferred stock). See paragraph (b)(1)(ii)(A) of this section. Therefore, after the application of paragraph (b) of this section, the share is still a loss share and, as such, subject to paragraph (c) of this section. No adjustment is required under paragraph (c) of this section because the net positive adjustment is $0. See paragraph (c)(3) of this section. Thus, after the application of paragraph (c) of this section, M's transfer of the S shares is still a transfer of loss shares and, accordingly, subject to this paragraph (d).

(C) Attribute reduction under this paragraph (d). Under this paragraph (d), S's attributes are reduced by S's attribute reduction amount. Paragraph (d)(3) of this section provides that S's attribute reduction amount is the lesser of the net stock loss and S's aggregate inside loss. The net stock loss is the excess of the $200 aggregate bases of the transferred shares over the $100 aggregate value of the transferred shares, or $100. S's aggregate inside loss is the excess of its $220 net inside attribute amount (the sum of the $100 basis in the land and the $120 loss carryover) over the $100 value of all outstanding S shares, or $120. The attribute reduction amount is therefore the lesser of the $100 net stock loss and the $120 aggregate inside loss, or $100. Under paragraph (d)(4) of this section, S's $100 attribute reduction amount is allocated and applied to reduce S's $120 loss carryover to $20. Under paragraph (d)(4)(iii) of this section, the reduction of the loss carryover is not a noncapital, nondeductible expense and has no effect on M's basis in the S stock.

(ii) Transfer of less than all S shares. (A) Facts. The facts are the same as in paragraph (i)(A) of this Example 1, except that M only sells 20 S shares to X. M's sale of the 20 S shares is a transfer of loss shares and therefore subject to this section. See paragraph (f)(10)(i)(A) and (f)(10)(i)(C) of this section. (There is no transfer of the remaining shares because S and M remain members of the same group.)

(B) Application of paragraphs (b) and (c) of this section. No adjustment is required under paragraph (b) or paragraph (c) of this section for the reasons set forth in paragraph (i)(B) of this Example 1. Thus, after the application of paragraph (c) of this section, M's transfer of the S shares is still a transfer of loss shares and, accordingly, subject to this paragraph (d).

(C) Attribute reduction under this paragraph (d). Under this paragraph (d), S's attributes are reduced by S's attribute reduction amount. Paragraph (d)(3) of this section provides that S's attribute reduction amount is the lesser of the net stock loss and S's aggregate inside loss. The net stock loss is $20, the excess of the $40 aggregate bases of the transferred shares over the $20 aggregate value of the transferred shares. S's aggregate inside loss is $120, the excess of its $220 net inside attribute amount (the sum of the $100 basis in the land and the $120 loss carryover) over the $100 value of all outstanding S shares. The attribute reduction amount is therefore $20, the lesser of the $20 net stock loss and the $120 aggregate inside loss. Under paragraph (d)(4) of this section, S's $20 attribute reduction amount is allocated and applied to reduce S's $120 loss carryover to $100.

Example (2). Proportionate allocation of attribute reduction amount. (i) Facts. M owns the sole outstanding share of S stock with a basis of $150. S owns land with a basis of $60, a factory with a basis of $30, publicly traded property with a basis of $30 and goodwill with a basis of $30. M sells its S share for $90. M's sale of the S share is a transfer of a loss share and therefore subject to this section. See paragraphs (f)(10)(i)(A), (f)(10)(i)(B), and (f)(10)(i)(C) of this section.

(ii) Application of paragraphs (b) and (c) of this section. Although the transfer is subject to this section, there is no basis redetermination under paragraph (b) of this section because there is only one share of S stock outstanding (and so there can be no disparity among members' bases in common shares and there are no outstanding preferred shares with respect to which there can be unrecognized gain or loss). See paragraph (b)(1)(ii)(A) of this section. Therefore, after the application of paragraph (b) of this section, the share is still a loss share and, as such, subject to paragraph (c) of this section. No adjustment is required under paragraph (c) of this section because both the disconformity amount and the net positive adjustment are $0. See paragraph (c)(3) of this section. Thus, after the application of paragraph (c) of this section, M's sale of the S share is still a transfer of a loss share and, accordingly, subject to this paragraph (d).

(iii) Attribute reduction under this paragraph (d). Under paragraph (d)(3) of this section, S's attribute reduction amount is determined to be $60, the lesser of the $60 net stock loss ($150 basis over $90 value) and S's $60 aggregate inside loss (the excess of S's $150 net inside attribute amount (the $60 basis of the land, plus the $30 basis of the factory, plus the $30 basis of the publicly traded property, plus the $30 basis of the goodwill) over the $90 value of the S share). Under paragraph (d)(4)(ii)(B)(2) of this section, the $60 attribute reduction amount is allocated and applied to reduce S's bases in its Category D assets, S's only attributes available for reduction, as follows:

Available attributes, basis in Category D assets	Attribute amount	Allocable portion of attribute reduction amount	Adjusted attribute amount
Class VII, Goodwill	$30	$30	$0
Class V:			
Land	60	(60/90 × 60) 40	20
Factory	30	(30/90 × 60) 20	10
Total Class V	90	60	30
Class II, publicly traded property	30	0	30
Totals	150	60	90

Example (3). Attribute reduction amount less than total attributes in Category A, Category B, and Category C. (i) No election to prescribe the allocation of S's attribute reduction amount. (A) Facts. P owns the sole outstanding share of M stock with a basis of $1,000 and M owns the sole outstanding share of S stock with a basis of $210. M sells its S share to X for $100. M's sale of the S share is a transfer of a loss share and therefore subject to this section. See paragraphs (f)(10)(i)(A), (f)(10)(i)(B), and (f)(10)(i)(C) of this section. At the time of the sale, S has no liabilities and the following attributes:

Category	Attribute	Attribute amount
Category A	Capital loss carryover	$10
Category B	NOL carryover	200
Category C	Deferred deductions	40
Category D, Class V	Basis in Land	50
Total Attributes		300

(B) Application of paragraphs (b) and (c) of this section. Although the transfer is subject to this section, there is no basis redetermination under paragraph (b) of this section because there is only one share of S stock outstanding (and so there can be no disparity among members' bases in common shares and there are no outstanding preferred shares with respect to which there can be unrecognized gain or loss). See paragraph (b)(1)(ii)(A) of this section. Therefore, after the application of paragraph (b) of this section, the share is still a loss share and, as such, subject to paragraph (c) of this section. No adjustment is required under paragraph (c) of this section because both the disconformity amount and the net positive adjustment are $0. See paragraph (c)(3) of this section. Thus, after the application of paragraph (c) of this section, M's transfer of the S share is still a transfer of a loss share and, accordingly, subject to this paragraph (d).

(C) Attribute reduction under this paragraph (d). (1) Computation of attribute reduction amount. Under paragraph (d)(3) of this section, S's attribute reduction amount is the lesser of the $110 net stock loss ($210 basis over $100 value) and S's aggregate inside loss. S's aggregate inside loss is $200 (S's $300 net inside attribute amount (the $10 capital loss carryover, plus the $200 NOL carryover, plus the $40 deferred deductions, plus the $50 basis in land) less the $100 value of all outstanding S shares). Thus, the attribute reduction amount is $110, the lesser of the $110 net stock loss and S's $200 aggregate inside loss. Under paragraph (d)(4)(ii)(A)(1) of this section, the $110 attribute reduction amount is allocated and applied to reduce S's attributes as follows:

Category	Attribute	Attribute amount	Allocation of attribute reduction amount	Adjusted attribute amount
Category A	Capital loss carryover	$10	$10	$0
Category B	NOL carryover	200	100	100
Category C	Deferred deductions	40	0	40
Category D, Class V	Basis in land	50	0	50
Totals		300	110	190

(ii) Election to prescribe the allocation of attribute reduction amount. (A) Facts. The facts are the same as in paragraph (i)(A) of this Example 3, except that P elects to allocate the attribute reduction amount to eliminate the Category C attributes, preserve the capital loss carryover, and reduce Category B attributes.

(B) Application of paragraphs (b) and (c) of this section. No adjustment is required under paragraph (b) or paragraph (c) of this section for the reasons set forth in paragraph (i)(B) of this Example 3. Thus, after the application of paragraph (c) of this section, M's sale of the S share is still a transfer of a loss share, and accordingly, subject to this paragraph (d).

(C) Attribute reduction under this paragraph (d). For the reasons set forth in paragraph (i)(C) of this Example 3, under this paragraph (d)(3), S's attribute reduction amount is determined to be $110. M elects to apply S's $110 attribute reduction amount as follows:

Category	Attribute	Attribute amount	Allocation of attribute reduction amount	Adjusted attribute amount
Category A	Capital loss carryover	$10	$0	$10
Category B	NOL carryover	200	70	130
Category C	Deferred deductions	40	40	0
Category D, Class V	Basis of land	50	0	50
Totals		300	110	190

Example (4). Attributes attributable to liability not taken into account. (i) S operates one business. (A) Facts. On January 1, year 1, M forms S by exchanging $150 for the sole outstanding share of S stock. In year 1, S earns $500, purchases land for $50, spends $100 to build a factory on that land, and then purchases publicly traded property for $250. In year 2, S earns a section 38 general business credit of $50. However, pollution generated by S's business gives rise to an environmental remediation liability under Federal law that would be required to be capitalized if a person purchased S's assets and assumed the liability. Before any amounts have been taken into account with respect to the environmental remediation liability, when the liability has a present value of $500, M sells its S share to X for $150. After giving effect to all other provisions of law, M's basis in the S share is $650 (the original basis of $150 increased under § 1.1502-32 by $500 for the income earned). The sale is therefore a transfer of a loss share of subsidiary stock and subject to this section. See paragraphs (f)(10)(i)(A), (f)(10)(i)(B), and (f)(10)(i)(C) of this section.

(B) Application of paragraphs (b) and (c) of this section. Although the transfer is subject to this section, there is no basis redetermination under paragraph (b) of this section because there is only one share of S stock outstanding (and so there can be no disparity among members' bases in common shares and there are no outstanding preferred shares with respect to which there can be unrecognized gain or loss). See paragraph (b)(1)(ii)(A) of this section. Therefore, after the application of paragraph (b) of this section, the share is still a loss share and, as such, subject to paragraph (c) of this section. No adjustment to basis is made under paragraph (c) of this section because, although the net positive adjustment is $500, the disconformity amount is $0. See paragraph (c)(3) of this section. Thus, after the application of paragraph (c) of this section, M's sale of the S share is still a transfer of a loss share and, accordingly, subject to this paragraph (d).

(C) Attribute reduction under this paragraph (d). (1) Under paragraph (d)(3) of this section, S's attribute reduction amount is the lesser of the $500 net stock loss ($650 basis over $150 value) and the aggregate inside loss. The aggregate inside loss is $500, computed as the excess of S's $650 net inside attribute amount (the sum of S's $100 basis in the factory, $50 basis in the land, $250 basis in the publicly traded property, and $250 cash remaining after the purchases) over the $150 value of the S share. Thus, S's attribute reduction amount is $500, the lesser of the $500 net stock loss and the $500 aggregate inside loss. Under paragraph (d)(4)(ii)(B)(2) of this section, S's $500 attribute reduction amount is allocated and applied to reduce S's attributes as follows:

Available attributes	Attribute amount	Allocable portion of attribute reduction amount	Adjusted attribute amount
Category D:			
Class V Assets:			
Basis of factory	$100	$100	$0
Basis of land	50	50	0
Class II Assets:			
Publicly traded property	250	250	0

(3) The remaining $100 attribute reduction amount is not applied to S's $250 cash (Class I asset) or to S's $50 general business tax credit. Under the general rule of this paragraph (d), that remaining $100 attribute reduction amount would have no further effect on S's attributes. However, S has a $500 liability that has not been taken into account. Therefore, under paragraph (d)(4)(ii)(C)(1) of this section, the remaining $100 attribute reduction amount is suspended and will be allocated and applied to reduce any amounts that become deductible or capitalizable as a result of the environmental remediation liability later being taken into account. If the liability is satisfied for an amount that is less than $100, under paragraph (d)(4)(ii)(C)(2) of this section the remaining portion of that $100 suspended attribute reduction amount is disregarded and has no further effect.

(ii) Lower-tier subsidiary with additional liability. (A) Facts. The facts are the same as in paragraph (i)(A) of Example 4, except that, in addition, S exchanged $50 for the sole outstanding share of stock of S1. S1 has $50 and equipment with an aggregate basis of $0. S1 also has employee medical expense liabilities that have not been taken into account and that would be required to be capitalized if a person purchased S1's assets and assumed the liabilities. At the time of the sale, S's environmental remediation liability had a present value of $475 and S1's employee medical expenses had a present value of $25. For the reasons set forth in paragraph (i)(A) of this Example 4, M's sale of the S share is a transfer of a loss share and therefore subject to this section.

(B) Application of paragraphs (b) and (c) of this section. No adjustment is made under paragraph (b) or paragraph (c) of this section for the reasons set forth in paragraph (i)(B) of this Example 4. Thus, after the application of paragraph (c) of this section, M's sale of the S share is still a transfer of a loss share and, accordingly, subject to this paragraph (d).

(C) Attribute reduction under this paragraph (d). (1) Computation of attribute reduction amount. Under paragraph (d)(3) of this section, S's attribute reduction amount is the lesser of the $500 net stock loss ($650 basis over $150 value) and the aggregate inside loss. The aggregate inside loss is the excess of S's net inside attribute amount over the value of the S share. Under paragraphs (d)(3)(iii)(B) and (d)(5)(i)(B) of this section, S's net inside attribute amount is determined by using S's $50 deemed basis in the S1 share (the greater of S's $50 actual basis in the share and S1's $50 net inside attribute amount). Accordingly, S's net inside attribute amount is $650 (the sum of its $100 basis in the factory, $50 basis in the land, $250 basis in the publicly traded property, $200 cash, and $50 deemed basis in its S1 share). The aggregate inside loss is $500, the excess of S's $650 net inside attribute amount over the $150 value of the S share. Thus, S's attribute reduction amount is $500, the lesser of the $500 net stock loss and S's $500 aggregate inside loss.

(2) Allocation, apportionment, and application of attribute reduction amount. Under paragraphs (d)(4) and (d)(5)(ii) of this section, S's $500 attribute reduction amount is allocated proportionately (by basis) between its S1 share and its non-stock Category D asset (consisting of all S's Category D assets other than its share of S1 stock, with a basis equal to $600, the aggregate basis of S's non-stock assets). However, under paragraph (d)(5)(ii) of this section, for purposes of allocating S's attribute reduction amount between its non-stock Category D asset and the S1 share, S's $50 deemed basis in its S1 share is treated as reduced by S1's $25 net non-loss assets (its Class I asset, $50 cash over S1's liabilities (which, for this purpose include the $25 of employee medical expense liabilities not taken into account as of the transfer)). As a result, S's attribute reduction amount is allocated $480 (600/625 x 500) to S's non-stock Category D asset and $20 (25/ 625 x 500) to the S1 share. The $480 attribute reduction

amount allocated to S's non-stock Category D asset produces the same reduction in the bases of S's assets (other than the S1 stock) as in paragraph (i)(C) of this Example 4; in addition, the $80 attribute reduction amount not applied to reduce S's attributes is suspended and applied to reduce any amounts that become deductible or capitalizable as a result of the environmental remediation liability later being taken into account. If the liability is satisfied for an amount that is less than $80, under paragraph (d)(4)(ii)(C)(2) of this section the remaining portion of that $80 suspended attribute reduction amount is disregarded and has no further effect. Because the S1 share is not transferred within the meaning of paragraph (f)(10) of this section, the allocated attribute reduction amount apportioned to the S1 share is applied fully to reduce the basis of the S1 share to $30. See paragraph (d)(5)(iii) of this section.

(D) Tier down of S's attribute reduction amount. The $20 portion of S's attribute reduction amount allocated to the S1 share is an attribute reduction amount of S1. Because S1 holds only cash, it has no attributes available for reduction under this paragraph (d). However, because S1 has a $25 liability not taken into account for tax purposes, paragraph (d)(4)(ii)(C)(1) of this section requires that $20 of the unapplied attribute reduction amount be suspended and then allocated and applied to reduce any amounts that become deductible or capitalizable as a result of the employee medical expense liabilities later being taken into account. If these liabilities are satisfied for an amount that is less than $20, under paragraph (d)(4)(ii)(C)(2) of this section the remaining portion of that $20 suspended attribute reduction amount is disregarded and has no further effect.

Example (5). Wholly owned lower-tier subsidiary (no lower-tier transfer). (i) Application of conforming limitation. (A) Facts. M owns the sole outstanding share of S stock with a basis of $250. S owns Asset with a basis of $100 and the only two outstanding shares of S1 stock (Share A has a basis of $40 and Share B has a basis of $60). S1 owns Asset 1 with a basis of $50. M sells its S share to P1, the common parent of another consolidated group, for $50. The sale is a transfer of a loss share and therefore subject to this section. See paragraphs (f)(10)(i)(A), (f)(10)(i)(B), and (f)(10)(i)(C) of this section.

(B) Application of paragraphs (b) and (c) of this section. Although the transfer is subject to this section, there is no basis redetermination under paragraph (b) of this section because there is only one share of S stock outstanding (and so there can be no disparity among members' bases in common shares and there are no outstanding preferred shares with respect to which there can be unrecognized gain or loss). See paragraph (b)(1)(ii)(A) of this section. Therefore, after the application of paragraph (b) of this section, the share is still a loss share and, as such, subject to paragraph (c) of this section. No adjustment is required under paragraph (c) of this section because, although there is a $50 disconformity amount, the net positive adjustment is $0. See paragraph (c)(3) of this section. Thus, after the application of paragraph (c) of this section, M's sale of the S share is still a transfer of a loss share and, accordingly, subject to this paragraph (d).

(C) Attribute reduction under this paragraph (d). (1) Computation of attribute reduction amount. Under paragraph (d)(3) of this section, S's attribute reduction amount is the lesser of M's net stock loss and S's aggregate inside loss. M's net stock loss is $200 ($250 basis over $50 value). S's aggregate inside loss is the excess of S's net inside attribute amount over the value of the S share. Under paragraphs (d)(3)(iii)(B) and (d)(5)(i)(B) of this section, S's net inside attribute amount is $200, computed as the sum of S's $100 basis in Asset and its $100 deemed basis in the deemed single share of S1 stock (computed as the greater of S's $100 aggregate basis in the S1 shares and S1's $50 basis in Asset 1). S's aggregate inside loss is therefore $150, $200 net inside attribute amount over the $50 value of the S share. Accordingly, S's attribute reduction amount is $150, the lesser of the $200 net stock loss and the $150 aggregate inside loss.

(2) Allocation, apportionment, and application of S's attribute reduction amount. Under paragraphs (d)(4) and (d)(5)(ii) of this section, S's $150 attribute reduction amount is allocated proportionately (by basis) between Asset (non-stock Category D asset) with a basis of $100, and the S1 stock (treated as a single share with a deemed basis of $100). Accordingly, $75 of the attribute reduction amount ($100/$200 x $150) is allocated to Asset and $75 of the attribute reduction amount ($100/$200 x $150) is allocated to the S1 stock. The $75 of the attribute reduction amount allocated to Asset is applied to reduce S's basis in Asset from $100 to $25. The $75 of the attribute reduction amount allocated to the S1 stock is first apportioned between the shares in a manner that reduces disparity to the greatest extent possible. Thus, of the total $75 allocated to the S1 stock, $27.50 is apportioned to Share A and $47.50 is apportioned to Share B. Because neither of the S1 shares is transferred within the meaning of paragraph (f)(10) of this section, the allocated attribute reduction amount apportioned to each of the individual S1 shares is applied fully to reduce the basis of each share to $12.50. See paragraph (d)(5)(iii) of this section. As a result, immediately after the allocation, apportionment, and application of S's attribute reduction amount, S's basis in Asset is $25 and S's basis in each of the S1 shares is $12.50.

(3) Tier down of S's attribute reduction amount, application of conforming limitation. Under paragraph (d)(5)(v)(A) of this section, the $75 portion of S's attribute reduction amount allocated to the S1 stock is an attribute reduction amount of S1 (regardless of the extent, if any, to which it is apportioned and applied to reduce the basis of any shares of S1 stock). Under the general rules of this paragraph (d), the $75 tier-down attribute reduction amount would be allocated and applied to reduce S1's basis in Asset 1 from $50 to $0. However, under paragraph (d)(5)(v)(B) of this section, S1's attributes can be reduced by only $25, the excess of the $50 portion of S1's net inside attribute amount that is allocable to all S1 shares held by members as of the transaction over $25, the aggregate amount of members' bases in nontransferred S1 shares after reduction under this paragraph (d). Thus, of S1's $75 tier-down attribute reduction amount, only $25 is applied to reduce S1's basis in Asset 1, from $50 to $25. The $50 unapplied portion of the tier-down attribute reduction amount subject to the conforming limitation has no further effect.

(ii) Application of basis restoration rule. (A) Facts. The facts are the same as in paragraph (i)(A) of this Example 5, except that S's basis in Share A is $15 and S's basis in Share B is $35, and S1's basis in Asset 1 is $100.

(B) Basis redetermination and basis reduction under paragraphs (b) and (c) of this section. No adjustment is required under paragraph (b) or paragraph (c) of this section for the reasons set forth in paragraph (i)(B) of this Example 5. Thus, after the application of paragraph (c) of this section, M's transfer of the S share is still a transfer of a loss share and, accordingly, subject to this paragraph (d).

(C) Attribute reduction under this paragraph (d). (1) Computation of attribute reduction amount. Under paragraph (d)(3) of this section, S's attribute reduction amount is the lesser of M's net stock loss and S's aggregate inside loss. M's net stock loss is $200 ($250 basis over $50 value). S's aggregate inside loss is the excess of S's net inside attribute amount over the value of the S share. Under paragraphs (d)(3)(iii)(B) and (d)(5)(i)(B) of this section, S's net inside attribute amount is $200, the sum of S's $100 basis in Asset and its $100 deemed basis in the deemed single share of S1 stock (computed as the greater of S's $50 aggregate basis in the S1 shares and S1's $100 basis in Asset 1). S's aggregate inside loss is therefore $150, $200 net inside attribute amount over the $50 value of the S share. Accordingly, S's attribute reduction amount is $150, the lesser of the $200 net stock loss and the $150 aggregate inside loss.

(2) Allocation, apportionment, and application of S's attribute reduction amount. Under paragraphs (d)(4) and (d)(5)(ii) of this section, S's $150 attribute reduction amount is allocated proportionately (by basis) between Asset (nonstock Category D asset) with a basis of $100, and the S1 stock (treated as a single share with a deemed basis of $100). Accordingly, $75 of the attribute reduction amount ($100/$200 x $150) is allocated to Asset and $75 of the attribute reduction amount ($100/$200 x $150) is allocated to the S1 stock. The $75 of the attribute reduction amount allocated to Asset is applied to reduce S's basis in Asset from $100 to $25. The $75 of the attribute reduction amount allocated to the S1 stock is first apportioned between the shares in a manner that reduces disparity to the greatest extent possible. Thus, of the total $75 allocated to the S1 stock, $27.50 is apportioned to Share A and $47.50 is apportioned to Share B. Because neither of the S1 shares is transferred within the meaning of paragraph (f)(10) of this section, the allocated attribute reduction amount apportioned to each of the individual S1 shares is applied fully to reduce the basis of each share to an excess loss account of $12.50. See paragraph (d)(5)(iii) of this section. As a result, immediately after the allocation, apportionment, and application of S's attribute reduction amount, S's basis in Asset is $25 and S's basis in each of the S1 shares is an excess loss account of $12.50.

(3) Tier down of S's attribute reduction amount. Under paragraph (d)(5)(v)(A) of this section, the $75 portion of S's attribute reduction amount allocated to S1 stock is an attribute reduction amount of S1 (regardless of the extent, if any, to which it is apportioned and applied to reduce the basis of any shares of S1 stock). Accordingly, under the general rules of this paragraph (d), the $75 tier-down attribute reduction amount is applied to reduce S1's basis in Asset 1 from $100 to $25.

(4) Basis restoration. Under paragraph (d)(5)(vi)(A) of this section, after this paragraph (d) has been applied with respect to all transfers of subsidiary stock, any reduction made to the basis of a share of lower-tier subsidiary stock under paragraph (d)(5)(iii) of this section is reversed to the extent necessary to conform the basis of that share to the share's allocable portion of the subsidiary's net inside attribute amount (after reduction). S1's net inside attribute amount after the application of this paragraph (d) is $25 and thus each of the two S1 share's allocable portion of S1's net inside attribute amount is $12.50. Accordingly, the reductions to Share A and to Share B under paragraph (d)(5)(iii) of this section are reversed to the extent necessary to restore the basis of each share to $12.50. Thus, $25 of the $27.50 of reduction to the basis of Share A, and $25 of the $47.50 of reduction to the basis of share B, is reversed, restoring the basis of each share to $12.50.

Example (6). Multiple blocks of lower-tier subsidiary stock outstanding. (i) Excess loss account taken into account (transfer of upper-tier share causes disposition within the meaning of § 1.1502-19(c)(1)(ii)(B)). (A) Facts. M owns the sole outstanding share of S stock with a basis of $200. S holds all five outstanding shares of S1 common stock (Shares A, B, C, D, and E). S has an excess loss account of $20 in Share A and a positive basis of $20 in each of the other shares. The only investment adjustment applied to any S1 share was a negative $20 investment adjustment applied to Share A when it was the only outstanding share, and this amount tiered up and adjusted M's basis in the S share. S1 owns one asset with a basis of $250. M sells its S share to P1, the common parent of a consolidated group, for $20. The sale of the S share is a disposition of Share A under § 1.1502-19(c)(1)(ii)(B) (S1 becomes a nonmember because it will have a separate return year as a member of the P1 group). Accordingly, under § 1.1502-19(b)(1)(i) and paragraph (a)(3)(i) of this section, before the application of this section, S's excess loss account in Share A is taken into account, increasing S's basis in Share A to $0 and M's basis in its S share to $220. After giving effect to the recognition of the excess loss account, M's sale of the S share is a transfer of a loss share and therefore subject to this section. See paragraphs (f)(10)(i)(A), (f)(10)(i)(B), and (f)(10)(i)(C) of this section.

(B) Basis redetermination and basis reduction under paragraphs (b) and (c) of this section. Although the transfer is subject to this section, there is no basis redetermination under paragraph (b) of this section because there is only one share of S stock outstanding (and so there can be no disparity among members' bases in common shares and there are no outstanding preferred shares with respect to which there can be unrecognized gain or loss). See paragraph (b)(1)(ii)(A) of this section. Therefore, after the application of paragraph (b) of this section, the share is still a loss share and, as such, subject to paragraph (c) of this section. No adjustment is made under paragraph (c) of this section because, even though there is a disconformity amount of $140, the net positive adjustment is $0. See paragraph (c)(3) of this section. Thus, after the application of paragraph (c) of this section, M's sale of the S share remains a transfer of a loss share and, accordingly, subject to this paragraph (d).

(C) Attribute reduction under this paragraph (d). (1) Computation of attribute reduction amount. Under paragraph (d)(3) of this section, S's attribute reduction amount is the lesser of M's net stock loss and S's aggregate inside loss. M's net stock loss is $200 ($220 basis over $20 value). S's aggregate inside loss is the excess of S's net inside attribute amount over the value of the S share. Under paragraphs (d)(3)(iii)(B) and (d)(5)(i)(B) of this section, S's net inside attribute amount is $250, S's $250 deemed basis in the deemed single share of S1 stock (computed as the greater of S's $80 aggregate basis in the S1 shares ($0 basis in Share A plus $20 basis in each of the four other shares) and S1's $250 basis in its asset). S's aggregate inside loss is therefore $230, $250 net inside attribute amount over the $20 value of the S share. Accordingly, S's attribute reduction amount is $200, the lesser of the $200 net stock loss and the $230 aggregate inside loss.

(2) Allocation, apportionment, and application of S's attribute reduction amount. Under paragraphs (d)(4) and (d)(5)(ii) of this section, S's $200 attribute reduction amount is allocated entirely to the S1 stock (treated as a single

share) and then apportioned among the shares in a manner that reduces disparity to the greatest extent possible. Thus, $24 is apportioned to Share A and $44 is apportioned to each of the other shares. Because none of the S1 shares are transferred within the meaning of paragraph (f)(10) of this section (notwithstanding that there is a disposition under § 1.1502-19(c)(1)(ii)(B)), the allocated attribute reduction amount apportioned to each of the individual S1 shares is applied fully to reduce the basis of each share to an excess loss account of $24. See paragraph (d)(5)(iii) of this section.

(3) Tier down of S's attribute reduction amount. Under paragraph (d)(5)(v)(A) of this section, the $200 of S's attribute reduction amount allocated to the S1 shares is an attribute reduction amount of S1 (regardless of the extent, if any, to which it is apportioned and applied to reduce the basis of any shares of S1 stock). Under the general rules of this paragraph (d), S1's $200 tier-down attribute reduction amount is allocated and applied to reduce S1's basis in its asset from $250 to $50.

(4) Basis restoration. Under paragraph (d)(5)(vi)(A) of this section, after this paragraph (d) has been applied with respect to all transfers of subsidiary stock, any reduction made to the basis of a share of lower-tier subsidiary stock under paragraph (d)(5)(iii) of this section is reversed to the extent necessary to conform the basis of that share to the share's allocable portion of the subsidiary's net inside attribute amount (after reduction). S1's net inside attribute amount after the application of this paragraph (d) is $50 and thus each of the five S1 share's allocable portion of S1's net inside attribute amount is $10. Accordingly, the reductions to the bases of S1 shares under paragraph (d)(5)(iii) of this section are reversed to the extent necessary to restore (to the extent possible) the basis of each share to $10. Thus, $24 of the $24 of reduction to the basis of Share A is reversed, restoring the basis of Share A to $0, and $34 of the $44 of reduction to the basis of each other share is reversed, restoring the basis of each of those shares to $10.

(ii) Sale of gain share to member. (A) Facts. The facts are the same as in paragraph (i)(A) of this Example 6, except that M owns Shares A, B, C, and D, S owns Share E, S has a liability of $20, and S1's basis in its asset is $500. Also, as part of the transaction, S sells Share E to M for $40. Unlike under the facts of paragraph (i)(A) of this Example 6, there is no disposition of Share A within the meaning of § 1.1502-19(c)(1)(ii)(B) (S1 continues to be a member of the group, and thus does not have a separate return year). As a result, the Share A excess loss account is not taken into account. Although S's sale of Share E is a transfer of that share, the share is not a loss share and thus the transfer is not subject to this section. M's sale of the S share, however, is a transfer of a loss share and therefore subject to this section. See paragraphs (f)(10)(i)(A), (f)(10)(i)(B), and (f)(10)(i)(C) of this section.

(B) Transfer in lowest tier (gain share). S's sale of Share E is the lowest-tier transfer in the transaction. Under paragraph (a)(3)(ii)(A) of this section, because there are no transfers of loss shares at that tier, no adjustments are required under paragraph (b) or (c) of this section. However, S's gain recognized on the transfer of Share E is computed and immediately adjusts members' bases in subsidiary stock under Sec. 1.1502-32 (because M and S are not members of the same group immediately after the transaction, the sale is not an intercompany transaction subject to Sec. 1.1502-13). Accordingly, M's basis in its S share is increased by $20, from $200 to $220.

(C) Transfers in next higher tier, application of paragraphs (b) and (c) of this section. The next higher tier transfer is M's sale of the S stock. The sale is a transfer of a loss share and therefore subject to this section. Although the transfer is subject to this section, there is no basis redetermination under paragraph (b) of this section because there is only one share of S stock outstanding (and so there can be no disparity among members' bases in common shares and there are no outstanding preferred shares with respect to which there can be unrecognized gain or loss). See paragraph (b)(1)(ii)(A) of this section. Therefore, after the application of paragraph (b) of this section, the share is still a loss share and, as such, subject to paragraph (c) of this section. Under paragraph (c) of this section, M's basis in its S share is decreased by $20, the lesser of S's $200 disconformity amount (computed as the excess of M's $220 basis in the S stock over S's $20 net inside attribute amount (computed as the $20 basis in Share E, increased by $20 to reflect the gain recognized with respect to the share, less the $20 liability)), and the $20 net positive adjustment. Thus, after the application of paragraph (c) of this section, M's basis in the S share is $200, and the sale remains a transfer of a loss share. There are no higher tier transfers and, therefore, M's transfer of the S share is then subject to this paragraph (d).

(D) Attribute reduction under this paragraph (d). (1) Computation of attribute reduction amount. Under paragraph (d)(3) of this section, S's attribute reduction amount is the lesser of M's net stock loss and S's aggregate inside loss. M's net stock loss is $180 ($200 basis over $20 value). S's aggregate inside loss is the excess of S's net inside attribute amount over the value of the S share. Under paragraphs (d)(3)(iii)(B) and (d)(5)(i)(B) of this section, S's net inside attribute amount is $80, computed as $100 (S's deemed basis in Share E (the greater of $40 (S's $20 basis in Share E, adjusted for the $20 gain recognized with respect to the share), and Share E's allocable portion of S1's net inside attribute amount of $100 (1/5 of S1's $500 basis in its asset)), less S's $20 liability. Accordingly, S's aggregate inside loss is $60 ($80 net inside attribute amount over the $20 value of the S stock). S's attribute reduction amount is therefore $60, the lesser of $180 net stock loss and $60 aggregate inside loss.

(2) Allocation, apportionment, and application of S's attribute reduction amount. Under paragraphs (d)(4) and (d)(5)(ii) of this section, S's $60 attribute reduction amount is allocated entirely to its S1 stock, Share E. However, because Share E was transferred within the meaning of paragraph (f)(10) of this section and gain was recognized on its transfer, none of the allocated amount is apportioned to, or applied to reduce the basis of Share E. See paragraph (d)(5)(iii)(A) of this section. Under paragraph (d)(5)(iv) of this section, the $60 allocated attribute reduction amount not apportioned or applied to Share E has no effect on S or S's attributes.

(3) Tier down of S's attribute reduction amount. Notwithstanding the fact that no portion of the allocated attribute reduction amount was apportioned to or applied to reduce the basis of Share E, the entire $60 allocated attribute reduction amount is an attribute reduction amount of S1. See paragraph (d)(5)(v)(A) of this section. Under the general rules of this paragraph (d), S1's $60 tier-down attribute reduction amount is allocated and applied to reduce S1's basis in its asset from $500 to $440.

(4) Basis restoration. Under paragraph (d)(5)(vi)(A) of this section, after this paragraph (d) has been applied with respect to all transfers of subsidiary stock, any reduction made

to the basis of a share of subsidiary stock under paragraph (d)(5)(iii) of this section is reversed to the extent necessary to conform the basis of that share to the share's allocable portion of the subsidiary's net inside attribute amount. No reduction was made to the basis of the S1 stock under paragraph (d)(5)(iii) of this section. Therefore, no stock basis is increased under the basis restoration rule in paragraph (d)(5)(vi)(A) of this section.

Example (7). Allocation of attribute reduction if lower-tier subsidiary has non-loss assets or liabilities. (i) S1 holds cash. (A) Facts. M owns the sole outstanding share of S stock with a basis of $800. S owns Asset with a basis of $400 and the sole outstanding share of S1 stock with a basis of $300. S1 holds Asset 1 with a basis of $50, and $100 cash. M sells its S share to P1, the common parent of a consolidated group, for $100. The sale is not a transfer of the S1 share because S and S1 are members of the same group following the transaction. However, the sale is a transfer of the S share, a loss share, and therefore subject to this section. See paragraphs (f)(10)(i)(A), (f)(10)(i)(B), and (f)(10)(i)(C) of this section.

(B) Application of paragraphs (b) and (c) of this section. Although the transfer is subject to this section, there is no basis redetermination under paragraph (b) of this section because there is only one share of S stock outstanding (and so there can be no disparity among members' bases in common shares and there are no outstanding preferred shares with respect to which there can be unrecognized gain or loss). See paragraph (b)(1)(ii)(A) of this section. Therefore, after the application of paragraph (b) of this section, the share is still a loss share and, as such, subject to the provisions of this paragraph (c). No adjustment is required under paragraph (c) of this section because, even though there is a disconformity amount of $100, the net positive adjustment is $0. See paragraph (c)(3) of this section. Thus, after the application of paragraph (c) of this section, M's sale of the S share is still a transfer of a loss share and, accordingly, subject to this paragraph (d).

(C) Attribute reduction under this paragraph (d). (1) Computation of attribute reduction amount. Under paragraph (d)(3) of this section, S's attribute reduction amount is the lesser of M's net stock loss and S's aggregate inside loss. M's net stock loss is $700 ($800 basis over $100 value). S's aggregate inside loss is the excess of S's net inside attribute amount over the value of the S share. Under paragraphs (d)(3)(iii)(B) and (d)(5)(i)(B) of this section, S's net inside attribute amount is $700, the sum of its $400 basis in Asset and its $300 deemed basis in the S1 share (computed as the greater of S's $300 basis in the S1 share and S1's $150 net inside attribute amount (reflecting the sum of S1's $50 basis in Asset 1 and S1's $100 cash)). Therefore, S's aggregate inside loss is $600 ($700 net inside attribute amount over the $100 value of the S stock). S's attribute reduction amount is $600, the lesser of the $700 net stock loss and the $600 aggregate inside loss.

(2) Allocation, apportionment, and application of S's attribute reduction amount. Under paragraphs (d)(4) and (d)(5)(ii) of this section, S's $600 attribute reduction amount is allocated proportionately (by basis) between S's $400 basis in Asset (non-stock Category D asset) and its deemed basis in the S1 share. However, under paragraph (d)(5)(ii) of this section, for purposes of allocating the attribute reduction amount, S's $300 deemed basis in the S1 share is treated as reduced by S1's net non-loss assets (its Class I asset, $100 cash) to $200. Thus, the $600 is allocated $400 to Asset ($400/$600 x $600) and $200 to the S1 share ($200/$600 x $600). The $400 allocated to Asset is applied to reduce S's basis in Asset from $400 to $0. Because the S1 share is not transferred within the meaning of paragraph (f)(10) of this section, the allocated attribute reduction amount apportioned to the S1 share is applied fully to reduce the basis of the S1 share to $100. See paragraph (d)(5)(iii) of this section.

(3) Tier down of S's attribute reduction amount. Under paragraph (d)(5)(v)(A) of this section, the $200 portion of S's attribute reduction amount allocated to the S1 stock is an attribute reduction amount of S1 (regardless of the extent, if any, to which it is apportioned and applied to reduce the basis of any shares of S1 stock). Under the general rules of this paragraph (d), S1's $200 tier-down attribute reduction amount is allocated and applied to reduce S1's basis in Asset 1 (S1's only attribute available for reduction) from $50 to $0. The $150 unapplied attribute reduction amount is disregarded and has no further effect.

(4) Basis restoration. Under paragraph (d)(5)(vi)(A) of this section, after this paragraph (d) has been applied with respect to all transfers of subsidiary stock, any reduction made to the basis of a share of subsidiary stock under paragraph (d)(5)(iii) of this section is reversed to the extent necessary to conform the basis of that share to the share's allocable portion of the subsidiary's net inside attribute amount. There is only one share of S1 stock outstanding and so S1's entire $100 net inside attribute amount is allocable to that share. Because S's $100 basis in the S1 share (as reduced under this paragraph (d)) is already conformed with its $100 allocable portion of S1's net inside attribute amount, there is no restoration under paragraph (d)(5)(vi)(A) of this section.

(ii) S1 borrows cash. The facts are the same as in paragraph (i)(A) of this Example 7 except that, in addition, S1 borrows $50 from X immediately before M sells the S share. The computation of the attribute reduction amount is the same as in paragraph (i)(C) of this Example 7 (the $50 cash from the loan proceeds and the $50 liability offset in the computation of S1's net inside attribute amount and so the net amount is unaffected, and the computation of S's deemed basis in the S1 stock is unaffected). Similarly, for purposes of allocating the attribute reduction amount between the non-stock Category D asset and the S1 stock, paragraph (d)(5)(ii) of this section requires S's deemed basis in the S1 share to be treated as reduced by S1's net non-loss assets (S1's non-loss assets over S1's liabilities). Accordingly, the additional $50 cash proceeds is offset by the $50 liability and there is no effect on the allocation of the attribute reduction amount. The results are the same as in paragraph (i) of this Example 7.

(iii) S1 has a liability not taken into account for tax purposes. (A) Facts. The facts are the same as in paragraph (ii) of this Example 7 except that, in addition, S1 has a $40 liability that is not taken into account for tax purposes as of the transfer and that would be required to be capitalized if a person purchased S1's assets and assumed the liability.

(B) Application of paragraphs (b) and (c) of this section. No adjustment is required under paragraph (b) or paragraph (c) of this section for the reasons set forth in paragraph (i)(B) of this Example 7. Thus, after the application of paragraph (c) of this section, P's sale of the S share is still a transfer of a loss share and, accordingly, subject to this paragraph (d).

(C) Attribute reduction under this paragraph (d). (1) Computation of attribute reduction amount. The attribute reduction amount is the same as computed in paragraph (i)(C)(1) of this Example 7 (under paragraph (f)(5) of this section, the term liability does not include liabilities not taken into account for tax purposes and so the additional $40 liability not yet taken into account for tax purposes does not affect the computation of S's attribute reduction amount).

(2) Allocation, apportionment, and application of S's attribute reduction amount. Under paragraphs (d)(4) and (d)(5)(ii) of this section, S's $600 attribute reduction amount is allocated proportionately (by basis) between S's $400 basis in Asset 1 (non-stock Category D asset) and its deemed basis in the S1 share. However, under paragraph (d)(5)(ii) of this section, for purposes of allocating the attribute reduction amount, S's $300 deemed basis in the S1 share is treated as reduced by S1's net non-loss assets (S1's non-loss assets over S1's liabilities). For this purpose, the term liabilities includes liabilities not taken into account for tax purposes, as described in paragraph (d)(4)(ii)(C)(1) of this section (generally, liabilities that, if assumed in a purchase, would give rise to a capitalized amount when satisfied). Thus, for this purpose, S's $300 deemed basis in the S1 share is reduced by S1's $60 net non-loss assets (the excess of S1's $150 non-loss assets (its Class I asset, $150 cash) over S1's $90 liabilities ($50 loan and $40 liability not yet taken into account for tax purposes)), to $240. Accordingly, S's $600 attribute reduction amount is allocated and applied $375 ($400/$640 x $600) to Asset (reducing S's basis in Asset from $400 to $25) and $225 ($240/$640 x $600) to the S1 share. Because the S1 share is not transferred within the meaning of paragraph (f)(10) of this section, the allocated attribute reduction amount apportioned to the S1 share is applied fully to reduce the basis of the S1 share to $75. See paragraph (d)(5)(iii) of this section.

(3) Tier down of S's attribute reduction amount, application of conforming limitation. Under paragraph (d)(5)(v)(A) of this section, the $225 portion of S's attribute reduction amount allocated to the S1 stock is an attribute reduction amount of S1 (regardless of the extent, if any, to which it is apportioned and applied to reduce the basis of any shares of S1 stock). Under the general rules of this paragraph (d), S1's $225 tier-down attribute reduction amount would be allocated and applied to reduce S1's attributes. However, under paragraph (d)(5)(v)(B) of this section, S1's attributes can be reduced by only $75, the excess of the $150 portion of S1's net inside attribute amount that is allocable to all S1 shares held by members as of the transaction over $75, the aggregate amount of members' bases in nontransferred S1 shares, after reduction under this paragraph (d). Thus, of S1's $225 tier-down attribute reduction amount, $50 is applied to reduce S1's basis in Asset 1, from $50 to $0. Although the $25 unapplied attribute reduction amount not subject to the conforming limitation would generally be disregarded without further effect, because S1 has a $40 liability not taken into account for tax purposes, paragraph (d)(4)(ii)(C)(1) of this section requires that the $25 of the unapplied attribute reduction amount not subject to the conforming limitation be suspended and then allocated and applied to reduce any amounts that become deductible or capitalizable as a result of that liability later being taken into account. If the liability is satisfied for an amount that is less than $25, under paragraph (d)(4)(ii)(C)(2) of this section the remaining portion of that $25 suspended attribute reduction amount is disregarded and has no further effect. The $150 unapplied portion of the tier-down attribute reduction amount subject to the conforming limitation has no further effect.

(4) Basis restoration. Under paragraph (d)(5)(vi)(A) of this section, after this paragraph (d) has been applied with respect to all transfers of subsidiary stock, any reduction made to the basis of a share of lower-tier subsidiary stock under paragraph (d)(5)(iii) of this section is reversed to the extent necessary to conform the basis of that share to the share's allocable portion of the subsidiary's net inside attribute amount. Paragraph (d)(5)(vi)(A) provides that, for this purpose, S1's net inside attribute amount is its net inside attribute amount, taking into account any reductions under this paragraph (d) and treating it as reduced by any attribute reduction amount suspended under paragraph (d)(4)(ii)(C)(1) of this section. Because S's $75 basis in its S1 stock (after application of this paragraph (d)) is already conformed with its $75 allocable portion of S1's net inside attribute amount ($100 net inside attributes after reduction, reduced by S1's $25 suspended attribute reduction amount), there is no restoration under paragraph (d)(5)(vi)(A) of this section.

Example (8). Election to reduce stock basis or reattribute attributes under paragraph (d)(6) of this section. (i) Deconsolidating sale. (A) Facts. P owns the sole outstanding share of M stock with a basis of $1,000. M owns all 100 outstanding shares of S stock with a basis of $2.10 per share ($210 total). M sells all its S shares to X for $1 per share ($100 total). M's sale of the S shares is a transfer of loss shares and therefore subject to this section. See paragraphs (f)(10)(i)(A), (f)(10)(i)(B), and (f)(10)(i)(C) of this section. At the time of the sale, S has no liabilities and the following:

Category	Attribute	Attribute amount
Category A	Capital loss carryover	$10
Category B	NOL carryover	90
Category C	Deferred deduction	40
Total Category A, Category B, and Category C Attributes		140
Category D, Class V	Basis in land	70
Total Attributes		210

(B) Application of paragraphs (b) and (c) of this section. Although the transfer is subject to this section, there is no basis redetermination under paragraph (b) of this section because there is no disparity among M's bases in shares of S common stock and there are no shares of S preferred stock outstanding (so there can be no unrecognized gain or loss with respect to preferred shares). See paragraph (b)(1)(ii)(A) of this section. No adjustment is required under paragraph (c) of this section because both the disconformity amount and the net positive adjustment are $0. See paragraph (c)(3) of this section. Thus, after the application of paragraph (c) of this section, M's transfer of the S shares is still a transfer of loss shares and, accordingly, subject to this paragraph (d).

(C) Attribute reduction under this paragraph (d). (1) Computation of attribute reduction amount. Under paragraph (d)(3) of this section, S's attribute reduction amount is the lesser of the $110 net stock loss ($210 aggregate basis over the $100 aggregate value) and S's aggregate inside loss. S's aggregate inside loss is $110 (S's $210 net inside attribute amount (the $10 capital loss carryover, plus the $90 NOL carryover, plus the $40 deferred deduction, plus the $70 basis in the land) over the $100 value of all outstanding S shares). S's attribute reduction amount is $110, the lesser of the $110 net stock loss and the $110 aggregate inside loss.

(2) Application of attribute reduction amount. (i) S's $110 attribute reduction amount is applied as follows:

Category	Attribute	Attribute amount	Allocation of attribute reduction amount	Adjusted attribute amount
Category A	Capital loss carryover	$10	$10	$0
Category B	NOL carryover	90	90	0
Category C	Deferred deduction	40	10	30
Category D, Class V	Basis in land	70	0	70
Totals		210	110	100

(ii) Alternatively, under paragraph (d)(4)(ii)(A)(1) of this section, P could specify the allocation of S's $110 attribute reduction amount among S's $10 capital loss carryover, S's $90 NOL carryover, and S's $40 deferred deduction.

(D) Results. The P group recognizes a $110 loss on M's sale of the S shares that is absorbed by the group, which reduces P's basis in the M share under § 1.1502-32 from $1,000 to $890. Immediately after the transaction, the entities own the following:

Entity	Asset	Basis
P	M share	$890
X	100 S shares	100
S	Category C, deferred deduction	30
	Category D, Class V Asset (land)	70

(E) Election to reduce stock basis. The facts are the same as in paragraph (i)(A) of this Example 8 except that P elects under paragraph (d)(6) of this section to reduce M's basis in the S shares by the full attribute reduction amount of $110, in lieu of S reducing its attributes. The election is effective for all transferred loss shares and is allocated to those shares in proportion to the loss in each. See paragraph (d)(6)(v)(A) of this section. Accordingly, the basis of each of the 100 transferred shares is reduced from $2.10 to $1.00. After giving effect to the election, the S shares are not loss shares and this section has no further application to the transfer. The $110 reduction in M's basis in the S shares pursuant to the election under paragraph (d)(6) of this section is a noncapital, nondeductible expense of M that will reduce P's basis in the M share. See paragraph (d)(6)(v)(A) of this section. Immediately after the transaction, the entities own the following:

Entity	Asset	Basis/attribute
P	M share	$890
X	100 S shares	100
S	Category A, capital loss carryover	10
	Category B, NOL carryover	90
	Category C, deferred deduction	40
	Category D, Class V asset (land)	70

(F) Election to reattribute losses. The facts are the same as in paragraph (i)(A) of this Example 8 except that P elects under paragraph (d)(6) of this section to reattribute S's attributes. S's attribute reduction amount is $110, and P can reattribute all or any portion of the attributes in Category A, Category B, and Category C to the extent of $110. P elects to reattribute the $90 NOL, and, as a result, S's NOL is $0. Under paragraph (d)(6)(iv)(A) of this section, the reattribution of the $90 NOL is a noncapital, nondeductible expense of S. Under Sec. 1.1502-32(c)(1)(ii)(A)(1) this $90 expense is allocated to the transferred loss shares of S stock in proportion to the loss in the shares, or $.90 per share. Further, this expense tiers up under § 1.1502-32 and reduces P's basis in the M stock by $90. After giving effect to the election, the P group would recognize a $20 loss on M's sale of the S shares, S would have an aggregate inside loss of $20 (S's $120 net inside attribute amount (the $10 capital loss carryover, plus the $40 deferred deduction, plus the $70 basis in the land) over the $100 value of all outstanding S shares), and S's attribute reduction amount would be $20 (applied $10 to the $10 capital loss carryover and $10 to the $40 deferred deduction). (Alternatively, under paragraph (d)(4)(ii)(A)(1) of this section, P could specify the allocation of S's $20 attribute reduction amount between S's $10 capital loss carryover and S's $40 deferred deduction. Further, P could elect to reduce M's remaining basis in the S shares by any amount up to the $20 attribute reduction amount, thereby reducing or eliminating S's attribute reduction amount.)

(ii) Nondeconsolidating sale. (A) Facts. The facts are the same as in paragraph (i)(A) of this Example 8, except that M only sells 20 S shares ($20 total).

(B) Application of paragraphs (b) and (c) of this section. No adjustment is required under paragraph (b) or paragraph (c) of this section for the reasons set forth in paragraph (i)(B) of this Example 8. Thus, after the application of paragraph (c) of this section, M's sale of the S shares is still a transfer of loss shares and, accordingly, subject to this paragraph (d).

(C) Attribute reduction under this paragraph (d). (1) Computation of attribute reduction amount. Under paragraph (d)(3) of this section, S's attribute reduction amount is the lesser of the $22 net stock loss ($42 aggregate basis over $20 aggregate value) and S's $110 aggregate inside loss (as calculated in paragraph (i)(C)(1) of this Example 8). S's attribute reduction amount is $22, the lesser of the $22 net stock loss and the $110 aggregate inside loss.

(2) Application of attribute reduction amount. (i) S's $22 attribute reduction amount is applied as follows:

Category	Attribute	Attribute amount	Allocation of attribute reduction amount	Adjusted attribute amount
Category A	Capital loss carryover	$10	$10	$0
Category B	NOL carryover	90	12	78
Category C	Deferred deduction	40	0	40
Category D, Class V	Land	70	0	70

(ii) Alternatively, under paragraph (d)(4)(ii)(A)(1) of this section, P could specify the allocation of S's $22 attribute reduction amount among S's $10 capital loss carryover, S's $90 NOL carryover, and S's $40 deferred deduction.

(D) Results. The P group recognizes a $22 loss on M's sale of the S shares that is absorbed by the group, which reduces P's basis in the M share under § 1.1502-32 from $1,000 to $978. Immediately after the transaction, the entities have the following:

Entity	Asset	Basis
P	M share	$978
X	20 S shares	20
S	Category B, NOL carryover	78
	Category C, deferred deduction	40
	Category D, Class V Asset (land)	70

(E) Election to reduce stock basis. The facts are the same as in paragraph (ii)(A) of this Example 8, except that P elects under paragraph (d)(6) of this section to reduce M's basis in the S shares by the full attribute reduction amount of $22, in lieu of S reducing its attributes. The election is effective for all transferred loss shares and is allocated to such shares in proportion to the loss in each share. See paragraph (d)(6)(v)(A) of this section. Accordingly, the basis of each of the 20 transferred shares is reduced from $2.10 to $1.00. After giving effect to the election, the transferred S shares are not loss shares and this section has no further application to the transfer. The $22 reduction in M's basis in the S shares pursuant to the election under paragraph (d)(6) of this section is a noncapital, nondeductible expense of M that will reduce P's basis in the M share. See paragraph (d)(6)(v)(A) of this section. Immediately after the transaction, the entities have the following:

Entity	Asset	Basis/attribute
P	M share	$978
M	80 S shares	168
X	20 S shares	20
S	Category A, capital loss carryover	10
	Category B, NOL	90
	Category C, deferred deduction	40
	Category D Class V Asset (land)	70

(F) Election to reattribute attributes. The facts are the same as in paragraph (ii)(A) of this Example 8. Because S remains a member of the same group as P following M's sale of S stock, P cannot elect under paragraph (d)(6) of this section to reattribute any portion of S's attributes in lieu of attribute reduction.

Example (9). Transfers at multiple tiers, gain and loss shares. (i) Facts. M owns the sole outstanding share of S stock with a basis of $700. S owns Asset 1 (basis of $170) and all ten outstanding shares of S1 common stock ($170 basis in share 1, $10 basis in share 2, and $15 basis in each of share 3 through share 10). S1 owns the sole outstanding share of S2 ($0 basis), the sole outstanding share of S3 ($60 basis), and the sole outstanding share of S4 ($100 basis). S2's sole asset is Asset 2 ($75 basis). S3's sole asset is Asset 3 ($75 basis). S4's sole asset is Asset 4 ($80 basis). In one transaction, M sells its S share to P1 (the common parent of a consolidated group) for $240, S sells S1 share 1 to X for $20, S contributes S1 share 2 to a partnership in a section 721 transaction, and S1 sells its S2 share to Y for $50. M's sale of the S share and S1's sale of the S2 share are transfers under paragraphs (f)(10)(i)(A), (f)(10)(i)(B), and (f)(10)(i)(C) of this section. S's sale of S1 share 1 to X is a transfer under paragraphs (f)(10)(i)(A) and (f)(10)(i)(C) of this section. S's contribution of S1 share 2 to the partnership is a transfer under paragraph (f)(10)(i)(C) of this section.

(ii) Transfer in lowest tier (gain share). However, S1's gain recognized on the transfer of the S2 share is computed and immediately adjusts members' bases in subsidiary stock under Sec. 1.1502-32. Under paragraph (a)(3)(ii)(A) of this section, because there are no transfers of loss shares at that tier, no adjustments are required under paragraph (b) or (c) of this section. However, S1's gain recognized on the transfer of the S2 share is computed and immediately adjusts members bases in subsidiary stock under § 1.1502-32. Accordingly, $5 is allocated to each of 10 S1 shares, increasing the basis of share 1 to $175, the basis of share 2 to $15, and the basis of each other share to $20. The $50 applied to S's bases in the S1 shares then tiers up to increase P's basis in the S share from $700 to $750.

(iii) Transfers in next highest tier (loss share). S's sale of the S1 share 1 and S's transfer of the S1 share 2 to a partnership are both transfers of stock in the next higher tier. However, only the S1 share 1 is a loss share and so this section only applies with respect to the transfer of that share.

(A) Basis redetermination under paragraph (b) of this section. Under paragraph (b)(2)(i)(A) of this section, members' bases in S1 shares are redetermined by first removing the positive investment adjustments applied to the bases of transferred loss common shares. Accordingly, the $5 positive investment adjustment applied to the basis of S1 share 1 is removed, reducing the basis of S1 share 1 from $175 to $170. Because there were no negative adjustments applied to the bases of S1 shares, there are no negative adjustments that can be reallocated to further reduce the basis of S1 share 1 under paragraph (b)(2)(i)(B) of this section. Finally, under paragraph (b)(2)(ii)(B) of this section, the $5 positive investment adjustment removed from S1 share 1 is reallocated and applied to increase the bases of other S1 common shares in a manner that reduces disparity to the greatest extent possible. Accordingly, the entire $5 investment adjustment removed from S1 share 1 is reallocated and applied to increase the basis of S1 share 2, from $15 to $20. After basis is redetermined under paragraph (b) of this section, the S1 share 1 is still a loss share and therefore subject to basis reduction under paragraph (c) of this section. (Because the S1 share 2 is not a loss share, this section does not apply with respect to the transfer of that share.)

(B) Basis reduction under paragraph (c) of this section. No adjustment is required to the basis of S1 share 1 under paragraph (c) of this section. The S1 share 1 has a disconformity amount of $149. This $149 disconformity amount is computed as the excess of the $170 basis in the S1 share 1 over the S1 share 1's $21 allocable portion (1/10) of S1's $210 net inside attribute amount. S1's $210 net inside attribute amount is determined under paragraph (c)(5) of this section as the sum of $50 (S1's $0 basis in the S2 share, adjusted for the $50 gain recognized with respect to that share), S1's $60 basis in the S3 stock, and S1's $100 basis in the S4 stock. (In computing the disconformity amount, the basis of the S2 share is not treated as tentatively reduced because that share is transferred in the transaction, and the bases of the S3 and S4 shares are not treated as tentatively reduced because no positive investment adjustments were applied to the bases of those shares.) However, the S1 share 1's net positive adjustment is $0 because the $5 positive investment adjustment originally allocated to S1 share 1 was reallocated to S1 share 2 under paragraph (b) of this section. See paragraph (c)(3) of this section. No adjustment is required to the basis of S1 share 2 under paragraph (c) of this section because S1 share 2 is not a loss share.

(C) Computation of loss, adjustments to stock basis. S recognizes a loss of $150 on the sale of the S1 share 1 ($170 basis over $20 amount realized) that is absorbed by the group. Under § 1.1502-32, M's basis in its S share is therefore decreased by $100, the net of the $150 loss recognized by S on the sale of the S1 share, and the $50 gain that tiered up from S1 (as a result of S1's sale of the S2 share). Following these adjustments, M's basis in the S share is $600 and the sale of the S share is still a transfer of a loss share.

(iv) Transfer in highest tier (loss share). The sale of the S share is a transfer in the next higher tier, which is the highest tier in this transaction. Because the sale is a transfer of a loss share, it is subject to this section.

(A) Basis redetermination and basis reduction under paragraphs (b) and (c) of this section. Although the transfer is subject to this section, there is no basis redetermination under paragraph (b) of this section because there is only one share of S stock outstanding (and so there can be no disparity among members' bases in common shares and there are no outstanding preferred shares with respect to which there can be unrecognized gain or loss). See paragraph (b)(1)(ii)(A) of this section. Therefore, after the application of paragraph (b) of this section, the share is still a loss share and, as such, subject to paragraph (c) of this section. In addition, no adjustment is required under paragraph (c) of this section. The S share has a disconformity amount of $230. This $230 disconformity amount is computed as the excess of the $600 basis in the S share over the S share's $370 allocable portion (1/1) of S's $370 net inside attribute amount. S's $370 net inside attribute amount is determined under paragraph (c)(5) of this section as the sum of $200 (S's $170 basis in the S1 share 1, adjusted for the $150 loss recognized with respect to that share, and S's $20 basis in each of S1 share 2 through share 10), and S's $170 basis in Asset 1. (In computing the disconformity amount, the bases of S1 share 1 and share 2 are not treated as tentatively reduced because those shares are transferred in the transaction, and the bases of S1 share 3 through share 10 are not treated as tentatively reduced because none of those shares have a disconformity amoun—each share has a basis of $20 and a $21 allocable portion (1/10) of S1's $210 net inside attribute amount, as determined in paragraph (iii)(B) of this Example 9.) However, the S share's net positive adjustment is $0 (the S share's net adjustment is negative $100). See paragraph (c)(3) of this section. Accordingly, the sale of the S share is still a transfer of a loss share. Because there are no higher-tier loss shares transferred in the transaction, this paragraph (d) then applies with respect to the transfer of the S share.

(B) Attribute reduction under this paragraph (d). (*1*) Computation of S's attribute reduction amount. Under paragraph (d)(3) of this section, S's attribute reduction amount is the lesser of P's net stock loss and S's aggregate inside loss. P's net stock loss is $360 ($600 basis over $240 amount realized). S's aggregate inside loss is the excess of S's net inside attribute amount over the value of the S share. S's net inside attribute amount is the sum of its bases in its assets, treating its S1 shares as a single share (the S1 stock) and treating S's deemed basis in the S1 stock as its basis in that stock. Under paragraph (d)(5)(i)(C) of this section, when subsidiaries are owned in multiple tiers, deemed basis is first determined for shares at the lowest tier, and then for stock in each next higher tier. Under paragraph (d)(5)(i)(B) of this section, S1's deemed basis in the S2 stock is $75 (computed as the greater of $50 (S1's $0 basis in the S2 share, adjusted for the $50 gain recognized with respect to the share) and $75 (S2's net inside attribute amount, the basis in Asset 2)). S1's deemed basis in the S3 stock is $75 (computed as the greater of $60 (S1's basis in the S3 share) and $75 (S3's net inside attribute amount, the basis in Asset 3)). S1's deemed basis in the S4 stock is $100 (computed as the greater of $100 (S1's basis in the S4 share) and $80 (S4's net inside attribute amount, the basis in Asset 4)). Accordingly, S1's net inside attribute amount is $250 ($75 deemed basis in the S2 stock plus $75 deemed basis in the S3 stock plus $100 deemed basis in the S4 stock). S's deemed basis in the S1 stock is the greater of the sum of S's actual basis in each share of S1 stock (adjusted for any gain or loss recognized) and S1's net inside attribute amount. S's actual basis in the S1 stock, adjusted for the loss recognized, is $200 (the sum of S's $170 basis in the S1 share 1, adjusted by the $150 loss recognized with respect to the share, and S's $20 basis in each of S1 share 2 through share 10). Thus, S's deemed basis in the S1 stock is $250, the greater of $200 (aggregate basis in S1 shares, adjusted for loss recognized) and $250 (S1's net inside attribute amount). As a result, S's net inside attribute amount is $420, the sum of S's $250 deemed basis in the S1 stock and S's $170 basis in Asset 1. Accordingly, the aggregate inside loss is $180, the excess of S's $420 net inside attribute amount over the $240 value of all of the S stock. S's attribute reduction amount is therefore $180, the lesser of the $360 net stock loss and the $180 aggregate inside loss.

(2) Allocation, apportionment, and application of S's attribute reduction amount. Under paragraphs (d)(4) and (d)(5)(ii) of this section, S's $180 attribute reduction amount is allocated proportionately (by basis) between Asset 1 (non-stock Category D asset) and the S1 stock. However, under paragraph (d)(5)(ii) of this section, for purposes of allocating S's $180 attribute reduction amount between S's non-stock Category D asset and the S1 stock, S's $250 deemed basis in the S1 stock is reduced by the $40 value of the transferred S1 shares (S1 share 1 and share 2) and the nontransferred S1 shares' $40 allocable portion (8/10) of S1's $50 net non-loss assets. S1's net non-loss assets is the $50 value of S1's transferred S2 shares. (S1 has no other non-loss assets, and there are no non-loss assets held by lower-tier subsidiaries.) Accordingly, for this purpose, S's deemed basis in the S1 stock is reduced by $80, from $250 to $170. Thus, $90 of the attribute reduction amount ($170/$340 x $180) is allocated to Asset 1 (reducing S's basis in Asset 1 from $170 to $80) and $90 of the attribute reduction amount ($170/$340 x $180) is allocated to the S1 stock. Under paragraph (d)(5)(iii)(A) of this section, none of the $90 allocated attribute reduction amount is apportioned to S1 share 1 because loss is recognized on the transfer of S1 share 1. Under paragraph (d)(5)(iii)(B) of this section, the $90 allocated attribute reduction amount is apportioned among the other nine shares of S1 common stock in a manner that reduces disparity to the greatest extent possible. Accordingly, of the total $90 allocated amount, $10 is apportioned to each of the remaining nine shares of S1 stock. Under paragraph (d)(5)(iii)(C) of this section, the allocated attribute reduction amount apportioned to an individual share cannot be applied to reduce the basis of the share below its value if the share is transferred other than in a recognition transfer. Because the S1 share 2 is transferred (contributed to the partnership) and the basis of S1 share 2 is already equal to its value, none of the $10 allocated attribute reduction amount apportioned to S1 share 2 is applied to reduce its basis. Because none of S1 share 3 through share 10 are transferred within the meaning of paragraph (f)(10) of this section, the $10 allocated attribute reduction amount apportioned to each of S1 share 3 through share 10 is applied fully to reduce the basis of each of those shares from $20 to $10. As a result, immediately after the allocation and application of S's attribute reduction amount, S's basis in Asset 1 is $80 ($170 minus $90), its bases in S1 share 1 and share 2 are not adjusted under paragraph (d)(5)(iii), and its basis in each of S1 share 3 through share 10 is $10. Under paragraph (d)(5)(v)(A) of this section, the entire $90 of S's attribute reduction amount that was allocated to the S1 stock is an attribute reduction amount of S1, regardless of the fact that none of the allocated amount was apportioned to S1 share 1 and none of the amount apportioned to S1 share 2 was applied to reduce the basis of S1 share 2.

(v) Attribute reduction under this paragraph (d) in next lower tier. (A) Computation of S1's attribute reduction amount. S's sale of S1 share 1 is a transfer of a loss share and it is in the next lower tier. Thus, this paragraph (d) next applies with respect to S's transfer of S1 share 1. S1's attribute reduction amount will include both the $90 attribute reduction amount that tiered down from S and any attribute reduction amount resulting from the application of this paragraph (d) with respect to S's transfer of S1 share 1 and share 2 (S1's direct attribute reduction amount). Under paragraph (d)(3) of this section, S1's direct attribute reduction amount is the lesser of the net stock loss on transferred S1 shares and S1's aggregate inside loss. The net stock loss on transferred S1 shares is $150, computed as the excess of S's $190 adjusted bases in transferred shares of S1 stock ($170 in S1 share 1 plus $20 in S1 share 2) over the $40 aggregate value of those shares. S1's aggregate inside loss is $50, the excess of S1's $250 net inside attribute amount (as calculated in paragraph (iv)(B)(1) of this Example 9) over the $200 value of all outstanding S1 shares. Therefore, S1's direct attribute reduction amount is $50, the lesser of the $150 net stock loss and S1's $50 aggregate inside loss. S1's total attribute reduction amount is thus $140, the sum of the $90 tier-down attribute reduction amount and the $50 direct attribute reduction amount.

(B) Allocation, apportionment, and application of S1's attribute reduction amount. Under paragraphs (d)(4) and (d)(5)(ii) of this section, S1's $140 attribute reduction amount is allocated proportionately (by basis) among the S2 stock, the S3 stock, and the S4 stock. However, under paragraph (d)(5)(ii) of this section, for purposes of allocating S1's $140 attribute reduction amount among S1's lower-tier subsidiary stock, S1's $75 deemed basis in the S2 stock is reduced by the $50 value of the transferred S2 share. Accordingly, for this purpose, S1's deemed basis in the S2 stock is reduced by $50, from $75 to $25. Thus, $17.50 of S1's attribute reduction amount ($25/$200 x $140) is allocated to the S2 stock, $52.50 of S1's attribute reduction amount ($75/$200 x $140) is allocated to the S3 stock, and $70 of S1's attribute reduction amount ($100/$200 x $140) is allocated to the S4 stock. Under paragraph (d)(5)(iii)(A) of this section, none of the $17.50 of S1's attribute reduction amount allocated to S2 stock is apportioned to the S2 share because gain was recognized on the transfer of the S2 share. Because neither the S3 share nor the S4 share is transferred within the meaning of paragraph (f)(10) of this section, the $52.50 of S1's attribute reduction amount allocated to the S3 stock, and the $70 of S1's attribute reduction amount allocated to the S4 stock, is apportioned to and applied fully to reduce the basis of such shares. Thus, S1's basis in the S3 share is reduced by $52.50, from $60 to $7.50, and S1's basis in the S4 stock is reduced by $70, from $100 to $30. (Note: The conforming limitation in paragraph (d)(5)(v)(B) of this section limits the application of the $90 tier down attribute reduction amount to $80, the amount by which the portion (10/10) S1's $250 net inside attribute amount attributable to S1 shares held by members exceeds $170 (the sum of the $50 direct attribute reduction amount, the $20 value of the S1 share 1 transferred in a recognition transfer, the

$20 basis (after reduction) in the S1 share 2 transferred other than in a recognition transfer, and the $80 aggregate basis (after reduction) in the nontransferred S1 shares held by members). However, the conforming limitation does not limit the application of S1's $90 tier-down attribute reduction amount because none of the $17.50 of S1's total attribute reduction amount allocated to the S2 share was applied to reduce the basis of the share. Accordingly, only $78.75 ($90--($17.50 x ($90/$140)) of the $90 tier-down attribute reduction was applied to reduce S1's attributes.) Under paragraph (d)(5)(v)(A) of this section, the attribute reduction amount allocated to the S2 stock, the S3 stock, and the S4 stock becomes an attribute reduction amount of S2, S3, and S4, respectively (even though the amount allocated to S2 stock was not apportioned to or applied to reduce the basis of the S2 share).

(vi) Attribute reduction under this paragraph (d) in lowest tier. Although the sale of the S2 share is a transfer of subsidiary stock at the next lower tier, the S2 share is not a loss share. Thus, this paragraph (d) does not apply with respect to that transfer. However, S2, S3, and S4 have attribute reduction amounts that tiered down from S1 and that are applied to reduce attributes under this paragraph (d).

(A) Tier down of S1's attribute reduction amount to S2. Under the general rules of this paragraph (d), S2's $17.50 tier-down attribute reduction amount is allocated and applied to reduce S2's basis in Asset 2 from $75 to $57.50.

(B) Tier down of S1's attribute reduction amount to S3. Under the general rules of this paragraph (d), S3's $52.50 tier-down attribute reduction amount is allocated and applied to reduce S3's basis in Asset 3 from $75 to $22.50.

(C) Tier down of S1's attribute reduction amount to S4, application of conforming limitation. Under the general rules of this paragraph (d), S4's $70 tier-down attribute reduction amount is allocated to, and would be applied to reduce, S4's basis in Asset 4. However, under paragraph (d)(5)(v)(B) of this section, the reduction is limited to the excess of S4's $80 net inside attribute amount over the $30 basis of the S4 share (after reduction under this paragraph (d)). As a result, only $50 (the excess of $80 over $30) of S4's $70 attribute reduction amount is applied to S4's basis in Asset 4, reducing it from $80 to $30. The $20 unapplied portion of S4's tier-down attribute reduction amount subject to the conforming limitation is disregarded and has no further effect.

(vii) Application of basis restoration rule. Under paragraph (d)(5)(vi)(A) of this section, after this paragraph (d) has been applied with respect to all transfers of subsidiary stock, any reduction made to the basis of a share of lower-tier subsidiary stock under paragraph (d)(5)(iii) of this section is reversed to the extent necessary to conform the basis of that share to the share's allocable portion of the subsidiary's net inside attribute amount. Restoration adjustments are first made at the lowest tier and then at each next higher tier successively.

(A) Basis restoration at lowest tier. The basis of the S2 share was not reduced under paragraph (d)(5)(iii) of this section and so there is no restoration of any basis in the S2 share. S3's $22.50 net inside attribute amount (after reduction under this paragraph (d)) exceeds S1's $7.50 basis in the S3 share (after reduction under this paragraph (d)) by $15. To conform S1's basis in the S3 share to S3's net inside attribute amount, the $52.50 reduction to the basis of the S3 share under paragraph (d)(5)(iii) of this section is reversed by $15 (restoring S1's basis in the S3 share to $22.50). The restoration of S1's basis in the S3 share does not tier up to affect the basis in stock of any other subsidiary. S1's $30 basis in the S4 share (after reduction under this paragraph (d)) is already conformed with S4's $30 net inside attribute amount (after reduction under this paragraph (d)) and so there is no restoration of any basis in the S4 share.

(B) Basis restoration at next higher tier. Each share of S1 stock has an allocable portion of S1's net inside attribute amount (after reduction) equal to $10.25 (1/10 x $102.50, the sum of S1's $0 basis in the S2 stock, adjusted for the $50 gain recognized with respect to the share, S1's $22.50 basis in the S3 stock (after restoration), and S1's $30 basis in the S4 stock). Neither S's basis in S1 share 1 nor S's basis in S1 share 2 was reduced under paragraph (d)(5)(iii) of this section. Accordingly, there is no restoration of any basis in either S1 share 1 or share 2. However, S's basis in each of S1 share 3 through share 10 was reduced under paragraph (d)(5)(iii) of this section by $10, from $20 to $10. Accordingly, the $10 reduction to the basis of each of those shares is reversed to the extent of $.25, to restore the basis of each such share to $10.25 (its allocable portion of S1's net inside attribute amount).

(viii) Results. After the application of this section, P recognizes a loss of $360 on the sale of the S share, S recognizes a loss of $150 on the sale of S1 share 1, and S1 recognizes a $50 gain on the sale of the S2 share. Immediately after the transaction, the entities each directly own the following:

Entity	Asset	Basis	Value
P1	S share	$240	$240
P	Proceeds of the sale of S share	240	240
S	Proceeds of sale of S1 share 1	20	20
	Partnership interest received for S1 share 2	20	20
	S1 share 3 through share 10	82 ($10.25 per share)	
	Asset 1	80	
S1	Proceeds of sale of S2 share	50	50
	The S3 share	22.50	
	The S4 share	30	
S2	Asset 2	57.50	
S3	Asset 3	22.50	
S4	Asset 4	30	
X	S1 share 1	20	20
Partnership	S1 share 2	20	20
Y	The S2 share	50	50

(e) Operating rules. *(1) Predecessors, successors.* This section applies to predecessor or successor persons, groups, and assets to the extent necessary to effectuate the purposes of this section.

(2) Adjustments for prior transactions that altered stock basis or other attributes. In certain situations, M's basis in S stock or S's attributes may be adjusted in a manner that alters the relationship between stock basis and inside attributes and prevents that relationship from identifying the extent to which stock basis reflects unrecognized gain and duplicated loss. The provisions of this paragraph (e)(2) modify the computations in paragraphs (c) and (d) of this section to adjust for the effects of such adjustments.

(i) Prior reductions to S's basis in assets or other attributes pursuant to section 362(e)(2)(A). If M transferred loss property to S in an intercompany transaction subject to section 362(e)(2) (for example, if the transfer was prior to September 17, 2008, no election was made to apply § 1.1502-80(h), and, as a result, S's attributes were reduced under section 362(e)(2)), then the disconformity amount of the S shares received in the section 362(e)(2) transaction is reduced by the amount that the basis in such shares would have been reduced under section 362(e)(2)(C) had such an election been made. In addition, for purposes of determining the attribute reduction amount under paragraph (d) of this section resulting from the transfer of any S shares received (or deemed received) in such a transfer, and for purposes of applying paragraph (d)(5)(v)(B) of this section (conforming limitation) to S, the bases in such shares is treated as reduced by the amount the bases in such shares would have been reduced under section 362(e)(2)(C) had such an election been made.

(ii) Prior reductions to the basis of any share of S stock pursuant to an election under section 362(e)(2)(C). If M transferred loss property to S in an intercompany transaction subject to section 362(e)(2) and the basis of any share of S stock was reduced as the result of an election under section 362(e)(2)(C) (including in the hands of a predecessor, to the extent that the effect of the election remains reflected in the basis of the S stock), then, for purposes of computing either any S share's disconformity amount or S's aggregate inside loss, and for purposes of applying paragraph (d)(5)(vi)(A) of this section (stock basis restoration) to S, S's net inside attribute amount is treated as reduced by the amount that S's attributes would have been reduced under section 362(e)(2)(A) in the absence of an election under section 362(e)(2)(C). Notwithstanding the general rule of this paragraph (e)(2)(ii), no reduction will be required to the extent that the group can establish that the net loss in the S shares transferred by M is no longer reflected in S's net inside attributes.

(iii) Other adjustments. Appropriate adjustments will be made in any other case in which an adjustment to S's net inside attributes or to M's basis in a share of S stock alters the relationship between such amounts, and the adjustment does not relate to the extent to which loss reflected in M's basis in S stock is noneconomic or duplicated within the meaning of this section.

(3) Special rules for subsidiary stock transferred in an intercompany transaction. (i) In general. This section applies with respect to M's transfer of a share of S stock to another member in an intercompany transaction in which M's intercompany item is deferred under § 1.1502-13 (and to any subsequent transfer of that share by a member) as of the time M's intercompany item is taken into account under § 1.1502-13. In determining the application of this section, all transferor-members are treated as divisions of a single corporation. Appropriate adjustments will be made to the intercompany item(s), any member's basis in an S share, to S's attributes, or any combination thereof, to further the purposes of this section and § 1.1502-13.

(ii) Certain prior intercompany transactions. If M transferred a share of S stock to another member before September 17, 2008 and M's intercompany item related to the transfer is taken into account on or after September 17, 2008, P may elect to apply this paragraph (e)(3) to the transfer. The election is made in the manner provided in paragraph (e)(5) of this section.

(iii) Examples. The application of this paragraph (e)(3) is illustrated by the following examples:

Example (1). Intercompany sale with duplicated loss. (i) Buying member later sells at gain. (A) Facts. M owns the sole outstanding share of stock of S with a basis of $100. S has one asset with a basis of $100. M sells the S share to M1 for $70, recognizing a loss of $30. While owned by M1, S recognizes $10 of depreciation deductions that are absorbed by the group. S's basis in the asset is reduced by $10 (from $100 to $90), and M1's basis in the S stock is reduced under § 1.1502-32 by $10 (from $70 to $60). Later, M1 sells the S share to X, an unrelated person, for $80.

(B) Analysis. M's sale of its S share to M1 is a transfer of the share, but this section applies as of the time M's intercompany item is taken into account under § 1.1502-13, as if M and M1 were divisions of a single corporation. If M and M1 were divisions of a single corporation, the S share's basis would be $90 ($100 reduced by $10 for the depreciation deductions absorbed by the group) and the group would recognize a $10 loss on the sale of the share that is potentially subject to this section. Thus, the sale would be a transfer of a loss share (to the extent of $10) and would be subject to this section (to the extent of that $10). Although the transfer would be subject to this section, there would be no adjustment under paragraph (b) of this section (S has only one share outstanding and so there is no disparity in bases of common shares and no unrecognized gain or loss with respect to preferred) or under paragraph (c) of this section (S has no net positive adjustment). Thus, after the application of paragraph (c) of this section, the share would still be a loss share and would therefore be subject to paragraph (d) of this section. Under paragraph (d) of this section, S would be subject to $10 of attribute reduction (the lesser of the $10 net stock loss and S's $10 aggregate inside loss), allocable to the basis in S's asset. Accordingly, S's basis in its asset is reduced by $10, from $90 to $80, M takes its $30 intercompany stock loss into account, and M1 recognizes a $20 stock gain.

(ii) Selling member deconsolidates. Assume the same facts as in paragraph (i)(A) of this Example 1, except that M1 does not sell the S share and M ceases to be a member of the group when the value of the S share is $80. Under § 1.1502-13, M's deconsolidation causes M's intercompany loss to be taken into account and this section applies at that time. At the time that M deconsolidates, if M and M1 were divisions of a single corporation, the basis in the S share would be $90 ($100 reduced by $10 for the depreciation deductions absorbed by the group) and the group would recognize a $10 loss on the sale of the share that is potentially subject to this section. Such a sale would be a transfer of a loss share (to the extent of $10) and would be subject to this section (to the extent of that $10). The analysis is then the same as in paragraph (i)(B) of this Example 1. As a result, S's basis in its asset is reduced from $90 to $80, M takes its $30 intercompany stock loss into account, and M1 holds the

S stock with a basis of $60 (and an unrecognized gain of $20).

(iii) M1 sells the S share at a loss. Assume the same facts as in paragraph (i)(A) of this Example 1, except that S declines in value and M1 sells the S share to X for $50, realizing a $10 loss. In this case, if M and M1 were divisions of a single corporation, the share's basis would be $90 ($100 reduced by $10 for the depreciation deductions absorbed by the group) and the group would recognize a $40 loss on the sale of the share that is potentially subject to this section. Thus, the sale would be a transfer of a loss share (to the extent of $40) and would be subject to this section (to the extent of that $40). Although the transfer would be subject to this section, for the reasons set forth in paragraph (i)(B) of this Example 1, there would be no adjustment under either paragraph (b) or paragraph (c) of this section. Thus, after the application of paragraph (c), the share would still be a loss share and would therefore be subject to paragraph (d) of this section. Under paragraph (d) of this section, S would be subject to $40 of attribute reduction (the lesser of the $40 net stock loss and S's $40 aggregate inside loss), allocable to the basis in S's asset. Accordingly, S's basis in its asset is reduced by $40, from $90 to $50, M takes its $30 intercompany stock loss into account, and M1 recognizes a $10 stock loss.

Example (2). Intercompany sale of built-in gain stock. (i) Facts. M owns the sole outstanding share of stock of S with a basis of $100. S's sole asset has a basis of $0. S sells its asset for $100 and recognizes a $100 gain that increases M's basis in its S share under § 1.1502-32 to $200. M sells the S share to M1 for $100 and recognizes a $100 intercompany loss. Later, M1 sells the S share to X, an unrelated person, for $120.

(ii) Analysis. M's sale of the S share to M1 is a transfer of the share, but this section applies as of the time M's intercompany item is taken into account under § 1.1502-13, as if M and M1 were divisions of a single corporation. If M and M1 were divisions of a single corporation, the S share's basis would be $200 ($100 increased by $100 for the gain recognized on the sale of the asset) and the group would recognize an $80 loss on the sale of the share that is potentially subject to this section. Thus, the sale would be a transfer of a loss share (to the extent of $80) and would be subject to this section (to the extent of that $80). Although the transfer would be subject to this section, there would be no adjustment under paragraph (b) of this section (S has only one share outstanding and so there is no disparity in bases of common shares and no unrecognized gain or loss with respect to preferred). Thus, after the application of paragraph (b), the share would still be a loss share and would therefore be subject to paragraph (c) of this section. Under paragraph (c) of this section, the basis in the S share would be reduced, but not below its $120 value, by the lesser of the $100 disconformity amount and the $100 net positive adjustment that was applied to the share when held by M. Accordingly, the basis in the S share would be reduced by $80, to $120. Because the S share would not be a loss share after the application of paragraph (c) of this section, paragraph (d) of this section would not apply to the transfer. As a result, because the positive adjustment was applied to the share when held by M, M's intercompany item is adjusted to reflect what it would have been had M's basis in its S share been reduced by $80 immediately before its sale to M1. Thus, M's intercompany loss is reduced to $20 and M takes this loss into account, and M1 recognizes a gain of $20.

Example (3). Intercompany sale creates built-in gain stock. (i) Facts. M owns the sole outstanding share of stock of S with a basis of $0. S's sole asset has a basis of $0. M sells the S share to M1 for $100 and recognizes a $100 intercompany gain. While owned by M1, S sells its asset for $100, recognizing a $100 gain that increases M1's basis in the S share under § 1.1502-32 to $200. Later, M1 sells the S share to X for $120.

(ii) Analysis. M's sale of its S share to M1 is a transfer of the share, but this section applies as of the time M's intercompany item is taken into account under § 1.1502-13, as if M and M1 were divisions of a single corporation. If M and M1 were divisions of a single corporation, the S share's basis would be $100 ($0 increased by $100 for the gain recognized on the sale of the asset) and the group would recognize a $20 gain on the sale of the share. Thus, the sale would not be a transfer of a loss share and this section would not apply to the transfer. Accordingly, under this paragraph (e)(3), no portion of M1's $80 loss is subject to this section. M takes its $100 intercompany stock gain into account, and M1 recognizes an $80 loss.

Example (4). Disparate bases in members' shares. (i) Facts. M holds Share A, one of the two outstanding shares of S stock, with a basis of $50 and M1 holds Share B, the other outstanding share of S stock with a basis of $0. S has $50 cash and an asset with a basis of $0. S sells the asset for $50, recognizing a $50 gain that increases M's basis in its S share under § 1.1502-32 by $25 (from $50 to $75) and increases M1's basis under § 1.1502-32 by $25 (from $0 to $25). Later, M sells its Share A to M1 for $50 and recognizes a $25 intercompany loss. Later, M1 sells both S shares to X for $100.

(ii) Analysis. M's sale of its Share A to M1 is a transfer of the share, but this section applies as of the time M's intercompany item is taken into account under § 1.1502-13, as if M and M1 were divisions of a single corporation. If M and M1 were divisions of a single corporation, the basis of Share A would be $75 ($50 increased by $25 for its share of the gain recognized on the sale of the asset), the basis of Share B would be $25, and the group would recognize a $25 loss on the sale of Share A that is potentially subject to this section and a $25 gain on the sale of Share B. Thus, the sale would be a transfer of a loss share (to the extent of $25) and would be subject to this section (to the extent of that $25). Although the transfer is subject to this section, there would be no adjustment under paragraph (b) of this section (all S shares held by members are transferred to a nonmember in one taxable transaction). Thus, after the application of paragraph (b), Share A would still be a loss share and therefore subject to paragraph (c) of this section. Under paragraph (c)(7) of this section, the basis of Share A would be treated as reduced by the gain recognized and taken into account with respect to the transfer of Share B in the same transaction, and so Share A would not be a loss share for purposes of paragraph (c) of this section. Although the share would be a loss share after the application of paragraph (c) of this section, no adjustment would be required under paragraph (d) of this section because there would be no net stock loss in the transaction. Because no adjustment would be made under this section if M and M1 were divisions of a single corporation, M takes its $25 intercompany stock loss into account and M1 recognizes a gain of $25. Alternatively, if the group elects to apply paragraph (b) of this section, M's intercompany item would be adjusted to reflect what it would have been had the $25 investment adjustment applied to Share A been reallocated to Share B, and M1's basis in Share B would be increased by that amount. If so, M's $25 intercompany loss would be reduced to zero, M1's basis in Share B would be increased from $25 to $50, and there would be no gain or loss recognized on either share.

Example (5). Subsidiary with built-in gain and built-in loss assets. (i) Facts. M owns the sole outstanding share of stock of S with a basis of $100. S has two assets, Asset 1 with a basis of $0 and Asset 2 with a basis of $80. M sells the S share to M1 for $90 and recognizes a $10 intercompany loss. While owned by M1, S sells Asset 1 for $60, recognizing a $60 gain that increases M1's basis in the S share under § 1.1502-32 to $150. Later, M1 sells the S share to X for $90.

(ii) Analysis. M's sale of the S share to M1 is a transfer of the share, but this section applies as of the time M's intercompany item is taken into account under § 1.1502-13, as if M and M1 were divisions of a single corporation. If M and M1 were divisions of a single corporation, the S share's basis would be $160 ($100 increased by $60 for the gain recognized on the sale of Asset 1) and the group would recognize a $70 loss on the sale of the share that is potentially subject to this section. Thus, the sale would be a transfer of a loss share (to the extent of $70) and would be subject to this section (to the extent of that $70). Although the transfer is subject to this section, there would be no adjustment under paragraph (b) of this section (S has only one share outstanding and so there is no disparity in bases of common shares and no unrecognized gain or loss with respect to preferred). Thus, after the application of paragraph (b), the share would still be a loss share and would therefore be subject to paragraph (c) of this section. Under paragraph (c) of this section, the basis in the S share would be reduced, but not below its $90 value, by the lesser of the $20 disconformity amount ($160 stock basis over $140 net inside attribute amount) and the $60 net positive adjustment that was applied to the share when held by M1. Accordingly, the basis in the S share would be reduced by $20, to $140. Because the S share would still be a loss share after the application of paragraph (c) of this section, paragraph (d) of this section would apply to the transfer. Under paragraph (d) of this section, S would have an attribute reduction amount of $50, the lesser of the $50 net stock loss ($140 basis over $90 value) and S's $50 aggregate inside loss (the excess of the sum of S's $80 basis in Asset 2 and S's $60 cash from the sale of Asset 1, over the $90 value of the S share). The adjustments required under this section are applied as follows: because the positive adjustment was applied to the share when held by M1, the $20 basis reduction required under paragraph (c) of this section is applied to M1's basis in its S share immediately before its sale to X, reducing it from $150 to $130. In addition, pursuant to paragraph (d) of this section, S's basis in Asset 2 is reduced by $50, from $80 to $30. M takes its $10 intercompany stock loss into account and M1 recognizes a loss of $40.

(iii) Allocation of basis reduction. Assume the same facts as in paragraph (i) of this Example 5, except that, while S is held by M, S earns $30 (consuming a portion of Asset 1) and, while S is held by M1, S earns $20 (consuming a portion of Asset 1) and sells Asset 1 for $10. Thus, M's basis in the S share immediately before the sale to M1 is $130, and M recognizes a $40 intercompany stock loss, and M1's basis in the S share immediately before the sale to X is $120. The analysis regarding the application of this section is the same as in paragraph (ii) of this Example 5. On a separate entity basis, M's basis in the S share would be subject to a $20 reduction under paragraph (c) of this section (at the time M transferred the S share the share had a $30 net positive adjustment and a $20 disconformity amount), and M1's basis in the S share would not be subject to reduction under paragraph (c) of this section (at the time M1 transferred the S share the share had a $30 net positive adjustment and a $20 negative disconformity amount). Therefore, the $20 basis reduction required under paragraph (c) of this section is allocated entirely to M. Accordingly, M's intercompany item is adjusted to reflect what it would have been had the entire $20 basis reduction been applied to the S share while held by M, and M1's basis in the S share is not reduced. Thus, M's intercompany stock loss is reduced by $20 to $20 and M takes this loss into account, and M1 recognizes a $30 loss. S's basis in Asset 2 is reduced by $50, from $80 to $30.

(4) Limited application to multiple-member section 332 liquidations. If more than one member owns shares of S stock, paragraphs (c) and (d) of this section do not apply to any transfer of S shares resulting from a liquidation of S to which section 332 applies.

(5) Form and manner of election(s) under this section. The elections provided in this section are irrevocable and made in the form of a statement titled "Section 1.1502-36 Statement." The statement must be included on or with the group's timely filed return (original or amended, if filed by the due date for the return, including extensions) for the taxable year of the transfer of the subsidiary stock to which the election relates or, in the case of an intercompany transfer, the year in which the intercompany item from the transfer is taken into account. The statement must include—

(i) The name and employer identification number (E.I.N.) of each subsidiary with respect to which an election is being made;

(ii) If P is electing under paragraph (b)(1)(ii) of this section to redetermine basis with respect to the transfer of stock of one or more subsidiaries, a statement that members' bases in shares of [name of subsidiary or subsidiaries] stock are being redetermined notwithstanding that all members' shares of [name of subsidiary or subsidiaries] are being transferred to one or more nonmembers in one fully taxable transaction;

(iii) If P is electing under paragraph (d)(2)(ii) of this section (attribute reduction amount less than five percent of value) to apply the attribute reduction provisions, a statement that paragraph (d) of this section is being applied to the transfer of shares of stock of [names of all subsidiaries whose shares are transferred] notwithstanding that the aggregate attribute reduction amount in the transaction is less than five percent of the aggregate value of the stock of [names of all subsidiaries whose shares are transferred] transferred by members in the transaction;

(iv) If P is electing under paragraph (d)(4)(ii)(A)(*1*) of this section to specify the allocation of the attribute reduction amount, a statement (for each subsidiary for which the election is being made) that the attribute reduction amount of [name of subsidiary] is being applied (or not applied) to reduce [identify the attributes in Category A, Category B, and Category C, and the amount of each, with respect to which the election is being made];

(v) If P is electing under paragraph (d)(5)(v)(B) of this section not to apply the conforming limitation on tier-down attribute reduction with respect to one or more subsidiaries, a statement that the conforming limitation in paragraph (d)(5)(v)(B) of this section is not being applied with respect to [name of subsidiary or subsidiaries];

(vi) If P is electing under paragraph (d)(5)(vi)(B) of this section not to restore lower-tier subsidiary stock basis with respect to one or more subsidiaries, a statement that members' bases in [name of subsidiary or subsidiaries] is not being restored under paragraph (d)(5)(vi)(A) of this section;

(vii) If P is electing under paragraph (d)(6) of this section to reattribute attributes, a statement (for each subsidiary for which the election is being made) that [identify the attributes in Category A, Category B, and Category C, and the amount of each or the amount in excess of an amount, with respect to which the election is being made] of [name of subsidiary] are being reattributed (or not) to P;

(viii) If P is electing under paragraph (d)(6) of this section to reduce stock basis, a statement (for each subsidiary for which the election is being made) that members' bases in shares of stock of [name of subsidiary] are being reduced by [specify amount or the amount in excess of an amount];

(ix) If P is electing under paragraph (e)(3)(ii) of this section to apply paragraph (e)(3) of this section to an intercompany transfer that occurred before September 17, 2008, a statement that paragraph (e)(3) of this section is being elected to apply to the transfer of stock of [name of subsidiary] by [name of transferor subsidiary] to [name of transferee subsidiary] on [date of transfer]; and

(x) If P is electing under § 1.1502-96(d)(5) to reattribute to itself all or any part of a section 382 limitation, a statement that P is electing to reattribute a section 382 limitation with respect to losses of [name of subsidiary or, if two or more subsidiaries are members of a loss subgroup, the name of each subsidiary in the loss subgroup]. A separate statement is made for each subsidiary or loss subgroup for which an election is being made. Each statement must include—

(A) The date of the ownership change giving rise to the separate section 382 limitation or subgroup section 382 limitation that is being apportioned;

(B) The amount of the separate (or subgroup) section 382 limitation for the taxable year in which the reattribution occurs (determined without reference to any apportionment under this section or § 1.1502-95(c)); and

(C) The amount of each net operating loss carryover, capital loss carryover, or deferred deduction, and the year in which it arose, of the subsidiary (or subsidiaries) that is subject to the separate section 382 limitation or subgroup section 382 limitation that is being apportioned to the common parent, and the amount of the value element and adjustment element of that limitation that is apportioned to the common parent.

(f) Definitions. In addition to the definitions in other paragraphs of this section and in other provisions of the regulations under section 1502, the following definitions apply for purposes of this section.

(1) Allocable portion has the same meaning as in § 1.1502-32(b)(4)(iii)(B). Thus, for example, within a class of stock, each share has the same allocable portion of the net inside attribute amount and, if there is more than one class of stock, the net inside attribute amount is allocated to each class by taking into account the terms of each class and all other facts and circumstances relating to the overall economic arrangement.

(2) Deferred deduction means any deduction for expenses or loss that would be taken into account under general tax accounting principles as of the time of the transfer of the share, but that is nevertheless not taken into account immediately after the transfer by reason of the application of a deferral provision. Such provisions include, for example, sections 267(f) and 469, and § 1.1502-13. "Deferred deduction" also includes S's portion of such consolidated tax attributes, for example consolidated excess charitable contributions that would be apportioned to S under the principles of § 1.1502-79(e) if S had a separate return year. Additionally, it includes amounts equivalent to deductions, such as negative adjustments under section 475 (mark to market accounting method for dealers in securities) and section 481 (adjustments required by changes in method of accounting).

(3) Distribution has the same meaning as in § 1.1502-32(b)(3)(v).

(4) Higher-tier, lower-tier. A subsidiary (S1) (and its shares of stock) is "higher-tier" with respect to another subsidiary (S2) (and its shares of stock) if investment adjustments made to the bases of shares of S2 stock under § 1.1502-32 affect the investment adjustments made to the bases of shares of S1 stock. A subsidiary (S1) (and its shares of stock) is "lower-tier" with respect to another subsidiary (S) (and its shares of stock) if investment adjustments made to the bases of shares of S1 stock affect the investment adjustments made to the bases of shares of S stock. The term lowest-tier subsidiary generally refers to a subsidiary that owns no stock of another subsidiary. The term highest-tier subsidiary generally refers to a subsidiary the stock of which is not lower tier to any shares transferred in the transaction.

(5) Liability means a liability that has been incurred within the meaning of section 461(h), except to the extent otherwise provided in paragraph (d)(4)(ii)(C)(1) of this section.

(6) Loss carryover means any net operating or capital loss carryover that is attributable to S, including any losses that would be apportioned to S under the principles of § 1.1502-21(b)(2) if S had a separate return year. However, solely for purposes of applying paragraph (d) of this section, loss carryovers do not include the amount of any losses waived under § 1.1502-32(b)(4).

(7) Loss share, gain share. A loss share is a share of stock with a basis that exceeds its value. A gain share is a share of stock with a value that exceeds its basis.

(8) Preferred stock, common stock. Preferred stock and common stock have the same meanings as in § 1.1502-32(d)(2) and (3), respectively.

(9) Transaction includes all the steps taken pursuant to the same plan or arrangement.

(10) Transfer. (i) Definition. Except as provided in paragraph (f)(10)(ii) of this section, for purposes of this section, M transfers a share of S stock on the earliest of—

(A) The date that M ceases to own the share as a result of a transaction in which, but for the application of this section (and notwithstanding the deferral of any amount recognized on the transfer, other than by reason of § 1.1502-13), M would recognize income, gain, loss or deduction with respect to the share (see paragraph (e)(3) of this section in the case of a transfer in an intercompany transaction);

(B) The date that M and S cease to be members of the same group;

(C) The date that a nonmember acquires the share from M; and

(D) The last day of the taxable year during which the share becomes worthless under section 165 (taking into account the provisions of § 1.1502-80(c)) if the share is treated as a capital asset, or the date the share becomes worthless (taking into account the provisions of § 1.1502-80(c)) if the share is not treated as a capital asset.

(ii) Excluded transactions. Notwithstanding paragraph (f)(10)(i) of this section, M does not transfer a share of S stock if—

(A) M ceases to own the share as a result of a transaction to which section 381(a) applies and in which either a member acquires assets from S or S acquires assets from M, provided that—

(1) M recognizes no income, gain, loss, or deduction with respect to the share, and

(2) If the transaction is a liquidation to which section 332 applies, M is the only member that owns shares of S stock (if another member owns shares of S stock, see paragraph (e)(4) of this section for a limitation on the application of this section); or

(B) M ceases to own the share as a result of a distribution of the share to a nonmember in a transaction to which section 355 applies, and in which the share is treated as qualified property for purposes of section 355(c) or section 361(c).

(11) Value means the amount realized, if any, or otherwise the fair market value.

(g) Anti-abuse rule. *(1) General rule.* If a taxpayer acts with a view to avoid the purposes of this section or to apply the rules of this section to avoid the purposes of any other rule of law, appropriate adjustments will be made to carry out the purposes of this section or such other rule of law.

(2) Examples. The following examples illustrate the principles of the anti-abuse rule in this paragraph (g). No implication is intended regarding the potential applicability of any other anti-abuse rules:

Example (1). Loss Trafficking. (i) Facts. M purchases the sole outstanding share of S stock for $100. At that time, S owns Asset 1 with a basis of $0. S sells Asset 1 for $100. Later, S purchases the sole outstanding share of X stock, a corporation with losses, with a view to liquidating X in a transaction to which section 332 applies in order to reduce S's disconformity amount. S purchases the X share for $1, and X has a $100 NOL and an asset with a basis of $1. Subsequently, M sells its S share for $100. After taking into account the effects of all applicable rules of law, M's basis in the S share is $200 (M's original $100 basis, increased under § 1.1502-32 to reflect the $100 gain recognized on the sale of Asset 1). M's sale of the S share is a transfer of a loss share and therefore subject to this section.

(ii) Analysis. Although M's transfer of the S share is subject to this section, there is no adjustment under paragraph (b) of this section (S has only one share outstanding and so there is no disparity in bases of common shares and no shares of S preferred stock outstanding (and so there is no unrecognized gain or loss on S preferred stock)). See paragraph (b)(1)(ii)(A) of this section. Accordingly, after the application of paragraph (b) of this section, M's sale of the S share is still a transfer of a loss share and therefore subject to paragraph (c) of this section. Under paragraph (c) of this section, M's $200 basis in the S share is reduced, but not below the share's $100 value, by the lesser of the share's net positive adjustment and disconformity amount. The share's net positive adjustment is $100, the positive adjustment attributable to the gain recognized on the sale of Asset 1. The share's disconformity amount is $0, the excess of M's $200 basis in the S share over S's $200 net inside attribute amount. Thus, the reduction to basis under paragraph (c) of this section would be $0. However, because S purchased the X stock and liquidated X with a view to avoiding the purposes of this section (by using X's attributes to minimize the disconformity amount of the S share), the attributes acquired from X are disregarded for purposes of applying this section. Accordingly, S's net inside attribute amount is limited to the $100 of attributes S would have had absent the purchase of the X stock, S's money ($100 from the sale of Asset 1). The loss share's disconformity amount is therefore the excess of $200 over $100, or $100. The lesser of the share's $100 net positive adjustment and $100 disconformity amount is $100. As a result, M's $200 basis in the S share is reduced by $100, to $100, and M recognizes no gain or loss on the sale of the S share.

Example (2). Use of a partnership to prevent current attribute reduction. (i) Facts. M owns all 5 outstanding shares of S common stock with a basis of $200 each. S owns Asset 1 with a basis of $1000. In year 1, with a view to preventing a current reduction in the basis of Asset 1, S contributes Asset 1 to a partnership in a transaction in which S recognizes no gain or loss. On December 31, year 2, M sells one S share for $20. After taking into account the effects of all applicable rules of law, M's basis in each S share is $200. M's sale of the S share is a transfer of a loss share and therefore subject to this section.

(i) Analysis. Although M's transfer of the S share is subject to this section, there is no basis redetermination under paragraph (b) of this section because there is no disparity among M's bases in its shares of S common stock and there are no shares of S preferred stock outstanding (and so there is no unrecognized gain or loss on S preferred stock). See paragraph (b)(1)(ii)(A) of this section. Accordingly, after the application of paragraph (b) of this section, M's sale of the S share is still a transfer of a loss share and therefore subject to paragraph (c) of this section. However, no adjustment is required under paragraph (c) of this section because both the disconformity amount and the net positive adjustment are $0. See paragraph (c)(3) of this section. Under paragraph (d) of this section, S's attribute reduction amount is $180 (the lesser of the $180 net stock loss and S's $900 aggregate inside loss ($1000 of attributes over $100 value of all of the S shares)). Absent the application of this paragraph (g), the $180 attribute reduction amount would be applied to reduce S's basis in the partnership interest. However, because S acted with a view to avoiding a current reduction in the basis of Asset 1 under paragraph (d) of this section, this section is applied by treating S as if it held Asset 1 at the time of the stock sale. The basis of Asset 1 is reduced by $180, to $820, effective immediately before the transfer to the partnership and, as a result, S's basis in its partnership interest is $820.

Example (3). Creation of an intercompany receivable to mitigate attribute reduction. (i) Facts. M owns all five outstanding shares of S common stock each with equal basis that exceeds value. S holds cash and Asset 1 with a basis that exceeds value. In year 1, with a view to mitigating a reduction in the basis of Asset 1, S lends the cash to M1. Asset 1 and the intercompany note received from M1 are assets of the same class under § 1.338-6(b)(2). On December 31, year 2, M sells one of its S shares and, without regard to this section, recognizes a loss. M's sale of the S share is a transfer of a loss share and therefore subject to this section.

(ii) Analysis. Although M's transfer of the S share is subject to this section, no adjustment is required under paragraph (b) of this section because there is no disparity among M's bases in shares of S common stock and there are no shares of S preferred stock outstanding (and so there is no unrecognized gain or loss on S preferred stock). See paragraph (b)(1)(ii)(A) of this section. Accordingly, after the application of paragraph (b) of this section, M's sale of the S shares is still a transfer of a loss share and therefore subject to paragraph (c) of this section. However, there is no adjustment under paragraph (c) of this section because the net positive adjustment is $0. See paragraph (c)(3) of this section. Under paragraph (d) of this section, S's attribute reduction amount would be applied to reduce S's basis in Asset 1 and the intercompany receivable in proportion to basis. However, because S acted with a view to mitigating the reduction in the basis of Asset 1 under paragraph (d) of this section, this section is applied without regard to the intercompany receivable. Accordingly, S's basis in Asset 1 is reduced by the full attribute reduction amount.

Example (4). Use of a partnership to reduce net stock loss. (i) Facts. M owns all ten outstanding shares of S common stock, one share (Share 1) has a basis of $0, and one share (Share 2) has a basis of $160. S has an aggregate inside loss of $80. In one transaction and with a view to mitigating a reduction in S's attributes, M contributes Share 1 to a partnership, recognizing no gain or loss, and sells Share 2 for $80. M's contribution of Share 1 to the partnership is a transfer, but the share is not a loss share and so the transfer is not subject to this section. M's sale of Share 2 is a transfer of a loss share and is therefore subject to this section.

(ii) Analysis. Although M's transfer of Share 2 is subject to this section, there is no adjustment under paragraph (b) of this section because there are no investment adjustments that have been applied to the shares. Accordingly, after the application of paragraph (b) of this section, M's sale of Share 2 is still a transfer of a loss share and therefore subject to paragraph (c) of this section. There is no adjustment under paragraph (c) of this section because the net positive adjustment is $0. See paragraph (c)(3) of this section. Accordingly, after the application of paragraph (c) of this section, M's sale of Share 2 is still a transfer of loss shares and therefore subject to paragraph (d) of this section. Under paragraph (d) of this section, the net stock loss would be determined to be $0, the excess of the $160 aggregate basis in all of the transferred shares over the $160 aggregate value of those shares. S's attribute reduction amount would be determined to be $0, the lesser of the $0 net stock loss and S's $80 aggregate inside loss. Thus, there would be no reduction of attributes under this paragraph (d) of this section. However, because M acted with a view to reducing the attribute reduction amount by transferring a gain share to a partnership while avoiding the recognition of the gain on the share, this section is applied without regard to the transfer of the gain share. Accordingly, the net stock loss is determined to be $80, and the attribute reduction amount is determined to be $80.

Example (5). Stuffing gain asset. (i) Facts. M owns the sole outstanding share of S stock (Share 1) with a basis of $100. S owns Asset 1 with a basis of $100 and a value of $20. With a view to avoid the purposes of this section, M transfers Asset 2 with a basis of $0 and a value of $80 to S in exchange for four additional shares of S stock (Share 2 through Share 5) in a transaction to which section 351 applies. M later sells Share 1 to X for $20. M's sale of Share 1 is a transfer of a loss share and therefore subject to this section.

(ii) Analysis. Although M's transfer of the Share 1 is subject to this section, there is no adjustment under paragraph (b) of this section because no investment adjustments have been applied to the basis of any S shares. Thus, after the application of paragraph (b) of this section, M's sale of the S share is still a transfer of a loss share and therefore subject to paragraph (c) of this section. There is no adjustment under paragraph (c) of this section because the net positive adjustment is $0. Accordingly, after the application of paragraph (c) of this section, M's sale of the S share is still a transfer of a loss share and therefore subject to paragraph (d) of this section. Under paragraph (d) of this section, S's attribute reduction amount would be $0, the lesser of the $80 net stock loss and S's $0 aggregate inside loss ($100 of attributes does not exceed the $100 value of all of the S shares). However, because M transferred Asset 2 to S with a view to avoid the purposes of this section, the application of this section to M's transfer of Share 1 is made without regard to the transfer of Asset 2. Accordingly, under paragraph (d) of this section, S's attribute reduction amount is $80, the lesser of the $80 net stock loss and S's $80 aggregate inside loss (computed without regard to Asset 2). S's basis in Asset 1 is therefore reduced by $80, from $100 to $20, under paragraph (d) of this section.

(iii) Transfer of all S shares. Assume the same facts as in paragraph (i) of this Example 5, except that M sells all five S shares to X, recognizing both the gain and the loss on the S shares. The transfer of Share 1 is still a transfer of a loss share and therefore subject to this section. However, because all the shares are transferred, the group's income is clearly reflected. Therefore, the purposes of this section are not avoided and this section applies without modification. S's attribute reduction amount is $0, the lesser of the $0 net stock loss and S's $0 aggregate inside loss.

(h) Effective/applicability date. This section applies to transfers of shares of subsidiary stock on or after September 17, 2008 unless the transfer was made pursuant to a binding agreement that was in effect prior to September 17, 2008 and at all times thereafter. For transfers of shares of subsidiary stock that are not subject to this section, see §§ 1.337(d)-2 and 1.1502-35.

T.D. 9424, 9/10/2008.

§ 1.1502-37 [Reserved]
§ 1.1502-38 [Reserved]
§ 1.1502-39 [Reserved]
§ 1.1502-40 [Reserved]

§ 1.1502-41A Determination of consolidated net long-term capital gain and consolidated net short-term capital loss generally applicable for consolidated return years beginning before January 1, 1997.

(a) Consolidated net long-term capital gain. The consolidated net long-term capital gain shall be determined by taking into account (1) those gains and losses to which § 1.1502-22A(a) applies which are treated as long term under section 1222, and (2) the consolidated section 1231 gain (computed in accordance with § 1.1502-23A).

(b) Consolidated net short-term capital loss. The consolidated net short-term capital loss shall be determined by taking into account (1) those gains and losses to which § 1.1502-22A(a) applies which are treated as short term under section 1222, and (2) the consolidated net capital loss carryovers and carrybacks to the taxable year (as determined under § 1.1502-22A(b)).

(c) Effective date. This section applies to any consolidated return years to which §§ 1.1502-21(h) or 1.1502-21T(g) in effect prior to June 25, 1999, as contained in 26 CFR part 1 revised April 1, 1999, as applicable does not apply. See §§ 1.1502-21(h) or 1.1502-21T(g) in effect prior to

June 25, 1999, as contained in 26 CFR part 1 revised April 1, 1999, as applicable for effective dates of these sections.

T.D. 6894, 9/7/66, amend T.D. 7637, 8/6/79, T.D. 8677, 6/26/96, T.D. 8823, 6/25/99.

§ 1.1502-42 Mutual savings banks, etc.

Caution: The Treasury has not yet amended Reg § 1.1502-42 to reflect changes made by P.L. 104-188.

(a) In general. This section applies to mutual savings banks and other institutions described in section 593(a).

(b) Total deposits. In computing for purposes of section 593(b)(1)(B)(ii) total deposits or withdrawable accounts at the close of the taxable year, the total deposits or withdrawable accounts of other members shall be excluded.

(c) Taxable income; taxable years for which the due date (without extensions) for filing returns is before March 15, 1983. For taxable years for which the due date (without extensions) for filing returns is before March 15, 1983, a member's taxable income for purposes of section 593(b)(2) is determined under § 1.1502-27(b) (computed without regard to any deduction under section 593(b)(2)). In addition, for taxable years beginning after July 11, 1969, taxable income as computed under the preceding sentence is subject to the adjustments provided in section 593(b)(2)(E). See § 1.593-6A(b)(5).

(d) Taxable income; taxable years for which the due date (without extensions) for filing returns is after March 14, 1983. *(1) In general.* For a taxable year for which the due date (without extensions) for filing returns is after March 14, 1983, a thrift's taxable income for purposes of section 593(b)(2) is its tentative taxable income (as defined in paragraph (e)(1) of this section).

(2) Definitions. For purposes of this section—

(i) A "thrift" is a member described in section 593(a).

(ii) A "nonthrift" is a member that is not a thrift.

(e) Tentative taxable income (or loss). *(1) Thrift.* For purposes of this section, a thrift's tentative taxable income (or loss) is its separate taxable income (determined under § 1.1502-12 without paragraph (q) thereof and without any deduction under section 593(b)), subject to the following adjustments in the following order:

(i) The adjustments described in paragraph (e)(3) of this section;

(ii) The adjustments described in section 593(b)(2)(E) for those thrifts with separate taxable income greater than zero (determined after the adjustments under paragraph (e)(3) of this section); and

(iii) The adjustments described in paragraph (f) of this section.

(2) Nonthrift. For purposes of this section, a nonthrift's tentative taxable income (or loss) is its separate taxable income (determined under § 1.1502-12), adjusted for the portion of the consolidated net operating loss deduction attributable to the member, the portion of the consolidated net capital loss carryover or carryback attributable to the member, and further adjusted as described in paragraph (e)(3) of this section.

(3) Adjustments for all members. For each member, the following adjustments taken into account in the computation of consolidated taxable income are included in determining its tentative taxable income (or loss) in order to adjust separate taxable income of the member to take into account certain consolidated items:

(i) The portions of the consolidated charitable contributions deduction and the consolidated dividends received deduction attributable to the member.

(ii) The member's capital gain net income, determined without any net capital loss carryover or carryback attributable to the member.

(iii) The member's net capital loss and section 1231 net loss, reduced by the portion of the consolidated net capital loss attributable to the member.

(f) Adjustments for thrifts. *(1) Reductions.* A thrift's separate taxable income (as adjusted under paragraph (e)(3) of this section) is reduced (but not below zero) by losses of thrifts and to the extent attributable to functionally related activities, losses of a nonthrift. Certain operating rules for determining the amount of the reductions are provided in paragraph (f)(4) of this section. The reductions are made in the following amounts in the following order:

(i) The thrift's allocable share (as determined under paragraph (h)(2) of this section) of another thrift's tentative taxable loss. That tentative taxable loss is determined by including a deduction under section 593(b) (other than paragraph (2) thereof) for the year in which the loss arises.

(ii) The thrift's allocable share (as determined under paragraph (h)(3) of this section) of the portion of the consolidated net operating loss deduction attributable to it or another thrift. That consolidated net operating loss deduction is determined by including a deduction under section 593(b) (other than paragraph (2) thereof) for the year in which the loss arose. The portion of a consolidated net operating loss deduction attributable to another thrift is computed by excluding losses arising in taxable years for which the due date (without extensions) for filing returns is before March 15, 1983.

(iii) The thrift's allocable share (as determined under paragraph (h)(4) of this section) of the loss attributable to functionally related activities of a nonthrift (as determined under paragraph (g) of this section). For a rule netting that share against certain income attributable to functionally related activities of that nonthrift, see paragraph (f)(4)(iv) of this section.

(iv) The thrift's allocable share (as determined under paragraph (h)(3) of this section) of the portion of the consolidated net operating loss deduction attributable to functionally related activities of a nonthrift (as determined under paragraph (h)(5) of this section). That consolidated net operating loss deduction is determined by excluding losses arising in taxable years for which the due date (without extensions) for filing returns is before March 15, 1983. For a rule netting that share against certain income attributable to functionally related activities of that nonthrift, see paragraph (f)(4)(iv) of this section.

(2) Increases. (i) A thrift's separate taxable income (as adjusted under paragraphs (e)(3) and (f)(1) of this section) is increased in a subsequent consolidated return year to restore reductions made in a prior consolidated return year to a thrift's separate taxable income by reason of losses of a nonthrift. This increase is the amount of the thrift's allocable share (as determined under paragraph (h)(6) of this section) of the income attributable to functionally related activities of a nonthrift in a consolidated return year and is made only in that year. This increase is made only if both the thrift and the nonthrift were members of the group in the consolidated

return years in which both the reduction and increase are made.

(ii) This subdivision (ii) limits the increases to a thrift's separate taxable income to assure that income of a particular nonthrift is used to restore reductions of a thrift only to the extent that such nonthrift's losses reduced the thrift's income. Therefore, as of the end of a consolidated return year, the cumulative increases to a thrift's tentative taxable income (by reason of income attributable to functionally related activities of a nonthrift) may not exceed the cumulative reductions to the thrift's separate taxable income made (by reason of the nonthrift's functionally related activities) under paragraph (f)(1)(iii) and (iv) of this section in the current and all prior consolidated return years during which both the thrift institution and the nonthrift institution were members of the group.

(iii) For a netting rule, see paragraph (f)(4)(iv) of this section.

(3) Special rule. (i) If a carryback to a thrift's separate taxable income diminishes the reduction to a thrift's separate taxable income for a prior consolidated return year otherwise required by paragraph (f)(1)(iii) or (iv) of this section, then any increases to a thrift's separate taxable income under paragraph (f)(2) of this section for an intervening consolidated return year must be recomputed to take into account the effect of such carryback. Thus, if a net operating loss attributable to a thrift is carried back and completely offsets the thrift's separate taxable income (before the reductions under paragraph (f)(1)(iii) or (iv) or this section), any increase to the thrift's separate taxable income under paragraph (f)(2) of this section (attributable to a reduction in the year to which the loss is carried) for an intervening consolidated return year will be eliminated. The recomputation required by this subparagraph (3) must be reflected on an amended return for the intervening consolidated return year for which the increase was previously reported. See example (2) in paragraph (j) of this section.

(ii) If a deficiency for an intervening consolidated return year results from the application of paragraph (f)(3)(i) of this section with respect to an item to which section 6501(h) applies, the deficiency may be assessed at any time within the period described in section 6501(h).

(iii) For purposes of chapter 67 of the Code (relating to interest), the last date prescribed for payment of any tax owed as a result of the application of paragraph (f)(3)(i) of this section is deemed to be the last day of the taxable year for which the item carried back arose.

(4) Operating rules. For purposes of paragraphs (d) through (j) of this section—

(i) The portion of a consolidated net operating loss deduction attributable to a member is determined as follows:

(A) First, determine under § 1.1502-79(a)(3) the portion of each consolidated net operating loss attributable to the member for the particular year in which the loss arose.

(B) Second, apply the anti-double-counting rule in paragraph (h)(3)(iii) of this section so as not to take the same loss into account twice.

(C) Finally, apply the loss absorption limit in paragraph (f)(4)(iii) of this section to the total amount of the consolidated net operating loss deduction from a particular loss year.

(ii) Capital loss carryovers and carrybacks shall be taken into account in a manner consistent with the principles of paragraphs (d) through (j) of this section.

(iii) This subdivision (iii) prescribes a loss absorption limit. The total amount of the consolidated net operating loss deduction from a given year (loss year) taken into account as reductions under paragraph (f)(1) of this section for another year (absorption year) shall not exceed the amount of the consolidated net operating loss deduction attributable to the loss year absorbed in computing consolidated taxable income for the absorption year. For this purpose, consolidated taxable income for the absorption year shall include a deduction under section 593(b) (other than paragraph (2) thereof) for each thrift member.

(iv) This subdivision (iv) prescribes a rule for netting in certain cases income attributable to functionally related activities of a nonthrift in a consolidated return year ("income year") against losses attributable to functionally related activities of that nonthrift which arise in a consolidated return year ("loss year"). That nonthrift's income is netted against the portion of that nonthrift's loss which would otherwise be applied in a consolidated return year ("reduction year") under paragraph (f)(1)(iii) or (iv) of this section to reduce a thrift's tentative taxable income, but—

(A) Only if the income year is not later than the loss year and the reduction year, and

(B) Only to the extent the income had not previously been taken into account under paragraph (f)(2) of this section or this subdivision (iv) as of the close of the later of the loss year and the reduction year.

(g) Income (or loss) attributable to functionally related activities of a nonthrift. *(1) In general.* For purposes of this section, the income (or loss) attributable to functionally related activities of a nonthrift is the income (or loss) of the nonthrift.

(i) Attributable to the provision of assets or the rendition of services to a thrift (such as the leasing of office space or providing computer or financial services), or

(ii) Derived from the assets described in section 7701(a)(19)(C)(iii) through (x), but only if such assets comprise 5 percent or more of the gross assets of the nonthrift.

(2) Amount of income (or loss). The amount of income (or loss) from such activities is the excess of (i) gross income from such activities over (ii) the deductions of the nonthrift allocable and apportionable to that gross income under the principles of § 1.861-8. The loss attributable to functionally related activities of a nonthrift is the excess (if any) of such deductions over such gross income. That loss, however, may not exceed the amount of the tentative taxable loss of that nonthrift (determined by excluding losses arising in taxable years for which the due date (without extensions) for filing returns is before March 15, 1983).

(h) Allocation of income and losses. *(1) In general.* Paragraph (h)(2)–(5) of this section provides rules for allocating different losses among thrifts that have tentative taxable income greater than zero. Generally, these allocations are made in the order listed in paragraph (f)(1) of this section and are based upon the relative tentative taxable income of the thrifts to which the particular loss is allocated. For purposes of each allocation under a subdivision of such paragraph (f)(1), the tentative taxable income of the thrifts used in making this allocation is reduced by the thrift's allocable share of losses allocated to the thrift under a prior subdivision of such paragraph (f)(1). Accordingly, for purposes of this paragraph (h), tentative taxable income is determined without regard to paragraph (f) of this section, except as otherwise provided. Paragraph (h)(6) of this section provides rules for allocating income attributable to functionally related activities of a nonthrift based upon the relative reductions to thrift income made on account of that nonthrift.

(2) Allocation of tentative taxable loss of other thrifts. For purposes of paragraph (f)(1)(i) of this section, a thrift's allocable share of another thrift's tentative taxable loss is the loss multiplied by a fraction. The numerator of the fraction is the tentative taxable income (if greater than zero) of the thrift, and the denominator is the aggregate of such tentative taxable income of each thrift.

(3) Allocation of portions of a consolidated net operating loss deduction. (i) For purposes of paragraph (f)(1)(ii) of this section, a first thrift's allocable share of the portion of the consolidated net operating loss deduction attributable to another thrift is determined under paragraph (h)(2) of this section as if that portion were a tentative taxable loss of that other thrift and by computing tentative taxable income under such paragraph (h)(2) by taking into account paragraph (f)(1)(i) of this section. A thrift's allocable share of the portion of the consolidated net operating loss deduction attributable to that thrift is equal to that entire portion.

(ii) For purposes of paragraph (f)(1)(iv) of this section, a thrift's allocable share of the portion of a consolidated net operating loss deduction attributable to functionally related activities of a nonthrift (determined under paragraph (h)(5) of this section) is determined under paragraph (h)(4) of this section as if that portion were a loss attributable to functionally related activities of the nonthrift and by computing tentative taxable income under such paragraph (h)(4) by taking into account paragraph (f)(1)(i), (ii), and (iii) of this section.

(iii) This subdivision (iii) prevents the "double-counting" of losses. The reduction to the tentative taxable income of a thrift is diminished to the extent the loss that gave rise to the reduction has previously been taken into account in reducing a thrift's tentative taxable income. Thus, any loss taken into account as a reduction to a thrift's separate taxable income under any subdivision of paragraph (f)(1) of this section shall be reduced (but not below zero) to the extent taken into account—

(A) In a prior consolidated return year under any subdivision of such paragraph (f)(1) or

(B) In the current consolidated return year under a previous subdivision of such paragraph (f)(1).

(4) Allocation of loss attributable to functionally related activities of a nonthrift. For purposes of paragraph (f)(1)(iii) of this section, a thrift's allocable share of a loss attributable to functionally related activities of a nonthrift is determined by multiplying the loss by a fraction. The numerator of the fraction is the tentative taxable income (if greater than zero) of the thrift (taking into account paragraph (f)(1)(i) and (ii) of this section) and the denominator is the aggregate of such tentative taxable income (so determined) of each thrift.

(5) Portion of the consolidated net operating loss deduction attributable to functionally related activities of a particular nonthrift. The portion of the consolidated net operating loss deduction attributable to functionally related activities of a particular nonthrift is the lesser of the following two amounts:

(i) The portion of the consolidated net operating loss deduction attributable to that nonthrift.

(ii) The aggregate of the losses attributable to functionally related activities of that nonthrift for the taxable years in which the consolidated net operating loss deduction arose.

(6) Allocation of income attributable to functionally related activities of a nonthrift. For purposes of paragraph (f)(2) of this section, a thrift institution's allocable share of the income attributable to functionally related activities of a nonthrift is determined by multiplying that income by a fraction. The numerator of the fraction is the amount of the cumulative reductions referred to in paragraph (f)(2)(ii) of this section (minus the cumulative increases under paragraph (f)(2) of this section) made on account of that nonthrift for the thrift and the denominator is the sum of such cumulative reductions (minus such cumulative increases) made on account of that nonthrift for all thrifts.

(7) Proper accounting The provisions of section 482 apply in determining a thrift institution's tentative taxable income, and in determining the gross income and deductions attributable to functionally related activities. For example, an expense such as the salary of an individual who performs services for both a thrift and a nonthrift must be allocated in a manner that fairly reflects the value of the services rendered to each.

(i) [Reserved]

(j) Examples. The provisions of this section may be illustrated by the following examples. In each example the letter "T" for a member denotes a thrift and the letters "NT" denote a nonthrift. Also, in each example, a thrift loss includes a bad debt deduction under section 593(b) (other than paragraph (2) thereof) for such year and a thrift with income would have such a bad debt deduction of zero.

Example (1). (a) In 1983, corporations T1, T2, NT1, and NT2 are formed. These corporations constitute an affiliated group that files a consolidated return on the basis of a calendar year. For 1983, 1984, and 1985, the tentative taxable income (or loss) of each member (before the application of paragraph (f) of this section) is as follows:

	1983	1984	1985
NT1	$ (60)	$(140)	$ 15
T1	1,000	500	750
NT2	(90)	(220)	150
T2	(300)	400	250

In 1983, NT1, in addition to its other business activities, acted as a collection agency for T1. Deductions attributable to those activities exceeded gross income attributable to those activities by $70. NT1's other activities generated a $10 gain. In 1984 and 1985, NT1 acted as a collection agency for T1 as its sole activity.

(b) The tentative taxable incomes of T1 and T2 for 1983 (determined under paragraph (e) of this section) as of the close of that year are adjusted by paragraph (f) of this section as follows:

T1's tentative taxable income (before the application of paragraph (f) of this section		$1,000
Less:		
T2's tentative taxable loss	$300	
NT1's functionally related loss (limited by NT1's overall loss)	60	360
T1's tentative taxable income for 1983		640

(ii) T2's tentative taxable income for 1983 is zero.

(c) The tentative taxable incomes of T1 and T2 for 1984 (determined under paragraph (e) of this section as of the close of that year) are adjusted by paragraph (f) of this section as follows:

(i) T1's tentative taxable income:

T1's tentative taxable income (before the application of paragraph (f) of this section)	$500
Less:	
T1's allocable portion of NT1's functionally related loss (140 × 500/(500 + 400))	78
T1's tentative taxable income for 1984	422

(ii) T2's tentative taxable income:

T2's tentative taxable income (before the application of paragraph (f) of this section ..	400
Less:	
T2's allocable portion of NT1's functionally related loss (140 × 400/(500 + 400))	62
T2's tentative taxable income for 1984	338

(d) For 1985, the amount under paragraph (f)(2) of this section for both T1 and T2 is $15 (NT1's tentative taxable income from functionally related activities for 1985). For 1983 and 1984, T1's tentative taxable income was reduced by a total of $138 (i.e., $60 + $78) due to NT1's losses from functionally related activities. For 1984, T2's tentative taxable income was reduced by $62 due to those losses. Accordingly, under paragraph (f)(2) of this section, T1's tentative taxable income for 1983 is increased by $10 (i.e. $15 income is increased by $5 (i.e., $15 × $62/($138

Example (2). (a) In 1983, corporations T, NT1, and NT2 are formed, these corporations constitute an affiliated group. NT2 provides computer services to T as its sole activity. For the calendar years 1983, 1984, and 1985, the group files a consolidated return. The tentative taxable income of each member (before the application of paragraph (f) of this section) is as follows:

	1983	1984	1985
T	$100	$0	$(200)
NT1	200	0	100
NT2	(20)	20	0

(b) Under paragraph (f)(1) of this section, T's tentative taxable income for 1983 (determined at the close of that year) is reduced to $80 (i.e., $100 less NT2's $20 loss). For 1984, under paragraph (f)(2) of this section, T's tentative taxable income is increased by $20. For 1985, the consolidated net operating loss of $100 (all of which is attributable to T) is carried back to 1983. That $100 carryback is not limited by paragraph (f)(4)(iii) of this section, since consolidated taxable income for 1983 available for absorption after a bad debt deduction of $0 under section 593(b) (other than paragraph (2) thereof) for that year is $280. Accordingly, under paragraph (f)(1)(ii) of this section, T's tentative taxable income is reduced by the full $100, which is taken into account before the previous reduction of T's tentative taxable income under paragraph (f)(1)(iii) of this section. In addition, under paragraph (f)(3)(i) of this section, the group must file an amended return for 1984 to eliminate the increase to T's bad debt deduction for 1984 by reason of the consolidated net operating loss carryback to 1983.

Example (3). (a) T and NT are formed in 1983 and are the only members of an affiliated group filing a consolidated return on a calendar year basis. NT provided computer services to T as its sole activity. For 1983, 1984, and 1985, the tentative taxable income of T and NT (before the application of paragraph (f) of this section) is as follows:

	1983	1984	1985
T	$100	$ 0	$ 0
NT	0	40	(40)

(b) At the close of 1983, T's tentative taxable income is $100. For 1985, however, the group has a consolidated net operating loss of $40, all of which is attributable to NT's functionally related activities and which is carried back to 1983. However, T's tentative taxable income for 1983 is not reduced under paragraph (f)(1)(iv) of this section, since under paragraph (f)(4)(iv) of this section, NT's 1984 income attributable to functionally related activities of $40 is netted against that $40 carryback.

Example (4). (a) In 1983, corporations T1, T2, NT1, and NT2 are formed. For calendar years 1983, 1984, and 1985, the affiliated group consisting of T1, T2, NT1, and NT2 filed a consolidated return. NT1 provided computer services to T1 as its sole activity. The tentative taxable income of each member (before the application of paragraph (f) of this section) is as follows:

	1983	1984	1985
T1	(50)	100	30
T2	(50)	(80)	(25)
NT1	(50)	(40)	(99)
NT2	120	30	100

(b) For 1983, the group has a consolidated net operating loss of $30, apportioned $10 each to T1, T2, and NT1 under § 1.1502-79A(a)(3). For 1984, the only thrift with tentative taxable income greater than zero (before applying paragraph (f) of this section) is T1. That tentative taxable income of $100 is first reduced to $20 by T2's $80 1984 loss under paragraph (f)(1)(i) of this section. Next, T1's remaining tentative taxable income of $20 is reduced to $10 by the portions attributable to T1 and T2 of the 1983 consolidated net operating loss carryover to 1984 under paragraph (f)(1)(ii) of this section. The sum of those portions is limited to $10 (i.e., $5 each) by paragraph (f)(4)(iii) of this section because 1984 consolidated taxable income available for absorption after a bad debt deduction under section 593(b) (other than paragraph (2) thereof) for each thrift member for that year is $10. For that reason, paragraph (f)(4)(iii) of this section also prevents any further portion of that carryover from being taken into account in 1984 as a reduction under paragraph (f)(1) of this section. T1's remaining tentative taxable income of $10 is reduced to zero, under paragraph (f)(1)(iii) of this section, by NT1's 1984 tentative taxable loss.

(c) For 1985, the only thrift with tentative taxable income greater than zero (before applying paragraph (f) of this section) is T1. T1's tentative taxable income for 1985 of $30 is reduced to $5 by T2's 1985 loss of $25 under paragraph (f)(1)(i) of this section. Next, the portions attributable to T1 and T2 of the consolidated net operating loss carryover from 1983 to 1985 for purposes of paragraph (f)(1)(ii) of this section must be determined. That determination is made without applying the rules for loss absorption in computing consolidated taxable income under § 1.1502-21A(b)(3). Those portions are instead determined in 3 steps under paragraph (f)(4)(i) of this section. The first of those steps is to determine each of T1's and T2's attributable portions of the 1983 consolidated net operating loss which under § 1.1502-79A(a)(3) is $10 or $20 for both thrifts. The second of those steps is to apply the anti-double counting rule under paragraph (h)(3)(iii) of this section to reduce that $20 amount by the $10 total of the two $5 portions attributable to T1 and T2 of the consolidated net operating loss carryover from 1983 to 1984 taken into account as reductions to T1's tentative taxable income for 1984 under paragraph (f)(1)(ii) of this section. That leaves a $10 total amount available to be taken into account as reductions to T1's remaining tentative taxable income of $5 for 1985 under paragraph (f)(1)(ii) of this section. Under the third of those steps that $10 amount, however, is limited, under the loss absorption limit of paragraph (f)(4)(iii) of this section, to the $6 of the 1983 consolidated net operating loss carryover to 1985 which is absorbed in computing consolidated taxable income for 1985 since 1985 consolidated taxable income available for absorption after a bad debt deduction under section 593(b) (other than paragraph (2) thereof) for that year is $6 (i.e., $30 + $100 − $99 − $25). Because separate taxable income cannot be reduced below zero under paragraph (f)(1) of this section, T1's remaining tentative taxable income of $5 is thus reduced to zero by the portions attributable to T1 and T2, respectively, of the consolidated net operating loss carryover from 1983 to 1985 under paragraph (f)(1)(ii) of this section.

T.D. 7246, 12/29/72, amend T.D. 7637, 8/6/79, T.D. 7815, 3/12/82, T.D. 7876, 3/14/83, T.D. 8677, 6/26/96.

§ 1.1502-43 Consolidated accumulated earnings tax.

(a) Group subject to tax. *(1) General rule.* For a group filing a consolidated return for the taxable year, the accumulated earnings tax under section 531 is imposed on consolidated accumulated taxable income (as defined in paragraph (b) of this section). This tax applies to any group that is formed or availed of to avoid or prevent the imposition of the individual income tax on the shareholders of either any of its members or any other corporation by permitting earnings and profits to accumulate instead of dividing or distributing them. Section 531 and this section do not apply to a group that is treated as a "personal holding company" under section 542(a)(1) as a result of the application of section 542(b)(1). Special rules are provided in this section for other groups which include one or more personal holding companies.

(2) Evidence of purpose to avoid income tax. (i) Under section 533(a), the fact that the group's earnings and profits are permitted to accumulate beyond the reasonable needs of its business is determinative of the purpose to avoid the income tax with respect to shareholders, unless the group by the preponderance of the evidence proves to the contrary.

(ii) The fact that a group is a mere holding or investment group is prima facie evidence of the group's purpose to avoid the income tax with respect to the shareholders. The activities of a member which is a personal holding company are not taken into account in determining if the group is a mere holding or investment group.

(3) Earnings and profits. For purposes of this paragraph (a) and paragraph (d) of this section, the following rules apply:

(i) If no member of the group is a personal holding company, the group's earnings and profits are the aggregate of the earnings and profits (or deficit) of each corporation that is a member at the close of the taxable year, determined in accordance with § 1.1502-33.

(ii) Earnings and profits resulting from the application of § 1.1502-33(b) are not taken into account.

(iii) Earnings and profits resulting from the disposition of a member's stock are determined without regard to the stock basis adjustments under §§ 1.1502-32 and 1.1502-33(c)(1).

(4) Reasonable needs of the business. The reasonable needs of the group's business include the reasonable needs of the business of any corporation (other than a personal holding company) that is a member at the close of the taxable year. Thus, the earnings and profits of one member may be accumulated with respect to the reasonable business needs of another member. If under § 1.537-3(b) the business of a nonmember corporation is considered the business of a member, then the earnings and profits of any member may be accumulated with respect to such nonmember's reasonable business needs.

(5) Burden of proof. The notification described in section 534(b) and the statement described in section 534(c) are made to or by the common parent corporation in accordance with § 1.1502-77.

(b) Consolidated accumulated taxable income. *(1) In general.* "Consolidated accumulated taxable income" is the group's consolidated taxable income determined under § 1.1502-11 adjusted in the manner provided in paragraph (b)(2) of this section, minus the sum of—

(i) The consolidated dividends paid deduction determined under paragraph (c) of this section and

(ii) The consolidated accumulated earnings credit determined under paragraph (d) of this section.

(2) Adjustments to consolidated taxable income. For purposes of paragraph (b)(1) of this section, consolidated taxable income is adjusted as follows:

(i) Under section 535(b)(1), the deduction for taxes is the excess of—

(A) The consolidated liability for tax determined without § 1.1502-2 (b) through (d) and without the foreign tax credit provided by section 33, over

(B) The consolidated foreign tax credit determined pursuant to § 1.1502-4. Foreign taxes deductible under § 1.535-2(a)(2) are also allowed as a deduction under section 535(b)(1).

(ii) The consolidated charitable contributions deduction under § 1.1502-24 does not apply. Under section 535(b)(2), there shall be allowed the aggregate charitable contributions of the members allowable under section 170, determined without section 170(b)(2) and (d)(2).

(iii) Under section 535(b)(3), the deductions provided in §§ 1.1502-26 and 1.1502-27 are not allowed.

(iv) Under section 535(b)(4), the consolidated net operating loss deduction described in §§ 1.1502-21(a) or 1.1502-21A(a), as appropriate is not allowed.

(v) Under section 535(b)(5), there is allowed as a deduction the consolidated net capital loss, determined under § 1.1502-22(a) or 1.1502-22A(a), as appropriate.

(vi) Under section 535(b)(6), there is allowed as a deduction an amount equal to (A) the excess of the consolidated net long-term capital gain (determined under §§ 1.1502-22(a) or 1.1502-41A, as appropriate) over the consolidated net short-term capital loss (determined under §§ 1.1502-22(a) or 1.1502-41A, as appropriate), minus (B) the taxes attributable to this excess. This consolidated net short-term capital loss is determined without the consolidated net capital loss carryovers or carrybacks to the taxable year.

(vii) Under section 535(b)(7), the consolidated net capital loss carryovers and carrybacks are not allowed. See §§ 1.1502-22(b) or 1.1502-22A(b), as appropriate.

(viii) Section 1.1502-15A (Limitations on built-in deductions not subject to § 1.1502-15) and 1.1502-15 do not apply.

(3) Personal holding company a member. If a member is a personal holding company for the taxable year—

(i) [Reserved]

(ii) In applying paragraph (b)(2)(i) of this section, consolidated liability for tax (as determined under that paragraph (b)(2)(i)) is reduced by the portion thereof allocable to that member under section 1552(a)(1), (2), (3), or (4) (or § 1.1502-33(d)), whichever is applicable. The consolidated foreign tax credit is computed by excluding the taxable income and any foreign taxes paid or accrued by that member, and foreign taxes deductible under § 1.535-2(a)(2) do not include foreign taxes attributable to that member.

(c) Consolidated dividends paid deduction. *(1) General rule.* For purposes of this section, the consolidated dividends paid deduction is the aggregate of the members' deductions under section 561(a)(1) and (2). This deduction is determined by excluding deductions for dividends paid to other members.

(2) Exception for certain personal holding companies. [Reserved]

(3) Dividends paid defined. For purposes of this paragraph (c), "dividends paid" and "dividend (or portion thereof) paid" include amounts treated as dividends paid during the taxable year under sections 562(b)(1), 563, and 565 (relating respectively to liquidating distributions, dividends paid after year end, and consent dividends).

(4) Examples. This paragraph (c) can be illustrated by the following examples:

Example (1). Corporations P and S constitute an affiliated group which files a consolidated return on a calendar year basis for 1984 and 1985. P owns all of S's stock and two individuals own all of P's stock. Neither member of the group is a personal holding company for 1984. Assume that on December 15, 1984, S pays a dividend (as defined in section 316(a)) of $2,000 to P, and P pays a dividend (as so defined) of $3,000 on January 15, 1985, to its individual shareholders. All dividends are paid in cash and are pro rata with no preference as to any shares or class of stock. For purposes of this paragraph (c), the consolidated dividends paid deduction for 1984 is $3,000, i.e., the dividend paid on January 15, 1985, by P to its nonmember shareholders. See section 563(a). The $2,000 dividend paid by S to P is not taken into account in computing the consolidated dividends paid deduction.

Example (2). [Reserved]

(d)

(1) In general. [Reserved]

(2) Special rule if a consolidated group is part of a controlled group. If a consolidated group is treated collectively as being one component member of a controlled group, or if each member of a consolidated group is treated as being a separate component member of a controlled group, see section 1561 for determining the portion of the accumulated earnings credit to be allocated to such group or to such members.

(e) Effective/applicability date. This section applies to any consolidated Federal income tax return due (without extensions) on or after December 21, 2009. However, a consolidated group may apply this section to any consolidated Federal income tax return filed on or after December 21, 2009. For returns due before December 21, 2009, see § 1.1502-43T as contained in 26 CFR part 1 in effect on April 1, 2009.

T.D. 7937, 1/26/84, amend T.D. 8560, 8/12/94, T.D. 8677, 6/26/96, T.D. 8823, 6/25/99, T.D. 9304, 12/21/2006, T.D. 9476, 12/22/2009.

§ 1.1502-44 Percentage depletion for independent producers and royalty owners.

(a) In general. The sum of the percentage depletion deductions for the taxable year for all oil or gas property owned by all members, plus any carryovers under section 613A(d)(1) or paragraph (d) of this section from a prior taxable year, may not exceed 65 percent of the group's adjusted consolidated taxable income (under paragraph (b) of this section) for the consolidated return year.

(b) Adjusted consolidated taxable income. For purposes of this section, adjusted consolidated taxable income is an amount (not less than zero) equal to the group's consolidated taxable income determined without—

(1) Any depletion with respect to an oil or gas property (other than a gas property with respect to which the depletion allowance for all production is determined pursuant to section 613A(b)) for which percentage depletion would exceed cost depletion in the absence of the depletable quantity limitations contained in section 613A(c)(1) and (6) and the consolidated taxable income limitation contained in paragraph (a) of this section.

(2) Any consolidated net operating loss carryback to the consolidated return year under §§ 1.1502-21 or 1.1502-21A (as appropriate), and

(3) Any consolidated net capital loss carryback to the consolidated return year under § 1.1502-22 or 1.1502-22A (as appropriate).

(c) Allocation to oil and gas properties. The maximum amount allowable as a deduction under section 613A(c), after the application of paragraph (a) of this section, is allocated to properties held by members in accordance with the regulations under section 613A(d). Those regulations provide for an initial allocation and possible reallocation of the maximum allowable percentage depletion deduction among oil and gas properties. Thus, if, after the initial allocation, cost depletion exceeds the percentage depletion that would be allowable for a particular oil or gas property, cost depletion must be used for that property and the maximum amount of percentage depletion allowable as a deduction for the group is reallocated among only the remaining properties held by all members.

(d) Carryover for disallowed amounts. *(1)* If any amount is disallowed as a deduction for the taxable year by reason of section 613A(d)(1) or paragraph (a) of this section, the disallowed amount for each oil or gas property is treated as an amount allowed as a deduction under section 613A(c), for the following taxable year for the member that owned the property, in accordance with the regulations under section 613A and paragraphs (a) and (d)(2) of this section.

(2) Any amount that was disallowed as a deduction in a separate return limitation year of a member may be carried to a consolidated return year only to the extent that 65 percent of the excess determined under paragraph (d)(3) of this section exceeds the sum of the otherwise allowable percentage depletion deductions for the member's oil and gas properties for the year.

(3) The excess determined in this subparagraph (3) for a member is the excess, if any, of adjusted consolidated taxable income for the year under paragraph (b) of this section over that income recomputed by excluding the items of income and deductions of the member.

(e) Effective date. This section applies to taxable years for which the due date (without extensions) for filing returns is after September 30, 1980.

T.D. 7725, 9/30/80, amend T.D. 8823, 6/25/99.

§ 5.1502-45 Limitation on losses to amount at risk.

(a) In general. *(1) Scope.* This section applies to a loss of any subsidiary if the common parent's stock meets the stock ownership requirement described in section 465(a)(1)(C).

(2) Limitation on use of losses. Except as provided in paragraph (a)(4) of this section, a loss from an activity of a subsidiary during a consolidated return year is includible in the computation of consolidated taxable income (or consolidated net operating loss) and consolidated capital gain net income (or consolidated net capital loss) only to the extent the loss does not exceed the amount that the parent is at risk in the activity at the close of that subsidiary's taxable year. In addition, the sum of a subsidiary's losses from all its activities is includible only to the extent that the parent is at risk in the subsidiary at the close of that year. Any excess may not be taken into account for the consolidated return year but will be treated as a deduction allocable to that activity of the subsidiary in the first succeeding taxable year.

(3) Amount parent is at risk in subsidiary's activity. The amount the parent is at risk in an activity of a subsidiary is the lesser of (i) the amount the parent is at risk in the subsidiary or (ii) the amount the subsidiary is at risk in the activity. These amounts are determined under paragraph (b) of this section and the principles of section 465. See section 465 and the regulations thereunder and the examples in paragraph (e) of this section.

(4) Excluded activities. The limitation on the use of losses in paragraph (a)(2) of this section does not apply to a loss attributable to an activity described in section 465(c)(3)(D).

(5) Substance over form. Any transaction or arrangement between members (or between a member and a person that is not a member) which does not cause the parent to be economically at risk in an activity of a subsidiary will be treated in accordance with the substance of the transaction or arrangement notwithstanding any other provision of this section.

(b) Rules for determining amount at risk. *(1) Excluded amounts.* The amount a parent is at risk in an activity of a subsidiary at the close of the subsidiary's taxable year does not include any amount which would not be taken into account under section 465 were the subsidiary not a separate corporation. Thus, for example, if the amount a parent is at risk in the activity of a subsidiary is attributable to nonrecourse financing, the amount at risk is not more than the fair market value of the property (other than the subsidiary's stock or debt or assets) pledged as security.

(2) Guarantees. If a parent guarantees a loan by a person other than a member to a subsidiary, the loan increases the amount the parent is at risk in the activity of the subsidiary.

(c) Application of section 465. This section applies in a manner consistent with the provisions of section 465. Thus, for example, the recapture of losses provided in section 465(e) applies if the amount the parent is at risk in the activity of a subsidiary is reduced below zero.

(d) Other consolidated return provisions unaffected. This section limits only the extent to which losses of a subsidiary may be used in a consolidated return year. This section does not apply for other purposes, such as § 1.1502-32 and § 1.1502-19, relating to investment in stock of a subsidiary and excess loss accounts, respectively. Thus, a loss which reduces a subsidiary's earnings and profits in a consolidated return year, but is disallowed as a deduction for the year by reason of this section, may nonetheless result in a negative adjustment to the basis of an owning member's stock in the subsidiary or create (or increase) an excess loss account.

(e) Examples. The provisions of this section may be illustrated by the examples in this paragraph (e). In each example, the stock ownership requirement of section 465(a)(1)(C) is met for the stock of the parent (P), and each affiliated group files a consolidated return on a calendar year basis and comprises only the members described.

Example (1). In 1979, P forms S with a contribution of $200 in exchange for all of S's stock. During the year, S borrows $400 from a commercial lender and P guarantees $100 of the loan. S uses $500 of its funds to acquire a motion picture film. S incurs a loss of $120 for the year with respect to the film. At the close of 1979, the amount P is at risk in S's activity is $300. If S has no gain or loss in 1980, and there are no contributions from or distributions to P, at the close of 1980 P's amount at risk in S's activity will be $180.

Example (2). P forms S-1 with a capital contribution of $1 on January 1, 1980. On February 1, 1980. S-1 borrows $100 with full recourse and contributes all $101 to its newly formed subsidiary S-2. S-2 uses the proceeds to explore for natural oil and gas resources. S-2 incurs neither gain nor loss from its explorations during the taxable year. As of December 31, 1980, P is at risk in the exploration activity of S-2 only to the extent of $1.

(f) Effective date. This section applies to consolidated return years ending on or after December 31, 1979.

T.D. 7685, 3/12/80.

§ 1.1502-47 Consolidated returns by life-nonlife groups.

Caution: The Treasury has not yet amended Reg § 1.1502-47 to reflect changes made by P.L. 99-514.

(a) Scope. *(1) In general.* Under section 1504(b)(2), insurance companies that are taxed under section 802 or 821 (relating respectively to life insurance companies and to certain mutual insurance companies) are not treated as includible corporations for purposes of determining under section 1504(a) the existence of an affiliated group and the composition of its membership. Section 1504(c)(2) provides an election whereby certain life insurance companies and mutual insurance companies may be treated as includible corporations, and thus members, of a group composed of other includible corporations. This section provides regulations for the making of this election and for the determination of an electing group's composition and its consolidated tax liability.

(2) General method of consolidation. (i) Subgroup method. The regulations adopt a subgroup method to determine consolidated taxable income. One subgroup is the group's nonlife companies (including those taxable under section 821). The other subgroup is the group's life insurance companies. Initially, the nonlife subgroup computes nonlife consolidated taxable income and the life subgroup computes consolidated partial life insurance company taxable income. A subgroup's income may in effect be reduced by a loss of the other subgroup. The life subgroup losses consist of consolidated loss from operations and life consolidated net capital loss. The nonlife subgroup losses consist of non-

life consolidated net operating loss and nonlife consolidated net capital loss. Consolidated taxable income is therefore defined in pertinent part as the sum of nonlife consolidated taxable income and consolidated partial life insurance company taxable income reduced by life subgroup losses or nonlife subgroup losses.

(ii) Subgroup loss. A subgroup loss does not actually affect the computation of nonlife consolidated taxable income or consolidated partial life insurance company taxable income. It merely constitutes a bottom-line adjustment in reaching consolidated taxable income. Furthermore, one subgroup's loss must first be carried back against income of the same subgroup before it may be used as a setoff against the second subgroup income in the taxable year the loss arose. (See section 1503(c)(1)). The carryback of the losses from one subgroup may not be used to offset income of the other subgroup in the year to which the loss is to be carried. This carryback of the first subgroup's loss may "bump" the second subgroup's loss that in effect previously reduced the income of the first subgroup. The second subgroup's loss that is bumped in appropriate cases may in effect reduce a succeeding year's income of the second or first subgroup. This approach gives the group the tax savings of the use of losses but the bumping rule assures that insofar as possible life deductions will be matched against life income and nonlife deductions against nonlife income.

(iii) Carryover of subgroup loss. A subgroup's loss may be used in a succeeding year, but in any particular succeeding year the loss must be used to reduce the income of the same subgroup before it may be used as a setoff against the other subgroup's income.

(3) Authority. This section is prescribed under the authority of sections 1502, 1503(c), 1504(c)(2), and 7805(b).

(4) Other provisions. The provisions of §§ 1.1502-1 through 1.1502-80 apply unless this section provides otherwise. Further, unless otherwise indicated in this section, a term used in this section has the same meaning as in sections 801-844.

(b) Effective dates. *(1) General rule.* This section is effective for taxable years for which the due date (without extensions) for filing returns is after March 14, 1983, except as provided in paragraph (b)(2) of this section.

(2) Tacking rule effective dates. (i) In general. Paragraph (d)(12)(v) of this section applies to any original consolidated Federal income tax return due (without extensions) after July 20, 2007.

(ii) Prior law. For original consolidated Federal income tax returns due (without extensions) after April 25, 2006, and on or before July 20, 2007, see § 1.1502-47T as contained in 26 CFR part 1 in effect on April 1, 2007. For original consolidated Federal income tax returns due (without extensions) on or before April 25, 2006, see § 1.1502-47 as contained in 26 CFR part 1 in effect on April 1, 2006.

(c) Cross references. The following table provides cross references for some of the definitions and operating rules that are relevant in making the election and determining the group's composition and its tax liability:

Item and Paragraph

—General definitions (d)

—Eligible corporation (Five-year rules) (d)(12)

—Election (e)

—Consolidated taxable income (g)

—Nonlife consolidated taxable income (h)

—Consolidated partial life insurance company taxable income (j)

—Nonlife subgroup losses (m)

—Life subgroup losses (n)

—Alternative tax (o)

(d) Definitions. For purposes of this section—

(1) Life insurance company. The term "life company" means a life insurance company as defined in section 801. Section 801 applies to each company separately.

(2) Mutual insurance company. The term "mutual company" means a mutual insurance company taxable under section 821(a)(1).

(3) Life insurance company taxable income. The term "life insurance company taxable income" is referred to as LICTI. The terms "TII", "GO", and "LO" refer, respectively, to taxable investment income (section 804), gain from operations (section 809), and loss from operations (section 812). The term "consolidated partial LICTI" refers to consolidated LICTI without section 802(b)(3).

(4) Group. The term "group" means an affiliated group of corporations (as defined in section 1504(a)). Unless otherwise indicated in this section, a group's composition is determined without section 1504(b)(2).

(5) Member. The term "member" means a corporation (including the common parent) that is an includible corporation in the group. A life company or mutual company is tentatively treated as a member for any taxable year for purposes of determining if it is an eligible corporation under paragraph (d)(12) of this section and therefore if it is an includible corporation under section 1504(c)(2). If such a company is eligible and includible (under section 1504(c)(2)), it will actually be treated as a member of the group.

(6) Life member. A life member is a member of the group that is a life company.

(7) Nonlife member. A nonlife member is a member of the group that is not a life company.

(8) Life subgroup. A life subgroup is composed of those members that are life members. If the group has only one life member, it constitutes a life subgroup.

(9) Nonlife subgroup. A nonlife subgroup is composed of those members that are nonlife members. If the group has only one nonlife member, it constitutes a nonlife subgroup.

(10) Separate return year. The term "separate return year" means a taxable year of a corporation for which it files a separate return or for which it joins in the filing of a consolidated return by another group. For purposes of this subparagraph (10), the term "group" is defined with regard to section 1504(b)(2) for years in which an election under section 1504(c)(2) is not in effect. Thus, a separate return year includes a taxable year for which that election is not in effect.

(11) Separate return limitation year. Section 1.1502-1(f)(2) provides exceptions to the definition of the term "separate return limitation year". For purposes of applying those exceptions to this section, for taxable years ending after December 31, 1980, the term "group" is defined without regard to section 1504(b)(2) and the definition in this subparagraph (11) applies separately to the nonlife subgroup in determining nonlife consolidated taxable income under paragraph (h) of this section and to the life subgroup in determining consolidated partial LICTI under paragraph (j) of this section. Paragraph (m)(3)(ix) of this section defines the term "separate return limitation year" for purposes of deter-

mining whether the losses of one subgroup may be used against the income of the other subgroup.

(12) Eligible corporations. (i) In general. A corporation is an eligible corporation for a taxable year of a group only if, throughout every day of the base period the corporation—

(A) Was in existence and a member of the group determined without the exclusions in section 1504(b)(2) (see paragraphs (d)(12)(iii)–(vi) of this section),

(B) Was engaged in the active conduct of a trade or business ("active business"),

(C) Did not experience a change in tax character (see paragraph (d)(12)(vii) of this section), and

(D) Did not undergo disproportionate asset acquisitions (see paragraph (d)(12)(viii) of this section).

(ii) Base period. The base period consists of the common parent's five taxable years immediately preceding the group's taxable year for which the consolidated return and the determination of eligibility are made. Eligibility is determined for each consolidated return year beginning with the first year for which the election under section 1504(c)(2) is effective.

(iii) In existence. Except as provided in paragraph (d)(12)(v) and (vi) of this section, a corporation organized after the base period begins is not eligible even though it is a member of the group immediately after its organization. For purposes of this subdivision (iii), a corporation that was a party to a reorganization described in section 368(a)(1)(F) shall be treated as the same entity both before and after the reorganization.

(iv) Membership period. Except as provided in paragraph (d)(12)(v) and (vi) of this section, a corporation must have been a member of the group throughout the base period to be eligible. Thus, an ineligible corporation includes one whose stock was acquired from outside the group at any time during the base period or one which was a member of a different group (whether by application of reverse acquisition rules in § 1.1502-75(d)(3) or otherwise) at any time during the base period. For purposes of this subdivision (iv), the common parent of a group is treated as constituting a group (and hence is a member) during any period when it was not a member of an affiliated group within the meaning of section 1504(a) (applied without section 1504(b)(2)).

(v) Tacking rule. The period during which an old corporation is in existence and a member of the group engaged in active business is included in (or tacks onto) the period for the new corporation if the following four conditions listed in this paragraph (d)(12)(v) are met. For purposes of this paragraph (d)(12)(v), a new corporation is a corporation (whether or not newly organized) during the period its eligibility depends upon the tacking rule. The four conditions are as follows—

(A) The first condition is that, at any time, 80 percent or more of the new corporation's assets it acquired (other than in the ordinary course of its trade or business) were acquired from the old corporation in one or more transactions described in section 351(a) or 381(a). This asset test is applied by using the fair market values of assets on the date they were acquired and without regard to liabilities. Assets acquired in the ordinary course of business will be excluded from total assets only if they were acquired after the new corporation became a member of the group (determined without section 1504(b)(2)). In addition, assets that the old corporation acquired from outside the group in transactions not conducted in the ordinary course of its trade or business are not included in the 80 percent (but are included in total assets) if the old corporation acquired those assets within five calendar years before the date of their transfer to the new corporation.

(B) The second condition is that at the end of the taxable year during which the first condition is first met, the old corporation and the new corporation must both have the same tax character. For purposes of this paragraph (d)(12), a corporation's tax character is the section under which it would be taxed (i.e., sections 11, 802, 821, or 831) if it filed a separate return. If the old corporation is not in existence (or adopts a plan of complete liquidation) at the end of that taxable year, this paragraph (d)(12)(v)(B) will apply to the old corporation's taxable year immediately preceding the beginning of the taxable year during which the first condition is first met.

(C) The third condition is that, at the end of the taxable year during which the first condition is first met, the new corporation does not undergo a disproportionate asset acquisition under paragraph (d)(12)(viii) of this section.

(D) The fourth condition is that, if there is more than one old corporation, the first two conditions apply to all of the corporations. Thus, the second condition (tax character) must be met by all of the old corporations transferring assets taken into account in meeting the test in paragraph (d)(12)(v)(A) of this section.

(vi) Old group remaining in existence. If the common parent of a group (or a new common parent) became the common parent in a transaction described in § 1.1502-75(d)(2) or (3) where a group remained in existence, then paragraph (d)(12)(ii)–(iv) of this section apply by treating that common parent as if it were also the previous common parent of the group that remains in existence. If this subdivision (vi) applies to a transaction, the tacking rule in paragraph (d)(12)(v) of this section does not apply to the transaction.

(vii) Change in tax character. A corporation must not experience during the base period a change in tax character (as defined in paragraph (d)(12)(v)(B) of this section) if the change is attributable to an acquisition of assets from outside the group in transactions not conducted in the ordinary course of its trade or business. However, if a new corporation relies on the tacking rules in paragraph (d)(12)(v) of this section, this subdivision (vii) shall apply during the base period and the current consolidated return year and even if the change in tax character is attributable to an asset acquisition from within the group.

(viii) Disproportionate asset acquisition. To be eligible, a corporation must not undergo during the base period disproportionate asset acquisitions which are attributable to an acquisition (or a series of acquisitions) of assets from outside the group in transactions not conducted in the ordinary course of its trade or business (special acquisition). Whether special acquisitions are disproportionate is determined at the end of each base period. Whether an acquisition results in a disproportionate asset acquisition depends on all of the facts and circumstances including the following factors and rules:

(A) One factor is the portion of the insurance reserves (i.e., total reserves in section 801(c)) of the acquiring company at the end of the base period which is attributable to special acquisitions.

(B) A second factor is the portion of the fair market value of the assets (without reduction for liabilities) of the acquiring company at the end of the base period that is attributable to special acquisitions.

(C) A third factor is the portion of the premiums generated during the last taxable year of the base period which are attributable to special acquisitions.

(D) A corporation will not experience a disproportionate asset acquisition unless 75 percent of one factor (whether or not listed in this subdivision (viii)) is attributable to special acquisitions.

(E) Money or other property contributed to a corporation by a shareholder that is not a member of the group (without section 1504(b)(2)) is not a special acquisition.

(F) If a new corporation relies on the tacking rules in paragraph (d)(12)(v) of this section, this subdivision (viii) applies to that corporation during a consolidated return year. Thus, if at any time during a consolidated return year, a new corporation undergoes a disproportionate asset acquisition, the corporation becomes ineligible at that time.

(13) Ineligible corporation. A corporation that is not an eligible corporation is ineligible. If a life company or mutual company is ineligible, it is not treated under section 1504(c)(2) as an includible corporation. Losses of a nonlife member arising in years when it is ineligible may not be used under section 1503(c)(2) and paragraph (m) of this section to set off the income of a life member. If a life or mutual company is ineligible and is the common parent of the group (without section 1504(b)(2)), the election under section 1504(c)(2) may not be made.

(14) Illustrations. The following examples illustrate this paragraph (d). In each example, L indicates a life company, another letter indicates a nonlife company, and each corporation uses the calendar year as its taxable year.

Example (1). P has owned all of the stock of S since 1913. On January 1, 1980, P purchased all of the stock of L_1 which owns all of the stock of L_2 and S_2. L_1 and L_2 are treated as members for purposes of determining if they are eligible for 1982. However, for 1982, L_1, L_2 and S_2 are ineligible because none of them has been a member of the group for P's five taxable years preceding 1982. For 1982, L_1 and L_2 may elect to file a consolidated return because they constitute an affiliated group under section 1504(c)(1), and P and S may file a consolidated return.

Example (2). Since 1974, P has been a mutual insurance company owning all the stock of L_1. In 1980, P transfers assets to S_1, a new stock casualty company subject to taxation under section 831(a). For 1982, only P and L_1 are eligible corporations. The tacking rule in paragraph (d)(12)(v) of this section does not apply in 1982 because the old corporation (P) and the new corporation (S_1) do do not have the same tax character. The result would be the same if P were a life company.

Example (3). Since 1974, L has owned all the stock of L_1 which has owned all the stock of S_1, a stock casualty company. L_1 writes some accident and health insurance business. In 1980, L_1 transfers this business, and S_1 transfers some of its business, to a new stock casualty company, S_2, in a transaction described in section 351(a). The property transferred to S_2 by L_1 had a fair market value of $50 million. The property transferred by S_1 had a fair market value of $40 million. S_2 is ineligible for 1982 because the tacking rule in paragraph (d)(12)(v) of this section does not apply. The old corporations (L_1 and S_1) and the new corporation (S_2) do not all have the same tax character. See subparagraph (d)(12)(v)(B) and (E) of this section. The result would be the same if L_1 transferred other property (e.g., stock and securities) with the same value, rather than accident and health insurance contracts, to S_2

Example (4). Since 1974, P has owned all the stock of S and L_1. L_1 is a large life company engaged in active business since 1974. On January 1, 1982, L_1 transfers in a section 351(a) transaction assets (not acquired from outside the group) to a new life company, L_2. For 1982, L_2 is eligible because under paragraph (d)(12)(v) of this section, L_2 is considered to have been in existence and a member of the group engaged in the active business since 1974 which is the period L_1 the old corporation, was in existence and a member of the group so engaged.

Example (5). The facts are the same as in example (4). Assume that the fair market value of the assets L_1 transferred to L_2 was $10 million on January 1, 1982 and that L_2 acquired no other assets prior to June 30, 1983. Assume further that on January 1, 1983, L_1 acquires (other than in the ordinary course of its trade or business) assets having a fair market value of $40 million from L_3, an unrelated life company. On June 30, 1983, L_1 transfers those assets to L_2. L_2 becomes ineligible on June 30, 1983. Since by fair market values, 80 percent (i.e., $^{40}/_{50}$) of L_2's assets are attributable to special acquisitions, L_2 has undergone a disproportionate asset acquisition at that time. See paragraph (d)(12)(viii)(B), (D), and (F) of this section.

Example (6). The facts are the same as in example (5) except that L_1 transfers assets (other than life insurance contracts) having a fair market value of $40 million to L_2 and L_2 purchases the assets of L_3 on June 30, 1983. The result of the 1983 acquisition is the same as in example (5).

Example (7). The facts are the same as in example (5) except the acquired assets acquired by L_2 in 1983 from L_1 have a fair market value of $20 million. In 1983, L_2 had $1 million of premiums on its pre-existing contracts but premiums generated by the acquired business for the entire year would have been $2 million. L_2 is eligible in 1983 because it did not experience a disproportionate asset acquisition on June 30, 1983.

Example (8). Since 1974, L_1 a State A corporation, has owned all of the stock of L_1 and S_1. On January 1, 1982, L merges into L_3, a smaller State B corporation, which owns the stock of S_2. The transaction is a reverse acquisition described in § 1.1502-75(d)(3) and the group of which L was the common parent remains in existence. Under paragraph (d)(12)(vi) of this section, L_3 is eligible for 1982. However, S_2 is ineligible in 1982 under paragraph (d)(12)(iv) of this section.

Example (9). The facts are the same as in example (8) except that L acquires the stock of L_3, L_3 and S_2 are both ineligible for 1982. On January 1, 1983, the fair market value of L_3's assets are $5 million (without liabilities) and on that date L transfers assets (not acquired from outside the group) having a fair market value of $95 million (without liabilities) to L_3. L and L_3 are life companies at the end of 1983. L_3 is eligible in 1983 under the tacking rule in paragraph (d)(12)(v) of this section. S_2 is ineligible in that year. The result would be the same if L was not a life company prior to January 1, 1983. See paragraph (d)(12)(v)(B) of this section.

Example (10). Since 1974, X, a foreign corporation, has owned all the stock of S_2 and S_1 and S_1 has owned all of the stock of L_1. On January 1, 1982, X incorporates a new U.S. company P, and transfers the stock of S_1 and S_2 to P. Assume that under § 1.1502-75(d)(3) (relating to reverse acquisitions), the S_1-L_1 affiliated group remains in existence. Under paragraph (d)(12)(vi) of this section, P, S_1 and L_1 are eligible but S_2 is ineligible. The result would be the same if X were an individual.

Example (11). The facts are the same as in Example (10) except that X owns all of the stock of S1, L1, and S2. In addition, on January 1, 1982, X transfers the stock of S1 and S2 to L1. L1 is eligible in 1982 under paragraph (d)(12)(iv) of this section. L1 would still be eligible even if it owned a subsidiary during the base period but sold the subsidiary prior to January 1, 1982. S1 and S2 are ineligible in 1982.

Example (12). Since 1974, S_1 has owned all of the stock of L_1. S_2, an unrelated company, has owned all of the stock of L_2 and S_3 for 10 years. S_1 and S_2 are active stock casualty companies and not holding companies. On January 1, 1982, S_1 and S_2 merge into a new casualty company, S, in a transaction described in § 1.1502-75(d)(3) so that the group of which S_1 was the common parent remains in existence. S and L_1 are eligible in 1982 under paragraph (d)(12)(vi) of this section. L_2 and S_3 are ineligible.

Example (13). The facts are the same as in Example (12) except that S2 (the first corporation in § 1.1502-75(d)(3)) acquires the stock of S1 in exchange for the stock of S2. The result is that only S2, S1, and L1 are eligible in 1982.

Example (14). Since 1974, S had owned all of the stock of L1. L1 is a large life company. On January 1, 1982, L1 incorporates L2 and transfers $40 million in cash and securities to L2 in a transaction described in section 351(a). On March 1, 1982, L2 purchases the assets of L3, an unrelated life company. The purchased assets have a fair market value (without liabilities) of $30 million on March 1, 1982. L2 is ineligible for 1982 because the tacking rule in § 1.1502-47T(d)(12)(v) does not apply. L2 experienced a disproportionate asset acquisition in 1982. See § 1.1502-47T(d)(12)(v)(C).

(e) Election. *(1) In general.* The election under section 1504(c)(2) may not be made if the group's common parent is an ineligible life company or an ineligible mutual company. The election under section 1504(c)(2) may only be made by the common parent of the group (as defined in section 1504(c)(2) without the exclusions in section 1504(b)(2)). For example, assume that P owns all of the stock of L_1, an eligible life company, which owns the stock of S_1. Assume further that P also owns the stock of L_2, an ineligible life member, which (for more than five years) has owned the stock of a nonlife company, S_2. Only P may make the election and, if it does so, P, L_1, and S_1 may file a consolidated return under this section. L_2 may not make the election under section 1504(c)(2) and may not file a consolidated return with S_2.

(2) How election is made. (i) General rule. The election under section 1504(c)(2) is generally made by the group's common parent in the same manner (and it has the same effect) as the election to file a consolidated return is made under § 1.1502-75(a) and (b) for a group which did not file a consolidated return for the immediately preceding taxable year. The procedure for making the election under section 1504(c)(2) is the same whether or not a consolidated return was filed by the life members or the nonlife members for the immediately preceding taxable year.

(ii) Special rule. Notwithstanding the general rule, however, if the nonlife members in the group filed a consolidated return for the immediately preceding taxable year and had executed and filed a Form 1122 that is effective for the preceding year, then such members will be treated as if they filed a Form 1122 when they join in the filing of a consolidated return under section 1504(c)(2) and they will be deemed to consent to the regulations under this section. However, an affiliation schedule (Form 851) must be filed by the group and the life members must execute a Form 1122 in the manner prescribed in § 1.1502-75(h)(2).

(3) Irrevocability. Except as provided in § 1.1502-75(c) and paragraph (e)(4) of this section, the election under section 1504(c)(2) is irrevocable.

(4) Permission to discontinue. (i) General rule. A "section 1504(c)(2) group" with a common parent that has made the election to file a consolidated return under section 1504(c)(2) in a previous taxable year is granted permission to elect (under § 1.1502-75(c)(2)(ii)) to discontinue filing such a consolidated return for that group's first taxable year for which the regulations under this section are effective. This election to discontinue shall be exercised in the time and manner prescribed in § 1.1502-75(c)(3), except that the group's common parent shall exercise this election to discontinue (and the other members of the section 1504(c)(2) group must comply with this election) by filing appropriate returns. For purposes of this paragraph (e)(4), an appropriate return is either a separate return or a consolidated return that is filed by newly exercising the privilege under § 1.1502-75(a)(1).

(ii) Types of groups. (A) A "section 1504(c)(2) group" is an affiliated group which files or filed a consolidated return pursuant to an election under section 1504(c)(2).

(B) A "limited group" is an affiliated group (determined without section 1504(c)(2)) having at least one member which was a member of a section 1504(c)(2) group on the date that the section 1504(c)(2) group elected to discontinue under paragraph (l)(4)(i) of this section.

(iii) Effect on restoration rules. If a group ceases to file a consolidated return or terminates or if a member leaves the group, certain items of income, gain, or loss on transactions between members are taken into account under §§ 1.1502-13, 1.1502-18, and 1.1502-19 ("restoration rules"). For purposes of applying these restoration rules solely by reason of an election under paragraph (e)(4)(i) or (e)(4)(v)(A) of this section to discontinue filing consolidated returns as a section 1504(c)(2) group, the following rules apply:

(A) The section 1504(c)(2) group shall not be considered to terminate and no member of that group shall be treated as ceasing to be a member.

(B) Members of that section 1504(c)(2) group that are included in the consolidated return of a limited group for the first taxable year for which the discontinuance is effective shall be considered to be filing a consolidated return as a continuation of the section 1504(c)(2) group. However, a corporation that is not a member of a particular limited group for that taxable year is considered to have a separate return year (and, for purposes of § 1.1502-19(c), not to be a member of a group filing a consolidated return) with respect to that limited group's members.

(C) Section 1.1502-13 shall be applied without regard to paragraph (f)(1)(vii).

(iv) Illustrations. The following examples illustrate paragraph (e)(4)(i)–(iii) of this section. In these examples, L indicates a life company and another letter indicates a nonlife company. All corporations use the calendar year as the taxable year. For all taxable years involved, P owns all the stock of L_1 and of S, L_1 owns all the stock of L_2, L_2 owns all the stock of L_3, and S owns all the stock of L_4. For 1981, P makes the life-nonlife election of section 1504(c)(2) and L_4 is an eligible corporation. For 1982, P makes the election to discontinue filing consolidated returns under section

1504(c)(2) in accordance with the permission granted in this paragraph (e)(4).

Example (1). L_1, L_2, and L_3 were eligible members. For 1982, P and S may either file separate returns or may file, as a limited group, a consolidated return. Similarly, L_1, L_2, and L_3 may either file separate returns or may file a consolidated return as a limited group under section 1504(c)(1). L_4 must file a separate return.

Example (2). For 1981, L_1 was an ineligible member and L_1, L_2 and L_3 filed a consolidated return under section 1504(c)(1). For 1982, L_1, L_2, and L_3 must continue filing a consolidated return under Section 1504(c)(1).

Example (3). For 1981, L_1 was an eligible member and L_2 and L_3 were ineligible members. For 1982, L_1, L_2, and L_3 either must each file a separate return or must file a consolidated return as a limited group under section 1504(c)(1) having L_1 as a common parent.

Example (4). The facts are the same as in example (3). Assume further that for 1981, L_2 and L_3 file a consolidated return. During 1981, intercompany transactions (see § 1.1502-13) occur in the life-nonlife group between P and L_1, between P and S, and between S and L_4 and occur in the ineligible life subgroup between L_2 and L_3. For 1982, the restoration rules of § 1.1502-13, as modified by paragraph (e)(4)(iii)(B) of this section, will be applicable as indicated in the following table:

Intercompany transactions between	§ 1.1502-13
P and L_1	Yes
P and S, if they file:	
Separate returns	Yes
A consolidated return	No
S and L_1	Yes
L_2 and L_3, if L_1, L_2 and L_3 file:	
Separate returns	Yes
A consolidated return	No

(v) Additional rules. (A) If a group with a taxable year ending in the month of December, 1982, had made the election under section 1504(c)(2) for a taxable year ending prior to December 1, 1982, and if that group meets the conditions of subdivision (vi) of this paragraph (e)(4), then the common parent may elect to discontinue filing a consolidated return for its taxable year ending in the month of December, 1982 (and other members of the section 1504(c)(2) group must comply with this election) by filing appropriate returns (see paragraph (e)(4)(i) of this section) before September 16, 1983.

(B) If a group made the election under section 1504(c)(2) for its taxable year ending in the month of December, 1982, and if that group meets the conditions of subdivision (vi) of this paragraph (e)(4), then the common parent may elect to withdraw the section 1504(c)(2) election (and all other members of the group determined without section 1504(b)(2) comply with the election) by filing before September 16, 1983, any returns for the appropriate taxable years that would have been filed had the section 1504(c)(2) election never been made.

(vi) A group referred to at subdivision (v)(A) or (B) of this paragraph (e)(4) meets the conditions of this subdivision (vi) if it—

(A) Filed before March 16, 1983, a return for its taxable year ending in the month of December, 1982, and

(B) Had not been granted an extension of time beyond March 15, 1983, for the filing of that return.

(vii) Interest. For purposes of section 6601(a), interest runs from the original due date (without extensions) for the filing of such returns as are filed pursuant to an election (to discontinue or withdraw as the case may be) under this paragraph (e)(4).

(5) Consent to regulations. If a group does not discontinue filing a consolidated return under paragraph (e)(4) of this section but continues to file a consolidated return for the group's first taxable year for which the regulations under this section are first effective, the members of the group will be deemed to have consented to the regulations under this section.

(6) Cross reference. If an election is made under section 1504(c)(2), see § 1.1502-75(e) and (f) for rules that apply for not including (or including) a member or a nonmember in the consolidated return.

(f) Effect of election. If the common parent makes the election under section 1504(c)(2), the following rules apply:

(1) Termination of group. A mere election under section 1504(c)(2) will not cause the creation of a new group or the termination of an affiliated group that files a consolidated return in the immediately preceding taxable year.

(2) Effect of eligibility. If a life member is eligible after an election under section 1504(c)(2), it may not be included as a member of an affiliated group as defined in section 1504(c)(1).

(3) Eligible and ineligible life companies. If any life company was a member of an affiliated group of life companies (as defined in section 1504(c)(1)) but is ineligible for a taxable year for which the election under section 1504(c)(2) is effective, that year is not a separate return year merely by reason of the election under section 1504(c)(2) in applying §§ 1.1502-13, 1.1502-18, and 1.1502-19 to transactions occurring in prior consolidated return years of that affiliated group. In addition, if more than one ineligible life member of the group (as defined in section 1504(c)(1)) joined in the filing of a consolidated return in the taxable year immediately preceding the year for which the election under section 1504(c)(2) is effective and, solely as a result of the election, one of the ineligible life members becomes the common parent of such a group (section 1504(c)(1)), the group must continue to file a consolidated return. For example, assume that L_1 owns all of the stock of S_1 and all of the stock of L_2. L_2 owns the stock of L_3. L_1, L_2 and L_3 are life companies and S_1 is a nonlife company. Assume further that in 1981, L_1, L_2 and L_3 file a consolidated return but L_1 makes the election under section 1504(c)(2) for 1982 and L_2 and L_3 are ineligible. L_2 and L_3 must continue to file a consolidated return in 1982. Moreover, L_2 could elect in 1982 to file a consolidated return (section 1504(c)(1)) with L_3 even if they did not file a consolidated return in 1981 with L_1.

(4) Inclusion of life company. If a life company is ineligible in the consolidated return year for which the election is effective, it will be treated as an includible corporation for the common parent's first taxable year in which the company becomes eligible.

(5) Dividends received deduction. Section 243(b)(5) defines the term affiliated group for purposes of the election to deduct 100 percent of the qualifying dividends received by a member from another member of the group. Section 246(b)(6) limits certain multiple tax benefits and the deduction itself. Section 243(b)(5) and (6) do not apply to the mutual companies and life companies that are eligible corpora-

tions. See section 1504(c)(2)(B)(i). Thus, the common parent of the group may elect to deduct 100 percent of the qualifying dividends received from an ineligible life company.

(6) Controlled group. Sections 1563(a)(4), (b)(2)(D), and (b)(3)(C) (insofar as it applies to corporations described in section 1563(b)(2)(D)) do not apply to any eligible or ineligible life company that is a member of the group for a taxable year during which the election is effective. See paragraph (d)(4) of this section for the definition of group.

(7) Consolidated tax. The tax liability of a group for a consolidated return year (before application of credits against that tax) is computed on a consolidated basis by adding together the following taxes:

(i) The tax imposed under section 11 on consolidated taxable income (as determined under paragraph (g) of this section). The taxes imposed under sections 802(a), 821(a), and 831(a) will each be treated as a tax imposed under section 11.

(ii) The tax imposed by section 1201 on consolidated net capital gain (as determined under paragraph (o) of this section) in lieu of the tax imposed under paragraph (f)(7)(i) of this section on that gain.

(iii) Any taxes described in § 1.1502-2 (other than by paragraphs (a), (f), and (h) thereof).

(g) Consolidated taxable income. The consolidated taxable income is the sum of the following three amounts:

(1) Nonlife consolidated taxable income. The nonlife consolidated taxable income (as defined in paragraph (h) of this section) of the nonlife subgroup, as set off by the life subgroup losses as provided in paragraph (n) of this section. The amount in this paragraph (g)(1) may not be less than zero.

(2) Consolidated partial LICTI. The consolidated partial LICTI (as defined in paragraph (j) of this section) of the life subgroup, as set off by the nonlife subgroup losses as provided in paragraph (m) of this section. The amount in this paragraph (g)(2) may not be less than zero.

(3) Surplus accounts. The sum of the amounts subtracted under section 815 from the policyholders' surplus accounts of the life members.

(h) Nonlife consolidated taxable income. *(1) In general.* Nonlife consolidated taxable income is the consolidated taxable income of the nonlife subgroup, computed under § 1.1502-11 as modified by this paragraph (h). For this purpose, separate taxable income of a member includes separate mutual insurance company taxable income (as defined in section 821(b)) and insurance company taxable income (as defined in section 832).

(2) Nonlife consolidated net operating loss deduction. (i) In general. In applying §§ 1.1502-21 or 1.1502-21A (as appropriate), the rules in this subparagraph (2) apply in determining for the nonlife subgroup the nonlife net operating loss and the portion of the nonlife net operating loss carryovers and carrybacks to the taxable year.

(ii) Nonlife CNOL. The nonlife consolidated net operating loss is determined under §§ 1.1502-21A(f) or 1.1502-21(e) (as appropriate) by treating the nonlife subgroup as the group.

(iii) Carryback. The nonlife consolidated net operating loss for the nonlife subgroup is carried back under §§ 1.1502-21A or 1.1502-21 (as appropriate) to the appropriate years (whether consolidated or separate) before the loss may be used as a nonlife subgroup loss under paragraphs (g)(2) and (m) of this section to set off consolidated partial LICTI in the year the loss arose. The election under section 172(b)(3)(C) to relinquish the entire carryback period for the net operating loss of the nonlife subgroup may be made by the common parent of the group. Furthermore, the election may be made even though the election under section 812(b)(3) and paragraph (l)(3)(iii) of this section is not made.

(iv) Subgroup rule. In determining the portion of the nonlife consolidated net operating loss that is absorbed when the loss is carried back to a consolidated return year beginning after December 31, 1981, §§ 1.1502-21A or 1.1502-21 (as appropriate) is applied by treating the nonlife subgroup as the group. Therefore, the absorption is determined without taking into account any life subgroup losses that were previously reported on a consolidated return as setting off nonlife consolidated taxable income for the year to which the nonlife loss is carried back.

(v) Carryover. The portion of the nonlife consolidated net operating loss that is not absorbed in a prior year as a carryback, or as a nonlife subgroup loss that set off consolidated partial LICTI for the year the loss arose, constitutes a nonlife carryover under this subparagraph (2) to reduce nonlife consolidated taxable income before that portion may constitute a nonlife subgroup loss that sets off consolidated partial LICTI for a particular year.

(vi) Transitional rules. The nonlife consolidated net operating loss deduction is subject to a transitional rule limitation in paragraph (h)(3) of this section.

(vii) Example. The following example illustrates this paragraph (h)(2). In the example, L indicates a life company, another letter indicates a nonlife company, and each corporation uses the calendar year as its taxable year.

Example. P owns all of the stock of S and L_1. L_1 owns all of the stock of L_2. For 1982, the group first files a consolidated return for which the election under section 1504(c)(2) is effective. P and S filed consolidated returns for 1979 through 1981. In 1982, the P−S group sustains a nonlife consolidated net operating loss. The loss is carried back to the consolidated return years 1979, 1980, and 1981 of P and S by using the principles of §§ 1.1502-21A and 1.1502-79A and, because the election in 1982 under section 1504(c)(2) does not result under paragraph (f)(1) of this section in the creation of a new group or the termination of the P−S nonlife group, the loss is absorbed on the consolidated return in those years without regard to whether the loss in 1982 is attributable to P or S and without regard to their contribution to consolidated taxable income in 1979, 1980, or 1981. The portion of the loss not absorbed in 1979, 1980, and 1981 may serve as a nonlife subgroup loss in 1982 that may set off the consolidated partial LICTI of L_1 and L_2 under paragraphs (g)(2) and (m) of this section.

(3) Transitional rule. (i) In general. The portion of the nonlife consolidated net operating loss deduction in a consolidated return year beginning after December 31, 1980 (referred to as "post-1980 year") attributable to net operating losses sustained in separate return years ending before January 1, 1981 (referred to as "pre-1981 year"), is subject to the rules and limitations in this subparagraph (3).

(ii) Separate nonlife groups. To determine the limitation, first, identify for the post-1980 year one or more separate affiliated groups of nonlife companies (as defined in section 1504 without section 1504(c)(2)). For this purpose, a single nonlife company may constitute a separate affiliated group if (A) it is not otherwise a member of a separate group or (B) it has a net operating loss sustained in the pre-1981 year that may be carried over and that year is a separate return limitation year (determined under § 1.1502-1(f) without paragraph (d)(11) of this section).

(iii) Carryover. Second, identify the pre-1981 year net operating losses that may be carried over and that are attributable to each separate affiliated group of nonlife companies. The separate return limitation year rules in §§ 1.1502-21A(c) or 1.1502-21(c) (as appropriate) do not apply to any of these carryovers.

(iv) Limitation. Third, treat the last taxable year ending before January 1, 1981, as if in that year there was a consolidated return change of ownership of each such separate affiliated group of nonlife companies and apply the consolidated return change of ownership limitation in § 1.1502-21A(d) to the losses of each group by treating the members of each separate group as old members.

(v) Examples. The following examples illustrate this paragraph (h)(3). In the examples L indicates a life company, another letter indicates a nonlife company, and each corporation uses the calendar year as its taxable year.

Example (1). Throughout all of 1982, P owns all of the stock of S and L_1 and L_1 owns all of the stock of L_2 which in turn owns all of the stock of S_1. Thus, for 1982, there are two nonlife subgroups under this subparagraph (3), P–S and S_1. For 1981, P and S did not file a consolidated return and for 1980 P has a net operating loss of $200,000. Assume that P had no income in 1981. For 1982, the group makes an election under section 1504(c)(2) to file a consolidated return and all corporations are eligible corporations. The consolidated taxable income for the nonlife subgroup for 1982 (determined without the consolidated net operating loss deduction) recomputed by including only items of income and deduction of P and S is $120,000. If $120,000 is the § 1.1502-21A(d)(2) amount for P and S, then the amount of P's net operating loss for 1980 that may be carried over to P and S for 1982 cannot exceed $120,000.

Example (2). (a) P owns all of the stock of S_1. On January 1, 1979, P purchased all of the stock of L_1 which owns all of the stock of L_2 and S_2. Prior to 1984, all of the corporations filed separate returns. For 1984, the group makes an election under section 1504(c)(2) to file a consolidated return.

(b) 1981, 1982, and 1983 are not treated under paragraph (d)(11) of this section as separate return limitation years of the P, S_1, and S_2 nonlife subgroup. However, P and S_1 will be treated as old members under paragraph (h)(3)(iv) of this section and under § 1.1502-21A(d) with respect to their losses in 1979 and 1980 (whether a consolidated return was filed or separate returns were filed) so that the portion of nonlife consolidated taxable income attributable to S_2 may not absorb the losses of P or S_1. The rules that apply to the $P-S_1$ nonlife subgroup for 1979 and 1980 apply in an identical way to S_2 by treating S_2 as a subgroup separate from the $P-S_1$ nonlife subgroup. See section 1507(c)(2)(A) of the Tax Reform Act of 1976.

(c) Similarly, L_1 and L_2 are treated as old members under paragraphs (1)(3) and (h)(3)(iv) of this section for losses arising in 1979 and 1980. However, since the L_1-L_2 subgroup is also the life subgroup under paragraph (d)(8) of this section, the limitation in paragraph (h)(3)(iv) of this section does not affect the computation of consolidated partial LICTI for the life subgroup.

(4) Nonlife consolidated capital gain net income or loss. (i) In general. In applying §§ 1.1502-22 or 1.1502-22A (as appropriate), the rules in this subparagraph (4) apply in determining for the nonlife subgroup the nonlife consolidated capital gain net income or loss and the portion of the nonlife net capital loss carryovers and carrybacks to the taxable year. In particular, the nonlife consolidated capital gain net income and nonlife consolidated net capital loss are determined under the principles of §§ 1.1502-22 or 1.1502-22A(a) (as appropriate) by treating the nonlife subgroup as the group.

(ii) Additional principles. In applying §§ 1.1502-22A or 1.1502-22 to nonlife consolidated net capital loss carryovers and carrybacks, the principles set forth in paragraph (h)(2)(iii) through (v) for applying §§ 1.1502-21 or 1.1502-21A (as appropriate) to nonlife consolidated net operating loss carryovers and carrybacks shall also apply. Further, the portion of nonlife consolidated net capital loss carryovers attributable to losses sustained in taxable years ending before January 1, 1981, is subject to the limitations in paragraph (h)(3) of this section applied by substituting "net capital loss" for the term "net operating loss" and "§ 1.1502-22A(d)" for "§ 1.1502-21A(d)".

(iii) Special rules. The nonlife consolidated net capital loss is reduced, for purposes of determining the carryovers and carrybacks under §§ 1.1502-22A(b)(1) or 1.1502-22(b) by the lesser of—

(A) The aggregate of the additional capital loss deductions allowed under section 822(c)(6) or section 832(c)(5), or

(B) The nonlife consolidated taxable income computed without capital gains and losses.

(i) [Reserved]

(j) Consolidated partial LICTI. [Reserved]

(k) Consolidated TII. *(1) General rule.* [Reserved]

(2) Separate TII. [Reserved]

(3) Company's share of investment yield. [Reserved]

(4) Life consolidated capital gain net income. [Reserved]

(5) Life consolidated net capital loss carryovers and carrybacks. The life consolidated net capital loss carryovers and carrybacks for the life subgroup are determined by applying the principles of §§ 1.1502-22 or 1.1502-22A (as appropriate) as modified by the following rules in this subparagraph (5):

(i) Life consolidated net capital loss is first carried back (or apportioned to the life members for separate return years) to be absorbed by life consolidated capital gain net income without regard to any nonlife subgroup capital losses and before the life consolidated net capital loss may serve as a life subgroup capital loss that sets off nonlife consolidated capital gain net income in the year the life consolidated net capital loss arose.

(ii) If a life consolidated net capital loss is not carried back or is not a life subgroup loss that sets off nonlife consolidated capital gain net income in the year the life consolidated net capital loss arose, then it is carried over to the particular year under this paragraph (k)(5) first against life consolidated capital gain net income before it may serve as a life subgroup capital loss that sets off nonlife consolidated capital gain net income in that particular year.

(iii) Section 818(f). Capital losses may not be deducted more than once and capital gain will not be included more than once. See section 818(e) and also section 818(f).

(iv) Capital loss carryovers are subject to the transitional rule in paragraph (k)(6) of this section.

(6) Transitional rule. The portion of the life consolidated capital loss carryovers attributable to the net capital losses of

the life members sustained in separate return years ending before January 1, 1981, is subject to the same limitations as the capital losses of nonlife members in paragraph (h)(4)(iii) of this section by applying the principles of paragraph (h)(3) of this section to each separate affiliated group of life companies.

(l) Consolidated GO or LO. *(1) General rule.* [Reserved]

(2) Separate GO. [Reserved]

(3) Consolidated operations loss deduction. (i) General rule. The consolidated operations loss deduction is an amount equal to the consolidated operations loss carryovers and carrybacks to the taxable year. The provisions of §§ 1.1502-21 or 1.1502-21A (as appropriate) and section 812 apply to the extent not inconsistent with this paragraph (l)(3).

(ii) Consolidated offset. For purposes of applying section 812(b) and (d), the term "consolidated offset" means the increase in the consolidated operations loss deduction which reduces consolidated partial LICTI to zero. For setoff of consolidated LO against nonlife consolidated taxable income, see paragraph (n)(2) of this section.

(iii) Carrybacks. A consolidated LO is first carried back to be absorbed by GO of a life member under section 809(d)(4) or consolidated partial LICTI (as the case may be under section 818(f)(2)) for prior consolidated return years (or apportioned to the life members for prior separate return years) without regard to any nonlife subgroup losses that were set off against consolidated partial LICTI and before the consolidated LO may serve as a life subgroup loss to be set off against nonlife consolidated taxable income in the year the consolidated LO arose. The election to relinquish the entire carryback period for the consolidated LO of the life subgroup may be made by the common parent of the group. See section 812(b)(3). Furthermore, the election may be made even though the election under section 172(b)(3)(C) and paragraph (h)(2)(iii) of this section is not made.

(iv) Carryovers. If a consolidated LO is not carried back or is not applied as a life subgroup loss that set off nonlife consolidated taxable income in the year the consolidated LO arose, then it is carried over to a particular year under this paragraph (l)(3) first against the GO of a life member under section 809(d)(4) or consolidated partial LICTI (as the case may be under section 818(f)(2)) before it may serve as a life subgroup loss that may be set off against nonlife consolidated taxable income for that particular year.

(v) Transitional rule. The portion of a consolidated operations loss deduction that is attributable to LO_8 sustained in separate return years ending before January 1, 1981, is subject to the same rules and limitations that the nonlife consolidated net operating loss deduction is subject to in paragraph (h)(3) of this section as applied by identifying separate affiliated groups of life companies.

(4) Life consolidated capital gain net income or loss. Life consolidated capital gain net income or loss is determined in the same manner as under paragraph (k)(4) of this section. However, a life member's company share is determined under section 809(a) and (b)(3).

(m) Consolidated partial LICTI setoff by nonlife subgroup losses. *(1) In general.* The nonlife subgroup losses consist of the nonlife consolidated net operating loss and the nonlife consolidated net capital loss. Under paragraph (g)(2) of this section, consolidated partial LICTI is set off by the amounts of these two consolidated losses specified in paragraph (m)(2) of this section. The setoff is subject to the rules and limitations in paragraph (m)(3) of this section.

(2) Amount of setoff. (i) Current year. Consolidated partial LICTI for the current taxable year is set off by the portion of the nonlife consolidated net operating loss and nonlife consolidated net capital loss arising in that year that cannot be carried back under paragraph (h) of this section to prior taxable years (whether consolidated or separate return years) of the nonlife subgroup.

(ii) Carryovers. The portion of the offsettable nonlife consolidated net operating loss or nonlife consolidated net capital loss that has not been used as a nonlife subgroup loss setoff against consolidated partial LICTI in the year it arose may be carried over to succeeding taxable years under the principles of §§ 1.1502-21 or 1.1502-21A (as appropriate) (relating to net operating loss deduction) or §§ 1.1502-22 or 1.1502-22A (as appropriate) (relating to net capital loss carryovers). However, in any particular succeeding year, the losses will be used under paragraph (h) of this section in computing nonlife consolidated taxable income before being used in that year as a nonlife subgroup loss that sets off consolidated partial LICTI.

(3) Nonlife subgroup loss rules and limitations. The nonlife subgroup losses are subject to the following operating rules and limitations:

(i) Separate return years. The carryovers in paragraph (m)(2)(ii) of this section may include net operating losses and net capital losses of the nonlife members arising in separate return years ending after December 31, 1980, that may be carried over to a succeeding year under the principles (including limitations) of §§ 1.1502-21 and 1.1502-22 (or §§ 1.1502-21A and 1.1502-22A, as appropriate). But see subdivision (ix) of this paragraph (m)(3).

(ii) Capital loss. Nonlife consolidated net capital loss sets off consolidated partial LICTI only to the extent of life consolidated capital gain net income (as determined under paragraph (l)(4) of this section) and this setoff applies before any nonlife consolidated net operating loss sets off consolidated partial LICTI.

(iii) Capital gain. Life consolidated capital gain net income is zero in any taxable year in which the life subgroup has a consolidated LO and, in any taxable year, it may not exceed consolidated partial LICTI.

(iv) Ordering rule. Consolidated partial LICTI for a consolidated return year is set off by nonlife subgroup losses for that year before being set off (under paragraph (m)(2)(ii) of this section) by a carryover of a nonlife subgroup loss to that year.

(v) Setoff at bottom line. The setoff of nonlife subgroup losses against consolidated partial LICTI does not affect life member deductions that depend in whole or in part on GO or TII. Thus, the setoff does not affect the amount of consolidated partial LICTI (as determined under paragraph (j) of this section) for any taxable year but it merely constitutes an adjustment in arriving at the group's consolidated taxable income under paragraph (g) of this section.

(vi) Ineligible nonlife member. (A) The offsetable nonlife consolidated net operating loss that arises in any consolidated return year (that may be set off against consolidated partial LICTI in the current taxable year or in a succeeding taxable year) is the amount computed under paragraph (h)(2)(ii) of this section reduced by the ineligible NOL. For purposes of this subparagraph (3), the "ineligible NOL" is in the year the loss arose the amount of the separate net operating loss (determined under § 1.1502-21(b)) of any nonlife member that is ineligible in that year (and not the portion of the nonlife consolidated net operating loss attributable under § 1.1502-21(b) to such a member).

(B) The carryovers of offsetable nonlife net operating losses under paragraph (m)(2)(ii) of this section do not include an ineligible NOL arising in a consolidated return year or a loss attributable to an ineligible member arising in a separate return year. See section 1503(c)(2).

(C) For absorption within the nonlife subgroup of an ineligible NOL arising in a consolidated return year or a loss of an ineligible member arising in a separate return year which is not a separate return limitation year under paragraph (m)(3)(ix) of this section, see paragraph (m)(3)(vii) of this section.

(vii) Absorption of ineligible NOL. (A) If all or a portion of a nonlife member's ineligible NOL (determined under paragraph (m)(3)(vi)(A) of this section) may be carried back or carried over under paragraph (h)(2) of this section to a particular consolidated return year of the nonlife subgroup (absorption year), then notwithstanding §§ 1.1502-21A(b)(3)(ii) or 1.1502-21(b), the amount carried to the absorption year will be absorbed by that member's contribution (to the extent thereof) to nonlife consolidated taxable income for that year.

(B) For purposes of (A) of this subdivision (vii), a member's contribution to nonlife consolidated taxable income for an absorption year is the amount of such income (computed without the portion of the nonlife consolidated net operating loss deduction attributable to taxable years subsequent to the year the loss arose), minus such consolidated taxable income recomputed by excluding both that member's items of income and deductions for the absorption year. The deductions of the member include the prior application of this paragraph (m)(3)(vii) to the absorption of the nonlife consolidated net operating loss deduction for losses arising in taxable years prior to the particular loss year.

(viii) Election to relinquish carryback. The offsetable nonlife consolidated net operating loss does not include the amount that could be carried back under paragraph (h)(2) of this section but for the common parent's election under section 172(b)(3)(C) to relinquish the carryback. See section 1503(c)(1).

(ix) Separate return limitation year. The offsetable nonlife consolidated net operating and capital loss carryovers do not include any losses attributable to a nonlife member that were sustained (A) in a separate return limitation year (determined without section 1504(b)(2)) of that member (or a predecessor), or (B) in a separate return year ending after December 31, 1980, in which an election was in effect under neither section 1504(c)(2) nor section 243(b)(2). For purposes of this paragraph (m), a separate return limitation year includes a taxable year ending before January 1, 1981. See section 1507(c)(2)(A) of the Tax Reform Act of 1976 and §§ 1.1502-15 and 1.1502-15A (including applicable exceptions thereto).

(x) Percentage limitation. The offsetable nonlife consolidated net operating losses that may be set off against consolidated partial LICTI in a particular year may not exceed a percentage limitation. This limitation is the applicable percentage in section 1503(c)(1) of the lesser of two amounts. The first amount is the sum of the offsetable nonlife consolidated net operating losses under paragraph (m)(2) of this section that may serve in the particular year (determined without this limitation) as a setoff against consolidated partial LICTI. The second amount is consolidated partial LICTI (as defined in paragraph (j) of this section) in the particular year reduced by any nonlife consolidated net capital loss that sets off consolidated partial LICTI in that year.

(xi) Further limitation. Any offsetable nonlife consolidated net operating loss remaining after applying the percentage limitation that is carried over to a succeeding taxable year may not be set off against the consolidated partial LICTI attributable to a life member that was not an eligible life member in the year the loss arose. See section 1503(c)(2).

(xii) Restoration rule. The carryback of a consolidated LO or life consolidated net capital loss under paragraph (l) of this section that reduces consolidated partial LICTI (or life consolidated capital gain net income) for a prior year may reduce the amount of nonlife subgroup losses that would offset consolidated partial LICTI in that prior year. Thus, that amount may be carried over under paragraph (h)(2) or (4) of this section from that prior year in determining nonlife consolidated taxable income in a succeeding year or serve as offsetable nonlife subgroup losses in a succeeding year.

(4) Acquired groups. [Reserved]

(5) Illustrations. The following examples illustrates this paragraph (m). In the examples, L indicates a life company, another letter indicates a nonlife company, and each corporation uses the calendar year as its taxable year.

Example (1). P owns all of the stock of L and S. S owns all of the stock of I, a nonlife member that is an ineligible corporation for 1982 under paragraph (d)(13) of this section. For 1982, the group elects under section 1504(c)(2) to file a consolidated return. For 1982, assume that any nonlife consolidated net operating loss may not be carried back to a prior taxable year. Other facts are summarized in the following table.

	Separate taxable income (loss)
P	$100
S	(100)
I	(100)
Nonlife consolidated net operating loss	(100)

Under paragraph (m)(3)(vi) of this section, P's separate income is considered to absorb the loss of S, an eligible member, first and the offsetable nonlife consolidated net operating loss is zero, i.e., the consolidated net operating loss ($100) reduced by I's loss ($100). The consolidated net operating loss ($100) may be carried over, but since it is entirely attributable to I (an ineligible member) its use is subject to the restrictions in paragraph (m)(3)(vi) of this section. The result would be the same if the group contained two additional members, S_1, an eligible member, and I_1, an ineligible member, where S_1 had a loss of ($100) and I_1 had income of $100.

Example (2). The facts are the same as in example (1) except that for 1982 S's separate net operating loss is $200. Assume further that L's consolidated partial LICTI is $200. Under paragraph (m)(3)(vi) of this section, the offsetable nonlife consolidated net operating loss is $100, i.e., the nonlife consolidated net operating loss computed under paragraph (h)(2)(ii) of this section ($200), reduced by the separate net operating loss of I ($100). The offsetable nonlife consolidated net operating loss that may be set off against consolidated partial LICTI in 1982 is $30, i.e., 30 percent of the lesser of the offsetable $100 or consolidated partial LICTI of $200. See paragraph (m)(3)(x) of this section. The nonlife subgroup may carry $170 to 1983 under paragraph (h)(2) of this section against nonlife consolidated taxable income, i.e., consolidated net operating loss ($200) less amount used in 1982 ($30). Under paragraph (m)(2)(ii) of this section, the offsetable nonlife consolidated net operating loss that may be carried to 1983 is $70, i.e., $100 minus $30. The facts and results are summarized in the table below.

	(Dollars Omitted)			
	Facts (a)	Offsetable (b)	Limit (c)	Unused loss (d)
1. P	100	—	—	—
2. S	(200)	(100)	—	(70)
3. I	(100)	—	—	(100)
4. Nonlife subgroup	(200)	(100)	(100)	(170)
5. L	200	—	200	—
6. 30% of lower of Line 4(c) or 5(c)	—	—	30	—
7. Unused offsetable loss	—	—	—	(70)

Accordingly, under paragraph (g) of this section (assuming no amount is withdrawn from L's surplus accounts), consolidated taxable income is $170, i.e., line 5(a) minus line 6(c)).

Example (3). The facts are the same as in example (2) with the following additions for 1983. The nonlife subgroup has nonlife consolidated taxable income of $50 (all of which is attributable to I) before the nonlife consolidated net operating loss deduction under paragraph (h)(2) of this section. Consolidated partial LICTI is $100. Under paragraph (h)(2) of this section, $50 of the nonlife consolidated net operating loss carryover ($170) is used in 1983 and, under paragraph (m)(3)(vi) and (vii) of this section, the portion used in 1982 is attributable to I, the ineligible nonlife member. Accordingly, the offsetable nonlife consolidated net operating loss from 1982 under paragraph (m)(3)(ii) of this section is $70, i.e., the unused loss from 1982. The offsetable nonlife consolidated net operating loss in 1983 is $24.50, i.e., 35 percent of the lesser of the offsetable loss of $70 or consolidated partial LICTI of $100. Accordingly, under paragraph (g) of this section (assuming no amount is withdrawn from L's surplus accounts), consolidated taxable income is $75.50, i.e., consolidated partial LICTI of $100 minus the offsetable loss of $24.50.

Example (4). P owns all of the stock of S and L. For 1982, all corporations are eligible corporations, and the group elects under section 1504(c)(2) to file a consolidated return, the nonlife consolidated net operating loss is $100, and the nonlife consolidated net capital loss is $50. Assume that the losses may not be carried back and the capital losses are not attributable to built-in deductions under paragraph (m)(3)(ix) of this section or under § 1.1502-15A. Other facts and the results are set forth in the following table:

	P-S	L
1. Nonlife consolidated net operating loss	($100)	
2. Nonlife consolidated capital loss	(50)	
3. Consolidated partial LICTI		$100
4. Life consolidated capital gain net income included in line 3		50
5. Offsetable:		
(a) 30% of lower of line 1 or line 3-4	(15)	
(b) Line 2	(50)	
(c) Total	(65)	
6. Unused losses available to be carried over:		
(a) From line 1 (line 1 minus line 5(a))	(85)	
(b) From line 2 (line 2 minus line 5(b))	0	

Accordingly, under paragraph (g) of this section consolidated taxable income is $35, i.e., line 3 minus line 5(c).

Example (5). The facts are the same as in example (4). Assume further that for 1983 L has an LO that is carried back to 1982 and the LO is large enough to reduce consolidated partial LICTI for 1982 to zero as determined before any setoff for nonlife losses. Under paragraph (m)(3)(xii) of this section, the nonlife consolidated net operating loss of $15 and the nonlife consolidated net capital loss of $50 that were set off in 1982 respectively against consolidated partial LICTI and life consolidated capital gain net income are restored. These restored amounts may constitute part of the nonlife consolidated net operating loss carryover to 1983 under paragraph (h)(2) of this section or part of the nonlife net capital loss carryover to 1983 under paragraph (h)(4) of this section.

Example (6). The facts are the same as in example (5) except that L's LO for 1983 as carried back reduces consolidated partial LICTI in 1982 from $100 to $25. Since consolidated partial LICTI of $100 in 1982 (before the carryback) included life consolidated capital gain net income of $50, under paragraph (m)(3)(iii) of this section, the life consolidated capital gain net income is $25, i.e., $50 but not more than $25. Therefore, under paragraph (m)(3)(ii) of this section, the offsetable nonlife capital loss in 1982 is $25 and, under paragraph (m)(3)(xii) of this section, $25 of the $50 nonlife consolidated net capital loss in 1982 may be carried under paragraph (h)(4) of this section to 1983. No nonlife consolidated net operating loss is used as a setoff against consolidated partial LICTI in 1982 under paragraph (m)(3)(xii) of this section by reason of the carryback of the consolidated LO from 1983 to 1982.

(n) Nonlife consolidated taxable income set off by life subgroup losses. *(1) In general.* The life subgroup losses consist of the consolidated LO and the life consolidated net capital loss (as determined under paragraph (l)(4) of this section). Under paragraph (g)(1) of this section, nonlife consolidated taxable income is set off by the amounts of these two consolidated losses specified in paragraph (n)(2) of this section.

(2) Amount of setoff. The portion of the consolidated LO or life consolidated net capital loss that may be set off against nonlife consolidated taxable income (determined under paragraph (h) of this section) is determined by applying the rules prescribed in paragraph (m)(2) and (3) of this section in the following manner:

(i) Substitute the term "life" for "nonlife", and vice versa.

(ii) Substitute the term "nonlife consolidated taxable income" for "consolidated partial LICTI", and vice versa.

(iii) Substitute the term "consolidated LO" for "nonlife consolidated net operating loss", "paragraph (l)" or "paragraph (j)" for "paragraph (h)", and "section 812(b)(3)" for "section 172(b)(3)(C)".

(iv) Paragraphs (m)(3)(vi), (vii), (x), and (xi) of this section do not apply to a consolidated LO.

(v) Capital losses may not be deducted more than once. See section 818(e) and also the requirements in section 818(f).

(vi) The setoff of life subgroup losses against nonlife consolidated taxable income does not affect nonlife member deductions that depend in whole or in part on taxable income.

(3) Illustrations. The following examples illustrate this paragraph (n). In the examples, L indicates a life company, another letter indicates a nonlife company, and each corporation uses the calendar year as its taxable year.

Example (1). P, S, L_1, and L_2 constitute a group that elects under section 1504(c)(2) to file a consolidated return for 1982. In 1982, the nonlife subgroup consolidated taxable income is $100 and there is $20 of nonlife consolidated net capital loss that cannot be carried back under paragraph (h) of this section to taxable years (whether consolidated or separate) preceding 1982. The nonlife subgroup has no carryover from years prior to 1982. Consolidated LO is $150 which under paragraph (l) of this section includes life consolidated capital gain net income of $25. The $150 LO is carried back under paragraph (l)(3) of this section to taxable years (whether consolidated or separate) preceding 1982 before it may offset in 1982 nonlife consolidated taxable income. Since life consolidated capital gain net income is zero for 1982, the nonlife capital loss offset is zero.

Example (2). The facts are the same as in example (1). Assume further that no part of the $150 consolidated LO for 1982 can be used by L_1 and L_2 in years prior to 1982. For 1982, $100 of consolidated LO sets off the $100 nonlife consolidated taxable income. The life subgroup carries under paragraph (l)(3) of this section to 1983 $50 of the consolidated LO ($150 minus $100). See paragraph (l)(3)(ii) of this section. The $50 carryover will be used in 1983 against life subgroup income before it may be used in 1983 to setoff nonlife consolidated taxable income.

Example (3). (a) The facts are the same as in example (1), except that for 1982 the nonlife consolidated taxable income is $150 and includes nonlife consolidated capital gain net income of $50, consolidated partial LICTI is $200, and a life consolidated net capital loss is $50. Assume that the $50 life consolidated net capital loss sets off the $50 nonlife consolidated capital gain net income. Consolidated taxable income under paragraph (g) of this section is $300, i.e., nonlife consolidated taxable income ($150) minus the setoff of the life consolidated net capital loss ($50), plus consolidated partial LICTI ($200).

(b) Assume that for 1983 the nonlife consolidated net operating loss is $150. Under paragraph (h)(2) of this section, the loss may be carried back to 1982 against nonlife consolidated taxable income. If P, the common parent, does not elect to relinquish the carryback under section 172(b)(3)(C), the entire $150 must be carried back reducing 1982 nonlife consolidated taxable income to zero and nonlife consolidated capital gain net income to zero. Under paragraph (m)(3)(xii) of this section, the setoff in 1982 of the nonlife consolidated capital gain net income ($50) by the life consolidated net capital loss ($50) is restored. Accordingly, the 1982 life consolidated net capital loss may be carried over by the life subgroup to 1983. Under paragraph (g) of this section, after the carryback consolidated taxable income for 1982 is $200, i.e., nonlife consolidated taxable income ($0) plus consolidated partial LICTI ($200).

Example (4). The facts are the same as in example (3), except that P elects under section 172(b)(3)(C) to relinquish the carryback of $150 arising in 1983. The setoff in part (a) of example (3) is not restored. However, the offsetable nonlife consolidated net operating loss for 1983 (or that may be carried forward from 1983) is zero. See paragraph (m)(3)(vii) of this section. Nevertheless, the $150 nonlife consolidated net operating loss may be carried forward to be used by the nonlife group.

Example (5). P owns all of the stock of S_1 and of L_1. On January 1, 1978, L_1 purchases all of the stock of L_1. For 1982, the group elects under section 1504(c)(2) to file a consolidated return. For 1982, L_1 is an eligible corporation under paragraph (d)(12) of this section but L_2 is ineligible. Thus, L_1 but not L_2 is a member for 1982. For 1982, L_2 sustains an LO that cannot be carried back. For 1982, L_2 is treated under paragraph (f)(6) of this section as a member of a controlled group of corporations under section 1563 with P, S, and L_1. For 1983, L_2 is eligible and is included on the group's consolidated return. L_2's LO for 1982 that may be carried to 1983 is not treated under paragraph (d)(11) of this section as having been sustained in a separate return limitation year for purposes of computing consolidated partial LICTI of the L_1-L_2 life subgroup for 1983. Furthermore, the portion of L_2's LO not used under paragraph (l)(3) of this section against life subgroup income in 1983 may be included in offsetable consolidated operations loss under paragraph (n)(2) and (m)(3)(i) of this section that reduces in 1983 nonlife consolidated taxable income because L_2's loss in 1982 was not sustained in a separate return limitation year under paragraph (n)(2) and (m)(3)(ix)(A) of this section or in a separate return year (1982) when an election was in effect neither under section 1504(c)(2) nor section 243(b)(2).

(o) Alternative tax. *(1) In general.* For purposes of the alternative tax under paragraph (f)(7)(ii) of this section, consolidated net capital gain is the sum of the following two amounts:

(i) The nonlife consolidated net capital gain reduced by any setoff of a life consolidated net capital loss.

(ii) The life consolidated net capital gain reduced by any setoff of a nonlife consolidated net capital loss.

(2) Net capital gain. For purposes of this paragraph (o)—

(i) Nonlife consolidated net capital gain is computed under §§ 1.1502-41A or 1.1502-22T (as appropriate) except that it may not exceed nonlife consolidated taxable income (computed under paragraph (h) of this section).

(ii) Life consolidated net capital gain is computed under §§ 1.1502-41A or 1.1502-22T (as appropriate), applied in a manner consistent with paragraph (l)(4) of this section, except that it may not exceed consolidated partial LICTI (as determined under paragraph (j) of this section).

(iii) Setoffs. Setoffs are determined under paragraphs (m) or (n) of this section (as the case may be).

(p) Transitional rule for credit carryovers. For limitations on credits arising in taxable years ending before January 1, 1981, that may be carried over to taxable years beginning on or after that date, section 1507(c)(2)(A) of the Tax Reform Act of 1976 and the principles in paragraph (h)(3) of this section (relating to limitations on loss carryovers) apply.

(q) Preemption. The rules in this section preempt any inconsistent rules in other sections (§ 1.1502-1 through 1.1502-80) of the consolidated return regulations. For example, the rules in paragraph (m)(3)(vi) apply notwithstanding §§ 1.1502-21A(b)(3) and 1.1502-79A(a)(3) or § 1.1502-21, as appropriate).

(r) Other consolidation principles. The fact that this section treats the life and nonlife members as separate groups in computing, respectively, consolidated partial LICTI (or LO) and nonlife consolidated taxable income (or loss) does not affect the usual rules in §§ 1.1502-0–1.1502-80 unless this section provides otherwise. Thus, the usual rules in § 1.1502-13 (relating to intercompany transactions) apply to both the life and nonlife members by treating them as members of one affiliated group.

(s) Filing requirements *(1) In general.* To file a consolidated income tax return for a life-nonlife consolidated group, the common parent shall—

(i) File the applicable consolidated corporate income tax return: a Form 1120-L, "U.S. Life Insurance Company Income Tax Return," where the common parent is a life insurance company; a Form 1120-PC, "U.S. Property and Casualty Insurance Company Income Tax Return," where the common parent is an insurance company, other than a life insurance company; or a Form 1120, "U.S. Corporation Income Tax Return," where the common parent is any other type of corporation;

(ii) Indicate clearly on the face of this return that such corporate tax return is a life-nonlife return;

(iii) Show any set offs required by paragraphs (g), (m), and (n) of this section;

(iv) Report separately the nonlife consolidated taxable income or loss, determined under paragraph (h) of this section, on a Form 1120 or 1120-PC (whether filed by the common parent or as an attachment to the consolidated return), as the case may be, of all nonlife members of the consolidated group; and

(v) Report separately the consolidated partial Life Insurance Company Taxable Income (as defined by paragraph (d)(3) of this section), determined under paragraph (j) of this section, on a Form 1120-L (whether filed by the common parent or as an attachment to the consolidated return), of all life members of the consolidated group.

(2) Cross reference. See § 1.1502-75(j), regarding the inclusion in a corporate tax return of the required statements and schedules for subsidiaries.

(t) Effective/applicability date. Paragraph (s) of this section applies to any consolidated Federal income tax return due (without extensions) on or after December 21, 2009. However, a consolidated group may apply paragraph (s) of this section to any consolidated Federal income tax return filed on or after December 21, 2009. For returns due before December 21, 2009, see § 1.1502-47T as contained in 26 CFR part 1 in effect on April 1, 2009.

T.D. 7877, 3/17/83, amend T.D. 7912, 9/1/83, T.D. 8560, 8/12/94, T.D. 8597, 7/12/95, T.D. 8677, 6/26/96, T.D. 8823, 6/25/99, T.D. 9258, 4/24/2006, T.D. 9304, 12/21/2006, T.D. 9342, 7/19/2007, T.D. 9476, 12/22/2009.

§ 1.1502-55 Computation of alternative minimum tax of consolidated groups.

(a) through (h)(3) [Reserved].

(h) *(4) Separate return year minimum tax credit.*

(i) and (ii) [Reserved].

(iii) (A) Limitation on portion of separate return year minimum tax credit arising in separate return limitation years. The aggregate of a member's minimum tax credits arising in SRLYs that are included in the consolidated minimum tax credits for all consolidated return years of the group may not exceed—

(1) The aggregate for all consolidated return years of the member's contributions to the consolidated section 53(c) limitation for each consolidated return year; reduced by

(2) The aggregate of the member's minimum tax credits arising and absorbed in all consolidated return years (whether or not absorbed by the member).

(B) Computational rules. (1) Member's contribution to the consolidated section 53(c) limitation. Except as provided in the special rule of paragraph (h)(4)(iii)(B)(2) of this section, a member's contribution to the consolidated section 53(c) limitation for a consolidated return year equals the member's share of the consolidated net regular tax liability minus its share of consolidated tentative minimum tax. The group computes the member's shares by applying to the respective consolidated amounts the principles of section 1552 and the percentage method under § 1.1502-33(d)(3), assuming a 100% allocation of any decreased tax liability. The group makes proper adjustments so that taxes and credits not taken into account in computing the limitation under section 53(c) are not taken into account in computing the member's share of the consolidated net regular tax, etc. (See, for example, the taxes described in section 26(b) that are disregarded in computing regular tax liability.)

(2) Adjustment for year in which alternative minimum tax is paid. For a consolidated return year for which consolidated tentative minimum tax is greater than consolidated regular tax liability, the group reduces the member's share of the consolidated tentative minimum tax by the member's share of the consolidated alternative minimum tax for the year. The group determines the member's share of consolidated alternative minimum tax for a year using the same method it uses to determine the member's share of the consolidated minimum tax credits for the year.

(3) Years included in computation. For purposes of computing the limitation under this paragraph (h)(4)(iii), the consolidated return years of the group include only those years, including the year to which a credit is carried, that the member has been continuously included in the group's consolidated return, but exclude any years after the year to which the credit is carried.

(4) Subgroup principles. The SRLY subgroup principles under § 1.1502-21(c)(2) apply for purposes of this paragraph (h)(4)(iii). The predecessor and successor principles under § 1.1502-21(f) also apply for purposes of this paragraph (h)(4)(iii).

(5) Overlap with section 383. The principles under § 1.1502-21(g) apply for purposes of this paragraph (h)(4)(iii). For example, an overlap of this paragraph (h)(4)(iii) and the application of section 383 with respect to a credit carryover occurs if a corporation becomes a member of a consolidated group (the SRLY event) within six months of the change date of an ownership change giving rise to a section 383 credit limitation with respect to that carryover (the section 383 event), with the result that the limitation of this paragraph (h)(4)(iii) does not apply. See §§ 1.1502-21(g)(2)(ii)(A) and 1.383-1; see also § 1.1502-21(g)(4) (subgroup rules).

(C) Effective date. (1) In general. This paragraph (h)(4)(iii) generally applies to consolidated return years for which the due date of the income tax return (without extensions) is after March 13, 1998. See § 1.1502-3(d)(4) for an optional effective date rule (generally making this paragraph (h)(4)(iii) also applicable to a consolidated return year beginning on or after January 1, 1997, if the due date of the income tax return (without extensions) was on or before March 13, 1998).

(i) Contribution years. In general, a group does not take into account a consolidated taxable year for which the due date of the income tax return (without extensions) is on or before March 13, 1998, in determining a member's (or subgroup's) contributions to the consolidated section 53(c) limitation under this paragraph (h)(4)(iii). However, if a consolidated group chooses to apply the optional effective date rule, the consolidated group shall not take into account a consolidated taxable year beginning before January 1, 1997 in determining a member's (or subgroup's) contributions to the consolidated section 53(c) limitation under this paragraph (h)(4)(iii).

(ii) Special subgroup rule. In the event that the principles of § 1.1502-21(g)(1) do not apply to a particular credit carryover in the current group, then solely for purposes of applying this paragraph (h)(4)(iii) to determine the limitation with respect to that carryover and with respect to which the SRLY register (the aggregate of the member's or subgroup's contribution to consolidated section 53(c) limitation reduced by the aggregate of the member's or subgroup's minimum tax credits arising and absorbed in all consolidated return years) began in a taxable year for which the due date of the return is on or before May 25, 2000, the principles of § 1.1502-21(c)(2) shall be applied without regard to the phrase "or for a carryover that was subject to the overlap rule described in paragraph (g) of this section or § 1.1502-15(g) with respect to another group (the former group)."

(2) Overlap rule. Paragraph (h)(4)(iii)(B)(5) of this section (relating to overlap with section 383) applies to taxable years for which the due date (without extensions) of the consolidated return is after May 25, 2000. For purposes of paragraph (h)(4)(iii)(B)(5) of this section, only an ownership change to which section 383, as amended by the Tax Reform Act of 1986 (100 Stat. 2095), applies and which results in a section 383 credit limitation shall constitute a section 383 event. The optional effective date rule of § 1.1502-3(d)(4) (generally making this paragraph (h)(4)(iii) also applicable to a consolidated return year beginning on or after January 1, 1997, if the due date of the income tax return (without extensions) was on or before March 13, 1998) does not apply with respect to paragraph (h)(4)(iii)(B)(5) of this section (relating to the overlap rule).

T.D. 8884, 5/24/2000.

PAR. 7. Section 1.1502-55 is added to read as follows:

Proposed § 1.1502-55 Computation of alternative minimum tax of consolidated groups. [*For Preamble, see ¶ 151,475*]

(a) In general. *(1) Overview.* This Section provides rules for determining a consolidated group's alternative minimum tax liability (its consolidated AMT) and for allocating various consolidated AMT attributes to members of the group. See also section 1561.

(2) Principles. The consolidated AMT is determined under an approach that generally parallels the determination of the group's consolidated regular tax liability. The statutory scheme and definitions in sections 55 through 59 apply in determining consolidated AMT. For example, section 55(b)(1) defines tentative minimum tax (TMT), and that term is modified under this section and referred to as "consolidated TMT." Generally, this section provides further refinements to the "consolidated" AMT terms only where necessary to illustrate the adjustments required to compute the consolidated AMT or to allocate consolidated AMT attributes among members.

(b) Consolidated AMTI. *(1) In general.* Consolidated alternative minimum taxable income (AMTI), computed in accordance with the principles of §§ 1.1502-11 and 1.1502-12 (relating to the computation of consolidated taxable income), equals consolidated pre-adjustment AMTI—

(i) Increased or decreased by the consolidated adjustment for adjusted current earnings (consolidated ACE adjustment), computed under paragraph (b)(3) of this section; and

(ii) Decreased by the consolidated alternative tax net operating loss deduction (consolidated ATNOL deduction), computed under paragraph (b)(4) of this section.

(2) Consolidated pre-adjustment AMTI. (i) In general. Consolidated pre-adjustment AMTI is determined in accordance with the principles of § 1.1502-11, taking into account the adjustments and preferences provided in sections 56 (excluding the section 56 (g) adjustment), 57, and 58. The consolidated NOL deduction, however, is not taken into account in computing consolidated pre-adjustment AMTI. In determining consolidated pre-adjustment AMTI, a consolidated appreciated property charitable deduction preference must be computed. The consolidated appreciated property charitable deduction preference is the amount by which the consolidated charitable contribution deduction determined under the principles of § 1.1502-24, computed by taking into account the adjustments provided in sections 56 (excluding the section 56(g) adjustment) and 58, would be reduced if all capital gain property of the group were taken into account at its adjusted basis.

(ii) Separate pre-adjustment AMTI. (A) In general. In computing consolidated pre-adjustment AMTI, each member must compute its separate pre-adjustment AMTI. The separate pre-adjustment AMTI of a member is determined in accordance with the principles of § 1.1502-12, taking into account the adjustments and preferences provided in sections 56 (excluding the section 56(g) adjustment), 57, and 58.

(B) Computation of member's section 57(a)(2) preference for excess IDCs. (1) In general. In computing separate pre-adjustment AMTI, a member's preference under section 57(a)(2) is the member's allocable share of the consolidated IDC preference. A member's allocable share of the consolidated IDC preference is determined by multiplying the consolidated IDC preference by a fraction, the numerator of which is the separate IDC preference of the member, and the denominator of which is the sum of the separate IDC preferences of all members that have a separate IDC preference.

(2) Consolidated IDC preference. The consolidated IDC preference is the excess of—

(i) The aggregate of each member's excess IDCs (as defined in section 57(a)(2)(B)) arising in the consolidated return year; over

(ii) 65 percent of the consolidated net income arising during the consolidated return year from all oil, gas, and geothermal properties (as defined in section 57(a)(2)(C)) of the group's members.

(3) Separate IDC preference. A member's separate IDC preference is the amount, if any, by which the member's ex-

cess IDCs arising in the taxable year from all properties of the member is greater than 65 percent of the net income from oil, gas and geothermal properties of the member for the taxable year.

(iii) Example. The following example illustrates the computation of consolidated pre-adjustment AMTI under this paragraph (b)(2).

Example. (i) P, S1, and S2 file a consolidated return, and have the following items of income and deduction for AMT purposes.

	P	S1	S2	Consolidated
Income	$1,000	$1,000	$1,000	
Depreciation	(300)	(100)	(200)	
Section 57(a)(2) IDC preference	240	-0-	160	
Section 57(a)(5) tax-exempt interest preference	100	50	-0-	
Separate pre-adjustment AMTI	$1,040	$ 950	$ 960	$2,950
AMT capital gains	300	150	100	550
Consolidated pre-adjustment AMTI				$3,500

(ii) Under paragraph (b)(2)(ii)(B) of this section, the section 57(a)(2) IDC preference for each of the members is computed as follows:

	P	S1	S2	Consolidated
IDCs	$460	$100	$395	$955
65% of net income from oil, gas, and geothermal properties	(160)	(200)	(195)	(555)
IDC preference	$300	$ -0-	$200	$400

(iii) The $400 consolidated IDC preference is allocated among the members that have a separate IDC preference (P and S2). Each member's allocable share of the consolidated IDC preference, which is included in its separate pre-adjustment AMTI, is computed as follows:

P

$$\$400 \text{ consolidated IDC preference} \times \frac{\$300, \text{ separate IDC preference}}{\$500, \text{ sum of separate IDC preferences of all members}} = \$240$$

S2

$$\$400 \text{ consolidated IDC preference} \times \frac{\$200, \text{ separate IDC preference}}{\$500, \text{ sum of separate IDC preferences of all members}} = \$160$$

(3) Consolidated ACE adjustment. (i) In general. In computing consolidated AMTI, subject to the limitation of paragraph (b)(3)(iii) of this section, consolidated pre-adjustment AMTI is increased (or decreased) by 75 percent of the excess (or deficit) for the consolidated return year of—

(A) The consolidated ACE (as defined in paragraph (b)(3)(ii) of this section) for the year; over

(B) The consolidated pre-adjustment AMTI (as defined in paragraph (b)(2) of this section) for the year.

(ii) Consolidated ACE. (A) In general. Consolidated ACE is determined in accordance with the principles of § 1.1502-11, taking into account the adjustments and preferences provided in sections 56, 57, and 58. The consolidated NOL deduction and the consolidated section 247 deduction, however, are not taken into account in computing consolidated ACE.

(B) Separate ACE. In computing consolidated ACE, each member must compute its separate ACE. The separate ACE of a member is the separate pre-adjustment AMTI of the member, as defined in paragraph (b)(2)(ii) of this section, adjusted as provided in section 56(g) and § 1.56(g)-1.

(iii) Limitation on consolidated negative ACE adjustments. (A) In general. Under the principles of section 56(g)(2)(B), the amount of the consolidated negative ACE adjustment for any consolidated return year is limited to the sum of—

(1) The consolidated return year cumulative ACE adjustment (as defined in paragraph (b)(3)(iii)(B)(1) of this section); and

(2) The separate return year cumulative ACE adjustment (as defined in paragraph (b)(3)(iii)(B)(2) of this section).

(B) Definitions. (1) Consolidated return year cumulative ACE adjustment. The consolidated return year cumulative ACE adjustment equals the excess, if any, of the consolidated positive ACE adjustments for prior consolidated return years, over the sum of—

(i) Consolidated negative ACE adjustments for prior consolidated return years (other than any portion of those consolidated negative ACE adjustments attributable to separate return year positive ACE adjustments, as determined under paragraph (b)(3)(iii)(C) of this section); and

(ii) Consolidated positive ACE adjustments for prior consolidated return years apportioned to a corporation that ceases to be a member and carried to its separate return years in accordance with paragraph (e)(2) of this section (or, for consolidated return years for which the due date of the income tax return (without regard to extensions) is before [the date that is sixty days after final regulations are filed with the FEDERAL REGISTER], in accordance with any reasonable method used by the group).

(2) Separate return year cumulative ACE adjustment. The separate return year cumulative ACE adjustment equals the excess, if any, of the separate return year positive ACE adjustments of the members for prior taxable years (as defined in paragraph (b)(3)(iii)(B)(3) of this section), over the sum of—

(i) The separate return year negative ACE adjustments of the members for prior taxable years (as defined in paragraph (b)(3)(iii)(B)(4) of this section); and

(ii) The portion of the consolidated negative ACE adjustments of the group for prior consolidated return years attributable to prior year separate return year positive ACE adjustments of the members (as determined under paragraph (b)(3)(iii)(C) of this section).

(3) Separate return year positive ACE adjustments. Separate return year positive ACE adjustments are—

(i) For each member, the increases in AMTI for prior separate return years (other than years for which the member joined in the filing of a consolidated return) due to the ACE adjustment under section 56(g); and

(ii) For any prior separate return years for which a member joined in the filing of a consolidated return with another group, the member's allocable share of that group's consolidated positive ACE adjustments determined under paragraph (e)(2) of this section (or, for taxable years for which the due date of the income tax return (without regard to extensions) is before [the date that is sixty days after final regulations are filed with the FEDERAL REGISTER], determined in accordance with any reasonable method used by that other group).

(4) Separate return year negative ACE adjustments. Separate return year negative ACE adjustments include the aggregate decreases in AMTI for prior separate return years (other than years for which the member joined in the filing of a consolidated return) due to the ACE adjustment under section 56(g).

(C) Consolidated negative ACE adjustments attributable to separate return year positive ACE adjustments. The portion of a consolidated negative ACE adjustment attributable to separate return year positive ACE adjustments is equal to the consolidated negative ACE adjustment multiplied by a fraction, the numerator of which is the separate return year cumulative ACE adjustment (as of the beginning of the consolidated return year) and the denominator of which is the aggregate of the separate return year cumulative ACE adjustment and the consolidated return year cumulative ACE adjustment (both determined as of the beginning of the consolidated return year).

(4) Consolidated ATNOL deduction. After taking into account the group's consolidated ACE adjustment for the year, the group takes the consolidated ATNOL deduction into account in computing consolidated AMTI. Subject to applicable limitations (e.g., section 382) and the provisions of section 56(d), the consolidated ATNOL deduction is the aggregate of the consolidated ATNOL carryovers and carrybacks determined under the principles of § 1.1502-21. The consolidated ATNOL for a consolidated return year is the consolidated net operating loss determined under the principles of § 1.1502-21(e) for the year, taking into account the adjustments and preferences provided in sections 56, 57, and 58 for that year.

(5) Example. The following example illustrates certain general principles of this paragraph (b).

Example. (i) Separate returns. P and S file separate returns. P's and S's items of income and deduction for regular tax (RT), AMT, and ACE purposes, and P's and S's tax liability are provided below. The effects of the lower section 11 brackets and the section 55(d) AMT exemption amount are ignored.

(A) P has pre-adjustment AMTI of $700 and ACE of $900, resulting in a $150 positive ACE adjustment (75 percent of the difference between P's ACE and P's pre-adjustment AMTI). P's ATNOL deduction ($100) reduces its AMTI to $750. P's TMT is therefore $150 (20 percent of AMTI). Thus, P has an AMT liability of $48, the difference between P's TMT ($150) and P's regular tax ($102).

P

	RT	AMT	ACE
Gross income	$1,000	$1,000	$ 1,000
Depreciation	(500)	(300)	(100)
Pre-adjustment AMTI		$ 700	
ACE			$ 900
ACE adjustment		150	
NOL deduction	(200)		
ATNOL deduction		(100)	
Taxable income	$ 300		
AMTI		$ 750	
TMT (20%)		$ 150	
RT liability (34%)	$ 102		
AMT		$ 48	

(B) S has pre-adjustment AMTI of $900 and ACE of $800, resulting in a $75 negative ACE adjustment (75 percent of the difference between S's pre-adjustment AMTI and S's ACE. (Assume that S may use the negative adjustment because of prior year positive ACE adjustments). S's ATNOL deduction ($200) reduces its AMTI to $625. Thus, S has no AMT liability because S's regular tax ($306) exceeds its TMT ($125).

S

	RT	AMT	ACE
Gross income	$1,000	$1,000	$ 1,000
Depreciation	0	(100)	(200)
Pre-adjustment AMTI		$ 900	
ACE			$ 800
ACE adjustment		(75)	
NOL deduction	(100)		
ATNOL deduction		(200)	
Taxable income	$ 900		
AMTI		$ 625	
TMT (20%)		$ 125	
RT liability (34%)	$ 306		
AMT		$ 0	

(ii) Consolidated return filed

(A) If F and S instead elect to file a consolidated return, the group would have the following results:

P group RT

	P	S	Consolidated
Gross income	$1,000	$1,000	$2,000
Depreciation	(500)	0	(500)
Aggregate separate taxable income	$ 500	$1,000	$1,500
Consolidated NOL deduction			(300)
Consolidated taxable income			$1,200
Consolidated RT (34%)			$ 408
AMT			
Gross income	$1,000	$1,000	$2,000
Depreciation	(300)	(100)	(400)
Consolidated pre-adjustment AMTI	700	900	$1,600
ACE depreciation adjustment	200	(100)	100
Consolidated ACE	$ 900	$ 800	$1,700
Consolidated ACE adjustment			75
Consolidated ATNOL deduction			(300)
Consolidated AMTI			$1,375
Consolidated TMT (20%)			$ 275
Consolidated AMT			$ 0

(B) The F group has consolidated pre-adjustment AMTI of $1,600. In addition, the group has consolidated ACE of $1,700, resulting in a $75 positive consolidated ACE adjustment (75 percent of the difference between the group's ACE and the group's pre-adjustment AMTI). The consolidated ATNOL deduction reduces consolidated AMTI to $1,375. The consolidated TMT is $275. Thus, the F group has no consolidated AMT liability because its consolidated regular tax ($408) exceeds its consolidated TMT ($275).

(c) Consolidated alternative minimum tax foreign tax credit. [Reserved]

(d) Separate return limitation years. [Reserved]

(e) Separate return years. *(1) Carryovers and carrybacks of consolidated AMT attributes to separate return years.* (i) In general. This paragraph (e)(1) provides principles under which various consolidated AMT attributes are allocated among members of a consolidated group, generally for purposes of apportioning the attribute to a corporation that ceases to be a member. The apportionment of consolidated AMT attributes that have regular tax counterparts is based on the principles applicable to the regular tax counterparts. See, e.g., § 1.1502-21(b) (principles applicable to consolidated net operating losses).

(ii) Examples. The following examples illustrate the application of this paragraph (e)(1).

Example (1). Allocation of consolidated ATNOL.

(i) P, S1, and S2 are members of a consolidated group. In 1993, the group has a consolidated ATNOL of $100. P has a separate ATNOL of $150, S1 has a separate ATNOL of $50, and S2 has separate AMTI of $100. The separate ATNOLs for P and S1 are determined by computing the consolidated ATNOL, taking into account only the member's income, gain, deduction, and loss, including the member's losses and deductions actually absorbed by the group in the taxable year (whether or not absorbed by the member). See § 1.1502-21(b)(2)(iv).

(ii) Under this paragraph (e)(1), the portion of the consolidated ATNOL allocable to each member is determined in accordance with the principles of the regulations relating to the carryover and carryback of the consolidated NOL to separate return years. See § 1.1502-21(b). Thus, the portion of the consolidated ATNOL allocable to P and S1 is determined by multiplying the consolidated ATNOL by a fraction, the numerator of which is the member's separate ATNOL and the denominator of which is the sum of all membersseparate ATNOLs. The portion of the consolidated ATNOL allocable to P is $75 ($100 multiplied by $150/$200). The portion of the consolidated ATNOL allocable to S1 is $25 ($100 multiplied by $50/$200). S2 is not allocated a portion of the consolidated ATNOL because S2 had no separate ATNOL.

Example (2). Allocation of consolidated ACE net capital loss.

(i) P, S1, and S2 are members of a consolidated group. In 1993, the group has a consolidated ACE net capital loss of $210. P has a separate ACE net capital loss of $90, 51 has a separate ACE net capital gain of $60, and S2 has a separate ACE net capital loss of $180. The separate ACE net capital losses for P and S2 are determined by computing the consolidated ACE net capital loss by taking into account only the member's gains and losses, including the member's losses actually absorbed by the group in the taxable year (whether or not absorbed by the member). See §§ 1.1502-22(b)(3) and 1.1502-21(b)(2)(iv).

(ii) Under this paragraph (e)(1), the portion of the consolidated ACE net capital loss allocable to each member is determined in accordance with the principles of the regulations relating to the carryover and carryback of the consolidated net capital loss to separate return years. See § 1.1502-22(b). Thus, the portion of the consolidated ACE net capital loss allocable to P and S2 is determined by multiplying the consolidated ACE net capital loss by a fraction, the numerator of which is the member's separate ACE net capital loss and the denominator of which is the sum of all membersseparate ACE net capital losses. The portion oy the consolidated ACE net capital loss allocable to P is $70 ($210 multiplied by $90/$270). The portion of the consolidated ACE net capital loss allocable to S2 is $140 ($210 multiplied by $180/$270). S1 is not allocated a portion of the consolidated ACE net capital loss because S1 had no separate ACE net capital loss.

(2) Carryover of consolidated positive ACE adjustments to separate return years. (i) In general. If a corporation ceases to be a member, the portion of the consolidated positive ACE adjustments allocated to the corporation is taken into account in its separate return years in accordance with the principles of §§ 1.56(g)-1(a)(2) and 1.1502-21(b). Any separate return year cumulative ACE adjustment attributable to a corporation as of the close of the taxable year in which the corporation ceases to be a member is also taken into account in its separate return year.

(ii) Portion of consolidated positive ACE adjustments allocable to a member. (A) In general. The portion of the consolidated positive ACE adjustments allocated to a member is the consolidated return year cumulative ACE adjustment as of the close of the consolidated return year in which the corporation ceases to be a member, multiplied by a fraction. The numerator of the fraction is the separate cumulative ACE adjustment of the member as of the close of the consolidated return year in which the corporation ceases to be a member, and the denominator of the fraction is the sum of the separate cumulative ACE adjustments of all members having separate cumulative ACE adjustments as of the close of the consolidated return year in which the corporation ceases to be a member.

(B) Separate cumulative ACE adjustment. The separate cumulative ACE adjustment of a member is the consolidated return year cumulative ACE adjustment, if any, taking into account only the member's items of income, gain, deduction, and loss, including the member's losses and deductions actually absorbed by the group (whether or not absorbed by the member).

(f) Deferral and restoration of gain or loss. The principles of the Internal Revenue Code and regulations that affect the timing of inclusion of items in consolidated taxable income generally apply for purposes of computing consolidated pre-adjustment AMTI and consolidated ACE. See, e.g., § 1.1502-13. Applicable adjustments and preferences provided in sections 56, 57, and 58 must be taken into account.

(g) Stock basis adjustments in computing consolidated AMT. *(1) Parallel approach.* The principles set forth in §§ 1.1502-19 and 1.1502-32 for determining the regular tax basis in (or the regular tax excess loss account with respect to) a member's stock generally apply in determining both the corresponding AMT stock basis (or AMT excess loss account) and ACE stock basis (or ACE excess loss account).

(2) Modifications to regular tax stock basis principles in computing consolidated pre-adjustment AMTI and consolidated ACE. The following modifications to the stock basis adjustment principles of §§ 1.1502-19 and 1.1502-32 apply for purposes of computing AMT stock basis (or AMT excess loss account) used in determining consolidated pre-adjustment AMTI and ACE stock basis (or ACE excess loss account) used in determining consolidated ACE—

(i) Adjustments may be determined annually but are required only if a difference between the regular tax and AMT or ACE basis in (or excess loss with respect to) a member's stock will affect the tax liability of any person (e.g., on a sale of the stock);

(ii) The annual reporting requirements of § 1.1502-32(g) do not apply under the AMT or ACE systems;

(iii) In determining the adjustments under § 1.1502-32(b)(3)(i), any section 57 preference items includible in AMTI are not taken into account (while tax-exempt interest described in section 57(a)(5) is not taken into account in determining the adjustments for AMTI under § 1.1502-32(b)(3)(i), it does result in a positive stock basis adjustment under § 1.1502-32(b)(3)(ii));

(iv) A member's portion of any disallowed consolidated negative ACE adjustment for a consolidated return year is treated as a non-capital, non-deductible expense under § 1.1502-32(b)(3)(iii) for purposes of determining the adjustments to another member's AMT basis in (or excess loss account with respect to) the stock of the member; and

(v) Solely for purposes of computing adjustments to the ACE basis in (or ACE excess loss account with respect to) the stock of a member, the member's excess of ACE deductions over ACE income for a consolidated return year is treated as a tax loss under § 1.1502-32(b)(3)(i) that is absorbed in the same year that it arises.

(3) Tax payments and refunds. The amount of any section 275 tax liability or refund of federal income tax taken into account under §§ 1.1502-19 and 1.1502-32 for regular tax purposes is also taken into account in computing AMT and ACE stock basis (or excess loss account).

(4) Example. The following example illustrates the principles of this paragraph (g).

Example. (i) Background.

(A) Corporations P and S file a consolidated return. On January 1, 1994, P has a $0 basis in S's stock. S has gross income for regular tax, AMT, and ACE purposes of $10,000 in 1994 and a loss from operations (before taking into account its depreciation deduction) for regular tax, AMT, and ACE purposes of $5,000 in 1995. The P group's tax liability (whether attributable to the regular tax or the AMT) is solely attributable to S, and the consolidated regular tax liability and consolidated AMT liability allocations under § 1.1552-1 are the same as the separate liabilities of S. Finally, the effects of the lower section 11 tax rate brackets and the section 55(d) AMT exemption amount are ignored.

(B) On December 31, 1995, P sells a portion of the S stock. Under paragraph (g)(2)(i) of this section, no adjustments to P's basis in S's stock are required for purposes of computing consolidated pre-adjustment AMTI and consolidated ACE in 1994. However, because there was a stock sale in 1995, P's basis in S's stock must be adjusted for AMT and ACE purposes in 1995 as follows:

(ii) Stock basis adjustments for 1994

(A) Adjustments—

	RT	AMT	ACE
Gross income	$10,000	$10,000	$ 10,000
Depreciation	(5,000)	(4,000)	(3,000)
Taxable income	$ 5,000		
Pre-adjustment AMTI		$ 6,000	
ACE			$ 7,000
ACE adjustment		750	
AMTI		$ 6,750	
TMT (20%)		$ 1,350	
RT liability (34%)	$ 1,700		
AMT		$ -0-	
(B) Stock basis adjustments—			
P's basis in S's stock on 1/1/94	$ -0-	$ -0-	$ -0-
Sec. 1.1502-32(b)(3)(i)	$ 5,000	6,750	7,000
Sec. 1.1502-32(b)(3)(iii)	(1,700)	(1,700)	(1,700)
P's Basis in S stock on 12/31/94	$ 3,300	$ 5,050	$ 5,300

(iii) (A) Stock basis adjustments for 1995.

	RT	AMT	ACE
Gross income	$ (5,000)	$(5,000)	$(5,000)
Depreciation	(5,000)	(4,000)	(3,000)
Taxable income	$(10,000)		
Pre-adjustment AMTI		$(9,000)	
ACE			$(8,000)
ACE adjustment		750)	
AMTI		$(8,250)	
TMT (20%)		$ -0-	
RT liability (34%)	$ -0-		
AMT		$ -0-	

Because of the section 56(d) 90-percent limitation on the amount of AMTI that may be offset by an ATNOL deduction, only $6,075 of the $8,250 ATNOL for 1995 is carried back to 1994 under the principles of § 1.1502-21(b). Thus, since all $5,000 of the 1994 regular taxable income was offset by the 1995 NOL, but only $6,075 of the 1994 AMTI was offset by the $135 results. Accordingly, only $1,565 of the $1,700 Federal income taxes paid in 1994 is refunded in 1995.

(B) Stock basis adjustments—

P's basis in S stock on 12/31/94	$3,300	$5,050	$ 5,300
Sec. 1.1502-32(b)(3)(i)	(5,000)	(6,075)	(8,000)
Sec. 1.1502-32(b)(3)(ii)	1,565	1,565	1,565
Sec. 1.1502-32(b)(3)(iii)	(-0-)	(-0-)	(-0-)
P's basis (ELA) in S stock when sold on 12/31/95	$ (135)	$ 540	$ (1,135)

(h) Consolidated MTC. *(1) Overview.* A group's consolidated minimum tax credit (MTC) is generally based on the consolidated adjusted net minimum tax for prior years. Adjustments are made to take into account a member's adjusted net minimum tax from prior separate return years. See paragraphs (h)(2) through (4) of this section. Adjustments are also made for the portion of the consolidated adjusted net minimum tax that is allocable to a corporation that ceases to be a member (and thus may be carried to the member's separate return years). See paragraph (h)(6) of this section.

(2) Computation of the consolidated MTC. The consolidated MTC available as of the beginning of any consolidated return year is the sum of—

(i) The consolidated return year MTC (as defined in paragraph (h)(3) of this section); and

(ii) The separate return year MTC (as defined in paragraph (h)(4) of this section).

(3) Consolidated return year MTC. (i) General rule. The consolidated return year MTC is the excess (if any) of—

(A) The consolidated adjusted net minimum tax (as defined in paragraph (h)(3)(ii) of this section) for all prior consolidated return years beginning after 1986; over

(B) The sum of—

(1) The amount of the consolidated adjusted net minimum tax for prior consolidated return years that is allowable as a consolidated MTC in prior years; and

(2) The amount of the consolidated adjusted minimum tax for prior consolidated return years that is allowed to be carried to a separate return year of a member in accordance with paragraph (h)(6) of this section (or, for consolidated return years for which the due date of the income tax return (without regard to extensions) is before [the date that is sixty days after the final regulations are filed with the FEDERAL REGISTER], in accordance with any reasonable method used by the group).

(ii) Consolidated adjusted net minimum tax. (A) In general. Except as provided in paragraphs (h)(3)(ii)(B) and (C) of this section, consolidated adjusted net minimum tax is the amount of the consolidated AMT.

(B) Exception for taxable years beginning after 1986 and before 1990. For taxable years beginning after December 31, 1986, and before January 1, 1990, consolidated adjusted net minimum tax is the amount of the consolidated AMT, reduced by the amount that would be the consolidated AMT for the taxable year if the only adjustments and tax preference items were those in section 56(c)(3), section 57(a)(1), section 57(a)(5), and section 57(a)(6).

(C) Special rule for groups with consolidated disallowed section 29 or section 28 credits. The amounts determined under paragraphs (h)(3)(ii)(A) and (B) of this section for a taxable year are increased by the amount, if any, of a group's consolidated disallowed section 29 credit or consolidated disallowed section 28 credit for the year. For this purpose, the consolidated disallowed section 29 credit is the sum of the section 29 credits of all the members that are not allowable under section 29 solely by reason of the application of section 29(b)(6)(B). The consolidated disallowed section 28 credit is the sum of the section 28 credits of all the members that are not allowable under section 28 solely by reason of the application of section 28(d)(2)(B).

(4) Separate return year MTC. (i) In general. The separate return year MTC is, subject to applicable limitations (e.g., section 383), the excess (if any) of—

(A) The adjusted net minimum tax (as defined in section 53(d)) for all prior separate return years of the group members beginning after 1986; over

(B) The sum of—

(1) The amount allowable as an MTC for such prior separate return years; and

(2) The amount described in paragraph (h)(4)(i)(A) of this section that is allowable as a consolidated MTC in prior years.

(ii) Adjusted net minimum tax arising in another consolidated group. In the case of a member that filed a consolidated return in a prior year with another group, the amount described in paragraph (h)(4)(i)(A) of this section includes any consolidated MTC of another group that is attributable to that member and that is apportioned to it and available in the consolidated return year in accordance with paragraph (h)(6) of this section (or, for taxable years for which the due date of the income tax return (without regard to extensions) is before [the date that is sixty days after final regulations are filed with the FEDERAL REGISTER], in accordance with any reasonable method used by that other group).

(iii) Limitation on portion of separate return year MTC arising in separate return limitation years. [Reserved]

(5) Limitation on allowable consolidated MTC. (i) In general. The available consolidated MTC allowable under this paragraph (h) for any consolidated return year is limited to the excess (if any) of—

(A) The modified consolidated regular tax liability (as defined in paragraph (h)(5)(ii) of this section) for the year; over

(B) The consolidated TMT for the year.

(ii) Modified consolidated regular tax liability. Modified consolidated regular tax liability is the consolidated regular tax liability, computed in accordance with section 26(b), reduced by the sum of the consolidated credits allowable under subparts A, B, D, E, and F of part III of subchapter A of chapter 1 of the Internal Revenue Code.

(6) Carryover of the consolidated MTC to separate return years. (i) In general. When a corporation ceases to be a member of a group, the group is required to allocate to that corporation a portion of the group's consolidated MTC. The allocation is generally based on the corporation's contributions to the group's consolidated adjusted net minimum tax during the consolidated return years for which the corporation was a member of the group. The amount of the consolidated MTC properly allocable to a departing member is

taken into account by the member in its succeeding separate return years.

(ii) Consolidated MTC allocable to a member. (A) In general. The amount of the consolidated MTC allocable to a corporation equals the corporation's allocable share of the consolidated MTC available as of the beginning of the consolidated return year in which the corporation ceases to be a member of a group—

(1) Increased by the corporation's allocable share of the consolidated adjusted net minimum tax, if any, for the consolidated return year in which the corporation ceases to be a member (as determined under paragraph (h)(6)(iii) of this section); and

(2) Decreased by the corporation's allocable share of any allowable consolidated MTC for the consolidated return year in which the corporation ceases to be a member (as determined under paragraphs (h)(6)(vi) and (7) of this section).

(B) Reference to rules for determining a member's allocable share. For purposes of determining a corporation's allocable share of the consolidated MTC available as of the beginning of the consolidated return year in which the corporation ceases to be a member of a group (as described in paragraph (h)(6)(ii)(A) of this section), the rules of paragraph (h)(6)(iii) of this section apply to determine the corporation's allocable share of consolidated adjusted net minimum tax in each prior consolidated return year, and the rules of paragraphs (h)(6)(vi) and (7) of this section apply to determine the corporation's allocable share of any allowable consolidated MTC in prior consolidated return years. The rules of paragraph (h)(7) of this section are also applicable in determining the remaining amount of the departing member's separate return year MTC (from years prior to joining the consolidated group) that is taken into account in succeeding separate return years.

(iii) Member's allocable share of consolidated adjusted net minimum tax. (A) In general. A member's allocable share of the consolidated adjusted net minimum tax for a consolidated return year is determined by multiplying the consolidated AMT for the year by a fraction, the numerator of which is the separate adjusted AMT of the member (as defined in paragraph (h)(6)(iv) of this section) for the year, and the denominator of which is the sum of the separate adjusted AMTs of each member for the year.

(B) Special allocation rule for groups with consolidated disallowed section 29 or section 28 credits. (1) General rule. In a consolidated return year in which the group has a consolidated disallowed section 29 or 28 credit, in addition to the amount determined under paragraph (h)(6)(iii)(A) of this section, a member's allocable share of consolidated adjusted net minimum tax for the year includes its allocable share of the consolidated disallowed section 29 or 28 credit.

(2) Allocable share of disallowed credit. A member's allocable share of the consolidated disallowed section 29 credit or consolidated disallowed section 28 credit for a consolidated return year is determined by multiplying the consolidated disallowed section 29 credit amount (or the consolidated disallowed section 28 credit amount) for the year by a fraction. The numerator of the fraction is the total section 29 credits (or section 28 credits) of the member for the taxable year, and the denominator is the total section 29 credits (or section 28 credits) of all members for the year.

(iv) Separate adjusted AMT. (A) In general. Subject to paragraph (h)(6)(iv)(B) of this section, the separate adjusted AMT of a member for a consolidated return year is the excess (if any) of—

(1) The consolidated AMT for the year; over

(2) The consolidated AMT for the year, computed by excluding the member's items of income, gain, deduction, and loss, and the member's credits.

(B) Special rule in computing separate adjusted AMT. If, in computing a member's separate adjusted AMT, there is no consolidated AMT computed without that member's items (i.e., the amount in paragraph (h)(6)(iv)(A)(2) of this section is zero), the amount determined under paragraph (h)(6)(iv)(A) of this section must be increased by the excess (if any) of the consolidated regular tax computed without the member's items, over consolidated TMT computed without the member's items.

(v) Examples. The provisions of paragraphs (h)(1) through (6)(iv) of this section are illustrated by the following examples. In the examples, corporations P, S1, and S2 file a consolidated return. In each example, the group has no consolidated disallowed section 28 or section 29 credits for the year. The effects of the lower section 11 brackets and the section 55(d) exemption amount are ignored.

Example (1). (i) 1993 regular tax and AMT computation.

	P	S1	S2	Consolidated
Taxable income	$1,200	$(200)	$3,000	$4,000
Adjustments and preferences	1,800	100	2,000	3,900
AMTI	$3,000	$(100)	$5,000	$7,900
TMT (20%)				$1,580
RT liability (34%)				1,360
AMT				$ 220

(ii) Computation of separate adjusted AMT.

(A) Computation of consolidated AMT excluding P's items:

Taxable income	$2,800
Adjustments and preferences	2,100
AMTI	$4,900
TMT (20%)	$ 980
RT liability (34%)	952
AMT	$ 28

Consolidatd AMT computed without P's items is $28. Accordingly, P's separate adjusted AMT is $192 ($220 − $28).

(B) Computation of consolidated AMT excluding S1's items:

Taxable income	$4,200
Adjustments and preferences	3,800
AMTI	$8,000
TMT (20%)	$1,600
RT liability (34%)	1,428
AMT	$ 172

Consolidated AMT computed without S1's items is $172. Accordingly, S1's separate adjusted AMT is $48 ($220 − $172).

(C) Computation of consolidated AMT excluding S2's items:

Taxable income	$1,000
Adjustments and preferences	1,900
AMTI	$2,900
TMT (20%)	$ 580
RT liability (34%)	340
AMT	$ 240

Consolidated AMT computed without S2's items is $240. Because consolidated AMT computed without S2's items more than that amount computed with S2's items, S2 has no separate adjusted AMT.

(iii) Allocation of 1993 consolidated adjusted net minimum tax to members of group. Under paragraph (h)(6)(iii)(A) of this section, the amount of the 1993 consolidated adjusted net minimum tax allocable to P and S1 is determined as follows (S2 is allocated no portion of the 1993 consolidated adjusted net minimum tax because S2 has no separate adjusted AMT):

P	$220 consolidated AMT	×	$192, P's separate adjusted AMT / $240, the sum of all members' separate adjusted AMTs = $176
S1	$220 consolidated AMT	×	$48, S1's separate adjusted AMT / $240, the sum of all members' separate adjusted AMTs = $44

Example (2). (i) 1994 regular tax and AMT computation.

	P	S1	S2	Consolidated
Taxable income	$5,000	$ -0-	$2,000	$ 7,000
Adjustments and preferences	(5,000)	8,000	3,400	6,400
AMTI	$ -0-	$8,000	$5,400	$13,400
TMT (20%)				$ 2,680
RT liability (34%)				2,380
AMT				$ 300

(ii) Computation of separate adjusted AMT.

(A) Computation of consolidated AMT excluding P's items:

Taxable income	$ 2,000
Adjustments and prefernces	11,400
AMTI	$13,400
TMT (20%)	$ 2,680
RT liability (34%)	680
AMT	$ 2,000

Consolidated AMT computed without P's items is $2,000. Because the consolidated AMT with P is only $300, P has no separate adjusted AMT.

(B) Computation of onsolidated AMT excluding S1's items:

Taxable income	$7,000
Adjustments and preferences	(1,600)
AMTI	$5,400
TMT (20%)	$1,080
RT liability (34%)	2,380
AMT	$ -0-

The group has no consolidated AMT if S1's items are excluded. Accordingly, under paragraph (h)(6)(iv)(B) of this section, S1's separate adjusted AMT is $1,600, the sum of $300 (consolidated AMT computed with S1's items minus consolidated AMT computed without S1's items), and $1,300 (the excess of the consolidated regular tax computed without S1's items ($2,380) over the consolidated TMT computed without S1's items ($1,080)).

(C) Computation of consolidated AMT excluding S2's items:

Taxable income	$5,000
Adjustments and preferences	3,000
AMTI	$8,000
TMT (20%)	1,600
RT liability (34%)	1,700
AMT	$ -0-

The group has no consolidated AMT if S2's items are excluded. Accordingly, under paragraph (h)(6)(iv)(B) of this section, S2's separate adjusted AMT is $400, the sum of $300 (consolidated AMT computed with S2's items minus consolidated AMT computed without S2's items), and $100 (the excess of the consolidated regular tax computed without

S2's items ($1,700) over the consolidated TMT computed without S2's items ($1,600)).

(iii) Allocation of 1994 consolidated MTC to members of the group. Under paragraph (h)(6)(iii)(A) of this section, the amount of the 1994 consolidated adjusted net minimum tax allocable to S1 and S2 is determined as follows (P is allocated no portion of the consolidated MTC because P has no separate adjusted AMT):

S1 $300 consolidated AMT	×	$1,600, S1's separate adjusted AMT = $225 ——— $2,000, the sum of all members' separate adjusted AMTs
S2 $300 consolidated AMT	×	$400, S2's separate adjusted AMT = $75 ——— $2,000, the sum of all members' separate adjusted AMTs

(vi) Member's allocable share of allowable consolidated MTC in a consolidated return year. (A) In general. For purposes of determining the amount of the consolidated MTC allocable to a member under this paragraph (h)(6), a member's allocable share of the consolidated adjusted net minimum tax for a consolidated return year must, as described in paragraph (h)(6)(ii) of this section, be reduced by the member's allocable share of that amount allowable in a subsequent consolidated return year as a consolidated MTC. The member's allocable share of consolidated adjusted net minimum tax for a year that is allowable as a consolidated MTC in a subsequent taxable year is determined by multiplying the consolidated adjusted net minimum tax for the year allowable as a consolidated MTC (taking into account the ordering rules of paragraph (h)(7) of this section) by a fraction, the numerator of which is the member's allocable share of that consolidated adjusted net minimum tax and the denominator of which is the total amount of that consolidated adjusted net minimum tax.

(B) Example. The provisions of this paragraph (h)(6)(vi) are illustrated by the following example.

Example. (i) P, S1, and S2 file a consolidated return. In 1994, the group has consolidated adjusted net minimum tax of $100. Pursuant to the allocation method provided in paragraph (h)(6)(iii) of this section, P's, S1's, and S2's allocable shares of the 1994 consolidated adjusted net minimum tax are $60, $30, and $10, respectively. The group has no separate return year MTC as defined in paragraph (h)(4) of this section.

(ii) In 1995, the group has an $80 excess of modified consolidated regular tax over consolidated tentative minimum tax. Accordingly, $80 of the 1994 consolidated adjusted net minimum tax is allowable as a consolidated MTC in 1995 to offset consolidated regular tax.

(iii) As described in paragraph (h)(6)(ii) of this section, each member's allocable share of the 1994 consolidated adjusted net minimum tax is reduced by its allocable share of that $80 amount allowable as a consolidated MTC in 1995. The reduction amount is, under paragraph (h)(6)(vi) of this section, determined by multiplying the consolidated adjusted net minimum tax allowable as a consolidated MTC by a fraction, the numerator of which is the member's allocable share of that consolidated adjusted net minimum tax and the denominator of which is the total amount of that consolidated adjusted net minimum tax. As provided above, P's allocable share of the consolidated adjusted net minimum tax is 60 percent (60/100), S1's allocable share is 30 percent (30/100), and S2's allocable share is 10 percent (10/100). Accordingly, P's allocable share of the consolidated adjusted net minimum tax is reduced by $48 ($80 multiplied by .60). S1's allocable share of the consolidated adjusted net minimum tax is reduced by $24 ($80 multiplied by .30). S2's allocable share of the consolidated adjusted net minimum tax is reduced by $8 ($80 multiplied by .10).

(7) Amount of adjusted net minimum tax allowable as a consolidated MTC. Under the rules provgded in paragraphs (h)(3)(i)(B)(1), (h)(4)(i)(B)(2), (h)(6)(ii), and (h)(6)(vi) of this section, adjusted net minimum tax, whether consolidated adjusted net minimum tax or adjusted net minimum tax from separate return years, must be reduced by the amount of that adjusted net minimum tax allowable in a subsequent consolidated return year as a consolidated MTC. For purposes of those rules, consolidated adjusted net minimum tax and adjusted net minimum tax from separate return years are allowable as a consolidated MTC in the order of the taxable year in which the adjusted net minimum tax is imposed, with the adjusted net minimum tax imposed in the taxable year with the earliest year end allowable first. Consolidated adjusted net minimum ax and adjusted net minimum tax from separate return years imposed in taxable years ending on the same date are considered to be allowable as a consolidated MTC in proportion to the total consolidated adjusted net minimum tax and adjusted net minimum tax from separate return years incurred in that same taxable year. If, however, there is a limitation on the use of a consolidated MTC (e.g., under section 383), the adjusted net minimum tax unable to be used as a credit because of the limitation is disregarded for purposes of the computation provided in this paragraph (h)(7).

(i) [Reserved]

(j) Successor and predecessor. For purposes of this section any reference to a corporation or member includes, as the context may require, a reference to a successor or predecessor.

(k) Effective date. This section applies to any consolidated return year for which the due date of the income tax return (without regard to extensions) is on or after [the date that is sixty days after final regulations are filed with the Federal Register].

§ 1.1502-75 Filing of consolidated returns.

(a) Privilege of filing consolidated returns. *(1) Exercise of privilege for first consolidated return year.* A group which did not file a consolidated return for the immediately preceding taxable year may file a consolidated return in lieu of separate returns for the taxable year, provided that each corporation which has been a member during any part of the taxable year for which the consolidated return is to be filed consents (in the manner provided in paragraph (b) of this section) to the regulations under section 1502. If a group wishes to exercise its privilege of filing a consolidated return, such consolidated return must be filed not later than the last day prescribed by law (including extensions of time) for the filing of the common parent's return. Such consolidated return may not be withdrawn after such last day (but the group may change the basis of its return at any time prior to such last day).

(2) Continued filing requirement. A group which filed (or was required to file) a consolidated return for the immediately preceding taxable year is required to file a consolidated return for the taxable year unless it has an election to discontinue filing consolidated returns under paragraph (c) of this section.

(b) How consent for first consolidated year exercised. *(1) General rule.* The consent of a corporation referred to in paragraph (a)(1) of this section shall be made by such corporation joining in the making of the consolidated return for such year. A corporation shall be deemed to have joined in the making of such return for such year if it files a Form 1122 in the manner specified in paragraph (h)(2) of this section.

(2) Consent under facts and circumstances. If a member of the group fails to file Form 1122, the Commissioner may under the facts and circumstances determine that such member has joined in the making of a consolidated return by such group. The following circumstances, among others, will be taken into account in making this determination:

(i) Whether or not the income and deductions of the member were included in the consolidated return;

(ii) Whether or not a separate return was filed by the member for that taxable year; and

(iii) Whether or not the member was included in the affiliations schedule, Form 851.

If the Commissioner determines that the member has joined in the making of the consolidated return, such member shall be treated as if it had filed a Form 1122 for such year for purposes of paragraph (h)(2) of this section.

(3) Failure to consent due to mistake. If any member has failed to join in the making of a consolidated return under either subparagraph (1) or (2) of this paragraph, then the tax liability of each member of the group shall be determined on the basis of separate returns unless the common parent corporation establishes to the satisfaction of the Commissioner that the failure of such member to join in the making of the consolidated return was due to a mistake of law or fact, or to inadvertence. In such case, such member shall be treated as if it had filed a Form 1122 for such year for purposes of paragraph (h)(2) of this section, and thus joined in the making of the consolidated return for such year.

(c) Election to discontinue filing consolidated returns. *(1) Good cause.* (i) In general. Notwithstanding that a consolidated return is required for a taxable year, the Commissioner, upon application by the common parent, may for good cause shown grant permission to a group to discontinue filing consolidated returns. Any such application shall be made to the Commissioner of Internal Revenue, Washington, D.C. 20224, and shall be made not later than the 90th day before the due date for the filing of the consolidated return (including extensions of time). In addition, if an amendment of the Code, or other law affecting the computation of tax liability, is enacted and the enactment is effective for a taxable year ending before or within 90 days after the date of enactment, then application for such a taxable year may be made not later than the 180th day after the date of enactment, and if the application is approved the permission to discontinue filing consolidated returns will apply to such taxable year notwithstanding that a consolidated return has already been filed for such year.

(ii) Substantial adverse change in law affecting tax liability. Ordinarily, the Commissioner will grant a group permission to discontinue filing consolidated returns if the net result of all amendments to the Code or regulations with effective dates commencing within the taxable year has a substantial adverse effect on the consolidated tax liability of the group for such year relative to what the aggregate tax liability would be if the members of the group filed separate returns for such year. Thus, for example, assume P and S filed a consolidated return for the calendar year 1966 and that the provisions of the Code have been amended by a bill which was enacted by Congress in 1966, but which is first effective for taxable years beginning on or after January 1, 1967. Assume further that P makes a timely application to discontinue filing consolidated returns. In order to determine whether the amendments have a substantial adverse effect on the consolidated tax liability for 1967, relative to what the aggregate tax liability would be if the members of the group filed separate returns for 1967, the difference between the tax liability of the group computed on a consolidated basis and taking into account the changes in the law effective for 1967 and the aggregate tax liability of the members of the group computed as if each such member filed separate returns for such year (also taking into account such changes) shall be compared with the difference between the tax liability of such group for 1967 computed on a consolidated basis without regard to the changes in the law effective in such year and the aggregate tax liability of the members of the group computed as if separate returns had been filed by such members for such year without regard to the changes in the law effective in such year.

(iii) Other factors. In addition, the Commissioner will take into account other factors in determining whether good cause exists for granting permission to discontinue filing consolidated returns beginning with the taxable year, including—

(a) Changes in law or circumstances, including changes which do not affect Federal income tax liability,

(b) Changes in law which are first effective in the taxable year and which result in a substantial reduction in the consolidated net operating loss (or consolidated unused investment credit) for such year relative to what the aggregate net operating losses (or investment credits) would be if the members of the group filed separate returns for such year, and

(c) Changes in the Code or regulations which are effective prior to the taxable year but which first have a substantial adverse effect on the filing of a consolidated return relative to the filing of separate returns by members of the group in such year.

(2) Discretion of Commissioner to grant blanket permission. (i) Permission to all groups. The Commissioner, in his discretion, may grant all groups permission to discontinue filing consolidated returns if any provision of the Code or regulations has been amended and such amendment is of the type which could have a substantial adverse effect on the filing of consolidated returns by substantially all groups, relative to the filing of separate returns. Ordinarily, the permission to discontinue shall apply with respect to the taxable year of each group which includes the effective date of such an amendment.

(ii) Permission to a class of groups. The Commissioner, in his discretion, may grant a particular class of groups permission to discontinue filing consolidated returns if any provision of the Code or regulations has been amended and such amendment is of the type which could have a substantial adverse effect on the filing of consolidated returns by substantially all such groups relative to the filing of separate returns. Ordinarily, the permission to discontinue shall apply with respect to the taxable year of each group within the class which includes the effective date of such an amendment.

(3) Time and manner for exercising election. If, under subparagraph (1) or (2) of this paragraph, a group has an election to discontinue filing consolidated returns for any taxable year and such group wishes to exercise such election, then the common parent must file a separate return for such year on or before the last day prescribed by law (including extensions of time) for the filing of the consolidated return for such year. See section 6081 (relating to extensions of time for filing returns).

(d) When group remains in existence. *(1) General rule.* A group remains in existence for a tax year if the common parent remains as the common parent and at least one subsidiary that was affiliated with it at the end of the prior year remains affiliated with it at the beginning of the year, whether or not one or more corporations have ceased to be subsidiaries at any time after the group was formed. Thus, for example, assume that corporation P acquires the sole outstanding share of stock of S on January 1, year 1, and that P and S file a consolidated return for the year 1 calendar year. On May 1, year 2, P acquires the sole outstanding share of stock of S1 and, on July 1, year 2, P sells the S share. The group (consisting originally of P and S) remains in existence in year 2 because P remained the common parent and, S, a subsidiary that was affiliated with P at the end of year 1, remained affiliated with P at the beginning of year 2.

(2) Common parent no longer in existence. (i) Mere change in identity. For purposes of this paragraph, the common parent corporation shall remain as the common parent irrespective of a mere change in identity, form, or place of organization of such common parent corporation (see section 368(a)(1)(F)).

(ii) Transfer of assets to subsidiary. The group shall be considered as remaining in existence notwithstanding that the common parent is no longer in existence if the members of the affiliated group succeed to and become the owners of substantially all of the assets of such former parent and there remains one or more chains of includible corporations connected through stock ownership with a common parent corporation which is an includible corporation and which was a member of the group prior to the date such former parent ceases to exist. For purposes of applying paragraph (f)(2)(i) of § 1.1502-1 to separate return years ending on or before the date on which the former parent ceases to exist, such former parent, and not the new common parent, shall be considered to be the corporation described in such paragraph.

(iii) Taxable years. If a transfer of assets described in subdivision (ii) of this subparagraph is an acquisition to which section 381(a) applies and if the group files a consolidated return for the taxable year in which the acquisition occurs, then for purposes of section 381—

(a) The former common parent shall not close its taxable year merely because of the acquisition, and all taxable years of such former parent ending on or before the date of acquisition shall be treated as taxable years of the acquiring corporation, and

(b) The corporation acquiring the assets shall close its taxable year as of the date of acquisition, and all taxable years of such corporation ending on or before the date of acquisition shall be treated as taxable years of the transferor corporation.

(iv) Exception. With respect to acquisitions occurring before January 1, 1971, subdivision (iii) of this subparagraph shall not apply if the group, in its income tax return, treats the taxable year of the former common parent as having closed as of the date of acquisition.

(3) Reverse acquisitions. (i) In general. If a corporation (hereinafter referred to as the "first corporation") or any member of a group of which the first corporation is the common parent acquires after October 1, 1965—

(a) Stock of another corporation (hereinafter referred to as the second corporation), and as a result the second corporation becomes (or would become but for the application of this subparagraph) a member of a group of which the first corporation is the common parent, or

(b) Substantially all the assets of the second corporation,

in exchange (in whole or in part) for stock of the first corporation, and the stockholders (immediately before the acquisition) of the second corporation, as a result of owning stock of the second corporation, own (immediately after the acquisition) more than 50 percent of the fair market value of the outstanding stock of the first corporation, then any group of which the first corporation was the common parent immediately before the acquisition shall cease to exist as of the date of acquisition, and any group of which the second corporation was the common parent immediately before the acquisition shall be treated as remaining in existence (with the first corporation becoming the common parent of the group). Thus, assume that corporations P and S comprised group PS (P being the common parent), that P was merged into corporation T (the common parent of a group composed of T and corporation U), and that the shareholders of P immediately before the merger, as a result of owning stock in P, own 90 percent of the fair market value of T's stock immediately after the merger. The group of which P was the common parent is treated as continuing in existence with T and U being added as members of the group, and T taking the place of P as the common parent. For purposes of determining under (a) of this subdivision whether the second corporation becomes (or would become) a member of the group of which the first corporation is the common parent, and for purposes of determining whether the former stockholders of the second corporation own more than 50 percent of the outstanding stock of the first corporation, there shall be taken into account any acquisitions or redemptions of the stock of either corporation which are pursuant to a plan of acquisition described in (a) or (b) of this subdivision.

(ii) Prior ownership of stock. For purposes of subdivision (i) of this subparagraph, if the first corporation, and any members of a group of which the first corporation is the common parent, have continuously owned for a period of at least 5 years ending on the date of the acquisition an aggregate of at least 25 percent of the fair market value of the outstanding stock of the second corporation, then the first corporation (and any subsidiary which owns stock of the second corporation immediately before the acquisition) shall, as a result of owning such stock, be treated as owning (immediately after the acquisition) a percentage of the fair market value of the first corporation's outstanding stock which bears the same ratio to (a) the percentage of the fair market value of all the stock of the second corporation owned immediately before the acquisition by the first corporation and its subsidiaries as (b) the fair market value of the total outstanding stock of the second corporation immediately before the acquisition bears to (c) the sum of (1) the fair market value, immediately before the acquisition, of the total outstanding stock of the first corporation, and (2) the fair market value, immediately before the acquisition, of the total outstanding stock of the second corporation (other than any such stock owned by the first corporation and any of its subsidiaries). For example, assume that corporation P owns stock in corporation T having a fair market value of $100,000, that P acquires the remaining stock of T from individuals in exchange for stock of P, that immediately before the acquisition the total outstanding stock of T had a fair market value of $150,000, and that immediately before the acquisition the total outstanding stock of P had a fair market value of $200,000. Assuming P owned at least 25 percent of the fair market value of T's stock for 5 years, then for purposes of this subparagraph, P is treated as owning (immediately after the acquisition) 40 percent of the fair market value of its own outstanding stock, determined as follows:

$$\frac{\$150,000}{\$200,000 + \$50,000} \times 66\tfrac{2}{3}\% = 40\%$$

Thus, if the former individual stockholders of T own, immediately after the acquisition more than 10 percent of the fair market value of the outstanding stock of P as a result of owning stock of T, the group of which T was the common parent is treated as continuing in existence with P as the common parent, and the group of which P was the common parent before the acquisition ceases to exist.

(iii) Election. The provisions of subdivision (ii) of this subparagraph shall not apply to any acquisition occurring in a taxable year ending after October 7, 1969, unless the first corporation elects to have such subdivision apply. The election shall be made by means of a statement, signed by any officer who is duly authorized to act on behalf of the first corporation, stating that the corporation elects to have the provisions of § 1.1502-75(d)(3)(ii) apply and identifying the acquisition to which such provisions will apply. The statement shall be filed, on or before the due date (including extensions of time) of the return for the group's first consolidated return year ending after the date of the acquisition, with the internal revenue officer with whom such return is required to be filed.

(iv) Transfer of assets to subsidiary. This subparagraph shall not apply to a transaction to which subparagraph (2)(ii) of this paragraph applies.

(v) Taxable years. If, in a transaction described in subdivision (i) of this subparagraph, the first corporation files a consolidated return for the first taxable year ending after the date of acquisition, then—

(a) The first corporation, and each corporation which, immediately before the acquisition, is a member of the group of which the first corporation is the common parent, shall close its taxable year as of the date of acquisition, and each such corporation shall, immediately after the acquisition, change to the taxable year of the second corporation, and

(b) If the acquisition is a transaction described in section 381(a)(2), then for purposes of section 381—

(1) All taxable years ending on or before the date of acquisition, of the first corporation and each corporation which, immediately before the acquisition, is a member of the group of which the first corporation is the common parent, shall be treated as taxable years of the transferor corporation, and

(2) The second corporation shall not close its taxable year merely because of such acquisition, and all taxable years ending on or before the date of acquisition, of the second corporation and each corporation which, immediately before the acquisition, is a member of any group of which the second corporation is the common parent, shall be treated as taxable years of the acquiring corporation.

(vi) Exception. With respect to acquisitions occurring before April 17, 1968, subdivision (v) of this subparagraph shall not apply if the parties to the transaction, in their income tax returns, treat subdivision (i) as not affecting the closing of taxable years or the operation of section 381.

(4) [Reserved]

(5) Coordination with section 833. (i) Election to continue old group. If, solely by reason of the enactment of section 833 (relating to certain Blue Cross or Blue Shield organizations and certain other health insurers), an organization to which section 833 applies (a "section 833 organization") became the new common parent of an old group on January 1, 1987, the old group may elect to continue in existence with that section 833 organization as its new common parent, provided all the old groups having the same section 833 organization as their new common parent elect to continue in existence. To revoke this election, see paragraph (d)(5)(x) of this section. To file as a new group, see paragraph (d)(5)(v) of this section.

(ii) Old group. For purposes of this paragraph (d)(5), an old group is a group which, for its last taxable year ending in 1986, either filed a consolidated return or was eligible to (but did not) file a consolidated return.

(iii) Manner of electing to continue. (A) Deemed election. If all the members of all the old groups having the same section 833 organization as their new common parent are included for the first taxable year beginning after December 31, 1986, on the same consolidated (or amended consolidated) return and a Form 1122 was not filed, the old groups are deemed to have elected under paragraph (d)(5)(i) of this section to continue in existence.

(B) Delayed election. If a deemed election to continue in existence was not made under paragraph (d)(5)(iii)(A) of this section, all the members of all the old groups having the same section 833 organization as their new common parent may make a delayed election under paragraph (d)(5)(i) of this section to continue in existence by

(1) filing an appropriate consolidated (or amended consolidated) return or returns for each taxable year beginning after December 31, 1986, (notwithstanding § 1.1502-75(a)(1)) on or before January 3, 1991 and

(2) on the top of any such return prominently affixing a statement containing the following declaration: "THIS RETURN" (or, if applicable, "AMENDED RETURN") "REFLECTS A DELAYED ELECTION TO CONTINUE UNDER § 1.1502-75T(d)(5)(iii)(B)". A delayed election to continue in existence automatically revokes a deemed election to file as a new group which was made under paragraph (d)(5)(vi) of this section.

(iv) Effects of election to continue in existence. If an old group or groups elect to continue in existence under paragraph (d)(5)(i) of this section, the following rules apply:

(A) Taxable years. Each member that filed returns other than on a calendar year basis shall close its taxable year on December 31, 1986, and change to a calendar year beginning on January 1, 1987. See section 843 and § 1.1502-76(a)(1).

(B) Carryovers from separate return limitation years. For purposes of applying the separate return limitation year rules to carryovers from taxable years beginning before 1987 to taxable years beginning after 1986, the following rules apply:

(1) Any taxable year beginning before 1987 of a corporation that was not a member of an old group (including a section 833 organization) will be treated as a separate return limitation year;

(2) Any taxable year beginning before 1987 of a corporation that was a member of an old group that, without regard to this section and the enactment of section 833, was a separate return limitation year will continue to be treated as a separate return limitation year;

(3) Any taxable year beginning before 1987 of a member of an old group (other than a separate return limitation year described in paragraph (d)(5)(iv)(B)(2) of this section) will not be treated as a separate return limitation year with respect to any corporation that was a member of such group for each day of that taxable year; and

(4) Any taxable year beginning before 1987 of a member of an old group will be treated as a separate return limitation year with respect to any corporation that was not a member of such group for each day of that taxable year (e.g., a corporation that was not a member of an old group, including a section 833 organization, or a corporation that was a member of another old group).

(c) Five-year rules for life-nonlife groups. Any life-nonlife election under section 1504(c)(2) in effect for an old group remains in effect. Any old group which was eligible to make a life-nonlife election will remain eligible to make the election. For purposes of section 1503(c), a nonlife member is treated as ineligible under § 1.1502-47(d)(13) with respect to a life member, unless both were members of the same affiliated group (determined without regard to the exclusions in section 1504(b)(1) and (2)) for five taxable years immediately preceding the taxable year in which the loss arose. See paragraph (d)(5)(ix) of this section for a tacking rule.

(v) Election to file as a new group. If, solely by reason of the enactment of section 833, a section 833 organization became the new common parent of an old group on January 1, 1987, the application of the five-year prohibition on reconsolidation in section 1504(a)(3)(A) to the old group is waived and the old group together with the new section 833 organization common parent may elect to file as a new group provided that all includible corporations elect to file a consolidated (or amended consolidated) return as a new group for the first taxable year beginning after December 31, 1986. To revoke this election, see paragraph (d)(5)(x) of this section.

(vi) Manner of electing to file as a new group. (A) Deemed election. The old group or groups and the section 833 organization are deemed to have elected under paragraph (d)(5)(v) of this section to file as a new group by filing, for the first taxable year beginning after December 31, 1986, a Form 1122 and a consolidated (or amended consolidated) tax return.

(B) Delayed election. If a deemed election to file is a new group was not made pursuant to paragraph (d)(5)(vi)(A) of this section, the old group or groups and the section 833 organization may make a delayed election under paragraph (d)(5)(v) of this section to file as a new group by

(1) filing an appropriate consolidated (or amended consolidated) return or returns for each taxable year beginning after December 31, 1986, (notwithstanding § 1.1502-75(a)(1)) on or before January 3, 1991 and

(2) on the top of any such return prominently affixing a statement containing the following declaration: "THIS RETURN" (or, if applicable, "AMENDED RETURN") "REFLECTS A DELAYED ELECTION TO FILE AS A NEW GROUP UNDER § 1.1502-75T(d)(5)(vi)(B)". A delayed election to file as a new group automatically revokes any deemed election to continue in existence which was made under paragraph (d)(5)(iii) of this section.

(vii) Effects of election to file as a new group. If an old group or groups elect to file as a new group under paragraph (d)(5)(v) of this section, the following rules apply:

(A) Termination. Each old group is treated as if it terminated on January 1, 1987, and the termination is not treated as resulting from the acquisition by a nonmember of all of the stock of the common parent.

(B) Taxable years. Each member that filed returns other than on a calendar year basis shall close its taxable year on December 31, 1986, and change to a calendar year beginning on January 1, 1987. See section 843 and § 1.1502-76(a)(1).

(C) Separate return limitation year and life-nonlife groups. For purposes of § 1.1502-1(f), sections 1503(c) and 1504(c), and § 1.1502-47, the group is treated as coming into existence as a new group on January 1, 1987. Thus, for example, paragraphs (d)(5)(iv)(B) and (C) of this section do not apply.

(viii) Earnings and profits. All distributions after January 1, 1987 by a corporation, whether or not such corporation was a member of an old group, to an existing Blue Cross or Blue Shield organization (as defined in section 833(c)(2)) out of earnings and profits accumulated before 1987 are deemed made out of earnings and profits accumulated in pre-affiliation years. See § 1.1502-32(h)(5).

(ix) Five-year tacking rules for certain life-nonlife groups. For purposes of applying § 1.1502-47(d)(5) and (12) to any taxable year ending after 1936 to a corporation, whether or not the corporation was a member of an old group, (A) the determination of whether the corporation was in existence and a member or tentatively treated as a member of a group, for taxable years ending before 1987, is made without regard to the exclusions under section 1504(b)(1) and (2) of any section 833 organization or life insurance company (as the case may be) and (B) a section 833 organization is not treated as having a change in tax character solely by reason of the loss of its tax-exempt status due to the enactment of section 833. This paragraph (d)(5)(ix) does not apply if an election to file as a new group under paragraph (d)(5)(v) of this section is made.

(x) Time to revoke elections made before September 5, 1990. An election by an old group to continue in existence or to file as a new group that was made (or deemed made) before September 5, 1990 may be revoked by filing an appropriate return (or returns) on or before January 3, 1991. For purposes of this paragraph (d)(5)(x), appropriate returns include separate returns filed by each member of the group or consolidated returns filed in accordance with a delayed election either under paragraph (d)(5)(iii)(B) or (vi)(B) of this section.

(xi) Examples. The following examples illustrate this paragraph (d)(5). In these examples, each corporation uses the calendar year as its taxable year.

Example (1). B is a section 833 organization. For several years, B has owned all of the outstanding stock of X, Y, and Z. X has owned all the outstanding stock of X_1 throughout X_1's existence and Y has owned all of the outstanding stock of Y_1 throughout Y_1's existence. For 1986, X and X_1 filed a consolidated federal income tax return but Y and Y_1 filed separate returns. Under paragraph (d)(5)(ii) of this section, X and X_1 and Y and Y_1 each constitute an old group because they either filed a consolidated return or were eligible to file a consolidated return for 1986. The X and Y groups may elect under paragraph (d)(5)(i) of this section to continue in existence. If they elect to continue, under paragraph (d)(5)(iv)(B) of this section, the separate return limitation year rules apply as follows: any taxable year of B or Z beginning before 1987 is treated as a separate return limitation year with respect to each other and to all other members of the group; any taxable year of X or X_1 beginning before 1987 is treated as a separate return limitation year with respect to B, Z, Y and Y_1, but not with respect to each other; and any taxable year of Y or Y_1 beginning before 1987 is treated as a separate return limitation year with respect to B, Z, X and X_1, but not with respect to each other.

Example (2). The facts are the same as in Example 1 except that B is owned by C, another section 833 organization. If the X and Y groups elect to continue, the results are the same as in Example 1, except that, under paragraph (d)(5)(iv)(B) *(1)* of this section, for purposes of applying the separate return limitation year rules, any taxable year of C beginning before 1987 is also treated as a separate return limitation year with respect to all other members of the group.

Example (3). The facts are the same as in Example 1 except that Y purchased Y_1 on January 1, 1985. If the X and Y groups elect to continue, the results are the same as in Example 1, except that, under paragraph (d)(5)(iv)(B)(2) of this section, for purposes of applying the separate return limitation year rules, any taxable year of Y_1 beginning before 1985 is treated as a separate return limitation year with respect to Y as well as with respect to all other members of the group.

Example (4). B, a section 833 organization, has owned all the stock of X since November 1984. X has owned all the stock of L, a life insurance company, throughout L's existence. In 1986, X and L properly filed a life-nonlife consolidated return. Under paragraph (d)(5)(i) of this section, the X group elects to continue in existence. Under paragraph (d)(5)(iv)(C) of this section, the life-nonlife election will remain in effect. However, losses of B which arise before 1990 cannot be used to offset the income of L. See section 1503(c)(2) and § 1.1502-47(d)(13) and paragraph (d)(5)(iv)(C) of this section. Under paragraph (d)(5)(iv)(B) of this section, the separate return limitation year rules apply as follows: any taxable year of B beginning before 1987 is treated as a separate return limitation year with respect to all other members of the group; and any taxable year of X or L beginning before 1987 is treated as a separate return limitation year with respect to B, but not with respect to each other.

Example (5). The facts are the same as Example 4 except that, on January 1, 1984, B formed L_1, a life insurance company. Under paragraph (d)(5)(ix) of this section and section 1504(c), the first year L_1 is eligible to join in B's life-nonlife election is 1989.

Example (6). The facts are the same as in Example 4 except that B and the X group elect under paragraph (d)(5)(v) of this section to file as a new group. The X group will be considered to have terminated under § 1.1502-75(d)(1) on December 31, 1986. X and L are each separately subject to the separate return limitation year rules of § 1.1502-1(f). The first year L and L_1 are eligible to join the new group in a life-nonlife election is 1992 (five years after the new group is formed). See section 1504(c)(2) and paragraphs (d)(5)(vii)(C) and (ix) of this section.

(e) Failure to include subsidiary. If a consolidated return is required for the taxable year under the provisions of paragraph (a)(2) of this section, the tax liability of all members of the group for such year shall be computed on a consolidated basis even though—

(1) Separate returns are filed by one or more members of the group, or

(2) There has been a failure to include in the consolidated return the income of any member of the group.

If subparagraph (1) of this paragraph applies, the amounts assessed or paid upon the basis of separate returns shall be considered as having been assessed or paid upon the basis of a consolidated return.

(f) Inclusion of one or more corporations not members of the group. *(1) Method of determining tax liability.* If a consolidated return includes the income of a corporation which was not a member of the group at any time during the consolidated return year, the tax liability of such corporation will be determined upon the basis of a separate return (or a consolidated return of another group, if paragraph (a)(2) or (b)(3) of this section applies), and the consolidated return will be considered as including only the income of the corporations which were members of the group during that taxable year. If a consolidated return includes the income of two or more corporations which were not members of the group but which constitute another group, the tax liability of such corporations will be computed in the same manner as if separate returns had been made by such corporations unless the Commissioner upon application approves the making of a consolidated return for the other group or unless under paragraph (a)(2) of this section a consolidated return is required for the other group.

(2) Allocation of tax liability. In any case in which amounts have been assessed and paid upon the basis of a consolidated return and the tax liability of one or more of the corporations included in the consolidated return is to be computed in the manner described in subparagraph (1) of this paragraph, the amounts so paid shall be allocated between the group composed of the corporations properly included in the consolidated return and each of the corporations the tax liability of which is to be computed on a separate basis (or on the basis of a consolidated return of another group) in such manner as the corporations which were included in the consolidated return may, subject to the approval of the Commissioner, agree upon or in the absence of an agreement upon the method used in allocating the tax liability of the members of the group under the provisions of section 1552(a).

(g) Computing periods of limitation. *(1) Income incorrectly included in consolidated return.* If—

(i) A consolidated return is filed by a group for the taxable year, and

(ii) The tax liability of a corporation whose income is included in such return must be computed on the basis of a separate return (or on the basis of a consolidated return with another group), then for the purpose of computing any period of limitation with respect to such separate return (or such other consolidated return), the filing of such consolidated return by the group shall be considered as the making of a return by such corporation.

(2) Income incorrectly included in separate returns. If a consolidated return is required for the taxable year under the provisions of paragraph (a)(2) of this section, the filing of separate returns by the members of the group for such year shall not be considered as the making of a return for the pur-

pose of computing any period of limitation with respect to such consolidated return unless there is attached to each such separate return a statement setting forth—

(i) The most recent taxable year of the member for which its income was included in a consolidated return, and

(ii) The reasons for the group's belief that a consolidated return is not required for the taxable year.

(h) Method of filing return and forms. *(1) Consolidated return made by common parent corporation.* The consolidated return shall be made on Form 1120 for the group by the common parent corporation. The consolidated return, with Form 851 (affiliations schedule) attached, shall be filed with the district director with whom the common parent would have filed a separate return.

(2) Filing of Form 1122 for first year. If, under the provisions of paragraph (a)(1) of this section, a group wishes to file a consolidated return for a taxable year, then a Form 1122 ("Authorization and Consent of Subsidiary Corporation To Be Included in a Consolidated Income Tax Return") must be executed by each subsidiary. For taxable years beginning before January 1, 2003, the executed Forms 1122 must be attached to the consolidated return for the taxable year. For taxable years beginning after December 31, 2002, the group must attach either executed Forms 1122 or unsigned copies of the completed Forms 1122 to the consolidated return. If the group submits unsigned Forms 1122 with its return, it must retain the signed originals in its records in the manner required by § 1.6001-1(e). Form 1122 is not required for a taxable year if a consolidated return was filed (or was required to be filed) by the group for the immediately preceding taxable year.

(3) Persons qualified to execute returns and forms. Each return or form required to be made or prepared by a corporation must be executed by the person authorized under section 6062 to execute returns of separate corporations.

(i) [Reserved]

(j) Statements and schedules for subsidiaries. The statement of gross income and deductions and the schedules required by the instructions on the return shall be prepared and filed in columnar form so that the details of the items of gross income, deductions and credits for each member may be readily audited. Such statements and schedules shall include in columnar form a reconciliation of surplus for each corporation, and a reconciliation of consolidated surplus. Consolidated balance sheets as of the beginning and close of the taxable year of the group, taken from the books of the members, shall accompany the consolidated return and shall be prepared in a form similar to that required for reconciliation of surplus.

(k) Cross-reference. See § 1.338(h)(10)-1T(d)(7) for special rules regarding filing consolidated returns when a section 338(h)(10) election is made for a target acquired from a selling consolidated group.

(l) Effective/applicability dates. Paragraph (d)(1) of this section applies to taxable years for which the due date of the original return (without regard to extensions) is on or after September 17, 2008.

T.D. 6894, 9/7/66, amend T.D. 7016, 10/6/69, T.D. 7024, 2/9/70, T.D. 7244, 12/29/72, T.D. 7246, 12/29/72, T.D. 8438, 9/24/92, T.D. 8515, 1/12/94, T.D. 8560, 8/12/94, T.D. 8858, 1/5/2000, T.D. 8940, 2/12/2001, T.D. 9100, 12/18/2003, T.D. 9300, 12/7/2006, T.D. 9424, 9/10/2008.

---

§ 1.1502-76 Taxable year of members of group.

(a) Taxable year of members of group. The consolidated return of a group must be filed on the basis of the common parent's taxable year, and each subsidiary must adopt the common parent's annual accounting period for the first consolidated return year for which the subsidiary's income is includible in the consolidated return. If any member is on a 52-53-week taxable year, the rule of the preceding sentence shall, with the advance consent of the Commissioner, be deemed satisfied if the taxable years of all members of the group end within the same 7-day period. Any request for such consent shall be filed with the Commissioner of Internal Revenue, Washington, DC 20224, not later than the 30th day before the due date (not including extensions of time) for the filing of the consolidated return.

(b) Items included in the consolidated return. *(1) General rules.* (i) In general. A consolidated return must include the common parent's items of income, gain, deduction, loss, and credit for the entire consolidated return year, and each subsidiary's items for the portion of the year for which it is a member. If the consolidated return includes the items of a corporation for only a portion of its tax year determined without taking this section into account, items for the portion of the year not included in the consolidated return must be included in a separate return (including the consolidated return of another group). The rules of this paragraph (b) must be applied to prevent the duplication or elimination of the corporation's items.

(ii) The day a corporation becomes or ceases to be a member. (A) End of the day rule. (1) In general. If a corporation (S), other than one described in paragraph (b)(1)(ii)(A)(2) of this section, becomes or ceases to be a member during a consolidated return year, it becomes or ceases to be a member at the end of the day on which its status as a member changes, and its tax year ends for all Federal income tax purposes at the end of that day. Appropriate adjustments must be made if another provision of the Internal Revenue Code or the regulations thereunder contemplates the event occurring before or after S's change in status. For example, S's items restored under § 1.1502-13 immediately before it becomes a nonmember are taken into account in determining the basis of S's stock under § 1.1502-32. On the other hand, if a section 338(g) election is made in connection with S becoming a member, the deemed asset sale under that section takes place before S becomes a member. See § 1.338-10(a)(5) (deemed sale excluded from purchasing corporation's consolidated return.)

(2) Special rule for former S corporations. If S becomes a member in a transaction other than in a qualified stock purchase for which an election under section 338(g) is made, and immediately before becoming a member an election under section 1362(a) was in effect, then S will become a member at the beginning of the day the termination of its S corporation election is effective. S's tax year ends for all Federal income tax purposes at the end of the preceding day. This paragraph (b)(1)(ii)(A)(2) applies to transactions occurring after November 10, 1999.

(B) Next day rule. If, on the day of S's change in status as a member, a transaction occurs that is properly allocable to the portion of S's day after the event resulting in the change, S and all persons related to S under section 267(b) immediately after the event must treat the transaction for all Federal income tax purposes as occurring at the beginning of the following day. A determination as to whether a transaction is properly allocable to the portion of S's day after the event will be respected if it is reasonable and consistently applied by all affected persons. In determining whether an allocation is reasonable, the following factors are among those to be considered—

(1) Whether income, gain, deduction, loss, and credit are allocated inconsistently (e.g., to maximize a seller's stock basis adjustments under § 1.1502-32);

(2) If the item is from a transaction with respect to S stock, whether it reflects ownership of the stock before or after the event (e.g., if a member transfers encumbered land to nonmember S in exchange for additional S stock in a transaction to which section 351 applies and the exchange results in S becoming a member of the consolidated group, the applicability of section 357(c) to the exchange must be determined under § 1.1502-80(d) by treating the exchange as occurring after the event; on the other hand, if S is a member but has a minority shareholder and becomes a nonmember as a result of its redemption of stock with appreciated property, S's gain under section 311 is treated as from a transaction occurring before the event);

(3) Whether the allocation is inconsistent with other requirements under the Internal Revenue Code and regulations promulgated thereunder (e.g., if a section 338(g) election is made in connection with a group's acquisition of S, the deemed asset sale must take place before S becomes a member and S's gain or loss with respect to its assets must be taken into account by S as a nonmember (but see § 1.338-1(d)), or if S realizes discharge of indebtedness income that is excluded from gross income under section 108(a) on the day it becomes a nonmember, the discharge of indebtedness income must be treated as realized by S as a member (see § 1.1502-28(b)(11))); and

(4) Whether other facts exist, such as a prearranged transaction or multiples changes in S's status, indicating that the transaction is not properly allocable to the portion of S's day after the event resulting in S's change.

(C) Successor corporations. For purposes of this paragraph (b)(1)(ii), any reference to a corporation includes a reference to a successor or predecessor as the context may require. A corporation is a successor if the basis of its assets is determined, directly or indirectly, in whole or in part, by reference to the basis of the assets of another corporation (the predecessor). For example, if a member forms S, S is treated as a member from the beginning of its existence.

(iii) Group structure changes. If the common parent ceases to be the common parent but the group remains in existence, adjustments must be made in accordance with the principles of § 1.1502-75(d)(2) and (3).

(2) Determination of items included in separate and consolidated returns. (i) In general. The returns for the years that end and begin with S becoming (or ceasing to be) a member are separate tax years for all Federal income tax purposes. The returns are subject to the rules of the Internal Revenue Code applicable to short periods, as if S ceased to exist on becoming a member (or first existed on becoming a nonmember). For example, cost recovery deductions under section 168 must be allocated for short periods. On the other hand, annualization under section 443 is not required of S solely because it has a short year as a result of becoming a member. (Similarly, section 443 applies with respect to a consolidated return only to the extent that the group's return is for a short period and section 443 applies without taking this paragraph (b) into account.)

(ii) Ratable allocation of a year's items. (A) Application. Although the periods ending and beginning with S's change in status are different tax years, items (other than extraordinary items) may be ratably allocated between the periods if—

(1) S is not required to change its annual accounting period or its method of accounting as a result of its change in status (e.g., because its stock is sold between consolidated groups that have the same annual accounting periods); and

(2) An irrevocable ratable allocation election is made under paragraph (b)(2)(ii)(D) of this section.

(B) General rule. (1) Allocation within original year. Under a ratable allocation election, paragraph (b)(2) of this section applies by allocating to each day of S's original year (S's tax year determined without taking this section into account) an equal portion of S's items taken into account in the original year, except that extraordinary items must be allocated to the day that they are taken into account. All persons affected by the election must take into account S's extraordinary items and the ratable allocation of S's remaining items in a manner consistent with the election.

(2) Items to be allocated. Under ratable allocation, the items to be allocated and their timing, location, character, and source are generally determined by treating the original year as a single tax year, and the items are not subject to the rules of the Internal Revenue Code applicable to short periods (unless the original year is a short period). However, the years ending and beginning with S's change in status are treated as different tax years (and as short periods) with respect to any item carried to or from these years (e.g., a net operating loss carried under section 172) and with respect to the application of section 481.

(3) Multiple applications. If this paragraph (b) applies more than once with respect to an original year, adjustments must be made in accordance with the principles of this paragraph (b). For example, if S becomes a member of two different consolidated groups during the same original year and ratable allocation is elected with respect to both groups, ratable allocation is generally determined for both groups by treating the original year as a single tax year; however, if ratable allocation is elected only with respect to the first group, the ratable allocation is determined by treating the original year as a short period that does not include the period that S is a member of the second group. Ratable allocation is not a method of accounting, and ratable allocation with respect to one application of this paragraph (b) to S does not require ratable allocation to be subsequently applied with respect to S.

(C) Extraordinary items. An extraordinary item is—

(1) Any item from the disposition or abandonment of a capital asset as defined in section 1221 (determined without the application of any other rules of law);

(2) Any item from the disposition or abandonment of property used in a trade or business as defined in section 1231(b) (determined without the application of any holding period requirement);

(3) Any item from the disposition or abandonment of an asset described in section 1221(1), (3), (4), or (5), if substantially all the assets in the same category from the same trade or business are disposed of or abandoned in one transaction (or series of related transactions);

(4) Any item from assets disposed of in an applicable asset acquisition under section 1060(c);

(5) Any item carried to or from any portion of the original year (e.g., a net operating loss carried under section 172), and any section 481(a) adjustment;

(6) The effects of any change in accounting method initiated by the filing of the appropriate form after S's change in status;

(7) Any item from the discharge or retirement of indebtedness (e.g., cancellation of indebtedness income or a deduction for retirement at a premium);

(8) Any item from the settlement of a tort or similar third-party liability;

(9) Any compensation-related deduction in connection with S's change in status (including, for example, deductions from bonus, severance, and option cancellation payments made in connection with S's change in status);

(10) Any dividend income from a nonmember that S controls within the meaning of section 304 at the time the dividend is taken into account;

(11) Any deemed income inclusion from a foreign corporation, or any deferred tax amount on an excess distribution from a passive foreign investment company under section 1291;

(12) Any interest expense allocable under section 172(h) to a corporate equity reduction transaction causing this paragraph (b) to apply;

(13) Any credit, to the extent it arises from activities or items that are not ratably allocated (e.g., the rehabilitation credit under section 47, which is based on placement in service); and

(14) Any item which, in the opinion of the Commissioner, would, if ratably allocated, result in a substantial distortion of income in any consolidated return or separate return in which the item is included.

(D) Election. (1) Statement. The election to ratably allocate items under this paragraph (b)(2)(ii) must be made in a separate statement entitled, "THIS IS AN ELECTION UNDER § 1.1502-76(b)(2)(ii) TO RATABLY ALLOCATE THE YEAR'S ITEMS OF]INSERT NAME AND EMPLOYER IDENTIFICATION NUMBER OF THE MEMBER]." The election must be filed by including a statement on or with the returns including the items for the years ending and beginning with S's change in status. If two or more members of the same consolidated group, as a consequence of the same plan or arrangement, cease to be members of that group and remain affiliated as members of another consolidated group, an election under this paragraph (b)(2)(ii)(D)(1) may be made only if it is made by each such member. Each statement must also indicate that an agreement, as described in paragraph (b)(2)(ii)(D)(2) of this section, has been entered into. Each party signing the agreement must retain either the original or a copy of the agreement as part of its records. See § 1.6001-1(e).

(2) Agreement. For each election under this paragraph (b)(2)(ii), the member and the common parent of each affected group must sign and date an agreement. The agreement must--

(i) Identify the extraordinary items, their amounts, and the separate or consolidated returns in which they are included;

(ii) Identify the aggregate amount to be ratably allocated, and the portion of the amount included in the separate and consolidated returns; and

(iii) Include the name and employer identification number of the common parent (if any) of each group that must take the items into account.

(iii) Ratable allocation of a month's items. If ratable allocation under paragraph (b)(2)(ii) of this section is not elected (e.g., because S is required to change its annual accounting period), this paragraph (b)(2)(iii) may be applied to ratably allocate only S's items taken into account in the month of its change in status, but only if the allocation is consistently applied by all affected persons. The ratable allocation is made by applying the principles of paragraph (b)(2)(ii) of this section under any reasonable method. For example, S may close its books both at the end of the preceding month and at the end of the month of the change, and allocate only its items (other than extraordinary items) from the month of the change. See paragraph (b)(1)(ii)(B) of this section for factors to be considered in determining whether the method is reasonable.

(iv) Taxes. To the extent properly taken into account during the member's tax year (determined without the application of this paragraph (b)), Federal, state, local, and foreign taxes are allocated under paragraph (b)(2) of this section on the basis of the items or activities to which the taxes relate. Thus, income tax is allocated based on the inclusion of the income (determined under the principles of this paragraph (b)) to which the tax relates. For example, if a calendar-year domestic corporation has $100 of foreign source dividend income (determined in accordance with United States tax accounting principles but without taking this paragraph (b) into account) that is passive income for purposes of section 904, and $60 of the income is allocated under this paragraph (b) to the period of the calendar year after it becomes a member of a consolidated group, then 60% of the corporation's deemed paid foreign tax credit associated with its dividend income for the calendar year is taken into account in computing the group's passive basket consolidated foreign tax credit. Similarly, property taxes relate to the ownership of property and are allocated over the period that the property is owned. This paragraph (b)(2)(iv) applies without regard to any determination or allocation by another taxing jurisdiction.

(v) Acquisition of S corporation. If a corporation is acquired in a transaction to which paragraph (b)(1)(ii)(A)(2) of this section applies, then paragraphs (b)(2)(ii) and (iii) of this section do not apply and items of income, gain, loss, deduction, and credit are assigned to each short taxable year on the basis of the corporation's normal method of accounting as determined under section 446. This paragraph (b)(2)(v) applies to transactions occurring after November 10, 1999.

(vi) Passthrough entities. (A) In general. If S is a partner in a partnership or an owner of a similar interest with respect to which items of the entity are taken into account by S, S is treated, solely for purposes of determining the year to which the entity's items are allocated under paragraph (b)(2) of this section, as selling or exchanging its entire interest in the entity immediately before S's change in status.

(B) Treatment as a conduit. For purposes of this paragraph (b)(2), if a member (together with other members) would be treated under section 318(a)(2) as owning an aggregate of at least 50% of any stock owned by the passthrough entity, the method that is used to determine the inclusion of the entity's items in the consolidated or separate return must be the same method that is used to determine the inclusion of the member's items in the consolidated or separate return.

(C) Exception for certain foreign entities. This paragraph (b)(2)(v) does not apply to any foreign corporation generating the deemed inclusion of income, or to any passive foreign investment company generating a deferred tax amount on an excess distribution under section 1291.

(3) Anti-avoidance rule. If any person acts with a principal purpose contrary to the purposes of this paragraph (b), to substantially reduce the Federal income tax liability of any

person, adjustments must be made as necessary to carry out the purposes of this section.

(4) Determination of due date for separate return. Paragraph (c) of this section contains rules for the filing of the separate return referred to in this paragraph (b). In applying paragraph (c) of this section, the due date for the filing of S's separate return shall also be determined without regard to the ending of the tax year under paragraph (b)(1)(ii) of this section or the deemed cessation of its existence under paragraph (b)(2)(i) of this section.

(5) Examples. For purposes of the examples in this paragraph (b), unless otherwise stated, P and X are common parents of calendar-year consolidated groups, P owns all of the only class of T's stock, T owns no stock of lower-tier members, all persons use the accrual method of accounting, the facts set forth the only corporate activity, all transactions are between unrelated persons, tax liabilities are disregarded, and any election required under paragraph (b)(2) of this section is properly made. The principles of this paragraph (b) are illustrated by the following examples.

Example (1). Items allocated between consolidated and separate returns.

(a) Facts. P and S are the only members of the P group. P sells all of S's stock to individual A on June 30, and therefore S becomes a nonmember on July 1 of Year 2.

(b) Analysis. Under paragraph (b)(1) of this section, the P group's consolidated return for Year 2 includes P's income for the entire tax year and S's income for the period from January 1 to June 30, and S must file a separate return for the period from July 1 to December 31.

(c) Acquisition of another subsidiary before end of tax year. The facts are the same as in paragraph (a) of this Example 1, except that on July 31 P acquires all the stock of T (which filed a separate return for its year ending on November 30 of Year 1) and T therefore becomes a member on August 1 of Year 2. Under § 1.1502-75(d) and paragraph (b)(1) of this section, the P group's consolidated return for Year 2 includes P's income for the entire year, S's income from January 1 to June 30, and T's income from August 1 to December 31. S must file a separate return that includes its income from July 1 to December 31, and T must file a separate return that includes its income from December 1 of Year 1 to July 31 of Year 2. (If P had acquired T after December 31, the P group that included S is a different group from the P group that includes T, and, for example, the P group that includes T must make a separate election under section 1501 and § 1.1502-75 if consolidated returns are to be filed).

Example (2). Group structure change.

(a) Facts. P owns all of the stock of S and T. Shortly after the beginning of Year 1, P merges into T in a reorganization described in section 368(a)(1)(A) (and in section 368(a)(1)(D)), and P's shareholders receive T's stock in exchange for all of P's stock. The P group is treated under § 1.1502-75(d)(2)(ii) as remaining in existence with T as its common parent.

(b) Analysis. Under paragraph (b)(1) of this section, the P group's return must include the common parent's items for the entire consolidated return year and, if the common parent ceases to be the common parent but the group remains in existence, appropriate adjustments must be made. Consequently, although P did not exist for all of Year 1, P's items for the portion of Year 1 ending with the merger are treated as the items of the common parent that must be included in the P group's return for Year 1.

(c) Reverse acquisition. Assume instead that X acquires all of P's assets in exchange for more than 50% of X's stock in a reorganization described in section 368(a)(1)(D). The reorganization constitutes a reverse acquisition under § 1.1502-75(d)(3), with the X group terminating and the P group surviving with X as its common parent. Consequently, P's items for the portion of Year 1 ending with the acquisition are treated as the items of the common parent that must be included in the P group's return for Year 1, and X's items are treated for purposes of paragraph (b)(1) of this section as the items of a subsidiary included in the P group's return for the portion of Year 1 for which X is a member.

Example (3). Ratable allocation.

(a) Facts. P sells all of T's stock to X, and T becomes a nonmember on July 1 of Year 1. T engages in the production and sale of merchandise throughout Year 1 and is required to use inventories. The sale is treated as causing T's tax year to end on June 30, and the periods beginning and ending with the sale are treated as two tax years for Federal income tax purposes.

(b) Analysis. If ratable allocation under paragraph (b)(2)(ii) of this section is not elected, T must perform an inventory valuation as of the acquisition and also as of the end of Year 1. If ratable allocation is elected, T must perform an inventory valuation only as of the close of Year 1, and T's income from inventory is ratably allocated, along with T's other items that are not extraordinary items, between the P and X consolidated returns.

(c) Merger into nonmember. Assume instead that T merges into a wholly owned subsidiary of X in a reorganization described in section 368(a)(2)(D), and P receives 10% of X's stock in exchange for all of T's stock. Under paragraph (b)(2)(ii)(B) of this section, because T's tax year ends on June 30 under section 381(b)(1), T's original year determined without taking paragraph (b) of this section into account also ends on June 30. Consequently, a ratable allocation under paragraph (b)(2)(ii) of this section is the same as an allocation based on closing the books.

Example (4). Net operating loss. P sells all of T's stock to X, T becomes a nonmember on June 30 of Year 1, and ratable allocation under paragraph (b)(2)(ii) of this section is elected. Under ratable allocation, the X group has a $100 consolidated net operating loss for Year 1, all of which is attributable to T. However, because of extraordinary items, T has $100 of income for the portion of Year 1 that T is a member of the P group. Under paragraph (b)(2)(ii)(B)(2) of this section, T's loss may be carried back from the X group to the portion of Year 1 that T was a member of the P group. See also section 172 and § 1.1502-21(b). Under paragraph (b)(2)(ii)(C)(5) of this section, any item carried to or from any portion of the original year is an extraordinary item, and the loss therefore is not taken into account again in determining the ratable allocation under paragraph (b)(2)(ii) of this section.

Example (5). Employee benefit plans.

(a) Facts. P sells all of T's stock to X, and T becomes a nonmember on June 30 of Year 1. On March 15 of Year 2, T contributes $100 to its retirement plan, which is a qualified plan under section 401(a). T is not required to make quarterly contributions to the plan for Year 1 under section 412(m). The contribution is made on account of T's taxable period beginning on July 1 of Year 1, and is deemed in accordance with section 404(a)(6) to have been made on the last day of T's taxable period beginning on July 1 of Year 1.

Ratable allocation under paragraph (b)(2)(ii) of this section is not elected.

(b) Analysis. Under paragraph (b) of this section, the sale is treated as causing T's tax year to end on June 30, and the period beginning on July 1 is treated as a separate annual accounting period for all Federal income tax purposes. T's income from January 1 to June 30 is included in the P group's Year 1 return, and T's income from July 1 to December 31 is included in the X group's Year 1 return. Thus, the $100 contribution is deductible by T for the period of Year 1 that it is a member of the X group, subject to the applicable limitations of section 404, if a contribution on the last day of that period would otherwise be deductible.

(c) The facts are the same as in paragraph (a) of this Example 5, except that, in accordance with section 404(a)(6), $40 of the $100 contribution is made on account of T's taxable period beginning on January 1 of Year 1 and is deemed to be made on the last day of T's taxable period beginning on January 1 of Year 1. The remaining $60 is made on account of T's taxable period beginning on July 1 of Year 1 and is deemed to be made on the last day of T's taxable period beginning on July 1 of Year 1. As in paragraph (b) of this Example 5, under paragraph (b) of this section, the sale is treated as causing T's tax year to end on June 30, and the period beginning on July 1 is treated as a separate annual accounting period for all Federal income tax purposes. The $40 portion of the contribution is deductible by T for the period of Year 1 that it is a member of the P group, subject to the applicable limitations of section 404 and provided that a $40 contribution on the last day of that period would otherwise be deductible for that period, and the $60 portion is deductible by T for the period of Year 1 that it is a member of the X group, subject to the same conditions.

(d) Ratable allocation. The facts are the same as in paragraph (a) of this Example 5, except that P, T, and X elect ratable allocation under paragraph (b)(2)(ii) of this section and T's deduction for the retirement plan contribution is not an extraordinary item. T's deduction may be ratably allocated, subject to the applicable limitations of section 404, and is allowable only if a contribution on the last day of Year 1 otherwise would be deductible for any period in the year. (The results would be the same if S were an unaffiliated corporation when acquired by X, and the due date of its last separate return (including extensions) were before the pension contribution was made on March 15 of Year 2).

Example (6). Allocation of partnership items.

(a) Facts. P sells all of T's stock to X, and T becomes a nonmember on June 30 of Year 1. T has a 10% interest in the capital and profits of a calendar-year partnership.

(b) Analysis. Under paragraph (b)(2)(vi)(A) of this section, T is treated, solely for purposes of determining T's tax year in which the partnership's items are included, as selling or exchanging its entire interest in the partnership as of P's sale of T's stock. Thus, the deemed disposition is not taken into account under section 708, it does not result in gain or loss being recognized by T, and T's holding period is unaffected. However, under section 706(a), in determining T's income, T is required to include its distributive share of partnership items for the partnership's year ending within or with T's tax year. Under section 706(c)(2), the partnership's tax year is treated as closing with respect to T for this purpose as of P's sale of T's stock. The allocation of T's distributive share of partnership items must be made under § 1.706-1(c)(2)(ii).

(c) Controlled partnership. The facts are the same as in paragraph (a) of this Example 6, except that T has a 75% interest in the capital and profits of the partnership. Under paragraph (b)(2)(vi)(B) of this section, T's distributive share of the partnership items is treated as T's items for purposes of paragraph (b)(2) of this section. Thus, if ratable allocation under paragraph (b)(2)(ii) of this section is not elected, T's distributive share of the partnership's items must be determined under § 1.706-1(c)(2)(ii) by an interim closing of the partnership's books. Similarly, if ratable allocation is elected for T's items that are not extraordinary items, T's distributive share of the partnership's nonextraordinary items must also be ratably allocated under § 1.706-1(c)(2)(ii).

Example (7). Acquisition of S corporation.

(a) Facts. Z is a small business corporation for which an election under section 1362(a) was in effect at all times since Year 1. At all times, Z had only 100 shares of stock outstanding, all of which were owned by individual A. On July 1 of Year 3, P acquired all of the Z stock. P does not make an election under section 338(g) with respect to its purchase of the Z stock.

(b) Analysis. As a result of P's acquisition of the Z stock, Z's election under section 1362(a) terminates. See sections 1361(b)(1)(B) and 1362(d)(2). Z is required to join in the filing of the P consolidated return. See § 1.1502-75. Z's tax year ends for all Federal income tax purposes on June 30 of Year 3. If no extension of time is sought, Z must file a separate return for the period from January 1 through June 30 of Year 3 on or before March 15 of Year 4. See paragraph (b)(4) of this section. Z will become a member of the P consolidated group as of July 1 of Year 3. See paragraph (b)(1)(ii)(A)(2) of this section. P group's Year 3 consolidated return will include Z's items from July 1 to December 31 of Year 3.

(6) Effective date. (i) General rule. Except as provided in paragraphs (b)(1)(ii) (A)(2) and (b)(2)(v) of this section, this paragraph (b) applies to corporations becoming or ceasing to be members of consolidated groups on or after January 1, 1995.

(ii) Prior law. For prior transactions, see prior regulations under section 1502 as in effect with respect to the transaction. See, e.g., § 1.1502-76(b) and (d) as contained in the 26 CFR part 1 edition revised as of April 1, 1994. However, § 1.1502-76(b)(5) and (6) as contained in the 26 CFR part 1 edition revised as of April 1, 1994 do not apply with respect to corporations becoming or ceasing to be members of consolidated groups on or after January 1, 1995. If both this paragraph (b) and prior law may apply to determine the inclusion of any amount in a return, appropriate adjustments must be made to prevent the omission or duplication of the amount.

(c) Time for making separate returns for periods not included in consolidated return. *(1) Consolidated return filed by due date for separate return.* If the group has filed a consolidated return on or before the due date for the filing of a subsidiary's separate return (including extensions of time and determined without regard to any change of its taxable year required under paragraph (a) of this section), then the separate return for any portion of the subsidiary's taxable year for which its income is not included in the consolidated return of the group must be filed no later than the due date of such consolidated return (including extensions of time).

(2) Consolidated return not filed by due date for separate return. If the group has not filed a consolidated return on or before the due date for the filing of a subsidiary corpora-

tion's separate return (including extensions of time and determined without regard to any change of its taxable year required under paragraph (a) of this section), then on or before such due date such subsidiary shall file a separate return either for the portion of its taxable year for which its income would not be included in a consolidated return if such a return were filed, or for its complete taxable year. However, if a separate return is filed for such portion of its taxable year and the group subsequently does not file a consolidated return, such subsidiary corporation shall file a substituted return for its complete taxable year not later than the due date (including extensions of time) prescribed for the filing of the common parent's return. On the other hand, if the return is filed for the subsidiary's complete taxable year and the group later files a consolidated return, such subsidiary must file an amended return not later than the due date (including extensions of time) for the filing of the consolidated return of the group. Such amended return shall be for that portion of such subsidiary's taxable year which is not included in the consolidated return. If, under this subparagraph, a substituted return must be filed, then the return previously filed shall not be considered a return within the meaning of section 6011. If, under this subparagraph, a substituted or amended return must be filed, then, for purposes of sections 6513(a) and 6601(a), the last date prescribed for payment of tax shall be the due date (not including extensions of time) for the filing of the subsidiary's separate return (determined without regard to this subparagraph and without regard to any change of its taxable year required under paragraph (a) of this section).

(3) Examples. The provisions of this paragraph may be illustrated by the following examples:

Example (1). Corporation P, which filed a separate return for the calendar year 1966, acquires all of the stock of corporation S as of the close of December 31, 1966. Corporation S reports its income on the basis of a fiscal year ending March 31. On June 15, 1967, the due date for the filing of a separate return by S (assuming no extensions of time), a consolidated return has not been filed for the group (P and S). On such date S may either file a return for the period April 1, 1966, through December 31, 1966, or it may file a return for the complete fiscal year ending March 31, 1967. If S files a return for the short period ending December 31, 1966, and if the group elects not to file a consolidated return for the calendar year 1967, S, on or before March 15, 1968 (the due date of P's return, assuming no extensions of time), must file a substituted return for the complete fiscal year ending March 31, 1967, in lieu of the return previously filed for the short period. Interest is computed from June 15, 1967. If, however, S files a return for the complete fiscal year ending March 31, 1967, and the group elects to file a consolidated return for the calendar year 1967, then S must file an amended return covering the period from April 1, 1966, through December 31, 1966, in lieu of the return previously filed for the complete fiscal year. Interest is computed from June 15, 1967.

Example (2). Assume the same facts as in example (1) except that corporation P acquires all of the stock of corporation S at the close of September 30, 1967, and that P files a consolidated return for the group for 1967 on March 15, 1968 (not having obtained any extensions of time). Since a consolidated return has been filed on or before the due date (June 15, 1968) for the filing of the separate return for the taxable year ending March 31, 1968, the return of S for the short taxable year beginning April 1, 1967, and ending September 30, 1967, should be filed no later than March 15, 1968.

(d) Effective/applicability date. *(1) Taxable years of members of group effective date.* (i) In general. Paragraph (a) of this section applies to any original consolidated Federal income tax return due (without extensions) after July 20, 2007.

(ii) Prior law. For original consolidated Federal income tax returns due (without extensions) after April 25, 2006, and on or before July 20, 2007, see § 1.1502-76T as contained in 26 CFR part 1 in effect on April 1, 2007. For original consolidated Federal income tax returns due (without extensions) on or before April 25, 2006, see § 1.1502-76 as contained in 26 CFR part 1 in effect on April 1, 2006.

(2) Election to ratably allocate items effective date. (i) In general. Paragraph (b)(2)(ii)(D) of this section applies to any original consolidated Federal income tax return due (without extensions) after July 20, 2007.

(ii) Prior law. For original consolidated Federal income tax returns due (without extensions) after May 30, 2006, and on or before July 20, 2007, see § 1.1502-76T as contained in 26 CFR part 1 in effect on April 1, 2007. For original consolidated Federal income tax returns due (without extensions) on or before May 30, 2006, see § 1.1502-76 as contained in 26 CFR part 1 in effect on April 1, 2006.

T.D. 6894, 9/7/66, amend T.D. 7244, 12/29/72, T.D. 7246, 12/29/72, T.D. 8560, 8/12/94, T.D. 8842, 11/9/99, T.D. 8858, 1/5/2000, T.D. 8940, 2/12/2001, T.D. 9192, 3/21/2005, T.D. 9258, 4/24/2006, T.D. 9264, 5/26/2006, T.D. 9342, 7/19/2007.

§ 1.1502-77 Agent for the group.

(a) Scope of agency *(1) In general* (i) Common parent. Except as provided in paragraphs (a)(3) and (6) of this section, the common parent (or a substitute agent described in paragraph (a)(1)(ii) of this section) for a consolidated return year is the sole agent (agent for the group) that is authorized to act in its own name with respect to all matters relating to the tax liability for that consolidated return year, for—

(A) Each member in the group; and

(B) Any successor (see paragraph (a)(1)(iii) of this section) of a member.

(ii) Substitute agents. For purposes of this section, any corporation designated as a substitute agent pursuant to paragraph (d) of this section to replace the common parent or a previously designated substitute agent acts as agent for the group to the same extent and subject to the same limitations as are applicable to the common parent, and any reference in this section to the common parent includes any such substitute agent.

(iii) Successor. For purposes of this section only, the term successor means an individual or entity (including a disregarded entity) that is primarily liable, pursuant to applicable law (including, for example, by operation of a state or Federal merger statute), for the tax liability of a member of the group. Such determination is made without regard to § 1.1502-1(f)(4) or 1.1502-6(a). (For inclusion of a successor in references to a subsidiary or member, see paragraph (c)(2) of this section.)

(iv) Disregarded entity. If a subsidiary of a group becomes, or its successor is or becomes, a disregarded entity for Federal tax purposes, the common parent continues to serve as the agent with respect to that subsidiary's tax liability under § 1.1502-6 for consolidated return years during which it was included in the group, even though the entity generally is not treated as a person separate from its owner for Federal tax purposes.

(v) Transferee liability. For purposes of assessing, paying and collecting transferee liability, any exercise of or reliance on the common parent's agency authority pursuant to this section is binding on a transferee (or subsequent transferees) of a member, regardless of whether the member's existence terminates prior to such exercise or reliance.

(vi) Purported common parent. If any corporation files a consolidated return purporting to be the common parent of a consolidated group but is subsequently determined not to have been the common parent of the claimed group, that corporation is treated, to the extent necessary to avoid prejudice to the Commissioner, as if it were the common parent.

(2) Examples of matters subject to agency. With respect to any consolidated return year for which it is the common parent—

(i) The common parent makes any election (or similar choice of a permissible option) that is available to a subsidiary in the computation of its separate taxable income, and any change in an election (or similar choice of a permissible option) previously made by or for a subsidiary, including, for example, a request to change a subsidiary's method or period of accounting;

(ii) All correspondence concerning the income tax liability for the consolidated return year is carried on directly with the common parent;

(iii) The common parent files for all extensions of time, including extensions of time for payment of tax under section 6164, and any extension so filed is considered as having been filed by each member;

(iv) The common parent gives waivers, gives bonds, and executes closing agreements, offers in compromise, and all other documents, and any waiver or bond so given, or agreement, offer in compromise, or any other document so executed, is considered as having also been given or executed by each member;

(v) The common parent files claims for refund, and any refund is made directly to and in the name of the common parent and discharges any liability of the Government to any member with respect to such refund;

(vi) The common parent takes any action on behalf of a member of the group with respect to a foreign corporation, for example, elections by, and changes to the method of accounting of, a controlled foreign corporation in accordance with § 1.964-1(c)(3);

(vii) Notices of claim disallowance are mailed only to the common parent, and the mailing to the common parent is considered as a mailing to each member;

(viii) Notices of deficiencies are mailed only to the common parent (except as provided in paragraph (b) of this section), and the mailing to the common parent is considered as a mailing to each member;

(ix) Notices of final partnership administrative adjustment under section 6223 with respect to any partnership in which a member of the group is a partner may be mailed to the common parent, and, if so, the mailing to the common parent is considered as a mailing to each member that is a partner entitled to receive such notice (for other rules regarding partnership proceedings, see paragraphs (a)(3)(v) and (a)(6)(iii) of this section);

(x) The common parent files petitions and conducts proceedings before the United States Tax Court, and any such petition is considered as also having been filed by each member;

(xi) Any assessment of tax may be made in the name of the common parent, and an assessment naming the common parent is considered as an assessment with respect to each member; and

(xii) Notice and demand for payment of taxes is given only to the common parent, and such notice and demand is considered as a notice and demand to each member.

(3) Matters reserved to subsidiaries. Except as provided in this paragraph (a)(3) and paragraph (a)(6) of this section, no subsidiary has authority to act for or to represent itself in any matter related to the tax liability for the consolidated return year. The following matters, however, are reserved exclusively to each subsidiary—

(i) The making of the consent required by § 1.1502-75(a)(1);

(ii) Any action with respect to the subsidiary's liability for a federal tax other than the income tax imposed by chapter 1 of the Internal Revenue Code (including, for example, employment taxes under chapters 21 through 25 of the Internal Revenue Code, and miscellaneous excise taxes under chapters 31 through 47 of the Internal Revenue Code);

(iii) The making of an election under section 936(e);

(iv) The making of an election to be treated as a DISC under § 1.992-2; and

(v) Any actions by a subsidiary acting as tax matters partner under sections 6221 through 6234 and the accompanying regulations (but see paragraph (a)(2)(ix) of this section regarding the mailing of a final partnership administrative adjustment to the common parent).

(4) Term of agency (i) In general. Except as provided in paragraph (a)(4)(iii) of this section, the common parent for the consolidated return year remains the agent for the group with respect to that year until the common parent's existence terminates, regardless of whether one or more subsidiaries in that year cease to be members of the group, whether the group files a consolidated return for any subsequent year, whether the common parent ceases to be the common parent or a member of the group in any subsequent year, or whether the group continues pursuant to § 1.1502-75(d) with a new common parent in any subsequent year.

(ii) Replacement of substitute agent designated by Commissioner. If the Commissioner replaces a previously designated substitute agent pursuant to paragraph (d)(3)(ii) of this section, the replaced substitute agent ceases to be the agent after the Commissioner designates another substitute agent.

(iii) New common parent after a group structure change. If the group continues in existence with a new common parent pursuant to § 1.1502-75(d) during a consolidated return year, the common parent at the beginning of the year is the agent for the group through the date of the § 1.1502-75(d) transaction, and the new common parent becomes the agent for the group beginning the day after the transaction, at which time it becomes the agent for the group with respect to the entire consolidated return year (including the period through the date of the transaction) and the former common parent is no longer the agent for that year.

(5) Identifying members in notice of a lien. Notwithstanding any other provisions of this paragraph (a), any notice of a lien, any levy or any other proceeding to collect the amount of any assessment, after the assessment has been made, must name the entity from which such collection is to be made.

(6) Direct dealing with a member. (i) Several liability. The Commissioner may, upon issuing to the common parent written notice that expressly invokes the authority of this provision, deal directly with any member of the group with respect to its liability under § 1.1502-6 for the consolidated tax of the group, in which event such member has sole authority to act for itself with respect to that liability. However, if the Commissioner believes or has reason to believe that the existence of the common parent has terminated, he may, if he deems it advisable, deal directly with any member with respect to that member's liability under § 1.1502-6 without giving the notice required by this provision.

(ii) Information requests. The Commissioner may, upon informing the common parent, request information relevant to the consolidated tax liability from any member of the group. However, if the Commissioner believes or has reason to believe that the existence of the common parent has terminated, he may request such information from any member of the group without informing the common parent.

(iii) Members as partners in partnerships. The Commissioner generally will deal directly with any member in its capacity as a partner of a partnership that is subject to the provisions of sections 6221 through 6234 and the accompanying regulations (but see paragraph (a)(2)(ix) of this section regarding the mailing of a final partnership administrative adjustment to the common parent). However, if requested to do so in accordance with the provisions of § 301.6223(c)-1(b) of this chapter, the Commissioner may deal with the common parent as agent for such member on any matter related to the partnership, except in regards to a settlement under section 6224(c) and except to the extent the member acts as tax matters partner of the partnership.

(b) Copy of notice of deficiency to entity that has ceased to be a member of the group. An entity that ceases to be a member of the group during or after a consolidated return year may file a written notice of that fact with the Commissioner and request a copy of any notice of deficiency with respect to the tax for a consolidated return year during which the entity was a member, or a copy of any notice and demand for payment of such deficiency, or both. Such filing does not limit the scope of the agency of the common parent provided for in paragraph (a) of this section. Any failure by the Commissioner to comply with such request does not limit an entity's tax liability under § 1.1502-6. For purposes of this paragraph (b), references to an entity include a successor of such entity.

(c) References to member or subsidiary. For purposes of this section, all references to a member or subsidiary for a consolidated return year include—

(1) Each corporation that was a member of the group during any part of such year (except that any reference to a subsidiary does not include the common parent);

(2) Except as indicated otherwise, a successor (as defined in paragraph (a)(1)(iii) of this section) of any corporation described in paragraph (c)(1) of this section; and

(3) Each corporation whose income was included in the consolidated return for such year, notwithstanding that the tax liability of such corporation should have been computed on the basis of a separate return, or as a member of another consolidated group, under the provisions of § 1.1502-75.

(d) Termination of common parent. *(1) Designation of substitute agent by common parent.* (i) If the common parent's existence terminates, it may designate a substitute agent for the group and notify the Commissioner, as provided in this paragraph (d)(1).

(A) Subject to the Commissioner's approval under paragraph (d)(1)(ii) of this section, before the common parent's existence terminates, the common parent may designate, for each consolidated return year for which it is the common parent and for which the period of limitations either for assessment, for collection after assessment, or for claiming a credit or refund has not expired, one of the following to act as substitute agent in its place—

(1) Any corporation that was a member of the group during any part of the consolidated return year and, except as provided in paragraph (e)(3)(ii) of this section, has not subsequently been disregarded as an entity separate from its owner or reclassified as a partnership for Federal tax purposes; or

(2) Any successor (as defined in paragraph (a)(1)(iii) of this section) of such a corporation or of the common parent that is a domestic corporation (and, except as provided in paragraph (e)(3)(ii) of this section, is not disregarded as an entity separate from its owner or classified as a partnership for Federal tax purposes), including a corporation that will become a successor at the time that the common parent's existence terminates.

(B) The common parent must notify the Commissioner in writing (under procedures prescribed by the Commissioner) of the designation and provide the following—

(1) An agreement executed by the designated corporation agreeing to serve as the group's substitute agent; and

(2) If the designated corporation was not itself a member of the group during the consolidated return year (because the designated corporation is a successor of a member of the group for the consolidated return year), a statement by the designated corporation acknowledging that it is or will be primarily liable for the consolidated tax as a successor of a member.

(ii) A designation under paragraph (d)(1)(i)(A) of this section does not apply unless and until it is approved by the Commissioner. The Commissioner's approval of such a designation is not effective before the existence of the common parent terminates.

(2) Default substitute agent. If the common parent fails to designate a substitute agent for the group before its existence terminates and if the common parent has a single successor that is a domestic corporation, such successor becomes the substitute agent for the group upon termination of the common parent's existence. However, see paragraph (d)(4) of this section regarding the consequences of the successor's failure to notify the Commissioner of its status as default substitute agent in accordance with procedures established by the Commissioner.

(3) Designation by the Commissioner. (i) In the event the common parent's existence terminates and no designation is made and approved under paragraph (d)(1) of this section and the Commissioner believes or has reason to believe that there is no successor of the common parent that satisfies the requirements of paragraph (d)(2) of this section (or the Commissioner believes or has reason to believe there is such a successor but has no last known address on file for such successor), the Commissioner may, at any time, with or without a request from any member of the group, designate a corporation described in paragraph (d)(1)(i)(A) of this section to act as the substitute agent. The Commissioner will notify the designated substitute agent in writing of its designation, and the designation is effective upon receipt by the designated substitute agent of such notice. The designated substitute agent must give notice of the designation to each corporation

that was a member of the group during any part of the consolidated return year, but a failure by the designated substitute agent to notify any such member of the group does not invalidate the designation.

(ii) At the request of any member, the Commissioner may, but is not required to, replace a substitute agent previously designated under paragraph (d)(3)(i) of this section with another corporation described in paragraph (d)(1)(i)(A) of this section.

(4) Absence of designation or notification of default substitute agent. Until a designation of a substitute agent for the group under paragraph (d)(1) of this section has become effective, the Commissioner has received notification in accordance with procedures established by the Commissioner that a successor qualifying under paragraph (d)(2) of this section has become the substitute agent by default, or the Commissioner has designated a substitute agent under paragraph (d)(3) of this section—

(i) Any notice of deficiency or other communication mailed to the common parent, even if no longer in existence, is considered as having been properly mailed to the agent for the group; and

(ii) The Commissioner is not required to act on any communication (including, for example, a claim for refund) submitted on behalf of the group by any person other than the common parent (including a successor of the common parent qualifying as a default substitute agent under paragraph (d)(2) of this section).

(e) Termination of a corporation's existence. *(1) In general.* For purposes of paragraphs (a)(1)(v), (a)(4)(i), (d), and (j) of this section, the existence of a corporation is deemed to terminate if—

(i) Its existence terminates under applicable law; or

(ii) Except as provided in paragraph (e)(3) of this section, it becomes, for Federal tax purposes, either—

(A) An entity that is disregarded as an entity separate from its owner; or

(B) An entity that is reclassified as a partnership.

(2) Purported agency. If the existence of the agent for the group terminates under circumstances described in paragraph (e)(1)(ii) of this section, until the Commissioner has approved the designation of a substitute agent for the group pursuant to paragraph (d)(1) of this section or the Commissioner designates a substitute agent and notifies the designated substitute agent pursuant to paragraph (d)(3) of this section, any post-termination action by that purported agent on behalf of the group has the same effect, to the extent necessary to avoid prejudice to the Commissioner, as if the agent's corporate existence had not terminated.

(3) Exceptions where no eligible corporation exists. (i) For purposes of the common parent's term as agent under paragraph (a)(4)(i) of this section and the term as agent of the substitute agent designated under paragraph (d) of this section, if a corporation either becomes disregarded as an entity separate from its owner or is reclassified as a partnership for Federal tax purposes, its existence is not deemed to terminate if the effect of such termination would be that no corporation remains eligible to serve as the substitute agent for the group's consolidated return year.

(ii) Similarly, for purposes of paragraph (d) of this section, an entity that is either disregarded as an entity separate from its owner or reclassified as a partnership for Federal tax purposes is not precluded from designation as a substitute agent merely because of such classification if the effect of the inability to make such designation would be that no corporation remains eligible to serve as the substitute agent for the group's consolidated return year.

(iii) Any entity described in paragraphs (e)(3)(i) or (ii) of this section that remains or becomes the agent for the group is treated as a corporation for purposes of this section.

(4) Exception for section 338 transactions. Notwithstanding section 338(a)(2), a target corporation for which an election is made under section 338 is not deemed to terminate for purposes of this section.

(f) Examples. The following examples illustrate the principles of this section. Unless otherwise indicated, each example addresses the question of which corporation is the proper party to execute a consent to waive the statute of limitations for Years 1 and 2 or the more general question of which corporation may be designated as a substitute agent for the group for Years 1 and 2. In each example, as of January 1 of Year 1, the P group consists of P and its two subsidiaries, S and S-1. P, as the common parent of the P group, files consolidated returns for the P group in Years 1 and 2. On January 1 of Year 1, domestic corporations S-2, U, V, W, W-1, X, Y, Z and Z-1 are not related to P or the members of the P group. All corporations are calendar year taxpayers. For none of the tax years at issue does the Commissioner exercise the authority under paragraph (a)(6) of this section to deal with any member separately. Any surviving corporation in a merger is a successor as described in paragraph (a)(1)(iii) of this section. Any notification to the Commissioner of the designation of the P group's substitute agent also contains a statement signed on behalf of the designated agent that it agrees to act as the group's substitute agent and, in the case of a successor, that it is primarily liable as a successor of a member. The examples are as follows:

Example (1). Disposition of all group members. On December 31 of Year 1, P sells all the stock of S-1 to X. On December 31 of Year 2, P distributes all the stock of S to P's shareholders. P files a separate return for Year 3. Although P is no longer a common parent after Year 2, P remains the agent for the P group for Years 1 and 2. For as long as P remains in existence, only P may execute a waiver of the period of limitations on assessment on behalf of the group for Years 1 and 2.

Example (2). Acquisition of common parent by another group. The facts are the same as in Example 1, except on January 1 of Year 3, all of the outstanding stock of P is acquired by Y. P thereafter joins in the Y group consolidated return as a member of Y group. Although P is a member of Y group in Year 3, P remains the agent for the P group for Years 1 and 2. For as long as P remains in existence, only P may execute a waiver of the period of limitations on assessment on behalf of the P group for Years 1 and 2.

Example (3). Merger of common parent—designation of remaining member as substitute agent. On December 31 of Year 1, P sells all the stock of S-1 to X. On July 1 of Year 2, P acquires all the stock of S-2. On November 30 of Year 2, P distributes all the stock of S to P's shareholders. On January 1 of Year 3, P merges into Y corporation. Just before the merger, P notifies the Commissioner in writing of the planned merger and of its designation of S as the substitute agent for the P group for Years 1 and 2. S is the only member that P can designate as the substitute agent for both Years 1 and 2 because it is the only subsidiary that was a member of the P group during part of both years. Although S-2 is the only remaining subsidiary of the P group when P merges into Y, S-2 was a member of the P group only in

Year 2. For that reason, S-2 cannot be the substitute agent for the P group for Year 1. Alternatively, P could designate a different substitute agent for each year, selecting S or S-1 as the substitute agent for Year 1, and S or S-2 as the substitute agent for Year 2. P could also designate its successor Y as the substitute agent for both Years 1 and 2.

Example (4). Forward triangular merger of common parent. On January 1 of Year 3, P merges with and into Z-1, a subsidiary of Z, in a forward triangular merger described in section 368(a)(1)(A) and (a)(2)(D). The transaction constitutes a reverse acquisition under § 1.1502-75(d)(3)(i) because P's shareholders receive more than 50% of Z's stock in exchange for all of P's stock. Just before the merger, P notifies the Commissioner in writing of the planned merger and its designation of Z-1, the corporation that will survive the planned merger, as the substitute agent of the P group for Years 1 and 2. Because Z-1 will be P's successor (within the meaning of paragraph (a)(1) of this section) after the planned merger, P may designate Z-1 as the substitute agent for the P group for Years 1 and 2, pursuant to paragraph (d)(1) of this section. Alternatively, P could have designated S or S-1 as the substitute agent for the P group for Years 1 and 2. Although Z is the new common parent of the P group, which continues pursuant to § 1.1502-75(d)(3)(i), P may not designate Z as the substitute agent for Years 1 and 2 because Z was not a member of the group during any part of Years 1 or 2 and is not a successor of P or any other member of P group.

Example (5). Reverse triangular merger of common parent. On March 1 of Year 3, W-1, a subsidiary of W, merges into P, in a reverse triangular merger described in section 368(a)(1)(A) and (a)(2)(E). P survives the merger with W-1. The transaction constitutes a reverse acquisition under § 1.1502-75(d)(3)(i) because P's shareholders receive more than 50% of W's stock in exchange for all of P's stock. Under paragraph (a) of this section, P remains the agent for the P group for Years 1 and 2, even though the P group continues with W as its new common parent pursuant to Sec. 1.1502-75(d)(3)(i). Because the transaction constitutes a reverse acquisition, the P group is treated as remaining in existence with W as its common parent. Before March 2 of Year 3, P is the agent for the P group for Year 3. Beginning on March 2 of Year 3, W becomes the agent for the P group with respect to all of Year 3 (including the period through March 1) and subsequent consolidated return years. For as long as P remains in existence, P remains the agent of the P group under paragraph (a) of this section for Years 1 and 2, and therefore only P may execute a waiver of the period of limitations on assessment on behalf of the P group for Years 1 and 2.

Example (6). Reverse triangular merger of common parent-subsequent spinoff of common parent. The facts are the same as in Example 5, except that on April 1 of Year 4, in a transaction unrelated to the Year 3 reverse acquisition, P distributes the stock of its subsidiaries S and S-1 to W, and W then distributes the stock of P to the W shareholders. Beginning on March 2 of Year 3, W becomes the agent for the P group with respect to Year 3 (including the period through March 1) and subsequent consolidated return years. Although P is no longer a member of the P group after the Year 4 spinoff, P remains the agent for the P group under paragraph (a) of this section for Years 1 and 2. Thus, for as long as P remains in existence, only P may execute a waiver of the period of limitations on assessment on behalf of the P group for Years 1 and 2.

Example (7). Qualified stock purchase and section 338 election. On March 31 of Year 2, V purchases the stock of P in a qualified stock purchase (within the meaning of section 338(d)(3)), and V makes a timely election pursuant to section 338(g) with respect to P. Although section 338(a)(2) provides that P is treated as a new corporation as of the beginning of the day after the acquisition date for purposes of subtitle A, paragraph (e)(4) of this section provides that P's existence is not deemed to terminate for purposes of this section notwithstanding the general rule of section 338(a)(2). Therefore, the election under section 338(g) does not result in a termination of P under paragraph (e) of this section, and new P remains the agent of the P group for Year 1 and the period ending March 31 of Year 2 (short Year 2). For as long as new P remains in existence, only new P may execute a waiver of the period of limitations on assessment on behalf of the P group for Year 1 and short Year 2.

Example (8). Fraudulent conveyance of assets. On March 15 of Year 2, P files a consolidated return that includes the income of S and S-1 for Year 1. On December 1 of Year 2, S-1 transfers assets having a fair market value of $100x to U in exchange for $10x. This transfer of assets for less than fair market value constitutes a fraudulent conveyance under applicable state law. On March 1 of Year 5, P executes a waiver extending to December 31 of Year 6 the period of limitations on assessment with respect to the group's Year 1 consolidated return. On February 1 of Year 6, the Commissioner issues a notice of deficiency to P asserting a deficiency of $30x for the P group's Year 1 consolidated tax liability. P does not file a petition for redetermination in the Tax Court, and the Commissioner makes a timely assessment against the P group. P, S and S-1 are all insolvent and are unable to pay the deficiency. On February 1 of Year 8, the Commissioner sends a notice of transferee liability to U, which does not file a petition in the Tax Court. On August 1 of Year 8, the Commissioner assesses the amount of the P group's deficiency against U. Under section 6901(c), the Commissioner may assess U's transferee liability within one year after the expiration of the period of limitations against the transferor S-1. By operation of section 6213(a) and 6503(a), the issuance of the notice of deficiency to P and the expiration of the 90-day period for filing a petition in the Tax Court have the effect of further extending by 150 days the P group's limitations period on assessment from the previously extended date of December 31 of Year 6 to May 30 of Year 7. Pursuant to paragraph (a)(1)(v) of this section, the waiver executed by P on March 1 of Year 5 to extend the period of limitations on assessment to December 31 of Year 6 and the further extension of the P group's limitations period to May 30 of Year 7 (by operation of sections 6213(a) and 6503(a)) have the derivative effect of extending the period of limitations on assessment of U's transferee liability to May 30 of Year 8. By operation of section 6901(f), the issuance of the notice of transferee liability to U and the expiration of the 90-day period for filing a petition in the Tax Court have the effect of further extending the limitations period on assessment of U's liability as a transferee by 150 days, from May 30 of Year 8 to October 27 of Year 8. Accordingly, the Commissioner may send a notice of transferee liability to U at any time on or before May 30 of Year 8 and assess the unpaid liability against U at any time on or before October 27 of Year 8. The result would be the same even if S-1 ceased to exist before March 1 of Year 5, the date P executed the waiver.

(g) Cross-reference. For further rules applicable to groups that include insolvent financial institutions, see § 301.6402-7 of this chapter.

(h) Effective date. *(1) Application.*

(i) In general. This section applies with respect to taxable years beginning on or after June 28, 2002.

(ii) Election to apply for prior taxable years. Notwithstanding paragraphs (h)(1)(i) and (h)(2) of this section, the common parent may elect to apply paragraph (d)(1) of this section in lieu of § 1.1502-77A(d) in designating a substitute agent for taxable years beginning before June 28, 2002. The common parent makes such an election by expressly referring to the election under this paragraph (h)(1)(ii) in notifying the Commissioner of the designation of the substitute agent. Once made, such election applies to any subsequent designation of a substitute agent for the consolidated return year(s) subject to the election.

(2) Prior law. For taxable years beginning before June 28, 2002, see § 1.1502-77A.

(3) Designation of a domestic substitute agent. (i) In general. The provisions of paragraphs (e)(1) and (j) of this section apply to taxable years for which the consolidated Federal income tax return is due (without extensions) after July 23, 2007.

(ii) Prior law. For taxable years for which the consolidated Federal income tax return is due (without extensions) on or before July 23, 2007, see § 1.1502-77(e)(1) as contained in the 26 CFR part 1 edition revised as of April 1, 2007. For taxable years for which the consolidated Federal income tax return is due (without extensions) after March 14, 2006, and on or before July 23, 2007, see § 1.1502-77T as contained in the 26 CFR part 1 edition revised as of April 1, 2007.

(i) [Reserved]

(j) Designation by Commissioner if common parent is treated as a domestic corporation under section 7874 or section 953(d). *(1) In general.* If the common parent is an entity created or organized under the law of a foreign country and is treated as a domestic corporation by reason of section 7874 (or regulations under that section) or a section 953(d) election (a foreign common parent), the Commissioner may at any time, with or without a request from any member of the group, designate another member of the group to act as the agent for the group (a domestic substitute agent) for any taxable year for which the consolidated Federal income tax return is due (without extensions) after July 23, 2007, and the foreign common parent would otherwise be the agent for the group. For each such year, the domestic substitute agent will be the sole agent for the group even though the foreign common parent remains in existence. The foreign common parent ceases to be the agent for the group when the Commissioner's designation of a domestic substitute agent becomes effective. The Commissioner may designate a domestic substitute agent for the term of a single taxable year, multiple years, or on a continuing basis.

(2) Domestic substitute agent. The domestic substitute agent, by designation or by succession, shall be a domestic corporation described in paragraph (d)(1)(i)(A) of this section (determined without regard to section 7874, a section 953(d) election or section 1504(d)).

(3) Designation by the Commissioner. The Commissioner will notify the domestic substitute agent in writing by mail or faxed transmission of the designation. The domestic substitute agent's designation is effective on the earliest of the 14th day following the date of a mailing, the 4th day following a faxed transmission, or the date the Commissioner receives written confirmation of the designation by a duly authorized officer of the domestic substitute agent (within the meaning of section 6062). The domestic substitute agent must give notice of its designation to the foreign common parent and each corporation that was a member of the group during any part of any consolidated return year for which the domestic substitute agent will be the agent. A failure of the domestic substitute agent to notify the foreign common parent or any member of the group does not invalidate the designation. The Commissioner will send a copy of the notification to the foreign common parent, and if applicable, to any domestic substitute agent the designation replaces; a failure to send a copy of the notification does not invalidate the designation.

(4) Term of agency. (i) Taxable years for which domestic substitute agent is the agent. If the Commissioner designates a domestic substitute agent for one or more taxable years, unless the designation is expressly limited to such term, such domestic substitute agent will continue as the group's sole agent for subsequent taxable years until the domestic substitute agent ceases to be a member of the continuing group, is replaced by a new domestic common parent (as provided in paragraph (j)(4)(iv)(A) of this section), is replaced by the Commissioner, or is replaced by a default substitute agent (as provided in paragraph (j)(5)(ii) of this section). If during the course of a consolidated return year the domestic substitute agent ceases to be a member of the continuing group or is replaced, it shall no longer act as agent for such taxable year or subsequent taxable years in any matter.

(ii) Continuing agency for prior taxable years. Unless replaced by a default substitute agent (as provided in paragraph (j)(5)(ii) of this section) or by the Commissioner, the domestic substitute agent at the end of a taxable year of the group will remain the agent for such year until its existence terminates, even if the group subsequently ceases to exist or the domestic substitute agent subsequently ceases to be a member of the group.

(iii) Replacement of a § 1.1502-77(d)(1) agent. If, pursuant to paragraph (d)(1) of this section, the common parent of the group designates a foreign common parent as the agent for the group for any taxable year, the Commissioner may, at any time, designate a domestic substitute agent to replace the foreign common parent, even if the Commissioner approved the terminating common parent's designation.

(iv) Group continues with a new common parent. (A) Year the new common parent becomes the common parent. If the group has a domestic substitute agent and the group continues in existence with a new common parent during a consolidated return year, and such new common parent is a domestic corporation (determined without regard to section 7874 or a section 953(d) election), the domestic substitute agent at the beginning of the year is the agent for the group through the date of the transaction in which the new common parent becomes the common parent, and the new common parent becomes the agent for the group beginning the day after the transaction, at which time it becomes the agent for the group with respect to the entire consolidated return year (including the period through the date of the transaction) and the former domestic substitute agent will no longer be the agent for the group for that year.

(B) Years preceding the year the new common parent becomes the common parent. If after the Commissioner's designation of a domestic substitute agent the group remains in existence with a new common parent, and such new common parent is a domestic corporation (determined without regard to section 7874 or a section 953(d) election), the

Commissioner may designate the new common parent as the sole agent for the group for any of the group's prior taxable years (for which the consolidated Federal income tax return is due (without extensions) after July 23, 2007) in which the new common parent was a member of the group. For this purpose, the new common parent is treated as having been a member of the group for any taxable year it is primarily liable for the group's income tax liability.

(v) Replacement of domestic substitute agent by the Commissioner. The Commissioner may at any time, with or without a request from any member of the group, designate a replacement for a domestic substitute agent (or a successor to such agent).

(5) Deemed § 1.1502-77(d) designation. (i) In general. If the Commissioner designates a domestic substitute agent under this paragraph (j), it will be treated as a designation of a substitute agent under paragraph (d) of this section.

(ii) Default substitute agent. If the domestic substitute agent's existence terminates and it has a single successor that is a domestic corporation (without regard to section 269B) that is eligible to be a domestic substitute agent, such successor becomes the domestic substitute agent and is treated as a default substitute agent under paragraph (d)(2) of this section. See paragraph (d)(4) of this section regarding the consequences of the successor's failure to notify the Commissioner of its status as a default substitute agent. The default substitute agent shall use procedures in section 9 of Rev. Proc. 2002-43 (2002-2 CB 99) or a corresponding provision of a successor revenue procedure for notification. (See § 601.601(d)(2)(ii)(b) of this chapter.)

(6) Request that IRS designate a domestic substitute agent. (i) Original designation. If the common parent of the group is a foreign common parent, and the IRS has not designated a domestic substitute agent, one or more members of the group may request the IRS to make a designation for taxable years for which the consolidated Federal income tax return is due (without extensions) after July 23, 2007. Such request is deemed to be a request under paragraph (d)(3)(i) of this section. Members of the group shall use the procedures in section 10 of Rev. Proc. 2002-43 (2002-2 CB 99) or a corresponding provision of a successor revenue procedure for this purpose. (See § 601.601(d)(2)(ii)(b) of this chapter.)

(ii) Request that IRS replace a previously designated substitute agent. If the IRS designates a domestic substitute agent pursuant to this paragraph (j), one or more members of the group may request that the IRS replace the designated domestic substitute agent with another member (or successor to another member). Such a request is deemed to be a request pursuant to paragraph (d)(3)(ii) of this section. Members of the group shall use the procedures in section 11 of Rev. Proc. 2002-43 (2002-2 CB 99) or a corresponding provision of a successor revenue procedure for this purpose. (See § 601.601(d)(2)(ii)(b) of this chapter.)

T.D. 9002, 6/27/2002, amend T.D. 9255, 3/9/2006, T.D. 9343, 7/20/2007.

§ 1.1502-77A Common parent agent for subsidiaries applicable for consolidated return years beginning before June 28, 2002.

(a) Scope of agency of common parent corporation. The common parent, for all purposes (other than the making of the consent required by paragraph (a)(1) of § 1.1502-75, the making of an election under section 936(e), the making of an election to be treated as a DISC under § 1.992-2, and a change of the annual accounting period pursuant to paragraph (b)(3)(ii) of § 1.991-1) shall be the sole agent for each subsidiary in the group, duly authorized to act in its own name in all matters relating to the tax liability for the consolidated return year. Except as provided in the preceding sentence, no subsidiary shall have authority to act for or to represent itself in any such matter. For example, any election available to a subsidiary corporation in the computation of its separate taxable income must be made by the common parent, as must any change in an election previously made by the subsidiary corporation; all correspondence will be carried on directly with the common parent; the common parent shall file for all extensions of time including extensions of time for payment of tax under section 6164; notices of deficiencies will be mailed only to the common parent, and the mailing to the common parent shall be considered as a mailing to each subsidiary in the group; notice and demand for payment of taxes will be given only to the common parent and such notice and demand will be considered as a notice and demand to each subsidiary; the common parent will file petitions and conduct proceedings before the Tax Court of the United States, and any such petition shall be considered as also having been filed by each such subsidiary. The common parent will file claims for refund or credit, and any refund will be made directly to and in the name of the common parent and will discharge any liability of the Government in respect thereof to any such subsidiary; and the common parent in its name will give waivers, give bonds, and execute closing agreements, offers in compromise, and all other documents, and any waiver or bond so given, or agreement, offer in compromise, or any other document so executed, shall be considered as having also been given or executed by each such subsidiary. Notwithstanding the provisions of this paragraph, any notice of deficiency, in respect of the tax for a consolidated return year, will name each corporation which was a member of the group during any part of such period (but a failure to include the name of any such member will not affect the validity of the notice of deficiency as to the other members); any notice and demand for payment will name each corporation which was a member of the group during any part of such period (but a failure to include the name of any such member will not affect the validity of the notice and demand as to the other members); and any levy, any notice of a lien, or any other proceeding to collect the amount of any assessment, after the assessment has been made, will name the corporation from which such collection is to be made. The provisions of this paragraph shall apply whether or not a consolidated return is made for any subsequent year, and whether or not one or more subsidiaries have become or have ceased to be members of the group at any time. Notwithstanding the provisions of this paragraph, the Commissioner may, upon notifying the common parent, deal directly with any member of the group in respect of its liability, in which event such member shall have full authority to act for itself.

(b) Notification of deficiency to corporation which has ceased to be a member of the group. If a subsidiary has ceased to be a member of the group and if such subsidiary files written notice of such cessation with the Commissioner, then the Commissioner upon request of such subsidiary will furnish it with a copy of any notice of deficiency in respect of the tax for a consolidated return year for which it was a member and a copy of any notice and demand for payment of such deficiency. The filing of such written notification and request by a corporation shall not have the effect of limiting the scope of the agency of the common parent provided for in paragraph (a) of this section and a failure by the Commissioner to comply with such written request shall not have the effect of limiting the tax liability of such corporation provided for in § 1.1502-6.

(c) Effect of waiver given by common parent. Unless the Commissioner agrees to the contrary, an agreement entered into by the common parent extending the time within which an assessment may be made or levy or proceeding in court begun in respect of the tax for a consolidated return year shall be applicable—

(1) To each corporation which was a member of the group during any part of such taxable year, and

(2) To each corporation the income of which was included in the consolidated return for such taxable year, notwithstanding that the tax liability of any such corporation is subsequently computed on the basis of a separate return under the provisions of § 1.1502-75.

(d) Effect of dissolution of common parent corporation. If the common parent corporation contemplates dissolution, or is about to be dissolved, or if for any other reason its existence is about to terminate, it shall forthwith notify the Commissioner of such fact and designate, subject to the approval of the Commissioner, another member to act as agent in its place to the same extent and subject to the same conditions and limitations as are applicable to the common parent. If the notice thus required is not given by the common parent, or the designation is not approved by the Commissioner, the remaining members may, subject to the approval of the Commissioner, designate another member to act as such agent, and notice of such designation shall be given to the Commissioner. Until a notice in writing designating a new agent has been approved by the Commissioner, any notice of deficiency or other communication mailed to the common parent shall be considered as having been properly mailed to the agent of the group; or, if the Commissioner has reason to believe that the existence of the common parent has terminated, he may, if he deems it advisable, deal directly with any member in respect of its liability.

(e) General rules. *(1) Scope.* This section applies if the corporation that is the common parent of the group ceases to be the common parent, whether or not the group remains in existence under § 1.1502-75(d).

(2) Notice of deficiency. A notice of deficiency mailed to any one or more corporations referred to in paragraph (a)(4) of this section is deemed for purposes of § 1.1502-77 to be mailed to the agent of the group. If the group has designated an agent that has been approved by the Commissioner under § 1.1502-77(d), a notice of deficiency shall be mailed to that designated agent in addition to any other corporation referred to in paragraph (a)(4) of this section. However, failure by the Commissioner to mail a notice of deficiency to that designated agent shall not invalidate the notice of deficiency mailed to any other corporation referred to in paragraph (a)(4) of this section.

(3) Waiver of statute of limitations. A waiver of the statute of limitations with respect to the group given by any one or more corporations referred to in paragraph (a)(4) of this section is deemed to be given by the agent of the group. *(4) Alternative agents.* The corporations referred to in paragraph (a)(2) and (3) of this section are—

(i) The common parent of the group for all or any part of the year to which the notice or waiver applies,

(ii) A successor to the former common parent in a transaction to which section 381(a) applies,

(iii) The agent designated by the group under § 1.1502-77(d), or

(iv) If the group remains in existence under § 1.1502-75(d)(2) or (3), the common parent of the group at the time the notice is mailed or the waiver given.

(f) Cross-reference. For further rules applicable to groups that include insolvent financial institutions, see § 301.6402-7 of this chapter.

(g) Effective date. This section applies to taxable years beginning before June 28, 2002, except paragraph (e) of this section applies to statutory notices and waivers of the statute of limitations for taxable years for which the due date (without extensions) of the consolidated return is after September 7, 1988, and which begin before June 28, 2002.

T.D. 6894, 9/7/66, amend T.D. 7323, 9/24/74, T.D. 7673, 2/7/80, T.D. 8226, 9/7/88, T.D. 8387, 12/30/91, T.D. 8446, 11/5/92, T.D. 9002, 6/27/2002.

§ 1.1502-78 Tentative carryback adjustments.

(a) General rule. If a group has a consolidated net operating loss, a consolidated net capital loss, or a consolidated unused business credit for any taxable year, then any application under section 6411 for a tentative carryback adjustment of the taxes for a consolidated return year or years preceding such year shall be made by the common parent corporation for the carryback year (or substitute agent designated under § 1.1502-77(d) for the carryback year) to the extent such loss or unused business credit is not apportioned to a corporation for a separate return year pursuant to § 1.1502-21(b), 1.1502-22(b), or 1.1502-79(c). In the case of the portion of a consolidated net operating loss or consolidated net capital loss or consolidated unused business credit to which the preceding sentence does not apply and that is to be carried back to a corporation that was not a member of a consolidated group in the carryback year, the corporation to which such loss or credit is attributable shall make any application under section 6411. In the case of a net capital loss or net operating loss or unused business credit arising in a separate return year that may be carried back to a consolidated return year, after taking into account the application of § 1.1502-21(b)(3)(ii)(B) with respect to any net operating loss arising in another consolidated group, the common parent for the carryback year (or substitute agent designated under § 1.1502-77(d) for the carryback year) shall make any application under section 6411.

(b) Special rules. *(1) Payment of refund.* Any refund allowable under an application referred to in paragraph (a) of this section shall be made directly to and in the name of the corporation filing the application, except that in all cases where a loss is deduced from the consolidated taxable income or a credit is allowed in computing the consolidated tax liability for a consolidated return year any refund shall be made directly to and in the name of the common parent corporation for the carryback year (or agent designated under § 1.1502-77(d) for the carryback year). The payment of any such refund shall discharge any liability of the Government with respect to such refund.

(2) Several liability. If a group filed a consolidated return for a taxable year for which there was an adjustment by reason of an application under section 6411, and if a deficiency is assessed against such group under section 6213(b)(3), then each member of such group shall be severally liable for such deficiency including any interest or penalty assessed in connection with such deficiency.

(3) Groups that include insolvent financial institutions. For further rules applicable to groups that include insolvent financial institutions, see § 301.6402-7 of this chapter.

(c) Examples. The provisions of paragraphs (a) and (b) of this section may be illustrated by the following examples:

Example (1). Corporations P, S, and S-1 filed a consolidated return for the calendar year 1966. P, S, and S-1 also filed a consolidated return for the calendar year 1969. The group incurred a consolidated net operating loss in 1969 attributable to S-1 which may be carried back to 1966 as a consolidated net operating loss carryback. If a tentative carryback adjustment is desired, P, the common parent for the carryback year, must file an application under section 6411 and any refund will be made to P.

Example (2). Assume the same facts as in example (1) except that P, S, and S-1 filed separate returns for the calendar year 1969, even though they were members of the same group for such year. S-1 incurred a net operating loss in 1969 which may be carried back to 1966. If a tentative carryback adjustment is desired, P must file an application under section 6411 and any refund from such application will be made to P.

Example (3). Corporations X, Y, and Z filed a consolidated return for the calendar year 1966. Z ceased to be a member of the group in 1967. Z filed a separate return for 1968 while X and Y filed a consolidated return for such year. The group incurred a consolidated net operating loss in 1968 attributable to Y, which may be carried back to 1966. Z also incurred a net operating loss for 1968 which may be carried back to 1966. If a tentative carryback adjustment is claimed with respect to the consolidated net operating loss, X, the common parent, must file an application under section 6411. If a tentative carryback adjustment is desired with respect to Z's loss, X must file an application. Any refunds attributable to either application will be made to X. If an assessment is made under section 6213(b)(3) to recover an excessive tentative allowance made with respect to calendar year 1966, X, Y, and Z are severally liable for such assessment.

Example (4). Corporations L and M filed a consolidated return for the calendar year 1966. Corporation N filed a separate return for such year. Later, N became a member of the group and filed a consolidated return with the group for the calendar year 1968. The group incurred a consolidated net operating loss in 1968 attributable to N which may be carried back to N's separate return for 1966. If a tentative carryback adjustment is desired, N must file an application under section 6411 and any refund will be made directly to N.

(d) Adjustments of overpayments of estimated income tax. If a group paid its estimated income tax on a consolidated basis, then any application under section 6425 for an adjustment of overpayment of estimated income tax shall be made by the common parent corporation. If the members of a group paid estimated income taxes on a separate basis, then any application under section 6425 shall be made by the member of the group which claims an overpayment on a separate basis. Any refund allowable under an application under section 6425 shall be made directly to and in the name of the corporation filing the application.

(e) Time for filing application. *(1) General rule.* The provisions of section 6411(a) apply to the filing of an application for a tentative carryback adjustment by a consolidated group.

(2) Special rule for new members. (i) New member. A new member is a corporation that, in the preceding taxable year, did not qualify as a member, as defined in § 1.1502-1(b), of the consolidated group that it now joins.

(ii) End of taxable year. Solely for the purpose of complying with the twelve-month requirement for making an application for a tentative carryback adjustment under section 6411(a), the separate return year of a qualified new member shall be treated as ending on the same date as the end of the current taxable year of the consolidated group that the qualified new member joins.

(iii) Qualified new member. A new member of a consolidated group qualifies for purposes of the provisions of this paragraph (e)(2) if, immediately prior to becoming a new member, either—

(A) It was the common parent of a consolidated group; or

(B) It was not required to join in the filing of a consolidated return.

(iv) Examples. The provisions of this paragraph (e)(2) may be illustrated by the following examples:

Example (1). Individual A owns 100 percent of the stock of X, a corporation that is not a member of a consolidated group and files separate tax returns on a calendar year basis. On January 31 of year 1, X becomes a member of the Y consolidated group, which also files returns on a calendar year basis. X is a qualified new member as defined in paragraph (e)(2)(iii)(B) of this section because, immediately prior to becoming a new member of the Y consolidated group, X was not required to join in the filing of a consolidated return. As a result of its becoming a new member of Group Y, X's separate return for the short taxable year (January 1 of year 1 through January 31 of year 1) is due September 15 of year 2 (with extensions). See § 1.1502-76(c). Group Y's consolidated return is also due September 15 of year 2 (with extensions). See § 1.1502-76(c). Solely for the purpose of complying with the twelve-month requirement for making an application for a tentative carryback adjustment under section 6411(a), X's taxable year for the separate return year is treated as ending on December 31 of year 1. X's application for a tentative carryback adjustment is therefore due on or before December 31 of year 2.

Example (2). Assume the same facts as in Example 1 except that immediately prior to becoming a new member of Group Y, X was a member of the Z consolidated group. Because X was required to join in the filing of the consolidated return for Group Z, X is not a qualified new member as defined in paragraph (e)(2)(iii) of this section. X's items for the one-month period will be included in the consolidated return for Group Z. Group Z's application for a tentative carryback adjustment, if any, continues to be due within 12 months of the end of its taxable year, which is not affected by X's change in status as a new member of Group Y.

(f) Effective date. *(1) In general.* This section applies to taxable years to which a loss or credit may be carried back and for which the due date (without extensions) of the original return is after June 28, 2002, except that the provisions of paragraph (e)(2) apply for applications by new members of consolidated groups for tentative carryback adjustments resulting from net operating losses, net capital losses, or unused business credits arising in separate return years of new members that begin on or after January 1, 2001.

(2) Prior law. For taxable years to which a loss or credit may be carried back and for which the due date (without extensions) of the original return is on or before June 28, 2002, see Sec. 1.1502-78 in effect prior to June 28, 2002, as contained in 26 CFR part 1 revised April 1, 2002.

T.D. 6894, 9/7/66, amend T.D. 7059, 9/16/70, T.D. 7246, 12/29/72, T.D. 8387, 12/20/91, T.D. 8446, 11/5/92, T.D. 8677, 6/26/96, T.D. 8823, 6/25/99, T.D. 8950, 6/21/2001, T.D. 9002, 6/27/2002.

§ 1.1502-79 Separate return years.

(a) Carryover and carryback of consolidated net operating losses to separate return years. For losses arising in consolidated return years beginning before January 1, 1997, see § 1.1502-79A(a). For later years, see § 1.1502-21(b).

(b) Carryover and carryback of consolidated net capital loss to separate return years. For losses arising in consolidated return years beginning before January 1, 1997, see § 1.1502-79A(b). For later years, see § 1.1502-22(b).

(c) Carryover and carryback of consolidated unused investment credit to separate return years. *(1) In general.* If a consolidated unused investment credit can be carried under the principles of section 46(b) and paragraph (b) of § 1.1502-3 to a separate return year of a corporation (or could have been so carried if such corporation were in existence) which was a member of the group in the year in which such unused credit arose, then the portion of such consolidated unused credit attributable to such corporation (as determined under subparagraph (2) of this paragraph) shall be apportioned to such corporation (and any successor to such corporation in a transaction to which section 381(a) applies) under the principles of § 1.1502-21(b) (or §§ 1.1502-79A(a)(1) and (2), as appropriate) of this section and shall be an investment credit carryover or carryback to such separate return year.

(2) Portion of consolidated unused investment credit attributable to a member. (i) *Investment credit carryback.*In the case of a consolidated unused credit which is an investment credit carryback, the portion of such consolidated unused credit attributable to a member of the group is an amount equal to such consolidated unused credit multiplied by a fraction, the numerator of which is the credit earned of such member for the consolidated unused credit year, and the denominator of which is the consolidated credit earned for such unused credit year.

(ii) Investment credit carryover. In the case of a consolidated unused credit which is an investment credit carryover, the portion of such consolidated unused credit attributable to a member of the group is an amount equal to such consolidated unused credit multiplied by a fraction, the numerator of which is the credit earned with respect to any section 38 property placed in service in the consolidated unused credit year and owned by such member (whether or not placed in service by such member) at the close of the last day as of which the taxable income of such member is included in a consolidated return filed by the group, and the denominator of which is the consolidated credit earned for such unused credit year.

(d) Carryover and carryback of consolidated unused foreign tax. *(1) In general.* If a consolidated unused foreign tax can be carried under the principles of section 904(d) and paragraph (e) of § 1.1502-4 to a separate return year of a corporation (or could have been so carried if such corporation were in existence) which was a member of the group in the year in which such unused foreign tax arose, then the portion of such consolidated unused foreign tax attributable to such corporation (as determined under subparagraph (2) of this paragraph) shall be apportioned to such corporation (and any successor to such corporation in a transaction to which section 381(a) applies) under the principles of § 1.1502-21(b) (or §§ 1.1502-79A(a)(1) and (2), as appropriate) and shall be deemed paid or accrued in such separate return year to the extent provided in section 904(d).

(2) Portion of consolidated unused foreign tax attributable to a member. The portion of a consolidated unused foreign tax for any year attributable to a member of a group is an amount equal to such consolidated unused foreign tax multiplied by a fraction, the numerator of which is the foreign taxes paid or accrued for such year (including those taxes deemed paid or accrued, other than by reason of section 904(d)) to each foreign country or possession (or to all foreign countries or possessions if the overall limitation is effective) by such member, and the denominator of which is the aggregate of all such taxes paid or accrued for such year (including those taxes deemed paid or accrued, other than by reason of section 904(d)) to each such foreign country or possession (or to all foreign countries or possessions if the overall limitation is effective) by all the members of the group.

(e) Carryover of consolidated excess charitable contributions to separate return years. *(1) In general.* If the consolidated excess charitable contributions for any taxable year can be carried under the principles of section 170(b)(2) and paragraph (b) of § 1.1502-24 to a separate return year of a corporation (or could have been so carried if such corporation were in existence) which was a member of the group in the year in which such excess contributions arose, then the portion of such consolidated excess charitable contributions attributable to such corporation (as determined under subparagraph (2) of this paragraph) shall be apportioned to such corporation (and any successor to such corporation in a transaction to which section 381(a) applies) under the principles of § 1.1502-21(b) (or §§ 1.1502-79A(a)(1) and (2), as appropriate) and shall be a charitable contribution carryover to such separate return year.

(2) Portion of consolidated excess charitable contributions attributable to a member. The portion of the consolidated excess charitable contributions attributable to a member of a group is an amount equal to such consolidated excess contributions multiplied by a fraction, the numerator of which is the charitable contributions paid by such member for the taxable year, and the denominator of which is the aggregate of all such charitable contributions paid for such year by all the members of the group.

T.D. 6894, 9/7/66, amend T.D. 7637, 8/6/79, T.D. 7728, 10/31/80, T.D. 8294, 3/9/90, T.D. 8319, 11/19/90, T.D. 8364, 9/13/91, T.D. 8597, 7/12/95, T.D. 8677, 6/26/96, T.D. 8823, 6/25/99.

§ 1.1502-79A Separate return years generally applicable for consolidated return years beginning before January 1, 1997.

(a) Carryover and carryback of consolidated net operating losses to separate return years. *(1) In general.* (i) If a consolidated net operating loss can be carried under the principles of section 172(b) and paragraph (b) of § 1.1502-21A to a separate return year of a corporation (or could have been so carried if such corporation were in existence) which was a member in the year in which such loss arose, then the portion of such consolidated net operating loss attributable to such corporation (as determined under subparagraph (3) of this paragraph) shall be apportioned to such corporation (and any successor to such corporation in a transaction to which section 381(a) applies) and shall be a net operating loss carryover or carryback to such separate return year; accordingly, such portion shall not be included in the consolidated net operating loss carryovers or carrybacks to the equivalent consolidated return year. Thus, for example, if a member filed a separate return for the third year preceding a consolidated return year in which a consolidated net operating loss was sustained and if any portion of such loss is apportioned to such member for such separate return year, such portion may not be carried back by the group to its third year preceding such consolidated return year.

(ii) If a corporation ceases to be a member during a consolidated return year, any consolidated net operating loss carryover from a prior taxable year must first be carried to such consolidated return year, notwithstanding that all or a portion of the consolidated net operating loss giving rise to the carryover is attributable to the corporation which ceases to be a member. To the extent not absorbed in such consolidated return year, the portion of the consolidated net operating loss attributable to the corporation ceasing to be a member shall then be carried to such corporation's first separate return year.

(iii) For rules permitting the reattribution of losses of a subsidiary to the common parent in the case of loss disallowance or basis reduction on the disposition or deconsolidation of stock of the subsidiary, see § 1.1502-20.

(2) Nonapportionment to certain members not in existence. Notwithstanding subparagraph (1) of this paragraph, the portion of a consolidated net operating loss attributable to a member shall not be apportioned to a prior separate return year for which such member was not in existence and shall be included in the consolidated net operating loss carrybacks to the equivalent consolidated return year of the group (or, if such equivalent year is a separate return year, then to such separate return year), provided that such member was a member of the group immediately after its organization.

(3) Portion of consolidated net operating loss attributable to a member. The portion of a consolidated net operating loss attributable to a member of a group is an amount equal to the consolidated net operating loss multiplied by a fraction, the numerator of which is the separate net operating loss of such corporation, and the denominator of which is the sum of the separate net operating losses of all members of the group in such year having such losses. For purposes of this subparagraph, the separate net operating loss of a member of the group shall be determined under § 1.1502-12 (except that no deduction shall be allowed under section 242), adjusted for the following items taken into account in the computation of the consolidated net operating loss:

(i) The portion of the consolidated dividends received deduction, the consolidated charitable contributions deductions, and the consolidated section 247 deduction, attributable to such member;

(ii) Such member's net capital gain (determined without regard to any net capital loss carryover attributable to such member);

(iii) Such member's net capital loss and section 1231 net loss, reduced by the portion of the consolidated net capital loss attributable to such member (as determined under paragraph (b)(2) if this section); and

(iv) The portion of any consolidated net capital loss carryover attributable to such member which is absorbed in the taxable year.

(4) Examples. The provisions of this paragraph may be illustrated by the following examples:

Example (1). (i) Corporation P was formed on January 1, 1966. P filed a separate return for the calendar year 1966. On March 15, 1967, P formed corporation S. P and S filed a consolidated return for 1967. On January 1, 1968, P purchased all the stock of corporation T, which had been formed in 1967 and had filed a separate return for its taxable year ending December 31, 1967.

(ii) P, S, and T join in the filing of a consolidated return for 1968, which return reflects a consolidated net operating loss of $11,000. $2,000 of such consolidated net operating loss is attributable to P, $3,000 to S, and $6,000 to T. Such apportionment of the consolidated net operating loss was made on the basis of the separate net operating losses of each member as determined under subparagraph (3) of this paragraph.

(iii) $5,000 of the 1968 consolidated net operating loss can be carried back to P's separate return for 1966. Such amount is the portion of the consolidated net operating loss attributable to P and S. Even though S was not in existence in 1966, the portion attributable to S can be carried back to P's separate return year, since S (unlike T) was a member of the group immediately after its organization. The 1968 consolidated net operating loss can be carried back against the group's income in 1967 except to the extent (i.e., $6,000) that it is apportioned to T for its 1967 separate return year and to the extent that it was absorbed in P's 1966 separate return year. The portion of the 1968 consolidated net operating loss attributable to T ($6,000) is a net operating loss carryback to its 1967 separate return.

Example (2). (i) Assume the same facts as in example (1). Assume further that on June 15, 1969, P sells all the stock of T to an outsider, that P and S file a consolidated return for 1969 (which includes the income of T for the period January 1, through June 15), and that T files a separate return for the period June 16 through December 31, 1969.

(ii) The 1968 consolidated net operating loss, to the extent not absorbed in prior years, must first be carried to the consolidated return year 1969. Any portion of the $6,000 amount attributable to T which is not absorbed in T's 1967 separate return year or in the 1969 consolidated return year shall then be carried to T's separate return year ending December 31, 1969.

(b) Carryover and carryback of consolidated net capital loss to separate return years. *(1) In general.* If a consolidated net capital loss can be carried under the principles of section 1212(a) and paragraph (b) of § 1.1502-22A to a separate return year of a corporation (or could have been so carried if such corporation were in existence) which was a member of the group in the year in which such consolidated net capital loss arose, then the portion of such consolidated net capital loss attributable to such corporation (as determined under subparagraph (2) of this paragraph) shall be apportioned to such corporation (and any successor to such corporation in a transaction to which section 381(a) applies) under the principles of paragraph (a)(1), (2) and (3) of this section and shall be a net capital loss carryback or carryover to such separate return year.

(2) Portion of consolidated net capital loss attributable to a member. The portion of a consolidated net capital loss attributable to a member of a group is an amount equal to such consolidated net capital loss multiplied by a fraction, the numerator of which is the net capital loss of such member, and the denominator of which is the sum of the net capital losses of those members of the group having net capital losses. For purposes of this subparagraph, the net capital loss of a member of the group shall be determined by taking into account the following:

(i) Such member's net capital gain or loss (determined without regard to any net capital loss carryover or carryback); and

(ii) Such member's section 1231 net loss, reduced by the portion of the consolidated section 1231 net loss attributable to such member.

(c) through (e) [Reserved]

(f) Effective date. Paragraphs (a) and (b) of this section apply to losses arising in consolidated return years to which § 1.1502-21T(g) does not apply. For this purpose net operating loss deductions, carryovers, and carrybacks arise in the year from which they are carried. See § 1.1502-21T(g) for effective dates of that section.

T.D. 8677, 6/26/96.

§ 1.1502-80 Applicability of other provisions of law.

(a) In general. *(1) Application of other provisions.* The Internal Revenue Code (Code), or other law, shall be applicable to the group to the extent the regulations do not exclude its application. To the extent not excluded, other rules operate in addition to, and may be modified by, these regulations. Thus, for example, in a transaction to which section 381(a) applies, the acquiring corporation will succeed to the tax attributes described in section 381(c). Furthermore, sections 269 and 482 apply for any consolidated return year. However, in a recognition transaction otherwise subject to section 1001, for example, the rules of section 1001 continue to apply, but may be modified by the intercompany transaction regulations under § 1.1502-13.

(2) No duplicative adjustments. Nothing in these regulations shall be interpreted or applied to require an adjustment, inclusion, or other item to the extent it would have the effect of duplicating any other adjustment, inclusion, or other item required under the Code or other rule of law, including other provisions of these regulations.

(3) Application of single-entity principles. If two or more adjustments, inclusions, or other items are subject to paragraph (a)(2) of this section, the determination of which adjustment, inclusion, or other item is treated as applied or taken into account is made by taking into account the purposes of the provisions and applying single-entity principles as appropriate.

(4) Effective/applicability dates. This paragraph (a) is applicable with respect to transactions and determinations on or after September 17, 2008.

(b) Non-applicability of section 304. Section 304 does not apply to any acquisition of stock of a corporation in an intercompany transaction or to any intercompany item from such transaction occurring on or after July 24, 1991.

(c) Deferral of section 165. *(1) General rule.* Subsidiary stock is not treated as worthless under section 165 until immediately before the earlier of the time—

(i) The stock is worthless within the meaning of § 1.1502-19(c)(1)(iii); or

(ii) The subsidiary for any reason ceases to be a member of the group.

(2) Cross reference. See § 1.1502-36 for additional rules relating to worthlessness of subsidiary stock on or after September 17, 2008.

(3) Effective/applicability date. This paragraph (c) applies to taxable years for which the original consolidated Federal income tax return is due (without extensions) after July 18, 2007. However, taxpayers may apply this paragraph (c) to taxable years beginning on or after January 1, 1995.

(d) Non-applicability of section 357(c). *(1) In general.* Section 357(c) does not apply to any transaction to which § 1.1502-13, § 1.1502-13T, § 1.1502-14, or § 1.1502-14T applies, if it occurs in a consolidated return year beginning on or after January 1, 1995. For example, P, S, and T are members of a consolidated group, P owns all of the stock of S and T with bases of $30 and $20, respectively, S has a $30 basis in its assets and $40 of liabilities, and S merges into T in a transaction described in section 368(a)(1)(A) (and in section 368(a)(1)(D)); section 357(c) does not apply to the merger, P's basis in T's stock increases to $50 ($30 plus $20), and T succeeds to S's $30 basis in the assets transferred subject to the $40 liability. Similarly, if S instead transferred its assets and liabilities to a newly formed subsidiary in a transaction to which section 351 applies, section 357(c) does not apply and S's basis in the subsidiary's stock is a $10 excess loss account. This paragraph (d) does not apply to a transaction if the transferor or transferee becomes a nonmember as part of the same plan or arrangement. The transferor (or transferee) is treated as becoming a nonmember once it is no longer a member of a consolidated group that includes the transferee (or transferor). For purposes of this paragraph (d), any reference to a transferor or transferee includes, as the context may require, a reference to a successor or predecessor.

(2) Prior period transactions. If, in a tax year beginning before January 1, 1995, a member's stock with an excess loss account is transferred in a transaction to which § 1.1502-13, § 1.1502-13T, § 1.1502-14, or § 1.1502-14T applies, paragraph (d)(1) of this section applies to the stock transfer to the extent that the income, gain, deduction, or loss (if any) is not taken into account in a tax year beginning before January 1, 1995. For example, if P, S, and T, are members of a consolidated group, T's stock has an excess loss account, and P transfers the T stock to S in 1993 in a transaction to which section 351 and § 1.1502-13 apply, section 357(c) applies to the transfer only to the extent P's gain is taken into account in tax years beginning before January 1, 1995.

(e) Non-applicability of section 163(e)(5). Section 163(e)(5) does not apply to any intercompany obligation (within the meaning of § 1.1502-13(g)) issued in a consolidated return year beginning on or after July 12, 1995.

(f) Non-applicability of section 1031. Section 1031 does not apply to any intercompany transaction occurring in consolidated return years beginning on or after July 12, 1995.

(g) Special rules for liquidations to which section 332 applies. Notwithstanding the general rule of section 381, if multiple members (distributee members) acquire assets of a corporation in a liquidation to which section 332 applies (regardless of whether any single member owns stock in the liquidating corporation meeting the requirements of section 1504(a)(2)), such members succeed to and take into account the items of the liquidating corporation (including items described in section 381(c), but excluding intercompany items under § 1.1502-13) as provided in this paragraph (g) to the extent not otherwise prohibited by any applicable provision of law. This paragraph (g) does not apply to the intercompany items of the liquidating corporation. See § 1.1502-13(j)(2)(ii).

(1) Income offset items and deferred income. Except as otherwise provided in this paragraph (g)(1), each distributee member succeeds to and takes into account the items of the liquidating corporation that could be used to offset the in-

come of the group or any member (including deferred deductions, net operating loss carryovers, and capital loss carryovers) (income offset items) to the extent that such items would have been reflected in investment adjustments to the stock of the liquidating corporation owned by such distributee member under § 1.1502-32(c) if, immediately prior to the liquidation, any stock of the liquidating corporation owned by nonmembers had been redeemed and then such items had been taken into account. However, each distributee member succeeds to the full amount of any deferred deduction or deferred income item attributable to the particular property or business operations distributed to such distributee in the liquidation to the extent that such item is not taken into account in the determination of the income or loss of the liquidating corporation with regard to the liquidation under chapter 1 of the Internal Revenue Code (Code). If the liquidating corporation is not a member of the group at the time of the liquidation, the rules of this paragraph (g)(1) are applied as if the liquidating corporation had been a member of the group.

(2) Accounting for deferred income items. Solely for the purpose of determining whether deferred income items of a liquidating corporation are taken into account under applicable principles of law as a result of a liquidation to which section 332 applies, the transfer of property to, and the assumption of liabilities by, a distributee member that does not own stock in the liquidating corporation meeting the requirements of section 1504(a)(2) without regard to the application of § 1.1502-34 immediately prior to the liquidation is not treated as part of a transaction to which section 381(a) applies. In addition, section 332(a) does not apply in determining the recognition or nonrecognition of any income realized by the distributee member under applicable principles of law on account of consideration received (or deemed received) on the assumption of the liquidating corporation's obligation or liability attributable to any deferred income item.

(3) Credits and earnings and profits. Each distributee member succeeds to and takes into account a percentage of each credit of the liquidating corporation equal to the value of the stock of the liquidating corporation owned by such distributee at the time of the liquidation divided by the total value of all the stock of the liquidating corporation owned by members of the group at the time of the liquidation. Except to the extent that the distributee member's earnings and profits already reflect the liquidating corporation's earnings and profits, each distributee member succeeds to and takes into account under the principles of § 1.1502-32(c) the earnings and profits, or deficit in earnings and profits, of the liquidating corporation (determined after taking into account the amount of earnings and profits properly applicable to distributions to non-member shareholders under § 1.381(c)(2)-1(c)(2)). If the liquidating corporation is not a member of the group at the time of the liquidation, the rules of this paragraph (g)(3) are applied as if the liquidating corporation had been a member of the group.

(4) Other items. With regard to items to which neither paragraph (g)(1) nor (g)(3) of this section applies, a distributee member that, immediately prior to the liquidation, owns stock in the liquidating corporation meeting the requirements of section 1504(a)(2) without regard to the application of § 1.1502-34 succeeds to the items of the liquidating corporation in accordance with section 381 and other applicable principles. A distributee member that, immediately prior to the liquidation, does not own stock in the liquidating corporation meeting the requirements of section 1504(a)(2) without regard to the application of § 1.1502-34 succeeds to the items of the liquidating corporation to the extent that it would have succeeded to those items if it had purchased, in a taxable transaction, the assets or businesses of the liquidating corporation that it received in the liquidation and had assumed the liabilities that it assumed in the liquidation.

(5) Determination of the items of a liquidating subsidiary. For purposes of this section, the items of a liquidating subsidiary include the amount of any consolidated tax attribute attributable to the liquidating subsidiary that is determined pursuant to the principles of § 1.1502-21(b)(2)(iv). In addition, if the liquidating subsidiary is a member of a separate return limitation year subgroup, the amount of a tax attribute that arose in a separate return limitation year that is attributable to that member shall also be determined pursuant to the principles of § 1.1502-21(b)(2)(iv).

(6) Examples. The following examples illustrate the application of this paragraph (g):

Example (1). Liquidation—80 percent distributee. (i) Facts. X has only common stock outstanding. On January 1 of year 1, X acquired equipment with a 10-year recovery period and elected to depreciate the equipment using the straight-line method of depreciation. On January 1 of year 7, M1 and M2 own 80 percent and 20 percent, respectively, of X's stock. X is a domestic corporation but is not a member of the group that includes M1 and M2. On that date, X distributes all of its assets to M1 and M2 in complete liquidation. The equipment is distributed to M1. Under section 334(b), M1's basis in the equipment is the same as it would be in X's hands. After computing its tax liability for the taxable year that includes the liquidation, X has net operating losses of $100, business credits of $40, and earnings and profits of $80.

(ii) Succession to items described in section 381(c). (A) Losses. Under paragraph (g)(1) of this section, each distributee member succeeds to X's items that could be used to offset the income of the group or any member to the extent that such items would have been reflected in investment adjustments to the stock of X it owned under § 1.1502-32(c) if, immediately prior to the liquidation, such items had been taken into account. Accordingly, M1 and M2 succeed to $80 and $20, respectively, of X's net operating loss.

(B) Credits and earnings and profits. Under paragraph (g)(3) of this section, because, immediately prior to the liquidation, M1 and M2 hold 80 percent and 20 percent, respectively, of the value of the stock of X, M1 and M2 succeed to $32 and $8, respectively, of X's $40 of business credits. In addition, because M1's and M2's earnings and profits do not reflect X's earnings and profits, X's earnings and profits are allocated to M1 and M2 under the principles of § 1.1502-32(c). Therefore, M1 and M2 succeed to $64 and $16, respectively, of X's earnings and profits.

(C) Depreciation of equipment's basis. Under paragraph (g)(4) of this section, because M1 owns stock in X meeting the requirements of section 1504(a)(2) without regard to the application of § 1.1502-34, M1 is required to continue to depreciate the equipment using the straight-line method of depreciation over the remaining recovery period of 4.5 years (assuming X used a half-year convention).

Example (2). Liquidation-no 80 percent distributee. (i) Facts. The facts are the same as in Example 1 except that M1 and M2 own 60 percent and 40 percent, respectively, of X's stock. In addition, on January 1 of year 6, X entered into a long-term contract with Y, an unrelated party. The total contract price is $1000, and X estimates the total allocable contract costs to be $500. At the time of the liquidation,

X had received $250 in progress payments under the contract and incurred costs of $125. X accounted for the contract under the percentage of completion method described in section 460(b). In the liquidation, M1 assumes X's contract obligations and rights.

(ii) Succession to items described in section 381(c). (A) Losses. Under paragraph (g)(1) of this section, each distributee member succeeds to X's items that could be used to offset the income of the group or any member to the extent that such items would have been reflected in investment adjustments to the stock of X it owned under § 1.1502-32(c) if, immediately prior to the liquidation, such items had been taken into account. Accordingly, M1 and M2 succeed to $60 and $40, respectively, of X's net operating loss.

(B) Credits and earnings and profits. Under paragraph (g)(3) of this section, because, immediately prior to the liquidation, M1 and M2 hold 60 percent and 40 percent, respectively, of the value of the stock of X, M1 and M2 succeed to $24 and $16, respectively, of X's $40 of business credits. In addition, because M1's and M2's earnings and profits do not reflect X's earnings and profits, X's earnings and profits are allocated to M1 and M2 under the principles of § 1.1502-32(c). Therefore, M1 and M2 succeed to $48 and $32, respectively, of X's earnings and profits.

(C) Depreciation of equipment's basis. Under section 334(a), M1's basis in the equipment is its fair market value at the time of the distribution. Pursuant to section 168(i)(7), to the extent that M1's basis in the equipment does not exceed X's adjusted basis in the equipment at the time of the transfer, M1 is required to continue to depreciate the equipment using the straight-line method of depreciation over the remaining recovery period of 4.5 years (assuming X used a half-year convention). Any portion of M1's basis in the equipment that exceeds X's adjusted basis in the equipment at the time of the transfer is treated as being placed in service by M1 in the year of the transfer. Thus, M1 may choose any applicable depreciation method, recovery period, and convention under section 168 for such excess basis.

(D) Method of accounting for long-term contract. Under paragraph (g)(4) of this section, M1 does not succeed to X's method of accounting for the contract. Rather, under § 1.460-4(k)(2), M1 is treated as having entered into a new contract on the date of the liquidation. Under § 1.460-4(k)(2)(iii), M1 must evaluate whether the new contract should be classified as a long-term contract within the meaning of § 1.460-1(b) and account for the contract under a permissible method of accounting.

Example (3). Liquidation—deferred items. (i) Facts. X has only common stock outstanding, and M1 and M2 (who are members of the same group) own 80 percent and 20 percent, respectively, of X's stock. X operates two divisions, each of which defers prepaid subscription income pursuant to an election under section 455. X distributes all of its assets in complete liquidation. M1 receives all of the assets of Division 1, including prepaid subscription income, and assumes X's liability to furnish or deliver the newspaper, magazine, or other periodical to which the prepaid subscription income received by M1 relates. M2 receives all of the assets of Division 2, including prepaid subscription income, and assumes X's liability to furnish or deliver the newspaper, magazine, or other periodical to which the prepaid subscription income received by M2 relates.

(ii) Acceleration of deferred income items and succession to other deferred items. Under paragraph (g)(1) of this section, M1 succeeds to the full amount of the deferred prepaid subscription income of X attributable to Division 1. Under applicable law, X does not recognize the deferred prepaid subscription income attributable to Division 1 because X's liability to furnish or deliver the newspaper, magazine, or other periodical ends as a result of a transaction to which section 381(a) applies. Under paragraph (g)(2) of this section, solely for purposes of determining whether the deferred income items of X attributable to Division 2 are taken into account as a result of the liquidation, the distribution of property to M2 is not treated as a transaction to which section 381(a) applies. Therefore, under applicable law, X's deferred prepaid subscription income attributable to Division 2 is taken into account in the determination of X's income or loss with regard to the liquidation. Further, under paragraph (g)(2) of this section, section 332(a) does not apply in determining the recognition or nonrecognition of any income that M2 realizes on account of consideration received (or deemed received) on its assumption of X's liability to furnish or deliver the newspaper, magazine, or other periodical to which the prepaid subscription income relates.

(7) Effective/applicability date. This paragraph (g) applies to transactions occurring after April 14, 2008.

(h) Non-applicability of section 362(e)(2). *(1) General rule.* Section 362(e)(2) does not apply to any intercompany transaction occurring on or after September 17, 2008. Taxpayers may apply this paragraph (h) to intercompany transactions occurring on or after October 22, 2004, and in such case, any election made under section 362(e)(2)(C) will have no effect. The purpose of this paragraph (h) is to facilitate the application of the consolidated return provisions addressing the duplication of loss between members of a consolidated group.

(2) Anti-abuse rule. (i) General rule. If a taxpayer engages in a transaction to which section 362(e)(2) would apply but for the application of paragraph (h)(1) of this section, and acts with a view to prevent the consolidated return provisions from properly addressing loss duplication, appropriate adjustments will be made to clearly reflect the income of the group.

(ii) Example. The following example illustrates the principle of the anti-abuse rule in this paragraph (h)(2).

Example. (A) Facts. P, the common parent of a consolidated group, owns the four outstanding shares of S stock (Share 1 through Share 4) with an aggregate basis of $0 and value of $80. S owns Asset 1 with a basis of $0 and a value of $80. With a view to prevent the consolidated return provisions from addressing the duplication of loss, P transfers Asset 2 with a basis of $100 and a value of $20 to S in exchange for an additional share of S stock (Share 5) in a transaction to which section 351 applies. P later sells Share 5 to X, an unrelated person, for $20 at a time when S's basis in Asset 2 was still $100. The sale is a transfer of a loss share and therefore subject to § 1.1502-36.

(B) Analysis. Although the sale would be subject to § 1.1502-36, that section would not prevent the stock loss or reduce S's attributes (to prevent duplication of the stock loss) because neither § 1.1502-36(b) nor § 1.1502-36(c) would adjust the basis of the transferred share (because there are no investment adjustments) and § 1.1502-36(d) would not reduce S's attributes (because S's aggregate inside loss is $0). However, because P acted with a view to prevent the consolidated return provisions from addressing the duplication of the loss on Asset 2, P's transfer of Asset 2 to S is subject to the anti-abuse rule in this paragraph (h)(2). Accordingly, effective immediately before the transfer of Share 5 to X, either P's basis in Share 5 or S's basis in Asset 2 must be adjusted to reflect what it would have been had section 362(e)(2) been applied at the time P transferred Asset 2 to S (taking into account the interim facts and circumstances). Accordingly, S must either reduce its basis in Asset 2 by $80 to $20 (eliminating the duplicated loss) or P must reduce its basis in Share 5 by $80 to $20 (eliminating the duplicated loss).

(C) Transfer of all S shares. Assume the same facts as those in paragraph (A) of this Example, except that P sells all five S shares to X. Although P's transfer of Asset 2 to S results in the duplication of an $80 loss, because all the shares are transferred, the transaction does not prevent the consolidated return provisions from properly addressing loss duplication. P's $80 duplicated loss is offset by an $80 duplicated gain, and the group recognizes the offsetting stock gain and loss. Accordingly, this paragraph (h)(2) does not apply to P's transfer of Asset 2 to S.

T.D. 6894, 9/7/66, amend T.D. 8402, 3/13/92, T.D. 8560, 8/12/94, T.D. 8597, 7/12/95, T.D. 8677, 6/26/96, T.D. 9048, 3/11/2003, T.D. 9118, 3/17/2004, T.D. 9192, 3/21/2005, T.D. 9254, 3/9/2006, T.D. 9341, 7/17/2007, T.D. 9376, 1/14/2008, T.D. 9424, 9/10/2008.

PAR. 4. In § 1.1502-80, paragraph (c) is revised to read as follows:

Proposed § 1.1502-80 Applicability of other provisions of law. [*For Preamble, see ¶ 152,509*]

(c) [The text of this proposed § 1.1502-80(c) is the same as the text of § 1.1502-80T(c) published elsewhere in this issue of the Federal Register].

PAR. 2. In § 1.1502-80, paragraph (d) is revised to read as follows:

Proposed § 1.1502-80 Applicability of other provisions of law. [*For Preamble, see ¶ 152,195*]

* * * * *

(d) Non-applicability of section 357(c). *(1) In general.* Section 357(c) does not apply to cause the transferor to recognize gain in any transaction to which § 1.1502-13 applies, if such transaction occurs in a consolidated return year beginning on or after the date these regulations are published as final regulations in the Federal Register. Notwithstanding the foregoing, for purposes of determining the transferor's basis in property under section 358(a) received in a transfer described in section 351, section 358(d)(2) shall operate to exclude liabilities described in section 357(c)(3)(A), other than those also described in section 357(c)(3)(B), from the computation of the amount of liabilities assumed that is treated as money received under section 358(d)(1), if such transfer occurs in a consolidated return year beginning on or after the date these regulations are published as final regulations in the Federal Register. This paragraph (d)(1) does not apply to a transaction if the transferor or transferee becomes a nonmember as part of the same plan or arrangement. The transferor (or transferee) is treated as becoming a nonmember once it is no longer a member of a consolidated group that includes the transferee (or transferor). For purposes of this paragraph (d)(1), any reference to a transferor or transferee includes, as the context may require, a reference to a successor or predecessor. For rules regarding the application of section 357(c) to transactions occurring in consolidated return years beginning on or after January 1, 1995, but before the date these regulations are published as final regulations in the Federal Register, see § 1.1502-80(d) in effect prior to the date these regulations are published as final regulations in the Federal Register (see 26 CFR part 1 revised April 1, 2001).

(2) Examples. The principles of paragraph (d)(1) of this section are illustrated by the following examples:

Example (1). P, S, and T are members of a consolidated group. P owns all of the stock of S and T with bases of $30 and $20, respectively. S has assets with a total fair market value equal to $100 and an aggregate basis of $30 and liabilities of $40. S merges into T in a transaction described in section 368(a)(1)(A) (and in section 368(a)(1)(D)). Section 357(c) does not apply to cause S to recognize gain in the merger. P's basis in T's stock increases to $50 ($30 plus $20), and T succeeds to S's $30 basis in the assets transferred and the $40 of liabilities.

Example (2). P owns all the stock of S1. S1 has assets with a total fair market value equal to $100 and an aggregate basis of $30. S1 has $40 of liabilities, $5 of which are described in section 357(c)(3)(A), but not section 357(c)(3)(B), and $35 of which are not described in section 357(c)(3)(A). S1 transfers its assets to a newly formed subsidiary, S2, in exchange for stock of S2 and S2's assumption of the liabilities of $40 in a transaction to which section 351 applies. Section 357(c) does not apply to cause S1 to recognize gain in connection with the transfer. For purposes of determining S1's basis in the S2 stock it received in the exchange, section 358(d)(2) operates to exclude $5 of the liabilities from the computation of the amount of liabilities assumed that are treated as money received under section 358(d)(1). S1's basis in the S2 stock received in the exchange is a $5 excess loss account (reflecting its $30 basis in the assets transferred reduced by $35, the amount of liabilities assumed that are not described in section 357(c)(3)(A)).

§ 1.1502-81T Alaska Native Corporations (Temporary).

(a) General rule. The application of section 60(b)(5) of the Tax Reform Act of 1984 and section 1804(e)(4) of the Tax Reform Act of 1986 (relating to Native Corporations established under the Alaska Native Claims Settlement Act (43 U.S.C. 1601 *et seq.*)) is limited to the use on a consolidated return of losses and credits of a Native Corporation, and of a corporation all of whose stock is owned directly by a Native Corporation, during any taxable year (beginning after the effective date of such sections and before 1992), or any part thereof, against the income and tax liability of a corporation affiliated with the Native Corporation. Thus, no other tax saving, tax benefit, or tax loss is intended to result from the application of section 60(b)(5) of the Tax Reform Act of 1984 and section 1804(e)(4) of the Tax Reform Act of 1986 to any person (whether or not such person is a member of an affiliated group of which a Native Corporation is the common parent). In particular, except as approved by the Secretary, no positive adjustment under § 1.1502-32(b) will be made with respect to the basis of stock of a corporation that is affiliated with a Native Corporation through application of section 60(b)(5) of the Tax Reform Act of 1984 and section 1804(e)(4) of the Tax Reform Act of 1986.

(b) Effective dates. This section applies to taxable years beginning after December 31, 1984.

T.D. 8130, 3/13/87, amend T.D. 8560, 8/12/94.

§ 1.1502-90 Table of contents.

The following list contains the major headings in §§ 1.1502-91 through 1.1502-99:

T.D. 8824, 6/25/99, amend T.D. 9304, 12/21/2006, T.D. 9329, 6/13/2007, T.D. 9424, 9/10/2008.

§ 1.1502-90A Table of contents (temporary).

The following list contains the major headings in §§ 1.1502-91A through 1.1502-99A:

T.D. 8678, 6/26/96, amend T.D. 8824, 6/25/99.

---

§ 1.1502-91 Application of section 382 with respect to a consolidated group.

(a) Determination and effect of an ownership change. *(1) In general.* This section and §§ 1.1502-92 and 1.1502-93 set forth the rules for determining an ownership change under section 382 for members of consolidated groups and the section 382 limitations with respect to attributes described in paragraphs (e) and (f) of this section. These rules generally provide that an ownership change and the section 382 limitation are determined with respect to these attributes for the group (or loss subgroup) on a single entity basis and not for its members separately. Following an ownership change of a loss group (or a loss subgroup) under § 1.1502-92, the amount of consolidated taxable income for any post-change year which may be offset by pre-change consolidated attributes (or pre-change subgroup attributes) shall not exceed the consolidated section 382 limitation (or subgroup section 382 limitation) for such year as determined under § 1.1502-93.

(2) Special rule for post-change year that includes the change date. If the post-change year includes the change date, section 382(b)(3)(A) is applied so that the consolidated section 382 limitation (or subgroup section 382 limitation) does not apply to the portion of consolidated taxable income that is allocable to the period in the year on or before the change date. See generally § 1.382-6 (relating to the allocation of income and loss). The allocation of consolidated taxable income for the post-change year that includes the change date must be made before taking into account any consolidated net operating loss deduction (as defined in § 1.1502-21(a)).

(3) Cross-reference. See §§ 1.1502-94 and 1.1502-95 for rules that apply section 382 to a corporation that becomes or ceases to be a member of a group or loss subgroup.

(b) Definitions and nomenclature. For purposes of this section and §§ 1.1502-92 through 1.1502-99, unless otherwise stated:

(1) The definitions and nomenclature contained in section 382 and the regulations thereunder (including the nomenclature and assumptions relating to the examples in § 1.382-2T(b)) and this section and §§ 1.1502-92 through 1.1502-99 apply.

(2) In all examples, all groups file consolidated returns, all corporations file their income tax returns on a calendar year basis, the only 5-percent shareholder of a corporation is a public group, the facts set forth the only owner shifts during the testing period, no election is made under paragraph (d)(4) of this section, and each asset of a corporation has a value equal to its adjusted basis.

(3) As the context requires, references to §§ 1.1502-91 through 1.1502-96 include references to corresponding provisions of §§ 1.1502-91A through 1.1502-96A. For example, a reference to an ownership change under §§ 1.1502-92 in § 1.1502-95(b) can include a reference to an ownership change under § 1.1502-92A.

(c) Loss group. *(1) Defined.* A loss group is a consolidated group that—

(i) Is entitled to use a net operating loss carryover to the taxable year that did not arise (and is not treated under § 1.1502-21(c) as arising) in a SRLY;

(ii) Has a consolidated net operating loss for the taxable year in which a testing date of the common parent occurs (determined by treating the common parent as a loss corporation); or

(iii) Has a net unrealized built-in loss (determined under paragraph (g) of this section by treating the date on which the determination is made as though it were a change date).

(2) Coordination with rule that ends separate tracking. A consolidated group may be a loss group because a member's losses that arose in (or are treated as arising in) a SRLY are treated as described in paragraph (c)(1)(i) of this section. See § 1.1502-96(a).

(3) Example. The following example illustrates the principles of this paragraph (c):

Example. Loss group.

(i) L and L1 file separate returns and each has a net operating loss carryover arising in Year 1 that is carried over to Year 2. A owns 40 shares and L owns 60 shares of the 100 outstanding shares of L1 stock. At the close of Year 1, L buys the 40 shares of L1 stock from A. For Year 2, L and L1 file a consolidated return. The following is a graphic illustration of these facts:

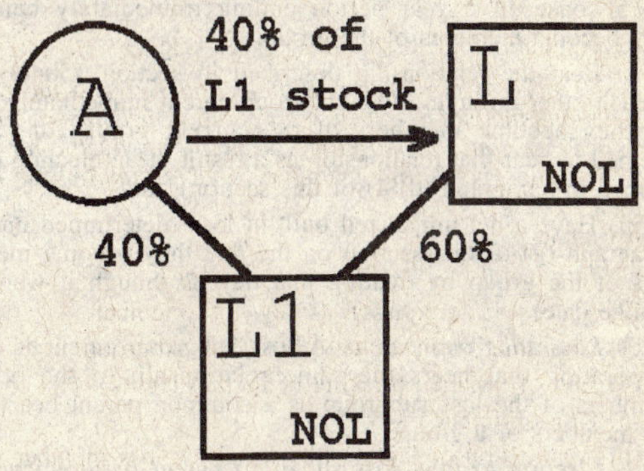

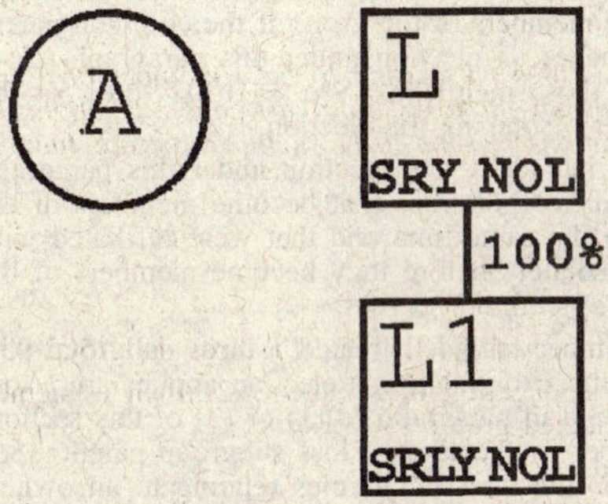

(ii) L and L1 become a loss group at the beginning of Year 2 because the group is entitled to use the Year 1 net operating loss carryover of L, the common parent, which did not arise (and is not treated under § 1.1502-21(c) as arising) in a SRLY. See § 1.1502-94 for rules relating to the application of section 382 with respect to L1's net operating loss carryover from Year 1 which did arise in a SRLY.

(d) Loss subgroup. *(1) Net operating loss carryovers.* Two or more corporations that become members of a consolidated group (the current group) compose a loss subgroup if—

(i) They were affiliated with each other in another group (the former group), whether or not the group was a consolidated group;

(ii) They bear the relationship described in section 1504(a)(1) to each other through a loss subgroup parent immediately after they become members of the current group (or are deemed to bear that relationship as a result of an election described in paragraph (d)(4) of this section); and

(iii) At least one of the members carries over a net operating loss that did not arise (and is not treated under § 1.1502-21(c) as arising) in a SRLY with respect to the former group.

(2) Net unrealized built-in loss. Two or more corporations that become members of a consolidated group compose a loss subgroup if they—

(i) Have been continuously affiliated with each other for the 5 consecutive year period ending immediately before they become members of the group;

(ii) Bear the relationship described in section 1504(a)(1) to each other through a loss subgroup parent immediately after they become members of the current group (or are deemed to bear that relationship as a result of an election described in paragraph (d)(4) of this section); and

(iii) Have a net unrealized built-in loss (determined under paragraph (g) of this section on the day they become members of the group by treating that day as though it were a change date).

(3) Loss subgroup parent. A loss subgroup parent is the corporation that bears the same relationship to the other members of the loss subgroup as a common parent bears to the members of a group.

(4) Election to treat loss subgroup parent requirement as satisfied. (i) In general. Solely for purposes of paragraphs (d)(1)(i) and (2)(ii) of this section, two or more corporations that become members of a consolidated group at the same time and that were affiliated with each other immediately before becoming members of the group are deemed to bear a section 1504(a)(1) relationship to each other immediately after they become members of the group if the common parent of that group makes an election under this paragraph (d)(4) with respect to those members. See § 1.1502-96(e) for the time and manner of making the election.

(ii) Members included. An election under this paragraph (d)(4) includes all corporations that become members of the current group at the same time and that were affiliated with each other immediately before they become members of the current group.

(iii) Each member included treated as loss subgroup parent. If the members to which this election applies are a loss subgroup described in paragraph (d)(1) or (2) of this section, then each member is treated as a loss subgroup parent. See § 1.1502-92(b)(1)(iii) for special rules relating to an ownership change of a loss subgroup if the election under this paragraph (d)(4) is made.

(5) Principal purpose of avoiding a limitation. The corporations described in paragraphs (d)(1) or (2) of this section do not compose a loss subgroup if any one of them is formed, acquired, or availed of with a principal purpose of avoiding the application of, or increasing any limitation under, section 382. Instead, § 1.1502-94 applies with respect to the attributes of each such corporation. Any member excluded from a loss subgroup, if excluded with a principal purpose of so avoiding or increasing any section 382 limitation, is treated as included in the loss subgroup. This paragraph (d)(5) does not apply solely because, in connection with becoming members of the group, the members of a group (or loss subgroup) are rearranged (or, in the case of the preceding sentence, are not rearranged) to bear a relationship to the other members described in section 1504(a)(1).

(6) Special rules. See § 1.1502-95(d) for rules concerning when a corporation ceases to be a member of a loss subgroup, and for certain exceptions that may apply if a member does not continue to satisfy the loss subgroup parent requirement within the current group. See also § 1.1502-96(a) for a special rule regarding the end of separate tracking of SRLY losses of a member that has an ownership change or that has been a member of a group for at least 5 consecutive years.

(7) Examples. The following examples illustrate the principles of this paragraph (d):

Example (1). Loss subgroup.

(i) P owns all the L stock and L owns all the L1 stock. The P group has a consolidated net operating loss arising in Year 1 that is carried to Year 2. On May 2, Year 2, P sells all the stock of L to A, and L and L1 thereafter file consolidated returns. A portion of the Year 1 consolidated net operating loss is apportioned under § 1.1502-21(b) to each of L and L1, which they carry over to Year 2. The following is a graphic illustration of these facts:

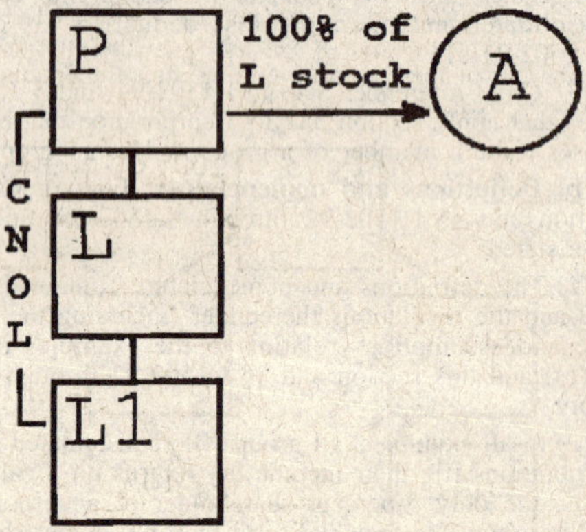

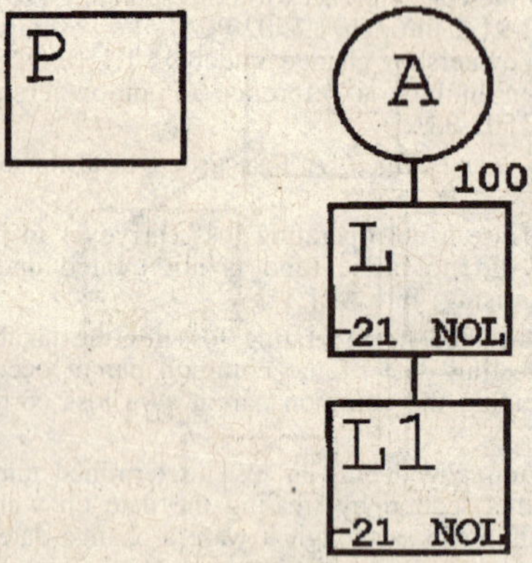

(ii) (a) L and L1 compose a loss subgroup within the meaning of paragraph (d)(1) of this section because—

(A) They were affiliated with each other in the P group (the former group);

(B) They bear a relationship described in section 1504(a)(1) to each other through a loss subgroup parent (L) immediately after they became members of the L group; and

(C) At least one of the members (here, both L and L1) carries over a net operating loss to the L group (the current group) that did not arise in a SRLY with respect to the P group.

(b) Under paragraph (d)(3) of this section, L is the loss subgroup parent of the L loss subgroup.

Example (2). Loss subgroup--section 1504(a)(1) relationship.

(i) P owns all the stock of L and L1. L owns all the stock of L2. L1 and L2 own 40 percent and 60 percent of the stock of L3, respectively. The P group has a consolidated net operating loss arising in Year 1 that is carried over to Year 2. On May 22, Year 2, P sells all the stock of L and L1 to P1, the common parent of another consolidated group. The Year 1 consolidated net operating loss is apportioned under § 1.1502-21(b), and each of L, L1, L2, and L3 carries over a portion of such loss to the first consolidated return year of the P1 group ending after the acquisition. The following is a graphic illustration of these facts:

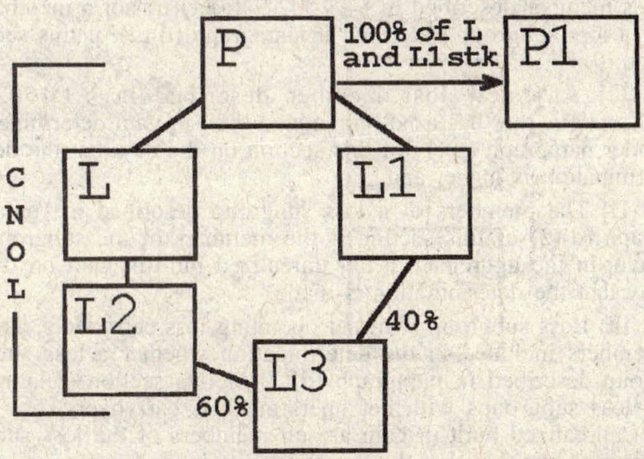

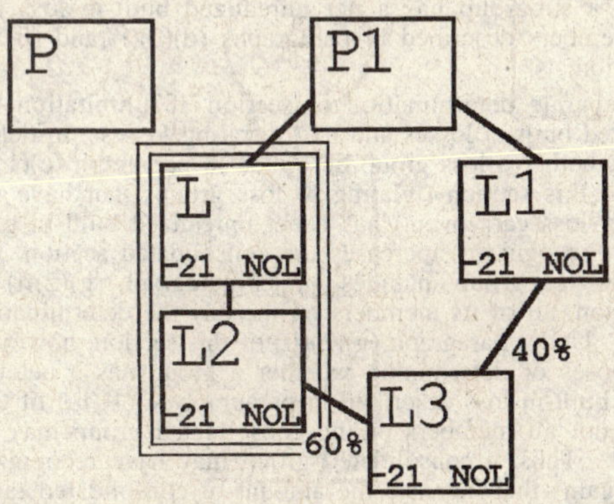

(ii) L and L2 compose a loss subgroup within the meaning of paragraph (d)(1) of this section. Neither L1 nor L3 is included in a loss subgroup because neither bears a relationship described in section 1504(a)(1) through a loss subgroup parent to any other member of the former group immediately after becoming members of the P1 group.

Example (3). Loss subgroup--section 1504(a)(1) relationship. The facts are the same as in Example 2, except that the stock of L1 is transferred to L in connection with the sale of the L stock to P1. L, L1, L2, and L3 compose a loss subgroup within the meaning of paragraph (d)(1) of this section because—

(i) They were affiliated with each other in the P group (the former group);

(ii) They bear a relationship described in section 1504(a)(1) to each other through a loss subgroup parent (L) immediately after they become members of the P1 group; and

(iii) At least one of the members (here, each of L, L1, L2, and L3) carries over a net operating loss to the P1 group (the current group).

Example (4). Loss subgroup—elective section 1504(a)(1) relationship. The facts are the same as in Example 2, except that P1 makes the election under paragraph (d)(4) of this section. The election includes L, L1, L2, and L3 (even though L and L2 would compose a loss subgroup without regard to the election) because they become members of the current group (the P1 group) at the same time and were affiliated with each other in the P group immediately before they became members of the P1 group. As a result of the election, L, L1, L2, and L3 are treated as satisfying the requirement that they bear the relationship described in section 1504(a)(1) to each other through a loss subgroup parent immediately after they become members of the P1 group. L, L1, L2, and L3 compose a loss subgroup within the meaning of paragraph (d)(1) of this section.

(e) Pre-change consolidated attribute. *(1) Defined.* A pre-change consolidated attribute of a loss group is—

(i) Any loss described in paragraph (c)(1)(i) or (ii) of this section (relating to the definition of loss group) that is allocable to the period ending on or before the change date; and

(ii) Any recognized built-in loss of the loss group.

(2) Example. The following example illustrates the principle of this paragraph (e):

Example. Pre-change consolidated attribute.

(i) The L group has a consolidated net operating loss arising in Year 1 that is carried over to Year 2. The L loss group has an ownership change at the beginning of Year 2.

(ii) The net operating loss carryover of the L loss group from Year 1 is a pre-change consolidated attribute because the L group was entitled to use the loss in Year 2 and therefore the loss was described in paragraph (c)(1)(i) of this section. Under paragraph (a)(2)(i) of this section, the amount of consolidated taxable income of the L group for Year 2 that may be offset by this loss carryover may not exceed the consolidated section 382 limitation of the L group for that year. See § 1.1502-93 for rules relating to the computation of the consolidated section 382 limitation.

(f) Pre-change subgroup attribute. *(1) Defined.* A pre-change subgroup attribute of a loss subgroup is—

(i) Any net operating loss carryover described in paragraph (d)(1)(iii) of this section (relating to the definition of loss subgroup); and

(ii) Any recognized built-in loss of the loss subgroup.

(2) Example. The following example illustrates the principle of this paragraph (f):

Example. Pre-change subgroup attribute.

(i) P is the common parent of a consolidated group. P owns all the stock of L, and L owns all the stock of L1. L2 is not a member of an affiliated group, and has a net operating loss arising in Year 1 that is carried over to Year 2. On December 11, Year 2, L1 acquires all the stock of L2, causing an ownership change of L2. During Year 2, the P group has a consolidated net operating loss that is carried over to Year 3. On November 2, Year 3, M acquires all the L stock from P. M, L, L1, and L2 thereafter file consolidated returns. All of the P group Year 2 consolidated net operating loss is apportioned under § 1.1502-21(b) to L and L2, which they carry over to the M group.

(ii) (a) L, L1, and L2 compose a loss subgroup because—

(1) They were affiliated with each other in the P group (the former group);

(2) They bear a relationship described in section 1504(a)(1) to each other through a loss subgroup parent (L) immediately after they became members of the L group; and

(3) At least one of the members (here, both L and L2) carries over a net operating loss to the M group (the current group) that is described in paragraph (d)(1)(iii) of this section.

(b) For this purpose, L2's loss from Year 1 that was a SRLY loss with respect to the P group (the former group) is described in paragraph (d)(1)(iii) of this section because L2 had an ownership change on becoming a member of the P group (see § 1.1502-96(a)) on December 11, Year 2. Starting on December 12, Year 2, the P group no longer separately tracked owner shifts of the stock of L1 with respect to the Year 1 loss. M's acquisition results in an ownership change of L, and therefore the L loss subgroup under § 1.1502-92(a)(2). See § 1.1502-93 for rules governing the computation of the subgroup section 382 limitation.

(iii) In the M group, L2's Year 1 loss continues to be subject to a section 382 limitation resulting from the ownership change that occurred on December 11, Year 2. See § 1.1502-96(c).

(g) Net unrealized built-in gain and loss. *(1) In general.* The determination whether a consolidated group (or loss subgroup) has a net unrealized built-in gain or loss under section 382(h)(3) is based on the aggregate amount of the separately computed net unrealized built-in gains or losses of each member that is included in the group (or loss subgroup) under paragraph (g)(2) of this section, including items of built-in income and deduction described in section 382(h)(6). Thus, for example, amounts deferred under section 267, or under § 1.1502-13 (other than amounts deferred with respect to the stock of a member (or an intercompany obligation) included in the group (or loss subgroup) under paragraph (g)(2) of this section) are built-in items. The threshold requirement under section 382(h)(3)(B) applies on an aggregate basis and not on a member-by-member basis. The separately computed amount of a member included in a group or loss subgroup does not include any unrealized built-in gain or loss on stock (including stock described in section 1504(a)(4) and § 1.382-2T(f)(18)(ii) and (iii)) of another member included in the group or loss subgroup (or an intercompany obligation). However, a member of a group or loss subgroup includes in its separately computed amount the unrealized built-in gain or loss on stock (but not on an intercompany obligation) of another member not included in the group or loss subgroup. If a member is not included in the determination whether a group (or subgroup) has a net unrealized built-in loss under paragraph (g)(2)(ii) or (iv) of this section, that member is not included in the loss group or loss subgroup. See § 1.1502-94(c) (relating to built-in gain or loss of a new loss member) and § 1.1502-96(a) (relating to the end of separate tracking of certain losses).

(2) Members included. (i) Consolidated group with a net operating loss. The members included in the determination whether a consolidated group described in paragraph (c)(1)(i) or (ii) of this section (relating to loss groups with net operating losses) has a net unrealized built-in gain are all members of the consolidated group on the day that the determination is made.

(ii) Determination whether a consolidated group has a net unrealized built-in loss. The members included in the determination whether a consolidated group is a loss group described in paragraph (c)(1)(iii) of this section are—

(A) The common parent and all other members that have been affiliated with the common parent for the 5 consecutive year period ending on the day that the determination is made;

(B) Any other member that has a net unrealized built-in loss determined under paragraph (g)(1) of this section on the date that the determination is made, and that is neither a new loss member described in § 1.1502-94(a)(1)(ii) nor a member of a loss subgroup described in paragraph (d)(2) of this section;

(C) Any new loss member described in § 1.1502-94(a)(1)(ii) that has a net unrealized built-in gain determined under paragraph (g)(1) of this section on the day that the determination is made; and

(D) The members of a loss subgroup described in paragraph (d)(2) of this section if the members of the subgroup have, in the aggregate, a net unrealized built-in gain on the day that the determination is made.

(iii) Loss subgroup with net operating loss carryovers. The members included in the determination whether a loss subgroup described in paragraph (d)(1) of this section (relating to loss subgroups with net operating loss carryovers) has a net unrealized built-in gain are all members of the loss subgroup on the day that the determination is made.

(iv) Determination whether subgroup has a net unrealized built-in loss. The members included in the determination whether a subgroup has a net unrealized built-in loss are those members described in paragraphs (d)(2)(i) and (ii) of this section.

(v) Separate determination of section 382 limitation for recognized built-in losses and net operating losses. In determining whether a loss group described in paragraph (c)(1)(i) or (ii) of this section (relating to loss groups that have net operating loss carryovers) has a net unrealized built-in gain which, if recognized, increases the consolidated section 382 limitation, the group includes, under paragraph (g)(2)(i) of this section, all of its members on the day the determination is made. Under paragraph (g)(2)(ii) of this section, however, for purposes of determining whether a group has a net unrealized built-in loss described in paragraph (c)(1)(iii) of this section, not all members of the consolidated group may be included. Thus, a consolidated group may have recognized built-in gains that increase the amount of consolidated taxable income that may be offset by its pre-change net operating loss carryovers that did not arise (and are not treated as arising) in a SRLY, and also may have recognized built-in losses the absorption of which is limited. Similar results may obtain for loss subgroups under paragraphs (g)(2)(iii) and (iv) of this section. See § 1.1502-93(c)(2) for rules prohibiting the use of recognized built-in gains to increase the amount of consolidated taxable income that can be offset by recognized built-in losses.

(3) Coordination with rule that ends separate tracking. See § 1.1502-96(a) for special rules relating to members (or loss subgroups) that have an ownership change within six months before, on, or after becoming a member of the group.

(4) Acquisitions of built-in gain or loss assets. A member of a consolidated group (or loss subgroup) may not, in determining its separately computed net unrealized built-in gain or loss, include any gain or loss with respect to assets acquired with a principal purpose to affect the amount of its net unrealized built-in gain or loss. A group (or loss subgroup) may not, in determining its net unrealized built-in gain or loss, include any gain or loss of a member acquired with a principal purpose to affect the amount of its net unrealized built-in gain or loss.

(5) Indirect ownership. A member's separately computed net unrealized built-in gain or loss is adjusted to the extent necessary to prevent any duplication of unrealized gain or loss attributable to the member's indirect ownership interest in another member through a nonmember if the member has a 5-percent or greater ownership interest in the nonmember.

(6) Common parent not common parent for five years. If the common parent has become the common parent of an existing group within the previous 5 year period in a transaction described in § 1.1502-75(d)(2)(ii) or (3), appropriate adjustments must be made in applying paragraph (g)(2)(ii)(A) of this section so that corporations that have not been members of the group for five years are not included. In such a case, references to the common parent in paragraph (g)(2)(ii)(A) of this section are to the former common parent. Thus, members of the group remaining in existence (including the new common parent) that have not been affiliated with the former common parent (or that have not been members of that group) for the five consecutive year period ending on the day that the determination is made are not included under paragraph (g)(2)(ii)(A) of this section. See, however, § 1.1502-96(a)(2) for special rules relating to members (or loss subgroups) that have an ownership change within six months before, on, or after the time that the member becomes a member of the group.

(h) Recognized built-in gain or loss. *(1) In general.* [Reserved].

(2) Disposition of stock or an intercompany obligation of a member. Gain or loss recognized by a member on the disposition of stock (including stock described in section 1504(a)(4) and § 1.382-2T(f)(18)(ii) and (iii)) of another member is treated as a recognized gain or loss for purposes of section 382(h)(2) (unless disallowed) even though gain or loss on such stock was not included in the determination of a net unrealized built-in gain or loss under paragraph (g)(1) of this section. Gain or loss recognized by a member with respect to an intercompany obligation is treated as recognized gain or loss only to the extent (if any) the transaction gives rise to aggregate income or loss within the consolidated group. The first sentence of this paragraph (h)(2) is applicable on or after September 17, 2008.

(3) Intercompany transactions. Gain or loss that is deferred under provisions such as section 267 and § 1.1502-13 is treated as recognized built-in gain or loss only to the extent taken into account by the group during the recognition period. See also § 1.1502-13(c)(7) Example 10.

(4) Exchanged basis property. If the adjusted basis of any asset is determined, directly or indirectly, in whole or in part, by reference to the adjusted basis of another asset held by the member at the beginning of the recognition period, the asset is treated, with appropriate adjustments, as held by the member at the beginning of the recognition period.

(i) [Reserved]

(j) Predecessor and successor corporations. A reference in this section and §§ 1.1502-92 through 1.1502-99 to a corporation, member, common parent, loss subgroup parent, or subsidiary includes, as the context may require, a reference to a predecessor or successor corporation as defined in § 1.1502-1(f)(4). For example, the determination whether a successor satisfies the continuous affiliation requirement of paragraph (d)(2)(i) or (g)(2)(ii) of this section is made by reference to its predecessor.

T.D. 8824, 6/25/99, amend T.D. 9048, 3/11/2003, T.D. 9187, 3/2/2005, T.D. 9254, 3/9/2006, T.D. 9424, 9/10/2008.

§ 1.1502-91A Application of section 382 with respect to a consolidated group generally applicable for testing dates before June 25, 1999.

(a) Determination and effect of an ownership change. *(1) In general.* This section and §§ 1.1502-92A and 1.1502-93A set forth the rules for determining an ownership change under section 382 for members of consolidated groups and the section 382 limitations with respect to attributes described in paragraphs (e) and (f) of this section. These rules generally provide that an ownership change and the section 382 limitation are determined with respect to these attributes for the group (or loss subgroup) on a single entity basis and not for its members separately. Following an ownership change of a loss group (or a loss subgroup) under § 1.1502-92A, the amount of consolidated taxable income for any post-change year which may be offset by pre-change consolidated attributes (or pre-change subgroup attributes) shall not exceed the consolidated section 382 limitation (or subgroup section 382 limitation) for such year as determined under § 1.1502-93A.

(2) Special rule for post-change year that includes the change date. If the post-change year includes the change date, section 382(b)(3)(A) is applied so that the consolidated section 382 limitation (or subgroup section 382 limitation) does not apply to the portion of consolidated taxable income that is allocable to the period in the year on or before the change date. See generally § 1.382-6 (relating to the allocation of income and loss). The allocation of consolidated taxable income for the post-change year that includes the change date must be made before taking into account any consolidated net operating loss deduction (as defined in §§ 1.1502-21(a) or 1.1502-21T(a) in effect prior to June 25, 1999, as contained in 26 CFR part 1 revised April 1, 1999, as applicable).

(3) Cross reference. See §§ 1.1502-94A and 1.1502-95A for rules that apply section 382 to a corporation that becomes or ceases to be a member of a group or loss subgroup.

(b) Definitions and nomenclature. For purposes of this section and §§ 1.1502-92A through 1.1502-99A, unless otherwise stated:

(1) The definitions and nomenclature contained in section 382 and the regulations thereunder (including the nomenclature and assumptions relating to the examples in § 1.382-2T(b)) and this section and §§ 1.1502-92A through 1.1502-99A apply; and

(2) In all examples, all groups file consolidated returns, all corporations file their income tax returns on a calendar year

basis, the only 5-percent shareholder of a corporation is a public group, the facts set forth the only owner shifts during the testing period, and each asset of a corporation has a value equal to its adjusted basis.

(c) Loss group. *(1) Defined.* A loss group is a consolidated group that:

(i) Is entitled to use a net operating loss carryover to the taxable year that did not arise (and is not treated under § 1.1502-21T(c) as arising) in a SRLY;

(ii) Has a consolidated net operating loss for the taxable year in which a testing date of the common parent occurs (determined by treating the common parent as a loss corporation); or

(iii) Has a net unrealized built-in loss (determined under paragraph (g) of this section by treating the date on which the determination is made as though it were a change date).

(2) Coordination with rule that ends separate tracking. A consolidated group may be a loss group because a member's losses that arose in (or are treated as arising in) a SRLY are treated as described in paragraph (c)(1)(i) of this section. See § 1.1502-96A(a).

(3) Example. The following example illustrates the principles of this paragraph (c).

Example. Loss group.

(a) L and L1 file separate returns and each has a net operating loss carryover arising in Year 1 that is carried over to Year 2. A owns 40 shares and L owns 60 shares of the 100 outstanding shares of L1 stock. At the close of Year 1, L buys the 40 shares of L1 stock from A. For Year 2, L and L1 file a consolidated return. The following is a graphic illustration of these facts:

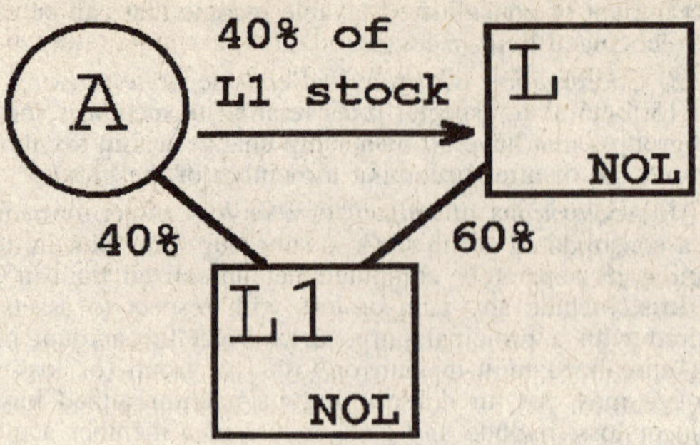

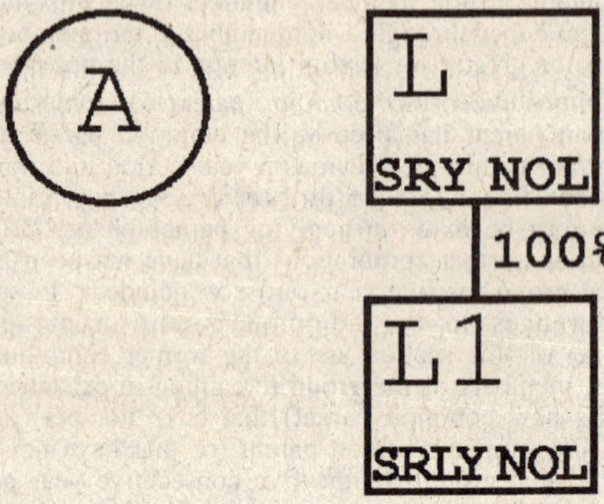

(b) L and L1 become a loss group at the beginning of Year 2 because the group is entitled to use the Year 1 net operating loss carryover of L, the common parent, which did not arise (and is not treated under §§ 1.1502-21(c) or 1.1502-21T(c) in effect prior to June 25, 1999, as contained in 26 CFR part 1 revised April 1, 1999, as applicable as arising) in a SRLY. See § 1.1502-94A for rules relating to the application of section 382 with respect to L1's net operating loss carryover from Year 1 which did arise in a SRLY.

(d) Loss subgroup. *(1) Net operating loss carryovers.* Two or more corporations that become members of a consolidated group (the current group) compose a loss subgroup if:

(i) They were affiliated with each other in another group (the former group), whether or not the group was a consolidated group;

(ii) They bear the relationship described in section 1504(a)(1) to each other through a loss subgroup parent immediately after they become members of the current group; and

(iii) At least one of the members carries over a net operating loss that did not arise (and is not treated under §§ 1.1502-21(c) or 1.1502-21T(c) in effect prior to June 25, 1999, as contained in 26 CFR part 1 revised April 1, 1999, as applicable as arising) in a SRLY with respect to the former group.

(2) Net unrealized built-in loss. Two or more corporations that become members of a consolidated group compose a loss subgroup if they:

(i) Have been continuously affiliated with each other for the 5 consecutive year period ending immediately before they become members of the group;

(ii) Bear the relationship described in section 1504(a)(1) to each other through a loss subgroup parent immediately after they become members of the current group; and

(iii) Have a net unrealized built-in loss (determined under paragraph (g) of this section on the day they become members of the group by treating that day as though it were a change date).

(3) Loss subgroup parent. A loss subgroup parent is the corporation that bears the same relationship to the other members of the loss subgroup as a common parent bears to the members of a group.

(4) Principal purpose of avoiding a limitation. The corporations described in paragraph (d)(1) or (2) of this section do not compose a loss subgroup if any one of them is formed, acquired, or availed of with a principal purpose of avoiding the application of, or increasing any limitation under, section 382. Instead, § 1.1502-94A applies with respect to the attributes of each such corporation. This paragraph (d)(4) does not apply solely because, in connection with becoming members of the group, the members of a group (or loss subgroup) are rearranged to bear a relationship to the other members described in section 1504(a)(1).

(5) Special rules. See § 1.1502-95A(d) for rules concerning when a corporation ceases to be a member of a loss subgroup. See also § 1.1502-96A(a) for a special rule regarding the end of separate tracking of SRLY losses of a member that has an ownership change or that has been a member of a group for at least 5 consecutive years.

(6) Examples. The following examples illustrate the principles of this paragraph (d).

Example (1). Loss subgroup.

(a) P owns all the L stock and L owns all the L1 stock. The P group has a consolidated net operating loss arising in Year 1 that is carried to Year 2. On May 2, Year 2, P sells all the stock of L to A, and L and L1 thereafter file consolidated returns. A portion of the Year 1 consolidated net operating loss is apportioned under §§ 1.1502-21(b) or 1.1502-21T(b) in effect prior to June 25, 1999, as contained in 26 CFR part 1 revised April 1, 1999, as applicable to each of L and L1, which they carry over to Year 2. The following is a graphic illustration of these facts:

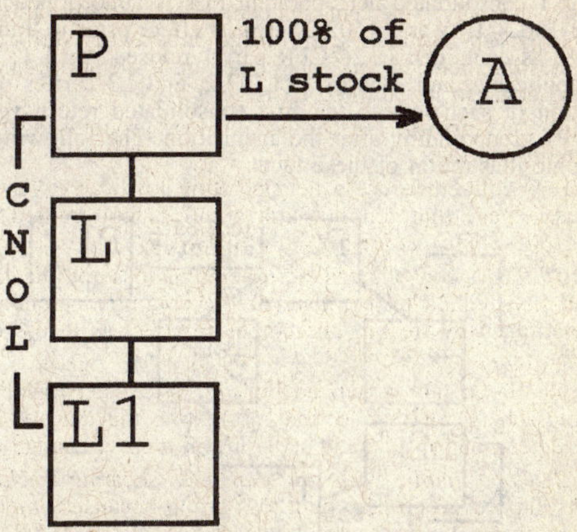

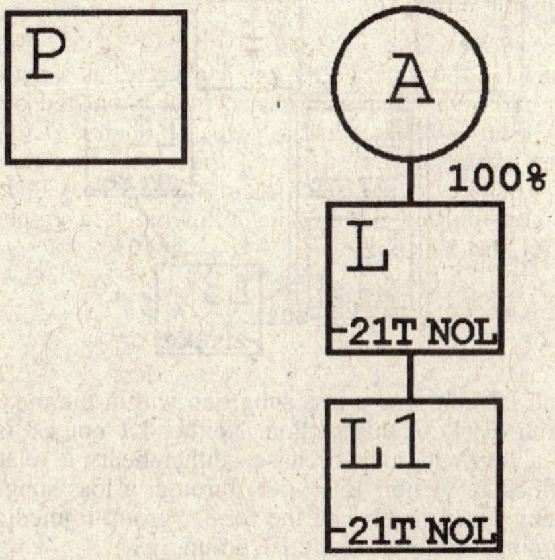

(b) (1) L and L1 compose a loss subgroup within the meaning of paragraph (d)(1) of this section because—

(i) They were affiliated with each other in the P group (the former group);

(ii) They bear a relationship described in section 1504(a)(1) to each other through a loss subgroup parent (L) immediately after they became members of the L group; and

(iii) At least one of the members (here, both L and L1) carries over a net operating loss to the L group (the current group) that did not arise in a SRLY with respect to the P group.

(2) Under paragraph (d)(3) of this section, L is the loss subgroup parent of the L loss subgroup.

Example (2). Loss subgroup - section 1504(a)(1) relationship.

(a) P owns all the stock of L and L1. L owns all the stock of L2. L1 and L2 own 40 percent and 60 percent of the stock of L3, respectively. The P group has a consolidated net operating loss arising in Year 1 that is carried over to Year 2. On May 22, Year 2, P sells all the stock of L and L1 to P1, the common parent of another consolidated group. The

Year 1 consolidated net operating loss is apportioned under §§ 1.1502-21(b) or 1.1502-21T(b) in effect prior to June 25, 1999, as contained in 26 CFR part 1 revised April 1, 1999, as applicable, and each of L, L1, L2, and L3 carries over a portion of such loss to the first consolidated return year of the P1 group ending after the acquisition. The following is a graphic illustration of these facts:

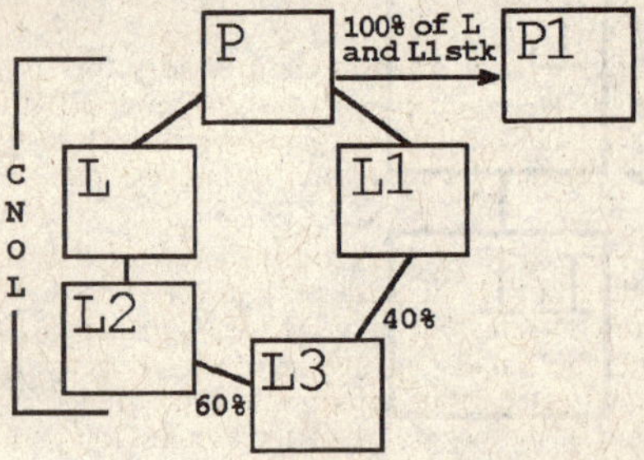

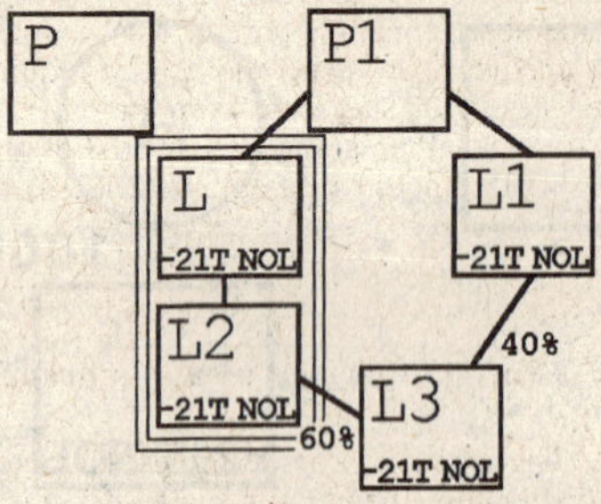

(b) L and L2 compose a loss subgroup within the meaning of paragraph (d)(1) of this section. Neither L1 nor L3 is included in a loss subgroup because neither bears a relationship described in section 1504(a)(1) through a loss subgroup parent to any other member of the former group immediately after becoming members of the P1 group.

Example (3). Loss subgroup—section 1504(a)(1) relationship. The facts are the same as in Example 2, except that the stock of L1 is transferred to L in connection with the sale of the L stock to P1. L, L1, L2, and L3 compose a loss subgroup within the meaning of paragraph (d)(1) of this section because—

(1) They were affiliated with each other in the P group (the former group);

(2) They bear a relationship described in section 1504(a)(1) to each other through a loss subgroup parent (L) immediately after they become members of the P1 group; and

(3) At least one of the members (here, each of L, L1, L2, and L3) carries over to the P1 group (the current group) a net operating loss that did not arise in a SRLY with respect to the P group (the former group).

(e) Pre-change consolidated attribute. *(1) Defined.* A pre-change consolidated attribute of a loss group is—

(i) Any loss described in paragraph (c)(1)(i) or (ii) of this section (relating to the definition of loss group) that is allocable to the period ending on or before the change date; and

(ii) Any recognized built-in loss of the loss group.

(2) Example. The following example illustrates the principle of this paragraph (e).

Example. Pre-change consolidated attribute.

(a) The L group has a consolidated net operating loss arising in Year 1 that is carried over to Year 2. The L loss group has an ownership change at the beginning of Year 2.

(b) The net operating loss carryover of the L loss group from Year 1 is a pre-change consolidated attribute because the L group was entitled to use the loss in Year 2, the loss did not arise in a SRLY with respect to the L group, and therefore the loss was described in paragraph (c)(1)(i) of this section. Under paragraph (a) of this section, the amount of consolidated taxable income of the L group for Year 2 that may be offset by this loss carryover may not exceed the consolidated section 382 limitation of the L group for that year. See § 1.1502-93A for rules relating to the computation of the consolidated section 382 limitation.

(f) Pre-change subgroup attribute. *(1) Defined.* A pre-change subgroup attribute of a loss subgroup is—

(i) Any net operating loss carryover described in paragraph (d)(1)(iii) of this section (relating to the definition of loss subgroup); and

(ii) Any recognized built-in loss of the loss subgroup.

(2) Example. The following example illustrates the principle of this paragraph (f).

Example. Pre-change subgroup attribute.

(a) P is the common parent of a consolidated group. P owns all the stock of L, and L owns all the stock of L1. L2 is not a member of an affiliated group, and has a net operating loss arising in Year 1 that is carried over to Year 2. On December 11, Year 2, L1 acquires all the stock of L2, causing an ownership change of L2. During Year 2, the P group has a consolidated net operating loss that is carried over to Year 3. On November 2, Year 3, M acquires all the L stock from P. M, L, L1, and L2 thereafter file consolidated returns. All of the P group Year 2 consolidated net operating loss is apportioned under §§ 1.1502-21(b) or 1.1502-21T(b) in effect prior to June 25, 1999, as contained in 26 CFR part 1 revised April 1, 1999, as applicable to L and L2, which they carry over to the M group.

(b) (1) L, L1, and L2 compose a loss subgroup because—

(i) They were affiliated with each other in the P group (the former group);

(ii) They bore a relationship described in section 1504(a)(1) to each other through a loss subgroup parent (L) immediately after they became members of the L group; and

(iii) At least one of the members (here, both L and L2) carries over a net operating loss to the M group (the current group) that is described in paragraph (d)(1)(iii) of this section.

(2) For this purpose, L2's loss from Year 1 that was a SRLY loss with respect to the P group (the former group) is treated as described in paragraph (d)(1)(iii) of this section because of the application of the principles of § 1.1502-96A(a). See paragraph (d)(5) of this section. M's acquisition results in an ownership change of L, and therefore the L loss subgroup under section § 1502-92A(a)(2). See § 1.1502-93A for rules governing the computation of the subgroup section 382 limitation.

(c) In the M group, L2's Year 1 loss continues to be subject to a section 382 limitation resulting from the ownership change that occurred on December 11, Year 2. See § 1.1502-96A(c).

(g) Net unrealized built-in gain and loss. *(1) In general.* The determination whether a consolidated group (or loss subgroup) has a net unrealized built-in gain or loss under section 382(h)(3) is based on the aggregate amount of the separately computed net unrealized built-in gains or losses of each member that is included in the group (or loss subgroup) under paragraph (g)(2) of this section, including items of built-in income and deduction described in section 382(h)(6). Thus, for example, amounts deferred under section 267, or under § 1.1502-13 (other than amounts deferred with respect to the stock of a member (or an intercompany obligation) included in the group (or loss subgroup) under paragraph (g)(2) of this section) are built-in items. The threshold requirement under section 382(h)(3)(B) applies on an aggregate basis and not on a member-by-member basis. The separately computed amount of a member included in a group or loss subgroup does not include any unrealized built-in gain or loss on stock (including stock described in section 1504(a)(4) and § 1.382-2T(f)(18)(ii) and (iii)) of another member included in the group or loss subgroup (or on an intercompany obligation). However, a member of a group or loss subgroup includes in its separately computed amount the unrealized built-in gain or loss on stock of another member (or on an intercompany obligation) not included in the group or loss subgroup. If a member is not included in a group (or loss subgroup) under paragraph (g)(2) of this section, the determination of whether the member has a net unrealized built-in gain or loss under section 382(h)(3) is made on a separate entity basis. See § 1.1502-94A(c) (relating to built-in gain or loss of a new loss member) and § 1.1502-96A(a) (relating to the end of separate tracking of certain losses).

(2) Members included. (i) Consolidated group. The members included in the determination whether a consolidated group has a net unrealized built-in gain or loss are all members of the group on the day that the determination is made other than—

(A) A new loss member with a net unrealized built-in loss described in § 1.1502-94A(a)(1)(ii); and

(B) Members included in a loss subgroup described in § 1.1502-91A(d)(2).

(ii) Loss subgroup. The members included in the determination whether a loss subgroup has a net unrealized built-in gain or loss are those members described in paragraphs (d)(2)(i) and (ii) of this section.

(3) Acquisitions of built-in gain or loss assets. A member of a consolidated group (or loss subgroup) may not, in determining its separately computed net unrealized built-in gain or loss, include any gain or loss with respect to assets acquired with a principal purpose to affect the amount of its net unrealized built-in gain or loss. A group (or loss subgroup) may not, in determining its net unrealized built-in gain or loss, include any gain or loss of a member acquired with a principal purpose to affect the amount of its net unrealized built-in gain or loss.

(4) Indirect ownership. A member's separately computed net unrealized built-in gain or loss is adjusted to the extent necessary to prevent any duplication of unrealized gain or loss attributable to the member's indirect ownership interest in another member through a nonmember if the member has a 5-percent or greater ownership interest in the nonmember.

(h) Recognized built-in gain or loss. *(1) In general.* [Reserved]

(2) Disposition of stock or an intercompany obligation of a member. Gain or loss recognized by a member on the disposition of stock (including stock described in section 1504(a)(4) and § 1.382-2T(f)(18)(ii) and (iii)) of another member (or an intercompany obligation disposed of before June 25, 1999) is treated as a recognized built-in gain or loss under section 382(h)(2) (unless disallowed under § 1.1502-20 or otherwise), even though gain or loss on such stock or obligation was not included in the determination of a net unrealized built-in gain or loss under paragraph (g)(1) of this section.

(3) Deferred gain or loss. Gain or loss that is deferred under provisions such as section 267 and § 1.1502-13 is treated as recognized built-in gain or loss only to the extent taken into account by the group during the recognition period.

(4) Exchanged basis property. If the adjusted basis of any asset is determined, directly or indirectly, in whole or in part, by reference to the adjusted basis of another asset held by the member at the beginning of the recognition period, the asset is treated, with appropriate adjustments, as held by the member at the beginning of the recognition period.

(i) [Reserved]

(j) Predecessor and successor corporations. A reference in this section and §§ 1.1502-92A through 1.1502-99A to a corporation, member, common parent, loss subgroup parent, or subsidiary includes, as the context may require, a reference to a predecessor or successor corporation. For example, the determination whether a successor satisfies the continuous affiliation requirement of paragraph (d)(2)(i) of this section is made by reference to its predecessor.

T.D. 8678, 6/26/96, amend T.D. 8823, 6/25/99, T.D. 8824, 6/25/99.

§ 1.1502-92 Ownership change of a loss group or a loss subgroup.

(a) Scope. This section provides rules for determining if there is an ownership change for purposes of section 382 with respect to a loss group or a loss subgroup. See § 1.1502-94 for special rules for determining if there is an ownership change with respect to a new loss member and § 1.1502-96(b) for special rules for determining if there is an ownership change of a subsidiary.

(b) Determination of an ownership change. *(1) Parent change method.* (i) Loss group. A loss group has an ownership change if the loss group's common parent has an ownership change under section 382 and the regulations thereunder. Solely for purposes of determining whether the common parent has an ownership change—

(A) The losses described in § 1.1502-91(c) are treated as net operating losses (or a net unrealized built-in loss) of the common parent; and

(B) The common parent determines the earliest day that its testing period can begin by reference to only the attributes that make the group a loss group under § 1.1502-91(c).

(ii) Loss subgroup. A loss subgroup has an ownership change if the loss subgroup parent has an ownership change under section 382 and the regulations thereunder. The principles of § 1.1502-95(b) (relating to ceasing to be a member of a consolidated group) apply in determining whether the loss subgroup parent has an ownership change. Solely for purposes of determining whether the loss subgroup parent has an ownership change—

(A) The losses described in § 1.1502-91(d) are treated as net operating losses (or a net unrealized built-in loss) of the loss subgroup parent;

(B) The day that the members of the loss subgroup become members of the group (or a loss subgroup) is treated as a testing date within the meaning of § 1.382-2(a)(4); and

(C) The loss subgroup parent determines the earliest day that its testing period can begin under § 1.382-2T(d)(3) by reference to only the attributes that make the members a loss subgroup under § 1.1502-91(d).

(iii) Special rule if election regarding section 1504(a)(1) relationship is made. (A) Ownership change of deemed loss subgroup parent is an ownership change of loss subgroup. If the common parent makes an election under § 1.1502-91(d)(4), each of the members in the loss subgroup is treated as the loss subgroup parent for purposes of determining whether the loss subgroup has an ownership change under section 382 and the regulations thereunder on or after the day the members become members of the group.

(B) Exception. Paragraph (b)(1)(iii)(A) of this section does not apply to cause an ownership change of a loss subgroup if a deemed loss subgroup parent has an ownership change upon (or after) ceasing to be a member of the current group.

(2) Examples. The following examples illustrate the principles of this paragraph (b):

Example (1). Loss group—ownership change of the common parent.

(i) A owns all the L stock. L owns 80 percent and B owns 20 percent of the L1 stock. For Year 1, the L group has a consolidated net operating loss that resulted from the operations of L1 and that is carried over to Year 2. The value of the L stock is $1000. The total value of the L1 stock is $600 and the value of the L1 stock held by B is $120. The L group is a loss group under § 1.1502-91(c)(1) because it is entitled to use its net operating loss carryover from Year 1. On August 15, Year 2, A sells 51 percent of the L stock to C. The following is a graphic illustration of these facts:

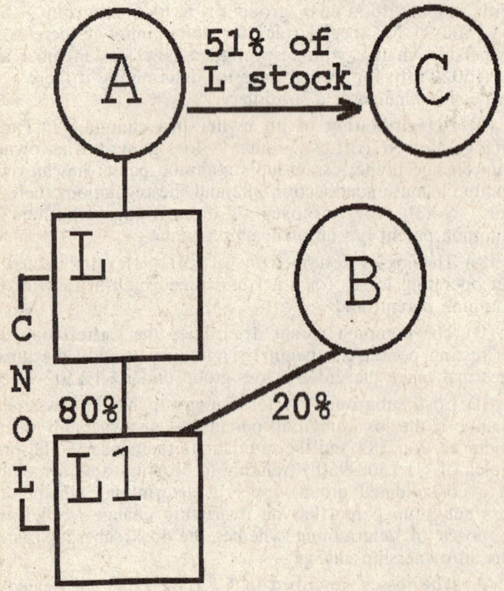

(ii) Under paragraph (b)(1)(i) of this section, section 382 and the regulations thereunder are applied to L to determine whether it (and therefore the L loss group) has an ownership change with respect to its net operating loss carryover from Year 1 attributable to L1 on August 15, Year 2. The sale of the L stock to C causes an ownership change of L under § 1.382-2T and of the L loss group under paragraph (b)(1)(i) of this section. The amount of consolidated taxable income of the L loss group for any post-change taxable year that may be offset by its pre-change consolidated attributes (that is, the net operating loss carryover from Year 1 attributable to L1) may not exceed the consolidated section 382 limitation for the L loss group for the taxable year.

Example (2). Loss group—owner shifts of subsidiaries disregarded.

(i) The facts are the same as in Example 1, except that on August 15, Year 2, A sells only 49 percent of the L stock to C and, on December 12, Year 3, in an unrelated transaction, B sells the 20 percent of the L1 stock to D. A's sale of the L stock to C does not cause an ownership change of L under § 1.382-2T nor of the L loss group under paragraph (b)(1)(i) of this section. The following is a graphic illustration of these facts:

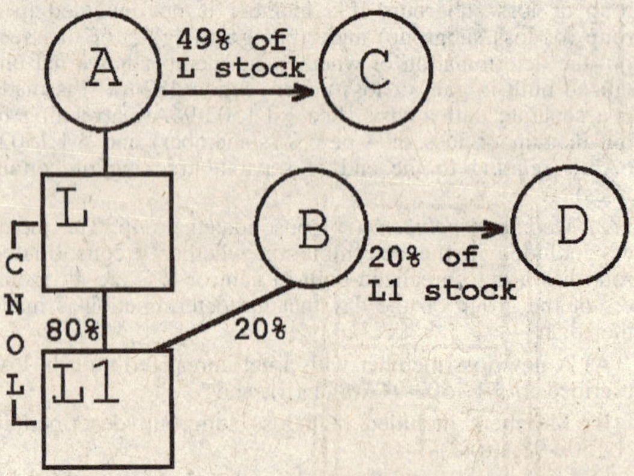

(ii) B's subsequent sale of L1 stock is not taken into account for purposes of determining whether the L loss group has an ownership change under paragraph (b)(1)(i) of this section, and, accordingly, there is no ownership change of the L loss group. See paragraph (c) of this section, however, for a supplemental ownership change method that would apply to cause an ownership change if the purchases by C and D were pursuant to a plan or arrangement and certain other conditions are satisfied.

Example (3). Loss subgroup—ownership change of loss subgroup parent controls.

(i) P owns all the L stock. L owns 80 percent and A owns 20 percent of the L1 stock. The P group has a consolidated net operating loss arising in Year 1 that is carried over to Year 2. On September 9, Year 2, P sells 51 percent of the L stock to B, and L1 is apportioned a portion of the Year 1 consolidated net operating loss under § 1.1502-21(b), which it carries over to its next taxable year. L and L1 file a consolidated return for their first taxable year ending after the sale to B. The following is a graphic illustration of these facts:

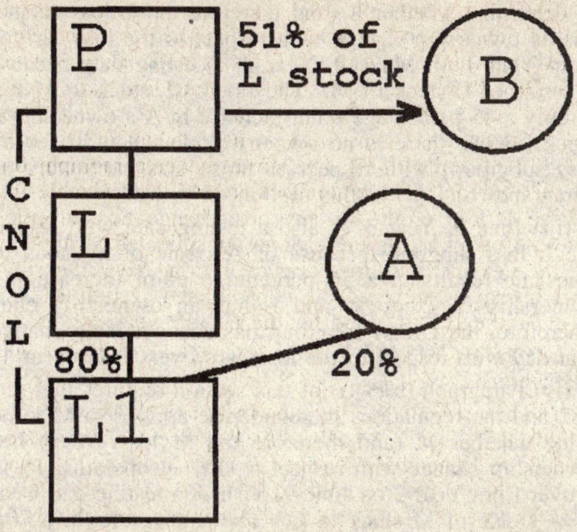

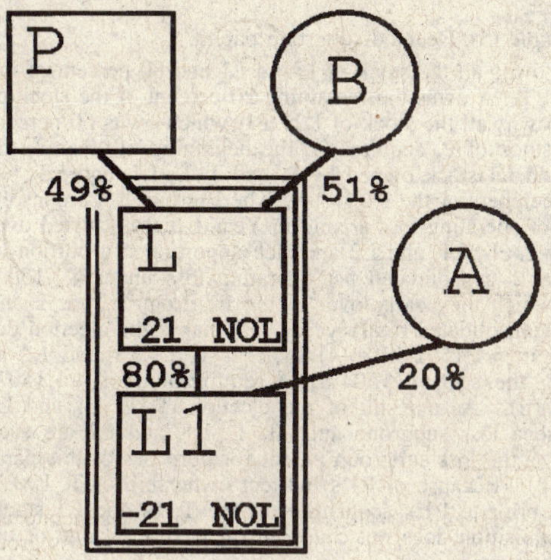

(ii) Under § 1.1502-91(d)(1), L and L1 compose a loss subgroup on September 9, Year 2, the day that they become members of the L group. Under paragraph (b)(1)(ii) of this section, section 382 and the regulations thereunder are applied to L to determine whether it (and therefore the L loss subgroup) has an ownership change with respect to the portion of the Year 1 consolidated net operating loss that is apportioned to L1 on September 9, Year 2. L has an ownership change resulting from P's sale of 51 percent of the L stock to A. Therefore, the L loss subgroup has an ownership change with respect to that loss.

Example (4). Loss group and loss subgroup—contemporaneous ownership changes.

(i) A owns all the stock of corporation M, M owns 35 percent and B owns 65 percent of the L stock, and L owns all the L1 stock. The L group has a consolidated net operating loss arising in Year 1 that is carried over to Year 2. On May 19, Year 2, B sells 45 percent of the L stock to M for cash. M, L, and L1 thereafter file consolidated returns. L and L1 are each apportioned a portion of the Year 1 consolidated net operating loss, which they carry over to the M group's Year 2 and Year 3 consolidated return years. The M group has a consolidated net operating loss arising in Year 2 that is carried over to Year 3. On June 9, Year 3, A sells 70 percent of the M stock to C. The following is a graphic illustration of these facts:

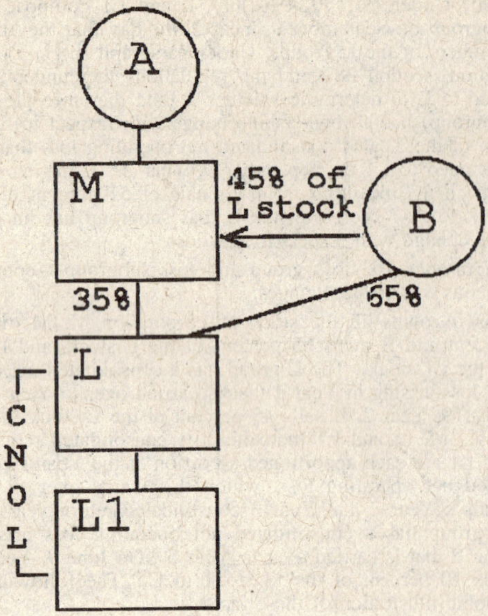

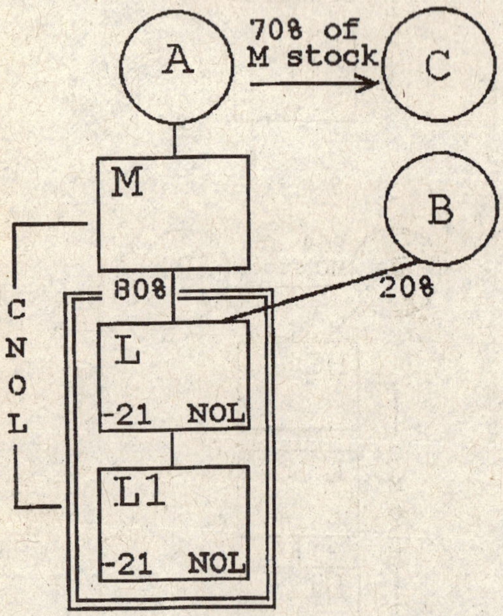

(ii) Under § 1.1502-91(d)(1), L and L1 compose a loss subgroup on May 19, Year 2, the day they become members of the M group. Under paragraph (b)(1)(ii) of this section, section 382 and the regulations thereunder are applied to L to determine whether L (and therefore the L loss subgroup) has an ownership change with respect to the loss carryovers from Year 1 on May 19, Year 2, a testing date because of B's sale of L stock to M. The sale of L stock to M results in only a 45 percentage point increase in A's ownership of L stock. Thus, there is no ownership change of L (or the L loss subgroup) with respect to those loss carryovers under paragraph (b)(1)(ii) of this section on that day.

(iii) June 9, Year 3, is also a testing date with respect to the L loss subgroup because of A's sale of M stock to C. The sale results in a 56 percentage point increase in C's ownership of L stock, and L has an ownership change. Therefore, the L loss subgroup has an ownership change on that day with respect to the loss carryovers from Year 1.

(iv) Paragraph (b)(1)(i) of this section requires that section 382 and the regulations thereunder be applied to M to determine whether M (and therefore the M loss group) has an ownership change with respect to the net operating loss carryover from Year 2 on June 9, Year 3, a testing date because of A's sale of M stock to C. The sale results in a 70 percentage point increase in C's ownership of M stock, and M has an ownership change. Therefore, the M loss group has an ownership change on that day with respect to that loss carryover.

Example (5). Deemed subgroup parent.

(i) P owns all the stock of L and L1 and 80 percent of the stock of T. A owns the remaining 20 percent of the stock of T. L1 owns all the stock of L2. P1, which owns 60 percent of the stock of P, acquires, at the beginning of Year 2, the T, L, and L1 stock owned by P, and T, L, L1, and L2 become members of the P1 group. The P group has a consolidated net operating loss arising in Year 1 that is carried over to Year 2. L, L1, and L2 are each apportioned a portion of the Year 1 consolidated net operating loss under § 1.1502-21(b), which they carry over to the P1 group's Year 2 and Year 3 consolidated return years. P1 makes the election described in § 1.1502-91(d)(4) to treat T, L, L1 and L2 as meeting the section 1504(a)(1) requirement of § 1.1502-91(d)(1)(ii). As a result of the election, T, L, L1 and L2 compose a loss subgroup and T, L, L1, and L2 are each treated as the loss subgroup parent for purposes of this paragraph (b). Because of P1's indirect ownership of T, L, L1, and L2 prior to P1's acquisition of the T, L, and L1 stock, P1's acquisition does not cause an ownership change of the loss subgroup.

(ii) On February 2, Year 3, L1 sells all of the stock of L2 to B. Although L2 is treated as a loss subgroup parent, the determination whether the loss subgroup comprised of T, L, and L1 has an ownership change under this paragraph (b) is made without regard to the sale of L2 because L2's ownership change occurred upon ceasing to be a member of the P1 group. See § 1.1502-95(b) to determine the application of section 382 to L2 when L2 ceases to be a member of the P1 group and the T, L, L1 and L2 loss subgroup.

(iii) On March 26, Year 3, A sells her 20 percent minority stock interest in T to C . C's purchase, together with the 32 percentage point owner shift effected by P1's acquisition of the T stock at the beginning of Year 2, causes an ownership change of T, and therefore of the loss subgroup comprised of T, L, and L1.

(3) Special adjustments. (i) Common parent succeeded by a new common parent. For purposes of determining if a loss group has an ownership change, if the common parent of a loss group is succeeded or acquired by a new common parent and the loss group remains in existence, the new

common parent is treated as a continuation of the former common parent with appropriate adjustments to take into account shifts in ownership of the former common parent during the testing period (including shifts that occur incident to the common parent's becoming the former common parent). A new common parent may be a continuation of the former common parent even if, under § 1.1502-91(g)(2)(ii), the new common parent is not included in determining whether the group has a net unrealized built-in loss.

(ii) Newly created loss subgroup parent. For purposes of determining if a loss subgroup has an ownership change, if the member that is the loss subgroup parent has not been the loss subgroup parent for at least 3 years as of a testing date, appropriate adjustments must be made to take into account owner shifts of members of the loss subgroup so that the structure of the loss subgroup does not have the effect of avoiding an ownership change under section 382. (See paragraph (b)(3)(iii), Example 3 of this section.)

(iii) Examples. The following examples illustrate the principles of this paragraph (b)(3):

Example (1). New common parent acquires old common parent.

(i) A, who owns all the L stock, sells 30 percent of the L stock to B on August 26, Year 1. L owns all the L1 stock. The L group has a consolidated net operating loss arising in Year 1 that is carried over to Year 3. On July 16, Year 2, A and B transfer their L stock to a newly created holding company, HC, in exchange for 70 percent and 30 percent, respectively, of the HC stock. HC, L, and L1 thereafter file consolidated returns. Under the principles of § 1.1502-75(d), the L loss group is treated as remaining in existence, with HC taking the place of L as the new common parent of the loss group. The following is a graphic illustration of these facts:

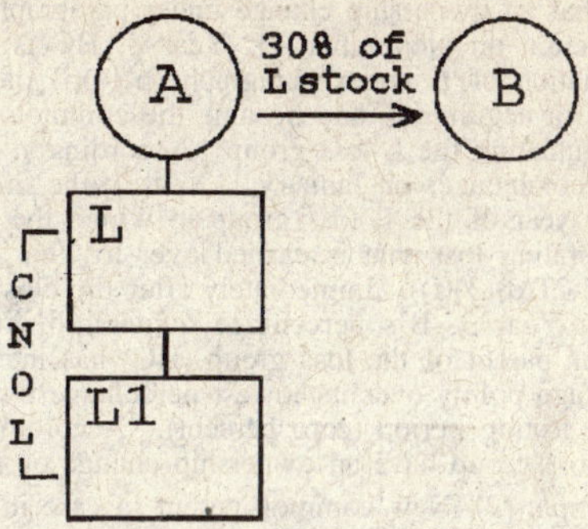

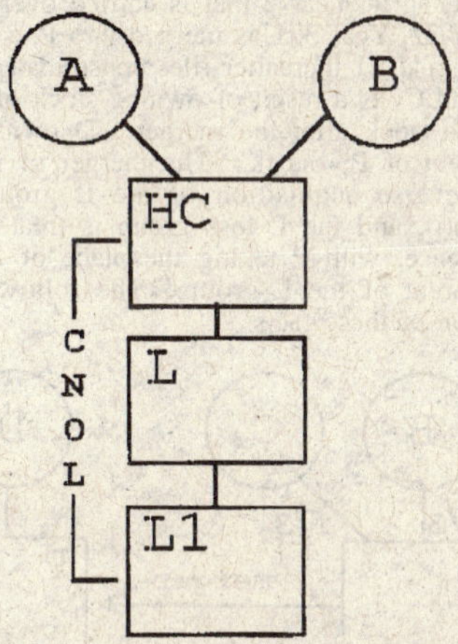

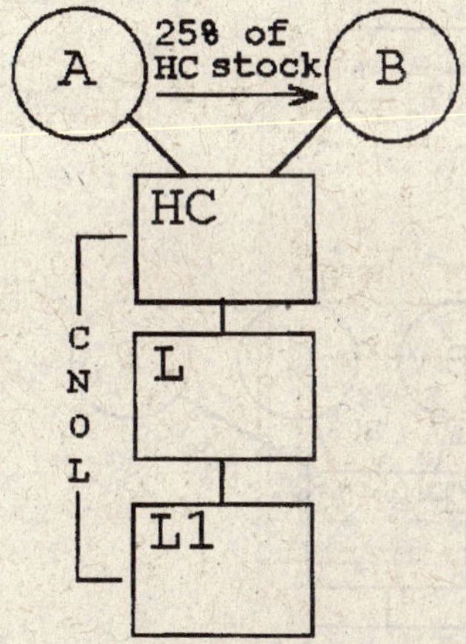

(ii) On November 11, Year 3, A sells 25 percent of the HC stock to B. For purposes of determining if the L loss group has an ownership change under paragraph (b)(1)(i) of this section on November 11, Year 3, HC is treated as a continuation of L under paragraph (b)(4)(i) of this section because it acquired L and became the common parent without terminating the L loss group. Accordingly, HC's testing period commences on January 1, Year 1, the first day of the taxable year of the L loss group in which the consolidated net operating loss that is carried over to Year 3 arose (see § 1.382-2T(d)(3)(i)). Immediately after the close of November 11, Year 3, B's percentage ownership interest in the common parent of the loss group (HC) has increased by 55 percentage points over its lowest percentage ownership during the testing period (zero percent). Accordingly, HC and the L loss group have an ownership change on that day.

Example (2). New common parent in case in which common parent ceases to exist.

(i) A, B, and C each own one-third of the L stock. L owns all the L1 stock. The L group has a consolidated net operating loss arising in Year 2 that is carried over to Year 3. On November 22, Year 3, L is merged into P, a corporation owned by D, and L1 thereafter files consolidated returns with P. A, B, and C, as a result of owning stock of L, own 90 percent of P's stock after the merger. D owns the remaining 10 percent of P's stock. The merger of L into P qualifies as a reverse acquisition of the L group under § 1.1502-75(d)(3)(i), and the L loss group is treated as remaining in existence, with P taking the place of L as the new common parent of the L group. The following is a graphic illustration of these facts:

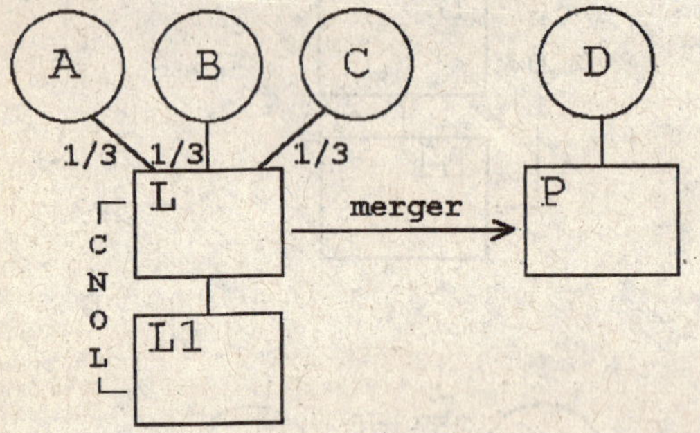

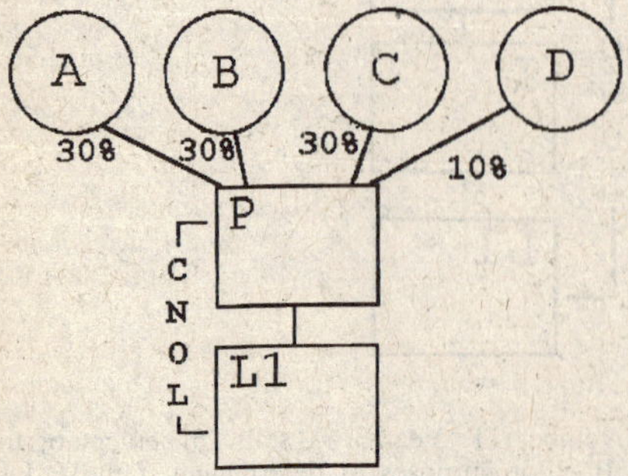

(ii) For purposes of determining if the L loss group has an ownership change on November 22, Year 3, the day of the merger, P is treated as a continuation of L so that the testing period for P begins on January 1, Year 2, the first day of the taxable year of the L loss group in which the consolidated net operating loss that is carried over to Year 3 arose. Immediately after the close of November 22, Year 3, D is the only 5-percent shareholder that has increased his ownership interest in P during the testing period (from zero to 10 percentage points).

(iii) The facts are the same as in paragraph (i) of this Example 2, except that A has held 23⅓ shares (23⅓ percent) of L's stock for five years, and A purchased an additional 10 shares of L stock from E two years before the merger. Immediately after the close of the day of the merger (a testing date), A's ownership interest in P, the common parent of the L loss group, has increased by 6⅔ percentage points over A's lowest percentage ownership during the testing period (23⅓ percent to 30 percent).

(iv) The facts are the same as in (i) of this Example 2, except that P has a net operating loss arising in Year 1 that is carried to the first consolidated return year ending after the day of the merger. Solely for purposes of determining whether the L loss group has an ownership change under paragraph (b)(1)(i) of this section, the testing period for P commences on January 1, Year 2. P does not determine the earliest day for its testing period by reference to its net operating loss carryover from Year 1, which §§ 1.1502-1(f)(3) and 1.1502-75(d)(3)(i) treat as arising in a SRLY. See § 1.1502-94 to determine the application of section 382 with respect to P's net operating loss carryover.

Example (3). Newly acquired loss subgroup parent.

(i) P owns all the L stock and L owns all the L1 stock. The P group has a consolidated net operating loss arising in Year 1 that is carried over to Year 3. On January 19, Year 2, L issues a 20 percent stock interest to B. On February 5, Year 3, P contributes its L stock to a newly formed subsidiary, HC, in exchange for all the HC stock, and distributes the HC stock to its sole shareholder A. HC, L, and L1 thereafter file consolidated returns. A portion of the P group's Year 1 consolidated net operating loss is apportioned to L and L1 under § 1.1502-21(b) and is carried over to the HC group's year ending after February 5, Year 3. HC, L, and L1 compose a loss subgroup within the meaning of § 1.1502-91(d) with respect to the net operating loss carryovers from Year 1. The following is a graphic illustration of these facts:

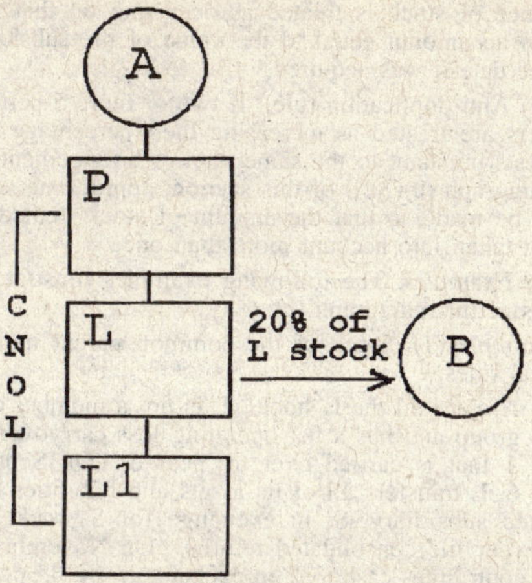

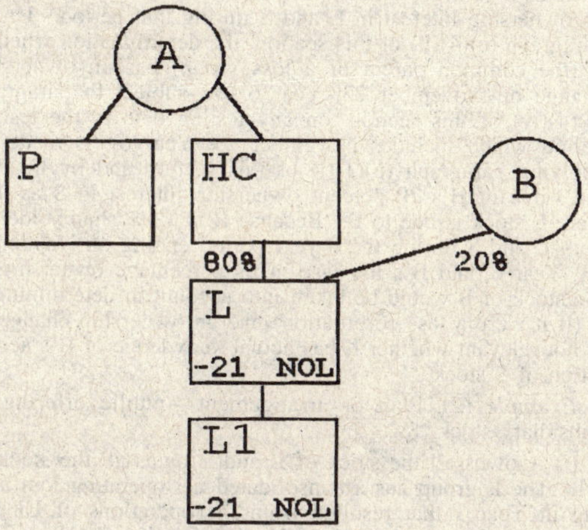

(ii) February 5, Year 3, is a testing date for HC as the loss subgroup parent with respect to the net operating loss carryovers of L and L1 from Year 1. See paragraph (b)(1)(ii)(B) of this section. For purposes of determining whether HC has an ownership change on the testing date, appropriate adjustments must be made with respect to the changes in the percentage ownership of the stock of HC because HC was not the loss subgroup parent for at least 3 years prior to the day on which it became a member of the HC loss subgroup (a testing date). The appropriate adjustments include adjustments so that HC succeeds to the owner shifts of other members of the former group. Thus, HC succeeds to the owner shift of L that resulted from the sale of the 20 percent interest to B in determining whether the HC loss subgroup has an ownership change on February 5, Year 3, and on any subsequent testing date that includes January 19, Year 2.

(4) End of separate tracking of certain losses. If § 1.1502-96(a) (relating to the end of separate tracking of attributes) applies to a loss subgroup, then, while one or more members that were included in the loss subgroup remain members of the consolidated group, there is an ownership change with respect to their attributes described in § 1.1502-96(a)(2) only if the consolidated group is a loss group and has an ownership change under paragraph (b)(1)(i) of this section (or such a member has an ownership change under § 1.1502-96(b) (relating to ownership changes of subsidiaries)). If, however, the loss subgroup has had an ownership change before § 1.1502-96(a) applies, see § 1.1502-96(c) for the continuing application of the subgroup's section 382 limitation with respect to its pre-change subgroup attributes.

(c) Supplemental rules for determining ownership change. *(1) Scope.* This paragraph (c) contains a supplemental rule for determining whether there is an ownership change of a loss group (or loss subgroup). It applies in addition to, and not instead of, the rules of paragraph (b) of this section. Thus, for example, if the common parent of the loss group has an ownership change under paragraph (b) of this section, the loss group has an ownership change even if, by applying this paragraph (c), the common parent would not have an ownership change. This paragraph (c) does not apply in determining an ownership change of a loss subgroup for which an election under § 1.1502-91(d)(4) is made.

(2) Cause for applying supplemental rule. This paragraph (c) applies to a loss group (or loss subgroup) if—

(i) Any 5-percent shareholder of the common parent (or loss subgroup parent) increases its percentage ownership interest in the stock of both—

(A) A subsidiary of the loss group (or loss subgroup) other than by a direct or indirect acquisition of stock of the common parent (or loss subgroup parent); and

(B) The common parent (or loss subgroup parent);

(ii) Those increases occur within a 3 year period ending on any day of a consolidated return year or, if shorter, the period beginning on the first day following the most recent ownership change of the loss group (or loss subgroup); and

(iii) Either—

(A) The common parent (or loss subgroup parent) has actual knowledge of the increase in the 5-percent shareholder's ownership interest in the stock of the subsidiary (or has actual knowledge of the plan or arrangement described in paragraph (c) (3)(i) of this section) before the date that the group's income tax return is filed for the taxable year that includes the date of that increase; or

(B) At any time during the period described in paragraph (c)(2)(ii) of this section, the 5-percent shareholder of the common parent is also a 5-percent shareholder of the subsidiary (determined without regard to paragraph (c)(3)(i) of this section) whose percentage increase in the ownership of the stock of the subsidiary would be taken into account in determining if the subsidiary has an ownership change (determined as if the subsidiary was a loss corporation and applying the principles of § 1.382-2T(k), including the principles relating to duty to inquire).

(3) Operating rules. Solely for purposes of this paragraph (c)—

(i) A 5-percent shareholder of the common parent (or loss subgroup parent) is treated as increasing its ownership interest in the stock of a subsidiary to the extent, if any, that another person or persons increases its percentage ownership interest in the stock of a subsidiary pursuant to a plan or arrangement under which the 5-percent shareholder increases its percentage ownership interest in the common parent (or loss subgroup parent);

(ii) The rules in section 382(l)(3) and §§ 1.382-2T(h) and 1.382-4(d) (relating to constructive ownership) apply with respect to the stock of the subsidiary by treating such stock as stock of a loss corporation; and

(iii) In the case of a loss subgroup, a subsidiary includes any member of the loss subgroup other than the loss subgroup parent. (A loss subgroup parent is, however, a subsidiary of the loss group of which it is a member.)

(4) Supplemental ownership change rules. The determination whether the common parent (or loss subgroup parent) has an ownership change is made by applying paragraph (b)(1) of this section as modified by the following additional rules:

(i) Additional testing dates for the common parent (or loss subgroup parent). A testing date for the common parent (or loss subgroup parent) also includes—

(A) Each day on which there is an increase in the percentage ownership of stock of a subsidiary as described in paragraph (c)(2) of this section; and

(B) The first day of the first consolidated return year for which the group is a loss group (or the members compose a loss subgroup).

(ii) Treatment of subsidiary stock as stock of the common parent (or loss subgroup parent). The common parent (or loss subgroup parent) is treated as though it had issued to the person acquiring (or deemed to acquire) the subsidiary stock an amount of its own stock (by value) that equals the value of the subsidiary stock represented by the percentage increase in that person's ownership of the subsidiary (determined on a separate entity basis). Similar principles apply if the increase in percentage ownership interest is effected by a redemption or similar transaction.

(iii) Different testing periods. Stock treated as issued under paragraph (c)(4)(ii) of this section on a testing date is not treated as so issued for purposes of applying the ownership change rules of this paragraph (c) and paragraph (b) (1) of this section in a testing period that does not include that testing date.

(iv) Disaffiliation of a subsidiary. If a deemed issuance of stock under paragraph (c)(4)(ii) of this section would not cause the loss group (or loss subgroup) to have an ownership change before the day (if any) on which the subsidiary ceases to be a member of the loss group (or subgroup), then paragraph (c)(4) of this section shall not apply.

(v) Subsidiary stock acquired first. If an increase of subsidiary stock described in paragraph (c)(2)(i)(A) of this section occurs before the date that the 5-percent shareholder increases its percentage ownership interest in the stock of the common parent (or loss subgroup parent), then the deemed issuance of stock is treated as occurring on that later date, but in an amount equal to the value of the subsidiary stock on the date it was acquired.

(vi) Anti-duplication rule. If two or more 5-percent shareholders are treated as increasing their percentage ownership interests pursuant to the same plan or arrangement described in paragraph (c)(3)(i) of this section, appropriate adjustments must be made so that the amount of stock treated as issued is not taken into account more than once.

(5) Examples. The following examples illustrate the principles of this paragraph (c):

Example (1). Stock of the common parent under supplemental rules.

(i) A owns all the L stock. L is not a member of an affiliated group and has a net operating loss carryover arising in Year 1 that is carried over to Year 6. On September 20, Year 6, L transfers all of its assets and liabilities to a newly created subsidiary, S, in exchange for S stock. L and S thereafter file consolidated returns. On November 23, Year 6, B contributes cash to L in exchange for a 45 percent ownership interest in L and contributes cash to S for a 20 percent ownership interest in S.

(ii) During the 3 year period ending on November 23, Year 6, B is a 5% shareholder of L and of S that increases its ownership interest in L and S during that period. Under paragraph (c)(4)(ii) of this section, the determination whether L (the common parent of a loss group) has an ownership change on November 23, Year 6 (or, subject to paragraph (c)(4)(iv) of this section, on any testing date in the testing period which includes November 23, Year 6), is made by applying paragraph (b)(1)(i) of this section and by treating the value of B's 20 percent ownership interest in S as if it were L stock issued to B. Because B is a 5% shareholder of both L and S during the 3 year period ending on November 23, Year 6, and B's increase in its percentage ownership in the stock of S would be taken into account in determining if S (if it were a loss corporation) had an ownership change, it is not relevant whether L has actual knowledge of B's acquisition of S stock.

Example (2). Plan or arrangement—public offering of subsidiary stock.

(i) A owns all the stock of L and L owns all the stock of L1. The L group has a consolidated net operating loss arising in Year 1 that resulted from the operations of L1 and that is carried over to Year 2. On October 7, Year 2, A sells 49 percent of the L stock to B. As part of a plan that includes the sale of L stock, A causes a public offering of L1 stock on November 6, Year 2. L has actual knowledge of the plan. The following is a graphic illustration of these facts:

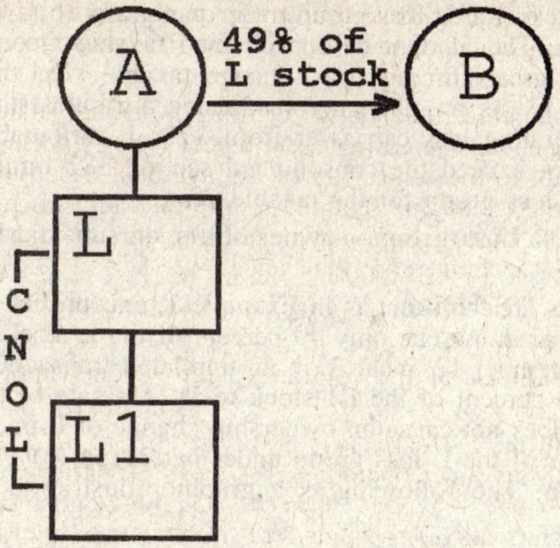

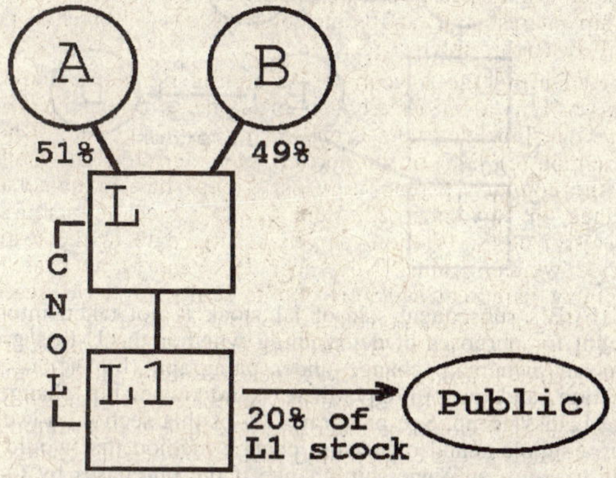

(ii) A's sale of the L stock to B does not cause an ownership change of the L loss group on October 7, Year 2, under the rules of § 1.382-2T and paragraph (b)(1)(i) of this section.

(iii) Because the issuance of L1 stock to the public occurs as part of the same plan as B's acquisition of L stock, and L has knowledge of the plan, paragraph (c)(4) of this section applies to determine whether the L loss group has an ownership change on November 6, Year 2 (or, subject to paragraph (c)(4)(iv) of this section, on any testing date for which the testing period includes November 6, Year 2).

(d) Testing period following ownership change under this section. If a loss group (or a loss subgroup) has had an ownership change under this section, the testing period for determining a subsequent ownership change with respect to pre-change consolidated attributes (or pre-change subgroup attributes) begins no earlier than the first day following the loss group's (or loss subgroup's) most recent change date.

(e) Information statements. *(1) Common parent of a loss group.* The common parent of a loss group must file the information statement required by § 1.382-11T(a) for a consolidated return year because of any owner shift, equity structure shift, or other transaction described in § 1.382-2T(a)(2)(i)—

(i) With respect to the common parent and with respect to any subsidiary stock subject to paragraph (c) of this section; and

(ii) With respect to an ownership change described in § 1.1502-96(b) (relating to ownership changes of subsidiaries).

(2) Abbreviated statement with respect to loss subgroups. The common parent of a consolidated group that has a loss subgroup during a consolidated return year must file the information statement required by § 1.382-11(a) because of any owner shift, equity structure shift, or other transaction described in § 1.382-2T(a)(2)(i) with respect to the loss subgroup parent and with respect to any subsidiary stock subject to paragraph (c) of this section. Instead of filing a separate statement for each loss subgroup parent, the common parent (which is treated as a loss corporation) may file the single statement described in paragraph (e)(1) of this section. In addition to the information concerning stock ownership of the common parent, the single statement must identify each loss subgroup parent and state which loss subgroups, if any, have had ownership changes during the consolidated return year. The loss subgroup parent is, however, still required to maintain the records necessary to determine if the loss subgroup has an ownership change. This paragraph (e)(2) applies with respect to the attributes of a loss subgroup until, under § 1.1502-96(a), the attributes are no longer treated as described in § 1.1502-91(d) (relating to the definition of loss subgroup). After that time, the information statement described in paragraph (e)(1) of this section must be filed with respect to those attributes.

T.D. 8824, 6/25/99, amend T.D. 9264, 5/26/2006, T.D. 9329, 6/13/2007.

§ 1.1502-92A Ownership change of a loss group or a loss subgroup generally applicable for testing dates before June 25, 1999.

(a) Scope. This section provides rules for determining if there is an ownership change for purposes of section 382 with respect to a loss group or a loss subgroup. See § 1.1502-94A for special rules for determining if there is an ownership change with respect to a new loss member and § 1.1502-96A(b) for special rules for determining if there is an ownership change of a subsidiary.

(b) Determination of an ownership change. *(1) Parent change method.* (i) Loss group. A loss group has an ownership change if the loss group's common parent has an ownership change under section 382 and the regulations thereunder. Solely for purposes of determining whether the common parent has an ownership change—

(A) The losses described in § 1.1502-91A(c) are treated as net operating losses (or a net unrealized built-in loss) of the common parent; and

(B) The common parent determines the earliest day that its testing period can begin by reference to only the attributes that make the group a loss group under § 1.1502-91A(c).

(ii) Loss subgroup. A loss subgroup has an ownership change if the loss subgroup parent has an ownership change under section 382 and the regulations thereunder. The principles of § 1.1502-95A(b) (relating to ceasing to be a member of a consolidated group) apply in determining whether the loss subgroup parent has an ownership change. Solely for purposes of determining whether the loss subgroup parent has an ownership change—

(A) The losses described in § 1.1502-91A(d) are treated as net operating losses (or a net unrealized built-in loss) of the loss subgroup parent;

(B) The day that the members of the loss subgroup become members of the group (or a loss subgroup) is treated as a testing date within the meaning of § 1.382-2(a)(4); and

(C) The loss subgroup parent determines the earliest day that its testing period can begin under § 1.382-2T(d)(3) by reference to only the attributes that make the members a loss subgroup under § 1.1502-91A(d).

(2) Examples. The following examples illustrate the principles of this paragraph (b).

Example (1). Loss group—ownership change of the common parent.

(a) A owns all the L stock. L owns 80 percent and B owns 20 percent of the L1 stock. For Year 1, the L group has a consolidated net operating loss that resulted from the operations of L1 and that is carried over to Year 2. The value of the L stock is $1000. The total value of the L1 stock is $600 and the value of the L1 stock held by B is $120. The L group is a loss group under § 1.1502-91A(c)(1) because it is entitled to use its net operating loss carryover from Year 1. On August 15, Year 2, A sells 51 percent of the L stock to C. The following is a graphic illustration of these facts:

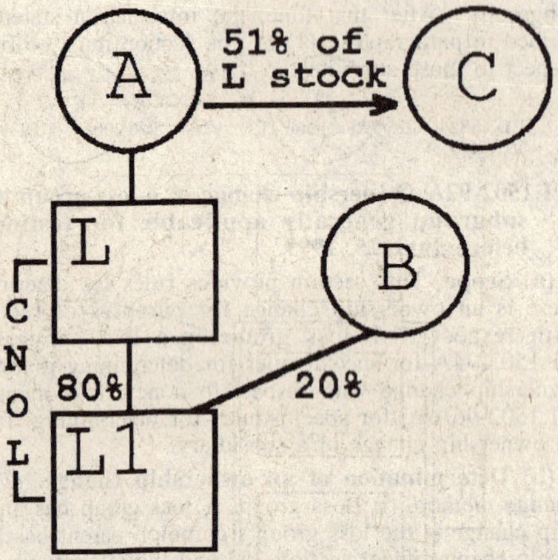

(b) Under paragraph (b)(1)(i) of this section, section 382 and the regulations thereunder are applied to L to determine whether it (and therefore the L loss group) has an ownership change with respect to its net operating loss carryover from Year 1 attributable to L1 on August 15, Year 2. The sale of the L stock to C causes an ownership change of L under § 1.382-2T and of the L loss group under paragraph (b)(1)(i) of this section. The amount of consolidated taxable income of the L loss group for any post-change taxable year that may be offset by its pre-change consolidated attributes (that is, the net operating loss carryover from Year 1 attributable to L1) may not exceed the consolidated section 382 limitation for the L loss group for the taxable year.

Example (2). Loss group—owner shifts of subsidiaries disregarded.

(a) The facts are the same as in Example 1, except that on August 15, Year 2, A sells only 49 percent of the L stock to C and, on December 12, Year 3, in an unrelated transaction, B sells the 20 percent of the L1 stock to D. A's sale of the L stock to C does not cause an ownership change of L under § 1.382-2T nor of the L loss group under paragraph (b)(1)(i) of this section. The following is a graphic illustration of these facts:

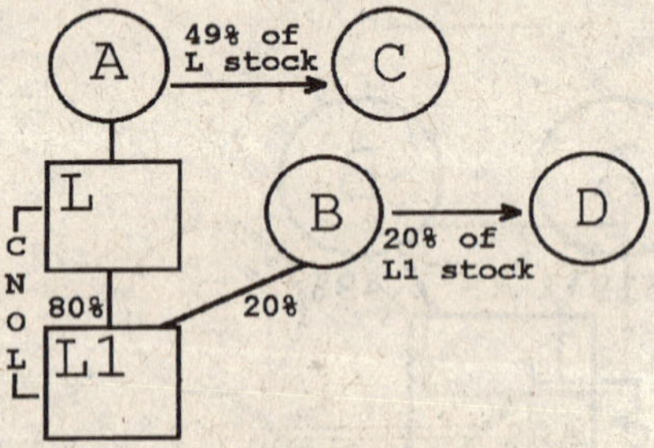

(b) B's subsequent sale of L1 stock is not taken into account for purposes of determining whether the L loss group has an ownership change under paragraph (b)(1)(i) of this section, and, accordingly, there is no ownership change of the L loss group. See paragraph (c) of this section, however, for a supplemental ownership change method that would apply to cause an ownership change if the purchases by C and D were pursuant to a plan or arrangement.

Example (3). Loss subgroup—ownership change of loss subgroup parent controls.

(a) P owns all the L stock. L owns 80 percent and A owns 20 percent of the L1 stock. The P group has a consolidated net operating loss arising in Year 1 that is carried over to Year 2. On September 9, Year 2, P sells 51 percent of the L stock to B, and L1 is apportioned a portion of the Year 1 consolidated net operating loss under §§ 1.1502-21(b) or 1.1502-21T(b) in effect prior to June 25, 1999, as contained in 26 CFR part 1 revised April 1, 1999, as applicable, which it carries over to its next taxable year. L and L1 file a consolidated return for their first taxable year ending after the sale to B. The following is a graphic illustration of these facts:

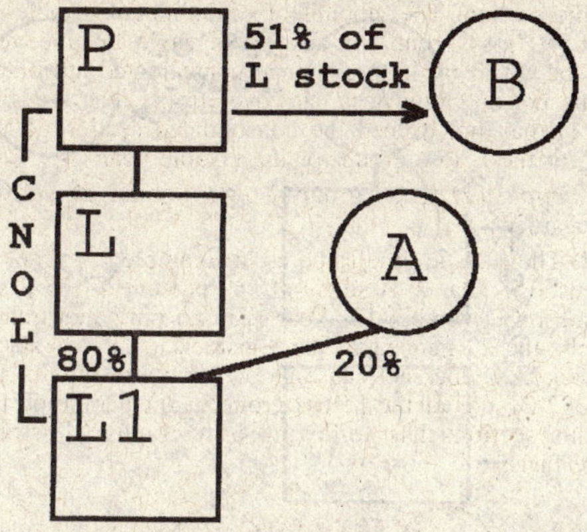

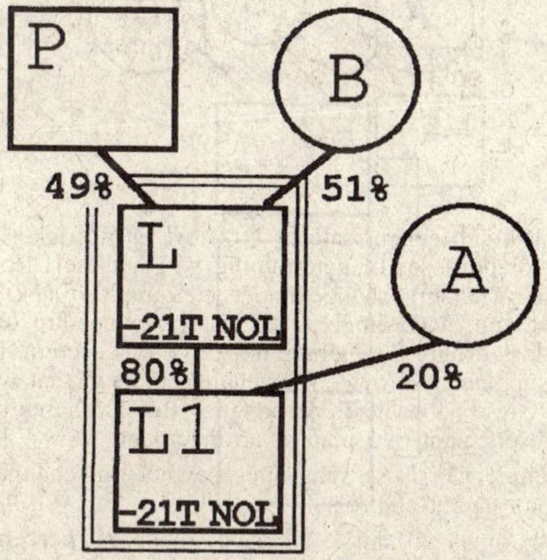

(b) Under § 1.1502-91A(d)(1), L and L1 compose a loss subgroup on September 9, Year 2, the day that they become members of the L group. Under paragraph (b)(1)(ii) of this section, section 382 and the regulations thereunder are applied to L to determine whether it (and therefore the L loss subgroup) has an ownership change with respect to the portion of the Year 1 consolidated net operating loss that is apportioned to L1 on September 9, Year 2. L has an ownership change resulting from P's sale of 51 percent of the L stock to A. Therefore, the L loss subgroup has an ownership change with respect to that loss.

Example (4). Loss group and loss subgroup—contemporaneous ownership changes.

(a) A owns all the stock of corporation M, M owns 35 percent and B owns 65 percent of the L stock, and L owns all the L1 stock. The L group has a consolidated net operating loss arising in Year 1 that is carried over to Year 2. On May 19, Year 2, B sells 45 percent of the L stock to M for cash. M, L, and L1 thereafter file consolidated returns. L and L1 are each apportioned a portion of the Year 1 consolidated net operating loss, which they carry over to the M group's Year 2 and Year 3 consolidated return years. The M group has a consolidated net operating loss arising in Year 2 that is carried over to Year 3. On June 9, Year 3, A sells 70 percent of the M stock to C. The following is a graphic illustration of these facts:

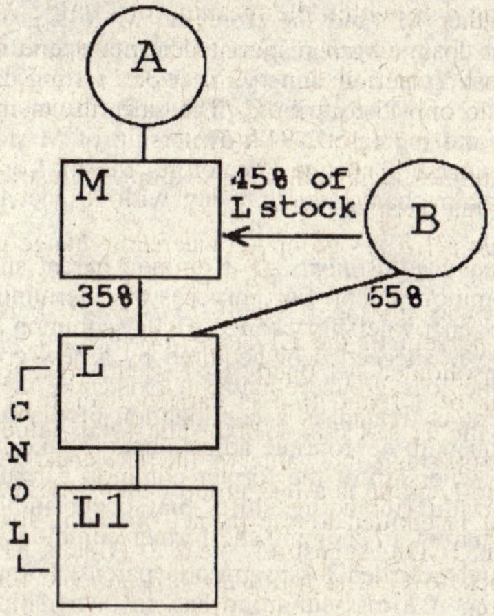

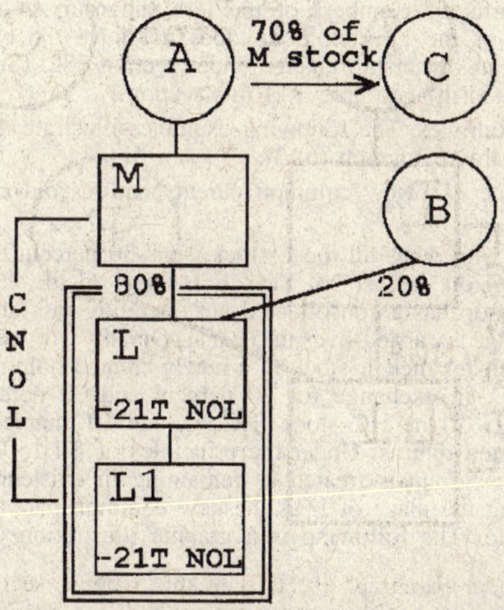

(b) Under § 1.1502-91A(d)(1), L and L1 compose a loss subgroup on May 19, Year 2, the day they become members of the M group. Under paragraph (b)(1)(ii) of this section, section 382 and the regulations thereunder are applied to L to determine whether L (and therefore the L loss subgroup) has an ownership change with respect to the loss carryovers from Year 1 on May 19, Year 2, a testing date because of B's sale of L stock to M. The sale of L stock to M results in only a 45 percentage point increase in A's ownership of L stock. Thus, there is no ownership change of L (or the L loss subgroup) with respect to those loss carryovers under paragraph (b)(1)(ii) of this section on that day.

(c) June 9, Year 3, is also a testing date with respect to the L loss subgroup because of A's sale of M stock to C. The sale results in a 56 percentage point increase in C's ownership of L stock, and L has an ownership change. Therefore, the L loss subgroup has an ownership change on that day with respect to the loss carryovers from Year 1.

(d) Paragraph (b)(1)(i) of this section requires that section 382 and the regulations thereunder be applied to M to determine whether M (and therefore the M loss group) has an ownership change with respect to the net operating loss carryover from Year 2 on June 9, Year 3, a testing date because of A's sale of M stock to C. The sale results in a 70 percentage point increase in C's ownership of M stock, and M has an ownership change. Therefore, the M loss group has an ownership change on that day with respect to that loss carryover.

(3) Special adjustments. (i) Common parent succeeded by a new common parent. For purposes of determining if a loss group has an ownership change, if the common parent of a loss group is succeeded or acquired by a new common parent and the loss group remains in existence, the new common parent is treated as a continuation of the former common parent with appropriate adjustments to take into account shifts in ownership of the former common parent during the testing period (including shifts that occur incident to the common parent's becoming the former common parent).

(ii) Newly created loss subgroup parent. For purposes of determining if a loss subgroup has an ownership change, if the member that is the loss subgroup parent has not been the loss subgroup parent for at least 3 years as of a testing date, appropriate adjustments must be made to take into account owner shifts of members of the loss subgroup so that the structure of the loss subgroup does not have the effect of avoiding an ownership change under section 382. (See paragraph (b)(3)(iii) Example 3 of this section.)

(iii) Examples. The following examples illustrate the principles of this paragraph (b)(3).

Example (1). New common parent acquires old common parent.

(a) A, who owns all the L stock, sells 30 percent of the L stock to B on August 26, Year 1. L owns all the L1 stock. The L group has a consolidated net operating loss arising in Year 1 that is carried over to Year 3. On July 16, Year 2, A and B transfer their L stock to a newly created holding company, HC, in exchange for 70 percent and 30 percent, respectively, of the HC stock. HC, L, and L1 thereafter file consolidated returns. Under the principles of § 1.1502-75(d), the L loss group is treated as remaining in existence, with HC taking the place of L as the new common parent of the loss group. The following is a graphic illustration of these facts:

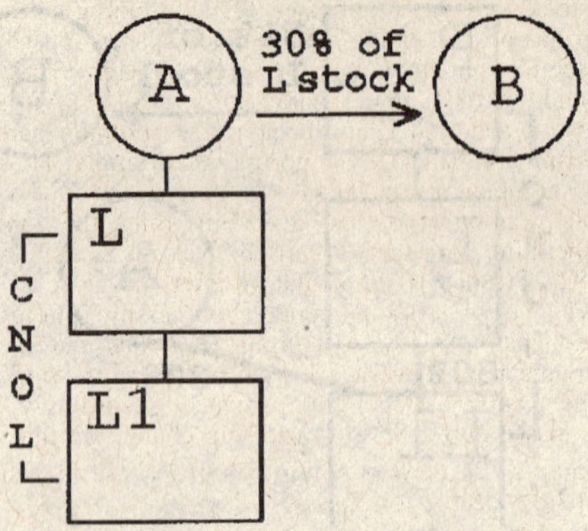

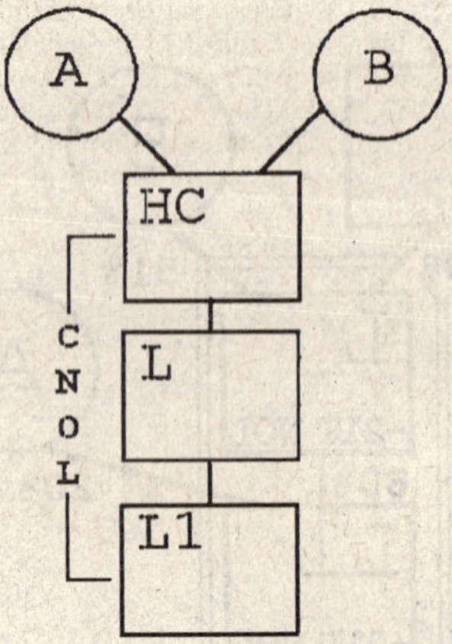

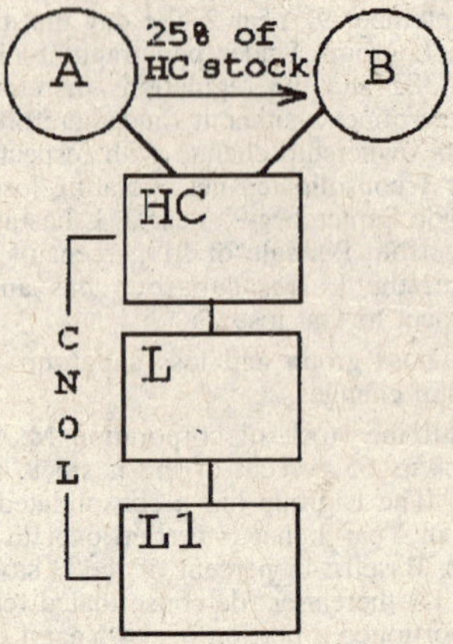

(b) On November 11, Year 3, A sells 25 percent of the HC stock to B. For purposes of determining if the L loss group has an ownership change under paragraph (b)(1)(i) of this section on November 11, Year 3, HC is treated as a continuation of L under paragraph (b)(3)(i) of this section because it acquired L and became the common parent without terminating the L loss group. Accordingly, HC's testing period commences on January 1, Year 1, the first day of the taxable year of the L loss group in which the consolidated net operating loss that is carried over to Year 3 arose (see § 1.382-2T(d)(3)(i)). Immediately after the close of November 11, Year 3, B's percentage ownership interest in the common parent of the loss group (HC) has increased by 55 percentage points over its lowest percentage ownership during the testing period (zero percent). Accordingly, HC and the L loss group have an ownership change on that day.

Example (2). New common parent in case in which common parent ceases to exist.

(a) A, B, and C each own one-third of the L stock. L owns all the L1 stock. The L group has a consolidated net operating loss arising in Year 2 that is carried over to Year 3. On November 22, Year 3, L is merged into P, a corporation owned by D, and L1 thereafter files consolidated returns with P. A, B, and C, as a result of owning stock of L, own 90 percent of P's stock after the merger. D owns the remaining 10 percent of P's stock. The merger of L into P qualifies as a reverse acquisition of the L group under § 1.1502-75(d)(3)(i), and the L loss group is treated as remaining in existence, with P taking the place of L as the new common parent of the L group. The following is a graphic illustration of these facts:

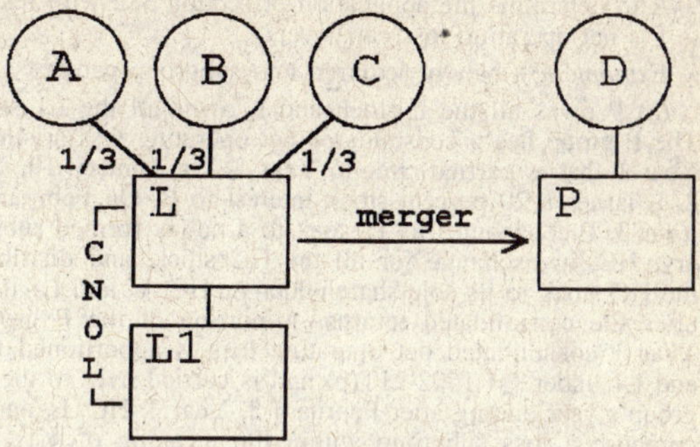

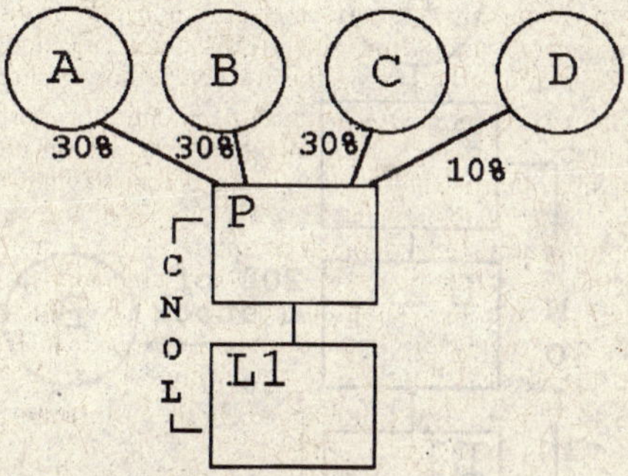

(b) For purposes of determining if the L loss group has an ownership change on November 22, Year 3, the day of the merger, P is treated as a continuation of L so that the testing period for P begins on January 1, Year 2, the first day of the taxable year of the L loss group in which the consolidated net operating loss that is carried over to Year 3 arose. Immediately after the close of November 22, Year 3, D is the only 5-percent shareholder that has increased his ownership interest in P during the testing period (from zero to 10 percentage points).

(c) The facts are the same as in paragraph (a) of this Example 2, except that A has held 23⅓ shares (23⅓ percent) of L's stock for five years, and A purchased an additional 10 shares of L stock from E two years before the merger. Immediately after the close of the day of the merger (a testing date), A's ownership interest in P, the common parent of the L loss group, has increased by 6⅔ percentage points over her lowest percentage ownership during the testing period (23⅓percent to 30 percent).

(d) The facts are the same as in (a) of this Example 2, except that P has a net operating loss arising in Year 1 that is carried to the first consolidated return year ending after the day of the merger. Solely for purposes of determining whether the L loss group has an ownership change under paragraph (b)(1)(i) of this section, the testing period for P commences on January 1, Year 2. P does not determine the earliest day for its testing period by reference to its net operating loss carryover from Year 1, which §§ 1502-1(f)(3) and 1.1502-75(d)(3)(i) treat as arising in a SRLY. See § 1.1502-

94A to determine the application of section 382 with respect to P's net operating loss carryover.

Example (3). Newly acquired loss subgroup parent.

(a) P owns all the L stock and L owns all the L1 stock. The P group has a consolidated net operating loss arising in Year 1 that is carried over to Year 3. On January 19, Year 2, L issues a 20 percent stock interest to B. On February 5, Year 3, P contributes its L stock to a newly formed subsidiary, HC, in exchange for all the HC stock, and distributes the HC stock to its sole shareholder A. HC, L, and L1 thereafter file consolidated returns. A portion of the P group's Year 1 consolidated net operating loss is apportioned to L and L1 under § 1.1502-21T(b) and is carried over to the HC group's year ending after February 5, Year 3. HC, L, and L1 compose a loss subgroup within the meaning of § 1.1502-91A(d) with respect to the net operating loss carryovers from Year 1. The following is a graphic illustration of these facts:

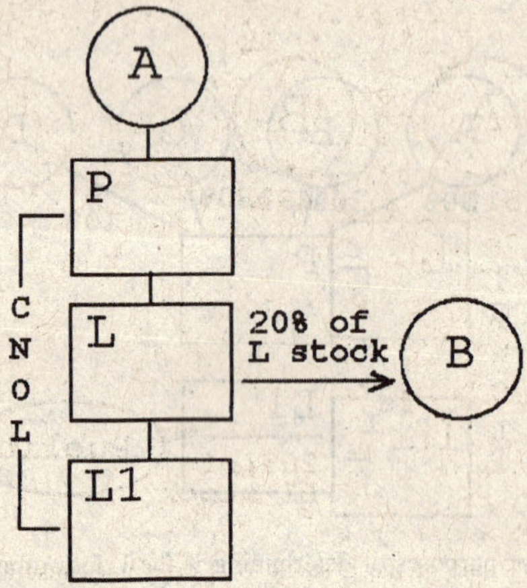

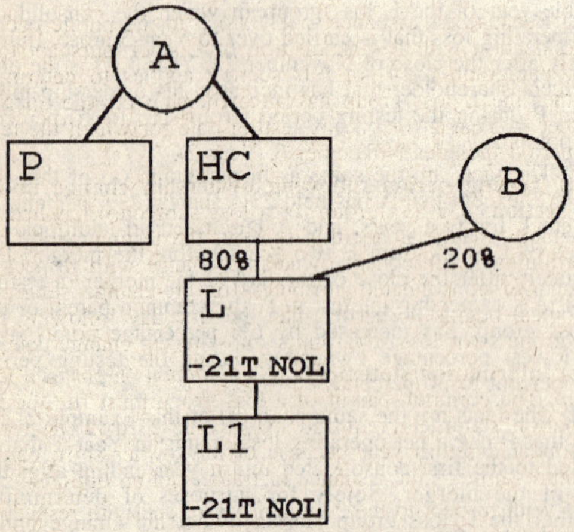

(b) February 5, Year 3, is a testing date for HC as the loss subgroup parent with respect to the net operating loss carryovers of L and L1 from Year 1. See paragraph (b)(1)(ii)(B) of this section. For purposes of determining whether HC has an ownership change on the testing date, appropriate adjustments must be made with respect to the changes in the percentage ownership of the stock of HC because HC was not the loss subgroup parent for at least 3 years prior to the day on which it became a member of the HC loss subgroup (a testing date). The appropriate adjustments include adjustments so that HC succeeds to the owner shifts of other members of the former group. Thus, HC succeeds to the owner shift of L that resulted from the sale of the 20 percent interest to B in determining whether the HC loss subgroup has an ownership change on February 5, Year 3, and on any subsequent testing date that includes January 19, Year 2.

(4) End of separate tracking of certain losses. If § 1.1502-96A(a) (relating to the end of separate tracking of attributes) applies to a loss subgroup, then, while one or more members that were included in the loss subgroup remain members of the consolidated group, there is an ownership change with respect to their attributes described in § 1.1502-96A(a)(2) only if the consolidated group is a loss group and has an ownership change under paragraph (b)(1)(i) of this section (or such a member has an ownership change under § 1.1502-96A(b) (relating to ownership changes of subsidiaries)). If, however, the loss subgroup has had an ownership change before § 1.1502-96A(a) applies, see § 1.1502-96A(c) for the continuing application of the subgroup's section 382 limitation with respect to its pre-change subgroup attributes.

(c) Supplemental rules for determining ownership change. *(1) Scope.* This paragraph (c) contains a supplemental rule for determining whether there is an ownership change of a loss group (or loss subgroup). It applies in addition to, and not instead of, the rules of paragraph (b) of this section. Thus, for example, if the common parent of the loss group has an ownership change under paragraph (b) of this section, the loss group has an ownership change even if, by applying this paragraph (c), the common parent would not have an ownership change.

(2) Cause for applying supplemental rule. This paragraph (c) applies to a loss group (or loss subgroup) if—

(i) Any 5-percent shareholder of the common parent (or loss subgroup parent) increases its percentage ownership interest in the stock of both—

(A) A subsidiary of the loss group (or loss subgroup) other than by a direct or indirect acquisition of stock of the common parent (or loss subgroup parent); and

(B) The common parent (or loss subgroup parent); and

(ii) Those increases occur within a 3 year period ending on any day of a consolidated return year or, if shorter, the period beginning on the first day following the most recent ownership change of the loss group (or loss subgroup).

(3) Operating rules. Solely for purposes of this paragraph (c)—

(i) A 5-percent shareholder of the common parent (or loss subgroup parent) is treated as increasing its percentage ownership interest in the common parent (or loss subgroup parent) or a subsidiary to the extent, if any, that any person acting pursuant to a plan or arrangement with the 5-percent shareholder increases its percentage ownership interest in the stock of that entity;

(ii) The rules in section 382(l)(3) and §§ 1.382-2T(h) and 1.382-4(d) (relating to constructive ownership) apply with respect to the stock of the subsidiary by treating such stock as stock of a loss corporation; and

(iii) In the case of a loss subgroup, a subsidiary includes any member of the loss subgroup other than the loss subgroup parent. (The loss subgroup parent is, however, a subsidiary of the loss group of which it is a member.)

(4) Supplemental ownership change rules. The determination whether the common parent (or loss subgroup parent) has an ownership change is made by applying paragraph (b)(1) of this section as modified by the following additional rules—

(i) Additional testing dates for the common parent (or loss subgroup parent). A testing date for the common parent (or loss subgroup parent) also includes—

(A) Each day on which there is an increase in the percentage ownership of stock of a subsidiary as described in paragraph (c)(2) of this section; and

(B) The first day of the first consolidated return year for which the group is a loss group (or the members compose a loss subgroup);

(ii) Treatment of subsidiary stock as stock of the common parent (or loss subgroup parent). The common parent (or loss subgroup parent) is treated as though it had issued to the person acquiring (or deemed to acquire) the subsidiary stock an amount of its own stock (by value) that equals the value of the subsidiary stock represented by the percentage increase in that person's ownership of the subsidiary (determined on a separate entity basis). A similar principle applies if the increase in percentage ownership interest is effected by a redemption or similar transaction; and

(iii) 5-percent shareholder of the common parent (or loss subgroup parent). Any person described in paragraph (c)(3)(i) of this section who is acting pursuant to the plan or arrangement is treated as a 5-percent shareholder of the common parent (or loss subgroup parent).

(5) Examples. The following examples illustrate the principles of this paragraph (c).

Example (1). Stock of the common parent under supplemental rules.

(a) A owns all the L stock. L is not a member of an affiliated group and has a net operating loss carryover arising in Year 1 that is carried over to Year 6. On September 20, Year 6, L transfers all of its assets and liabilities to a newly created subsidiary, S, in exchange for S stock. L and S thereafter file consolidated returns. On November 23, Year 6, B contributes cash to L in exchange for a 45 percent ownership interest in L and contributes cash to S for a 20 percent ownership interest in S.

(b) B is a 5-percent shareholder of L who increases his percentage ownership interest in L and S during the 3 year period ending on November 23, Year 6. Under paragraph (c)(4)(ii) of this section, the determination whether L (the common parent of a loss group) has an ownership change on November 23, Year 6 (or on any testing date in the testing period which includes November 23, Year 6), is made by applying paragraph (b)(1)(i) of this section and by treating the value of B's 20 percent ownership interest in S as if it were L stock issued to B.

Example (2). Plan or arrangement—public offering of subsidiary stock.

(a) A owns all the stock of L and L owns all the stock of L1. The L group has a consolidated net operating loss arising in Year 1 that resulted from the operations of L1 and that is carried over to Year 2. As part of a plan, A sells 49 percent of the L stock to B on October 7, Year 2, and L1 issues new stock representing a 20 percent ownership interest in L1 to the public on November 6, Year 2. The following is a graphic illustration of these facts:

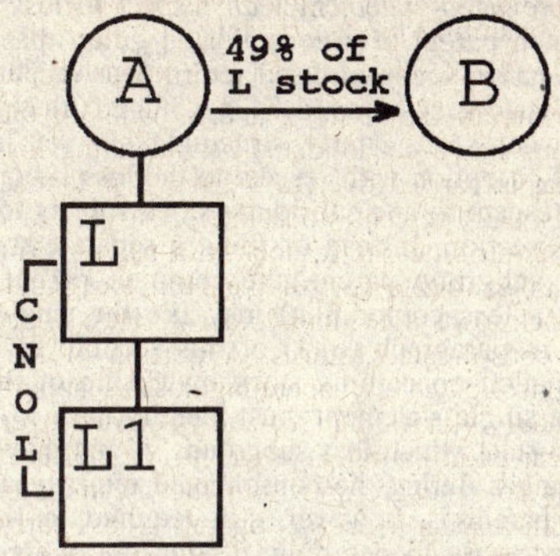

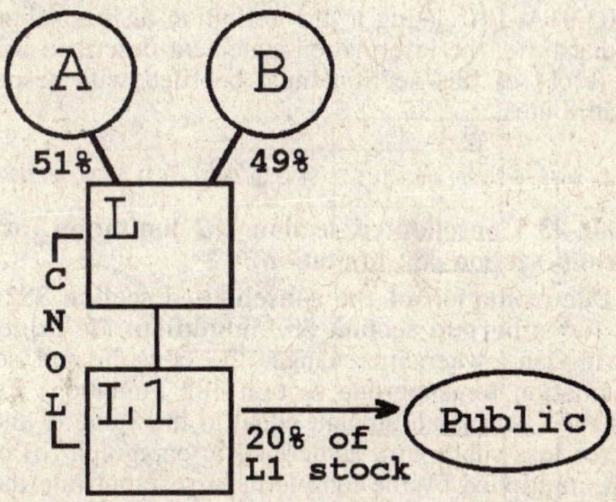

(b) A's sale of the L stock to B does not cause an ownership change of the L loss group on October 7, Year 2, under the rules of § 1.382-2T and paragraph (b)(1)(i) of this section.

(c) Because the issuance of L1 stock to the public occurs in connection with B's acquisition of L stock pursuant to a plan, paragraph (c)(4) of this section applies to determine whether the L loss group has an ownership change on November 6, Year 2 (or on any testing date for which the testing period includes November 6, Year 2).

(d) Testing period following ownership change under this section. If a loss group (or a loss subgroup) has had an ownership change under this section, the testing period for determining a subsequent ownership change with respect to pre-change consolidated attributes (or pre-change subgroup attributes) begins no earlier than the first day following the loss group's (or loss subgroup's) most recent change date.

(e) Information statements. *(1) Common parent of a loss group.* The common parent of a loss group must file the information statement required by § 1.382-2T(a)(2)(ii) for a consolidated return year because of any owner shift, equity structure shift, or the issuance or transfer of an option—

(i) With respect to the common parent and with respect to any subsidiary stock subject to paragraph (c) of this section; and

(ii) With respect to an ownership change described in § 1.1502-96A(b) (relating to ownership changes of subsidiaries).

(2) Abbreviated statement with respect to loss subgroups. The common parent of a consolidated group that has a loss subgroup during a consolidated return year must file the information statement required by § 1.382-2T(a)(2)(ii) because of any owner shift, equity structure shift, or issuance or transfer of an option with respect to the loss subgroup parent and with respect to any subsidiary stock subject to paragraph (c) of this section. Instead of filing a separate statement for each loss subgroup parent, the common parent (which is treated as a loss corporation) may file the single statement described in paragraph (e)(1) of this section. In addition to the information concerning stock ownership of the common parent, the single statement must identify each loss subgroup parent and state which loss subgroups, if any, have had ownership changes during the consolidated return year. The loss subgroup parent is, however, still required to maintain the records necessary to determine if the loss subgroup has an ownership change. This paragraph (e)(2) applies with respect to the attributes of a loss subgroup until, under § 1.1502-96A(a), the attributes are no longer treated as described in § 1.1502-91A(d) (relating to the definition of loss subgroup). After that time, the information statement described in paragraph (e)(1) of this section must be filed with respect to those attributes.

T.D. 8678, 6/26/96, amend T.D. 8823, 6/25/99, T.D. 8824, 6/25/99.

§ 1.1502-93 Consolidated section 382 limitation (or subgroup section 382 limitation).

(a) Determination of the consolidated section 382 limitation (or subgroup section 382 limitation. *(1) In general.* Following an ownership change, the consolidated section 382 limitation (or subgroup section 382 limitation) for any post-change year is an amount equal to the value of the loss group (or loss subgroup), as defined in paragraph (b) of this section, multiplied by the long-term tax-exempt rate that applies with respect to the ownership change, and adjusted as required by section 382 and the regulations thereunder. See, for example, section 382(b)(2) (relating to the carryforward of unused section 382 limitation), section 382(b)(3)(B) (relating to the section 382 limitation for the post-change year that includes the change date), section 382(h) (relating to recognized built-in gains and section 338 gains), and section 382(m)(2) (relating to short taxable years). For special rules relating to the recognized built-in gains of a loss group (or loss subgroup), see paragraph (c)(2) of this section.

(2) Coordination with apportionment rule. For special rules relating to apportionment of a consolidated section 382 limitation (or a subgroup section 382 limitation) or net unrealized built-in gain when one or more corporations cease to be members of a loss group (or a loss subgroup) and to aggregation of amounts so apportioned, see § 1.1502-95(c).

(b) Value of the loss group (or loss subgroup). *(1) Stock value immediately before ownership change.* Subject to any adjustment under paragraph (b)(2) of this section, the value of the loss group (or loss subgroup) is the value, immediately before the ownership change, of the stock of each member, other than stock that is owned directly or indirectly by another member. For this purpose—

(i) Ownership is determined under § 1.382-2T;

(ii) A member is considered to indirectly own stock of another member through a nonmember only if the member has a 5-percent or greater ownership interest in the nonmember; and

(iii) Stock includes stock described in section 1504(a)(4) and § 1.382-2T(f)(18)(ii) and (iii).

(2) Adjustment to value. (i) In general. The value of the loss group (or loss subgroup), as determined under paragraph (b)(1) of this section, is adjusted under any rule in section 382 or the regulations thereunder requiring an adjustment to such value for purposes of computing the amount of the section 382 limitation. See, for example, section 382(e)(2) (redemptions and corporate contractions), section 382(l)(1) (certain capital contributions) and section 382(l)(4) (ownership of substantial nonbusiness assets). For purposes of section 382(e)(2), redemptions and corporate contractions that do not effect a transfer of value outside of the loss group (or loss subgroup) are disregarded. For purposes of section 382(l)(1), capital contributions between members of the loss group (or loss subgroup)(or a contribution of stock to a member made solely to satisfy the loss subgroup parent requirement of paragraph (d)(1)(ii) or (2)(ii) of this section), are not taken into account. Also, the substantial nonbusiness asset test of section 382(l)(4) is applied on a group (or subgroup) basis, and is not applied separately to its members.

(ii) Anti-duplication. Appropriate adjustments must be made to the extent necessary to prevent any duplication of the value of the stock of a member, even though corporations that do not file consolidated returns may not be required to make such an adjustment. In making these adjustments, the group (or loss subgroup) may apply the principles of § 1.382-8 (relating to controlled groups of corporations) in determining the value of a loss group (or loss subgroup) even if that section would not apply if separate returns were filed. Also, the principles of § 1.382-5(d)(relating to successive ownership changes and absorption of a section 382 limitation) may apply to adjust the consolidated section 382 limitation (or subgroup section 382 limitation) of a loss group (or loss subgroup) to avoid a duplication of value if there are simultaneous (rather than successive) ownership changes.

(3) Examples. The following examples illustrate the principles of this paragraph (b):

Example (1). Basic case.

(i) L, L1, and L2 compose a loss group. L has outstanding common stock, the value of which is $100. L1 has outstanding common stock and preferred stock that is described in section 1504(a)(4). L owns 90 percent of the L1 common stock, and A owns the remaining 10 percent of the L1 common stock plus all the preferred stock. The value of the L1 common stock is $40, and the value of the L1 preferred stock is $30. L2 has outstanding common stock, 50 percent of which is owned by L and 50 percent by L1. The L group has an ownership change. The following is a graphic illustration of these facts:

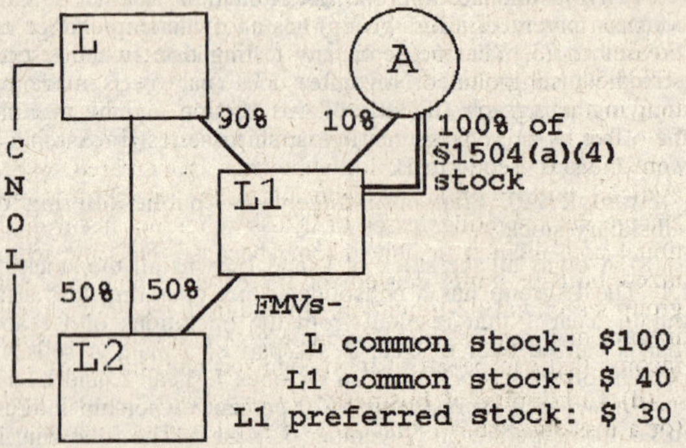

(ii) Under paragraph (b)(1) of this section, the L group does not include the value of the stock of any member that is owned directly or indirectly by another member in computing its consolidated section 382 limitation. Accordingly, the value of the stock of the loss group is $134, the sum of the value of—

(a) The common stock of L ($100);

(b) The 10 percent of the L1 common stock ($4) owned by A; and

(c) The L1 preferred stock ($30) owned by A.

Example (2). Indirect ownership.

(i) L and L1 compose a consolidated group. L's stock has a value of $100. L owns 80 shares (worth $80) and corporation M owns 20 shares (worth $20) of the L1 stock. L also owns 79 percent of the stock of corporation M. The L group has an ownership change. The following is a graphic illustration of these facts:

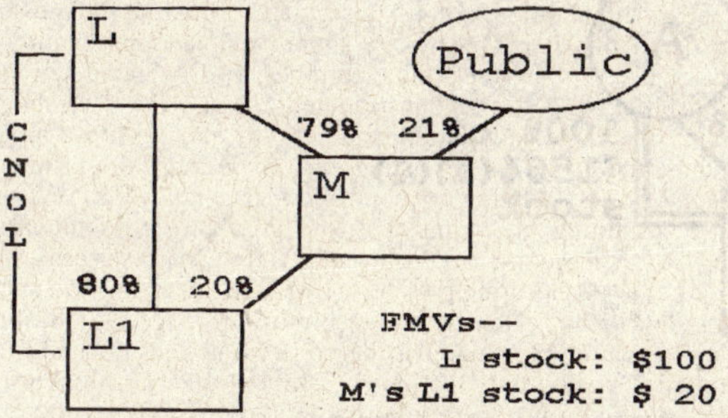

(ii) Under paragraph (b)(1) of this section, because of L's more than 5 percent ownership interest in M, a nonmember, L is considered to indirectly own 15.8 shares of the L1 stock held by M (79% × 20 shares). The value of the L loss group is $104.20, the sum of the values of—

(a) The L stock ($100); and

(b) The L1 stock not owned directly or indirectly by L (21% × $20, or $4.20).

(c) Recognized built-in gain of a loss group or loss subgroup. *(1) In general.* If a loss group (or loss subgroup) has a net unrealized built-in gain, any recognized built-in gain of the loss group (or loss subgroup) is taken into account under section 382(h) in determining the consolidated section 382 limitation (or subgroup section 382 limitation).

(1) Adjustments. Appropriate adjustments must be made so that any recognized built-in gain of a member that increases more than one section 382 limitation (whether consolidated, subgroup, or separate) does not effect a duplication in the amount of consolidated taxable income that can be offset by pre-change net operating losses. For example, a consolidated section 382 limitation that is increased by recognized built-in gains is reduced to the extent that pre-change net operating losses of a loss subgroup absorb additional consolidated taxable income because the same recognized built-in gains caused an increase in that loss subgroup's section 382 limitation. In addition, recognized built-in gain may not increase the amount of consolidated taxable income that can be offset by recognized built-in losses.

(d) Continuity of business. *(1) In general.* A loss group (or a loss subgroup) is treated as a single entity for purposes of determining whether it satisfies the continuity of business enterprise requirement of section 382(c)(1).

(2) Example. The following example illustrates the principle of this paragraph (d):

Example. Continuity of business enterprise. L owns all the stock of two subsidiaries, L1 and L2. The L group has an ownership change. It has pre-change consolidated attributes attributable to L2. Each of the members has historically conducted a separate line of business. Each line of business is approximately equal in value. One year after the ownership change, L discontinues its separate business and the business of L2. The separate business of L1 is continued for the remainder of the 2 year period following the ownership change. The continuity of business enterprise requirement of section 382(c)(1) is met even though the separate businesses of L and L2 are discontinued.

(e) Limitations of losses under other rules. If a section 382 limitation for a post-change year exceeds the consolidated taxable income that may be offset by pre-change attributes for any reason, including the application of the limitation of § 1.1502-21(c), the amount of the excess is carried forward under section 382(b)(2) (relating to the carryforward of unused section 382 limitation).

T.D. 8824, 6/25/99.

---

§ 1.1502-93A Consolidated section 382 limitation (or subgroup section 382 limitation), generally applicable for testing dates before June 25, 1999.

(a) Determination of the consolidated section 382 limitation (or subgroup section 382 limitation). *(1) In general.* Following an ownership change, the consolidated section 382 limitation (or subgroup section 382 limitation) for any post-change year is an amount equal to the value of the loss group (or loss subgroup), as defined in paragraph (b) of this section, multiplied by the long-term tax-exempt rate that applies with respect to the ownership change, and adjusted as required by section 382 and the regulations thereunder. See, for example, section 382(b)(2) (relating to the carryforward of unused section 382 limitation), section 382(b)(3)(B) (relating to the section 382 limitation for the post-change year that includes the change date), section 382(m)(2) (relating to short taxable years), and section 382(h) (relating to recognized built-in gains and section 338 gains).

(2) Coordination with apportionment rule. For special rules relating to apportionment of a consolidated section 382 limitation (or a subgroup section 382 limitation) when one or more corporations cease to be members of a loss group (or a loss subgroup) and to aggregation of amounts so apportioned, see § 1.1502-95A(c).

(b) Value of the loss group (or loss subgroup). *(1) Stock value immediately before ownership change.* Subject to any adjustment under paragraph (b)(2) of this section, the value of the loss group (or loss subgroup) is the value, immediately before the ownership change, of the stock of each member, other than stock that is owned directly or indirectly by another member. For this purpose—

(i) Ownership is determined under § 1.382-2T;

(ii) A member is considered to indirectly own stock of another member through a nonmember only if the member has a 5-percent or greater ownership interest in the nonmember; and

(iii) Stock includes stock described in section 1504(a)(4) and § 1.382-2T(f)(18)(ii) and (iii).

(2) Adjustment to value. The value of the loss group (or loss subgroup), as determined under paragraph (b)(1) of this section, is adjusted under any rule in section 382 or the regulations thereunder requiring an adjustment to such value for purposes of computing the amount of the section 382 limitation. See, for example, section 382(e)(2) (redemptions and corporate contractions), section 382(l)(1) (certain capital contributions) and section 382(l)(4) (ownership of substantial nonbusiness assets). The value of the loss group (or loss subgroup) determined under this paragraph (b) is also adjusted to the extent necessary to prevent any duplication of the value of the stock of a member. For example, the principles of § 1.382-8 (relating to controlled groups of corporations) apply in determining the value of a loss group (or loss subgroup) if, under § 1.1502-91A(g)(2), members are not included in the determination whether the group (or loss subgroup) has a net unrealized built-in loss.

(3) Examples. The following examples illustrate the principles of this paragraph (b).

Example (1). Basic case.

(a) L, L1, and L2 compose a loss group. L has outstanding common stock, the value of which is $100. L1 has outstanding common stock and preferred stock that is described in section 1504(a)(4). L owns 90 percent of the L1 common stock, and A owns the remaining 10 percent of the L1 common stock plus all the preferred stock. The value of the L1 common stock is $40, and the value of the L1 preferred stock is $30. L2 has outstanding common stock, 50 percent of which is owned by L and 50 percent by L1. The L group has an ownership change. The following is a graphic illustration of these facts:

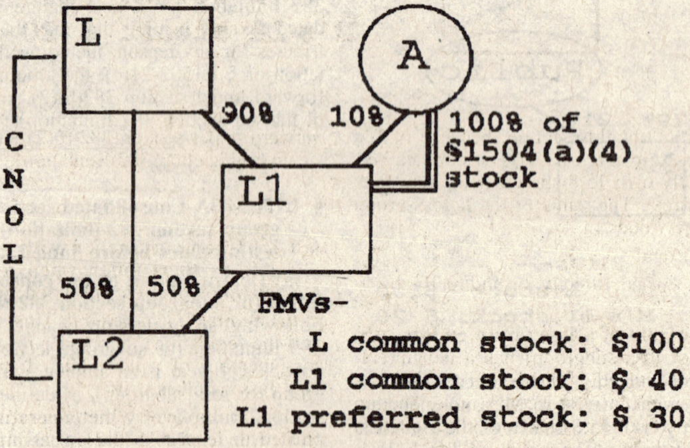

(b) Under paragraph (b)(1) of this section, the L group does not include the value of the stock of any member that is owned directly or indirectly by another member in computing its consolidated section 382 limitation. Accordingly, the value of the stock of the loss group is $134, the sum of the value of—

(1) The common stock of L ($100);

(2) the 10 percent of the L1 common stock ($4) owned by A; and

(3) The L1 preferred stock ($30) owned by A.

Example (2). Indirect ownership.

(a) L and L1 compose a consolidated group. L's stock has a value of $100. L owns 80 shares (worth $80) and corporation M owns 20 shares (worth $20) of the L1 stock. L also owns 79 percent of the stock of corporation M. The L group has an ownership change. The following is a graphic illustration of these facts:

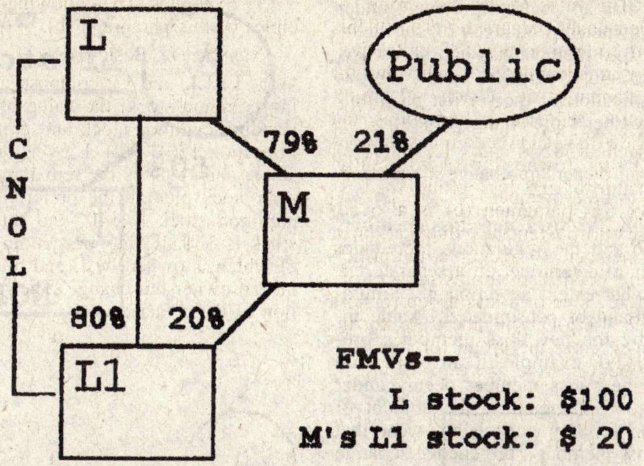

(b) Under paragraph (b)(1) of this section, because of L's more than 5 percent ownership interest in M, a nonmember, L is considered to indirectly own 15.8 shares of the L1 stock held by M (79% × 20 shares). The value of the L loss group is $104.20, the sum of the values of—

(1) The L stock ($100); and

(2) The L1 stock not owned directly or indirectly by L (21% × $20, or $4.20).

(c) Recognized built-in gain of a loss group or loss subgroup. If a loss group (or loss subgroup) has a net unrealized built-in gain, any recognized built-in gain of the loss group (or loss subgroup) is taken into account under section 382(h) in determining the consolidated section 382 limitation (or subgroup section 382 limitation). See § 1.1502-99A(a)(2) for a special rule relating to the application of § 1.1502-93(c)(2) to consolidated return years for which the return date is after June 25, 1999.

(d) Continuity of business. *(1) In general.* A loss group (or a loss subgroup) is treated as a single entity for purposes of determining whether it satisfies the continuity of business enterprise requirement of section 382(c)(1).

(2) Example. The following example illustrates the principle of this paragraph (d).

Example. Continuity of business enterprise. L owns all the stock of two subsidiaries, L1 and L2. The L group has an ownership change. It has pre-change consolidated attributes attributable to L2. Each of the members has historically conducted a separate line of business. Each line of business is approximately equal in value. One year after the ownership change, L discontinues its separate business and the business of L2. The separate business of L1 is continued for the remainder of the 2 year period following the ownership change. The continuity of business enterprise requirement of section 382(c)(1) is met even though the separate businesses of L and L2 are discontinued.

(e) Limitations of losses under other rules. If a section 382 limitation for a post-change year exceeds the consolidated taxable income that may be offset by pre-change attributes for any reason, including the application of the limitation of §§ 1.1502-21(c) or 1.1502-21T(c) in effect prior to June 25, 1999, as contained in 26 CFR part 1 revised April 1, 1999, as applicable, the amount of the excess is carried forward under section 382(b)(2) (relating to the carryforward of unused section 382 limitation).

T.D. 8678, 6/26/96, amend T.D. 8823, 6/25/99, T.D. 8824, 6/25/99.

§ 1.1502-94 Coordination with section 382 and the regulations thereunder when a corporation becomes a member of a consolidated group.

(a) Scope. *(1) In general.* This section applies section 382 and the regulations thereunder to a corporation that is a new loss member of a consolidated group. A corporation is a new loss member if it--

(i) Carries over a net operating loss that arose (or is treated under § 1.1502-21(c) as arising) in a SRLY with respect to the current group, and that is not described in § 1.1502-91(d)(1); or

(ii) Has a net unrealized built-in loss (determined under paragraph (c) of this section immediately before it becomes a member of the current group by treating that day as a change date) that is not taken into account under § 1.1502-91(d)(2) in determining whether two or more corporations compose a loss subgroup.

(2) Successor corporation as new loss member. A new loss member also includes any successor to a corporation that has a net operating loss carryover arising in a SRLY and that is treated as remaining in existence under § 1.382-2(a)(1)(ii) following a transaction described in section 381(a).

(3) Coordination in the case of a loss subgroup. For rules regarding the determination of whether there is an ownership change of a loss subgroup with respect to a net operating loss or a net unrealized built-in loss described in § 1.1502-91(d) (relating to the definition of loss subgroup) and the computation of a subgroup section 382 limitation following such an ownership change, see §§ 1.1502-92 and 1.1502-93.

(4) End of separate tracking of certain losses. If § 1.1502-96(a) (relating to the end of separate tracking of attributes) applies to a new loss member, then, while that member remains a member of the consolidated group, there is an ownership change with respect to its attributes described in § 1.1502-96(a)(2) only if the consolidated group is a loss group and has an ownership change under § 1.1502-

92(b)(1)(i) (or that member has an ownership change under § 1.1502-96(b) (relating to ownership changes of subsidiaries)). If, however, the new loss member has had an ownership change before § 1.1502-96(a) applies, see § 1.1502-96(c) for the continuing application of the section 382 limitation with respect to the member's pre-change losses.

(5) Cross-reference. See section 382(a) and § 1.1502-96(c) for the continuing effect of an ownership change after a corporation becomes or ceases to be a member.

(b) Application of section 382 to a new loss member. *(1) In general.* Section 382 and the regulations thereunder apply to a new loss member to determine, on a separate entity basis, whether and to what extent a section 382 limitation applies to limit the amount of consolidated taxable income that may be offset by the new loss member's pre-change separate attributes. For example, if an ownership change with respect to the new loss member occurs under section 382 and the regulations thereunder, the amount of consolidated taxable income for any post-change year that may be offset by the new loss member's pre-change separate attributes shall not exceed the section 382 limitation as determined separately under section 382(b) with respect to that member for such year. If the post-change year includes the change date, section 382(b)(3)(A) is applied so that the section 382 limitation of the new loss member does not apply to the portion of the taxable income for such year that is allocable to the period in such year on or before the change date. See generally § 1.382-6 (relating to the allocation of income and loss).

(2) Adjustment to value. Appropriate adjustments must be made to the extent necessary to prevent any duplication of the value of the stock of a member, even though corporations that do not file consolidated returns may not be required to make such an adjustment. For example, the principles of § 1.1502-93(b)(2)(ii) (relating to adjustments to value) apply in determining the value of a new loss member.

(3) Pre-change separate attribute defined. A pre-change separate attribute of a new loss member is—

(i) Any net operating loss carryover of the new loss member described in paragraph (a)(1) of this section; and

(ii) Any recognized built-in loss of the new loss member.

(4) Examples. The following examples illustrate the principles of this paragraph (b):

Example (1). Basic case.

(i) A and P each own 50 percent of the L stock. On December 19, Year 6, P purchases 30 percent of the L stock from A for cash. L has net operating losses arising in Year 1 and Year 2 that it carries over to Year 6 and Year 7. The following is a graphic illustration of these facts:

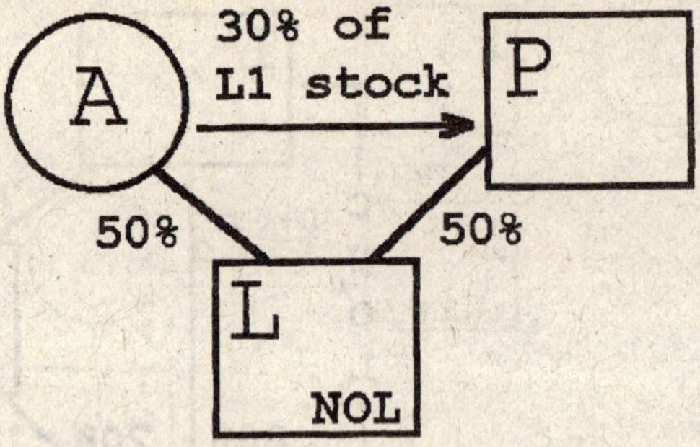

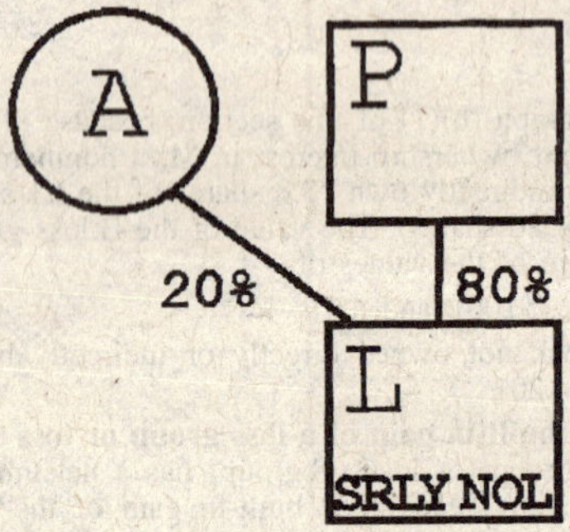

(ii) L is a new loss member because it has net operating loss carryovers that arose in a SRLY with respect to the P group and L is not a member of a loss subgroup under § 1.1502-91(d). Under section 382 and the regulations thereunder, L is a loss corporation on December 19, Year 6, that day is a testing date for L, and the testing period for L commences on December 20, Year 3.

(iii) P's purchase of L stock does not cause an ownership change of L on December 19, Year 6, with respect to the net operating loss carryovers from Year 1 and Year 2 under section 382 and § 1.382-2T. The use of the loss carryovers, however, is subject to limitation under § 1.1502-21(c).

Example (2). Multiple new loss members.

(i) The facts are the same as in Example 1, and, on December 31, Year 6, L purchases all the stock of L1 from B for cash. L1 has a net operating loss of $40 arising in Year 3 that it carries over to Year 7. The following is a graphic illustration of these facts:

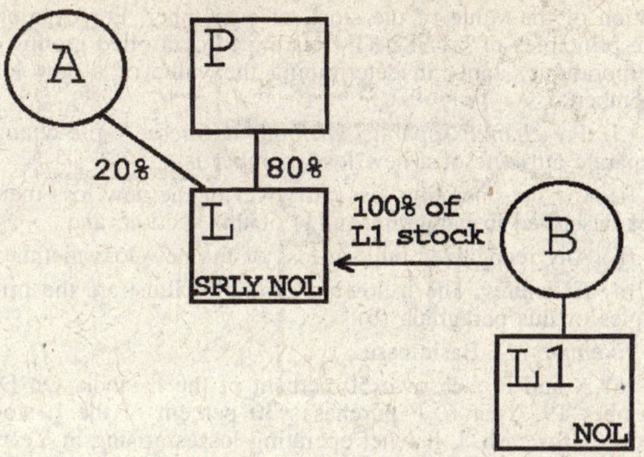

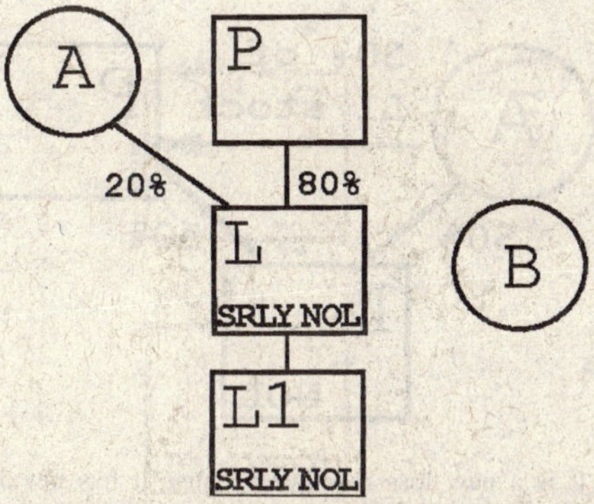

(ii) L1 is a new loss member because it has a net operating loss carryover from Year 3 that arose in a SRLY with respect to the P group and L1 is not a member of a loss subgroup under § 1.1502-91(d)(1).

(iii) L's purchase of all the stock of L1 causes an ownership change of L1 on December 31, Year 6, under section 382 and § 1.382-2T. Accordingly, a section 382 limitation based on the value of the L1 stock immediately before the ownership change limits the amount of consolidated taxable income of the P group for any post-change year that may be offset by L1's loss from Year 3.

(iv) L1's ownership change upon becoming a member of the P group is an ownership change described in § 1.1502-96(a). Thus, starting on January 1, Year 7, the P group no longer separately tracks owner shifts of the stock of L1 with respect to L1's loss from Year 3, and the P group is a loss group because L1's Year 3 loss is treated as a loss described in § 1.1502-91(c).

Example (3). Ownership changes of new loss members.

(i) The facts are the same as in Example 2, and, on July 30, Year 7, C purchases all the stock of P for cash.

(ii) L is a new loss member on July 30, Year 7, because its Year 1 and Year 2 losses arose in SRLYs with respect to the P group and it is not a member of a loss subgroup under § 1.1502-91(d)(1). The testing period for L commences on August 1, Year 4. C's purchase of all the P stock causes an ownership change of L on July 30, Year 7, under section 382 and § 1.382-2T with respect to its Year 1 and Year 2 losses. Accordingly, a section 382 limitation based on the value of the L stock immediately before the ownership change limits the amount of consolidated taxable income of the P group for any post-change year that may be offset by L's Year 1 and Year 2 losses. See § 1.1502-21(c) for rules relating to an additional limitation.

(iii) The P group is a loss group on July 30, Year 7, because it is entitled to use L1's loss from Year 3, and such loss is no longer treated as a loss of a new loss member starting the day after L1's ownership change on December 31, Year 6. See §§ 1.1502-96(a) and 1.1502-91(c)(2). C's purchase of all the P stock causes an ownership change of P, and therefore the P loss group, on July 30, Year 7, with respect to L1's Year 3 loss. Accordingly, a consolidated section 382 limitation based on the value of the P stock immediately before the ownership change limits the amount of consolidated taxable income of the P group for any post-change year that may be offset by L1's Year 3 loss.

(c) Built-in gains and losses. As the context may require, the principles of §§ 1.1502-91(g) and (h) and 1.1502-93(c) (relating to built-in gains and losses) apply to a new loss member on a separate entity basis. See § 1.1502-91(g)(4). See § 1.1502-13 (including Example 10 of § 1.1502-13(c)(7)) for rules relating to the treatment of intercompany transactions.

(d) Information statements. The common parent of a consolidated group that has a new loss member subject to paragraph (b)(1) of this section during a consolidated return year must file the information statement required by § 1.382-11(a) because of any owner shift, equity structure shift, or other transaction described in § 1.382-2T(a)(2)(i). Instead of filing a separate statement for each new loss member, the common parent may file a single statement described in § 1.382-11(a) with respect to the stock ownership of the common parent (which is treated as a loss corporation). In addition to the information concerning stock ownership of the common parent, the single statement must identify each new loss member and state which new loss members, if any, have had ownership changes during the consolidated return year. The new loss member is, however, required to maintain the records necessary to determine if it has an ownership change. This paragraph (d) applies with respect to the attributes of a new loss member until an event occurs which ends separate tracking under § 1.1502-96(a). After that time, the information statement described in § 1.1502-92(e)(1) must be filed with respect to these attributes.

T.D. 8824, 6/25/99, amend T.D. 9264, 5/26/2006, T.D. 9329, 6/13/2007.

§ 1.1502-94A Coordination with section 382 and the regulations thereunder when a corporation becomes a member of a consolidated group generally applicable for corporations becoming members of a group before June 25, 1999.

(a) Scope. *(1) In general.* This section applies section 382 and the regulations thereunder to a corporation that is a new loss member of a consolidated group. A corporation is a new loss member if it—

(i) Carries over a net operating loss that arose (or is treated under §§ 1.1502-21(c) or 1.1502-21T(c) in effect prior to June 25, 1999, as contained in 26 CFR part 1 revised April 1, 1999, as applicable as arising) in a SRLY with respect to the current group, and that is not described in § 1.1502-91A(d)(1); or

(ii) Has a net unrealized built-in loss (determined under paragraph (c) of this section on the day it becomes a member of the current group by treating that day as a change date) that is not taken into account under § 1.1502-91A(d)(2) in determining whether two or more corporations compose a loss subgroup.

(2) Successor corporation as new loss member. A new loss member also includes any successor to a corporation that has a net operating loss carryover arising in a SRLY and that is treated as remaining in existence under § 1.382-2(a)(1)(ii) following a transaction described in section 381(a).

(3) Coordination in the case of a loss subgroup. For rules regarding the determination of whether there is an ownership change of a loss subgroup with respect to a net operating loss or a net unrealized built-in loss described in § 1.1502-91A(d) (relating to the definition of loss subgroup) and the computation of a subgroup section 382 limitation following such an ownership change, see §§ 1.1502-92A and 1.1502-93A.

(4) End of separate tracking of certain losses. If § 1.1502-96A(a) (relating to the end of separate tracking of attributes) applies to a new loss member, then, while that member remains a member of the consolidated group, there is an ownership change with respect to its attributes described in § 1.1502-96A(a)(2) only if the consolidated group is a loss group and has an ownership change under § 1.1502-92A(b)(1)(i) (or that member has an ownership change under § 1.1502-96A(b) (relating to ownership changes of subsidiaries)). If, however, the new loss member has had an ownership change before § 1.1502-96A(a) applies, see § 1.1502-96A(c) for the continuing application of the section 382 limitation with respect to the member's pre-change losses.

(5) Cross-reference.

See section 382(a) and § 1.1502-96A(c) for the continuing effect of an ownership change after a corporation becomes or ceases to be a member.

(b) Application of section 382 to a new loss member *(1) In general.* Section 382 and the regulations thereunder apply to a new loss member to determine, on a separate entity basis, whether and to what extent a section 382 limitation applies to limit the amount of consolidated taxable income that may be offset by the new loss member's pre-change separate attributes. For example, if an ownership change with respect to the new loss member occurs under section 382 and the regulations thereunder, the amount of consolidated taxable income for any post-change year that may be offset by the new loss member's pre-change separate attributes shall not exceed the section 382 limitation as determined separately under section 382(b) with respect to that member for such year. If the post-change year includes the change date, section 382(b)(3)(A) is applied so that the section 382 limitation of the new loss member does not apply to the portion of the taxable income for such year that is allocable to the period in such year on or before the change date. See generally § 1.382-6 (relating to the allocation of income and loss).

(2) Adjustment to value. The value of the new loss member is adjusted to the extent necessary to prevent any duplication of the value of the stock of a member. For example, the principles of § 1.382-8T (relating to controlled groups of corporations) apply in determining the value of a new loss member.

(3) Pre-change separate attribute defined. A pre-change separate attribute of a new loss member is—

(i) Any net operating loss carryover of the new loss member described in paragraph (a)(1) of this section; and

(ii) Any recognized built-in loss of the new loss member.

(4) Examples. The following examples illustrate the principles of this paragraph (b).

Example (1). Basic case.

(a) A and P each own 50 percent of the L stock. On December 19, Year 6, P purchases 30 percent of the L stock from A for cash. L has net operating losses arising in Year 1 and Year 2 that it carries over to Year 6 and Year 7. The following is a graphic illustration of these facts:

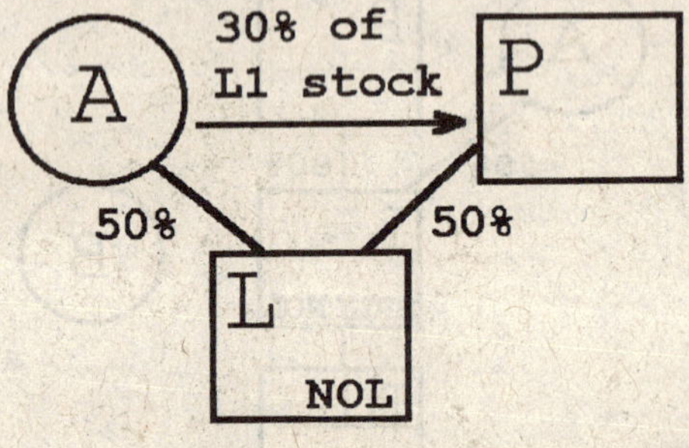

(b) L is a new loss member because it has net operating loss carryovers that arose in a SRLY with respect to the P group and L is not a member of a loss subgroup under § 1.1502-91A(d). Under section 382 and the regulations thereunder, L is a loss corporation on December 19, Year 6, that day is a testing date for L, and the testing period for L commences on December 20, Year 3.

(c) P's purchase of L stock does not cause an ownership change of L on December 19, Year 6, with respect to the net operating loss carryovers from Year 1 and Year 2 under section 382 and § 1.382-2T. The use of the loss carryovers, however, is subject to limitation under §§ 1.1502-21(c) or 1.1502-21T(c) in effect prior to June 25, 1999, as contained in 26 CFR part 1 revised April 1, 1999, as applicable.

Example (2). Multiple new loss members.

(a) The facts are the same as in Example 1, and, on December 31, Year 6, L purchases all the stock of L1 from B for cash. L1 has a net operating loss of $40 arising in Year 3 that it carries over to Year 7. The following is a graphic illustration of these facts:

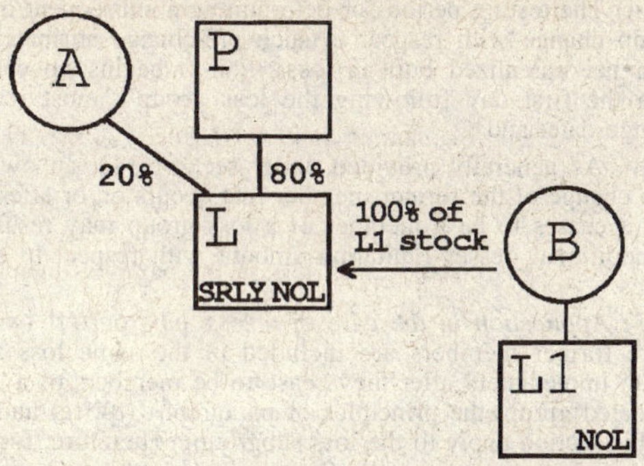

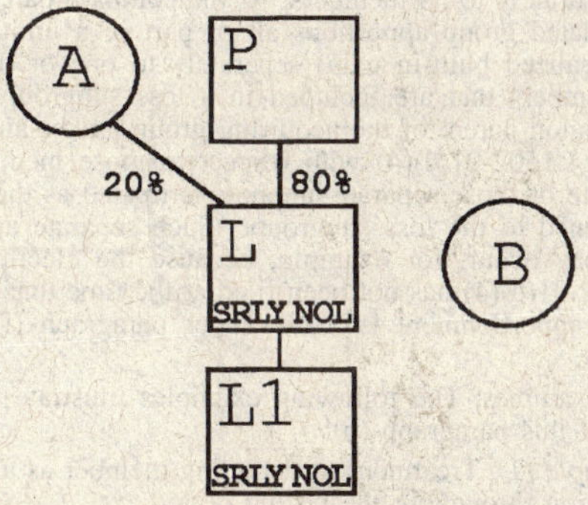

(b) L1 is a new loss member because it has a net operating loss carryover from Year 3 that arose in a SRLY with respect to the P group and L1 is not a member of a loss subgroup under § 1.1502-91A(d)(1).

(c) L's purchase of all the stock of L1 causes an ownership change of L1 on December 31, Year 6, under section 382 and § 1.382-2T. Accordingly, a section 382 limitation based on the value of the L1 stock immediately before the ownership change limits the amount of consolidated taxable income of the P group for any post-change year that may be offset by L1's loss from Year 3.

(d) L1's ownership change in connection with its becoming a member of the P group is an ownership change described in § 1.1502-96A(a). Thus, starting on January 1, Year 7, the P group no longer separately tracks owner shifts of the stock of L1 with respect to L1's loss from Year 3. Instead, the P group is a loss group because of such loss under § 1.1502-91A(c).

Example (3). Ownership changes of new loss members.

(a) The facts are the same as in Example 2, and, on April 30, Year 7, C purchases all the stock of P for cash.

(b) L is a new loss member on April 30, Year 7, because its Year 1 and Year 2 losses arose in SRLYs with respect to the P group and it is not a member of a loss subgroup under § 1.1502-91A(d)(1). The testing period for L commences on May 1, Year 4. C's purchase of all the P stock causes an ownership change of L on April 30, Year 7, under section 382 and § 1.382-2T with respect to its Year 1 and Year 2 losses. Accordingly, a section 382 limitation based on the value of the L stock immediately before the ownership change limits the amount of consolidated taxable income of the P group for any post-change year that may be offset by L's Year 1 and Year 2 losses. See also § 1.1502-21T in effect prior to June 25, 1999, contained in 26 CFR Part 1, revised April 1, 1999, or § 1.1502-21, as applicable.

(c) The P group is a loss group on April 30, Year 7, because it is entitled to use L1's loss from Year 3, and such loss is no longer treated as a loss of a new loss member starting the day after L1's ownership change on December 31, Year 6. See §§ 1.1502-96A(a) and 1.1502-91A(c)(2). C's purchase of all the P stock causes an ownership change of P, and therefore the P loss group, on April 30, Year 7, with respect to L1's Year 3 loss. Accordingly, a consolidated section 382 limitation based on the value of the P stock immediately before the ownership change limits the amount of consolidated taxable income of the P group for any post-change year that may be offset by L1's Year 3 loss.

(c) Built-in gains and losses. As the context may require, the principles of §§ 1.1502-91A(g) and (h) and 1.1502-93A(c) (relating to built-in gains and losses) apply to a new loss member on a separate entity basis. See § 1.1502-91A(g)(3).

(d) Information statements. The common parent of a consolidated group that has a new loss member subject to paragraph (b)(1) of this section during a consolidated return year must file the information statement required by § 1.382-2T(a)(2)(ii) because of any owner shift, equity structure shift, or issuance or transfer of an option with respect to the new loss member. Instead of filing a separate statement for each new loss member the common parent may file a single statement described in § 1.382-2T(a)(2)(ii) with respect to the stock ownership of the common parent (which is treated as a loss corporation). In addition to the information concerning stock ownership of the common parent, the single statement must identify each new loss member and state which new loss members, if any, have had ownership changes during the consolidated return year. The new loss member is, however, required to maintain the records necessary to determine if it has an ownership change. This paragraph (d) applies with respect to the attributes of a new loss member until an event occurs which ends separate tracking under § 1.1502-96A(a). After that time, the information statement described in § 1.1502-92A(e)(1) must be filed with respect to these attributes.

T.D. 8678, 6/26/96, amend T.D. 8823, 6/25/99, T.D. 8824, 6/25/99.

§ 1.1502-95 Rules on ceasing to be a member of a consolidated group (or loss subgroup).

(a) In general. *(1) Consolidated group.* This section provides rules for applying section 382 on or after the day that a member ceases to be a member of a consolidated group (or loss subgroup). The rules concern how to determine whether an ownership change occurs with respect to losses of the member, and how a consolidated section 382 limitation (or subgroup section 382 limitation) and a loss group's (or loss subgroup's) net unrealized built-in gain or loss is apportioned to the member. As the context requires, a reference in this section to a loss group, a member, or a corporation also includes a reference to a loss subgroup, and a reference to a consolidated section 382 limitation also includes a reference to a subgroup section 382 limitation.

(2) Election by common parent. Only the common parent (not the loss subgroup parent) may make the election under paragraph (c) of this section to apportion a consolidated section 382 limitation (or subgroup section 382 limitation) or a loss group's (or loss subgroup's) net unrealized built-in gain.

(3) Coordination with §§ 1.1502-91 through 1.1502-93. For rules regarding the determination of whether there is an ownership change of a loss subgroup and the computation of a subgroup section 382 limitation following such an ownership change, see §§ 1.1502-91 through 1.1502-93.

(b) Separate application of section 382 when a member leaves a consolidated group. *(1) In general.* Except as provided in §§ 1.1502-91 through 1.1502-93 (relating to rules applicable to loss groups and loss subgroups), section 382 and the regulations thereunder apply to a corporation on a separate entity basis after it ceases to be a member of a consolidated group (or loss subgroup). Solely for purposes of determining whether a corporation has an ownership change—

(i) Any portion of a consolidated net operating loss that is apportioned to the corporation under § 1.1502-21(b) is treated as a net operating loss of the corporation beginning on the first day of the taxable year in which the loss arose;

(ii) The testing period may include the period during which (or before which) the corporation was a member of the group (or loss subgroup); and

(iii) Except to the extent provided in § 1.1502-96(d) (relating to reattributed losses), the day it ceases to be a member of a consolidated group is treated as a testing date of the corporation within the meaning of § 1.382-2(a)(4).

(2) Effect of a prior ownership change of the group. If a loss group has had an ownership change under § 1.1502-92 before a corporation ceases to be a member of a consolidated group (the former member)—

(i) Any pre-change consolidated attribute that is subject to a consolidated section 382 limitation continues to be treated as a pre-change loss with respect to the former member after it is apportioned to the former member and, if any net unrealized built-in loss is allocated to the former member under paragraph (e) of this section, any recognized built-in loss of the former member is a pre-change loss of the member;

(ii) The section 382 limitation with respect to such pre-change attribute is zero unless the common parent, under paragraph (c) of this section, apportions to the former member all or part of the consolidated section 382 limitation applicable to such attribute. The limitation applicable to a pre-change attribute other than a recognized built-in loss may be increased to the extent that the common parent has apportioned all or part of the loss group's net unrealized built-in gain to the former member, and the former member recognizes built-in gain during the recognition period;

(iii) The testing period for determining a subsequent ownership change with respect to such pre-change attribute (or such net unrealized built-in loss, if any) begins no earlier than the first day following the loss group's most recent change date; and

(iv) As generally provided under section 382, an ownership change of the former member that occurs on or after the day it ceases to be a member of a loss group may result in an additional, lesser limitation amount with respect to such losses.

(3) Application in the case of a loss subgroup. If two or more former members are included in the same loss subgroup immediately after they cease to be members of a consolidated group, the principles of paragraphs (b), (c) and (e) of this section apply to the loss subgroup. Therefore, for example, an apportionment by the common parent under paragraph (c) of this section is made to the loss subgroup rather than separately to its members. If the common parent of the consolidated group apportions all or part of a limitation (or net unrealized built-in gain) separately to one or more former members that are included in a loss subgroup because the common parent of the acquiring group makes an election under § 1.1502-91(d)(4) with respect to those members, the aggregate of those separate amounts is treated as the amount apportioned to the loss subgroup. Such separate apportionment may occur, for example, because the election under § 1.1502-91(d)(4) has not been filed at the time that the election of apportionment is made under paragraph (f) of this section.

(4) Examples. The following examples illustrate the principles of this paragraph (b):

Example (1). Treatment of departing member as a separate corporation throughout the testing period.

(i) A owns all the L stock. L owns all the stock of L1 and L2. The L group has a consolidated net operating loss arising in Year 1 that is carried over to Year 3. On January 12, Year 2, A sells 30 percent of the L stock to B. On February 7, Year 3, L sells 40 percent of the L2 stock to C, and L2 ceases to be a member of the group. A portion of the Year 1 consolidated net operating loss is apportioned to L2 under § 1.1502-21(b) and is carried to L2's first separate return year, which ends December 31, Year 3. The following is a graphic illustration of these facts:

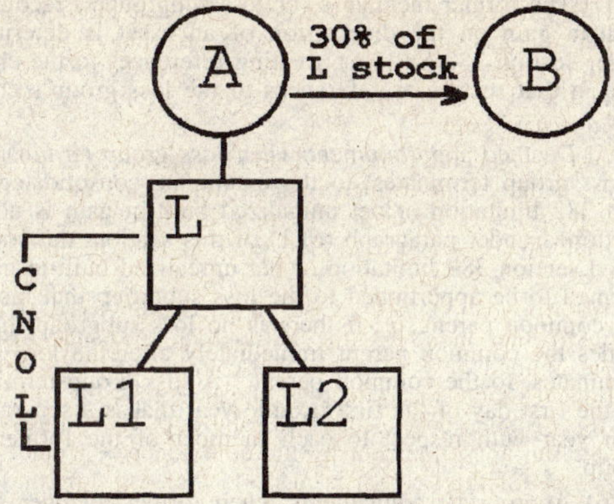

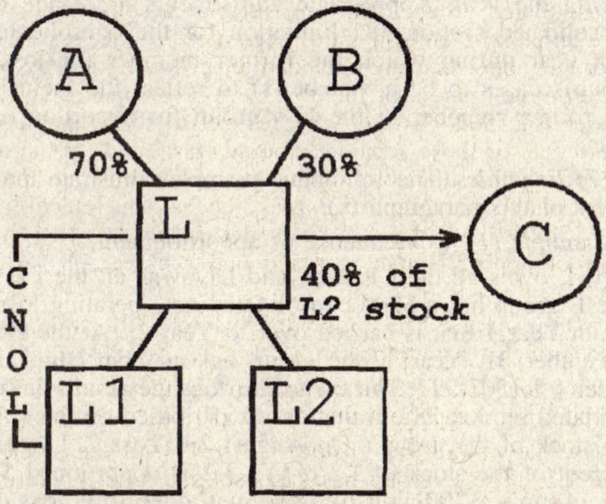

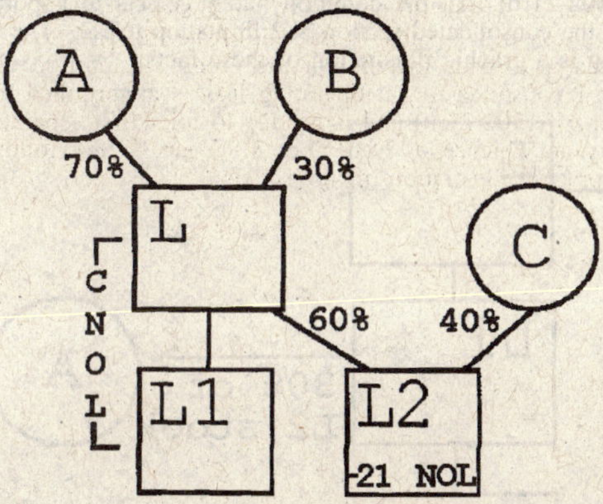

(ii) Under paragraph (b)(1) of this section, L2 is a loss corporation on February 7, Year 3. Under paragraph (b)(1)(iii) of this section, February 7, Year 3, is a testing date. Under paragraph (b)(1)(ii) of this section, the testing period for L2 with respect to this testing date commences on January 1, Year 1, the first day of the taxable year in which the portion of the consolidated net operating loss apportioned to L2 arose. Therefore, in determining whether L2 has an ownership change on February 7, Year 3, B's purchase of 30 percent of the L stock and C's purchase of 40 percent of the L2 stock are each owner shifts. L2 has an ownership change under section 382(g) and § 1.382-2T because B and C have increased their ownership interests in L2 by 18 and 40 percentage points, respectively, during the testing period.

Example (2). Effect of prior ownership change of loss group.

(i) L owns all the L1 stock and L1 owns all the L2 stock. The L loss group had an ownership change under § 1.1502-92 in Year 2 with respect to a consolidated net operating loss arising in Year 1 and carried over to Year 2 and Year 3. The consolidated section 382 limitation computed solely on the basis of the value of the stock of L is $100. On December 31, Year 2, L1 sells 25 percent of the stock of L2 to B. L2 is apportioned a portion of the Year 1 consolidated net operating loss which it carries over to its first separate return year ending after December 31, Year 2. L2's separate section 382 limitation with respect to this loss is zero unless L elects to apportion all or a part of the consolidated section 382 limitation to L2. (See paragraph (c) of this section for rules regarding the apportionment of a consolidated section 382 limitation.) L apportions $50 of the consolidated section 382 limitation to L2, and the remaining $50 of the consolidated section 382 limitation stays with the loss group composed of L and L1.

(ii) On December 31, Year 3, L1 sells its remaining 75 percent stock interest in L2 to C, resulting in an ownership change of L2. L2's section 382 limitation computed on the change date with respect to the value of its stock is $30. Accordingly, L2's section 382 limitation for post-change years ending after December 31, Year 3, with respect to its pre-change losses, including the consolidated net operating losses apportioned to it from the L group, is $30, adjusted for a short taxable year, carryforward of unused limitation, or any other adjustment required under section 382.

(c) Apportionment of a consolidated section 382 limitation. *(1) In general.* The common parent may elect to apportion all or any part of a consolidated section 382 limitation to a former member (or loss subgroup). The common parent also may elect to apportion all or any part of the loss group's net unrealized built-in gain to a former member (or loss subgroup).

(2) Amount which may be apportioned. (i) Consolidated section 382 limitation. The common parent may apportion all or part of each element of the consolidated section 382 limitation determined under § 1.1502-93. For this purpose, the consolidated section 382 limitation consists of two elements—

(A) The value element, which is the element of the limitation determined under section 382(b)(1) (relating to value multiplied by the long-term tax-exempt rate) without regard to such adjustments as those described in section 382(b)(2) (relating to the carryforward of unused section 382 limitation), section 382(b)(3)(B)(relating to the section 382 limitation for the post-change year that includes the change date), section 382(h)(relating to built-in gains and section 338 gains), and section 382(m)(2)(relating to short taxable years); and

(B) The adjustment element, which is so much (if any) of the limitation for the taxable year during which the former member ceases to be a member of the consolidated group that is attributable to a carryover of unused limitation under section 382(b)(2) or to recognized built-in gains under 382(h).

(ii) Net unrealized built-in gain. The aggregate amount of the loss group's net unrealized built-in gain that may be apportioned to one or more former members that cease to be members during the same consolidated return year cannot exceed the loss group's excess, immediately after the close of that year, of net unrealized built-in gain over recognized built-in gain, determined under section 382(h)(1)(A)(ii) (relating to a limitation on recognized built-in gain). For this purpose, net unrealized built-in gain apportioned to former members in prior consolidated return years is treated as recognized built-in gain in those years.

(3) Effect of apportionment on the consolidated group. (i) Consolidated section 382 limitation. The value element of the consolidated section 382 limitation for any post-change year ending after the day that a former member (or loss subgroup) ceases to be a member(s) is reduced to the extent that it is apportioned under this paragraph (c). The consolidated section 382 limitation for the post-change year in which the former member (or loss subgroup) ceases to be a member(s) is also reduced to the extent that the adjustment element for that year is apportioned under this paragraph (c).

(ii) Net unrealized built-in gain. The amount of the loss group's net unrealized built-in gain that is apportioned to the former member (or loss subgroup) is treated as recognized built-in gain for a prior taxable year ending in the recognition period for purposes of applying the limitation of section 382(h)(1)(A)(ii) to the loss group's recognition period taxable years beginning after the consolidated return year in which the former member (or loss subgroup) ceases to be a member.

(4) Effect on corporations to which an apportionment is made. (i) Consolidated section 382 limitation. The amount of the value element that is apportioned to a former member (or loss subgroup) is treated as the amount determined under section 382(b)(1) for purposes of determining the amount of that corporation's (or loss subgroup's) section 382 limitation for any taxable year ending after the former member (or loss subgroup) ceases to be a member(s). Appropriate adjustments must be made to the limitation based on the value element so apportioned for a short taxable year, carryforward of unused limitation, or any other adjustment required under section 382. The adjustment element apportioned to a former member (or loss subgroup) is treated as an adjustment under section 382(b)(2) or section 382(h), as appropriate, for the first taxable year after the member (or members) ceases to be a member (or members).

(ii) Net unrealized built-in gain. For purposes of determining the amount by which the former member's (or loss subgroup's) section 382 limitation for any taxable year beginning after the former member (or loss subgroup) ceases to be a member(s) is increased by its recognized built-in gain—

(A) The amount of net unrealized built-in gain apportioned to a former member (or loss subgroup) is treated as if it were an amount of net unrealized built-in gain determined under section 382(h)(1)(A)(i)(without regard to the threshold of section 382(h)(3)(B)) with respect to such member or loss subgroup, and that amount is not reduced under section 382(h)(1)(A)(ii) by the loss group's recognized built-in gain;

(B) The former member's (or loss subgroup's) 5 year recognition period begins on the loss group's change date;

(C) In applying section 382(h)(1)(A)(ii), the former member (or loss subgroup) takes into account only its prior taxable years that begin after it ceases to be a member of the loss group; and

(D) The former member's (or loss subgroup's) recognized built-in gain on the disposition of an asset is determined under section 382(h)(2)(A), treating references to the change date in that section as references to the loss group's change date.

(5) Deemed apportionment when loss group terminates. If a loss group terminates, to the extent the consolidated section 382 limitation or net unrealized built-in gain is not apportioned under paragraph (c)(1) of this section, the consolidated section 382 limitation or net unrealized built-in gain is deemed to be apportioned to the loss subgroup that includes the common parent, or, if there is no loss subgroup that includes the common parent immediately after the loss group terminates, to the common parent. A loss group terminates on the first day of the first taxable year that is a separate return year with respect to each member of the former loss group.

(6) Appropriate adjustments when former member leaves during the year. Appropriate adjustments are made to the consolidated section 382 limitation for the consolidated return year during which the former member (or loss subgroup) ceases to be a member(s) to reflect the inclusion of the former member in the loss group for a portion of that year.

(7) Examples. The following examples illustrate the principles of this paragraph (c):

Example (1). Consequence of apportionment.

(i) L owns all the L1 stock and L1 owns all the L2 stock. The L group has a $200 consolidated net operating loss arising in Year 1 that is carried over to Year 2. At the close of December 31, Year 1, the group has an ownership change under § 1.1502-92. The ownership change results in a consolidated section 382 limitation of $10 based on the value of the stock of the group. On August 29, Year 2, L1 sells 30 percent of the stock of L2 to A. L2 is apportioned $90 of the group's $200 consolidated net operating loss under § 1.1502-21(b). L, the common parent, elects to apportion $6 of the consolidated section 382 limitation to L2. The following is a graphic illustration of these facts:

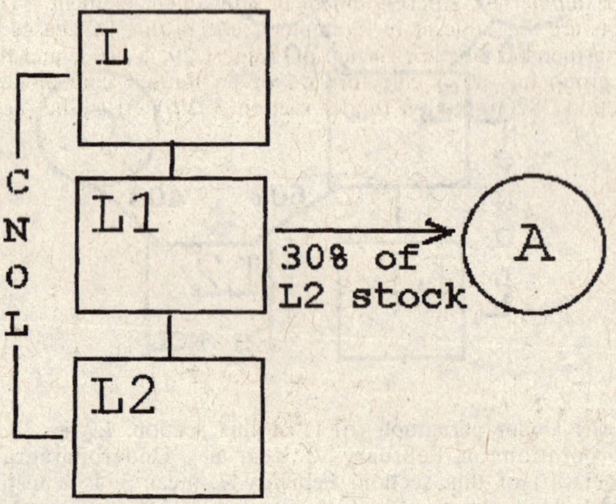

(ii) For its separate return years ending after December 31, Year 2, L2's section 382 limitation with respect to the $90 of the group's net operating loss apportioned to it is $6, adjusted, as appropriate, for any short taxable year, unused section 382 limitation, or other adjustment. For its consolidated return year ending December 31, Year 2 the L group's consolidated section 382 limitation with respect to the remaining $110 of pre-change consolidated attribute is $4 ($10 minus the $6 value element apportioned to L2), adjusted, as appropriate, for any short taxable year, unused section 382 limitation, or other adjustment.

(iii) For the L group's consolidated return year ending December 31, Year 2, the value element of its consolidated section 382 limitation is increased by $4 (rounded to the nearest dollar), to account for the period during which L2 was a member of the L group ($6, the consolidated section 382 limitation apportioned to L2, times 241/365, the ratio of the number of days during Year 2 that L2 is a member of the group to the number of days in the group's consolidated return year). See paragraph (c)(6) of this section. Therefore, the value element of the consolidated section 382 limitation for Year 2 of the L group is $8 (rounded to the nearest dollar).

(iv) The section 382 limitation for L2's short taxable year ending December 31, Year 2, is $2 (rounded to the nearest dollar), which is the amount that bears the same relationship to $6, the value element of the consolidated section 382 limitation apportioned to L2, as the number of days during that short taxable year, 124 days, bears to 365. See § 1.382-5(c).

Example (2). Consequence of no apportionment. The facts are the same as in Example 1, except that L does not elect to apportion any portion of the consolidated section 382 limitation to L2. For its separate return years ending after August 29, Year 2, L2's section 382 limitation with respect to the $90 of the group's pre-change consolidated attribute apportioned to L2 is zero under paragraph (b)(2)(ii) of this section. Thus, the $90 consolidated net operating loss apportioned to L2 cannot offset L2's taxable income in any of its separate return years ending after August 29, Year 2. For its consolidated return years ending after August 29, Year 2, the L group's consolidated section 382 limitation with respect to the remaining $110 of pre-change consolidated attribute is $10, adjusted, as appropriate, for any short taxable year, unused section 382 limitation, or other adjustment.

Example (3). Apportionment of adjustment element. The facts are the same as in Example 1, except that L2 ceases to be a member of the L group on August 29, Year 3, and the L group has a $4 carryforward of an unused consolidated section 382 limitation (under section 382(b)(2)) to the Year 3 consolidated return year. The carryover of unused limitation increases the consolidated section 382 limitation for the Year 3 consolidated return year from $10 to $14. L may elect to apportion all or any portion of the $10 value element and all or any portion of the $4 adjustment element to L2.

(d) Rules pertaining to ceasing to be a member of a loss subgroup. *(1) In general.* A corporation ceases to be a member of a loss subgroup on the earlier of—

(i) The first day of the first taxable year for which it files a separate return; or

(ii) The first day that it ceases to bear a relationship described in section 1504(a)(1) to the loss subgroup parent (treating for this purpose the loss subgroup parent as the common parent described in section 1504(a)(1)(A)).

(2) Exceptions. Paragraph (d)(1)(ii) of this section does not apply to a member of a loss subgroup while that member remains a member of the current group—

(i) If an election under § 1.1502-91(d)(4) (relating to treating the subgroup parent requirement as satisfied) applies to the members of the loss subgroup;

(ii) Starting on the day after the change date (but not earlier than the date the loss subgroup becomes a member of the group), if there is an ownership change of the loss subgroup within six months before, on, or after becoming members of the group; or

(iii) Starting the day after the period of 5 consecutive years following the day that the loss subgroup become members of the group during which the loss subgroup has not had an ownership change.

(3) Examples. The principles of this paragraph (d) are illustrated by the following examples:

Example (1). Basic case.

(i) P owns all the L stock, L owns all the L1 stock and L1 owns all the L2 stock. The P group has a consolidated net operating loss arising in Year 1 that is carried over to Year 2. On December 11, Year 2, P sells all the stock of L to corporation M. Each of L, L1, and L2 is apportioned a portion of the Year 1 consolidated net operating loss, and thereafter each joins with M in filing consolidated returns. Under § 1.1502-92, the L loss subgroup has an ownership change on December 11, Year 2. The L loss subgroup has a subgroup section 382 limitation of $100. The following is a graphic illustration of these facts:

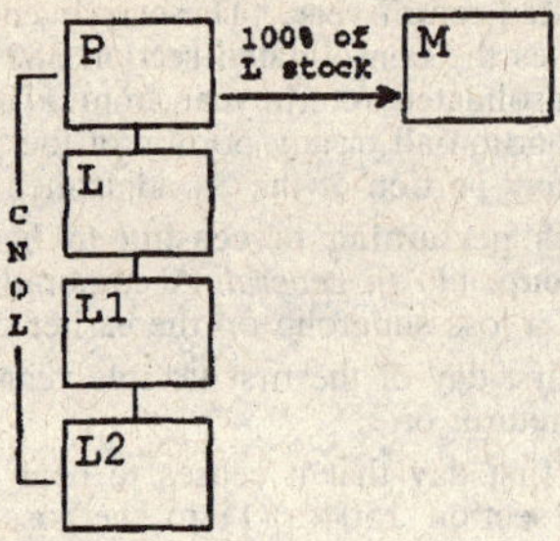

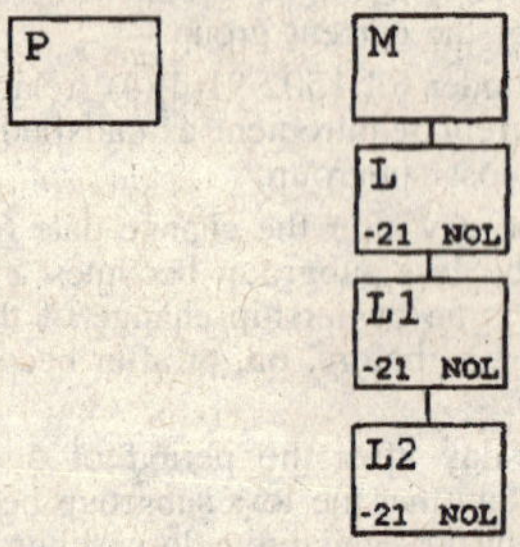

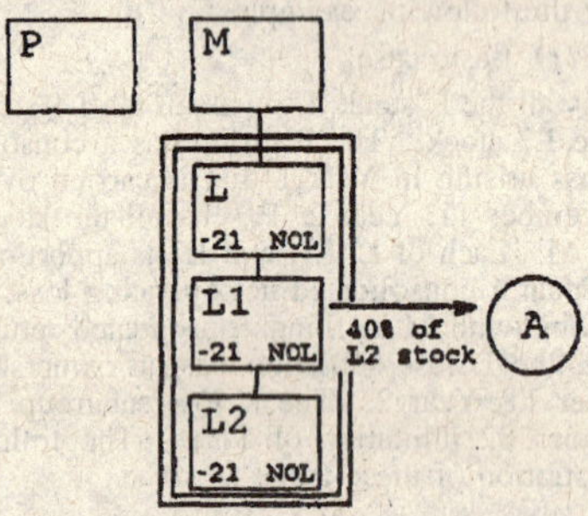

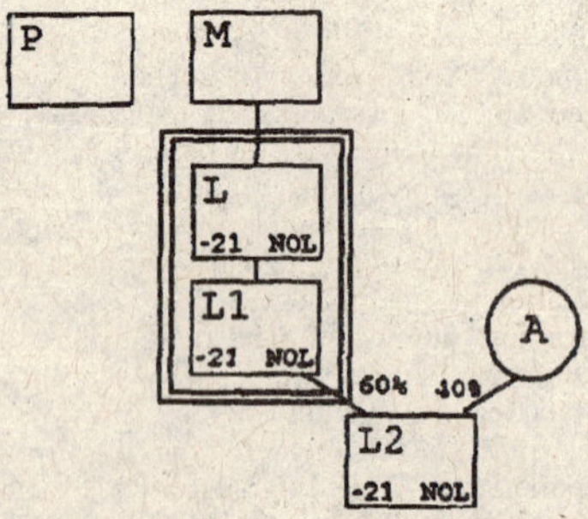

(ii) On May 22, Year 3, L1 sells 40 percent of the L2 stock to A. L2 carries over a portion of the P group's net operating loss from Year 1 to its separate return year ending December 31, Year 3. Under paragraph (d)(1) of this section, L2 ceases to be a member of the L loss subgroup on May 22, Year 3, which is both (1) the first day of the first taxable year for which it files a separate return and (2) the day it ceases to bear a relationship described in section 1504(a)(1) to the loss subgroup parent, L. The net operating loss of L2 that is carried over from the P group is treated as a pre-change loss of L2 for its separate return years ending after May 22, Year 3. Under paragraphs (a)(2) and (b)(2) of this section, the separate section 382 limitation with respect to this loss is zero unless M elects to apportion all or a part of the subgroup section 382 limitation of the L loss subgroup to L2.

Example (2). Formation of a new loss subgroup. The facts are the same as in Example 1, except that A purchases 40 percent of the L1 stock from L rather than purchasing L2 stock from L1. L1 and L2 file a consolidated return for their first taxable year ending after May 22, Year 3, and each of L1 and L2 carries over a part of the net operating loss of the P group that arose in Year 1. Under paragraph (d)(1) of this section, L1 and L2 cease to be members of the L loss subgroup on May 22, Year 3. The net operating losses carried over from the P group are treated as pre-change subgroup attributes of the loss subgroup composed of L1 and L2. The subgroup section 382 limitation with respect to those losses is zero unless M elects to apportion all or part of the subgroup section 382 limitation of the L loss subgroup to the L1 loss subgroup. The following is a graphic illustration of these facts:

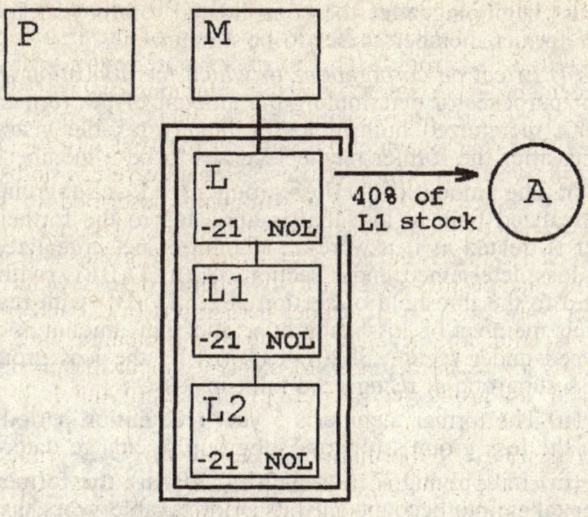

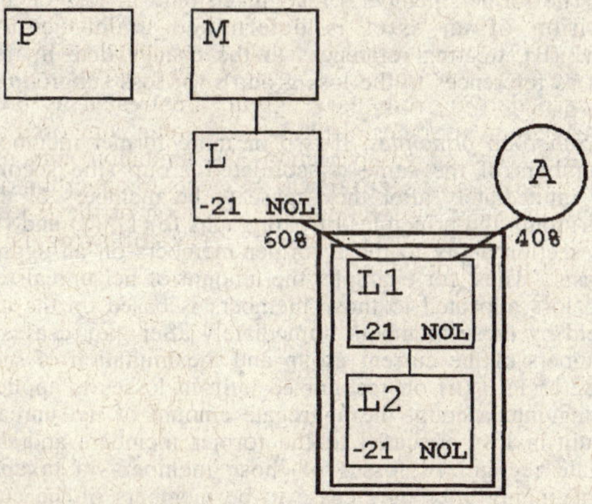

Example (3). Ownership change upon becoming members of the group.

(i) A owns all the stock of P, and P owns all the stock of L1 and L2. The P group has a consolidated net operating loss arising in Year 1 that is carried over to Year 3 and Year 4. Corporation M acquires all the stock of P on November 11, Year 3, and P, L1, and L2 thereafter file consolidated returns with M. M's acquisition results in an ownership change of the P loss subgroup under § 1.1502-92(b)(1)(ii).

(ii) P distributes the L2 stock to M on October 7, Year 4, and L2 ceases to bear the relationship described in section 1504(a)(1) to P, the P loss subgroup parent. However, under paragraph (d)(2) of this section, L2 does not cease to be a member of the P loss subgroup because the P loss subgroup had an ownership change upon becoming members of the M group and L2 remains in the M group.

Example (4). Ceasing to bear a section 1504 (a)(1) to the loss subgroup parent.

(i) A owns all the stock of P, and P owns all the stock of L1 and L2. The P group has a consolidated net operating loss arising in Year 1 that is carried over to Year 7. At the close of Year 2, X acquires all of the stock of P, causing an ownership change of the loss subgroup composed of P, L1 and L2 under § 1.1502-92(b)(1)(ii). In Year 4, M, which is owned by the same person that owns X, acquires all of the stock of P, and the M acquisition does not cause a second ownership change of the P loss subgroup.

(ii) P distributes the L2 stock to M on February 3, Year 6 (less than 5 years after the P loss subgroup became members of the M group) and L2 ceases to bear the relationship described in section 1504(a)(1) to P, the loss subgroup parent. Thus, the section 382 limitation from the Year 2 ownership change that applies with respect to the pre-change attributes attributable to L2 is zero except to the extent M elects to apportion all or part of the P loss subgroup section 382 limitation to L2.

Example (5). Relationship through a successor. The facts are the same as in Example 3, except that M's acquisition of the P stock does not result in an ownership change of the P loss subgroup, and, instead of P's distributing the stock of L2, L2 merges into L1 on October 7, Year 4. L1 (as successor to L2 in the merger within the meaning of § 1.1502-1(f)(4)) continues to bear a relationship described in section 1504(a)(1) to P, the loss subgroup parent. Thus, L2 does not cease to be a member of the P loss subgroup as a result of the merger.

Example (6). Reattribution of net operating loss carryover under § 1.1502-36(d)(6). The facts are the same as in Example 3, except that, instead of distributing the L2 stock to M, P sells that stock to B, and, under § 1.1502-36(d)(6), M reattributes $10 of L2's net operating loss carryover to itself. Under § 1.1502-36(d)(6)(iv)(A), M succeeds to the reattributed loss as if the loss were succeeded to in a transaction to which section 381(a) applies. M, as successor to L2, does not cease to be a member of the P loss subgroup.

(e) Allocation of net unrealized built-in loss. *(1) In general.* This paragraph (e) provides rules for the allocation of a loss group's (or loss subgroup's) net unrealized built-in loss if a member ceases to be a member of a loss group (or loss subgroup). This paragraph (e) applies if—

(i) A loss group (or loss subgroup) has a net unrealized built-in loss on a change date; and

(ii) Immediately after the close of the consolidated return year in which the departing member ceases to be a member, the amount of the loss group's (or loss subgroup's) excess of net unrealized built-in loss over recognized built-in loss, determined under section 382(h)(1)(B)(ii) (relating to a limitation on recognized built-in loss), is greater than zero. (The amount of such excess is referred to as the remaining NUBIL balance.) In applying section 382(h)(1)(B)(ii) for this purpose, net unrealized built-in loss allocated to departing members in prior consolidated return years is treated as recognized built-in loss in those years.

(2) Amount of allocation. (i) In general. The amount of net unrealized built-in loss allocated to a departing member is equal to the remaining NUBIL balance, multiplied by a fraction. The numerator of the fraction is the amount of the built-in loss, taken into account on the change date under § 1.1502-91(g), in the assets held by the departing member immediately after the member ceases to be a member of the loss group (or loss subgroup). The denominator of the fraction is the sum of the numerator, plus the amount of the built-in loss, taken into account under § 1.1502-91(g) on the change date, in the assets held by the loss group (or loss subgroup) immediately after the close of the taxable year in which the departing member ceases to be a member. (Fluctuations in value of the assets between the change date and the date that the member ceases to be a member of the group (or loss subgroup), or the close of the taxable year in

which the member ceases to be a member of the loss group, are disregarded.) Because the amount of built-in loss on the change date with respect to a departing member's assets is taken into account (rather than that member's separately computed net unrealized built-in loss on the change date), a departing member can be apportioned all or part of the loss group's net unrealized built-in loss, even if the departing member had a separately computed net unrealized built-in gain on the change date. Amounts taken into account under section 382(h)(6)(C) (relating to certain deduction items) are treated as if they were assets in determining the numerator and denominator of the fraction.

(ii) Transferred basis property and deferred gain or loss. For purposes of paragraph (b)(2)(i) of this section, assets held by the departing member immediately after it ceases to be a member of the group (or by other members immediately after the close of the taxable year) include—

(A) Assets held at that time that are transferred basis property that was held by any member of the group (or loss subgroup) on the change date; and

(B) Assets held at that time by any member of the consolidated group with respect to which gain or loss of the group member or loss subgroup member at issue has been deferred in an intercompany transaction and has not been taken into account.

(iii) Assets for which gain or loss has been recognized. For purposes of paragraph (b)(2)(i) of this section, assets held by the departing member immediately after it ceases to be a member of the group (or by other members immediately after the close of the taxable year) do not include assets with respect to which gain or loss has previously been recognized and taken into account during the recognition period (including gain or loss recognized in an intercompany transaction and taken into account immediately before the member leaves the group). Appropriate adjustments must be made if gain or loss on an asset has been only partially recognized and taken into account.

(iv) Exchanged basis property. The rules of § 1.1502-91(h) apply for purposes of this paragraph (e) (disregarding stock received from the departing member or another member that is a member immediately after the close of the taxable year).

(v) Two or more members depart during the same year. If two or more members cease to be members during the same consolidated return year, appropriate adjustments must be made to the denominator of the fraction for each departing member by treating the other departing members as if they had not ceased to be members during that year and as if the assets held by those other departing members immediately after they cease to be members of the group (or loss subgroup) are assets held by the group immediately after the close of the taxable year.

(vi) Anti-abuse rule. If assets are transferred between members or a member ceases to be a member with a principal purpose of causing or affecting the allocation of amounts under this paragraph (e), appropriate adjustments must be made to eliminate any benefit of such acquisition, disposition, or allocation.

(3) Effect of allocation on the consolidated group. The amount of the net unrealized built-in loss that is allocated to the former member is treated as recognized built-in loss for a prior taxable year ending in the recognition period for purposes applying the limitation of section 382(h)(1)(B)(ii) to a loss group's (or loss subgroup's) recognition period taxable years beginning after the consolidated return year in which the former member ceases to be a member.

(4) Effect on corporations to which the allocation is made. For purposes of determining the amount of the former member's recognized built-in losses in any taxable year beginning after the former member ceases to be a member—

(i) The amount of the loss group's (or loss subgroup's) net unrealized built-in loss that is allocated to the former member is treated as if it were an amount of net unrealized built-in loss determined under section 382(h)(1)(B)(i) (without regard to the threshold of section 382(h)(3)(B)) with respect to such member or loss subgroup, and that amount is not reduced under section 382(h)(1)(B)(ii) by the loss group's (or loss subgroup's) recognized built-in losses;

(ii) The former member's 5 year recognition period begins on the loss group's (or loss subgroup's) change date;

(iii) In applying section 382(h)(1)(B)(ii), the former member takes into account only its prior taxable years that begin after it ceases to be a member of the loss group (or loss subgroup); and

(iv) The former member's recognized built-in loss on the disposition of an asset is determined under section 382(h)(2)(B), treating references to the change date in that section as references to the loss group's (or loss subgroup's) change date.

(5) Subgroup principles. If two or more former members are members of the same consolidated group (the second group) immediately after they cease to be members of the current group, the principles of paragraphs (e)(1), (2) and (4) of this section apply to those former members on an aggregate basis. Thus, for example, the amount of net unrealized built-in loss allocated to those members is based on the assets held by those members immediately after they cease to be members of the current group and the limitation of section 382(h)(1)(B)(ii) on recognized built-in losses is applied by taking into account the aggregate amount of net unrealized built-in loss allocated to the former members and the aggregate recognized losses of those members in taxable years beginning after they cease to be members of the current group. If one or more of such members cease to be members of the second group, the principles of this paragraph (e) are applied with respect to those members to allocate to them all or part of any remaining unrecognized amount of net unrealized built-in loss allocated to the members that became members of the second group.

(6) Apportionment of consolidated section 382 limitation (or subgroup section 382 limitation).

(i) In general. For rules relating to the apportionment of a consolidated section 382 limitation (or subgroup section 382 limitation) to a former member, see paragraph (c) of this section.

(ii) Special rule for former members that become members of the same consolidated group. If recognized built-in losses of one or more former members would be subject to a consolidated section 382 limitation (or subgroup section 382 limitation) if recognized immediately before the member (or members) cease to be members of the group, an apportionment of that limitation may be made, under paragraph (c) of this section, to a loss subgroup that includes such member (or members), and the recognized built-in losses (if any) of that member (or members) will be subject to that apportioned limitation. If two or more of such former members are not included in a loss subgroup immediately after they cease to be members of the group (for example, because they do not have net operating loss carryovers or, in the aggregate, a net unrealized built-in loss), but are members of the same consolidated group, an apportionment of the consolidated section 382 limitation (or subgroup section 382 limitation) may be made to them as if they were a loss subgroup.

(7) Examples. The following examples illustrate the principles of this paragraph (e):

Example (1). Basic allocation case. (i) P owns all of the stock of L1 and L2. On September 4, Year 1, A purchases all of the P stock, causing an ownership change of the P group. On that date P has two assets (other than the L1 and L2 stock), asset 1 with an adjusted basis of $40 and a fair market value of $15 and asset 2 with an adjusted basis of $50 and a fair market value of $100. L1 has two assets, asset 3 , with a fair market value of $50 and an adjusted basis of $100, and asset 4, with an adjusted basis of $125 and a fair market value of $75. L2 has two assets, asset 5, with a fair market value of $150 and an adjusted basis of $100, and asset 6, with an adjusted basis of $90 and a fair market value of $40. Thus, the P loss group has a net unrealized built-in loss of $75.

On March 19, Year 3, P sells all of the L2 stock to M. At that time, asset 5, which has appreciated in value, has a fair market value of $250 and an adjusted basis of $100. Asset 6, which has declined in value, has an adjusted basis of $90 and a fair market value of $10.

(iii) On April 8, Year 3, P sells asset 1, and has a recognized built-in loss of $25 that is subject to the P group's section 382 limitation. On November 11, Year 4, L2 sells asset 6 for its then fair market value, $10, recognizing a loss of $80. On June 3, Year 5, L1 sells asset 4, recognizing a loss of $50.

(iv) Immediately after the close of Year 3, the P loss group's remaining NUBIL balance is $50 ($75 net unrealized built-in loss reduced by the $25 recognized built-in loss of P). The portion of the remaining NUBIL balance that is allocated to L2 is $17 (rounded to the nearest dollar). Seventeen dollars is the product obtained by multiplying $50 (the remaining NUBIL balance) by $50/$150. The numerator of the fraction ($50) is the amount of built-in loss in asset 6, taken into account on the change date under § 1.1502-91(g). The denominator ($150) is the sum of the numerator ($50) and the amount of built-in loss in assets 3 and 4, taken into account on the change date under § 1.1502-91(g) ($100). The built-in loss in asset 1 is not included in the denominator of the fraction because it is not held by the P group immediately after the close of Year 3.

(v) Seventeen dollars of L2's $80 loss on the sale of asset 6 is a recognized built-in loss and subject to a section 382 limitation of zero, unless P apportions some or all of the P group's consolidated section 382 limitation to L2 (adjusted for a short taxable year, carryover of unused limitation, or any other adjustment required under section 382).

(vi) Thirty-three dollars of L1's $50 loss on the sale of asset 4 is subject to the P group's consolidated section 382 limitation, reduced by the amount of such limitation apportioned to L2, and adjusted for any short taxable year, a carryforward of unused limitation, or other adjustment. (In applying section 382(h)(1)(B)(ii) with respect to Year 5, the P group's net unrealized built-in loss is reduced by P's $25 recognized built-in loss in Year 3 and the $17 of net unrealized built-in loss allocated to L2, thus limiting the P group's recognized built-in loss in Year 5 to $33.)

Example (2). Two members depart in the same year. The facts are the same as in Example 1, except that P sells all of the stock of L1 to C on November 1, Year 3. The amount of net unrealized built-in loss apportioned to L2 (rounded to the nearest dollar) is $17 ($50 remaining NUBIL balance × $50/$150). The amount of net unrealized built-in loss apportioned to L1 (rounded to the nearest dollar) is $33 ($50 remaining NUBIL balance × $100/$150).

(8) Reporting requirements. (i) Common Parent. Except as provided in paragraph (e)(8)(iii) of this section, if a net unrealized built-in loss is allocated under paragraph (e) of this section, the common parent must include a statement entitled, "STATEMENT OF NET UNREALIZED BUILT-IN LOSS ALLOCATION PURSUANT TO § 1.1502-95(e)," on or with its income tax return for the taxable year in which the former member(s) (or a new loss subgroup that includes that member) ceases to be a member. The statement must include—

(A) The name and employer identification number of the departing member;

(B) The amount of the remaining NUBIL balance for the taxable year in which the member departs;

(C) The amount of the net unrealized built-in loss allocated to the departing member; and

(D) A representation that the common parent has delivered a copy of the statement to the former member (or the common parent of the group of which the former member is a member) on or before the day the group files its income tax return for the consolidated return year that the former member ceases to be a member.

(ii) Former member. Except as provided in paragraph (e)(8)(iii) of this section, the former member must include a statement on or with its first income tax return (or the first return in which the former member joins) that is filed after the close of the consolidated return year of the group of which the former member (or a new loss subgroup that includes that member) ceases to be a member. The statement will be identical to the statement filed by the common parent under paragraph (e)(8)(i) of this section except that instead of including the information described in paragraph (e)(8)(i)(A) of this section the former member must provide the name, employer identification number and tax year of the former common parent, and instead of the representation described in paragraph (e)(8)(i)(D) of this section the former member must represent that it has received and retained the copy of the statement delivered by the common parent as part of its records. See § 1.6001-1(e).

(iii) Exception. This paragraph (e)(8) does not apply if the required information (other than the amount of the remaining NUBIL balance) is included in a statement of election under paragraph (f) of this section (relating to apportioning a section 382 limitation).

(f) Filing the election to apportion the section 382 limitation and net unrealized built-in gain. *(1) Form of the election to apportion.* (i) Statement. An election under paragraph (c) of this section must be made in the form set forth in this paragraph (f)(1)(i). The election must be made by the common parent and the party described in paragraph (f)(2) of this section. It must be filed in accordance with paragraph (f)(3) of this section and be entitled, "THIS IS AN ELECTION UNDER § 1.1502-95 TO APPORTION ALL OR PART OF THE [INSERT THE CONSOLIDATED SECTION 382 LIMITATION, THE SUBGROUP SECTION 382 LIMITATION, THE LOSS GROUP'S NET UNREALIZED BUILT-IN GAIN, OR THE LOSS SUBGROUP'S NET UNREALIZED BUILT-IN GAIN, AS APPROPRIATE] IN THE AMOUNT OF [INSERT THE AMOUNT OF THE

LOSS LIMITATION OR NET UNREALIZED BUILT-IN GAIN] TO [INSERT NAME(S) AND EMPLOYER IDENTIFICATION NUMBER(S) OF THE CORPORATION (OR THE CORPORATIONS THAT COMPOSE A NEW LOSS SUBGROUP) TO WHICH ALLOCATION IS MADE]." The statement must also indicate that an agreement, as described in paragraph (f)(1)(ii) of this section, has been entered into.

(ii) Agreement. Both the common parent and the party described in paragraph (f)(2) of this section must sign and date the agreement. The agreement must include, as appropriate—

(A) The date of the ownership change that resulted in the consolidated section 382 limitation (or subgroup section 382 limitation) or the loss group's (or loss subgroup's) net unrealized built-in gain;

(B) The amount of the departing member's (or loss subgroup's) pre-change net operating loss carryovers and the taxable years in which they arose that will be subject to the limitation that is being apportioned to that member (or loss subgroup);

(C) The amount of any net unrealized built-in loss allocated to the departing member (or loss subgroup) under paragraph (e) of this section, which, if recognized, can be a pre-change attribute subject to the limitation that is being apportioned;

(D) If a consolidated section 382 limitation (or subgroup section 382 limitation) is being apportioned, the amount of the consolidated section 382 limitation (or subgroup section 382 limitation) for the taxable year during which the former member (or new loss subgroup) ceases to be a member of the consolidated group (determined without regard to any apportionment under this section);

(E) If any net unrealized built-in gain is being apportioned, the amount of the loss group's (or loss subgroup's) net unrealized built-in gain (as determined under paragraph (c)(2)(ii) of this section) that may be apportioned to members that ceased to be members during the consolidated return year;

(F) The amount of the value element and adjustment element of the consolidated section 382 limitation (or subgroup section 382 limitation) that is apportioned to the former member (or new loss subgroup) pursuant to paragraph (c) of this section;

(G) The amount of the loss group's (or loss subgroup's) net unrealized built-in gain that is apportioned to the former member (or new loss subgroup) pursuant to paragraph (c) of this section;

(H) If the former member is allocated any net unrealized built-in loss under paragraph (e) of this section, the amount of any adjustment element apportioned to the former member that is attributable to recognized built-in gains (determined in a manner that will enable both the group and the former member to apply the principles of § 1.1502-93(c)); and

(I) The name and employer identification number of the common parent making the apportionment.

(2) Signing the agreement. The agreement must be signed by both the common parent and the former member (or, in the case of a loss subgroup, the common parent and the loss subgroup parent) by persons authorized to sign their respective income tax returns. If the allocation is made to a loss subgroup for which an election under § 1.1502-91(d)(4) is made, and not separately to its members, the agreement under this paragraph (f) must be signed by the common parent and any member of the new loss subgroup by persons authorized to sign their respective income tax returns. Each party signing the agreement must retain either the original or a copy of the agreement as part of its records. See § 1.6001-1(e).

(3) Filing of the election. (i) Filing by the common parent. The election must be filed by the common parent of the group that is apportioning the consolidated section 382 limitation (or the subgroup section 382 limitation) or the loss group's net unrealized built-in gain (or loss subgroup's net unrealized built-in gain) by including the statement on or with its income tax return for the taxable year in which the former member (or new loss subgroup) ceases to be a member.

(ii) Filing by the former member. An identical statement must be included on or with the first return of the former member (or the first return in which the former member, or the members of a new loss subgroup, join) that is filed after the close of the consolidated return year of the group of which the former member (or the members of a new loss subgroup) ceases to be a member.

(4) Revocation of election. An election statement made under paragraph (c) of this section is revocable only with the consent of the Commissioner.

(g) Effective/applicability date. Paragraphs (e)(8) and (f) of this section apply to any original consolidated Federal income tax return due (without extensions) after June 14, 2007. For original consolidated Federal income tax returns due (without extensions) after May 30, 2006, and on or before June 14, 2007, see § 1.1502-95T as contained in 26 CFR part 1 in effect on April 1, 2007. For original consolidated Federal income tax returns due (without extensions) on or before May 30, 2006, see § 1.1502-95 as contained in 26 CFR part 1 in effect on April 1, 2006.

T.D. 8824, 6/25/99, amend T.D. 9264, 5/26/2006, T.D. 9329, 6/13/2007, T.D. 9424, 9/10/2008.

§ 1.1502-95A Rules on ceasing to be a member of a consolidated group generally applicable for corporation ceasing to be members before June 25, 1999.

(a) In general. *(1) Consolidated group.* This section provides rules for applying section 382 on or after the day that a member ceases to be a member of a consolidated group (or loss subgroup). The rules concern how to determine whether an ownership change occurs with respect to losses of the member, and how a consolidated section 382 limitation (or subgroup section 382 limitation) is apportioned to the member. As the context requires, a reference in this section to a loss group, a member, or a corporation also includes a reference to a loss subgroup, and a reference to a consolidated section 382 limitation also includes a reference to a subgroup section 382 limitation.

(2) Election by common parent. Only the common parent (not the loss subgroup parent) may make the election under paragraph (c) of this section to apportion either a consolidated section 382 limitation or a subgroup section 382 limitation.

(3) Coordination with §§ 1.1502-91A through 1.1502-93A. For rules regarding the determination of whether there is an ownership change of a loss subgroup and the computation of a subgroup section 382 limitation following such an ownership change, see §§ 1.1502-91A through 1.1502-93A.

(b) Separate application of section 382 when a member leaves a consolidated group. *(1) In general.* Except as provided in §§ 1.1502-91A through 1.1502-93A (relating to rules applicable to loss groups and loss subgroups), section 382 and the regulations thereunder apply to a corporation on a separate entity basis after it ceases to be a member of a consolidated group (or loss subgroup). Solely for purposes of determining whether a corporation has an ownership change—

(i) Any portion of a consolidated net operating loss that is apportioned to the corporation under §§ 1.1502-21(b) or 1.1502-21T(b) in effect prior to June 25, 1999, as contained in 26 CFR part 1 revised April 1, 1999, as applicable is treated as a net operating loss of the corporation beginning on the first day of the taxable year in which the loss arose;

(ii) The testing period may include the period during which (or before which) the corporation was a member of the group (or loss subgroup); and

(iii) Except to the extent provided in § 1.1502-20(g) (relating to reattributed losses), the day it ceases to be a member of a consolidated group is treated as a testing date of the corporation within the meaning of § 1.382-2(a)(4).

(2) Effect of a prior ownership change of the group. If a loss group has had an ownership change under § 1.1502-92A before a corporation ceases to be a member of a consolidated group (the former member)—

(i) Any pre-change consolidated attribute that is subject to a consolidated section 382 limitation continues to be treated as a pre-change loss with respect to the former member after the attribute is apportioned to the former member;

(ii) The former member's section 382 limitation with respect to such attribute is zero except to the extent the common parent apportions under paragraph (c) of this section all or a part of the consolidated section 382 limitation to the former member;

(iii) The testing period for determining a subsequent ownership change with respect to such attribute begins no earlier than the first day following the loss group's most recent change date; and

(iv) As generally provided under section 382, an ownership change of the former member that occurs on or after the day it ceases to be a member of a loss group may result in an additional, lesser limitation amount with respect to such loss.

(3) Application in the case of a loss subgroup. If two or more former members are included in the same loss subgroup immediately after they cease to be members of a consolidated group, the principles of paragraphs (b) and (c) of this section apply to the loss subgroup. Therefore, for example, an apportionment by the common parent under paragraph (c) of this section is made to the loss subgroup rather than separately to its members.

(4) Examples. The following examples illustrate the principles of this paragraph (b).

Example (1). Treatment of departing member as a separate corporation throughout the testing period.

(a) A owns all the L stock. L owns all the stock of L1 and L2. The L group has a consolidated net operating loss arising in Year 1 that is carried over to Year 3. On January 12, Year 2, A sells 30 percent of the L stock to B. On February 7, Year 3, L sells 40 percent of the L2 stock to C, and L2 ceases to be a member of the group. A portion of the Year 1 consolidated net operating loss is apportioned to L2 under §§ 1.1502-21(b) or 1.1502-21T(b) in effect prior to June 25, 1999, as contained in 26 CFR part 1 revised April 1, 1999, as applicable and is carried to L2's first separate return year, which ends December 31, Year 3. The following is a graphic illustration of these facts:

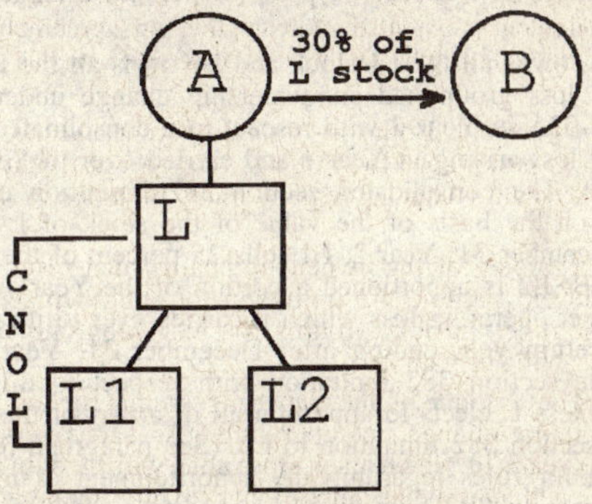

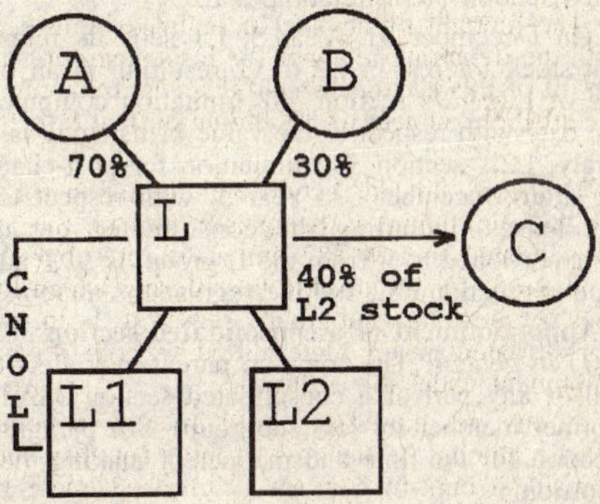

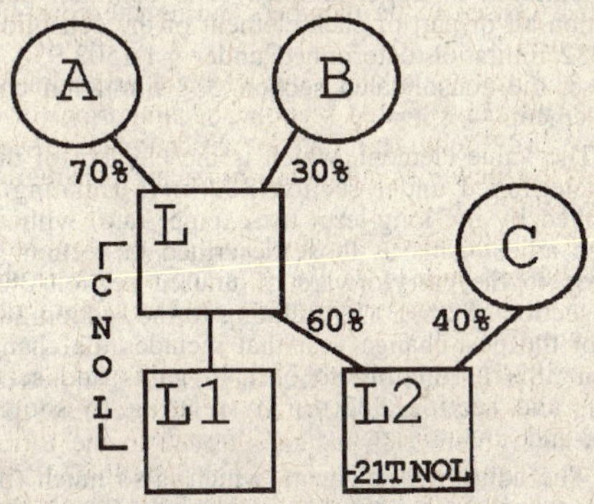

(b) Under paragraph (b)(1) of this section, L2 is a loss corporation on February 7, Year 3. Under paragraph (b)(1)(iii) of this section, February 7, Year 3, is a testing date. Under paragraph (b)(1)(ii) of this section, the testing period for L2 with respect to this testing date commences on January 1, Year 1, the first day of the taxable year in which the portion of the consolidated net operating loss apportioned to L2 arose. Therefore, in determining whether L2 has an ownership change on February 7, Year 3, B's purchase of 30 percent of the L stock and C's purchase of 40 percent of the L2 stock are each owner shifts. L2 has an ownership change under section 382(g) and § 1.382-2T because B and C have increased their ownership interests in L2 by 18 and 40 percentage points, respectively, during the testing period.

Example (2). Effect of prior ownership change of loss group.

(a) L owns all the L1 stock and L1 owns all the L2 stock. The L loss group had an ownership change under section 1.1502-92A in Year 2 with respect to a consolidated net operating loss arising in Year 1 and carried over to Year 2 and Year 3. The consolidated section 382 limitation computed solely on the basis of the value of the stock of L is $100. On December 31, Year 2, L1 sells 25 percent of the stock of L2 to B. L2 is apportioned a portion of the Year 1 consolidated net operating loss which it carries over to its first separate return year ending after December 31, Year 2. L2's separate section 382 limitation with respect to this loss is zero unless L elects to apportion all or a part of the consolidated section 382 limitation to L2. (See paragraph (c) of this section for rules regarding the apportionment of a consolidated section 382 limitation.) L apportions $50 of the consolidated section 382 limitation to L2.

(b) On December 31, Year 3, L1 sells its remaining 75 percent stock interest in L2 to C, resulting in an ownership change of L2. L2's section 382 limitation computed on the change date with respect to the value of its stock is $30. Accordingly, L2's section 382 limitation for post-change years ending after December 31, Year 3, with respect to its pre-change losses, including the consolidated net operating losses apportioned to it from the L group, is $30, adjusted as required by section 382 and the regulations thereunder.

(c) Apportionment of a consolidated section 382 limitation. *(1) In general.* The common parent may elect to apportion all or any part of a consolidated section 382 limitation to a former member (or loss subgroup). See paragraph (e) of this section for the time and manner of making the election to apportion.

(2) Amount of apportionment. The common parent may apportion all or part of each element of the consolidated section 382 limitation determined under § 1.1502-93A. For this purpose, the consolidated section 382 limitation consists of two elements—

(i) The value element, which is the element of the limitation determined under section 382(b)(1) (relating to value multiplied by the long-term tax-exempt rate) without regard to such adjustments as those described in section 382(b)(2) (relating to the carryforward of unused section 382 limitation), section 382(b)(3)(B) (relating to the section 382 limitation for the post-change year that includes the change date), section 382(h) (relating to built-in gains and section 338 gains), and section 382(m)(2) (relating to short taxable years); and

(ii) The adjustment element, which is so much (if any) of the limitation for the taxable year during which the former member ceases to be a member of the consolidated group that is attributable to a carryover of unused limitation under section 382(b)(2) or to recognized built-in gains under 382(h).

(3) Effect of apportionment on the consolidated section 382 limitation. The value element of the consolidated section 382 limitation for any post-change year ending after the day that a former member (or loss subgroup) ceases to be a member(s) is reduced to the extent that it is apportioned under this paragraph (c). The consolidated section 382 limitation for the post-change year in which the former member (or loss subgroup) ceases to be a member(s) is also reduced to the extent that the adjustment element for that year is apportioned under this paragraph (c).

(4) Effect on corporations to which the consolidated section 382 limitation is apportioned. The amount of the value element that is apportioned to a former member (or loss subgroup) is treated as the amount determined under section 382(b)(1) for purposes of determining the amount of that corporation's (or loss subgroup's) section 382 limitation for any taxable year ending after the former member (or loss subgroup) ceases to be a member(s). Appropriate adjustments must be made to the limitation based on the value element so apportioned for a short taxable year, carryforward of unused limitation, or any other adjustment required under section 382. The adjustment element apportioned to a former member (or loss subgroup) is treated as an adjustment under section 382(b)(2) or section 382(h), as appropriate, for the first taxable year after the member (or members) ceases to be a member (or members).

(5) Deemed apportionment when loss group terminates. If a loss group terminates, to the extent the consolidated section 382 limitation is not apportioned under paragraph (c)(1) of this section, the consolidated section 382 limitation is deemed to be apportioned to the loss subgroup that includes the common parent, or, if there is no loss subgroup that includes the common parent immediately after the loss group terminates, to the common parent. A loss group terminates on the first day of the first taxable year that is a separate return year with respect to each member of the former loss group.

(6) Appropriate adjustments when former member leaves during the year. Appropriate adjustments are made to the consolidated section 382 limitation for the consolidated return year during which the former member (or loss subgroup) ceases to be a member(s) to reflect the inclusion of the former member in the loss group for a portion of that year.

(7) Examples. The following examples illustrate the principles of this paragraph (c).

Example (1). Consequence of apportionment.

(a) L owns all the L1 stock and L1 owns all the L2 stock. The L group has a $200 consolidated net operating loss arising in Year 1 that is carried over to Year 2. At the close of December 31, Year 1, the group has an ownership change under § 1.1502-92A. The ownership change results in a consolidated section 382 limitation of $10 based on the value of the stock of the group. On August 29, Year 2, L1 sells 30 percent of the stock of L2 to A. L2 is apportioned $90 of the group's $200 consolidated net operating loss under §§ 1.1502-21(b) or 1.1502-21T(b) in effect prior to June 25, 1999, as contained in 26 CFR part 1 revised April 1, 1999, as applicable. L, the common parent, elects to apportion $6 of the consolidated section 382 limitation to L2. The following is a graphic illustration of these facts:

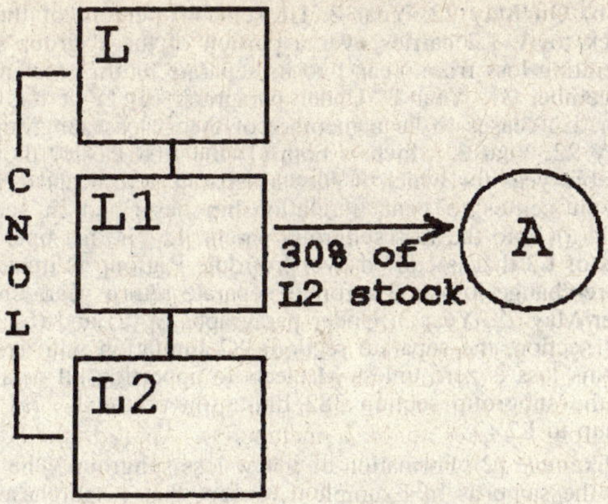

(b) For its separate return years ending after August 29, Year 2 (other than the taxable year ending December 31, Year 2), L2's section 382 limitation with respect to the $90 of the group's net operating loss apportioned to it is $6, adjusted, as appropriate, for any short taxable year, unused section 382 limitation, or other adjustment. For its consolidated return years ending after August 29, Year 2, (other than the year ending December 31, Year 2) the L group's consolidated section 382 limitation with respect to the remaining $110 of pre-change consolidated attribute is $4 ($10 minus the $6 value element apportioned to L2), adjusted, as appropriate, for any short taxable year, unused section 382 limitation, or other adjustment.

(c) For the L group's consolidated return year ending December 31, Year 2, the value element of its consolidated section 382 limitation is increased by $4 (rounded to the nearest dollar), to account for the period during which L2 was a member of the L group ($6, the consolidated section 382 limitation apportioned to L2, times 241/365, the ratio of the number of days during Year 2 that L2 is a member of the group to the number of days in the group's consolidated return year). See paragraph (c)(6) of this section. Therefore, the value element of the consolidated section 382 limitation for Year 2 of the L group is $8 (rounded to the nearest dollar).

(d) The section 382 limitation for L2's short taxable year ending December 31, Year 2, is $2 (rounded to the nearest dollar), which is the amount that bears the same relationship to $6, the value element of the consolidated section 382 limitation apportioned to L2, as the number of days during that short taxable year, 124 days, bears to 365. See § 1.382-4(c).

Example (2). Consequence of no apportionment. The facts are the same as in Example 1, except that L does not elect to apportion any portion of the consolidated section 382 limitation to L2. For its separate return years ending after August 29, Year 2, L2's section 382 limitation with respect to the $90 of the group's pre-change consolidated attribute apportioned to L2 is zero under paragraph (b)(2)(ii) of this section. Thus, the $90 consolidated net operating loss apportioned to L2 cannot offset L2's taxable income in any of its separate return years ending after August 29, Year 2. For its consolidated return years ending after August 29, Year 2, the L group's consolidated section 382 limitation with respect to the remaining $110 of pre-change consolidated attribute is $10, adjusted, as appropriate, for any short taxable year, unused section 382 limitation, or other adjustment.

Example (3). Apportionment of adjustment element. The facts are the same as in Example 1, except that L2 ceases to be a member of the L group on August 29, Year 3, and the L group has a $4 carryforward of an unused consolidated section 382 limitation (under section 382(b)(2)) to the 1993 consolidated return year. The carryover of unused limitation increases the consolidated section 382 limitation for the Year 3 consolidated return year from $10 to $14. L may elect to apportion all or any portion of the $10 value element and all or any portion of the $4 adjustment element to L2.

(d) Rules pertaining to ceasing to be a member of a loss subgroup. *(1) In general.* A corporation ceases to be a member of a loss subgroup—

(i) On the first day of the first taxable year for which it files a separate return; or

(ii) The first day that it ceases to bear a relationship described in section 1504(a)(1) to the loss subgroup parent (treating for this purpose the loss subgroup parent as the common parent described in section 1504(a)(1)(A)).

(2) Examples. The principles of this paragraph (d) are illustrated by the following examples.

Example (1). Basic case.

(a) P owns all the L stock, L owns all the L1 stock and L1 owns all the L2 stock. The P group has a consolidated net operating loss arising in Year 1 that is carried over to Year 2. On December 11, Year 2, P sells all the stock of L to corporation M. Each of L, L1, and L2 is apportioned a portion of the Year 1 consolidated net operating loss, and thereafter each joins with M in filing consolidated returns. Under § 1.1502-92A, the L loss subgroup has an ownership change on December 11, Year 2. The L loss subgroup has a subgroup section 382 limitation of $100. The following is a graphic illustration of these facts:

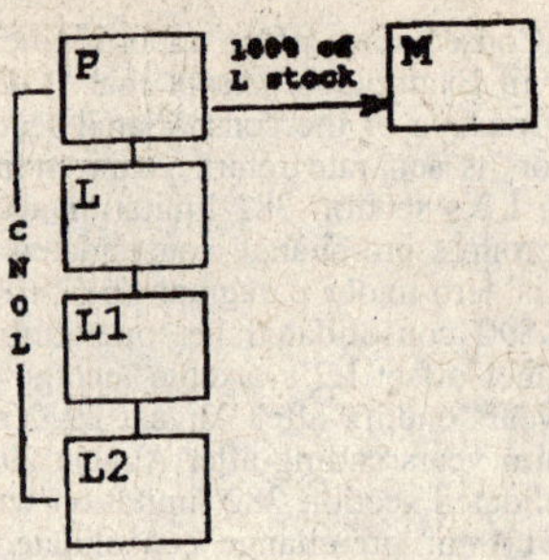

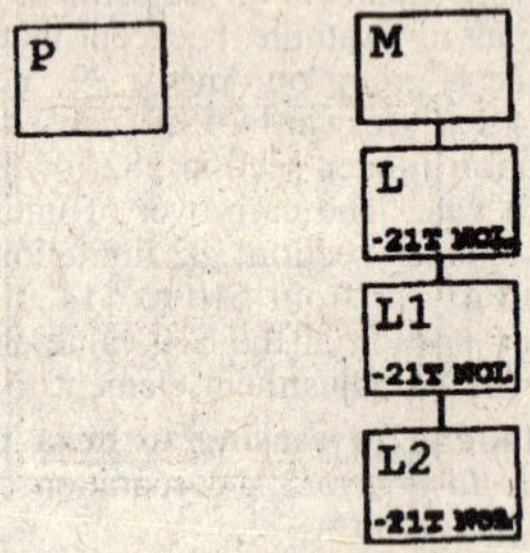

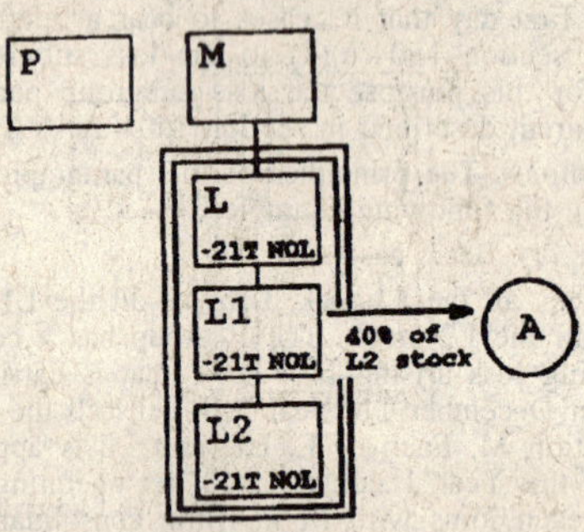

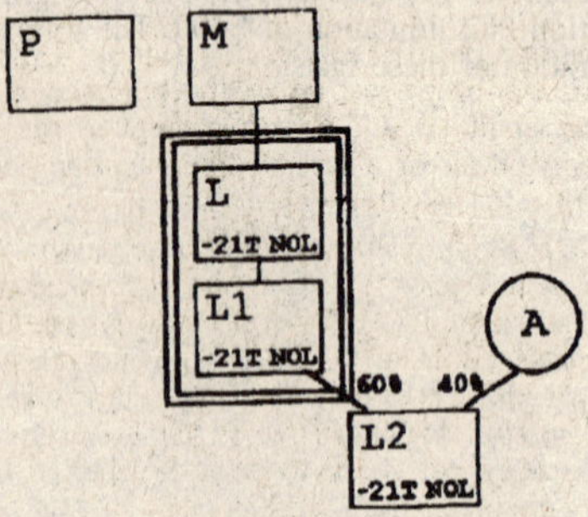

(b) On May 22, Year 3, L1 sells 40 percent of the L2 stock to A. L2 carries over a portion of the P group's net operating loss from Year 1 to its separate return year ending December 31, Year 3. Under paragraph (d)(1) of this section, L2 ceases to be a member of the L loss subgroup on May 22, Year 3, which is both (1) the first day of the first taxable year for which it files a separate return and (2) the day it ceases to bear a relationship described in section 1504(a)(1) to the loss subgroup parent, L. The net operating loss of L2 that is carried over from the P group is treated as a pre-change loss of L2 for its separate return years ending after May 22, Year 3. Under paragraphs (a)(2) and (b)(2) of this section, the separate section 382 limitation with respect to this loss is zero unless M elects to apportion all or a part of the subgroup section 382 limitation of the L loss subgroup to L2.

Example (2). Formation of a new loss subgroup. The facts are the same as in Example 1, except that A purchases 40 percent of the L1 stock from L rather than purchasing L2 stock from L1. L1 and L2 file a consolidated return for their first taxable year ending after May 22, Year 3, and each of L1 and L2 carries over a part of the net operating loss of the P group that arose in Year 1. Under paragraph (d)(1) of this section, L1 and L2 cease to be members of the L loss subgroup on May 22, Year 3. The net operating losses carried over from the P group are treated as pre-change subgroup attributes of the loss subgroup composed of L1 and L2. The subgroup section 382 limitation with respect to those losses is zero unless M elects to apportion all or part of the subgroup section 382 limitation of the L loss subgroup to the L1 loss subgroup. The following is a graphic illustration of these facts:

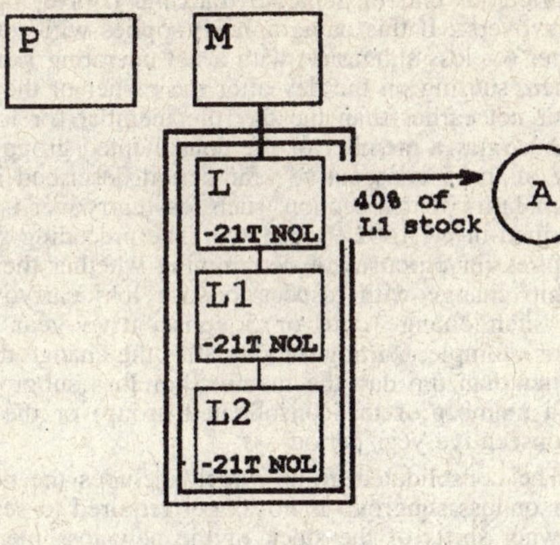

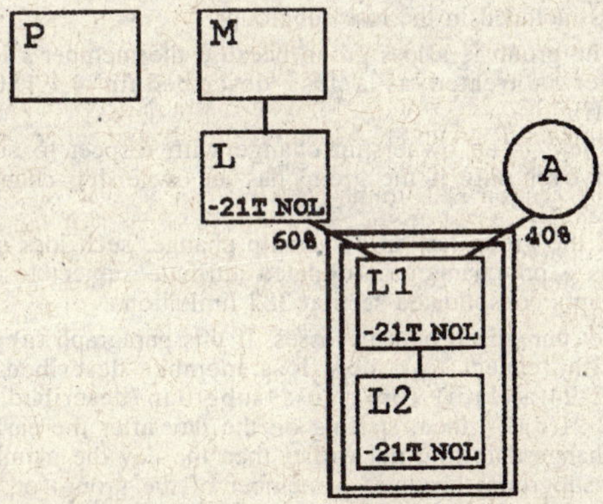

Example (3). Ceasing to bear a section 1504(a)(1) relationship to a loss subgroup parent.

(a) A owns all the stock of P, and P owns all the stock of L1 and L2. The P group has a consolidated net operating loss arising in Year 1 that is carried over to Year 3 and Year 4. Corporation M acquires all the stock of P on November 11, Year 3, and P, L1, and L2 thereafter file consolidated returns with M. M's acquisition results in an ownership change of the P loss subgroup under § 1.1502-92A(b)(1)(ii). The following is a graphic illustration of these facts:

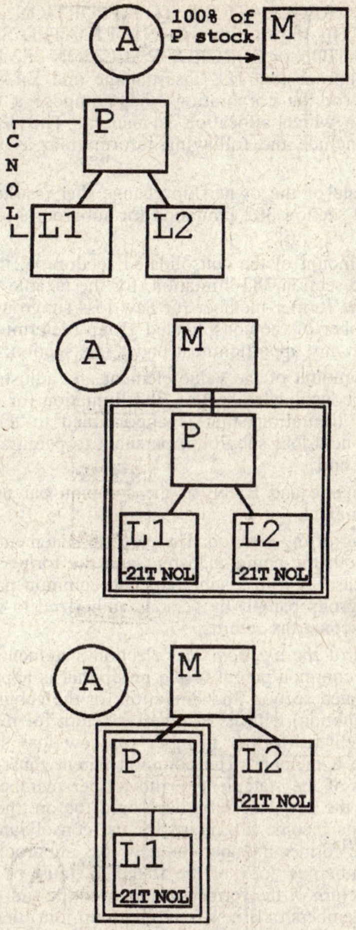

(b) P distributes the L2 stock to M on October 7, Year 4. L2 ceases to be a member of the P loss subgroup on October 7, Year 4, the first day that it ceases to bear the relationship described in section 1504(a)(1) to P, the P loss subgroup parent. See paragraph (d)(1)(ii) of this section. Thus, the section 382 limitation with respect to the pre-change subgroup attributes attributable to L2 is zero except to the extent M elects to apportion all or a part of the subgroup section 382 limitation of the P loss subgroup to L2.

Example (4). Relationship through a successor. The facts are the same as in Example 3, except that, instead of P's distributing the stock of L2, L2 merges into L1 on October 7, Year 4. L1 (as successor to L2 in the merger within the meaning of § 1.382-2T(f)(4)) continues to bear a relationship described in section 1504(a)(1) to P, the loss subgroup parent. Thus, L2 does not cease to be a member of the P loss subgroup as a result of the merger.

(e) Filing the election to apportion. *(1) Form of the election to apportion.* An election under paragraph (c) of this section must be made by the common parent. The election must be made in the form of the following statement: "THIS IS AN ELECTION UNDER § 1.1502-95A OF THE IN-

COME TAX REGULATIONS TO APPORTION ALL OR PART OF THE [insert either CONSOLIDATED SECTION 382 LIMITATION or SUBGROUP SECTION 382 LIMITATION, as appropriate] TO [insert name and E.I.N. of the corporation (or the corporations that compose a new loss subgroup) to which allocation is made]." The declaration must also include the following information, as appropriate—

(i) The date of the ownership change that resulted in the consolidated section 382 limitation (or subgroup section 382 limitation);

(ii) The amount of the consolidated section 382 limitation (or subgroup section 382 limitation) for the taxable year during which the former member (or new loss subgroup) ceases to be a member of the consolidated group (determined without regard to any apportionment under this section;

(iii) The amount of the value element and adjustment element of the consolidated section 382 limitation (or subgroup section 382 limitation) that is apportioned to the former member (or new loss subgroup) pursuant to paragraph (c) of this section; and

(iv) The name and E.I.N. of the common parent making the apportionment.

(2) Signing of the election. The election statement must be signed by both the common parent and the former member (or, in the case of a loss subgroup, the common parent and the loss subgroup parent) by persons authorized to sign their respective income tax returns.

(3) Filing of the election. The election statement must be filed by the common parent of the group that is apportioning the consolidated section 382 limitation (or the subgroup section 382 limitation) with its income tax return for the taxable year in which the former member (or new loss subgroup) ceases to be a member. The common parent must also deliver a copy of the statement to the former member (or the members of the new loss subgroup) on or before the day the group files its income tax return for the consolidated return year that the former member (or new loss subgroup) ceases to be a member. A copy of the statement must be attached to the first return of the former member (or the first return in which the members of a new loss subgroup join) that is filed after the close of the consolidated return year of the group of which the former member (or the members of a new loss subgroup) ceases to be a member.

(4) Revocation of election. An election statement made under paragraph (c) of this section is revocable only with the consent of the Commissioner.

T.D. 8678, 6/26/96, amend T.D. 8823, 6/25/99, T.D. 8824, 6/25/99.

§ 1.1502-96 Miscellaneous rules.

(a) End of separate tracking of losses. *(1) Application.* This paragraph (a) applies to a member (or a loss subgroup) with a net operating loss carryover that arose (or is treated under § 1.1502-21(c) as arising) in a SRLY, or a member (or loss subgroup) with a net unrealized built-in loss determined at the time that the member (or loss subgroup) becomes a member of the consolidated group if there is—

(i) An ownership change of the member (or loss subgroup) within six months before, on, or after becoming a member of the group; or

(ii) A period of 5 consecutive years following the day that the member (or loss subgroup) becomes a member of a group during which the member (or loss subgroup) has not had an ownership change.

(2) Effect of end of separate tracking. (i) Net operating loss carryovers. If this paragraph (a) applies with respect to a member (or loss subgroup) with a net operating loss carryover, then, starting on the day after the earlier of the change date (but not earlier than the day the member (or loss subgroup) becomes a member of the consolidated group) or the last day of the 5 consecutive year period described in paragraph (a)(1)(ii) of this section, such loss carryover is treated as described in § 1.1502-91(c)(1)(i). The preceding sentence also applies for purposes of determining whether there is an ownership change with respect to such loss carryover following such change date or 5 consecutive year period. Thus, for example, starting the day after the change date (but not earlier than the day the member (or loss subgroup) becomes a member of the consolidated group) or the end of the 5 consecutive year period—

(A) The consolidated group which includes the new loss member or loss subgroup is no longer required to separately track owner shifts of the stock of the new loss member or subgroup parent to determine if an ownership change occurs with respect to the loss carryover of the new loss member or members included in the loss subgroup;

(B) The group is a loss group because the member's loss carryover is treated as a loss described in § 1.1502-91(c)(1)(i);

(C) There is an ownership change with respect to such loss carryover only if the group has an ownership change; and

(D) If the group has an ownership change, such loss carryover is a pre-change consolidated attribute subject to the loss group's consolidated section 382 limitation.

(ii) Net unrealized built-in losses. If this paragraph (a) applies with respect to a new loss member described in § 1.1502-94(a)(1)(ii) (or a loss subgroup described in § 1.1502-91(d)(2)) then, starting on the day after the earlier of the change date (but not earlier than the day the member (or loss subgroup) becomes a member of the group) or the last day of the 5 consecutive year period described in paragraph (a)(1)(ii) of this section, the member (or members of the loss subgroup) are treated, for purposes of applying § 1.1502-91(g)(2)(ii), as if they have been affiliated with the common parent for 5 consecutive years. Starting on that day, the member's (or the members of the loss subgroup's) separately computed net unrealized built-in loss is included in the determination whether the group has a net unrealized built-in loss, and there is an ownership change with respect to the member's separately computed net unrealized built-in loss only if the group (including the member) has a net unrealized built-in loss and has an ownership change. Thus, for example, starting the day after the change date (but not earlier than the day the member (or loss subgroup) becomes a member of the consolidated group), or the end of the 5 consecutive period—

(A) The consolidated group which includes the new loss member or loss subgroup is no longer required to separately track owner shifts of the stock of the new loss member or subgroup parent to determine if an ownership change occurs with respect to the net unrealized built-in loss of the new loss member or members of the loss subgroup;

(B) The group includes the member's (or the loss subgroup members') separately computed net unrealized built-in loss in determining whether it is a loss group under § 1.1502-91(c)(1)(iii);

(C) There is an ownership change with respect to such net unrealized built-in loss only if the group is a loss group and has an ownership change; and

(D) If the group has an ownership change, the member's separately computed net unrealized built-in loss and its assets are taken into account in determining the group's pre-change consolidated attributes described in § 1.1502-91(e)(1) (relating to recognized built-in losses) that are subject to the group's consolidated section 382 limitation.

(iii) Common parent not common parent for five years. If the common parent has become the common parent of an existing group within the previous 5-year period in a transaction described in § 1.1502-75(d)(2)(ii) or (3), appropriate adjustments must be made in applying paragraphs (a)(2)(ii) and (3) of this section. In such a case, as the context requires, references to the common parent are to the former common parent.

(3) Continuing effect of end of separate tracking. (i) In general. As the context may require, a current group determines which of its members are included in a loss subgroup on any testing date by taking into account the application of this section in the former group. See the example in § 1.1502-91(f)(2). For this purpose, corporations that are treated under paragraph (a)(2)(ii) of this section as having been affiliated with the common parent of the former group for 5 consecutive years are also treated as having been affiliated with any other members that have been (or are treated as having been) affiliated with the common parent. The corporations are treated as having been affiliated with such other members for the same period of time that those members have been (or are treated as having been) affiliated with the common parent. If two or more corporations become members of the group at the same time, but paragraph (a)(1) of this section does not apply to every such corporation, then immediately after the corporations become members of the group, the corporations to which paragraph (a)(1) of this section applied are treated as not having been previously affiliated, for purposes of applying this paragraph (a)(3), with the corporations to which paragraph (a)(2)(ii) of this section did not apply.

(ii) Example. The following example illustrates the principles of this paragraph (a)(3):

Example. (i) L has owned all the stock of L1 for three years. At the close of December 31, Year 1, the M group purchases all the L stock, and L and L1 become members of the M group. Other than the stock of L1, L has one asset (the L loss asset) with a net unrealized built-in loss of $200 on this date. L1 has one asset with a net unrealized built-in gain of $50 (the L1 gain asset). L and L1 do not compose a loss subgroup because they do not meet the five year affiliation requirement of § 1.1502-91(d)(2)(i). L is a new loss member, and M's purchase of L causes an ownership change of L. At the close of December 31, Year 4, at a time when L1 has been affiliated with the M group for three years and has been affiliated with L for six years, the S group purchases all the M stock. On this date, the L loss asset has a net unrealized built-in loss of $300, the L1 gain asset has a net unrealized built-in gain of $80, and M, the common parent of the M group, has one asset with a net unrealized built-in gain of $200.

(ii) Paragraph (a)(1) of this section applies to L because L is a new loss member described in § 1.1502-94(a)(1)(ii) that has an ownership change upon becoming a member of the M group on December 31, Year 1. Accordingly, L is treated as having been affiliated with M for 5 consecutive years, and the L loss asset with a net unrealized built-in loss of $300 is included in the determination whether the M group has a net unrealized built-in loss.

(iii) The S group determines which of its members are included in a loss subgroup by taking into account application of paragraph (a) of this section in the M group. For this purpose, application of paragraph (a) of this section causes L to be treated as having been affiliated with M (or as having been a member of the M group) for 5 consecutive years as of January 1, Year 2. Therefore, the S group includes L in the determination whether the M subgroup acquired by S on December 31, Year 4, has a net unrealized built-in loss.

(iv) Because paragraph (a)(1) of this section applied to L when L became a member of the M group, but did not apply to L1, L is treated as not having been affiliated with L1 before L and L1 joined the M group. Also, L1 is not included in the determination whether the M subgroup has a net unrealized built-in loss because L1 has not been continuously affiliated with members of the M group for the five consecutive year period ending immediately before they become members of the S group. See § 1.1502-91(g)(2).

(4) Special rule for testing period. For purposes of determining the beginning of the testing period for a loss group, the member's (or loss subgroup's) net operating loss carryovers (or net unrealized built-in loss) described in paragraph (a)(2) of this section are considered to arise—

(i) In a case described in paragraph (a)(1)(i) of this section, in a taxable year that begins not earlier than the later of the day following the change date or the day that the member becomes a member of the group; and

(ii) In a case described in paragraph (a)(1)(ii) of this section, in a taxable year that begins 3 years before the end of the 5 consecutive year period.

(5) Limits on effects of end of separate tracking. The rule contained in this paragraph (a) applies solely for purposes of §§ 1.1502-91 through 1.1502-95 and this section (other than paragraph (b)(2)(ii)(B) of this section (relating to the definition of pre-change attributes of a subsidiary)) and § 1.1502-98, and not for purposes of other provisions of the consolidated return regulations. However, the rule contained in this paragraph (a) does apply in §§ 1.1502-15(g), 1.1502-21(g) and 1.1502-22(g) for purposes of determining the composition of loss subgroups defined in § 1.1502-91(d). See also paragraph (c) of this section for the continuing effect of an ownership change with respect to pre-change attributes.

(b) Ownership change of subsidiary. *(1) Ownership change of a subsidiary because of options or plan or arrangement.* Notwithstanding § 1.1502-92, a subsidiary may have an ownership change for purposes of section 382 with respect to its attributes which a group or loss subgroup includes in making a determination under § 1.1502-91(c)(1) (relating to the definition of loss group) or § 1.1502-91(d) (relating to the definition of loss subgroup). The subsidiary has such an ownership change if it has an ownership change under the principles of § 1.1502-95(b) and section 382 and the regulations thereunder (determined on a separate entity basis by treating the subsidiary as not being a member of a consolidated group) in the event of—

(i) The deemed exercise under § 1.382-4(d) of an option or options (other than an option with respect to stock of the common parent) held by a person (or persons acting pursuant to a plan or arrangement) to acquire more than 20 percent of the stock of the subsidiary; or

(ii) An increase by 1 or more 5-percent shareholders, acting pursuant to a plan or arrangement to avoid an ownership change of a subsidiary, in their percentage ownership interest in the subsidiary by more than 50 percentage points during the testing period of the subsidiary through the acquisition (or deemed acquisition pursuant to § 1.382-4(d)) of ownership interests in the subsidiary and in higher-tier members with respect to the subsidiary.

(2) Effect of the ownership change. (i) In general. If a subsidiary has an ownership change under paragraph (b)(1) of this section, the amount of consolidated taxable income for any post-change year that may be offset by the pre-change losses of the subsidiary shall not exceed the section 382 limitation for the subsidiary. For purposes of this limitation, the value of the subsidiary is determined solely by reference to the value of the subsidiary's stock.

(ii) Pre-change losses. The pre-change losses of a subsidiary are—

(A) Its allocable part of any consolidated net operating loss which is attributable to it under § 1.1502-21(b) (determined on the last day of the consolidated return year that includes the change date) that is not carried back and absorbed in a taxable year prior to the year including the change date;

(B) Its net operating loss carryovers that arose (or are treated under § 1.1502-21(c) as having arisen) in a SRLY; and

(C) Its recognized built-in loss with respect to its separately computed net unrealized built-in loss, if any, determined on the change date.

(3) Coordination with §§ 1.1502-91, 1.1502-92, and 1.1502-94. If an increase in percentage ownership interest causes an ownership change with respect to an attribute under this paragraph (b) and under § 1.1502-92 on the same day, the ownership change is considered to occur only under § 1.1502-92 and not under this paragraph (b). See § 1.1502-94 for anti-duplication rules relating to value.

(4) Example. The following example illustrates paragraph (b)(1)(ii) of this section:

Example. Plan to avoid an ownership change of a subsidiary.

(i) L owns all the stock of L1, L1 owns all the stock of L2, L2 owns all the stock of L3, and L3 owns all the stock of L4. The L group has a consolidated net operating loss arising in Year 1 that is carried over to Year 2. L has assets other than its L1 stock with a value of $900. L1, L2, and L3 own no assets other than their L2, L3, and L4 stock. L4 has assets with a value of $100. During Year 2, A, B, C, and D, acting pursuant to a plan to avoid an ownership change of L4, acquire the following ownership interests in the members of the L loss group: (A) on September 11, Year 2, A acquires 20 percent of the L1 stock from L and B acquires 20 percent of the L2 stock from L1; and (B) on September 20, Year 2, C acquires 20 percent of the stock of L3 from L2 and D acquires 20 percent of the stock of L4 from L3.

(ii) The acquisitions by A, B, C, and D pursuant to the plan have increased their respective percentage ownership interests in L4 by approximately 10, 13, 16, and 20 percentage points, for a total of approximately 59 percentage points during the testing period. This more than 50 percentage point increase in the percentage ownership interest in L4 causes an ownership change of L4 under paragraph (b)(2) of this section.

(c) Continuing effect of an ownership change. A loss corporation (or loss subgroup) that is subject to a limitation under section 382 with respect to its pre-change losses continues to be subject to the limitation regardless of whether it becomes a member or ceases to be a member of a consolidated group. See § 1.382-5(d) (relating to successive ownership changes and absorption of a section 382 limitation).

(d) Losses reattributed under § 1.1502-36(d)(6). *(1) In general.* This paragraph (d) contains rules relating to net operating carryovers, capital loss carryovers, and deferred deductions (collectively, loss or losses) that are reattributed to the common parent under § 1.1502-36(d)(6). References in this paragraph (d) to a subsidiary are references to the subsidiary (or lower-tier subsidiary) whose loss is reattributed to the common parent.

(2) Deemed section 381(a) transaction. Under § 1.1502-36(d)(6)(iv)(A), the common parent succeeds to the reattributed losses as if the losses were succeeded to in a transaction to which section 381(a) applies. In general, §§ 1.1502-91 through 1.1502-95, this section, and § 1.1502-98 are applied to the reattributed losses in accordance with that characterization. See generally, § 1.382-2(a)(1)(ii) (relating to distributor or transferor loss corporations in transactions under section 381), § 1.1502-1(f)(4) (relating to the definition of predecessor and successor) and § 1.1502-91(j) (relating to predecessor and successor corporations). For example, if the reattributed loss is a pre-change attribute subject to a section 382 limitation, it remains subject to that limitation following the reattribution. In certain cases, the limitation applicable to the reattributed loss is zero unless the common parent apportions all or part of the limitation to itself. (See paragraph (d)(4) of this section.)

(3) Rules relating to owner shifts. (i) In general. Any owner shift of the subsidiary (including any deemed owner shift resulting from section 382(g)(4)(D) or 382(l)(3)) in connection with the disposition of the stock of the subsidiary is not taken into account in determining whether there is an ownership change with respect to the reattributed loss. However, any owner shift with respect to the successor corporation that is treated as continuing in existence under § 1.382-2(a)(1)(ii) must be taken into account for such purpose if such owner shift is effected by the reattribution and an owner shift of the stock of the subsidiary not held directly or indirectly by the common parent would have been taken into account if such shift had occurred immediately before the reattribution. See paragraph (d)(3)(ii) Example 2 of this section.

(ii) Examples. The following examples illustrate the principles of this paragraph (d)(3):

Example (1). No owner shift for reattributed loss. (i) Facts. P, the common parent of a consolidated group, owns 60% of the stock of L, and B owns the remaining 40%. L has a net operating loss carryover of $100 from year 1 that it carries over to years 2, 3, and 4. At the beginning of year 2, P purchases 40% of the L stock from B, which does not cause an ownership change of L. On December 31, year 3, P sells all of the L stock to M. Pursuant to § 1.1502-36(d)(6), P reattributes $10 of L's $100 net operating loss carryover to itself, and L carries $90 of its net operating loss carryover to its year 4.

(ii) Analysis. The sale of the L stock to M does not cause an owner shift that is taken into account in determining if there is an ownership change with respect to the $10 reattributed loss. Following the reattribution, § 1.1502-94(b) continues to apply to determine if there is an ownership change with respect to the $10 reattributed loss, until, under paragraph (a) of this section, the loss is treated as described in § 1.1502-91(c)(1)(i). In applying § 1.1502-94(b), the 40 percentage point increase by the P shareholders prior to the reattribution is taken into account. The sale of the L stock to

M does cause an ownership change of L with respect to the $90 of its net operating loss that it carries over to year 4.

Example (2). Owner shift for reattributed loss. The facts are the same as in Example 1, except that P only purchases 20% of the L stock from B and sells 80% of the L stock to M. L is a new loss member, and, under § 1.1502-94(b)(1), an owner shift of the stock of L not held directly or indirectly by the common parent (the 20% of L stock still held by B) would have been taken into account if such shift had occurred immediately before the reattribution. Following the reattribution, § 1.1502-94(b) continues to apply to determine if there is an ownership change with respect to the $10 reattributed loss, until, under paragraph (a) of this section, the loss is treated as described in § 1.1502-91(c)(1)(i). With respect to the $10 reattributed loss, the P shareholders have increased their percentage ownership interest by 40 percentage points. The P shareholders have increased their ownership interests by 20 percentage points as a result of P's purchase of stock from B, and, under § 1.382-2(a)(1)(ii), are treated as increasing their interests by an additional 20 percentage points as a result of the reattribution. (The acquisition of the L stock by M does not, however, effect an owner shift for the $10 of reattributed loss.) The sale of the L stock to M causes an ownership change of L with respect to the $90 of net operating loss that L carries over to Year 4.

(4) Rules relating to the section 382 limitation. (i) Reattributed loss is a pre-change separate attribute of a new loss member. If the reattributed loss is a pre-change separate attribute of a new loss member that is subject to a separate section 382 limitation prior to the disposition of subsidiary stock, the common parent's limitation with respect to that loss is zero, except to the extent that the common parent apportions to itself, under paragraph (d)(5) of this section, all or part of such limitation. A separate section 382 limitation is the limitation described in § 1.1502-94(b) that applies to a pre-change separate attribute.

(ii) Reattributed loss is a pre-change subgroup attribute. If the reattributed loss is a pre-change subgroup attribute subject to a subgroup section 382 limitation prior to the disposition of subsidiary stock, and, immediately after the reattribution, the common parent is not a member of the loss subgroup, the section 382 limitation with respect to that loss is zero, except to the extent that the common parent apportions to itself, under paragraph (d)(5) of this section, all or part of the subgroup section 382 limitation. See, however, § 1.1502-95(d)(3) Example 6, for an illustration of a case where the common parent, as successor to the subsidiary, is a member of the loss subgroup immediately after the reattribution.

(iii) Potential application of section 382(l)(1). In general, the value of the stock of the common parent is used to determine the section 382 limitation for an ownership change with respect to the reattributed loss that occurs at the time of, or after, the reattribution. For example, if the loss is a pre-change consolidated attribute, the value of the stock of the common parent is used to determine the section 382 limitation, and no adjustment to that value is required because of the deemed section 381(a) transaction. However, if the loss is a pre-change separate attribute of a new loss member (or is a pre-change attribute of a loss subgroup member and the common parent was not the loss subgroup parent immediately before the reattribution), the deemed section 381(a) transaction is considered to constitute a capital contribution with respect to the new loss member (or loss subgroup member) for purposes of section 382(l)(1). Accordingly, if that section applies because the deemed capital contribution is (or is considered under section 382(l)(1)(B) to be) part of a plan described in section 382(l)(1)(A), the value of the stock of the common parent after the deemed section 381(a) transaction must be adjusted to reflect the capital contribution. Ordinarily, this will require the value of the stock of the common parent to be reduced to an amount that represents the value of the stock of the subsidiary (or loss subgroup of which the subsidiary was a member) when the reattribution occurred.

(iv) Duplication or omission of value. In determining any section 382 limitation with respect to the reattributed loss and with respect to other pre-change losses, appropriate adjustments must be made so that value is not improperly omitted or duplicated as a result of the reattribution. For example, if the subsidiary has an ownership change upon its departure, and the common parent (as successor) has an ownership change with respect to the reattributed pre-change separate attribute upon its reattribution under paragraph (d)(3)(i) of this section, proper adjustments must be made so that the value of the subsidiary is not taken into account more than once in determining the section 382 limitation for the reattributed loss and the loss that is not reattributed.

(v) Special rule for continuity of business requirement. If the reattributed loss is a pre-change attribute of new loss member and the reattribution occurs within the two-year period beginning on the change date, then, starting immediately after the reattribution, the continuity of business requirement of section 382(c)(1) is applied with respect to the business enterprise of the common parent. Similar principles apply if the reattributed loss is a pre-change subgroup attribute and, on the day after the reattribution, the common parent is not a member of the loss subgroup.

(5) Election to reattribute section 382 limitation. (i) Effect of election. The common parent may elect to apportion to itself all or part of any separate section 382 limitation or subgroup section 382 limitation to which the loss is subject immediately before the reattribution. However, no net unrealized built-in gain of the member (or loss subgroup) whose loss is reattributed can be apportioned to the common parent. The principles of § 1.1502-95(c) apply to the apportionment, treating, as the context requires, references to the former member as references to the common parent, and references to the consolidated section 382 limitation as references to the separate section 382 limitation (or subgroup section 382 limitation) that is being apportioned. Thus, for example, the common parent can reattribute to itself all or part of the value element or adjustment element of the limitation, and any part of such element that is apportioned requires a corresponding reduction in such element of the separate section 382 limitation of the subsidiary whose loss is reattributed (or in the subgroup section 382 limitation if the reattributed loss is a pre-change subgroup attribute). Appropriate adjustments must be made to the separate section 382 limitation (or subgroup section 382 limitation) for the consolidated return year in which the reattribution is made to reflect that the reattributed loss is an attribute acquired by the common parent during the year in a transaction to which section 381(a) applies. The election is made by the common parent as part of the election to reattribute the loss. See § 1.1502-36(e)(5)(x) for the time and manner of making the election.

(ii) Examples. The following examples illustrate the principles of this paragraph (d)(5):

Example (1). Consequence of apportionment. (i) Facts. P, the common parent of a consolidated group, purchases all of the stock of L on December 31, year 1. L carries over a net operating loss arising in year 1 to each of the next 5 taxable years. The purchase of the L stock causes an ownership change of L, and results in a separate section 382 limitation of $10 for L's net operating loss carryover based on the value of the L stock. On July 2, year 3, P sells 30% of the L stock to A. Under § 1.1502-36(d)(6), P elects to reattribute to itself $110 of L's $200 net operating loss carryover. P also elects to apportion to itself $6 of the $10 value element of the separate section 382 limitation.

(ii) Analysis. (A) P's separate section 382 limitation. For the consolidated return years ending after December 31, year 3, P's separate section 382 limitation with respect to the reattributed net operating loss carryover is $6, adjusted as appropriate for any short taxable year, unused section 382 limitation, or other adjustment. For the P group's consolidated return year ending December 31, year 3, the separate section 382 limitation for L's net operating loss carryover is $8, the sum of $5 and $3. Five dollars of the limitation is the amount that bears the same relationship to $10 as the number of days in the period ending with the deemed section 381(a) transaction, 183 days, bears to 365. Three dollars of the limitation is the amount that bears the same relationship to $6 as the number of days in the period between July 3 and December 31, 182, bears to 365.

(B) L's separate section 382 limitation. For L's taxable years ending after December 31, year 3, L's separate section 382 limitation for its $90 of net operating loss carryover that was not reattributed to P is $4, adjusted as appropriate for any short taxable year, unused section 382 limitation, or other adjustment. For L's short taxable year ending December 31, year 3, the section 382 limitation for its $90 of net operating loss carryover is $2, the amount that bears the same relationship to $4 (the portion of the value element that was not apportioned to P), as the number of days during the short taxable year, 182 days, bears to 365. See § 1.382-5(c).

Example (2). No apportionment required for consolidated pre-change attribute. (i) Facts. P, the common parent of a consolidated group, forms L. For year 1, L has an operating loss of $70 that is not absorbed and is included in the group's consolidated net operating loss that is carried over to subsequent years. On January 1 of year 3, A buys all of the P stock and the P group has an ownership change. The consolidated section 382 limitation based on the value of the P stock is $10.

(ii) Analysis. On April 13 of year 4, P sells all of the stock of L to B and, under § 1.1502-36(d)(6), elects to reattribute to itself $45 of L's net operating loss carryover. Following the reattribution, the $45 portion of the year 1 net operating loss carryover retains its character as a pre-change consolidated attribute, and remains subject to so much of the $10 consolidated section 382 limitation as P does not elect to apportion to L under § 1.1502-95(c).

(e) Time and manner of making election under § 1.1502-91(d)(4). *(1) In general.* This paragraph (e) prescribes the time and manner of making the election under § 1.1502-91(d)(4), relating to treating two or more corporations as treating the section 1504(a)(1) requirement of § 1.1502-91(d)(1)(ii) and (d) (2)(ii) as satisfied.

(2) Election statement. An election under § 1.1502-91(d)(4) must be made by the common parent. The election must be made in the form of the following statement: "THIS IS AN ELECTION UNDER § 1.1502-91(d)(4) TO TREAT THE FOLLOWING CORPORATIONS AS MEETING THE REQUIREMENTS OF § 1.1502-91(d)(1)(ii) AND (d)(2)(ii) IMMEDIATELY AFTER THEY BECAME MEMBERS OF THE GROUP." [List separately the name of each corporation, its E.I.N., and the date that it became a member of the group]. If separate elections are being made for corporations that became members at different times or that were acquired from different affiliated groups, provide a separate statement and list for each election.

(3) The election statement must be filed by the common parent with its income tax return for the consolidated return year in which the members with respect to which the election is made become members of the group. Such election must be filed on or before the due date for such income tax return, including extensions.

(4) An election made under this paragraph (e) is irrevocable.

T.D. 8824, 6/25/99, amend T.D. 9424, 9/10/2008.

§ 1.1502-96A Miscellaneous rules generally applicable for testing dates before June 25, 1999.

(a) End of separate tracking of losses. *(1) Application.* This paragraph (a) applies to a member (or a loss subgroup) with a net operating loss carryover that arose (or is treated under §§ 1.1502-21(c) or 1.1502-21T(c) in effect prior to June 25, 1999, as contained in 26 CFR part 1 revised April 1, 1999, as applicable as arising) in a SRLY (or a net unrealized built-in gain or loss determined at the time that the member (or loss subgroup) becomes a member of the consolidated group if there is—

(i) An ownership change of the member (or loss subgroup in connection with, or after, becoming a member of the group; or

(ii) A period of 5 consecutive years following the day that the member (or loss subgroup) becomes a member of a group during which the member (or loss subgroup) has not had an ownership change.

(2) Effect of end of separate tracking. If this paragraph (a) applies with respect to a member (or loss subgroup), then, starting on the day after the earlier of the change date (but not earlier than the day the member (or loss subgroup) becomes a member of the consolidated group) or the last day of the 5 consecutive year period described in paragraph (a)(1)(ii) of this section, the member's net operating loss carryover that arose (or is treated under §§ 1.1502-21(c) or 1.1502-21T(c) in effect prior to June 25, 1999, as contained in 26 CFR part 1 revised April 1, 1999, as applicable as arising) in a SRLY, is treated as described in § 1.1502-91A(c)(1)(i). Also, the member's separately computed net unrealized built-in gain or loss is included in the determination whether the group has a net unrealized built-in gain or loss. The preceding sentences also apply for purposes of determining whether there is an ownership change with respect to such attributes following such change date (or earlier day) or 5 consecutive year period. Thus, for example, starting the day after the change date or the end of the 5 consecutive year period—

(i) The consolidated group which includes the new loss member or loss subgroup is no longer required to separately track owner shifts of the stock of the new loss member or loss subgroup parent to determine if an ownership change occurs with respect to the attributes of the new loss member or members included in the loss subgroup;

(ii) The group includes the member's attributes in determining whether it is a loss group under § 1.1502-91A(c);

(iii) There is an ownership change with respect to such attributes only if the group is a loss group and has an ownership change; and

(iv) If the group has an ownership change, such attributes are pre-change consolidated attributes subject to the loss group's consolidated section 382 limitation.

(3) Continuing effect of end of separate tracking. As the context may require, a current group determines which of its members are included in a loss subgroup on any testing date by taking into account the application of this section in the former group. See the example in § 1.1502-91A(f)(2).

(4) Special rule for testing period. For purposes of determining the beginning of the testing period for a loss group, the member's (or loss subgroup's) net operating loss carryovers (or net unrealized built-in gain or loss) described in paragraph (a)(2) of this section are considered to arise—

(i) in a case described in paragraph (a)(1)(i) of this section, in a taxable year that begins not earlier than the later of the day following the change date or the day that the member becomes a member of the group; and

(ii) in a case described in paragraph (a)(1)(ii) of this section, in a taxable year that begins 3 years before the end of the 5 consecutive year period.

(5) Limits on effects of end of separate tracking. The rule contained in this paragraph (a) applies solely for purposes of §§ 1.1502-91A through 1.1502-95A and this section (other than paragraph (b)(2)(ii)(B) of this section (relating to the definition of pre-change attributes of a subsidiary)) and § 1.1502-98A, and not for purposes of other provisions of the consolidated return regulations, including, for example, §§ 1.1502-15 and 1.1502-21 (or § 1.1502-15T in effect prior to June 25, 1999, as contained in 26 CFR part 1 revised April 1, 1999 and § 1.1502-21T in effect prior to June 25, 1999, as contained in 26 CFR part 1 revised April 1, 1999, as applicable) (relating to the consolidated net operating loss deduction). See also paragraph (c) of this section for the continuing effect of an ownership change with respect to pre-change attributes.

(b) Ownership change of subsidiary. *(1) Ownership change of a subsidiary because of options or plan or arrangement.* Notwithstanding § 1.1502-92A, a subsidiary may have an ownership change for purposes of section 382 with respect to its attributes which a group or loss subgroup includes in making a determination under § 1.1502-91A(c)(1) (relating to the definition of loss group) or § 1.1502-91A(d) (relating to the definition of loss subgroup). The subsidiary has such an ownership change if it has an ownership change under the principles of § 1.1502-95A(b) and section 382 and the regulations thereunder (determined on a separate entity basis by treating the subsidiary as not being a member of a consolidated group) in the event of—

(i) The deemed exercise under § 1.382-4(d) of an option or options (other than an option with respect to stock of the common parent) held by a person (or persons acting pursuant to a plan or arrangement) to acquire more than 20 percent of the stock of the subsidiary; or

(ii) An increase by 1 or more 5-percent shareholders, acting pursuant to a plan or arrangement to avoid an ownership change of a subsidiary, in their percentage ownership interest in the subsidiary by more than 50 percentage points during the testing period of the subsidiary through the acquisition (or deemed acquisition pursuant to § 1.382-4(d)) of ownership interests in the subsidiary and in higher-tier members with respect to the subsidiary.

(2) Effect of the ownership change. (i) In general. If a subsidiary has an ownership change under paragraph (b)(1) of this section, the amount of consolidated taxable income for any post-change year that may be offset by the pre-change losses of the subsidiary shall not exceed the section 382 limitation for the subsidiary. For purposes of this limitation, the value of the subsidiary is determined solely by reference to the value of the subsidiary's stock.

(ii) Pre-change losses. The pre-change losses of a subsidiary are—

(A) Its allocable part of any consolidated net operating loss which is attributable to it under §§ 1.1502-21(b) or 1.1502-21T(b) in effect prior to June 25, 1999, as contained in 26 CFR part 1 revised April 1, 1999, as applicable (determined on the last day of the consolidated return year that includes the change date) that is not carried back and absorbed in a taxable year prior to the year including the change date;

(B) Its net operating loss carryovers that arose (or are treated under §§ 1.1502-21(c) or 1.1502-21T(c) in effect prior to June 25, 1999, as contained in 26 CFR part 1 revised April 1, 1999, as applicable as having arisen) in a SRLY; and

(C) Its recognized built-in loss with respect to its separately computed net unrealized built-in loss, if any, determined on the change date.

(3) Coordination with §§ 1.1502-91A, 1.1502-92A, and 1.1502-94A. If an increase in percentage ownership interest causes an ownership change with respect to an attribute under this paragraph (b) and under § 1.1502-92A on the same day, the ownership change is considered to occur only under § 1.1502-92A and not under this paragraph (b). See § 1.1502-94A for anti-duplication rules relating to value.

(4) Example. The following example illustrates paragraph (b)(1)(ii) of this section.

Example. Plan to avoid an ownership change of a subsidiary. (a) L owns all the stock of L1, L1 owns all the stock of L2, L2 owns all the stock of L3, and L3 owns all the stock of L4. The L group has a consolidated net operating loss arising in Year 1 that is carried over to Year 2. L has assets other than its L1 stock with a value of $900. L1, L2, and L3 own no assets other than their L2, L3, and L4 stock. L4 has assets with a value of $100. During Year 2, A, B, C, and D, acting pursuant to a plan to avoid an ownership change of L4, acquire the following ownership interests in the members of the L loss group: (A) on September 11, Year 2, A acquires 20 percent of the L1 stock from L and B acquires 20 percent of the L2 stock from L1; and (B) on September 20, Year 2, C acquires 20 percent of the stock of L3 from L2 and D acquires 20 percent of the stock of L4 from L3. The following is a graphic illustration of these facts:

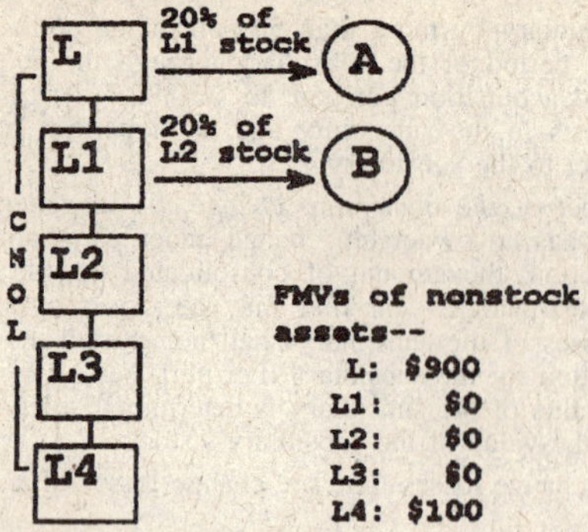

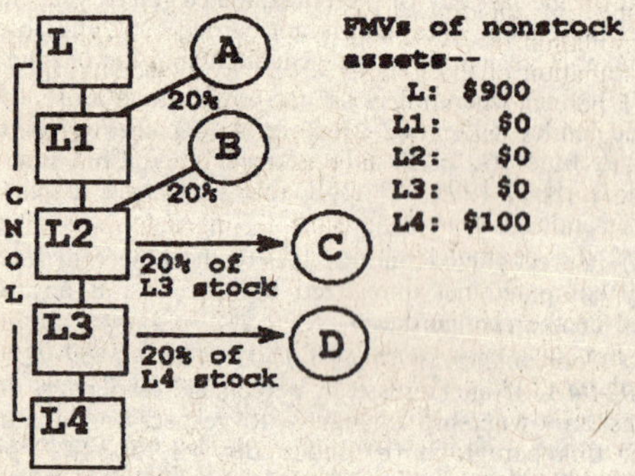

(b) The acquisitions by A, B, C, and D pursuant to the plan have increased their respective percentage ownership interests in L4 by approximately 10, 13, 16, and 20 percentage points, for a total of approximately 59 percentage points during the testing period. This more than 50 percentage point increase in the percentage ownership interest in L4 causes an ownership change of L4 under paragraph (b)(2) of this section.

(c) Continuing effect of an ownership change. A loss corporation (or loss subgroup) that is subject to a limitation under section 382 with respect to its pre-change losses continues to be subject to the limitation regardless of whether it becomes a member or ceases to be a member of a consolidated group. See § 1.382-5(d) (relating to successive ownership changes and absorption of a section 382 limitation).

T.D. 8678, 6/26/96, amend T.D. 8823, 6/25/99, T.D. 8824, 6/25/99.

§ 1.1502-97 Special rules under section 382 for members under the jurisdiction of a court in a title 11 or similar case [Reserved].

T.D. 8824, 6/25/99.

§ 1.1502-97A Special rules under section 382 for members under the jurisdiction of a court in a title 11 or similar case. [Reserved].

T.D. 8678, 6/26/96, amend T.D. 8824, 6/25/99.

§ 1.1502-98 Coordination with section 383.

The rules contained in §§ 1.1502-91 through 1.1502-96 also apply for purposes of section 383, with appropriate adjustments to reflect that section 383 applies to credits and net capital losses. For example, subgroups with respect to the carryover of general business credits, minimum tax credits, unused foreign tax, and net capital loss are determined by applying the principles of § 1.1502-91(d)(1). Similarly, in the case of net capital losses, general business credits, and excess foreign taxes that are pre-change attributes, § 1.383-1 applies the principles of §§ 1.1502-91 through 1.1502-96. For example, if a loss group has an ownership change under § 1.1502-92 and has a carryover of unused general business credits from a pre-change consolidated return year to a post-change consolidated return year, the amount of the group's regular tax liability for the post-change year that can be offset by the carryover cannot exceed the consolidated section 383 credit limitation for that post-change year, determined by applying the principles of §§ 1.383-1(c)(6) and 1.1502-93 (relating to the computation of the consolidated section 382 limitation).

T.D. 8824, 6/25/99, amend T.D. 8884, 5/24/2000.

§ 1.1502-98A Coordination with section 383 generally applicable for testing dates (or members joining or leaving a group) before June 25, 1999.

The rules contained in §§ 1.1502-91A through 1.1502-96A also apply for purposes of section 383, with appropriate adjustments to reflect that section 383 applies to credits and net capital losses. Similarly, in the case of net capital losses, general business credits, and excess foreign taxes that are pre-change attributes, § 1.383-1 applies the principles of §§ 1.1502-91A through 1.1502-96A. For example, if a loss group has an ownership change under § 1.1502-92A and has a carryover of unused general business credits from a pre-change consolidated return year to a post-change consolidated return year, the amount of the group's regular tax liability for the post-change year that can be offset by the carryover cannot exceed the consolidated section 383 credit limitation for that post-change year, determined by applying the principles of §§ 1.383-1(c)(6) and 1.1502-93A (relating to the computation of the consolidated section 382 limitation).

T.D. 8678, 6/26/96, amend T.D. 8824, 6/25/99.

§ 1.1502-99 Effective dates.

(a) In general. Except as provided in paragraphs (b) and (c) of this section, §§ 1.1502-91 through 1.1502-96 and § 1.1502-98 apply to any testing date on or after June 25, 1999. Sections 1.1502-94 through 1.1502-96 also apply to a corporation that becomes a member of a group or ceases to be a member of a group (or loss subgroup) on any date on or after June 25, 1999.

(b) Special rules. *(1) Election to treat subgroup parent requirement as satisfied.* Section 1.1502-91(d)(4), § 1.1502-91(d)(7), Example 4, § 1.1502-92(b)(1)(iii), § 1.1502-92(b)(2), Example 5, the last two sentences of § 1.1502-95(b)(3), § 1.1502-95(d)(2)(i), and § 1.1502-96(e) (all of which relate to the election under § 1.1502-91(d)(4) to treat the loss subgroup parent requirement as satisfied) apply to corporations that become members of a consolidated group in taxable years for which the due date of the income tax return (without extensions) is after June 25, 1999.

(2) Principal purpose of avoiding a limitation. The third sentence of § 1.1502-91(d)(5) (relating to members excluded from a loss subgroup) applies to corporations that become members of a consolidated group on or after June 25, 1999.

(3) Ceasing to be a member of a loss subgroup. (i) Ownership change of a loss subgroup. Section 1.1502-95(d)(2)(ii) and § 1.1502-95(d)(3), Example 3 apply to corporations that cease to bear a relationship described in section 1504(a)(1) to a loss subgroup parent in taxable years for which the due date of the income tax return (without extensions) is after June 25, 1999.

(ii) Expiration of 5-year period. Section 1.1502-95(d)(2)(iii) applies with respect to the day after the last day of any 5 consecutive year period described in that section that ends in a taxable year for which the due date of the income tax return (without extensions) is after June 25, 1999.

(4) Reattribution of losses under § 1.1502-36(d)(6). Section 1.1502-96(d) applies to reattributions of net operating loss carryovers, capital loss carryovers, and deferred deductions in connection with a transfer of stock to which § 1.1502-36 applies, and the election under § 1.1502-96(d)(5) (relating to an election to reattribute section 382 limitation) can be made with an election under § 1.1502-36(d)(6) to reattribute a loss to the common parent that is filed at the time and in the manner provided in § 1.1502-36(e)(5)(x).

(5) Election to apportion net unrealized built-in gain. In the case of corporations that cease to be members of a loss group (or loss subgroup) before June 25, 1999 in a taxable year for which the due date of the income tax return (without extensions) is after June 25, 1999, § 1.1502-95(a), (b), (c), and (f) apply to those corporations if the common parent makes the election described in the second sentence of paragraph (c)(1) of § 1.1502-95 in the time and manner prescribed in paragraph (f) of § 1.1502-95.

(c) Testing period may include a period beginning before June 25, 1999. *(1) In general.* A testing period for purposes of §§ 1.1502-91 through 1.1502-96 and 1.1502-98 may include a period beginning before June 25, 1999. Thus, for example, in applying § 1.1502-92(b)(1)(i) (relating to the determination of an ownership change of a loss group), the determination of the lowest percentage of ownership interest of any 5-percent shareholder of the common parent during a testing period ending on a testing date occurring on or after June 25, 1999 takes into account the period beginning before June 25, 1999, except to the extent that the period is more than 3 years before the testing date or is otherwise before the beginning of the testing period. See § 1.1502-92(b)(1).

(2) Transition rule for net unrealized built-in loss. A loss group (or loss subgroup) that has a net unrealized built-in loss on a testing date on or after June 25, 1999 may apply § 1.1502-91A(g) (and § 1.1502-96A(a) as it relates to § 1.1502-91A(g)) for the period ending on the day before June 25, 1999 to determine under § 1.382-2T(d)(ii)(A) the earliest date that its testing period begins (treating the day before June 25, 1999 as the end of a taxable year.) Thus, for example, if a consolidated group with no net operating losses has a net unrealized built-in loss determined under § 1.1502-91(g) on a testing date after June 25, 1999, but, under § 1.1502-91A(g), does not have a net unrealized built-in loss for the period ending on the day before June 25, 1999, the group's testing period begins no earlier than June 25, 1999.

T.D. 8824, 6/25/99, amend T.D. 9424, 9/10/2008.

§ 1.1502-99A Effective dates.

(a) Effective date. *(1) In general.* Except as provided in § 1.1502-99(b), §§ 1.1502-91A through 1.1502-96A and 1.1502-98A apply to any testing date on or after January 1, 1997, and before June 25, 1999. Sections 1.1502-94A through 1.1502-96A also apply on any date on or after January 1, 1997, and before June 25, 1999, on which a corporation becomes a member of a group or on which a corporation ceases to be a member of a loss group (or a loss subgroup).

(2) Anti-duplication rules for recognized built-in gain. Section 1.1502-93(c)(2) (relating to recognized built-in gain of a loss group or loss subgroup) applies to taxable years for which the due date for income tax returns (without extensions) is after June 25, 1999.

(b) Testing period may include a period beginning before January 1, 1997. A testing period for purposes of §§ 1.1502-91A through 1.1502-96A and 1.1502-98A may include a period beginning before January 1, 1997. Thus, for example, in applying § 1.1502-92A(b)(1)(i) (relating to the determination of an ownership change of a loss group), the determination of the lowest percentage ownership interest of any 5-percent shareholder of the common parent during a testing period ending on a testing date occurring on or after January 1, 1997, takes into account the period beginning before January 1, 1997, except to the extent that the period is more than 3 years before the testing date or is otherwise before the beginning of the testing period. See § 1.1502-92A(b)(1).

(c) Transition rules. *(1) Methods permitted.* (i) In general. For the period ending before January 1, 1997, a consolidated group is permitted to use any method described in paragraph (c)(2) of this section which is consistently applied to determine if an ownership change occurred with respect to a consolidated net operating loss, a net operating loss carryover (including net operating loss carryovers arising in SRLYs), or a net unrealized built-in loss. If an ownership change occurred during that period, the group is also permitted to use any method described in paragraph (c)(2) of this section which is consistently applied to compute the amount of the section 382 limitation that applies to limit the use of taxable income in any post-change year ending before, on, or after January 1, 1997. The preceding sentence does not preclude the imposition of an additional, lesser limitation due to a subsequent ownership change nor, except as provided in paragraph (c)(1)(iii) of this section, does it permit the beginning of a new testing period for the loss group.

(ii) Adjustments to offset excess limitation. If an ownership change occurred during the period ending before January 1, 1997, and a method described in paragraph (c)(2) of this section was not used for a post-change year, the members (or group) must reduce the section 382 limitation for post-change years for which an income tax return is filed after January 1, 1997, to offset, as quickly as possible, the effects of any section 382 limitation that members took into account in excess of the amount that would have been allowable under §§ 1.1502-91A through 1.1502-96A and 1.1502-98A.

(iii) Coordination with effective date. Notwithstanding that a group may have used a method described in paragraph (c)(2)(ii) or (iii) of this section for the period before January 1, 1997, §§ 1.1502-91A through 1.1502-96A and 1.1502-98A apply to any testing date occurring on or after January 1, 1997, for purposes of determining whether there is an ownership change with respect to any losses and, if so, the collateral consequences. Any ownership change of a member other than the common parent pursuant to a method described in paragraph (c)(2)(ii) or (iii) of this section does not cause a new testing period of the loss group to begin for purposes of applying § 1.1502-92A on or after January 1, 1997.

(2) Permitted methods. The methods described in this paragraph (c)(2) are:

(i) A method that does not materially differ from the rules in §§ 1.1502-91A through 1.1502-96A and 1.1502-98A (other than those in § 1.1502-95A(c) and (b)(2)(ii) (relating to the apportionment of a section 382 limitation) as they would apply to a corporation that ceases to be a member of the group before January 1, 1997). As the context requires, the method must treat references to rules in current regulations as references to rules in regulations generally effective for taxable years before January 1, 1997. Thus, for example, the taxpayer must treat a reference to § 1.382-4(d) (relating to options) as a reference to § 1.382-2T(h)(4) for any testing date to which § 1.382-2T(h)(4) applies. Similarly, a reference to §§ 1.1502-21(c) or 1.1502-21T(c) in effect prior to June 25, 1999, as contained in 26 CFR part 1 revised April 1, 1999, as applicable may be a reference to § 1.1502-21A(c), as appropriate. Furthermore, the method must treat all corporations that were affiliated on January 1, 1987, and continuously thereafter as having met the 5 consecutive year requirement of § 1.1502-91A(d)(2)(i) on any day before January 1, 1992, on which the determination of net unrealized built-in gain or loss of a loss subgroup is made;

(ii) A reasonable application of the rules in section 382 and the regulations thereunder applied to each member on a separate entity basis, treating each member's allocable part of a consolidated net operating loss which is attributable to it under §§ 1.1502-21(b) or 1.1502-21T(b) in effect prior to June 25, 1999, as contained in 26 CFR part 1 revised April 1, 1999, as applicable as a net operating loss of that member and applying rules similar to § 1.382-8 to avoid duplication of value in computing the section 382 limitation for the member (see § 1.382-8(h) (relating to the effective date and transition rules regarding controlled groups)); or

(iii) A method approved by the Commissioner upon application by the common parent.

(d) Amended returns. A group may file an amended return in connection with an ownership change occurring before January 1, 1997, to modify the amount of a section 382 limitation with respect to a consolidated net operating loss, a net operating loss carryover (including net operating loss carryovers arising in SRLYs), or a recognized built-in loss (or gain) only if it files amended returns:

(1) For the earliest taxable year ending after December 31, 1986, in which it had an ownership change, if any, under § 1.1502-92A;

(2) For all subsequent taxable years for which returns have already been filed as of the date of the amended return;

(3) The modification with respect to all members for all taxable years ending in 1987 and thereafter complies with §§ 1.1502-91A through 1.1502-96A and 1.1502-98A; and

(4) The amended return(s) permitted by the applicable statute of limitations is/are filed before Tuesday, September 24, 1996.

(e) Section 383. This section also applies for the purposes of section 383, with appropriate adjustments to reflect that section 383 applies to credits and net capital losses.

T.D. 8679, 6/26/96, amend T.D. 8823, 6/25/99, T.D. 8824, 6/25/99.

§ 1.1502-100 Corporations exempt from tax.

(a) In general. *(1) Computation of tax liability.* The tax liability for a consolidated return year of a group of two or more corporations described in section 1504(e) which are exempt from taxation under section 501 (hereinafter referred to in this section as "exempt group") shall be determined on a consolidated basis by applying the provisions of subchapter F of chapter 1 of the Code in the manner provided in this section. See section 1504(e) for tax-exempt corporations eligible to file a consolidated return.

(2) Applicability of other consolidated return provisions. The provisions of § 1.1502-1 through § 1.1502-80 shall be applicable to an exempt group to the extent they are not inconsistent with the provisions of this section or the provisions of subchapter F of chapter 1 of the Code. For purposes of applying the provisions of § 1.1502-1 through § 1.1502-80 to an exempt group, the following substitutions shall be made—

(i) The term "exempt group" shall be substituted for the term "group",

(ii) The terms "unrelated business taxable income", "separate unrelated business taxable income", and "consolidated unrelated business taxable income" shall be substituted for the terms "taxable income", "separate taxable income", and "consolidated taxable income", and

(iii) The term "consolidated liability for tax determined under § 1.1502-2" (or an equivalent term) shall mean the consolidated liability for tax of an exempt group determined under paragraph (b) of this section.

(b) Consolidated liability for tax. The tax liability for a consolidated return year of an exempt group is the tax imposed by section 511(a) or section 1201(a) on the consolidated unrelated business taxable income for the year (determined under paragraph (c) of this section), and by allowing the credits and surtax exemption provided in § 1.1502-2.

(c) Consolidated unrelated business taxable income. The consolidated unrelated business taxable income for a consolidated return year shall be determined by taking into account—

(1) The separate unrelated business taxable income of each member of the exempt group (determined under paragraph (d) of this section);

(2) Any consolidated net operating loss deduction (determined under §§ 1.1502-21A or 1.1502-21 (as appropriate)) subject to the limitations provided in section 512(b)(6);

(3) Any consolidated charitable contribution deduction (determined under § 1.1502-24) subject to the limitations provided in section 512(b)(10); and

(4) Any consolidated net gain or net loss from the disposition of debt-financed property (as defined in section 514(b)) taken into account as provided by section 514(a), or from the cutting of timber to which section 631 applies.

(d) Separate unrelated business taxable income. The separate unrelated business taxable income of a member of an exempt group shall be computed in accordance with the provisions of section 512 covering the determination of unrelated business taxable income of separate corporations, except that—

(1) The provisions of paragraphs (a) through (k) and (o) of § 1.1502-12 shall apply; and

(2) No charitable contributions deduction shall be taken into account under section 512(b)(10).

See sections 511(c) and 512(a)(3)(C) for special rules applicable to organizations described in section 501(c)(2).

T.D. 7183, 4/20/72, amend T.D. 7595, 2/16/79, T.D. 8823, 6/25/99.

§ 1.1503-1 Computation and payment of tax.

Caution: The Treasury has not yet amended Reg § 1.1503-1 to reflect changes made by P.L. 101-239, P.L. 100-647, P.L. 99-514, P.L. 98-369, P.L. 94-455.

(a) General rule. In any case in which a consolidated return is filed or required to be filed, the tax shall be determined, computed, assessed, collected, and adjusted in accordance with the regulations prescribed under section 1502 promulgated prior to the last date prescribed by law for the filing of such return.

(b) Limitation. If the affiliated group includes one or more Western Hemisphere trade corporations (as defined in section 921) or one or more regulated public utilities (as defined in section 1503(c)), the increase in tax described in section 1503(a) shall be applied in a manner provided in the regulations under section 1502.

T.D. 6140, 8/29/55, amend T.D. 7244, 12/30/72.

§ 1.1503-2 Dual consolidated loss.

(a) Purpose and scope. This section provides rules for the application of section 1503(d), concerning the determination and use of dual consolidated losses. Paragraph (b) of this section provides a general rule prohibiting a dual consolidated loss from offsetting the taxable income of a domestic affiliate. Paragraph (c) of this section provides definitions of the terms used in this section. Paragraph (d) of this section provides rules for calculating the amount of a dual consolidated loss and for adjusting the basis of stock of a dual resident corporation. Paragraph (e) of this section contains an anti-avoidance provision. Paragraph (f) of this section applies the rules of paragraph (d) of this section to the computation of foreign tax credit limitations. Paragraph (g) of this section provides certain exceptions to the limitation rule of paragraph (b) of this section. Finally, paragraph (h) of this section provides the effective date of the regulations and a provision for the retroactive application of the regulations to qualifying taxpayers.

(b) In general. *(1) Limitation on the use of a dual consolidated loss to offset income of a domestic affiliate.* Except as otherwise provided in this section, a dual consolidated loss of a dual resident corporation cannot offset the taxable income of any domestic affiliate in the taxable year in which the loss is recognized or in any other taxable year, regardless of whether the loss offsets income of another person under the income tax laws of a foreign country and regardless of whether the income that the loss may offset in the foreign country is, has been, or will be subject to tax in the United States. Pursuant to paragraph (c)(1) and (2) of this section, the same limitation shall apply to a dual consolidated loss of a separate unit of a domestic corporation as if the separate unit were a wholly owned subsidiary of such corporation.

(2) Limitation on the use of a dual consolidated loss to offset income of a successor-in-interest. A dual consolidated loss of a dual resident corporation also cannot be used to offset the taxable income of another corporation by means of a transaction in which the other corporation succeeds to the tax attributes of the dual resident corporation under section 381 of the Code. Similarly, a dual consolidated loss of a separate unit of a domestic corporation cannot be used to offset income of the domestic corporation following the termination, liquidation, sale, or other disposition of the separate unit. However, if a dual resident corporation transfers its assets to another corporation in a transaction subject to section 381, and the acquiring corporation is a dual resident corporation of the same foreign country of which the transferor dual resident corporation is a resident, or a domestic corporation that carries on the business activities of the transferor dual resident corporation as a separate unit, then income generated by the transferee dual resident corporation, or separate unit, may be offset by the carryover losses of the transferor dual resident corporation. In addition, if a domestic corporation transfers a separate unit to another domestic corporation in a transaction subject to section 381, the income generated by the separate unit following the transfer may be offset by the carryover losses of the separate unit.

(3) Application of rules to multiple tiers of separate units. If a separate unit of a domestic corporation is owned indirectly through another separate unit, the principles of paragraph (b)(1) and (2) of this section shall apply as if the upper-tier separate unit were a subsidiary of the domestic corporation and the lower-tier separate unit were a lower-tier subsidiary.

(4) Examples. The following examples illustrate the application of this paragraph (b).

Example (1). P, a domestic corporation, owns all of the outstanding stock of DRC, a domestic corporation. P and DRC file a consolidated U.S. income tax return. DRC is managed and controlled in Country W, a country that determines the tax residence of corporations according to their place of management and control. Therefore, DRC is a dual resident corporation and any net operating loss it incurs is a dual consolidated loss. In Years 1 through 3, DRC incurs dual consolidated losses. Under this paragraph (b), the dual consolidated losses may not be used to offset P's income on the group's consolidated U.S. income tax return. At the end of Year 3, DRC sells all of its assets and discontinues its business operations. DRC is then liquidated into P, pursuant to the provisions of section 332. Normally, under section 381, P would succeed to, and be permitted to utilize, DRC's net operating loss carryovers. However, this paragraph (b) prohibits the dual consolidated losses of DRC from reducing P's income for U.S. tax purposes. Therefore, DRC's net operating loss carryovers will not be available to offset P's income.

Example (2). The facts are the same as in Example 1, except that DRC does not sell its assets and, following the liquidation of DRC, P continues to operate DRC's business as a separate unit (e.g., a branch). DRC's loss carryovers are available to offset P's income generated by the assets previously owned by DRC and now held by the separate unit.

(c) Definitions. The following definitions shall apply for purposes of this section.

(1) Domestic corporation. The term "domestic corporation" has the meaning assigned to it by section 7701(a)(3) and (4). The term also includes any corporation otherwise treated as a domestic corporation by the Code, including, but not limited to, sections 269B, 953(d), and 1504(d). For purposes of this section, any separate unit of a domestic corporation, as defined in paragraph (c)(3) and (4) of this section, shall be treated as a separate domestic corporation.

(2) Dual resident corporation. A dual resident corporation is a domestic corporation that is subject to the income tax of a foreign country on its worldwide income or on a residence basis. A corporation is taxed on a residence basis if it is

taxed as a resident under the laws of the foreign country. An S corporation, as defined in section 1361, is not a dual resident corporation. For purposes of this section, any separate unit of a domestic corporation, as defined in paragraph (c)(3) and (4) of this section, shall be treated as a dual resident corporation. Unless otherwise indicated, any reference in this section to a dual resident corporation refers also to a separate unit.

(3) Separate unit. (i) The term "separate unit" shall mean any of the following:

(A) A foreign branch, as defined in § 1.367(a)-6T(g) (or a successor regulation), that is owned either directly by a domestic corporation or indirectly by a domestic corporation through ownership of a partnership or trust interest (regardless of whether the partnership or trust is a United States person);

(B) an interest in a partnership; or

(C) an interest in a trust.

(ii) If two or more foreign branches located in the same foreign country are owned by a single domestic corporation and the losses of each branch are made available to offset the income of the other branches under the tax laws of the foreign country, within the meaning of paragraph (c)(15)(ii) of this section, then the branches shall be treated as one separate unit.

(4) Hybrid entity separate unit. The term "separate unit" includes an interest in an entity that is not taxable as an association for U.S. income tax purposes but is subject to income tax in a foreign country as a corporation (or otherwise at the entity level) either on its worldwide income or on a residence basis.

(5) Dual consolidated loss. (i) In general. The term "dual consolidated loss" means the net operating loss (as defined in section 172(c) and the regulations thereunder) of a domestic corporation incurred in a year in which the corporation is a dual resident corporation. The dual consolidated loss shall be computed under paragraph (d)(1) of this section. The fact that a particular item taken into account in computing a dual resident corporation's net operating loss is not taken into account in computing income subject to a foreign country's income tax shall not cause such item to be excluded from the calculation of the dual consolidated loss.

(ii) Exceptions. A dual consolidated loss shall not include the following—

(A) A net operating loss incurred by a dual resident corporation in a foreign country whose income tax laws—

(1) Do not permit the dual resident corporation to use its losses, expenses or deductions to offset the income of any other person that is recognized in the same taxable year in which the losses, expenses or deductions are incurred; and

(2) Do not permit the losses, expenses or deductions of the dual resident corporation to be carried over or back to be used, by any means, to offset the income of any other person in other taxable years; or

(B) A net operating loss incurred during that portion of the taxable year prior to the date on which the domestic corporation becomes a dual resident corporation or subsequent to the date on which the domestic corporation ceases to be a dual resident corporation. For purposes of determining the amount of the net operating loss incurred in that portion of the taxable year prior to the date on which the domestic corporation becomes a dual resident corporation or subsequent to the date on which the domestic corporation ceases to be a dual resident corporation, in no event shall more than the aggregate of the equal daily portion of the net operating loss commensurate with the portion of the taxable year during which the domestic corporation was not a dual resident corporation be allocated to that portion of the taxable year in which the domestic corporation was not a dual resident corporation.

(iii) Dual consolidated losses of separate units that are partnership interests, including interests in hybrid entities. [Reserved]

(6) Subject to tax. For purposes of determining whether a domestic corporation is subject to the income tax of a foreign country on its income, the fact that the corporation has no actual income tax liability to the foreign country for a particular taxable year shall not be taken into account.

(7) Foreign country. For purposes of this section, possessions of the United States shall be considered foreign countries.

(8) Consolidated group. The term "consolidated group" means an affiliated group, as defined in section 1504(a), with which a dual resident corporation or domestic owner files a consolidated U.S. income tax return.

(9) Domestic owner. The term "domestic owner" means a domestic corporation that owns one or more separate units.

(10) Affiliated dual resident corporation or affiliated domestic owner. The term "affiliated dual resident corporation" or "affiliated domestic owner" means a dual resident corporation or domestic owner that is a member of a consolidated group.

(11) Unaffiliated dual resident corporation or unaffiliated domestic owner. The term "unaffiliated dual resident corporation" or "unaffiliated domestic owner" means a dual resident corporation or domestic owner that is an unaffiliated domestic corporation.

(12) Successor-in-interest. The term "successor-in-interest means an acquiring corporation that succeeds to the tax attributes of an acquired corporation by means of a transaction subject to section 381.

(13) Domestic affiliate. The term "domestic affiliate" means any member of an affiliated group, without regard to the exceptions contained in section 1504(b) (other than section 1504(b)(3)) relating to includible corporations.

(14) Unaffiliated domestic corporation. The term "unaffiliated domestic corporation" means a domestic corporation that is not a member of an affiliated group.

(15) Use of loss to offset income of a domestic affiliate or another person. (i) A dual consolidated loss shall be deemed to offset income of a domestic affiliate in the year it is included in the computation of the consolidated taxable income of a consolidated group. The fact that no tax benefit results from the inclusion of the dual consolidated loss in the computation of the group's consolidated taxable income in the taxable year shall not be taken into account.

(ii) Except as provided in paragraph (c)(15)(iii) of this section, a loss, expense, or deduction taken into account in computing a dual consolidated loss shall be deemed to offset income of another person under the income tax laws of a foreign country in the year it is made available for such offset. The fact that the other person does not have sufficient income in that year to benefit from such an offset shall not be taken into account. However, where the laws of a foreign country provide an election that would enable a dual resident corporation or separate unit to use its losses, expenses, or deductions to offset income of another person, the losses, expenses, or deductions shall be considered to offset such income only if the election is made.

(iii) The losses, expenses, or deductions taken into account in computing a dual resident corporation's or separate unit's dual consolidated loss shall not be deemed to offset income of another person under the income tax laws of a foreign country for purposes of this section, if under the laws of the foreign country the losses, expenses, or deductions of the dual resident corporation or separate unit are used to offset the income of another dual resident corporation or separate unit within the same consolidated group (or income of another separate unit that is owned by the unaffiliated domestic owner of the first separate unit). If the losses, expenses, or deductions of a dual resident corporation or separate unit are made available under the laws of a foreign country to offset the income of other dual resident corporations or separate units within the same consolidated group (or other separate units owned by the unaffiliated domestic owner of the first separate unit), as well as the income of another person, and the laws of the foreign country do not provide applicable rules for determining which person's income is offset by the losses, expenses, or deductions, then for purposes of this section, the losses, expenses or deductions shall be deemed to offset the income of the other dual resident corporations or separate units, to the extent of such income, before being considered to offset the income of the other person.

(iv) Except to the extent paragraph (g)(1) of this section applies, where the income tax laws of a foreign country deny the use of losses, expenses, or deductions of a dual resident corporation to offset the income of another person because the dual resident corporation is also subject to income taxation by another country on its worldwide income or on a residence basis, the dual resident corporation shall be treated as if it actually had offset its dual consolidated loss against the income of another person in such foreign country.

(16) Examples. The following examples illustrate this paragraph (c).

Example (1). X, a member of a consolidated group, conducts business through a branch in Country Y. Under Country Y's income tax laws, the branch is taxed as a permanent establishment and its losses may be used under the Country Y form of consolidation to offset the income of Z, a Country Y affiliate of X. In Year 1, the branch of X incurs an overall loss that would be treated as a net operating loss if the branch were a separate domestic corporation. Under paragraph (c)(3) of this section, the branch of X is treated as a separate domestic corporation and a dual resident corporation. Thus, under paragraph (c)(5), its loss constitutes a dual consolidated loss. Unless X qualifies for an exception under paragraph (g) of this section, paragraph (b) of this section precludes the use of the branch's loss to offset any income of X not derived from the branch operations or any income of a domestic affiliate of X.

Example (2). A and B are members of a consolidated group. FC is a Country X corporation that is wholly owned by B. A and B organize a partnership, P, under the laws of Country X. P conducts business in Country X and its business activity constitutes a foreign branch within the meaning of paragraph (c)(3)(i)(A) of this section. P also earns U.S. source income that is unconnected with the branch operations and, therefore, is not subject to tax by Country X. Under the laws of Country X, the branch can consolidate with FC. The interests in P held by A and B are each treated as a dual resident corporation. The branch is also treated as a separate dual resident corporation. Unless an exception under paragraph (g) of this section applies, any dual consolidated loss incurred by P's branch cannot offset the U.S. source income earned by P or any other income of A or B.

Example (3). X is classified as a partnership for U.S. income tax purposes. A, B and C are the sole partners of X. A and B are domestic corporations and C is a Country Y corporation. For U.S. income tax purposes, each partner has an equal interest in each item of partnership profit or loss. Under Country Y's law, X is classified as a corporation and its income and losses may be used under the Country Y form of consolidation to offset the income of companies that are affiliates of X. Under paragraph (c)(3) and (4) of this section, the partnership interests held by A and B are treated as separate domestic corporations and as dual resident corporations. Unless an exception under paragraph (g) of this section applies, losses allocated to A and B can only be used to offset profits of X allocated to A and B, respectively.

Example (4). P, a domestic corporation, files a consolidated U.S. income tax return with its two wholly-owned domestic subsidiaries, DRC1 and DRC2. Each subsidiary is also treated as a Country Y resident for Country Y tax purposes. Thus, DRC1 and DRC2 are dual resident corporations. DRC1 owns FC, a Country Y corporation. Country Y's tax laws permit affiliated resident corporations to file a form of consolidated return. In Year 1, DRC1 incurs a $200 net operating loss for both U.S. and Country Y tax purposes, while DRC2 recognizes $200 of income under the tax laws of each country. FC also earns $200 of income for Country Y tax purposes. DRC1, DRC2, and FC file a Country Y consolidated return. However, Country Y has no applicable rules for determining which income is offset by DRC1's $200 loss. Under paragraph (c)(15)(iii) of this section, the loss shall be treated as offsetting DRC2's $200 of income. Because DRC1 and DRC2 are members of the same consolidated group, for purposes of this section, the offset of DRC1's loss against the income of DRC2 is not considered a use of the loss against the income of another person under the laws of a foreign country.

Example (5). DRC, a domestic corporation, files a consolidated U.S. income tax return with its parent, P. DRC is also subject to tax in Country Y on its worldwide income. Therefore, DRC is a dual resident corporation and any net operating loss incurred by DRC is a dual consolidated loss. Country Y's tax laws permit corporations that are subject to tax on their worldwide income to use the Country Y form of consolidation, thus enabling eligible corporations to use their losses to offset income of affiliates. However, to prevent corporations like DRC from offsetting losses against income of affiliates in Country Y and then again offsetting the losses against income of foreign affiliates under the tax laws of another country, Country Y prevents a corporation that is also subject to the income tax of another country on its worldwide income or on a residence basis from using the Country Y form of consolidation. There is no agreement, as described in paragraph (g)(1) of this section, between the United States and Country Y. Because of Country Y's statute, DRC will be treated as having actually offset its losses against the income of affiliates in Country Y under paragraph (c)(15)(iv) of this section. Therefore, DRC will not be able to file an agreement described in paragraph (g)(2) of this section and offset its losses against the income of P or any other domestic affiliate.

(d) Special rules for accounting for dual consolidated losses. *(1) Determination of amount of dual consolidated loss.* (i) Dual resident corporation that is a member of a consolidated group. For purposes of determining whether a dual resident corporation that is a member of a consolidated group has a dual consolidated loss for the taxable year, the dual resident corporation shall compute its taxable income (or loss) in accordance with the rules set forth in the regulations under section 1502 governing the computation of consolidated taxable income, taking into account only the dual resident corporation's items of income, gain, deduction, and loss for the year. However, for purposes of this computation, the following items shall not be taken into account:

(A) Any net capital loss of the dual resident corporation; and

(B) Any carryover or carryback losses.

(ii) Dual resident corporation that is a separate unit of a domestic corporation. For purposes of determining whether a separate unit has a dual consolidated loss for the taxable year, the separate unit shall compute its taxable income (or loss) as if it were a separate domestic corporation and a dual resident corporation in accordance with the provisions of paragraph (d)(1)(i) of this section, using only those items of income, expense, deduction, and loss that are otherwise attributable to such separate unit.

(2) Effect of a dual consolidated loss. For any taxable year in which a dual resident corporation or separate unit has a dual consolidated loss to which paragraph (b) of this section applies, the following rules shall apply.

(i) If the dual resident corporation is a member of a consolidated group, the group shall compute its consolidated taxable income without taking into account the items of income, loss, or deduction taken into account in computing the dual consolidation loss. The dual consolidated loss may be carried over or back for use in other taxable years as a separate net operating loss carryover or carryback of the dual resident corporation arising in the year incurred. It shall be treated as a loss incurred by the dual resident corporation in a separate return limitation year and (without regard to whether the dual resident corporation is a common parent) shall be subject to all of the limitations of §§ 1.1502-21A(c) or 1.1502-21(c), as appropriate (relating to limitations on net operating loss carryovers and carrybacks from separate return limitation years).

(ii) The unaffiliated domestic owner of a separate unit, or the consolidated group of an affiliated domestic owner, shall compute its taxable income without taking into account the items of income, loss or deduction taken into account in computing the separate unit's dual consolidated loss. The dual consolidated loss shall be treated as a loss incurred by a separate corporation and its use shall be subject to all of the limitations of §§ 1.1502-21A(c) or 1.1502-21(c), as appropriate, as if the separate unit were filing a consolidated return with the unaffiliated domestic owner or with the consolidated group of the affiliated domestic owner.

(3) Basis adjustments for dual consolidated losses. (i) Dual resident corporation that is a member of an affiliated group. When a dual resident corporation is a member of a consolidated group, each other member owning stock in the dual resident corporation shall adjust the basis of the stock in the following manner.

(A) Positive adjustments. Positive adjustments shall be made in accordance with the principles of § 1.1502-32(b)(1), except that there shall be no positive adjustment under § 1.1502-32(b)(1)(ii) for any amount of the dual consolidated loss that is not absorbed as a result of the application of paragraph (b) of this section. In addition, there shall be no positive adjustment for any amount included in income pursuant to paragraph (g)(2)(vii) of this section.

(B) Negative adjustments. Negative adjustments shall be made in accordance with the principles of § 1.1502-32(b)(2), except that there shall be no negative adjustment under § 1.1502-32(b)(2)(ii) for the amount of the dual consolidated loss subject to paragraph (b) of this section that is absorbed in a carryover year.

(ii) Dual resident corporation that is a separate unit arising from an interest in a partnership. Where a separate unit is an interest in a partnership, the domestic owner shall adjust its basis in the separate unit in accordance with section 705, except that no increase in basis shall be permitted for any amount included as income pursuant to paragraph (g)(2)(vii) of this section.

(4) Examples. The following examples illustrate this paragraph (d).

Example (1). (i) P, S1, S2, and T are domestic corporations. P owns all of the stock of S1 and S2. S2 owns all of the stock of T. T is a resident of Country FC for Country FC income tax purposes. Therefore, T is a dual resident corporation. P, S1, S2, and T file a consolidated U.S. income tax return. X and Y are corporations that are not members of the consolidated group.

(ii) At the beginning of Year 1, P has a basis of $1000 in the stock of S2. S2 has a $500 basis in the stock of T.

(iii) In Year 1, T incurs interest expense in the amount of $100. In addition, T sells a noncapital asset, u, in which it has a basis of $10, to S1 for $50. T also sells a noncapital asset, v, in which it has a basis of $200, to S1 for $100. The sales of u and v are intercompany transactions described in § 1.1502-13. T also sells a capital asset, z, in which it has a basis of $180, to Y for $90. In Year 1, S1 earns $200 of separate taxable income, calculated in accordance with § 1.1502-12, as well as $90 of capital gain from a sale of an asset to X. P and S2 have no items of income, loss, or deduction for Year 1.

(iv) In Year 1, T has a dual consolidated loss of $100 (attributable to its interest expense). T's $90 capital loss is not included in the computation of the dual consolidated loss. Instead, T's capital loss is included in the computation of the consolidated group's capital gain net income under § 1.1502-22(c) and is used to offset S1's $90 capital gain.

(v) No elective agreement, as described in paragraph (g)(1) of this section, exists between the United States and Country FC. For Country FC tax purposes, T's $100 loss is offset against the income of a Country FC affiliate. Therefore, T is not eligible for the exception provided in paragraph (g)(2) of this section.

(vi) Because T has a dual consolidated loss for the year, the consolidated taxable income of the consolidated group is calculated without regard to T's items of income, loss or deduction taken into account in computing the dual consolidated loss. Therefore, the consolidated taxable income of the consolidated group is $200 (the sum of $200 of separate taxable income earned by S1 plus $90 of capital gain earned by S1 minus $90 of capital loss incurred by T). The $40 gain recognized by T upon the sale of item u to S1 and the $100 loss recognized by T upon the sale of item v to S1 are deferred pursuant to § 1.1502-13(c)(1).

(vii) S2 may not make the positive adjustment provided for in § 1.1502-32(b)(1)(ii) to its basis in the stock of T for the $100 dual consolidated loss incurred by T. In addition, no positive adjustment in the basis of the stock is required for T's $90 capital loss because the loss has been absorbed by the consolidated group. S2, however, must make the negative adjustment provided for in § 1.1502-32(b)(2)(i) for its allocable part of T's deficit in earnings and profits for the taxable year attributable to both T's $100 dual consolidated loss and T's $90 capital loss. Thus, as provided in § 1.1502-32(e)(1), S2 must make a $190 net negative adjustment to its basis in the stock of T, reducing its basis to $310. As provided in § 1.1502-33(c)(4)(ii)(a), S2's earnings and profits for Year 1 will reflect S2's decrease in its basis in T stock for the taxable year. Since S2 has no other earnings and profits for the taxable year, S2 has a $190 deficit in earnings and profits for the year. As provided in § 1.1502-32(b)(2)(i), P must make a negative adjustment to its basis in the stock of S2 for its allocable part of S2's deficit in earnings and profits for the taxable year. Thus, P must make a $190 net negative adjustment to its basis in S2 stock, reducing its basis to $810.

Example (2). (i) The facts are the same as in Example 1, except that in Year 2, S1 sells items u and v to X for no gain or loss. The disposition of items u and v outside of the consolidated group restores the deferred loss and gain to T. T also incurs $100 of interest expense in Year 2. In addition, T sells a noncapital asset, r, in which it has a basis of $100, to Y for $300. P and S2 have no items of income, loss, or deduction for Year 2.

(ii) T has $40 of separate taxable income in Year 2, computed as follows:

($100)	interest expense
($100)	sale of item v to S1
$ 40	sale of item u to S1
$200	sale of item r to Y
$ 40	

Thus, T has no dual consolidated loss for the year.

(iii) Since T does not have a dual consolidated loss for the taxable year, the group's consolidated taxable income is calculated in accordance with the general rule of § 1.1502-11 and not in accordance with paragraph (d)(2) of this section. T is the only member of the consolidated group that has any income or loss for the taxable year. Thus, the consolidated taxable income of the group, computed without regard to T's dual consolidated loss carryover, is $40.

(iv) As provided by § 1.1502-21A(c), the amount of the dual consolidated loss arising in Year 1 that is included in the group's consolidated net operating loss deduction for Year 2 is $40 (that is, the consolidated taxable income computed without regard to the consolidated net operating loss deduction minus such consolidated taxable income recomputed by excluding the items of income and deduction of T). Thus, the group has no consolidated taxable income for the year.

(v) S2 must make the positive adjustment provided for in § 1.1502-32(b)(1)(i) to its basis in T stock for its allocable part of T's undistributed earnings and profits for the taxable year. S2 cannot make the negative adjustment provided for in § 1.1502-32(b)(2)(ii) for the dual consolidated loss of T incurred in Year 1 and absorbed in Year 2. Thus, as provided in § 1.1502-32(e)(2), S2 must make a $40 net positive adjustment to its basis in T stock, increasing its basis to $350. As provided in § 1.1502-33(c)(4)(ii)(a), S2's earnings and profits for Year 2 will reflect S2's increase in its basis in T stock for the taxable year. Since S2 has no other earnings and profits for the taxable year, S2 has $40 of earnings and profits for the year. As provided in § 1.1502-32(b)(1)(i), P must make a positive adjustment to its basis in the stock of S2 for its allocable part of the undistributed earnings and profits of S2 for the taxable year. Thus, P must make a $40 net positive adjustment to its basis in S2 stock, increasing its basis to $850.

(e) Special rule for use of dual consolidated loss to offset tainted income. *(1) In general.* The dual consolidated loss of any dual resident corporation that ceases to be a dual resident corporation shall not be used to offset income of such corporation to the extent that such income is tainted income, as defined in paragraph (e)(2) of this section.

(2) Tainted income defined. Tainted income is any income derived from tainted assets, as defined in paragraph (e)(3) of this section, beginning on the date such assets are acquired by the dual resident corporation. In the absence of evidence establishing the actual amount of income that is attributable to the tainted assets, the portion of a corporation's income in a particular taxable year that is treated as tainted income shall be an amount equal to the corporation's taxable income for the year multiplied by a fraction, the numerator of which is the fair market value of the tainted asset at the end of the taxable year and the denominator of which is the fair market value of the total assets owned by the corporation at the end of the taxable year. Documentation submitted to establish the actual amount of income that is attributable to the tainted assets must be attached to the consolidated group's or unaffiliated dual resident corporation's timely filed tax return for the taxable year in which the income is recognized.

(3) Tainted assets defined. Tainted assets are any assets acquired by a dual resident corporation in a nonrecognition transaction, as defined in section 7701(a)(45), or any assets otherwise transferred to the corporation as a contribution to capital, at any time during the three taxable years immediately preceding the taxable year in which the corporation ceases to be a dual resident corporation or at any time thereafter. Tainted assets shall not include assets that were acquired by such dual resident corporation on or before December 31, 1986.

(4) Exceptions. Income derived from assets acquired by a dual resident corporation shall not be subject to the limitation described in paragraph (e)(1) of this section, if—

(i) For the taxable year in which the assets were acquired, the corporation did not have a dual consolidated loss (or a carry forward of a dual consolidated loss to such year); or

(ii) The assets were acquired as replacement property in the ordinary course of business.

(f) Computation of foreign tax credit limitations. If a dual resident corporation or separate unit is subject to paragraph (d)(2) of this section, the consolidated group or unaffiliated domestic owner shall compute its foreign tax credit limitation by applying the limitations of paragraph (d)(2). Thus, the dual consolidated loss is not taken into account until the year in which it is absorbed.

(g) Exception. *(1) Elective agreement in place between the United States and a foreign country.* Paragraph (b) of this section shall not apply to a dual consolidated loss to the extent the dual resident corporation, or domestic owner of a separate unit, elects to deduct the loss in the United States pursuant to an agreement entered into between the United States and a foreign country that puts into place an elective procedure through which losses offset income in only one country.

(2) Elective relief provision. (i) In general. Paragraph (b) of this section shall not apply to a dual consolidated loss if the consolidated group, unaffiliated dual resident corporation, or unaffiliated domestic owner elects to be bound by the provisions of this paragraph (g)(2). In order to elect relief under this paragraph (g)(2), the consolidated group, un-

affiliated dual resident corporation, or unaffiliated domestic owner must attach to its timely filed (including extensions) U.S. income tax return for the taxable year in which the dual consolidated loss is incurred an agreement described in paragraph (g)(2)(i)(A) of this section. The agreement must be signed under penalties of perjury by the person who signs the return. For taxable years beginning after December 31, 2002, the agreement attached to the income tax return of the consolidated group, unaffiliated dual resident corporation or unaffiliated domestic owner pursuant to the preceding sentence may be an unsigned copy. If an unsigned copy is attached to the return, the consolidated group, unaffiliated dual resident corporation, or unaffiliated domestic owner must retain the original in its records in the manner specified by § 1.6001-1(e). The agreement must include the following items, in paragraphs labeled to correspond with the items set forth in paragraph (g)(2)(i)(A) through (F) of this section.

(A) A statement that the document submitted is an election and an agreement under the provisions of paragraph (g)(2) of this section.

(B) The name, address, identifying number, and place and date of incorporation of the dual resident corporation, and the country or countries that tax the dual resident corporation on its worldwide income or on a residence basis, or, in the case of a separate unit, identification of the separate unit, including the name under which it conducts business, its principal activity, and the country in which its principal place of business is located.

(C) An agreement by the consolidated group, unaffiliated dual resident corporation, or unaffiliated domestic owner to comply with all of the provisions of § 1.1503-2(g)(2)(iii)-(vii).

(D) A statement of the amount of the dual consolidated loss covered by the agreement.

(E) A certification that no portion of the dual resident corporation's or separate unit's losses, expenses, or deductions taken into account in computing the dual consolidated loss has been, or will be, used to offset the income of any other person under the income tax laws of a foreign country.

(F) A certification that arrangements have been made to ensure that no portion of the dual consolidated loss will be used to offset the income of another person under the laws of a foreign country and that the consolidated group, unaffiliated dual resident corporation, or unaffiliated domestic owner will be informed of any such foreign use of any portion of the dual consolidated loss.

(ii) Consistency rule. (A) If any loss, expense, or deduction taken into account in computing the dual consolidated loss of a dual resident corporation or separate unit is used under the laws of a foreign country to offset the income of another person, then the following other dual consolidated losses (if any) shall be treated as also having been used to offset income of another person under the laws of such foreign country, but only if the income tax laws of the foreign country permit any loss, expense, or deduction taken into account in computing the other dual consolidated loss to be used to offset the income of another person in the same taxable year:

(1) Any dual consolidated loss of a dual resident corporation that is a member of the same consolidated group of which the first dual resident corporation or domestic owner is a member, if any loss, expense, or deduction taken into account in computing such dual consolidated loss is recognized under the income tax laws of such country in the same taxable year; and

(2) Any dual consolidated loss of a separate unit that is owned by the same domestic owner that owns the first separate unit, or that is owned by any member of the same consolidated group of which the first dual resident corporation or domestic owner is a member, if any loss, expense, or deduction taken into account in computing such dual consolidated loss is recognized under the income tax laws of such country in the same taxable year.

(B) The following examples illustrate the application of this paragraph (g)(2)(ii).

Example (1). P, a domestic corporation, owns A and B, which are domestic corporations, and C, a Country X corporation. A is subject to the income tax laws of Country X on a residence basis and, thus, is a dual resident corporation. B conducts business in Country X through a branch, which is a separate unit under paragraph (c)(3) of this section. The income tax laws of Country X permit branches of foreign corporations to elect to file consolidated returns with Country X affiliates. In Year 1, A incurs a dual consolidated loss, which is used to offset the income of C under the Country X form of consolidation. The branch of B also incurs a net operating loss. However, B elects not to use the loss on a Country X consolidated return to offset the income of foreign affiliates. The use of A's loss to offset the income of C in Country X will cause the separate unit of B to be treated as if it too had used its dual consolidated loss to offset the income of an affiliate in Country X. Therefore, an election and agreement under this paragraph (g)(2) cannot be made with respect to the separate unit's dual consolidated loss.

Example (2). The facts are the same as in Example 1, except that the income tax laws of Country X do not permit branches of foreign corporations to file consolidated income tax returns with Country X affiliates. Therefore, an election and agreement described in this paragraph (g)(2) may be made for the dual consolidated loss incurred by the separate unit of B.

(iii) Triggering events requiring the recapture of dual consolidated losses. (A) The consolidated group, unaffiliated dual resident corporation, or unaffiliated domestic owner must agree that, if there is a triggering event described in this paragraph (g)(2)(iii), and no exception applies under paragraph (g)(2)(iv) of this section, the consolidated group, unaffiliated dual resident corporation, or unaffiliated domestic owner will recapture and report as income the amount of the dual consolidated loss provided in paragraph (g)(2)(vii) of this section on its tax return for the taxable year in which the triggering event occurs (or, when the triggering event is a use of the loss for foreign purposes, the taxable year that includes the last day of the foreign tax year during which such use occurs). In addition, the consolidated group, unaffiliated dual resident corporation, or unaffiliated domestic owner must pay any applicable interest charge required by paragraph (g)(2)(vii) of this section. For purposes of this section, any of the following events shall constitute a triggering event:

(1) In any taxable year up to and including the 15th taxable year following the year in which the dual consolidated loss that is the subject of the agreement filed under this paragraph (g)(2) was incurred, any portion of the losses, expenses, or deductions taken into account in computing the dual consolidated loss is used by any means to offset the income of any other person under the income tax laws of a foreign country;

(2) An affiliated dual resident corporation or affiliated domestic owner ceases to be a member of the consolidated group that filed the election. For purposes of this paragraph

(g)(2)(iii)(A)(2), a dual resident corporation or domestic owner shall be considered to cease to be a member of the consolidated group if it is no longer a member of the group within the meaning of § 1.1502-1(b), or if the group ceases to exist because the common parent is no longer in existence or is no longer a common parent or the group no longer files on the basis of a consolidated return. Such disaffiliation, however, shall not constitute a triggering event if the taxpayer demonstrates, to the satisfaction of the Commissioner, that the dual resident corporation's or separate unit's losses, expenses, or deductions cannot be used to offset income of another person under the laws of a foreign country at any time after the affiliated dual resident corporation or affiliated domestic owner ceases to be a member of the consolidated group.

(3) An unaffiliated dual resident corporation or unaffiliated domestic owner becomes a member of a consolidated group. Such affiliation of the dual resident corporation or domestic owner, however, shall not constitute a triggering event if the taxpayer demonstrates, to the satisfaction of the Commissioner, that the losses, expenses, or deductions of the dual resident corporation or separate unit cannot be used to offset the income of another person under the laws of a foreign country at any time after the dual resident corporation or domestic owner becomes a member of the consolidated group.

(4) A dual resident corporation transfers assets in a transaction that results, under the laws of a foreign country, in a carryover of its losses, expenses, or deductions. For purposes of this paragraph (g)(2)(iii)(A)(4), a transfer, either in a single transaction or a series of transactions within a twelve-month period, of 50% or more of the dual resident corporation's assets (measured by the fair market value of the assets at the time of such transfer (or for multiple transactions, at the time of the first transfer)) shall be deemed a triggering event, unless the taxpayer demonstrates, to the satisfaction of the Commissioner, that the transfer of assets did not result in a carryover under foreign law of the dual resident corporation's losses, expenses, or deductions to the transferee of the assets;

(5) A domestic owner of a separate unit transfers assets of the separate unit in a transaction that results, under the laws of a foreign country, in a carryover of the separate unit's losses, expenses, or deductions. For purposes of this paragraph (g)(2)(iii)(A)(5), a transfer, either in a single transaction or a series of transactions over a twelve-month period, of 50% or more of the separate unit's assets (measured by the fair market value of the assets at the time of the transfer (or for multiple transfers, at the time of the first transfer)), shall be deemed a triggering event, unless the taxpayer demonstrates, to the satisfaction of the Commissioner, that the transfer of assets did not result in a carryover under foreign law of the separate unit's losses, expenses, or deductions to the transferee of the assets;

(6) An unaffiliated dual resident corporation or unaffiliated domestic owner becomes a foreign corporation by means of a transaction (e.g., a reorganization) that, for foreign tax purposes, is not treated as involving a transfer of assets (and carryover of losses) to a new entity. Such a transaction, however, shall not constitute a triggering event if the taxpayer demonstrates, to the satisfaction of the Commissioner, that the dual resident corporation's or separate unit's losses, expenses, or deductions cannot be used to offset income of another person under the laws of the foreign country at any time after the unaffiliated dual resident corporation or unaffiliated domestic owner becomes a foreign corporation.

(7) A domestic owner of a separate unit, either in a single transaction or a series of transactions within a twelve-month period, sells, or otherwise disposes of, 50% or more of the interest in the separate unit (measured by voting power or value) owned by the domestic owner on the last day of the taxable year in which the dual consolidated loss was incurred. For purposes of this paragraph (g)(2)(iii)(A)(7), the domestic owner shall be deemed to have disposed of its entire interest in a hybrid entity separate unit if such hybrid entity becomes classified as a foreign corporation for U.S. tax purposes. The disposition of 50% or more of the interest in a separate unit, however, shall not constitute a triggering event if the taxpayer demonstrates, to the satisfaction of the Commissioner, that the losses, expenses, or deductions of the separate unit cannot be used to offset income of another person under the laws of the foreign country at any time after the disposition of the interest in the separate unit; or

(8) The consolidated group, unaffiliated dual resident corporation, or unaffiliated domestic owner fails to file a certification required under paragraph (g)(2)(vi)(B) of this section.

(B) A taxpayer wishing to rebut the presumption of a triggering event described in paragraphs (g)(2)(iii)(A)(2) through (7) of this section, by demonstrating that the losses, expenses, or deductions of the dual resident corporation or separate unit cannot be carried over or otherwise used under the laws of the foreign country, must attach documents demonstrating such facts to its timely filed U.S. income tax return for the year in which the presumed triggering event occurs.

(C) The following example illustrates this paragraph (g)(2)(iii).

Example. DRC, a domestic corporation, is a member of CG, a consolidated group. DRC is a resident of Country Y for Country Y income tax purposes. Therefore, DRC is a dual resident corporation. In Year 1, DRC incurs a dual consolidated loss of $100. CG files an agreement described in paragraph (g)(2) of this section and, thus, the $100 dual consolidated loss is included in the computation of CG's consolidated taxable income. In Year 6, all of the stock of DRC is sold to P, a domestic corporation that is a member of NG, another consolidated group. The sale of DRC to P is a triggering event under paragraph (g)(2)(iii)(A) of this section, requiring the recapture of the dual consolidated loss. However, the laws of Country Y provide for a five-year carryover period for losses. At the time of DRC's disaffiliation from CG, the losses, expenses and deductions that were included in the computation of the dual consolidated loss had expired for Country Y purposes. Therefore, upon adequate documentation that the losses, expenses, or deductions have expired for Country Y purposes, CG can rebut the presumption that a triggering event has occurred.

(iv) Exceptions. (A) Acquisition by a member of the consolidated group. The following events shall not constitute triggering events, requiring the recapture of the dual consolidated loss under paragraph (g)(2)(vii) of this section:

(1) An affiliated dual resident corporation or affiliated domestic owner ceases to be a member of a consolidated group solely by reason of a transaction in which a member of the same consolidated group succeeds to the tax attributes of the dual resident corporation or domestic owner under the provisions of section 381;

(2) Assets of an affiliated dual resident corporation or assets of a separate unit of an affiliated domestic owner are ac-

quired by a member of its consolidated group in any other transaction; or

(3) An affiliated domestic owner of a separate unit transfers its interest in the separate unit to another member of its consolidated group.

(B) Acquisition by an unaffiliated domestic corporation or a new consolidated group. (1) If all the requirements of paragraph (g)(2)(iv)(B)(3) of this section are met, the following events shall not constitute triggering events requiring the recapture of the dual consolidated loss under paragraph (g)(2)(vii) of this section:

(i) An affiliated dual resident corporation or affiliated domestic owner becomes an unaffiliated domestic corporation or a member of a new consolidated group (other than in a transaction described in paragraph (g)(2)(iv)(B)(2)(ii) of this section);

(ii) Assets of a dual resident corporation or a separate unit are acquired by an unaffiliated domestic corporation or a member of a new consolidated group; or

(iii) A domestic owner of a separate unit transfers its interest in the separate unit to an unaffiliated domestic corporation or to a member of a new consolidated group.

(2) If the requirements of paragraph (g)(2)(iv)(B)(3)(iii) of this section are met, the following events shall not constitute triggering events requiring the recapture of the dual consolidated loss under paragraph (g)(2)(vii) of this section—

(i) An unaffiliated dual resident corporation or unaffiliated domestic owner becomes a member of a consolidated group;

(ii) A consolidated group that filed an agreement under this paragraph (g)(2) ceases to exist as a result of a transaction described in § 1.1502-13(j)(5)(i) (other than a transaction in which any member of the terminating group, or the successor-in-interest of such member, is not a member of the surviving group immediately after the terminating group ceases to exist).

(3) If the following requirements (as applicable) are satisfied, the events listed in paragraphs (g)(2)(iv)(B)(1) and (2) of this section shall not constitute triggering events requiring recapture under paragraph (g)(2)(vii) of this section.

(i) The consolidated group, unaffiliated dual resident corporation, or unaffiliated domestic owner that filed the agreement under this paragraph (g)(2) and the unaffiliated domestic corporation or new consolidated group must enter into a closing agreement with the Internal Revenue Service providing that the consolidated group, unaffiliated dual resident corporation, or unaffiliated domestic owner and the unaffiliated domestic corporation or new consolidated group will be jointly and severally liable for the total amount of the recapture of dual consolidated loss and interest charge required in paragraph (g)(2)(vii) of this section, if there is a triggering event described in paragraph (g)(2)(iii) of this section;

(ii) The unaffiliated domestic corporation or new consolidated group must agree to treat any potential recapture amount under paragraph (g)(2)(vii) of this section as unrealized built-in gain for purposes of section 384(a), subject to any applicable exceptions thereunder;

(iii) The unaffiliated domestic corporation or new consolidated group must file, with its timely filed (including extensions) income tax return for the taxable year in which the event described in paragraph (g)(2)(iv)(B)(1) or (2) of this section occurs, an agreement described in paragraph (g)(2)(i) of this section (new (g)(2)(i) agreement), whereby it assumes the same obligations with respect to the dual consolidated loss as the corporation or consolidated group that filed the original (g)(2)(i) agreement with respect to that loss. The new (g)(2)(i) agreement must be signed under penalties of perjury by the person who signs the return and must include a reference to this paragraph (g)(2)(iv)(B)(3)(iii). For taxable years beginning after December 31, 2002, the agreement attached to the return pursuant to the preceding sentence may be an unsigned copy. If an unsigned copy is attached to the return, the corporation or consolidated group must retain the original in its records in the manner specified by § 1.6001-1(e).

(C) Subsequent triggering events. Any triggering event described in paragraph (g)(2)(iii) of this section that occurs subsequent to one of the transactions described in paragraph (g)(2)(iv)(A) or (B) of this section and does not fall within the exceptions provided in paragraph (g)(2)(iv)(A) or (B) of this section shall require recapture under paragraph (g)(2)(vii) of this section.

(D) Example. The following example illustrates the application of paragraph (g)(2)(iv)(B)(2)(ii) of this section:

Example. (i) Facts. C is the common parent of a consolidated group (the C Group) that includes DRC, a domestic corporation. DRC is a dual resident corporation and incurs a dual consolidated loss in its taxable year ending December 31, Year 1. The C Group elects to be bound by the provisions of this paragraph (g)(2) with respect to the Year 1 dual consolidated loss. No member of the C Group incurs a dual consolidated loss in Year 2. On December 31, Year 2, stock of C is acquired by D in a transaction described in § 1.1502-13(j)(5)(i). As a result of the acquisition, all the C Group members, including DRC, become members of a consolidated group of which D is the common parent (the D Group).

(ii) Acquisition not a triggering event. Under paragraph (g)(2)(iv)(B)(2)(ii) of this section, the acquisition by D of the C Group is not an event requiring the recapture of the Year 1 dual consolidated loss of DRC, or the payment of an interest charge, as described in paragraph (g)(2)(vii) of this section, provided that the D Group files the new (g)(2)(i) agreement described in paragraph (g)(2)(iv)(B)(3)(iii) of this section.

(iii) Subsequent event. A triggering event occurs on December 31, Year 3, that requires recapture by the D Group of the dual consolidated loss that DRC incurred in Year 1, as well as the payment of an interest charge, as provided in paragraph (g)(2)(vii) of this section. Each member of the D Group, including DRC and the other former members of the C Group, is severally liable for the additional tax (and the interest charge) due upon the recapture of the dual consolidated loss of DRC.

(v) Ordering rules for determining the foreign use of losses. If the laws of a foreign country provide for the use of losses of a dual resident corporation to offset the income of another person but do not provide applicable rules for determining the order in which such losses are used to offset the income of another person in a taxable year, then for purposes of this section, the following rules shall govern:

(A) If under the laws of the foreign country the dual resident corporation has losses from different taxable years, the dual resident corporation shall be deemed to use first the losses from the earliest taxable year from which a loss may be carried forward or back for foreign law purposes.

(B) Any net loss, or income, that the dual resident corporation has in a taxable year shall first be used to offset net income, or loss, recognized by affiliates of the dual resident corporation in the same taxable year before any carryover of the dual resident corporation's losses is considered to be used to offset any income from the taxable year.

(C) Where different losses, expenses, or deductions (e.g., capital losses and ordinary losses) of a dual resident corporation incurred in the same taxable year are available to offset the income of another person, the different losses shall be deemed to offset such income on a pro rata basis.

Example. DRC, a domestic corporation, is taxed as a resident under the tax laws of Country Y. Therefore, DRC is a dual resident corporation. FA is a Country Y affiliate of DRC. Country Y's tax laws permit affiliated corporations to file a form of consolidated return. In Year 1, DRC incurs a capital loss of $80 which, for Country Y purposes, offsets completely $30 of capital gain recognized by FA. Neither corporation has any other taxable income or loss for the year. In Year 1 (and in other years), DRC recognizes the same amount of income for U.S. purposes as it does for Country Y purposes. Under paragraph (d)(1)(i) of this section, however, DRC's $80 capital loss is not a dual consolidated loss. In Year 2, DRC incurs a net operating loss of $100, while FA incurs a net operating loss of $50. DRC's $100 loss is a dual consolidated loss. Since the dual consolidated loss is not used to offset the income of another person under Country Y law, DRC is permitted to file an agreement described in this paragraph (g)(2). In Year 3, DRC has a net operating loss of $10 and FA has capital gains of $60. For Country Y purposes, DRC's $10 net operating loss is used to offset $10 of FA's $60 capital gain. DRC's $10 loss is a dual consolidated loss. Because the loss is used to offset FA's income, DRC will not be able to file an agreement under this paragraph (g)(2) with respect to the loss. Country Y permits FA's remaining $50 of Year 3 income to be offset by carryover losses. However, Country Y has no applicable rules for determining which carryover losses from Years 1 and 2 are used to offset such income. Under the ordering rules of paragraph (g)(2)(v)(A) of this section, none of DRC's $100 Year 2 loss will be deemed to offset FA's remaining $50 of Year 3 income. Instead, the $50 of capital loss carryover from Year 1 will be considered to offset the income.

(vi) Reporting requirements. (A) In general. The consolidated group, unaffiliated dual resident corporation, or unaffiliated domestic owner must answer the applicable questions regarding dual consolidated losses on its U.S. income tax return filed for the year in which the dual consolidated loss is incurred and for each of the following fifteen taxable years.

(B) Annual certification. Except as provided in § 1.1503-2(g)(2)(vi)(C), until and unless Form 1120 or the Schedules thereto contain questions pertaining to dual consolidated losses, the consolidated group, unaffiliated dual resident corporation, or unaffiliated domestic owner must file with its income tax return for each of the 15 taxable years following the taxable year in which the dual consolidated loss is incurred a certification that the losses, expenses, or deductions that make up the dual consolidated loss have not been used to offset the income of another person under the tax laws of a foreign country. For taxable years beginning before January 1, 2003, the annual certification must be signed under penalties of perjury by a person authorized to sign the agreement described in § 1.1503-2(g)(2)(i). For taxable years beginning after December 31, 2002, the certification is verified by signing the return with which the certification is filed. The certification for a taxable year must identify the dual consolidated loss to which it pertains by setting forth the taxpayer's year in which the loss was incurred and the amount of such loss. In addition, the certification must warrant that arrangements have been made to ensure that the loss will not be used to offset the income of another person under the laws of a foreign country and that the taxpayer will be informed of any such foreign use of any portion of the loss. If dual consolidated losses of more than one taxable year are subject to the rules of this paragraph (g)(2)(vi)(B), the certifications for those years may be combined in a single document but each dual consolidated loss must be separately identified.

(C) Exception. A consolidated group or unaffiliated domestic owner is not required to file annual certifications under paragraph (g)(2)(vi)(B) of this section with respect to a dual consolidated loss of any separate unit other than a hybrid entity separate unit.

(vii) Recapture of loss and interest charge. (A) Presumptive rule. (1) Amount of recapture. Except as otherwise provided in this paragraph (g)(2)(vii), upon the occurrence of a triggering event described in paragraph (g)(2)(iii) of this section, the taxpayer shall recapture and report as gross income the total amount of the dual consolidated loss to which the triggering event applies on its income tax return for the taxable year in which the triggering event occurs (or, when the triggering event is a use of the loss for foreign tax purposes, the taxable year that includes the last day of the foreign tax year during which such use occurs).

(2) Interest charge. In connection with the recapture, the taxpayer shall pay an interest charge. Except as otherwise provided in this paragraph (g)(2)(vii), such interest shall be determined under the rules of section 6601(a) as if the additional tax owed as a result of the recapture had accrued and been due and owing for the taxable year in which the losses, expenses, or deductions taken into account in computing the dual consolidated loss gave rise to a tax benefit for U.S. income tax purposes. For purposes of this paragraph (g)(2)(vii)(A)(2), a tax benefit shall be considered to have arisen in a taxable year in which such losses, expenses or deductions reduced U.S. taxable income.

(B) Rebuttal of presumptive rule. (1) Amount of recapture. The amount of dual consolidated loss that must be recaptured under this paragraph (g)(2)(vii) may be reduced if the taxpayer demonstrates, to the satisfaction of the Commissioner, the offset permitted by this paragraph (g)(2)(vii)(B). The reduction in the amount of recapture is the amount by which the dual consolidated loss would have offset other taxable income reported on a timely filed U.S. income tax return for any taxable year up to and including the year of the triggering event if such loss had been subject to the restrictions of paragraph (b) of this section (and therefore had been subject to the separate return limitation year restrictions of §§ 1.1502-21A(c) or 1.1502-21(c) (as appropriate)) commencing in the taxable year in which the loss was incurred. A taxpayer utilizing this rebuttal rule must attach to its timely filed U.S. income tax return a separate accounting showing that the income for each year that offsets the dual resident corporation's or separate unit's recapture amount is attributable only to the dual resident corporation or separate unit.

(2) Interest charge. The interest charge imposed under this paragraph (g)(2)(vii) may be appropriately reduced if the taxpayer demonstrates, to the satisfaction of the Commissioner, that the net interest owed would have been less than that provided in paragraph (g)(2)(vii)(A)(2) of this section if the taxpayer had filed an amended return for the year in which the loss was incurred, and for any other affected years up to and including the year of recapture, treating the dual consolidated loss as a loss subject to the restrictions of para-

graph (b) of this section (and therefore subject to the separate return limitation year restrictions of §§ 1.1502-21A(c) or 1.1502-21(c) (as appropriate)). A taxpayer utilizing this rebuttal rule must attach to its timely filed U.S. income tax return a computation demonstrating the reduction in the net interest owed as a result of treating the dual consolidated loss as a loss subject to the restrictions of paragraph (b) of this section.

(C) Computation of taxable income in year of recapture. (1) Presumptive rule. Except as otherwise provided in paragraph (g)(2)(vii)(C)(2) of this section, for purposes of computing the taxable income for the year of recapture, no current, carryover or carryback losses of the dual resident corporation or separate unit, of other members of the consolidated group, or of the domestic owner that are not attributable to the separate unit, may offset and absorb the recapture amount.

(2) Rebuttal of presumptive rule. The recapture amount included in gross income may be offset and absorbed by that portion of the taxpayer's (consolidated or separate) net operating loss carryover that is attributable to the dual consolidated loss being recaptured, if the taxpayer demonstrates, to the satisfaction of the Commissioner, the amount of such portion of the carryover. A taxpayer utilizing this rebuttal rule must attach to its timely filed U.S. income tax return a computation demonstrating the amount of net operating loss carryover that, under this paragraph (g)(2)(vii)(C)(2), may absorb the recapture amount included in gross income.

(D) Character and source of recapture income. The amount recaptured under this paragraph (g)(2)(vii) shall be treated as ordinary income in the year of recapture. The amount recaptured shall be treated as income having the same source and falling within the same separate category for purposes of section 904 as the dual consolidated loss being recaptured.

(E) Reconstituted net operating loss. Commencing in the taxable year immediately following the year in which the dual consolidated loss is recaptured, the dual resident corporation or separate unit shall be treated as having a net operating loss in an amount equal to the amount actually recaptured under paragraph (g)(2)(vii)(A) or (B) of this section. This reconstituted net operating loss shall be subject to the restrictions of paragraph (b) of this section (and therefore, the separate return limitation year restrictions of §§ 1.1502-21A(c) or 1.1502-21T(c) (as appropriate)). The net operating loss shall be available only for carryover, under section 172(b), to taxable years following the taxable year of recapture. For purposes of determining the remaining carryover period, the loss shall be treated as if it had been recognized in the taxable year in which the dual consolidated loss that is the basis of the recapture amount was incurred.

(F) Consequences of failing to comply with recapture provisions. (1) In general. If the taxpayer fails to comply with the recapture provisions of this paragraph (g)(2)(vii) upon the occurrence of a triggering event, then the dual resident corporation or separate unit that incurred the dual consolidated loss (or a successor-in-interest) shall not be eligible for the relief provided in paragraph (g)(2) of this section with respect to any dual consolidated losses incurred in the five taxable years beginning with the taxable year in which recapture is required.

(2) Exceptions. In the case of a triggering event other than a use of the losses, expenses, or deductions taken into account in computing the dual consolidated loss to offset income of another person under the income tax laws of a foreign country, this rule shall not apply in the following circumstances:

(i) The failure to recapture is due to reasonable cause; or

(ii) A taxpayer seeking to rebut the presumption of a triggering event satisfies the filing requirements of paragraph (g)(2)(iii)(B) of this section.

(G) Examples. The following examples illustrate this paragraph (g)(2)(vii).

Example (1). P, a domestic corporation, files a consolidated return with DRC, a dual resident corporation. In Year 1, DRC incurs a dual consolidated loss of $100 and P earns $100. P files an agreement under this paragraph (g)(2). Therefore, the consolidated group is permitted to offset P's $100 of income with DRC's $100 loss. In Year 2, DRC earns $30, which is completely offset by a $30 net operating loss incurred by P. In Year 3, DRC earns income of $25 while P recognizes no income or loss. In addition, there is a triggering event in Year 3. Therefore, under the presumptive rule of paragraph (g)(2)(vii)(A) of this section, DRC must recapture $100. However, the $100 recapture amount may be reduced by $25 (the amount by which the dual consolidated loss would have offset other taxable income if it had been subject to the separate return limitation year restrictions from Year 1) upon adequate documentation of such offset under paragraph (g)(2)(vii)(B)(1) of this section. Commencing in Year 4, the $100 (or $75) recapture amount is treated as a loss incurred by DRC in a separate return limitation year, subject to the restrictions of §§ 1.1502-21A(c) or 1.1502-21(c), as appropriate. The carryover period of the loss, for purposes of section 172(b), will start from Year 1, when the dual consolidated loss was incurred.

Example (2). The facts are the same as in Example 1, except that in Year 2, DRC earns $75 and P earns $50. In Year 3, DRC earns $25 while P earns $30. A triggering event occurs in Year 3. The $100 presumptive amount of recapture can be reduced to zero by the $75 and $25 earned by DRC in Years 2 and 3, respectively, upon adequate documentation of such offset under paragraph (g)(2)(vii)(B)(1) of this section. Nevertheless, an interest charge will be owed. Under the presumptive rule of paragraph (g)(2)(vii)(A)(2) of this section, interest will be charged on the additional tax owed on the $100 of recapture income as if the tax had accrued in Year 1 (the year in which the dual consolidated loss reduced the income of P). However, the net interest will be reduced to the amount that would have been owed if the consolidated group had filed amended returns, treating the dual consolidated loss as a loss subject to the separate return limitation year restrictions of §§ 1.1502-21A(c) or 1.1502-21(c), as appropriate, upon adequate documentation of such reduction of interest under paragraph (g)(2)(vii)(B)(2) of this section.

Example (3). P, a domestic corporation, owns DRC, a domestic corporation that is subject to the income tax laws of Country Z on a residence basis. DRC owns FE, a Country Z corporation. In Year 1, DRC incurs a net operating loss for U.S. tax purposes. Under the tax laws of Country Z, the loss is not recognized until Year 3. The Year 1 net operating loss is a dual consolidated loss under paragraph (c)(5) of this section. The consolidated group elects relief under paragraph (g)(2) of this section by filing the appropriate agreement and uses the dual consolidated loss on its U.S. income tax return. In Year 3, the dual consolidated loss is used under the laws of Country Z to offset the income of FE, which is a triggering event under paragraph (g)(2)(iii) of this section. However, the consolidated group does not recapture the dual consolidated loss. The consolidated group's failure to comply with the recapture provisions of this paragraph (g)(2)(vii) prevents DRC from being eligible for the relief provided under paragraph (g)(2) of this section for any dual consolidated losses incurred in Years 3 through 7, inclusive.

(h) Effective date. *(1) In general.* These regulations are effective for taxable years beginning on or after October 1, 1992. Section 1.1503-2A is effective for taxable years beginning after December 31, 1986, and before October 1, 1992. Paragraph (g)(2)(iv)(B)(2) of this section shall apply with respect to transactions otherwise constituting triggering events occurring on or after January 1, 2002.

(2) Taxpayers that have filed for relief under § 1.1503-2A. (i) In general. Except as provided in paragraph (h)(2)(ii) of this section, taxpayers that have filed agreements described in § 1.1503-2A(c)(3) or certifications described in § 1.1503-2A(d)(3) shall continue to be subject to the provisions of such agreements or certifications, including the amended return or recapture requirements applicable in the event of a triggering event, for the remaining term of such agreements or certifications.

(ii) Special transition rule. A taxpayer that has filed an agreement described in § 1.1503-2A(c)(3) or a certification described in § 1.1503-2A(d)(3) and that is in compliance with the provisions of § 1.1503-2A may elect to replace such agreement or certification with an agreement described in paragraph (g)(2)(i) of this section. However, a taxpayer making this election must replace all agreements and certifications filed under § 1.1503-2A. If the taxpayer is a consolidated group, the election must be made with respect to all dual resident corporations or separate units within the group. Likewise, if the taxpayer is an unaffiliated domestic owner, the election must be made with respect to all separate units of the domestic owner. The taxpayer must file the replacement agreement with its timely filed income tax return for its first taxable year commencing on or after October 1, 1992, stating that such agreement is a replacement for the agreement filed under § 1.1503-2A(c)(3) or the certification filed under § 1.1503-2A(d)(3) and identifying the taxable year for which the original agreement or certification was filed. A single agreement described in paragraph (g)(2)(i) of this section may be filed to replace more than one agreement or certification filed under § 1.1503-2A; however, each dual consolidated loss must be separately identified. A taxpayer may also elect to apply § 1.1503-2 for all open years, with respect to agreements filed under § 1.1503-2A(c)(3) or certifications filed under § 1.1503-2A(d)(3), in cases where the agreement or certification is no longer in effect and the taxpayer has complied with the provisions of § 1.1503-2A. For example, a taxpayer may have had a triggering event under § 1.1503-2A that is not a triggering event under § 1.1503-2. If the taxpayer fully complied with the requirements of the agreement entered into under § 1.1503-2A(c)(3) and filed amended U.S. income tax returns within the time required under § 1.1503-2A(c)(3), the taxpayer may file amended U.S. income tax returns consistent with the position that the earlier triggering event is no longer a triggering event.

(3) Taxpayers that are in compliance with § 1.1503-2A but have not filed for relief thereunder. A taxpayer that is in compliance with the provisions of § 1.1503-2A but has not filed an agreement described in § 1.1503-2A(c)(3) or a certification described in § 1.1503-2A(d)(3) may elect to have the provisions of § 1.1503-2 apply for any open year. In particular, a taxpayer may elect to apply the provisions of § 1.1503-2 in a case where the dual consolidated loss has been subjected to the separate return limitation year restrictions of §§ 1.1502-21A(c) or 1.1502-21(c) (as appropriate) but the losses, expenses, or deductions taken into account in computing the dual consolidated loss have not been used to offset the income of another person for foreign tax purposes. However, if a taxpayer is a consolidated group, the election must be made with respect to all dual resident corporations or separate units within the group. Likewise, if the taxpayer is an unaffiliated domestic owner, the election must be made with respect to all separate units of the domestic owner.

T.D. 8434, 9/4/92, amend T.D. 8597, 7/12/95, T.D. 8677, 6/26/96, T.D. 8823, 6/25/99, T.D. 9084, 7/29/2003, T.D. 9100, 12/18/2003, T.D. 9300, 12/7/2006.

§ 1.1503(d)-0 Table of contents.

This section lists the captions contained in §§ 1.1503(d)-1 through 1.1503(d)-8.

(1) Rebuttals, exceptions to triggering events, and recapture.

(2) Termination of ability for foreign use.

(i) In general.

(ii) Statement.

(3) Agreements filed in connection with stand-alone exception.

§ 1.1503(d)-7 Examples.

(a) In general.

(b) Presumed facts for examples.

(c) Examples.

§ 1.1503(d)-8 Effective dates.

(a) General rule.

(b) Special rules.

(1) Reduction of term of agreements filed under §§ 1.1503-2A(c)(3), 1.1503-2A(d)(3), 1.1503-2(g)(2)(i), or 1.1503-2T(g)(2)(i).

(2) Reduction of term of agreements filed under §§ 1.1503-2(g)(2)(iv)(B)(2)(i) (1992), 1.1503-2(g)(2)(iv)(B)(3)(i), or Rev. Proc. 2000-42.

(3) Relief for untimely filings.

(i) General rule.

(ii) Closing agreements.

(iii) Pending requests for relief.

(4) Multiple-party event exception to triggering events.

(5) Basis adjustment rules.

T.D. 9315, 3/16/2007.

§ 1.1503(d)-1 Definitions and special rules for filings under section 1503(d).

(a) In general. This section and §§ 1.1503(d)-2 through 1.1503(d)-8 provide rules concerning the determination and use of dual consolidated losses pursuant to section 1503(d). Paragraph (b) of this section provides definitions that apply for purposes of this section and §§ 1.1503(d)-2 through 1.1503(d)-8. Paragraph (c) of this section provides a reasonable cause exception and a signature requirement for filings.

(b) Definitions. The following definitions apply for purposes of this section and §§ 1.1503(d)-2 through 1.1503(d)-8:

(1) Domestic corporation means an entity classified as a domestic corporation under section 7701(a)(3) and (4) or otherwise treated as a domestic corporation by the Internal Revenue Code, including, but not limited to, sections 269B, 953(d), 1504(d), and 7874. However, solely for purposes of section 1503(d), the term domestic corporation shall not include a regulated investment company as defined in section 851, a real estate investment trust as defined in section 856, or an S corporation as defined in section 1361.

(2) Dual resident corporation means—

(i) A domestic corporation that is subject to an income tax of a foreign country on its worldwide income or on a residence basis. A corporation is taxed on a residence basis if it is taxed as a resident under the laws of the foreign country; and

(ii) A foreign insurance company that makes an election to be treated as a domestic corporation pursuant to section 953(d) and is treated as a member of an affiliated group for purposes of chapter 6, even if such company is not subject to an income tax of a foreign country on its worldwide income or on a residence basis. See section 953(d)(3).

(3) Hybrid entity means an entity that is not taxable as an association for Federal tax purposes, but is subject to an income tax of a foreign country as a corporation (or otherwise at the entity level) either on its worldwide income or on a residence basis.

(4) Separate unit. (i) In general. The term separate unit means either of the following that is carried on or owned, as applicable, directly or indirectly, by a domestic corporation (including a dual resident corporation):

(A) Except to the extent provided in paragraph (b)(4)(iii) of this section, a business operation outside the United States that, if carried on by a U.S. person, would constitute a foreign branch as defined in § 1.367(a)-6T(g)(1) (foreign branch separate unit).

(B) An interest in a hybrid entity (hybrid entity separate unit).

(ii) Separate unit combination rule. Except as otherwise provided in this paragraph, if a domestic owner, or two or more domestic owners that are members of the same consolidated group, have two or more separate units (individual separate units), then all such individual separate units that are located (in the case of a foreign branch separate unit) or subject to an income tax either on their worldwide income or on a residence basis (in the case of a hybrid entity an interest in which is a hybrid entity separate unit) in the same foreign country shall be treated as one separate unit (combined separate unit). See § 1.1503(d)-7(c) Example 1. Separate units of a foreign insurance company that is a dual resident corporation under paragraph (b)(2)(ii) of this section, however, shall not be combined with separate units of any other domestic corporation. Except as specifically provided in this section or §§ 1.1503(d)-2 through 1.1503(d)-8, any individual separate unit composing a combined separate unit loses its character as an individual separate unit.

(iii) Business operations that do not constitute a permanent establishment. A business operation carried on by a domestic corporation that is not a dual resident corporation shall not constitute a foreign branch separate unit, provided the business operation:

(A) Is not carried on indirectly through a hybrid entity or a transparent entity; and

(B) Is conducted in a country with which the United States has entered into an income tax convention and is not treated as a permanent establishment pursuant to that convention, or is not otherwise subject to tax on a net basis under that convention. See § 1.1503(d)-7(c) Example 2.

(iv) Foreign branch separate units held by dual resident corporations or hybrid entities in the same foreign country. A foreign branch separate unit may be owned by a dual resident corporation, or through a hybrid entity (an interest in which is a separate unit), even where the foreign branch is located in the same foreign country that subjects such dual resident corporation or hybrid entity to tax on its worldwide income or on a residence basis. But see the rule under paragraph (b)(4)(ii) of this section that combines certain same-country hybrid entity separate units and foreign branch separate units. See also § 1.1503(d)-7(c) Example 1.

(5) Dual consolidated loss means—

(i) In the case of a dual resident corporation, and except to the extent provided in § 1.1503(d)-5(b), the net operating loss (as defined in section 172(c) and the related regulations) incurred in a year in which the corporation is a dual resident corporation; and

(ii) In the case of a separate unit, the net loss attributable to the separate unit under § 1.1503(d)-5(c) through (e).

(6) Subject to tax. For purposes of determining whether a domestic corporation or another entity is subject to an income tax of a foreign country on its income, the fact that it has no actual income tax liability to the foreign country for a particular taxable year shall not be taken into account.

(7) Foreign country includes any possession of the United States.

(8) Consolidated group has the meaning provided in § 1.1502-1(h).

(9) Domestic owner means—

(i) A domestic corporation (including a dual resident corporation) that has one or more separate units or interests in a transparent entity; and

(ii) In the case of a combined separate unit, a domestic corporation (including a dual resident corporation) that has one or more individual separate units that are treated as part of the combined separate unit under paragraph (b)(4)(ii) of this section.

(10) Affiliated dual resident corporation and affiliated domestic owner mean a dual resident corporation and a domestic owner, respectively, that is a member of a consolidated group.

(11) Unaffiliated dual resident corporation, unaffiliated domestic corporation, and unaffiliated domestic owner mean a dual resident corporation, domestic corporation, and domestic owner, respectively, that is not a member of a consolidated group.

(12) Domestic affiliate means—

(i) A member of an affiliated group, without regard to the exceptions contained in section 1504(b) (other than section 1504(b)(3)) relating to includible corporations;

(ii) A domestic owner;

(iii) A separate unit; or

(iv) An interest in a transparent entity, as defined in paragraph (b)(16) of this section.

(13) Domestic use. See § 1.1503(d)-2.

(14) Foreign use. See § 1.1503(d)-3.

(15) Grantor trust means a trust, any portion of which is treated as being owned by the grantor or another person under subpart E of subchapter J of this chapter.

(16) Transparent entity. (i) In general. The term transparent entity means an entity described in this paragraph (b)(16) where all or a portion of its interests are owned, directly or indirectly, by a domestic corporation. An entity is described in this paragraph (b)(16) if the entity—

(A) Is not taxable as an association for Federal tax purposes;

(B) Is not subject to income tax in a foreign country as a corporation (or otherwise at the entity level) either on its worldwide income or on a residence basis; and

(C) Is not a pass-through entity under the laws of the applicable foreign country. For purposes of applying the preceding sentence, the applicable foreign country is the foreign country in which the relevant foreign branch separate unit is located, or the foreign country that subjects the relevant hybrid entity (an interest in which is a separate unit) or dual resident corporation to an income tax either on its worldwide income or on a residence basis.

(ii) Example. A U.S. limited liability company (LLC) does not elect to be taxed as an association for Federal tax purposes and is not subject to income tax in a foreign country as a corporation (or otherwise at the entity level) either on its worldwide income or on a residence basis. The LLC is owned by a hybrid entity (an interest in which is a separate unit) that is the relevant hybrid entity. Provided the LLC is not treated as a pass-through entity by the applicable foreign country that subjects the relevant hybrid entity to an income tax either on its worldwide income or on a residence basis, the LLC would qualify as a transparent entity. See also § 1.1503(d)-7(c) Example 26.

(17) Disregarded entity means an entity that is disregarded as an entity separate from its owner, under §§ 301.7701-1 through 301.7701-3 of this chapter, for Federal tax purposes.

(18) Partnership means an entity that is classified as a partnership, under §§ 301.7701-1 through 301.7701-3 of this chapter, for Federal tax purposes.

(19) Indirectly, when used in reference to ownership, means ownership through a partnership, a disregarded entity, or a grantor trust, regardless of whether the partnership, disregarded entity, or grantor trust is a U.S. person.

(20) Certification period means the period of time up to and including the fifth taxable year following the year in which the dual consolidated loss that is the subject of a domestic use agreement (as described in § 1.1503(d)-6(d)(1)) was incurred.

(c) Special rules for filings under section 1503(d). *(1) Reasonable cause exception.* A person that is permitted or required to file an election, agreement, statement, rebuttal, computation, or other information pursuant to section 1503(d) and these regulations, that fails to make such filing in a timely manner, shall be considered to have satisfied the timeliness requirement with respect to such filing if the person is able to demonstrate, to the Area Director, Field Examination, Small Business/Self Employed or the Director of Field Operations, Large and Mid-Size Business (Director) having jurisdiction of the taxpayer's tax return for the taxable year, that such failure was due to reasonable cause and not willful neglect. In determining whether the taxpayer has reasonable cause, the Director shall consider whether the taxpayer acted reasonably and in good faith. In general, the taxpayer must demonstrate that it exercised ordinary care and prudence in meeting its tax obligations but nonetheless did not comply with the prescribed duty within the prescribed time. Whether the taxpayer acted reasonably and in good faith will be determined after considering all the facts and circumstances. The Director shall notify the person in writing within 120 days of the filing if it is determined that the failure to comply was not due to reasonable cause, or if additional time will be needed to make such determination. For this purpose, the 120-day period shall begin on the date the taxpayer is notified in writing that the request has been received and assigned for review. If, once such period commences, the taxpayer is not again notified within 120 days, then the taxpayer shall be deemed to have established reasonable cause. The reasonable cause exception of this paragraph (c) shall only apply if, once the person becomes aware of its failure to file the election, agreement, statement, rebuttal, computation or other information in a timely manner, the person complies with the requirements of paragraph (c)(2) of this section.

(2) Requirements for reasonable cause relief. (i) Time of submission. Requests for reasonable cause relief will only be considered if once the person becomes aware of the failure to file the election, agreement, statement, rebuttal, computa-

tion or other information, the person attaches all the documents that should have been filed, as well as a written statement setting forth the reasons for the failure to timely comply, to an amended return that amends the return to which the documents should have been attached pursuant to the rules of section 1503(d) and these regulations.

(ii) Notice requirement. In addition to the requirements of paragraph (c)(2)(i) of this section, the taxpayer must provide a copy of the amended return and all required attachments to the Director as follows:

(A) If the taxpayer is under examination for any taxable year when the taxpayer requests relief, the taxpayer must provide a copy of the amended return and attachments to the personnel conducting the examination.

(B) If the taxpayer is not under examination for any taxable year when the taxpayer requests relief, the taxpayer must provide a copy of the amended return and attachments to the Director having jurisdiction of the taxpayer's return.

(3) Signature requirement. When an election, agreement, statement, rebuttal, computation, or other information is required pursuant to section 1503(d) and these regulations to be attached to and filed by the due date (including extensions) of a U.S. tax return and signed under penalties of perjury by the person who signs the return, the attachment and filing of an unsigned copy is considered to satisfy such requirement, provided the taxpayer retains the original in its records in the manner specified by § 1.6001-1(e).

T.D. 9315, 3/16/2007.

§ 1.1503(d)-2 Domestic use.

A domestic use of a dual consolidated loss shall be deemed to occur when the dual consolidated loss is made available to offset, directly or indirectly, the income of a domestic affiliate (other than the dual resident corporation or separate unit that, in each case, incurred the dual consolidated loss) in the taxable year in which the dual consolidated loss is recognized, or in any other taxable year, regardless of whether the dual consolidated loss offsets income under the income tax laws of a foreign country and regardless of whether any income that the dual consolidated loss may offset in the foreign country is, has been, or will be subject to tax in the United States. A domestic use shall be deemed to occur in the year the dual consolidated loss is included in the computation of the taxable income of a consolidated group, unaffiliated dual resident corporation, or an unaffiliated domestic owner, as applicable, even if no tax benefit results from such inclusion in that year. See § 1.1503(d)-7(c) Examples 2 through 4.

T.D. 9315, 3/16/2007.

§ 1.1503(d)-3 Foreign use.

(a) Foreign use. *(1) In general.* Except as provided in paragraph (c) of this section, a foreign use of a dual consolidated loss shall be deemed to occur when any portion of a deduction or loss taken into account in computing the dual consolidated loss is made available under the income tax laws of a foreign country to offset or reduce, directly or indirectly, any item that is recognized as income or gain under such laws and that is, or would be, considered under U.S. tax principles to be an item of—

(i) A foreign corporation as defined in section 7701(a)(3) and (a)(5); or

(ii) A direct or indirect owner of an interest in a hybrid entity, provided such interest is not a separate unit. See § 1.1503(d)-7(c) Examples 5 through 10 and 37.

(2) Indirect use. (i) General rule. Except to the extent provided in paragraph (a)(2)(ii) of this section, an item of deduction or loss shall be deemed to be made available indirectly if—

(A) One or more items are taken into account as deductions or losses for foreign tax purposes, but do not give rise to corresponding items of income or gain for U.S. tax purposes; and

(B) The item or items described in paragraph (a)(2)(i)(A) of this section have the effect of making an item of deduction or loss composing the dual consolidated loss available for a foreign use as described in paragraph (a)(1) of this section.

(ii) Exception. The general rule provided in paragraph (a)(2)(i) of this section shall not apply if the consolidated group, unaffiliated domestic owner, or unaffiliated dual resident corporation demonstrates, to the satisfaction of the Commissioner, that the item or items described in paragraph (a)(2)(i)(A) of this section that gave rise to the indirect foreign use—

(A) Were not incurred, or taken into account, with a principal purpose of avoiding the provisions of section 1503(d). For purposes of this paragraph (a)(2)(ii), an item incurred or taken into account as interest for foreign tax purposes, but disregarded for U.S. tax purposes, shall be deemed to have been incurred, or taken into account, with a principal purpose of avoiding the provisions of section 1503(d). Similarly, for purposes of this paragraph (a)(2)(ii), an item incurred or taken into account as the result of an instrument that is treated as debt for foreign tax purposes and equity for U.S. tax purposes, shall be deemed to have been incurred, or taken into account, with a principal purpose of avoiding the provisions of section 1503(d); and

(B) Were incurred, or taken into account, in the ordinary course of the dual resident corporation's or separate unit's trade or business.

(iii) Examples. See § 1.1503(d)-7(c) Examples 6 through 8.

(3) Deemed use. See paragraph (e) of this section for a deemed foreign use pursuant to the mirror legislation rule.

(b) Available for use. A foreign use shall be deemed to occur in the year in which any portion of a deduction or loss taken into account in computing the dual consolidated loss is made available for an offset described in paragraph (a) of this section, regardless of whether it actually offsets or reduces any items of income or gain under the income tax laws of the foreign country in such year, and regardless of whether any of the items that may be so offset or reduced are regarded as income under U.S. tax principles.

(c) Exceptions. *(1) In general.* Paragraphs (c)(2) through (9) of this section provide exceptions to the general definition of foreign use set forth in paragraphs (a) and (b) of this section. These exceptions only apply to a foreign use that occurs solely as a result of the conditions or circumstances described therein, and do not apply if a foreign use occurs in any other case or by any other means. For example, the exception under paragraph (c)(4) of this section (regarding certain interests in partnerships or grantor trusts) shall not apply where the item of deduction or loss is made available through a foreign consolidation regime (or similar method). In addition, these exceptions do not apply when attempting to demonstrate that no foreign use of a dual consolidated loss can occur in any other year by any means under § 1.1503(d)-6(c), (e)(2)(i), or (j)(2). But see § 1.1503(d)-6(e)(2)(ii), which takes into account the exception under paragraph (c)(7) of this section for purposes of rebutting certain asset transfers.

(2) Election or merger required to enable foreign use. Where the laws of a foreign country provide an election that would enable a foreign use, a foreign use shall be considered to occur only if the election is made. Similarly, where the laws of a foreign country would enable a foreign use through a sale, merger, or similar transaction, a foreign use shall be considered to occur only if the sale, merger, or similar transaction occurs.

(3) Presumed use where no foreign country rule for determining use. This paragraph (c)(3) applies if the losses or deductions composing the dual consolidated loss are made available under the laws of a foreign country both to offset income that would constitute a foreign use and to offset income that would not constitute a foreign use, and the laws of the foreign country do not provide applicable rules for determining which income is offset by the losses or deductions. In such a case, the losses or deductions shall be deemed to be made available to offset the income that does not constitute a foreign use, to the extent of such income, before being considered to be made available to offset the income that does constitute a foreign use. See § 1.1503(d)-7(c) Example 11.

(4) Certain interests in partnerships or grantor trusts. (i) General rule. Except to the extent provided in paragraph (c)(4)(iii) of this section, this paragraph (c)(4)(i) applies to a dual consolidated loss attributable to an interest in a hybrid entity partnership or a hybrid entity grantor trust, or to a separate unit owned indirectly through a partnership or grantor trust. In such a case, a foreign use will not be considered to occur if the foreign use is solely the result of another person's ownership of an interest in the partnership or grantor trust, as applicable, and the allocation or carry forward of an item of deduction or loss composing such dual consolidated loss as a result of such ownership. See § 1.1503(d)-7(c) Example 13.

(ii) Combined separate unit. This paragraph applies to a dual consolidated loss attributable to a combined separate unit that includes an individual separate unit to which paragraph (c)(4)(i) of this section would apply, but for the application of the separate unit combination rule provided under § 1.1503(d)-1(b)(4)(ii). In such a case, paragraph (c)(4)(i) of this section shall apply to the portion of the dual consolidated loss of such combined separate unit that is attributable, as provided under § 1.1503(d)-5(c) through (e), to the individual separate unit (otherwise described in paragraph (c)(4)(i) of this section) that is a component of the combined separate unit. See § 1.1503(d)-7(c) Example 14.

(iii) Reduction in interest. The exception under paragraph (c)(4)(i) of this section shall not apply if, at any time following the year in which the dual consolidated loss is incurred, there is more than a de minimis reduction in the domestic owner's percentage interest in the partnership or grantor trust, as applicable, as described in paragraph (c)(5) of this section. In such a case, a foreign use shall be deemed to occur at the time the reduction in interest exceeds the de minimis amount. See § 1.1503(d)-7(c) Example 13.

(5) De minimis reduction of an interest in a separate unit. (i) General rule. This paragraph applies to a de minimis reduction of a domestic owner's interest in a separate unit (including an interest described in paragraph (c)(4)(i) of this section). Except to the extent provided in paragraph (c)(5)(ii) of this section, no foreign use shall be considered to occur with respect to a dual consolidated loss as a result of an item of deduction or loss composing such dual consolidated loss being made available solely as a result of a reduction in the domestic owner's interest in the separate unit, as provided under paragraph (c)(5)(iii) of this section. See § 1.1503(d)-7(c) Example 5.

(ii) Limitations. The exception provided in paragraph (c)(5)(i) of this section shall not apply if—

(A) During any 12-month period the domestic owner's percentage interest in the separate unit is reduced by 10 percent or more, as determined by reference to the domestic owner's interest at the beginning of the 12-month period; or

(B) At any time the domestic owner's percentage interest in the separate unit is reduced by 30 percent or more, as determined by reference to the domestic owner's interest at the end of the taxable year in which the dual consolidated loss was incurred.

(iii) Reduction in interest. The following rules apply for purposes of paragraphs (c)(4) and (5) of this section. A reduction of a domestic owner's interest in a separate unit shall include a reduction resulting from another person acquiring through sale, exchange, contribution, or other means, an interest in the foreign branch or hybrid entity, as applicable. A reduction may occur either directly or indirectly, including through an interest in a partnership, a disregarded entity, or a grantor trust through which a separate unit is carried on or owned. In the case of an interest in a hybrid entity partnership or a separate unit all or a portion of which is carried on or owned through a partnership, an interest in such separate unit (or portion of such separate unit) is determined by reference to the owner's interest in the profits or the capital in the separate unit. In the case of an interest in a hybrid entity grantor trust or a separate unit all or a portion of which is carried on or owned through a grantor trust, an interest in such separate unit (or portion of such separate unit) is determined by reference to the domestic owner's share of the assets and liabilities of the separate unit.

(iv) Examples and coordination with exceptions to other triggering events. See § 1.1503(d)-7(c) Examples 5, 13, and 14. See also § 1.1503(d)-6(f)(3) and (f)(5) for rules that coordinate the de minimis exception to foreign use with exceptions to other triggering events described in § 1.1503(d)-6(e)(1), and provide an exception to foreign use following certain compulsory transfers.

(6) Certain asset basis carryovers. No foreign use shall be considered to occur with respect to a dual consolidated loss solely as a result of items of deduction or loss composing such dual consolidated loss being made available as a result of the transfer of assets of a dual resident corporation or separate unit, provided—

(i) Such items of loss and deduction are made available solely as a result of the basis of the transferred assets being determined, under foreign law, in whole or in part by reference to the basis of the assets in the hands of the dual resident corporation or separate unit;

(ii) The aggregate adjusted basis, as determined under U.S. tax principles, of all the assets so transferred during any 12-month period is less than 10 percent of the aggregate adjusted basis, as determined under U.S. tax principles, of all the dual resident corporation's or separate unit's assets, determined by reference to the assets held at the beginning of such 12-month period; and

(iii) The aggregate adjusted basis, as determined under U.S. tax principles, of all the assets so transferred at any time is less than 30 percent of the aggregate adjusted basis, as determined under U.S. tax principles, of all the dual resident corporation's or separate unit's assets, determined by reference to the assets held at the end of the taxable year in which the dual consolidated loss was generated. See § 1.1503(d)-7(c) Example 15.

(7) Assumption of certain liabilities. (i) In general. Except to the extent provided in paragraph (c)(7)(ii) of this section, no foreign use shall be considered to occur with respect to any dual consolidated loss solely as a result of an item of deduction or loss composing such dual consolidated loss being made available following the assumption of liabilities of a dual resident corporation or separate unit, provided such availability arises solely as the result of an item of deduction or loss incurred with respect to, or as a result of, such liabilities. See § 1.1503(d)-7(c) Example 16.

(ii) Ordinary course limitation. Paragraph (c)(7)(i) of this section shall apply only to the extent the liabilities assumed were incurred in the ordinary course of the dual resident corporation's, or separate unit's, trade or business. For purposes of this paragraph, liabilities incurred in the ordinary course of a trade or business shall include debt incurred to finance the trade or business of the dual resident corporation or separate unit.

(8) Multiple-party events. This paragraph applies to a transaction that qualifies for the triggering event exception described in § 1.1503(d)-6(f)(2)(i)(B) where the acquiring unaffiliated domestic corporation or consolidated group owns, directly or indirectly, more than 90 percent, but less than 100 percent, of the transferred assets or interests immediately after the transaction. In such a case, no foreign use shall be considered to occur with respect to a dual consolidated loss of the dual resident corporation or separate unit whose assets or interests were acquired, solely as a result of the less than 10 percent direct or indirect ownership of the acquired assets or interests by persons other than the acquiring unaffiliated domestic corporation or consolidated group, as applicable, immediately after the transaction. See § 1.1503(d)-7(c) Example 37.

(9) Additional guidance. The Commissioner may provide, by guidance published in the Internal Revenue Bulletin, that certain events or transactions do or do not result in a foreign use. Such guidance may also modify the triggering events and rebuttals described in § 1.1503(d)-6(e), and the exceptions thereto under § 1.1503(d)-6(f), as appropriate.

(d) Ordering rules for determining the foreign use of losses. If the laws of a foreign country provide for the foreign use of losses of a dual resident corporation or a separate unit, but do not provide applicable rules for determining the order in which such losses are used in a taxable year, the following rules shall apply:

(1) Any net loss, or net income, that the dual resident corporation or separate unit has in a taxable year shall first be used to offset net income, or loss, recognized by its affiliates in the same taxable year before any carry over of its losses is considered to be used to offset any income from the taxable year.

(2) If under the laws of the foreign country the dual resident corporation or separate unit has losses from different taxable years, it shall be deemed to use first the losses which would not constitute a triggering event that would result in the recapture of a dual consolidated loss pursuant to § 1.1503(d)-6(h). Thereafter, it shall be deemed to use first the losses from the most recent taxable year from which a loss may be carried forward or back for foreign law purposes.

(3) Where different losses or deductions (for example, capital losses and ordinary losses) of a dual resident corporation or separate unit incurred in the same taxable year are available for foreign use, the different losses shall be deemed to be used on a pro rata basis. See § 1.1503(d)-7(c) Example 12.

(e) Mirror legislation rule. *(1) In general.* Except as provided in paragraph (e)(2) of this section and § 1.1503(d)-6(b) (relating to agreements entered into between the United States and a foreign country), a foreign use shall be deemed to occur if the income tax laws of a foreign country would deny any opportunity for the foreign use of the dual consolidated loss in the year in which the dual consolidated loss is incurred (mirror legislation), determined by assuming that such foreign country had recognized the dual consolidated loss in such year, for any of the following reasons:

(i) The dual resident corporation or separate unit that incurred the loss is subject to income taxation by another country (for example, the United States) on its worldwide income or on a residence basis.

(ii) The loss may be available to offset income (other than income of the dual resident corporation or separate unit) under the laws of another country (for example, the United States).

(iii) The deductibility of any portion of a deduction or loss taken into account in computing the dual consolidated loss depends on whether such amount is deductible under the laws of another country (for example, the United States). See § 1.1503(d)-7(c) Examples 17 through 19.

(2) Stand-alone exception. (i) In general. This paragraph (e)(2) applies if, in the absence of the mirror legislation described in paragraph (e)(1) of this section, no item of deduction or loss composing the dual consolidated loss of such dual resident corporation or separate unit would otherwise be available for a foreign use in the taxable year in which such dual consolidated loss is incurred. This determination is made without regard to whether such availability is limited by election (or other similar procedure). However, for purposes of this paragraph (e)(2)(i), no item of deduction or loss composing the dual consolidated loss of a dual resident corporation or separate unit is considered to be made available for foreign use solely because the laws of a foreign country would enable a foreign use through a sale, merger, or similar transaction (provided no such sale, merger, or similar transaction actually occurs). In such a case, no foreign use shall be considered to occur pursuant to paragraph (e)(1) of this section with respect to the dual consolidated loss, provided the requirements of paragraph (e)(2)(ii) of this section are satisfied. See § 1.1503(d)-7(c) Examples 17 through 19.

(ii) Stand-alone domestic use agreement. In order to qualify for the exception under paragraph (e)(2)(i) of this section, the consolidated group, unaffiliated dual resident corporation, or unaffiliated domestic owner, as the case may be, must enter into a domestic use agreement in accordance with the provisions of § 1.1503(d)-6(d) and, in addition, must include the following items in such domestic use agreement:

(A) A statement that the document is also being submitted under the provisions of paragraph (e)(2) of this section.

(B) A certification that the conditions of paragraph (e)(2)(i) of this section are satisfied during the taxable year in which the dual consolidated loss is incurred.

(C) An agreement to include with each annual certification required under § 1.1503(d)-6(g), a certification that the conditions described in paragraph (e)(2)(i) of this section are satisfied during the taxable year of each such certification.

(iii) Termination of stand-alone domestic use agreement. This paragraph (e)(2)(iii) applies to a consolidated group, unaffiliated dual resident corporation, or unaffiliated domestic owner, as the case may be, that entered into a domestic use agreement pursuant to paragraph (e)(2)(ii) of this section, with respect to a dual consolidated loss, and which subsequently makes an election pursuant to § 1.1503(d)-6(b) (relating to agreements entered into between the United States and a foreign country) with respect to such dual consolidated loss. In such a case, the dual consolidated loss shall be subject to the election under § 1.1503(d)-6(b) (and any related agreements, representations and conditions), and the domestic use agreement entered into pursuant to paragraph (e)(2)(ii) of this section shall terminate and have no further effect.

T.D. 9315, 3/16/2007.

§ 1.1503(d)-4 Domestic use limitation and related operating rules.

(a) Scope. This section prescribes rules that apply when the general limitation on the domestic use of a dual consolidated loss under paragraph (b) of this section applies. Thus, the rules of this section do not apply when an exception to the domestic use limitation applies (for example, as a result of a domestic use election under § 1.1503(d)-6(d)). In general, when the domestic use limitation applies, the dual consolidated loss of a dual resident corporation or separate unit is subject to the separate return limitation year (SRLY) provisions of § 1.1502-21(c), as modified under this section. Paragraph (c) of this section provides rules that determine the effect of a dual consolidated loss on a consolidated group, an unaffiliated dual resident corporation, or an unaffiliated domestic owner. Paragraph (d) of this section provides rules that eliminate dual consolidated losses following certain transactions or events. Paragraph (e) of this section contains provisions that prevent dual consolidated losses from offsetting tainted income. Finally, paragraph (f) of this section provides rules for computing foreign tax credits.

(b) Limitation on domestic use of a dual consolidated loss. Except as provided in § 1.1503(d)-6, the domestic use of a dual consolidated loss is not permitted. See § 1.1503(d)-2 for the definition of a domestic use. See also § 1.1503(d)-7(c) Examples 2 through 4.

(c) Effect of a dual consolidated loss on a consolidated group, unaffiliated dual resident corporation, or unaffiliated domestic owner. For any taxable year in which a dual resident corporation or separate unit has a dual consolidated loss that is subject to the domestic use limitation of paragraph (b) of this section, the following rules shall apply:

(1) Dual resident corporation. This paragraph (c)(1) applies to a dual consolidated loss of a dual resident corporation. The unaffiliated dual resident corporation, or consolidated group that includes the dual resident corporation, shall compute its taxable income (or loss), or consolidated taxable income (or loss), respectively, without taking into account those items of deduction and loss that compose the dual resident corporation's dual consolidated loss. For this purpose, the dual consolidated loss shall be treated as composed of a pro rata portion of each item of deduction and loss of the dual resident corporation taken into account in calculating the dual consolidated loss. The dual consolidated loss is subject to the limitations on its use contained in paragraph (c)(3) of this section and, subject to such limitations, may be carried over or back for use in other taxable years as a separate net operating loss carryover or carryback of the dual resident corporation arising in the year incurred. If the dual resident corporation owns a separate unit or an interest in a transparent entity, the limitations contained in paragraph (c)(3) of this section shall apply to the dual resident corporation as if the separate unit or interest in a transparent entity were a separate domestic corporation that filed a consolidated return with the unaffiliated dual resident corporation, or with the consolidated group of the affiliated dual resident corporation, as applicable.

(2) Separate unit. This paragraph (c)(2) applies to a dual consolidated loss that is attributable to a separate unit. The unaffiliated domestic owner of a separate unit, or the consolidated group of an affiliated domestic owner of a separate unit, shall compute its taxable income (or loss) or consolidated taxable income (or loss), respectively, without taking into account those items of deduction and loss that compose the separate unit's dual consolidated loss. For this purpose, the dual consolidated loss shall be treated as composed of a pro rata portion of each item of deduction and loss of the separate unit taken into account in calculating the dual consolidated loss. The dual consolidated loss is subject to the limitations contained in paragraph (c)(3) of this section as if the separate unit to which the dual consolidated loss is attributable were a separate domestic corporation that filed a consolidated return with its unaffiliated domestic owner or with the consolidated group of its affiliated domestic owner, as applicable. Subject to such limitations, the dual consolidated loss may be carried over or back for use in other taxable years as a separate net operating loss carryover or carryback of the separate unit arising in the year incurred. See § 1.1503(d)-7(c) Examples 29 and 38.

(3) SRLY limitation. The dual consolidated loss shall be treated as a loss incurred by the dual resident corporation or separate unit in a separate return limitation year and shall be subject to all of the limitations of § 1.1502-21(c) (SRLY limitation), subject to the following modifications—

(i) Notwithstanding § 1.1502-1(f)(2)(i), the SRLY limitation is applied to any dual consolidated loss of a common parent that is a dual resident corporation, or any dual consolidated loss attributable to a separate unit of a common parent;

(ii) The SRLY limitation is applied without regard to § 1.1502-21(c)(2) (SRLY subgroup limitation) and 1.1502-21(g) (overlap with section 382);

(iii) For purposes of calculating the general SRLY limitation under § 1.1502-21(c)(1)(i), the calculation of aggregate consolidated taxable income shall only include items of income, gain, deduction, and loss generated—

(A) In the case of a hybrid entity separate unit, in years in which the hybrid entity (an interest in which is a separate unit) is taxed as a corporation (or otherwise at the entity level) either on its worldwide income or as a resident in the same foreign country in which it was so taxed during the year in which the dual consolidated loss was generated; and

(B) In the case of a foreign branch separate unit, in years in which the foreign branch qualified as a separate unit in the same foreign country in which it so qualified during the year in which the dual consolidated loss was generated.

(iv) For purposes of calculating the general SRLY limitation under § 1.1502-21(c)(1)(i), the calculation of aggregate consolidated taxable income shall not include any amount included in income pursuant to § 1.1503(d)-6(h) (relating to the recapture of a dual consolidated loss).

(4) Items of a dual consolidated loss used in other taxable years. A pro rata portion of each item of deduction or loss that composes the dual consolidated loss shall be considered to be used when the dual consolidated loss is used in other taxable years. See § 1.1503(d)-7(c) Examples 29 and 38.

(5) Reconstituted net operating losses. For additional rules and limitations that apply to reconstituted net operating losses, see § 1.1503(d)-6(h)(6).

(d) Elimination of a dual consolidated loss after certain transactions. *(1) General rule.* In general, a dual resident corporation has a net operating loss (and, therefore, a dual consolidated loss) only if it sustains such loss, or succeeds to such loss as a result of acquiring the assets of a corporation that sustained the loss in a transaction described in section 381(a). Similarly, a net loss generally is attributable to a separate unit of a domestic owner (and therefore is a dual consolidated loss) only if the domestic owner incurs the deductions or losses, or succeeds to such deductions or losses in a transaction described in section 381(a). Except as provided in § 1.1503(d)-6(h)(6)(iii), section 1503(d) and these regulations do not alter these general rules. Thus, the provisions of §§ 1.1503(d)-1 through 1.1503(d)-8 generally do not cause a corporation to have a dual consolidated loss if it did not sustain (or inherit) the loss. Instead, these regulations either eliminate a dual consolidated loss that a corporation sustained (or inherited), or prevent the carryover of a dual consolidated loss under section 381 that would ordinarily occur, as a result of certain transactions.

(i) Transactions described in section 381(a). This paragraph (d)(1)(i) applies to a dual consolidated loss of a dual resident corporation, or of a domestic owner attributable to a separate unit, that is subject to the domestic use limitation rule of paragraph (b) of this section. In such a case, and except as provided in paragraph (d)(2) of this section, the dual consolidated loss shall not carry over to another corporation in a transaction described in section 381(a) and, as a result, shall be eliminated. See § 1.1503(d)-7(c) Example 20.

(ii) Cessation of separate unit status. This paragraph (d)(1)(ii) applies when a separate unit of an unaffiliated domestic owner ceases to be a separate unit of its domestic owner, or when a separate unit of an affiliated domestic owner ceases to be a separate unit with respect to its domestic owner and all other members of the affiliated domestic owner's consolidated group. In such a case, and except as provided in paragraph (d)(2)(iii) of this section, a dual consolidated loss of the domestic owner attributable to such separate unit, that is subject to the domestic use limitation of paragraph (b) of this section, shall be eliminated. For purposes of this paragraph (d)(1)(ii), a separate unit may cease to be a separate unit if, for example, such separate unit is terminated, dissolved, liquidated, sold, or otherwise disposed of. See § 1.1503(d)-7(c) Example 21.

(2) Exceptions. (i) Certain section 368(a)(1)(F) reorganizations. Paragraph (d)(1)(i) of this section (relating to transactions described in section 381(a)) shall not apply to a dual consolidated loss of a dual resident corporation that undergoes a reorganization described in section 368(a)(1)(F) in which the resulting corporation is a domestic corporation. In such a case, the dual consolidated loss of the resulting corporation continues to be subject to the limitations of paragraphs (b) and (c) of this section, applied as if the resulting corporation incurred the dual consolidated loss.

(ii) Acquisition of a dual resident corporation by another dual resident corporation. If a dual resident corporation transfers its assets to another dual resident corporation in a transaction described in section 381(a), and the transferee corporation is a resident of (or is taxed on its worldwide income by) the same foreign country of which the transferor was a resident (or was taxed on its worldwide income), then paragraph (d)(1)(i) of this section shall not apply with respect to dual consolidated losses of the dual resident corporation, and income generated by the transferee may be offset by the carryover dual consolidated losses of the transferor, subject to the limitations of paragraphs (b) and (c) of this section applied as if the transferee incurred the dual consolidated loss. Dual consolidated losses of the transferor dual resident corporation may not, however, be used to offset income attributable to separate units or interests in transparent entities owned by the transferee because they constitute domestic affiliates under § 1.1503(d)-1(b)(12)(iii) and (iv), respectively.

(iii) Acquisition of a separate unit by a domestic corporation. This paragraph (d)(2)(iii) provides exceptions to the general rules in paragraphs (d)(1)(i) and (ii) of this section that eliminate the dual consolidated loss of a domestic owner that is attributable to a separate unit following certain transactions or events. The exceptions set forth in this paragraph (d)(2)(iii) shall only apply where a domestic owner transfers its assets to a domestic corporation (transferee corporation) in a transaction described in section 381(a).

(A) Acquisition by a corporation that is not a member of the same consolidated group. (1) General rule. If a domestic owner transfers either an individual separate unit or a combined separate unit to a transferee corporation that is not a member of its consolidated group in a transaction described in section 381(a), and the transferee corporation, or a member of the transferee's consolidated group, is a domestic owner of the transferred separate unit immediately after the transaction, then paragraphs (d)(1)(i) and (ii) of this section shall not apply to such transfer. In addition, income of the transferee, or a member of the transferee's consolidated group, that is attributable to the transferred separate unit may be offset by the carryover dual consolidated losses of the transferor domestic owner that were attributable to the transferred separate unit, subject to the limitations of paragraphs (b) and (c) of this section applied as if the transferee incurred the dual consolidated losses and such losses were attributable to the separate unit. See § 1.1503(d)-7(c) Example 21.

(2) Combination with separate units of the transferee. This paragraph (d)(2)(iii)(A)(2) applies to a transaction described in paragraph (d)(2)(iii)(A)(1) of this section where the transferred separate unit is combined with another separate unit of the transferee, or another member of the transferee's consolidated group, immediately after the transfer as provided under § 1.1503(d)-1(b)(4)(ii). In such a case, income generated by the transferee, or another member of the transferee's consolidated group, that is attributable to the combined separate unit may be offset by the carryover dual consolidated losses that were attributable to the transferred separate unit, subject to the limitations of paragraphs (b) and (c) of this section, applied as if the transferee incurred the dual consolidated losses and such losses were attributable to the combined separate unit.

(B) Acquisition by a member of the same consolidated group. If an affiliated domestic owner transfers its assets to another member of its consolidated group in a transaction described in section 381(a), and the transferee corporation or another member of such consolidated group is a domestic owner of the separate unit to which the dual consolidated loss was attributable, then paragraphs (d)(1)(i) and (ii) of this section shall not apply. In addition, income generated by the transferee that is attributable to the transferred separate unit may be offset by the carryover dual consolidated losses that were attributable to the transferred separate unit, subject to the limitations of paragraphs (b) and (c) of this section, applied as if the transferee incurred the dual consolidated losses and such losses were attributable to the separate unit. See § 1.1503(d)-7(c) Example 21.

(iv) Special rules for foreign insurance companies. See § 1.1503(d)-6(a) for additional limitations that apply where the transferor is a foreign insurance company that is a dual resident corporation under § 1.1503(d)-1(b)(2)(ii).

(e) Special rule denying the use of a dual consolidated loss to offset tainted income. *(1) In general.* Dual consolidated losses incurred by a dual resident corporation that are subject to the domestic use limitation rule under paragraph (b) of this section shall not be used to offset income it earns after it ceases to be a dual resident corporation to the extent that such income is tainted income.

(2) Tainted income. (i) Definition. For purposes of paragraph (e)(1) of this section, the term tainted income means—

(A) Income or gain recognized on the sale or other disposition of tainted assets; and

(B) Income derived as a result of holding tainted assets.

(ii) Income presumed to be derived from holding tainted assets. In the absence of evidence establishing the actual amount of income that is attributable to holding tainted assets, the portion of a corporation's income in a particular taxable year that is treated as tainted income derived as a result of holding tainted assets shall be an amount equal to the corporation's taxable income for the year (other than income described in paragraph (e)(2)(i)(A) of this section) multiplied by a fraction, the numerator of which is the fair market value of all tainted assets acquired by the corporation (determined at the time such assets were so acquired) and the denominator of which is the fair market value of the total assets owned by the corporation at the end of such taxable year. To establish the actual amount of income that is attributable to holding tainted assets, documentation must be attached to, and filed by the due date (including extensions) of, the domestic corporation's tax return or the consolidated tax return of an affiliated group of which it is a member, as the case may be, for the taxable year in which the income is generated. See § 1.1503(d)-7(c) Example 22.

(3) Tainted assets defined. For purposes of paragraph (e)(2) of this section, tainted assets are any assets acquired by a domestic corporation in a nonrecognition transaction, as defined in section 7701(a)(45), any assets otherwise transferred to the corporation as a contribution to capital, or any assets otherwise received from a separate unit or a transparent entity owned by such domestic corporation, at any time during the three taxable years immediately preceding the taxable year in which the corporation ceases to be a dual resident corporation or at any time thereafter.

(4) Exceptions. Income derived from assets acquired by a domestic corporation shall not be subject to the limitation described in paragraph (e)(1) of this section, and in addition shall not be treated as tainted assets as defined in paragraph (e)(3) of this section, if—

(i) For the taxable year in which the assets were acquired, the corporation did not have a dual consolidated loss (or a carryforward of a dual consolidated loss to such year); or

(ii) The assets were acquired as replacement property in the ordinary course of business.

(f) Computation of foreign tax credit limitation. If a dual consolidated loss is subject to the domestic use limitation rule under paragraph (b) of this section, the consolidated group, unaffiliated dual resident corporation, or unaffiliated domestic owner shall compute its foreign tax credit limitation by applying the limitations of paragraph (c) of this section. Thus, the items constituting the dual consolidated loss are not taken into account until the year in which such items are absorbed.

T.D. 9315, 3/16/2007.

§ 1.1503(d)-5 Attribution of items and basis adjustments.

(a) In general. This section provides rules for determining the amount of income or dual consolidated loss of a dual resident corporation. This section also provides rules for determining the income or dual consolidated loss attributable to a separate unit, as well as the income or loss attributable to an interest in a transparent entity. Paragraph (b) of this section provides rules with respect to dual resident corporations. Paragraph (c) of this section provides rules with respect to separate units and interests in transparent entities. These determinations are required for various purposes under section 1503(d). For example, it is necessary for purposes of applying the domestic use limitation rule under § 1.1503(d)-4(b) to a dual consolidated loss, and for determining the extent to which a dual consolidated loss is available to offset income as provided under § 1.1503(d)-4(c). These determinations are also necessary for purposes of determining whether the amount subject to recapture may be reduced pursuant to § 1.1503(d)-6(h)(2). Paragraph (d) of this section provides rules with respect to the foreign tax treatment of items. Paragraph (e) of this section provides rules regarding the treatment of items where a dual resident corporation, separate unit, or transparent entity only qualified as such during a portion of a taxable year. Paragraph (f) of this section provides rules for determining the assets and liabilities of a separate unit. Finally, paragraph (g) of this section provides rules for making basis adjustments to stock of certain members of a consolidated group and to certain interests in partnerships. The rules in this section apply for purposes of §§ 1.1503(d)-1 through 1.1503(d)-7.

(b) Determination of amount of income or dual consolidated loss of a dual resident corporation. *(1) In general.* For purposes of determining whether a dual resident corporation has income or a dual consolidated loss for the taxable year, and except as provided in paragraph (b)(2) of this section, the dual resident corporation shall compute its income or dual consolidated loss taking into account only those items of income, gain, deduction, and loss from such year (including any items recognized by such corporation as a result of an election under section 338). In the case of an affiliated dual resident corporation, such calculation shall be made in accordance with the rules set forth in the regulations under section 1502 governing the computation of consolidated taxable income. See also paragraphs (d) and (e) of this section.

(2) Exceptions. For purposes of determining the income or dual consolidated loss of a dual resident corporation, the following shall not be taken into account—

(i) Any net capital loss of the dual resident corporation;

(ii) Any carryover or carryback losses; or

(iii) Any items of income, gain, deduction, and loss that are attributable to a separate unit or an interest in a transparent entity of the dual resident corporation.

(c) Determination of amount of income or dual consolidated loss attributable to a separate unit, and income or loss attributable to an interest in a transparent entity. *(1) In general.* (i) Scope and purpose. Paragraphs (c) through (e) of this section apply for purposes of determining the income or dual consolidated loss attributable to a separate unit, and the income or loss attributable to an interest in a transparent entity, for the taxable year. In the case of an affiliated domestic owner, this determination shall be made in accordance with the rules set forth in the regulations under section 1502 governing the computation of consolidated taxable income. These rules apply solely for purposes of section 1503(d).

(ii) Only items of domestic owner taken into account. The computation made under paragraphs (c) through (e) of this section shall be made using only those existing items of income, gain, deduction, and loss of the separate unit's or transparent entity's domestic owner (or owners, in the case of certain combined separate units), as determined for U.S. tax purposes. These items must be translated into U.S. dollars (if necessary) at the appropriate exchange rate provided under section 989(b), as modified by regulations. The computation shall be made as if the separate unit or interest in a transparent entity were a domestic corporation, using items that are attributable to the separate unit or interest in a transparent entity. However, for purposes of making this computation, net capital losses, and carryover or carryback losses, of the domestic owner shall not be taken into account. Items of income, gain, deduction, and loss that are otherwise disregarded for U.S. tax purposes shall not be regarded or taken into account for purposes of this section. See § 1.1503(d)-7(c) Examples 6 and 23 through 25.

(iii) Separate application. The attribution rules of this section shall apply separately to each separate unit or interest in a transparent entity. Thus, an item of income, gain, deduction, or loss shall not be considered attributable to more than one separate unit or interest in a transparent entity. In addition, for purposes of this section items of income, gain, deduction, and loss attributable to a separate unit or an interest in a transparent entity shall not offset items of income, gain, deduction, and loss of another separate unit or interest in a transparent entity. See § 1.1503(d)-7(c) Example 24. See also the separate unit combination rule in § 1.1503(d)-1(b)(4)(ii).

(2) Foreign branch separate unit. (i) In general. Except to the extent provided in paragraph (c)(4) of this section, for purposes of determining the items of income, gain, deduction (other than interest), and loss of a domestic owner that are attributable to the domestic owner's foreign branch separate unit, the principles of section 864(c)(2), (c)(4), and (c)(5), as set forth in § 1.864-4(c), and §§ 1.864-5 through 1.864-7, shall apply. The principles apply without regard to limitations imposed on the effectively connected treatment of income, gain, or loss under the trade or business safe harbors in section 864(b) and the limitations for treating foreign source income as effectively connected under section 864(c)(4)(D). Except as provided in paragraph (c)(2)(iii) of this section, for purposes of determining the domestic owner's interest expense that is attributable to a foreign branch separate unit, the principles of § 1.882-5, as modified in paragraph (c)(2)(ii) of this section, shall apply. When applying the principles of section 864(c) (as modified by this paragraph) and § 1.882-5 (as modified in paragraph (c)(2)(ii) of this section), the foreign branch separate unit's domestic owner shall be treated as a foreign corporation, the foreign branch separate unit shall be treated as a trade or business within the United States, and the other assets of the domestic owner shall be treated as assets that are not U.S. assets.

(ii) Principles of § 1.882-5. For purposes of paragraph (c)(2)(i) of this section, the principles of § 1.882-5 shall be applied, subject to the following modifications—

(A) Except as otherwise provided in this section, only the assets, liabilities, and interest expense of the domestic owner shall be taken into account in the § 1.882-5 formula;

(B) Except as provided under paragraph (c)(2)(ii)(C) of this section, a taxpayer may use the alternative tax book value method under § 1.861-9(i) for purposes of determining the value of its U.S. assets pursuant to § 1.882-5(b)(2) and its worldwide assets pursuant to § 1.882-5(c)(2);

(C) For purposes of determining the value of a U.S. asset pursuant to § 1.882-5(b)(2), and worldwide assets pursuant to § 1.882-5(c)(2), the taxpayer must use the same methodology under § 1.861-9T(g) (that is, tax book value, alternative tax book value, or fair market value) that the taxpayer uses for purposes of allocating and apportioning interest expense for the taxable year under section 864(e);

(D) Asset values shall be determined pursuant to § 1.861-9T(g)(2); and

(E) For purposes of determining the step-two U.S. connected liabilities, the amounts of worldwide assets and liabilities under § 1.882-5(c)(2)(iii) and (iv) must be determined in accordance with U.S. tax principles, rather than substantially in accordance with U.S. tax principles.

(iii) Exception where foreign country attributes interest expense solely by reference to books and records. The principles of § 1.882-5 shall not apply if the foreign country in which the foreign branch separate unit is located determines, for purposes of computing taxable income (or loss) of a permanent establishment or branch of a nonresident corporation under the laws of the foreign country, the interest expense of the foreign branch separate unit by taking into account only the items of interest expense reflected on the foreign branch separate unit's books and records. In such a case, only those items of the domestic owner's interest expense reflected on the foreign branch separate unit's books and records (as provided in paragraph (c)(3)(i) of this section), adjusted to conform to U.S. tax principles, shall be attributable to the foreign branch separate unit. This paragraph shall not apply where the foreign country does not use a method of attributing interest based solely on the interest that is reflected on the books and records. For example, this paragraph does not apply if the foreign country uses a method for attributing interest expense similar to § 1.882-5 or that set forth in the Organization for Economic Co-operation and Development Report on the Attribution of Profits to Permanent Establishments, Part II (Banks), December 2006. See http://www.oecd.org.

(3) Hybrid entity separate unit and an interest in a transparent entity. (i) General rule. This paragraph (c)(3) applies to determine the items of income, gain, deduction, and loss of a domestic owner that are attributable to a hybrid entity separate unit, or an interest in a transparent entity, of such domestic owner. Except to the extent provided in paragraph (c)(4) of this section, the domestic owner's items of income, gain, deduction, and loss are attributable to the extent they are reflected on the books and records of the hybrid entity or transparent entity, as applicable, as adjusted to conform to

U.S. tax principles. See § 1.1503(d)-7(c) Examples 23 through 26. For purposes of this paragraph (c)(3), the term "books and records" has the meaning provided under § 1.989(a)-1(d). The treatment of items for foreign tax purposes, including under any type of foreign anti-deferral regime, is not relevant for purposes of determining whether items are reflected on the books and records of the entity, or for purposes of making adjustments to such items to conform to U.S. tax principles. The method described in the second sentence of this paragraph shall not apply to the extent that the Commissioner determines that booking practices are employed with a principal purpose of avoiding the principles of section 1503(d), including inconsistently treating the same or similar items of income, gain, deduction, and loss. In such a case, the Commissioner may reallocate the items of income, gain, deduction, and loss between or among a domestic owner, its hybrid entities, its transparent entities (and interests therein), its separate units, or any other entity, as applicable, in a manner consistent with the principles of section 1503(d) and which properly reflects income (or loss).

(ii) Interests in certain disregarded entities, partnerships, and grantor trusts owned by a hybrid entity or transparent entity. This paragraph (c)(3)(ii) applies if a hybrid entity or transparent entity to which paragraph (c)(3)(i) of this section applies owns, directly or indirectly (other than through a hybrid entity or transparent entity), an interest in an entity that is treated as a disregarded entity, partnership, or grantor trust for U.S. tax purposes, but is not a hybrid entity or a transparent entity. For example, the rules of this paragraph would apply when a hybrid entity holds an interest in a limited partnership created in the United States and, for both U.S. and foreign tax purposes the entity is considered a partnership. In such a case, and except to the extent provided in paragraph (c)(4) of this section, items of income, gain, deduction, and loss that are reflected on the books and records of such disregarded entity, partnership or grantor trust, as determined under paragraph (c)(3)(i) of this section, shall be treated as being reflected on the books and records of the hybrid entity or transparent entity for purposes of applying paragraph (c)(3)(i) of this section. See § 1.1503(d)-7(c) Example 26.

(4) Special rules. The following special rules shall apply for purposes of attributing items to separate units or interests in transparent entities under this section:

(i) Allocation of items between certain tiered separate units and interests in transparent entities. (A) Foreign branch separate unit. This paragraph (c)(4)(i) applies where a hybrid entity or transparent entity owns directly or indirectly (other than through a hybrid entity or a transparent entity), a foreign branch separate unit. For purposes of determining items of income, gain, deduction, and loss of the domestic owner that are attributable to the domestic owner's foreign branch separate unit described in the preceding sentence, only items of income, gain, deduction, and loss that are attributable to the domestic owner's interest in the hybrid entity, or transparent entity, as provided in paragraph (c)(3) of this section, shall be taken into account. Further, only assets, liabilities, and activities of the domestic owner's interest in the hybrid entity or the transparent entity shall be taken into account under paragraph (c)(2) of this section when applying the principles of 864(c)(2), (c)(4), (c)(5) (as set forth in § 1.864-4(c), and §§ 1.864-5 through 1.864-7), and § 1.882-5 (as modified in paragraph (c)(2)(ii) of this section). See § 1.1503(d)-7(c) Examples 25 and 26.

(B) Hybrid entity separate unit or interest in a transparent entity. For purposes of determining items of income, gain, deduction, and loss that are attributable to a hybrid entity separate unit or an interest in a transparent entity described in paragraph (c)(3) of this section, such items shall not be taken into account to the extent they are attributable to a foreign branch separate unit pursuant to paragraph (c)(4)(i)(A) of this section. See § 1.1503(d)-7(c) Examples 25 and 26.

(ii) Combined separate unit. If two or more individual separate units defined in § 1.1503(d)-1(b)(4)(i) are treated as one combined separate unit pursuant to § 1.1503(d)-1(b)(4)(ii), the items of income, gain, deduction, and loss that are attributable to the combined separate unit shall be determined as follows:

(A) Items of income, gain, deduction, and loss are first attributed to each individual separate unit without regard to § 1.1503(d)-1(b)(4)(ii), pursuant to the rules of paragraphs (c) through (e) of this section.

(B) The combined separate unit then takes into account all of the items of income, gain, deduction, and loss attributable to its individual separate units pursuant to paragraph (c)(4)(ii)(A) of this section. See § 1.1503(d)-7(c) Examples 25 and 26.

(iii) Gain or loss on the direct or indirect disposition of a separate unit or an interest in a transparent entity. (A) In general. This paragraph (c)(4)(iii) applies for purposes of attributing items of income, gain, deduction, and loss that are recognized on the sale, exchange, or other disposition of a separate unit or an interest in a transparent entity (or an interest in a disregarded entity, partnership, or grantor trust that owns, directly or indirectly, a separate unit or an interest in a transparent entity). For purposes of this paragraph (c)(4)(iii), items taken into account on the sale, exchange, or other disposition include loss recapture income or gain under section 367(a)(3)(C) or 904(f)(3), and gain or loss recognized by the domestic owner as the result of an election under section 338. In cases where this paragraph (c)(4)(iii)(A) applies, items taken into account on the sale, exchange, or other disposition shall be attributable to the separate unit or the interest in the transparent entity to the extent of gain or loss that would have been recognized had the separate unit or transparent entity sold all its assets (as determined in paragraph (f) of this section) in a taxable exchange, immediately before the sale, exchange, or other disposition (deemed sale). For purposes of a deemed sale described in this paragraph (c)(4)(iii), the assets are treated as being sold for an amount equal to their fair market value, plus the assumption of the liabilities of the separate unit or interest in a transparent entity (as determined in paragraph (f) of this section). See § 1.1503(d)-7(c) Example 27.

(B) Multiple separate units or interests in transparent entities. This paragraph (c)(4)(iii)(B) applies to a sale, exchange, or other disposition described in paragraph (c)(4)(iii)(A) of this section that results in more than one separate unit or interest in a transparent entity being, directly or indirectly, disposed of. In such a case, items of income, gain, deduction, and loss recognized on such sale, exchange, or other disposition are allocated and attributed to each separate unit or interest in a transparent entity, based on the relative gain or loss that would have been recognized by each separate unit or interest in a transparent entity pursuant to a deemed sale of their assets. See § 1.1503(d)-7(c) Example 28.

(iv) Inclusions on stock. Any amount included in income of a domestic owner arising from ownership of stock in a foreign corporation (for example, under sections 78, 951, or 986(c)) through a separate unit, or interest in a transparent entity, shall be attributable to the separate unit or interest in a transparent entity, if an actual dividend from such foreign corporation would have been so attributed. See § 1.1503(d)-7(c) Example 24.

(v) Foreign currency gain or loss recognized under section 987. Foreign currency gain or loss of a domestic owner recognized under section 987 as a result of a transfer or remittance shall not be attributable to a separate unit or an interest in a transparent entity.

(vi) Recapture of dual consolidated loss. If all or a portion of a dual consolidated loss that was attributable to a separate unit is included in the gross income of a domestic owner under the recapture provisions of § 1.1503(d)-6(h), such amount shall be attributable to the separate unit that incurred the dual consolidated loss being recaptured. See § 1.1503(d)-7(c) Examples 38 and 40.

(d) Foreign tax treatment disregarded. The fact that a particular item taken into account in computing the income or dual consolidated loss of a dual resident corporation or a separate unit, or the income or loss of an interest in a transparent entity, is not taken into account in computing income (or loss) subject to a foreign country's income tax shall not cause such item to be excluded from being taken into account under paragraph (b), (c), or (e) of this section.

(e) Items generated or incurred while a dual resident corporation, a separate unit, or a transparent entity. For purposes of determining the amount of the dual consolidated loss of a dual resident corporation for the taxable year, only the items of income, gain, deduction, and loss generated or incurred during the period the dual resident corporation qualified as such shall be taken into account. For purposes of determining the amount of income of a dual resident corporation for the taxable year, all the items of income, gain, deduction, and loss generated or incurred during the year shall be taken into account. For purposes of determining the amount of the income or dual consolidated loss attributable to a separate unit, or the income or loss attributable to an interest in a transparent entity, for the taxable year, only the items of income, gain, deduction, and loss generated or incurred during the period the separate unit or the interest in the transparent entity qualified as such shall be taken into account. For purposes of this paragraph (e), the allocation of items to periods shall be made under the principles of § 1.1502-76(b).

(f) Assets and liabilities of a separate unit or an interest in a transparent entity. A separate unit or an interest in a transparent entity shall be treated as owning assets to the extent items of income, gain, deduction, and loss from such assets would be attributable to the separate unit or interest in the transparent entity under paragraphs (c) through (e) of this section. Similarly, liabilities shall be treated as liabilities of a separate unit, or an interest in a transparent entity, to the extent interest expense incurred on such liabilities would be attributable to the separate unit, or the interest in a transparent entity, under paragraphs (c) through (e) of this section.

(g) Basis adjustments. *(1) Affiliated dual resident corporation or affiliated domestic owner.* If a member of a consolidated group owns stock in an affiliated dual resident corporation or an affiliated domestic owner that is a member of the same consolidated group, the member shall adjust the basis of the stock in accordance with the provisions of § 1.1502-32. Corresponding adjustments shall be made to the stock of other members in accordance with the provisions of § 1.1502-32. In the case where two or more individual separate units are treated as a combined separate unit pursuant to § 1.1503(d)-1(b)(4)(ii), see paragraph (g)(3) of this section.

(2) Interests in hybrid entities that are partnerships or interests in partnerships through which a separate unit is owned indirectly. (i) Scope. This paragraph (g)(2) applies for purposes of determining the adjusted basis of an interest in—

(A) A hybrid entity that is a partnership; and

(B) A partnership through which a domestic owner indirectly owns a separate unit.

(ii) Determination of basis of partner's interest. The adjusted basis of an interest described in paragraph (g)(2)(i) of this section shall be adjusted in accordance with section 705 and this paragraph (g)(2). The adjusted basis shall not be decreased for any amount of a dual consolidated loss that is attributable to the partnership interest, or separate unit owned indirectly through the partnership interest, as applicable, that is not absorbed as a result of the application of § 1.1503(d)-4(b) and (c). The adjusted basis shall, however, be decreased for the amount of such dual consolidated loss that is absorbed in a carryover or carryback taxable year. The adjusted basis shall be increased for any amount included in income pursuant to § 1.1503(d)-6(h) as a result of the recapture of a dual consolidated loss that was attributable to the interest in the hybrid partnership, or separate unit owned indirectly through the partnership interest, as applicable.

(3) Combined separate units. This paragraph (g)(3) applies where two or more individual separate units of one or more affiliated domestic owners are treated as one combined separate unit pursuant to § 1.1503(d)-1(b)(4)(ii). In such a case, a member owning stock in an affiliated domestic owner of the combined separate unit shall adjust the basis in the stock of such domestic owner as provided in paragraph (g)(1) of this section, and an affiliated domestic owner shall adjust its basis in a partnership, as provided in paragraph (g)(2) of this section, taking into account only those items of income, gain, deduction, or loss attributable to each individual separate unit, prior to combination. For purposes of this rule, if the dual consolidated loss attributable to a combined separate unit is subject to the domestic use limitation of § 1.1503(d)-4(b), then for purposes of this paragraph (g) and § 1.1502-32, the dual consolidated loss shall be allocated to an individual separate unit to the extent such individual separate unit contributed items of deduction or loss giving rise to the dual consolidated loss. In addition, if one or more affiliated domestic owners are required to recapture all or a portion of a dual consolidated loss pursuant to paragraph (h) of this section, such recapture amount shall be allocated to the affiliated domestic owner of the individual separate units composing the combined separate unit, to the extent such individual separate units contributed items of deduction or loss giving rise to the recaptured dual consolidated loss.

T.D. 9315, 3/16/2007.

§ 1.1503(d)-6 Exceptions to the domestic use limitation rule.

(a) In general. *(1) Scope and purpose.* This section provides certain exceptions to the domestic use limitation rule of § 1.1503(d)-4(b). Paragraph (b) of this section provides an exception for bilateral elective agreements. Paragraph (c) of this section provides rules regarding an exception that applies when there is no possibility of a foreign use. Paragraphs (d) through (h) of this section provide rules for an exception where a domestic use election is made. Paragraph (e) of this section provides rules with respect to triggering events, and paragraph (f) of this section provides rules regarding exceptions to triggering events. Paragraph (g) of this section provides rules with respect to the annual certification reporting requirement. Paragraph (h) of this section provides rules regarding the recapture of dual consolidated losses. Finally, paragraph (j) of this section provides rules regarding the termination of domestic use agreements and the annual certification requirement.

(2) Absence of foreign affiliate or foreign consolidation regime. The absence of a foreign affiliate or a foreign consolidation regime alone does not constitute an exception to the domestic use limitation rule. This is the case because it is still possible that all or a portion of the dual consolidated loss may be put to a foreign use. For example, there may be a foreign use with respect to an affiliate acquired in a year subsequent to the year in which the dual consolidated loss was incurred. In addition, a foreign use may occur in the absence of a foreign consolidation regime through a sale, merger, or similar transaction. See § 1.1503(d)-7(c) Example 2.

(3) Foreign insurance companies treated as domestic corporations. The exceptions contained in this section shall not apply to losses of a foreign insurance company that is a dual resident corporation under § 1.1503(d)-1(b)(2)(ii), or to losses attributable to any separate unit of such foreign insurance company. In addition, these exceptions shall not apply to losses described in the preceding sentence that, subject to the rules of § 1.1503(d)-4(d), carry over to a domestic corporation pursuant to a transaction described in section 381(a).

(b) Elective agreement in place between the United States and a foreign country. *(1) In general.* The domestic use limitation rule of § 1.1503(d)-4(b) shall not apply to a dual consolidated loss to the extent the consolidated group, unaffiliated dual resident corporation, or unaffiliated domestic owner, as the case may be, elects to deduct the loss in the United States pursuant to an agreement entered into between the United States and a foreign country that puts into place an elective procedure through which losses in a particular year may be used to offset income in only one country. This exception shall apply only if all the terms and conditions required under such agreement are satisfied, including any reporting or filing requirements. See § 1.1503(d)-3(e)(2)(iii) for the effect of an agreement described in this paragraph on a stand-alone domestic use agreement.

(2) Application to combined separate units. This paragraph (b)(2) applies where two or more individual separate units are treated as one combined separate unit pursuant to § 1.1503(d)-1(b)(4)(ii), and an agreement described in paragraph (b)(1) of this section would apply to at least one of the individual separate units. In such a case, and except to the extent provided in the agreement, the consolidated group, unaffiliated dual resident corporation, or unaffiliated domestic owner, as the case may be, may apply the agreement to the individual separate units, as applicable, provided the terms and conditions of the agreement are otherwise satisfied. See § 1.1503(d)-7(c) Example 19.

(c) No possibility of foreign use. *(1) In general.* The domestic use limitation rule of § 1.1503(d)-4(b) shall not apply to a dual consolidated loss if the consolidated group, unaffiliated dual resident corporation, or unaffiliated domestic owner, as the case may be—

(i) Demonstrates, to the satisfaction of the Commissioner, that no foreign use (as defined in § 1.1503(d)-3) of the dual consolidated loss occurred in the year in which it was incurred, and that no foreign use can occur in any other year by any means; and

(ii) Prepares a statement described in paragraph (c)(2) of this section that is attached to, and filed by the due date (including extensions) of, its U.S. income tax return for the taxable year in which the dual consolidated loss is incurred. See § 1.1503(d)-7(c) Examples 2, 30, and 31.

(2) Statement. The statement described in this paragraph (c)(2) must be signed under penalties of perjury by the person who signs the tax return. The statement must be labeled "No Possibility of Foreign Use of Dual Consolidated Loss Statement" at the top of the page and must include the following items, in paragraphs labeled to correspond with the items set forth in paragraphs (c)(2)(i) through (iv) of this section:

(i) A statement that the document is submitted under the provisions of paragraph (c) of this section.

(ii) The name, address, taxpayer identification number, and place and date of incorporation of the dual resident corporation, and the country or countries that tax the dual resident corporation on its worldwide income or on a residence basis, or, in the case of a separate unit, identification of the separate unit, including the name under which it conducts business, its principal activity, and the country in which its principal place of business is located. In the case of a combined separate unit, such information must be provided for each individual separate unit that is treated as part of the combined separate unit under § 1.1503(d)-1(b)(4)(ii).

(iii) A statement of the amount of the dual consolidated loss at issue.

(iv) An analysis, in reasonable detail and specificity, of the treatment of the losses and deductions composing the dual consolidated loss under the relevant facts. The analysis must include the reasons supporting the conclusion that no foreign use of the dual consolidated loss can occur as described in paragraph (c)(1)(i) of this section. The analysis must be supported with official or certified English translations of the relevant provisions of foreign law. The analysis may, for example, be based on the taxpayer's interpretation of foreign law, on advice received from local tax advisers in an opinion, or on a ruling from local country tax authorities. In all cases, however, the determination must be made to the satisfaction of the Commissioner.

(d) Domestic use election. *(1) In general.* The domestic use limitation rule of § 1.1503(d)-4(b) shall not apply to a dual consolidated loss if an election to be bound by the provisions of paragraphs (d) through (j) of this section is made by the consolidated group, unaffiliated dual resident corporation, or unaffiliated domestic owner, as the case may be (elector). In order to elect such relief, an agreement described in this paragraph (d)(1) (domestic use agreement) must be attached to, and filed by the due date (including extensions) of, the U.S. income tax return of the elector for the taxable year in which the dual consolidated loss is incurred. The domestic use agreement must be signed under penalties of perjury by the person who signs the return. If dual consolidated losses of more than one dual resident corporation or separate unit requires the filing of domestic use agreements by the same elector, the agreements may be combined in a single document, but the information required by paragraphs (d)(1)(ii) and (iv) of this section must be provided separately with respect to each dual consolidated loss. The domestic use agreement must be labeled "Domestic Use Election and Agreement" at the top of the page and must include the following items, in paragraphs labeled to correspond with the following:

(i) A statement that the document submitted is an election and an agreement under the provisions of paragraph (d) of this section.

(ii) The information required by paragraph (c)(2)(ii) of this section.

(iii) An agreement by the elector to comply with all of the provisions of paragraphs (d) through (j) of this section, as applicable.

(iv) A statement of the amount of the dual consolidated loss at issue.

(v) A certification that there has not been, and will not be, a foreign use (as defined in § 1.1503(d)-3) during the certification period (as defined in § 1.1503(d)-1(b)(20)).

(vi) A certification that arrangements have been made to ensure that there will be no foreign use of the dual consolidated loss during the certification period, and that the elector will be informed of any such foreign use of the dual consolidated loss during such period.

(vii) If applicable, a notification that an excepted triggering event under paragraph (f)(2) of this section has occurred with respect to the dual consolidated loss within the taxable year in which the loss is incurred. See paragraph (g) of this section for notification of excepted triggering events occurring during the certification period.

(2) No domestic use election available if there is a triggering event in the year the dual consolidated loss is incurred. Except as otherwise provided in this section, if a dual resident corporation or separate unit incurs a dual consolidated loss in a taxable year and a triggering event, as described in paragraph (e)(1) of this section, occurs (and no exception applies) with respect to the dual consolidated loss in such taxable year, then the consolidated group, unaffiliated dual resident corporation, or unaffiliated domestic owner, as the case may be, may not make a domestic use election with respect to such dual consolidated loss and the loss will be subject to the domestic use limitation rule of § 1.1503(d)-4(b). See § 1.1503(d)-7(c) Examples 5 through 7. See also § 1.1503(d)-4(d) for rules that eliminate a dual consolidated loss after certain transactions.

(e) Triggering events requiring the recapture of a dual consolidated loss. *(1) Events.* Except as provided under paragraphs (e)(2) (rebuttal of triggering events) and (f) (exceptions to triggering events) of this section, if there is a triggering event described in this paragraph (e)(1) with respect to a dual consolidated loss of a dual resident corporation or a separate unit during the certification period (as defined in § 1.1503(d)-1(b)(20)), the elector will recapture and report as ordinary income the amount of such dual consolidated loss as provided in paragraph (h) of this section on its tax return for the taxable year in which the triggering event occurs (or, when the triggering event is a foreign use of the dual consolidated loss, the taxable year that includes the last day of the foreign taxable year during which such use occurs). In addition, the elector must pay any applicable interest charge required by paragraph (h) of this section. For purposes of this section, any of the following events shall constitute a triggering event:

(i) Foreign use. A foreign use (as defined in § 1.1503(d)-3) of the dual consolidated loss. See § 1.1503(d)-3(c) for exceptions to foreign use.

(ii) Disaffiliation. An affiliated dual resident corporation or affiliated domestic owner that incurred directly or through a separate unit, respectively, a dual consolidated loss that is subject to a domestic use election, ceases to be a member of the consolidated group that made the domestic use election. For purposes of this paragraph (e)(1)(ii), an affiliated dual resident corporation or affiliated domestic owner shall be considered to cease to be a member of the consolidated group if it is no longer a member of the group within the meaning of § 1.1502-1(b), or if the group ceases to exist (for example, when the group no longer files a consolidated return). See § 1.1503(d)-7(c) Example 34. Any consequences resulting from this triggering event (for example, recapture of a dual consolidated loss) shall be taken into account on the tax return of the consolidated group for the taxable year that includes the date on which the affiliated dual resident corporation or affiliated domestic owner ceases to be a member of the consolidated group. This paragraph (e)(1)(ii) shall not apply to an acquisition described in § 1.1502-75(d)(3) where the consolidated group that includes the affiliated dual resident corporation or affiliated domestic owner, as applicable, is treated as remaining in existence.

(iii) Affiliation. An unaffiliated dual resident corporation or unaffiliated domestic owner becomes a member of a consolidated group. Any consequences resulting from this triggering event (for example, recapture of a dual consolidated loss) shall be taken into account on the tax return of the unaffiliated dual resident corporation or unaffiliated domestic owner for the taxable year that ends at the end of the day on which such corporation becomes a member of the consolidated group.

(iv) Transfer of assets. Fifty percent or more of the dual resident corporation's or separate unit's gross assets (measured by the fair market value of the assets at the time of such transaction or, for multiple transactions, at the time of the first transaction) is sold or otherwise disposed of in either a single transaction or a series of transactions within a twelve-month period. See § 1.1503(d)-7(c) Examples 5 and 35 through 37. In determining whether fifty percent or more of such assets is sold or otherwise disposed of, any dispositions occurring in the ordinary course of the dual resident corporation's or separate unit's trade or business shall be disregarded. In addition, for purposes of this paragraph (e)(1)(iv), an interest in another separate unit and the shares of a dual resident corporation shall not be treated as assets of a separate unit or a dual resident corporation.

(v) Transfer of an interest in a separate unit. Fifty percent or more of the interest in a separate unit (measured by voting power or value at the time of such transaction, or for multiple transactions, at the time of the first transaction) of the domestic owner, as determined by reference to such domestic owner's percentage interest on the last day of the taxable year in which the dual consolidated loss was incurred, is sold or otherwise disposed of either in a single transaction or a series of transactions within a twelve-month period. See § 1.1503(d)-7(c) Examples 5 and 35 through 37.

(vi) Conversion to a foreign corporation. An unaffiliated dual resident corporation, unaffiliated domestic owner, or hybrid entity an interest in which is a separate unit, that incurred the dual consolidated loss, becomes a foreign corporation (for example, as a result of a reorganization or an election to be classified as a corporation under § 301.7701-3(c) of this chapter).

(vii) Conversion to a regulated investment company, a real estate investment trust, or an S corporation. An unaffiliated dual resident corporation or unaffiliated domestic owner elects to be a regulated investment company pursuant to section 851(b)(1), a real estate investment trust pursuant to section 856(c)(1), or an S corporation pursuant to section 1362(a).

(viii) Failure to certify. The elector fails to file a certification with respect to a dual consolidated loss as required under paragraph (g) of this section.

(ix) Cessation of stand-alone status. In the case of a dual consolidated loss that is subject to the stand-alone exception described in § 1.1503(d)-3(e)(2), the conditions described in § 1.1503(d)-3(e)(2)(i) are no longer satisfied. See § 1.1503(d)-7(c) Example 18.

(2) Rebuttal. (i) General rule. An event described in paragraph (e)(1) of this section shall not constitute a triggering event if the elector demonstrates, to the satisfaction of the Commissioner, that there can be no foreign use (as defined in § 1.1503(d)-3) of the dual consolidated loss during the remaining certification period by any means. See paragraph (j)(1) of this section for rules regarding the termination of domestic use agreements and annual certifications following rebuttals under this general rule.

(ii) Certain asset transfers. An event described in paragraph (e)(1)(iv) of this section shall not constitute a triggering event if the elector demonstrates, to the satisfaction of the Commissioner, that the transfer of assets did not result in a carryover under foreign law of the dual resident corporation's, or separate unit's, losses, expenses, or deductions to the transferee of the assets. For purposes of this determination, the exception to foreign use in § 1.1503(d)-3(c)(7) shall be taken into account. Following rebuttal under this paragraph (e)(2)(ii), the domestic use agreement continues in effect.

(iii) Reporting. In order to satisfy the requirements of paragraph (e)(2)(i) or (ii) of this section, the elector must prepare a statement, labeled "Rebuttal of Triggering Event" at the top of the page, that indicates that it is submitted under the provisions of this paragraph (e)(2). The statement must include the information described in paragraphs (c)(2)(ii) and (iii) of this section. The statement must also include the information described in paragraph (c)(2)(iv) of this section that supports the conclusions under paragraph (e)(2)(i) or (ii) of this section, as applicable. The statement must be attached to, and filed by the due date (including extensions) of, the elector's income tax return for the taxable year in which the presumed triggering event occurs.

(iv) Examples. See § 1.1503(d)-7(c) Examples 32 and 33.

(f) Triggering event exceptions. *(1) Continuing ownership of assets or interests.* The following events shall not constitute triggering events, requiring the recapture of the dual consolidated loss under paragraph (h) of this section:

(i) Disaffiliation as a result of a transaction described in section 381. An affiliated dual resident corporation or affiliated domestic owner ceases to be a member of a consolidated group solely by reason of a transaction in which a member of the same consolidated group succeeds to the tax attributes of the dual resident corporation or domestic owner under the provisions of section 381.

(ii) Continuing ownership by consolidated group. This paragraph (f)(1)(ii) applies when assets of an affiliated dual resident corporation, or assets of, or interests in, a separate unit of an affiliated domestic owner are sold or otherwise disposed of. In such a case, the sale or disposition shall not be treated as a triggering event to the extent the assets or interests are acquired by one or more members of the consolidated group that includes the affiliated dual resident corporation or affiliated domestic owner, or by a partnership or a grantor trust, but only if immediately after the acquisition more than 90 percent of the partnership's or grantor trust's interests is owned, directly or indirectly, by members of such consolidated group.

(iii) Continuing ownership by unaffiliated dual resident corporation or unaffiliated domestic owner. This paragraph (f)(1)(iii) applies when assets of an unaffiliated dual resident corporation, or assets of, or interests in, a separate unit of an unaffiliated domestic owner, are sold or otherwise disposed of. In such a case, the sale or disposition shall not be a triggering event to the extent such assets or interests are acquired by the unaffiliated dual resident corporation, or unaffiliated domestic owner, as applicable, or by a partnership or grantor trust, but only if immediately after the acquisition more than 90 percent of the partnership's or grantor trust's interests is owned, directly or indirectly, by the unaffiliated dual resident corporation or unaffiliated domestic owner. For example, this paragraph (f)(1)(iii) applies when an unaffiliated domestic owner acquires direct ownership of the assets of a separate unit that it had immediately before owned indirectly through a partnership.

(2) Transactions requiring a new domestic use agreement. (i) Multiple-party events. If all the requirements of paragraph (f)(2)(iii) of this section are satisfied, the following events shall not constitute triggering events requiring the recapture of the dual consolidated loss under paragraph (h) of this section:

(A) An affiliated dual resident corporation or affiliated domestic owner becomes an unaffiliated domestic corporation or a member of a new consolidated group (other than in a transaction described in paragraph (f)(2)(ii)(B) of this section).

(B) Assets of a dual resident corporation or assets of, or interests in, a separate unit, are sold or otherwise disposed of in a transaction in which such assets or interests are acquired by an unaffiliated domestic corporation, one or more members of a new consolidated group, or by a partnership or grantor trust, but only if immediately after the sale or disposition more than 90 percent of the partnership's or grantor trust's interests is owned, directly or indirectly, by the unaffiliated domestic owner or by members of a new consolidated group, as applicable. See the related exception to foreign use provided under § 1.1503(d)-3(c)(8). See also § 1.1503(d)-7(c) Examples 36 and 37.

(ii) Events resulting in a single consolidated group. If the requirements of paragraph (f)(2)(iii)(A) of this section are satisfied, the following events shall not constitute triggering events requiring the recapture of the dual consolidated loss under paragraph (h) of this section:

(A) An unaffiliated dual resident corporation or unaffiliated domestic owner becomes a member of a consolidated group.

(B) A consolidated group ceases to exist as a result of a transaction described in § 1.1502-13(j)(5)(i) (relating to acquisitions of the common parent of the consolidated group), other than a transaction in which any member of the terminating group, or the successor-in-interest of such member, is not a member of the surviving group immediately after the terminating group ceases to exist. See § 1.1503(d)-7(c) Example 34.

(iii) Requirements. (A) New domestic use agreement. The unaffiliated domestic corporation or new consolidated group (subsequent elector) must file an agreement described in paragraph (d)(1) of this section (new domestic use agreement). The new domestic use agreement must be labeled "New Domestic Use Agreement" at the top of the page, and must be attached to and filed by the due date (including extensions) of, the subsequent elector's income tax return for the taxable year in which the event described in paragraph (f)(2)(i) or (f)(2)(ii) of this section occurs. The new domestic use agreement must be signed under penalties of perjury by the person who signs the return and must include the following items:

(1) A statement that the document submitted is an election and agreement under the provisions of paragraph (f)(2) of this section.

(2) An agreement to assume the same obligations with respect to the dual consolidated loss as the unaffiliated dual resident corporation, unaffiliated domestic owner, or consolidated group, as applicable, that filed the original domestic use agreement (original elector) with respect to that loss. In such a case, obligations of an elector provided under this section shall also be considered to be obligations of a subsequent elector.

(3) In the event of a transaction described in section 384(a) involving the subsequent elector, an agreement to treat any potential recapture amount under paragraph (h) of this section with respect to the dual consolidated loss as unrealized built-in gain for purposes of section 384(a), subject to any applicable exceptions (for example, the threshold requirements under section 382(h)(3)(B)). The potential recapture amount treated as unrealized built-in gain under this paragraph (f)(2)(iii)(A)(3) may be reduced to the extent permitted by paragraph (h)(2)(i) of this section.

(4) In the case of a multiple-party event described in paragraph (f)(2)(i) of this section, an agreement to be subject to the rules provided in paragraph (h)(3) of this section.

(5) The name, U.S. taxpayer identification number, and address of the original elector and prior subsequent electors, if any, with respect to the dual consolidated loss.

(B) Statement filed by original elector. In the case of a multiple-party event described in paragraph (f)(2)(i) of this section, the original elector must file a statement that is attached to and filed by the due date (including extensions) of its income tax return for the taxable year in which the event occurs. The statement must be labeled "Original Elector Statement" at the top of the page, must be signed under penalties of perjury by the person who signs the tax return, and must include the following items:

(1) A statement that the document submitted is an election and agreement under the provisions of paragraph (f)(2) of this section.

(2) An agreement to be subject to the rules provided in paragraph (h)(3) of this section.

(3) The name, U.S. taxpayer identification number, and address of the subsequent elector.

(3) Certain transfers qualifying for the de minimis exception to foreign use. If a transaction or event qualifies for the de minimis exception to foreign use described in § 1.1503(d)-3(c)(5), the transaction or event shall not constitute a triggering event under paragraph (e)(1)(iv) (transfers of assets) or (v) (transfers of an interest in a separate unit) of this section. For purposes of the preceding sentence, the transaction or event shall include deemed transfers that occur as a result of the transaction or event. See, for example, deemed transfers occurring pursuant to Rev. Rul. 99-5 (1999-1 CB 434), see § 601.601(d)(2)(ii)(b), and section 708 and the related regulations. See also § 1.1503(d)-7 Example 5. This paragraph (f)(3) only applies if the entire transaction or event qualifies for the de minimis exception to foreign use. For example, if a domestic owner sells five percent of a separate unit to a foreign corporation, which would qualify for the de minimis exception to foreign use if it were the only transfer, but pursuant to the same transaction also sells 70 percent of the same separate unit to another corporation in a manner that results in a triggering event under paragraph (e)(1)(v) of this section, this paragraph shall not apply to prevent the transaction from resulting in a triggering event.

(4) Deemed transactions as a result of certain transfers that do not result in a foreign use. The rules in this paragraph (f)(4) apply where the assets of, or the interests in, a separate unit are transferred in a transaction that would not result in a foreign use and, but for resulting deemed transactions or events, would not result in a triggering event described in paragraph (e)(1) of this section. For purposes of this paragraph (f)(4), deemed transactions or events shall include transactions or events that are deemed to occur pursuant to Rev. Rul. 99-5 and section 708 and the related regulations. In such a case, the deemed transactions shall not result in a triggering event under paragraph (e)(1)(iv) (transfers of assets) or (v) (transfers of an interest in a separate unit) of this section. See also § 1.1503(d)-7 Example 35.

(5) Compulsory transfers. Transfers of the assets or stock of a dual resident corporation, or of the assets or interests in a separate unit, shall not constitute a triggering event (including a foreign use that occurs as a result of, or following, the transfer) if such transfers are—

(i) Legally required by a foreign government as a necessary condition of doing business in a foreign country;

(ii) Compelled by a genuine threat of immediate expropriation by a foreign government; or

(iii) The result of the expropriation of assets by the foreign government.

(6) Subsequent triggering events. Any triggering event described in paragraph (e) of this section that occurs subsequent to one of the transactions described in this paragraph (f), and that itself does not meet any of the exceptions provided in this paragraph (f), shall require recapture under paragraph (h) of this section by the elector or subsequent elector, as applicable.

(g) Annual certification reporting requirement. Unless and until the domestic use agreement is terminated pursuant to paragraph (j) of this section, the elector must file a certification, labeled "Certification of Dual Consolidated Loss" at the top of the page, that is attached to, and filed by the due date (including extensions) of, its income tax return for each taxable year during the certification period. The certification must provide that there has been no foreign use of the dual consolidated loss. The certification must identify the dual consolidated loss to which it pertains by setting forth the elector's year in which the loss was incurred and the amount of such loss. In addition, the certification must warrant that arrangements have been made to ensure that there will be no foreign use of the dual consolidated loss and that the elector will be informed of any such foreign use. If applicable, the certification must include a notification that an excepted triggering event under paragraph (f)(2) of this section has occurred with respect to the dual consolidated loss within the taxable year being certified. If dual consolidated losses of more than one taxable year are subject to the rules of this paragraph (g), the certification for those years may be combined in a single document, but each dual consolidated loss must be separately identified. See § 1.1503(d)-3(e)(2)(ii) for additional certifications required where taxpayers elect the stand-alone exception of § 1.1503(d)-3(e)(2).

(h) Recapture of dual consolidated loss and interest charge. *(1) Presumptive rules.* (i) Amount of recapture. Except as otherwise provided in this section, upon the occurrence of a triggering event described in paragraph (e) of this section that does not meet any of the exceptions provided in paragraph (f) of this section, the dual resident corporation or domestic owner of the separate unit shall recapture as gross income the total amount of the dual consolidated loss to which the triggering event applies on its income tax return for the taxable year in which the triggering event occurs (or, when the triggering event is a foreign use of the dual consolidated loss, the taxable year that includes the last day of the foreign taxable year during which such foreign use occurs). See § 1.1503(d)-5(c)(4)(vi) for rules with respect to the attribution of recapture income to a separate unit. See also § 1.1503(d)-7 Examples 38 through 40.

(ii) Interest charge. In connection with the recapture, the elector shall pay an interest charge. An interest charge may be due even if the amount of recapture income is reduced to zero pursuant to paragraph (h)(2)(i) of this section. See § 1.1503(d)-7(c) Example 39. Except as otherwise provided in this section, the amount of the interest shall be computed under the rules of section 6601(a) by treating the additional tax resulting from the recapture as though it had been due and unpaid as of the date for payment of the tax for the taxable year in which the taxpayer received a tax benefit from the dual consolidated loss. For purposes of this paragraph (h)(1)(ii), a tax benefit shall be considered to have arisen in a taxable year in which the losses or deductions taken into account in computing the dual consolidated loss reduced U.S. taxable income. For the purpose of computing the interest charge, the additional tax resulting from the recapture is determined by treating the recapture income as the last income earned in the year of recapture. The interest shall be computed to the date for payment of the tax for the year of recapture and the interest thus computed becomes a part of the tax liability for that taxable year. See section 6601 for the computation of interest on a tax liability that it is not paid timely. The recapture interest charge shall be deductible to the same extent as interest under section 6601.

(2) Reduction of presumptive recapture amount and presumptive interest charge. (i) Amount of recapture. The dual resident corporation or domestic owner may recapture an amount less than the total dual consolidated loss if the elector demonstrates, to the satisfaction of the Commissioner, the lesser amount described in this paragraph (h)(2)(i). The reduction in the amount of recapture is the amount by which the dual consolidated loss would have offset other taxable income reported on a timely filed U.S. income tax return for any taxable year up to and including the taxable year of the triggering event (or, when the triggering event is a foreign use of the dual consolidated loss, the taxable year that includes the last day of the foreign taxable year during which such foreign use occurs) if no domestic use election had been made for the loss such that it was subject to the domestic use limitation of § 1.1503(d)-4(b) (and therefore subject to the limitation under § 1.1503(d)-4(c)). For this purpose, the rules for attributing items of income, gain, deduction, and loss under § 1.1503(d)-5 shall apply. An elector using this rebuttal rule must prepare a separate accounting showing the income for each year that would have offset the dual resident corporation's or separate unit's recapture amount if no domestic use election had been made for the dual consolidated loss. The separate accounting must be signed under penalties of perjury by the person who signs the elector's tax return, must be labeled "Reduction of Recapture Amount" at the top of the page, and must indicate that it is submitted under the provisions of this paragraph (h)(2)(i). The accounting must be attached to, and filed by the due date (including extensions) of, the elector's income tax return for the taxable year in which the triggering event occurs. See § 1.1503(d)-7(c) Examples 38 through 40.

(ii) Interest charge. The interest charge imposed under this section may be reduced if the elector demonstrates, to the satisfaction of the Commissioner, that the net interest owed would have been less than that provided in paragraph (h)(1)(ii) of this section if the elector had filed an amended return for the taxable year in which the recaptured dual consolidated loss was incurred, and for any other affected taxable years up to and including the taxable year of recapture, if no domestic use election had been made for the dual consolidated loss such that it had been subject to the restrictions of § 1.1503(d)-4(b) (and therefore subject to the limitations under § 1.1503(d)-4(c)). An elector using this rebuttal rule must prepare a computation demonstrating the reduction in the net interest owed as a result of treating the dual consolidated loss as a loss subject to the restrictions of § 1.1503(d)-4(b) (and therefore subject to the limitations under § 1.1503(d)-4(c)). The computation must be labeled "Reduction of Interest Charge" at the top of the page and must indicate that it is submitted under the provisions of this paragraph (h)(2)(ii). The computation must be signed under penalties of perjury by the person who signs the elector's tax return, and must be attached to, and filed by the due date (including extensions) of, the elector's income tax return for the taxable year in which the triggering event occurs. See § 1.1503(d)-7(c) Examples 39 and 40.

(3) Rules regarding multiple-party event exceptions to triggering events. (i) Scope. The rules of this paragraph (h)(3) apply when, after a triggering event described in paragraph (e) of this section with respect to which the requirements of paragraph (f)(2)(i) of this section were met (excepted event), a triggering event under paragraph (e) of this section occurs, and no exception applies to such triggering event under paragraph (f) of this section (subsequent triggering event). See § 1.1503(d)-7(c) Examples 36 and 37.

(ii) Original elector and prior subsequent electors not subject to recapture or interest charge. (A) Except to the extent otherwise provided in this paragraph (h)(3), neither the original elector nor any prior subsequent elector shall be subject to the rules of this paragraph (h) with respect to dual consolidated losses subject to the original domestic use agreement.

(B) In the case of a dual consolidated loss with respect to which multiple excepted events have occurred, only the subsequent elector that owns the dual resident corporation or separate unit at the time of the subsequent triggering event shall be subject to the recapture rules of this paragraph (h). For purposes of this paragraph (h), the term prior subsequent elector refers to all other subsequent electors.

(iii) Recapture tax amount and required statement. (A) In general. If a subsequent triggering event occurs, the subsequent elector shall take into account the recapture tax amount as determined under paragraph (h)(3)(iii)(B) of this section. The subsequent elector must prepare a statement that computes the recapture tax amount, as provided under paragraph (h)(3)(iii)(B) of this section, with respect to the dual consolidated loss subject to the new domestic use agreement. This statement must be attached to, and filed by the due date (including extensions) of, the subsequent elector's income tax return for the taxable year in which the subsequent triggering event occurs (or, when the subsequent triggering event is a foreign use of the dual consolidated loss, the taxable year that includes the last day of the foreign taxable year during which such foreign use occurs). The statement must be signed under penalties of perjury by the person who signs the return. The statement must be labeled "Statement Identifying Liability" at the top and, in addition to the calculation of the recapture tax amount, must include the following items, in paragraphs labeled to correspond with the items set forth in paragraphs (h)(3)(iii)(A)(1) through (3) of this section:

(1) A statement that the document is submitted under the provisions of § 1.1503(d)-6(h)(3)(iii).

(2) A statement identifying the amount of the dual consolidated losses at issue and the taxable years in which they were used.

(3) The name, address, and taxpayer identification number of the original elector and all prior subsequent electors.

(B) Recapture tax amount. The recapture tax amount equals the excess (if any) of—

(1) The income tax liability of the subsequent elector for the taxable year that includes the amount of recapture and related interest charge with respect to the dual consolidated losses that are recaptured as a result of the subsequent triggering event, as provided under paragraphs (h)(1) and (h)(2) of this section; over

(2) The income tax liability of the subsequent elector for such taxable year, computed by excluding the amount of recapture and related interest charge described in paragraph (h)(3)(iii)(B)(1) of this section.

(iv) Tax assessment and collection procedures. (A) In general. (1) Subsequent elector. An assessment identifying an income tax liability of the subsequent elector is considered an assessment of the recapture tax amount where the recapture tax amount is part of the income tax liability being assessed and the recapture tax amount is reflected in a statement attached to the subsequent elector's income tax return as provided under paragraph (h)(3)(iii) of this section.

(2) Original elector and prior subsequent electors. The assessment of the recapture tax amount as set forth in paragraph (h)(3)(iv)(A)(1) of this section shall be considered as having been properly assessed as an income tax liability of the original elector and of each prior subsequent elector, if any. The date of such assessment shall be the date the income tax liability of the subsequent elector was properly assessed. The Commissioner may collect all or a portion of such recapture tax amount from the original elector and/or the prior subsequent electors under the circumstances set forth in paragraph (h)(3)(iv)(B) of this section.

(B) Collection from original elector and prior subsequent electors; joint and several liability. (1) In general. If the subsequent elector does not pay in full the income tax liability that includes a recapture tax amount, the Commissioner may collect that portion of the unpaid balance of such income tax liability attributable to the recapture tax amount in full or in part from the original elector and/or from any prior subsequent elector, provided that the following conditions are satisfied with respect to such elector:

(i) The Commissioner properly has assessed the recapture tax amount pursuant to paragraph (h)(3)(iv)(A)(1) of this section.

(ii) The Commissioner has issued a notice and demand for payment of the recapture tax amount to the subsequent elector in accordance with § 301.6303-1 of this chapter.

(iii) The subsequent elector has failed to pay all of the recapture tax amount by the date specified in such notice and demand.

(iv) The Commissioner has issued a notice and demand for payment of the unpaid portion of the recapture tax amount to the original elector, or prior subsequent elector (as the case may be), in accordance with § 301.6303-1 of this chapter.

(2) Joint and several liability. The liability imposed under this paragraph (h)(3)(iv)(B) on the original elector and each prior subsequent elector shall be joint and several.

(C) Allocation of partial payments of tax. If the subsequent elector's income tax liability for a taxable period includes a recapture tax amount, and if such income tax liability is satisfied in part by payment, credit, or offset, such payment, credit or offset shall be allocated first to that portion of the income tax liability that is not attributable to the recapture tax amount, and then to that portion of the income tax liability that is attributable to the recapture tax amount.

(D) Refund. If the Commissioner makes a refund of any income tax liability that includes a recapture tax amount, the Commissioner shall allocate and pay the refund to each elector who paid a portion of such income tax liability as follows:

(1) The Commissioner shall first determine the total amount of recapture tax paid by and/or collected from the original elector and from any prior subsequent electors. The Commissioner shall then allocate and pay such refund to the original elector and prior subsequent electors, with each such elector receiving an amount of such refund on a pro rata basis, not to exceed the amount of recapture tax paid by and/or collected from such elector.

(2) The Commissioner shall pay the balance of such refund, if any, to the subsequent elector.

(v) Definition of income tax liability. Solely for purposes of paragraph (h)(3) of this section, the term income tax liability means the income tax liability imposed on a domestic corporation under Title 26 of the United States Code for a taxable year, including additions to tax, additional amounts, penalties, and any interest charge related to such income tax liability.

(vi) Example. See § 1.1503(d)-7(c) Example 36.

(4) Computation of taxable income in year of recapture. (i) Presumptive rule. Except to the extent provided in paragraph (h)(4)(ii) of this section, for purposes of computing the taxable income for the year of recapture, no current, carryover or carryback losses may offset and absorb the recapture amount.

(ii) Exception to presumptive rule. The recapture amount included in gross income may be offset and absorbed by that portion of the elector's net operating loss carryover that is attributable to the dual resident corporation or separate unit that incurred the dual consolidated loss being recaptured, if the elector demonstrates, to the satisfaction of the Commissioner, the amount of such portion of the carryover. The principles of § 1.1502-21(b)(2)(iv) shall apply for purposes of determining whether any portion of a net operating loss carryover is attributable to the dual resident corporation or separate unit. In the case of a separate unit, such determination shall be made by treating the separate unit as a domestic corporation and a member of the consolidated group composing its unaffiliated domestic owner, or members of the consolidated group of which its affiliated domestic owner is a member, as appropriate. An elector utilizing this rebuttal rule must prepare a computation demonstrating the amount of net operating loss carryover that, under this paragraph (h)(4)(ii), may absorb the recapture amount included in gross income. Such computation must be signed under penalties of perjury and attached to and filed by the due date (including extensions) of, the income tax return for the taxable year in which the triggering event occurs (or, when the triggering event is a foreign use of the dual consolidated loss, the taxable year that includes the last day of the foreign taxable year during which such foreign use occurs).

(5) Character and source of recapture income. The amount recaptured under this paragraph (h) shall be treated as ordinary income. Except as provided in the prior sentence, such income shall be treated, as applicable, as income from the same source, having the same character, and falling within the same separate category, for all purposes, including sections 904(d) and 907, to which the items of deduction or loss composing the dual consolidated loss were allocated and apportioned, as provided under sections 861(b), 862(b), 863(a), 864(e), 865, and the related regulations. For this determination, the pro rata computation of the items of deduction or loss composing the dual consolidated loss as described in § 1.1503(d)-4(c)(4) shall apply. See § 1.1503(d)-7(c) Example 38.

(6) Reconstituted net operating loss. (i) General rule. Except as provided in paragraphs (h)(6)(ii) and (iii) of this section, commencing in the taxable year immediately following the year in which the dual consolidated loss is recaptured, the dual resident corporation, or the domestic owner of the separate unit, that incurred the dual consolidated loss that is recaptured shall be treated as having a net operating loss (reconstituted net operating loss) in an amount equal to the amount actually recaptured under this paragraph (h). If a domestic corporation (transferee) acquires the assets of the dual resident corporation or domestic owner in a transaction described in section 381(a), the preceding sentence shall be applied by treating the transferee as the dual resident corporation or domestic owner, as applicable. In a case to which this paragraph (h)(6) applies, the transferee corporation shall be treated as having a reconstituted net operating loss in an amount equal to the amount actually recaptured under this paragraph (h). In no event, however, shall more than one corporation be treated as having a reconstituted net operating loss as a result of a single dual consolidated loss being recaptured. A reconstituted net operating loss of a domestic owner shall be attributable under § 1.1503(d)-5 to the separate unit that incurred the dual consolidated loss that was recaptured. Moreover, a reconstituted net operating loss shall be subject to the domestic use limitation of § 1.1503(d)-4(b) (and therefore subject to the limitation under § 1.1503(d)-4(c)), without regard to the exceptions contained in paragraphs (b) through (d) of this section (relating to elective agreements in place between the United States and a foreign country, the ability to demonstrate no possibility of a foreign use, and a domestic use election, respectively). The reconstituted net operating loss shall be available only for carryover, under section 172(b), to taxable years following the taxable year of recapture. For purposes of determining the remaining carryover period, the reconstituted net operating loss shall be treated as if it had been recognized in the taxable year in which the dual consolidated loss that is the basis of the recapture amount was incurred. See § 1.1503(d)-7(c) Examples 36, 38, and 40.

(ii) Exception. Paragraph (h)(6)(i) of this section shall not apply to the extent the dual consolidated loss that is the basis of the recapture amount would have been eliminated pursuant to § 1.1503(d)-4(d) if no domestic use election had been made for such loss. See § 1.1503(d)-7(c) Example 40.

(iii) Special rule for recapture following multiple-party event exception to a triggering event. This paragraph applies to an excepted event described in paragraph (f)(2)(i)(B) of this section that is followed by a subsequent triggering event requiring recapture as described in paragraph (f)(6) of this section. In such a case, the domestic corporation that owns, directly or indirectly, the assets of the dual resident corporation, or the assets of or the interests in a separate unit, immediately following the excepted event shall be treated as if it incurred the dual consolidated loss that is recaptured for purposes of applying paragraph (h)(6)(i) of this section. See § 1.1503(d)-7(c) Example 36.

(i) [Reserved].

(j) Termination of domestic use agreement and annual certifications. *(1) Rebuttals, exceptions to triggering events, and recapture.* The domestic use agreement filed with respect to a dual consolidated loss shall terminate prior to the end of the certification period and have no further effect if—

(i) An elector is able to rebut the presumption of a triggering event pursuant to the general rule in paragraph (e)(2)(i) of this section;

(ii) An event described in paragraph (e)(1) of this section is not a triggering event as a result of the application of paragraphs (f)(2)(i) or (ii) (relating to events requiring a new domestic use agreement) of this section; this paragraph (j)(1)(ii) does not, however, apply to terminate the new domestic use agreement filed in connection with the event pursuant to paragraph (f)(2)(iii)(A) of this section. See also paragraph (h)(3)(iv) of this section regarding collection from the original elector and prior subsequent electors in certain cases; or

(iii) A dual consolidated loss is recaptured pursuant to paragraph (h) of this section. See § 1.1503(d)-7(c) Examples 32 through 34.

(2) Termination of ability for foreign use. (i) In general. A domestic use agreement filed with respect to a dual consolidated loss shall terminate and have no further effect as of the end of a taxable year if the elector—

(A) Demonstrates, to the satisfaction of the Commissioner, that as of the end of such taxable year no foreign use (as defined in § 1.1503(d)-3) of the dual consolidated loss can occur in any other year by any means; and

(B) Prepares a statement described in paragraph (j)(2)(ii) of this section that is attached to, and filed by the due date (including extensions) of, its U.S. income tax return for such taxable year.

(ii) Statement. The statement described in this paragraph (j)(2)(ii) must be signed under penalties of perjury by the person who signs the return. The statement must be labeled "Termination of Ability for Foreign Use" at the top of the page and must include the following information, in paragraphs labeled to correspond with the following:

(A) A statement that the document is submitted under the provisions of paragraph (j)(2) of this section.

(B) The information required by paragraph (c)(2)(ii) of this section.

(C) A statement of the amount of the dual consolidated loss at issue and the year in which such dual consolidated loss was incurred.

(D) The information described in paragraph (c)(2)(iv) of this section that supports the conclusion that no foreign use can occur as provided in paragraph (j)(2)(i)(A) of this section.

(3) Agreements filed in connection with stand-alone exception. See § 1.1503(d)-3(e)(2)(iii) for the termination of domestic use agreements filed in connection with the stand-alone exception to the mirror legislation rule when a subsequent election is made under paragraph (b) of this section (relating to agreements entered into between the United States and a foreign country).

T.D. 9315, 3/16/2007.

§ 1.1503(d)-7 Examples.

(a) In general. This section provides examples that illustrate the application of §§ 1.1503(d)-1 through 1.1503(d)-6. This section also provides facts that are presumed for such examples.

(b) Presumed facts for examples. For purposes of the examples in this section, unless otherwise indicated, the following facts are presumed:

(1) Each entity has only a single class of equity outstanding, all of which is held by a single owner.

(2) P, a domestic corporation and the common parent of the P consolidated group, owns S, a domestic corporation and a member of the P consolidated group.

(3) DRCX, a domestic corporation, is subject to Country X tax on its worldwide income or on a residence basis, and is a dual resident corporation.

(4) DE1X and DE2X are both Country X entities, subject to Country X tax on their worldwide income or on a residence basis, and disregarded as entities separate from their owners for U.S. tax purposes. DE3Y is a Country Y entity, subject to Country Y tax on its worldwide income or on a residence basis, and disregarded as an entity separate from its owner for U.S. tax purposes. All the interests in DE1X, DE2X, and DE3Y constitute hybrid entity separate units.

(5) FBX is a Country X business operation that, if carried on by a U.S. person, would constitute a foreign branch, as defined in § 1.367(a)-6T(g)(1), and is a Country X foreign branch separate unit.

(6) Neither the assets nor the activities of an entity constitute a foreign branch separate unit.

(7) FSX is a Country X entity that is subject to Country X tax on its worldwide income or on a residence basis and is classified as a foreign corporation for U.S. tax purposes.

(8) The applicable foreign country has a consolidation regime that--

(i) Includes as members of a consolidated group any commonly controlled branches and permanent establishments in such jurisdiction, and entities that are subject to tax in such jurisdiction on their worldwide income or on a residence basis; and

(ii) Allows the losses of members of consolidated groups to offset income of other members.

(9) There is no mirror legislation, within the meaning of § 1.1503(d)-3(e)(1), in the applicable foreign country.

(10) There is no elective agreement described in § 1.1503(d)-6(b) between the United States and the applicable foreign country.

(11) There is no income tax convention between the United States and the applicable foreign country.

(12) If a domestic use election, within the meaning of § 1.1503(d)-6(d), is made, all the necessary filings related to such election are properly completed on a timely basis.

(13) If there is a triggering event requiring recapture of a dual consolidated loss, the amount of recapture is not reduced pursuant to § 1.1503(d)-6(h)(2).

(14) There are no other items of income, gain, deduction, and loss. In addition, the United States and the applicable foreign country recognize the same items of income, gain, deduction, and loss in each taxable year.

(15) All taxpayers use the calendar year as their taxable year.

(c) Examples. The following examples illustrate the application of §§ 1.1503(d)-1 through 1.1503(d)-6:

Example (1). Separate unit combination rule. (i) Facts. P owns DE3Y which, in turn, owns DE1X. DE1X owns FBX. PRS, an entity treated as a partnership for both U.S. and Country X tax purposes, is owned 50 percent by P and 50 percent by an unrelated foreign person. PRS carries on a business operation in Country X that, if carried on by a U.S. person, would constitute a foreign branch within the meaning of § 1.367(a)-6T(g)(1). In addition, P owns DRCX, a member of the consolidated group of which P is the parent, which carries on business operations in Country X that constitute a foreign branch within the meaning of § 1.367(a)-6T(g)(1). S owns DE2X.

(ii) Result. Pursuant to § 1.1503(d)-1(b)(4)(ii), the interest in DE1X, the interest in DE2X, FBX, P's share of the Country X business operations carried on by PRS (which is owned by P indirectly through its interest in PRS), and DRCX's Country X business operations are combined and treated as a single separate unit of the consolidated group of which P is the parent. This is the case regardless of whether the losses of each individual separate unit are made available to offset the income of the other individual separate units under Country X tax laws. Because DRCX is a dual resident corporation, it is not combined and treated as part of this combined separate unit and, as a result, DRCx's income or dual consolidated loss is not taken into account in determining the income or dual consolidated loss of the combined separate unit. In addition, P's interest in DE3Y is not combined and is another separate unit because it is subject to tax in Country Y, rather than Country X.

Example (2). Definition of a separate unit and application of domestic use limitation--foreign branch separate unit. (i) Facts. P carries on business operations in Country X that constitute a permanent establishment under the U.S.-Country X income tax convention. In year 1, a loss is attributable to P's Country X permanent establishment, as determined under § 1.1503(d)-5.

(ii) Result. Under §§ 1.1503(d)-1(b)(4)(i)(A) and 1.367(a)-6T(g)(1), P's Country X permanent establishment constitutes a foreign branch separate unit. Therefore, the year 1 loss attributable to the foreign branch separate unit constitutes a dual consolidated loss pursuant to § 1.1503(d)-1(b)(5)(ii). The dual consolidated loss rules apply to the dual consolidated loss even though there is no affiliate of the foreign branch separate unit in Country X, because it is still possible that all or a portion of the dual consolidated loss can be put to a foreign use. For example, there may be a foreign use with respect to a Country X affiliate acquired in a year subsequent to the year in which the dual consolidated loss was incurred. See § 1.1503(d)-6(a)(2). Accordingly, unless an exception under § 1.1503(d)-6 applies (such as a domestic use election), the year 1 dual consolidated loss attributable to P's

Country X permanent establishment is subject to the domestic use limitation rule of § 1.1503(d)-4(b). As a result, pursuant to § 1.1503(d)-4(c), the year 1 dual consolidated loss cannot offset income of P that is not attributable to its Country X foreign branch separate unit, nor can it offset income of any other domestic affiliate. The loss can, however, offset income of the Country X foreign branch separate unit, subject to the application of § 1.1503(d)-4(c). The result would be the same even if Country X did not have a consolidation regime that includes as members of consolidated groups Country X branches or permanent establishments of nonresident corporations. The dual consolidated loss rules apply even in the absence of a consolidation regime in the foreign country because it is possible that all or a portion of a dual consolidated loss can be put to a foreign use by other means, such as through a sale, merger, or similar transaction. See § 1.1503(d)-6(a)(2).

(iii) Alternative facts. The facts are the same as in paragraph (i) of this Example 2, except that P's Country X business operations constitute a foreign branch as defined in § 1.367(a)-6T(g)(1), but do not constitute a permanent establishment under the U.S.-Country X income tax convention. Although the activities carried on by P in Country X would otherwise constitute a foreign branch separate unit as described in § 1.1503(d)-1(b)(4)(i)(A), the exception under § 1.1503(d)-1(b)(4)(iii) applies because the activities do not constitute a permanent establishment under the U.S.-Country X income tax convention. Thus, the Country X business operations do not constitute a foreign branch separate unit, and the year 1 loss is not subject to the dual consolidated loss rules. If P instead carried on its Country X business operations through DE1X, then the exception under § 1.1503(d)-1(b)(4)(iii) would not apply because P carries on the business operations through a hybrid entity and, as a result, the business operations would constitute a foreign branch separate unit. Thus, in such a case the year 1 loss would be subject to the dual consolidated loss rules.

Example (3). Domestic use limitation--foreign branch separate unit owned through a partnership. (i) Facts. P and S organize a partnership, PRSX, under the laws of Country X. PRSX is treated as a partnership for both U.S. and Country X tax purposes. PRSX owns FBX. PRSX earns U.S. source income that is unconnected with its FBX branch operations, and such income is not subject to tax by Country X. In addition, such U.S. source income is not attributable to FBX under § 1.1503(d)-5.

(ii) Result. Under § 1.1503(d)-1(b)(4)(i)(A), P's and S's shares of FBX owned indirectly through their interests in PRSX are individual foreign branch separate units. Pursuant to § 1.1503(b)-1(b)(4)(ii), these individual separate units are combined and treated as a single separate unit of the consolidated group of which P is the parent. Unless an exception under § 1.1503(d)-6 applies, any dual consolidated loss attributable to FBX cannot offset income of P or S (other than income attributable to FBX, subject to the application of § 1.1503(d)-4(c)), including their distributive share of the U.S. source income earned through their interests in PRSX, nor can it offset income of any other domestic affiliates.

Example (4). Definition of a separate unit and domestic use limitation--interest in hybrid entity partnership and indirectly owned foreign branch separate unit. (i) Facts. HPSX is a Country X entity that is subject to Country X tax on its worldwide income. HPSX is classified as a partnership for Federal tax purposes. P, S, and FSX, are the sole partners of HPSX. For U.S. tax purposes, P, S, and FSX each has an equal interest in each item of HPSX's profit or loss. HPSX carries on operations in Country Y that, if carried on by a U.S. person, would constitute a foreign branch within the meaning of § 1.367(a)-6T(g)(1).

(ii) Result. Under § 1.1503(d)-1(b)(4)(i)(B), the partnership interests in HPSX held by P and S are individual hybrid entity separate units. These individual separate units are combined into a single separate unit under § 1.1503(d)-1(b)(4)(ii). In addition, P's and S's share of the Country Y operations owned indirectly through their interests in HPSX are individual foreign branch separate units under § 1.1503(d)-1(b)(4)(i)(B). These individual separate units are also combined into a single separate unit under § 1.1503(d)-1(b)(4)(ii). Unless an exception under § 1.1503(d)-6 applies, dual consolidated losses attributable to P's and S's combined interests in HPSX can only be used to offset income attributable to their combined interests in HPSX (other than income attributable to P's and S's combined interests in the Country Y foreign branch separate unit), subject to the application of § 1.1503(d)-4(c). Similarly, dual consolidated losses attributable to P's and S's combined interests in the Country Y operations of HPSX can only be used to offset income attributable to their combined interests in such Country Y operations, subject to the application of § 1.1503(d)-4(c). Neither FSX's interest in HPSX, nor its share of the Country Y operations owned by HPSX, is a separate unit because FSX is not a domestic corporation.

Example (5). Foreign use--general rule and de minimis reduction exception. (i) Facts. P owns DE1X. DE1X owns FSX. In year 1, there is a $100x loss attributable to P's interest in DE1X that is a dual consolidated loss. Also in year 1, FSX earns $200x of income. DE1X and FSX file a Country X consolidated tax return. For Country X tax purposes, the year 1 $100x loss of DE1X is used to offset $100x of year 1 income generated by FSX. Under Country X tax law, unused losses are carried forward and available to offset income in subsequent taxable years.

(ii) Result. The $100x loss attributable to P's interest in DE1X is available to, and in fact does, offset FSX's income under the laws of Country X. In addition, under U.S. tax principles, such income is considered to be an item of FSX, a foreign corporation. As a result, under § 1.1503(d)-3(a), there has been a foreign use of the year 1 dual consolidated loss attributable to P's interest in DE1X. Therefore, P cannot make a domestic use election with respect to the loss as provided under § 1.1503(d)-6(d)(2), and such loss will be subject to the domestic use limitation rule of § 1.1503(d)-4(b). The result would be the same even if FSX, under Country X tax law, had no income against which the dual consolidated loss of DE1X could be offset (unless FSX's ability to use the loss under Country X tax law requires an election, and no such election is made).

(iii) Alternative facts. The facts are the same as in paragraph (i) of this Example 5, except that FSX cannot use the loss of DE1X under Country X tax law without an election, and no such election is made. Pursuant to the exception in § 1.1503(d)-3(c)(2), there is no foreign use of the year 1 dual consolidated loss attributable to P's interest in DE1X. In addition, P files a domestic use election with respect to the year 1 dual consolidated loss attributable to its interest in DE1X and, at the beginning of year 3, P sells its interest in DE1X to F, a Country Y entity that is a foreign corporation. The sale of the interest in DE1X to F results in a foreign use triggering event pursuant to § 1.1503(d)-6(e)(1)(i) because, immediately after the sale, the loss attributable to the interest in DE1X carries over under Country X law and, therefore, is available under U.S. tax principles to offset income of the owner of the interest in DE1X which, in the hands of F, is not a separate unit. It is also a foreign use because the loss is available under U.S. tax principles to offset the income of F, a foreign corporation. See § 1.1503(d)-3(a)(1). Finally, the transfer is a triggering event pursuant to § 1.1503(d)-6(e)(1)(iv) and (v).

(iv) Alternative facts. The facts are the same as in paragraph (iii), of this Example 5, except that P only sells 5 percent of its interest in DE1X to F. Pursuant to Rev. Rul. 99-5 (1999-1 CB 434), see § 601.601(d)(2)(ii)(b) of this chapter, the transaction is treated as if P sold 5 percent of its interest in each of DE1X's assets to F, and then immediately thereafter P and F transferred their interests in the assets of DE1X to a partnership in exchange for an ownership interest therein. The sale of the 5 percent interest in DE1X generally results in a foreign use triggering event because a portion of the dual consolidated loss carries over under Country X tax law and is available under U.S. tax principles to offset income of the owner of the interest in DE1X, a hybrid entity, which in the hands of F is not a separate unit. It is also a foreign use because the loss is available under U.S. tax principles to offset the income of F, a foreign corporation. See § 1.1503(d)-3(a)(1). However, pursuant to the exception under § 1.1503(d)-3(c)(5) (relating to a de minimis reduction of an interest in a separate unit), such availability does not result in a foreign use. In addition, pursuant to § 1.1503(d)-6(f)(1) and (3), the deemed transfers pursuant to Rev. Rul. 99-5 as a result of the sale are not treated as triggering events described in § 1.1503(d)-6(e)(1)(iv) or (v).

Example (6). Foreign use and indirect foreign use--foreign reverse hybrid structure and disregarded payments. (i) Facts. P owns DE1X. DE1X owns 99 percent and S owns 1 percent of FRHX, a Country X partnership that elected to be treated as a corporation for U.S. tax purposes. FRHX conducts a trade or business in Country X. In year 1, DE1X incurs interest expense on a third-party loan, which constitutes a dual consolidated loss attributable to P's interest in DE1X. In year 1, for Country X tax purposes, DE1X takes into account its distributive share of income generated by FRHX and offsets such income with its interest expense.

(ii) Result. In year 1, the dual consolidated loss attributable to P's interest in DE1X is available to, and in fact does, offset income recognized in Country X and, under U.S. tax principles, the income is considered to be income of FRHX, a foreign corporation. Accordingly, pursuant to § 1.1503(d)-3(a)(1), there is a foreign use of the dual consolidated loss. Therefore, P cannot make a domestic use election with respect to the year 1 dual consolidated loss attributable to its interest in DE1X, as provided under § 1.1503(d)-6(d)(2), and such loss will be subject to the domestic use limitation rule of § 1.1503(d)-4(b).

(iii) Alternative facts. (A) The facts are the same as in paragraph (i) of this Example 6, except as follows. Instead of owning DE1X, P owns DE3Y which, in turn, owns DE1X. In addition, DE3Y, rather than DE1X, is the obligor on the third-party loan and therefore incurs the interest expense on such loan. Finally, DE3Y on-lends the loan proceeds from the third-party loan to DE1X, and DE1X pays interest to DE3Y on such loan that is generally disregarded for U.S. tax purposes.

(B) Pursuant to § 1.1503(d)-5(c)(1)(ii), for purposes of calculating income or a dual consolidated loss, DE3Y and DE1X do not take into account interest income or interest expense, respectively, with respect to amounts paid on the disregarded loan from DE3Y to DE1X. As a result, such items neither create a dual consolidated loss with respect to the interest in DE1X, nor do they reduce (or eliminate) the dual consolidated loss attributable to the interest in DE3Y. Thus, in year 1, there is a dual consolidated loss attributable to P's interest in DE3Y, but not to P's indirect interest in DE1X.

(C) In year 1, interest expense paid by DE1X to DE3Y on the disregarded loan is taken into account as a deduction in computing DE1X's taxable income for Country X tax purposes, but does not give rise to a corresponding item of income or gain for U.S. tax purposes (because it is generally disregarded). In addition, such interest has the effect of making an item of deduction or loss composing the dual consolidated loss attributable to P's interest in DE3Y available for a foreign use. This is the case because it may reduce or offset items of deduction or loss composing the dual consolidated loss for foreign tax purposes, and creates another deduction or loss that may reduce or offset income of DE1X for foreign tax purposes that, under U.S. tax principles, is treated as income of FRHX, a foreign corporation. Moreover, because the disregarded item is incurred or taken into account as interest for foreign tax purposes, it is deemed to have been incurred or taken into account with a principal purpose of avoiding the provisions of section 1503(d). Accordingly, there is an indirect foreign use of the year 1 dual consolidated loss attributable to P's interest in DE3Y, and P cannot make a domestic use election with respect to such loss as provided under § 1.1503(d)-6(d)(2). Thus, the loss will be subject to the domestic use limitation rule of § 1.1503(d)-4(b).

Example (7). Indirect foreign use--hybrid instrument. (i) Facts. P owns DE1X which, in turn, owns FSX. DE1X borrows cash from an unrelated lender and transfers the cash to FSX in exchange for an instrument (hybrid instrument). The hybrid instrument is treated as equity for U.S. tax purposes and debt for Country X tax purposes. Interest expense on the loan from the unrelated lender results in a dual consolidated loss being attributable to P's interest in DE1X in year 1. DE1X does not elect under Country X law to consolidate with FSX. In year 1, FSX distributes its stock as a payment on the hybrid instrument to DE1X. For U.S. tax purposes, such payment is excluded from P's gross income under section 305. However, for Country X tax purposes, such payment is treated as interest and gives rise to a deduction taken into account in computing FSX's Country X tax liability; the payment also gives rise to interest income to DE1X for Country X tax purposes.

(ii) Result. The payment on the hybrid instrument does not give rise to an item of income or gain for U.S. tax purposes and therefore does not reduce (or eliminate) the dual consolidated loss attributable to P's interest in DE1X. In addition, such payment is taken into account as a deduction in computing FSX's taxable income for Country X tax purposes. Moreover, such payment has the effect of making an item of deduction or loss composing the dual consolidated loss attributable to P's interest in DE1X available for a foreign use. This is the case because it may reduce or offset items of deduction or loss composing the dual consolidated loss for foreign tax purposes, and creates a deduction that reduces or offsets income of FSX for foreign tax purposes that, under U.S. tax principles, is income of a foreign corporation. Further, because the item is incurred, or taken into account, using an instrument that is treated as equity for U.S. tax purposes and debt for foreign tax purposes, it is deemed to have been engaged in with the principal purpose of avoiding the provisions of section 1503(d). As a result, there has been an indirect foreign use of the year 1 dual consolidated loss, and P cannot make a domestic use election with respect to such loss, as provided under § 1.1503(d)-6(d)(2). Thus, the year 1 dual consolidated loss will be subject to the domestic use limitation rule of § 1.1503(d)-4(b).

Example (8). No indirect foreign use--transaction entered into in the ordinary course of business. (i) Facts. P owns DE1X and FBY. FBY is a foreign branch separate unit located in Country Y. DE1X owns FBX and FSX. P's interest in DE1X and FBX are combined and treated as a single separate unit (Country X separate unit) pursuant to § 1.1503(d)-1(b)(4)(ii). Under Country X tax laws, DE1X elects to consolidate with FSX. FBY engages in the business of providing services and, in connection with its ordinary course of business, provides services to unrelated third parties and to DE1X. As compensation for services, DE1X makes a payment to FBY. Under Country X tax law, the payment is deductible. However, the payment is generally disregarded for U.S. tax purposes and, pursuant to § 1.1503(d)-5(c)(1)(ii), is not taken into account in calculating the income or dual consolidated loss attributable to the Country X separate unit or FBY. In year 1, the Country X separate unit and FBY each has a dual consolidated loss. The dual consolidated loss attributable to the Country X separate unit is subject to the domestic use limitation under § 1.1503(d)-4(b) because DE1X and FSX elect to consolidate and, as a result, the dual consolidated loss is put to a foreign use.

(ii) Result. The payment made by DE1X to FBY in connection with the performance of services is taken into account as a deduction in computing DE1X's taxable income for Country X tax purposes, but does not give rise to an item of income or gain for U.S. tax purposes. In addition, such payment has the effect of making an item of deduction or loss composing the dual consolidated loss attributable to FBY available for a foreign use. This is the case because it may reduce or offset items of deduction or loss composing the dual consolidated loss of FBY for foreign tax purposes, and creates another deduction that reduces or offsets income of FSX for foreign tax purposes (because DE1X and FSX elect to file a consolidated return) that, under U.S. tax principles, is income of a foreign corporation. However, the transaction between DE1X and FBY was entered into in the ordinary course of FBY's trade or business. As a result, if P can demonstrate to the satisfaction of the Commissioner that the transaction was not entered into with a principal purpose of avoiding the provisions of section 1503(d), FBY's year 1 dual consolidated loss will not be treated as having been made available for an indirect foreign use. In such a case, P would be entitled to make a domestic use election with respect to such loss.

Example (9). Foreign use--dual resident corporation with hybrid entity joint venture. (i) Facts. P owns DRCX, a member of the P consolidated group. DRCX owns 80 percent of HPSX, a Country X entity that is subject to Country X tax on its worldwide income. HPSX is classified as a partnership for U.S. tax purposes. FSX owns the remaining 20 percent of HPSX. In year 1, DRCX generates a $100x net operating loss (without regard to items attributable to DRCX's interest in HPSX). Also in year 1, HPSX generates $100x of income, $80x of which is attributable to DRCX's interest in HPSX. DRCX and HPSX file a consolidated tax return for Country X tax purposes, and HPSX offsets its $100x of income with the $100x loss generated by DRCX.

(ii) Result. DRCX and its interest in HPSX are not combined because DRCX is a dual resident corporation and the combination rule under § 1.1503(d)-1(b)(4)(ii) only applies to separate units. The $100x year 1 net operating loss incurred by DRCX (without regard to items attributable to DRCX's interest in HPSX) is a dual consolidated loss. In addition, HPSX is a hybrid entity and DRCX's interest in HPSX is a hybrid entity separate unit; however, there is no dual consolidated loss attributable to such separate unit in year 1 (instead, there is $80x of income attributable to such separate unit). DRCX's year 1 dual consolidated loss offsets $100x of income for Country X purposes, and $20x of such income is, under U.S. tax principles, income of FSX, which owns an interest in HPSX that is not a separate unit (in addition, FSX is a foreign corporation). As a result, pursuant to § 1.1503(d)-3(a), there is a foreign use of the year 1 dual consolidated loss of DRCX, and P cannot make a domestic use election with respect to such loss pursuant to § 1.1503(d)-6(d)(2). Therefore, such loss will be subject to the domestic use limitation rule of § 1.1503(d)-4(b). The result would be the same even if HPSX, under Country X laws, had no income against which the dual consolidated loss could be offset (unless the ability to use the loss under Country X laws required an election, and no such election is made).

Example (10). Foreign use--foreign parent corporation. (i) Facts. F1 and F2, nonresident alien individuals, each owns 50 percent of FPX, a Country X entity that is subject to Country X tax on its worldwide income. FPX is classified as a foreign corporation for U.S. tax purposes. FPX owns DRCX. DRCX is the parent of a consolidated group that includes as a member DS, a domestic corporation. In year 1, DRCX incurs a dual consolidated loss of $100x and, for Country X tax purposes, FPX generates $100x of income. In year 1, FPX elects to consolidate with DRCX for Country X tax purposes, and the $100x year 1 loss of DRCX is used to offset the income of FPX under the laws of Country X. For U.S. tax purposes, the items of FPX do not constitute items of income in year 1.

(ii) Result. The year 1 dual consolidated loss of DRCX offsets the income of FPX under the laws of Country X. Pursuant to § 1.1503(d)-3(a), the offset constitutes a foreign use because the items constituting such income are considered under U.S. tax principles to be items of a foreign corporation. This is the case even though the United States does not recognize such items as income in year 1. Therefore, DRCX cannot make a domestic use election with respect to its year 1 dual consolidated loss pursuant to § 1.1503(d)-6(d)(2). As a result, such loss will be subject to the domestic use limitation rule of § 1.1503(d)-4(b).

(iii) Alternative facts. The facts are the same as in paragraph (i) of this Example 10, except that FPX is classified as a partnership for U.S. tax purposes. The result would be the same as in paragraph (ii) of this Example 10, because the offset of the income generated by FPX is a foreign use pursuant to § 1.1503(d)-3(a). This is the case because the items constituting such income are considered under U.S. tax principles to be items of F1 and F2, the owners of interests in FPX (a hybrid entity), that are not separate units. Moreover, the result would be the same if F1 and F2 owned their interests in FPX indirectly through another partnership.

Example (11). No foreign use--absence of foreign loss allocation rules. (i) Facts. P owns DE1X and DRCX. DRCX is a member of the P consolidated group and owns FSX. DE1X owns FBX. P's interest in DE1X and P's indirect interest in FBX are individual separate units that are combined into a single separate unit (Country X separate unit) pursuant to § 1.1503(d)-1(b)(4)(ii). In year 1, DRCX incurs a $200x net operating loss and $200x of income is attributable to P's Country X separate unit. The $200x net operating loss incurred by DRCX is a dual consolidated loss. FSX also earns $200x of income in year 1. DRCX, DE1X, and FSX file a Country X consolidated tax return. However, Country X has no applicable rules for determining which income is offset by DRCX's year 1 $200x loss.

(ii) Result. Under § 1.1503(d)-3(c)(3), DRCX's $200x loss shall be treated as having been made available to offset the $200x of income attributable to P's Country X separate unit. P's Country X separate unit is not, under U.S. tax principles, a foreign corporation, and there is no interest in DE1X (which is a hybrid entity) that is not a separate unit. As a result, DRCX's loss being made available to offset the income attributable to P's Country X separate unit is not considered a foreign use of such loss. Therefore, P can make a domestic use election with respect to DRCX's year 1 dual consolidated loss.

(iii) Alternative facts. The facts are the same as in paragraph (i) of this Example 11, except that in year 1 only $150x of income is attributable to P's Country X separate unit. Because only $150x of income is attributed to P's Country X separate unit, $50x of DRCX's year 1 dual consolidated loss is treated as being made available to offset the income of FSX, a foreign corporation, and therefore constitutes a foreign use. As a result, DRCX cannot make a domestic use election with respect to its year 1 dual consolidated loss pursuant to § 1.1503(d)-6(d)(2), and such loss will be subject to the domestic use limitation rule of § 1.1503(d)-4(b).

Example (12). No foreign use--absence of foreign loss usage ordering rules. (i) Facts. (A) P owns DRCX, a member of the P consolidated group. DRCX owns FSX. Under the Country X consolidation regime, a consolidated group may elect in any given year to use all or a portion of the losses of one consolidated group member to offset income of other consolidated group members. If no such election is made in a year in which losses are generated by a consolidated member, such losses carry forward and are available, at the election of the consolidated group, to offset income of consolidated group members in subsequent taxable years. Country X law does not provide ordering rules for determining when a loss from a particular taxable year is used because, under Country X law, losses never expire. In addition, Country X law does not provide ordering rules for determining when a particular type of loss (for example, capital or ordinary) is used.

(B) In year 1, DRCX incurs a capital loss of $80x which, under § 1.1503(d)-5(b)(2), is not a dual consolidated loss. DRCX also incurs a net operating loss of $80x in year 1 which is a dual consolidated loss. FSX generates $60x of capital gain in year 1 which, for Country X purposes, can be offset by capital losses and net operating losses. Under the laws of Country X, DRCX elects to use $60x of its total year 1 loss of $160x to offset the $60x of capital gain generated by FSX in year 1; the remaining $100x of year 1 loss carries forward. In both year 2 and year 3, DRCX incurs a net operating loss of $100x, while FSX incurs no income or loss in years 2 and 3. DRCX's $100x losses incurred in year 2 and year 3 are dual consolidated losses. Because DRCX does not elect under the laws of Country X to use all or a portion of its year 2 or year 3 net operating losses of $100x to offset the income of other members of the Country X consolidated group, P is permitted to make (and in fact does make) a domestic use election with respect to both the year 2 and year 3 dual consolidated losses of DRCX. In year 4, DRCX has a net operating loss of $10x and FSX generates $125x of income. Country X law permits, upon an election, FSX's $125x of income generated in year 4 to be offset by losses (including carryover losses from prior years) of other group members. Accordingly, in year 4, DRCX elects to use $125x of its accumulated losses to offset the $125x of year 4 income generated by FSX.

(ii) Result. (A) Under the ordering rules of § 1.1503(d)-3(d)(3), a pro rata amount of DRCX's year 1 net operating loss ($30x) and capital loss ($30x) is considered to be used to offset FSX's year 1 $60x capital gain. As a result, P cannot make a domestic use election with respect to DRCX's year 1 $80x dual consolidated loss because a portion of such loss is put to a foreign use.

(B) DRCX's $10x year 4 net operating loss is also a dual consolidated loss. Under the ordering rules of § 1.1503(d)-3(d)(1), such loss is considered to be used to offset $10x of FSX's year 4 $125x of income. Consequently, P cannot make a domestic use election with respect to such loss. Under the ordering rules of § 1.1503(d)-3(d)(2), $50x of capital loss carryover and $50x of ordinary loss from year 1 will be considered to offset $100x of FSX's year 4 income because the income is first deemed to have been offset by losses the use of which would not constitute a triggering event that would result in the recapture of a dual consolidated loss. The remaining $15x of FSX's year 4 income is considered to be offset by losses from year 3 because it is the most recent taxable year from which a loss may be carried forward. Thus, a portion of the year 3 dual consolidated loss has been put to a foreign use and the entire year 3 dual consolidated loss is recaptured. However, none of DRCX's $100x year 2 net operating loss will be deemed to offset FSX's year 4 income. As a result, DRCX's year 2 dual consolidated loss will not be recaptured.

Example (13). Exception to foreign use through partnership interest. (i) Facts. (A) P owns 80 percent of HPSX, a Country X entity subject to Country X tax on its worldwide income. FSZ, an unrelated foreign corporation, owns the remaining 20 percent of HPSX. HPSX is classified as a partnership for Federal tax purposes and carries on operations in Country X that, if carried on by a U.S. person, would constitute a foreign branch within the meaning of § 1.367(a)-6T(g)(1). P's interest in HPSX and P's indirect interest in the Country X branch are individual separate units that are combined into a single separate unit (Country X separate unit) pursuant to § 1.1503(d)-1(b)(4)(ii).

(B) In year 1, HPSX incurs a loss of $100x, $80x of which is attributable to P's Country X separate unit. The $80x of loss attributable to P's Country X separate unit constitutes a dual consolidated loss and P makes a domestic use election with respect to such loss. In year 2, HPSX generates $50x of income, $40x of which is attributable to P's interest in the Country X separate unit. Under Country X income tax laws, the $100x of year 1 loss incurred by HPSX is carried forward and offsets the $50x of income generated by HPSX in year 2; the remaining $50x of loss is carried forward and is available to offset income generated by HPSX in subsequent years. P and FSZ maintain their ownership interests in HPSX throughout years 1 and 2.

(ii) Result. In year 2, under the laws of Country X, the $100x of year 1 loss, which includes the $80x dual consolidated loss attributable to P's Country X separate unit, is made available to offset income of HPSX. Such income is attributable to P's interest in HPSX, which is a separate unit. Such income also is income of FSZ, a foreign corporation that is an owner of an interest in HPSX, which is not a separate unit. However, pursuant to § 1.1503(d)-3(c)(4), there is no foreign use of the year 1 dual consolidated loss in year 2.

This is the case because P's interest in HPSX as of the end of year 1 has not been reduced by more than a de minimis amount, and the portion of the $80x dual consolidated loss was made available for a foreign use in year 2 solely as a result of FSZ's ownership in HPSX and the allocation or carry forward of the dual consolidated loss as a result of such ownership.

(iii) Alternative facts. The facts are the same as in paragraph (i) of this Example 13, except that P also owns FSX. In addition, FSX and HPSX elect to file a consolidated return under Country X law. The exception to foreign use under § 1.1503(d)-3(c)(4) does not apply because there is a foreign use other than by reason of the dual consolidated loss being made available as a result of FSZ's ownership in HPSX and the allocation or carry forward of the dual consolidated loss as a result of such ownership. That is, the exception does not apply because there is also a foreign use of the dual consolidated loss as a result of FSX and HPSX filing a consolidated return under Country X law.

(iv) Alternative facts. The facts are the same as in paragraph (i) of this Example 13, except that at the end of year 2, FSZ contributes cash to HPSX in exchange for additional equity of HPSX. As a result of the contribution, FSZ's interest in HPSX increases from 20 percent to 30 percent, and P's interest in HPSX decreases from 80 percent to 70 percent. P's interest in HPSX is reduced within a single 12-month period by 12.5 percent (10/80), as compared to P's interest in HPSX as of the beginning of such 12-month period. Accordingly, pursuant to § 1.1503(d)-3(c)(4)(iii), the exception to foreign use provided under § 1.1503(d)-3(c)(4)(i) does not apply. Therefore, in year 2 there is a foreign use of the $80x year 1 dual consolidated loss attributable to P's Country X separate unit. Such foreign use constitutes a triggering event in year 2 and the $80x year 1 dual consolidated loss is recaptured. Alternatively, if FSZ were a domestic corporation, there would not be a foreign use of the $80x year 1 dual consolidated loss because the loss would not be available to offset income that, under U.S. tax principles, is income of a foreign corporation or a direct or indirect owner of an interest in a hybrid entity that is not a separate unit.

Example (14). Exception to foreign use through partnership interest--combination rule. (i) Facts. (A) P and FSX form PRSX. P and FSX each own 50 percent of PRSX throughout years 1 and 2. PRSX is treated as a partnership for both U.S. and Country X tax purposes. PRSX owns DEY. DEY is a Country Y entity subject to Country Y tax on its worldwide income and disregarded as an entity separate from its owner for U.S. tax purposes. DEY conducts business operations in Country Y that, if carried on by a U.S. person, would constitute a foreign branch as defined in § 1.367(a)-6T(g)(1). P's interest in the Country Y operations conducted by DEY is an individual foreign branch separate unit. P's interest in DEY, owned indirectly through PRSX, is a hybrid entity individual separate unit. P also owns FBY, a Country Y foreign branch individual separate unit. Under § 1.1503(d)-1(b)(4)(ii), FBY and P's indirect interests in DEY and DEY's Country Y business operations are treated as a combined separate unit (Country Y separate unit).

(B) In year 1, there is a $100x loss attributable to the Country Y business operations conducted by DEY. Thus, there is a $50x loss attributable to P's interest in DEY's Country Y business operations in year 1. Also in year 1, there is a $200x loss attributable to FBY. No income or loss is attributable to P's interest in DEY in year 1. Under § 1.1503(d)-5(c)(4)(ii), the dual consolidated loss attributable to P's combined Country Y separate unit is $250x ($50x loss attributable to P's indirect interest in DEY's Country Y operations, plus $200x loss attributable to FBY). In year 2, neither DEY nor DEY's Country Y operations generates income or loss. Under Country Y law, the $100x of year 1 loss incurred by DEY is carried forward and is available to offset income of DEY in year 2.

(ii) Result. As a result of the carryover of the year 1 $100x loss (which includes $50x of the year 1 dual consolidated loss) under Country Y law, a portion of such loss will be available to offset income of DEY that is attributable to P's interest in DEY owned indirectly through PRSX. A portion of such loss will also be available to offset income of DEY that is attributable to FSX's indirect ownership of DEY. Accordingly, under § 1.1503(d)-3(a), there would be a foreign use of a portion of P's $250x year 1 dual consolidated loss because it is available to offset an item of income of the owner of an interest in a hybrid entity, which is not a separate unit (there would also be a foreign use in this case because FSX is a foreign corporation). However, there has not been a reduction of P's interest in DEY, DEY has not consolidated under the laws of Country Y, and there has not been any other foreign use of the dual consolidated losses. As a result, no foreign use occurs as a result of the carryforward pursuant to § 1.1503(d)-3(c)(4)(i) and (ii).

Example (15). No foreign use--asset basis carryover exception. (i) Facts. P owns FBX and FSX. In year 1, there is a dual consolidated loss attributable to FBX. P's items of income, gain, deduction, and loss that are taken into account in calculating FBX's dual consolidated loss include depreciation deductions attributable to FBX's assets. P makes a domestic use election under § 1.1503(d)-6(d) with respect to the year 1 dual consolidated loss of FBX. At the end of year 2, P contributes a portion of FBX's assets to FSX, in exchange for stock in FSX. The aggregate adjusted basis of the assets transferred by P to FSX is less than 10 percent of the aggregate adjusted basis of all of FBX's assets held at the beginning of year 2. In addition, no other assets of FBX are transferred during the certification period. Under Country X law, FSX's basis in the transferred assets is determined by reference to P's basis in such assets. In addition, under Country X law, a portion of the depreciation deductions that were taken into account in year 1 for U.S. tax purposes, are taken into account in year 2 for Country X tax purposes.

(ii) Result. As a result of the transfer of assets from P to FSX, a portion of the year 1 dual consolidated loss is available for a foreign use. This is the case because a portion of the basis in FBX's assets, which gave rise to depreciation deductions that were taken into account in computing the year 1 dual consolidated loss, will give rise to a depreciation deduction under Country X laws that will be available, under U.S. tax principles, to offset the income of FSX, a foreign corporation, in year 2. However, the aggregate adjusted basis of all the assets transferred by P to FSX, within the 12-month period ending at the end of year 2, is less than 10 percent of the aggregate adjusted basis of all of FBX's assets at the beginning of such 12-month period. Moreover, the aggregate adjusted basis of the assets transferred by P to FSX at any time during the certification period is less than 30 percent of the aggregate adjusted basis of FBX's assets held at the end of year 1. In addition, the item of deduction giving rise to the foreign use is being made available solely as a result of the adjusted basis of the transferred assets being determined in whole, or in part, by reference to the adjusted basis of such transferred assets in the hands of FBX. As a result, this transfer will not result in a foreign use pursuant to § 1.1503(d)-3(c)(6).

Example (16). No foreign use--liability assumption exception. (i) Facts. P owns FBX. In year 1, there is a dual consolidated loss attributable to FBX for which P makes a domestic use election under § 1.1503(d)-6(d). The dual consolidated loss includes a deduction for salary expense that was deductible for U.S. tax purposes at the end of year 1, even though it was not paid until year 2. The deduction was incurred in the ordinary course of FBX's trade or business. During year 2, and before the accrued salary expense liability was paid, P sells all the assets of FBX to FSX in exchange for cash and FSX's assumption of the liabilities of the FBX trade or business, including the obligation to pay the accrued salary expense. Under Country X law, the accrued salary expense of FBX is deductible, and is taken into account for purposes of computing the taxable income of FBX, when paid. FBX pays the accrued salary expense after the sale of FBX to FSX.

(ii) Result. (A) As a result of FSX's assumption of the FBX liabilities, including the accrued salary expense, a portion of the dual consolidated loss is available for a foreign use in year 2. This is the case because the deduction that was taken into account in year 1 in computing the dual consolidated loss under U.S. tax principles will, under Country X tax law, be taken into account and will be available to offset the income of FSX, a foreign corporation, in year 2. However, because this item of expense is made available solely as a result of the assumption of a liability of FBX, and such liability was incurred in the ordinary course of FBX's trade or business, there will not be a foreign use of the year 1 dual consolidated loss pursuant to § 1.1503(d)-3(c)(7).

(B) The transfer of all the assets of FBX to FSX is a triggering event under § 1.1503(d)-6(e)(1)(iv), unless P can rebut the triggering event under § 1.1503(d)-6(e)(2). For purposes of determining whether, under § 1.1503(d)-6(e)(2)(ii), the transfer of assets resulted in a carryover under foreign law of FBX's losses, expenses, or deductions, the exception to foreign use for the assumption of liabilities is taken into account. However, the other exceptions to foreign use do not apply for this purpose (or for purposes of demonstrating that no foreign use of a dual consolidated loss can occur in any other year under § 1.1503(d)-6(c), (e)(2)(i) or (j)(2)). See § 1.1503(d)-3(c)(1). Provided the other requirements of § 1.1503(d)-6(e)(2)(ii) and (iii) are satisfied, P may be able to rebut the occurrence of a triggering event upon the transfer of FBX's assets to FSX.

Example (17). Mirror legislation rule--dual resident corporation and hybrid entity separate unit. (i) Facts. P owns DRCX, a member of the P consolidated group. DRCX owns FSX. In year 1, DRCX incurs a $100x net operating loss that is a dual consolidated loss. To prevent corporations like DRCX from offsetting losses both against income of affiliates in Country X and against income of foreign affiliates under the tax laws of another country, Country X mirror legislation prevents a corporation that is subject to the income tax of another country on its worldwide income or on a residence basis from using the Country X form of consolidation. Accordingly, the Country X mirror legislation prevents the loss of DRCX from being made available to offset income of FSX.

(ii) Result. Under § 1.1503(d)-3(e), because the losses of DRCX are subject to Country X's mirror legislation, there is a deemed foreign use of DRCX's year 1 dual consolidated loss. The stand-alone exception to the mirror rule in § 1.1503(d)-3(e)(2) does not apply because, absent the mirror legislation, DRCX's year 1 dual consolidated loss would be available for a foreign use (as defined in § 1.1503(d)-3), without regard to whether such availability is limited by election or similar procedure. That is, absent the mirror legislation, all or a portion of the dual consolidated loss would be available to offset the income of FSX under the Country X consolidation regime. This is the case even if Country X did not recognize DRCX as having a loss in year 1. Therefore, P may not make a domestic use election with respect to DRCX's year 1 dual consolidated loss pursuant to § 1.1503(d)-3(d)(2).

(iii) Alternative facts. The facts are the same as in paragraph (i) of this Example 17, except that P owns DE1X (rather than DRCX) and, in year 1, there is a $100 dual consolidated loss attributable to P's interest in DE1X (rather than of DRCX). The Country X mirror legislation only applies to Country X dual resident corporations and, therefore, does not apply to losses attributable to P's interest in DE1X. As a result, the mirror legislation rule under § 1.1503(d)-3(e) would not deny the opportunity of such loss from being put to a foreign use (for example, by offsetting the income of FSX through the Country X consolidation regime). Therefore, a domestic use election can be made with respect to the dual consolidated loss (provided the conditions for such an election are otherwise satisfied).

Example (18). Mirror legislation rule--standalone foreign branch separate unit. (i) Facts. P owns FBX. In year 1, there is a $100x dual consolidated loss attributable to FBX. Country X enacted mirror legislation to prevent Country X branches and permanent establishments of nonresident corporations from offsetting losses both against income of Country X affiliates and against other income of its owner (or foreign affiliates thereof) under the tax laws of another country. The Country X mirror legislation prevents a Country X branch or permanent establishment of a nonresident corporation from offsetting its losses against the income of Country X affiliates if such losses may be deductible against income (other than income of the Country X branch or permanent establishment) under the laws of another country.

(ii) Result. In general, under § 1.1503(d)-3(e), because the losses of FBX are subject to Country X's mirror legislation, there is a deemed foreign use of FBX's year 1 dual consolidated loss. However, in the absence of the Country X mirror legislation, no item of deduction or loss composing FBX's year 1 dual consolidated loss would be available in the year incurred for a foreign use (as defined in § 1.1503(d)-3), without regard to whether such availability is limited by election or otherwise. This is the case because there is no Country X entity through which the dual consolidated loss could be put to a foreign use (absent a sale, merger, or similar transaction involving FBX). As a result, the stand-alone exception in § 1.1503(d)-3(e)(2) may apply, provided P complies with the requirements of § 1.1503(d)-3(e)(2)(ii). Accordingly, P may make a domestic use election with respect to the year 1 dual consolidated loss of FBX pursuant to § 1.1503(d)-6(d). If, however, any item of the dual consolidated loss would otherwise be available for a foreign use during the certification period (for example, as a result of P acquiring a foreign corporation that is organized under the laws of Country X such that losses of FBX could be put to a foreign use through consolidation or similar means), then such loss would be recaptured pursuant to § 1.1503(d)-6(e)(1)(ix).

(iii) Alternative facts. The facts are the same as in paragraph (i) of this Example 18, except that the Country X mirror legislation operates in a manner similar to the rules under section 1503(d). That is, it allows the taxpayer to elect to use the loss to either offset income of an affiliate in Country X, or income of an affiliate (or other income of the owner of the Country X branch or permanent establishment) in the other country, but not both. Because the Country X mirror legislation permits the taxpayer to choose to put the dual consolidated loss to a foreign use, it does not deny the opportunity to put the loss to a foreign use. Therefore, there is no deemed foreign use of the dual consolidated loss pursuant to § 1.1503(d)-4(e) and a domestic use election can be made for such loss.

Example (19). Application of mirror legislation rule to combined separate unit. (i) Facts. P owns FBX, FSX, and DE1X. In year 1, there is a $50x dual consolidated loss attributable to FBX and $10x of income attributable to P's interest in DE1X. FSX has income of $100x. Pursuant to § 1.1503(d)-1(b)(4)(ii), FBX and P's interest in DE1X are combined and treated as a single separate unit (Country X separate unit) which has a year 1 dual consolidated loss of $40x. Country X enacted mirror legislation to prevent Country X branches or permanent establishments of nonresident corporations from offsetting losses both against income of Country X affiliates and against other income of its owner (or foreign affiliates thereof) under the tax laws of another country. The Country X mirror legislation prevents a Country X branch or permanent establishment of a nonresident corporation from offsetting its losses against the income of Country X affiliates if such losses may be deductible against income (other than income of the Country X branch or permanent establishment) under the laws of another country. However, the United States and Country X have entered into an agreement described in § 1.1503(d)-6(b) pursuant to the U.S.-Country X income tax convention (mirror agreement). The mirror agreement applies to Country X foreign branch separate units of domestic corporations, but not to Country X hybrid entity separate units. The mirror agreement provides that neither the Country X mirror legislation nor the mirror legislation rule under § 1.1503(d)-3(e) will apply to losses attributable to Country X foreign branch separate units, provided certain conditions and reporting requirements are satisfied (including a domestic use election, if the loss is to be used to offset income of a domestic affiliate). Thus, losses attributable to Country X foreign branch separate units can, subject to the requirements of the mirror agreement, be used to offset income of a domestic affiliate or a Country X affiliate (but not both).

(ii) Result. The Country X mirror legislation only applies to Country X foreign branch separate units and does not apply to hybrid entity separate units. In addition, if P complies with the terms and conditions of the mirror agreement, the Country X mirror legislation would not apply to FBX. As a result, the income tax laws of Country X would not deny the opportunity of a loss of either individual separate unit that composes P's combined Country X separate unit from being put to a foreign use. Therefore, notwithstanding § 1.1503(d)-3(e), a domestic use election can be made with respect to the dual consolidated loss attributable to P's Country X separate unit, provided the terms and conditions of the mirror agreement are satisfied. See § 1.1503(d)-6(b)(2).

(iii) Alternative facts. The facts are the same as in paragraph (i) of this Example 19, except that the Country X mirror legislation also applies to losses attributable to DE1X, but the mirror agreement does not apply to such losses. The mirror legislation rule would apply with respect to P's interest in DE1X and, as a result, there is a deemed foreign use of the dual consolidated loss attributable to the Country X separate unit and a domestic use election cannot be made for such loss. This is the case even though, pursuant to § 1.1503(d)-5(c)(4)(ii)(A), P's interest in DE1X (which is subject to the Country X mirror legislation) does not, as an individual separate unit, have a dual consolidated loss in year 1. Further, the stand-alone exception to the mirror legislation rule in § 1.1503(d)-3(e)(2) does not apply because, absent the mirror legislation, the Country X combined separate unit's dual consolidated loss would be available in the year incurred for a foreign use (as defined in § 1.1503(d)-3) because it could be used to offset income of FSX under the Country X consolidation regime. This is the case even if Country X requires an election to consolidate and no such election is made. The result would be the same even if Country X did not recognize DE1X as having a loss.

Example (20). Dual consolidated loss limitation after section 381 transaction--disposition of assets and subsequent liquidation of dual resident corporation. (i) Facts. P owns DRCX, a member of the P consolidated group. In year 1, DRCX incurs a dual consolidated loss and P does not make a domestic use election with respect to such loss. Under § 1.1503(d)-4(b), DRCX's year 1 dual consolidated loss is subject to the limitations under § 1.1503(d)-4(c) and, therefore, may not be used to offset the income of P or S (or any other domestic affiliate) on the group's U.S. income tax return. At the beginning of year 2, DRCX sells all of its assets for cash and distributes the cash to P pursuant to a liquidation that qualifies under section 332.

(ii) Result. In general, under section 381, P would succeed to, and be permitted to use, DRCX's net operating loss carryover. However, § 1.1503(d)-4(d)(1)(i) prohibits the dual consolidated loss of DRCX from carrying over to P. Therefore, DRCX's year 1 net operating loss carryover is eliminated.

Example (21). Dual consolidated loss limitation applied to a separate unit transferred in a section 381 transaction. (i) Facts. S owns DE1X which, in turn, owns FBX. S's interest in DE1X and its indirect interest in FBX are combined and treated as a single separate unit (Country X separate unit) pursuant to § 1.1503(d)-1(b)(4)(ii). In year 1, a dual consolidated loss is attributable to the Country X separate unit, and P does not make a domestic use election with respect to such loss. Under § 1.1503(d)-4(b), the year 1 dual consolidated loss attributable to the Country X separate unit may not be used to offset the income of P or S (other than income attributable to the Country X separate unit, subject to the application of § 1.1503(d)-4(c)) on the group's consolidated U.S. income tax return (nor may it be used to offset the income of any other domestic affiliates). At the beginning of year 2, S transfers its entire interest in DE1X, and thus its entire indirect interest in FBX, to FSX in a transaction described in section 381.

(ii) Result. Section 1.1503(d)-4(d)(1)(ii) provides that the dual consolidated loss attributable to a separate unit that is subject to the domestic use limitation under § 1.1503(d)-4(b) is eliminated if the separate unit ceases to be a separate unit of its affiliated domestic owner and all other members of the affiliated domestic owner's separate group. As a result of the transfer of the Country X separate unit to FSX, the Country X separate unit ceases to be a separate unit of S, and is not a separate unit of any other member of the P consolidated group. In addition, the exceptions in § 1.1503(d)-4(d)(2)(iii) do not apply because FSX is not a domestic corporation. Thus, the year 1 dual consolidated loss attributable to the Country X separate unit is eliminated.

(iii) Alternative facts. Assume the same facts as in paragraph (i) of this Example 21, except S transfers its assets to DC, a domestic corporation that is not a member of the P consolidated group, in a transaction described in section 381(a). Immediately after the transaction, the Country X separate unit is a separate unit of DC. Under § 1.1503(d)-4(d)(1)(ii), the year 1 dual consolidated loss of the Country X separate unit would be eliminated because it ceases to be a separate unit of S, and is not a separate unit of any other member of the P consolidated group. However, because the transferee is a domestic corporation and the Country X separate unit is a separate unit in the hands of DC immediately after the transaction, the exception under § 1.1503(d)-4(d)(2)(iii)(A) applies. As a result, the year 1 dual consolidated loss of the Country X separate unit is not eliminated and any income generated by DC that is attributable to the Country X separate unit following the transfer may be offset by the carryover dual consolidated losses attributable to the Country X separate unit, subject to the limitations of § 1.1503(d)-4(b) and (c) applied as if DC generated the dual consolidated loss and such loss was attributable to the Country X separate unit.

(iv) Alternative facts. Assume the same facts as in paragraph (iii) of this Example 21, except that P owns DE2X and the interest in DE2X is combined with and therefore included in the Country X separate unit. In addition, a portion of the dual consolidated loss of the Country X separate unit is attributable to P's interest in DE2X. Pursuant to § 1.1503(d)-4(d)(2)(iii)(A), the result would be the same as in paragraph (iii) of this Example 21, with respect to the portion of the dual consolidated loss attributable to the combined separate unit that is succeeded to and taken into account by DC pursuant to section 381. The portion of the dual consolidated loss attributable to P's interest in DE2X, however, does not carry over to DC but is retained by P and continues to be subject to the limitations of § 1.1503(d)-4(b) and (c) with respect to P's interest in DE2X.

(v) Alternative facts. Assume the same facts as in paragraph (iv) of this Example 21, except that DC is a member of the P consolidated group. Pursuant to § 1.1503(d)-4(d)(2)(iii)(B), the dual consolidated loss of the Country X separate unit is not eliminated and income attributable to the Country X separate unit may continue to be offset by the dual consolidated loss that is succeeded to and taken into account by DC pursuant to section 381, subject to the limitations of § 1.1503(d)-4(b) and (c). The result would be the same even if the interest in DE1X ceased to be a separate unit in the hands of DC (for example, because it dissolved under Country X law in connection with the transaction), provided P, or another member of the P consolidated group, continued to own a portion of the Country X separate unit.

Example (22). Tainted income. (i) Facts. P owns 100 percent of DRCZ, a domestic corporation that is included as a member of the P consolidated group. DRCZ conducts a business in the United States. During year 1, DRCZ was managed and controlled in Country Z and therefore was subject to tax as a resident of Country Z and was a dual resident corporation. In year 1, DRCZ incurred a dual consolidated loss of $200x, and P did not make a domestic use election with respect to such loss. As a result, such loss is subject to the domestic use limitation rule of § 1.1503(d)-4(b). At the end of year 1, DRCZ moved its management and control to the United States and, as a result, ceased being a dual resident corporation. At the beginning of year 2, P transferred asset A, a non-depreciable asset, to DRCZ in exchange for common stock in a transaction that qualified for nonrecognition under section 351. At the time of the transfer, P's tax basis in asset A equaled $50x and the fair market value of asset A equaled $100x. The tax basis of asset A in the hands of DRCZ immediately after the transfer equaled $50x pursuant to section 362. Asset A did not constitute replacement property acquired in the ordinary course of business. DRCZ did not generate income or gain during years 2, 3, or 4. On June 30, year 5, DRCZ sold asset A to a third party for $100x, its fair market value at the time of the sale, and recognized $50x of income on such sale. In addition to the $50x income generated on the sale of asset A, DRCZ generated $100x of operating income in year 5. At the end of year 5, the fair market value of all the assets of DRCZ was $400x.

(ii) Result. DRCZ ceased being a dual resident corporation at the end of year 1. Therefore, its year 1 dual consolidated loss cannot be offset by tainted income. Asset A is a tainted asset because it was acquired in a nonrecognition transaction after DRCZ ceased being a dual resident corporation (and was not replacement property acquired in the ordinary course of business). As a result, the $50x of income recognized by DRCZ on the disposition of asset A is tainted income and cannot be offset by the year 1 dual consolidated loss of DRCZ. In addition, absent evidence establishing the actual amount of tainted income, $25x of the $100x year 5 operating income of DRCZ (($100x/$400x) x $100x) also is treated as tainted income and cannot be offset by the year 1 dual consolidated loss of DRCZ under § 1.1503(d)-4(e)(2)(ii). Therefore, $75x of the $150x year 5 income of DRCZ constitutes tainted income and may not be offset by the year 1 dual consolidated loss of DRCZ; however, the remaining $75x of year 5 income of DRCZ may be offset by such dual consolidated loss. The result would be the same if, instead of P transferring asset A to DRCZ, such asset was received from a separate unit or a transparent entity of DRCZ.

Example (23). Treatment of disregarded item and books and records of a hybrid entity. (i) Facts. P owns DE1X which, in turn, owns FSX. In year 1, P borrows from a third party and on-lends the proceeds to DE1X. In year 1, P incurs interest expense attributable to the third-party loan. Also in year 1, DE1X incurs interest expense attributable to its loan from P, but such expense is generally disregarded for U.S. tax purposes because DE1X is disregarded as an entity separate from P. The third-party loan and related interest expense are reflected on the books and records of P (and not on the books and records of DE1X). The loan from P to DE1X and related interest expense are reflected on the books and records of DE1X. There are no other items of income, gain, deduction, or loss reflected on the books and records of DE1X in year 1.

(ii) Result. Because the interest expense on P's third-party loan is not reflected on the books and records of DE1X, no portion of such expense is attributable to P's interest in DE1X pursuant to § 1.1503(d)-5(c)(3) for purposes of calculating the year 1 dual consolidated loss, if any, attributable to such interest. In addition, even though P's interest in DE1X is treated as a separate domestic corporation for purposes of determining the amount of income or dual consolidated loss attributable to it pursuant to § 1.1503(d)-5(c)(1)(ii), such treatment does not cause the interest expense incurred on the loan from P to DE1X that is generally disregarded for U.S. tax purposes to be regarded for purposes of calculating the year 1 dual consolidated loss, if any, attributable to P's interest in DE1X. As a result, even though the disregarded interest expense is reflected on the books and records of DE1X, it is not taken into account for purposes of calculating income or a dual consolidated loss. Therefore, there is no dual consolidated loss attributable to P's interest in DE1X in year 1.

Example (24). Dividend income attributable to a separate unit. (i) Facts. P owns DE1X which, in turn, owns FBX. P's interest in DE1X and its indirect interest in FBX are combined and treated as a single separate unit (Country X separate unit) pursuant to § 1.1503(d)-1(b)(4)(ii). DE1X owns DE3Y. DE3Y owns the stock of FSX. P's Country X separate unit would, without regard to year 1 dividend income (or related section 78 gross-up) received from FSX, have a dual consolidated loss of $75x in year 1. In year 1, FSX distributes $50x to DE3Y that is taxable as a dividend. DE3Y distributes the same amount to DE1X. P computes foreign taxes deemed paid on the dividend under section 902 of $25x and includes that amount in gross income under section 78.

(ii) Result. The $50x dividend is reflected on the books and records of DE3Y and, therefore, is attributable to P's interest in DE3Y pursuant to § 1.1503(d)-5(c)(3)(i). In addition, the $25x section 78 gross-up is attributable to P's interest in DE3Y pursuant to § 1.1503(d)-5(c)(4)(iv). The distribution of $50x from DE3Y to DE1X is generally disregarded for U.S. tax purposes and, therefore, does not give rise to an item that is taken into account for purposes of calculating income or a dual consolidated loss. This is the case even though the item would be reflected on the books and records of DE1X. In addition, pursuant to § 1.1503(d)-5(c)(1)(iii), each separate unit must calculate its own income or dual consolidated loss, and each item of income, gain, deduction, and loss must be taken into account only once. As a result, the dual consolidated loss of $75x attributable to P's Country X separate unit in year 1 is not reduced by the amount of dividend income attributable to P's indirect interest in DE3Y.

Example (25). Items reflected on books and records of a combined separate unit. (i) Facts. P owns DE1X which, in turn, owns FBX. P's interest in DE1X and its indirect interest in FBX are combined and treated as a single separate unit (Country X separate unit) pursuant to § 1.1503(d)-1(b)(4)(ii). The following items are reflected on the books and records of DE1X in year 1: Sales, depreciation expense, a political contribution, royalty expense paid to P, repairs and maintenance expense paid to a third party, and Country X income tax expense. The amount of sales under U.S. tax principles equals the amount of sales reported for accounting purposes. The depreciation expense is calculated on a straight-line basis over the useful life of the asset for accounting purposes, but is subject to accelerated depreciation for U.S. tax purposes. In addition, the repairs and maintenance expense, which is deducted when paid for accounting purposes, is properly capitalized and amortized over five years for U.S. tax purposes. Finally, P elects to claim as a credit under section 901 the Country X income tax expense that was paid in year 1.

(ii) Result. (A) For purposes of determining the income or dual consolidated loss attributable to P's Country X separate unit, items of income, gain, deduction, and loss must first be attributed to the individual separate units (that is, P's interest in DE1X and its indirect interest in FBX). For purposes of attributing items to P's interest in DE1X, P's items that are reflected on DE1X's books and records, as adjusted to conform to U.S. tax principles, are taken into account. See § 1.1503(d)-5(c)(3)(i). For purposes of attributing items (other than interest expense) to FBX, the principles of section 864(c)(2), (c)(4), and (c)(5) (as set forth in § 1.864-4(c) and §§ 1.864-5 through 1.864-7) must be applied and, for interest expense, the principles of § 1.882-5, as modified under § 1.1503(d)-5(c)(2)(ii), must be applied; however, for these purposes, pursuant to § 1.1503(d)-5(c)(4)(i)(A), FBX only takes into account items attributable to P's interest in DE1X and the assets, liabilities, and activities of such interest. In addition, to the extent such items are taken into account by FBX, they are not taken into account in determining the items attributable to P's interest in DE1X. § 1.1503(d)-5(c)(4)(i)(B). Because P's interest in DE1X has no assets or liabilities, and conducts no activities, other than through its ownership of FBX, all of the items that are reflected on the books and records of DE1X, as adjusted to conform to U.S. tax principles, are attributable to FBX; no items are attributable to P's interest in DE1X.

(B) The items reflected on the books and records of DE1X must be adjusted to conform to U.S. tax principles. No adjustment is required to sales because the amount of sales under U.S. tax principles equals the amount of sales for accounting purposes. The amount of straight-line depreciation expense reflected on DE1X's books and records must be adjusted to reflect the amount of depreciation on the asset that is allowable for U.S. tax purposes. The political contribution is not taken into account because it is not deductible for U.S. tax purposes. Similarly, because the royalty expense is paid to P, and therefore is generally disregarded for U.S. tax purposes, it is not taken into account. The repair and maintenance expense that is deducted in year 1 for accounting purposes also must be adjusted to conform to U.S. tax principles. Thus, the repair and maintenance expense will be taken into account in computing the income or dual consolidated loss attributable to P's Country X separate unit over five years (even though no item related to such expense would be reflected on the books and records of DE1X for years 2 through 5). Finally, because P elected to claim as a credit the Country X foreign taxes paid during year 1, no deduction is allowed for such amount pursuant to section 275(a)(4) and, therefore, the Country X tax expense is not taken into account.

(C) Pursuant to § 1.1503(d)-5(c)(4)(ii)(B), the combined Country X separate unit of P calculates its income or dual consolidated loss by taking into account all the items of income, gain, deduction, and loss that were separately attributable to P's interest in DE1X and FBX. However, in this case, there are no items attributable to P's interest in DE1X. Therefore, the items attributable to the Country X separate unit are the items attributable to FBX.

Example (26). Items attributable to a combined separate unit. (i) Facts. P owns DE1X. DE1X owns a 50 percent interest in PRSZ, a Country Z entity that is classified as a partnership both for Country Z tax purposes and for U.S. tax purposes. FSX, which is unrelated to P, owns the remaining 50 percent interest in PRSZ. PRSZ carries on operations in Country X that, if carried on by a U.S. person, would constitute a foreign branch as defined in § 1.367(a)-6T(g)(1). Therefore, P's share of the Country X operations carried on by PRSZ constitutes a foreign branch separate unit. PRSZ also owns assets that do not constitute a part of its Country X branch, including all of the interests in TET, a disregarded entity. TET is an entity incorporated under the laws of Country T, a country that does not have an income tax. Under the laws of Country X, an interest holder of TET does not take into account on a current basis the interest holder's share of items of income, gain, deduction, and loss of TET.

(ii) Result. (A) Pursuant to § 1.1503(d)-1(b)(4)(ii), P's interest in DE1X, and P's indirect ownership of a portion of the Country X operations carried on by PRSZ, are combined and treated as a single separate unit (Country X separate unit). Pursuant to § 1.1503(d)-5(c)(4)(ii)(A), for purposes of determining P's items of income, gain, deduction, and loss attributable to the Country X separate unit, the items of P are first attributed to each separate unit that composes the Country X separate unit.

(B) Pursuant to § 1.1503(d)-5(c)(2)(i), the principles of section 864(c)(2), (c)(4), and (c)(5) (as set forth in § 1.864-4(c) and §§ 1.864-5 through 1.864-7), apply for purposes of determining P's items of income, gain, deduction (other than interest expense), and loss that are attributable to P's indirect interest in the Country X operations carried on by PRSZ. For purposes of determining P's interest expense that is attributable to P's indirect interest in the Country X operations carried on by PRSZ, the principles of § 1.882-5, as modified under § 1.1503(d)-5(c)(2)(ii), shall apply. For purposes of applying these rules, P is treated as a foreign corporation, the Country X operations carried on by PRSZ are treated as a trade or business within the United States, and the assets of P (including its share of the PRSZ assets, other than those of the Country X operations) are treated as assets that are not U.S. assets. In addition, because P carries on its share of the Country X operations through DE1X, a hybrid entity, § 1.1503(d)-5(c)(4)(i)(A) provides that only the items attributable to P's interest in DE1X, and only the assets, liabilities, and activities of P's interest in DE1X, are taken into account for purposes of this determination.

(C) TET is a transparent entity as defined in § 1.1503(d)-1(b)(16) because it is not taxable as an association for Federal tax purposes, is not subject to income tax in a foreign country as a corporation (or otherwise at the entity level) either on its worldwide income or on a residence basis, and is not treated as a pass-through entity under the laws of Country X (the applicable foreign country). TET is not a pass-through entity under the laws of Country X because a Country X holder of an interest in TET does not take into account on a current basis the interest holder's share of items of income, gain, deduction, and loss of TET. For purposes of determining P's items of income, gain, deduction, and loss that are attributable to P's interest in TET, only those items of P that are reflected on the books and records of TET, as adjusted to conform to U.S. tax principles, are taken into account. § 1.1503(d)-5(c)(3)(i). Because the interest in TET is not a separate unit, a loss attributable to such interest is not a dual consolidated loss and is not subject to section 1503(d) and these regulations. Items must nevertheless be attributed to the interests in TET. For example, such attribution is required for purposes of calculating the income or dual consolidated loss attributable to the Country X separate unit, and for purposes of applying the domestic use limitation under § 1.1503(d)-4(b) to a dual consolidated loss attributable to the Country X separate unit.

(D) For purposes of determining P's items of income, gain, deduction, and loss that are attributable to P's interest in DE1X, only those items of P that are reflected on the books and records of DE1X, as adjusted to conform to U.S. tax principles, are taken into account. § 1.1503(d)-5(c)(3)(i). For this purpose, DE1X's distributive share of the items of income, gain, deduction, and loss that are reflected on the books and records of PRSZ, as adjusted to conform to U.S. tax principles, are treated as being reflected on the books and records of DE1X, except to the extent such items are taken into account by the Country X operations of PRSZ. See § 1.1503(d)-5(c)(3)(ii) and (4)(i)(B). Because TET is a transparent entity, the items reflected on its books and records are not treated as being reflected on the books and records of DE1X.

(E) Pursuant to § 1.1503(d)-5(c)(4)(ii)(B), the combined Country X separate unit of P calculates its income or dual consolidated loss by taking into account all the items of income, gain, deduction, and loss that were separately attributable to P's interest in DE1X and the Country X operations of PRSZ owned indirectly by P.

Example (27). Sale of separate unit by another separate unit. (i) Facts. P owns DE3Y which, in turn, owns DE1X. DE3Y also owns other assets that do not constitute a foreign branch separate unit. DE1X owns FBX. Pursuant to § 1.1503(d)-1(b)(4)(ii), P's indirect interests in DE1X and FBX are combined and treated as one Country X separate unit (Country X separate unit). DE3Y sells its interest in DE1X at the end of year 1 to an unrelated foreign person for cash. The sale results in an ordinary loss of $30x. Items of income, gain, deduction, and loss derived from the assets that gave rise to the $30x loss would be attributable to the Country X separate unit under § 1.1503(d)-5(c) through (e). Without regard to the sale of DE1X, no items of income, gain, deduction, and loss are attributable to P's Country X separate unit in year 1.

(ii) Result. Pursuant to § 1.1503(d)-5(c)(4)(iii)(A), the $30x ordinary loss recognized on the sale is attributable to the Country X separate unit, and not P's interest in DE3Y. This is the case because the Country X separate unit is treated as owning the assets that gave rise to the loss under § 1.1503(d)-5(f). Thus, the loss attributable to the sale creates a year 1 dual consolidated loss attributable to the Country X separate unit. In addition, pursuant to § 1.1503(d)-6(d)(2), P cannot make a domestic use election with respect to the dual consolidated loss because the sale of the interest in DE1X is a triggering event described in § 1.1503(d)-6(e)(1)(iv) and (v). Further, although the year 1 dual consolidated loss would otherwise be subject to the domestic use limitation rule of § 1.1503(d)-4(b), it is eliminated pursuant to § 1.1503(d)-4(d)(1)(ii). Finally, if there were a dual consolidated loss attributable to P's interest in DE3Y, the sale of the interest in DE1X would not be taken into account for purposes of determining whether there is an asset triggering event with respect to such dual consolidated loss under § 1.1503(d)-6(e)(1)(iv).

Example (28). Gain on sale of tiered separate units. (i) Facts. P owns 75 percent of HPSX, a Country X entity subject to Country X tax on its worldwide income. FSX owns the remaining 25 percent of HPSX. HPSX is classified as a partnership for Federal tax purposes. HPSX carries on operations in Country Y that, if carried on by a U.S. person, would constitute a foreign branch within the meaning of § 1.367(a)-6T(g)(1). HPSX also owns assets that do not constitute a part of its Country Y operations and would not themselves constitute a foreign branch within the meaning of § 1.367(a)-6T(g)(1) if owned by a U.S. person. Neither HPSX nor the Country Y operations has liabilities. P's indirect interest in the Country Y operations carried on by HPSX, and P's interest in HPSX, are each separate units. P sells its interest in HPSX and recognizes a gain of $150x on such sale. Immediately prior to P's sale of its interest in HPSX, P's portion of the assets of the Country Y operations (that is, assets the income, gain, deduction and loss from which would be attributable to P's Country Y foreign branch separate unit) had a built-in gain of $200x, and P's portion of HPSX's other assets (that is, assets the income, gain, deduction and loss from which would be attributable to P's interest in HPSX) had a built-in gain of $100x.

(ii) Result. Pursuant to § 1.1503(d)-5(c)(4)(iii)(B), $100x of the total $150x of gain recognized ($200x/$300x x $150x) is attributable to P's indirect interest in its share of the Country Y operations carried on by HPSX. Similarly, $50x of such gain ($100x/$300x x $150x) is attributable to P's interest in HPSX.

Example (29). Effect on domestic affiliate. (i) Facts. (A) P owns DE1X which, in turn, owns FBX. P's interest in DE1X and its indirect interest in FBX are combined and treated as a single separate unit (Country X separate unit) pursuant to § 1.1503(d)-1(b)(4)(ii). In years 1 and 2, the items of income, gain, deduction, and loss that are attributable to P's Country X separate unit pursuant to § 1.1503(d)-5 are as follows:

Item	Year 1	Year 2
Sales income	$100x	$160x
Salary expense	($75x)	($75x)
Research and experimental expense	($50x)	($50x)
Interest expense	($25x)	($25x)
Income/(dual consolidated loss)	($50x)	$10x

(B) P does not make a domestic use election with respect to the year 1 dual consolidated loss attributable to its Country X separate unit. Pursuant to § 1.1503(d)-4(b) and (c)(2), the year 1 dual consolidated loss of $50x is treated as a loss incurred by a separate domestic corporation and is subject to the limitations under § 1.1503(d)-4(c)(3). The P consolidated group has $100x of consolidated taxable income in year 2.

(ii) Result. (A) P must compute its taxable income for year 1 without taking into account the $50x dual consolidated loss, pursuant to § 1.1503(d)-4(c)(2). Such amount consists of a pro rata portion of the expenses that were taken into account in calculating the year 1 dual consolidated loss. Thus, the items of the dual consolidated loss that are not taken into account by P in computing its taxable income are as follows: $25x of salary expense ($75x/$150x x $50x); $16.67x of research and experimental expense ($50x/$150x x $50x); and $8.33x of interest expense ($25x/$150x x $50x). The remaining amounts of each of these items, together with the $100x of sales income, are taken into account by P in computing its taxable income for year 1 as follows: $50x of salary expense ($75x - $25x); $33.33x of research and experimental expense ($50x - $16.67x); and $16.67x of interest expense ($25x - $8.33x).

(B) Subject to the limitations provided under § 1.1503(d)-4(c), the year 1 $50x dual consolidated loss is carried forward and is available to offset the $10x of income attributable to the Country X separate unit in year 2. Pursuant to § 1.1503(d)-4(c)(4), a pro rata portion of each item of deduction or loss included in such dual consolidated loss is considered to be used to offset the $10x of income, as follows: $5x of salary expense ($25x/ $50x x $10x); $3.33x of research and experimental expense ($16.67x/ $50x x $10x); and $1.67x of interest expense ($8.33x/$50x x $10x). The remaining amount of each item shall continue to be subject to the limitations under § 1.1503(d)-4(c).

Example (30). Exception to domestic use limitation--no possibility of foreign use because items are not deducted or capitalized under foreign law. (i) Facts. P owns DE1X which, in turn, owns FSX. In year 1, the sole item of income, gain, deduction, and loss attributable to P's interest in DE1X, as provided under § 1.1503(d)-5, is $100x of interest expense paid on a loan to an unrelated lender. For Country X tax purposes, the $100x interest expense attributable to P's interest in DE1X in year 1 is treated as a repayment of principal and therefore cannot be deducted (at any time) or capitalized.

(ii) Result. The $100x of interest expense attributable to P's interest in DE1X constitutes a dual consolidated loss. However, because the sole item constituting the dual consolidated loss cannot be deducted or capitalized (at any time) for Country X tax purposes, P can demonstrate that there can be no foreign use of the dual consolidated loss at any time. As a result, pursuant to § 1.1503(d)-6(c)(1), if P prepares a statement described in § 1.1503(d)-6(c)(2) and attaches it to its timely filed tax return, the year 1 dual consolidated loss attributable to P's interest in DE1X will not be subject to the domestic use limitation rule of § 1.1503(d)-4(b).

Example (31). No exception to domestic use limitation--inability to demonstrate no possibility of foreign use. (i) Facts. P owns DE1X which, in turn, owns FBX. P's interest in DE1X and its indirect interest in FBX are combined and treated as a single separate unit (Country X separate unit) pursuant to § 1.1503(d)-1(b)(4)(ii). In year 1, the sole items of income, gain, deduction, and loss attributable to P's Country X separate unit, as provided under § 1.1503(d)-5, are $75x of sales income and $100x of depreciation expense. For Country X tax purposes, DE1X also generates $75x of sales income in year 1, but the $100x of depreciation expense is not deductible until year 2.

(ii) Result. The year 1 $25x net loss attributable to P's interest in the Country X separate unit constitutes a dual consolidated loss. In addition, even though DE1X has positive income in year 1 for Country X tax purposes, P cannot demonstrate that there is no possibility of foreign use with respect to the Country X separate unit's dual consolidated loss as provided under § 1.1503(d)-6(c)(1)(i). P cannot make such a demonstration because the depreciation expense, an item composing the year 1 dual consolidated loss, is deductible (in a later year) for Country X tax purposes and, therefore, may be available to offset or reduce income for Country X purposes that would constitute a foreign use. For example, if DE1X elected to be classified as a corporation pursuant to § 301.7701-3(c) of this chapter effective as of the end of year 1, and the deferred depreciation expense were available for Country X tax purposes to offset year 2 income of DE1X, an entity treated as a foreign corporation in year 2 for U.S. tax purposes, there would be a foreign use.

(iii) Alternative facts. (A) The facts are the same as in paragraph (i) of this Example 31, except as follows. In year 1, the sole items of income, gain, deduction, and loss attributable to P's Country X separate unit, as provided in § 1.1503(d)-5, are $75x of sales income, $100x of interest expense, and $25x of depreciation expense. For Country X tax purposes, DE1X generates $75x of sales income in year

1; the $100x interest expense is treated as a repayment of principal and therefore cannot be deducted or capitalized (at any time); and the $25x of depreciation expense is not deductible in year 1, but is deductible in year 2.

(B) In year 1, the $50x net loss attributable to P's Country X separate unit constitutes a dual consolidated loss. Even though the $100x interest expense, a nondeductible and noncapital item for Country X tax purposes, exceeds the $50x year 1 dual consolidated loss attributable to P's Country X separate unit, P cannot demonstrate that there is no possibility of foreign use of the dual consolidated loss as provided under § 1.1503(d)-6(c)(1)(i). P cannot make such a demonstration because the $25x depreciation expense, an item of deduction or loss composing the year 1 dual consolidated loss, is deductible under Country X law (in year 2) and, therefore, may be available to offset or reduce income for Country X tax purposes that would constitute a foreign use.

Example (32). Triggering event rebuttal--expiration of losses in foreign country. (i) Facts. P owns DRCX, a member of the P consolidated group. In year 1, DRCX incurs a dual consolidated loss of $100x. P makes a domestic use election with respect to DRCX's year 1 dual consolidated loss and such loss therefore is included in the computation of the P group's consolidated taxable income. DRCX has no income or loss in year 2 through year 5. In year 5, P sells the stock of DRCX to FSX. At the time of the sale of the stock of DRCX, all of the losses and deductions that were included in the computation of the year 1 dual consolidated loss of DRCX had expired for Country X tax purposes because the laws of Country X only provide for a three-year carryover period for such items.

(ii) Result. The sale of DRCX to FSX generally would be a triggering event under § 1.1503(d)-6(e)(1)(ii), which would require DRCX to recapture the year 1 dual consolidated loss (and pay an applicable interest charge) on the P consolidated group's tax return for the year that includes the date on which DRCX ceases to be a member of the P consolidated group. However, upon adequate documentation that the losses and deductions have expired for Country X tax purposes, P can rebut the presumption that a triggering event has occurred pursuant to § 1.1503(d)-6(e)(2)(i). If the triggering event presumption is rebutted, the domestic use agreement filed by the P consolidated group with respect to the year 1 dual consolidated loss of DRCX is terminated and has no further effect pursuant to § 1.1503(d)-6(j)(1)(i). If the presumptive triggering event is not rebutted, the domestic use agreement would terminate and have no further effect pursuant to § 1.1503(d)-6(j)(1)(iii) because the dual consolidated loss would be recaptured.

Example (33). Triggering events and rebuttals--tax basis carryover transaction. (i) Facts. (A) P owns DE1X. DE1X's sole asset is A, which it acquired at the beginning of year 1 for $100x. DE1X does not have any liabilities. For U.S. tax purposes, DE1X's tax basis in A at the beginning of year 1 is $100x and DE1X's sole item of income, gain, deduction, and loss for year 1 is a $20x depreciation deduction attributable to A. As a result, the $20x depreciation deduction constitutes a dual consolidated loss attributable to P's interest in DE1X. P makes a domestic use election with respect to the year 1 dual consolidated loss.

(B) For Country X tax purposes, DE1X has a $100x tax basis in A at the beginning of year 1, but A is not a depreciable asset. As a result, DE1X does not have any items of income, gain, deduction, and loss in year 1 for Country X tax purposes.

(C) During year 2, P sells its interest in DE1X to FSX for $80x. P's disposition of its interest in DE1X constitutes a presumptive triggering event under § 1.1503(d)-6(e)(1)(iv) and (v) requiring the recapture of the year 1 $20x dual consolidated loss (plus the applicable interest charge). For Country X tax purposes, DE1X retains its tax basis of $100x in A following the sale.

(ii) Result. The year 1 dual consolidated loss is a result of the $20x depreciation deduction attributable to A. Although no item of deduction or loss was recognized by DE1X at the time of the sale for Country X tax purposes, the deduction composing the dual consolidated loss was retained by DE1X after the sale in the form of tax basis in A. As a result, a portion of the dual consolidated loss may be available to offset income for Country X tax purposes in a manner that would constitute a foreign use. For example, if DE1X were to dispose of A, the amount of gain recognized by DE1X would be reduced (or an amount of loss recognized by DE1X would be increased) and, therefore, an item composing the dual consolidated loss would be available, under U.S. tax principles, to reduce income of a foreign corporation (and an owner of an interest in a hybrid entity that is not a separate unit). Thus, P cannot demonstrate pursuant to § 1.1503(d)-6(e)(2)(i) that there can be no foreign use of the year 1 dual consolidated loss following the triggering event, and must recapture the year 1 dual consolidated loss. Pursuant to § 1.1503(d)-6(j)(1)(iii), the domestic use agreement filed by the P consolidated group with respect to the year 1 dual consolidated loss is terminated and has no further effect.

(iii) Alternative facts. The facts are the same as paragraph (i) of this Example 33, except that instead of P selling its interest in DE1X to FSX, DE1X sells asset A to FSX for $80x and, for Country X tax purposes, FSX's tax basis in A immediately after the sale is $80x. P's disposition of Asset A constitutes a presumptive triggering event under § 1.1503(d)-6(e)(1)(iv) requiring the recapture of the year 1 $20x dual consolidated loss (plus the applicable interest charge). For Country X tax purposes, FSX's tax basis in A was not determined, in whole or in part, by reference to the basis of A in the hands of DE1X. As a result, the deduction composing the dual consolidated loss will not give rise to an item of deduction or loss in the form of tax basis for Country X tax purposes (for example, when FSX disposes of A). Therefore, P may be able to demonstrate (for example, by obtaining the opinion of a Country X tax advisor) pursuant to § 1.1503(d)-6(e)(2)(i) that there can be no foreign use of the year 1 dual consolidated loss and, thus, would not be required to recapture the year 1 dual consolidated loss.

Example (34). Triggering event resulting in a single consolidated group where acquirer files a new domestic use agreement. (i) Facts. P owns DRCX, a member of the P consolidated group. In year 1, DRCX incurs a dual consolidated loss and P makes a domestic use election with respect to such loss. No member of the P consolidated group incurs a dual consolidated loss in year 2. At the end of year 2, T, the parent of the T consolidated group, acquires all the stock of P, and all the members of the P group, including DRCX, become members of a consolidated group of which T is the common parent.

(ii) Result. (A) Under § 1.1503(d)-6(f)(2)(ii)(B), the acquisition by T of the P consolidated group is not an event described in § 1.1503(d)-6(e)(1)(ii) requiring the recapture of the year 1 dual consolidated loss of DRCX (and the payment of an interest charge), provided that the T consolidated group files a new domestic use agreement described in §

1.1503(d)-6(f)(2)(iii)(A). If a new domestic use agreement is filed, then pursuant to § 1.1503(d)-6(j)(1)(ii), the domestic use agreement filed by the P consolidated group with respect to the year 1 dual consolidated loss of DRCX is terminated and has no further effect.

(B) Assume that T files a new domestic use agreement and a triggering event occurs at the end of year 3. As a result, the T consolidated group must recapture the dual consolidated loss that DRCX incurred in year 1 (and pay an interest charge), as provided in § 1.1503(d)-6(h). Each member of the T consolidated group, including DRCX and any former members of the P consolidated group, is severally liable for the additional tax (and the interest charge) due upon the recapture of the dual consolidated loss of DRCX. In addition, pursuant to § 1.1503(d)-6(j)(1)(iii), the new domestic use agreement filed by the T group with respect to the year 1 dual consolidated loss of DRCX is terminated and has no further effect.

Example (35). Triggering event exceptions for certain deemed transfers. (i) Facts. P owns DE1X. In year 1, there is a $100x dual consolidated loss attributable to P's interest in DE1X. P files a domestic use agreement under § 1.1503(d)-6(d) with respect to such loss. During year 2, P sells 33 percent of its interest in DE1X to T, an unrelated domestic corporation.

(ii) Result. Pursuant to Rev. Rul. 99-5, the transaction is treated as if P sold 33 percent of its interest in each of DE1X's assets to T and then immediately thereafter P and T transferred their interests in the assets of DE1X to a partnership in exchange for an ownership interest therein. Upon the transfer of 33 percent of P's interest to T, a domestic corporation, no foreign use occurs and, therefore, there is no foreign use triggering event. However, P's deemed transfer of 67 percent of its interest in the assets of DE1X to a partnership is nominally a triggering event under § 1.1503(d)-6(e)(1)(iv). Because the initial transfer of 33 percent of DE1X's interest was to a domestic corporation and there is only a triggering event because of the deemed transfer under Rev. Rul. 99-5, the deemed asset transfer is not treated as resulting in a triggering event pursuant to § 1.1503(d)-6(f)(4).

(iii) Alternative facts. The facts are the same as in paragraph (i) of this Example 35, except that P sells 60 percent (rather than 33 percent) of its interest in DE1X to T. The sale is a triggering event under § 1.1503(d)-6(e)(1)(iv) and (v) without regard to the occurrence of a deemed transaction. Therefore, § 1.1503(d)-6(f)(4) does not apply.

Example (36). Triggering event exception involving multiple parties. (i) Facts. P owns DE1X which, in turn, owns FBX. P's interest in DE1X and its indirect interest in FBX are combined and treated as a single separate unit (Country X separate unit) pursuant to § 1.1503(d)-1(b)(4)(ii). In year 1, there is a $100x dual consolidated loss attributable to P's Country X separate unit and P makes a domestic use election with respect to such loss. No member of the P consolidated group incurs a dual consolidated loss in year 2. At the end of year 2, T, the parent of the T consolidated group, acquires all of P's interest in DE1X for cash.

(ii) Result. (A) Under § 1.1503(d)-6(f)(2)(i)(B), the acquisition by T of the interest in DE1X is not an event described in § 1.1503(d)-6(e)(1)(iv) or (v) requiring the recapture of the year 1 dual consolidated loss attributable to the Country X separate unit (and the payment of an interest charge), provided: (1) the T consolidated group files a new domestic use agreement described in § 1.1503(d)-6(f)(2)(iii)(A) with respect to the year 1 dual consolidated loss of the Country X separate unit; and (2) the P consolidated group files a statement described in § 1.1503(d)-6(f)(2)(iii)(B) with respect to the year 1 dual consolidated loss. If these requirements are satisfied, then pursuant to § 1.1503(d)-6(j)(1)(ii) the domestic use agreement filed by the P consolidated group with respect to the year 1 dual consolidated loss is terminated and has no further effect (if these requirements are not satisfied such that the P consolidated group recaptures the dual consolidated loss, the domestic use agreement would terminate pursuant to § 1.1503(d)-6(j)(1)(iii)).

(B) Assume a triggering event occurs at the end of year 3 that requires recapture by the T consolidated group of the year 1 dual consolidated loss, as well as the payment of an interest charge, as provided in § 1.1503(d)-6(h). T continues to own the Country X separate unit after the triggering event. In that case, each member of the T consolidated group is severally liable for the additional tax (and the interest charge) due upon the recapture of the year 1 dual consolidated loss. The T consolidated group must prepare a statement that computes the recapture tax amount as provided under § 1.1503(d)-6(h)(3)(iii). Pursuant to § 1.1503(d)-6(h)(3)(iv)(A), the recapture tax amount is assessed as an income tax liability of the T consolidated group and is considered as having been properly assessed as an income tax liability of the P consolidated group. If the T consolidated group does not pay in full the income tax liability attributable to the recapture tax amount, the unpaid balance of such recapture tax amount may be collected from the P consolidated group in accordance with the provisions of § 1.1503(d)-6(h)(3)(iv)(B). Pursuant to § 1.1503(d)-6(j)(1)(iii), the new domestic use agreement filed by the T consolidated group is terminated and has no further effect. Finally, pursuant to § 1.1503(d)-6(h)(6)(iii), T is treated as if it incurred the dual consolidated loss that is recaptured for purposes of applying § 1.1503(d)-6(h)(6)(i). Thus, T has a reconstituted net operating loss equal to the amount of the year 1 dual consolidated loss that was recaptured, and such loss is attributable to the Country X separate unit (and subject to the rules and limitations under § 1.1503(d)-6(h)(6)(i)). Because T is treated as if it incurred the year 1 dual consolidated loss, P shall not be treated as having a net operating loss under § 1.1503(d)-6(h)(6)(i).

Example (37). No foreign use following multiple-party event exception to triggering event. (i) Facts. P owns DE1X which, in turn, owns FBX. P's interest in DE1X and its indirect interest in FBX are combined and treated as a single separate unit (Country X separate unit) pursuant to § 1.1503(d)-1(b)(4)(ii). In year 1, there is a $100x dual consolidated loss attributable to P's Country X separate unit and P makes a domestic use election with respect to such loss. T, a domestic corporation unrelated to P, owns 95 percent of PRS, a partnership. FSX owns the remaining 5 percent of PRS. At the beginning of year 3, PRS purchases 100 percent of the interest in DE1X from P for cash. For Country X tax purposes, the $100x loss incurred by DE1X in year 1 carries forward and is available to offset income of DE1X in subsequent years.

(ii) Result. P's sale of its interest in DE1X is a triggering event under § 1.1503(d)-6(e)(1)(iv) and (v). However, if P and T comply with the requirements under § 1.1503(d)-6(f)(2)(iii), the sale would qualify for the multiple-party event exception under § 1.1503(d)-6(f)(2)(i). In addition, because the $100x loss of DE1X carries forward to subsequent years for Country X purposes and is available to offset income of DE1X, there would be a foreign use of the dual consolidated loss immediately after the sale pursuant to § 1.1503(d)-3(a)(1). This is the case because the dual consolidated loss would be available to offset or reduce income that is considered, under U.S. tax principles, to be an item of FSX, a foreign corporation (it would also be a foreign use because FSX is an indirect owner of an interest in a hybrid entity that is not a separate unit). However, there is no foreign use in this case as a result of FSX's 5 percent interest in DE1X pursuant to § 1.1503(d)-3(c)(8).

Example (38). Character and source of recapture income. (i) Facts. (A) P owns FBX. In year 1, the items of income, gain, deduction, and loss that are attributable to FBX for purposes of determining whether it has a dual consolidated loss are as follows:

Sales income	$100x
Salary expense	($75x)
Interest expense	($50x)
Dual consolidated loss	($25x)

(B) P makes a domestic use election with respect to the year 1 dual consolidated loss attributable to FBX and, thus, the $25x dual consolidated loss is used to offset the P group's consolidated taxable income.

(C) Pursuant to § 1.861-8, the $75x of salary expense incurred by FBX is allocated and apportioned entirely to foreign source general limitation income. Pursuant to § 1.861-9T, $25x of the $50x interest expense attributable to FBX is allocated and apportioned to domestic source income, $15x of such interest expense is allocated and apportioned to foreign source general limitation income, and the remaining $10x of such interest expense is allocated and apportioned to foreign source passive income.

(D) During year 2, $5x of income is attributable to FBX under the rules of § 1.1503(d)-5, and the P consolidated group has $100x of consolidated taxable income. At the end of year 2, FBX undergoes a triggering event described in § 1.1503(d)-6(e)(1), and P continues to own FBX following the triggering event. Pursuant to § 1.1503(d)-6(h)(2)(i), P is able to demonstrate to the satisfaction of the Commissioner that the $25x dual consolidated loss attributable to FBX in year 1 would have offset the $5x of income attributable to FBX in year 2, if no domestic use election were made with respect to the year 1 loss such that it was subject to the limitations of § 1.1503(d)-4(b) and (c).

(ii) Result. P must recapture and report as ordinary income $20x ($25x - $5x) of FBX's year 1 dual consolidated loss, plus applicable interest. The $20x recapture income is attributable to FBX pursuant to § 1.1503(d)-5(c)(4)(vi). Pursuant to § 1.1503(d)-6(h)(5), the recapture income is treated as ordinary income whose source and character (including section 904 separate limitation character) is determined by reference to the manner in which the recaptured items of expense or loss taken into account in calculating the dual consolidated loss were allocated and apportioned. Further, pursuant to § 1.1503(d)-6(h)(5), the pro rata computation described in § 1.1503(d)-4(c)(4) shall apply. Thus, the character and source of the recapture income is determined in the same proportion as each item of deduction or loss that contributed to the dual consolidated loss being recaptured. Accordingly, P's $20x of recapture income is characterized and sourced as follows: $4x of domestic source income (($25x/$125x) x $20x); $14.4x of foreign source general limitation income (($75x + $15x)/$125x) x $20x); and $1.6x of foreign source passive income (($10x/$125x) x $20x). Pursuant to § 1.1503(d)-6(h)(6)(i), commencing in year 3, the $20x recapture amount is reconstituted and treated as a net operating loss incurred by FBX in a separate return limitation year, subject to the limitation under § 1.1503(d)-4(b) (and therefore subject to the restrictions of § 1.1503(d)-4(c)). Pursuant to § 1.1503(d)-6(j)(1)(iii), the domestic use agreement filed by the P consolidated group with respect to the year 1 dual consolidated loss of FBX is terminated and has no further effect.

Example (39). Interest charge without recapture. (i) Facts. P owns DE1X which, in turn, owns FBX. P's interest in DE1X and its indirect interest in FBX are combined and treated as a single separate unit (Country X separate unit) pursuant to § 1.1503(d)-1(b)(4)(ii). In year 1, a dual consolidated loss of $100x is attributable to P's Country X separate unit. P makes a domestic use election with respect to such loss and uses the loss to offset the P group's consolidated taxable income. In year 2, there is $100x of income attributable to P's Country X separate unit and the P consolidated group has $200x of consolidated taxable income. At the end of year 2, the Country X separate unit undergoes a triggering event within the meaning of § 1.1503(d)-6(e)(1). P demonstrates, to the satisfaction of the Commissioner, that if no domestic use election were made with respect to the year 1 dual consolidated loss such that it was subject to the limitations of § 1.1503(d)-4(b) and (c), the year 1 $100x dual consolidated loss would have been offset by the $100x of year 2 income.

(ii) Result. There is no recapture of the year 1 dual consolidated loss attributable to P's Country X separate unit because it is reduced to zero under § 1.1503(d)-6(h)(2)(i). However, P is liable for one year of interest charge under § 1.1503(d)-6(h)(1)(ii), even though P's recapture amount is zero. This is the case because the P consolidated group had the benefit of the dual consolidated loss in year 1, and the income that offset the recapture income was not recognized until year 2. Pursuant to § 1.1503(d)-6(j)(1)(iii), the domestic use agreement filed by the P consolidated group with respect to the year 1 dual consolidated loss is terminated and has no further effect.

Example (40). Reduced recapture and interest charge, and reconstituted dual consolidated loss. (i) Facts. S owns DE1X which, in turn, owns FBX. S's interest in DE1X and its indirect interest in FBX are combined and treated as a single separate unit (Country X separate unit) pursuant to § 1.1503(d)-1(b)(4)(ii). In year 1, there is a $100x dual consolidated loss attributable to S's Country X separate unit, and P earns $100x. P makes a domestic use election with respect to the Country X separate unit's year 1 dual consolidated loss. Therefore, the consolidated group is permitted to offset P's $100x of income with the Country X separate unit's $100x dual consolidated loss. In year 2, $30x of income is attributable to the Country X separate unit under the rules of § 1.1503(d)-5 and such income is offset by a $30x net operating loss incurred by P in such year. In year 3, $25x of income is attributable to the Country X separate unit under the rules of § 1.1503(d)-5, and P earns $15x of income. In addition, at the end of year 3 there is a foreign use of the year 1 dual consolidated loss that constitutes a triggering event. S continues to own the Country X separate unit after the triggering event.

(ii) Result. (A) Under the presumptive rule of § 1.1503(d)-6(h)(1)(i), S must recapture $100x (plus applicable interest). However, under § 1.1503(d)-6(h)(2)(i), S may be able to demonstrate that a lesser amount is subject to recapture. The lesser amount is the amount of the $100x dual consolidated loss that would have remained subject to § 1.1503(d)-4(c) at the time of the foreign use triggering event if a domestic use election had not been made for such loss.

(B) Although the combined separate unit earned $30x of income in year 2, there was no consolidated taxable income in such year. As a result, as of the end of year 2 the $100x dual consolidated loss would continue to be subject to § 1.1503(d)-4(c) if a domestic use election had not been made for such loss. However, the $30x earned in year 2 can be carried forward to subsequent taxable years and may reduce the recapture income to the extent of consolidated taxable income generated in subsequent years. In year 3, $25x of income was attributable to the Country X separate unit and P earns $15x of income. Thus, the P consolidated group has $40x of consolidated taxable income in year 3. As a result, the $100x of recapture income can be reduced by $40x. This is the case because if a domestic use election had not been made for the $100x year 1 dual consolidated loss such that it was subject to the limitations of § 1.1503(d)-4(b) and (c), only $60x of the loss would have remained subject to such limitations at the time of the foreign use triggering event. Accordingly, if S can adequately document the lesser amount, the amount of recapture income is $60x ($100x - $40x). The $60x recapture income is attributable to the Country X separate unit pursuant to § 1.1503(d)-5(c)(4)(vi).

(C) Pursuant to § 1.1503(d)-6(h)(6)(i), commencing in year 4, the $60x recapture amount is reconstituted and treated as a net operating loss incurred by the Country X separate unit of S in a separate return limitation year, subject to the limitation under § 1.1503(d)-4(b) (and therefore subject to the restrictions of § 1.1503(d)-4(c)). The loss is only available for carryover to taxable years after year 3 (and is not available for carryback). The carryover period of the loss, for purposes of section 172(b), will start from year 1, when the dual consolidated loss that was subject to recapture was incurred. In addition, such reconstituted net operating loss is not eligible for the exceptions contained in § 1.1503(d)-6(b) through (d). Pursuant to § 1.1503(d)-6(j)(1)(iii), the domestic use agreement filed by the P consolidated group with respect to the year 1 dual consolidated loss of the Country X separate unit is terminated and has no further effect.

(iii) Alternative facts. The facts are the same as in paragraph (i) of this Example 40, except that the triggering event that occurs at the end of year 3 is a sale by S of its entire interest in DE1X to B, an unrelated domestic corporation. The sale does not qualify as a transaction described in section 381. The results are the same as in paragraph (ii) of this Example 40, except that pursuant to § 1.1503(d)-6(h)(6)(ii) the $60x net operating loss is not reconstituted (with respect to either S or B). The loss is not reconstituted with respect to S because the Country X separate unit ceases to be a separate unit of S (or any other member of the consolidated group that includes S) and therefore would have been eliminated pursuant to § 1.1503(d)-4(d)(1)(ii) if no domestic use election had been made with respect to such loss. The loss is not reconstituted with respect to B because B was not the domestic owner of the combined separate unit when the dual consolidated loss that is recaptured was incurred, and B did not acquire the Country X separate unit in a section 381 transaction.

T.D. 9315, 3/16/2007.

§ 1.1503(d)-8 Effective dates.

(a) General rule. Except as provided in paragraph (b) of this section, this paragraph (a) provides the dates of applicability of §§ 1.1503(d)-1 through 1.1503(d)-7. Sections 1.1503(d)-1 through 1.1503(d)-7 shall apply to dual consolidated losses incurred in taxable years beginning on or after April 18, 2007. However, a taxpayer may apply §§ 1.1503(d)-1 through 1.1503(d)-7, in their entirety, to dual consolidated losses incurred in taxable years beginning on or after January 1, 2007, by filing its return and attaching to such return the domestic use agreements, certifications, or other information in accordance with these regulations. For purposes of this section, the term application date means either April 18, 2007, or, if the taxpayer applies these regulations pursuant to the preceding sentence, January 1, 2007. Section 1.1503-2 applies for dual consolidated losses incurred in taxable years beginning on or after October 1, 1992, and before the application date.

(b) Special rules. *(1) Reduction of term of agreements filed under §§ 1.1503-2A(c)(3), 1.1503-2A(d)(3), 1.1503-2(g)(2)(i), or 1.1503-2T(g)(i).* If an agreement is filed in accordance with §§ 1.1503-2A(c)(3), 1.1503-2A(d)(3), 1.1503-2(g)(2)(i), or 1.1503-2T(g)(2)(i) with respect to a dual consolidated loss incurred in a taxable year beginning prior to the application date and an event requiring recapture with respect to the dual consolidated loss subject to the agreement has not occurred as of the application date, then such agreement will be considered by the Internal Revenue Service to apply only for any taxable year up to and including the fifth taxable year following the year in which the dual consolidated loss that is the subject of the agreement was incurred and thereafter will have no effect.

(2) Reduction of term of agreements filed under §§ 1.1503-2(g)(2)(iv)(B)(2)(i) (1992), 1.1503-2(g)(2)(iv)(B)(3)(i), or Rev. Proc. 2000-42. Taxpayers subject to the terms of a closing agreement entered into with the Internal Revenue Service pursuant to §§ 1.1503-2(g)(2)(iv)(B)(2)(i) (1992), 1.1503-2(g)(2)(iv)(B)(3)(i), or Rev. Proc. 2000-42 (2000-2 CB 394), see § 601.601(d)(2)(ii)(b) of this chapter, will be deemed to have satisfied the closing agreement's fifteen-year certification period requirement if the five-year certification period specified in § 1.1503(d)-1(b)(20) has elapsed, provided such closing agreement is still in effect as of the application date, and provided the dual consolidated losses have not been recaptured. For example, if a calendar year taxpayer that has a January 1, 2007, application date entered into a closing agreement with respect to a dual consolidated loss incurred in 2003 and, as of January 1, 2007, the closing agreement is still in effect and the dual consolidated loss subject to the closing agreement has not been recaptured, then the closing agreement's fifteen-year certification period will be deemed satisfied when the five-year certification period described in § 1.1503(d)-1(b)(20) has elapsed. Thus, the dual consolidated loss will be subject to the recapture and certification provisions of the closing agreement in such a case only through December 31, 2008. Alternatively, if a calendar year taxpayer that has a January 1, 2007, application date entered into a closing agreement with respect to a dual consolidated loss incurred in 2000 and, as of January 1, 2007, the closing agreement is still in effect and the dual consolidated loss

subject to the closing agreement has not been recaptured, then the certification period is deemed to be satisfied.

(3) Relief for untimely filings. Paragraphs (b)(3)(i) through (iii) of this section set forth the effective dates for rules that provide relief for the failure to make timely filings of an election, agreement, statement, rebuttal, computation, closing agreement, or other information, pursuant to section 1503(d) and these regulations.

(i) General rule. Except as provided in paragraphs (b)(3)(ii) and (iii) of this section, the reasonable cause relief standard of § 1.1503(d)-1(c) applies for all untimely filings with respect to dual consolidated losses, including with respect to dual consolidated losses incurred in taxable years beginning before the application date.

(ii) Closing agreements. Solely with respect to closing agreements described in § 1.1503-2(g)(2)(iv)(B)(3)(i) and Rev. Proc. 2000-42, taxpayers must request relief for untimely requests through the process provided under §§ 301.9100-1 through 301.9100-3 of this chapter. See paragraph (b)(4) of this section for rules that permit the multiple-party event exception, rather than closing agreements, for certain triggering events.

(iii) Pending requests for relief. Taxpayers that have letter ruling requests under §§ 301.9100-1 through 301.9100-3 of this chapter pending as of March 19, 2007 (other than requests under paragraph (b)(3)(ii) of this section) are not required to use the reasonable cause procedure under § 1.1503(d)-1(c); however, if such taxpayers have not yet received a determination of their request, they may withdraw their request consistent with the procedures contained in Rev. Proc. 2007-1 (2007-1 IRB 1), see § 601.601(d)(2)(ii)(b) of this chapter, (or any succeeding document) and use the reasonable cause procedure set forth in § 1.1503(d)-1(c). In that event, the Internal Revenue Service will refund the taxpayer's user fee.

(4) Multiple-party event exception to triggering events. This paragraph (b)(4) applies to events described in § 1.1503-2(g)(2)(iv)(B)(1)(i) through (iii) that occur after April 18, 2007 and that are with respect to dual consolidated losses that were incurred in taxable years beginning on or after October 1, 1992, and before the application date. The events described in the previous sentence are not eligible for the exception described in § 1.1503-2(g)(2)(iv)(B)(1), but instead are eligible for the multiple-party event exception described in § 1.1503(d)-6(f)(2)(i), as modified by this paragraph (b)(4). Thus, such events are not eligible for a closing agreement described in § 1.1503-2(g)(2)(iv)(B)(3)(i) and Rev. Proc. 2000-42. For purposes of applying § 1.1503(d)-6(f)(2)(i) to transactions covered by this paragraph, agreements described in § 1.1503-2(g)(2)(i) (rather than domestic use agreements) shall be filed, and subsequent triggering events and exceptions thereto have the meaning provided in § 1.1503-2(g)(2)(iii)(A) and (iv) (other than the exception provided under § 1.1503-2(g)(2)(iv)(B)(1)). For example, if a calendar year taxpayer that has a January 1, 2007, application date filed an election under § 1.1503-2(g)(2)(i) with respect to a dual consolidated loss that was incurred in 2004, and a triggering event described in § 1.1503-2(g)(2)(iv)(B)(1)(ii) occurs with respect to such dual consolidated loss after April 18, 2007, then the event is eligible for the multiple-party event exception under § 1.1503(d)-6(f)(2)(i) (and not the exception under § 1.1503-2(g)(2)(iv)(B)(1)). However, in order to comply with § 1.1503(d)-6(f)(2)(iii)(A), the subsequent elector must file a new agreement described in § 1.1503-2(g)(2)(i) (rather than a new domestic use agreement). In addition, for purposes of determining whether there is a subsequent triggering event, and exceptions thereto, pursuant to such new agreement, § 1.1503-2(g)(2)(iii)(A) and (iv) (other than the exception provided under § 1.1503-2(g)(2)(iv)(B)(1)) shall apply. Notwithstanding the general application of this paragraph (b)(4) to events described in § 1.1503-2(g)(2)(iv)(B)(1)(i) through (iii) that occur after April 18, 2007, a taxpayer may choose to apply this paragraph (b)(4) to events described in § 1.1503-2(g)(2)(iv)(B)(1)(i) through (iii) that occur after March 19, 2007 and on or before April 18, 2007.

(5) Basis adjustment rules. Taxpayers may apply the basis adjustment rules of § 1.1503(d)-5(g) for all open years in which such basis is relevant, even if the basis adjustment is attributable to a dual consolidated loss incurred (or recaptured) in a closed taxable year. Taxpayers applying the provisions of § 1.1503(d)-5(g), however, must do so consistently for all open years.

T.D. 9315, 3/16/2007.

§ 1.1504-0 Outline of provisions.

In order to facilitate the use of §§ 1.1504-1 through 1.1504-4, this section lists the captions contained in §§ 1.1504-1 through 1.1504-4.

§ 1.1504-1 Definitions.

§ 1.1504-2 [Reserved]

§ 1.1504-3 [Reserved]

§ 1.1504-4 Treatment of warrants, options, convertible obligations, and other similar interests.

(a) Introduction.

(1) General rule.

(2) Exceptions.

(b) Options not treated as stock or as exercised.

(1) General rule.

(2) Options treated as exercised.

(i) In general.

(ii) Aggregation of options.

(iii) Effect of treating option as exercised.

(A) In general.

(B) Cash settlement options, phantom stock, stock appreciation rights, or similar interests.

(iv) Valuation.

(3) Example.

(c) Definitions.

(1) Issuing corporation.

(2) Related or sequential option.

(3) Related persons.

(4) Measurement date.

(i) General rule.

(ii) Issuances, transfers, or adjustments not treated as measurement dates.

(iii) Transactions increasing likelihood of exercise.

(iv) Measurement date for options issued pursuant to a plan.

(v) Measurement date for related or sequential options.

(vi) Example.

(5) In-the-money.

(d) Options.

T.D. 8462, 12/28/92.

§ 1.1504-1 Definitions.

The privilege of filing consolidated returns is extended to all includible corporations constituting affiliated groups as defined in section 1504. See the regulations under § 1.1502 for a description of an affiliated group and the corporations which may be considered as includible corporations.

T.D. 6140, 8/29/55.

§ 1.1504-2 [Reserved]

§ 1.1504-3 [Reserved]

§ 1.1504-4 Treatment of warrants, options, convertible obligations, and other similar interests.

(a) Introduction. *(1) General rule.* This section provides regulations under section 1504(a)(5)(A) and (B) regarding the circumstances in which warrants, options, obligations convertible into stock, and other similar interests are treated as exercised for purposes of determining whether a corporation is a member of an affiliated group. The fact that an instrument may be treated as an option under these regulations does not prevent such instrument from being treated as stock under general principles of law. Except as provided in paragraph (a)(2) of this section, this section applies to all provisions under the Internal Revenue Code and the regulations to which affiliation within the meaning of section 1504(a) (with or without the exceptions in section 1504(b)) is relevant, including those provisions that refer to section 1504(a)(2) (with or without the exceptions in section 1504(b)) without referring to affiliation, provided that the 80 percent voting power and 80 percent value requirements of section 1504(a)(2) are not modified therein.

(2) Exceptions. This section does not apply to sections 163(j), 864(e), or 904(i) or to the regulations thereunder. This section also does not apply to any other provision specified by the Internal Revenue Service in regulations, a revenue ruling, or revenue procedure. See § 601.601(d)(2)(ii)(b) of this chapter.

(b) Options not treated as stock or as exercised. *(1) General rule.* Except as provided in paragraph (b)(2) of this section, an option is not considered either as stock or as exercised. Thus, options are disregarded in determining whether a corporation is a member of an affiliated group unless they are described in paragraph (b)(2) of this section.

(2) Options treated as exercised. (i) In general. Solely for purposes of determining whether a corporation is a member of an affiliated group, an option is treated as exercised if, on a measurement date with respect to such option—

(A) It could reasonably be anticipated that, if not for this section, the issuance or transfer of the option in lieu of the issuance, redemption, or transfer of the underlying stock would result in the elimination of a substantial amount of federal income tax liability (as described in paragraphs (e) and (f) of this section); and

(B) It is reasonably certain that the option will be exercised (as described in paragraph (g) of this section).

(ii) Aggregation of options. All options with the same measurement date are aggregated in determining whether the issuance or transfer of an option in lieu of the issuance, redemption, or transfer of the underlying stock would result in the elimination of a substantial amount of federal income tax liability.

(iii) Effect of treating option as exercised. (A) In general. An option that is treated as exercised is treated as exercised for purposes of determining the percentage of the value of stock owned by the holder and other parties, but is not treated as exercised for purposes of determining the percentage of the voting power of stock owned by the holder and other parties.

(B) Cash settlement options, phantom stock, stock appreciation rights, or similar interests. If a cash settlement option, phantom stock, stock appreciation right, or similar interest is treated as exercised, the option is treated as having been converted into stock of the issuing corporation. If the amount to be received upon the exercise of such an option is determined by reference to a multiple of the increase in the value of a share of the issuing corporation's stock on the exercise date over the value of a share of the stock on the date the option is issued, the option is treated as converted into a corresponding number of shares of such stock. Appropriate adjustments must be made in any situation in which the amount to be received upon exercise of the option is determined in another manner.

(iv) Valuation. For purposes of section 1504(a)(2)(B) and this section, all shares of stock within a single class are considered to have the same value. Thus, control premiums and minority and blockage discounts within a single class are not taken into account.

(3) Example. The provisions of paragraph (b)(2) of this section may be illustrated by the following example:

Example. (i) Corporation P owns all 100 shares of the common stock of Corporation S, the only class of S stock outstanding. Each share of S stock has a fair market value of $10 and has one vote. On June 30, 1992, P issues to Corporation X an option to acquire 80 shares of the S stock from P.

(ii) If, under the provisions of this section, the option is treated as exercised, then, solely for purposes of determining affiliation, P is treated as owning only 20 percent of the value of the outstanding S stock and X is treated as owing the remaining 80 percent of the value of the S stock. P is still treated as owning all of the voting power of S. Accordingly, because P is treated as owning less than 80 percent of the value of the outstanding S stock, P and S are no longer affiliated. However, because X is not treated as owning any of the voting power of S, X and S are also not affiliated.

(c) Definitions. For purposes of this section—

(1) Issuing corporation. "Issuing corporation" means the corporation whose stock is subject to an option.

(2) Related or sequential option. "Related or sequential option" means an option that is one of a series of options issued to the same or related persons. For purposes of this section, any options issued to the same person or related persons within a two year period are presumed to be part of a series of options. This presumption may be rebutted if the facts and circumstances clearly establish that the options are not part of a series of options. Any options issued to the same person or related persons more than two years apart are presumed not to be part of a series of options. This presumption may be rebutted if the facts and circumstances clearly establish that the options are part of a series of options.

(3) Related persons. Persons are related if they are related within the meaning of section 267(b) (without the application of sections 267(c) and 1563(e)(1)) or 707(b)(1), substituting "10 percent" for "50 percent" wherever it appears.

(4) Measurement date. (i) General rule. "Measurement date" means a date on which an option is issued or transferred or on which the terms of an existing option or the underlying stock are adjusted (including an adjustment pursuant to the terms of the option or the underlying stock).

(ii) Issuances, transfers, or adjustments not treated as measurement dates. A measurement date does not include a date on which—

(A) An option is issued or transferred by gift, at death, or between spouses or former spouses under section 1041;

(B) An option is issued or transferred—

(1) Between members of an affiliated group (determined with the exceptions in section 1504(b) and without the application of this section); or

(2) Between persons none of which is a member of the affiliated group (determined without the exceptions in section 1504(b) and without the application of this section), if any, of which the issuing corporation is a member, unless—

(i) Any such person is related to (or acting in concert with) the issuing corporation or any member of its affiliated group; and

(ii) The issuance or transfer is pursuant to a plan a principal purpose of which is to avoid the application of section 1504 and this section;

(C) An adjustment occurs in the terms or pursuant to the terms of an option or the underlying stock that does not materially increase the likelihood that the option will be exercised; or

(D) A change occurs in the exercise price of an option or in the number of shares that may be issued or transferred pursuant to the option as determined by a bona fide, reasonable, adjustment formula that has the effect of preventing dilution of the interests of the holders of the options.

(iii) Transactions increasing likelihood of exercise. If a change or alteration referred to in this paragraph (c)(4)(iii) is made for a principal purpose of increasing the likelihood that an option will be exercised, a measurement date also includes any date on which—

(A) The capital structure of the issuing corporation is changed; or

(B) The fair market value of the stock of the issuing corporation is altered through a transfer of assets to or from the issuing corporation (other than regular, ordinary dividends) or by any other means.

(iv) Measurement date for options issued pursuant to a plan. In the case of options issued pursuant to a plan, a measurement date for any of the options constitutes a measurement date for all options issued pursuant to the plan that are outstanding on the measurement date.

(v) Measurement date for related or sequential options. In the case of related or sequential options, a measurement date for any of the options constitutes a measurement date for all related or sequential options that are outstanding on the measurement date.

(vi) Example. The provisions of paragraph (c)(4)(v) of this section may be illustrated by the following example.

Example. (i) Corporation P owns all 80 shares of the common stock of Corporation S, the only class of S stock outstanding. On January 1, 1992, S issues a warrant, exercisable within 3 years, to U, an unrelated corporation, to acquire 10 newly issued shares of S common stock. On July 1, 1992, S issues a second warrant to U to acquire 10 additional newly issued shares of S common stock. On January 1, 1993, S issues a third warrant to T, a wholly owned subsidiary of U, to acquire 10 newly issued shares of S common stock. Assume that the facts and circumstances do not clearly establish that the options are not part of a series of options.

(ii) January 1, 1992, July 1, 1992, and January 1, 1993, constitute measurement dates for the first warrant, the second warrant, and the third warrant, respectively, because the warrants were issued on those dates.

(iii) Because the first and second warrants were issued within two years of each other, and both warrants were issued to U, the warrants constitute related or sequential options. Accordingly, July 1, 1992, constitutes a measurement date for the first warrant as well as for the second warrant.

(iv) Because the first, second, and third warrants were all issued within two years of each other, and were all issued to the same or related persons, the warrants constitute related or sequential options. Accordingly, January 1, 1993, constitutes a measurement date for the first and second warrants, as well as for the third warrant.

(5) In-the-money. "In-the-money" means the exercise price of the option is less than (or in the case of an option to sell stock, greater than) the fair market value of the underlying stock.

(d) Options. *(1) Instruments treated as options.* For purposes of this section, except to the extent otherwise provided in this paragraph (d), the following are treated as options:

(i) A call option, warrant, convertible obligation, put option, redemption agreement (including a right to cause the redemption of stock), or any other instrument that provides for the right to issue, redeem, or transfer stock (including an option on an option); and

(ii) A cash settlement option, phantom stock, stock appreciation right, or any other similar interest (except for stock).

(2) Instruments generally not treated as options. For purposes of this section, the following will not be treated as options:

(i) Options on section 1504(a)(4) stock. Options on stock described in section 1504(a)(4);

(ii) Certain publicly traded options. (A) General rule. Options which on the measurement date are traded on (or subject to the rules of) a qualified board or exchange as defined in section 1256(g)(7), or on any other exchange, board of trade, or market specified by the Internal Revenue Service in regulations, a revenue ruling, or revenue procedure. See § 601.601(d)(2)(ii)(b) of this chapter;

(B) Exception. Paragraph (d)(2)(ii)(A) of this section does not apply to options issued, transferred, or listed with a principal purpose of avoiding the application of section 1504 and this section. For example, a principal purpose of avoiding the application of section 1504 and this section may exist if warrants, convertible or exchangeable debt instruments, or other similar instruments have an exercise price (or, in the case of convertible or exchangeable instruments, a conversion or exchange premium) that is materially less than, or a term that is materially longer than, those that are customary for publicly traded instruments of their type. A principal purpose may also exist if a large percentage of an issuance of an instrument is placed with one investor (or group of investors) and a very small percentage of the issuance is traded on a qualified board or exchange;

(iii) Stock purchase agreements. Stock purchase agreements or similar arrangements whose terms are commercially reasonable and in which the parties' obligations to complete the transaction are subject only to reasonable closing conditions;

(iv) Escrow, pledge, or other security agreements. Agreements for holding stock in escrow or under a pledge or other security agreement that are part of a typical commercial transaction and that are subject to customary commercial conditions;

(v) Compensatory options. (A) General rule. Stock appreciation rights, warrants, stock options, phantom stock, or other similar instruments provided to employees, directors, or independent contractors in connection with the performance of services for the corporation or a related corporation (and that is not excessive by reference to the services performed) and which—

(1) Are nontransferable within the meaning of § 1.83-3(d); and

(2) Do not have a readily ascertainable fair market value as defined in § 1.83-7(b) on the measurement date;

(B) Exceptions. (1) Paragraph (d)(2)(v)(A) of this section does not apply to options issued or transferred with a principal purpose of avoiding the application of section 1504 and this section; and

(2) Paragraph (d)(2)(v)(A) of this section ceases to apply to options that become transferable;

(vi) Options granted in connection with a loan. Options granted in connection with a loan if the lender is actively and regularly engaged in the business of lending and the options are issued in connection with a loan to the issuing corporation that is commercially reasonable. This paragraph (d)(2)(vi) continues to apply if the option is transferred with the loan (or if a portion of the option is transferred with a corresponding portion of the loan). However, if the option is transferred without a corresponding portion of the loan, this paragraph (d)(2)(vi) ceases to apply;

(vii) Options created pursuant to a title 11 or similar case. Options created by the solicitation or receipt of acceptances to a plan of reorganization in a title 11 or similar case (within the meaning of section 368(a)(3)(A)), the option created by the confirmation of the plan, and any option created under the plan prior to the time the plan becomes effective;

(viii) Convertible preferred stock. Convertible preferred stock, provided the terms of the conversion feature do not permit or require the tender of any consideration other than the stock being converted; and

(ix) Other enumerated instruments. Any other instruments specified by the Internal Revenue Service in regulations, a revenue ruling, or revenue procedure. See § 601.601(d)(2)(ii)(b) of this chapter.

(e) Elimination of federal income tax liability. For purposes of this section, the elimination of federal income tax liability includes the elimination or deferral of federal income tax liability. In determining whether there is an elimination of federal income tax liability, the tax consequences to all involved parties are considered. Examples of elimination of federal income tax liability include the use of a loss or deduction that would not otherwise be utilized, the acceleration of a loss or deduction to a year earlier than the year in which the loss or deduction would otherwise be utilized, the deferral of gain or income to a year later than the year in which the gain or income would otherwise be reported, and the acceleration of gain or income to a year earlier than the year in which the gain or income would otherwise be reported, if such gain or income is offset by a net operating loss or net capital loss that would otherwise expire unused. The elimination of federal income tax liability does not include the deferral of gain with respect to the stock subject to the option that would be recognized if such stock were sold on a measurement date.

(f) Substantial amount of federal income tax liability. The determination of what constitutes a substantial amount of federal income tax liability is based on all the facts and circumstances, including the absolute amount of the elimination, the amount of the elimination relative to overall tax liability, and the timing of items of income and deductions, taking into account present value concepts.

(g) Reasonable certainty of exercise. *(1) Generally.* The determination of whether, as of a measurement date, an option is reasonably certain to be exercised is based on all the facts and circumstances, including:

(i) Purchase price. The purchase price of the option in absolute terms and in relation to the fair market value of the stock or the exercise price of the option;

(ii) In-the-money option. Whether and to what extent the option is in-the-money on the measurement date;

(iii) Not in-the-money option. If the option is not in-the-money on the measurement date, the amount or percentage by which the exercise price of the option is greater than (or in the case of an option to sell stock, is less than) the fair market value of the underlying stock;

(iv) Exercise price. Whether the exercise price of the option is fixed or fluctuates depending on the earnings, value, or other indication of economic performance of the issuing corporation;

(v) Time of exercise. The time at which, or the period of time during which, the option can be exercised;

(vi) Related or sequential options. Whether the option is one in a series of related or sequential options;

(vii) Stockholder rights. The existence of an arrangement (either within the option agreement or in a related agreement) that, directly or indirectly, affords managerial or economic rights in the issuing corporation that ordinarily would be afforded to owners of the issuing corporation's stock (e.g., voting rights, dividend rights, or rights to proceeds on liquidation) to the person who would acquire the stock upon exercise of the option or a person related to such person. For this purpose, managerial or economic rights in the issuing corporation possessed because of actual stock ownership in the issuing corporation are not taken into account;

(viii) Restrictive covenants. The existence of restrictive covenants or similar arrangements (either within the option agreement or in a related agreement) that, directly or indirectly, prevent or limit the ability of the issuing corporation to undertake certain activities while the option is outstanding (e.g., covenants limiting the payment of dividends or borrowing of funds);

(ix) Intention to alter value. Whether it was intended that through a change in the capital structure of the issuing corporation or a transfer of assets to or from the issuing corporation (other than regular, ordinary dividends) or by any other means, the fair market value of the stock of the issuing corporation would be altered for a principal purpose of increasing the likelihood that the option would be exercised; and

(x) Contingencies. Any contingency (other than the mere passage of time) to which the exercise of the option is subject (e.g., a public offering of the issuing corporation's stock or reaching a certain level of earnings).

(2) Cash settlement options, phantom stock, stock appreciation rights, or similar interests. A cash settlement option, phantom stock, stock appreciation right, or similar interest is treated as reasonably certain to be exercised if it is reasonably certain that the option will have value at some time during the period in which the option may be exercised.

(3) Safe harbors. (i) Options to acquire stock. Except as provided in paragraph (g)(3)(iv) of this section, an option to acquire stock is not considered reasonably certain, as of a measurement date, to be exercised if—

(A) The option may be exercised no more than 24 months after the measurement date and the exercise price is equal to or greater than 90 percent of the fair market value of the underlying stock on the measurement date; or

(B) The terms of the option provide that the exercise price of the option is equal to or greater than the fair market value of the underlying stock on the exercise date.

(ii) Options to sell stock. Except as provided in paragraph (g)(3)(iv) of this section, an option to sell stock is not considered reasonably certain, as of a measurement date, to be exercised if—

(A) The option may be exercised no more than 24 months after the measurement date and the exercise price is equal to or less than 110 percent of the fair market value of the underlying stock on the measurement date; or

(B) The terms of the option provide that the exercise price of the option is equal to or less than the fair market value of the underlying stock on the exercise date.

(iii) Options exercisable at fair market value. For purposes of paragraphs (g)(3)(i)(B) and (g)(3)(ii)(B) of this section, an option whose exercise price is determined by a formula is considered to have an exercise price equal to the fair market value of the underlying stock on the exercise date if the formula is agreed upon by the parties when the option is issued in a bona fide attempt to arrive at fair market value on the exercise date and is to be applied based upon the facts in existence on the exercise date.

(iv) Exceptions. The safe harbors of this paragraph (g)(3) do not apply if—

(A) An arrangement exists that provides the holder or a related party with stockholder rights described in paragraph (g)(1)(vii) of this section (except for rights arising upon a default under the option or a related agreement);

(B) It is intended that through a change in the capital structure of the issuing corporation or a transfer of assets to or from the issuing corporation (other than regular, ordinary dividends) or by any other means, the fair market value of the stock of the issuing corporation will be altered for a principal purpose of increasing the likelihood that the option will be exercised; or

(C) The option is one in a series of related or sequential options, unless all such options satisfy paragraph (g)(3)(i) or (ii) of this section.

(v) Failure to satisfy safe harbor. Failure of an option to satisfy one of the safe harbors of this paragraph (g)(3) does not affect the determination of whether an option is treated as reasonably certain to be exercised.

(h) Examples. The provisions of this section may be illustrated by the following examples. These examples assume that the measurement dates set forth in the examples are the only measurement dates that have taken place or will take place.

Example (1). (i) P is the common parent of a consolidated group, consisting of P, S, and T. P owns all 100 shares of S's only class of stock, which is voting common stock. P also owns all the stock of T. On June 30, 1992, when the fair market value of the S stock is $40 per share, P sells to U, an unrelated corporation, an option to acquire 40 shares of the S stock that P owns at an exercise price of $30 per share, exercisable at any time within 3 years after the granting of the option. P and T have had substantial losses for 5 consecutive years while S has had substantial income during the same period. Because P, S, and T have been filing consolidated returns, P and T have been able to use all of their losses to offset S's income. It is anticipated that P, S, and T will continue their earnings histories for several more years. On July 31, 1992, S declares and pays a dividend of $1 per share to P.

(ii) If P, S, and T continue to file consolidated returns after June 30, 1992, it could reasonably be anticipated that P, S, and T would eliminate a substantial amount of federal income tax liability by using P's and T's future losses to offset S's income in consolidated returns. Furthermore, based on the difference between the exercise price of the option and the fair market value of the S stock, it is reasonably certain, on June 30, 1992, a measurement date, that the option will be exercised. Therefore, the option held by U is treated as exercised. As a result, for purposes of determining whether P and S are affiliated, P is treated as owning only 60 percent of the value of outstanding shares of S stock and U is treated as owning the remaining 40 percent. P is still treated as owning 100 percent of the voting power. Because members of the P group are no longer treated as owning stock possessing 80 percent of the total value of the S stock as of June 30, 1992, S is no longer a member of the P group. Additionally, P is not entitled to a 100 percent dividends received deduction under section 243(a)(3) because P and S are also treated as not affiliated for purposes of section 243. P is only entitled to an 80 percent dividends received deduction under section 243(c).

Example (2). (i) The facts are the same as in Example 1 except that rather than P issuing an option to acquire 40 shares of S stock to U on June 30, 1992, P, pursuant to a plan, issues an option to U1 on July 1, 1992, to acquire 20 shares of S stock, and issues an option to U2 on July 2, 1992, to acquire 20 shares of S stock.

(ii) Because the options issued to U1 and U2 were issued pursuant to a plan, July 2, 1992, constitutes a measurement date for both options. Therefore, both options are aggregated in determining whether the issuance of the options, rather than the sale of the S stock, would result in the elimination of a substantial amount of federal income tax liability. Accordingly, as in Example 1, because the continued affiliation of P, S, and T could reasonably be anticipated to result in the elimination of a substantial amount of federal income tax liability and the options are reasonably certain to be exercised, the options are treated as exercised for purposes of determining whether P and S are affiliated, and P and S are no longer affiliated as of July 2, 1992.

Example (3). (i) The facts are the same as in Example 1 except that the option gives U the right to acquire all 100 shares of the S stock, and U is the common parent of a consolidated group. The U group has had substantial losses for 5 consecutive years and it is anticipated that the U group will continue its earnings history for several more years.

(ii) If P sold the S stock, in lieu of the option, to U, S would become a member of the U group. Because the U group files consolidated returns, if P sold the S stock to U, U would be able to use its future losses to offset future income of S. When viewing the transaction from the effect on all parties, the sale of the option, in lieu of the underlying S stock, does not result in the elimination of federal income tax liability because S's income would be offset by the losses of members of either the P or U group. Accordingly, the option is disregarded and S remains a member of the P group.

Example (4). (i) P is the common parent of a consolidated group, consisting of P and S. P owns 90 of the 100 outstanding shares of S's only class of stock, which is voting common stock, and U, an unrelated corporation, owns the remaining 10 shares. On August 31, 1992, when the fair market value of the S stock is $100 per share, P sells a call option to U that entitles U to purchase 20 shares of S stock from P, at any time before August 31, 1993, at an exercise price of $115 per share. The call option does not provide U with any voting rights, dividend rights, or any other managerial or economic rights ordinarily afforded to owners of the S stock. There is no intention on August 31, 1992, to alter the value of S to increase the likelihood of the exercise of the call option.

(ii) Because the exercise price of the call option is equal to or greater than 90 percent of the fair market value of the S stock on August 31, 1992, a measurement date, the option may be exercised no more than 24 months after the measurement date, and none of the items described in paragraph (g)(3)(iv) of this section that preclude application of the safe harbor are present, the safe harbor of paragraph (g)(3)(i) of this section applies and the call option is treated as if it is not reasonably certain to be exercised. Therefore, regardless of whether the continued affiliation of P and S would result in the elimination of a substantial amount of federal income tax liability, the call option is disregarded in determining whether S remains a member of the P group.

Example (5). (i) The facts are the same as in Example 4 except that the call option gives U the right to vote similar to that of a shareholder.

(ii) Under paragraph (g)(3)(iv) of this section, the safe harbor of paragraph (g)(3)(i) of this section does not apply because the call option entitles U to voting rights equivalent to that of a shareholder. Accordingly, all of the facts and circumstances surrounding the sale of the call option must be taken into consideration in determining whether it is reasonably certain that the call option will be exercised.

Example (6). (i) In 1992, two unrelated corporations, X and Y, decide to engage jointly in a new business venture. To accomplish this purpose, X organizes a new corporation, S, on September 30, 1992. X acquires 100 shares of the voting common stock of S, which are the only shares of S stock outstanding. Y acquires a debenture of S which is convertible, on September 30, 1995, into 100 shares of S common stock. If the conversion right is not exercised, X will have the right, on September 30, 1995, to put 50 shares of its S stock to Y in exchange for 50 percent of the debenture held by Y. The likelihood of the success of the venture is uncertain. It is anticipated that S will generate substantial losses in its early years of operation. X expects to have substantial taxable income during the three years following the organization of S.

(ii) Under the terms of this arrangement, it is reasonably certain, on September 30, 1992, a measurement date, that on September 30, 1995, either through Y's exercise of its conversion right or X's right to put S stock to Y, that Y will own 50 percent of the S stock. Additionally, it could reasonably be anticipated, on September 30, 1992, a measurement date, that the affiliation of X and S would result in the elimination of a substantial amount of federal income tax liability. Accordingly, for purposes of determining whether X and S are affiliated, X is treated as owning only 50 percent of the value of the S stock as of September 30, 1992, a measurement date, and S is not a member of the X affiliated group.

Example (7). (i) The facts are the same as in Example 6 except that rather than acquiring 100 percent of the S stock and the right to put S stock to Y, X acquires only 80 percent of the S stock, while S, rather than acquiring a convertible debenture, acquires 20 percent of the S stock, and an option to acquire an additional 30 percent of the S stock. The terms of the option are such that the option will only be exercised if the new business venture succeeds.

(ii) In contrast to Example 6, because of the true business risks involved in the start-up of S and whether the business venture will ultimately succeed, along with the fact that X does not have an option to put S stock to Y, it is not reasonably certain on September 30, 1992, a measurement date, that the option will be exercised and that X will only own 50 percent of the S stock on September 30, 1995. Accordingly, the option is disregarded in determining whether S is a member of the X group.

(i) Effective date. This section applies, generally, to options with a measurement date on or after February 28, 1992. This section does not apply to options issued prior to February 28, 1992, which have a measurement date on or after February 28, 1992, if the measurement date for the option occurs solely because of an adjustment in the terms of the option pursuant to the terms of the option as it existed on February 28, 1992. Paragraph (b)(2)(iv) of this section applies to stock outstanding on or after February 28, 1992.

T.D. 8462, 12/28/92.

§ 1.1551-1 Disallowance of surtax exemption and accumulated earnings credit.

Caution: The Treasury has not yet amended Reg § 1.1551-1 to reflect changes made by P.L. 99-514, P.L. 97-34.

(a) In general. **If—**

(1) Any corporation transfers, on or after January 1, 1951, and before June 13, 1963, all or part of its property (other than money) to a transferee corporation,

(2) Any corporation transfers, directly or indirectly, after June 12, 1963, all or part of its property (other than money) to a transferee corporation, or

(3) Five or fewer individuals are in control of a corporation and one or more of them transfer, directly or indirectly, after June 12, 1963, property (other than money) to a transferee corporation,

and the transferee was created for the purpose of acquiring such property or was not actively engaged in business at the time of such acquisition, and if after such transfer the transferor or transferors are in control of the transferee during any part of the taxable year of the transferee, then for such taxable year of the transferee the Secretary or his delegate may disallow the surtax exemption defined in section 11(d) or the accumulated earnings credit of $150,000 ($100,000 in the case of taxable years beginning before January 1, 1975) provided in paragraph (2) or (3) of section 535(c), unless the transferee establishes by the clear preponderance of the evidence that the securing of such exemption or credit was not a major purpose of the transfer.

(b) Purpose of section 1551. The purpose of section 1551 is to prevent avoidance or evasion of the surtax imposed by section 11(c) or of the accumulated earnings tax imposed by section 531. It is not intended, however, that section 1551 be interpreted as delimiting or abrogating any principle of law established by judicial decision, or any existing provisions of the Code, such as sections 269 and 482, which have the effect of preventing the avoidance or evasion of income taxes. Such principles of law and such provisions of the Code, including section 1551, are not mutually exclusive, and in appropriate cases they may operate together or they may operate separately.

(c) Application of section 269(b) to cases covered by section 1551. The provisions of section 269(b) and the authority of the district director thereunder, to the extent not inconsistent with the provisions of section 1551, are applicable to cases covered by section 1551. Pursuant to the authority provided in section 269(b) the district director may allow to the transferee any part of a surtax exemption or accumulated earnings credit for a taxable year for which such exemption or credit would otherwise be disallowed under section 1551(a); or he may apportion such exemption or credit among the corporations involved. For example, corporation A transfers on January 1, 1955, all of its property to corporations B and C in exchange for all of the stock of such corporations. Immediately thereafter, corporation A is dissolved and its stockholders become the sole stockholders of corporations B and C. Assuming that corporations B and C are unable to establish by the clear preponderance of the evidence that the securing of the surtax exemption defined in section 11(d) or the accumulated earnings credit provided in section 535, or both, was not a major purpose of the transfer, the district director is authorized under sections 1551(c) and 269(b) to allow one such exemption and credit and to apportion such exemption and credit between corporations B and C.

(d) Actively engaged in business. For purposes of this section, a corporation maintaining an office for the purpose of preserving its corporate existence is not considered to be "actively engaged in business" even though such corporation may be deemed to be "doing business" for other purposes. Similarly, for purposes of this section, a corporation engaged in winding up its affairs, prior to an acquisition to which section 1551 is applicable, is not considered to be "actively engaged in business."

(e) Meaning and application of the term "control." *(1) In general.* For purposes of this section, the term "control" means—

(i) With respect to a transferee corporation described in paragraph (a)(1) or (2) of this section, the ownership by the transferor corporation, its shareholders, or both, of stock possessing either (a) at least 80 percent of the total combined voting power of all classes of stock entitled to vote, or (b) at least 80 percent of the total value of shares of all classes of stock.

(ii) With respect to each corporation described in paragraph (a)(3) of this section, the ownership by five or fewer individuals of stock possessing (a) at least 80 percent of the total combined voting power of all classes of stock entitled to vote or at least 80 percent of the total value of shares of all classes of the stock of each corporation, and *(b)* more than 50 percent of the total combined voting power of all classes of stock entitled to vote or more than 50 percent of the total value of shares of all classes of stock of each corporation, taking into account the stock ownership of each such individual only to the extent such stock ownership is identical with respect to each such corporation.

(2) Special rules. In determining for purposes of this section whether stock possessing at least 80 percent (or more than 50 percent in the case of subparagraph (1)(ii)(b) of this paragraph) of the total combined voting power of all classes of stock entitled to vote is owned, all classes of such stock shall be considered together; it is not necessary that at least 80 percent (or more than 50 percent) of each class of voting stock be owned. Likewise, in determining for purposes of this section whether stock possessing at least 80 percent (or more than 50 percent) of the total value of shares of all classes of stock is owned, all classes of stock of the corporation shall be considered together; it is not necessary that at least 80 percent (or more than 50 percent) of the value of shares of each class be owned. The fair market value of a share shall be considered as the value to be used for purposes of this computation. With respect to transfers described in paragraph (a)(2) or (3) of this section, the ownership of stock shall be determined in accordance with the provisions of section 1563(e) and the regulations thereunder. With respect to transfers described in paragraph (a)(1) of this section, the ownership of stock shall be determined in accordance with the provisions of section 544 and the regulations thereunder, except that constructive ownership under section 544(a)(2)

shall be determined only with respect to the individual's spouse and minor children. In determining control, no stock shall be excluded because such stock was acquired before January 1, 1951 (the effective date of section 1551(a)(1)), or June 13, 1963 (the effective date of section 1551(a)(2) and (3)).

(3) Example. This paragraph may be illustrated by the following example:

Example. On January 1, 1964, individual A, who owns 50 percent of the voting stock of corporation X, and individual B, who owns 30 percent of such voting stock, transfer property (other than money) to corporation Y (newly created for the purpose of acquiring such property) in exchange for all of Y's voting stock. After the transfer, A and B own the voting stock of corporations X and Y in the following proportions:

Individual	Corporation X	Corporation Y	Identical ownership
A	50	30	30
B	30	50	30
Total	80	80	60

The transfer of property by A and B to corporation Y is a transfer described in paragraph (a)(3) of this section since (i) A and B own at least 80 percent of the voting stock of corporations X and Y, and (ii) taking into account each such individual's stock ownership only to the extent such ownership is identical with respect to each such corporation, A and B own more than 50 percent of the voting stock of corporations X and Y.

(f) Taxable year of allowance or disallowance. *(1) In general.* The district director's authority with respect to cases covered by section 1551 is not limited to the taxable year of the transferee corporation in which the transfer of property occurs. Such authority extends to the taxable year in which the transfer occurs or any subsequent taxable year of the transferee corporation if, during any part of such year, the transferor or transferors are in control of the transferee.

(2) Examples. This paragraph may be illustrated by the following examples:

Example (1). On January 1, 1955, corporation D transfers property (other than money) to corporation E, a corporation not actively engaged in business at the time of the acquisition of such property, in exchange for 60 percent of the voting stock of E. During a later taxable year of E, corporation D acquires an additional 20 percent of such voting stock. As a result of such additional acquisition, D owns 80 percent of the voting stock of E. Accordingly, section 1551(a)(1) is applicable for the taxable year in which the later acquisition of stock occurred and for each taxable year thereafter in which the requisite control continues.

Example (2). On June 20, 1963, individual A, who owns all of the stock of corporation X, transfers property (other than money) to corporation Y, a corporation not actively engaged in business at the time of the acquisition of such property, in exchange for 60 percent of the voting stock of Y. During a later taxable year of Y, A acquires an additional 20 percent of such voting stock. After such acquisition A owns at least 80 percent of the voting stock of corporations X and Y. Accordingly, section 1551(a)(3) is applicable for the taxable year in which the later acquisition of stock occurred and for each taxable year thereafter in which the requisite control continues.

Example (3). Individuals A and B each owns 50 percent of the stock of corporation X. On January 15, 1964, A transfers property (other than money) to corporation Y (newly created by A for the purpose of acquiring such property) in exchange for all the stock of Y. In a subsequent taxable year of Y, individual B buys 50 percent of the stock which A owns in Y (or he transfers money to Y in exchange for its stock, as a result of which he owns 50 percent of Y's stock). Immediately thereafter the stock ownership of A and B in corporation Y is identical to their stock ownership in corporation X. Accordingly, section 1551(a)(3) is applicable for the taxable year in which B acquires stock in corporation Y (see paragraph (g)(3) of this section) and for each taxable year thereafter in which the requisite control continues. Moreover, if B's acquisition of stock in Y is pursuant to a preexisting agreement with A, A's transfer to Y and B's acquisition of Y's stock are considered a single transaction and section 1551(a)(3) also would be applicable for the taxable year in which A's transfer to Y took place and for each taxable year thereafter in which the requisite control continues.

(g) Nature of transfer. *(1) Corporate transfers before June 13, 1963.* A transfer made before June 13, 1963, by any corporation of all or part of its assets, whether or not such transfer qualifies as a reorganization under section 368, is within the scope of section 1551(a)(1), except that section 1551(a)(1) does not apply to a transfer of money only. For example, the transfer of cash for the purpose of expanding the business of the transfer or corporation through the formation of a new corporation is not a transfer within the scope of section 1551(a)(1), irrespective of whether the new corporation uses the cash to purchase from the transferor corporation stock in trade or similar property.

(2) Corporate transfers after June 12, 1963. A direct or indirect transfer made after June 12, 1963, by any corporation of all or part of its assets to a transferee corporation, whether or not such transfer qualifies as a reorganization under section 368, is within the scope of section 1551(a)(2) except that section 1551(a)(2) does not apply to a transfer of money only. For example, if a transferor corporation transfers property to its shareholders or to a subsidiary, the transfer of that property by the shareholders or the subsidiary to a transferee corporation as part of the same transaction is a transfer of property by the transferor corporation to which section 1551(a)(2) applies. A transfer of property pursuant to a purchase by a transferee corporation from a transferor corporation controlling the transferee is within the scope of section 1551(a)(2), whether or not the purchase follows a transfer of cash from the controlling corporation.

(3) Other transfers after June 12, 1963. A direct or indirect transfer made after June 12, 1963, by five or fewer individuals to a transferee corporation, whether or not such transfer qualifies under one or more other provisions of the Code (for example, section 351), is within the scope of section 1551(a)(3) except that section 1551(a)(3) does not apply to a transfer of money only. Thus, if one of five or fewer individuals who are in control of a corporation transfers property (other than money) to a controlled transferee corporation, the transfer is within the scope of section 1551(a)(3) notwithstanding that the other individuals transfer nothing or transfer only money.

(4) Examples. This paragraph may be illustrated by the following examples:

Example (1). Individuals A and B each owns 50 percent of the voting stock of corporation X. On January 15, 1964, A and B each acquires property (other than money) from X and, as part of the same transaction, each transfers such property to his wholly owned corporation (newly created for the purpose of acquiring such property). A and B retain substantial continuing interests in corporation X. The transfers to the two newly created corporations are within the scope of section 1551(a)(2).

Example (2). Corporation W organizes corporation X, a wholly owned subsidiary, for the purpose of acquiring the properties of corporation Y. Pursuant to a reorganization qualifying under section 368(a)(1)(C), substantially all of the properties of corporation Y are transferred on June 15, 1963, to corporation X solely in exchange for voting stock of corporation W. There is a transfer of property from W to X within the meaning of section 1551(a)(2).

Example (3). Individuals A and B, each owning 50 percent of the voting stock of corporation X, organize corporation Y to which each transfers money only in exchange for 50 percent of the stock of Y. Subsequently, Y uses such money to acquire other property from A and B after June 12, 1963. Such acquisition is within the scope of section 1551(a)(3).

Example (4). Individual A owns 55 percent of the stock of corporation X. Another 25 percent of corporation X's stock is owned in the aggregate by individuals B, C, D, and E. On June 15, 1963, individual A transfers property to corporation Y (newly created for the purpose of acquiring such property) in exchange for 60 percent of the stock of Y, and B, C, and D acquire all of the remaining stock of Y. The transfer is within the scope of section 1551(a)(3).

(h) Purpose of transfer. In determining, for purposes of this section, whether the securing of the surtax exemption or accumulated earnings credit constituted "a major purpose" of the transfer, all circumstances relevant to the transfer shall be considered. A "major purpose" will not be inferred from the mere purchase of inventory by a subsidiary from a centralized warehouse maintained by its parent corporation or by another subsidiary of the parent corporation. For disallowance of the surtax exemption and accumulated earnings credit under section 1551, it is not necessary that the obtaining of either such credit or exemption, or both, have been the sole or principal purpose of the transfer of the property. It is sufficient if it appears, in the light of all the facts and circumstances, that the obtaining of such exemption or credit or both, was one of the major considerations that prompted the transfer. Thus, the securing of the surtax exemption or the accumulated earnings credit may constitute "a major purpose" of the transfer, notwithstanding that such transfer was effected for a valid business purpose and qualified as a reorganization within the meaning of section 368. The taxpayer's burden of establishing by the clear preponderance of the evidence that the securing of either such exemption or credit or both was not "a major purpose" of the transfer may be met, for example, by showing that the obtaining of such exemption, or credit, or both, was not a major factor in relationship to the other consideration or considerations which prompted the transfer.

T.D. 6140, 8/29/55, amend T.D. 6377, 5/12/59, T.D. 6412, 9/10/59, T.D. 6911, 2/23/67, T.D. 7376, 9/15/75.

§ 1.1552-1 Earnings and profits.

(a) General rule. For the purpose of determining the earnings and profits of each member of an affiliated group which is required to be included in a consolidated return for such group filed for a taxable year beginning after December 31, 1953, and ending after August 16, 1954, the tax liability of the group shall be allocated among the members of the group in accordance with one of the following methods, pursuant to an election under paragraph (c) of this section:

(1) (i) The tax liability of the group shall be apportioned among the members of the group in accordance with the ratio which that portion of the consolidated taxable income attributable to each member of the group having taxable income bears to the consolidated taxable income.

(ii) For consolidated return years beginning after December 31, 1965, a member's portion of the tax liability of the group under the method of allocation provided by subdivision (i) of this subparagraph is an amount equal to the tax liability of the group multiplied by a fraction, the numerator of which is the taxable income of such member, and the denominator of which is the sum of the taxable incomes of all the members. For purposes of this subdivision the taxable income of a member shall be the separate taxable income determined under § 1.1502-12, adjusted for the following items taken into account in the computation of consolidated taxable income:

(a) The portion of the consolidated net operating loss deduction, the consolidated charitable contributions deduction, the consolidated dividends received deduction, the consolidated section 247 deduction, the consolidated section 582(c) net loss and the consolidated section 922 deduction, attributable to such member;

(b) Such member's capital gain net income (net capital gain for taxable years beginning before January 1, 1977) (determined without regard to any net capital loss carryover attributable to such member);

(c) Such member's net capital loss and section 1231 net loss, reduced by the portion of the consolidated net capital loss attributable to such member; and

(d) The portion of any consolidated net capital loss carryover attributable to such member which is absorbed in the taxable year. If the computation of the taxable income of a member under this subdivision results in an excess of deductions over gross income, then for purposes of this subdivision such member's taxable income shall be zero.

(2) (i) The tax liability of the group shall be allocated to the several members of the group on the basis of the percentage of the total tax which the tax of such member if computed on a separate return would bear to the total amount of the taxes for all members of the group so computed.

(ii) For consolidated return years beginning after December 31, 1965, a member's portion of the tax liability of the group under the method of allocation provided by subdivision (i) of this subparagraph is an amount equal to the tax liability of the group multiplied by a fraction, the numerator of which is the separate return tax liability of such member, and the denominator of which is the sum of the separate return tax liabilities of all the members. For purposes of this subdivision the separate return tax liability of a member is its tax liability computed as if it has filed a separate return for the year except that—

(a) Gains and losses on intercompany transactions shall be taken into account as provided in § 1.1502-13 as if a consolidated return had been filed for the year;

(b) Gains and losses relating to inventory adjustments shall be taken into account as provided in § 1.1502-18 as if a consolidated return had been filed for the year;

(c) Transactions with respect to stock, bonds, or other obligations of members shall be reflected as provided in

§ 1.1502-13(f) and (g) as if a consolidated return had been filed for the year;

(d) Excess losses shall be included in income as provided in § 1.1502-19 as if a consolidated return had been filed for the year;

(e) In the computation of the deduction under section 167, property shall not lose its character as new property as a result of a transfer from one member to another member during the year;

(f) A dividend distributed by one member to another member during the year shall not be taken into account in computing the deductions under section 243(a)(1), 244(a), 245, or 247 (relating to deductions with respect to dividends received and dividends paid);

(g) Basis shall be determined under §§ 1.1502-31 and 1.1502-32, and earnings and profits shall be determined under § 1.1502-33, as if a consolidated return had been filed for the year;

(h) Subparagraph (2) of § 1.1502-3(f) shall apply as if a consolidated return had been filed for the year; and

(i) For purposes of subtitle A of the Code, the surtax exemption of the member shall be an amount equal to $25,000 ($50,000 in the case of a taxable year ending in 1975), divided by the number of members (or such portion of $25,000 or $50,000 which is apportioned to the member pursuant to a schedule attached to the consolidated return for the taxable year). (However, if for the taxable year some or all of the members are component members of a controlled group of corporations (within the meaning of section 1563) and if there are other such component members which do not join in filing the consolidated return for such year, the amount to be divided among the members filing the consolidated return shall be (in lieu of $25,000 or $50,000) the sum of the amounts apportioned to the component members which join in filing the consolidated return (as determined for taxable years beginning after December 31, 1974, under § 1.1561-2(a)(2) or § 1.1561-3, whichever is applicable, and for taxable years beginning before January 1, 1975, under § 1.1561-2A(a)(2) or § 1.1561-3A, whichever is applicable).)

If the computation of the separate return tax liability of a member under this subdivision does not result in a positive tax liability, then for purposes of this subdivision such member's separate return tax liability shall be zero.

(3) (i) The tax liability of the group (excluding the tax increases arising from the consolidation) shall be allocated on the basis of the contribution of each member of the group to the consolidated taxable income of the group. Any tax increases arising from the consolidation shall be distributed to the several members in direct proportion to the reduction in tax liability resulting to such members from the filing of the consolidated return as measured by the difference between their tax liabilities determined on a separate return basis and their tax liabilities (determined without regard to the 2-percent increase provided by section 1503(a) and paragraph (a) of § 1.1502-30A (as contained in the 26 C.F.R. edition revised as of April 1, 1996) for taxable years beginning before Jan. 1, 1964) based on their contributions to the consolidated taxable income.

(ii) For consolidated return years beginning after December 31, 1965, a member's portion of the tax liability of the group under the method of allocation provided by subdivision (i) of this subparagraph shall be determined by—

(a) Allocating the tax liability of the group in accordance with subparagraph (1)(ii) of this paragraph, but

(b) The amount of tax liability allocated to any member shall not exceed the separate return tax liability of such member, determined in accordance with subparagraph (2)(ii) of this paragraph, and

(c) The sum of the amounts which would be allocated to the members but for (b) of this subdivision (ii) shall be apportioned among the other members in direct proportion to, but limited to, the reduction in tax liability resulting to such other members. Such reduction for any member shall be the excess, if any, of (1) its separate return tax liability determined in accordance with subparagraph (2)(ii) of this paragraph, over (2) the amount allocated to such member under (a) of this subdivision (ii).

If any amount remains after being apportioned among members with a reduction in tax liability to the extent of such reduction, as provided in (c) of this subdivision (ii), such remaining amount shall, notwithstanding (b) of this subdivision (ii), be allocated to the members in accordance with the fractions determined under subparagraph (1)(ii) of this paragraph.

(4) The tax liability of the group shall be allocated in accordance with any other method selected by the group with the approval of the Commissioner. No method of allocation may be approved under this subparagraph which may result in the allocation of a positive tax liability for a taxable year, among the members who are allocated a positive tax liability for such year, in a total amount which is more or less than the tax liability of the group for such year. (However, see paragraph (d) of § 1.1502-33.)

(b) Application of rules. *(1) Tax liability of the group.* For purposes of section 1552 and this section, the tax liability of the group for a taxable year shall consist of the Federal income tax liability of the group for such year determined in accordance with § 1.1502-2 or § 1.1502-30A (as contained in the 26 C.F.R. edition revised as of April 1, 1996), whichever is applicable. Thus, in the case of a carryback of a loss or credit to such year, although the earnings and profits of the members of the group may not be adjusted until the subsequent taxable year from which the loss or credit was carried back, the effect of the carryback, for purposes of this section, shall be determined by allocating the amount of the adjustment as a part of the tax liability of the group for the taxable year to which the loss or credit is carried. For example, if a consolidated net operating loss is carried back from 1969 to 1967, the allocation of the tax liability of the group for 1967 shall be recomputed in accordance with the method of allocation used for 1967, and the changes resulting from such recomputation shall, for accrual method taxpayers, be reflected in the the earnings and profits of the appropriate members in 1969.

(2) Effect of allocation. The amount of tax liability allocated to a corporation as its share of the tax liability of the group, pursuant to this section, shall (i) result in a decrease in the earnings and profits of such corporation in such amount, and (ii) be treated as a liability of such corporation for such amount. If the full amount of such liability is not paid by such corporation, pursuant to an agreement among the members of the group or otherwise, the amount which is not paid will generally be treated as a distribution with respect to stock, a contribution to capital, or a combination thereof, as the case may be.

(c) Method of election. *(1)* The election under paragraph (a) (1), (2), or (3) of this section shall be made not later than the time prescribed by law for filing the first consolidated return of the group for a taxable year beginning after December 31, 1953, and ending after August 16, 1954 (including extensions thereof). If the group elects to allocate its tax liability in accordance with the method prescribed in paragraph (a)(1), (2), or (3) of this section, a statement shall be attached to the return stating which method is elected. Such statement shall be made by the common parent corporation and shall be binding upon all members of the group. In the event that the group desires to allocate its tax liability in accordance with any other method pursuant to paragraph (a)(4) of this section, approval of such method by the Commissioner must be obtained within the time prescribed above. If such approval is not obtained in such time, the group shall allocate in accordance with the method prescribed in paragraph (a)(1) of this section. The request shall state fully the method which the group wishes to apply in apportioning the tax liability. Except as provided in subparagraph (2) of this paragraph, an election once made shall be irrevocable and shall be binding upon the group with respect to the year for which made and for all future years for which a consolidated return is filed or required to be filed unless the Commissioner authorizes a change to another method prior to the time prescribed by law for filing the return for the year in which such change is to be effective.

(2) Each group may make a new election to use any one of the methods prescribed in paragraph (a)(1), (2), or (3) of this section for its first consolidated return year beginning after December 31, 1965, or in conjunction with an election under paragraph (d) of § 1.1502-33, or may request the Commissioner's approval of a method under paragraph (a)(4) of this section for its first consolidated return year beginning after December 31, 1965, irrespective of its previous method of allocation under this section. If such new election is not made in conjunction with an election under paragraph (d) of § 1.1502-33, it shall be effective for the first consolidated return year beginning after December 31, 1965, and all succeeding years. (See § 1.1502-33 for the method of making such new election in conjunction with an election under paragraph (d) of § 1.1502-33.) Any other such new election (or request for the Commissioner's approval of a method under paragraph (a)(4) of this section) shall be made within the time prescribed by law for filing the consolidated return for the first taxable year beginning after December 31, 1965 (including extensions thereof), or within 60 days after July 3, 1968, whichever is later. Such new election shall be made by attaching a statement to the consolidated return for the first taxable year beginning after December 31, 1965, or if such election is made within the time prescribed above but after such return is filed, by filing a statement with the internal revenue officer with whom such return was filed.

(d) Failure to elect. If a group fails to make an election in its first consolidated return, or any other election, in accordance with paragraph (c) of this section, the method prescribed under paragraph (a)(1) of this section shall be applicable and shall be binding upon the group in the same manner as if an election has been made to so allocate.

(e) Definitions. Except as otherwise provided in this section, the terms used in this section shall have the same meaning as provided in the regulations under section 1502.

(f) Example. The provisions of this section may be illustrated by the following example:

Example. Corporation P is the common parent owning all of the stock of corporations S1 and S2, members of an affiliated group. A consolidated return is filed for the taxable year ending December 31, 1966, by P, S1, and S2. For 1966 such corporations had the following taxable incomes or losses computed in accordance with paragraph (a) (1)(ii) of this section:

P	0
S1	$2,000
S2	(1,000)

The group has not made an election under paragraph (c) of this section or paragraph (d) of § 1.1502-33. Accordingly, the method of allocation provided by paragraph (a)(1) of this section is in effect for the group. Assuming that the consolidated taxable income is equal to the sum of the members' taxable income and losses, or $1,000 the tax liability of the group for the year (assuming a 22-percent rate) is $220, all of which is allocated to S1. S1 accordingly reduces its earnings and profits in the amount of $220, irrespective of who actually pays the tax liability. If S1 pays the $220 tax liability there will be no further effect upon the income, earnings and profits, or the basis of stock of any member. If, however, P pays the $220 tax liability (and such payment is not in fact a loan from P to S1), then P shall be treated as having made a contribution to the capital of S1 in the amount of $220. On the other hand, if S2 pays the $220 tax liability (and such payment is not in fact a loan from S2), then S2 shall be treated as having made a distribution with respect to its stock to P in the amount of $220, and P shall be treated as having made a contribution to the capital of S1 in the amount of $220.

T.D. 6140, 8/29/55, amend T.D. 6962, 7/2/68, T.D. 7528, 12/27/77, T.D. 7728, 10/31/80, T.D. 8560, 8/12/94, T.D. 8597, 7/12/95, T.D. 8677, 6/26/96.

PAR. 8. Section 1.1552-1 is amended by adding paragraphs (g) through (j) to read as follows:

Proposed § 1.1552-1 Earnings and profits. [*For Preamble, see ¶ 151,475*]

* * * * *

(g) Allocation of consolidated AMT and allowable consolidated MTC to members. *(1) In general.* For purposes of determining the earnings and profits of each member of a consolidated group, the consolidated AMT and allowable consolidated MTC (computed under § 1.1502-55) must be allocated among the members in accordance with this paragraph (g).

(2) Amount of consolidated AMT allocated to a member. The amount of consolidated AMT allocated to a member is determined by multiplying the consolidated AMT by a fraction, the numerator of which is the separate adjusted AMT (as defined in § 1.1502-55(h)(6)(iv)) of the member for the year, and the denominator of which is the sum of each member's separate adjusted AMT for the year.

(3) Amount of allowable consolidated MTC allocated to a member. The amount of allowable consolidated MTC in a taxable year must be allocated among the consolidated group members in accordance with t he principles of § 1.1502-55(h)(6)(vi) and (7).

(4) Effective date. Paragraph (g) of this section applies to any consolidated return year for which the due date of the income tax return (without regard to extensions) is on or after [the date that is sixty days after final regulations are filed with the FEDERAL REGISTER].

(h) Allocation of consolidated environmental tax. *(1) In general.* For purposes of determining the earnings and profits of each member of a consolidated group, the consolidated environmental tax (as defined in paragraph (h)(2) of this section) must be allocated among the members in accordance with paragraph (h)(3) of this section.

(2) Consolidated environmental tax. (i) In general. The consolidated environmental tax is equal to 0.12 percent of the excess of—

(A) Consolidated modified AMTI; over

(B) $2,000,000.

(ii) Consolidated modified AMTI. For purposes of determining the consolidated environmental tax, consolidated modified AMTI is equal to the consolidated AMTI (as defined in § 1.1502-55(b)), but determined without taking into account—

(A) The consolidated ATNOL deduction (as defined in § 1.1502-55(b)(4)); and

(B) The deduction for the payment of an environmental tax under section 164(a)(5).

(3) Amount of consolidated environmental tax to be allocated to a member. (i) In general. The amount of consolidated environmental tax to be allocated to a member is determined by multiplying the consolidated environmental tax by a fraction, the numerator of which is the separate modified AMTI of the member, and denominator of which is the sum of each member's separate modified AMTI.

(ii) Separate modified AMTI. For purposes of the allocation of consolidated environmental tax, separate modified AMTI of a member is the consolidated modified AMTI determined by taking into account only the member's items of income, gain, deduction, and loss, including the member's losses and deductions actually absorbed by the group in the taxable year (whether or not absorbed by the member). For purposes of this allocation, a member is considered to have separate modified AMTI only if the computation in this paragraph (h)(3)(ii) produces a number that is greater than zero.

(4) Effective date. Paragraph (h) of this section applies to any consolidated return year for which the due date of the income tax return (without regard to extensions) is on or after [the date that is sixty days after final regulations are filed with the FEDERAL REGISTER].

(i) [Reserved]

(j) Allocation of consolidated additional taxes to members. For purposes of determining the earnings and profits of each member of a consolidated group, the consolidated additional taxes (as defined in § 1.1502-2(b)) are allocated to the members in accordance with any reasonable method used by the group. This paragraph (j) applies to any consolidated return year for which the due date of the income tax return (without regard to extensions) is on or after [the date that is sixty days after final regulations are filed with the FEDERAL REGISTER].

§ 1.1561-0 Table of contents.

This section lists the table of contents for §§ 1.1561-1 through 1.1561-3.

T.D. 9476, 12/22/2009.

Proposed § 1.1561-0 Table of contents. [*For Preamble, see ¶ 152,943*]

• ***Caution:*** This Notice of Proposed Rulemaking was partially finalized by TD 9451, 05/26/2009. Reg. §§ 1.1561-0 and 1.1561-2 remain proposed.

[The text of the proposed § 1.1561-0 is the same as the text for § 1.1561-0T published elsewhere in this issue of the Federal Register]. [*See T.D. 9369, 12/21/2007, 72 Fed. Reg. 246.*]

§ 1.1561-1 General rules regarding certain tax benefits available to the component members of a controlled group of corporations.

(a) In general. *(1) Limitation.* Part II (section 1561 and following) of subchapter B of chapter 6 of the Internal Revenue Code (Code) (part II) provides rules to limit the amounts of certain specified tax benefit items of component members of a controlled group of corporations for their tax years which include a particular December 31st date, or, in the case of a short taxable year member (see section 1561(b) and § 1.1561-2(e)), the date substituted for that December 31st date. The amount of the tax items enumerated in section 1561(a) available to any of the component members of a controlled group shall be determined for purposes of subtitle A of the Code as if the component members were a single corporation. Certain other tax items also set forth in section 1561(a) (for example, the additional tax imposed by section 11(b)(1) and the section 55(d)(3) phase out of the alternative minimum tax exemption amount) will be determined by combining the positive taxable income or positive alternative minimum taxable income of the component members of such a group and then allocating the amount of such items among those members.

(2) Definitions. For certain definitions (including the definition of a controlled group of corporations and a component member) and special rules for purposes of this part II see section 1563.

(b) Special rules. *(1) S Corporation.* For purposes of this part II, the term corporation includes a small business corporation (as defined in section 1361). However, for the treatment of such a corporation as an excluded member of a controlled group of corporations see § 1.1563-1(b)(2)(ii)(C).

(2) 52-53-week taxable year. In the case of corporations electing a 52-53-week taxable year under section 441(f)(1), the provisions of this part II shall be applied in accordance with the special rule of section 441(f)(2)(A). See § 1.441-2.

(c) Tax avoidance. The provisions of this part II do not delimit or abrogate any principle of law established by judicial decision, or any existing provisions of the Code, such as sections 269, 482, and 1551, which serve to prevent any avoidance or evasion of income taxes.

(d) Effective/applicability date. This section applies to any tax year beginning on or after December 21, 2009. However, taxpayers may apply this section to any Federal income tax return filed on or after December 21, 2009. For tax years beginning before December 21, 2009, see § 1.1561-1T as contained in 26 CFR part 1 in effect on April 1, 2009.

T.D. 9476, 12/22/2009.

PAR. 2. In the list below, for each section indicated in the left column, remove the old language in the middle column and add the new language in the right column.

Affected Section	Remove	Add
1.46-1(p)(2)(iv)	paragraph (b)(1) of § 1.441-2	§ 1.441-2
1.48-3(d)(1)(iii)	paragraph (b)(1) of § 1.441-2	§ 1.441-2
1.280H-1T(a), last sentence	§ 1.441-4T(d)	§ 1.441-3(c)
1.443-1(b)(1)(ii)	and paragraph (c)(5) of § 1.441-2	and § 1.441-1(b)(2)(ii).
1.444-1T(a)(1), first sentence	§ 1.444-4T(d)	§ 1.441-3(c)
1.444-2T(a), last sentence	§ 1.441-4T(d)	§ 1.441-3(c)
1.448-1(h)(2)(ii)(B)(1)	§ 1.441-2T(b)(1)	§ 1.441-2(c)
1.469-1(h)(4)(ii)(D)	§ 1.441-4T(f)	§ 1.441-3(e)
1.469-1T(g)(2)(i)	§ 1.441-4T(d)	§ 1.441-2
1.1561-1(c)(2)	See paragraph (b)(1) of § 1.441-2	See § 1.441-2
1.6654-2(a), concluding text	paragraph (b) of § 1.441-2	§ 1.441-2(c)
1.6655-2(a)(4), first sentence	paragraph (b) of § 1.441-2	§ 1.441-1(b)

Proposed § 1.1561-1 [*For Preamble, see ¶ 152,177*]

• ***Caution:*** This Notice of Proposed Rulemaking was partially finalized by T.D. 8996, issued on 5/16/2002. Proposed regulation §§ 1.46-1, 1.48-3, 1.280H-1T, 1.443-1, 1.444-1T, 1.444-2T, 1.448-1, 1.469-1, 1.469-1T, 1.898-4, 1.1561-1, 1.6654-2, 1.6655-2 and 301.7701(b)-6 remains in effect.

§ 1.1561-2 Special rules for allocating reductions of certain section 1561(a) tax-benefit items.

(a) Additional tax. *(1) Calculation.* (i) In general. For the purpose of determining the amount, if any, of the additional tax imposed by section 11(b)(1) (the additional tax), the taxable incomes of all of the component members of a controlled group of corporations shall be combined to determine whether either of the income thresholds for imposing the additional tax have been attained.

(ii) Special rules. For purposes of paragraph (a)(1)(i) of this section—

(A) Component member means a corporation that is apportioned some part of any applicable tax bracket amount; and

(B) Taxable income means the positive taxable income of a component member for its entire tax year (even if it was not a member of the group for each day of that tax year) that includes the same December 31st testing date, which is also applicable to the other component members of that same controlled group.

(2) Apportionment. (i) Any additional tax determined under paragraph (a)(1) of this section shall be apportioned among such members in the same manner as the corresponding tax bracket of section 11(b)(1) is apportioned. For rules to apportion the section 11(b)(1) tax brackets among the component members of a controlled group, see § 1.1561-3(b) or (c).

(ii) Apportionment methods. Unless the component members of a controlled group elect to use the first-in-first-out (FIFO) method described in paragraph (a)(2)(ii)(B) of this section, such members are required to apportion the amount of the additional tax using the proportionate method described in paragraph (a)(2)(ii)(A) of this section. These component members may elect the FIFO method by specifically adopting such method in their apportionment plan.

(A) Proportionate method. Under the proportionate method, the additional tax is allocated to each component member in the same proportion as the portion of the tax-benefit amount that inured to a member from utilizing lower tax brackets bears to the amount of the group's total tax-benefit amount inuring to it from utilizing those lower tax brackets. The tax-benefit amount that inures to a corporation from using a particular tax bracket is the tax savings that such corporation realizes from having a portion of its taxable income taxed at the lower rate attributed to that tax bracket instead of the high tax rates to which it would otherwise be subject. The steps for applying the proportionate method of allocation are as follows:

(1) Step 1. The regular tax (not including the additional tax) owed by a component member under a particular tax bracket is divided by the total tax owed by all component members under that tax bracket;

(2) Step 2. The percentage calculated under Step 1 is multiplied by the total tax-benefit amount inuring to all the members of the group from their use of this tax bracket. This computed amount equals the portion of the group's tax-benefit amount that inured to such member from using its portion of this tax bracket;

(3) Step 3. The amount determined under Step 2 is divided by the total tax-benefit amount, inuring to all the component members of the group from using all the tax brackets to which any component member's income was subject;

(4) Step 4. The percentage calculated under Step 3 is multiplied by the amount of the group's additional tax. The amount determined under this Step 4 equals the amount of the additional tax apportioned to such member for that tax bracket; and

(5) Step 5. If a component member is liable for regular tax (not including the additional tax) under more than one tax bracket, that member must calculate the amount of the additional tax apportioned to it with respect to each tax bracket. Accordingly, steps 1 through 4 must be applied for each tax bracket applicable to that member. The sum of all the apportioned amounts of additional tax from each tax bracket for which the member is subject is the total amount of the additional tax apportioned to that member.

(B) FIFO method. Under the FIFO method, the first dollars of the additional tax are to be allocated proportionately to the members starting with the lowest tax bracket (that is, the first tax bracket), up to the amount of the tax benefit inuring to those members from using that tax bracket. Any remaining amount of additional tax is then allocated proportionately among the component members who use the next higher tax bracket, and so on, until the entire amount of the additional tax has been fully apportioned among the members. For example, the first $9,500 of the additional tax liability of a controlled group is apportioned entirely to the member(s) that availed themselves of the benefit of the 15 percent tax bracket.

(3) Examples. The provisions of this paragraph (a) may be illustrated by the following examples:

Example (1). (i) Facts. A controlled group of corporations consists of three members: X, Y and Z. X owns all the stock of Y and Z. Each corporation files its separate return on a calendar year basis. For calendar year 2007, the component members of the controlled group have an apportionment plan in effect. The members apportioned 80% of the 15 percent tax-bracket amount ($40,000) to X and the remaining 10% ($10,000) to Y. The members apportioned 100% of the 25 percent tax-bracket amount ($25,000) to Y. However, these members have not adopted the FIFO method for apportioning the additional taxes. Therefore, they must follow the proportionate method. For 2007, X had taxable income (TI) of $40,000, Y had TI of $60,000 and Z had TI of $100,000. Thus the total TI of the group is $200,000.

(ii) Calculating the tax from the tax brackets and the tax benefit derived from such tax. (A) Regular tax of group subject to a 15 percent tax rate. (1) Calculating the group's tax which resulted from applying a 15 percent tax rate. The amount of tax under the 15 percent tax bracket is $7,500 (15% x $50,000).

(2) The tax-benefit amount inuring to the group from using the 15 percent tax bracket. A tax benefit inures to those members of the group who avail themselves of the 15 percent tax bracket. That tax benefit results from having the first $50,000 of its income taxed at the 15 percent tax rate, instead of at the 34 percent tax rate. Thus, the tax-benefit amount inuring to this group from using the 15 percent tax bracket is $9,500 ($17,000 (34% x $50,000) minus $7,500 (15% x $50,000)).

(B) Regular tax of group subject to a 25 percent tax rate. (1) Calculating the group's tax which resulted from applying a 25 percent tax rate. The amount of tax under the 25 percent tax bracket is $6,250 (25% x $25,000 ($75,000 - $50,000)).

(2) The tax-benefit amount inuring to the group from using the 25 percent tax bracket. A tax benefit inures to those members of the group who avail themselves of the 25 percent tax bracket. That tax benefit results from having $25,000 of its income taxed at the 25 percent tax rate, instead of at the 34 percent tax rate. Thus, the tax-benefit amount inuring to this group from using the 25 percent tax bracket is $2,250 ($8,500 (34% x $25,000) minus $6,250 (25% x $25,000)).

(C) Regular tax of group subject to a 34 percent tax rate. (1) Calculating the group's tax which resulted from applying a 34 percent tax rate. The amount of tax under the 34 percent tax bracket is $42,500 (34% x $125,000 ($200,000 (total TI) - $75,000) (amount taxed at lower rates)).

(2) The tax-benefit amount inuring to the group from using the 34 percent tax bracket. The group's total TI of $200,000 is less than the $15,000,000 income threshold for imposing any 3 percent additional tax on the group. Therefore, there is no tax benefit inuring to the members of this group for using the 34 percent tax bracket.

(D) The computation of the additional tax. Since the combined TI of the group exceeds $100,000, a 5 percent additional tax is imposed on the group. That 5 percent additional tax is the lesser amount of 5 percent of the group's taxable income exceeding $100,000 or $11,750. Five percent of that excess amount of taxable income is $5,000 (5% x $100,000 ($200,000 - $100,000)). Since $5,000 is less than $11,750, the group's 5 percent additional tax is $5,000.

(iii) Apportioning the amount of additional tax to each applicable tax bracket.

(2) The apportioned tax under each bracket. The amount of tax owed by each member under each tax bracket pursuant to the apportionment plan is as follows:

Name of component member	Amount of tax owed under the 15% tax bracket	Amount of tax owed under the 25% tax bracket	Amount of tax owed under the 34% tax bracket
X	$6,000	0	0
Y	$1,500	$6,250	$8,500
Z	0	0	$34,000

(B) Apportioning the 5 percent additional tax among the component members of the controlled group. Since the group did not elect to adopt the FIFO method of apportionment, it is required to apportion the $5,000 of its 5 percent additional tax pursuant to the proportionate method in the following manner:

(1) Amount of the additional tax apportioned to X. Pursuant to the plan, X was liable for $6,000 of the group's $7,500 regular tax (80%) owed under the 15 percent tax bracket (and X is not liable for any regular tax under any higher tax bracket). See Step 1 of paragraph (a)(2)(ii)(A) of this section. X's portion of the group's tax benefit which it derived from using the 15 percent tax rate is $7,600 (0.8 x $9,500). See Step 2. The tax benefit inuring to the entire group from using the 15 percent and 25 percent tax brackets is $11,750 ($9,500 (from the 15 percent tax bracket) + $2,250 (from the 25 percent tax bracket)). So, X's percentage portion of the group's total tax benefit is $7,600/$11,750 (64.68%). See Step 3. Thus, X's allocated portion of the 5 percent additional tax from using the 15 percent tax bracket is $3,234 (0.6468 x $5,000). See Step 4.

(2) Amount of the additional tax apportioned to Y. (i) Regular tax apportioned to Y from using the 15 percent tax bracket. Pursuant to the plan, Y was liable for the remaining $1,500 of the group's $7,500 regular tax (20%) owed under the 15 percent tax bracket. See Step 1. Y's portion of the group's tax benefit which it derived from using the 15 percent tax rate is $1,900 ($9,500 - $7,600, or 0.2 x $9,500). See Step 2. So, Y's percentage portion of the group's total tax benefit is $1,900/$11,750 (16.17%). See Step 3. Thus, Y's allocated portion of the 5 percent additional tax from using the 15 percent tax bracket is $809 (0.1617 x $5,000). See Step 4. (ii) Regular tax apportioned to Y from using the 25 percent tax bracket. Pursuant to the plan, Y was liable for 100% of the group's regular tax owed under the 25 percent tax bracket, an amount of $6,250. See Step 1. Y is, therefore, entitled to 100% of the group's tax benefit which it derived from using this tax bracket, an amount of $2,250. See Step 2. So, Y's percentage portion of the group's total tax benefit is $2,250/$11,750 (19.15%). See Step 3. Thus, Y's allocated portion of the 5 percent additional tax from using the 25 percent tax bracket is $957 (0.1915 x $5,000). See Step 4. Y's total allocated portion of the additional tax is $1,766 ($809 + $957). See Step 5.

Example (2). (i) Facts. The facts are the same as in Example 1, except that on August 31, 2007, X of the X-Y-Z controlled group sold all of the stock of Z to M of the M-N controlled group, a pair of corporations unrelated to the X-Y group. Pursuant to the terms of the sales agreement, the members of the M-N group properly notified the members of the X-Y group on a timely basis that Z's taxable income for its 2007 tax year, as based on the group's December 31st testing date, was $100,000.

(ii) Controlled group analysis. On December 31st , 2007, X and Y are members of the selling controlled group and M, N and Z are members of the buying controlled group. However, pursuant to section 1563(b)(3), Z is treated as an additional member of the X-Y group on December31st 2007, since it was a member for at least one-half the number of days (243 out of 364) during the period beginning on January 1 and ending on December 30, 2007. Conversely, pursuant to section 1563(b)(2)(A), Z is treated as an excluded member of the M-N controlled group. Therefore, on December 31st, 2007, X, Y and Z qualify as component members of the selling group, and only M and N qualify as component members of the buying group.

(iii) Additional tax analysis. With regard to X and Y's 2007 tax years, X and Y together owed $5,000 of additional tax, as calculated in Example 1. X's allocated portion of the additional tax is $3,234, as calculated in the manner set forth in Example 1. Y's allocated portion of the additional tax is $1,766, also as calculated in the manner set forth in Example 1.

Example (3). (i) The facts are the same as in Example 2, except that in 2012, pursuant to an IRS audit, Z's 2007 taxable income was re-determined. It was adjusted by an income increase of $10,000. Pursuant to the terms of the sales agreement, the members of the M-N group timely notified the members of the X-Y group of Z's income adjustment.

(ii) Additional tax analysis. For 2007 the X-Y-Z group owed a revised additional tax in the amount of $5,500, allocated as follows: $3,557.40 to X and $1,942.60 to Y. X and Y each filed an amended 2007 tax return to report their portions of the $500 increase to the group's additional tax. Pursuant to their apportionment plan for allocating their regular tax, and as a result of defaulting to the proportionate method for allocating the group's additional tax, X reported $323.40 as its share of the group's increase to its additional tax and Y reported $176.60 as its share of the group's increase to its additional tax.

Example (4). The facts are the same as in Example 1, except that the members elected in their apportionment plan to adopt the FIFO method for apportioning the additional tax. Under the FIFO method, the 5 percent additional tax amount of $5,000 will be apportioned entirely to those members who would benefit from using the 15 percent tax bracket, by reason that $5,000 of the group's additional tax is less than $9,500, which is the full tax-benefit amount inuring to a controlled group from having a 15 percent tax rate applied to the full income bracket subject to that rate. Since X derived 80 percent of the group's tax benefit by its use of the 15 percent tax bracket, its share of the group's 5 percent additional tax is $4,000 (80% x $5,000), and Y's share of the group's 5 percent additional tax is, therefore, $1,000, which is the remaining amount of the group's 5 percent additional tax, attributable to the 15 percent tax bracket.

(b) Reduction to the amount exempted from the alternative minimum tax. *(1) Calculation.* The alternative minimum taxable incomes of the component members of a controlled group of corporations shall be taken into account in calculating the reduction set forth in section 55(d)(3) to the amount exempted from the alternative minimum tax (the exemption amount). For purposes of the preceding sentence, alternative minimum taxable income means the positive alternative minimum taxable income of a component member for its entire tax year (even if it was not a member of the group for each day of that tax year) that includes the same December 31st testing date, which is also applicable to the other component members of that same controlled group.

(2) Apportionment. Any reduction to the exemption amount shall be apportioned to the component members of a controlled group in the same manner that the amount of the exemption (provided in section 55(d)(2)) to the alternative minimum tax was allocated under section 1561(a). For rules to apportion the section 55(d)(2) exemption amount among the component members of a controlled group, see § 1.1561-3(b) or (c).

(3) Examples. The provisions of this paragraph (b) may be illustrated by the following example:

Example. (i) Facts. A controlled group of corporations consists of three members: X, Y and Z. X owns all of the stock of Y and Z. Each corporation files its separate return on a calendar year basis. For calendar year 2007, the component members of this controlled group have an apportionment plan in effect. The group has chosen to apportion the entire section 55(d)(2) exemption amount of $40,000 to Z. For 2007, X had alternative minimum taxable income (AMTI) of $40,000, Y had AMTI of $60,000 and Z had AMTI of $100,000. Thus the total AMTI of the group is $200,000.

(ii) Calculating the reduction to the exemption amount. Section 55(d)(3)(A) provides that the section 55(d)(2) exemption amount shall be reduced (but not below zero) by an amount equal to 25 percent of the amount by which the AMTI of a corporation exceeds $150,000. For the purpose of computing the group's AMTI, the AMTI of each of the component members, for their tax years that have the same December 31st testing date, shall be taken into account. In accordance with these provisions, the $40,000 exemption amount is reduced by $12,500 (25% × $50,000 ($200,000 - $150,000)). Pursuant to the group's allocation plan, the entire $12,500 reduction to the exemption amount is allocated to Z. Thus, after such allocation, Z's $40,000 exemption amount is reduced to $27,500 ($40,000 - $12,500).

(c) Accumulated earnings credit. The component members of a controlled group of corporations are permitted to allocate the amount of the accumulated earnings credit unequally if they have an apportionment plan in effect.

(d) [Reserved].

(e) Short taxable years not including a December 31st date. *(1) General rule.* If a corporation has a short taxable year not including a December 31st date and, after applying the rules of section 1561(b) and paragraph (e)(2)(i) of this section, it qualifies as a component member of the group with respect to its short taxable year (short-year member), then, for purposes of subtitle A of the Internal Revenue Code, the amount of any tax-benefit item described in section 1561(b) allocated to that component member's short taxable year shall be the amount specified in section 1561(a) for that item, divided by the number of corporations which are component members of that group on the last day of that component member's short taxable year. The component members of such group may not apportion, by an apportionment plan, an amount of such tax-benefit item to any short-year member that differs from equal apportionment of that item.

(2) Additional rules. For purposes of paragraph (e)(1) of this section—

(i) Section 1563(b) shall be applied as if the last day of the taxable year of a short-year member were substituted for December 31st; and

(ii) The term short taxable year does not refer to any portion of a tax year of a corporation for which its income is required to be included in a consolidated return pursuant to § 1.1502-76(b).

(3) Calculation of the additional tax. A short-year member (as defined in paragraph (e)(1) of this section) for its short taxable year calculates its additional tax liability imposed by section 11(b)(1) only on its own income, and therefore the subsequent calculation of the additional tax liability with regard to the remaining members of the group will not include the income of this short-year member.

(4) Calculation of the alternative minimum tax. If a component member has a tax year of less than 12 months, whether or not such tax year includes a December 31st date, see section 443(d) for the annualization method required for calculating the alternative minimum tax.

(5) Examples. The provisions of this paragraph (e) may be illustrated by the following examples:

Example (1). Formation of a new member of a controlled group. (i) Facts. On January 2, 2007, corporation X transfers cash to newly formed corporation Y (which begins business on that date) and receives all of the stock of Y in return. X also owns all of the stock of corporation Z on each day of 2006 and 2007. X, Y and Z have an apportionment plan in effect, apportioning the 15 percent tax-bracket amount as follows: 40% ($20,000) to each of X and Y and 20% ($10,000) to Z. X, Y and Z each file a separate return with respect to the group's December 31st 2007 testing date. X is on a calendar tax year and Z is on a fiscal tax year ending on March 31. Y adopts a fiscal year ending on June 30 and timely files a tax return for its short taxable year beginning on January 2, 2007, and ending on June 30, 2007.

(ii) Y's short taxable year. On June 30, 2007, Y is a component member of a parent-subsidiary controlled group of corporations composed of X, Y and Z. Pursuant to paragraph (e)(1) of this section, the group may not apportion any amount of the 15 percent tax bracket to Y's short taxable year ending on June 30, 2007. Rather, Y is entitled to exactly ⅓ of such bracket amount, or $16,667.

(iii) The members' subsequent tax years. On December 31st, 2007, X, Y and Z are component members of a parent-subsidiary controlled group of corporations. For their tax years that include December 31st, 2007 (X's calendar year ending December 31st, 2007, Z's fiscal year ending March 31, 2008 and Y's fiscal year ending June 30, 2008), X, Y and Z apportion among themselves the full amount of all of the applicable tax brackets pursuant to their apportionment plan. For example, 40% of the 15 percent tax-bracket amount, or $20,000, was apportioned to each of X and Y, and the remaining 10%, or $10,000, was apportioned to Z.

Example (2). Allocating a tax bracket to the short taxable year of a liquidated member of a controlled group. (i) Facts. On January 1, 2007, corporation P owns all of the stock of corporations S1, S2 and S3 (the P group). Each of these four component members of the P group, with respect to the group's December 31st, 2007 testing date, files its separate return on a calendar year basis. These members have an apportionment plan in effect (the P group plan) under which S1 and S2 are each entitled to 40% of the 15 percent tax-bracket amount ($20,000), and P and S3 are each entitled to 10% of the 15 percent tax-bracket amount ($5,000). On May 31, 2007, S1 liquidates and therefore files a return for the short taxable year beginning on January 1, 2007, and ending on May 31, 2007. On July 31, 2007, S2 liquidates and therefore files a return for the short taxable year beginning on January 1, 2007 and ending on July 31, 2007. P and S3 each file a return for their 2007 calendar tax years.

(ii) Apportionment of the 15 percent tax bracket to S1 for its short taxable year. On May 31, 2007, S1 is a component member of the P group composed of P, S1, S2 and S3. Pursuant to paragraph (e)(1) of this section, the group may not apportion any amount of the 15 percent tax bracket to S1's short taxable year ending on June 30, 2007. Rather, S1 is entitled to exactly ¼ of such bracket amount, or $12,500.

(iii) Apportionment of the 15 percent tax bracket to S2 for its short taxable year. On July 31, 2007, S2 is a component member of the P group composed of P, S2 and S3. Pursuant to paragraph (e)(1) of this section, the group may not apportion any amount of the 15 percent tax bracket to S2's short taxable year ending on June 30, 2007. Rather, S2 is entitled to exactly ⅓ of such bracket amount, or $16,667.

(iv) Apportionment of the 15 percent tax bracket to P and S3 for each of their calendar tax years. On December 31st, 2007, P and S3 are component members of the P group. Accordingly, for P and S3's 2007 calendar tax year, they are each apportioned $25,000 of the 15 percent tax bracket, pursuant to the applicable P group plan.

Example (3). Liquidation of member after its transfer to another controlled group. (i) Facts. The facts are the same as in Example 2, except that P, on April 30, 2007, sold all of the stock of S2 to the M-N controlled group. At the time of the sale, M and N are both unrelated to any members of the P group. As in Example 2, S2 liquidates on July 31, 2007, and therefore files a tax return for its short taxable year beginning on January 1, 2007, and ending on July 31, 2007. Pursuant to the sales agreement, the N-M group timely notified P that S2 had liquidated.

(ii) Controlled group analysis. On April 30, 2007, the date of the sale of S2, the P group reasonably expected that S2 would be treated as an excluded member with respect to its December 31st, 2007 testing date. On that April 30th date, S2 had been a member of the P group for less than one-half the number of days of what it expected would be a full 2007 calendar tax year preceding December 31st, 2007 (120 days (January 1-April 30) out of 364 days (January 1-December 30)). Yet, as a result of S2's subsequent liquidation by the M-N group prior to December 31st, 2007, S2 became a component member of the P group with respect to the P group's December 31st, 2007 testing date. With respect to that December 31st testing date, S2 thus was a member of the P group for more than one-half of the number of days of its tax year ending on July 31, 2007, which days proceeded December 31st, 2007 (120 days (January 1-April 30 of 2007) out of 211 days (January 1-July 30 of 2007)). The allocation of the 15 percent tax-bracket amount to the P group members is determined in the same manner as in Example 2 and, therefore, the bracket amounts allocated to P, S1, S2 and S3 are the same as determined in Example 2. The allocation of the bracket amounts would be the same if, at the time P sold all of the S2 stock, the parties had made a section 338(h)(10) election.

Example (4). Short taxable year including a December 31st date. Corporation X owns all of the stock of corporations Y and Z. X, Y and Z each file separate returns. X and Y are on a calendar tax year and Z is on a fiscal tax year beginning October 1 and ending September 30. On January 2, 2007, Z liquidates. Because Z's final tax year (beginning on October 1, 2006 and ending on January 2, 2007) includes a December 31st date, that is, December 31, 2006, it is therefore not subject to the short taxable year rule provided by section 1561(b) and paragraph (e) of this section. Accordingly, Z is a component member of the X-Y-Z group, for the group's December 31st , 2006 testing date. Thus, the rules of this paragraph (e) do not limit the amount of any of the tax-benefit items of section 1561(a) available to Z or to this controlled group.

(f) Effective/applicability date. This section applies to any tax year beginning on or after December 21, 2009. However, taxpayers may apply this section to any Federal income tax return filed on or after December 21, 2009. For tax years beginning before December 21, 2009, see § 1.1561-2T as contained in 26 CFR part 1 in effect on April 1, 2009.

T.D. 9476, 12/22/2009.

Proposed § 1.1561-2 Special rules for allocating reductions to certain section 1561(a) tax-benefit items. [*For Preamble, see ¶ 152,943*]

• ***Caution:*** This Notice of Proposed Rulemaking was partially finalized by TD 9451, 05/26/2009. Reg. §§ 1.1561-0 and 1.1561-2 remain proposed.

[The text of the proposed § 1.1561-2 is the same as the text for § 1.1561-2T(a) through (f)(1) published elsewhere in this issue of the Federal Register]. [*See T.D. 9369, 12/21/2007, 72 Fed. Reg. 246.*]

§ 1.1561-3 Allocation of the section 1561(a) tax items.

(a) Filing of form. *(1) In general.* For each tax year that a corporation is a component member of the same controlled group of corporations on a December 31st (its testing date), or, in the case of a short-year member (see section 1561(b) and § 1.1561-2(e)), the date substituted for that December 31st date (its testing date), such corporation and all the other component members of such group each must file the required form (that is, Schedule O or any successor form) with the Federal income tax return for that component member's tax year that includes a particular testing date. Each such corporation must file that form with its return whether or not—

(i) An apportionment plan is in effect; or

(ii) Any change is made to the group's apportionment of its section 1561(a) tax benefit items from the previous year.

(2) Exception for component members that are members of a consolidated group. If any of the component members of a controlled group of corporations are also members of a consolidated group, the parent of such consolidated group shall file only one form on behalf of all such members. Such form shall contain the information required for each such member.

(b) No apportionment plan in effect. If the component members of a controlled group of corporations do not have an apportionment plan in effect, the amounts of the section 1561(a) items must be divided equally among all such members. For purposes of the preceding sentence, if any of the component members of a controlled group of corporations are also members of a consolidated group, such members will each be treated as a separate component member of the controlled group.

(c) Apportionment plan in effect. *(1) Adoption of plan.* The component members of a controlled group of corporations consent to the adoption (or amendment) of an apportionment plan by checking the box to that effect on such form. For purposes of this paragraph (c)—

(i) An apportionment plan that is adopted (including a plan that has been amended) continues in effect until it is terminated;

(ii) A consolidated group is treated collectively as one component member of such group. This treatment occurs even where a member of that consolidated group has joined or left the group, if after such corporation joins or leaves the consolidated group, that group remains in existence, pursuant to § 1.1502-75(d); and

(iii) The members must allocate the amounts of the section 1561(a) items between/among themselves as described in the plan.

(2) Limitation on adopting a plan. (i) Sufficient statute of limitations period for making an assessment of tax. The members may only adopt or amend such a plan if there is at least one year remaining in the statutory period (including any extensions thereof) for the assessment of a deficiency against every member the tax liability of which would be increased by the adoption of such a plan.

(ii) Insufficient statute of limitations period for making an assessment of tax. If any member cannot satisfy the requirement of paragraph (c)(2)(i) of this section, the members may not adopt or amend such a plan unless the member not satisfying such requirement has entered into an agreement with the Internal Revenue Service to extend the statute of limitations for the limited purpose of assessing any deficiency against such member attributable to the adoption of such a plan.

(3) Termination of plan. An apportionment plan that is in effect for the component members of a controlled group with respect to a particular December 31 is terminated with respect to a succeeding December 31 if—

(i) Each member of such group consents to the termination of such a plan for the current December 31st by checking the box to that effect on its form;

(ii) The controlled group ceases to remain in existence (within the meaning of section 1563(a)) during the calendar year ending on the current December 31st;

(iii) Any corporation which was a component member of such group on the preceding December 31st is not a component member of such group on the current December 31st; or

(iv) Any corporation which was not a component member of such group on the preceding December 31st is a component member of such group on the current December 31st.

(d) Effective/applicability date. This section applies to any tax year beginning on or after December 21, 2009. However, taxpayers may apply this section to any Federal income tax return filed on or after December 21, 2009. For tax years beginning before December 21, 2009, see § 1.1561-3T as contained in 26 CFR part 1 in effect on April 1, 2009.

T.D. 9476, 12/22/2009.

§ 1.1563-1 Definition of controlled group of corporations and component members and related concepts.

(a) Controlled group of corporations. *(1) In general.* (i) Types of controlled groups. For purposes of sections 1561 through 1563, the term controlled group of corporations means any group of corporations which is—

(A) A parent-subsidiary controlled group (as defined in paragraph (a)(2) of this section);

(B) A brother-sister controlled group (as defined in paragraph (a)(3)(i) of this section);

(C) A combined group (as defined in paragraph (a)(4) of this section); or

(D) A life insurance controlled group (as defined in paragraph (a)(5) of this section).

(ii) Cross reference. For the exclusion of certain stock for purposes of applying the definitions contained in this paragraph, see section 1563(c) and § 1.1563-2.

(2) Parent-subsidiary controlled group. (i) Definition. The term parent-subsidiary controlled group means one or more chains of corporations connected through stock ownership with a common parent corporation if—

(A) Stock possessing at least 80 percent of the total combined voting power of all classes of stock entitled to vote or at least 80 percent of the total value of shares of all classes of stock of each of the corporations, except the common parent corporation, is owned (directly and with the application of § 1.1563-3(b)(1), relating to options) by one or more of the other corporations; and

(B) The common parent corporation owns (directly and with the application of § 1.1563-3(b)(1), relating to options) stock possessing at least 80 percent of the total combined voting power of all classes of stock entitled to vote or at least 80 percent of the total value of shares of all classes of stock of at least one of the other corporations, excluding, in computing such voting power or value, stock owned directly by such other corporations.

(ii) Examples. The definition of a parent-subsidiary controlled group of corporations may be illustrated by the following examples:

Example (1). P Corporation owns stock possessing 80 percent of the total combined voting power of all classes of stock entitled to vote of S Corporation. P is the common parent of a parent-subsidiary controlled group consisting of member corporations P and S.

Example (2). Assume the same facts as in Example 1. Assume further that S owns stock possessing 80 percent of the total value of shares of all classes of stock of X Corporation. P is the common parent of a parent-subsidiary controlled group consisting of member corporations P, S, and X. The result would be the same if P, rather than S, owned the X stock.

Example (3). P Corporation owns 80 percent of the only class of stock of S Corporation and S, in turn, owns 40 percent of the only class of stock of X Corporation. P also owns 80 percent of the only class of stock of Y Corporation and Y, in turn, owns 40 percent of the only class of stock of X. P is the common parent of a parent-subsidiary controlled group consisting of member corporations P, S, X, and Y.

Example (4). P Corporation owns 75 percent of the only class of stock of Y and Z Corporations; Y owns all the remaining stock of Z; and Z owns all the remaining stock of Y. Since intercompany stockholdings are excluded (that is, are not treated as outstanding) for purposes of determining whether P owns stock possessing at least 80 percent of the voting power or value of at least one of the other corporations, P is treated as the owner of stock possessing 100 percent of the voting power and value of Y and of Z for purposes of paragraph (a)(2)(i)(B) of this section. Also, stock possessing 100 percent of the voting power and value of Y and Z is owned by the other corporations in the group within the meaning of paragraph (a)(2)(i)(A) of this section. (P and Y together own stock possessing 100 percent of the voting power and value of Z, and P and Z together own stock possessing 100 percent of the voting power and value of Y.) Therefore, P is the common parent of a parent-subsidiary controlled group of corporations consisting of member corporations P, Y, and Z.

(3) Brother-sister controlled group. (i) Definition. The term brother-sister controlled group means two or more corporations if the same five or fewer persons who are individuals, estates, or trusts own (directly and with the application of the rules contained in § 1.1563-3(b)) stock possessing more than 50 percent of the total combined voting power of all classes of stock entitled to vote or more than 50 percent of the total value of shares of all classes of stock of each corporation, taking into account the stock ownership of each such person only to the extent such stock ownership is identical with respect to each such corporation.

(ii) Additional stock ownership requirement for purposes of certain other provisions of law. For purposes of any provision of law (other than sections 1561 through 1563) that incorporates the section 1563(a) definition of a controlled group, the term brother-sister controlled group means two or more corporations if the same five or fewer persons who are individuals, estates, or trusts own (directly and with the application of the rules contained in § 1.1563-3(b)) stock possessing—

(A) At least 80 percent of the total combined voting power of all classes of stock entitled to vote or at least 80 percent of the total value of shares of all classes of stock of each corporation (the 80 percent requirement);

(B) More than 50 percent of the total combined voting power of all classes of stock entitled to vote or more than 50 percent of the total value of shares of all classes of stock of each corporation, taking into account the stock ownership of each such person only to the extent such stock ownership is identical with respect to each such corporation (the more-than-50 percent identical ownership requirement); and

(C) The five or fewer persons whose stock ownership is considered for purposes of the 80 percent requirement must be the same persons whose stock ownership is considered for purposes of the more-than-50 percent identical ownership requirement.

(iii) Examples. The principles of paragraph (a)(3)(ii) of this section may be illustrated by the following examples:

Example (1). (i) The outstanding stock of corporations P, W, X, Y, and Z, which have only one class of stock outstanding, is owned by the following unrelated individuals:

Individuals	P (%)	W (%)	X (%)	Y (%)	Z (%)	Identical ownership
A	55	51	55	55	55	51.
B	45	49				(45% in P & W).
C			45			
D				45		
E					45	
Total	100	100	100	100	100	

(ii) Corporations P and W are members of a brother-sister controlled group of corporations. Although the more-than-50 percent identical ownership requirement is met for all 5 corporations, corporations X, Y, and Z are not members because at least 80 percent of the stock of each of those corporations is not owned by the same 5 or fewer persons whose stock ownership is considered for purposes of the more-than-50 percent identical ownership requirement.

Example (2). (i) The outstanding stock of corporations X and Y, which have only one class of stock outstanding, is owned by the following unrelated individuals:

Individuals	Corporations X (%)	Y (%)
A	12	12
B	12	12
C	12	12
D	12	12
E	13	13
F	13	13
G	13	13
H	13	13
Total	100	100

(ii) Any group of five of the shareholders will own more than 50 percent of the stock in each corporation, in identical holdings. However, X and Y are not members of a brother-sister controlled group because at least 80 percent of the stock of each corporation is not owned by the same five or fewer persons.

Example (3). (i) Corporation X and Y each have two classes of stock outstanding, voting common and non-voting common. (None of this stock is excluded from the definition of stock under section 1563(c).) Unrelated individuals A and B own the following percentages of the class of stock entitled to vote (voting) and of the total value of shares of all classes of stock (value) in each of corporations X and Y:

Individuals	Corporations	
	X	Y
A	100% voting, 60% value	75% voting, 60% value
B	0% voting, 10% value	25% voting, 10% value

(ii) No other shareholder of X owns (or is considered to own) any stock in Y. X and Y are a brother-sister controlled group of corporations. The group meets the more-than-50 percent identical ownership requirement because A and B own more than 50 percent of the total value of shares of all classes of stock of X and Y in identical holdings. (The group also meets the more-than-50 percent identical ownership requirement because of A's voting stock ownership.) The group meets the 80 percent requirement because A and B own at least 80 percent of the total combined voting power of all classes of stock entitled to vote.

Example (4). Assume the same facts as in Example 3 except that the value of the stock owned by A and B is not more than 50 percent of the total value of shares of all classes of stock of each corporation in identical holdings. X and Y are not a brother-sister controlled group of corporations. The group meets the more-than-50 percent identical ownership requirement because A owns more than 50 percent of the total combined voting power of the voting stock of each corporation. For purposes of the 80 percent requirement, B's voting stock in Y cannot be combined with A's voting stock in Y since B, who does not own any voting stock in X, is not a person whose ownership is considered for purposes of the more-than-50 percent identical ownership requirement. Because no other shareholder owns stock in both X and Y, these other shareholders' stock ownership is not counted towards meeting either the more-than-50 percent identical ownership requirement or the 80 percent ownership requirement.

(iv) Special rule if prior law applies. Paragraph (a)(3)(ii) of this section, as amended by TD 8179, applies to taxable years ending on or after December 31, 1970. See, however, the transitional rule in paragraph (d) of this section.

(4) Combined group. (i) Definition. The term combined group means any group of three or more corporations if—

(A) Each such corporation is a member of either a parent-subsidiary controlled group of corporations or a brother-sister controlled group of corporations; and

(B) At least one of such corporations is the common parent of a parent-subsidiary controlled group and also is a member of a brother-sister controlled group.

(ii) Examples. The definition of a combined group of corporations may be illustrated by the following examples:

Example (1). A, an individual, owns stock possessing 80 percent of the total combined voting power of all classes of the stock of corporations X and Y. Y, in turn, owns stock possessing 80 percent of the total combined voting power of all classes of the stock of corporation Z. X, Y, and Z are members of the same combined group since—

(i) X, Y, and Z are each members of either a parent-subsidiary or brother-sister controlled group of corporations; and

(ii) Y is the common parent of a parent-subsidiary controlled group of corporations consisting of Y and Z, and also is a member of a brother-sister controlled group of corporations consisting of X and Y.

Example (2). Assume the same facts as in Example 1, and further assume that corporation X owns 80 percent of the total value of shares of all classes of stock of corporation S. X, Y, Z, and S are members of the same combined group.

(5) Life insurance controlled group. (i) Definition. The term life insurance controlled group means two or more life insurance companies each of which is a member of a controlled group of corporations described in paragraph (a)(2), (a)(3)(i), or (a)(4) of this section and to which § 1.1502-47(f)(6) does not apply. Such insurance companies shall be treated as a controlled group of corporations separate from any other corporations which are members of a controlled group described in such paragraph (a)(2), (a)(3)(i), or (a)(4) of this section. For purposes of this section, the common parent of the controlled group described in paragraph (a)(2) of this section shall be referred to as the common parent of the life insurance controlled group.

(ii) Examples. The following examples illustrate the definition of a life insurance controlled group. In these examples, L indicates a life company, another letter indicates a nonlife company and each corporation uses the calendar year as its taxable year:

Example (1). Since January 1, 1999, corporation P has owned all the stock of corporations L 1 and Y, and L 1 has owned all the stock of corporation X. On January 1, 2005, Y acquired all of the stock of corporation L 2. Since L 1 and L 2 are members of a parent-subsidiary controlled group of corporations, such companies are treated as members of a life insurance controlled group separate from the parent-subsidiary controlled group consisting of P, X and Y. For purposes of this section, P is referred to as the common parent of the life insurance controlled group even though P is not a member of such group.

Example (2). The facts are the same as in Example 1, except that, beginning with the 2005 tax year, the P affiliated group elected to file a consolidated return and P made a section 1504(c)(2) election. Pursuant to paragraph (a)(5)(i) of this section, L 1 and L 2 are not members of a separate life insurance controlled group. Instead, P, X, Y, L 1 and L 2 constitute one controlled group. See § 1.1502-47(f)(6).

(6) Voting power of stock. For purposes of this section, and §§ 1.1563-2 and 1.1563-3, in determining whether the stock owned by a person (or persons) possesses a certain percentage of the total combined voting power of all classes of stock entitled to vote of a corporation, consideration will be given to all the facts and circumstances of each case. A share of stock will generally be considered as possessing the voting power accorded to such share by the corporate charter, by-laws, or share certificate. On the other hand, if there is any agreement, whether express or implied, that a shareholder will not vote his stock in a corporation, the formal voting rights possessed by his stock may be disregarded in determining the percentage of the total combined voting power possessed by the stock owned by other shareholders in the corporation, if the result is that the corporation becomes a component member of a controlled group of corporations. Moreover, if a shareholder agrees to vote his stock in a corporation in the manner specified by another shareholder in the corporation, the voting rights possessed by the stock owned by the first shareholder may be considered to be possessed by the stock owned by such other shareholder

if the result is that the corporation becomes a component member of a controlled group of corporations.

(b) Component members. *(1) In general.* (i) Definition. For purposes of sections 1561 through 1563, a corporation is with respect to its taxable year a component member of a controlled group of corporations for the group's testing date if such corporation—

(A) Is a member of such controlled group on such testing date and is not treated as an excluded member under paragraph (b)(2) of this section; or

(B) Is not a member of such controlled group on such testing date but is treated as an additional member under paragraph (b)(3) of this section.

(ii) Member of a controlled group of corporations. For purposes of sections 1561 through 1563, a member of a controlled group is a corporation connected with other member(s) of a controlled group under the stock ownership rules and the stock qualification rules set forth in section 1563. Under these rules, for a corporation to qualify as a component member of the group with respect to a group's December 31st testing date (or the short-year testing date for a short-year member), that corporation does not have to be a member of that group on that group's testing date. In addition, a corporation that is a member of a controlled group on the group's testing date does not necessarily qualify as a component member of that group with respect to that testing date.

(iii) Additional concepts used in applying the controlled group rules.

(A) The term testing date means the date used for determining the status of controlled group members as either component members or excluded members. That testing date is then also used to determine which taxable years of those component members are to be subjected to the controlled group rules. Generally, a member's testing date is the December 31st date included within that member's taxable year, whether such member is on a calendar or fiscal taxable year. However, if a component member of a controlled group has a short taxable year that does not include a December 31st date, then the last day of that short taxable year becomes that member's testing date.

(B) The term testing period means the time period used for determining the status of controlled group members as either component members or excluded members. The testing period begins on the first day of a member's taxable year and ends on the day before its testing date. (Generally, the testing date is December 31st, but for a component member having a short taxable year not ending on December 31st, the testing date for the short taxable year of that member (and only that member) becomes the last day of that member's short taxable year.) Thus, for a member on a fiscal taxable year, the portion of its taxable year beginning on December 31st and ending on the last day of its taxable year is not taken into account for determining its status as a component member or an excluded member.

(2) Excluded members. (i) Temporal test. A corporation, which is a member of a controlled group of corporations on the group's testing date, a date included within that member's taxable year, but who was a member of such group for less than one-half of the number of days of its testing period, shall be treated as an excluded member of such group for that group's testing date.

(ii) Qualification test. A corporation which is a member of a controlled group of corporations on a testing date shall be treated as an excluded member of such group on such date if, for its taxable year including such date, such corporation is—

(A) Exempt from taxation under section 501(a) (except a corporation which is subject to tax on its unrelated business taxable income under section 511) or 521 for such taxable year;

(B) A foreign corporation not subject to taxation under section 882(a) for the taxable year;

(C) An S corporation (as defined in section 1361) for purposes of any tax benefit item described in section 1561(a) to which it is not subject;

(D) A franchised corporation (as defined in section 1563(f)(4) and § 1.1563-4); or

(E) An insurance company subject to taxation under section 801, unless such insurance company (without regard to this paragraph (b)(2)(ii)(E)) is a component member of a life insurance controlled group described in paragraph (a)(5)(i) of this section or unless § 1.1502-47(f)(6) applies (which treats a life insurance company, for which a section 1504(c)(2) election is effective, as a member (whether eligible or ineligible) of a life-nonlife affiliated group).

(3) Additional members. A corporation shall be treated as an additional member of a controlled group of corporations, that is, an additional component member, on the group's testing date if it—

(i) Is not a member of such group on such date;

(ii) Is not described, with respect to such taxable year, in paragraph (b)(2)(ii)(A), (b)(2)(ii)(B), (b)(2)(ii)(C), (b)(2)(ii)(D), or (b)(2)(ii)(E) of this section; and

(iii) Was a member of such group for one-half (or more) of the number of days in its testing period.

(4) Examples. The provisions of this paragraph (b) may be illustrated by the following examples:

Example (1). B, an individual, owns all of the stock of corporations W and X on each day of 1964. W and X each use the calendar year as their taxable year. On January 1, 1964, B also owns all the stock of corporation Y (a fiscal year corporation with a taxable year beginning on July 1, 1964, and ending on June 30, 1965), which stock he sells on October 15, 1964. On December 1, 1964, B purchases all the stock of corporation Z (a fiscal year corporation with a taxable year beginning on September 1, 1964, and ending on August 31, 1965). On December 31, 1964, W, X, and Z are members of the same controlled group. However, the component members of the group on such December 31st are W, X, and Y. Under paragraph (b)(2)(i) of this section, Z is treated as an excluded member of the group on December 31, 1964, since Z was a member of the group for less than one-half of the number of days (29 out of 121 days) during the period beginning on September 1, 1964 (the first day of its taxable year) and ending on December 30, 1964. Under paragraph (b)(3) of this section, Y is treated as an additional member of the group on December 31, 1964, since Y was a member of the group for at least one-half of the number of days (107 out of 183 days) during the period beginning on July 1, 1964 (the first day of its taxable year) and ending on December 30, 1964.

Example (2). On January 1, 1964, corporation P owns all the stock of corporation S, which in turn owns all the stock of corporation S-1. On November 1, 1964, P purchases all of the stock of corporation X from the public and sells all of the stock of S to the public. Corporation X owns all the stock of corporation Y during 1964. P, S, S-1, X, and Y file their returns on the basis of the calendar year. On December

31, 1964, P, X, and Y are members of a parent-subsidiary controlled group of corporations; also, corporations S and S-1 are members of a different parent-subsidiary controlled group on such date. However, since X and Y have been members of the parent-subsidiary controlled group of which P is the common parent for less than one-half the number of days during the period January 1 through December 30, 1964, they are not component members of such group on such date. On the other hand, X and Y have been members of a parent-subsidiary controlled group of which X is the common parent for at least one-half the number of days during the period January 1 through December 30, 1964, and therefore they are component members of such group on December 31, 1964. Also since S and S-1 were members of the parent-subsidiary controlled group of which P is the common parent for at least one-half the number of days in the taxable years of each such corporation during the period January 1 through December 30, 1964, P, S, and S-1 are component members of such group on December 31, 1964.

Example (3). Throughout 1964, corporation M owns all the stock of corporation F which, in turn, owns all the stock of corporations L1, L2, X, and Y. M is a domestic mutual insurance company subject to taxation under section 821, F is a foreign corporation not engaged in a trade or business within the United States, L1 and L2 are domestic life insurance companies subject to taxation under section 802, and X and Y are domestic corporations subject to tax under section 11 of the Code. Each corporation uses the calendar year as its taxable year. On December 31, 1964, M, F, L1, L2, X, and Y are members of a parent-subsidiary controlled group of corporations. However, under paragraph (b)(2)(ii) of this section, M, F, L1, and L2 are treated as excluded members of the group on December 31, 1964. Thus, on December 31, 1964, the component members of the parent-subsidiary controlled group of which M is the common parent include only X and Y.

Furthermore, since paragraph (b)(2)(ii)(E) of this section does not result in L1 and L2 being treated as excluded members of a life insurance controlled group, L1 and L2 are component members of a life insurance controlled group on December 31, 1964.

(5) Application of constructive ownership rules. For purposes of paragraphs (b)(2)(i) and (b)(3)(iii) of this section, it is necessary to determine whether a corporation was a member of a controlled group of corporations for one-half (or more) of the number of days in its taxable year which precede the December 31st falling within such taxable year. Therefore, the constructive ownership rules contained in § 1.1563-3(b) (to the extent applicable in making such determination) must be applied on a day-by-day basis. For example, if P Corporation owns all the stock of X Corporation on each day of 1964, and on December 30, 1964, acquires an option to purchase all the stock of Y Corporation (a calendar-year taxpayer which has been in existence on each day of 1964), the application of § 1.1563-3(b)(1) on a day-by-day basis results in Y being a member of the brother-sister controlled group on only one day of Y's 1964 year which precedes December 31, 1964. Accordingly, since Y is not a member of such group for one-half or more of the number of days in its 1964 year preceding December 31, 1964, Y is treated as an excluded member of such group on December 31, 1964.

(c) Overlapping groups. *(1) In general.* If on a December 31st a corporation is a component member of a controlled group of corporations by reason of ownership of stock possessing at least 80 percent of the total value of shares of all classes of stock of the corporation, and if on such December 31st such corporation is also a component member of another controlled group of corporations by reason of ownership of other stock (that is, stock not used to satisfy the at-least-80 percent total value test) possessing at least 80 percent of the total combined voting power of all classes of stock of the corporation entitled to vote, then such corporation shall be treated as a component member only of the controlled group of which it is a component member by reason of the ownership of at least 80 percent of the total value of its shares.

(2) Brother-sister controlled groups. (i) One corporation. If on a December 31st, a corporation would, without the application of this paragraph (c)(2), be a component member of more than one brother-sister controlled group on such date, the corporation will be treated as a component member of only one such group on such date. Such corporation may elect the group in which it is to be included by including on or with its income tax return for the taxable year that includes such date a statement entitled, "STATEMENT TO ELECT CONTROLLED GROUP PURSUANT TO § 1.1563-1(c)(2)." This statement must include—

(A) A description of each of the controlled groups in which the corporation could be included. The description must include the name and employer identification number of each component member of each such group and the stock ownership of the component members of each such group; and

(B) The following representation: [INSERT NAME AND EMPLOYER IDENTIFICATION NUMBER OF CORPORATION] ELECTS TO BE TREATED AS A COMPONENT MEMBER OF THE [INSERT DESIGNATION OF GROUP].

(ii) Multiple corporations. If more than one corporation would, without the application of this paragraph (c)(2), be a component member of more than one controlled group, those corporations electing to be component members of the same group must file a single statement. The statement must contain the information described in paragraph (c)(2)(i) of this section, plus the names and employer identification numbers of all other corporations designating the same group. The original statement must be included on or with the original Federal income tax return (including any amended return filed on or before the due date (including extensions) of such return) of the corporation that, among those corporations which would (without the application of this paragraph (c)(2)) belong to more than one group, has the taxable year including such December 31st which ends on the earliest date. That corporation must provide a copy of the statement to each other corporation included in the statement and represent in its statement that it has done so. Either the original or a copy of the statement must be retained by each corporation as part of its records. See § 1.6001-1(e) of this chapter.

(iii) Election. (A) An election filed under this paragraph (c)(2) is irrevocable and effective until a change in the stock ownership of the corporation results in termination of membership in the controlled group in which such corporation has been included.

(B) In the event no election is filed in accordance with the provisions of this paragraph (c)(2), then the Internal Revenue Service will determine the group in which such corporation is to be included. Such determination will be binding for all subsequent years unless the corporation files a valid election with respect to any such subsequent year or until a change in the stock ownership of the corporation results in termination of membership in the controlled group in which such corporation has been included.

(iv) Examples. The provisions of this paragraph (c)(2) may be illustrated by the following examples (in which it is assumed that all the individuals are unrelated):

Example (1). (i) On each day of 1970 all the outstanding stock of corporations X, Y, and Z is held in the following manner:

Individuals	Corporations		
	X (%)	Y (%)	Z (%)
A	55	40	5
B	40	20	40
C	5	40	55

(ii) Since the more-than-50 percent identical ownership requirement of section 1563(a)(2) is met with respect to corporations X and Y and with respect to corporations Y and Z, but not with respect to corporations X, Y, and Z, corporation Y would, without the application of this paragraph (c)(2), be a component member on December 31, 1970, of overlapping groups consisting of X and Y and of Y and Z. If Y does not file an election in accordance with paragraph (c)(2)(i) of this section, the Internal Revenue Service will determine the group in which Y is to be included.

Example (2). (i) On each day of 1970, all the outstanding stock of corporations V, W, X, Y, and Z is held in the following manner:

Individuals	Corporations				
	V	W	X	Y	Z
D	52	52	52	52	52
E..........................	40	2	2	2	2
F..........................	2	40	2	2	2
G	2	2	40	2	2
H	2	2	2	40	2
I	2	2	2	2	40

(ii) On December 31, 1970, the more-than-50 percent identical ownership requirement of section 1563(a)(2) may be met with regard to any combination of the corporations but all five corporations cannot be included as component members of a single controlled group because the inclusion of all the corporations in a single group would be dependent upon taking into account the stock ownership of more than five persons. Therefore, if the corporations do not file a statement in accordance with paragraph (c)(2)(ii) of this section, the Internal Revenue Service will determine the group in which each corporation is to be included. The corporations or the Internal Revenue Service, as the case may be, may designate that three corporations be included in one group and two corporations in another, or that any four corporations be included in one group and that the remaining corporation not be included in any group.

(d) Transitional rules. *(1) In general.* Treasury decision 8179 amended paragraph (a)(3)(ii) of this section to revise the definition of a brother-sister controlled group of corporations. In general, those amendments are effective for taxable years ending on or after December 31, 1970.

(2) Limited nonretroactivity. (i) Old group. Under the authority of section 7805(b), the Internal Revenue Service will treat an old group as a brother-sister controlled group corporations for purposes of applying sections 401, 404(a), 408(k), 409A, 410, 411, 412, 414, 415, and 4971 of the Internal Revenue Code (Code) and sections 202, 203, 204, and 302 of the Employment Retirement Income Security Act of 1974 (ERISA) in a plan year or taxable year beginning before March 2, 1988, to the extent necessary to prevent an adverse effect on any old member (or any other corporation), or on any plan or other entity described in such sections (including plans, etc., of corporations not part of such old group), that would result solely from the retroactive effect of the amendment to this section by TD 8179. An adverse effect includes the disqualification of a plan or the disallowance of a deduction or credit for a contribution to a plan. The Internal Revenue Service, however, will not treat an old member as a member of an old group to the extent that such treatment will have an adverse effect on that old member.

(ii) Old member of old group. Section 7805(b) will not be applied pursuant to paragraph (d)(2)(i) of this section to treat an old member of an old group as a member of a brother-sister controlled group to prevent an adverse effect for a taxable year if, for that taxable year, that old member treats or has treated itself as not being a member of that old group for purposes of sections 401, 404(a), 408(k), 409A, 410, 411, 412, 414, 415, and 4971 of the Code and sections 202, 203, 204, and 302 and Title IV of ERISA for such taxable year (such as by filing, with respect to such taxable year, a return, amended return, or claim for credit or refund in which the amount of any deduction, credit, limitation, or tax due is determined by treating itself as not being a member of the old group for purposes of those sections). However, the fact that one or more (but not all) of the old members do not qualify for section 7805(b) treatment because of the preceding sentence will not preclude that old member (or members) from being treated as a member of the old group under paragraph (d)(2)(i) of this section in order to prevent the disallowance of a deduction or credit of another old member (or other corporation) or to prevent the disqualification of, or other adverse effect on, another old member's plan (or other entity) described in the sections of the Code and ERISA enumerated in such paragraph.

(3) Election of general nonretroactivity. In the case of a taxable year ending on or after December 31, 1970, and before March 2, 1988, an old group will be treated as a brother-sister controlled group of corporations for all purposes of the Code for such taxable year if—

(i) Each old member files a statement consenting to such treatment for such taxable year with the District Director having audit jurisdiction over its return within six months after March 2, 1988; and

(ii) No old member—

(A) Files or has filed, with respect to such taxable year, a return, amended return, or claim for credit or refund in which the amount of any deduction, credit, limitation, or tax due is determined by treating any old member as not a member of the old group; or

(B) Treats the employees of all members of the old group as not being employed by a single employer for purposes of sections 401, 404(a), 408(k), 409A, 410, 411, 412, 414, 415, and 4971 of the Code and sections 202, 203, 204, and 302 of ERISA for such taxable year.

(4) Definitions. For purposes of this paragraph (d)—

(i) An old group is a brother-sister controlled group of corporations, determined by applying paragraph (a)(3)(ii) of this section as in effect before the amendments made by TD 8179, that is not a brother-sister controlled group of corporations, determined by applying paragraph (a)(3)(ii) of this section as amended by such Treasury decision; and

(ii) An old member is any corporation that is a member of an old group.

(5) Election to choose between membership in more than one controlled group. (i) In general. A corporation may make an election under paragraph (c)(2) of this section by filing an amended return on or before September 2, 1988 if—

(A) An old member has filed an election under paragraph (c)(2) of this section to be treated as a component member of an old group for a December 31st before March 2, 1988; and

(B) That corporation would (without regard to such paragraph (c)(2)) be a component member of more than one brother-sister controlled group (not including an old group) on December 31st.

(ii) Exception. This paragraph (d)(5) does not apply to a corporation that is treated as a member of an old group under paragraph (d)(3) of this section.

(6) Refunds. See section 6511(a) for period of limitation on filing claims for credit or refund.

(e) Effective/applicability date. This section applies to taxable years beginning on or after May 26, 2009. However, taxpayers may apply this section to taxable years beginning before May 26, 2009. For taxable years beginning before May 26, 2009, see § 1.1563-1T as contained in 26 CFR part 1 in effect on April 1, 2009.

T.D. 9451, 5/26/2009.

PAR. 2. Section 1.1563-1 is amended by:

1. Redesignating paragraph (a)(1)(ii) as paragraph (a)(1)(iii) and adding paragraph (a)(1)(ii).

2. Adding Example 4 to paragraph (b)(4).

3. Adding a sentence at the end of paragraph (e).

The additions to read as follows:

Proposed § 1.1563-1 Definition of controlled group of corporations and component members and related concepts. [*For Preamble, see ¶ 153,133*]

(a) * * *

(1) * * *

(ii) Special rules. In determining whether a corporation is included in a controlled group of corporations, section 1563(b) shall not be taken into account. For rules defining a component member of a controlled group of corporations, including rules defining an excluded member and an additional member, see section 1563(b) and paragraph (b) of this section.

* * * * *

(b) * * *

(4) * * *

Example (4). Individual A owns all of the stock of corporations X, Y and Z. Each of these corporations is an S corporation. X, Y, and Z are each members of a brother-sister controlled group, even though each such corporation is treated as an excluded member of such group. See § 1.1563-1(b)(2)(ii)(C).

* * * * *

(e) * * * Paragraph (a)(1)(ii) of this section applies to taxable years beginning on or after the date of publication in the Federal Register of the Treasury decision adopting these rules as final regulations.

PAR. 22. Section 1.1563-1 is amended by revising paragraph (c)(2)(i) through (iii) and adding paragraph (e) to read as follows:

Proposed § 1.1563-1 Definition of controlled group of corporations and component members. [*For Preamble, see ¶ 152,759*]

• ***Caution:*** This Notice of Proposed Rulemaking was partially finalized by TD 9329, 06/13/2007 and TD 9342, 07/19/2007. Prop. Reg. 1.1563-1 remains proposed.

[The text of the proposed amendment to § 1.1563-1 is the same as the text for § 1.1563-1T published elsewhere in this issue of the Federal Register]. [See T.D. 9264, 05/26/2006, 71 Fed. Reg. 103.]

§ 1.1563-2 Excluded stock.

(a) Certain stock excluded. For purposes of sections 1561 through 1563 and the regulations thereunder, the term "stock" does not include—

(1) Nonvoting stock which is limited and preferred as to dividends, and

(2) Treasury stock.

(b) Stock treated as excluded stock. *(1) Parent-subsidiary controlled group.* If a corporation (hereinafter in this paragraph referred to as "parent corporation") owns 50 percent or more of the total combined voting power of all classes of stock entitled to vote or 50 percent or more of the total value of shares of all classes of stock in another corporation (hereinafter in this paragraph referred to as "subsidiary corporation"), the provisions of subparagraph (2) of this paragraph shall apply. For purposes of this subparagraph, stock owned by a corporation means stock owned directly plus stock owned with the application of the constructive ownership rules of paragraph (b)(1) and (4) of § 1.1563-3, relating to options and attribution from corporations. In determining whether the stock owned by a corporation possesses the requisite percentage of the total combined voting power of all classes of stock entitled to vote of another corporation, see paragraph (a)(6) of § 1.1563-1.

(2) Stock treated as not outstanding. If the provisions of this subparagraph apply, then for purposes of determining whether the parent corporation or the subsidiary corporation is a member of a parent-subsidiary controlled group of corporations within the meaning of paragraph (a)(2) of § 1.1563-1, the following stock of the subsidiary corporation

shall, except as otherwise provided in paragraph (c) of this section, be treated as if it were not outstanding:

(i) Plan of deferred compensation. Stock in the subsidiary corporation held by a trust which is part of a plan of deferred compensation for the benefit of the employees of the parent corporation or the subsidiary corporation. The term "plan of deferred compensation" shall have the same meaning such term has in section 406(a)(3) and the regulations thereunder.

(ii) Principal stockholders and officers. Stock in the subsidiary corporation owned (directly and with the application of the rules contained in paragraph (b) of § 1.1563-3) by an individual who is a principal stockholder or officer of the parent corporation. A principal stockholder of the parent corporation is an individual who owns (directly and with the application of the rules contained in paragraph (b) of § 1.1563-3) 5 percent or more of the total combined voting power of all classes of stock entitled to vote or 5 percent or more of the total value of shares of all classes of stock of the parent corporation. An officer of the parent corporation includes the president, vice-presidents, general manager, treasurer, secretary, and comptroller of such corporation, and any other person who performs duties corresponding to those normally performed by persons occupying such positions.

(iii) Employees. Stock in the subsidiary corporation owned (directly and with the application of the rules contained in paragraph (b) of § 1.1563-3) by an employee of the subsidiary corporation if such stock is subject to conditions which substantially restrict or limit the employee's right (or if the employee constructively owns such stock, the direct owner's right) to dispose of such stock and which run in favor of the parent or subsidiary corporation. In general, any condition which extends, directly or indirectly, to the parent corporation or the subsidiary corporation preferential rights with respect to the acquisition of the employee's (or direct owner's) stock will be considered to be a condition described in the preceding sentence. It is not necessary, in order for a condition to be considered to be in favor of the parent corporation or the subsidiary corporation, that the parent or subsidiary be extended a discriminatory concession with respect to the price of the stock. For example, a condition whereby the parent corporation is given a right of first refusal with respect to any stock of the subsidiary corporation offered by an employee for sale is a condition which substantially restricts or limits the employee's right to dispose of such stock and runs in favor of the parent corporation. Moreover, any legally enforceable condition which prohibits the employee from disposing of his stock without the consent of the parent (or a subsidiary of the parent) will be considered to be a substantial limitation running in favor of the parent corporation.

(iv) Controlled exempt organization. Stock in the subsidiary corporation owned (directly and with the application of the rules contained in paragraph (b) of § 1.1563-3) by an organization (other than the parent corporation)—

(a) To which section 501 (relating to certain educational and charitable organizations which are exempt from tax) applies, and

(b) Which is controlled directly or indirectly by the parent corporation or subsidiary corporation, by an individual, estate, or trust that is a principal stockholder of the parent corporation, by an officer of the parent corporation, or by any combination thereof.

The terms "principal stockholder of the parent corporation" and "officer of the parent corporation" shall have the same meanings in this subdivision as in subdivision (ii) of this subparagraph. The term "control" as used in this subdivision means control in fact and the determination of whether the control requirement of (b) of this subdivision is met will depend upon all the facts and circumstances of each case, without regard to whether such control is legally enforceable and irrespective of the method by which such control is exercised or exercisable.

(3) Brother-sister controlled group. If five or fewer persons (hereinafter referred to as common owners) who are individuals, estates, or trusts own (directly and with the application of the rules contained in paragraph (b) of § 1.1563-3) stock possessing 50 percent or more of the total combined voting power of all classes of stock entitled to vote or 50 percent or more of the total value of shares of all classes of stock in a corporation, the provisions of subparagraph (4) of this paragraph shall apply. In determining whether the stock owned by such person or persons possesses the requisite percentage of the total combined voting power of all classes of stock entitled to vote of a corporation, see paragraph (a)(6) of § 1.1563-1.

(4) Stock treated as not outstanding. If the provisions of this subparagraph apply, then for purposes of determining whether a corporation is a member of a brother-sister controlled group of corporations within the meaning of paragraph (a)(3) of § 1.1563-1, the following stock of such corporation shall, except as otherwise provided in paragraph (c) of this section, be treated as if it were not outstanding:

(i) Exempt employees' trust. Stock in such corporation held by an employees' trust described in section 401(a) which is exempt from tax under section 501(a), if such trust is for the benefit of the employees of such corporation.

(ii) Employees. Stock in such corporation owned (directly and with the application of the rules contained in paragraph (b) of § 1.1563-3) by an employee of such corporation if such stock is subject to conditions which run in favor of a common owner of such corporation (or in favor of such corporation) and which substantially restrict or limit the employee's right (or if the employee constructively owns such stock, the record owner's right) to dispose of such stock. The principles of subparagraph (2)(iii) of this paragraph shall apply in determining whether a condition satisfies the requirements of the preceding sentence. Thus, in general, a condition which extends, directly or indirectly, to the common owner or such corporation preferential rights with respect to the acquisition of the employee's (or record owner's) stock will be considered to be a condition which satisfies such requirements. For purposes of this subdivision, if a condition which restricts or limits an employee's right (or the direct owner's right) to dispose of his stock also applies to the stock in such corporation held by the common owner pursuant to a bona fide reciprocal stock purchase arrangement, such condition shall not be treated as one which restricts or limits the employee's right to dispose of such stock. An example of a reciprocal stock purchase arrangement is an agreement whereby the common owner and the employee are given a right of first refusal with respect to stock of the employer corporation owned by the other party. If, however, the agreement also provides that the common owner has the right to purchase the stock of the employer corporation owned by the employee in the event that the corporation should discharge the employee for reasonable cause, the purchase arrangement would not be reciprocal within the meaning of this subdivision.

(iii) Controlled exempt organization. Stock in such corporation owned (directly and with the application of the rules contained in paragraph (b) of § 1.1563-3) by an organization—

(a) To which section 501(c)(3) (relating to certain educational and charitable organizations which are exempt from tax) applies, and

(b) Which is controlled directly or indirectly by such corporation, by an individual, estate, or trust that is a principal stockholder of such corporation, by an officer of such corporation, or by any combination thereof.

The term "principal stockholder" and "officer" shall have the same meanings in this subdivision as in subparagraph (2)(ii) of this paragraph. The term "control" as used in this subdivision means control in fact and the determination of whether the control requirement of (b) of this subdivision is met will depend upon all the facts and circumstances of each case, without regard to whether such control is legally enforceable and irrespective of the method by which such control is exercised or exercisable.

(5) Other controlled groups. The provisions of subparagraphs (1), (2), (3), and (4) of this paragraph shall apply in determining whether a corporation is a member of a combined group (within the meaning of paragraph (a)(4) of § 1.1563-1) or an insurance group (within the meaning of paragraph (a)(5) of § 1.1563-1). For example, under paragraph (a)(4) of § 1.1563-1, in order for a corporation to be a member of a combined group such corporation must be a member of a parent-subsidiary group or a brother-sister group. Accordingly, the excluded stock rules provided by this paragraph are applicable in determining whether the corporation is a member of such group.

(6) Meaning of employee. For purposes of this section §§ 1.1563-3 and 1.1563-4, the term "employee" has the same meaning such term is given in section 3306(i) of the Code (relating to definitions for purposes of the Federal Unemployment Tax Act. Accordingly, the term employee as used in such sections includes an officer of a corporation.

(7) Examples. The provisions of this paragraph may be illustrated by the following examples:

Example (1). Corporation P owns 70 of the 100 shares of the only class of stock of corporation S. The remaining shares of S are owned as follows: 4 shares by Jones (the general manager of P), and 26 shares by Smith (who also owns 5 percent of the total combined voting power of the stock of P). P satisfies the 50 percent stock ownership requirement of subparagraph (1) of this paragraph with respect to S. Since Jones is an officer of P and Smith is a principal stockholder of P, under subparagraph (2)(ii) of this paragraph the S stock owned by Jones and Smith is treated as not outstanding for purposes of determining whether P and S are members of a parent-subsidiary controlled group of corporations within the meaning of paragraph (a)(2) of § 1.1563-1. Thus, P is considered to own stock possessing 100 percent (70 ÷ 70) of the total voting power and value of all the S stock. Accordingly, P and S are members of a parent-subsidiary controlled group of corporations.

Example (2). Assume the same facts as in example (1) and further assume that Jones owns 15 shares of the 100 shares of the only class of stock of corporation S-1, and corporation S owns 75 shares of such stock. P satisfies the 50 percent stock ownership requirement of subparagraph (1) of this paragraph with respect to S-1 since P is considered as owning 52.5 percent (70 percent × 75 percent) of the S-1 stock with the application of paragraph (b)(4) of § 1.1563-3. Since Jones is an officer of P, under subparagraph (2)(ii) of this paragraph, the S-1 stock owned by Jones is treated as not outstanding for purposes of determining whether S-1 is a member of the parent-subsidiary controlled group of corporations. Thus, S is considered to own stock possessing 88.2 percent (75 ÷ 85) of the voting power and value of the S-1 stock. Accordingly, P, S, and S-1 are members of a parent-subsidiary controlled group of corporations.

Example (3). Corporation X owns 60 percent of the only class of stock of corporation Y. Davis, the president of Y, owns the remaining 40 percent of the stock of Y. Davis has agreed that if he offers his stock in Y for sale he will first offer the stock to X at a price equal to the fair market value of the stock on the first date the stock is offered for sale. Since Davis is an employee of Y within the meaning of section 3306(i) of the Code, and his stock in Y is subject to a condition which substantially restricts or limits his right to dispose of such stock and runs in favor of X, under subparagraph (2)(iii) of this paragraph such stock is treated as if it were not outstanding for purposes of determining whether X and Y are members of a parent-subsidiary controlled group of corporations. Thus, X is considered to own stock possessing 100 percent of the voting power and value of the stock of Y. Accordingly, X and Y are members of a parent-subsidiary controlled group of corporations. The result would be the same if Davis's wife, instead of Davis, owned directly the 40 percent stock interest in Y and such stock was subject to a right of first refusal running in favor of X.

(c) Exception. *(1) General.* If stock of a corporation is owned by a person directly or with the application of the rules contained in paragraph (b) of § 1.1563-3 and such ownership results in the corporation being a component member of a controlled group of corporations on a December 31, then the stock shall not be treated as excluded stock under the provisions of paragraph (b) of this section if the result of applying such provisions is that such corporation is not a component member of a controlled group of corporations on such December 31.

(2) Illustration. The provisions of this paragraph may be illustrated by the following example:

Example. On each day of 1965, corporation P owns directly 50 of the 100 shares of the only class of stock of corporation S. Jones, an officer of P, owns directly 30 shares of S stock and P has an option to acquire such 30 shares from Jones. The remaining shares of S are owned by unrelated persons. If, pursuant to the provisions of paragraph (b)(2)(ii) of this section, the 30 shares of S stock owned directly by Jones is treated as not outstanding, the result is that P would be treated as owning stock possessing only 71 percent (50 ÷ 70) of the total voting power and value of S stock, and S would not be a component member of a controlled group of corporations on December 31, 1965. However, since P is considered as owning the 30 shares of S stock with the application of paragraph (b)(1) of this section, and such ownership plus the S stock directly owned by P (50 shares) results in S being a component member of a controlled group of corporations on December 31, 1965, the provisions of this paragraph apply. Therefore, the provisions of paragraph (b)(2)(ii) of this section do not apply with respect to the 30 shares of S stock, and on December 31, 1965, S is a component member of a controlled group of corporations consisting of P and S.

T.D. 6845, 8/4/65, amend T.D. 7181, 4/24/72.

§ 1.1563-3 Rules for determining stock ownership.

(a) In general. In determining stock ownership for purposes of §§ 1.1562-5, 1.1563-1, 1.1563-2, and this section, the constructive ownership rules of paragraph (b) of this section apply to the extent such rules are referred to in such sections. The application of such rules shall be subject to the operating rules and special rules contained in paragraphs (c) and (d) of this section.

(b) Constructive ownership. *(1) Options.* If a person has an option to acquire any outstanding stock of a corporation, such stock shall be considered as owned by such person. For purposes of this subparagraph, an option to acquire such an option, and each one of a series of such options, shall be considered as an option to acquire such stock. For example, assume Smith owns an option to purchase 100 shares of the outstanding stock of M Corporation. Under this subparagraph, Smith is considered to own such 100 shares. The result would be the same if Smith owned an option to acquire the option (or one of a series of options) to purchase 100 shares of M stock.

(2) Attribution from partnerships. (i) Stock owned, directly or indirectly, by or for a partnership shall be considered as owned by any partner having an interest of 5 percent or more in either the capital or profits of the partnership in proportion to his interest in capital or profits, whichever such proportion is the greater.

(ii) The provisions of this subparagraph may be illustrated by the following example:

Example. Green, Jones, and White, unrelated individuals, are partners in the GJW partnership. The partners' interests in the capital and profits of the partnership are as follows:

Partner	Capital Percent	Profits Percent
Green	36	25
Jones	60	71
White	4	4

The GJW partnership owns the entire outstanding stock (100 shares) of X Corporation. Under this subparagraph, Green is considered to own the X stock owned by the partnership in proportion to his interest in capital (36 percent) or profits (25 percent), whichever such proportion is the greater. Therefore, Green is considered to own 36 shares of the X stock. However, since Jones has a greater interest in the profits of the partnership, he is considered to own the X stock in proportion to his interest in such profits. Therefore, Jones is considered to own 71 shares of the X stock. Since White does not have an interest of 5 percent or more in either the capital or profits of the partnership, he is not considered to own any shares of the X stock.

(3) Attribution from estates or trusts. (i) Stock owned, directly or indirectly, by or for an estate or trust shall be considered as owned by any beneficiary who has an actuarial interest of 5 percent or more in such stock, to the extent of such actuarial interest. For purposes of this subparagraph, the actuarial interest of each beneficiary shall be determined by assuming the maximum exercise of discretion by the fiduciary in favor of such beneficiary and the maximum use of such stock to satisfy his rights as a beneficiary. A beneficiary of an estate or trust who cannot under any circumstances receive any interest in stock held by the estate or trust, including the proceeds from the disposition thereof, or the income therefrom, does not have an actuarial interest in such stock. Thus, where stock owned by a decedent's estate has been specifically bequeathed to certain beneficiaries and the remainder of the estate is bequeathed to other beneficiaries, the stock is attributable only to the beneficiaries to whom it is specifically bequeathed. Similarly, a remainderman of a trust who cannot under any circumstances receive any interest in the stock of a corporation which is a part of the corpus of the trust (including any accumulated income therefrom or the proceeds from a disposition thereof) does not have an actuarial interest in such stock. However, an income beneficiary of a trust does have an actuarial interest in stock if he has any right to the income from such stock even though under the terms of the trust instrument such stock can never be distributed to him. The factors and methods prescribed in § 20.2031-7 of this chapter (Estate Tax Regulations) for use in ascertaining the value of an interest in property for estate tax purposes shall be used for purposes of this subdivision in determining a beneficiary's actuarial interest in stock owned directly or indirectly by or for a trust.

(ii) For the purposes of this subparagraph, property of a decedent shall be considered as owned by his estate if such property is subject to administration by the executor or administrator for the purposes of paying claims against the estate and expenses of administration notwithstanding that, under local law, legal title to such property vests in the decedent's heirs, legatees or devisees immediately upon death. With respect to an estate, the term "beneficiary" includes any person entitled to receive property of the decedent pursuant to a will or pursuant to laws of descent and distribution. A person shall no longer be considered a beneficiary of an estate when all the property to which he is entitled has been received by him, when he no longer has a claim against the estate arising out of having been a beneficiary, and when there is only a remote possibility that it will be necessary for the estate to seek the return of property or to seek payment from him by contribution or otherwise to satisfy claims against the estate or expenses of administration. When pursuant to the preceding sentence, a person ceases to be a beneficiary, stock owned by the estate shall not thereafter be considered owned by him.

(iii) Stock owned, directly or indirectly, by or for any portion of a trust of which a person is considered the owner under subpart E, part I, subchapter J of the Code (relating to grantors and others treated as substantial owners) is considered as owned by such person.

(iv) This subparagraph does not apply to stock owned by any employees' trust described in section 401(a) which is exempt from tax under section 501(a).

(4) Attribution from corporations. (i) Stock owned, directly or indirectly, by or for a corporation shall be considered as owned by any person who owns (within the meaning of section 1563(d)) 5 percent or more in value of its stock in that proportion which the value of the stock which such person so owns bears to the value of all the stock in such corporation.

(ii) The provisions of this subparagraph may be illustrated by the following example:

Example. Brown, an individual, owns 60 shares of the 100 shares of the only class of outstanding stock of corporation P. Smith, an individual, owns 4 shares of the P stock, and corporation X owns 36 shares of the P stock. Corporation P owns, directly and indirectly, 50 shares of the stock of corporation S. Under this subparagraph, Brown is considered to own 30 shares of the S stock ($^{60}/_{100} \times 50$), and X is considered to own 18 shares of the S stock ($^{36}/_{100} \times 50$). Since Smith does not own 5 percent or more in value of the P stock, he is not considered as owning any of the S stock owned by P. If, in this example, Smith's wife had owned directly 1 share of the P stock, Smith (and his wife) would each own 5 shares of the P stock, and therefore Smith (and his wife) would be considered as owning 2.5 shares of the S stock (5/100 × 50).

(5) Spouse. (i) Except as provided in subdivision (ii) of this subparagraph, an individual shall be considered to own the stock owned, directly or indirectly, by or for his spouse, other than a spouse who is legally separated from the individual under a decree of divorce, whether interlocutory or final, or a decree of separate maintenance.

(ii) An individual shall not be considered to own stock in a corporation owned, directly or indirectly, by or for his spouse on any day of a taxable year of such corporation, provided that each of the following conditions are satisfied with respect to such taxable year:

(a) Such individual does not, at any time during such taxable year, own directly any stock in such corporation.

(b) Such individual is not a member of the board of directors or an employee of such corporation and does not participate in the management of such corporation at any time during such taxable year.

(c) Not more than 50 percent of such corporation's gross income for such taxable year was derived from royalties, rents, dividends, interest, and annuities.

(d) Such stock in such corporation is not, at any time during such taxable year, subject to conditions which substantially restrict or limit the spouse's right to dispose of such stock and which run in favor of the individual or his children who have not attained the age of 21 years. The principles of paragraph (b)(2)(iii) of § 1.1563-2 shall apply in determining whether a condition is a condition described in the preceding sentence.

(iii) For purposes of subdivision (ii)(c) of this subparagraph, the gross income of a corporation for a taxable year shall be determined under section 61 and the regulations thereunder. The terms "royalties", "rents", "dividends" , "interest", and "annuities" shall have the same meanings such terms are given for purposes of section 1244(c). See paragraph (e)(1)(ii), (iii), (iv), (v), and (vi) of § 1.1244(c)-1.

(6) Children, grandchildren, parents, and grandparents. (i) An individual shall be considered to own the stock owned, directly or indirectly, by or for his children who have not attained the age of 21 years, and, if the individual has not attained the age of 21 years, the stock owned, directly or indirectly, by or for his parents.

(ii) If an individual owns (directly, and with the application of the rules of this paragraph but without regard to this subdivision) stock possessing more than 50 percent of the total combined voting power of all classes of stock entitled to vote or more than 50 percent of the total value of shares of all classes of stock in a corporation, then such individual shall be considered to own the stock in such corporation owned, directly or indirectly, by or for his parents, grandparents, grandchildren, and children who have attained the age of 21 years. In determining whether the stock owned by an individual possesses the requisite percentage of the total combined voting power of all classes of stock entitled to vote of a corporation, see paragraph (a)(6) of § 1.1563-1.

(iii) For purposes of section 1563, and §§ 1.1563-1 through 1.563-4, a legally adopted child of an individual shall be treated as a child of such individual by blood.

(iv) The provisions of this subparagraph may be illustrated by the following example:

Example. (a) Facts. Individual F owns directly 40 shares of the 100 shares of the only class of stock of Z Corporation. His son, M (20 years of age), owns directly 30 shares of such stock, and his son, A (30 years of age), owns directly 20 shares of such stock. The remaining 10 shares of the Z stock are owned by an unrelated person.

(b) F's ownership. Individual F owns 40 shares of the Z stock directly and is considered to own the 30 shares of Z stock owned directly by M. Since, for purposes of the more-than-50-percent stock ownership test contained in subdivision (ii) of this subparagraph, F is treated as owning 70 shares or 70 percent of the total voting power and value of the Z stock, he is also considered as owning the 20 shares owned by his adult son, A. Accordingly, F is considered as owning a total of 90 shares of the Z stock.

(c) M's ownership. Minor son, M, owns 30 shares of the Z stock directly, and is considered to own the 40 shares of Z stock owned directly by his father, F. However, M is not considered to own the 20 shares of Z stock owned directly by his brother, A, and constructively by F, because stock constructively owned by F by reason of family attribution is not considered as owned by him for purposes of making another member of his family the constructive owner of such stock. See paragraph (c)(2) of this section. Accordingly, M owns and is considered as owning a total of 70 shares of the Z stock.

(d) A's ownership. Adult son, A, owns 20 shares of the Z stock directly. Since, for purposes of the more-than-50-percent stock ownership test contained in subdivision (ii) of this subparagraph, A is treated as owning only the Z stock which he owns directly, he does not satisfy the condition precedent for the attribution of Z stock from his father. Accordingly, A is treated as owning only the 20 shares of Z stock which he owns directly.

(c) Operating rules and special rules. *(1) In general.* Except as provided in subparagraph (2) of this paragraph, stock constructively owned by a person by reason of the application of subparagraph (1), (2), (3), (4), (5), or (6) of paragraph (b) of this section shall, for purposes of applying such subparagraphs, be treated as actually owned by such person.

(2) Members of family. Stock constructively owned by an individual by reason of the application of subparagraph (5) or (6) of paragraph (b) of this section shall not be treated as owned by him for purposes of again applying such subparagraphs in order to make another the constructive owner of such stock.

(3) Precedence of option attribution. For purposes of this section, if stock may be considered as owned by a person under subparagraph (1) of paragraph (b) of this section (relating to option attribution) and under any other subparagraph of such paragraph, such stock shall be considered as owned by such person under subparagraph (1) of such paragraph.

(4) Examples. The provisions of this paragraph may be illustrated by the following examples:

Example (1). A, 30 years of age, has a 90 percent interest in the capital and profits of a partnership. The partnership owns all the outstanding stock of corporation X and X owns 60 shares of the 100 outstanding shares of corporation Y. Under subparagraph (1) of this paragraph, the 60 shares of Y constructively owned by the partnership by reason of subparagraph (4) of paragraph (b) of this section is treated as actually owned by the partnership for purposes of applying subparagraph (2) of paragraph (b) of this section. Therefore, A is considered as owning 54 shares of the Y stock (90 percent of 60 shares).

Example (2). Assume the same facts as in example (1). Assume further that B, who is 20 years of age and the brother of A, directly owns 40 shares of Y stock. Although the stock of Y owned by B is considered as owned by C (the father of A and B) under paragraph (b)(6)(i) of this section, under subparagraph (2) of this paragraph such stock may not be treated as owned by C for purposes of applying paragraph (b)(6)(ii) of this section in order to make A the constructive owner of such stock.

Example (3). Assume the same facts assumed for purposes of example (2), and further assume that C has an option to acquire the 40 shares of Y stock owned by his son, B. The rule contained in subparagraph (2) of this paragraph does not prevent the reattribution of such 40 shares to A because, under subparagraph (3) of this paragraph, C is considered as owning the 40 shares by reason of option attribution and not by reason of family attribution. Therefore, since A satisfies the more-than-50-percent stock ownership test contained in paragraph (b)(6)(ii) of this section with respect to Y, the 40 shares of Y stock constructively owned by C are reattributed to A, and A is considered as owning a total of 94 shares of Y stock.

(d) Special rule of section 1563(f)(3)(B). *(1) In general.* If the same stock of a corporation is owned (within the meaning of section 1563(d)) by two or more persons, then such stock shall be treated as owned by the person whose ownership of such stock results in the corporation being a component member of a controlled group on a December 31 which has at least one other component member of such date.

(2) Component member of more than one group. (i) If, by reason of subparagraph (1) of this paragraph, a corporation would (but for this subparagraph) become a component member of more than one controlled group on a December 31, such corporation shall be treated as a component member of only one such controlled group on such date. The determination as to which group such corporation is treated as a component member of shall be made in accordance with the rules contained in paragraphs (d)(2)(ii), (iii) and (iv) of this section.

(ii) In any case in which a corporation is a component member of a controlled group of corporations on a December 31 as a result of treating each share of its stock as owned only by the person who owns such share directly, then each such share shall be treated as owned by the person who owns such share directly.

(iii) If the application of subdivision (ii) of this subparagraph does not result in a corporation being treated as a component member of only one controlled group on a December 31, then the stock of such corporation described in subparagraph (1) of this paragraph shall be treated as owned by the one person described in such subparagraph who owns, directly and with the application of the rules contained in paragraph (b)(1), (2), (3), and (4) of this section, the stock possessing the greatest percentage of the total value of shares of all classes of stock of the corporation.

(iv) Statement. If the application of paragraph (d)(2)(ii) or (iii) of this section does not result in a corporation being treated as a component member of only one controlled group of corporations on a December 31, then such corporation will be treated as a component member of only one such group on such date. Such corporation may elect the group in which it is to be included by including on or with its income tax return a statement entitled, "STATEMENT TO ELECT CONTROLLED GROUP PURSUANT TO § 1.1563-3(d)(2)(iv)." The statement must include—

(A) A description of each of the controlled groups in which the corporation could be included. The description must include the name and employer identification number of each component member of each such group and the stock ownership of the component members of each such group; and

(B) The following representation: [INSERT NAME AND EMPLOYER IDENTIFICATION NUMBER OF CORPORATION] ELECTS TO BE TREATED AS A COMPONENT MEMBER OF THE [INSERT DESIGNATION OF GROUP].

(v) Election. (A) Election filed. An election filed under paragraph (d)(2)(iv) of this section is irrevocable and effective until paragraph (d)(2)(ii) or (iii) of this section applies or until a change in the stock ownership of the corporation results in termination of membership in the controlled group in which such corporation has been included.

(B) Election not filed. In the event no election is filed in accordance with the provisions of paragraph (d)(2)(iv) of this section, then the Internal Revenue Service will determine the group in which such corporation is to be included. Such determination will be binding for all subsequent years unless the corporation files a valid election with respect to any such subsequent year or until a change in the stock ownership of the corporation results in termination of membership in the controlled group in which such corporation has been included.

(3) Examples. The provisions of this paragraph may be illustrated by the following examples, in which each corporation referred to uses the calendar year as its taxable year and the stated facts are assumed to exist on each day of 1970 (unless otherwise provided in the example):

Example (1). Jones owns all the stock of corporation X and has an option to purchase from Smith all the outstanding stock of corporation Y. Smith owns all the outstanding stock of corporation Z. Since the Y stock is considered as owned by two or more persons, under subparagraph (2)(ii) of this paragraph the Y stock is treated as owned only by Smith since he has direct ownership of such stock. Therefore, on December 31, 1970, Y and Z are component members of the same brother-sister controlled group. If, however, Smith had owned his stock in corporation Z for less than one-half of the number of days of Z's 1970 taxable year, then under subparagraph (1) of this paragraph the Y stock would be treated as owned only by Jones since his ownership results in Y being a component member of a controlled group on December 31, 1970.

Example (2). Individual H owns directly all the outstanding stock of corporation M. W (the wife of H) owns directly all the outstanding stock of corporation N. Neither spouse is considered as owning the stock directly owned by the other because each of the conditions prescribed in paragraph (b)(5)(ii) of this section is satisfied with respect to each corporation's 1970 taxable year. H owns directly 60 percent of the only class of stock of corporation P and W owns the remaining 40 percent of the P stock. Under subparagraph (2)(iii) of this paragraph, the stock of P is treated as owned only by H since H owns (directly and with the application of the rules contained in paragraph (b)(1), (2), (3), and (4) of this section) the stock possessing the greatest percentage of the total value of shares of all classes of stock of P. Accordingly, on December 31, 1970, P is treated as a component member of a brother-sister group consisting of M and P.

Example (3). Unrelated individuals A and B each own 49 percent of all the outstanding stock of corporation R, which in turn owns 70 percent of the only class of outstanding stock of corporation S. The remaining 30 percent of the stock of corporation S is owned by unrelated individual C. C also owns the remaining 2 percent of the stock of corporation R. Under the attribution rule of paragraph (b)(4) of this section A and B are each considered to own 34.3 percent of the stock of corporation S. Accordingly, since five or fewer persons own at least 80 percent of the stock of corporations R and S and also own more than 50 percent identically (A's and B's identical ownership each is 34.3 percent, C's identical ownership is 2 percent), on December 31, 1970, corporations R and S are treated as component members of the same brother-sister controlled group for purposes of paragraph (a)(3)(ii) of § 1.1563-1.

(e) Effective/applicability date. Paragraph (d)(2)(iv) and (v) of this section apply to any taxable year beginning on or after May 30, 2006. However, taxpayers may apply paragraph (d)(2)(iv) and (v) of this section to any original Federal income tax return (including any amended return filed on or before the due date (including extensions) of such original return) timely filed on or after May 30, 2006. For taxable years beginning before May 30, 2006, see § 1.1563-3 as contained in 26 CFR part 1 in effect on April 1, 2006.

T.D. 6845, 8/4/65, amend T.D. 7181, 4/24/72, T.D. 7779, 6/1/81, T.D. 8179, 3/1/88, T.D. 9264, 5/26/2006, T.D. 9304, 12/21/2006, T.D. 9329, 6/13/2007, T.D. 9451, 5/26/2009.

§ 1.1563-4 Franchised corporations.

(a) In general. For purposes of paragraph (b)(2)(ii)(d) of § 1.1563-1, a member of a controlled group of corporations shall be considered to be a franchised corporation for a taxable year if each of the following conditions is satisfied for one-half (or more) of the number of days preceding the December 31 included within such taxable year (or, if such taxable year does not include a December 31, for one-half or more of the number of days in such taxable year preceding the last day of such year):

(1) Such member is franchised to sell the products of another member, or the common owner, of such controlled group.

(2) More than 50 percent (determined on the basis of cost) of all the goods held by such member primarily for sale to its customers are acquired from members or the common owner of the controlled group, or both.

(3) The stock of such member is to be sold to an employee (or employees) of such member pursuant to a bona fide plan designed to eliminate the stock ownership of the parent corporation (as defined in paragraph (b)(1) of § 1.1563-2) or of the common owner (as defined in paragraph (b)(3) of § 1.1563-2) in such member.

(4) Such employee owns (or such employees in the aggregate own) directly more than 20 percent of the total value of shares of all classes of stock of such member. For purposes of this subparagraph, the determination of whether an employee (or employees) owns the requisite percentage of the total value of the stock of the member shall be made without regard to paragraph (b) of § 1.1563-2, relating to certain stock treated as excluded stock. Furthermore, if the corporation has more than one class of stock outstanding, the relative voting rights as between each such class of stock shall be disregarded in making such determination.

(b) Plan for elimination of stock ownership. *(1)* A plan referred to in paragraph (a)(3) of this section must—

(i) Provide a reasonable selling price for the stock of the member, and

(ii) Require that a portion of the employee's compensation or dividends, or both, from such member be applied to the purchase of such stock (or to the purchase of notes, bonds, debentures, or similar evidences of indebtedness of such member held by the parent corporation or the common owner).

It is not necessary, in order to satisfy the requirements of subdivision (ii) of this subparagraph, that the plan require that a percentage of every dollar of the compensation and dividends be applied to the purchase of the stock (or the indebtedness). The requirements of such subdivision are satisfied if an otherwise qualified plan provides that under certain specified conditions (such as a requirement that the member earn a specified profit) no portion of the compensation and/or dividends need be applied to the purchase of the stock (or indebtedness), provided such conditions are reasonable.

(2) A plan for the elimination of the stock ownership of the parent corporation or of the common owner will satisfy the requirements of paragraph (a)(3) of this section and subparagraph (1) of this paragraph even though it does not require that the stock of the member be sold to an employee (or employees) if it provides for the redemption of the stock of the member held by the parent or common owner and under the plan the amount of such stock to be redeemed during any period is calculated by reference to the profits of such member during such period.

T.D. 6845, 8/4/65.

§ 20.0-1 Introduction.

(a) In general. *(1)* The regulations in this part (Part 20, Subchapter B, Chapter I, Title 26, Code of Federal Regulations) are designated "Estate Tax Regulations." These regulations pertain to (i) the Federal estate tax imposed by chapter 11 of subtitle B of the Internal Revenue Code on the transfer of estates of decedents dying after August 16, 1954, and (ii) certain related administrative provisions of subtitle F of the Code. It should be noted that the application of many of the provisions of these regulations may be affected by the provisions of an applicable death tax convention with a foreign country. Unless otherwise indicated, references in the regulations to the "Internal Revenue Code" or the "Code" are references to the Internal Revenue Code of 1954, as amended, and references to a section or other provision of law are references to a section or other provision of the Internal Revenue Code of 1954, as amended. Unless otherwise provided, the Estate Tax Regulations are applicable to the estates of decedents dying after August 16, 1954, and supersede the regulations contained in Part 81, Subchapter B, Chapter I, Title 26, Code of Federal Regulations (1939) (Regulations 105, Estate Tax), as prescribed and made applicable to the Internal Revenue Code of 1954 by Treasury Decision 6091, signed August 16, 1954 (19 F.R. 5167, Aug. 17, 1954). The regulations in this part do not reflect the amendments made by the Foreign Investors Tax Act of 1966 (80 Stat. 1539).

(2) Section 2208 makes the provisions of chapter 11 of the Code apply to the transfer of the estates of certain decedents dying after September 2, 1958, who were citizens of the United States and residents of a possession thereof at the

time of death. Section 2209 makes the provisions of chapter 11 apply to the transfer of the estates of certain other decedents dying after September 14, 1960, who were citizens of the United States and residents of a possession thereof at the time of death. See §§ 20.2208-1 and 20.2209-1. Except as otherwise provided in §§ 20.2208-1 and 20.2209-1, the provisions of these regulations do not apply to the estates of such decedents.

(b) Scope of regulations. *(1) Estates of citizens or residents.* Subchapter A of chapter 11 of the Code pertains to the taxation of the estate of a person who was a citizen or a resident of the United States at the time of his death. A "resident" decedent is a decedent who, at the time of his death, had his domicile in the United States. The term "United States", as used in the estate tax regulations, includes only the States and the District of Columbia. The term also includes the Territories of Alaska and Hawaii prior to their admission as States. See section 7701(a)(9). A person acquires a domicile in a place by living there, for even a brief period of time, with no definite present intention of later removing therefrom. Residence without the requisite intention to remain indefinitely will not suffice to constitute domicile, nor will intention to change domicile effect such a change unless accompanied by actual removal. For the meaning of the term "citizen of the United States" as applied in a case where the decedent was a resident of a possession of the United States, see § 20.2208-1. The regulations pursuant to subchapter A are set forth in §§ 20.2001 to 20.2056(d)-1.

(2) Estates of nonresidents not citizens. Subchapter B of chapter 11 of the Code pertains to the taxation of the estate of a person who was a nonresident not a citizen of the United States at the time of his death. A "nonresident" decedent is a decedent who, at the time of his death, had his domicile outside the United States under the principles set forth in subparagraph (1) of this paragraph. (See, however, section 2202 with respect to missionaries in foreign service.) The regulations pursuant to subchapter B are set forth in §§ 20.2101 to 20.2108.

(3) Miscellaneous substantive provisions. Subchapter C of chapter 11 of the Code contains a number of miscellaneous substantive provisions. The regulations pursuant to subchapter C are set forth in §§ 20.2201-1 to 20.2209-1.

(4) Procedure and administration provisions. Subtitle F of the Internal Revenue Code contains some sections which are applicable to the Federal estate tax. The regulations pursuant to those sections are set forth in §§ 20.6001 to 20.7404. Such regulations do not purport to be all the regulations on procedure and administration which are pertinent to estate tax matters. For the remainder of the regulations on procedure and administration which are pertinent to estate tax matters, see Part 301 (Regulations on Procedure and Administration) of this chapter.

(c) Arrangement and numbering. Each section of the regulations in this part (other than this section and § 20.0-2) is designated by a number composed of the part number followed by a decimal point (20.); the section of the Internal Revenue Code which it interprets; a hyphen (-); and a number identifying the section. By use of these designations one can ascertain the sections of the regulations relating to a provision of the Code. For example, the regulations pertaining to section 2012 of the Code are designated § 20.2012-1.

T.D. 6296, 6/23/58, amend T.D. 6526, 1/18/61, T.D. 7238, 12/28/72, T.D. 7296, 12/11/73, T.D. 7665, 1/24/80, T.D. 8522, 2/28/94.

§ 20.0-2 General description of tax.

(a) Nature of tax. The Federal estate tax is neither a property tax nor an inheritance tax. It is a tax imposed upon the transfer of the entire taxable estate and not upon any particular legacy, devise, or distributive share. Escheat of a decedent's property to the State for lack of heirs is a transfer which causes the property to be included in the decedent's gross estate.

(b) Method of determining tax; estate of citizen or resident. *(1) In general.* Subparagraphs (2) to (5) of this paragraph contain a general description of the method to be used in determining the Federal estate tax imposed upon the transfer of the estate of a decedent who was a citizen or resident of the United States at the time of his death.

(2) Gross estate. The first step in determining the tax is to ascertain the total value of the decedent's gross estate. The value of the gross estate includes the value of all property to the extent of the interest therein of the decedent at the time of his death. (For certain exceptions in the case of real property situated outside the United States, see paragraphs (a) and (c) of § 20.2031-1.) In addition, the gross estate may include property in which the decedent did not have an interest at the time of his death. A decedent's gross estate for Federal estate tax purposes may therefore be very different from the same decedent's estate for local probate purposes. Examples of items which may be included in a decedent's gross estate and not in his probate estate are the following: certain property transferred by the decedent during his lifetime without adequate consideration; property held jointly by the decedent and others; property over which the decedent had a general power of appointment; proceeds of certain policies of insurance on the decedent's life; annuities; and dower or curtesy of a surviving spouse or a statutory estate in lieu thereof. For a detailed explanation of the method of ascertaining the value of the gross estate, see sections 2031 through 2044, and the regulations thereunder.

(3) Taxable estate. The second step in determining the tax is to ascertain the value of the decedent's taxable estate. The value of the taxable estate is determined by subtracting from the value of the gross estate the authorized exemption and deductions. Under various conditions and limitations, deductions are allowable for expenses, indebtedness, taxes, losses, charitable transfers, and transfers to a surviving spouse. For a detailed explanation of the method of ascertaining the value of the taxable estate, see sections 2051 through 2056, and the regulations thereunder.

(4) Gross estate tax. The third step is the determination of the gross estate tax. This is accomplished by the application of certain rates to the value of the decedent's taxable estate. In this connection, see section 2001 and the regulations thereunder.

(5) Net estate tax payable. The final step is the determination of the net estate tax payable. This is done by subtracting from the gross estate tax the authorized credits against tax. Under certain conditions and limitations, credits are allowable for the following (computed in the order stated below):

(i) State death taxes paid in connection with the decedent's estate (section 2011);

(ii) Gift taxes paid on inter-vivos transfers by the decedent of property included in his gross estate (section 2012);

(iii) Foreign death taxes paid in connection with the decedent's estate (section 2014); and

(iv) Federal estate taxes paid on transfers of property to the decedent (section 2013).

Sections 2015 and 2016 contain certain further rules for the application of the credits for State and foreign death taxes. Sections 25.2701-5 and 25.2702-6 of this chapter contain rules that provide additional adjustments to mitigate double taxation in cases where the amount of the decedent's gift was previously determined under the special valuation provisions of sections 2701 and 2702. For a detailed explanation of the credits against tax, see sections 2011 through 2016 and the regulations thereunder.

(c) Method of determining tax; estate of nonresident not a citizen. In general, the method to be used in determining the Federal estate tax imposed upon the transfer of an estate of a decedent who was a nonresident not a citizen of the United States is similar to that described in paragraph (b) of this section with respect to the estate of a citizen or resident. Briefly stated, the steps are as follows: First, ascertain the sum of the value of that part of the decedent's "entire gross estate" which at the time of his death was situated in the United States (see §§ 20.2103-1 and 20.2104-1) and, in the case of an estate of an expatriate to which section 2107 applies, any amounts includible in his gross estate under section 2107(b) (see paragraph (b) of § 20.2107-1); second, determine the value of the taxable estate by subtracting from the amount determined under the first step in amount of the allowable deductions (see § 20.2106-1); third, compute the gross estate tax on the taxable estate (see § 20.2101-1); and fourth, subtract from the gross estate tax the total amount of any allowable credits in order to arrive at the net estate tax payable (see § 20.2102-1 and paragraph (c) of § 20.2107-1).

T.D. 6296, 6/23/58, amend T.D. 6684, 10/23/63, T.D. 7296, 12/11/73, T.D. 8395, 1/28/92.

§ 20.2001-1 Valuation of adjusted taxable gifts and section 2701(d) taxable events.

(a) Adjusted taxable gifts made prior to August 6, 1997. For purposes of determining the value of adjusted taxable gifts as defined in section 2001(b), if the gift was made prior to August 6, 1997, the value of the gift may be adjusted at any time, even if the time within which a gift tax may be assessed has expired under section 6501. This paragraph (a) also applies to adjustments involving issues other than valuation for gifts made prior to August 6, 1997.

(b) Adjusted taxable gifts and section 2701(d) taxable events occurring after August 5, 1997. For purposes of determining the amount of adjusted taxable gifts as defined in section 2001(b), if, under section 6501, the time has expired within which a gift tax may be assessed under chapter 12 of the Internal Revenue Code (or under corresponding provisions of prior laws) with respect to a gift made after August 5, 1997, or with respect to an increase in taxable gifts required under section 2701(d) and § 25.2701-4 of this chapter, then the amount of the taxable gift will be the amount as finally determined for gift tax purposes under chapter 12 of the Internal Revenue Code and the amount of the taxable gift may not thereafter be adjusted. The rule of this paragraph (b) applies to adjustments involving all issues relating to the gift, including valuation issues and legal issues involving the interpretation of the gift tax law.

(c) Finally determined. For purposes of paragraph (b) of this section, the amount of a taxable gift as finally determined for gift tax purposes is—

(1) The amount of the taxable gift as shown on a gift tax return, or on a statement attached to the return, if the Internal Revenue Service does not contest such amount before the time has expired under section 6501 within which gift taxes may be assessed;

(2) The amount as specified by the Internal Revenue Service before the time has expired under section 6501 within which gift taxes may be assessed on the gift, if such specified amount is not timely contested by the taxpayer;

(3) The amount as finally determined by a court of competent jurisdiction; or

(4) The amount as determined pursuant to a settlement agreement entered into between the taxpayer and the Internal Revenue Service.

(d) Definitions. For purposes of paragraph (b) of this section, the amount is finally determined by a court of competent jurisdiction when the court enters a final decision, judgment, decree or other order with respect to the amount of the taxable gift that is not subject to appeal. See, for example, section 7481 regarding the finality of a decision by the U.S. Tax Court. Also, for purposes of paragraph (b) of this section, a settlement agreement means any agreement entered into by the Internal Revenue Service and the taxpayer that is binding on both. The term includes a closing agreement under section 7121, a compromise under section 7122, and an agreement entered into in settlement of litigation involving the amount of the taxable gift.

(e) Expiration of period of assessment. For purposes of determining if the time has expired within which a tax may be assessed under chapter 12 of the Internal Revenue Code, see § 301.6501(c)-1(e) and (f) of this chapter.

(f) Effective dates. Paragraph (a) of this section applies to transfers of property by gift made prior to August 6, 1997, if the estate tax return for the donor/decedent's estate is filed after December 3, 1999. Paragraphs (b) through (e) of this section apply to transfers of property by gift made after August 5, 1997, if the gift tax return for the calendar period in which the gift is made is filed after December 3, 1999.

T.D. 6296, 6/23/58, amend T.D. 8845, 12/2/99.

§ 20.2002-1 Liability for payment of tax.

The Federal estate tax imposed both with respect to the estates of citizens or residents and with respect to estates of nonresidents not citizens is payable by the executor or administrator of the decedent's estate. This duty applies to the entire tax, regardless of the fact that the gross estate consists in part of property which does not come within the possession of the executor or administrator. If there is no executor or administrator appointed, qualified and acting in the United States, any person in actual or constructive possession of any property of the decedent is required to pay the entire tax to the extent of the value of the property in his possession. See section 2203, defining the term "executor". The personal liability of the executor or such other person is described in section 3467 of the Revised Statutes (31 U.S.C. 192) as follows:

> Every executor, administrator, or assignee, or other person, who pays, in whole or in part, any debt due by the person or estate for whom or for which he acts before he satisfies and pays the debts due to the United States from such person or estate, shall become answerable in his own person and estate to the extent of such payments for the debts so due to the United States, or for so much thereof as may remain due and unpaid.

As used in said section, the word "debt" includes a beneficiary's distributive share of an estate. Thus, if the executor pays a debt due by the decedent's estate or distributes any portion of the estate before all the estate tax is paid, he is personally liable, to the extent of the payment or distribution, for so much of the estate tax as remains due and unpaid. In addition, section 6324(a)(2) provides that if the estate tax is not paid when due, then the spouse, transferee, trustee (except the trustee of an employee's trust which meets the requirements of section 401(a)), surviving tenant, person in possession of the property by reason of the exercise, nonexercise, or release of a power of appointment, or beneficiary, who receives, or has on the date of the decedent's death, property included in the gross estate under sections 2034 through 2042, is personally liable for the tax to the extent of the value, at the time of the decedent's death, of such property. See also the following related sections of the Internal Revenue Code: Section 2204, discharge of executor from personal liability; section 2205, reimbursement out of estate; sections 2206 and 2207, liability of life insurance beneficiaries and recipients of property over which decedent had power of appointment; sections 6321 through 6325, concerning liens for taxes; and section 6901(a)(1), concerning the liabilities of transferees and fiduciaries.

T.D. 6296, 6/23/58.

§ 20.2011-1 Credit for State death taxes.

Caution: The Treasury has not yet amended Reg § 20.2011-1 to reflect changes made by P.L. 107-16, P.L. 94-455.

(a) In general. A credit is allowed under section 2011 against the Federal estate tax for estate, inheritance, legacy or succession taxes actually paid to any State, Territory, or the District of Columbia, or, in the case of decedents dying before September 3, 1958, any possession of the United States (hereafter referred to as "State death taxes"). The credit, however, is allowed only for State death taxes paid (1) with respect to property included in the decedent's gross estate, and (2) with respect to the decedent's estate. The amount of the credit is subject to the limitation described in paragraph (b) of this section. It is subject to further limitations described in § 20.2011-2 if a deduction is allowed under section 2053(d) for State death taxes paid with respect to a charitable gift. See paragraph (a) of § 20.2014-1 as to the allowance of a credit for death taxes paid to a possession of the United States in a case where the decedent died after September 2, 1958.

(b) Amount of credit. *(1)* If the decedent's taxable estate does not exceed $40,000, the credit for State death taxes is zero. If the decedent's taxable estate does exceed $40,000, the credit for State death taxes is limited to an amount computed in accordance with the following table:

Table for Computation of Maximum Credit for State Death Taxes

(A) Taxable estate equal to or more than—	(B) Taxable estate less than—	(C) Credit on amount in column (A)	(D) Rates of credit on excess over amount in column (A)
			Per cent
$40,000	$90,000		0.8
90,000	140,000	$400	1.6
140,000	240,000	1,200	2.4
240,000	440,000	3,600	3.2
440,000	640,000	10,000	4.0
640,000	840,000	18,000	4.8
840,000	1,040,000	27,600	5.6
1,040,000	1,540,000	38,800	6.4
1,540,000	2,040,000	70,800	7.2
2,040,000	2,540,000	106,800	8.0
2,540,000	3,040,000	146,800	8.8
3,040,000	3,540,000	190,800	9.6
3,540,000	4,040,000	238,800	10.4
4,040,000	5,040,000	290,800	11.2
5,040,000	6,040,000	402,800	12.0
6,040,000	7,040,000	522,800	12.8
7,040,000	8,040,000	650,800	13.6
8,040,000	9,040,000	786,800	14.4
9,040,000	10,040,000	930,800	15.2
10,040,000		1,082,800	16.0

(2) Subparagraph (1) of this paragraph may be illustrated by the following example:

Example. (i) The decedent died January 1, 1955, leaving a taxable estate of $150,000. On January 1, 1956, inheritance taxes totalling $2,500 were actually paid to a State with respect to property included in the decedent's gross estate. Reference to the table discloses that the specified amount in column (A) nearest to but less than the value of the decedent's taxable estate is $140,000. The maximum credit in respect of this amount, as indicated in column (C), is $1,200. The amount by which the taxable estate exceeds the same specified amount is $10,000. The maximum credit in respect of this amount, computed at the rate of 2.4 percent indicated in column (D), is $240. Thus, the maximum credit in respect of the decedent's taxable estate of $150,000 is $1,440, even though $2,500 in inheritance taxes was actually paid to the State.

(ii) If, in subdivision (i) of this example, the amount actually paid to the State was $950, the credit for State death taxes would be limited to $950. If, in subdivision (i) of this example, the decedent's taxable estate was $35,000, no credit for State death taxes would be allowed.

(c) Miscellaneous limitations and conditions to credit. *(1) Period of limitations.* The credit for State death taxes is limited under section 2011(c) to those taxes which were actually paid and for which a credit was claimed within four years after the filing of the estate tax return for the decedent's estate. If, however, a petition has been filed with the Tax Court of the United States for the redetermination of a deficiency within the time prescribed in section 6213(a), the credit is limited to those taxes which were actually paid and for which a credit was claimed within four years after the filing of the return or within 60 days after the decision of the Tax Court becomes final, whichever period is the last to expire. Similarly, if an extension of time has been granted under section 6161 for payment of the tax shown on the return, or of a deficiency, the credit is limited to those taxes which were actually paid and for which a credit was claimed within four years after the filing of the return, or before the date of the expiration of the period of the extension, whichever period is last to expire. If a claim for refund or credit of an overpayment of the Federal estate tax is filed within the time prescribed in section 6511, the credit for State death taxes is limited to such taxes as were actually paid and credit therefor claimed within four years after the filing of the return or before the expiration of 60 days from the date of mailing by certified or registered mail by the district director to the taxpayer of a notice of disallowance of any part of the claim, or before the expiration of 60 days after a decision by any court of competent jurisdiction becomes final with respect to a timely suit instituted upon the claim, whichever period is the last to expire. See section 2015 for the applicable period of limitations for credit for State death taxes on reversionary or remainder interests if an election is made under section 6163(a) to postpone payment of the estate tax attributable to reversionary or remainder interests. If a claim for refund based on the credit for State death taxes is filed within the applicable period described in this subparagraph, a refund may be made despite the general limitation provisions of sections 6511 and 6512. Any refund based on the credit described in this section shall be made without interest.

(2) Submission of evidence. Before the credit for State death taxes is allowed, evidence that such taxes have been paid must be submitted to the district director. The district director may require the submission of a certificate from the proper officer of the taxing State, Territory, or possession of the United States, or the District of Columbia, showing: (i) The total amount of tax imposed (before adding interest and penalties and before allowing discount); (ii) the amount of any discount allowed; (iii) the amount of any penalties and interest imposed or charged; (iv) the total amount actually paid in cash; and (v) the date or dates of payment. If the amount of these taxes has been redetermined, the amount finally determined should be stated. The required evidence should be filed with the return, but if that is not convenient or possible, then it should be submitted as soon thereafter as practicable. The district director may require the submission of such additional proof as is deemed necessary to establish the right to the credit. For example, he may require the submission of a certificate of the proper officer of the taxing jurisdiction showing (vi) whether a claim for refund of any part of the State death tax is pending and (vii) whether a refund of any part thereof has been authorized, and if a refund has been made, its date and amount, and a description of the property or interest in respect of which the refund was made. The district director may also require an itemized list of the property in respect of which State death taxes were imposed, certified by the officer having custody of the records pertaining to those taxes. In addition, he may require the executor to submit a written statement (containing a declaration that it is made under penalties of perjury) stating whether, to his knowledge, any person has instituted litigation or taken an appeal (or contemplates doing so), the final determination of which may affect the amount of those taxes. See section 2016 concerning the redetermination of the estate tax if State death taxes claimed as credit are refunded.

(d) Definition of "basic estate tax". Section 2011(d) provides definitions of the terms "basic estate tax" and "additional estate tax", used in the Internal Revenue Code of 1939, and "estate tax imposed by the Revenue Act of 1926", for the purpose of supplying a means of computing State death taxes under local statutes using those terms, and for use in determining the exemption provided for in section 2201 for estates of certain members of the Armed Forces. See section 2011(e)(3) for a modification of these definitions if a deduction is allowed under section 2053(d) for State death taxes paid with respect to a charitable gift.

T.D. 6296, 6/23/58, amend T.D. 6526, 1/18/61.

§ 20.2011-2 Limitation on credit if a deduction for State death taxes is allowed under section 2053(d).

Caution: The Treasury has not yet amended Reg § 20.2011-2 to reflect changes made by P.L. 107-16, P.L. 94-455.

If a deduction is allowed under section 2053(d) for State death taxes paid with respect to a charitable gift, the credit for State death taxes is subject to special limitations. Under these limitations, the credit cannot exceed the least of the following:

(a) The amount of State death taxes paid other than those for which a deduction is allowed under section 2053(d);

(b) The amount indicated in section 2011(b) to be the maximum credit allowable with respect to the decedent's taxable estate; or

(c) An amount, A, which bears the same ratio to B (the amount which would be the maximum credit allowable under section 2011(b) if the deduction under section 2053(d) for State death taxes were not allowed in computing the decedent's taxable estate) as C (the amount of State death taxes paid other than those for which a deduction is allowed under section 2053(d)) bears to D (the total amount of State death taxes paid). For the purpose of this computation, in determining what the decedent's taxable estate would be if the deduction for State death taxes under section 2053(d) were not allowed, adjustment must be made for the decrease in the deduction for charitable gifts under section 2055 or 2106(a)(2) (for estates of nonresidents not citizens) by reason of any increase in Federal estate tax which would be charged against the charitable gifts.

The application of this section may be illustrated by the following example:

Example. The decedent died January 1, 1955, leaving a gross estate of $925,000. Expenses, indebtedness, etc., amounted to $25,000. The decedent bequeathed $400,000 to his son with the direction that the son bear the State death taxes on the bequest. The residuary estate was left to a charitable organization. Except as noted above, all Federal and State death taxes were payable out of the residuary estate. The State imposed death taxes of $60,000 on the son's bequest and death taxes of $75,000 on the bequest to charity. No death taxes were imposed by a foreign country with respect to any property in the gross estate. The decedent's taxable estate (determined without regard to the limitation imposed by section 2011(e)(2)(B)) is computed as follows:

Gross estate				$925,000.00
Expenses, indebtedness, etc.			$25,000.00	
Exemption			60,000.00	
Deduction under section 2053(d)			75,000.00	
Charitable deduction:				
Gross estate		$925,000.00		
Expenses, etc.	$25,000.00			
Bequest to son	400,000.00			
State death tax paid from residue	75,000.00			
Federal estate tax paid from residue	122,916.67	622,916.67	302,083.33	462,083.33
Taxable estate				462,916.67

If the deduction under section 2053(d) were not allowed, the decedent's taxable estate would be computed as follows:

Gross estate				$925,000.00
Expenses, indebtedness, etc.			$25,000.00	
Exemption			60,000.00	
Charitable deduction:				
Gross estate		$925,000.00		
Expenses, etc.	$25,000.00			
Bequest to son	400,000.00			
State death tax paid from residue	75,000.00			
Federal estate tax paid from residue	155,000.00	655,000.00	270,000.00	355,000.00
Taxable estate				570,000.00

On a taxable estate of $570,000, the maximum credit allowable under section 2011(b) would be $15,200. Under these facts, the credit for State death taxes is determined as follows:

(1) Amount of State death taxes paid other than those for which a deduction is allowed under section 2053(d) ($135,000 − $75,000)	$60,000.00
(2) Amount indicated in section 2011(b) to be the maximum credit allowable with respect to the decedent's taxable estate of $462,916.67	10,916.67
(3) Amount determined by use of the ratio described in paragraph (c) above $\left(\frac{\$60,000}{\$135,000} \times \$15,000\right)$	6,755.56
(4) Credit for State death taxes (least of subparagraphs (1) through (3) above)	6,755.56

T.D. 6296, 6/23/58, amend T.D. 6600, 5/28/62.

§ 20.2012-1 Credit for gift tax.

Caution: The Treasury has not yet amended Reg § 20.2012-1 to reflect changes made by P.L. 94-455.

(a) In general. With respect to gifts made before 1977, a credit is allowed under section 2012 against the Federal estate tax for gift tax paid under chapter 12 of the Internal Revenue Code, or corresponding provisions of prior law, on a gift by the decedent of property subsequently included in the decedent's gross estate. The credit is allowed even though the gift tax is paid after the decedent's death and the amount of the gift tax is deductible from the gross estate as a debt of the decedent.

(b) Limitations on credit. The credit for gift tax is limited to the smaller of the following amounts:

(1) The amount of gift tax paid on the gift, computed as set forth in paragraph (c) of this section, or

(2) The amount of the estate tax attributable to the inclusion of the gift in the gross estate, computed as set forth in paragraph (d) of this section.

When more than one gift is included in the gross estate, a separate computation of the two limitations on the credit is to be made for each gift.

(c) "First limitation". The amount of the gift tax paid on the gift is the "first limitation". Thus, if only one gift was made during a certain calendar quarter or calendar year if the gift was made before January 1, 1971, and the gift is wholly included in the decedent's gross estate for the purpose of the estate tax, the credit with respect to the gift is limited to the amount of the gift tax paid for that calendar quarter or calendar year. On the other hand, if more than one gift was made during a certain calendar quarter or calendar year, the credit with respect to any such gift which is included in the decedent's gross estate is limited under section 2012(d) to an amount, A, which bears the same ratio to B (the total gift tax paid for that calendar quarter or calendar year,) as C (the "amount of the gift", computed as described below) bears to D (the total taxable gifts for the calendar quarter or the calendar year computed without deduction of the gift tax specific exemption). Stated algebraically, the "first limitation" (A) equals

$$\frac{\text{“Amount of the gift” (C)}}{\text{Total taxable gifts, plus specific exemption allowed (D)}} \times \text{Total gift tax paid (B).}$$

For purposes of the ratio stated above, the "amount of the gift" referred to as factor "C" is the value of the gift reduced by any portion excluded or deducted under sections 2503(b) (annual exclusion), 2522 (charitable deduction), or 2523 (marital deduction) of the Internal Revenue Code or corresponding provisions of prior law. In making the computations described in this paragraph, the values to be used are those finally determined for the purpose of the gift tax, irrespective of the values determined for the purpose of the estate tax. A similar computation is made in case only a portion of any gift is included in the decedent's gross estate. The application of this paragraph may be illustrated by the following example:

Example. The donor made gifts during the calendar year 1955 on which a gift tax was determined as shown below:

Gift of property to son on February 1		$13,000
Gift of property to wife on May 1		86,000
Gift of property to charitable organization on May 15		10,000
Total gifts		109,000
Less exclusions ($3,000 for each gift)		9,000
Total included amount of gifts		100,000
Marital deduction (for gift to wife)	$43,000	
Charitable deduction	7,000	
Specific exemption ($30,000 less $20,000 used in prior years)	10,000	
Total deductions		60,000
Taxable gifts		40,000
Total gift tax paid for calendar year 1955		3,600

The donor's gift to his wife was made in contemplation of death and was thereafter included in his gross estate. Under the "first limitation", the credit with respect to that gift cannot exceed

$$\frac{\text{\$86,000 − \$3,000 − \$43,000 (gift to wife, less annual exclusion and marital deduction)}}{\text{\$40,000 + \$10,000 (taxable gifts, plus specific exemption allowed)}} \times \text{\$3,600 (total gift tax paid) = \$2,880.}$$

(d) "Second limitation". *(1)* The amount of the estate tax attributable to the inclusion of the gift in the gross estate is the "second limitation". Thus, the credit with respect to any gift of property included in the gross estate is limited to an amount, E, which bears the same ratio to F (the gross estate tax, reduced by any credit for State death taxes under section 2011) as G (the "value of the gift", computed as described in subparagraph (2) of this paragraph) bears to H (the value of entire gross estate, reduced by the total deductions allowed under sections 2055 or 2106(a)(2) (charitable deduction) and 2056 (marital deduction)). Stated algebraically, the "second limitation" (E) equals

$$\frac{\text{“Value of the gift” (G)}}{\text{Value of gross estate, less marital and charitable deductions (H)}} \times \text{Gross estate tax, less credit for State death taxes (F).}$$

(2) For purposes of the ratio stated in subparagraph (1) of this paragraph, the "value of the gift" referred to as factor "G" is the value of the property transferred by gift and included in the gross estate, as determined for the purpose of the gift tax or for the purpose of the estate tax, whichever is lower, and adjusted as follows:

(i) The appropriate value is reduced by all or a portion of any annual exclusion allowed for gift tax purposes under section 2503(b) of the Internal Revenue Code or corresponding provisions of prior law. If the gift tax value is lower than the estate tax value, it is reduced by the entire amount of the exclusion. If the estate tax value is lower than the gift tax value, it is reduced by an amount which bears the same ratio to the estate tax value as the annual exclusion bears to the total value of the property as determined for gift tax purposes. To illustrate: In 1955, a donor, in contemplation of death, transferred certain property to his five children which was valued at $300,000 for the purpose of the gift tax. Thereafter, the same property was included in his gross estate at a value of $270,000. In computing his gift tax, the donor was allowed annual exclusions totalling $15,000. The reduction provided for in this subdivision is

$$\frac{\$15{,}000 \text{ (annual exclusions allowed)}}{\$300{,}000 \text{ (value of transferred property for the purpose of the gift tax)}} \times \$270{,}000 \text{ (value of transferred property for the purpose of the estate tax)} = \$13{,}500.$$

(ii) The appropriate value is further reduced if any portion of the value of the property is allowed as a marital deduction under section 2056 or as a charitable deduction under section 2055 or section 2106(a)(2) (for estates of nonresidents not citizens). The amount of the reduction is an amount which bears the same ratio to the value determined under subdivision (i) of this subparagraph as the portion of the property allowed as a marital deduction or as a charitable deduction bears to the total value of the property as determined for the purpose of the estate tax. Thus, if a gift is made solely to the decedent's surviving spouse and is subsequently included in the decedent's gross estate decedent's surviving spouse and is subsequently included in the decedent's gross estate as having been made in contemplation of death, but a marital deduction is allowed under section 2056 for the full value of the gift, no credit for gift tax on the gift will be allowed since the reduction under this subdivision together with the reduction under subdivision (i) of this subparagraph will have the effect of reducing the factor "G" of the ratio in subparagraph (1) of this paragraph to zero.

(e) Credit for "split gifts". If a decedent made a gift of property which is thereafter included in his gross estate, and, under the provisions of section 2513 of the Internal Revenue Code of 1954 or section 1000(f) of the Internal Revenue Code of 1939, the gift was considered as made one-half by the decedent and one-half by his spouse, credit against the estate tax is allowed for the gift tax paid with respect to both halves of the gift. The "first limitation" is to be separately computed with respect to each half of the gift in accordance with the principles stated in paragraph (c) of this section. The "second limitation" is to be computed with respect to the entire gift in accordance with the principles stated in paragraph (d) of this section. To illustrate: A donor, in contemplation of death, transferred property valued at $106,000 to his son on January 1, 1955, and he and his wife consented that the gift should be considered as made one-half by him and one-half by her. The property was thereafter included in the donor's gross estate. Under the "first limitation", the amount of the gift tax of the donor paid with respect to the one-half of the gift considered as made by him is determined to be $11,250, and the amount of the gift tax of his wife paid with respect to the one-half of the gift considered as made by her is determined to be $1,200. Under the "second limitation", the amount of the estate tax attributable to the property is determined to be $28,914. Therefore, the credit for gift tax allowed is $12,450 ($11,250 plus $1,200).

T.D. 6296, 6/23/58, amend T.D. 7238, 12/28/72, T.D. 8522, 2/28/94.

§ 20.2013-1 Credit for tax on prior transfers.

Caution: The Treasury has not yet amended Reg § 20.2013-1 to reflect changes made by P.L. 94-455.

(a) In general. A credit is allowed under section 2013 against the Federal estate tax imposed on the present decedent's estate for Federal estate tax paid on the transfer of property to the present decedent from a transferor who died within ten years before, or within two years after, the present decedent's death. See § 20.2013-5 for definition of the terms "property" and "transfer". There is no requirement that the transferred property be identified in the estate of the present decedent or that the property be in existence at the time of the decedent's death. It is sufficient that the transfer of the property was subjected to Federal estate tax in the estate of the transferor and that the transferor died within the prescribed period of time. The executor must submit such proof as may be requested by the district director in order to establish the right of the estate to the credit.

(b) Limitations on credit. The credit for tax on prior transfers is limited to the smaller of the following amounts:

(1) The amount of the Federal estate tax attributable to the transferred property in the transferor's estate, computed as set forth in § 20.2013-2; or

(2) The amount of the Federal estate tax attributable to the transferred property in the decedent's estate, computed as set forth in § 20.2013-3.

Rules for valuing property for purposes of the credit are contained in § 20.2013-4.

(c) Percentage reduction. If the transferor died within the two years before, or within the two years after, the present decedent's death, the credit is the smaller of the two limitations described in paragraph (b) of this section. If the transferor predeceased the present decedent by more than two years, the credit is a certain percentage of the smaller of the two limitations described in paragraph (b) of this section, determined as follows:

(1) 80 percent, if the transferor died within the third or fourth years preceding the present decedent's death;

(2) 60 percent, if the transferor died within the fifth or sixth years preceding the present decedent's death;

(3) 40 percent, if the transferor died within the seventh or eighth years preceding the present decedent's death; and

(4) 20 percent, if the transferor died within the ninth or tenth years preceding the present decedent's death.

The word "within" as used in this paragraph means "during". Therefore, if a death occurs on the second anniversary of another death, the first death is considered to have occurred within the two years before the second death. If the credit for tax on prior transfers relates to property received from two or more transferors, the provisions of this paragraph are to be applied separately with respect to the property received from each transferor. See paragraph (d) of example (2) in § 20.2013-6.

(d) Examples. For illustrations of the application of this section, see examples (1) and (2) set forth in § 20.2013-6.

T.D. 6296, 6/23/58.

§ 20.2013-2 "First limitation".

(a) The amount of the Federal estate tax attributable to the transferred property in the transferor's estate is the "first limitation." Thus, the credit is limited to an amount, A, which bears the same ratio to B (the "transferor's adjusted Federal estate tax", computed as described in paragraph (b) of this section) as C (the value of the property transferred (see § 20.2013-4)) bears to D (the "transferor's adjusted taxable estate", computed as described in paragraph (c) of this section). Stated algebraically, the "first limitation" (A) equals

$$\frac{\text{Value of transferred property (C)}}{\text{“Transferor's adjusted taxable estate” (D)}} \times \text{“Transferor's adjusted Federal estate tax” (B).}$$

(b) For purposes of the ratio stated in paragraph (a) of this section, the "transferor's adjusted Federal estate tax" referred to as factor "B" is the amount of the Federal estate tax paid with respect to the transferor's estate plus:

(1) Any credit allowed the transferor's estate for gift tax under section 2012, or the corresponding provisions of prior law; and

(2) Any credit allowed the transferor's estate, under section 2013, for tax on prior transfers, but only if the transferor acquired property from a person who died within 10 years before the death of the present decedent.

(c) *(1)* For purposes of the ratio stated in paragraph (a) of this section, the "transferor's adjusted taxable estate" referred to as factor "D" is the amount of the transferor's taxable estate (or net estate) decreased by the amount of any "death taxes" paid with respect to his gross estate and increased by the amount of the exemption allowed in computing his taxable estate (or net estate). The amount of the transferor's taxable estate (or net estate) is determined in accordance with the provisions of § 20.2051-1 in the case of a citizen or resident of the United States or of § 20.2106-1 in the case of a nonresident not a citizen of the United States (or the corresponding provisions of prior regulations). The term "death taxes" means the Federal estate tax plus all other estate, inheritance, legacy, succession, or similar death taxes imposed by, and paid to, any taxing authority, whether within or without the United States. However, only the net amount of such taxes paid is taken into consideration.

(2) The amount of the exemption depends upon the citizenship and residence of the transferor at the time of his death. Except in the case of a decedent described in section 2209 (relating to certain residents of possessions of the United States who are considered nonresidents not citizens), if the decedent was a citizen or resident of the United States, the exemption is the $60,000 authorized by section 2052 (or the corresponding provisions of prior law). If the decedent was a nonresident not a citizen of the United States, or is considered under section 2209 to have been such a nonresident, the exemption is the $30,000 or $2,000, as the case may be, authorized by section 2106(a)(3) (or the corresponding provisions of prior law), or such larger amount as is authorized by section 2106(a)(3)(B) or may have been allowed as an exemption pursuant to the prorated exemption provisions of an applicable death tax convention. See § 20.2052-1 and paragraph (a)(3) of § 20.2106-1.

(d) If the credit for tax on prior transfers relates to property received from two or more transferors, the provisions of this section are to be applied separately with respect to the property received from each transferor. See paragraph (b) of example (2) in § 20.2013-6.

(e) For illustrations of the application of this section, see examples (1) and (2) set forth in § 20.2013-6.

T.D. 6296, 6/23/58, amend T.D. 7296, 12/11/73.

§ 20.2013-3 "Second limitation".

(a) The amount of the Federal estate tax attributable to the transferred property in the present decedent's estate is the "second limitation". Thus, the credit is limited to the difference between—

(1) The net estate tax payable (see paragraph (b)(5) or (c), as the case may be, of § 20.0-2) with respect to the present decedent's estate, determined without regard to any credit for tax on prior transfers under section 2013 or any credit for foreign death taxes claimed under the provisions of a death tax convention, and

(2) The net estate tax determined as provided in subparagraph (1) of this paragraph but computed by subtracting from the present decedent's gross estate the value of the property transferred (see § 20.2013-4), and by making only the adjustment indicated in paragraph (b) of this section if a charitable deduction is allowable to the estate of the present decedent.

(b) If a charitable deduction is allowable to the estate of the present decedent under the provisions of section 2055 or section 2106(a)(2) (for estates of nonresidents not citizens), for purposes of determining the tax described in paragraph (a)(2) of this section, the charitable deduction otherwise allowable is reduced by an amount, E, which bears the same ratio to F (the charitable deduction otherwise allowable) as G (the value of the transferred property (see § 20.2013-4)) bears to H (the value of the present decedent's gross estate reduced by the amount of the deductions for expenses, indebtedness, taxes, losses, etc., allowed under the provisions of sections 2053 and 2054 or section 2106(a)(1) (for estates of nonresidents not citizens)). See paragraph (c)(2) of example (1) and paragraph (c)(2) of example (2) in § 20.2013-6.

(c) If the credit for tax on prior transfers relates to property received from two or more transferors, the property received from all transferors is aggregated in determining the limitation on credit under this section (the "second limitation"). However, the limitation so determined is apportioned to the property received from each transferor in the ratio that the property received from each transferor bears to the total property received from all transferors. See paragraph (c) of example (2) in § 20.2013-6.

(d) For illustrations of the application of this section, see examples (1) and (2) set forth in § 20.2013-6.

T.D. 6296, 6/23/58, amend T.D. 7296, 12/11/73.

§ 20.2013-4 Valuation of property transferred.

(a) For purposes of section 2013 and §§ 20.2013 to 20.2013-6, the value of the property transferred to the decedent is the value at which the property was included in the transferor's gross estate for the purpose of the Federal estate tax (see sections 2031, 2032, 2103, and 2107, and the regulations thereunder) reduced as indicated in paragraph (b) of this section. If the decedent received a life estate or a remainder or other limited interest in property that was included in a transferor decedent's gross estate, the value of the interest is determined as of the date of the transferor's death on the basis of recognized valuation principles (see §§ 20.2031-7 (or for certain prior periods, § 20.2031-7A) and 20.7520-1 through 20.7520-4). The application of this paragraph may be illustrated by the following examples:

Example (1). A died on January 1, 1953, leaving Blackacre to B. The property was included in A's gross estate at a value of $100,000. On January 1, 1955, B sold Blackacre to C for $150,000. B died on February 1, 1955. For purposes of computing the credit against the tax imposed on B's estate, the value of the property transferred to B is $100,000.

Example (2). A died on January 1, 1953, leaving Blackacre to B for life and, upon B's death, remainder to C. At the time of A's death, B was 56 years of age. The property was included in A's gross estate at a value of $100,000. The part of that value attributable to the life estate is $44,688 and the part of that value attributable to the remainder is $55,312 (see § 20.2031-7A(b)). B died on January 1, 1955, and C died on January 1, 1956. For purposes of computing the credit against the tax imposed on B's estate, the value of the property transferred to B is $44,688. For purposes of computing the credit against the tax imposed on C's estate, the value of the property transferred to C is $55,312.

(b) In arriving at the value of the property transferred to the decedent, the value at which the property was included in the transferor's gross estate (see paragraph (a) of this section) is reduced as follows:

(1) By the amount of the Federal estate tax and any other estate, inheritance, legacy, or succession taxes which were payable out of the property transferred to the decedent or which were payable by the decedent in connection with the property transferred to him. For example, if under the transferor's will or local law all death taxes are to be paid out of other property with the result that the decedent receives a bequest free and clear of all death taxes, no reduction is to be made under this subparagraph;

(2) By the amount of any marital deduction allowed the transferor's estate under section 2056 (or under section 812(e) of the Internal Revenue Code of 1939) if the decedent was the spouse of the transferor at the time of the transferor's death;

(3) (i) By the amount of administration expenses in accordance with the principles of § 20.2056(b)-4(d).

(ii) This paragraph (b)(3) applies to transfers from estates of decedents dying on or after December 3, 1999; and

(4) (i) By the amount of any encumbrance on the property or by the amount of any obligation imposed by the transferor and incurred by the decedent with respect to the property, to the extent such charges would be taken into account if the amount of a gift to the decedent of such property were being determined.

(ii) For purposes of this subparagraph, an obligation imposed by the transferor and incurred by the decedent with respect to the property includes a bequest, etc., in lieu of the interest of the surviving spouse under community property laws, unless the interest was, immediately prior to the transferor's death, a mere expectancy. However, an obligation imposed by the transferor and incurred by the decedent with respect to the property does not include a bequest, devise, or other transfer in lieu of dower, curtesy, or of a statutory estate created in lieu of dower or curtesy, or of other marital rights in the transferor's property or estate.

(iii) The application of this subparagraph may be illustrated by the following examples:

Example (1). The transferor devised to the decedent real estate subject to a mortgage. The value of the property transferred to the decedent does not include the amount of the mortgage. If, however, the transferor by his will directs the executor to pay off the mortgage, such payment constitutes an additional amount transferred to the decedent.

Example (2). The transferor bequeathed certain property to the decedent with a direction that the decedent pay $1,000 to X. The value of the property transferred to the decedent is the value of the property reduced by $1,000.

Example (3). The transferor bequeathed certain property to his wife the decedent, in lieu of her interest in property held by them as community property under the law of the State of their residence. The wife elected to relinquish her community property interest and to take the bequest. The value of the property transferred to the decedent is the value of the property reduced by the value of the community property interest relinquished by the wife.

Example (4). The transferor bequeathed to the decedent his entire residuary estate, out of which certain claims were to be satisfied. The entire distributable income of the transferor's estate (during the period of its administration) was applied toward the satisfaction of these claims and the remaining portion of the claims was satisfied by the decedent out of his own funds. Thus, the decedent received a larger sum upon settlement of the transferor's estate than he was actually bequeathed. The value of the property transferred to the decedent is the value at which such property was included in the transferor's gross estate, reduced by the amount of the estate income and the decedent's own funds paid out in satisfaction of the claims.

T.D. 7077, 12/1/70, amend T.D. 7296, 12/11/73, T.D. 8522, 2/28/94, T.D. 8540, 6/9/94, T.D. 8846, 12/2/99.

§ 20.2013-5 "Property" and "transfer" defined.

(a) For purposes of section 2013 and §§ 20.2013-1 to 20.2013-6, the term "property" means any beneficial interest in property, including a general power of appointment (as defined in section 2041) over property. Thus, the term does not include an interest in property consisting merely of a bare legal title, such as that of a trustee. Nor does the term include a power of appointment over property which is not a general power of appointment (as defined in section 2041). Examples of property, as described in this paragraph, are annuities, life estates, estates for terms of years, vested or contingent remainders and other future interests.

(b) In order to obtain the credit for tax on prior transfers, there must be a transfer of property described in paragraph (a) of this section by or from the transferor to the decedent. The term "transfer" of property by or from a transferor means any passing of property or an interest in property under circumstances which were such that the property or interest was included in the gross estate of the transferor. In this connection, if the decedent receives property as a result of the exercise or nonexercise of a power of appointment, the donee of the power (and not the creator) is deemed to be the transferor of the property if the property subject to the power is includible in the donee's gross estate under section 2041 (relating to powers of appointment). Thus, notwithstanding the designation by local law of the capacity in which the decedent takes, property received from the transferor includes interests in property held by or devolving upon the decedent: (1) As spouse under dower or curtesy law or laws creating an estate in lieu of dower or curtesy; (2) as surviving tenant of a tenancy by the entirety or joint tenancy with survivorship rights; (3) as beneficiary of the proceeds of life insurance; (4) as survivor under an annuity contract; (5) as donee (possessor) of a general power of appointment (as defined in section 2041); (6) as appointee under the exercise of a general power of appointment (as defined in section 2041); or (7) as remainderman under the release or nonexercise of a power of appointment by reason of which the property is included in the gross estate of the donee of the power under section 2041.

(c) The application of this section may be illustrated by the following example:

Example. A devises Blackacre to B, as trustee, with directions to pay the income therefrom to C, his son, for life. Upon C's death, Blackacre is to be sold. C is given a general testamentary power, to appoint one-third of the proceeds, and a testamentary power, which is not a general power, to appoint the remaining two-thirds of the proceeds, to such of the issue of his sister D as he should choose. D has a daughter, E, and a son, F. Upon his death, C exercised his general power by appointing one-third of the proceeds to D and his special power by appointing two-thirds of the proceeds to E. Since B's interest in Blackacre as a trustee is not a beneficial interest, no part of it is "property" for purpose of the credit in B's estate. On the other hand, C's life estate and his testamentary power over the one-third interest in the remainder constitute "property" received from A for purpose of the credit in C's estate. Likewise, D's one-third interest in the remainder received through the exercise of C's general power of appointment is "property" received from C for purpose of the credit in D's estate. No credit is allowed E's estate for the property which passed to her from C since the property was not included in C's gross estate. On the other hand, no credit is allowed in E's estate for property passing to her from A since her interest was not susceptible of valuation at the time of A's death (see § 20.2013-4).

T.D. 6296, 6/23/58.

§ 20.2013-6 Examples.

Caution: The Treasury has not yet amended Reg § 20.2013-6 to reflect changes made by P.L. 94-455.

The application of §§ 20.2013-1 to 20.2013-5 may be further illustrated by the following examples:

Example (1). (a) A died December 1, 1953, leaving a gross estate of $1,000,000. Expenses, indebtedness, etc., amounted to $90,000. A bequeathed $200,000 to B, his wife, $100,000 of which qualifies for the marital deduction. B died November 1, 1954, leaving a gross estate of $500,000. Expenses, indebtedness, etc., amounted to $40,000. B bequeathed $150,000 to charity. A and B were both citizens of the United States. The estates of A and B both paid State death taxes equal to the maximum credit allowable for State death taxes. Death taxes were not a charge on the bequest to B.

(b) "First limitation" on credit for B's estate (§ 20.2013-2):

A's gross estate		$1,000,000.00
Expenses, indebtedness, etc		90,000.00
A's adjusted gross estate		910,000.00
Marital deduction	$100,000.00	
Exemption	60,000.00	
		160,000.00
A's taxable estate		750,000.00
A's gross estate tax		233,200.00
Credit for State death taxes		23,280.00
A's net estate tax payable		209,920.00

"First limitation" = $209,920.00 (§ 20.2013-2(b)) ×

$$\frac{\$200,000.00 - \$100,000.00 \text{ (§ 20.2013-4)}}{\$750,000.00 - \$209,920.00 - \$23,280.00 + \$60,000.00 \text{ (§ 20.213-2(c))}} \ldots\ldots \$\ 36,393.90$$

(c) "Second limitation" on credit for B's estate (§ 20.2013-3):

(1) B's net estate tax payable as described in § 20.2013-3(a)(1) (previously taxed transfer included):

B's gross estate		$500,000.00
Expenses, indebtedness, etc	$ 40,000.00	
Charitable deduction	150,000.00	
Exemption	60,000.00	
		250,000.00
B's taxable estate		250,000.00
B's gross estate tax		65,700.00
Credit for State death taxes		3,920.00
B's net estate tax payable		61,780.00

(2) B's net estate tax payable as described in § 20.2013-3(a)(2) (previously taxed transfer excluded):

B's gross estate		$400,000.00
Expenses, indebtedness, etc	$ 40,000.00	
Charitable deduction (§ 20.2013-3(b)) = $150,000.00 − ($150,000.00 × $\frac{\$200,000.00 - \$100,000.00)}{\$500,000.00 - \$40,000.00)}$	117,391.30	
Exemption	60,000.00	217,391.30
B's taxable estate		182,608.70
B's gross estate tax		45,482.61
Credit for State death taxes		2,221.61
B's net estate tax payable		43,260.00

(3) "Second limitation":

Subparagraph (1)	$61,780.00	
Less: Subparagraph (2)	43,260.00	
		18,520.00

(d) Credit of B's estate for tax on prior transfers (§ 20.2013-1(c)):

Credit for tax on prior transfers− $18,520.00 (lower of paragraphs (b) and (c)) × 100 percent (percentage to be taken into account under § 20.2013-1(c)) $18,520.00

Example (2). (a) The facts are the same as those contained in example (1) of this paragraph with the following additions. C died December 1, 1950, leaving a gross estate of $250,000. Expenses, indebtedness, etc., amounted to $50,000. C bequeathed $50,000 to B. C was a citizen of the United States. His estate paid State death taxes equal to the maximum credit allowable for State death taxes. Death taxes were not a charge on the bequest to B.

(b) "First limitation" on credit for B's estate (§ 20.2013-2(d))—

(1) With respect to the property received from A: "First limitation" = $36,393.90 (this computation is identical with the one contained in paragraph (b) of example (1) of this section).

(2) With respect to the property received from C:

C's gross estate		$250,000.00
Expenses, indebtedness, etc	$50,000.00	
Exemption	60,000.00	
		110,000.00
C's taxable estate		140,000.00
C's gross estate tax		$ 32,700.00
Credit for State death taxes		1,200.00
C's net estate tax payable		31,500.00

"First limitation" = $31,500.00 (§ 20.2013-2(b)) ×

$$\frac{\$50,000\ (\S\ 20.2013\text{-}4)}{\$140,000.00 - \$31,500.00 - \$1,200.00 + \$60,000.00\ (\S\ 2020.13\text{-}2(c))} \quad 9,414.23$$

(c) "Second limitation" on credit for B's estate (§ 20.2013-3(c)):

(1) B's net estate tax payable as described in § 20.2013-3(a)(1) (previously taxed transfers included) = $61,780.00 (this computation is identical with the one contained in paragraph (c)(1) of example (1) of this section).

(2) B's net estate tax payable as described in § 20.2013-3(a)(2) (previously taxed transfers excluded):

B's gross estate		$350,000.00
Expenses, indebtedness, etc.	$40,000.00	
Charitable deduction (§ 20.2013-3(b)) = $150,000.00 − $\left(\$150,000.00 \times \frac{\$200,000.00 - \$100,000.00 + \$50,000.00}{\$500,000.00 - \$40,000.00}\right)$	101,086.96	
Exemption	60,000.00	
		201,086.96
B's taxable estate		148,913.04
B's gross estate tax		35,373.91
Credit for State death taxes		1,413.91
B's net estate tax payable		33,960.00

(3) "Second limitation":

Subparagraph (1)	$61,780.00	
Less: Subparagraph (2)	33,960.00	
		27,820.00

(4) Apportionment of "second limitation" on credit:

Transfer from A (§ 20.2013-4)	100,000.00
Transfer from C (§ 20.2013-4)	50,000.00
Total	150,000.00
Portion of "second limitation" attributable to transfer from A$\frac{100}{150}$ of $27,820.00)	18,546.67
Portion of "second limitation" attributable to transfer from C$\frac{50}{150}$ of $27,820.00)	9,273.33

(d) Credit of B's estate for tax on prior transfers (§ 20.2013-1(c)):

Credit for tax on transfer from A= $18,546.67 (lower of "first limitation" computed in paragraph (b)(1) and "second limitation" apportioned to A's transfer in paragraph (c)(4)) × 100 percent (percentage to be taken into account under § 20.2013-1(c))	$18,546.67
Credit for tax on transfer from C= $9,273.33 (lower of "first limitation" computed in paragraph (b)(2) and "second limitation" apportioned to B's transfer in paragraph (c)(4)) × 80 percent (percentage to be taken into account under § 20.2013-1(c))	7,418.66
Total credit for tax on prior transfers	25,965.33

T.D. 6296, 6/23/58.

§ 20.2014-1 Credit for foreign death taxes.

Caution: The Treasury has not yet amended Reg § 20.2014-1 to reflect changes made by P.L. 94-455.

(a) In general. *(1)* A credit is allowed under section 2014 against the Federal estate tax for any estate, inheritance, legacy, or succession taxes actually paid to any foreign country (hereinafter referred to as "foreign death taxes"). The credit is allowed only for foreign death taxes paid (i) with respect to property situated within the country to which the tax is paid, (ii) with respect to property included in the decedent's gross estate, and (iii) with respect to the decedent's estate. The credit is allowable to the estate of a decedent who was a citizen of the United States at the time of his death. The credit is also allowable, as provided in paragraph (c) of this section, to the estate of a decedent who was a resident but not a citizen of the United States at the time of his death. The credit is not allowable to the estate of a decedent who was neither a citizen nor a resident of the United States at the time of his death. See paragraph (b)(1) of § 20.0-1 for the meaning of the term "resident" as applied to a decedent. The credit is allowable not only for death taxes paid to foreign countries which are states in the international sense, but also for death taxes paid to possessions or political subdivisions of foreign states. With respect to the estate of a decedent dying after September 2, 1958, the term "foreign country", as used in this section and §§ 20.2014-2 to 20.2014-6, includes a possession of the United States. See §§ 20.2011-1 and 20.2011-2 for the allowance of a credit for death taxes paid to a possession of the United States in the case of a decedent dying before September 3, 1958. No credit is allowable for interest or penalties paid in connection with foreign death taxes.

(2) In addition to the credit for foreign death taxes under section 2014, similar credits are allowed under death tax conventions with certain foreign countries. If credits against the Federal estate tax are allowable under section 2014, or under section 2014 and one or more death tax conventions, for death taxes paid to more than one country, the credits are combined and the aggregate amount is credited against the Federal estate tax, subject to the limitation provided for in paragraph (c) of § 20.2014-4. For application of the credit in cases involving a death tax convention, see § 20.2014-4.

(3) No credit is allowable under section 2014 in connection with property situated outside of the foreign country imposing the tax for which credit is claimed. However, such a credit may be allowable under certain death tax conventions. In the case of a tax imposed by a political subdivision of a foreign country, credit for the tax shall be allowed with respect to property having a situs in that foreign country, even

though, under the principles described in this subparagraph, the property has a situs in a political subdivision different from the one imposing the tax. Whether or not particular property of a decedent is situated in the foreign country imposing the tax is determined in accordance with the same principles that would be applied in determining whether or not similar property of a nonresident decedent not a citizen of the United States is situated within the United States for Federal estate tax purposes. See §§ 20.2104-1 and 20.2105-1. For example, under § 20.2104-1 shares of stock are deemed to be situated in the United States only if issued by a domestic corporation. Thus, a share of corporate stock is regarded as situated in the foreign country imposing the tax only if the issuing corporation is incorporated in that country. Further, under § 20.2105-1 amounts receivable as insurance on the life of a nonresident not a citizen of the United States at the time of his death are not deemed situated in the United States. Therefore, in determining the credit under section 2014 in the case of a decedent who was a citizen or resident of the United States, amounts receivable as insurance on the life of the decedent and payable under a policy issued by a corporation incorporated in a foreign country are not deemed situated in such foreign country. In addition, under § 20.2105-1 in the case of an estate of a nonresident not a citizen of the United States who died on or after November 14, 1966, a debt obligation of a domestic corporation is not considered to be situated in the United States if any interest thereon would be treated under section 862(a)(1) as income from sources without the United States by reason of section 861(a)(1)(B) (relating to interest received from a domestic corporation less than 20 percent of whose gross income for a 3-year period was derived from sources within the United States). Accordingly, a debt obligation the primary obligor on which is a corporation incorporated in the foreign country imposing the tax is not considered to be situated in that country if, under circumstances corresponding to those described in § 20.2105-1 less than 20 percent of the gross income of the corporation for the 3-year period was derived from sources within that country. Further, under § 20.2104-1 in the case of an estate of a nonresident not a citizen of the United States who died before November 14, 1966, a bond for the payment of money is not situated within the United States unless it is physically located in the United States. Accordingly, in the case of the estate of a decedent dying before November 14, 1966, a bond is deemed situated in the foreign country imposing the tax only if it is physically located in that country. Finally, under § 20.2105-1 moneys deposited in the United States with any person carrying on the banking business by or for a nonresident not a citizen of the United States who died before November 14, 1966, and who was not engaged in business in the United States at the time of death are not deemed situated in the United States. Therefore, an account with a foreign bank in the foreign country imposing the tax is not considered to be situated in that country under corresponding circumstances.

(4) Where a deduction is allowed under section 2053(d) for foreign death taxes paid with respect to a charitable gift, the credit for foreign death taxes is subject to further limitations as explained in § 20.2014-7.

(b) Limitations on credit. The credit for foreign death taxes is limited to the smaller of the following amounts:

(1) The amount of a particular foreign death tax attributable to property situated in the country imposing the tax and included in the decedent's gross estate for Federal estate tax purposes, computed as set forth in § 20.2014-2; or

(2) The amount of the Federal estate tax attributable to particular property situated in a foreign country, subjected to foreign death tax in that country, and included in the decedent's gross estate for Federal estate tax purposes, computed as set forth in § 20.2014-3.

(c) Credit allowable to estate of resident not a citizen. *(1)* In the case of an estate of a decedent dying before November 14, 1966, who was a resident but not a citizen of the United States, a credit is allowed to the estate under section 2014 only if the foreign country of which the decedent was a citizen or subject, in imposing foreign death taxes, allows a similar credit to the estates of citizens of the United States who were resident in that foreign country at the time of death.

(2) In the case of an estate of a decedent dying on or after November 14, 1966, who was a resident but not a citizen of the United States, a credit is allowed to the estate under section 2014 without regard to the similar credit requirement of subparagraph (1) of this paragraph unless the decedent was a citizen or subject of a foreign country with respect to which there is in effect at the time of the decedent's death a Presidential proclamation, as authorized by section 2014(h), reinstating the similar credit requirement. In the case of an estate of a decedent who was a resident of the United States and a citizen or subject of a foreign country with respect to which such a proclamation has been made, and who dies while the proclamation is in effect, a credit is allowed under section 2014 only if that foreign country, in imposing foreign death taxes, allows a similar credit to the estates of citizens of the United States who were resident in that foreign country at the time of death. The proclamation authorized by section 2014(h) for the reinstatement of the similar credit requirement with respect to the estates of citizens or subjects of a specific foreign country may be made by the President whenever he finds that—

(i) The foreign country, in imposing foreign death taxes, does not allow a similar credit to the estates of citizens of the United States who were resident in the foreign country at the time of death,

(ii) The foreign country, after having been requested to do so, has not acted to provide a similar credit to the estates of such citizens, and

(iii) It is in the public interest to allow the credit under section 2014 to the estates of citizens or subjects of the foreign country only if the foreign country allows a similar credit to the estates of citizens of the United States who were resident in the foreign country at the time of death.

The proclamation for the reinstatement of the similar credit requirement with respect to the estates of citizens or subjects of a specific foreign country may be revoked by the President. In that case, a credit is allowed under section 2014, to the estate of a decedent who was a citizen or subject of that foreign country and a resident of the United States at the time of death without regard to the similar credit requirement if the decedent dies after the proclamation reinstating the similar credit requirement has been revoked.

T.D. 6296, 6/23/58, amend T.D. 6526, 1/18/61, T.D. 6600, 5/28/62, T.D. 7296, 12/11/73.

§ 20.2014-2 "First limitation".

(a) The amount of a particular foreign death tax attributable to property situated in the country imposing the tax and included in the decedent's gross estate for Federal estate tax purposes is the "first limitation." Thus, the credit for any foreign death tax is limited to an amount, A, which bears the same ratio to B (the amount of the foreign death tax without allowance of credit, if any, for Federal estate tax) as C (the value of the property situated in the country imposing the foreign death tax, subjected to the foreign death tax, included in the gross estate and for which a deduction is not allowed under section 2053(d)) bears to D (the value of all property subjected to the foreign death tax). Stated algebraically, the "first limitation" (A) equals—

$$\frac{\text{Value of property in foreign country subjected to foreign death tax, included in gross estate and for which a deduction is not allowed under section 2053(d) (C)}}{\text{Value of all property subjected to foreign death tax (D)}} \times \text{Amount of foreign death tax (B)}$$

The values used in this proportion are the values determined for the purpose of the foreign death tax. The amount of the foreign death tax for which credit is allowable must be converted into United States money. The application of this paragraph may be illustrated by the following example:

Example. At the time of his death on June 1, 1966, the decedent, a citizen of the United States, owned stock in X Corporation (a corporation organized under the laws of Country Y) valued at $80,000. In addition, he owned bonds issued by Country Y valued at $80,000. The stock and bond certificates were in the United States. Decedent left by will $20,000 of the stock and $50,000 of the Country Y bonds to his surviving spouse. He left the rest of the stock and bonds to his son. Under the situs rules referred to in paragraph (a)(3) of § 20.2014-1 the stock is deemed situated in Country Y while the bonds are deemed to have their situs in the United States. (The bonds would be deemed to have their situs in Country Y if the decedent had died on or after November 14, 1966.) There is no death tax convention in existence between the United States and Country Y. The laws of Country Y provide for inheritance taxes computed as follows:

Inheritance tax of surviving spouse:	
Value of stock	$20,000
Value of bonds	50,000
Total value	70,000
Tax (16 percent rate)	11,200
Inheritance tax of son:	
Value of stock	60,000
Value of bonds	30,000
Total value	90,000
Tax (16 percent rate)	14,400

The "first limitation" on the credit for foreign death taxes is:

$$\frac{\$20{,}000 + \$60{,}000 \text{ (factor C of the ratio stated at § 20.2014-2(a))}}{\$70{,}000 + \$90{,}000 \text{ (factor D of the ratio stated at § 20.2014-2(a))}} \times (\$11{,}200 + \$14{,}400) \text{ (factor B of the ratio stated at the § 20.2014-2(a))} = 12{,}800$$

(b) If a foreign country imposes more than one kind of death tax or imposes taxes at different rates upon the several shares of an estate, or if a foreign country and a political subdivision or possession thereof each imposes a death tax, a "first limitation" is to be computed separately for each tax or rate and the results added in order to determine the total "first limitation." The application of this paragraph may be illustrated by the following example:

Example. The facts are the same as those contained in the example set forth in paragraph (a) of this section, except that the tax of the surviving spouse was computed at a 10 percent rate and amounted to $7,000, and the tax of the son was computed at a 20 percent rate and amounted to $18,000. In this case, the "first limitation" on the credit for foreign death taxes is computed as follows:

"First limitation" with respect to inheritance tax of surviving spouse:

$$\frac{\$20{,}000 \text{ (factor C of the ratio stated at § 20.2014-2(a))}}{\$70{,}000 \text{ (factor D of the ratio stated at § 20.2014-2(a))}} \times \$7{,}000 \text{ (factor B of the ratio stated at § 20.2014-2(a))} = \$\ 2{,}000$$

"First limitation" with respect to inheritance tax of son:

$$\frac{\$60{,}000 \text{ (factor C of the ratio stated at § 20.2014-2(a))}}{\$90{,}000 \text{ (factor D of the ratio stated at § 20.2014-2(a))}} \times \$18{,}000 \text{ (factor B of the ratio stated at § 20.2014-2(a))} = \$12{,}000$$

Total "first limitation" on the credit for foreign death taxes	14,000

T.D. 6296, 6/23/58, amend T.D. 6600, 5/28/62, T.D. 6684, 10/23/63, T.D. 7296, 12/11/73.

§ 20.2014-3 "Second limitation".

Caution: The Treasury has not yet amended Reg § 20.2014-3 to reflect changes made by P.L. 94-455.

(a) The amount of the Federal estate tax attributable to particular property situated in a foreign country, subjected to foreign death tax in that country, and included in the decedent's gross estate for Federal estate tax purposes is the "second limitation." Thus, the credit is limited to an amount, E, which bears the same ratio to F (the gross Federal estate tax, reduced by any credit for State death taxes under section 2011 and by any credit for gift tax under section 2012) as G (the "adjusted value of the property situated in the foreign country, subjected to foreign death tax, and included in the gross estate", computed as described in paragraph (b) of this section) bears to H (the value of the entire gross estate, reduced by the total amount of the deductions allowed under sections 2055 (charitable deduction) and 2056 (marital deduction)). Stated algebraically, the "second limitation" (E) equals

$$\frac{\text{“Adjusted value of the property situated in the foreign country, subjected to foreign death taxes, and included in the gross estate” (G)}}{\text{Value of entire gross estate, less charitable and marital deductions (H)}} \times \text{Gross Federal estate tax, less credits for State death taxes and gift tax (F)}$$

The values used in this proportion are the values determined for the purpose of the Federal estate tax.

(b) Adjustment is required to factor "G" of the ratio stated in paragraph (a) of this section if a deduction for foreign death taxes under section 2053(d), a charitable deduction under section 2055, or a marital deduction under section 2056 is allowed with respect to the foreign property. If a deduction for foreign death taxes is allowed, the value of the property situated in the foreign country, subjected to foreign death tax, and included in the gross estate does not include the value of any property in respect of which the deduction for foreign death taxes is allowed. See § 20.2014-7. If a charitable deduction or a marital deduction is allowed, the value of such foreign property (after exclusion of the value of any property in respect of which the deduction for foreign death taxes is allowed) is reduced as follows:

(1) If a charitable deduction or a marital deduction is allowed to a decedent's estate with respect to any part of the foreign property, except foreign property in respect of which a deduction for foreign death taxes is allowed, specifically bequeathed, devised, or otherwise specifically passing to a charitable organization or to the decedent's spouse, the value of the foreign property is reduced by the amount of the charitable deduction or marital deduction allowed with respect to such specific transfer. See example (1) of paragraph (c) of this section.

(2) If a charitable deduction or a marital deduction is allowed to a decedent's estate with respect to a bequest, devise or other transfer of an interest in a group of assets including both the foreign property and other property, the value of the foreign property is reduced by an amount, I, which bears the same ratio to J (the amount of the charitable deduction or marital deduction allowed with respect to such transfer of an interest in a group of assets) as K (the value of the foreign property, except foreign property in respect of which a deduction for foreign death taxes is allowed, included in the group of assets) bears to L (the value of the entire group of assets). As used in this subparagraph, the term "group of assets" has reference to those assets which, under applicable law, are chargeable with the charitable or marital transfer. See example (2) of paragraph (c) of this section.

Any reduction described in paragraph (b)(1) or (b)(2) of this section on account of the marital deduction must proportionately take into account, if applicable, the limitation on the aggregate amount of the marital deduction contained in § 20.2056(a)-1(c). See § 20.2014-3(c), Example 3.

(c) The application of paragraphs (a) and (b) of this section may be illustrated by the following examples. In each case, the computations relate to the amount of credit under section 2014 without regard to the amount of credit which may be allowable under an applicable death tax convention.

Example (1). (i) Decedent, a citizen and resident of the United States at the time of his death on February 1, 1967, left a gross estate of $1,000,000 which includes the following: shares of stock issued by a domestic corporation, valued at $750,000; bonds issued in 1960 by the United States and physically located in foreign Country X, valued at $50,000; and shares of stock issued by a Country X corporation, valued at $200,000, with respect to which death taxes were paid to Country X. Expenses, indebtedness, etc., amounted to $60,000. Decedent specifically bequeathed $40,000 of the stock issued by the Country X corporation to a U.S. charity and left the residue of his estate, in equal shares, to his son and daughter. The gross Federal estate tax is $266,500, and the credit for State death taxes is $27,600. Under the situs rules referred to in paragraph (a)(3) of § 20.2014-1, the shares of stock issued by the Country X corporation comprise the only property deemed to be situated in Country X. (The bonds also would be deemed to have their situs in Country X if the decedent had died before November 14, 1966.)

(ii) The "second limitation" on the credit for foreign death taxes is:

$$\frac{\text{\$200,000 − \$40,000 (factor G of the ratio stated at § 20.2014-3(a); see also § 20.2014-3(b)(1))}}{\text{\$1,000,000 − \$40,000 (factor H of the ratio stated at § 20.2014-3(a))}} \times \text{(\$266,500 − \$27,600) (factor F of the ratio stated at § 20.2014-3(a)) = \$39,816.67.}$$

The lesser of this amount and the amount of the "first limitation" (computed under § 20.2014-2) is the credit for foreign death taxes.

Example (2). (i) Decedent, a citizen and resident of the United States at the time of his death, left a gross estate of $1,000,000 which includes: shares of stock issued by a United States corporation, valued at $650,000; shares of stock issued by a Country X corporation, valued at $200,000; and life insurance, in the amount of $150,000, payable to a son. Expenses, indebtedness, etc., amounted to $40,000. The decedent made a specific bequest of $25,000 of the Country X corporation stock to Charity A and a general bequest of $100,000 to Charity B. The residue of his estate was left to his daughter. The gross Federal estate tax is $242,450 and the credit for State death taxes is $24,480. Under these facts and applicable law, neither the stock of the Country X corporation specifically bequeathed to Charity A nor the insurance payable to the son could be charged with satisfying the bequest to Charity B. Therefore, the "group of assets" which could be so charged is limited to stock of the Country X corporation valued at $175,000 and stock of the United States corporation valued at $650,000.

(ii) Factor "G" of the ratio which is used in determining the "second limitation" is computed as follows:

Value of property situated in Country X		$200,000.00
Less:		
Reduction described in § 20.2014-3(b)(1)	$ 25,000.00	
Reduction described in § 20.2014-3(b)(2) = $\frac{\$175{,}000 \text{ (factor K of the ratio stated at § 20.2014-3(b)(2))}}{\$175{,}000 + \$650{,}000 \text{ (factor L of the ratio stated at § 20.2014-3(b)(2))}} \times$ $100,000 (factor J of the ratio stated at § 20.2014-3(b)(2)) =	21,212.12	
		46,212.12
Factor "G" of the ratio		153,787.88

(iii) In this case, the "second limitation" on the credit for foreign death taxes is:

$$\frac{\$153{,}787.88 \text{ (factor G of the ratio stated at § 20.2014-3(a); see also subdivision (ii) above)}}{\$1{,}000{,}000 - \$125{,}000 \text{ (factor H of the ratio stated at § 20.2014-3(a))}} \times (\$242{,}450 - \$24{,}480) \text{ (factor F of the ratio stated at § 20.2014-3(a))} = \$38{,}309.88.$$

Example (3). (i) Decedent, a citizen and resident of the United States at the time of his death, left a gross estate of $850,000 which includes: shares by United States corporations, valued at $440,000; real estate located in the United States, valued at $110,000; and shares of stock issued by Country X corporations, valued at $300,000. Expenses, indebtedness, etc., amounted to $50,000. Decedent devised $40,000 in real estate to a United States charity. In addition, he bequeathed to his wife $200,000 in United States stocks and $300,000 in Country X stocks. The residue of his estate passed to his children. The gross Federal estate tax is $81,700 and the credit for State death taxes is $5,520.

(ii) Decedent's adjusted gross estate is $800,000 (i. e., $850,000, gross estate less $50,000, expenses, indebtedness, etc.). Assume that the limitation imposed by section 2056(c), as in effect before 1982, is applicable so that the aggregate allowable marital deduction is limited to one-half the adjusted gross estate, or $400,000 (which is 50 percent of $800,000). Factor "G" of the ratio which is used in determining the "second limitation" is computed as follows:

Value of property situated in Country X		$300,000
Less: Reduction described in § 20.2014-3(b)(1) determined as follows (see also end of Sec. 20.2014-3(b))—		
Total amount of bequests which qualify for the marital deduction:		
Specific bequest of Country X stock	$300,000	
Specific bequest of United States stock	200,000	
	500,000	
Limitation on aggregate marital deduction under section 2056(c)	400,000	
Part of specific bequest of Country X stock with respect to which the marital deduction is allowed— $\left(\frac{\$400{,}000}{\$500{,}000} \times \$300{,}000\right)$		240,000
Factor "G" of the ratio		60,000

(iii) Thus, the "second limitation" on the credit for foreign death taxes is

$$\frac{\$60{,}000 \text{ (factor G of the ratio stated at § 20.2014-3(a); see also subdivision (ii) above)}}{\$850{,}000 - \$40{,}000 - \$400{,}000 \text{ (factor H of the ratio stated at § 20.2014-3(a))}} \times (\$81{,}700 - \$5{,}520) \text{ (factor F of the ratio stated at § 20.2014-3(a))} = \$11{,}148.29.$$

(d) If the foreign country imposes more than one kind of death tax or imposes taxes at different rates upon the several shares of an estate, or if the foreign country and a political subdivision or possession thereof each imposes a death tax, the "second limitation" is still computed by applying the ratio set forth in paragraph (a) of this section. Factor "G" of the ratio is determined by taking into consideration the combined value of the foreign property which is subjected to each different tax or different rate. The combined value, however, cannot exceed the value at which such property was included in the gross estate for Federal estate tax purposes. Thus, if Country X imposes a tax on the inheritance of a surviving spouse at a 10-percent rate and on the inheritance of a son at a 20-percent rate, the combined value of their inheritances is taken into consideration in determining factor "G" of the ratio, which is then used in computing the "second limitation." However, the "first limitation" is computed as provided in paragraph (b) of § 20.2014-2. The lesser of the "first limitation" and the "second limitation" is the credit for foreign death taxes.

T.D. 6296, 6/23/58, amend T.D. 6600, 5/28/62, T.D. 7296, 12/11/73, T.D. 8522, 2/28/94.

§ 20.2014-4 Application of credit in cases involving a death tax convention.

Caution: The Treasury has not yet amended Reg § 20.2014-4 to reflect changes made by P.L. 94-455.

(a) In general. *(1)* If credit for a particular foreign death tax is authorized by a death tax convention, there is allowed either the credit provided for by the convention or the credit provided for by section 2014, whichever is the more beneficial to the estate. For cases where credit may be taken under both the death tax convention and section 2014, see paragraph (b) of this section. The application of this paragraph may be illustrated by the following example:

Example. (i) Decedent, a citizen of the United States and a domiciliary of foreign Country X at the time of his death on December 1, 1966, left a gross estate of $1 million which includes the following: Shares of stock issued by a Country X corporation, valued at $400,000; bonds issued in 1962 by the United States and physically located in Country X, valued at $350,000; and real estate located in the United States, valued at $250,000. Expenses, indebtedness, etc., amounted to $50,000. Decedent left his entire estate to his son. There is in effect a death tax convention between the United States and Country X which provides for the allowance of credit by the United States for succession duties imposed by the national government of Country X. The gross Federal estate tax is $307,200, and the credit for State death taxes is $33,760. Country X imposed a net succession duty on the stocks and bonds of $180,000. Under the situs rules referred to in paragraph (a)(3) of § 20.2014-1, the shares of stock comprise the only property deemed to be situated in Country X. (If the decedent had died before November 14, 1966, the bonds also would be deemed to have their situs in Country X.) Under the convention, both the stocks and the bonds are deemed to be situated in Country X. In this example all figures are rounded to the nearest dollar.

(ii) (a) The credit authorized by the convention for death taxes imposed by Country X is computed as follows:

(1) Country X tax attributable to property situated in Country X and subjected to tax by both countries

$$\left(\frac{\$750{,}000}{\$750{,}000} \times 180{,}000\right) \ldots\ldots\ldots\ \$180{,}000$$

(2) Federal estate tax attributable to property situated in Country X and subjected to tax by both countries

$$\left(\frac{\$750{,}000}{\$1{,}000{,}000} \times \$273{,}440\right) \ldots\ldots\ldots\ 205{,}080$$

(3) Credit (Subdivision (1) or (2), whichever is less) $180,000

(b) The credit authorized by section 2014 for death taxes imposed by Country X is computed as follows:

(1) "First limitation" computed under § 20.2014-2

$$\left(\frac{\$400{,}000}{\$750{,}000} \times \$180{,}000\right) \ldots\ldots\ldots\ \$96{,}000$$

(2) "Second limitation" computed under § 20.2014-3

$$\left(\frac{\$400{,}000}{\$1{,}000{,}000} \times \$273{,}440\right) \ldots\ldots\ldots\ 109{,}376$$

(3) Credit (subdivision (1) or (2), whichever is less) $96,000

(iii) On the basis of the facts contained in this example, the credit of $180,000 authorized by the convention is the more beneficial to the estate.

(2) It should be noted that the greater of the treaty credit and the statutory credit is not necessarily the more beneficial to the estate. Such is the situation, for example, in those cases which involve both a foreign death tax credit and a credit under section 2013 for tax on prior transfers. The reason is that the amount of the credit for tax on prior transfers may differ depending upon whether the credit for foreign death tax is taken under the treaty or under the statute. Therefore, under certain circumstances, the advantage of taking the greater of the treaty credit and the statutory credit may be more than offset by a resultant smaller credit for tax on prior transfers. The solution is to compute the net estate tax payable first on the assumption that the treaty credit will be taken and then on the assumption that the statutory credit will be taken. Such computations will indicate whether the treaty credit or the statutory credit is in fact the more beneficial to the estate.

(b) Taxes imposed by both a foreign country and a political subdivision thereof. If death taxes are imposed by both a foreign country with which the United States has entered into a death tax convention and one or more of its possessions or political subdivisions, there is allowed, against the tax imposed by section 2001—

(1) A credit for the combined death taxes paid to the foreign country and its political subdivisions or possessions as provided for by the convention, or

(2) A credit for the combined death taxes paid to the foreign country and its political subdivisions or possessions as determined under section 2014, or

(3) (i) A credit for that amount of the combined death taxes paid to the foreign country and its political subdivisions or possessions as is allowable under the convention, and

(ii) A credit under section 2014 for the death taxes paid to each political subdivision or possession, but only to the extent such death taxes are not directly or indirectly creditable under the convention,

whichever is the most beneficial to the estate. The application of this paragraph may be illustrated by the following example:

Example. (1) Decedent, a citizen of the United States and a domiciliary of Province Y of foreign Country X at the time of his death on February 1, 1966, left a gross estate of $250,000 which includes the following: Bonds issued by Country X physically located in Province Y, valued at $75,000; bonds issued by Province Z of Country X and physically located in the United States, valued at $50,000; and shares of stock issued by a domestic corporation, valued at $125,000. Decedent left his entire estate to his son. Expenses, indebtedness etc., amounted to $26,000. The Federal estate tax after allowance of the credit for State death taxes is $38,124. Province Y imposed a death tax of 8 percent on the Country X bonds located therein which amounted to $6,000. No death tax was imposed by Province Z. Country X imposed a death tax of 15 percent on the Country X bonds and the Province Z bonds which amounted to $18,750 before allowance of any credit for the death tax of Province Y. Country X allows against its death taxes a credit for death taxes paid to any of its provinces on property which it also taxes, but only to the extent of one-half of the Country X death tax attributable to the property, or the amount of death taxes paid to its province, whichever is less. Country X, therefore, allowed a credit of $5,625 for the death taxes paid to Province Y. There is in effect a death tax convention between the United States and Country X which provides for allowance of credit by the United States for death taxes imposed by the national government of Country X. The death tax convention provides that in computing the "first limitation" for the credit under the convention, the tax of Country X is not to be reduced by the amount of the credit allowed for provincial taxes. Under the situs rules described in paragraph (a)(3) of § 20.2014-1, only the Country X bonds located in Province Y are deemed situated in Country X. (The bonds issued by Province Z also would be deemed to have their situs in Country X if the decedent had died on or after November 14, 1966.) Under the convention, both the Country X bonds and the Province Z bonds are deemed to be situated in Country X. In this example all figures are rounded to the nearest dollar.

(2) (i) The credit authorized by section 2014 for death taxes imposed by Country X (which includes death taxes imposed by Province Y according to § 20.2014-1(a)(1)) is computed as follows:

(a) "first limitation" with respect to tax imposed by national government of Country X (computed under paragraph (b) of § 20.2014-2)

(1) Gross Country X death tax attributable to Country X bonds (before allowance of provincial death taxes)

$\frac{\$75{,}000}{\$125{,}000} \times \$18{,}750$ $11,250

(2) Less credit for Province Y death taxes on such bonds 5,625

(3) Net Country X death tax attributable to such bonds 5,625

(b) "First limitation" with respect to tax imposed by Province Y (computed under paragraph (b) of § 20.2014-2)

$\frac{\$75{,}000}{\$75{,}000} \times \$6{,}000$ 6,000

(c) Total "first limitation" 11,625

(d) "Second limitation" (computed under paragraph (d) of § 20.2014-3)

$\frac{\$75{,}000}{\$250{,}000} \times \$38{,}124$ 11,437

(e) Credit (subdivision (c) or (d), whichever is less) 11,437

(ii) The credit authorized under the death tax convention between the United States and Country X is computed as follows:

(a) Country X tax attributable to property situated in Country X and subject to tax by both countries

$\frac{\$125{,}000}{\$125{,}000} \times \$18{,}750$ $18,750

(b) Federal estate tax attributable to property situated in Country X and subjected to tax by both countries

$\frac{\$125{,}000}{\$250{,}000} \times 38{,}124$ 19,062

(c) Credit (subdivision (a) or (b), whichever is less) 18,750

(3) If the estate takes a credit for death taxes under the convention, it would receive a credit of $18,750 which would include an indirect credit of $5,625 for death taxes paid to Province Y. The death tax of Province Y which was not directly or indirectly creditable under the convention is $375 ($6,000 − $5,625). A credit for this tax would also be allowed under section 2014 but only to the extent of $187, as the amount of credit for the combined foreign death taxes is limited to the amount of Federal estate tax attributable to the property, determined in accordance with the rules prescribed for computing the "second limitation" under section 2014. In this case, the "second limitation" under section 2014 on the taxes attributable to the Country X bonds is $11,437 (see computation set forth in (2)(i)(d) of this example). The amount of credit under the convention for taxes attributable to Country X bonds is $11,250 ($75,000/$125,000 × $18,750). Inasmuch as the "second limitation" under section 2014 in respect of the Country X bonds ($11,437) exceeds the amount of the credit allowed under the convention in respect of the Country X bonds ($11,250) by $187, the additional credit allowable under section 2014 for the death taxes paid to Province Y not directly or indirectly creditable under the convention is limited to $187.

(c) Taxes imposed by two foreign countries with respect to the same property. It is stated as a general rule in paragraph (a)(2) of § 20.2014-1 that if credits against the Federal estate tax are allowable under section 2014, or under section 2014 and one or more death tax conventions, for death taxes paid to more than one country, the credits are combined and the aggregate amount is credited against the Federal estate tax. This rule may result in credit being allowed for taxes imposed by two different countries upon the same item of property. If such is the case, the total amount of the credits with respect to such property is limited to the amount of the Federal estate tax attributable to the property, determined in accordance with the rules prescribed for computing the "second limitation" set forth in § 20.2014-3. The application of this section may be illustrated by the following example:

Example. The decedent, a citizen of the United States and a domiciliary of Country X at the time of his death on May 1, 1967, left a taxable estate which included bonds issued by Country Z and physically located in Country X. Each of the three countries involved imposed death taxes on the Country Z bonds. Assume that under the provisions of a treaty between the United States and Country X the estate is entitled to a credit against the Federal estate tax for death taxes imposed by Country X on the bonds in the maximum amount of $20,000. Assume, also, that since the decedent died after November 13, 1966, so that under the situs rules referred to in paragraph (a)(3) of § 20.2014-1 the bonds are deemed to have their situs in Country Z, the estate is entitled to a credit against the Federal estate tax for death taxes imposed by Country Z on the bonds in the maximum amount of $10,000. Finally, assume that the Federal estate tax attributable to the bonds is $25,000. Under these circumstances, the credit allowed the estate with respect to the bonds would be limited to $25,000.

T.D. 6296, 6/23/58, amend T.D. 6742, 6/22/64, T.D. 7296, 12/11/73.

§ 20.2014-5 Proof of credit.

(a) If the foreign death tax has not been determined and paid by the time the Federal estate tax return required by section 6018 is filed, credit may be claimed on the return in an estimated amount. However, before credit for the foreign death tax is finally allowed, satisfactory evidence, such as a statement by an authorized official of each country, possession or political subdivision thereof imposing the tax, must be submitted on Form 706CE certifying: (1) The full amount of the tax (exclusive of any interest or penalties), as computed before allowance of any credit, remission, or relief; (2) the amount of any credit, allowance, remission, or relief, and other pertinent information, including the nature of the allowance and a description of the property to which it pertains; (3) the net foreign death tax payable after any such allowance; (4) the date on which the death tax was paid, or if not all paid at one time, the date and amount of each partial payment; and (5) a list of the property situated in the foreign country and subjected to its tax, showing a description and the value of the property. Satisfactory evidence must also be submitted showing that no refund of the death tax is pending and none is authorized or, if any refund is pending or has been authorized, its amount and other pertinent information. See also section 2016 and § 20.2016-1 for requirements if foreign death taxes claimed as a credit are subsequently recovered.

(b) The following information must also be submitted whenever applicable:

(1) If any of the property subjected to the foreign death tax was situated outside of the country imposing the tax, the description of each item of such property and its value.

(2) If more than one inheritance or succession is involved with respect to which credit is claimed, or if the foreign country, possession or political subdivision thereof imposes more than one kind of death tax, or if both the foreign country and a possession or political subdivision thereof each imposes a death tax, a separate computation with respect to each inheritance or succession tax.

(c) In addition to the information required under paragraphs (a) and (b) of this section, the district director may require the submission of any further proof deemed necessary to establish the right to the credit.

T.D. 6296, 6/23/58.

§ 20.2014-6 Period of limitations on credit.

The credit for foreign death taxes under section 2014 is limited to those taxes which were actually paid and for which a credit was claimed within four years after the filing of the estate tax return for the decedent's estate. If, however, a petition has been filed with The Tax Court of the United States for the redetermination of a deficiency within the time prescribed in section 6213(a), the credit is limited to those taxes which were actually paid and for which a credit was claimed within four years after the filing of the return, or before the expiration of 60 days after the decision of the Tax Court becomes final, whichever period is the last to expire. Similarly, if an extension of time has been granted under section 6161 for payment of the tax shown on the return, or of a deficiency, the credit is limited to those taxes which were actually paid and for which a credit was claimed within four years after the filing of the return, or before the date of the expiration of the period of the extension, whichever period is the last to expire. See section 2015 for the applicable period of limitations for credit for foreign death taxes on reversionary or remainder interests if an election is made under section 6163(a) to postpone payment of the estate tax attributable to reversionary or remainder interests. If a claim for refund based on the credit for foreign death taxes is filed within the applicable period described in this section, a refund may be made despite the general limitation provisions of sections 6511 and 6512. Any refund based on the credit for foreign death taxes shall be made without interest.

T.D. 6296, 6/23/58.

§ 20.2014-7 Limitation on credit if a deduction for foreign death taxes is allowed under section 2053(d).

Caution: The Treasury has not yet amended Reg § 20.2014-7 to reflect changes made by P.L. 94-455.

If a deduction is allowed under section 2053(d) for foreign death taxes paid with respect to a charitable gift, the credit for foreign death taxes is subject to special limitations. In such a case the property described in subparagraphs (A), (B), and (C) of paragraphs (1) and (2) of section 2014(b) shall not include any property with respect to which a deduction is allowed under section 2053(d). The application of this section may be illustrated by the following example:

Example. The decedent, a citizen of the United States, died July 1, 1955, leaving a gross estate of $1,200,000 consisting of: Shares of stock issued by United States corporations, valued at $600,000; bonds issued by the United States Government physically located in the United States, valued at $300,000; and shares of stock issued by a Country X corporation, valued at $300,000. Expenses, indebtedness, etc., amounted to $40,000. The decedent made specific bequests of $400,000 of the United States corporation stock to a niece and $100,000 of the Country X corporation stock to a nephew. The residue of his estate was left to charity. There is no death tax convention in existence between the United States and Country X. The Country X tax imposed was at a 50-percent rate on all beneficiaries. A State inheritance tax of $20,000 was imposed on the niece and nephew. The decedent did not provide in his will for the payment of the death taxes, and under local law the Federal estate tax is payable from the general estate, the same as administration expenses.

Distribution of the Estate

Gross estate		$1,200,000.00
Debts and charges	$ 40,000.00	
Bequest of U.S. corporation stock to niece	400,000.00	
Bequest of country X corporation stock to nephew	100,000.00	
Net Federal estate tax	136,917.88	676,917.88
Residue before country X tax		523,082.12
Country X succession tax on charity		100,000.00
Charitable deduction		423,082.12

Taxable Estate and Federal Estate Tax

Gross estate		$1,200,000.00
Debts and charges	$ 40,000.00	
Deduction of foreign death tax under section 2053(d)	100,000.00	
Charitable deduction	423,082.12	
Exemption	60,000.00	623,082.12
Taxable estate		576,917.88
Gross estate tax		172,621.26
Credit for State death taxes		15,476.72
Gross estate tax less credit for State death taxes		157,144.54
Credit for foreign death taxes		20,226.66
Net Federal estate tax		136,917.88

Credit for Foreign Death Taxes
Country X Tax

Succession tax on nephew:	
Value of stock of country X corporation	$ 100,000
Tax (50% rate)	50,000
Succession tax on charity:	
Value of stock of country X corporation	200,000
Tax (50% rate)	100,000

Computation of Exclusion Under Section 2014(b)

Value of property situated in country X	$ 300,000
Value of property in respect of which a deduction is allowed under section 2053(d)	200,000
Value of property situated within country X, subjected to tax, and included in gross estate as limited by section 2014(f)	100,000

First Limitation, § 20.2014-2(a)

$100,000 (factor C of the ratio stated at § 20.2014-2(a)) / $100,000 + $200,000 (factor D of the ratio stated at § 20.2014-2(a)) × ($50,000 + $100,000) (factor B of the ratio stated at § 20.2014-2(a)) = $ 50,000.00

Second Limitation, § 20.2014-3(a)

$100,000 (factor G of the ratio stated at § 20.2014-3(a)) (as limited by section 2014(f)) / $1,200,000 − $423,082.12 (factor H of the ratio stated at § 20.2014-3(a)) × (172,621.26 − $15,476.72) (factor F of the ratio stated at § 20.2014-3(a)) = $ 20,226.66

T.D. 6600, 5/28/62.

§ 20.2015-1 Credit for death taxes on remainders.

(a) If the executor of an estate elects under section 6163(a) to postpone the time for payment of any portion of the Federal estate tax attributable to a reversionary or remainder interest in property, credit is allowed under sections 2011 and 2014 against that portion of the Federal estate tax for State death taxes and foreign death taxes attributable to the reversionary or remainder interest if the State death taxes or foreign death taxes are paid and if credit therefor is claimed either—

(1) Within the time provided for in sections 2011 and 2014, or

(2) Within the time for payment of the tax imposed by section 2001 or 2101 as postponed under section 6163(a) and as extended under section 6163(b) (on account of undue hardship) or, if the precedent interest terminated before July

5, 1958, within 60 days after the termination of the preceding interest or interests in the property. The allowance of credit, however, is subject to the other limitations contained in sections 2011 and 2014 and, in the case of the estate of a decedent who was a nonresident not a citizen of the United States, in section 2102(b).

(b) In applying the rule stated in paragraph (a) of this section, credit for State death taxes or foreign death taxes paid within the time provided in sections 2011 and 2014 is applied first to the portion of the Federal estate tax payment of which is not postponed, and any excess is applied to the balance of the Federal estate tax. However, credit for State death taxes or foreign death taxes not paid within the time provided in section 2011 or 2014 is allowable only against the portion of the Federal estate tax attributable to the reversionary or remainder interest, and only for State or foreign death taxes attributable to that interest. If a State death tax or a foreign death tax is imposed upon both a reversionary or remainder interest and upon other property, without a definite apportionment of the tax, the amount of the tax deemed attributable to the reversionary or remainder interest is an amount which bears the same ratio to the total tax as the value of the reversionary or remainder interest bears to the value of the entire property with respect to which the tax was imposed. In applying this ratio, adjustments consistent with those required under paragraph (c) of § 20.6163-1 must be made.

(c) The application of this section may be illustrated by the following examples:

Example (1). One-third of the Federal estate tax was attributable to a remainder interest in real property located in State Y, and two-thirds of the Federal estate tax was attributable to other property located in State X. The payment of the tax attributable to the remainder interest was postponed under the provisions of section 6163(a). The maximum credit allowable for State death taxes under the provisions of section 2011 is $12,000. Therefore, of the maximum credit allowable, $4,000 is attributable to the remainder interest and $8,000 is attributable to the other property. Within the 4-year period provided for in section 2011, inheritance tax in the amount of $9,000 was paid to State X in connection with the other property. With respect to this $9,000, $8,000 (the maximum amount allowable) is allowed as a credit against the Federal estate tax attributable to the other property, and $1,000 is allowed as a credit against the postponed tax. The life estate or other precedent interest expired after July 4, 1958. After the expiration of the 4-year period but before the expiration of the period of postponement elected under section 6163(a) and of the period of extension granted under section 6163(b) for payment of the tax, inheritance tax in the amount of $5,000 was paid to State Y in connection with the remainder interest. As the maximum credit allowable with respect to the remainder interest is $4,000 and $1,000 has already been allowed as a credit, an additional $3,000 will be credited against the Federal estate tax attributable to the remainder interest. It should be noted that if the life estate or other precedent interest had expired after the expiration of the 4-year period but before July 5, 1958, the same result would be reached only if the inheritance tax had been paid to State Y before the expiration of 60 days after the termination of the life estate or other precedent interest.

Example (2). The facts are the same as in example (1), except that within the 4-year period inheritance tax in the amount of $2,500 was paid to State Y with respect to the remainder interest and inheritance tax in the amount of $7,500 was paid to State X with respect to the other property. The amount of $8,000 is allowed as a credit against the Federal estate tax attributable to the other property and the amount of $2,000 is allowed as a credit against the postponed tax. The life estate or other precedent interest expired after July 4, 1958. After the expiration of the 4-year period but before the expiration of the period of postponement elected under section 6163(a) and of the period of extension granted under section 6163(b) for payment of the tax, inheritance tax in the amount of $5,000 was paid to State Y in connection with the remainder interest. As the maximum credit allowable with respect to the remainder interest is $4,000 and $2,000 already has been allowed as a credit, an additional $2,000 will be credited against the Federal estate tax attributable to the remainder interest. It should be noted that if the life estate or other precedent interest had expired after the expiration of the 4-year period but before July 5, 1958, the same result would be reached only if the inheritance tax had been paid to State Y before the expiration of 60 days after the termination of the life estate or other precedent interest.

Example (3). The facts are the same as in example (2), except that no payment was made to State Y within the 4-year period. The amount of $7,500 is allowed as a credit against the Federal estate tax attributable to the other property. After termination of the life interest additional credit will be allowed in the amount of $4,000 against the Federal estate tax attributable to the remainder interest. Since the payment of $5,000 was made to State Y following the expiration of the 4-year period, no part of the payment may be allowed as a credit against the Federal estate tax attributable to the other property.

T.D. 6296, 6/23/58, amend T.D. 6526, 1/18/61, T.D. 7296, 12/11/73.

§ 20.2016-1 Recovery of death taxes claimed as credit.

In accordance with the provisions of section 2016, the executor (or any other person) receiving a refund of any State death taxes or foreign death taxes claimed as a credit under section 2011 or section 2014 shall notify the district director of the refund within 30 days of its receipt. The notice shall contain the following information:

(a) The name of the decedent;

(b) The date of the decedent's death;

(c) The property with respect to which the refund was made;

(d) The amount of the refund, exclusive of interest;

(e) The date of the refund; and

(f) The name and address of the person receiving the refund.

If the refund was in connection with foreign death taxes claimed as a credit under section 2014, the notice shall also contain a statement showing the amount of interest, if any, paid by the foreign country on the refund. Finally, the person filing the notice shall furnish the district director such additional information as he may request. Any Federal estate tax found to be due by reason of the refund is payable by the person or persons receiving it, upon notice and demand, even though the refund is received after the expiration of the period of limitations set forth in section 6501 (see section 6501(c)(5)). If the tax found to be due results from a refund of foreign death tax claimed as a credit under section 2014, such tax shall not bear interest for any period before the receipt of the refund, except to the extent that interest was paid by the foreign country on the refund.

T.D. 6296, 6/23/58.

§ 20.2031-0 Table of contents.

This section lists the section headings and undesignated center headings that appear in the regulations under section 2031.

T.D. 8540, 6/9/94, amend T.D. 8819, 4/29/99, T.D. 8886, 6/9/2000, T.D. 9448, 5/1/2009.

§ 20.2031-1 Definition of gross estate; valuation of property.

(a) Definition of gross estate. Except as otherwise provided in this paragraph the value of the gross estate of a decedent who was a citizen or resident of the United States at the time of his death is the total value of the interests described in sections 2033 through 2044. The gross estate of a decedent who died before October 17, 1962, does not include real property situated outside the United States (as defined in paragraph (b)(1) of § 20.0-1). Except as provided in paragraph (c) of this section (relating to the estates of decedents dying after October 16, 1962, and before July 1, 1964), in the case of a decedent dying after October 16, 1962, real property situated outside the United States which comes within the scope of sections 2033 through 2044 is included in the gross estate to the same extent as any other property coming within the scope of those sections. In arriving at the value of the gross estate the interests described in sections 2033 through 2044 are valued as described in this section, §§ 20.2031-2 through 20.2031-9 and § 20.2032-1. The contents of sections 2033 through 2044 are, in general, as follows:

(1) Sections 2033 and 2034 are concerned mainly with interests in property passing through the decedent's probate estate. Section 2033 includes in the decedent's gross estate any interest that the decedent had in property at the time of his death. Section 2034 provides that any interest of the decedent's surviving spouse in the decedent's property, such as dower or curtesy, does not prevent the inclusion of such property in the decedent's gross estate.

(2) Sections 2035 through 2038 deal with interests in property transferred by the decedent during his life under such circumstances as to bring the interests within the decedent's gross estate. Section 2035 includes in the decedent's gross estate property transferred in contemplation of death, even though the decedent had no interest in, or control over, the property at the time of his death. Section 2036 provides for the inclusion of transferred property with respect to which the decedent retained the income or the power to designate who shall enjoy the income. Section 2037 includes in the decedent's gross estate certain transfers under which the beneficial enjoyment of the property could be obtained only by surviving the decedent. Section 2038 provides for the inclusion of transferred property if the decedent had at the time of his death the power to change the beneficial enjoyment of the property. It should be noted that there is considerable overlap in the application of sections 2036 through 2038 with respect to reserved powers, so that transferred property may be includible in the decedent's gross estate in varying degrees under more than one of those sections.

(3) Sections 2039 through 2042 deal with special kinds of property and powers. Sections 2039 and 2040 concern annuities and jointly held property respectively. Section 2041 deals with powers held by the decedent over the beneficial enjoyment of property not originating with the decedent. Section 2042 concerns insurance under policies on the life of the decedent.

(4) Section 2043 concerns the sufficiency of consideration for transfers made by the decedent during his life. This has a bearing on the amount to be included in the decedent's gross estate under sections 2035 through 2038, and 2041. Section 2044 deals with retroactivity.

(b) Valuation of property in general. The value of every item of property includible in a decedent's gross estate under sections 2031 through 2044 is its fair market value at the time of the decedent's death, except that if the executor elects the alternate valuation method under section 2032, it is the fair market value thereof at the date, and with the adjustments, prescribed in that section. The fair market value is the price at which the property would change hands between a willing buyer and a willing seller, neither being under any compulsion to buy or to sell and both having reasonable knowledge of relevant facts. The fair market value of a particular item of property includible in the decedent's gross estate is not to be determined by a forced sale price. Nor is the fair market value of an item of property to be determined by the sale price of the item in a market other than that in which such item is most commonly sold to the public, taking into account the location of the item wherever appropriate. Thus, in the case of an item of property includible in the decedent's gross estate, which is generally obtained by the public in the retail market, the fair market value of such an item of property is the price at which the item or a comparable item would be sold at retail. For example, the fair market value of an automobile (an article generally obtained by the public in the retail market) includible in the decedent's gross estate is the price for which an automobile of the same or approximately the same description, make, model, age, condition, etc., could be purchased by a member of the general public and not the price for which the particular automobile of the decedent would be purchased by a dealer in used automobiles. Examples of items of property which are generally sold to the public at retail may be found in §§ 20.2031-6 and 20.2031-8. The value is generally to be determined by ascertaining as a basis the fair market value as of the applicable valuation date of each unit of property. For example, in the case of shares of stock or bonds, such unit of property is generally a share of stock or a bond. Livestock, farm machinery, harvested and growing crops must generally be itemized and the value of each item separately returned. Property shall not be returned at the value at which it is assessed for local tax purposes unless that value represents the fair market value as of the applicable valuation date. All relevant facts and elements of value as of the applicable valuation date shall be considered in every case. The value of items of property which were held by the decedent for sale in the course of a business generally should be reflected in the value of the business. For valuation of interests in businesses, see § 20.2031-3. See § 20.2031-2 and §§ 20.2031-4 through 20.2031-8 for further information concerning the valuation of other particular kinds of property. For certain circumstances under which the sale of an item of property at a price below its fair market value may result in a deduction for the estate, see paragraph (d)(2) of § 20.2053-3.

(c) Real property situated outside the United States; gross estate of decedent dying after October 16, 1962, and before July 1, 1964. *(1) In general.* In the case of a decedent dying after October 16, 1962, and before July 1, 1964, the value of real property situated outside the United States (as defined in paragraph (b)(1) of § 20.0-1) is not included in the gross estate of the decedent—

(i) Under section 2033, 2034, 2035(a), 2036(a), 2037(a), or 2038(a) to the extent the real property, or the decedent's interest in it, was acquired by the decedent before February 1, 1962;

(ii) Under section 2040 to the extent such property or interest was acquired by the decedent before February 1, 1962, or was held by the decedent and the survivor in a joint tenancy or tenancy by the entirety before February 1, 1962; or

(iii) Under section 2041(a) to the extent that before February 1, 1962, such property or interest was subject to a general power of appointment (as defined in section 2041) possessed by the decedent.

(2) Certain property treated as acquired before February 1, 1962. For purposes of this paragraph real property situated outside the United States (including property held by the decedent and the survivor in a joint tenancy or tenancy by the entirety), or an interest in such property or a general power of appointment in respect of such property, which was acquired by the decedent after January 31, 1962, is treated as acquired by the decedent before February 1, 1962, if

(i) Such property, interest, or power was acquired by the decedent by gift within the meaning of section 2511, or from a prior decedent by devise or inheritance, or by reason of death, form of ownership, or other conditions (including the exercise or nonexercise of a power of appointment); and

(ii) Before February 1, 1962, the donor or prior decedent had acquired the property or his interest therein or had possessed a power of appointment in respect thereof.

(3) Certain property treated as acquired after January 31, 1962. For purposes of this paragraph that portion of capital additions or improvements made after January 31, 1962, to real property situated outside the United States is, to the extent that it materially increases the value of the property, treated as real property acquired after January 31, 1962. Accordingly, the gross estate may include the value of improvements on unimproved real property, such as office buildings, factories, houses, fences, drainage ditches, and other capital items, and the value of capital additions and improvements to existing improvements, placed on real property after January 31, 1962, whether or not the value of such real property or existing improvements is included in the gross estate.

T.D. 6296, 6/23/58, amend T.D. 6684, 10/23/63, T.D. 6826, 6/14/65.

§ 20.2031-2 Valuation of stocks and bonds.

(a) In general. The value of stocks and bonds is the fair market value per share or bond on the applicable valuation date.

(b) Based on selling prices. *(1)* In general, if there is a market for stocks or bonds, on a stock exchange, in an over-the-counter market, or otherwise, the mean between the highest and lowest quoted selling prices on the valuation date is the fair market value per share or bond. If there were no sales on the valuation date but there were sales on dates within a reasonable period both before and after the valuation date, the fair market value is determined by taking a weighted average of the means between the highest and lowest sales on the nearest date before and the nearest date after the valuation date. The average is to be weighted inversely by the respective numbers of trading days between the selling dates and the valuation date. If the stocks or bonds are listed on more than one exchange, the records of the exchange where the stocks or bonds are principally dealt in should be employed if such records are available in a generally available listing or publication of general circulation. In the event that such records are not so available and such stocks or bonds are listed on a composite listing of combined exchanges available in a generally available listing or publication of general circulation, the records of such combined exchanges should be employed. In valuing listed securities, the executor should be careful to consult accurate records to obtain values as of the applicable valuation date. If quotations of unlisted securities are obtained from brokers, or evidence as to their sale is obtained from officers of the issuing companies, copies of the letters furnishing such quotations or evidence of sale should be attached to the return.

(2) If it is established with respect to bonds for which there is a market on a stock exchange, that the highest and lowest selling prices are not available for the valuation date in a generally available listing or publication of general circulation but that closing selling prices are so available, the fair market value per bond is the mean between the quoted closing selling price on the valuation date and the quoted closing selling price on the trading day before the valuation date. If there were no sales on the trading day before the valuation date but there were sales on date within a reasonable period before the valuation date, the fair market value is determined by taking a weighted average of the quoted closing selling price on the valuation date and the quoted closing selling price on the nearest date before the valuation date. The closing selling price for the valuation date is to be weighted by the number of trading days between the previous selling date and the valuation date. If there were no sales within a reasonable period before the valuation date but there were sales on the valuation date, the fair market value is the closing selling price on such valuation date. If there were no sales on the valuation date but there were sales on dates within a reasonable period both before and after the valuation date, the fair market value is determined by taking a weighted average of the quoted closing selling prices on the nearest date before and the nearest date after the valuation date. The average is to be weighted inversely by the respective numbers of trading days between the selling dates

and the valuation date. If the bonds are listed on more than one exchange, the records of the exchange where the bonds are principally dealt in should be employed. In valuing listed securities, the executor should be careful to consult accurate records to obtain values as of the applicable valuation date.

(3) The application of this paragraph may be illustrated by the following examples:

Example (1). Assume that sales of X Company common stock nearest the valuation date (Friday, June 15) occurred two trading days before (Wednesday, June 13) and three trading days after (Wednesday, June 20) and on these days the mean sale prices per share were $10 and $15, respectively. The price of $12 is taken as representing the fair market value of a share of X Company common stock as of the valuation date

$$\frac{(3 \times 10) + (2 \times 15)}{5}$$

Example (2). Assume the same facts as in example (1) except that the mean sale prices per share on June 13 and June 20 were $15 and $10, respectively. The price of $13 is taken as representing the fair market value of a share of X Company common stock as of the valuation date

$$\frac{(3 \times 15) + (2 \times 10)}{5}$$

Example (3). Assume the decedent died on Sunday, October 7, and that Saturday and Sunday were not trading days. If sales of X Company common stock occurred on Friday, October 5, at mean sale prices per share of $20 and on Monday, October 8, at mean sale prices per share of $23, the price of $21.50 is taken as representing the fair market value of a share of X Company common stock as of the valuation date

$$\frac{(1 \times 20) + (23 \times 1)}{2}$$

Example (4). Assume that on the valuation date (Tuesday, April 3, 1973) the closing selling price of a listed bond was $25 per bond and that the highest and lowest selling prices are not available in a generally available listing or publication of general circulation for that date. Assume further, that the closing selling price of the same listed bond was $21 per bond on the day before the valuation date (Monday, April 2, 1973). Thus, under paragraph (b)(2) of this section the price of $23 is taken as representing the fair market value per bond as of the valuation date

$$\frac{(25 + 21)}{2}$$

Example (5). Assume the same facts as in example (4) except that there were no sales on the day before the valuation date. Assume further, that there were sales on Thursday, March 29, 1973, and that the closing selling price on that day was $23. The price of $24.50 is taken as representing the fair market value per bond as of the valuation date

$$\frac{((1 \times 23) + (3 \times 25))}{4}$$

Example (6). Assume that no bonds were traded on the valuation date (Friday, April 20). Assume further, that sales of bonds nearest the valuation date occurred two trading days before (Wednesday, April 18) and three trading days after (Wednesday, April 25) the valuation date and that on these two days the closing selling prices per bond were $29 and $22, respectively. The highest and lowest selling prices are not available for these dates in a generally available listing or publication of general circulation. Thus, under paragraph (b)(2) of this section, the price of $26.20 is taken as representing the fair market value of a bond as of the valuation date

$$\frac{((3 \times 29) + (2 \times 22))}{5}$$

(c) Based on bid and asked prices. If the provisions of paragraph (b) of this section are inapplicable because actual sales are not available during a reasonable period beginning before and ending after the valuation date, the fair market value may be determined by taking the mean between the bona fide bid and asked prices on the valuation date, or if none, by taking a weighted average of the means between the bona fide bid and asked prices on the nearest trading date before and the nearest trading date after the valuation date, if both such nearest dates are within a reasonable period. The average is to be determined in the manner described in paragraph (b) of this section.

(d) Based on incomplete selling prices or bid and asked prices. If the provisions of paragraph (b) and (c) of this section are inapplicable because no actual sale prices or bona fide bid and asked prices are available on a date within a reasonable period before the valuation date, but such prices are available on a date within a reasonable period after the valuation date, or vice versa, then the mean between the highest and lowest available sale prices or bid and asked prices may be taken as the value.

(e) Where selling prices or bid and asked prices do not reflect fair market value. If it is established that the value of any bond or share of stock determined on the basis of selling or bid and asked prices as provided under paragraphs (b), (c), and (d) of this section does not reflect the fair market value thereof, then some reasonable modification of that basis or other relevant facts and elements of value are considered in determining the fair market value. Where sales at or near the date of death are few or of a sporadic nature, such sales alone may not indicate fair market value. In certain exceptional cases, the size of the block of stock to be valued in relation to the number of shares changing hands in sales may be relevant in determining whether selling prices reflect the fair market value of the block of stock to be valued. If the executor can show that the block of stock to be valued is so large in relation to the actual sales on the existing market that it could not be liquidated in a reasonable time without depressing the market, the price at which the block could be sold as such outside the usual market, as through an underwriter, may be a more accurate indication of value than market quotations. Complete data in support of any allowance claimed due to the size of the block of stock being valued shall be submitted with the return. On the other hand, if the block of stock to be valued represents a controlling interest, either actual or effective, in a going business, the price at which other lots change hands may have little relation to its true value.

(f) Where selling prices or bid and asked prices are unavailable. If the provisions of paragraphs (b), (c), and (d) of this section are inapplicable because actual sale prices and bona fide bid and asked prices are lacking, then the fair market value is to be determined by taking the following factors into consideration:

(1) In the case of corporate or other bonds, the soundness of the security, the interest yield, the date of maturity, and other relevant factors; and

(2) In the case of shares of stock, the company's net worth, prospective earning power and dividend-paying capacity, and other relevant factors.

Some of the "other relevant factors" referred to in subparagraphs (1) and (2) of this paragraph are: The good will of the business; the economic outlook in the particular industry; the company's position in the industry and its management; the degree of control of the business represented by the block of stock to be valued; and the values of securities of corporations engaged in the same or similar lines of business which are listed on a stock exchange. However, the weight to be accorded such comparisons or any other evidentiary factors considered in the determination of a value depends upon the facts of each case. In addition to the relevant factors described above, consideration shall also be given to nonoperating assets, including proceeds of life insurance policies payable to or for the benefit of the company, to the extent such nonoperating assets have not been taken into account in the determination of net worth, prospective earning power and dividend-earning capacity. Complete financial and other data upon which the valuation is based should be submitted with the return, including copies of reports of any examinations of the company made by accountants, engineers, or any technical experts as of or near the applicable valuation date.

(g) **Pledged securities.** The full value of securities pledged to secure an indebtedness of the decedent is included in the gross estate. If the decedent had a trading account with a broker, all securities belonging to the decedent and held by the broker at the date of death must be included at their fair market value as of the applicable valuation date. Securities purchased on margin for the decedent's account and held by a broker must also be returned at their fair market value as of the applicable valuation date. The amount of the decedent's indebtedness to a broker or other person with whom securities were pledged is allowed as a deduction from the gross estate in accordance with the provisions of § 20.2053-1 or § 20.2106-1 (for estates of nonresidents not citizens).

(h) Securities subject to an option or contract to purchase. Another person may hold an option or a contract to purchase securities owned by a decedent at the time of his death. The effect, if any, that is given to the option or contract price in determining the value of the securities for estate tax purposes depends upon the circumstances of the particular case. Little weight will be accorded a price contained in an option or contract under which the decedent is free to dispose of the underlying securities at any price he chooses during his lifetime. Such is the effect, for example, of an agreement on the part of a shareholder to purchase whatever shares of stock the decedent may own at the time of his death. Even if the decedent is not free to dispose of the underlying securities at other than the option or contract price, such price will be disregarded in determining the value of the securities unless it is determined under the circumstances of the particular case that the agreement represents a bona fide business arrangement and not a device to pass the decedent's shares to the natural objects of his bounty for less than an adequate and full consideration in money or money's worth. See section 2703 and the regulations at § 25.2703 of this chapter for special rules involving options and agreements (including contracts to purchase) entered into (or substantially modified after) October 8, 1990.

(i) Stock sold "ex-dividend." In any case where a dividend is declared on a share of stock before the decedent's death but payable to stockholders of record on a date after his death and the stock is selling "ex-dividend" on the date of the decedent's death, the amount of the dividend is added to the ex-dividend quotation in determining the fair market value of the stock as of the date of the decedent's death.

(j) Application of chapter 14. See section 2701 and the regulations at § 25.2701 of this chapter for special rules for valuing the transfer of an interest in a corporation and for the treatment of unpaid qualified payments at the death of the transferor or an applicable family member. See section 2704(b) and the regulations at § 25.2704-2 of this chapter for special valuation rules involving certain restrictions on liquidation rights created after October 8, 1990.

T.D. 6296, 6/23/58, amend T.D. 6826, 6/14/65, T.D. 7312, 4/26/74, T.D. 7327, 9/30/74, T.D. 7432, 9/10/76, T.D. 8395, 1/28/92.

§ 20.2031-3 Valuation of interests in businesses.

The fair market value of any interest of a decedent in a business, whether a partnership or a proprietorship, is the net amount which a willing purchaser, whether an individual or a corporation, would pay for the interest to a willing seller, neither being under any compulsion to buy or to sell and both having reasonable knowledge of relevant facts. The net value is determined on the basis of all relevant factors including—

(a) A fair appraisal as of the applicable valuation date of all the assets of the business, tangible and intangible, including good will;

(b) The demonstrated earning capacity of the business; and

(c) The other factors set forth in paragraphs (f) and (h) of § 20.2031-2 relating to the valuation of corporate stock, to the extent applicable.

Special attention should be given to determining an adequate value of the good will of the business in all cases in which the decedent has not agreed, for an adequate and full consideration in money or money's worth, that his interest passes at his death to, for example, his surviving partner or partners. Complete financial and other data upon which the valuation is based should be submitted with the return, including copies of reports of examinations of the business made by accountants, engineers, or any technical experts as of or near the applicable valuation date. See section 2701 and the regulations at § 25.2701 of this chapter for special rules for valuing the transfer of an interest in a partnership and for the treatment of unpaid qualified payments that the death of the transferor or an applicable family member. See section 2703 and the regulations at § 25.2703 of this chapter for special rules involving options and agreements (including contracts to purchase) entered into (or substantially modified after) October 8, 1990. See section 2704(b) and the regulations at § 25.2704-2 of this chapter for special valuation rules involving certain restrictions on liquidation rights created after October 8, 1990.

T.D. 6296, 6/23/58, amend T.D. 8395, 1/28/92.

§ 20.2031-4 Valuation of notes.

The fair market value of notes, secured or unsecured, is presumed to be the amount of unpaid principal, plus interest accrued to the date of death, unless the executor establishes that the value is lower or that the notes are worthless. However, items of interest shall be separately stated on the estate tax return. If not returned at face value, plus accrued interest, satisfactory evidence must be submitted that the note is worth less than the unpaid amount (because of the interest rate, date of maturity, or other cause), or that the note is uncollectible, either in whole or in part (by reason of the insolvency of the party or parties liable, or for other cause), and that any property pledged or mortgaged as security is insufficient to satisfy the obligation.

T.D. 6296, 6/23/58.

PAR. 7.

Section 20.2031-4 is amended by adding a new sentence at the end to read as follows:

Proposed § 20.2031-4 Valuation of notes. [*For Preamble, see ¶ 151,027*]

* * * See § 20.7872-1 for special rules in the case of gift loans (within the meaning of § 1.7872-4(b)) made after June 6, 1984.

§ 20.2031-5 Valuation of cash on hand or on deposit.

The amount of cash belonging to the decedent at the date of his death, whether in his possession or in the possession of another, or deposited with a bank, is included in the decedent's gross estate. If bank checks outstanding at the time of the decedent's death and given in discharge of bona fide legal obligations of the decedent incurred for an adequate and full consideration in money or money's worth are subsequently honored by the bank and charged to the decedent's account, the balance remaining in the account may be returned, but only if the obligations are not claimed as deductions from the gross estate.

T.D. 6296, 6/23/58.

§ 20.2031-6 Valuation of household and personal effects.

(a) General rule. The fair market value of the decedent's household and personal effects is the price which a willing buyer would pay to a willing seller, neither being under any compulsion to buy or to sell and both having reasonable knowledge of relevant facts. A room by room itemization of household and personal effects is desirable. All the articles should be named specifically, except that a number of articles contained in the same room, none of which has a value in excess of $100, may be grouped. A separate value should be given for each article named. In lieu of an itemized list, the executor may furnish a written statement, containing a declaration that it is made under penalties of perjury, setting forth the aggregate value as appraised by a competent appraiser or appraisers of recognized standing and ability, or by a dealer or dealers in the class of personalty involved.

(b) Special rule in cases involving a substantial amount of valuable articles. Notwithstanding the provisions of paragraph (a) of this section, if there are included among the household and personal effects articles having marked artistic or intrinsic value of a total value in excess of $3,000 (e. g., jewelry, furs, silverware, paintings, etchings, engravings, antiques, books, statuary, vases, oriental rugs, coin or stamp collections), the appraisal of an expert or experts, under oath, shall be filed with the return. The appraisal shall be accompanied by a written statement of the executor containing a declaration that it is made under the penalties of perjury as to the completeness of the itemized list of such property and as to the disinterested character and the qualifications of the appraiser or appraisers.

(c) Disposition of household effects prior to investigation. If it is desired to effect distribution or sale of any portion of the household or personal effects of the decedent in advance of an investigation by an officer of the Internal Revenue Service, information to that effect shall be given to the district director. The statement to the district director shall be accompanied by an appraisal of such property, under oath, and by a written statement of the executor, containing a declaration that it is made under the penalties of perjury, regarding the completeness of the list of such property and the qualifications of the appraiser, as heretofore described. If a personal inspection by an officer of the Internal Revenue Service is not deemed necessary, the executor will be so advised. This procedure is designed to facilitate disposition of such property and to obviate future expense and inconvenience to the estate by affording the district director an opportunity to make an investigation should one be deemed necessary prior to sale or distribution.

(d) Additional rules if an appraisal involved. If, pursuant to paragraphs (a), (b), and (c) of this section, expert appraisers are employed, care should be taken to see that they are reputable and of recognized competency to appraise the particular class of property involved. In the appraisal, books in sets by standard authors should be listed in separate groups. In listing paintings having artistic value, the size subject, and artist's name should be stated. In the case of oriental rugs, the size, make, and general condition should be given. Sets of silverware should be listed in separate groups. Groups or individual pieces of silverware should be weighed and the weights given in troy ounces. In arriving at the value of silverware, the appraisers should take into consideration its antiquity, utility, desirability, condition, and obsolescence.

T.D. 6296, 6/23/58.

§ 20.2031-7 Valuation of annuities, interests for life or term of years, and remainder or reversionary interests.

(a) In general. Except as otherwise provided in paragraph (b) of this section and § 20.7520-3(b) (pertaining to certain limitations on the use of prescribed tables), the fair market value of annuities, life estates, terms of years, remainders, and reversionary interests for estates of decedents is the present value of such interests, determined under paragraph (d) of this section. The regulations in this and in related sections provide tables with standard actuarial factors and examples that illustrate how to use the tables to compute the present value of ordinary annuity, life, and remainder interests in property. These sections also refer to standard and special actuarial factors that may be necessary to compute the present value of similar interests in more unusual fact situations.

(b) Commercial annuities and insurance contracts. The value of annuities issued by companies regularly engaged in their sale, and of insurance policies on the lives of persons other than the decedent, is determined under § 20.2031-8. See § 20.2042-1 with respect to insurance policies on the decedent's life.

(c) through (d)(5) [Reserved]. For further guidance, see § 20.2031-7T(c) through (d)(5).

(6) Actuarial Table B, Table J, and Table K where the valuation date is after April 30, 1989. Except as provided in § 20.7520-3(b) (pertaining to certain limitations on prescribed tables), for determination of the present value of an interest that is dependent on a term of years, the tables in this paragraph (d)(6) must be used in the application of the provisions of this section when the section 7520 interest rate component is between 4.2 and 14 percent.

TABLE B

TERM CERTAIN REMAINDER FACTORS APPLICABLE AFTER APRIL 30, 1989

	INTEREST RATE									
YEARS	4.2%	4.4%	4.6%	4.8%	5.0%	5.2%	5.4%	5.6%	5.8%	6.0%
1	.959693	.957854	.956023	.954198	.952381	.950570	.948767	.946970	.945180	.943396
2	.921010	.917485	.913980	.910495	.907029	.903584	.900158	.896752	.893364	.889996
3	.883887	.878817	.873786	.868793	.863838	.858920	.854040	.849197	.844390	.839619
4	.848260	.841779	.835359	.829001	.822702	.816464	.810285	.804163	.798100	.792094
5	.814069	.806302	.798623	.791031	.783526	.776106	.768771	.761518	.754348	.747258
6	.781257	.772320	.763501	.754801	.746215	.737744	.729384	.721135	.712994	.704961
7	.749766	.739770	.729925	.720230	.710681	.701277	.692015	.682893	.673908	.665057
8	.719545	.708592	.697825	.687242	.676839	.666613	.656561	.646679	.636964	.627412
9	.690543	.678728	.667137	.655765	.644609	.633663	.622923	.612385	.602045	.591898
10	.662709	.650122	.637798	.625730	.613913	.602341	.591009	.579910	.569041	.558395
11	.635997	.622722	.609750	.597071	.584679	.572568	.560729	.549157	.537846	.526788
12	.610362	.596477	.582935	.569724	.556837	.544266	.532001	.520035	.508361	.496969
13	.585760	.571339	.557299	.543630	.530321	.517363	.504745	.492458	.480492	.468839
14	.562150	.547259	.532790	.518731	.505068	.491790	.478885	.466343	.454151	.442301
15	.539491	.524195	.509360	.494972	.481017	.467481	.454350	.441612	.429255	.417265
16	.517746	.502102	.486960	.472302	.458112	.444374	.431072	.418194	.405723	.393646
17	.496877	.480941	.465545	.450670	.436297	.422408	.408987	.396017	.383481	.371364
18	.476849	.460671	.445071	.430028	.415521	.401529	.388033	.375016	.362458	.350344
19	.457629	.441256	.425498	.410332	.395734	.381681	.368153	.355129	.342588	.330513
20	.439183	.422659	.406786	.391538	.376889	.362815	.349291	.336296	.323807	.311805
21	.421481	.404846	.388897	.373605	.358942	.344881	.331396	.318462	.306056	.294155
22	.404492	.387783	.371794	.356494	.341850	.327834	.314417	.301574	.289278	.277505
23	.388188	.371440	.355444	.340166	.325571	.311629	.298309	.285581	.273420	.261797
24	.372542	.355785	.339813	.324586	.310068	.296225	.283025	.270437	.258431	.246979
25	.357526	.340791	.324869	.309719	.295303	.281583	.268525	.256096	.244263	.232999
26	.343115	.326428	.310582	.295533	.281241	.267664	.254768	.242515	.230873	.219810
27	.329285	.312670	.296923	.281998	.267848	.254434	.241715	.229654	.218216	.207368
28	.316012	.299493	.283866	.269082	.255094	.241857	.229331	.217475	.206253	.195630
29	.303275	.286870	.271382	.256757	.242946	.229902	.217582	.205943	.194947	.184557
30	.291051	.274780	.259447	.244997	.231377	.218538	.206434	.195021	.184260	.174110
31	.279319	.263199	.248038	.233776	.220359	.207736	.195858	.184679	.174158	.164255
32	.268061	.252106	.237130	.223069	.209866	.197468	.185823	.174886	.164611	.154957
33	.257256	.241481	.226702	.212852	.199873	.187707	.176303	.165612	.155587	.146186
34	.246887	.231304	.216732	.203103	.190355	.178429	.167270	.156829	.147058	.137912
35	.236935	.221556	.207201	.193801	.181290	.169609	.158701	.148512	.138996	.130105

TABLE B

TERM CERTAIN REMAINDER FACTORS APPLICABLE AFTER APRIL 30, 1989

	INTEREST RATE									
YEARS	4.2%	4.4%	4.6%	4.8%	5.0%	5.2%	5.4%	5.6%	5.8%	6.0%
36	.227385	.212218	.198089	.184924	.172657	.161225	.150570	.140637	.131376	.122741
37	.218220	.203274	.189377	.176454	.164436	.153256	.142856	.133179	.124174	.115793
38	.209424	.194707	.181049	.168373	.156605	.145681	.135537	.126116	.117367	.109239
39	.200983	.186501	.173087	.160661	.149148	.138480	.128593	.119428	.110933	.103056
40	.192882	.178641	.165475	.153302	.142046	.131635	.122004	.113095	.104851	.097222
41	.185107	.171112	.158198	.146281	.135282	.125128	.115754	.107098	.099103	.091719
42	.177646	.163900	.151241	.139581	.128840	.118943	.109823	.101418	.093670	.086527
43	.170486	.156992	.144590	.133188	.122704	.113064	.104197	.096040	.088535	.081630
44	.163614	.150376	.138231	.127088	.116861	.107475	.098858	.090947	.083682	.077009
45	.157019	.144038	.132152	.121267	.111297	.102163	.093793	.086124	.079094	.072650
46	.150690	.137968	.126340	.115713	.105997	.097113	.088988	.081557	.074758	.068538
47	.144616	.132153	.120784	.110413	.100949	.092312	.084429	.077232	.070660	.064658
48	.138787	.126583	.115473	.105356	.096142	.087749	.080103	.073136	.066786	.060998
49	.133193	.121248	.110395	.100530	.091564	.083412	.075999	.069258	.063125	.057546
50	.127824	.116138	.105540	.095926	.087204	.079289	.072106	.065585	.059665	.054288
51	.122672	.111243	.100898	.091532	.083051	.075370	.068411	.062107	.056394	.051215
52	.117728	.106555	.096461	.087340	.079096	.071644	.064907	.058813	.053302	.048316
53	.112982	.102064	.092219	.083340	.075330	.068103	.061581	.055695	.050380	.045582
54	.108428	.097763	.088164	.079523	.071743	.064737	.058426	.052741	.047618	.043001

55	.104058	.093642	.084286	.075880	.068326	.061537	.055433	.049944	.045008	.040567
56	.099864	.089696	.080580	.072405	.065073	.058495	.052593	.047296	.042541	.038271
57	.095839	.085916	.077036	.069089	.061974	.055604	.049898	.044787	.040208	.036105
58	.091976	.082295	.073648	.065924	.059023	.052855	.047342	.042412	.038004	.034061
59	.088268	.078826	.070409	.062905	.056212	.050243	.044916	.040163	.035921	.032133
60	.084710	.075504	.067313	.060024	.053536	.047759	.042615	.038033	.033952	.030314

TABLE B

TERM CERTAIN REMAINDER FACTORS APPLICABLE AFTER APRIL 30, 1989

				INTEREST RATE						
YEARS	6.2%	6.4%	6.6%	6.8%	7.0%	7.2%	7.4%	7.6%	7.8%	8.0%
1	.941620	.939850	.938086	.936330	.934579	.932836	.931099	.929368	.927644	.925926
2	.886647	.883317	.880006	.876713	.873439	.870183	.866945	.863725	.860523	.857339
3	.834885	.830185	.825521	.820892	.816298	.811738	.807211	.802718	.798259	.793832
4	.786144	.780249	.774410	.768626	.762895	.757218	.751593	.746021	.740500	.735030
5	.740248	.733317	.726464	.719687	.712986	.706360	.699808	.693328	.686920	.680583
6	.697032	.689208	.681486	.673864	.666342	.658918	.651590	.644357	.637217	.630170
7	.656339	.647752	.639292	.630959	.622750	.614662	.606694	.598845	.591111	.583490
8	.618022	.608789	.599711	.590786	.582009	.573379	.564892	.556547	.548340	.540269
9	.581942	.572170	.562581	.553170	.543934	.534868	.525971	.517237	.508664	.500249
10	.547968	.537754	.527750	.517950	.508349	.498944	.489731	.480704	.471859	.463193
11	.515977	.505408	.495075	.484972	.475093	.465433	.455987	.446750	.437717	.428883
12	.485854	.475007	.464423	.454093	.444012	.434173	.424569	.415196	.406046	.397114
13	.457490	.446436	.435669	.425181	.414964	.405012	.395316	.385870	.376666	.367698
14	.430781	.419582	.408695	.398109	.387817	.377810	.368078	.358615	.349412	.340461
15	.405632	.394344	.383391	.372762	.362446	.352434	.342717	.333285	.324130	.315242
16	.381951	.370624	.359654	.349028	.338735	.328763	.319103	.309745	.300677	.291890
17	.359653	.348331	.337386	.326805	.316574	.306682	.297117	.287867	.278921	.270269
18	.338656	.327379	.316498	.305997	.295864	.286084	.276645	.267534	.258739	.250249
19	.318885	.307687	.296902	.286514	.276508	.266870	.257584	.248638	.240018	.231712
20	.300268	.289179	.278520	.268272	.258419	.248946	.239836	.231076	.222651	.214548
21	.282739	.271785	.261276	.251191	.241513	.232225	.223311	.214755	.206541	.198656
22	.266232	.255437	.245099	.235197	.225713	.216628	.207925	.199586	.191596	.183941
23	.250689	.240073	.229924	.220222	.210947	.202078	.193598	.185489	.177733	.170315
24	.236054	.225632	.215689	.206201	.197147	.188506	.180259	.172387	.164873	.157699
25	.222273	.212060	.202334	.193072	.184249	.175845	.167839	.160211	.152943	.146018
26	.209297	.199305	.189807	.180779	.172195	.164035	.156275	.148895	.141877	.135202
27	.197078	.187317	.178056	.169269	.160930	.153017	.145507	.138379	.131611	.125187
28	.185572	.176049	.167031	.158491	.150402	.142740	.135482	.128605	.122088	.115914
29	.174739	.165460	.156690	.148400	.140563	.133153	.126147	.119521	.113255	.107328
30	.164537	.155507	.146989	.138951	.131367	.124210	.117455	.111079	.105060	.099377
31	.154932	.146154	.137888	.130104	.122773	.115868	.109362	.103233	.097458	.092016
32	.145887	.137362	.129351	.121820	.114741	.108085	.101827	.095942	.090406	.085200
33	.137370	.129100	.121342	.114064	.107235	.100826	.094811	.089165	.083865	.078889
34	.129350	.121335	.113830	.106802	.100219	.094054	.088278	.082867	.077797	.073045
35	.121798	.114036	.106782	.100001	.093663	.087737	.082196	.077014	.072168	.067635

TABLE B

TERM CERTAIN REMAINDER FACTORS APPLICABLE AFTER APRIL 30, 1989

				INTEREST RATE						
YEARS	6.2%	6.4%	6.6%	6.8%	7.0%	7.2%	7.4%	7.6%	7.8%	8.0%
36	.114688	.107177	.100171	.093634	.087535	.081844	.076532	.071574	.066946	.062625
37	.107992	.100730	.093969	.087673	.081809	.076347	.071259	.066519	.062102	.057986
38	.101688	.094671	.088151	.082090	.076457	.071219	.066349	.061821	.057609	.053690
39	.095751	.088977	.082693	.076864	.071455	.066436	.061778	.057454	.053440	.049713
40	.090161	.083625	.077573	.071970	.066780	.061974	.057521	.053396	.049573	.046031
41	.084897	.078595	.072770	.067387	.062412	.057811	.053558	.049625	.045987	.042621
42	.079941	.073867	.068265	.063097	.058329	.053929	.049868	.046120	.042659	.039464
43	.075274	.069424	.064038	.059079	.054513	.050307	.046432	.042862	.039572	.036541
44	.070880	.065248	.060074	.055318	.050946	.046928	.043233	.039835	.036709	.033834
45	.066742	.061323	.056354	.051796	.047613	.043776	.040254	.037021	.034053	.031328
46	.062845	.057635	.052865	.048498	.044499	.040836	.037480	.034406	.031589	.029007
47	.059176	.054168	.049592	.045410	.041587	.038093	.034898	.031976	.029303	.026859
48	.055722	.050910	.046522	.042519	.038867	.035535	.032493	.029717	.027183	.024869

49	.052469	.047848	.043641	.039812	.036324	.033148	.030255	.027618	.025216	.023027
50	.049405	.044970	.040939	.037277	.033948	.030922	.028170	.025668	.023392	.021321
51	.046521	.042265	.038405	.034903	.031727	.028845	.026229	.023855	.021699	.019742
52	.043805	.039722	.036027	.032681	.029651	.026907	.024422	.022170	.020129	.018280
53	.041248	037333	.033796	.030600	.027711	.025100	.022739	.020604	.018673	.016925
54	038840	.035087	.031704	.028652	.025899	.023414	.021172	.019149	.017322	.015672
55	.036572	.032977	.029741	.026828	.024204	.021842	.019714	.017796	.016068	.014511
56	.034437	.030993	.027900	.025119	.022621	.020375	.018355	.016539	.014906	.013436
57	.032427	.029129	.026172	.023520	.021141	.019006	.017091	.015371	.013827	.012441
58	.030534	.027377	.024552	.022023	.019758	.017730	.015913	.014285	.012827	.011519
59	.028751	.025730	.023032	.020620	.018465	.016539	.014817	.013276	.011899	.010666
60	.027073	.024183	.021606	.019307	.017257	.015428	.013796	.012339	.011038	.009876

TABLE B

TERM CERTAIN REMAINDER FACTORS APPLICABLE AFTER APRIL 30, 1989

				INTEREST RATE						
YEARS	8.2%	8.4%	8.6%	8.8%	9.0%	9.2%	9.4%	9.6%	9.8%	10.0%
1	.924214	.922509	.920810	.919118	.917431	.915751	.914077	.912409	.910747	.909091
2	.854172	.851023	.847892	.844777	.841680	.838600	.835536	.832490	.829460	.826446
3	.789438	.785077	.780747	.776450	.772183	.767948	.763744	.759571	.755428	.751315
4	.729610	.724241	.718920	.713649	.708425	.703250	.698121	.693039	.688003	.683013
5	.674316	.668119	.661989	.655927	.649931	.644001	.638136	.632335	.626597	.620921
6	.623213	.616346	.609566	.602874	.596267	.589745	.583305	.576948	.570671	.564474
7	.575982	.568585	.561295	.554112	.547034	.540059	.533186	.526412	.519737	.513158
8	.532331	.524524	.516846	.509294	.501866	.494560	.487373	.480303	.473349	.466507
9	.491988	.483879	.475917	.468101	.460428	.452894	.445496	.438233	.431101	.424098
10	.454703	.446383	.438230	.430240	.422411	.414738	.407218	.399848	.392624	.385543
11	.420243	.411792	.403526	.395441	.387533	.379797	.372228	.364824	.357581	.350494
12	.388394	.379882	.371571	.363457	.355535	.347799	.340245	.332869	.325666	.318631
13	.358960	.350445	.342147	.334060	.326179	.318497	.311010	.303713	.296599	.289664
14	.331756	.323288	.315052	.307040	.299246	.291664	.284287	.277110	.270127	.263331
15	.306613	.298236	.290103	.282206	.274538	.267092	.259860	.252838	.246017	.239392
16	.283376	.275126	.267130	.259381	.251870	.244589	.237532	.230691	.224059	.217629
17	.261901	.253806	.245976	.238401	.231073	.223983	.217123	.210485	.204061	.197845
18	.242052	.234139	.226497	.219119	.211994	.205113	.198467	.192048	.185848	.179859
19	223708	.215995	.208561	.201396	.194490	.187832	.181414	.175226	.169260	.163508
20	.206754	.199257	.192045	.185107	.178431	.172007	.165826	.159878	.154153	.148644
21	.191085	.183817	.176837	.170135	.163698	.157516	.151578	.145874	.140395	.135131
22	.176604	.169573	.162834	.156374	.150182	.144245	.138554	.133097	.127864	.122846
23	.163220	.156432	.149939	.143726	.137781	.132093	.126649	.121439	.116452	.111678
24	.150850	.144310	.138065	.132101	.125405	.120964	.115767	.110802	.106058	.101526
25	.139418	.133128	.127132	.121416	.115968	.110773	.105820	.101097	.096592	.092296
26	.128852	.122811	.117064	.111596	.106393	.101441	.096727	.092241	.087971	.083905
27	.119087	.113295	.107794	.102570	.097608	.092894	.088416	.084162	.080119	.076278
28	.110062	.104515	.099258	.094274	.089548	.085068	.080819	.076790	.072968	.069343
29	.101721	.096416	.091398	.086649	.082155	.077901	.073875	.070064	.066456	.063039
30	.094012	.088945	.084160	.079640	.075371	.071338	.067527	.063927	.060524	.057309
31	.086887	.082053	.077495	.073199	.069148	.065328	.061725	.058327	.055122	.052099
32	.080302	.075694	.071358	.067278	.063438	.059824	.056422	.053218	.050202	.047362
33	.074216	.069829	.065708	.061837	.058200	.054784	.051574	.048557	.045722	.043057
34	.068592	.064418	.060504	.056835	.053395	.050168	.047142	.044304	.041641	.039143
35	.063394	.059426	.055713	.052238	.048986	.045942	.043092	.040423	.037924	.035584

TABLE B

TERM CERTAIN REMAINDER FACTORS APPLICABLE AFTER APRIL 30, 1989

				INTEREST RATE						
YEARS	8.2%	8.4%	8.6%	8.8%	9.0%	9.2%	9.4%	9.6%	9.8%	10.0%
36	.058589	.054821	.051301	.048013	.044941	.042071	.039389	.036882	.034539	.032349
37	.054149	.050573	.047239	.044130	.041231	.038527	.036005	.033652	.031457	.029408
38	.050045	.046654	.043498	.040560	.037826	.035281	.032911	.030704	.028649	.026735
39	.046253	.043039	.040053	.037280	.034703	.032309	.030083	.028015	.026092	.024304
40	.042747	.039703	.036881	.034264	.031838	.029587	.027498	.025561	.023763	.022095
41	.039508	.036627	.033961	.031493	.029209	.027094	.025136	.023322	.021642	.020086
42	.036514	.033789	.031271	.028946	.026797	.024811	.022976	.021279	.019711	.018260

43	.033746	.031170	.028795	.026605	.024584	.022721	.021002	.019415	.017951	.016600
44	.031189	.028755	.026515	.024453	.022555	.020807	.019197	.017715	.016349	.015091
45	.028825	.026527	.024415	.022475	.020692	.019054	.017548	.016163	.014890	.013719
46	.026641	.024471	.022482	.020657	.018984	.017449	.016040	.014747	.013561	.012472
47	.024622	.022575	.020701	.018986	.017416	.015978	.014662	.013456	.012351	.011338
48	.022756	.020825	.019062	.017451	.015978	.014632	.013402	.012277	.011248	.010307
49	.021031	.019212	.017552	.016039	.014659	.013400	.012250	.011202	.010244	.009370
50	.019437	.017723	.016163	.014742	.013449	.012271	.011198	.010221	.009330	.008519
51	.017964	.016350	.014883	.013550	.012338	.011237	.010236	.009325	.008497	.007744
52	.016603	.015083	.013704	.012454	.011319	.010290	.009356	.008508	.007739	.007040
53	015345	.013914	.012619	.011446	.010385	.009423	.008552	.007763	.007048	.006400
54	.014182	.012836	.011620	.010521	.009527	.008629	.007817	.007083	.006419	.005818
55	.013107	.011841	.010699	.009670	.008741	.007902	.007146	.006463	.005846	.005289
56	.012114	.010923	.009852	.008888	.008019	.007237	.006532	.005897	.005324	.004809
57	.011196	.010077	.009072	.008169	.007357	.006627	.005971	.005380	.004849	.004371
58	.010347	.009296	.008354	.007508	.006749	.006069	.005458	.004909	.004416	.003974
59	.009563	.008576	.007692	.006901	.006192	.005557	.004989	.004479	.004022	.003613
60	.008838	.007911	.007083	.006343	.005681	.005089	.004560	.004087	.003663	.003284

TABLE B

TERM CERTAIN REMAINDER FACTORS APPLICABLE AFTER APRIL 30, 1989

				INTEREST RATE						
YEARS	10.2%	10.4%	10.6%	10.8%	11.0%	11.2%	11.4%	11.6%	11.8%	12.0%
1	.907441	.905797	.904159	.902527	.900901	.899281	.897666	.896057	.894454	.892857
2	.823449	.820468	.817504	.814555	.811622	.808706	.805804	.802919	.800049	.797194
3	.747232	.743178	.739153	.735158	.731191	.727253	.723343	.719461	.715607	.711780
4	.678069	.673168	.668312	.663500	.658731	.654005	.649321	.644679	.640078	.635518
5	.615307	.609754	.604261	.598827	.593451	.588134	.582873	.577669	.572520	.567427
6	.558355	.552313	.546348	.540457	.534641	.528897	.523225	.517625	.512093	.506631
7	.506674	.500284	.493985	.487777	.481658	.475627	.469682	.463821	.458044	.452349
8	.459777	.453156	.446641	.440232	.433926	.427722	.421617	.415610	.409700	.403883
9	.417221	.410467	.403835	.397322	.390925	.384642	.378472	.372411	.366458	.360610
10	.378603	.371800	.365131	.358593	.352184	.345901	.339741	.333701	.327780	.321973
11	.343560	.336775	.330137	.323640	.317283	.311062	.304974	.299016	.293184	.287476
12	.311760	.305050	.298496	.292094	.285841	.279732	.273765	.267935	.262240	.256675
13	.282904	.276313	.269888	.263623	.257514	.251558	.245749	.240085	.234561	.229174
14	.256719	.250284	.244022	.237927	.231995	.226221	.220601	.215130	.209804	.204620
15	.232957	.226706	.220634	.214735	.209004	.203436	.198026	.192769	.187661	.182696
16	.211395	.205350	.199489	.193804	.188292	.182946	.177761	.172732	167854	.163122
17	.191828	.186005	.180369	.174914	.169633	.164520	.159570	.154778	.150138	.145644
18	.174073	.168483	.163083	.157864	.152822	.147950	.143241	.138690	.134291	.130040
19	157961	.152612	.147453	.142477	.137678	.133048	.128582	.124274	.120117	.116107
20	.143340	.138235	.133321	.128589	.124034	.119648	.115424	.111357	.107439	.103667
21	.130073	.125213	.120543	.116055	.111742	.107597	.103612	.099782	.096100	.092560
22	.118033	.113418	.108990	.104743	.100669	.096760	.093009	.089410	.085957	.082643
23	.107108	.102733	.098544	.094533	.090693	.087014	.083491	.080117	.076884	.073788
24	.097195	.093056	.089100	.085319	.081705	.078250	.074947	.071789	.068770	.065882
25	.088198	.084289	.080560	.077003	.073608	.070369	.067278	.064327	.061511	.058823
26	.080035	.076349	.072839	.069497	.066314	.063281	.060393	.057641	.055019	.052521
27	.072627	.069157	.065858	.062723	.059742	.056908	.054213	.051650	.049212	.046894
28	.065905	.062642	.059547	.056609	.053822	.051176	.048665	.046281	.044018	.041869
29	.059804	.056741	.053840	.051091	.048488	.046022	.043685	.041470	.039372	.037383
30	.054269	.051396	.048680	.046111	.043683	.041386	.039214	.037160	.035216	.033378
31	.049246	.046554	.044014	.041617	.039354	.037218	.035201	.033297	.031500	.029802
32	.044688	.042169	.039796	.037560	.035454	.033469	.031599	.029836	.028175	.026609
33	.040552	.038196	.035982	.033899	.031940	.030098	.028365	.026735	.025201	.023758
34	.036798	.034598	.032533	.030595	.028775	.027067	.025463	.023956	.022541	.021212
35	.033392	.031339	.029415	.027613	.025924	.024341	.022857	.021466	.020162	.018940

TABLE B

TERM CERTAIN REMAINDER FACTORS APPLICABLE AFTER APRIL 30, 1989

	INTEREST RATE									
YEARS	10.2%	10.4%	10.6%	10.8%	11.0%	11.2%	11.4%	11.6%	11.8%	12.0%
36	.030301	.028387	.026596	.024921	.023355	.021889	.020518	.019235	.018034	.016910
37	.027497	.025712	.024047	.022492	.021040	.019684	.018418	.017236	.016131	.015098
38	.024952	.023290	.021742	.020300	.018955	.017702	.016533	.015444	.014428	.013481
39	.022642	.021096	.019658	.018321	.017077	.015919	.014841	.013839	.012905	.012036
40	.020546	.019109	.017774	.016535	.015384	.014316	.013323	.012400	.011543	.010747
41	.018645	.017309	.016071	.014923	.013860	.012874	.011959	.011111	.010325	.009595
42	.016919	.015678	.014531	.013469	.012486	.011577	.010735	.009956	.009235	.008567
43	.015353	.014201	.013138	.012156	.011249	.010411	.009637	.008922	.008260	.007649
44	.013932	.012864	.011879	.010971	.010134	.009362	.008651	.007994	.007389	.006830
45	.012642	.011652	.010740	.009902	.009130	.008419	.007765	.007163	.006609	.006098
46	.011472	.010554	.009711	.008937	.008225	.007571	.006971	.006419	.005911	.005445
47	.010410	.009560	.008780	.008065	.007410	.006809	.006257	.005752	.005287	.004861
48	.009447	.008659	.007939	.007279	.006676	.006123	.005617	.005154	.004729	.004340
49	.008572	.007844	.007178	.006570	.006014	.005506	.005042	.004618	.004230	.003875
50	.007779	.007105	.006490	.005929	.005418	.004952	.004526	.004138	.003784	.003460
51	.007059	.006435	.005868	.005351	.004881	.004453	.004063	.003708	.003384	.003089
52	.006406	.005829	.005306	.004830	.004397	.004005	.003647	.003322	.003027	.002758
53	.005813	.005280	.004797	.004359	.003962	.003601	.003274	.002977	.002708	.002463
54	005275	.004783	.004337	.003934	.003569	.003238	.002939	.002668	.002422	.002199
55	.004786	.004332	.003922	.003551	.003215	.002912	.002638	.002390	.002166	.001963
56	.004343	.003924	.003546	.003205	.002897	.002619	.002368	.002142	.001938	.001753
57	.003941	.003554	.003206	.002892	.002610	.002355	.002126	.001919	.001733	.001565
58	.003577	.003220	.002899	.002610	.002351	.002118	.001908	.001720	.001550	.001398
59	.003246	.002916	.002621	.002356	.002118	.001905	.001713	.001541	.001387	.001248
60	.002945	.002642	.002370	.002126	.001908	.001713	.001538	.001381	.001240	.001114

TABLE B

TERM CERTAIN REMAINDER FACTORS APPLICABLE AFTER APRIL 30, 1989

	INTEREST RATE									
YEARS	12.2%	12.4%	12.6%	12.8%	13.0%	13.2%	13.4%	13.6%	13.8%	14.0%
1	.891266	.889680	.888099	.886525	.884956	.883392	.881834	.880282	.878735	.877193
2	.794354	.791530	.788721	.785926	.783147	.780382	.777632	.774896	.772175	.769468
3	.707981	.704208	.700462	.696743	.693050	.689383	.685742	.682127	.678536	.674972
4	.630999	.626520	.622080	.617680	.613319	.608996	.604711	.600464	.596254	.592080
5	.562388	.557402	.552469	.547589	.542760	.537982	.533255	.528577	.523949	.519369
6	.501237	.495909	.490648	.485451	.480319	.475249	.470242	.465297	.460412	.455587
7	.446735	.441200	.435744	.430364	.425061	.419831	.414676	.409592	.404580	.399637
8	.398160	.392527	.386984	.381529	.376160	.370876	.365675	.360557	.355518	.350559
9	.354866	.349223	.343680	.338235	.332885	.327629	.322465	.317391	.312406	.307508
10	.316280	.310697	.305222	.299853	.294588	.289425	.284361	.279394	.274522	.269744
11	.281889	.276421	.271068	.265827	.260698	.255676	.250759	.245945	.241232	.236617
12	.251238	.245926	.240735	.235663	.230706	.225862	.221128	.216501	.211979	.207559
13	.223920	.218795	.213797	.208921	.204165	.199525	.194998	.190582	.186273	.182069
14	.199572	.194658	.189873	.185213	.180677	.176258	.171956	.167766	.163685	.159710
15	.177872	.173183	.168626	.164196	.159891	.155705	.151637	.147681	.143835	.140096
16	.158531	.154077	.149757	.145564	.141496	.137549	.133718	.130001	.126393	.122892
17	.141293	.137080	.132999	.129046	.125218	.121510	.117917	.114438	.111066	.107800
18	.125930	.121957	.118116	.114403	.110812	.107341	.103984	.100737	.097598	.094561
19	.112237	.108503	.104899	.101421	.098064	.094824	.091696	.088677	.085762	.082948
20	.100033	.096533	.093161	.089912	.086782	.083767	.080861	.078061	.075362	.072762
21	.089156	.085883	.082736	.079709	.076798	.073999	.071306	.068716	.066224	.063826
22	.079462	.076408	.073478	.070664	.067963	.065370	.062880	.060489	.058193	.055988
23	.070821	.067979	.065255	.062646	.060144	.057747	.055450	.053247	.051136	.049112
24	.063121	.060480	.057953	.055537	.053225	.051014	.048898	.046873	.044935	.043081
25	.056257	.053807	.051468	.049235	.047102	.045065	.043119	.041261	.039486	.037790
26	.050140	.047871	.045709	.043648	.041683	.039810	.038024	.036321	.034698	.033149
27	.044688	.042590	.040594	.038695	.036888	.035168	.033531	.031973	.030490	.029078
28	.039829	.037892	.036052	.034304	.032644	.031067	.029569	.028145	.026793	.025507
29	.035498	.033711	.032017	.030411	.028889	.027444	.026075	.024776	.023544	.022375

30	.031638	.029992	.028435	.026960	.025565	.024244	.022994	.021810	.020689	.019627
31	.028198	.026684	.025253	.023901	.022624	.021417	.020277	.019199	.018180	.017217
32	.025132	.023740	.022427	.021189	.020021	.018920	.017881	.016900	.015975	.015102
33	.022399	.021121	.019917	.018785	.017718	.016714	.015768	.014877	.014038	.013248
34	.019964	.018791	.017689	.016653	.015680	.014765	.013905	.013096	.012336	.011621
35	.017793	.016718	.015709	.014763	.013876	.013043	.012261	.011528	.010840	.010194

TABLE B

TERM CERTAIN REMAINDER FACTORS APPLICABLE AFTER APRIL 30, 1989

				INTEREST RATE						
YEARS	12.2%	12.4%	12.6%	12.8%	13.0%	13.2%	13.4%	13.6%	13.8%	14.0%
36	.015858	.014873	.013951	.013088	.012279	.011522	.010813	.010148	.009525	.008942
37	.014134	.013233	.012390	.011603	.010867	.010178	.009535	.008933	.008370	.007844
38	.012597	.011773	.011004	.010286	.009617	.008992	.008408	.007864	.007355	.006880
39	.011227	.010474	.009772	.009119	.008510	.007943	.007415	.006922	.006463	.006035
40	.010007	.009319	.008679	.008084	.007531	.007017	.006538	.006093	.005679	.005294
41	.008919	.008291	.007708	.007167	.006665	.006199	.005766	.005364	.004991	.004644
42	.007949	.007376	.006845	.006354	.005898	.005476	.005085	.004722	.004386	.004074
43	.007084	.006562	.006079	.005633	.005219	.004837	.004484	.004157	.003854	.003573
44	.006314	.005838	.005399	.004993	.004619	.004273	.003954	.003659	.003386	.003135
45	.005628	.005194	.004795	.004427	.004088	.003775	.003487	.003221	.002976	.002750
46	.005016	.004621	.004258	.003924	.003617	.003335	.003075	.002835	.002615	.002412
47	.004470	.004111	.003782	.003479	.003201	.002946	.002711	.002496	.002298	.002116
48	.003984	.003658	.003359	.003084	.002833	.002602	.002391	.002197	.002019	.001856
49	.003551	.003254	.002983	.002734	.002507	.002299	.002108	.001934	.001774	.001628
50	.003165	.002895	.002649	.002424	.002219	.002031	.001859	.001702	.001559	.001428
51	.002821	.002576	.002353	.002149	.001963	.001794	.001640	.001499	.001370	.001253
52	.002514	.002292	.002089	.001905	.001737	.001585	.001446	.001319	.001204	.001099
53	.002241	.002039	.001856	.001689	.001538	.001400	.001275	.001161	.001058	.000964
54	.001997	.001814	.001648	.001497	.001361	.001237	.001124	.001022	.000930	.000846
55	.001780	.001614	.001463	.001327	.001204	.001093	.000991	.000900	.000817	.000742
56	.001586	.001436	.001300	.001177	.001066	.000965	.000874	.000792	.000718	.000651
57	.001414	.001277	.001154	.001043	.000943	.000853	.000771	.000697	.000631	.000571
58	.001260	.001136	.001025	.000925	.000835	.000753	.000680	.000614	.000554	.000501
59	.001123	.001011	.000910	.000820	.000739	.000665	.000600	.000540	.000487	.000439
60	.001001	.000900	.000809	.000727	.000654	.000588	.000529	.000476	.000428	.000385

TABLE J

ADJUSTMENT FACTORS FOR TERM CERTAIN ANNUITIES PAYABLE AT THE BEGINNING OF EACH INTERVAL APPLICABLE AFTER APRIL 30, 1989

	Frequency Of Payments				
Interest Rate	Annually	Semi Annually	Quarterly	Monthly	Weekly
4.2	1.0420	1.0314	1.0261	1.0226	1.0213
4.4	1.0440	1.0329	1.0274	1.0237	1.0223
4.6	1.0460	1.0344	1.0286	1.0247	1.0233
4.8	1.0480	1.0359	1.0298	1.0258	1.0243
5.0	1.0500	1.0373	1.0311	1.0269	1.0253
5.2	1.0520	1.0388	1.0323	1.0279	1.0263
5.4	1.0540	1.0403	1.0335	1.0290	1.0273
5.6	1.0560	1.0418	1.0348	1.0301	1.0283
5.8	1.0580	1.0433	1.0360	1.0311	1.0293
6.0	1.0600	1.0448	1.0372	1.0322	1.0303
6.2	1.0620	1.0463	1.0385	1.0333	1.0313
6.4	1.0640	1.0478	1.0397	1.0343	1.0323
6.6	1.0660	1.0492	1.0409	1.0354	1.0333
6.8	1.0680	1.0507	1.0422	1.0365	1.0343
7.0	1.0700	1.0522	1.0434	1.0375	1.0353
7.2	1.0720	1.0537	1.0446	1.0386	1.0363
7.4	1.0740	1.0552	1.0458	1.0396	1.0373
7.6	1.0760	1.0567	1.0471	1.0407	1.0383
7.8	1.0780	1.0581	1.0483	1.0418	1.0393
8.0	1.0800	1.0596	1.0495	1.0428	1.0403
8.2	1.0820	1.0611	1.0507	1.0439	1.0413

8.4	1.0840	1.0626	1.0520	1.0449	1.0422
8.6	1.0860	1.0641	1.0532	1.0460	1.0432
8.8	1.0880	1.0655	1.0544	1.0471	1.0442
9.0	1.0900	1.0670	1.0556	1.0481	1.0452
9.2	1.0920	1.0685	1.0569	1.0492	1.0462
9.4	1.0940	1.0700	1.0581	1.0502	1.0472
9.6	1.0960	1.0715	1.0593	1.0513	1.0482
9.8	1.0980	1.0729	1.0605	1.0523	1.0492
10.0	1.1000	1.0744	1.0618	1.0534	1.0502
10.2	1.1020	1.0759	1.0630	1.0544	1.0512
10.4	1.1040	1.0774	1.0642	1.0555	1.0521
10.6	1.1060	1.0788	1.0654	1.0565	1.0531
10.8	1.1080	1.0803	1.0666	1.0576	1.0541
11.0	1.1100	1.0818	1.0679	1.0586	1.0551

TABLE J

ADJUSTMENT FACTORS FOR TERM CERTAIN ANNUITIES PAYABLE AT THE BEGINNING OF EACH INTERVAL APPLICABLE AFTER APRIL 30, 1989

	Frequency Of Payments				
Interest Rate	Annually	Semi Annually	Quarterly	Monthly	Weekly
11.2	1.1120	1.0833	1.0691	1.0597	1.0561
11.4	1.1140	1.0847	1.0703	1.0607	1.0571
11.6	1.1160	1.0862	1.0715	1.0618	1.0581
11.8	1.1180	1.0877	1.0727	1.0628	1.0590
12.0	1.1200	1.0892	1.0739	1.0639	1.0600
12.2	1.1220	1.0906	1.0752	1.0649	1.0610
12.4	1.1240	1.0921	1.0764	1.0660	1.0620
12.6	1.1260	1.0936	1.0776	1.0670	1.0630
12.8	1.1280	1.0950	1.0788	1.0681	1.0639
13.0	1.1300	1.0965	1.0800	1.0691	1.0649
13.2	1.1320	1.0980	1.0812	1.0701	1.0659
13.4	1.1340	1.0994	1.0824	1.0712	1.0669
13.6	1.1360	1.1009	1.0836	1.0722	1.0679
13.8	1.1380	1.1024	1.0849	1.0733	1.0688
14.0	1.1400	1.1039	1.0861	1.0743	1.0698

TABLE K

ADJUSTMENT FACTORS FOR ANNUITIES PAYABLE AT THE END OF EACH INTERVAL APPLICABLE AFTER APRIL 30, 1989

	Frequency Of Payments				
Interest Rate	Annually	Semi Annually	Quarterly	Monthly	Weekly
4.2	1.0000	1.0104	1.0156	1.0191	1.0205
4.4	1.0000	1.0109	1.0164	1.0200	1.0214
4.6	1.0000	1.0114	1.0171	1.0209	1.0224
4.8	1.0000	1.0119	1.0178	1.0218	1.0234
5.0	1.0000	1.0123	1.0186	1.0227	1.0243
5.2	1.0000	1.0128	1.0193	1.0236	1.0253
5.4	1.0000	1.0133	1.0200	1.0245	1.0262
5.6	1.0000	1.0138	1.0208	1.0254	1.0272
5.8	1.0000	1.0143	1.0215	1.0263	1.0282
6.0	1.0000	1.0148	1.0222	1.0272	1.0291
6.2	1.0000	1.0153	1.0230	1.0281	1.0301
6.4	1.0000	1.0158	1.0237	1.0290	1.0311
6.6	1.0000	1.0162	1.0244	1.0299	1.0320
6.8	1.0000	1.0167	1.0252	1.0308	1.0330
7.0	1.0000	1.0172	1.0259	1.0317	1.0339
7.2	1.0000	1.0177	1.0266	1.0326	1.0349
7.4	1.0000	1.0182	1.0273	1.0335	1.0358
7.6	1.0000	1.0187	1.0281	1.0344	1.0368
7.8	1.0000	1.0191	1.0288	1.0353	1.0378
8.0	1.0000	1.0196	1.0295	1.0362	1.0387
8.2	1.0000	1.0201	1.0302	1.0370	1.0397

8.4	1.0000	1.0206	1.0310	1.0379	1.0406
8.6	1.0000	1.0211	1.0317	1.0388	1.0416
8.8	1.0000	1.0215	1.0324	1.0397	1.0425
9.0	1.0000	1.0220	1.0331	1.0406	1.0435
9.2	1.0000	1.0225	1.0339	1.0415	1.0444
9.4	1.0000	1.0230	1.0346	1.0424	1.0454
9.6	1.0000	1.0235	1.0353	1.0433	1.0463
9.8	1.0000	1.0239	1.0360	1.0442	1.0473
10.0	1.0000	1.0244	1.0368	1.0450	1.0482
10.2	1.0000	1.0249	1.0375	1.0459	1.0492
10.4	1.0000	1.0254	1.0382	1.0468	1.0501
10.6	1.0000	1.0258	1.0389	1.0477	1.0511
10.8	1.0000	1.0263	1.0396	1.0486	1.0520
11.0	1.0000	1.0268	1.0404	1.0495	1.0530

TABLE K

ADJUSTMENT FACTORS FOR ANNUITIES PAYABLE AT THE END OF EACH INTERVAL APPLICABLE AFTER APRIL 30, 1989

	Frequency Of Payments				
Interest Rate	Annually	Semi Annually	Quarterly	Monthly	Weekly
11.2	1.0000	1.0273	1.0411	1.0503	1.0539
11.4	1.0000	1.0277	1.0418	1.0512	1.0549
11.6	1.0000	1.0282	1.0425	1.0521	1.0558
11.8	1.0000	1.0287	1.0432	1.0530	1.0568
12.0	1.0000	1.0292	1.0439	1.0539	1.0577
12.2	1.0000	1.0296	1.0447	1.0548	1.0587
12.4	1.0000	1.0301	1.0454	1.0556	1.0596
12.6	1.0000	1.0306	1.0461	1.0565	1.0605
12.8	1.0000	1.0310	1.0468	1.0574	1.0615
13.0	1.0000	1.0315	1.0475	1.0583	1.0624
13.2	1.0000	1.0320	1.0482	1.0591	1.0634
13.4	1.0000	1.0324	1.0489	1.0600	1.0643
13.6	1.0000	1.0329	1.0496	1.0609	1.0652
13.8	1.0000	1.0334	1.0504	1.0618	1.0662
14.0	1.0000	1.0339	1.0511	1.0626	1.0671

(7) [Reserved]. For further guidance, see § 20.2031-7T(d)(7).

(e) Effective/applicability dates. This section applies after April 30, 1999, and before May 1, 2009.

T.D. 8540, 6/9/94, amend T.D. 8819, 4/29/99, T.D. 8886, 6/9/2000, T.D. 9448, 5/1/2009.

PAR. 7. Section 20.2031-7 is amended by revising paragraphs (c), (d)(1), (d)(2), (d)(3), (d)(4), (d)(5), (d)(7), and (e) to read as follows:

Proposed § 20.2031-7 Valuation of annuities, interests for life or term of years, and remainder or reversionary interests. [*For Preamble, see ¶ 153,105*]

* * * * *

(c) [The text of this proposed paragraph (c) is the same as the text of § 20.2031-7T(c) published elsewhere in this issue of the Federal Register]. [*See T.D. 9448, 05/07/2009, 74 Fed. Reg. 87.*]

(d) [The text of this proposed paragraph (d)(1) through (d)(5) is the same as the text of § 20.2031-7T(d)(1) through (d)(5) published elsewhere in this issue of the Federal Register]. [*See T.D. 9448, 05/07/2009, 74 Fed. Reg. 87.*]

* * * * *

(7) [The text of this proposed paragraph (d)(7) is the same as the text of § 20.2031-7T(d)(7) published elsewhere in this issue of the Federal Register]. [*See T.D. 9448, 05/07/2009, 74 Fed. Reg. 87.*]

(e) [The text of this proposed paragraph (e) is the same as the text of § 20.2031-7T(e) published elsewhere in this issue of the Federal Register]. [*See T.D. 9448, 05/07/2009, 74 Fed. Reg. 87.*]

§ 20.2031-7A Valuation of annuities, interests for life or term of years, and remainder or reversionary interests for estates of decedents for which the valuation date of the gross estate is before May 1, 2009.

(a) Valuation of annuities, interests for life or term of years, and remainder or reversionary interests for estates of decedents for which the valuation date of the gross estate is before January 1, 1952. Except as otherwise provided in § 20.2031-7(b), if the valuation date of the decedent's gross estate is before January 1, 1952, the present value of annuities, life estates, terms for years, remainders, and reversions is their present value determined under this section. If the valuation of the interest involved is dependent upon the continuation or termination of one or more lives or upon a term certain concurrent with one or more lives, the factor for the present value is computed on the basis of interest at the rate of 4 percent a year, compounded annually, and life contingencies as to each life involved from values that are based on the Actuaries' or Combined Experience

Table of Mortality, as extended. This table and related factors are described in former section 81.10 (as contained in the 26 CFR Part 81 edition revised as of April 1, 1958). The present value of an interest measured by a term of years is computed on the basis of interest at the rate of 4 percent a year.

(b) Valuation of annuities, interests for life or term of years, and remainder or reversionary interests for estates of decedents for which the valuation date of the gross estate is after December 31, 1951, and before January 1, 1971. Except as otherwise provided in § 20.2031-7(b), if the valuation date for the decedent's gross estate is after December 31, 1951, and before January 1, 1971, the present value of annuities, life estates, terms of years, remainders, and reversions is their present value determined under this section. If the valuation of the interest involved is dependent upon the continuation or termination of one or more lives, or upon a term certain concurrent with one or more lives, the factor for the present value is computed on the basis of interest at the rate of 3½ percent a year, compounded annually, and life contingencies as to each life involved are taken from U.S. Life Table 38. This table and related factors are set forth in former § 20.2031-7 (as contained in the 26 CFR Part 20 edition revised as of April 1, 1984). Special factors involving one and two lives may be found in or computed with the use of tables contained in the publication entitled "Actuarial Values for Estate and Gift Tax," Internal Revenue Service Publication Number 11 (Rev. 5-59). This publication is no longer available for purchase from the Superintendent of Documents. However, it may be obtained by requesting a copy from: CC:DOM:CORP:T:R (IRS Publication 11), room 5228, Internal Revenue Service, POB 7604, Ben Franklin Station, Washington, DC 20044. The present value of an interest measured by a term of years is computed on the basis of interest at the rate of 3½ percent a year.

(c) Valuation of annuities, interests for life or term of years, and remainder or reversionary interests for estates of decedents for which the valuation date of the gross estate is after December 31, 1970, and before December 1, 1983. Except as otherwise provided in § 20.2031-7(b), if the valuation date of the decedent's gross estate is after December 31, 1970, and before December 1, 1983, the present value of annuities, life estates, terms of years, remainders, and reversions is their present value determined under this section. If the valuation of the interest involved is dependent upon the continuation of or termination of one or more lives or upon a term certain concurrent with one or more lives, the factor for the present value is computed on the basis of interest at the rate of 6 percent a year, compounded annually, and life contingencies are determined as to each male and female life involved, from values that are set forth in Table LN. Table LN contains values that are taken from the life table for total males and the life table for total females appearing as Tables 2 and 3, respectively, in United States Life Tables: 1959-1960, published by the Department of Health and Human Services, Public Health Service. Table LN and related factors are set forth in former § 20.2031-10 (as contained in the 26 CFR Part 20 edition revised as of April 1, 1994). Special factors involving one and two lives may be found in or computed with the use of tables contained in Internal Revenue Service Publication 723, "Actuarial Values I: Valuation of Last Survivor Charitable Remainders," (12-70), and Internal Revenue Service Publication 723A, "Actuarial Values II: Factors at 6 Percent Involving One and Two Lives," (12-70). These publications are no longer available for purchase from the Superintendent of Documents. However, a copy of each may be obtained from: CC:DOM:CORP:T:R (IRS Publication 723/723A), room 5228, Internal Revenue Service, POB 7604, Ben Franklin Station, Washington, DC 20044.

(d) Valuation of annuities, interests for life or term of years, and remainder or reversionary interests for estates of decedents for which the valuation date of the gross estate is after November 30, 1983, and before May 1, 1989. *(1) In general.* (i) Except as otherwise provided in § 20.2031-7(b), if the decedent died after November 30, 1983, and the valuation date for the gross estate is before May 1, 1989, the fair market value of annuities, life estates, terms of years, remainders, and reversions is their present value determined under this section. If the decedent died after November 30, 1983, and before August 9, 1984, or, in cases where the valuation date of the decedent's gross estate is before May 1, 1989, if, on December 1, 1983, the decedent was mentally incompetent so that the disposition of the decedent's property could not be changed, and the decedent died on or after December 1, 1983, without having regained competency to dispose of the decedent's property, or if the decedent died within 90 days of the date on which the decedent first regained competency, the fair market value of annuities, life estates, terms for years, remainders, and reversions included in the gross estate of such decedent is their present value determined under either this section or § 20.2031-7A(c), at the option of the taxpayer. The value of annuities issued by companies regularly engaged in their sale, and of insurance policies on the lives of persons other than the decedent, is determined under § 20.2031-8. The fair market value of a remainder interest in a charitable remainder unitrust, as defined in § 1.664-3 of this chapter, is its present value determined under § 1.664-4 of this chapter. The fair market value of a life interest or term for years in a charitable remainder unitrust is the fair market value of the property as of the date of valuation less the fair market value of the remainder interest on such date determined under § 1.664-4 of this chapter. The fair market value of the interests in a pooled income fund, as defined in § 1.642(c)-5 of this chapter, is their value determined under § 1.642(c)-6 of this chapter.

(ii) The present value of an annuity, life estate, remainder, or reversion determined under this section which is dependent on the continuation or termination of the life of one person is computed by the use of Table A in paragraph (d)(6) of this section. The present value of an annuity, term for years, remainder, or reversion dependent on a term certain is computed by the use of Table B in paragraph (d)(6) of this section. If the interest to be valued is dependent upon more than one life or there is a term certain concurrent with one or more lives, see paragraph (d)(5) of this section. For purposes of the computations described in this section, the age of a person is to be taken as the age of that person at his or her nearest birthday.

(iii) In all examples set forth in this section, the decedent is assumed to have died on or after August 9, 1984, with the valuation date of the decedent's gross estate before May 1, 1989, and to have been competent to change the disposition of the property on December 1, 1983.

(2) Annuities. (i) If an annuity is payable annually at the end of each year during the life of an individual (as for example if the first payment is due one year after the decedent's death), the amount payable annually is multiplied by the figure in column 2 of Table A opposite the number of years in column 1 nearest the age of the individual whose life measures the duration of the annuity. If the annuity is

payable annually at the end of each year for a definite number of years, the amount payable annually is multiplied by the figure in column 2 of Table B opposite the number of years in column 1 representing the duration of the annuity. The application of this paragraph (d)(2)(i) may be illustrated by the following examples:

Example (1). The decedent received, under the terms of the decedent's father's will an annuity of $10,000 a year payable annually for the life of the decedent's elder brother. At the time the decedent died, an annual payment had just been made. The brother at the decedent's death was 40 years eight months old. By reference to Table A, the figure in column 2 opposite 41 years, the number nearest to the brother's actual age, is found to be 9.1030. The present value of the annuity at the date of the decedent's death is, therefore, $91,030 ($10,000 × 9.1030).

Example (2). The decedent was entitled to receive an annuity of $10,000 a year payable annually throughout a term certain. At the time the decedent died, the annual payment had just been made and five more annual payments were still to be made. By reference to Table B, it is found that the figure in column 2 opposite five years is 3.7908. The present value of the annuity is, therefore, $37,908 ($10,000 × 3.7808).

(ii) If an annuity is payable at the end of semiannual, quarterly, monthly, or weekly periods during the life of an individual (as for example if the first payment is due one month after the decedent's death), the aggregate amount to be paid within a year is first multiplied by the figure in column 2 of Table A opposite the number of years in column 1 nearest the age of the individual whose life measures the duration of the annuity. The product so obtained is then multiplied by whichever of the following factors is appropriate:

1.0244 for semiannual payments,

1.0368 for quarterly payments,

1.0450 for monthly payments,

1.0482 for weekly payments.

If the annuity is payable at the end of semiannual, quarterly, monthly, or weekly periods for a definite number of years, the aggregate amount to be paid within a year is first multiplied by the figure in column 2 of Table B opposite the number of years in column 1 representing the duration of the annuity. The product so obtained is then multiplied by whichever of the above factors is appropriate. The application of this paragraph (d)(2)(ii) may be illustrated by the following example:

Example. The facts are the same as those contained in example (1) set forth in paragraph (d)(2)(i) of this section, except that the annuity is payable semiannually. The aggregate annual amount, $10,000, is multiplied by the factor 9.1030 and the product multiplied by 1.0244. The present value of the annuity at the date of the decedent's death is, therefore, $93,251.13 ($10,000 × 9.1030 × 1.0244).

(iii) (A) If the first payment of an annuity for the life of an individual is due at the beginning of the annual or other payment period rather than at the end (as for example if the first payment is to be made immediately after the decedent's death), the value of the annuity is the sum of (A) the first payment plus (B) the present value of a similar annuity, the first payment of which is not to be made until the end of the payment period, determined as provided in paragraphs (d)(2)(i) or (ii) of this section, the application of this paragraph (d)(2)(iii)(A) may be illustrated by the following example:

Example. The decedent was entitled to receive an annuity of $50 a month during the life of another person. The decedent died on the date the payment was due. At the date of the decedent's death, the person whose life measures the duration of the annuity was 50 years of age. The value of the annuity at the date of the decedent's death is $50 plus the product of $50 × 12 × 8.4743 (see Table A) × 1.0450 (See paragraph (d)(2)(ii) of this section). That is $50 plus $5,313.39, or $5,363.39.

Example. The facts are the same as those contained in example (1) set forth in paragraph (b)(1) of this section, except that the annuity is payable semiannually. The aggregate annual amount, $10,000, is multiplied by the factor 9.1030 and the product multiplied by 1.0244. The present value of the annuity at the date of the decedent's death is, therefore, $93,251.13 ($10,000 × 9.1030 × 1.0244).

(B) If the first payment of an annuity for a definite number of years is due at the beginning of the annual or other payment period, the applicable factor is the product of the factor shown in Table B multiplied by whichever of the following factors is appropriate:

1.1000 for annual payments,

1.0744 for semiannual payments,

1.0618 for quarterly payments,

1.0534 for monthly payments,

1.0502 for weekly payments.

The application of this paragraph (d)(2)(iii)(B) may be illustrated by the following example:

Example. The decedent was the beneficiary of an annuity of $50 a month. On the day a payment was due, the decedent died. There were 300 payments to be made, including the payment due. The value of the annuity as of the date of decedent's death is the product of $50 × 12 × 9.0770 (see Table B) × 1.0534, or $5,737.03.

(3) Life estates and terms for years. If the interest to be valued is the right of a person for his or her life, or for the life of another person, to receive the income of certain property or to use nonincome-producing property, the value of the interest is the value of the property multiplied by the figure in column 3 of Table A opposite the number of years nearest to the actual age of the measuring life. If the interest to be valued is the right to receive income of property or to use nonincome-producing property for a term of years, column 3 of Table B is used. The application of this paragraph (d)(3) may be illustrated by the following example:

Example. The decedent or the decedent's estate was entitled to receive the income from a fund of $50,000 during the life of the decedent's elder brother. Upon the brother's death, the remainder is to go to B. The brother was 31 years, five months old at the time of decedent's death. By reference to Table A the figure in column 3 opposite 31 years is found to be 0.95254. The present value of the decedent's interest is, therefore, $47,627 ($50,000 × 0.95254).

(4) Remainders or reversionary interests. If a decedent had, at the time of the decedent's death, a remainder or a reversionary interest in property to take effect after an estate for the life of another, the present value of the decedent's interest is obtained by multiplying the value of the property by the figure in column 4 of Table A opposite the number of years nearest to the actual age of the person whose life measures the preceding estate. If the remainder or reversion is to take effect at the end of the term for years, column 4 of Table B is used. The application of this paragraph (d)(4) may be illustrated by the following example:

Example. The decedent was entitled to receive certain property worth $50,000 upon the death of the decedent's elder sister, to whom the income was bequeathed for life. At the time of the decedent's death, the elder sister was 31 years five months old. By reference to Table A the figure in column 4 opposite 31 years is found to be .04746. The present value of the remainder interest at the date of the decedent's death is, therefore, $2,373 ($50,000 × .04746).

(5) Actuarial computations by the Internal Revenue Service. If the valuation of the interest involved is dependent upon the continuation or the termination of more than one life or upon a term certain concurrent with one or more lives a special factor must be used. The factor is to be computed on the basis of interest at the rate of 10 percent a year, compounded annually, and life contingencies determined, as to each person involved, from the values of LX that are set forth in column 2 of Table LN of paragraph (d)(6). Table LN contains values of LX taken from the life table for the total population appearing as Table 1 of United States Life Tables: 1969–71, published by the Department of Health and Human Services, Public Health Service. Many special factors involving one and two lives may be found in or computed with the use of the tables contained in Internal Revenue Service Publication 723E, "Actuarial Values II: Factors at 10 Percent Involving One and Two Lives," (12-83). This publication is no longer available for purchase from the Superintendent of Documents. However, it may be obtained by requesting a copy from: CC:DOM:CORP:T:R (IRS Publication 723E), room 5228, Internal Revenue Service, POB 7604, Ben Franklin Station, Washington DC 20044. The request must be accompanied by a statement of the date of birth of each person, the duration of whose life may affect the value of the interest, and by copies of the relevant instruments. Special factors are not furnished for prospective transfers.

(6) Tables. The following tables shall be used in the application of the provisions of this section:

Table A—Single Life, Unisex, 10 Percent—Table Showing the Present Worth of an Annuity, of a Life Estate, and a Remainder Interest—Applicable for Transfers After November 30, 1983, and Before May 1, 1989

Age (1)	Annuity (2)	Life Estate (3)	Remainder (4)
0	9.7188	.97188	.02812
1	9.8988	.98988	.01012
2	9.9017	.99017	.00983
3	9.9008	.99008	.00992
4	9.8981	.98981	.01019
5	9.8938	.98938	.01062
6	9.8884	.98884	.01116
7	9.8822	.98822	.01178
8	9.8748	.98748	.01252
9	9.8663	.98663	.01337
10	9.8565	.98565	.01435
11	9.8453	.98453	.01547
12	9.8329	.98329	.01671
13	9.8198	.98198	.01802
14	9.8066	.98066	.01934
15	9.7937	.97937	.02063
16	9.7815	.97815	.02185
17	9.7700	.97700	.02300
18	9.7590	.97590	.02410
19	9.7480	.97480	.02520
20	9.7365	.97365	.02635
21	9.7245	.97245	.02755
22	9.7120	.97120	.02880
23	9.6986	.96986	.03014
24	9.6841	.96841	.03159
25	9.6678	.96678	.03322
26	9.6495	.96495	.03505
27	9.6290	.96290	.03710
28	9.6062	.96062	.03938
29	9.5813	.95813	.04187
30	9.5543	.95543	.04457
31	9.5254	.95254	.04746
32	9.4942	.94942	.05058
33	9.4608	.94608	.05392
34	9.4250	.94250	.05750
35	9.3868	.93868	.06132
36	9.3460	.93460	.06540
37	9.3026	.93026	.06974
38	9.2567	.92567	.07433
39	9.2083	.92083	.07917
40	9.1571	.91571	.08429
41	9.1030	.91030	.08970
42	9.0457	.90457	.09543
43	8.9855	.89855	.10145
44	8.9221	.89221	.10779
45	8.8558	.88558	.11442
46	8.7863	.87863	.12137
47	8.7137	.87137	.12863
48	8.6374	.86374	.13626
49	8.5578	.85578	.14422
50	8.4743	.84743	.15257
51	8.3874	.83874	.16126
52	8.2969	.82969	.17031
53	8.2028	.82028	.17972
54	8.1054	.81054	.18946
55	8.0046	.80046	.19954
56	7.9006	.79006	.20994
57	7.7931	.77931	.22069
58	7.6822	.76822	.23178
59	7.5675	.75675	.24325
60	7.4491	.74491	.25509
61	7.3267	.73267	.26733
62	7.2002	.72002	.27998
63	7.0696	.70696	.29304
64	6.9352	.69352	.30648
65	6.7970	.67970	.32030
66	6.6551	.66551	.33449
67	6.5098	.65098	.34902
68	6.3610	.63610	.36390
69	6.2086	.62086	.37914
70	6.0522	.60522	.39478
71	5.8914	.58914	.41086
72	5.7261	.57261	.42739
73	5.5571	.55571	.44429
74	5.3862	.53862	.46138

Age (1)	Annuity (2)	Life Estate (3)	Remainder (4)
75	5.2149	.52149	.47851
76	5.0441	.50441	.49559
77	4.8742	.48742	.51258
78	4.7049	.47049	.52951
79	4.5357	.45357	.54643
80	4.3659	.43659	.56341
81	4.1967	.41967	.58033
82	4.0295	.40295	.59705
83	3.8642	.38642	.61358
84	3.6998	.36998	.63002
85	3.5359	.35359	.64641
86	3.3764	.33764	.66236
87	3.2262	.32262	.67738
88	3.0859	.30859	.69141
89	2.9526	.29526	.70474
90	2.8221	.28221	.71779
91	2.6955	.26955	.73045
92	2.5771	.25771	.74229
93	2.4692	.24692	.75308
94	2.3728	.23728	.76272
95	2.2887	.22887	.77113
96	2.2181	.22181	.77819
97	2.1550	.21550	.78450
98	2.1000	.21000	.79000
99	2.0486	.20486	.79514
100	1.9975	.19975	.80025
101	1.9532	.19532	.80468
102	1.9054	.19054	.80946
103	1.8437	.18437	.81563
104	1.7856	.17856	.82144
105	1.6962	.16962	.83038
106	1.5488	.15488	.84512
107	1.3409	.13409	.86591
108	1.0068	.10068	.89932
109	.4545	.04545	.95455

Table B—Term Certain, Unisex, 10 Percent—Table Showing the Present Worth of an Annuity for a Term Certain, of an Income Interest for a Term Certain, and of a Remainder Interest Postponed for a Term Certain—Applicable for Transfers After November 30, 1983, and Before May 1, 1989

(1) Number of Years	(2) Annuity	(3) Term Certain	(4) Remainder
1	.9091	.090909	.909091
2	1.7355	.173554	.826446
3	2.4869	.248685	.751315
4	3.1699	.316987	.683013
5	3.7908	.379079	.620921
6	4.3553	.435526	.564474
7	4.8684	.486842	.513158
8	5.3349	.533493	.466507
9	5.7590	.575902	.424098
10	6.1446	.614457	.385543
11	6.4951	.649506	.350494
12	6.8137	.681369	.318631
13	7.1034	.710336	.289664
14	7.3667	.736669	.263331
15	7.6061	.760608	.239392
16	7.8237	.782371	.217629
17	8.0216	.802155	.197845
18	8.2014	.820141	.179859
19	8.3649	.836492	.163508
20	8.5136	.851356	.148644
21	8.6487	.864869	.135131
22	8.7715	.877154	.122846
23	8.8832	.888322	.111678
24	8.9847	.898474	.101526
25	9.0770	.907704	.092296
26	9.1609	.916095	.083905
27	9.2372	.923722	.076278
28	9.3066	.930657	.069343
29	9.3696	.936961	.063039
30	9.4269	.942691	.057309
31	9.4790	.947901	.052099
32	9.5264	.952638	.047362
33	9.5694	.956943	.043057
34	9.6086	.960857	.039143
35	9.6442	.964416	.035584
36	9.6765	.967651	.032349
37	9.7059	.970592	.029408
38	9.7327	.973265	.026735
39	9.7570	.975686	.024304
40	9.7791	.977905	.022095
41	9.7991	.979914	.020096
42	9.8174	.981740	.018260
43	9.8340	.983400	.016600
44	9.8491	.984909	.015091
45	9.8628	.986281	.013718
46	9.8753	.987528	.012472
47	9.8866	.988662	.011338
48	9.8969	.989693	.010307
49	9.9063	.990630	.009370
50	9.9148	.991481	.008519
51	9.9226	.992256	.007744
52	9.9296	.992960	.007040
53	9.9360	.993600	.006400
54	9.9418	.994182	.005818
55	9.9471	.994711	.005289
56	9.9519	.995191	.004809
57	9.9563	.995629	.004371
58	9.9603	.996026	.003974
59	9.9639	.996387	.003613
60	9.9672	.996716	.003284

Table LN—Applicable for Transfers After November 30, 1983, and Before May 1, 1989

Age X (1)	lx (2)	Age X (1)	lx (2)	Age X (1)	lx (2)	Age X (1)	lx (2)	Age X (1)	lx (2)
0	100000	23	96292	46	91144	69	64166	92	6070
1	97998	24	96145	47	90662	70	61984	93	4773
2	97876	25	96000	48	90142	71	59715	94	3682
3	97792	26	95859	49	89579	72	57360	95	2786
4	97724	27	95721	50	88972	73	54913	96	2068
5	97668	28	95586	51	88315	74	52363	97	1511
6	97619	29	95448	52	87605	75	49705	98	1087
7	97573	30	95307	53	86838	76	46946	99	772
8	97531	31	95158	54	86007	77	44101	100	542
9	97494	32	95003	55	85110	78	41192	101	375
10	97460	33	94840	56	84142	79	38245	102	257
11	97430	34	94666	57	83103	80	35285	103	175
12	97401	35	94482	58	81988	81	32323	104	117
13	97367	36	94285	59	80798	82	29375	105	78
14	97322	37	94073	60	79529	83	26469	106	52
15	97261	38	93843	61	78181	84	23638	107	34
16	97181	39	93593	62	76751	85	20908	108	22
17	97083	40	93322	63	75236	86	18282	109	14
18	96970	41	93028	64	73631	87	15769	110	0
19	96846	42	92712	65	71933	88	13407		
20	96716	43	92368	66	70139	89	11240		
21	96580	44	91995	67	68246	90	9297		
22	96438	45	91587	68	66254	91	7577		

(e) Valuation of annuities, interests for life or term of years, and remainder or reversionary interests for estates of decedents for which the valuation date of the gross estate is after April 30,1989, and before May 1, 1999. *(1) In general.* Except as otherwise provided in § 20.2031-7(b) and § 20.7520-3(b) (pertaining to certain limitations on the use of prescribed tables), if the valuation date for the gross estate of the decedent is after April 30, 1989, and before May 1, 1999, the fair market value of annuities, life estates, terms of years, remainders, and reversionary interests is the present value of the interests determined by use of standard or special section 7520 actuarial factors and the valuation methodology described in § 20.2031-7(d). These factors are derived by using the appropriate section 7520 interest rate and, if applicable, the mortality component for the valuation date of the interest that is being valued. See §§ 20.7520-1 through 20.7520-4. See paragraph (e)(4) of this section for determination of the appropriate table for use in valuing these interests.

(2) Transitional rule. (i) If the valuation date is after April 30, 1989, and before June 10, 1994, a taxpayer can rely on Notice 89-24 (1989-1 C.B. 660), or Notice 89-60 (1989-1 C.B. 700). See § 601.601(d)(2)(ii)(b) of this chapter.

(ii) If a decedent dies after April 30, 1989, and if on May 1, 1989, the decedent was mentally incompetent so that the disposition of the decedent's property could not be changed, and the decedent dies without having regained competency to dispose of the decedent's property or dies within 90 days of the date on which the decedent first regains competency, the fair market value of annuities, life estates, terms for years, remainders, and reversions included in the gross estate of the decedent is their present value determined either under this section or under the corresponding section applicable at the time the decedent became mentally incompetent, at the option of the decedent's executor. For example, see paragraph (d) of this section.

(3) Publications and actuarial computations by the Internal Revenue Service. Many standard actuarial factors not included in paragraph (e)(4) of this section or in § 20.2031-7(d)(6) are included in Internal Revenue Service Publication 1457, "Actuarial Values, Alpha Volume," (8-89). Publication 1457 also includes examples that illustrate how to compute many special factors for more unusual situations. Publication 1457 is no longer available for purchase from the Superintendent of Documents, United States Government Printing Office, Washington, DC 20402. However, pertinent factors in this publication may be obtained from: CC:DOM:CORP:R (IRS Publication 1457), room 5226, Internal Revenue Service, POB 7604, Ben Franklin Station, Washington, DC 20044. If a special factor is required in the case of an actual decedent, the Internal Revenue Service may furnish the factor to the executor upon a request for a ruling. The request for a ruling must be accompanied by a recitation of the facts including a statement of the date of birth for each measuring life, the date of the decedent's death, any other applicable dates, and a copy of the will, trust, or other relevant documents. A request for a ruling must comply with the instructions for requesting a ruling published periodically in the Internal Revenue Bulletin (see §§ 601.201 and 601.601(d)(2)(ii)(b) of this chapter) and include payment of the required user fee.

(4) Actuarial tables. Except as provided in § 20.7520-3(b) (pertaining to certain limitations on the use of prescribed tables), Life Table 80CNSMT and Table S (Single life remainder factors applicable where the valuation date is after April 30, 1989, and before May 1, 1999), contained in this paragraph (e)(4), and Table B, Table J, and Table K set forth in § 20.2031-7(d)(6) must be used in the application of the provisions of this section when the section 7520 interest rate

component is between 4.2 and 14 percent. Table S and Table 80CNSMT are as follows:

TABLE S

BASED ON LIFE TABLE 80CNSMT SINGLE LIFE REMAINDER FACTORS APPLICABLE AFTER APRIL 30, 1989 AND BEFORE MAY 1, 1999

					Interest Rate					
AGE	4.2%	4.4%	4.6%	4.8%	5.0%	5.2%	5.4%	5.6%	5.8%	6.0%
0	.07389	.06749	.06188	.05695	.05261	.04879	.04541	.04243	.03978	.03744
1	.06494	.05832	.05250	.04738	.04287	.03889	.03537	.03226	.02950	.02705
2	.06678	.05999	.05401	.04874	.04410	.03999	.03636	.03314	.03028	.02773
3	.06897	.06200	.05587	.05045	.04567	.04143	.03768	.03435	.03139	.02875
4	.07139	.06425	.05796	.05239	.04746	.04310	.03922	.03578	.03271	.02998
5	.07401	.06669	.06023	.05451	.04944	.04494	.04094	.03738	.03421	.03137
6	.07677	.06928	.06265	.05677	.05156	.04692	.04279	.03911	.03583	.03289
7	.07968	.07201	.06521	.05918	.05381	.04903	.04477	.04097	.03757	.03453
8	.08274	.07489	.06792	.06172	.05621	.05129	.04689	.04297	.03945	.03630
9	.08597	.07794	.07079	.06443	.05876	.05370	.04917	.04511	.04148	.03821
10	.08936	.08115	.07383	.06730	.06147	.05626	.05159	.04741	.04365	.04027
11	.09293	.08453	.07704	.07035	.06436	.05900	.05419	.04988	.04599	.04250
12	.09666	.08807	.08040	.07354	.06739	.06188	.05693	.05248	.04847	.04486
13	.10049	.09172	.08387	.07684	.07053	.06487	.05977	.05518	.05104	.04731
14	.10437	.09541	.08738	.08017	.07370	.06788	.06263	.05791	.05364	.04978
15	.10827	.09912	.09090	.08352	.07688	.07090	.06551	.06064	.05623	.05225
16	11220	.10285	.09445	.08689	.08008	.07394	.06839	.06337	.05883	.05472
17	.11615	.10661	.09802	.09028	.08330	.07699	.07129	.06612	.06144	.05719
18	.12017	.11043	.10165	.09373	.08656	.08009	.07422	.06890	.06408	.05969
19	.12428	.11434	.10537	.09726	.08992	.08327	.07724	.07177	.06679	.06226
20	.12850	.11836	.10919	.10089	.09337	.08654	.08035	.07471	.06959	.06492
21	.13282	.12248	.11311	.10462	.09692	.08991	.08355	.07775	.07247	.06765
22	.13728	.12673	.11717	.10848	.10059	.09341	.08686	.08090	.07546	.07049
23	.14188	.13113	.12136	.11248	.10440	.09703	.09032	.08418	.07858	.07345
24	.14667	.13572	.12575	.11667	.10839	.10084	.09395	.08764	.08187	.07659
25	.15167	.14051	.13034	.12106	.11259	.10486	.09778	.09130	.08536	.07991
26	.15690	.14554	.13517	.12569	.11703	.10910	.10184	.09518	.08907	.08346
27	.16237	.15081	.14024	.13056	.12171	.11359	.10614	.09930	.09302	.08724
28	.16808	.15632	.14555	.13567	.12662	.11831	.11068	.10366	.09720	.09125
29	.17404	.16208	.15110	.14104	.13179	.12329	.11547	.10827	.10163	.09551
30	.18025	.16808	.15692	.14665	.13721	.12852	.12051	.11313	.10631	.10002
31	.18672	.17436	.16300	.15255	.14291	.13403	.12584	.11827	.11127	.10480
32	.19344	.18090	.16935	.15870	.14888	.13980	.13142	.12367	.11650	.10985
33	.20044	.18772	.17598	.16514	.15513	.14587	.13730	.12936	.12201	.11519
34	.20770	.19480	.18287	.17185	.16165	.15221	.14345	.13533	.12780	.12080

TABLE S

BASED ON LIFE TABLE 80CNSMT SINGLE LIFE REMAINDER FACTORS APPLICABLE AFTER APRIL 30, 1989 AND BEFORE MAY 1, 1999

					Interest Rate					
AGE	4.2%	4.4%	4.6%	4.8%	5.0%	5.2%	5.4%	5.6%	5.8%	6.0%
35	.21522	.20215	.19005	.17884	.16846	.15883	.14989	.14159	.13388	.12670
36	.22299	.20974	.19747	.18609	.17552	.16571	.15660	.14812	.14022	.13287
37	.23101	.21760	.20516	.19360	.18286	.17288	.16358	.15492	.14685	.13933
38	.23928	.22572	.21311	.20139	.19048	.18032	.17085	.16201	.15377	.14607
39	.24780	.23409	.22133	.20945	.19837	.18804	.17840	.16939	.16097	.15310
40	.25658	.24273	.22982	.21778	.20654	.19605	.18624	.17706	.16847	.16043
41	.26560	.25163	.23858	.22639	.21499	.20434	.19436	.18502	.17627	.16806
42	.27486	.26076	.24758	.23525	.22370	.21289	.20276	.19326	.18434	.17597
43	.28435	.27013	.25683	.24436	.23268	.22172	.21143	.20177	.19270	.18416
44	.29407	.27975	.26633	.25373	.24191	.23081	.22038	.21057	.20134	.19265
45	.30402	.28961	.27608	.26337	.25142	.24019	.22962	.21966	.21028	.20144
46	.31420	.29970	.28608	.27326	.26120	.24983	.23913	.22904	.21951	.21053
47	.32460	.31004	.29632	.28341	.27123	.25975	.24892	.23870	.22904	.21991
48	.33521	.32058	.30679	.29379	.28151	.26992	.25897	.24862	.23883	.22957
49	.34599	.33132	.31746	.30438	.29201	.28032	.26926	.25879	.24888	.23949

50	.35695	.34224	.32833	.31518	.30273	.29094	.27978	.26921	.25918	.24966
51	.36809	.35335	.33940	.32619	.31367	.30180	.29055	.27987	.26973	.26010
52	.37944	.36468	.35070	.33744	.32486	.31292	.30158	.29081	.28057	.27083
53	.39098	.37622	.36222	.34892	.33629	.32429	.31288	.30203	.29170	.28186
54	.40269	.38794	.37393	.36062	.34795	.33590	.32442	.31349	.30308	.29316
55	.41457	.39985	.38585	.37252	.35983	.34774	.33621	.32522	.31474	.30473
56	.42662	.41194	.39796	.38464	.37193	.35981	.34824	.33720	.32666	.31658
57	.43884	.42422	.41028	.39697	.38426	.37213	.36053	.34945	.33885	.32872
58	.45123	.43668	.42279	.40951	.39682	.38468	.37307	.36196	.35132	.34114
59	.46377	.44931	.43547	.42224	.40958	.39745	.38584	.37471	.36405	.35383
60	.47643	.46206	.44830	.43513	.42250	.41040	.39880	.38767	.37699	.36674
61	.48916	.47491	.46124	.44814	.43556	.42350	.41192	.40080	.39012	.37985
62	.50196	.48783	.47427	.46124	.44874	.43672	.42518	.41408	.40340	.39314
63	.51480	.50081	.48736	.47444	.46201	.45006	.43856	.42749	.41684	.40658
64	.52770	.51386	.50054	.48773	.47540	.46352	.45208	.44105	.43043	.42019
65	.54069	.52701	.51384	.50115	.48892	.47713	.46577	.45480	.44422	.43401
66	.55378	.54029	.52727	.51472	.50262	.49093	.47965	.46876	.45824	.44808
67	.56697	.55368	.54084	.52845	.51648	.50491	.49373	.48293	.47248	.46238
68	.58026	.56717	.55453	.54231	.53049	.51905	.50800	.49729	.48694	.47691
69	.59358	.58072	.56828	.55624	.54459	.53330	.52238	.51179	.50154	.49160
70	.60689	.59427	.58205	.57021	.55874	.54762	.53683	.52638	.51624	.50641

TABLE S

BASED ON LIFE TABLE 80CNSMT SINGLE LIFE REMAINDER FACTORS APPLICABLE AFTER APRIL 30, 1989 AND BEFORE MAY 1, 1999

	Interest Rate									
AGE	4.2%	4.4%	4.6%	4.8%	5.0%	5.2%	5.4%	5.6%	5.8%	6.0%
71	.62014	.60778	.59578	.58415	.57287	.56193	.55131	.54100	.53099	.52126
72	.63334	.62123	.60948	.59808	.58700	.57624	.56579	.55563	.54577	.53617
73	.64648	.63465	.62315	.61198	.60112	.59056	.58029	.57030	.56059	.55113
74	.65961	.64806	.63682	.62590	.61527	.60492	.59485	.58504	.57550	.56620
75	.67274	.66149	.65054	.63987	.62948	.61936	.60950	.59990	.59053	.58140
76	.68589	.67495	.66429	.65390	.64377	.63390	.62427	.61487	.60570	.59676
77	.69903	.68841	.67806	.66796	.65811	.64849	.63910	.62993	.62097	.61223
78	.71209	.70182	.69179	.68199	.67242	.66307	.65393	.64501	.63628	.62775
79	.72500	.71507	.70537	.69588	.68660	.67754	.66867	.65999	.65151	.64321
80	.73768	.72809	.71872	.70955	.70058	.69180	.68320	.67479	.66655	.65849
81	.75001	.74077	.73173	.72288	.71422	.70573	.69741	.68926	.68128	.67345
82	.76195	.75306	.74435	.73582	.72746	.71926	.71123	.70335	.69562	.68804
83	.77346	.76491	.75654	.74832	.74026	.73236	.72460	.71699	.70952	.70219
84	.78456	.77636	.76831	.76041	.75265	.74503	.73756	.73021	.72300	.71592
85	.79530	.78743	.77971	.77212	.76466	.75733	.75014	.74306	.73611	.72928
86	.80560	.79806	.79065	.78337	.77621	.76917	.76225	.75544	.74875	.74216
87	.81535	.80813	.80103	.79404	.78717	.78041	.77375	.76720	.76076	.75442
88	.82462	.81771	.81090	.80420	.79760	.79111	.78472	.77842	.77223	.76612
89	.83356	.82694	.82043	.81401	.80769	.80147	.79533	.78929	.78334	.77747
90	.84225	.83593	.82971	.82357	.81753	.81157	.80570	.79991	.79420	.78857
91	.85058	.84455	.83861	.83276	.82698	.82129	.81567	.81013	.80466	.79927
92	.85838	.85263	.84696	.84137	.83585	.83040	.82503	.81973	.81449	.80933
93	.86557	.86009	.85467	.84932	.84405	.83884	.83370	.82862	.82360	.81865
94	.87212	.86687	.86169	.85657	.85152	.84653	.84160	.83673	.83192	.82717
95	.87801	.87298	.86801	.86310	.85825	.85345	.84872	.84404	.83941	.83484
96	.88322	.87838	.87360	.86888	.86420	.85959	.85502	.85051	.84605	.84165
97	.88795	.88328	.87867	.87411	.86961	.86515	.86074	.85639	.85208	.84782
98	.89220	.88769	.88323	.87883	.87447	.87016	.86589	.86167	.85750	.85337
99	.89612	.89176	.88745	.88318	.87895	.87478	.87064	.86656	.86251	.85850
100	.89977	.89555	.89136	.88722	.88313	.87908	.87506	.87109	.86716	.86327
101	.90326	.89917	.89511	.89110	.88712	.88318	.87929	.87543	.87161	.86783
102	.90690	.90294	.89901	.89513	.89128	.88746	.88369	.87995	.87624	.87257
103	.91076	.90694	.90315	.89940	.89569	.89200	.88835	.88474	.88116	.87760
104	.91504	.91138	.90775	.90415	.90058	.89704	.89354	.89006	.88661	.88319
105	.92027	.91681	.91337	.90996	.90658	.90322	.89989	.89659	.89331	.89006
106	.92763	.92445	.92130	.91816	.91506	.91197	.90890	.90586	.90284	.89983
107	.93799	.93523	.93249	.92977	.92707	.92438	.92170	.91905	.91641	.91378
108	.95429	.95223	.95018	.94814	.94611	.94409	.94208	.94008	.93809	.93611

109	.97985	.97893	.97801	.97710	.97619	.97529	.97438	.97348	.97259	.97170

TABLE S

BASED ON LIFE TABLE 80CNSMT SINGLE LIFE REMAINDER FACTORS APPLICABLE AFTER APRIL 30, 1989 AND BEFORE MAY 1, 1999

				Interest Rate						
AGE	6.2%	6.4%	6.6%	6.8%	7.0%	7.2%	7.4%	7.6%	7.8%	8.0%
0	.03535	.03349	.03183	.03035	.02902	.02783	.02676	.02579	.02492	.02413
1	.02486	.02292	.02119	.01963	.01824	.01699	.01587	.01486	.01395	.01312
2	.02547	.02345	.02164	.02002	.01857	.01727	.01609	.01504	.01408	.01321
3	.02640	.02429	.02241	.02073	.01921	.01785	.01662	.01552	.01451	.01361
4	.02753	.02535	.02339	.02163	.02005	.01863	.01735	.01619	.01514	.01418
5	.02883	.02656	.02453	.02269	.02105	.01956	.01822	.01700	.01590	.01490
6	.03026	.02790	.02578	.02387	.02215	.02060	.01919	.01792	.01677	.01572
7	.03180	.02935	.02714	.02515	.02336	.02174	.02027	.01894	.01773	.01664
8	.03347	.03092	.02863	.02656	.02469	.02300	.02146	.02007	.01881	.01766
9	.03528	.03263	.03025	.02810	.02615	.02438	.02278	.02133	.02000	.01880
10	.03723	.03449	.03201	.02977	.02774	.02590	.02423	.02271	.02133	.02006
11	.03935	.03650	.03393	.03160	.02949	.02757	.02583	.02424	.02279	.02147
12	.04160	.03865	.03598	.03356	.03136	.02936	.02755	.02589	.02438	.02299
13	.04394	.04088	.03811	.03560	.03331	.03123	.02934	.02761	.02603	.02458
14	.04629	.04312	.04025	.03764	.03527	.03311	.03113	.02933	.02768	.02617
15	.04864	.04536	.04238	.03968	.03721	.03496	.03290	.03103	.02930	.02773
16	.05099	.04759	.04451	.04170	.03913	.03679	.03466	.03270	.03090	.02926
17	.05333	.04982	.04662	.04370	.04104	.03861	.03638	.03434	.03247	.03075
18	.05570	.05207	.04875	.04573	.04296	.04044	.03812	.03599	.03404	.03225
19	.05814	.05438	.05095	.04781	.04494	.04231	.03990	.03769	.03565	.03378
20	.06065	.05677	.05321	.04996	.04698	.04424	.04173	.03943	.03731	.03535
21	.06325	.05922	.05554	.05217	.04907	.04623	.04362	.04122	.03901	.03697
22	.06594	.06178	.05797	.05447	.05126	.04831	.04559	.04309	.04078	.03865
23	.06876	.06446	.06051	.05688	.05355	.05048	.04766	.04505	.04265	.04042
24	.07174	.06729	.06321	.05945	.05599	.05281	.04987	.04715	.04465	.04233
25	.07491	.07031	.06609	.06219	.05861	.05530	.05224	.04941	.04680	.04438
26	.07830	.07355	.06918	.06515	.06142	.05799	.05481	.05187	.04915	.04662
27	.08192	.07702	.07250	.06832	.06446	.06090	.05759	.05454	.05170	.04906
28	.08577	.08071	.07603	.07171	.06772	.06402	.06059	.05740	.05445	.05170
29	.08986	.08464	.07981	.07534	.07120	.06736	.06380	.06049	.05742	.05456
30	.09420	.08882	.08383	.07921	.07492	.07095	.06725	.06381	.06061	.05763
31	.09881	.09327	.08812	.08335	.07891	.07479	.07095	.06738	.06405	.06095
32	.10369	.09797	.09267	.08774	.08315	.07888	.07491	.07120	.06774	.06451
33	.10885	.10297	.09750	.09241	.08767	.08325	.07913	.07529	.07170	.06834
34	.11430	.10824	.10261	.09736	.09246	.08790	.08363	.07964	.07592	.07243

TABLE S

BASED ON LIFE TABLE 80CNSMT SINGLE LIFE REMAINDER FACTORS APPLICABLE AFTER APRIL 30, 1989 AND BEFORE MAY 1, 1999

				Interest Rate						
AGE	6.2%	6.4%	6.6%	6.8%	7.0%	7.2%	7.4%	7.6%	7.8%	8.0%
35	.12002	.11380	.10800	.10259	.09754	.09282	.08841	.08428	.08041	.07679
36	.12602	.11963	.11366	.10809	.10288	.09800	.09344	.08917	.08516	.08140
37	.13230	.12574	.11961	.11387	.10850	.10347	.09876	.09433	.09018	.08628
38	.13887	.13214	.12584	.11994	.11441	.10922	.10436	.09978	.09549	.09145
39	.14573	.13883	.13237	.12630	.12061	.11527	.11025	.10553	.10109	.09690
40	.15290	.14583	.13920	.13297	.12712	.12162	.11644	.11157	.10698	.10266
41	.16036	.15312	.14633	.13994	.13393	.12827	.12294	.11792	.11318	.10871
42	.16810	.16071	.15375	.14720	.14103	.13522	.12973	.12456	.11967	.11505
43	.17614	.16858	.16146	.15475	.14842	.14245	.13682	.13149	.12645	.12169
44	.18447	.17675	.16948	.16261	.15613	.15000	.14421	.13873	.13355	.12864
45	.19310	.18524	.17780	.17078	.16414	.15787	.15192	.14630	.14096	.13591
46	.20204	.19402	.18644	.17926	.17247	.16604	.15995	.15418	.14870	.14350
47	.21128	.20311	.19538	.18806	.18112	.17454	.16830	.16238	.15676	.15141
48	.22080	.21249	.20462	.19716	.19007	.18335	.17696	.17090	.16513	.15964
49	.23059	.22214	.21413	.20653	.19930	.19244	.18591	.17970	.17379	.16816
50	.24063	.23206	.22391	.21617	.20881	.20180	.19514	.18879	.18274	.17697

51	25095	.24225	.23398	.22610	.21861	.21147	.20466	.19818	.19199	.18609
52	.26157	.25275	.24436	.23636	.22874	.22147	.21453	.20791	.20159	.19556
53	.27249	.26357	.25505	.24694	.23919	.23180	.22474	.21799	.21154	.20537
54	.28369	.27466	.26604	.25782	.24995	.24244	.23526	.22839	.22181	.21552
55	.29518	.28605	.27734	.26900	.26103	.25341	.24611	.23912	.23243	.22601
56	.30695	.29774	.28893	.28050	.27242	.26469	.25728	.25019	.24338	.23685
57	.31902	.30973	.30084	.29232	.28415	.27632	.26881	.26161	.25469	.24805
58	.33138	.32203	.31306	.30446	.29621	.28829	.28069	.27339	.26637	.25962
59	.34402	.33461	.32558	.31691	.30859	.30059	.29290	.28550	.27839	.27155
60	.35690	.34745	.33836	.32963	.32124	.31317	.30540	.29792	.29073	.28379
61	.36999	.36050	.35137	.34259	.33414	.32601	.31817	.31062	.30334	.29633
62	.38325	.37374	.36458	.35576	.34726	.33907	.33117	.32356	.31621	.30912
63	.39669	.38717	.37799	.36913	.36060	.35236	.34441	.33674	.32933	.32217
64	.41031	.40078	.39159	.38272	.37415	.36588	.35789	.35016	.34270	.33548
65	.42416	.41464	.40545	.39656	.38798	.37968	.37166	.36390	.35639	.34912
66	.43825	.42876	.41958	.41070	.40211	.39380	.38576	.37797	.37043	.36312
67	.45260	.44315	.43399	.42513	.41655	.40824	.40019	.39238	.38482	.37749
68	.46720	.45779	.44868	.43985	.43129	.42299	.41494	.40713	.39956	.39221
69	.48197	.47263	.46357	.45478	.44625	.43798	.42995	.42215	.41458	.40722
70	.49686	.48760	.47861	.46988	.46140	.45316	.44516	.43738	.42983	.42248

TABLE S

BASED ON LIFE TABLE 80CNSMT SINGLE LIFE REMAINDER FACTORS APPLICABLE AFTER APRIL 30, 1989 AND BEFORE MAY 1, 1999

	Interest Rate									
AGE	6.2%	6.4%	6.6%	6.8%	7.0%	7.2%	7.4%	7.6%	7.8%	8.0%
71	.51182	.50265	.49374	.48508	.47666	.46847	.46051	.45276	.44523	.43790
72	.52685	.51778	.50896	.50038	.49203	.48390	.47599	.46829	.46079	.45349
73	.54194	.53298	.52426	.51578	.50751	.49946	.49161	.48397	.47652	.46926
74	.55714	.54832	.53972	.53134	.52317	.51520	.50744	.49986	.49247	.48527
75	.57250	.56382	.55536	.54710	.53904	.53118	.52351	.51601	.50870	.50156
76	.58803	.57951	.57120	.56308	.55515	.54740	.53984	.53245	.52522	.51817
77	.60369	.59535	.58720	.57923	.57144	.56383	.55639	.54912	.54200	.53504
78	.61942	.61126	.60329	.59549	.58787	.58040	.57310	.56596	.55896	.55212
79	.63508	.62713	.61935	.61174	.60428	.59698	.58983	.58283	.57597	.56925
80	.65059	.64285	.63527	.62785	.62058	.61345	.60646	.59961	.59290	.58632
81	.66579	.65827	.65090	.64368	.63659	.62965	.62283	.61615	.60959	.60316
82	.68061	.67332	.66616	.65914	.65226	.64550	.63886	.63235	.62595	.61968
83	.69499	.68793	.68099	.67418	.66749	.66092	.65447	.64813	.64191	.63579
84	.70896	.70213	.69541	.68881	.68233	.67595	.66969	.66353	.65748	.65153
85	.72256	.71596	.70947	.70308	.69681	.69063	.68456	.67859	.67271	.66693
86	.73569	.72931	.72305	.71688	.71081	.70484	.69896	.69318	.68748	.68188
87	74818	.74204	.73599	.73003	.72417	.71839	.71271	.70711	70159	.69616
88	.76011	.75419	.74836	.74261	.73695	.73137	.72588	.72046	.71512	.70986
89	.77169	.76599	.76037	.75484	.74938	.74400	.73870	.73347	.72831	.72323
90	.78302	.77755	.77215	.76683	.76158	.75640	.75129	.74625	.74128	.73638
91	.79395	.78870	.78352	.77842	.77337	.76840	.76349	.75864	.75385	.74913
92	.80423	.79920	.79423	.78933	.78449	.77971	.77499	.77033	.76572	.76118
93	.81377	.80894	.80417	.79946	.79481	.79022	.78568	.78120	.77677	.77239
94	.82247	.81784	.81325	.80873	.80425	.79983	.79547	.79115	.78688	.78266
95	.83033	.82586	.82145	.81709	.81278	.80852	.80431	.80014	.79602	.79195
96	.83729	.83298	.82872	.82451	.82034	.81622	.81215	.80812	.80414	.80019
97	.84361	.83944	.83532	.83124	.82721	.82322	.81927	.81537	.81151	.80769
98	.84929	.84525	.84126	.83730	.83339	.82952	.82569	.82190	.81815	.81443
99	.85454	.85062	.84674	.84290	.83910	.83534	.83161	.82792	.82427	.82066
100	.85942	.85561	.85184	.84810	.84440	.84074	.83711	.83352	.82997	.82644
101	.86408	.86037	.85670	.85306	.84946	.84589	.84236	.83886	.83539	.83196
102	.86894	.86534	.86177	.85823	.85473	.85126	.84782	.84442	.84104	.83770
103	.87408	.87060	.86714	.86371	.86032	.85695	.85362	.85031	.84703	.84378
104	.87980	.87644	.87311	.86980	.86653	.86328	.86005	.85686	.85369	.85054
105	.88684	.88363	.88046	.87731	.87418	.87108	.86800	.86494	.86191	.85890
106	.89685	.89389	.89095	.88804	.88514	.88226	.87940	.87656	.87374	.87094
107	.91117	.90858	.90600	.90344	.90089	.89836	.89584	.89334	.89085	.88838
108	.93414	.93217	.93022	.92828	.92634	.92442	.92250	.92060	.91870	.91681
109	.97081	.96992	.96904	.96816	.96729	.96642	.96555	.96468	.96382	.96296

TABLE S

BASED ON LIFE TABLE 80CNSMT SINGLE LIFE REMAINDER FACTORS APPLICABLE AFTER APRIL 30, 1989 AND BEFORE MAY 1, 1999

	Interest Rate									
AGE	8.2%	8.4%	8.6%	8.8%	9.0%	9.2%	9.4%	9.6%	9.8%	10.0%
0	.02341	.02276	.02217	.02163	.02114	.02069	.02027	.01989	.01954	.01922
1	.01237	.01170	.01108	.01052	.01000	.00953	.00910	.00871	.00834	.00801
2	.01243	.01172	.01107	.01048	.00994	.00944	.00899	.00857	.00819	.00784
3	.01278	.01203	.01135	.01073	.01016	.00964	.00916	.00872	.00832	.00795
4	.01332	.01253	.01182	.01116	.01056	.01001	.00951	.00904	.00862	.00822
5	.01400	.01317	.01241	.01172	.01109	.01051	.00998	.00949	.00904	.00862
6	.01477	.01390	.01310	.01238	.01171	.01110	.01054	.01002	.00954	.00910
7	.01563	.01472	.01389	.01312	.01242	.01178	.01118	.01064	.01013	.00966
8	.01660	.01564	.01477	.01396	.01322	.01254	.01192	.01134	.01081	.01031
9	.01770	.01669	.01577	.01492	.01414	.01342	.01276	.01216	.01159	.01107
10	.01891	.01785	.01688	.01599	.01517	.01442	.01372	.01308	.01249	.01194
11	.02026	.01915	.01814	.01720	.01634	.01555	.01481	.01414	.01351	.01293
12	.02173	.02056	.01950	.01852	.01761	.01678	.01601	.01529	.01463	.01402
13	.02326	.02204	.02092	.01989	.01895	.01807	.01726	.01651	.01582	.01517
14	.02478	.02351	.02234	.02126	.02027	.01935	.01850	.01771	.01698	.01630
15	.02628	.02495	.02372	.02259	.02155	.02058	.01969	.01886	.01810	.01738
16	.02774	.02635	.02507	.02388	.02279	.02178	.02084	.01997	.01917	.01842
17	.02917	.02772	.02637	.02513	.02399	.02293	.02194	.02103	.02018	.01940
18	.03059	.02907	.02767	.02637	.02517	.02406	.02302	.02207	.02118	.02035
19	.03205	.03046	.02899	.02763	.02637	.02521	.02412	.02312	.02218	.02131
20	.03355	.03188	.03035	.02892	.02760	.02638	.02524	.02419	.02320	.02229
21	.03509	.03334	.03173	.03024	.02886	.02758	.02638	.02527	.02424	.02328
22	.03669	.03487	.03318	.03162	.03017	.02882	.02757	.02640	.02532	.02430
23	.03837	.03646	.03470	.03306	.03154	.03013	.02881	.02759	.02644	.02538
24	.04018	.03819	.03634	.03463	.03303	.03155	.03016	.02888	.02767	.02655
25	.04214	.04006	.03812	.03633	.03465	.03309	.03164	.03029	.02902	.02784
26	.04428	.04210	.04008	.03820	.03644	.03481	.03328	.03186	.03052	.02928
27	.04662	.04434	.04223	.04025	.03841	.03670	.03509	.03360	.03219	.03088
28	.04915	.04677	.04456	.04249	.04056	.03876	.03708	.03550	.03403	.03264
29	.05189	.04941	.04709	.04493	.04291	.04102	.03925	.03760	.03604	.03458
30	.05485	.05226	.04984	.04757	.04546	.04348	.04162	.03988	.03825	.03671
31	.05805	.05535	.05282	.05045	.04824	.04616	.04421	.04238	.04067	.03905
32	.06149	.05867	.05603	.05356	.05124	.04906	.04702	.04510	.04329	.04160
33	.06520	.06226	.05950	.05692	.05449	.05221	.05007	.04806	.04616	.04438
34	.06916	.06609	.06322	.06052	.05799	.05560	.05336	.05125	.04926	.04738

TABLE S

BASED ON LIFE TABLE 80CNSMT SINGLE LIFE REMAINDER FACTORS APPLICABLE AFTER APRIL 30, 1989 AND BEFORE MAY 1, 1999

	Interest Rate									
AGE	8.2%	8.4%	8.6%	8.8%	9.0%	9.2%	9.4%	9.6%	9.8%	10.0%
35	.07339	.07020	.06720	.06439	.06174	.05925	.05690	.05469	.05260	.05063
36	.07787	.07455	.07143	.06850	.06573	.06313	.06068	.05836	.05617	.05411
37	.08262	.07917	.07593	.07287	.06999	.06727	.06470	.06228	.05999	.05783
38	.08765	.08407	.08069	.07751	.07451	.07167	.06899	.06646	.06407	.06180
39	.09296	.08925	.08574	.08243	.07931	.07635	.07356	.07092	.06841	.06604
40	.09858	.09472	.09109	.08765	.08440	.08132	.07841	.07565	.07303	.07055
41	.10449	.10050	.09673	.09316	.08978	.08658	.08355	.08067	.07794	.07535
42	.11069	.10656	.10265	.09895	.09544	.09212	.08896	.08596	.08312	.08041
43	.11718	.11291	.10887	.10503	.10140	.09794	.09466	.09154	.08858	.08576
44	.12399	.11958	.11540	.11143	.10766	.10407	.10067	.09743	.09434	.09141
45	.13111	.12656	.12224	.11814	.11423	.11052	.10699	.10362	.10042	.09736
46	.13856	.13387	.12941	.12516	.12113	.11728	.11362	.11013	.10680	.10363
47	.14633	.14150	.13690	.13252	.12835	.12438	.12059	.11697	.11352	.11022
48	.15442	.14945	.14471	.14020	.13589	.13179	.12787	.12412	.12055	.11713
49	.16280	.15769	.15281	.14816	.14373	.13949	.13544	.13157	.12787	.12433
50	.17147	.16622	.16121	.15643	.15186	.14749	.14331	.13931	.13548	.13182
51	18045	.17507	.16993	.16501	.16030	.15580	.15150	.14737	.14342	.13963

52	.18979	.18427	.17899	.17394	.16911	.16448	.16004	.15579	.15172	.14780
53	.19947	.19383	.18842	.18324	.17828	.17352	.16896	.16458	.16038	.15635
54	.20950	.20372	.19819	.19288	.18779	.18291	.17822	.17372	.16940	.16524
55	.21986	.21397	.20831	.20288	.19767	.19266	.18785	.18322	.17878	.17450
56	.23058	.22457	.21879	.21324	.20791	.20278	.19785	.19310	.18854	.18414
57	.24167	.23554	.22965	.22399	.21854	.21329	.20824	.20338	.19870	.19419
58	.25314	.24690	.24090	.23512	.22956	.22420	.21904	.21407	.20927	.20464
59	.26497	.25863	.25252	.24664	.24097	.23550	.23023	.22515	.22024	.21551
60	.27712	.27068	.26448	.25849	.25272	.24716	.24178	.23659	.23158	.22674
61	.28956	.28304	.27674	.27067	.26480	.25913	.25366	.24837	.24325	.23831
62	.30228	.29567	.28929	.28312	.27717	.27141	.26584	.26045	.25524	.25020
63	.31525	.30857	.30211	.29586	.28982	.28397	.27832	.27284	.26754	.26240
64	.32851	.32176	.31522	.30890	.30278	.29685	.29111	.28555	.28016	.27493
65	.34209	.33528	.32868	.32229	.31610	.31010	.30429	.29865	.29317	.28787
66	.35604	.34918	.34253	.33609	.32983	.32377	.31788	.31217	.30663	.30124
67	.37037	.36347	.35678	.35028	.34398	.33786	.33191	.32614	.32053	.31508
68	.38508	.37815	.37142	.36489	.35854	.35237	.34638	.34055	.33488	.32937
69	.40008	.39313	.38638	.37982	.37344	.36724	.36120	.35533	.34961	.34405
70	.41533	.40838	.40162	.39504	.38864	.38241	.37634	.37043	.36468	.35907

TABLE S

BASED ON LIFE TABLE 80CNSMT SINGLE LIFE REMAINDER FACTORS APPLICABLE AFTER APRIL 30, 1989 AND BEFORE MAY 1, 1999

				Interest Rate						
AGE	8.2%	8.4%	8.6%	8.8%	9.0%	9.2%	9.4%	9.6%	9.8%	10.0%
71	.43076	.42382	.41705	.41047	.40405	.39780	.39171	.38578	.38000	.37436
72	.44638	.43945	.43269	.42611	.41969	.41344	.40733	.40138	.39558	.38991
73	.46218	.45527	.44854	.44197	.43556	.42931	.42321	.41725	.41143	.40575
74	.47823	.47137	.46466	.45812	.45173	.44549	.43940	.43345	.42763	.42195
75	.49459	.48777	.48112	.47462	.46826	.46205	.45598	.45004	.44424	.43856
76	.51127	.50452	.49793	.49148	.48517	.47900	.47297	.46706	.46129	.45563
77	.52823	.52157	.51505	.50867	.50243	.49632	.49033	.48447	.47873	.47311
78	.54541	.53885	.53242	.52613	.51996	.51392	.50800	.50220	.49652	.49094
79	.56267	.55621	.54989	.54369	.53762	.53166	.52582	.52009	.51448	.50897
80	.57987	.57354	.56733	.56125	.55527	.54941	.54366	.53802	.53248	.52705
81	.59685	.59065	.58457	.57860	.57274	.56699	.56134	.55579	.55035	.54499
82	.61351	.60746	.60151	.59567	.58993	.58429	.57875	.57331	.56796	.56270
83	.62978	.62387	.61806	.61236	.60675	.60123	.59581	.59047	.58523	.58007
84	.64567	.63992	.63426	.62869	.62321	.61783	.61253	.60731	.60218	.59713
85	.66125	.65565	.65014	.64472	.63938	.63413	.62896	.62387	.61886	.61392
86	.67636	.67092	.66557	.66030	.65511	.65000	.64496	.64000	.63511	.63030
87	69081	.68554	.68034	.67522	.67018	.66520	.66031	.65548	.65071	64602
88	.70468	.69957	.69453	.68956	.68466	.67983	.67507	.67037	.66574	.66117
89	.71821	.71326	.70838	.70357	.69882	.69414	.68952	.68495	.68045	.67601
90	.73153	.72676	.72204	.71739	.71280	.70827	.70379	.69938	.69502	.69071
91	.74447	.73986	.73532	.73083	.72640	.72202	.71770	.71343	.70921	.70504
92	.75669	.75225	.74787	.74354	.73927	.73504	.73087	.72674	.72267	.71864
93	.76807	.76379	.75957	.75540	.75127	.74719	.74317	.73918	.73524	.73135
94	.77849	.77437	.77030	.76627	.76229	.75835	.75446	.75061	.74680	.74303
95	.78792	.78394	.78001	.77611	.77226	.76845	.76468	.76096	.75727	.75362
96	.79630	.79244	.78863	.78485	.78112	.77742	.77377	.77015	.76657	.76303
97	.80391	.80016	.79646	.79280	.78917	.78559	.78203	.77852	.77504	.77160
98	.81076	.80712	.80352	.79996	.79643	.79294	.78948	.78606	.78267	.77931
99	.81709	.81354	.81004	.80657	.80313	.79972	.79635	.79302	.78971	.78644
100	.82296	.81950	.81609	.81270	.80934	.80602	.80273	.79947	.79624	.79304
101	.82855	.82518	.82185	.81854	.81526	.81201	.80880	.80561	.80245	.79932
102	.83438	.83110	.82785	.82462	.82142	.81826	.81512	.81200	.80892	.80586
103	.84056	.83737	.83420	.83106	.82795	.82487	.82181	.81878	.81577	.81279
104	.84743	.84433	.84127	.83822	.83521	.83221	.82924	.82630	.82338	.82048
105	.85591	.85295	.85001	.84709	.84419	.84132	.83846	.83563	.83282	.83003
106	.86816	.86540	.86266	.85993	.85723	.85454	.85187	.84922	.84659	.84397
107	.88592	.88348	.88105	.87863	.87623	.87384	.87147	.86911	.86676	.86443
108	.91493	.91306	.91119	.90934	.90749	.90566	.90383	.90201	.90020	.89840
109	.96211	.96125	.96041	.95956	.95872	.95788	.95704	.95620	.95537	.95455

TABLE S

BASED ON LIFE TABLE 80CNSMT SINGLE LIFE REMAINDER FACTORS APPLICABLE AFTER APRIL 30, 1989 AND BEFORE MAY 1, 1999

	Interest Rate									
AGE	10.2%	10.4%	10.6%	10.8%	11.0%	11.2%	11.4%	11.6%	11.8%	12.0%
0	.01891	.01864	.01838	.01814	.01791	.01770	.01750	.01732	.01715	.01698
1	.00770	.00741	.00715	.00690	.00667	.00646	.00626	.00608	.00590	.00574
2	.00751	.00721	.00693	.00667	.00643	.00620	.00600	.00580	.00562	.00544
3	.00760	.00728	.00699	.00671	.00646	.00622	.00600	.00579	.00560	.00541
4	.00786	.00752	.00721	.00692	.00665	.00639	.00616	.00594	.00573	.00554
5	.00824	.00788	.00755	.00724	.00695	.00668	.00643	.00620	.00598	.00578
6	.00869	.00832	.00796	.00764	.00733	.00705	.00678	.00654	.00630	.00608
7	.00923	.00883	.00846	.00811	.00779	.00749	.00720	.00694	.00669	.00646
8	.00986	.00943	.00904	.00867	.00833	.00801	.00771	.00743	.00716	.00692
9	.01059	.01014	.00972	.00933	.00897	.00863	.00831	.00801	.00773	.00747
10	.01142	.01095	.01051	.01009	.00971	.00935	.00901	.00869	.00840	.00812
11	.01239	.01189	.01142	.01098	.01057	.01019	.00983	.00950	.00918	.00889
12	.01345	.01292	.01243	.01197	.01154	.01113	.01075	.01040	.01007	.00975
13	.01457	.01401	.01349	.01300	.01255	.01212	.01172	.01135	.01100	.01067
14	.01567	.01508	.01453	.01402	.01354	.01309	.01267	.01227	.01190	.01155
15	.01672	.01610	.01552	.01498	.01448	.01400	.01356	.01314	.01275	.01238
16	01772	.01707	.01646	.01589	.01536	.01486	.01439	.01396	.01354	.01315
17	.01866	.01798	.01734	.01674	.01618	.01566	.01516	.01470	.01427	.01386
18	.01958	.01886	.01818	.01755	.01697	.01641	.01590	.01541	.01495	.01452
19	.02050	.01974	.01903	.01837	.01775	.01717	.01662	.01611	.01563	.01517
20	.02143	.02064	.01989	.01919	.01854	.01793	.01735	.01681	.01630	.01582
21	.02238	.02154	.02075	.02002	.01933	.01868	.01807	.01750	.01696	.01646
22	.02336	.02247	.02164	.02087	.02014	.01946	.01882	.01821	.01764	.01711
23	.02438	.02345	.02257	.02176	.02099	.02027	.01959	.01895	.01835	.01778
24	.02550	.02451	.02359	.02273	.02192	.02115	.02044	.01976	.01913	.01853
25	.02673	.02569	.02472	.02381	.02295	.02214	.02138	.02067	.01999	.01936
26	.02811	.02701	.02598	.02502	.02411	.02326	.02246	.02170	.02098	.02031
27	.02965	.02849	.02741	.02639	.02543	.02452	.02367	.02287	.02211	.02140
28	.03134	.03013	.02898	.02790	.02689	.02593	.02503	.02418	.02338	.02262
29	.03322	.03193	.03072	.02958	.02851	.02750	.02654	.02564	.02479	.02398
30	.03527	.03391	.03264	.03143	.03030	.02923	.02821	.02726	.02635	.02550
31	.03753	.03610	.03475	.03348	.03228	.03115	.03008	.02907	.02811	.02720
32	.04000	.03849	.03707	.03573	.03446	.03326	.03213	.03105	.03004	.02907
33	.04269	.04111	.03961	.03819	.03685	.03558	.03438	.03325	.03217	.03115
34	.04561	.04394	.04236	.04087	.03946	.03812	.03685	.03565	.03451	.03342

TABLE S

BASED ON LIFE TABLE 80CNSMT SINGLE LIFE REMAINDER FACTORS APPLICABLE AFTER APRIL 30, 1989 AND BEFORE MAY 1, 1999

	Interest Rate									
AGE	10.2%	10.4%	10.6%	10.8%	11.0%	11.2%	11.4%	11.6%	11.8%	12.0%
35	.04877	.04702	.04535	.04378	.04229	.04087	.03953	.03826	.03706	.03591
36	.05215	.05031	.04856	.04690	.04533	.04384	.04242	.04108	.03980	.03859
37	.05578	.05384	.05200	.05025	.04860	.04703	.04553	.04411	.04276	.04148
38	.05965	.05761	.05568	.05385	.05211	.05045	.04888	.04738	.04595	.04460
39	.06379	.06165	.05962	.05770	.05587	.05412	.05247	.05089	.04939	.04795
40	.06820	.06596	.06383	.06181	.05989	.05806	.05631	.05465	.05307	.05155
41	.07288	.07054	.06832	.06620	.06418	.06226	.06042	.05868	.05701	.05541
42	.07784	.07539	.07306	.07085	.06873	.06671	.06479	.06295	.06119	.05952
43	.08308	.08052	.07808	.07576	.07355	.07143	.06941	.06748	.06564	.06387
44	.08861	.08594	.08340	.08097	.07865	.07644	.07432	.07230	.07036	.06851
45	.09445	.09167	.08901	.08648	.08406	.08174	.07953	.07741	.07538	.07343
46	.10060	.09770	.09494	.09230	.08977	.08735	.08503	.08281	.08068	.07865
47	.10707	.10406	.10119	.09843	.09579	.09327	.09085	.08853	.08630	.08417
48	.11386	.11073	.10774	.10487	.10213	.09949	.09697	.09455	.09222	.08999
49	.12094	.11769	.11458	.11160	.10874	.10600	.10337	.10084	.09842	.09609
50	.12831	.12494	.12172	.11862	.11565	.11280	.11006	.10743	.10490	.10247
51	13600	.13251	.12917	.12596	.12288	.11991	.11706	.11432	.11169	.10915

52	.14405	.14044	.13698	.13366	.13046	.12738	.12442	.12157	.11883	.11619
53	.15247	.14875	.14517	.14172	.13841	.13522	.13215	.12919	.12635	.12360
54	.16124	.15740	.15370	.15014	.14671	.14341	.14023	.13717	.13421	.13136
55	.17039	.16642	.16261	.15893	.15539	.15198	.14868	.14551	.14244	.13948
56	.17991	.17583	.17190	.16811	.16445	.16092	.15752	.15423	.15106	.14799
57	.18984	.18564	.18160	.17769	.17392	.17029	.16677	.16338	.16010	.15692
58	.20018	.19587	.19172	.18770	.18382	.18007	.17645	.17295	.16956	.16628
59	.21093	.20652	.20225	.19812	.19414	.19028	.18655	.18294	.17945	.17606
60	.22206	.21753	.21316	.20893	.20483	.20087	.19703	.19332	.18972	.18624
61	.23353	.22890	.22442	.22009	.21589	.21182	.20788	.20407	.20037	.19678
62	.24532	.24059	.23601	.23158	.22728	.22311	.21907	.21515	.21135	.20767
63	.25742	.25260	.24793	.24339	.23900	.23473	.23060	.22658	.22268	.21890
64	.26987	.26495	.26019	.25556	.25107	.24671	.24248	.23837	.23438	.23050
65	.28271	.27771	.27286	.26815	.26357	.25912	.25480	.25059	.24651	.24254
66	.29601	.29093	.28600	.28120	.27654	.27200	.26760	.26331	.25913	.25507
67	.30978	.30462	.29961	.29474	.29000	.28539	.28090	.27653	.27227	.26813
68	.32401	.31879	.31371	.30877	.30396	.29927	.29471	.29027	.28593	.28171
69	.33863	.33336	.32822	.32322	.31835	.31359	.30896	.30445	.30005	.29576
70	.35361	.34829	.34310	.33804	.33311	.32830	.32361	.31903	.31457	.31021

TABLE S

BASED ON LIFE TABLE 80CNSMT SINGLE LIFE REMAINDER FACTORS APPLICABLE AFTER APRIL 30, 1989 AND BEFORE MAY 1, 1999

				Interest Rate						
AGE	10.2%	10.4%	10.6%	10.8%	11.0%	11.2%	11.4%	11.6%	11.8%	12.0%
71	.36886	.36349	.35826	.35316	.34818	.34332	.33858	.33394	.32942	.32500
72	.38439	.37899	.37373	.36858	.36356	.35866	.35387	.34919	.34461	.34015
73	.40021	.39479	.38950	.38432	.37927	.37433	.36950	.36478	.36016	.35565
74	.41639	.41096	.40565	.40046	.39538	.39042	.38556	.38081	.37616	.37161
75	.43301	.42758	.42226	.41706	.41198	.40699	.40212	.39734	.39267	.38809
76	.45009	.44467	.43937	.43417	.42908	.42410	.41921	.41443	.40974	.40514
77	.46761	.46221	.45693	.45175	.44667	.44170	.43682	.43203	.42734	.42274
78	.48548	.48013	.47488	.46973	.46468	.45972	.45486	.45009	.44541	.44082
79	.50356	.49826	.49306	.48795	.48294	.47802	.47319	.46845	.46379	.45922
80	.52171	.51647	.51133	.50628	.50132	.49644	.49166	.48695	.48233	.47779
81	.53974	.53457	.52950	.52451	.51961	.51479	.51006	.50541	.50083	.49633
82	.55753	.55245	.54745	.54254	.53771	.53296	.52828	.52369	.51917	.51472
83	.57500	.57001	.56510	.56026	.55551	.55083	.54623	.54170	.53724	.53285
84	.59216	.58726	.58245	.57770	.57304	.56844	.56391	.55945	.55506	.55074
85	.60906	.60428	.59956	.59492	.59034	.58583	.58139	.57702	.57270	.56845
86	.62555	.62088	.61627	.61173	.60725	.60284	.59849	.59420	.58997	.58580
87	.64139	.63683	.63233	.62790	.62352	.61921	.61495	.61076	.60661	.60253
88	.65666	.65221	.64783	.64350	.63923	.63502	.63086	.62675	.62270	.61871
89	.67163	.66730	.66304	.65882	.65466	.65055	.64650	.64249	.63854	.63463
90	.68646	.68226	.67812	.67402	.66998	.66599	.66204	.65814	.65430	.65049
91	.70093	.69686	.69285	.68888	.68496	.68108	.67725	.67347	.66973	.66604
92	.71466	.71073	.70684	.70300	.69920	.69545	.69173	.68806	.68444	.68085
93	.72750	.72370	.71994	.71622	.71254	.70890	.70530	.70174	.69822	.69474
94	.73931	.73562	.73198	.72838	.72481	.72129	.71780	.71434	.71093	.70755
95	.75001	.74644	.74291	.73941	.73595	.73253	.72914	.72579	.72247	.71919
96	.75953	.75606	.75262	.74923	.74586	.74253	.73924	.73598	.73275	.72955
97	.76819	.76481	.76147	.75816	.75489	.75165	.74844	.74526	.74211	.73899
98	.77599	.77270	.76944	.76621	.76302	.75986	.75672	.75362	.75054	.74750
99	.78319	.77998	.77680	.77365	.77053	.76744	.76437	.76134	.75833	.75535
100	.78987	.78673	.78362	.78054	.77748	.77446	.77146	.76849	.76555	.76263
101	.79622	.79315	.79010	.78708	.78409	.78113	.77819	.77528	.77239	.76953
102	.80283	.79983	.79685	.79390	.79097	.78807	.78519	.78234	.77951	.77671
103	.80983	.80690	.80399	.80111	.79825	.79541	.79260	.78981	.78705	.78430
104	.81760	.81475	.81192	.80912	.80633	.80357	.80083	.79810	.79541	.79273
105	.82726	.82451	.82178	.81907	.81638	.81371	.81106	.80843	.80582	.80322
106	.84137	.83879	.83623	.83368	.83115	.82863	.82614	.82366	.82119	.81874
107	.86211	.85981	.85751	.85523	.85297	.85071	.84847	.84624	.84403	.84182
108	.89660	.89481	.89304	.89127	.88950	.88775	.88601	.88427	.88254	.88081
109	.95372	.95290	.95208	.95126	.95045	.94964	.94883	.94803	.94723	.94643

TABLE S

BASED ON LIFE TABLE 80CNSMT SINGLE LIFE REMAINDER FACTORS APPLICABLE AFTER APRIL 30, 1989 AND BEFORE MAY 1, 1999

	Interest Rate									
AGE	12.2%	12.4%	12.6%	12.8%	13.0%	13.2%	13.4%	13.6%	13.8%	14.0
0	.01683	.01669	.01655	.01642	.01630	.01618	.01607	.01596	.01586	.01576
1	.00559	.00544	.00531	.00518	.00506	.00494	.00484	.00473	.00464	.00454
2	.00528	.00513	.00499	.00485	.00473	.00461	.00449	.00439	.00428	.00419
3	.00524	.00508	.00493	.00479	.00465	.00453	.00441	.00429	.00419	.00408
4	.00536	.00519	.00503	.00488	.00473	.00460	.00447	.00435	.00423	.00412
5	.00558	.00540	.00523	.00507	.00492	.00477	.00464	.00451	.00439	.00427
6	.00588	.00569	.00550	.00533	.00517	.00502	.00487	.00473	.00460	.00448
7	.00624	.00604	.00584	.00566	.00549	.00532	.00517	.00502	.00488	.00475
8	.00668	.00646	.00626	.00606	.00588	.00570	.00554	.00538	.00523	.00509
9	.00722	.00699	.00677	.00656	.00636	.00617	.00600	.00583	.00567	.00552
10	.00785	.00761	.00737	.00715	.00694	.00674	.00655	.00637	.00620	.00604
11	.00861	.00835	.00810	.00786	.00764	.00743	.00723	.00704	.00686	.00668
12	.00946	.00918	.00891	.00866	.00843	.00820	.00799	.00779	.00760	.00741
13	.01035	.01006	.00978	.00951	.00927	.00903	.00880	.00859	.00839	.00819
14	.01122	.01091	.01061	.01034	.01007	.00982	.00958	.00936	.00914	.00894
15	.01203	.01171	.01140	.01110	.01082	.01056	.01031	.01007	.00985	.00963
16	.01279	.01244	.01211	.01181	.01151	.01123	.01097	.01072	.01048	.01025
17	.01347	.01311	.01276	.01244	.01213	.01184	.01156	.01130	.01104	.01081
18	.01411	.01373	.01336	.01302	.01270	.01239	.01210	.01182	.01155	.01130
19	.01474	.01434	.01396	.01359	.01325	.01293	.01262	.01233	.01205	.01178
20	.01537	.01494	.01454	.01415	.01379	.01345	.01313	.01282	.01252	.01224
21	.01598	.01553	.01510	.01470	.01432	.01396	.01361	.01329	.01298	.01268
22	.01660	.01613	.01568	.01525	.01485	.01446	.01410	.01375	.01343	.01312
23	.01725	.01674	.01627	.01581	.01539	.01498	.01460	.01423	.01388	.01355
24	.01796	.01742	.01692	.01644	.01599	.01556	.01515	.01476	.01439	.01404
25	.01876	.01819	.01765	.01714	.01666	.01621	.01577	.01536	.01497	.01460
26	.01967	.01907	.01850	.01796	.01745	.01696	.01650	.01606	.01565	.01525
27	.02072	.02008	.01948	.01890	.01836	.01784	.01735	.01688	.01644	.01601
28	.02190	.02122	.02057	.01996	.01938	.01883	.01831	.01781	.01734	.01689
29	.02322	.02249	.02181	.02116	.02054	.01996	.01940	.01887	.01836	.01788
30	.02469	.02392	.02319	.02250	.02184	.02122	.02062	.02006	.01952	.01900
31	.02634	.02552	.02475	.02401	.02331	.02264	.02201	.02140	.02083	.02028
32	.02816	.02729	.02647	.02568	.02494	.02423	.02355	.02291	.02229	.02170
33	.03018	.02926	.02838	.02755	.02675	.02600	.02528	.02459	.02393	.02331
34	.03239	.03142	.03048	.02960	.02875	.02795	.02718	.02645	.02575	.02508

TABLE S

BASED ON LIFE TABLE 80CNSMT SINGLE LIFE REMAINDER FACTORS APPLICABLE AFTER APRIL 30, 1989 AND BEFORE MAY 1, 1999

	Interest Rate									
Age	12.2%	12.4%	12.6%	12.8%	13.0%	13.2%	13.4%	13.6%	13.8%	14.0
35	.03482	.03378	.03279	.03185	.03095	.03009	.02928	.02850	.02775	.02704
36	.03743	.03633	.03528	.03428	.03333	.03242	.03155	.03072	.02992	.02916
37	.04026	.03909	.03798	.03692	.03591	.03494	.03401	.03313	.03228	.03147
38	.04330	.04207	.04089	.03977	.03869	.03767	.03668	.03574	.03484	.03398
39	.04658	.04528	.04403	.04284	.04170	.04061	.03957	.03857	.03762	.03670
40	.05011	.04873	.04741	.04615	.04495	.04379	.04269	.04163	.04061	.03964
41	.05389	.05244	.05104	.04971	.04844	.04721	.04604	.04492	.04384	.04281
42	.05791	.05638	.05491	.05350	.05216	.05086	.04962	.04844	.04729	.04620
43	.06219	.06057	.05902	.05754	.05612	.05475	.05344	.05218	.05098	.04981
44	.06673	.06503	.06340	.06184	.06034	.05890	.05752	.05619	.05491	.05368
45	.07157	.06978	.06806	.06642	.06484	.06332	.06186	.06046	.05911	.05781
46	.07669	.07481	.07301	.07128	.06962	.06802	.06649	.06501	.06358	.06221
47	.08212	.08015	.07826	.07645	.07470	.07302	.07140	.06984	.06834	.06690
48	.08784	.08578	.08380	.08190	.08006	.07830	.07660	.07496	.07338	.07186
49	.09384	.09169	.08961	.08762	.08570	.08384	.08206	.08034	.07868	.07708
50	.10013	.09787	.09570	.09361	.09160	.08966	.08779	.08598	.08424	.08256
51	10671	.10436	.10209	.09991	.09780	.09577	.09381	.09192	.09009	.08832

52	.11365	.11120	.10883	.10655	.10435	.10222	.10017	.09819	.09628	.09442
53	.12095	.11840	.11593	.11355	.11126	.10904	.10689	.10482	.10282	.10088
54	.12860	.12595	.12338	.12090	.11851	.11619	.11396	.11179	.10970	.10767
55	.13663	.13386	.13120	.12862	.12613	.12372	.12138	.11912	.11694	.11482
56	.14503	.14217	.13940	.13672	.13413	.13162	.12919	.12683	.12456	.12235
57	.15385	.15089	.14801	.14523	.14254	.13994	.13741	.13496	.13259	.13029
58	.16311	.16004	.15706	.15418	.15139	.14868	.14606	.14352	.14105	.13866
59	.17279	.16961	.16654	.16355	.16066	.15786	.15514	.15250	.14994	.14745
60	.18286	.17958	.17640	.17332	.17033	.16743	.16462	.16188	.15922	.15664
61	.19330	.18992	.18665	.18347	.18038	.17738	.17447	.17164	.16889	.16622
62	.20409	.20061	.19724	.19396	.19078	.18768	.18467	.18175	.17891	.17614
63	.21522	.21165	.20818	.20480	.20152	.19833	.19523	.19221	.18928	.18642
64	.22672	.22306	.21949	.21602	.21265	.20937	.20617	.20306	.20003	.19708
65	.23867	.23491	.23125	.22769	.22423	.22085	.21757	.21437	.21125	.20821
66	.25112	.24727	.24353	.23988	.23632	.23286	.22948	.22619	.22299	.21986
67	.26409	.26016	.25633	.25260	.24896	.24541	.24195	.23857	.23528	.23206
68	.27760	.27359	.26968	.26586	.26214	.25851	.25497	.25151	.24814	.24484
69	.29157	.28748	.28350	.27961	.27581	.27211	.26849	.26495	.26150	.25812
70	.30596	.30181	.29775	.29379	.28992	.28614	.28245	.27884	.27532	.27187

TABLE S

BASED ON LIFE TABLE 80CNSMT SINGLE LIFE REMAINDER FACTORS APPLICABLE AFTER APRIL 30, 1989 AND BEFORE MAY 1, 1999

				Interest Rate						
Age	12.2%	12.4%	12.6%	12.8%	13.0%	13.2%	13.4%	13.6%	13.8%	14.0
71	.32069	.31648	.31236	.30833	.30440	.30055	.29679	.29312	.28952	.28600
72	.33578	.33151	.32733	.32325	.31925	.31535	.31152	.30778	.30412	.30054
73	.35123	.34691	.34269	.33855	.33450	.33054	.32666	.32286	.31914	.31550
74	.36715	.36279	.35852	.35434	.35024	.34623	.34230	.33845	.33468	.33098
75	.38360	.37921	.37491	.37069	.36656	.36250	.35853	.35464	.35082	.34708
76	.40064	.39623	.39190	.38765	.38349	.37941	.37540	.37148	.36762	.36384
77	.41823	.41381	.40947	.40521	.40103	.39692	.39290	.38895	.38507	.38126
78	.43632	.43189	.42755	.42329	.41910	.41499	.41095	.40698	.40309	.39926
79	.45473	.45032	.44599	.44173	.43755	.43344	.42940	.42543	.42153	.41770
80	.47333	.46894	.46463	.46040	.45623	.45213	.44811	.44414	.44025	.43642
81	.49191	.48755	.48328	.47907	.47493	.47085	.46684	.46290	.45902	.45520
82	.51034	.50603	.50179	.49762	.49351	.48947	.48549	.48157	.47772	.47392
83	.52852	.52427	.52008	.51595	.51189	.50788	.50394	.50006	.49623	.49246
84	.54648	.54228	.53815	.53407	.53006	.52610	.52221	.51836	.51458	.51084
85	.56426	.56013	.55606	.55205	.54810	.54420	.54035	.53656	.53282	.52913
86	.58169	.57764	.57364	.56970	.56581	.56197	.55818	.55445	.55076	.54713
87	.59850	.59452	.59060	.58673	.58291	.57913	.57541	.57174	.56811	.56453
88	.61476	.61086	.60702	.60322	.59947	.59577	.59212	.58851	.58494	.58142
89	.63078	.62697	.62321	.61950	.61583	.61220	.60862	.60508	.60159	.59813
90	.64674	.64302	.63935	.63573	.63215	.62861	.62511	.62165	.61823	.61485
91	.66238	.65877	.65520	.65167	.64819	.64474	.64133	.63795	.63462	.63132
92	.67730	.67379	.67032	.66689	.66350	.66014	.65682	.65354	.65029	.64708
93	.69130	.68789	.68452	.68119	.67789	.67463	.67140	.66820	.66504	.66191
94	.70421	.70090	.69762	.69438	.69118	.68800	.68486	.68175	.67867	.67563
95	.71594	.71272	.70954	.70639	.70326	.70017	.69712	.69409	.69109	.68812
96	.72638	.72325	.72014	.71707	.71403	.71101	.70803	.70507	.70215	.69925
97	.73590	.73285	.72982	.72682	.72385	.72090	.71799	.71510	.71224	.70941
98	.74448	.74149	.73853	.73560	.73269	.72981	.72696	.72414	.72134	.71856
99	.75240	.74948	.74658	.74371	.74086	.73805	.73525	.73248	.72974	.72702
100	.75974	.75687	.75403	.75121	.74842	.74566	.74292	.74020	.73751	.73484
101	.76669	.76388	.76109	.75833	.75559	.75287	.75018	.74751	.74486	.74223
102	.77393	.77117	.76844	.76573	.76304	.76037	.75773	.75511	.75251	.74993
103	.78158	.77888	.77620	.77355	.77091	.76830	.76571	.76313	.76058	.75805
104	.79007	.78743	.78482	.78222	.77964	.77709	.77455	.77203	.76953	.76705
105	.80065	.79809	.79556	.79304	.79054	.78805	.78559	.78314	.78071	.77829
106	.81631	.81389	.81149	.80911	.80674	.80438	.80204	.79972	.79741	.79511
107	.83963	.83745	.83529	.83313	.83099	.82886	.82674	.82463	.82254	.82045
108	.87910	.87739	.87569	.87400	.87232	.87064	.86897	.86731	.86566	.86401
109	.94563	.94484	.94405	.94326	.94248	.94170	.94092	.94014	.93937	.93860

TABLE 80CNSMT

APPLICABLE AFTER APRIL 30, 1989, AND BEFORE MAY 1, 1999

Age x (1)	l(x) (2)	Age x (1)	l(x) (2)	Age x (1)	l(x) (2)
0	100000	37	95492	74	59279
1	98740	38	95317	75	56799
2	98648	39	95129	76	54239
3	98584	40	94926	77	51599
4	98535	41	94706	78	48878
5	98495	42	94465	79	46071
6	98459	43	94201	80	43180
7	98426	44	93913	81	40208
8	98396	45	93599	82	37172
9	98370	46	93256	83	34095
10	98347	47	92882	84	31012
11	98328	48	92472	85	27960
12	98309	49	92021	86	24961
13	98285	50	91526	87	22038
14	98248	51	90986	88	19235
15	98196	52	90402	89	16598
16	98129	53	89771	90	14154
17	98047	54	89087	91	11908
18	97953	55	88348	92	9863
19	97851	56	87551	93	8032
20	97741	57	86695	94	6424
21	97623	58	85776	95	5043
22	97499	59	84789	96	3884
23	97370	60	83726	97	2939
24	97240	61	82581	98	2185
25	97110	62	81348	99	1598
26	96982	63	80024	100	1150
27	96856	64	78609	101	815
28	96730	65	77107	102	570
29	96604	66	75520	103	393
30	96477	67	73846	104	267
31	96350	68	72082	105	179
32	96220	69	70218	106	119
33	96088	70	68248	107	78
34	95951	71	66165	108	51
35	95808	72	63972	109	33
36	95655	73	61673	110	0

(f) Valuation of annuities, interests for life or term of years, and remainder or reversionary interests for estates of decedents for which the valuation date of the gross estate is after April 30,1999, and before May 1, 2009. *(1) In general.* Except as otherwise provided in § 20.2031-7(b) and § 20.7520-3(b) (pertaining to certain limitations on the use of prescribed tables), if the valuation date for the gross estate of the decedent is after April 30, 1999, and before May 1, 2009, the fair market value of annuities, life estates, terms of years, remainders, and reversionary interests is the present value of the interests determined by use of standard or special section 7520 actuarial factors and the valuation methodology described in § 20.2031-7T(d). These factors are derived by using the appropriate section 7520 interest rate and, if applicable, the mortality component for the valuation date of the interest that is being valued. See §§ 20.7520-1 through 20.7520-4. See paragraph (f)(4) of this section for determination of the appropriate table for use in valuing these interests.

(2) Transitional rule. (i) If a decedent dies after April 30, 1999, and if on May 1, 1999, the decedent was mentally incompetent so that the disposition of the decedent's property could not be changed, and the decedent dies without having regained competency to dispose of the decedent's property or dies within 90 days of the date on which the decedent first regains competency, the fair market value of annuities, life estates, terms for years, remainders, and reversions included in the gross estate of the decedent is their present value determined either under this section or under the corresponding section applicable at the time the decedent became mentally incompetent, at the option of the decedent's executor. For example, see paragraph (d) of this section.

(ii) If a decedent dies after April 30, 1999, and before July 1, 1999, the fair market value of annuities, life estates, remainders, and reversions based on one or more measuring lives included in the gross estate of the decedent is their present value determined under this section by use of the section 7520 interest rate for the month in which the valuation date occurs (see §§ 20.7520-1(b) and 20.7520-2(a)(2)) and the appropriate actuarial tables under either paragraph (e)(4) or paragraph (f)(4) of this section, at the option of the decedent's executor.

(iii) For purposes of paragraphs (f)(2)(i) and (f)(2)(ii) of this section, where the decedent's executor is given the option to use the appropriate actuarial tables under either paragraph (e)(4) or paragraph (f)(4) of this section, the decedent's executor must use the same actuarial table with respect to each individual transaction and with respect to all transfers occurring on the valuation date (for example, gift and income tax charitable deductions with respect to the same transfer must be determined based on the same tables, and all assets includible in the gross estate and/or estate tax deductions claimed must be valued based on the same tables).

(3) Publications and actuarial computations by the Internal Revenue Service. Many standard actuarial factors not included in paragraph (f)(4) of this section or in § 20.2031-7(d)(6) are included in Internal Revenue Service Publication 1457, "Actuarial Values, Book Aleph," (7-99). Publication 1457 also includes examples that illustrate how to compute many special factors for more unusual situations. Publication 1457 is no longer available for purchase from the Superintendent of Documents, United States Government Printing Office. However, pertinent factors in this publication may be obtained from: CC:PA:LPD:PR (IRS Publication 1457), Room 5205, Internal Revenue Service, P.O. Box 7604, Ben Franklin Station, Washington, DC 20044. If a special factor is required in the case of an actual decedent, the Internal Revenue Service may furnish the factor to the executor upon a request for a ruling. The request for a ruling must be accompanied by a recitation of the facts including a statement of the date of birth for each measuring life, the date of the decedent's death, any other applicable dates, and a copy of the will, trust, or other relevant documents. A request for a ruling must comply with the instructions for requesting a ruling published periodically in the Internal Revenue Bulletin (see §§ 601.201 and 601.601(d)(2)(ii)(b)) and include payment of the required user fee.

(4) Actuarial tables. Except as provided in § 20.7520-3(b) (pertaining to certain limitations on the use of prescribed tables), Life Table 90CM and Table S (Single life remainder factors applicable where the valuation date is after April 30, 1999, and before May 1, 2009), contained in this paragraph (f)(4), and Table B, Table J, and Table K set forth in § 20.2031-7(d)(6) must be used in the application of the provisions of this section when the section 7520 interest rate component is between 4.2 and 14 percent. Table S and Table 90CM are as follows:

Table S.--Based on Life on Life Table 90CM Single Life Remainder Factors

[Applicable After April 30, 1999, and Before May 1, 2009]

	[Interest rate]									
Age	4.2%	4.4%	4.6%	4.8%	5.0%	5.2%	5.4%	5.6%	5.8%	6.0%
0	.06752	.06130	.05586	.05109	.04691	.04322	.03998	.03711	.03458	.03233
1	.06137	.05495	.04932	.04438	.04003	.03620	.03283	.02985	.02721	.02487
2	.06325	.05667	.05088	.04580	.04132	.03737	.03388	.03079	.02806	.02563
3	.06545	.05869	.05275	.04752	.04291	.03883	.03523	.03203	.02920	.02668
4	.06784	.06092	.05482	.04944	.04469	.04048	.03676	.03346	.03052	.02791
5	.07040	.06331	.05705	.05152	.04662	.04229	.03845	.03503	.03199	.02928
6	.07310	.06583	.05941	.05372	.04869	.04422	.04025	.03672	.03357	.03076
7	.07594	.06849	.06191	.05607	.05089	.04628	.04219	.03854	.03528	.03236
8	.07891	.07129	.06453	.05853	.05321	.04846	.04424	.04046	.03709	.03407
9	.08203	.07423	.06731	.06115	.05567	.05079	.04643	.04253	.03904	.03592
10	.08532	.07734	.07024	.06392	.05829	.05326	.04877	.04474	.04114	.03790
11	.08875	.08059	.07331	.06683	.06104	.05587	.05124	.04709	.04336	.04002
12	.09233	.08398	.07653	.06989	.06394	.05862	.05385	.04957	.04572	.04226
13	.09601	.08748	.07985	.07304	.06693	.06146	.05655	.05214	.04816	.04458
14	.09974	.09102	.08322	.07624	.06997	.06435	.05929	.05474	.05064	.04694
15	.10350	.09460	.08661	.07946	.07303	.06725	.06204	.05735	.05312	.04930
16	.10728	.09818	.09001	.08268	.07608	.07014	.06479	.05996	.05559	.05164
17	.11108	.10179	.09344	.08592	.07916	.07306	.06755	.06257	.05807	.05399
18	.11494	.10545	.09691	.08921	.08227	.07601	.07034	.06521	.06057	.05636
19	.11889	.10921	.10047	.09259	.08548	.07904	.07322	.06794	.06315	.05880
20	.12298	.11310	.10417	.09610	.08881	.08220	.07622	.07078	.06584	.06135
21	.12722	.11713	.10801	.09976	.09228	.08550	.07935	.07375	.06866	.06403
22	.13159	.12130	.11199	.10354	.09588	.08893	.08260	.07685	.07160	.06682
23	.13613	.12563	.11612	.10748	.09964	.09250	.08601	.08009	.07468	.06975
24	.14084	.13014	.12043	.11160	.10357	.09625	.08958	.08349	.07793	.07284
25	.14574	.13484	.12493	.11591	.10768	.10018	.09334	.08708	.08135	.07611
26	.15084	.13974	.12963	.12041	.11199	.10431	.09728	.09085	.08496	.07956
27	.15615	.14485	.13454	.12513	.11652	.10865	.10144	.09484	.08878	.08322
28	.16166	.15016	.13965	.13004	.12124	.11319	.10580	.09901	.09279	.08706
29	.16737	.15567	.14497	.13516	.12617	.11792	.11035	.10339	.09699	.09109
30	.17328	.16138	.15048	.14047	.13129	.12286	.11510	.10796	.10138	.09532
31	.17938	.16728	.15618	.14599	.13661	.12799	.12004	.11272	.10597	.09974
32	.18568	.17339	.16210	.15171	.14214	.13333	.12520	.11769	.11076	.10435
33	.19220	.17972	.16824	.15766	.14790	.13889	.13058	.12289	.11578	.10920
34	.19894	.18627	.17460	.16383	.15388	.14468	.13618	.12831	.12102	.11426
35	.20592	.19307	.18121	.17025	.16011	.15073	.14204	.13399	.12652	.11958
36	.21312	.20010	.18805	.17691	.16658	.15701	.14814	.13990	.13225	.12514
37	.22057	.20737	.19514	.18382	.17331	.16356	.15450	.14608	.13825	.13096

Age	4.2%	4.4%	4.6%	4.8%	5.0%	5.2%	5.4%	5.6%	5.8%	6.0%
	[Interest rate]									
38	.22827	.21490	.20251	.19100	.18031	.17038	.16113	.15253	.14452	.13705
39	.23623	.22270	.21013	.19845	.18759	.17747	.16805	.15927	.15108	.14344
40	.24446	.23078	.21805	.20620	.19516	.18487	.17527	.16631	.15795	.15013
41	.25298	.23915	.22626	.21425	.20305	.19259	.18282	.17368	.16514	.15715
42	.26178	.24782	.23478	.22262	.21125	.20062	.19069	.18138	.17267	.16450
43	.27087	.25678	.24360	.23129	.21977	.20898	.19888	.18941	.18053	.17220
44	.28025	.26603	.25273	.24027	.22860	.21766	.20740	.19777	.18873	.18023
45	.28987	.27555	.26212	.24953	.23772	.22664	.21622	.20644	.19724	.18858
46	.29976	.28533	.27179	.25908	.24714	.23591	.22536	.21542	.20606	.19725
47	.30987	.29535	.28171	.26889	.25682	.24546	.23476	.22468	.21518	.20621
48	.32023	.30563	.29190	.27897	.26678	.25530	.24447	.23425	.22460	.21549
49	.33082	.31615	.30234	.28931	.27702	.26543	.25447	.24412	.23434	.22509
50	.34166	.32694	.31306	.29995	.28756	.27586	.26479	.25432	.24441	.23502
51	.35274	.33798	.32404	.31085	.29838	.28658	.27541	.26482	.25479	.24528
52	.36402	.34924	.33525	.32200	.30946	.29757	.28630	.27561	.26547	.25584
53	.37550	.36070	.34668	.33339	.32078	.30882	.29746	.28667	.27643	.26669
54	.38717	.37237	.35833	.34500	.33234	.32031	.30888	.29801	.28766	.27782
55	.39903	.38424	.37019	.35683	.34413	.33205	.32056	.30961	.29918	.28925
56	.41108	.39631	.38227	.36890	.35617	.34405	.33250	.32149	.31099	.30097
57	.42330	.40857	.39455	.38118	.36844	.35629	.34469	.33363	.32306	.31297
58	.43566	.42098	.40699	.39364	.38089	.36873	.35710	.34600	.33538	.32522
59	.44811	.43351	.41956	.40623	.39350	.38133	.36968	.35855	.34789	.33768
60	.46066	.44613	.43224	.41896	.40624	.39408	.38243	.37127	.36058	.35033
61	.47330	.45887	.44505	.43182	.41914	.40699	.39535	.38418	.37347	.36318
62	.48608	.47175	.45802	.44485	.43223	.42011	.40848	.39732	.38660	.37629
63	.49898	.48478	.47115	.45807	.44550	.43343	.42184	.41069	.39997	.38966
64	.51200	.49793	.48442	.47143	.45895	.44694	.43539	.42427	.41357	.40326
65	.52512	.51121	.49782	.48495	.47255	.46062	.44912	.43805	.42738	.41709
66	.53835	.52461	.51137	.49862	.48634	.47449	.46307	.45206	.44143	.43118
67	.55174	.53818	.52511	.51250	.50034	.48860	.47727	.46633	.45576	.44556
68	.56524	.55188	.53899	.52654	.51452	.50291	.49168	.48083	.47034	.46020
69	.57882	.56568	.55299	.54071	.52885	.51737	.50627	.49552	.48513	.47506
70	.59242	.57951	.56703	.55495	.54325	.53193	.52096	.51034	.50004	.49007
71	.60598	.59332	.58106	.56918	.55767	.54651	.53569	.52520	.51503	.50516
72	.61948	.60707	.59504	.58338	.57206	.56108	.55043	.54009	.53004	.52029
73	.63287	.62073	.60895	.59751	.58640	.57561	.56513	.55495	.54505	.53543
74	.64621	.63435	.62282	.61162	.60073	.59015	.57985	.56984	.56009	.55061
75	.65953	.64796	.63671	.62575	.61510	.60473	.59463	.58480	.57523	.56591
76	.67287	.66160	.65063	.63995	.62954	.61940	.60952	.59989	.59050	.58135
77	.68622	.67526	.66459	.65419	.64404	.63415	.62450	.61509	.60590	.59694
78	.69954	.68892	.67856	.66845	.65858	.64895	.63955	.63036	.62140	.61264
79	.71278	.70250	.69246	.68265	.67308	.66372	.65457	.64563	.63690	.62836
80	.72581	.71588	.70618	.69668	.68740	.67833	.66945	.66077	.65227	.64396
81	.73857	.72899	.71962	.71045	.70147	.69268	.68408	.67566	.66741	.65933
82	.75101	.74178	.73274	.72389	.71522	.70672	.69840	.69024	.68225	.67441
83	.76311	.75423	.74553	.73700	.72864	.72044	.71240	.70451	.69678	.68919
84	.77497	.76645	.75809	.74988	.74183	.73393	.72618	.71857	.71110	.70377
85	.78665	.77848	.77047	.76260	.75487	.74728	.73982	.73250	.72530	.71823
86	.79805	.79025	.78258	.77504	.76764	.76036	.75320	.74617	.73925	.73245
87	.80904	.80159	.79427	.78706	.77998	.77301	.76615	.75940	.75277	.74624
88	.81962	.81251	.80552	.79865	.79188	.78521	.77865	.77220	.76584	.75958
89	.82978	.82302	.81636	.80980	.80335	.79699	.79072	.78455	.77847	.77248
90	.83952	.83309	.82676	.82052	.81437	.80831	.80234	.79645	.79064	.78492
91	.84870	.84260	.83658	.83064	.82479	.81902	.81332	.80771	.80217	.79671
92	.85716	.85136	.84563	.83998	.83441	.82891	.82348	.81812	.81283	.80761
93	.86494	.85942	.85396	.84858	.84326	.83801	.83283	.82771	.82266	.81767
94	.87216	.86690	.86170	.85657	.85149	.84648	.84153	.83664	.83181	.82704
95	.87898	.87397	.86902	.86412	.85928	.85450	.84977	.84510	.84049	.83592
96	.88537	.88060	.87587	.87121	.86659	.86203	.85751	.85305	.84864	.84427
97	.89127	.88672	.88221	.87775	.87335	.86898	.86467	.86040	.85618	.85200
98	.89680	.89245	.88815	.88389	.87968	.87551	.87138	.86730	.86326	.85926
99	.90217	.89803	.89393	.88987	.88585	.88187	.87793	.87402	.87016	.86633
100	.90738	.90344	.89953	.89567	.89183	.88804	.88428	.88056	.87687	.87322

Age	4.2%	4.4%	4.6%	4.8%	5.0%	5.2%	5.4%	5.6%	5.8%	6.0%
	[Interest rate]									
101	.91250	.90876	.90504	.90137	.89772	.89412	.89054	.88699	.88348	.88000
102	.91751	.91396	.91045	.90696	.90350	.90007	.89668	.89331	.88997	.88666
103	.92247	.91912	.91579	.91249	.90922	.90598	.90276	.89957	.89640	.89326
104	.92775	.92460	.92148	.91839	.91532	.91227	.90924	.90624	.90326	.90031
105	.93290	.92996	.92704	.92415	.92127	.91841	.91558	.91276	.90997	.90719
106	.93948	.93680	.93415	.93151	.92889	.92628	.92370	.92113	.91857	.91604
107	.94739	.94504	.94271	.94039	.93808	.93579	.93351	.93124	.92899	.92675
108	.95950	.95767	.95585	.95404	.95224	.95045	.94867	.94689	.94512	.94336
109	.97985	.97893	.97801	.97710	.97619	.97529	.97438	.97348	.97259	.97170

Age	6.2%	6.4%	6.6%	6.8%	7.0%	7.2%	7.4%	7.6%	7.8%	8.0%
0	.03034	.02857	.02700	.02559	.02433	.02321	.02220	.02129	.02047	.01973
1	.02279	.02094	.01929	.01782	.01650	.01533	.01427	.01331	.01246	.01168
2	.02347	.02155	.01983	.01829	.01692	.01569	.01458	.01358	.01268	.01187
3	.02444	.02243	.02065	.01905	.01761	.01632	.01516	.01412	.01317	.01232
4	.02558	.02349	.02163	.01996	.01846	.01712	.01590	.01481	.01382	.01292
5	.02686	.02469	.02275	.02101	.01945	.01804	.01677	.01562	.01458	.01364
6	.02825	.02600	.02398	.02217	.02053	.01906	.01773	.01653	.01544	.01445
7	.02976	.02742	.02532	.02343	.02172	.02019	.01880	.01754	.01640	.01536
8	.03137	.02894	.02675	.02479	.02301	.02140	.01995	.01864	.01744	.01635
9	.03311	.03059	.02832	.02627	.02442	.02274	.02122	.01985	.01859	.01745
10	.03499	.03237	.03001	.02788	.02595	.02420	.02262	.02118	.01987	.01867
11	.03700	.03428	.03183	.02961	.02760	.02578	.02413	.02262	.02125	.02000
12	.03913	.03632	.03377	.03146	.02937	.02748	.02575	.02418	.02275	.02144
13	.04135	.03843	.03579	.03339	.03122	.02924	.02744	.02580	.02431	.02294
14	.04359	.04057	.03783	.03534	.03308	.03102	.02915	.02744	.02587	.02444
15	.04584	.04270	.03986	.03728	.03493	.03279	.03083	.02905	.02742	.02593
16	.04806	.04482	.04187	.03919	.03674	.03452	.03248	.03063	.02892	.02736
17	.05029	.04692	.04387	.04108	.03855	.03623	.03411	.03218	.03040	.02877
18	.05253	.04905	.04588	.04299	.04036	.03795	.03574	.03373	.03187	.03017
19	.05484	.05124	.04796	.04496	.04222	.03972	.03742	.03532	.03339	.03161
20	.05726	.05354	.05013	.04702	.04418	.04158	.03919	.03700	.03498	.03313
21	.05980	.05595	.05242	.04920	.04625	.04354	.04105	.03877	.03667	.03473
22	.06246	.05847	.05482	.05147	.04841	.04559	.04301	.04063	.03844	.03642
23	.06524	.06112	.05734	.05387	.05069	.04777	.04508	.04260	.04032	.03821
24	.06819	.06392	.06001	.05642	.05312	.05008	.04728	.04470	.04232	.04012
25	.07131	.06690	.06285	.05913	.05570	.05255	.04964	.04695	.04447	.04218
26	.07460	.07005	.06586	.06200	.05845	.05518	.05215	.04936	.04677	.04438
27	.07810	.07340	.06907	.06508	.06140	.05800	.05485	.05195	.04925	.04676
28	.08179	.07693	.07246	.06833	.06451	.06098	.05772	.05469	.05189	.04929
29	.08566	.08065	.07603	.07176	.06780	.06414	.06075	.05761	.05469	.05198
30	.08973	.08456	.07978	.07536	.07127	.06748	.06396	.06069	.05766	.05483
31	.09398	.08865	.08372	.07915	.07491	.07098	.06733	.06394	.06078	.05785
32	.09843	.09294	.08785	.08313	.07875	.07468	.07089	.06737	.06409	.06103
33	.10310	.09745	.09220	.08732	.08279	.07858	.07466	.07100	.06759	.06441
34	.10799	.10217	.09676	.09173	.08705	.08269	.07862	.07483	.07129	.06798
35	.11314	.10715	.10157	.09638	.09155	.08704	.08283	.07890	.07522	.07179
36	.11852	.11236	.10662	.10127	.09628	.09162	.08726	.08319	.07938	.07581
37	.12416	.11783	.11193	.10641	.10126	.09645	.09194	.08772	.08377	.08006
38	.13009	.12359	.11751	.11183	.10652	.10155	.09689	.09253	.08843	.08459
39	.13629	.12962	.12338	.11753	.11206	.10693	.10212	.09761	.09337	.08938
40	.14281	.13597	.12955	.12355	.11791	.11262	.10766	.10299	.09860	.09447
41	.14966	.14264	.13606	.12989	.12409	.11864	.11352	.10870	.10417	.09989
42	.15685	.14966	.14291	.13657	.13061	.12500	.11972	.11475	.11006	.10564
43	.16437	.15702	.15010	.14360	.13747	.13171	.12627	.12115	.11631	.11174
44	.17224	.16472	.15764	.15098	.14469	.13876	.13317	.12789	.12290	.11819
45	.18042	.17274	.16550	.15867	.15223	.14615	.14040	.13496	.12982	.12496
46	.18893	.18110	.17370	.16671	.16011	.15387	.14796	.14238	.13708	.13207
47	.19775	.18975	.18220	.17505	.16830	.16190	.15584	.15010	.14466	.13950
48	.20688	.19873	.19102	.18373	.17682	.17027	.16406	.15817	.15258	.14727
49	.21633	.20804	.20018	.19274	.18568	.17898	.17262	.16658	.16084	.15539
50	.22612	.21769	.20969	.20210	.19490	.18805	.18155	.17536	.16948	.16388
51	.23625	.22769	.21955	.21182	.20448	.19749	.19084	.18452	.17849	.17275

Age	6.2%	6.4%	6.6%	6.8%	7.0%	7.2%	7.4%	7.6%	7.8%	8.0%
52	.24669	.23799	.22973	.22186	.21438	.20726	.20047	.19400	.18784	.18196
53	.25742	.24861	.24022	.23222	.22461	.21735	.21043	.20383	.19753	.19151
54	.26845	.25952	.25101	.24290	.23516	.22777	.22072	.21399	.20756	.20140
55	.27978	.27074	.26212	.25389	.24604	.23853	.23136	.22450	.21793	.21166
56	.29140	.28227	.27355	.26522	.25725	.24963	.24233	.23535	.22867	.22227
57	.30333	.29411	.28529	.27686	.26879	.26106	.25365	.24656	.23976	.23324
58	.31551	.30621	.29731	.28878	.28061	.27278	.26528	.25807	.25116	.24453
59	.32790	.31854	.30956	.30095	.29269	.28477	.27716	.26986	.26284	.25610
60	.34050	.33107	.32202	.31334	.30500	.29699	.28929	.28190	.27478	.26794
61	.35331	.34384	.33473	.32598	.31757	.30948	.30170	.29422	.28701	.28007
62	.36639	.35688	.34772	.33892	.33044	.32229	.31443	.30687	.29958	.29255
63	.37974	.37020	.36101	.35216	.34363	.33542	.32750	.31986	.31250	.30539
64	.39334	.38378	.37456	.36568	.35711	.34884	.34087	.33317	.32574	.31857
65	.40718	.39761	.38838	.37947	.37087	.36257	.35455	.34681	.33932	.33208
66	.42128	.41172	.40249	.39357	.38496	.37663	.36858	.36079	.35326	.34597
67	.43569	.42616	.41694	.40803	.39941	.39107	.38299	.37518	.36761	.36028
68	.45038	.44089	.43170	.42281	.41419	.40585	.39777	.38994	.38235	.37499
69	.46531	.45587	.44672	.43786	.42927	.42094	.41286	.40503	.39743	.39006
70	.48040	.47103	.46194	.45312	.44456	.43626	.42820	.42038	.41278	.40540
71	.49558	.48629	.47727	.46851	.46000	.45174	.44371	.43591	.42832	.42095
72	.51082	.50162	.49268	.48399	.47554	.46733	.45934	.45157	.44401	.43666
73	.52607	.51697	.50813	.49952	.49114	.48299	.47506	.46733	.45981	.45249
74	.54139	.53241	.52367	.51515	.50686	.49879	.49092	.48325	.47578	.46849
75	.55683	.54798	.53936	.53095	.52276	.51477	.50698	.49938	.49197	.48474
76	.57243	.56373	.55524	.54696	.53888	.53100	.52330	.51579	.50846	.50130
77	.58819	.57965	.57132	.56318	.55523	.54747	.53988	.53247	.52523	.51815
78	.60408	.59572	.58755	.57957	.57177	.56414	.55668	.54939	.54225	.53527
79	.62001	.61184	.60385	.59604	.58840	.58092	.57360	.56644	.55943	.55256
80	.63582	.62786	.62007	.61244	.60497	.59765	.59048	.58347	.57659	.56985
81	.65142	.64367	.63608	.62864	.62135	.61421	.60721	.60034	.59361	.58701
82	.66673	.65920	.65182	.64458	.63748	.63052	.62368	.61698	.61041	.60395
83	.68175	.67444	.66728	.66024	.65334	.64656	.63991	.63338	.62696	.62066
84	.69657	.68950	.68256	.67574	.66904	.66246	.65599	.64964	.64340	.63727
85	.71128	.70446	.69775	.69116	.68467	.67830	.67204	.66587	.65982	.65386
86	.72576	.71919	.71272	.70636	.70010	.69394	.68789	.68193	.67606	.67029
87	.73981	.73349	.72726	.72114	.71511	.70917	.70333	.69757	.69190	.68632
88	.75342	.74735	.74137	.73548	.72968	.72396	.71833	.71279	.70732	.70194
89	.76658	.76076	.75503	.74938	.74381	.73832	.73290	.72757	.72231	.71712
90	.77928	.77371	.76823	.76281	.75748	.75221	.74702	.74190	.73684	.73186
91	.79131	.78600	.78075	.77557	.77046	.76542	.76044	.75553	.75068	.74589
92	.80246	.79737	.79235	.78740	.78250	.77767	.77290	.76818	.76353	.75893
93	.81274	.80788	.80307	.79832	.79363	.78899	.78441	.77989	.77542	.77100
94	.82232	.81766	.81306	.80850	.80401	.79956	.79517	.79082	.78653	.78228
95	.83141	.82695	.82254	.81818	.81387	.80961	.80539	.80122	.79710	.79302
96	.83996	.83569	.83147	.82729	.82316	.81907	.81503	.81103	.80707	.80315
97	.84787	.84378	.83973	.83573	.83176	.82784	.82396	.82012	.81632	.81255
98	.85530	.85138	.84750	.84366	.83985	.83609	.83236	.82867	.82502	.82140
99	.86255	.85880	.85508	.85140	.84776	.84415	.84057	.83703	.83353	.83005
100	.86960	.86601	.86246	.85894	.85546	.85200	.84858	.84519	.84183	.83849
101	.87655	.87313	.86974	.86638	.86305	.85975	.85648	.85324	.85003	.84684
102	.88338	.88012	.87689	.87369	.87052	.86738	.86426	.86116	.85809	.85505
103	.89015	.88706	.88399	.88095	.87793	.87494	.87197	.86903	.86611	.86321
104	.89737	.89446	.89157	.88871	.88586	.88304	.88024	.87745	.87469	.87195
105	.90443	.90170	.89898	.89628	.89360	.89094	.88830	.88568	.88307	.88049
106	.91351	.91101	.90852	.90605	.90359	.90115	.89873	.89632	.89392	.89154
107	.92452	.92230	.92010	.91791	.91573	.91356	.91141	.90927	.90714	.90502
108	.94161	.93987	.93814	.93641	.93469	.93298	.93128	.92958	.92790	.92622
109	.97081	.96992	.96904	.96816	.96729	.96642	.96555	.96468	.96382	.96296

Age	8.2%	8.4%	8.6%	8.8%	9.0%	9.2%	9.4%	9.6%	9.8%	10.0%
0	.01906	.01845	.01790	.01740	.01694	.01652	.01613	.01578	.01546	.01516
1	.01098	.01034	.00977	.00924	.00876	.00833	.00793	.00756	.00722	.00691
2	.01113	.01046	.00986	.00930	.00880	.00834	.00791	.00753	.00717	.00684
3	.01155	.01084	.01020	.00962	.00909	.00860	.00816	.00775	.00737	.00702

Age	8.2%	8.4%	8.6%	8.8%	9.0%	9.2%	9.4%	9.6%	9.8%	10.0%
4	.01211	.01137	.01069	.01008	.00952	.00900	.00853	.00810	.00770	.00733
5	.01279	.01201	.01130	.01065	.01006	.00952	.00902	.00856	.00814	.00775
6	.01356	.01274	.01199	.01131	.01068	.01011	.00959	.00910	.00865	.00824
7	.01442	.01356	.01277	.01205	.01140	.01079	.01023	.00972	.00925	.00881
8	.01536	.01446	.01363	.01287	.01218	.01154	.01096	.01041	.00991	.00945
9	.01641	.01546	.01460	.01380	.01307	.01240	.01178	.01120	.01068	.01019
10	.01758	.01659	.01567	.01484	.01407	.01336	.01270	.01210	.01154	.01103
11	.01886	.01781	.01686	.01598	.01517	.01442	.01373	.01310	.01251	.01196
12	.02024	.01915	.01814	.01721	.01636	.01558	.01485	.01419	.01357	.01299
13	.02168	.02054	.01948	.01851	.01762	.01679	.01603	.01533	.01467	.01407
14	.02313	.02193	.02083	.01981	.01887	.01801	.01721	.01646	.01578	.01514
15	.02456	.02330	.02214	.02107	.02009	.01918	.01834	.01756	.01684	.01617
16	.02593	.02462	.02340	.02229	.02126	.02030	.01942	.01860	.01785	.01714
17	.02728	.02590	.02463	.02346	.02238	.02138	.02046	.01960	.01880	.01806
18	.02861	.02717	.02584	.02462	.02348	.02243	.02146	.02056	.01972	.01894
19	.02998	.02847	.02708	.02580	.02461	.02351	.02249	.02154	.02066	.01984
20	.03142	.02984	.02839	.02704	.02580	.02465	.02357	.02258	.02165	.02079
21	.03295	.03130	.02978	.02837	.02706	.02585	.02473	.02368	.02271	.02180
22	.03455	.03283	.03124	.02976	.02839	.02712	.02594	.02484	.02382	.02286
23	.03626	.03446	.03279	.03124	.02981	.02847	.02723	.02608	.02500	.02400
24	.03809	.03620	.03446	.03283	.03133	.02993	.02863	.02741	.02628	.02522
25	.04005	.03808	.03625	.03456	.03298	.03151	.03014	.02887	.02768	.02656
26	.04216	.04010	.03819	.03641	.03476	.03322	.03178	.03044	.02919	.02802
27	.04444	.04229	.04029	.03843	.03670	.03508	.03357	.03217	.03085	.02962
28	.04687	.04463	.04254	.04059	.03877	.03708	.03550	.03402	.03263	.03133
29	.04946	.04712	.04493	.04289	.04099	.03922	.03756	.03600	.03455	.03318
30	.05221	.04976	.04748	.04534	.04335	.04149	.03975	.03812	.03659	.03515
31	.05511	.05255	.05017	.04794	.04585	.04390	.04208	.04037	.03876	.03725
32	.05818	.05551	.05302	.05069	.04851	.04647	.04455	.04276	.04107	.03948
33	.06144	.05866	.05606	.05363	.05135	.04921	.04720	.04532	.04355	.04188
34	.06489	.06200	.05928	.05674	.05436	.05212	.05002	.04805	.04619	.04444
35	.06857	.06555	.06273	.06007	.05758	.05524	.05304	.05097	.04902	.04718
36	.07246	.06932	.06638	.06361	.06101	.05856	.05626	.05409	.05205	.05012
37	.07659	.07332	.07025	.06737	.06466	.06210	.05969	.05742	.05528	.05325
38	.08098	.07758	.07439	.07138	.06855	.06588	.06336	.06099	.05874	.05662
39	.08563	.08210	.07878	.07565	.07270	.06992	.06729	.06480	.06245	.06023
40	.09059	.08692	.08347	.08021	.07714	.07423	.07149	.06889	.06643	.06411
41	.09586	.09206	.08848	.08509	.08189	.07886	.07600	.07329	.07072	.06828
42	.10147	.09753	.09381	.09029	.08696	.08381	.08083	.07800	.07531	.07277
43	.10742	.10334	.09948	.09583	.09237	.08909	.08598	.08304	.08024	.07758
44	.11373	.10950	.10551	.10172	.09813	.09472	.09148	.08841	.08549	.08272
45	.12035	.11599	.11185	.10792	.10420	.10066	.09730	.09410	.09106	.08817
46	.12732	.12281	.11853	.11447	.11061	.10694	.10345	.10013	.09696	.09395
47	.13460	.12995	.12553	.12133	.11733	.11353	.10991	.10646	.10317	.10004
48	.14223	.13743	.13287	.12853	.12439	.12046	.11671	.11313	.10972	.10646
49	.15020	.14526	.14056	.13608	.13181	.12774	.12385	.12015	.11661	.11322
50	.15855	.15347	.14862	.14401	.13960	.13540	.13138	.12754	.12388	.12037
51	.16727	.16205	.15707	.15232	.14777	.14344	.13929	.13532	.13153	.12789
52	.17634	.17098	.16587	.16097	.15630	.15183	.14755	.14345	.13953	.13577
53	.18576	.18027	.17501	.16999	.16518	.16057	.15616	.15194	.14789	.14400
54	.19552	.18990	.18451	.17935	.17441	.16968	.16514	.16078	.15661	.15260
55	.20564	.19989	.19437	.18908	.18402	.17915	.17449	.17001	.16571	.16157
56	.21613	.21025	.20461	.19919	.19400	.18901	.18422	.17962	.17519	.17093
57	.22698	.22098	.21522	.20968	.20436	.19925	.19434	.18961	.18507	.18069
58	.23816	.23204	.22616	.22051	.21507	.20984	.20481	.19996	.19530	.19080
59	.24962	.24339	.23740	.23163	.22608	.22073	.21558	.21062	.20584	.20123
60	.26136	.25502	.24892	.24304	.23738	.23192	.22666	.22158	.21669	.21196
61	.27339	.26695	.26075	.25477	.24900	.24343	.23806	.23288	.22787	.22304
62	.28578	.27925	.27295	.26687	.26100	.25533	.24985	.24456	.23945	.23451
63	.29854	.29192	.28553	.27935	.27339	.26762	.26205	.25666	.25145	.24641
64	.31164	.30494	.29846	.29221	.28615	.28030	.27463	.26915	.26384	.25870
65	.32508	.31831	.31177	.30543	.29930	.29336	.28761	.28203	.27663	.27140
66	.33891	.33208	.32547	.31906	.31285	.30684	.30101	.29536	.28987	.28456
67	.35318	.34630	.33963	.33316	.32689	.32081	.31491	.30918	.30363	.29823
68	.36785	.36093	.35422	.34770	.34138	.33524	.32928	.32349	.31787	.31240

Age	8.2%	8.4%	8.6%	8.8%	9.0%	9.2%	9.4%	9.6%	9.8%	10.0%
69	.38290	.37595	.36920	.36265	.35628	.35009	.34408	.33824	.33256	.32703
70	.39823	.39127	.38450	.37791	.37151	.36529	.35924	.35335	.34762	.34204
71	.41378	.40681	.40003	.39343	.38701	.38076	.37467	.36875	.36298	.35736
72	.42950	.42253	.41575	.40914	.40271	.39644	.39034	.38438	.37858	.37293
73	.44535	.43840	.43162	.42502	.41858	.41231	.40619	.40022	.39440	.38872
74	.46139	.45446	.44771	.44112	.43469	.42842	.42230	.41632	.41049	.40479
75	.47769	.47080	.46408	.45752	.45111	.44485	.43874	.43277	.42693	.42123
76	.49430	.48747	.48079	.47427	.46790	.46167	.45558	.44963	.44380	.43811
77	.51123	.50447	.49786	.49139	.48506	.47888	.47282	.46690	.46111	.45543
78	.52845	.52177	.51523	.50884	.50257	.49645	.49044	.48457	.47881	.47317
79	.54584	.53926	.53282	.52650	.52032	.51426	.50833	.50251	.49681	.49122
80	.56325	.55678	.55044	.54423	.53813	.53216	.52630	.52056	.51492	.50939
81	.58054	.57419	.56797	.56186	.55587	.54999	.54422	.53856	.53300	.52754
82	.59762	.59140	.58530	.57931	.57343	.56766	.56198	.55641	.55094	.54557
83	.61448	.60840	.60243	.59657	.59081	.58515	.57958	.57411	.56874	.56346
84	.63124	.62531	.61949	.61376	.60813	.60259	.59715	.59179	.58652	.58134
85	.64800	.64224	.63657	.63099	.62550	.62010	.61478	.60955	.60441	.59934
86	.66461	.65902	.65351	.64810	.64276	.63751	.63233	.62724	.62222	.61728
87	.68083	.67541	.67008	.66483	.65965	.65455	.64953	.64458	.63970	.63489
88	.69663	.69140	.68624	.68116	.67615	.67121	.66634	.66154	.65680	.65213
89	.71201	.70696	.70199	.69708	.69224	.68747	.68276	.67811	.67353	.66900
90	.72694	.72209	.71730	.71257	.70791	.70330	.69876	.69427	.68984	.68547
91	.74117	.73650	.73190	.72735	.72286	.71842	.71404	.70972	.70545	.70123
92	.75439	.74991	.74548	.74110	.73678	.73251	.72829	.72412	.72000	.71593
93	.76664	.76233	.75806	.75385	.74969	.74557	.74150	.73748	.73350	.72957
94	.77809	.77394	.76983	.76578	.76177	.75780	.75388	.75000	.74616	.74237
95	.78899	.78500	.78106	.77715	.77329	.76947	.76569	.76195	.75826	.75460
96	.79928	.79544	.79165	.78790	.78418	.78050	.77686	.77326	.76970	.76617
97	.80883	.80514	.80149	.79787	.79430	.79075	.78725	.78377	.78033	.77693
98	.81781	.81427	.81075	.80727	.80382	.80041	.79703	.79368	.79036	.78708
99	.82661	.82320	.81982	.81648	.81316	.80988	.80662	.80340	.80020	.79704
100	.83519	.83192	.82868	.82547	.82228	.81913	.81600	.81290	.80982	.80678
101	.84368	.84055	.83744	.83437	.83131	.82829	.82529	.82231	.81936	.81643
102	.85203	.84904	.84607	.84313	.84021	.83731	.83444	.83159	.82876	.82596
103	.86034	.85748	.85465	.85184	.84906	.84629	.84355	.84082	.83812	.83544
104	.86923	.86653	.86385	.86119	.85855	.85593	.85333	.85074	.84818	.84563
105	.87792	.87537	.87283	.87032	.86782	.86534	.86287	.86042	.85799	.85557
106	.88918	.88683	.88450	.88218	.87987	.87758	.87530	.87304	.87079	.86855
107	.90291	.90082	.89873	.89666	.89460	.89255	.89051	.88849	.88647	.88447
108	.92455	.92288	.92123	.91958	.91794	.91630	.91468	.91306	.91145	.90984
109	.96211	.96125	.96041	.95956	.95872	.95788	.95704	.95620	.95537	.95455

Age	10.2%	10.4%	10.6%	10.8%	11.0%	11.2%	11.4%	11.6%	11.8%	12.0%
0	.01488	.01463	.01439	.01417	.01396	.01377	.01359	.01343	.01327	.01312
1	.00662	.00636	.00612	.00589	.00568	.00548	.00530	.00513	.00497	.00482
2	.00654	.00626	.00600	.00576	.00554	.00533	.00514	.00496	.00479	.00463
3	.00670	.00641	.00613	.00588	.00564	.00542	.00522	.00502	.00484	.00468
4	.00699	.00668	.00639	.00612	.00587	.00563	.00542	.00521	.00502	.00484
5	.00739	.00706	.00675	.00646	.00620	.00595	.00571	.00550	.00529	.00510
6	.00786	.00751	.00718	.00687	.00659	.00633	.00608	.00585	.00563	.00543
7	.00841	.00803	.00769	.00736	.00706	.00678	.00652	.00627	.00604	.00582
8	.00902	.00863	.00826	.00791	.00759	.00730	.00702	.00675	.00651	.00628
9	.00973	.00931	.00892	.00856	.00822	.00790	.00760	.00733	.00706	.00682
10	.01055	.01010	.00969	.00930	.00894	.00861	.00829	.00799	.00772	.00746
11	.01146	.01099	.01055	.01014	.00976	.00940	.00907	.00875	.00846	.00818
12	.01246	.01196	.01150	.01106	.01066	.01028	.00993	.00960	.00928	.00899
13	.01351	.01298	.01249	.01204	.01161	.01121	.01084	.01049	.01016	.00985
14	.01455	.01400	.01348	.01300	.01255	.01213	.01173	.01136	.01102	.01069
15	.01555	.01497	.01443	.01392	.01345	.01300	.01259	.01220	.01183	.01148
16	.01648	.01587	.01530	.01477	.01427	.01380	.01336	.01295	.01257	.01220
17	.01737	.01673	.01612	.01556	.01504	.01455	.01408	.01365	.01324	.01286
18	.01822	.01754	.01691	.01632	.01576	.01525	.01476	.01430	.01387	.01347
19	.01908	.01837	.01770	.01708	.01650	.01595	.01544	.01495	.01450	.01407
20	.01999	.01924	.01854	.01788	.01726	.01669	.01615	.01564	.01516	.01471

Age	10.2%	10.4%	10.6%	10.8%	11.0%	11.2%	11.4%	11.6%	11.8%	12.0%
21	.02096	.02017	.01943	.01874	.01809	.01748	.01691	.01637	.01586	.01539
22	.02197	.02114	.02036	.01963	.01895	.01830	.01770	.01713	.01660	.01610
23	.02306	.02218	.02136	.02059	.01987	.01919	.01855	.01795	.01739	.01686
24	.02424	.02331	.02245	.02163	.02087	.02016	.01948	.01885	.01825	.01769
25	.02552	.02455	.02364	.02278	.02197	.02122	.02051	.01984	.01920	.01861
26	.02692	.02589	.02493	.02403	.02318	.02238	.02162	.02091	.02025	.01961
27	.02846	.02738	.02636	.02541	.02451	.02367	.02287	.02212	.02141	.02074
28	.03012	.02898	.02791	.02690	.02595	.02506	.02422	.02342	.02267	.02196
29	.03190	.03070	.02957	.02851	.02751	.02656	.02567	.02483	.02404	.02329
30	.03381	.03254	.03135	.03023	.02917	.02817	.02723	.02634	.02551	.02471
31	.03583	.03450	.03324	.03206	.03094	.02989	.02890	.02796	.02707	.02623
32	.03799	.03659	.03527	.03402	.03284	.03173	.03068	.02968	.02874	.02785
33	.04031	.03883	.03744	.03612	.03488	.03371	.03260	.03155	.03055	.02961
34	.04279	.04123	.03976	.03838	.03707	.03583	.03465	.03354	.03249	.03149
35	.04545	.04382	.04227	.04081	.03943	.03812	.03688	.03571	.03459	.03354
36	.04830	.04658	.04495	.04341	.04196	.04058	.03927	.03803	.03685	.03573
37	.05134	.04953	.04782	.04620	.04467	.04321	.04183	.04052	.03928	.03809
38	.05462	.05272	.05092	.04921	.04760	.04606	.04461	.04322	.04191	.04066
39	.05812	.05613	.05424	.05245	.05075	.04913	.04760	.04614	.04475	.04343
40	.06190	.05981	.05782	.05594	.05415	.05245	.05083	.04929	.04783	.04643
41	.06597	.06378	.06170	.05972	.05784	.05605	.05435	.05272	.05118	.04970
42	.07035	.06806	.06587	.06380	.06182	.05994	.05815	.05644	.05481	.05326
43	.07505	.07265	.07036	.06818	.06611	.06414	.06225	.06045	.05874	.05710
44	.08008	.07757	.07518	.07290	.07072	.06865	.06667	.06478	.06298	.06125
45	.08542	.08279	.08029	.07791	.07563	.07346	.07138	.06940	.06750	.06569
46	.09108	.08834	.08573	.08324	.08085	.07858	.07640	.07432	.07233	.07043
47	.09705	.09419	.09147	.08886	.08637	.08399	.08172	.07954	.07745	.07545
48	.10335	.10038	.09754	.09482	.09222	.08973	.08735	.08507	.08288	.08078
49	.10999	.10690	.10394	.10111	.09840	.09581	.09332	.09093	.08864	.08644
50	.11701	.11380	.11073	.10778	.10496	.10225	.09965	.09716	.09477	.09247
51	.12441	.12108	.11789	.11482	.11189	.10907	.10636	.10376	.10126	.09886
52	.13217	.12871	.12540	.12222	.11916	.11623	.11341	.11071	.10810	.10560
53	.14028	.13670	.13327	.12997	.12680	.12375	.12082	.11801	.11529	.11268
54	.14875	.14505	.14150	.13808	.13480	.13163	.12859	.12566	.12284	.12012
55	.15760	.15378	.15011	.14657	.14317	.13989	.13674	.13370	.13077	.12794
56	.16684	.16290	.15911	.15546	.15194	.14855	.14528	.14213	.13909	.13615
57	.17648	.17242	.16851	.16474	.16111	.15760	.15422	.15096	.14781	.14477
58	.18647	.18229	.17827	.17438	.17064	.16702	.16353	.16015	.15689	.15374
59	.19678	.19249	.18835	.18435	.18049	.17676	.17316	.16968	.16631	.16305
60	.20740	.20300	.19875	.19464	.19066	.18682	.18311	.17952	.17604	.17268
61	.21837	.21385	.20949	.20527	.20119	.19724	.19341	.18971	.18613	.18266
62	.22973	.22511	.22064	.21631	.21212	.20807	.20414	.20033	.19664	.19306
63	.24152	.23680	.23222	.22779	.22350	.21934	.21530	.21139	.20760	.20392
64	.25372	.24890	.24422	.23969	.23529	.23103	.22690	.22289	.21899	.21521
65	.26633	.26141	.25664	.25201	.24752	.24316	.23893	.23482	.23083	.22695
66	.27940	.27439	.26953	.26481	.26023	.25577	.25145	.24724	.24316	.23918
67	.29299	.28790	.28296	.27815	.27348	.26894	.26453	.26024	.25606	.25200
68	.30709	.30193	.29691	.29202	.28728	.28265	.27816	.27378	.26952	.26537
69	.32166	.31643	.31134	.30639	.30157	.29687	.29230	.28785	.28351	.27928
70	.33661	.33133	.32618	.32116	.31628	.31152	.30688	.30235	.29794	.29364
71	.35188	.34654	.34134	.33627	.33133	.32651	.32181	.31722	.31275	.30838
72	.36742	.36204	.35679	.35168	.34668	.34181	.33706	.33241	.32788	.32345
73	.38317	.37776	.37248	.36733	.36229	.35738	.35257	.34788	.34330	.33882
74	.39923	.39380	.38849	.38330	.37823	.37328	.36844	.36370	.35908	.35455
75	.41566	.41021	.40489	.39968	.39459	.38961	.38474	.37997	.37531	.37074
76	.43254	.42709	.42176	.41655	.41144	.40645	.40156	.39677	.39208	.38749
77	.44988	.44444	.43912	.43391	.42880	.42380	.41891	.41411	.40940	.40479
78	.46765	.46224	.45694	.45174	.44665	.44166	.43677	.43197	.42726	.42265
79	.48574	.48037	.47510	.46993	.46487	.45990	.45502	.45024	.44554	.44094
80	.50397	.49865	.49343	.48830	.48327	.47834	.47349	.46873	.46406	.45947
81	.52219	.51693	.51176	.50669	.50171	.49682	.49201	.48729	.48265	.47809
82	.54029	.53510	.53000	.52499	.52007	.51523	.51047	.50580	.50120	.49667
83	.55826	.55315	.54813	.54319	.53834	.53356	.52886	.52424	.51969	.51522
84	.57624	.57123	.56629	.56144	.55666	.55195	.54732	.54277	.53828	.53386
85	.59435	.58944	.58460	.57984	.57516	.57054	.56599	.56151	.55710	.55275

Age	10.2%	10.4%	10.6%	10.8%	11.0%	11.2%	11.4%	11.6%	11.8%	12.0%
86	.61241	.60762	.60289	.59824	.59365	.58913	.58468	.58029	.57596	.57170
87	.63015	.62548	.62087	.61633	.61185	.60744	.60309	.59880	.59456	.59039
88	.64753	.64299	.63851	.63409	.62973	.62543	.62118	.61700	.61287	.60879
89	.66454	.66013	.65579	.65150	.64726	.64308	.63895	.63488	.63086	.62689
90	.68115	.67689	.67268	.66853	.66442	.66037	.65637	.65241	.64851	.64465
91	.69706	.69294	.68887	.68486	.68089	.67696	.67309	.66925	.66547	.66173
92	.71190	.70792	.70399	.70011	.69627	.69247	.68872	.68501	.68134	.67771
93	.72569	.72184	.71804	.71429	.71057	.70689	.70326	.69967	.69611	.69259
94	.73861	.73490	.73123	.72759	.72400	.72044	.71692	.71344	.71000	.70659
95	.75097	.74739	.74384	.74033	.73686	.73342	.73002	.72665	.72331	.72001
96	.76267	.75922	.75579	.75240	.74905	.74572	.74243	.73917	.73595	.73275
97	.77356	.77022	.76691	.76363	.76039	.75718	.75399	.75084	.74772	.74463
98	.78382	.78059	.77740	.77423	.77110	.76799	.76491	.76186	.75884	.75584
99	.79390	.79079	.78771	.78465	.78162	.77862	.77565	.77270	.76978	.76688
100	.80376	.80076	.79779	.79485	.79193	.78904	.78617	.78333	.78051	.77771
101	.81353	.81066	.80780	.80497	.80217	.79938	.79662	.79388	.79117	.78847
102	.82318	.82042	.81768	.81496	.81227	.80960	.80694	.80431	.80170	.79911
103	.83278	.83014	.82752	.82491	.82233	.81977	.81723	.81470	.81220	.80971
104	.84310	.84059	.83810	.83563	.83317	.83073	.82831	.82591	.82352	.82115
105	.85318	.85079	.84843	.84607	.84374	.84142	.83911	.83682	.83455	.83229
106	.86633	.86413	.86193	.85975	.85758	.85543	.85329	.85116	.84904	.84694
107	.88247	.88049	.87852	.87656	.87460	.87266	.87073	.86881	.86690	.86500
108	.90825	.90666	.90507	.90350	.90193	.90037	.89881	.89727	.89572	.89419
109	.95372	.95290	.95208	.95126	.95045	.94964	.94883	.94803	.94723	.94643

Age	12.2%	12.4%	12.6%	12.8%	13.0%	13.2%	13.4%	13.6%	13.8%	14.0%
0	.01298	.01285	.01273	.01261	.01250	.01240	.01230	.01221	.01212	.01203
1	.00468	.00455	.00443	.00431	.00420	.00410	.00400	.00391	.00382	.00374
2	.00448	.00435	.00421	.00409	.00398	.00387	.00376	.00366	.00357	.00348
3	.00452	.00437	.00423	.00410	.00398	.00386	.00375	.00365	.00355	.00345
4	.00468	.00452	.00437	.00423	.00410	.00397	.00386	.00375	.00364	.00354
5	.00493	.00476	.00460	.00445	.00431	.00418	.00405	.00393	.00382	.00371
6	.00524	.00506	.00489	.00473	.00458	.00444	.00430	.00418	.00406	.00394
7	.00562	.00543	.00525	.00508	.00492	.00477	.00462	.00449	.00436	.00423
8	.00606	.00586	.00566	.00548	.00531	.00515	.00499	.00485	.00471	.00458
9	.00659	.00637	.00616	.00597	.00579	.00561	.00545	.00529	.00514	.00500
10	.00721	.00698	.00676	.00655	.00636	.00617	.00600	.00583	.00567	.00552
11	.00792	.00767	.00744	.00722	.00701	.00682	.00663	.00645	.00628	.00612
12	.00871	.00845	.00821	.00797	.00775	.00754	.00735	.00716	.00698	.00681
13	.00955	.00928	.00902	.00877	.00854	.00831	.00810	.00790	.00771	.00753
14	.01038	.01009	.00981	.00955	.00930	.00907	.00885	.00864	.00843	.00824
15	.01116	.01085	.01056	.01028	.01002	.00977	.00954	.00932	.00910	.00890
16	.01186	.01153	.01123	.01094	.01066	.01040	.01015	.00992	.00969	.00948
17	.01250	.01215	.01183	.01152	.01124	.01096	.01070	.01045	.01022	.00999
18	.01308	.01272	.01238	.01206	.01175	.01147	.01119	.01093	.01068	.01044
19	.01367	.01329	.01293	.01259	.01227	.01196	.01167	.01140	.01113	.01088
20	.01428	.01388	.01350	.01314	.01280	.01248	.01217	.01188	.01161	.01134
21	.01494	.01451	.01411	.01373	.01337	.01303	.01271	.01240	.01211	.01183
22	.01562	.01517	.01475	.01435	.01397	.01361	.01326	.01294	.01263	.01233
23	.01635	.01588	.01543	.01501	.01460	.01422	.01386	.01351	.01319	.01287
24	.01716	.01665	.01618	.01573	.01530	.01489	.01451	.01415	.01380	.01347
25	.01804	.01751	.01701	.01653	.01608	.01565	.01524	.01485	.01448	.01413
26	.01902	.01845	.01792	.01741	.01693	.01648	.01604	.01563	.01524	.01487
27	.02011	.01951	.01895	.01841	.01790	.01742	.01696	.01652	.01610	.01571
28	.02129	.02066	.02006	.01949	.01895	.01844	.01795	.01748	.01704	.01662
29	.02258	.02191	.02127	.02067	.02009	.01955	.01903	.01853	.01806	.01762
30	.02396	.02325	.02257	.02193	.02132	.02074	.02019	.01966	.01916	.01869
31	.02543	.02467	.02396	.02328	.02263	.02201	.02143	.02087	.02034	.01983
32	.02701	.02621	.02545	.02472	.02404	.02338	.02276	.02217	.02160	.02106
33	.02871	.02786	.02706	.02629	.02556	.02487	.02420	.02357	.02297	.02240
34	.03054	.02964	.02879	.02797	.02720	.02646	.02576	.02509	.02445	.02383
35	.03253	.03158	.03067	.02981	.02898	.02820	.02745	.02674	.02606	.02541
36	.03467	.03366	.03269	.03178	.03090	.03007	.02928	.02852	.02779	.02710
37	.03697	.03590	.03488	.03391	.03298	.03209	.03125	.03044	.02967	.02893

Age	12.2%	12.4%	12.6%	12.8%	13.0%	13.2%	13.4%	13.6%	13.8%	14.0%
38	.03947	.03833	.03725	.03622	.03524	.03430	.03340	.03254	.03172	.03094
39	.04217	.04096	.03982	.03873	.03768	.03669	.03573	.03482	.03395	.03312
40	.04510	.04383	.04262	.04146	.04035	.03930	.03828	.03732	.03639	.03550
41	.04830	.04695	.04567	.04445	.04327	.04215	.04108	.04005	.03907	.03812
42	.05177	.05035	.04900	.04770	.04646	.04527	.04413	.04304	.04200	.04100
43	.05553	.05404	.05261	.05123	.04992	.04866	.04746	.04630	.04520	.04413
44	.05960	.05802	.05651	.05506	.05368	.05235	.05107	.04985	.04867	.04754
45	.06395	.06229	.06069	.05917	.05770	.05630	.05495	.05365	.05241	.05121
46	.06860	.06685	.06517	.06356	.06202	.06053	.05911	.05774	.05643	.05516
47	.07353	.07169	.06992	.06823	.06660	.06504	.06353	.06209	.06070	.05936
48	.07877	.07684	.07498	.07320	.07149	.06984	.06826	.06673	.06527	.06385
49	.08433	.08231	.08036	.07849	.07669	.07495	.07329	.07168	.07013	.06864
50	.09026	.08814	.08609	.08413	.08224	.08042	.07867	.07698	.07535	.07378
51	.09655	.09433	.09219	.09013	.08815	.08624	.08440	.08262	.08091	.07926
52	.10318	.10086	.09863	.09647	.09439	.09239	.09046	.08860	.08680	.08506
53	.11017	.10774	.10541	.10315	.10098	.09888	.09686	.09491	.09302	.09120
54	.11750	.11498	.11254	.11019	.10792	.10572	.10361	.10156	.09958	.09767
55	.12522	.12258	.12005	.11759	.11522	.11294	.11072	.10859	.10652	.10451
56	.13332	.13059	.12794	.12539	.12292	.12054	.11823	.11599	.11383	.11174
57	.14183	.13899	.13624	.13359	.13102	.12853	.12613	.12380	.12154	.11936
58	.15070	.14775	.14490	.14215	.13948	.13689	.13439	.13197	.12962	.12734
59	.15990	.15685	.15389	.15103	.14826	.14558	.14298	.14046	.13801	.13564
60	.16942	.16626	.16321	.16024	.15737	.15459	.15189	.14927	.14673	.14426
61	.17929	.17603	.17287	.16981	.16684	.16395	.16115	.15844	.15580	.15324
62	.18960	.18623	.18297	.17980	.17673	.17375	.17085	.16803	.16530	.16264
63	.20035	.19688	.19352	.19025	.18708	.18400	.18100	.17809	.17525	.17250
64	.21154	.20797	.20451	.20114	.19787	.19469	.19159	.18859	.18566	.18281
65	.22318	.21951	.21595	.21249	.20912	.20584	.20265	.19955	.19652	.19358
66	.23532	.23156	.22790	.22434	.22088	.21751	.21422	.21102	.20791	.20487
67	.24804	.24419	.24044	.23679	.23324	.22977	.22640	.22311	.21990	.21678
68	.26133	.25740	.25356	.24983	.24618	.24263	.23917	.23579	.23250	.22929
69	.27516	.27114	.26723	.26341	.25969	.25605	.25251	.24905	.24567	.24237
70	.28945	.28536	.28137	.27747	.27367	.26996	.26633	.26279	.25934	.25596
71	.30412	.29996	.29590	.29193	.28806	.28427	.28057	.27696	.27343	.26998
72	.31913	.31491	.31078	.30675	.30281	.29895	.29519	.29150	.28790	.28438
73	.33444	.33016	.32597	.32188	.31788	.31396	.31013	.30638	.30271	.29913
74	.35012	.34579	.34155	.33741	.33335	.32938	.32549	.32168	.31795	.31430
75	.36628	.36190	.35762	.35343	.34932	.34530	.34136	.33750	.33372	.33001
76	.38299	.37858	.37427	.37004	.36589	.36183	.35784	.35394	.35011	.34636
77	.40028	.39585	.39151	.38725	.38307	.37898	.37496	.37103	.36716	.36337
78	.41812	.41368	.40933	.40506	.40086	.39675	.39271	.38874	.38485	.38103
79	.43641	.43198	.42762	.42334	.41914	.41502	.41096	.40698	.40308	.39924
80	.45496	.45054	.44619	.44192	.43772	.43360	.42954	.42556	.42164	.41779
81	.47360	.46920	.46487	.46061	.45643	.45231	.44827	.44429	.44038	.43653
82	.49223	.48785	.48355	.47932	.47516	.47106	.46703	.46307	.45916	.45532
83	.51081	.50648	.50221	.49802	.49388	.48982	.48581	.48187	.47799	.47416
84	.52951	.52523	.52101	.51686	.51277	.50874	.50477	.50086	.49701	.49321
85	.54847	.54425	.54009	.53600	.53196	.52798	.52406	.52019	.51638	.51262
86	.56749	.56335	.55926	.55523	.55126	.54734	.54348	.53966	.53591	.53220
87	.58627	.58221	.57820	.57425	.57035	.56650	.56270	.55895	.55526	.55161
88	.60477	.60079	.59688	.59301	.58919	.58542	.58170	.57802	.57439	.57081
89	.62297	.61909	.61527	.61149	.60776	.60408	.60044	.59685	.59330	.58979
90	.64084	.63707	.63335	.62968	.62604	.62246	.61891	.61540	.61194	.60851
91	.65803	.65437	.65076	.64719	.64366	.64017	.63672	.63330	.62993	.62659
92	.67412	.67058	.66707	.66360	.66017	.65678	.65342	.65010	.64682	.64357
93	.68911	.68567	.68227	.67890	.67557	.67227	.66901	.66578	.66258	.65942
94	.70321	.69988	.69657	.69330	.69006	.68686	.68369	.68055	.67744	.67437
95	.71674	.71351	.71031	.70713	.70399	.70088	.69781	.69476	.69174	.68875
96	.72959	.72646	.72335	.72028	.71724	.71422	.71123	.70828	.70534	.70244
97	.74156	.73853	.73552	.73254	.72959	.72666	.72376	.72089	.71804	.71522
98	.75287	.74993	.74702	.74413	.74126	.73842	.73561	.73282	.73006	.72732
99	.76401	.76117	.75834	.75555	.75277	.75002	.74730	.74459	.74191	.73926
100	.77494	.77219	.76946	.76676	.76408	.76142	.75878	.75616	.75357	.75099
101	.78580	.78315	.78052	.77791	.77532	.77275	.77021	.76768	.76517	.76268
102	.79654	.79399	.79146	.78894	.78645	.78397	.78152	.77908	.77666	.77426

Age	12.2%	12.4%	12.6%	12.8%	13.0%	13.2%	13.4%	13.6%	13.8%	14.0%
103	.80724	.80479	.80236	.79994	.79755	.79517	.79280	.79046	.78813	.78582
104	.81879	.81646	.81413	.81183	.80954	.80726	.80501	.80276	.80054	.79832
105	.83005	.82782	.82560	.82340	.82121	.81904	.81688	.81474	.81260	.81049
106	.84485	.84277	.84071	.83866	.83662	.83459	.83257	.83057	.82857	.82659
107	.86311	.86124	.85937	.85751	.85566	.85382	.85199	.85017	.84835	.84655
108	.89266	.89114	.88963	.88812	.88662	.88513	.88364	.88216	.88068	.87922
109	.94563	.94484	.94405	.94326	.94248	.94170	.94092	.94014	.93937	.93860

Table 90CM.—Life Table Applicable After April 30, 1999

Age x (1)	l(x) (2)	Age x (1)	l(x) (2)	Age x (1)	l(x) (2)
0	100000	38	95780	75	60449
1	99064	39	95581	76	57955
2	98992	40	95373	77	55373
3	98944	41	95156	78	52704
4	98907	42	94928	79	49943
5	98877	43	94687	80	47084
6	98850	44	94431	81	44129
7	98826	45	94154	82	41091
8	98803	46	93855	83	37994
9	98783	47	93528	84	34876
10	98766	48	93173	85	31770
11	98750	49	92787	86	28687
12	98734	50	92370	87	25638
13	98713	51	91918	88	22658
14	98681	52	91424	89	19783
15	98635	53	90885	90	17046
16	98573	54	90297	91	14466
17	98497	55	89658	92	12066
18	98409	56	88965	93	9884
19	98314	57	88214	94	7951
20	98215	58	87397	95	6282
21	98113	59	86506	96	4868
22	98006	60	85537	97	3694
23	97896	61	84490	98	2745
24	97784	62	83368	99	1999
25	97671	63	82169	100	1424
26	97556	64	80887	101	991
27	97441	65	79519	102	672
28	97322	66	78066	103	443
29	97199	67	76531	104	284
30	97070	68	74907	105	175
31	96934	69	73186	106	105
32	96791	70	71357	107	60
33	96642	71	69411	108	33
34	96485	72	67344	109	17
35	96322	73	65154	110	0
36	96150	74	62852		
37	95969				

(5) Effective/applicability dates. Paragraphs (f)(1) through (f)(4) apply after April 30, 1999, and before May 1, 2009.

T.D. 6296, 6/23/58, amend T.D. 7077, 12/1/70, T.D. 7955, 5/11/84, T.D. 8540, 6/9/94, T.D. 8819, 4/29/99, T.D. 8886, 6/9/2000, T.D. 9448, 5/1/2009.

§ 20.2031-7T Valuation of annuities, interests for life or term of years, and remainder or reversionary interests (temporary).

(a) through (b) [Reserved]. For further information see § 20.2031-7(a) through (b).

(c) Actuarial valuations. The present value of annuities, life estates, terms of years, remainders, and reversions for estates of decedents for which the valuation date of the gross estate is on or after May 1, 2009, is determined under paragraph (d) of this section. The present value of annuities, life estates, terms of years, remainders, and reversions for estates of decedents for which the valuation date of the gross estate is before May 1, 2009, is determined under the following sections:

Valuation dates		Applicable Regulations
After	Before	
	01-01-52	20.2031-7A(a)
12-31-51	01-01-71	20.2031-7A(b)
12-31-70	12-01-83	20.2031-7A(c)
11-30-83	05-01-89	20.2031-7A(d)
04-30-89	05-01-99	20.2031-7A(e)
04-30-99	05-01-09	20.2031-7A(f)

(d) Actuarial valuations on or after May 1, 2009. *(1) In general.* Except as otherwise provided in paragraph (b) of this section and § 20.7520-3(b) (pertaining to certain limitations on the use of prescribed tables), if the valuation date for the gross estate of the decedent is on or after May 1, 2009, the fair market value of annuities, life estates, terms of years, remainders, and reversionary interests is the present value determined by use of standard or special section 7520 actuarial factors. These factors are derived by using the appropriate section 7520 interest rate and, if applicable, the mortality component for the valuation date of the interest that is being valued. For purposes of the computations described in this section, the age of an individual is the age of that individual at the individual's nearest birthday. See §§ 20.7520-1 through 20.7520-4.

(2) Specific interests. (i) Charitable remainder trusts. The fair market value of a remainder interest in a pooled income fund, as defined in § 1.642(c)-5, is its value determined under § 1.642(c)-6T(e). The fair market value of a remainder interest in a charitable remainder annuity trust, as defined in § 1.664-2(a), is the present value determined under § 1.664-2(c). The fair market value of a remainder interest in a charitable remainder unitrust, as defined in § 1.664-3, is its present value determined under § 1.664-4T(e). The fair market value of a life interest or term of years in a charitable remainder unitrust is the fair market value of the property as of the date of valuation less the fair market value of the remainder interest on that date determined under § 1.664-4T(e)(4) and (5).

(ii) Ordinary remainder and reversionary interests. If the interest to be valued is to take effect after a definite number of years or after the death of one individual, the present value of the interest is computed by multiplying the value of the property by the appropriate remainder interest actuarial factor (that corresponds to the applicable section 7520 interest rate and remainder interest period) in Table B (for a term certain) or the appropriate Table S (for one measuring life), as the case may be. Table B is contained in § 20.2031-7(d)(6) and Table S (for one measuring life when the valuation date is on or after May 1, 2009) is contained in paragraph (d)(7) of this section and in Internal Revenue Service Publication 1457. See § 20.2031-7A containing Table S for valuation of interests before May 1, 2009. For information about obtaining actuarial factors for other types of remainder interests, see paragraph (d)(4) of this section.

(iii) Ordinary term-of-years and life interests. If the interest to be valued is the right of a person to receive the income of certain property, or to use certain nonincome-producing property, for a term of years or for the life of one individual, the present value of the interest is computed by multiplying the value of the property by the appropriate term-of-years or life interest actuarial factor (that corresponds to the applicable section 7520 interest rate and term-of-years or life interest period). Internal Revenue Service Publication 1457 includes actuarial factors for a remainder interest after a term of years in Table B and after the life of one individual in Table S (for one measuring life when the valuation date is on or after May 1, 2009). However, term-of-years and life interest actuarial factors are not included in Table B in § 20.2031-7(d)(6) or Table S in paragraph (d)(7) of this section (or in § 20.2031-7A). If Internal Revenue Service Publication 1457 (or any other reliable source of term-of-years and life interest actuarial factors) is not conveniently available, an actuarial factor for the interest may be derived mathematically. This actuarial factor may be derived by subtracting the correlative remainder factor (that corresponds to the applicable section 7520 interest rate and the term of years or the life) in Table B (for a term of years) in § 20.2031-7(d)(6) or in Table S (for the life of one individual) in paragraph (d)(7) of this section, as the case may be, from 1.000000. For information about obtaining actuarial factors for other types of term-of-years and life interests, see paragraph (d)(4) of this section.

(iv) Annuities. (A) If the interest to be valued is the right of a person to receive an annuity that is payable at the end of each year for a term of years or for the life of one individual, the present value of the interest is computed by multiplying the aggregate amount payable annually by the appropriate annuity actuarial factor (that corresponds to the applicable section 7520 interest rate and annuity period). Internal Revenue Publication 1457 includes actuarial factors for a remainder interest in Table B (after an annuity payable for a term of years) and in Table S (after an annuity payable for the life of one individual when the valuation date is on or after May 1, 2009). However, annuity actuarial factors are not included in Table B in § 20.2031-7(d)(6) or Table S in paragraph (d)(7) of this section (or in § 20.2031-7A). If Internal Revenue Service Publication 1457 (or any other reliable source of annuity actuarial factors) is not conveniently available, a required annuity factor for a term of years or for one life may be mathematically derived. This annuity factor may be derived by subtracting the applicable remainder factor (that corresponds to the applicable section 7520 interest rate and annuity period) in Table B (in the case of a term-of-years annuity) in § 20.2031-7(d)(6) or in Table S (in the case of a one-life annuity when the valuation date is on or after May 1, 2009) in paragraph (d)(7) of this section, as the case may be, from 1.000000 and then dividing the result by the applicable section 7520 interest rate expressed as a decimal number.

(B) If the annuity is payable at the end of semiannual, quarterly, monthly, or weekly periods, the product obtained by multiplying the annuity factor by the aggregate amount payable annually is then multiplied by the applicable adjustment factor as contained in Table K in § 20.2031-7(d)(6) for payments made at the end of the specified periods. The provisions of this paragraph (d)(2)(iv)(B) are illustrated by the following example:

Example. At the time of the decedent's death, the survivor/ annuitant, age 72, is entitled to receive an annuity of $15,000 a year for life payable in equal monthly installments at the end of each period. The section 7520 rate for the month in which the decedent died is 5.6 percent. Under Table S in paragraph (d)(7) of this section, the remainder factor at 5.6 percent for an individual aged 72 is .53243. By converting the remainder factor to an annuity factor, as described above, the annuity factor at 5.6 percent for an individual aged 72 is 8.3495 (1.00000 minus .53243, divided by .056). Under Table K in § 20.2031-7(d)(6), the adjustment factor under the column for payments made at the end of each monthly period at the rate of 5.6 percent is 1.0254. The aggregate annual amount, $15,000, is multiplied by the factor 8.3495 and the product multiplied by 1.0254. The present value of the annuity at the date of the decedent's death is, therefore, $128,423.66 ($15,000 x 8.3495 x 1.0254).

(C) If an annuity is payable at the beginning of annual, semiannual, quarterly, monthly, or weekly periods for a term of years, the value of the annuity is computed by multiplying the aggregate amount payable annually by the annuity factor described in paragraph (d)(2)(iv)(A) of this section; and the product so obtained is then multiplied by the adjustment factor in Table J in § 20.2031-7(d)(6) at the appropriate interest rate component for payments made at the beginning of specified periods. If an annuity is payable at the beginning of annual, semiannual, quarterly, monthly, or weekly periods for one or more lives, the value of the annuity is the sum of the first payment plus the present value of a similar annuity, the first payment of which is not to be made until the end of the payment period, determined as provided in this paragraph (d)(2)(iv).

(v) Annuity and unitrust interests for a term of years or until the prior death of an individual. See § 25.2512-5T(d)(2)(v) for examples explaining how to compute the present value of an annuity or unitrust interest that is payable until the earlier of the lapse of a specific number of years or the death of an individual.

(3) Transitional rule. (i) If a decedent dies on or after May 1, 2009, and if on May 1, 2009, the decedent was mentally incompetent so that the disposition of the decedent's property could not be changed, and the decedent dies without having regained competency to dispose of the decedent's property or dies within 90 days of the date on which the decedent first regains competency, the fair market value of annuities, life estates, terms for years, remainders, and reversions included in the gross estate of the decedent is their present value determined either under this section or under the corresponding section applicable at the time the decedent became mentally incompetent, at the option of the decedent's executor. For examples, see § 20.2031-7A(d).

(ii) If a decedent dies on or after May 1, 2009, and before July 1, 2009, the fair market value of annuities, life estates, remainders, and reversions based on one or more measuring lives included in the gross estate of the decedent is their present value determined under this section by use of the section 7520 interest rate for the month in which the valuation date occurs (see §§ 20.7520-1(b) and 20.7520-2(a)(2)) and the appropriate actuarial tables under either paragraph (d)(7) of this section or § 20.2031-7A(f)(4), at the option of the decedent's executor.

(iii) For purposes of paragraphs (d)(3)(i) and (d)(3)(ii) of this section, where the decedent's executor is given the option to use the appropriate actuarial tables under either paragraph (d)(7) of this section or § 20.2031-7A(f)(4), the decedent's executor must use the same actuarial table with respect to each individual transaction and with respect to all transfers occurring on the valuation date (for example, gift and income tax charitable deductions with respect to the same transfer must be determined based on the same tables, and all assets includible in the gross estate and/or estate tax deductions claimed must be valued based on the same tables).

(4) Publications and actuarial computations by the Internal Revenue Service. Many standard actuarial factors not included in § 20.2031-7(d)(6) or in paragraph (d)(7) of this section are included in Internal Revenue Service Publication 1457, "Actuarial Valuations Version 3A" (2009). Publication 1457 also includes examples that illustrate how to compute many special factors for more unusual situations. This publication will be available beginning May 1, 2009, at no charge, electronically via the Internal Revenue Service Internet site at http:/ /www.irs.gov. If a special factor is required in the case of an actual decedent, the Internal Revenue Service may furnish the factor to the executor upon a request for a ruling. The request for a ruling must be accompanied by a recitation of the facts including a statement of the date of birth for each measuring life, the date of the decedent's death, any other applicable dates, and a copy of the will, trust, or other relevant documents. A request for a ruling must comply with the instructions for requesting a ruling published periodically in the Internal Revenue Bulletin (see §§ 601.201 and 601.601(d)(2)(ii)(b)) and include payment of the required user fee.

(5) Examples. The provisions of this section are illustrated by the following examples:

Example (1). Remainder payable at an individual's death. The decedent, or the decedent's estate, was entitled to receive certain property worth $50,000 upon the death of A, to whom the income was bequeathed for life. At the time of the decedent's death, A was 47 years and 5 months old. In the month in which the decedent died, the section 7520 rate was 6.2 percent. Under Table S in paragraph (d)(7) of this section, the remainder factor at 6.2 percent for determining the present value of the remainder interest due at the death of a person aged 47, the number of years nearest A's actual age at the decedent's death, is .18672. The present value of the remainder interest at the date of the decedent's death is, therefore, $9,336.00 ($50,000 x .18672).

Example (2). Income payable for an individual's life. A's parent bequeathed an income interest in property to A for life, with the remainder interest passing to B at A's death. At the time of the parent's death, the value of the property was $50,000 and A was 30 years and 10 months old. The section 7520 rate at the time of the parent's death was 6.2 percent. Under Table S in paragraph (d)(7) of this section, the remainder factor at 6.2 percent for determining the present value of the remainder interest due at the death of a person aged 31, the number of years closest to A's age at the decedent's death, is .08697. Converting this remainder factor to an income factor, as described in paragraph (d)(2)(iii) of this section, the factor for determining the present value of an income interest for the life of a person aged 31 is .91303. The present value of A's interest at the time of the parent's death is, therefore, $45,651.50 ($50,000 x .91303).

Example (3). Annuity payable for an individual's life. A purchased an annuity for the benefit of both A and B. Under the terms of the annuity contract, at A's death, a survivor annuity of $10,000 per year payable in equal semiannual installments made at the end of each interval is payable to B for life. At A's death, B was 45 years and 7 months old. Also, at A's death, the section 7520 rate was 4.8 percent. Under Table S in paragraph (d)(7) of this section, the factor at 4.8 percent for determining the present value of the remainder interest at the death of a person age 46 (the number of years nearest B's actual age) is .24774. By converting the factor to an annuity factor, as described in paragraph (d)(2)(iv)(A) of this section, the factor for the present value of an annuity payable until the death of a person age 46 is 15.6721 (1.00000 minus .24774, divided by .048). The adjustment factor from Table K in § 20.2031-7(d)(6) at an interest rate of 4.8 percent for semiannual annuity payments made at the end of the period is 1.0119. The present value of the annuity at the date of A's death is, therefore, $158,585.98 ($10,000 x 15.6721 x 1.0119).

Example (4). Annuity payable for a term of years. The decedent, or the decedent's estate, was entitled to receive an annuity of $10,000 per year payable in equal quarterly installments at the end of each quarter throughout a term certain. At the time of the decedent's death, the section 7520 rate was 9.8 percent. A quarterly payment had just been made prior to the decedent's death and payments were to continue for 5 more years. Under Table B in § 20.2031-7(d)(6) for the interest rate of 9.8 percent, the factor for the present value of a remainder interest due after a term of 5 years is .626597. Converting the factor to an annuity factor, as described in paragraph (d)(2)(iv)(A) of this section, the factor for the present value of an annuity for a term of 5 years is 3.8102 (1.00000 minus .626597, divided by .098). The adjustment factor from Table K in § 20.2031-7(d)(6) at an interest rate of 9.8 percent for quarterly annuity payments made at the end of the period is 1.0360. The present value of the annuity is, therefore, $39,473.67 ($10,000 x 3.8102 x 1.0360).

(6) [Reserved]. For further guidance, see § 20.2031-7(d)(6).

(7) Actuarial Table S and Table 2000CM where the valuation date is on or after May 1, 2009. Except as provided in § 20.7520-2(b) (pertaining to certain limitations on the use of prescribed tables), for determination of the present value of an interest that is dependent on the termination of a life interest, Table 2000CM and Table S (single life remainder factors applicable where the valuation date is on or after May 1, 2009) contained in this paragraph (d)(7) and Table J and Table K contained in § 20.2031-7(d)(6), must be used in the application of the provisions of this section when the section 7520 interest rate component is between 0.2 and 14 percent.

Table S
Based on Life Table 2000CM
Single Life Remainder Factors
Applicable on or After May 1, 2009
Interest Rate

AGE	0.2%	0.4%	0.6%	0.8%	1.0%	1.2%	1.4%	1.6%	1.8%	2.0%
0	.85816	.73751	.63478	.54723	.47252	.40872	.35416	.30747	.26745	.23313
1	.85889	.73863	.63604	.54844	.47355	.40948	.35459	.30752	.26711	.23239
2	.86054	.74145	.63968	.55260	.47802	.41409	.35922	.31209	.27155	.23664
3	.86221	.74433	.64339	.55687	.48263	.41887	.36404	.31685	.27619	.24112
4	.86390	.74725	.64716	.56121	.48733	.42374	.36898	.32175	.28098	.24575
5	.86560	.75018	.65097	.56561	.49209	.42871	.37401	.32675	.28588	.25050
6	.86731	.75314	.65482	.57006	.49692	.43375	.37913	.33186	.29090	.25538
7	.86902	.75611	.65868	.57454	.50180	.43885	.38432	.33704	.29601	.26035
8	.87073	.75909	.66258	.57907	.50674	.44403	.38960	.34233	.30122	.26544
9	.87246	.76209	.66651	.58364	.51173	.44928	.39497	.34771	.30654	.27064
10	.87419	.76511	.67046	.58826	.51679	.45459	.40042	.35319	.31197	.27596
11	.87592	.76814	.67445	.59291	.52190	.45998	.40596	.35876	.31750	.28139
12	.87766	.77119	.67845	.59761	.52706	.46544	.41157	.36443	.32313	.28693
13	.87939	.77424	.68247	.60232	.53225	.47094	.41723	.37015	.32884	.29255
14	.88112	.77728	.68649	.60704	.53746	.47646	.42293	.37592	.33460	.29823
15	.88284	.78031	.69050	.61176	.54267	.48199	.42865	.38172	.34038	.30394
16	.88455	.78333	.69449	.61647	.54788	.48752	.43437	.38752	.34619	.30968
17	.88625	.78633	.69848	.62117	.55309	.49307	.44012	.39336	.35203	.31546
18	.88795	.78933	.70246	.62588	.55830	.49863	.44589	.39923	.35791	.32129
19	.88964	.79232	.70644	.63059	.56354	.50422	.45170	.40514	.36385	.32719
20	.89132	.79532	.71044	.63534	.56882	.50987	.45757	.41114	.36987	.33317
21	.89301	.79832	.71445	.64010	.57413	.51555	.46350	.41719	.37597	.33925
22	.89470	.80133	.71847	.64488	.57947	.52129	.46948	.42332	.38216	.34541
23	.89639	.80434	.72251	.64970	.58486	.52708	.47554	.42954	.38844	.35168
24	.89808	.80737	.72658	.65456	.59031	.53295	.48169	.43586	.39484	.35809
25	.89978	.81042	.73068	.65947	.59583	.53890	.48795	.44230	.40137	.36464
26	.90149	.81349	.73482	.66443	.60141	.54494	.49430	.44886	.40804	.37134
27	.90320	.81657	.73899	.66944	.60707	.55107	.50076	.45554	.41484	.37819
28	.90492	.81968	.74319	.67450	.61278	.55728	.50733	.46233	.42178	.38520
29	.90665	.82279	.74741	.67960	.61856	.56356	.51398	.46924	.42884	.39233
30	.90837	.82591	.75165	.68473	.62438	.56990	.52070	.47623	.43601	.39959
31	.91010	.82904	.75592	.68989	.63024	.57631	.52751	.48333	.44329	.40698
32	.91182	.83218	.76020	.69509	.63616	.58278	.53440	.49052	.45068	.41449
33	.91355	.83532	.76449	.70031	.64212	.58931	.54137	.49780	.45818	.42213
34	.91527	.83847	.76880	.70556	.64811	.59589	.54839	.50516	.46578	.42988

Table S
Based on Life Table 2000CM
Single Life Remainder Factors
Applicable on or After May 1, 2009
Interest Rate

AGE	0.2%	0.4%	0.6%	0.8%	1.0%	1.2%	1.4%	1.6%	1.8%	2.0%
35	.91700	.84162	.77312	.71082	.65414	.60253	.55549	.51261	.47347	.43774
36	.91872	.84477	.77744	.71611	.66021	.60921	.56266	.52014	.48127	.44572
37	.92043	.84792	.78178	.72142	.66631	.61594	.56989	.52774	.48916	.45381
38	.92215	.85107	.78613	.72675	.67244	.62272	.57718	.53544	.49715	.46201
39	.92386	.85422	.79048	.73210	.67860	.62955	.58453	.54320	.50523	.47032
40	.92557	.85736	.79483	.73746	.68479	.63641	.59194	.55104	.51340	.47873
41	.92727	.86050	.79918	.74283	.69100	.64331	.59940	.55894	.52165	.48724
42	.92896	.86364	.80354	.74820	.69723	.65024	.60690	.56691	.52998	.49585
43	.93065	.86677	.80789	.75359	.70348	.65721	.61447	.57495	.53840	.50457
44	.93234	.86990	.81225	.75899	.70976	.66422	.62208	.58305	.54690	.51338
45	.93402	.87302	.81660	.76439	.71605	.67125	.62973	.59122	.55547	.52228
46	.93569	.87613	.82095	.76980	.72236	.67832	.63743	.59945	.56413	.53129
47	.93735	.87924	.82530	.77521	.72867	.68541	.64517	.60773	.57286	.54037
48	.93901	.88233	.82964	.78062	.73501	.69253	.65295	.61606	.58166	.54955
49	.94065	.88541	.83397	.78604	.74135	.69967	.66077	.62446	.59053	.55882
50	.94229	.88849	.83830	.79145	.74771	.70684	.66864	.63292	.59949	.56819
51	.94393	.89156	.84263	.79688	.75409	.71404	.67655	.64143	.60852	.57766
52	.94556	.89462	.84695	.80230	.76048	.72127	.68450	.65001	.61763	.58722
53	.94717	.89767	.85126	.80772	.76687	.72852	.69249	.65863	.62680	.59687
54	.94878	.90070	.85555	.81313	.77326	.73577	.70050	.66730	.63603	.60658
55	.95037	.90371	.85983	.81853	.77964	.74302	.70851	.67598	.64530	.61635
56	.95195	.90670	.86406	.82388	.78599	.75024	.71651	.68465	.65457	.62613
57	.95351	.90965	.86827	.82920	.79230	.75744	.72448	.69332	.66384	.63593
58	.95505	.91257	.87243	.83447	.79857	.76459	.73242	.70195	.67309	.64573
59	.95657	.91546	.87655	.83970	.80479	.77170	.74033	.71057	.68233	.65553
60	.95807	.91832	.88064	.84490	.81098	.77879	.74822	.71918	.69158	.66534
61	.95955	.92115	.88469	.85005	.81713	.78584	.75608	.72776	.70081	.67515
62	.96101	.92395	.88869	.85515	.82323	.79283	.76388	.73630	.71001	.68494
63	.96245	.92670	.89265	.86020	.82926	.79977	.77164	.74479	.71917	.69470
64	.96387	.92942	.89655	.86518	.83524	.80665	.77933	.75323	.72828	.70443
65	.96527	.93210	.90040	.87011	.84116	.81346	.78697	.76162	.73735	.71411
66	.96665	.93476	.90423	.87502	.84706	.82027	.79461	.77002	.74645	.72385
67	.96802	.93739	.90803	.87990	.85292	.82705	.80223	.77841	.75554	.73359
68	.96937	.93999	.91179	.88472	.85874	.83378	.80980	.78676	.76461	.74331
69	.97070	.94255	.91549	.88949	.86449	.84044	.81731	.79504	.77362	.75299
70	.97200	.94506	.91914	.89419	.87016	.84702	.82473	.80326	.78256	.76260

Table S
Based on Life Table 2000CM
Single Life Remainder Factors
Applicable on or After May 1, 2009
Interest Rate

AGE	0.2%	0.4%	0.6%	0.8%	1.0%	1.2%	1.4%	1.6%	1.8%	2.0%
71	.97328	.94754	.92273	.89882	.87577	.85353	.83209	.81140	.79143	.77215
72	.97453	.94997	.92626	.90338	.88129	.85996	.83935	.81945	.80021	.78162
73	.97576	.95234	.92972	.90785	.88671	.86627	.84651	.82739	.80888	.79098
74	.97695	.95466	.93310	.91223	.89202	.87247	.85353	.83518	.81741	.80019
75	.97811	.95692	.93638	.91649	.89720	.87851	.86039	.84281	.82577	.80923
76	.97924	.95910	.93957	.92063	.90224	.88440	.86708	.85026	.83393	.81807
77	.98033	.96122	.94267	.92465	.90715	.89013	.87360	.85753	.84191	.82671
78	.98138	.96327	.94567	.92855	.91190	.89571	.87995	.86461	.84968	.83515
79	.98239	.96526	.94857	.93233	.91652	.90112	.88611	.87149	.85725	.84337
80	.98337	.96717	.95138	.93598	.92098	.90635	.89208	.87817	.86460	.85135
81	.98431	.96901	.95408	.93951	.92529	.91141	.89786	.88463	.87172	.85910
82	.98521	.97077	.95667	.94290	.92944	.91629	.90344	.89088	.87861	.86660
83	.98608	.97247	.95917	.94616	.93343	.92099	.90882	.89691	.88526	.87385
84	.98691	.97409	.96156	.94928	.93727	.92551	.91399	.90271	.89166	.88084
85	.98770	.97565	.96384	.95228	.94094	.92984	.91895	.90828	.89782	.88757
86	.98845	.97713	.96602	.95514	.94446	.93398	.92371	.91362	.90373	.89402

87	.98917	.97854	.96810	.95786	.94781	.93794	.92825	.91873	.90939	.90021
88	.98985	.97988	.97008	.96046	.95100	.94171	.93258	.92361	.91479	.90612
89	.99049	.98115	.97196	.96292	.95404	.94530	.93671	.92826	.91994	.91176
90	.99110	.98235	.97373	.96526	.95691	.94871	.94062	.93267	.92484	.91713
91	.99168	.98348	.97541	.96747	.95964	.95193	.94434	.93686	.92949	.92223
92	.99222	.98455	.97700	.96955	.96222	.95498	.94785	.94083	.93390	.92707
93	.99273	.98556	.97849	.97152	.96464	.95786	.95117	.94457	.93806	.93163
94	.99321	.98651	.97989	.97337	.96692	.96057	.95429	.94810	.94199	.93595
95	.99366	.98739	.98121	.97510	.96907	.96312	.95724	.95143	.94569	.94002
96	.99408	.98822	.98244	.97673	.97108	.96551	.95999	.95454	.94916	.94384
97	.99447	.98900	.98359	.97825	.97297	.96774	.96258	.95747	.95242	.94742
98	.99483	.98973	.98467	.97967	.97473	.96984	.96500	.96021	.95547	.95078
99	.99518	.99040	.98568	.98101	.97638	.97180	.96727	.96278	.95834	.95394
100	.99549	.99103	.98661	.98224	.97791	.97362	.96937	.96516	.96100	.95687
101	.99579	.99162	.98750	.98340	.97935	.97534	.97136	.96742	.96351	.95964
102	.99607	.99217	.98831	.98448	.98068	.97692	.97319	.96950	.96583	.96220
103	.99634	.99271	.98911	.98553	.98199	.97848	.97500	.97155	.96812	.96473
104	.99659	.99320	.98984	.98651	.98320	.97992	.97666	.97344	.97023	.96705
105	.99683	.99369	.99056	.98747	.98439	.98134	.97830	.97530	.97231	.96934
106	.99713	.99429	.99146	.98865	.98586	.98309	.98033	.97760	.97488	.97218
107	.99747	.99496	.99246	.98998	.98751	.98506	.98262	.98020	.97779	.97539
108	.99800	.99602	.99404	.99208	.99012	.98818	.98624	.98431	.98240	.98049
109	.99900	.99801	.99702	.99603	.99505	.99407	.99310	.99213	.99116	.99020

Table S
Based on Life Table 2000CM
Single Life Remainder Factors
Applicable on or After May 1, 2009
Interest Rate

AGE	2.2%	2.4%	2.6%	2.8%	3.0%	3.2%	3.4%	3.6%	3.8%	4.0%
0	.20365	.17830	.15648	.13767	.12144	.10741	.09528	.08476	.07564	.06772
1	.20251	.17677	.15458	.13542	.11885	.10451	.09209	.08131	.07194	.06379
2	.20656	.18060	.15817	.13877	.12197	.10740	.09476	.08376	.07420	.06586
3	.21084	.18466	.16200	.14236	.12533	.11054	.09767	.08647	.07670	.06817
4	.21527	.18888	.16600	.14613	.12887	.11385	.10076	.08935	.07938	.07066
5	.21984	.19324	.17013	.15004	.13255	.11730	.10399	.09237	.08220	.07329
6	.22454	.19773	.17440	.15408	.13636	.12089	.10736	.09553	.08515	.07605
7	.22933	.20233	.17879	.15824	.14030	.12460	.11085	.09880	.08822	.07892
8	.23425	.20705	.18330	.16254	.14436	.12844	.11447	.10221	.09142	.08193
9	.23930	.21191	.18795	.16697	.14857	.13243	.11824	.10576	.09476	.08507
10	.24446	.21689	.19273	.17153	.15292	.13655	.12214	.10945	.09824	.08835
11	.24975	.22200	.19764	.17623	.15740	.14081	.12619	.11328	.10187	.09177
12	.25515	.22724	.20268	.18107	.16202	.14521	.13037	.11724	.10563	.09533
13	.26064	.23256	.20782	.18600	.16674	.14972	.13466	.12132	.10949	.09900
14	.26620	.23796	.21303	.19101	.17154	.15430	.13903	.12547	.11344	.10273
15	.27179	.24340	.21829	.19607	.17639	.15894	.14344	.12968	.11743	.10652
16	.27742	.24887	.22358	.20117	.18128	.16361	.14790	.13391	.12145	.11034
17	.28309	.25439	.22893	.20632	.18622	.16834	.15241	.13821	.12554	.11421
18	.28881	.25997	.23434	.21154	.19123	.17314	.15699	.14258	.12969	.11815
19	.29461	.26563	.23983	.21684	.19633	.17803	.16167	.14703	.13393	.12218
20	.30050	.27139	.24543	.22226	.20156	.18304	.16646	.15161	.13829	.12633
21	.30649	.27726	.25114	.22779	.20689	.18817	.17138	.15631	.14277	.13060
22	.31259	.28323	.25697	.23344	.21235	.19342	.17642	.16114	.14739	.13500
23	.31879	.28934	.26293	.23923	.21795	.19882	.18161	.16612	.15215	.13955
24	.32515	.29559	.26904	.24519	.22372	.20440	.18699	.17128	.15710	.14429
25	.33166	.30201	.27534	.25133	.22969	.21018	.19256	.17665	.16226	.14924
26	.33833	.30861	.28182	.25767	.23586	.21616	.19835	.18224	.16764	.15440
27	.34517	.31538	.28849	.26420	.24224	.22236	.20436	.18804	.17324	.15980
28	.35217	.32233	.29535	.27093	.24882	.22877	.21058	.19407	.17907	.16542
29	.35932	.32944	.30237	.27784	.25558	.23537	.21701	.20031	.18511	.17126
30	.36661	.33670	.30956	.28492	.26253	.24216	.22362	.20674	.19135	.17730
31	.37403	.34411	.31691	.29217	.26965	.24914	.23044	.21338	.19779	.18355
32	.38160	.35167	.32442	.29960	.27697	.25631	.23745	.22022	.20445	.19002
33	.38930	.35939	.33211	.30721	.28447	.26368	.24467	.22727	.21133	.19671
34	.39713	.36724	.33993	.31497	.29213	.27123	.25207	.23451	.21839	.20360

Table S
Based on Life Table 2000CM
Single Life Remainder Factors
Applicable on or After May 1, 2009
Interest Rate

AGE	2.2%	2.4%	2.6%	2.8%	3.0%	3.2%	3.4%	3.6%	3.8%	4.0%
35	.40509	.37523	.34792	.32290	.29998	.27896	.25967	.24195	.22567	.21070
36	.41318	.38337	.35606	.33100	.30800	.28688	.26746	.24961	.23317	.21803
37	.42139	.39165	.36435	.33927	.31621	.29499	.27546	.25746	.24087	.22557
38	.42974	.40008	.37281	.34771	.32460	.30330	.28366	.26554	.24880	.23334
39	.43821	.40864	.38141	.35631	.33316	.31179	.29205	.27381	.25694	.24133
40	.44679	.41734	.39016	.36507	.34189	.32046	.30064	.28229	.26529	.24954
41	.45549	.42616	.39906	.37399	.35080	.32932	.30942	.29097	.27386	.25797
42	.46430	.43511	.40809	.38307	.35987	.33836	.31840	.29986	.28264	.26662
43	.47324	.44421	.41729	.39232	.36913	.34760	.32758	.30897	.29165	.27552
44	.48229	.45343	.42663	.40172	.37857	.35702	.33697	.31829	.30088	.28465
45	.49144	.46277	.43611	.41128	.38817	.36663	.34655	.32782	.31033	.29400
46	.50072	.47225	.44574	.42101	.39796	.37644	.35634	.33757	.32002	.30360
47	.51009	.48185	.45550	.43089	.40791	.38642	.36633	.34753	.32992	.31343
48	.51958	.49158	.46540	.44093	.41803	.39660	.37652	.35770	.34006	.32351
49	.52917	.50143	.47545	.45113	.42833	.40696	.38691	.36810	.35043	.33383
50	.53888	.51141	.48566	.46150	.43883	.41754	.39754	.37874	.36106	.34442
51	.54871	.52153	.49602	.47204	.44951	.42832	.40838	.38961	.37194	.35528
52	.55865	.53179	.50653	.48276	.46038	.43931	.41945	.40073	.38307	.36641
53	.56869	.54217	.51718	.49363	.47143	.45050	.43074	.41208	.39446	.37781
54	.57882	.55265	.52796	.50465	.48265	.46186	.44222	.42364	.40607	.38945
55	.58902	.56322	.53884	.51579	.49400	.47338	.45387	.43540	.41789	.40131
56	.59926	.57383	.54978	.52701	.50544	.48501	.46565	.44729	.42987	.41335
57	.60951	.58449	.56078	.53830	.51698	.49675	.47755	.45932	.44201	.42555
58	.61978	.59517	.57182	.54964	.52858	.50858	.48956	.47147	.45427	.43790
59	.63007	.60589	.58290	.56105	.54027	.52050	.50167	.48375	.46668	.45041
60	.64039	.61665	.59405	.57254	.55205	.53253	.51392	.49617	.47925	.46310
61	.65072	.62743	.60524	.58409	.56390	.54465	.52627	.50872	.49196	.47595
62	.66104	.63822	.61645	.59566	.57581	.55683	.53870	.52136	.50478	.48892
63	.67133	.64900	.62766	.60726	.58774	.56907	.55120	.53409	.51770	.50200
64	.68161	.65977	.63887	.61887	.59970	.58134	.56375	.54688	.53071	.51519
65	.69186	.67053	.65009	.63049	.61170	.59367	.57637	.55976	.54381	.52849
66	.70216	.68136	.66140	.64223	.62383	.60615	.58916	.57283	.55713	.54203
67	.71250	.69224	.67277	.65405	.63605	.61874	.60208	.58605	.57062	.55575
68	.72283	.70312	.68416	.66590	.64833	.63140	.61509	.59938	.58423	.56963
69	.73312	.71398	.69553	.67776	.66062	.64409	.62815	.61277	.59793	.58360
70	.74335	.72479	.70688	.68959	.67291	.65680	.64124	.62621	.61168	.59764

Table S
Based on Life Table 2000CM
Single Life Remainder Factors
Applicable on or After May 1, 2009
Interest Rate

AGE	2.2%	2.4%	2.6%	2.8%	3.0%	3.2%	3.4%	3.6%	3.8%	4.0%
71	.75353	.73556	.71819	.70141	.68519	.66951	.65434	.63968	.62549	.61176
72	.76364	.74626	.72945	.71318	.69744	.68220	.66745	.65317	.63933	.62593
73	.77365	.75686	.74061	.72487	.70962	.69484	.68051	.66662	.65315	.64009
74	.78350	.76733	.75164	.73643	.72167	.70735	.69346	.67997	.66688	.65417
75	.79318	.77761	.76249	.74781	.73355	.71971	.70625	.69318	.68048	.66813
76	.80266	.78769	.77314	.75899	.74524	.73187	.71886	.70621	.69390	.68192
77	.81194	.79756	.78358	.76997	.75672	.74382	.73127	.71904	.70713	.69553
78	.82100	.80722	.79380	.78072	.76798	.75556	.74346	.73166	.72016	.70894
79	.82984	.81664	.80378	.79124	.77900	.76706	.75542	.74405	.73296	.72213
80	.83843	.82582	.81351	.80149	.78976	.77830	.76711	.75618	.74550	.73507
81	.84678	.83474	.82298	.81148	.80025	.78927	.77853	.76803	.75777	.74773
82	.85487	.84339	.83217	.82119	.81045	.79994	.78966	.77959	.76974	.76009
83	.86269	.85177	.84107	.83060	.82035	.81030	.80047	.79083	.78139	.77214
84	.87024	.85986	.84968	.83970	.82993	.82035	.81095	.80174	.79271	.78385
85	.87751	.86765	.85798	.84849	.83919	.83005	.82110	.81230	.80368	.79521
86	.88450	.87515	.86597	.85696	.84811	.83942	.83089	.82251	.81428	.80619

87	.89119	.88234	.87363	.86508	.85668	.84843	.84031	.83234	.82450	.81679
88	.89760	.88922	.88099	.87289	.86492	.85708	.84938	.84180	.83434	.82700
89	.90372	.89580	.88801	.88034	.87280	.86537	.85806	.85087	.84378	.83681
90	.90954	.90207	.89471	.88746	.88032	.87329	.86637	.85954	.85282	.84620
91	.91508	.90803	.90109	.89424	.88750	.88085	.87429	.86783	.86146	.85518
92	.92033	.91369	.90714	.90068	.89432	.88803	.88184	.87572	.86969	.86374
93	.92530	.91904	.91287	.90678	.90078	.89484	.88899	.88321	.87751	.87188
94	.92999	.92411	.91830	.91256	.90690	.90130	.89578	.89032	.88493	.87961
95	.93442	.92889	.92342	.91802	.91269	.90741	.90220	.89706	.89197	.88694
96	.93858	.93338	.92824	.92316	.91813	.91316	.90825	.90340	.89859	.89385
97	.94248	.93759	.93276	.92798	.92325	.91857	.91395	.90937	.90484	.90036
98	.94614	.94155	.93701	.93252	.92807	.92367	.91931	.91500	.91073	.90650
99	.94959	.94528	.94101	.93679	.93260	.92846	.92436	.92030	.91628	.91229
100	.95278	.94874	.94473	.94075	.93682	.93292	.92906	.92523	.92144	.91769
101	.95581	.95201	.94824	.94451	.94081	.93715	.93352	.92992	.92635	.92281
102	.95860	.95503	.95149	.94798	.94450	.94105	.93763	.93424	.93088	.92754
103	.96136	.95802	.95470	.95142	.94816	.94492	.94171	.93853	.93538	.93224
104	.96390	.96077	.95766	.95458	.95152	.94848	.94547	.94248	.93951	.93657
105	.96640	.96347	.96057	.95769	.95483	.95199	.94917	.94637	.94359	.94083
106	.96950	.96684	.96420	.96157	.95896	.95636	.95379	.95123	.94868	.94616
107	.97301	.97064	.96829	.96595	.96362	.96131	.95901	.95672	.95445	.95219
108	.97859	.97670	.97482	.97295	.97109	.96923	.96739	.96555	.96373	.96191
109	.98924	.98828	.98733	.98638	.98544	.98450	.98356	.98263	.98170	.98077

Table S
Based on Life Table 2000CM
Single Life Remainder Factors
Applicable on or After May 1, 2009
Interest Rate

AGE	4.2%	4.4%	4.6%	4.8%	5.0%	5.2%	5.4%	5.6%	5.8%	6.0%
0	.06083	.05483	.04959	.04501	.04101	.03749	.03441	.03170	.02931	.02721
1	.05668	.05049	.04507	.04034	.03618	.03254	.02934	.02652	.02403	.02183
2	.05858	.05222	.04665	.04178	.03750	.03373	.03042	.02750	.02492	.02264
3	.06072	.05420	.04848	.04346	.03904	.03516	.03173	.02871	.02603	.02366
4	.06303	.05634	.05046	.04530	.04075	.03674	.03319	.03006	.02729	.02483
5	.06547	.05861	.05258	.04726	.04258	.03844	.03478	.03153	.02866	.02610
6	.06805	.06102	.05482	.04935	.04453	.04026	.03647	.03312	.03014	.02749
7	.07074	.06353	.05717	.05155	.04658	.04217	.03826	.03479	.03171	.02895
8	.07356	.06617	.05964	.05386	.04875	.04421	.04017	.03658	.03338	.03053
9	.07651	.06895	.06225	.05631	.05105	.04637	.04220	.03849	.03518	.03222
10	.07960	.07185	.06499	.05889	.05347	.04865	.04435	.04052	.03709	.03402
11	.08283	.07490	.06786	.06160	.05603	.05106	.04663	.04267	.03912	.03594
12	.08620	.07808	.07087	.06444	.05871	.05360	.04903	.04494	.04127	.03798
13	.08967	.08137	.07397	.06738	.06149	.05623	.05152	.04729	.04351	.04010
14	.09321	.08472	.07715	.07038	.06433	.05892	.05406	.04971	.04579	.04227
15	.09680	.08812	.08036	.07342	.06721	.06164	.05664	.05214	.04810	.04445
16	.10041	.09154	.08360	.07649	.07011	.06438	.05923	.05459	.05041	.04664
17	.10409	.09502	.08689	.07960	.07305	.06716	.06185	.05707	.05276	.04886
18	.10782	.09855	.09024	.08276	.07604	.06998	.06452	.05959	.05514	.05111
19	.11164	.10217	.09366	.08600	.07910	.07288	.06726	.06218	.05758	.05341
20	.11559	.10592	.09721	.08937	.08228	.07589	.07010	.06487	.06012	.05582
21	.11965	.10977	.10087	.09283	.08557	.07900	.07305	.06765	.06276	.05831
22	.12383	.11376	.10465	.09642	.08897	.08223	.07610	.07055	.06550	.06090
23	.12817	.11789	.10859	.10016	.09252	.08559	.07930	.07358	.06837	.06363
24	.13270	.12221	.11270	.10408	.09625	.08914	.08267	.07678	.07141	.06651
25	.13744	.12674	.11703	.10821	.10019	.09289	.08625	.08018	.07465	.06960
26	.14239	.13149	.12158	.11256	.10435	.09686	.09003	.08380	.07810	.07288
27	.14758	.13647	.12636	.11714	.10873	.10106	.09405	.08764	.08177	.07639
28	.15300	.14169	.13137	.12195	.11335	.10549	.09829	.09171	.08567	.08012
29	.15864	.14712	.13660	.12698	.11819	.11013	.10275	.09598	.08977	.08406
30	.16448	.15275	.14203	.13222	.12323	.11498	.10742	.10047	.09408	.08820
31	.17053	.15861	.14769	.13768	.12849	.12006	.11230	.10517	.09860	.09255
32	.17680	.16468	.15357	.14336	.13398	.12535	.11741	.11009	.10335	.09712
33	.18330	.17099	.15968	.14927	.13970	.13088	.12275	.11525	.10832	.10192
34	.19000	.17750	.16599	.15539	.14562	.13661	.12829	.12061	.11350	.10693

Table S
Based on Life Table 2000CM
Single Life Remainder Factors
Applicable on or After May 1, 2009
Interest Rate

AGE	4.2%	4.4%	4.6%	4.8%	5.0%	5.2%	5.4%	5.6%	5.8%	6.0%
35	.19692	.18423	.17253	.16174	.15178	.14258	.13408	.12621	.11892	.11217
36	.20407	.19119	.17931	.16833	.15818	.14879	.14009	.13204	.12457	.11764
37	.21144	.19838	.18631	.17515	.16481	.15523	.14635	.13811	.13046	.12335
38	.21904	.20582	.19357	.18222	.17170	.16193	.15287	.14444	.13661	.12932
39	.22687	.21348	.20105	.18952	.17882	.16887	.15962	.15102	.14300	.13554
40	.23493	.22137	.20878	.19707	.18619	.17606	.16663	.15784	.14965	.14201
41	.24322	.22950	.21674	.20487	.19381	.18350	.17390	.16493	.15656	.14873
42	.25173	.23786	.22494	.21290	.20168	.19120	.18141	.17227	.16372	.15572
43	.26049	.24648	.23342	.22122	.20982	.19918	.18922	.17990	.17118	.16301
44	.26950	.25535	.24214	.22979	.21824	.20742	.19730	.18781	.17892	.17057
45	.27874	.26447	.25112	.23862	.22692	.21595	.20566	.19600	.18694	.17843
46	.28824	.27385	.26038	.24774	.23589	.22476	.21431	.20450	.19527	.18659
47	.29798	.28349	.26989	.25712	.24513	.23386	.22326	.21328	.20390	.19505
48	.30797	.29338	.27967	.26678	.25466	.24325	.23250	.22238	.21283	.20383
49	.31822	.30355	.28974	.27674	.26449	.25294	.24206	.23179	.22210	.21294
50	.32876	.31401	.30011	.28701	.27465	.26298	.25196	.24156	.23172	.22242
51	.33958	.32477	.31079	.29759	.28513	.27335	.26221	.25168	.24170	.23226
52	.35068	.33582	.32178	.30851	.29595	.28407	.27282	.26216	.25206	.24249
53	.36206	.34717	.33308	.31974	.30710	.29513	.28378	.27301	.26279	.25309
54	.37371	.35880	.34467	.33127	.31857	.30651	.29507	.28420	.27388	.26406
55	.38559	.37067	.35652	.34308	.33032	.31820	.30668	.29572	.28529	.27537
56	.39765	.38275	.36859	.35512	.34232	.33014	.31855	.30751	.29699	.28697
57	.40990	.39502	.38086	.36739	.35455	.34233	.33068	.31957	.30898	.29887
58	.42231	.40747	.39333	.37985	.36700	.35474	.34304	.33188	.32121	.31103
59	.43490	.42011	.40600	.39253	.37968	.36740	.35567	.34446	.33374	.32348
60	.44768	.43296	.41890	.40546	.39261	.38033	.36858	.35733	.34656	.33625
61	.46064	.44600	.43200	.41860	.40578	.39351	.38175	.37048	.35968	.34933
62	.47373	.45920	.44527	.43194	.41915	.40690	.39514	.38387	.37305	.36267
63	.48696	.47253	.45870	.44544	.43271	.42049	.40876	.39749	.38666	.37625
64	.50030	.48601	.47229	.45911	.44645	.43428	.42258	.41133	.40051	.39010
65	.51377	.49963	.48603	.47295	.46037	.44827	.43662	.42540	.41460	.40420
66	.52750	.51352	.50007	.48711	.47464	.46262	.45103	.43987	.42911	.41872
67	.54144	.52765	.51436	.50154	.48919	.47727	.46578	.45468	.44397	.43363
68	.55554	.54196	.52885	.51619	.50398	.49218	.48079	.46978	.45915	.44887
69	.56976	.55640	.54349	.53102	.51896	.50731	.49603	.48513	.47458	.46438
70	.58407	.57095	.55826	.54598	.53410	.52260	.51147	.50069	.49025	.48013

Table S
Based on Life Table 2000CM
Single Life Remainder Factors
Applicable on or After May 1, 2009
Interest Rate

AGE	4.2%	4.4%	4.6%	4.8%	5.0%	5.2%	5.4%	5.6%	5.8%	6.0%
71	.59848	.58561	.57316	.56109	.54940	.53808	.52710	.51646	.50615	.49614
72	.61294	.60035	.58815	.57632	.56484	.55371	.54291	.53243	.52225	.51237
73	.62741	.61512	.60318	.59160	.58035	.56943	.55882	.54851	.53849	.52876
74	.64183	.62983	.61818	.60686	.59586	.58516	.57476	.56464	.55480	.54523
75	.65612	.64444	.63309	.62204	.61129	.60083	.59065	.58074	.57109	.56169
76	.67026	.65891	.64786	.63710	.62661	.61640	.60646	.59676	.58731	.57810
77	.68423	.67321	.66248	.65201	.64181	.63186	.62215	.61269	.60345	.59444
78	.69800	.68733	.67692	.66676	.65684	.64717	.63772	.62849	.61948	.61068
79	.71156	.70124	.69116	.68132	.67170	.66230	.65312	.64414	.63537	.62680
80	.72487	.71490	.70516	.69563	.68632	.67721	.66830	.65959	.65106	.64272
81	.73791	.72830	.71890	.70970	.70069	.69188	.68325	.67481	.66654	.65844
82	.75065	.74140	.73235	.72348	.71479	.70628	.69794	.68977	.68176	.67391
83	.76308	.75419	.74548	.73695	.72858	.72037	.71232	.70443	.69669	.68909
84	.77516	.76664	.75828	.75008	.74203	.73413	.72638	.71877	.71130	.70396
85	.78689	.77873	.77072	.76285	.75512	.74753	.74008	.73275	.72556	.71849
86	.79825	.79044	.78278	.77524	.76783	.76055	.75340	.74636	.73944	.73264

87	.80921	.80176	.79443	.78722	.78014	.77316	.76630	.75956	.75292	.74638
88	.81978	.81268	.80569	.79880	.79203	.78536	.77880	.77234	.76598	.75971
89	.82994	.82317	.81651	.80995	.80349	.79712	.79085	.78467	.77859	.77259
90	.83967	.83324	.82690	.82065	.81450	.80843	.80244	.79655	.79073	.78500
91	.84898	.84288	.83685	.83091	.82505	.81928	.81358	.80795	.80241	.79693
92	.85787	.85208	.84636	.84072	.83515	.82966	.82423	.81888	.81360	.80838
93	.86632	.86083	.85541	.85006	.84477	.83955	.83440	.82931	.82428	.81931
94	.87435	.86915	.86402	.85894	.85393	.84898	.84409	.83925	.83447	.82975
95	.88197	.87705	.87219	.86739	.86265	.85795	.85331	.84872	.84419	.83970
96	.88915	.88451	.87991	.87537	.87088	.86643	.86203	.85768	.85338	.84912
97	.89593	.89154	.88720	.88290	.87865	.87444	.87028	.86616	.86208	.85804
98	.90232	.89818	.89408	.89002	.88600	.88202	.87808	.87418	.87031	.86649
99	.90835	.90444	.90057	.89674	.89294	.88918	.88546	.88177	.87811	.87449
100	.91397	.91028	.90663	.90301	.89942	.89587	.89234	.88885	.88539	.88196
101	.91930	.91583	.91238	.90897	.90558	.90223	.89890	.89560	.89233	.88908
102	.92424	.92096	.91771	.91448	.91128	.90811	.90496	.90184	.89875	.89568
103	.92914	.92605	.92300	.91996	.91695	.91397	.91100	.90806	.90514	.90225
104	.93364	.93074	.92786	.92501	.92217	.91935	.91656	.91379	.91103	.90830
105	.93809	.93537	.93266	.92998	.92731	.92467	.92204	.91943	.91683	.91426
106	.94365	.94115	.93867	.93621	.93376	.93133	.92892	.92651	.92413	.92176
107	.94994	.94771	.94549	.94328	.94108	.93890	.93673	.93457	.93242	.93028
108	.96010	.95830	.95651	.95472	.95295	.95118	.94942	.94767	.94593	.94420
109	.97985	.97893	.97801	.97710	.97619	.97529	.97438	.97348	.97259	.97170

Table S
Based on Life Table 2000CM
Single Life Remainder Factors
Applicable on or After May 1, 2009
Interest Rate

AGE	6.2%	6.4%	6.6%	6.8%	7.0%	7.2%	7.4%	7.6%	7.8%	8.0%
0	.02534	.02370	.02223	.02093	.01978	.01874	.01782	.01699	.01625	.01559
1	.01989	.01817	.01664	.01528	.01406	.01298	.01202	.01115	.01037	.00967
2	.02061	.01882	.01722	.01580	.01454	.01340	.01239	.01148	.01066	.00993
3	.02156	.01969	.01802	.01654	.01521	.01403	.01297	.01201	.01115	.01038
4	.02264	.02069	.01896	.01741	.01602	.01478	.01367	.01267	.01176	.01095
5	.02383	.02180	.01999	.01838	.01693	.01563	.01446	.01341	.01246	.01161
6	.02512	.02301	.02113	.01944	.01793	.01657	.01535	.01424	.01325	.01235
7	.02650	.02430	.02234	.02058	.01900	.01758	.01630	.01514	.01410	.01315
8	.02798	.02570	.02365	.02182	.02017	.01868	.01734	.01613	.01503	.01404
9	.02957	.02720	.02507	.02316	.02143	.01988	.01848	.01721	.01606	.01502
10	.03128	.02881	.02659	.02460	.02280	.02118	.01971	.01838	.01718	.01608
11	.03309	.03053	.02823	.02615	.02428	.02258	.02105	.01966	.01839	.01725
12	.03503	.03237	.02997	.02781	.02585	.02408	.02248	.02103	.01971	.01850
13	.03704	.03428	.03179	.02954	.02750	.02565	.02398	.02246	.02108	.01982
14	.03909	.03623	.03364	.03130	.02918	.02726	.02551	.02392	.02248	.02116
15	.04117	.03820	.03551	.03308	.03087	.02886	.02704	.02538	.02387	.02249
16	.04324	.04016	.03737	.03484	.03254	.03046	.02855	.02682	.02524	.02379
17	.04533	.04214	.03924	.03661	.03422	.03205	.03007	.02826	.02661	.02509
18	.04746	.04415	.04114	.03841	.03592	.03366	.03159	.02970	.02798	.02639
19	.04963	.04620	.04309	.04025	.03766	.03530	.03315	.03117	.02937	.02772
20	.05191	.04835	.04512	.04217	.03948	.03702	.03478	.03272	.03083	.02910
21	.05427	.05058	.04723	.04416	.04137	.03881	.03647	.03432	.03235	.03054
22	.05672	.05291	.04943	.04625	.04334	.04067	.03823	.03599	.03394	.03205
23	.05930	.05535	.05174	.04844	.04542	.04265	.04010	.03777	.03562	.03364
24	.06204	.05795	.05421	.05078	.04764	.04476	.04211	.03967	.03743	.03536
25	.06497	.06074	.05687	.05331	.05005	.04705	.04429	.04174	.03940	.03724
26	.06811	.06373	.05972	.05603	.05264	.04952	.04665	.04400	.04155	.03929
27	.07146	.06694	.06278	.05895	.05543	.05219	.04920	.04644	.04389	.04153
28	.07503	.07036	.06605	.06209	.05844	.05507	.05196	.04908	.04642	.04396
29	.07881	.07398	.06953	.06542	.06163	.05814	.05490	.05191	.04913	.04656
30	.08279	.07780	.07319	.06894	.06502	.06138	.05802	.05491	.05202	.04933
31	.08697	.08182	.07707	.07267	.06860	.06483	.06134	.05810	.05509	.05229
32	.09137	.08606	.08115	.07660	.07239	.06848	.06485	.06148	.05835	.05543
33	.09601	.09053	.08546	.08075	.07639	.07234	.06858	.06508	.06182	.05878
34	.10084	.09520	.08996	.08511	.08059	.07640	.07249	.06886	.06547	.06231

Table S
Based on Life Table 2000CM
Single Life Remainder Factors
Applicable on or After May 1, 2009
Interest Rate

AGE	6.2%	6.4%	6.6%	6.8%	7.0%	7.2%	7.4%	7.6%	7.8%	8.0%
35	.10590	.10009	.09470	.08968	.08501	.08067	.07662	.07285	.06933	.06605
36	.11120	.10522	.09966	.09448	.08966	.08517	.08098	.07706	.07341	.06999
37	.11674	.11059	.10486	.09952	.09454	.08990	.08556	.08150	.07771	.07416
38	.12254	.11621	.11032	.10481	.09968	.09487	.09039	.08618	.08225	.07856
39	.12857	.12208	.11601	.11035	.10505	.10009	.09545	.09110	.08702	.08320
40	.13487	.12820	.12196	.11613	.11067	.10555	.10076	.09626	.09204	.08807
41	.14142	.13458	.12817	.12217	.11655	.11127	.10632	.10167	.09730	.09319
42	.14823	.14122	.13464	.12848	.12269	.11725	.11214	.10734	.10282	.09856
43	.15535	.14816	.14141	.13508	.12913	.12353	.11826	.11330	.10863	.10422
44	.16274	.15538	.14847	.14196	.13585	.13008	.12466	.11954	.11472	.11016
45	.17042	.16290	.15581	.14914	.14286	.13694	.13135	.12608	.12110	.11640
46	.17842	.17073	.16348	.15664	.15020	.14411	.13836	.13293	.12780	.12294
47	.18672	.17886	.17145	.16445	.15784	.15159	.14568	.14010	.13481	.12980
48	.19534	.18732	.17974	.17258	.16581	.15940	.15334	.14759	.14215	.13699
49	.20429	.19612	.18838	.18106	.17413	.16757	.16134	.15544	.14984	.14453
50	.21362	.20529	.19740	.18993	.18284	.17612	.16974	.16368	.15793	.15247
51	.22332	.21484	.20680	.19917	.19194	.18506	.17853	.17232	.16642	.16080
52	.23341	.22479	.21660	.20883	.20144	.19442	.18774	.18138	.17533	.16957
53	.24388	.23513	.22681	.21889	.21136	.20419	.19737	.19087	.18467	.17876
54	.25473	.24585	.23739	.22935	.22168	.21437	.20741	.20076	.19442	.18837
55	.26593	.25693	.24835	.24017	.23238	.22494	.21784	.21105	.20458	.19838
56	.27742	.26831	.25962	.25132	.24340	.23583	.22860	.22169	.21508	.20875
57	.28922	.28001	.27121	.26280	.25476	.24707	.23971	.23267	.22593	.21947
58	.30129	.29199	.28309	.27457	.26642	.25862	.25114	.24398	.23712	.23053
59	.31367	.30428	.29529	.28667	.27842	.27051	.26293	.25565	.24867	.24197
60	.32638	.31691	.30784	.29914	.29079	.28278	.27509	.26771	.26062	.25380
61	.33940	.32987	.32073	.31195	.30352	.29542	.28763	.28015	.27295	.26603
62	.35269	.34311	.33391	.32506	.31656	.30837	.30050	.29293	.28564	.27862
63	.36625	.35663	.34738	.33847	.32990	.32165	.31370	.30604	.29867	.29155
64	.38007	.37043	.36113	.35218	.34356	.33524	.32723	.31950	.31204	.30484
65	.39417	.38451	.37519	.36620	.35753	.34917	.34110	.33330	.32577	.31850
66	.40871	.39905	.38972	.38071	.37201	.36361	.35550	.34765	.34006	.33273
67	.42365	.41400	.40468	.39567	.38696	.37853	.37038	.36250	.35487	.34749
68	.43892	.42931	.42001	.41101	.40230	.39387	.38570	.37780	.37014	.36272
69	.45450	.44493	.43567	.42670	.41800	.40958	.40141	.39350	.38582	.37837
70	.47033	.46083	.45162	.44269	.43403	.42563	.41748	.40957	.40189	.39443

Table S
Based on Life Table 2000CM
Single Life Remainder Factors
Applicable on or After May 1, 2009
Interest Rate

AGE	6.2%	6.4%	6.6%	6.8%	7.0%	7.2%	7.4%	7.6%	7.8%	8.0%
71	.48644	.47702	.46788	.45901	.45040	.44203	.43391	.42602	.41835	.41090
72	.50278	.49347	.48441	.47562	.46707	.45877	.45069	.44284	.43520	.42776
73	.51930	.51010	.50115	.49245	.48399	.47575	.46774	.45994	.45234	.44494
74	.53591	.52684	.51802	.50943	.50106	.49291	.48497	.47724	.46970	.46235
75	.55253	.54361	.53492	.52645	.51820	.51015	.50230	.49465	.48719	.47991
76	.56912	.56036	.55182	.54349	.53536	.52742	.51968	.51213	.50475	.49754
77	.58565	.57706	.56868	.56050	.55251	.54471	.53708	.52964	.52236	.51525
78	.60209	.59369	.58549	.57747	.56963	.56197	.55448	.54715	.53999	.53298
79	.61841	.61021	.60219	.59435	.58668	.57917	.57182	.56463	.55760	.55071
80	.63456	.62657	.61875	.61109	.60359	.59625	.58906	.58202	.57512	.56836
81	.65050	.64273	.63512	.62766	.62034	.61318	.60616	.59927	.59252	.58590
82	.66621	.65867	.65127	.64401	.63690	.62992	.62308	.61636	.60977	.60330
83	.68164	.67433	.66716	.66012	.65321	.64642	.63976	.63322	.62680	.62050
84	.69676	.68969	.68275	.67593	.66923	.66265	.65618	.64983	.64358	.63745
85	.71154	.70472	.69801	.69141	.68493	.67856	.67229	.66613	.66007	.65412
86	.72595	.71937	.71290	.70654	.70028	.69412	.68806	.68210	.67623	.67046

87	.73995	.73362	.72740	.72127	.71523	.70929	.70344	.69768	.69201	.68642
88	.75354	.74746	.74148	.73558	.72978	.72406	.71842	.71287	.70739	.70200
89	.76668	.76085	.75511	.74945	.74387	.73837	.73295	.72761	.72234	.71714
90	.77934	.77377	.76827	.76284	.75749	.75222	.74701	.74188	.73681	.73181
91	.79153	.78620	.78094	.77575	.77063	.76558	.76059	.75566	.75080	.74600
92	.80323	.79814	.79312	.78816	.78326	.77843	.77365	.76894	.76428	.75967
93	.81440	.80956	.80477	.80004	.79536	.79074	.78618	.78166	.77721	.77280
94	.82508	.82047	.81591	.81140	.80694	.80253	.79817	.79387	.78961	.78539
95	.83526	.83088	.82654	.82225	.81800	.81380	.80965	.80554	.80148	.79746
96	.84491	.84074	.83662	.83254	.82850	.82450	.82055	.81663	.81276	.80892
97	.85405	.85009	.84617	.84230	.83846	.83466	.83089	.82717	.82348	.81982
98	.86270	.85895	.85523	.85155	.84791	.84430	.84072	.83718	.83367	.83019
99	.87090	.86735	.86382	.86033	.85687	.85345	.85005	.84668	.84335	.84004
100	.87856	.87519	.87185	.86854	.86526	.86201	.85878	.85559	.85242	.84927
101	.88587	.88268	.87952	.87638	.87327	.87019	.86713	.86409	.86109	.85810
102	.89263	.88961	.88662	.88364	.88069	.87777	.87487	.87199	.86913	.86629
103	.89938	.89653	.89370	.89089	.88810	.88534	.88259	.87987	.87717	.87448
104	.90558	.90289	.90021	.89756	.89492	.89231	.88971	.88713	.88456	.88202
105	.91170	.90916	.90664	.90413	.90164	.89917	.89672	.89428	.89186	.88945
106	.91940	.91706	.91474	.91242	.91013	.90784	.90558	.90332	.90108	.89885
107	.92816	.92605	.92395	.92186	.91978	.91772	.91567	.91362	.91159	.90957
108	.94247	.94075	.93904	.93734	.93565	.93396	.93229	.93062	.92895	.92730
109	.97081	.96992	.96904	.96816	.96729	.96642	.96555	.96468	.96382	.96296

Table S
Based on Life Table 2000CM
Single Life Remainder Factors
Applicable on or After May 1, 2009
Interest Rate

AGE	8.2%	8.4%	8.6%	8.8%	9.0%	9.2%	9.4%	9.6%	9.8%	10.0%
0	.01498	.01444	.01395	.01351	.01310	.01273	.01240	.01209	.01181	.01155
1	.00904	.00847	.00796	.00749	.00707	.00668	.00633	.00601	.00572	.00545
2	.00926	.00866	.00812	.00763	.00718	.00677	.00640	.00606	.00575	.00547
3	.00968	.00905	.00848	.00796	.00748	.00705	.00666	.00630	.00597	.00567
4	.01021	.00955	.00894	.00839	.00789	.00744	.00702	.00664	.00629	.00597
5	.01083	.01013	.00949	.00891	.00839	.00790	.00746	.00706	.00669	.00635
6	.01153	.01080	.01012	.00951	.00895	.00844	.00798	.00755	.00715	.00679
7	.01229	.01151	.01081	.01016	.00957	.00903	.00854	.00808	.00767	.00728
8	.01314	.01232	.01157	.01089	.01026	.00969	.00917	.00869	.00825	.00784
9	.01407	.01321	.01242	.01170	.01104	.01044	.00989	.00938	.00891	.00848
10	.01509	.01418	.01335	.01259	.01190	.01126	.01068	.01014	.00965	.00919
11	.01620	.01525	.01437	.01358	.01285	.01218	.01156	.01099	.01047	.00998
12	.01740	.01640	.01549	.01465	.01388	.01317	.01252	.01192	.01137	.01086
13	.01867	.01762	.01665	.01577	.01496	.01422	.01353	.01290	.01231	.01177
14	.01995	.01885	.01784	.01691	.01606	.01527	.01455	.01389	.01327	.01270
15	.02123	.02007	.01901	.01803	.01714	.01632	.01556	.01485	.01420	.01360
16	.02247	.02126	.02015	.01913	.01818	.01732	.01652	.01578	.01509	.01446
17	.02371	.02244	.02127	.02020	.01921	.01830	.01746	.01668	.01596	.01529
18	.02494	.02361	.02239	.02126	.02022	.01926	.01838	.01756	.01680	.01610
19	.02620	.02480	.02352	.02234	.02125	.02024	.01931	.01844	.01764	.01690
20	.02751	.02605	.02471	.02346	.02232	.02126	.02028	.01937	.01853	.01775
21	.02888	.02735	.02593	.02463	.02343	.02231	.02128	.02032	.01944	.01861
22	.03030	.02870	.02722	.02585	.02458	.02341	.02233	.02132	.02038	.01951
23	.03181	.03013	.02858	.02714	.02581	.02458	.02344	.02237	.02139	.02047
24	.03345	.03169	.03006	.02855	.02715	.02586	.02465	.02353	.02249	.02152
25	.03524	.03340	.03169	.03010	.02863	.02727	.02600	.02482	.02373	.02270
26	.03720	.03527	.03348	.03181	.03027	.02884	.02750	.02626	.02510	.02402
27	.03934	.03732	.03544	.03370	.03208	.03057	.02916	.02786	.02664	.02549
28	.04167	.03955	.03759	.03576	.03406	.03247	.03099	.02962	.02833	.02713
29	.04417	.04196	.03990	.03798	.03619	.03453	.03298	.03153	.03017	.02890
30	.04684	.04452	.04237	.04036	.03848	.03674	.03510	.03358	.03215	.03081
31	.04969	.04727	.04501	.04291	.04094	.03911	.03739	.03579	.03428	.03287
32	.05272	.05019	.04783	.04563	.04357	.04165	.03984	.03816	.03657	.03509
33	.05595	.05331	.05085	.04854	.04639	.04437	.04248	.04070	.03904	.03748
34	.05936	.05661	.05403	.05162	.04936	.04725	.04527	.04341	.04166	.04001

Table S
Based on Life Table 2000CM
Single Life Remainder Factors
Applicable on or After May 1, 2009
Interest Rate

AGE	8.2%	8.4%	8.6%	8.8%	9.0%	9.2%	9.4%	9.6%	9.8%	10.0%
35	.06297	.06010	.05741	.05489	.05253	.05032	.04824	.04629	.04445	.04272
36	.06679	.06380	.06100	.05837	.05590	.05358	.05140	.04935	.04742	.04561
37	.07083	.06771	.06479	.06204	.05947	.05704	.05476	.05261	.05059	.04868
38	.07511	.07186	.06881	.06595	.06326	.06072	.05834	.05609	.05397	.05196
39	.07961	.07623	.07306	.07007	.06726	.06462	.06212	.05977	.05754	.05544
40	.08434	.08083	.07753	.07442	.07149	.06873	.06612	.06366	.06133	.05913
41	.08932	.08568	.08225	.07901	.07596	.07308	.07035	.06778	.06534	.06304
42	.09455	.09077	.08720	.08384	.08066	.07766	.07481	.07213	.06958	.06717
43	.10007	.09615	.09245	.08895	.08564	.08251	.07955	.07674	.07408	.07156
44	.10586	.10180	.09796	.09433	.09089	.08763	.08454	.08162	.07884	.07621
45	.11195	.10774	.10376	.09999	.09642	.09303	.08982	.08677	.08387	.08112
46	.11835	.11400	.10987	.10596	.10225	.09873	.09539	.09222	.08920	.08633
47	.12505	.12055	.11629	.11224	.10839	.10474	.10126	.09796	.09482	.09182
48	.13209	.12745	.12303	.11884	.11485	.11106	.10746	.10402	.10075	.09764
49	.13948	.13469	.13013	.12579	.12167	.11774	.11400	.11043	.10703	.10379
50	.14727	.14233	.13762	.13314	.12887	.12481	.12093	.11723	.11370	.11033
51	.15546	.15037	.14551	.14089	.13648	.13228	.12826	.12443	.12077	.11726
52	.16407	.15884	.15384	.14907	.14452	.14018	.13603	.13206	.12826	.12463
53	.17312	.16774	.16260	.15769	.15300	.14852	.14423	.14012	.13620	.13243
54	.18259	.17707	.17179	.16674	.16191	.15729	.15286	.14862	.14456	.14067
55	.19247	.18680	.18139	.17620	.17123	.16648	.16192	.15755	.15335	.14933
56	.20270	.19690	.19135	.18602	.18092	.17603	.17134	.16684	.16251	.15836
57	.21329	.20736	.20167	.19622	.19099	.18596	.18114	.17650	.17205	.16777
58	.22422	.21816	.21235	.20677	.20140	.19625	.19130	.18653	.18195	.17754
59	.23553	.22935	.22341	.21770	.21221	.20693	.20185	.19696	.19225	.18772
60	.24725	.24095	.23489	.22906	.22345	.21805	.21285	.20783	.20300	.19834
61	.25937	.25296	.24679	.24084	.23511	.22959	.22427	.21914	.21419	.20941
62	.27185	.26534	.25906	.25300	.24716	.24153	.23609	.23084	.22577	.22088
63	.28469	.27808	.27169	.26553	.25959	.25384	.24830	.24294	.23776	.23275
64	.29789	.29119	.28471	.27845	.27240	.26656	.26091	.25544	.25016	.24504
65	.31148	.30468	.29812	.29177	.28563	.27969	.27394	.26837	.26299	.25777
66	.32564	.31877	.31213	.30570	.29948	.29345	.28761	.28195	.27647	.27115
67	.34034	.33341	.32671	.32021	.31391	.30780	.30188	.29614	.29057	.28517
68	.35552	.34855	.34179	.33523	.32887	.32270	.31671	.31089	.30524	.29976
69	.37115	.36414	.35734	.35073	.34432	.33809	.33204	.32616	.32045	.31489
70	.38719	.38016	.37332	.36668	.36023	.35396	.34786	.34193	.33616	.33054

Table S
Based on Life Table 2000CM
Single Life Remainder Factors
Applicable on or After May 1, 2009
Interest Rate

AGE	8.2%	8.4%	8.6%	8.8%	9.0%	9.2%	9.4%	9.6%	9.8%	10.0%
71	.40366	.39662	.38977	.38311	.37663	.37032	.36419	.35821	.35240	.34674
72	.42053	.41350	.40665	.39998	.39349	.38716	.38100	.37500	.36916	.36346
73	.43774	.43073	.42389	.41723	.41074	.40441	.39824	.39222	.38636	.38063
74	.45519	.44821	.44140	.43476	.42829	.42197	.41580	.40979	.40391	.39818
75	.47280	.46587	.45910	.45250	.44605	.43975	.43360	.42759	.42173	.41599
76	.49051	.48364	.47693	.47037	.46396	.45770	.45158	.44560	.43975	.43403
77	.50830	.50150	.49486	.48836	.48201	.47580	.46972	.46377	.45795	.45225
78	.52613	.51942	.51286	.50644	.50015	.49400	.48797	.48208	.47630	.47064
79	.54396	.53736	.53089	.52456	.51835	.51227	.50632	.50048	.49476	.48915
80	.56174	.55525	.54888	.54265	.53653	.53054	.52466	.51890	.51325	.50770
81	.57941	.57305	.56681	.56068	.55467	.54878	.54299	.53731	.53174	.52627
82	.59696	.59073	.58461	.57861	.57272	.56693	.56125	.55566	.55018	.54480
83	.61430	.60822	.60224	.59637	.59061	.58494	.57937	.57389	.56851	.56322
84	.63142	.62549	.61966	.61393	.60830	.60276	.59731	.59196	.58669	.58150
85	.64825	.64249	.63682	.63124	.62575	.62035	.61503	.60980	.60465	.59958
86	.66477	.65918	.65367	.64825	.64291	.63765	.63248	.62738	.62236	.61741

87	.68092	.67550	.67016	.66490	.65972	.65462	.64959	.64463	.63975	.63493
88	.69669	.69145	.68628	.68119	.67618	.67123	.66635	.66154	.65680	.65212
89	.71201	.70696	.70198	.69706	.69221	.68742	.68270	.67805	.67345	.66892
90	.72688	.72201	.71721	.71246	.70779	.70317	.69861	.69411	.68966	.68528
91	.74126	.73658	.73196	.72739	.72289	.71844	.71404	.70970	.70541	.70117
92	.75513	.75063	.74620	.74181	.73748	.73320	.72897	.72479	.72066	.71657
93	.76844	.76414	.75988	.75568	.75152	.74741	.74334	.73932	.73535	.73142
94	.78123	.77711	.77303	.76901	.76502	.76108	.75718	.75332	.74951	.74573
95	.79348	.78954	.78565	.78179	.77798	.77421	.77047	.76677	.76312	.75950
96	.80513	.80137	.79765	.79397	.79032	.78671	.78314	.77960	.77610	.77263
97	.81621	.81262	.80908	.80556	.80208	.79864	.79522	.79184	.78849	.78517
98	.82674	.82333	.81995	.81660	.81328	.80999	.80673	.80351	.80031	.79713
99	.83677	.83352	.83030	.82711	.82395	.82082	.81771	.81463	.81158	.80855
100	.84616	.84307	.84001	.83697	.83396	.83097	.82801	.82507	.82216	.81927
101	.85514	.85221	.84930	.84641	.84355	.84070	.83788	.83509	.83231	.82956
102	.86348	.86069	.85792	.85517	.85245	.84974	.84706	.84439	.84175	.83912
103	.87182	.86918	.86655	.86395	.86136	.85880	.85625	.85372	.85121	.84872
104	.87950	.87699	.87450	.87203	.86957	.86713	.86471	.86231	.85992	.85755
105	.88706	.88468	.88232	.87998	.87765	.87534	.87304	.87076	.86849	.86624
106	.89664	.89444	.89225	.89008	.88792	.88577	.88364	.88152	.87941	.87731
107	.90756	.90557	.90358	.90160	.89964	.89768	.89574	.89380	.89188	.88997
108	.92565	.92401	.92238	.92075	.91914	.91753	.91592	.91433	.91274	.91116
109	.96211	.96125	.96041	.95956	.95872	.95788	.95704	.95620	.95537	.95455

Table S
Based on Life Table 2000CM
Single Life Remainder Factors
Applicable on or After May 1, 2009
Interest Rate

AGE	10.2%	10.4%	10.6%	10.8%	11.0%	11.2%	11.4%	11.6%	11.8%	12.0%
0	.01132	.01110	.01089	.01071	.01053	.01037	.01022	.01008	.00995	.00983
1	.00520	.00497	.00476	.00457	.00439	.00423	.00407	.00393	.00379	.00367
2	.00521	.00496	.00474	.00454	.00435	.00417	.00401	.00385	.00371	.00358
3	.00539	.00513	.00490	.00468	.00447	.00429	.00411	.00395	.00380	.00366
4	.00567	.00540	.00515	.00492	.00470	.00450	.00432	.00414	.00398	.00383
5	.00603	.00574	.00547	.00523	.00500	.00478	.00459	.00440	.00423	.00407
6	.00646	.00615	.00587	.00560	.00536	.00513	.00492	.00472	.00453	.00436
7	.00693	.00660	.00630	.00602	.00576	.00551	.00529	.00508	.00488	.00469
8	.00747	.00712	.00680	.00650	.00622	.00596	.00572	.00549	.00528	.00509
9	.00808	.00771	.00737	.00705	.00675	.00648	.00622	.00598	.00576	.00555
10	.00877	.00838	.00801	.00767	.00736	.00707	.00679	.00654	.00630	.00608
11	.00954	.00912	.00873	.00838	.00804	.00773	.00744	.00717	.00692	.00668
12	.01038	.00994	.00953	.00915	.00880	.00847	.00816	.00788	.00761	.00735
13	.01127	.01081	.01038	.00998	.00960	.00925	.00893	.00862	.00833	.00806
14	.01217	.01168	.01122	.01080	.01040	.01003	.00969	.00937	.00906	.00878
15	.01305	.01253	.01205	.01160	.01118	.01079	.01042	.01008	.00976	.00946
16	.01387	.01333	.01282	.01234	.01190	.01149	.01110	.01074	.01040	.01009
17	.01467	.01409	.01356	.01306	.01259	.01216	.01175	.01137	.01101	.01067
18	.01544	.01484	.01427	.01374	.01325	.01279	.01236	.01195	.01157	.01122
19	.01621	.01557	.01497	.01442	.01390	.01341	.01295	.01253	.01213	.01175
20	.01702	.01634	.01571	.01512	.01457	.01406	.01357	.01312	.01270	.01230
21	.01784	.01713	.01646	.01584	.01526	.01471	.01420	.01372	.01327	.01285
22	.01870	.01794	.01724	.01658	.01596	.01539	.01485	.01434	.01386	.01342
23	.01961	.01881	.01807	.01737	.01672	.01611	.01554	.01500	.01449	.01402
24	.02062	.01977	.01899	.01825	.01756	.01691	.01630	.01573	.01520	.01469
25	.02175	.02085	.02002	.01924	.01851	.01782	.01718	.01657	.01600	.01547
26	.02301	.02207	.02119	.02036	.01958	.01886	.01817	.01753	.01692	.01635
27	.02443	.02343	.02250	.02162	.02080	.02003	.01930	.01862	.01798	.01737
28	.02600	.02495	.02396	.02303	.02216	.02134	.02057	.01985	.01916	.01852
29	.02771	.02660	.02555	.02457	.02365	.02278	.02197	.02120	.02047	.01979
30	.02956	.02838	.02728	.02624	.02526	.02434	.02348	.02266	.02189	.02116
31	.03155	.03031	.02914	.02804	.02701	.02604	.02512	.02425	.02344	.02266
32	.03370	.03239	.03115	.02999	.02890	.02787	.02690	.02598	.02511	.02429
33	.03601	.03463	.03333	.03210	.03095	.02985	.02883	.02785	.02693	.02606
34	.03847	.03701	.03564	.03434	.03312	.03197	.03088	.02985	.02887	.02795

Table S
Based on Life Table 2000CM
Single Life Remainder Factors
Applicable on or After May 1, 2009
Interest Rate

AGE	10.2%	10.4%	10.6%	10.8%	11.0%	11.2%	11.4%	11.6%	11.8%	12.0%
35	.04109	.03956	.03811	.03675	.03546	.03424	.03308	.03199	.03096	.02998
36	.04390	.04228	.04076	.03932	.03795	.03667	.03545	.03429	.03320	.03216
37	.04688	.04518	.04358	.04206	.04062	.03926	.03798	.03676	.03560	.03450
38	.05007	.04829	.04660	.04500	.04349	.04205	.04069	.03940	.03818	.03701
39	.05346	.05158	.04981	.04812	.04653	.04502	.04358	.04222	.04092	.03969
40	.05705	.05508	.05321	.05144	.04976	.04817	.04666	.04522	.04385	.04255
41	.06086	.05879	.05683	.05497	.05320	.05152	.04993	.04841	.04697	.04559
42	.06488	.06271	.06066	.05870	.05684	.05508	.05340	.05180	.05028	.04882
43	.06917	.06690	.06474	.06269	.06074	.05888	.05711	.05543	.05382	.05229
44	.07370	.07132	.06906	.06691	.06486	.06291	.06105	.05928	.05759	.05598
45	.07850	.07602	.07365	.07139	.06924	.06719	.06524	.06338	.06160	.05990
46	.08360	.08100	.07852	.07616	.07390	.07176	.06970	.06775	.06587	.06409
47	.08897	.08626	.08367	.08120	.07884	.07659	.07443	.07238	.07041	.06853
48	.09466	.09183	.08912	.08654	.08407	.08172	.07946	.07730	.07524	.07326
49	.10069	.09774	.09492	.09222	.08964	.08717	.08481	.08255	.08038	.07831
50	.10711	.10403	.10109	.09827	.09558	.09300	.09053	.08816	.08589	.08371
51	.11392	.11072	.10765	.10472	.10191	.09921	.09663	.09415	.09178	.08950
52	.12116	.11783	.11464	.11159	.10866	.10585	.10315	.10057	.09808	.09569
53	.12883	.12538	.12206	.11889	.11584	.11291	.11010	.10740	.10481	.10231
54	.13694	.13336	.12992	.12662	.12345	.12041	.11748	.11467	.11196	.10936
55	.14547	.14176	.13820	.13478	.13149	.12832	.12528	.12235	.11953	.11682
56	.15437	.15054	.14685	.14330	.13989	.13661	.13345	.13040	.12747	.12464
57	.16365	.15969	.15588	.15221	.14868	.14527	.14199	.13883	.13578	.13284
58	.17330	.16921	.16528	.16149	.15783	.15431	.15091	.14763	.14447	.14141
59	.18335	.17914	.17508	.17117	.16739	.16375	.16023	.15684	.15356	.15039
60	.19385	.18952	.18534	.18131	.17741	.17365	.17001	.16650	.16311	.15982
61	.20480	.20035	.19605	.19189	.18788	.18400	.18025	.17662	.17311	.16971
62	.21615	.21158	.20717	.20290	.19877	.19477	.19090	.18716	.18354	.18003
63	.22791	.22323	.21870	.21431	.21007	.20596	.20198	.19812	.19439	.19077
64	.24009	.23530	.23066	.22616	.22181	.21758	.21349	.20953	.20568	.20195
65	.25271	.24781	.24306	.23846	.23400	.22967	.22547	.22139	.21744	.21360
66	.26600	.26100	.25615	.25145	.24688	.24245	.23814	.23396	.22990	.22596
67	.27992	.27483	.26989	.26509	.26043	.25590	.25150	.24722	.24306	.23901
68	.29443	.28926	.28423	.27934	.27459	.26997	.26548	.26110	.25685	.25271
69	.30950	.30424	.29914	.29417	.28934	.28463	.28005	.27559	.27125	.26703
70	.32508	.31976	.31459	.30955	.30464	.29986	.29520	.29067	.28625	.28194

Table S
Based on Life Table 2000CM
Single Life Remainder Factors
Applicable on or After May 1, 2009
Interest Rate

AGE	10.2%	10.4%	10.6%	10.8%	11.0%	11.2%	11.4%	11.6%	11.8%	12.0%
71	.34122	.33585	.33062	.32552	.32054	.31570	.31097	.30637	.30187	.29749
72	.35790	.35249	.34721	.34205	.33703	.33213	.32734	.32268	.31812	.31367
73	.37505	.36960	.36428	.35909	.35403	.34908	.34425	.33953	.33492	.33042
74	.39258	.38711	.38177	.37655	.37145	.36647	.36160	.35684	.35219	.34764
75	.41039	.40491	.39956	.39432	.38921	.38420	.37931	.37452	.36983	.36525
76	.42843	.42296	.41760	.41236	.40724	.40222	.39731	.39250	.38779	.38318
77	.44668	.44122	.43588	.43065	.42552	.42050	.41559	.41077	.40605	.40143
78	.46510	.45967	.45435	.44914	.44403	.43902	.43411	.42930	.42458	.41995
79	.48365	.47826	.47298	.46780	.46271	.45773	.45284	.44804	.44333	.43871
80	.50226	.49693	.49169	.48655	.48150	.47655	.47169	.46692	.46224	.45763
81	.52090	.51562	.51044	.50536	.50036	.49546	.49064	.48590	.48125	.47668
82	.53951	.53431	.52920	.52418	.51924	.51439	.50963	.50494	.50033	.49580
83	.55802	.55291	.54788	.54294	.53808	.53329	.52859	.52396	.51941	.51493
84	.57640	.57139	.56645	.56159	.55681	.55210	.54747	.54291	.53843	.53401
85	.59459	.58968	.58484	.58008	.57539	.57077	.56623	.56175	.55733	.55298
86	.61254	.60774	.60302	.59836	.59377	.58925	.58479	.58040	.57607	.57180

87	.63019	.62551	.62090	.61635	.61187	.60745	.60309	.59880	.59456	.59038
88	.64751	.64296	.63847	.63405	.62968	.62537	.62112	.61693	.61279	.60871
89	.66444	.66003	.65567	.65137	.64712	.64293	.63880	.63471	.63068	.62670
90	.68094	.67667	.67244	.66827	.66415	.66009	.65607	.65210	.64818	.64431
91	.69699	.69285	.68877	.68473	.68074	.67680	.67291	.66906	.66526	.66150
92	.71254	.70855	.70460	.70071	.69685	.69304	.68928	.68555	.68187	.67823
93	.72753	.72369	.71989	.71613	.71242	.70874	.70510	.70150	.69794	.69442
94	.74200	.73830	.73464	.73103	.72745	.72390	.72040	.71693	.71350	.71010
95	.75591	.75236	.74885	.74538	.74194	.73853	.73516	.73182	.72851	.72524
96	.76920	.76580	.76243	.75909	.75579	.75252	.74928	.74607	.74289	.73974
97	.78188	.77863	.77540	.77220	.76904	.76590	.76279	.75971	.75665	.75363
98	.79399	.79088	.78779	.78473	.78170	.77869	.77571	.77276	.76983	.76693
99	.80555	.80257	.79962	.79670	.79380	.79092	.78807	.78525	.78244	.77966
100	.81641	.81357	.81075	.80796	.80518	.80243	.79971	.79700	.79432	.79165
101	.82683	.82412	.82144	.81877	.81612	.81350	.81089	.80831	.80574	.80320
102	.83652	.83394	.83137	.82882	.82630	.82379	.82130	.81883	.81637	.81394
103	.84624	.84379	.84135	.83892	.83652	.83413	.83176	.82941	.82707	.82475
104	.85519	.85285	.85053	.84822	.84593	.84365	.84139	.83915	.83692	.83470
105	.86400	.86178	.85957	.85737	.85519	.85302	.85087	.84873	.84660	.84449
106	.87523	.87316	.87110	.86905	.86702	.86500	.86299	.86099	.85900	.85703
107	.88806	.88617	.88429	.88242	.88055	.87870	.87686	.87502	.87320	.87139
108	.90958	.90802	.90646	.90490	.90336	.90182	.90028	.89876	.89724	.89573
109	.95372	.95290	.95208	.95126	.95045	.94964	.94883	.94803	.94723	.94643

Table S
Based on Life Table 2000CM
Single Life Remainder Factors
Applicable on or After May 1, 2009
Interest Rate

AGE	12.2%	12.4%	12.6%	12.8%	13.0%	13.2%	13.4%	13.6%	13.8%	14.0%
0	.00972	.00961	.00951	.00941	.00932	.00924	.00916	.00908	.00901	.00894
1	.00355	.00345	.00334	.00325	.00316	.00307	.00299	.00292	.00285	.00278
2	.00346	.00334	.00323	.00313	.00303	.00294	.00286	.00278	.00270	.00263
3	.00353	.00340	.00329	.00318	.00307	.00298	.00289	.00280	.00272	.00264
4	.00369	.00356	.00343	.00332	.00321	.00310	.00300	.00291	.00283	.00274
5	.00392	.00377	.00364	.00352	.00340	.00329	.00318	.00308	.00299	.00290
6	.00420	.00405	.00391	.00377	.00365	.00353	.00342	.00331	.00321	.00311
7	.00452	.00436	.00421	.00406	.00393	.00380	.00368	.00357	.00346	.00336
8	.00490	.00473	.00457	.00441	.00427	.00413	.00400	.00388	.00376	.00365
9	.00535	.00517	.00499	.00483	.00467	.00453	.00439	.00426	.00413	.00402
10	.00587	.00567	.00548	.00531	.00514	.00499	.00484	.00470	.00456	.00444
11	.00645	.00624	.00605	.00586	.00568	.00551	.00536	.00521	.00506	.00493
12	.00711	.00689	.00668	.00648	.00629	.00611	.00595	.00579	.00563	.00549
13	.00781	.00757	.00735	.00714	.00694	.00675	.00657	.00640	.00624	.00609
14	.00851	.00826	.00802	.00780	.00759	.00739	.00720	.00702	.00684	.00668
15	.00918	.00891	.00866	.00842	.00820	.00799	.00779	.00759	.00741	.00724
16	.00979	.00950	.00924	.00899	.00875	.00853	.00832	.00811	.00792	.00774
17	.01035	.01006	.00978	.00951	.00926	.00902	.00880	.00859	.00838	.00819
18	.01088	.01057	.01027	.00999	.00973	.00948	.00924	.00901	.00880	.00860
19	.01139	.01106	.01075	.01045	.01017	.00990	.00965	.00942	.00919	.00898
20	.01192	.01157	.01124	.01092	.01063	.01035	.01008	.00983	.00959	.00936
21	.01245	.01208	.01173	.01139	.01108	.01078	.01050	.01023	.00998	.00974
22	.01300	.01260	.01222	.01187	.01154	.01122	.01092	.01064	.01037	.01011
23	.01357	.01315	.01275	.01238	.01202	.01168	.01137	.01106	.01078	.01051
24	.01422	.01377	.01334	.01294	.01257	.01221	.01187	.01155	.01124	.01095
25	.01496	.01448	.01403	.01361	.01320	.01282	.01246	.01212	.01180	.01149
26	.01582	.01531	.01483	.01438	.01395	.01354	.01316	.01279	.01244	.01211
27	.01680	.01626	.01575	.01527	.01481	.01437	.01396	.01357	.01320	.01285
28	.01791	.01734	.01679	.01628	.01579	.01533	.01489	.01447	.01408	.01370
29	.01914	.01853	.01795	.01740	.01688	.01639	.01592	.01548	.01505	.01465
30	.02048	.01982	.01921	.01862	.01807	.01754	.01704	.01657	.01612	.01569
31	.02193	.02124	.02058	.01996	.01937	.01881	.01828	.01777	.01729	.01683
32	.02351	.02278	.02208	.02142	.02079	.02019	.01962	.01908	.01857	.01808
33	.02523	.02445	.02371	.02300	.02234	.02170	.02109	.02052	.01997	.01944
34	.02707	.02624	.02545	.02470	.02399	.02331	.02267	.02205	.02146	.02091

Table S
Based on Life Table 2000CM
Single Life Remainder Factors
Applicable on or After May 1, 2009
Interest Rate

AGE	12.2%	12.4%	12.6%	12.8%	13.0%	13.2%	13.4%	13.6%	13.8%	14.0%
35	.02905	.02817	.02733	.02653	.02577	.02505	.02436	.02371	.02308	.02249
36	.03117	.03024	.02935	.02850	.02769	.02693	.02619	.02550	.02483	.02419
37	.03345	.03246	.03151	.03061	.02976	.02894	.02816	.02742	.02671	.02603
38	.03590	.03485	.03385	.03289	.03198	.03112	.03029	.02950	.02874	.02802
39	.03852	.03740	.03634	.03533	.03436	.03344	.03256	.03172	.03092	.03015
40	.04131	.04013	.03900	.03793	.03690	.03593	.03499	.03410	.03324	.03242
41	.04428	.04303	.04184	.04070	.03962	.03858	.03759	.03664	.03573	.03486
42	.04744	.04612	.04486	.04366	.04250	.04140	.04035	.03934	.03838	.03745
43	.05083	.04943	.04810	.04683	.04561	.04444	.04333	.04226	.04123	.04025
44	.05443	.05296	.05155	.05021	.04892	.04768	.04650	.04537	.04428	.04324
45	.05827	.05672	.05523	.05381	.05245	.05114	.04989	.04869	.04754	.04643
46	.06237	.06074	.05917	.05767	.05623	.05485	.05352	.05225	.05103	.04986
47	.06673	.06500	.06335	.06177	.06025	.05879	.05739	.05605	.05475	.05351
48	.07137	.06955	.06781	.06614	.06454	.06300	.06152	.06010	.05874	.05742
49	.07632	.07441	.07258	.07082	.06913	.06750	.06595	.06444	.06300	.06161
50	.08162	.07962	.07769	.07584	.07407	.07236	.07071	.06913	.06760	.06614
51	.08731	.08520	.08318	.08124	.07937	.07757	.07583	.07416	.07256	.07101
52	.09340	.09119	.08907	.08703	.08507	.08317	.08135	.07959	.07790	.07627
53	.09991	.09760	.09538	.09324	.09118	.08919	.08728	.08543	.08365	.08193
54	.10685	.10443	.10211	.09987	.09771	.09562	.09361	.09167	.08980	.08799
55	.11420	.11168	.10925	.10690	.10464	.10246	.10035	.09832	.09635	.09445
56	.12191	.11928	.11675	.11430	.11193	.10965	.10745	.10531	.10325	.10126
57	.13001	.12727	.12462	.12207	.11960	.11721	.11491	.11268	.11052	.10843
58	.13846	.13561	.13286	.13020	.12762	.12513	.12273	.12040	.11814	.11595
59	.14732	.14436	.14150	.13873	.13605	.13346	.13095	.12851	.12616	.12388
60	.15665	.15358	.15060	.14772	.14494	.14224	.13962	.13709	.13463	.13225
61	.16642	.16324	.16016	.15717	.15428	.15147	.14875	.14611	.14355	.14107
62	.17663	.17333	.17014	.16704	.16404	.16113	.15830	.15556	.15290	.15031
63	.18726	.18385	.18055	.17734	.17423	.17121	.16828	.16544	.16267	.15999
64	.19833	.19481	.19140	.18809	.18487	.18175	.17871	.17576	.17289	.17010
65	.20987	.20624	.20273	.19931	.19598	.19275	.18961	.18656	.18358	.18069
66	.22213	.21840	.21478	.21125	.20783	.20449	.20125	.19809	.19501	.19202
67	.23508	.23125	.22753	.22390	.22037	.21694	.21360	.21034	.20716	.20407
68	.24868	.24476	.24094	.23722	.23359	.23006	.22662	.22327	.22000	.21681
69	.26291	.25889	.25498	.25117	.24745	.24383	.24030	.23685	.23349	.23020
70	.27773	.27364	.26964	.26574	.26194	.25823	.25461	.25107	.24762	.24425

Table S
Based on Life Table 2000CM
Single Life Remainder Factors
Applicable on or After May 1, 2009
Interest Rate

AGE	12.2%	12.4%	12.6%	12.8%	13.0%	13.2%	13.4%	13.6%	13.8%	14.0%
71	.29321	.28904	.28496	.28099	.27710	.27331	.26961	.26599	.26246	.25900
72	.30933	.30508	.30094	.29689	.29294	.28907	.28530	.28160	.27799	.27446
73	.32602	.32171	.31751	.31340	.30938	.30545	.30160	.29784	.29416	.29056
74	.34319	.33884	.33458	.33042	.32634	.32236	.31845	.31463	.31089	.30723
75	.36076	.35637	.35207	.34786	.34374	.33970	.33575	.33188	.32808	.32437
76	.37867	.37425	.36991	.36567	.36151	.35744	.35344	.34953	.34569	.34192
77	.39690	.39245	.38810	.38383	.37964	.37554	.37151	.36756	.36369	.35989
78	.41541	.41096	.40659	.40231	.39811	.39398	.38993	.38596	.38206	.37823
79	.43418	.42973	.42536	.42107	.41686	.41272	.40866	.40467	.40075	.39691
80	.45311	.44868	.44432	.44003	.43582	.43169	.42763	.42363	.41971	.41585
81	.47219	.46777	.46343	.45916	.45497	.45084	.44679	.44280	.43888	.43502
82	.49135	.48696	.48265	.47841	.47424	.47014	.46610	.46213	.45822	.45437
83	.51052	.50618	.50191	.49771	.49357	.48950	.48549	.48154	.47766	.47383
84	.52966	.52537	.52115	.51700	.51291	.50887	.50490	.50099	.49714	.49334
85	.54870	.54448	.54032	.53622	.53218	.52820	.52428	.52041	.51660	.51284
86	.56759	.56344	.55935	.55532	.55135	.54742	.54356	.53974	.53598	.53227

87	.58626	.58219	.57818	.57422	.57031	.56646	.56266	.55891	.55521	.55155
88	.60468	.60070	.59677	.59290	.58907	.58529	.58157	.57788	.57425	.57066
89	.62277	.61888	.61505	.61126	.60753	.60383	.60018	.59658	.59302	.58950
90	.64048	.63670	.63296	.62927	.62563	.62202	.61846	.61494	.61146	.60803
91	.65778	.65411	.65048	.64689	.64334	.63983	.63636	.63293	.62954	.62619
92	.67462	.67106	.66754	.66406	.66061	.65720	.65383	.65050	.64720	.64393
93	.69094	.68749	.68408	.68071	.67737	.67406	.67079	.66756	.66435	.66118
94	.70673	.70340	.70011	.69685	.69362	.69042	.68725	.68412	.68102	.67794
95	.72199	.71878	.71560	.71246	.70934	.70625	.70319	.70016	.69716	.69419
96	.73662	.73353	.73047	.72743	.72443	.72145	.71850	.71557	.71268	.70981
97	.75063	.74766	.74471	.74180	.73890	.73604	.73319	.73038	.72758	.72482
98	.76405	.76120	.75837	.75557	.75279	.75003	.74730	.74459	.74190	.73923
99	.77690	.77417	.77146	.76877	.76610	.76345	.76083	.75822	.75564	.75308
100	.78901	.78639	.78379	.78121	.77866	.77612	.77360	.77110	.76862	.76616
101	.80067	.79816	.79568	.79321	.79076	.78832	.78591	.78351	.78114	.77877
102	.81152	.80912	.80674	.80438	.80203	.79970	.79738	.79508	.79280	.79054
103	.82245	.82016	.81789	.81563	.81339	.81116	.80895	.80676	.80458	.80241
104	.83250	.83031	.82814	.82599	.82384	.82171	.81960	.81750	.81541	.81334
105	.84239	.84030	.83823	.83617	.83412	.83209	.83006	.82806	.82606	.82407
106	.85507	.85311	.85117	.84924	.84733	.84542	.84352	.84164	.83976	.83790
107	.86958	.86779	.86600	.86422	.86246	.86070	.85895	.85721	.85548	.85376
108	.89422	.89272	.89123	.88974	.88826	.88679	.88533	.88386	.88241	.88096
109	.94563	.94484	.94405	.94326	.94248	.94170	.94092	.94014	.93937	.93860

Table 2000CM

Age x	lx	Age x	lx	Age x	lx
0	100000	37	96921	74	66882
1	99305	38	96767	75	64561
2	99255	39	96600	76	62091
3	99222	40	96419	77	59476
4	99197	41	96223	78	56721
5	99176	42	96010	79	53833
6	99158	43	95782	80	50819
7	99140	44	95535	81	47694
8	99124	45	95268	82	44475
9	99110	46	94981	83	41181
10	99097	47	94670	84	37837
11	99085	48	94335	85	34471
12	99073	49	93975	86	31114
13	99057	50	93591	87	27799
14	99033	51	93180	88	24564
15	98998	52	92741	89	21443
16	98950	53	92270	90	18472
17	98891	54	91762	91	15685
18	98822	55	91211	92	13111
19	98745	56	90607	93	10773
20	98664	57	89947	94	8690
21	98577	58	89225	95	6871
22	98485	59	88441	96	5315
23	98390	60	87595	97	4016
24	98295	61	86681	98	2959
25	98202	62	85691	99	2122
26	98111	63	84620	100	1477
27	98022	64	83465	101	997
28	97934	65	82224	102	650
29	97844	66	80916	103	410
30	97750	67	79530	104	248
31	97652	68	78054	105	144
32	97549	69	76478	106	81
33	97441	70	74794	107	43
34	97324	71	73001	108	22
35	97199	72	71092	109	11
36	97065	73	69056	110	0

(e) Effective/applicability date. This section applies on or after May 1, 2009.

(f) Expiration date. This section expires on or before May 1, 2012.

T.D. 9448, 5/1/2009.

§ 20.2031-8 Valuation of certain life insurance and annuity contracts; valuation of shares in an open-end investment company.

(a) Valuation of certain life insurance and annuity contracts. *(1)* The value of a contract for the payment of an annuity, or an insurance policy on the life of a person other than the decedent, issued by a company regularly engaged in the selling of contracts of that character is established through the sale by that company of comparable contracts. An annuity payable under a combination annuity contract and life insurance policy on the decedent's life (e.g., a "retirement income" policy with death benefit) under which there was no insurance element at the time of the decedent's death (see paragraph (d) of § 20.2039-1) is treated like a contract for the payment of an annuity for purposes of this section.

(2) As valuation of an insurance policy through sale of comparable contracts is not readily ascertainable when, at the date of the decedent's death, the contract has been in force for some time and further premium payments are to be made, the value may be approximate by adding to the interpolated terminal reserve at the date of the decedent's death the proportionate part of the gross premium last paid before the date of the decedent's death which covers the period extending beyond that date. If, however, because of the unusual nature of the contract such an approximation is not reasonably close to the full value of the contract, this method may not be used.

(3) The application of this section may be illustrated by the following examples. In each case involving an insurance contract, it is assumed that there are no accrued dividends or outstanding indebtedness on the contract.

Example (1). X purchased from a life insurance company a joint and survivor annuity contract under the terms of which X was to receive payments of $1,200 annually for his life and, upon X's death, his wife was to receive payments of $1,200 annually for her life. Five years after such purchase, when his wife was 50 years of age, X died. The value of the annuity contract at the date of X's death is the amount which the company would charge for an annuity providing for the payment of $1,200 annually for the life of a female 50 years of age.

Example (2). Y died holding the incidents of ownership in a life insurance policy on the life of his wife. The policy was one on which no further payments were to be made to the company (e.g., a single premium policy or a paid-up policy). The value of the insurance policy at the date of Y's death is the amount which the company would charge for a single premium contract of the same specified amount on the life of a person of the age of the insured.

Example (3). Z died holding the incidents of ownership in a life insurance policy on the life of his wife. The policy was an ordinary life policy issued nine years and four months prior to Z's death and at a time when Z's wife was 35 years of age. The gross annual premium is $2,811 and the decedent died four months after the last premium due date. The value of the insurance policy at the date of Z's death is computed as follows:

Terminal reserve at end of tenth year	$14,601.00
Terminal reserve at end of ninth year	12,965.00
Increase	1,636.00
One-third of such increase (Z having died four months following the last preceding premium due date) is	545.33
Terminal reserve at end of ninth year	12,965.00
Interpolated terminal reserve at date of Z's death	13,510.33
Two-thirds of gross premium ⅔ × $2,811)	1,874.00
Value of the insurance policy	15,384.33

(b) Valuation of shares in an open-end investment company. *(1)* The fair market value of a share in an open-end investment company (commonly known as a "mutual fund") is the public redemption price of a share. In the absence of an affirmative showing of the public redemption price in effect at the time of death, the last public redemption price quoted by the company for the date of death shall be presumed to be the applicable redemption price. If the alternate valuation method under 2032 is elected, the last public redemption price quoted by the company for the alternate valuation date shall be the applicable redemption price. If there is no public redemption price quoted by the company for the applicable valuation date (e.g., the valuation date is a Saturday, Sunday, or holiday), the fair market value of the mutual fund share is the last public redemption price quoted by the company for the first day preceding the applicable valuation date for which there is a quotation. In any case where a dividend is declared on a share in an open-end investment company before the decedent's death but payable to shareholders of record on a date after his death and the share is quoted "ex-dividend" on the date of the decedent's death, the amount of the dividend is added to the ex-dividend quotation in determining the fair market value of the share as of the date of the decedent's death. As used in this paragraph, the term "open-end investment company" includes only a company which on the applicable valuation date was engaged in offering its shares to the public in the capacity of an open-end investment company.

(2) The provisions of this paragraph shall apply with respect to estates of decedents dying after August 16, 1954.

T.D. 6296, 6/23/58, amend T.D. 6680, 10/9/63, T.D. 7319, 7/22/74.

§ 20.2031-9 Valuation of other property.

The valuation of any property not specifically described in §§ 20.2031-2 to 20.2031-8 is made in accordance with the general principles set forth in § 20.2031-1. For example, a future interest in property not subject to valuation in accordance with the actuarial principles set forth in § 20.2031-7 is to be valued in accordance with the general principles set forth in § 20.2031-1.

T.D. 6296, 6/23/58.

§ 20.2032-1 Alternate valuation.

Caution: The Treasury has not yet amended Reg § 20.2032-1 to reflect changes made by P.L. 97-34, P.L. 94-455.

(a) In general. In general, section 2032 provides for the valuation of a decedent's gross estate at a date other than the date of the decedent's death. More specifically, if an executor elects the alternate valuation method under section 2032, the property included in the decedent's gross estate on the date of his death is valued as of whichever of the following dates is applicable:

(1) Any property distributed, sold, exchanged, or otherwise disposed of within 6 months (1 year, if the decedent died on or before December 31, 1970) after the decedent's death is valued as of the date on which it is first distributed, sold, exchanged, or otherwise disposed of;

(2) Any property not distributed, sold, exchanged, or otherwise disposed of within 6 months (1 year, if the decedent died on or before December 31, 1970) after the decedent's death is valued as of the date 6 months (1 year, if the decedent died on or before December 31, 1970) after the date of the decedent's death;

(3) Any property, interest, or estate which is affected by mere lapse of time is valued as of the date of the decedent's death, but adjusted for any difference in its value not due to mere lapse of time as of the date 6 months (1 year, if the decedent died on or before December 31, 1970) after the decedent's death, or as of the date of its distribution, sale, exchange, or other disposition, whichever date first occurs.

(b) Method and effect of election. *(1) In general.* The election to use the alternate valuation method is made on the return of tax imposed by section 2001. For purposes of this paragraph (b), the term return of tax imposed by section 2001 means the last estate tax return filed by the executor on or before the due date of the return (including extensions of time to file actually granted) or, if a timely return is not filed, the first estate tax return filed by the executor after the due date, provided the return is filed no later than 1 year after the due date (including extensions of time to file actually granted). Once the election is made, it is irrevocable, provided that an election may be revoked on a subsequent return filed on or before the due date of the return (including extensions of time to file actually granted). The election may be made only if it will decrease both the value of the gross estate and the sum (reduced by allowable credits) of the estate tax and the generation-skipping transfer tax payable by reason of the decedent's death with respect to the property includible in the decedent's gross estate. If the election is made, the alternate valuation method applies to all property included in the gross estate and cannot be applied to only a portion of the property.

(2) Protective election. If, based on the return of tax as filed, use of the alternate valuation method would not result in a decrease in both the value of the gross estate and the sum (reduced by allowable credits) of the estate tax and the generation-skipping transfer tax liability payable by reason of the decedent's death with respect to the property includible in the decedent's gross estate, a protective election may be made to use the alternate valuation method if it is subsequently determined that such a decrease would occur. A protective election is made on the return of tax imposed by section 2001. The protective election is irrevocable as of the due date of the return (including extensions of time actually granted). The protective election becomes effective on the date on which it is determined that use of the alternate valuation method would result in a decrease in both the value of the gross estate and in the sum (reduced by allowable credits) of the estate tax and generation-skipping transfer tax liability payable by reason of the decedent's death with respect to the property includible in the decedent's gross estate.

(3) Requests for extension of time to make the election. A request for an extension of time to make the election or protective election pursuant to §§ 301.9100-1 and 301.9100-3 of this chapter will not be granted unless the return of tax imposed by section 2001 is filed no later than 1 year after the due date of the return (including extensions of time actually granted).

(c) Meaning of "distributed, sold, exchanged, or otherwise disposed of." *(1)* The phrase "distributed, sold, exchanged, or otherwise disposed of" comprehends all possible ways by which property ceases to form a part of the gross estate. For example, money on hand at the date of the decedent's death which is thereafter used in the payment of funeral expenses, or which is thereafter invested, falls within the term "otherwise disposed of." The term also includes the surrender of a stock certificate for corporate assets in complete or partial liquidation of a corporation pursuant to section 331. The term does not, however, extend to transactions which are mere changes in form. Thus, it does not include a transfer of assets to a corporation in exchange for its stock in a transaction with respect to which no gain or loss would be recognizable for income tax purposes under section 351. Nor does it include an exchange of stock or securities in a corporation for stock or securities in the same corporation or another corporation in a transaction, such as a merger, recapitalization, reorganization or other transaction described in section 368(a) or 355, with respect to which no gain or loss is recognizable for income tax purposes under section 354 or 355.

(2) Property may be "distributed" either by the executor, or by a trustee of property included in the gross estate under sections 2035 through 2038, or section 2041. Property is considered as "distributed" upon the first to occur of the following:

(i) The entry of an order or decree of distribution, if the order or decree subsequently becomes final;

(ii) The segregation or separation of the property from the estate or trust so that it becomes unqualifiedly subject to the demand or disposition of the distributee; or

(iii) The actual paying over or delivery of the property to the distributee.

(3) Property may be "sold, exchanged, or otherwise disposed of" by: (i) The executor; (ii) a trustee or other donee to whom the decedent during his lifetime transferred property included in his gross estate under sections 2035 through 2038, or section 2041; (iii) an heir or devisee to whom title to property passes directly under local law; (iv) a surviving joint tenant or tenant by the entirety; or (v) any other person. If a binding contract for the sale, exchange, or other disposition of property is entered into, the property is considered as sold, exchanged, or otherwise disposed of on the effective date of the contract, unless the contract is not subsequently carried out substantially in accordance with its terms. The effective date of a contract is normally the date it is entered into (and not the date it is consummated, or the date legal title to the property passes) unless the contract specifies a different effective date.

(d) "Included property" and "excluded property". If the executor elects the alternate valuation method under section 2032, all property interests existing at the date of decedent's death which form a part of his gross estate as determined under sections 2033 through 2044 are valued in accordance with the provisions of this section. Such property interests are referred to in this section as "included property". Furthermore, such property interests remain "included property" for the purpose of valuing the gross estate under the alternate valuation method even though they change in form during the alternate valuation period by being actually received, or disposed of, in whole or in part, by the estate. On the other hand, property earned or accrued (whether received or not) after the date of the decedent's death and during the alternate valuation period with respect to any property interest existing at the date of the decedent's death, which does not represent a form of "included property" itself or the receipt of "included property" is excluded in valuing the gross estate under the alternate valuation method. Such property is referred to in this section as "excluded property". Illustrations of "included property" and "excluded property" are contained in the subparagraphs (1) to (4) of this paragraph:

(1) Interest-bearing obligations. Interest-bearing obligations, such as bonds or notes, may comprise two elements of "included property" at the date of the decedent's death, namely, (i) the principal of the obligation itself, and (ii) interest accrued to the date of death. Each of these elements is to be separately valued as of the applicable valuation date. Interest accrued after the date of death and before the subsequent valuation date constitutes "excluded property". However, any part payment of principal made between the date of death and the subsequent valuation date, or any advance payment of interest for a period after the subsequent valuation date made during the alternate valuation period which has the effect of reducing the value of the principal obligation as of the subsequent valuation date, will be included in the gross estate, and valued as of the date of such payment.

(2) Leased property. The principles set forth in subparagraph (1) of this paragraph with respect to interest-bearing obligations also apply to leased realty or personalty which is included in the gross estate and with respect to which an obligation to pay rent has been reserved. Both the realty or personalty itself and the rents accrued to the date of death constitute "included property", and each is to be separately valued as of the applicable valuation date. Any rent accrued after the date of death and before the subsequent valuation date is "excluded property". Similarly, the principle applicable with respect to interest paid in advance is equally applicable with respect to advance payments of rent.

(3) Noninterest-bearing obligations. In the case of noninterest-bearing obligations sold at a discount, such as savings bonds, the principal obligation and the discount amortized to the date of death are property interests existing at the date of death and constitute "included property". The obligation itself is to be valued at the subsequent valuation date without regard to any further increase in value due to amortized discount. The additional discount amortized after death and during the alternate valuation period is the equivalent of interest accruing during that period and is, therefore, not to be included in the gross estate under the alternate valuation method.

(4) Stock of a corporation. Shares of stock in a corporation and dividends declared to stockholders of record on or before the date of the decedent's death and not collected at the date of death constitute "included property" of the estate. On the other hand, ordinary dividends out of earnings and profits (whether in cash, shares of the corporation, or other property) declared to stockholders of record after the date of the decedent's death are "excluded property" and are not to be valued under the alternate valuation method. If, however, dividends are declared to stockholders of record after the date of the decedent's death with the effect that the shares of stock at the subsequent valuation date do not reasonably represent the same "included property" of the gross estate as existed at the date of the decedent's death, the dividends are "included property", except to the extent that they are out of earnings of the corporation after the date of the decedent's death. For example, if a corporation makes a distribution in partial liquidation to stockholders of record during the alternate valuation period which is not accompanied by a surrender of a stock certificate for cancellation, the amount of the distribution received on stock included in the gross estate is itself "included property", except to the extent that the distribution was out of earnings and profits since the date of the decedent's death. Similarly, if a corporation, in which the decedent owned a substantial interest and which possessed at the date of the decedent's death accumulated earnings and profits equal to its paid-in capital, distributed all of its accumulated earnings and profits as a cash dividend to shareholders of record during the alternate valuation period, the amount of the dividends received on stock includible in the gross estate will be included in the gross estate under the alternate valuation method. Likewise, a stock dividend distributed under such circumstances is "included property".

(e) Illustrations of "included property" and "excluded property". The application of paragraph (d) of this section may be further illustrated by the following example in which it is assumed that the decedent died on January 1, 1955:

Description	Subsequent valuation date	Alternate value	Value at date of death
Bond, par value $1,000 bearing interest at 4 percent payable quarterly on Feb. 1, May 1, Aug. 1, and Nov. 1. Bond distributed to legatee on Mar. 1, 1955	Mar. 1, 1955	$ 1,000.00	$ 1,000.00
Interest coupon of $10 attached to bond and not cashed at date of death although due and payable Nov. 1, 1954. Cashed by executor on Feb. 1, 1955	Feb. 1, 1955	10.00	10.00
Interest accrued from Nov. 1, 1954, to Jan. 1, 1955, collected on Feb. 1, 1955	Feb. 1, 1955	6.67	6.67
Real estate, not disposed of within year following death. Rent of $300 due at the end of each quarter, Feb. 1, May 1, Aug. 1, and Nov. 1	Jan. 1, 1956	11,000.00	12,000.00
Rent due for quarter ending Nov. 1, 1954, but not collected until Feb. 1, 1955	Feb. 1, 1955	300.00	300.00
Rent accrued for November and December 1954, collected on Feb. 1, 1955	Feb. 1, 1955	200.00	200.00
Common stock, X Corporation, 500 shares, not disposed of within year following decedent's death	Jan. 1, 1956	47,500.00	50,000.00
Dividend of $2 per share declared Dec. 10, 1954, and paid on Jan. 10, 1955, to holders of record on Dec. 30, 1954	Jan. 10, 1955	1,000.00	1,000.00

(f) Mere lapse of time. In order to eliminate changes in value due only to mere lapse of time, section 2032(a)(3) provides that any interest or estate "affected by mere lapse of time" is included in a decedent's gross estate under the alternate valuation method at its value as of the date of the decedent's death, but with adjustment for any difference in its value as of the subsequent valuation date not due to mere lapse of time. Properties, interests, or estates which are "affected by mere lapse of time" include patents, estates for the life of a person other than the decedent, remainders, reversions, and other like properties, interests, or estates. The phrase "affected by mere lapse of time" has no reference to obligations for the payment of money, whether or not interest-bearing, the value of which changes with the passing of time. However, such an obligation, like any other property, may become affected by lapse of time when made the subject of a bequest or transfer which itself is creative of an interest or estate so affected. The application of this paragraph is illustrated in subparagraphs (1) and (2) of this paragraph:

(1) [Reserved]. Further guidance, see § 20.2032-1T(f)(1).

(2) Patents. To illustrate the alternate valuation of a patent, assume that the decedent owned a patent which, on the date of the decedent's death, had an unexpired term of ten years and a value of $78,000. Six months after the date of the decedent's death, the patent was sold, because of lapse of time and other causes, for $60,000. The alternate value thereof would be obtained by dividing $60,000 by 0.95 (ratio of the remaining life of the patent at the alternate date to the remaining life of the patent at the date of the decedent's death), and would, therefore, be $63,157.89.

(g) Effect of election on deductions. If the executor elects the alternate valuation method under section 2032, any deduction for administration expenses under section 2053(b) (pertaining to property not subject to claims) or losses under section 2054 (or section 2106(a)(1), relating to estates of nonresidents not citizens) is allowed only to the extent that it is not otherwise in effect allowed in determining the value of the gross estate. Furthermore, the amount of any charitable deduction under section 2055 (or section 2106(a)(2), relating to the estates of nonresidents not citizens) or the amount of any marital deduction under section 2056 is determined by the value of the property with respect to which the deduction is allowed as of the date of the decedent's death, adjusted, however, for any difference in its value as of the date 6 months (1 year, if the decedent died on or before December 31, 1970) after death, or as of the date of its distribution, sale, exchange, or other disposition, whichever first occurs. However, no such adjustment may take into account any difference in value due to lapse of time or to the occurrence or nonoccurrence of a contingency.

(h) Effective date. Paragraph (b) of this section is applicable to decedents dying on or after January 4, 2005. However, pursuant to section 7805(b)(7), taxpayers may elect to apply paragraph (b) of this section retroactively if the period of limitations for filing a claim for a credit or refund of Federal estate or generation-skipping transfer tax under section 6511 has not expired.

T.D. 6296, 6/23/58, amend T.D. 7238, 12/28/72, T.D. 7955, 5/11/84, T.D. 8540, 6/9/94, T.D. 8819, 4/29/99, T.D. 9172, 1/3/2005, T.D. 9448, 5/1/2009.

PAR. 8. Section 20.2032-1 is amended by revising paragraphs (f)(1) and (h) to read as follows:

Proposed § 20.2032-1 Alternate valuation. [*For Preamble, see ¶ 153,105*]

* * * * *

(f) * * *

(1) [The text of this proposed paragraph (f)(1) is the same as the text of § 20.2032-1T(f)(1) published elsewhere in this issue of the Federal Register]. [*See T.D. 9448, 05/07/2009, 74 Fed. Reg. 87.*]

* * * * *

(h) [The text of this proposed paragraph (h) is the same as the text of § 20.2032-1T(h) published elsewhere in this issue of the Federal Register]. [*See T.D. 9448, 05/07/2009, 74 Fed. Reg. 87.*]

PAR. 2. Section 20.2032-1 is amended as follows:

1. Paragraph (f)(1) is redesignated as paragraph (f)(2)(i).

2. Paragraph (f)(2) is redesignated as paragraph (f)(2)(ii).

3. Paragraph (f) introductory text is redesignated as paragraph (f)(2) introductory text and the last sentence is revised.

4. New paragraphs (f)(1) and (f)(3) are added.

5. The heading for paragraph (h) is revised and four sentences are added at the end of the paragraph.

The additions and revisions read as follows.

Proposed § 20.2032-1 Alternate valuation. [*For Preamble, see ¶ 152,993*]

* * * * *

(f) Post-death market conditions and other post-death events. *(1) In general.* The election to use the alternate valuation method under section 2032 permits the property included in the gross estate to be valued as of the alternate valuation date to the extent that the change in value during the alternate valuation period is the result of market conditions. The term market conditions is defined as events outside of the control of the decedent (or the decedent's executor or trustee) or other person whose property is being valued that affect the fair market value of the property being valued. Changes in value due to mere lapse of time or to other post-death events other than market conditions will be ignored in determining the value of decedent's gross estate under the alternate valuation method.

(2) Mere lapse of time. * * * The application of this paragraph (f)(2) is illustrated in paragraphs (f)(2)(i) and (f)(2)(ii) of this section:

* * * * *

(3) Post-death events. (i) In general. In order to eliminate changes in value due to post-death events other than market conditions, any interest or estate affected by post-death events other than market conditions is included in a decedent's gross estate under the alternate valuation method at its value as of the date of the decedent's death, with adjustment for any change in value that is due to market conditions. The term post-death events includes, but is not limited to, a reorganization of an entity (for example, corporation, partnership, or limited liability company) in which the estate holds an interest, a distribution of cash or other property to the estate from such entity, or one or more distributions by the estate of a fractional interest in such entity.

(ii) Examples. The following examples illustrate the application of this paragraph (f)(3). In each example, decedent's (D's) estate elects to value D's gross estate under the alternate valuation method, so that the valuation date of the property included in D's gross estate as of D's date of death is either the date the property is distributed, sold, exchanged, or disposed of under section 2032(a)(1) (the date of distribution (distribution date)) or the date that is 6 months after the date of the decedent's death under section 2032(a)(2) (the six month alternate valuation date (AVD)).

Example (1). At D's death, D owned common stock in Corporation, a closely-held subchapter C corporation. At that time, the common stock was not subject to transfer restrictions. D's stock was valued at $50X at the date of death. Two months after D's death, D's estate participated in a tax-free reorganization of Corporation that qualified under section 368(a) with respect to which no gain or loss was recognized for income tax purposes under section 354 or 355. Pursuant to the reorganization, D's estate opted to exchange its stock for stock subject to transfer restrictions. Although the value of the stock did not change during the alternate valuation period, discounts for lack of marketability and lack of control (totaling $20X) were applied in determining the value of the stock held by D's estate on the AVD, and D's estate reported the value of the stock on the AVD as $30X. Because the claimed reduction in value is not attributable to market conditions, the discounts may not be taken into account in determining the value of the stock on the AVD. Accordingly, the value on the AVD is $50X.

Example (2). The facts are the same as in Example 1 except that the value of the stock declined from $50X to $40X during the alternate valuation period because of changes in market conditions during that period. D's estate may report the value of the stock as $40X on the AVD. As in Example 1, however, no discounts resulting from the reorganization are allowed in computing the value on the AVD.

Example (3). At D's death, D owned property valued at $100X. Two months after D's death, the executor of D's estate and other family members formed four limited partnerships. The estate contributed the estate's property to the partnerships in exchange for a 25% interest in each partnership. Discounts for lack of marketability and lack of control (totaling $25X) were applied in determining the value of the estate's partnership interests, and the estate reported $75X as the total value of the estate's partnership interests on the AVD. Because the reduction in value is not attributable to market conditions, the discounts for lack of marketability and control may not be taken into account in determining the value of the partnership interests on the AVD. The result would be the same if the limited partnerships were formed prior to D's death, and the estate transferred property into the partnerships after D's death but prior to the AVD.

Example (4). At D's death, D owned 100% of the units of a limited liability company (LLC). The executor elected the alternative valuation method. During the 6 months following D's death and in accordance with D's will, the executor made 6 distributions, each to a different residuary legatee on a different date and each of a 10% interest in the LLC. Pursuant to section 2032(a)(1), each distribution is valued on the distribution date. On the AVD, the estate held 40% of the units in the LLC. Pursuant to section 2032(a)(2), the 40% is valued on the AVD. In valuing the 10% interests distributed and the 40% interest held on the AVD, discounts for lack of control and lack of marketability were applied. The reduction in value of the units is not attributable to market conditions. Accordingly, the discounts for lack of marketability and control may not be taken into account in determining the value of the units distributed or held by the estate. The value of each 10% distribution is determined by taking 10% of the value on the distribution date of the units (100%) owned by the estate at D's death. The value of the units held by the estate on the AVD is determined by taking 40% of the value on the AVD of all of the units (100%) owned by the estate at D's death. If because of market conditions, the units had declined in value as of each distribution date or as of the AVD, D's estate would take such reduction in value into account.

Example (5). D died owning 100% of Blackacre. D's will directs that Blackacre be divided between two trusts, 70% to Trust A for the benefit of S, D's surviving spouse, and 30% to Trust B for the benefit of C, D's surviving child. The executor of D's estate distributed a 70% interest in Blackacre to Trust A three months after D's death, and distributed a 30% interest in Blackacre to Trust B four months after D's death. On the estate tax return, the executor elected to value the estate's property under the alternate valuation method under section 2032. There was no change in the value of Blackacre during the four-month period following D's death. The 70% interest in Blackacre is to be valued as of the distribution date to Trust A, and that value is determined by taking 70% of the value of all (100%) of Blackacre as of the distribution date. The 30% interest in Blackacre is to be valued as of the distribution date to Trust B, and that value is determined by taking 30% of the value of all (100%) of Blackacre as of the distribution date. If, however, because of market conditions such as a decline in the real estate market, Blackacre's value had declined by 10% between D's date of death and the distribution date of the 30% interest, the value of the 30% interest would be determined by ascertaining 30% of the value of all (100%) of Blackacre as of the distribution date, which would equal 30% of 90% of the date of death value of Blackacre.

* * * * *

(h) Effective/applicability date. * * * The fourth sentence of paragraph (f)(2)(i) of this section is applicable to decedents dying after May 1, 1999, subject to transition rules for certain incapacitated individuals. The fifth sentence of paragraph (f)(2)(i) of this section is applicable to decedents dying after November 30, 1983, subject to transition rules for certain incapacitated individuals. The first, second, and third sentences of paragraph (f)(2)(i), paragraph (f)(2)(ii), and all but the last sentence in paragraph (f)(2) of this section are applicable to decedents dying after August 16, 1954. When adopted as final regulations, the rules contained in paragraphs (f)(1), (f)(3), and the last sentence of paragraph (f)(2) of this section, will be made applicable to estates of decedents dying on or after April 25, 2008.

* * * * *

§ 20.2032-1T Alternate valuation.

(a) through (e) [Reserved]. For further guidance, see § 20.2032-1(a) through (e).

(f) [Reserved]. For further guidance, see § 20.2032-1(f).

(1) Life estates, remainders, and similar interests. The values of life estates, remainders, and similar interests are to be obtained by applying the methods prescribed in § 20.2031-7, using (i) the age of each person, the duration of whose life may affect the value of the interest, as of the date of the decedent's death, and (ii) the value of the property as of the alternate valuation date. For example, assume that the decedent, or the decedent's estate, was entitled to receive certain property worth $50,000 upon the death of A, who was entitled to the income for life. At the time of the decedent's death, on or after May 1, 2009, A was 47 years and 5 months old. In the month in which the decedent died, the section 7520 rate was 6.2 percent. The value of the decedent's remainder interest at the date of the decedent's death would, as illustrated in Example 1 of § 20.2031-7T(d)(5), be $9,336.00 ($50,000 x .18672). If, because of economic conditions, the property declined in value and was worth only

$40,000 on the date that was 6 months after the date of the decedent's death, the value of the remainder interest would be $7,468.80 ($40,000 x .18672), even though A would be 48 years old on the alternate valuation date.

(2) through (g) [Reserved]. For further guidance, see § 20.2032-1(f)(2) through (g).

(h) Effective/applicability date. Paragraph (f)(1) applies on or after May 1, 2009.

(i) Expiration date. Paragraph (f)(1) expires on or before May 1, 2012.

T.D. 9448, 5/1/2009.

§ 22.0 Certain elections under the Economic Recovery Tax Act of 1981.

(a) Election of special rules for woodlands. *(1) In general.* This paragraph applies to the election of special rules for woodlands under section 2032A(e)(13) of the Code, as added by section 421(h) of the Economic Recovery Tax Act of 1981. The executor shall make this election for an estate by attaching to the estate tax return a statement that—

(i) Contains the decedent's name and taxpayer identification number as they appear on the estate tax return,

(ii) Identifies the election as an election under section 2032A(e)(13) of the Code,

(iii) Specifies the property with respect to which the election is made, and

(iv) Provides all information necessary to show that the executor is entitled to make the election.

(2) Additional information required. If later regulations issued under section 2032A(e)(13) require the executor to furnish information in addition to that required under paragraph (a)(1) of this section and an office of the Internal Revenue Service requests the executor to furnish the additional information, the executor shall furnish the additional information in a statement filed with that office of the Internal Revenue Service within 60 days after the request is made. The statement shall also contain the information required by paragraph (a)(1)(i), (ii), and (iii) of this section. If the additional information is not provided within 60 days after the request is made, the election may, at the discretion of the Commissioner, be held invalid.

(b) Election of special use valuation for qualified real property. This paragraph applies to the election of special use valuation for qualified real property under section 2032A(d)(1) of the Code, as amended by section 421(j)(3) of the Economic Recovery Tax Act of 1981. This election shall be made in the manner prescribed in § 20.2032A-8(a)(3), except that the election shall be valid even if the estate tax return is not timely filed.

(c) Elections irrevocable. Elections to which this section applies may not be revoked.

(d) Effective date. The elections described in this section are available with respect to the estates of decedents dying after 1981.

T.D. 7793, 11/2/81.

§ 20.2032A-3 Material participation requirements for valuation of certain farm and closely-held business real property.

Caution: The Treasury has not yet amended Reg § 20.2032A-3 to reflect changes made by P.L. 97-34.

(a) In general. Under section 2032A, an executor may, for estate tax purposes, make a special election concerning valuation of qualified real property (as defined in section 2032A(b)) used as a farm for farming purposes or in another trade or business. If this election is made, the property will be valued on the basis of its value for its qualified use in farming or the other trade or business, rather than its fair market value determined on the basis of highest and best use (irrespective of whether its highest and best use is the use in farming or other business). For the special valuation rules of section 2032A to apply, the deceased owner and/or a member of the owner's family (as defined in section 2032A(e)(2)) must materially participate in the operation of the farm or other business. Whether the required material participation occurs is a factual determination, and the types of activities and financial risks which will support such a finding will vary with the mode of ownership of both the property itself and of any business in which it is used. Passively collecting rents, salaries, draws, dividends, or other income from the farm or other business is not sufficient for material participation, nor is merely advancing capital and reviewing a crop plan or other business proposal and financial reports each season or business year.

(b) Types of qualified property. *(1) In general.* Real property valued under section 2032A must pass from the decendent to a qualified heir or be acquired from the decedent by a qualified heir. The real property may be owned directly or may be owned indirectly through ownership of an interest in a corporation, a partnership, or a trust. Where the ownership is indirect, however, the decedent's interest in the business must, in addition to meeting the tests for qualification under section 2032A, qualify under the tests of section 6166(b)(1) as an interest in a closely-held business on the date of the decedent's death and for sufficient other time (combined with periods of direct ownership) to equal at least 5 years of the 8 year period preceding the death. All specially valued property must be used in a trade or business. Directly owned real property that is leased by a decedent to a separate closely held business is considered to be qualified real property, but only if the separate business qualifies as a closely held business under section 6166(b)(1) with respect to the decedent on the date of his or her death and for sufficient other time (combined with periods during which the property was operated as a proprietorship) to equal at least 5 years of the 8 year period preceding the death. For example, real property owned by the decedent and leased to a farming corporation or partnership owned and operated entirely by the decedent and fewer than 15 members of the decedent's family is eligible for special use valuation. Under section 2032A, the term trade or business applies only to an active business such as a manufacturing, mercantile, or service enterprise, or to the raising of agricultural or horticultural commodities, as distinguished from passive investment activities. The mere passive rental of property to a party other than a member of the decedent's family will not qualify. The decedent or a member of the decedent's family must own an equity interest in the farm operation. A trade or business is not necessarily present even though an office and regular hours are maintained for management of income producing assets, as the term "business" is not as broad under section 2032A as under section 162. Additionally, no trade or business is present in the case of activities not engaged in for profit. See section 183.

(2) Structures and other real property improvements. Qualified real property includes residential buildings and other structures and real property improvements occupied or used

on a regular basis by the owner or lessee of real property (or by employees of the owner or lessee) for the purpose of operating the farm or other closely held business. A farm residence occupied by the decedent owner of the specially valued property is considered to be occupied for the purpose of operating the farm even though a family member (not the decedent) was the person materially participating in the operation of the farm as required under section 2032A(b)(1)(C).

(c) Period material participation must last. The required participation must last—

(1) For periods totalling 5 years or more during the 8 years immediately preceding the date of the decedent's death; and

(2) For periods totalling 5 years or more during any 8 year period ending after the date of the decedent's death (up to a maximum of 15 years after decedent's death, when the additional estate tax provisions of section 2032A(c) cease to apply).

In determining whether the material participation requirement is satisfied, no exception is made for periods during which real property is held by the decedent's estate. Additionally, contemporaneous material participation by 2 or more family members during a period totalling a year will not result in that year being counted as 2 or more years for purposes of satisfying the requirements of this paragraph (c). Death of a qualified heir (as defined in section 2032A(e)(1)) before the requisite time has passed ends any material participation requirement for that heir's portion of the property as to the original decedent's estate if the heir received a separate, joint or other undivided property interest from the decedent. If qualified heirs receive successive interests in specially valued property (e.g., life estate and remainder interests) from the decedent, the material participation requirement does not end with respect to any part of the property until the death of the last qualified heir (or, if earlier, the expiration of 15 years from the date of the decedent's death). The requirements of section 2032A will fully apply to an heir's estate if an election under this section is made for the same property by the heir's executor. In general, to determine whether the required participation has occurred, brief periods (e.g., periods of 30 days or less) during which there was no material participation may be disregarded. This is so only if these periods were both preceded and followed by substantial periods (e.g., periods of more than 120 days) in which there was uninterrupted material participation. See paragraph (e)(1) of this section which provides a special rule for periods when little or no activity is necessary to manage fully a farm.

(d) Period property must be owned by decedent and family members. Only real property which is actually owned by any combination of the decedent, members of the decedent's family, and qualified closely held businesses for periods totalling at least 5 of the 8 years preceding the date of decedent's death may be valued under section 2032A. For example, replacement property acquired in like-kind exchange under section 1031 is considered to be owned only from the date on which the replacement property is actually acquired. On the other hand, replacement property acquired as a result of an involuntary conversion in a transfer that would meet the requirements of section 2032A(h) if it occurred after the date of the decedent's death is considered to have been owned from the date in which the involuntarily converted property was acquired. Property transferred from a proprietorship to a corporation or a partnership during the 8-year period ending on the date of the decedent's death is considered to be continuously owned to the extent of the decedent's equity interest in the corporation or partnership if, (1) the transfer meets the requirements of section 351 or 721, respectively, and (2) the decedent's interest in the corporation or partnership meets the requirements for indirectly held property contained in paragraph (b)(1) of this section. Likewise, property transferred to a trust is considered to be continuously owned if the beneficial ownership of the trust property is such that the requirements of section 6166(b)(1)(C) would be so satisfied if the property were owned by a corporation and all beneficiaries having vested interests in the trust were shareholders in the corporation. Any periods following the transfer during which the interest in the corporation, partnership, or trust does not meet the requirements of section 6166(b)(1) may not be counted for purposes of satisfying the ownership requirements of this paragraph (d).

(e) Required activities. *(1) In general.* Actual employment of the decedent (or of a member of the decedent's family) on a substantially full-time basis (35 hours a week or more) or to any lesser extent necessary personally to manage fully the farm or business in which the real property to be valued under section 2032A is used constitutes material participation. For example, many farming operations require only seasonal activity. Material participation is present as long as all necessary functions are performed even though little or no actual activity occurs during nonproducing seasons. In the absence of this direct involvement in the farm or other business, the activities of either the decedent or family members must meet the standards prescribed in this paragraph and those prescribed in the regulations issued under section 1402(a)(1). Therefore, if the participant (or participants) is self-employed with respect to the farm or other trade or business, his or her income from the farm or other business must be earned income for purposes of the tax on self-employment income before the participant is considered to be materially participating under section 2032A. Payment of the self-employment tax is not conclusive as to the presence of material participation. If no self-employment taxes have been paid, however, material participation is presumed not to have occurred unless the executor demonstrates to the satisfaction of the Internal Revenue Service that material participation did in fact occur and informs the Service of the reason no such tax was paid. In addition, all such taxes (including interest and penalties) determined to be due must be paid. In determining whether the material participation requirement is satisfied, the activities of each participant are viewed separately from the activities of all other participants, and at any given time, the activities of at least one participant must be material. If the involvement is less than full-time, it must be pursuant to an arrangement providing for actual participation in the production or management of production where the land is used by any nonfamily member, or any trust or business entity, in farming or another business. The arrangement may be oral or written, but must be formalized in some manner capable of proof. Activities not contemplated by the arrangement will not support a finding of material participation under section 2032A, and activities of any agent or employee other than a family member may not be considered in determining the presence of material participation. Activities of family members are considered only if the family relationship existed at the time the activities occurred.

(2) Factors considered. No single factor is determinative of the presence of material participation, but physical work and participation in management decisions are the principal

factors to be considered. As a minimum, the decedent and/or a family member must regularly advise or consult with the other managing party on the operation of the business. While they need not make all final management decisions alone, the decedent and/or family members must participate in making a substantial number of these decisions. Additionally, production activities on the land should be inspected regularly by the family participant, and funds should be advanced and financial responsibility assumed for a substantial portion of the expense involved in the operation of the farm or other business in which the real property is used. In the case of a farm, the furnishing by the owner or other family members of a substantial portion of the machinery, implements, and livestock used in the production activities is an important factor to consider in finding material participation. With farms, hotels, or apartment buildings, the operation of which qualifies as a trade or business, the participating decedent or heir's maintaining his or her principal place of residence on the premises is a factor to consider in determining whether the overall participation is material. Retention of a professional farm manager will not by itself prevent satisfaction of the material participation requirement by the decedent and family members. However, the decedent and/or a family member must personally materially participate under the terms of arrangement with the professional farm manager to satisfy this requirement.

(f) Special rules for corporations, partnerships, and trusts. *(1) Required arrangement.* With indirectly owned property as with property that is directly owned, there must be an arrangement calling for material participation in the business by the decedent owner or a family member. Where the real property is indirectly owned, however, even full-time involvement must be pursuant to an arrangement between the entity and the decedent or family member specifying the services to be performed. Holding an office in which certain material functions are inherent may constitute the necessary arrangement for material participation. Where property is owned by a trust, the arrangement will generally be found in one or more of four situations. First, the arrangement may result from appointment as a trustee. Second, the arrangement may result from an employer-employee relationship in which the participant is employed by a qualified closely held business owned by the trust in a position requiring his or her material participation in its activities. Third, the participants may enter into a contract with the trustees to manage, or take part in managing, the real property for the trust. Fourth, where the trust agreement expressly grants the management rights to the beneficial owner, that grant is sufficient to constitute the arrangement required under this section.

(2) Required activities. The same participation standards apply under section 2032A where property is owned by a qualified closely held business as where the property is directly owned. In the case of a corporation, a partnership, or a trust where the participating decedent and/or family members are employees and thereby not subject to self-employment income taxes, they are to be viewed as if they were self-employed, and their activities must be activities that would subject them to self-employment income taxes were they so. Where property is owned by a corporation, a partnership or a trust, participation in the management and operation of the real property itself as a component of the closely held business is the determinative factor. Nominally holding positions as a corporate officer or director and receiving a salary therefrom or merely being listed as a partner and sharing in profits and losses will not alone support a finding of material participation. This is so even though, as partners, the participants pay self-employment income taxes on their distributive shares of partnership earnings under § 1.1402(a)-2. Further, it is especially true for corporate directors in states where the board of directors need not be an actively functioning entity or need only act informally. Corporate offices held by an owner are, however, factors to be considered with all other relevant facts in judging the degree of participation. When real property is directly owned and is leased to a corporation or partnership in which the decedent owns an interest which qualified as an interest in a trade or business within the meaning of section 6166(b)(1), the presence of material participation is determined by looking at the activities of the participant with regard to the property in whatever capacity rendered. During any periods when qualified real property is held by an estate, material participation is to be determined in the same manner as if the property were owned by a trust.

(g) Examples. The rules for determining material participation may be illustrated by the following examples. Additional illustrations may be found in examples (1) through (6) in § 1.1402(a)-4.

Example (1). A, the decedent, actively operated his 100-acre farm on a full-time basis for 20 years. He then leased it to B for the 10 years immediately preceding his death. By the terms of the lease, A was to consult with B on where crops were to be planted, to supervise marketing of the crop, and to share equally with B in expenses and earnings. A was present on the farm each spring for consultation; however, once planting was completed, he left for his retirement cottage where he remained until late summer, at which time he returned to the farm to supervise the marketing operation. A at all times maintained the farm home in which he had lived for the time he had owned the farm and lived there when at the farm. In light of his activities, assumption of risks, and valuable knowledge of proper techniques for the particular land gained over 20 years of full-time farming on the land involved, A is deemed to have materially participated in the farming business.

Example (2). D is the 70-year old widow of farmer C. She lives on a farm for which special valuation has been elected and has lived there for 20 years. D leases the land to E under an arrangement calling for her participation in the operation of the farm. D annually raises a vegetable garden, chickens, and hogs. She also inspects the tobacco fields (which produce approximately 50 percent of farm income) weekly and informs E if she finds any work that needs to be done. D and E share expenses and income equally. Other decisions such as what fields to plant and when to plant and harvest crops are left to E, but D does occasionally make suggestions. During the harvest season, D prepares and serves meals for all temporary farm help. D is deemed to participate materially in the farm operations based on her farm residence and her involvement with the main money crop.

Example (3). Assume that D in example (2) moved to a nursing home 1 year after her husband's death. E completely operated the farm for her for 6 years following her move. If E is not a member of D's family, material participation ceases when D moves; however, if E is a member of D's family, E's material participation will prevent disqualification even if D owns the property. Further, upon D's death, the section 2032A valuation could be elected for her estate if E were a member of her family and the other requirements of section 2032A were satisfied.

Example (4). F, a qualified heir, owned a specially valued farm. He contracted with G to manage the farm for him as F, a lawyer, lived and worked 15 miles away in a nearby town. F supplied all machinery and equipment and assumed financial responsibility for the expenses of the farm operation. The contract specified that G was to submit a crop plan and a list of expenses and earnings for F's approval. It also called for F to inspect the farm regularly and to approve all expenditures over $100. In practice, F visited the farm weekly during the growing season to inspect and discuss operations. He actively participated in making important management decisions such as what fields to plant or pasture and how to utilize the subsidy program. F is deemed to have materially participated in the farm operation as his personal involvement amounted to more than managing an investment. Had F not regularly inspected the farm and participated in management decisions, however, he would not be considered to be materially participating. This would be true even though F did assume financial responsibility for the operation and did review annual crop plans.

Example (5). Decedent I owned 90 percent of all outstanding stock of X Corporation, a qualified closely-held business which owns real property to be specially valued. I held no formal position in the corporation and there was no arrangement for him to participate in daily business operations. I regularly spent several hours each day at the corporate offices and made decisions on many routine matters. I is not deemed to have materially participated in the X Corporation despite his activity because there was no arrangement requiring him to act in the manner in which he did.

Example (6). Decedent J was a senior partner in the law firm of X, Y, and Z, which is a qualified closely held business owning the building in which its offices are located. J ceased to practice law actively 5 years before his death in 1977; however, he remained a full partner and annually received a share of firm profits. J is not deemed to have materially participated under section 2032A even though he still may have reported his distributive share of partnership income for self-employment income tax purposes if the payments were not made pursuant to any retirement agreement. This is so because J does not meet the requirement of actual personal material participation.

Example (7). K, the decedent, owned a tree farm. He contracted with L, a professional forester, to manage the property for him as K, a doctor, lived and worked in a town 50 miles away. The activities of L are not considered in determining whether K materially participated in the tree farm operation. During the 5 years preceding K's death, there was no need for frequent inspections of the property or consultation concerning it, inasmuch as most of the land had been reforested and the trees were in the beginning stages of their growing cycle. However, once every year, L submitted for K's approval a proposed plan for the management of the property over the next year. K actively participated in making important management decisions, such as where and whether a pre-commercial thinning should be conducted, whether the timber was adequately protected from fire and disease, whether fire lines needed to be plowed around the new trees, and whether boundary lines were properly maintained around the property. K inspected the property at least twice every year and assumed financial responsibility for the expenses of the tree farm. K also reported his income from the tree farm as earned income for purposes of the tax on self-employment income. Over a period of several years, K had harvested and marketed timber from certain tracts of the tree farm and had supervised replanting of the areas where trees were removed. K's history of harvesting, marketing, and replanting of trees showed him to be in the business of tree farming rather than merely passively investing in timber land. If the history of K's tree farm did not show such an active business operation, however, the tree farm would not qualify for special use valuation. In light of all these facts, K is deemed to have materially participated in the farm as his personal involvement amounted to more than managing an investment.

Example (8). Decedent M died on January 1, 1978, owning a farm for which special use valuation under section 2032A has been elected. M owned the farm real property for 15 years before his death. During the 4 years preceding M's death (January 1, 1974 through December 31, 1977), the farm was rented to N, a non-family member, and neither M nor any member of his family materially participated in the farming operation. From January 1, 1970, until December 31, 1973, both M and his daughter, O, materially participated in the farming operation. The material participation requirement of section 2032A(b)(1)(C)(ii) is not satisfied because material participation did not occur for periods aggregating at least 5 different years of the 8 years preceding M's death.

T.D. 7710, 7/28/80, amend T.D. 7786, 8/25/81.

§ 20.2032A-4 Method of valuing farm real property.

Caution: The Treasury has not yet amended Reg § 20.2032A-4 to reflect changes made by P.L. 97-34.

(a) In general. Unless the executor of the decedent's estate elects otherwise under section 2032A(e)(7)(B)(ii) or fails to document comparable rented farm property meeting the requirements of this section, the value of the property which is used for farming purposes and which is subject to an election under section 2032A is determined by—

(1) Subtracting the average annual state and local real estate taxes on actual tracts of comparable real property in the same locality from the average annual gross cash rental for that same comparable property, and

(2) Dividing the result so obtained by the average annual effective interest rate charged on new Federal land bank loans.

The computation of each average annual amount is to be based on the 5 most recent calendar years ending before the date of the decedent's death.

(b) Gross cash rental. *(1) Generally.* Gross cash rental is the total amount of cash received for the use of actual tracts of comparable farm real property in the same locality as the property being specially valued during the period of one calendar year. This amount is not diminished by the amount of any expenses or liabilities associated with the farm operation or the lease. See, paragraph (d) of this section for a definition of comparable property and rules for property on which buildings or other improvements are located and farms including multiple property types. Only rentals from tracts of comparable farm property which are rented solely for an amount of cash which is not contingent upon production are acceptable for use in valuing real property under section 2032A(e)(7). The rentals considered must result from an arm's-length transaction as defined in this section. Additionally, rentals received under leases which provide for payment solely in cash are not acceptable as accurate measures of cash rental value if involvement by the lessor (or a member of the lessor's family who is other than a lessee) in the management or operation of the farm to an extent which amounts to material participation under the rules of section 2032A is contemplated or actually occurs. In general, therefore, rentals for any property which qualifies for special use valuation cannot be used to compute gross cash rentals under this section because the total amount received by the lessor does not reflect the true cash rental value of the real property.

(2) Special rules. (i) Documentation required of executor. The executor must identify to the Internal Revenue Service actual comparable property for all specially valued property and cash rentals from that property if the decedent's real property is valued under section 2032A(e)(7). If the executor does not identify such property and cash rentals, all specially valued real property must be valued under the rules of section 2032A(e)(8) if special use valuation has been elected. See, however, § 20.2032A-8(d) for a special rule for estates electing section 2032A treatment on or before August 30, 1980.

(ii) Arm's-length transaction required. Only those cash rentals which result from a lease entered into in an arm's-length transaction are acceptable under section 2032A(e)(7). For these purposes, lands leased from the Federal government, or any state or local government, which are leased for less than the amount that would be demanded by a private individual leasing for profit are not leased in an arm's-length transaction. Additionally, leases between family members (as defined in section 2032A(e)(2)) which do not provide a return on the property commensurate with that received under leases between unrelated parties in the locality are not acceptable under this section.

(iii) In-kind rents, statements of appraised rental value, and area averages. Rents which are paid wholly or partly in kind (e.g., crop shares) may not be used to determine the value of real property under section 2032A(e)(7). Likewise, appraisals or other statements regarding rental value as well as area-wide averages of rentals (i.e., those compiled by the United States Department of Agriculture) may not be used under section 2032A(e)(7) because they are not true measures of the actual cash rental value of comparable property in the same locality as the specially valued property.

(iv) Period for which comparable real property must have been rented solely for cash. Comparable real property rented solely for cash must be identified for each of the five calendar years preceding the year of the decedent's death if section 2032A(e)(7) is used to value the decedent's real property. Rentals from the same tract of comparable property need not be used for each of these 5 years, however, provided an actual tract of property meeting the requirements of this section is identified for each year.

(v) Leases under which rental of personal property is included. No adjustment to the rents actually received by the lessor is made for the use of any farm equipment or other personal property the use of which is included under a lease for comparable real property unless the lease specifies the amount of the total rental attributable to the personal property and that amount is reasonable under the circumstances.

(c) State and local real estate taxes. For purposes of the farm valuation formula under section 2032A(e)(7) state and local taxes are taxes which are assessed by a state or local government and which are allowable deductions under section 164. However, only those taxes on the comparable real property from which cash rentals are determined may be used in the formula valuation.

(d) Comparable real property defined. Comparable real property must be situated in the same locality as the specially valued property. This requirement is not to be viewed in terms of mileage or political divisions alone, but rather is to be judged according to generally accepted real property valuation rules. The determination of properties which are comparable is a factual one and must be based on numerous factors, no one of which is determinative. It will, therefore, frequently be necessary to value farm property in segments where there are different uses or land characteristics included in the specially valued farm. For example, if section 2032A(e)(7) is used, rental property on which comparable buildings or improvements are located must be identified for specially valued property on which buildings or other real property improvements are located. In cases involving multiple areas or land characteristics, actual comparable property for each segment must be used, and the rentals and taxes from all such properties combined (using generally accepted real property valuation rules) for use in the valuation formula given in this section. However, any premium or discount resulting from the presence of multiple uses or other characteristics in one farm is also to be reflected. All factors generally considered in real estate valuation are to be considered in determining comparability under section 2032A. While not intended as an exclusive list, the following factors are among those to be considered in determining comparability—

(1) Similarity of soil as determined by any objective means, including an official soil survey reflected in a soil productivity index;

(2) Whether the crops grown are such as would deplete the soil in a similar manner;

(3) The types of soil conservation techniques that have been practiced on the two properties;

(4) Whether the two properties are subject to flooding;

(5) The slope of the land;

(6) In the case of livestock operations, the carrying capacity of the land;

(7) Where the land is timbered, whether the timber is comparable to that on the subject property;

(8) Whether the property as a whole is unified or whether it is segmented, and where segmented, the availability of the means necessary for movement among the different segments;

(9) The number, types, and conditions of all buildings and other fixed improvements located on the properties and their location as it affects efficient management and use of property and value per se; and

(10) Availability of, and type of, transportation facilities in terms of costs and of proximity of the properties to local markets.

(e) Effective interest rate defined. *(1) Generally.* The annual effective interest rate on new Federal land bank loans is the average billing rate charged on new agricultural loans to farmers and ranchers in the farm credit district in which the real property to be valued under section 2032A is located, adjusted as provided in paragraph (e)(2) of this section. This rate is to be a single rate for each district covering the period of one calendar year and is to be computed to the nearest one-hundredth of one percent. In the event that the district billing rates of interest on such new agricultural loans change during a year, the rate for that year is to be weighted to reflect the portion of the year during which each such rate was charged. If a district's billing rate on such new agricultural loans varies according to the amount of the loan, the rate applicable to a loan in an amount resulting from dividing the total dollar amount of such loans closed during the year by the total number of the loans closed is to be used under section 2032A. Applicable rates may be obtained from the district director of internal revenue.

(2) Adjustment to billing rate of interest. The billing rate of interest determined under this paragraph is to be adjusted to reflect the increased cost of borrowing resulting from the required purchase of land bank association stock. For section 2032A purposes, the rate of required stock investment is the average of the percentages of the face amount of new agricultural loans to farmers and ranchers required to be invested in such stock by the applicable district bank during the year. If this percentage changes during a year, the average is to be adjusted to reflect the period when each percentage requirement was effective. The percentage is viewed as a reduction in the loan proceeds actually received from the amount upon which interest is charged.

(3) Example. The determination of the effective interest rate for any year may be illustrated as follows:

Example. District X of the Federal land bank system charged an 8 percent billed interest rate on new agricultural loans for 8 months of the year, 1976, and an 8.75 percent rate for 4 months of the year. The average billing rate was, therefore, 8.25 percent $[(1.08 \times 8/12) + (1.0875 \times 4/12) = 1.0825]$. The district required stock equal to 5 percent of the face amount of the loan to be purchased as a precondition to receiving a loan. Thus, the borrower only received 95 percent of the funds upon which he paid interest. The applicable annual interest rate for 1976 of 8.68 percent is computed as follows:

8.25 percent × 1.00 (total loan amount) = 8.25 percent (billed interest rate) divided by 0.95 (percent of loan proceeds received by borrower) = 8.68 percent (effective interest rate for 1976).

T.D. 7710, 7/28/80.

§ 20.2032A-8 Election and agreement to have certain property valued under section 2032A for estate tax purposes.

Caution: The Treasury has not yet amended Reg § 20.2032A-8 to reflect changes made by P.L. 105-34, P.L. 97-34.

(a) Election of special use valuation. *(1) In general.* An election under section 2032A is made as prescribed in paragraph (a)(3) of this section and on Form 706, United States Estate Tax Return. Once made, this election is irrevocable; however, see paragraph (d) of this section for a special rule for estates for which elections are made on or before August 30, 1980. Under section 2032A(a)(2), special use valuation may not reduce the value of the decedent's estate by more than $500,000. This election is available only if, at the time of death, the decedent was a citizen or resident of the United States.

(2) Elections to specially value less than all qualified real property included in an estate. An election under section 2032A need not include all real property included in an estate which is eligible for special use valuation, but sufficient property to satisfy the threshold requirements of section 2032A(b)(1)(B) must be specially valued under the election. If joint or undivided interests (e.g. interests as joint tenants or tenants in common) in the same property are received from a decedent by qualified heirs, an election with respect to one heir's joint or undivided interest need not include any other heir's interest in the same property if the electing heir's interest plus other property to be specially valued satisfy the requirements of section 2032A(b)(1)(B). If successive interests (e.g. life estates and remainder interests) are created by a decedent in otherwise qualified property, an election under section 2032A is available only with respect to that property (or portion thereof) in which qualified heirs of the decedent receive all of the successive interests, and such an election must include the interests of all of those heirs. For example, if a surviving spouse receives a life estate in otherwise qualified property and the spouse's brother receives a remainder interest in fee, no part of the property may be valued pursuant to an election under section 2032A. Where successive interests in specially valued property are created, remainder interests are treated as being received by qualified heirs only if such remainder interests are not contingent upon surviving a nonfamily member or are not subject to divestment in favor of a nonfamily member.

(3) Time and manner of making election. An election under this section is made by attaching to a timely filed estate tax return the agreement described in paragraph (c)(1) of this section and a notice of election which contains the following information:

(i) The decedent's name and taxpayer identification number as they appear on the estate tax return;

(ii) The relevant qualified use;

(iii) The items of real property shown on the estate tax return to be specially valued pursuant to the election (identified by schedule and item number);

(iv) The fair market value of the real property to be specially valued under section 2032A and its value based on its qualified use (both values determined without regard to the adjustments provided by section 2032A(b)(3)(B));

(v) The adjusted value (as defined in section 2032A(b)(3)(B)) of all real property which is used in a qualified use and which passes from the decedent to a qualified heir and the adjusted value of all real property to be specially valued;

(vi) The items of personal property shown on the estate tax return that pass from the decedent to a qualified heir and are used in a qualified use under section 2032A (identified by schedule and item number) and the total value of such personal property adjusted as provided under section 2032A (b)(3)(B);

(vii) The adjusted value of the gross estate, as defined in section 2032A (b)(3)(A);

(viii) The method used in determining the special value based on use;

(ix) Copies of written appraisals of the fair market value of the real property;

(x) A statement that the decedent and/or a member of his or her family has owned all specially valued real property for at least 5 years of the 8 years immediately preceding the date of the decedent's death;

(xi) Any periods during the 8-year period preceding the date of the decedent's death during which the decedent or a member of his or her family did not own the property, use it in a qualified use, or materially participate in the operation of the farm or other business within the meaning of section 2032A(e)(6);

(xii) The name, address, taxpayer identification number, and relationship to the decedent of each person taking an interest in each item of specially valued property, and the value of the property interests passing to each such person based on both fair market value and qualified use;

(xiii) Affidavits describing the activities constituting material participation and the identity of the material participant or participants; and

(xiv) A legal description of the specially valued property. If neither an election nor a protective election is timely made, special use valuation is not available to the estate. See section 2032A(d)(1), 6075(a), and 6081(a).

(b) Protective election. A protective election may be made to specially value qualified real property. The availability of special use valuation pursuant to this election is contingent upon values as finally determined (or agreed to following examination of a return) meeting the requirements of section 2032A. A protective election does not, however, extend the time for payment of any amount of tax. Rules for such extensions are contained in sections 6161, 6163, 6166, and 6166A. The protective election is to be made by a notice of election filed with a timely estate tax return stating that a protective election under section 2032A is being made pending final determination of values. This notice is to include the following information:

(1) The decedent's name and taxpayer identification number as they appear on the estate tax return;

(2) The relevant qualified use; and

(3) The items of real and personal property shown on the estate tax return which are used in a qualified use, and which pass to qualified heirs (identified by schedule and item number).

If it is found that the estate qualifies for special use valuation based upon values as finally determined (or agreed to following examination of a return), an additional notice of election must be filed within 60 days after the date of such determination. This notice must set forth the information required under paragraph (a)(3) of this section and is to be attached, together with the agreement described in paragraph (c)(1) of this section, to an amended estate tax return. The new return is to be filed with the Internal Revenue Service office where the original return was filed.

(c) Agreement to special valuation by persons with an interest in property. *(1) In general.* The agreement required under section 2032A(a)(1)(B) and (d)(2) must be executed by all parties who have any interest in the property being valued based on its qualified use as of the date of the decedent's death. In the case of a qualified heir, the agreement must express consent to personal liability under section 2032A(c) in the event of certain early dispositions of the property or early cessation of the qualified use. See section 2032A(c)(6). In the case of parties (other than qualified heirs) with interests in the property, the agreement must express consent to collection of any additional estate tax imposed under section 2032A(c) from the qualified property. The agreement is to be in a form that is binding on all parties having an interest in the property. It must designate an agent with satisfactory evidence of authority to act for the parties to the agreement in all dealings with the Internal Revenue Service on matters arising under section 2032A and must indicate the address of that agent.

(2) Persons having an interest in designated property. An interest in property is an interest which, as of the date of the decedent's death, can be asserted under applicable local law so as to affect the disposition of the specially valued property by the estate. Any person in being at the death of the decedent who has any such interest in the property, whether present or future, or vested or contingent, must enter into the agreement. Included among such persons are owners of remainder and executory interests, the holders of general or special powers of appointment, beneficiaries of a gift over in default of exercise of any such power, co-tenants, joint tenants and holders of other undivided interests when the decedent held only a joint or undivided interest in the property or when only an undivided interest is specially valued, and trustees of trusts holding any interest in the property. An heir who has the power under local law to caveat (challenge) a will and thereby affect disposition of the property is not, however, considered to be a person with an interest in property under section 2032A solely by reason of that right. Likewise, creditors of an estate are not such persons solely by reason of their status as creditors.

(3) Consent on behalf of interested party. If any person required to enter into the agreement provided for by paragraph (c)(1) either desires that an agent act for him or her or cannot legally bind himself or herself due to infancy or other incompetency, or to death before the election under section 2032A is timely exercised, a representative authorized under local law to bind such person in an agreement of this nature is permitted to sign the agreement on his or her behalf.

(4) Duties of agent designated in agreement. The Internal Revenue Service will contact the agent designated in the agreement under paragraph (c)(1) on all matters relating to continued qualification under section 2032A of the specially valued real property and on all matters relating to the special lien arising under section 6324B. It is the duty of the agent as attorney-in-fact for the parties with interests in the specially valued property to furnish the Service with any requested information and to notify the Service of any disposition or cessation of qualified use of any part of the property.

(d) Special rule for estates for which elections under section 2032A are made on or before August 30, 1980. An election to specially value real property under section 2032A that is made on or before August 30, 1980, may be revoked. To revoke an election, the executor must file a notice of revocation with the Internal Revenue Service office where the original estate tax return was filed on or before January 31, 1981 (or if earlier, the date on which the period of limitation for assessment expires). This notice of revocation must contain the decedent's name, date of death, and taxpayer identification number, and is to be accompanied by remittance of any additional amount of estate tax and interest determined to be due as a result of valuation of the qualified property based upon its fair market value. Elections that are made on or before August 30, 1980, that do not comply with this section as proposed on July 13, 1978 (43 FR 30070), and amended on December 21, 1978 (43 FR 59517), must be conformed to this final regulation by means of an amended return before the original estate tax return can be finally accepted by the Internal Revenue Service.

T.D. 7710, 7/28/80, amend T.D. 7786, 8/25/81.

§ 20.2033-1 Property in which the decedent had an interest.

(a) In general. The gross estate of a decedent who was a citizen or resident of the United States at the time of his death includes under section 2033 the value of all property, whether real or personal, tangible or intangible, and wherever situated, beneficially owned by the decedent at the time of his death. (For certain exceptions in the case of real property situated outside the United States, see paragraphs (a) and (c) of § 20.2031-1.) Real property is included whether it came into the possession and control of the executor or administrator or passed directly to heirs or devisees. Various statutory provisions which exempt bonds, notes, bills, and certificates of indebtedness of the Federal Government or its agencies and the interest thereon from taxation are generally not applicable to the estate tax, since such tax is an excise tax on the transfer of property at death and is not a tax on the property transferred.

(b) Miscellaneous examples. A cemetery lot owned by the decedent is part of his gross estate, but its value is limited to the salable value of that part of the lot which is not designed for the interment of the decedent and the members of his family. Property subject to homestead or other exemptions under local law is included in the gross estate. Notes or other claims held by the decedent are likewise included even though they are cancelled by the decedent's will. Interest and rents accrued at the date of the decedent's death constitute a part of the gross estate. Similarly, dividends which are payable to the decedent or his estate by reason of the fact that on or before the date of the decedent's death he was a stockholder of record (but which have not been collected at death) constitute a part of the gross estate.

T.D. 6296, 6/23/58, amend T.D. 6684, 10/23/63.

§ 20.2034-1 Dower or curtesy interests.

A decedent's gross estate includes under section 2034 any interest in property of the decedent's surviving spouse existing at the time of the decedent's death as dower or curtesy, or any interest created by statute in lieu thereof (although such other interest may differ in character from dower or curtesy). Thus, the full value of property is included in the decedent's gross estate, without deduction of such an interest of the surviving husband or wife, and without regard to when the right to such an interest arose.

T.D. 6296, 6/23/58.

§ 20.2036-1 Transfers with retained life estate.

Caution: The Treasury has not yet amended Reg § 20.2036-1 to reflect changes made by P.L. 100-203, P.L. 95-600, P.L. 94-455.

(a) In general. A decedent's gross estate includes under section 2036 the value of any interest in property transferred by the decedent after March 3, 1931, whether in trust or otherwise, except to the extent that the transfer was for an adequate and full consideration in money or money's worth (see § 20.2043-1), if the decedent retained or reserved--

(1) For his life;

(2) For any period not ascertainable without reference to his death (if the transfer was made after June 6, 1932); or

(3) For any period which does not in fact end before his death:

(i) The use, possession, right to income, or other enjoyment of the transferred property.

(ii) The right, either alone or in conjunction with any other person or persons, to designate the person or persons who shall possess or enjoy the transferred property or its income (except that, if the transfer was made before June 7, 1932, the right to designate must be retained by or reserved to the decedent alone).

(b) Meaning of terms. *(1)* A reservation by the decedent "for any period not ascertainable without reference to his death" may be illustrated by the following examples:

(i) A decedent reserved the right to receive the income from transferred property in quarterly payments, with the proviso that no part of the income between the last quarterly payment and the date of the decedent's death was to be received by the decedent or his estate; and

(ii) A decedent reserved the right to receive the income from transferred property after the death of another person who was in fact enjoying the income at the time of the decedent's death. In such a case, the amount to be included in the decedent's gross estate under this section does not include the value of the outstanding income interest of the other person. It may be noted that if the other person predeceased the decedent, the reservation by the decedent may be considered to be either for his life, or for a period which does not in fact end before his death.

(2) The "use, possession, right to the income, or other enjoyment of the transferred property" is considered as having been retained by or reserved to the decedent to the extent that the use, possession, right to the income, or other enjoyment is to be applied toward the discharge of a legal obligation of the decedent, or otherwise for his pecuniary benefit. The term "legal obligation" includes a legal obligation to support a dependent during the decedent's lifetime.

(3) The phrase "right . . . to designate the person or persons who shall possess or enjoy the transferred property or the income therefrom" includes a reserved power to designate the person or persons to receive the income from the transferred property, or to possess or enjoy nonincome-producing property, during the decedent's life or during any other period described in paragraph (a) of this section. With respect to such a power, it is immaterial (i) whether the power was exercisable alone or only in conjunction with another person or persons, whether or not having an adverse interest; (ii) in what capacity the power was exercisable by the decedent or by another person or persons in conjunction with the decedent; and (iii) whether the exercise of the power was subject to a contingency beyond the decedent's control which did not occur before his death (e.g., the death of another person during the decedent's lifetime). The phrase, however, does not include a power over the transferred property itself which does not affect the enjoyment of the income received or earned during the decedent's life. (See, however, section 2038 for the inclusion of property in the gross estate on account of such a power.) Nor does the phrase apply to a power held solely by a person other than the decedent. But, for example, if the decedent reserved the unrestricted power to remove or discharge a trustee at any time and appoint himself as trustee, the decedent is considered as having the powers of the trustee.

(c) Retained or reserved interest. *(1) Amount included in gross estate.* (i) In general. If the decedent retained or reserved an interest or right with respect to all of the property transferred by him, the amount to be included in his gross estate under section 2036 is the value of the entire property, less only the value of any outstanding income interest which is not subject to the decedent's interest or right and which is actually being enjoyed by another person at the time of the decedent's death. If the decedent retained or reserved an interest or right with respect to a part only of the property transferred by him, the amount to be included in his gross estate under section 2036 is only a corresponding proportion of the amount described in the preceding sentence. An interest or right is treated as having been retained or reserved if at the time of the transfer there was an understanding, express or implied, that the interest or right would later be conferred.

(ii) Examples. The application of paragraph (c)(1)(i) of this section is illustrated in the following examples:

Example (1). [Reserved].

Example (2). D transferred D's personal residence to D's child (C), but retained the right to use the residence for a term of years. D dies during the term. At D's death, the fair market value of the personal residence is includible in D's gross estate under section 2036(a)(1) because D retained the right to use the residence for a period that did not in fact end before D's death.

(2) Retained annuity, unitrust, and other income interests in trusts. (i) In general. This paragraph (c)(2) applies to a grantor's retained use of an asset held in trust or a retained annuity, unitrust, or other interest in any trust (other than a trust constituting an employee benefit) including without limitation the following (collectively referred to in this paragraph (c)(2) as "trusts"): Certain charitable remainder trusts (collectively CRTs) such as a charitable remainder annuity trust (CRAT) within the meaning of section 664(d)(1), a charitable remainder unitrust (CRUT) within the meaning of section 664(d)(2) or (d)(3), and any charitable remainder trust that does not qualify under section 664(d), whether because the CRT was created prior to 1969, there was a defect in the drafting of the CRT, there was no intention to qualify the CRT for the charitable deduction, or otherwise; other trusts established by a grantor (collectively GRTs) such as a grantor retained annuity trust (GRAT) paying out a qualified annuity interest within the meaning of § 25.2702-3(b) of this chapter, a grantor retained unitrust (GRUT) paying out a qualified unitrust interest within the meaning of § 25.2702-3(c) of this chapter; and various other forms of grantor retained income trusts (GRITs) whether or not the grantor's retained interest is a qualified interest as defined in section 2702(b), including without limitation a qualified personal residence trust (QPRT) within the meaning of § 25.2702-5(c) of this chapter and a personal residence trust (PRT) within the meaning of § 25.2702-5(b) of this chapter. If a decedent transferred property into such a trust and retained or reserved the right to use such property, or the right to an annuity, unitrust, or other interest in such trust with respect to the property decedent so transferred for decedent's life, any period not ascertainable without reference to the decedent's death, or for a period that does not in fact end before the decedent's death, then the decedent's right to use the property or the retained annuity, unitrust, or other interest (whether payable from income and/or principal) constitutes the retention of the possession or enjoyment of, or the right to the income from, the property for purposes of section 2036. The portion of the trust's corpus includible in the decedent's gross estate for Federal estate tax purposes is that portion of the trust corpus necessary to provide the decedent's retained use or retained annuity, unitrust, or other payment (without reducing or invading principal) as determined in accordance with § 20.2031-7 (or § 20.2031-7A, if applicable). The portion of the trust's corpus includible in the decedent's gross estate under section 2036, however, shall not exceed the fair market value of the trust's corpus at the decedent's date of death.

(ii) Graduated retained interests. [Reserved].

(iii) Examples. The application of paragraphs (c)(2)(i) and (c)(2)(ii) of this section are illustrated in the following examples:

Example (1). (i) Decedent (D) transferred $100,000 to an inter vivos trust that qualifies as a CRAT under section 664(d)(1). The trust agreement provides for an annuity of $7,500 to be paid each year to D for D's life, then to D's child (C) for C's life, with the remainder to be distributed upon the survivor's death to N, a charitable organization described in sections 170(c), 2055(a), and 2522(a). The annuity is payable to D or C, as the case may be, annually on each December 31st. D dies in September 2006, survived by C who was then age 40. On D's death, the value of the trust assets was $300,000 and the section 7520 interest rate was 6 percent. D's executor does not elect to use the alternate valuation date.

(ii) The amount of corpus with respect to which D retained the right to the income, and thus the amount includible in D's gross estate under section 2036, is that amount of corpus necessary to yield the annual annuity payment to D (without reducing or invading principal). In this case, the formula for determining the amount of corpus necessary to yield the annual annuity payment to D is: annual annuity / section 7520 interest rate = amount includible under section 2036. The amount of corpus necessary to yield the annual annuity is $7,500 / .06 = $125,000. Therefore, $125,000 is includible in D's gross estate under section 2036(a)(1). (The result would be the same if D had retained an interest in the CRAT for a term of years and had died during the term. The result also would be the same if D had irrevocably relinquished D's annuity interest less than 3 years prior to D's death because of the application of section 2035.) If, instead, the trust agreement had provided that D could revoke C's annuity interest or change the identity of the charitable remainderman, see section 2038 with regard to the portion of the trust to be included in the gross estate on account of such a retained power to revoke. Under the facts presented, section 2039 does not apply to include any amount in D's gross estate by reason of this retained annuity. See § 20.2039-1(e).

Example (2). (i) D transferred $100,000 to a GRAT in which D's annuity is a qualified interest described in section 2702(b). The trust agreement provides for an annuity of $12,000 per year to be paid to D for a term of ten years or until D's earlier death. The annuity amount is payable in twelve equal installments at the end of each month. At the expiration of the term of years or on D's earlier death, the remainder is to be distributed to D's child (C). D dies prior to the expiration of the ten-year term. On the date of D's death, the value of the trust assets is $300,000 and the section 7520 interest rate is 6 percent. D's executor does not elect to use the alternate valuation date.

(ii) The amount of corpus with respect to which D retained the right to the income, and thus the amount includible in D's gross estate under section 2036, is that amount of corpus necessary to yield the annual annuity payment to D (without reducing or invading principal). In this case, the formula for determining the amount of corpus necessary to yield the annual annuity payment to D is: annual annuity (adjusted for monthly payments) / section 7520 interest rate = amount includible under section 2036. The Table K adjustment factor for monthly annuity payments in this case is 1.0272. Thus, the amount of corpus necessary to yield the annual annuity is ($12,000 x 1.0272) / .06 = $205,440. Therefore, $205,440 is includible in D's gross estate under section 2036(a)(1). If, instead, the trust agreement had provided that the annuity was to be paid to D during D's life and to D's estate for the balance of the 10-year term if D died during that term, then the portion of trust corpus includible in D's gross estate would still be as calculated in this paragraph. It is not material whether payments are made to D's estate after D's death. Under the facts presented, section

2039 does not apply to include any amount in D's gross estate by reason of this retained annuity. See § 20.2039-1(e).

Example (3). (i) In 2000, D created a CRUT within the meaning of section 664(d)(2). The trust instrument directs the trustee to hold, invest, and reinvest the corpus of the trust and to pay to D for D's life, and then to D's child (C) for C's life, in equal quarterly installments payable at the end of each calendar quarter, an amount equal to 6 percent of the fair market value of the trust as valued on December 15 of the prior taxable year of the trust. At the termination of the trust, the then-remaining corpus, together with any and all accrued income, is to be distributed to N, a charitable organization described in sections 170(c), 2055(a), and 2522(a). D dies in 2006, survived by C, who was then age 55. The value of the trust assets on D's death was $300,000. D's executor does not elect to use the alternate valuation date and, as a result, D's executor does not choose to use the section 7520 interest rate for either of the two months prior to D's death.

(ii) The amount of the corpus with respect to which D retained the right to the income, and thus the amount includible in D's gross estate under section 2036(a)(1), is that amount of corpus necessary to yield the unitrust payments. In this case, such amount of corpus is determined by dividing the trust's equivalent income interest rate by the section 7520 rate (which was 6 percent at the time of D's death). The equivalent income interest rate is determined by dividing the trust's adjusted payout rate by the excess of 1 over the adjusted payout rate. Based on § 1.664-4(e)(3) of this chapter, the appropriate adjusted payout rate for the trust at D's death is 5.786 percent (6 percent x .964365). Thus, the equivalent income interest rate is 6.141 percent (5.786 percent / (1--5.786 percent)). The ratio of the equivalent interest rate to the assumed interest rate under section 7520 is 102.35 percent (6.141 percent / 6 percent). Because this exceeds 100 percent, D's retained payout interest exceeds a full income interest in the trust, and D effectively retained the income from all the assets transferred to the trust. Accordingly, because D retained for life an interest at least equal to the right to all income from all the property transferred by D to the CRUT, the entire value of the corpus of the CRUT is includible in D's gross estate under section 2036(a)(1). (The result would be the same if D had retained, instead, an interest in the CRUT for a term of years and had died during the term.) Under the facts presented, section 2039 does not apply to include any amount in D's gross estate by reason of D's retained unitrust interest. See § 20.2039-1(e).

(iii) If, instead, D had retained the right to a unitrust amount having an adjusted payout for which the corresponding equivalent interest rate would have been less than the 6 percent assumed interest rate of section 7520, then a correspondingly reduced proportion of the trust corpus would be includible in D's gross estate under section 2036(a)(1). Alternatively, if the interest retained by D was instead only one-half of the 6 percent unitrust interest, then the amount included in D's estate would be the amount needed to produce a 3 percent unitrust interest. All of the results in this Example 3 would be the same if the trust had been a GRUT instead of a CRUT.

Example (4). During life, D established a 15-year GRIT for the benefit of individuals who are not members of D's family within the meaning of section 2704(c)(2). D retained the right to receive all of the net income from the GRIT, payable annually, during the GRIT's term. D dies during the GRIT's term. D's executor does not elect to use the alternate valuation date. In this case, the GRIT's corpus is includible in D's gross estate under section 2036(a)(1) because D retained the right to receive all of the income from the GRIT for a period that did not in fact end before D's death. If, instead, D had retained the right to receive 60 percent of the GRIT's net income, then 60 percent of the GRIT's corpus would have been includible in D's gross estate under section 2036. Under the facts presented, section 2039 does not apply to include any amount in D's gross estate by reason of D's retained interest. See § 20.2039-1(e).

Example (5). In 2003, D transferred $10X to a pooled income fund that conforms to Rev. Proc. 88-53, 1988-2 CB 712 (1988) in exchange for 1 unit in the fund. D is to receive all of the income from that 1 unit during D's life. Upon D's death, D's child (C), is to receive D's income interest for C's life. In 2008, D dies. D's executor does not elect to use the alternate valuation date. In this case, the fair market value of D's 1 unit in the pooled income fund is includible in D's gross estate under section 2036(a)(1) because D retained the right to receive all of the income from that unit for a period that did not in fact end before D's death. See § 601.601(d)(2)(ii)(b) of this chapter.

Example (6). D transferred D's personal residence to a trust that met the requirements of a qualified personal residence trust (QPRT) as set forth in § 25.2702-5(c) of this chapter. Pursuant to the terms of the QPRT, D retained the right to use the residence for 10 years or until D's prior death. D dies before the end of the term. D's executor does not elect to use the alternate valuation date. In this case, the fair market value of the QPRT's assets on the date of D's death are includible in D's gross estate under section 2036(a)(1) because D retained the right to use the residence for a period that did not in fact end before D's death.

(3) Effective/applicability dates. Paragraphs (a) and (c)(1)(i) of this section are applicable to the estates of decedents dying after August 16, 1954. Paragraphs (c)(1)(ii) and (c)(2) of this section apply to the estates of decedents dying on or after July 14, 2008.

T.D. 6296, 6/23/58, amend T.D. 6501, 11/15/60, T.D. 9414, 7/11/2008.

PAR. 2. Section 20.2036-1 is amended by:

1. Revising paragraph (b)(1)(ii) and paragraph (c)(1)(ii) introductory text.

2. Adding paragraphs (c)(1)(ii) Example 1, (c)(2)(ii), (c)(2)(iii) Example 7, and two sentences at the end of paragraph (c)(3).

The revisions and additions read as follows:

Proposed § 20.2036-1 Transfers with retained life estate.
[*For Preamble, see ¶ 153,101*]

* * * * *

(b) * * * *(1)* * * *

(ii) A decedent reserved the right to receive the income, annuity, or other payment from transferred property after the death of another person who was in fact enjoying the income, annuity, or other payment at the time of the decedent's death. In such a case, the amount to be included in the decedent's gross estate under this section does not include the value of the outstanding interest of the other person. If the other person predeceased the decedent, the reservation by the decedent may be considered to be either for life, or for a period which does not in fact end before death. If the decedent retained the right to receive an annuity or other payment (rather than income) after the death of the current recipient of that interest, then the amount includible in the decedent's gross estate under section 2036 is the amount of trust corpus required to produce sufficient income to satisfy the entire annuity or other payment the decedent would have been entitled to receive if the decedent had survived the current recipient (thus, also including the portion of that entire amount payable to the decedent before the current recipient's death), reduced by the present value of the current recipient's interest. However, the amount includible shall not be less than the amount of corpus required to produce sufficient income to satisfy the annuity or other payment the decedent was entitled, at the time of the decedent's death, to receive for each year. In no event, however, shall the amount includible exceed the value of the trust corpus on the date of death. The following steps implement this computation.

(A) Step 1: Determine the fair market value of the trust corpus on the date of death.

(B) Step 2: Determine, in accordance with paragraph (c)(2)(i) of this section, the amount of corpus required to generate sufficient income to pay the annuity, unitrust, or other payment (determined on the date of the decedent's death) payable to the decedent for the trust year in which the decedent's death occurred.

(C) Step 3: Determine, in accordance with paragraph (c)(2)(i) of this section, the amount of corpus required to generate sufficient income to pay the annuity, unitrust, or other payment that the decedent would have been entitled to receive for each trust year if the decedent had survived the current recipient.

(D) Step 4: Determine the present value of the current recipient's annuity, unitrust, or other payment.

(E) Step 5: Reduce the amount determined in Step 3 by the amount determined in Step 4, but not to below the amount determined in Step 2.

(F) Step 6: The amount includible in the decedent's gross estate under section 2036 is the lesser of the amounts determined in Step 5 and Step 1.

* * * * *

(c) * * * *(1)* * * *

(ii) Examples. The application of paragraphs (b)(1)(ii) and (c)(1)(i) of this section is illustrated in the following examples:

Example (1). (i) In 2001, Decedent (D) creates an irrevocable inter vivos trust. The terms of the trust provide that all of the trust income is to be paid to D and C, D's child, in equal shares during their joint lives and, on the death of the first to die of D and C, all of the trust income is to be paid to the survivor. On the death of the survivor of D and C, the remainder is to be paid to another individual, F. In 2009, D dies survived by C. Fifty percent of the value of the trust corpus is includible in D's gross estate under section 2036(a)(1) because, under the terms of the trust, D retained the right to receive one-half of the trust income for D's life. In addition, the value of the remaining 50 percent of the trust corpus, less the present value of C's outstanding life estate, also is includible in D's gross estate under section 2036(a)(1), because D retained the right to receive all of the trust income for such time as D survived C. If C had predeceased D, then 100 percent of the trust corpus would have been includible in D's gross estate.

(ii) Assume the same facts as above, except that the trust provides that, rather than all the income, an annuity of $10,000 per year is to be paid to D and C in equal shares during their joint lives and, on the death of the first to die of D and C, the entire $10,000 annuity is to be paid to the survivor for life. On D's date of death, the fair market value of the trust is $120,000 and the section 7520 rate is 7 percent. At the date of death, the amount of trust corpus needed to produce D's annuity interest ($5,000 per year) is $71,429 ($5,000/.07). In addition, assume the present value of C's right to receive $5,000 annually for the remainder of C's life is $40,000. The portion of the trust corpus includible in D's gross estate under section 2036(a)(1) is $102,857, determined as follows:

(A) Step 1: Fair market value of corpus	$120,000
(B) Step 2: Corpus required to produce D's date of death annuity ($5,000÷.07)	71,429
(C) Step 3: Corpus required to produce D's annuity if D had survived C ($10,000÷.07)	142,857
(D) Step 4: Present value of C's interest	40,000
(E) Step 5: The amount determined in Step 3 reduced by the amount determined in Step 4, but not to below the amount determined in Step 2 ($142,857—$40,000, but not less than $71,429)	102,857
(F) Step 6: The lesser of the amounts determined in Steps 5 and 1 ($102,857 or $120,000)	102,857

* * * * *

(2) * * *

(ii) Graduated retained interests. (A) In general. For purposes of this section, a graduated retained interest is the grantor's reservation of a right to receive an annuity, unitrust, or other payment as described in paragraph (c)(2)(i) of this section, payable at least annually, that increases (but does not decrease) over a period of time, not more often than annually.

(B) Other definitions. (1) Base amount. The base amount is the amount of corpus required to generate the annuity, unitrust, or other payment payable for the trust year in which the decedent's death occurs. See paragraph (c)(2)(i) of this section for the calculation of the base amount.

(2) Periodic addition. The periodic addition in a graduated retained interest for each year after the year in which decedent's death occurs is the amount (if any) by which the annuity, unitrust, or other payment that would have been payable for that year if the decedent had survived exceeds the total amount of payments for the year immediately preceding that year. For example, assume the trust instrument provides that the grantor is to receive an annual annuity payable to the grantor or his estate for a 5-year term. The initial annual payment is $100,000, and each succeeding annual payment is to be 120 percent of the amount payable for the preceding year. Assuming the grantor dies in the second year of the trust (whether before or after the due date of the second annual payment), the periodic additions for years 3, 4, and 5 of the trust are as follows:

	(1) Annual payment	(2) Prior year payment	(1−2) Periodic addition
Year 3	144,000	120,000	24,000
Year 4	172,800	144,000	28,800
Year 5	207,360	172,800	34,560

(3) Corpus amount. For each trust year in which a periodic addition occurs (increase year), the corpus amount is the amount of trust corpus which, starting from the decedent's date of death, is necessary to generate an amount of income sufficient to pay the periodic addition, beginning in the increase year and continuing in perpetuity, without reducing or invading principal. For each year with a periodic addition, the corpus amount required as of the date of death is the product of two factors: the first is the result of dividing the periodic addition (adjusted for payments made more frequently than annually, if applicable, and for payments due at the beginning, rather than the end, of a payment period (see Table K or J of § 20.2031-7(d)(6))) by the section 7520 rate (periodic addition/rate); and the second is 1 divided by the sum of 1 and the section 7520 rate raised to the T power (1/(1 + rate)[supcaret]T).

(i) That formula is:

$$\frac{\text{(Periodic Addition)} \times \text{(Adjustment Factor)}}{\text{Section 7520 Rate}} \times \frac{1}{(1 + \text{Section 7520 Rate})^{t}}$$

(ii) Where adjustment factor, if applicable, is the factor for payments made more frequently than annually and for payments due at the beginning, rather than the end, of a calendar period (See Table K or J of § 20.2031-7(d)(6)) and T equals the time period in years from the date of death through the last day of the trust year immediately before the year for which the periodic addition is first payable.

(C) Amount includible. The amount includible in the gross estate in the case of a graduated retained interest is the sum of the base amount and the corpus amount for each year for which a periodic addition is first payable. The sum of these amounts represents the amount of trust principal that would be necessary to generate the annual payments that would have been paid to the decedent if the decedent had survived and had continued to receive the reserved graduated retained interest. The amount of trust corpus includible in a decedent's gross estate under this section, however, shall not exceed the fair market value of the trust corpus on the decedent's date of death. The provisions of this section also apply to graduated retained interests in transferred property not held in trust.

(iii) * * *

* * * * *

Example (7). (i) On November 1, year N, D transfers assets valued at $2,000,000 to a GRAT. Under the terms of the GRAT, the trustee is to pay to D an annuity for a 5-year term that qualifies as a qualified interest described in section 2702(b). The annuity amount is to be paid annually at the end of each trust year, on October 31st. The first annual payment is to be $100,000. Each succeeding payment is to be 120 percent of the amount paid in the preceding year. Income not distributed in any year is to be added to principal. If D dies during the 5-year term, the payments are to be made to D's estate for the balance of the GRAT term. At the end of the 5-year term, the trust is to terminate and the corpus is to be distributed to C, D's child. D dies on January 31st of the third year of the GRAT term. On the date of D's death, the value of the trust corpus is $3,200,000 and the section 7520 interest rate is 6.8 percent. D's executor does not elect to value the gross estate as of the alternate valuation date.

(ii) The amount includible in D's gross estate under section 2036(a)(1) is determined and illustrated as follows using the methodology contained in paragraph (c)(2)(ii)(C) of this section:

A GRAT Year	B Annual annuity payment	C Periodic addition	D Required principal: C × Adj. factor/ 0.068	E Deferral period: death to GRAT Year	F Present value factor: 1/(1+.068)^E	G Corpus amount at death: D × F
3	144,000	n/a	2,117,647	n/a	n/a	2,117,647
4	172,800	28,800	423,529	0.747945	0.951985	403,193
5	207,360	34,560	508,235	1.747945	0.891372	453,026
Total	......	......	......	......	......	2,973,866

(iii) An illustration of the amount of trust corpus (as of the decedent's death) necessary to produce the scheduled payments is as follows:

		Year 3	Year 4	Year 5	Amount required to generate annuity
Additional Annuity	$ 34,560	Deferral Period		$453,026	$ 453,026
Additional Annuity	28,800	Deferral Period	$403,193		403,193
Annuity in year of death	144,000	$2,117,647			2,117,647
Total amount (sum) included in gross estate					2,973,866

(iv) A total corpus amount (as defined in paragraph (c)(2)(ii)(B)(3) of this section) of $2,973,866 constitutes the principal required as of D's date of death to produce (without reducing or invading principal) the annual payments that D would have received if D had survived and continued to receive the retained annuity. Therefore, $2,973,866 of the trust corpus is includible in D's gross estate under section 2036(a)(1). The remaining $226,134 of the trust corpus is not includible in D's gross estate under section 2036(a)(1). The result would be the same if D's retained annuity instead had been payable to D for a term of 5 years, or until D's prior death, at which time the GRAT would have terminated and the trust corpus would have become payable to another.

(v) If, instead, D's annuity was to have been paid on a monthly or quarterly basis, then the periodic addition would have to be adjusted as provided in paragraph (c)(2)(ii)(B)(3) of this section. Specifically, in Column D of the Table for years 4 and 5 in this example, the amount of the principal required would be computed by multiplying the periodic addition by the appropriate factor from Table K or J of § 20.2036-7(d)(6) before dividing as indicated and computing the amounts in Columns E through G. In addition, Column D in year 3 also would have to be so adjusted. Under the facts presented, section 2039 does not apply to include any amount in D's gross estate by reason of this retained interest. See § 20.2039-1(e).

(3) * * * Paragraph (b)(1)(ii) of this section is applicable to estates of decedents dying on or after the date of publication in the Federal Register of the Treasury decision adopting these rules as final regulations. The introductory text of paragraph (c)(1)(ii) of this section, Example 1 of paragraph (c)(1)(ii) of this section, all of paragraph (c)(2)(ii) of this section, and Example 7 of paragraph (c)(2)(iii) of this section, are applicable to estates of decedents dying on or after the date of publication in the Federal Register of the Treasury decision adopting these rules as final regulations.

Proposed § 20.2036-2 Special treatment of retained voting rights. [*For Preamble, see ¶ 150,877*]

(a) In general. For purposes of section 2036(a)(1) and § 20.2036-1(a), the retention of the right to vote (directly or indirectly) shares of stock of a controlled corporation is a retention of the enjoyment of the transferred property if:

(1) The transfer was made after June 22, 1976;

(2) The corporation was a controlled corporation at any time after transfer of that stock; and

(3) The corporation was a controlled corporation at any time during the three-year period ending on the decedent's death.

The rule of this section does not require inclusion of stock in the gross estate if the transferred stock has not voting rights or if the donor has not retained voting rights in the stock transferred. Thus, for example, if a person owning 100 percent of the voting and nonvoting stock of a corporation transfers the nonvoting stock, that person shall not be treated as having retained the enjoyment of the property transferred merely because of voting rights in the stock retained. Stock carrying voting rights that will vest only when conditions occur, such as preferred stock which gains voting rights only if no dividends are paid, is subject to this section. However, if the decedent's right to vote such stock is only in a fiduciary capacity (e.g., because the decedent is trustee of a trust to which the stock has been transferred), such stock is subject to this section only if, after the transfer by the decedent, the conditions occur that give the decedent the right to vote the stock. Stock that possesses voting rights in only extraordinary matters, such as mergers or liquidations shall be subject to this section unless the decedent's retention of voting rights is only in a fiduciary capacity.

(b) Relinquishment or cessation of voting rights within three years of death. In general, the relinquishment or cessation of retained voting rights shall be treated as a "transfer of property" for purposes of section 2035 (transfer within three years of death) if:

(1) The voting rights were retained in a transfer made after June 22, 1976; and

(2) The corporation was a controlled corporation at some point in time occurring after the transfer, before the relinquishment or cessation of voting rights, and within three years of death.

However, to the extent that a relinquishment of voting rights is in exchange for voting rights in another controlled corporation, the relinquishment shall not be treated as a "transfer of property" for purposes of section 2035. See paragraph (e)(3) of this section for the treatment of voting rights in such other corporation.

(c) Meaning of right to vote. For purposes of this section, the term " right to vote" means the power to vote, whether exercisable alone or in conjunction with other persons. The capacity in which the decedent can exercise voting power is immaterial. Accordingly, a fiduciary power exercisable as trustee, co-trustee, or as officer of a corporation is a right to vote stock within the meaning of this section. For purposes of section 2036(b)(1) and § 20.2036-2(a), the constructive ownership rules of section 318 shall not be used to attribute the retention of voting rights to the decedent. Therefore, the fact that a relative of the decedent is trustee of a trust to which the decedent has transferred stock shall not in itself require a finding that the decedent indirectly retained the right to vote that stock. However, any arrangement to shift formal voting power away from the decedent will not be treated for this purpose as a relinquishment of all voting rights if, in substance, the decedent has retained voting power. Moreover, voting power shall be deemed retained in cases where there is any agreement with the decedent, express or implied, that the shareholder, or other holder of the power to vote stock, either will vote the stock in a specified manner or will not vote the stock. If the decedent has the power to obtain the right to vote, such as where he may appoint himself as trustee of a trust holding the stock, the decedent has retained the right to vote for purposes of section 2036.

(d) Meaning of controlled corporation *(1) In general.* For purposes of this section, the term " controlled corporation" means a corporation in which the decedent, with application of the constructive ownership rules of section 318, is deemed to own or have a right to vote stock possessing at least 20 percent of the total combined voting power of all classes of stock.

(2) Computations. (i) Total combined voting power of all classes of stock. For purposes of this paragraph, the total combined voting power of all classes of stock shall include only stock that currently has voting power. Stock that may vote only on extraordinary matters, such as mergers or liquidations, shall be disregarded. Similarly, treasury stock and stock that is authorized but unissued shall be disregarded.

(ii) Decedent's percentage of total combined voting power. For purposes of this paragraph, in determining whether the voting power possessed by the decedent is a least 20 percent of the total combined voting power of all classes of stock, consideration will be given to all the facts and circumstances. Generally, the percentage of voting power possessed by a person in a corporation may be determined by reference to the power of stock to vote for the election of directors. Instruments that do not have voting rights shall be disregarded. Instruments having no voting rights but which may be converted into voting stock shall be disregarded until such conversion occurs. Instruments carrying voting rights that will vest only when conditions, the occurrence of which is indeterminate, have been met will be disregarded until the conditions have occurred which cause the voting rights to vest. An example of such an instrument is preferred stock which gains voting rights only if no dividends are paid.

(iii) Example. The following example illustrates the application of paragraphs (d)(1) through (d)(2)(ii) of this section.

Example. A corporation has three classes of stock outstanding, consisting of 40 shares of class A voting stock, 50 shares of class B voting stock, and 60 shares of class C preferred stock which is nonvoting except for extraordinary matters or unless the arrearages in dividends exceed a specified amount. Assume for purposes of this example that except for extraordinary business matters, the voting stock's only voting power is the right to vote in the election of directors. The class A stockholders are entitled to elect 7 of the 10 corporate directors, and the class B stockholders are entitled to elect the other 3 of the 10 directors. Thus, the class A stock (as a class) possesses 70 percent of the total combined voting power of all classes of stock, and the class B stock (as a class) possesses 30 percent of such voting power. At the time of D's death, D has voting rights in 9 shares of class A stock directly; and with the constructive ownership rules of section 318. D is deemed to have voting rights in 3 additional shares of class A stock. D has no interest in the class B stock and owns all 60 shares of the class C stock. Thus, D is deemed to possess 21 percent ((9 + 3) shares/40 shares × 70 percent) of the total combined voting power of all classes of stock. By reason of such voting power, the corporation is a controlled corporation within the meaning of this section.

(e) Direct versus indirect retention of voting rights. *(1) Direct transfers.* Subject to the limitations contained in paragraph (a) of this section, if the decedent transfers stock of a controlled corporation (except in case of a bona fide sale for adequate and full consideration in money or money's worth), the retention of voting rights in the stock transferred shall require a portion of the fair market value of the stock to be included in the gross estate. For purposes of this paragraph (e)(1), transfers of stock in exchange for, in whole or in part, either property donated by the decedent or property for which the decedent supplied the purchase consideration, will not be considered a bona fide sale for adequate and full consideration. The amount included in the gross estate under this paragraph (e)(1) shall be an amount, not less than zero, equal to the fair market value at death of the stock transferred less the value of any consideration the decedent received in exchange.

(2) Indirect transfer. Section 2036 applies to indirect as well as direct transfers. The acquisition of voting rights in stock acquired through the exercise of other instruments transferred by the decedent (such as through the exercise of warrants or options, or the conversion rights on convertible nonvoting stock or indebtedness) shall cause the stock to be treated as acquired with consideration furnished by the decedent and an indirect transfer by the decedent. If a third party makes a transfer to the trust and the consideration for the transfer was furnished by the decedent, the transfer by the third party to the trust will be treated as a transfer by the decedent to the trust. In addition, if the decedent makes a transfer by gift to a trust, and the trust subsequently acquires stock in which the decedent has voting rights, then for purposes of section 2036(a), the transaction will be treated as an indirect transfer of stock by the decedent (irrespective of whether the acquisition of the stock can be traced to the gift). The amount included in the gross estate in such a case is equal to the fair market value at death of the portion of the stock acquired with funds provided by the decedent. In the case of a purchase of stock from a third party by a trust, the stock shall be treated as purchased with funds provided by the decedent to the extent there are funds in the trust treated as provided by the decedent. For this purpose, the portion of the funds in the trust treated as provided by the decedent shall be determined after each addition to the trust and is equal to a fraction. The numerator of the fraction is the sum of—

(i) The total value of the trust immediately prior to the latest addition multiplied by the fraction of such value treated as provided by the decedent because of prior additions, and

(ii) The amount of the latest addition to the extent provided by the decedent.

The denominator of the fraction is the total value of the trust immediately after the latest addition.

(3) Exchange of voting rights. For purposes of this section, if a decedent is deemed to have retained the right to vote shares of stock of a controlled corporation in a transfer occurring after June 22, 1976, the subsequent relinquishment of those voting rights in exchange for voting rights in other stock of a controlled corporation, shall be treated as a retention of voting rights in such other stock. Furthermore, for purposes of section 2036(a), such other stock shall be treated as property transferred by the decedent. For example, if a person transfers stock in ABC Corporation (a controlled corporation) after June 22, 1976, to a trust for which that person is a trustee—thus retaining voting rights in a fiduciary capacity—and the trust later sells the ABC Corporation stock, using the proceeds to purchase stock in XYZ Corpora-

tion (a controlled corporation), that person will be treated as having retained the right to vote the shares of XYZ Corporation. In such a transaction, the shares of XYZ Corporation shall be treated as transferred by that person. If the stock in XYZ Corporation is acquired directly from the decedent, the amount included in the gross estate shall be determined under paragraph (e)(1) of this section. If the stock in XYZ Corporation is acquired from someone other than the decedent, the amount included in the decedent's gross estate shall be determined under paragraph (e)(2) of this section.

(4) Examples. The following examples illustrate the application of section 2043 and paragraphs (e)(1) and (e)(2) of this section.

Example (1). During 1977, D transferred by gift $100,000 cash to a trust. During 1979, D transferred to the trust 1000 shares of ABC Corporation voting stock worth $100,000. The 1979 transfer was in exchange for $50,000 cash and D retained voting rights in all the stock transferred. Assume that at some time after the stock transfer, ABC Corporation is a controlled corporation within the meaning of this section. D dies during 1981, at which time the stock is worth $150,000. As a result of the stock transfer, the amount included in D's gross estate under section 2036 is $100,000, computed as follows:

Fair market value of instruments at death	$150,000
Less consideration received by D	50,000
Amount included in D's gross estate	100,000

Example (2). The facts are the same as in *example (1)* except that the 1979 transfer to the trust (1000 shares of ABC Corporation) was in exchange for $100,000 cash. As a result of the stock transfer, the amount included in D's gross estate under section 2036 is $50,000, computed as follows:

Fair market value of instruments at death	$150,000
Less consideration received by D	100,000
Amount included in D's gross estate	50,000

The 1979 transfer is not considered a bona fide sale for adequate and full consideration in money or money's worth since D provided the consideration by virtue of his 1977 transfer to the trust.

Example (3). During 1979, D transferred by gift 1000 shares of ABC Corporation voting stock worth $100,000 to his wife W. During 1980, W made a gift of the same stock to a trust. Assume that D becomes trustee of the trust and hence acquires the right to vote the stock in that capacity. Assume further that, at some time after D's transfer, ABC Corporation is a controlled corporation within the meaning of this section. D dies during 1981, at which time the stock is worth $150,000. The full $150,000 is included in D's gross estate under section 2036.

Example (4). During 1979, D transferred by gift $90,000 to a trust that already had $90,000 of funds, all of which is attributable to contributions by persons other than D. During 1980, the trust purchased at full fair market value 1000 shares of ABC Corporation voting stock worth $100,000, at which time, because of appreciation, the value of the trust was $210,000. Assume that D acquires the right to vote the stock as trustee of the trust and that at some time after the stock purchase, ABC Corporation is a controlled corporation within the meaning of this section. D dies during 1981, at which time the stock is worth $150,000. Pursuant to paragraph (e)(2) of this section, at the time of the stock purchase, $105,000 (50 percent of $210,000) of funds in the trust were funds supplied by D, $100,000 of which are treated as used to purchase the stock. Accordingly, the amount included in D's gross estate under section 2036, $150,000, is the value at death of the portion of the stock acquired with funds provided by D.

§ 20.2037-1 Transfers taking effect at death.

(a) In general. A decedent's gross estate includes under section 2037 the value of any interest in property transferred by the decedent after September 7, 1916, whether in trust or otherwise, except to the extent that the transfer was for an adequate and full consideration in money or money's worth (see § 20.2043-1), if—

(1) Possession or enjoyment of the property could, through ownership of the interest, have been obtained only by surviving the decedent,

(2) The decedent had retained a possibility (referred to in this section as a "reversionary interest") that the property, other than the income alone, would return to the decedent or his estate or would be subject to a power of disposition by him, and

(3) The value of the reversionary interest immediately before the decedent's death exceeded 5 percent of the value of the entire property.

However, if the transfer was made before October 8, 1949, section 2037 is applicable only if the reversionary interest arose by the express terms of the instrument of transfer and not by operation of law (see paragraph (f) of this section). See also paragraph (g) of this section with respect to transfers made between November 11, 1935, and January 29, 1940. The provisions of section 2037 do not apply to transfers made before September 8, 1916.

(b) Condition of survivorship. As indicated in paragraph (a) of this section, the value of an interest in transferred property is not included in a decedent's gross estate under section 2037 unless possession or enjoyment of the property could, through ownership of such interest, have been obtained only by surviving the decedent. Thus, property is not included in the decedent's gross estate if, immediately before the decedent's death, possession or enjoyment of the property could have been obtained by any beneficiary either by surviving the decedent or through the occurrence of some other event such as the expiration of a term of years. However, if a consideration of the terms and circumstances of the transfer as a whole indicates that the "other event" is unreal and if the death of the decedent does, in fact, occur before the "other event", the beneficiary will be considered able to possess or enjoy the property only by surviving the decedent. Notwithstanding the foregoing, an interest in transferred property is not includible in a decedent's gross estate under section 2037 if possession or enjoyment of the property could have been obtained by any beneficiary during the decedent's life through the exercise of a general power of appointment (as defined in section 2041) which in fact was exercisable immediately before the decedent's death. See examples (5) and (6) in paragraph (e) of this section.

(c) Retention of reversionary interest. *(1)* As indicated in paragraph (a) of this section, the value of an interest in transferred property is not included in a decedent's gross estate under section 2037 unless the decedent had retained a reversionary interest in the property, and the value of the reversionary interest immediately before the death of the decedent exceeded 5 percent of the value of the property.

(2) For purposes of section 2037, the term "reversionary interest" includes a possibility that property transferred by the decedent may return to him or his estate and a possibility that property transferred by the decedent may become sub-

ject to a power of disposition by him. The term is not used in a technical sense, but has reference to any reserved right under which the transferred property shall or may be returned to the grantor. Thus, it encompasses an interest arising either by the express terms of the instrument of transfer or by operation of law. (See, however, paragraph (f) of this section with respect to transfers made before October 8, 1949.) The term "reversionary interest" does not include rights to income only, such as the right to receive the income from a trust after the death of another person. (However, see section 2036 for the inclusion of property in the gross estate on account of such rights.) Nor does the term "reversionary interest" include the possibility that the decedent during his lifetime might have received back an interest in transferred property by inheritance through the estate of another person. Similarly, a statutory right of a spouse to receive a portion of whatever estate a decedent may leave at the time of his death is not a "reversionary interest".

(3) For purposes of this section, the value of the decedent's reversionary interest is computed as of the moment immediately before his death, without regard to whether or not the executor elects the alternate valuation method under section 2032 and without regard to the fact of the decedent's death. The value is ascertained in accordance with recognized valuation principles for determining the value for estate tax purposes of future or conditional interests in property. (See §§ 20.2031-1, 20.2031-7, and 20.2031-9.) For example, if the decedent's reversionary interest was subject to an outstanding life estate in his wife, his interest is valued according to the actuarial rules set forth in § 20.2031-7. On the other hand, if the decedent's reversionary interest was contingent on the death of his wife without issue surviving and if it cannot be shown that his wife is incapable of having issue (so that his interest is not subject to valuation according to the actuarial rules in § 20.2031-7), his interest is valued according to the general rules set forth in § 20.2031-1. A possibility that the decedent may be able to dispose of property under certain conditions is considered to have the same value as a right of the decedent to the return of the property under those same conditions.

(4) In order to determine whether or not the decedent retained a reversionary interest in transferred property of a value in excess of 5 percent, the value of the reversionary interest is compared with the value of the transferred property, including interests therein which are not dependent upon survivorship of the decedent. For example, assume that the decedent, A, transferred property in trust with the income payable to B for life and with the remainder payable to C if A predeceases B, but with the property to revert to A if B predeceases A. Assume further that A does, in fact, predecease B. The value of A's reversionary interest immediately before his death is compared with the value of the trust corpus, without deduction of the value of B's outstanding life estate. If, in the above example, A had retained a reversionary interest in one-half only of the trust corpus, the value of his reversionary interest would be compared with the value of one-half of the trust corpus, again without deduction of any part of the value of B's outstanding life estate.

(d) Transfers partly taking effect at death. If separate interests in property are transferred to one or more beneficiaries, paragraphs (a) to (c) of this section are to be separately applied with respect to each interest. For example, assume that the decedent transferred an interest in Blackacre to A which could be possessed or enjoyed only by surviving the decedent, and that the decedent transferred an interest in Blackacre to B which could be possessed or enjoyed only on the occurrence of some event unrelated to the decedent's death. Assume further that the decedent retained a reversionary interest in Blackacre of a value in excess of 5 percent. Only the value of the interest transferred to A is includible in the decedent's gross estate. Similar results would obtain if possession or enjoyment of the entire property could have been obtained only by surviving the decedent, but the decedent had retained a reversionary interest in a part only of such property.

(e) Examples. The provisions of paragraphs (a) to (d) of this section may be further illustrated by the following examples. It is assumed that the transfers were made on or after October 8, 1949; for the significance of this date, see paragraphs (f) and (g) of this section:

Example (1). The decedent transferred property in trust with the income payable to his wife for life and, at her death, remainder to the decedent's then surviving children, or if none, to the decedent or his estate. Since each beneficiary can possess or enjoy the property without surviving the decedent, no part of the property is includible in the decedent's gross estate under section 2037, regardless of the value of the decedent's reversionary interest. (However, see section 2033 for inclusion of the value of the reversionary interest in the decedent's gross estate.)

Example (2). The decedent transferred property in trust with the income to be accumulated for the decedent's life, and at his death, principal and accumulated income to be paid to the decedent's then surviving issue, or, if none, to A or A's estate. Since the decedent retained no reversionary interest in the property, no part of the property is includible in the decedent's gross estate, even though possession or enjoyment of the property could be obtained by the issue only by surviving the decedent.

Example (3). The decedent transferred property in trust with the income payable to his wife for life and with the remainder payable to the decedent or, if he is not living at his wife's death, to his daughter or her estate. The daughter cannot obtain possession or enjoyment of the property without surviving the decedent. Therefore, if the decedent's reversionary interest immediately before his death exceeded 5 percent of the value of the property, the value of the property, less the value of the wife's outstanding life estate, is includible in the decedent's gross estate.

Example (4). The decedent transferred property in trust with the income payable to his wife for life and with the remainder payable to his son or, if the son is not living at the wife's death, to the decedent or, if the decedent is not then living, to X or X's estate. Assume that the decedent was survived by his wife, his son, and X. Only X cannot obtain possession or enjoyment of the property without surviving the decedent. Therefore, if the decedent's reversionary interest immediately before his death exceeded 5 percent of the value of the property, the value of X's remainder interest (with reference to the time immediately after the decedent's death) is includible in the decedent's gross estate.

Example (5). The decedent transferred property in trust with the income to be accumulated for a period of 20 years or until the decedent's prior death, at which time the principal and accumulated income was to be paid to the decedent's son if then surviving. Assume that the decedent does, in fact, die before the expiration of the 20-year period. If, at the time of the transfer, the decedent was 30 years of age, in good health, etc., the son will be considered able to possess or enjoy the property without surviving the decedent. If, on the other hand, the decedent was 70 years of age at the time of the transfer, the son will not be considered able to possess or enjoy the property without surviving the decedent. In this latter case, if the value of the decedent's reversionary interest (arising by operation of law) immediately before his death exceeded 5 percent of the value of the property, the value of the property is includible in the decedent's gross estate.

Example (6). The decedent transferred property in trust with the income to be accumulated for his life and, at his death, the principal and accumulated income to be paid to the decedent's then surviving children. The decedent's wife was given the unrestricted power to alter, amend, or revoke the trust. Assume that the wife survived the decedent but did not, in fact, exercise her power during the decedent's lifetime. Since possession or enjoyment of the property could have been obtained by the wife during the decedent's lifetime under the exercise of a general power of appointment, which was, in fact, exercisable immediately before the decedent's death, no part of the property is includible in the decedent's gross estate.

(f) Transfers made before October 8, 1949. *(1)* Notwithstanding any provisions to the contrary contained in paragraphs (a) to (e) of this section, the value of an interest in property transferred by a decedent before October 8, 1949, is included in his gross estate under section 2037 only if the decedent's reversionary interest arose by the express terms of the instrument and not by operation of law. For example, assume that the decedent, on January 1, 1947, transferred property in trust with the income payable to his wife for the decedent's life and, at his death, remainder to his then surviving descendants. Since no provision was made for the contingency that no descendants of the decedent might survive him, a reversion to the decedent's estate existed by operation of law. The descendants cannot obtain possession or enjoyment of the property without surviving the decedent. However, since the decedent's reversionary interest arose by operation of law, no part of the property is includible in the decedent's gross estate under section 2037. If, in the above example, the transfer had been made on or after October 8, 1949, and if the decedent's reversionary interest immediately before his death exceeded 5 percent of the value of the property, the value of the property would be includible in the decedent's gross estate.

(2) The decedent's reversionary interest will be considered to have arisen by the express terms of the instrument of transfer and not by operation of law if the instrument contains an express disposition which affirmatively creates the reversionary interest, even though the terms of the disposition do not refer to the decedent or his estate, as such. For example, where the disposition is, in its terms, to the next of kin of the decedent and such a disposition, under applicable local law, constitutes a reversionary interest in the decedent's estate, the decedent's reversionary interest will be considered to have arisen by the express terms of the instrument of transfer and not by operation of law.

(g) Transfers made after November 11, 1935, and before January 29, 1940. The provisions of paragraphs (a) to (f) of this section are fully applicable to transfers made after November 11, 1935 (the date on which the Supreme Court decided Helvering v. St. Louis Union Trust Co. (296 U. S. 39) and Becker v. St. Louis Union Trust Co. (296 U. S. 48)), and before January 29, 1940 (the date on which the Supreme Court decided Helvering v. Hallock and companion cases (309 U. S. 106)), except that the value of an interest in property transferred between these dates is not included in a decedent's gross estate under section 2037 if—

(1) The Commissioner, whose determination shall be final, determines that the transfer is classifiable with the transfers involved in the St. Louis Union Trust Co. cases, rather than with the transfer involved in the case of Klein v. United States (283 U. S. 231), previously decided by the Supreme Court, and

(2) The transfer shall have been finally treated for all gift tax purposes, both as to the calendar year of the transfer and as to subsequent calendar years, as a gift in an amount measured by the value of the property undiminished by reason of a provision in the instrument of transfer by which the property, in whole or in part, is to revert to the decedent should he survive the donee or another person, or the reversion is conditioned upon some other contingency terminable by the decedent's death.

T.D. 6296, 6/23/58.

---

§ 20.2038-1 Revocable transfers.

Caution: The Treasury has not yet amended Reg § 20.2038-1 to reflect changes made by P.L. 94-455.

(a) In general. A decedent's gross estate includes under section 2038 the value of any interest in property transferred by the decedent, whether in trust or otherwise, if the enjoyment of the interest was subject at the date of the decedent's death to any change through the exercise of a power by the decedent to alter, amend, revoke, or terminate, or if the decedent relinquished such a power in contemplation of death. However, section 2038 does not apply—

(1) To the extent that the transfer was for an adequate and full consideration in money or money's worth (see § 20.2043-1);

(2) If the decedent's power could be exercised only with the consent of all parties having an interest (vested or contingent) in the transferred property, and if the power adds nothing to the rights of the parties under local law; or

(3) To a power held solely by a person other than the decedent. But, for example, if the decedent had the unrestricted power to remove or discharge a trustee at any time and appoint himself trustee, the decedent is considered as having the powers of the trustee. However, this result would not follow if he only had the power to appoint himself trustee under limited conditions which did not exist at the time of his death. (See last two sentences of paragraph (b) of this section.)

Except as provided in this paragraph, it is immaterial in what capacity the power was exercisable by the decedent or by another person or persons in conjunction with the decedent; whether the power was exercisable alone or only in conjunction with another person or persons, whether or not having an adverse interest (unless the transfer was made before June 2, 1924; see paragraph (d) of this section); and at what time or from what source the decedent acquired his power (unless the transfer was made before June 23, 1936; see paragraph (c) of this section). Section 2038 is applicable to any power affecting the time or manner of enjoyment of property or its income, even though the identity of the beneficiary is not affected. For example, section 2038 is applicable to a power reserved by the grantor of a trust to accumulate income or distribute it to A, and to distribute corpus to A, even though the remainder is vested in A or his estate, and no other person has any beneficial interest in the trust. However, only the value of an interest in property subject to a power to which section 2038 applies is included in the decedent's gross estate under section 2038.

(b) Date of existence of power. A power to alter, amend, revoke, or terminate will be considered to have existed at the date of the decedent's death even though the exercise of the power was subject to a precedent giving of notice or even though the alteration, amendment, revocation, or termination would have taken effect only on the expiration of a stated period after the exercise of the power, whether or not on or before the date of the decedent's death notice had been given or the power had been exercised. In determining the value of the gross estate in such cases, the full value of the property transferred subject to the power is discounted for the period required to elapse between the date of the decedent's death and the date upon which the alteration, amendment, revocation, or termination could take effect. In this connection, see especially § 20.2031-7. However, section 2038 is not applicable to a power the exercise of which was subject to a contingency beyond the decedent's control which did not occur before his death (e.g., the death of another person during the decedent's life). See, however, section 2036(a)(2) for the inclusion of property in the decedent's gross estate on account of such a power.

(c) Transfers made before June 23, 1936. Notwithstanding anything to the contrary in paragraphs (a) and (b) of this section, the value of an interest in property transferred by a decedent before June 23, 1936, is not included in his gross estate under section 2038 unless the power to alter, amend, revoke, or terminate was reserved at the time of the transfer. For purposes of this paragraph, the phrase "reserved at the time of the transfer" has reference to a power (arising either by the express terms of the instrument of transfer or by operation of law) to which the transfer was subject when made and which continued to the date of the decedent's death (see paragraph (b) of this section) to be exercisable by the decedent alone or by the decedent in conjunction with any other person or persons. The phrase also has reference to any understanding, express or implied, had in connection with the making of the transfer that the power would later be created or conferred.

(d) Transfers made before June 2, 1924. Notwithstanding anything to the contrary in paragraphs (a) to (c) of this section, if an interest in property was transferred by a decedent before the enactment of the Revenue Act of 1924 (June 2, 1924, 4:01 p. m., eastern standard time), and if a power reserved by the decedent to alter, amend, revoke, or terminate was exercisable by the decedent only in conjunction with a person having a substantial adverse interest in the transferred property, or in conjunction with several persons some or all of whom held such an adverse interest, there is included in the decedent's gross estate only the value of any interest or interests held by a person or persons not required to join in the exercise of the power plus the value of any insubstantial adverse interest or interests of a person or persons required to join in the exercise of the power.

(e) Powers relinquished in contemplation of death. *(1) In general.* If a power to alter, amend, revoke, or terminate would have resulted in the inclusion of an interest in property in a decedent's gross estate under section 2038 if it had been held until the decedent's death, the relinquishment of the power in contemplation of the decedent's death within 3 years before his death results in the inclusion of the same interest in property in the decedent's gross estate, except to the extent that the power was relinquished for an adequate and full consideration in money or money's worth (see § 20.2043-1). For the meaning of the phrase "in contemplation of death", see paragraph (c) of § 20.2035-1.

(2) Transfers before June 23, 1936. In the case of a transfer made before June 23, 1936, section 2038 applies only to a relinquishment made by the decedent. However, in the case of a transfer made after June 22, 1936, section 2038 also applies to a relinquishment made by a person or persons holding the power in conjunction with the decedent, if the relinquishment was made in contemplation of the decedent's death and had the effect of extinguishing the power.

(f) Effect of disability to relinquish power in certain cases. Notwithstanding anything to the contrary in paragraphs (a) through (e) of this section the provisions of this section do not apply to a transfer if—

(1) The relinquishment on or after January 1, 1940, and on or before December 31, 1947, of the power would, by reason of section 1000(e), of the Internal Revenue Code of 1939, be deemed not a transfer of property for the purpose of the gift tax under chapter 4 of the Internal Revenue Code of 1939, and

(2) The decedent was, for a continuous period beginning on or before September 30, 1947, and ending with his death, after August 16, 1954, under a mental disability to relinquish a power.

For the purpose of the foregoing provision, the term "mental disability" means mental incompetence, in fact, to release the power whether or not there was an adjudication of incompetence. Such provision shall apply even though a guardian could have released the power for the decedent. No interest shall be allowed or paid on any overpayment allowable under section 2038(c) with respect to amounts paid before August 7, 1959.

T.D. 6296, 6/23/58, amend T.D. 6600, 5/28/62.

§ 20.2039-1 Annuities.

(a) In general. In general. A decedent's gross estate includes under section 2039(a) and (b) the value of an annuity or other payment receivable by any beneficiary by reason of surviving the decedent under certain agreements or plans to the extent that the value of the annuity or other payment is attributable to contributions made by the decedent or his employer. Sections 2039(a) and (b), however, have no application to an amount which constitutes the proceeds of insurance under a policy on the decedent's life. Paragraph (b) of this section describes the agreements or plans to which section 2039(a) and (b) applies; paragraph (c) of this section provides rules for determining the amount includible in the decedent's gross estate; paragraph (d) of this section distinguishes proceeds of life insurance; and paragraph (e) of this section distinguishes annuity, unitrust, and other interests retained by a decedent in certain trusts.

The fact that an annuity or other payment is not includible in a decedent's gross estate under section 2039(a) and (b) does not mean that it is not includible under some other section of part III of subchapter A of chapter 11. However, see section 2039(c) and (d) and § 20.2039-2 for rules relating to the exclusion from a decedent's gross estate of annuities and other payments under certain "qualified plans." Further, the fact that an annuity or other payment may be includible under section 2039(a) will not preclude the application of another section of chapter 11 with regard to that interest. For annuity interests in trust, see paragraph (e)(1) of this section.

(b) Agreements or plans to which section 2039(a) and (b) applies. *(1)* Section 2039(a) and (b) applies to the value of an annuity or other payment receivable by any beneficiary under any form of contract or agreement entered into after March 3, 1931, under which—

(i) An annuity or other payment was payable to the decedent, either alone or in conjunction with another person or persons, for his life or for any period not ascertainable without reference to his death or for any period which does not in fact end before his death, or

(ii) The decedent possessed, for his life or for any period not ascertainable without reference to his death or for any period which does not in fact end before his death, the right to receive such an annuity or other payment, either alone or in conjunction with another person or persons. The term "annuity or other payment" as used with respect to both the decedent and the beneficiary has reference to one or more payments extending over any period of time. The payments may be equal or unequal, conditional or unconditional, periodic or sporadic. The term "contract or agreement" includes any arrangement, understanding or plan, or any combination of arrangements, understandings or plans arising by reason of the decedent's employment. An annuity or other payment "was payable" to the decedent if, at the time of his death, the decedent was in fact receiving an annuity or other payment, whether or not he had an enforceable right to have payments continued. The decedent "possessed the right to receive" an annuity or other payment if, immediately before his death, the decedent had an enforceable right to receive payments at some time in the future, whether or not, at the time of his death, he had a present right to receive payments. In connection with the preceding sentence, the decedent will be regarded as having had "an enforceable right to receive payments at some time in the future" so long as he had complied with his obligations under the contract or agreement up to the time of his death. For the meaning of the phrase "for his life or for any period not ascertainable without reference to his death or for any period which does not in fact end before his death", see section 2036 and § 20.2036-1.

(2) The application of this paragraph is illustrated and more fully explained in the following examples. In each example: (i) It is assumed that all transactions occurred after March 3, 1931, and (ii) the amount stated to be includible in the decedent's gross estate is determined in accordance with the provisions of paragraph (c) of this section.

Example (1). The decedent purchased an annuity contract under the terms of which the issuing company agreed to pay an annuity to the decedent for his life and, upon his death, to pay a specified lump sum to his designated beneficiary. The decedent was drawing his annuity at the time of his death. The amount of the lump sum payment to the beneficiary is includible in the decedent's gross estate under section 2039(a) and (b).

Example (2). Pursuant to a retirement plan, the employer made contributions to a fund which was to provide the employee, upon his retirement at age 60, with an annuity for life, and which was to provide the employee's wife, upon his death after retirement, with a similar annuity for life. The benefits under the plan were completely forfeitable during the employees' life, but upon his death after retirement, the benefits to the wife were forfeitable only upon her remarriage. The employee had no right to originally designate or to ever change the employer's designation of the surviving beneficiary. The retirement plan at no time met the requirements of section 401(a) (relating to qualified plans). Assume that the employee died at age 61 after the employer started payment of his annuity as described above. The value of the wife's annuity is includible in the decedent's gross estate under section 2039(a) and (b). Includibility in this case is based on the fact that the annuity to the decedent "was payable" at the time of his death. The fact that the decedent's annuity was forfeitable is of no consequence since, at the time of his death, he was in fact receiving payments under the plan. Nor is it important that the decedent had no right to choose the surviving beneficiary. The element of forfeitability in the wife's annuity may be taken into account only with respect to the valuation of the annuity in the decedent's gross estate.

Example (3). Pursuant to a retirement plan, the employer made contributions to a fund which was to provide the employee, upon his retirement at age 60, with an annuity of $100 per month for life, and which was to provide his designated beneficiary, upon the employee's death after retirement, with a similar annuity for life. The plan also provided that (a) upon the employee's separation from service before retirement, he would have a nonforfeitable right to receive a reduced annuity starting at age 60, and (b) upon the employee's death before retirement, a lump sum payment representing the amount of the employer's contributions credited to the employee's account would be paid to the designated beneficiary. The plan at no time met the requirements of section 401(a) (relating to qualified plans). Assume that the employee died at age 49 and that the designated beneficiary was paid the specified lump sum payment. Such amount is includible in the decedent's gross estate under section 2039(a) and (b). Since, immediately before his death, the employee had an enforceable right to receive an annuity commencing at age 60, he is considered to have "possessed the right to receive" an annuity as that term is used in section 2039(a). If, in this example, the employee would not be entitled to any benefits in the event of his separation from service before retirement for any reason other than death, the result would be the same so long as the decedent had complied with his obligations under the contract up to the time of his death. In such case, he is considered to have had, immediately before his death, an enforceable right to receive an annuity commencing at age 60.

Example (4). Pursuant to a retirement plan, the employer made contributions to a fund which was to provide the employee, upon his retirement at age 60, with an annuity for life, and which was to provide his designated beneficiary, upon the employee's death after retirement, with a similar annuity for life, and which was to provide his designated beneficiary, upon the employee's death after retirement, with a similar annuity for life. The plan provided, however, that no benefits were payable in the event of the employee's death before retirement. The retirement plan at no time met the requirements of section 401(a) (relating to qualified plans). Assume that the employee died at age 59 but that the employer nevertheless started payment of an annuity in a slightly reduced amount to the designated beneficiary. The value of the annuity is not includible in the decedent's gross estate under section 2039(a) and (b). Since the employee died before reaching the retirement age, the employer was under no obligation to pay the annuity to the employee's designated beneficiary. Therefore, the annuity was not paid under a "contract or agreement" as that term is used in section 2039(a). If, however, it can be established that the employer has consistently paid an annuity under such circumstances, the annuity will be considered as having been paid under a "contract or agreement".

Example (5). The employer made contributions to a retirement fund which were credited to the employee's individual account. Under the plan, the employee was to receive one-half the amount credited to his account upon his retirement at age 60, and his designated beneficiary was to receive the other one-half upon the employee's death after retirement. If the employee should die before reaching the retirement age, the entire amount credited to his account at such time was to be paid to the designated beneficiary. The retirement plan at no time met the requirements of section 401(a) (relating to qualified plans). Assume that the employee received one-half the amount credited to his account upon reaching the retirement age and that he died shortly thereafter. Since the employee received all that he was entitled to receive under the plan before his death, no amount was payable to him for his life or for any period not ascertainable without reference to his death, or for any period which did not in fact end before his death. Thus, the amount of the payment to the designated beneficiary is not includible in the decedent's gross estate under section 2039(a) and (b). If, in this example, the employee died before reaching the retirement age, the amount of the payment to the designated beneficiary would be includible in the decedent's gross estate under section 2039(a) and (b). In this latter case, the decedent possessed the right to receive a lump sum payment for a period which did not in fact end before his death.

Example (6). The employer made contributions to two different funds set up under two different plans. One plan was to provide the employee, upon his retirement at age 60, with an annuity for life, and the other plan was to provide the employee's designated beneficiary, upon the employee's death, with a similar annuity for life. Each plan was established at a different time and each plan was administered separately in every respect. Neither plan at any time met the requirements of section 401(a) (relating to qualified plans). The value of the designated beneficiary's annuity is includible in the employee's gross estate. All rights and benefits accruing to an employee and to others by reason of the employment (except rights and benefits accruing under certain plans meeting the requirements of section 401(a) (see § 20.2039-2)) are considered together in determining whether or not section 2039(a) and (b) applies. The scope of section 2039(a) and (b) cannot be limited by indirection.

(c) Amount includible in the gross estate. The amount to be included in a decedent's gross estate under section 2039(a) and (b) is an amount which bears the same ratio to the value at the decedent's death of the annuity or other payment receivable by the beneficiary as the contribution made by the decedent, or made by his employer (or former employer) for any reason connected with his employment, to the cost of the contract or agreement bears to its total cost. In applying this ratio, the value at the decedent's death of the annuity or other payment is determined in accordance with the rules set forth in §§ 20.2031-1, 20.2031-7, 20.2031-8, and 20.2031-9. The application of this paragraph may be illustrated by the following examples:

Example (1). On January 1, 1945, the decedent and his wife each contributed $15,000 to the purchase price of an annuity contract under the terms of which the issuing company agreed to pay an annuity to the decedent and his wife for their joint lives and to continue the annuity to the survivor for his life. Assume that the value of the survivor's annuity at the decedent's death (computed under § 20.2031-8) is $20,000. Since the decedent contributed one-half of the cost of the contract, the amount to be included in his gross estate under section 2039(a) and (b) is $10,000.

Example (2). Under the terms of an employment contract entered into on January 1, 1945, the employer and the employee made contributions to a fund which was to provide the employee, upon his retirement at age 60, with an annuity for life, and which was to provide his designated beneficiary, upon the employee's death after retirement, with a similar annuity for life. The retirement fund at no time formed part of a plan meeting the requirements of section 401(a) (relating to qualified plans). Assume that the employer and the employee each contributed $5,000 to the retirement fund. Assume, further, that the employee died after retirement at which time the value of the survivor's annuity was $8,000. Since the employer's contributions were made by reason of the decedent's employment, the amount to be included in his gross estate under section 2039(a) and (b) is the entire $8,000. If, in the above example, only the employer made contributions to the fund, the amount to be included in the gross estate would still be $8,000.

(d) Insurance under policies on the life of the decedent. If an annuity or other payment receivable by a beneficiary under a contract or agreement is in substance the proceeds of insurance under a policy on the life of the decedent, section 2039(a) and (b) does not apply. For the extent to which such an annuity or other payment is includible in a decedent's gross estate, see section 2042 and § 20.2042-1. A combination annuity contract and life insurance policy on the decedent's life (e.g., a "retirement income" policy with death benefits) which matured during the decedent's lifetime so that there was no longer an insurance element under the contract at the time of the decedent's death is subject to the provisions of section 2039(a) and (b). On the other hand, the treatment of a combination annuity contract and life insurance policy on the decedent's life which did not mature during the decedent's lifetime depends upon the nature of the contract at the time of the decedent's death. The nature of the contract is generally determined by the relation of the reserve value of the policy to the value of the death benefit at the time of the decedent's death. If the decedent dies before the reserve value equals the death benefit, there is still an insurance element under the contract. The contract is therefore considered, for estate tax purposes, to be an insurance policy subject to the provisions of section 2042. However, if the decedent dies after the reserve value equals the death benefit, there is no longer an insurance element under the contract. The contract is therefore considered to be a contract for an annuity or other payment subject to the provisions of section 2039(a) and (b) or some other section of part III of subchapter A of chapter 11. Notwithstanding the relation of the reserve value to the value of the death benefit, a contract under which the death benefit could never exceed the total premiums paid, plus interest, contains no insurance element.

Example. Pursuant to a retirement plan established January 1, 1945, the employer purchased a contract from an insurance company which was to provide the employee, upon his retirement at age 65, with an annuity of $100 per month for life, and which was to provide his designated beneficiary, upon the employee's death after retirement, with a similar annuity for life. The contract further provided that if the employee should die before reaching the retirement age, a lump sum payment of $20,000 would be paid to his designated beneficiary in lieu of the annuity described above. The plan at no time met the requirements of section 401(a) (relating to qualified plans). Assume that the reserve value of the contract at the retirement age would be $20,000. If the employee died after reaching the retirement age, the death benefit to the designated beneficiary would constitute an annuity, the value of which would be includible in the employee's gross estate under section 2039(a) and (b). If, on the other hand, the employee died before reaching his retirement age, the death benefit to the designated beneficiary would constitute insurance under a policy on the life of the decedent since the reserve value would be less than the death benefit. Accordingly, its includibility would depend upon section 2042 and § 20.2042-1.

(e) No application to certain trusts. Section 2039 shall not be applied to include in a decedent's gross estate all or any portion of a trust (other than a trust constituting an employee benefit, but including those described in the following sentence) if the decedent retained a right to use property of the trust or retained an annuity, unitrust, or other interest in the trust, in either case as described in section 2036. Such trusts include without limitation the following (collectively referred to in this paragraph (e) as "trusts"): Certain charitable remainder trusts (collectively CRTs) such as a charitable remainder annuity trust (CRAT) within the meaning of section 664(d)(1), a charitable remainder unitrust (CRUT) within the meaning of section 664(d)(2) or (d)(3), and any other charitable remainder trust that does not qualify under section 664(d), whether because the CRT was created prior to 1969, there was a defect in the drafting of the CRT, there was no intention to qualify the CRT for the charitable deduction, or otherwise; other trusts established by a grantor (collectively GRTs) such as a grantor retained annuity trust (GRAT) paying out a qualified annuity interest within the meaning of § 25.2702-3(b) of this chapter, a grantor retained unitrust (GRUT) paying out a qualified unitrust interest within the meaning of § 25.2702-3(c) of this chapter; and various forms of grantor retained income trusts (GRITs) whether or not the grantor's retained interest is a qualified interest as defined in section 2702(b), including without limitation a qualified personal residence trust (QPRT) within the meaning of § 25.2702-5(c) of this chapter and a personal residence trust (PRT) within the meaning of § 25.2702-5(b) of this chapter. For purposes of determining the extent to which a retained interest causes all or a portion of a trust to be included in a decedent's gross estate, see § 20.2036-1(c)(1), (2), and (3).

(f) Effective/applicability dates. The first, second, and fourth sentences in paragraph (a) of this section are applicable to the estates of decedents dying after August 16, 1954. The fifth sentence of paragraph (a) of this section is applicable to the estates of decedents dying on or after October 27, 1972, and to the estates of decedents for which the period for filing a claim for credit or refund of an estate tax overpayment ends on or after October 27, 1972. The third, sixth, and seventh sentences of paragraph (a) of this section and all of paragraph (e) of this section are applicable to the estates of decedents dying on or after July 14, 2008.

T.D. 6296, 6/23/58, amend T.D. 7416, 4/5/76, T.D. 9414, 7/11/2008.

§ 20.2039-1T Limitations and repeal of estate tax exclusion for qualified plans and individual retirement plans (IRAs) (Temporary).

Q-1. Are there any exceptions to the general effective dates of the $100,000 limitation and the repeal of the estate tax exclusion for the value of interests under qualified plans and IRAs described in section 2039(c) and (e)?

A-1. (a) Yes. Section 245 of the Tax Equity and Fiscal Responsibility Act of 1982 (TEFRA) limited the estate tax exclusion to $100,000 for estates of decedents dying after December 31, 1982. Section 525 of the Tax Reform Act of 1984 (TRA of 1984) repealed the exclusion for estates of decedents dying after December 31, 1984.

(b) Section 525(b)(3) of the TRA of 1984 amended section 245 of TEFRA to provide that the $100,000 limitation on the exclusion for the value of a decedent's interest in a plan or IRA will not apply to the estate of any decedent dying after December 31, 1982, to the extent that the decedent-participant was in pay status on December 31, 1982, with respect to such interest and irrevocably elected the form of benefit payable under the plan or IRA (including the form of any survivor benefits) with respect to such interest before January 1, 1983.

(c) Similarly, the TRA of 1984 provides that the repeal of the estate tax exclusion for the value of a decedent's interest in a plan or IRA will not apply to the estate of a decedent dying after December 31, 1984, to the extent that the decedent-participant was in pay status on December 31, 1984, with respect to such interest and irrevocably elected the form of benefit payable under the plan or IRA (including the form of any survivor benefits) with respect to such interest before July 18, 1984.

Q-2. What is the meaning of "in pay status" on the applicable date?

A-2. A participant was in pay status on the applicable date with respect to a portion of his or her interest in a plan or IRA if such portion is to be paid in a benefit form that has been elected on or before such date and the participant has received, on or before such date, at least one payment under such benefit form.

Q-3. What is required for an election of the form of benefit payable under the plan to have been irrevocable as of any applicable date?

A-3. As of any applicable date, an election of the form of benefit payable under a plan is irrevocable if, as of such date, it was a written irrevocable election that, with respect to all payments to be received after such date, specified the form of distribution (e.g., lump sum, level dollar annuity, formula annuity) and the period over which the distribution would be made (e.g., single life, joint and survivor, term certain). An election is not irrevocable as of any applicable date if, on or after such date, the form or period of the distribution could be determined or altered by any person or persons. An election does not fail to be irrevocable as of an applicable date merely because the beneficiaries were not designated as of such date or could be changed after such date. If any interest in any IRA may not, by law or contract, be subject to an irrevocable election described in this section, any election of the form of benefit payable under the IRA does not satisfy the requirement that an irrevocable election have been made.

T.D. 8073, 1/29/86.

§ 20.2039-2 Annuities under "qualified plans" and section 403(b) annuity contracts.

Caution: The Treasury has not yet amended Reg § 20.2039-2 to reflect changes made by P.L. 98-369, P.L. 97-448, P.L. 97-248, P.L. 97-34.

(a) Section 2039(c) exclusion. In general, in the case of a decedent dying after December 31, 1953, the value of an annuity or other payment receivable under a plan or annuity contract described in paragraph (b) of this section is excluded from the decedent's gross estate to the extent provided in paragraph (c) of this section. In the case of a plan described in paragraph (b)(1) or (2) of this section (a "qualified plan"), the exclusion is subject to the limitation described in § 20.2039-3 (relating to lump sum distributions paid with respect to a decedent dying after December 31, 1976, and before January 1, 1979) or § 20.2039-4 (relating to lump sum distributions paid with respect to a decedent dying after December 31, 1978).

(b) Plans and annuity contracts to which section 2039(c) applies. Section 2039(c) excludes from a decedent's gross estate, to the extent provided in paragraph (c) of this section, the value of an annuity or other payment receivable by any beneficiary (except the value of an annuity or other payment receivable by or for the benefit of the decedent's estate) under—

(1) An employees' trust (or under a contract purchased by an employees' trust) forming part of a pension, stock bonus, or profit-sharing plan which, at the time of the decedent's separation from employment (whether by death or otherwise), or at the time of the earlier termination of the plan, met the requirements of section 401(a);

(2) A retirement annuity contract purchased by an employer (and not by an employees' trust) pursuant to a plan which, at the time of decedent's separation from employment (by death or otherwise), or at the time of the earlier termination of the plan, was a plan described in section 403(a);

(3) In the case of a decedent dying after December 31, 1957, a retirement annuity contract purchased for an employee by an employer which, for its taxable year in which the purchase occurred, is an organization referred to in section 170(b)(1)(A)(ii) or (vi) or which is a religious organization (other than a trust) and is exempt from tax under 501(a);

(4) In the case of a decedent dying after December 31, 1965, an annuity under chapter 73 of title 10 of the United States Code (10 U.S.C. 1431, *et seq.*); or

(5) In the case of a decedent dying after December 31, 1962, a bond purchase plan described in section 405.

For the meaning of the term "annuity or other payment", see paragraph (b) of § 20.2039-1. For the meaning of the phrase "receivable by or for the benefit of the decedent's estate", see paragraph (b) of § 20.2042-1. The application of this paragraph may be illustrated by the following examples in each of which it is assumed that the amount stated to be excludable from the decedent's gross estate is determined in accordance with paragraph (c) of this section:

Example (1). Pursuant to a pension plan, the employer made contributions to a trust which was to provide the employee, upon his retirement at age 60, with an annuity for life, and which was to provide his wife, upon the employee's death after retirement, with a similar annuity for life. At the time of the employee's retirement, the pension trust formed part of a plan meeting the requirements of section 401(a). Assume that the employee died at age 61 after the trustee started payment of his annuity as described above. Since the wife's annuity was receivable under a qualified pension plan, no part of the value of such annuity is includible in the decedent's gross estate by reason of the provisions of section 2039(c). If, in this example, the employer provided other benefits under nonqualified plans, the result would be the same since the exclusion under section 2039(c) is confined to the benefits provided for under the qualified plan.

Example (2). Pursuant to a profit-sharing plan, the employer made contributions to a trust which were allocated to the employee's individual account. Under the plan, the employee would, upon retirement at age 60, receive a distribution of the entire amount credited to the account. If the employee should die before reaching retirement age, the amount credited to the account would be distributed to the employee's designated beneficiary. Assume that the employee died before reaching the retirement age and that at such time the plan met the requirements of section 401(a). Since the payment to the designated beneficiary is receivable under qualified profit-sharing plan, the provisions of section 2039(c) apply. However, if the payment is a lump sum distribution to which § 20.2039-3 or § 20.2039-4 applies, the payment is excludable from the decedent's gross estate only as provided in such section.

Example (3). Pursuant to a pension plan, the employer made contributions to a trust which were used by the trustee to purchase a contract from an insurance company for the benefit of an employee. The contract was to provide the employee, upon retirement at age 65, with an annuity of $100 per month for life, and was to provide the employee's designed beneficiary upon the employee's death after retirement, with a similar annuity for life. The contract further provided that if the employee should die before reaching retirement age, a lump sum payment equal to the greater of (a) $10,000 or (b) the reserve value of the policy would be paid to the designated beneficiary in lieu of the annuity. Assume that the employee died before reaching the retirement age and that at such time the plan met the requirements of section 401(a). Since the payment to the designated beneficiary is receivable under a qualified pension plan, the provisions of section 2039(c) apply. However, if the payment is a lump sum distribution to which § 20.2039-3 or § 20.2039-4 applies, the payment is excludable from the decedent's gross estate only as provided in such section. It should be noted that for purposes of the exclusion under section 2039(c) it is immaterial whether or not the payment constitutes the proceeds of life insurance under the principles set forth in § 20.2039-1(d).

Example (4). Pursuant to a profit-sharing plan, the employer made contributions to a trust which were allocated to the employee's individual account. Under the plan, the employee would, upon his retirement at age 60, be given the option to have the amount credited to his account (a) paid to him in a lump sum, (b) used to purchase a joint and survivor annuity for him and his designated beneficiary, or (c) left with the trustee under an arrangement whereby interest would be paid to him for his lifetime with the principal to be paid, at his death, to his designated beneficiary. The plan further provided that, if the third method of settlement were selected, the employee would retain the right to have the principal paid to himself in a lump sum up to the time of his death. At the time of the employee's retirement, the profit-sharing plan met the requirements of section 401(a). Assume that the employee, upon reaching his retirement age, elected to have the amount credited to his account left with the trustee under the interest arrangement. Assume, further, that the employee did not exercise his right to have such amount paid to him before his death. Under such circumstances, the employee is considered as having constructively received the amount credited to his account upon his retirement. Thus, such amount is not considered as receivable by the designated beneficiary under the profit-sharing plan and the exclusion of section 2039(c) is not applicable.

Example (5). An employer purchased a retirement annuity contract for an employee which was to provide the employee, upon his retirement at age 60, with an annuity for life and which was to provide his wife, upon the employee's death after retirement, with a similar annuity for life. The employer, for its taxable year in which the annuity contract was purchased, was an organization referred to in section 170(b)(1)(A)(ii), and was exempt from tax under section 501(a). The entire amount of the purchase price of the annuity contract was excluded from the employee's gross income under section 403(b). No part of the value of the survivor annuity payable after the employee's death is includible in the decedent's gross estate by reason of the provisions of section 2039(c); or

(c) Amounts excludable from the gross estate. *(1)* The amount to be excluded from a decedent's gross estate under section 2039(c) is an amount which bears the same ratio to the value at the decedent's death of an annuity or other payment receivable by the beneficiary as the employer's contribution (or a contribution made on the employer's behalf) on the employee's account to the plan or towards the purchase of the annuity contract bears to the total contributions on the employee's account to the plan or towards the purchase of the annuity contract. In applying this ratio—

(i) Payments or contributions made by or on behalf of the employer towards the purchase of an annuity contract described in paragraph (b)(3) of this section are considered to include only such payments or contributions as are, or were, excludable from the employee's gross income under section 403(b).

(ii) In the case of a decedent dying before January 1, 1977, payments or contributions made under a plan described in paragraph (b)(1), (2) or (5) of this section on behalf of the decedent for a period for which the decedent was self-employed, within the meaning of section 401(c)(1), with respect to the plan are considered payments or contributions made by the decedent and not by the employer.

(iii) In the case of a decedent dying after December 31, 1976, however, payments or contributions made under a plan described in paragraph (b)(1), (2) or (5) of this section on behalf of the decedent for a period for which the decedent was self-employed, within the meaning of section 401(c)(1), with respect to the plan are considered payments or contributions made by the employer to the extent the payments or contributions are, or were, deductible under section 404 or 405(c). Contributions or payments attributable to that period which are not, or were not, so deductible are considered made by the decedent.

(iv) In the case of a plan described in paragraph (b)(1) or (2) of this section, a rollover contribution described in section 402(a)(5), 403(a)(4), 409(d)(3)(A)(ii) or 409(b)(3)(C) is considered an amount contributed by the employer.

(v) In the case of an annuity contract described in paragraph (b)(3) of this section, a rollover contribution described in section 403(b)(8) is considered an amount contributed by the employer.

(vi) In the case of a plan described in paragraph (b)(1), (2) or (5) of this section, an amount includable in the gross income of an employee under section 1379(b) (relating to shareholder-employee beneficiaries under certain qualified plans) is considered an amount paid or contributed by the decedent.

(vii) Amounts payable under paragraph (b)(4) of this section are attributable to payments or contributions made by the decedent only to the extent of amounts deposited by the decedent pursuant to section 1438 or 1452(d) of Title 10 of the United States Code.

(viii) The value at the decedent's death of the annuity or other payment is determined under the rules of §§ 20.2031-1 and 20.2031-7 or, for certain prior periods, § 20.2031-7A.

(2) In certain cases, the employer's contribution (or a contribution made on his behalf) to a plan on the employee's account and thus the total contributions to the plan on the employee's account cannot be readily ascertained. In order to apply the ratio stated in subparagraph (1) of this paragraph in such a case, the method outlined in the following two sentences must be used unless a more precise method is presented. In such a case, the total contributions to the plan on the employee's account is the value of any annuity or other payment payable to the decedent and his survivor computed as of the time the decedent's rights first mature (or as of the time the survivor's rights first mature if the decedent's rights never mature) and computed in accordance with the rules set forth in §§ 20.2031-1, 20.2031-7, 20.2031-8, and 20.2031-9. By subtracting from such value the amount of the employee's contribution to the plan, the amount of the employer's contribution to the plan on the employee's account may be obtained. The application of this paragraph may be illustrated by the following example:

Example. Pursuant to a pension plan, the employer and the employee contributed to a trust which was to provide the employee, upon his retirement at age 60, with an annuity for life, and which was to provide his wife, upon the employee's death after retirement, with a similar annuity for life. At the time of the employee's retirement, the pension trust formed part of a plan meeting the requirements of section 401(a). Assume the following: (i) That the employer's contributions to the fund were not credited to the accounts of individual employees; (ii) that the value of the employee's annuity and his wife's annuity, computed as of the time of the decedent's retirement, was $40,000; (iii) that the employee contributed $10,000 to the plan; and (iv) that the value at the decedent's death of the wife's annuity was $16,000. On the basis of these facts, the total contributions to the fund on the employee's account are presumed to be $30,000 ($40,000 less $10,000). Since the wife's annuity was receivable under a qualified pension plan, that part of the value of such annuity which is attributable to the employer's contributions

$$\left(\frac{\$30,000}{\$40,000} \times \$16,000, \text{ or } \$12,000\right)$$

is excludable from the decedent's gross estate by reason of the provisions of section 2039(c). Compare this result with the results reached in the examples set forth in paragraph (b) of this section in which all contributions to the plans were made by the employer.

(d) Exclusion of certain annuity interests created by community property laws. *(1)* In the case of an employee on whose behalf contributions or payments were made by his employer or former employer under an employees' trust forming part of a pension, stock bonus, or profit-sharing plan described in section 2039(c)(1), under an employee's retirement annuity contract described in section 2039(c)(2), or toward the purchase of an employee's retirement annuity contract described in section 2039(c)(3), which under section 2039(c) are not considered as contributed by the employee, if the spouse of such employee predeceases him, then, notwithstanding the provisions of section 2039 or of any other provision of law, there shall be excluded from the gross estate of such spouse the value of any interest of such spouse in such plan or trust or such contract, to the extent such interest—

(i) Is attributable to such contributions or payments, and

(ii) Arises solely by reason of such spouse's interest in community income under the community property laws of a State.

(2) Section 2039(d) and this paragraph do not provide any exclusion for such spouse's property interest in the plan, trust or contract to the extent it is attributable to the contributions of the employee spouse. Thus, the decedent's community property interest in the plan, trust, or contract which is attributable to contributions made by the employee spouse are includible in the decedent's gross estate. See paragraph (c) of this section.

(3) Section 2039(d) and this paragraph apply to the estate of a decedent who dies on or after October 27, 1972, and to the estate of a decedent who died before October 27, 1972, if the period for filing a claim for credit or refund of an overpayment of the estate tax ends on or after October 27, 1972. Interest will not be allowed or paid on any overpayment of tax resulting from the application of section 2039(d) and this paragraph for any period prior to April 26, 1973.

T.D. 6296, 6/23/58, amend T.D. 6526, 1/18/61, T.D. 6666, 7/15/63, T.D. 7043, 6/1/70, T.D. 7416, 4/5/76, T.D. 7428, 8/13/76, T.D. 7562, 8/30/78, T.D. 7761, 1/21/81, T.D. 8540, 6/9/94.

PAR. 10. Section 20.2039-2 is amended by adding a new subdivision (ix) to paragraph (c)(1) to read as follows:

Proposed § 20.2039-2 Annuities under "qualified plans" and section 403(b) annuity contracts. [*For Preamble, see ¶ 150,933*] * * *

(c) Amounts excludable from the gross estate.

(1) * * *

(ix) Any deductible employee contributions (within the meaning of section 72(o)(5)) are considered amounts contributed by the employer.

* * * * *

§ 20.2039-3 Lump sum distributions under "qualified plans;" decedents dying after December 31, 1976, and before January 1, 1979.

(a) Limitation of section 2039(c) exclusion. This section applies in the case of a decedent dying after December 31, 1976, and before January 1, 1979. If a lump sum distribution is paid with respect to the decedent under a plan described in § 20.2039-2(b)(1) or (2) (a "qualified plan"), no amount payable with respect to the decedent under the plan is excludable from the decedent's gross estate under § 20.2039-2.

(b) "Lump sum distribution" defined. For purposes of this section the term "lump sum distribution" means a lump sum distribution defined in section 402(e)(4)(A) that satisfies the requirements of section 402(e)(4)(C), relating to the aggregation of certain trusts and plans. The distribution of an annuity contract is not a lump sum distribution for purposes of this section, and § 20.2039-2 will apply with respect to the distribution of an annuity contract without regard to whether the contract is included in a distribution that is otherwise a lump sum distribution under this paragraph (b). A distribution is a lump sum distribution for purposes of this section without regard to the election described in section 402(e)(4)(B).

(c) Amounts payable as a lump sum distribution. If on the date the estate tax return is filed, an amount under a qualified plan is payable with respect to the decedent as a lump sum distribution (whether at the election of a beneficiary or otherwise), for purposes of this section the amount is deemed paid as a lump sum distribution no later than on such date. Accordingly, no portion of the amount payable under the plan is excludable from the value of the decedent's gross estate under § 20.2039-2. If, however, the amount payable as a lump sum distribution is not, in fact, thereafter paid as a lump sum distribution, there shall be allowed a credit or refund of any tax paid which is attributable to treating such amount as a lump sum distribution under this paragraph. Any claim for credit or refund filed under this paragraph must be filed within the time prescribed by section 6511, and must provide satisfactory evidence that the amount originally payable as a lump sum distribution is no longer payable in such form.

(d) Filing date. For purposes of paragraph (c) of this section, "the date the estate tax return is filed" means the earlier of—

(1) The date the estate tax return is actually filed, or

(2) The date nine months after the decedent's death, plus any extension of time for filing the estate tax return granted under section 6081.

T.D. 7761, 1/21/81.

§ 20.2039-4 Lump sum distributions from "qualified plans;" decedents dying after December 31, 1978.

Caution: The Treasury has not yet amended Reg § 20.2039-4 to reflect changes made by P.L. 98-369, P.L. 97-448, P.L. 97-248, P.L. 97-34.

(a) Limitation on section 2039(c) exclusion. This section applies in the case of a decedent dying after December 31, 1978. If a lump sum distribution is paid or payable with respect to a decedent under a plan described in § 20.2039-2(b)(1) or (2) (a "qualified plan"), no amount paid or payable with respect to the decedent under the plan is excludable from the decedent's gross estate under § 20.2039-2, unless the recipient of the distribution makes the section 402(a)/403(a) taxation election described in paragraph (c) of this section. For purposes of this section, an amount is payable as a lump sum distribution under a plan if, as of the date the estate tax return is filed (as determined under § 20.2039-3(d)), it is payable as a lump sum distribution at the election of the recipient or otherwise.

(b) "Lump sum distribution" defined; treatment of annuity contracts. For purposes of this section the term "lump sum distribution" means a lump sum distribution defined in section 402(e)(4)(A) that satisfies the requirement of section 402(e)(4)(C), relating to the aggregation of certain trusts and plans. A distribution is a lump sum distribution for purposes of this section without regard to the election described in section 402(e)(4)(B). The distribution of an annuity contract is not a lump sum distribution for purposes of this section, and the limitation described in this section does not apply to an annuity contract distributed under a plan. Accordingly, if the amount payable with respect to a decedent under a plan is paid to a recipient partly by the distribution of an annuity contract, and partly by the distribution of an amount that is a lump sum distribution within the meaning of this paragraph (b), § 20.2039-2 shall apply with respect to the annuity contract without regard to whether the recipient makes the section 402(a)/403(a) taxation election with respect to the remainder of the distribution.

(c) Recipient's section 402(a)/403(a) taxation election. The section 402(a)/403(a) taxation election is the election by the recipient of a lump sum distribution to treat the distribution as—

(1) Taxable under section 402(a), without regard to section 402(a)(2), to the extent includable in gross income (in the case of a distribution under a qualified plan described in § 20.2039-2(b)(1)),

(2) Taxable under section 403(a), without regard to section 403(a)(2), to the extent includable in gross income (in the case of a distribution under a qualified annuity contract described in § 20.2039-2(b)(2)), or

(3) A rollover contribution, in whole or in part, under section 402(a)(7) (relating to rollovers by a decedent's surviving spouse).

Accordingly, if a recipient makes the election, no portion of the distribution is taxable to the recipient under the 10-year averaging provisions of section 402(e) or as long-term capital gain under section 402(a)(2). However, a recipient's election under this paragraph (c) does not preclude the application of section 402(e)(4)(J) to any securities of the employer corporation included in the distribution.

(d) Method of election. *(1) General rule.* The recipient of a lump sum distribution shall make the section 402(a)/403(a) taxation election by:

(i) Determining the income tax liability on the income tax return (or amended return) for the taxable year of the distribution in a manner consistent with paragraph (c)(1) or (2) of this section,

(ii) Rolling over all or any part of the distribution under section 402(a)(7), or

(iii) Filing a section 2039(F)(2) election statement described in paragraph (d)(2) of this section.

(2) Election statement. A recipient may file a section 2039(f)(2) election statement indicating that the recipient elects to treat a lump sum distribution in the manner described in paragraph (c) of this section. The statement must be filed where the recipient would file the income tax return for the taxable year of the distribution. The statement must be signed by the recipient and include the individual's name, address, social security number, the name of the decedent, and a statement indicating the election is being made. A section 2039(f)(2) election statement may be filed at any time prior to making the election under paragraph (d)(1)(i) or (ii) of this section.

(3) Effect on estate tax return. If the date the estate tax return is filed precedes the date on which the recipient makes the section 402(a)/403(a) taxation election with respect to a lump sum distribution, the estate tax return may not reflect the election. However, if after the estate tax return is filed, the recipient makes the section 402(a)/403(a) taxation election, the executor of the estate may file a claim for refund or credit of an overpayment of the Federal estate tax within the time prescribed in section 6511. See also, § 20.6031-1 for rules relating to obtaining an extension of time for filing the estate tax return.

(e) Election irrevocable. If a recipient of a lump sum distribution files a section 2039(f)(2) election statement, an income tax return (or amended return) or makes a rollover contribution that constitutes the section 402(a)/403(a) taxation election described in paragraphs (c) and (d), the election may not be revoked. Accordingly, a subsequent and amended income tax return filed by the recipient that is inconsistent with the prior election will not be given effect for purposes of section 2039 and section 402 or 403.

(f) Lump sum distribution to multiple recipients. In the case of a lump sum distribution paid or payable under a qualified plan with respect to the decedent to more than one recipient, the exclusion under § 20.2039-2 applies to so much of the distribution as is paid or payable to a recipient who makes the section 402(a)/403(a) taxation election.

(g) Distributions of annuity contracts included in multiple distributions. Notwithstanding that a recipient makes the section 402(a)/403(a) taxation election with respect to a lump sum distribution that includes the distribution of an annuity contract, the distribution of an annuity contract is to be taken into account by the recipient for purposes of the multiple distribution rules under section 402(e).

T.D. 7761, 1/21/81, amend T.D. 7956, 5/11/84.

PAR. 11. Section 20.2039-4 is amended by adding a new paragraph (h) to read as follows:

Proposed § 20.2039-4 Lump sum distributions from "qualified plans;" decedents dying after December 31, 1978. [*For Preamble, see ¶ 150,933*]

* * * * *

(h) Accumulated deductible employee contributions. For purposes of this section, a lump sum distribution includes an amount attributable to accumulated deductible employee contributions (as defined in section 72(o)(5)(B)) in any qualified plan taken into account for purposes of determining whether any distribution from that qualified plan is a lump sum distribution as determined under paragraph (b) of this section. Thus, amounts attributable to accumulated deductible employee contributions in a qualified plan under which amounts are payable in a lump sum distribution are not excludible from the decedent's gross estate under § 20.2039-2, unless the recipient makes the section 402(a)/403(c) taxation election with respect to a lump sum distribution payable from that qualified plan.

§ 20.2039-5 Annuities under individual retirement plans.

Caution: The Treasury has not yet amended Reg § 20.2039-5 to reflect changes made by P.L. 98-369, P.L. 97-448, P.L. 97-248, P.L. 97-34.

(a) Section 2039(e) exclusion. *(1) In general.* In the case of a decedent dying after December 31, 1976, section 2039(e) excludes from the decedent's gross estate, to the extent provided in paragraph (c) of this section, the value of a "qualifying annuity" receivable by a beneficiary under an individual retirement plan. The term "individual retirement plan" means—

(i) An individual retirement account described in section 408(a).

(ii) An individual retirement annuity described in section 408(b), or

(iii) A retirement bond described in section 409(a).

(2) Limitations. (i) Section 2039(e) applies only with respect to the gross estate of a decedent on whose behalf the individual retirement plan was established. Accordingly, section 2039(e) does not apply with respect to the estate of a decedent who was only a beneficiary under the plan.

(ii) Section 2039(e) does not apply to an annuity receivable by or for the benefit of the decedent's estate. For the meaning of the term "receivable by or for the benefit of the decedent's estate," see § 20.2042-1(b).

(b) Qualifying annuity. For purposes of this section, the term "qualifying annuity" means an annuity contract or other arrangement providing for a series of substantially equal periodic payments to be made to a beneficiary for the beneficiary's life or over a period ending at least 36 months after the decedent's death. The term "annuity contract" includes an annuity purchased for a beneficiary and distributed to the beneficiary, if under section 408 the contract is not included in the gross income of the beneficiary upon distribution. The term "other arrangement" includes any arrangement arising by reason of the decedent's participation in the program providing the individual retirement plan. Payments shall be considered "periodic" if under the arrangement or contract (including a distributed contract) payments are to be made to the beneficiary at regular intervals. If the contract or arrangement provides optional payment provisions, not all of which provide for periodic payments, payments shall be considered periodic only if an option providing periodic payments is elected not later than the date the estate tax return is filed (as determined under § 20.2039-3(d)). For this purpose, the right to surrender a contract (including a distributed contract) for a cash surrender value will not be considered an optional payment provision. Payments shall be considered "substantially equal" even though the amounts receivable by the beneficiary may vary. Payments shall not be considered substantially equal, however, if more than 40% of the total amount payable to the beneficiary under the individual retirement plan, determined as of the date of the decedent's death and excluding any postmortem increase, is payable to the beneficiary in any 12-month period.

(c) Amount excludible from gross estate. *(1) In general.* Except as otherwise described in this paragraph (c), the amount excluded from the decedent's gross estate under section 2039(e) is the entire value of the qualifying annuity (as determined under §§ 20.2031-1 and 20.2031-7 or, for certain prior periods, § 20.2031-7A) payable under the individual retirement plan.

(2) Excess contribution. In any case in which there exists, on the date of the decedent's death, an excess contribution (as defined in section 4973(b)) with respect to the individual retirement plan, the amount excluded from the value of the decedent's gross estate is determined under the following formula:

$$E = A - A(X \div C - R)$$

Where:

E =the amount excluded from the decedent's gross estate under section 2039(e).

A =the value of the qualifying annuity at the decedent's death (as determined under §§ 20.2031-1 and 20.2031-7 or, for certain prior periods, § 20.2031-7A),

X =the amount which is an excess contribution at the decedent's death (as determined under section 4973(b)),

C =the total amount contributed by or on behalf of the decedent to the individual retirement plan, and

R =the total of amounts paid or distributed from the individual retirement plan before the death of the decedent which were either includable in the gross income of the recipient under section 408(d)(1) and represented the payment or distribution of an excess represented the payment or distribution of an excess contribution, or were payments or distributions described in section 408(d)(4) or (5) (relating to returned excess contributions).

(3) Certain section 403(b)(8) rollover contributions. This subparagraph (3) applies if the decedent made a rollover contribution to the individual retirement plan under section 403(b)(8), and the contribution was attributable to a distribution under an annuity contract other than an annuity contract described in § 20.2039-2(b)(3). If such a rollover contribution was the only contribution made to the plan, no part of the value of the qualifying annuity payable under the plan is excluded from the decedent's gross estate under section 2039(e). If a contribution other than such a rollover contribution was made to the plan, the amount excluded from the decedent's gross estate is determined under the formula described in subparagraph (2) of this paragraph, except that for purposes of that formula, X includes the amount that was a rollover contribution under section 403(b)(8) attributable to a distribution under an annuity contract not described in § 20.2039-2(b)(3).

(4) Surviving spouse's rollover contribution. This subparagraph (4) applies if the decedent made a rollover contribution to the individual retirement plan under section 402(a)(7), relating to rollovers by a surviving spouse. If the rollover contribution under section 402(a)(7) was the only contribution made by the decedent to the plan, no part of the value of the qualifying annuity payable under the plan is excluded from the decedent's gross estate under section 2039(e). If a contribution other than a rollover contribution under section 402(a)(7) was made by the decedent to the plan, the amount excluded from the decedent's gross estate is determined under the formula described in subparagraph (2) of this paragraph, except that for purposes of that formula, X includes the amount that was a rollover contribution under section 402(a)(7).

(5) Election under § 1.408-2(b)(7)(ii). This subparagraph (5) applies if the decedent at any time made the election described in § 1.408-2(b)(7)(ii) with respect to an amount in the individual retirement plan. If this subparagraph (5) applies, the amount excluded from the decedent's gross estate is determined under the formula described in subparagraph (2), except that for purposes of that formula, X and C include the amount with respect to which the election was made.

(6) Plan-to-plan rollovers. (i) This subparagraph (6) applies if the individual retirement plan is a transferee plan. A "transferee plan" is a plan that was the recipient of a contribution described in section 408(d)(3)(A)(i) or 409(b)(3)(C) (relating to rollovers from one individual retirement plan to another) made by the decedent. The amount of the contribution described in section 408(d)(3)(A)(i) or 409(b)(3)(C) is the "rollover amount." The plan from which the rollover amount was paid or distributed to the decedent is the "transferor plan."

(ii) If the decedent made a contribution described in subparagraph (3) or (4) to the transferor plan, the amount excluded from the decedent's gross estate with respect to the transferee plan is determined under the formula described in subparagraph (2), except that for purposes of that formula, X includes so much of the rollover amount as was attributable to the contribution to the transferor plan that was described in subparagraph (3) or (4). The extent to which a rollover amount is attributable to a contribution described in subparagraph (3) or (4) that was made to the transferor plan is determined by multiplying the rollover amount by a fraction, the numerator of which is the amount of such contribution, and the denominator of which is the sum of all amounts contributed by the decedent to the transferor plan (if not returned as described under R in subparagraph (2)), and any amount in the transferor plan to which the election described in subparagraph (5) applied.

(iii) If the decedent made the election described in subparagraph (5) with respect to an amount in the transferor plan, the amount excluded from the decedent's gross estate with respect to the transferee plan is determined under the formula described in subparagraph (2), except that for purposes of that formula, X includes so much of the rollover amount as was attributable to the amount in the transferor plan to which the election applied. The extent to which a rollover amount is attributable to an amount in the transferor plan to which the election applied is determined by multiplying the rollover amount by a fraction, the numerator of which is the amount to which the election applied, and the denominator of which is the sum of all amounts contributed by the decedent to the transferor plan (if not returned as described under R in subparagraph (2)), and the amount in the transferor plan to which the election applied.

(iv) If a transferor plan described in this subparagraph (6) was also a transferee plan, then the rules described in this subparagraph (6) are to be applied with respect to both the rollover amount paid to the plan and the rollover amount thereafter paid from the plan.

(d) Examples. The provisions of this section are illustrated by the following examples:

Example (1). (1) A establishes an individual retirement account described in section 408(a) on January 1, 1976, when A is age 65. A's only contribution to the account is a rollover contribution described in section 402(a)(5). The trust agreement provides that A may at any time elect to have the balance in the account distributed in one of the following methods:

(i) A single sum payment of the account,

(ii) Equal or substantially equal semiannual payments over a period equal to A's life expectancy, or

(iii) Equal or substantially equal semiannual payments over a period equal to the life expectancy of A and A's spouse.

(2) The trust agreement further provides that although semiannual payments have commenced under option (ii) or (iii), A (or A's surviving spouse) may, by written notice to the trustee, receive all or a part of the balance remaining in the account. In addition, under option (ii), any balance remaining in the account at A's death is payable in a single sum to A's designated beneficiary. Under option (iii), any balance remaining in the account at the death of the survivor of A or A's spouse is payable in a single sum to a beneficiary designated by A or A's surviving spouse.

(3) A elects option (iii), and the first semiannual payment is made to A on July 1, 1976. On that date, A's life expectancy is 15 years, and that of A's spouse is 22 years. Under option (iii), the semiannual payments to A or A's surviving spouse will continue until July 1, 1998.

(4) A dies on November 20, 1978. On December 15, 1978, the trust agreement is modified so that A's surviving spouse no longer may elect to receive all or part of the balance remaining in the account. The value of the semiannual payments payable to A's spouse is excluded from A's gross estate under section 2039(e).

(5) A's spouse dies July 12, 1981, and the single sum payment payable on account of the death of A's spouse is paid to the designated beneficiary on August 1, 1981. Notwithstanding that the balance in the account was paid to the designated beneficiary within 36 months after A's death, the value of the semiannual payments payable to A's spouse are excluded from A's gross estate, since at A's death those semiannual payments were to be paid over a period extending beyond 36 months. Section 2039(e) does not apply to exclude any amount from the estate of A's spouse, because A's spouse was only a beneficiary and not the individual on whose behalf the account was established.

Example (2). Assume the same facts as in example (1), except that the trust agreement is not modified so that A's surviving spouse no longer may elect to receive all or part of the balance remaining in the account (see (2) and (4) in example (1)). Instead, the balance of the account is applied toward the purchase of a contract providing an immediate annuity, the contract is distributed to A's surviving spouse on December 15, 1978, and under section 408 the contract is not included in the gross income of the spouse upon its distribution. The value of the annuity contract is excluded from A's gross estate, if the contract provides for a series of substantially equal periodic payments (within the meaning of paragraph (b) of this section) to be made over the life of A's surviving spouse or over a period not ending before the date 36 months after A's death.

Example (3). (1) B establishes an individual retirement plan described in section 408(a) ("IRA B") on February 6, 1981, in order to receive a $220,000 rollover contribution from a qualified plan, as described in section 402(a)(5). B dies August 14, 1981. C, an individual, is the sole beneficiary under IRA B. The amount in IRA B ($238,000) is payable to C in whole or part as C may elect. Because the amount in IRA B is payable to C as other than a qualifying annuity, within the meaning of paragraph (b) of this section, no amount is excluded from B's gross estate under section 2039(e).

(2) On October 17, 1981, C contributes $1,500 on C's own behalf to IRA B. Under § 1.408-2(b)(7)(ii), C's contribution will cause IRA B to be treated as being maintained by and on behalf of C ("IRA C") and C's making the contribution constitutes an election to which paragraph (c)(5) of this section applies. The balance in IRA C immediately before C's contribution is $240,000. Accordingly, the amount with respect to which C made the election is $240,000.

(3) C dies January 19, 1982. E, an individual, is the sole beneficiary under the plan, and the amounts payable to E ($242,000) are payable as a qualifying annuity, within the meaning of paragraph (b) of this section.

(4) The rules described in section 2039(e) and this section are applied with respect to the gross estate of C without regard to whether amounts now payable under IRA C were or were not excluded from B's gross estate. Under paragraph (c) of this section, the amount not excluded from C's gross estate is the value of the qualifying annuity payable to E ($242,000), multiplied by the fraction $240,000/($240,000 + $1,500). Thus, the amount not excluded from C's gross estate is $240,497. [($242,000) ($240,000 ($240,000 + $1,500)) = $240,497.] The amount excluded is therefore $1,503 ($242,000 − $240,497).

Example (4). (1) F, an individual, establishes an individual retirement plan ("IRA F1") in 1977 and makes $1,250 annual contributions for 1977, 1978, 1979 and 1980 (4 × $1,250 = $5,000), each of which is deducted by F under section 219. In February 1980, F receives and $85,000 distribution on account of the death of G, F's spouse, from the qualified plan of G's former employer, and rolls it over into IRA F1, under section 402(a)(7). Because IRA F1 includes a rollover contribution under section 402(a)(7), paragraph (c)(4) of this section applies. In 1981, F's entire interest in IRA F1, $100,000, is paid to F and contributed to another individual retirement plan ("IRA F2") under section 408(d)(3)(A)(i). IRA F2 is a transferee plan to which paragraph (c)(6) of this section applies because of the rollover. F makes a $1,500 deductible contribution to IRA F2 for 1981.

(2) F dies in 1984. The balance in IRA F2 ($146,000) is payable to G, an individual, as a qualifying annuity, within the meaning of paragraph (b) of this section.

(3) Under paragraph (c) of this section, the amount *not* excluded from F's gross estate is the value of the qualifying annuity payable under IRA F2 multiplied by the fraction $96,700/$101,500. Accordingly, the amount not excluded is $139,096. [($146,000) ($96,700/$101,500) = $139,096.] The amount excluded is $6,904 ($146,000 − $139,096).

(4) The numerator of the fraction ($96,700) is determined by multiplying the amount rolled over from IRA F1 to IRA F2 ($100,000)) by a fraction, the numerator of which is the amount of the rollover contribution to IRA F1 ($85,000), and the denominator of which is the total contributions to IRA F1 ($85,000 + $5,000 = $90,000). [($100,000) ($85,000/$90,000) = $96,700.]

(5) The denominator of the fraction ($101,500) is the sum of the contributions to IRA F2 (the $100,000 rollover contribution from IRA F1, and the $1,500 annual contribution to IRA F2).

T.D. 7761, 1/21/81, amend T.D. 8540, 6/9/94.

§ 20.2040-1 Joint interests.

Caution: The Treasury has not yet amended Reg § 20.2040-1 to reflect changes made by P.L. 97-34, P.L. 96-222, P.L. 95-600, P.L. 94-455.

(a) In general. A decedent's gross estate includes under section 2040 the value of property held jointly at the time of the decedent's death by the decedent and another person or persons with right of survivorship, as follows:

(1) To the extent that the property was acquired by the decedent and the other joint owner or owners by gift, devise, bequest, or inheritance, the decedent's fractional share of the property is included.

(2) In all other cases, the entire value of the property is included except such part of the entire value as is attributable to the amount of the consideration in money or money's worth furnished by the other joint owner or owners. See § 20.2043-1 with respect to adequacy of consideration. Such part of the entire value is that portion of the entire value of the property at the decedent's death (or at the alternate valuation date described in section 2032 which the consideration in money or money's worth furnished by the other joint owner or owners bears to the total cost of acquisition and capital additions. In determinating the consideration furnished by the other joint owner or owners, there is taken into account only that portion of such consideration which is shown not to be attributable to money or other property acquired by the other joint owner or owners from the decedent for less than a full and adequate consideration in money or money's worth.

The entire value of jointly held property is included in a decedent's gross estate unless the executor submits facts sufficient to show that property was not acquired entirely with consideration furnished by the decedent, or was acquired by the decedent and the other joint owner or owners by gift, bequest, devise, or inheritance.

(b) Meaning of "property held jointly". Section 2040 specifically covers property held jointly by the decedent and any other person (or persons), property held by the decedent and spouse as tenants by the entirety, and a deposit of money, or a bond or other instrument, in the name of the decedent and any other person and payable to either or the survivor. The section applies to all classes of property, whether real or personal, and regardless of when the joint interests were created. Furthermore, it makes no difference that the survivor takes the entire interest in the property by right of survivorship and that no interest therein forms a part of the decedent's estate for purposes of administration. The section has no application to property held by the decedent and any other person (or persons) as tenants in common.

(c) Examples. The application of this section may be explained in the following examples in each of which it is assumed that the other joint owner or owners survived the decedent:

(1) If the decedent furnished the entire purchase price of the jointly held property, the value of the entire property is included in his gross estate;

(2) If the decedent furnished a part only of the purchase price, only a corresponding portion of the value of the property is so included;

(3) If the decedent furnished no part of the purchase price, no part of the value of the property is so included;

(4) If the decedent, before the acquisition of the property by himself and the other joint owner, gave the latter a sum of money or other property which thereafter became the other joint owner's entire contribution to the purchase price, then the value of the entire property is so included, notwithstanding the fact that the other property may have appreciated in value due to market conditions between the time of the gift and the time of the acquisition of the jointly held property;

(5) If the decedent, before the acquisition of the property by himself and the other joint owner, transferred to the latter for less than an adequate and full consideration in money or money's worth other income-producing property, the income from which belonged to and became the other joint owner's entire contribution to the purchase price, then the value of the jointly held property less that portion attributable to the income which the other joint owner did furnish is included in the decedent's gross estate;

(6) If the property originally belonged to the other joint owner and the decedent purchased his interest from the other joint owner, only that portion of the value of the property attributable to the consideration paid by the decedent is included;

(7) If the decedent and his spouse acquired the property by will or gift as tenants by the entirety, one-half of the value of the property is included in the decedent's gross estate; and

(8) If the decedent and his two brothers acquired the property by will or gift as joint tenants, one-third of the value of the property is so included.

T.D. 6296, 6/23/58.

§ 20.2041-1 Powers of appointment; in general.

(a) Introduction. A decedent's gross estate includes under section 2041 the value of property in respect of which the decedent possessed, exercised, or released certain powers of appointment. This section contains rules of general application; § 20.2041-2 contains rules specifically applicable to general powers of appointment created on or before October 21, 1942; and § 20.2041-3 sets forth specific rules applicable to powers of appointment created after October 21, 1942.

(b) Definition of "power of appointment". *(1) In general.* The term "power of appointment" includes all powers which are in substance and effect powers of appointment regardless of the nomenclature used in creating the power and regardless of local property law connotations. For example, if a trust instrument provides that the beneficiary may appropriate or consume the principal of the trust, the power to consume or appropriate is a power of appointment. Similarly, a power given to a decedent to affect the beneficial enjoyment of trust property or its income by altering, amending, or revoking the trust instrument or terminating the trust is a power of appointment. If the community property laws of a State confer upon the wife a power of testamentary disposition over property in which she does not have a vested interest she is considered as having a power of appointment. A power in a donee to remove or discharge a trustee and appoint himself may be a power of appointment. For example, if under the terms of a trust instrument, the trustee or his successor has the power to appoint the principal of the trust for the benefit of individuals including himself, and the decedent has the unrestricted power to remove or discharge the trustee at any time and appoint any other person including himself, the decedent is considered as having a power of appointment. However, the decedent is not considered to have a power of appointment if he only had the power to appoint a successor, including himself, under limited conditions which did not exist at the time of his death, without an accompanying unrestricted power of removal. Similarly, a power to amend only the administrative provisions of a trust instrument, which cannot substantially affect the beneficial enjoyment of the trust property or income, is not a power of appointment. The mere power of management, investment, custody of assets, or the power to allocate receipts and disbursements as between income and principal, exercisable in a fiduciary capacity, whereby the holder has no power to enlarge or shift any of the beneficial interests therein except as an incidental consequence of the discharge of such fiduciary duties is not a power of appointment. Further, the right in a beneficiary of a trust to assent to a periodic accounting, thereby relieving the trustee from further accountability, is not a power of appointment if the right of assent does not consist of any power or right to enlarge or shift the beneficial interest of any beneficiary therein.

(2) Relation to other sections. For purposes of §§ 20.2041-1 to 20.2041-3, the term "power of appointment" does not include powers reserved by the decedent to himself within the concept of sections 2036 through 2038. (See §§ 20.2036-1 to 20.2038-1.) No provision of section 2041 or of §§ 20.2041-1 to 20.2041-3 is to be construed as in any way limiting the application of any other section of the Internal Revenue Code or of these regulations. The power of the owner of a property interest already possessed by him to dispose of his interest, and nothing more, is not a power of appointment, and the interest is includible in his gross estate to the extent it would be includible under section 2033 or some other provision of part III of subchapter A of chapter 11. For example, if a trust created by S provides for payment of the income to A for life with power in A to appoint the remainder by will and, in default of such appointment for payment of the income to A's widow, W, for her life and for payment of the remainder to A's estate, the value of A's interest in the remainder is includible in his gross estate under section 2033 regardless of its includibility under section 2041.

(3) Powers over a portion of property. If a power of appointment exists as to part of an entire group of assets or only over a limited interest in property, section 2041 applies only to such part or interest. For example, if a trust created by S provides for the payment of income to A for life, then to W for life, with power in A to appoint the remainder by will and in default of appointment for payment of the remainder to B or his estate, and if A dies before W, section 2041 applies only to the value of the remainder interest excluding W's life estate. If A dies after W, section 2041 would apply to the value of the entire property. If the power were only over one-half the remainder interest, section 2041 would apply only to one-half the value of the amounts described above.

(c) Definition of "general power of appointment". *(1) In general.* The term "general power of appointment" as defined in section 2041(b)(1) means any power of appointment exercisable in favor of the decedent, his estate, his creditors, or the creditors of his estate, except (i) joint powers, to the extent provided in §§ 20.2041-2 and 20.2041-3, and (ii) certain powers limited by an ascertainable standard, to the extent provided in subparagraph (2) of this paragraph. A power of appointment exercisable to meet the estate tax, or any other taxes, debts, or charges which are enforceable against the estate, is included within the meaning of a power of appointment exercisable in favor of the decedent's estate, his creditors, or the creditors of his estate. A power of appointment exercisable for the purpose of discharging a legal obligation of the decedent or for his pecuniary benefit is considered a power of appointment exercisable in favor of the decedent or his creditors. However, for purposes of §§ 20.2041-1 to 20.2041-3, a power of appointment not otherwise considered to be a general power of appointment is not treated as a general power of appointment merely by reason of the fact that an appointee may, in fact, be a creditor of the decedent or his estate. A power of appointment is not a general power if by its terms it is either—

(a) Exercisable only in favor of one or more designated persons or classes other than the decedent or his creditors, or the decedent's estate or the creditors of his estate, or

(b) Expressly not exercisable in favor of the decedent or his creditors, or the decedent's estate or the creditors of his estate.

A decedent may have two powers under the same instrument, one of which is a general power of appointment and the other of which is not. For example, a beneficiary may have a power to withdraw trust corpus during his life, and a testamentary power to appoint the corpus among his descendants. The testamentary power is not a general power of appointment.

(2) Powers limited by an ascertainable standard. A power to consume, invade, or appropriate income or corpus, or both, for the benefit of the decedent which is limited by an ascertainable standard relating to the health, education, support, or maintenance of the decedent is, by reason of section 2041(b)(1)(A), not a general power of appointment. A power is limited by such a standard if the extent of the holder's duty to exercise and not to exercise the power is reasonably measurable in terms of his needs for health, education, or support (or any combination of them). As used in this subparagraph, the words "support" and "maintenance" are synonymous and their meaning is not limited to the bare necessities of life. A power to use property for the comfort, welfare, or happiness of the holder of the power is not limited by the requisite standard. Examples of powers which are limited by the requisite standard are powers exercisable for the holder's "support," "support in reasonable comfort," "maintenance in health and reasonable comfort," "support in his accustomed manner of living," "education, including college and professional education," "health," and "medical, dental, hospital and nursing expenses and expenses of invalidism." In determining whether a power is limited by an ascertainable standard, it is immaterial whether the beneficiary is required to exhaust his other income before the power can be exercised.

(3) Certain powers under wills of decedents dying between January 1 and April 2, 1948. Section 210 of the Technical Changes Act of 1953 provides that if a decedent died after December 31, 1947, but before April 3, 1948, certain property interests described therein may, if the decedent's surviving spouse so elects, be accorded special treatment in the determination of the marital deduction to be allowed the decedent's estate under the provisions of section 812(e) of the Internal Revenue Code of 1939. See § 81.47a(h) of Regulations 105 (26 CFR (1939) 81.47a(h)). The section further provides that property affected by the election shall, for the purpose of inclusion in the surviving spouse's gross estate, be considered property with respect to which she has a general power of appointment. Therefore, notwithstanding any other provision of law or of §§ 20.2041-1 to 20.2041-3, if the present decedent (in her capacity as surviving spouse of a prior decedent) has made an election under section 210 of the Technical Changes Act of 1953, the property which was the subject of the election shall be considered as property with respect to which the present decedent has a general power of appointment created after October 21, 1942, exercisable by deed or will, to the extent it was treated as an interest passing to the surviving spouse and not passing to any other person for the purpose of the marital deduction in the prior decedent's estate.

(d) Definition of "exercise". Whether a power of appointment is in fact exercised may depend upon local law. For example, the residuary clause of a will may be considered under local law as an exercise of a testamentary power of appointment in the absence of evidence of a contrary intention drawn from the whole of the testator's will. However, regardless of local law, a power of appointment is considered as exercised for purposes of section 2041 even though the exercise is in favor of the taker in default of appointment, and irrespective of whether the appointed interest and the interest in default of appointment are identical or whether the appointee renounces any right to take under the appointment. A power of appointment is also considered as exercised even though the disposition cannot take effect until the occurrence of an event after the exercise takes place, if the exercise is irrevocable and, as of the time of the exercise, the condition was not impossible of occurrence. For example, if property is left in trust to A for life, with a power in B to appoint the remainder by will, and B dies before A, exercising his power by appointing the remainder to C if C survives A, B is considered to have exercised his power if C is living at B's death. On the other hand, a testamentary power of appointment is not considered as exercised if it is exercised subject to the occurrence during the decedent's life of an express or implied condition which did not in fact occur. Thus, if in the preceding example, C dies before B, B's power of appointment would not be considered to have been exercised. Similarly, if a trust provides for income to A for life, remainder as A appoints by will, and A appoints a life estate in the property to B and does not otherwise exercise his power, but B dies before A, A's power is not considered to have been exercised.

(e) Time of creation of power. A power of appointment created by will is, in general, considered as created on the date of the testator's death. However, section 2041(b)(3) provides that a power of appointment created by a will executed on or before October 21, 1942, is considered a power created on or before that date if the testator dies before July 1, 1949, without having republished the will, by codicil or otherwise, after October 21, 1942. A power of appointment created by an inter vivos instrument is considered as created on the date the instrument takes effect. Such a power is not considered as created at some future date merely because it is not exercisable on the date the instrument takes effect, or because it is revocable, or because the identity of its holders is not ascertainable until after the date the instrument takes effect. However, if the holder of a power exercises it by creating a second power, the second power is considered as created at the time of the exercise of the first. The application of this paragraph may be illustrated by the following examples:

Example (1). A created a revocable trust before October 22, 1942, providing for payment of income to B for life with remainder as B shall appoint by will. Even though A dies after October 21, 1942, without having exercised his power of revocation, B's power of appointment is considered a power created before October 22, 1942.

Example (2). C created an irrevocable inter vivos trust before October 22, 1942, naming T as trustee and providing for payment of income to D for life with remainder to E. T was given the power to pay corpus to D and the power to appoint a successor trustee. If T resigns after October 21, 1942, and appoints D as successor trustee, D is considered to have a power of appointment created before October 22, 1942.

Example (3). F created an irrevocable inter vivos trust before October 22, 1942, providing for payment of income to G for life with remainder as G shall appoint by will, but in default of appointment income to H for life with remainder as H shall appoint by will. If G died after October 21, 1942, without having exercised his power of appointment, H's power of appointment is considered a power created before October 22, 1942, even though it was only a contingent interest until G's death.

Example (4). If in example (3) above G had exercised his power of appointment by creating a similar power in J, J's power of appointment would be considered a power created after October 21, 1942.

T.D. 6296, 6/23/58, amend T.D. 6582, 12/11/61.

§ 20.2041-2 Powers of appointment created on or before October 21, 1942.

(a) In general. Property subject to a general power of appointment created on or before October 21, 1942, is includible in the gross estate of the holder of the power under section 2041 only if he exercised the power under specified circumstances. Section 2041(a)(1) requires that there be included in the gross estate of a decedent the value of property subject to such a power only if the power is exercised by the decedent either (1) by will, or (2) by a disposition which is of such nature that if it were a transfer of property owned by the decedent, the property would be includible in the decedent's gross estate under section 2035 (relating to transfers in contemplation of death), 2036 (relating to transfers with retained life estate), 2037 (relating to transfers taking effect at death), or 2038 (relating to revocable transfers). See paragraphs (b), (c), and (d) of § 20.2041-1 for the definition of various terms used in this section.

(b) Joint powers created on or before October 21, 1942. Section 2041(b)(1)(B) provides that a power created on or before October 21, 1942, which at the time of the exercise is not exercisable by the decedent except in conjunction with another person, is not deemed a general power of appointment.

(c) Exercise during life. The circumstances under which section 2041 applies to the exercise other than by will of a general power of appointment created on or before October 21, 1942, are set forth in paragraph (a) of this section. In this connection, the rules of sections 2035 through 2038 which are to be applied are those in effect on the date of the decedent's death which are applicable to transfers made on the date when the exercise of the power occurred. Those rules are to be applied in determining the extent to which and the conditions under which a disposition is considered a transfer of property. The application of this paragraph may be illustrated by the following examples:

Example (1). A decedent in 1951 exercised a general power of appointment created in 1940, reserving no interest in or power over the property subject to the general power. The decedent died in 1956. Since the exercise was not made within three years before the decedent's death, no part of the property is includible in his gross estate. See section 2035(b), relating to transfers in contemplation of death.

Example (2). S created a trust in 1930 to pay the income to A for life, remainder as B appoints by an instrument filed with the trustee during B's lifetime, and in default of appointment remainder to C. B exercised the power in 1955 by directing that after A's death the income be paid to himself for life with remainder to C. If B dies after A, the entire value of the trust property would be included in B's gross estate, since such a disposition if it were a transfer of property owned by B would cause the property to be included in his gross estate under section 2036(a)(1). If B dies before A, the value of the trust property less the value of A's life estate would be included in B's gross estate for the same reason.

Example (3). S created a trust in 1940 to pay the income to A for life, remainder as A appoints by an instrument filed with the trustee during A's lifetime. A exercised the power in 1955, five years before his death, reserving the right of revocation. The exercise, if not revoked before death, will cause the property subject to the power to be included in A's gross estate under section 2041(a)(1), since such a disposition if it were a transfer of property owned by A would cause the property to be included in his gross estate under section 2038. However, if the exercise were completely revoked, so that A died still possessed of the power, the property would not be included in A's gross estate for the reason that the power will not be treated as having been exercised.

Example (4). A decedent exercised a general power of appointment created in 1940 by making a disposition in trust under which possession or enjoyment of the property subject to the exercise could be obtained only by surviving the decedent and under which the decedent retained a reversionary interest in the property of a value of more than five percent. The exercise will cause the property subject to the power to be included in the decedent's gross estate, since such a disposition if it were a transfer of property owned by the decedent would cause the property to be included in his gross estate under section 2037.

(d) Release or lapse. A failure to exercise a general power of appointment created on or before October 21, 1942, or a complete release of such a power is not considered to be an exercise of a general power of appointment. The phrase "a complete release" means a release of all powers over all or a portion of the property subject to a power of appointment, as distinguished from the reduction of a power of appointment to a lesser power. Thus, if the decedent completely relinquished all powers over one-half of the property subject to a power of appointment, the power is completely released as to that one-half. If at or before the time a power of appointment is relinquished, the holder of the power exercises the power in such a manner or to such an extent that the relinquishment results in the reduction, enlargement, or shift in a beneficial interest in property, the relinquishment will be considered to be an exercise and not a release of the power. For example, assume that A created a trust in 1940 providing for payment of the income to B for life and, upon B's death, remainder to C. Assume further that B was given the unlimited power to amend the trust instrument during his lifetime. If B amended the trust in 1948 by providing that upon his death the remainder was to be paid to D, and if he further amended the trust in 1950 by deleting his power to amend the trust, such relinquishment will be considered an exercise and not a release of a general power of appointment. On the other hand, if the 1948 amendment became ineffective before or at the time of the 1950 amendment, or if B in 1948 merely amended the trust by changing the purely ministerial powers of the trustee, his relinquishment of the power in 1950 will be considered as a release of a power of appointment.

(e) Partial release. If a general power of appointment created on or before October 21, 1942, is partially released so that it is not thereafter a general power of appointment, a subsequent exercise of the partially released power is not an exercise of a general power of appointment if the partial release occurs before whichever is the later of the following dates:

(1) November 1, 1951, or

(2) If the decedent was under a legal disability to release the power on October 21, 1942, the day after the expiration of 6 months following the termination of such legal disability.

However, if a general power created on or before October 21, 1942, is partially released on or after the later of these dates, a subsequent exercise of the power will cause the property subject to the power to be included in the holder's gross estate, if the exercise is such that if it were a disposition of property owned by the decedent it would cause the property to be included in his gross estate. The legal disability referred to in this paragraph is determined under local law and may include the disability of an insane person, a minor, or an unborn child, the fact that the type of general power of appointment possessed by the decedent actually was not generally releasable under the local law does not place the decedent under a legal disability within the meaning of this paragraph. In general, however, it is assumed that all general powers of appointment are releasable, unless the local law on the subject is to the contrary, and it is presumed that the method employed to release the power is effective, unless it is not in accordance with the local law relating specifically to releases or, in the absence of such local law, is not in accordance with the local law relating to similar transactions.

(f) Partial exercise. If a general power of appointment created on or before October 21, 1942, is exercised only as to a portion of the property subject to the power, section 2041 is applicable only to the value of that portion. For example, if a decedent had a general power of appointment exercisable by will created on or before October 21, 1942, over a trust fund valued at $200,000 at the date of his death, and if the decedent exercised his power either to the extent of directing the distribution of one-half of the trust property to B or of directing the payment of $100,000 to B, the trust property would be includible in the decedent's gross estate only to the extent of $100,000.

T.D. 6296, 6/23/58.

§ 20.2041-3 Powers of appointment created after October 21, 1942.

(a) In general. *(1)* Property subject to a power of appointment created after October 21, 1942, is includible in the gross estate of the holder of the power under varying conditions depending on whether the power is (i) general in nature, (ii) possessed at death, or (iii) exercised or released. See paragraphs (b), (c), and (d) of § 20.2041-1 for the definition of various terms used in this section. See paragraph (c) of this section for the rules applicable to determine the extent to which joint powers created after October 21, 1942, are to be treated as general powers of appointment.

(2) If the power is a general power of appointment, the value of an interest in property subject to such a power is includible in a decedent's gross estate under section 2041(a)(2) if either—

(i) The decedent has the power at the time of his death (and the interest exists at the time of his death), or

(ii) The decedent exercised or released the power, or the power lapsed, under the circumstances and to the extent described in paragraph (d) of this section.

(3) If the power is not a general power of appointment, the value of property subject to the power is includible in the holder's gross estate under section 2041(a)(3) only if it is exercised to create a further power under certain circumstances (see paragraph (e) of this section).

(b) Existence of power at death. For purposes of section 2041(a)(2), a power of appointment is considered to exist on the date of a decedent's death even though the exercise of the power is subject to the precedent giving of notice, or even though the exercise of the power takes effect only on the expiration of a stated period after its exercise, whether or not on or before the decedent's death notice has been given or the power has been exercised. However, a power which by its terms is exercisable only upon the occurrence during the decedent's lifetime of an event or a contingency which did not in fact take place or occur during such time is not a power in existence on the date of the decedent's death. For example, if a decedent was given a general power of appointment exercisable only after he reached a certain age, only if he survived another person, or only if he died without descendants, the power would not be in existence on the date of the decedent's death if the condition precedent to its exercise had not occurred.

(c) Joint powers created after October 21, 1942. The treatment of a power of appointment created after October 21, 1942, which is exercisable only in conjunction with another person is governed by section 2041(b)(1)(C), which provides as follows:

(1) Such a power is not considered a general power of appointment if it is not exercisable by the decedent except with the consent or joinder of the creator of the power.

(2) Such power is not considered a general power of appointment if it is not exercisable by the decedent except with the consent or joinder of a person having a substantial interest in the property subject to the power which is adverse to the exercise of the power in favor of the decedent, his estate, his creditors, or the creditors of his estate. An interest adverse to the exercise of a power is considered as substantial if its value in relation to the total value of the property subject to the power is not insignificant. For this purpose, the interest is to be valued in accordance with the actuarial principles set forth in § 20.2031-7 or, if it is not susceptible to valuation under those provisions, in accordance with the general principles set forth in § 20.2031-1. A taker in default of appointment under a power has an interest which is adverse to an exercise of the power. A coholder of the power has no adverse interest merely because of his joint possession of the power nor merely because he is a permissible appointee under a power. However, a coholder of a power is considered as having an adverse interest where he may possess the power after the decedent's death and may exercise it at that time in favor of himself, his estate, his creditors, or the creditors of his estate. Thus, for example, if X, Y, and Z held a power jointly to appoint among a group of persons which includes themselves and if on the death of X the power will pass to Y and Z jointly, then Y and Z are considered to have interests adverse to the exercise of the power in favor of X. Similarly, if on Y's death the power will pass to Z, Z is considered to have an interest adverse to the exercise of the power in favor of Y. The application of this subparagraph may be further illustrated by the following additional examples in each of which it is assumed that the value of the interest in question is substantial:

Example (1). The decedent and R were trustees of a trust under the terms of which the income was to be paid to the decedent for life and then to M for life, and the remainder was to be paid to R. The trustees had power to distribute corpus to the decedent. Since R's interest was substantially adverse to an exercise of the power in favor of the decedent the latter did not have a general power of appointment. If M and the decedent were the trustees, M's interest would likewise have been adverse.

Example (2). The decedent and L were trustees of a trust under the terms of which the income was to be paid to L for life and then to M for life, and the remainder was to be paid to the decedent. The trustees had power to distribute corpus to the decedent during L's life. Since L's interest was adverse to an exercise of the power in favor of the decedent, the decedent did not have a general power of appointment. If the decedent and M were the trustees, M's interest would likewise have been adverse.

Example (3). The decedent and L were trustees of a trust under the terms of which the income was to be paid to L for life. The trustees could designate whether corpus was to be distributed to the decedent or to A after L's death. L's interest was not adverse to an exercise of the power in favor of the decedent, and the decedent therefore had a general power of appointment.

(3) A power which is exercisable only in conjunction with another person, and which after application of the rules set forth in subparagraphs (1) and (2) of this paragraph constitutes a general power of appointment, will be treated as though the holders of the power who are permissible appointees of the property were joint owners of property subject to the power. The decedent, under this rule, will be treated as possessed of a general power of appointment over an aliquot share of the property to be determined with reference to the number of joint holders, including the decedent, who (or whose estates or creditors) are permissible appointees. Thus, for example, if X, Y, and Z hold an unlimited power jointly to appoint among a group of persons, including themselves, but on the death of X the power does not pass to Y and Z jointly, then Y and Z are not considered to have interests adverse to the exercise of the power in favor of X. In this case X is considered to possess a general power of appointment as to one-third of the property subject to the power.

(d) Releases, lapses, and disclaimers of general powers of appointment. *(1)* Property subject to a general power of appointment created after October 21, 1942, is includible in the gross estate of a decedent under section 2041(a)(2) even though he does not have the power at the date of his death, if during his life he exercised or released the power under circumstances such that, if the property subject to the power had been owned and transferred by the decedent, the property would be includible in the decedent's gross estate under section 2035, 2036, 2037, or 2038. Further, section 2041(b)(2) provides that the lapse of a power of appointment is considered to be a release of the power to the extent set forth in subparagraph (3) of this paragraph. A release of a power of appointment need not be formal or express in character. The principles set forth in § 20.2041-2 for determining the application of the pertinent provisions of sections 2035 through 2038 to a particular exercise of a power of appointment are applicable for purposes of determining whether or not an exercise or release of a power of appointment created after October 21, 1942, causes the property to be included in a decedent's gross estate under section 2041(a)(2). If a general power of appointment created after October 21, 1942, is partially released, a subsequent exercise or release of the power under circumstances described in the first sentence of this subparagraph, or its possession at death will nevertheless cause the property subject to the power to be included in the gross estate of the holder of the power.

(2) Section 2041(a)(2) is not applicable to the complete release of a general power of appointment created after October 21, 1942, whether exercisable during life or by will, if the release was not made in contemplation of death within the meaning of section 2035, and if after the release the holder of the power retained no interest in or control over the property subject to the power which would cause the property to be included in his gross estate under sections 2036 through 2038 if the property had been transferred by the holder.

(3) The failure to exercise a power of appointment created after October 21, 1942, within a specified time, so that the power lapses, constitutes a release of the power. However, section 2041(b)(2) provides that such a lapse of a power of appointment during any calendar year during the decedent's life is treated as a release for purposes of inclusion of property in the gross estate under section 2041(a)(2) only to the extent that the property which could have been appointed by exercise of the lapsed power exceeds the greater of (i) $5,000 or (ii) 5 percent of the aggregate value, at the time of the lapse, of the assets out of which, or the proceeds of which, the exercise of the lapsed power could have been satisfied. For example, assume that A transferred $200,000 worth of securities in trust providing for payment of income to B for life with remainder to B's issue. Assume further that B was given a noncumulative right to withdraw $10,000 a year from the principal of the trust fund (which neither increased nor decreased in value prior to B's death). In such case, the failure of B to exercise his right of withdrawal will not result in estate tax with respect to the power to withdraw $10,000 which lapses each year before the year of B's death. At B's death there will be included in his gross estate the $10,000 which he was entitled to withdraw for the year in which his death occurs less any amount which he may have taken during that year. However, if in the above example B had possessed the right to withdraw $15,000 of the principal annually, the failure to exercise such power in any year will be considered a release of the power to the extent of the excess of the amount subject to withdrawal over 5 percent of the trust fund (in this example, $5,000, assuming that the trust fund is worth $200,000 at the time of the lapse). Since each lapse is treated as though B had exercised dominion over the trust property by making a transfer of principal reserving the income therefrom for his life, the value of the trust property (but only to the extent of the excess of the amount subject to withdrawal over 5 percent of the trust fund) is includible in B's gross estate (unless before B's death he has disposed of his right to the income under circumstances to which sections 2035 through 2038 would not be applicable). The extent to which the value of the trust property is included in the decedent's gross estate is determined as provided in subparagraph (4) of this paragraph.

(4) The purpose of section 2041(b)(2) is to provide a determination, as of the date of the lapse of the power, of the proportion of the property over which the power lapsed which is an exempt disposition for estate tax purposes and the proportion which, if the other requirements of sections 2035 through 2038 are satisfied, will be considered as a taxable disposition. Once the taxable proportion of any disposition at the date of the lapse has been determined, the valuation of that proportion as of the date of the decedent's death (or, if the executor has elected the alternate valuation method under section 2032, the value as of the date therein provided), is to be ascertained in accordance with the principles which are applicable to the valuation of transfers of property by the decedent under the corresponding provisions of sections 2035 through 2038. For example, if the life beneficiary of a trust had a right exercisable only during one calendar year to draw down $50,000 from the corpus of a trust, which he did not exercise, and if at the end of the year the corpus was worth $800,000, the taxable portion over which the power lapsed is $10,000 (the excess of $50,000 over 5 percent of the corpus), or 1/80 of the total value. On the decedent's death, if the total value of the corpus of the trust (excluding income accumulated after the lapse of the power) on the applicable valuation date was $1,200,000, $15,000 (1/80 of $1,200,000) would be includible in the decedent's gross estate. However, if the total value was then $600,000, only $7,500 (1/80 of $600,000) would be includible.

(5) If the failure to exercise a power, such as a right of withdrawal, occurs in more than a single year, the proportion of the property over which the power lapsed which is treated as a taxable disposition will be determined separately for each such year. The aggregate of the taxable proportions for all such years, valued in accordance with the above principles, will be includible in the gross estate by reason of the lapse. The includible amount, however, shall not exceed the aggregate value of the assets out of which, or the proceeds of which, the exercise of the power could have been satisfied, valued as of the date of the decedent's death (or, if the executor has elected the alternate valuation method under section 2032, the value as of the date therein provided).

(6) (i) A disclaimer or renunciation of a general power of appointment created in a transfer made after December 31, 1976, is not considered to be the release of the power if the disclaimer or renunciation is a qualified disclaimer as described in section 2518 and the corresponding regulations. For rules relating to when the transfer creating the power occurs, see § 25.2518-2(c)(3) of this chapter. If the disclaimer or renunciation is not a qualified disclaimer, it is considered a release of the power by the disclaimant.

(ii) The disclaimer or renunciation of a general power of appointment created in a taxable transfer before January 1, 1977, in the person disclaiming is not considered to be a release of the power. The disclaimer or renunciation must be unequivocal and effective under local law. A disclaimer is a complete and unqualified refusal to accept the rights to which one is entitled. There can be no disclaimer or renunciation of a power after its acceptance. In the absence of facts to the contrary, the failure to renounce or disclaim within a reasonable time after learning of its existence will be presumed to constitute an acceptance of the power. In any case where a power is purported to be disclaimed or renounced as to only a portion of the property subject to the power, the determination as to whether or not there has been a complete and unqualified refusal to accept the rights to which one is entitled will depend on all the facts and circumstances of the particular case, taking into account the recognition and effectiveness of such a disclaimer under local law. Such rights refer to the incidents of the power and not to other interests of the decedent in the property. If effective under local law, the power may be disclaimed or renounced without disclaiming or renouncing such other interests.

(iii) The first and second sentences of paragraph (d)(6)(i) of this section are applicable for transfers creating the power to be disclaimed made on or after December 31, 1997.

(e) Successive powers. *(1)* Property subject to a power of appointment created after October 21, 1942, which is not a general power, is includible in the gross estate of the holder of the power under section 2041(a)(3) if the power is exercised, and if both of the following conditions are met:

(i) If the exercise is (a) by will, or (b) by a disposition which is of such nature that if it were a transfer of property owned by the decedent, the property would be includible in the decedent's gross estate under sections 2035 through 2037; and

(ii) If the power is exercised by creating another power of appointment which, under the terms of the instruments creating and exercising the first power and under applicable local law, can be validly exercised so as to (a) postpone the vesting of any estate or interest in the property for a period ascertainable without regard to the date of the creation of the first power, or (b) (if the applicable rule against perpetuities is stated in terms of suspension of ownership or of the power of alienation, rather than of vesting) suspend the absolute ownership or the power of alienation of the property for a period ascertainable without regard to the date of the creation of the first power.

(2) For purposes of the application of section 2041(a)(3), the value of the property subject to the second power of appointment is considered to be its value unreduced by any precedent or subsequent interest which is not subject to the second power. Thus, if a decedent has a power to appoint by will $100,000 to a group of persons consisting of his children and grandchildren and exercises the power by making an outright appointment of $75,000 and by giving one appointee a power to appoint $25,000, no more than $25,000 will be includible in the decedent's gross estate under section 2041(a)(3). If, however, the decedent appoints the income from the entire fund to a beneficiary for life with power in the beneficiary to appoint the remainder by will, the entire $100,000 will be includible in the decedent's gross estate under section 2041(a)(3) if the exercise of the second power can validly postpone the vesting of any estate or interest in the property or can suspend the absolute ownership or power of alienation of the property for a period ascertainable without regard to the date of the creation of the first power.

(f) Examples. The application of this section may be further illustrated by the following examples, in each of which it is assumed, unless otherwise stated, that S has transferred property in trust after October 21, 1942, with the remainder payable to R at L's death, and that neither L nor R has any interest in or power over the enjoyment of the trust property except as is indicated separately in each example:

Example (1). Income is directed to be paid to L during his lifetime at the end of each year, if living. L has an unrestricted power during his lifetime to cause the income to be distributed to any other person, but no power to cause it to be accumulated. At L's death, no part of the trust property is includible in L's gross estate since L had a power to dispose of only his income interest, a right otherwise possessed by him.

Example (2). Income is directed to be accumulated during L's life but L has a noncumulative power to distribute $10,000 of each year's income to himself. Unless L's power is limited by an ascertainable standard (relating to his health, etc.), as defined in paragraph (c)(2) of § 20.2041-1, he has a general power of appointment over $10,000 of each year's income, the lapse of which may cause a portion of any income not distributed to be included in his gross estate under section 2041. See subparagraphs (3), (4), and (5) of paragraph (d) of this section. Thus, if the trust income during the year amounts to $20,000, L's failure to distribute any of the income to himself constitutes a lapse as to $5,000 (i.e., the amount by which $10,000 exceeds $5,000). If L's power were cumulative (i.e., if the power did not lapse at the end of each year but lapsed only by reason of L's death), the total accumulations which L chose not to distribute to himself immediately before his death would be includible in his gross estate under section 2041.

Example (3). L is entitled to all the income during his lifetime and has an unrestricted power to cause corpus to be distributed to himself. L had a general power of appointment over the corpus of the trust, and the entire corpus as of the time of his death is includible in his gross estate under section 2041.

Example (4). Income was payable to L during his lifetime. R has an unrestricted power to cause corpus to be distributed to L. R dies before L. In such case, R has only a power to dispose of his remainder interest, the value of which is includible in his gross estate under section 2033, and nothing in addition would be includible under section 2041. If in this example R's remainder were contingent on his surviving L, nothing would be includible in his gross estate under either section 2033 or 2041. While R would have a power of appointment, it would not be a general power.

Example (5). Income was payable to L during his lifetime. R has an unrestricted power to cause corpus to be distributed to himself. R dies before L. While the value of R's remainder interest is includible in his gross estate under section 2033, R also has a general power of appointment over the entire trust corpus. Under such circumstances, the entire value of the trust corpus is includible in R's gross estate under section 2041.

T.D. 6296, 6/23/58, amend T.D. 8095, 8/6/86, T.D. 8744, 12/30/97.

§ 20.2042-1 Proceeds of life insurance.

(a) In general. *(1)* Section 2042 provides for the inclusion in a decedent's gross estate of the proceeds of insurance on the decedent's life (i) receivable by or for the benefit of the estate (see paragraph (b) of this section), and (ii) receivable by other beneficiaries (see paragraph (c) of this section). The term "insurance" refers to life insurance of every description, including death benefits paid by fraternal beneficial societies operating under the lodge system.

(2) Proceeds of life insurance which are not includible in the gross estate under section 2042 may, depending upon the facts of the particular case, be includible under some other section of part III of subchapter A of chapter 11. For example, if the decedent possessed incidents of ownership in an insurance policy on his life but gratuitously transferred all rights in the policy in contemplation of death, the proceeds would be includible under section 2035. Section 2042 has no application to the inclusion in the gross estate of the value of rights in an insurance policy on the life of a person other than the decedent, or the value of rights in a combination annuity contract and life insurance policy on the decedent's life (i.e., a "retirement income" policy with death benefit or an "endowment" policy) under which there was no insurance element at the time of the decedent's death (see paragraph (d) of § 20.2039-1).

(3) Except as provided in paragraph (c)(6), the amount to be included in the gross estate under section 2042 is the full amount receivable under the policy. If the proceeds of the policy are made payable to a beneficiary in the form of an annuity for life or for a term of years, the amount to be included in the gross estate is the one sum payable at death under an option which could have been exercised either by the insured or by the beneficiary, or if no option was granted, the sum used by the insurance company in determining the amount of the annuity.

(b) Receivable by or for the benefit of the estate. *(1)* Section 2042 requires the inclusion in the gross estate of the proceeds of insurance on the decedent's life receivable by the executor or administrator, or payable to the decedent's estate. It makes no difference whether or not the estate is specifically named as the beneficiary under the terms of the policy. Thus, if under the terms of an insurance policy the proceeds are receivable by another beneficiary but are subject to an obligation, legally binding upon the other beneficiary, to pay taxes, debts, or other charges enforceable against the estate, then the amount of such proceeds required for the payment in full (to the extent of the beneficiary's obligation) of such taxes, debts, or other charges is includible in the gross estate. Similarly, if the decedent purchased an insurance policy in favor of another person or a corporation as collateral security for a loan or other accommodation, its proceeds are considered to be receivable for the benefit of the estate. The amount of the loan outstanding at the date of the decedent's death, with interest accrued to that date, will be deductible in determining the taxable estate. See § 20.2053-4.

(2) If the proceeds of an insurance policy made payable to the decedent's estate are community assets under the local community property law and, as a result, one-half of the proceeds belongs to the decedent's spouse, then only one-half of the proceeds is considered to be receivable by or for the benefit of the decedent's estate.

(c) Receivable by other beneficiaries. *(1)* Section 2042 requires the inclusion in the gross estate of the proceeds of insurance on the decedent's life not receivable by or for the benefit of the estate if the decedent possessed at the date of his death any of the incidents of ownership in the policy, exercisable either alone or in conjunction with any other person. However, if the decedent did not possess any of such incidents of ownership at the time of his death nor transfer them in contemplation of death, no part of the proceeds would be includible in his gross estate under section 2042. Thus, if the decedent owned a policy of insurance on his life and, 4 years before his death, irrevocably assigned his entire interest in the policy to his wife retaining no reversionary interest therein (see subparagraph (3) of this paragraph), the proceeds of the policy would not be includible in his gross estate under section 2042.

(2) For purposes of this paragraph, the term "incidents of ownership" is not limited in its meaning to ownership of the policy in the technical legal sense. Generally speaking, the term has reference to the right of the insured or his estate to the economic benefits of the policy. Thus, it includes the power to change the beneficiary, to surrender or cancel the policy, to assign the policy, to revoke an assignment, to pledge the policy for a loan, or to obtain from the insurer a loan against the surrender value of the policy, etc. See subparagraph (6) of this paragraph for rules relating to the circumstances under which incidents of ownership held by a corporation are attributable to a decedent through his stock ownership.

(3) The term "incidents of ownership" also includes a reversionary interest in the policy or its proceeds, whether arising by the express terms of the policy or other instrument or by operation of law, but only if the value of the reversionary interest immediately before the death of the decedent exceeded 5 percent of the value of the policy. As used in this subparagraph, the term "reversionary interest" includes a possibility that the policy or its proceeds may return to the decedent or his estate and a possibility that the policy or its proceeds may become subject to a power of disposition by him. In order to determine whether or not the value of a reversionary interest immediately before the death of the decedent exceeded 5 percent of the value of the policy, the principles contained in paragraph (c)(3) and (4) of § 20.2037-1, insofar as applicable, shall be followed under this subparagraph. In that connection, there must be specifically taken into consideration any incidents of ownership held by others immediately before the decedent's death which would affect the value of the reversionary interest. For example, the decedent would not be considered to have a reversionary interest in the policy of a value in excess of 5 percent if the power to obtain the cash surrender value existed in some other person immediately before the decedent's death and was exercisable by such other person alone and in all events. The terms "reversionary interest" and "incidents of ownership" do not include the possibility that the decedent might receive a policy or its proceeds by inheritance through the estate of another person, or as a surviving spouse under a statutory right of election or a similar right.

(4) A decedent is considered to have an "incident of ownership" in an insurance policy on his life held in trust if, under the terms of the policy, the decedent (either alone or in conjunction with another person or persons) has the power (as trustee or otherwise) to change the beneficial ownership in the policy or its proceeds, or the time or manner of enjoyment thereof, even though the decedent has no beneficial interest in the trust. Moreover, assuming the decedent created the trust, such a power may result in the inclusion in the decedent's gross estate under section 2036 or 2038 of other property transferred by the decedent to the trust if, for example, the decedent has the power to surrender the insurance policy and if the income otherwise used to pay premiums on the policy would become currently payable to a beneficiary of the trust in the event that the policy were surrendered.

(5) As an additional step in determining whether or not a decedent possessed any incidents of ownership in a policy or any part of a policy, regard must be given to the effect of the State or other applicable law upon the terms of the policy. For example, assume that the decedent purchased a policy of insurance on his life with funds held by him and his

surviving wife as community property, designating their son as beneficiary but retaining the right to surrender the policy. Under the local law, the proceeds upon surrender would have inured to the marital community. Assuming that the policy is not surrendered and that the son receives the proceeds on the decedent's death, the wife's transfer of her one-half interest in the policy was not considered absolute before the decedent's death. Upon the wife's prior death, one-half of the value of the policy would have been included in her gross estate. Under these circumstances, the power of surrender possessed by the decedent as agent for his wife with respect to one-half of the policy is not, for purposes of this section, an "incident of ownership", and the decedent is, therefore, deemed to possess an incident of ownership in only one-half of the policy.

(6) In the case of economic benefits of a life insurance policy on the decedent's life that are reserved to a corporation of which the decedent is the sole or controlling stockholder, the corporation's incidents of ownership will not be attributed to the decedent through his stock ownership to the extent the proceeds of the policy are payable to the corporation. Any proceeds payable to a third party for a valid business purpose, such as in satisfaction of a business debt of the corporation, so that the net worth of the corporation is increased by the amount of such proceeds, shall be deemed to be payable to the corporation for purposes of the preceding sentence. See § 20.2031-2(f) for a rule providing that the proceeds of certain life insurance policies shall be considered in determining the value of the decedent's stock. Except as hereinafter provided with respect to a group-term life insurance policy, if any part of the proceeds of the policy are not payable to or for the benefit of the corporation, and thus are not taken into account in valuing the decedent's stock holdings in the corporation for purposes of section 2031, any incidents of ownership held by the corporation as to that part of the proceeds will be attributed to the decedent through his stock ownership where the decedent is the sole or controlling stockholder. Thus, for example, if the decedent is the controlling stockholder in a corporation, and the corporation owns a life insurance policy on his life, the proceeds of which are payable to the decedent's spouse, the incidents of ownership held by the corporation will be attributed to the decedent through his stock ownership and the proceeds will be included in his gross estate under section 2042. If in this example the policy proceeds had been payable 40 percent to decedent's spouse and 60 percent to the corporation, only 40 percent of the proceeds would be included in decedent's gross estate under section 2042. For purposes of this subparagraph, the decedent will not be deemed to be the controlling stockholder of a corporation unless, at the time of his death, he owned stock possessing more than 50 percent of the total combined voting power of the corporation. Solely for purposes of the preceding sentence, a decedent shall be considered to be the owner of only the stock with respect to which legal title was held, at the time of his death, by (i) the decedent (or his agent or nominee); (ii) the decedent and another person jointly (but only the proportionate number of shares which corresponds to the portion of the total consideration which is considered to be furnished by the decedent for purposes of section 2040 and the regulations thereunder); and (iii) by a trustee of a voting trust (to the extent of the decedent's beneficial interest therein) or any other trust with respect to which the decedent was treated as an owner under subpart E, part I, subchapter J, chapter 1 of the Code immediately prior to his death. In the case of group-term life insurance, as defined in the regulations under section 79, the power to surrender or cancel a policy held by a corporation shall not be attributed to any decedent through his stock ownership.

T.D. 6296, 6/23/58, amend T.D. 7312, 4/26/74, T.D. 7623, 5/14/79.

§ 20.2043-1 Transfers for insufficient consideration.

(a) In general. The transfers, trusts, interests, rights or powers enumerated and described in sections 2035 through 2038 and section 2041 are not subject to the Federal estate tax if made, created, exercised, or relinquished in a transaction which constituted a bona fide sale for an adequate and full consideration in money or money's worth. To constitute a bona fide sale for an adequate and full consideration in money or money's worth, the transfer must have been made in good faith, and the price must have been an adequate and full equivalent reducible to a money value. If the price was less than such a consideration, only the excess of the fair market value of the property (as of the applicable valuation date) over the price received by the decedent is included in ascertaining the value of his gross estate.

(b) Marital rights and support obligations. For purposes of chapter 11, a relinquishment or promised relinquishment of dower, curtesy, or of a statutory estate created in lieu of dower or curtesy, or of other marital rights in the decedent's property or estate, is not to any extent a consideration in "money or money's worth."

T.D. 6296, 6/23/58.

§ 20.2044-1 Certain property for which marital deduction was previously allowed.

(a) In general. Section 2044 generally provides for the inclusion in the gross estate of property in which the decedent had a qualifying income interest for life and for which a deduction was allowed under section 2056(b)(7) or 2523(f). The value of the property included in the gross estate under section 2044 is not reduced by the amount of any section 2503(b) exclusion that applied to the transfer creating the interest. See section 2207A, regarding the right of recovery against the persons receiving the property that is applicable in certain cases.

(b) Passed from. For purposes of section 1014 and chapters 11 and 13 of subtitle B of the Internal Revenue Code, property included in a decedent's gross estate under section 2044 is considered to have been acquired from or to have passed from the decedent to the person receiving the property upon the decedent's death. Thus, for example, the property is treated as passing from the decedent for purposes of determining the availability of the charitable deduction under section 2055, the marital deduction under section 2056, and special use valuation under section 2032A. In addition, the tax imposed on property includible under section 2044 is eligible for the installment payment of estate tax under section 6166.

(c) Presumption. Unless established to the contrary, section 2044 applies to the entire value of the trust at the surviving spouse's death. If a marital deduction is taken on either the estate or gift tax return with respect to the transfer which created the qualifying income interest, it is presumed that the deduction was allowed for purposes of section 2044. To avoid the inclusion of property in the decedent-spouse's gross estate under this section, the executor of the spouse's estate must establish that a deduction was not taken for the transfer which created the qualifying income interest. For example, to establish that a deduction was not taken, the executor may produce a copy of the estate or gift tax return filed with respect to the transfer by the first spouse or the first spouse's estate establishing that no deduction was taken under section 2523(f) or section 2056(b)(7). In addition, the executor may establish that no return was filed on the original transfer by the decedent because the value of the first spouse's gross estate was below the threshold requirement for filing under section 6018. Similarly, the executor could establish that the transfer creating the decedent's qualifying income interest for life was made before the effective date of section 2056(b)(7) or section 2523(f).

(d) Amount included. *(1) In general.* The amount included under this section is the value of the entire interest in which the decedent had a qualifying income interest for life, determined as of the date of the decedent's death (or the alternate valuation date, if applicable). If, in connection with the transfer of property that created the decedent's qualifying income interest for life, a deduction was allowed under section 2056(b)(7) or section 2523(f) for less than the entire interest in the property (i.e., for a fractional or percentage share of the entire interest in the transferred property), the amount includible in the decedent's gross estate under this section is equal to the fair market value of the entire interest in the property on the date of the decedent's death (or the alternate valuation date, if applicable) multiplied by the fractional or percentage share of the interest for which the deduction was taken.

(2) Inclusion of income. If any income from the property for the period between the date of the transfer creating the decedent-spouse's interest and the date of the decedent-spouse's death has not been distributed before the decedent-spouse's death, the undistributed income is included in the decedent-spouse's gross estate under this section to the extent that the income is not so included under any other section of the Internal Revenue Code.

(3) Reduction of includible share in certain cases. If only a fractional or percentage share is includible under this section, the includible share is appropriately reduced if—

(i) The decedent-spouse's interest was in a trust and distributions of principal were made to the spouse during the spouse's lifetime;

(ii) The trust provides that the distributions are to be made from the qualified terminable interest share of the trust; and

(iii) The executor of the decedent-spouse's estate can establish the reduction in that share based on the fair market value of the trust assets at the time of each distribution.

(4) Interest in previously severed trust. If the decedent-spouse's interest was in a trust consisting of only qualified terminable interest property and the trust was severed (in compliance with § 20.2056(b)-7(b) or § 25.2523(f)-1(b) of this chapter) from a trust that, after the severance, held only property that was not qualified terminable interest property, only the value of the property in the severed portion of the trust is includible in the decedent-spouse's gross estate.

(e) Examples. The following examples illustrate the principles in paragraphs (a) through (d) of this section, where the decedent, D, was survived by spouse, S.

Example (1). Inclusion of trust subject to election. Under D's will, assets valued at $800,000 in D's gross estate (net of debts, expenses and other charges, including death taxes, payable from the property) passed in trust with income payable to S for life. Upon S's death, the trust principal is to be distributed to D's children. D's executor elected under section 2056(b)(7) to treat the entire trust property as qualified terminable interest property and claimed a marital deduction of $800,000. S made no disposition of the income interest during S's lifetime under section 2519. On the date of S's death, the fair market value of the trust property was $740,000. S's executor did not elect the alternate valuation date. The amount included in S's gross estate pursuant to section 2044 is $740,000.

Example (2). Inclusion of trust subject to partial election. The facts are the same as in Example 1, except that D's executor elected under section 2056(b)(7) with respect to only 50 percent of the value of the trust ($400,000). Consequently, only the equivalent portion of the trust is included in S's gross estate; i.e., $370,000 (50 percent of $740,000).

Example (3). Spouse received qualifying income interest in a fraction of trust income. Under D's will, assets valued at $800,000 in D's gross estate (net of debts, expenses and other charges, including death taxes, payable from the property) passed in trust with 20 percent of the trust income payable to S for S's life. The will provides that the trust principal is to be distributed to D's children upon S's death. D's executor elected to deduct, pursuant to section 2056(b)(7), 50 percent of the amount for which the election could be made; i.e., $80,000 (50 percent of 20 percent of $800,000). Consequently, on the death of S, only the equivalent portion of the trust is included in S's gross estate; i.e., $74,000 (50 percent of 20 percent of $740,000).

Example (4). Distribution of corpus during spouse's lifetime. The facts are the same as in Example 3, except that S was entitled to receive all the trust income but the executor of D's estate elected under section 2056(b)(7) with respect to only 50 percent of the value of the trust ($400,000). Pursuant to authority in the will, the trustee made a discretionary distribution of $100,000 of principal to S in 1995 and charged the entire distribution to the qualified terminable interest share. Immediately prior to the distribution, the fair market value of the trust property was $1,100,000 and the qualified terminable interest portion of the trust was 50 percent. Immediately after the distribution, the qualified terminable interest portion of the trust was 45 percent ($450,000 divided by $1,000,000). Provided S's executor can establish the relevant facts, the amount included in S's gross estate is $333,000 (45 percent of $740,000).

Example (5). Spouse assigns a portion of income interest during life. Under D's will, assets valued at $800,000 in D's gross estate (net of debts, expenses and other charges, including death taxes, payable from the property) passed in trust with all the income payable to S, for S's life. The will provides that the trust principal is to be distributed to D's children upon S's death. D's executor elected under section 2056(b)(7) to treat the entire trust property as qualified terminable interest property and claimed a marital deduction of $800,000. During the term of the trust, S transfers to C the right to 40 percent of the income from the trust for S's life. Because S is treated as transferring the entire remainder interest in the trust corpus under section 2519 (as well as 40 percent of the income interest under section 2511), no part of the trust is includible in S's gross estate under section 2044. However, if S retains until death an income interest in 60 percent of the trust corpus (which corpus is treated pursuant to section 2519 as having been transferred by S for both gift and estate tax purposes), 60 percent of the property will be includible in S's gross estate under section 2036(a) and a corresponding adjustment is made in S's adjusted taxable gifts.

Example (6). Inter vivos trust subject to election under section 2523(f). D transferred $800,000 to a trust providing that trust income is to be paid annually to S, for S's life. The trust provides that upon S's death, $100,000 of principal is to be paid to X charity and the remaining principal distributed to D's children. D elected to treat all of the property transferred to the trust as qualified terminable interest property under section 2523(f). At the time of S's death, the fair market value of the trust is $1,000,000. S's executor does not elect the alternate valuation date. The amount included in S's gross estate is $1,000,000; i.e., the fair market value at S's death of the entire trust property. The $100,000 that passes to X charity on S's death is treated as a transfer by S to X charity for purposes of section 2055. Therefore, S's estate is allowed a charitable deduction for the $100,000 transferred from the trust to the charity to the same extent that a deduction would be allowed by section 2055 for a bequest by S to X charity.

Example (7). Spousal interest in the form of an annuity. D died prior to October 24, 1992, the effective date of the Energy Policy Act of 1992 (Pub. L. 102-486). See § 20.2056(b)-7(e). Under D's will, assets valued at $500,000 in D's gross estate (net of debts, expenses and other charges, including death taxes, payable from the property) passed in trust pursuant to which an annuity of $20,000 a year was payable to S for S's life. Trust income not paid to S as an annuity is to be accumulated in the trust and may not be distributed during S's lifetime. D's estate deducted $200,000 under section 2056(b)(7) and § 20.2056(b)-7(e)(2). S did not assign any portion of S's interest during S's life. At the time of S's death, the value of the trust property is $800,000. S's executor does not elect the alternate valuation date. The amount included in S's gross estate pursuant to section 2044 is $320,000 ([$200,000/$500,000] × $800,000).

Example (8). Inclusion of trust property when surviving spouse dies before first decedent's estate tax return is filed. D dies on July 1, 1997. Under the terms of D's will, a trust is established for the benefit of D's spouse, S. The will provides that S is entitled to receive the income from that portion of the trust that the executor elects to treat as qualified terminable interest property. The remaining portion of the trust passes as of D's date of death to a trust for the benefit of C, D's child. The trust terms otherwise provide S with a qualifying income interest for life under section 2056(b)(7)(B)(ii). S dies on February 10, 1998. On April 1, 1998, D's executor files D's estate tax return on which an election is made to treat a portion of the trust as qualified terminable interest property under section 2056(b)(7). S's estate tax return is filed on November 10, 1998. The value on the date of S's death of the portion of the trust for which D's executor made a QTIP election is includible in S's gross estate under section 2044.

T.D. 8522, 2/28/94, amend T.D. 8779, 8/18/98.

PAR. 2. In § 20.2044-1, paragraph (e) Example 8 is added to read as follows:

Proposed § 20.2044-1 Certain property for which marital deduction was previously allowed. [*For Preamble, see ¶ 151,799*]

[The text of paragraph (e) Example 8 as proposed is the same as the text of § 20.2044-1T(e) Example 8 published elsewhere in this issue of the Federal Register]. *See T.D. 8714, 2/18/1997, 62 Fed. Reg. 32.*]

§ 20.2044-2 Effective dates.

Except as specifically provided in Example 7 of § 20.2044-1(e), the provisions of § 20.2044-1 are effective with respect to estates of a decedent-spouse dying after March 1, 1994. With respect to estates of decedent-spouses dying on or before such date, taxpayers may rely on any reasonable interpretation of the statutory provisions. For these purposes, the provisions of § 20.2044-1 (as well as project LR-211-76, 1984-1 C.B., page 598, see section 601.601(d)(2)(ii)(b) of this chapter), are considered a reasonable interpretation of the statutory provisions.

T.D. 8522, 2/28/94.

§ 20.2045-1 Applicability to pre-existing transfers or interests.

Sections 2034 through 2042 are applicable regardless of when the interests and events referred to in those sections were created or took place, except as otherwise provided in those sections and the regulations thereunder.

T.D. 6296, 6/23/58, amend T.D. 8522, 2/28/94.

§ 20.2046-1 Disclaimed property.

(a) This section shall apply to the disclaimer or renunciation of an interest in the person disclaiming by a transfer made after December 31, 1976. For rules relating to when the transfer creating the interest occurs, see § 25.2518-2(c)(3) and (c)(4) of this chapter. If a qualified disclaimer is made with respect to such a transfer, the Federal estate tax provisions are to apply with respect to the property interest disclaimed as if the interest had never been transferred to the person making the disclaimer. See section 2518 and the corresponding regulations for rules relating to a qualified disclaimer.

(b) The first and second sentences of this section are applicable for transfers creating the interest to be disclaimed made on or after December 31, 1997.

T.D. 8095, 8/6/86, amend T.D. 8744, 12/30/97.

§ 20.2051-1 Definition of taxable estate.

Caution: The Treasury has not yet amended Reg § 20.2051-1 to reflect changes made by P.L. 95-600, P.L. 94-455.

(a) General rule. The taxable estate of a decedent who was a citizen or resident (see § Sec. 20.0-1(b)(1)) of the United States at death is determined by subtracting the total amount of the deductions authorized by sections 2053 through 2058 from the total amount which must be included in the gross estate under sections 2031 through 2044. These deductions are in general as follows—

(1) Funeral and administration expenses and claims against the estate (including certain taxes and charitable pledges) (section 2053).

(2) Losses from casualty or theft during the administration of the estate (section 2054).

(3) Charitable transfers (section 2055).

(4) The marital deduction (section 2056).

(5) Qualified domestic trusts (section 2056A).

(6) Family-owned business interests (section 2057) to the extent applicable to estates of decedents.

(7) State death taxes (section 2058) to the extent applicable to estates of decedents.

(b) Special rules. See section 2106 and the corresponding regulations for special rules regarding the computation of the taxable estate of a decedent who was not a citizen or resident of the United States. See also § 1.642(g)-1 of this chapter concerning the disallowance for income tax purposes of certain deductions allowed for estate tax purposes.

(c) Effective/applicability date. This section applies to the estates of decedents dying on or after October 20, 2009.

T.D. 6296, 6/23/58, T.D. 9468, 10/16/2009.

§ 20.2052-1 Exemption.

Caution: The Treasury has not yet amended Reg § 20.2052-1 to reflect changes made by P.L. 94-455.

An exemption of $60,000 is allowed as a deduction under section 2052 from the gross estate of a decedent who was a citizen or resident of the United States at the time of his death. For the amount of the exemption allowed as a deduction from the gross estate of a decedent who was a nonresident not a citizen of the United States, see paragraph (a)(3) of § 20.2106-1.

T.D. 6296, 6/23/58.

§ 20.2053-1 Deductions for expenses, indebtedness, and taxes; in general.

(a) General rule. In determining the taxable estate of a decedent who was a citizen or resident of the United States at death, there are allowed as deductions under section 2053(a) and (b) amounts falling within the following two categories (subject to the limitations contained in this section and in §§ 20.2053-2 through 20.2053-10)—

(1) First category. Amounts which are payable out of property subject to claims and which are allowable by the law of the jurisdiction, whether within or without the United States, under which the estate is being administered for—

(i) Funeral expenses;

(ii) Administration expenses;

(iii) Claims against the estate (including taxes to the extent set forth in § 20.2053-6 and charitable pledges to the extent set forth in § 20.2053-5); and

(iv) Unpaid mortgages on, or any indebtedness in respect of, property, the value of the decedent's interest in which is included in the value of the gross estate undiminished by the mortgage or indebtedness.

As used in this subparagraph, the phrase "allowable by the law of the jurisdiction" means allowable by the law governing the administration of decedents' estates. The phrase has no reference to amounts allowable as deductions under a law which imposes a State death tax. See further §§ 20.2053-2 through 20.2053-7.

(2) Second category. Amounts representing expenses incurred in administering property which is included in the gross estate but which is not subject to claims and which—

(i) Would be allowed as deductions in the first category if the property being administered were subject to claims; and

(ii) Were paid before the expiration of the period of limitation for assessment provided in section 6501.

See further § 20.2053-8.

(b) Provisions applicable to both categories. *(1) In general.* If the item is not one of those described in paragraph (a) of this section, it is not deductible merely because payment is allowed by the local law. If the amount which may be expended for the particular purpose is limited by the local law no deduction in excess of that limitation is permissible.

(2) Bona fide requirement. (i) In general. Amounts allowed as deductions under section 2053(a) and (b) must be expenses and claims that are bona fide in nature. No deduction is permissible to the extent it is founded on a transfer that is essentially donative in character (a mere cloak for a gift or bequest) except to the extent the deduction is for a claim that would be allowable as a deduction under section 2055 as a charitable bequest.

(ii) Claims and expenses involving family members. Factors indicative (but not necessarily determinative) of the bona fide nature of a claim or expense involving a family member of a decedent, a related entity, or a beneficiary of a decedent's estate or revocable trust, in relevant instances, may include, but are not limited to, the following—

(A) The transaction underlying the claim or expense occurs in the ordinary course of business, is negotiated at arm's length, and is free from donative intent.

(B) The nature of the claim or expense is not related to an expectation or claim of inheritance.

(C) The claim or expense originates pursuant to an agreement between the decedent and the family member, related entity, or beneficiary, and the agreement is substantiated with contemporaneous evidence.

(D) Performance by the claimant is pursuant to the terms of an agreement between the decedent and the family member, related entity, or beneficiary and the performance and the agreement can be substantiated.

(E) All amounts paid in satisfaction or settlement of a claim or expense are reported by each party for Federal income and employment tax purposes, to the extent appropriate, in a manner that is consistent with the reported nature of the claim or expense.

(iii) Definitions. The following definitions apply for purposes of this paragraph (b)(2):

(A) Family members include the spouse of the decedent; the grandparents, parents, siblings, and lineal descendants of the decedent or of the decedent's spouse; and the spouse and lineal descendants of any such grandparent, parent, and sibling. Family members include adopted individuals.

(B) A related entity is an entity in which the decedent, either directly or indirectly, had a beneficial ownership interest at the time of the decedent's death or at any time during the three-year period ending on the decedent's date of death. Such an entity, however, shall not include a publicly-traded entity nor shall it include a closely-held entity in which the combined beneficial interest, either direct or indirect, of the decedent and the decedent's family members, collectively, is less than 30 percent of the beneficial ownership interests (whether voting or non-voting and whether an interest in stock, capital and/or profits), as determined at the time a claim described in this section is being asserted. Notwithstanding the foregoing, an entity in which the decedent, directly or indirectly, had any managing interest (for example, as a general partner of a partnership or as a managing member of a limited liability company) at the time of the decedent's death shall be considered a related entity.

(C) Beneficiaries of a decedent's estate include beneficiaries of a trust of the decedent.

(3) Court decrees and settlements. (i) Court decree. If a court of competent jurisdiction over the administration of an estate reviews and approves expenditures for funeral expenses, administration expenses, claims against the estate, or unpaid mortgages (referred to in this section as a "claim or expense"), a final judicial decision in that matter may be re-

lied upon to establish the amount of a claim or expense that is otherwise deductible under section 2053 and these regulations provided that the court actually passes upon the facts on which deductibility depends. If the court does not pass upon those facts, its decree may not be relied upon to establish the amount of the claim or expense that is otherwise deductible under section 2053. It must appear that the court actually passed upon the merits of the claim. This will be presumed in all cases of an active and genuine contest. If the result reached appears to be unreasonable, this is some evidence that there was not such a contest, but it may be rebutted by proof to the contrary. Any amount meeting the requirements of this paragraph (b)(3)(i) is deductible to the extent it actually has been paid or will be paid, subject to any applicable limitations in this section.

(ii) Claims and expenses where court approval not required under local law. A deduction for the amount of a claim or expense that is otherwise deductible under section 2053 and these regulations will not be denied under section 2053 solely because a local court decree has not been entered with respect to such amount, provided that no court decree is required under applicable law to determine the amount or allowability of the claim or expense.

(iii) Consent decree. A local court decree rendered by consent may be relied on to establish the amount of a claim or expense that is otherwise deductible under section 2053 and these regulations provided that the consent resolves a bona fide issue in a genuine contest. Consent given by all parties having interests adverse to that of the claimant will be presumed to resolve a bona fide issue in a genuine contest. Any amount meeting the requirements of this paragraph (b)(3)(iii) is deductible to the extent it actually has been paid or will be paid, subject to any applicable limitations in this section.

(iv) Settlements. A settlement may be relied on to establish the amount of a claim or expense (whether contingent or noncontingent) that is otherwise deductible under section 2053 and these regulations, provided that the settlement resolves a bona fide issue in a genuine contest and is the product of arm's-length negotiations by parties having adverse interests with respect to the claim or expense. A deduction will not be denied for a settlement amount paid by an estate if the estate can establish that the cost of defending or contesting the claim or expense, or the delay associated with litigating the claim or expense, would impose a higher burden on the estate than the payment of the amount paid to settle the claim or expense. Nevertheless, no deduction will be allowed for amounts paid in settlement of an unenforceable claim. For this purpose, to the extent a claim exceeds an applicable limit under local law, the claim is deemed to be unenforceable. However, as long as the enforceability of the claim is at issue in a bona fide dispute, the claim will not be deemed to be unenforceable for this purpose. Any amount meeting the requirements of this paragraph (b)(3)(iv) is deductible to the extent it actually has been paid or will be paid, subject to any applicable limitations in this section.

(v) Additional rules. Notwithstanding paragraph (b)(3)(i) through (iv) of this section, additional rules may apply to the deductibility of certain claims and expenses. See § 20.2053-2 for additional rules regarding the deductibility of funeral expenses. See § 20.2053-3 for additional rules regarding the deductibility of administration expenses. See § 20.2053-4 for additional rules regarding the deductibility of claims against the estate. See § 20.2053-7 for additional rules regarding the deductibility of unpaid mortgages.

(4) Examples. Unless otherwise provided, assume that the amount of any claim or expense is paid out of property subject to claims and is paid within the time prescribed for filing the "United States Estate (and Generation-Skipping Transfer) Tax Return," Form 706. The following examples illustrate the application of this paragraph (b):

Example (1). Consent decree at variance with the law of the State. Decedent's (D's) estate is probated in State. D's probate estate is valued at $100x. State law provides that the executor's commission shall not exceed 3 percent of the probate estate. A consent decree is entered allowing the executor's commission in the amount of $5x. The estate pays the executor's commission in the amount of $5x. For purposes of section 2053, the executor may deduct only $3x of the $5x expense paid for the executor's commission because the amount approved by the consent decree in excess of $3x is in excess of the applicable limit for executor's commissions under local law. Therefore, for purposes of section 2053, the consent decree may not be relied upon to establish the amount of the expense for the executor's commission.

Example (2). Decedent's (D's) estate is probated in State. State law grants authority to an executor to administer an estate without court approval, so long as notice of and a right to object to a proposed action is provided to interested persons. The executor of D's estate (E) proposes to sell property of the estate in order to pay the debts of D. E gives requisite notice to all interested parties and no interested person objects. E sells the real estate and pays a real estate commission of $20x to a professional real estate agent. The amount of the real estate commission paid does not exceed the applicable limit under State law. Provided that the sale of the property was necessary to pay D's debts, expenses of administration, or taxes, to preserve the estate, or to effect distribution, the executor may deduct the $20x expense for the real estate commission under section 2053 even though no court decree was entered approving the expense.

Example (3). Claim by family member. For a period of three years prior to D's death, D's niece (N) provides accounting and bookkeeping services on D's behalf. N is a CPA and provides similar accounting and bookkeeping services to unrelated clients. At the end of each month, N presents an itemized bill to D for services rendered. The fees charged by N conform to the prevailing market rate for the services rendered and are comparable to the fees N charges other clients for similar services. The amount due is timely paid each month by D and is properly reported for Federal income and employment tax purposes by N. In the six months prior to D's death, D's poor health prevents D from making payments to N for the amount due. After D's death, N asserts a claim against the estate for $25x, an amount representing the amount due for the six-month period prior to D's death. D's estate pays $25x to N in satisfaction of the claim before the return is timely filed and N properly reports the $25x received by E for income tax purposes. Barring any other relevant facts or circumstances, E may rely on the following factors to establish that the claim is bona fide: (1) N's claim for services rendered arose in the ordinary course of business, as N is a CPA performing similar services for other clients; (2) the fees charged were deemed to be negotiated at arm's length, as the fees were consistent with the fees N charged for similar services to unrelated clients; (3) the billing records and the records of D's timely payments to N constitute contemporaneous evidence of an agreement between D and N for N's bookkeeping services; and (4) the amount of the payments to N is properly reported by N for

Federal income and employment tax purposes. E may deduct the amount paid to N in satisfaction of the claim.

(c) Provision applicable to first category only. Deductions of the first category (described in paragraph (a)(1) of this section) are limited under section 2053(a) to amounts which would be properly allowable out of property subject to claims by the law of the jurisdiction under which the decedent's estate is being administered. Further, the total allowable amount of deductions of the first category is limited by section 2053(c)(2) to the sum of—

(1) The value of property included in the decedent's gross estate and subject to claims, plus

(2) Amounts paid, out of property not subject to claims against the decedent's estate, within 9 months (15 months in the case of the estate of a decedent dying before January 1, 1971) after the decedent's death (the period within which the estate tax return must be filed under section 6075), or within any extension of time for filing the return granted under section 6081.

The term "property subject to claims" is defined in section 2053(c)(2) as meaning the property includible in the gross estate which, or the avails of which, under the applicable law, would bear the burden of the payment of these deductions in the final adjustment and settlement of the decedent's estate. However, for the purposes of this definition, the value of property subject to claims is first reduced by the amount of any deduction allowed under section 2054 for any losses from casualty or theft incurred during the settlement of the estate attributable to such property. The application of this paragraph may be illustrated by the following examples:

Example (1). The only item in the gross estate is real property valued at $250,000 which the decedent and his surviving spouse held as tenants by the entirety. Under the local law this real property is not subject to claims. Funeral expenses of $1,200 and debts of the decedent in the amount of $1,500 are allowable under local law. Before the prescribed date for filing the estate tax return, the surviving spouse paid the funeral expenses and $1,000 of the debts. The remaining $500 of the debts was paid by her after the prescribed date for filing the return. The total amount allowable as deductions under section 2053 is limited to $2,200, the amount paid prior to the prescribed date for filing the return.

Example (2). The only two items in the gross estate were a bank deposit of $20,000 and insurance in the amount of $150,000. The insurance was payable to the decedent's surviving spouse and under local law was not subject to claims. Funeral expenses of $1,000 and debts in the amount of $29,000 were allowable under local law. A son was executor of the estate and before the prescribed date for filing the estate tax return he paid the funeral expenses and $9,000 of the debts, using therefor $5,000 of the bank deposit and $5,000 supplied by the surviving spouse. After the prescribed date for filing the return, the executor paid the remaining $20,000 of the debts, using for that purpose the $15,000 left in the bank account plus an additional $5,000 supplied by the surviving spouse. The total amount allowable as deductions under section 2053 is limited to $25,000 ($20,000 of property subject to claims plus the $5,000 additional amount which, before the prescribed date for filing the return, was paid out of property not subject to claims).

(d) Amount deductible. *(1) General rule.* To take into account properly events occurring after the date of a decedent's death in determining the amount deductible under section 2053 and these regulations, the deduction for any claim or expense described in paragraph (a) of this section is limited to the total amount actually paid in settlement or satisfaction of that item (subject to any applicable limitations in this section). However, see paragraph (d)(4) of this section for the rules for deducting certain ascertainable amounts; see § 20.2053-4(b) and (c) for the rules regarding the deductibility of certain claims against the estate; and see § 20.2053-7 for the rules regarding the deductibility of unpaid mortgages and other indebtedness.

(2) Application of post-death events. In determining whether and to what extent a deduction under section 2053 is allowable, events occurring after the date of a decedent's death will be taken into consideration—

(i) Until the expiration of the applicable period of limitations on assessment prescribed in section 6501 (including without limitation at all times during which the running of the period of limitations is suspended); and

(ii) During subsequent periods, in determining the amount (if any) of an overpayment of estate tax due in connection with a claim for refund filed within the time prescribed in section 6511(a).

(3) Reimbursements. A deduction is not allowed to the extent that a claim or expense described in paragraph (a) of this section is or could be compensated for by insurance or otherwise could be reimbursed. If the executor is able to establish that only a partial reimbursement could be collected, then only that portion of the potential reimbursement that reasonably could have been expected to be collected will reduce the estate's deductible portion of the total claim or expense. An executor may certify that the executor neither knows nor reasonably should have known of any available reimbursement for a claim or expense described in section 2053(a) or (b) on the estate's United States Estate (and Generation-Skipping Transfer) Tax Return (Form 706), in accordance with the instructions for that form. A potential reimbursement will not reduce the deductible amount of a claim or expense to the extent that the executor, on Form 706 and in accordance with the instructions for that form, provides a reasonable explanation for his or her reasonable determination that the burden of necessary collection efforts in pursuit of a right of reimbursement would outweigh the anticipated benefit from those efforts. Nevertheless, even if a reasonable explanation is provided, subsequent events (including without limitation an actual reimbursement) occurring within the period described in § 20.2053-1(d)(2) will be considered in determining the amount (if any) of a reduction under this paragraph (d)(3) in the deductible amount of a claim or expense.

(4) Exception for certain ascertainable amounts. (i) General rule. A deduction will be allowed for a claim or expense that satisfies all applicable requirements even though it is not yet paid, provided that the amount to be paid is ascertainable with reasonable certainty and will be paid. For example, executors' commissions and attorneys' fees that are not yet paid, and that meet the requirements for deductibility under § 20.2053-3(b) and (c), respectively, are deemed to be ascertainable with reasonable certainty and may be deducted if such expenses will be paid. However, no deduction may be taken upon the basis of a vague or uncertain estimate. To the extent a claim or expense is contested or contingent, such a claim or expense cannot be ascertained with reasonable certainty.

(ii) Effect of post-death events. A deduction under this paragraph (d)(4) will be allowed to the extent the Commissioner is reasonably satisfied that the amount to be paid is ascertainable with reasonable certainty and will be paid. In making this determination, the Commissioner will take into account events occurring after the date of a decedent's death. To the extent the amount for which a deduction was claimed does not satisfy the requirements of this paragraph (d)(4), and is not otherwise deductible, the deduction will be disallowed by the Commissioner. If a deduction is claimed on Form 706 for an amount that is not yet paid and the deduction is disallowed in whole or in part (or if no deduction is claimed on Form 706), then if the claim or expense subsequently satisfies the requirements of this paragraph (d)(4) or is paid, relief may be sought by filing a claim for refund. To preserve the estate's right to claim a refund for amounts becoming deductible after the expiration of the period of limitation for the filing of a claim for refund, a protective claim for refund may be filed in accordance with paragraph (d)(5) of this section.

(5) Protective claim for refund. (i) In general. A protective claim for refund under this section may be filed at any time before the expiration of the period of limitation prescribed in section 6511(a) for the filing of a claim for refund to preserve the estate's right to claim a refund by reason of claims or expenses that are not paid or do not otherwise meet the requirements of deductibility under section 2053 and these regulations until after the expiration of the period of limitation for filing a claim for refund. Such a protective claim shall be made in accordance with guidance that may be provided from time to time by publication in the Internal Revenue Bulletin (see § 601.601(d)(2)(ii)(b)). Although the protective claim need not state a particular dollar amount or demand an immediate refund, a protective claim must identify each outstanding claim or expense that would have been deductible under section 2053(a) or (b) if such item already had been paid and must describe the reasons and contingencies delaying the actual payment of the claim or expense. Action on protective claims will proceed after the executor has notified the Commissioner within a reasonable period that the contingency has been resolved and that the amount deductible under § 20.2053-1 has been established.

(ii) Effect on marital and charitable deduction. To the extent that a protective claim for refund is filed with respect to a claim or expense that would have been deductible under section 2053(a) or (b) if such item already had been paid and that is payable out of a share that meets the requirements for a charitable deduction under section 2055 or a marital deduction under section 2056 or section 2056A, or from a combination thereof, neither the charitable deduction nor the marital deduction shall be reduced by the amount of such claim or expense until the amount is actually paid or meets the requirements of paragraph (d)(4) of this section for deducting certain ascertainable amounts or the requirements of § 20.2053-4(b) or (c) for deducting certain claims against the estate.

(6) [Reserved].

(7) Examples. Assume that the amounts described in section 2053(a) are payable out of property subject to claims and are allowable by the law of the jurisdiction governing the administration of the estate, whether the applicable jurisdiction is within or outside of the United States. Assume that the claims against the estate are not deductible under § 20.2053-4(b) or (c). Also assume, unless otherwise provided, that none of the limitations on the amount of the deduction described in this section apply to the deduction claimed under section 2053. The following examples illustrate the application of this paragraph (d):

Example (1). Amount of expense ascertainable. Decedent's (D's) estate was probated in State. State law provides that the personal representative shall receive compensation equal to 2.5 percent of the value of the probate estate. The executor (E) may claim a deduction for estimated fees equal to 2.5 percent of D's probate estate on the Form 706 filed for D's estate under the rule for deducting certain ascertainable amounts set forth in paragraph (d)(4) of this section, provided that the estimated amount will be paid. However, the Commissioner will disallow the deduction upon examination of the estate's Form 706 to the extent that the amount for which a deduction was claimed no longer satisfies the requirements of paragraph (d)(4) of this section. If this occurs, E may file a protective claim for refund in accordance with paragraph (d)(5) of this section in order to preserve the estate's right to claim a refund for the amount of the fee that is subsequently paid or that subsequently meets the requirements of paragraph (d)(4) of this section for deducting certain ascertainable amounts.

Example (2). Amount of claim not ascertainable. Prior to death, Decedent (D) is sued by Claimant (C) for $100x in a tort proceeding and responds asserting affirmative defenses available to D under applicable local law. C and D are unrelated. D subsequently dies and D's Form 706 is due before a final judgment is entered in the case. The executor of D's estate (E) may not claim a deduction with respect to C's claim on D's Form 706 under the special rule contained in paragraph (d)(4) of this section because the deductible amount cannot be ascertained with reasonable certainty. However, E may file a timely protective claim for refund in accordance with paragraph (d)(5) of this section in order to preserve the estate's right to subsequently claim a refund at the time a final judgment is entered in the case and the claim is either paid or meets the requirements of paragraph (d)(4) of this section for deducting certain ascertainable amounts.

Example (3). Amount of claim payable out of property qualifying for marital deduction. The facts are the same as in Example 2 except that the applicable credit amount, under section 2010, against the estate tax was fully consumed by D's lifetime gifts, D is survived by Spouse (S), and D's estate passes entirely to S in a bequest that qualifies for the marital deduction under section 2056. Even though any amount D's estate ultimately pays with respect to C's claim will be paid from the assets qualifying for the marital deduction, in filing Form 706, E need not reduce the amount of the marital deduction claimed on D's Form 706. Instead, pursuant to the protective claim for refund filed by E, the marital deduction will be reduced by the claim once a final judgment is entered in the case. At that time, a deduction will be allowed for the amount that is either paid or meets the requirements of paragraph (d)(4) of this section for deducting certain ascertainable amounts.

(e) Disallowance of double deductions. See section 642(g) and § 1.642(g)-1 with respect to the disallowance for income tax purposes of certain deductions unless the right to take such deductions for estate tax purposes is waived.

(f) Effective/applicability date. This section applies to the estates of decedents dying on or after October 20, 2009.

T.D. 6296, 6/23/58, amend T.D. 7238, 12/28/72, T.D. 9468, 10/16/2009.

§ 20.2053-2 Deduction for funeral expenses.

Such amounts for funeral expenses are allowed as deductions from a decedent's gross estate as (a) are actually expended, (b) would be properly allowable out of property subject to claims under the laws of the local jurisdiction, and (c) satisfy the requirements of paragraph (c) of § 20.2053-1.

A reasonable expenditure for a tombstone, monument, or mausoleum, or for a burial lot, either for the decedent or his family, including a reasonable expenditure for its future care, may be deducted under this heading, provided such an expenditure is allowable by the local law. Included in funeral expenses is the cost of transportation of the person bringing the body to the place of burial.

T.D. 6296, 6/23/58.

§ 20.2053-3 Deduction for expenses of administering estate.

(a) In general. The amounts deductible from a decedent's gross estate as "administration expenses" of the first category (see paragraphs (a) and (c) of § 20.2053-1) are limited to such expenses as are actually and necessarily incurred in the administration of the decedent's estate; that is, in the collection of assets, payment of debts, and distribution of property to the persons entitled to it. The expenses contemplated in the law are such only as attend the settlement of an estate and the transfer of the property of the estate to individual beneficiaries or to a trustee, whether the trustee is the executor or some other person. Expenditures not essential to the proper settlement of the estate, but incurred for the individual benefit of the heirs, legatees, or devisees, may not be taken as deductions. Administration expenses include (1) executor's commissions; (2) attorney's fees; and (3) miscellaneous expenses. Each of these classes is considered separately in paragraphs (b) through (d) of this section.

(b) Executor's commissions. *(1)* Executors' commissions are deductible to the extent permitted by § 20.2053-1 and this section, but no deduction may be taken if no commissions are to be paid. In addition, the amount of the commissions claimed as a deduction must be in accordance with the usually accepted standards and practice of allowing such an amount in estates of similar size and character in the jurisdiction in which the estate is being administered, or any deviation from the usually accepted standards or range of amounts (permissible under applicable local law) must be justified to the satisfaction of the Commissioner.

(2) A bequest or devise to the executor in lieu of commissions is not deductible. If, however, the terms of the will set forth the compensation payable to the executor for services to be rendered in the administration of the estate, a deduction may be taken to the extent that the amount so fixed does not exceed the compensation allowable by the local law or practice and to the extent permitted by § 20.2053-1.

(3) Except to the extent that a trustee is in fact performing services with respect to property subject to claims which would normally be performed by an executor, amounts paid as trustees' commissions do not constitute expenses of administration under the first category, and are only deductible as expenses of the second category to the extent provided in § 20.2053-8.

(c) Attorney's fees. *(1)* Attorney's fees are deductible to the extent permitted by § 20.2053-1 and this section. Further, the amount of the fees claimed as a deduction may not exceed a reasonable remuneration for the services rendered, taking into account the size and character of the estate, the law and practice in the jurisdiction in which the estate is being administered, and the skill and expertise of the attorneys.

(2) A deduction for attorneys' fees incurred in contesting an asserted deficiency or in prosecuting a claim for refund should be claimed at the time the deficiency is contested or the refund claim is prosecuted. A deduction for reasonable attorney's fees actually incurred in contesting an asserted deficiency or in prosecuting a claim for refund will be allowed to the extent permitted by § 20.2053-1 even though the deduction, as such, was not claimed on the estate tax return or in the claim for refund. A deduction for these fees shall not be denied, and the sufficiency of a claim for refund shall not be questioned, solely by reason of the fact that the amount of the fees to be paid was not established at the time that the right to the deduction was claimed.

(3) Attorneys' fees incurred by beneficiaries incident to litigation as to their respective interests are not deductible if the litigation is not essential to the proper settlement of the estate within the meaning of paragraph (a) of this section. An attorney's fee not meeting this test is not deductible as an administration expense under section 2053 and this section, even if it is approved by a probate court as an expense payable or reimbursable by the estate.

(d) Miscellaneous administration expenses. *(1)* Miscellaneous administration expenses include such expenses as court costs, surrogates' fees, accountants' fees, appraisers' fees, clerk hire, etc. Expenses necessarily incurred in preserving and distributing the estate, including the cost of storing or maintaining property of the estate if it is impossible to effect immediate distribution to the beneficiaries, are deductible to the extent permitted by § 20.2053-1. Expenses for preserving and caring for the property may not include outlays for additions or improvements; nor will such expenses be allowed for a longer period than the executor is reasonably required to retain the property.

(2) Expenses for selling property of the estate are deductible to the extent permitted by § 20.2053-1 if the sale is necessary in order to pay the decedent's debts, expenses of administration, or taxes, to preserve the estate, or to effect distribution. The phrase "expenses for selling property" includes brokerage fees and other expenses attending the sale, such as the fees of an auctioneer if it is reasonably necessary to employ one. Where an item included in the gross estate is disposed of in a bona fide sale (including a redemption) to a dealer in such items at a price below its fair market value, for purposes of this paragraph there shall be treated as an expense for selling the item whichever of the following amounts is the lesser: (i) The amount by which the fair market value of the property on the applicable valuation date exceeds the proceeds of the sale, or (ii) the amount by which the fair market value of the property on the date of the sale exceeds the proceeds of the sale. The principles used in determining the value at which an item of property is included in the gross estate shall be followed in arriving at the fair market value of the property for purposes of this paragraph. See §§ 20.2031-1 through 20.2031-9.

(3) Expenses incurred in defending the estate against claims described in section 2053(a)(3) are deductible to the extent permitted by § 20.2053-1 if the expenses are incurred incident to the assertion of defenses to the claim available under the applicable law, even if the estate ultimately does not prevail. For purposes of this paragraph (d)(3), "expenses incurred in defending the estate against claims'' include costs relating to the arbitration and mediation of contested issues, costs associated with defending the estate against claims (whether or not enforceable), and costs associated with reaching a negotiated settlement of the issues.

(e) Effective/applicability date. This section applies to the estates of decedents dying on or after October 20, 2009.

T.D. 6296, 6/23/58, amend T.D. 6826, 6/14/65, T.D. 7612, 4/19/79, T.D. 9468, 10/16/2009.

§ 20.2053-4 Deduction for claims against the estate.

(a) In general. *(1) General rule.* For purposes of this section, liabilities imposed by law or arising out of contracts or torts are deductible if they meet the applicable requirements set forth in § 20.2053-1 and this section. To be deductible, a claim against a decedent's estate must represent a personal obligation of the decedent existing at the time of the decedent's death. Except as otherwise provided in paragraphs (b) and (c) of this section and to the extent permitted by § 20.2053-1, the amounts that may be deducted as claims against a decedent's estate are limited to the amounts of bona fide claims that are enforceable against the decedent's estate (and are not unenforceable when paid) and claims that—

(i) Are actually paid by the estate in satisfaction of the claim; or

(ii) Meet the requirements of § 20.2053-1(d)(4) for deducting certain ascertainable amounts.

(2) Effect of post-death events. Events occurring after the date of a decedent's death shall be considered in determining whether and to what extent a deduction is allowable under section 2053. See § 20.2053-1(d)(2).

(b) Exception for claims and counterclaims in related matter. *(1) General rule.* If a decedent's gross estate includes one or more claims or causes of action and there are one or more claims against the decedent's estate in the same or a substantially-related matter, or, if a decedent's gross estate includes a particular asset and there are one or more claims against the decedent's estate integrally related to that particular asset, the executor may deduct on the estate's United States Estate (and Generation-Skipping Transfer) Tax Return (Form 706) the current value of the claim or claims against the estate, even though payment has not been made, provided that—

(i) Each such claim against the estate otherwise satisfies the applicable requirements set forth in § 20.2053-1;

(ii) Each such claim against the estate represents a personal obligation of the decedent existing at the time of the decedent's death;

(iii) Each such claim is enforceable against the decedent's estate (and is not unenforceable when paid);

(iv) The value of each such claim against the estate is determined from a "qualified appraisal'' performed by a "qualified appraiser'' within the meaning of section 170 of the Internal Revenue Code and the corresponding regulations;

(v) The value of each such claim against the estate is subject to adjustment for post-death events; and

(vi) The aggregate value of the related claims or assets included in the decedent's gross estate exceeds 10 percent of the decedent's gross estate.

(2) Limitation on deduction. The deduction under this paragraph (b) is limited to the value of the related claims or particular assets included in decedent's gross estate.

(3) Effect of post-death events. If, under this paragraph (b), a deduction is claimed on Form 706 for a claim against the estate and, during the period described in § 20.2053-1(d)(2), the claim is paid or meets the requirements of § 20.2053-1(d)(4) for deducting certain ascertainable amounts, the claimed deduction is subject to adjustment to reflect, and may not exceed, the amount paid on the claim or the amount meeting the requirements of § 20.2053-1(d)(4). If, under this paragraph (b), a deduction is claimed on Form 706 for a claim against the estate and, during the period described in § 20.2053-1(d)(2), the claim remains unpaid (and does not meet the requirements of § 20.2053-1(d)(4) for deducting certain ascertainable amounts), the claimed deduction is subject to adjustment to reflect, and may not exceed, the current valuation of the claim. A valuation of the claim will be considered current if it reflects events occurring after the decedent's death. With regard to any amount in excess of the amount deductible under this paragraph (b), an estate may preserve the estate's right to claim a refund for claims that are paid or that meet the requirements of § 20.2053-1(d)(4) after the expiration of the period of limitation for filing a claim for refund by filing a protective claim for refund in accordance with the rules in § 20.2053-1(d)(5).

(c) Exception for claims totaling not more than $500,000. *(1) General rule.* An executor may deduct on Form 706 the current value of one or more claims against the estate even though payment has not been made on the claim or claims to the extent that—

(i) Each such claim against the estate otherwise satisfies the applicable requirements for deductibility set forth in § 20.2053-1;

(ii) Each such claim against the estate represents a personal obligation of the decedent existing at the time of the decedent's death;

(iii) Each such claim is enforceable against the decedent's estate (and is not unenforceable when paid);

(iv) The value of each such claim against the estate is determined from a "qualified appraisal" performed by a "qualified appraiser" within the meaning of section 170 of the Internal Revenue Code and the corresponding regulations;

(v) The total amount deducted by the estate under this paragraph (c) does not exceed $500,000;

(vi) The full value of each claim, rather than just a portion of that amount, must be deductible under this paragraph (c) and, for this purpose, the full value of each such claim is deemed to be the unpaid amount of that claim that is not deductible after the application of §§ 20.2053-1 and 20.2053-4(b); and

(vii) The value of each claim deducted under this paragraph (c) is subject to adjustment for post-death events.

(2) Effect of post-death events. If, under this paragraph (c), a deduction is claimed for a claim against the estate and, during the period described in § 20.2053-1(d)(2), the claim is paid or meets the requirements of § 20.2053-1(d)(4) for deducting certain ascertainable amounts, the amount of the allowable deduction for that claim is subject to adjustment to reflect, and may not exceed, the amount paid on the claim or the amount meeting the requirements of § 20.2053-1(d)(4). If, under this paragraph (c), a deduction is claimed for a claim against the estate and, during the period described in § 20.2053-1(d)(2), the claim remains unpaid (and does not meet the requirements of § 20.2053-1(d)(4) for deducting certain ascertainable amounts), the amount of the allowable deduction for that claim is subject to adjustment to reflect, and may not exceed, the current value of the claim. The value of the claim will be considered current if it reflects events occurring after the decedent's death. To claim a deduction for amounts in excess of the amount deductible under this paragraph (c), the estate may preserve the estate's right to claim a refund for claims that are not paid or that do not meet the requirements of § 20.2053-1(d)(4) until after the expiration of the period of limitation for the filing of a claim for refund by filing a protective claim for refund in accordance with the rules in § 20.2053-1(d)(5).

(3) Examples. The following examples illustrate the application of this paragraph (c). Assume that the value of each

claim is determined from a "qualified appraisal" performed by a "qualified appraiser" and reflects events occurring after the death of the decedent (D). Also assume that each claim represents a personal obligation of D that existed at D's death, that each claim is enforceable against the decedent's estate (and is not unenforceable when paid), and that each claim otherwise satisfies the requirements for deductibility of § 20.2053-1.

Example (1). There are three claims against the estate of the decedent (D) that are not paid and are not deductible under § 20.2053-1(d)(4) or paragraph (b) of this section: $25,000 of Claimant A, $35,000 of Claimant B, and $1,000,000 of Claimant C. The executor of D's estate (E) may not claim a deduction under this paragraph with respect to any portion of the claim of Claimant C because the value of that claim exceeds $500,000. E may claim a deduction under this paragraph for the total amount of the claims filed by Claimant A and Claimant B ($60,000) because the aggregate value of the full amount of those claims does not exceed $500,000.

Example (2). There are three claims against the estate of the decedent (D) that are not paid and are not deductible under § 20.2053-1(d)(4) or paragraph (b) of this section; specifically, a separate $200,000 claim of each of three claimants, A, B and C. The executor of D's estate (E) may claim a deduction under this paragraph for any two of these three claims because the aggregate value of the full amount of any two of the claims does not exceed $500,000. E may not deduct any part of the value of the remaining claim under this paragraph because the aggregate value of the full amount of all three claims would exceed $500,000.

Example (3). As a result of an automobile accident involving the decedent (D) and A, D's gross estate includes a claim against A that is valued at $750,000. In the same matter, A files a counterclaim against D's estate that is valued at $1,000,000. A's claim against D's estate is not paid and is not deductible under § 20.2053-1(d)(4). All other section 2053 claims and expenses of D's estate have been paid and are deductible. The executor of D's estate (E) deducts $750,000 of A's claim against the estate under § 20.2053-4(b). E may claim a deduction under this paragraph (c) for the total value of A's claim not deducted under § 20.2053-4(b), or $250,000. If, instead, the value of A's claim against D's estate is $1,500,000, so that the amount not deductible under § 20.2053-4(b) exceeds $500,000, no deduction is available under this paragraph (c).

(d) Special rules.

(1) Potential and unmatured claims. Except as provided in § 20.2053-1(d)(4) and in paragraphs (b) and (c) of this section, no estate tax deduction may be taken for a claim against the decedent's estate while it remains a potential or unmatured claim. Claims that later mature may be deducted (to the extent permitted by § 20.2053-1) in connection with a timely claim for refund. To preserve the estate's right to claim a refund for claims that mature and become deductible after the expiration of the period of limitation for filing a claim for refund, a protective claim for refund may be filed in accordance with § 20.2053-1(d)(5). See § 20.2053-1(b)(3) for rules relating to the treatment of court decrees and settlements.

(2) Contested claims. Except as provided in paragraphs (b) and (c) of this section, no estate tax deduction may be taken for a claim against the decedent's estate to the extent the estate is contesting the decedent's liability. Contested claims that later mature may be deducted (to the extent permitted by § 20.2053-1) in connection with a claim for refund filed within the time prescribed in section 6511(a). To preserve the estate's right to claim a refund for claims that mature and become deductible after the expiration of the period of limitation for filing a claim for refund, a protective claim for refund may be filed in accordance with § 20.2053-1(d)(5). See § 20.2053-1(b)(3) for rules relating to the treatment of court decrees and settlements.

(3) Claims against multiple parties. If the decedent or the decedent's estate is one of two or more parties against whom the claim is being asserted, the estate may deduct only the portion of the total claim due from and paid by the estate, reduced by the total of any reimbursement received from another party, insurance, or otherwise. The estate's deductible portion also will be reduced by the contribution or other amount the estate could have collected from another party or an insurer but which the estate declines or fails to attempt to collect. See further § 20.2053-1(d)(3).

(4) Unenforceable claims. Claims that are unenforceable prior to or at the decedent's death are not deductible, even if they are actually paid. Claims that become unenforceable during the administration of the estate are not deductible to the extent that they are paid (or will be paid) after they become unenforceable. However, see § 20.2053-1(b)(3)(iv) regarding a claim whose enforceability is at issue.

(5) Claims founded upon a promise. Except with regard to pledges or subscriptions (see § 20.2053-5), section 2053(c)(1)(A) provides that the deduction for a claim founded upon a promise or agreement is limited to the extent that the promise or agreement was bona fide and in exchange for adequate and full consideration in money or money's worth; that is, the promise or agreement must have been bargained for at arm's length and the price must have been an adequate and full equivalent reducible to a money value.

(6) Recurring payments.

(i) Noncontingent obligations. If a decedent is obligated to make recurring payments on an enforceable and certain claim that satisfies the requirements for deductibility under this section and the payments are not subject to a contingency, the amount of the claim will be deemed ascertainable with reasonable certainty for purposes of the rule for deducting certain ascertainable amounts set forth in § 20.2053-1(d)(4). If the recurring payments will be paid, a deduction will be allowed under the rule for deducting certain ascertainable amounts set forth in § 20.2053-1(d)(4) (subject to any applicable limitations in § 20.2053-1). Recurring payments for purposes of this section exclude those payments made in connection with a mortgage or indebtedness described in and governed by § 20.2053-7. If a decedent's obligation to make a recurring payment is contingent on the death or remarriage of the claimant and otherwise satisfies the requirements of this paragraph (d)(6)(i), the amount of the claim (measured according to actuarial principles, using factors set forth in the transfer tax regulations or otherwise provided by the IRS) will be deemed ascertainable with reasonable certainty for purposes of the rule for deducting certain ascertainable amounts set forth in § 20.2053-1(d)(4).

(ii) Contingent obligations. If a decedent has a recurring obligation to pay an enforceable and certain claim but the decedent's obligation is subject to a contingency or is not otherwise described in paragraph (d)(6)(i) of this section, the amount of the claim is not ascertainable with reasonable certainty for purposes of the rule for deducting certain ascertainable amounts set forth in § 20.2053-1(d)(4). Accordingly, the amount deductible is limited to amounts actually paid by the estate in satisfaction of the claim in accordance with § 20.2053-1(d)(1) (subject to any applicable limitations in § 20.2053-1).

(iii) Purchase of commercial annuity to satisfy recurring obligation to pay. If a decedent has a recurring obligation (whether or not contingent) to pay an enforceable and certain claim and the estate purchases a commercial annuity from an unrelated dealer in commercial annuities in an arm's-length transaction to satisfy the obligation, the amount deductible by the estate (subject to any applicable limitations in § 20.2053-1) is the sum of—

(A) The amount paid for the commercial annuity, to the extent that the amount paid is not refunded, or expected to be refunded, to the estate;

(B) Any amount actually paid to the claimant by the estate prior to the purchase of the commercial annuity; and

(C) Any amount actually paid to the claimant by the estate in excess of the annuity amount as is necessary to satisfy the recurring obligation.

(7) Examples. The following examples illustrate the application of paragraph (d) of this section. Except as is otherwise provided in the examples, assume—

(i) A claim satisfies the applicable requirements set forth in § 20.2053-1 and paragraph (a) of this section, is payable from property subject to claims, and the amount of the claim is not subject to any other applicable limitations in § 20.2053-1;

(ii) A claim is not deductible under paragraphs (b) or (c) of this section as an exception to the general rule contained in paragraph (a) of this section; and

(iii) The claimant (C) is not a family member, related entity or beneficiary of the estate of decedent (D) and is not the executor (E).

Example (1). Contested claim, single defendant, no decision. D is sued by C for $100x in a tort proceeding and responds asserting affirmative defenses available to D under applicable local law. D dies and E is substituted as defendant in the suit. D's Form 706 is due before a judgment is reached in the case. D's gross estate exceeds $100x. E may not take a deduction on Form 706 for the claim against the estate. However, E may claim a deduction under § 20.2053-3(c) or § 20.2053-3(d)(3) for expenses incurred in defending the estate against the claim if the expenses have been paid in accordance with § 20.2053-1(d)(1) or if the expenses meet the requirements of § 20.2053-1(d)(4) for deducting certain ascertainable amounts. E may file a protective claim for refund before the expiration of the period of limitation prescribed in section 6511(a) in order to preserve the estate's right to claim a refund, if the amount of the claim will not be paid or cannot be ascertained with reasonable certainty by the expiration of this limitation period. If payment is subsequently made pursuant to a court decision or a settlement, the payment, as well as expenses incurred incident to the claim and not previously deducted, may be deducted and relief may be sought in connection with a timely-filed claim for refund.

Example (2). Contested claim, single defendant, final court decree and payment. The facts are the same as in Example 1 except that, before the Form 706 is timely filed, the court enters a decision in favor of C, no timely appeal is filed, and payment is made. E may claim a deduction on Form 706 for the amount paid in satisfaction of the claim against the estate pursuant to the final decision of the local court, including any interest accrued prior to D's death. In addition, E may claim a deduction under § 20.2053-3(c) or § 20.2053-3(d)(3) for expenses incurred in defending the estate against the claim and in processing payment of the claim if the expenses have been paid in accordance with § 20.2053-1(d)(1) or if the expenses meet the requirements of § 20.2053-1(d)(4) for deducting certain ascertainable amounts.

Example (3). Contested claim, single defendant, settlement and payment. The facts are the same as in Example 1 except that a settlement is reached between E and C for $80x and payment is made before Form 706 is timely filed. E may claim a deduction on Form 706 for the amount paid to C ($80x) in satisfaction of the claim against the estate. In addition, E may claim a deduction under § 20.2053-3(c) or § 20.2053-3(d)(3) for expenses incurred in defending the estate, reaching a settlement, and processing payment of the claim if the expenses have been paid in accordance with § 20.2053-1(d)(1) or if the expenses meet the requirements of § 20.2053-1(d)(4) for deducting certain ascertainable amounts.

Example (4). Contested claim, multiple defendants. The facts are the same as in Example 1 except that the suit filed by C lists D and an unrelated third-party (K) as defendants. If the claim against the estate is not resolved prior to the time the Form 706 is filed, E may not take a deduction for the claim on Form 706. If payment is subsequently made of D's share of the claim pursuant to a court decision holding D liable for 40 percent of the amount due and K liable for 60 percent of the amount due, then E may claim a deduction for the amount paid in satisfaction of the claim against the estate representing D's share of the liability as assigned by the court decree ($40x), plus any interest on that share accrued prior to D's death. If the court decision finds D and K jointly and severally liable for the entire $100x and D's estate pays the entire $100x but could have reasonably collected $50x from K in reimbursement, E may claim a deduction of $50x together with the interest on $50x accrued prior to D's death. In both instances, E also may claim a deduction under § 20.2053-3(c) or § 20.2053-3(d)(3) for expenses incurred and not previously deducted in defending the estate against the claim and processing payment of the amount due from D if the expenses have been paid in accordance with § 20.2053-1(d)(1) or if the expenses meet the requirements of § 20.2053-1(d)(4) for deducting certain ascertainable amounts.

Example (5). Contested claim, multiple defendants, settlement and payment. The facts are the same as in Example 1 except that the suit filed by C lists D and an unrelated third-party (K) as defendants. D's estate settles with C for $10x and payment is made before Form 706 is timely filed. E may take a deduction on Form 706 for the amount paid to C ($10x) in satisfaction of the claim against the estate. In addition, E may claim a deduction under § 20.2053-3(c) or § 20.2053-3(d)(3) for expenses incurred in defending the estate, reaching a settlement, and processing payment of the claim if the expenses have been paid in accordance with § 20.2053-1(d)(1) or if the expenses meet the requirements of § 20.2053-1(d)(4) for deducting certain ascertainable amounts.

Example (6). Mixed claims. During life, D contracts with C to perform specific work on D's home for $75x. Under the contract, additional work must be approved in advance by D. C performs additional work and sues D for $100x for work completed including the $75x agreed to in the contract. D dies and D's Form 706 is due before a judgment is reached in the case. E accepts liability of $75x but contests liability of $25x. E may take a deduction of $75x on Form 706 if the amount has been paid or meets the requirements of § 20.2053-1(d)(4) for deducting certain ascertainable amounts. In addition, E may claim a deduction under § 20.2053-3(c) or § 20.2053-3(d)(3) for expenses incurred in defending the estate against the claim if the expenses have been paid or if the expenses meet the requirements of § 20.2053-1(d)(4) for deducting certain ascertainable amounts. E may file a protective claim for refund before the expiration of the period of limitation prescribed in section 6511(a) in order to preserve the estate's right to claim a refund for any amount in excess of $75x that is subsequently paid to resolve the claim against the estate. To the extent that any unpaid expenses incurred in defending the estate against the claim are not deducted as an ascertainable amount pursuant to § 20.2053-1(d)(4), they may be included in the protective claim for refund.

Example (7). Claim having issue of enforceability. D is sued by C for $100x in a tort proceeding in which there is an issue as to whether the claim is barred by the applicable period of limitations. After D's death but prior to the decision of the court, a settlement meeting the requirements of § 20.2053-1(b)(3)(iv) is reached between E and C in the amount of $50x. E pays C this amount before the Form 706 is timely filed. E may take a deduction on Form 706 for the amount paid to C ($50x) in satisfaction of the claim. If, subsequent to E's payment to C, facts develop to indicate that the claim was, in fact, unenforceable, the deduction will not be denied provided the enforceability of the claim was at issue in a bona dispute at the time of the payment. See § 20.2053-1(b)(3)(iv). A deduction may be available under § 20.2053-3(d)(3) for expenses incurred in defending the estate, reaching a settlement, and processing payment of the claim if the expenses have been paid in accordance with § 20.2053-1(d)(1) or if the expenses meet the requirements of § 20.2053-1(d)(4) for deducting certain ascertainable amounts.

Example (8). Noncontingent and recurring obligation to pay, binding on estate. D's property settlement agreement incident to D's divorce, signed three years prior to D's death, obligates D or D's estate to pay to S, D's former spouse, $20x per year until S's death or remarriage. Prior to D's death, D made payments in accordance with the agreement and, after D's death, E continues to make the payments in accordance with the agreement. D's obligation to pay S under the property settlement agreement is deemed to be a claim against the estate that is ascertainable with reasonable certainty for purposes of § 20.2053-1(d)(4). To the extent the obligation to make the recurring payment is a claim that will be paid, E may deduct the amount of the claim (measured according to actuarial principles, using factors set forth in the transfer tax regulations or otherwise provided by the IRS) under the rule for deducting certain ascertainable amounts set forth in § 20.2053-1(d)(4).

Example (9). Recurring obligation to pay, estate purchases a commercial annuity in satisfaction. D's settlement agreement with T, the claimant in a suit against D, signed three years prior to D's death, obligates D or D's estate to pay to T $20x per year for 10 years, provided that T does not reveal the details of the claim or of the settlement during that period. D dies in Year 1. In Year 2, D's estate purchases a commercial annuity from an unrelated issuer of commercial annuities, XYZ, to fund the obligation to T. E may deduct the entire amount paid to XYZ to obtain the annuity, even though the obligation to T was contingent.

(e) Interest on claim. *(1)* Subject to any applicable limitations in § 20.2053-1, the interest on a deductible claim is itself deductible as a claim under section 2053 to the extent of the amount of interest accrued at the decedent's death (even if the executor elects the alternate valuation method under section 2032), but only to the extent of the amount of interest actually paid or meeting the requirements of § 20.2053-1(d)(4) for deducting certain ascertainable amounts.

(2) Post-death accrued interest may be deductible in appropriate circumstances either as an estate tax administration expense under section 2053 or as an income tax deduction.

(f) Effective/applicability date. This section applies to the estates of decedents dying on or after October 20, 2009.

T.D. 6296, 6/23/58, T.D. 9468, 10/16/2009.

§ 20.2053-5 Deductions for charitable, etc., pledges or subscriptions.

(a) A pledge or a subscription, evidenced by a promissory note or otherwise, even though enforceable against the estate, is deductible (subject to any applicable limitations in Sec. 20.2053-1) only to the extent that—

(1) Liability therefore was contracted bona fide and for an adequate and full consideration in cash or its equivalent, or

(2) It would have constituted an allowable deduction under section 2055 (relating to charitable, etc., deductions) if it had been a bequest.

(b) Effective/applicability date. This section applies to the estates of decedents dying on or after October 20, 2009.

T.D. 6296, 6/23/58, T.D. 9468, 10/16/2009.

§ 20.2053-6 Deduction for taxes.

(a) In general. *(1)* Taxes are deductible in computing a decedent's gross estate—

(i) Only as claims against the estate (except to the extent that excise taxes may be allowable as administration expenses);

(ii) Only to the extent not disallowed by section 2053(c)(1)(B) and this section; and

(iii) Subject to any applicable limitations in § 20.2053-1.

(2) See §§ 20.2053-9 and 20.2053-10 with respect to the deduction allowed for certain state and foreign death taxes.

(b) Property taxes. Property taxes are not deductible unless they accrued before the decedent's death. However, they are not deductible merely because they have accrued in an accounting sense. Property taxes in order to be deductible must be an enforceable obligation of the decedent at the time of his death.

(c) Death taxes. *(1)* For the estates of decedents dying on or before December 31, 2004, no estate, succession, legacy or inheritance tax payable by reason of the decedent's death is deductible, except as provided in §§ 20.2053-9 and 20.2053-10 with respect to certain state and foreign death taxes on transfers for charitable, etc., uses. However, see sections 2011 and 2014 and the corresponding regulations with respect to credits for death taxes.

(1) For the estates of decedents dying after December 31, 2004, see section 2058 to determine the deductibility of state death taxes.

(d) Gift taxes. Unpaid gift taxes on gifts made by a decedent before his death are deductible. If a gift is considered as made one-half by the decedent and one-half by his spouse under section 2513, the entire amount of the gift tax, unpaid at the decedent's death, attributable to a gift in fact made by the decedent is deductible. No portion of the tax attributable to a gift in fact made by the decedent's spouse is deductible except to the extent that the obligation is enforced against the decedent's estate and his estate has no effective right of contribution against his spouse. (See section 2012 and § 20.2012-1 with respect to credit for gift taxes paid upon gifts of property included in a decedent's gross estate.)

(e) Excise taxes. Excise taxes incurred in selling property of a decedent's estate are deductible as an expense of administration if the sale is necessary in order to (1) pay the decedent's debts, expenses of administration, or taxes, (2) preserve the estate, or (3) effect distribution. Excise taxes incurred in distributing property of the estate in kind are also deductible.

(f) Income taxes. Unpaid income taxes are deductible if they are on income properly includible in an income tax return of the decedent for a period before his death. Taxes on income received after the decedent's death are not deductible. If income received by a decedent during his lifetime is included in a joint income tax return filed by the decedent and his spouse, or by the decedent's estate and his surviving spouse, the portion of the joint liability for the period covered by the return for which a deduction will be allowed is the amount for which the decedent's estate would be liable under local law, as between the decedent and his spouse, after enforcement of any effective right of reimbursement or contribution. In the absence of evidence to the contrary, the deductible amount is presumed to be an amount bearing the same ratio to the total joint tax liability for the period covered by the return that the amount of income tax for which the decedent would have been liable if he had filed a separate return for that period bears to the total of the amounts for which the decedent and his spouse would have been liable if they had both filed separate returns for that period. Thus, in the absence of evidence to the contrary, the deductible amount equals

$$\frac{\text{Decedent's separate tax}}{\text{Both separate taxes}} \times \text{Joint tax}$$

However, the deduction cannot in any event exceed the lesser of—

(1) The decedent's liability for the period (as determined in this paragraph) reduced by the amounts already contributed by the decedent toward payment of the joint liability, or

(2) If there is an enforceable agreement between the decedent and his spouse or between the executor and the spouse relative to the payment of the joint liability, the amount which pursuant to the agreement is to be contributed by the estate toward payment of the joint liability.

If the decedent's estate and his surviving spouse are entitled to a refund on account of an overpayment of a joint income tax liability, the overpayment is an asset includible in the decedent's gross estate under section 2033 in the amount to which the estate would be entitled under local law, as between the estate and the surviving spouse. In the absence of evidence to the contrary, the includible amount is presumed to be the amount by which the decedent's contributions toward payment of the joint tax exceeds his liability determined in accordance with the principles set forth in this paragraph (other than subparagraph (1) of this paragraph).

(g) Post-death adjustments of deductible tax liability. Post-death adjustments increasing a tax liability accrued prior to the decedent's death, including increases of taxes deducted under this section, will increase the amount of the deduction available under section 2053(a)(3) for that tax liability. Similarly, any refund subsequently determined to be due to and received by the estate or its successor in interest with respect to taxes deducted by the estate under this section reduce the amount of the deduction taken for that tax liability under section 2053(a)(3). Expenses associated with defending the estate against the increase in tax liability or with obtaining the refund may be deductible under § 20.2053-3(d)(3). A protective claim for refund of estate taxes may be filed before the expiration of the period of limitation for filing a claim for refund in order to preserve the estate's right to claim a refund if the amount of a deductible tax liability may be affected by such an adjustment or refund. The application of this section may be illustrated by the following examples:

Example (1). Increase in tax due. After the decedent's death, the Internal Revenue Service examines the gift tax return filed by the decedent in the year before the decedent's death and asserts a deficiency of $100x. The estate pays attorney's fees of $30x in a non-frivolous defense against the increased deficiency. The final determination of the deficiency, in the amount of $90x, is paid by the estate prior to the expiration of the limitation period for filing a claim for refund. The estate may deduct $90x under section 2053(a)(3) and $30x under § 20.2053-3(c)(2) or (d)(3) in connection with a timely claim for refund.

Example (2). Refund of taxes paid. Decedent's estate timely files D's individual income tax return for the year in which the decedent died. The estate timely pays the entire amount of the tax due, $50x, as shown on that return. The entire $50x was attributable to income received prior to the decedent's death. Decedent's estate subsequently discovers an error on the income tax return and timely files a claim for refund of income tax. Decedent's estate receives a refund of $10x. The estate is allowed a deduction of only $40x under section 2053(a)(3) for the income tax liability accrued prior to the decedent's death. If D's estate had claimed a deduction of $50x on D's United States Estate (and Generation-Skipping Transfer) Tax Return (Form 706), the deduction claimed under section 2053(a)(3) will be allowed only to the extent of $40x upon examination by the Commissioner.

(h) Effective/applicability date. This section applies to the estates of decedents dying on or after October 20, 2009.

T.D. 6296, 6/23/58, T.D. 9468, 10/16/2009.

§ 20.2053-7 Deduction for unpaid mortgages.

A deduction is allowed from a decedent's gross estate of the full unpaid amount of a mortgage upon, or of any other indebtedness in respect of, any property of the gross estate, including interest which had accrued thereon to the date of death, provided the value of the property, undiminished by the amount of the mortgage or indebtedness, is included in the value of the gross estate. If the decedent's estate is liable for the amount of the mortgage or indebtedness, the full value of the property subject to the mortgage or indebtedness must be included as part of the value of the gross estate; the amount of the mortgage or indebtedness being in such case allowed as a deduction. But if the decedent's estate is not so liable, only the value of the equity of redemption (or the value of the property, less the mortgage or indebtedness) need be returned as part of the value of the gross estate. In no case may the deduction on account of the mortgage or indebtedness exceed the liability therefor contracted bona fide and for an adequate and full consideration in money or money's worth. See § 20.2043-1. Only interest accrued to the date of the decedent's death is allowable even though the alternate valuation method under section 2032 is selected. In any case where real property situated outside the United States does not form a part of the gross estate, no deduction may be taken of any mortgage thereon or any other indebtedness in respect thereof.

T.D. 6296, 6/23/58, amend T.D. 6684, 10/23/63.

§ 20.2053-8 Deduction for expenses in administering property not subject to claims.

(a) Expenses incurred in administering property included in a decedent's gross estate but not subject to claims fall within the second category of deductions set forth in § 20.2053-1, and may be allowed as deductions if they—

(1) Would be allowed as deductions in the first category if the property being administered were subject to claims; and

(2) Were paid before the expiration of the period of limitation for assessment provided in section 6501.

Usually, these expenses are incurred in connection with the administration of a trust established by a decedent during his lifetime. They may also be incurred in connection with the collection of other assets or the transfer or clearance of title to other property included in a decedent's gross estate for estate tax purposes but not included in his probate estate.

(b) These expenses may be allowed as deductions only to the extent that they would be allowed as deductions under the first category if the property were subject to claims. See § 20.2053-3. The only expenses in administering property not subject to claims which are allowed as deductions are those occasioned by the decedent's death and incurred in settling the decedent's interest in the property or vesting good title to the property in the beneficiaries. Expenses not coming within the description in the preceding sentence but incurred on behalf of the transferees are not deductible.

(c) The principles set forth in paragraphs (b), (c), and (d) of § 20.2053-3 (relating to the allowance of executor's commissions, attorney's fees, and miscellaneous administration expenses of the first category) are applied in determining the extent to which trustee's commissions, attorney's and accountant's fees, and miscellaneous administration expenses are allowed in connection with the administration of property not subject to claims.

(d) The application of this section may be illustrated by the following examples:

Example (1). In 1940, the decedent made an irrevocable transfer of property to the X Trust Company, as trustee. The instrument of transfer provided that the trustee should pay the income from the property to the decedent for the duration of his life and, upon his death, distribute the corpus of the trust among designated beneficiaries. The property was included in the decedent's gross estate under the provisions of section 2036. Three months after the date of death, the trustee distributed the trust corpus among the beneficiaries, except for $6,000 which it withheld. The amount withheld represented $5,000 which it retained as trustee's commissions in connection with the termination of the trust and $1,000 which it had paid to an attorney for representing it in connection with the termination. Both the trustee's commissions and the attorney's fees were allowable under the law of the jurisdiction in which the trust was being administered, were reasonable in amount, and were in accord with local custom. Under these circumstances, the estate is allowed a deduction of $6,000.

Example (2). In 1945, the decedent made an irrevocable transfer of property to Y Trust Company, as trustee. The instrument of transfer provided that the trustee should pay the income from the property to the decedent during his life. If the decedent's wife survived him, the trust was to continue for the duration of her life, with Y Trust Company and the decedent's son as co-trustees, and with income payable to the decedent's wife for the duration of her life. Upon the death of both the decedent and his wife, the corpus is to be distributed among designated remaindermen. The decedent was survived by his wife. The property was included in the decedent's gross estate under the provisions of section 2036. In accordance with local custom, the trustee made an accounting to the court as of the date of the decedent's death. Following the death of the decedent, a controversy arose among the remaindermen as to their respective rights under the instrument of transfer, and a suit was brought in court to which the trustee was made a party. As a part of the accounting, the court approved the following expenses which the trustee had paid within 3 years following the date of death: $10,000, trustee's commissions; $5,000, accountant's fees; $25,000, attorney's fees; and $2,500, representing fees paid to the guardian of a remainderman who was a minor. The trustee's commissions and accountant's fees were for services in connection with the usual issues involved in a trust accounting as also were one-half of the attorney's and guardian's fees. The remainder of the attorney's and guardian's fees were for services performed in connection with the suit brought by the remaindermen. The amount allowed as a deduction is the $28,750 ($10,000, trustee's commissions; $5,000, accountant's fees; $12,500, attorney's fees; and $1,250, guardian's fees) incurred as expenses in connection with the usual issues involved in a trust accounting. The remaining expenses are not allowed as deductions since they were incurred on behalf of the transferees.

Example (3). Decedent in 1950 made an irrevocable transfer of property to the Z Trust Company, as trustee. The instrument of transfer provided that the trustee should pay the income from the property to the decedent's wife for the duration of her life. If the decedent survived his wife the trust corpus was to be returned to him but if he did not survive her, then upon the death of the wife, the trust corpus was to be distributed among their children. The decedent predeceased his wife and the transferred property, less the value of the wife's outstanding life estate, was included in his gross estate under the provisions of section 2037 since his reversionary interest therein immediately before his death was in excess of 5 percent of the value of the property. At the wife's request, the court ordered the trustee to render an accounting of the trust property as of the date of the decedent's death. No deduction will be allowed the decedent's estate for any of the expenses incurred in connection with the trust accounting, since the expenses were incurred on behalf of the wife.

Example (4). If, in the preceding example, the decedent died without other property and no executor or administrator of his estate was appointed, so that it was necessary for the trustee to prepare an estate tax return and participate in its audit, or if the trustee required accounting proceedings for its own protection in accordance with local custom, trustees attorneys and guardians' fees in connection with the estate tax or accounting proceedings would be deductible to the same extent that they would be deductible if the property were subject to claims. Deductions incurred under similar circumstances by a surviving joint tenant or the recipient of life insurance proceeds would also be deductible.

T.D. 6296, 6/23/58.

§ 20.2053-9 Deduction for certain State death taxes.

(a) General rule. A deduction is allowed a decedent's estate under section 2053(d) for the amount of any estate, succession, legacy, or inheritance tax imposed by a State, Territory, or the District of Columbia, or, in the case of a decedent dying before September 3, 1958, a possession of the United States upon a transfer by the decedent for charitable, etc., uses described in section 2055 or 2106(a)(2) (relating to the estates of nonresidents not citizens), but only if (1) the conditions stated in paragraph (b) of this section are met, and (2) an election is made in accordance with the provisions of paragraph (c) of this section. See section 2011(e) and § 20.2011-2 for the effect which the allowance of this deduction has upon the credit for State death taxes. However, see section 2058 to determine the deductibility of state death taxes by estates to which section 2058 is applicable.

(b) Condition for allowance of deduction. *(1)* The deduction is not allowed unless either—

(i) The entire decrease in the Federal estate tax resulting from the allowance of the deduction inures solely to the benefit of a charitable, etc., transferee described in section 2055 or 2106(a)(2), or

(ii) The Federal estate tax is equitably apportioned among all the transferees (including the decedent's surviving spouse and the charitable, etc., transferees) of property included in the decedent's gross estate.

For allowance of the credit, it is sufficient if either of these conditions is satisfied. Thus, in a case where the entire decrease in Federal estate tax inures to the benefit of a charitable transferee, the deduction is allowable even though the Federal estate tax is not equitably apportioned among all the transferees of property included in the decedent's gross estate. Similarly, if the Federal estate tax is equitably apportioned among all the transferees of property included in the decedent's gross estate, the deduction is allowable even though a noncharitable transferee receives some benefit from the allowance of the deduction.

(2) For purposes of this paragraph, the Federal estate tax is considered to be equitably apportioned among all the transferees (including the decedent's surviving spouse and the charitable, etc., transferees) of property included in the decedent's gross estate only if each transferee's share of the tax is based upon the net amount of his transfer subjected to the tax (taking into account any exemptions, credits, or deductions allowed by chapter 11). See examples (2) through (5) of paragraph (e) of this section.

(c) Exercise of election. The election to take a deduction for a state death tax imposed upon a transfer for charitable, etc., uses shall be exercised by the executor by the filing of a written notification to that effect with the Commissioner. The notification shall be filed before the expiration of the period of limitation for assessment provided in section 6501 (usually 3 years from the last day for filing the return). The election may be revoked by the executor by the filing of a written notification to that effect with the Commissioner at any time before the expiration of such period.

(d) Amount of State death tax imposed upon a transfer. If a State death tax is imposed upon the transfer of the decedent's entire estate and not upon the transfer of a particular share thereof, the State death tax imposed upon a transfer for charitable, etc., uses is deemed to be an amount, E, which bears the same ratio to F (the amount of the State death tax imposed with respect to the transfer of the entire estate) as G (the value of the charitable, etc., transfer, reduced as provided in the next sentence) bears to H (the total value of the properties, interests, and benefits subjected to the State death tax received by all persons interested in the estate, reduced as provided in the last sentence of this paragraph). In arriving at amount G of the ratio, the value of the charitable, etc., transfer is reduced by the amount of any deduction or exclusion allowed with respect to such property in determining the amount of the State death tax. In arriving at amount H of the ratio, the total value of the properties, interests, and benefits subjected to State death tax received by all persons interests in the estate is reduced by the amount of all deductions and exclusions allowed in determining the amount of the State death tax on account of the nature of a beneficiary or a beneficiary's relationship to the decedent.

(e) Examples. The application of this section may be illustrated by the following examples:

Example (1). The decedent's gross estate was valued at $200,000. He bequeathed $90,000 to a nephew, $10,000 to Charity A, and the remainder of his estate to Charity B. State inheritance tax in the amount of $13,500 was imposed upon the bequest to the nephew, $1,500 upon the bequest to Charity A, and $15,000 upon the bequest to Charity B. Under the will and local law, each legatee is required to pay the State inheritance tax on his bequest, and the Federal estate tax is to be paid out of the residuary estate. Since the entire burden of paying the Federal estate tax falls on Charity B, it follows that the decrease in the Federal estate tax resulting from the allowance of deductions for State death taxes in the amounts of $1,500 and $15,000 would inure solely for the benefit of Charity B. Therefore, deductions of $1,500 and $15,000 are allowable under section 2053(d). If, in this example, the State death taxes as well as the Federal estate tax were to be paid out of the residuary estate, the result would be the same.

Example (2). The decedent's gross estate was valued at $350,000. Expenses, indebtedness, etc., amounted to $50,000. The entire estate was bequeathed in equal shares to a son, a daughter, and Charity C. State inheritance tax in the amount of $2,000 was imposed upon the bequest to the son, $2,000 upon the bequest to the daughter, and $5,000 upon the bequest to Charity C. Under the will and local law, each legatee is required to pay his own State inheritance tax and his proportionate share of the Federal estate tax determined by taking into consideration the net amount of his bequest subjected to the tax. Since each legatee's share of the Federal estate tax is based upon the net amount of his bequest subjected to the tax (note that the deductions under sections 2053(d) and 2055 will have the effect of reducing Charity C's proportionate share of the tax), the tax is considered to be equitably apportioned. Thus, a deduction of $5,000 is allowable under section 2053(d). This deduction together with a deduction of $95,000 under section 2055 (charitable deduction) will mean that none of Charity C's bequest is subjected to Federal estate tax. Hence, the son and the daughter will bear the entire estate tax.

Example (3). The decedent bequeathed his property in equal shares, after payment of all expenses, to a son, a daughter, and a charity. State inheritance tax of $2,000 was imposed upon the bequest to the son, $2,000 upon the bequest to the daughter, and $15,000 upon the bequest to the charity. Under the will and local law, each beneficiary pays the State inheritance tax on his bequest and the Federal estate tax is to be paid out of the estate as an administration expense. If the deduction for State death tax on the charitable bequest is allowed in this case, some portion of the decrease in the Federal estate tax would inure to the benefit of the son and the daughter. The Federal estate tax is not considered to be equitably apportioned in this case since each legatee's share of the Federal estate tax is not based upon the net amount of his bequest subjected to the tax (note that the deductions under sections 2053(d) and 2055 will not have the effect of reducing the charity's proportionate share of the tax). Inasmuch as some of the decrease in the Federal estate tax payable would inure to the benefit of the son and the daughter, and inasmuch as there is no equitable apportionment of the tax, no deduction is allowable under section 2053(d).

Example (4). The decedent bequeathed his entire residuary estate in trust to pay the income to X for life with remainder to charity. The State imposed inheritance taxes of $2,000 upon the bequest to X and $10,000 upon the bequest to charity. Under the will and local law, all State and Federal taxes are payable out of the residuary estate and therefore they would reduce the amount which would become the corpus of the trust. If the deduction for the State death tax on the charitable bequest is allowed in this case, some portion of the decrease in the Federal estate tax would inure to the benefit of X since the allowance of the deduction would increase the size of the corpus from which X is to receive the income for life. Also, the Federal estate tax is not considered to be equitably apportioned in this case since each legatee's share of the Federal estate tax is not based upon the net amount of his bequest subjected to the tax (note that the deductions under sections 2053(d) and 2055 will not have the effect of reducing the charity's proportionate share of the tax). Inasmuch as some of the decrease in the Federal estate tax payable would inure to the benefit of X, and inasmuch as there is no equitable apportionment of the tax, no deduction is allowable under section 2053(d).

Example (5). The decedent's gross estate was valued at $750,000. Expenses, indebtedness, etc., amounted to $50,000. The decedent bequeathed $350,000 of his estate to his surviving spouse and the remainder of his estate equally to his son and Charity D. State inheritance tax in the amount of $7,000 was imposed upon the bequest to the surviving spouse, $26,250 upon the bequest to the son, and $26,250 upon the bequest to Charity D. The will was silent concerning the payment of taxes. In such a case, the local law provides that each legatee shall pay his own State inheritance tax. The local law further provides for an apportionment of the Federal estate tax among the legatees of the estate. Under the apportionment provisions, the surviving spouse is not required to bear any part of the Federal estate tax with respect to her $350,000 bequest. It should be noted, however, that the marital deduction allowed to the decedent's estate by reason of the bequest to the surviving spouse is limited to $343,000 ($350,000 bequest less $7,000 State inheritance tax payable by the surviving spouse). Thus, the bequest to the surviving spouse is subjected to the Federal estate tax in the net amount of $7,000. If the deduction for State death tax on the charitable bequest is allowed in this case, some portion of the decrease in the Federal estate tax would inure to the benefit of the son. The Federal estate tax is not considered to be equitably apportioned in this case since each legatee's share of the Federal estate tax is not based upon the net amount of his bequest subjected to the tax (note that the surviving spouse is to pay no tax). Inasmuch as some of the decrease in the Federal estate tax payable would inure to the benefit of the son, and inasmuch as there is no equitable apportionment of the tax, no deduction is allowable under section. 2053(d).

(f) Effective/applicability date. *(1)* The last sentence of paragraph (a) of this section applies to the estates of decedents dying on or after October 20, 2009, to which section 2058 is applicable.

(2) The other provisions of this section apply to the estates of decedents dying on or after October 20, 2009, to which section 2058 is not applicable.

T.D. 6296, 6/23/58, amend T.D. 6526, 1/18/61, T.D. 6666, 7/15/63, T.D. 9468, 10/16/2009.

§ 20.2053-10 Deduction for certain foreign death taxes.

(a) General rule. A deduction is allowed the estate of a decedent dying on or after July 1, 1955, under section 2053(d) for the amount of any estate, succession, legacy, or inheritance tax imposed by and actually paid to any foreign country, in respect of any property situated within such foreign country and included in the gross estate of a citizen or resident of the United States, upon a transfer by the decedent for charitable, etc., uses described in section 2055, but only if (1) the conditions stated in paragraph (b) of this section are met, and (2) an election is made in accordance with the provisions of paragraph (c) of this section. The determination of the country within which property is situated is made in accordance with the rules contained in §§ 20.2104 and 20.2105 in determining whether property is situated within or without the United States. See section 2014(f) and § 20.2014-7 for the effect which the allowance of this deduction has upon the credit for foreign death taxes.

(b) Condition for allowance of deduction. *(1)* The deduction is not allowed unless either—

(i) The entire decrease in the Federal estate tax resulting from the allowance of the deduction inures solely to the benefit of a charitable, etc., transferee described in section 2055, or

(ii) The Federal estate tax is equitably apportioned among all the transferees (including the decedent's surviving spouse and the charitable, etc., transferees) of property included in the decedent's gross estate.

For allowance of the deduction, it is sufficient if either of these conditions is satisfied. Thus, in a case where the entire decrease in Federal estate tax inures to the benefit of a charitable transferee, the deduction is allowable even though the Federal estate tax is not equitably apportioned among all the transferees of property included in the decedent's gross estate. Similarly, if the Federal estate tax is equitably apportioned among all the transferees of property included in the decedent's gross estate, the deduction is allowable even though a noncharitable transferee receives some benefit from the allowance of the deduction.

(2) For purposes of this paragraph, the Federal estate tax is considered to be equitably apportioned among all the transferees (including the decedent's surviving spouse and the charitable, etc., transferees) of property included in the decedent's gross estate only if each transferee's share of the tax is based upon the net amount of his transfer subjected to the tax (taking into account any exemptions, credits, or deductions allowed by chapter 11). See examples (2) through (5) of paragraph (e) of § 20.2053-9.

(c) Exercise of election. The election to take a deduction for a foreign death tax imposed upon a transfer for charitable, etc. uses shall be exercised by the executor by the filing of a written notification to that effect with the Commissioner of internal revenue in whose district the estate tax return for the decedent's estate was filed. An election to take the deduction for foreign death taxes is deemed to be a waiver of the right to claim a credit under a treaty with any foreign country for any tax or portion thereof claimed as a deduction under this section. The notification shall be filed before the expiration of the period of limitation for assessment provided in section 6501 (usually 3 years from the last day for filing the return). The election may be revoked by the executor by the filing of a written notification to that effect with the Commissioner at any time before the expiration of such period.

(d) Amount of foreign death tax imposed upon a transfer. If a foreign death tax is imposed upon the transfer of the entire part of the decedent's estate subject to such tax and not upon the transfer of a particular share thereof, for foreign death tax imposed upon a transfer for charitable, etc., uses is deemed to be an amount, J, which bears the same ratio to K (the amount of the foreign death tax imposed with respect to the transfer of the entire part of the decedent's estate subject to such tax) as M (the value of the charitable, etc., transfer, reduced as provided in the next sentence) bears to N (the total value of the properties, interests, and benefits subjected to the foreign death tax received by all persons interested in the estate, reduced as provided in the last sentence of this paragraph). In arriving at amount M of the ratio, the value of the charitable, etc., transfer is reduced by the amount of any deduction or exclusion allowed with respect to such property in determining the amount of the foreign death tax. In arriving at amount N of the ratio, the total value of the properties, interests, and benefits subjected to foreign death tax received by all persons interested in the estate is reduced by the amount of all deductions and exclusions allowed in determining the amount of the foreign death tax on account of the nature of a beneficiary or a beneficiary's relationship to the decedent.

(e) Effective/applicability date. This section applies to the estates of decedents dying on or after October 20, 2009.

T.D. 6600, 5/28/62, T.D. 9468, 10/16/2009.

§ 20.2054-1 Deduction for losses from casualties or theft.

A deduction is allowed for losses incurred during the settlement of the estate arising from fires, storms, shipwrecks, or other casualties, or from theft, if the losses are not compensated for by insurance or otherwise. If the loss is partly compensated for, the excess of the loss over the compensation may be deducted. Losses which are not of the nature described are not deductible. In order to be deductible a loss must occur during the settlement of the estate. If a loss with respect to an asset occurs after its distribution to the distributee it may not be deducted. Notwithstanding the foregoing, no deduction is allowed under this section if the estate has waived its right to take such a deduction pursuant to the provisions of section 642(g) in order to permit its allowance for income tax purposes. See further § 1.642(g)-1.

T.D. 6296, 6/23/58.

PAR. 2.

Section 20.2055 is amended.

Proposed § 20.2055 Statutory provisions; transfers for public, charitable and religious uses. [*For Preamble, see ¶ 150,177*]

[Code Sec. 2055]

§ 20.2055-1 Deduction for transfers for public, charitable, and religious uses; in general.

Caution: The Treasury has not yet amended Reg § 20.2055-1 to reflect changes made by P.L. 105-34.

(a) General rule. A deduction is allowed under section 2055(a) from the gross estate of a decedent who was a citizen or resident of the United States at the time of his death for the value of property included in the decedent's gross estate and transferred by the decedent during his lifetime or by will—

(1) To or for the use of the United States, any State, Territory, any political subdivision thereof, or the District of Columbia, for exclusively public purposes;

(2) To or for the use of any corporation or association organized and operated exclusively for religious, charitable, scientific, literary, or educational purposes (including the encouragement of art and for the prevention of cruelty to children or animals), if no part of the net earnings of the corporation or association inures to the benefit of any private stockholder or individual (other than as a legitimate object of such purposes), if the organization is not disqualified for tax exemption under section 501(c)(3) by reason of attempting to influence legislation, and if, in the case of transfers made after December 31, 1969, it does not participate in, or intervene in (including the publishing or distributing of statements), any political campaign on behalf of or in opposition to any candidate for public office.[;]

(3) To a trustee or trustees, or a fraternal society, order, or association operating under the lodge system, if the transferred property is to be used exclusively for religious, charitable, scientific, literary, or educational purposes (or for the prevention of cruelty to children or animals), if no substantial part of the activities of such transferee is carrying on propaganda, or otherwise attempting, to influence legislation, and if, in the case of transfers made after December 31, 1969, such transferee does not participate in, or intervene in (including the publishing or distributing of statements), any political campaign on behalf of any candidate for public office; or

(4) To or for the use of any veterans' organization incorporated by act of Congress, or of any of its departments, local chapters, or posts, no part of the net earnings of which inures to the benefit of any private shareholder or individual.

The deduction is not limited, in the case of estates of citizens or residents of the United States, to transfers to domestic corporations or associations, or to trustees for use within the United States. Nor is the deduction subject to percentage limitations such as are applicable to the charitable deduction under the income tax. An organization will not be considered to meet the requirements of subparagraph (2) or (3) of this paragraph if such organization engages in any activity which would cause it to be classified as an "action" organization under paragraph (c)(3) of § 1.501(c)(3)-1 of this chapter (Income Tax Regulations). See § 20.2055-4 and § 20.2055-5 for rules relating to the disallowance of deductions to trusts and organizations which engage in certain prohibited transactions or whose governing instruments do not contain certain specified requirements.

(b) Powers of appointment. *(1) General rule.* A deduction is allowable under section 2055(b) for the value of property passing to or for the use of a transferee described in paragraph (a) of this section by the exercise, failure to exercise, release or lapse of a power of appointment by reason of which the property is includible in the decedent's gross estate under section 2041.

(2) Certain bequests subject to power of appointment. For the allowance of a deduction in the case of a bequest in trust where the decedent's surviving spouse (i) was over 80 years of age at the date of decedent's death, (ii) was entitled for life to all of the net income from the trust, and (iii) had a power of appointment over the corpus of the trust exercisable by will in favor of, among others, a charitable organization, see section 2055(b)(2). See also section 6503(e) for suspension of the period of limitations for assessment or collection of any deficiency attributable to the allowance of the deduction.

(c) Submission of evidence. In establishing the right of the estate to the deduction authorized by section 2055, the executor should submit the following with the return:

(1) A copy of any instrument in writing by which the decedent made a transfer of property in his lifetime the value of which is required by statute to be included in his gross estate, for which a deduction under section 2055 is claimed. If the instrument is of record the copy should be certified, and if not of record, the copy should be verified.

(2) A written statement by the executor containing a declaration that it is made under penalties of perjury and stating whether any action has been instituted to construe or to contest the decedent's will or any provision thereof affecting the charitable deduction claimed and whether, according to his information and belief, any such action is designed or contemplated.

The executor shall also submit such other documents or evidence as may be requested by the district director.

(d) Cross references. *(1)* See section 2055(f) for certain cross references relating to section 2055.

(2) For treatment of bequests accepted by the Secretary of State or the Secretary of Commerce, for the purpose of organizing and holding an international conference to negotiate a Patent Corporation Treaty, as bequests to or for the use of the United States, see section 3 of Joint Resolution of December 24, 1969 (P.L. 91-160, 83 Stat. 443).

(3) For treatment of bequests accepted by the Secretary of the Department of Housing and Urban Development, for the purpose of aiding or facilitating the work of the Department, as bequests to or for the use of the United States, see section 7(k) of the Department of Housing and Urban Development Act (42 U.S.C. 3535), as added by section 905 of P.L. 91-609 (84 Stat. 1809).

(4) For treatment of certain property accepted by the Chairman of the Administrative Conference of the United States, for the purpose of aiding and facilitating the work of the Conference, as a devise or bequest to the United States, see 5 U.S.C. 575(c)(12), as added by section 1(b) of the Act of October 21, 1972 (Pub. L. 92-526, 86 Stat. 1048) [1972-2 C.B. 701].

(5) For treatment of the Board for International Broadcasting as a corporation described in Section 2055(a)(2), see section 7 of the Board for International Broadcasting Act of 1973 (Public Law 93-129, 87 Stat. 459).

T.D. 6296, 6/23/58, amend T.D. 7318, 7/10/74, T.D. 8308, 8/30/90.

§ 20.2055-2 Transfers not exclusively for charitable purposes.

Caution: The Treasury has not yet amended Reg § 20.2055-2 to reflect changes made by P.L. 105-34.

(a) Remainders and similar interests. If a trust is created or property is transferred for both a charitable and a private purpose, deduction may be taken of the value of the charitable beneficial interest only insofar as that interest is presently ascertainable, and hence severable from the noncharitable interest. Thus, in the case of decedents dying before January 1, 1970, if money or property is placed in trust to pay the income to an individual during his life, or for a term of years, and then to pay the principal to a charitable organization, the present value of the remainder is deductible. See paragraph (e) of this section for limitations applicable to decedents dying after December 31, 1969. See paragraph (f) of this section for rules relating to valuation of partial interests in property passing for charitable purposes.

(b) Transfers subject to a condition or a power. *(1)* If, as of the date of a decedent's death, a transfer for charitable purposes is dependent upon the performance of some act or the happening of a precedent event in order that it might become effective, no deduction is allowable unless the possibility that the charitable transfer will not become effective is so remote as to be negligible. If an estate or interest has passed to, or is vested in, charity at the time of a decedent's death and the estate or interest would be defeated by the subsequent performance of some act or the happening of some event, the possibility of occurrence of which appeared at the time of the decedent's death to be so remote as to be negligible, the deduction is allowable. If the legatee, devisee, donee, or trustee is empowered to divert the property or fund, in whole or in part, to a use or purpose which would have rendered it, to the extent that it is subject to such power, not deductible had it been directly so bequeathed, devised, or given by the decedent, the deduction will be limited to that portion, if any, of the property or fund which is exempt from an exercise of the power.

(2) The application of this paragraph may be illustrated by the following examples:

Example (1). In 1965, A dies leaving certain property in trust in which charity is to receive the income for the life of his widow. The assets placed in trust by the decedent consist of stock in a corporation the fiscal policies of which are controlled by the decedent and his family. The trustees of the trust and the remaindermen are members of the decedent's family, and the governing instrument contains no adequate guarantee of the requisite income to the charitable organization. Under such circumstances, no deduction will be allowed. Similarly, if the trustees are not members of the decedent's family but have no power to sell or otherwise dispose of the closely held stock, or otherwise insure the requisite enjoyment of income to the charitable organization, no deduction will be allowed.

Example (2). C dies leaving a tract of land to a city government for as long as the land is used by the city for a public park. If the city accepts the tract and if, on the date of C's death, the possibility that the city will not use the land for a public park is so remote as to be negligible, a deduction will be allowed.

(c) Disclaimers. *(1) Decedents dying after December 31, 1976.* In the case of a bequest, devise, or transfer made by a decedent dying after December 31, 1976, the amount of a bequest, devise or transfer for which a deduction is allowable under section 2055 includes an interest which falls into the bequest, devise or transfer as the result of either—

(i) A qualified disclaimer (see section 2518 and the corresponding regulations for rules relating to a qualified disclaimer), or

(ii) The complete termination of a power to consume, invade, or appropriate property for the benefit of an individual by reason of the death of such individual or for any other reason, if the termination occurs within the period of time (including extensions) for filing the decedent's Federal estate tax return and before such power has been exercised.

(2) Decedents dying before January 1, 1977. In the case of a bequest, devise or transfer made by a decedent dying before January 1, 1977, the amount of a bequest, devise or transfer, for which a deduction is allowable under section 2055 includes an interest which falls into the bequest, devise or transfer as a result of either—

(i) A disclaimer of a bequest, devise, transfer, or power, if the disclaimer is made within 9 months (15 months if the decedent died on or before December 31, 1970) after the decedent's death (the period of time within which the estate tax return must be filed under section 6075) or within any extension of time for filing the return granted pursuant to section 6081, and the disclaimer is irrevocable at the time the deduction is allowed, or

(ii) The complete termination of a power to consume, invade, or appropriate property for the benefit of an individual (whether the termination occurs by reason of the death of the individual, or otherwise) if the termination occurs within the period described in paragraph (c)(2)(i) of this section and before the power has been exercised. Ordinarily, a disclaimer made by a person not under any legal disability will be considered irrevocable when filed with the probate court. A disclaimer is a complete and unqualified refusal to accept the right to which one is entitled. Thus, if a beneficiary uses these rights for his own purposes, as by receiving a consideration for his formal disclaimer, he has not refused the rights to which he was entitled. There can be no disclaimer after an acceptance of these rights, expressly or impliedly. The disclaimer of a power is to be distinguished from the release or exercise of a power. The release or exercise of a power by the donee of the power in favor of a person or object described in paragraph (a) of § 20.2055-1 does not result in any deduction under section 2055 in the estate of the donor of a power (but see paragraph (b)(1) of § 20.2055-1 with respect to the donee's estate).

(d) Payments in compromise. If a charitable organization assigns or surrenders a part of a transfer to it pursuant to a compromise agreement in settlement of a controversy, the amount so assigned or surrendered is not deductible as a transfer to that charitable organization.

(e) Limitation applicable to decedents dying after December 31, 1969. *(1) Disallowance of deduction.* (i) In general. In the case of decedents dying after December 31, 1969, where an interest in property passes or has passed from the decedent for charitable purposes and an interest (other than an interest which is extinguished upon the decedent's death) in the same property passes or has passed from the decedent for private purposes (for less than an adequate and full consideration in money or money's worth) after October 9, 1969, no deduction is allowed under section 2055 for the value of the interest which passes or has passed for charitable purposes unless the interest in property is a deductible interest described in subparagraph (2) of this paragraph. The principles of section 2056 and the regulations thereunder shall apply for purposes of determining under this paragraph (e)(1)(i) whether an interest in property passes or has passed from the decedent. If however, as of the date of a decedent's death, a transfer for a private purpose is dependent upon the performance of some act or the happening of a precedent event in order that it might become effective, an interest in property will be considered to pass for a private purpose unless the possibility of occurrence of such act or event is so remote as to be negligible. The application of this paragraph (e)(1)(i) may be illustrated by the following examples, in each of which it is assumed that the interest in property which passes for private purposes does not pass for an adequate and full consideration in money or money's worth:

Example (1). In 1973, H creates a trust which is to pay the income of the trust to W for her life, the reversionary interest in the trust being retained by H. H predeceases W in 1975. H's will provide that the residue of his estate (including the reversionary interest in the trust) is to be transferred to charity. For purposes of this paragraph (e)(1)(i), interests in the same property have passed from H for charitable purposes and for private purposes.

Example (2). In 1973, H creates a trust which is to pay the income of a trust to W for her life and upon termination of the life estate to transfer the remainder to S. S predeceases W in 1975. S's will provides that the residue of his estate (including the remainder interest in the trust) is to be transferred to charity. For purposes of this paragraph (e)(1)(i), interests in the same property have not passed from H or S for charitable purposes and for private purposes.

Example (3). H transfers Blackacre to A by gift, reserving the right to the rentals of Blackacre for a term of 20 years. H dies within the 20-year term, bequeathing the right to the remaining rentals to charity. For purposes of this paragraph (e)(1)(i) the term "property" refers to Blackacre, and the right to rentals from Blackacre consist of an interest in Blackacre. An interest in Blackacre has passed from H for charitable purposes and for private purposes.

Example (4). H bequeaths the residue of his estate in trust for the benefit of A and a charity. An annuity of $5,000 a year is to be paid to charity for 20 years. Upon termination of the 20-year term the corpus is to be distributed to A if living. However, if A should die during the 20-year term, the corpus is to be distributed to charity upon termination of the term. An interest in the residue of the estate has passed from H for charitable purposes. In addition, an interest in the residue of the estate has passed from H for private purposes, unless the possibility that A will survive the 20-year term is so remote as to be negligible.

Example (5). H bequeaths the residue of his estate in trust. Under the terms of the trust an annuity of $5,000 a year is to be paid to charity for 20 years. Upon termination of the term, the corpus is to pass to such of A's children and their issue as A may appoint. However, if A should die during the 20-year term without exercising the power of appointment, the corpus is to be distributed to charity upon termination of the term. Since the possible appointees include private persons, an interest in the residue of the estate is considered to have passed from H for private purposes.

Example (6). H devises Blackacre to X Charity. Under applicable local law, W, H's widow, is entitled to elect a dower interest in Blackacre. W elects to take her dower interest in Blackacre. For purposes of this paragraph (e)(1)(i), interests in the same property have passed from H for charitable purposes and for private purposes. If, however, W does not elect to take her dower interest in Blackacre, then, for purposes of this paragraph (e)(1)(i), interests in the same property have not passed from H for charitable purposes and for private purposes.

(ii) Works of art and copyrights treated as separate properties. (a) In general. For purposes of paragraphs (e)(1)(i) and (e)(2) of this section, in the case of decedents dying after December 31, 1981, if a decedent makes a qualified contribution of a work of art, the work of art and the copyright on such work of art shall be treated as separate properties. Thus, a deduction is allowable under section 2055 for a qualified contribution of a work of art, whether or not the related copyright is simultaneously transferred to a charitable organization.

(b) Work of art defined. for purposes of paragraph (e)(1)(ii) *(a)* of this section, the term "work of art" means any tangible personal property with respect to which a copyright exists under Federal law.

(c) Qualified contribution defined. For purposes of paragraph (e)(1)(ii) *(a)* of this section, the term "qualified contribution" means any transfer of property to a qualified organization (as defined in paragraph (e)(1)(ii) *(d)* of this section) if the use of the property by the organization is related to the purpose or function constituting the basis for its exemption under section 501. The rules contained in § 1.170A-4(b)(3) shall apply in determining if the use of property by an organization is related to such purpose or function.

(d) Qualified organization defined. For purposes of paragraph (e)(1)(ii) *(c)* of this section, the term "qualified organization" means any organization described in section 501(c)(3) other than a private foundation (as defined in section 509). A private operating foundation (as defined in section 4942(j)(3)) shall be considered a qualified organization under this paragraph.

(e) Examples. The application of paragraphs (e)(1)(i) and (e)(1)(ii) *(a)*through *(d)* of this section may be illustrated by the following examples:

Example (1). A, an artist, died in 1983. A work of art created by A and the copyright interest in that work of art were included in A's estate. Under the terms of A's will, the work of art is transferred to X charity, the only charitable beneficiary under A's will. X has no suitable use for the work of art and sells it. It is determined under the rules of § 1.170A-4(b)(3) that the property is put to an unrelated use by X charity. Therefore, the rule of paragraph (e)(1)(ii) *(a)*, which treats works of art and their copyrights as separate properties, does not apply because the transfer of the work of art to X is not a qualified contribution. To determine whether paragraph (e)(1)(i) of this section applies to disallow a deduction under section 2055, it must be determined which interests are treated as passing to X under local law.

(i) If under local law A's will is treated as fully transferring both the work of art and the copyright interest to X, then paragraph (e)(1)(i) of this section does not apply to disallow a deduction under section 2055 for the value of the work of art and the copyright interest.

(ii) If under local law A's will is treated as transferring only the work of art to X, and the copyright interest is treated as part of the residue of the estate, no deduction is allowable under section 2055 to A's estate for the value of the work of art because the transfer of the work of art is not a qualified contribution and paragraph (e)(1)(i) of this section applies to disallow the deduction.

Example (2). B, a collector of art, purchased a work of art from an artist who retained the copyright interest. B died in 1983. Under the terms of B's will the work of art is given to Y charity. Since B did not own the copyright interest, paragraph (e)(1)(i) of this section does not apply to disallow a deduction under section 2055 for the value of the work of art, regardless of whether or not the contribution is a qualified contribution under paragraph (e)(1)(ii) *(c)* of this section.

(2) Deductible interests. A deductible interest for purposes of subparagraph (1) of this paragraph is a charitable interest in property where—

(i) Undivided portion of decedent's entire interest. The charitable interest is an undivided portion, not in trust, of the decedent's entire interest in property. An undivided portion of a decedent's entire interest in property must consist of a fraction or percentage of each and every substantial interest or right owned by the decedent in such property and must extend over the entire term of the decedent's interest in such property and in other property into which such property is converted. For example, if the decedent transferred a life estate in an office building to his wife for her life and retained a reversionary interest in the office building, the devise by the decedent of one-half of that reversionary interest to charity while his wife is still alive will not be considered the transfer of a deductible interest; because an interest in the same property has already passed from the decedent for private purposes, the reversionary interest will not be considered the decedent's entire interest in the property. If, on the other hand, the decedent had been given a life estate in Blackacre for the life of his wife and the decedent had no other interest in Blackacre at any time during his life, the devise by the decedent of one-half of that life estate to charity would be considered the transfer of a deductible interest; because the life estate would be considered the decedent's entire interest in the property, the devise would be of an undivided portion of such entire interest. An undivided portion of a decedent's entire interest in the property includes an interest in property whereby the charity is given the right, as a tenant in common with the decedent's devisee or legatee, to possession, dominion, and control of the property for a portion of each year appropriate to its interest in such property. However, except as provided in paragraphs (e)(2)(ii), (iii), and (iv) of this section, for purposes of this subdivision a charitable contribution of an interest in property not in trust where the decedent transfers some specific rights to one party and transfers other substantial rights to another party will not be considered a contribution of an undivided portion of the decedent's entire interest in property. A bequest to charity made on or before December 17, 1980, of an open space easement in gross in perpetuity shall be considered the transfer to charity of an undivided portion of the decedent's entire interest in the property. For the definition of an open space easement in gross in perpetuity, see § 1.170A-7(b)(1)(ii) of this chapter (Income Tax Regulations).

(ii) Remainder interest in personal residence. The charitable interest is a remainder interest, not in trust, in a personal residence. Thus, for example, if the decedent devises to charity a remainder interest in a personal residence and bequeaths to his surviving spouse a life estate in such property, the value of the remainder interest is deductible under section 2055. For purposes of this subdivision, the term "personal residence" means any property which was used by the decedent as his personal residence even though it was not used as his principal residence. For example, a decedent's vacation home may be a personal residence for purposes of this subdivision. The term "personal residence" also includes stock owned by the decedent as a tenant-stockholder in a cooperative housing corporation (as those terms are defined in section 216(b)(1) and (2) if the dwelling which the decedent was entitled to occupy as such stockholder was used by him as his personal residence.

(iii) Remainder interest in a farm. The charitable interest is a remainder interest, not in trust, in a farm. Thus, for example, if the decedent devises to charity a remainder interest in a farm and bequeaths to his daughter a life estate in such property, the value of the remainder interest is deductible under section 2055. For purposes of this subdivision, the term "farm" means any land used by the decedent or his tenant for the production of crops, fruits, or other agricultural products or for the sustenance of livestock. The term "livestock" includes cattle, hogs, horses, mules, donkeys, sheep, goats, captive furbearing animals, chickens, turkeys, pigeons, and other poultry. A farm includes the improvements thereon.

(iv) Qualified conservation contribution. The charitable interest is a qualified conservation contribution. For the definition of a qualified conservation contribution, see § 1.170A-14.

(v) Charitable remainder trusts and pooled income funds. The charitable interest is a remainder interest in a trust which is a charitable remainder annuity trust, as defined in section 664(d)(1) and § 1.664-2 of this chapter; a charitable remainder unitrust, as defined in section 664(d)(2) and (3) and § 1.664-3 of this chapter; or a pooled income fund, as defined in section 642(c)(5) and § 1.642(c)-5 of this chapter. The charitable organization to or for the use of which the remainder interest passes must meet the requirements of both section 2055(a) and section 642(c)(5)(A), section 664(d)(1)(C), or section 664(d)(2)(C), whichever applies. For example, the charitable organization to which the remainder interest in a charitable remainder annuity trust passes may not be a foreign corporation.

(vi) Guaranteed annuity interest. (a) The charitable interest is a guaranteed annuity interest, whether or not such interest is in trust. For purposes of this subdivision (vi), the term "guaranteed annuity interest" means the right pursuant to the instrument of transfer to receive a guaranteed annuity. A guaranteed annuity is an arrangement under which a determinable amount is paid periodically, but not less often than annually, for a specified term of years or for the life or lives of certain individuals, each of whom must be living at the date of death of the decedent and can be ascertained at such date. Only one or more of the following individuals may be used as measuring lives: the decedent's spouse, and an individual who, with respect to all remainder beneficiaries (other than charitable organizations described in section 170, 2055, or 2522), is either a lineal ancestor or the spouse of a lineal ancestor of those beneficiaries. A trust will satisfy the requirement that all noncharitable remainder beneficiaries are lineal descendants of the individual who is the measuring life, or that individual's spouse, if there is less than a 15% probability that individuals who are not lineal descendants will receive any trust corpus. This probability must be computed, based on the current applicable Life Table contained in § 20.2031-7, as of the date of the decedent's death taking into account the interests of all primary and contingent remainder beneficiaries who are living at that time. An interest payable for a specified term of years can qualify as a guaranteed annuity interest even if the governing instrument contains a savings clause intended to ensure compliance with a rule against perpetuities. The savings clause must utilize a period for vesting of 21 years after the deaths of measuring lives who are selected to maximize, rather than limit, the term of the trust. The rule in this paragraph that a charitable interest may be payable for the life or lives of only certain specified individuals does not apply in the case of a charitable guaranteed annuity interest payable under a charitable remainder trust described in section 664. An amount is determinable if the exact amount which must be paid under the conditions specified in the instrument of transfers can be ascertained as of the appropriate valuation date. For example, the amount to be paid may be a stated sum for a term of years, or for the life of the decedent's spouse, at the expiration of which it may be changed by a specified amount, but it may not be redetermined by reference to a fluctuating index such as the cost of living index. In further illustration, the amount to be paid may be expressed in terms of a fraction or a percentage of the net fair market value, as finally determined for Federal estate tax purposes, of the residue of the estate on the appropriate valuation date, or it may be expressed in terms of a fraction or percentage of the cost of living index on the appropriate valuation date.

(b) A charitable interest is a guaranteed annuity interest only if it is a guaranteed annuity interest in every respect. For example, if the charitable interest is the right to receive from a trust each year a payment equal to the lesser of a sum certain or a fixed percentage of the net fair market value of the trust assets, determined annually, such interest is not a guaranteed annuity interest.

(c) Where a charitable interest in the form of a guaranteed annuity interest is not in trust, the interest will be considered a guaranteed annuity interest only if it is to be paid by an insurance company or by an organization regularly engaged in issuing annuity contracts.

(d) Where a charitable interest in the form of a guaranteed annuity interest is in trust, the governing instrument of the trust may provide that income of the trust which is in excess of the amount required to pay the guaranteed annuity interest shall be paid to or for the use of a charity. Nevertheless, the amount of the deduction under section 2055 shall be limited to the fair market value of the guaranteed annuity interest as determined under paragraph (f)(2)(iv) of this section.

(e) Where a charitable interest in the form of a guaranteed annuity interest is in trust and the present value, on the appropriate valuation date, of all the income interests for a charitable purpose exceeds 60 percent of the aggregate fair market value of all amounts in such trust (after the payment of estate taxes and all other liabilities), the charitable interest will not be considered a guaranteed annuity interest unless the governing instrument of the trust prohibits both the acquisition and the retention of assets which would give rise to a tax under section 4944 if the trustee had acquired such assets.

(f) Where a charitable interest in the form of a guaranteed annuity interest is in trust, the charitable interest generally is not a guaranteed annuity interest if any amount may be paid by the trust for a private purpose before the expiration of all the charitable annuity interests. There are two exceptions to this general rule. First, the charitable interest is a guaranteed annuity interest if the amount payable for a private purpose is in the form of a guaranteed annuity interest and the trust's governing instrument does not provide for any preference or priority in the payment of the private annuity as opposed to the charitable annuity. Second, the charitable interest is a guaranteed annuity interest if under the trust's governing instrument the amount that may be paid for a private purpose is payable only from a group of assets that are devoted exclusively to private purposes and to which section 4947(a)(2) is inapplicable by reason of section 4947(a)(2)(B). For purposes of this paragraph (e)(2)(vi)(f), an amount is not paid for a private purpose if it is paid for an adequate and full consideration in money or money's worth. See § 53.4947-1(c) of this chapter for rules relating to the inapplicability of section 4947(a)(2) to segregated amounts in a split-interest trust.

(g) Neither the requirement in *(e)* of this subdivision (vi) for a prohibition in the governing instrument against the retention of assets which would give rise to a tax under section 4944 if the trustee had acquired the assets nor the provisions of *(f)* of this subdivision (v) shall apply to—

(l) A trust executed on or before May 21, 1972, if—

(i) The trust is irrevocable on such date,

(ii) The trust is revocable on such date and the decedent dies within 3 years after such date without having amended any dispositive provision of the trust after such date, or

(iii) The trust is revocable on such date and no dispositive provision of the trust is amended within a period ending 3 years after such date and the decedent is, at the end of such 3-year period and at all times thereafter, under a mental disability (as defined in § 1.642(c)-2(b)(3)(ii) of this chapter) to amend the trust, or

(2) A will executed on or before May 21, 1972, if—

(i) The testator dies within 3 years after such date without having amended any dispositive provision of the will after such date, by codicil or otherwise,

(ii) The testator at no time after such date has the right to change the provisions of the will which pertain to the trust, or

(iii) No dispositive provision of the will is amended by the decedent, by codicil or otherwise, within a period ending 3 years after such date and the decedent is, at the end of such 3-year period and at all times thereafter, under a mental disability (as defined in § 1.642(c)-2(b)(3)(ii) of this chapter) to amend the will by codicil or otherwise.

(h) For purposes of this subdivision (vi) and paragraph (f) of this section, the term "appropriate valuation date" means the date of death or the alternate valuation date determined pursuant to an election under section 2032.

(i) For rules relating to certain governing instrument requirements and to the imposition of certain excise taxes where the guaranteed annuity interest is in trust and for rules governing payment of private income interests by split-interest trusts, see section 4947(a)(2) and (b)(3)(A), and the regulations thereunder.

(vii) Unitrust interest. (a) The charitable interest is a unitrust interest, whether or not such interest is in trust. For purposes of this subdivision (vii), the term "unitrust interest" means the right pursuant to the instrument of transfer to receive payment, not less often than annually, of a fixed percentage of the net fair market value, determined annually, of the property which funds the unitrust interest. In computing the net fair market value of the property which funds the unitrust interest, all assets and liabilities shall be taken into account without regard to whether particular items are taken into account in determining the income from the property. The net fair market value of the property which funds the unitrust interest may be determined on any one date during the year or by taking the average of valuations made on more than one date during the year, provided that the same valuation date or dates and valuation methods are used each year. Where the charitable interest is a unitrust interest to be paid by a trust and the governing instrument of the trust does not specify the valuation date or dates, the trustee shall select such date or dates and shall indicate his selection on the first return on Form 1041 which the trust is required to file. Payments under a unitrust interest may be paid for a specified term of years or for the life or lives of certain individuals, each of whom must be living at the date of death of the decedent and can be ascertained at such date. Only one or more of the following individuals may be used as measuring lives: the decedent's spouse, and an individual who, with respect to all remainder beneficiaries (other than charitable organizations described in section 170, 2055, or 2522), is either a lineal ancestor or the spouse of a lineal ancestor of those beneficiaries. A trust will satisfy the requirement that all noncharitable remainder beneficiaries are lineal descendants of the individual who is the measuring life, or that individual's spouse, if there is less than a 15% probability that individuals who are not lineal descendants will receive any trust corpus. This probability must be computed, based on the current applicable Life Table contained in § 20.2031-7, as of the date of the decedent's death taking into account the interests of all primary and contingent remainder beneficiaries who are living at that time. An interest payable for a specified term of years can qualify as a unitrust interest even if the governing instrument contains a savings clause intended to ensure compliance with a rule against perpetuities. The savings clause must utilize a period for vesting of 21 years after the deaths of measuring lives who are selected to maximize, rather than limit, the term of the trust. The rule in this paragraph that a charitable interest may be payable for the life or lives of only certain specified individuals does not apply in the case of a charitable unitrust interest payable under a charitable remainder trust described in section 664.

(b) A charitable interest is a unitrust interest only if it is a unitrust interest in every respect. For example, if the charitable interest is the right to receive from a trust each year a payment equal to the lesser of a sum certain or a fixed percentage of the net fair market value of the trust assets, determined annually, such interest is not a unitrust interest.

(c) Where a charitable interest in the form of a unitrust interest is not in trust, the interest will be considered a unitrust interest only if it is to be paid by an insurance company or by an organization regularly engaged in issuing interests otherwise meeting the requirements of a unitrust interest.

(d) Where a charitable interest in the form of a unitrust interest is in trust, the governing instrument of the trust may provide that income of the trust which is in excess of the amount required to pay the unitrust interest shall be paid to or for the use of a charity. Nevertheless, the amount of the deduction under section 2055 shall be limited to the fair market value of the unitrust interest as determined under paragraph (f)(2)(v) of this section.

(e) Where a charitable interest in the form of a unitrust interest is in trust, the charitable interest generally is not a unitrust interest if any amount may be paid by the trust for a private purpose before the expiration of all the charitable unitrust interests. There are two exceptions to this general rule. First, the charitable interest is a unitrust interest if the amount payable for a private purpose is in the form of a unitrust interest and the trust's governing instrument does not provide for any preference or priority in the payment of the private unitrust interest as opposed to the charitable unitrust interest. Second, the charitable interest is a unitrust interest if under the trust's governing instrument the amount that may be paid for a private purpose is payable only from a group of assets that are devoted exclusively to private purposes and to which section 4947(a)(2) is inapplicable by reason of section 4947(a)(2)(B). For purposes of this paragraph (e)(2)(vii)(e), an amount is not paid for a private purpose if it is paid for an adequate and full consideration in money or money's worth. See § 53.4947-1(c) of this chapter for rules relating to the inapplicability of section 4947(a)(2) to segregated amounts in a split-interest trust.

(f) For rules relating to certain governing instrument requirements and to the imposition of certain excise taxes where the unitrust interest is in trust and for rules governing payment of private income interests by a split-interest trust, see section 4947(a)(2) and (b)(3)(A), and the regulations thereunder.

(3) Effective/applicability date. The provisions of this paragraph apply only in the case of decedents dying after December 31, 1969, except that they do not apply—

(i) In the case of property passing under the terms of a will executed on or before October 9, 1969—

(a) If the decedent dies after October 9, 1969, but before October 9, 1972, without having amended any dispositive provision of the will after October 9, 1969, by codicil or otherwise,

(b) If the decedent dies after October 9, 1969, and at no time after that date had the right to change the portions of the will which pertain to the passing of the property to, or for the use of, an organization described in section 2055(a), or

(c) If no dispositive provision of the will is amended by the decedent, by codicil or otherwise, after October 9, 1969, and before October 9, 1972, and the decedent is on October 9, 1972, and at all times thereafter under a mental disability (as defined in § 1.642(c)-2(b)(3)(ii) of this chapter (Income Tax Regulations)) to amend the will by codicil or otherwise, or

(ii) In the case of property transferred in trust on or before October 9, 1969—

(a) If the decedent dies after October 9, 1969, but before October 9, 1972, without having amended, after October 9, 1969, any dispositive provision of the instrument governing the disposition of the property,

(b) If the property transferred was an irrevocable interest to, or for the use of, an organization described in section 2055(a), or

(c) If no dispositive provision of the instrument governing the disposition of the property is amended by the decedent after October 9, 1969, and before October 9, 1972, and the decedent is on October 9, 1972, and at all times thereafter under a mental disability (as defined in § 1.642(c)-2(b)(3)(ii) of this chapter) to change the disposition of the property, and

(iii)

[Reserved]. For further guidance, see § 20.2055-2T(e)(3)(iii).

(4) Amendment of dispositive provisions. For purposes of subparagraphs (2) and (3) of this paragraph, an amendment shall generally be considered as one which amends the dispositive provisions of a will or trust if it results in a change in the persons to whom the funds are to be given or makes changes in the conditions under which the funds are given. Examples of amendments which do not amend the dispositive provisions of a will or trust include the substitution of one fiduciary for another to act in the capacity of executor or trustee and the change in the name of a legatee or beneficiary by reason of the legatee's or beneficiary's marriage. On the other hand, examples of amendments which do amend the dispositive provisions of a will or trust include an increase or decrease in the amount of a general bequest, an amendment which increases or decreases the power of a trustee to determine an allocation of income or corpus in such a way as to change the beneficiaries of the funds or a beneficiary's share of the funds, or a change in the allocation of, or in the right to allocate, receipts and expenditures between income and principal in such a way as to change the beneficiaries of the funds or a beneficiary's share of the funds.

(5) Amendment of wills providing for pour-over into trusts. For purposes of subparagraphs (2) and (3) of this paragraph, an amendment of a dispositive provision of a trust to which assets are to be transferred under a will shall be considered a dispositive amendment of such will.

(f) Valuation of charitable interest. *(1) In general.* The amount of the deduction in the case of a contribution of a partial interest in property to which this section applies is the fair market value of the partial interest at the appropriate valuation date, as defined in paragraph (e)(2)(vi) *(h)* of this section. The fair market value of an annuity, life estate, term for years, remainder, reversion, (or) unitrust interest is its present value.

(2) Certain decedents dying after July 31, 1969. In the case of a transfer of an interest described in subdivision (v), (vi) or (vii) of paragraph (e)(2) of this section by decedents dying after July 31, 1969, the present value of such interest is to be determined under the following rules:

(i) The present value of a remainder interest in a charitable remainder annuity trust is to be determined under § 1.664-2(c) of this chapter (Income Tax Regulations).

(ii) The present value of a remainder interest in a charitable remainder unitrust is to be determined under § 1.664-4 of this chapter.

(iii) The present value of a remainder interest in a pooled income fund is to be determined under § 1.642(c)-6 of this chapter.

(iv) The present value of a guaranteed annuity interest described in paragraph (e)(2)(vi) of this section is to be determined under § 20.2031-7 or, for certain prior periods, § 20.2031-7A except that, if the annuity is issued by a company regularly engaged in the sale of annuities, the present value is to be determined under § 20.2031-8. If by reason of all the conditions and circumstances surrounding a transfer of an income interest in property in trust it appears that the charity may not receive the beneficial enjoyment of the interest, a deduction will be allowed under section 2055 only for the minimum amount it is evident the charity will receive.

Example (1). In 1975, B dies bequeathing $20,000 in trust with the requirement that a designated charity be paid a guaranteed annuity interest (as defined in paragraph (e)(2)(vi) of this section) of $4,100 a year, payable annually at the end of each year, for a period of 6 years and that the remainder be paid to his children. The fair market value of an annuity of $4,100 a year for a period of 6 years is $20,160.93 ($4,100 × 4.9173), as determined under Table B in § 20.2031-7A(d). The deduction with respect to the guaranteed annuity interest will be limited to $20,000, which is the minimum amount it is evident the charity will receive.

Example (2). In 1975, C dies bequeathing $40,000 in trust with the requirement that D, an individual, and X Charity, be paid simultaneously guaranteed annuity interests (as defined in paragraph (e)(2)(vi) of this section) of $5,000 a year each, payable annually at the end of each year, for a period of 5 years and that the remainder be paid to C's children. The fair market value of two annuities of $5,000 each a year for a period of 5 years is $42,124 ([$5,000 × 4.2124] × 2), as determined under Table B in § 20.2031-7A(d). The trust instrument provides that in the event the trust fund is insufficient to pay both annuities in a given year, the trust fund will be evenly divided between the charitable and private annuitants. The deduction with respect to the charitable annuity will be limited to $20,000, which is the minimum amount it is evident the charity will receive.

Example (3). In 1975, D dies bequeathing $65,000 in trust with the requirement that a guaranteed annuity interest (as defined in paragraph (e)(2)(vi) of this section) of $5,000 a year, payable annually at the end of each year, be paid to Y Charity for a period of 10 years and that a guaranteed annuity interest (as defined in paragraph (e)(2)(vi) of this section) of $5,000 a year, payable annually at the end of each year, be paid to W, his widow, aged 62, for 10 years or until her prior death. The annuities are to be paid simultaneously, and the remainder is to be paid to D's children. The fair market value of the private annuity is $33,877 ($5,000 × 6.7754), as determined pursuant to § 20.2031-7A(c) and by the use of factors involving one life and a term of years as published in Publication 723A (12–70). The fair market value of the charitable annuity is $36,800.50 ($5,000 × 7.3601), as determined under Table B in § 20.2031-7A(d). It is not evident from the governing instrument of the trust or from local law that the trustee would be required to apportion the trust fund between the widow and charity in the event the fund were insufficient to pay both annuities in a given year. Accordingly, the deduction with respect to the charitable annuity will be limited to $31,123 ($65,000 less $33,877 [the value of the private annuity]), which is the minimum amount it is evident the charity will receive.

(v) The present value of a unitrust interest described in paragraph (e)(2)(vii) of this section is to be determined by subtracting the present value of all interests in the transferred property other than the unitrust interest from the fair market value of the transferred property.

(3) Certain decedents dying before August 1, 1969. In the case of decedents dying before August 1, 1969, the present value of an interest described in subparagraph (2) of this paragraph is to be determined under § 20.2031-7 except that, if the interest is an annuity issued by a company regularly engaged in the sale of annuities, the present value is to be determined under § 20.2031-8.

(4) [Reserved]. For further guidance, see § 20.2055-2T(f)(4).

(5) Special computations. If the interest transferred is such that its present value is to be determined by a special computation, a request for a special factor, accompanied by a statement of the date of birth and sex of each individual the duration of whose life may affect the value of the interest, and by copies of the relevant instruments, may be submitted by the fiduciary to the Commissioner who may, if conditions permit, supply the factor requested. If the Commissioner furnishes the factor, a copy of the letter supplying the factor must be attached to the tax return in which the deduction is claimed. If the Commissioner does not furnish the factor, the claim for deduction must be supported by a full statement of the computation of the present value made in accordance with the principles set forth in this paragraph.

T.D. 6296, 6/23/58, amend T.D. 7238, 12/28/72, T.D. 7318, 7/10/74, T.D. 7340, 1/6/75, T.D. 7955, 5/11/84, T.D. 7957, 5/16/84, T.D. 8069, 1/13/86, T.D. 8095, 8/6/86, T.D. 8540, 6/9/94, T.D. 8819, 4/29/99, T.D. 8886, 6/9/2000, T.D. 8923, 1/4/2001, T.D. 9068, 7/3/2003, T.D. 9448, 5/1/2009.

PAR. 9. Section 20.2055-2 is amended by revising paragraphs (e)(3)(iii) and (f)(4) to read as follows:

Proposed § 20.2055-2 Transfers not exclusively for charitable purposes. [*For Preamble, see ¶ 153,105*]

* * * * *

(e) * * *

(3) * * *

(iii) [The text of this proposed paragraph (e)(3)(iii) is the same as the text of § 20.2055-2T(e)(3)(iii) published elsewhere in this issue of the Federal Register]. [*See T.D. 9448, 05/07/2009, 74 Fed. Reg. 87.*]

* * * * *

(f) * * *

(4) [The text of this proposed paragraph (f)(4) is the same as the text of § 20.2055-2T(f)(4) published elsewhere in this issue of the Federal Register]. [*See T.D. 9448, 05/07/2009, 74 Fed. Reg. 87.*]

PAR. 3. § 20.2055-2 is amended by adding a sentence at the end of paragraph (a) and by adding a new paragraph (g) immediately following § 20.2055-2(f). These added and amended provisions read as follows:

Proposed § 20.2055-2 Transfers not exclusively for charitable purposes. [*For Preamble, see ¶ 150,177*]

(a) Remainders and similar interests. * * * See paragraph (g) of this section for special rules relating to certain wills and trusts in existence on September 21, 1974.

* * * * *

(g) Special rules applicable in the case of certain wills and trusts in existence on September 21, 1974. *(1)* In general, in the case of a will executed before September 21, 1974, or a trust created (within the meaning of applicable local law) after July 31, 1969, and before September 21, 1974, if—

(i) At the time of the decedent's death a deduction is not allowable solely because of the failure of an interest in property which passes or has passed from the decedent to a person, or for a use, described in section 2055(a) to meet the requirements of section 2055(e)(2)(A), and

(ii) The governing instrument is amended or conformed in accordance with this paragraph so that the interest is in a trust which is a charitable remainder annuity trust or a charitable remainder unitrust (described in section 664) or a pooled income fund (described in section 642(c)(5)), or the governing instrument is treated under paragraph (g)(8) of this section as if it were amended, a deduction shall nevertheless be allowed.

(2) An amendment or conformation pursuant to this paragraph must be made before January 1, 1976, or, if later, on or before the 30th day after the date on which judicial proceedings begun before January 1, 1976 (which are required to amend or conform the governing instrument) become final.

(3) A governing instrument may be amended or conformed under this paragraph only where:

(i) The transfer is not in trust but passes under a will executed before September 21, 1974;

(ii) The transfer is in the form of a testamentary trust created under a will executed before September 21, 1974;

(iii) The transfer was in trust, which was created (within the meaning of applicable local law) after July 31, 1969, and before September 21, 1974, but only if, at the time of the creation of the trust, the governing instrument provides that an organization described in section 170(c) receives an irrevocable remainder interest in such trust;

(iv) Property was transferred inter vivos after July 31, 1969, and before October 18, 1971, to a trust created (within the meaning of applicable local law) before August 1, 1969, which trust provides that an organization described in section 170(c) receives an irrevocable remainder interest in such trust, and the transferred property and any undistributed income therefrom is severed and placed in a separate trust before the applicable date specified in paragraph (g)(2) of this section. An instrument governing a transfer under this subdivision (iv), which is amended pursuant to this paragraph, shall be treated as having made such transfer to a trust deemed created on the date of such transfer;

(v) In the case of a transfer to a pooled income fund made before September 21, 1974 (or a transfer made under a will which was executed before September 21, 1974), the instrument governing the transfer fails to satisfy the requirements of § 1.642(c)-5(b).

However, a governing instrument may not be amended pursuant to this paragraph unless, at the time of the decedent's death, the interest is an irrevocable remainder interest for which a deduction, but for section 2055(e)(2)(A), would be allowable under section 2055(a) and the regulations thereunder. The provisions of section 508(d)(2)(A) (relating to disallowance of certain charitable, etc., deductions) shall not apply to such interest if the governing instrument is amended so as to comply with the requirements of section 508(e) (relating to governing instruments) by the applicable date described in paragraph (g)(2) of this section.

(4) The decree resulting from any judicial proceedings begun to amend a governing instrument pursuant to paragraph (g)(1) of this section must be binding, under local law, on all parties having an interest in the bequest or transfer as well as the fiduciary of the decedent's estate and trustee of the trust to be amended. In the event local law does not require judicial proceedings to amend or conform a governing instrument, a deduction may nevertheless be allowed if the governing instrument is amended or conformed by nonjudicial agreement between all parties having an interest in the bequest or transfer as well as the fiduciary of the decedent's estate and trustee of the trust to be amended, provided that the agreement is binding, under local law, on all such parties. The judicial proceedings or nonjudicial agreement must also account for any distributions made from the deemed date of creation to the date of the amendment in the following manner:

(i) Where the amount of the distributions which would have been made by the trust to a recipient had the amendment pursuant to paragraph (g)(1) of this section been in effect since the creation of the trust exceeds the amount of the distributions made by the trust prior to the amendment, the trust must pay an amount equal to such excess to the recipient;

(ii) Where the amount of the distributions made to the recipient prior to the amendment pursuant to paragraph (g)(1) of this section exceeds the amount of the distributions which would have been made by such trust if the amended provisions of such trust had been in effect from the time of creation of such trust, the recipient must pay an amount equal to such excess to the trust.

See § 1.664-1(d)(4) for rules relating to the year of inclusion in the case of an underpayment to a recipient and the allowance of a deduction in the case of an overpayment to a recipient.

(5) Where a charitable remainder trust (as described in § 1.664-1 (a)(1)(iii)(a)) results from an amendment pursuant to this paragraph, the trust will be treated as a charitable remainder trust for all purposes from the date it would be deemed created under § 1.664-1(a)(4) and (5), whether or not such date is after September 20, 1974. Subject to the limitations imposed by section 6511, the estate tax charitable deduction is allowable and the charitable remainder trust is exempt from Federal income taxation. For the application of certain excise taxes pursuant to section 4947(a)(2) see § 53.4947-1(c)(1)(iii) and (c)(6). In amending a governing instrument pursuant to paragraph (g)(1) of this section, the exchange of a noncharit beneficiary's interest in an unqualified transfer in trust for an interest in a qualified transfer in trust will not be treated as an act of self-dealing (described in section 4941) or a taxable expenditure (described in section 4945).

(6) If, on the due date for filing the estate tax return (including any extensions thereof), proceedings to amend or conform a governing instrument pursuant to paragraph (g)(1) of this section have not become final, such return shall be filed with the tax computed as if no deduction were allowable under this paragraph. When the proceedings to amend or conform such instrument have become final (within the applicable date described in paragraph (g)(2) of this section), a deduction shall be allowed upon the filing of a claim for credit or refund (within the limitations of section 6511). In the case of a credit or refund as a result of an amendment or conformation made pursuant to this paragraph, no interest shall be allowed for the period prior to the expiration of the 180th day after the date on which the claim for credit or refund is filed.

(7) If a governing instrument is amended under this paragraph, then, except as provided in paragraph (g)(8)(ii) of this section, the amount of the deduction allowable under this section shall be the amount that equals the value of the interest which, under the rules of section 2055 (including the rules governing disclaimers) passes to, or for the use of, an organization described in section 2055(a).

(8) (i) In the case of a will executed before September 21, 1974, or a trust created (within the meaning of applicable local law) before such date and after July 31, 1969, that creates an interest for which a deduction would be allowable under section 2055(a) but for section 2055(e)(2)(A), if the date of death of the decedent is prior to January 1, 1976, and if on or before the filing date of the estate tax return (including any extension thereof)—

(A) The interest is in a charitable trust which, if a deduction under section 2055(a) had been allowed, would be in a trust described in section 4947(a)(1), or

(B) Such interest passes directly to a person or for a use described in section 2055(a) (as, for example, by reason of the termination of an intervening interest),

the governing instrument shall be treated as if it were amended or conformed pursuant to paragraph (g)(1) of this section and a deduction shall be allowed. See section 508(d)(2) and § 1.508-2(b) for the disallowance of such a deduction in the case of an interest in a trust described in section 4947(a)(1) if the governing instrument fails to meet the requirements of section 508(e) by the end of the taxable year of the trust in which the filing date of the estate tax return occurs. A governing instrument treated as amended under this subdivision (i) may not thereafter be amended.

The provisions of this subparagraph shall not apply if the requirements of subdivision (A) or (B) of this subdivision (ii) are satisfied as a result of an amendment of a dispositive provision of the governing instrument occuring since the date of death of the decedent.

(ii) The amount of the deduction for a transfer which is treated under this paragraph as if it were amended will be determined as if the transfer were a charitable remainder annuity trust which provides an annuity of 6 percent of the initial fair market value payable from the date of death—

(A) In the case of a transfer providing a life estate, for the expected lives of the noncharitable beneficiaries as determined on the date of death of the decedent, or

(B) In the case of a transfer providing a term of years, for the term of years as expressed in the governing instrument, but not to exceed 20 years.

Any distributions made to a recipient from the date of death of the decedent to the date on which the transfer is deemed to be amended (i.e., the date the transfer satisfies the requirement of paragraph (g)(8)(i) of this section) must be taken into account under this subdivision (ii) in determining the amount of the deduction, to the extent that the adjustments in such distributions required by paragraph (g)(4) of this section, determined as if the charitable remainder annuity trust were deemed created at the date of death of the decedent, have not been made on or before the filing date of the estate tax return.

§ 20.2055-2T Transfers not exclusively for charitable purposes.

(a) through (e)(3)(ii). [Reserved]. For further guidance see § 20.2055-2(a) through (e)(3)(ii).

(e) *(3)* (iii) The rule in paragraphs (e)(2)(vi)(a) and (e)(2)(vii)(a) of this section that guaranteed annuity interests or unitrust interests, respectively, may be payable for a specified term of years or for the life or lives of only certain individuals is generally effective in the case of transfers pursuant to wills and revocable trusts when the decedent dies on or after April 4, 2000. Two exceptions from the application of this rule in paragraphs (e)(2)(vi)(a) and (e)(2)(vii)(a) of this section are provided in the case of transfers pursuant to a will or revocable trust executed on or before April 4, 2000. One exception is for a decedent who dies on or before July 5, 2001, without having republished the will (or amended the trust) by codicil or otherwise. The other exception is for a decedent who was on April 4, 2000, under a mental disability that prevented a change in the disposition of the decedent's property, and who either does not regain competence to dispose of such property before the date of death, or dies prior to the later of 90 days after the date on which the decedent first regains competence, or July 5, 2001, without having republished the will (or amended the trust) by codicil or otherwise. If a guaranteed annuity interest or unitrust interest created pursuant to a will or revocable trust when the decedent dies on or after April 4, 2000, uses an individual other than one permitted in paragraphs (e)(2)(vi)(a) and (vii)(a) of this section, and the interest does not qualify for this transitional relief, the interest may be reformed into a lead interest payable for a specified term of years. The term of years is determined by taking the factor for valuing the annuity or unitrust interest for the named individual measuring life and identifying the term of years (rounded up to the next whole year) that corresponds to the equivalent term of years factor for an annuity or unitrust interest. For example, in the case of an annuity interest payable for the life of an individual age 40 at the time of the transfer on or after May 1, 2009, assuming an interest rate of 7.4 percent under section 7520, the annuity factor from column 1 of Table S(7.4), contained in IRS Publication 1457, Actuarial Valuations Version 3A, for the life of an individual age 40 is 12.1519 (1.00000 minus .10076, divided by .074). Based on Table B(7.4), contained in Publication 1457, Actuarial Valuations Version 3A, the factor 12.1519 corresponds to a term of years between 32 and 33 years. Accordingly, the annuity interest must be reformed into an interest payable for a term of 33 years. A judicial reformation must be commenced prior to the later of July 5, 2001, or the date prescribed by section 2055(e)(3)(C)(iii). Any judicial reformation must be completed within a reasonable time after it is commenced. A non-judicial reformation is permitted if effective under state law, provided it is completed by the date on which a judicial reformation must be commenced. In the alternative, if a court, in a proceeding that is commenced on or before July 5, 2001, declares any transfer made pursuant to a will or revocable trust where the decedent dies on or after April 4, 2000, and on or before March 6, 2001, null and void ab initio, the Internal Revenue Service will treat such transfers in a manner similar to that described in section 2055(e)(3)(J).

(4) through (f)(3). [Reserved]. For further guidance see § 20.2055-2(e)(4) through (f)(3).

(f) *(4) Other decedents.* The present value of an interest not described in paragraph (f)(2) of this section is to be determined under § 20.2031-7T(d) in the case of decedents where the valuation date of the gross estate is on or after May 1, 2009, or under § 20.2031-7A in the case of decedents where the valuation date of the gross estate is before May 1, 2009.

(5) [Reserved]. For further guidance see § 20.2055-2(f)(5).

(6) Effective/applicability date. Paragraphs (e)(3)(iii) and (f)(4) apply on or after May 1, 2009.

(7) Expiration date. Paragraphs (e)(3)(iii) and (f)(4) expire on or before May 1, 2012.

T.D. 9448, 5/1/2009.

---

§ 20.2055-3 Effect of death taxes and administration expenses.

(a) Death taxes. *(1)* If under the terms of the will or other governing instrument, the law of the jurisdiction under which the estate is administered, or the law of the jurisdiction imposing the particular tax, the Federal estate tax, or any estate, succession, legacy, or inheritance tax is payable in whole or in part out of any property the transfer of which would otherwise be allowable as a deduction under section 2055, section 2055(c) provides that the sum deductible is the amount of the transferred property reduced by the amount of the tax. Section 2055(c) in effect provides that the deduction is based on the amount actually available for charitable uses, that is, the amount of the fund remaining after the payment of all death taxes. Thus, if $50,000 is bequeathed for a charitable purpose and is subjected to a State inheritance tax of $5,000, payable out of the $50,000, the amount deductible is $45,000. If a life estate is bequeathed to an individual with remainder over to a charitable organization, and by the local law the inheritance tax upon the life estate is paid out of the corpus with the result that the charitable organization will be entitled to receive only the amount of the fund less the tax, the deduction is limited to the present value, as of the date of the testator's death, of the remainder of the fund so reduced. If a testator bequeaths his residuary estate, or a portion of it, to charity, and his will contains a direction that certain inheritance taxes, otherwise payable from legacies upon which they were imposed, shall be payable out of the residuary estate, the deduction may not exceed the bequest to charity thus reduced pursuant to the direction of the will. If a residuary estate, or a portion of it, is bequested to charity, and by the local law the Federal estate tax is payable out of the residuary estate, the deduction may not exceed that portion of the residuary estate bequeathed to charity as reduced by the Federal estate tax. The return should fully disclose the computation of the amount to be deducted. If the amount to be deducted is dependent upon the amount of any death tax which has not been paid before the filing of the return, there should be submitted with the return a computation of that tax.

(2) It should be noted that if the Federal estate tax is payable out of a charitable transfer so that the amount of the transfer otherwise passing to charity is reduced by the amount of the tax, the resultant decrease in the amount passing to charity will further reduce the allowable deduction. In such a case, the amount of the charitable deduction can be obtained only by a series of trial-and-error computations, or by a formula. If, in addition, interdependent State and Federal taxes are involved, the computation becomes highly complicated. Examples of methods of computation of the charitable deduction and the marital deduction (with which similar problems are encountered) in various situations are contained in supplemental instructions to the estate tax return.

(3) For the allowance of a deduction to a decedent's estate for certain State death taxes imposed upon charitable transfers, see section 2053(d) and § 20.2053-9.

(b) Administration expenses. *(1) Definitions.* (i) Management expenses. Estate management expenses are expenses that are incurred in connection with the investment of estate assets or with their preservation or maintenance during a reasonable period of administration. Examples of these expenses could include investment advisory fees, stock brokerage commissions, custodial fees, and interest.

(ii) Transmission expenses. Estate transmission expenses are expenses that would not have been incurred but for the decedent's death and the consequent necessity of collecting the decedent's assets, paying the decedent's debts and death taxes, and distributing the decedent's property to those who are entitled to receive it. Estate transmission expenses include any administration expense that is not a management expense. Examples of these expenses could include executor commissions and attorney fees (except to the extent of commissions or fees specifically related to investment, preservation, or maintenance of the assets), probate fees, expenses incurred in construction proceedings and defending against will contests, and appraisal fees.

(iii) Charitable share. The charitable share is the property or interest in property that passed from the decedent for which a deduction is allowable under section 2055(a) with respect to all or part of the property interest. The charitable share includes, for example, bequests to charitable organizations and bequests to a charitable lead unitrust or annuity trust, a charitable remainder unitrust or annuity trust, and a pooled income fund, described in section 2055(e)(2). The charitable share also includes the income produced by the property or interest in property during the period of administration if the income, under the terms of the governing instrument or applicable local law, is payable to the charitable organization or is to be added to the principal of the property interest passing in whole or in part to the charitable organization.

(2) Effect of transmission expenses. For purposes of determining the charitable deduction, the value of the charitable share shall be reduced by the amount of the estate transmission expenses paid from the charitable share.

(3) Effect of management expenses attributable to the charitable share. For purposes of determining the charitable deduction, the value of the charitable share shall not be reduced by the amount of the estate management expenses attributable to and paid from the charitable share. Pursuant to section 2056(b)(9), however, the amount of the allowable charitable deduction shall be reduced by the amount of any such management expenses that are deducted under section 2053 on the decedent's federal estate tax return.

(4) Effect of management expenses not attributable to the charitable share. For purposes of determining the charitable deduction, the value of the charitable share shall be reduced by the amount of the estate management expenses paid from the charitable share but attributable to a property interest not included in the charitable share.

(5) Example. The following example illustrates the application of this paragraph (b):

Example. The decedent, who dies in 2000, leaves his residuary estate, after the payment of debts, expenses, and estate taxes, to a charitable remainder unitrust that satisfies the requirements of section 664(d). During the period of administration, the estate incurs estate transmission expenses of $400,000. The residue of the estate (the charitable share) must be reduced by the $400,000 of transmission expenses and by the Federal and State estate taxes before the present value of the remainder interest passing to charity can be determined in accordance with the provisions of § 1.664-4 of this chapter. Because the estate taxes are payable out of the residue, the computation of the estate taxes and the allowable charitable deduction are interrelated. See paragraph (a)(2) of this section.

(6) Cross reference. See § 20.2056(b)-4(d) for additional examples applicable to the treatment of administration expenses under this paragraph (b).

(7) Effective date. The provisions of this paragraph (b) apply to estates of decedents dying on or after December 3, 1999.

T.D. 6296, 6/23/58, amend T.D. 8846, 12/2/99.

§ 20.2055-4 Disallowance of charitable, etc., deductions because of "prohibited transactions" in the case of decedents dying before January 1, 1970.

(a) Sections 503(e) and 681(b)(5) provide that no deduction which would otherwise be allowable under section 2055 for the value of property transferred by the decedent during his lifetime or by will for religious, charitable, scientific, literary, or educational purposes (including the encouragement of art and the prevention of cruelty to children or animals) is allowed if (1) the transfer is made in trust, and, for income tax purposes for the taxable year of the trust in which the transfer is made, the deduction otherwise allowable to the trust under section 642(c) is limited by section 681(b)(1) by reason of the trust having engaged in a prohibited transaction described in section 681(b)(2), or (2) the transfer is made to a corporation, community chest, fund or foundation which, for its taxable year in which the transfer is made, is not exempt from income tax under section 501(a) by reason of having engaged in a prohibited transaction described in section 503(c).

(b) For purposes of section 681(b)(5) and section 503(e), the term "transfer" includes any gift, contribution, bequest, devise, legacy, or other disposition. In applying such sections for estate tax purposes, a transfer, whether made during the decedent's lifetime or by will, is considered as having been made at the moment of the decedent's death.

(c) The income tax regulations contain the rules for the determination of the taxable year of the trust for which the deduction under section 642(c) is limited by section 681(b) and for the determination of the taxable year of the organization for which an exemption is denied under section 503(a). Generally, such taxable year is a taxable year subsequent to the taxable year during which the trust or organization has been notified by the Commissioner of Internal Revenue that it has engaged in a prohibited transaction. However, if the trust or organization during or prior to the taxable year entered into the prohibited transaction for the purpose of diverting its corpus or income from the charitable or other purposes by reason of which it is entitled to a deduction or exemption, and the transaction involves a substantial part of the income or corpus, then the deduction of the trust under section 642(c) for such taxable year is limited by section 681(b), or exemption of the organization for such taxable year is denied under section 503(a), whether or not the organization has previously received notification by the Commissioner of Internal Revenue that it is engaged in a prohibited transaction. In certain cases, the limitation of sections 681 or 503 may be removed or the exemption may be reinstated for certain subsequent taxable years under the rules set forth in the income tax regulations under sections 681 and 503. In cases in which prior notification by the Commissioner of Internal Revenue is not required in order to limit the deduction of the trust under section 681(b) or to deny exemption of the organization under section 503, the deduction otherwise allowable under section 2055 is not disallowed in respect of transfers made during the same taxable year of the trust or organization in which a prohibited transaction occurred or in a prior taxable year unless the decedent or a member of his family was a party to the prohibited transaction. For the purpose of the preceding sentence, the members of the decedent's family include only his brothers and sisters, whether by whole or half blood, spouse, ancestors, and lineal descendants.

(d) This section applies only in the case of decedents dying before January 1, 1970. In the case of decedents dying after December 31, 1969, see § 20.2055-5.

T.D. 6296, 6/23/58, amend T.D. 7318, 7/10/74.

§ 20.2055-5 Disallowance of charitable, etc., deductions in the case of decedents dying after December 31, 1969.

(a) Organizations subject to section 507(c) tax. Section 508(d)(1) provides that, in the case of decedents dying after December 31, 1969, a deduction which would otherwise be allowable under section 2055 for the value of property transferred by the decedent to or for the use of an organization upon which the tax provided by section 507(c) has been imposed shall not be allowed if the transfer is made by the decedent after notification is made under section 507(a) or if the decedent is a substantial contributor (as defined in section 507(d)(2)) who dies on or after the first day on which action is taken by such organization that culminates in the imposition of the tax under section 507(c). This paragraph does not apply if the entire amount of the unpaid portion of the tax imposed by section 507(c) is abated under section 507(g) by the Commissioner or his delegate.

(b) Taxable private foundations, section 4947 trusts, etc. *(1) In general.* Section 508(d)(2) provides that, in the case of decedents dying after December 31, 1969, a deduction which would otherwise be allowable under section 2055 for the value of property transferred by the decedent shall not be allowed if the transfer is made to or for the use of—

(i) A private foundation or a trust described in section 4947(a)(2) in a taxable year of such organization for which such organization fails to meet the governing instrument requirements of section 508(e) (determined without regard to section 508(e)(2)(B) and (C)), or

(ii) Any organization in a period for which it is not treated as an organization described in section 501(c)(3) by reason of its failure to give notification under section 508(a) of its status to the Commissioner.

For additional rules, see § 1.508-2(b)(1) of this chapter (Income Tax Regulations).

(2) Transfers not covered by section 508(d)(2)(A). (i) In general. Any deduction which would otherwise be allowable under section 2055 for the value of property transferred by a decedent dying after December 31, 1969, will not be disallowed under section 508(d)(2)(A) and subparagraph (1)(i) of this paragraph—

(a) In the case of property passing under the terms of a will executed on or before October 9, 1969—

(1) If the decedent dies after October 9, 1969, but before October 9, 1972, without having amended any dispositive provision of the will after October 9, 1969, by codicil or otherwise.

(2) If the decedent dies after October 9, 1969, and at no time after that date had the right to change the portions of the will which pertain to the passing of the property to, or for the use of, an organization described in section 2055(a), or

(3) If no dispositive provision of the will is amended by the decedent, by codicil or otherwise, after October 9, 1969, and before October 9, 1972, and the decedent is on October 9, 1972, and at all times thereafter under a mental disability (as defined in § 1.642(c)-2(b)(3)(ii) of this chapter) to amend the will by codicil or otherwise, or

(b) In the case of property transferred in trust on or before October 9, 1969—

(1) If the decedent dies after October 9, 1969, but before October 9, 1972, without having amended, after October 9, 1969, any dispositive provision of the instrument governing the disposition of the property,

(2) If the property transferred was an irrevocable interest to, or for the use of, an organization described in section 2055(a), or

(3) If no dispositive provision of the instrument governing the disposition of the property is amended by the decedent after October 9, 1969, and before October 9, 1972, and the decedent is on October 9, 1972, and at all times thereafter under a mental disability (as defined in § 1.642(c)-2(b)(3)(ii) of this chapter) to change the disposition of the property.

(ii) Amendment of dispositive provisions. For purposes of subdivision (i) of this subparagraph, the provisions of paragraph (e)(4) and (5) of § 20.2055-2 shall apply in determining whether an amendment will be considered as one which amends the dispositive provisions of a will or trust.

(c) Foreign organization with substantial support from foreign sources. Section 4948(c)(4) provides that, in the case of decedents dying after December 31, 1969, a deduction which would otherwise be allowable under section 2055 for the value of property transferred by the decedent to or for the use of a foreign organization which has received substantially all of its support (other than gross investment income) from sources without the United States shall not be allowed if the transfer is made (1) after the date on which the Commissioner has published notice that he has notified such organization that it has engaged in a prohibited transaction, or (2) in a taxable year of such organization for which it is not exempt from taxation under section 501(a) because it has engaged in a prohibited transaction after December 31, 1969.

T.D. 7318, 7/10/74.

§ 20.2055-6 Disallowance of double deduction in the case of qualified terminable interest property.

No deduction is allowed from the decedent's gross estate under section 2055 for property with respect to which a deduction is allowed by reason of section 2056(b)(7). See section 2056(b)(9) and § 20.2056(b)-9.

T.D. 8522, 2/28/94.

§ 20.2056-0 Table of contents.

This section lists the captions that appear in the regulations under §§ 20.2056(a)-1 through 20.2056(d)-2.

T.D. 8522, 2/28/94, amend T.D. 8612, 8/21/95.

§ 20.2056(a)-1 Marital deduction; in general.

(a) In general. A deduction is allowed under section 2056 from the gross estate of a decedent for the value of any property interest which passes from the decedent to the decedent's surviving spouse if the interest is a deductible interest as defined in § 20.2056(a)-2. With respect to decedents dying in certain years, a deduction is allowed under section 2056 only to the extent that the total of the deductible interests does not exceed the applicable limitations set forth in paragraph (c) of this section. The deduction allowed under section 2056 is referred to as the marital deduction. See also sections 2056(d) and 2056A for special rules applicable in the case of decedents dying after November 10, 1988, if the decedent's surviving spouse is not a citizen of the United States at the time of the decedent's death. In such cases, the marital deduction may not be allowed unless the property passes to a qualified domestic trust as described in section 2056A(a).

(b) Requirements for marital deduction. *(1) In general.* To obtain the marital deduction with respect to any property interest, the executor must establish the following facts—

(i) The decedent was survived by a spouse (see § 20.2056(c)-2(e));

(ii) The property interest passed from the decedent to the spouse (see §§ 20.2056(b)-5 through 20.2056(b)-8 and 20.2056(c)-1 through 20.2056(c)-3);

(iii) The property interest is a deductible interest (see § 20.2056(a)-2); and

(iv) The value of the property interest (see § 20.2056(b)-4).

(2) Burden of establishing requisite facts. The executor must provide the facts relating to any applicable limitation on the amount of the allowable marital deduction under § 20.2056(a)-1(c), and must submit proof necessary to establish any fact required under paragraph (b)(1), including any evidence requested by the district director.

(c) Marital deduction; limitation on aggregate deductions. *(1) Estates of decedents dying before 1977.* In the case of estates of decedents dying before January 1, 1977, the marital deduction is limited to one-half of the value of the adjusted gross estate, as that term was defined under section 2056(c)(2) prior to repeal by the Economic Recovery Tax Act of 1981.

(2) Estates of decedents dying after December 31, 1976, and before January 1, 1982. Except as provided in § 2002(d)(1) of the Tax Reform Act of 1976 (Pub. L. 94-455), in the case of decedents dying after December 31, 1976, and before January 1, 1982, the marital deduction is limited to the greater of—

(i) $250,000; or

(ii) One-half of the value of the decedent's adjusted gross estate, adjusted for intervivos gifts to the spouse as prescribed by section 2056(c)(1)(B) prior to repeal by the Economic Recovery Tax Act of 1981 (Pub. L. 97-34).

(3) Estates of decedents dying after December 31, 1981. In the case of estates of decedents dying after December 31, 1981, the marital deduction is limited as prescribed in paragraph (c)(2) of this section if the provisions of § 403(e)(3) of Pub. L. 97-34 are satisfied.

T.D. 6296, 6/23/58, amend T.D. 8095, 8/6/86, T.D. 8522, 2/28/94.

§ 20.2056(a)-2 Marital deduction; deductible interests and nondeductible interests.

Caution: The Treasury has not yet amended Reg § 20.2056(a)-2 to reflect changes made by P.L. 97-34.

(a) In general. Property interests which passed from a decedent to his surviving spouse fall within two general categories: (1) Those with respect to which the marital deduction is authorized, and (2) those with respect to which the marital deduction is not authorized. These categories are referred to in this section and other sections of the regulations under section 2056 as "deductible interests" and "nondeductible interests", respectively (see paragraph (b) of this section). Subject to any applicable limitations set forth in § 20.2056(a)-1(c), the amount of the marital deduction is the aggregate value of the deductible interests.

(b) Deductible interests. An interest passing to a decedent's surviving spouse is a "deductible interest" if it does not fall within one of the following categories of "nondeductible interests":

(1) Any property interest which passed from the decedent to his surviving spouse is a "nondeductible interest" to the extent it is not included in the decedent's gross estate.

(2) If a deduction is allowed under section 2053 (relating to deductions for expenses and indebtedness) by reason of the passing of a property interest from the decedent to his surviving spouse, such interest is, to the extent of the deduction under section 2053, a "nondeductible interest". Thus, a property interest which passed from the decedent to his surviving spouse in satisfaction of a deductible claim of the spouse against the estate is, to the extent of the claim, a "nondeductible interest" (see § 20.2056(b)-4). Similarly, amounts deducted under section 2053(a)(2) for commissions allowed to the surviving spouse as executor are "nondeductible interests". As to the valuation, for the purpose of the marital deduction, of any property interest which passed from the decedent to his surviving spouse subject to a mortgage or other encumbrance, see § 20.2056(b)-4.

(3) If during settlement of the estate a loss deductible under section 2054 occurs with respect to a property interest, then that interest is, to the extent of the deductible loss, a "nondeductible interest" for the purpose of the marital deduction.

(4) A property interest passing to a decedent's surviving spouse which is a "terminable interest", as defined in § 20.2056(b)-1, is a "nondeductible interest" to the extent specified in that section.

T.D. 6296, 6/23/58, amend T.D. 8522, 2/28/94.

§ 20.2056(b)-1 Marital deduction; limitation in case of life estate or other terminable interest.

Caution: The Treasury has not yet amended Reg § 20.2056(b)-1 to reflect changes made by P.L. 97-34.

(a) In general. Section 2056(b) provides that no marital deduction is allowed with respect to certain property interests, referred to generally as "terminable interests", passing from a decedent to his surviving spouse. The phrase "terminable interest" is defined in paragraph (b) of this section. However, the fact that an interest in property passing to a decedent's surviving spouse is a "terminable interest" makes it nondeductible only (1) under the circumstances described in paragraph (c) of this section, and (2) if it does not come within one of the exceptions referred to in paragraph (d) of this section.

(b) "Terminable interests". A "terminable interest" in property is an interest which will terminate or fail on the lapse of time or on the occurrence or the failure to occur of some contingency. Life estates, terms for years, annuities, patents, and copyrights are therefore terminable interests. However, a bond, note, or similar contractual obligation, the discharge of which would not have the effect of an annuity or a term for years, is not a terminable interest.

(c) Nondeductible terminable interests. *(1)* A property interest which constitutes a terminable interest, as defined in paragraph (b) of this section, is nondeductible if—

(i) Another interest in the same property passed from the decedent to some other person for less than an adequate and full consideration in money or money's worth, and

(ii) By reason of its passing, the other person or his heirs or assigns may possess or enjoy any part of the property after the termination or failure of the spouse's interest.

(2) Even though a property interest which constitutes a terminable interest is not nondeductible by reason of the rules stated in subparagraph (1) of this paragraph, such an interest is nondeductible if—

(i) The decedent has directed his executor or a trustee to acquire such an interest for the decedent's surviving spouse (see further paragraph (f) of this section), or

(ii) Such an interest passing to the decedent's surviving spouse may be satisfied out of a group of assets which includes a nondeductible interest (see further § 20.2056(b)-2). In this case, however, full nondeductibility may not result.

(d) Exceptions. A property interest passing to a decedent's surviving spouse is deductible (if it is not otherwise disqualified under § 20.2056(a)-2) even though it is a terminable interest, and even though an interest therein passed from the decedent to another person, if it is a terminable interest only because—

(1) It is conditioned on the spouse's surviving for a limited period, in the manner described in § 20.2056(b)-3;

(2) It is a right to income for life with a general power of appointment, meeting the requirements set forth in § 20.2056(b)-5;

(3) It consists of life insurance or annuity payments held by the insurer with a general power of appointment in the spouse, meeting the requirements set forth in § 20.2056(b)-6;

(4) It is qualified terminable interest property, meeting the requirements set forth in § 20.2056(b)-7; or

(5) It is an interest in a qualified charitable remainder trust in which the spouse is the only noncharitable beneficiary, meeting the requirements set forth in § 20.2056(b)-8.

(e) Miscellaneous principles. *(1)* In determining whether an interest passed from the decedent to some other person, it is immaterial whether interests in the same property passed to the decedent's spouse and another person at the same time, or under the same instrument.

(2) In determining whether an interest in the same property passed from the decedent both to his surviving spouse and to some other person, a distinction is to be drawn between "property", as such term is used in section 2056, and an "interest in property". The term "property" refers to the underlying property in which various interests exist; each such interest is not for this purpose to be considered as "property".

(3) Whether or not an interest is nondeductible because it is a terminable interest is to be determined by reference to the property interests which actually passed from the decedent. Subsequent conversions of the property are immaterial for this purpose. Thus, where a decedent bequeathed his estate to his wife for life with remainder to his children, the interest which passed to his wife is a nondeductible interest, even though the wife agrees with the children to take a fractional share of the estate in fee in lieu of the life interest in the whole, or sells the life estate for cash, or acquires the remainder interest of the children either by purchase or gift.

(4) The terms passed from the decedent, passed from the decedent to his surviving spouse and passed from the decedent to a person other than his surviving spouse are defined in §§ 20.2056(c)-1 through 20.2056(c)-3.

(f) Direction to acquire a terminable interest. No marital deduction is allowed with respect to a property interest which a decedent directs his executor or a trustee to convert after his death into a terminable interest for his surviving spouse. The marital deduction is not allowed even though no interest in the property subject to the terminable interest passes to another person and even though the interest would otherwise come within the exceptions described in §§ 20.2056(b)-5 and 20.2056(b)-6 (relating to life estates and life insurance and annuity payments with powers of appointment). However, a general investment power, authorizing investments in both terminable interests and other property, is not a direction to invest in a terminable interest.

(g) Examples. The application of this section may be illustrated by the following examples. In each example, it is assumed that the executor made no election under section 2056(b)(7) (even if under the specific facts the election would have been available), that any property interest passing from the decedent to a person other than the surviving spouse passed for less than full and adequate consideration in money or money's worth, and that section 2056(b)(8) is inapplicable.

Example (1). H (the decedent) devised real property to W (his surviving wife) for life, with remainder to A and his heirs. The interest which passed from H to W is a nondeductible interest since it will terminate upon her death and A (or his heirs or assigns) will thereafter possess or enjoy the property.

Example (2). H bequeathed the residue of his estate in trust for the benefit of W and A. The trust income is to be paid to W for life, and upon her death the corpus is to be distributed to A or his issue. However, if A should die without issue, leaving W surviving, the corpus is then to be distributed to W. The interest which passed from H to W is a nondeductible interest since it will terminate in the event of her death if A or his issue survive, and A or his issue will thereafter possess or enjoy the property.

Example (3). H during his lifetime purchased an annuity contract providing for payments to himself for life and then to W for life if she should survive him. Upon the death of the survivor of H and W, the excess, if any, of the cost of the contract over the annuity payments theretofore made was to be refunded to A. The interest which passed from H to W is a nondeductible interest since A may possess or enjoy a part of the property following the termination of the interest of W. If, however, the contract provided for no refund upon the death of the survivor of H and W, or provided that any refund was to go to the estate of the survivor, then the interest which passed from H to W is (to the extent it is included in H's gross estate) a deductible interest.

Example (4). H, in contemplation of death, transferred a residence to A for life with remainder to W provided W survives A, but if W predeceases A, the property is to pass to B and his heirs. If it is assumed that H died during A's lifetime, and the value of the residence was included in determining the value of his gross estate, the interest which passed from H to W is a nondeductible interest since it will terminate if W predeceases A and the property will thereafter be possessed or enjoyed by B (or his heirs or assigns). This result is not affected by B's assignment of his interest during H's lifetime, whether made in favor of W or another person, since the term "assigns" (as used in section 2056(b)(1)(B)) includes such an assignee. However, if it is assumed that A predeceased H, the interest of B in the property was extinguished, and, viewed as of the time of the subsequent death of H, the interest which passed from him to W is the entire interest in the property and, therefore, a deductible interest.

Example (5). H transferred real property to A by gift, reserving the right to the rentals of the property for a term of 20 years. H died within the 20-year term, bequeathing the right to the remaining rentals to a trust for the benefit of W. The terms of the trust satisfy the five conditions stated in § 20.2056(b)-5, so that the property interest which passed in trust is considered to have passed from H to W. However, the interest is a nondeductible interest since it will terminate upon the expiration of the term and A will thereafter possess or enjoy the property.

Example (6). H bequeathed a patent to W and A as tenants in common. In this case, the interest of W will terminate upon the expiration of the term of the patent, but possession or enjoyment of the property by A must necessarily cease at the same time. Therefore, since A's possession or enjoyment cannot outlast the termination of W's interest, the latter is a deductible interest.

Example (7). A decedent bequeathed $100,000 to his wife, subject to a direction to his executor to use the bequest for the purchase of an annuity for the wife. The bequest is a nondeductible interest.

Example (8). Assume that pursuant to local law an allowance for support is payable to the decedent's surviving spouse during the period of the administration of the decedent's estate, but that upon her death or remarriage during such period her right to any further allowance will terminate. Assume further that the surviving spouse is sole beneficiary of the decedent's estate. Under such circumstances, the allowance constitutes a deductible interest since any part of the allowance not receivable by the surviving spouse during her lifetime will pass to her estate under the terms of the decedent's will. If, in this example, the decedent bequeathed only one-third of his residuary estate to his surviving spouse, then two-thirds of the allowance for support would constitute a nondeductible terminable interest.

T.D. 6296, 6/23/58, amend T.D. 8522, 2/28/94.

§ 20.2056(b)-2 Marital deduction; interest in unidentified assets.

(a) In general. Section 2056(b)(2) provides that if an interest passing to a decedent's surviving spouse may be satisfied out of assets (or their proceeds) which include a particular asset that would be a nondeductible interest if it passed from the decedent to his spouse, the value of the interest passing to the spouse is reduced, for the purpose of the marital deduction, by the value of the particular asset.

(b) Application of section 2056(b)(2). In order for section 2056(b)(2) to apply, two circumstances must coexist, as follows:

(1) The property interest which passed from the decedent to his surviving spouse must be payable out of a group of assets included in the gross estate. Examples of property interests payable out of a group of assets are a general legacy, a bequest of the residue of the decedent's estate or of a proportion of the residue, and a right to a share of the corpus of a trust upon its termination.

(2) The group of assets out of which the property interest is payable must include one or more particular assets which, if passing specifically to the surviving spouse, would be nondeductible interests. Therefore, section 2056(b)(2) is not applicable merely because the group of assets includes a terminable interest, but would only be applicable if the terminable interest were nondeductible under the provisions of § 20.2056(b)-1.

(c) Interest nondeductible if circumstances present. If both of the circumstances set forth in paragraph (b) of this section are present, the property interest payable out of the group of assets is (except as to any excess of its value over the aggregate value of the particular asset or assets which would not be deductible if passing specifically to the surviving spouse) a nondeductible interest.

(d) Example. The application of this section may be illustrated by the following example:

Example. A decedent bequeathed one-third of the residue of his estate to his wife. The property passing under the decedent's will included a right to the rentals of an office building for a term of years, reserved by the decedent under a deed of the building by way of gift to his son. The decedent did not make a specific bequest of the right to such rentals. Such right, if passing specifically to the wife, would be a nondeductible interest (see example (5) of paragraph (g) of § 20.2056(b)-1). It is assumed that the value of the bequest of one-third of the residue of the estate to the wife was $85,000, and that the right to the rentals was included in the gross estate at a value of $60,000. If the decedent's executor had the right under the decedent's will or local law to assign the entire lease in satisfaction of the bequest, the bequest is a nondeductible interest to the extent of $60,000. If the executor could only assign a one-third interest in the lease in satisfaction of the bequest, the bequest is a nondeductible interest to the extent of $20,000. If the decedent's will provided that his wife's bequest could not be satisfied with a nondeductible interest, the entire bequest is a deductible interest. If, in this example, the asset in question had been foreign real estate not included in the decedent's gross estate, the results would be the same.

T.D. 6296, 6/23/58, amend T.D. 8522, 2/28/94.

§ 20.2056(b)-3 Marital deduction; interest of spouse.

Caution: The Treasury has not yet amended Reg § 20.2056(b)-3 to reflect changes made by P.L. 97-34.

(a) In general. Generally, no marital deduction is allowable if the interest passing to the surviving spouse is a terminable interest as defined in paragraph (b) of § 20.2056(b)-1. However, section 2056(b)(3) provides an exception to this rule so as to allow a deduction if (1) the only condition under which it will terminate is the death of the surviving spouse within 6 months after the decedent's death, or her death as a result of a common disaster which also resulted in the decedent's death, and (2) the condition does not in fact occur.

(b) Six months survival. If the only condition which will cause the interest taken by the surviving spouse to terminate is the death of the surviving spouse and the condition is of such nature that it can occur only within 6 months following the decedent's death, the exception provided by section 2056(b)(3) will apply, provided the condition does not in fact occur. However, if the condition (unless it relates to death as a result of a common disaster) is one which may occur either within the 6-month period or thereafter, the exception provided by section 2056(b)(3) will not apply.

(c) Common disaster. If a property interest passed from the decedent to his surviving spouse subject to the condition that she does not die as a result of a common disaster which also resulted in the decedent's death, the exception provided by section 2056(b)(3) will not be applied in the final audit of the return if there is still a possibility that the surviving spouse may be deprived of the property interest by operation of the common disaster provision as given effect by the local law.

(d) Examples. The application of this section may be illustrated by the following examples:

Example (1). A decedent bequeathed his entire estate to his spouse on condition that she survive him by 6 months. In the event his spouse failed to survive him by 6 months, his estate was to go to his niece and her heirs. The decedent was survived by his spouse. It will be observed that, as of the time of the decedent's death, it was possible that the niece would, by reason of the interest which passed to her from the decedent, possess or enjoy the estate after the termination of the interest which passed to the spouse. Hence, under the general rule set forth in § 20.2056(b)-1, the interest which passed to the spouse would be regarded as a nondeductible interest. If the surviving spouse in fact died within 6 months after the decedent's death, that general rule is to be applied, and the interest which passed to the spouse is a nondeductible interest. However, if the spouse in fact survived the decedent by 6 months, thus extinguishing the interest of the niece, the case comes within the exception provided by section 2056(b)(3), and the interest which passed to the spouse is a deductible interest. (It is assumed for the purpose of this example that no other factor which would cause the interest to be nondeductible is present.)

Example (2). The facts are the same as in example (1) except that the will provided that the estate was to go to the niece either in case the decedent and his spouse should both die as a result of a common disaster, or in case the spouse should fail to survive the decedent by 3 months. It is assumed that the decedent was survived by his spouse. In this example, the interest which passed from the decedent to his surviving spouse is to be regarded as a nondeductible interest if the surviving spouse in fact died either within 3 months after the decedent's death or as a result of a common disaster which also resulted in the decedent's death. However, if the spouse in fact survived the decedent by 3 months, and did not thereafter die as a result of a common disaster which also resulted in the decedent's death, the exception provided under section 2056(b)(3) will apply and the interest will be deductible.

Example (3). The facts are the same as in example (1) except that the will provided that the estate was to go to the niece if the decedent and his spouse should both die as a result of a common disaster and if the spouse failed to survive the decedent by 3 months. If the spouse in fact survived the decedent by 3 months, the interest of the niece is extinguished, and the interest passing to the spouse is a deductible interest.

Example (4). A decedent devised and bequeathed his residuary estate to his wife if she was living on the date of distribution of his estate. The devise and bequest is a nondeductible interest even though distribution took place within 6 months after the decedent's death and the surviving spouse in fact survived the date of distribution.

T.D. 6296, 6/23/58.

§ 20.2056(b)-4 Marital deduction; valuation of interest passing to surviving spouse.

(a) In general. The value, for the purpose of the marital deduction, of any deductible interest which passed from the decedent to his surviving spouse is to be determined as of the date of the decedent's death, except that if the executor elects the alternate valuation method under section 2032 the valuation is to be determined as of the date of the decedent's death but with the adjustment described in paragraph (a)(3) of § 20.2032-1. The marital deduction may be taken only with respect to the net value of any deductible interest which passed from the decedent to his surviving spouse, the same principles being applicable as if the amount of a gift to the spouse were being determined.

(b) Property interest subject to an encumbrance or obligation. If a property interest passed from the decedent to his surviving spouse subject to a mortgage or other encumbrance, or if an obligation is imposed upon the surviving spouse by the decedent in connection with the passing of a property interest, the value of the property interest is to be reduced by the amount of the mortgage, other encumbrance, or obligation. However, if under the terms of the decedent's will or under local law the executor is required to discharge, out of other assets of the decedent's estate, a mortgage or other encumbrance on property passing from the decedent to his surviving spouse, or is required to reimburse the surviving spouse for the amount of the mortgage or other encumbrance, the payment or reimbursement constitutes an additional interest passing to the surviving spouse. The passing of a property interest subject to the imposition of an obligation by the decedent does not include a bequest, devise, or transfer in lieu of dower, curtesy, or of a statutory estate created in lieu of dower or curtesy, or of other marital rights in the decedent's property or estate. The passing of a property interest subject to the imposition of an obligation by the decedent does, however, include a bequest, etc., in lieu of the interest of his surviving spouse under community property laws unless such interest was, immediately prior to the decedent's death, a mere expectancy. The following examples are illustrative of property interests which passed from the decedent to his surviving spouse subject to the imposition of an obligation by the decedent:

Example (1). A decedent devised a residence valued at $25,000 to his wife, with a direction that she pay $5,000 to his sister. For the purpose of the marital deduction, the value of the property interest passing to the wife is only $20,000.

Example (2). A decedent devised real property to his wife in satisfaction of a debt owing to her. The debt is a deductible claim under section 2053. Since the wife is obligated to relinquish the claim as a condition to acceptance of the devise, the value of the devise is, for the purpose of the marital deduction, to be reduced by the amount of the claim.

Example (3). A decedent bequeathed certain securities to his wife in lieu of her interest in property held by them as community property under the law of the State of their residence. The wife elected to relinquish her community property interest and to take the bequest. For the purpose of the marital deduction, the value of the bequest is to be reduced by the value of the community property interest relinquished by the wife.

(c) Effect of death taxes. *(1)* In the determination of the value of any property interest which passed from the decedent to his surviving spouse, there must be taken into account the effect which the Federal estate tax, or any estate, succession, legacy, or inheritance tax, has upon the net value to the surviving spouse of the property interest.

(2) For example, assume that the only bequest to the surviving spouse is $100,000 and the spouse is required to pay a State inheritance tax in the amount of $1,500. If no other death taxes affect the net value of the bequest, the value, for the purpose of the marital deduction, is $98,500.

(3) As another example, assume that a decedent devised real property to his wife having a value for Federal estate tax purposes of $100,000 and also bequeathed to her a nondeductible interest for life under a trust. The State of residence valued the real property at $90,000 and the life interest at $30,000, and imposed an inheritance tax (at graduated rates) of $4,800 with respect to the two interests. If it is assumed that the inheritance tax on the devise is required to be paid by the wife, the amount of tax to be ascribed to the devise is

$$\frac{90{,}000}{120{,}000} \times \$4{,}800 = \$3{,}600$$

Accordingly, if no other death taxes affect the net value of the bequest, the value, for the purpose of the marital deduction, is $100,000 less $3,600, or $96,400.

(4) If the decedent bequeaths his residuary estate, or a portion of it, to his surviving spouse, and his will contains a direction that all death taxes shall be payable out of the residuary estate, the value of the bequest, for the purpose of the marital deduction, is based upon the amount of the residue as reduced pursuant to such direction. If the residuary estate, or a portion of it, is bequeathed to the surviving spouse, and by the local law the Federal estate tax is payable out of the residuary estate, the value of the bequest, for the purpose of the marital deduction, may not exceed its value as reduced by the Federal estate tax. Methods of computing the deduction, under such circumstances, are set forth in supplemental instructions to the estate tax return.

(d) Effect of administration expenses. *(1) Definitions.* (i) Management expenses. Estate management expenses are expenses that are incurred in connection with the investment of estate assets or with their preservation or maintenance during a reasonable period of administration. Examples of these expenses could include investment advisory fees, stock brokerage commissions, custodial fees, and interest.

(ii) Transmission expenses. Estate transmission expenses are expenses that would not have been incurred but for the decedent's death and the consequent necessity of collecting the decedent's assets, paying the decedent's debts and death taxes, and distributing the decedent's property to those who are entitled to receive it. Estate transmission expenses include any administration expense that is not a management expense. Examples of these expenses could include executor commissions and attorney fees (except to the extent of commissions or fees specifically related to investment, preservation, or maintenance of the assets), probate fees, expenses incurred in construction proceedings and defending against will contests, and appraisal fees.

(iii) Marital share. The marital share is the property or interest in property that passed from the decedent for which a deduction is allowable under section 2056(a). The marital share includes the income produced by the property or interest in property during the period of administration if the income, under the terms of the governing instrument or applicable local law, is payable to the surviving spouse or is to be added to the principal of the property interest passing to, or for the benefit of, the surviving spouse.

(2) Effect of transmission expenses. For purposes of determining the marital deduction, the value of the marital share shall be reduced by the amount of the estate transmission expenses paid from the marital share.

(3) Effect of management expenses attributable to the marital share. For purposes of determining the marital deduction, the value of the marital share shall not be reduced by the amount of the estate management expenses attributable to and paid from the marital share. Pursuant to section 2056(b)(9), however, the amount of the allowable marital deduction shall be reduced by the amount of any such management expenses that are deducted under section 2053 on the decedent's Federal estate tax return.

(4) Effect of management expenses not attributable to the marital share. For purposes of determining the marital deduction, the value of the marital share shall be reduced by the amount of the estate management expenses paid from the marital share but attributable to a property interest not included in the marital share.

(5) Examples. The following examples illustrate the application of this paragraph (d):

Example (1). The decedent dies after 2006 having made no lifetime gifts. The decedent makes a bequest of shares of ABC Corporation stock to the decedent's child. The bequest provides that the child is to receive the income from the shares from the date of the decedent's death. The value of the bequeathed shares on the decedent's date of death is $3,000,000. The residue of the estate is bequeathed to a trust for which the executor properly makes an election under section 2056(b)(7) to treat as qualified terminable interest property. The value of the residue on the decedent's date of death, before the payment of administration expenses and Federal and State estate taxes, is $6,000,000. Under applicable local law, the executor has the discretion to pay administration expenses from the income or principal of the residuary estate. All estate taxes are to be paid from the residue. The State estate tax equals the State death tax credit available under section 2011.

During the period of administration, the estate incurs estate transmission expenses of $400,000, which the executor charges to the residue. For purposes of determining the marital deduction, the value of the residue is reduced by the Federal and State estate taxes and by the estate transmission expenses. If the transmission expenses are deducted on the Federal estate tax return, the marital deduction is $3,500,000 ($6,000,000 minus $400,000 transmission expenses and minus $2,100,000 Federal and State estate taxes). If the transmission expenses are deducted on the estate's Federal income tax return rather than on the estate tax return, the marital deduction is $3,011,111 ($6,000,000 minus $400,000 transmission expenses and minus $2,588,889 Federal and State estate taxes).

Example (2). The facts are the same as in Example 1, except that, instead of incurring estate transmission expenses, the estate incurs estate management expenses of $400,000 in connection with the residue property passing for the benefit of the spouse. The executor charges these management expenses to the residue. In determining the value of the residue passing to the spouse for marital deduction purposes, a reduction is made for Federal and State estate taxes payable from the residue but no reduction is made for the estate management expenses. If the management expenses are deducted on the estate's income tax return, the net value of the property passing to the spouse is $3,900,000 ($6,000,000 minus $2,100,000 Federal and State estate taxes). A marital deduction is claimed for that amount, and the taxable estate is $5,100,000.

Example (3). The facts are the same as in Example 1, except that the estate management expenses of $400,000 are incurred in connection with the bequest of ABC Corporation stock to the decedent's child. The executor charges these management expenses to the residue. For purposes of determining the marital deduction, the value of the residue is reduced by the Federal and State estate taxes and by the management expenses. The management expenses reduce the value of the residue because they are charged to the property passing to the spouse even though they were incurred with respect to stock passing to the child. If the management expenses are deducted on the estate's Federal income tax return, the marital deduction is $3,011,111 ($6,000,000 minus $400,000 management expenses and minus $2,588,889 Federal and State estate taxes). If the management expenses are deducted on the estate's Federal estate tax return, rather than on the estate's Federal income tax return, the marital deduction is $3,500,000 ($6,000,000 minus $400,000 management expenses and minus $2,100,000 in Federal and State estate taxes).

Example (4). The decedent, who dies in 2000, has a gross estate of $3,000,000. Included in the gross estate are proceeds of $150,000 from a policy insuring the decedent's life and payable to the decedent's child as beneficiary. The applicable credit amount against the tax was fully consumed by the decedent's lifetime gifts. Applicable State law requires the child to pay any estate taxes attributable to the life insurance policy. Pursuant to the decedent's will, the rest of the decedent's estate passes outright to the surviving spouse. During the period of administration, the estate incurs estate management expenses of $150,000 in connection with the property passing to the spouse. The value of the property passing to the spouse is $2,850,000 ($3,000,000 less the insurance proceeds of $150,000 passing to the child). For purposes of determining the marital deduction, if the management expenses are deducted on the estate's income tax return, the marital deduction is $2,850,000 ($3,000,000 less $150,000) and there is a resulting taxable estate of $150,000 ($3,000,000 less a marital deduction of $2,850,000). Suppose, instead, the management expenses of $150,000 are deducted on the estate's estate tax return under section 2053 as expenses of administration. In such a situation, claiming a marital deduction of $2,850,000 would be taking a deduction for the same $150,000 in property under both sections 2053 and 2056 and would shield from estate taxes the $150,000 in insurance proceeds passing to the decedent's child. Therefore, in accordance with section 2056(b)(9), the marital deduction is limited to $2,700,000, and the resulting taxable estate is $150,000.

Example (5). The decedent dies after 2006 having made no lifetime gifts. The value of the decedent's residuary estate on the decedent's date of death is $3,000,000, before the payment of administration expenses and Federal and State estate taxes. The decedent's will provides a formula for dividing the decedent's residuary estate between two trusts to reduce the estate's Federal estate taxes to zero. Under the formula, one trust, for the benefit of the decedent's child, is to be funded with that amount of property equal in value to so much of the applicable exclusion amount under section 2010 that would reduce the estate's Federal estate tax to zero. The other trust, for the benefit of the surviving spouse, satisfies the requirements of section 2056(b)(7) and is to be funded with the remaining property in the estate. The State estate tax equals the State death tax credit available under section 2011. During the period of administration, the estate incurs transmission expenses of $200,000. The transmission expenses of $200,000 reduce the value of the residue to $2,800,000. If the transmission expenses are deducted on the Federal estate tax return, then the formula divides the residue so that the value of the property passing to the child's trust is $1,000,000 and the value of the property passing to the marital trust is $1,800,000. The allowable marital deduction is $1,800,000. The applicable exclusion amount shields from Federal estate tax the entire $1,000,000 passing to the child's trust so that the amount of Federal and State estate taxes is zero. Alternatively, if the transmission expenses are deducted on the estate's Federal income tax return, the formula divides the residue so that the value of the property passing to the child's trust is $800,000 and the value of the property passing to the marital trust is $2,000,000. The allowable marital deduction is $2,000,000. The applicable exclusion amount shields from Federal estate tax the entire $800,000 passing to the child's trust so that the amount of Federal and State estate taxes remains zero.

Example (6). The facts are the same as in Example 5, except that the decedent's will provides that the child's trust is to be funded with that amount of property equal in value to the applicable exclusion amount under section 2010 allowable to the decedent's estate. The residue of the estate, after the payment of any debts, expenses, and Federal and State estate taxes, is to pass to the marital trust. The applicable exclusion amount in this case is $1,000,000, so the value of the property passing to the child's trust is $1,000,000. After deducting the $200,000 of transmission expenses, the residue of the estate is $1,800,000 less any estate taxes. If the transmission expenses are deducted on the Federal estate tax return, the allowable marital deduction is $1,800,000, the taxable estate is zero, and the Federal and State estate taxes are zero. Alternatively, if the transmission expenses are deducted on the estate's Federal income tax return, the net value of the property passing to the spouse is $1,657,874 ($1,800,000 minus $142,106 estate taxes). A marital deduction is claimed for that amount, the taxable estate is $1,342,106, and the Federal and State estate taxes total $142,106.

Example (7). The decedent, who dies in 2000, makes an outright pecuniary bequest of $3,000,000 to the decedent's surviving spouse, and the residue of the estate, after the payment of all debts, expenses, and Federal and State estate taxes, passes to the decedent's child. Under the terms of the governing instrument and applicable local law, a beneficiary of a pecuniary bequest is not entitled to any income on the bequest. During the period of administration, the estate pays estate transmission expenses from the income earned by the property that will be distributed to the surviving spouse in satisfaction of the pecuniary bequest. The income earned on this property is not part of the marital share. Therefore, the allowable marital deduction is $3,000,000, unreduced by the amount of the estate transmission expenses.

(6) Effective date. The provisions of this paragraph (d) apply to estates of decedents dying on or after December 3, 1999.

(e) Remainder interests. If the income from property is made payable to another individual for life, or for a term of years, with remainder absolutely to the surviving spouse or to her estate, the marital deduction is based upon the present value of the remainder. The present value of the remainder is to be determined in accordance with the rules stated in § 20.2031-7. For example, if the surviving spouse is to receive $50,000 upon the death of a person aged 31 years, the present value of the remainder is $14,466. If the remainder is such that its value is to be determined by a special computation (see paragraph (b) of § 20.2031-7), a request for a specific factor may be submitted to the Commissioner. The request should be accompanied by a statement of the date of birth of each person, the duration of whose life may affect the value of the remainder, and copies of the relevant instruments. The Commissioner may, if conditions permit, supply the factor requested. If the Commissioner does not furnish the factor, the claim for deduction must be supported by a full statement of the computation of the present value made in accordance with the principles set forth in the applicable paragraphs of § 20.2031-7.

T.D. 6296, 6/23/58, amend T.D. 8522, 2/28/94, T.D. 8540, 6/9/94, T.D. 8846, 12/2/99.

§ 20.2056(b)-5 Marital deduction; life estate with power of appointment in surviving spouse.

(a) In general. Section 2056(b)(5) provides that if an interest in property passes from the decedent to his surviving spouse (whether or not in trust) and the spouse is entitled for life to all the income from the entire interest or all the income from a specific portion of the entire interest, with a power in her to appoint the entire interest or the specific portion, the interest which passes to her is a deductible interest, to the extent that it satisfies all five of the conditions set forth below (see paragraph (b) of this section if one or more of the conditions is satisfied as to only a portion of the interest):

(1) The surviving spouse must be entitled for life to all of the income from the entire interest or a specific portion of the entire interest, or to a specific portion of all the income from the entire interest.

(2) The income payable to the surviving spouse must be payable annually or at more frequent intervals.

(3) The surviving spouse must have the power to appoint the entire interest or the specific portion to either herself or her estate.

(4) The power in the surviving spouse must be exercisable by her alone and (whether exercisable by will or during life) must be exercisable in all events.

(5) The entire interest or the specific portion must not be subject to a power in any other person to appoint any part to any person other than the surviving spouse.

(b) Specific portion; deductible amount. If either the right to income or the power of appointment passing to the surviving spouse pertains only to a specific portion of a property interest passing from the decedent, the marital deduction is allowed only to the extent that the rights in the surviving spouse meet all of the five conditions described in paragraph (a) of this section. While the rights over the income and the power must coexist as to the same interest in property, it is not necessary that the rights over the income or the power as to such interest be in the same proportion. However, if the rights over income meeting the required conditions set forth in paragraph (a)(1) and (2) of this section extend over a smaller share of the property interest than the share with respect to which the power of appointment requirements set forth in paragraph (a)(3) through (5) of this section are satisfied, the deductible interest is limited to the smaller share. Correspondingly, if a power of appointment meeting all the requirements extends to a smaller portion of the property interest than the portion over which the income rights pertain, the deductible interest cannot exceed the value of the portion to which such power of appointment applies. Thus, if the decedent leaves to his surviving spouse the right to receive annually all of the income from a particular property interest and a power of appointment meeting the specifications prescribed in paragraph (a)(3) through (5) of this section as to only one-half of the property interest, then only one-half of the property interest is treated as a deductible interest. Correspondingly, if the income interest of the spouse satisfying the requirements extends to only one-fourth of the property interest and a testamentary power of appointment satisfying the requirements extends to all of the property interest, then only one-fourth of the interest in the spouse qualifies as a deductible interest. Further, if the surviving spouse has no right to income from a specific portion of a property interest but a testamentary power of appointment which meets the necessary conditions over the entire interest, then none of the interest qualifies for the deduction. In addition, if, from the time of the decedent's death, the surviving spouse has a power of appointment meeting all of the required conditions over three-fourths of the entire property interest and the prescribed income rights over the entire interest, but with a power in another person to appoint one-half of the entire interest, the value of the interest in the surviving spouse over only one-half of the property interest will qualify as a deductible interest.

(c) Meaning of specific portion. *(1) In general.* Except as provided in paragraphs (c)(2) and (c)(3) of this section, a partial interest in property is not treated as a specific portion of the entire interest. In addition, any specific portion of an entire interest in property is nondeductible to the extent the specific portion is subject to invasion for the benefit of any person other than the surviving spouse, except in the case of a deduction allowable under section 2056(b)(5), relating to the exercise of a general power of appointment by the surviving spouse.

(2) Fraction or percentage share. Under section 2056(b)(10), a partial interest in property is treated as a specific portion of the entire interest if the rights of the surviving spouse in income, and the required rights as to the power described in § 20.2056(b)-5(a), constitute a fractional or percentage share of the entire property interest, so that the surviving spouse's interest reflects its proportionate share of the increase or decrease in the value of the entire property interest to which the income rights and the power relate. Thus, if the spouse's right to income and the spouse's power extend to a specified fraction or percentage of the property, or the equivalent, the interest is in a specific portion of the property. In accordance with paragraph (b) of this section, if the spouse has the right to receive the income from a specific portion of the trust property (after applying paragraph (c)(3) of this section) but has a power of appointment over a different specific portion of the property (after applying paragraph (c)(3) of this section), the marital deduction is limited to the lesser specific portion.

(3) Special rule in the case of estates of decedents dying on or before October 24, 1992, and certain decedents dying after October 24, 1992, with wills or revocable trusts executed on or prior to that date. (i) In the case of estates of decedents within the purview of the effective date and transitional rules contained in paragraphs (c)(3)(ii) and (iii) of this section:

(A) A specific sum payable annually, or at more frequent intervals, out of the property and its income that is not limited by the income of the property is treated as the right to receive the income from a specific portion of the property. The specific portion, for purposes of paragraph (c)(2) of this section, is the portion of the property that, assuming the interest rate generally applicable for the valuation of annuities at the time of the decedent's death, would produce income equal to such payments. However, a pecuniary amount payable annually to a surviving spouse is not treated as a right to the income from a specific portion of the trust property for purposes of this paragraph (c)(3)(i)(A) if any person other than the surviving spouse may receive, during the surviving spouse's lifetime, any distribution of the property. To determine the applicable interest rate for valuing annuities, see sections 2031 and 7520 and the regulations under those sections.

(B) The right to appoint a pecuniary amount out of a larger fund (or trust corpus) is considered the right to appoint a specific portion of such fund or trust for purposes of paragraph (c)(2) in an amount equal to such pecuniary amount.

(ii) The rules contained in paragraphs (c)(3)(i)(A) and (B) of this section apply with respect to estates of decedents dying on or before October 24, 1992.

(iii) The rules contained in paragraphs (c)(3)(i)(A) and (B) of this section apply in the case of decedents dying after October 24, 1992, if property passes to the spouse pursuant to a will or revocable trust agreement executed on or before October 24, 1992, and either—

(A) On that date, the decedent was under a mental disability to change the disposition of the property and did not regain competence to dispose of such property before the date of death; or

(B) The decedent dies prior to October 24, 1995.

(iv) Notwithstanding paragraph (c)(3)(iii) of this section, paragraphs (c)(3)(i)(A) and (B) of this section do not apply if the will or revocable trust is amended after October 24, 1992, in any respect that increases the amount of the transfer qualifying for the marital deduction or alters the terms by which the interest so passes to the surviving spouse of the decedent.

(4) Local law. A partial interest in property is treated as a specific portion of the entire interest if it is shown that the surviving spouse has rights under local law that are identical to those the surviving spouse would have acquired had the partial interest been expressed in terms satisfying the requirements of paragraph (c)(2) (or paragraph (c)(3) if applicable) of this section.

(5) Examples. The following examples illustrate the application of paragraphs (a) through (c)(4) of this section:

Example (1). Spouse entitled to the lesser of an annuity or a fraction of trust income. The decedent, D, died prior to October 24, 1992. D bequeathed in trust 500 identical shares of X company stock, valued for estate tax purposes at $500,000. The trust provides that during the lifetime of D's spouse, S, the trustee is to pay annually to S the lesser of one-half of the trust income or $20,000. Any trust income not paid to S is to be accumulated in the trust and may not be distributed during S's lifetime. S has a testamentary general power of appointment over the entire trust principal. The applicable interest rate for valuing annuities as of D's date of death under section 7520 is 10 percent. For purposes of paragraphs (a) through (c) of this section, S is treated as receiving all of the income from the lesser of—

(i) One half of the stock ($250,000); or

(ii) $200,000, the specific portion of the stock which, as determined in accordance with § 20.2056(b)-5(c)(3)(i)(A), would produce annual income of $20,000 (20,000/.10). Accordingly, the marital deduction is limited to $200,000 (200,000/500,000 or ⅖ of the value of the trust).

Example (2). Spouse possesses power and income interest over different specific portions of trust. The facts are the same as in Example 1 except that S's testamentary general power of appointment is exercisable over only ¼ of the trust principal. Consequently, under section 2056(b)(5), the marital deduction is allowable only for the value of ¼of the trust ($125,000); i.e., the lesser of the value of the portion with respect to which S is deemed to be entitled to all of the income (⅖ of the trust or $200,000), or the value of the portion with respect to which S possesses the requisite power of appointment (¼ of the trust or $125,000).

Example (3). Power of appointment over pecuniary amount. The decedent, D, died prior to October 24, 1992. D bequeathed property valued at $400,000 for estate tax purposes in trust. The trustee is to pay annually to D's spouse, S, one-fourth of the trust income. Any trust income not paid to S is to be accumulated in the trust and may not be distributed during S's lifetime. The will gives S a testamentary general power of appointment over the sum of $160,000. Because D died prior to October 24, 1992, S's power of appointment over $160,000 is treated as a power of appointment over a specific portion of the entire trust interest. The marital deduction allowable under section 2056(b)(5) is limited to $100,000; that is, the lesser of—

(1) The value of the trust corpus ($400,000);

(2) The value of the trust corpus over which S has a power of appointment ($160,000); or

(3) That specific portion of the trust with respect to which S is entitled to all the income ($100,000).

Example (4). Power of appointment over shares of stock constitutes a power over a specific portion. Under D's will, 250 shares of Y company stock were bequeathed in trust pursuant to which all trust income was payable annually to S, D's spouse, for life. S was given a testamentary general power of appointment over 100 shares of stock. The trust provides that if the trustee sells the Y company stock, S's general power of appointment is exercisable with respect to the sale proceeds or the property in which the proceeds are reinvested. Because the amount of property represented by a single share of stock would be altered if the corporation split its stock, issued stock dividends, made a distribution of capital, etc., a power to appoint 100 shares at the time of S's death is not necessarily a power to appoint the entire interest that the 100 shares represented on the date of D's death. If it is shown that, under local law, S has a general power to appoint not only the 100 shares designated by D but also 100/250 of any distributions by the corporation that are included in trust principal, the requirements of paragraph (c)(2) of this section are satisfied and S is treated as having a general power to appoint 100/250 of the entire interest in the 250 shares. In that case, the marital deduction is limited to 40 percent of the trust principal. If local law does not give S that power, the 100 shares would not constitute a specific portion under § 20.2056(b)-5(c) (including § 20.2056(b)-5(c)(3)(i)(B)). The nature of the asset is such that a change in the capitalization of the corporation could cause an alteration in the original value represented by the shares at the time of D's death and, thus, it does not represent a specific portion of the trust.

(d) Meaning of entire interest. Because a marital deduction is allowed for each separate qualifying interest in property passing from the decedent to the decedent's surviving spouse (subject to any applicable limitations in § 20.2056(a)-1(c)), for purposes of paragraphs (a) and (b) of this section, each property interest with respect to which the surviving spouse received any rights is considered separately in determining whether the surviving spouse's rights extend to the entire interest or to a specific portion of the entire interest. A property interest which consists of several identical units of property (such as a block of 250 shares of stock, whether the ownership is evidenced by one or several certificates) is considered one property interest, unless certain of the units are to be segregated and accorded different treatment, in which case each segregated group of items is considered a separate property interest. The bequest of a specified sum of money constitutes the bequest of a separate property interest if immediately following distribution by the executor and thenceforth it, and the investments made with it, must be so segregated or accounted for as to permit its identification as a separate item of property. The application of this paragraph may be illustrated by the following examples:

Example (1). The decedent transferred to a trustee three adjoining farms, Blackacre, Whiteacre, and Greenacre. His will provided that during the lifetime of the surviving spouse the trustee should pay her all of the income from the trust. Upon her death, all of Blackacre, a one-half interest in Whiteacre, and a one-third interest in Greenacre were to be distributed to the person or persons appointed by her in her will. The surviving spouse is considered as being entitled to all of the income from the entire interest in Blackacre, all of the income from the entire interest in Whiteacre, and all of the income from the entire interest in Greenacre. She also is considered as having a power of appointment over the entire interest in Blackacre, over one-half of the entire interest in Whiteacre, and over one-third of the entire interest in Greenacre.

Example (2). The decedent bequeathed $250,000 to C, as trustee. C is to invest the money and pay all of the income from the investments to W, the decedent's surviving spouse, annually. W was given a general power, exercisable by will, to appoint one-half of the corpus of the trust. Here, immediately following distribution by the executor, the $250,000 will be sufficiently segregated to permit its identification as a separate item, and the $250,000 will constitute an entire property interest. Therefore, W has a right to income and a power of appointment such that one-half of the entire interest is a deductible interest.

Example (3). The decedent bequeathed 100 shares of Z Corporation stock to D, as trustee. W, the decedent's surviving spouse, is to receive all of the income of the trust annually and is given a general power, exercisable by will, to appoint out of the trust corpus the sum of $25,000. In this case the $25,000 is not, immediately following distribution, sufficiently segregated to permit its identification as a separate item of property in which the surviving spouse has the entire interest. Therefore, the $25,000 does not constitute the entire interest in a property for the purpose of paragraphs (a) and (b) of this section.

(e) Application of local law. In determining whether or not the conditions set forth in paragraph (a)(1) through (5) of this section are satisfied by the instrument of transfer, regard is to be had to the applicable provisions of the law of the jurisdiction under which the interest passes and, if the transfer is in trust, the applicable provisions of the law governing the administration of the trust. For example, silence of a trust instrument as to the frequency of payment will not be regarded as a failure to satisfy the condition set forth in paragraph (a)(2) of this section that income must be payable to the surviving spouse annually or more frequently unless the applicable law permits payment to be made less frequently than annually. The principles outlined in this paragraph and paragraphs (f) and (g) of this section which are applied in determining whether transfers in trust meet such conditions are equally applicable in ascertaining whether, in the case of interests not in trust, the surviving spouse has the equivalent in rights over income and over the property.

(f) Right to income. *(1)* If an interest is transferred in trust, the surviving spouse is "entitled for life to all of the income from the entire interest or a specific portion of the entire interest", for the purpose of the condition set forth in paragraph (a)(1) of this section, if the effect of the trust is to give her substantially that degree of beneficial enjoyment of the trust property during her life which the principles of the law of trusts accord to a person who is unqualifiedly designated as the life beneficiary of a trust. Such degree of enjoyment is given only if it was the decedent's intention, as manifested by the terms of the trust instrument and the surrounding circumstances, that the trust should produce for the surviving spouse during her life such an income, or that the spouse should have such use of the trust property as is consistent with the value of the trust corpus and with its preservation. The designation of the spouse as sole income beneficiary for life of the entire interest or a specific portion of the entire interest will be sufficient to qualify the trust unless the terms of the trust and the surrounding circumstances considered as a whole evidence an intention to deprive the spouse of the requisite degree of enjoyment. In determining whether a trust evidences that intention, the treatment required or permitted with respect to individual items must be considered in relation to the entire system provided for the administration of the trust. In addition, the surviving spouse's interest shall meet the condition set forth in paragraph (a)(1) of this section if the spouse is entitled to income as determined by applicable local law that provides for a reasonable apportionment between the income and remainder beneficiaries of the total return of the trust and that meets the requirements of § 1.643(b)-1 of this chapter.

(2) If the over-all effect of a trust is to give to the surviving spouse such enforceable rights as will preserve to her the requisite degree of enjoyment, it is immaterial whether that result is effected by rules specifically stated in the trust instrument, or, in their absence, by the rules for the management of the trust property and the allocation of receipts and expenditures supplied by the State law. For example, a provision in the trust instrument for amortization of bond premium by appropriate periodic charges to interest will not disqualify the interest passing in trust even though there is no State law specifically authorizing amortization, or there is a State law denying amortization which is applicable only in the absence of such a provision in the trust instrument.

(3) In the case of a trust, the rules to be applied by the trustee in allocation of receipts and expenses between income and corpus must be considered in relation to the nature and expected productivity of the assets passing in trust, the nature and frequency of occurrence of the expected receipts, and any provisions as to change in the form of investments. If it is evident from the nature of the trust assets and the rules provided for management of the trust that the allocation to income of such receipts as rents, ordinary cash dividends, and interest will give to the spouse the substantial enjoyment during life required by the statute, provisions that such receipts as stock dividends and proceeds from the conversion of trust assets shall be treated as corpus will not disqualify the interest passing in trust. Similarly, provision for a depletion charge against income in the case of trust assets which are subject to depletion will not disqualify the interest passing in trust, unless the effect is to deprive the spouse of the requisite beneficial enjoyment. The same principle is applicable in the case of depreciation, trustees' commissions, and other charges.

(4) Provisions granting administrative powers to the trustee will not have the effect of disqualifying an interest passing in trust unless the grant of powers evidences the intention to deprive the surviving spouse of the beneficial enjoyment required by the statute. Such an intention will not be considered to exist if the entire terms of the instrument are such that the local courts will impose reasonable limitations upon the exercise of the powers. Among the powers which if subject to reasonable limitations will not disqualify the interest passing in trust are the power to determine the allocation or apportionment of receipts and disbursements between income and corpus, the power to apply the income or corpus for the benefit of the spouse, and the power to retain the assets passing to the trust. For example, a power to retain trust assets which consist substantially of unproductive property will not disqualify the interest if the applicable rules for the administration of the trust require, or permit the spouse to require, that the trustee either make the property productive or convert it within a reasonable time. Nor will such a power disqualify the interest if the applicable rules for administration of the trust require the trustee to use the degree of judgment and care in the exercise of the power which a prudent man would use if he were owner of the trust assets. Further, a power to retain a residence or other property for the personal use of the spouse will not disqualify the interest passing in trust.

(5) An interest passing in trust will not satisfy the condition set forth in paragraph (a)(1) of this section that the surviving spouse be entitled to all the income if the primary purpose of the trust is to safeguard property without providing the spouse with the required beneficial enjoyment. Such trusts include not only trusts which expressly provide for the accumulation of the income but also trusts which indirectly accomplish a similar purpose. For example, assume that the corpus of a trust consists substantially of property which is not likely to be income producing during the life of the surviving spouse and that the spouse cannot compel the trustee to convert or otherwise deal with the property as described in subparagraph (4) of this paragraph. An interest passing to such a trust will not qualify unless the applicable rules for the administration require, or permit the spouse to require, that the trustee provide the required beneficial enjoyment, such as by payments to the spouse out of other assets of the trust.

(6) If a trust is created during the decedent's life, it is immaterial whether or not the interest passing in trust satisfied the conditions set forth in paragraph (a)(1) through (5) of this section prior to the decedent's death. If a trust may be terminated during the life of the surviving spouse, under her exercise of a power of appointment or by distribution of the corpus to her, the interest passing in trust satisfies the condition set forth in paragraph (a)(1) of this section (that the spouse be entitled to all the income) if she (i) is entitled to the income until the trust terminates, or (ii) has the right, ex-

ercisable in all events, to have the corpus distributed to her at any time during her life.

(7) An interest passing in trust fails to satisfy the conditions set forth in paragraph (a)(1) of this section, that the spouse be entitled to all the income, to the extent that the income is required to be accumulated in whole or in part or may be accumulated in the discretion of any person other than the surviving spouse; to the extent that the consent of any person other than the surviving spouse is required as a condition precedent to distribution of the income; or to the extent that any person other than the surviving spouse has the power to alter the terms of the trust so as to deprive her of her right to the income. An interest passing in trust will not fail to satisfy the condition that the spouse be entitled to all the income merely because its terms provide that the right of the surviving spouse to the income shall not be subject to assignment, alienation, pledge, attachment or claims of creditors.

(8) In the case of an interest passing in trust, the terms "entitled for life" and "payable annually or at more frequent intervals," as used in the conditions set forth in paragraph (a)(1) and (2) of this section, require that under the terms of the trust the income referred to must be currently (at least annually; see paragraph (e) of this section) distributable to the spouse or that she must have such command over the income that it is virtually hers. Thus, the conditions in paragraph (a)(1) and (2) of this section are satisfied in this respect if, under the terms of the trust instrument, the spouse has the right exercisable annually (or more frequently) to require distribution to herself of the trust income, and otherwise the trust income is to be accumulated and added to corpus. Similarly, as respects the income for the period between the last distribution date and the date of the spouse's death, it is sufficient if that income is subject to the spouse's power to appoint. Thus, if the trust instrument provides that income accrued or undistributed on the date of the spouse's death is to be disposed of as if it had been received after her death, and if the spouse has a power of appointment over the trust corpus, the power necessarily extends to the undistributed income.

(9) An interest is not to be regarded as failing to satisfy the conditions set forth in paragraph (a)(1) and (2) of this section (that the spouse be entitled to all the income and that it be payable annually or more frequently) merely because the spouse is not entitled to the income from estate assets for the period before distribution of those assets by the executor, unless the executor is, by the decedent's will, authorized or directed to delay distribution beyond the period reasonably required for administration of the decedent's estate. As to the valuation of the property interest passing to the spouse in trust where the right to income is expressly postponed, see § 20.2056(b)-4.

(g) Power of appointment in surviving spouse. *(1)* The conditions set forth in paragraph (a)(3) and (4) of this section, that is, that the surviving spouse must have a power of appointment exercisable in favor of herself or her estate and exercisable alone and in all events, are not met unless the power of the surviving spouse to appoint the entire interest or a specific portion of it falls within one of the following categories:

(i) A power so to appoint fully exercisable in her own favor at any time following the decedent's death (as, for example, an unlimited power to invade); or

(ii) A power so to appoint exercisable in favor of her estate. Such a power, if exercisable during life, must be fully exercisable at any time during life, or, if exercisable by will, must be fully exercisable irrespective of the time of her death (subject in either case to the provisions of § 20.2053(b)-3, relating to interests conditioned on survival for a limited period); or

(iii) A combination of the powers described under subdivisions (i) and (ii) of this subparagraph. For example, the surviving spouse may, until she attains the age of 50 years, have a power to appoint to herself and thereafter have a power to appoint to her estate. However, the condition that the spouse's power must be exercisable in all events is not satisfied unless irrespective of when the surviving spouse may die the entire interest or a specific portion of it will at the time of her death be subject to one power or the other (subject to the exception in § 20.2053(b)-3, relating to interests contingent on survival for a limited period).

(2) The power of the surviving spouse must be a power to appoint the entire interest or a specific portion of it as unqualified owner (and free of the trust if a trust is involved, or free of the joint tenancy if a joint tenancy is involved) or to appoint the entire interest or a specific portion of it as a part of her estate (and free of the trust if a trust is involved), that is, in effect, to dispose of it to whomsoever she pleases. Thus, if the decedent devised property to a son and the surviving spouse as joint tenants with right of survivorship and under local law the surviving spouse has a power of severance exercisable without consent of the other joint tenant, and by exercising this power could acquire a one-half interest in the property as a tenant in common, her power of severance will satisfy the condition set forth in paragraph (a)(3) of this section that she have a power of appointment in favor of herself or her estate. However, if the surviving spouse entered into a binding agreement with the decedent to exercise the power only in favor of their issue, that condition is not met. An interest passing in trust will not be regarded as failing to satisfy the condition merely because takers in default of the surviving spouse's exercise of the power are designated by the decedent. The decedent may provide that, in default of exercise of the power, the trust shall continue for an additional period.

(3) A power is not considered to be a power exercisable by a surviving spouse alone and in all events as required by paragraph (a)(4) of this section if the exercise of the power in the surviving spouse to appoint the entire interest or a specific portion of it to herself or to her estate requires the joinder or consent of any other person. The power is not "exercisable in all events", if it can be terminated during the life of the surviving spouse by any event other than her complete exercise or release of it. Further, a power is not "exercisable in all events" if it may be exercised for a limited purpose only. For example, a power which is not exercisable in the event of the spouse's remarriage is not exercisable in all events. Likewise, if there are any restrictions, either by the terms of the instrument or under applicable local law, on the exercise of a power to consume property (whether or not held in trust) for the benefit of the spouse, the power is not exercisable in all events. Thus, if a power of invasion is exercisable only for the spouse's support, or only for her limited use, the power is not exercisable in all events. In order for a power of invasion to be exercisable in all events, the surviving spouse must have the unrestricted power exercisable at any time during her life to use all or any part of the property subject to the power, and to dispose of it in any manner, including the power to dispose of it by gift (whether or not she has power to dispose of it by will).

(4) The power in the surviving spouse is exercisable in all events only if it exists immediately following the decedent's

death. For example, if the power given to the surviving spouse is exercisable during life, but cannot be effectively exercised before distribution of the assets by the executor, the power is not exercisable in all events. Similarly, if the power is exercisable by will, but cannot be effectively exercised in the event the surviving spouse dies before distribution of the assets by the executor, the power is not exercisable in all events. However, an interest will not be disqualified by the mere fact that, in the event the power is exercised during administration of the estate, distribution of the property to the appointee will be delayed for the period of administration. If the power is in existence at all times following the decedent's death, limitations of a formal nature will not disqualify an interest. Examples of formal limitations on a power exercisable during life are requirements that an exercise must be in a particular form, that it must be filed with a trustee during the spouse's life, that reasonable notice must be given, or that reasonable intervals must elapse between successive partial exercises. Examples of formal limitations on a power exercisable by will are that it must be exercised by a will executed by the surviving spouse after the decedent's death or that exercise must be by specific reference to the power.

(5) If the surviving spouse has the requisite power to appoint to herself or her estate, it is immaterial that she also has one or more lesser powers. Thus, if she has a testamentary power to appoint to her estate, she may also have a limited power of withdrawal or of appointment during her life. Similarly, if she has an unlimited power of withdrawal, she may have a limited testamentary power.

(h) Requirement of survival for a limited period. A power of appointment in the surviving spouse will not be treated as failing to meet the requirements of paragraph (a)(3) of this section even though the power may terminate, if the only conditions which would cause the termination are those described in paragraph (a) of § 20.2056(b)-3, and if those conditions do not in fact occur. Thus, the entire interest or a specific portion of it will not be disqualified by reason of the fact that the exercise of the power in the spouse is subject to a condition of survivorship described in § 20.2056(b)-3 if the terms of the condition, that is, the survivorship of the surviving spouse, or the failure to die in a common disaster, are fulfilled.

(i) [Reserved]

(j) Existence of a power in another. Paragraph (a)(5) of this section provides that a transfer described in paragraph (a) is nondeductible to the extent that the decedent created a power in the trustee or in any other person to appoint a part of the interest to any person other than the surviving spouse. However, only powers in other persons which are in opposition to that of the surviving spouse will cause a portion of the interest to fail to satisfy the condition set forth in paragraph (a)(5) of this section. Thus, a power in a trustee to distribute corpus to or for the benefit of a surviving spouse will not disqualify the trust. Similarly, a power to distribute corpus to the spouse for the support of minor children will not disqualify the trust if she is legally obligated to support such children. The application of this paragraph may be illustrated by the following examples:

Example (1). Assume that a decedent created a trust, designating his surviving spouse as income beneficiary for life with an unrestricted power in the spouse to appoint the corpus during her life. The decedent further provided that in the event the surviving spouse should die without having exercised the power, the trust should continue for the life of his son with a power in the son to appoint the corpus. Since the power in the son could become exercisable only after the death of the surviving spouse, the interest is not regarded as failing to satisfy the condition set forth in paragraph (a)(5) of this section.

Example (2). Assume that the decedent created a trust, designating his surviving spouse as income beneficiary for life and as donee of a power to appoint by will the entire corpus. The decedent further provided that the trustee could distribute 30 percent of the corpus to the decedent's son when he reached the age of 35 years. Since the trustee has a power to appoint 30 percent of the entire interest for the benefit of a person other than the surviving spouse, only 70 percent of the interest placed in trust satisfied the condition set forth in paragraph (a)(5) of this section. If, in this case, the surviving spouse had a power, exercisable by her will, to appoint only one-half of the corpus as it was constituted at the time of her death, it should be noted that only 35 percent of the interest placed in the trust would satisfy the condition set forth in paragraph (a)(3) of this section.

T.D. 6296, 6/23/58, amend T.D. 8522, 2/28/94, T.D. 9102, 12/30/2003.

---

§ 20.2056(b)-6 Marital deduction; life insurance or annuity payments with power of appointment in surviving spouse.

(a) In general. Section 2056(b)(6) provides that an interest in property passing from a decedent to his surviving spouse, which consists of proceeds held by an insurer under the terms of a life insurance, endowment, or annuity contract, is a "deductible interest" to the extent that it satisfied all five of the following conditions (see paragraph (b) of this section if one or more of the conditions is satisfied as to only a portion of the proceeds):

(1) The proceeds, or a specific portion of the proceeds, must be held by the insurer subject to an agreement either to pay the entire proceeds or a specific portion thereof in installments, or to pay interest thereon, and all or a specific portion of the installments or interest payable during the life of the surviving spouse must be payable only to her.

(2) The installments or interest payable to the surviving spouse must be payable annually, or more frequently, commencing not later than 13 months after the decedent's death.

(3) The surviving spouse must have the power to appoint all or a specific portion of the amounts so held by the insurer to either herself or her estate.

(4) The power in the surviving spouse must be exercisable by her alone and (whether exercisable by will or during life) must be exercisable in all events.

(5) The amounts or the specific portion of the amounts payable under such contract must not be subject to a power in any other person to appoint any part thereof to any person other than the surviving spouse.

(b) Specific portion; deductible interest. If the right to receive interest or installment payments or the power of appointment passing to the surviving spouse pertains only to a specific portion of the proceeds held by the insurer, the marital deduction is allowed only to the extent that the rights of the surviving spouse in the specific portion meet the five conditions described in paragraph (a) of this section. While the rights to interest, or to receive payment in installments, and the power must coexist as to the proceeds of the same contract, it is not necessary that the rights to each be in the same proportion. If the rights to interest meeting the required conditions set forth in paragraph (a)(1) and (2) of this section extend over a smaller share of the proceeds than the share with respect to which the power of appointment requirements set forth in paragraph (a)(3) through (5) of this section are satisfied, the deductible interest is limited to the smaller share. Similarly, if the portion of the proceeds payable in installments is a smaller portion of the proceeds than the portion to which the power of appointment meeting such requirements relates, the deduction is limited to the smaller portion. In addition, if a power of appointment meeting all the requirements extends to a smaller portion of the proceeds than the portion over which the interest or installment rights pertain, the deductible interest cannot exceed the value of the portion to which such power of appointment applies. Thus, if the contract provides that the insurer is to retain the entire proceeds and pay all of the interest thereon annually to the surviving spouse and if the surviving spouse has a power of appointment meeting the specifications prescribed in paragraph (a)(3) through (5) of this section, as to only one-half of the proceeds held, then only one-half of the proceeds may be treated as a deductible interest. Correspondingly, if the rights of the spouse to receive installment payments or interest satisfying the requirements extend to only one-fourth of the proceeds and a testamentary power of appointment satisfying the requirements of paragraph (a)(3) through (5) of this section extends to all of the proceeds, then only one-fourth of the proceeds qualifies as a deductible interest. Further, if the surviving spouse has no right to installment payments (or interest) over any portion of the proceeds but a testamentary power of appointment which meets the necessary conditions over the entire remaining proceeds, then none of the proceeds qualifies for the deduction. In addition, if, from the time of the decedent's death, the surviving spouse has a power of appointment meeting all of the required conditions over three-fourths of the proceeds and the right to receive interest from the entire proceeds, but with a power in another person to appoint one-half of the entire proceeds, the value of the interest in the surviving spouse over only one-half of the proceeds will qualify as a deductible interest.

(c) Applicable principles. *(1)* The principles set forth in paragraph (c) of § 20.2056(b)-5 for determining what constitutes a "specific portion of the entire interest" for the purpose of section 2056(b)(5) are applicable in determining what constitutes a "specific portion of all such amounts" for the purpose of section 2056(b)(6). However, the interest in the proceeds passing to the surviving spouse will not be disqualified by the fact that the installment payments or interest to which the spouse is entitled or the amount of the proceeds over which the power of appointment is exercisable may be expressed in terms of a specific sum rather than a fraction or a percentage of the proceeds provided it is shown that such sums are a definite or fixed percentage or fraction of the total proceeds.

(2) The provisions of paragraph (a) of this section are applicable with respect to a property interest which passed from the decedent in the form of proceeds of a policy of insurance upon the decedent's life, a policy of insurance upon the life of a person who predeceased the decedent, a matured endowment policy, or an annuity contract, but only in case the proceeds are to be held by the insurer. With respect to proceeds under any such contract which are to be held by a trustee, with power of appointment in the surviving spouse, see § 20.2056(b)-5. As to the treatment of proceeds not meeting the requirements of § 20.2056(b)-5 or of this section, see § 20.2056(a)-2.

(3) In the case of a contract under which payments by the insurer commenced during the decedent's life, it is immaterial whether or not the conditions in subparagraphs (1) through (5) of paragraph (a) of this section were satisfied prior to the decedent's death.

(d) Payments of installments or interest. The conditions in subparagraphs (1) and (2) of paragraph (a) of this section relative to the payments of installments or interest to the surviving spouse are satisfied if, under the terms of the contract, the spouse has the right exercisable annually (or more frequently) to require distribution to herself of installments of the proceeds or a specific portion thereof, as the case may be, and otherwise such proceeds or interest are to be accumulated and held by the insurer pursuant to the terms of the contract. A contract which otherwise requires the insurer to make annual or more frequent payments to the surviving spouse following the decedent's death, will not be disqualified merely because the surviving spouse must comply with certain formalities in order to obtain the first payment. For example, the contract may satisfy the conditions in subparagraphs (1) and (2) of paragraph (a) of this section even though it requires the surviving spouse to furnish proof of death before the first payment is made. The condition in paragraph (a)(1) of this section is satisfied where interest on the proceeds or a specific portion thereof is payable, annually or more frequently, for a term, or until the occurrence of a specified event, following which the proceeds or a specific portion thereof are to be paid in annual or more frequent installments.

(e) Powers of appointment. *(1)* In determining whether the terms of the contract satisfy the conditions in subparagraph (3), (4), or (5) of paragraph (a) of this section relating to a power of appointment in the surviving spouse or any other person, the principles stated in § 20.2056(b)-5 are applicable. As stated in § 20.2056(b)-5, the surviving spouse's power to appoint is "exercisable in all events" only if it is in existence immediately following the decedent's death, subject, however, to the operation of § 20.2056(b)-3 relating to interests conditioned on survival for a limited period.

(2) For examples of formal limitations on the power which will not disqualify the contract, see paragraph (g)(4) of § 20.2056(b)-5. If the power is exercisable from the moment of the decedent's death, the contract is not disqualified merely because the insurer may require proof of the decedent's death as a condition to making payment to the appointee. If the submission of proof of the decedent's death is a condition to the exercise of the power, the power will not be considered "exercisable in all events" unless in the event the surviving spouse had died immediately following the decedent, her power to appoint would have been considered to exist at the time of her death, within the meaning of section 2041(a)(2). See paragraph (b) of § 20.2041-3.

(3) It is sufficient for the purposes of the condition in paragraph (a)(3) of this section that the surviving spouse have the power to appoint amounts held by the insurer to herself or her estate if the surviving spouse has the unqualified power, exercisable in favor of herself or her estate, to appoint amounts held by the insurer which are payable after her death. Such power to appoint need not extend to installments or interest which will be paid to the spouse during her life. Further, the power to appoint need not be a power to require payment in a single sum. For example, if the proceeds of a policy are payable in installments, and if the surviving spouse has the power to direct that all installments payable after her death be paid to her estate, she has the requisite power.

(4) It is not necessary that the phrase "power to appoint" be used in the contract. For example, the condition in paragraph (a)(3) of this section that the surviving spouse have the power to appoint amounts held by the insurer to herself or her estate is satisfied by terms of a contract which give the surviving spouse a right which is, in substance and effect, a power to appoint to herself or her estate, such as a right to withdraw the amount remaining in the fund held by the insurer, or a right to direct that any amount held by the insurer under the contract at her death shall be paid to her estate.

T.D. 6296, 6/23/58.

§ 20.2056(b)-7 Election with respect to life estate for surviving spouse.

(a) In general. Subject to section 2056(d), a marital deduction is allowed under section 2056(b)(7) with respect to estates of decedents dying after December 31, 1981, for qualified terminable interest property as defined in paragraph (b) of this section. All of the property for which a deduction is allowed under this paragraph (a) is treated as passing to the surviving spouse (for purposes of § 20.2056(a)-1), and no part of the property is treated as passing to any person other than the surviving spouse (for purposes of § 20.2056(b)-1).

(b) Qualified terminable interest property. *(1) In general.* Section 2056(b)(7)(B)(i) provides the definition of qualified terminable interest property.

(i) Terminable interests described in section 2056(b)(1)(C) cannot qualify as qualified terminable interest property. Thus, if the decedent directs the executor to purchase a terminable interest with estate assets, the terminable interest acquired will not qualify as qualified terminable interest property.

(ii) For purposes of section 2056(b)(7)(B)(i), the term property generally means the entire interest in property (within the meaning of § 20.2056(b)-5(d)) or a specific portion of the entire interest (within the meaning of § 20.2056(b)-5(c)).

(2) Property for which an election may be made. (i) In general. The election may relate to all or any part of property that meets the requirements of section 2056(b)(7)(B)(i), provided that any partial election must be made with respect to a fractional or percentage share of the property so that the elective portion reflects its proportionate share of the increase or decrease in value of the entire property for purposes of applying sections 2044 or 2519. The fraction or percentage may be defined by formula.

(ii) Division of trusts. (A) In general. A trust may be divided into separate trusts to reflect a partial election that has been made, or is to be made, if authorized under the governing instrument or otherwise permissible under local law. Any such division must be accomplished no later than the end of the period of estate administration. If, at the time of the filing of the estate tax return, the trust has not yet been divided, the intent to divide the trust must be unequivocally signified on the estate tax return.

(B) Manner of dividing and funding trust. The division of the trust must be done on a fractional or percentage basis to reflect the partial election. However, the separate trusts do not have to be funded with a pro rata portion of each asset held by the undivided trust.

(C) Local law. A trust may be divided only if the fiduciary is required, either by applicable local law or by the express or implied provisions of the governing instrument, to divide the trust on the basis of the fair market value of the assets of the trust at the time of the division.

(3) Persons permitted to make the election. The election referred to in section 2056(b)(7)(B)(i)(III) must be made by the executor that is appointed, qualified, and acting within the United States, within the meaning of section 2203, regardless of whether the property with respect to which the election is to be made is in the executor's possession. If there is no executor appointed, qualified, and acting within the United States, the election may be made by any person with respect to property in the actual or constructive possession of that person and may also be made by that person with respect to other property not in the actual or constructive possession of that person if the person in actual or constructive possession of such other property does not make the election. For example, in the absence of an appointed executor, the trustee of an intervivos trust (that is included in the gross estate of the decedent) can make the election.

(4) Manner and time of making the election.. (i) In general. The election referred to in section 2056(b)(7)(B)(i)(III) and (v) is made on the return of tax imposed by section 2001 (or section 2101). For purposes of this paragraph, the term return of tax imposed by section 2001 means the last estate tax return filed by the executor on or before the due date of the return, including extensions or, if a timely return is not filed, the first estate tax return filed by the executor after the due date.

(ii) Election irrevocable. The election, once made, is irrevocable, provided that an election may be revoked or modified on a subsequent return filed on or before the due date of the return, including extensions actually granted. If an executor appointed under local law has made an election on the return of tax imposed by section 2001 (or section 2101) with respect to one or more properties, no subsequent election may be made with respect to other properties included in the gross estate after the return of tax imposed by section 2001 is filed. An election under section 2056(b)(7)(B)(v) is separate from any elections made under section 2056A(a)(3).

(c) Protective elections. *(1) In general.* A protective election may be made to treat property as qualified terminable interest property only if, at the time the federal estate tax return is filed, the executor of the decedent's estate reasonably believes that there is a bona fide issue that concerns whether an asset is includible in the decedent's gross estate, or the amount or nature of the property the surviving spouse is entitled to receive, i.e., whether property that is includible is eligible for the qualified terminable interest property election. The protective election must identify either the specific asset, group of assets, or trust to which the election applies and the specific basis for the protective election.

(2) Protective election irrevocable. The protective election, once made on the return of tax imposed by section 2001, cannot be revoked. For example, if a protective election is made on the basis that a bona fide question exists regarding the inclusion of a trust corpus in the gross estate and it is later determined that the trust corpus is so includible, the protective election becomes effective with respect to the trust corpus and cannot thereafter be revoked.

(d) Qualifying income interest for life. *(1) In general.* Section 2056(b)(7)(B)(ii) provides the definition of qualifying income interest for life. For purposes of section 2056(b)(7)(B)(ii)(II), the surviving spouse is included within the prohibited class of powerholders referred to therein. A power under applicable local law that permits the trustee to adjust between income and principal to fulfill the trustee's duty of impartiality between the income and remainder beneficiaries that meets the requirements of § 1.643(b)-1 of this chapter will not be considered a power to appoint trust property to a person other than the surviving spouse.

(2) Entitled for life to all income. The principles of § 20.2056(b)-5(f), relating to whether the spouse is entitled for life to all of the income from the entire interest, or a specific portion of the entire interest, apply in determining whether the surviving spouse is entitled for life to all of the income from the property regardless of whether the interest passing to the spouse is in trust.

(3) Contingent income interests. (i) An income interest for a term of years, or a life estate subject to termination upon the occurrence of a specified event (e.g., remarriage), is not a qualifying income interest for life. However, a qualifying income interest for life that is contingent upon the executor's election under section 2056(b)(7)(B)(v) will not fail to be a qualifying income interest for life because of such contingency or because the portion of the property for which the election is not made passes to or for the benefit of persons other than the surviving spouse. This paragraph (d)(3)(i) applies with respect to estates of decedents whose estate tax returns are due after February 18, 1997. This paragraph (d)(3)(i) also applies to estates of decedents whose estate tax returns were due on or before February 18, 1997, that meet the requirements of paragraph (d)(3)(ii) of this section.

(ii) Estates of decedents whose estate tax returns were due on or before February 18, 1997, that did not make the election under section 2056(b)(7)(B)(v) because the surviving spouse's income interest in the property was contingent upon the election or because the nonelected portion of the property was to pass to a beneficiary other than the surviving spouse are granted an extension of time to make the QTIP election if the following requirements are satisfied:

(A) The period of limitations on filing a claim for credit or refund under section 6511(a) has not expired.

(B) A claim for credit or refund is filed on Form 843 with a revised Recapitulation and Schedule M, Form 706 (or 706NA) that signifies the QTIP election. Reference to this section should be made on the Form 843.

(C) The following statement is included with the Form 843: "The undersigned certifies that the property with respect to which the QTIP election is being made will be included in the gross estate of the surviving spouse as provided in section 2044 of the Internal Revenue Code, in determining the federal estate tax liability on the spouse's death." The statement must be signed, under penalties of perjury, by the surviving spouse, the surviving spouse's legal representative (if the surviving spouse is legally incompetent), or the surviving spouse's executor (if the surviving spouse is deceased).

(4) Income between last distribution date and date of spouse's death. An income interest does not fail to constitute a qualifying income interest for life solely because income between the last distribution date and the date of the surviving spouse's death is not required to be distributed to the surviving spouse or to the estate of the surviving spouse. See § 20.2044-1 relating to the inclusion of such undistributed income in the gross estate of the surviving spouse.

(5) Pooled income funds. An income interest in a pooled income fund described in section 642(c)(5) constitutes a qualifying income interest for life for purposes of section 2056(b)(7)(B)(ii).

(6) Power to distribute principal to spouse. An income interest in a trust will not fail to constitute a qualifying income interest for life solely because the trustee has a power to distribute principal to or for the benefit of the surviving spouse. The fact that property distributed to a surviving spouse may be transferred by the spouse to another person does not result in a failure to satisfy the requirement of section 2056(b)(7)(B)(ii)(II). However, if the surviving spouse is legally bound to transfer the distributed property to another person without full and adequate consideration in money or money's worth, the requirement of section 2056(b)(7)(B)(ii)(II) is not satisfied.

(e) Annuities payable from trusts in the case of estates of decedents dying on or before October 24, 1992, and certain decedents dying after October 24, 1992, with wills or revocable trusts executed on or prior to that date. *(1) In general.* In the case of estates of decedents within the purview of the effective date and transitional rules contained in § 20.2056(b)-7(e)(5), a surviving spouse's lifetime annuity interest payable from a trust or other group of assets passing from the decedent is treated as a qualifying income interest for life for purposes of section 2056(b)(7)(B)(ii).

(2) Deductible interest. The deductible interest, for purposes of § 20.2056(a)-2(b), is the specific portion of the property that, assuming the applicable interest rate for valuing annuities, would produce income equal to the minimum amount payable annually to the surviving spouse. If, based on the applicable interest rate, the entire property from which the annuity may be satisfied is insufficient to produce income equal to the minimum annual payment, the value of the deductible interest is the entire value of the property. The value of the deductible interest may not exceed the value of the property from which the annuity is payable. If the annual payment may increase, the increased amount is not taken into account in valuing the deductible interest.

(3) Distributions permissible only to surviving spouse. An annuity interest is not treated as a qualifying income interest for life for purposes of section 2056(b)(7)(B)(ii) if any person other than the surviving spouse may receive, during the surviving spouse's lifetime, any distribution of the property or its income (including any distribution under an annuity contract) from which the annuity is payable.

(4) Applicable interest rate. To determine the applicable interest rate for valuing annuities, see sections 2031 and 7520 and the regulations under those sections.

(5) Effective dates. (i) The rules contained in § 20.2056(b)-7(e) apply with respect to estates of decedents dying on or before October 24, 1992.

(ii) The rules contained in § 20.2056(b)-7(e) apply in the case of decedents dying after October 24, 1992, if property passes to the spouse pursuant to a will or revocable trust executed on or before October 24, 1992, and either—

(A) On that date, the decedent was under a mental disability to change the disposition of his property and did not regain his competence to dispose of such property before the date of death; or

(B) The decedent dies prior to October 24, 1995.

(iii) Notwithstanding the foregoing, the rules contained in § 20.2056(b)-7(e) do not apply if the will or revocable trust is amended after October 24, 1992, in any respect that increases the amount of the transfer qualifying for the marital deduction or alters the terms by which the interest so passes to the surviving spouse.

(f) Joint and survivor annuities. [Reserved]

(g) Application of local law. The provisions of local law are taken into account in determining whether the conditions of section 2056(b)(7)(B)(ii)(I) are satisfied. For example, silence of a trust instrument as to the frequency of payment is not regarded as a failure to satisfy the requirement that the income must be payable to the surviving spouse annually or more frequently unless applicable local law permits payments less frequently.

(h) Examples. The following examples illustrate the application of paragraphs (a) through (g) of this section. In each example, it is assumed that the decedent, D, was survived by S, D's spouse and that, unless stated otherwise, S is not the trustee of any trust established for S's benefit.

Example (1). Life estate in residence. D owned a personal residence valued at $250,000 for estate tax purposes. Under D's will, the exclusive and unrestricted right to use the residence (including the right to continue to occupy the property as a personal residence or to rent the property and receive the income) passes to S for life. At S's death, the property passes to D's children. Under applicable local law, S must consent to any sale of the property. If the executor elects to treat all of the personal residence as qualified terminable interest property, the deductible interest is $250,000, the value of the residence for estate tax purposes.

Example (2). Power to make property productive. D's will established a trust funded with property valued for estate tax purposes at $500,000. The assets include both income producing assets and non-productive assets. S was given the power, exercisable annually, to require distribution of all of the trust income to herself. No trust property may be distributed during S's lifetime to any person other than S. Applicable local law permits S to require that the trustee either make the trust property productive or sell the property and reinvest in productive property within a reasonable time after D's death. If the executor elects to treat all of the trust as qualified terminable interest property, the deductible interest is $500,000. If the executor elects to treat only 20 percent of the trust as qualified terminable interest property, the deductible interest is $100,000, i.e., 20 percent of $500,000.

Example (3). Power of distribution over fraction of trust income. The facts are the same as in Example 2 except that S is given the right exercisable annually for S's lifetime to require distribution to herself of only 50 percent of the trust income for life. The remaining trust income is to be accumulated or distributed among S and the decedent's children in the trustee's discretion. The maximum amount that D's executor may elect to treat as qualified terminable interest property is $250,000; i.e., the estate tax value of the trust ($500,000) multiplied by the percentage of the trust in which S has a qualifying income interest for life (50 percent). If D's executor elects to treat only 20 percent of the portion of the trust in which S has a qualifying income interest as qualified terminable interest property, the deductible interest is $50,000, i.e., 20 percent of $250,000.

Example (4). Power to distribute trust corpus to other beneficiaries. D's will established a trust providing that S is entitled to receive at least annually all the trust income. The trustee is given the power to use annually during S's lifetime $5,000 from the trust for the maintenance and support of S's minor child, C. Any such distribution does not necessarily relieve S of S's obligation to support and maintain C. S does not have a qualifying income interest for life in any portion of the trust because the bequest fails to satisfy the condition that no person have a power, other than a power the exercise of which takes effect only at or after S's death, to appoint any part of the property to any person other than S. The trust would also be nondeductible under section 2056(b)(7) if S, rather than the trustee, held the power to appoint a portion of the principal to C. However, in the latter case, if S made a qualified disclaimer (within the meaning of section 2518) of the power to appoint to C, the trust could qualify for the marital deduction pursuant to section 2056(b)(7), assuming that the power is personal to S and S's disclaimer terminates the power. Similarly, in either case, if C made a qualified disclaimer of C's right to receive distributions from the trust, the trust would qualify under section 2056(b)(7), assuming that C's disclaimer effectively negates the trustee's power under local law.

Example (5). Spouse's income interest terminable on remarriage. D's will established a trust providing that all of the trust income is payable at least annually to S for S's lifetime, provided that, if S remarries, S's interest in the trust will pass to X. The trust is not deductible under section 2056(b)(7). S's income interest is not a qualifying income interest for life because it is not for life but, rather, is terminable upon S's remarriage.

Example (6). Spouse's qualifying income interest for life contingent on executor's election. D's will established a trust providing that S is entitled to receive the income, payable at least annually, from that portion of the trust that the executor elects to treat as qualified terminable interest property. The portion of the trust which the executor does not elect to treat as qualified terminable interest property passes as of D's date of death to a trust for the benefit of C, D's child. Under these facts, the executor is not considered to have a power to appoint any part of the trust property to any person other than S during S's life.

Example (7). Formula partial election. D's will established a trust funded with the residue of D's estate. Trust income is to be paid annually to S for life, and the principal is to be distributed to D's children upon S's death. S has the power to require that all the trust property be made productive. There is no power to distribute trust property during S's lifetime to any person other than S. D's executor elects to deduct a fractional share of the residuary estate under section 2056(b)(7). The election specifies that the numerator of the fraction is the amount of deduction necessary to reduce the Federal estate tax to zero (taking into account final estate tax values) and the denominator of the fraction is the final estate tax value of the residuary estate (taking into account any specific bequests or liabilities of the estate paid out of the residuary estate). The formula election is of a fractional share. The value of the share qualifies for the marital deduction even though the executor's determinations to claim administration expenses as estate or income tax deductions and the final estate tax values will affect the size of the fractional share.

Example (8). Formula partial election. The facts are the same as in Example 7 except that, rather than defining a fraction, the executor's formula states: "I elect to treat as qualified terminable interest property that portion of the residuary trust, up to 100 percent, necessary to reduce the Federal estate tax to zero, after taking into account the available unified credit, final estate tax values and any liabilities and specific bequests paid from the residuary estate." The formula election is of a fractional share. The share is equivalent to the fractional share determined in Example 7.

Example (9). Severance of QTIP trust. D's will established a trust funded with the residue of D's estate. Trust income is to be paid annually to S for life, and the principal is to be distributed to D's children upon S's death. S has the power to require that all of the trust property be made productive. There is no power to distribute trust property during S's lifetime to any person other than S. D's will authorizes the executor to make the election under section 2056(b)(7) only with respect to the minimum amount of property necessary to reduce estate taxes on D's estate to zero, authorizes the executor to divide the residuary estate into two separate trusts to reflect the election, and authorizes the executor to charge any payment of principal to S to the qualified terminable interest trust. S is the sole beneficiary of both trusts during S's lifetime. The authorizations in the will do not adversely affect the allowance of the marital deduction. Only the property remaining in the marital deduction trust, after payment of principal to S, is subject to inclusion in S's gross estate under section 2044 or subject to gift tax under section 2519.

Example (10). Payments to spouse from individual retirement account. S is the life beneficiary of sixteen remaining annual installments payable from D's individual retirement account. The terms of the account provide for the payment of the account balance in nineteen annual installments that commenced when D reached age 70½. Each installment is equal to all the income earned on the remaining principal in the account plus a share of the remaining principal equal to 1/19 in the first year, 1/18 in the second year, 1/17 in the third year, etc. Under the terms of the account, S has no right to withdraw any other amounts from the account. Any payments remaining after S's death pass to D's children. S's interest in the account qualifies as a qualifying income interest for life under section 2056(b)(7)(B)(ii), without regard to the provisions of section 2056(b)(7)(C).

Example (11). Spouse's interest in trust in the form of an annuity. D died prior to October 24, 1992. D's will established a trust funded with income producing property valued at $500,000 for estate tax purposes. The trustee is required by the trust instrument to pay $20,000 a year to S for life. Trust income in excess of the annuity amount is to be accumulated in the trust and may not be distributed during S's lifetime. S's lifetime annuity interest is treated as a qualifying income interest for life. If the executor elects to treat the entire portion of the trust in which S has a qualifying income interest as qualified terminable interest property, the value of the deductible interest is (assuming that 10 percent is the applicable interest rate under section 7520 for valuing annuities on the appropriate valuation date) $200,000, because that amount would yield an income to S of $20,000 a year.

Example (12). Value of spouse's annuity exceeds value of trust corpus. The facts are the same as in Example 11 except that the trustee is required to pay S $70,000 a year for life. If the executor elects to treat the entire portion of the trust in which S has a qualifying income interest as qualified terminable interest property, the value of the deductible interest is $500,000, which is the lesser of the entire value of the property ($500,000), or the amount of property that (assuming a 10 percent interest rate) would yield an income to S of $70,000 a year ($700,000).

Example (13). Pooled income fund. D's will provides for a bequest of $200,000 to a pooled income fund described in section 642(c)(5), designating S as the income beneficiary for life. If D's executor elects to treat the entire $200,000 as qualified terminable interest property, the deductible interest is $200,000.

Example (14). Funding severed QTIP trusts. D's will established a trust satisfying the requirements of section 2056(b)(7). Pursuant to the authority in D's will and § 20.2056(b)-7(b)(2)(ii), D's executor indicates on the Federal estate tax return that an election under section 2056(b)(7) is being made with respect to 50 percent of the trust, and that the trust will subsequently be divided to reflect the partial election on the basis of the fair market value of the property at the time of the division. D's executor funds the trust at the end of the period of estate administration. At that time, the property available to fund the trusts consists of 100 shares of X Corporation stock with a current value of $400,000 and 200 shares of Y Corporation stock with a current value of $400,000. D may fund each trust with the stock of either or both corporations, in any combination, provided that the aggregate value of the stock allocated to each trust is $400,000.

T.D. 8522, 2/28/94, amend T.D. 8779, 8/18/98, T.D. 9102, 12/30/2003.

PAR. 3. Section 20.2056(b)-7 is amended to read as follows:

Proposed § 20.2056(b)-7 Election with respect to life estate for surviving spouse. [*For Preamble, see ¶ 151,799*]

[The text of paragraphs (d)(3), and (h) Example 6 is the same as the text of § 20.2056(b)-7T(d)(3)(ii), and (h) Example 6 published elsewhere in this issue of the Federal Register]. *See T.D. 8714, 2/18/1997, 62 Fed. Reg. 32.*]

§ 20.2056(b)-8 Special rule for charitable remainder trusts.

(a) In general. *(1) Surviving spouse only noncharitable beneficiary.* With respect to estates of decedents dying after December 31, 1981, subject to section 2056(d), if the surviving spouse of the decedent is the only noncharitable beneficiary of a charitable remainder annuity trust or a charitable remainder unitrust described in section 664 (qualified charitable remainder trust), section 2056(b)(1) does not apply to the interest in the trust that is transferred to the surviving spouse. Thus, the value of the annuity or unitrust interest passing to the spouse qualifies for a marital deduction under section 2056(b)(8) and the value of the remainder interest qualifies for a charitable deduction under section 2055. If an interest in property qualifies for a marital deduction under section 2056(b)(8), no election may be made with respect to the property under section 2056(b)(7). For purposes of this section, the term non-charitable beneficiary means any beneficiary of the qualified charitable remainder trust other than an organization described in section 170(c).

(2) Interest for life or term of years. The surviving spouse's interest need not be an interest for life to qualify for a marital deduction under section 2056(b)(8). However, for purposes of section 664, an annuity or unitrust interest payable to the spouse for a term of years cannot be payable for a term that exceeds 20 years.

(3) Payment of state death taxes. A deduction is allowed under section 2056(b)(8) even if the transfer to the surviving spouse is conditioned on the spouse's payment of state death taxes, if any, attributable to the qualified charitable remainder trust. See § 20.2056(b)-4(c) for the effect of such a condition on the amount of the deduction allowable.

(b) Charitable remainder trusts where the surviving spouse is not the only noncharitable beneficiary. In the case of a charitable remainder trust where the decedent's spouse is not the only noncharitable beneficiary (for example, where the noncharitable interest is payable to the decedent's spouse for life and then to another individual for life), the qualification of the interest as qualified terminable interest property is determined solely under section 2056(b)(7) and not under section 2056(b)(8). Accordingly, if the decedent died on or before October 24, 1992, or the trust otherwise comes within the purview of the transitional rules contained in § 20.2056(b)-7(e)(5), the spousal annuity or unitrust interest may qualify under § 20.2056(b)-(7)(e) as a qualifying income interest for life.

T.D. 8522, 2/28/94.

§ 20.2056(b)-9 Denial of double deduction.

The value of an interest in property may not be deducted for Federal estate tax purposes more than once with respect to the same decedent. For example, where a decedent transfers a life estate in a farm to the spouse with a remainder to charity, the entire property is, pursuant to the executor's election under section 2056(b)(7), treated as passing to the spouse. The entire value of the property qualifies for the marital deduction. No part of the value of the property qualifies for a charitable deduction under section 2055 in the decedent's estate.

T.D. 8522, 2/28/94.

§ 20.2056(b)-10 Effective dates.

Except as specifically provided in §§ 20.2056(b)-5(c)(3)(ii) and (iii), 20.2056(b)-7(d)(3), 20.2056(b)-7(e)(5), and 20.2056(b)-8(b), the provisions of §§ 20.2056(b)-5(c), 20.2056(b)-7, 20.2056(b)-8, and 20.2056(b)-9 are applicable with respect to estates of decedents dying after March 1, 1994. With respect to decedents dying on or before such date, the executor of the decedent's estate may rely on any reasonable interpretation of the statutory provisions. In addition, the rule in the last sentence of § 20.2056(b)-5(f)(1) and the rule in the last sentence of § 20.2056(b)-7(d)(1) regarding the effect on the spouse's right to income if applicable local law provides for the reasonable apportionment between the income and remainder beneficiaries of the total return of the trust are applicable with respect to trusts for taxable years ending after January 2, 2004.

T.D. 8522, 2/28/94, amend T.D. 8779, 8/18/98, T.D. 9102, 12/30/2003.

PAR. 4.

Section 20.2056(b)-10 is revised to read as follows:

Proposed § 20.2056(b)-10 Effective dates. [*For Preamble, see ¶ 151,799*]

Except as specifically provided in §§ 20.2056(b)-5(c)(3)(ii) and (iii), 20.2056(b)-7T(d)(3), 20.2056(b)-7(e)(5), and 20.2056(b)-8(b), the provisions of §§ 20.2056(b)-5(c), 20.2056(b)-7, 20.2056(b)-8, and 20.2056(b)-9 are effective with respect to estates of decedents dying after March 1, 1994. With respect to decedents dying on or before March 1, 1994, the executor of the decedent's estate may rely on any reasonable interpretation of the statutory provisions. For these purposes, the provisions of §§ 20.2056(b)-5(c), 20.2056(b)-7, 20.2056(b)-8, and 20.2056(b)-9 (as well as project LR-211-76 (1984-1 C.B. 598), see § 601.601(d)(2)(ii)(b) of this chapter), are considered a reasonable interpretation of the statutory provisions.

§ 20.2056(c)-1 Marital deduction; definition of passed from the decedent.

(a) In general. The following rules are applicable in determining the person to whom any property interest "passed from the decedent":

(1) Property interests devolving upon any person (or persons) as surviving co-owner with the decedent under any form of joint ownership under which the right of survivorship existed are considered as having passed from the decedent to such person (or persons).

(2) Property interests at any time subject to the decedent's power to appoint (whether alone or in conjunction with any person) are considered as having passed from the decedent to the appointee under his exercise of the power, or, in case of the lapse, release or nonexercise of the power, as having passed from the decedent to the taker in default of exercise.

(3) The dower or curtesy interest (or statutory interest in lieu thereof) of the decedent's surviving spouse is considered as having passed from the decedent to his spouse.

(4) The proceeds of insurance upon the life of the decedent are considered as having passed from the decedent to the person who, at the time of the decedent's death, was entitled to receive the proceeds.

(5) Any property interest transferred during life, bequeathed or devised by the decedent, or inherited from the decedent, is considered as having passed to the person to whom he transferred, bequeathed, or devised the interest, or to the person who inherited the interest from him.

(6) The survivor's interest in an annuity or other payment described in section 2039 (see §§ 20.2039-1 and 20.2039-2) is considered as having passed from the decedent to the survivor only to the extent that the value of such interest is included in the decedent's gross estate under that section. If only a portion of the entire annuity or other payment is included in the decedent's gross estate and the annuity or other payment is payable to more than one beneficiary, then the value of the interest considered to have passed to each beneficiary is that portion of the amount payable to each beneficiary that the amount of the annuity or other payment included in the decedent's gross estate bears to the total value of the annuity or other payment payable to all beneficiaries.

(b) Expectant interest in property under community property laws. If before the decedent's death the decedent's surviving spouse had merely an expectant interest in property held by her and the decedent under community property laws, that interest is considered as having passed from the decedent to the spouse.

T.D. 6296, 6/23/58, amend T.D. 8522, 2/28/94.

§ 20.2056(c)-2 Marital deduction; definition of passed from the decedent to his surviving spouse.

(a) In general. In general, the definition stated in § 20.2056(c)-1 is applicable in determining the property interests which "passed from the decedent to his surviving spouse". Special rules are provided, however, for the following:

(1) In the case of certain interests with income for life to the surviving spouse with power of appointment in her (see § 20.2056(b)-5);

(2) In the case of certain interests with income for life to the surviving spouse that the executor elects to treat as qualified terminable interest property (see § 20.2056(b)-7);

(3) In the case of proceeds held by the insurer under a life insurance, endowment, or annuity contract with power of appointment in the surviving spouse (see § 20.2056(b)-6);

(4) In case of the disclaimer of an interest by the surviving spouse or by any other person (see § 20.2056(d)-1);

(5) In case of an election by the surviving spouse (see paragraph (c) of this section); and

(6) In case of a controversy involving the decedent's will, see paragraph (d) of this section.

A property interest is treated as passing to the surviving spouse only if it passes to the spouse as beneficial owner, except to the extent otherwise provided in §§ 20.2056(b)-5 and 20.2056(b)-7. For this purpose, where a property interest passed from the decedent in trust, such interest is considered to have passed from him to his surviving spouse to the extent of her beneficial interest therein. The deduction may not be taken with respect to a property interest which passed to such spouse merely as trustee, or subject to a binding agreement by the spouse to dispose of the interest in favor of a third person. An allowance or award paid to a surviving spouse pursuant to local law for her support during the administration of the decedent's estate constitutes a property interest passing from the decedent to his surviving spouse. In determining whether or not such an interest is deductible, however, see generally the terminable interest rules of § 20.2056(b)-1 and especially example (8) of paragraph (g) of that section.

(b) Examples. The following illustrate the provisions of paragraph (a) of this section:

(1) A property interest bequeathed in trust by H (the decedent) is considered as having passed from him to W (his surviving spouse)—

(i) If the trust income is payable to W for life and upon her death the corpus is distributable to her executors or administrators;

(ii) If W is entitled to the trust income for a term of years following which the corpus is to be paid to W or her estate;

(iii) If the trust income is to be accumulated for a term of years or for W's life and the augmented fund paid to W or her estate; or

(iv) If the terms of the transfer satisfy the requirements of § 20.2056(b)-5 or 20.2056(b)-7.

(2) If H devised property—

(i) To A for life with remainder absolutely to W or her estate, the remainder interest is considered to have passed from H to W;

(ii) To W for life with remainder to her estate, the entire property is considered as having passed from H to W; or

(iii) Under conditions which satisfy the provisions of § 20.2056(b)-5 or 20.2056(b)-7, the entire property is considered as having passed from H to W.

(3) Proceeds of insurance upon the life of H are considered as having passed from H to W if the terms of the contract—

(i) Meet the requirements of § 20.2056(b)-6;

(ii) Provide that the proceeds are payable to W in a lump sum;

(iii) Provide that the proceeds are payable in installments to W for life and after her death any remaining installments are payable to her estate;

(iv) Provide that interest on the proceeds is payable to W for life and upon her death the principal amount is payable to her estate; or

(v) Provide that the proceeds are payable to a trustee under an arrangement whereby the requirements of § 20.2056(b)-5 or 20.2056(b)-7 are satisfied.

(c) Effect of election by surviving spouse. This paragraph contains rules applicable if the surviving spouse may elect between a property interest offered to her under the decedent's will or other instrument and a property interest to which she is otherwise entitled (such as dower, a right in the decedent's estate, or her interest under community property laws) of which adverse disposition was attempted by the decedent under the will or other instrument. If the surviving spouse elects to take against the will or other instrument, then the property interests offered thereunder are not considered as having "passed from the decedent to his surviving spouse" and the dower or other property interest retained by her is considered as having so passed (if it otherwise so qualifies under this section). If the surviving spouse elects to take under the will or other instrument, then the dower or other property interest relinquished by her is not considered as having "passed from the decedent to his surviving spouse" (irrespective of whether it otherwise comes within the definition stated in paragraph (a) of this section) and the interest taken under the will or other instrument is considered as having so passed (if it otherwise so qualifies). As to the valuation of the property interest taken under the will or other instrument, see paragraph (b) of § 20.2056(b)-4.

(d) Will contests. *(1)* If as a result of a controversy involving the decedent's will, or involving any bequest or devise thereunder, his surviving spouse assigns or surrenders a property interest in settlement of the controversy, the interest so assigned or surrendered is not considered as having "passed from the decedent to his surviving spouse."

(2) If as a result of the controversy involving the decedent's will, or involving any bequest or devise thereunder, a property interest is assigned or surrendered to the surviving spouse, the interest so acquired will be regarded as having "passed from the decedent to his surviving spouse" only if the assignment or surrender was a bona fide recognition of enforceable rights of the surviving spouse in the decedent's estate. Such a bona fide recognition will be presumed where the assignment or surrender was pursuant to a decision of a local court upon the merits in an adversary proceeding following a genuine and active contest. However, such a decree will be accepted only to the extent that the court passed upon the facts upon which deductibility of the property interests depends. If the assignment or surrender was pursuant to a decree rendered by consent, or pursuant to an agreement not to contest the will or not to probate the will, it will not necessarily be accepted as a bona fide evaluation of the rights of the spouse.

(e) Survivorship. If the order of deaths of the decedent and his spouse cannot be established by proof, a presumption (whether supplied by local law, the decedent's will, or otherwise) that the decedent was survived by his spouse will be recognized as satisfying paragraph (b)(1) of § 20.2056(a)-1, but only to the extent that it has the effect of giving to the spouse an interest in property includible in her gross estate under part III of subchapter A of chapter 11. Under these circumstances, if an estate tax return is required to be filed for the estate of the decedent's spouse, the marital deduction will not be allowed in the final audit of the estate tax return of the decedent's estate with respect to any property interest which has not been finally determined to be includible in the gross estate of his spouse.

T.D. 6296, 6/23/58, amend T.D. 8522, 2/28/94.

§ 20.2056(c)-3 Marital deduction; definition of "passed from the decedent to a person other than his surviving spouse".

The expression "passed from the decedent to a person other than his surviving spouse" refers to any property interest which, under the definition stated in § 20.2056(c)-1 is considered as having "passed from the decedent" and which under the rules referred to in § 20.2056(c)-2 is not considered as having "passed from the decedent to his surviving spouse." Interests which passed to a person other than the surviving spouse include interests so passing under the decedent's exercise, release, or nonexercise of a nontaxable power to appoint. It is immaterial whether the property interest which passed from the decedent to a person other than his surviving spouse is included in the decedent's gross estate. The term "person other than his surviving spouse" includes the possible unascertained takers of a property interest, as, for example, the members of a class to be ascertained in the future. As another example, assume that the decedent created a power of appointment over a property interest, which does not come within the purview of § 20.2056(b)-5 or § 20.2056(b)-6. In such a case, the term "person other than his surviving spouse" refers to the possible appointees and possible takers in default (other than the spouse) of such property interest. Whether or not there is a possibility that the "person other than his surviving spouse" (or the heirs or assigns of such person) may possess or enjoy the property following termination or failure of the interest therein which passed from the decedent to his surviving spouse is to be determined as of the time of the decedent's death.

T.D. 6296, 6/23/58, amend T.D. 8522, 2/28/94.

§ 20.2056(d)-1 Marital deduction; special rules for marital deduction if surviving spouse is not a United States citizen.

Rules pertaining to the application of section 2056(d), including certain transition rules, are contained in §§ 20.2056A-1 through 20.2056A-13.

T.D. 8612, 8/21/95.

§ 20.2056(d)-2 Marital deduction; effect of disclaimers of post-December 31, 1976 transfers.

(a) Disclaimer by a surviving spouse. If a surviving spouse disclaims an interest in property passing to such spouse from the decedent, which interest was created in a transfer made after December 31, 1976, the effectiveness of the disclaimer will be determined by section 2518 and the corresponding regulations. For rules relating to when the transfer creating the interest occurs, see § 25.2518-2(c)(3) and (c)(4) of this chapter. If a qualified disclaimer is determined to have been made by the surviving spouse, the property interest disclaimed is treated as if such interest had never been transferred to the surviving spouse.

(b) Disclaimer by a person other than a surviving spouse. If an interest in property passes from a decedent to a person other than the surviving spouse, and the interest is created in a transfer made after December 31, 1976, and—

(1) The person other than the surviving spouse makes a qualified disclaimer with respect to such interest; and

(2) The surviving spouse is entitled to such interest in property as a result of such disclaimer, the disclaimed interest is treated as passing directly from the decedent to the surviving spouse. For rules relating to when the transfer creating the interest occurs, see § 25.2518-2(c)(3) and (c)(4) of this chapter.

(c) Effective date. The first and second sentences of paragraphs (a) and (b) of this section are applicable for transfers creating the interest to be disclaimed made on or after December 31, 1997.

T.D. 6296, 6/23/58, amend T.D. 8095, 8/6/86, T.D. 8612, 8/21/95, T.D. 8744, 12/30/97.

§ 20.2056(d)-3 Marital deduction; effect of disclaimers of pre-January 1, 1977 transfers.

(a) Disclaimer by a surviving spouse. If an interest in property passes to a decedent's surviving spouse in a taxable transfer made by a decedent dying before January 1, 1977, and the decedent's surviving spouse makes a disclaimer of this property interest the disclaimed interest is considered as passing from the decedent to the person or persons entitled to receive the interest as a result of the disclaimer. A disclaimer is a complete and unqualified refusal to accept the rights to which one is entitled. It is, therefore, necessary to distinguish between the surviving spouse's disclaimer of a property interest and such surviving spouse's acceptance and subsequent disposal of a property interest. For example, if proceeds of insurance are payable to the surviving spouse and the proceeds are refused so that they consequently pass to an alternate beneficiary designated by the decedent, the proceeds are considered as having passed from the decedent to the alternate beneficiary. On the other hand, if the insurance company is directed by the surviving spouse to hold the proceeds at interest during such spouse's life and, upon this spouse's death, to pay the principal sum to another person designated by the surviving spouse, thus effecting a transfer of a remainder interest, the proceeds are considered as having passed from the decedent to the surviving spouse. See paragraph (c) of § 20.2056(e)-2 with respect to a spouse's exercise or failure to exercise a right to take against a decedent's will.

(b) Disclaimer by a person other than a surviving spouse. *(1) Decedents dying after October 3, 1966 and before January 1, 1977.* This paragraph (b)(1) applies in the case of a disclaimer of property passing to one other than the surviving spouse from a decedent dying after October 3, 1966 and before January 1, 1977. If a surviving spouse is entitled to receive property from the decedent as a result of the timely disclaimer made by the disclaimant, the property received by the surviving spouse is to be treated as passing to the surviving spouse from the decedent. Both a disclaimer of property passing by the laws of intestacy or otherwise, as by insurance or by trust, and a disclaimer of bequests and devises under the will of a decedent are to be fully effective for purposes of computing the marital deduction under section 2056. A disclaimer is a complete and unqualified refusal to accept some or all of the rights to which one is entitled. It must be a valid refusal under State law and must be made without consideration. For example, a disclaimer for the benefit of a surviving spouse who promises to give or bequeath property to a child of the person who disclaims is not a disclaimer within the meaning of this paragraph (b)(1). The disclaimer must be made before the person disclaiming accepts any property under the disclaimed interest. In the case of property transferred by a decedent dying after December 31, 1970, and before January 1, 1977, the disclaimer must be made within 9 months after the decedent's death (or within any extension of time for filing the estate tax return granted pursuant to section 6081). In the case of property transferred by a decedent dying after October 3, 1966, and before January 1, 1971, the disclaimer must be made within 15 months after the decedent's death (or within any extension of time for filing the estate tax return granted pursuant to section 6081). If the disclaimer does not satisfy the requirements of this paragraph (b)(1), for the purpose of the marital deduction, the property is considered as passing from the decedent to the person who made the disclaimer as if the disclaimer had not been made.

(2) Decedents dying after September 30, 1963 and before October 4, 1966. This paragraph (b)(2) applies in the case of a disclaimer of property passing to one other than the surviving spouse from a decedent dying after September 30, 1963 and before October 4, 1966. If, as a result of the disclaimer by the disclaimant, the surviving spouse is entitled to receive the disclaimed property interest, then such interest shall, for the purposes of this paragraph (b)(2), be considered as passing from the decedent to the surviving spouse if the following conditions are met. First, the interest disclaimed was bequeathed or devised to the disclaimant. Second, the disclaimant disclaimed all bequests and devises under the will before the date prescribed for the filing of the estate tax return. Third, the disclaimant did not accept any property under the bequest or devise before making the disclaimer.

The interests passing by disclaimer to the surviving spouse under this paragraph (b)(2) are to qualify for the marital deduction only to the extent that, when added to any other allowable marital deduction without regard to this paragraph (b)(2), they do not exceed the greater of the deductions which would be allowable for the marital deduction without regard to the disclaimer if the surviving spouse exercised the election under State law to take against the will, or an amount equal to one-third of the decedent's adjusted gross estate. If the disclaimer does not satisfy the requirements of this paragraph (b)(2), the property is treated as passing from the decedent to the person who made the disclaimer, in the same manner as if the disclaimer had not been made.

(3) Decedents dying before October 4, 1966. Unless the rule of paragraph (b)(2) of this section applies, this paragraph (b)(3) applies in the case of a disclaimer of property passing to one other than the surviving spouse from a decedent dying before October 4, 1966. For the purpose of these transfers, it is unnecessary to distinguish for the purpose of the marital deduction between a disclaimer by a person other than the surviving spouse and a transfer by such person. If the surviving spouse becomes entitled to receive an interest in property from the decedent as a result of a disclaimer made by some other person, the interest is, nevertheless, considered as having passed from the decedent, not to the surviving spouse, but to the person who made the disclaimer, as though the disclaimer had not been made. If, as a result of a disclaimer made by a person other than the surviving spouse, a property interest passes to the surviving spouse under circumstances which meet the conditions set forth in § 20.2056(b)-5 (relating to a life estate with a power of appointment), the rule stated in the preceding sentence applies, not only with respect to the portion of the interest which beneficially vests in the surviving spouse, but also with respect to the portion over which such spouse acquires a power to appoint. The rule applies also in the case of proceeds under a life insurance, endowment, or annuity contract which, as a result of a disclaimer made by a person other than the surviving spouse, are held by the insurer subject to the conditions set forth in § 20.2056(b)-6.

T.D. 8095, 8/6/86, amend T.D. 8612, 8/21/95.

§ 20.2056A-0 Table of contents.

This section lists the captions that appear in the final regulations under §§ 20.2056A-1 through 20.2056A-13.

T.D. 8612, 8/21/95, amend T.D. 8686, 11/27/96.

§ 20.2056A-1 Restrictions on allowance of marital deduction if surviving spouse is not a United States citizen.

(a) General rule. Subject to the special rules provided in section 7815(d)(14) of the Omnibus Budget Reconciliation Act of 1989 (Pub. L. 101-239; 103 Stat. 2106), in the case of a decedent dying after November 10, 1988, the federal estate tax marital deduction is not allowed for property passing to or for the benefit of a surviving spouse who is not a United States citizen at the date of the decedent's death (whether or not the surviving spouse is a resident of the United States) unless—

(1) The property passes from the decedent to (or pursuant to)—

(i) A qualified domestic trust (QDOT) described in section 2056A and § 20.2056A-2;

(ii) A trust that, although not meeting all of the requirements for a QDOT, is reformed after the decedent's death to meet the requirements of a QDOT (see § 20.2056A-4(a));

(iii) The surviving spouse not in trust (e.g., by outright bequest or devise, by operation of law, or pursuant to the terms of an annuity or other similar plan or arrangement) and, prior to the date that the estate tax return is filed and on or before the last date prescribed by law that the QDOT election may be made (no more than one year after the time prescribed by law, including extensions, for filing the return), the surviving spouse either actually transfers the property to a QDOT or irrevocably assigns the property to a QDOT (see § 20.2056A-4(b)); or

(iv) A plan or other arrangement that would have qualified for the marital deduction but for section 2056(d)(1)(A), and whose payments are not assignable or transferable to a QDOT, if the requirements of § 20.2056A-4(c) are met; and

(2) The executor makes a timely QDOT election under section 20.2056A-3.

(b) Marital deduction allowed if resident spouse becomes citizen. For purposes of section 2056(d)(1) and paragraph (a) of this section, the surviving spouse is treated as a citizen of the United States at the date of the decedent's death if the requirements of section 2056(d)(4) are satisfied. For purposes of section 2056(d)(4)(A) and notwithstanding § 20.2056A-3(a), a return filed prior to the due date (including extensions) is considered filed on the last date that the return is required to be filed (including extensions), and a late return filed at any time after the due date is considered filed on the date that it is actually filed. A surviving spouse is a resident only if the spouse is a resident under chapter 11 of the Internal Revenue Code. See § 20.0-1(b)(1). The status of the spouse as a resident under section 7701(b) is not relevant to this determination except to the extent that the income tax residency of the spouse is pertinent in applying § 20.0-1(b)(1).

(c) Special rules in the case of certain transfers subject to estate and gift tax treaties. Under section 7815(d)(14) of the Omnibus Budget Reconciliation Act of 1989 (Pub. L. 101-239, 103 Stat. 2106) certain special rules apply in the case of transfers governed by certain estate and gift tax treaties to which the United States is a party. In the case of the estate of, or gift by, an individual who was not a citizen or resident of the United States but was a resident of a foreign country with which the United States has a tax treaty with respect to estate, inheritance, or gift taxes, the amendments made by section 5033 of the Technical and Miscellaneous Revenue Act of 1988 (Pub. L. 100-647, 102 Stat. 3342) do not apply to the extent such amendments would be inconsistent with the provisions of such treaty relating to estate, inheritance, or gift tax marital deductions. Under this rule, the estate may choose either the statutory deduction under section 2056A or the marital deduction allowed under the treaty. Thus, the estate may not avail itself of both the marital deduction under the treaty and the marital deduction under the QDOT provisions of section 2056A and chapter 11 of the Internal Revenue Code with respect to the remainder of the marital property that is not deductible under the treaty.

T.D. 8612, 8/21/95.

§ 20.2056A-2 Requirements for qualified domestic trust.

Caution: The Treasury has not yet amended Reg § 20.2056A-2 to reflect changes made by P.L. 105-34.

(a) In general. In order to qualify as a qualified domestic trust (QDOT), the requirements of paragraphs (b) and (c) of this section, and the requirements of § 20.2056A-2T(d), must be satisfied. The executor of the decedent's estate and the U.S. Trustee shall establish in such manner as may be prescribed by the Commissioner on the estate tax return and applicable instructions that these requirements have been satisfied or are being complied with. In order to constitute a QDOT, the trust must be maintained under the laws of a state of the United States or the District of Columbia, and the administration of the trust must be governed by the laws of a particular state of the United States or the District of Columbia. For purposes of this paragraph, a trust is maintained under the laws of a state of the United States or the District of Columbia if the records of the trust (or copies thereof) are kept in that state (or the District of Columbia). The trust may be established pursuant to an instrument executed under either the laws of a state of the United States or the District of Columbia or pursuant to an instrument executed under the laws of a foreign jurisdiction, such as a foreign will or trust, provided that such foreign instrument designates the law of a particular state of the United States or the District of Columbia as governing the administration of the trust, and such designation is effective under the law of the designated jurisdiction. In addition, the trust must constitute an ordinary trust, as defined in § 301.7701-4(a) of this chapter, and not any other type of entity. For purposes of this paragraph (a), a trust will not fail to constitute an ordinary trust solely because of the nature of the assets transferred to that trust, regardless of its classification under sections 301.7701-2 through 301.7701-4 of this chapter.

(b) Qualified marital interest requirements. *(1) Property passing to QDOT.* If property passes from a decedent to a QDOT, the trust must qualify for the federal estate tax marital deduction under section 2056(b)(5) (life estate with power of appointment), section 2056(b)(7) (qualified terminable interest property, including joint and survivor annuities under section 2056(b)(7)(C)), or section 2056(b)(8) (surviving spouse is the only noncharitable beneficiary of a charitable remainder trust), or meet the requirements of an estate trust as defined in § 20.2056(c)-2(b)(1)(i) through (iii).

(2) Property passing outright to spouse. If property does not pass from a decedent to a QDOT, but passes to a noncitizen surviving spouse in a form that meets the requirements for a marital deduction without regard to section 2056(d)(1)(A), and that is not described in paragraph (b)(1) of this section, the surviving spouse must either actually transfer the property, or irrevocably assign the property, to a trust (whether created by the decedent, the decedent's executor or by the surviving spouse) that meets the requirements of paragraph (c) of this section and the requirements of § 20.2056A-2T(d) (pertaining, respectively, to statutory requirements and regulatory requirements imposed to ensure collection of tax) prior to the filing of the estate tax return for the decedent's estate and on or before the last date prescribed by law that the QDOT election may be made (see § 20.2056A-3(a)).

(3) Property passing under a nontransferable plan or arrangement. If property does not pass from a decedent to a QDOT, but passes under a plan or other arrangement that meets the requirements for a marital deduction without regard to section 2056(d)(1)(A) and whose payments are not assignable or transferable (see § 20.2056A-4(c)), the property is treated as meeting the requirements of this section, and the requirements of section 20.2056A-2T(d), if the requirements of § 20.2056A-4(c) are satisfied. In addition, where an annuity or similar arrangement is described above except that it is assignable or transferable, see § 20.2056A-4(b)(7).

(c) Statutory requirements. The requirements of section 2056A(a)(1)(A) and (B) must be satisfied. For purposes of that section, a domestic corporation is a corporation that is created or organized under the laws of the United States or under the laws of any state of the United States or the District of Columbia. The trustee required under that section is referred to herein as the "U.S. Trustee".

(d) Additional requirements to ensure collection of the section 2056A estate tax. *(1) Security and other arrangements for payment of estate tax imposed under section 2056A(b)(1).* (i) QDOTs with assets in excess of $2 million. If the fair market value of the assets passing, treated, or deemed to have passed to the QDOT (or in the form of a QDOT), determined without reduction for any indebtedness with respect to the assets, as finally determined for federal estate tax purposes, exceeds $2 million as of the date of the decedent's death or, if applicable, the alternate valuation date (adjusted as provided in paragraph (d)(1)(iii) of this section), the trust instrument must meet the requirements of either paragraph (d)(1)(i)(A), (B), or (C) of this section at all times during the term of the QDOT. The QDOT may alternate between any of the arrangements provided in paragraphs (d)(1)(i)(A), (B), and (C) of this section provided that, at any given time, one of the arrangements must be operative. See paragraph (d)(1)(iii) of this section for the definition of finally determined. The QDOT may provide that the trustee has the discretion to use any one of the security arrangements or may provide that the trustee is limited to using only one or two of the arrangements specified in the trust instrument. A trust instrument that specifically states that the trust must be administered in compliance with paragraph (d)(1)(i)(A), (B), or (C) of this section is treated as meeting the requirements of paragraphs (d)(1)(i)(A), (B), or (C) for purposes of paragraphs (d)(1)(i) and, if applicable, (d)(1)(ii) of this section.

(A) Bank trustee. Except as otherwise provided in paragraph (d)(6)(ii) or (iii) of this section, the trust instrument must provide that whenever the Bank Trustee security alternative is used for the QDOT, at least one U.S. Trustee must be a bank as defined in section 581. Alternatively, except as otherwise provided in paragraph (d)(6)(ii) or (iii) of this section, at least one trustee must be a United States branch of a foreign bank, provided that, in such cases, during the entire term of the QDOT a U.S. Trustee must act as a trustee with the foreign bank trustee.

(B) Bond. Except as otherwise provided in paragraph (d)(6)(ii) or (iii) of this section, the trust instrument must provide that whenever the bond security arrangement alternative is used for the QDOT, the U.S. Trustee must furnish a bond in favor of the Internal Revenue Service in an amount equal to 65 percent of the fair market value of the trust assets (determined without regard to any indebtedness with respect to the assets) as of the date of the decedent's death (or alternate valuation date, if applicable), as finally determined for federal estate tax purposes (and as further adjusted as provided in paragraph (d)(1)(iv) of this section). If, after examination of the estate tax return, the fair market value of the trust assets, as originally reported on the estate tax return, is adjusted (pursuant to a judicial proceeding or otherwise) resulting in a final determination of the value of the assets as reported on the return, the U.S. Trustee has a reasonable period of time (not exceeding sixty days after the conclusion of the proceeding or other action resulting in a final determination of the value of the assets) to adjust the amount of the bond accordingly. But see, paragraph (d)(1)(i)(D) of this section for a special rule in the case of a substantial undervaluation of QDOT assets. Unless an alternate arrangement under paragraph (d)(1)(i)(A), (B), or (C) of this section, or an arrangement prescribed under paragraph (d)(4) of this section, is provided, or the trust is otherwise no longer subject to the requirements of section 2056A pursuant to section 2056A(b)(12), the bond must remain in effect until the trust ceases to function as a QDOT and any tax liability finally determined to be due under section 2056A(b) is paid, or is finally determined to be zero.

(1) Requirements for the bond. The bond must be with a satisfactory surety, as prescribed under section 7101 and § 301.7101-1 of this chapter (Regulations on Procedure and Administration), and is subject to Internal Revenue Service review as may be prescribed by the Commissioner. The bond may not be cancelled. The bond must be for a term of at least one year and must be automatically renewable at the end of that term, on an annual basis thereafter, unless notice of failure to renew is mailed to t he U.S. Trustee and the Internal Revenue Service at least 60 days prior to the end of the term, including periods of automatic extensions. Any notice of failure to renew required to be sent to the Internal Revenue Service must be sent to the Estate and Gift Tax Group in the District Office of the Internal Revenue Service that has examination jurisdiction over the decedent's estate (Internal Revenue Service, District Director, [specify location] District Office, Estate and Gift Tax Examination Group, [specify Street Address, City, State, Zip Code]) (or in the case of noncitizen decedents and United States citizens who die domiciled outside the United States, Estate Tax Group, Assistant Commissioner (International), 950 L'Enfant Plaza, CP:IN:D:C:EX:HQ:1114, Washington, DC 20024). The Internal Revenue Service will not draw on the bond if, within 30 days of receipt of the notice of failure to renew, the U.S. Trustee notifies the Internal Revenue Service (at the same address to which notice of failure to renew is to be sent) that an alternate arrangement under paragraph (d)(1)(i)(A), (B), or (C) or (d)(4) of this section, has been secured and that the arrangement will take effect immediately prior to or upon expiration of the bond.

(2) Form of bond. The bond must be in the following form (or in a form that is the same as the following form in all material respects), or in such alternative form as the Commissioner may prescribe by guidance published in the Internal Revenue Bulletin (see section 601.601(d)(2) of this chapter):

Bond in Favor of the Internal Revenue Service to Secure Payment of Section 2056A Estate Tax Imposed Under Section 2056A(b) of the Internal Revenue Code.

KNOW ALL PERSONS BY THESE PRESENTS, That the undersigned, ________, the SURETY, and ________, the PRINCIPAL, are irrevocably held and firmly bound to pay the tax up to *$[amount determined under paragraph (d)(1)(i)(B) of this section]*, imposed under section 2056A(b)(1) of the Internal Revenue Code (including penalties and interest on said tax) determined by the Internal Revenue Service to be payable with respect to the principal as trustee for: *[Identify trust and governing instrument, name and address of trustee]*, a qualified domestic trust as defined in section 2056A(a) of the Internal Revenue Code, for the payment of which the said Principal and said Surety, bind themselves, their heirs, executors, administrators, successors and assigns, jointly and severally, firmly by these presents.

WHEREAS, The Internal Revenue Service may demand payment under this bond at any time if the Internal Revenue Service in its sole discretion determines that a taxable event with respect to the trust has occurred; the trust no longer qualifies as a qualified domestic trust as described in section 2056A(a) of the Internal Revenue Code and the regulations promulgated thereunder, or a distribution subject to the tax imposed under section 2056A(b)(1) has been made. Demand by the Internal Revenue Service for payment may be made whether or not the tax and tax return (Form 706-QDT) with respect to the taxable event is due at the time of such demand, or an assessment has been made by the Internal Revenue Service with respect to the tax.

NOW THEREFORE, The condition of this obligation is such that it must not be cancelled and, if payment of all tax liability finally determined to be imposed under section 2056A(b) is made, then this obligation shall be null and void; otherwise, this obligation is to remain in full force and effect for one year from its effective date and is to be automatically renewable on an annual basis unless, at least 60 days prior to the expiration date, including periods of automatic renewals, the surety mails to the U.S. Trustee and the Internal Revenue Service by Registered or Certified Mail, return receipt requested, notice of the failure to renew. Receipt of this notice of failure to renew by the Internal Revenue Service may be considered a taxable event. The Internal Revenue service will not draw upon the bond if, within 30 days of receipt of the notice of failure to renew, the trustee notifies the Internal Revenue Service that an alternate security arrangement has been secured and that the arrangement will take effect immediately prior to or upon expiration of the bond. The surety remains liable for all taxable events occurring prior to the date of expiration. All notices required to be sent to the Internal Revenue Service under this instrument should be sent to District Director, *[specify location]* District Office, Estate and Gift Tax Examination Group, Street Address, City, State, Zip Code. (In the case of nonresident noncitizen decedents and United States citizens who die domiciled outside the United States, all notices should be sent to Estate Tax Group, Assistant Commissioner (International), 950 L'Enfant Plaza, CP:IN:D:C:EX:HQ:1114, Washington, DC 20024).

This bond shall be effective as of ________.

Principal ____________ Date ________

Surety ____________ Date ________

(3) Additional governing instrument requirements. The trust instrument must provide that in the event the Internal Revenue Service draws on the bond, in accordance with its terms, neither the U.S. Trustee nor any other person will seek a return of any part of the remittance until after April 15th of the calendar year following the year in which the bond is drawn upon. After that date, any such remittance will be treated as a deposit and returned (without interest) upon request of the U.S. Trustee, unless it is determined that assessment or collection of the tax imposed by section 2056A(b)(1) is in jeopardy, within the meaning of section 6861. If an assessment under section 6861 is made, the remittance will first be credited to any tax liability reported on the Form 706-QDT, then to any unpaid balance of a section 2056A(b)(1)(A) tax liability (plus interest and penalties) for any prior taxable years, and any balance will then be returned to the U.S. Trustee.

(4) Procedure. The bond is to be filed with the decedent's federal estate tax return, Form 706 or 706NA (unless an extension for filing the bond is granted under section 301.9100 of this chapter). The U.S. Trustee must provide a written statement with the bond that provides a list of the assets that will be used to fund the QDOT and the respective values of the assets. The written statement must also indicate whether any exclusions under paragraph (d)(1)(iv) of this section are claimed.

(C) Letter of credit. Except as otherwise provided in paragraph (d)(6)(ii) or (iii) of this section, the trust instrument must provide that whenever the letter of credit security arrangement is used for the QDOT, the U.S. Trustee must furnish an irrevocable letter of credit issued by a bank as defined in section 581, a United States branch of a foreign bank, or a foreign bank with a confirmation by a bank as defined in section 581. The letter of credit must be for an amount equal to 65 percent of the fair market value of the trust assets (determined without regard to any indebtedness with respect to the assets) as of the date of the decedent's death (or alternate valuation date, if applicable), as finally determined for federal estate tax purposes (and as further adjusted as provided in paragraph (d)(1)(iv) of this section). If, after examination of the estate tax return, the fair market value of the trust assets, as originally reported on the estate tax return, is adjusted (pursuant to a judicial proceeding or otherwise) resulting in a final determination of the value of the assets as reported on the return, the U.S. Trustee has a reasonable period of time (not exceeding 60 days after the conclusion of the proceeding or other action resulting in a final determination of the value of the assets) to adjust the amount of the letter of credit accordingly. But see, paragraph (d)(1)(i)(D) of this section for a special rule in the case of a substantial undervaluation of QDOT assets. Unless an alternate arrangement under paragraph (d)(1)(i)(A), (B), or (C) of this section, or an arrangement prescribed under paragraph (d)(4) of this section, is provided, or the trust is otherwise no longer subject to the requirements of section 2056A pursuant to section 2056A(b)(12), the letter of credit must remain in effect until the trust ceases to function as a QDOT and any tax liability finally determined to be due under section 2056A(b) is paid or is finally determined to be zero.

(1) Requirements for the letter of credit. The letter of credit must be irrevocable and provide for sight payment. The letter of credit must have a term of at least one year and must be automatically renewable at the end of the term, at least on an annual basis, unless notice of failure to renew is mailed to the U.S. Trustee and the Internal Revenue Service at least sixty days prior to the end of the term, including periods of automatic renewals. If the letter of credit is issued by the U.S. branch of a foreign bank and the U.S. branch is closing, the branch (or foreign bank) must notify the U.S. Trustee and the Internal Revenue Service of the closure and the notice of closure must be mailed at least 60 days prior to the date of closure. Any notice of failure to renew or closure of a U.S. branch of a foreign bank required to be sent to the Internal Revenue Service must be sent to the Estate and Gift Tax Group in the District Office of the Internal Revenue Service that has examination jurisdiction over the decedent's estate (Internal Revenue Service, District Director, [specify location] District Office, Estate and Gift Tax Examination Group, [Street Address, City State, Zip Code]) (or in the case of noncitizen decedents and United States citizens who die domiciled outside the United States, Estate Tax, Assistant Commissioner (International), 950 L'Enfant Plaza, CP:IN:D:C:EX:HQ:1114, Washington, DC 20024). The Internal Revenue Service will not draw on the letter of credit if, within 30 days of receipt of the notice of failure to renew or closure of the U.S. branch of a foreign bank, the U.S. Trustee notifies the Internal Revenue Service (at the same address to which notice is to be sent) that an alternate arrangement under paragraph (d)(1)(i)(A), (B), or (C), or (d)(4) of this section, has been secured and that the arrangement will take effect immediately prior to or upon expiration of the letter of credit or closure of the U.S. branch of the foreign bank.

(2) Form of letter of credit. The letter of credit must be made in the following form (or in a form that is the same as the following form in all material respects), or an alternative form that the Commissioner prescribes by guidance published in the Internal Revenue Bulletin (see section 601.601(d)(2) of this chapter):

[Issue Date]

To: Internal Revenue Service

Attention: District Director, *[specify location]*

District Office

Estate and Gift Tax Examination Group

[Street Address, City, State, ZIP Code]

[Or in the case of nonresident noncitizen decedents and United States citizens who die domiciled outside the United States,

To: Estate Tax Group,

Assistant Commissioner (International)

950 L'Enfant Plaza

CP:IN:D:C:EX:HQ:1114

Washington, DC 20024].

Dear Sirs:

We hereby confirm our irrevocable Letter of Credit No.___ in your favor for drawings up to U.S. $ [*Applicant should provide bank with amount which Applicant determined under paragraph (d)(1)(i)(C)*] effective immediately. This Letter of Credit is issued, presentable and payable at our office at ____________ and expires at 3:00 p.m. [EDT, EST, CDT, CST, MDT, MST, PDT, PST] on ________ at said office.

For information and reference only, we are informed that this Letter of Credit relates to [*Applicant should provide bank with the identity of qualified domestic trust and governing instrument*], and the name, address, and identifying number of the trustee is [*Applicant should provide bank with the trustee name, address and the QDOT's TIN number, if any*].

Drawings on this Letter of Credit are available upon presentation of the following documents:

1. Your draft drawn at sight on us bearing our Letter of Credit No. ______; and
2. Your signed statement as follows:

The amount of the accompanying draft is payable under [*identify bank*] irrevocable Letter of Credit No. ______ pursuant to section 2056A of the Internal Revenue Code and the regulations promulgated thereunder, because the Internal Revenue Service in its sole discretion has determined that a "taxable event" with respect to the trust has occurred; e.g., the trust no longer qualifies as a qualified domestic trust as described in section 2056A of the Internal Revenue Code and regulations promulgated thereunder, or a distribution subject to the tax imposed under section 2056A(b)(1) of the Internal Revenue Code has been made.

Except as expressly stated herein, this undertaking is not subject to any agreement, requirement or qualification. The obligation of [*Name of Issuing Bank*] under this Letter of Credit is the individual obligation of [*Name of Issuing Bank*] and is in no way contingent upon reimbursement with respect thereto.

It is a condition of this Letter of Credit that it is deemed to be automatically extended without amendment for a period of one year from the expiration date hereof, or any future expiration date, unless at least 60 days prior to any expiration date, we mail to you and to the U.S. Trustee notice by Registered Mail or Certified Mail, return receipt requested, or by courier to your and the trustee's address indicated above, that we elect not to consider this Letter of Credit renewed for any such additional period. Upon receipt of such notice, you may draw hereunder on or before the then current expiration date, by presentation of your draft and statement as stipulated above.

[In the case of a letter of credit issued by a U.S. branch of a foreign bank the following language must be added]. It is a further condition of this Letter of Credit that if the U.S. branch of [*name of foreign bank*] is to be closed, that at least sixty days prior to closing, we mail to you and the U.S. Trustee notice by Registered Mail or Certified Mail, return receipt requested, or by courier to your and the U.S. Trustees's address indicated above, that this branch will be closing. This notice will specify the actual date of closing. Upon receipt of the notice, you may draw hereunder on or before the date of closure, by presentation of your draft and statement as stipulated above.

Except where otherwise stated herein, this Letter of Credit is subject to the Uniform Customs and Practice for Documentary Credits, 1993 Revision, ICC Publication No. 500. If we notify you of our election not to consider this Letter of Credit renewed and the expiration date occurs during an interruption of business described in Article 17 of said Publication 500, unless you had consented to cancellation prior to the expiration date, the bank hereby specifically agrees to effect payment if this Letter of Credit is drawn against within 30 days after the resumption of business.

Except as stated herein, this Letter of Credit cannot be modified or revoked without your consent.

Authorized Signature __________ Date ____

(3) Form of confirmation. If the requirements of this paragraph (d)(1)(i)(C) are satisfied by the issuance of a letter of credit by a foreign bank with confirmation by a bank as defined in section 581, the confirmation must be made in the following form (or in a form that is the same as the following form in all material respects), or an alternative form as the Commissioner prescribes by guidance published in the Internal Revenue Bulletin (see § 602.101(d)(2) of this chapter):

[Issue Date]

To: Internal Revenue Service

Attention: District Director, [*specify location*]

District Office

Estate and Gift Tax Examination Group

[State Address, City, State, ZIP Code]

[or in the case of nonresident noncitizen decedents and United States citizens who die domiciled outside the United States,

To: Estate Tax Group,

Assistant Commissioner (International)

950 L'Enfant Plaza

CP:IN:D:C:EX:HQ:1114

Washington, DC 20024].

Dear Sirs:

We hereby confirm the enclosed irrevocable Letter of Credit No. ____, and amendments thereto, if any, in your favor by ______ [Issuing Bank] for drawings up to U.S. $ ____ [same amount as in initial Letter of Credit] effective immediately. This confirmation is issued, presentable and payable at our office at __________ and expires at 3:00 p.m. [EDT, EST, CDT, CST, MDT, MST, PDT, PST] on ______ at said office.

For information and reference only, we are informed that this Confirmation relates to [Applicant should provide bank with the identity of qualified domestic trust and governing instrument], and the name, address, and identifying number of the trustee is [Applicant should provide bank with the trustee name, address and the QDOT's TIN number, if any].

We hereby undertake to honor your sight draft(s) drawn as specified in the Letter of Credit.

Except as expressly stated herein, this undertaking is not subject to any agreement, condition or qualification. The obligation of [*Name of Confirming Bank*] under this Confirmation is the individual obligation of [*Name of Confirming Bank*] and is in no way contingent upon reimbursement with respect thereto.

It is a condition of this Confirmation that it is deemed to be automatically extended without amendment for a period of one year from the expiry date hereof, or any future expiration date, unless at least sixty days prior to the expiration date, we send to you and to the U.S. Trustee notice by Registered Mail or Certified Mail, return receipt requested, or by courier to your and the trustee's addresses, respectively, indicated above, that we elect not to consider this Confirmation renewed for any additional period. Upon receipt of this notice by you, you may draw hereunder on or before the then current expiration date, by presentation of your draft and statement as stipulated above.

Except where otherwise stated herein, this Confirmation is subject to the Uniform Customs and Practice for Documentary Credits, 1993 Revision, ICC Publication No. 500. If we notify you of our election not to consider this Confirmation renewed and the expiration date occurs during an interruption of business described in Article 17 of said Publication 500, unless you had consented to cancellation prior to the expiration date, the bank hereby specifically agrees to effect payment if this Confirmation is drawn against within 30 days after the resumption of business.

Except as stated herein, this Confirmation cannot be modified or revoked without your consent.

Authorized Signature __________ Date ______

(4) Additional governing instrument requirements. The trust instrument must provide that if the Internal Revenue Service draws on the letter of credit (or confirmation) in accordance with its terms, neither the U.S. Trustee nor any other person will seek a return of any part of the remittance until April 15th of the calendar year following the year in which the letter of credit (or confirmation) is drawn upon. After that date, any such remittance will be treated as a deposit and returned (without interest) upon request of the U.S. Trustee after the date specified above, unless it is determined that assessment or collection of the tax imposed by section 2056A(b)(1) is in jeopardy, within the meaning of section 6861. If an assessment under section 6861 is made, the remittance will first be credited to any tax liability reported on the Form 706-QDT, then to any unpaid balance of a section 2056A(b)(1)(A) tax liability (plus interest and penalties) for any prior taxable years, and any balance will then be returned to the U.S. Trustee.

(5) Procedure. The letter of credit (and confirmation, if applicable) is to be filed with the decedent's federal estate tax return, Form 706 or 706NA (unless an extension for filing the letter of credit is granted under § 301.9100 of this chapter). The U.S. Trustee must provide a written statement with the letter of credit that provides a list of the assets that will be used to fund the QDOT and the respective values of the assets. The written statement must also indicate whether any exclusions under paragraph (d)(1)(iv) of this section are claimed.

(D) Disallowance of marital deduction for substantial undervaluation of QDOT property in certain situations. (1) If either—

(i) The bond or letter of credit security arrangement under paragraph (d)(1)(i)(B) or (C) of this section is chosen by the U.S. Trustee; or

(ii) The QDOT property as originally reported on the decedent's estate tax return is valued at $2 million or less but, as finally determined for federal estate tax purposes, the QDOT property is determined to be in excess of $2 million, then the marital deduction will be disallowed in its entirety for failure to comply with the requirements of section 2056A if the value of the QDOT property reported on the estate tax return is 50 percent or less of the amount finally determined to be the correct value of the property for federal estate tax purposes.

(2) The preceding sentence does not apply if—

(i) There was reasonable cause for the undervaluation; and

(ii) The fiduciary of the estate acted in good faith with respect to the undervaluation. For this purpose, § 1.6664-4(b) of this chapter applies, to the extent applicable, with respect to the facts and circumstances to be taken into account in making this determination.

(ii) QDOTs with assets of $2 million or less. If the fair market value of the assets passing, treated, or deemed to have passed to the QDOT (or in the form of a QDOT), determined without reduction for any indebtedness with respect to the assets, as finally determined for federal estate tax purposes, is $2 million or less as of the date of the decedent's death or, if applicable, the alternate valuation date (adjusted as provided in paragraph (d)(1)(iv) of this section), the trust instrument must provide that either no more than 35 percent of the fair market value of the trust assets, determined annually on the last day of the taxable year of the trust (or on the last day of the calendar year if the QDOT does not have a taxable year), will consist of real property located outside of the United States, or the trust will meet the requirements prescribed by paragraph (d)(1)(i)(A), (B), or (C) of this section. See paragraph (d)(1)(ii)(D) of this section for special rules in the case of principal distributions from a QDOT, fluctuations in the value of foreign real property held by a QDOT due to changes in value of foreign currency, and fluctuations in the fair market value of assets held by the QDOT. See paragraph (d)(1)(iv) of this section for a special rule for personal residences. If the fair market value, as originally reported on the decedent's estate tax return, of the assets passing or deemed to have passed to the QDOT (determined without reduction for any indebtedness with respect to the assets) is $2 million or less, but the fair market value of the assets as finally determined for federal estate tax purposes is more than $2 million, the U.S. Trustee has a reasonable period of time (not exceeding sixty days after the conclusion of the proceeding or other action resulting in a final determination of the value of the assets) to meet the requirements prescribed by paragraph (d)(1)(i)(A), (B), or (C) of this section. However, see paragraph (d)(1)(i)(D) of this section in the case of a substantial undervaluation of QDOT assets. See § 20.2056A-2(d)(1)(iii) for the definition of finally determined.

(A) Multiple QDOTs. For purposes of this paragraph (d)(1)(ii), if more than one QDOT is established for the benefit of the surviving spouse, the fair market value of all the QDOTs are aggregated in determining whether the $2 million threshold under this paragraph (d)(1)(ii) is exceeded.

(B) Look-through rule. For purposes of determining whether no more than 35 percent of the fair market value of the QDOT assets consists of foreign real property, if the QDOT owns more than 20% of the voting stock or value in a corporation with 15 or fewer shareholders, or more than 20% of the capital interest of a partnership with 15 or fewer partners, then all assets owned by the corporation or partnership are deemed to be owned directly by the QDOT to the extent of the QDOT's pro rata share of the as sets of that corporation or partnership. For a partnership, the QDOT partner's pro rata share is based on the greater of its interest in the capital or profits of the partnership. For purposes of this paragraph, all stock in the corporation, or interests in the partnership, as the case may be, owned by or held for the benefit of the surviving spouse, or any members of the surviving spouse's family (within the meaning of section 267(c)(4)), are treated as owned by the QDOT solely for purposes of determining the number of partners or shareholders in the entity and the QDOT's percentage voting interest or value in the corporation or capital interest in the partnership, but not for the purpose of determining the QDOT's pro rata share of the assets of the entity.

(C) Interests in other entities. Interests owned by the QDOT in other entities (such as an interest in a trust) are accorded treatment consistent with that described in paragraph (d)(1)(ii)(B) of this section.

(D) Special rule for foreign real property. For purposes of this paragraph (d)(1)(ii), if, on the last day of any taxable year during the term of the QDOT (or the last day of the calendar year if the QDOT does not have a taxable year), the value of foreign real property owned by the QDOT exceeds 35 percent of the fair market value of the trust assets due to: distributions of QDOT principal during that year; fluctuations in the value of the foreign currency in the jurisdiction where the real estate is located; or fluctuations in the fair market value of any assets held in the QDOT, then the QDOT will not be treated as failing to meet the requirements of this paragraph (d)(1). Accordingly, the QDOT will not cease to be a QDOT within the meaning of section 20.2056A-5(b)(3) if, by the end of the taxable year (or the last day of the calendar year if the QDOT does not have a taxable year) of the QDOT immediately following the year in which the 35 percent limit was exceeded, the value of the foreign real property held by the QDOT does not exceed 35 percent of the fair market value of the trust assets or, alternatively, the QDOT meets the requirements of either paragraph (d)(1)(i)(A), (B), or (C) of this section on or before the close of that succeeding year.

(iii) Definition of finally determined. For purposes of § 20.2056A-2(d)(1)(i) and (ii), the fair market value of assets will be treated as finally determined on the earliest to occur of—

(A) The entry of a decision, judgment, decree, or other order by any court of competent jurisdiction that has become final;

(B) The execution of a closing agreement made under section 7121;

(C) Any final disposition by the Internal Revenue Service of a claim for refund;

(D) The issuance of an estate tax closing letter (Form L-154 or equivalent) if no claim for refund is filed; or

(E) The expiration of the period of assessment.

(iv) Special rules for personal residence and related personal effects. (A) Two million dollar threshold. For purposes of determining whether the $2 million threshold under paragraphs (d)(1)(i) and (ii) of this section has been exceeded, the executor of the estate may elect to exclude up to $600,000 in value attributable to real property (and related furnishings) owned directly by the QDOT that is used by, or held for the use of the surviving spouse as a personal residence and that passes, or is treated as passing, to the QDOT under section 2056(d). The election may be made regardless of whether the real property is situated within or without the United States. The election is made by attaching to the estate tax return on which the QDOT election is made a written statement claiming the exclusion. The statement must clearly identify the property or properties (i.e. address and location) for which the election is being made.

(B) Security requirement. For purposes of determining the amount of the bond or letter of credit required when paragraph (d)(1)(i)(B) or (C) of this section applies, the executor of the estate may elect to exclude, during the term of the QDOT, up to $600,000 in value attributable to real property (and related furnishings) owned directly by the QDOT that is used by, or held for the use of the surviving spouse as a personal residence and that passes, or is treated as passing, to the QDOT under section 2056(d). The election may be made regardless of whether the real property is situated within or without the United States. The election is made by attaching to the estate tax return on which the QDOT election is made a written statement claiming the exclusion. If an election is not made on the decedent's estate tax return, the election may be made, prospectively, at any time, during the term of the QDOT, by attaching to the Form 706-QDT a written statement claiming the exclusion. A statement may also be attached to the Form 706-QDT that cancels a prior election of the personal residence exclusion that was made under this paragraph, either on the decedent's estate tax return or on a Form 706-QDT.

(C) Foreign real property limitation. The special rules of this paragraph (d)(1)(iv) do not apply for purposes of determining whether more than 35 percent of the QDOT assets consist of foreign real property under paragraph (d)(1)(ii) of this section.

(D) Personal residence. For purposes of this paragraph (d)(1)(iv), a personal residence is either the principal residence of the surviving spouse within the meaning of section 1034 or one other residence of the surviving spouse. In order to be used by or held for the use of the spouse as a personal residence, the residence must be available at all times for use by the surviving spouse. The residence may not be rented to another party, even when not occupied by the spouse. A personal residence may include appurtenant structures used by the surviving spouse for residential purposes and adjacent land not in excess of that which is reasonably appropriate for residential purposes (taking into account the residence's size and location).

(E) Related furnishings. The term related furnishings means furniture and commonly included items such as appliances, fixtures, decorative items and china, that are not beyond the value associated with normal household and decorative use. Rare artwork, valuable antiques, and automobiles of any kind or class are not within the meaning of this term.

(F) Required statement. If one or both of the exclusions provided in paragraph (d)(1)(iv)(A) or (B) of this section are elected by the executor of the estate and the personal residence is later sold or ceases to be used, or held for use as a personal residence, the U.S. Trustee must file the statement that is required under paragraph (d)(3) of this section at the time and in the manner provided in paragraphs (d)(3)(ii) and (iii) of this section.

(G) Cessation of use. Except as provided in this paragraph (d)(1)(iv)(G), if the residence ceases to be used by, or held for the use of, the spouse as a personal residence of the spouse, or if the residence is sold during the term of the QDOT, the exclusions provided in paragraphs (d)(1)(iv)(A) and (B) of this section cease to apply. However, if the residence is sold, the exclusion continues to apply if, within 12 months of the date of sale, the amount of the adjusted sales price (as defined in section 1034(b)(1)) is reinvested to purchase a new personal residence for the spouse. If less than the amount of the adjusted sales price is reinvested, the amount of the exclusion equals the amount reinvested in the new residence plus any amount previously allocated to a residence that continues to qualify for the exclusion, up to a total of $600,000. If the QDOT ceases to qualify for all or any portion of the initially claimed exclusions, paragraph (d)(1)(i) of this section, if applicable (determined as if the portion of the exclusions disallowed had not been initially claimed by the QDOT), must be complied with no later than 120 days after the effective date of the cessation. In addition, if a residence ceases to be used by, or held for the use of the spouse as a personal residence of the spouse or if the personal residence is sold during the term of the QDOT, the personal residence exclusion may be allocated to another residence that is held in either the same QDOT or in another QDOT that is established for the surviving spouse, if the other residence qualifies as being used by, or held for the use of the spouse as a personal residence. The trustee may allocate up to $600,000 to the new personal residence (less the amount previously allocated to a residence that continues to qualify for the exclusion) even if the entire $600,000 exclusion was not previously utilized with respect to the original personal residence(s).

(v) Anti-abuse rule. Regardless of whether the QDOT designates a bank as the U.S. Trustee under paragraph (d)(1)(i)(A) of this section (or otherwise complies with paragraph (d)(1)(i)(A) of this section by naming a foreign bank with a United States branch as a trustee to serve with the U.S. Trustee), complies with paragraph (d)(1)(i)(B) or (C) of this section, or is subject to and complies with the foreign real property requirements of paragraph (d)(1)(ii) of this section, the trust immediately ceases to qualify as a QDOT if the trust utilizes any device or arrangement that has, as a principal purpose, the avoidance of liability for the estate tax imposed under section 2056A(b)(1), or the prevention of the collection of the tax. For example, the trust may become subject to this paragraph (d)(1)(v) if the U.S. Trustee that is selected is a domestic corporation established with insubstantial capitalization by the surviving spouse or members of the spouse's family.

(2) Individual trustees. If the U.S. Trustee is an individual United States citizen, the individual must have a tax home (as defined in section 911(d)(3)) in the United States.

(3) Annual reporting requirements. (i) In general. The U.S. Trustee must file a written statement described in paragraph (d)(3)(iii) of this section, if the QDOT satisfies any one of the following criteria for the applicable reporting years—

(A) The QDOT directly owns any foreign real property on the last day of its taxable year (or the last day of the calendar year if it has no taxable year), and the QDOT does not satisfy the requirements of paragraph (d)(1)(i)(A), (B), or (C) or (d)(4) of this section by employing a bank as trustee or providing security; or

(B) The personal residence previously subject to the exclusion under paragraph (d)(1)(iv) of this section is sold, or that personal residence ceases to be used, or held for use, as a personal residence, during the taxable year (or during the calendar year if the QDOT does not have a taxable year); or

(C) After the application of the look-through rule contained in paragraph (d)(1)(ii)(B) of this section, the QDOT is treated as owning any foreign real property on the last day of the taxable year (or the last day of the calendar year if the QDOT has no taxable year), and the QDOT does not satisfy the requirements of paragraph (d)(1)(A), (B), (C) or (d)(4) of this section by employing a bank as trustee or providing security.

(ii) Time and manner of filing. The written statement, containing the information described in paragraph (d)(3)(iii) of this section, is to be filed for the taxable year of the QDOT (calendar year if the QDOT does not have a taxable year) for which any of the events or conditions requiring the filing of a statement under paragraph (d)(3)(i) of this section have occurred or have been satisfied. The written statement is to be submitted to the Internal Revenue Service by filing a Form 706-QDT, with the statement attached, no later than April 15th of the calendar year following the calendar year in which or with which the taxable year of the QDOT ends (or by April 15th of the following year if the QDOT has no taxable year), unless an extension of time is obtained under § 20.2056A-11(a). The Form 706-QDT, with attached statement, must be filed regardless of whether the Form 706-QDT is otherwise required to be filed under the provisions of this chapter. Failure to file timely the statement may subject the QDOT to the rules of paragraph (d)(1)(v) of this section.

(iii) Contents of statement. The written statement must contain the following information—

(A) The name, address, and taxpayer identification number, if any, of the U.S. Trustee and the QDOT; and

(B) A list summarizing the assets held by the QDOT, together with the fair market value of each listed QDOT asset, determined as of the last day of the taxable year (December 31 if the QDOT does not have a taxable year) for which the written statement is filed. If the look-through rule contained in paragraph (d)(1)(ii)(B) of this section applies, then the partnership, corporation, trust or other entity must be identified and the QDOT's pro rata share of the foreign real property and other assets owned by that entity must be listed on the statement as if directly owned by the QDOT; and

(C) If a personal residence previously subject to the exclusion under paragraph (d)(1)(iv) of this section is sold during the taxable year (or during the calendar year if the QDOT does not have a taxable year), the statement must provide the date of sale, the adjusted sales price (as defined in section 1034(b)(1)), the extent to which the amount of the adjusted sales price has been or will be used to purchase a new personal residence and, if not timely reinvested, the steps that will or have been taken to comply with paragraph (d)(1)(i) of this section, if applicable; and

(D) If the personal residence ceases to be used, or held for use, as a personal residence by the surviving spouse during the taxable year (or during the calendar year if the QDOT does not have a taxable year), the written statement must describe the steps that will or have been taken to comply with paragraph (d)(1)(i) of this section, if applicable.

(4) Request for alternate arrangement or waiver. If the Commissioner provides guidance published in the Internal Revenue Bulletin (see § 601.601(d)(2) of this chapter) pursuant to which a testator, executor, or the U.S. Trustee may adopt an alternate plan or arrangement to assure collection of the section 2056A estate tax, and if the alternate plan or arrangement is adopted in accordance with the published guidance, then the QDOT will be treated, subject to paragraph (d)(1)(v) of this section, as meeting the requirements of paragraph (d)(1) of this section. Until this guidance is published in the Internal Revenue Bulletin (see § 601.601(d)(2) of this chapter), taxpayers may submit a request for a private letter ruling for the approval of an alternate plan or arrangement proposed to be adopted to assure collection of the section 2056A estate tax in lieu of the requirements prescribed in this paragraph (d)(4).

(5) Adjustment of dollar threshold and exclusion. The Commissioner may increase or decrease the dollar amounts referred to in paragraph (d)(1)(i), (ii) or (iv) of this section in accordance with guidance published in the Internal Revenue Bulletin (see § 601.601(d)(2) of this chapter).

(6) Effective date and special rules. (i) This paragraph (d) is effective for estates of decedents dying after February 19, 1996.

(ii) Special rule in the case of incompetency. A revocable trust or a trust created under the terms of a will is deemed to meet the governing instrument requirements of this paragraph (d) notwithstanding that the requirements are not contained in the governing instrument (or otherwise incorporated by reference) if the trust instrument (or will) was executed on or before November 20, 1995, and—

(A) The testator or settlor dies after February 19, 1996;

(B) The testator or settlor is, on November 20, 1995, and at all times thereafter, under a legal disability to amend the will or trust instrument;

(C) The will or trust instrument does not provide the executor or the U.S. Trustee with a power to amend the instrument in order to meet the requirements of section 2056A; and

(D) The U.S. Trustee provides a written statement with the federal estate tax return (Form 706 or 706NA) that the trust is being administered (or will be administered) so as to be in actual compliance with the requirements of this paragraph (d) and will continue to be administered so as to be in actual compliance with this paragraph (d) for the duration of the trust. This statement must be binding on all successor trustees.

(iii) Special rule in the case of certain irrevocable trusts. An irrevocable trust is deemed to meet the governing instrument requirements of this paragraph (d) notwithstanding that the requirements are not contained in the governing instrument (or otherwise incorporated by reference) if the trust was executed on or before November 20, 1995, and:

(A) The settlor dies after February 19, 1996;

(B) The trust instrument does not provide the U.S. Trustee with a power to amend the trust instrument in order to meet the requirements of section 2056A; and

(C) The U.S. Trustee provides a written statement with the decedent's federal estate tax return (Form 706 or 706NA) that the trust is being administered in actual compliance with the requirements of this paragraph (d) and will continue to be administered so as to be in actual compliance with this paragraph (d) for the duration of the trust. This statement must be binding on all successor trustees.

T.D. 8612, 8/21/95, amend T.D. 8686, 11/27/96.

§ 20.2056A-3 QDOT election.

(a) General rule. Subject to the time period prescribed in section 2056A(d), the election to treat a trust as a QDOT must be made on the last federal estate tax return filed before the due date (including extensions of time to file actually granted) or, if a timely return is not filed, on the first federal estate tax return filed after the due date. The election, once made, is irrevocable.

(b) No partial elections. An election to treat a trust as a QDOT may not be made with respect to a specific portion of an entire trust that would otherwise qualify for the marital deduction but for the application of section 2056(d). However, if the trust is actually severed in accordance with the applicable requirements of § 20.2056(b)-7(b)(2)(ii) prior to the due date for the election, a QDOT election may be made for any one or more of the severed trusts.

(c) Protective elections. A protective election may be made to treat a trust as a QDOT only if at the time the federal estate tax return is filed, the executor of the decedent's estate reasonably believes that there is a bona fide issue that concerns either the residency or citizenship of the decedent, the citizenship of the surviving spouse, whether an asset is includible in the decedent's gross estate, or the amount or nature of the property the surviving spouse is entitled to receive. For example, if at the time the federal estate tax return is filed either the estate is involved in a bona fide will contest, there is uncertainty regarding the inclusion in the gross estate of an asset which, if includible, would be eligible for the QDOT election, or there is uncertainty regarding the status of the decedent as a resident alien or a nonresident alien for estate tax purposes, or a similar uncertainty regarding the citizenship status of the surviving spouse, a protective QDOT election may be made. The protective election is in addition to, and is not in lieu of, the requirements set forth in § 20.2056A-4. The protective QDOT election must be made on a written statement signed by the executor under penalties of perjury and must be attached to the return described in paragraph (a) of this section, and must identify the specific assets to which the protective election refers and the specific basis for the protective election. However, the protective election may otherwise be defined by means of a formula (such as the minimum amount necessary to reduce the estate tax to zero). Once made, the protective election is irrevocable. For example, if a protective election is made because a bona fide question exists as to the includibility of an asset in the decedent's gross estate and it is later finally determined that the asset is so includible, the protective election becomes effective with respect to the asset and cannot thereafter be revoked.

(d) Manner of election. The QDOT election under paragraph (a) of this section is made in the form and manner set forth in the decedent's estate tax return, including applicable instructions.

T.D. 8612, 8/21/95.

§ 20.2056A-4 Procedures for conforming marital trusts and nontrust marital transfers to the requirements of a qualified domestic trust.

(a) Marital trusts. *(1) In general.* If an interest in property passes from the decedent to a trust for the benefit of a noncitizen surviving spouse and if the trust otherwise qualifies for a marital deduction but for the provisions of section 2056(d)(1)(A), the property interest is treated as passing to the surviving spouse in a QDOT if the trust is reformed, either in accordance with the terms of the decedent's will or trust agreement or pursuant to a judicial proceeding, to meet the requirements of a QDOT. For this purpose, the requirements of a QDOT include all of the applicable requirements set forth in § 20.2056A-2, and the requirements of § 20.2056A-2T(d). A reformation pursuant to the terms of the decedent's will or trust instrument must be completed by the time prescribed (including extensions) for filing the decedent's estate tax return. For purposes of this paragraph (a), a return filed prior to the due date (including extensions) is considered filed on the last date that the return is required to be filed (including extensions), and a late return filed at any time after the due date is considered filed on the date that it is actually filed.

(2) Judicial reformations. In general, a reformation pursuant to a judicial proceeding is permitted under this section if the reformation is commenced on or before the due date (determined with regard to extensions actually granted) for filing the return of tax imposed by chapter 11 of the Internal Revenue Code, regardless of the date that the return is actually filed. The reformation (either pursuant to a judicial proceeding or otherwise) must result in a trust that is effective under local law. The reformed trust may be revocable by the spouse, or otherwise be subject to the spouse's general power of appointment, provided that no person (including the spouse) has the power to amend the trust during the continued existence of the trust such that it would no longer qualify as a QDOT. Prior to the time that the judicial reformation is completed, the trust must be treated as a QDOT. Thus, the trustee of the trust is responsible for filing the Form 706-QDT, paying any section 2056A estate tax that

becomes due, and filing the annual statement required under § 20.2056A-2T(d)(3), if applicable. Failure to comply with these requirements may cause the trust to be subject to the anti-abuse rule under § 20.2056A-2T(d)(1)(iv). In addition, if the judicial reformation is terminated prior to the time that the reformation is completed, the estate of the decedent is required to pay the increased estate tax imposed on the decedent's estate (plus interest and any applicable penalties) that becomes due at the time of such termination as a result of the failure of the trust to comply with section 2056(d). See section 6511 as to applicable time periods for credit or refund of tax.

(3) Tolling of statutory assessment period. For the tolling of the statute of limitations in the case of a judicial reformation, see section 2056(d)(5)(B).

(b) Nontrust marital transfers. *(1) In general.* Under section 2056(d)(2)(B), if an interest in property passes outright from a decedent to a noncitizen surviving spouse either by testamentary bequest or devise, by operation of law, or pursuant to an annuity or other similar plan or arrangement, and such property interest otherwise qualifies for a marital deduction except that it does not pass in a QDOT, solely for purposes of section 2056(d)(2)(A), the property is treated as passing to the surviving spouse in a QDOT if the property interest is either actually transferred to a QDOT before the estate tax return is filed and on or before the last date prescribed by law that the QDOT election may be made, or is assigned to a QDOT under an enforceable and irrevocable written assignment made on or before the date on which the return is filed and on or before the last date prescribed by law that the QDOT election may be made. The transfer or assignment of property to a QDOT may be made by the surviving spouse, the surviving spouse's legal representative (if the surviving spouse is incompetent), or the personal representative of the surviving spouse's estate (if the surviving spouse has died). The QDOT to which the property is transferred may be created by the decedent (during life or by will), by the surviving spouse, or by the executor. For purposes of section 2056(d)(2)(B), if no property other than the property passing to the surviving spouse from the decedent is transferred to the QDOT, the transferee QDOT need not be in a form such that the property transferred to the QDOT would qualify for a marital deduction under section 2056(a). However, if other property is or has been transferred to the QDOT, 100 percent of the value of the transferee QDOT must qualify for the marital deduction under section 2056. For example, if the decedent, a U.S. citizen, bequeaths property to a trust that does not satisfy the requirements of section 2056(b)(5) or (7), or to a trust that does not qualify as an estate trust under § 20.2056(c)-2(b)(1)(i)-(iii), that trust cannot be used as a transferee QDOT by the surviving spouse, since after that trust is fully funded the portion of the value of the trust attributable to property bequeathed to the trust by the decedent will not qualify for a marital deduction under section 2056. Similarly, if the decedent, a nonresident not a citizen of the United States, bequeaths foreign situs assets to a trust created under his will, the surviving spouse may not transfer U.S. situs assets passing to the spouse outside of the will to that trust under this paragraph. See § 20.2056A-3(c) with respect to protective elections. See § 20.2056A-3(a) with respect to the time limitations for making the QDOT election.

(2) Form of transfer or assignment. A transfer or assignment of property to a QDOT must be in writing and otherwise be in accordance with all local law requirements for such assignment or transfer. The transfer or assignment may be of a specific asset or a group of assets, or a fractional share of either, or may be of a pecuniary amount. A transfer or assignment of less than an entire interest in an asset or a group of assets may be expressed by means of a formula (such as the minimum amount necessary to reduce the estate tax to zero). In the case of a transfer, a copy of the trust instrument evidencing the transfer must be submitted with the decedent's estate tax return. In the case of an assignment, a copy of the assignment must be submitted with the decedent's estate tax return.

(3) Assets eligible for transfer or assignment. If a transfer or assignment is of a specific asset or group of assets, only assets included in the decedent's gross estate and passing from the decedent to the spouse (or the proceeds from the sale, exchange or conversion of such assets) may be transferred or assigned to the QDOT. The noncitizen surviving spouse may not transfer or assign to the QDOT property owned by the surviving spouse at the time of the decedent's death in lieu of property included in the decedent's gross estate that passes to the spouse (or in lieu of the proceeds from the sale, exchange or conversion of such includible assets). In addition, if only a portion of an asset is includible in the decedent's gross estate, the spouse may only transfer the portion that is so includible to the transferee trust under this paragraph (b)(3).

(4) Pecuniary assignment—Special rules. If the assignment is expressed in the form of a pecuniary amount (such as a fixed dollar amount or a formula designed to reduce the decedent's estate tax to zero), the assignment must specify that—

(i) Assets actually transferred to the QDOT in satisfaction of the assignment have an aggregate fair market value on the date of actual transfer to the QDOT amounting to no less than the amount of the pecuniary transfer or assignment; or

(ii) The assets actually transferred to the QDOT be fairly representative of appreciation or depreciation in the value of all property available for transfer to the QDOT between the valuation date and the date of actual transfer to the QDOT, if the assignment is to be satisfied by accounting for the assets on the basis of their fair market value as of some date before the date of actual transfer to the QDOT.

(5) Transfer tax treatment of transfer or assignment. Property assigned or transferred to a QDOT pursuant to section 2056(d)(2)(B) is treated as passing from the decedent to a QDOT solely for purposes of section 2056(d)(2)(A). For all other purposes (e.g., income, gift, estate, generation-skipping transfer tax, and section 1491 excise tax), the surviving spouse is treated as the transferor of the property to the QDOT. However, the spouse is not considered the transferor of property to a QDOT if the transfer by the spouse constitutes a transfer that satisfies the requirements of section 2518(c)(3). For a special exception to the valuation rules of section 2702 in the case of a transfer by the surviving spouse to a QDOT, see § 25.2702-1(c)(8) of this chapter.

(6) Period for completion of transfer. Property irrevocably assigned but not actually transferred to the QDOT before the estate tax return is filed must actually be conveyed and transferred to the QDOT under applicable local law before the administration of the decedent's estate is completed. If there is no administration of the decedent's estate (because for example, none of the decedent's assets are subject to probate under local law), the conveyance must be made on or before the date that is one year after the due date (including extensions) for filing the decedent's estate tax return. If an actual transfer to the QDOT is not timely made, section 2056(d)(1)(A) applies and the marital deduction is not al-

lowed. The executor of the decedent's estate (or other authorized legal representative) may request a private letter ruling from the Internal Revenue Service requesting an extension of the time for completing the conveyance or waiving the actual conveyance under specified circumstances under § 301.9100-1(a) of this chapter.

(7) Retirement accounts and annuities. (i) In general. An assignment otherwise in compliance with this paragraph (b) of rights under annuities or other similar arrangements that are assignable and thus, are not described in paragraph (c) of this section, is treated as a transfer of such property to the QDOT regardless of the method of payment actually elected under such annuity or plan.

(ii) Individual retirement annuities. Individual retirement annuities described in section 408(b) are not assignable pursuant to section 408(b)(1) and thus, do not come within the purview of this paragraph (b)(7). See the procedures provided in paragraph (c) of this section.

(iii) Individual retirement accounts. Unless the terms of the account provide otherwise, individual retirement accounts described in section 408(a) are assignable and subject to the provisions of this paragraph (b)(7). However, under paragraph (c) of this section, the surviving spouse may treat an individual retirement account as nonassignable and, therefore, eligible for the procedures in paragraph (c) of this section if the spouse timely complies with the requirements in paragraph (c) of this section.

(iv) Other effects of assignment. The provisions of this paragraph (b)(7) apply solely for purposes of qualifying the annuity or account under the rules of § 20.2056A-2 and this section. See, for example, section 408(d) and 4980A regarding the consequences of an assignment for purposes other than this paragraph (b)(7).

(8) Protective assignment. A protective assignment of property to a QDOT may be made only if, at the time the federal estate tax return is filed, the executor of the decedent's estate reasonably believes that there is a bona fide issue that concerns either the residency or citizenship of the decedent, the citizenship of the surviving spouse, whether all or a portion of an asset is includible in the decedent's gross estate, or the amount or nature of the property the surviving spouse is entitled to receive. For example, if at the time the federal estate tax return is filed, either the estate is involved in a bona fide will contest, there is uncertainty regarding the inclusion in the gross estate of an asset which, if includible, would be eligible for the QDOT election, or there is uncertainty regarding the status of the decedent as a resident alien or a nonresident alien for estate tax purposes, or a similar uncertainty regarding the citizenship status of the surviving spouse, a protective assignment may be made. The protective assignment must be made on a written statement signed by the assignor under penalties of perjury on or before the date prescribed under paragraph (b)(1) of this section, and must identify the specific assets to which the assignment refers and the specific basis for the protective assignment. However, the protective assignment may otherwise be defined by means of a formula (such as the minimum amount necessary to reduce the estate tax to zero). Once made, the protective assignment cannot be revoked. For example, if a protective assignment is made because a bona fide question exists as to the includibility of an asset in the decedent's gross estate and it is later finally determined that the asset is so includible, the protective assignment becomes effective with respect to the asset and cannot thereafter be revoked. Protective assignments are, in all events, subject to paragraph (b)(6) of this section. A copy of the protective assignment must be submitted with the decedent's estate tax return.

(c) Nonassignable annuities and other arrangements. *(1) Definition and general rule.* For purposes of this section, a nonassignable annuity or other arrangement means a plan, annuity, or other arrangement (whether qualified or not qualified under part I of subchapter D of chapter 1 of subtitle A of the Internal Revenue Code) that qualifies for the marital deduction but for section 2056(d)(1)(A), and whose payments are not assignable or transferable to the QDOT under either federal law (see, e.g., section 401(a)(13)), state law, foreign law, or the terms of the plan or arrangement itself. For purposes of this paragraph (c), a surviving spouse's interest as beneficiary of an individual retirement annuity described in section 408(b) is a nonassignable annuity or other arrangement. See section 408(b)(1). For purposes of this paragraph (c), a surviving spouse's interest as beneficiary of an individual retirement account described in section 408(a), although assignable under that section, is considered to be a nonassignable annuity or other arrangement eligible for the procedures contained in this paragraph (c), at the option of the surviving spouse, if the requirements of this paragraph are otherwise satisfied. See paragraph (b)(7) of this section if the spouse elects to treat the account as assignable. In the case of a plan, annuity, or other arrangement which is not assignable or transferable (or is treated as such), the property passing under the plan from the decedent is treated as meeting the requirements § 20.2056A-2, and the requirements of § 20.2056A-2T(d) (pertaining, respectively, to general requirements, qualified marital interest requirements, statutory requirements, and requirements to ensure collection of the tax) if the requirements of either paragraph (c)(2) or (3) of this section are satisfied. Thus, the property will be treated as passing in the form of a QDOT, notwithstanding that the spouse does not irrevocably transfer or assign the annuity or other payment to the QDOT as provided in paragraph (b) of this section. The Commissioner will prescribe by administrative guidance the extent, if any, to which the provisions of this paragraph (c) apply to a rollover from a qualified trust to an eligible retirement plan within the meaning of section 402(c) or a distribution from an individual retirement account or an individual retirement annuity that is paid into an individual retirement account or an individual retirement annuity within the meaning of section 408(d)(3).

(2) Agreement to remit section 2056A estate tax on corpus portion of each annuity payment. The requirements of this paragraph (c)(2) are satisfied if—

(i) The noncitizen surviving spouse agrees to pay on an annual basis, as described in paragraph (c)(6)(i) of this section, the estate tax imposed under section 2056A(b)(1) due on the corpus portion, as defined in paragraph (c)(4) of this section, of each nonassignable annuity or other payment received under the plan or arrangement. However, for purposes of this paragraph (c)(2), if the financial circumstances of the spouse are such that an amount equal to all or a portion of the corpus portion of a nonassignable annuity payment received by the spouse would be subject to a hardship exemption (as defined in § 20.2056A-5(c)) if paid from a QDOT, then all or a corresponding part of the corpus portion will be exempt from the tax payment requirement under this paragraph (c)(2);

(ii) The executor of the decedent's estate files with the estate tax return the Information Statement described in paragraph (c)(5) of this section;

(iii) The executor files with the estate tax return the Agreement To Pay Section 2056A Estate Tax described in paragraph (c)(6) of this section; and

(iv) The executor makes the election under § 20.2056A-3 with respect to the nonassignable annuity or other payment.

(3) Agreement to roll over corpus portion of annuity payment to QDOT. The requirements of this paragraph (c)(3) are satisfied if—

(i) The noncitizen surviving spouse agrees to roll over and transfer, within the time prescribed under paragraph (c)(7)(i) of this section, the corpus portion of each annuity payment to a QDOT, whether the QDOT is created by the decedent's will, the executor of the decedent's estate, or the surviving spouse. However, for purposes of this section, if the financial circumstances of the spouse are such that an amount equal to all or a portion of the corpus portion of a nonassignable annuity payment received by the spouse would be subject to a hardship exemption (as defined in § 20.2056A-5(c)) if paid from a QDOT, then all or a corresponding part of the corpus portion will be exempt from the rollover requirement under this paragraph (c)(3);

(ii) A QDOT for the benefit of the surviving spouse is established prior to the date that the estate tax return is filed and on or prior to the last date prescribed by law that the QDOT election may be made;

(iii) The executor of the decedent's estate files with the estate tax return the Information Statement described in paragraph (c)(5) of this section;

(iv) The executor files with the estate tax return the Agreement To Roll Over Annuity Payments described in paragraph (c)(7) of this section; and

(v) The executor makes the election under § 20.2056A-3 with respect to the nonassignable annuity or other payment. See § 20.2056A-5(c)(3)(iv)(A), regarding distributions from the QDOT reimbursing the spouse for income taxes paid (either by actual payment or withholding) by the spouse with respect to amounts transferred to the QDOT pursuant to this paragraph (c)(3).

(4) Determination of corpus portion. (i) Corpus portion. For purposes of this paragraph (c), the corpus portion of each nonassignable annuity or other payment is the corpus amount of the annual payment divided by the total annual payment.

(ii) Corpus amount. (A) The corpus amount of the annual payment is determined in accordance with the following formula:

$$\text{Corpus Amount} = \frac{\text{Total present value of annuity or other payment}}{\text{Expected annuity term}}$$

(B) [Reserved]. For further guidance, see § 20.2056A-4T(c)(4)(ii)(B).

(5) Information statement. (i) In general. In order for a nonassignable annuity or other payment described in this paragraph (c) to qualify under either paragraph (c)(2) or (3) of this section, the Information Statement described in paragraph (c)(5)(ii) of this section must be filed with the decedent's federal estate tax return. The Information Statement must be signed under penalties of perjury by both the executor of the decedent's estate and by the surviving spouse of the decedent (or by the legal representative of the surviving spouse if the surviving spouse is legally incompetent to sign the statement). The Statement must contain all of the information prescribed by this paragraph (c)(5).

(ii) Annuity source information. (A) Employment-related annuity. If the nonassignable annuity or other payment is employment-related, the following information must be provided—

(1) The name and address of the employer;

(2) The date of retirement or other separation from employment of the decedent;

(3) The name and address of the pension fund, insurance company, or other obligor that is paying the annuity (or similar payment); and

(4) The identification number, if any, that the obligor has assigned to the annuity or other payment.

(B) Annuity not employment-=related. If the nonassignable annuity or other payment is not employment-related, the following information must be provided—

(1) The name and address of the person or entity paying the nonassignable annuity or other payment;

(2) The date of acquisition of the nonassignable annuity contract by the decedent or by the decedent and the surviving spouse; and

(3) The identification number, if any, that the obligor has assigned to the nonassignable annuity or other payment.

(iii) The total annuity amount payable each year. The total amount payable annually under the nonassignable annuity or other arrangement, including a description of whether the annuity is payable monthly, quarterly, or at some other interval, and a description of any scheduled changes in the annuity payout amount.

(iv) The duration of the annuity. A description of the term of the nonassignable annuity or other payment in years, if it is determined by a term certain, and the name, address, and birthdate of any measuring life if the nonassignable annuity or other payment is determined by one or more lives.

(v) The market interest rate under section 7520. The applicable interest rate as determined under section 7520.

(vi) Determination of corpus portion of each payment (In accordance with paragraph (c)(4) of this section). The following items are required in order to determine the corpus portion of each payment—

(A) The present value of the nonassignable annuity or other payment as of the decedent's death;

(B) The expected annuity term;

(C) The corpus amount of the annual annuity payments (paragraph (c)(5)(vi)(A) of this section divided by paragraph (c)(5)(vi)(B) of this section); and

(D) The corpus portion of the annual payments (paragraph (c)(5)(vi)(C) of this section divided by the total amount payable annually).

(vii) Recipient QDOT. In the case of an agreement to rollover under paragraph (c)(3) of this section, the following must be provided—

(A) The name and address of the trustee of the QDOT who is the U.S. Trustee; and

(B) The name and taxpayer identification number of the QDOT.

(viii) Certification statement. The executor of the decedent's estate and the surviving spouse of the decedent (or the legal representative of the surviving spouse if the surviving spouse is legally incompetent to so certify) must each sign a Certification Statement as follows:

Under penalties of perjury, I hereby certify that, to the best of my knowledge and belief, the information reported in this Information Statement is true, correct and complete.

(6) Agreement to pay section 2056A estate tax. (i) Payment of section 2056A estate tax. The tax payable under paragraph (c)(2) of this section is payable on an annual basis, commencing in the calendar year following the calendar year of the receipt by the surviving spouse of the spouse's first annuity payment. Form 706QDT and the payment are due on April 15th of each year following the calendar year in which an annuity payment is received except that, in the year of the deceased spouse's death, the Form 706-QDT and the payment are not due prior to the due date, including extensions, for filing the deceased spouse's estate tax return, or if no return is filed, no later than 9 months from the date of the deceased spouse's death; and, in the year of the surviving spouse's death, the Form 706-QDT must be filed and the payment made no later than 9 months from the date of the surviving spouse's death. See § 20.2056A-11 for extensions of time for filing Form 706-QDT and paying the section 2056A estate tax.

(ii) Agreement. In order for a nonassignable annuity or other payment described in this paragraph (c) to qualify under paragraph (c)(2) of this section, the executor of the decedent's estate must file with the estate tax return the following Agreement To Pay Section 2056A Estate Tax, which must be signed by the surviving spouse of the decedent (or by the surviving spouse's legal representative if the surviving spouse is legally incompetent to sign the agreement):

I [*name*] hereby agree that I will report all annuity payments received under the [*name of plan or arrangement*] on Form 706-QDT for the calendar year and remit, on an annual basis, to the Internal Revenue Service the estate tax that is imposed under section 2056A(b)(1) of the Internal Revenue Code on the corpus portion of each annuity payment (as defined in § 20.2056A-4(c)(4) of the Estate Tax Regulations) received under the plan during the calendar year. I also agree that Form 706-QDT is to be filed no later than April 15th of the year following the calendar year in which any annuity payments are received except that: in the case of annuity payments received in the year of my spouse's death, Form 706-QDT and the payment shall not be due prior to the due date, including extensions, for filing my spouse's estate tax return or, if no return is filed, no later than 9 months from the date of my spouse's death (except if I am granted an extension of time to file Form 706-QDT under the provisions of § 20.2056A-11); and in the year of my death, the Form 706-QDT must be filed and the payment made no later than the date my estate tax return is filed (or if no return is filed, no later than 9 months from the date of my death). I further agree that if I fail to timely file Form 706-QDT or to timely pay the tax imposed on the corpus portion of any annuity payment (determined after any extensions of time to pay granted to me under the provisions of § 20.2056A-11), I may become immediately liable to pay the amount of the tax determined by application of section 2056A(b)(1) on the entire remaining present value of the annuity, calculated as of the beginning of the year in which the payment was received with respect to which I failed to timely pay the tax or failed to timely file the return. However, I may make an application for relief under § 301.9100-1 of the Procedure and Administration Regulations, from the consequences of failing to timely file the Form 706-QDT or failing to timely pay the tax on the corpus portion. [The following sentence is applicable only in cases where the plan or arrangement is established and administered by a person or an entity that is located outside of the United States.] I agree, at the request of the District Director, [or the Assistant Commissioner (International) in the case of a surviving spouse of a nonresident noncitizen decedent or a surviving spouse of a United States citizen who died domiciled outside the United States] to enter into a security agreement to secure my undertakings under this agreement.

(7) Agreement to roll over annuity payments. (i) Roll over of corpus portion. Beginning in the calendar year of the receipt by the surviving spouse of the spouse's first annuity payment, the corpus portion of each annuity payment, as determined under paragraph (c)(4) of this section, must, within 60 days of receipt, be transferred to a QDOT. In addition, all annuity payments received during the calendar year must be reported on Form 706-QDT no later than April 15th of the year following the year in which the annuity payments are received, except that in the year of the surviving spouse's death, the Form 706-QDT must be filed no later than the date the estate tax return is filed (or if no return is filed, no later than 9 months from the date of the surviving spouse's death). See § 20.2056A-11 for extensions of time for filing Form 706-QDT.

(ii) Agreement. In order for a nonassignable annuity or other payment described in this paragraph (c) to qualify under paragraph (c)(3) of this section, the executor of the decedent's estate must file with the estate tax return the following Agreement To Roll Over Annuity Payments, which must be signed by the surviving spouse of the decedent (or by the legal representative of the surviving spouse if the surviving spouse is legally incompetent to sign the agreement):

I [*name*] hereby agree that within 60 days of receipt of each annuity payment paid under the [*name of plan or arrangement*], I will transfer an amount equal to ______ percent (the corpus portion determined under § 20.2056A-4(c)(4) of the Estate Tax Regulations) of each annuity payment to [*identify the QDOT*]. Further, I will report all annuity payments received during the calendar year under the [*name of plan or arrangement*] on Form 706-QDT including a schedule of transfers to the [identify the QDOT]. I also agree that Form 706-QDT is to be filed no later than April 15th of the year following the year in which any annuity payments are received except that: in the case of annuity payments received in the year of my spouse's death, Form 706-QDT shall not be due prior to the due date, including extensions, for filing my spouse's estate tax return, or, if no return is filed, no later than 9 months from the date of my spouse's death (except if I am granted an extension of time to file Form 706-QDT under the provisions of § 20.2056A-11); and in the year of my death, the Form 706-QDT must be filed no later than the date my estate tax return is filed (or if no return is filed, no later than 9 months from the date of my death), and except if I am granted an extension of time to file Form 706-QDT under the provisions of § 20.2056A-11. I further agree that if I fail to timely transfer any required amount with respect to any annuity payment, or fail to timely file Form 706-QDT reporting the transfers for any year, I may become immediately liable to pay the amount of the tax determined by application of section 2056A(b)(1) on the entire remaining present value of the annuity, calculated as of the beginning of the year in which the payment was received with respect to which I failed to make the timely transfer or timely file a return. However, I may make an application for relief under § 301.9100-1 of the Procedure and Administration Regulations, from the consequences of failing to timely file Form 706-QDT or failing to timely transfer the corpus portion of any annuity payment to the QDOT. [The following sentence is applicable only in cases where the plan or arrangement is established and administered by a person or an entity that is located outside of the United States.] I agree, at the request of the District Director [or the Assistant Commissioner (International) in the case of a surviving spouse of a nonresident noncitizen decedent or a surviving spouse of a United States citizen who died domiciled outside the United States] to enter into a security agreement to secure my undertakings under this agreement.

(d) Examples. The provisions of this section are illustrated by the following examples. In each of the following examples the decedent, D, a citizen of the United States, died after August 22, 1995, and D's surviving spouse, S, is not a United States citizen at the time of D's death.

Example (1). Transfer and assignment of probate and nonprobate property to QDOT.

(i) S is the beneficiary of the following probate and nonprobate assets included in D's gross estate:

D's gross estate:	
Pecuniary bequest under will	$ 400,000
Proceeds of life insurance	200,000
D's interest in property owned jointly with S includible in the gross estate under § 2040(a)	300,000
Devise of real property under will	100,000
Total	$1,000,000

(ii) Before the estate tax return for D's estate is filed and before the date that the QDOT election must be made, S creates a QDOT pursuant to which all income is payable to S for life and the remainder is distributable to S's children. S retains a power of appointment over the disposition of the remainder to ensure that S does not make an immediate gift of the remainder of the trust. Also, before the estate tax return is filed and before the date that the QDOT election must be made, S transfers the life insurance proceeds and the specifically devised real property to the QDOT. S decides not to transfer the property that had been jointly owned to the QDOT. Because S has not received distribution of the pecuniary bequest before D's estate tax return is filed and before the date that the QDOT election must be made, S irrevocably assigns the interest in the pecuniary bequest to the QDOT. Assume that the pecuniary bequest is in fact transferred by S to the QDOT before the estate administration is concluded. D's executor makes a QDOT election on the estate tax return for the $700,000 in property that S has transferred and assigned to the QDOT. A marital deduction of $700,000 is allowed to D's estate assuming the estate tax return is filed and the QDOT election is made within the time limitation prescribed in § 20.2056A-3(a). No marital deduction is allowed for the $300,000 interest in jointly-owned property not transferred to the QDOT.

Example (2). Formula assignment. Under the terms of D's will, the entire probate estate passes outright to S. Prior to the date D's estate tax return is filed and before the date that the QDOT election must be made, S establishes a QDOT and S executes an irrevocable assignment in which S assigns to the QDOT, "that portion of the gross estate necessary to reduce the estate tax to zero, taking into account all available credits and deductions." The assignment meets the requirements of paragraph (b) of this section, assuming that the QDOT is funded by the time that administration of D's estate is completed.

Example (3). Jointly owned property. At the time of D's death, D and S hold real property as joint tenants with right of survivorship. In accordance with section 2056(d)(1)(B), section 2040(a), and § 20.2056A-8(a), 60 percent of the value of the property is included in D's gross estate. S establishes a QDOT and, prior to the date the estate tax return is filed and before the date that the QDOT election must be made, S transfers a 60 percent interest in the real property to the QDOT. The transfer satisfies the requirements of paragraph (b) of this section.

Example (4). [Reserved]. For further guidance, see § 20.2056A-4T(d) Example 4.

Example (5). Transfer to QDOT subject to gift tax. D's will bequeaths $700,000 outright to S. The bequest qualifies for a marital deduction under section 2056(a) except that it does not pass in a QDOT. S creates an irrevocable trust that meets the requirements for a QDOT and transfers the $700,000 to the QDOT. The QDOT instrument provides that S is entitled to all the income from the QDOT payable at least annually and that, upon the death of S, the property remaining in the QDOT is to be distributed to the grandchildren of D and S in equal shares. The trust instrument contains all other provisions required to qualify as a QDOT. On D's estate tax return, D's executor makes a QDOT election under section 2056A(a)(3). Solely for purposes of the marital deduction, the property is deemed to pass from D to the QDOT. D's estate is entitled to a marital deduction for the $700,000 value of the property passing from D to S. S's transfer of property to the QDOT is treated as a gift of the remainder interest for gift tax purposes because S's transfer creates a vested remainder interest in the grandchildren of D and S. Accordingly, as of the date that S transfers the property to the QDOT, a gift tax is imposed on the present value of the remainder interest. See § 25.2702-1(c)(8) of this chapter exempting S's transfer from the special valuation rules contained in section 2702. At S's death, S is treated as the transferor of the property into the trust for estate tax and generation-skipping transfer tax purposes. See, e.g., sections 2036 and 2652(a)(1). The trust is not eligible for a reverse QTIP election by D's estate under section 2652(a)(3) because a QTIP election cannot be made for the QDOT. This is so because the marital deduction is allowed under section 2056(a) for the outright bequest to the spouse and the spouse is then separately treated as the transferor of the property to the QDOT.

T.D. 8612, 8/21/95, amend T.D. 8819, 4/29/99, T.D. 9448, 5/1/2009.

PAR. 10. Section 20.2056A-4 is amended by revising paragraph (c)(4)(ii)(B) and Example 4 in paragraph (d) to read as follows:

Proposed § 20.2056A-4 Procedures for conforming marital trusts and nontrust marital transfers to the requirements of a qualified domestic trust. [*For Preamble, see ¶ 153,105*]

* * * * *

(c) * * *

(4) * * *

(ii) * * *

(B) [The text of this proposed paragraph (c)(4)(ii)(B) is the same as the text of § 20.2056A-4T(c)(4)(ii)(B) published elsewhere in this issue of the Federal Register]. [*See T.D. 9448, 05/07/2009, 74 Fed. Reg. 87.*]

* * * * *

(d) * * *

Example (4). [The text of this proposed paragraph (d), Example 4 is the same as the text of Example 4 in § 20.2056A-4T(d) published elsewhere in this issue of the Federal Register]. [*See T.D. 9448, 05/07/2009, 74 Fed. Reg. 87.*]

§ 20.2056A-4T Procedures for conforming marital trusts and nontrust marital transfers to the requirements of a qualified domestic trust (temporary).

(a) through (c)(4)(ii)(A). [Reserved]. For further guidance see § 20.2056A-4(a) through (c)(4)(ii)(A).

(c) *(4)* (ii) (B) The total present value of the annuity or other payment is the present value of the nonassignable annuity or other payment as of the date of the decedent's death, determined in accordance with the interest rates and mortality data prescribed by section 7520. The expected annuity term is the number of years that would be required for the scheduled payments to exhaust a hypothetical fund equal to the present value of the scheduled payments. This is determined by first dividing the total present value of the payments by the annual payment. From the quotient so obtained, the expected annuity term is derived by identifying the term of years that corresponds to the annuity factor equal to the quotient. This is determined by using column 1 of Table B, for the applicable interest rate, contained in Publication 1457, Actuarial Valuations Version 3A. A copy of this publication is available beginning May 1, 2009, at no charge, electronically via the IRS Internet site at http://www.irs.gov. If the quotient obtained falls between two terms, the longer term is used.

(5) through (c)(7). [Reserved]. For further guidance see § 20.2056A-4(c)(5) through (c)(7).

(d)

Example (1). through 3. [Reserved]. For further guidance see § 20.2056A-4(d) Examples 1 through 3.

Example (4). Computation of corpus portion of annuity payment. (i) At the time of D's death on or after May 1, 2009, D is a participant in an employees' pension plan described in section 401(a). On D's death, D's spouse S, a resident of the United States, becomes entitled to receive a survivor's annuity of $72,000 per year, payable monthly, for life. At the time of D's death, S is age 60. Assume that under section 7520, the appropriate discount rate to be used for valuing annuities in the case of this decedent is 6.0 percent. The annuity factor at 6.0 percent for a person age 60 is 11.0625 (1.0000 minus .33625, divided by .06). The adjustment factor at 6.0 percent in Table K for monthly payments is 1.0272. Accordingly, the right to receive $72,000 per year on a monthly basis is equal to the right to receive $73,958.40 ($72,000 x 1.0272) on an annual basis.

(ii) The corpus portion of each annuity payment received by S is determined as follows. The first step is to determine the annuity factor for the number of years that would be required to exhaust a hypothetical fund that has a present value and a payout corresponding to S's interest in the payments under the plan, determined as follows:

(A) Present value of S's annuity: $73,958.40 x 11.0625 = $818,164.80.

(B) Annuity Factor for Expected Annuity Term: $818,164.80/$73,958.40 = 11.0625

(iii) The second step is to determine the number of years that would be required for S 's annuity to exhaust a hypothetical fund of $818,164.80. The term certain annuity factor of 11.0625 falls between the annuity factors for 18 and 19 years in a 6.0 percent term certain annuity table (Column 1 of Table B, Publication 1457 Actuarial Valuations Version 3A, which may be obtained on the IRS Internet site). Accordingly, the expected annuity term is 19 years.

(iv) The third step is to determine the corpus amount by dividing the expected term of 19 years into the present value of the hypothetical fund as follows:

Corpus amount of annual payment: $818,164.80/19 = $43,061.31

(v) In the fourth step, the corpus portion of each annuity payment is determined by dividing the corpus amount of each annual payment by the annual annuity payment (adjusted for payments more frequently than annually as in (i) of this Example 4) as follows:

Corpus portion of each annuity payment: $43,061.31/$73,958.40 = .58

(vi) Accordingly, 58 percent of each payment to S is deemed to be a distribution of corpus. A marital deduction is allowed for $818,164.80, the present value of the annuity as of D's date of death, if either: S agrees to roll over the corpus portion of each payment to a QDOT and the executor files the Information Statement described in paragraph (c)(5) of this section and the Roll Over Agreement described in paragraph (c)(7) of this section; or S agrees to pay the tax due on the corpus portion of each payment and the executor files the Information Statement described in paragraph (c)(5) of this section and the Payment Agreement described in paragraph (c)(6) of this section.

Example (5). [Reserved]. For further guidance see § 20.2056A-4(d) Example 5.

(e) Effective/applicability date. Paragraph (c)(4)(ii)(B) and Example 4 in paragraph (d) of this section are applicable with respect to decedents dying on or after May 1, 2009.

(f) Expiration date. Paragraph (c)(4)(ii)(B) and Example 4 in paragraph (d) of this section expire on or before May 1, 2012.

T.D. 9448, 5/1/2009.

§ 20.2056A-5 Imposition of section 2056A estate tax.

(a) In general. An estate tax is imposed under section 2056A(b)(1) on the occurrence of a taxable event, as defined in section 2056A(b)(9). The tax is generally equal to the amount of estate tax that would have been imposed if the amount involved in the taxable event had been included in the decedent's taxable estate and had not been deductible under section 2056. See section 2056A(b)(3) and paragraph (c) of this section for certain exceptions from taxable events.

(b) Amounts subject to tax *(1) Distribution of principal during the spouse's lifetime.* If a taxable event occurs during the noncitizen surviving spouse's lifetime, the amount on which the section 2056A estate tax is imposed is the amount of money and the fair market value of the property that is the subject of the distribution (including property distributed from the trust pursuant to the exercise of a power of appointment), including any amount withheld from the distribution by the U.S. Trustee to pay the tax. If, however, the tax is not withheld by the U.S. Trustee but is paid by the U.S. Trustee out of other assets of the QDOT, an amount equal to the tax so paid is treated as an additional distribution to the spouse in the year that the tax is paid.

(2) Death of surviving spouse. If a taxable event occurs as a result of the death of the surviving spouse, the amount subject to tax is the fair market value of the trust assets on the date of the spouse's death (or alternate valuation date if applicable). See also section 2032A. Any corpus portion amounts, within the meaning of § 20.2056A-4(c)(4)(i), remaining in a QDOT upon the surviving spouse's death, are subject to tax under section 2056A(b)(1)(B), as well as any residual payments resulting from a nonassignable plan or arrangement that, upon the surviving spouse's death, are payable to the spouse's estate or to successor beneficiaries.

(3) Trust ceases to qualify as QDOT. If a taxable event occurs as a result of the trust ceasing to qualify as a QDOT (for example, the trust ceases to have at least one U.S. Trustee), the amount subject to tax is the fair market value of the trust assets on the date of disqualification.

(c) Distributions and dispositions not subject to tax. *(1) Distributions of principal on account of hardship.* Section 2056A(b)(3)(B) provides an exemption from the section 2056A estate tax for distributions to the surviving spouse on account of hardship. A distribution of principal is treated as made on account of hardship if the distribution is made to the spouse from the QDOT in response to an immediate and substantial financial need relating to the spouse's health, maintenance, education, or support, or the health, maintenance, education, or support of any person that the surviving spouse is legally obligated to support. A distribution is not treated as made on account of hardship if the amount distributed may be obtained from other sources that are reasonably available to the surviving spouse; e.g., the sale by the surviving spouse of personally owned, publicly traded stock or the cashing in of a certificate of deposit owned by the surviving spouse. Assets such as closely held business interests, real estate and tangible personalty are not considered sources that are reasonably available to the surviving spouse. Although a hardship distribution of principal is exempt from the section 2056A estate tax, it must be reported on Form 706-QDT even if it is the only distribution that occurred during the filing period. See § 20.2056A-11 regarding filing requirements for Form 706-QDT.

(2) Distributions of income to the surviving spouse. Section 2056A(b)(3)(A) provides an exemption from the section 2056A estate tax for distributions of income to the surviving spouse. In general, for purposes of section 2056A(b)(3)(A), the term income has the same meaning as is provided in section 643(b), except that income does not include capital gains. In addition, income does not include any other item that would be allocated to corpus under applicable local law governing the administration of trusts irrespective of any specific trust provision to the contrary. However, distributions made to the surviving spouse as the income beneficiary in conformance with applicable local law that defines the term income as a unitrust amount (or permits a right to income to be satisfied by such an amount), or that permits the trustee to adjust between principal and income to fulfill the trustee's duty of impartiality between income and principal beneficiaries, will be considered distributions of trust income if applicable local law provides for a reasonable apportionment between the income and remainder beneficiaries of the total return of the trust and meets the requirements of § 1.643(b)-1 of this chapter. In cases where there is no specific statutory or case law regarding the allocation of such items under the law governing the administration of the QDOT, the allocation under this paragraph (c)(2) will be governed by general principles of law (including but not limited to any uniform state acts, such as the Uniform Principal and Income Act, or any Restatements of applicable law). Further, except as provided in this paragraph (c)(2) or in administrative guidance published by the Internal Revenue Service, income does not include items constituting income in respect of a decedent (IRD) under section 691. However, in cases where a QDOT is designated by the decedent as a beneficiary of a pension or profit sharing plan described in section 401(a) or an individual retirement account or annuity described in section 408, the proceeds of which are payable to the QDOT in the form of an annuity, any payments received by the QDOT may be allocated between income and corpus using the method prescribed under § 20.2056A-4(c) for determining the corpus and income portion of an annuity payment.

(3) Certain miscellaneous distributions and dispositions. Certain miscellaneous distributions and dispositions of trust assets are exempt from the section 2056A estate tax, including but not limited to the following—

(i) Payments for ordinary and necessary expenses of the QDOT (including bond premiums and letter of credit fees);

(ii) Payments to applicable governmental authorities for income tax or any other applicable tax imposed on the QDOT (other than a payment of the section 2056A estate tax due on the occurrence of a taxable event as described in paragraph (b) of this section);

(iii) Dispositions of trust assets by the trustees (such as sales, exchanges, or pledging as collateral) for full and adequate consideration in money or money's worth; and

(iv) Pursuant to section 2056A(b)(15), amounts paid from the QDOT to reimburse the surviving spouse for any tax imposed on the spouse under Subtitle A of the Internal Revenue Code on any item of income of the QDOT to which the surviving spouse is not entitled under the terms of the trust. Such distributions include (but are not limited to) amounts paid from the QDOT to reimburse the spouse for income taxes paid by the spouse (either by actual payment or through withholding) with respect to amounts received from a nonassignable annuity or other arrangement that are transferred by the spouse to a QDOT pursuant to § 20.2056A-4(c)(3); and income taxes paid by the spouse (either by actual payment or through withholding) with respect to amounts received in a lump sum distribution from a qualified plan if the lump sum distribution is assigned by the surviving spouse to a QDOT. For purposes of this paragraph (c)(3)(iv), the amount of attributable tax eligible for reimbursement is the difference between the actual income tax liability of the spouse and the spouse's income tax liability determined as if the item had not been included in the spouse's gross income in the applicable taxable year.

T.D. 8612, 8/21/95, amend T.D. 9102, 12/30/2003.

§ 20.2056A-6 Amount of tax.

(a) Definition of tax. Section 2056A(b)(2) provides for the computation of the section 2056A estate tax. For purposes of sections 2056A(b)(2)(A)(i) and (ii), in determining the tax that would have been imposed under section 2001 on the estate of the first decedent, the rates in effect on the date of the first decedent's death are used. For this purpose, the provisions of section 2001(c)(2) (pertaining to phaseout of graduated rates and unified credit) apply. In addition, for purposes of sections 2056A(b)(2)(A)(i) and (ii), *the tax which would have been imposed by section 2001 on the estate of the decedent* means the net tax determined under section 2001 or 2101, as the case may be, after allowance of any allowable credits, including the unified credit allowable under section 2010, the credit for state death taxes under section 2011, the credit for tax on prior transfers under section 2013, and the credit for foreign death taxes under section 2014. See paragraph (b)(4) of this section regarding the application of the credits under sections 2011 and 2014. In the case of a decedent nonresident not a citizen of the United States, the applicable credits are determined under section 2102. The estate tax (net of any applicable credits) imposed under section 2056A(b)(1) constitutes an estate tax for purposes of section 691(c)(2)(A).

(b) Benefits allowed in determining amount of section 2056A estate tax. *(1) General rule.* Section 2056A(b)(10) provides for the allowance of certain benefits in computing the section 2056A estate tax. Except as provided in this section, the rules of each of the credit, deduction and deferral provisions, as provided in the Internal Revenue Code must be complied with.

(2) Treatment as resident. For purposes of section 2056A(b)(10)(A), a noncitizen spouse is treated as a resident of the United States for purposes of determining whether the QDOT property is includible in the spouse's gross estate under chapter 11 of the Internal Revenue Code, and for purposes of determining whether any of the credits, deductions or deferral provisions are allowable with respect to the QDOT property to the estate of the spouse.

(3) Special rule in the case of trusts described in section 2056(b)(8). In the case of a QDOT in which the spouse's interest qualifies for a marital deduction under section 2056(b)(8), the provisions of section 2056A(b)(10)(A) apply in determining the allowance of a charitable deduction in computing the section 2056A estate tax, notwithstanding that the QDOT is not includible in the spouse's gross estate.

(4) Credit for state and foreign death taxes. If the assets of the QDOT are included in the surviving spouse's gross estate for federal estate tax purposes, or would have been so includible if the spouse had been a United States resident, and state or foreign death taxes are paid by the spouse's estate with respect to the QDOT, the taxes paid by the spouse's estate with respect to the QDOT are creditable, to the extent allowable under section 2011 or 2014, as applicable, in computing the section 2056A estate tax. In addition, state or foreign death taxes previously paid by the decedent/transferor's estate are also creditable in computing the section 2056A estate tax to the extent allowable under sections 2011 and 2014. Specifically, the tax that would have been imposed on the decedent's estate if the taxable estate had been increased by the value of the QDOT assets on the spouse's death plus the amount involved in prior taxable events (section 2056A(b)(2)(A)(i)), is determined after allowance of a credit equal to the lesser of the state or foreign death tax previously paid by the decedent's estate, or the amount prescribed under section 2011(b) or 2014(b) computed based on a taxable estate increased by such amounts. Similarly, the tax that would have been imposed on the decedent's estate if the taxable estate had been increased only by the amount involved in prior taxable events (section 2056A(b)(2)(A)(ii)) is determined after allowance of a credit equal to the lesser of the state or foreign death tax previously paid by the decedent's estate, or the amount prescribed under section 2011(b) or 2014(b) computed based on a taxable estate increased by the amount involved in such prior taxable events. See paragraph (d), Example 2, of this section.

(5) Alternate valuation and special use valuation. (i) In general. In order to claim the benefits of alternate valuation under section 2032, or special use valuation under section 2032A, for purposes of computing the section 2056A estate tax, an election must be made on the Form 706-QDT that is filed with respect to the balance remaining in the QDOT upon the death of the surviving spouse. In addition, the separate requirements for making the section 2032 and/or section 2032A elections under those sections and the regulations thereunder must be complied with except that, for this purpose, the surviving spouse is treated as a resident of the United States regardless of the surviving spouse's actual residency status. Solely for purposes of this paragraph (b)(5), the citizenship of the first decedent is immaterial.

(ii) Alternate valuation. For purposes of the alternate valuation election under section 2032, the election may not be made unless the election decreases both the value of the property remaining in the QDOT upon the death of the surviving spouse and the net amount of section 2056A estate tax due. Once made, the election is irrevocable.

(iii) Special use valuation. For purposes of section 2032A, the Designated Filer (in the case of multiple QDOTs) or the U.S. Trustee may elect to value certain farm and closely held business real property at its farm or business use value, rather than its fair market value, if all of the requirements under section 2032A and the applicable regulations are met, except that, for this purpose, the surviving spouse is treated as a resident of the United States regardless of the spouse's actual residency status. The total value of property valued under section 2032A in the QDOT cannot be decreased from fair market value by more than $750,000.

(c) Miscellaneous rules. See sections 2056A(b)(2)(B)(i) and 2056A(b)(2)(C) for special rules regarding the appropriate rate of tax. See section 2056A(b)(2)(B)(ii) for provisions regarding a credit or refund with respect to the section 2056A estate tax.

(d) Examples. The rules of this section are illustrated by the following examples.

Example (1). (i) D, a United States citizen, dies in 1995 a resident of State X, with a gross estate of $1,200,000. Under D's will, a pecuniary bequest of $700,000 passes to a QDOT for the benefit of D's spouse S, who is a resident but not a citizen of the United States. D's estate tax is computed as follows:

Gross estate	$1,200,000	
Marital Deduction	(700,000)	
Taxable Estate	$ 500,000	
Gross Tax		$ 155,800
Less: Unified Credit		(155,800)
Net tax		0

(ii) S dies in 1997 at which time S is still a resident of the United States and the value of the assets of the QDOT is $700,000. Assuming there were no taxable events during S's lifetime with respect to the QDOT, the estate tax imposed under section 2056A(b)(1)(B) is $235,000, computed as follows:

D's actual taxable estate	$ 500,000	
QDOT property	700,000	
Total	$1,200,000	
Gross Tax		$ 427,800
Less: Unified Credit		(192,800)
Net Tax		$ 235,000
Less: Tax that would have been imposed on D's actual taxable estate of $500,000		0
Section 2056A Estate Tax		$ 235,000

Example (2). (i) The facts are the same as in Example 1, except that D's gross estate was $2,000,000 and D's estate paid $70,000 in state death taxes to State X. D's estate tax is computed as follows:

Gross Estate	$2,000,000		
Marital Deduction	(700,000)		
Taxable Estate	$1,300,000		
Gross Tax			$ 469,800
Less: Unified Credit		192,800	
State Death Tax Limitation (lesser of $51,000 or $70,000 tax paid)		51,600	(244,400)
Estate Tax			$ 225,400

(ii) S dies in 1997 at which time S is still a resident of the United States and the value of the assets of the QDOT is $800,000. S's estate pays $40,000 in State X death taxes with respect to the inclusion of the QDOT in S's gross estate for state death tax purposes. Assuming there were no taxable events during S's lifetime with respect to the QDOT, the estate tax imposed under section 2056A(b)(1)(B) is $ 304,800 computed as follows:

D's actual Taxable Estate	$1,300,000	
QDOT Property	800,000	
Total	$2,100,000	
Gross Tax		$ 829,800
Less: Unified Credit		(192,800)
Pre-2011 section 2056A estate tax		$ 637,000
(A) State Death Tax Credit Computation:		
(1) State death tax paid by S's estate with respect to the QDOT [$40,000] plus state death tax previously paid by D's estate [$70,000] = $110,000.		
(2) Credit limit under section 2011(b) (based on D's adjusted taxable estate of $2,040,000 under sections 2056A(b)(2)(A) and 2011(b)) = $106,800.		
(B) State death tax credit allowable against section 2056A estate tax (lesser of paragraph (ii)(A)(1) or (2) of this Example 2.		(106,800)
Net Tax		$ 530,200
Less: Tax that would have been imposed on D's taxable estate of $1,300,000		225,400
Section 2056A Estate Tax		$ 304,800

T.D. 8612, 8/21/95.

§ 20.2056A-7 Allowance of prior transfer credit under section 2013.

(a) Property subject to QDOT election. Section 2056(d)(3) provides special rules for computing the section 2013 credit allowed with respect to property subject to a QDOT election. In computing the credit under section 2013, the amount of the credit is determined under section 2013 and the regulations thereunder, except that—

(1) The first limitation as described in section 2013(b) and § 20.2013-2 is the amount of the estate tax imposed under section 2056A(b)(1)(A), with respect to distributions during the spouse's life, and under section 2056A(b)(1)(B), with respect to the value of the QDOT assets on the spouse's death;

(2) In computing the second limitation as described in section 2013(c) and § 20.2013-3, the value of the property transferred to the decedent (as defined in section 2013(d) and § 20.2013-4) is deemed to be the value of the QDOT assets on the date of death of the surviving spouse. The value as so determined is not reduced by the section 2056A estate tax imposed at the time of the spouse's death; and

(3) The amount of the credit is determined without regard to the percentage limitations contained in section 2013(a).

(b) Property not subject to QDOT election. If property includible in a decedent's gross estate passes to a noncitizen surviving spouse (the transferee) and no deduction is allowed to the decedent's estate for that interest in property under section 2056(a) solely because the requirements of section 2056(d)(2) are not satisfied, and the transferee spouse dies with an estate that is subject to tax under section 2001 or 2101, as the case may be, any credit for tax on prior transfers allowable to the estate of the transferee spouse under section 2013 with respect to such interest in property is determined in accordance with the rules of section 2013 and the regulations thereunder, except that the amount of the credit is determined without regard to the percentage limitations contained in section 2013(a).

(c) Example. The application of this section may be illustrated by the following example:

Example. The facts are the same as in § 20.2056A-6, Example 2(ii). D, a United States citizen, dies in 1994, a resident of State X, with a gross estate of $2,000,000. Under D's will, a pecuniary bequest of $700,000 passes to a QDOT for the benefit of D's spouse S, who is a resident but not a citizen of the United States. S dies in 1997 at which time S is still a resident of the United States and the value of the assets of the QDOT is $800,000. There were no taxable events during S's lifetime. An estate tax of $304,800 is imposed under section 2056A(b)(1)(B). S's taxable estate, including the value of the QDOT ($800,000), is $1,500,000.

(i) Under paragraph (a)(1) of this section, the first limitation for purposes of section 2013(b) is $304,800, the amount of the section 2056A estate tax.

(ii) Under paragraph (a)(2) of this section, the second limitation for purposes of section 2013(c) is computed as follows:

(A) S's net estate tax payable under § 20.2013-3(a)(1), as modified under paragraph (a)(2) of this section, is computed as follows:

Taxable estate		$1,500,000
Gross estate tax		555,800
Less: Unified credit	$ 192,800	
Credit for state death taxes	64,400	257,200
Pre-2013 net estate tax payable		$ 298,600

(B) S's net estate tax payable under § 20.2013-3(a)(2), as modified under paragraph (a)(2) of this section, is computed as follows:

Taxable estate		$ 700,000
Gross estate tax		229,800
Less: Unified credit	$ 192,800	
Credit for state death taxes	18,000	210,800
Net tax payable		$ 19,000
(C) Second Limitation:		
Paragraph (ii)(A) of this Example	$ 298,600	
Less: Paragraph (ii)(B) of this Example	$ 19,000	
		$ 279,600

(iii) Credit for tax on prior transfers = $279,600 (lesser of paragraphs (i) or (ii) of this Example.

T.D. 8612, 8/21/95.

§ 20.2056A-8 Special rules for joint property.

(a) Inclusion in gross estate. *(1) General rule.* If property is held by the decedent and the surviving spouse of the decedent as joint tenants with right of survivorship, or as tenants by the entirety, and the surviving spouse is not a United States citizen (or treated as a United States citizen) at the time of the decedent's death, the property is subject to inclusion in the decedent's gross estate in accordance with the rules of section 2040(a) (general rule for includibility of joint interests), and section 2040(b) (special rule for includibility of certain joint interests of husbands and wives) does not apply. Accordingly, the rules contained in section 2040(a) and § 20.2040-1 govern the extent to which such joint interests are includible in the gross estate of a decedent who was a citizen or resident of the United States. Under § 20.2040-1(a)(2), the entire value of jointly held property is included in the decedent's gross estate unless the executor submits facts sufficient to show that property was not entirely acquired with consideration furnished by the decedent, or was acquired by the decedent and the other joint owner by gift, bequest, devise or inheritance. If the decedent is a nonresident not a citizen of the United States, the rules of this paragraph (a)(1) apply pursuant to sections 2103, 2031, 2040(a), and 2056(d)(1)(B).

(2) Consideration furnished by surviving spouse. For purposes of applying section 2040(a), in determining the amount of consideration furnished by the surviving spouse, any consideration furnished by the decedent with respect to the property before July 14, 1988, is treated as consideration furnished by the surviving spouse to the extent that the consideration was treated as a gift to the spouse under section 2511, or to the extent that the decedent elected to treat the transfer as a gift to the spouse under section 2515 (to the extent applicable). For purposes of determining whether the consideration was a gift by the decedent under section 2511, it is presumed that the decedent was a citizen of the United States at the time the consideration was so furnished to the spouse. The special rule of this paragraph (a)(2) is applicable only if the donor spouse predeceases the donee spouse and not if the donee spouse predeceases the donor spouse. In cases where the donee spouse predeceases the donor spouse, any portion of the consideration treated as a gift to the donee spouse/decedent on the creation of the tenancy (or subsequently thereafter), regardless of the date the tenancy was created, is not treated as consideration furnished by the donee spouse/decedent for purposes of section 2040(a).

(3) Amount allowed to be transferred to QDOT. If, as a result of the application of the rules described above, only a portion of the value of a jointly-held property interest is includible in a decedent's gross estate, only that portion that is so includible may be transferred to a QDOT under section 2056(d)(2). See § 20.2056A-4(b)(1) and (d), Example 3.

(b) Surviving spouse becomes citizen. Paragraph (a) of this section does not apply if the surviving spouse meets the requirements of section 2056(d)(4). For the definition of resident in applying section 2056(d)(4), see § 20.0-1(b).

(c) Examples. The provisions of this section are illustrated by the following examples:

Example (1). In 1987, D, a United States citizen, purchases real property and takes title in the names of D and S, D's spouse (a noncitizen, but a United States resident), as joint tenants with right of survivorship. In accordance with § 25.2511-1(h)(5) of this chapter, one-half of the value of the property is a gift to S. D dies in 1995. Because S is not a United States citizen, the provisions of section 2040(a) are determinative of the extent to which the real property is includible in D's gross estate. Because the joint tenancy was established before July 14, 1988, and under the applicable provisions of the Internal Revenue Code and regulations the transfer was treated as a gift of one-half of the property, one-half of the value of the property is deemed attributable to consideration furnished by S for purposes of section 2040(a). Accordingly, only one-half of the value of the property is includible in D's gross estate under section 2040(a).

Example (2). The facts are the same as in Example 1, except that S dies in 1995 survived by D who is not a citizen of the United States. For purposes of applying section 2040(a), D's gift to S on the creation of the tenancy is not treated as consideration furnished by S toward the acquisition of the property. Accordingly, since S made no other contributions with respect to the property, no portion of the property is includible in S's gross estate.

Example (3). The facts are the same as in Example 1, except that D and S purchase real property in 1990 making the down payment with funds from a joint bank account. All subsequent mortgage payments and improvements are paid from the joint bank account. The only funds deposited in the joint bank account are the earnings of D and S. It is established that D earned approximately 60% of the funds and S earned approximately 40% of the funds. D dies in 1995. The establishment of S's contribution to the joint bank account is sufficient to show that S contributed 40% of the consideration for the property. Thus, under paragraph § 20.2040-1(a)(2), 60% of the value of the property is includible in D's gross estate.

T.D. 8612, 8/21/95.

§ 20.2056A-9 Designated filer.

Section 2056A(b)(2)(C) provides special rules where more than one QDOT is established with respect to a decedent. The designation of a person responsible for filing a return under section 2056A(b)(2)(C)(i) (the Designated Filer) must be made on the decedent's federal estate tax return, or on the first Form 706-QDT that is due and is filed by its prescribed date, including extensions. The Designated Filer must be a U.S. Trustee. If the U.S. Trustee is an individual, that individual must have a tax home (as defined in section 911(d)(3)) in the United States. At least sixty days before the due date for filing the tax returns for all of the QDOTs, the U.S. Trustee(s) of each of the QDOTs must provide to the Designated Filer all of the necessary information relating to distributions from their respective QDOTs. The section 2056A estate tax due from each QDOT is allocated on a pro rata basis (based on the ratio of the amount of each respective distribution constituting a taxable event to the amount of all such distributions), unless a different allocation is required under the terms of the governing instrument or under local law. Unless the decedent has provided for a successor Designated Filer, if the Designated Filer ceases to qualify as a U.S. Trustee, or otherwise becomes unable to serve as the Designated Filer, the remaining trustees of each QDOT must select a qualifying successor Designated Filer (who is also a U.S. Trustee) prior to the due date for the filing of Form 706-QDT (including extensions). The selection is to be indicated on the Form 706-QDT. Failure to select a successor Designated Filer will result in the application of section 2056A(b)(2)(C).

T.D. 8612, 8/21/95.

§ 20.2056A-10 Surviving spouse becomes citizen after QDOT established.

(a) Section 2056A estate tax no longer imposed under certain circumstances. Section 2056A(b)(12) provides that a QDOT is no longer subject to the imposition of the section 2056A estate tax if the surviving spouse becomes a citizen of the United States and the following conditions are satisfied—

(1) The spouse either was a United States resident (for the definition of resident for this purpose, see § 20.2056A-1(b)) at all times after the death of the decedent and before becoming a United States citizen, or no taxable distributions are made from the QDOT before the spouse becomes a United States citizen (regardless of the residency status of the spouse); and

(2) The U.S. Trustee(s) of the QDOT notifies the Internal Revenue Service and certifies in writing that the surviving spouse has become a United States citizen. Notice is to be made by filing a final Form 706-QDT on or before April 15th of the calendar year following the year in which the surviving spouse becomes a United States citizen, unless an extension of time for filing is granted under section 6081.

(b) Special election by spouse. If the surviving spouse becomes a United States citizen and the spouse is not a United States resident at all times after the death of the decedent and before becoming a United States citizen, and a tax was previously imposed under section 2056A(b)(1)(A) with respect to any distribution from the QDOT before the surviving spouse becomes a United States citizen, the estate tax imposed under section 2056A(b)(1) does not apply to distributions after the spouse becomes a citizen if—

(1) The spouse elects to treat any taxable distribution from the QDOT prior to the spouse's election as a taxable gift made by the spouse for purposes of section 2001(b)(1)(B) (referring to adjusted taxable gifts), and for purposes of determining the amount of the tax imposed by section 2501 on actual taxable gifts made by the spouse during the year in which the spouse becomes a citizen or in any subsequent year;

(2) The spouse elects to treat any previous reduction in the section 2056A estate tax by reason of the decedent's unified credit (under either section 2010 or section 2102(c)) as a reduction in the spouse's unified credit under section 2505 for purposes of determining the amount of the credit allowable with respect to taxable gifts made by the surviving spouse during the taxable year in which the spouse becomes a citizen, or in any subsequent year; and

(3) The elections referred to in this paragraph (b) are made by timely filing a Form 706-QDT on or before April 15th of the year following the year in which the surviving spouse becomes a citizen (unless an extension of time for filing is granted under section 6081) and attaching notification of the election to the return.

T.D. 8612, 8/21/95.

§ 20.2056A-11 Filing requirements and payment of the section 2056A estate tax.

(a) Distributions during surviving spouse's life. Section 2056A(b)(5)(A) provides the due date for payment of the section 2056A estate tax imposed on distributions during the spouse's lifetime. An extension of not more than 6 months may be obtained for the filing of Form 706-QDT under section 6081(a) if the conditions specified therein are satisfied. See also § 20.2056A-5(c)(1) regarding the requirements for filing a Form 706-QDT in the case of a distribution to the surviving spouse on account of hardship, and § 20.2056A-2T(d)(3) regarding the requirements for filing Form 706-QDT in the case of the required annual statement.

(b) Tax at death of surviving spouse. Section 2056A(b)(5)(B) provides the due date for payment of the section 2056A estate tax imposed on the death of the spouse under section 2056A(b)(1)(B). An extension of not more than 6 months may be obtained for the filing of the Form 706-QDT under section 6081(a), if the conditions specified therein are satisfied. The obtaining of an extension of time to file under section 6081(a) does not extend the time to pay the section 2056A estate tax as prescribed under section 2056A(b)(5)(B).

(c) Extension of time for paying section 2056A estate tax. *(1) Extension of time for paying tax under section 6161(a)(2).* Pursuant to sections 2056A(b)(10)(C) and 6161(a)(2), upon a showing of reasonable cause, an extension of time for a reasonable period beyond the due date may be granted to pay any part of the estate tax that is imposed upon the surviving spouse's death under section 2056A(b)(1)(B) and shown on the final Form 706-QDT, or any part of any installments of such tax payable under section 6166 (including any part of a deficiency prorated to any installment under such section). The extension may not exceed 10 years from the date prescribed for payment of the tax (or in the case of an installment or part of a deficiency prorated to an installment, if later, not beyond the date that is 12 months after the due date for the last installment). Such extension may be granted by the district director or the director of the service center where the Form 706-QDT is filed.

(2) Extension of time for paying tax under section 6161(a)(1). An extension of time beyond the due date to pay any part of the estate tax imposed on lifetime distributions under section 2056A(b)(1)(A), or imposed at the death of the surviving spouse under section 2056A(b)(1)(B), may be granted for a reasonable period of time, not to exceed 6 months (12 months in the case of the estate tax imposed under section 2056A(b)(1)(B) at the surviving spouse's death), by the district director or the director of the service center where the Form 706-QDT is filed.

(d) Liability for tax. Under section 2056A(b)(6), each trustee (and not solely the U.S. Trustee(s)) of a QDOT is personally liable for the amount of the estate tax imposed in the case of any taxable event under section 2056A(b)(1). In the case of multiple QDOTs with respect to the same decedent, each trustee of a QDOT is personally liable for the amount of the section 2056A estate tax imposed on any taxable event with respect to that trustee's QDOT, but is not personally liable for tax imposed with respect to taxable events involving QDOTs of which that person is not a trustee. However, the assets of any QDOT are subject to collection by the Internal Revenue Service for any tax resulting from a taxable event with respect to any other QDOT established with respect to the same decedent. The trustee may also be personally liable as a withholding agent under section 1461 or other applicable provisions of the Internal Revenue Code.

T.D. 8612, 8/21/95.

§ 20.2056A-12 Increased basis for section 2056A estate tax paid with respect to distribution from a QDOT.

Under section 2056A(b)(13), in the case of any distribution from a QDOT on which an estate tax is imposed under section 2056A(b)(1)(A), the distribution is treated as a transfer by gift for purposes of section 1015, and any estate tax paid under section 2056A(b)(1)(A) is treated as a gift tax. See § 1.1015-5(c)(4) and (5) of this chapter for rules for determining the amount by which the basis of the distributed property is increased.

T.D. 8612, 8/21/95.

§ 20.2056A-13 Effective dates.

Except as provided in this section, the provisions of §§ 20.2056A-1 through 20.2056A-12 are applicable with respect to estates of decedents dying after August 22, 1995. The rule in the fourth sentence of § 20.2056A-5(c)(2) regarding unitrusts and distributions of income to the surviving spouse in conformance with applicable local law is applicable to trusts for taxable years ending after January 2, 2004.

T.D. 8612, 8/21/95, amend T.D. 9102, 12/30/2003.

§ 20.2101-1 Estates of nonresidents not citizens; tax imposed.

(a) Imposition of tax. Section 2101 imposes a tax on the transfer of the taxable estate of a nonresident who is not a citizen of the United States at the time of death. In the case of estates of decedents dying after November 10, 1988, the tax is computed at the same rates as the tax that is imposed on the transfer of the taxable estate of a citizen or resident of the United States in accordance with the provisions of sections 2101(b) and (c). For the meaning of the terms resident, nonresident, and United States, as applied to a decedent for purposes of the estate tax, see § 20.0-1(b)(1) and (2). For the liability of the executor for the payment of the tax, see section 2002. For special rules as to the phaseout of the graduated rates and unified credit, see sections 2001(c)(2) and 2101(b).

(b) Special rates in the case of certain decedents. In the case of an estate of a nonresident who was not a citizen of the United States and who died after December 31, 1976, and on or before November 10, 1988, the tax on the nonresident's taxable estate is computed using the formula provided under section 2101(b), except that the rate schedule in paragraph (c) of this section is to be used in lieu of the rate schedule in section 2001(c).

(c) Rate schedule for decedents dying before December 31, 1976 and on or before November 10, 1988.

If the amount for which the tentative tax to be computed is:	The tentative tax is:
Not over $100,000	6% of such amount.
Over $100,000 but not over $500,000	$6,000, plus 12% of excess over $100,000.
Over $500,000 but not over $1,000,000	$54,000, plus 18% of excess over $500,000.
Over $1,000,000 but not over $2,000,000	$144,000, plus 24% of excess over $1,000,000.
Over $2,000,000	$384,000, plus 30% of excess over $2,000,000.

T.D. 6296, 6/23/59, amend T.D. 7296, 12/11/73, T.D. 8612, 8/21/95.

§ 20.2102-1 Estates of nonresidents not citizens; credits against tax.

Caution: The Treasury has not yet amended Reg § 20.2102-1 to reflect changes made by P.L. 105-34.

(a) In general. In arriving at the net estate tax payable with respect to the transfer of an estate of a nonresident who was not a citizen of the United States at the time of his death, the following credits are subtracted from the tax imposed by section 2101:

(1) The State death tax credit under section 2011, to the extent permitted by section 2102(b) and paragraph (b) of this section;

(2) The gift tax credit under section 2012; and

(3) The credit under section 2013 for tax on prior transfers.

Except as provided in section 2102(b) and paragraph (b) of this section (relating to a special limitation on the amount of the credit for State death taxes), the amount of each of these credits is determined in the same manner as that prescribed for its determination in the case of estates of citizens or residents of the United States. See §§ 20.2011 through 20.2013-6. Subject to the additional special limitation contained in section 2102(b) in the case of section 2015, the provisions of sections 2015 and 2016, relating respectively to the credit for death taxes on remainders and the recovery of taxes claimed as a credit, are applicable with respect to the credit for State death taxes in the case of the estates of nonresidents not citizens. However, no credit is allowed under section 2014 for foreign death taxes.

(b) Special limitation. *(1) In general.* In the case of estates of decedents dying on or after November 14, 1966, other than estates the estate tax treatment of which is subject to a Presidential proclamation made pursuant to section 2103(a), the maximum credit allowable under section 2011 for State death taxes against the tax imposed by section 2101 on the transfer of estates of nonresidents not citizens of the United States is an amount which bears the same ratio to the maximum credit computed as provided in section 2011(b) (and without regard to this special limitation) as the value of the property (determined in the same manner as that prescribed in paragraph (b) of § 20.2031-1 for the estates of citizens or residents of the United States) in respect of which a State death tax was actually paid and which is included in the gross estate under section 2103 or, if applicable, section 2107(b) bears to the value (as so determined) of the total gross estate under section 2103 or 2107(b). For purposes of this special limitation, the term "State death taxes" means the taxes described in section 2011(a) and paragraph (a) of § 20.2011-1.

(2) Illustrations. The application of this paragraph may be illustrated by the following examples:

Example (1). A, a nonresident not a citizen of the United States, died on February 15, 1967, owning real property in State Z valued at $50,000 and stock in various domestic corporations valued at $100,000 and not subject to death taxes in any State. State Z's inheritance tax actually paid with respect to the real property in State Z is $2,000. A's taxable estate for Federal estate tax purposes is $110,000, in respect of which the maximum credit under section 2011 would be $720 in the absence of the special limitation contained in section 2102(b). However, under section 2102(b) and this paragraph the amount of the maximum credit allowable in respect to A's estate for State death taxes is limited to the amount which bears the same ratio to $720 (the maximum credit computed as provided in section 2011(b)) as $50,000 (the value of the property in respect of which a State death tax was actually paid and which is included in A's gross estate under section 2103) bears to $150,000 (the value of A's total gross estate under section 2103). Accordingly, the maximum credit allowable under section 2102 and this section for all State death taxes actually paid is $240 ($720 × $50,000/$150,000).

Example (2). B, a nonresident not a citizen of the United States, died on January 15, 1967, owning real property in State X valued at $100,000, real property in State Y valued at $200,000, and stock in various domestic corporations valued at $300,000 and not subject to death taxes in any State. States X and Y both impose inheritance taxes. State X has, in addition to its inheritance tax, an estate tax equal to the amount by which the maximum State death tax credit allowable to an estate against its Federal estate tax exceeds the amount of the inheritance tax imposed by State X plus the amount of death taxes paid to other States. State Y has no estate tax. The amount of the inheritance tax actually paid to State X with respect to the real property situated in State X is $4,000; the amount of the inheritance tax actually paid to State Y with respect to the real property situated in State Y is $9,000. B's taxable estate for Federal estate tax purposes is $550,000, in respect of which the maximum credit under section 2011 would be $14,400 in the absence of the special limitation contained in section 2102(b). However, under section 2102(b) and this paragraph the amount of the maximum credit allowable in respect of B's estate for State death taxes is limited to the amount which bears the same ratio to $14,400 (the maximum credit computed as provided in section 2011(b)) as $300,000 (the value of the property in respect of which a State death tax was actually paid and which is included in B's gross estate under section 2103) bears to $600,000 (the value of B's total gross estate under section 2103). Accordingly, the maximum credit allowable under section 2102 and this section for all State death taxes actually paid is $7,200 ($14,400 × $300,000/$600,000), and the estate tax of State X is not applicable to B's estate.

(c) Unified credit. *(1) In general.* Subject to paragraph (c)(2) of this section, in the case of estates of decedents dying after November 10, 1988, a unified credit of $13,000 is allowed against the tax imposed by section 2101 subject to the limitations of section 2102(c).

(2) When treaty is applicable. To the extent required under any treaty obligation of the United States, the estate of a nonresident not a citizen of the United States is allowed the unified credit permitted to a United States citizen or resident of $192,800, multiplied by the proportion that the total gross estate of the decedent situated in the United States bears to the decedent's total gross estate wherever situated.

(3) Certain residents of possessions. In the case of a decedent who is considered to be a nonresident not a citizen of the United States under section 2209, there is allowed a unified credit equal to the greater of $13,000, or $46,800 multiplied by the proportion that the decedent's gross estate situated in the United States bears to the total gross estate of the decedent wherever situated.

T.D. 6296, 6/23/58, amend T.D. 7296, 12/11/73, T.D. 8612, 8/21/95.

§ 20.2103-1 Estates of nonresidents not citizens; "entire gross estate".

The "entire gross estate" wherever situated of a nonresident who was not a citizen of the United States at the time of his death is made up in the same way as the "gross estate" of a citizen or resident of the United States. See §§ 20.2031 through 20.2044-1. See paragraphs (a) and (c) of § 20.2031-1 for the circumstances under which real property situated outside the United States is excluded from the gross estate of a citizen or resident of the United States. However, except as provided in § 2107(b) with respect to the estates of certain expatriates, in the case of a nonresident not a citizen, only that part of the entire gross estate which on the date of the decedent's death is situated in the United States is included in his taxable estate. In fact, property situated outside the United States need not be disclosed on the return unless § 2107 is applicable, certain deductions are claimed, or information is specifically requested. See §§ 20.2106-1, 20.2106-2, and 20.2107-1. For a description of property considered to be situated in the United States, see § 20.2104-1. For a description of property considered to be situated outside the United States, see § 20.2105-1.

T.D. 6296, 6/23/58, amend T.D. 6684, 10/23/63, T.D. 7296, 12/11/73.

§ 20.2104-1 Estates of nonresidents not citizens; property within the United States.

(a) In general. Property of a nonresident who was not a citizen of the United States at the time of his death is considered to be situated in the United States if it is—

(1) Real property located in the United States.

(2) Tangible personal property located in the United States, except certain works of art on loan for exhibition (see paragraph (b) of § 20.2105-1).

(3) In the case of an estate of a decedent dying before November 14, 1966, written evidence of intangible personal property which is treated as being the property itself, such as a bond for the payment of money, if it is physically located in the United States; except that this subparagraph shall not apply to obligations of the United States (but not its instrumentalities) issued before March 1, 1941, if the decedent was not engaged in business in the United States at the time of his death. See § 2106(c).

(4) Except as specifically provided otherwise in this section or in § 20.2105-1 (which specific exceptions, in the case of estates of decedents dying on or after November 14, 1966, cause this subparagraph to have relatively limited ap-

plicability), intangible personal property the written evidence of which is not treated as being the property itself, if it is issued by or enforceable against a resident of the United States or a domestic corporation or governmental unit.

(5) Shares of stock issued by a domestic corporation, irrespective of the location of the certificates (see, however, paragraph (i) of § 20.2105-1 for a special rule with respect to certain withdrawable accounts in savings and loan or similar associations).

(6) In the case of an estate of a decedent dying before November 14, 1966, moneys deposited in the United States by or for the decedent with any person carrying on the banking business, if the decedent was engaged in business in the United States at the time of his death.

(7) In the case of an estate of a decedent dying on or after November 14, 1966, except as specifically provided otherwise in paragraph (d), (i), (j), (l) or (m) of § 20.2105-1, any debt obligation, including a bank deposit, the primary obligor of which is—

(i) A United States person (as defined in § 7701(a)(30)), or

(ii) The United States, a State or any political subdivision thereof, the District of Columbia, or any agency or instrumentality of any such government.

This paragraph applies irrespective of whether the written evidence of the debt obligation is treated as being the property itself or whether the decedent was engaged in business in the United States at the time of his death. For purposes of this subparagraph and paragraphs (k), (l) and (m) of § 20.2105-1, a debt obligation on which there are two or more primary obligors shall be apportioned among such obligors, taking into account to the extent appropriate under all the facts and circumstances any choate or inchoate rights of contribution existing among such obligors with respect to the indebtedness. The term "agency or instrumentality", as used in paragraph (a)(r)(ii) of this section does not include a possession of the United States or an agency or instrumentality of a possession. Currency is not a debt obligation for purposes of this subparagraph.

(8) In the case of an estate of a decedent dying on or after January 1, 1970, except as specifically provided otherwise in paragraph (i) or (l) of § 20.2105-1, deposits with a branch in the United States of a foreign corporation, if the branch is engaged in the commercial banking business, whether or not the decedent was engaged in business in the United States at the time of his death.

(b) Transfers. Property of which the decedent has made a transfer taxable under §§ 2035 through 2038 is deemed to be situated in the United States if it is determined, under the provisions of paragraph (a) of this section, to be so situated either at the time of the transfer or at the time of the decedent's death. See §§ 20.2035-1 through 20.2038-1.

(c) Death tax convention. It should be noted that the situs rules described in this section may be modified for various purposes under the provisions of an applicable death tax convention with a foreign country.

T.D. 6296, 6/23/58, amend T.D. 7296, 12/11/73, T.D. 7321, 8/15/74.

§ 20.2105-1 Estates of nonresidents not citizens; property without the United States.

Caution: The Treasury has not yet amended Reg § 20.2105-1 to reflect changes made by P.L. 105-34, P.L. 103-66.

Property of a nonresident who was not a citizen of the United States at the time of his death is considered to be situated outside the United States if it is—

(a) *(1)* Real property located outside the United States, except to the extent excludable from the entire gross estate wherever situated under § 20.2103-1.

(2) Tangible personal property located outside the United States.

(b) Works of art owned by the decedent if they were—

(1) Imported into the United States solely for exhibition purposes,

(2) Loaned for those purposes to a public gallery or museum, no part of the net earnings of which inures to the benefit of any private shareholder or individual, and

(3) At the time of the death of the owner, on exhibition, or enroute to or from exhibition, in such a public gallery or museum.

(c) In the case of an estate of a decedent dying before November 14, 1966, written evidence of intangible personal property which is treated as being the property itself, such as a bond for the payment of money, if it is not physically located in the United States.

(d) Obligations of the United States issued before March 1, 1941, even though physically located in the United States, if the decedent was not engaged in business in the United States at the time of his death.

(e) Except as specifically provided otherwise in this section or in § 20.2104-1, intangible personal property the written evidence of which is not treated as being the property itself, if it is not issued by or enforceable against a resident of the United States or a domestic corporation or governmental unit.

(f) Shares of stock issued by a corporation which is not a domestic corporation, regardless of the location of the certificates.

(g) Amounts receivable as insurance on the decedent's life.

(h) In the case of an estate of a decedent dying before November 14, 1966, moneys deposited in the United States by or for the decedent with any person carrying on the banking business, if the decedent was not engaged in business in the United States at the time of his death.

(i) In the case of an estate of a decedent dying on or after November 14, 1966, and before January 1, 1976, any amount deposited in the United States which is described in § 861(c) (relating to certain bank deposits, withdrawable accounts, and amounts held by an insurance company under an agreement to pay interest), if any interest thereon, were such interest received by the decedent at the time of his death, would be treated under § 862(a)(1) as income from sources without the United States by reason of § 861(a)(1)(A) (relating to interest on amounts described in § 861(c) which is not effectively connected with the conduct of a trade or business within the United States) and the regulations thereunder. If such interest would be treated by reason of those provisions as income from sources without the United States only in part, the amount described in § 861(c) shall be considered situated outside the United States in the same proportion as the part of the interest which would be treated as income from sources without the United States bears to the total amount of the interest. This paragraph applies whether or not the decedent was engaged in business in the United States at the time of his death, and, except with respect to amounts described in § 861(c)(3) (relating to amounts held by an insurance company under an agreement to pay interest), whether or not the deposit or other amount is in fact interest-bearing.

(j) In the case of an estate of a decedent dying on or after November 14, 1966, deposits with a branch outside of the United States of a domestic corporation or domestic partnership, if the branch is engaged in the commercial banking business. This paragraph applies whether or not the decedent was engaged in business in the United States at the time of his death, and whether or not the deposits, upon withdrawal, are payable in currency of the United States.

(k) In the case of an estate of a decedent dying on or after November 14, 1966, except as specifically provided otherwise in paragraph (a)(8) of § 20.2104-1 with respect to estates of decedents dying on or after January 1, 1970, any debt obligation, including a bank deposit, the primary obligor of which is neither—

(1) A United States person (as defined in § 7701(a)(30)), nor

(2) The United States, a State or any political subdivision thereof, the District of Columbia, or any agency or instrumentality of any such government.

This paragraph applies irrespective of whether the written evidence of the debt obligation is treated as being the property itself or whether the decedent was engaged in business in the United States at the time of his death. See paragraph (a)(7) of § 20.2104-1 for the treatment of a debt obligation on which there are two or more primary obligors. The term "agency or instrumentality," as used in subparagraph (2) of this paragraph, does not include a possession of the United States or an agency or instrumentality of a possession. Currency is not a debt obligation for purposes of this paragraph.

(l) In the case of an estate of a decedent dying on or after November 14, 1966, any debt obligation to the extent that the primary obligor on the debt obligation is a domestic corporation, if any interest thereon, were the interest received from such obligor by the decedent at the time of his death, would be treated under § 862(a)(1) as income from sources without the United States by reason of § 861(a)(1)(B) (relating to interest received from a domestic corporation less than 20 percent of whose gross income for a 3-year period was derived from sources within the United States) and the regulations thereunder. For such purposes the 3-year period referred to in § 861(a)(1)(B) is the period of 3 years ending with the close of the domestic corporation's last taxable year terminating before the decedent's death. This paragraph applies whether or not (1) the obligation is in fact interest-bearing, (2) the written evidence of the debt obligation is treated as being the property itself, or (3) the decedent was engaged in business in the United States at the time of his death. See paragraph (a)(7) of § 20.2104-1 for the treatment of a debt obligation on which there are two or more primary obligors.

(m) *(1)* In the case of an estate of a decedent dying after December 31, 1972, except as otherwise provided in paragraph (m)(2) of this section any debt obligation to the extent that the primary obligor on the debt obligation is a domestic corporation or domestic partnership, if any interest thereon, were the interest received from such obligor by the decedent at the time of his death, would be treated under § 862(a)(1) as income from sources without the United States by reason of § 861(a)(1)(G) (relating to interest received on certain debt obligations with respect to which elections have been made under § 4912(c)) and the regulations thereunder. This paragraph applies whether or not (i) the obligation is in fact interest bearing, (ii) the written evidence of the debt obligation is treated as being the property itself, or (iii) the decedent was engaged in business in the United States at the time of his death. See paragraph (a)(7) of § 20.2104-1 for the treatment of a debt obligation on which there are two or more primary obligors.

(2) In the case of an estate of a decedent dying before January 1, 1974, this paragraph does not apply to any debt obligation of a foreign corporation assumed by a domestic corporation which is treated under § 4912(c)(2) as issued by such domestic corporation during 1973.

T.D. 6296, 6/23/58, amend T.D. 6684, 10/23/63, T.D. 7296, 12/11/73, T.D. 7321, 8/15/74.

§ 20.2106-1 Estates of nonresidents not citizens; taxable estate; deductions in general.

(a) The taxable estate of a nonresident who was not a citizen of the United States at the time of his death is determined by adding the value of that part of his gross estate which, at the time of his death, is situated in the United States and, in the case of an estate to which section 2107 (relating to expatriation to avoid tax) applies, any amounts includible in his gross estate under section 2107(b), and then subtracting from the sum thereof the total amount of the following deductions:

(1) The deductions allowed in the case of estates of decedents who were citizens or residents of the United States under sections 2053 and 2054 (see §§ 20.2053-1 through 20.2053-9 and § 20.2054-1) for expenses, indebtedness and taxes, and for losses, to the extent provided in § 20.2106-2.

(2) A deduction computed in the same manner as the one allowed under section 2055 (see §§ 20.2055-1 through 20.2055-5) for charitable, etc., transfers, except—

(i) That the deduction is allowed only for transfers to corporations and associations created or organized in the United States, and to trustees for use within the United States, and

(ii) That the provisions contained in paragraph (c)(2) of § 20.2055-2 relating to termination of a power to consume are not applicable.

(3) Subject to the special rules set forth at § 20.2056A-1(c), the amount which would be deductible with respect to property situated in the United States at the time of the decedent's death under the principles of section 2056. Thus, if the surviving spouse of the decedent is a citizen of the United States at the time of the decedent's death, a marital deduction is allowed with respect to the estate of the decedent if all other applicable requirements of section 2056 are satisfied. If the surviving spouse of the decedent is not a citizen of the United States at the time of the decedent's death, the provisions of section 2056, including specifically the provisions of section 2056(d) and (unless section 2056(d)(4) applies) the provisions of section 2056A (QDOTs) must be satisfied.

(b) Section 2106(b) provides that no deduction is allowed under paragraph (a)(1) or (2) of this section unless the executor discloses in the estate tax return the value of that part of the gross estate not situated in the United States. See § 20.2105-1. Such part must be valued as of the date of the decedent's death, or if the alternate valuation method under section 2032 is elected, as of the applicable valuation date.

T.D. 6296, 6/23/58, amend T.D. 6526, 1/18/61, T.D. 7296, 12/11/73, T.D. 7321, 8/15/74, T.D. 8612, 8/21/95.

§ 20.2106-2 Estates of nonresidents not citizens; deductions for expenses, losses, etc.

(a) In computing the taxable estate of a nonresident who was not a citizen of the United States at the time of his death, deductions are allowed under sections 2053 and 2054 for expenses, indebtedness and taxes, and for losses, to the following extent:

(1) A pledge or subscription is deductible if it is an enforceable claim against the estate and if it would constitute an allowable deduction under paragraph (a)(2) of § 20.2106-1, relating to charitable, etc., transfers, if it had been a bequest.

(2) That proportion of other deductions under sections 2053 and 2054 is allowed which the value of that part of the decedent's gross estate situated in the United States at the time of his death bears to the value of the decedent's entire gross estate wherever situated. It is immaterial whether the amounts to be deducted were incurred or expended within or without the United States. For purposes of this subparagraph, an amount which is includible in the decedent's gross estate under section 2107(b) with respect to stock in a foreign corporation shall be included in the value of the decedent's gross estate situated in the United States.

No deduction is allowed under this paragraph unless the value of the decedent's entire gross estate is disclosed in the estate tax return. See paragraph (b) of § 20.2106-1.

(b) In order that the Internal Revenue Service may properly pass upon the items claimed as deductions, the executor should submit a certified copy of the schedule of liabilities, claims against the estate, and expenses of administration filed under any applicable foreign death duty act. If no such schedule was filed, the executor should submit a certified copy of the schedule of these liabilities, claims and expenses filed with the foreign court in which administration was had. If the items of deduction allowable under section 2106(a)(1) were not included in either such schedule, or if no such schedules were filed, then there should be submitted a written statement of the foreign executor containing a declaration that it is made under the penalties of perjury setting forth the facts relied upon as entitling the estate to the benefit of the particular deduction or deductions.

(c) [Reserved]

T.D. 6296, 6/23/58, amend T.D. 7294, 12/11/73, T.D. 8612, 8/21/95.

§ 20.2107-1 Expatriation to avoid tax.

Caution: The Treasury has not yet amended Reg § 20.2107-1 to reflect changes made by P.L. 110-245, P.L. 105-34, P.L. 104-191, P.L. 97-34, P.L. 94-455.

(a) Rate of tax. The tax imposed by § 2107(a) on the transfer of the taxable estates of certain nonresident expatriate decedents who were formerly citizens of the United States is computed in accordance with the table contained in § 2001, relating to the rate of the tax imposed on the transfer of the taxable estates of decedents who were citizens or residents of the United States. Except for any amounts included in the gross estate solely by reason of § 2107(b) and paragraph (b)(1)(ii) and (iii) of this section, the value of the taxable estate to be used in this computation is determined as provided in § 2106 and § 20.2106-1. The decedents to which § 2107(a) and this section apply are described in paragraph (d) of this section.

(b) Gross estate. *(1) Determination of value.* (i) General rule. Except as provided in subdivision (ii) of this subparagraph with respect to stock in certain foreign corporations, for purposes of the tax imposed by § 2107(a), the value of the gross estate of every estate the transfer of which is subject to the tax imposed by that section is determined as provided in § 2103 and § 20.2103-1.

(ii) Amount includible with respect to stock in certain foreign corporations. If at the time of his death a nonresident expatriate decedent the transfer of whose estate is subject to the tax imposed by § 2107(a)—

(a) Owned (within the meaning of § 958(a) and the regulations thereunder) 10 percent or more of the total combined voting power of all classes of stock entitled to vote in a foreign corporation, and

(b) Owned (within the meaning of § 958(a) and the regulations thereunder), or is considered to have owned (by applying the ownership rules of § 958(b) and the regulations thereunder), more than 50 percent of the total combined voting power of all classes of stock entitled to vote in such foreign corporation,

then § 2107(b) requires the inclusion in the decedent's gross estate, in addition to amounts otherwise includible therein under subdivision (i) of this subparagraph of an amount equal to that proportion of the fair market value (determined at the time of the decedent's death or, if so elected by the executor of the decedent's estate, on the alternate valuation date as provided in § 2032) of the stock in such foreign corporation owned (within the meaning of § 958(a) and the regulations thereunder) by the decedent at the time of his death, which the fair market value of any assets owned by such foreign corporation and situated in the United States, at the time of his death, bears to the total fair market value of all assets owned by such foreign corporation at the time of his death.

(iii) Rules of application. (a) In determining the proportion of the fair market value of the stock which is includible in the gross estate under subdivision (ii) of this subparagraph, the fair market value of the foreign corporation's assets situated in the United States and of its total assets shall be determined without reduction for any outstanding liabilities of the corporation.

(b) For purposes of subdivision (ii) of this subparagraph, the foreign corporation's assets which are situated in the United States shall be all its property which, by applying the provisions of §§ 2104, 2105, and §§ 20.2104-1 and 20.2105-1, would be considered to be situated in the United States if such property were property of a nonresident who was not a citizen of the United States.

(c) For purposes of subdivision (ii)(a) of this subparagraph, a decedent is treated as owning stock in a foreign corporation at the time of his death to the extent he owned (within the meaning of § 958(a) and the regulations thereunder) the stock at the time he made a transfer of the stock in a transfer described in §§ 2035 to 2038, inclusive (relating respectively to transfers made in contemplation of death, transfers with a retained life estate, transfers taking effect at death, and revocable transfers). For purposes of subdivision (ii)(b) of this subparagraph, a decedent is treated as owning stock in a foreign corporation at the time of his death to the extent he owned (within the meaning of § 958(a) and the regulations thereunder), or is considered to have owned (by applying the ownership rules of § 958(b) and the regulations thereunder), the stock at the time he made a transfer of the stock in a transfer described in §§ 2035 to 2038, inclusive.

In applying the proportion rule of § 2107(b) and subdivision (ii) of this subparagraph where a decedent is treated as owning stock in a foreign corporation at the time of his death by reason of having transferred his interest in such stock in a transfer described in §§ 2035 to 2038, inclusive, the proportionate value of the interest includible in his gross estate is based upon the value as of the applicable valuation date described in § 2031 or 2032 of the amount, determined as of the date of transfer, of his interest in the stock. See example (2) in subparagraph (2) of this paragraph.

(d) For purposes of applying subdivision (ii) *(b)* of this subparagraph, the same shares of stock may not be counted more than once. See example (2) in subparagraph (2) of this paragraph.

(e) The principles applied in paragraph (b) of § 1.957-1 of this chapter (Income Tax Regulations) for determining what constitutes total combined voting power of all classes of stock entitled to vote in a foreign corporation for purposes of § 957(a) shall be applied in determining what constitutes total combined voting power of all classes of stock entitled to vote in a foreign corporation for purposes of § 2107(b) and subdivision (ii) of this subparagraph. In applying such principles under this paragraph changes in language shall be made, where necessary, in order to treat the nonresident expatriate decedent, rather than U.S. shareholders, as owning such total combined voting power.

(2) Illustrations. The application of this paragraph may be illustrated by the following examples:

Example (1). (a) At the time of his death, H, a nonresident expatriate decedent the transfer of whose estate is subject to the tax imposed by § 2107(a), owned a 60-percent interest in M Company, a foreign partnership, which in turn owned stock issued by N Corporation, a foreign corporation. The stock in N Corporation held by M Company, which constituted 50 percent of the total combined voting power of all classes of stock entitled to vote in N Corporation, was valued at $50,000 at the time of H's death. In addition, W, H's wife, also a nonresident not a citizen of the United States, owned at the time of H's death stock in N Corporation constituting 25 percent of the total combined voting power of all classes of stock entitled to vote in that corporation. The fair market value of the assets of N Corporation which, at the time of H's death, were situated in the United States constituted 40 percent of the fair market value of all assets of that corporation. It is assumed for purposes of this example that the executor of H's estate has not elected to value the estate on the alternate valuation date provided in § 2032.

(b) The test contained in subparagraph (1)(ii)*(a)* of this paragraph is met since at the time of his death H indirectly owned (within the meaning of § 958(a) and the regulations thereunder) 30 percent (60 percent of 50 percent) of the total combined voting power of all classes of stock entitled to vote in N Corporation; and the test contained in subparagraph (1)(ii) *(b)* of this paragraph is met since at such time H owned or is considered to have owned (within the meaning of § 958(a) and (b) and the regulations thereunder) 55 percent of the total combined voting power of all classes of stock entitled to vote in N Corporation (having constructive ownership of his wife's 25 percent, in addition to his own indirect ownership of 30 percent, of the total combined voting power). Accordingly, $12,000 is included in H's gross estate by reason of § 2107(b) and this paragraph. This $12,000 is the amount which is equal to 40 percent (the percentage of the fair market value of N Corporation's assets which were situated within the United States at H's death) of $30,000 (the fair market value of the stock then owned by H within the meaning of § 958(a) and the regulations thereunder, *i.e.,* H's 60-percent interest in the $50,000 fair market value of stock held by M Company).

Example (2). (a) Assume the same facts as those given in example (1) except that H made a transfer to W in contemplation of his death (within the meaning of § 2035), of his 60-percent interest in M Company, that on the date of the transfer held stock in N Corporation constituting 80 percent of the total combined voting power of all classes of stock entitled to vote in that corporation (rather than the 50 percent of total combined voting power held by M Company on the date of H's death), and that the 80 percent of total combined voting power owned by M Company on the date of the transfer is valued at $70,000 on that date and at $85,000 at the time of H's death. It is assumed for purposes of this example that the 60-percent interest in M Company was held by W at the time of H's death.

(b) The test contained in subparagraph (1)(ii)*(a)* of this paragraph is met since, under subparagraph (1)(iii) *(c)* of this paragraph, H is treated as owning (within the meaning of § 958(a) and the regulations thereunder), at the time of his death, the 48 percent (60 percent of 80 percent) of the total combined voting power of all classes of stock entitled to vote in N Corporation represented by his transferred interest in M Company; and the test contained in subparagraph (1)(ii) *(b)* of this paragraph is met since, under that subparagraph and subparagraph (1)(iii) *(c)* of this paragraph, H is treated as owning (within the meaning of § 958(a) or (b)), at the time of his death, 73 percent (48 percent plus 25 percent) of the total combined voting power of all classes of stock entitled to vote in N Corporation. Accordingly, $20,400 is included in H's gross estate by reason of § 2107(b) and this paragraph. This $20,400 is the amount which is equal to 40 percent (the percentage of the fair market value of N Corporation's assets which were situated within the United States at H's death) of $51,000 (the fair market value at the time of H's death of the transferred interest which under subparagraph (1)(iii) *(e)* of this paragraph H is considered to own within the meaning of § 958(a) and the regulations thereunder at that time, *i.e.,* the 60 percent interest in the $85,000 fair market value at that time of the 80-percent total combined voting power held by M Company on the date of transfer).

(c) The fact that the stock in N Corporation owned by M Company is considered under subparagraph (1)(ii) *(b)* of this paragraph to be owned by H for two independent reasons (i.e., under § 958(a) and the regulations thereunder, because H transferred his 60-percent interest in M Company to W in contemplation of death, and under § 958(b) and the regulations thereunder, because H is considered to own the stock in N Corporation indirectly owned by his wife, W, by reason of her ownership of such transferred interest) does not cause the shares of stock represented by the transferred interest in M Company to be counted twice in determining whether the test contained in that subparagraph is met. See subparagraph (1)(iii) *(d)* of this paragraph.

Example (3). (a) At the time of his death, H, a nonresident expatriate decedent the transfer of whose estate is subject to the tax imposed by § 2107(a), owned a 40-percent beneficial interest in a domestic trust; at that time he also directly owned stock in P Corporation, a foreign corporation, constituting 15 percent of the total combined voting power of all classes of stock entitled to vote in that corporation. The trust owned stock in P Corporation constituting 51 percent of the total combined voting power of all classes of stock entitled to vote in that corporation. The stock in P Corporation owned directly by H was valued at $20,000 on the alternate valuation date determined pursuant to an election under § 2032. The fair market value of the assets of P Corporation which, at the time of H's death were situated in the United States constituted 20 percent of the fair market value of all assets of that corporation.

(b) By reason of § 958(b)(2) and the regulations thereunder, the trust is considered to own all the stock entitled to vote in P Corporation since it owns more than 50 percent of the total combined voting power of all classes of stock entitled to vote in that corporation. The test contained in subparagraph (1)(ii) *(a)* of this paragraph is met since at the time of his death H owned (within the meaning of § 958(a) and the regulations thereunder) 15 percent of the total combined voting power of all classes of stock entitled to vote in P Corporation; the stock in P Corporation owned by the trust is not considered to have been owned by H under § 958(a)(2) since the trust is not a foreign trust. In addition, the test contained in subparagraph (1)(ii) *(b)* of this paragraph is met since at the time of his death H owned or is considered to have owned (within the meaning of § 958(a) and (b) and the regulations thereunder) 55 percent of the total combined voting power of all classes of stock entitled to vote in that corporation (his 15 percent directly owned plus his 40 percent (40 percent of 100 percent) considered to be owned). Accordingly, $4,000 is included in H's gross estate by reason of § 2107(b) and this paragraph. This $4,000 is the amount which is equal to 20 percent (the percentage of the fair market value of P Corporation's assets which were situated within the United States at H's death) of $20,000 (the fair market value of the stock then owned by H within the meaning of § 958(a) and the regulations thereunder). In addition, the value of H's interest in the domestic trust is included in his gross estate under § 2103 to the extent it constitutes property having a situs in the United States.

(c) Credits. Credits against the tax imposed by § 2107(a) are allowed for any amounts determined in accordance with § 2102 and § 20.2102-1 (relating to credits against the estate tax for State death taxes, gift tax, and tax on prior transfers). In computing the special limitation on the credit for State death taxes contained in § 2102(b) and paragraph (b) of § 20.2102-1, amounts included in the gross estate under § 2107(b) and paragraph (b)(1) of this section are to be taken into account.

(d) Decedents to whom the tax imposed by § 2107(a) applies. *(1) General rule.* The tax imposed by § 2107(a) applies to the transfer of the taxable estate of every decedent nonresident not a citizen of the United States dying on or after November 14, 1966, who lost his U. S. citizenship after March 8, 1965, and within the 10-year period ending with the date of his death, except in the case of the estate of a decedent whose loss of U. S. citizenship either—

(i) Resulted from the application of § 301(b), 350, or 355 of the Immigration and Nationality Act as amended (8 USC 1401(b), 1482, or 1487); or

(ii) Did not have for one of its principal purposes (but not necessarily its only principal purpose) the avoidance of Federal income, estate, or gift tax.

Section 301(b) of the Immigration and Nationality Act provides generally that a U. S. citizen, who is born outside the United States of parents one of whom is an alien and the other is a U. S. citizen who was physically present in the United States for a specified period, shall lose his U. S. citizenship, if, within a specified period preceding the age of 28 years, he fails to be continuously physically present in the United States for at least 5 years. Section 350 of that Act provides that under certain circumstances a person, who at birth acquired the nationality of the United States and of a foreign country and who has voluntarily sought or claimed benefits of the nationality of any foreign country, shall lose his U. S. nationality if, after attaining the age of 22 years, he has a continuous residence for 3 years in the foreign country of which he is a national by birth. Section 355 of that Act provides that a person having U. S. nationality, who is under 21 years of age and whose residence is in a foreign country with or under the legal custody of a parent who loses his U. S. nationality under specified circumstances, shall lose his U. S. nationality if he has or acquires the nationality of that foreign country and attains the age of 25 years without having established his residence in the United States. Section 2107 and this section do not apply to the transfer of any estate the estate tax treatment of which is subject to a Presidential proclamation made pursuant to § 2108(a) (relating to the application of pre-1967 estate tax provisions in the case of a foreign country which imposes a more burdensome tax than the United States).

(2) Burden of proof. (i) General rule. In determining for purposes of subparagraph (1)(ii) of this paragraph whether a principal purpose for the loss of U. S. citizenship by a decedent was the avoidance of Federal income, estate, or gift tax, the Commissioner must first establish that it is reasonable to believe that the decedent's loss of U. S. citizenship would, but for § 2107 and this section, result in a substantial reduction in the sum of *(a)* the Federal estate tax and *(b)* all estate, inheritance, legacy, and succession taxes imposed by foreign countries and political subdivisions thereof, in respect of the transfer of the decedent's estate. Once the Commissioner has so established, the burden of proving that the loss of citizenship by the decedent did not have for one of its principal purposes the avoidance of Federal income, estate, or gift tax shall be on the executor of the decedent's estate.

(ii) Tentative determination of substantial reduction in Federal and foreign death taxes. In the absence of complete factual information, the Commissioner may make a tentative determination, based on the information available, that the decedent's loss of U.S. citizenship would, but for § 2107 and this section, result in a substantial reduction in the sum of the Federal and foreign death taxes described in subdivision (i) *(a)* and *(b)* of this subparagraph. This tentative determination may be based upon the fact that the laws of the foreign country of which the decedent became a citizen and the laws of the foreign country of which the decedent was a resident at the time of his death, including the laws of any political subdivisions of those foreign countries, would ordinarily result, in the case of an estate of a nonexpatriate decedent having the same citizenship and residence as the decedent, in liability for total death taxes under such laws substantially lower than the amount of the Federal estate tax which would be imposed on the transfer of a comparable estate of a citizen of the United States. In the absence of a preponderance of evidence to the contrary, this tentative determination shall be sufficient to establish that it is reasonable to believe that the decedent's loss of U. S. citizenship would, but for § 2107 and this section, result in a substantial reduction in the sum of the Federal and foreign death taxes described in subdivision (i) *(a)* and *(b)* of this subparagraph.

T.D. 7296, 12/11/73.

§ 20.2201-1 Members of the Armed Forces dying during an induction period.

Caution: The Treasury has not yet amended Reg § 20.2201-1 to reflect changes made by P.L. 104-117, P.L. 93-597.

(a) The additional estate tax as defined in § 2011(d) does not apply to the transfer of the taxable estate of a citizen or resident of the United States dying during an induction period as defined in § 112(c)(5) (see paragraph (b) of this section) and while in active service as a member of the Armed Forces of the United States, if the decedent—

(1) Was killed in action while serving in a combat zone, as determined under § 112(c)(2) and (3) (see paragraph (c) of this section), or

(2) Died as a result of wounds, disease, or injury suffered while serving in such a combat zone and while in line of duty, by reason of a hazard to which he was subject as an incident of such service.

(b) Section 112(c)(5) defines the term "induction period" as meaning any period during which individuals are liable for induction, for reasons other than prior deferment, for training and service in the Armed Forces of the United States.

(c) Section 112(c)(2) and (3) provides that service is performed in a combat zone only—

(1) If it is performed in an area which the President of the United States has designated by Executive order for purposes of § 112(c) as an area in which the Armed Forces of the United States are, or have, engaged in combat, and

(2) If it is performed on or after the date designated by the President by Executive order as the date of the commencing of combatant activities in such zone and on or before the date designated by the President by Executive order as the date of termination of combatant activities in such zone.

(d) If the official record of the branch of the Armed Forces of which the decedent was a member at the time of his death states that the decedent was killed in action while serving in a combat zone, or that death resulted from wounds or injuries received or disease contracted while in line of duty in a combat zone, this fact shall, in the absence of evidence establishing to the contrary, be presumed to be established for the purposes of the exemption. Moreover, wounds, injuries or disease suffered while in line of duty will be considered to have been caused by a hazard to which the decedent was subjected as an incident of service as a member of the Armed Forces, unless the hazard which caused the wounds, injuries, or disease was clearly unrelated to such service.

(e) A person was in active service as a member of the Armed Forces of the United States if he was at the time of his death actually serving in such forces. A member of the Armed Forces in active service in a combat zone who thereafter becomes a prisoner of war or missing in action, and occupies such status at death or when the wounds, disease, or injury resulting in death were incurred, is considered for purposes of this section as serving in a combat zone.

(f) The exemption from tax granted by § 2201 does not apply to the basic estate tax as defined in § 2011(d).

T.D. 6296, 6/23/58.

§ 20.2202-1 Missionaries in foreign service.

Caution: The Treasury has not yet amended Reg § 20.2202-1 to reflect changes made by P.L. 94-455.

Section 2202 provides that a duly commissioned missionary, dying while in foreign missionary service under a board of foreign missions of a religious denomination in the United States, is presumed to have retained a United States residence (see paragraph (b)(1) of § 20.0-1) held at the time of his commission and departure for foreign service, in the absence of relevant facts other than his intention to remain permanently in such foreign service.

T.D. 6296, 6/23/58.

§ 20.2203-1 Definition of executor.

The term "executor" means the executor or administrator of the decedent's estate. However, if there is no executor or administrator appointed, qualified and acting within the United States, the term means any person in actual or constructive possession of any property of the decedent. The term "person in actual or constructive possession of any property of the decedent" includes, among others, the decedent's agents and representatives; safe-deposit companies, warehouse companies, and other custodians of property in this country; brokers holding, as collateral, securities belonging to the decedent; and debtors of the decedent in this country.

T.D. 6296, 6/23/58.

§ 20.2204-1 Discharge of executor from personal liability.

(a) General rule. The executor of a decedent's estate may make written application to the applicable internal revenue officer with whom the estate tax return is required to be filed, as provided in § 20.6091-1, for a determination of the Federal estate tax and for a discharge of personal liability therefrom. Within 9 months after receipt of the application, or if the application is made before the return is filed then within 9 months after the return is filed, the executor will be notified of the amount of the tax and, upon payment thereof, he will be discharged from personal liability for any deficiency in the tax thereafter found to be due. If no such notification is received, the executor is discharged at the end of such 9 month period from personal liability for any deficiency thereafter found to be due. The discharge of the executor from personal liability under this section applies only to him in his personal capacity and to his personal assets. The discharge is not applicable to his liability as executor to the extent of the assets of the estate in his possession or control. Further, the discharge is not to operate as a release of any part of the gross estate from the lien for estate tax for any deficiency that may thereafter be determined to be due.

(b) Special rule in the case of extension of time for payment of tax. In addition to the provisions of paragraph (a) of this section, an executor of the estate of a decedent dying after December 31, 1970, may make written application to be discharged from personal liability for the amount of Federal estate tax for which the time for payment has been extended under § 6161, 6163, or 6166. In such a case, the executor will be notified of the amount of bond, if any, to be furnished within 9 months after receipt of the application, or, if the application is made before the return is filed, within 9 months after the return is filed. The amount of any bond required under the provisions of this paragraph shall not exceed the amount of tax the payment of which has been extended. Upon furnishing the bond in the form required under § 301.7101-1 of this chapter (Regulations on Procedure and Administration), or upon receipt of the notification that no bond is required, the executor will be discharged from personal liability for the tax the payment of which has been extended. If no notification is received, the executor is discharged at the end of such 9 month period from personal liability for the tax the payment of which has been extended.

T.D. 6296, 6/23/58, amend T.D. 7238, 12/28/72, T.D. 7941, 2/6/84.

§ 20.2204-2 Discharge of fiduciary other than than executor from personal liability.

Caution: The Treasury has not yet amended Reg § 20.2204-2 to reflect changes made by P.L. 94-455.

(a) A fiduciary (not including a fiduciary of the estate of a nonresident decedent), other than the executor, who as a fiduciary holds, or has held at any time since the decedent's death, property transferred to the fiduciary from a decedent dying after December 31, 1970, or his estate, may make written application to the applicable internal revenue officer with whom the estate tax return is required to be filed, as provided in § 20.6091-1, for a determination of the Federal estate tax liability with respect to such property and for a discharge of personal liability therefrom. The application must be accompanied by a copy of the instrument, if any, under which the fiduciary is acting, a description of all the property transferred to the fiduciary from the decedent or his estate, and any other information that would be relevant to a determination of the fiduciary's tax liability.

(b) Upon the discharge of the executor from personal liability under § 20.2204-1, or, if later, within 6 months after the receipt of the application filed by a fiduciary pursuant to the provisions of paragraph (a) of this section, such fiduciary will be notified either (1) of the amount of tax for which it has been determined the fiduciary is liable, or (2) that it has been determined that the fiduciary is not liable for any such tax. The fiduciary will also be notified of the amount of bond, if any, to be furnished for any Federal estate tax for which the time for payment has been extended under § 6161, 6163, or 6166. The amount of any bond required under the provisions of this paragraph shall not exceed the amount of tax the payment of which has been so extended. Upon payment of the amount for which it has been determined the fiduciary is liable, and upon furnishing any bond required under this paragraph in the form specified under § 301.7101-1 of this chapter (Regulations on Procedure and Administration), or upon receipt by the fiduciary of notification of a determination that he is not liable for such tax or that a bond is not required, the fiduciary will be discharged from personal liability for any deficiency in the tax thereafter found to be due. If no such notification is received, the fiduciary is discharged at the end of such 6 months (or upon discharge of the executor, if later) from personal liability for any deficiency thereafter found to be due. The discharge of the fiduciary from personal liability under this section applies only to him in his personal capacity and to his personal assets. The discharge is not applicable to his liability as a fiduciary (such as a trustee) to the extent of the assets of the estate in his possession or control. Further, the discharge is not to operate as a release of any part of the gross estate from the lien for estate tax for any deficiency that may thereafter be determined to be due.

T.D. 7238, 12/28/72.

§ 20.2204-3 Special rules for estates of decedents dying after December 31, 1976; special lien under § 6324A.

For purposes of §§ 20.2204-1(b) and 20.2204-2(b), in the case of a decedent dying after December 31, 1976, if the executor elects a special lien in favor of the United States under § 6324A, relating to special lien for estate taxes deferred under §§ 6166 or 6166A (as in effect prior to its repeal by the Economic Recovery Tax Act of 1981), such lien shall be treated as the furnishing of a bond with respect to the amount for which the time for payment has been extended under § 6166. If an election has been made under § 6324A, the executor may not thereafter substitute a bond pursuant to § 2204 in lieu of that lien. If a bond has been supplied under § 2204, however, the executor may, by filing a proper notice of election and agreement, substitute a lien under § 6324A for any part or all of such bond. See §§ 20.6324A-1 and 301.6324A-1 for rules relating to a special lien under § 6324A.

T.D. 7941, 2/6/84.

§ 20.2205-1 Reimbursement out of estate.

If any portion of the tax is paid by or collected out of that part of the estate passing to, or in the possession of, any person other than the duly qualified executor or administrator, that person may be entitled to reimbursement, either out of the undistributed estate or by contribution from other beneficiaries whose shares or interests in the estate would have been reduced had the tax been paid before distribution of the estate, or whose shares or interests are subject either to an equal or prior liability for the payment of taxes, debts, or other charges against the estate. For specific provisions giving the executor the right to reimbursement from life insurance beneficiaries and from recipients of property over which the decedent had a power of appointment, see §§ 2206 and 2207. These provisions, however, are not designed to curtail the right of the district director to collect the tax from any person, or out of any property, liable for its payment. The district director cannot be required to apportion the tax among the persons liable nor to enforce any right of reimbursement or contribution.

T.D. 6296, 6/23/58.

§ 20.2206-1 Liability of life insurance beneficiaries.

With respect to the right of the district director to collect the tax without regard to the provisions of § 2206, see § 20.2205-1.

T.D. 6296, 6/23/58.

§ 20.2207-1 Liability of recipient of property over which decedent had power of appointment.

With respect to the right of the district director to collect the tax without regard to the provisions of § 2207, see § 20.2205-1.

T.D. 6296, 6/23/58.

§ 20.2207A-1 Right of recovery of estate taxes in the case of certain marital deduction property.

Caution: The Treasury has not yet amended Reg § 20.2207A-1 to reflect changes made by P.L. 105-34.

(a) In general. *(1) Right of recovery from person receiving the property.* If the gross estate includes the value of property that is includible by reason of § 2044 (relating to certain property in which the decedent had a qualifying income interest for life under §§ 2056(b)(7) or 2523(f)), the estate of the surviving spouse is entitled to recover from the person receiving the property (as defined in paragraph (d) of this section) the amount of Federal estate tax attributable to that property. The right of recovery arises when the Federal estate tax with respect to the property includible in the gross estate by reason of § 2044 is paid by the estate. There is no right of recovery from any person for the property received by that person for which a deduction was allowed from the gross estate if no tax is attributable to that property.

(2) Failure to exercise right of recovery. Failure of an estate to exercise a right of recovery under this section upon a transfer subject to § 2044 is treated as a transfer for Federal gift tax purposes of the unrecovered amounts from the persons who would benefit from the recovery to the persons from whom the recovery could have been obtained. See § 25.2511-1 of this chapter. The transfer is considered made when the right of recovery is no longer enforceable under applicable law. A delay in the exercise of the right of recovery without payment of sufficient interest is a below-market loan. Section 1.7872-5T of the Temporary Income Tax regulations describes factors that are used to determine, based on the facts and circumstances of a particular case, whether a loan otherwise subject to imputation under section 7872 (relating to the treatment of below-market loans) is exempted from its provisions.

(3) Waiver of right of recovery. The provisions of § 20.2207A-1(a)(2) do not apply to the extent that the surviving spouse's will provides that a recovery shall not be made or to the extent that the beneficiaries cannot otherwise compel recovery. Thus, e.g., if the surviving spouse gives the executor of the estate discretion to waive the right of recovery and the executor waives the right, no gift occurs under § 25.2511-1 of this chapter if the persons who would benefit from the recovery cannot compel the executor to exercise the right of recovery.

(b) Amount of estate tax attributable to property includible under § 2044. The amount of Federal estate tax attributable to property includible in the gross estate under § 2044 is the amount by which the total Federal estate tax (including penalties and interest attributable to the tax) under chapter 11 of the Internal Revenue Code that has been paid, exceeds the total Federal estate tax (including penalties and interest attributable to the tax) under chapter 11 of the Internal Revenue Code that would have been paid if the value of the property includible in the gross estate by reason of § 2044 had not been so included.

(c) Amount of estate tax attributable to a particular property. An estate's right of recovery with respect to a particular property is an amount equal to the amount determined in paragraph (b) of this section multiplied by a fraction. The numerator of the fraction is the value for Federal estate tax purposes of the particular property included in the gross estate by reason of § 2044, less any deduction allowed with respect to the property. The denominator of the fraction is the total value of all properties included in the gross estate by reason of § 2044, less any deductions allowed with respect to those properties.

(d) Person receiving the property. If the property is in a trust at the time of the decedent's death, the person receiving the property is the trustee and any person who has received a distribution of the property prior to the expiration of the right of recovery if the property does not remain in trust. This paragraph (d) does not affect the right, if any, under local law, of any person with an interest in property to reimbursement or contribution from another person with an interest in the property.

(e) Example. The following example illustrates the application of paragraphs (a) through (d) of this section.

Example. D died in 1994. D's will created a trust funded with certain income producing assets included in D's gross estate at $1,000,000. The trust provides that all the income is payable to D's wife, S, for life, remainder to be divided equally among their four children. In computing D's taxable estate, D's executor deducted, pursuant to § 2056(b)(7), $1,000,000. Assume that S received no other property from D and that S died in 1996. Assume further that S made no § 2519 disposition of the property, that the property was included in S's gross estate at a value of $1,080,000, and that S's will contained no provision regarding § 2207A(a). The tax attributable to the property is equal to the amount by which the total Federal estate tax (including penalties and interest) paid by S's estate exceeds the Federal estate tax (including penalties and interest) that would have been paid if S's gross estate had been reduced by $1,080,000. That amount of tax may be recovered by S's estate from the trust. If, at the time S's estate seeks reimbursement, the trust has been distributed to the four children, S's estate is also entitled to recover the tax from the children.

T.D. 8522, 2/28/94, amend T.D. 9077, 7/17/2003.

§ 25.2207A-1 Right of recovery of gift taxes in the case of certain marital deduction property.

(a) In general. If an individual is treated as transferring an interest in property by reason of § 2519, the individual or the individual's estate is entitled to recover from the person receiving the property (as defined in paragraph (e) of this section) the amount of gift tax attributable to that property. The value of property to which this paragraph (a) applies is the value of all interests in the property other than the qualifying income interest. There is no right of recovery from any person for the property received by that person for which a deduction was allowed from the total amount of gifts, if no Federal gift tax is attributable to the property. The right of recovery arises at the time the Federal gift tax is actually paid by the transferor subject to § 2519.

(b) Failure of a person to exercise the right of recovery. *(1)* The failure of a person to exercise a right of recovery provided by section 2207A(b) upon a lifetime transfer subject to section 2519 is treated as a transfer for Federal gift tax purposes of the unrecovered amounts to the person(s) from whom the recovery could have been obtained. See § 25.2511-1. The transfer is considered to be made when the right to recovery is no longer enforceable under applicable law and is treated as a gift even if recovery is impossible. A delay in the exercise of the right of recovery without payment of sufficient interest is a below-market loan. Section 1.7872-5T of this chapter describes factors that are used to determine, based on the facts and circumstances of a particular case, whether a loan otherwise subject to imputation under section 7872 (relating to the treatment of below-market loans) is exempted from its provisions.

(2) The transferor subject to section 2519 may execute a written waiver of the right of recovery arising under section 2207A before that right of recovery becomes unenforceable. If a waiver is executed, the transfer of the unrecovered

amounts by the transferor is considered to be made on the later of—

(i) The date of the valid and irrevocable waiver rendering the right of recovery no longer enforceable; or

(ii) The date of the payment of the tax by the transferor.

(c) Amount of gift tax attributable to all properties. The amount of Federal gift tax attributable to all properties includible in the total amount of gifts under § 2519 made during the calendar year is the amount by which the total Federal gift tax for the calendar year (including penalties and interest attributable to the tax) under chapter 12 of the Internal Revenue Code which has been paid, exceeds the total Federal gift tax for the calendar year (including penalties and interest attributable to the tax) under chapter 12 of the Internal Revenue Code which would have been paid if the value of the properties includible in the total amount of gifts by reason of § 2519 had not been included.

(d) Amount of gift tax attributable to a particular property. A person's right of recovery with respect to a particular property is an amount equal to the amount determined in paragraph (c) of this section multiplied by a fraction. The numerator of the fraction is the value of the particular property included in the total amount of gifts made during the calendar year by reason of § 2519, less any deduction allowed with respect to the property. The denominator of the fraction is the total value of all properties included in the total amount of gifts made during the calendar year by reason of § 2519, less any deductions allowed with respect to those properties.

(e) Person receiving the property. If the property is in a trust at the time of the transfer, the person receiving the property is the trustee, and any person who has received a distribution of the property prior to the expiration of the right of recovery if the property does not remain in trust. This paragraph (e) does not affect the right, if any, under local law, of any person with an interest in property to reimbursement or contribution from another person with an interest in the property.

(f) Example. The following example illustrates the application of paragraphs (a) through (e) of this section.

Example. D created an inter vivos trust during 1994 with certain income producing assets valued at $1,000,000. The trust provides that all income is payable to D's wife, S, for S's life, with the remainder at S's death to be divided equally among their four children. In computing taxable gifts during calendar year 1994, D deducted, pursuant to § 2523(f), $1,000,000 from the total amount of gifts made. In addition, assume that S received no other transfers from D and that S made a gift during 1996 of the entire life interest to one of the children, at which time the value of trust assets was $1,080,000 and the value of S's life interest was $400,000. Although the entire value of the trust assets ($1,080,000) is, pursuant to §§ 2511 and 2519, included in the total amount of S's gifts for calendar year 1996, S is only entitled to reimbursement for the Federal gift tax attributable to the value of the remainder interest, that is, the Federal gift tax attributable to $680,000 ($1,080,000 less $400,000). The Federal gift tax attributable to $680,000 is equal to the amount by which the total Federal gift tax (including penalties and interest) paid for the calendar year exceeds the federal gift tax (including penalties and interest) that would have been paid if the total amount of gifts during 1996 had been reduced by $680,000. That amount of tax may be recovered by S from the trust.

T.D. 8522, 2/28/94, amend T.D. 9077, 7/17/2003.

§ 20.2207A-2 Effective date.

The provisions of § 20.2207A-1 are effective with respect to estates of decedents dying after March 1, 1994. With respect to estates of decedent dying on or before such date, the executor of the decedent's estate may rely on any reasonable interpretation of the statutory provisions. For these purposes, the provisions of § 20.2207A-1 (as well as project LR-211-76, 1984-1 C.B., page 598, see § 601.601(d)(2)(ii)(b) of this chapter), are considered a reasonable interpretation of the statutory provisions.

T.D. 8522, 2/28/94.

§ 25.2207A-2 Effective date.

The provisions of § 25.2207A-1 are effective with respect to dispositions made after March 1, 1994. With respect to gifts made on or before such date, the donor may rely on any reasonable interpretation of the statutory provisions. For these purposes, the provisions of § 25.2207A-1 (as well as project LR-211-76, 1984-1 C.B., page 598, see § 601.601(d)(2)(ii)(b) of this chapter), are considered a reasonable interpretation of the statutory provisions.

T.D. 8522, 2/28/94.

§ 20.2208-1 Certain residents of possessions considered citizens of the United States.

As used in this part, the term "citizen of the United States" is considered to include a decedent dying after September 2, 1958, who, at the time of his death, was domiciled in a possession of the United States and was a United States citizen, and who did not acquire his United States citizenship solely by reason of his being a citizen of such possession or by reason of his birth or residence within such possession. The estate of such a decedent is, therefore, subject to the tax imposed by § 2001. See paragraph (a)(2) of § 20.0-1 and § 20.2209-1 for further information relating to the application of the Federal estate tax to the estates of decedents who were residents of possessions of the United States. The application of this section may be illustrated by the following example and the examples set forth in § 20.2209-1:

Example. A, a citizen of the United States by reason of his birth in the United States at San Francisco, established residence in Puerto Rico and acquired a Puerto Rican citizenship. A died on September 4, 1958, while a citizen and domiciliary of Puerto Rico. A's estate is, by reason of the provisions of § 2208, subject to the tax imposed by § 2001 inasmuch as his United States citizenship is based on birth in the United States and is not based solely on being a citizen of a possession or solely on birth or residence in a possession.

T.D. 6526, 1/18/61.

§ 20.2209-1 Certain residents of possessions considered nonresidents not citizens of the United States.

As used in this part, the term "nonresident not a citizen of the United States" is considered to include a decedent dying after September 14, 1960, who, at the time of his death, was domiciled in a possession of the United States and was a United States citizen, and who acquired his United States citizenship solely by reason of his being a citizen of such possession or by reason of his birth or residence within such possession. The estate of such a decedent is, therefore, subject to the tax imposed by § 2101 which is the tax applicable in the case of a "nonresident not a citizen of the United States." See paragraph (a)(2) of § 20.0-1 and § 20.2208-1 for further information relating to the application of the Federal estate tax to the estates of decedents who were residents of possessions of the United States. The application of this section may be illustrated by the following examples and the example set forth in § 20.2208-1. In each of the following examples the decedent is deemed a "nonresident not a citizen of the United States" and his estate is subject to the tax imposed by § 2101 since the decedent died after September 14, 1960, but would not have been so deemed and subject to such tax if the decedent had died on or before September 14, 1960.

Example (1). C, who acquired his United States citizenship under § 5 of the Act of March 2, 1917 (39 Stat. 953), by reason of being a citizen of Puerto Rico, died in Puerto Rico on October 1, 1960, while domiciled therein. C is considered to have acquired his United States citizenship solely by reason of his being a citizen of Puerto Rico.

Example (2). E, whose parents were United States citizens by reason of their birth in Boston, was born in the Virgin Islands on March 1, 1927. On September 30, 1960, he died in the Virgin Islands while domiciled therein. E is considered to have acquired his United States citizenship solely by reason of his birth in the Virgin Islands (§ 306 of the Immigration and Nationality Act (66 Stat. 237, 8 USC 1406)).

Example (3). N, who acquired United States citizenship by reason of being a native of the Virgin Islands and a resident thereof on June 28, 1932 (§ 306 of the Immigration and Nationality Act (66 Stat. 237, 8 USC 1406)), died on October 1, 1960, while domiciled in the Virgin Islands. N is considered to have acquired his United States citizenship solely by reason of his birth or residence in the Virgin Islands.

Example (4). P, a former Danish citizen, who on January 17, 1917, resided in the Virgin Islands, made the declaration to preserve his Danish citizenship required by Article 6 of the treaty entered into on August 4, 1916, between the United States and Denmark. Subsequently P acquired United States citizenship when he renounced such declaration before a court of record (§ 306 of the Immigration and Nationality Act (66 Stat. 237, 8 USC 1406)). P died on October 1, 1960, while domiciled in the Virgin Islands. P is considered to have acquired his United States citizenship solely by reason of his birth or residence in the Virgin Islands.

Example (5). R, a former French citizen, acquired his United States citizenship through naturalization proceedings in a court located in the Virgin Islands after having qualified for citizenship by residing in the Virgin Islands for 5 years. R died on October 1, 1960, while domiciled in the Virgin Islands. R is considered to have acquired his United States citizenship solely by reason of his birth or residence within the Virgin Islands.

T.D. 6526, 1/18/61.

§ 25.0-1 Introduction.

(a) In general. *(1)* The regulations in this part are designated "Gift Tax Regulations." These regulations pertain to (i) the gift tax imposed by chapter 12 of subtitle B of the Internal Revenue Code on the transfer of property by gift by individuals in the calendar year 1955, in subsequent calendar years beginning before the calendar year 1971, in calendar quarters beginning with the first calendar of calendar year 1971 through the last calendar quarter of the calendar year 1981, and in calendar years beginning with the calendar year 1982, and (ii) certain related administrative provisions of subtitle F of the Code. It should be noted that the application of some of the provisions of these regulations may be affected by the provisions of an applicable gift tax convention with a foreign country. Unless otherwise indicated, references in these regulations as to the "Internal Revenue Code" or the "Code" are references to the Internal Revenue Code of 1954, as amended, and references to a section or other provision of law are references to a section or other provision of the Internal Revenue Code of 1954, as amended. The Gift Tax Regulations are applicable to the transfer of property by gift by individuals in calendar years 1955 through 1970, in calendar quarters beginning with the first calendar quarter of calendar year 1971 through the last calendar quarter of the calendar year 1981, and in calendar years beginning with the calendar year 1982, and supersede the regulations contained in Part 86, Subchapter B, Chapter 1, Title 26, Code of Federal Regulations (1939) (Regulations 108, Gift Tax (8 FR 10858)), as prescribed and made applicable to the Internal Revenue Code of 1954 by Treasury Decision 6091, signed August 16, 1954 (19 FR 5167, Aug. 17, 1954).

(2) Section 2501(b) makes the provisions of chapter 12 of the Code apply in the case of gifts made after September 2, 1958, by certain citizens of the United States who were residents of a possession thereof at the time the gifts were made. Section 2501(c) makes the provisions of chapter 12 apply in the case of gifts made after September 14, 1960, by certain other citizens of the United States who were residents of a possession thereof at the time the gifts were made. See paragraphs (c) and (d) of § 25.2501-1. Except as otherwise provided in paragraphs (c) and (d) of § 25.2501-1, the provisions of these regulations do not apply to the making of gifts by such citizens.

(b) Nature of tax. The gift tax is not a property tax. It is a tax imposed upon the transfer of property by individuals. It is not applicable to transfers by corporations or persons other than individuals. However, see paragraph (h)(1) of § 25.2511-1 with respect to the extent to which a transfer by or to a corporation is considered a transfer by or to its shareholders.

(c) Scope of regulations. *(1) Determination of tax liability.* Subchapter A of chapter 12 of the Code pertains to the determination of tax liability. The regulations pursuant to subchapter A are set forth in §§ 25.2501-1 through 25.2504-2. Sections 25.2701-5 and 25.2702-6 contain rules that provide additional adjustments to mitigate double taxation where the amount of the transferor's property was previously determined under the special valuation provisions of sections 2701 and 2702.

(2) Transfer. Subchapter B of chapter 12 and chapter 14 of the Internal Revenue Code pertain to the transfers which constitute the making of gifts and the valuation of those transfers. The regulations pursuant to subchapter B are set forth in §§ 25.2511-1 through 25.2518-3. The regulations pursuant to chapter 14 are set forth in §§ 25.2701-1 through 25.2704-3.

(3) Deductions. Subchapter C of chapter 12 of the Code pertains to the deductions which are allowed in determining the amount of taxable gifts. The regulations pursuant to subchapter C are set forth in §§ 25.2521-1 through 25.2524-1.

(4) Procedure and administration provisions. Subtitle F of the Internal Revenue Code contains some sections which are applicable to the gift tax. The regulations pursuant to those

sections are set forth in §§ 25.6001-1 through 25.7101-1. Such regulations do not purport to be all the regulations on procedure and administration which are pertinent to gift tax matters. For the remainder of the regulations on procedure and administration which are pertinent to gift tax matters, see Part 301 of this chapter (Regulations on Procedure and Administration).

(d) Arrangement and numbering. Each section of the regulations in this part (other than this section) is designated by a number composed of the part number followed by a decimal point (25.); the section of the Internal Revenue code which it interprets; a hyphen (-); and a number identifying the section. By use of these designations one can ascertain the sections of the regulations relating to a provision of the Code. For example, the regulations pertaining to section 2521 of the Code are designated § 25.2521-1.

T.D. 6334, 11/14/58, amend T.D. 6542, 1/19/61, T.D. 7238, 12/28/72, T.D. 7296, 12/11/73, T.D. 7665, 1/24/80, T.D. 7910, 9/6/83, T.D. 8395, 1/28/92.

§ 25.2501-1 Imposition of tax.

Caution: The Treasury has not yet amended Reg § 25.2501-1 to reflect changes made by P.L. 110-245, P.L. 104-191.

(a) In general. *(1)* The tax applies to all transfers by gift of property, wherever situated, by an individual who is a citizen or resident of the United States, to the extent the value of the transfers exceeds the amount of the exclusions authorized by section 2503 and the deductions authorized by sections 2521 (as in effect prior to its repeal by the Tax Reform Act of 1976), 2522, and 2523. For each "calendar period" (as defined in § 25.2502-1(c)(1)), the tax described in this paragraph (a) is imposed on the transfer of property by gift during such calendar period.

(2) The tax does not apply to a transfer by gift of intangible property before January 1, 1967, by a nonresident not a citizen of the United States, unless the donor was engaged in business in the United States during the calendar year in which the transfer was made.

(3) (i) The tax does not apply to any transfer by gift of intangible property on or after January 1, 1967, by a nonresident not a citizen of the United States (whether or not he was engaged in business in the United States), unless the donor is an expatriate who lost his U.S. citizenship after March 8, 1965, and within the 10-year period ending with the date of transfer, and the loss of citizenship—

(a) Did not result from the application of section 301(b), 350, or 355 of the Immigration and Nationality Act, as amended (8 U.S.C. 1401(b), 1482, or 1487) (For a summary of these sections, see paragraph (d)(1) of § 20.2107-1 of this chapter (estate tax regulations)), and

(b) Had for one of its principal purposes (but not necessarily its only principal purpose) the avoidance of Federal income, estate, or gift tax.

(ii) In determining for purposes of subdivision (i)*(b)* of this subparagraph whether a principal purpose for the loss of U.S. citizenship by a donor was the avoidance of Federal income, estate, or gift tax, the Commissioner must first establish that it is reasonable to believe that the donor's loss of U.S. citizenship would, but for section 2501(a)(3) and this subparagraph, result in a substantial reduction for the "calendar period" [as defined in § 25.2502-1(c)(1)] in the sum of *(a)* the Federal gift tax and *(b)* all gift taxes imposed by foreign countries and political subdivisions thereof, in respect of the transfer of property by gift. Once the Commissioner has so established, the burden of proving that the loss of citizenship by the donor did not have for one of its principal purposes the avoidance of Federal income estate, or gift tax shall be on the donor. In the absence of complete factual information, the Commissioner may make a tentative determination, based on the information available, that the donor's loss of U.S. citizenship would, but for section 2501(a)(3) and this subparagraph, result in a substantial reduction for the calendar period in the sum of the Federal and foreign gift taxes described in *(a)* and *(b)* of this subdivision on the transfer of property by gift. This tentative determination may be based upon the fact that the laws of the foreign country of which the donor became a citizen and the laws of the foreign country of which the donor was a resident at the time of the transfer, including the laws of any political subdivision of those foreign countries, would ordinarily result in the case of a nonexpatriate donor having the same citizenship and residence as the donor, in liability for total gift taxes under such laws for the calendar period substantially lower than the amount of the Federal gift tax which would be imposed for such period on an amount of comparable gifts by a citizen of the United States. In the absence of a preponderance of evidence to the contrary; this tentative determination shall be sufficient to establish that it is reasonable to believe that the donor's loss of U.S. citizenship would, but for section 250(a)(3) and this subparagraph, result in a substantial reduction for the calendar period in the sum of the Federal and foreign gift taxes described in *(a)* and *(b)* of this subdivision on the transfer of property by gift.

(4) For additional rules relating to the application of the tax to transfers by nonresidents not citizens of the United States, see section 2511 and § 25.2511-3.

(5) The general rule of this paragraph (a) shall not apply to a transfer after May 7, 1974, of money or other property to a political organization for the use of that organization. However, this exception to the general rule applies solely to a transfer to a political organization as defined in section 527(e)(1) and including a newsletter fund to the extent provided under section 527(g). The general rule governs a transfer of property to an organization other than a political organization as so defined.

(b) Resident. A resident is an individual who has his domicile in the United States at the time of the gift. For this purpose the United States includes the States and the District of Columbia. The term also includes the Territories of Alaska and Hawaii prior to admission as a State. See section 7701(a)(9). All other individuals are non-residents. A person acquires a domicile in a place by living there, for even a brief period of time with no definite present intention of moving therefrom. Residence without the requisite intention to remain indefinitely will not constitute domicile nor will intention to change domicile effect such a change unless accompanied by actual removal.

(c) Certain residents of possessions considered citizens of the United States. As used in this part, the term "citizen of the United States" includes a person who makes a gift after September 2, 1958 and who, at the time of making the gift was domiciled in a possession of the United States and was a United States citizen, and who did not acquire his United States citizenship solely by reason of his being a citizen of such possession or by reason of his birth or residence within such possession. The gift of such a person is, therefore, subject to the tax imposed by section 2501 in the same manner in which a gift made by resident of the United States is subject to the tax. See paragraph (a) of § 25.0-1 and paragraph (d) of this section for further information relating to the application of the Federal gift tax to gifts made by persons who were residents of possessions of the United States. The application of this paragraph may be illustrated by the following example and the examples set forth in paragraph (d) of this section:

Example. A, a citizen of the United States by reason of his birth in the United States at San Francisco, established residence in Puerto Rico and acquired Puerto Rican citizenship. A makes a gift of stock of a Spanish corporation on September 4, 1958, while a citizen and domiciliary of Puerto Rico. A's gift is, by reason of the provisions of section 2501(b) subject to the tax imposed by section 2501 inasmuch as his United States citizenship is based on birth in the United States and is not based solely on being a citizen of a possession or solely on birth or residence in a possession.

(d) Certain residents of possessions considered nonresidents not citizens of the United States. As used in this part, the term "nonresident not a citizen of the United States" includes a person who makes a gift after September 14, 1960, and who at the time of making the gift, was domiciled in a possession of the United States and was a United States citizen, and who acquired his United States citizenship solely by reason of his being a citizen of such possession or by reason of his birth or residence within such possession. The gift of such a person is, therefore, subject to the tax imposed by section 2501 in the same manner in which a gift is subject to the tax when made by a donor who is a "nonresident not a citizen of the United States." See paragraph (a) of § 25.0-1 and paragraph (c) of this section for further information relating to the application of the Federal gift tax to gifts made by persons who were residents of possessions of the United States. The application of this paragraph may be illustrated by the following examples and the example set forth in paragraph (c) of this section. In each of the following examples the person who makes the gift is deemed a "nonresident not a citizen of the United States" and his gift is subject to the tax imposed by section 2501 in the same manner in which a gift is subject to the tax when made by a donor who is a nonresident not a citizen of the United States, since he made the gift after September 14, 1960, but would not have been so deemed and subject to such tax if the person who made the gift had made it on or before September 14, 1960.

Example (1). C, who acquired his United States citizenship under section 5 of the Act of March 2, 1917 (39 Stat. 953), by reason of being a citizen of Puerto Rico, while domiciled in Puerto Rico makes a gift on October 1, 1960, of real estate located in New York. C is considered to have acquired his United States citizenship solely by reason of his being a citizen of Puerto Rico.

Example (2). E, whose parents were United States citizens by reason of their birth in Boston, was born in the Virgin Islands on March 1, 1927. On September 30, 1960, while domiciled in the Virgin Islands, he made a gift of tangible personal property situated in Kansas. E is considered to have acquired his United States citizenship solely by reason of his birth in the Virgin Islands (section 306 of the Immigration and Nationality Act (66 Stat. 237, 8 U.S.C. 1406)).

Example (3). N, who acquired United States citizenship by reason of being a native of the Virgin Islands and a resident thereof on June 28, 1932 (section 306 of the Immigration and Nationality Act (66 Stat. 237, 8 U.S.C. 1406)), made a gift on October 1, 1960, at which time he was domiciled in the Virgin Islands, of tangible personal property situated in Wisconsin. N is considered to have acquired his United States citizenship solely by reason of his birth or residence in the Virgin Islands.

Example (4). P, a former Danish citizen, who on January 17, 1917, resided in the Virgin Islands, made the declaration to preserve his Danish citizenship required by Article 6 of the treaty entered into on August 4, 1916, between the United States and Denmark. Subsequently P acquired United States citizenship when he renounced such declaration before a court of record (section 306 of the Immigration and Nationality Act (66 Stat. 237, 8 U.S.C. 1406)). P, while domiciled in the Virgin Islands, made a gift on October 1, 1960, of tangible personal property situated in California. P is considered to have acquired his United States citizenship solely by reason of his birth or residence in the Virgin Islands.

Example (5). R, a former French citizen, acquired his United States citizenship through naturalization proceedings in a court located in the Virgin Islands after having qualified for citizenship by residing in the Virgin Islands for 5 years. R, while domiciled in the Virgin Islands, made a gift of tangible personal property situated in Hawaii on October 1, 1960. R is considered to have acquired his United States citizenship solely by reason of his birth or residence within the Virgin Islands.

T.D. 6334, 11/14/58, amend T.D. 6542, 1/19/61, T.D. 7238, 12/28/72, T.D. 7296, 12/11/73, T.D. 7671, 2/5/80, T.D. 7910, 9/6/83.

---

§ 25.2502-1 Rate of tax.

Caution: The Treasury has not yet amended Reg § 25.2502-1 to reflect changes made by P.L. 100-203.

(a) Computation of tax. The rate of tax is determined by the total of all gifts made by the donor during the calendar period and all the preceding calendar periods since June 6, 1932. See § 25.2502-1(c)(1) for the definition of "calendar period" and § 25.2502-1(c)(2) for the definition of "preceding calendar periods." The following six steps are to be followed in computing the tax:

(1) First step. Ascertain the amount of the "taxable gifts" (as defined in § 25.2503-1) for the calendar period for which the return is being prepared.

(2) Second step. Ascertain "the aggregate sum of the taxable gifts for each of the preceding calendar periods" (as defined in § 25.2504-1), considering only those gifts made after June 6, 1932.

(3) Third step. Ascertain the total amount of the taxable gifts which is the sum of the amounts determined in the first and second steps. See § 25.2702-6 for an adjustment to the total amount of an individual's taxable gifts where the individual's current taxable gifts include the transfer of certain interests in trust that were previously valued under the provisions of section 2702.

(4) Fourth step. Compute the tentative tax on the total amount of taxable gifts (as determined in the third step) using the rate schedule in effect at the time the gift (for which the return is being filed) is made.

(5) Fifth step. Compute the tentative tax on the aggregate sum of the taxable gifts for each of the preceding calendar periods (as determined in the second step), using the same rate schedule set forth in the fourth step of this paragraph (a).

(6) Sixth step. Subtract the amount determined in the fifth step from the amount determined in the fourth step. The

amount remaining is the gift tax for the calendar period for which the return is being prepared.

(b) Rate of tax. The tax is computed in accordance with the rate schedule in effect at the time the gift was made as set forth in section 2001(c) or corresponding provisions of prior law.

(c) Definitions. *(1)* The term "calendar period" means:

(i) Each calendar year for the calendar years 1932 (but only that portion of such year after June 6, 1932) through 1970;

(ii) Each calendar quarter for the first calendar quarter of the calendar year 1971 through the last calendar quarter of calendar year 1981; or

(iii) Each calendar year for the calendar year 1982 and each succeeding calendar year.

(2) The term "preceding calendar periods" means all calendar periods ending prior to the calendar period for which the tax is being computed.

(d) Examples. The following examples illustrate the application of this section with respect to gifts made by citizens or residents of the United States:

Example (1). Assume that in 1955 the donor made taxable gifts, as ascertained under the first step (paragraph (a)(2) of this section), of $62,500 and that there were no taxable gifts for prior years, with the result that the amount ascertainable under the third step is $62,500. Under the fourth step a tax is computed on this amount. Reference to the tax rate schedule in effect in the year 1955 discloses that the tax on this amount is $7,650.

Example (2). A donor makes gifts (other than gifts of future interests in property) during the calendar year 1955 of $30,000 to A and $33,000 to B. Two exclusions of $3,000 each are allowable, in accordance with the provisions of section 2503(b), which results in included gifts for 1955 of $57,000. Specific exemption was claimed and allowed in a total amount of $50,000 in the donor's gift tax returns for the calendar years 1934 and 1935 so there remains no specific exemption available for the donor to claim for 1955. The total amount of gifts made by the donor during preceding years, after excluding $5,000 for each donee for each calendar year in accordance with the provisions of section 1003(b)(1) of the 1939 Code, is computed as follows:

Calendar year 1934	$120,000
Calendar year 1935	25,000
Total amount of included gifts for preceding calendar years	145,000

The aggregate sum of the taxable gifts for preceding calendar years is $115,000, which is determined by deducting a specific exemption of $30,000 from $145,000, the total amount of included gifts for preceding calendar years. The deduction from the 1934 and 1935 gifts for the specific exemption cannot exceed $30,000 for purposes of computing the tax on the 1955 gifts even though a specific exemption in a total amount of $50,000 was allowed in computing the donor's gift tax liability for 1934 and 1935. (See paragraph (b) of § 25.2504-1.) The computation of the tax for the calendar year 1955 (following the steps set forth in paragraph (a) of this section) is shown below:

(1) Amount of taxable gifts for year	$ 57,000
(2) Total amount of taxable gifts for preceding years	115,000
(3) Total taxable gifts	172,000
(4) Tax computed on item 3 (in accordance with the rate schedule in effect for the year 1955)	31,725
(5) Tax computed on item 2 (using same rate schedule)	18,900
(6) Tax for year 1955 (item 4 minus item 5)	12,825

Example (3). (i) Facts. During the calendar year 1955, H makes the following gifts of present interests:

To his daughter	$40,000
To his son	5,000
To W, his wife	5,000
To a charitable organization	10,000

The gifts to W qualify for the marital deduction, and, pursuant to the provisions of section 2513 (see § 25.2513-1), H and W consent to treat the gifts to third parties as having been made one-half by each spouse. The amount of H's taxable gifts for preceding years is $50,000. Only $25,000 of H's specific exemption provided under section 2521, which was in effect at the time was claimed and allowed in preceding years. H's remaining specific exemption of $5,000 is claimed for the calendar year 1955. See § 25.2521-1. W made no gifts during the calendar year 1955 nor during any preceding calendar year. W claims sufficient specific exemption on her return to eliminate tax liability.

(ii) Computation of H's tax for the calendar year 1955.

(a) H's taxable gifts for year.

Total gifts of H		$60,000
Less: Portion of items to be reported by spouse (one-half of total gifts to daughter, son and charity)		27,500
Balance		32,500
Less: Exclusions (three of $3,000 each for daughter, wife and charity and one of $2,500 for son)		11,500
Total included amount of gifts for year		
Less: Deductions:		
Charity	$2,000	
Marital	2,000	
Specific exemption	5,000	
Total deductions		$ 9,000
Amount of taxable gifts for year		12,000

(b) Computation of tax. The steps set forth in paragraph (a) of this section are followed.

(1) Amount of taxable gifts for year	$12,000
(2) Total taxable gifts for preceding years	50,000
(3) Total taxable gifts (item (1) plus item (2))	62,000
(4) Tax computed on item (3) in accordance with the rate schedule in effect for the year 1955	7,545
(5) Tax computed on item (2) in accordance with the rate schedule in effect for the year 1955	5,250
(6) Tax for the calendar year (item (4) minus item (5))	2,295

(iii) Computation of W's tax for calendar year 1955. (a) W's taxable gifts for year.

Total gifts of W	$ 0
Less: Portion of items to be reported by spouse	0
Balance	0
Gifts of spouse to be included	27,500
Total gifts for year	27,500
Less: Exclusions (two of $3,000 each for daughter and charity and one of $2,500 for son)	8,500

Balance		19,000
Less—Deductions:		
Charity	$2,000	
Marital	0	
Specific exemption	17,000	
Total deductions		19,000
Amount of taxable gifts for year		0

(b) Computation of tax. Since W had no "taxable gifts" during the year, there is no tax.

Example (4). (i) Facts. The facts are the same as in example (3) except that W made outright gifts of $10,000 to her niece and $20,000 to H at various times during the year. The amount of taxable gifts made by W in preceding calendar years is $75,000, and only $20,000 of her specific exemption provided under section 2521, which was in effect at the time, was claimed and allowed for preceding years. See § 25.2521-1. The remaining specific exemption of $10,000 is claimed for the calendar year 1955.

(ii) Computation of H's tax for the calendar year 1955. (a) H's taxable gifts for year.

Total gifts of H		$60,000
Less: Portion of items to be reported by spouse		27,500
Balance		32,500
Gifts of spouse to be included		5,000
Total gifts for year		37,500
Less: Exclusions ($11,500 as shown in example (3) plus $3,000 exclusion for gift to niece)		14,500
Total included amount of gifts for year		23,000
Deductions:		
Charity	$ 2,000	
Marital	2,000	
Specific exemption	5,000	
Total deductions		$ 9,000
Amount of taxable gifts for year		14,000

(b) Computation of tax.

(1) Amount of taxable gifts for year	14,000
(2) Total taxable gifts for preceding years	50,000
(3) Total taxable gifts (item (1) plus item (2))	$64,000
(4) Tax computed on item (3)	7,965
(5) Tax computed on item (2)	5,250
(6) Tax for year (item (4) minus item (5))	2,715

(iii) Computation of W's tax for the calendar year 1955.

(a) W's taxable gifts for year.

Total gifts of W		$30,000
Less: Portion of items to be reported by spouse (one-half of gift to niece)		5,000
Balance		25,000
Gifts of spouse to be included		27,500
Total gifts for year		52,500
Less: Exclusions (fourth of $3,000 each for daughter, husband, niece and charity, and one of $2,500 for son)		14,500
Total included amount of gifts for year		38,000
Deductions:		
Charity	$ 2,000	
Marital	10,000	
Specific exemption	10,000	
Total deductions		22,000
Amount of taxable gifts for year		16,000

(b) Computation of tax.

(1) Amount of taxable gifts for year	16,000
(2) Total taxable gifts for preceding years	75,000
(3) Total taxable gifts	91,000
(4) Tax computed on item (3)	13,635
(5) Tax computed on item (2)	10,275
(6) Tax for year (item (4) minus item (5))	3,360

Example (5). A makes gifts (other than gifts of future interests in property) to B in the first quarter of 1971 of $43,000 and in the second quarter of 1971 of $60,000. A gave to C in the second quarter of 1971 land valued at $11,000. The full amount of A's specific exemption provided under section 2521 was claimed and allowed in 1956. In 1966, A made taxable gifts totaling $21,000 on which gift tax was timely paid and no other taxable gifts were made by A in any other year preceding 1971. The gift tax return due for the first calendar quarter of 1971 was timely filed and the tax paid. With respect to the gifts made to B in 1971, the $3,000 annual gift tax exclusion provided by section 2503(b) is applied in its entirety against the $43,000 gift made to B in the first quarter and therefore is not available to offset the $60,000 gift made to B in the second quarter. (See § 25.2503-2(b).) A further $3,000 annual gift tax exclusion is available, however, to offset the $11,000 gift made to C in the second quarter of 1971. The computation of the gift tax for the second calendar quarter of 1971 due on August 15, 1971 (following the steps set forth in paragraph (a) of this section) is shown below:

(1) Amount of taxable gifts for the second calendar quarter of 1971 ($60,000 + $11,000 – $3,000)	$ 68,000
(2) Total amount of taxable gifts for preceding calendar periods ($43,000 – $3,000 + $21,000)	61,000
(3) Total taxable gifts	129,000
(4) Tax computed on item 3 in accordance with the rate schedule in effect for the year 1971	22,050
(5) Tax computed on item 2 (using same rate schedule)	7,335
(6) Tax for second calendar quarter of 1971 (item 4 minus item 5)	14,715

Example (6). A makes gifts (other than gifts of future interests in property) during the calendar year 1982 of $160,000 to B and $100,000 to C. Two exclusions of $10,000 each are allowable, in accordance with the provisions of section 2503(b), which results in taxable gifts for 1982 of $240,000. In the first calendar quarter of 1978, A made taxable gifts totaling $100,000 on which gift tax was paid. For the calendar year 1969, A made taxable gifts totaling $50,000. The full amount of A's specific exemption provided under section 2521, which was in effect at the time, was claimed and allowed in 1968. The computation of the gift tax for the calendar period 1982 (following the steps set forth in paragraph (a) of this section) is shown below.

(1) Amount of taxable gifts for the calendar year 1982, $240,000.

(2) Total amount of taxable gifts for preceding calendar periods ($100,000 + $50,000), $150,000.

(3) Total taxable gifts, $390,000.

(4) Tax computed on item 3 (in accordance with the rate schedule in effect for the year 1982), $118,400.

(5) Tax computed on item 2 (using same rate schedule), $38,800.

(6) Tax for year 1982 (Item 4 minus item 5), $79,600.

T.D. 6334, 11/14/58, amend T.D. 7238, 12/28/72, T.D. 7910, 9/6/83, T.D. 8395, 1/28/92.

§ 25.2502-2 Donor primarily liable for tax.

Caution: The Treasury has not yet amended Reg § 25.2502-2 to reflect changes made by P.L. 97-34.

Section 2502(d) provides that the donor shall pay the tax. If the donor dies before the tax is paid the amount of the tax is a debt due the United States from the decedent's estate and his executor or administrator is responsible for its payment out of the estate. (See § 25.6151-1 for the time and place for paying the tax.) If there is no duly qualified executor or administrator, the heirs, legatees, devisees and distributees are liable for and required to pay the tax to the extent of the value of their inheritances, bequests, devises or distributive shares of the donor's estate. If a husband and wife effectively signify consent, under section 2513, to have gifts made to a third party during any "calendar period" (as defined in § 25.2502-1(c)(1)) considered as made one-half by each, the liability with respect to the gift tax of each spouse for that calendar period is joint and several (see § 25.2513-4). As to the personal liability of the donee, see paragraph (b) of § 301.6324-1 of this chapter (Regulations on Procedure and Administration). As to the personal liability of the executor or administrator, see section 3467 of the Revised Statutes (31 U.S.C. 192), which reads as follows:

Every executor, administrator, or assignee, or other person, who pays, in whole or in part, any debt due by the person or estate for whom or for which he acts before he satisfies and pays the debts due to the United States from such person or estate, shall become answerable in his own person and estate to the extent of such payments for the debts so due to the United States, or for so much thereof as may remain due and unpaid.

As used in such section 3467, the word "debt" includes a beneficiary's distributive share of an estate. Thus if an executor pays a debt due by the estate which is being administered by him or distributes any portion of the estate before there is paid all of the gift tax which he has a duty to pay, the executor is personally liable, to the extent of the payment or distribution, for so much of the gift tax as remains due and unpaid.

T.D. 6334, 11/14/58, amend T.D. 7238, 12/28/72, T.D. 7910, 9/6/83.

§ 25.2503-1 General definitions of "taxable gifts" and of "total amount of gifts."

Caution: The Treasury has not yet amended Reg § 25.2503-1 to reflect changes made by P.L. 99-514, P.L. 97-34.

The term "taxable gifts" means the "total amount of gifts" made by the donor during the "calendar period" (as defined in § 25.2502-1(c)(1)) less the deductions provided for in sections 2521 (as in effect before its repeal by the Tax Reform Act of 1976), 2522, and 2523 (specific exemption, charitable, etc., gifts and the marital deduction, respectively). The term "total amount of gifts" means the sum of the values of the gifts made during the calendar period less the amounts excludable under section 2503(b). See § 25.2503-2. The entire value of any gift of a future interest in property must be included in the total amount of gifts for the calendar period in which the gift is made. See § 25.2503-3.

T.D. 6334, 11/14/58, amend T.D. 7238, 12/28/72, T.D. 7910, 9/6/83.

§ 25.2503-2 Exclusions from gifts.

Caution: The Treasury has not yet amended Reg § 25.2503-2 to reflect changes made by P.L. 105-34.

(a) Gifts made after December 31, 1981. Except as provided in paragraph (f) of this section (involving gifts to a noncitizen spouse), the first $10,000 of gifts made to any one donee during the calendar year 1982 or any calendar year thereafter, except gifts of future interests in property as defined in §§ 25.2503-3 and 25.2503-4, is excluded in determining the total amount of gifts for the calendar year. In the case of a gift in trust the beneficiary of the trust is the donee.

(b) Gifts made after December 31, 1970 and before January 1, 1982. In computing taxable gifts for the calendar quarter, in the case of gifts (other than gifts of future interests in property) made to any person by the donor during any calendar quarter of the calendar year 1971 or any subsequent calendar year, $3,000 of such gifts to such person less the aggregate of the amounts of such gifts to such person during all preceding calendar quarters of any such calendar year shall not be included in the total amount of gifts made during such quarter. Thus, the first $3,000 of gifts made to any one donee during the calendar year 1971 or any calendar year thereafter, except gifts of future interests in property as defined in §§ 25.2503-3 and 25.2503-4, is excluded in determining the total amount of gifts for a calendar quarter. In the case of a gift in trust the beneficiary of the trust is the donee. The application of this paragraph may be illustrated by the following examples:

Example (1). A made a gift of $3,000 to B on January 8, 1971, and on April 20, 1971, gave B an additional gift of $10,000. A made no other gifts in 1971. The total amount of gifts made by A during the second quarter of 1971 is $10,000 because the $3,000 exclusion provided by section 2503(b) is first applied to the January 8th gift.

Example (2). A gave $2,000 to B on January 8, 1971, and on April 20, 1971, gave him $10,000. The total amount of gifts made by A during the second quarter of 1971 is $9,000 because only $2,000 of the $3,000 exclusion provided by section 2503(b) was applied against the January 8th gift; $1,000 was available to offset other gifts (except gifts of a future interest) made to B during 1971.

(c) Gifts made before January 1, 1971. The first $3,000 of gifts made to any one donee during the calendar year 1955, or 1970, or any calendar year intervening between calendar year 1955 and calendar year 1970, except gifts of future interests in property as defined in §§ 25.2503-3 and 25.2503-4, is excluded in determining the total amount of gifts for the calendar year. In the case of a gift in trust the beneficiary of the trust is the donee.

(d) Transitional rule. The increased annual gift tax exclusion as defined in section 2503(b) shall not apply to any gift subject to a power of appointment granted under an instrument executed before September 12, 1981, and not amended on or after that date, provided that: (1) The power is exercisable after December 31, 1981, (2) the power is expressly defined in terms of, or by reference to, the amount of the gift tax exclusion under section 2503(b) (or the corresponding provision of prior law), and (3) there is not enacted a State law applicable to such instrument which construes the power of appointment as referring to the increased annual gift tax exclusion provided by the Economic Recovery Tax Act of 1981.

(e) Examples. The provisions of paragraph (d) of this section may be illustrated by the following examples:

Example (1). A executed an instrument to create a trust for the benefit of B on July 2, 1981. The trust granted to B the power, for a period of 90 days after any transfer of cash to the trust, to withdraw from the trust the lesser of the amount of the transferred cash or the amount equal to the section 2503(b) annual gift tax exclusion. The trust was not amended on or after September 12, 1981. No state statute has been enacted which construes the power of appointment as referring to the increased annual gift tax exclusion provided by the Economic Recovery Tax Act of 1981. Accordingly, the maximum annual gift tax exclusion applicable to any gift subject to the exercise of the power of appointment is $3,000.

Example (2). Assume the same facts as in example (1) except that the power of appointment granted in the trust refers to section 2503(b) as amended at any time. The maximum annual gift tax exclusion applicable to any gift subject to the exercise of the power of appointment is $10,000.

(f) Special rule in the case of gifts made on or after July 14, 1988, to a spouse who is not a united states citizen. *(1) In general.* Subject to the special rules set forth at § 20.2056A-1(c) of this chapter, in the case of gifts made on or after July 14, 1988, if the donee of the gift is the donor's spouse and the donee spouse is not a citizen of the United States at the time of the gift, the first $100,000 of gifts made during the calendar year to the donee spouse (except gifts of future interests) is excluded in determining the total amount of gifts for the calendar year. The rule of this paragraph (f) applies regardless of whether the donor is a citizen or resident of the United States for purposes of chapter 12 of the Internal Revenue Code.

(2) Gifts made after June 29, 1989. In the case of gifts made after June 29, 1989, the $100,000 exclusion provided in paragraph (f)(1) of this section applies only if the gift in excess of the otherwise applicable annual exclusion is in a form that qualifies for the gift tax marital deduction under section 2523(a) but for the provisions of section 2523(i)(1) (disallowing the marital deduction if the donee spouse is not a United States citizen.) See § 25.2523(i)-1(d), Example 4.

(3) Effective date. This paragraph (f) is effective with respect to gifts made after August 22, 1995.

T.D. 6334, 11/14/58, amend T.D. 7238, 12/28/72, T.D. 7910, 9/6/83, T.D. 7978 9/28/84, T.D. 8612, 8/21/95.

§ 25.2503-3 Future interests in property.

Caution: The Treasury has not yet amended Reg § 25.2503-3 to reflect changes made by P.L. 97-34, P.L. 95-600.

(a) No part of the value of a gift of a future interest may be excluded in determining the total amount of gifts made during the "calendar period" [as defined in § 25.2502-1(c)(1)]. "Future interest" is a legal term, and includes reversions, remainders, and other interests or estates, whether vested or contingent, and whether or not ported by a particular interest or estate, which are limited to commence in use, possession, or enjoyment at some future date or time. The term has no reference to such contractual rights as exist in a bond, note (though bearing no interest until maturity), or in a policy of life insurance, the obligations of which are to be discharged by payments in the future. But a future interest or interests in such contractual obligations may be created by the limitations contained in a trust or other instrument of transfer used in effecting a gift.

(b) An unrestricted right to the immediate use, possession, or enjoyment of property or the income from property (such as a life estate or term certain) is a present interest in property. An exclusion is allowable with respect to a gift of such an interest (but not in excess of the value of the interest). If a donee has received a present interest in property, the possibility that such interest may be diminished by the transfer of a greater interest in the same property to the donee through the exercise of a power is disregarded in computing the value of the present interest, to the extent that no part of such interest will at any time pass to any other person (see example (4) of paragraph (c) of this section). For an exception to the rule disallowing an exclusion for gifts of future interests in the case of certain gifts to minors, see § 25.2503-4.

(c) The operation of this section may be illustrated by the following examples:

Example (1). Under the terms of a trust created by A the trustee is directed to pay the net income to B, so long as B shall live. The trustee is authorized in his discretion to withhold payments of income during any period he deems advisable and add such income to the trust corpus. Since B's right to receive the income payments is subject to the trustee's discretion, it is not a present interest and no exclusion is allowable with respect to the transfer in trust.

Example (2). C transfers certain insurance policies on his own life to a trust created for the benefit of D. Upon C's death the proceeds of the policies are to be invested and the net income therefrom paid to D during his lifetime. Since the income payments to D will not begin until after C's death the transfer in trust represents a gift of a future interest in property against which no exclusion is allowable.

Example (3). Under the terms of a trust created by E the net income is to be distributed to E's three children in such shares as the trustee, in his uncontrolled discretion, deems advisable. While the terms of the trust provide that all of the net income is to be distributed, the amount of income any one of the three beneficiaries will receive rests entirely within the trustee's discretion and cannot be presently ascertained. Accordingly, no exclusions are allowable with respect to the transfers to the trust.

Example (4). Under the terms of a trust the net income is to be paid to F for life, with the remainder payable to G on F's death. The trustee has the uncontrolled power to pay over the corpus to F at any time. Although F's present right to receive the income may be terminated, no other person has the right to such income interest. Accordingly, the power in the trustee is disregarded in determining the value of F's present interest. The power would not be disregarded to the extent that the trustee during F's life could distribute corpus to persons other than F.

Example (5). The corpus of a trust created by J consists of certain real property, subject to a mortgage. The terms of the trust provide that the net income from the property is to be used to pay the mortgage. After the mortgage is paid in full the net income is to be paid to K during his lifetime. Since K's right to receive the income payments will not begin until after the mortgage is paid in full the transfer in trust represents a gift of a future interest in property against which no exclusion is allowable.

Example (6). L pays premiums on a policy of insurance on his life, all the incidents of ownership in the policy (including the right to surrender the policy) are vested in M. The payment of premiums by L constitutes a gift of a present interest in property.

T.D. 6334, 11/14/58, amend T.D. 7238, 12/28/72, T.D. 7910, 9/6/83.

§ 25.2503-4 Transfer for the benefit of a minor.

(a) Section 2503(c) provides that no part of a transfer for the benefit of a donee who has not attained the age of 21 years on the date of the gift will be considered a gift of a future interest in property if the terms of the transfer satisfy all of the following conditions:

(1) Both the property itself and its income may be expended by or for the benefit of the donee before he attains the age of 21 years;

(2) Any portion of the property and its income not disposed of under subparagraph (1) of this paragraph will pass to the donee when he attains the age of 21 years; and

(3) Any portion of the property and its income not disposed of under subparagraph (1) of this paragraph will be payable either to the estate of the donee or as he may appoint under a general power of appointment as defined in section 2514(c) if he dies before attaining the age of 21 years.

(b) Either a power of appointment exercisable by the donee by will or a power of appointment exercisable by the donee during his lifetime will satisfy the conditions set forth in paragraph (a)(3) of this section. However, if the transfer is to qualify for the exclusion under this section, there must be no restrictions of substance (as distinguished from formal restrictions of the type described in paragraph (g)(4) of § 25.2523(e)-1) by the terms of the instrument of transfer on the exercise of the power by the donee. However, if the minor is given a power of appointment exercisable during lifetime or is given a power of appointment exercisable by will, the fact that under the local law a minor is under a disability to exercise an inter vivos power or to execute a will does not cause the transfer to fail to satisfy the conditions of section 2503(c). Further, a transfer does not fail to satisfy the conditions of section 2503(c) by reason of the mere fact that—

(1) There is left to the discretion of a trustee the determination of the amounts, if any, of the income or property to be expended for the benefit of the minor and the purpose for which the expenditure is to be made, provided there are no substantial restrictions under the terms of the trust instrument on the exercise of such discretion;

(2) The donee, upon reaching age 21, has the right to extend the term of the trust; or

(3) The governing instrument contains a disposition of the property or income not expended during the donee's minority to persons other than the donee's estate in the event of the default of appointment by the donee.

(c) A gift to a minor which does not satisfy the requirements of section 2503(c) may be either a present or a future interest under the general rules of § 25.2503-3. Thus, for example, a transfer of property in trust with income required to be paid annually to a minor beneficiary and corpus to be distributed to him upon his attaining the age of 25 is a gift of a present interest with respect to the right to income but is a gift of a future interest with respect to the right to corpus.

T.D. 6334, 11/14/58.

Proposed § 25.2503-5 Individual retirement plan for spouse. [*For Preamble, see ¶ 150,703*]

(a) In general. For purposes of section 2503(b), any payment made by an individual for the benefit of his or her spouse—

(1) To individual retirement account described in section 408(a),

(2) To an individual retirement subaccount described in § 1.220-1(b)(3),

(3) For an individual retirement annuity described in section 408(b), or

(4) For a retirement bond described in section 409,

shall not be considered a gift of a future interest in property to the extent that such payment is allowable as a deduction under section 220 for the taxable year for which the contribution is made. Thus, for example, if individual A paid $900 to an individual retirement account for 1980 on behalf of A's spouse, B, of which $875 was deductible, $875 would not be a gift of a future interest.

(b) Effective date. Paragraph (a) of this section is effective for transfers made after December 31, 1976.

§ 25.2503-6 Exclusion for certain qualified transfer for tuition or medical expenses.

(a) In general. Section 2503(e) provides that any qualified transfer after December 31, 1981, shall not be treated as a transfer of property by gift for purposes of chapter 12 of subtitle B of the Code. Thus, a qualified transfer on behalf of any individual is excluded in determining the total amount of gifts in calendar year 1982 and subsequent years. This exclusion is available in addition to the $10,000 annual gift tax exclusion. Furthermore, an exclusion for a qualified transfer is permitted without regard to the relationship between the donor and the donee.

(b) Qualified transfers. *(1) Definition.* For purposes of this paragraph, the term "qualified transfer" means any amount paid on behalf of an individual—

(i) As tuition to a qualifying educational organization for the education or training of that individual, or (ii) To any person who provides medical care with respect to that individual as payment for the qualifying medical expenses arising from such medical care.

(2) Tuition expenses. For purposes of paragraph (b)(1)(i) of this section, a qualifying educational organization is one which normally maintains a regular faculty and curriculum and normally has a regularly enrolled body of pupils or students in attendance at the place where its educational activities are regularly carried on. See Section 170(b)(1)(A)(ii) and the regulations thereunder. The unlimited exclusion is permitted for tuition expenses of full-time or part-time students paid directly to the qualifying educational organization providing the education. No unlimited exclusion is permitted for amounts paid for books, supplies, dormitory fees, board, or other similar expenses which do not constitute direct tuition costs.

(3) Medical expenses. For purposes of paragraph (b)(1)(ii) of this section, qualifying medical expenses are limited to those expenses defined in section 213(d) (section 213(e) prior to January 1, 1984) and include expenses incurred for the diagnosis, cure, mitigation, treatment or prevention of disease, or for the purpose of affecting any structure or function of the body or for transportation primarily for and es-

sential to medical care. In addition, the unlimited exclusion from the gift tax includes amounts paid for medical insurance on behalf of any individual. The unlimited exclusion from the gift tax does not apply to amounts paid for medical care that are reimbursed by the donee's insurance. Thus, if payment for a medical expense is reimbursed by the donee's insurance company, the donor's payment for that expense, to the extent of the reimbursed amount, is not eligible for the unlimited exclusion from the gift tax and the gift is treated as having been made on the date the reimbursement is received by the donee.

(c) Examples. The provisions of paragraph (b) of this section may be illustrated by the following examples.

Example (1). In 1982, A made a tuition payment directly to a foreign university on behalf of B. A had no legal obligation to make this payment. The foreign university is described in section 170(b)(1)(A)(ii) of the Code. A's tuition payment is exempt from the gift tax under section 2503(e) of the Code.

Example (2). A transfers $100,000 to a trust the provisions of which state that the funds are to be used for tuition expenses incurred by A's grandchildren. A's transfer to the trust is a completed gift for Federal gift tax purposes and is not a direct transfer to an educational organization as provided in paragraph (b)(2) of this section and does not qualify for the unlimited exclusion from gift tax under section 2503(e).

Example (3). C was seriously injured in an automobile accident in 1982. D, who is unrelated to C, paid C's various medical expenses by checks made payable to the physician. D also paid the hospital for C's hospital bills. These medical and hospital expenses were types described in section 213 of the Code and were not reimbursed by insurance or otherwise. Because the medical and hospital bills paid in 1982 for C were medical expenses within the meaning of section 213 of the Code, and since they were paid directly by D to the person rendering the medical care, they are not treated as transfers subject to the gift tax.

Example (4). Assume the same facts as in example (2) except that instead of making the payments directly to the medical service provider, D reimbursed C for the medical expenses which C had previously paid. The payments made by D to C do not qualify for the exclusion under section 2503(e) of the Code and are subject to the gift tax on the date the reimbursement is received by C to the extent the reimbursement and all other gifts from D to C during the year of the reimbursement exceed the $10,000 annual exclusion provided in section 2503(b).

T.D. 7978, 9/28/84.

§ 25.2504-1 Taxable gifts for preceding calendar periods.

(a) In order to determine the correct gift tax liability for any calendar period it is necessary to ascertain the correct amount, if any, of the aggregate sum of the taxable gifts for each of the "preceding calendar periods" (as defined in § 25.2502-1(c)(2)). See paragraph (a) of § 25.2502-1. The term "aggregate sum of the taxable gifts for each of the preceding calendar periods" means the correct aggregate of such gifts, not necessarily that returned for those calendar periods and in respect of which tax was paid. All transfers that constituted gifts in prior calendar periods under the laws, including the provisions of law relating to exclusions from gifts, in effect at the time the transfers were made are included in determining the amount of taxable gifts for preceding calendar periods. The deductions other than for the specific exemption (see paragraph (b) of this section) allowed by the laws in effect at the time the transfers were made also are taken into account in determining the aggregate sum of the taxable gifts for preceding calendar periods. (The allowable exclusion from a gift is $5,000 for years before 1939, $4,000 for the calendar years 1939 through 1942, $3,000 for the calendar years 1943 through 1981, and $10,000 thereafter.)

(b) In determining the aggregate sum of the taxable gifts for the "preceding calendar periods" (as defined in § 25.2502-1(c)(2)), the total of the amounts allowed as deductions for the specific exemption, under section 2521 (as in effect prior to its repeal by the Tax Reform Act of 1976) and the corresponding provisions of prior laws, shall not exceed $30,000. Thus, if the only prior gifts by a donor were made in 1940 and 1941 (at which time the specific exemption allowable was $40,000), and if in the donor's returns for those years the donor claimed deductions totaling $40,000 for the specific exemption and reported taxable gifts totaling $110,000, then in determining the aggregate sum of the taxable gifts for the preceding calendar periods: the deductions for the specific exemption cannot exceed $30,000, and the donor's taxable gifts for such periods will be $120,000 (instead of the $110,000 reported on the donor's returns). (The allowable deduction for the specific exemption was $50,000 for calendar years before 1936, $40,000 for calendar years 1936 through 1942, and $30,000 for 1943 through 1976.)

(c) If the donor and the donor's spouse consented to have gifts made to third parties considered as made one-half by each spouse, pursuant to the provisions of section 2513 or section 1000(f) of the Internal Revenue Code of 1939 (which corresponds to Section 2513), these provisions shall be taken into account in determining the aggregate sum of the taxable gifts for the preceding calendar periods (under paragraph (a) of this section).

(d) If interpretations of the gift tax law in preceding calendar periods resulted in the erroneous inclusion of property for gift tax purposes that should have been excluded, or the erroneous exclusion of property that should have been included, adjustments must be made in order to arrive at the correct aggregate of taxable gifts for the preceding calendar periods (under paragraph (a) of this section). However, see section 1000(e) and (g) of the 1939 Code relating to certain discretionary trusts and reciprocal trusts. However, see § 25.2504-2(b) regarding certain gifts made after August 5, 1997.

T.D. 6334, 11/14/58, amend T.D. 7238, 12/28/72, T.D. 7910, 9/6/83, T.D. 8845, 12/2/99.

§ 25.2504-2 Determination of gifts for preceding calendar periods.

(a) Gifts made before August 6, 1997. If the time has expired within which a tax may be assessed under chapter 12 of the Internal Revenue Code (or under corresponding provisions of prior laws) on the transfer of property by gift made during a preceding calendar period, as defined in § 25.2502-1(c)(2), the gift was made prior to August 6, 1997, and a tax has been assessed or paid for such prior calendar period, the value of the gift, for purposes of arriving at the correct amount of the taxable gifts for the preceding calendar periods (as defined under § 25.2504-1(a)), is the value used in computing the tax for the last preceding calendar period for which a tax was assessed or paid under chapter 12 of the Internal Revenue Code or the corresponding provisions of prior laws. However, this rule does not apply where no tax was paid or assessed for the prior calendar period.

Furthermore, this rule does not apply to adjustments involving issues other than valuation. See § 25.2504-1(d).

(b) Gifts made or section 2701(d) taxable events occurring after August 5, 1997. If the time has expired under section 6501 within which a gift tax may be assessed under chapter 12 of the Internal Revenue Code (or under corresponding provisions of prior laws) on the transfer of property by gift made during a preceding calendar period, as defined in § 25.2502-1(c)(2), or with respect to an increase in taxable gifts required under section 2701(d) and § 25.2701-4, and the gift was made, or the section 2701(d) taxable event occurred, after August 5, 1997, the amount of the taxable gift or the amount of the increase in taxable gifts, for purposes of determining the correct amount of taxable gifts for the preceding calendar periods (as defined in § 25.2504-1(a)), is the amount that is finally determined for gift tax purposes (within the meaning of § 20.2001-1(c) of this chapter) and such amount may not be thereafter adjusted. The rule of this paragraph (b) applies to adjustments involving all issues relating to the gift including valuation issues and legal issues involving the interpretation of the gift tax law. For purposes of determining if the time has expired within which a gift tax may be assessed, see § 301.6501(c)-1(e) and (f) of this chapter.

(c) Examples. The following examples illustrate the rules of paragraphs (a) and (b) of this section:

Example (1). (i) Facts. In 1996, A transferred closely-held stock in trust for the benefit of B, A's child. A timely filed a Federal gift tax return reporting the 1996 transfer to B. No gift tax was assessed or paid as a result of the gift tax annual exclusion and the application of A's available unified credit. In 2001, A transferred additional closely-held stock to the trust. A's Federal gift tax return reporting the 2001 transfer was timely filed and the transfer was adequately disclosed under § 301.6501(c)-1(f)(2) of this chapter. In computing the amount of taxable gifts, A claimed annual exclusions with respect to the transfers in 1996 and 2001. In 2003, A transfers additional property to B and timely files a Federal gift tax return reporting the gift.

(ii) Application of the rule limiting adjustments to prior gifts. Under section 2504(c), in determining A's 2003 gift tax liability, the amount of A's 1996 gift can be adjusted for purposes of computing prior taxable gifts, since that gift was made prior to August 6, 1997, and therefore, the provisions of paragraph (a) of this section apply. Adjustments can be made with respect to the valuation of the gift and legal issues presented (for example, the availability of the annual exclusion with respect to the gift). However, A's 2001 transfer was adequately disclosed on a timely filed gift tax return and, thus, under paragraph (b) of this section, the amount of the 2001 taxable gift by A may not be adjusted (either with respect to the valuation of the gift or any legal issue) for purposes of computing prior taxable gifts in determining A's 2003 gift tax liability.

Example (2). (i) Facts. In 1996, A transferred closely-held stock to B, A's child. A timely filed a Federal gift tax return reporting the 1996 transfer to B and paid gift tax on the value of the gift reported on the return. On August 1, 1997, A transferred additional closely-held stock to B in exchange for a promissory note signed by B. Also, on September 10, 1997, A transferred closely-held stock to C, A's other child. On April 15, 1998, A timely filed a gift tax return for 1997 reporting the September 10, 1997, transfer to C and, under § 301.6501(c)-1(f)(2) of this chapter, adequately disclosed that transfer and paid gift tax with respect to the transfer. However, A believed that the transfer to B on August 1, 1997, was for full and adequate consideration and A did not report the transfer to B on the 1997 Federal gift tax return. In 2002, A transfers additional property to B and timely files a Federal gift tax return reporting the gift.

(ii) Application of the rule limiting adjustments to prior gifts. Under section 2504(c), in determining A's 2002 gift tax liability, the value of A's 1996 gift cannot be adjusted for purposes of computing the value of prior taxable gifts, since that gift was made prior to August 6, 1997, and a timely filed Federal gift tax return was filed on which a gift tax was assessed and paid. However, A's prior taxable gifts can be adjusted to reflect the August 1, 1997, transfer because, although a gift tax return for 1997 was timely filed and gift tax was paid, under § 301.6501(c)-1(f) of this chapter the period for assessing gift tax with respect to the August 1, 1997, transfer did not commence to run since that transfer was not adequately disclosed on the 1997 gift tax return. Accordingly, a gift tax may be assessed with respect to the August 1, 1997, transfer and the amount of the gift would be reflected in prior taxable gifts for purposes of computing A's gift tax liability for 2002. A's September 10, 1997, transfer to C was adequately disclosed on a timely filed gift tax return and, thus, under paragraph (b) of this section, the amount of the September 10, 1997, taxable gift by A may not be adjusted for purposes of computing prior taxable gifts in determining A's 2002 gift tax liability.

Example (3). (i) Facts. In 1994, A transferred closely-held stock to B and C, A's children. A timely filed a Federal gift tax return reporting the 1994 transfers to B and C and paid gift tax on the value of the gifts reported on the return. Also in 1994, A transferred closely-held stock to B in exchange for a bona fide promissory note signed by B. A believed that the transfer to B in exchange for the promissory note was for full and adequate consideration and A did not report that transfer to B on the 1994 Federal gift tax return. In 2002, A transfers additional property to B and timely files a Federal gift tax return reporting the gift.

(ii) Application of the rule limiting adjustments to prior gifts. Under section 2504(c), in determining A's 2002 gift tax liability, the value of A's 1994 gifts cannot be adjusted for purposes of computing prior taxable gifts because those gifts were made prior to August 6, 1997, and a timely filed Federal gift tax return was filed with respect to which a gift tax was assessed and paid, and the period of limitations on assessment has expired. The provisions of paragraph (a) of this section apply to the 1994 transfers. However, for purposes of determining A's adjusted taxable gifts in computing A's estate tax liability, the gifts may be adjusted. See § 20.2001-1(a) of this chapter.

(d) Effective dates. Paragraph (a) of this section applies to transfers of property by gift made prior to August 6, 1997. Paragraphs (b) and (c) of this section apply to transfers of property by gift made after August 5, 1997, if the gift tax return for the calendar period in which the transfer is reported is filed after December 3, 1999.

T.D. 6334, 11/14/58, amend T.D. 7238, 12/28/72, T.D. 7910, 9/6/83, T.D. 8845, 12/2/99.

§ 25.2511-1 Transfers in general.

> ***Caution:*** The Treasury has not yet amended Reg § 25.2511-1 to reflect changes made by P.L. 107-147.

(a) The gift tax applies to a transfer by way of gift whether the transfer is in trust or otherwise, whether the gift is direct or indirect, and whether the property is real or personal, tangible or intangible. For example, a taxable transfer may be effected by the creation of a trust, the forgiving of a debt, the assignment of a judgment, the assignment of the benefits of an insurance policy, or the transfer of cash, certificates of deposit, or Federal, State or municipal bonds. Statutory provisions which exempt bonds, notes, bills and certificates of indebtedness of the Federal Government or its agencies and the interest thereon from taxation are not applicable to the gift tax, since the gift tax is an excise tax on the transfer, and is not a tax on the subject of the gift.

(b) In the case of a gift by a nonresident not a citizen of the United States—

(1) If the gift was made on or after January 1, 1967, by a donor who was not an expatriate to whom section 2501(a)(2) was inapplicable on the date of the gift by reason of section 2501(a)(3) and paragraph (a)(3) of § 25.2501-1, or

(2) If the gift was made before January 1, 1967, by a donor who was not engaged in business in the United States during the calendar year in which the gift was made,

the gift tax applies only if the gift consisted of real property or tangible personal property situated within the United States at the time of the transfer. See §§ 25.2501-1 and 25.2511-3.

(c) *(1)* The gift tax also applies to gifts indirectly made. Thus, any transaction in which an interest in property is gratuitously passed or conferred upon another, regardless of the means or device employed, constitutes a gift subject to tax. See further § 25.2512-8 relating to transfers for insufficient consideration. However, in the case of a transfer creating an interest in property (within the meaning of § 25.2518-2(c)(3) and (c)(4)) made after December 31, 1976, this paragraph (c)(1) shall not apply to the donee if, as a result of a qualified disclaimer by the donee, the interest passes to a different donee. Nor shall it apply to a donor if, as a result of a qualified disclaimer by the donee, a completed transfer of an interest in property is not effected. See section 2518 and the corresponding regulations for rules relating to a qualified disclaimer.

(2) In the case of taxable transfers creating an interest in the person disclaiming made before January 1, 1977, where the law governing the administration of the decedent's estate gives a beneficiary, heir, or next-of-kin a right completely and unqualifiedly to refuse to accept ownership of property transferred from a decedent (whether the transfer is effected by the decedent's will or by the law of descent and distribution), a refusal to accept ownership does not constitute the making of a gift if the refusal is made within a reasonable time after knowledge of the existence of the transfer. The refusal must be unequivocal and effective under the local law. There can be no refusal of ownership of property after its acceptance. In the absence of the facts to the contrary, if a person fails to refuse to accept a transfer to him of ownership of a decedent's property within a reasonable time after learning of the existence of the transfer, he will be presumed to have accepted the property. Where the local law does not permit such a refusal, any disposition by the beneficiary, heir, or next-of-kin whereby ownership is transferred gratuitously to another constitutes the making of a gift by the beneficiary, heir, or next-of-kin. In any case where a refusal is purported to relate to only a part of the property, the determination of whether or not there has been a complete and unqualified refusal to accept ownership will depend on all of the facts and circumstances in each particular case, taking into account the recognition and effectiveness of such a purported refusal under the local law. In illustration, if Blackacre was devised to A under the decedent's will (which also provided that all lapsed legacies and devises shall go to B, the residuary beneficiary), and under the local law A could refuse to accept ownership in which case title would be considered as never having passed to A, A's refusal to accept Blackacre within a reasonable time of learning of a devise will not constitute the making of a gift by A to B. However, if a decedent who owned Greenacre died intestate with C and D as his only heirs, and under local law the heir of a decedent cannot, by refusal to accept, prevent himself from becoming an owner of intestate property, any gratuitous disposition by C (by whatever term it is known) whereby he gives up his ownership of a portion of Greenacre and D acquires the whole thereof constitutes the making of a gift by C to D.

(3) The fourth sentence of paragraph (c)(1) of this section is applicable for transfers creating an interest to be disclaimed made on or after December 31, 1997.

(d) If a joint income tax return is filed by a husband and wife for a taxable year, the payment by one spouse of all or part of the income tax liability for such year is not treated as resulting in a transfer which is subject to gift tax. The same rule is applicable to the payment of gift tax for a "calendar period" [as defined in § 25.2502-1(c)(1)] in the case of a husband and wife who have consented to have the gifts made considered as made half by each of them in accordance with the provisions of section 2513.

(e) If a donor transfers by gift less than his entire interest in property, the gift tax is applicable to the interest transferred. The tax is applicable, for example, to the transfer of an undivided half interest in property, or to the transfer of a life estate when the grantor retains the remainder interest, or vice versa. However, if the donor's retained interest is not susceptible of measurement on the basis of generally accepted valuation principles, the gift tax is applicable to the entire value of the property subject to the gift. Thus, if a donor, aged 65 years, transfers a life estate in property to A, aged 25 years, with remainder to A's issue, or in default of issue, with reversion to the donor, the gift tax will normally be applicable to the entire value of the property.

(f) If a donor is the owner of only a limited interest in property, and transfers his entire interest, the interest is in every case to be valued by the rules set forth in §§ 25.2512-1 through 25.2512-7. If the interest is a remainder or reversion or other future interest, it is to be valued on the basis of actuarial principles set forth in § 25.2412-5, or if it is not susceptible of valuation in that manner, in accordance with the principles set forth in § 25.2512-1.

(g) *(1)* Donative intent on the part of the transferor is not an essential element in the application of the gift tax to the transfer. The application of the tax is based on the objective facts of the transfer and the circumstances under which it is made, rather than on the subjective motives of the donor. However, there are certain types of transfers to which the tax is not applicable. It is applicable only to a transfer of a beneficial interest in property. It is not applicable to a transfer of bare legal title to a trustee. A transfer by a trustee of trust property in which he has no beneficial interest does not constitute a gift by the trustee (but such a transfer may constitute a gift by the creator of the trust, if until the transfer he had the power to change the beneficiaries by amending or revoking the trust). The gift tax is not applicable to a transfer for a full and adequate consideration in money or money's worth, or to ordinary business transactions, described in § 25.2512-8.

(2) If a trustee has a beneficial interest in trust property, a transfer of the property by the trustee is not a taxable trans-

fer if it is made pursuant to a fiduciary power the exercise or nonexercise of which is limited by a reasonably fixed or ascertainable standard which is set forth in the trust instrument. A clearly measurable standard under which the holder of a power is legally accountable is such a standard for this purpose. For instance, a power to distribute corpus for the education, support, maintenance, or health of the beneficiary; for his reasonable support and comfort; to enable him to maintain his accustomed standard of living; or to meet an emergency, would be such a standard. However, a power to distribute corpus for the pleasure, desire, or happiness of a beneficiary is not such a standard. The entire context of a provision of a trust instrument granting a power must be considered in determining whether the power is limited by a reasonably definite standard. For example, if a trust instrument provides that the determination of the trustee shall be conclusive with respect to the exercise or nonexercise of a power, the power is not limited by a reasonably definite standard. However, the fact that the governing instrument is phrased in discretionary terms is not in itself an indication that no such standard exists.

(h) The following are examples of transactions resulting in taxable gifts and in each case it is assumed that the transfers were not made for an adequate and full consideration in money or money's worth:

(1) A transfer of property by a corporation to B is a gift to B from the stockholders of the corporation. If B himself is a stockholder, the transfer is a gift to him from the other stockholders but only to the extent it exceeds B's own interest in such amount as a shareholder. A transfer of property by B to a corporation generally represents gifts by B to the other individual shareholders of the corporation to the extent of their proportionate interests in the corporation. However, there may be an exception to this rule, such as a transfer made by an individual to a charitable, public, political or similar organization which may constitute a gift to the organization as a single entity, depending upon the facts and circumstances in the particular case.

(2) The transfer of property to B if there is imposed upon B the obligation of paying a commensurate annuity to C is a gift to C.

(3) The payment of money or the transfer of property to B in consideration of B's promise to render a service to C is a gift to C, or to both B and C, depending on whether the service to be rendered to C is or is not an adequate and full consideration in money or money's worth for that which is received by B. See section 2512(b) and the regulations thereunder.

(4) If A creates a joint bank account for himself and B (or a similar type of ownership by which A can regain the entire fund without B's consent), there is a gift to B when B draws upon the account for his own benefit, to the extent of the amount drawn without any obligation to account for a part of the proceeds to A. Similarly, if A purchases a United States savings bond registered as payable to "A or B," there is a gift to B when B surrenders the bond for cash without any obligation to account for a part of the proceeds to A.

(5) If A with his own funds purchases property and has the title conveyed to himself and B as joint owners, with rights of survivorship (other than a joint ownership described in example (4)) but which rights may be defeated by either party severing his interest, there is a gift to B in the amount of half the value of the property. However, see § 25.2515-1 relative to the creation of a joint tenancy (or tenancy by the entirety) between husband and wife in real property with rights of survivorship which, unless the donor elects otherwise is not considered as a transfer includible for Federal gift tax purposes at the time of the creation of the joint tenancy. See § 25.2515-2 with respect to determining the extent to which the creation of a tenancy by the entirety constitutes a taxable gift if the donor elects to have the creation of the tenancy so treated. See also § 25.2523(d)-1 with respect to the marital deduction allowed in the case of the creation of a joint tenancy or a tenancy by the entirety.

(6) If A is possessed of a vested remainder interest in property, subject to being divested only in the event he should fail to survive one or more individuals or the happening of some other event, an irrevocable assignment of all or any part of his interest would result in a transfer includible for Federal gift tax purposes. See especially § 25.2512-5 for the valuation of an interest of this type.

(7) If A, without retaining a power to revoke the trust or to change the beneficial interests therein, transfers property in trust whereby B is to receive the income for life and at his death the trust is to terminate and the corpus is to be returned to A, provided A survives, but if A predeceases B the corpus is to pass to C, A has made a gift equal to the total value of the property less the value of his retained interest. See § 25.2512-5 for the valuation of the donor's retained interest.

(8) If the insured purchases a life insurance policy, or pays a premium on a previously issued policy, the proceeds of which are payable to a beneficiary or beneficiaries other than his estate, and with respect to which the insured retains no reversionary interest in himself or his estate and no power to revest the economic benefits in himself or his estate or to change the beneficiaries or their proportionate benefits (or if the insured relinquishes by assignment, by designation of a new beneficiary or otherwise, every such power that was retained in a previously issued policy), the insured has made a gift of the value of the policy, or to the extent of the premium paid, even though the right of the assignee or beneficiary to receive the benefits is conditioned upon his surviving the insured. For the valuation of life insurance policies see § 25.2512-6.

(9) Where property held by a husband and wife as community property is used to purchase insurance upon the husband's life and a third person is revocably designated as beneficiary and under the State law the husband's death is considered to make absolute the transfer by the wife, there is a gift by the wife at the time of the husband's death of half the amount of the proceeds of such insurance.

(10) If under a pension plan (pursuant to which he has an unqualified right to an annuity) an employee has an option to take either a retirement annuity for himself alone or a smaller annuity for himself with a survivorship annuity payable to his wife, an irrevocable election by the employee to take the reduced annuity in order that an annuity may be paid, after the employee's death, to his wife results in the making of a gift. However, see section 2517 and the regulations thereunder for the exemption from gift tax of amounts attributable to employers' contributions under qualified plans and certain other contracts.

T.D. 6334, 11/14/58, amend T.D. 6542, 1/19/61, T.D. 7150, 12/1/71, T.D. 7238, 12/28/72, T.D. 7296, 12/11/73, T.D. 7910, 9/6/83, T.D. 8095, 8/6/86, T.D. 8540, 6/9/94, T.D. 8744, 12/30/97.

---

§ 25.2511-2 Cessation of donor's dominion and control.

Caution: The Treasury has not yet amended Reg § 25.2511-2 to reflect changes made by P.L. 107-147.

(a) The gift tax is not imposed upon the receipt of the property by the donee, nor is it necessarily determined by the measure of enrichment resulting to the donee from the transfer, nor is it conditioned upon ability to identify the donee at the time of the transfer. On the contrary, the tax is a primary and personal liability of the donor, is an excise upon his act of making the transfer, is measured by the value of the property passing from the donor, and attaches regardless of the fact that the identity of the donee may not then be known or ascertainable.

(b) As to any property, or part thereof or interest therein, of which the donor has so parted with dominion and control as to leave in him no power to change its disposition, whether for his own benefit or for the benefit of another, the gift is complete. But if upon a transfer of property (whether in trust or otherwise) the donor reserves any power over its disposition, the gift may be wholly incomplete, or may be partially complete and partially incomplete, depending upon all the facts in the particular case. Accordingly, in every case of a transfer of property subject to a reserved power, the terms of the power must be examined and its scope determined. For example, if a donor transfers property to another in trust to pay the income to the donor or accumulate it in the discretion of the trustee, and the donor retains a testamentary power to appoint the remainder among his descendants, no portion of the transfer is a completed gift. On the other hand, if the donor had not retained the testamentary power of appointment, but instead provided that the remainder should go to X or his heirs, the entire transfer would be a completed gift. However, if the exercise of the trustee's power in favor of the grantor is limited by a fixed or ascertainable standard (see paragraph (g)(2) of § 25.2511-1), enforceable by or on behalf of the grantor, then the gift is incomplete to the extent of the ascertainable value of any rights thus retained by the grantor.

(c) A gift is incomplete in every instance in which a donor reserves the power to revest the beneficial title to the property in himself. A gift is also incomplete if and to the extent that a reserved power gives the donor the power to name new beneficiaries or to change the interests of the beneficiaries as between themselves unless the power is a fiduciary power limited by a fixed or ascertainable standard. Thus, if an estate for life is transferred but, by an exercise of a power, the estate may be terminated or cut down by the donor to one of less value, and without restriction upon the extent to which the estate may be so cut down, the transfer constitutes an incomplete gift. If in this example the power was confined to the right to cut down the estate for life to one for a term of five years, the certainty of an estate for not less than that term results in a gift to that extent complete.

(d) A gift is not considered incomplete, however, merely because the donor reserves the power to change the manner or time of enjoyment. Thus, the creation of a trust the income of which is to be paid annually to the donee for a period of years, the corpus being distributable to him at the end of the period, and the power reserved by the donor being limited to a right to require that, instead of the income being so payable, it should be accumulated and distributed with the corpus to the donee at the termination of the period, constitutes a completed gift.

(e) A donor is considered as himself having a power if it is exercisable by him in conjunction with any person not having a substantial adverse interest in the disposition of the transferred property or the income therefrom. A trustee, as such, is not a person having an adverse interest in the disposition of the trust property or its income.

(f) The relinquishment or termination of a power to change the beneficiaries of transferred property, occurring otherwise than by the death of the donor (the statute being confined to transfers by living donors), is regarded as the event which completes the gift and causes the tax to apply. For example, if A transfers property in trust for the benefit of B and C but reserves the power as trustee to change the proportionate interests of B and C, and if A thereafter has another person appointed trustee in place of himself, such later relinquishment of the power by A to the new trustee completes the gift of the transferred property, whether or not the new trustee has a substantial adverse interest. The receipt of income or of other enjoyment of the transferred property by the transferee or by the beneficiary (other than by the donor himself) during the interim between the making of the initial transfer and the relinquishment or termination of the power operates to free such income or other enjoyment from the power, and constitutes a gift of such income or of such other enjoyment taxable as of the "calendar period" as defined in § 25.2502-1(c)(1)] of its receipt. If property is transferred in trust to pay the income to A for life with remainder to B, powers to distribute corpus to A, and to withhold income from A for future distribution to B, are powers to change the beneficiaries of the transferred property.

(g) If a donor transfers property to himself as trustee (or to himself and some other person, not possessing a substantial adverse interest, as trustees), and retains no beneficial interest in the trust property and no power over it except fiduciary powers, the exercise or nonexercise of which is limited by a fixed or ascertainable standard, to change the beneficiaries of the transferred property, the donor has made a completed gift and the entire value of the transferred property is subject to the gift tax.

(h) If a donor delivers a properly indorsed stock certificate to the donee or the donee's agent, the gift is completed for gift tax purposes on the date of delivery. If the donor delivers the certificate to his bank or broker as his agent, or to the issuing corporation or its transfer agent, for transfer into the name of the donee, the gift is completed on the date the stock is transferred on the books of the corporation.

(i) [Reserved]

(j) If the donor contends that a power is of such nature as to render the gift incomplete, and hence not subject to the tax as of the calendar period (as defined in § 25.2502-1(c)(1)) of the initial transfer, see § 301.6501(c)-1(f)(5) of this chapter.

T.D. 6334, 11/14/58, amend T.D. 7238, 12/28/72, T.D. 7910, 9/6/83, T.D. 8845, 12/2/99.

§ 25.2511-3 Transfers by nonresidents not citizens.

(a) In general. Sections 2501 and 2511 contain rules relating to the taxation of transfers of property by gift by a donor who is a nonresident not a citizen of the United States. (See paragraph (b) of § 25.2501-1 for the definition of the term "resident" for purposes of the gift tax.) As combined these rules are:

(1) The gift tax applies only to the transfer of real property and tangible personal property situated in the United States at the time of the transfer if either—

(i) The gift was made on or after January 1, 1967, by a nonresident not a citizen of the United States who was not an expatriate to whom § 2501(a)(2) was inapplicable on the date of the gift by reason of § 2501(a)(3) and paragraph (a)(3) of § 25.2501-1, or

(ii) The gift was made before January 1, 1967, by a nonresident not a citizen of the United States who was not engaged in business in the United States during the calendar year in which the gift was made.

(2) The gift tax applies to the transfer of all property (whether real or personal, tangible or intangible) situated in the United States at the time of the transfer if either—

(i) The gift was made on or after January 1, 1967, by a nonresident not a citizen of the United States who was an expatriate to whom § 2501(a)(2) was inapplicable on the date of the gift by reason of § 2501(a)(3) and paragraph (a)(3) of § 25.2501-1, or

(ii) The gift was made before January 1, 1967, by a nonresident not a citizen of the United States who was engaged in business in the United States during the calendar year in which the gift was made.

(b) Situs of property. For purposes of applying the gift tax to the transfer of property owned and held by a nonresident not a citizen of the United States at the time of the transfer—

(1) Real-property and tangible personal property. Real property and tangible personal property constitute property within the United States only if they are physically situated therein.

(2) Intangible personal property. Except as provided otherwise in subparagraphs (3) and (4) of this paragraph, intangible personal property constitutes property within the United States if it consists of a property right issued by or enforceable against a resident of the United States or a domestic corporation (public or private), irrespective of where the written evidence of the property is physically located at the time of the transfer.

(3) Shares of stock. Irrespective of where the stock certificates are physically located at the time of the transfer—

(i) Shares of stock issued by a domestic corporation constitute property within the United States, and

(ii) Shares of stock issued by a corporation which is not a domestic corporation constitute property situated outside the United States

(4) Debt obligations. (i) In the case of gifts made on or after January 1, 1967, a debt obligation, including a bank deposit, the primary obligor of which is a United States person (as defined in § 7791(a)(30)), the United States, a State, or any political subdivision thereof, the District of Columbia, or any agency or instrumentality of any such government constitutes property situated within the United States. This subdivision applies—

(a) In the case of a debt obligation of a domestic corporation, whether or not any interest on the obligation would be treated under § 862(a)(1) as income from sources without the United States by reason of § 861(a)(1)(B) (relating to interest received from a domestic corporation less than 20 percent of whose gross income for a 3-year period was derived from sources within the United States) and the regulations thereunder:

(b) In the case of an amount described in § 861(c) (relating to certain bank deposits, withdrawable accounts, and amounts held by an insurance company under an agreement to pay interest), whether or not any interest thereon would be treated under § 862(a)(1) as income from sources without the United States by reason of § 861(a)(1)(A) (relating to interest on amounts described in § 861(c) which is not effectively connected with the conduct of a trade or business within the United States) and the regulations thereunder:

(c) In the case of a deposit with a domestic corporation or domestic partnership, whether or not the deposit is with a foreign branch thereof engaged in the commercial banking business; and

(d) Irrespective of where the written evidence of the debt obligation is physically located at the time of the transfer.

For purposes of this subdivision, a debt obligation on which there are two or more primary obligors shall be apportioned among such obligors, taking into account to the extent appropriate under all the facts and circumstances any choate or inchoate rights of contribution existing among such obligors with respect to the indebtedness. The term "agency or instrumentality", as used in this subdivision, does not include a possession of the United States or an agency or instrumentality of a possession.

(ii) In the case of gifts made on or after January 1, 1967, a debt obligation, including a bank deposit, not deemed under subdivision (i) of this subparagraph to be situated within the United States, constitutes property situated outside the United States.

(iii) In the case of gifts made before January 1, 1967, a debt obligation the written evidence of which is treated as being the property itself constitutes property situated within the United States if the written evidence of the obligation is physically located in the United States at the time of the transfer, irrespective of who is the primary obligor on the debt. If the written evidence of the obligation is physically located outside the United States, the debt obligation constitutes property situated outside the United States.

(iv) Currency is not a debt obligation for purposes of this subparagraph.

T.D. 6334, 11/14/58, amend T.D. 6542, 1/19/61, T.D. 7238, 12/28/72, T.D. 7296, 12/11/73.

---

§ 25.2512-0 Table of contents.

This section lists the section headings that appear in the regulations under section 2512.

T.D. 8540, 6/9/94, amend T.D. 8819, 4/29/99, T.D. 8886, 6/9/2000, T.D. 9448, 5/1/2009.

---

§ 25.2512-1 Valuation of property; in general.

Caution: The Treasury has not yet amended Reg § 25.2512-1 to reflect changes made by P.L. 94-455.

Section 2512 provides that if a gift is made in property, its value at the date of the gift shall be considered the amount of the gift. The value of the property is the price at which such property would change hands between a willing buyer and a willing seller, neither being under any compulsion to buy or to sell, and both having reasonable knowledge of relevant facts. The value of a particular item of property is not the price that a forced sale of the property would produce. Nor is the fair market value of an item of property the sale price in a market other than that in which such item is most commonly sold to the public, taking into account the location of the item wherever appropriate. Thus, in the case of an item of property made the subject of a gift, which is generally obtained by the public in the retail market, the fair market value of such an item of property is the price at which the item or a comparable item would be sold at retail. For example, the value of an automobile (an article generally obtained by the public in the retail market) which is the subject of a gift, is the price for which an automobile of the same or approximately the same description, make, model, age, condition, etc., could be purchased by a member of the general public and not the price for which the particular automobile of the donor would be purchased by a dealer in used automobiles. Examples of items of property which are generally sold to the public at retail may be found in § 25.2512-6. The value is generally to be determined by ascertaining as a basis the fair market value at the time of the gift of each unit of the property. For example, in the case of shares of stocks or bonds, such unit of property is generally a share or a bond. Property shall not be returned at the value at which it is assessed for local tax purposes unless that value represents the fair market value thereof on the date of the gift. All relevant facts and elements of value as of the time of the gift shall be considered. Where the subject of a gift is an interest in a business, the value of items of property in the inventory of the business generally should be reflected in the value of the business. For valuation of interests in businesses, see § 25.2512-3. See § 25.2512-2 and §§ 25.2512-4 through 25.2512-6 for further information concerning the valuation of other particular kinds of property. See section 2701 and the regulations at § 25.2701 for special rules for valuing transfers of an interest in a corporation or a partnership and for the treatment of unpaid qualified payments at the subsequent transfer of an applicable retained interest by the transferor or by an applicable family member. See section 2704(b) and the regulations at § 25.2704-2 for special valuation rules where an interest in property is subject to an applicable restriction.

T.D. 6334, 11/14/58, amend T.D. 6826, 6/14/65, T.D. 8395, 1/28/92.

§ 25.2512-2 Stocks and bonds.

(a) In general. The value of stocks and bonds is the fair market value per share or bond on the date of the gift.

(b) Based on selling prices. *(1)* In general, if there is a market for stocks or bonds, on a stock exchange, in an over-the-counter market or otherwise, the mean between the highest and lowest quoted selling prices on the date of the gift is the fair market value per share or bond. If there were no sales on the date of the gift but there were sales on dates within a reasonable period both before and after the date of the gift, the fair market value is determined by taking a weighted average of the means between the highest and lowest sales on the nearest date before and the nearest date after the date of the gift. The average is to be weighted inversely by the respective numbers of trading days between the selling dates and the date of the gift. If the stocks or bonds are listed on more than one exchange, the records of the exchange where the stocks or bonds are principally dealt in should be employed if such records are available in a generally available listing or publication of general circulation. In the event that such records are not so available and such stocks or bonds are listed on a composite listing of combined exchanges available in a generally available listing or publication of general circulation, the records of such combined exchanges should be employed. In valuing listed securities, the donor should be careful to consult accurate records to obtain values as of the date of the gift. If quotations of unlisted securities are obtained from brokers, or evidence as to their sale is obtained from the officers of the issuing companies, copies of letters furnishing such quotations or evidence of sale should be attached to the return.

(2) If it is established with respect to bonds for which there is a market on a stock exchange, that the highest and lowest selling prices are not available for the date of the gift in a generally available listing or publication of general circulation but that closing prices are so available, the fair market value per bond is the mean between the quoted closing selling price on the date of the gift and the quoted closing selling price on the trading day before the date of the gift. If there were no sales on the trading day before the date of the gift but there were sales on dates within a reasonable period before the date of the gift, the fair market value is determined by taking a weighted average of the quoted closing selling prices on the date of the gift and the nearest date before the date of the gift. The closing selling price for the date of the gift is to be weighted by the respective number of trading days between the previous selling date and the date of the gift. If there were no sales within a reasonable period before the date of the gift but there were sales on the date of the gift, the fair market value is the closing selling price on the date of the gift. If there were no sales on the date of the gift but there were sales within a reasonable period both before and after the date of the gift, the fair market value is determined by taking a weighted average of the quoted closing selling prices on the nearest date before and the nearest date after the date of the gift. The average is to be weighed inversely by the respective numbers of trading days between the selling dates and the date of the gift. If the bonds are listed on more than one exchange, the records of the exchange where the bonds are principally dealt in should be employed. In valuing listed securities, the donor should be careful to consult accurate records to obtain values as of the date of the gift.

(3) The application of this paragraph may be illustrated by the following examples:

Example (1). Assume that sales of stock nearest the date of the gift (Friday, June 15) occurred two trading days before (Wednesday, June 13) and three trading days after (Wednesday, June 20) and on these days the mean sale prices per share were $10 and $15, respectively. The price of $12 is taken as representing the fair market value of a share of stock as of the date of the gift.

$$\frac{((3 \times 10) + (2 \times 15))}{5}$$

Example (2). Assume the same facts as in example 1 except that the mean sale prices per share on June 13 and June

20 were $15 and $10 respectively. The price of $13 is taken as representing the fair market value of a share of stock as of the date of the gift.

$$\frac{(3 \times 15) + (2 \times 10)}{5}$$

Example (3). Assume that on the date of the gift (Tuesday, April 3, 1973) the closing selling price of certain listed bonds was $25 per bond and that the highest and lowest selling prices are not available in a generally available listing or publication of general circulation for that date. Assume further, that the closing selling price of such bonds was $21 per bond on the day before the date of the gift (Monday, April 2, 1973). Thus, under paragraph (b)(2) of this section, the price of $23 is taken as representing the fair market value per bond as of the date of the gift.

$$\frac{(25 + 21)}{2}$$

Example (4). Assume the same facts as in example 3 except that there were no sales on the day before the date of the gift. Assume further, that there were sales on Thursday, March 29, 1973, and that the closing selling price on that day was $23. The price of $24.50 is taken as representing the fair market value per bond as of the date of the gift.

$$\frac{((1 \times 23) + (3 \times 25)).}{4}$$

Example (5). Assume that no bonds were traded on the date of the gift (Friday, April 20). Assume further, that sales of bonds nearest the date of the gift occurred two trading days before (Wednesday, April 18) and three trading days after (Wednesday, April 25) the date of the gift and that on these two days the closing selling prices per bond were $29 and $22, respectively. The highest and lowest selling prices are not available for these dates in a generally available listing or publication of general circulation. Thus, under paragraph (b)(2) of this section the price of $26.20 is taken as representing the fair market value of a bond as of the date of the gift.

$$\frac{((3 \times 29) + (2 \times 22))}{5}$$

(c) Based on bid and asked prices. If the provisions of paragraph (b) of this section are inapplicable because actual sales are not available during a reasonable period beginning before and ending after the date of the gift, the fair market value may be determined by taking the mean between the bona fide bid and asked prices on the date of the gift, or if none, by taking a weighted average of the means between the bona fide bid and asked prices on the nearest trading date before and the nearest trading date after the date of the gift, if both such nearest dates are within a reasonable period. The average is to be determined in the manner described in paragraph (b) of this section.

(d) Where selling prices and bid and asked prices are not available for dates both before and after the date of gift. If the provisions of paragraphs (b) and (c) of this section are inapplicable because no actual sale prices or quoted bona fide bid and asked prices are available on a date within a reasonable period before the date of the gift, but such prices are available on a date within a reasonable period after the date of the gift, or vice versa, then the mean between the highest and lowest available sale prices or bid and asked prices may be taken as the value.

(e) Where selling prices or bid and asked prices do not represent fair market value. In cases in which it is established that the value per bond or share of any security determined on the basis of the selling or bid and asked prices as provided under paragraphs (b), (c), and (d) of this section does not represent the fair market value thereof, then some reasonable modification of the value determined on that basis or other relevant facts and elements of value shall be considered in determining fair market value. Where sales at or near the date of the gift are few or of a sporadic nature, such sales alone may not indicate fair market value. In certain exceptional cases, the size of the block of securities made the subject of each separate gift in relation to the number of shares changing hands in sales may be relevant in determining whether selling prices reflect the fair market value of the block of stock to be valued. If the donor can show that the block of stock to be valued, with reference to each separate gift, is so large in relation to the actual sales on the existing market that it could not be liquidated in a reasonable time without depressing the market, the price at which the block could be sold as such outside the usual market, as through an underwriter, may be a more accurate indication of value than market quotations. Complete data in support of any allowance claimed due to the size of the block of stock being valued should be submitted with the return. On the other hand, if the block of stock to be valued represents a controlling interest, either actual or effective, in a going business, the price at which other lots change hands may have little relation to its true value.

(f) Where selling prices or bid and asked prices are unavailable. If the provisions of paragraphs (b), (c), and (d) of this section are inapplicable because actual sale prices and bona fide bid and asked prices are lacking, then the fair market value is to be determined by taking the following factors into consideration:

(1) In the case of corporate or other bonds, the soundness of the security, the interest yield, the date of maturity, and other relevant factors; and

(2) In the case of shares of stock, the company's net worth, prospective earning power and dividend-paying capacity, and other relevant factors.

Some of the "other relevant factors" referred to in subparagraphs (1) and (2) of this paragraph are: The goodwill of the business; the economic outlook in the particular industry; the company's position in the industry and its management; the degree of control of the business represented by the block of stock to be valued; and the values of securities of corporations engaged in the same or similar lines of business which are listed on a stock exchange. However, the weight to be accorded such comparisons or any other evidentiary factors considered in the determination of a value depends upon the facts of each case. Complete financial and other data upon which the valuation is based should be submitted with the return, including copies of reports of any examinations of the company made by accountants, engineers, or any technical experts as of or near the date of the gift.

T.D. 6334, 11/14/58, amend T.D. 7327, 9/27/74, T.D. 7432, 9/10/76.

§ 25.2512-3 Valuation of interests in businesses.

(a) Care should be taken to arrive at an accurate valuation of any interest in a business which the donor transfers without an adequate and full consideration in money or money's worth. The fair market value of any interest in a business, whether a partnership or a proprietorship, is the net amount which a willing purchaser, whether an individual or a corporation, would pay for the interest to a willing seller, neither being under any compulsion to buy or to sell and both having reasonable knowledge of the relevant facts. The net value is determined on the basis of all relevant factors including—

(1) A fair appraisal as of the date of the gift of all the assets of the business, tangible and intangible, including good will;

(2) The demonstrated earning capacity of the business; and

(3) The other factors set forth in paragraph (f) of § 25.2512-2 relating to the valuation of corporate stock, to the extent applicable.

Special attention should be given to determining an adequate value of the good will of the business. Complete financial and other data upon which the valuation is based should be submitted with the return, including copies of reports of examinations of the business made by accountants, engineers, or any technical experts as of or near the date of the gift.

T.D. 6334, 11/14/58.

§ 25.2512-4 Valuation of notes.

The fair market value of notes, secured or unsecured, is presumed to be the amount of unpaid principal, plus accrued interest to the date of the gift, unless the donor establishes a lower value. Unless returned at face value, plus accrued interest, it must be shown by satisfactory evidence that the note is worth less than the unpaid amount (because of the interest rate, or date of maturity, or other cause), or that the note is uncollectible in part (by reason of the insolvency of the party or parties liable, or for other cause), and that the property, if any, pledged or mortgaged as security is insufficient to satisfy it.

T.D. 6334, 11/14/58.

PAR. 43.

Section 25.2512-4 is revised to read as follows:

Proposed § 25.2512-4 Valuation of notes. [*For Preamble, see ¶ 151,065*]

• ***Caution:*** Prop reg § 1.482-2 was finalized by T.D. 8204, 5/20/88. Prop regs §§ 1.163-7, 1.446-2, 1.483-1 through -5, 1.1001-1, 1.1012-1, 1.1271 through -3, 1.1272-1, 1.1273-1, 1.1273-2, 1.1274-1 throught -7, 1.1274A-1, 1.1275-1 through -3, and 1.1275-5 were withdrawn by the Treasury on 12/22/92, 57 Fed. Reg. 67050. Prop reg § 1.1275-4 was superseded by the Treasury on 12/16/94, Fed. Reg. 59, 64884, which was finalized by T.D. 8674, 6/11/96.

The fair market value of notes, secured or unsecured, is presumed to be the amount of unpaid principal, plus accrued interest to the date of the gift, unless the donor establishes a lower value. The fair market value of a debt instrument (as defined in § 1.1275-1(b)) whose issue price is determined under section 1273(b)(1), (2), or (3), or section 1274 is presumed to be its revised issue price (as defined in § 1.1275-1(h)). Unless returned at this value, it must be shown by satisfactory evidence that the note is worth less than the unpaid amount (because of the interest rate, or date of maturity, or other cause), or that the note is uncollectible in part (by reason of the insolvency of the party or parties liable, or for other cause), and that the property, if any, pledged or mortgaged as security is insufficient to satisfy it. See § 25.2512-8 and § 1.1012-2 for special rules relating to certain sales or exchanges of property. See § 25.7872-1 for special rules in the case of gift loans (within the meaning of § 1.7872-4(b)) made after June 6, 1984.

PAR. 4.

Section 25.2512-4 is amended by adding a new sentence at the end to read as follows:

Proposed § 25.2512-4 Valuation of notes. [*For Preamble, see ¶ 151,027*]

* * * See § 25.7872-1 for special rules in the case of gift loans (within the meaning of § 1.7872-4(b)) made after June 6, 1984.

§ 25.2512-5 Valuation of annuities, unitrust interests, interests for life or term of years, and remainder or reversionary interests.

(a) In general. Except as otherwise provided in paragraph (b) of this section and § 25.7520-3(b), the fair market value of annuities, unitrust interests, life estates, terms of years, remainders, and reversions transferred by gift is the present value of the interests determined under paragraph (d) of this section. Section 20.2031-7 of this chapter (Estate Tax Regulations) and related sections provide tables with standard actuarial factors and examples that illustrate how to use the tables to compute the present value of ordinary annuity, life, and remainder interests in property. These sections also refer to standard and special actuarial factors that may be necessary to compute the present value of similar interests in more unusual fact situations. These factors and examples are also generally applicable for gift tax purposes in computing the values of taxable gifts.

(b) Commercial annuities and insurance contracts. The value of life insurance contracts and contracts for the payment of annuities issued by companies regularly engaged in their sale is determined under § 25.2512-6.

(c) and **(d)** [Reserved]. For further guidance, see § 25.2512-5T(c) and (d).

(e) Effective/applicability dates. This section applies after April 30, 1999, and before May 1, 2009.

T.D. 8540, 6/9/94, amend T.D. 8819, 4/29/99, T.D. 8886, 6/9/2000, T.D. 9448, 5/1/2009.

PAR. 13. Section 25.2512-5 is amended by revising paragraphs (c), (d) and (e) to read as follows:

Proposed § 25.2512-5 Valuation of annuities, unitrust interest, interests for life or term of years, and remainder or reversionary interests. [*For Preamble, see ¶ 153,105*]

* * * * *

(c) [The text of this proposed paragraph (c) is the same as the text of § 25.2512-5T(c) published elsewhere in this issue of the Federal Register]. [*See T.D. 9448, 05/07/2009, 74 Fed. Reg. 87.*]

(d) [The text of this proposed paragraph (d) is the same as the text of § 25.2512-5T(d) published elsewhere in this issue of the Federal Register]. [*See T.D. 9448, 05/07/2009, 74 Fed. Reg. 87.*]

(e) [The text of this proposed paragraph (e) is the same as the text of § 25.2512-5T(e) published elsewhere in this issue of the Federal Register]. [*See T.D. 9448, 05/07/2009, 74 Fed. Reg. 87.*]

§ 25.2512-5A Valuation of annuities, unitrust interests, interests for life or term of years, and remainder or reversionary interests transferred before May 1, 2009.

(a) Valuation of annuities, interests for life or term of years, and remainder or reversionary interests transferred before January 1, 1952. Except as otherwise provided in § 25.2512-5(b), if the transfer was made before January 1, 1952, the present value of annuities, life estates, terms of years, remainders, and reversions is their present value determined under this section. If the valuation of the interest involved is dependent upon the continuation or termination of one or more lives or upon a term certain concurrent with one or more lives, the factor for the present value is computed on the basis of interest at the rate of 4 percent a year, compounded annually, and life contingencies for each life involved from values that are based upon the "Actuaries' or Combined Experience Table of Mortality, as extended." This table and many additional factors are described in former § 86.19 (as contained in the 26 CFR Part 81 edition revised as of April 1, 1958). The present value of an interest measured by a term of years is computed on the basis of interest at the rate of 4 percent a year.

(b) Valuation of annuities, interests for life or term of years, and remainder or reversionary interests transferred after December 31, 1951, and before January 1, 1971. Except as otherwise provided in § 25.2512-5(b), the present value of annuities, life estates, terms of years, remainders, and reversions transferred after December 31, 1951, and before January 1, 1971, is the present value of such interests determined under this section. If the value of the interest involved is dependent upon the continuation or termination of one or more lives, the factor for the present value is computed on the basis of interest at the rate of 3 ½ percent a year, compounded annually, and life contingencies for each life involved from U.S. Life Table 38. This table and many accompanying factors are set forth in former § 25.2512-5 (as contained in the 26 CFR Part 25 edition revised as of April 1, 1984). Special factors involving one and two lives may be found in or computed with the use of tables contained in Internal Revenue Service Publication Number 11, "Actuarial Values for Estate and Gift Tax," (Rev. 5-59). This publication is no longer available for purchase from the Superintendent of Documents. However, it may be obtained by requesting a copy from: CC:DOM:CORP:T:R (IRS Publication 11), room 5228, Internal Revenue Service, POB 7604, Ben Franklin Station, Washington, DC 20044. The present value of an interest measured by a term of years is computed on the basis of interest at the rate of 3½ percent a year.

(c) Valuation of annuities, interests for life or term of years, and remainder or reversionary interests transferred after December 31, 1970, and before December 1, 1983. Except as otherwise provided in § 25.2512-5(b), the present value of annuities, life estates, terms of years, remainders, and reversions transferred after December 31, 1970, and before December 1, 1983, is the present value of such interests determined under this section. If the interest to be valued is dependent upon the continuation or termination of one or more lives or upon a term certain concurrent with one or more lives, the factor for the present value is computed on the basis of interest at the rate of 6 percent a year, compounded annually, and life contingencies determined for each male and female life involved, from the values that are set forth in Table LN. Table LN contains values that are taken from the life table for total males and the life table for total females appearing as Tables 2 and 3, respectively, in United States Life Tables: 1959-61, published by the Department of Health and Human Services, Public Health Service. Table LN and accompanying factors are set forth in former § 25.2512-9 (as contained in the 26 CFR Part 25 edition revised as of April 1, 1994). Special factors involving one and two lives may be found in or computed with the use of tables contained in Internal Revenue Service Publication 723, entitled "Actuarial Values I: Valuation of Last Survivor Charitable Remainders" (12-70), and Internal Revenue Service Publication 723A, entitled "Actuarial Values II: Factors at 6 Percent Involving One and Two Lives" (12-70). These publications are no longer available for purchase from the Superintendent of Documents. However, a copy of each may be obtained from: CC:DOM:CORP:T:R (IRS Publication 723/723A), room 5228, Internal Revenue Service, POB 7604, Ben Franklin Station, Washington, DC 20044. The present value of an interest measured by a term of years is computed on the basis of interest at the rate of 6 percent a year.

(d) Valuation of annuities, interests for life or term of years, and remainder or reversionary interests transferred after November 30, 1983, and before May 1, 1989. *(1) In general.* (i) (A) Except as otherwise provided in this paragraph (d)(1)(i)(A), the fair market value of annuities, life estates, terms of years, remainders, and reversions transferred after November 30, 1983, and before May 1, 1989, is the present value determined under this section. The value of annuities issued by companies regularly engaged in their sale and of insurance policies issued by companies regularly engaged in their sale is determined under § 25.2512-6. The fair market value of a remainder interest in a charitable remainder unitrust, as defined in § 1.664-3, is its present value determined under § 1.664-4. The fair market value of a life interest or term for years in a charitable remainder unitrust is the fair market value of the property as of the date of transfer less the fair market value of the remainder interest on such date determined under § 1.664-4. The fair market value of interests in a pooled income fund, as defined in § 1.642(c)-5, is their value determined under § 1.642(c)-6. Where the donor transfers property in trust or otherwise and retains an interest therein, the value of the gift is the value of the property transferred less the value of the donor's retained interest. See section 2702 and the regulations at § 25.2702 for special rules for valuing transfers of interests in trust after October 8, 1990. See § 25.2512-9 with respect to the valuation of annuities, life estates, terms for years, remainders, and reversions transferred after December 31, 1970, and before December 1, 1983.

(B) If the donor transfers in December of 1983, either—

(1) A remainder or a reversion subject to a life interest or a term for years where the life interest or term for years was transferred by the donor after December 31, 1982, and before December 1, 1983, or

(2) A life interest or term for years, the remainder interest of which was transferred by the donor after December 31, 1982, and before December 1, 1983,

the donor shall make an election. The donor may elect to value both interests transferred in 1983 under § 25.2512-5A(c) as if such section applied to all transfers made before January 1, 1984, or the donor may elect to have both transfers valued under this section. The donor shall indicate the election being made in a statement attached to the donor's gift tax return for 1983.

(C) If the donor transfers in calendar year 1984, either—

(*1*) A remainder on a reversion subject to a life interest or a term for years where the life interest or term for years was transferred by the donor in the first eleven months of 1983, or

(*2*) A life interest or term for years, the remainder interest of which was transferred by the donor in the first eleven months of 1983,

the donor shall make an election. The donor may elect to value the interest transferred in 1984 under § 25.2512-5A(c) as if such section applied to all transfers made before January 1, 1985, or the donor may elect to have the transfer valued under this section. If the donor elects to value the interest transferred in 1984 under § 25.2512-5A(c), the donor shall indicate that the election is being made by attaching a statement to the donor's gift tax return for 1984. If the donor elects to value the interest transferred in 1984 under this section the election shall not be effective unless the donor declares, in a statement attached to the donor's gift tax return for 1984, that the donor has filed an amended gift tax return for 1983, in which the donor has revalued the transfers made in the first eleven months of 1983 under this section as if this section applied to transfers made after December 31, 1982.

(ii) The present value of an annuity, life estate, remainder, or reversion determined under this section which is dependent on the continuation or termination of the life of one person is computed by the use of Table A in paragraph (d)(6) of this section. The present value of an annuity, term for years, remainder, or reversion dependent on a term certain is computed by the use of Table B in paragraph (d)(6) of this section. If the interest to be valued is dependent upon more than one life or there is a term certain concurrent with one or more lives, see paragraph (d)(5) of this section. For purposes of the computations described in this section, the age of the person is to be taken at his or her nearest birthday.

(iii) In all examples set forth in this section, the interest is assumed to have been transferred after November 30, 1983, and before May 1, 1989.

(2) Annuities. (i) If an annuity is payable annually at the end of each year during the life of an individual (as for example if the first payment is due one year after the date of the gift), the amount payable annually is multiplied by the figure in column 2 of Table A opposite the number of years in column 1 nearest the age of the individual whose life measures the duration of the annuity. If the annuity is payable annually at the end of each year for a definite number of years, the amount payable annually is multiplied by the figure in column 2 of Table B opposite the number of years in column 1 representing the duration of the annuity.

The application of this paragraph (d)(2)(i) may be illustrated by the following examples:

Example (1). The donor assigns an annuity of $10,000 a year payable annually during the donor's life immediately after an annual payment has been made. The age of the donor on the date of assignment is 40 years and eight months. By reference to Table A, it is found that the figure in column 2 opposite 41 years is 9.1030. The value of the gift is, therefore $91,030 ($10,000 multiplied by 9.1030).

Example (2). The donor was entitled to receive an annuity of $10,000 a year payable annually at the end of annual periods throughout a term of 20 years. The donor, when 15 years have elapsed, makes a gift thereof to the donor's son. By reference to Table B, it is found that the figure in column 2 opposite five years, the unexpired portion of the 20-year period, is 3.7908. The present value of the annuity is, therefore, $37,908 (10,000 multiplied by 3.7908).

(ii) If an annuity is payable at the end of semiannual, quarterly, monthly, or weekly periods during the life of an individual (as for example if the first payment is due one month after the date of the gift), the aggregate amount to be paid within a year is first multiplied by the figure in column 2 of Table A opposite the number of years in column 1 nearest the age of the individual whose life measures the duration of the annuity. The product so obtained is then multiplied by whichever of the following factors is appropriate:

1.0244 for semiannual payments,

1.0368 for quarterly payments,

1.0450 for monthly payments,

1.0482 for weekly payments.

If the annuity is payable at the end of semiannual, quarterly, monthly, or weekly periods for a definite number of years the aggregate amount to be paid within a year is first multiplied by the figure in column 2 of Table B opposite the number of years in column 1 representing the duration of the annuity. The product so obtained is then multiplied by whichever of the above factors is appropriate. The application of this paragraph (d)(2)(ii) may be illustrated by the following example:

Example. The facts are the same as those contained in example (1) set forth in paragraph (d)(2)(i) above, except that the annuity is payable semiannually. The aggregate annual amount, $10,000 is multiplied by the factor 9.1030, and the product multiplied by 1.0244. The value of the gift is, therefore, $93,251.13 ($10,000 × 9.1030 × 1.0244).

(iii) (A) If the first payment of an annuity for the life of an individual is due at the beginning of the annual or other payment period rather than at the end (as for example if the first payment is to be made immediately after the date of the gift), the value of the annuity is the sum of (A) the first payment plus (B) the present value of a similar annuity, the first payment of which is not to be made until the end of the payment period, determined as provided in paragraphs (d)(2)(i) or (ii) of this section. The application of this paragraph (d)(2)(iii)(A) may be illustrated by the following example:

Example. The donee is made the beneficiary for life of an annuity of $50 a month from the income of a trust, subject to the right reserved by the donor to cause the annuity to be paid for the donor's own benefit or for the benefit of another. On the day a payment is due, the donor relinquishes the reserved power. The donee is then 50 years of age. The value of the gift is $50 plus the product of $50 × 12 × 8.4743 (see Table A) × 1.0450. That is, $50 plus $5,313.39, or $5,363.39.

(B) If the first payment of an annuity for a definite number of years is due at the beginning of the annual or other payment period, the applicable factor is the product of the factor shown in Table B multiplied by whichever of the following factors is appropriate:

1.1000 for annual payments,

1.0744 for semiannual payments,

1.0618 for quarterly payments,

1.0534 for monthly payments, or

1.0502 for weekly payments.

The application of this paragraph (d)(2)((ii))(B) may be illustrated by the following example:

Example. The donee is the beneficiary of an annuity of $50 a month, subject to a reserved right in the donor to cause the annuity or the cash value thereof to be paid for the donor's own benefit or the benefit of another. On the day a payment is due, the donor relinquishes the power. There are 300 payments to be made covering a period of 25 years, including the payment due. The value of the gift is the product of $50 × 12 × 9.0770 (factor for 25 years Table B) × 1.0534, or $5,737.03.

(3) Life estates and terms for years. If the interest to be valued is the right of a person for his or her life, or for the life of another person, to receive the income of certain property or to use non-income-producing property, the value of the interest is the value of the property multiplied by the figure in column 3 of Table A opposite the number of years nearest to the actual age of the measuring life. If the interest to be valued is the right to receive income of property or to use nonincome-producing property for a term of years, column 3 of Table B is used. The application of this paragraph (d)(3) may be illustrated by the following example:

Example. The donor who during the donor's life is entitled to receive the income from property worth $50,000, makes a gift of such interest. The donor is 31 years old on the date of the gift. The value of the gift is $47,627 ($50,000 × .95254).

(4) Remainders or reversionary interests. If the interest to be valued is a remainder or reversionary interest subject to a life estate, the value of the interest should be obtained by multiplying the value of the property at the date of the gift by the figure in column 4 of Table A opposite the number of years nearest the age of the life tenant. If the remainder or reversion is to take effect at the end of a term for years, column 4 of Table B should be used. The application of this paragraph (d)(4) may be illustrated by the following example:

Example. The donor transfers by gift a remainder interest in property worth $50,000, subject to the donor's sister's right to receive the income therefrom for her life. The sister at the date of the gift is 31 years of age. By reference to Table A it is found that the figure in column 4 opposite age 31 is .04746. The value of the gift is, therefore $2,373 ($50,000 × .04746).

(5) Actuarial computations by the Internal Revenue Service. If the interest to be valued is dependent upon the continuation or termination of more than one life, or there is a term certain concurrent with one or more lives, or if the retained interest of the donor is conditioned upon survivorship, a special factor is necessary. The factor is to be computed on the basis of interest at the rate of 10 percent a year, compounded annually, and life contingencies are determined for each person involved from the values of *lx* that are set forth in column 2 of Table LN in § 20.2031-7A(d)(6) of this chapter. Table LN contains values of *lx* taken from life table for the total population appearing as Table 1 in the United States Life Tables: 1969-71, published by the Department of Health and Human Services, Public Health Service. A copy of the publication containing many such special factors, may be purchased from the Superintendent of Documents, United States Government Printing Office, Washington, D.C. 20402. However, if a special factor is required in the case of an actual gift, the Commissioner will furnish the factor to the donor upon request. The request must be accompanied by a statement of the date of birth of each person the duration of whose life may affect the value of the interest, and by copies of the relevant instruments. Special factors are not furnished for prospective transfers.

(6) Tables. (i) For actuarial factors showing the present worth at 10 percent of a single life annuity, a life interest, and a remainder interest postponed for a single life, see § 20.2031-7A(d)(6) of this chapter, Table A, of the Estate Tax Regulations.

(ii) For actuarial factors showing the present worth at 10 percent of an annuity for a term certain, an income interest for a term certain, and a remainder interest postponed for a term certain, see § 20.2031-7A(d)(6) of this chapter, Table B, of the Estate Tax Regulations.

(e) Valuation of annuities, unitrust interests, interests for life or term of years, and remainder or reversionary interests transferred after April 30, 1989, and before May 1, 1999. *(1) In general.* Except as otherwise provided in §§ 25.2512-5(b) and 25.7520-3(b) (pertaining to certain limitations on the use of prescribed tables), if the valuation date of the transferred interest is after April 30, 1989, and before May 1, 1999, the fair market value of annuities, unitrust interests, life estates, terms of years, remainders, and reversions transferred by gift is the present value of the interests determined by use of standard or special section 7520 actuarial factors and the valuation methodology described in § 25.2512-5(d). Sections 20.2031-7(d)(6) and 20.2031-7A(e)(4) of this chapter and related sections provide tables with standard actuarial factors and examples that illustrate how to use the tables to compute the present value of ordinary annuity, life, and remainder interests in property. These sections also refer to standard and special actuarial factors that may be necessary to compute the present value of similar interests in more unusual fact situations. These factors and examples are also generally applicable for gift tax purposes in computing the values of taxable gifts.

(2) Transitional rule. (i) If the valuation date of a transfer of an interest in property by gift is after April 30, 1989, and before June 10, 1994, a donor can rely on Notice 89-24 (1989-1 C.B. 660), or Notice 89-60 (1989-1 C.B. 700), in valuing the transferred interest. (See § 601.601(d)(2)(ii)(b) of this chapter.)

(ii) If a donor transferred an interest in property by gift after December 31, 1988, and before May 1, 1989, retaining an interest in the same property, and after April 30, 1989, and before January 1, 1990, transferred the retained interest in property, the donor may, at the option of the donor, value the transfer of the retained interest under this paragraph (e) or paragraph (d) of this section.

(3) Publications and actuarial computations by the Internal Revenue Service. Many standard actuarial factors not included in §§ 20.2031-7(d)(6) and 20.2031-7A(e)(4) of this chapter are included in Internal Revenue Service Publication 1457, "Actuarial Values, Alpha Volume," (8-89). Internal Revenue Service Publication 1457 also includes examples that illustrate how to compute many special factors for more unusual situations. Publication 1457 is no longer available for purchase from the Superintendent of Documents, United States Government Printing Office, Washington, DC 20402. However, pertinent factors in this publication may be obtained from: CC:DOM:CORP:R (IRS Publication 1457), room 5226, Internal Revenue Service, POB 7604, Ben Franklin Station, Washington, DC 20044. If a special factor is required in the case of a completed gift, the Internal Revenue Service may furnish the factor to the donor upon a request for a ruling. The request for a ruling must be accompanied by a recitation of the facts including a statement of the date of birth for each measuring life, the date of the gift, any other applicable dates, and a copy of the will, trust, or other relevant documents. A request for a ruling must com-

ply with the instructions for requesting a ruling published periodically in the Internal Revenue Bulletin (see §§ 601.201 and 601.601(d)(2)(ii)(b) of this chapter) and include payment of the required user fee.

(f) Valuation of annuities, unitrust interests, interests for life or term of years, and remainder or reversionary interests transferred after April 30, 1999, and before May 1, 2009. *(1) In general.* Except as otherwise provided in §§ 25.2512-5(b) and 25.7520-3(b) (pertaining to certain limitations on the use of prescribed tables), if the valuation date of the transferred interest is after April 30, 1999, and before May 1, 2009, the fair market value of annuities, unitrust interests, life estates, terms of years, remainders, and reversions transferred by gift is the present value of the interests determined by use of standard or special section 7520 actuarial factors and the valuation methodology described in § 25.2512-5T(d). Sections 20.2031-7(d)(6) and 20.2031-7A(f)(4) and related sections provide tables with standard actuarial factors and examples that illustrate how to use the tables to compute the present value of ordinary annuity, life, and remainder interests in property. These sections also refer to standard and special actuarial factors that may be necessary to compute the present value of similar interests in more unusual fact situations. These factors and examples are also generally applicable for gift tax purposes in computing the values of taxable gifts.

(2) Transitional rule. If the valuation date of a transfer of property by gift is after April 30, 1999, and before July 1, 1999, the fair market value of the interest transferred is determined by use of the section 7520 interest rate for the month in which the valuation date occurs (see §§ 25.7520-1(b) and 25.7520-2(a)(2)) and the appropriate actuarial tables under either § 20.2031-7A(e)(4) or § 20.2031-7A(f)(4), at the option of the donor. However, with respect to each individual transaction and with respect to all transfers occurring on the valuation date, the donor must use the same actuarial tables (for example, gift and income tax charitable deductions with respect to the same transfer must be determined based on the same tables, and all transfers made on the same date must be valued based on the same tables).

(3) Publications and actuarial computations by the Internal Revenue Service. Many standard actuarial factors not included in §§ 20.2031-7(d)(6) and 20.2031-7A(f)(4) are included in Internal Revenue Service Publication 1457, "Actuarial Values, Book Aleph," (7-99). Internal Revenue Service Publication 1457 also includes examples that illustrate how to compute many special factors for more unusual situations. Publication 1457 is no longer available for purchase from the Superintendent of Documents, United States Government Printing Office. However, pertinent factors in this publication may be obtained from: CC:PA:LPD:PR (IRS Publication 1457), Room 5205, Internal Revenue Service, P.O.Box 7604, Ben Franklin Station, Washington, DC 20044. If a special factor is required in the case of a completed gift, the Internal Revenue Service may furnish the factor to the donor upon a request for a ruling. The request for a ruling must be accompanied by a recitation of the facts including a statement of the date of birth for each measuring life, the date of the gift, any other applicable dates, and a copy of the will, trust, or other relevant documents. A request for a ruling must comply with the instructions for requesting a ruling published periodically in the Internal Revenue Bulletin (see §§ 601.201 and 601.601(d)(2)(ii)(b)) and include payment of the required user fee.

(4) Effective/applicability dates. Paragraphs (f)(1) through (f)(3) apply after April 30, 1999, and before May 1, 2009.

T.D. 6334, 11/14/58, amend T.D. 7077, 12/1/70, T.D. 7955, 5/11/84, T.D. 8395, 1/28/92, T.D. 8540, 6/9/94, T.D. 8819, 4/29/99, T.D. 8886, 6/9/2000, T.D. 9448, 5/1/2009.

§ 25.2512-5T Valuation of annuities, unitrust interests, interests for life or term of years, and remainder or reversionary interests (temporary).

(a) and (b) [Reserved]. For further guidance, see § 25.2512-5(a) and (b).

(c) Actuarial valuations. The present value of annuities, unitrust interests, life estates, terms of years, remainders, and reversions transferred by gift on or after May 1, 2009, is determined under paragraph (d) of this section. The present value of annuities, unitrust interests, life estates, terms of years, remainders, and reversions transferred by gift before May 1, 2009, is determined under the following sections:

Transfers		Applicable Regulations
After	Before	
	01-01-52	25.2512-5A(a)
12-31-51	01-01-71	25.2512-5A(b)
12-31-70	12-01-83	25.2512-5A(c)
11-30-83	05-01-89	25.2512-5A(d)
04-30-89	05-01-99	25.2512-5A(e)
04-30-99	05-01-09	25.2512-5A(f)

(d) Actuarial valuations on or after May 1, 2009. *(1) In general.* Except as otherwise provided in paragraph (b) of this section and § 25.7520-3(b) (relating to exceptions to the use of prescribed tables under certain circumstances), if the valuation date for the gift is on or after May 1, 2009, the fair market value of annuities, life estates, terms of years, remainders, and reversions transferred on or after May 1, 2009, is the present value of such interests determined under paragraph (d)(2) of this section and by use of standard or special section 7520 actuarial factors. These factors are derived by using the appropriate section 7520 interest rate and, if applicable, the mortality component for the valuation date of the interest that is being valued. See §§ 25.7520-1 through 25.7520-4. The fair market value of a qualified annuity interest described in section 2702(b)(1) and a qualified unitrust interest described in section 2702(b)(2) is the present value of such interests determined under § 25.7520-1(c).

(2) Specific interests. When the donor transfers property in trust or otherwise and retains an interest therein, generally, the value of the gift is the value of the property transferred less the value of the donor's retained interest. However, if the donor transfers property after October 8, 1990, to or for the benefit of a member of the donor's family, the value of the gift is the value of the property transferred less the value of the donor's retained interest as determined under section 2702. If the donor assigns or relinquishes an annuity, life estate, remainder, or reversion that the donor holds by virtue of a transfer previously made by the donor or another, the value of the gift is the value of the interest transferred. However, see section 2519 for a special rule in the case of the assignment of an income interest by a person who received the interest from a spouse.

(i) Charitable remainder trusts. The fair market value of a remainder interest in a pooled income fund, as defined in § 1.642(c)-5, is its value determined under § 1.642(c)-6T(e) (see § 1.642(c)-6A for certain prior periods). The fair market value of a remainder interest in a charitable remainder annuity trust, as described in § 1.664-2(a), is its present value determined under § 1.664-2(c). The fair market value of a remainder interest in a charitable remainder unitrust, as defined in § 1.664-3, is its present value determined under § 1.664-4T(e). The fair market value of a life interest or term for years in a charitable remainder unitrust is the fair market value of the property as of the date of transfer less the fair market value of the remainder interest, determined under § 1.664-4T(e)(4) and (5).

(ii) Ordinary remainder and reversionary interests. If the interest to be valued is to take effect after a definite number of years or after the death of one individual, the present value of the interest is computed by multiplying the value of the property by the appropriate remainder interest actuarial factor (that corresponds to the applicable section 7520 interest rate and remainder interest period) in Table B (for a term certain) or the appropriate Table S (for one measuring life), as the case may be. Table B is contained in § 20.2031-7(d)(6) and Table S (for one measuring life when the valuation date is on or after May 1, 2009) is included in § 20.2031-7T(d)(7) and Internal Revenue Service Publication 1457. See § 20.2031-7A containing Table S for valuation of interests before May 1, 2009. For information about obtaining actuarial factors for other types of remainder interests, see paragraph (d)(4) of this section.

(iii) Ordinary term-of-years and life interests. If the interest to be valued is the right of a person to receive the income of certain property, or to use certain nonincome-producing property, for a term of years or for the life of one individual, the present value of the interest is computed by multiplying the value of the property by the appropriate term-of-years or life interest actuarial factor (that corresponds to the applicable section 7520 interest rate and term-of-years or life interest period). Internal Revenue Service Publication 1457 includes actuarial factors for a remainder interest after a term of years in Table B and after the life of one individual in Table S (for one measuring life when the valuation date is on or after May 1, 2009). However, term-of-years and life interest actuarial factors are not included in Table B in § 20.2031-7(d)(6) or Table S in § 20.2031-7T(d)(7) (or in § 20.2031-7A). If Internal Revenue Service Publication 1457 (or any other reliable source of term-of-years and life interest actuarial factors) is not conveniently available, an actuarial factor for the interest may be derived mathematically. This actuarial factor may be derived by subtracting the correlative remainder factor (that corresponds to the applicable section 7520 interest rate) in Table B (for a term of years) in § 20.2031-7(d)(6) or in Table S (for the life of one individual) in § 20.2031-7T(d)(7), as the case may be, from 1.000000. For information about obtaining actuarial factors for other types of term-of-years and life interests, see paragraph (d)(4) of this section.

(iv) Annuities. (A) If the interest to be valued is the right of a person to receive an annuity that is payable at the end of each year for a term of years or for the life of one individual, the present value of the interest is computed by multiplying the aggregate amount payable annually by the appropriate annuity actuarial factor (that corresponds to the applicable section 7520 interest rate and annuity period). Internal Revenue Service Publication 1457 includes actuarial factors in Table B (for a remainder interest after an annuity payable for a term of years) and in Table S (for a remainder interest after an annuity payable for the life of one individual when the valuation date is on or after May 1, 2009). However, annuity actuarial factors are not included in Table B in § 20.2031-7(d)(6) or Table S in § 20.2031-7T(d)(7) (or in § 20.2031-7A). If Internal Revenue Service Publication 1457 (or any other reliable source of annuity actuarial factors) is not conveniently available, an annuity factor for a term of years or for one life may be derived mathematically. This annuity factor may be derived by subtracting the applicable remainder factor (that corresponds to the applicable section 7520 interest rate and annuity period) in Table B (in the case of a term-of-years annuity) in § 20.2031-7(d)(6) or in Table S (in the case of a one-life annuity) in § 20.2031-7T(d)(7), as the case may be, from 1.000000 and then dividing the result by the applicable section 7520 interest rate expressed as a decimal number. See § 20.2031-7T(d)(2)(iv) for an example that illustrates the computation of the present value of an annuity.

(B) If the annuity is payable at the end of semiannual, quarterly, monthly, or weekly periods, the product obtained by multiplying the annuity factor by the aggregate amount payable annually is then multiplied by the applicable adjustment factor set forth in Table K in § 20.2031-7(d)(6) at the appropriate interest rate component for payments made at the end of the specified periods. The provisions of this paragraph (d)(2)(iv)(B) are illustrated by the following example:

Example. In July of a year after 2008, the donor agreed to pay the annuitant the sum of $10,000 per year, payable in equal semiannual installments at the end of each period. The semiannual installments are to be made on each December 31st and June 30th. The annuity is payable until the annuitant's death. On the date of the agreement, the annuitant is 68 years and 5 months old. The donee annuitant's age is treated as 68 for purposes of computing the present value of the annuity. The section 7520 rate on the date of the agreement is 6.6 percent. Under Table S in § 20.2031-7T(d)(7), the factor at 6.6 percent for determining the present value of a remainder interest payable at the death of an individual aged 68 is .42001. Converting the remainder factor to an annuity factor, as described above, the annuity factor for determining the present value of an annuity transferred to an individual age 68 is 8.7877 (1.00000 minus .42001 divided by .066). The adjustment factor from Table K in § 20.2031-7(d)(6) in the column for payments made at the end of each semiannual period at the rate of 6.6 percent is 1.0162. The aggregate annual amount of the annuity, $10,000, is multiplied by the factor 8.7877 and the product is multiplied by 1.0162. The present value of the donee's annuity is, therefore, $89,300.61 ($10,000 x 8.7877 x 1.0162).

(C) If an annuity is payable at the beginning of annual, semiannual, quarterly, monthly, or weekly periods for a term of years, the value of the annuity is computed by multiplying the aggregate amount payable annually by the annuity factor described in paragraph (d)(2)(iv)(A) of this section; and the product so obtained is then multiplied by the adjustment factor in Table J in § 20.2031-7(d)(6) at the appropriate interest rate component for payments made at the beginning of specified periods. If an annuity is payable at the beginning of annual, semiannual, quarterly, monthly, or weekly periods for one or more lives, the value of the annuity is the sum of the first payment and the present value of a similar annuity, the first payment of which is not to be made until the end of the payment period, determined as provided in paragraph (d)(2)(iv)(B) of this section.

(v) Annuity and unitrust interests for a term of years or until the prior death of an individual. (A) Annuity interests. The present value of an annuity interest that is payable until the earlier to occur of the lapse of a specific number of years or the death of an individual may be computed with values from the tables in §§ 20.2031-7(d)(6) and 20.2031-7T(d)(7) as described in the following example:

Example. The donor transfers $100,000 into a trust on or after May 1, 2009, and retains the right to receive an annuity from the trust in the amount of $6,000 per year, payable in equal semiannual installments at the end of each period. The semiannual installments are to be made on each June 30th and December 31st. The annuity is payable for 10 years or until the donor's prior death. At the time of the transfer, the donor is 59 years and 6 months old. The donor's age is deemed to be 60 for purposes of computing the present value of the retained annuity. The section 7520 rate for the month in which the transfer occurred is 5.8 percent. The present value of the donor's retained interest is $42,575.65, determined as follows

TABLE S value at 5.8 percent, age 60	.34656
TABLE S value at 5.8 percent, age 70	.49025
TABLE 2000CM value at age 70	74794
TABLE 2000CM value at age 60	.87595
TABLE B value at 5.8 percent, 10 years	.569041
TABLE K value at 5.8 percent	1.0143

Factor for donor's retained interest at 5.8 percent:

$$\frac{(1.00000-.34656)-(.569041\times(74794\ /\ \times 87595)(1.00000-.49025))}{.058} = 6.9959$$

Present value of donor's retained interest:

($6,000 × 6.9959 × 1.0143) $42,575.65:

(B) Unitrust interests. The present value of a unitrust interest that is payable until the earlier to occur of the lapse of a specific number of years or the death of an individual may be computed with values from the tables in §§ 1.664-4(e)(6) and 1.664-4T(e)(7) as described in the following example:

Example. The donor who, as of the nearest birthday, is 60 years old, transfers $100,000 to a unitrust on January 1st of a year after 2009. The trust instrument requires that each year the trust pay to the donor, in equal semiannual installments on June 30th and December 31st, 6 percent of the fair market value of the trust assets, valued as of January 1st each year, for 10 years or until the prior death of the donor. The section 7520 rate for the January in which the transfer occurred is 6.6 percent. Under Table F(6.6) in § 1.664-4(e)(6), the appropriate adjustment factor is .953317 for semiannual payments payable at the end of the semiannual period. The adjusted payout rate is 5.720 percent (6% x .953317). The present value of the donor's retained interest is $41,920.00 determined as follows:

TABLE U(1) value at 5.6 percent, age 60	.33970
TABLE U(1) value at 5.6 percent, age 70	.48352
TABLE 2000CM value at age 70	74794
TABLE 2000CM value at age 60	87595
TABLE D value at 5.6 percent, 10 years	.561979

Factor for donor's retained interest at 5.6 percent:

(1.000000 − .33970) − (.561979 × (74794/87595) × (1.000000 − .48352)) = .41247

TABLE U(1) value at 5.8 percent, age 60	.32846
TABLE U(1) value at 5.8 percent, age 70	.47241
TABLE 2000CM value at age 70	74794
TABLE 2000CM value at age 60	87595
TABLE D value at 5.8 percent, 10 years	550185

Factor for donor's retained interest at 5.8 percent:

(1.000000 − .32846) − (.550185 × (74974/87595) × (1.000000 − .47241)) = .42369

Difference-.01122

Interpolation adjustment:

$$\frac{5.720\% - 5.6\%}{0.2\%} = \frac{x}{.01122}$$

x = .00673

Factor at 5.6 percent, age 60	.41247
Plus: Interpolation adjustment	.00673
Interpolated Factor	.41920
Present value of donor's retained interest:	
($100,000 × .41920)	$41,920.00

(3) Transitional rule. If the valuation date of a transfer of property by gift is on or after May 1, 2009, and before July 1, 2009, the fair market value of the interest transferred is determined by use of the section 7520 interest rate for the month in which the valuation date occurs (see §§ 25.7520-1(b) and 25.7520-2(a)(2)) and the appropriate actuarial tables under either § 20.2031-7T(d)(7) or § 20.2031-7A(f)(4), at the option of the donor. However, with respect to each individual transaction and with respect to all transfers occurring on the valuation date, the donor must use the same actuarial tables (for example, gift and income tax charitable deductions with respect to the same transfer must be determined based on the same tables, and all transfers made on the same date must be valued based on the same tables).

(4) Publications and actuarial computations by the Internal Revenue Service. Many standard actuarial factors not included in § 20.2031-7(d)(6) or § 20.2031-7T(d)(7) are included in Internal Revenue Service Publication 1457, "Actuarial Valuations Version 3A" (2009). Internal Revenue Service Publication 1457 also includes examples that illustrate how to compute many special factors for more unusual situations. A copy of this publication is available beginning May 1, 2009, at no charge, electronically via the IRS Internet site at http:// www.irs.gov. If a special factor is required in the case of a completed gift, the Internal Revenue Service may furnish the factor to the donor upon a request for a ruling. The request for a ruling must be accompanied by a recitation of the facts including a statement of the date of birth for each measuring life, the date of the gift, any other applicable dates, and a copy of the will, trust, or other relevant documents. A request for a ruling must comply with the instructions for requesting a ruling published periodically in the Internal Revenue Bulletin (see §§ 601.201 and 601.601(d)(2)(ii)(b)) and include payment of the required user fee.

(e) Effective/applicability date. This section applies on or after May 1, 2009.

(f) Expiration date. This section expires on or before May 1, 2012.

T.D. 9448, 5/1/2009.

§ 25.2512-6 Valuation of certain life insurance and annuity contracts; valuation of shares in an open-end investment company.

(a) Valuation of certain life insurance and annuity contracts. The value of a life insurance contract or of a contract for the payment of an annuity issued by a company regularly engaged in the selling of contracts of that character is established through the sale of the particular contract by the company, or through the sale by the company of comparable contracts. As valuation of an insurance policy through sale of comparable contracts is not readily ascertainable when the gift is of a contract which has been in force for some time and on which further premium payments are to be made, the value may be approximated by adding to the interpolated terminal reserve at the date of the gift the proportionate part of the gross premium last paid before the date of the gift which covers the period extending beyond that date. If, however, because of the unusual nature of the contract such approximation is not reasonably close to the full value, this method may not be used. The following examples, so far as relating to life insurance contracts, are of gifts of such contracts on which there are no accrued dividends or outstanding indebtedness.

Example (1). A donor purchases from a life insurance company for the benefit of another a life insurance contract or a contract for the payment of an annuity. The value of the gift is the cost of the contract.

Example (2). An annuitant purchased from a life insurance company a single payment annuity contract by the terms of which he was entitled to receive payments of $1,200 annually for the duration of his life. Five years subsequent to such purchase, and when of the age of 50 years, he gratuitously assigns the contract. The value of the gift is the amount which the company would charge for an annuity contract providing for the payment of $1,200 annually for the life of a person 50 years of age.

Example (3). A donor owning a life insurance policy on which no further payments are to be made to the company (e.g., a single premium policy or paid-up policy) makes a gift of the contract. The value of the gift is the amount which the company would charge for a single premium contract of the same specified amount on the life of a person of the age of the insured.

Example (4). A gift is made four months after the last premium due date of an ordinary life insurance policy issued nine years and four months prior to the gift thereof by the insured, who was 35 years of age at date of issue. The gross annual premium is $2,811. The computation follows:

Terminal reserve at end of tenth year	$14,601.00
Terminal reserve at end of ninth year	12,965.00
Increase	1,636.00
One-third of such increase (the gift having been made four months following the last preceding premium due date), is	545.33
Terminal reserve at end of ninth year	12,965.00
Interpolated terminal reserve at date of gift	13,510.33
Two-thirds of gross premium ($2,811)	1,874.00
Value of the gift	15,384.33

Example (5). A donor purchases from a life insurance company for $ 15,198, a joint and survivor annuity contract which provides for the payment of $ 60 a month to the donor during his lifetime, and then to his sister for such time as she may survive him. The premium which would have been charged by the company for an annuity of $ 60 monthly payable during the life of the donor alone is $ 10,690. The value of the gift is $ 4,508 ($ 15,198 less $ 10,690).

(b) Valuation of shares in an open-end investment company. *(1)* The fair market value of a share in an open-end investment company (commonly known as a "mutual fund") is the public redemption price of a share. In the absence of an affirmative showing of the public redemption price quoted by the company for the date of the gift shall be presumed to be the applicable public redemption price. If there is no public redemption price quoted by the company for the date of the gift (e.g., the date of the gift is a Saturday, Sunday, or holiday), the fair market value of the mutual fund share is the last public redemption price quoted by the company for the first day preceding the date of the gift for which there is a quotation. As used in this paragraph, the term "open-end investment company" includes only a company which on the date of the gift was engaged in offering its shares to the public in the capacity of an open-end investment company.

(2) The provisions of this paragraph shall apply with respect to gifts made after December 31, 1954.

T.D. 6334, 11/14/58, amend T.D. 6542, 1/19/61, T.D. 6680, 10/9/63, T.D. 7319, 7/22/74.

§ 25.2512-7 Effect of excise tax.

If jewelry, furs or other property, the purchase of which is subject to an excise tax, is purchased at retail by a taxpayer and made the subject of gifts within a reasonable time after purchase, the purchase price, including the excise tax, is considered to be the fair market value of the property on the date of the gift, in the absence of evidence that the market price of similar articles has increased or decreased in the meantime. Under other circumstances, the excise tax is taken into account in determining the fair market value of property to the extent, and only to the extent, that it affects the price at which the property would change hands between a willing buyer and a willing seller, as provided in § 25.2512-1.

T.D. 6334, 11/14/58.

§ 25.2512-8 Transfers for insufficient consideration.

Transfers reached by the gift tax are not confined to those only which, being without a valuable consideration, accord with the common law concept of gifts, but embrace as well sales, exchanges, and other dispositions of property for a consideration to the extent that the value of the property transferred by the donor exceeds the value in money or money's worth of the consideration given therefor. However, a sale, exchange, or other transfer of property made in the ordinary course of business (a transaction which is bona fide, at arm's length, and free from any donative intent), will be considered as made for an adequate and full consideration in money or money's worth. A consideration not reducible to a value in money or money's worth, as love and affection, promise of marriage, etc., is to be wholly disregarded, and the entire value of the property transferred constitutes the amount of the gift. Similarly, a relinquishment or promised relinquishment of dower or curtesy, or of a statutory estate created in lieu of dower or curtesy, or of other marital rights in the spouse's property or estate, shall not be considered to any extent a consideration "in money or money's worth."

See, however, section 2516 and the regulations thereunder with respect to certain transfers incident to a divorce. See also sections 2701, 2702, 2703 and 2704 and the regulations at § 25.2701-0 through 25.2704-3 for special rules for valuing transfers of business interests, transfers in trust, and transfers pursuant to options and purchase agreements.

T.D. 6334, 11/14/58, amend T.D. 8395, 1/28/92.

PAR. 44.

Section 25.2512-8 is revised to read as follows:

Proposed § 25.2512-8 Transfers for insufficient or excessive consideration. [*For Preamble, see ¶ 151,065*]

• ***Caution:*** Prop reg § 1.482-2 was finalized by T.D. 8204, 5/20/88. Prop regs §§ 1.163-7, 1.446-2, 1.483-1 through -5, 1.1001-1, 1.1012-1, 1.1271 through -3, 1.1272-1, 1.1273-1, 1.1273-2, 1.1274-1 throught -7, 1.1274A-1, 1.1275-1 through -3, and 1.1275-5 were withdrawn by the Treasury on 12/22/92, 57 Fed. Reg. 67050. Prop reg § 1.1275-4 was superseded by the Treasury on 12/16/94, Fed. Reg. 59, 64884, which was finalized by T.D. 8674, 6/11/96.

Transfers reached by the gift tax are not confined to those only which, being without a valuable consideration, accord with the common law concept of gifts, but embrace as well sales, exchanges, and other dispositions of property for a consideration to the extent that the value of the property transferred by the donor differs from the value in money or money's worth of the consideration given therefor. However, a sale, exchange, or other transfer of property made in the ordinary course of business (a transaction which is bona fide, at arm's length, and free from any donative intent), will be considered as made for consideration in money or money's worth equal to the value of the property transferred. If the buyer issues one or more debt instruments as all or a part of the consideration for the property, then the property and the debt instruments shall be valued in accordance with the rules set forth in § 1.1012-2. A consideration not reducible to a value in money or money's worth, as love and affection, promise of marriage, etc., is to be wholly disregarded, and the entire value of the property transferred constitutes the amount of the gift. Similarly, a relinquishment or promised relinquishment of dower or curtesy, or of a statutory estate created in lieu of dower or curtesy, or of other material rights in the spouse's property or estate, shall not be considered to any extent a consideration "in money or money's worth." See, however, section 2516 and the regulations thereunder with respect to certain transfers incident to a divorce.

* * * * *

§ 25.2513-1 Gifts by husband or wife to third party considered as made one-half by each.

(a) A gift made by one spouse to a person other than his (or her) spouse may, for the purpose of the gift tax, be considered as made one-half by his spouse, but only if at the time of the gift each spouse was a citizen or resident of the United States. For purposes of this section, an individual is to be considered as the spouse of another individual only if he was married to such individual at the time of the gift and does not remarry during the remainder of the "calendar period" [as defined in § 25.2502-1(c)(1)].

(b) The provisions of this section will apply to gifts made during a particular "calendar period" [as defined in 25.2502-1(c)(1)] only if both spouses signify their consent to treat all gifts made to third parties during that calendar quarter (or calendar year) by both spouses while married to each other as having been made one-half by each spouse. As to the manner and time for signifying consent, see § 25.2513-2. Such consent, if signified with respect to any calendar period is effective with respect to all gifts made to third parties during such calendar period except as follows:

(1) If the consenting spouses were not married to each other during a portion of the calendar period, the consent is not effective with respect to any gifts made during such portion of the calendar period. Where the consent is signified by an executor or administrator of a deceased spouse, the consent is not effective with respect to gifts made by the surviving spouse during the portion of the calendar period that his spouse was deceased.

(2) If either spouse was a nonresident not a citizen of the United States during any portion of the calendar period, the consent is not effective with respect to any gift made during that portion of the calendar period.

(3) The consent is not effective with respect to a gift by one spouse of a property interest over which he created in his spouse a general power of appointment (as defined in section 2514(c)).

(4) If one spouse transferred property in part to his spouse and in part to third parties, the consent is effective with respect to the interest transferred to third parties only insofar as such interest is ascertainable at the time of the gift and hence severable from the interest transferred to his spouse. See § 25.2512-5 for the principles to be applied in the valuation of annuities, life estates, terms for years, remainders and reversions.

(5) The consent applies alike to gifts made by one spouse alone and to gifts made partly by each spouse, provided such gifts were to third parties and do not fall within any of the exceptions set forth in subparagraphs (1) through (4) of this paragraph. The consent may not be applied only to a portion of the property interest constituting such gifts. For example, a wife may not treat gifts made by her spouse from his separate property to third parties as having been made one-half by her if her spouse does not consent to treat gifts made by her to third parties during the same calendar period as having been made one-half by him. If the consent is effectively signified on either the husband's return or the wife's return, all gifts made by the spouses to third parties (except as described in subparagraphs (1) through (4) of this paragraph), during the calendar period will be treated as having been made one-half by each spouse.

(c) If a husband and wife consent to have the gifts made to third party donees considered as made one-half by each spouse, and only one spouse makes gifts during the "calendar period" (as defined in § 25.2502-1(c)(1)), the other spouse is not required to file a gift tax return provided: (1) The total value of the gifts made to each third party donee since the beginning of the calendar year is not in excess of $20,000 ($6,000 for calendar years prior to 1982), and (2) no portion of the property transferred constitutes a gift of a future interest. If a transfer made by either spouse during the calendar period to a third-party represents a gift of a future interest in property and the spouses consent to have the gifts considered as made one-half by each, a gift tax return for such calendar period must be filed by each spouse regardless of the value of the transfer. (See § 25.2503-3 for the definition of a future interest.)

(d) The following examples illustrate the application of this section relating to the requirements for the filing of a return, assuming that a consent was effectively signified:

(1) A husband made gifts valued at $7,000 during the second quarter of 1971 to a third party and his wife made no gifts during this time. Each spouse is required to file a return for the second calendar quarter of 1971.

(2) A husband made gifts valued at $5,000 to each of two third parties during the year 1970 and his wife made no gifts. Only the husband is required to file a return. (See § 25.6019-2.)

(3) During the third quarter of 1971, a husband made gifts valued at $5,000 to a third party, and his wife made gifts valued at $2,000 to the same third party. Each spouse is required to file a return for the third calendar quarter of 1971.

(4) A husband made gifts valued at $5,000 to a third party and his wife made gifts valued at $3,000 to another third party during the year 1970. Only the husband is required to file a return for the calendar year 1970. (See § 25.6019-2).

(5) A husband made gifts valued at $2,000 during the first quarter of 1971 to third parties which represented gifts of future interests in property (see § 25.2503-3), and his wife made no gifts during such calendar quarter. Each spouse is required to file a return for the first calendar quarter of 1971.

T.D. 6334, 11/14/58, amend T.D. 7238, 12/28/72, T.D. 7910, 9/6/83.

§ 25.2513-2 Manner and time of signifying consent.

(a) *(1)* Consent to the application of the provisions of section 2513 with respect to a "calendar period" [as defined in § 25.2502-1(c)(1)] shall, in order to be effective, be signified by both spouses. If both spouses file tax returns within the time for signifying consent, it is sufficient if—

(i) The consent of the husband is signified on the wife's return, and the consent of the wife is signified on the husband's return;

(ii) The consent of each spouse is signified on his own return; or

(iii) The consent of both spouses is signified on one of the returns.

If only one spouse files a gift tax return within the time provided for signifying consent, the consent of both spouses shall be signified on that return. However, wherever possible, the notice of the consent is to be shown on both returns and it is preferred that the notice be executed in the manner described in subdivision (i) of this subparagraph. The consent may be revoked only as provided in § 25.2513-3. If one spouse files more than one gift tax return for a calendar period on or before the due date of the return, the last return so filed shall, for the purpose of determining whether a consent has been signified, be considered as the return. (See §§ 25.6075-1 and 25.6075-2 for the due date of a gift tax return.)

(2) For gifts made after December 31, 1970, and before January 1, 1982 subject to the limitations of paragraph (b) of this section, the consent signified on a return filed for a calendar quarter will be effective for a previous calendar quarter of the same calendar year for which no return was filed because the gifts made during such previous calendar quarter did not exceed the annual exclusion provided by section 2503(b), if the gifts in such previous calendar quarter are listed on that return. Thus, for example, if A gave $2,000 to his son in the first quarter of 1972 (and filed no return because of section 2503(b)) and gave a further $4,000 to such son in the last quarter of the year, A and his spouse could signify consent to the application of section 2513 on the return filed for the fourth quarter and have it apply to the first quarter as well, provided that the $2,000 gift is listed on such return.

(b) *(1)* With respect to gifts made after December 31, 1981, or before January 1, 1971, the consent may be signified at any time following the close of the calendar year, subject to the following limitations:

(i) The consent may not be signified after the 15th day of April following the close of the calendar year, unless before such 15th day no return has been filed for the year by either spouse, in which case the consent may not be signified after a return for the year is filed by either spouse; and

(ii) The consent may not be signified for a calendar year after a notice of deficiency in gift tax for that year has been sent to either spouse in accordance with the provisions of section 6212(a).

(2) With respect to gifts made after December 31, 1970, and before January 1, 1982 the consent may be signified at any time following the close of the calendar quarter in which the gift was made, subject to the following limitations:

(i) The consent may not be signified after the 15th day of the second month following the close of such calendar quarter, unless before such 15th day, no return has been filed for such calendar quarter by either spouse, in which case the consent may not be signified after a return for such calendar quarter is filed by either spouse; and

(ii) The consent may not be signified after a notice of deficiency with respect to the tax for such calendar quarter has been sent to either spouse in accordance with section 6212(a).

(c) The executor or administrator of a deceased spouse, or the guardian or committee of a legally incompetent spouse, as the case may be, may signify the consent.

(d) If the donor and spouse consent to the application of section 2513, the return or returns for the "calendar period" [as defined in § 25.2502-1(c)(1)] must set forth, to the extent provided thereon, information relative to the transfers made by each spouse.

T.D. 6334, 11/14/58, amend T.D. 7238, 12/28/72, T.D. 7910, 9/6/83.

§ 25.2513-3 Revocation of consent.

Caution: The Treasury has not yet amended Reg § 25.2513-3 to reflect changes made by P.L. 97-34.

(a) *(1)* With respect to gifts made after December 31, 1981, or before January 1, 1971, if the consent to the application of the provisions of section 2513 for a calendar year was effectively signified on or before the 15th day of April following the close of the calendar year, either spouse may revoke the consent by filing in duplicate a signed statement of revocation, but only if the statement is filed on or before such 15th day of April. Therefore, a consent that was not effectively signified until after the 15th day of April following the close of the calendar year to which it applies may not be revoked.

(2) With respect to gifts made after December 31, 1970 as before January 1, 1982 if the consent to the application of the provisions of section 2513 for a calendar quarter was effectively signified on or before the 15th day of the second month following the close of such calendar quarter, either spouse may revoke the consent by filing in duplicate a signed statement of revocation, but only if the statement is filed on or before such 15th day of the second month following the close of such calendar quarter. Therefore, a consent that was not effectively signified until after the 15th day of the second month following the close of the calendar quarter to which it applies may not be revoked.

(b) Except as provided in paragraph (b) of § 301.6091-1 of this chapter (relating to hand-carried documents), the statement referred to in paragraph (a) of this section shall be filed with the internal revenue officer with whom the gift tax return is required to be filed, or with whom the gift tax return would be required to be filed if a return were required.

T.D. 6334, 11/14/58, amend T.D. 7012, 5/14/69, T.D. 7238, 12/28/72, T.D. 7910, 9/6/83.

§ 25.2513-4 Joint and several liability for tax.

If consent to the application of the provisions of section 2513 is signified as provided in § 25.2513-2, and not revoked as provided in § 25.2513-3, the liability with respect to the entire gift tax of each spouse for such "calendar period" [as defined in § 25.2502(c)(1)] is joint and several. See paragraph (d) of § 25.2511-1.

T.D. 6334, 11/14/58, amend T.D. 7238, 12/28/72, T.D. 7910, 9/6/83.

§ 25.2514-1 Transfers under power of appointment.

(a) Introductory. Section 2514 treats the exercise of a general power of appointment created on or before October 21, 1942, as a transfer of property for purposes of the gift tax. The section also treats as a transfer of property the exercise or complete release of a general power of appointment created after October 21, 1942, and under certain circumstances the exercise of a power of appointment (not a general power of appointment) created after October 21, 1942, by the creation of another power of appointment. See paragraph (d) of § 25.2514-3. Under certain circumstances, also, the failure to exercise a power of appointment created after October 21, 1942, within a specified time, so that the power lapses, constitutes a transfer of property. Paragraphs (b) through (e) of this section contain definitions of certain terms used in §§ 25.2514-2 and 25.2514-3. See § 25.2514-2 for specific rules applicable to certain powers created on or before October 21, 1942. See § 25.2514-3 for specific rules applicable to powers created after October 21, 1942.

(b) Definition of "power of appointment". *(1) In general.* The term "power of appointment" includes all powers which are in substance and effect powers of appointment received by the donee of the power from another person, regardless of the nomenclature used in creating the power and regardless of local property law connotations. For example, if a trust instrument provides that the beneficiary may appropriate or consume the principal of the trust, the power to consume or appropriate is a power of appointment. Similarly, a power given to a donee to affect the beneficial enjoyment of a trust property or its income by altering, amending or revoking the trust instrument or terminating the trust is a power of appointment. A power in a donee to remove or discharge a trustee and appoint himself may be a power of appointment. For example, if under the terms of a trust instrument, the trustee or his successor has the power to appoint the principal of the trust for the benefit of individuals including himself, and A, another person, has the unrestricted power to remove or discharge the trustee at any time and appoint any other person, including himself, A is considered as having a power of appointment. However, he would not be considered to have a power of appointment if he only had the power to appoint a successor, including himself, under limited conditions which did not exist at the time of exercise, release or lapse of the trustee's power, without an accompanying unrestricted power of removal. Similarly, a power to amend only the administrative provisions of a trust instrument, which cannot substantially affect the beneficial enjoyment of the trust property or income, is not a power of appointment. The mere power of management, investment, custody of assets, or the power to allocate receipts and disbursements as between income and principal, exercisable in a fiduciary capacity, whereby the holder has no power to enlarge or shift any of the beneficial interests therein except as an incidental consequence of the discharge of such fiduciary duties is not a power of appointment. Further, the right in a beneficiary of a trust to assent to a periodic accounting, thereby relieving the trustee from further accountability, is not a power of appointment if the right of assent does not consist of any power or right to enlarge or shift the beneficial interest of any beneficiary therein.

(2) Relation to other sections. For purposes of §§ 25.2514-1 through 25.2514-3, the term "power of appointment" does not include powers reserved by a donor to himself. No provision of section 2514 or of §§ 25.2514-1 through 25.2514-3 is to be construed as in any way limiting the application of any other section of the Internal Revenue Code or of these regulations. The power of the owner of a property interest already possessed by him to dispose of his interest, and nothing more, is not a power of appointment, and the interest is includible in the amount of his gifts to the extent it would be includible under section 2511 or other provisions of the Internal Revenue Code. For example, if a trust created by S provides for payment of the income to A for life with power in A to appoint the entire trust property by deed during her lifetime to a class consisting of her children, and a further power to dispose of the entire corpus by will to anyone, including her estate, and A exercises the inter vivos power in favor of her children, she has necessarily made a transfer of her income interest which constitutes a taxable gift under section 2511(a), without regard to section 2514. This transfer also results in a relinquishment of her general power to appoint by will, which constitutes a transfer under section 2514 if the power was created after October 21, 1942.

(3) Powers over a portion of property. If a power of appointment exists as to part of an entire group of assets or only over a limited interest in property, section 2514 applies only to such part or interest.

(c) Definition of "general power of appointment". *(1) In general.* The term "general power of appointment" as defined in section 2514(c) means any power of appointment exercisable in favor of the person possessing the power (referred to as the "possessor"), his estate, his creditors, or the creditors of his estate, except (i) joint powers, to the extent provided in §§ 25.2514-2 and 25.2514-3 and (ii) certain powers limited by an ascertainable standard, to the extent provided in subparagraph (2) of this paragraph. A power of appointment exercisable to meet the estate tax, or any other taxes, debts, or charges which are enforceable against the possessor or his estate, is included within the meaning of a power of appointment exercisable in favor of the possessor, his estate, his creditors, or the creditors of his estate. A power of appointment exercisable for the purpose of discharging a legal obligation of the possessor or for his pecuniary benefit is considered a power of appointment exercisable in favor of the possessor or his creditors. However, for purposes of §§ 25.2514-1 through 25.2514-3, a power of appointment not otherwise considered to be a general power of appointment is not treated as a general power of appointment merely by reason of the fact that an appointee may, in fact, be a creditor of the possessor or his estate. A power of appointment is not a general power if by its terms it is either—

(a) Exercisable only in favor of one or more designated persons or classes other than the possessor or his creditors, or the possessor's estate, or the creditors of his estate, or

(b) Expressly not exercisable in favor of the possessor or his creditors, the possessor's estate, or the creditors of his estate.

A beneficiary may have two powers under the same instrument, one of which is a general power of appointment and the other of which is not. For example, a beneficiary may have a general power to withdraw a limited portion of trust corpus during his life, and a further power exercisable during his lifetime to appoint the corpus among his children. The latter power is not a general power of appointment (but its exercise may result in the exercise of the former power; see paragraph (d) of this section).

(2) Powers limited by an ascertainable standard. A power to consume, invade, or appropriate income or corpus, or both, for the benefit of the possessor which is limited by an ascertainable standard relating to the health, education, support, or maintenance of the possessor is, by reason of section 2514(c)(1), not a general power of appointment. A power is limited by such a standard if the extent of the possessor's duty to exercise and not to exercise the power is reasonably measurable in terms of his needs for health, education, or support (or any combination of them). As used in this subparagraph, the words "support" and "maintenance" are synonymous and their meaning is not limited to the bare necessities of life. A power to use property for the comfort, welfare, or happiness of the holder of the power is not limited by the requisite standard. Examples of powers which are limited by the requisite standard are powers exercisable for the holder's "support," "support in reasonable comfort," "maintenance in health and reasonable comfort," "support in his accustomed manner of living," "education, including college and professional education," "health," and "medical, dental, hospital and nursing expenses and expenses of invalidism." In determining whether a power is limited by an ascertainable standard, it is immaterial whether the beneficiary is required to exhaust his other income before the power can be exercised.

(3) Certain powers under wills of decedents dying between January 1 and April 2, 1948. Section 210 of the Technical Changes Act of 1953 provides that if a decedent died after December 31, 1947, but before April 3, 1948, certain property interests described therein may, if the decedent's surviving spouse so elects, be accorded special treatment in the determination of the marital deduction to be allowed the decedent's estate under the provisions of section 812(e) of the Internal Revenue Code of 1939. See paragraph (h) of § 81.47a of Regulations 105 (26 CFR (1939) 81.47a(h)). The section further provides that property affected by the election shall be considered property with respect to which the surviving spouse has a general power of appointment. Therefore, notwithstanding any other provision of law or of §§ 25.2514-1 through 25.2514-3, if the surviving spouse has made an election under section 210 of the Technical Changes Act of 1953, the property which was the subject of the election shall be considered as property with respect to which she has a general power of appointment created after October 21, 1942, exercisable by deed or will, to the extent it was treated as an interest passing to the surviving spouse and not passing to any other person for the purpose of the marital deduction in the prior decedent's estate.

(d) Definition of "exercise." Whether a power of appointment is in fact exercised may depend upon local law. However, regardless of local law, a power of appointment is considered as exercised for purposes of section 2514 even though the exercise is in favor of the taker in default of appointment, and irrespective of whether the appointed interest and the interest in default of appointment are identical of whether the appointee renounces any right to take under the appointment. A power of appointment is also considered as exercised even though the disposition cannot take effect until the occurrence of an event after the exercise takes place, if the exercise is irrevocable and, as of the time of the exercise, the condition was not impossible of occurrence. For example, if property is left in trust to A for life, with a power in A to appoint the remainder by an instrument filed with the trustee during his life, and A exercises his power by appointing the remainder to B in the event that B survives A, A is considered to have exercised his power if the exercise was irrevocable.

Furthermore, if a person holds both a presently exercisable general power of appointment and a presently exercisable nongeneral power of appointment over the same property, the exercise of the nongeneral power is considered the exercise of the general power only to the extent that immediately after the exercise of the nongeneral power the amount of money or property subject to being transferred by the exercise of the general power is decreased. For example, assume A has a noncumulative annual power to withdraw the greater of $5,000 or 5 percent of the value of a trust having a value of $300,000 and a lifetime nongeneral power to appoint all or a portion of the trust corpus to A's child or grandchildren. If A exercises the nongeneral power by appointing $150,000 to A's child, the exercise of the nongeneral power is treated as the exercise of the general power to the extent of $7,500 (maximum exercise of general power before the exercise of the nongeneral power, 5% of $300,000 or $15,000, less maximum exercise of the general power after the exercise of the nongeneral power, 5% of $150,000 or $7,500).

(e) Time of creation of power. A power of appointment created by will is, in general, considered as created on the date of the testator's death. However, section 2514(f) provides that a power of appointment created by a will executed on or before October 21, 1942, is considered a power created on or before that date if the testator dies before July 1, 1949, without having republished the will, by codicil or otherwise, after October 21, 1942. A power of appointment created by an inter vivos instrument is considered as created on the date the instrument takes effect. Such a power is not considered as created at some future date merely because it is not exercisable on the date the instrument takes effect, or because it is revocable, or because the identity of its holders is not ascertainable until after the date the instrument takes effect. However, if the holder of a power exercises it by creating a second power, the second power is considered as created at the time of the exercise of the first. The application of this paragraph may be illustrated by the following examples:

Example (1). A created a revocable trust before October 22, 1942, providing for payment of income to B for life with remainder as B shall appoint by deed or will. Even though A dies after October 21, 1942, without having exercised his power of revocation, B's power of appointment is considered a power created before October 22, 1942.

Example (2). C created an irrevocable inter vivos trust before October 22, 1942, naming T as trustee and providing for payment of income to D for life with remainder to E. T was given the power to pay corpus to D and the power to appoint a successor trustee. If T resigns after October 21, 1942, and appoints D as successor trustee, D is considered to have a power of appointment created before October 22, 1942.

Example (3). F created an irrevocable inter vivos trust before October 22, 1942, providing for payment of income to G for life with remainder as G shall appoint by deed or will, but in default of appointment income to H for life with remainder as H shall appoint by deed or will. If G died after October 21, 1942, without having exercised his power of appointment, H's power of appointment is considered a power created before October 22, 1942, even though it was only a contingent interest until G's death.

Example (4). If in example (3) above G had exercised by will his power of appointment, by creating a similar power in J, J's power of appointment would be considered a power created after October 21, 1942.

T.D. 6334, 11/14/58, amend T.D. 6582, 12/11/61, T.D. 7757, 1/14/81.

§ 25.2514-2 Powers of appointment created on or before October 21, 1942.

(a) In general. The exercise of a general power of appointment created on or before October 21, 1942, is deemed to be a transfer of property by the individual possessing the power.

(b) Joint powers created on or before October 21, 1942. Section 2514(c)(2) provides that a power created on or before October 21, 1942, which at the time of the exercise is not exercisable by the possessor except in conjunction with another person, is not deemed a general power of appointment.

(c) Release or lapse. A failure to exercise a general power of appointment created on or before October 21, 1942, or a complete release of such a power is not considered to be an exercise of a general power of appointment. The phrase "a complete release" means a release of all powers over all or a portion of the property subject to a power of appointment, as distinguished from the reduction of a power of appointment to a lesser power. Thus, if the possessor completely relinquished all powers over one-half of the property subject to a power of appointment, the power is completely released as to that one-half. If at or before the time a power of appointment is relinquished, the holder of the power exercises the power in such a manner or to such an extent that the relinquishment results in the reduction, enlargement or shift in a beneficial interest in property, the relinquishment will be considered to be an exercise and not a release of the power. For example, assume that A created a trust in 1940 providing for payment of the income to B for life with the power in B to amend the trust, and for payment of the remainder to such persons as B shall appoint or, upon default of appointment, to C. If B amended the trust in 1948 by providing that upon his death the remainder was to be paid to D, and if he further amended the trust in 1955 by deleting his power to amend the trust, such relinquishment will be considered an exercise and not a release of a general power of appointment. On the other hand, if the 1948 amendment became ineffective before or at the time of the 1955 amendment, or if B in 1948 merely amended the trust by changing the purely ministerial powers of the trustee, his relinquishment of the power in 1955 will be considered as release of a power of appointment.

(d) Partial release. If a general power of appointment created on or before October 21, 1942, is partially released so that it is not thereafter a general power of appointment, a subsequent exercise of the partially released power is not an exercise of a general power of appointment if the partial release occurs before whichever is the later of the following dates:

(1) November 1, 1951; or

(2) If the possessor was under a legal disability to release the power on October 21, 1942, the day after the expiration of 6 months following the termination of such legal disability.

However, if a general power created on or before October 21, 1942, is partially released on or after the later of those dates, a subsequent exercise of the power will constitute an exercise of a general power of appointment. The legal disability referred to in this paragraph is determined under local law and may include the disability of an insane person, a minor, or an unborn child. The fact that the type of general power of appointment possessed by the holder actually was not generally releasable under the local law does not place the holder under a legal disability within the meaning of this paragraph. In general, however, it is assumed that all general powers of appointment are releasable, unless the local law on the subject is to the contrary, and it is presumed that the method employed to release the power is effective, unless it is not in accordance with the local law relating specifically to releases or, in the absence of such local law, is not in accordance with the local law relating to similar transactions.

(e) Partial exercise. If a general power of appointment created on or before October 21, 1942, is exercised only as to a portion of the property subject to the power, the exercise is considered to be a transfer only as to the value of that portion.

T.D. 6334, 11/14/58.

§ 25.2514-3 Powers of appointment created after October 21, 1942.

(a) In general. The exercise, release, or lapse (except as provided in paragraph (c) of this section) of a general power of appointment created after October 21, 1942, is deemed to be a transfer of property by the individual possessing the power. The exercise of a power of appointment that is not a general power is considered to be a transfer if it is exercised to create a further power under certain circumstances (see paragraph (d) of this section). See paragraph (c) of § 25.2514-1 for the definition of various terms used in this section. See paragraph (b) of this section for the rules applicable to determine the extent to which joint powers created after October 21, 1942, are to be treated as general powers of appointment.

(b) Joint powers created after October 21, 1942. The treatment of a power of appointment created after October 21, 1942, which is exercisable only in conjunction with another person is governed by section 2514(c)(3), which provides as follows:

(1) Such a power is not considered as a general power of appointment if it is not exercisable by the possessor except with the consent or joinder of the creator of the power.

(2) Such power is not considered as a general power of appointment if it is not exercisable by the possessor except with the consent or joinder of a person having a substantial interest in the property subject to the power which is adverse to the exercise of the power in favor of the possessor, his estate, his creditors, or the creditors of his estate. An interest adverse to the exercise of a power is considered as substantial if its value in relation to the total value of the property subject to the power is not insignificant. For this purpose, the interest is to be valued in accordance with the actuarial principles set forth in § 25.2512-5 or, if it is not susceptible to valuation under those provisions, in accordance with the general principles set forth in § 25.2512-1. A taker in default of appointment under a power has an interest which is adverse to an exercise of the power. A coholder of the power has no adverse interest merely because of his joint possession of the power nor merely because he is a permissible appointee under a power. However, a coholder of a power is considered as having an adverse interest where he may possess the power after the possessor's death and may exercise it at that time in favor of himself, his estate, his creditors, or the creditors of his estate. Thus, for example, if X, Y, and Z held a power jointly to appoint among a group of persons which includes themselves and if on the death of X the power will pass to Y and Z jointly, then Y and Z are considered to have interests adverse to the exercise of the power in favor of X. Similarly, if on Y's death the power will pass to Z. Z is considered to have an interest adverse to the exercise of the power in favor of Y. The application of this subparagraph may be further illustrated by the following examples in each of which it is assumed that the value of the interest in question is substantial:

Example (1). The taxpayer and R are trustees of a trust under which the income is to be paid to the taxpayer for life and then to M for life, and R is remainderman. The trustees have power to distribute corpus to the taxpayer. Since R's interest is substantially adverse to an exercise of the power in favor of the taxpayer, the latter does not have a general power of appointment. If M and the taxpayer were trustees, M's interest would likewise be adverse.

Example (2). The taxpayer and L are trustees of a trust under which the income is to be paid to L for life and then to M for life, and the taxpayer is remainderman. The trustees have power to distribute corpus to the taxpayer during L's life. Since L's interest is adverse to an exercise of the power in favor of the taxpayer, the taxpayer does not have a general power of appointment. If the taxpayer and M were trustees, M's interest would likewise be adverse.

Example (3). The taxpayer and L are trustees of a trust under which the income is to be paid to L for life. The trustees can designate whether corpus is to be distributed to the taxpayer or to A after L's death. L's interest is not adverse to an exercise of the power in favor of the taxpayer, and the taxpayer therefore has a general power of appointment.

(3) A power which is exercisable only in conjunction with another person, and which after application of the rules set forth in subparagraphs (1) and (2) of this paragraph, constitutes a general power of appointment, will be treated as though the holders of the power who are permissible appointees of the property were joint owners of property subject to the power. The possessor, under this rule, will be treated as possessed of a general power of appointment over an aliquot share of the property to be determined with reference to the number of joint holders, including the possessor, who (or whose estates or creditors) are permissible appointees. Thus, for example, if X, Y, and Z hold an unlimited power jointly to appoint among a group of persons, including themselves, but on the death of X the power does not pass to Y and Z jointly, then Y and Z are not considered to have interests adverse to the exercise of the power in favor of X. In this case, X is considered to possess a general power of appointment as to one-third of the property subject to the power.

(c) Partial releases, lapses, and disclaimers of general powers of appointment created after October 21, 1942. *(1) Partial release of power.* The general principles set forth in § 25.2511-2 for determining whether a donor of property (or of a property right or interest) has divested himself of all or any portion of his interest therein to the extent necessary to effect a completed gift are applicable in determining whether a partial release of a power of appointment constitutes a taxable gift. Thus, if a general power of appointment is partially released so that thereafter the donor may still appoint among a limited class of persons not including himself the partial release does not effect a complete gift, since the possessor of the power has retained the right to designate the ultimate beneficiaries of the property over which he holds the power and since it is only the termination of such control which completes a gift.

(2) Power partially released before June 1, 1951. If a general power of appointment created after October 21, 1942, was partially released prior to June 1, 1951, so that it no longer represented a general power of appointment, as defined in paragraph (c) of § 25.2514-1, the subsequent exercise, release, or lapse of the partially released power at any time thereafter will not constitute the exercise or release of a general power of appointment. For example, assume that A created a trust in 1943 under which B possessed a general power of appointment. By an instrument executed in 1948 such general power of appointment was reduced in scope by B to an excepted power. The inter vivos exercise in 1955, or in any "calendar period" [as defined in § 25.2502-1(c)(1)] thereafter, of such excepted power is not considered an exercise or release of a general power of appointment for purposes of the gift tax.

(3) Power partially released after May 31, 1951. If a general power of appointment created after October 21, 1942, was partially released after May 31, 1951, the subsequent exercise, release or a lapse of the power at any time thereafter, will constitute the exercise or release of a general power of appointment for gift tax purposes.

(4) Release or lapse of power. A release of a power of appointment need not be formal or express in character. For example, the failure to exercise a general power of appointment created after October 21, 1942, within a specified time so that the power lapses, constitutes a release of the power. In any case where the possessor of a general power of appointment is incapable of validly exercising or releasing a power, by reason of minority, or otherwise, and the power may not be validly exercised or released on his behalf, the failure to exercise or release the power is not a lapse of the power. If a trustee has in his capacity as trustee a power which is considered as a general power of appointment, his resignation or removal as trustee will cause a lapse of his power. However, section 2514(e) provides that a lapse during any calendar year is considered as a release so as to be subject to the gift tax only to the extent that the property which could have been appointed by exercise of the lapsed

power of appointment exceeds the greater of (i) $5,000, or (ii) 5 percent of the aggregate value, at the time of the lapse, of the assets out of which, or the proceeds of which, the exercise of the lapsed power could be satisfied. For example, if an individual has a noncumulative right to withdraw $10,000 a year from the principal of a trust fund, the failure to exercise this right of withdrawal in a particular year will not constitute a gift if the fund at the end of the year equals or exceeds $200,000. If, however, at the end of the particular year the fund should be worth only $100,000, the failure to exercise the power will be considered a gift to the extent of $5,000, the excess of $10,000 over 5 percent of a fund of $100,000. Where the failure to exercise a power, such as a right of withdrawal, occurs in more than a single year, the value of the taxable transfer will be determined separately for each year.

(5) Disclaimer of power created after December 31, 1976. A disclaimer or renunciation of a general power of appointment created in a transfer made after December 31, 1976, is not considered a release of the power for gift tax purposes if the disclaimer or renunciation is a qualified disclaimer as described in section 2518 and the corresponding regulations. For rules relating to when a transfer creating the power occurs, see § 25.2518-2(c)(3). If the disclaimer or renunciation is not a qualified disclaimer, it is considered a release of the power.

(6) Disclaimer of power created before January 1, 1977. A disclaimer or renunciation of a general power of appointment created in a taxable transfer before January 1, 1977, in the person disclaiming is not considered a release of the power. The disclaimer or renunciation must be unequivocal and effective under local law. A disclaimer is a complete and unqualified refusal to accept the rights to which one is entitled. There can be no disclaimer or renunciation of a power after its acceptance. In the absence of facts to the contrary, the failure to renounce or disclaim within a reasonable time after learning of the existence of a power shall be presumed to constitute an acceptance of the power. In any case where a power is purported to be disclaimed or renounced as to only a portion of the property subject to the power, the determination as to whether there has been a complete and unqualified refusal to accept the rights to which one is entitled will depend on all the facts and circumstances of the particular case, taking into account the recognition and effectiveness of such a disclaimer under local law. Such rights refer to the incidents of the power and not to other interests of the possessor of the power in the property. If effective under local law, the power may be disclaimed or renounced without disclaiming or renouncing such other interests.

(7) The first and second sentences of paragraph (c)(5) of this section are applicable for transfers creating the power to be disclaimed made on or after December 31, 1997.

(d) Creation of another power in certain cases. Paragraph (d) of section 2514 provides that there is a transfer for purposes of the gift tax of the value of property (or of property rights or interests) with respect to which a power of appointment, which is not a general power of appointment, created after October 21, 1942, is exercised by creating another power of appointment which, under the terms of the instruments creating and exercising the first power and under applicable local law, can be validly exercised so as to (1) postpone the vesting of any estate or interest in the property for a period ascertainable without regard to the date of the creation of the first power, or (2) (if the applicable rule against perpetuities is stated in terms of suspension of ownership or of the power of alienation, rather than of vesting) suspend the absolute ownership or the power of alienation of the property for a period ascertainable without regard to the date of the creation of the first power. For the purpose of section 2514(d), the value of the property subject to the second power of appointment is considered to be its value unreduced by any precedent or subsequent interest which is not subject to the second power. Thus, if a donor has a power to appoint $100,000 among a group consisting of his children or grandchildren and during his lifetime exercises the power by making an outright appointment of $75,000 and by giving one appointee a power to appoint $25,000, no more than $25,000 will be considered a gift under section 2514(d). If, however, the donor appoints the income from the entire fund to a beneficiary for life with power in the beneficiary to appoint the remainder, the entire $100,000 will be considered a gift under section 2514(d), if the exercise of the second power can validly postpone the vesting of any estate or interest in the property or can suspend the absolute ownership or power of alienation of the property for a period ascertainable without regard to the date of the creation of the first power.

(e) Examples. The application of this section may be further illustrated by the following examples in each of which it is assumed, unless otherwise stated, that S has transferred property in trust after October 21, 1942, with the remainder payable to R at L's death, and that neither L nor R has any interest in or power over the enjoyment of the trust property except as is indicated separately in each example:

Example (1). The income is payable to L for life. L has the power to cause the income to be paid to R. The exercise of the right constitutes the making of a transfer of property under section 2511. L's power does not constitute a power of appointment since it is only a power to dispose of his income interest, a right otherwise possessed by him.

Example (2). The income is to be accumulated during L's life. L has the power to have the income distributed to himself. If L's power is limited by an ascertainable standard (relating to health etc.) as defined in paragraph (c)(2) of § 25.2514-1, the lapse of such power will not constitute a transfer of property for gift tax purposes. If L's power is not so limited, its lapse or release during L's lifetime may constitute a transfer of property for gift tax purposes. See especially paragraph (c)(4) of § 25.2514-3.

Example (3). The income is to be paid to L for life. L has a power, exercisable at any time, to cause the corpus to be distributed to himself. L has a general power of appointment over the remainder interest, the release of which constitutes a transfer for gift tax purposes of the remainder interest. If in this example L had a power to cause the corpus to be distributed only to X, L would have a power of appointment which is not a general power of appointment, the exercise or release of which would not constitute a transfer of property for purposes of the gift tax. Although the exercise or release of the nongeneral power is not taxable under this section, see § 25.2514-1(b)(2) for the gift tax consequences of the transfer of the life income interest.

Example (4). The income is payable to L for life. R has the right to cause the corpus to be distributed to L at any time. R's power is not a power of appointment, but merely a right to dispose of his remainder interest, a right already possessed by him. In such a case, the exercise of the right constitutes the making of a transfer of property under section 2511 of the value, if any, of his remainder interest. See paragraph (e) of § 25.2511-1.

Example (5). The income is to be paid to L. R has the right to appoint the corpus to himself at any time. R's general power of appointment over the corpus includes a general power to dispose of L's income interest therein. The lapse or release of R's general power over the income interest during his life may constitute the making of a transfer of property. See especially paragraph (c)(4) of § 25.2514-3.

T.D. 6334, 11/14/58, amend T.D. 7238, 12/28/72, T.D. 7776, 5/20/81, T.D. 7910, 9/6/83, T.D. 8095, 8/6/86, T.D. 8744, 12/30/97.

§ 25.2515-1 Tenancies by the entirety; in general.

(a) Scope. *(1) In general.* This section and §§ 25.2515-2 through 25.2515-4 do not apply to the creation of a tenancy by the entirety after December 31, 1981, and do not reflect changes made to the Internal Revenue Code by sections 702(k)(1)(A) of the Revenue Act of 1978, or section 2002(c)(2) of the Tax Reform Act of 1976.

(2) Special rule in the case of tenancies created after July 13, 1988, if the donee spouse is not a United States citizen. Under section 2523(i)(3), applicable (subject to the special treaty rule contained in Public Law 101-239, section 7815(d)(14)) in the case of tenancies by the entirety and joint tenancies created between spouses after July 13, 1988, if the donee spouse is not a citizen of the United States, the principles contained in section 2515 and §§ 25.2515-1 through 25.2515-4 apply in determining the gift tax consequences with respect to the creation and termination of the tenancy, except that the election provided in section 2515(a) (prior to repeal by the Economic Recovery Tax Act of 1981) and § 25.2515-2 (relating to the donor's election to treat the creation of the tenancy as a transfer for gift tax purposes) does not apply.

(3) Nature of. An estate by the entirety in real property is essentially a joint tenancy between husband and wife with the right of survivorship. As used in this section and §§ 25.2515-2 through 25.2515-4, the term "tenancy by the entirety" includes a joint tenancy between husband and wife in real property with right of survivorship, or a tenancy which accords to the spouses rights equivalent thereto regardless of the term by which such a tenancy is described in local property law.

(b) Gift upon creation of tenancy by the entirety; in general. During calendar years prior to 1955 the contribution made by a husband or wife in the creation of a tenancy by the entirety constituted a gift to the extent that the consideration furnished by either spouse exceeded the value of the rights retained by that spouse. The contribution made by either or both spouses in the creation of such a tenancy during the calendar year 1955, any calendar year beginning before January 1, 1971, or any calendar quarter beginning after December 31, 1970, is not deemed a gift by either spouse, regardless of the proportion of the total consideration furnished by either spouse, unless the donor spouse elects (see § 25.2515-2) under section 2515(c) to treat such transaction as a gift in the calendar quarter or calendar year in which the transaction is effected. See § 25.2502-1(c)(1) for the definition of calendar quarter. However, there is a gift upon the termination of such a tenancy, other than by the death of a spouse, if the proceeds received by one spouse on termination of the tenancy are larger than the proceeds allocable to the consideration furnished by that spouse to the tenancy. The creation of a tenancy by the entirety takes place if (1) a husband or his wife purchases property and causes the title thereto to be conveyed to themselves as tenants by the entirety, (2) both join in such a purchase, or (3) either or both cause to be created such a tenancy in property already owned by either or both of them. The rule prescribed herein with respect to the creation of a tenancy by the entirety applies also to contributions made in the making of additions to the value of such a tenancy (in the form of improvements, reductions in the indebtedness, or otherwise), regardless of the proportion of the consideration furnished by each spouse. See § 25.2516-1 for transfers made pursuant to a property settlement agreement incident to divorce.

(c) Consideration. *(1) In general.* (i) The consideration furnished by a person in the creation of a tenancy by the entirety or the making of additions to the value thereof is the amount contributed by him in connection therewith. The contribution may be made by either spouse or by a third party. It may be furnished in the form of money, other property, or an interest in property. If it is furnished in the form of other property or an interest in property, the amount of the contribution is the fair market value of the property or interest at the time it was transferred to the tenancy or was exchanged for the property which became the subject of the tenancy. For example, if a decedent devised real property to the spouses as tenants by the entirety and the fair market value of the property was $30,000 at the time of the decedent's death, the amount of the decedent's contribution to the creation of the tenancy was $30,000. As another example, assume that in 1950 the husband purchased real property for $25,000, taking it in his own name as sole owner, and that in 1956 when the property had a fair market value of $40,000 he caused it to be transferred to himself and his wife as tenants by the entirety. Here, the amount of the husband's contribution to the creation of the tenancy was $40,000 (the fair market value of the property at the time it was transferred to the tenancy). Similarly, assume that in 1950 the husband purchased, as sole owner, corporate shares for $25,000 and in 1956, when the shares had a fair market value of $35,000, he exchanged them for real property which was transferred to the husband and his wife as tenants by the entirety. The amount of the husband's contribution to the creation of the tenancy was $35,000 (the fair market value of the shares at the time he exchanged them for the real property which became the subject of the tenancy).

(ii) Whether consideration derived from third-party sources is deemed to have been furnished by a third party or to have been furnished by the spouses will depend upon the terms under which the transfer is made. If a decedent devises real property to the spouses as tenants by the entirety, the decedent, and not the spouses, is the person who furnished the consideration for the creation of the tenancy. Likewise, if a decedent in his will directs his executor to discharge an indebtedness of the tenancy, the decedent, and not the spouses, is the person who furnished the consideration for the addition to the value of the tenancy. However, if the decedent bequeathed a general legacy to the husband and the wife and they used the legacy to discharge an indebtedness of the tenancy, the spouses, and not the decedent, are the persons who furnished the consideration for the addition to the value of the tenancy. The principles set forth in this subdivision with respect to transfers by decedents apply equally well to inter vivos transfers by third parties.

(iii) Where a tenancy is terminated in part (e.g., where a portion of the property subject to the tenancy is sold to a third party, or where the original property is disposed of and in its place there is substituted other property of lesser value acquired through reinvestment under circumstances which satisfy the requirements of paragraph (d)(2)(ii) of this section), the proportionate contribution of each person to the remaining tenancy is in general the same as his proportionate contribution to the original tenancy, and the character of his contribution remains the same. These proportions are applied to the cost of the remaining or substituted property. Thus, if the total contribution to the cost of the property was $20,000 and a fourth of the property was sold, the contribution to the remaining portion of the tenancy is normally $15,000. However, if it is shown that at the time of the contribution more or less than one-fourth thereof was attributable to the portion sold, the contribution is divided between the portion sold and the portion retained in the proper proportion. If the portion sold was acquired as a separate tract, it is treated as a separate tenancy. As another example of the application of this subdivision, assume that in 1950 X (a third party) gave to H and W (H's wife), as tenants by the entirety, real property then having a value of $15,000. In 1955, H spent $5,000 thereon in improvements and under section 2515(e) elected to treat his contribution as a gift. In 1956 W spent $10,000 in improving the property but did not elect to treat her contribution as a gift. Between 1957 and 1960 the property appreciated in value by $30,000. In 1960, the property was sold for $60,000, and $45,000 of the proceeds if the sale were, under circumstances that satisfy the requirements of paragraph (d)(2)(ii) of this section, reinvested in other real property. Since X contributed one-half of the total consideration for the original property and the additions to its value he is considered as having furnished $22,500 (one half of $45,000) toward the creation of the remaining portion of the tenancy and the making of additions to the value thereof. Similarly, H is considered as having furnished $7,500 (one-sixth of $45,000) which was treated as a gift in the year furnished, and W is considered as having furnished $15,000 (one-third of $45,000) which was not treated as a gift in the year furnished.

(2) Proportion of consideration attributable to appreciation. Any general appreciation (appreciation due to fluctuations in market value) in the value of the property occurring between two successive contribution dates which can readily be measured and which can be determined with reasonable certainty to be allocable to any particular contribution or contributions previously furnished is to be treated, for the purpose of the computation in §§ 25.2515-3 and 25.2515-4, as though it were additional consideration furnished by the person who furnished the prior consideration. Any general depreciation in value is treated in a comparable manner. For the purpose of the first sentence of this subparagraph, successive contribution dates are the two consecutive dates on which any contributions to the tenancy are made, not necessarily by the same party. Further, appreciation allocable to the prior consideration falls in the same class as the prior consideration to which it relates. The application of this subparagraph may be illustrated by the following examples:

Example (1). In 1940, H purchased real property for $15,000 which he caused to be transferred to himself and W (his wife) as tenants by the entirety. In 1956 when the fair market value of the property was $30,000, W made $5,000 improvements to the property. In 1957 the property was sold for $35,000. The general appreciation of $15,000 which occurred between the date of purchase and the date of W's improvements to the property constitutes an additional contribution by H, having the same characteristics as his original contribution of $15,000.

Example (2). In 1955 real property was purchased by H and W and conveyed to them as tenants by the entirety. The purchase price of the property was $15,000 of which H contributed $10,000 and W, $5,000. In 1960 when the fair market value of the property is $21,000, W makes improvements thereto of $5,000. The property then is sold for $26,000. The appreciation in value of $6,000 results in an additional contribution of $4,000 (10,000/15,000 × $6,000) by H, and an additional contribution by W of $2,000 (5,000/15,000 × $6,000). H's total contribution to the tenancy is $14,000 ($10,000 + $4,000) and W's total contribution is $12,000 ($5,000 + $2,000 + $5,000).

Example (3). In 1956 real property was purchased by H and W and conveyed to them as tenants by the entirety. The purchase price of the property was $15,000, on which a down payment of $3,000 was made. The remaining $12,000 was to be paid in monthly installments over a period of 15 years. H furnished $2,000 of the down payment and W, $1,000. H paid all the monthly installments. During the period 1956 to 1971 the property gradually appreciates in value to $24,000. Here, the appreciation is so gradual and the contributions so numerous that the amount allocable to any particular contribution cannot be ascertained with any reasonable certainty. Accordingly, in such a case the appreciation in value may be disregarded in determining the amount of consideration furnished in making the computations provided for in §§ 25.2515-3 and 25.2515-4.

(d) Gift upon termination of tenancy by the entirety. *(1) In general.* Upon the termination of the tenancy, whether created before, during, or subsequent to the calendar year 1955, a gift may result, depending upon the disposition made of the proceeds of the termination (whether the proceeds be in the form of cash, property, or interests in property). A gift may result notwithstanding the fact that the contribution of either spouse to the tenancy was treated as a gift. See § 25.2515-3 for the method of determining the amount of any gift that may result from the termination of the tenancy in those cases in which no portion of the consideration contributed was treated as a gift by the spouses in the calendar quarter or calendar year in which it was furnished. See § 25.2514-4 for the method of determining the amount of any gift that may result from the termination of the tenancy in those cases in which all or a portion of the consideration contributed was treated as constituting a gift by the spouses in the calendar quarter or calendar year in which it was furnished. See § 25.2515-2 for the procedure to be followed by a donor who elects under section 2515(c) to treat the creation of a tenancy by the entirety (or the making of additions to its value) as a transfer subject to the gift tax in the calendar quarter (calendar year with respect to such transfers made before January 1, 1971) in which the transfer is made, and for the method of determining the amount of the gift. See § 25.2502-1(c)(1) for the definition of calendar quarter.

(2) Termination. (i) In general. Except as indicated in subdivision (ii) of this subparagraph, a termination of a tenancy is effected when all or a portion of the property so held by the spouses is sold, exchanged, or otherwise disposed of, by gift or in any other manner, or when the spouses through any form of conveyance or agreement become tenants in common of the property or otherwise alter the nature of their respective interests in the property formerly held by them as tenants by the entirety. In general, any increase in the indebtedness on a tenancy constitutes a termination of the tenancy to the extent of the increase in the indebtedness. However, such an increase will not constitute a termination of the tenancy to the extent that the increase is offset by additions to the tenancy within a reasonable time after such increase. Such additions (to the extent of the increase in the indebted-

ness) shall not be treated by the spouses as contributions within the meaning of paragraph (c) of this section.

(ii) Exchange or reinvestment. A termination is not considered as effected to the extent that the property subject to the tenancy is exchanged for other real property, the title to which is held by the spouses in an identical tenancy. For this purpose, a tenancy is considered identical if the proportionate values of the spouses' respective rights (other than any change in the proportionate values resulting solely from the passing of time) are identical to those held in the property which was sold. In addition the sale, exchange (other than an exchange described above), or other disposition of property held as tenants by the entirety is not considered as a termination if all three of the following conditions are satisfied:

(a) There is no division of the proceeds of the sale, exchange or other disposition of the property held as tenants by the entirety;

(b) On or before the due date for the filing of a gift tax return for the calendar quarter or calendar year (see § 25.6075-1 for the time for filing gift tax returns) in which the property held as tenants by the entirety was sold, exchanged, or otherwise disposed of, the spouses enter into a binding contract for the purchase of other real property; and

(c) After the sale, exchange, or other disposition of the former property and within a reasonable time after the date of the contract referred to in (b) of this subdivision, such other real property actually is acquired by the spouses and held by them in an identical tenancy.

To the extent that all three of the conditions set forth in this subdivision are not met (whether by reason of the death of one of the spouses or for any other reason), the provisions of the preceding sentence shall not apply, and the sale, exchange or other disposition of the property will constitute a termination of the tenancy. As used in subdivision (c) the expression "a reasonable time" means the time which, under the particular facts in each case, is needed for those matters which are incident to the acquisition of the other property (i.e., perfecting of title, arranging for financing, construction, etc.). The fact that proceeds of a sale are deposited in the name of one tenant or of both tenants separately or jointly as a convenience does not constitute a division within the meaning of subdivision (a) if the other requirements of this subdivision are met. The proceeds of a sale, exchange, or other disposition of property held as tenants by the entirety will be deemed to have been used for the purchase of other real property if applied to the purchase or construction of improvements which themselves constitute real property and which are additions to other real property held by the spouses in a tenancy identical to that in which they held the property which was sold, exchanged, or otherwise disposed of.

(3) Proceeds of termination. (i) The proceeds of termination may be received by a spouse in the form of money, property, or an interest in property. Where the proceeds are received in the form of property (other than money) or an interest in property, the value of the proceeds received by that spouse is the fair market value, on the date of termination of the tenancy by the entirety, of the property or interest received. Thus, if a tenancy by the entirety is terminated so that thereafter each spouse owns an undivided half interest in the property as tenant in common, the value of the proceeds of termination received by each spouse is one-half the value of the property at the time of the termination of the tenancy by the entirety. If under local law one spouse, without the consent of the other, can bring about a severance of his or her interest in a tenancy by the entirety and does so by making a gift of his or her interest to a third party, that spouse is considered as having received proceeds of termination in the amount of the fair market value, at the time of the termination, of his severable interest determined in accordance with the rules prescribed in § 25.2512-5. He has, in addition, made a gift to the third party of the fair market value of the interest conveyed to the third party. In such a case, the other spouse also is considered as having received as proceeds of termination the fair market value, at the time of termination, of the interest which she thereafter holds in the property as tenant in common with the third party. However, since section 2515(b) contemplates that the spouses may divide the proceeds of termination in some proportion other than that represented by the values of their respective legal interests in the property, if both spouses join together in making a gift to a third party of property held by them as tenants by the entirety, the value of the proceeds of termination which will be treated as received by each is the amount which each reports (on his or her gift tax return filed for the calendar quarter or calendar year in which the termination occurs) as the value of his or her gift to the third party. This amount is the amount which each reports without regard to whether the spouses elect under section 2513 to treat the gifts as made one-half by each. For example, assume that H and W (his wife) hold real property as tenants by the entirety; that in the first calendar quarter of 1972, when the property has a fair market value of $60,000, they give it to their son; and that on their gift tax returns for such calendar quarter. H reports himself as having made a gift to the son of $36,000 and W reports herself as having made a gift to the son of $24,000. Under these circumstances, H is considered as having received proceeds of termination valued at $36,000, and W is considered as having received proceeds of termination valued at $24,000.

(ii) Except as provided otherwise in subparagraph (2)(ii) of this paragraph (under which certain tenancies by the entirety are considered not to be terminated), where the proceeds of a sale, exchange, or other disposition of the property are not actually divided between the spouses but are held (whether in a bank account or otherwise) in their joint names or in the name of one spouse as custodian or trustee for their joint interests, each spouse is presumed, in the absence of a showing to the contrary, to have received, as of the date of termination proceeds of termination equal in value to the value of his or her enforceable property rights in respect of the proceeds.

T.D. 6334, 11/14/58, amend T.D. 7238, 12/28/72, T.D. 8522, 2/28/94.

§ 25.2515-2 Tenancies by the entirety; transfers treated as gifts; manner of election and valuation.

(a) The election to treat the creation of a tenancy by the entirety in real property, or additions made to its value, as constituting a gift in the calendar quarter or calendar year in which effected, shall be exercised by including the value of such gifts in the gift tax return of the donor for such calendar quarter or calendar year in which the tenancy was created, or the additions in value were made to the property. See section 6019 and the regulations thereunder. The election may be exercised only in a return filed within the time prescribed by law, or before the expiration of any extension of time granted pursuant to law for the filing of the return. See section 6075 for the time for filing the gift tax return and section 6081 for extensions of time for filing the return, together with the regulations thereunder. In order to make the election, a gift tax return must be filed for the calendar quarter or calendar year in which the tenancy was created, or additions in value thereto made, even though the value of the gift involved does not exceed the amount of the exclusion provided by section 2503(b). See § 25.2502-1(c)(1) for the definition of calendar quarter.

(b) If the donor spouse exercises the election as provided in paragraph (a) of this section, the amount of the gift at the creation of the tenancy is the amount of his contribution to the tenancy less the value of his retained interest in it, determined as follows:

(1) If under the law of the jurisdiction governing the rights of the spouses, either spouse, acting alone, can bring about a severance of his or her interest in the property, the value of the donor's retained interest is one-half the value of the property.

(2) If, under the law of the jurisdiction governing the rights of the spouses each is entitled to share in the income or other enjoyment of the property but neither, acting alone, may defeat the right of the survivor of them to the whole of the property, the amount of retained interest of the donor is determined by use of the appropriate actuarial factors for the spouses at their respective attained ages at the time the transaction is effected.

(c) Factors representing the respective interests of the spouses, under a tenancy by the entirety, at their attained ages at the time of the transaction may be readily computed based on the method described in § 25.2512-5. State law may provide that the husband only is entitled to all of the income or other enjoyment of the real property held as tenants by the entirety, and the wife's interest consists only of the right of survivorship with no right of severance. In such a case, a special factor may be needed to determine the value of the interests of the respective spouses. See § 25.2512-5(d)(4) for the procedure for obtaining special factors from the Internal Revenue Service in appropriate cases.

(d) The application of this paragraph may be illustrated by the following example:

Example. A husband with his own funds acquires real property valued at $10,000 and has it conveyed to himself and his wife as tenants by the entirety. Under the law of the jurisdiction governing the rights of the parties, each spouse is entitled to share in the income from the property but neither spouse acting alone could bring about a severance of his or her interest. The husband elects to treat the transfer as a gift in the year in which effected. At the time of transfer, the ages of the husband and wife are 45 and 40, respectively, on their birthdays nearest to the date of transfer. The value of the gift to the wife is $5,502.90, computed as follows:

Value of property transferred	$10,000.00
Less $10,000 × 0.44971 (factor for value of donor's retained rights)	4,497.10
Value of gift	$ 5,502.90

T.D. 6334, 11/14/58, amend T.D. 7150, 12/1/71, T.D. 7238, 12/28/72, T.D. 8540, 6/9/94.

§ 25.2515-3 Termination of tenancy by the entirety; cases in which entire value of gift is determined under section 2515(b).

Caution: The Treasury has not yet amended Reg § 25.2515-3 to reflect changes made by P.L. 97-34.

(a) In any case in which—

(1) The creation of a tenancy by the entirety (including additions in value thereto) was not treated as a gift, and

(2) The entire consideration for the creation of the tenancy, and any additions in value thereto, was furnished solely by the spouses (see paragraph (c)(1)(ii) of § 25.2515-1),

the termination of the tenancy (other than by the death of a spouse) always results in the making of a gift by a spouse who receives a smaller share of the proceeds of the termination (whether received in cash, property or interests in property) than the share of the proceeds attributable to the total consideration furnished by him. See paragraph (c) of § 25.2515-1 for a discussion of what constitutes consideration and the value thereof. Thus, a gift is effected at the time of termination of the tenancy by the spouse receiving less than one-half of the proceeds of termination if such spouse (regardless of age) furnished one-half or more of the total consideration for the purchase and improvements, if any, of the property held in the tenancy. Also, if one spouse furnished the entire consideration, a gift is made by such spouse to the extent that the other spouse receives any portion of the proceeds of termination. See § 25.2515-4 for determination of the amount of the gift, if any, in cases in which the creation of the tenancy was treated as a gift or a portion of the consideration was furnished by a third person. See paragraph (d)(2) of § 25.2515-1 as to the acts which effect a termination of the tenancy.

(b) In computing the value of the gift under the circumstances described in paragraph (a) of this section, it is first necessary to determine the spouse's share of the proceeds attributable to the consideration furnished by him. This share is computed by multiplying the total value of the proceeds of the termination by a fraction, the numerator of which is the total consideration furnished by the donor spouse and the denominator of which is the total consideration furnished by both spouses. From this amount there is subtracted the value of the proceeds of termination received by the donor spouse. The amount remaining is the value of the gift. In arriving at the "total consideration furnished by the donor spouse" and the "total consideration furnished by both spouses", for purposes of the computation provided for in this paragraph, the consideration furnished (see paragraph (c) of § 25.2515-1) is not reduced by any amounts which otherwise would have been excludable under section 2503(b) in determining the amounts of taxable gifts for calendar quarters or calendar years in which the consideration was furnished. (See § 25.2502-1(c)(1) for the definition of calendar quarter.) As an example assume that in 1955, real property was purchased for $30,000, the husband and wife each contributing $12,000 and the remaining $6,000 being obtained through a mortgage on the property. In each of the years 1956 and 1957, the husband paid $3,000 on the principal of the indebtedness, but did not disclose the value of these transfers on his gift tax returns for those years. The total consideration furnished by the husband is $18,000, the total consideration furnished by the wife is $12,000, and the total consideration furnished by both spouses is $30,000.

(c) The application of this section may be illustrated by the following examples:

Example (1). In 1956 the husband furnished $30,000 and his wife furnished $10,000 of the consideration for the purchase and subsequent improvement of real property held by them as tenants by the entirety. The husband did not elect to treat the consideration furnished as a gift. The property later is sold for $60,000, the husband receiving $35,000 and his wife receiving $25,000 of the proceeds of the termination. The termination of the tenancy results in a gift of $10,000 by the husband to his wife, computed as follows:

$30,000 (consideration furnished by husband before sale)
× $60,000 (proceeds of termination) = $45,000
$40,000 (total consideration furnished by both spouses)
× $60,000 (proceeds of termination) = $45,000

$45,000 − $35,000 (proceeds received by husband) = $10,000 gift by husband to wife.

Example (2). In 1950 the husband purchased shares of X Company for $10,000. In 1955 when those shares had a fair market value of $30,000, he and his wife purchased real property from A and had it conveyed to them as tenants by the entirety. In payment for the real property, the husband transferred his shares of X Company to A and the wife paid A the sum of $10,000. They later sold the real property for $60,000, divided $24,000 (each taking $12,000) and reinvested the remaining $36,000 in other real property under circumstances that satisfied the conditions set forth in paragraph (d)(2)(ii) of § 25.2515-1. The tenancy was terminated only with respect to the $24,000 divided between them. This termination of the tenancy resulted in a gift of $6,000 by the husband to the wife, computed as follows:

$30,000 (consideration furnished by husband before sale) / $40,000 (total consideration furnished by both spouses) × $24,000 (proceeds of termination) = $18,000

$18,000 − $12,000 (proceeds received by husband) = $6,000 gift by husband to wife.

Since the tenancy was terminated only in part, with respect to the remaining portion of the tenancy each spouse is considered as having furnished that proportion of the total consideration for the remaining portion of the tenancy as the consideration furnished by him before the sale bears to the total consideration furnished by both spouses before the sale. See paragraph (c) of § 25.2515-1. The consideration furnished by the husband for the reduced tenancy is $27,000, computed as follows:

$30,000 (consideration furnished by husband before sale) / $40,000 (total consideration furnished by both spouses before sale) × $36,000 (consideration for reduced tenancy) = $27,000

The consideration furnished by the wife is $9,000, computed in a similar manner.

T.D. 6334, 11/14/58, amend T.D. 7238, 12/28/72.

§ 25.2515-4 Termination of tenancy by entirety; cases in which none, or a portion only, of value of gift is determined under section 2516(b).

Caution: The Treasury has not yet amended Reg § 25.2515-4 to reflect changes made by P.L. 97-34.

(a) In general. The rules provided in section 2515(b) (see § 25.2515-3) are not applied in determining whether a gift has been made at the termination of a tenancy to the extent that the consideration furnished for the creation of the tenancy was treated as a gift or if the consideration for the creation of the tenancy was furnished by a third party. Consideration furnished for the creation of the tenancy was treated as a gift if it was furnished either *(1)* during calendar years prior to 1955, or *(2)* during the calendar year 1955 and subsequent years and the donor spouse exercised the election to treat the furnishing of consideration as a gift. (For the definition of calendar quarter see § 25.2502-1(c)(1).) See paragraph (b) of this section for the manner of computing the value of gifts resulting from the termination of the tenancy under these circumstances. See paragraph (c) of this section for the rules to be applied where part of the total consideration for the creation of the tenancy and additions to the value thereof was not treated as a gift and part either was treated as a gift or was furnished by a third party.

(b) Value of gift when entire consideration is of the type described in paragraph (a) of this section. If the entire consideration for the creation of a tenancy by the entirety was treated as a gift or contributed by a third party, the determination of the amount, if any, of a gift made at the termination of the tenancy will be made by the application of the general principles set forth in § 25.2511-1. Under those principles, when a spouse surrenders a property interest in a tenancy, the creation of which was treated as a gift, and in return receives an amount (whether in the form of cash, property, or an interest in property) less than the value of the property interest surrendered, that spouse is deemed to have made a gift in an amount equal to the difference between the value, at the time of termination, of the property interest surrendered by such spouse and the amount received in exchange. Thus, if the husband's interest in such a tenancy at the time of termination is worth $44,971 and the wife's interest therein at the time is worth $55,029, the property is sold for $100,000, and each spouse receives $50,000 out of the proceeds of the sale, the wife has made a gift to the husband of $5,029. The principles applied in paragraph (c) of § 25.2515-2 for the method of determining the value of the respective interests of the spouses at the time of the creation of a tenancy by the entirety are equally applicable in determining the value of each spouse's interest in the tenancy at termination, except that the actuarial factors to be applied are those for the respective spouses at the ages attained at the date of termination.

(c) Valuation of gift where both types of consideration are involved. If the consideration furnished consists in part of the type described in paragraph (a) of § 25.2515-3 (consideration furnished by the spouses after 1954, and not treated as a gift in the calendar quarter or calendar year in which it was furnished) and in part of the type described in paragraph (a) of this section (consideration furnished by the spouses and treated as a gift or furnished by a third party), the amount of the gift is determined as follows:

(1) By applying the principles set forth in paragraph (b) of § 25.2515-3 to that portion of the total proceeds of termination which the consideration described in paragraph (a) of § 25.2515-3 bears to the total consideration furnished;

(2) By applying the principles set forth in paragraph (b) of this section to the remaining portion of the total proceeds of termination; and

(3) By subtracting the proceeds of termination received by the donor from the total of the amounts which under the principles referred to in subparagraphs (1) and (2) of this paragraph are to be compared with the proceeds of termination received by a spouse in determining whether a gift was made by that spouse.

For example assume that consideration of $30,000 was furnished by the husband in 1954. Assume also that on February 1, 1955, the husband contributed $12,000 and the wife $8,000, the husband's contribution not being treated as a gift (see paragraph (b) of § 25.2515-1). Assume further that between 1957 and 1965 the property appreciated in value by $40,000 and was sold in 1965 for $90,000 (of which the husband received $40,000 and the wife $50,000). The principles set forth in paragraph (b) of § 25.2515-3 are applied to $36,000 (20,000/50,000 × $90,000) in arriving at the amount which is compared with the proceeds of termination received by a spouse. Applying the principles set forth in paragraph (b) of § 25.2515-3, this amount in the case of the husband is $21,600 (12,000/20,000 × $36,000). Similarly, the principles set forth in paragraph (b) of this section are applied to $54,000 ($90,000 − 36,000), the remaining portion of the proceeds of termination, in arriving at the amount which is compared with the proceeds of termination received by a spouse. If in this case either spouse, without the consent of the other spouse, can bring about a severance of his interest in the tenancy, the amount determined under paragraph (b) of this section in the case of the husband would be $27,000½ of $54,000). The total of the two amounts which are to be compared with the proceeds of termination received by the husband is $48,600 ($21,600 + 27,000). This sum of $48,600 is then compared with the $40,000 proceeds received by the husband, and the termination of the tenancy has resulted, for gift tax purposes, in a transfer of $8,600 by the husband to his wife in 1965. See paragraph (d) of this section for an additional example illustrating the application of this paragraph.

(d) The application of paragraph (c) of this section may further be illustrated by the following example:

Example. X died in 1948 and devised real property to Y and Z (Y's wife) as tenants by the entirety. Under the law of the jurisdiction, both spouses are entitled to share equally in the income from, or the enjoyment of, the property, but neither spouse, acting alone, may defeat the right of the survivor of them to the whole of the property. The fair market value of the property at the time of X's death was $100,000 and this amount is the consideration which X furnished toward the creation of the tenancy. In 1955, at which time the fair market value of the property was the same as at the time of X's death, improvements of $50,000 were made to the property, of which Y furnished $40,000 out of his own funds and Z furnished $10,000 out of her own funds. Y did not elect to treat his transfer to the tenancy as resulting in the making of a gift in 1955. In 1956 the property was sold for $300,000 and Y and Z each received $150,000 of the proceeds. At the time the property was sold Y and Z were 45 and 40 years of age, respectively, on their birthdays nearest the date of sale. The value of the gift made by Y to Z is $19,942, computed as follows:

Amount determined under principles set forth in § 25.2515-3:

$$\frac{\$50{,}000 \text{ (consideration not treated as gift in year furnished)}}{\$150{,}000 \text{ (total consideration furnished)}} \times \$300{,}000 \text{ (proceeds of termination)}$$

$$= \$100{,}000 \text{ (Proceeds of termination to which principles set forth in § 25.2515-3 apply)}$$

$$\frac{\$40{,}000 \text{ (consideration furnished by H and not treated as gift)}}{\$50{,}000 \text{ (total consideration not treated as gift)}} \times \$100{,}000 = \$80{,}000$$

Amount determined under principles set forth in paragraph (b) of this section:
$300,000 (total proceeds of termination) − $100,000 (proceeds to which principles set forth in § 25.2515-3 apply) = $200,000 (proceeds to which principles set forth in paragraph (b) apply) 0.44971 (factor for Y's interest) × $200,000 = $89,942

Amount of gift:	
Amount determined under § 25.2515-3	$ 80,000
Amount determined under paragraph (b)	89,942
Total	169,942
Less: Proceeds received by Y	150,000
Amount of gift made by Y to Z	19,942

T.D. 6334, 11/14/58, amend T.D. 7238, 12/28/72.

§ 25.2516-1 Certain property settlements.

Caution: The Treasury has not yet amended Reg § 25.2516-1 to reflect changes made by P.L. 98-369.

(a) Section 2516 provides that transfers of property or interests in property made under the terms of a written agreement between spouses in settlement of their marital or property rights are deemed to be for an adequate and full consideration in money or money's worth and, therefore, exempt from the gift tax (whether or not such agreement is approved by a divorce decree), if the spouses obtain a final decree of divorce from each other within two years after entering into the agreement.

(b) See paragraph (b) of § 25.6019-3 for the circumstances under which information relating to property settlements must be disclosed on the transferor's gift tax return for the "calendar period" [as defined in § 25-2502-1(c)(1)] in which the agreement becomes effective.

T.D. 6334, 11/14/58, amend T.D. 7238, 12/28/72, T.D. 7910, 9/6/83.

§ 25.2516-2 Transfers in settlement of support obligations.

Transfers to provide a reasonable allowance for the support of children (including legally adopted children) of a marriage during minority are not subject to the gift tax if made pursuant to an agreement which satisfies the requirements of section 2516.

T.D. 6334, 11/14/58.

PAR. 12.

Section 25.2517-1 is amended by adding a new subdivision (viii) to paragraph (c)(1) to read as follows:

Proposed § 25.2517-1 Employees' annuities. [*For Preamble, see ¶ 150,933*]

Caution: The Treasury has not yet amended Reg § 25.2517-1 to reflect changes made by P.L. 99-514.

* * * * *

(c) Limitation on amount excludable from gift.

(1) * * *

(viii) Any deductible employee contributions (within the meaning of section 72(o)(5)) are considered amounts contributed by the employer.

* * * * *

§ 25.2518-1 Qualified disclaimers of property; in general.

(a) Applicability. *(1) In general.* The rules described in this section, § 25.2518-2, and § 25.2518-3 apply to the qualified disclaimer of an interest in property which is created in the person disclaiming by a transfer made after December 31, 1976. In general, a qualified disclaimer is an irrevocable and unqualified refusal to accept the ownership of an interest in property. For rules relating to the determination of when a transfer creating an interest occurs, see § 25.2518-2(c)(3) and (4).

(2) Example. The provisions of paragraph (a)(1) of this section may be illustrated by the following example:

Example. W creates an irrevocable trust on December 10, 1968, and retains the right to receive the income for life. Upon the death of W, which occurs after December 31, 1976, the trust property is distributable to W's surviving issue, per stirpes. The transfer creating the remainder interest in the trust occurred in 1968. See § 25.2511-1(c)(2). Therefore, section 2518 does not apply to the disclaimer of the remainder interest because the transfer creating the interest was made prior to January 1, 1977. If, however, W had caused the gift to be incomplete by also retaining the power to designate the person or persons to receive the trust principal at death, and, as a result, no transfer (within the meaning of § 25.2511-1(c)(2)) of the remainder interest was made at the time of the creation of the trust, section 2518 would apply to any disclaimer made after W's death with respect to an interest in the trust property.

(3) Paragraph (a)(1) of this section is applicable for transfers creating the interest to be disclaimed made on or after December 31, 1997.

(b) Effect of a qualified disclaimer. If a person makes a qualified disclaimer as described in section 2518(b) and § 25.2518-2, for purposes of the Federal estate, gift, and generation-skipping transfer tax provisions, the disclaimed interest in property is treated as if it had never been transferred to the person making the qualified disclaimer. Instead, it is considered as passing directly from the transferor of the property to the person entitled to receive the property as a result of the disclaimer. Accordingly, a person making a qualified disclaimer is not treated as making a gift. Similarly, the value of a decedent's gross estate for purposes of the Federal estate tax does not include the value of property with respect to which the decedent, or the decedent's executor or administrator on behalf of the decedent, has made a qualified disclaimer. If the disclaimer is not a qualified disclaimer, for the purposes of the Federal estate, gift, and generation-skipping transfer tax provisions, the disclaimer is disregarded and the disclaimant is treated as having received the interest.

(c) Effect of local law. *(1) In general.* (i) Interests created before 1982. A disclaimer of an interest created in a taxable transfer before 1982 which otherwise meets the requirements of a qualified disclaimer under section 2518 and the corresponding regulations but which, by itself, is not effective under applicable local law to divest ownership of the disclaimed property from the disclaimant and vest it in another, is nevertheless treated as a qualified disclaimer under section 2518 if, under applicable local law, the disclaimed interest in property is transferred, as a result of attempting the disclaimer, to another person without any direction on the part of the disclaimant. An interest in property will not be considered to be transferred without any direction on the part of the disclaimant if, under applicable local law, the disclaimant has any discretion (whether or not such discretion is exercised) to determine who will receive such interest. Actions by the disclaimant which are required under local law merely to divest ownership of the property from the disclaimant and vest ownership in another person will not disqualify the disclaimer for purposes of section 2518(a). See § 25.2518-2(d)(1) for rules relating to the immediate vesting of title in the disclaimant.

(ii) Interests created after 1981. [Reserved].

(2) Creditor's claims. The fact that a disclaimer is voidable by the disclaimant's creditors has no effect on the determination of whether such disclaimer constitutes a qualified disclaimer. However, a disclaimer that is wholly void or that is voided by the disclaimant's creditors cannot be a qualified disclaimer.

(3) Examples. The provisions of paragraphs (c)(1) and (2) of this section may be illustrated by the following examples:

Example (1). F dies testate in State Y on June 17, 1978. G and H are beneficiaries under the will. The will provides that any disclaimed property is to pass to the residuary estate. H has no interest in the residuary estate. Under the applicable laws of State Y, a disclaimer must be made within 6 months of the death of the testator. Seven months after F's death, H disclaimed the real property H received under the will. The disclaimer statute of State Y has a provision stating that an untimely disclaimer will be treated as an assignment of the interest disclaimed to those persons who would have taken had the disclaimer been valid. Pursuant to this provision, the disclaimed property became part of the residuary estate. Assuming the remaining requirements of section 2518 are met, H has made a qualified disclaimer for purposes of section 2518(a).

Example (2). Assume the same facts as in example (1) except that the law of State Y does not treat an ineffective disclaimer as a transfer to alternative takers. H assigns the disclaimed interest by deed to those who would have taken had the disclaimer been valid. Under these circumstances, H has not made a qualified disclaimer for purposes of section 2518(a) because the disclaimant directed who would receive the property.

Example (3). Assume the same facts as in example (1) except that the law of State Y requires H to pay a transfer tax in order to effectuate the transfer under the ineffective disclaimer provision. H pays the transfer tax. H has made a qualified disclaimer for purposes of section 2518(a).

(d) Cross-reference. For rules relating to the effect of qualified disclaimers on the estate tax charitable and marital deductions, see §§ 20.2055-2(c) and 20.2056(d)-1 respectively. For rules relating to the effect of a qualified disclaimer of a general power of appointment, see § 20.2041-3(d).

T.D. 8095, 8/6/86, amend T.D. 8744, 12/30/97.

§ 25.2518-2 Requirements for a qualified disclaimer.

(a) In general. For the purposes of section 2518(a), a disclaimer shall be a qualified disclaimer only if it satisfies the requirements of this section. In general, to be a qualified disclaimer—

(1) The disclaimer must be irrevocable and unqualified;

(2) The disclaimer must be in writing;

(3) The writing must be delivered to the person specified in paragraph (b)(2) of this section within the time limitations specified in paragraph (c)(1) of this section;

(4) The disclaimant must not have accepted the interest disclaimed or any of its benefits; and

(5) The interest disclaimed must pass either to the spouse of the decedent or to a person other than the disclaimant without any direction on the part of the person making the disclaimer.

(b) Writing. *(1) Requirements.* A disclaimer is a qualified disclaimer only if it is in writing. The writing must identify the interest in property disclaimed and be signed either by the disclaimant or by the disclaimant's legal representative.

(2) Delivery. The writing described in paragraph (b)(1) of this section must be delivered to the transferor of the interest, the transferor's legal representative, the holder of the legal title to the property to which the interest relates, or the person in possession of such property.

(c) Time limit. *(1) In general.* A disclaimer is a qualified disclaimer only if the writing described in paragraph (b)(1) of this section is delivered to the persons described in paragraph (b)(2) of this section no later than the date which is 9 months after the later of—

(i) The date on which the transfer creating the interest in the disclaimant is made, or

(ii) The day on which the disclaimant attains age 21.

(2) A timely mailing of a disclaimer treated as a timely delivery. Although section 7502 and the regulations under that section apply only to documents to be filed with the Service, a timely mailing of a disclaimer to the person described in paragraph (b)(2) of this section is treated as a timely delivery if the mailing requirements under paragraphs (c)(1), (c)(2) and (d) of § 301.7502-1 are met. Further, if the last day of the period specified in paragraph (c)(1) of this section falls on Saturday, Sunday or a legal holiday (as defined in paragraph (b) of § 301.7503-1), then the delivery of the writing described in paragraph (b)(1) of this section shall be considered timely if delivery is made on the first succeeding day which is not Saturday, Sunday or a legal holiday. See paragraph (d)(3) of this section for rules applicable to the exception for individuals under 21 years of age.

(3) Transfer. (i) For purposes of the time limitation described in paragraph (c)(1)(i) of this section, the 9-month period for making a disclaimer generally is to be determined with reference to the transfer creating the interest in the disclaimant. With respect to inter vivos transfers, a transfer creating an interest occurs when there is a completed gift for Federal gift tax purposes regardless of whether a gift tax is imposed on the completed gift. Thus, gifts qualifying for the gift tax annual exclusion under section 2503(b) are regarded as transfers creating an interest for this purpose. With respect to transfers made by a decedent at death or transfers that become irrevocable at death, the transfer creating the interest occurs on the date of the decedent's death, even if an estate tax is not imposed on the transfer. For example, a bequest of foreign-situs property by a nonresident alien decedent is regarded as a transfer creating an interest in property even if the transfer would not be subject to estate tax. If there is a transfer creating an interest in property during the transferor's lifetime and such interest is later included in the transferor's gross estate for estate tax purposes (or would have been included if such interest were subject to estate tax), the 9-month period for making the qualified disclaimer is determined with reference to the earlier transfer creating the interest. In the case of a general power of appointment, the holder of the power has a 9-month period after the transfer creating the power in which to disclaim. If a person to whom any interest in property passes by reason of the exercise, release, or lapse of a general power desires to make a qualified disclaimer, the disclaimer must be made within a 9-month period after the exercise, release, or lapse regardless of whether the exercise, release, or lapse is subject to estate or gift tax. In the case of a nongeneral power of appointment, the holder of the power, permissible appointees, or takers in default of appointment must disclaim within a 9-month period after the original transfer that created or authorized the creation of the power. If the transfer is for the life of an income beneficiary with succeeding interests to other persons, both the life tenant and the other remaindermen, whether their interests are vested or contingent, must disclaim no later than 9 months after the original transfer creating an interest. In the case of a remainder interest in property which an executor elects to treat as qualified terminable interest property under section 2056(b)(7), the remainderman must disclaim within 9 months of the transfer creating the interest, rather than 9 months from the date such interest is subject to tax under section 2044 or 2519. A person who receives an interest in property as the result of a qualified disclaimer of the interest must disclaim the previously disclaimed interest no later than 9 months after the date of the transfer creating the interest in the preceding disclaimant. Thus, if A were to make a qualified disclaimer of a specific bequest and as a result of the qualified disclaimer the property passed as part of the residue, the beneficiary of the residue could make a qualified disclaimer no later than 9 months after the date of the testator's death. See paragraph (d)(3) of this section for the time limitation rule with reference to recipients who are under 21 years of age.

(ii) Sentences 1 through 10 and 12 of paragraph (c)(3)(i) of this section are applicable for transfers creating the interest to be disclaimed made on or after December 31, 1997.

(4) Joint property. (i) Interests in joint tenancy with right of survivorship or tenancies by the entirety. Except as provided in paragraph (c)(4)(iii) of this section (with respect to joint bank, brokerage, and other investment accounts), in the case of an interest in a joint tenancy with right of survivorship or a tenancy by the entirety, a qualified disclaimer of the interest to which the disclaimant succeeds upon creation of the tenancy must be made no later than 9 months after the creation of the tenancy regardless of whether such interest can be unilaterally severed under local law. A qualified disclaimer of the survivorship interest to which the survivor succeeds by operation of law upon the death of the first joint tenant to die must be made no later than 9 months after the death of the first joint tenant to die regardless of whether such interest can be unilaterally severed under local law and, except as provided in paragraph (c)(4)(ii) of this section (with respect to certain tenancies created on or after July 14, 1988), such interest is deemed to be a one-half interest in the property. (See, however, section 2518(b)(2)(B) for a special rule in the case of disclaimers by persons under age 21.) This is the case regardless of the portion of the property attributable to consideration furnished by the disclaimant and regardless of the portion of the property that is included in the decedent's gross estate under section 2040 and regardless of whether the interest can be unilaterally severed under local law. See paragraph (c)(5), Examples (7) and (8), of this section.

(ii) Certain tenancies in real property between spouses created on or after July 14, 1988. In the case of a joint tenancy between spouses or a tenancy by the entirety in real property created on or after July 14, 1988, to which section 2523(i)(3) applies (relating to the creation of a tenancy where the spouse of the donor is not a United States citizen), the surviving spouse may disclaim any portion of the joint interest that is includible in the decedent's gross estate under section 2040. See paragraph (c)(5), Example (9), of this section.

(iii) Special rule for joint bank, brokerage, and other investment accounts (e.g., accounts held at mutual funds) established between spouses or between persons other than husband and wife. In the case of a transfer to a joint bank, brokerage, or other investment account (e.g., an account held at a mutual fund), if a transferor may unilaterally regain the transferor's own contributions to the account without the consent of the other cotenant, such that the transfer is not a completed gift under § 25.2511-1(h)(4), the transfer creating the survivor's interest in the decedent's share of the account occurs on the death of the deceased cotenant. Accordingly, if a surviving joint tenant desires to make a qualified disclaimer with respect to funds contributed by a deceased cotenant, the disclaimer must be made within 9 months of the cotenant's death. The surviving joint tenant may not disclaim any portion of the joint account attributable to consideration furnished by that surviving joint tenant. See paragraph (c)(5), Examples (12), (13), and (14), of this section, regarding the treatment of disclaimed interests under sections 2518, 2033 and 2040.

(iv) Effective date. This paragraph (c)(4) is applicable for disclaimers made on or after December 31, 1997.

(5) Examples. The provisions of paragraphs (c)(1) through (c)(4) of this section may be illustrated by the following examples. For purposes of the following examples, assume that all beneficiaries are over 21 years of age.

Example (1). On May 13, 1978, in a transfer which constitutes a completed gift for Federal gift tax purposes, A creates a trust in which B is given a lifetime interest in the income from the trust. B is also given a nongeneral testamentary power of appointment over the corpus of the trust. The power of appointment may be exercised in favor of any of the issue of A and B. If there are no surviving issue at B's death or if the power is not exercised, the corpus is to pass to E. On May 13, 1978, A and B have two surviving children, C and D. If A, B, C or D wishes to make a qualified disclaimer, the disclaimer must be made no later than 9 months after May 13, 1978.

Example (2). Assume the same facts as in example (1) except that B is given a general power of appointment over the corpus of the trust. B exercises the general power of appointment in favor of C upon B's death on June 17, 1989. C may make a qualified disclaimer no later than 9 months after June 17, 1989. If B had died without exercising the general power of appointment, E could have made a qualified disclaimer no later than 9 months after June 17, 1989.

Example (3). F creates a trust on April 1, 1978, in which F's child G is to receive the income from the trust for life. Upon G's death, the corpus of the trust is to pass to G's child H. If either G or H wishes to make a qualified disclaimer, it must be made no later than 9 months after April 1, 1978.

Example (4). A creates a trust on February 15, 1978, in which B is named the income beneficiary for life. The trust further provides that upon B's death the proceeds of the trust are to pass to C, if then living. If C predeceases D, the proceeds shall pass to D or D's estate. To have timely disclaimers for purposes of section 2518, B, C, and D must disclaim their respective interests no later than 9 months after February 15, 1978.

Example (5). A, a resident of State Q, dies on January 10, 1979, devising certain real property to B. The disclaimer laws of State Q require that a disclaimer be made within a reasonable time after a transfer. B disclaims the entire interest in real property on November 10, 1979. Although B's disclaimer may be effective under State Q law, it is not a qualified disclaimer under section 2518 because the disclaimer was made later than 9 months after the taxable transfer to B.

Example (6). A creates a revocable trust on June 1, 1980, in which B and C are given the income interest for life. Upon the death of the last income beneficiary, the remainder interest is to pass to D. The creation of the trust is not a completed gift for Federal gift tax purposes, but each distribution of trust income to B and C is a completed gift at the date of distribution. B and C disclaim each income distribution no later than 9 months after the date of the particular distribution. In order to disclaim an income distribution in the form of a check, the recipient must return the check to the trustee uncashed along with a written disclaimer. A dies on September 1, 1982, causing the trust to become irrevocable, and the trust corpus is includible in A's gross estate for Federal estate tax purposes under section 2038. If B or C wishes to make a qualified disclaimer of his income interest, he must do so no later than 9 months after September 1, 1982. If D wishes to make a qualified disclaimer of his remainder interest, he must do so no later than 9 months after September 1, 1982.

Example (7). On February 1, 1990, A purchased real property with A's funds. Title to the property was conveyed to "A and B, as joint tenants with right of survivorship." Under applicable state law, the joint interest is unilaterally severable by either tenant. B dies on May 1, 1998, and is survived by A. On January 1, 1999, A disclaims the one-half survivorship interest in the property to which A succeeds as a result of B's death. Assuming that the other requirements of section 2518(b) are satisfied, A has made a qualified disclaimer of the one-half survivorship interest (but not the interest retained by A upon the creation of the tenancy, which may not be disclaimed by A). The result is the same whether or not A and B are married and regardless of the proportion of consideration furnished by A and B in purchasing the property.

Example (8). Assume the same facts as in Example (7) except that A and B are married and title to the property was conveyed to "A and B, as tenants by the entirety." Under applicable state law, the tenancy cannot be unilaterally severed by either tenant. Assuming that the other requirements of section 2518(b) are satisfied, A has made a qualified disclaimer of the one-half survivorship interest (but not the interest retained by A upon the creation of the tenancy, which may not be disclaimed by A). The result is the same regardless of the proportion of consideration furnished by A and B in purchasing the property.

Example (9). On March 1, 1989, H and W purchase a tract of vacant land which is conveyed to them as tenants by the entirety. The entire consideration is paid by H. W is not a United States citizen. H dies on June 1, 1998. W can disclaim the entire joint interest because this is the interest includible in H's gross estate under section 2040(a). Assuming that W's disclaimer is received by the executor of H's estate no later than 9 months after June 1, 1998, and the other requirements of section 2518(b) are satisfied, W's disclaimer of the property would be a qualified disclaimer. The result would be the same if the property was held in joint tenancy with right of survivorship that was unilaterally severable under local law.

Example (10). In 1986, spouses A and B purchased a personal residence taking title as tenants by the entirety. B dies on July 10, 1998. A wishes to disclaim the one-half undivided interest to which A would succeed by right of survivorship. If A makes the disclaimer, the property interest would pass under B's will to their child C. C, an adult, and A resided in the residence at B's death and will continue to reside there in the future. A continues to own a one-half undivided interest in the property. Assuming that the other requirements of section 2518(b) are satisfied, A may make a qualified disclaimer with respect to the one-half undivided survivorship interest in the residence if A delivers the written disclaimer to the personal representative of B's estate by April 10, 1999, since A is not deemed to have accepted the interest or any of its benefits prior to that time and A's occupancy of the residence after B's death is consistent with A's retained undivided ownership interest. The result would be the same if the property was held in joint tenancy with right of survivorship that was unilaterally severable under local law.

Example (11). H and W, husband and wife, reside in state X, a community property state. On April 1, 1978, H and W purchase real property with community funds. The property is not held by H and W as jointly owned property with rights of survivorship. H and W hold the property until January 3, 1985, when H dies. H devises his portion of the property to W. On March 15, 1985, W disclaims the portion of the property devised to her by H. Assuming all the other requirements of section 2518(b) have been met, W has made a qualified disclaimer of the interest devised to her by H. However, W could not disclaim the interest in the property that she acquired on April 1, 1978.

Example (12). On July 1, 1990, A opens a bank account that is held jointly with B, A's spouse, and transfers $50,000 of A's money to the account. A and B are United States citizens. A can regain the entire account without B's consent, such that the transfer is not a completed gift under § 25.2511-1(h)(4). A dies on August 15, 1998, and B disclaims the entire amount in the bank account on October 15, 1998. Assuming that the remaining requirements of section 2518(b) are satisfied, B made a qualified disclaimer under section 2518(a) because the disclaimer was made within 9 months after A's death at which time B had succeeded to full dominion and control over the account. Under state law, B is treated as predeceasing A with respect to the disclaimed interest. The disclaimed account balance passes through A's probate estate and is no longer joint property includible in A's gross estate under section 2040. The entire account is, instead, includible in A's gross estate under section 2033. The result would be the same if A and B were not married.

Example (13). The facts are the same as Example (12), except that B, rather than A, dies on August 15, 1998. A may not make a qualified disclaimer with respect to any of the funds in the bank account, because A furnished the funds for the entire account and A did not relinquish dominion and control over the funds.

Example (14). The facts are the same as Example (12), except that B disclaims 40 percent of the funds in the account. Since, under state law, B is treated as predeceasing A with respect to the disclaimed interest, the 40 percent portion of the account balance that was disclaimed passes as part of A's probate estate, and is no longer characterized as joint property. This 40 percent portion of the account balance is, therefore, includible in A's gross estate under section 2033. The remaining 60 percent of the account balance that was not disclaimed retains its character as joint property and, therefore, is includible in A's gross estate as provided in section 2040(b). Therefore, 30 percent ($\frac{1}{2} \times 60$ percent) of the account balance is includible in A's gross estate under section 2040(b), and a total of 70 percent of the aggregate account balance is includible in A's gross estate. If A and B were not married, then the 40 percent portion of the account subject to the disclaimer would be includible in A's gross estate as provided in section 2033 and the 60 percent portion of the account not subject to the disclaimer would be includible in A's gross estate as provided in section 2040(a), because A furnished all of the funds with respect to the account.

(d) No acceptance of benefits. *(1) Acceptance.* A qualified disclaimer cannot be made with respect to an interest in property if the disclaimant has accepted the interest or any of its benefits, expressly or impliedly, prior to making the disclaimer. Acceptance is manifested by an affirmative act which is consistent with ownership of the interest in property. Acts indicative of acceptance include using the property or the interest in property; accepting dividends, interest, or rents from the property; and directing others to act with respect to the property or interest in property. However, merely taking delivery of an instrument of title, without more, does not constitute acceptance. Moreover, a disclaimant is not considered to have accepted property merely because under applicable local law title to the property vests immediately in the disclaimant upon the death of a decedent. The acceptance of one interest in property will not, by itself, constitute an acceptance of any other separate interests created by the transferor and held by the disclaimant in the same property. In the case of residential property, held in joint tenancy by some or all of the residents, a joint tenant will not be considered to have accepted the joint interest merely because the tenant resided on the property prior to disclaiming his interest in the property. The exercise of a power of appointment to any extent by the donee of the power is an acceptance of its benefits. In addition, the acceptance of any consideration in return for making the disclaimer is an acceptance of the benefits of the entire interest disclaimed.

(2) Fiduciaries. If a beneficiary who disclaims an interest in property is also a fiduciary, actions taken by such person in the exercise of fiduciary powers to preserve or maintain the disclaimed property shall not be treated as an acceptance of such property or any of its benefits. Under this rule, for example, an executor who is also a beneficiary may direct the harvesting of a crop or the general maintenance of a home. A fiduciary, however, cannot retain a wholly discretionary power to direct the enjoyment of the disclaimed interest. For example, a fiduciary's disclaimer of a beneficial interest does not meet the requirements of a qualified disclaimer if the fiduciary exercised or retains a discretionary power to allocate enjoyment of that interest among members of a designated class. See paragraph (e) of this section for rules relating to the effect of directing the redistribution of disclaimed property.

(3) Under 21 years of age. A beneficiary who is under 21 years of age has until 9 months after his twenty-first birthday in which to make a qualified disclaimer of his interest in property. Any actions taken with regard to an interest in property by a beneficiary or a custodian prior to the beneficiary's twenty-first birthday will not be an acceptance by the beneficiary of the interest.

(4) Examples. The provisions of paragraphs (d)(1), (2) and (3) of this section may be illustrated by the following examples:

Example (1). On April 9, 1977, A established a trust for the benefit of B, then age 22. Under the terms of the trust, the current income of the trust is to be paid quarterly to B. Additionally, one half the principal is to be distributed to B when B attains the age of 30 years. The balance of the principal is to be distributed to B when B attains the age of 40 years. Pursuant to the terms of the trust, B received a distribution of income on June 30, 1977. On August 1, 1977, B disclaimed B's right to receive both the income from the trust and the principal of the trust. B's disclaimer of the income interest is not a qualified disclaimer for purposes of section 2518(a) because B accepted income prior to making the disclaimer. B's disclaimer of the principal, however, does satisfy section 2518(b)(3). See also § 25.2518-3 for rules relating to the disclaimer of less than an entire interest in property.

Example (2). B is the recipient of certain property devised to B under the will of A. The will stated that any disclaimed property was to pass to C. B and C entered into negotiations in which it was decided that B would disclaim all interest in the real property that was devised to B. In exchange, C promised to let B live in the family home for life. B's disclaimer is not a qualified disclaimer for purposes of section 2518(a) because B accepted consideration for making the disclaimer.

Example (3). A received a gift of Blackacre on December 25, 1978. A never resided on Blackacre but when property taxes on Blackacre became due on July 1, 1979, A paid them out personal funds. On August 15, 1979, A disclaimed the gift of Blackacre. Assuming all the requirements of section 2518(b) have been met, A has made a qualified disclaimer of Blackacre. Merely paying the property taxes does not constitute an acceptance of Blackacre even though A's personal funds were used to pay the taxes.

Example (4). A died on February 15, 1978. Pursuant to A's will, B received a farm in State Z. B requested the executor to sell the farm and to give the proceeds to B. The executor then sold the farm pursuant to B's request. B then disclaimed $50,000 of the proceeds from the sale of the farm. B's disclaimer is not a qualified disclaimer. By requesting the executor to sell the farm B accepted the farm even though the executor may not have been legally obligated to comply with B's request. See also § 25.2518-3 for rules relating to the disclaimer of less than an entire interest in property.

Example (5). Assume the same facts as in example (4) except that instead of requesting the executor to sell the farm, B pledged the farm as security for a short-term loan which was paid off prior to distribution of the estate. B then disclaimed his interest in the farm. B's disclaimer is not a qualified disclaimer. By pledging the farm as security for the loan, B accepted the farm.

Example (6). A delivered 1,000 shares of stock in Corporation X to B as a gift on February 1, 1980. A had the shares registered in B's name on that date. On April 1, 1980, B disclaimed the interest in the 1,000 shares. Prior to making the disclaimer, B did not pledge the shares, accept any dividends or otherwise commit any acts indicative of acceptance. Assuming the remaining requirements of section 2518 are satisfied, B's disclaimer is a qualified disclaimer.

Example (7). On January 1, 1980, A created an irrevocable trust in which B was given a testamentary general power of appointment over the trust's corpus. B executed a will on June 1, 1980, in which B provided for the exercise of the power of appointment. On September 1, 1980, B disclaimed the testamentary power of appointment. Assuming the remaining requirements of section 2518(b) are satisfied, B's disclaimer of the testamentary power of appointment is a qualified disclaimer.

Example (8). H and W reside in X, a community property state. On January 1, 1981, H and W purchase a residence with community funds. They continue to reside in the house until H dies testate on February 1, 1990. Although H could devise his portion of the residence to any person, H devised his portion of the residence to W. On September 1, 1990, W disclaims the portion of the residence devised to her pursuant to H's will but continues to live in the residence. Assuming the remaining requirements of section 2518(b) are satisfied, W's disclaimer is a qualified disclaimer under section 2518(a). W's continued occupancy of the house prior to making the disclaimer will not by itself be treated as an acceptance of the benefits of the portion of the residence devised to her by H.

Example (9). In 1979, D established a trust for the benefit of D's minor children E and F. Under the terms of the trust, the trustee is given the power to make discretionary distributions of current income and corpus to both children. The corpus of the trust is to be distributed equally between E and F when E becomes 35 years of age. Prior to attaining the age of 21 years on April 8, 1982, E receives several distributions of income from the trust. E receives no distributions of income between April 8, 1982 and August 15, 1982, which is the date on which E disclaims all interest in the income from the trust. As a result of the disclaimer the income will be distributed to F. If the remaining requirements of section 2518 are met, E's disclaimer is a qualified disclaimer under section 2518(a). To have a qualified disclaimer of the interest in corpus, E must disclaim the interest no later than 9 months after April 8, 1982, E's 21st birthday.

Example (10). Assume the same facts as in example (9) except that E accepted a distribution of income on May 13, 1982. E's disclaimer is not a qualified disclaimer under section 2518 because by accepting an income distribution after attaining the age of 21, E accepted benefits from the income interest.

Example (11). F made a gift of 10 shares of stock to G as custodian for H under the State X Uniform Gifts to Minors Act. At the time of the gift, H was 15 years old. At age 18, the local age of majority, the 10 shares were delivered to and registered in the name of H. Between the receipt of the shares and H's 21st birthday, H received dividends from the shares. Within 9 months of attaining age 21, H disclaimed the 10 shares. Assuming H did not accept any dividends from the shares after attaining age 21, the disclaimer by H is a qualified disclaimer under section 2518.

(e) Passage without direction by the disclaimant of beneficial enjoyment of disclaimed interest. *(1) In general.* A disclaimer is not a qualified disclaimer unless the disclaimed interest passes without any direction on the part of the disclaimant to a person other than the disclaimant (except as provided in paragraph (e)(2) of this section). If there is an express or implied agreement that the disclaimed interest in property is to be given or bequeathed to a person specified by the disclaimant, the disclaimant shall be treated as directing the transfer of the property interest. The requirements of a qualified disclaimer under section 2518 are not satisfied if—

(i) The disclaimant, either alone or in conjunction with another, directs the redistribution or transfer of the property or interest in property to another person (or has the power to direct the redistribution or transfer of the property or interest in property to another person unless such power is limited by an ascertainable standard); or

(ii) The disclaimed property or interest in property passes to or for the benefit of the disclaimant as a result of the disclaimer (except as provided in paragraph (e)(2) of this section).

If a power of appointment is disclaimed, the requirements of this paragraph (e)(1) are satisfied so long as there is no direction on the part of the disclaimant with respect to the transfer of the interest subject to the power or with respect to the transfer of the power to another person. A person may make a qualified disclaimer of a beneficial interest in property even if after such disclaimer the disclaimant has a fiduciary power to distribute to designated beneficiaries, but only if the power is subject to an ascertainable standard. See examples (11) and (12) of paragraph (e)(5) of this section.

(2) Disclaimer by surviving spouse. In the case of a disclaimer made by a decedent's surviving spouse with respect to property transferred by the decedent, the disclaimer satisfies the requirements of this paragraph (e) if the interest passes as a result of the disclaimer without direction on the part of the surviving spouse either to the surviving spouse or to another person. If the surviving spouse, however, retains the right to direct the beneficial enjoyment of the disclaimed property in a transfer that is not subject to Federal estate and gift tax (whether as trustee or otherwise), such spouse will be treated as directing the beneficial enjoyment of the disclaimed property, unless such power is limited by an ascertainable standard. See examples (4), (5), and (6) in paragraph (e)(5) of this section.

(3) Partial failure of disclaimer. If a disclaimer made by a person other than the surviving spouse is not effective to pass completely an interest in property to a person other than the disclaimant because—

(i) The disclaimant also has a right to receive such property as an heir at law, residuary beneficiary, or by any other means; and

(ii) The disclaimant does not effectively disclaim these rights, the disclaimer is not a qualified disclaimer with respect to the portion of the disclaimed property which the disclaimant has a right to receive. If the portion of the disclaimed interest in property which the disclaimant has a right to receive is not severable property or an undivided portion of the property, then the disclaimer is not a qualified disclaimer with respect to any portion of the property. Thus, for example, if a disclaimant who is not a surviving spouse receives a specific bequest of a fee simple interest in property and as a result of the disclaimer of the entire interest, the property passes to a trust in which the disclaimant has a remainder interest, then the disclaimer will not be a qualified disclaimer unless the remainder interest in the property is also disclaimed. See § 25.2518-3(a)(1)(ii) for the definition of severable property.

(4) Effect of precatory language. Precatory language in a disclaimer naming takers of disclaimed property will not be considered as directing the redistribution or transfer of the property or interest in property to such persons if the applicable State law gives the language no legal effect.

(5) Examples. The provisions of this paragraph (e) may be illustrated by the following examples:

Example (1). A, a resident of State X, died on July 30, 1978. Pursuant to A's will, B, A's son and heir at law, received the family home. In addition, B and C each received 50 percent of A's residuary estate. B disclaimed the home. A's will made no provision for the distribution of property in the case of a beneficiary's disclaimer. Therefore, pursuant to the disclaimer laws of State X, the disclaimed property became part of the residuary estate. Because B's 50 percent share of the residuary estate will be increased by 50 percent of the value of the family home, the disclaimed property will not pass solely to another person. Consequently, B's disclaimer of the family home is a qualified disclaimer only with respect to the 50 percent portion that passes solely to C. Had B also disclaimed B's 50 percent interest in the residuary estate, the disclaimer would have been a qualified disclaimer under section 2518 of the entire interest in the home (assuming the remaining requirements of a qualified disclaimer were satisfied). Similarly, if under the laws of State X, the disclaimer has the effect of divesting B of all interest in the home, both as devisee and as a beneficiary of the residuary estate, including any property resulting from its sale, the disclaimer would be a qualified disclaimer of B's entire interest in the home.

Example (2). D, a resident of State Y, died testate on June 30, 1978. E, an heir at law of D, received specific bequests of certain severable personal property from D. E disclaimed the property transferred by D under the will. The will made no provision for the distribution of property in the case of a beneficiary's disclaimer. The disclaimer laws of State Y provide that such property shall pass to the decedent's heirs at law in the same manner as if the disclaiming beneficiary had died immediately before the testator's death. Because State Y's law treats E as predeceasing D, the property disclaimed by E does not pass to E as an heir at law or otherwise. Consequently, if the remaining requirements of section 2518(b) are satisfied, E's disclaimer is a qualified disclaimer under section 2518(a).

Example (3). Assume the same facts as in example (2) except that State Y has no provision treating the disclaimant as predeceasing the testator. E's disclaimer satisfies section 2518(b)(4) only to the extent that E does not have a right to receive the property as an heir at law. Had E disclaimed both the share E received under D's will and E's intestate share, the requirement of section 2518(b)(4) would have been satisfied.

Example (4). B died testate on February 13, 1980. B's will established both a marital trust and a nonmarital trust. The decedent's surviving spouse, A, is an income beneficiary of the marital trust and has a testamentary general power of appointment over its assets. A is also an income beneficiary of the nonmarital trust, but has no power to appoint or invade the corpus. The provisions of the will specify that any portion of the marital trust disclaimed is to be added to the nonmarital trust. A disclaimed 30 percent of the marital trust. (See § 25.2518-3(b) for rules relating to the disclaimer of an undivided portion of an interest in property.) Pursuant to the will, this portion of the marital trust property was transferred to the nonmarital trust without any direction on the part of A. This disclaimer by A satisfies section 2518(b)(4).

Example (5). Assume the same facts as in example (4) except that A, the surviving spouse, has both an income interest in the nonmarital trust and a testamentary nongeneral power to appoint among designated beneficiaries. This power is not limited by an ascertainable standard. The requirements of section 2518(b)(4) are not satisfied unless A also disclaims the nongeneral power to appoint the portion of the trust corpus that is attributable to the property that passed to the nonmarital trust as a result of A's disclaimer. Assuming that the fair market value of the disclaimed property on the date of the disclaimer is $250,000 and that the fair market value of the nonmarital trust (including the disclaimed property) immediately after the disclaimer is $750,000, A must disclaim the power to appoint one-third of the nonmarital trust's corpus. The result is the same regardless of whether the nongeneral power is testamentary or inter vivos.

Example (6). Assume the same facts as in example (4) except that A has both an income interest in the nonmarital trust and a power to invade corpus if needed for A's health or maintenance. In addition, an independent trustee has power to distribute to A any portion of the corpus which the trustee determines to be desirable for A's happiness. Assuming the other requirements of section 2518 are satisfied. A may make a qualified disclaimer of interests in the marital trust without disclaiming any of A's interests in the nonmarital trust.

Example (7). B died testate on June 1, 1980. B's will created both a marital trust and a nonmarital trust. The decedent's surviving spouse, C, is an income beneficiary of the marital trust and has a testamentary general power of appointment over its assets. C is an income beneficiary of the nonmarital trust, and additionally has the noncumulative right to withdraw yearly the greater of $5,000 or 5 percent of the aggregate value of the principal. The provisions of the will specify that any portion of the marital trust disclaimed is to be added to the nonmarital trust. C disclaims 50 percent of the marital trust corpus. Pursuant to the will, this amount is transferred to the nonmarital trust. Assuming the remaining requirements of section 2518(b) are satisfied, C's disclaimer is a qualified disclaimer.

Example (8). A, a resident of State X, died on July 19, 1979. A was survived by a spouse B, and three children, C, D, and E. Pursuant to A's will, B received one-half of A's estate and the children received equal shares of the remaining one-half of the estate. B disclaimed the entire interest B had received. The will made no provisions for the distribution of property in the case of a beneficiary's disclaimer. The disclaimer laws of State X provide that under these circumstances disclaimed property passes to the decedent's heirs at law in the same manner as if the disclaiming beneficiary had died immediately before the testator's death. As a result, C, D, and E are A's only remaining heirs at law, and will divide the disclaimed property equally among themselves. B's disclaimer includes language stating that "it is my intention that C, D, and E will share equally in the division of this property as a result of my disclaimer." State X considers these to be precatory words and gives them no legal effect. B's disclaimer meets all other requirements imposed by State X on disclaimers, and is considered an effective disclaimer under which the property will vest solely in C, D, and E in equal shares without any further action required by B. Therefore, B is not treated as directing the redistribution or transfer of the property. If the remaining requirements of section 2518 are met, B's disclaimer is a qualified disclaimer.

Example (9). C died testate on January 1, 1979. According to C's will, D was to receive ⅓ of the residuary estate with any disclaimed property going to E. D was also to receive a second ⅓ of the residuary estate with any disclaimed property going to F. Finally, D was to receive a final ⅓ of the residuary estate with any disclaimed property going to G. D specifically states that he is disclaiming the interest in which the disclaimed property is designated to pass to E. D has effectively directed that the disclaimed property will pass to E and therefore D's disclaimer is not a qualified disclaimer under section 2518(a).

Example (10). Assume the same facts as in example (9) except that C's will also states that D was to receive Blackacre and Whiteacre. C's will further provides that if D disclaimed Blackacre then such property was to pass to E and that if D disclaimed Whiteacre then Whiteacre was to pass to F. D specifically disclaims Blackacre with the intention that it pass to E. Assuming the other requirements of section 2518 are met, D has made a qualified disclaimer of Blackacre. Alternatively, D could disclaim an undivided portion of both Blackacre and Whiteacre. Assuming the other requirements of section 2518 are met, this would also be a qualified disclaimer.

Example (11). G creates an irrevocable trust on February 16, 1983, naming H, I and J as the income beneficiaries for life and F as the remainderman. F is also named the trustee and as trustee has the discretionary power to invade the corpus and make discretionary distributions to H, I or J during their lives. F disclaims the remainder interest on August 8, 1983, but retains his discretionary power to invade the corpus. F has not made a qualified disclaimer because F retains the power to direct enjoyment of the corpus and the retained fiduciary power is not limited by an ascertainable standard.

Example (12). Assume the same facts as in example (11) except that F may only invade the corpus to make distributions for the health, maintenance or support of H, I or J during their lives. If the other requirements of section 2518(b) are met, F has made a qualified disclaimer of the remainder interest because the retained fiduciary power is limited by an ascertainable standard.

T.D. 8095, 8/6/86, amend T.D. 8744, 12/30/97.

§ 25.2518-3 Disclaimer of less than an entire interest.

(a) Disclaimer of a partial interest. *(1) In general.* (i) Interest. If the requirements of this section are met, the disclaimer of all or an undivided portion of any separate interest in property may be a qualified disclaimer even if the disclaimant has another interest in the same property. In general, each interest in property that is separately created by the transferor is treated as a separate interest. For example, if an income interest in securities is bequeathed to A for life, then to B for life, with the remainder interest in such securities bequeathed to A's estate, and if the remaining requirements of section 2518(b) are met, A could make a qualified disclaimer of either the income interest or the remainder, or an undivided portion of either interest. A could not, however, make a qualified disclaimer of the income interest for a certain number of years. Further, where local law merges interests separately created by the transferor, a qualified disclaimer will be allowed only if there is a disclaimer of the entire merged interest or an undivided portion of such merged interest. See example (12) in paragraph (d) of this section. See § 25.2518-3(b) for rules relating to the disclaimer of an undivided portion. Where the merger of separate interests would occur but for the creation by the transferor of a nominal interest (as defined in paragraph (a)(1)(iv) of this section), a qualified disclaimer will be allowed only if there is a disclaimer of all the separate interests, or an undivided portion of all such interests, which would have merged but for the nominal interest.

(ii) Severable property. A disclaimant shall be treated as making a qualified disclaimer of a separate interest in property if the disclaimer relates to severable property and the disclaimant makes a disclaimer which would be a qualified disclaimer if such property were the only property in which the disclaimant had an interest. If applicable local law does not recognize a purported disclaimer of severable property, the disclaimant must comply with the requirements of paragraph (c)(1) of § 25.2518-1 in order to make a qualified disclaimer of the severable property. Severable property is property which can be divided into separate parts each of which, after severance, maintains a complete and independent existence. For example, a legatee of shares of corporate stock may accept some shares of the stock and make a qualified disclaimer of the remaining shares.

(iii) Powers of appointment. A power of appointment with respect to property is treated as a separate interest in such property and such power of appointment with respect to all or an undivided portion of such property may be disclaimed independently from any other interests separately created by the transferor in the property if the requirements of section 2518(b) are met. See example (21) of paragraph (d) of this section. Further, a disclaimer of a power of appointment with respect to property is a qualified disclaimer only if any right to direct the beneficial enjoyment of the property which is retained by the disclaimant is limited by an ascertainable standard. See example (9) of paragraph (d) of this section.

(iv) Nominal interest. A nominal interest is an interest in property created by the transferor that—

(A) Has an actuarial value (as determined under § 20.2031-7) of less than 5 percent of the total value of the property at the time of the taxable transfer creating the interest,

(B) Prevents the merger under local law or two or more other interests created by the transferor, and

(C) Can be clearly shown from all the facts and circumstances to have been created primarily for the purpose of preventing the merger of such other interests.

Factors to be considered in determining whether an interest is created primarily for the purpose of preventing merger include (but are not limited to) the following: the relationship between the transferor and the interest holder; the age difference between the interest holder and the beneficiary whose interests would have merged; the interest holder's state of health at the time of the taxable transfer; and, in the case of a contingent remainder, any other factors which indicate that the possibility of the interest vesting as a fee simple is so remote as to be negligible.

(2) In trust. A disclaimer is not a qualified disclaimer under section 2518 if the beneficiary disclaims income derived from specific property transferred in trust while continuing to accept income derived from the remaining properties in the same trust unless the disclaimer results in such property being removed from the trust and passing, without any direction on the part of the disclaimant, to persons other than the disclaimant or to the spouse of the decedent. Moreover, a disclaimer of both an income interest and a remainder interest in specific trust assets is not a qualified disclaimer if the beneficiary retains interests in other trust property unless, as a result of the disclaimer, such assets are removed from the trust and pass, without any direction on the part of the disclaimant, to persons other than the disclaimant or to the spouse of the decedent. The disclaimer of an undivided portion of an interest in a trust may be a qualified disclaimer. See also paragraph (b) of this section for rules relating to the disclaimer of an undivided portion of an interest in property.

(b) Disclaimer of undivided portion. A disclaimer of an undivided portion of a separate interest in property which meets the other requirements of a qualified disclaimer under section 2518(b) and the corresponding regulations is a qualified disclaimer. An undivided portion of a disclaimant's separate interest in property must consist of a fraction or percentage of each and every substantial interest or right owned by the disclaimant in such property and must extend over the entire term of the disclaimant's interest in such property and in other property into which such property is converted. A disclaimer of some specific rights while retaining other rights with respect to an interest in the property is not a qualified disclaimer of an undivided portion of the disclaimant's interest in property. Thus, for example, a disclaimer made by the devisee of a fee simple interest in Blackacre is not a qualified disclaimer if the disclaimant disclaims a remainder interest in Blackacre but retains a life estate.

(c) Disclaimer of a pecuniary amount. A disclaimer of a specific pecuniary amount out of a pecuniary or nonpecuniary bequest or gift which satisfies the other requirements of a qualified disclaimer under section 2518(b) and the corresponding regulations is a qualified disclaimer provided that no income or other benefit of the disclaimed amount inures to the benefit of the disclaimant either prior to or subsequent to the disclaimer. Thus, following the disclaimer of a specific pecuniary amount from a bequest or gift, the amount disclaimed and any income attributable to such amount must be segregated from the portion of the gift or bequest that was not disclaimed. Such a segregation of assets making up the disclaimer of a pecuniary amount must be made on the basis of the fair market value of the assets on the date of the disclaimer or on a basis that is fairly representative of value changes that may have occurred between the date of transfer and the date of the disclaimer. A pecuniary amount distributed to the disclaimant from the bequest or gift prior to the disclaimer shall be treated as a distribution of corpus from the bequest or gift. However, the acceptance of a distribution from the gift or bequest shall also be considered to be an acceptance of a proportionate amount of income earned by the bequest or gift. The proportionate share of income considered to be accepted by the disclaimant shall be determined at the time of the disclaimer according to the following formula:

$$\frac{\text{Total amount of distributions received by the disclaimant out of the gift or bequest}}{\text{Total value of the gift or bequest on the date of transfer}} \times \text{Total amount of income earned by the gift or bequest between date of transfer and date of disclaimer}$$

See examples (17), (18), and (19) in § 25.2518-3(d) for illustrations of the rules set forth in this paragraph (c).

(d) Examples. The provisions of this section may be illustrated by the following examples:

Example (1). A, a resident of State Q, died on August 1, 1978. A's will included specific bequests of 100 shares of stock in X corporation; 200 shares of stock in Y corporation; 500 shares of stock in Z corporation; personal effects consisting of paintings, home furnishings, jewelry, and silver, and a 500 acre farm consisting of a residence, various outbuildings, and 500 head of cattle. The laws of State Q provide that a disclaimed interest passes in the same manner as if the disclaiming beneficiary had died immediately before the testator's death. Pursuant to A's will, B was to receive both the personal effects and the farm. C was to receive all the shares of stock in Corporation X and Y and D was to receive all the shares of stock in Corporation Z. B disclaimed 2 of the paintings and all the jewelry, C disclaimed 50 shares of Y corporation stock, and D disclaimed 100 shares of Z corporation stock. If the remaining requirements of section 2518(b) and the corresponding regulations are met, each of these disclaimers is a qualified disclaimer for purposes of section 2518(a).

Example (2). Assume the same facts as in example (1) except that D disclaimed the income interest in the shares of Z corporation stock while retaining the remainder interest in such shares. D's disclaimer is not a qualified disclaimer.

Example (3). Assume the same facts as in example (1) except that B disclaimed 300 identified acres of the 500 acres. Assuming that B's disclaimer meets the remaining requirements of section 2518(b), it is a qualified disclaimer.

Example (4). Assume the same facts as in example (1) except that A devised the income from the farm to B for life and the remainder interest to C. B disclaimed 40 percent of the income from the farm. Assuming that it meets the remaining requirements of section 2518(b), B's disclaimer of an undivided portion of the income is a qualified disclaimer.

Example (5). E died on September 13, 1978. Under the provisions of E's will, E's shares of stock in X, Y, and Z corporations were to be transferred to a trust. The trust provides that all income is to be distributed currently to F and G in equal parts until F attains the age of 45 years. At that time the corpus of the trust is to be divided equally between F and G. F disclaimed the income arising from the shares of X stock. G disclaimed 20 percent of G's interest in the trust. F's disclaimer is not a qualified disclaimer because the X stock remains in the trust. If the remaining requirements of section 2518(b) are met, G's disclaimer is a qualified disclaimer.

Example (6). Assume the same facts as in example (5) except that F disclaimed both the income interest and the remainder interest in the shares of X stock. F's disclaimer results in the X stock being transferred out of the trust to G without any direction on F's part. F's disclaimer is a qualified disclaimer under section 2518(b).

Example (7). Assume the same facts as in example (5) except that F is only an income beneficiary of the trust. The X stock remains in the trust after F's disclaimer of the income arising from the shares of X stock. F's disclaimer is not a qualified disclaimer under section 2518.

Example (8). Assume the same facts as in example (5) except that F disclaimed the entire income interest in the trust while retaining the interest F has in corpus. Alternatively, assume that G disclaimed G's entire corpus interest while retaining G's interest in the income from the trust. If the remaining requirements of section 2518(b) are met, either disclaimer will be a qualified disclaimer.

Example (9). G creates an irrevocable trust on May 13, 1980, with H, I, and J as the income beneficiaries. In addition, H, who is the trustee, holds the power to invade corpus for H's health, maintenance, support and happiness and a testamentary power of appointment over the corpus. In the absence of the exercise of the power of appointment, the property passes to I and J in equal shares. H disclaimed the power to invade corpus for H's health, maintenance, support and happiness. Because H retained the testamentary power to appoint the property in the corpus, H's disclaimer is not a qualified disclaimer. If H also disclaimed the testamentary power of appointment, H's disclaimer would have been a qualified disclaimer.

Example (10). E creates an irrevocable trust on May 1, 1980, in which D is the income beneficiary for life. Subject to the trustee's discretion, E's children, A, B, and C, have the right to receive corpus during D's lifetime. The remainder passes to D if D survives A, B, C, and all their issue. D also holds an inter vivos power to appoint the trust corpus to A, B, and C. On September 1, 1980, D disclaimed the remainder interest. D's disclaimer is not a qualified disclaimer because D retained the power to direct the use and enjoyment of corpus during D's life.

Example (11). Under H's will, a trust is created from which W is to receive all of the income for life. The trustee has the power to invade the trust corpus for the support or maintenance of D during the life of W. The trust is to terminate at W's death, at which time the trust property is to be distributed to D. D makes a timely disclaimer of the right to corpus during W's lifetime, but does not disclaim the remainder interest. D's disclaimer is a qualified disclaimer assuming the remaining requirements of section 2518 are met.

Example (12). Under the provisions of G's will A received a life estate in a farm, and was the sole beneficiary of property in the residuary estate. The will also provided that the remainder interest in the farm pass to the residuary estate. Under local law A's interests merged to give A a fee simple in the farm. A made a timely disclaimer of the life estate. A's disclaimer of a partial interest is not a qualified disclaimer under section 2518(a). If A makes a disclaimer of the entire merged interest in the farm or an undivided portion of such merged interest then A would be making a qualified disclaimer assuming all the other requirements of section 2518(b) are met.

Example (13). A, a resident of State Z, dies on September 3, 1980. Under A's will, Blackacre is devised to C for life, then to D for 1 month, remainder to C. Had A not created D's interest, State Z law would have merged C's life estate and the remainder to C to create a fee simple interest in C. Assume that the actuarial value of D's interest is less than 5 percent of the total value of Blackacre on the date of A's death. Further assume that facts and circumstances (particularly the duration of D's interest) clearly indicate that D's interest was created primarily for the purpose of preventing the merger of C's two interests in Blackacre. D's interest in Blackacre is a nominal interest and C's two interests will, for purposes of making a qualified disclaimer, be considered to have merged. Thus, C cannot make a qualified disclaimer of his remainder while retaining the life estate. C can, however, make a qualified disclaimer of both of these interests entirely or an undivided portion of both.

Example (14). A, a resident of State X, dies on October 12, 1978. Under A's will, Blackacre was devised to B for life, then to C for life if C survives B, remainder to B's estate. On the date of A's death, B and C are both 8 year old grandchildren of A. In addition, C is in good health. The actual value of C's interest is less than 5 percent of the total value of Blackacre on the date of A's death. No facts are present which would indicate that the possibility of C's contingent interest vesting is so remote as to be negligible. Had C's contingent life estate not been created, B's life estate and remainder interests would have merged under local law to give B a fee simple interest in Blackacre. Although C's interest prevents the merger of B's two interests and has an actual value of less than 5 percent, C's interest is not a nominal interest within the meaning of § 25.2518-3(a)(1)(iv) because the facts and circumstances do not clearly indicate that the interest was created primarily for the purpose of preventing the merger of other interests in the property. Assuming all the other requirements of section 2518(b) are met, B can make a qualified disclaimer of the remainder while retaining his life estate.

Example (15). In 1981, A transfers $60,000 to a trust created for the benefit of B who was given the income interest for life and who also has a testamentary nongeneral power of appointment over the corpus. A transfers an additional $25,000 to the trust on June 1, 1984. At that time the trust corpus (exclusive of the $25,000 transfer) has a fair market value of $75,000. On January 1, 1985, B disclaims the right to receive income attributable to 25 percent of the corpus

$$\left(\frac{\$25{,}000 \text{ (1984 transfer)}}{\$100{,}000 \text{ (Fair market value of corpus immediately after the 1984 transfer)}} = 25\%.\right)$$

Assuming that no distributions were made to B attributable to the $25,000, B's disclaimer is a qualified disclaimer for purposes of section 2518(a) if all the remaining requirements of section 2518(b) are met.

Example (16). Under the provisions of B's will, A is left an outright cash legacy of $50,000 and has no other interest in B's estate. A timely disclaimer by A of any stated dollar amount is a qualified disclaimer under section 2518(a).

Example (17). D bequeaths his brokerage account to E. The account consists of stocks and bonds and a cash amount earning interest. The total value of the cash and assets in the account on the date of D's death is $100,000. Four months after D's death, E makes a withdrawal of cash from the account for personal use amounting to $40,000. Eight months after D's death, E disclaims $60,000 of the account without specifying any particular assets or cash. The cumulative fair market value of the stocks and bonds in the account on the date of the disclaimer is equal to the value of such stocks and bonds on the date of D's death. The income earned by the account between the date of D's death and the date of E's disclaimer was $20,000. The amount of income earned by the account that E accepted by withdrawing $40,000 from the account prior to the disclaimer is determined by applying the formula set forth in § 25.2518-3(c) as follows:

$$\frac{\$\,40{,}000}{\$100{,}000} \times \$20{,}000 = \$8{,}000$$

E is considered to have accepted $8,000 of the income earned by the account. If (i) the $60,000 disclaimed by E and the $12,000 of income earned prior to the disclaimer which is attributable to that amount are segregated from the $8,000 of income E is considered to have accepted, (ii) E does not accept any benefits of the $72,000 so segregated, and (iii) the other requirements of section 2518(b) are met, then E's disclaimer of $60,000 from the account is a qualified disclaimer.

Example (18). A bequeathed his residuary estate to B. The residuary estate had a value of $1 million on the date of A's death. Six months later, B disclaimed $200,000 out of this bequest. B received distributions of all the income from the entire estate during the period of administration. When the estate was distributed, B received the entire residuary estate except for $200,000 in cash. B did not make a qualified disclaimer since he accepted the benefits of the $200,000 during the period of estate administration.

Example (19). Assume the same facts as in example (18) except that no income was paid to B and the value of the residuary estate on the date of the disclaimer (including interest earned from date of death) was $1.5 million. In addition, as soon as B's disclaimer was made, the executor of A's estate set aside assets worth $300,000

$$\left(\frac{\$200{,}000}{\$1{,}000{,}000} \times \$1{,}500{,}000\right)$$

and the interest earned after the disclaimer on that amount in a separate fund so that none of the income was paid to B. B's disclaimer is a qualified disclaimer under section 2518(a).

Example (20). A bequeathed his residuary estate to B. B disclaims a fractional share of the residuary estate. Any disclaimed property will pass to A's surviving spouse, W. The numerator of the fraction disclaimed is the smallest amount which will allow A's estate to pass free of Federal estate tax and the denominator is the value of the residuary estate. B's disclaimer is a qualified disclaimer.

Example (21). A created a trust on July 1, 1979. The trust provides that all current income is to be distributed equally between B and C for the life of B. B also is given a testamentary general power of appointment over the corpus. If the power is not exercised, the corpus passes to C or C's heirs. B disclaimed the testamentary power to appoint an undivided one-half of the trust corpus. Assuming the remaining requirements of section 2518(b) are satisfied, B's disclaimer is a qualified disclaimer under section 2518(a).

T.D. 8095, 8/6/86, amend T.D. 8540, 6/9/94.

§ 25.2519-1 Dispositions of certain life estates.

(a) In general. If a donee spouse makes a disposition of all or part of a qualifying income interest for life in any property for which a deduction was allowed under section

2056(b)(7) or section 2523(f) for the transfer creating the qualifying income interest, the donee spouse is treated for purposes of chapters 11 and 12 of subtitle B of the Internal Revenue Code as transferring all interests in property other than the qualifying income interest. For example, if the donee spouse makes a disposition of part of a qualifying income interest for life in trust corpus, the spouse is treated under section 2519 as making a transfer subject to chapters 11 and 12 of the entire trust other than the qualifying income interest for life. Therefore, the donee spouse is treated as making a gift under section 2519 of the entire trust less the qualifying income interest, and is treated for purposes of section 2036 as having transferred the entire trust corpus, including that portion of the trust corpus from which the retained income interest is payable. A transfer of all or a portion of the income interest of the spouse is a transfer by the spouse under section 2511. See also section 2702 for special rules applicable in valuing the gift made by the spouse under section 2519.

(b) Presumption. Unless the donee spouse establishes to the contrary, section 2519 applies to the entire trust at the time of the disposition. If a deduction is taken on either the estate or gift tax return with respect to the transfer which created the qualifying income interest, it is presumed that the deduction was allowed for purposes of section 2519. To avoid the application of section 2519 upon a transfer of all or part of the donee spouse's income interest, the donee spouse must establish that a deduction was not taken for the transfer of property which created the qualifying income interest. For example, to establish that a deduction was not taken, the donee spouse may produce a copy of the estate or gift tax return filed with respect to the transfer creating the qualifying income interest for life establishing that no deduction was taken under section 2056(b)(7) or section 2523(f). In addition, the donee spouse may establish that no return was filed on the original transfer by the donor spouse because the value of the first spouse's gross estate was below the threshold requirement for filing under section 6018. Similarly, the donee spouse could establish that the transfer creating the qualifying income interest for life was made before the effective date of section 2056(b)(7) or section 2523(f), whichever is applicable.

(c) Amount treated as a transfer. *(1) In general.* The amount treated as a transfer under this section upon a disposition of all or part of a qualifying income interest for life in qualified terminable interest property is equal to the fair market value of the entire property subject to the qualifying income interest, determined on the date of the disposition (including any accumulated income and not reduced by any amount excluded from total gifts under section 2503(b) with respect to the transfer creating the interest), less the value of the qualifying income interest in the property on the date of the disposition. The gift tax consequences of the disposition of the qualifying income interest are determined separately under § 25.2511-2. See paragraph (c)(4) of this section for the effect of gift tax that the donee spouse is entitled to recover under section 2207A.

(2) Disposition of interest in property with respect to which a partial election was made. If, in connection with the transfer of property that created the spouse's qualifying income interest for life, a deduction was allowed under section 2056(b)(7) or section 2523(f) for less than the entire interest in the property (i.e., for a fractional or percentage share of the entire interest in the transferred property) the amount treated as a transfer by the donee spouse under this section is equal to the fair market value of the entire property subject to the qualifying income interest on the date of the disposition, less the value of the qualifying income interest for life, multiplied by the fractional or percentage share of the interest for which the deduction was taken.

(3) Reduction for distributions charged to nonelective portion of trust. The amount determined under paragraph (c)(2) of this section (if applicable) is appropriately reduced if—

(i) The donee spouse's interest is in a trust and distributions of principal have been made to the donee spouse;

(ii) The trust provides that distributions of principal are made first from the qualified terminable interest share of the trust; and

(iii) The donee spouse establishes the reduction in that share based on the fair market value of the trust assets at the time of each distribution.

(4) Effect of gift tax entitled to be recovered under section 2207A on the amount of the transfer. The amount treated as a transfer under paragraph (c)(1) of this section is further reduced by the amount the donee spouse is entitled to recover under section 2207A(b) (relating to the right to recover gift tax attributable to the remainder interest). If the donee spouse is entitled to recover gift tax under section 2207A(b), the amount of gift tax recoverable and the value of the remainder interest treated as transferred under section 2519 are determined by using the same interrelated computation applicable for other transfers in which the transferee assumes the gift tax liability. The gift tax consequences of failing to exercise the right of recovery are determined separately under § 25.2207A-1(b).

(5) Interest in previously severed trust. If the donee spouse's interest is in a trust consisting of only qualified terminable interest property, and the trust was previously severed (in compliance with § 20.2056(b)-7(b)(2)(ii) of this chapter or § 25.2523(f)-1(b)(3)(ii) from a trust that, after the severance, held only property that was not qualified terminable interest property, only the value of the property in the severed portion of the trust at the time of the disposition is treated as transferred under this section.

(d) Identification of property transferred. If only part of the property in which a donee spouse has a qualifying income interest for life is qualified terminable interest property, the donee spouse is, in the case of a disposition of all or part of the income interest within the meaning of section 2519, deemed to have transferred a pro rata portion of the entire qualified terminable interest property for purposes of this section.

(e) Exercise of power of appointment. The exercise by any person of a power to appoint qualified terminable interest property to the donee spouse is not treated as a disposition under section 2519, even though the donee spouse subsequently disposes of the appointed property.

(f) Conversion of qualified terminable interest property. The conversion of qualified terminable interest property into other property in which the donee spouse has a qualifying income interest for life is not, for purposes of this section, treated as a disposition of the qualifying income interest. Thus, the sale and reinvestment of assets of a trust holding qualified terminable interest property is not a disposition of the qualifying income interest, provided that the donee spouse continues to have a qualifying income interest for life in the trust after the sale and reinvestment. Similarly, the sale of real property in which the spouse possesses a legal life estate and thus meets the requirements of qualified terminable interest property, followed by the transfer of the proceeds into a trust which also meets the requirements of qualified terminable interest property, or by the reinvestment of the proceeds in income producing property in which the donee spouse has a qualifying income interest for life, is not considered a disposition of the qualifying income interest. On the other hand, the sale of qualified terminable interest property, followed by the payment to the donee spouse of a portion of the proceeds equal to the value of the donee spouse's income interest, is considered a disposition of the qualifying income interest.

(g) **Examples.** The following examples illustrate the application of paragraphs (a) through (f) of this section. Except as provided otherwise in the examples, assume that the decedent, D, was survived by spouse, S, that in each example the section 2503(b) exclusion has already been fully utilized for each year with respect to the donee in question, that section 2503(e) is not applicable to the amount deemed transferred, and that the gift taxes on the amount treated as transferred under paragraph (c) are offset by S's unified credit. The examples are as follows:

Example (1). Transfer of the spouse's life estate in residence. Under D's will, a personal residence valued for estate tax purposes at $250,000 passes to S for life, and after S's death to D's children. D's executor made a valid election to treat the property as qualified terminable interest property. During 1995, when the fair market value of the property is $300,000 and the value of S's life interest in the property is $100,000, S makes a gift of S's entire interest in the property to D's children. Pursuant to section 2519, S makes a gift in the amount of $200,000 (i.e., the fair market value of the qualified terminable interest property of $300,000 less the fair market value of S's qualifying income interest in the property of $100,000). In addition, under section 2511, S makes a gift of $100,000 (i.e., the fair market value of S's income interest in the property). See § 25.2511-2.

Example (2). Sale of spouse's life estate. The facts are the same as in Example 1 except that during 1995, S sells S's interest in the property to D's children for $100,000. Pursuant to section 2519, S makes a gift of $200,000 ($300,000 less $100,000 value of the qualifying income interest in the property). S does not make a gift of the income interest under section 2511, because the consideration received for S's income interest is equal to the value of the income interest.

Example (3). Transfer of income interest in trust subject to partial election. D's will established a trust valued for estate tax purposes at $500,000, all of the income of which is payable annually to S for life. After S's death, the principal of the trust is to be distributed to D's children. Assume that only 50 percent of the trust was treated as qualified terminable interest property. During 1995, S makes a gift of all of S's interest in the trust to D's children at which time the fair market value of the trust is $400,000 and the fair market value of S's life income interest in the trust is $100,000. Pursuant to section 2519, S makes a gift of $150,000 (the fair market value of the qualified terminable interest property, 50 percent of $400,000, less the $50,000 income interest in the qualified terminable interest property). S also makes a gift pursuant to section 2511 of $100,000 (i.e., the fair market value of S's life income interest).

Example (4). Transfer of a portion of income interest in trust subject to a partial election. The facts are the same as in Example 3 except that S makes a gift of only 40 percent of S's interest in the trust. Pursuant to section 2519, S makes a gift of $150,000 (i.e., the fair market value of the qualified terminable interest property, 50 percent of $400,000, less the $50,000 value of S's qualified income interest in the qualified terminable interest property). S also makes a gift pursuant to section 2511 of $40,000 (i.e., the fair market value of 40 percent of S's life income interest). See also section 2702 for additional rules that may affect the value of the total amount of S's gift under section 2519 to take into account the fact that S's 30 percent retained income interest attributable to the qualifying income interest is valued at zero under that section, thereby increasing the value of S's section 2519 gift to $180,000. In addition, under § 25.2519-1(d), S's disposition of 40 percent of the income interest is deemed to be a transfer of a pro rata portion of the qualified terminable interest property. Thus, assuming no further lifetime dispositions by S, 30 percent (60 percent of 50 percent) of the trust property is included in S's gross estate under section 2036 and an adjustment is made to S's adjusted taxable gifts under section 2001(b)(1)(B). If S later disposes of all or a portion of the retained income interest, see § 25.2702-6.

Example (5). Transfer of a portion of spouse's interest in a trust from which corpus was previously distributed to the spouse. D's will established a trust valued for estate tax purposes at $500,000, all of the income of which is payable annually to S for life. The trustee is granted the discretion to distribute trust principal to S. All appointments of principal must be made from the portion of the trust subject to the section 2056(b)(7) election. After S's death, the principal of the trust is to be distributed to D's children. The executor makes the section 2056(b)(7) election with respect to 50 percent of the trust. In 1994, pursuant to the terms of D's will, the trustee distributed $50,000 of principal to S and charged the entire distribution to the qualified terminable interest portion of the trust.

Immediately prior to the distribution, the value of the entire trust was $550,000 and the value of the qualified terminable interest portion was $275,000 (50 percent of $550,000). Provided S can establish the above facts, the qualified terminable interest portion of the trust immediately after the distribution is $225,000 or 45 percent of the value of the trust ($225,000/$500,000). In 1996, when the value of the trust is $400,000 and the value of S's income interest is $100,000, S makes a transfer of 40 percent of S's income interest. S's gift under section 2519 is $135,000; i.e., the fair market value of the qualified terminable interest property, 45 percent of $400,000 ($180,000), less the value of the income interest in the qualified terminable interest property, $45,000 (45 percent of $100,000). S also makes a gift under section 2511 of $40,000; i.e., the fair market value of 40 percent of S's income interest. S's disposition of 40 percent of the income interest is deemed to be a transfer under section 2519 of the entire 45 percent portion of the remainder subject to the section 2056(b)(7) election. Since S retained 60 percent of the income interest, 27 percent (60 percent of 45 percent) of the trust property is includible in S's gross estate under section 2036. See also section 2702 and Example 4 as to the principles applicable in valuing S's gift under section 2702 and adjusted taxable gifts upon S's subsequent death.

Example (6). Transfer of spousal annuity payable from trust. D died prior to October 24, 1992. D's will established a trust valued for estate tax purposes at $500,000. The trust instrument required the trustee to pay an annuity to S of $20,000 a year for life. All the trust income other than the amounts paid to S as an annuity are to be accumulated in the trust and may not be distributed during S's lifetime to any person other than S. After S's death, the principal of the trust is to be distributed to D's children. Because D died prior to the effective date of section 1941 of the Energy Policy Act of 1992, S's annuity interest qualifies as a qualifying income interest for life. Under § 20.2056(b)-7(e) of this chapter, based on an applicable 10 percent interest rate, 40 percent of the property, or $200,000, is the value of the deductible interest. During 1996, S makes a gift of the annuity interest to D's children at which time the fair market value of the trust is $800,000 and the fair market value of S's annuity interest in the trust is $100,000. Pursuant to section 2519, S is treated as making a gift of $220,000 (the fair market value of the qualified terminable interest property, 40 percent of $800,000 ($320,000), less the $100,000 annuity interest in the qualified terminable interest property). S is also treated pursuant to section 2511 as making a gift of $100,000 (the fair market value of S's annuity interest).

T.D. 8522, 2/28/94, amend T.D. 9077, 7/17/2003.

§ 25.2519-2 Effective date.

Except as specifically provided in § 25.2519-1(g), Example 6, the provisions of § 25.2519-1 are effective with respect to gifts made after March 1, 1994. With respect to gifts made on or before such date, the donee spouse of a section 2056(b)(7) or section 2523(f) transfer may rely on any reasonable interpretation of the statutory provisions. For these purposes, the provisions of § 25.2519-1 (as well as project LR-211-76, 1984-1 C.B., page 598, see § 601.601(d)(2)(ii)(b) of this chapter), are considered a reasonable interpretation of the statutory provisions.

T.D. 8522, 2/28/94.

§ 25.2521-1 Specific exemption.

Caution: The Treasury has not yet amended Reg § 25.2521-1 to reflect changes made by P.L. 94-455.

(a) In determining the amount of taxable gifts for the calendar quarter (calendar year with respect to gifts made before January 1, 1971) there may be deducted, if the donor was a resident or citizen of the United States at the time the gifts were made, a specific exemption of $30,000, less the sum of the amounts claimed and allowed as an exemption in prior calendar quarters or calendar years. The exemption, at the option of the donor, may be taken in the full amount of $30,000 in a single calendar quarter or calendar year, or be spread over a period of time in such amounts as the donor sees fit, but after the limit has been reached no further exemption is allowable. Except as otherwise provided in a tax convention between the United States and another country, a donor who was a nonresident not a citizen of the United States at the time the gift or gifts were made is not entitled to this exemption. For the definition of calendar quarter see § 25.2502-1(c)(1).

(b) No part of a donor's lifetime specific exemption of $30,000 may be deducted from the value of a gift attributable to his spouse where a husband and wife consent, under the provisions of section 2513, to have the gifts made during a calendar quarter or calendar year considered as made one-half by each of them. The "gift-splitting" provisions of section 2513 do not authorize the filing of a joint gift tax return nor permit a donor to claim any of his spouse's specific exemption. For example, if a husband has no specific exemption remaining available, but his wife does, and the husband makes a gift to which his wife consents under the provisions of section 2513, the specific exemption remaining available may be claimed only on the return of the wife with respect to one-half of the gift. The husband may not claim any specific exemption since he has none available.

(c) *(1)* With respect to gifts made after December 31, 1970, the amount by which the specific exemption claimed and allowed in gift tax returns for prior calendar quarters and calendar years exceeds $30,000 is includible in determining the aggregate sum of the taxable gifts for preceding calendar years and calendar quarters. See paragraph (b) of § 25.2504-1.

(2) With respect to gifts made before January 1, 1971, the amount by which the specific exemption claimed and allowed in gift tax returns for prior calendar years exceeds $30,000 is includible in determining the aggregate sum of the taxable gifts for preceding calendar years. See paragraph (b) of § 25.2504-1.

T.D. 6334, 11/14/58, amend T.D. 7238, 12/28/72.

§ 25.2522(a)-1 Charitable and similar gifts; citizens or residents.

(a) In determining the amount of taxable gifts for the "calendar period" (as defined in § 25.2502-1(c)(1)) there may be deducted in the case of a donor who was a citizen or resident of the United States at the time the gifts were made, all gifts included in the "total amount gifts" made by the donor during the calendar period (see section 2503 and the regulations thereunder) and made to or for the use of:

(1) The United States, any State, Territory, or any political subdivision thereof, or the District of Columbia, for exclusively public purposes.

(2) Any corporation, trust, community chest, fund, or foundation organized and operated exclusively for religious, charitable, scientific, literary, or educational purposes, including the encouragement of art and the prevention of cruelty to children or animals, if no part of the net earnings of the organization inures to the benefit of any private shareholder or individual, if it is not disqualified for tax exemption under section 501(c)(3) by reason of attempting to influence legislation, and if, in the case of gifts made after December 31, 1969, it does not participate in, or intervene in (including the publishing or distributing of statements), any political campaign on behalf of or in opposition to any candidate for public office.

(3) A fraternal society, order, or association, operating under the lodge system, provided the gifts are to be used by the society, order or association exclusively for one or more of the purposes set forth in subparagraph (2) of this paragraph.

(4) Any post or organization of war veterans or auxiliary unit or society thereof, if organized in the United States or any of its possessions, and if no part of its net earnings inures to the benefit of any private shareholder or individual.

The deduction is not limited to gifts for use within the United States, or to gifts to or for the use of domestic corporations, trusts, community chests, funds, or foundations, or fraternal societies, orders, or associations operating under the lodge system. An organization will not be considered to meet the requirements of subparagraph (2) of this paragraph, or of paragraph (b)(2) or (3) of this section, if such organization engages in any activity which would cause it to be classified as an "action" organization under paragraph (c)(3) of § 1.501(c)(3)-1 of this chapter (Income Tax Regulations). For the deductions for charitable and similar gifts made by a nonresident who was not a citizen of the United States at the time the gifts were made, see § 25.2522(b)-1. See §§ 25.2522(c)-1 and 25.2522(c)-2 for rules relating to the disallowance of deductions to trusts and organizations which engage in certain prohibited transactions or whose governing instruments do not contain certain specified requirements.

(b) The deduction under section 2522 is not allowed for a transfer to a corporation, trust, community chest, fund, or foundation unless the organization or trust meets the following four tests:

(1) It must be organized and operated exclusively for one or more of the specified purposes.

(2) It must not be disqualified for tax exemption under section 501(c)(3) by reason of attempting to influence legislation.

(3) In the case of gifts made after December 31, 1969, it must not participate in, or intervene in (including the publishing or distributing of statements), any political campaign on behalf of any candidate for public office.

(4) Its net earnings must not inure in whole or in part to the benefit of private shareholders or individuals other than as legitimate objects of the exempt purposes.

(c) In order to prove the right to the charitable, etc., deduction provided by section 2522 the donor must submit such data as may be requested by the Internal Revenue Service. As to the extent the deductions provided by this section are allowable, see section 2524.

T.D. 6334, 11/14/58, amend T.D. 7012, 5/14/69, T.D. 7238, 12/28/72, T.D. 7318, 7/10/74, T.D. 7910, 9/6/83, T.D. 8308, 8/30/90.

§ 25.2522(a)-2 Transfers not exclusively for charitable, etc., purposes in the case of gifts made before August 1, 1969.

(a) Remainders and similar interests. If a trust is created or property is transferred for both a charitable and a private purpose, deduction may be taken of the value of the charitable beneficial interest only insofar as that interest is presently ascertainable, and hence severable from the noncharitable interest. The present value of a remainder or other deferred payment to be made for a charitable purpose is to be determined in accordance with the rules stated in § 25.2512-5. Thus, if money or property is placed in trust to pay the income to an individual during his life, or for a term of years, and then to pay the principal to a charitable organization, the present value of the remainder is deductible. If the interest involved is such that its value is to be determined by a special computation, see § 25.2512-5(d)(4), a request for a specific factor accompanied by a statement of the date of birth of each person, the duration of whose life may affect the value of the remainder, and by copies of the relevant instruments may be submitted by the donor to the Commissioner, who may, if conditions permit, supply the factor requested. If the Commissioner does not furnish the factor, the claim for deduction must be supported by a full statement of the computation of the present value made in accordance with the principles set forth in the applicable paragraph of § 25.2512-5.

(b) Transfers subject to a condition or a power. If, as of the date of the gift, a transfer for charitable purposes is dependent upon the performance of some act or the happening of a precedent event in order that it might become effective, no deduction is allowable unless the possibility that the charitable transfer will not become effective is so remote as to be negligible. If an estate or interest passes to or is vested in charity on the date of the gift and the estate or interest would be defeated by the performance of some act or the happening of some event, the occurrence of which appeared to have been highly improbable on the date of the gift, the deduction is allowable. If the donee or trustee is empowered to divert the property or fund, in whole or in part, to a use or purpose which would have rendered it, to the extent that it is subject to such power, not deductible had it been directly so given by the donor, the deduction will be limited to that portion of the property or fund which is exempt from the exercise of the power. The deduction is not allowed in the case of a transfer in trust conveying to charity a present interest in income if by reason of all the conditions and circumstances surrounding the transfer it appears that the charity may not receive the beneficial enjoyment of the interest. For example, assume that assets placed in trust by the donor consist of stock in a corporation, the fiscal policies of which are controlled by the donor and his family, that the trustees and remaindermen are likewise members of the donor's family, and that the governing instrument contains no adequate guarantee of the requisite income to the charitable organization. Under such circumstances, no deduction will be allowed. Similarly, if the trustees are not members of the donor's family but have no power to sell or otherwise dispose of closely held stock, or otherwise insure the requisite enjoyment of income to the charitable organization, no deduction will be allowed.

(c) Effective date. This section applies only to gifts made before August 1, 1969. In the case of gifts made after July 31, 1969, see § 25.2522(c)-2.

T.D. 6334, 11/14/58, amend T.D. 7318, 7/10/74, T.D. 8540, 6/9/94.

§ 25.2522(b)-1 Charitable and similar gifts; non-residents not citizens.

(a) The deduction for charitable and similar gifts, in the case of a nonresident who was not a citizen of the United States at the time he made the gifts, is governed by the same rules as those applying to gifts by citizens or residents, subject, however, to the following exceptions:

(1) If the gifts are made to or for the use of a corporation, the corporation must be one created or organized under the laws of the United States or of any State or Territory thereof.

(2) If the gifts are made to or for the use of a trust, community chest, fund or foundation, or a fraternal society, order or association operating under the lodge system, the gifts must be for use within the United States exclusively for religious, charitable, scientific, literary or educational purposes, including the encouragement of art and the prevention of cruelty to children or animals.

T.D. 6334, 11/14/58.

§ 25.2522(c)-1 Disallowance of charitable, etc., deductions because of "prohibited transactions" in the case of gifts made before January 1, 1970.

(a) Sections 503(e) and 681(b)(5) provide that no deduction which would otherwise be allowable under section 2522 for a gift for religious, charitable, scientific, literary or educational purposes, including the encouragement of art and the prevention of cruelty to children or animals, is allowed if—

(1) The gift is made in trust and, for income tax purposes for the taxable year of the trust in which the gift is made, the deduction otherwise allowable to the trust under section 642(c) is limited by section 681(b)(1) by reason of the trust having engaged in a prohibited transaction described in section 681(b)(2); or

(2) The gift is made to any corporation, community chest, fund or foundation which, for its taxable year in which the gift is made is not exempt from income tax under section 501(a) by reason of having engaged in a prohibited transaction described in section 503(c).

(b) For purposes of section 503(e) and section 681(b)(5) the term "gift" includes any gift, contribution, or transfer without adequate consideration.

(c) Regulations relating to the income tax contain the rules for the determination of the taxable year of the trust for which the deduction under section 642(c) is limited by section 681(b), and for the determination of the taxable year of the organization for which an exemption is denied under section 503(a). Generally, such taxable year is a taxable year subsequent to the taxable year during which the trust or organization has been notified by the Internal Revenue Service that it has engaged in a prohibited transaction. However, if the trust or organization during or prior to the taxable year entered into the prohibited transaction for the purpose of diverting its corpus or income from the charitable or other purposes by reason of which it is entitled to a deduction or exemption, and the transaction involves a substantial part of such income or corpus, then the deduction of the trust under section 642(c) for such taxable year is limited by section 681(b), or the exemption of the organization for such taxable year is denied under section 503(a), whether or not the organization has previously received notification by the Internal Revenue Service that it has engaged in a prohibited transaction. In certain cases, the limitation of section 503 or 681 may be removed or the exemption may be reinstated for certain subsequent taxable years under the rules set forth in the income tax regulations under sections 503 and 681.

(d) In cases in which prior notification by the Internal Revenue Service is not required in order to limit the deduction of the trust under section 681(b), or to deny exemption of the organization under section 503, the deduction otherwise allowable under § 25.2522(a)-1 is not disallowed with respect to gifts made during the same taxable year of the trust or organization in which a prohibited transaction occurred, or in a prior taxable year, unless the donor or a member of his family was a party to the prohibited transaction. For purposes of the preceding sentence, the members of the donor's family include only his brothers and sisters (whether by whole or half blood), spouse, ancestors, and lineal descendants.

(e) This section applies only to gifts made before January 1, 1970. In the case of gifts made after December 31, 1969, see § 25.2522(c)-2.

T.D. 6334, 11/14/58, amend T.D. 7318, 7/10/74.

§ 25.2522(c)-2 Disallowance of charitable, etc., deductions in the case of gifts made after December 31, 1969.

(a) Organizations subject to section 507(c) tax. Section 508(d)(1) provides that, in the case of gifts made after December 31, 1969, a deduction which would otherwise be allowable under section 2522 for a gift to or for the use of an organization upon which the tax provided by section 507(c) has been imposed shall not be allowed if the gift is made by the donor after notification is made under section 507(a) or if the donor is a substantial contributor (as defined in section 507(d)(2)) who makes such gift in his taxable year (as defined in section 441) which includes the first day on which action is taken by such organization that culminates in the imposition of the tax under section 507(c) and any subsequent taxable year. This paragraph does not apply if the entire amount of the unpaid portion of the tax imposed by section 507(c) is abated under section 507(g) by the Commissioner or his delegate.

(b) Taxable private foundations, section 4947 trusts, etc. Section 508(d)(2) provides that, in the case of gifts made after December 31, 1969, a deduction which would otherwise be allowable under section 2522 shall not be allowed if the gift is made to or for the use of—

(1) A private foundation or a trust described in section 4947(a)(2) in a taxable year of such organization for which such organization fails to meet the governing instrument requirements of section 508(e) (determined without regard to section 508(e)(2)(B) and (C)), or

(2) Any organization in a period for which it is not treated as an organization described in section 501(c)(3) by reason of its failure to give notification under section 508(a) of its status to the Commissioner.

For additional rules, see § 1.508-2(b)(1) of this chapter (Income Tax Regulations)

(c) Foreign organizations with substantial support from foreign sources. Section 4948(c)(4) provides that, in the case of gifts made after December 31, 1969, a deduction which would otherwise be allowable under section 2522 for a gift to or for the use of a foreign organization which has received substantially all of its support (other than gross investment income) from sources without the United States shall not be allowed if the gift is made (1) after the date on which the Commissioner has published notice that he has notified such organization that it has engaged in a prohibited transaction, or (2) in a taxable year of such organization for which it is not exempt from taxation under section 501(a) because it has engaged in a prohibited transaction after December 31, 1969.

T.D. 7318, 7/10/74.

§ 25.2522(c)-3 Transfers not exclusively for charitable, etc., purposes in the case of gifts made after July 31, 1969.

(a) Remainders and similar interests. If a trust is created or property is transferred for both a charitable and a private purpose, deduction may be taken of the value of the charitable beneficial interest only insofar as that interest is presently ascertainable, and hence severable from the noncharitable interest.

(b) Transfers subject to a condition or a power. *(1)* If, as of the date of the gift, a transfer for charitable purposes is dependent upon the performance of some act or of the happening of a precedent event in order that it might become effective, no deduction is allowable unless the possibility that the charitable transfer will not become effective is so remote as to be negligible. If an estate or interest has passed to, or is vested in, charity on the date of the gift and the estate or interest would be defeated by the performance of some act or the happening of some event, the possibility of occurrence of which appeared on such date to be so remote as to be negligible, the deduction is allowable. If the donee or trustee is empowered to divert the property or fund, in whole or in part, to a use or purpose which would have rendered it, to the extent that it is subject to such power, not deductible had it been directly so given by the donor, the deduction will be limited to that portion, if any, of the property or fund which is exempt from an exercise of the power.

(2) The application of this paragraph may be illustrated by the following examples:

Example (1). In 1965, A transfers certain property in trust in which charity is to receive the income for his life. The assets placed in trust by the donor consist of stock in a corporation the fiscal policies of which are controlled by the donor and his family. The trustees of the trust and the remainderman are members of the donor's family and the governing instrument contains no adequate guarantee of the requisite income to the charitable organization. Under such circumstances, no deduction will be allowed. Similarly, if the trustees are not members of the donor's family but have no power to sell or otherwise dispose of the closely held stock, or otherwise insure the requisite enjoyment of income to the charitable organization, no deduction will be allowed.

Example (2). C transfers a tract of land to a city government for as long as the land is used by the city for a public park. If on the date of gift the city does plan to use the land for a public park and the possibility that the city will not use the land for a public park is so remote as to be negligible, a deduction will be allowed.

(c) Transfers of partial interests in property. *(1) Disallowance of deduction.* (i) In general. If a donor transfers an interest in property after July 31, 1969, for charitable purposes and an interest in the same property is retained by the donor, or is transferred or has been transferred for private purposes after such date (for less than an adequate and full consideration in money or money's worth), no deduction is allowed under section 2522 for the value of the interest which is transferred or has been transferred for charitable purposes unless the interest in property is a deductible interest described in subparagraph (2) of this paragraph. The principles that are used in applying section 2523 and the regulations thereunder shall apply for purposes of determining under this paragraph(c)(1)(i) whether an interest in property is retained by the donor, or is transferred or has been transferred by the donor. If, however, as of the date of the gift, a retention of an interest by a donor, or a transfer for a private purpose, is dependent upon the performance of some act or the happening of a precedent event in order that it may become effective, an interest in property will be considered retained by the donor, or transferred for a private purpose, unless the possibility of occurrence of such act or event is so remote as to be negligible. The application of this paragraph(c)(1)(i) may be illustrated by the following examples, in each of which it is assumed that the property interest which is transferred for private purposes is not transferred for an adequate and full consideration in money or money's worth:

Example (1). In 1973, H creates a trust which is to pay the income of the trust to W for her life, the reversionary interest in the trust being retained by H. In 1975, H gives the reversionary interest to charity, while W is still living. For purposes of this paragraph(c)(1)(i), interests in the same property have been transferred by H for charitable purposes and for private purposes.

Example (2). In 1973, H creates a trust which is to pay the income of the trust to W for her life and upon termination of the life estate to transfer the remainder to S. In 1975, S gives his remainder interest to charity, while W is still living. For purposes of this paragraph(c)(1)(i), interests in the same property have not been transferred by H or S for charitable purposes and for private purposes.

Example (3). H transfers Blackacre to A by gift, reserving the right to the rentals of Blackacre for a term of 20 years. After 4 years H transfers the right to the remaining rentals to charity. For purposes of this paragraph(c)(1)(i) the term "property" refers to Blackacre, and the right to rentals from Blackacre consist of an interest in Blackacre. An interest in Blackacre has been transferred by H for charitable purposes and for private purposes.

Example (4). H transfers property in trust for the benefit of A and a charity. An annuity of $5,000 a year is to be paid to charity for 20 years. Upon termination of the 20-year term the corpus is to be distributed to A if living. However, if A should die during the 20-year term, the corpus is to be distributed to charity upon termination of the term. An interest in property has been transferred by H for charitable purposes. In addition, an interest in the same property has been transferred by H for private purposes unless the possibility that A will survive the 20-year term is so remote as to be negligible.

Example (5). H transfers property in trust, under the terms of which an annuity of $5,000 a year is to be paid to charity for 20 years. Upon termination of the term, the corpus is to pass to such of A's children and their issue as A may appoint. However, if A should die during the 20-year term without exercising the power of appointment, the corpus is to be distributed to charity upon termination of the term. Since the possible appointees include private persons, an interest in the corpus of the trust is considered to have been transferred by H for private purposes.

(ii) Works of art and copyright treated as separate properties. For purposes of paragraphs (c)(1)(i) and (c)(2) of this section, rules similar to the rules in § 20.2055-2(e)(1)(ii) shall apply in the case of transfers made after December 31, 1981.

(2) Deductible interests. A deductible interest for purposes of subparagraph (1) of this paragraph is a charitable interest in property where—

(i) Undivided portion of donor's entire interest. The charitable interest is an undivided portion, not in trust, of the donor's entire interest in property. An undivided portion of a donor's entire interest in property must consist of a fraction or percentage of each and every substantial interest or right owned by the donor in such property and must extend over the entire term of the donor's interest in such property and in other property into which such property is converted. For example, if the donor gave a life estate in an office building to his wife for her life and retained a reversionary interest in the office building, the gift by the donor of one-half of that reversionary interest to charity while his wife is still alive will not be considered the transfer of a deductible interest; because an interest in the same property has already passed from the donor for private purposes, the reversionary interest will not be considered the donor's entire interest in the property. If, on the other hand, the donor had been given a life estate in Blackacre for the life of his wife and the donor had no other interest in Blackacre on or before the time of gift, the gift by the donor of one-half of that life estate to charity would be considered the transfer of a deductible interest; because the life estate would be considered the donor's entire interest in the property, the gift would be of an undivided portion of such entire interest. An undivided portion of a donor's entire interest in property includes an interest in property whereby the charity is given the right, as a tenant in common with the donor, to possession, dominion, and control of the property for a portion of each year appropriate to its interest in such property. However, except as provided in paragraphs (c)(2)(ii), (iii), and (iv) of this section, for purposes of this subdivision a charitable contribution of an interest in property not in trust where the decedent transfers some specific rights to one party and transfers other substantial rights to another party will not be considered a contribution of a undivided portion of the decedent's entire interest in property. A gift of an open space easement in gross in perpetuity shall be considered a gift of an undivided portion of the donor's entire interest in property. A gift to charity made on or before December 17, 1980, of an open space easement in gross in perpetuity shall be considered the transfer to charity of an undivided portion of the donor's entire interest in property.

(ii) Remainder interest in a personal residence. The charitable interest is an irrevocable remainder interest, not in trust, in a personal residence. Thus, for example, if the donor gives to charity a remainder interest in a personal residence and retains an estate in such property for life or a term of years the value of such remainder interest is deductible under section 2522. For purposes of this subdivision, the term "personal residence" means any property which is used by the donor as his personal residence even though it is not used as his principal residence. For example, a donor's vacation home may be a personal residence for purposes of this subdivision. The term "personal residence" also includes stock owned by the donor on the date of gift as a tenant-stockholder in a cooperative housing corporation (as those terms are defined in section 216(b)(1) and (2)) if the dwelling which the donor is entitled to occupy as such stockholder is used by him as his personal residence.

(iii) Remainder interest in a farm. The charitable interest is an irrevocable remainder interest, not in trust, in a farm. Thus, for example, if the donor gives to charity a remainder interest in a farm and retains an estate in such property for life or a term of years, the value of such remainder interest is deductible under section 2522. For purposes of this subdivision, the term "farm" means any land used by the donor or his tenant for the production of crops, fruits, or other agricultural products or for the sustenance of livestock. The term "livestock" includes cattle, hogs, horses, mules, donkeys, sheep, goats, captive furbearing animals, chickens, turkeys, pigeons, and other poultry. A farm includes the improvements thereon.

(iv) Qualified Conservation Contribution. The charitable interest is a qualified conservation contribution. For the definition of a qualified conservation contribution, see § 1.170-A-14.

(v) Charitable remainder trust and pooled income funds. The charitable interest is a remainder interest in a trust which is a charitable remainder annuity trust, as defined in section 664(d)(1) and § 1.664-2 of this chapter; a charitable remainder unitrust, as defined in section 664(d)(2) and (3) and § 1.664-3 of this chapter; or a pooled income fund, as defined in section 642(c)(5) and § 1.642(c)-5 of this chapter. The charitable organization to or for the use of which the remainder interest is transferred must meet the requirements of both section 2522(a) or (b) and section 642(c)(5)(A), section 664(d)(1)(C), or section 664(d)(2)(C), whichever applies. For example, the charitable organization to which the remainder interest in a charitable remainder annuity trust is transferred may not be a foreign corporation.

(vi) Guaranteed annuity interest. (a) The charitable interest is a guaranteed annuity interest, whether or not such interest is in trust. For purposes of this paragraph (c)(2)(vi), the term "guaranteed annuity interest" means an irrevocable right pursuant to the instrument of transfer to receive a guaranteed annuity. A guaranteed annuity is an arrangement under which a determinable amount is paid periodically, but not less often than annually, for a specified term of years or for the life or lives of certain individuals, each of whom must be living at the date of the gift and can be ascertained at such date. Only one or more of the following individuals may be used as measuring lives: the donor, the donor's spouse, and an individual who, with respect to all remainder beneficiaries (other than charitable organizations described in section 170, 2055, or 2522), is either a lineal ancestor or the spouse of a lineal ancestor of those beneficiaries. A trust will satisfy the requirement that all noncharitable remainder beneficiaries are lineal descendants of the individual who is the measuring life, or that individual's spouse, if there is less than a 15% probability that individuals who are not lineal descendants will receive any trust corpus. This probability must be computed, based on the current applicable Life Table contained in § 20.2031-7, at the time property is transferred to the trust taking into account the interests of all primary and contingent remainder beneficiaries who are living at that time. An interest payable for a specified term of years can qualify as a guaranteed annuity interest even if the governing instrument contains a savings clause intended to ensure compliance with a rule against perpetuities. The savings clause must utilize a period for vesting of 21 years after the deaths of measuring lives who are selected to maximize, rather than limit, the term of the trust. The rule in this paragraph that a charitable interest may be payable for the life or lives of only certain specified individuals does not apply in the case of a charitable guaranteed annuity interest payable under a charitable remainder trust described in section 664. An amount is determinable if the exact amount which must be paid under the conditions specified in the instrument of transfer can be ascertained as of the date of gift. For example, the amount to be paid may be a stated sum for a term of years, or for the life of the donor, at the expiration of which it may be changed by a specified amount, but it may not be redetermined by reference to a fluctuating index such as the cost of living index. In further illustration, the amount to be paid may be expressed as a fraction or percentage of the cost of living index on the date of gift.

(b) A charitable interest is a guaranteed annuity interest only if it is a guaranteed annuity interest in every respect. For example, if the charitable interest is the right to receive from a trust each year a payment equal to the lesser of a sum certain or a fixed percentage of the net fair market value of the trust assets, determined annually, such interest is not a guaranteed annuity interest.

(c) Where a charitable interest in the form of a guaranteed annuity interest is not in trust, the interest will be considered a guaranteed annuity interest only if it is to be paid by an insurance company or by an organization regularly engaged in issuing annuity contracts.

(d) Where a charitable interest in the form of a guaranteed annuity interest is in trust, the governing instrument of the trust may provide that income of the trust which is in excess of the amount required to pay the guaranteed annuity interest shall be paid to or for the use of a charity. Nevertheless, the amount of the deduction under section 2522 shall be limited to the fair market value of the guaranteed annuity interest as determined under paragraph (d)(2)(iv) of this section.

(e) Where a charitable interest in the form of a guaranteed annuity interest is in trust and the present value on the date of gift of all income interests for a charitable purpose exceeds 60 percent of the aggregate fair market value of all amounts in such trust (after the payment of liabilities), the charitable interest will not be considered a guaranteed annuity interest unless the governing instrument of the trust prohibits both the acquisition and the retention of assets which would give rise to a tax under section 4944 if the trustee had acquired such assets. The requirement in this *(e)* for a prohibition in the governing instrument against the retention of assets which would give rise to a tax under section 4944 if the trustee had acquired the assets shall not apply to a gift made on or before May 21, 1972.

(f) Where a charitable interest in the form of a guaranteed annuity interest is in trust, and the gift of such interest is made after May 21, 1972, the charitable interest generally is not a guaranteed annuity interest if any amount may be paid by the trust for a private purpose before the expiration of all the charitable annuity interests. There are two exceptions to this general rule. First, the charitable interest is a guaranteed annuity interest if the amount payable for a private purpose is in the form of a guaranteed annuity interest and the trust's governing instrument does not provide for any preference or priority in the payment of the private annuity as opposed to the charitable annuity. Second, the charitable interest is a guaranteed annuity interest if under the trust's governing instrument the amount that may be paid for a private purpose is payable only from a group of assets that are devoted exclusively to private purposes and to which section 4947(a)(2) is inapplicable by reason of section 4947(a)(2)(B). For purposes of this paragraph (c)(2)(vi)(f), an amount is not paid for a private purpose if it is paid for an adequate and full consideration in money or money's worth. See § 53.4947-1(c) of this chapter for rules relating to the inapplicability of section 4947(a)(2) to segregated amounts in a split-interest trust.

(g) For rules relating to certain governing instrument requirements and to the imposition of certain excise taxes where the guaranteed annuity interest is in trust and for rules governing payment of private income interests by a split-interest trust, see section 4947(a)(2) and (b)(3)(A), and the regulations thereunder.

(vii) Unitrust interest. (a) The charitable interest is a unitrust interest, whether or not such interest is in trust. For purposes of this paragraph (c)(2)(vii), the term "unitrust interest" means an irrevocable right pursuant to the instrument of transfer to receive payment, not less often than annually, of a fixed percentage of the net fair market value, determined annually, of the property which funds the unitrust interest. In computing the net fair market value of the property which funds the unitrust interest, all assets and liabilities shall be taken into account without regard to whether particular items are taken into account in determining the income from the property. The net fair market value of the property which funds the unitrust interest may be determined on any one date during the year or by taking the average of valuations made on more than one date during the year, provided that the same valuation date or dates and valuation methods are used each year. Where the charitable interest is a unitrust interest to be paid by a trust and the governing instrument of the trust does not specify the valuation date or dates, the trustee shall select such date or dates and shall indicate his selection on the first return on Form 1041 which the trust is required to file. Payments under a unitrust interest may be paid for a specified term of years or for the life or lives of certain individuals, each of whom must be living at the date of the gift and can be ascertained at such date. Only one or more of the following individuals may be used as measuring lives: the donor, the donor's spouse, and an individual who, with respect to all remainder beneficiaries (other than charitable organizations described in section 170, 2055, or 2522), is either a lineal ancestor or the spouse of a lineal ancestor of those beneficiaries. A trust will satisfy the requirement that all noncharitable remainder beneficiaries are lineal descendants of the individual who is the measuring life, or that individual's spouse, if there is less than a 15% probability that individuals who are not lineal descendants will receive any trust corpus. This probability must be computed, based on the current applicable Life Table contained in § 20.2031-7, at the time property is transferred to the trust taking into account the interests of all primary and contingent remainder beneficiaries who are living at that time. An interest payable for a specified term of years can qualify as a unitrust interest even if the governing instrument contains a savings clause intended to ensure compliance with a rule against perpetuities. The savings clause must utilize a period for vesting of 21 years after the deaths of measuring lives who are selected to maximize, rather than limit, the term of the trust. The rule in this paragraph that a charitable interest may be payable for the life or lives of only certain specified individuals does not apply in the case of a charitable unitrust interest payable under a charitable remainder trust described in section 664.

(b) A charitable interest is a unitrust interest only if it is a unitrust interest in every respect. For example, if the charitable interest is the right to receive from a trust each year a payment equal to the lesser of a sum certain or a fixed percentage of the net fair market value of the trust assets, determined annually, such interest is not a unitrust interest.

(c) Where a charitable interest in the form of a unitrust interest is not in trust, the interest will be considered a unitrust interest only if it is to be paid by an insurance company or by an organization regularly engaged in issuing interests otherwise meeting the requirements of a unitrust interest.

(d) Where a charitable interest in the form of a unitrust interest is in trust, the governing instrument of the trust may provide that income of the trust which is in excess of the amount required to pay the unitrust interest shall be paid to or for the use of a charity. Nevertheless, the amount of the deduction under section 2522 shall be limited to the fair market value of the unitrust interest as determined under paragraph (d)(2)(v) of this section.

(e) Where a charitable interest in the form of a unitrust interest is in trust, the charitable interest generally is not a unitrust interest if any amount may be paid by the trust for a private purpose before the expiration of all the charitable unitrust interests. There are two exceptions to this general rule. First, the charitable interest is a unitrust interest if the amount payable for a private purpose is in the form of a unitrust interest and the trust's governing instrument does not provide for any preference or priority in the payment of the private unitrust interest as opposed to the charitable unitrust interest. Second, the charitable interest is a unitrust interest if under the trust's governing instrument the amount that may be paid for a private purpose is payable only from a group of assets that are devoted exclusively to private purposes and to which section 4947(a)(2) is inapplicable by reason of section 4947(a)(2)(B). For purposes of this paragraph (c)(2)(vii)(e), an amount is not paid for a private purpose if it is paid for an adequate and full consideration in money or money's worth. See § 53.4947-1(c) of this chapter for rules relating to the inapplicability of section 4947(a)(2) to segregated amounts in a split-interest trust.

(f) For rules relating to certain governing instrument requirements and to the imposition of certain excise taxes where the unitrust interest is in trust and for rules governing payment of private income interests by a split-interest trust, see sections 4947(a)(2) and (b)(3)(A), and the regulations thereunder.

(d) Valuation of charitable interest. *(1) In general.* The amount of the deduction in the case of a contribution of a partial interest in property to which this section applies is the fair market value of the partial interest on the date of gift. The fair market value of an annuity, life estate, term for years, remainder, reversion or unitrust interest is its present value.

(2) Certain transfers after July 31, 1969. In the case of a transfer after July 31, 1969, of an interest described in paragraph (c)(2)(v), (vi), or (vii) of this section, the present value of such interest is to be determined under the following rules:

(i) The present value of a remainder interest in a charitable remainder annuity trust is to be determined under § 1.664-2(c) of this chapter (Income Tax Regulations).

(ii) The present value of a remainder interest in a charitable remainder unitrust is to be determined under § 1.664-4 of this chapter.

(iii) The present value of a remainder interest in a pooled income fund is to be determined under § 1.642(c)-6 of this chapter.

(iv) The present value of a guaranteed annuity interest described in paragraph (c)(2)(vi) of this section is to be determined under § 25.2512-5 except that, if the annuity is issued by a company regularly engaged in the sale of annuities, the present value is to be determined under § 25.2512-6. If by reason of all the conditions and circumstances surrounding a transfer of an income interest in property in trust it appears that the charity may not receive the beneficial enjoyment of the interest, a deduction will be allowed under section 2522 only for the minimum amount it is evident the charity will receive.

Example (1). In 1975, B transfers $20,000 in trust with the requirement that a designated charity be paid a guaranteed annuity interest (as defined in paragraph (c)(2)(vi) of this section) of $4,100 a year, payable annually at the end of each year for a period of 6 years and that the remainder be paid to his children. The fair market value of an annuity of $4,100 a year for a period of 6 years is $20,160.93 ($4,100 × 4.9173), as determined under § 25.2512-5A(c). The deduction with respect to the guaranteed annuity interest will be limited to $20,000, which is the minimum amount it is evident the charity will receive.

Example (2). In 1975, C transfers $40,000 in trust with the requirement that D, an individual, and X Charity be paid simultaneously guaranteed annuity interests (as defined in paragraph (c)(2)(vi) of this section) of $5,000 a year each, payable annually at the end of each year, for a period of 5 years and that the remainder be paid to C's children. The fair market value of two annuities of $5,000 each a year for a period of 5 years is $42,124 ([$5,000 × 4.2124] × 2), as determined under § 25.2512-5A(c). The trust instrument provides that in the event the trust fund is insufficient to pay both annuities in a given year, the trust fund will be evenly divided between the charitable and private annuitants. The deduction with respect to the charitable annuity will be limited to $20,000, which is the minimum amount it is evident the charity will receive.

Example (3). In 1975, D transfers $65,000 in trust with the requirement that a guaranteed annuity interest (as defined in paragraph (c)(2)(vi) of this section) of $5,000 a year, payable annually at the end of each year, be paid to Y Charity for a period of 10 years and that a guaranteed annuity interest (as defined in paragraph (c)(2)(vi) of this section) of $5,000 a year, payable annually at the end of each year, be paid to W, his wife, aged 62, for 10 years or until her prior death. The annuities are to be paid simultaneously, and the remainder is to be paid to D's children. The fair market value of the private annuity is $33,877 ($5,000 × 6.7754), as determined pursuant to § 25.2512-5A(c) and by the use of factors involving one life and a term of years as published in Publication 723A (12-70). The fair market value of the charitable annuity is $36,800.50 ($5,000 × 7.3601), as determined under § 25.2512-5A(c). It is not evident from the governing instrument of the trust or from local law that the trustee would be required to apportion the trust fund between the wife and charity in the event the fund were insufficient to pay both annuities in a given year. Accordingly, the deduction with respect to the charitable annuity will be limited to $31,123 ($65,000 less $33,877 [the value of the private annuity]), which is the minimum amount it is evident the charity will receive.

(v) The present value of a unitrust interest described in paragraph (c)(2)(vii) of this section is to be determined by subtracting the present value of all interests in the transferred property other than the unitrust interest from the fair market value of the transferred property.

(3) Other transfers. The present value of an interest not described in paragraph (d)(2) of this section is to be determined under § 25.2512-5.

(4) Special computations. If the interest transferred is such that its present value is to be determined by a special computation, a request for a special factor, accompanied by a statement of the date of birth and sex of each individual the duration of whose life may affect the value of the interest, and by copies of the relevant instruments, may be submitted by the donor to the Commissioner who may, if conditions permit, supply the factor requested. If the Commissioner furnishes the factor, a copy of the letter supplying the factor must be attached to the tax return in which the deduction is claimed. If the Commissioner does not furnish the factor, the claim for deduction must be supported by a full statement of the computation of the present value made in accordance with the principles set forth in this paragraph.

(e) [Reserved]. For further guidance, see § 25.2522(c)-3T(e).

T.D. 7318, 7/10/74, amend T.D. 7340, 1/6/75, T.D. 7955, 5/11/84, T.D. 8069, 1/13/86, T.D. 8540, 6/9/94, T.D. 8630, 12/12/95, T.D. 8923, 1/4/2001, T.D. 9068, 7/3/2003, T.D. 9448, 5/1/2009.

PAR. 14. Section 25.2522(c)-3 is amended by revising paragraph (e) to read as follows:

Proposed § 25.2522(c)-3 Transfers not exclusively for charitable, etc., purposes in the case of gifts made after July 31, 1969. [*For Preamble, see ¶ 153,105*]

* * * * *

(e) [The text of this proposed paragraph (e) is the same as the text of § 25.2522(c)-3T(e) published elsewhere in this issue of the Federal Register]. [*See T.D. 9448, 05/07/2009, 74 Fed. Reg. 87.*]

§ 25.2522(c)-3T Transfers not exclusively for charitable, etc., purposes in the case of gifts made after July 31, 1969 (temporary).

(a) through (d) [Reserved]. For further guidance, see § 25.2522(c)-3(a) through (d).

(e) Effective/applicability date. This section applies only to gifts made after July 31, 1969. In addition, the rule in paragraphs (c)(2)(vi)(a) and (c)(2)(vii)(a) of this section that guaranteed annuity interests or unitrust interests, respectively, may be payable for a specified term of years or for the life or lives of only certain individuals applies to transfers made on or after April 4, 2000. If a transfer is made on or after April 4, 2000, that uses an individual other than one permitted in paragraphs (c)(2)(vi)(a) and (c)(2)(vii)(a) of this section, the interest may be reformed into a lead interest payable for a specified term of years. The term of years is determined by taking the factor for valuing the annuity or unitrust interest for the named individual measuring life and identifying the term of years (rounded up to the next whole year) that corresponds to the equivalent term of years factor for an annuity or unitrust interest. For example, in the case of an annuity interest payable for the life of an individual age 40 at the time of the transfer on or after May 1, 2009, assuming an interest rate of 7.4 percent under section 7520, the annuity factor from column 1 of Table S(7.4), contained in IRS Publication 1457, Actuarial Valuations Version 3A, for the life of an individual age 40 is 12.1519 (1--.10076/.074). Based on Table B(7.4), contained in Publication 1457, Actuarial Valuations Version 3A, the factor 12.1519 corresponds to a term of years between 32 and 33 years. Accordingly, the annuity interest must be reformed into an interest payable for a term of 33 years. A judicial reformation must be commenced prior to October 15th of the year following the year in which the transfer is made and must be completed within a reasonable time after it is commenced. A non-judicial reformation is permitted if effective under state law, provided it is completed by the date on which a judicial reformation must be commenced. In the alternative, if a court, in a proceeding that is commenced on or before July 5, 2001, declares any transfer, made on or after April 4, 2000, and on or before March 6, 2001, null and void ab initio, the Internal Revenue Service will treat such transfers in a manner similar to that described in section 2055(e)(3)(J).

T.D. 9448, 5/1/2009.

§ 25.2522(c)-4 Disallowance of double deduction in the case of qualified terminable interest property.

No deduction is allowed under section 2522 for the transfer of an interest in property if a deduction is taken from the total amount of gifts with respect to that property by reason of section 2523(f). See § 25.2523(h)-1.

T.D. 8522, 2/28/94.

§ 25.2522(d)-1 Additional cross references.

Caution: The Treasury has not yet amended Reg § 25.2522(d)-1 to reflect changes made by P.L. 98-369, P.L. 97-473, P.L. 94-455.

(a) See section 14 of the Wild and Scenic Rivers Act (Public Law 90-542, 82 Stat 918) for provisions relating to the claim and allowance of the value of certain easements as a gift under section 2522.

(b) For treatment of gifts accepted by the Secretary of State or the Secretary of Commerce, for the purpose of organizing and holding an international conference to negotiate a Patent Corporation Treaty, as gifts to or for the use of the United States, see section 3 of Joint Resolution of December 24, 1969 (Public Law 91-160, 83 Stat. 443).

(c) For treatment of gifts accepted by the Secretary of the Department of Housing and Urban Development, for the purpose of aiding or facilitating the work of the Department, as gifts to or for the use of the United States, see section 7(k) of the Department of Housing and Urban Development Act (42 U.S.C. 3535), as added by section 905 of Public Law 91-609 (84 Stat. 1809).

(d) For treatment of certain property accepted by the Chairman of the Administrative Conference of the United States, for the purpose of aiding and facilitating the work of the Conference, as gifts to the United States, see 5 U.S.C. 575(c)(12), as added by section 1(b) of the Act of October 21, 1972 (Public Law 92-526, 86 Stat. 1048).

(e) For treatment of the Board for International Broadcasting as a corporation described in section 2522(a)(2), see section 7 of the Board for International Broadcasting Act of 1973 (Public Law 93-129, 87 Stat 459).

T.D. 7318, 7/10/74.

§ 25.2523(a)-1 Gift to spouse; in general.

(a) In general. In determining the amount of taxable gifts for the calendar quarter (with respect to gifts made after December 31, 1970, and before January 1, 1982), or calendar year (with respect to gifts made before January 1, 1971, or after December 31, 1981), a donor may deduct the value of any property interest transferred by gift to a donee who at the time of the gift is the donor's spouse, except as limited by paragraphs (b) and (c) of this section. See § 25.2502-1(c)(1) for the definition of calendar quarter. This deduction is referred to as the marital deduction. In the case of gifts made prior to July 14, 1988, no marital deduction is allowed with respect to a gift if, at the time of the gift, the donor is a nonresident not a citizen of the United States. Further, in the case of gifts made on or after July 14, 1988, no marital deduction is allowed (regardless of the donor's citizenship or residence) for transfers to a spouse who is not a citizen of the United States at the time of the transfer. However, for certain special rules applicable in the case of estate and gift tax treaties, see section 7815(d)(14) of Public Law 101-239. The donor must submit any evidence necessary to establish the donor's right to the marital deduction.

(b) "Deductible interests" and "non-deductible interests". *(1) In general.* The property interests transferred by a donor to his spouse consist of either transfers with respect to which the marital deduction is authorized (as described in subparagraph (2) of this paragraph) or transfers with respect to which the marital deduction is not authorized (as described in subparagraph (3) of this paragraph). These transfers are referred to in this section and in §§ 25.2523(b)-1 through 25.2523(f)-1 as "deductible interests" and "nondeductible interests", respectively.

(2) "Deductible interest". A property interest transferred by a donor to his spouse is a "deductible interest" if it does not fall within either class of "nondeductible interests" described in subparagraph (3) of this paragraph.

(3) "Nondeductible interests". (i) A property interest transferred by a donor to his spouse which is a "terminable interest", as defined in § 25.2523(b)-1, is a "nondeductible interest" to the extent specified in that section.

(ii) Any property interest transferred by a donor to the donor's spouse is a nondeductible interest to the extent it is not required to be included in a gift tax return for a calendar quarter (for gifts made after December 31, 1970, and before January 1, 1982) or calendar year (for gifts made before January 1, 1971, or after December 31, 1981).

(c) Computation. *(1) In general.* The amount of the marital deduction depends upon when the interspousal gifts are made, whether the gifts are terminable interests, whether the limitations of § 25.2523(f)-1A (relating to gifts of community property before January 1, 1982) are applicable, and whether § 25.2523(f)-1 (relating to the election with respect to life estates) is applicable, and (with respect to gifts made on or after July 14, 1988) whether the donee spouse is a citizen of the United States (see section 2523(i)).

(2) Gifts prior to January 1, 1977. Generally, with respect to gifts made during a calendar quarter prior to January 1, 1977, the marital deduction allowable under section 2523 is 50 percent of the aggregate value of the deductible interests. See section 2524 for an additional limitation on the amount of the allowable deduction.

(3) Gifts after December 31, 1976, and before January 1, 1982. Generally, with respect to gifts made during a calendar quarter beginning after December 31, 1976, and ending prior to January 1, 1982, the marital deduction allowable under section 2523 is computed as a percentage of the deductible interests in those gifts. If the aggregate amount of deductions for such gifts is $100,000 or less, a deduction is allowed for 100 percent of the deductible interests. No deduction is allowed for otherwise deductible interests in an aggregate amount that exceeds $100,000 and is equal to or less than $200,000. For deductible interests in excess of $200,000, the deduction is limited to 50 percent of such deductible interests. If a donor remarries, the computations in this paragraph (c)(3) are made on the basis of aggregate gifts to all persons who at the time of the gifts are the donor's spouse. See section 2524 for an additional limitation on the amount of the allowable deduction.

(4) Gifts after December 31, 1981. Generally, with respect to gifts made during a calendar year beginning after December 31, 1981 (other than gifts made on or after July 14, 1988, to a spouse who is not a United States citizen on the date of the transfer), the marital deduction allowable under section 2523 is 100 percent of the aggregate value of the deductible interests. See section 2524 for an additional limitation on the amount of the allowable deduction, and section 2523(i) regarding disallowance of the marital deduction for gifts to a spouse who is not a United States citizen.

(d) Examples. The following examples (in which it is assumed that the donors have previously utilized any specific exemptions provided by section 2521 for gifts prior to January 1, 1977) illustrate the application of paragraph (c) of this section and the interrelationship of sections 2523 and 2503.

Example (1). A donor made a transfer by gift of $6,000 cash to his spouse on December 25, 1971. The donor made no other transfers during 1971. The amount of the marital deduction for the fourth calendar quarter of 1971 is $3,000 (one-half of $6,000); the amount of the annual exclusion under section 2503(b) is $3,000; and the amount of taxable gifts is zero ($6,000 – $3,000 (annual exclusion) – $3,000 (marital deduction)).

Example (2). A donor made transfers by gift to his spouse of $3,000 cash on January 1, 1971, and $3,000 cash on May 1, 1971. The donor made no other transfers during 1971. For the first calendar quarter of 1971 the marital deduction is zero because the amount excluded under section 2503(b) is $3,000, and the amount of taxable gifts is also zero. For the second calendar quarter of 1971 the marital deduction is $1,500 (one-half of $3,000), and the amount of taxable gifts is $1,500 ($3,000 – $1,500 (marital deduction)). Under section 2503(b) no amount of the second $3,000 gift may be excluded because the entire $3,000 annual exclusion was applied against the gift made in the first calendar quarter of 1971.

Example (3). A donor made a transfer by gift to his spouse of $10,000 cash on April 1, 1972. The donor made no other transfers during 1972. For the second calendar quarter of 1972 the amount of the marital deduction is $5,000 (one-half of $10,000); the amount excluded under section 2503(b) is $3,000; the amount of taxable gifts is $2,000 ($10,000 – $3,000 (annual exclusion) – $5,000 (marital deduction)).

Example (4). A donor made transfers by gift to his spouse of $2,000 cash on January 1, 1971, $2,000 cash on April 5, 1971, and $10,000 cash on December 1, 1971. The donor made no other transfers during 1971. For the first calendar quarter of 1971 the marital deduction is zero because the amount excluded under section 2503(b) is $2,000 and the amount of taxable gifts is also zero. For the second calendar quarter of 1971 the marital deduction is $1,000 (one-half of $2,000) (see section 2524); the amount excluded under section 2503(b) is $1,000 because $2,000 of the $3,000 annual exclusion was applied against the gift made in the first calendar quarter of 1971; and the amount of taxable gifts is zero ($2,000 – $1,000 (annual exclusion) – $1,000 (marital deduction)). For the fourth calendar quarter of 1971, the marital deduction is $5,000 (one-half of $10,000); the amount excluded under section 2503(b) is zero because the entire $3,000 annual exclusion was applied against the gifts made in the first and second calendar quarters of 1971; and the amount of taxable gifts is $5,000 ($10,000 – $5,000 (marital deduction)).

Example (5). A donor made transfers by gift to his spouse of $2,000 cash on January 10, 1972, $2,000 cash on May 1, 1972, and a remainder interest valued at $16,000 on June 1, 1972. The donor made no other transfers during 1972. For the first calendar quarter of 1972, the marital deduction is zero because $2,000 is excluded under section 2503(b), and the amount of taxable gifts is also zero. For the second calendar quarter of 1972 the marital deduction is $9,000 (one-half of $16,000 plus one-half of $2,000); the amount excluded under section 2503(b) is $1,000 because $2,000 of the $3,000 annual exclusion was applied against the gift made in the first calendar quarter of 1971; and the amount of taxable gifts is $8,000 ($18,000 – $1,000 (annual exclusion) – $9,000 (marital deduction)).

Example (6). A donor made transfers by gift to his spouse of $2,000 cash on January 1, 1972, a remainder interest valued at $16,000 on January 5, 1972, and $2,000 cash on April 30, 1972. The donor made no other transfers during 1972. For the first calendar quarter of 1972, the marital deduction is $9,000 (one-half of $16,000 plus one-half of $2,000); the amount excluded under section 2503(b) is $2,000; and the amount of taxable gifts is $7,000 ($18,000 – $2,000 (annual exclusion) – $9,000 (marital deduction)). For the second calendar quarter of 1972 the marital deduction is $1,000 (one-half of $2,000); the amount excluded under section 2503(b) is $1,000 because $2,000 of the $3,000 annual exclusion was applied against the gift of the present interest in the first calendar quarter of 1971; and the amount of taxable gifts is zero ($2,000 – $1,000 (annual exclusion) – $1,000 (marital deduction)).

Example (7). A donor made a transfer by gift to his spouse of $12,000 cash on July 1, 1955. The donor made no other transfers during 1955. For the calendar year 1955 the amount of the marital deduction is $6,000 (one-half of $12,000); the amount excluded under section 2503(b) is $3,000; and the amount of taxable gifts is $3,000 ($12,000 – $3,000 (annual exclusion) – $6,000 (marital deduction)).

Example (8). A donor made a transfer by gift to the donor's spouse, a United States citizen, of $200,000 cash on January 1, 1995. The donor made no other transfers during 1995. For calendar year 1995, the amount excluded under section 2503(b) is $10,000; the marital deduction is $190,000; and the amount of taxable gifts is zero ($200,000 – $10,000 (annual exclusion) – $190,000 (marital deduction)).

(e) Valuation. If the income from property is made payable to the donor or another individual for life or for a term of years, with remainder to the donor's spouse or to the estate of the donor's spouse, the marital deduction is computed (pursuant to § 25.2523(a)-1(c)) with respect to the present value of the remainder, determined under section 7520. The present value of the remainder (that is, its value as of the date of gift) is to be determined in accordance with the rules stated in § 25.2512-5 or, for certain prior periods, § 25.2512-5A. See the example in paragraph (d) of § 25.2512-5. If the remainder is such that its value is to be determined by a special computation, a request for a specific factor, accompanied by a statement of the dates of birth of each person, the duration of whose life may affect the value of the remainder, and by copies of the relevant instruments may be submitted by the donor to the Commissioner who, if conditions permit, may supply the factor requested. If the Commissioner does not furnish the factor, the claim for deduction must be supported by a full statement of the computation of the present value, made in accordance with the principles set forth in § 25.2512-5(d) or, for certain prior periods, § 25.2512-5A.

T.D. 6334, 11/14/58, amend T.D. 7012, 5/14/69, T.D. 7238, 12/28/72, T.D. 7955, 5/11/84, T.D. 8522, 2/28/94, T.D. 8540, 6/9/94.

§ 25.2523(b)-1 Life estate or other terminable interest.

(a) In general. *(1)* The provisions of section 2523(b) generally disallow a marital deduction with respect to certain property interests (referred to generally as terminable interests and defined in paragraph (a)(3) of this section) transferred to the donee spouse under the circumstances described in paragraph (a)(2) of this section, unless the transfer comes within the purview of one of the exceptions set forth in § 25.2523(d)-1 (relating to certain joint interests); § 25.2523(e)-1 (relating to certain life estates with powers of appointment; § 25.2523(f)-1 (relating to certain qualified terminable interest property); or § 25.2523(g)-1 (relating to certain qualified charitable remainder trusts).

(2) If a donor transfers a terminable interest in property to the donee spouse, the marital deduction is disallowed with respect to the transfer if the donor spouse also—

(i) Transferred an interest in the same property to another donee (see paragraph (b) of this section), or

(ii) Retained an interest in the same property in himself (see paragraph (c) of this section), or

(iii) Retained a power to appoint an interest in the same property (see paragraph (d) of this section).

Notwithstanding the preceding sentence, the marital deduction is disallowed under these circumstances only if the other donee, the donor, or the possible appointee, may, by reason of the transfer or retention, possess or enjoy any part of the property after the termination or failure of the interest therein transferred to the donee spouse.

(3) For purposes of this section, a distinction is to be drawn between "property," as such term is used in section 2523 and an "interest, in property." The "property" referred to is the underlying property in which various interests exist; each such interest is not, for this purpose, to be considered as "property." A "terminable interest" in property is an interest which will terminate or fail on the lapse of time or on the occurrence or failure to occur of some contingency. Life estates, terms for years, annuities, patents, and copyrights are therefore terminable interests. However, a bond, note, or similar contractual obligation, the discharge of which would not have the effect of an annuity or term for years, is not a terminable interest.

(b) Interest in property which another donee may possess or enjoy. *(1)* Section 2523(b) provides that no marital deduction shall be allowed with respect to the transfer to the donee spouse of a "terminable interest" in property, in case—

(i) The donor transferred (for less than an adequate and full consideration in money or money's worth) an interest in the same property to any person other than the donee spouse (or the estate of such spousé), and

(ii) By reason of such transfer, such person (or his heirs or assigns) may possess or enjoy any part of such property after the termination or failure of the interest therein transferred to the donee spouse.

(2) In determining whether the donor transferred an interest in property to any person other than the donee spouse, it is immaterial whether the transfer to the person other than the donee spouse was made at the same time as the transfer to such spouse, or at any earlier time.

(3) Except as provided in § 25.2523(e)-1 or 25.2523(f)-1, if at the time of the transfer it is impossible to ascertain the particular person or persons who may receive a property interest transferred by the donor, such interest is considered as transferred to a person other than the donee spouse for the purpose of section 2523(b). This rule is particularly applicable in the case of the transfer of a property interest by the donor subject to a reserve power. See § 25.2511-2. Under this rule, any property interest over which the donor reserved a power to revest the beneficial title in himself, or over which the donor reserved the power to name new beneficiaries or to change the interests of the beneficiaries as between themselves, is for the purpose of section 2523(b), considered as transferred to a "person other than the donee spouse." The following examples, in which it is assumed that the donor did not make an election under sections 2523(f)(2)(C) and (f)(4), illustrate the application of the provisions of this paragraph (b)(3):

Example (1). If a donor transferred property in trust naming his wife as the irrevocable income beneficiary for 10 years, and providing that, upon the expiration of that term, the corpus should be distributed among his wife and children in such proportions as the trustee should determine, the right to the corpus, for the purpose of the marital deduction, is considered as transferred to a "person other than the donee spouse."

Example (2). If, in the above example, the donor had provided that, upon the expiration of the 10-year term, the corpus was to be paid to his wife, but also reserved the power to revest such corpus in himself the right to corpus, for the purpose of the marital deduction, is considered as transferred to a "person other than the donee spouse."

(4) The term "person other than the donee spouse" includes the possible unascertained takers of a property interest, as, for example, the members of a class to be ascertained in the future. As another example, assume that the donor created a power of appointment over a property interest, which does not come within the purview of

§ 25.2523(e)-1. In such a case, the term "person other than the donee spouse" refers to the possible appointees and takers in default (other than the spouse) of such property interest.

(5) An exercise or release at any time by the donor (either alone or in conjunction with any person) of a power to appoint an interest in property, even though not otherwise a transfer by him is considered as a transfer by him in determining, for the purpose of section 2523(b), whether he transferred an interest in such property to a person other than the donee spouse.

(6) The following examples illustrate the application of this paragraph. In each example, it is assumed that the donor made no election under sections 2523(f)(2)(C) and (f)(4) and that the property interest that the donor transferred to a person other than the donee spouse is not transferred for adequate and full consideration in money or money's worth:

Example (1). H (the donor) transferred real property to W (his wife) for life, with remainder to A and his heirs. No marital deduction may be taken with respect to the interest transferred to W, since it will terminate upon her death and A (or his heirs or assigns) will thereafter possess or enjoy the property.

Example (2). H transferred property for the benefit of W and A. The income was payable to W for life and upon her death the principal was to be distributed to A or his issue. However, if A should die without issue, leaving W surviving, the principal was then to be distributed to W. No marital deduction may be taken with respect to the interest transferred to W, since it will terminate in the event of her death if A or his issue survive, and A or his issue will thereafter possess or enjoy the property.

Example (3). H purchased for $100,000 a life annuity for W. If the annuity payments made during the life of W should be less than $100,000, further payments were to be made to A. No marital deduction may be taken with respect to the interest transferred to W, since A may possess or enjoy a part of the property following the termination of W's interest. If, however, the contract provided for no continuation of payments, and provided for no refund upon the death of W, or provided that any refund was to go to the estate of W, then a marital deduction may be taken with respect to the gift.

Example (4). H transferred property to A for life with remainder to W provided W survives A, but if W predeceases A, the property is to pass to B and his heirs. No marital deduction may be taken with respect to the interest transferred to W.

Example (5). H transferred real property to A, reserving the right to the rentals of the property for a term of 20 years. H later transferred the right to the remaining rentals to W. No marital deduction may be taken with respect to the interest since it will terminate upon the expiration of the balance of the 20-year term and A will thereafter possess or enjoy the property.

Example (6). H transferred a patent to W and A as tenants in common. In this case, the interest of W will terminate upon the expiration of the term of the patent, but possession and enjoyment of the property by A must necessarily cease at the same time. Therefore, since A's possession or enjoyment cannot outlast the termination of W's interest, the provisions of section 2523(b) do not disallow the marital deduction with respect to the interest.

(c) Interest in property which the donor may possess or enjoy. *(1)* Section 2523(b) provides that no marital deduction is allowed with respect to the transfer to the donee spouse of a "terminable interest" in property, if—

(i) The donor retained in himself an interest in the same property, and

(ii) By reason of such retention, the donor (or his heirs or assigns may possess or enjoy any part of the property after the termination or failure of the interest transferred to the donee spouse. However, as to a transfer to the donee spouse as sole joint tenant with the donor or as tenant by the entirety, see § 25.2523(d)-1.

(2) In general, the principles illustrated by the examples under paragraph (b) of this section are applicable in determining whether the marital deduction may be taken with respect to a property interest transferred to the donee spouse subject to the retention by the donor of an interest in the same property. The application of this paragraph may be further illustrated by the following example, in which it is assumed that the donor made no election under sections 2523(f)(2)(C) and (f)(4).

Example. The donor purchased three annuity contracts for the benefit of his wife and himself. The first contract provided for payments to the wife for life, with refund to the donor in case the aggregate payments made to the wife were less than the cost of the contract. The second contract provided for payments to the donor for life, and then to the wife for life if she survived the donor. The third contract provided for payments to the donor and his wife for their joint lives and then to the survivor of them for life. No marital deduction may be taken with respect to the gifts resulting from the purchases of the contracts since, in the case of each contract, the donor may possess or enjoy a part of the property after the termination or failure of the interest transferred to the wife.

(d) Interest in property over which the donor retained a power to appoint. *(1)* Section 2523(b) provides that no marital deduction is allowed with respect to the transfer to the donee spouse of a "terminable interest" in property if—

(i) The donor had, immediately after the transfer, a power to appoint an interest in the same property, and

(ii) The donor's power was exercisable (either alone or in conjunction with any person) in such manner that the appointee may possess or enjoy any part of the property after the termination or failure of the interest transferred to the donee spouse.

(2) For the purposes of section 2523(b), the donor is to be considered as having, immediately after the transfer to the donee spouse, such a power to appoint even though the power cannot be exercised until after the lapse of time, upon the occurrence of an event or contingency, or upon the failure of an event or contingency to occur. It is immaterial whether the power retained by the donor was a taxable power of appointment under section 2514.

(3) The principles illustrated by the examples under paragraph (b) of this section are generally applicable in determining whether the marital deduction may be taken with respect to a property interest transferred to the donee spouse subject to retention by the donor of a power to appoint an interest in the same property. The application of this paragraph may be further illustrated by the following example:

Example. The donor, having a power of appointment over certain property, appointed a life estate to his spouse. No marital deduction may be taken with respect to such transfer, since, if the retained power to appoint the remainder interest is exercised, the appointee thereunder may possess or enjoy the property after the termination or failure of the interest taken by the donee spouse.

T.D. 6334, 11/14/58, amend T.D. 8522, 2/28/94.

§ 25.2523(c)-1 Interest in unidentified assets.

(a) Section 2523(c) provides that if an interest passing to a donee spouse may be satisfied out of a group of assets (or their proceeds) which include a particular asset that would be a nondeductible interest if it passed from the donor to his spouse, the value of the interest passing to the spouse is reduced, for the purpose of the marital deduction, by the value of the particular asset.

(b) In order for this section to apply, two circumstances must coexist, as follows:

(1) The property interest transferred to the donee spouse must be payable out of a group of assets. An example of a property interest payable out of a group of assets is a right to a share of the corpus of a trust upon its termination.

(2) The group of assets out of which the property interest is payable must include one or more particular assets which, if transferred by the donor to the donee spouse, would not qualify for the marital deduction. Therefore, section 2523(c) is not applicable merely because a group of assets includes a terminable interest, but would only be applicable if the terminable interest were nondeductible under the provisions of § 25.2523(b)-1.

(c) If both of the circumstances set forth in paragraph (b) of this section exist, only a portion of the property interest passing to the spouse is a deductible interest. The portion qualifying as a deductible interest is an amount equal to the excess, if any, of the value of the property interest passing to the spouse over the aggregate value of the asset (or assets) that if transferred to the spouse would not qualify for the marital deduction. See paragraph (c) of § 25.2523(a)-1 to determine the percentage of the deductible interest allowable as a marital deduction. The application of this section may be illustrated by the following example:

Example. H was absolute owner of a rental property and on July 1, 1950, transferred it to A by gift, reserving the income for a period of 20 years. On July 1, 1955, he created a trust to last for a period of 10 years. H was to receive the income from the trust and at the termination of the trust the trustee is to turn over to H's wife, W, property having a value of $100,000. The trustee has absolute discretion in deciding which properties in the corpus he shall turn over to W in satisfaction of the gift to her. The trustee received two items of property from H. Item (1) consisted of shares of corporate stock. Item (2) consisted of the right to receive the income from the rental property during the unexpired portion of the 20-year term. Assume that at the termination of the trust on July 1, 1965, the value of the right to the rental income for the then unexpired term of 5 years (item (2)) will be $30,000. Since item (2) is a nondeductible interest and the trustee can turn it over to W in partial satisfaction of her gift, only $70,000 of the $100,000 receivable by her on July 1, 1965, will be considered as property with respect to which a marital deduction is allowable. The present value on July 1, 1955, of the right to receive $70,000 at the end of 10 years is $49,624.33 as determined under § 25.2512-5A(c). The value of the property qualifying for the marital deduction, therefore, is $49,624.33 and a marital deduction is allowed for one-half of that amount, or $24,812.17.

T.D. 6334, 11/14/58, amend T.D. 8522, 2/28/94, T.D. 8540, 6/9/94.

§ 25.2523(d)-1 Joint interests.

Section 2523(d) provides that if a property interest is transferred to the donee spouse as sole joint tenant with the donor or as a tenant by the entirety, the interest of the donor in the property which exists solely by reason of the possibility that the donor may survive the donee spouse, or that there may occur a severance of the tenancy, is not for the purposes of section 2523(b), to be considered as an interest retained by the donor in himself. Under this provision, the fact that the donor may, as surviving tenant, possess or enjoy the property after the termination of the interest transferred to the donee spouse does not preclude the allowance of the marital deduction with respect to the latter interest. Thus, if the donor purchased real property in the name of the donor and the donor's spouse as tenants by the entirety or as joint tenants with right of survivorship, a marital deduction is allowable with respect to the value of the interest of the donee spouse in the property (subject to the limitations set forth in § 25.2523(a)-1). See paragraph (c) of § 25.2523(b)-1, and section 2524.

T.D. 6334, 11/14/58, amend T.D. 7238, 12/28/72, T.D. 8522, 2/28/94.

§ 25.2523(e)-1 Marital deduction; life estate with power of appointment in donee spouse.

(a) In general. Section 2523(e) provides that if an interest in property is transferred by a donor to his spouse (whether or not in trust) and the spouse is entitled for life to all the income from the entire interest or all the income from a specific portion of the entire interest, with a power in her to appoint the entire interest or the specific portion, the interest transferred to her is a deductible interest, to the extent that it satisfies all five of the conditions set forth below (see paragraph (b) of this section if one or more of the conditions is satisfied as to only a portion of the interest):

(1) The donee spouse must be entitled for life to all of the income from the entire interest or a specific portion of the entire interest, or to a specific portion of all the income from the entire interest.

(2) The income payable to the donee spouse must be payable annually or at more frequent intervals.

(3) The donee spouse must have the power to appoint the entire interest or the specific portion to either herself or her estate.

(4) The power in the donee spouse must be exercisable by her alone and (whether exercisable by will or during life) must be exercisable in all events.

(5) The entire interest or the specific portion must not be subject to a power in any other person to appoint any part to any person other than the donee spouse.

(b) Specific portion; deductible amount. If either the right to income or the power of appointment given to the donee spouse pertains only to a specific portion of a property interest, the portion of the interest which qualifies as a deductible interest is limited to the extent that the rights in the donee spouse meet all of the five conditions described in paragraph (a) of this section. While the rights over the income and the power must coexist as to the same interest in property, it is not necessary that the rights over the income or the power as to such interest be in the same proportion. However, if the rights over income meeting the required conditions set forth in paragraph (a)(1) and (2) of this section extend over a smaller share of the property interest than the share with respect to which the power of appointment requirements set forth in paragraph (a)(3) through (5) of this section are satisfied, the deductible interest is limited to the smaller share. Conversely, if a power of appointment meeting all the requirements extends to a smaller portion of the property interest than the portion over which the income rights pertain, the deductible interest cannot exceed the value of the portion to which such power of appointment applies. Thus, if the donor gives to the donee spouse the right to receive annually all of the income from a particular property interest and a power of appointment meeting the specifications prescribed in paragraph (a)(3) through (5) of this section as to only one-half of the property interest, then only one-half of the property interest is treated as a deductible interest. Correspondingly, if the income interest of the spouse satisfying the requirements extends to only one-fourth of the property interest and a testamentary power of appointment satisfying the requirements extends to all of the property interest, then only one-fourth of the interest in the spouse qualifies as a deductible interest. Further, if the donee spouse has no right to income from a specific portion of a property interest but a testamentary power of appointment which meets the necessary conditions over the entire interest, then none of the interest qualifies for the deduction. In addition, if, from the time of the transfer, the donee spouse has a power of appointment meeting all of the required conditions over three-fourths of the entire property interest and the prescribed income rights over the entire interest, but with a power in another person to appoint one-half of the entire interest, the value of the interest in the donee spouse over only one-half of the property interest will qualify as a deductible interest.

(c) Meaning of specific portion. *(1) In general.* Except as provided in paragraphs (c)(2) and (c)(3) of this section, a partial interest in property is not treated as a specific portion of the entire interest. In addition, any specific portion of an entire interest in property is nondeductible to the extent the specific portion is subject to invasion for the benefit of any person other than the donee spouse, except in the case of a deduction allowable under section 2523(e), relating to the exercise of a general power of appointment by the donee spouse.

(2) Fraction or percentage share. Under section 2523(e), a partial interest in property is treated as a specific portion of the entire interest if the rights of the donee spouse in income, and the required rights as to the power described in § 25.2523(e)-1(a), constitute a fractional or percentage share of the entire property interest, so that the donee spouse's interest reflects its proportionate share of the increase or decrease in the value of the entire property interest to which the income rights and the power relate. Thus, if the spouse's right to income and the spouse's power extend to a specified fraction or percentage of the property, or its equivalent, the interest is in a specific portion of the property. In accordance with paragraph (b) of this section, if the spouse has the right to receive the income from a specific portion of the trust property (after applying paragraph (c)(3) of this section) but has a power of appointment over a different specific portion of the property (after applying paragraph (c)(3) of this section), the marital deduction is limited to the lesser specific portion.

(3) Special rule in the case of gifts made on or before October 24, 1992. In the case of gifts within the purview of the effective date rule contained in paragraph (c)(3)(iii) of this section:

(i) A specific sum payable annually, or at more frequent intervals, out of the property and its income that is not limited by the income of the property is treated as the right to receive the income from a specific portion of the property. The specific portion, for purposes of paragraph (c)(2) of this section, is the portion of the property that, assuming the interest rate generally applicable for the valuation of annuities at the time of the donor's gift, would produce income equal to such payments. However, a pecuniary amount payable annually to a donee spouse is not treated as a right to the income from a specific portion of trust property for purposes of this paragraph (c)(3)(i) if any person other than the donee spouse may receive, during the donee spouse's lifetime, any distribution of the property. To determine the applicable interest rate for valuing annuities, see sections 2512 and 7520 and the regulations under those sections.

(ii) The right to appoint a pecuniary amount out of a larger fund (or trust corpus) is considered the right to appoint a specific portion of such fund or trust in an amount equal to such pecuniary amount.

(iii) The rules contained in paragraphs(c)(3)(i) and (ii) of this section apply with respect to gifts made on or before October 24, 1992.

(4) Local law. A partial interest in property is treated as a specific portion of the entire interest if it is shown that the donee spouse has rights under local law that are identical to those the donee spouse would have acquired had the partial interest been expressed in terms satisfying the requirements of paragraph (c)(2) of this section (or paragraph (c)(3) of this section if applicable).

(5) Examples. The following examples illustrate the application of paragraphs (b) and (c) of this section, where D, the donor, transfers property to D's spouse, S:

Example (1). Spouse entitled to the lesser of an annuity or a fraction of trust income. Prior to October 24, 1992, D transferred in trust 500 identical shares of X Company stock, valued for gift tax purposes at $500,000. The trust provided that during the lifetime of D's spouse, S, the trustee is to pay annually to S the lesser of one-half of the trust income or $20,000. Any trust income not paid to S is to be accumulated in the trust and may not be distributed during S's lifetime. S has a testamentary general power of appointment over the entire trust principal. The applicable interest rate for valuing annuities as of the date of D's gift under section 7520 is 10 percent. For purposes of paragraphs (a) through (c) of this section, S is treated as receiving all of the income from the lesser of one-half of the stock ($250,000), or $200,000, the specific portion of the stock which, as determined in accordance with § 25.2523(e)-1(c)(3)(i) of this chapter, would produce annual income of $20,000 (20,000/.10). Accordingly, the marital deduction is limited to $200,000 (200,000/500,000 or ⅖ of the value of the trust.)

Example (2). Spouse possesses power and income interest over different specific portions of trust. The facts are the same as in Example 1 except that S's testamentary general power of appointment is exercisable over only ¼ of the trust principal. Consequently, under section 2523(e), the marital deduction is allowable only for the value of ¼of the trust ($125,000); i.e., the lesser of the value of the portion with respect to which S is deemed to be entitled to all of the income (⅖ of the trust or $200,000), or the value of the portion with respect to which S possesses the requisite power of appointment (¼ of the trust or $125,000).

Example (3). Power of appointment over shares of stock constitutes a power over a specific portion. D transferred 250 identical shares of Y company stock to a trust under the terms of which trust income is to be paid annually to S, during S's lifetime. S was given a testamentary general power of appointment over 100 shares of stock. The trust provides that if the trustee sells the Y company stock, S's general power of appointment is exercisable with respect to the sale proceeds or the property in which the proceeds are reinvested. Because the amount of property represented by a single share of stock would be altered if the corporation split its stock, issued stock dividends, made a distribution of capital, etc., a power to appoint 100 shares at the time of S's death is not necessarily a power to appoint the entire interest that the 100 shares represented on the date of D's gift. If it is shown that, under local law, S has a general power to appoint not only the 100 shares designated by D but also 100/250 of any distributions by the corporation that are included in trust principal, the requirements of paragraph (c)(2) of this section are satisfied and S is treated as having a general power to appoint 100/250 of the entire interest in the 250 shares. In that case, the marital deduction is limited to 40 percent of the trust principal. If local law does not give S that power, the 100 shares would not constitute a specific portion under § 25.2523(e)-1(c) (including § 25.2523(e)-1(c)(3)(ii)). The nature of the asset is such that a change in the capitalization of the corporation could cause an alteration in the original value represented by the shares at the time of the transfer and is thus not a specific portion of the trust.

(d) Definition of "entire interest". Since a marital deduction is allowed for each qualifying separate interest in property transferred by the donor to the donee spouse, for purposes of paragraphs (a) and (b) of this section, each property interest with respect to which the donee spouse received some rights is considered separately in determining whether her rights extend to the entire interest or to a specific portion of the entire interest. A property interest which consists of several identical units of property (such as a block of 250 shares of stock, whether the ownership is evidenced by one or several certificates) is considered one property interest, unless certain of the units are to be segregated and accorded different treatment, in which case each segregated group of items is considered a separate property interest. The bequest of a specified sum of money constitutes the bequest of a separate property interest if immediately following the transfer and thenceforth it, and the investments made with it, must be so segregated or accounted for as to permit its identification as a separate item of property. The application of this paragraph may be illustrated by the following examples:

Example (1). The donor transferred to a trustee three adjoining farms, Blackacre, Whiteacre, and Greenacre. The trust instrument provided that during the lifetime of the donee spouse the trustee should pay her all of the income from the trust. Upon her death, all of Blackacre, a one-half interest in Whiteacre, and a one-third interest in Greenacre were to be distributed to the person or persons appointed by her in her will. The donee spouse is considered as being entitled to all of the income from the entire interest in Blackacre, all of the income from the entire interest in Whiteacre, and all of the income from the entire interest in Greenacre. She also is considered as having a power of appointment over the entire interest in Blackacre, over one-half of the entire interest in Whiteacre, and over one-third of the entire interest in Greenacre.

Example (2). The donor transferred $250,000 to C, as trustee. C is to invest the money and pay all of the income from the investments to W, the donor's spouse, annually. W was given a general power, exercisable by will, to appoint one-half of the corpus of the trust. Here, immediately following establishment of the trust, the $250,000 will be sufficiently segregated to permit its identification as a separate item, and the $250,000 will constitute an entire property interest. Therefore, W has a right to income and a power of appointment such that one-half of the entire interest is a deductible interest.

Example (3). The donor transferred 100 shares of Z Corporation stock to D, as trustee. W, the donor's spouse, is to receive all of the income of the trust annually and is given a general power, exercisable by will, to appoint out of the trust corpus the sum of $25,000. In this case the $25,000 is not, immediately following establishment of the trust, sufficiently segregated to permit its identification as a separate item of property in which the donee spouse has the entire interest. Therefore, the $25,000 does not constitute the entire interest in a property for the purpose of paragraphs (a) and (b) of this section.

(e) Application of local law. In determining whether or not the conditions set forth in paragraph (a)(1) through (5) of this section are satisfied by the instrument of transfer, regard is to be had to the applicable provisions of the law of the jurisdiction under which the interest passes and, if the transfer is in trust, the applicable provisions of the law governing the administration of the trust. For example, silence of a trust instrument as to the frequency of payment will not be regarded as a failure to satisfy the condition set forth in paragraph (a)(2) of this section that income must be payable to the donee spouse annually or more frequently unless the applicable law permits payment to be made less frequently than annually. The principles outlined in this paragraph and paragraphs (f) and (g) of this section which are applied in determining whether transfers in trust meet such conditions are equally applicable in ascertaining whether, in the case of interests not in trust, the donee spouse has the equivalent in rights over income and over the property.

(f) Right to income. *(1)* If an interest is transferred in trust, the donee spouse is "entitled for life to all of the income from the entire interest or a specific portion of the entire interest," for the purpose of the condition set forth in paragraph (a)(1) of this section, if the effect of the trust is to give her substantially that degree of beneficial enjoyment of the trust property during her life which the principles of the law of trusts accord to a person who is unqualifiedly designated as the life beneficiary of a trust. Such degree of enjoyment is given only if it was the donor's intention, as manifested by the terms of the trust instrument and the surrounding circumstances, that the trust should produce for the donee spouse during her life such an income, or that the spouse should have such use of the trust property as is consistent with the value of the trust corpus and with its preservation. The designation of the spouse as sole income beneficiary for life of the entire interest or a specific portion of the entire interest will be sufficient to qualify the trust unless the terms of the trust and the surrounding circumstances considered as a whole evidence an intention to deprive the spouse of the requisite degree of enjoyment. In determining whether a trust evidences that intention, the treatment required or permitted with respect to individual items must be considered in relation to the entire system provided for the administration of the trust. In addition, the spouse's interest shall meet the condition set forth in paragraph (a)(1) of this section if the spouse is entitled to income as defined or determined by applicable local law that provides for a reasonable apportionment between the income and remainder beneficiaries of the total return of the trust and that meets the requirements of § 1.643(b)-1 of this chapter.

(2) If the over-all effect of a trust is to give to the donee spouse such enforceable rights as will preserve to her the requisite degree of enjoyment, it is immaterial whether that result is effected by rules specifically stated in the trust instrument, or, in their absence, by the rules for the management of the trust property and the allocation of receipts and expenditures supplied by the State law. For example, a provision in the trust instrument for amortization of bond premium by appropriate periodic charges to interest will not disqualify the interest transferred in trust even though there is no State law specifically authorizing amortization or there is a State law denying amortization which is applicable only in the absence of such a provision in the trust instrument.

(3) In the case of a trust, the rules to be applied by the trustee in allocation of receipts and expenses between income and corpus must be considered in relation to the nature and expected productivity of the assets transferred in trust, the nature and frequency of occurrence of the expected receipts, and any provisions as to change in the form of investments. If it is evident from the nature of the trust assets and the rules provided for management of the trust that the allocation to income of such receipts as rents, ordinary cash dividends and interest will give to the spouse the substantial enjoyment during life required by the statute, provisions that such receipts as stock dividends and proceeds from the conversion of trust assets shall be treated as corpus will not disqualify the interest transferred in trust. Similarly, provision for a depletion charge against income in the case of trust assets which are subject to depletion will not disqualify the interest transferred in trust, unless the effect is to deprive the spouse of the requisite beneficial enjoyment. The same principle is applicable in the case of depreciation, trustees' commissions, and other charges.

(4) Provisions granting administrative powers to the trustees will not have the effect of disqualifying an interest transferred in trust unless the grant of powers evidences the intention to deprive the donee spouse of the beneficial enjoyment required by the statute. Such an intention will not be considered to exist if the entire terms of the instrument are such that the local courts will impose reasonable limitations upon the exercise of the powers. Among the powers which if subject to reasonable limitations will not disqualify the interest transferred in trust are the power to determine the allocation or apportionment of receipts and disbursements between income and corpus, the power to apply the income or corpus for the benefit of the spouse, and the power to retain the assets transferred to the trust. For example, a power to retain trust assets which consist substantially of unproductive property will not disqualify the interest if the applicable rules for the administration of the trust require, or permit the spouse to require, that the trustee either make the property productive or convert it within a reasonable time. Nor will such a power disqualify the interest if the applicable rules for administration of the trust require the trustee to use the degree of judgment and care in the exercise of the power which a prudent man would use if he were owner of the trust assets. Further, a power to retain a residence for the spouse or other property for the personal use of the spouse will not disqualify the interest transferred in trust.

(5) An interest transferred in trust will not satisfy the condition set forth in paragraph (a)(1) of this section that the donee spouse be entitled to all the income if the primary purpose of the trust is to safeguard property without providing the spouse with the required beneficial enjoyment. Such trusts include not only trusts which expressly provide for the accumulation of the income but also trusts which indirectly accomplish a similar purpose. For example, assume that the corpus of a trust consists substantially of property which is not likely to be income producing during the life of the donee spouse and that the spouse cannot compel the trustee to convert or otherwise deal with the property as described in subparagraph (4) of this paragraph. An interest transferred to such a trust will not qualify unless the applicable rules for the administration require, or permit the spouse to require, that the trustee provide the required beneficial enjoyment, such as by payments to the spouse out of other assets of the trust.

(6) If a trust may be terminated during the life of the donee spouse, under her exercise of a power of appointment or by distribution of the corpus to her, the interest transferred in trust satisfies the condition set forth in paragraph (a)(1) of this section (that the spouse be entitled to all the income) if she (i) is entitled to the income until the trust terminates, or (ii) has the right, exercisable in all events, to have the corpus distributed to her at any time during her life.

(7) An interest transferred in trust fails to satisfy the condition set forth in paragraph (a)(1) of this section, that the spouse be entitled to all the income, to the extent that the income is required to be accumulated in whole or in part or may be accumulated in the discretion of any person other than the donee spouse; to the extent that the consent of any person other than the donee spouse is required as a condition precedent to distribution of the income; or to the extent that any person other than the donee spouse has the power to alter the terms of the trust so as to deprive her of her right to the income. An interest transferred in trust will not fail to satisfy the condition that the spouse be entitled to all the income merely because its terms provide that the right of the donee spouse to the income shall not be subject to assignment, alienation, pledge, attachment or claims of creditors.

(8) In the case of an interest transferred in trust, the terms "entitled for life" and "payable annually or at more frequent intervals", as used in the conditions set forth in paragraph (a)(1) and (2) of this section, require that under the terms of the trust the income referred to must be currently (at least annually; see paragraph (e) of this section) distributable to the spouse or that she must have such command over the income that it is virtually hers. Thus, the conditions in paragraph (a)(1) and (2) of this section are satisfied in this respect if, under the terms of the trust instrument, the donee spouse has the right exercisable annually (or more frequently) to require distribution to herself of the trust income, and otherwise the trust income is to be accumulated and added to corpus. Similarly, as respects the income for the period between the last distribution date and the date of the spouse's death, it is sufficient if that income is subject to the spouse's power to appoint. Thus, if the trust instrument provides that income accrued or undistributed on the date of the spouse's death is to be disposed of as if it had been received after her death, and if the spouse has a power of appointment over the trust corpus, the power necessarily extends to the undistributed income.

(g) Power of appointment in donee spouse. *(1)* The conditions set forth in paragraph (a)(3) and (4) of this section, that is, that the donee spouse must have a power of appointment exercisable in favor of herself or her estate and exercisable alone and in all events, are not met unless the power of the donee spouse to appoint the entire interest or a specific portion of it falls within one of the following categories:

(i) A power so to appoint fully exercisable in her own favor at any time during her life (as, for example, an unlimited power to invade); or

(ii) A power so to appoint exercisable in favor of her estate. Such a power, if exercisable during life, must be fully exercisable at any time during life, or, if exercisable by will, must be fully exercisable irrespective of the time of her death; or

(iii) A combination of the powers described under subdivisions (i) and (ii) of this subparagraph. For example, the donee spouse may, until she attains the age of 50 years, have a power to appoint to herself and thereafter have a power to appoint to her estate. However, the condition that the spouse's power must be exercisable in all events is not satisfied unless irrespective of when the donee spouse may die the entire interest or a specific portion of it will at the time of her death be subject to one power or the other.

(2) The power of the donee spouse must be a power to appoint the entire interest or a specific portion of it as unqualified owner (and free of the trust if a trust is involved, or free of the joint tenancy if a joint tenancy is involved) or to appoint the entire interest or a specific portion of it as a part of her estate (and free of the trust if a trust is involved), that is, in effect, to dispose of it to whomsoever she pleases. Thus, if the donor transferred property to a son and the donee spouse as joint tenants with right of survivorship and under local law the donee spouse has a power of severance exercisable without consent of the other joint tenant, and by exercising this power could acquire a one-half interest in the property as a tenant in common, her power of severance will satisfy the condition set forth in paragraph (a)(3) of this section that she have a power of appointment in favor of herself or her estate. However, if the donee spouse entered into a binding agreement with the donor to exercise the power only in favor of their issue, that condition is not met. An interest transferred in trust will not be regarded as failing to satisfy the condition merely because takers in default of the donee spouse's exercise of the power are designated by the donor. The donor may provide that, in default of exercise of the power, the trust shall continue for an additional period.

(3) A power is not considered to be a power exercisable by a donee spouse alone and in all events as required by paragraph (a)(4) of this section if the exercise of the power in the donee spouse to appoint the entire interest or a specific portion of it to herself or to her estate requires the joinder or consent of any other person. The power is not "exercisable in all events", if it can be terminated during the life of the donee spouse by any event other than her complete exercise or release of it. Further, a power is not "exercisable in all events" if it may be exercised for a limited purpose only. For example, a power which is not exercisable in the event of the spouse's remarriage is not exercisable in all events. Likewise, if there are any restrictions, either by the terms of the instrument or under applicable local law, on the exercise of a power to consume property (whether or not held in trust) for the benefit of the spouse, the power is not exercisable in all events. Thus, if a power of invasion is exercisable only for the spouse's support, or only for her limited use, the power is not exercisable in all events. In order for a power of invasion to be exercisable in all events, the donee spouse must have the unrestricted power exercisable at any time during her life to use all or any part of the property subject to the power, and to dispose of it in any manner, including the power to dispose of it by gift (whether or not she has power to dispose of it by will).

(4) If the power is in existence at all times following the transfer of the interest, limitations of a formal nature will not disqualify the interest. Examples of formal limitations on a power exercisable during life are requirements that an exercise must be in a particular form, that it must be filed with a trustee during the spouse's life, that reasonable notice must be given, or that reasonable intervals must elapse between successive partial exercises. Examples of formal limitations on a power exercisable by will are that it must be exercised by a will executed by the donee spouse after the making of the gift or that exercise must be by specific reference to the power.

(5) If the donee spouse has the requisite power to appoint to herself or her estate, it is immaterial that she also has one or more lesser powers. Thus, if she has a testamentary power to appoint to her estate, she may also have a limited power of withdrawal or of appointment during her life. Similarly, if she has an unlimited power of withdrawal, she may have a limited testamentary power.

(h) Existence of a power in another. Paragraph (a)(5) of this section provides that a transfer described in paragraph (a) is nondeductible to the extent that the donor created a power in the trustee or in any other person to appoint a part of the interest to any person other than the donee spouse. However, only powers in other persons which are in position to that of the donee spouse will cause a portion of the interest to fail to satisfy the condition set forth in paragraph (a)(5) of this section. Thus, a power in a trustee to distribute corpus to or for the benefit of the donee spouse will not disqualify the trust. Similarly, a power to distribute corpus to the spouse for the support of minor children will not disqualify the trust if she is legally obligated to support such children. The application of this paragraph may be illustrated by the following examples:

Example (1). Assume that a donor created a trust, designating his spouse as income beneficiary for life with an unrestricted power in the spouse to appoint the corpus during her life. The donor further provided that in the event the donee spouse should die without having exercised the power, the trust should continue for the life of his son with a power in the son to appoint the corpus. Since the power in the son could become exercisable only after the death of the donee spouse, the interest is not regarded as failing to satisfy the condition set forth in paragraph (a)(5) of this section.

Example (2). Assume that the donor created a trust, designating his spouse as income beneficiary for life and as donee of a power to appoint by will the entire corpus. The donor further provided that the trustee could distribute 30 percent of the corpus to the donor's son when he reached the age of 35 years. Since the trustee has a power to appoint 30 percent of the entire interest for the benefit of a person other than the donee spouse, only 75 percent of the interest placed in trust satisfied the condition set forth in paragraph (a)(5) of this section. If, in this case, the donee spouse had a power, exercisable by her will, to appoint only one-half of the corpus as it was constituted at the time of her death, it should be noted that only 35 percent of the interest placed in the trust would satisfy the condition set forth in paragraph (a)(3) of this section.

T.D. 6334, 11/14/58, amend T.D. 6542, 1/19/61, T.D. 8522, 2/28/94, T.D. 9102, 12/30/2003.

§ 25.2523(f)-1 Election with respect to life estate transferred to donee spouse.

(a) In general. *(1)* With respect to gifts made after December 31, 1981, subject to section 2523(i), a marital deduction is allowed under section 2523(a) for transfers of qualified terminable interest property. Qualified terminable interest property is terminable interest property described in section 2523(b)(1) that satisfies the requirements of section 2523(f)(2) and this section. Terminable interests that are described in section 2523(b)(2) cannot qualify as qualified terminable interest property. Thus, if the donor retains a power described in section 2523(b)(2) to appoint an interest in qualified terminable interest property, no deduction is allowable under section 2523(a) for the property.

(2) All of the property for which a deduction is allowed under this paragraph (a) is treated as passing to the donee spouse (for purposes of § 25.2523(a)-1), and no part of the property is treated as retained by the donor or as passing to any person other than the donee spouse (for purposes of § 25.2523(b)-1(b)).

(b) Qualified terminable interest property. *(1) Definition.* Section 2523(f)(2) provides the definition of qualified terminable interest property.

(2) Meaning of property. For purposes of section 2523(f)(2), the term property generally means an entire interest in property (within the meaning of § 25.2523(e)-1(d)) or a specific portion of the entire interest (within the meaning of § 25.2523(e)-1(c)).

(3) Property for which the election may be made. (i) In general. The election may relate to all or any part of property that meets the requirements of section 2523(f)(2)(A) and (B), provided that any partial election must be made with respect to a fractional or percentage share of the property so that the elective portion reflects its proportionate share of the increase or decrease in the entire property for purposes of applying sections 2044 or 2519. Thus, if the interest of the donee spouse in a trust (or other property in which the spouse has a qualifying income interest) meets the requirements of this section, the election may be made under section 2523(f)(2)(C) with respect to a part of the trust (or other property) only if the election relates to a defined fraction or percentage of the entire trust (or other property) or specific portion thereof within the meaning of § 25.2523(e)-1(c). The fraction or percentage may be defined by formula.

(ii) Division of trusts. If the interest of the donee spouse in a trust meets the requirements of this section, the trust may be divided into separate trusts to reflect a partial election that has been made, if authorized under the terms of the governing instrument or otherwise permissible under local law. A trust may be divided only if the fiduciary is required, either by applicable local law or by the express or implied provisions of the governing instrument, to divide the trust according to the fair market value of the assets of the trust at the time of the division. The division of the trusts must be done on a fractional or percentage basis to reflect the partial election. However, the separate trusts do not have to be funded with a pro rata portion of each asset held by the undivided trust.

(4) Manner and time of making election. (i) An election under section 2523(f)(2)(C) (other than a deemed election with respect to a joint and survivor annuity as described in section 2523(f)(6)), is made on a gift tax return for the calendar year in which the interest is transferred. The return must be filed within the time prescribed by section 6075(b) (determined without regard to section 6019(a)(2)), including any extensions authorized under section 6075(b)(2) (relating to an automatic extension of time for filing a gift tax return where the donor is granted an extension of time to file the income tax return).

(ii) If the election is made on a return for the calendar year that includes the date of death of the donor, the return (as prescribed by section 6075(b)(3)) must be filed no later than the time (including extensions) for filing the estate tax return. The election, once made, is irrevocable.

(c) Qualifying income interest for life. *(1) In general.* For purposes of this section, the term qualifying income interest for life is defined as provided in section 2056(b)(7)(B)(ii) and § 20.2056(b)-7(d)(1).

(i) Entitled for life to all the income. The principles outlined in § 25.2523(e)-1(f) (relating to whether the spouse is entitled for life to all of the income from the entire interest or a specific portion of the entire interest) apply in determining whether the donee spouse is entitled for life to all the income from the property, regardless of whether the interest passing to the donee spouse is in trust. An income interest granted for a term of years, or a life estate subject to termination upon the occurrence of a specified event (e.g., divorce) is not a qualifying income interest for life.

(ii) Income between last distribution date and date of spouse's death. An income interest does not fail to constitute a qualifying income interest for life solely because income for the period between the last distribution date and the date of the donee spouse's death is not required to be distributed to the estate of the donee spouse. See § 20.2044-1 of this chapter relating to the inclusion of such undistributed income in the gross estate of the donee spouse.

(iii) Pooled income funds. An income interest in a pooled income fund described in section 642(c)(5) constitutes a qualifying income interest for life for purposes of this section.

(iv) Distribution of principal for the benefit of the donee spouse. An income interest does not fail to constitute a qualifying income interest for life solely because the trustee has a power to distribute principal to or for the benefit of the donee spouse. The fact that property distributed to a donee spouse may be transferred by the spouse to another person does not result in a failure to satisfy the requirement of section 2056(b)(7)(B)(ii)(II). However, if the governing instrument requires the donee spouse to transfer the distributed property to another person without full and adequate consideration in money or money's worth, the requirement of section 2056(b)(7)(B)(ii)(II) is not satisfied.

(2) Immediate right to income. In order to constitute a qualifying income interest for life, the donee spouse must be granted the immediate right to receive the income from the property. Thus, an income interest does not constitute a qualifying income interest for life if the donee spouse receives the right to trust income commencing at some time in the future, e.g., on the termination of a preceding life income interest of the donor spouse.

(3) Annuities payable from trusts in the case of gifts made on or before October 24, 1992. (i) In the case of gifts made on or before October 24, 1992, a donee spouse's lifetime annuity interest payable from a trust or other group of assets passing from the donor is treated as a qualifying income interest for life for purposes of section 2523(f)(2)(B). The deductible interest, for purposes of § 25.2523(a)-1(b), is the specific portion of the property that, assuming the applicable interest rate for valuing annuities at the time the annuity interest is transferred, would produce income equal to the min-

imum amount payable annually to the donee spouse. If, based on the applicable interest rate, the entire property from which the annuity may be satisfied is insufficient to produce income equal to the minimum annual payment, the value of the deductible interest is the entire value of the property. The value of the deductible interest may not exceed the value of the property from which the annuity is payable. If the annual payment may increase, the increased amount is not taken into account in valuing the deductible interest.

(ii) An annuity interest is not treated as a qualifying income interest for life for purposes of section 2523(f)(2)(B) if any person other than the donee spouse may receive during the donee spouse's lifetime, any distribution of the property or its income from which the annuity is payable.

(iii) To determine the applicable interest rate for valuing annuities, see sections 2512 and 7520 and the regulations under those sections.

(4) Joint and survivor annuities. [Reserved]

(d) Treatment of interest retained by the donor spouse. *(1) In general.* Under section 2523(f)(5)(A), if a donor spouse retains an interest in qualified terminable interest property, any subsequent transfer by the donor spouse of the retained interest in the property is not treated as a transfer for gift tax purposes. Further, the retention of the interest until the donor spouse's death does not cause the property subject to the retained interest to be includible in the gross estate of the donor spouse.

(2) Exception. Under section 2523(f)(5)(B), the rule contained in paragraph (d)(1) of this section does not apply to any property after the donee spouse is treated as having transferred the property under section 2519, or after the property is includible in the gross estate of the donee spouse under section 2044.

(e) Application of local law. The provisions of local law are taken into account in determining whether or not the conditions of section 2523(f)(2)(A) and (B), and the conditions of paragraph (c) of this section, are satisfied. For example, silence of a trust instrument on the frequency of payment is not regarded as a failure to satisfy the requirement that the income must be payable to the donee spouse annually or more frequently unless applicable local law permits payments less frequently to the donee spouse.

(f) Examples. The following examples illustrate the application of this section, where D, the donor, transfers property to D's spouse, S. Unless stated otherwise, it is assumed that S is not the trustee of any trust established for S's benefit:

Example (1). Life estate in residence. D transfers by gift a personal residence valued at $250,000 on the date of the gift to S and D's children, giving S the exclusive and unrestricted right to use the property (including the right to continue to occupy the property as a personal residence or rent the property and receive the income for her lifetime). After S's death, the property is to pass to D's children. Under applicable local law, S's consent is required for any sale of the property. If D elects to treat all of the transferred property as qualified terminable interest property, the deductible interest is $250,000, the value of the property for gift tax purposes.

Example (2). Power to make property productive. D transfers assets having a fair market value of $500,000 to a trust pursuant to which S is given the right exercisable annually to require distribution of all the trust income to S. No trust property may be distributed during S's lifetime to any person other than S. The assets used to fund the trust include both income producing assets and nonproductive assets. Applicable local law permits S to require that the trustee either make the trust property productive or sell the property and reinvest the proceeds in productive property within a reasonable time after the transfer. If D elects to treat the entire trust as qualified terminable interest property, the deductible interest is $500,000. If D elects to treat only 20 percent of the trust as qualified terminable interest property, the deductible interest is $100,000; i.e., 20 percent of $500,000.

Example (3). Power of distribution over fraction of trust income. The facts are the same as in Example 2 except that S is given the power exercisable annually to require distribution to S of only 50 percent of the trust income for life. The remaining trust income may be accumulated or distributed among D's children and S in the trustee's discretion. The maximum amount that D may elect to treat as qualified terminable interest property is $250,000; i.e., the value of the trust for gift tax purposes ($500,000) multiplied by the percentage of the trust in which S has a qualifying income interest for life (50 percent). If D elects to treat only 20 percent of the portion of the trust in which S has a qualifying income interest as qualified terminable interest property, the deductible interest is $50,000; i.e, 20 percent of $250,000.

Example (4). Power to distribute trust corpus to other beneficiaries. D transfers $500,000 to a trust providing that all the trust income is to be paid to D's spouse, S, during S's lifetime. The trustee is given the power to use annually $5,000 from the trust for the maintenance and support of S's minor child, C. Any such distribution does not necessarily relieve S of S's obligation to support and maintain C. S does not have a qualifying income interest for life in any portion of the trust because the gift fails to satisfy the condition in sections 2523(f)(3) and 2056(b)(7)(B)(ii)(II) that no person have a power, other than a power the exercise of which takes effect only at or after S's death, to appoint any part of the property to any person other than S. The trust would also be nondeductible under section 2523(f) if S, rather than the trustee, were given the power to appoint a portion of the principal to C. However, in the latter case, if S made a qualified disclaimer (within the meaning of section 2518) of the power to appoint to C, the trust could qualify for the marital deduction pursuant to section 2523(f), assuming that the power was personal to S and S's disclaimer terminates the power. Similarly, if C made a qualified disclaimer of the right to receive distributions from the trust, the trust would qualify under section 2523(f) assuming that C's disclaimer effectively negates the trustee's power under local law.

Example (5). Spouse's interest terminable on divorce. The facts are the same as in Example 3 except that if S and D divorce, S's interest in the trust will pass to C. S's income interest is not a qualifying income interest for life because it is terminable upon S's divorce. Therefore, no portion of the trust is deductible under section 2523(f).

Example (6). Spouse's interest in trust in the form of an annuity. Prior to October 24, 1992, D established a trust funded with income producing property valued for gift tax purposes at $800,000. The trustee is required by the trust instrument to pay $40,000 a year to S for life. Any income in excess of the annuity amount is to be accumulated in the trust and may not be distributed during S's lifetime. S's lifetime annuity interest is treated as a qualifying income interest for life. If D elects to treat the entire portion of the trust in which S has a qualifying income interest as qualified terminable interest property, the value of the deductible interest is $400,000, because that amount would yield an income to S of $40,000 a year (assuming a 10 percent interest rate applies in valuing annuities at the time of the transfer).

Example (7). Value of spouse's annuity exceeds value of trust corpus. The facts are the same as in Example 6, except that the trustee is required to pay S $100,000 a year for S's life. If D elects to treat the entire portion of the trust in which S has a qualifying income interest for life as qualified terminable interest property, the value of the deductible interest is $800,000, which is the lesser of the entire value of the property ($800,000) or the amount of property that (assuming a 10 percent interest rate) would yield an income to S of $100,000 a year ($1,000,000).

Example (8). Transfer to pooled income fund. D transfers $200,000 on June 1, 1994, to a pooled income fund (described in section 642(c)(5)) designating S as the only life income beneficiary. If D elects to treat the entire $200,000 as qualified terminable interest property, the deductible interest is $200,000.

Example (9). Retention by donor spouse of income interest in property. On October 1, 1994, D transfers property to an irrevocable trust under the terms of which trust income is to be paid to D for life, then to S for life and, on S's death, the trust corpus is to be paid to D's children. Because S does not possess an immediate right to receive trust income, S's interest does not qualify as a qualifying income interest for life under section 2523(f)(2). Further, under section 2702(a)(2) and § 25.2702-2(b), D is treated for gift tax purposes as making a gift with a value equal to the entire value of the property. If D dies in 1996 survived by S, the trust corpus will be includible in D's gross estate under section 2036. However, in computing D's estate tax liability, D's adjusted taxable gifts under section 2001(b)(1)(B) are adjusted to reflect the inclusion of the gifted property in D's gross estate. In addition, if S survives D, the trust property is eligible for treatment as qualified terminable interest property under section 2056(b)(7) in D's estate.

Example (10). Retention by donor spouse of income interest in property. On October 1, 1994, D transfers property to an irrevocable trust under the terms of which trust income is to be paid to S for life, then to D for life and, on D's death, the trust corpus is to be paid to D's children. D elects under section 2523(f) to treat the property as qualified terminable interest property. D dies in 1996, survived by S. S subsequently dies in 1998. Under § 2523(f)-1(d)(1), because D elected to treat the transfer as qualified terminable interest property, no part of the trust corpus is includible in D's gross estate because of D's retained interest in the trust corpus. On S's subsequent death in 1998, the trust corpus is includible in S's gross estate under section 2044.

Example (11). Retention by donor spouse of income interest in property. The facts are the same as in Example 10, except that S dies in 1996 survived by D, who subsequently dies in 1998. Because D made an election under section 2523(f) with respect to the trust, on S's death the trust corpus is includible in S's gross estate under section 2044. Accordingly, under section 2044(c), S is treated as the transferor of the property for estate and gift tax purposes. Upon D's subsequent death in 1998, because the property was subject to inclusion in S's gross estate under section 2044, the exclusion rule in § 25.2523(f)-1(d)(1) does not apply under § 25.2523(f)-1(d)(2). However, because S is treated as the transferor of the property, the property is not subject to inclusion in D's gross estate under section 2036 or section 2038. If the executor of S's estate made a section 2056(b)(7) election with respect to the trust, the trust is includible in D's gross estate under section 2044 upon D's later death.

T.D. 8522, 2/28/94.

---

§ 25.2523(f)-1A Special rule applicable to community property transferred prior to January 1, 1982.

(a) In general. With respect to gifts made prior to January 1, 1982, the marital deduction is allowable with respect to any transfer by a donor to the donor's spouse only to the extent that the transfer is shown to represent a gift of property that was not, at the time of the gift, held as community property, as defined in paragraph (b) of this section. The burden of establishing the extent to which a transfer represents a gift of property not so held rests upon the donor.

(b) Definition of "community property." *(1)* For the purpose of paragraph (a) of this section, the term "community property" is considered to include—

(i) Any property held by the donor and his spouse as community property under the law of any State, Territory, or possession of the United States, or of any foreign country, except property in which the donee spouse had at the time of the gift merely an expectant interest. The donee spouse is regarded as having, at any particular time, merely an expectant interest in property held at that time by the donor and herself as community property under the law of any State, Territory, or possession of the United States, or of any foreign country, if, in case such property were transferred by gift into the separate property of the donee spouse, the entire value of such property (and not merely one-half of it), would be treated as the amount of the gift.

(ii) Separate property acquired by the donor as a result of a "conversion", after December 31, 1941, of property held by him and the donee spouse as a community property under the law of any State, Territory, or possession of the United States, or of any foreign country (except such property in which the donee spouse had at the time of the "conversion" merely an expectant interest), into their separate property, subject to the limitation with respect to value contained in subparagraph (5) of this paragraph.

(iii) Property acquired by the donor in exchange (by one exchange or a series of exchanges) for separate property resulting from such "conversion."

(2) The characteristics of property which acquired a noncommunity instead of a community status by reason of an agreement (whether antenuptial or postnuptial) are such that section 2523(f) classifies the property as community property of the donor and his spouse in the computation of the marital deduction. In distinguishing property which thus acquired a noncommunity status from property which acquired such a status solely by operation of the community property law, section 2523(f) refers to the former category of property as "separate property" acquired as a result of a "conversion" of "property held as such community property." As used in section 2523(f) the phrase "property held as such community property" is used to denote the body of property comprehended within the community property system; the expression "separate property" includes any noncommunity property, whether held in joint tenancy, tenancy by the entirety, tenancy in common, or otherwise; and the term "conversion" includes any transaction or agreement which transforms property from a community status into a noncommunity status.

(3) The separate property which section 2523(f) classifies as community property is not limited to that which was in existence at the time of the convention. The following are illustrative of the scope of section 2523(f):

(i) A partition of community property between husband and wife, whereby a portion of the property became the separate property of each, is a conversion of community property.

(ii) A transfer of community property into some other form of co-ownership, such as a joint tenancy, is a conversion of the property.

(iii) An agreement (whether made before or after marriage) that future earnings and gains which would otherwise be community property shall be shared by the spouses as separate property effects a conversion of such earnings and gains.

(iv) A change in the form of ownership of property which causes future rentals, which would otherwise have been acquired as community property, to be acquired as separate property effects a conversion of the rentals.

(4) The rules of section 2523(f) are applicable, however, only if the conversion took place after December 31, 1941, and only to the extent stated in this section.

(5) If the value of the separate property acquired by the donor as a result of a conversion did not exceed the value of the separate property thus acquired by the donee spouse, the entire separate property thus acquired by the donor is to be considered, for the purposes of this section, as held by him and the donee spouse as community property. If the value (at the time of conversion) of the separate property so acquired by the donor exceeded the value (at that time) of the separate property so acquired by the donee spouse, only a part of the separate property so acquired by the donor (and only the same fractional part of property acquired by him in exchange for such separate property) is to be considered, for purposes of this section, as held by him and the donee spouse as community property. The part of such separate property (or property acquired in exchange for it) which is considered as so held is the same proportion of it which the value (at the time of the conversion) of the separate property so acquired by the donee spouse is of the value (at that time) of the separate property so acquired by the donor. The following example illustrates the application of the provisions of this paragraph:

Example. During 1942 the donor and his spouse partitioned certain real property held by them under community property laws. The real property then had a value of $224,000. A portion of the property, then having a value of $160,000, was converted into the donor's separate property, and the remaining portion, then having a value of $64,000, was converted into his spouse's separate property. In 1955 the donor made a gift to his spouse of the property acquired by him as a result of the partition, which property then had a value of $200,000. The portion of the property transferred by gift which is considered as community property is

$$\frac{\$64{,}000 \text{ (value of property acquired by donee spouse)}}{\$160{,}000 \text{ (value of property acquired by donor spouse)}} \times \$200{,}000 = \$80{,}000.$$

The marital deduction with respect to the gift is, therefore, limited to one-half of $120,000 (the difference between $200,000, the value of the gift, and $80,000, the portion of the gift considered to have been of "community property"). The marital deduction with respect to the gift is, therefore, $60,000.

T.D. 6334, 11/14/58, amend T.D. 8522, 2/28/94.

§ 25.2523(g)-1 Special rule for charitable remainder trusts.

(a) In general. *(1)* With respect to gifts made after December 31, 1981, subject to section 2523(i), if the donor's spouse is the only noncharitable beneficiary (other than the donor) of a charitable remainder annuity trust or charitable remainder unitrust described in section 664 (qualified charitable remainder trust), section 2523(b) does not apply to the interest in the trust transferred to the donee spouse. Thus, the value of the annuity or unitrust interest passing to the spouse qualifies for a marital deduction under section 2523(g) and the value of the remainder interest qualifies for a charitable deduction under section 2522.

(2) A marital deduction for the value of the donee spouse's annuity or unitrust interest in a qualified charitable remainder trust to which section 2523(g) applies is allowable only under section 2523(g). Therefore, if an interest in property qualifies for a marital deduction under section 2523(g), no election may be made with respect to the property under section 2523(f).

(3) The donee spouse's interest need not be an interest for life to qualify for a marital deduction under section 2523(g). However, for purposes of section 664, an annuity or unitrust interest payable to the spouse for a term of years cannot be payable for a term that exceeds 20 years or the trust does not qualify under section 2523(g).

(4) A deduction is allowed under section 2523(g) even if the transfer to the donee spouse is conditioned on the donee spouse's payment of state death taxes, if any, attributable to the qualified charitable remainder trust.

(5) For purposes of this section, the term noncharitable beneficiary means any beneficiary of the qualified charitable remainder trust other than an organization described in section 170(c).

(b) Charitable remainder trusts where the donee spouse and the donor are not the only noncharitable beneficiaries. In the case of a charitable remainder trust where the donor and the donor's spouse are not the only noncharitable beneficiaries (for example, where the noncharitable interest is payable to the donor's spouse for life and then to another individual (other than the donor) for life), the qualification of the interest as qualified terminable interest property is determined solely under section 2523(f) and not under section 2523(g). Accordingly, if the transfer to the trust is made prior to October 24, 1992, the spousal annuity or unitrust interest may qualify under § 25.2523(f)-(1)(c)(3) as a qualifying income interest for life.

T.D. 8522, 2/28/94.

§ 25.2523(h)-1 Denial of double deduction.

The value of an interest in property may not be deducted for Federal gift tax purposes more than once with respect to the same donor. For example, assume that D, a donor, transferred a life estate in a farm to D's spouse, S, with a remainder to charity and that D elects to treat the property as qualified terminable interest property. The entire value of the property is deductible under section 2523(f). No part of the value of the property qualifies for a charitable deduction under section 2522 for gift tax purposes.

T.D. 8522, 2/28/94.

§ 25.2523(h)-2 Effective dates.

Except as specifically provided, in §§ 25.2523(e)-1(c)(3), 25.2523(f)-1(c)(3), and 25.2523(g)-1(b), the provisions of §§ 25.2523(e)-1(c), 25.2523(f)-1, 25.2523(g)-1, and 25.2523(h)-1 are effective with respect to gifts made after March 1, 1994. With respect to gifts made on or before such date, donors may rely on any reasonable interpretation of the statutory provisions. For these purposes, the provisions of §§ 25.2523(e)-1(c), 25.2523(f)-1, 25.2523(g)-1, and 25.2523(h)-1, (as well as project LR-211-76, 1984-1 C.B., page 598, see § 601.601(d)(2)(ii)(b) of this chapter), are considered a reasonable interpretation of the statutory provisions. In addition, the rule in the last sentence of § 25.2523(e)-1(f)(1) regarding the determination of income under applicable local law applies to trusts for taxable years ending after January 2, 2004.

T.D. 8522, 2/28/94, amend T.D. 9102, 12/30/2003.

§ 25.2523(i)-1 Disallowance of marital deduction when spouse is not a United States citizen.

(a) In general. Subject to § 20.2056A-1(c) of this chapter, section 2523(i)(1) disallows the marital deduction if the spouse of the donor is not a citizen of the United States at the time of the gift. If the spouse of the donor is a citizen of the United States at the time of the gift, the gift tax marital deduction under section 2523(a) is allowed regardless of whether the donor is a citizen or resident of the United States at the time of the gift, subject to the otherwise applicable rules of section 2523.

(b) Exception for certain joint and survivor annuities. Paragraph (a) does not apply to disallow the marital deduction with respect to any transfer resulting in the acquisition of rights by a noncitizen spouse under a joint and survivor annuity described in section 2523(f)(6).

(c) Increased annual exclusion. *(1) In general.* In the case of gifts made from a donor to the donor's spouse for which a marital deduction is not allowable under this section, if the gift otherwise qualifies for the gift tax annual exclusion under section 2503(b), the amount of the annual exclusion under section 2503(b) is $100,000 in lieu of $10,000. However, in the case of gifts made after June 29, 1989, in order for the increased annual exclusion to apply, the gift in excess of the otherwise applicable annual exclusion under section 2503(b) must be in a form that qualifies for the marital deduction but for the disallowance provision of section 2523(i)(1). See paragraph (d), Example 4, of this section.

(2) Status of donor. The $100,000 annual exclusion for gifts to a noncitizen spouse is available regardless of the status of the donor. Accordingly, it is immaterial whether the donor is a citizen, resident or a nonresident not a citizen of the United States, as long as the spouse of the donor is not a citizen of the United States at the time of the gift and the conditions for allowance of the increased annual exclusion have been satisfied. See § 25.2503-2(f).

(d) Examples. The principles outlined in this section are illustrated in the following examples. Assume in each of the examples that the donee, S, is D's spouse and is not a United States citizen at the time of the gift.

Example (1). Outright transfer of present interest. In 1995, D, a United States citizen, transfers to S, outright, 100 shares of X corporation stock valued for federal gift tax purposes at $130,000. The transfer is a gift of a present interest in property under section 2503(b). Additionally, the gift qualifies for the gift tax marital deduction except for the disallowance provision of section 2523(i)(1). Accordingly, $100,000 of the $130,000 gift is excluded from the total amount of gifts made during the calendar year by D for gift tax purposes.

Example (2). Transfer of survivor benefits. In 1995, D, a United States citizen, retires from employment in the United States and elects to receive a reduced retirement annuity in order to provide S with a survivor annuity upon D's death. The transfer of rights to S in the joint and survivor annuity is a gift by D for gift tax purposes. However, under paragraph (b) of this section, the gift qualifies for the gift tax marital deduction even though S is not a United States citizen.

Example (3). Transfer of present interest in trust property. In 1995, D, a resident alien, transfers property valued at $500,000 in trust to S, who is also a resident alien. The trust instrument provides that the trust income is payable to S at least quarterly and S has a testamentary general power to appoint the trust corpus. The transfer to S qualifies for the marital deduction under section 2523 but for the provisions of section 2523(i)(1). Because S has a life income interest in the trust, S has a present interest in a portion of the trust. Accordingly, D may exclude the present value of S's income interest (up to $100,000) from D's total 1995 calendar year gifts.

Example (4). Transfer of present interest in trust property. The facts are the same as in Example 3, except that S does not have a testamentary general power to appoint the trust corpus. Instead, D's child, C, has a remainder interest in the trust. If S were a United States citizen, the transfer would qualify for the gift tax marital deduction if a qualified terminable interest property election was made under section 2523(f)(4). However, because S is not a U.S. citizen, D may not make a qualified terminable interest property election. Accordingly, the gift does not qualify for the gift tax marital deduction but for the disallowance provision of section 2523(i)(1). The $100,000 annual exclusion under section 2523(i)(2) is not available with respect to D's transfer in trust and D may not exclude the present value of S's income interest in excess of $10,000 from D's total 1995 calendar year gifts.

Example (5). Spouse becomes citizen after transfer. D, a United States citizen, transfers a residence valued at $350,000 on December 20, 1995, to D's spouse, S, a resident alien. On January 31, 1996, S becomes a naturalized United States citizen. On D's federal gift tax return for 1995, D must include $250,000 as a gift ($350,000 transfer less $100,000 exclusion). Although S becomes a citizen in January, 1996, S is not a citizen of the United States at the time the transfer is made. Therefore, no gift tax marital deduction is allowable. However, the transfer does qualify for the $100,000 annual exclusion.

T.D. 8612, 8/21/95.

§ 25.2523(i)-2 Treatment of spousal joint tenancy property where one spouse is not a United States citizen.

(a) In general. In the case of a joint tenancy with right of survivorship between spouses, or a tenancy by the entirety, where the donee spouse is not a United States citizen, the gift tax treatment of the creation and termination of the tenancy (regardless of whether the donor is a citizen, resident or nonresident not a citizen of the United States at such time), is governed by the principles of sections 2515 and 2515A (as such sections were in effect before their repeal by the Economic Recovery Tax Act of 1981). However, in applying these principles, the donor spouse may not elect to treat the creation of a tenancy in real property as a gift, as provided in section 2515(c) (prior to its repeal by the Economic Recovery Tax Act of 1981, Pub. L. 97-34, 95 Stat. 172).

(b) Tenancies by the entirety and joint tenancies in real property. *(1) Creation of the tenancy on or after July 14, 1988.* Under the principles of section 2515 (without regard to section 2515(c)), the creation of a tenancy by the entirety (or joint tenancy) in real property (either by one spouse alone or by both spouses), and any additions to the value of the tenancy in the form of improvements, reductions in indebtedness thereon, or otherwise, is not deemed to be a transfer of property for purposes of the gift tax, regardless of the proportion of the consideration furnished by each spouse, but only if the creation of the tenancy would otherwise be a gift to the donee spouse who is not a citizen of the United States at the time of the gift.

(2) Termination. (i) Tenancies created after December 31, 1954 and before January 1, 1982 not subject to an election under section 2515(c), and tenancies created on or after July 14, 1988. When a tenancy to which this paragraph (b) applies is terminated on or after July 14, 1988, other than by reason of the death of a spouse, then, under the principles of section 2515, a spouse is deemed to have made a gift to the extent that the proportion of the total consideration furnished by the spouse, multiplied by the proceeds of the termination (whether in the form of cash, property, or interests in property), exceeds the value of the proceeds of termination received by the spouse. See section 2523(i), and § 25.2523(i)-1 and § 25.2503-2(f) as to certain of the tax consequences that may result upon termination of the tenancy. This paragraph (b)(2)(i) applies to tenancies created after December 31, 1954, and before January 1, 1982, not subject to an election under section 2515(c), and to tenancies created on or after July 14, 1988.

(ii) Tenancies created after December 31, 1954 and before January 1, 1982 subject to an election under section 2515(c) and tenancies created after December 31, 1981 and before July 14, 1988. When a tenancy to which this paragraph (a) applies is terminated on or after July 14, 1988, other than by reason of the death of a spouse, then, under the principles of section 2515, a spouse is deemed to have made a gift to the extent that the proportion of the total consideration furnished by the spouse, multiplied by the proceeds of the termination (whether in the form of cash, property, or interests in property), exceeds the value of the proceeds of termination received by the spouse. See section 2523(i), and §§ 25.2523(i)-1 and 25.2503-2(f) as to certain of the tax consequences that may result upon termination of the tenancy. In the case of tenancies to which this paragraph applies, if the creation of the tenancy was treated as a gift to the noncitizen donee spouse under section 2515(c) (in the case of tenancies created prior to 1982) or section 2511 (in the case of tenancies created after December 31, 1981 and before July 14, 1988), then, upon termination of the tenancy, for purposes of applying the principles of section 2515 and the regulations thereunder, the amount treated as a gift on creation of the tenancy is treated as consideration originally belonging to the noncitizen spouse and never acquired by the noncitizen spouse from the donor spouse. This paragraph (b)(2)(ii) applies to tenancies created after December 31, 1954, and before January 1, 1982, subject to an election under section 2515(c), and to tenancies created after December 31, 1981, and before July 14, 1988.

(3) Miscellaneous provisions. (i) Tenancy by the entirety. For purposes of this section, tenancy by the entirety includes a joint tenancy between husband and wife with right of survivorship.

(ii) No election to treat as gift. The regulations under section 2515 that relate to the election to treat the creation of a tenancy by the entirety as constituting a gift and the consequences of such an election upon termination of the tenancy (§§ 25.2515-2 and 25.2515-4) do not apply for purposes of section 2523(i)(3).

(4) Examples. The application of this section may be illustrated by the following examples:

Example (1). In 1992, A, a United States citizen, furnished $200,000 and A's spouse B, a resident alien, furnished $50,000 for the purchase and subsequent improvement of real property held by them as tenants by the entirety. The property is sold in 1998 for $300,000. A receives $225,000 and B receives $75,000 of the sales proceeds. The termination results in a gift of $15,000 by A to B, computed as follows:

$$\frac{\$200{,}000 \text{ (consideration furnished by A)}}{\$250{,}000 \text{ (total consideration furnished by both spouses)}} \times \$300{,}000 \text{ (proceeds of termination)} = \$240{,}000 \text{ (Proceeds of termination attributable to A.)}$$

$240,000 – $225,000 (proceeds received by A) = $15,000 gift by A to B.

Example (2). In 1986, A purchased real property for $300,000 and took title in the names of A and B, A's spouse, as joint tenants. Under section 2511 and § 25.2511-1(h)(1) of the regulations, A was treated as making a gift of one-half of the value of the property ($150,000) to B. In 1995, the real property is sold for $400,000 and B receives the entire proceeds of sale. For purposes of determining the amount of the gift on termination of the tenancy under the principles of section 2515 and the regulations thereunder, the amount treated as a gift to B on creation of the tenancy under section 2511 is treated as B's contribution towards the purchase of the property. Accordingly, the termination of the tenancy results in a gift of $200,000 from A to B determined as follows:

$$\frac{\$150{,}000 \text{ (consideration furnished by A)}}{\$300{,}000 \text{ (total consideration deemed furnished by both spouses)}} \times \$400{,}000 \text{ (proceeds of termination)} = \$200{,}000 \text{ (Proceeds of termination attributable to A.)}$$

$200,000 – 0 (proceeds received by A) = $200,000 gift by A to B.

(c) Tenancies by the entirety in personal property where one spouse is not a United States citizen. *(1) In general.* In the case of the creation (either by one spouse alone or by both spouses where at least one of the spouses is not a United States citizen) of a joint interest in personal property with right of survivorship, or additions to the value thereof in the form of improvements, reductions in the indebtedness thereof, or otherwise, the retained interest of each spouse, solely for purposes of determining whether there has been a gift by the donor to the spouse who is not a citizen of the United States at the time of the gift, is treated as one-half of the value of the joint interest. See section 2523(i) and §§ 25.2523(i)-1 and 25.2503-2(f) as to certain of the tax consequences that may result upon creation and termination of the tenancy.

(2) Exception. The rule provided in paragraph (c)(1) of this section does not apply with respect to any joint interest in property if the fair market value of the interest in property (determined as if each spouse had a right to sever) cannot reasonably be ascertained except by reference to the life expectancy of one or both spouses. In these cases, actuarial principles may need to be resorted to in determining the gift tax consequences of the transaction.

T.D. 8612, 8/21/95.

§ 25.2523(i)-3 Effective date.

The provisions of §§ 25.2523(i)-1 and 25.2523(i)-2 are effective in the case of gifts made after August 22, 1995.

T.D. 8612, 8/21/95.

§ 25.2524-1 Extent of deductions.

Under the provisions of section 2524, the charitable deduction provided for in section 2522 and the marital deduction provided for in section 2523 are allowable only to the extent that the gifts with respect to which those deductions are authorized, are included in the "total amount of gifts" made during the "calendar period" (as defined in § 25.2502-1(c)(1)) computed as provided in section 2503 and § 25.2503-1 (i.e., the total gifts less exclusions). The following examples (in both of which it is assumed that the donor has previously utilized his entire $30,000 specific exemption provided by section 2521 which was in effect at the time) illustrate the application of the provisions of this section:

Example (1). A donor made transfers by gift to his spouse of $5,000 cash on January 1, 1971, and $1,000 cash on April 5, 1971. The donor made no other transfers during 1971. The first $3,000 of such gifts for the calendar year is excluded under the provisions of section 2503(b) in determining the "total amount of gifts" made during the first calendar quarter of 1971. The marital deduction for the first calendar quarter of $2,500 (one-half of $5,000) otherwise allowable is limited by section 2524 to $2,000. The amount of taxable gifts is zero ($5,000 – $3,000 (annual exclusion) – $2,000 (marital deduction)). For the second calendar quarter of 1971, the marital deduction is $500 (one-half of $1,000); the amount excluded under section 2503(b) is zero because the entire $3,000 annual exclusion was applied against the gift in the first calendar quarter of 1971; and the amount of taxable gifts is $500 ($1,000 – $500 (marital deduction)).

Example (2). The only gifts made by a donor to his spouse during calendar year 1969 were a gift of $2,400 in May and a gift of $3,000 in August. The first $3,000 of such gifts is excluded under the provisions of section 2503(b) in determining the "total amount of gifts" made during the calendar year. The marital deduction for 1969 of $2,700 (one-half of $2,400 plus one-half $3,000) otherwise allowable is limited by section 2524 to $2,400. The amount of taxable gifts is zero ($5,400 – $3,000 (annual exclusion) – $2,400 (marital deduction)).

T.D. 6334, 11/14/58, amend T.D. 7238, 12/28/72, T.D. 7910, 9/5/83.

§ 26.2600-1 Table of contents.

T.D. 8187, 3/14/88, amend T.D. 8644, 12/26/95, T.D. 8912, 12/19/2000, T.D. 9208, 6/28/2005, T.D. 9214, 7/15/2005, T.D. 9348, 8/1/2007, T.D. 9421, 7/30/2008.

PAR. 2. In § 26.2600-1, the table of contents is amended by adding the entry for § 26.2642-6(h) to read as follows:

Proposed § 26.2600-1 Table of contents. [*For Preamble, see ¶ 152,895*]

* * * * *

§ 26.2642-6 Qualified severance.

* * * * *

(h) Treatment of trusts resulting from a severance that is not a qualified severance.

* * * * *

§ 26.2601-1 Effective dates.

(a) Transfers subject to the generation-skipping transfer tax. *(1) In general.* Except as otherwise provided in this section, the provisions of chapter 13 of the Internal Revenue Code of 1986 (Code) apply to any generation-skipping transfer (as defined in section 2611) made after October 22, 1986.

(2) Certain transfers treated as if made after October 22, 1986. Solely for purposes of chapter 13, an inter vivos transfer is treated as if it were made on October 23, 1986, if it was—

(i) Subject to chapter 12 (regardless of whether a tax was actually incurred or paid); and

(ii) Made after September 25, 1985, but before October 23, 1986. For purposes of this paragraph, the value of the property transferred shall be the value of the property on the date the property was transferred.

(3) Certain trust events treated as if occurring after October 22, 1986. For purposes of chapter 13, if an inter vivos transfer is made to a trust after September 25, 1985, but before October 23, 1986, any subsequent distribution from the trust or termination of an interest in the trust that occurred before October 23, 1986, is treated as occurring immediately after the deemed transfer on October 23, 1986. If more than one distribution or termination occurs with respect to a trust, the events are treated as if they occurred on October 23, 1986, in the same order as they occurred. See paragraph (b)(1)(iv)(B) of this section for rules determining the portion of distributions and terminations subject to tax under chapter 13. This paragraph (a)(3) does not apply to transfers to trusts not subject to chapter 13 by reason of the transition rules in paragraphs (b)(2) and (3) of this section. The provisions of this paragraph (a)(3) do not apply in determining the value of the property under chapter 13.

(4) Example. The following example illustrates the principle that paragraph (a)(2) of this section is not applicable to transfers under a revocable trust that became irrevocable by reason of the transferor's death after September 25, 1985, but before October 23, 1986:

Example. T created a revocable trust on September 30, 1985, that became irrevocable when T died on October 10, 1986. Although the trust terminated in favor of a grandchild of T, the transfer to the grandchild is not treated as occurring on October 23, 1986, pursuant to paragraph (a)(2) of this section because it is not an inter vivos transfer subject to chapter 12. The transfer is not subject to chapter 13 because it is in the nature of a testamentary transfer that occurred prior to October 23, 1986.

(b) Exceptions. *(1) Irrevocable trusts.* (i) In general. The provisions of chapter 13 do not apply to any generation-skipping transfer under a trust (as defined in section 2652(b)) that was irrevocable on September 25, 1985. The rule of the preceding sentence does not apply to a pro rata portion of any generation-skipping transfer under an irrevocable trust if additions are made to the trust after September 25, 1985. See paragraph (b)(1)(iv) of this section for rules for determining the portion of the trust that is subject to the provisions of chapter 13. Further, the rule in the first sentence of this paragraph (b)(1)(i) does not apply to a transfer of property pursuant to the exercise, release, or lapse of a general power of appointment that is treated as a taxable transfer under chapter 11 or chapter 12. The transfer is made by the person holding the power at the time the exercise, release, or lapse of the power becomes effective, and is not considered a transfer under a trust that was irrevocable on September 25, 1985. See paragraph (b)(1)(v)(B) of this section regarding the treatment of the release, exercise, or lapse of a power of appointment that will result in a constructive addition to a trust. See § 26.2652-1(a) for the definition of a transferor.

(ii) Irrevocable trust defined. (A) In general. Unless otherwise provided in either paragraph (b)(1)(ii)(B) or (C) of this section, any trust (as defined in section 2652(b)) in existence on September 25, 1985, is considered an irrevocable trust.

(B) Property includible in the gross estate under section 2038. For purposes of this chapter a trust is not an irrevocable trust to the extent that, on September 25, 1985, the settlor held a power with respect to such trust that would have caused the value of the trust to be included in the settlor's gross estate for Federal estate tax purposes by reason of section 2038 (without regard to powers relinquished before September 25, 1985) if the settlor had died on September 25, 1985. A trust is considered subject to a power on September 25, 1985, even though the exercise of the power was subject to the precedent giving of notice, or even though the exercise could take effect only on the expiration of a stated period, whether or not on or before September 25, 1985, notice had been given or the power had been exercised. A trust is not considered subject to a power if the power is, by its terms, exercisable only on the occurrence of an event or contingency not subject to the settlor's control (other than the death of the settlor) and if the event or contingency had not in fact taken place on September 25, 1985.

(C) Property includible in the gross estate under section 2042. A policy of insurance on an individual's life that is treated as a trust under section 2652(b) is not considered an irrevocable trust to the extent that, on September 25, 1985, the insured possessed any incident of ownership (as defined in § 20.2042-1(c) of this chapter, and without regard to any incidents of ownership relinquished before September 25, 1985), that would have caused the value of the trust, (i.e., the insurance proceeds) to be included in the insured's gross estate for Federal estate tax purposes by reason of section 2042, if the insured had died on September 25, 1985.

(D) Examples. The following examples illustrate the application of this paragraph (b)(1):

Example (1). Section 2038 applicable. On September 25, 1985, T, the settlor of a trust that was created before September 25, 1985, held a testamentary power to add new beneficiaries to the trust. T held no other powers over any portion of the trust. The testamentary power held by T would have caused the trust to be included in T's gross estate under section 2038 if T had died on September 25, 1985. Therefore, the trust is not an irrevocable trust for purposes of this section.

Example (2). Section 2038 not applicable when power held by a person other than settlor. On September 25, 1985, S, the spouse of the settlor of a trust in existence on that date, had an annual right to withdraw a portion of the principal of the trust. The trust was otherwise irrevocable on that date. Because the power was not held by the settlor of the trust, it is not a power described in section 2038. Thus, the trust is considered an irrevocable trust for purposes of this section.

Example (3). Section 2038 not applicable. In 1984, T created a trust and retained the right to expand the class of remaindermen to include any of T's afterborn grandchildren. As of September 25, 1985, all of T's grandchildren were named remaindermen of the trust. Since the exercise of T's power was dependent on there being afterborn grandchildren who were not members of the class of remaindermen, a contingency that did not exist on September 25, 1985, the trust is not considered subject to the power on September 25, 1985, and is an irrevocable trust for purposes of this section. The result is not changed even if grandchildren are born after September 25, 1985, whether or not T exercises the power to expand the class of remaindermen.

Example (4). Section 2042 applicable. On September 25, 1985, T purchased an insurance policy on T's own life and designated child, C, and grandchild, GC, as the beneficiaries. T retained the power to obtain from the insurer a loan against the surrender value of the policy. T's insurance policy is a trust (as defined in section 2652(b)) for chapter 13 purposes. The trust is not considered an irrevocable trust because, on September 25, 1985, T possessed an incident of ownership that would have caused the value of the policy to be included in T's gross estate under section 2042 if T had died on that date.

Example (5). Trust partially irrevocable. In 1984, T created a trust naming T's grandchildren as the income and remainder beneficiaries. T retained the power to revoke the trust as to one-half of the principal at any time prior to T's death. T retained no other powers over the trust principal. T did not die before September 25, 1985, and did not exercise or release the power before that date. The half of the trust not subject to T's power to revoke is an irrevocable trust for purposes of this section.

(iii) Trust containing qualified terminable interest property. (A) In general. For purposes of chapter 13, a trust described in paragraph (b)(1)(ii) of this section that holds qualified terminable interest property by reason of an election under section 2056(b)(7) or section 2523(f) (made either on, before or after September 25, 1985) is treated in the same manner as if the decedent spouse or the donor spouse (as the case may be) had made an election under section 2652(a)(3). Thus, transfers from such trusts are not subject to chapter 13, and the decedent spouse or the donor spouse (as the case may be) is treated as the transferor of such property. The rule of this paragraph (b)(1)(iii) does not apply to that portion of the trust that is subject to chapter 13 by reason of an addition to the trust occurring after September 25, 1985. See section 26.2652-2(a) for rules where an election under section 2652(a)(3) is made. See § 26.2652-2(c) for rules where a portion of a trust is subject to an election under section 2652(a)(3).

(B) Examples. The following examples illustrate the application of this paragraph (b)(1)(iii):

Example (1). QTIP election made after September 25, 1985. On March 28, 1985, T established a trust. The trust instrument provided that the trustee must distribute all income annually to T's spouse, S, during S's life. Upon S's death, the remainder is to be distributed to GC, the grandchild of T and S. On April 15, 1986, T elected under section 2523(f) to treat the property in the trust as qualified terminable interest property. On December 1, 1987, S died and soon thereafter the trust assets were distributed to GC. Because the trust was irrevocable on September 25, 1985, the transfer to GC is not subject to tax under chapter 13. T is treated as the transferor with respect to the transfer of the trust assets to GC in the same manner as if T had made an election under section 2652(a)(3) to reverse the effect of the section 2523(f) election for chapter 13 purposes.

Example (2). Section 2652(a)(3) election deemed to have been made. Assume the same facts as in Example 1, except the trust instrument provides that after S's death all income is to be paid annually to C, the child of T and S. Upon C's death, the remainder is to be distributed to GC. C died on October 1, 1992, and soon thereafter the trust assets are distributed to GC. Because the trust was irrevocable on September 25, 1985, the termination of C's interest is not subject to chapter 13.

(iv) Additions to irrevocable trusts. (A) In general. If an addition is made after September 25, 1985, to an irrevocable trust which is excluded from chapter 13 by reason of paragraph (b)(1) of this section, a pro rata portion of subsequent distributions from (and terminations of interests in property held in) the trust is subject to the provisions of chapter 13. If an addition is made, the trust is thereafter deemed to consist of two portions, a portion not subject to chapter 13 (the non-chapter 13 portion) and a portion subject to chapter 13 (the chapter 13 portion), each with a separate inclusion ratio (as defined in section 2642(a)). The non-chapter 13 portion represents the value of the assets of the trust as it existed on September 25, 1985. The applicable fraction (as defined in section 2642(a)(2)) for the non-chapter 13 portion is deemed to be 1 and the inclusion ratio for such portion is 0. The chapter 13 portion of the trust represents the value of all additions made to the trust after September 25, 1985. The inclusion ratio for the chapter 13 portion is determined under section 2642. This paragraph (b)(1)(iv)(A) requires separate portions of one trust only for purposes of determining inclusion ratios. For purposes of chapter 13, a constructive addition under paragraph (b)(1)(v) of this section is treated as an addition. See paragraph (b)(4) of this section for exceptions to the additions rule of this paragraph (b)(1)(iv). See § 26.2654-1(a)(2) for rules treating additions to a trust by an individual other than the initial transferor as a separate trust for purposes of chapter 13.

(B) Terminations of interests in and distributions from trusts. Where a termination or distribution described in section 2612 occurs with respect to a trust to which an addition has been made, the portion of such termination or distribution allocable to the chapter 13 portion is determined by reference to the allocation fraction, as defined in paragraph (b)(1)(iv)(C) of this section. In the case of a termination described in section 2612(a) with respect to a trust, the portion of such termination that is subject to chapter 13 is the product of the allocation fraction and the value of the trust (to the extent of the terminated interest therein). In the case of a distribution described in section 2612(b) from a trust, the portion of such distribution that is subject to chapter 13 is the product of the allocation fraction and the value of the property distributed.

(C) Allocation fraction. (1) In general. The allocation fraction allocates appreciation and accumulated income between the chapter 13 and non-chapter 13 portions of a trust. The numerator of the allocation fraction is the amount of the addition (valued as of the date the addition is made), determined without regard to whether any part of the transfer is subject to tax under chapter 11 or chapter 12, but reduced by the amount of any Federal or state estate or gift tax imposed and subsequently paid by the recipient trust with respect to the addition. The denominator of the allocation fraction is the total value of the entire trust immediately after the addition. For purposes of this paragraph (b)(1)(iv)(C), the total value of the entire trust is the fair market value of the property held in trust (determined under the rules of section 2031), reduced by any amount attributable to or paid by the trust and attributable to the transfer to the trust that is similar to an amount that would be allowable as a deduction under section 2053 if the addition had occurred at the death of the transferor, and further reduced by the same amount that the numerator was reduced to reflect Federal or state estate or gift tax incurred by and subsequently paid by the recipient trust with respect to the addition. Where there is more than one addition to principal after September 25, 1985, the portion of the trust subject to chapter 13 after each such addition is determined pursuant to a revised fraction. In each case, the numerator of the revised fraction is the sum of the value of the chapter 13 portion of the trust immediately before the latest addition, and the amount of the latest addition. The denominator of the revised fraction is the total value of the entire trust immediately after the addition. If the transfer to the trust is a generation-skipping transfer, the numerator and denominator are reduced by the amount of the generation-skipping transfer tax, if any, that is imposed by chapter 13 on the transfer and actually recovered from the trust. The allocation fraction is rounded off to five decimal places (.00001).

(2) Examples. The following examples illustrate the application of paragraph (b)(1)(iv) of this section. In each of the examples, assume that the recipient trust does not pay any Federal or state transfer tax by reason of the addition.

Example (1). Post September 25, 1985, addition to trust.

(i) On August 16, 1980, T established an irrevocable trust. Under the trust instrument, the trustee is required to distribute the entire income annually to T's child, C, for life, then to T's grandchild, GC, for life. Upon GC's death, the remainder is to be paid to GC's issue. On October 1, 1986, when the total value of the entire trust is \$400,000, T transfers \$100,000 to the trust. The allocation fraction is computed as follows:

$$\frac{\text{Value of addition}}{\text{Total value of trust}} = \frac{\$100{,}000}{\$400{,}000 + \$100{,}000} = .2$$

(ii) Thus, immediately after the transfer, 20 percent of the value of future generation-skipping transfers under the trust will be subject to chapter 13.

Example (2). Effect of expenses. Assume the same facts as in Example 1, except immediately prior to the transfer on October 1, 1986, the fair market value of the individual assets in the trust totaled \$400,000. Also, assume that the trust had accrued and unpaid debts, expenses, and taxes totaling \$300,000. Assume further that the entire \$300,000 represented amounts that would be deductible under section 2053 if the trust were includible in the transferor's gross estate. The numerator of the allocation fraction is \$100,000 and the denominator of the allocation fraction is \$200,000 ((\$400,000 − \$300,000) + \$100,000). Thus, the allocation fraction is .5 ($100,000/$200,000) and 50 percent of the value of future generation-skipping transfers will be subject to chapter 13.

Example (3). Multiple additions.

(i) Assume the same facts as in Example 1, except on January 30, 1988, when the total value of the entire trust is $600,000, T transfers an additional $40,000 to the trust. Before the transfer, the value of the portion of the trust that was attributable to the prior addition was $120,000 ($600,000 × .2). The new allocation fraction is computed as follows:

$$\frac{\text{Total value of additions}}{\text{Total value of trust}} = \frac{\$120{,}000 + \$40{,}000}{\$600{,}000 + \$40{,}000} = \frac{\$160{,}000}{\$640{,}000} = .25$$

(ii) Thus, immediately after the transfer, 25 percent of the value of future generation-skipping transfers under the trust will be subject to chapter 13.

Example (4). Allocation fraction at time of generation-skipping transfer. Assume the same facts as in Example 3, except on March 1, 1989, when the value of the trust is $800,000, C dies. A generation-skipping transfer occurs at C's death because of the termination of C's life estate. Therefore, $200,000 ($800,000 × .25) is subject to tax under chapter 13.

(v) Constructive additions. (A) Powers of appointment. Except as provided in paragraph (b)(1)(v)(B) of this section, where any portion of a trust remains in the trust after the post-September 25, 1985, release, exercise, or lapse of a power of appointment over that portion of the trust, and the release, exercise, or lapse is treated to any extent as a taxable transfer under chapter 11 or chapter 12, the value of the entire portion of the trust subject to the power that was released, exercised, or lapsed is treated as if that portion had been withdrawn and immediately retransferred to the trust at the time of the release, exercise, or lapse. The creator of the power will be considered the transferor of the addition except to the extent that the release, exercise, or lapse of the power is treated as a taxable transfer under chapter 11 or chapter 12. See section 26.2652-1 for rules for determining the identity of the transferor of property for purposes of chapter 13.

(B) Special rule for certain powers of appointment. The release, exercise, or lapse of a power of appointment (other than a general power of appointment as defined in section 2041(b)) is not treated as an addition to a trust if—

(1) Such power of appointment was created in an irrevocable trust that is not subject to chapter 13 under paragraph (b)(1) of this section; and

(2) In the case of an exercise, the power of appointment is not exercised in a manner that may postpone or suspend the vesting, absolute ownership or power of alienation of an interest in property for a period, measured from the date of creation of the trust, extending beyond any life in being at the date of creation of the trust plus a period of 21 years plus, if necessary, a reasonable period of gestation (the perpetuities period). For purposes of this paragraph (b)(1)(v)(B)(2), the exercise of a power of appointment that validly postpones or suspends the vesting, absolute ownership or power of alienation of an interest in property for a term of years that will not exceed 90 years (measured from the date of creation of the trust) will not be considered an exercise that postpones or suspends vesting, absolute ownership or the power of alienation beyond the perpetuities period. If a power is exercised by creating another power, it is deemed to be exercised to whatever extent the second power may be exercised.

(C) Constructive addition if liability is not paid out of trust principal. Where a trust described in paragraph (b)(1) of this section is relieved of any liability properly payable out of the assets of such trust, the person or entity who actually satisfies the liability is considered to have made a constructive addition to the trust in an amount equal to the liability. The constructive addition occurs when the trust is relieved of liability (e.g., when the right of recovery is no longer enforceable). But see section 26.2652-1(a)(3) for rules involving the application of section 2207A in the case of an election under section 2652(a)(3).

(D) Examples. The following examples illustrate the application of this paragraph (b)(1)(v):

Example (1). Lapse of a power of appointment. On June 19, 1980, T established an irrevocable trust with a corpus of $500,000. The trust instrument provides that the trustee shall distribute the entire income from the trust annually to T's spouse, S, during S's life. At S's death, the remainder is to be distributed to T and S's grandchild, GC. T also gave S a general power of appointment over one-half of the trust assets. On December 21, 1989, when the value of the trust corpus is $1,500,000, S died without having exercised the general power of appointment. The value of one-half of the trust corpus, $750,000 ($1,500,000 × .5) is included in S's gross estate under section 2041(a) and is subject to tax under Chapter 11. Because the value of one-half of the trust corpus is subject to tax under Chapter 11 with respect to S's estate, S is treated as the transferor of that property for purposes of Chapter 13 (see section 2652(a)(1)(A)). For purposes of the generation-skipping transfer tax, the lapse of S's power of appointment is treated as if $750,000 ($1,500,000 × .5) had been distributed to S and then transferred back to the trust. Thus, S is considered to have added $750,000 ($1,500,000 × .5) to the trust at the date of S's death. Because this constructive addition occurred after September 25, 1985, 50 percent of the corpus of the trust became subject to Chapter 13 at S's death.

Example (2). Multiple actual additions. On June 19, 1980, T established an irrevocable trust with a principal of $500,000. The trust instrument provides that the trustee shall distribute the entire income from the trust annually to T's spouse, S, during S's life. At S's death, the remainder is to be distributed to GC, the grandchild of T and S. On October 1, 1985, when the trust assets were valued at $800,000, T added $200,000 to the trust. After the transfer on October 1, 1985, the allocation fraction was .2 ($200,000/$1,000,000). On December 21, 1989, when the value of the trust principal is $1,000,000, T adds $1,000,000 to the trust. After this addition, the new allocation fraction is 0.6 ($1,200,000/$2,000,000). The numerator of the fraction is the value of that portion of trust assets that were subject to chapter 13 immediately prior to the addition (by reason of the first addition), $200,000 (.2 × $1,000,000), plus the value of the second transfer, $1,000,000, which equals $1,200,000. The denominator of the fraction, $2,000,000, is the total value of the trust assets immediately after the second transfer. Thus, 60 percent of the principal of the trust becomes subject to chapter 13.

Example (3). Entire portion of trust subject to lapsed power is treated as an addition. On September 25, 1985, B possessed a general power of appointment over the assets of an irrevocable trust that had been created by T in 1980. Under the terms of the trust, B's power lapsed on July 20,

1987. For Federal gift tax purposes, B is treated as making a gift of ninety-five percent (100% – 5%) of the value of the principal (see section 2514). However, because the entire trust was subject to the power of appointment, 100 percent (that portion of the trust subject to the power) of the assets of the trust are treated as a constructive addition. Thus, the entire amount of all generation-skipping transfers occurring pursuant to the trust instrument after July 20, 1987, are subject to chapter 13.

Example (4). Exercise of power of appointment in favor of another trust. On March 1, 1985, T established an irrevocable trust as defined in paragraph (b)(1)(ii) of this section. Under the terms of the trust instrument, the trustee is required to distribute the entire income annually to T's child, C, for life, then to T's grandchild, GC, for life. GC has the power to appoint any or all of the trust assets to Trust 2 which is an irrevocable trust (as defined in paragraph (b)(1)(ii) of this section) that was established on August 1, 1985. The terms of Trust 2's governing instrument provide that the trustee shall pay income to T's great grandchild, GGC, for life. Upon GGC's death, the remainder is to be paid to GGC's issue. GGC was alive on March 1, 1985, when Trust 1 was created. C died on April 1, 1986. On July 1, 1987, GC exercised the power of appointment. The exercise of GC's power does not subject future transfers from Trust 2 to tax under chapter 13 because the exercise of the power in favor of Trust 2 does not suspend the vesting, absolute ownership, or power of alienation of an interest in property for a period, measured from the date of creation of Trust 1, extending beyond the life of GGC (a beneficiary under Trust 2 who was in being at the date of creation of Trust 1) plus a period of 21 years. The result would be the same if Trust 2 had been created after the effective date of chapter 13.

Example (5). Exercise of power of appointment in favor of another trust. Assume the same facts as in Example 4, except that GGC was born on March 28, 1986. The valid exercise of GC's power in favor of Trust 2 causes the principal of Trust 1 to be subject to chapter 13, because GGC was not born until after the creation of Trust 1. Thus, such exercise may suspend the vesting, absolute ownership, or power of alienation of an interest in the trust principal for a period, measured from the date of creation of Trust 1, extending beyond the life of GGC (a beneficiary under Trust 2 who was not a life in being at the date of creation of Trust 1).

Example (6). Extension for the longer of two periods. Prior to the effective date of chapter 13, GP established an irrevocable trust under which the trust income was to be paid to GP's child, C, for life. C was given a testamentary power to appoint the remainder in further trust for the benefit of C's issue. In default of C's exercise of the power, the remainder was to pass to charity. C died on February 3, 1995, survived by a child who was alive when GP established the trust. C exercised the power in a manner that validly extends the trust in favor of C's issue until the later of May 15, 2064 (80 years from the date the trust was created), or the death of C's child plus 21 years. C's exercise of the power is a constructive addition to the trust because the exercise may extend the trust for a period longer than the permissible periods of either the life of C's child (a life in being at the creation of the trust) plus 21 years or a term not more than 90 years measured from the creation of the trust. On the other hand, if C's exercise of the power could extend the trust based only on the life of C's child plus 21 years or only for a term of 80 years from the creation of the trust (but not the later of the two periods) then the exercise of the power would not have been a constructive addition to the trust.

Example (7). Extension for the longer of two periods. The facts are the same as in Example 6 except local law provides that the effect of C's exercise is to extend the term of the trust until May 15, 2064, whether or not C's child predeceases that date by more than 21 years. C's exercise is not a constructive addition to the trust because C exercised the power in a manner that cannot postpone or suspend vesting, absolute ownership, or power of alienation for a term of years that will exceed 90 years. The result would be the same if the effect of C's exercise is either to extend the term of the trust until 21 years after the death of C's child or to extend the term of the trust until the first to occur of May 15, 2064 or 21 years after the death of C's child.

(vi) Appreciation and income. Except to the extent that the provisions of paragraphs (b)(1)(iv) and (v) of this section allocate subsequent appreciation and accumulated income between the original trust and additions thereto, appreciation in the value of the trust and undistributed income added thereto are not considered an addition to the principal of a trust.

(2) Transition rule for wills or revocable trusts executed before October 22, 1986. (i) In general. The provisions of chapter 13 do not apply to any generation-skipping transfer under a will or revocable trust executed before October 22, 1986, provided that—

(A) The document in existence on October 21, 1986, is not amended at any time after October 21, 1986, in any respect which results in the creation of, or an increase in the amount of, a generation-skipping transfer;

(B) In the case of a revocable trust, no addition is made to the revocable trust after October 21, 1986, that results in the creation of, or an increase in the amount of, a generation-skipping transfer; and

(C) The decedent dies before January 1, 1987.

(ii) Revocable trust defined. For purposes of this section, the term revocable trust means any trust (as defined in section 2652(b)) except to the extent that, on October 22, 1986, the trust—

(A) Was an irrevocable trust described in paragraph (b)(1) of this section; or

(B) Would have been an irrevocable trust described in paragraph (b)(1) of this section had it not been created or become irrevocable after September 25, 1985, and before October 22, 1986.

(iii) Will or revocable trust containing qualified terminable interest property. The rules contained in paragraph (b)(1)(iii) of this section apply to any will or revocable trust within the scope of the transition rule of this paragraph (b)(2).

(iv) Amendments to will or revocable trust. For purposes of this paragraph (b)(2), an amendment to a will or a revocable trust in existence on October 21, 1986, is not considered to result in the creation of, or an increase in the amount of, a generation-skipping transfer where the amendment is—

(A) Basically administrative or clarifying in nature and only incidentally increases the amount transferred; or

(B) Designed to ensure that an existing bequest or transfer qualifies for the applicable marital or charitable deduction for estate, gift, or generation-skipping transfer tax purposes and only incidentally increases the amount transferred to a skip person or to a generation-skipping trust.

(v) Creation of, or increase in the amount of, a GST. In determining whether a particular amendment to a will or revocable trust creates, or increases the amount of, a generation-skipping transfer for purposes of this paragraph (b)(2), the effect of the instrument(s) in existence on October 21, 1986, is measured against the effect of the instrument(s) in existence on the date of death of the decedent or on the date of any prior generation-skipping transfer. If the effect of an amendment cannot be immediately determined, it is deemed to create, or increase the amount of, a generation-skipping transfer until a determination can be made.

(vi) Additions to revocable trusts. Any addition made after October 21, 1986, but before the death of the settlor, to a revocable trust subjects all subsequent generation-skipping transfers under the trust to the provisions of chapter 13. Any addition made to a revocable trust after the death of the settlor (if the settlor dies before January 1, 1987) is treated as an addition to an irrevocable trust. See paragraph (b)(1)(v) of this section for rules involving constructive additions to trusts. See paragraph (b)(1)(v)(B) of this section for rules providing that certain transfers to trusts are not treated as additions for purposes of this section.

(vii) Examples. The following examples illustrate the application of paragraph (b)(2)(iv) of this section:

(A) Facts applicable to Examples 1 through 5. In each of Examples 1 through 5 assume that T executed a will prior to October 22, 1986, and that T dies on December 31, 1986.

Example (1). Administrative change. On November 1, 1986, T executes a codicil to T's will removing one of the co-executors named in the will. Although the codicil may have the effect of lowering administrative costs and thus increasing the amount transferred, it is considered administrative in nature and thus does not cause generation-skipping transfers under the will to be subject to chapter 13.

Example (2). Effect of amendment not immediately determinable. On November 1, 1986, T executes a codicil to T's will revoking a bequest of $100,000 to C, a non-skip person (as defined under section 2613(b)) and causing that amount to be added to a residuary trust held for a skip person. The amendment is deemed to increase the amount of a generation-skipping transfer and prevents any transfers under the will from qualifying under paragraph (b)(2)(i) of this section. If, however, C dies before T and under local law the property would have been added to the residue in any event because the bequest would have lapsed, the codicil is not considered an amendment that increases the amount of a generation-skipping transfer.

Example (3). Refund of tax paid because of amendment. T's will provided that an amount equal to the maximum allowable marital deduction would pass to T's spouse with the residue of the estate passing to a trust established for the benefit of skip persons. On October 23, 1986, the will is amended to provide that the marital share passing to T's spouse shall be the lesser of the maximum allowable marital deduction or the minimum amount that will result in no estate tax liability for T's estate. The amendment may increase the amount of a generation-skipping transfer. Therefore, any generation-skipping transfers under the will are subject to tax under chapter 13. If it becomes apparent that the amendment does not increase the amount of a generation-skipping transfer, a claim for refund may be filed with respect to any generation-skipping transfer tax that was paid within the period set forth in section 6511. For example, it would become apparent that the amendment did not result in an increase in the residue if it is subsequently determined that the maximum marital deduction and the minimum amount that will result in no estate tax liability are equal in amount.

Example (4). An amendment that increases a generation-skipping transfer causes complete loss of exempt status. T's will provided for the creation of two trusts for the benefit of skip persons. On November 1, 1986, T executed a codicil to the will specifically increasing the amount of a generation-skipping transfer under the will. All transfers made pursuant to the will or either of the trusts created thereunder are precluded from qualifying under the transition rule of paragraph (b)(2)(i) of this section and are subject to tax under chapter 13.

Example (5). Corrective action effective. Assume that T in Example 4 later executes a second codicil deleting the increase to the generation-skipping transfer. Because the provision increasing a generation-skipping transfer does not become effective, it is not considered an amendment to a will in existence on October 22, 1986.

(B) Facts applicable to Examples 6 through 8. T created a trust on September 30, 1985, in which T retained the power to revoke the transfer at any time prior to T's death. The trust provided that, upon the death of T, the income was to be paid to T's spouse, W, for life and then to A, B, and C, the children of T's sibling, S, in equal shares for life, with one-third of the principal to be distributed per stirpes to each child's surviving issue upon the death of the child. The trustee has the power to make discretionary distributions of trust principal to T's sibling, S.

Example (6). Amendment that affects only a person who is not a skip person. A became disabled, and T modified the trust on December 1, 1986, to increase A's share of the income. Since the amendment does not result in the creation of, or increase in the amount of, a generation-skipping transfer, transfers pursuant to the trust are not subject to chapter 13.

Example (7). Amendment that adds a skip person. Assume that T amends the trust to add T's grandchild, D, as an income beneficiary. The trust will be subject to the provisions of chapter 13 because the amendment creates a generation-skipping transfer.

Example (8). Refund of tax paid during interim period when effect of amendment is not determinable. Assume that T amends the trust to provide that the issue of S are to take a one-fourth share of the principal per stirpes upon S's death. Because the distribution to be made upon S's death may involve skip persons, the amendment is considered an amendment that creates or increases the amount of a generation-skipping transfer until a determination can be made. Accordingly, any distributions from (or terminations of interests in) such trust are subject to chapter 13 until it is determined that no skip person has been added to the trust. At that time, a claim for refund may be filed within the period set forth in section 6511 with respect to any generation-skipping transfer tax that was paid.

(3) Transition rule in the case of mental incompetency. (i) In general. If an individual was under a mental disability to change the disposition of his or her property continuously from October 22, 1986, until the date of his or her death, the provisions of chapter 13 do not apply to any generation-skipping transfer—

(A) Under a trust (as defined in section 2652(b)) to the extent such trust consists of property, or the proceeds of property, the value of which was included in the gross estate of the individual (other than property transferred by or on behalf of the individual during the individual's life after October 22, 1986); or

(B) Which is a direct skip (other than a direct skip from a trust) that occurs by reason of the death of the individual.

(ii) Mental disability defined. For purposes of this paragraph (b)(2), the term mental disability means mental incompetence to execute an instrument governing the disposition of the individual's property, whether or not there was an adjudication of incompetence and regardless of whether there has been an appointment of a guardian, fiduciary, or other person charged with either the care of the individual or the care of the individual's property.

(iii) Decedent who has not been adjudged mentally incompetent. (A) If there has not been a court adjudication that the decedent was mentally incompetent on or before October 22, 1986, the executor must file, with Form 706, either—

(1) A certification from a qualified physician stating that the decedent was—

(i) mentally incompetent at all times on and after October 22, 1986; and

(ii) did not regain competence to modify or revoke the terms of the trust or will prior to his or her death; or

(2) Sufficient other evidence demonstrating that the decedent was mentally incompetent at all times on and after October 22, 1986, as well as a statement explaining why no certification is available from a physician; and

(3) Any judgement or decree relating to the decedent's incompetency that was made after October 22, 1986.

(B) Such items in paragraphs (b)(3)(iii)(A)(1), (2), and (3) of this section will be considered relevant, but not determinative, in establishing the decedent's state of competency.

(iv) Decedent who has been adjudged mentally incompetent. If the decedent has been adjudged mentally incompetent on or before October 22, 1986, a copy of the judgment or decree, and any modification thereof, must be filed with the Form 706.

(v) Rule applies even if another person has power to change trust terms. In the case of a transfer from a trust, this paragraph (b)(3) applies even though a person charged with the care of the decedent or the decedent's property has the power to revoke or modify the terms of the trust, provided that the power is not exercised after October 22, 1986, in a manner that creates, or increases the amount of, a generation-skipping transfer. See paragraph (b)(2)(iv) of this section for rules concerning amendments that create or increase the amount of a generation-skipping transfer.

(vi) Example. The following example illustrates the application of paragraph (b)(3)(v) of this section:

Example. T was mentally incompetent on October 22, 1986, and remained so until death in 1993. Prior to becoming incompetent, T created a revocable generation-skipping trust that was includible in T's gross estate. Prior to October 22, 1986, the appropriate court issued an order under which P, who was thereby charged with the care of T's property, had the power to modify or revoke the revocable trust. Although P exercised the power after October 22, 1986, and while T was incompetent, the power was not exercised in a manner that created, or increased the amount of, a generation-skipping transfer. Thus, the existence and exercise of P's power did not cause the trust to lose its exempt status under paragraph (b)(3) of this section. The result would be the same if the court order was issued after October 22, 1986.

(4) Retention of trust's exempt status in the case of modifications, etc.. (i) In general. This paragraph (b)(4) provides rules for determining when a modification, judicial construction, settlement agreement, or trustee action with respect to a trust that is exempt from the generation-skipping transfer tax under paragraph (b)(1), (2), or (3) of this section (hereinafter referred to as an exempt trust) will not cause the trust to lose its exempt status. In general, unless specifically provided otherwise, the rules contained in this paragraph are applicable only for purposes of determining whether an exempt trust retains its exempt status for generation-skipping transfer tax purposes. Thus (unless specifically noted), the rules do not apply in determining, for example, whether the transaction results in a gift subject to gift tax, or may cause the trust to be included in the gross estate of a beneficiary, or may result in the realization of gain for purposes of section 1001.

(A) Discretionary powers. The distribution of trust principal from an exempt trust to a new trust or retention of trust principal in a continuing trust will not cause the new or continuing trust to be subject to the provisions of chapter 13, if—

(1) Either—

(i) The terms of the governing instrument of the exempt trust authorize distributions to the new trust or the retention of trust principal in a continuing trust, without the consent or approval of any beneficiary or court; or

(ii) at the time the exempt trust became irrevocable, state law authorized distributions to the new trust or retention of principal in the continuing trust, without the consent or approval of any beneficiary or court; and

(2) The terms of the governing instrument of the new or continuing trust do not extend the time for vesting of any beneficial interest in the trust in a manner that may postpone or suspend the vesting, absolute ownership, or power of alienation of an interest in property for a period, measured from the date the original trust became irrevocable, extending beyond any life in being at the date the original trust became irrevocable plus a period of 21 years, plus if necessary, a reasonable period of gestation. For purposes of this paragraph (b)(4)(i)(A), the exercise of a trustee's distributive power that validly postpones or suspends the vesting, absolute ownership, or power of alienation of an interest in property for a term of years that will not exceed 90 years (measured from the date the original trust became irrevocable) will not be considered an exercise that postpones or suspends vesting, absolute ownership, or the power of alienation beyond the perpetuities period. If a distributive power is exercised by creating another power, it is deemed to be exercised to whatever extent the second power may be exercised.

(B) Settlement. A court-approved settlement of a bona fide issue regarding the administration of the trust or the construction of terms of the governing instrument will not cause an exempt trust to be subject to the provisions of chapter 13, if—

(1) The settlement is the product of arm's length negotiations; and

(2) The settlement is within the range of reasonable outcomes under the governing instrument and applicable state law addressing the issues resolved by the settlement. A settlement that results in a compromise between the positions of the litigating parties and reflects the parties' assessments of the relative strengths of their positions is a settlement that is within the range of reasonable outcomes.

(C) Judicial construction. A judicial construction of a governing instrument to resolve an ambiguity in the terms of the instrument or to correct a scrivener's error will not cause an exempt trust to be subject to the provisions of chapter 13, if—

(1) The judicial action involves a bona fide issue; and

(2) The construction is consistent with applicable state law that would be applied by the highest court of the state.

(D) Other changes.

(1) A modification of the governing instrument of an exempt trust (including a trustee distribution, settlement, or construction that does not satisfy paragraph (b)(4)(i)(A), (B), or (C) of this section) by judicial reformation, or nonjudicial reformation that is valid under applicable state law, will not cause an exempt trust to be subject to the provisions of chapter 13, if the modification does not shift a beneficial interest in the trust to any beneficiary who occupies a lower generation (as defined in section 2651) than the person or persons who held the beneficial interest prior to the modification, and the modification does not extend the time for vesting of any beneficial interest in the trust beyond the period provided for in the original trust.

(2) For purposes of this section, a modification of an exempt trust will result in a shift in beneficial interest to a lower generation beneficiary if the modification can result in either an increase in the amount of a GST transfer or the creation of a new GST transfer. To determine whether a modification of an irrevocable trust will shift a beneficial interest in a trust to a beneficiary who occupies a lower generation, the effect of the instrument on the date of the modification is measured against the effect of the instrument in existence immediately before the modification. If the effect of the modification cannot be immediately determined, it is deemed to shift a beneficial interest in the trust to a beneficiary who occupies a lower generation (as defined in section 2651) than the person or persons who held the beneficial interest prior to the modification. A modification that is administrative in nature that only indirectly increases the amount transferred (for example, by lowering administrative costs or income taxes) will not be considered to shift a beneficial interest in the trust. In addition, administration of a trust in conformance with applicable local law that defines the term income as a unitrust amount (or permits a right to income to be satisfied by such an amount) or that permits the trustee to adjust between principal and income to fulfill the trustee's duty of impartiality between income and principal beneficiaries will not be considered to shift a beneficial interest in the trust, if applicable local law provides for a reasonable apportionment between the income and remainder beneficiaries of the total return of the trust and meets the requirements of § 1.643(b)-1 of this chapter.

(E) Examples. The following examples illustrate the application of this paragraph (b)(4). In each example, assume that the trust established in 1980 was irrevocable for purposes of paragraph (b)(1)(ii) of this section and that there have been no additions to any trust after September 25, 1985. The examples are as follows:

Example (1). Trustee's power to distribute principal authorized under trust instrument. In 1980, Grantor established an irrevocable trust (Trust) for the benefit of Grantor's child, A, A's spouse, and A's issue. At the time Trust was established, A had two children, B and C. A corporate fiduciary was designated as trustee. Under the terms of Trust, the trustee has the discretion to distribute all or part of the trust income to one or more of the group consisting of A, A's spouse or A's issue. The trustee is also authorized to distribute all or part of the trust principal to one or more trusts for the benefit of A, A's spouse, or A's issue under terms specified by the trustee in the trustee's discretion. Any trust established under Trust, however, must terminate 21 years after the death of the last child of A to die who was alive at the time Trust was executed. Trust will terminate on the death of A, at which time the remaining principal will be distributed to A's issue, per stirpes. In 2002, the trustee distributes part of Trust's principal to a new trust for the benefit of B and C and their issue. The new trust will terminate 21 years after the death of the survivor of B and C, at which time the trust principal will be distributed to the issue of B and C, per stirpes. The terms of the governing instrument of Trust authorize the trustee to make the distribution to a new trust without the consent or approval of any beneficiary or court. In addition, the terms of the governing instrument of the new trust do not extend the time for vesting of any beneficial interest in a manner that may postpone or suspend the vesting, absolute ownership or power of alienation of an interest in property for a period, measured from the date of creation of Trust, extending beyond any life in being at the date of creation of Trust plus a period of 21 years, plus if necessary, a reasonable period of gestation. Therefore, neither Trust nor the new trust will be subject to the provisions of chapter 13 of the Internal Revenue Code.

Example (2). Trustee's power to distribute principal pursuant to state statute. In 1980, Grantor established an irrevocable trust (Trust) for the benefit of Grantor's child, A, A's spouse, and A's issue. At the time Trust was established, A had two children, B and C. A corporate fiduciary was designated as trustee. Under the terms of Trust, the trustee has the discretion to distribute all or part of the trust income or principal to one or more of the group consisting of A, A's spouse or A's issue. Trust will terminate on the death of A, at which time, the trust principal will be distributed to A's issue, per stirpes. Under a state statute enacted after 1980 that is applicable to Trust, a trustee who has the absolute discretion under the terms of a testamentary instrument or irrevocable inter vivos trust agreement to invade the principal of a trust for the benefit of the income beneficiaries of the trust, may exercise the discretion by appointing so much or all of the principal of the trust in favor of a trustee of a trust under an instrument other than that under which the power to invade is created, or under the same instrument. The trustee may take the action either with consent of all the persons interested in the trust but without prior court approval, or with court approval, upon notice to all of the parties. The exercise of the discretion, however, must not reduce any fixed income interest of any income beneficiary of the trust and must be in favor of the beneficiaries of the trust. Under state law prior to the enactment of the state statute, the trustee did not have the authority to make distributions in trust. In 2002, the trustee distributes one-half of Trust's principal to a new trust that provides for the payment of trust income to A for life and further provides that, at A's death, one-half of the trust remainder will pass to B or B's issue and one-half of the trust will pass to C or C's issue. Because the state statute was enacted after Trust was created and requires the consent of all of the parties, the transaction constitutes a modification of Trust. However, the modification does not shift any beneficial interest in Trust to a beneficiary or beneficiaries who occupy a lower generation than the person or persons who held the beneficial interest prior to the modification. In addition, the modification does not extend the time for vesting of any beneficial interest in Trust beyond the period provided for in the original trust. The new trust will terminate at the same date provided under Trust. Therefore, neither Trust nor the new trust will be subject to the provisions of chapter 13 of the Internal Revenue Code.

Example (3). Construction of an ambiguous term in the instrument. In 1980, Grantor established an irrevocable trust for the benefit of Grantor's children, A and B, and their issue. The trust is to terminate on the death of the last to die of A and B, at which time the principal is to be distributed to their issue. However, the provision governing the termination of the trust is ambiguous regarding whether the trust principal is to be distributed per stirpes, only to the children of A and B, or per capita among the children, grandchildren, and more remote issue of A and B. In 2002, the trustee files a construction suit with the appropriate local court to resolve the ambiguity. The court issues an order construing the instrument to provide for per capita distributions to the children, grandchildren, and more remote issue of A and B living at the time the trust terminates. The court's construction resolves a bona fide issue regarding the proper interpretation of the instrument and is consistent with applicable state law as it would be interpreted by the highest court of the state. Therefore, the trust will not be subject to the provisions of chapter 13 of the Internal Revenue Code.

Example (4). Change in trust situs. In 1980, Grantor, who was domiciled in State X, executed an irrevocable trust for the benefit of Grantor's issue, naming a State X bank as trustee. Under the terms of the trust, the trust is to terminate, in all events, no later than 21 years after the death of the last to die of certain designated individuals living at the time the trust was executed. The provisions of the trust do not specify that any particular state law is to govern the administration and construction of the trust. In State X, the common law rule against perpetuities applies to trusts. In 2002, a State Y bank is named as sole trustee. The effect of changing trustees is that the situs of the trust changes to State Y, and the laws of State Y govern the administration and construction of the trust. State Y law contains no rule against perpetuities. In this case, however, in view of the terms of the trust instrument, the trust will terminate at the same time before and after the change in situs. Accordingly, the change in situs does not shift any beneficial interest in the trust to a beneficiary who occupies a lower generation (as defined in section 2651) than the person or persons who held the beneficial interest prior to the transfer. Furthermore, the change in situs does not extend the time for vesting of any beneficial interest in the trust beyond that provided for in the original trust. Therefore, the trust will not be subject to the provisions of chapter 13 of the Internal Revenue Code. If, in this example, as a result of the change in situs, State Y law governed such that the time for vesting was extended beyond the period prescribed under the terms of the original trust instrument, the trust would not retain exempt status.

Example (5). Division of a trust. In 1980, Grantor established an irrevocable trust for the benefit of his two children, A and B, and their issue. Under the terms of the trust, the trustee has the discretion to distribute income and principal to A, B, and their issue in such amounts as the trustee deems appropriate. On the death of the last to die of A and B, the trust principal is to be distributed to the living issue of A and B, per stirpes. In 2002, the appropriate local court approved the division of the trust into two equal trusts, one for the benefit of A and A's issue and one for the benefit of B and B's issue. The trust for A and A's issue provides that the trustee has the discretion to distribute trust income and principal to A and A's issue in such amounts as the trustee deems appropriate. On A's death, the trust principal is to be distributed equally to A's issue, per stirpes. If A dies with no living descendants, the principal will be added to the trust for B and B's issue. The trust for B and B's issue is identical (except for the beneficiaries), and terminates at B's death at which time the trust principal is to be distributed equally to B's0 issue, per stirpes. If B dies with no living descendants, principal will be added to the trust for A and A's issue. The division of the trust into two trusts does not shift any beneficial interest in the trust to a beneficiary who occupies a lower generation (as defined in section 2651) than the person or persons who held the beneficial interest prior to the division. In addition, the division does not extend the time for vesting of any beneficial interest in the trust beyond the period provided for in the original trust. Therefore, the two partitioned trusts resulting from the division will not be subject to the provisions of chapter 13 of the Internal Revenue Code.

Example (6). Merger of two trusts. In 1980, Grantor established an irrevocable trust for Grantor's child and the child's issue. In 1983, Grantor's spouse also established a separate irrevocable trust for the benefit of the same child and issue. The terms of the spouse's trust and Grantor's trust are identical. In 2002, the appropriate local court approved the merger of the two trusts into one trust to save administrative costs and enhance the management of the investments. The merger of the two trusts does not shift any beneficial interest in the trust to a beneficiary who occupies a lower generation (as defined in section 2651) than the person or persons who held the beneficial interest prior to the merger. In addition, the merger does not extend the time for vesting of any beneficial interest in the trust beyond the period provided for in the original trust. Therefore, the trust that resulted from the merger will not be subject to the provisions of chapter 13 of the Internal Revenue Code.

Example (7). Modification that does not shift an interest to a lower generation. In 1980, Grantor established an irrevocable trust for the benefit of Grantor's grandchildren, A, B, and C. The trust provides that income is to be paid to A, B, and C, in equal shares for life. The trust further provides that, upon the death of the first grandchild to die, one-third of the principal is to be distributed to that grandchild's issue, per stirpes. Upon the death of the second grandchild to die, one-half of the remaining trust principal is to be distributed to that grandchild's issue, per stirpes, and upon the death of the last grandchild to die, the remaining principal is to be distributed to that grandchild's issue, per stirpes. In 2002, A became disabled. Subsequently, the trustee, with the consent of B and C, petitioned the appropriate local court and the court approved a modification of the trust that increased A's share of trust income. The modification does not shift a beneficial interest to a lower generation beneficiary because the modification does not increase the amount of a GST transfer under the original trust or create the possibility that new GST transfers not contemplated in the original trust may be made. In this case, the modification will increase the amount payable to A who is a member of the same generation as B and C. In addition, the modification does not extend the time for vesting of any beneficial interest in the trust beyond the period provided for in the original trust. Therefore, the trust as modified will not be subject to the provisions of chapter 13 of the Internal Revenue Code. However, the modification increasing A's share of trust income is a transfer by B and C to A for Federal gift tax purposes.

Example (8). Conversion of income interest into unitrust interest. In 1980, Grantor established an irrevocable trust under the terms of which trust income is payable to A for life and, upon A's death, the remainder is to pass to A's issue, per stirpes. In 2002, the appropriate local court approves a modification to the trust that converts A's income interest into the right to receive the greater of the entire income of the trust or a fixed percentage of the trust assets valued annually (unitrust interest) to be paid each year to A for life. The modification does not result in a shift in beneficial interest to a beneficiary who occupies a lower generation (as defined in section 2651) than the person or persons who held the beneficial interest prior to the modification. In this case, the modification can only operate to increase the amount distributable to A and decrease the amount distributable to A's issue. In addition, the modification does not extend the time for vesting of any beneficial interest in the trust beyond the period provided for in the original trust. Therefore, the trust will not be subject to the provisions of chapter 13 of the Internal Revenue Code.

Example (9). Allocation of capital gain to income. In 1980, Grantor established an irrevocable trust under the terms of which trust income is payable to Grantor's child, A, for life, and upon A's death, the remainder is to pass to A's issue, per stirpes. Under applicable state law, unless the governing instrument provides otherwise, capital gain is allocated to principal. In 2002, the trust is modified to allow the trustee to allocate capital gain to the income. The modification does not shift any beneficial interest in the trust to a beneficiary who occupies a lower generation (as defined in section 2651) than the person or persons who held the beneficial interest prior to the modification. In this case, the modification can only have the effect of increasing the amount distributable to A, and decreasing the amount distributable to A's issue. In addition, the modification does not extend the time for vesting of any beneficial interest in the trust beyond the period provided for in the original trust. Therefore, the trust will not be subject to the provisions of chapter 13 of the Internal Revenue Code.

Example (10). Administrative change to terms of a trust. In 1980, Grantor executed an irrevocable trust for the benefit of Grantor's issue, naming a bank and five other individuals as trustees. In 2002, the appropriate local court approves a modification of the trust that decreases the number of trustees which results in lower administrative costs. The modification pertains to the administration of the trust and does not shift a beneficial interest in the trust to any beneficiary who occupies a lower generation (as defined in section 2651) than the person or persons who held the beneficial interest prior to the modification. In addition, the modification does not extend the time for vesting of any beneficial interest in the trust beyond the period provided for in the original trust. Therefore, the trust will not be subject to the provisions of chapter 13 of the Internal Revenue Code.

Example (11). Conversion of income interest to unitrust interest under state statute. In 1980, Grantor, a resident of State X, established an irrevocable trust for the benefit of Grantor's child, A, and A's issue. The trust provides that trust income is payable to A for life and upon A's death the remainder is to pass to A's issue, per stirpes. In 2002, State X amends its income and principal statute to define income as a unitrust amount of 4% of the fair market value of the trust assets valued annually. For a trust established prior to 2002, the statute provides that the new definition of income will apply only if all the beneficiaries who have an interest in the trust consent to the change within two years after the effective date of the statute. The statute provides specific procedures to establish the consent of the beneficiaries. A and A's issue consent to the change in the definition of income within the time period, and in accordance with the procedures, prescribed by the state statute. The administration of the trust, in accordance with the state statute defining income to be a 4% unitrust amount, will not be considered to shift any beneficial interest in the trust. Therefore, the trust will not be subject to the provisions of chapter 13 of the Internal Revenue Code. Further, under these facts, no trust beneficiary will be treated as having made a gift for federal gift tax purposes, and neither the trust nor any trust beneficiary will be treated as having made a taxable exchange for federal income tax purposes. Similarly, the conclusions in this example would be the same if the beneficiaries' consent was not required, or, if the change in administration of the trust occurred because the situs of the trust was changed to State X from a state whose statute does not define income as a unitrust amount or if the situs was changed to such a state from State X.

Example (12). Equitable adjustments under state statute. The facts are the same as in Example 11, except that in 2002, State X amends its income and principal statute to permit the trustee to make adjustments between income and principal when the trustee invests and manages the trust assets under the state's prudent investor standard, the trust describes the amount that shall or must be distributed to a beneficiary by referring to the trust's income, and the trustee after applying the state statutory rules regarding allocation of receipts between income and principal is unable to administer the trust impartially. The provision permitting the trustees to make these adjustments is effective in 2002 for trusts created at any time. The trustee invests and manages the trust assets under the state's prudent investor standard, and pursuant to authorization in the state statute, the trustee allocates receipts between the income and principal accounts in a manner to ensure the impartial administration of the trust. The administration of the trust in accordance with the state statute will not be considered to shift any beneficial interest in the trust. Therefore, the trust will not be subject to the provisions of chapter 13 of the Internal Revenue Code. Further, under these facts, no trust beneficiary will be treated as having made a gift for federal gift tax purposes, and neither the trust nor any trust beneficiary will be treated as having made a taxable exchange for federal income tax purposes. Similarly, the conclusions in this example would be the same if the change in administration of the trust occurred because the situs of the trust was changed to State X from a state whose statute does not authorize the trustee to make adjustments between income and principal or if the situs was changed to such a state from State X.

(ii) Effective dates. The rules in this paragraph (b)(4) are generally applicable on and after December 20, 2000. However, the rule in the last sentence of paragraph (b)(4)(i)(D)(2) of this section and Example 11 and Example 12 in paragraph (b)(4)(i)(E) of this section regarding the administration of a trust and the determination of income in conformance with applicable state law applies to trusts for taxable years ending after January 2, 2004.

(5) Exceptions to additions rule. (i) In general. Any addition to a trust made pursuant to an instrument or arrangement covered by the transition rules in paragraph (b)(1), (2) or (3) of this section is not treated as an addition for purposes of this section. Moreover, any property transferred inter vivos to a trust is not treated as an addition if the same property would have been added to the trust pursuant to an instrument covered by the transition rules in paragraph (b)(2) or (3) of this section.

(ii) Examples. The following examples illustrate the application of paragraph (b)(4)(i) of this section:

Example (1). Addition pursuant to terms of exempt instrument. On December 31, 1980, T created an irrevocable trust having a principal of $100,000. Under the terms of the trust, the principal was to be held for the benefit of T's grandchild, GC. Pursuant to the terms of T's will, a document entitled to relief under the transition rule of paragraph (b)(2) of this section, the residue of the estate was paid to the trust. Because the addition to the trust was paid pursuant to the terms of an instrument (T's will) that is not subject to the provisions of chapter 13 because of paragraph (b)(2) of this section, the payment to the trust is not considered an addition to the principal of the trust. Thus, distributions to or for the benefit of GC, are not subject to the provisions of chapter 13.

Example (2). Property transferred inter vivos that would have been transferred to the same trust by the transferor's will. T is the grantor of a trust that was irrevocable on September 25, 1985. T's will, which was executed before October 22, 1986, and not amended thereafter, provides that, upon T's death, the entire estate will pour over into T's trust. On October 1, 1985, T transfers $100,000 to the trust. While T's will otherwise qualifies for relief under the transition rule in paragraph (b)(2) of this section, the transition rule is not applicable unless T dies prior to January 1, 1987. Thus, if T dies after December 31, 1986, the transfer is treated as an addition to the trust for purposes of any distribution made from the trust after the transfer to the trust on October 1, 1985. If T dies before January 1, 1987, the entire trust (as well as any distributions from or terminations of interests in the trust prior to T's death) is exempt, under paragraph (b)(2) of this section, from chapter 13 because the $100,000 would have been added to the trust under a will that would have qualified under paragraph (b)(2) of this section. In either case, for any generation-skipping transfers made after the transfer to the trust on October 1, 1985, but before T's death, the $100,000 is treated as an addition to the trust and a proportionate amount of the trust is subject to chapter 13.

Example (3). Pour over to a revocable trust. T and S are the settlors of separate revocable trusts with equal values. Both trusts were established for the benefit of skip persons (as defined in section 2613). S dies on December 1, 1985, and under the provisions of S's trust, the principal pours over into T's trust. If T dies before January 1, 1987, the entire trust is excluded under paragraph (b)(2) of this section from the operation of chapter 13. If T dies after December 31, 1986, the entire trust is subject to the generation-skipping transfer tax provisions because T's trust is not a trust described in paragraph (b)(1) or (2) of this section. In the latter case, the fact that S died before January 1, 1987, is irrelevant because the principal of S's trust was added to a trust that never qualified under the transition rules of paragraph (b)(1) or (2) of this section.

Example (4). Pour over to exempt trust. Assume the same facts as in Example 3, except upon the death of S on December 1, 1985, S's trust continues as an irrevocable trust and that the principal of T's trust is to be paid over upon T's death to S's trust. Again, if T dies before January 1, 1987, S's entire trust falls within the provisions of paragraph (b)(2) of this section. However, if T dies after December 31, 1986, the pour-over is considered an addition to the trust. Therefore, S's trust is not a trust excluded under paragraph (b)(2) of this section because an addition is made to the trust.

Example (5). Lapse of a general power of appointment. S, the spouse of the settlor of an irrevocable trust that was created in 1980, had, on September 25, 1985, a general power of appointment over the trust assets. The trust provides that should S fail to exercise the power of appointment the property is to remain in the trust. On October 21, 1986, S executed a will under which S failed to exercise the power of appointment. If S dies before January 1, 1987, without having exercised the power in a manner which results in the creation of, or increase in the amount of, a generation-skipping transfer (or amended the will in a manner that results in the creation of, or increase in the amount of, a generation-skipping transfer), transfers pursuant to the trust or the will are not subject to chapter 13 because the trust is an irrevocable trust and the will qualifies under paragraph (b)(2) of this section.

Example (6). Lapse of general power of appointment held by intestate decedent. Assume the same facts as in Example 5, except on October 22, 1986, S did not have a will and that S dies after that date. Upon S's death, or upon the prior exercise or release of the power, the value of the entire trust is treated as having been distributed to S, and S is treated as having made an addition to the trust in the amount of the entire principal. Any distribution or termination pursuant to the trust occurring after S's death is subject to chapter 13. It is immaterial whether S's death occurs before January 1, 1987, since paragraph (b)(2) of this section is only applicable where a will or revocable trust was executed before October 22, 1986.

(c) Additional effective dates. Except as otherwise provided, the regulations under §§ 26.2611-1, 26.2612-1, 26.2613-1, 26.2632-1, 26.2641-1, 26.2642-1, 26.2642-2, 26.2642-3, 26.2642-4, 26.2642-5, 26.2652-1, 26.2652-2, 26.2653-1, 26.2654-1, 26.2663-1, and 26.2663-2 are effective with respect to generation-skipping transfers as defined in § 26.2611-1 made on or after December 27, 1995. However, taxpayers may, at their option, rely on these regulations in the case of generation-skipping transfers made, and trusts that became irrevocable, after December 23, 1992, and before December 27, 1995. The last four sentences in paragraph (b)(1)(i) of this section are applicable on and after November 18, 1999.

T.D. 7812, 3/2/82, amend T.D. 8187, 3/14/88, T.D. 8644, 12/26/95, T.D. 8912, 12/19/2000, T.D. 9102, 12/30/2003.

§ 26.2611-1 Generation-skipping transfer defined.

A generation-skipping transfer (GST) is an event that is either a direct skip, a taxable distribution, or a taxable termination. See § 26.2612-1 for the definition of these terms. The determination as to whether an event is a GST is made by reference to the most recent transfer subject to the estate or gift tax. See § 26.2652-1(a)(2) for determining whether a transfer is subject to Federal estate or gift tax.

T.D. 8644, 12/26/95.

§ 26.2612-1 Definitions.

Caution: The Treasury has not yet amended Reg § 26.2612-1 to reflect changes made by P.L. 105-34.

(a) Direct skip. In general. A direct skip is a transfer to a skip person that is subject to Federal estate or gift tax. If property is transferred to a trust, the transfer is a direct skip only if the trust is a skip person. Only one direct skip occurs when a single transfer of property skips two or more generations. See paragraph (d) of this section for the definition of skip person. See § 26.2652-1(b) for the definition of trust. See § 26.2632-1(c)(4) for the time that a direct skip occurs if the transferred property is subject to an estate tax inclusion period.

(b) Taxable termination. *(1) In general.* Except as otherwise provided in this paragraph (b), a taxable termination is a termination (occurring for any reason) of an interest in trust unless—

(i) A transfer subject to Federal estate or gift tax occurs with respect to the property held in the trust at the time of the termination;

(ii) Immediately after the termination, a person who is not a skip person has an interest in the trust; or

(iii) At no time after the termination may a distribution, other than a distribution the probability of which occurring is so remote as to be negligible (including a distribution at the termination of the trust) be made from the trust to a skip person. For this purpose, the probability that a distribution will occur is so remote as to be negligible only if it can be ascertained by actuarial standards that there is less than a 5 percent probability that the distribution will occur.

(2) Partial termination. If a distribution of a portion of trust property is made to a skip person by reason of a termination occurring on the death of a lineal descendant of the transferor, the termination is a taxable termination with respect to the distributed property.

(3) Simultaneous termination. A simultaneous termination of two or more interests creates only one taxable termination.

(c) Taxable distribution. *(1) In general.* A taxable distribution is a distribution of income or principal from a trust to a skip person unless the distribution is a taxable termination or a direct skip. If any portion of GST tax (including penalties and interest thereon) imposed on a distributee is paid from the distributing trust, the payment is an additional taxable distribution to the distributee. For purposes of chapter 13, the additional distribution is treated as having been made on the last day of the calendar year in which the original taxable distribution is made. If Federal estate or gift tax is imposed on any individual with respect to an interest in property held by a trust, the interest in property is treated as having been distributed to the individual to the extent that the value of the interest is subject to Federal estate or gift tax. See § 26.2652-1(a)(6) Example 5, regarding the treatment of the lapse of a power of appointment as a transfer to a trust.

(2) Look-through rule not to apply. Solely for purposes of determining whether any transfer from a trust to another trust is a taxable distribution, the rules of section 2651(e)(2) do not apply. If the transferring trust and the recipient trust have the same transferor, see § 26.2642-4(a)(1) and (2) for rules for recomputing the applicable fraction of the recipient trust.

(d) Skip person. A skip person is—

(1) An individual assigned to a generation more than one generation below that of the transferor (determined under the rules of section 2651); or

(2) A trust if—

(i) All interests in the trust are held by skip persons; or

(ii) No person holds an interest in the trust and no distributions, other than a distribution the probability of which occurring is so remote as to be negligible (including distributions at the termination of the trust), may be made after the transfer to a person other than a skip person. For this purpose, the probability that a distribution will occur is so remote as to be negligible only if it can be ascertained by actuarial standards that there is less than a 5 percent probability that the distribution will occur.

(e) Interest in trust. *(1) In general.* An interest in trust is an interest in property held in trust as defined in section 2652(c) and these regulations. An interest in trust exists if a person—

(i) Has a present right to receive trust principal or income;

(ii) Is a permissible current recipient of trust principal or income and is not described in section 2055(a); or

(iii) Is described in section 2055(a) and the trust is a charitable remainder annuity trust or unitrust (as defined in section 664(d)) or a pooled income fund (as defined in section 642(c)(5)).

(2) Exceptions. (i) Support obligations. In general, an individual has a present right to receive trust income or principal if trust income or principal may be used to satisfy the individual's support obligations. However, an individual does not have an interest in a trust merely because a support obligation of that individual may be satisfied by a distribution that is either within the discretion of a fiduciary or pursuant to provisions of local law substantially equivalent to the Uniform Gifts (Transfers) to Minors Act.

(ii) Certain interests disregarded. An interest which is used primarily to postpone or avoid the GST tax is disregarded for purposes of chapter 13. An interest is considered as used primarily to postpone or avoid the GST tax if a significant purpose for the creation of the interest is to postpone or avoid the tax.

(3) Disclaimers. An interest does not exist to the extent it is disclaimed pursuant to a disclaimer that constitutes a qualified disclaimer under section 2518.

(f) Examples. The following examples illustrate the provisions of this section.

Example (1). Direct skip. T gratuitously conveys Blackacre to T's grandchild. Because the transfer is a transfer to a skip person of property subject to Federal gift tax, it is a direct skip.

Example (2). Direct skip of more than one generation. T gratuitously conveys Blackacre to T's great-grandchild. The transfer is a direct skip. Only one GST tax is imposed on the direct skip although two generations are skipped by the transfer.

Example (3). Withdrawal power in trust. T transfers $50,000 to a new trust providing that trust income is to be paid to T's child, C, for life and, on C's death, the trust principal is to be paid to T's descendants. Under the terms of the trust, T grants four grandchildren the right to withdraw $10,000 from the trust for a 60 day period following the transfer. Since C, who is not a skip person, has an interest in the trust, the trust is not a skip person. T's transfer to the trust is not a direct skip.

Example (4). Taxable termination. T establishes an irrevocable trust under which the income is to be paid to T's child, C, for life. On the death of C, the trust principal is to be paid to T's grandchild, GC. Since C has an interest in the trust, the trust is not a skip person and the transfer to the trust is not a direct skip. If C dies survived by GC, a taxable termination occurs at C's death because C's interest in the trust terminates and thereafter the trust property is held by a skip person who occupies a lower generation than C.

Example (5). Direct skip of property held in trust. T establishes a testamentary trust under which the income is to be paid to T's surviving spouse, S, for life and the remainder is to be paid to a grandchild of T and S. T's executor elects to treat the trust as qualified terminable interest property under section 2056(b)(7). The transfer to the trust is not a direct skip because S, a person who is not a skip person, holds a present right to receive income from the trust. Upon S's death, the trust property is included in S's gross estate under section 2044 and passes directly to a skip person. The GST occurring at that time is a direct skip because it is a transfer subject to chapter 11. The fact that the interest created by T is terminated at S's death is immaterial because S becomes the transferor at the time of the transfer subject to chapter 11.

Example (6). Taxable termination. T establishes an irrevocable trust for the benefit of T's child, C, T's grandchild, GC, and T's great-grandchild, GGC. Under the terms of the trust, income and principal may be distributed to any or all of the living beneficiaries at the discretion of the trustee. Upon the death of the second beneficiary to die, the trust principal is to be paid to the survivor. C dies first. A taxable termination occurs at that time because, immediately after C's interest terminates, all interests in the trust are held by skip persons (GC and GGC).

Example (7). Taxable termination resulting from distribution. The facts are the same as in Example 6, except twenty years after C's death the trustee exercises its discretionary power and distributes the entire principal to GGC. The distribution results in a taxable termination because GC's interest in the trust terminates as a result of the distribution of the entire trust property to GGC, a skip person. The result would be the same if the trustee retained sufficient funds to pay the GST tax due by reason of the taxable termination, as well as any expenses of winding up the trust.

Example (8). Simultaneous termination of interests of more than one beneficiary. T establishes an irrevocable trust for the benefit of T's child, C, T's grandchild, GC, and T's great-grandchild, GGC. Under the terms of the trust, income and principal may be distributed to any or all of the living beneficiaries at the discretion of the trustee. Upon the death of C, the trust property is to be distributed to GGC if then living. If C is survived by both GC and GGC, both C's and GC's interests in the trust will terminate on C's death. However, because both interests will terminate at the same time and as a result of one event, only one taxable termination occurs.

Example (9). Partial taxable termination. T creates an irrevocable trust providing that trust income is to be paid to T's children, A and B, in such proportions as the trustee determines for their joint lives. On the death of the first child to die, one-half of the trust principal is to be paid to T's then living grandchildren. The balance of the trust principal is to be paid to T's grandchildren on the death of the survivor of A and B. If A predeceases B, the distribution occurring on the termination of A's interest in the trust is a taxable termination and not a taxable distribution. It is a taxable termination because the distribution is a distribution of a portion of the trust that occurs as a result of the death of A, a lineal descendant of T. It is immaterial that a portion of the trust continues and that B, a person other than a skip person, thereafter holds an interest in the trust.

Example (10). Taxable distribution. T establishes an irrevocable trust under which the trust income is payable to T's child, C, for life. When T's grandchild, GC, attains 35 years of age, GC is to receive one-half of the principal. The remaining one-half of the principal is to be distributed to GC on C's death. Assume that C survives until GC attains age 35. When the trustee distributes one-half of the principal to GC on GC's 35th birthday, the distribution is a taxable distribution because it is a distribution to a skip person and is neither a taxable termination nor a direct skip.

Example (11). Exercise of withdrawal right as taxable distribution. The facts are the same as in Example 10, except GC holds a continuing right to withdraw trust principal and after one year GC withdraws $10,000. The withdrawal by GC is not a taxable termination because the withdrawal does not terminate C's interest in the trust. The withdrawal by GC is a taxable distribution to GC.

Example (12). Interest in trust. T establishes an irrevocable trust under which the income is to be paid to T's child, C, for life. On the death of C, the trust principal is to be paid to T's grandchild, GC. Because C has a present right to receive income from the trust, C has an interest in the trust. Because GC cannot currently receive distributions from the trust, GC does not have an interest in the trust.

Example (13). Support obligation. T establishes an irrevocable trust for the benefit of T's grandchild, GC. The trustee has discretion to distribute property for GC's support without regard to the duty or ability of GC's parent, C, to support GC. Because GC is a permissible current recipient of trust property, GC has an interest in the trust. C does not have an interest in the trust because the potential use of the trust property to satisfy C's support obligation is within the discretion of a fiduciary. C would be treated as having an interest in the trust if the trustee was required to distribute trust property for GC's support.

T.D. 8644, 12/26/95, amend T.D. 9214, 7/15/2005.

§ 26.2613-1 Skip person.

For the definition of *skip person* see § 26.2612-1(d).

T.D. 8644, 12/26/95.

§ 26a.2621-1 Generation-skipping transfer tax return requirements.

Caution: The Treasury has not yet amended Reg § 26a.2621-1 to reflect changes made by P.L. 94-455.

(a) In general. Chapter 13 of the Code imposes a tax on generation-skipping transfers, as defined in section 2611. The tax applies to both taxable distributions and terminations of either interests in property or powers over property. For purposes of this part, the term "distributee" means a younger generation beneficiary who actually receives money or property (or has money or property applied for his benefit) from a generation-skipping trust or trust equivalent. This section contains rules for making the required tax return.

(b) Person required to make returns—. *(1) In general.* Except as otherwise provided in this section, the following person must make the required tax return, Form 706-B, Generation-Skipping Transfer Tax Return—

(i) The distributee in a taxable distribution, as defined in section 2613 (a),

(ii) The trustee in the case of a taxable termination, as defined in section 2613(b), or

(iii) The distributee in the case of a generation-skipping transfer involving a generation-skipping trust equivalent.

(2) Entity. If a trust, estate, corporation or partnership is the recipient of money or property in a taxable distribution, then those persons who are assigned to a generation under section 2611(c)(7) shall be treated as distributees to the extent of their interest in the entity and are responsible for filing the return and paying the tax.

(3) Exceptions. (i) Minors. If a distributee is otherwise required to make a return, but the distributee is a minor, a re-

turn must be made by the minor or must be made for the minor by the minor's guardian or other person charged with the care of the minor's person or property.

(ii) Returns made by agents. The return of tax may be made by an agent if, by reason of disease, injury, illness or absence from the country, the person liable for making the return is unable to make it. Mere convenience is not sufficient reason for authorizing an agent to make the return. If the return is made by an agent, the return must be ratified by the principal within a reasonable time after such person becomes able to do so. If not ratified, it will not be the return required by the statute. The ratification must be in the form of a statement executed under penalties of perjury by the principal and filed with the Internal Revenue Service office with which the return was filed. It must state specifically that the return made by the agent has been carefully examined and that the principal ratifies the return. If a return is signed by an agent, a statement fully explaining the inability of the principal must accompany the return.

(iii) Returns filed by fiduciary or executor on behalf of distributee. A fiduciary acting as the guardian or committee of an insane person must make the required return. If a distributee who would be required to make the return for a transfer dies after the transfer occurs but before the return is filed, the executor or other person in possession of the decedent's assets is required to make the return.

(4) Special rules. (i) Joint and undivided interests with distributees making return. If paragraph (b)(1) of this section requires the distributee to make the tax return and if more than one distributee of a deemed transferor receives an interest in or power over property jointly, or simultaneously receives other undivided interests in property, all of the distributees must jointly make the return. Should any distributee fail to join in making the return, the remaining distributees must make a return for the entire transfer. This return must identify the distributee not joining in it and the property interests passing to that distributee. The tax is to be computed on the entire transfer and is to be paid in full by the distributees making the return, unless their liability under paragraph (h)(1) of this section is less than that amount, in which case an amount equal to their full liability must be remitted. This payment does not, however, relieve the non-filing distributee of any liability under state law to the person who filed the return for tax attributable to property received by the non-filing distributee.

(ii) Multiple trustees. In the case of a taxable termination, if there is more than one trustee of a generation-skipping trust, the return may be made by any one of them. The return must identify the trustees not joining in it. Payment of the entire amount of tax is due with the return.

(c) Time and manner of filing return. *(1) In general.* Form 706-B must be filed with the Internal Revenue Service office with which an estate or gift tax return of the deemed transferor must be filed. It must be filed—

(i) Except as provided in paragraph (c)(1)(ii) of this section, in the case of a taxable distribution or termination that occurs before the death of the deemed transferor, on or before the expiration of 6 months after the close of the taxable year of the trust (or in the case of a trust equivalent, the close of the deemed transferor's taxable year in which the transfer occurred).

(ii) In the case of a taxable distribution or termination that occurs within the same taxable year as the death of the deemed transferor, or any time after the death of the deemed transferor, on or before the later of the expiration of 6 months after the last day allowed for filing the estate tax return (including extensions), or 6 months after the close of the taxable year of the trust (or in the case of a trust equivalent, the close of the distributee's taxable year in which the transfer occurred).

When, under section 2613(b), any transfer is deemed to occur later than it actually does, the time for filing the return is to be measured from the date on which the transfer is deemed to occur (see also paragraph (k) of this section for initial filing date).

(2) Transfers within 3 years of death of deemed transferor. If a deemed transferor dies within 3 years after a generation-skipping transfer has occurred, an amended return must be filed for the transfer. The due date for the return is determined as if the prior transfer occurred at the same time as the deemed transferor's death and the tax must be recomputed as if the transfer had occurred immediately after the deemed transferor's death. Only one amended return need be filed by each distributee who filed previously. It must include all transfers that occurred within 3 years prior to the deemed transferor's death and any increase in tax must be paid by that distributee. If the rules under § 26a.2621-1(g)(2) (relating to a distribution and a termination occurring during the same taxable year) apply, then those persons required to file a return under § 26a.2621-1(b) because of a distribution in a short period (described in paragraph (g)(2) of this section) and an amended return for transfers within 3 years of death are required to file only one return which includes all the transfers that occurred during the 3-year period.

(d) Form of return. Form 706-B must be filed in accordance with its instructions.

(e) Requirement of return where no tax is due. A return of tax for every generation-skipping transfer, as defined in section 2611(a), and every transfer that would be a generation-skipping transfer but for the application of section 2613(a)(4)(A) or (b)(5)(A), must be made as provided in this section. This is so even if no tax liability arises from a given transfer.

(f) Information return. *(1) General rule.* In the case of a generation-skipping transfer, the trustee must complete and file Form 706-B(1), Information Return by Trustee for a Taxable Distribution or Termination From a Generation-Skipping Trust, with the same Internal Revenue Service Center with which the distributee must file Form 706-B. Only one Form 706-B is required to be filed for younger generation beneficiaries having the same deemed transferor. In addition, the trustee must complete and send Form 706-B(2), Beneficiary's Share of a Taxable Distribution From a Generation-Skipping Trust, to each distributee required to file Form 706-B within the time the trustee is required to file Form 706-B(1).

(2) Time for filing. If the due date of the 706-B is determined under § 26a.2621-1(c)(1)(i), then Form 706-B(1) must be filed on or before the fifteenth day of the third month following the close of the taxable year of the trust. If the due date of Form 706-B is determined under § 26a.2621-1(c)(1)(ii), then Form 706-B(1) must be filed on or before the later of the fifteenth day of the third month following the close of the taxable year of the trust, or the fifteenth day of the third month following the last day allowed for filing the estate tax return.

(g) Taxable distributions. *(1) Annual return.* The return required by this section must include all taxable distributions received by the distributee from a trust that occurred during the taxable year of the trust. For the sole purpose of determining the rate at which a taxable distribution is taxed, all taxable distributions that relate to the same deemed transferor and that are from the same or different trusts which have the same taxable year are treated as occurring simultaneously during the taxable year (or short period) and the rules under section 2602 apply in computing the tax on each.

(2) Exception. If, in addition to taxable distributions occurring during the taxable year of the trust, there is also a taxable termination which is not the result of the death of the deemed transferor, then for the purpose of determining whether distributions exceed the amount of section 643(b) income, section 643(b) income is computed separately for each of two periods. The first period begins on the first day of the taxable year of the trust and ends on the day immediately preceding the day on which the taxable termination occurs (or is deemed to occur). The second begins the day the taxable termination occurs (or is deemed to occur) and ends on the last day of the taxable year. If the termination is the result of the death of a deemed transferor, the first period ends immediately before the termination occurs (or is deemed to occur) and the second period begins immediately after the termination occurs (or is deemed to occur). The amount of section 643(b) income for each period is then determined as if each short period were a short taxable year. If after computing section 643(b) income for each period, distributions during a period exceed section 643(b) income for that period, then the return must be filed for the year if the distribution of the money or property meets the definition of a taxable distribution. If after computing section 643(b) income for the first short period the income exceeds the amount distributed, then the excess is treated as earned during the second short period.

(3) Examples. This paragraph may be illustrated by the following examples.

Example (1). Assume A creates a generation-skipping trust with the income and/or corpus payable to his child B and his grandchildren C and D (the children of B) for their joint lives and the life of the survivor, and upon the death of the last survivor to the grandchildren of B per stirpes. Assume that the grandchild exclusion has been utilized and that all section 643(b) income has been distributed previously. During the year 1990 C received $40,000 from the trust and D received $110,000. B has made no gifts during his lifetime and there have been no other generation-skipping transfers. Since C and D both have the same deemed transferor, the transfers are treated as occurring simultaneously and the tax is computed in the following manner:

(1) Fair market value of property transferred to C & D	$150,000
(2) Prior generation-skipping transfers	0
(3) Adjusted taxable gifts	0
(4) Taxable estate	0
(5) Total	$150,000
(6) Tax on amount on line 5	$ 38,800
(7) Tax due from C (40,000)/(150,000) × 38,800	$ 10,347
(8) Tax due from D (110,000)/(150,000) × 38,800	$ 28,453

Example (2). Assume A creates a generation-skipping trust with the income and/or corpus payable in the sole discretion of the trustee to his child B, grandchild C, and great grandchild D for their joint lives and for the lives of the survivors. Upon the death of the last survivor the trust corpus is to be distributed to A's great great grandchildren per stirpes. The trust is a calendar year taxpayer. On January 1, 1990, the trustee distributes $20,000 to C. On June 1, 1990, B dies. Section 643(b) income for the full year is $30,000, one-half ($15,000) of which was earned between Jan. 1, 1990, and June 1, 1990. Thus, under paragraph (c) $5,000 ($20,000 minus $15,000) of the $20,000 distribution is a taxable distribution.

(h) Liability for tax. *(1) Distributee.* If the tax imposed is not paid when due, each distributee (whether or not required to file a return) that receives property from the trust at the same time as or any time after a generation-skipping transfer is personally liable for the tax under section 2603(a)(1)(B) as a distributee to the extent of an amount equal to the fair market value of the property received determined as of the date of the distribution.

(2) Trustees. In the case of a taxable termination, if a trustee is required to make the return, the trustee is personally liable for the tax imposed on the transfer if the tax is not paid when due.

This liability applies whether or not a trustee joins in making the tax return in situations involving multiple trustees or makes the return when it is the sole trustee. If a trustee pays the tax determined to be due based on written data furnished by the Service, the trustee is not personally liable for any tax exceeding the amount determined to be due based on that data. This limit on a trustee's personal liability applies only if all the required information that was furnished to the Service by the trustee (or trustees) was accurate and complete. An increase in tax based on a higher property valuation than that claimed by the trustee is, for example, the result of inaccurate information and therefore the trustee will be liable for any increase in tax.

(3) Lien on property. The tax imposed by section 2601 is a lien on all property transferred in a generation-skipping transfer until the tax is fully paid or becomes unenforceable by reason of lapse of time. The lien attaches at the time of the generation-skipping transfer and is in addition to the lien for taxes under section 6321. Thus, for example, if property passes to more than one person in a simultaneous transfer as described in section 2602(b), the property passing to each person is liable for the full amount of tax caused by the total transfer.

(i) This designation is not used.

(j) Request to Internal Revenue Service for information. *(1) In general.* A trustee or distributee may, before making a generation-skipping transfer tax return, request in writing that the Internal Revenue Service supply it with a statement showing—

(i) The amount of the deemed transferor's adjusted taxable gifts within the meaning of section 2001(b) as modified by section 2001(e),

(ii) The amount of the deemed transferor's taxable estate and the estate tax thereon before allowance of any credits,

(iii) The amount of prior generation-skipping transfers with respect to the deemed transferor,

(iv) The amount of prior generation-skipping transfers that occurred within three years prior to the deemed transferor's death and the amount of the generation-skipping transfer tax paid with respect to these transfers,

(v) The amount of generation-skipping transfer tax imposed before the allowance of any credits with respect to prior generation-skipping transfers,

(vi) The amount of State death tax credit allowed on the deemed transferor's estate tax return and the amount of State death tax credit allowed on prior generation-skipping transfer tax returns,

(vii) The amounts necessary to complete Schedule F, Credit for Tax on Prior Transfers,

(viii) The amount of the grandchild exclusion that has been used for transfers to a grandchild of the grantor,

(ix) The amount of any taxable distributions or taxable terminations that occurred during the same taxable year and that were made from other trusts having the same deemed transferor, and

(x) Any other data that may be needed to complete Form 706-B, Generation-Skipping Transfers Tax Return.

(2) Filing of request. The request for the information specified in paragraph (j)(1) of this section must be in writing and signed by any person required to file the return. It must be addressed to the Internal Revenue Service office with which an estate or gift tax return of the deemed transferor would be filed. It should be filed not less than 90 days before the due date of the generation-skipping tax return for the transfer involved. If the request is filed less than 90 days before the due date of the return, the failure to obtain the information will not be considered reasonable cause for failing to file a timely return or to pay the tax under section 6651. The written request should include the following information:

(i) The name and taxpayer identification number of the deemed transferor and of the grantor;

(ii) A statement of the specific information requested from the Service;

(iii) In the case of a trustee or other agent, a certified copy of its appointment.

(k) Initial filing date. Notwithstanding any other provision of these regulations, the time for filing Form 706-B shall be the date determined under paragraph (c) of this section or December 31, 1982, whichever is later. The due date for Forms 706-B(1) and (2) shall be the date determined under paragraph (f) of this section or August 14, 1981, whichever is later.

T.D. 7711, 8/4/80, amend T.D. 7769, 2/2/81, T.D. 7792, 11/2/81, T.D. 7818, 6/2/82.

§ 26.2632-1 Allocation of GST exemption.

Caution: The Treasury has not yet amended Reg § 26.2632-1 to reflect changes made by P.L. 107-16.

(a) General rule. Except as otherwise provided in this section, an individual or the individual's executor may allocate the individual's $1 million GST exemption at any time from the date of the transfer through the date for filing the individual's Federal estate tax return (including any extensions for filing that have been actually granted). If no estate tax return is required to be filed, the GST exemption may be allocated at any time through the date a Federal estate tax return would be due if a return were required to be filed (including any extensions actually granted). If property is held in trust, the allocation of GST exemption is made to the entire trust rather than to specific trust assets. If a transfer is a direct skip to a trust, the allocation of GST exemption to the transferred property is also treated as an allocation of GST exemption to the trust for purposes of future GSTs with respect to the trust by the same transferor.

(b) Lifetime allocations. *(1) Automatic allocation to direct skips.* (i) In general. If a direct skip occurs during the transferor's lifetime, the transferor's GST exemption not previously allocated (unused GST exemption) is automatically allocated to the transferred property (but not in excess of the fair market value of the property on the date of the transfer). The transferor may prevent the automatic allocation of GST exemption by describing on a timely-filed United States Gift (and Generation-Skipping Transfer) Tax Return (Form 709) the transfer and the extent to which the automatic allocation is not to apply. In addition, a timely-filed Form 709 accompanied by payment of the GST tax (as shown on the return with respect to the direct skip) is sufficient to prevent an automatic allocation of GST exemption with respect to the transferred property. See paragraph (c)(4) of this section for special rules in the case of direct skips treated as occurring at the termination of an estate tax inclusion period.

(ii) Time for filing Form 709. A Form 709 is timely filed if it is filed on or before the date required for reporting the transfer if it were a taxable gift (i.e., the date prescribed by section 6075 (b), including any extensions to file actually granted (the due date)). Except as provided in paragraph (b)(1)(iii) of this section, the automatic allocation of GST exemption (or the election to prevent the allocation, if made) is irrevocable after the due date. An automatic allocation of GST exemption is effective as of the date of the transfer to which it relates. Except as provided above, a Form 709 need not be filed to report an automatic allocation.

(iii) Transitional rule. An election to prevent an automatic allocation of GST exemption filed on or before January 26, 1996, becomes irrevocable on July 24, 1996.

(2) Automatic allocation to indirect skips made after December 31, 2000. (i) In general. An indirect skip is a transfer of property to a GST trust as defined in section 2632(c)(3)(B) provided that the transfer is subject to gift tax and does not qualify as a direct skip. In the case of an indirect skip made after December 31, 2000, to which section 2642(f) (relating to transfers subject to an estate tax inclusion period (ETIP)) does not apply, the transferor's unused GST exemption is automatically allocated to the property transferred (but not in excess of the fair market value of the property on the date of the transfer). The automatic allocation pursuant to this paragraph is effective whether or not a Form 709 is filed reporting the transfer, and is effective as of the date of the transfer to which it relates. An automatic allocation is irrevocable after the due date of the Form 709 for the calendar year in which the transfer is made. In the case of an indirect skip to which section 2642(f) does apply, the indirect skip is deemed to be made at the close of the ETIP and the GST exemption is deemed to be allocated at that time. In either case, except as otherwise provided in paragraph (b)(2)(ii) of this section, the automatic allocation of exemption applies even if an allocation of exemption is made to the indirect skip in accordance with section 2632(a).

(ii) Prevention of automatic allocation. Except as otherwise provided in forms or other guidance published by the Service, the transferor may prevent the automatic allocation of GST exemption with regard to an indirect skip (including indirect skips to which section 2642(f) may apply) by making an election, as provided in paragraph (b)(2)(iii) of this section. Notwithstanding paragraph (b)(2)(iii)(B) of this section, the transferor may also prevent the automatic allocation of GST exemption with regard to an indirect skip by making an affirmative allocation of GST exemption on a Form 709 filed at any time on or before the due date for timely filing (within the meaning of paragraph (b)(1)(ii) of this section) of an amount that is less than (but not equal to) the value of the property transferred as reported on that return, in accordance with the provisions of paragraph (b)(4) of this section. See paragraph (b)(4)(iii) Example 6 of this section. Any election out of the automatic allocation rules under this section has no effect on the application of the automatic allocation rules applicable after the transferor's death under section 2632(e) and paragraph (d) of this section.

(iii) Election to have automatic allocation rules not apply. (A) In general. A transferor may prevent the automatic allocation of GST exemption (elect out) with respect to any transfer or transfers constituting an indirect skip made to a trust or to one or more separate shares that are treated as separate trusts under § 26.2654-1(a)(1) (collectively referred to hereinafter as a trust). In the case of a transfer treated under section 2513 as made one-half by the transferor and one-half by the transferor's spouse, each spouse shall be treated as a separate transferor who must satisfy separately the requirements of paragraph (b)(2)(iii)(B) to elect out with respect to the transfer. A transferor may elect out with respect to—

(1) One or more prior-year transfers subject to section 2642(f) (regarding ETIPs) made by the transferor to a specified trust or trusts;

(2) One or more (or all) current-year transfers made by the transferor to a specified trust or trusts;

(3) One or more (or all) future transfers made by the transferor to a specified trust or trusts;

(4) All future transfers made by the transferor to all trusts (whether or not in existence at the time of the election out); or

(5) Any combination of paragraphs (b)(2)(iii)(A)(1) through (4) of this section.

(B) Manner of making an election out. Except as otherwise provided in forms or other guidance published by the IRS, an election out is made as described in this paragraph (b)(2)(iii)(B). To elect out, the transferor must attach a statement (election out statement) to a Form 709 filed within the time period provided in paragraph (b)(2)(iii)(C) of this section (whether or not any transfer was made in the calendar year for which the Form 709 was filed, and whether or not a Form 709 otherwise would be required to be filed for that year). See paragraph (b)(4)(iv) Example 7 of this section. The election out statement must identify the trust (except for an election out under paragraph (b)(2)(iii)(A)(4) of this section), and specifically must provide that the transferor is electing out of the automatic allocation of GST exemption with respect to the described transfer or transfers. Prior-year transfers that are subject to section 2642(f), and to which the election out is to apply, must be specifically described or otherwise identified in the election out statement. Further, unless the election out is made for all transfers made to the trust in the current year and/or in all future years, the current-year transfers and/or future transfers to which the election out is to apply must be specifically described or otherwise identified in the election out statement.

(C) Time for making an election out. To elect out, the Form 709 with the attached election out statement must be filed on or before the due date for timely filing (within the meaning of paragraph (b)(1)(ii) of this section) of the Form 709 for the calendar year in which—

(1) For a transfer subject to section 2642(f), the ETIP closes; or

(2) For all other elections out, the first transfer to be covered by the election out was made.

(D) Effect of election out. An election out does not affect the automatic allocation of GST exemption to any transfer not covered by the election out statement. Except for elections out for transfers described in paragraph (b)(2)(iii)(A)(1) of this section that are specifically described in an election out statement, an election out does not apply to any prior-year transfer to a trust, including any transfer subject to an ETIP (even if the ETIP closes after the election is made). An election out does not prevent the transferor from allocating the transferor's available GST exemption to any transfer covered by the election out, either on a timely filed Form 709 reporting the transfer or at a later date in accordance with the provisions of paragraph (b)(4) of this section. An election out with respect to future transfers remains in effect unless and until terminated. Once an election out with respect to future transfers is made, a transferor need not file a Form 709 in future years solely to prevent the automatic allocation of the GST exemption to any future transfer covered by the election out.

(E) Termination of election out. Except as otherwise provided in forms or other guidance published by the IRS, an election out may be terminated as described in this paragraph (b)(2)(iii)(E). Pursuant to this section, a transferor may terminate an election out made on a Form 709 for a prior year, to the extent that election out applied to future transfers or to a transfer subject to section 2642(f). To terminate an election out, the transferor must attach a statement (termination statement) to a Form 709 filed on or before the due date of the Form 709 for the calendar year in which is made the first transfer to which the election out is not to apply (whether or not any transfer was made in the calendar year for which the Form 709 was filed, and whether or not a Form 709 otherwise would be required to be filed for that year). The termination statement must identify the trust (if applicable), describe the prior election out that is being terminated, specifically provide that the prior election out is being terminated, and either describe the extent to which the prior election out is being terminated or describe any current-year transfers to which the election out is not to apply. Consequently, the automatic allocation rules contained in section 2632(c)(1) will apply to any current-year transfer described on the termination statement and, except as otherwise provided in this paragraph, to all future transfers that otherwise would have been covered by the election out. The termination of an election out does not affect any transfer, or any election out, that is not described in the termination statement. The termination of an election out will not revoke the election out for any prior-year transfer, except for a prior-year transfer subject to section 2642(f) for which the election out is revoked on a timely filed Form 709 for the calendar year in which the ETIP closes or for any prior calendar year. The termination of an election out does not preclude the transferor from making another election out in the same or any subsequent year.

(3) Election to treat trust as a GST trust. (i) In general. A transferor may elect to treat any trust as a GST trust (GST trust election), without regard to whether the trust is subject to section 2642(f), with respect to—

(A) Any current-year transfer (or any or all current-year transfers) by the electing transferor to the trust;

(B) Any selected future transfers by the electing transferor to the trust;

(C) All future transfers by the electing transferor to the trust; or

(D) Any combination of paragraphs (b)(3)(i)(A) through (C) of this section.

(ii) Time and manner of making GST trust election. Except as otherwise provided in forms or other guidance published by the Internal Revenue Service, a GST trust election is made as described in this paragraph (b)(3)(ii). To make a GST trust election, the transferor must attach a statement (GST trust election statement) to a Form 709 filed on or before the due date for timely filing (within the meaning of paragraph (b)(1)(ii) of this section) of the Form 709 for the calendar year in which the first transfer to be covered by the GST trust election is made (whether or not any transfer was made in the calendar year for which the Form 709 was filed, and whether or not a Form 709 otherwise would be required to be filed for that year). The GST trust election statement must identify the trust, specifically describe or otherwise clearly identify the transfers to be covered by the election, and specifically provide that the transferor is electing to have the trust treated as a GST trust with respect to the covered transfers.

(iii) Effect of GST trust election. Except as otherwise provided in this paragraph, a GST trust election will cause all transfers made by the electing transferor to the trust that are subject to the election to be deemed to be made to a GST trust as defined in section 2632(c)(3)(B). Thus, the electing transferor's unused GST exemption may be allocated automatically to such transfers in accordance with paragraph (b)(2) of this section. A transferor may prevent the automatic allocation of GST exemption to future transfers to the trust either by terminating the GST trust election in accordance with paragraph (b)(3)(iv) of this section (in the case of trusts that would not otherwise be treated as GST trusts) or by electing out of the automatic allocation of GST exemption in accordance with paragraph (b)(2) of this section.

(iv) Termination of GST trust election. Except as otherwise provided in forms or other guidance published by the Service, a GST trust election may be terminated as described in this paragraph (b)(3)(iv). A transferor may terminate a GST trust election made on a Form 709 for a prior year, to the extent that election applied to future transfers or to a transfer subject to section 2642(f). To terminate a GST trust election, the transferor must attach a statement (termination statement) to a Form 709 filed on or before the due date for timely filing (within the meaning of paragraph (b)(1)(ii) of this section) a Form 709 for the calendar year: in which is made the electing transferor's first transfer to which the GST trust election is not to apply; or that is the first calendar year for which the GST trust election is not to apply, even if no transfer is made to the trust during that year. The termination statement must identify the trust, describe the current-year transfer (if any), and provide that the prior GST trust election is terminated. Accordingly, if the trust otherwise does not satisfy the definition of a GST trust, the automatic allocation rules contained in section 2632(c)(1) will not apply to the described current-year transfer or to any future transfers made by the transferor to the trust, unless and until another election under this paragraph (b)(3) is made.

(4) Allocation to other transfers. (i) In general. An allocation of GST exemption to property transferred during the transferor's lifetime, other than in a direct skip, is made on Form 709. The allocation must clearly identify the trust to which the allocation is being made, the amount of GST exemption allocated to it, and if the allocation is late or if an inclusion ratio greater than zero is claimed, the value of the trust assets at the effective date of the allocation. See paragraph (b)(4)(ii) of this section. The allocation should also state the inclusion ratio of the trust after the allocation. Except as otherwise provided in this paragraph, an allocation of GST exemption may be made by a formula; e.g., the allocation may be expressed in terms of the amount necessary to produce an inclusion ratio of zero. However, formula allocations made with respect to charitable lead annuity trusts are not valid except to the extent they are dependent on values as finally determined for Federal estate or gift tax purposes. With respect to a timely allocation, an allocation of GST exemption becomes irrevocable after the due date of the return. Except as provided in § 26.2642-3 (relating to charitable lead annuity trusts), an allocation of GST exemption to a trust is void to the extent the amount allocated exceeds the amount necessary to obtain an inclusion ratio of zero with respect to the trust. See § 26.2642-1 for the definition of inclusion ratio. An allocation is also void if the allocation is made with respect to a trust that has no GST potential with respect to the transferor making the allocation, at the time of the allocation. For this purpose, a trust has GST potential even if the possibility of a GST is so remote as to be negligible.

(ii) Effective date of allocation. (A) In general. (1) Except as otherwise provided, an allocation of GST exemption is effective as of the date of any transfer as to which the Form 709 on which it is made is a timely filed return (a timely allocation). If more than one timely allocation is made, the earlier allocation is modified only if the later allocation clearly identifies the transfer and the nature and extent of the modification. Except as provided in paragraph (d)(1) of this section, an allocation to a trust made on a Form 709 filed after the due date for reporting a transfer to the trust (a late allocation) is effective on the date the Form 709 is filed and is deemed to precede in point of time any taxable event occurring on such date. For purposes of this paragraph (b)(4)(ii), the Form 709 is deemed filed on the date it is postmarked to the Internal Revenue Service address as directed in forms or other guidance published by the Service. See § 26.2642-2 regarding the effect of a late allocation in determining the inclusion ratio, etc. See paragraph (c)(1) of this section regarding allocation of GST exemption to property subject to an estate tax inclusion period. If it is unclear whether an allocation of GST exemption on a Form 709 is a late or a timely allocation to a trust, the allocation is effective in the following order—

(i) To any transfer to the trust disclosed on the return as to which the return is a timely return;

(ii) As a late allocation; and

(iii) To any transfer to the trust not disclosed on the return as to which the return would be a timely return.

(2) A late allocation to a trust may be made on a Form 709 that is timely filed with respect to another transfer. A late allocation is irrevocable when made.

(B) Amount of allocation. If other transfers exist with respect to which GST exemption could be allocated under paragraphs (b)(4)(ii)(A)(1)(ii) and (iii), any GST exemption allocated under paragraph (b)(4)(ii)(A)(1)(i) of this section is allocated in an amount equal to the value of the transferred property as reported on the Form 709. Thus, if the GST exemption allocated on the Form 709 exceeds the value of the transfers reported on that return that have generation-skipping potential, the initial allocation under paragraph (b)(4)(ii)(A)(1)(i) of this section is in the amount of the value of those transfers as reported on that return. Any remaining amount of GST exemption allocated on that return is then allocated pursuant to paragraphs (b)(4)(ii)(A)(1)(ii) and (iii) of this section, notwithstanding any subsequent upward adjustment in value of the transfers reported on the return.

(iii) Examples. The following examples illustrate the provisions of this paragraph (b):

Example (1). Modification of allocation of GST exemption. On December 1, 2003, T transfers $100,000 to an irrevocable GST trust described in section 2632(c)(3)(B). The transfer to the trust is not a direct skip. The date prescribed for filing the gift tax return reporting the taxable gift is April 15, 2004. On February 10, 2004, T files a Form 709 on which T properly elects out of the automatic allocation rules contained in section 2632(c)(1) with respect to the transfer in accordance with paragraph (b)(2)(iii) of this section, and allocates $50,000 of GST exemption to the trust. On April 13th of the same year, T files an additional Form 709 on which T confirms the election out of the automatic allocation rules contained in section 2632(c)(1) and allocates $100,000 of GST exemption to the trust in a manner that clearly indicates the intention to modify and supersede the prior allocation with respect to the 2003 transfer. The allocation made on the April 13 return supersedes the prior allocation because it is made on a timely-filed Form 709 that clearly identifies the trust and the nature and extent of the modification of GST exemption allocation. The allocation of $100,000 of GST exemption to the trust is effective as of December 1, 2003. The result would be the same if the amended Form 709 decreased the amount of the GST exemption allocated to the trust.

Example (2). Modification of allocation of GST exemption. The facts are the same as in Example 1 except, on July 8, 2004, T files a Form 709 attempting to reduce the earlier allocation. The return filed on July 8, 2004, is not a timely filed return. The $100,000 GST exemption allocated to the trust, as amended on April 13, 2004, remains in effect because an allocation, once made, is irrevocable and may not be modified after the last date on which a timely filed Form 709 may be filed.

Example (3). Effective date of late allocation of GST exemption. On November 15, 2003, T transfers $100,000 to an irrevocable GST trust described in section 2632(c)(3)(B). The transfer to the trust is not a direct skip. The date prescribed for filing the gift tax return reporting the taxable gift is April 15, 2004. On February 10, 2004, T files a Form 709 on which T properly elects out of the automatic allocation rules contained in section 2632(c)(1) in accordance with paragraph (b)(2)(iii) of this section with respect to that transfer. On December 1, 2004, T files a Form 709 and allocates $50,000 to the trust. The allocation is effective as of December 1, 2004.

Example (4). Effective date of late allocation of GST exemption. T transfers $100,000 to an irrevocable GST trust on December 1, 2003, in a transfer that is not a direct skip. On April 15, 2004, T files a Form 709 on which T properly elects out of the automatic allocation rules contained in section 2632(c)(1) with respect to the entire transfer in accordance with paragraph (b)(2)(iii) of this section and T does not make an allocation of any GST exemption on the Form 709. On September 1, 2004, the trustee makes a taxable distribution from the trust to T's grandchild in the amount of $30,000. Immediately prior to the distribution, the value of the trust assets was $150,000. On the same date, T allocates GST exemption to the trust in the amount of $50,000. The allocation of GST exemption on the date of the transfer is treated as preceding in point of time the taxable distribution. At the time of the GST, the trust has an inclusion ratio of .6667 (1--(50,000/150,000)).

Example (5). Automatic allocation to split-gift. On December 1, 2003, T transfers $50,000 to an irrevocable GST Trust described in section 2632(c)(3)(B). The transfer to the trust is not a direct skip. On April 30, 2004, T and T's spouse, S, each files an initial gift tax return for 2003, on which they consent, pursuant to section 2513, to have the gift treated as if one-half had been made by each. In spite of being made on a late-filed gift tax return for 2003, the election under section 2513 is valid because neither spouse had filed a timely gift tax return for that year. Previously, neither T nor S filed a timely gift tax return electing out of the automatic allocation rules contained in section 2632(c)(1). As a result of the election under section 2513, which is retroactive to the date of T's transfer, T and S are each treated as the transferor of one-half of the property transferred in the indirect skip. Thus, $25,000 of T's unused GST exemption and $25,000 of S's unused GST exemption is automatically allocated to the trust. Both allocations are effective on and after the date that T made the transfer. The result would be the same if T's transfer constituted a direct skip subject to the automatic allocation rules contained in section 2632(b).

Example (6). Partial allocation of GST exemption. On December 1, 2003, T transfers $100,000 to an irrevocable GST trust described in section 2632(c)(3)(B). The transfer to the trust is not a direct skip. The date prescribed for filing the gift tax return reporting the taxable gift is April 15, 2004. On February 10, 2004, T files a Form 709 on which T allocates $40,000 of GST exemption to the trust. By filing a timely Form 709 on which a partial allocation is made of $40,000, T effectively elected out of the automatic allocation rules for the remaining value of the transfer for which T did not allocate GST exemption.

(iv) Example. The following example illustrates language that may be used in the statement required under paragraph (b)(2)(iii) of this section to elect out of the automatic allocation rules under various scenarios:

Example (1). On March 1, 2006, T transfers $100,000 to Trust B, a GST trust described in section 2632(c)(3)(B). Subsequently, on September 15, 2006, T transfers an additional $75,000 to Trust B. No other transfers are made to Trust B in 2006. T attaches an election out statement to a timely filed Form 709 for calendar year 2006. Except with regard to paragraph (v) of this Example 1, the election out statement identifies Trust B as required under paragraph (b)(2)(iii)(B) of this section, and contains the following alternative election statements:

(i) "T hereby elects that the automatic allocation rules will not apply to the $100,000 transferred to Trust B on March 1, 2006." The election out of the automatic allocation rules will be effective only for T's March 1, 2006, transfer and will not apply to T's $75,000 transfer made on September 15, 2006.

(ii) "Thereby elects that the automatic allocation rules will not apply to any transfers to Trust B in 2006." The election out of the automatic allocation rules will be effective for T's transfers to Trust B made on March 1, 2006, and September 15, 2006.

(iii) "Thereby elects that the automatic allocation rules will not apply to any transfers to Trust B made by T in 2006 or to any additional transfers T may make to Trust B in subsequent years." The election out of the automatic allocation rules will be effective for T's transfers to Trust B in 2006 and for all future transfers to be made by T to Trust B, unless and until T terminates the election out of the automatic allocation rules.

(iv) "Thereby elects that the automatic allocation rules will not apply to any transfers T has made or will make to Trust B in the years 2006 through 2008." The election out of the automatic allocation rules will be effective for T's transfers to Trust B in 2006 through 2008. T's transfers to Trust B after 2008 will be subject to the automatic allocation rules, unless T elects out of those rules for one or more years after 2008. T may terminate the election out of the automatic allocation rules for 2007, 2008, or both in accordance with the termination rules of paragraph (b)(2)(iii)(E) of this section. T may terminate the election out for one or more of the transfers made in 2006 only on a later but still timely filed Form 709 for calendar year 2006.

(v) "Thereby elects that the automatic allocation rules will not apply to any current or future transfer that T may make to any trust." The election out of the automatic allocation rules will be effective for all of T's transfers (current-year and future) to Trust B and to any and all other trusts (whether such trusts exist in 2006 or are created in a later year), unless and until T terminates the election out of the automatic allocation rules. T may terminate the election out with regard to one or more (or all) of the transfers covered by the election out in accordance with the termination rules of paragraph (b)(2)(iii)(E) of this section.

(c) Special rules during an estate tax inclusion period. *(1) In general.* (i) Automatic allocations with respect to direct skips and indirect skips. A direct skip or an indirect skip that is subject to an estate tax inclusion period (ETIP) is deemed to have been made only at the close of the ETIP. The transferor may prevent the automatic allocation of GST exemption to a direct skip or an indirect skip by electing out of the automatic allocation rules at any time prior to the due date of the Form 709 for the calendar year in which the close of the ETIP occurs (whether or not any transfer was made in the calendar year for which the Form 709 was filed, and whether or not a Form 709 otherwise would be required to be filed for that year). See paragraph (b)(2)(i) of this section regarding the automatic allocation of GST exemption to an indirect skip subject to an ETIP.

(ii) Other allocations. An affirmative allocation of GST exemption cannot be revoked, but becomes effective as of (and no earlier than) the date of the close of the ETIP with respect to the trust. If an allocation has not been made prior to the close of the ETIP, an allocation of exemption is effective as of the close of the ETIP during the transferor's lifetime if made by the due date for filing the Form 709 for the calendar year in which the close of the ETIP occurs (timely ETIP return). An allocation of exemption is effective in the case of the close of the ETIP by reason of the death of the transferor as provided in paragraph (d) of this section.

(iii) Portion of trust subject to ETIP. If any part of a trust is subject to an ETIP, the entire trust is subject to the ETIP. See § 26.2642-1(b)(2) for rules determining the inclusion ratio applicable in the case of GSTs during an ETIP.

(2) Estate tax inclusion period defined. (i) In general. An ETIP is the period during which, should death occur, the value of transferred property would be includible (other than by reason of section 2035) in the gross estate of—

(A) The transferor; or

(B) The spouse of the transferor.

(ii) Exceptions. (A) For purposes of paragraph (c)(2) of this section, the value of transferred property is not considered as being subject to inclusion in the gross estate of the transferor or the spouse of the transferor if the possibility that the property will be included is so remote as to be negligible. A possibility is so remote as to be negligible if it can be ascertained by actuarial standards that there is less than a 5 percent probability that the property will be included in the gross estate.

(B) For purposes of paragraph (c)(2) of this section, the value of transferred property is not considered as being subject to inclusion in the gross estate of the spouse of the transferor, if the spouse possesses with respect to any transfer to the trust, a right to withdraw no more than the greater of $5,000 or 5 percent of the trust corpus, and such withdrawal right terminates no later than 60 days after the transfer to the trust.

(C) The rules of this paragraph (c)(2) do not apply to qualified terminable interest property with respect to which the special election under § 26.2652-2 has been made.

(3) Termination of an ETIP. An ETIP terminates on the first to occur of—

(i) The death of the transferor;

(ii) The time at which no portion of the property is includible in the transferor's gross estate (other than by reason of section 2035) or, in the case of an individual who is a transferor solely by reason of an election under section 2513, the time at which no portion would be includible in the gross estate of the individual's spouse (other than by reason of section 2035);

(iii) The time of a GST, but only with respect to the property involved in the GST; or

(iv) In the case of an ETIP arising by reason of an interest or power held by the transferor's spouse under subsection (c)(2)(i)(B) of this section, at the first to occur of—

(A) The death of the spouse; or

(B) The time at which no portion of the property would be includible in the spouse's gross estate (other than by reason of section 2035).

(4) Treatment of direct skips. If property transferred to a skip person is subject to an ETIP, the direct skip is treated as occurring on the termination of the ETIP.

(5) Examples. The following examples illustrate the rules of this section as they apply to the termination of an ETIP during the lifetime of the transferor. In each example assume that T transfers $100,000 to an irrevocable trust:

Example (1). Allocation of GST exemption during ETIP. The trust instrument provides that trust income is to be paid to T for 9 years or until T's prior death. The trust principal is to be paid to T's grandchild on the termination of T's income interest. If T dies within the 9-year period, the value of the trust principal is includible in T's gross estate under section 2036(a). Thus, the trust is subject to an ETIP. T files a timely Form 709 reporting the transfer and allocating $100,000 of GST exemption to the trust. The allocation of GST exemption to the trust is not effective until the termination of the ETIP.

Example (2). Effect of prior allocation on termination of ETIP. The facts are the same as in Example 1, except the trustee has the power to invade trust principal on behalf of T's grandchild, GC, during the term of T's income interest. In year 4, when the value of the trust is $200,000, the trustee distributes $15,000 to GC. The distribution is a taxable distribution. The ETIP with respect to the property distributed to GC terminates at the time of the taxable distribution. See paragraph (c)(3)(iii) of this section. Solely for purposes of determining the trust's inclusion ratio with respect to the taxable distribution, the prior $100,000 allocation of GST exemption (as well as any additional allocation made on a timely ETIP return) is effective immediately prior to the taxable distribution. See § 26.2642-1(b)(2). The trust's inclusion ratio with respect to the taxable distribution is therefore .50 (1−(100,000/200,000)).

Example (3). Split-gift transfers subject to ETIP. The trust instrument provides that trust income is to be paid to T for 9 years or until T's prior death. The trust principal is to be paid to T's grandchild on the termination of T's income interest. T files a timely Form 709 reporting the transfer. T's spouse, S, consents to have the gift treated as made one-half by S under section 2513. Because S is treated as transferring one-half of the property to T's grandchild, S becomes the transferor of one-half of the trust for purposes of chapter 13. Because the value of the trust would be includible in T's gross estate if T died immediately after the transfer, S's transfer is subject to an ETIP. If S should die prior to the termination of the trust, S's executor may allocate S's GST exemption to the trust, but only to the portion of the trust for which S is treated as the transferor. However, the allocation does not become effective until the earlier of the expiration of T's income interest or T's death.

Example (4). Transfer of retained interest as ETIP termination. The trust instrument provides that trust income is to be paid to T for 9 years or until T's prior death. The trust principal is to be paid to T's grandchild on the termination of T's income interest. Four years after the initial transfer, T transfers the income interest to T's sibling. The ETIP with respect to the trust terminates on T's transfer of the income interest because, after the transfer, the trust property would not be includible in T's gross estate (other than by reason of section 2035) if T died at that time.

Example (5). Election out of automatic allocation of GST exemption for trust subject to an ETIP. On December 1, 2003, T transfers $100,000 to Trust A, an irrevocable GST trust described in section 2632(c)(3) that is subject to an estate tax inclusion period (ETIP). T made no other gifts in 2003. The ETIP terminates on December 31, 2008. T timely files a gift tax return (Form 709) reporting the gift on April 15, 2004. On May 15, 2006, T files a Form 709 on which T properly elects out of the automatic allocation rules contained in section 2632(c)(1) with respect to the December 1, 2003, transfer to Trust A in accordance with paragraph (b)(2)(iii) of this section. Because the indirect skip is not deemed to occur until December 31, 2008, T's election out of automatic GST allocation filed on May 15, 2006, is timely, and will be effective as of December 31, 2008 (unless revoked on a Form 709 filed on or before the due date of a Form 709 for calendar year 2008).

(d) Allocations after the transferor's death. *(1) Allocation by executor.* Except as otherwise provided in this paragraph (d), an allocation of a decedent's unused GST exemption by the executor of the decedent's estate is made on the appropriate United States Estate (and Generation-Skipping Transfer) Tax Return (Form 706 or Form 706NA) filed on or before the date prescribed for filing the return by section 6075(a) (including any extensions actually granted (the due date)). An allocation of GST exemption with respect to property included in the gross estate of a decedent is effective as of the date of death. A timely allocation of GST exemption by an executor with respect to a lifetime transfer of property that is not included in the transferor's gross estate is made on a Form 709. A late allocation of GST exemption by an executor, other than an allocation that is deemed to be made under section 2632(b)(1) or (c)(1), with respect to a lifetime transfer of property is made on Form 706, Form 706NA, or Form 709 (filed on or before the due date of the transferor's estate tax return) and applies as of the date the allocation is filed. An executor may allocate the decedent's GST exemption by use of a formula. For purposes of this section, an allocation is void if the allocation is made for a trust that has no GST potential with respect to the transferor for whom the allocation is being made, as of the date of the transferor's death. For this purpose, a trust has GST potential even if the possibility of a GST is so remote as to be negligible.

(2) Automatic allocation after death. A decedent's unused GST exemption is automatically allocated on the due date for filing Form 706 or Form 706NA to the extent not otherwise allocated by the decedent's executor on or before that date. The automatic allocation occurs whether or not a return is actually required to be filed. Unused GST exemption is allocated pro rata (subject to the rules of § 26.2642-2(b)), on the basis of the value of the property as finally determined for purposes of chapter 11 (chapter 11 value), first to direct skips treated as occurring at the transferor's death. The balance, if any, of unused GST exemption is allocated pro rata (subject to the rules of § 26.2642-2(b)) on the basis of the chapter 11 value of the nonexempt portion of the trust property (or in the case of trusts that are not included in the gross estate, on the basis of the date of death value of the trust) to trusts with respect to which a taxable termination may occur or from which a taxable distribution may be made. The automatic allocation of GST exemption is irrevocable, and an allocation made by the executor after the automatic allocation is made is ineffective. No automatic allocation of GST exemption is made to a trust that will have a new transferor with respect to the entire trust prior to the occurrence of any GST with respect to the trust. In addition, no automatic allocation of GST exemption is made to a trust if, during the nine month period ending immediately after the death of the transferor—

(i) No GST has occurred with respect to the trust; and

(ii) At the end of such period no future GST can occur with respect to the trust.

(e) Effective dates. This section is applicable as provided in § 26.2601-1(c), with the following exceptions:

(1) Paragraphs (b)(2) and (b)(3), the third sentence of paragraph (b)(4)(i), the fourth sentence of paragraph (b)(4)(ii)(A)(1), paragraphs (b)(4)(iii) and (b)(4)(iv), and the fourth sentence of paragraph (d)(1) of this section, which will apply to elections made on or after July 13, 2004; and

(2) Paragraph (c)(1), and Example 5 of paragraph (c)(5), which will apply to elections made on or after June 29, 2005.

T.D. 8644, 12/26/95, amend T.D. 9208, 6/28/2005.

§ 26.2641-1 Applicable rate of tax.

The rate of tax applicable to any GST (applicable rate) is determined by multiplying the maximum Federal estate tax rate in effect at the time of the GST by the inclusion ratio (as defined in § 26.2642-1). For this purpose, the maximum Federal estate tax rate is the maximum rate set forth under section 2001(c) (without regard to section 2001(c)(2)).

T.D. 8644, 12/26/95.

§ 26.2642-1 Inclusion ratio.

(a) In general. Except as otherwise provided in this section, the inclusion ratio is determined by subtracting the applicable fraction (rounded to the nearest one-thousandth (.001)) from 1. In rounding the applicable fraction to the nearest one-thousandth, any amount that is midway between one one-thousandth and another one-thousandth is rounded up to the higher of those two amounts.

(b) Numerator of applicable fraction. *(1) In general.* Except as otherwise provided in this paragraph (b), and in §§ 26.2642-3 (providing a special rule for charitable lead annuity trusts) and 26.2642-4 (providing rules for the redetermination of the applicable fraction), the numerator of the applicable fraction is the amount of GST exemption allocated to the trust (or to the transferred property in the case of a direct skip not in trust).

(2) GSTs occurring during an ETIP. (i) In general. For purposes of determining the inclusion ratio with respect to a taxable termination or a taxable distribution that occurs during an ETIP, the numerator of the applicable fraction is the sum of—

(A) The GST exemption previously allocated to the trust (including any allocation made to the trust prior to any taxable termination or distribution) reduced (but not below zero) by the nontax amount of any prior GSTs with respect to the trust; and

(B) Any GST exemption allocated to the trust on a timely ETIP return filed after the termination of the ETIP. See § 26.2632-1(c)(5) Example 2.

(ii) Nontax amount of a prior GST. (1) The nontax amount of a prior GST with respect to the trust is the amount of the GST multiplied by the applicable fraction attributable to the trust at the time of the prior GST.

(2) For rules regarding the allocation of GST exemption to property during an ETIP, see § 26.2632-1(c).

(c) Denominator of applicable fraction. *(1) In general.* Except as otherwise provided in this paragraph (c) and in §§ 26.2642-3 and 26.2642-4, the denominator of the applicable fraction is the value of the property transferred to the trust (or transferred in a direct skip not in trust) (as determined under § 26.2642-2) reduced by the sum of—

(i) Any Federal estate tax and any State death tax incurred by reason of the transfer that is chargeable to the trust and is actually recovered from the trust;

(ii) The amount of any charitable deduction allowed under section 2055, 2106, or 2522 with respect to the transfer; and

(iii) In the case of a direct skip, the value of the portion of the transfer that is a nontaxable gift. See paragraph (c)(3) of this section for the definition of nontaxable gift.

(2) Zero denominator. If the denominator of the applicable fraction is zero, the inclusion ratio is zero.

(3) Nontaxable gifts. Generally, for purposes of chapter 13, a transfer is a nontaxable gift to the extent the transfer is excluded from taxable gifts by reason of section 2503(b) (after application of section 2513) or section 2503(e). However, a transfer to a trust for the benefit of an individual is not a nontaxable gift for purposes of this section unless—

(i) Trust principal or income may, during the individual's lifetime, be distributed only to or for the benefit of the individual; and

(ii) The assets of the trust will be includible in the gross estate of the individual if the individual dies before the trust terminates.

(d) Examples. The following examples illustrate the provisions of this section. See § 26.2652-2(d) Examples 2 and 3 for illustrations of the computation of the inclusion ratio where the special (reverse QTIP) election may be applicable.

Example (1). Computation of the inclusion ratio. T transfers $100,000 to a newly-created irrevocable trust providing that income is to be accumulated for 10 years. At the end of 10 years, the accumulated income is to be distributed to T's child, C, and the trust principal is to be paid to T's grandchild. T allocates $40,000 of T's GST exemption to the trust on a timely-filed gift tax return. The applicable fraction with respect to the trust is .40 ($40,000 (the amount of GST exemption allocated to the trust) over $100,000 (the value of the property transferred to the trust)). The inclusion ratio is .60 (1 − .40). If the maximum Federal estate tax rate is 55 percent at the time of a GST, the rate of tax applicable to the transfer (applicable rate) will be .333 (55 percent (the maximum estate tax rate) × .60 (the inclusion ratio)).

Example (2). Gift entirely nontaxable. On December 1, 1996, T transfers $10,000 to an irrevocable trust for the benefit of T's grandchild, GC. GC possesses a right to withdraw any contributions to the trust such that the entire transfer qualifies for the annual exclusion under section 2503(b). Under the terms of the trust, the income is to be paid to GC for 10 years or until GC's prior death. Upon the expiration of GC's income interest, the trust principal is payable to GC or GC's estate. The transfer to the trust is a direct skip. T made no prior gifts to or for the benefit of GC during 1996. The entire $10,000 transfer is a nontaxable transfer. For purposes of computing the tax on the direct skip, the denominator of the applicable fraction is zero, and thus, the inclusion ratio is zero.

Example (3). Gift nontaxable in part. T transfers $12,000 to an irrevocable trust for the benefit of T's grandchild, GC. Under the terms of the trust, the income is to be paid to GC for 10 years or until GC's prior death. Upon the expiration of GC's income interest, the trust principal is payable to GC or GC's estate. Further, GC has the right to withdraw $10,000 of any contribution to the trust such that $10,000 of the transfer qualifies for the annual exclusion under section 2503(b). The amount of the nontaxable transfer is $10,000. Solely for purposes of computing the tax on the direct skip, T's transfer is divided into two portions. One portion is equal to the amount of the nontaxable transfer ($10,000) and has a zero inclusion ratio; the other portion is $2,000 ($12,000 − $10,000). With respect to the $2,000 portion, the denominator of the applicable fraction is $2,000. Assuming that T has sufficient GST exemption available, the numerator of the applicable fraction is $2,000 (unless T elects to have the automatic allocation provisions not apply). Thus, assuming T does not elect to have the automatic allocation not apply, the applicable fraction is one ($2,000/$2,000 = 1) and the inclusion ratio is zero (1 − 1 = 0).

Example (4). Gift nontaxable in part. Assume the same facts as in Example 3, except T files a timely Form 709 electing that the automatic allocation of GST exemption not apply to the $12,000 transferred in the direct skip. T's transfer is divided into two portions, a $10,000 portion with a zero inclusion ratio and a $2,000 portion with an applicable fraction of zero (0/$2,000 = 0) and an inclusion ratio of one (1 − 0 = 1).

T.D. 8644, 12/26/95.

§ 26.2642-2 Valuation.

Caution: The Treasury has not yet amended Reg § 26.2642-2 to reflect changes made by P.L. 107-16.

(a) Lifetime transfers. *(1) In general.* For purposes of determining the denominator of the applicable fraction, the value of property transferred during life is its fair market value on the effective date of the allocation of GST exemption. In the case of a timely allocation under § 26.2632-1(b)(2)(ii), the denominator of the applicable fraction is the fair market value of the property as finally determined for purposes of chapter 12.

(2) Special rule for late allocations during life. If a transferor makes a late allocation of GST exemption to a trust, the value of the property transferred to the trust is the fair market value of the trust assets determined on the effective date of the allocation of GST exemption. Except as otherwise provided in this paragraph (a)(2), if a transferor makes a late allocation of GST exemption to a trust, the transferor may, solely for purposes of determining the fair market value of the trust assets, elect to treat the allocation as having been made on the first day of the month during which the late allocation is made (valuation date). An election under this paragraph (a)(2) is not effective with respect to a life insurance policy or a trust holding a life insurance policy, if the insured individual has died. An allocation subject to the election contained in this paragraph (a)(2) is not effective until it is actually filed with the Internal Revenue Service. The election is made by stating on the Form 709 on which the allocation is made—

(i) That the election is being made;

(ii) The applicable valuation date; and

(iii) The fair market value of the trust assets on the valuation date.

(b) Transfers at death. *(1) In general.* Except as provided in paragraphs (b)(2) and (3) of this section, in determining the denominator of the applicable fraction, the value of property included in the decedent's gross estate is its value for purposes of chapter 11. In the case of qualified real property with respect to which the election under section 2032A is made, the value of the property is the value determined under section 2032A provided the recapture agreement described in section 2032A(d)(2) filed with the Internal Revenue Service specifically provides for the signatories' consent to the imposition of, and personal liability for, additional GST tax in the event an additional estate tax is imposed under section 2032A(c). See § 26.2642-4(a)(4). If the recapture agreement does not contain these provisions, the value of qualified real property as to which the election under section 2032A is made is the fair market value of the property determined without regard to the provisions of section 2032A.

(2) Special rule for pecuniary payments. (i) In general. If a pecuniary payment is satisfied with cash, the denominator of the applicable fraction is the pecuniary amount. If property other than cash is used to satisfy a pecuniary payment, the denominator of the applicable fraction is the pecuniary amount only if payment must be made with property on the basis of the value of the property on—

(A) The date of distribution; or

(B) A date other than the date of distribution, but only if the pecuniary payment must be satisfied on a basis that fairly reflects net appreciation and depreciation (occurring between the valuation date and the date of distribution) in all of the assets from which the distribution could have been made.

(ii) Other pecuniary amounts payable in kind. The denominator of the applicable fraction with respect to any property used to satisfy any other pecuniary payment payable in kind is the date of distribution value of the property.

(3) Special rule for residual transfers after payment of a pecuniary payment. (i) In general. Except as otherwise provided in this paragraph (b)(3), the denominator of the applicable fraction with respect to a residual transfer of property after the satisfaction of a pecuniary payment is the estate tax value of the assets available to satisfy the pecuniary payment reduced, if the pecuniary payment carries appropriate interest (as defined in paragraph (b)(4) of this section), by the pecuniary amount. The denominator of the applicable fraction with respect to a residual transfer of property after the satisfaction of a pecuniary payment that does not carry appropriate interest is the estate tax value of the assets available to satisfy the pecuniary payment reduced by the present value of the pecuniary payment. For purposes of this paragraph (b)(3)(i), the present value of the pecuniary payment is determined by using—

(A) The interest rate applicable under section 7520 at the death of the transferor; and

(B) The period between the date of the transferor's death and the date the pecuniary amount is paid.

(ii) Special rule for residual transfers after pecuniary payments payable in kind. The denominator of the applicable fraction with respect to any residual transfer after satisfaction of a pecuniary payment payable in kind is the date of distribution value of the property distributed in satisfaction of the residual transfer, unless the pecuniary payment must be satisfied on the basis of the value of the property on—

(A) The date of distribution; or

(B) A date other than the date of distribution, but only if the pecuniary payment must be satisfied on a basis that fairly reflects net appreciation and depreciation (occurring between the valuation date and the date of distribution) in all of the assets from which the distribution could have been made.

(4) Appropriate interest. (i) In general. For purposes of this section and § 26.2654-1 (relating to certain trusts treated as separate trusts), appropriate interest means that interest must be payable from the date of death of the transferor (or from the date specified under applicable State law requiring the payment of interest) to the date of payment at a rate—

(A) At least equal to—

(1) The statutory rate of interest, if any, applicable to pecuniary bequests under the law of the State whose law governs the administration of the estate or trust; or

(2) If no such rate is indicated under applicable State law, 80 percent of the rate that is applicable under section 7520 at the death of the transferor; and

(B) Not in excess of the greater of—

(1) The statutory rate of interest, if any, applicable to pecuniary bequests under the law of the State whose law governs the administration of the trust; or

(2) 120 percent of the rate that is applicable under section 7520 at the death of the transferor.

(ii) Pecuniary payments deemed to carry appropriate interest. For purposes of this paragraph (b)(4), if a pecuniary payment does not carry appropriate interest, the pecuniary payment is considered to carry appropriate interest to the extent—

(A) The entire payment is made or property is irrevocably set aside to satisfy the entire pecuniary payment within 15 months of the transferor's death; or

(B) The governing instrument or applicable local law specifically requires the executor or trustee to allocate to the pecuniary payment a pro rata share of the income earned by the fund from which the pecuniary payment is to be made between the date of death of the transferor and the date of payment. For purposes of paragraph (b)(4)(ii)(A) of this section, property is irrevocably set aside if it is segregated and held in a separate account pending distribution.

(c) Examples. The following examples illustrate the provisions of this section:

Example (1). T transfers $100,000 to a newly-created irrevocable trust on December 15, 1996. The trust provides that income is to be paid to T's child for 10 years. At the end of the 10-year period, the trust principal is to be paid to T's grandchild. T does not allocate any GST exemption to the trust on the gift tax return reporting the transfer. On November 15, 1997, T files a Form 709 allocating $50,000 of GST exemption to the trust. Because the allocation was made on a late filed return, the value of the property transferred to the trust is determined on the date the allocation is filed (unless an election is made pursuant to paragraph (a)(2) of this section to value the trust property as of the first day of the month in which the allocation document is filed with the Internal Revenue Service). On November 15, 1997, the value of the trust property is $150,000. Effective as of November 15, 1997, the applicable fraction with respect to the trust is .333 ($50,000 (the amount of GST exemption allocated to the trust) over $150,000 (the value of the trust principal on the effective date of the GST exemption allocation)), and the inclusion ratio is .667 (1.0 – .333).

Example (2). The facts are the same as in Example 1, except the value of the trust property is $80,000 on November 15, 1997. The applicable fraction is .625 ($50,000 over $80,000) and the inclusion ratio is .375 (1.0 – .625).

Example (3). T transfers $100,000 to a newly-created irrevocable trust on December 15, 1996. The trust provides that income is to be paid to T's child for 10 years. At the end of the 10-year period, the trust principal is to be paid to T's grandchild. T does not allocate any GST exemption to the trust on the gift tax return reporting the transfer. On November 15, 1997, T files a Form 709 allocating $50,000 of GST exemption to the trust. T elects to value the trust principal on the first day of the month in which the allocation is made pursuant to the election provided in paragraph (a)(2) of this section. Because the late allocation is made in November, the value of the trust is determined as of November 1, 1997.

T.D. 8644, 12/26/95.

§ 26.2642-3 Special rule for charitable lead annuity trusts.

(a) In general. In determining the applicable fraction with respect to a charitable lead annuity trust—

(1) The numerator is the adjusted generation-skipping transfer tax exemption (adjusted GST exemption); and

(2) The denominator is the value of all property in the trust immediately after the termination of the charitable lead annuity.

(b) Adjusted GST exemption defined. The adjusted GST exemption is the amount of GST exemption allocated to the trust increased by an amount equal to the interest that would accrue if an amount equal to the allocated GST exemption were invested at the rate used to determine the amount of the estate or gift tax charitable deduction, compounded annually, for the actual period of the charitable lead annuity. If a late allocation is made to a charitable lead annuity trust, the adjusted GST exemption is the amount of GST exemption allocated to the trust increased by the interest that would accrue if invested at such rate for the period beginning on the date of the late allocation and extending for the balance of the actual period of the charitable lead annuity. The amount of GST exemption allocated to a charitable lead annuity trust is not reduced even though it is ultimately determined that the allocation of a lesser amount of GST exemption would have resulted in an inclusion ratio of zero. For purposes of chapter 13, a charitable lead annuity trust is any trust providing an interest in the form of a guaranteed annuity described in § 25.2522(c)-3(c)(2)(vi) of this chapter for which the transferor is allowed a charitable deduction for Federal estate or gift tax purposes.

(c) Example. The following example illustrates the provisions of this section:

Example. T creates a charitable lead annuity trust for a 10-year term with the remainder payable to T's grandchild. T timely allocates an amount of GST exemption to the trust which T expects will ultimately result in a zero inclusion ratio. However, at the end of the charitable lead interest, because the property has not appreciated to the extent T anticipated, the numerator of the applicable fraction is greater than the denominator. The inclusion ratio for the trust is zero. No portion of the GST exemption allocated to the trust is restored to T or to T's estate.

T.D. 8644, 12/26/95.

§ 26.2642-4 Redetermination of applicable fraction.

(a) In general. The applicable fraction for a trust is redetermined whenever additional exemption is allocated to the trust or when certain changes occur with respect to the principal of the trust. Except as otherwise provided in this paragraph (a), the numerator of the redetermined applicable fraction is the sum of the amount of GST exemption currently being allocated to the trust (if any) plus the value of the nontax portion of the trust, and the denominator of the redetermined applicable fraction is the value of the trust principal immediately after the event occurs. The nontax portion of a trust is determined by multiplying the value of the trust assets, determined immediately prior to the event, by the then applicable fraction.

(1) Multiple transfers to a single trust. If property is added to an existing trust, the denominator of the redetermined applicable fraction is the value of the trust immediately after the addition reduced as provided in § 26.2642-1(c).

(2) Consolidation of separate trusts. If separate trusts created by one transferor are consolidated, a single applicable fraction for the consolidated trust is determined. The numerator of the redetermined applicable fraction is the sum of the nontax portions of each trust immediately prior to the consolidation.

(3) Property included in transferor's gross estate. If the value of property held in a trust created by the transferor, with respect to which an allocation was made at a time that the trust was not subject to an ETIP, is included in the transferor's gross estate, the applicable fraction is redetermined if additional GST exemption is allocated to the property. The numerator of the redetermined applicable fraction is an amount equal to the nontax portion of the property immediately after the death of the transferor increased by the amount of GST exemption allocated by the executor of the transferor's estate to the trust. If additional GST exemption is not allocated to the trust, then, except as provided in this paragraph (a)(3), the applicable fraction immediately before death is not changed, if the trust was not subject to an ETIP at the time GST exemption was allocated to the trust. In any event, the denominator of the applicable fraction is reduced

to reflect any federal or state, estate or inheritance taxes paid from the trust.

(4) Imposition of recapture tax under section 2032A. (i) If an additional estate tax is imposed under section 2032A and if the section 2032A election was effective (under § 26.2642-2(b)) for purposes of the GST tax, the applicable fraction with respect to the property is redetermined as of the date of death of the transferor. In making the redetermination, any available GST exemption not allocated at the death of the transferor (or at a prior recapture event) is automatically allocated to the property. The denominator of the applicable fraction is the fair market value of the property at the date of the transferor's death reduced as provided in § 26.2642-1(c) and further reduced by the amount of the additional GST tax actually recovered from the trust.

(ii) The GST tax imposed with respect to any taxable termination, taxable distribution, or direct skip occurring prior to the recapture event is recomputed based on the applicable fraction as redetermined. Any additional GST tax as recomputed is due and payable on the date that is six months after the event that causes the imposition of the additional estate tax under section 2032A. The additional GST tax is remitted with Form 706-A and is reported by attaching a statement to Form 706-A showing the computation of the additional GST tax.

(iii) The applicable fraction, as redetermined under this section, is also used in determining any GST tax imposed with respect to GSTs occurring after the date of the recapture event.

(b) Examples. The following examples illustrate the principles of this section:

Example (1). Allocation of additional exemption. T transfers $200,000 to an irrevocable trust under which the income is payable to T's child, C, for life. Upon the termination of the trust, the remainder is payable to T's grandchild, GC. At a time when no ETIP exists with respect to the trust property, T makes a timely allocation of $100,000 of GST exemption, resulting in an inclusion ratio of .50. Subsequently, when the entire trust property is valued at $500,000, T allocates an additional $100,000 of T's unused GST exemption to the trust. The inclusion ratio of the trust is recomputed at that time. The numerator of the applicable fraction is $350,000 ($250,000 (the nontax portion as of the date of the allocation) plus $100,000 (the GST exemption currently being allocated)). The denominator is $500,000 (the date of allocation fair market value of the trust). The inclusion ratio is .30 (1 − .70).

Example (2). Multiple transfers to a trust, allocation both timely and late. On December 10, 1993, T transfers $10,000 to an irrevocable trust that does not satisfy the requirements of section 2642(c)(2). T makes identical transfers to the trust on December 10, 1994, 1995, 1996, and on January 15, 1997. Immediately after the transfer on January 15, 1997, the value of the trust principal is $40,000. On January 14, 1998, when the value of the trust principal is $50,000, T allocates $30,000 of GST exemption to the trust. T discloses the 1997 transfer on the Form 709 filed on January 14, 1998. Thus, T's allocation is a timely allocation with respect to the transfer in 1997, $10,000 of the allocation is effective as of the date of that transfer, and, on and after January 15, 1997, the inclusion ratio of the trust is .75 (1 − ($10,000/$40,000)). The balance of the allocation is a late allocation with respect to prior transfers to the trust and is effective as of January 14, 1998. In redetermining the inclusion ratio as of that date, the numerator of the redetermined applicable fraction is $32,500 ($12,500 (.25 × $50,000), the nontax portion of the trust on January 14, 1998) plus $20,000 (the amount of GST exemption allocated late to the trust). The denominator of the new applicable fraction is $50,000 (the value of the trust principal at the time of the late allocation).

Example (3). Excess allocation. (i) T creates an irrevocable trust for the benefit of T's child and grandchild in 1996 transferring $50,000 to the trust on the date of creation. T allocates no GST exemption to the trust on the Form 709 reporting the transfer. On July 1, 1997 (when the value of the trust property is $60,000), T transfers an additional $40,000 to the trust.

(ii) On April 15, 1998, when the value of the trust is $150,000, T files a Form 709 reporting the 1997 transfer and allocating $150,000 of GST exemption to the trust. The allocation is a timely allocation of $40,000 with respect to the 1997 transfer and is effective as of that date. Thus, the applicable fraction for the trust as of July 1, 1997 is .40 ($40,000/$100,000 ($40,000 + $60,000)).

(iii) The allocation is also a late allocation of $90,000, the amount necessary to attain a zero inclusion ratio on April 15, 1998, computed as follows: $60,000 (the nontax portion immediately prior to the allocation (.40 × $150,000)) plus $90,000 (the additional allocation necessary to produce a zero inclusion ratio based on a denominator of $150,000)/$150,000 equals one and, thus, an inclusion ratio of zero. The balance of the allocation, $20,000 ($150,000 less the timely allocation of $40,000 less the late allocation of $90,000) is void.

Example (4). Undisclosed transfer. (i) The facts are the same as in Example 3, except that on February 1, 1998 (when the value of the trust is $150,000), T transfers an additional $50,000 to the trust and the value of the entire trust corpus on April 15, 1998 is $220,000. The Form 709 filed on April 15, 1998 does not disclose the 1998 transfer. Under the rule in § 26.2632-1(b)(2)(ii), the allocation is effective first as a timely allocation to the 1997 transfer; second, as a late allocation to the trust as of April 15, 1998; and, finally as a timely allocation to the February 1, 1998 transfer. As of April 15, 1998, $55,000, a pro rata portion of the trust assets, is considered to be the property transferred to the trust on February 1, 1998 (($50,000/$200,000) × $220,000). The balance of the trust, $165,000, represents prior transfers to the trust.

(ii) As in Example 3, the allocation is a timely allocation as to the 1997 transfer (and the applicable fraction as of July 1, 1997 is .40) and a late allocation as of 1998. The amount of the late allocation is $99,000, computed as follows: (.40 × $165,000 plus $99,000)/$165,000 = one.

(iii) The balance of the allocation, $11,000 ($150,000 less the timely allocation of $40,000 less the late allocation of $99,000) is a timely allocation as of February 1, 1998. The applicable fraction with respect to the trust, as of February 1, 1998, is .355, computed as follows: $60,000 (the nontax portion of the trust immediately prior to the February 1, 1998 transfer (.40 × $150,000)) plus $11,000 (the amount of the timely allocation to the 1998 transfer)/$200,000 (the value of the trust on February 1, 1998, after the transfer on that date) = $71,000/$200,000 = .355.

(iv) The applicable fraction with respect to the trust, as of April 15, 1998, is .805 computed as follows: $78,100 (the nontax portion immediately prior to the allocation (.355 × $220,000)) plus $99,000 (the amount of the late allocation)/$220,000 = $177,100/$220,000 = .805.

Example (5). Redetermination of inclusion ratio on ETIP termination. (i) T transfers $100,000 to an irrevocable trust. The trust instrument provides that trust income is to be paid to T for 9 years or until T's prior death. The trust principal is to be paid to T's grandchild, GC, on the termination of T's income interest. The trustee has the power to invade trust principal for the benefit of GC during the term of T's income interest. The trust is subject to an ETIP while T holds the retained income interest. T files a timely Form 709 reporting the transfer and allocates $100,000 of GST exemption to the trust. In year 4, when the value of the trust is $200,000, the trustee distributes $15,000 to GC. The distribution is a taxable distribution. Because of the existence of the ETIP, the inclusion ratio with respect to the taxable distribution is determined immediately prior to the occurrence of the GST. Thus, the inclusion ratio applicable to the year 4 GST is .50 (1 − ($100,000/$200,000)).

(ii) In year 5, when the value of the trust is again $200,000, the trustee distributes another $15,000 to GC. Because the trust is still subject to the ETIP in year 5, the inclusion ratio with respect to the year 5 GST is again computed immediately prior to the GST. In computing the new inclusion ratio, the numerator of the applicable fraction is reduced by the nontax portion of prior GSTs occurring during the ETIP. Thus, the numerator of the applicable fraction with respect to the GST in year 5 is $92,500 ($100,000 − (.50 × $15,000)) and the inclusion ratio applicable with respect to the GST in year 5 is .537 (1 − ($92,500/$200,000) = .463). Any additional GST exemption allocated on a timely ETIP return with respect to the GST in year 5 is effective immediately prior to the transfer.

T.D. 8644, 12/26/95.

§ 26.2642-5 Finality of inclusion ratio.

(a) Direct skips. The inclusion ratio applicable to a direct skip becomes final when no additional GST tax (including additional GST tax payable as a result of a cessation, etc. of qualified use under section 2032A(c)) may be assessed with respect to the direct skip.

(b) Other GSTs. With respect to taxable distributions and taxable terminations, the inclusion ratio for a trust becomes final, on the later of—

(1) The expiration of the period for assessment with respect to the first GST tax return filed using that inclusion ratio (unless the trust is subject to an election under section 2032A in which case the applicable date under this subsection is the expiration of the period of assessment of any additional GST tax due as a result of a cessation, etc. of qualified use under section 2032A); or

(2) The expiration of the period for assessment of Federal estate tax with respect to the estate of the transferor. For purposes of this paragraph (b)(2), if an estate tax return is not required to be filed, the period for assessment is determined as if a return were required to be filed and as if the return were timely filed within the period prescribed by section 6075(a).

T.D. 8644, 12/26/95.

§ 26.2642-6 Qualified severance.

(a) In general. If a trust is divided in a qualified severance into two or more trusts, the separate trusts resulting from the severance will be treated as separate trusts for generation-skipping transfer (GST) tax purposes and the inclusion ratio of each new resulting trust may differ from the inclusion ratio of the original trust. Because the post-severance resulting trusts are treated as separate trusts for GST tax purposes, certain actions with respect to one resulting trust will generally have no GST tax impact with respect to the other resulting trust(s). For example, GST exemption allocated to one resulting trust will not impact on the inclusion ratio of the other resulting trust(s); a GST tax election made with respect to one resulting trust will not apply to the other resulting trust(s); the occurrence of a taxable distribution or termination with regard to a particular resulting trust will not have any GST tax impact on any other trust resulting from that severance. In general, the rules in this section are applicable only for purposes of the GST tax and are not applicable in determining, for example, whether the resulting trusts may file separate income tax returns or whether the severance may result in a gift subject to gift tax, may cause any trust to be included in the gross estate of a beneficiary, or may result in a realization of gain for purposes of section 1001. See § 1.1001-1(h) of this chapter for rules relating to whether a qualified severance will constitute an exchange of property for other property differing materially either in kind or in extent.

(b) Qualified severance defined. A qualified severance is a division of a trust (other than a division described in § 26.2654-1(b)) into two or more separate trusts that meets each of the requirements in paragraph (d) of this section.

(c) Effective date of qualified severance. A qualified severance is applicable as of the date of the severance, as defined in § 26.2642-6(d)(3), and the resulting trusts are treated as separate trusts for GST tax purposes as of that date.

(d) Requirements for a qualified severance. For purposes of this section, a qualified severance must satisfy each of the following requirements:

(1) The single trust is severed pursuant to the terms of the governing instrument, or pursuant to applicable local law.

(2) The severance is effective under local law.

(3) The date of severance is either the date selected by the trustee as of which the trust assets are to be valued in order to determine the funding of the resulting trusts, or the court-imposed date of funding in the case of an order of the local court with jurisdiction over the trust ordering the trustee to fund the resulting trusts on or as of a specific date. For a date to satisfy the definition in the preceding sentence, however, the funding must be commenced immediately upon, and funding must occur within a reasonable time (but in no event more than 90 days) after, the selected valuation date.

(4) The single trust (original trust) is severed on a fractional basis, such that each new trust (resulting trust) is funded with a fraction or percentage of the original trust, and the sum of those fractions or percentages is one or one hundred percent, respectively. For this purpose, the fraction or percentage may be determined by means of a formula (for example, that fraction of the trust the numerator of which is equal to the transferor's unused GST tax exemption, and the denominator of which is the fair market value of the original trust's assets on the date of severance). The severance of a trust based on a pecuniary amount does not satisfy this requirement. For example, the severance of a trust is not a qualified severance if the trust is divided into two trusts, with one trust to be funded with $1,500,000 and the other trust to be funded with the balance of the original trust's assets. With respect to the particular assets to be distributed to each separate trust resulting from the severance, each such trust may be funded with the appropriate fraction or percent-

age (pro rata portion) of each asset held by the original trust. Alternatively, the assets may be divided among the resulting trusts on a non-pro rata basis, based on the fair market value of the assets on the date of severance. However, if a resulting trust is funded on a non-pro rata basis, each asset received by a resulting trust must be valued, solely for funding purposes, by multiplying the fair market value of the asset held in the original trust as of the date of severance by the fraction or percentage of that asset received by that resulting trust. Thus, the assets must be valued without taking into account any discount or premium arising from the severance, for example, any valuation discounts that might arise because the resulting trust receives less than the entire interest held by the original trust. See paragraph (j), Example 6 of this section.

(5) The terms of the resulting trusts must provide, in the aggregate, for the same succession of interests of beneficiaries as are provided in the original trust. This requirement is satisfied if the beneficiaries of the separate resulting trusts and the interests of the beneficiaries with respect to the separate trusts, when the separate trusts are viewed collectively, are the same as the beneficiaries and their respective beneficial interests with respect to the original trust before severance. With respect to trusts from which discretionary distributions may be made to any one or more beneficiaries on a non-pro rata basis, this requirement is satisfied if—

(i) The terms of each of the resulting trusts are the same as the terms of the original trust (even though each permissible distributee of the original trust is not a beneficiary of all of the resulting trusts);

(ii) Each beneficiary's interest in the resulting trusts (collectively) equals the beneficiary's interest in the original trust, determined by the terms of the trust instrument or, if none, on a per-capita basis. For example, in the case of the severance of a discretionary trust established for the benefit of A, B, and C and their descendants with the remainder to be divided equally among those three families, this requirement is satisfied if the trust is divided into three separate trusts of equal value with one trust established for the benefit of A and A's descendants, one trust for the benefit of B and B's descendants, and one trust for the benefit of C and C's descendants;

(iii) The severance does not shift a beneficial interest in the trust to any beneficiary in a lower generation (as determined under section 2651) than the person or persons who held the beneficial interest in the original trust; and

(iv) The severance does not extend the time for the vesting of any beneficial interest in the trust beyond the period provided for in (or applicable to) the original trust.

(6) In the case of a qualified severance of a trust with an inclusion ratio as defined in § 26.2642-1 of either one or zero, each trust resulting from the severance will have an inclusion ratio equal to the inclusion ratio of the original trust.

(7)

(i) In the case of a qualified severance occurring after GST tax exemption has been allocated to the trust (whether by an affirmative allocation, a deemed allocation, or an automatic allocation pursuant to the rules contained in section 2632), if the trust has an inclusion ratio as defined in § 26.2642-1 that is greater than zero and less than one, then either paragraph (d)(7)(ii) or (iii) of this section must be satisfied.

(ii) The trust is severed initially into only two resulting trusts. One resulting trust must receive that fractional share of the total value of the original trust as of the date of severance that is equal to the applicable fraction, as defined in § 26.2642-1(b) and (c), used to determine the inclusion ratio of the original trust immediately before the severance. The other resulting trust must receive that fractional share of the total value of the original trust as of the date of severance that is equal to the excess of one over the fractional share described in the preceding sentence. The trust receiving the fractional share equal to the applicable fraction shall have an inclusion ratio of zero, and the other trust shall have an inclusion ratio of one. If the applicable fraction with respect to the original trust is .50, then, with respect to the two equal trusts resulting from the severance, the trustee may designate which of the resulting trusts will have an inclusion ratio of zero and which will have an inclusion ratio of one. Each separate trust resulting from the severance then may be further divided in accordance with the rules of this section. See paragraph (j), Example 7, of this section.

(iii) The trust is severed initially into more than two resulting trusts. One or more of the resulting trusts in the aggregate must receive that fractional share of the total value of the original trust as of the date of severance that is equal to the applicable fraction used to determine the inclusion ratio of the original trust immediately before the severance. The trust or trusts receiving such fractional share shall have an inclusion ratio of zero, and each of the other resulting trust or trusts shall have an inclusion ratio of one. (If, however, two or more of the resulting trusts each receives the fractional share of the total value of the original trust equal to the applicable fraction, the trustee may designate which of those resulting trusts will have an inclusion ratio of zero and which will have an inclusion ratio of one.) The resulting trust or trusts with an inclusion ratio of one must receive in the aggregate that fractional share of the total value of the original trust as of the date of severance that is equal to the excess of one over the fractional share described in the second sentence of this paragraph. See paragraph (j), Example 9, of this section.

(e) Reporting a qualified severance. *(1) In general.* A qualified severance is reported by filing Form 706-GS(T), "Generation-Skipping Transfer Tax Return for Terminations," (or such other form as may be provided from time to time by the Internal Revenue Service (IRS) for the purpose of reporting a qualified severance). Unless otherwise provided in the applicable form or instructions, the IRS requests that the filer write "Qualified Severance" at the top of the form and attach a Notice of Qualified Severance (Notice). The return and attached Notice should be filed by April 15th of the year immediately following the year during which the severance occurred or by the last day of the period covered by an extension of time, if an extension of time is granted, to file such form.

(2) Information concerning the original trust. The Notice should provide, with respect to the original trust that was severed—

(i) The name of the transferor;

(ii) The name and date of creation of the original trust;

(iii) The tax identification number of the original trust; and

(iv) The inclusion ratio before the severance.

(3) Information concerning each new trust. The Notice should provide, with respect to each of the resulting trusts created by the severance—

(i) The name and tax identification number of the trust;

(ii) The date of severance (within the meaning of paragraph (c) of this section);

(iii) The fraction of the total assets of the original trust received by the resulting trust;

(iv) Other details explaining the basis for the funding of the resulting trust (a fraction of the total fair market value of the assets on the date of severance, or a fraction of each asset); and

(v) The inclusion ratio.

(f) Time for making a qualified severance. *(1)* A qualified severance of a trust may occur at any time prior to the termination of the trust. Thus, provided that the separate resulting trusts continue in existence after the severance, a qualified severance may occur either before or after—

(i) GST tax exemption has been allocated to the trust;

(ii) A taxable event has occurred with respect to the trust; or

(iii) An addition has been made to the trust.

(2) Because a qualified severance is effective as of the date of severance, a qualified severance has no effect on a taxable termination as defined in section 2612(a) or a taxable distribution as defined in section 2612(b) that occurred prior to the date of severance. A qualified severance shall be deemed to occur before a taxable termination or a taxable distribution that occurs by reason of the qualified severance. See paragraph (j) Example 8 of this section.

(g) Trusts that were irrevocable on September 25, 1985. *(1) In general.* See § 26.2601-1(b)(4) for rules regarding severances and other actions with respect to trusts that were irrevocable on September 25, 1985.

(2) Trusts in receipt of a post-September 25, 1985, addition. A trust described in § 26.2601-1(b)(1)(iv)(A) that is deemed for GST tax purposes to consist of one separate share not subject to GST tax (the non-chapter 13 portion) with an inclusion ratio of zero, and one separate share subject to GST tax (the chapter 13 portion) with an inclusion ratio determined under section 2642, may be severed into two trusts in accordance with § 26.2654-1(a)(3). One resulting trust will hold the non-chapter 13 portion of the original trust (the non-chapter 13 trust) and will not be subject to GST tax, and the other resulting trust will hold the chapter 13 portion of the original trust (the chapter 13 trust) and will have the same inclusion ratio as the chapter 13 portion immediately prior to the severance. The chapter 13 trust may be further divided in a qualified severance in accordance with the rules of this section. The non-chapter 13 trust may be further divided in accordance with the rules of § 26.2601-1(b)(4).

(h) Treatment of trusts resulting from a severance that is not a qualified severance. Trusts resulting from a severance (other than a severance recognized for GST tax purposes under § 26.2654-1) that does not meet the requirements of a qualified severance under paragraph (b) of this section will be treated, after the date of severance, as separate trusts for purposes of the GST tax, provided that the trusts resulting from such severance are recognized as separate trusts under applicable state law. The post-severance treatment of the resulting trusts as separate trusts for GST tax purposes generally permits the allocation of GST tax exemption, the making of various elections permitted for GST tax purposes, and the occurrence of a taxable distribution or termination with regard to a particular resulting trust, with no GST tax impact on any other trust resulting from that severance. Each trust resulting from a severance described in this paragraph (h), however, will have the same inclusion ratio immediately after the severance as that of the original trust immediately before the severance. (See § 26.2654-1 for the inclusion ratio of each trust resulting from a severance described in that section.) Further, any trust resulting from a nonqualified severance may be severed subsequently, pursuant to a qualified severance described in this § 26.2642-6.

(i) [Reserved].

(j) Examples. The rules of this section are illustrated by the following examples:

Example (1). Succession of interests. T dies in 2006. T's will establishes a testamentary trust (Trust) providing that income is to be paid to T's sister, S, for her life. On S's death, one-half of the corpus is to be paid to T's child, C (or to C's estate if C fails to survive S), and one-half of the corpus is to be paid to T's grandchild, GC (or to GC's estate if GC fails to survive S). On the Form 706, "United States Estate (and Generation-Skipping Transfer) Tax Return," filed for T's estate, T's executor allocates all of T's available GST tax exemption to other transfers and trusts, such that Trust's inclusion ratio is 1. Subsequent to filing the Form 706 in 2007 and in accordance with applicable state law, the trustee divides Trust into two separate trusts, Trust 1 and Trust 2, with each trust receiving 50 percent of the value of the assets of the original trust as of the date of severance. Trust 1 provides that trust income is to be paid to S for life with remainder to C or C's estate, and Trust 2 provides that trust income is to be paid to S for life with remainder to GC or GC's estate. Because Trust 1 and Trust 2 provide for the same succession of interests in the aggregate as provided in the original trust, the severance constitutes a qualified severance, provided that all other requirements of section 2642(a)(3) and this section are satisfied.

Example (2). Succession of interests in discretionary trust. In 2006, T establishes Trust, an irrevocable trust providing that income may be paid from time to time in such amounts as the trustee deems advisable to any one or more members of the group consisting of T's children (A and B) and their respective descendants. In addition, the trustee may distribute corpus to any trust beneficiary in such amounts as the trustee deems advisable. On the death of the last to die of A and B, the trust is to terminate and the corpus is to be distributed in two equal shares, one share to the then-living descendants of each child, per stirpes. T elects, under section 2632(c)(5), to not have the automatic allocation rules contained in section 2632(c) apply with respect to T's transfers to Trust, and T does not otherwise allocate GST tax exemption with respect to Trust. As a result, Trust has an inclusion ratio of one. In 2008, the trustee of Trust, pursuant to applicable state law, divides Trust into two equal but separate trusts, Trust 1 and Trust 2, each of which has terms identical to the terms of Trust except for the identity of the beneficiaries. Trust 1 and Trust 2 each has an inclusion ratio of one. Trust 1 provides that income is to be paid in such amounts as the trustee deems advisable to A and A's descendants. In addition, the trustee may distribute corpus to any trust beneficiary in such amounts as the trustee deems advisable. On the death of A, Trust 1 is to terminate and the corpus is to be distributed to the then-living descendants of A, per stirpes, but, if A dies with no living descendants, the principal will be added to Trust 2. Trust 2 contains identical provisions, except that B and B's descendants are the trust beneficiaries and, if B dies with no living descendants, the principal will be added to Trust 1. Trust 1 and Trust 2 in the aggregate provide for the same beneficiaries and the same succession of interests as provided in Trust, and the severance does not shift any beneficial interest to a beneficiary who occupies a lower generation than the person or persons who held the beneficial interest in Trust. Accordingly, the severance constitutes a qualified severance, provided that all other requirements of section 2642(a)(3) and this section are satisfied.

Example (3). Severance based on actuarial value of beneficial interests. In 2004, T establishes Trust, an irrevocable trust providing that income is to be paid to T's child C during C's lifetime. Upon C's death, Trust is to terminate and the assets of Trust are to be paid to GC, C's child, if living, or, if GC is not then living, to GC's estate. T properly elects, under section 2632(c)(5), not to have the automatic allocation rules contained in section 2632(c) apply with respect to T's transfers to Trust, and T does not otherwise allocate GST tax exemption with respect to Trust. Thus, Trust has an inclusion ratio of one. In 2009, the trustee of Trust, pursuant to applicable state law, divides Trust into two separate trusts, Trust 1 for the benefit of C (and on C's death to C's estate), and Trust 2 for the benefit of GC (and on GC's death to GC's estate). The document severing Trust directs that Trust 1 is to be funded with an amount equal to the actuarial value of C's interest in Trust prior to the severance, determined under section 7520 of the Internal Revenue Code. Similarly, Trust 2 is to be funded with an amount equal to the actuarial value of GC's interest in Trust prior to the severance, determined under section 7520. Trust 1 and Trust 2 do not provide for the same succession of interests as provided under the terms of the original trust. Therefore, the severance is not a qualified severance. Furthermore, because the severance results in no non-skip person having an interest in Trust 2, Trust 2 constitutes a skip person under section 2613 and, therefore, the severance results in a taxable termination subject to GST tax.

Example (4). Severance of a trust with a 50% inclusion ratio. On September 1, 2006, T transfers $100,000 to a trust for the benefit of T's grandchild, GC. On a timely filed Form 709, "United States Gift (and Generation-Skipping Transfer) Tax Return," reporting the transfer, T allocates all of T's remaining GST tax exemption ($50,000) to the trust. As a result of the allocation, the applicable fraction with respect to the trust is .50 [$50,000 (the amount of GST tax exemption allocated to the trust) divided by $100,000 (the value of the property transferred to the trust)]. The inclusion ratio with respect to the trust is .50 [1-.50]. In 2007, pursuant to authority granted under applicable state law, the trustee severs the trust into two trusts, Trust 1 and Trust 2, each of which is identical to the original trust and each of which receives a 50 percent fractional share of the total value of the original trust, valued as of the date of severance. Because the applicable fraction with respect to the original trust is .50 and the trust is severed into two equal trusts, the trustee may designate which resulting trust has an inclusion ratio of one, and which resulting trust has an inclusion ratio of zero. Accordingly, in the Notice of Qualified Severance reporting the severance, the trustee designates Trust 1 as having an inclusion ratio of zero, and Trust 2 as having an inclusion ratio of one. The severance constitutes a qualified severance, provided that all other requirements of section 2642(a)(3) and this section are satisfied.

Example (5). Funding of severed trusts on a non-pro rata basis. T's will establishes a testamentary trust (Trust) for the benefit of T's descendants, to be funded with T's stock in Corporation A and Corporation B, both publicly traded stocks. T dies on May 1, 2004, at which time the Corporation A stock included in T's gross estate has a fair market value of $100,000 and the stock of Corporation B included in T's gross estate has a fair market value of $200,000. On a timely filed Form 706, T's executor allocates all of T's remaining GST tax exemption ($270,000) to Trust. As a result of the allocation, the applicable fraction with respect to Trust is .90 [$270,000 (the amount of GST tax exemption allocated to the trust) divided by $300,000 (the value of the property transferred to the trust)]. The inclusion ratio with respect to Trust is .10 [1-.90]. On August 1, 2008, in accordance with applicable local law, the trustee executes a document severing Trust into two trusts, Trust 1 and Trust 2, each of which is identical to Trust. The instrument designates August 3, 2008, as the date of severance (within the meaning of paragraph (d)(3) of this section). The terms of the instrument severing Trust provide that Trust 1 is to be funded on a non-pro rata basis with assets having a fair market value on the date of severance equal to 90% of the value of Trust's assets on that date, and Trust 2 is to be funded with assets having a fair market value on the date of severance equal to 10% of the value of Trust's assets on that date. On August 3, 2008, the value of the Trust assets totals $500,000, consisting of Corporation A stock worth $450,000 and Corporation B stock worth $50,000. On August 4, 2008, the trustee takes all action necessary to transfer all of the Corporation A stock to Trust 1 and to transfer all of the Corporation B stock to Trust 2. On August 6, 2008, the stock transfers are completed and the stock is received by the appropriate resulting trust. Accordingly, Trust 1 is funded with assets having a value equal to 90% of the value of Trust as of the date of severance, August 3, 2008, and Trust 2 is funded with assets having a value equal to 10% of the value of Trust as of the date of severance. Therefore, the severance constitutes a qualified severance, provided that all other requirements of section 2642(a)(3) and this section are satisfied. Trust 1 will have an inclusion ratio of zero and Trust 2 will have an inclusion ratio of one.

Example (6). Funding of severed trusts on a non-pro rata basis. (i) T's will establishes an irrevocable trust (Trust) for the benefit of T's descendants. As a result of the allocation of GST tax exemption, the applicable fraction with respect to Trust is .60 and Trust's inclusion ratio is .40 [1-.60]. Pursuant to authority granted under applicable state law, on August 1, 2008, the trustee executes a document severing Trust into two trusts, Trust 1 and Trust 2, each of which is identical to Trust. The instrument of severance provides that the severance is intended to qualify as a qualified severance within the meaning of section 2642(a)(3) and designates August 3, 2008, as the date of severance (within the meaning of paragraph (d)(3) of this section). The instrument further provides that Trust 1 and Trust 2 are to be funded on a non-pro rata basis with Trust 1 funded with assets having a fair market value on the date of severance equal to 40% of the value of Trust's assets on that date and Trust 2 funded with assets having a fair market value equal to 60% of the value of Trust's assets on that date. The fair market value of the assets used to fund each trust is to be determined in compliance with the requirements of paragraph (d)(4) of this section.

(ii) On August 3, 2008, the fair market value of the Trust assets totals $4,000,000, consisting of 52% of the outstanding common stock in Company, a closely-held corporation, valued at $3,000,000 and $1,000,000 in cash and marketable securities. Trustee proposes to divide the Company stock equally between Trust 1 and Trust 2, and thus transfer 26% of the Company stock to Trust 1 and 26% of the stock to Trust 2. In addition, the appropriate amount of cash and marketable securities will be distributed to each trust. In accordance with paragraph (d)(4) of this section, for funding purposes, the interest in the Company stock distributed to each trust is valued as a pro rata portion of the value of the 52% interest in Company held by Trust before severance, without taking into account, for example, any valuation discount that might otherwise apply in valuing the noncontrolling interest distributed to each resulting trust.

(iii) Accordingly, for funding purposes, each 26% interest in Company stock distributed to Trust 1 and Trust 2 is valued at $1,500,000 (.5 x $3,000,000). Therefore, Trust 1, which is to be funded with $1,600,000 (.40 x $4,000,000), receives $100,000 in cash and marketable securities valued as of August 3, 2008, in addition to the Company stock, and Trust 2, which is to be funded with $2,400,000 (.60 x $4,000,000), receives $900,000 in cash and marketable securities in addition to the Company stock. Therefore, the severance is a qualified severance, provided that all other requirements of section 2642(a)(3) and this section are satisfied.

Example (7). Statutory qualified severance. T dies on October 1, 2004. T's will establishes a testamentary trust (Trust) to be funded with $1,000,000. Trust income is to be paid to T's child, S, for S's life. The trustee may also distribute trust corpus from time to time, in equal or unequal shares, for the benefit of any one or more members of the group consisting of S and T's three grandchildren (GC1, GC2, and GC3). On S's death, Trust is to terminate and the assets are to be divided equally among GC1, GC2, and GC3 (or their respective then-living descendants, per stirpes). On a timely filed Form 706, T's executor allocates all of T's remaining GST tax exemption ($300,000) to Trust. As a result of the allocation, the applicable fraction with respect to the trust is .30 [$300,000 (the amount of GST tax exemption allocated to the trust) divided by $1,000,000 (the value of the property transferred to the trust)]. The inclusion ratio with respect to the trust is .70 [1-.30]. On June 1, 2007, the trustee determines that it is in the best interest of the beneficiaries to sever Trust to provide a separate trust for each of T's three grandchildren and their respective families. The trustee severs Trust into two trusts, Trust 1 and Trust 2, each with terms and beneficiaries identical to Trust and thus each providing that trust income is to be paid to S for life, trust principal may be distributed for the benefit of any or all members of the group consisting of S and T's grandchildren, and, on S's death, the trust is to terminate and the assets are to be divided equally among GC1, GC2, and GC3 (or their respective then-living descendants, per stirpes). The instrument severing Trust provides that Trust 1 is to receive 30% of Trust's assets and Trust 2 is to receive 70% of Trust's assets. Further, each such trust is to be funded with a pro rata portion of each asset held in Trust. The trustee then severs Trust 1 into three equal trusts, Trust GC1, Trust GC2, and Trust GC3. Each trust is named for a grandchild of T and provides that trust income is to be paid to S for life, trust principal may be distributed for the benefit of S and T's grandchild for whom the trust is named, and, on S's death, the trust is to terminate and the trust proceeds distributed to the respective grandchild for whom the trust is named. If that grandchild has predeceased the termination date, the trust proceeds are to be distributed to that grandchild's then-living descendants, per stirpes, or, if none, then equally to the other two trusts resulting from the severance of Trust 1. Each such resulting trust is to be funded with a pro rata portion of each Trust 1 asset. The trustee also severs Trust 2 in a similar manner, into Trust GC1(2), Trust GC2(2), and Trust GC3(2). The severance of Trust into Trust 1 and Trust 2, the severance of Trust 1 into Trust GC1, Trust GC2, Trust GC3, and the severance of Trust 2 into Trust GC1(2), Trust GC2(2) and Trust GC3(2), constitute qualified severances, provided that all other requirements of section 2642(a)(3) and this section are satisfied with respect to each severance. Trust GC1, Trust GC2, Trust GC3 will each have an inclusion ratio of zero and Trust GC1(2), Trust GC2(2), and Trust GC3(2) will each have an inclusion ratio of one.

Example (8). Qualified severance deemed to precede a taxable termination. In 2004, T establishes an inter vivos irrevocable trust (Trust) for a term of 10 years providing that Trust income is to be paid annually in equal shares to T's child C and T's grandchild GC (the child of another then-living child of T). If either C or GC dies prior to the expiration of the 10-year term, the deceased beneficiary's share of Trust's income is to be paid to that beneficiary's then-living descendants, per stirpes, for the balance of the trust term. At the expiration of the 10-year trust term, the corpus is to be distributed equally to C and GC; if either C or GC is not then living, then such decedent's share is to be distributed instead to such decedent's then-living descendants, per stirpes. T allocates T's GST tax exemption to Trust such that Trust's applicable fraction is .50 and Trust's inclusion ratio is .50 [1-.50]. In 2006, pursuant to applicable state law, the trustee severs the trust into two equal trusts, Trust 1 and Trust 2. The instrument severing Trust provides that Trust 1 is to receive 50% of the Trust assets, and Trust 2 is to receive 50% of Trust's assets. Both resulting trusts are identical to Trust, except that each has different beneficiaries: C and C's descendants are designated as the beneficiaries of Trust 1, and GC and GC's descendants are designated as the beneficiaries of Trust 2. The severance constitutes a qualified severance, provided all other requirements of section 2642(a)(3) and this section are satisfied. Because the applicable fraction with respect to Trust is .50 and Trust was severed into two equal trusts, the trustee may designate which resulting trust has an inclusion ratio of one, and which has an inclusion ratio of zero. Accordingly, in the Notice of Qualified Severance reporting the severance, the trustee designates Trust 1 as having an inclusion ratio of one, and Trust 2 as having an inclusion ratio of zero. Because Trust 2 is a skip person under section 2613, the severance of Trust resulting in the distribution of 50% of Trust's corpus to Trust 2 would constitute a taxable termination or distribution (as described in section 2612(a)) of that 50% of Trust for GST tax purposes, but for the rule that a qualified severance is deemed to precede a taxable termination that is caused by the qualified severance. Thus, no GST tax will be due with regard to the creation and funding of Trust 2 because the inclusion ratio of Trust 2 is zero.

Example (9). Regulatory qualified severance. (i) In 2004, T establishes an inter vivos irrevocable trust (Trust) providing that trust income is to be paid annually in equal shares to T's children, A and B, for 10 years. Trust provides that the trustee has discretion to make additional distributions of principal to A and B during the 10-year term without adjustments to their shares of income or the trust remainder. If either (or both) dies prior to the expiration of the 10-year term, the deceased child's share of trust income is to be paid to the child's then living descendants, per stirpes, for the balance of the trust term. At the expiration of the 10-year term, the corpus is to be distributed equally to A and B; if A and B (or either or them) is not then living, then such decedent's share is to be distributed instead to such decedent's then living descendants, per stirpes. T allocates GST tax exemption to Trust such that Trust's applicable fraction is .25 and its inclusion ratio is .75.

(ii) In 2006, pursuant to applicable state law, the trustee severs the trust into three trusts: Trust 1, Trust 2, and Trust 3. The instrument severing Trust provides that Trust 1 is to receive 50% of Trust's assets, Trust 2 is to receive 25% of Trust's assets, and Trust 3 is to receive 25% of Trust's assets. All three resulting trusts are identical to Trust, except that each has different beneficiaries: A and A's issue are designated as the beneficiaries of Trust 1, and B and B's issue are designated as the beneficiaries of Trust 2 and Trust 3. The severance constitutes a qualified severance, provided that all other requirements of section 2642(a)(3) and this section are satisfied. Trust 1 will have an inclusion ratio of 1. Because both Trust 2 and Trust 3 have each received the fractional share of Trust's assets equal to Trust's applicable fraction of .25, trustee designates that Trust 2 will have an inclusion ratio of one and that Trust 3 will have an inclusion ratio of zero.

Example (10). Beneficiary's interest dependent on inclusion ratio. On August 8, 2006, T transfers $1,000,000 to Trust and timely allocates $400,000 of T's remaining GST tax exemption to Trust. As a result of the allocation, the applicable fraction with respect to Trust is .40 [$400,000 divided by $1,000,000] and Trust's inclusion ratio is .60 [1-.40]. Trust provides that all income of Trust will be paid annually to C, T's child, for life. On C's death, the corpus is to pass in accordance with C's exercise of a testamentary limited power to appoint the corpus of Trust to C's lineal descendants. However, Trust provides that if, at the time of C's death, Trust's inclusion ratio is greater than zero, then C may also appoint that fraction of the trust corpus equal to the inclusion ratio to the creditors of C's estate. On May 3, 2008, pursuant to authority granted under applicable state law, the trustee severs Trust into two trusts. Trust 1 is funded with 40% of Trust's assets, and Trust 2 is funded with 60% of Trust's assets in accordance with the requirements of this section. Both Trust 1 and Trust 2 provide that all income of Trust will be paid annually to C during C's life. On C's death, Trust 1 corpus is to pass in accordance with C's exercise of a testamentary limited power to appoint the corpus to C's lineal descendants. Trust 2 is to pass in accordance with C's exercise of a testamentary power to appoint the corpus of Trust to C's lineal descendants and to the creditors of C's estate. The severance constitutes a qualified severance, provided that all other requirements of section 2642(a)(3) and this section are satisfied. No additional contribution or allocation of GST tax exemption is made to either Trust 1 or Trust 2 prior to C's death. Accordingly, the inclusion ratio with respect to Trust 1 is zero. The inclusion ratio with respect to Trust 2 is one until C's death, at which time C will become the transferor of Trust 2 for GST tax purposes. (Some or all of C's GST tax exemption may be allocated to Trust 2 upon C's death.)

Example (11). Date of severance. Trust is an irrevocable trust that has both skip person and non-skip person beneficiaries. Trust holds two parcels of real estate, Property A and Property B, stock in Company X, a publicly traded company, and cash. On June 16, 2008, the local court with jurisdiction over Trust issues an order, pursuant to the trustee's petition authorized under state law, severing Trust into two resulting trusts of equal value, Trust 1 and Trust 2. The court order directs that Property A will be distributed to Trust 1 and Property B will be distributed to Trust 2, and that an appropriate amount of stock and cash will be distributed to each trust such that the total value of property distributed to each trust as of the date of severance will be equal. The court order does not mandate a particular date of funding. Trustee receives notice of the court order on June 24, and selects July 16, 2008, as the date of severance. On June 26, 2008, Trustee commences the process of transferring title to Property A and Property B to the appropriate resulting trust(s), which process is completed on July 8, 2008. Also on June 26, the Trustee hires a professional appraiser to value Property A and Property B as of the date of severance and receives the appraisal report on Friday, October 3, 2008. On Monday, October 6, 2008, Trustee commences the process of transferring to Trust 1 and Trust 2 the appropriate amount of Company X stock valued as of July 16, 2008, and that transfer (as well as the transfer of Trust's cash) is completed by October 9, 2008. Under the facts presented, the funding of Trust 1 and Trust 2 occurred within 90 days of the date of severance selected by the trustee, and within a reasonable time after the date of severance taking into account the nature of the assets involved and the need to obtain an appraisal. Accordingly, the date of severance for purposes of this section is July 16, 2008, the resulting trusts are to be funded based on the value of the original trust assets as of that date, and the severance is a qualified severance assuming that all other requirements of section 2642(a)(3) and this section are met. (However, if Trust had contained only marketable securities and cash, then in order to satisfy the reasonable time requirement, the stock transfer would have to have been commenced, and generally completed, immediately after the date of severance, and the cash distribution would have to have been made at the same time.)

Example (12). Other severance that does not meet the requirements of a qualified severance. (i) In 2004, T establishes an irrevocable inter vivos trust (Trust) providing that Trust income is to be paid to T's children, A and B, in equal shares for their joint lives. Upon the death of the first to die of A and B, all Trust income will be paid to the survivor of A and B. At the death of the survivor, the corpus is to be distributed in equal shares to T's grandchildren, W and X (with any then-deceased grandchild's share being paid in accordance with that grandchild's testamentary general power of appointment). W is A's child and X is B's child. T elects under section 2632(c)(5) not to have the automatic allocation rules contained in section 2632(c) apply with respect to T's transfers to Trust, but T allocates GST tax exemption to Trust resulting in Trust having an inclusion ratio of .30.

(ii) In 2009, the trustee of Trust, as permitted by applicable state law, divides Trust into two separate trusts, Trust 1 and Trust 2. Trust 1 provides that trust income is to be paid to A for life and, on A's death, the remainder is to be distributed to W (or pursuant to W's testamentary general power of appointment). Trust 2 provides that trust income is to be paid to B for life and, on B's death, the remainder is to be distributed to X (or pursuant to X's testamentary general power of appointment). Because Trust 1 and Trust 2 do not provide A and B with the contingent survivor income interests that were provided to A and B under the terms of Trust, Trust 1 and Trust 2 do not provide for the same succession of interests in the aggregate as provided by Trust. Therefore, the severance does not satisfy the requirements of this section and is not a qualified severance. Provided that Trust 1 and Trust 2 are recognized as separate trusts under applicable state law, Trust 1 and Trust 2 will be recognized as separate trusts for GST tax purposes pursuant to paragraph (h) of this section, prospectively from the date of the severance. However, Trust 1 and Trust 2 each have an inclusion ratio of .30 immediately after the severance, the same as the inclusion ratio of Trust prior to severance.

Example (13). Qualified severance following a non-qualified severance. Assume the same facts as in Example 12, except that, as of November 4, 2010, the trustee of Trust 1 severs Trust 1 into two trusts, Trust 3 and Trust 4, in accordance with applicable local law. The instrument severing Trust 1 provides that both resulting trusts have provisions identical to Trust 1. The terms of the instrument severing Trust 1 further provide that Trust 3 is to be funded on a pro rata basis with assets having a fair market value as of the date of severance equal to 70% of the value of Trust 1's assets on that date, and Trust 4 is to be funded with assets having a fair market value as of the date of severance equal to 30% of the value of Trust 1's assets on that date. The severance constitutes a qualified severance, provided that all other requirements of section 2642(a)(3) and this section are satisfied. Trust 3 will have an inclusion ratio of zero and Trust 4 will have an inclusion ratio of one.

(k) Effective/applicability date. *(1) In general.* Except as otherwise provided in this paragraph (k), this section applies to severances occurring on or after August 2, 2007. Paragraph (d)(7)(iii), paragraph (h), and Examples 9, 12 and 13 of paragraph (j) of this section apply to severances occurring on or after September 2, 2008.

(2) Transition rule. In the case of a qualified severance occurring after December 31, 2000, and before August 2, 2007, taxpayers may rely on any reasonable interpretation of section 2642(a)(3) as long as reasonable notice concerning the qualified severance and identification of the trusts involved has been given to the IRS. For this purpose, the proposed regulations (69 FR 51967) are treated as a reasonable interpretation of the statute. For purposes of the reporting provisions of § 26.2642-6(e), notice to the IRS should be mailed by the due date of the gift tax return (including extensions granted) for gifts made during the year in which the severance occurred. If no gift tax return is filed, notice to the IRS should be mailed by April 15th of the year immediately following the year during which the severance occurred. For severances occurring between December 31, 2000, and January 1, 2007, notification should be mailed to the IRS as soon as reasonably practicable after August 2, 2007, if sufficient notice has not already been given.

T.D. 9348, 8/1/2007, amend T.D. 9421, 7/30/2008.

PAR. 3. Section 26.2642-6 is amended as follows:

1. Paragraphs (d)(4) and (d)(7) are revised.
2. Paragraph (h) is added.
3. Paragraph (j) Examples 6, 9, 12 and 13 are added.
4. Paragraph (k)(1) is revised.

The additions and revisions read as follows:

Proposed § 26.2642-6 Qualified severance. [*For Preamble, see ¶ 152,895*]

* * * * *

(d) * * *

(4) The single trust (original trust) is severed on a fractional basis, such that each new trust (resulting trust) is funded with a fraction or percentage of the original trust, and the sum of those fractions or percentages is one or one hundred percent, respectively. For this purpose, the fraction or percentage may be determined by means of a formula (for example, that fraction of the trust the numerator of which is equal to the transferor's unused GST tax exemption, and the denominator of which is the fair market value of the original trust's assets on the date of severance). The severance of a trust based on a pecuniary amount does not satisfy this requirement. For example, the severance of a trust is not a qualified severance if the trust is divided into two trusts, with one trust to be funded with $1,500,000 and the other trust to be funded with the balance of the original trust's assets. With respect to the particular assets to be distributed to each resulting trust, each resulting trust may be funded with the appropriate fraction or percentage (pro rata portion) of each asset held by the original trust. Alternatively, the assets may be divided among the resulting trusts on a non-pro rata basis, based on the fair market value of the assets on the date of severance. However, if a resulting trust is funded on a non-pro rata basis, each asset received by a resulting trust must be valued, solely for funding purposes, by multiplying the fair market value of the asset held in the original trust as of the date of severance by the fraction or percentage of that asset received by that resulting trust. Thus, the assets must be valued without taking into account any discount or premium arising from the severance, for example, any valuation discounts that might arise because the resulting trust receives less than the entire interest held by the original trust. See paragraph (j), Example 6 of this section.

* * * * *

(7) In the case of a qualified severance occurring after GST tax exemption has been allocated to the trust (whether by an affirmative allocation, a deemed allocation, or an automatic allocation pursuant to the rules contained in section 2632), if the trust has an inclusion ratio as defined in § 26.2642-1 that is greater than zero and less than one, then either paragraph (d)(7)(i) or (ii) of this section must be satisfied.

(i) The trust is severed initially into only two resulting trusts. One resulting trust must receive that fractional share of the total value of the original trust as of the date of severance that is equal to the applicable fraction, as defined in § 26.2642-1(b) and (c), used to determine the inclusion ratio of the original trust immediately before the severance. The other resulting trust must receive that fractional share of the total value of the original trust as of the date of severance that is equal to the excess of one over the fractional share described in the preceding sentence. The trust receiving the fractional share equal to the applicable fraction shall have an inclusion ratio of zero, and the other trust shall have an inclusion ratio of one. If the applicable fraction with respect to the original trust is .50, then, with respect to the two equal trusts resulting from the severance, the Trustee may designate which of the resulting trusts will have an inclusion ratio of zero and which will have an inclusion ratio of one. Each separate trust resulting from the severance then may be further divided in accordance with the rules of this section. See paragraph (j), Example 7 of this section.

(ii) The trust is severed initially into more than two resulting trusts. One or more of the resulting trusts in the aggregate must receive that fractional share of the total value of the original trust as of the date of severance that is equal to the applicable fraction used to determine the inclusion ratio of the original trust immediately before the severance. The trust or trusts receiving such fractional share shall have an inclusion ratio of zero, and each of the other resulting trust or trusts shall have an inclusion ratio of one. (If, however, two or more of the resulting trusts each receives the fractional share of the total value of the original trust equal to the applicable fraction, the trustee may designate which of those resulting trusts will have an inclusion ratio of zero and which will have an inclusion ratio of one.) The resulting trust or trusts with an inclusion ratio of one must receive in the aggregate that fractional share of the total value of the original trust as of the date of severance that is equal to the excess of one over the fractional share described in the second sentence of this paragraph. See paragraph (j), Example 9 of this section.

* * * * *

(h) Treatment of trusts resulting from a severance that is not a qualified severance. Trusts resulting from a severance (other than a severance under § 26.2654-1) that does not meet the requirements of a qualified severance under paragraph (b) of this section will be treated, after the date of severance, as separate trusts for purposes of the generation-skipping transfer (GST) tax, provided that the trusts resulting from such severance are recognized as separate trusts under applicable state law. The post-severance treatment of the resulting trusts as separate trusts for GST tax purposes generally permits the allocation of GST tax exemption, the making of various elections permitted for GST tax purposes, and the occurrence of a taxable distribution or termination with regard to a particular resulting trust, with no GST tax impact on any other trust resulting from that severance. Each trust resulting from a severance described in this paragraph, however, will have the same inclusion ratio immediately after the severance as that of the original trust immediately before the severance. (See § 26.2654-1 for the inclusion ratio of each trust resulting from a severance described in that section.)

* * * * *

(j) * * *

Example (6). Funding of severed trusts on a non-pro rata basis. T's will establishes an irrevocable trust, Trust, for the benefit of T's descendants. As a result of the allocation of GST tax exemption, the applicable fraction with respect to Trust is .60 and Trust's inclusion ratio is .40 [1-.60]. Pursuant to authority granted under applicable state law, on August 1, 2008, the trustee executes a document severing Trust into two trusts, Trust 1 and Trust 2, each of which is identical to Trust. The instrument of severance provides that the severance is intended to qualify as a qualified severance within the meaning of section 2642(a)(3) and designates August 3, 2008, as the date of severance (within the meaning of paragraph (d)(3) of this section). The instrument further provides that Trust 1 and Trust 2 are to be funded on a non-pro rata basis with Trust 1 funded with assets having a fair market value on the date of severance equal to 40% of the value of Trust's assets on that date and Trust 2 funded with assets having a fair market value equal to 60% of the value of Trust's assets on that date. The fair market value of the assets used to fund each trust is to be determined in compliance with the requirements of paragraph (d)(4) of this section. On August 3, 2008, the fair market value of the Trust assets totals $4,000,000, consisting of 52% of the outstanding common stock in Company, a closely-held corporation, valued at $3,000,000 and $1,000,000 in cash and marketable securities. Trustee proposes to divide the Company stock equally between Trust 1 and Trust 2, and thus transfer 26% of the Company stock to Trust 1 and 26% of the stock to Trust 2. In addition, the appropriate amount of cash and marketable securities will be distributed to each trust. In accordance with paragraph (d)(4) of this section, for funding purposes, the interest in the Company stock distributed to each trust is valued as a pro rata portion of the value of the 52% interest in Company held by Trust before severance, without taking into account, for example, any valuation discount that might otherwise apply in valuing the noncontrolling interest distributed to each resulting trust. Accordingly, for funding purposes, each 26% interest in Company stock distributed to Trust 1 and Trust 2 is valued at $1,500,000 (.5 x $3,000,000). Therefore, Trust 1, which is to be funded with $1,600,000 (.40 x $4,000,000), receives $100,000 in cash and marketable securities valued as of August 3, 2008, in addition to the Company stock, and Trust 2, which is to be funded with $2,400,000 (.60 x $4,000,000), receives $900,000 in cash and marketable securities in addition to the Company stock. Therefore, the severance is a qualified severance, provided that all other requirements of section 2642(a)(3) and this section are satisfied.

* * * * *

Example (9). Regulatory qualified severance. In 2004, T establishes an inter vivos irrevocable trust (Trust) providing that Trust income is to be paid annually in equal shares to T's children, A and B, for 10 years. If either (or both) dies prior to the expiration of the 10-year term, the deceased child's share of trust income is to be paid to the child's then living descendants, per stirpes, for the balance of the trust term. At the expiration of the 10-year trust term, the corpus is to be distributed equally to A and B; if A and B (or either or them) is not then living, then such decedent's share is to be distributed instead to such decedent's then living descendants, per stirpes. T allocates GST tax exemption to Trust such that Trust's applicable fraction is .25 and its inclusion ratio is .75. In 2006, pursuant to applicable state law, the trustee severs the trust into three trusts: Trust 1, Trust 2, and Trust 3. The instrument severing Trust provides that Trust 1 is to receive 50% of Trust's assets, Trust 2 is to receive 25% of Trust's assets, and Trust 3 is to receive 25% of Trust's assets. All three resulting trusts are identical to Trust, except that each has different beneficiaries: A and A's issue are designated as the beneficiaries of Trust 1, and B and B's issue are designated as the beneficiaries of Trust 2 and Trust 3. The severance constitutes a qualified severance, provided that all other requirements of section 2642(a)(3) and this section are satisfied. Trust 1 will have an inclusion ratio of 1. Because both Trust 2 and Trust 3 have each received the fractional share of Trust's assets equal to Trust's applicable fraction of .25, trustee designates that Trust 2 will have an inclusion ratio of one and that Trust 3 will have an inclusion ratio of zero.

* * * * *

Example (12). Mandatory severance that does not qualify as a qualified severance. In 1996, T creates an irrevocable inter vivos trust (Trust) that provides the trustee with the discretionary power to distribute income or corpus from time to time to one or more of T's children and grandchildren. Trust provides that, when T's youngest child reaches age 30, Trust is to be divided equally into separate trusts (resulting trusts), with one resulting trust for each child of T who is then living, and one resulting trust for each child of T who is then deceased and who has then living descendants. The income from a child's resulting trust will be paid to that child during the child's life, with the remainder passing to such child's descendants (grandchildren and younger generation descendants of T). On a timely filed Form 709, "United States Gift (and Generation-Skipping Transfer) Tax Return," reporting the transfer, T allocates all of T's remaining GST tax exemption to Trust. As a result of the allocation, the applicable fraction with respect to Trust is .20, so Trust's inclusion ratio is .80 [1 -.20]. T's youngest child reaches age 30 in 2008. (No additional gifts are made through 2008 and Trust's inclusion ratio does not change.) In accordance with

Trust's terms, Trust is divided in 2008 into three separate trusts (Trust 1, Trust 2, and Trust 3), one trust for each of T's three children, each of whom is then living. Trust 1, Trust 2, and Trust 3 are each recognized as a separate trust under applicable state law. With the consent of all interested parties, each resulting trust is funded with assets different from the assets distributed to the other two resulting trusts in a manner that does not meet the requirements of paragraph (d)(3) of this section. As a result, the severance does not satisfy the requirements of a qualified severance under this section. Under paragraph (h) of this section, however, Trust 1, Trust 2, and Trust 3 are each recognized as a separate trust for GST tax purposes prospectively from the date of severance, because the severance was effective to create three separate trusts under applicable state law. Therefore, after the severance, if T becomes entitled to any additional GST tax exemption pursuant to subsequent changes in applicable Federal tax law, T may allocate that additional GST tax exemption to any one or more of these three resulting trusts. Because the severance is not a qualified severance, however, the inclusion ratio of each of the three new trusts immediately after the severance will be .80, the same as Trust's inclusion ratio immediately before the severance.

Example (13). Other severance that does not qualify as a qualified severance. In 2004, T establishes an irrevocable inter vivos trust (Trust) providing that Trust income is to be paid to T's children, A and B, in equal shares for their joint lives. Upon the death of the first to die of A and B, all Trust income will be paid to the survivor of A and B. At the death of the survivor, the corpus is to be distributed in equal shares to T's grandchildren, W and X (with any then-deceased grandchild's share being paid in accordance with that grandchild's testamentary general power of appointment). W is A's child and X is B's child. T elects under section 2632(c)(5) not to have the automatic allocation rules contained in section 2632(c) apply with respect to T's transfers to Trust, and T does not otherwise allocate GST tax exemption to Trust. In 2006, the trustee of Trust, as permitted by applicable state law, divides Trust into two separate trusts, Trust 1 and Trust 2. Trust 1 provides that trust income is to be paid to A for life and, on A's death, the remainder is to be distributed to W (or pursuant to W's testamentary general power of appointment). Trust 2 provides that trust income is to be paid to B for life and, on B's death, the remainder is to be distributed to X (or pursuant to X's testamentary general power of appointment). Because Trust 1 and Trust 2 do not provide A and B with the contingent survivor income interests that were provided to A and B under the terms of Trust, Trust 1 and Trust 2 do not provide for the same succession of interests in the aggregate as provided by Trust. Therefore, the severance does not satisfy the requirements of this section and is not a qualified severance. However, under paragraph (h) of this section, provided that Trust 1 and Trust 2 are recognized as separate trusts under applicable state law, Trust 1 and Trust 2 will be recognized as separate trusts for GST tax purposes, prospectively from the date of the severance. Trust 1 and Trust 2 each have the same inclusion ratio immediately after the severance as Trust's inclusion ratio immediately before the severance.

(k) * * * *(1) In general.* Except as otherwise provided, this section applies to severances occurring on or after August 2, 2007. Paragraph (d)(7)(ii), paragraph (h), and Examples 9, 12, and 13 of paragraph (j) of this section apply to severances occurring on or after August 2, 2007. Paragraph (d)(4) and Example 6 of paragraph (j) apply to severances occurring on or after August 2, 2007.

Proposed § 26.2642-7 Relief under section 2642(g)(1).
[*For Preamble, see ¶ 152,987*]

(a) In general. Under section 2642(g)(1)(A), the Secretary has the authority to issue regulations describing the circumstances in which a transferor, as defined in section 2652(a), or the executor of a transferor's estate, as defined in section 2203, will be granted an extension of time to allocate generation-skipping transfer (GST) exemption as described in sections 2642(b)(1) and (2). The Secretary also has the authority to issue regulations describing the circumstances under which a transferor or the executor of a transferor's estate will be granted an extension of time to make the elections described in section 2632(b)(3) and (c)(5). Section 2632(b)(3) provides that an election may be made by or on behalf of a transferor not to have the transferor's GST exemption automatically allocated under section 2632(b)(1) to a direct skip, as defined in section 2612(c), made by the transferor during life. Section 2632(c)(5)(A)(i) provides that an election may be made by or on behalf of a transferor not to have the transferor's GST exemption automatically allocated under section 2632(c)(1) to an indirect skip, as defined in section 2632(c)(3)(A), or to any or all transfers made by such transferor to a particular trust. Section 2632(c)(5)(A)(ii) provides that an election may be made by or on behalf of a transferor to treat any trust as a GST trust, as defined in section 2632(c)(3)(B), for purposes of section 2632(c) with respect to any or all transfers made by that transferor to the trust. This section generally describes the factors that the Internal Revenue Service (IRS) will consider when an extension of time is sought by or on behalf of a transferor to timely allocate GST exemption and/or to make an election under section 2632(b)(3) or (c)(5). Relief provided under this section will be granted through the IRS letter ruling program. See paragraph (h) of this section.

(b) Effect of Relief. If an extension of time to allocate GST exemption is granted under this section, the allocation of GST exemption will be considered effective as of the date of the transfer, and the value of the property transferred for purposes of chapter 11 or chapter 12 will determine the amount of GST exemption to be allocated. If an extension of time to elect out of the automatic allocation of GST exemption under section 2632(b)(3) or (c)(5) is granted under this section, the election will be considered effective as of the date of the transfer. If an extension of time to elect to treat any trust as a GST trust under section 2632(c)(5)(A)(ii) is granted under this section, the election will be considered effective as of the date of the first (or each) transfer covered by that election.

(c) Limitation on relief. The amount of GST exemption that may be allocated to a transfer as the result of relief granted under this section is limited to the amount of the transferor's unused GST exemption under section 2631(c) as of the date of the transfer. Thus, if, by the time of the making of the allocation or election pursuant to relief granted under this section, the GST exemption amount under section 2631(c) has increased to an amount in excess of the amount in effect for the date of the transfer, no portion of the increased amount may be applied to that earlier transfer by reason of the relief granted under this section.

(d) Basis for determination. *(1) In general.* Requests for relief under this section will be granted when the transferor or the executor of the transferor's estate provides evidence (including the affidavits described in paragraph (h) of this section) to establish to the satisfaction of the IRS that the transferor or the executor of the transferor's estate acted reasonably and in good faith, and that the grant of relief will not prejudice the interests of the Government. Paragraphs (d)(2) and (d)(3) of this section set forth nonexclusive lists of factors the IRS will consider in determining whether this standard of reasonableness, good faith, and lack of prejudice to the interests of the Government has been met so that such relief will be granted. In making this determination, IRS will consider these factors, as well as all other relevant facts and circumstances. Paragraph (e) of this section sets forth situations in which this standard has not been met and, as a result, in which relief under this section will not be granted.

(2) Reasonableness and good faith. The following is a nonexclusive list of factors that will be considered to determine whether the transferor or the executor of the transferor's estate acted reasonably and in good faith for purposes of this section:

(i) The intent of the transferor to timely allocate GST exemption to a transfer or to timely make an election under section 2632(b)(3) or (c)(5), as evidenced in the trust instrument, the instrument of transfer, or other relevant documents contemporaneous with the transfer, such as Federal gift and estate tax returns and correspondence. This may include evidence of the intended GST tax status of the transfer or the trust (for example, exempt, non-exempt, or partially exempt), or more explicit evidence of intent with regard to the allocation of GST exemption or the election under section 2632(b)(3) or (c)(5).

(ii) Intervening events beyond the control of the transferor or of the executor of the transferor's estate as the cause of the failure to allocate GST exemption to a transfer or the failure to make an election under section 2632(b)(3) or (c)(5).

(iii) Lack of awareness by the transferor or the executor of the transferor's estate of the need to allocate GST exemption to the transfer, despite the exercise of reasonable diligence, taking into account the experience of the transferor or the executor of the transferor's estate and the complexity of the GST issue, as the cause of the failure to allocate GST exemption to a transfer or to make an election under section 2632(b)(3) or (c)(5).

(iv) Consistency by the transferor with regard to the allocation of the transferor's GST exemption (for example, the transferor's consistent allocation of GST exemption to transfers to skip persons or to a particular trust, or the transferor's consistent election not to have the automatic allocation of GST exemption apply to transfers to one or more trusts or skip persons pursuant to section 2632(b)(3) or (c)(5)). Evidence of consistency may be less relevant if there has been a change of circumstances or change of trust beneficiaries that would otherwise explain a deviation from prior GST exemption allocation decisions.

(v) Reasonable reliance by the transferor or the executor of the transferor's estate on the advice of a qualified tax professional retained or employed by one or both of them and, in reliance on or consistent with that advice, the failure of the transferor or the executor to allocate GST exemption to the transfer or to make an election described in section 2632(b)(3) or (c)(5). Reliance on a qualified tax professional will not be considered to have been reasonable if the transferor or the executor of the transferor's estate knew or should have known that the professional either—

(A) Was not competent to render advice on the GST exemption; or

(B) Was not aware of all relevant facts.

(3) Prejudice to the interests of the Government. The following is a nonexclusive list of factors that will be considered to determine whether the interests of the Government would be prejudiced for purposes of this section:

(i) The interests of the Government would be prejudiced to the extent to which the request for relief is an effort to benefit from hindsight. The interests of the Government would be prejudiced if the IRS determines that the requested relief is an attempt to benefit from hindsight rather than to achieve the result the transferor or the executor of the transferor's estate intended at the time when the transfer was made. A factor relevant to this determination is whether the grant of the requested relief would permit an economic advantage or other benefit that would not have been available if the allocation or election had been timely made. Similarly, there would be prejudice if a grant of the requested relief would permit an economic advantage or other benefit that results from the selection of one out of a number of alternatives (other than whether or not to make an allocation or election) that were available at the time the allocation or election could have been timely made, if hindsight makes the selected alternative more beneficial than the other alternatives. Finally, in a situation where the only choices were whether or not to make a timely allocation or election, prejudice would exist if the transferor failed to make the allocation or election in order to wait to see (thus, with the benefit of hindsight) whether or not the making of the allocation of exemption or election would be more beneficial.

(ii) The timing of the request for relief will be considered in determining whether the interests of the Government would be prejudiced by granting relief under this section. The interests of the Government would be prejudiced if the transferor or the executor of the transferor's estate delayed the filing of the request for relief with the intent to deprive the IRS of sufficient time to challenge the claimed identity of the transferor of the transferred property that is the subject of the request for relief, the value of that transferred property for Federal gift or estate tax purposes, or any other aspect of the transfer that is relevant for Federal gift or estate tax purposes. The fact that any period of limitations on the assessment or collection of transfer taxes has expired prior to the filing of a request for relief under this section, however, will not by itself prohibit a grant of relief under this section. Similarly, the combination of the expiration of any such period of limitations with the fact that the asset or interest was valued for transfer tax purposes with the use of a valuation discount will not by itself prohibit a grant of relief under this section.

(iii) The occurrence and effect of an intervening taxable termination or taxable distribution will be considered in determining whether the interests of the Government would be prejudiced by granting relief under this section. The interests of the Government may be prejudiced if a taxable termination or taxable distribution occurred between the time for making a timely allocation of GST exemption or a timely election described in section 2632(b)(3) or (c)(5) and the time at which the request for relief under this section was filed. The impact of a grant of relief on (and the difficulty of adjusting) the GST tax consequences of that intervening termination or distribution will be considered in determining whether the occurrence of a taxable termination or taxable distribution constitutes prejudice.

(e) Situations in which the standard of reasonableness, good faith, and lack of prejudice to the interests of the Government has not been met. Relief under this section will not be granted if the IRS determines that the transferor or the executor of the transferor's estate has not acted reasonably and in good faith, and/or that the grant of relief would prejudice the interests of the Government. The following situations provide illustrations of some circumstances under which the standard of reasonableness, good faith, and lack of prejudice to the interests of the Government has not been met, and as a result, in which relief under this section will not be granted:

(1) Timely allocations and elections. Relief will not be granted under this section to decrease or revoke a timely allocation of GST exemption as described in § 26.2632-1(b)(4)(ii)(A)(1), or to revoke an election under section 2632(b)(3) or (c)(5) made on a timely filed Federal gift or estate tax return.

(2) Timing. Relief will not be granted if the transferor or executor delayed the filing of the request for relief with the intent to deprive the IRS of sufficient time to challenge the claimed identity of the transferor or the valuation of the transferred property for Federal gift or estate tax purposes. (However, see paragraph (d)(3)(ii) of this section for examples of facts which alone do not constitute prejudice.)

(3) Failure after being accurately informed. Relief will not be granted under this section if the decision made by the transferor or the executor of the transferor's estate (who had been accurately informed in all material respects by a qualified tax professional retained or employed by either (or both) of them with regard to the allocation of GST exemption or an election described in section 2632(b)(3) or (c)(5)) was reflected or implemented by the action or inaction that is the subject of the request for relief.

(4) Hindsight. Relief under this section will not be granted if the IRS determines that the requested relief is an attempt to benefit from hindsight rather than an attempt to achieve the result the transferor or the executor of the transferor's estate intended when the transfer was made. One factor that will be relevant to this determination is whether the grant of relief will give the transferor the benefit of hindsight by providing an economic advantage that may not have been available if the allocation or election had been timely made. Thus, relief will not be granted if that relief will shift GST exemption from one trust to another trust unless the beneficiaries of the two trusts, and their respective interests in those trusts, are the same. Similarly, relief will not be granted if there is evidence that the transferor or executor had not made a timely allocation of the exemption in order to determine which of the various trusts achieved the greatest asset appreciation before selecting the trust that should have a zero inclusion ratio.

(f) Period of limitations under section 6501. A request for relief under this section does not reopen, suspend, or extend the period of limitations on assessment or collection of any estate, gift, or GST tax under section 6501. Thus, the IRS may request that the transferor or the transferor's executor consent, under section 6501(c)(4), to an extension of the period of limitation on assessment or collection of any or all gift and GST taxes for the transfer(s) that are the subject of the requested relief. The transferor or the transferor's executor has the right to refuse to extend the period of limitations, or to limit such extension to particular issues or to a particular period of time. See section 6501(c)(4)(B).

(g) Refunds. The filing of a request for relief under section 2642(g)(1) with the IRS does not constitute a claim for refund or credit of an overpayment and no implied right to refund will arise from the filing of such a request for relief. Similarly, the filing of such a request for relief does not extend the period of limitations under section 6511 for filing a claim for refund or credit of an overpayment. In the event the grant of relief under section 2642(g)(1) results in a potential claim for refund or credit of an overpayment, no such refund or credit will be allowed to the taxpayer or to the taxpayer's estate if the period of limitations under section 6511 for filing a claim for a refund or credit of the Federal gift, estate, or GST tax that was reduced by the granted relief has expired. The period of limitations under section 6511 is generally the later of three years from the time the original return is filed or two years from the time the tax was paid. If the IRS and the taxpayer agree to extend the period for assessment of tax, the period for filing a claim for refund or credit will be extended. Section 6511(c). The taxpayer or the taxpayer's estate is responsible for preserving any potential claim for refund or credit. A taxpayer who seeks and is granted relief under section 2642(g)(1) will not be regarded as having filed a claim for refund or credit by requesting such relief. In order to preserve a right of refund or credit, the taxpayer or the executor of the taxpayer's estate also must file before the expiration of the period of limitations under section 6511 for filing such a claim any required forms for requesting a refund or credit in accordance with the instructions to such forms and applicable regulations.

(h) Procedural requirements. *(1) Letter ruling program.* The relief described in this section is provided through the IRS's private letter ruling program. See Revenue Procedure 2008-1 (2008-1 IRB 1), or its successor, (which are available at http://www.irs.gov). Requests for relief under this section that do not meet the requirements of § 301.9100-2 of this chapter must be made under the rules of this section.

(2) Affidavit and declaration of transferor or the executor of the transferor's estate. (i) The transferor or the executor of the transferor's estate must submit a detailed affidavit describing the events that led to the failure to timely allocate GST exemption to a transfer or the failure to timely elect under section 2632(b)(3) or (c)(5), and the events that led to the discovery of the failure. If the transferor or the executor of the transferor's estate relied on a tax professional for advice with respect to the allocation or election, the affidavit must describe—

(A) The scope of the engagement;

(B) The responsibilities the transferor or the executor of the transferor's estate believed the professional had assumed, if any; and

(C) The extent to which the transferor or the executor of the transferor's estate relied on the professional.

(ii) Attached to each affidavit must be copies of any writing (including, without limitation, notes and e-mails) and other contemporaneous documents within the possession of the affiant relevant to the transferor's intent with regard to the application of GST tax to the transaction for which relief under this section is being requested.

(iii) The affidavit must be accompanied by a dated declaration, signed by the transferor or the executor of the transferor's estate that states: "Under penalties of perjury, I declare that I have examined this affidavit, including any attachments thereto, and to the best of my knowledge and belief, this affidavit, including any attachments thereto, is true, correct, and complete. In addition, under penalties of perjury, I declare that I have examined all the documents included as part of this request for relief, and, to the best of my knowledge and belief, these documents collectively contain all the relevant facts relating to the request for relief, and such facts are true, correct, and complete."

(3) Affidavits and declarations from other parties. (i) The transferor or the executor of the transferor's estate must submit detailed affidavits from individuals who have knowledge

or information about the events that led to the failure to allocate GST exemption or to elect under section 2632(b)(3) or (c)(5), and/or to the discovery of the failure. These individuals may include individuals whose knowledge or information is not within the personal knowledge of the transferor or the executor of the transferor's estate. The individuals described in paragraph (h)(3)(i) of this section must include—

(A) Each agent or legal representative of the transferor who participated in the transaction and/or the preparation of the return for which relief is being requested;

(B) The preparer of the relevant Federal estate and/or gift tax return(s);

(C) Each individual (including an employee of the transferor or the executor of the transferor's estate) who made a substantial contribution to the preparation of the relevant Federal estate and/or gift tax return(s); and

(D) Each tax professional who advised or was consulted by the transferor or the executor of the transferor's estate with regard to any aspect of the transfer, the trust, the allocation of GST exemption, and/or the election under section 2632(b)(3) or (c)(5).

(ii) Each affidavit must describe the scope of the engagement and the responsibilities of the individual as well as the advice or service(s) the individual provided to the transferor or the executor of the transferor's estate.

(iii) Attached to each affidavit must be copies of any writing (including, without limitation, notes and e-mails) and other contemporaneous documents within the possession of the affiant relevant to the transferor's intent with regard to the application of GST tax to the transaction for which relief under this section is being requested.

(iv) Each affidavit also must include the name, and current address of the individual, and be accompanied by a dated declaration, signed by the individual that states: "Under penalties of perjury, I declare that I have personal knowledge of the information set forth in this affidavit, including any attachments thereto. In addition, under penalties of perjury, I declare that I have examined this affidavit, including any attachments thereto, and, to the best of my knowledge and belief, the affidavit contains all the relevant facts of which I am aware relating to the request for relief filed by or on behalf of [transferor or the executor of the transferor's estate], and such facts are true, correct, and complete."

(v) If an individual who would be required to provide an affidavit under paragraph (h)(3)(i) of this section has died or is not competent, the affidavit required under paragraph (h)(2) of this section must include a statement to that effect, as well as a statement describing the relationship between that individual and the transferor or the executor of the transferor's estate and the information or knowledge the transferor or the executor of the transferor's estate believes that individual had about the transfer, the trust, the allocation of exemption, or the election. If an individual who would be required to provide an affidavit under paragraph (h)(3)(i) of this section refuses to provide the transferor or the executor of the transferor's estate with such an affidavit, the affidavit required under paragraph (h)(2) of this section must include a statement that the individual has refused to provide the affidavit, a description of the efforts made to obtain the affidavit from the individual, the information or knowledge the transferor or the executor of the transferor's estate believes the individual had about the transfer, and the relationship between the individual and the transferor or the executor of the transferor's estate.

(i) Effective/applicability date. Section 26.2642-7 applies to requests for relief filed on or after the date of publication of the Treasury decision adopting these proposed rules as final regulations in the Federal Register.

§ 26.2651-1 Generation assignment.

(a) Special rule for persons with a deceased parent. *(1) In general.* This paragraph (a) applies for purposes of determining whether a transfer to or for the benefit of an individual who is a descendant of a parent of the transferor (or the transferor's spouse or former spouse) is a generation-skipping transfer. If that individual's parent, who is a lineal descendant of the parent of the transferor (or the transferor's spouse or former spouse), is deceased at the time the transfer (from which an interest of such individual is established or derived) is subject to the tax imposed on the transferor by chapter 11 or 12 of the Internal Revenue Code, the individual is treated as if that individual were a member of the generation that is one generation below the lower of—

(i) The transferor's generation; or

(ii) The generation assignment of the individual's youngest living lineal ancestor who is also a descendant of the parent of the transferor (or the transferor's spouse or former spouse).

(2) Special rules. (i) Corresponding generation adjustment. If an individual's generation assignment is adjusted with respect to a transfer in accordance with paragraph (a)(1) of this section, a corresponding adjustment with respect to that transfer is made to the generation assignment of each—

(A) Spouse or former spouse of that individual;

(B) Descendant of that individual; and

(C) Spouse or former spouse of each descendant of that individual.

(ii) Continued application of generation assignment. If a transfer to a trust would be a generation-skipping transfer but for paragraph (a)(1) of this section, any generation assignment determined under this paragraph (a) continues to apply in determining whether any subsequent distribution from (or termination of an interest in) the portion of the trust attributable to that transfer is a generation-skipping transfer.

(iii) Ninety-day rule. For purposes of paragraph (a)(1) of this section, any individual who dies no later than 90 days after a transfer occurring by reason of the death of the transferor is treated as having predeceased the transferor.

(iv) Local law. A living person is not treated as having predeceased the transferor solely by reason of a provision of applicable local law; e.g., an individual who disclaims is not treated as a predeceased parent solely because state law treats a disclaimant as having predeceased the transferor for purposes of determining the disposition of the disclaimed property.

(3) Established or derived. For purposes of section 2651(e) and paragraph (a)(1) of this section, an individual's interest is established or derived at the time the transferor is subject to transfer tax on the property. See § 26.2652-1(a) for the definition of a transferor. If the same transferor, on more than one occasion, is subject to transfer tax imposed by either chapter 11 or 12 of the Internal Revenue Code on the property so transferred (whether the same property, reinvestments thereof, income thereon, or any or all of these), then the relevant time for determining whether paragraph (a)(1) of this section applies is the earliest time at which the transferor is subject to the tax imposed by either chapter 11 or 12 of the Internal Revenue Code. For purposes of section 2651(e) and paragraph (a)(1) of this section, the interest of a

remainder beneficiary of a trust for which an election under section 2523(f) or section 2056(b)(7) (QTIP election) has been made will be deemed to have been established or derived, to the extent of the QTIP election, on the date as of which the value of the trust corpus is first subject to tax under section 2519 or section 2044. The preceding sentence does not apply to a trust, however, to the extent that an election under section 2652(a)(3) (reverse QTIP election) has been made for the trust because, to the extent of a reverse QTIP election, the spouse who established the trust will remain the transferor of the trust for generation-skipping transfer tax purposes.

(4) Special rule in the case of additional contributions to a trust. If a transferor referred to in paragraph (a)(1) of this section contributes additional property to a trust that existed before the application of paragraph (a)(1), then the additional property is treated as being held in a separate trust for purposes of chapter 13 of the Internal Revenue Code. The provisions of § 26.2654-1(a)(2), regarding treatment as separate trusts, apply as if different transferors had contributed to the separate portions of the single trust. Additional subsequent contributions from that transferor will be added to the new share that is treated as a separate trust.

(b) Limited application to collateral heirs. Paragraph (a) of this section does not apply in the case of a transfer to any individual who is not a lineal descendant of the transferor (or the transferor's spouse or former spouse) if the transferor has any living lineal descendant at the time of the transfer.

(c) Examples. The following examples illustrate the provisions of this section:

Example (1). T establishes an irrevocable trust, Trust, providing that trust income is to be paid to T's grandchild, GC, for 5 years. At the end of the 5-year period or on GC's prior death, Trust is to terminate and the principal is to be distributed to GC if GC is living or to GC's children if GC has died. The transfer that occurred on the creation of the trust is subject to the tax imposed by chapter 12 of the Internal Revenue Code and, at the time of the transfer, T's child, C, who is a parent of GC, is deceased. GC is treated as a member of the generation that is one generation below T's generation. As a result, GC is not a skip person and Trust is not a skip person. Therefore, the transfer to Trust is not a direct skip. Similarly, distributions to GC during the term of Trust and at the termination of Trust will not be GSTs.

Example (2). On January 1, 2004, T transfers $100,000 to an irrevocable inter vivos trust that provides T with an annuity payable for four years or until T's prior death. The annuity satisfies the definition of a qualified interest under section 2702(b). When the trust terminates, the corpus is to be paid to T's grandchild, GC. The transfer is subject to the tax imposed by chapter 12 of the Internal Revenue Code and, at the time of the transfer, T's child, C, who is a parent of GC, is living. C dies in 2006. In this case, C was alive at the time the transfer by T was subject to the tax imposed by chapter 12 of the Internal Revenue Code. Therefore, section 2651(e) and paragraph (a)(1) of this section do not apply. When the trust subsequently terminates, the distribution to GC is a taxable termination that is subject to the GST tax to the extent the trust has an inclusion ratio greater than zero. See section 2642(a).

Example (3). T dies testate in 2002, survived by T's spouse, S, their children, C1 and C2, and C1's child, GC. Under the terms of T's will, a trust is established for the benefit of S and of T and S's descendants. Under the terms of the trust, all income is payable to S during S's lifetime and the trustee may distribute trust corpus for S's health, support and maintenance. At S's death, the corpus is to be distributed, outright, to C1 and C2. If either C1 or C2 has predeceased S, the deceased child's share of the corpus is to be distributed to that child's then-living descendants, per stirpes. The executor of T's estate makes the election under section 2056(b)(7) to treat the trust property as qualified terminable interest property (QTIP) but does not make the election under section 2652(a)(3) (reverse QTIP election). In 2003, C1 dies survived by S and GC. In 2004, S dies, and the trust terminates. The full fair market value of the trust is includible in S's gross estate under section 2044 and S becomes the transferor of the trust under section 2652(a)(1)(A). GC's interest is considered established or derived at S's death, and because C1 is deceased at that time, GC is treated as a member of the generation that is one generation below the generation of the transferor, S. As a result, GC is not a skip person and the transfer to GC is not a direct skip.

Example (4). The facts are the same as in Example 3. However, the executor of T's estate makes the election under section 2652(a)(3) (reverse QTIP election) for the entire trust. Therefore, T remains the transferor because, for purposes of chapter 13 of the Internal Revenue Code, the election to be treated as qualified terminable interest property is treated as if it had not been made. In this case, GC's interest is established or derived on T's death in 2002. Because C1 was living at the time of T's death, the predeceased parent rule under section 2651(e) does not apply, even though C1 was deceased at the time the transfer from S to GC was subject to the tax under chapter 11 of the Internal Revenue Code. When the trust terminates, the distribution to GC is a taxable termination that is subject to the GST tax to the extent the trust has an inclusion ratio greater than zero. See section 2642(a).

Example (5). T establishes an irrevocable trust providing that trust income is to be paid to T's grandniece, GN, for 5 years or until GN's prior death. At the end of the 5-year period or on GN's prior death, the trust is to terminate and the principal is to be distributed to GN if living, or if GN has died, to GN's then-living descendants, per stirpes. S is a sibling of T and the parent of N. N is the parent of GN. At the time of the transfer, T has no living lineal descendant, S is living, N is deceased, and the transfer is subject to the gift tax imposed by chapter 12 of the Internal Revenue Code. GN is treated as a member of the generation that is one generation below T's generation because S, GN's youngest living lineal ancestor who is also a descendant of T's parent, is in T's generation. As a result, GN is not a skip person and the transfer to the trust is not a direct skip. In addition, distributions to GN during the term of the trust and at the termination of the trust will not be GSTs.

Example (6). On January 1, 2004, T transfers $50,000 to a great-grandniece, GGN, who is the great-grandchild of B, a brother of T. At the time of the transfer, T has no living lineal descendants and B's grandchild, GN, who is a parent of GGN and a child of B's living child, N, is deceased. GGN will be treated as a member of the generation that is one generation below the lower of T's generation or the generation assignment of GGN's youngest living lineal ancestor who is also a descendant of the parent of the transferor. In this case, N is GGN's youngest living lineal ancestor who is also a descendant of the parent of T. Because N's generation assignment is lower than T's generation, GGN will be treated as a member of the generation that is one generation below N's generation assignment (i.e., GGN will be treated as a member of her parent's generation). As a result, GGN remains a skip person and the transfer to GGN is a direct skip.

Example (7). T has a child, C. C and C's spouse, S, have a 20-year-old child, GC. C dies and S subsequently marries S2. S2 legally adopts GC. T transfers $100,000 to GC. Under section 2651(b)(1), GC is assigned to the generation that is two generations below T. However, since GC's parent, C, is deceased at the time of the transfer, GC will be treated as a member of the generation that is one generation below T. As a result, GC is not a skip person and the transfer to GC is not a direct skip.

T.D. 9214, 7/15/2005.

§ 26.2651-2 Individual assigned to more than 1 generation.

(a) In general. Except as provided in paragraph (b) or (c) of this section, an individual who would be assigned to more than 1 generation is assigned to the youngest of the generations to which that individual would be assigned.

(b) Exception. Notwithstanding paragraph (a) of this section, an adopted individual (as defined in this paragraph) will be treated as a member of the generation that is one generation below the adoptive parent for purposes of determining whether a transfer to the adopted individual from the adoptive parent (or the spouse or former spouse of the adoptive parent, or a lineal descendant of a grandparent of the adoptive parent) is subject to chapter 13 of the Internal Revenue Code. For purposes of this paragraph (b), an adopted individual is an individual who is—

(1) Legally adopted by the adoptive parent;

(2) A descendant of a parent of the adoptive parent (or the spouse or former spouse of the adoptive parent);

(3) Under the age of 18 at the time of the adoption; and

(4) Not adopted primarily for the purpose of avoiding GST tax. The determination of whether an adoption is primarily for GST tax-avoidance purposes is made based upon all of the facts and circumstances. The most significant factor is whether there is a bona fide parent/child relationship between the adoptive parent and the adopted individual, in which the adoptive parent has fully assumed all significant responsibilities for the care and raising of the adopted child. Other factors may include (but are not limited to), at the time of the adoption—

(i) The age of the adopted individual (for example, the younger the age of the adopted individual, or the age of the youngest of siblings who are all adopted together, the more likely the adoption will not be considered primarily for GST tax-avoidance purposes); and

(ii) The relationship between the adopted individual and the individual's parents (for example, objective evidence of the absence or incapacity of the parents may indicate that the adoption is not primarily for GST tax-avoidance purposes).

(c) Special rules. *(1) Corresponding generation adjustment.* If an individual's generation assignment is adjusted with respect to a transfer in accordance with paragraph (b) of this section, a corresponding adjustment with respect to that transfer is made to the generation assignment of each—

(i) Spouse or former spouse of that individual;

(ii) Descendant of that individual; and

(iii) Spouse or former spouse of each descendant of that individual.

(2) Continued application of generation assignment. If a transfer to a trust would be a generation-skipping transfer but for paragraph (b) of this section, any generation assignment determined under paragraph (b) or (c) of this section continues to apply in determining whether any subsequent distribution from (or termination of an interest in) the portion of the trust attributable to that transfer is a generation-skipping transfer.

(d) Example. The following example illustrates the provisions of this section:

Example. T has a child, C. C has a 20-year-old child, GC. T legally adopts GC and transfers $100,000 to GC. GC's generation assignment is determined by section 2651(b)(1) and GC is assigned to the generation that is two generations below T. In addition, because T has legally adopted GC, GC is generally treated as a child of T under state law. Under these circumstances, GC is an individual who is assigned to more than one generation and the exception in § 26.2651-2(b) does not apply. Thus, the special rule under section 2651(f)(1) applies and GC is assigned to the generation that is two generations below T. GC remains a skip person with respect to T and the transfer to GC is a direct skip.

T.D. 9214, 7/15/2005.

§ 26.2651-3 Effective dates.

(a) In general. The rules of §§ 26.2651-3 and 26.2651-2 are applicable for terminations, distributions, and transfers occurring on or after July 18, 2005.

(b) Transition rule. In the case of transfers occurring after December 31, 1997, and before July 18, 2005, taxpayers may rely on any reasonable interpretation of section 2651(e). For this purpose, these final regulations, as well as the proposed regulations issued on September 3, 2004, (69 FR 53862) are treated as a reasonable interpretation of the statute.

T.D. 9214, 7/15/2005.

§ 26.2652-1 Transferor defined; other definitions.

Caution: The Treasury has not yet amended Reg § 26.2652-1 to reflect changes made by P.L. 105-34.

(a) Transferor defined. *(1) In general.* Except as otherwise provided in paragraph (a)(3) of this section, the individual with respect to whom property was most recently subject to Federal estate or gift tax is the transferor of that property for purposes of chapter 13. An individual is treated as transferring any property with respect to which the individual is the transferor. Thus, an individual may be a transferor even though there is no transfer of property under local law at the time the Federal estate or gift tax applies. For purposes of this paragraph, a surviving spouse is the transferor of a qualified domestic trust created by the deceased spouse that is included in the surviving spouse's gross estate, provided the trust is not subject to the election described in § 26.2652-2 (reverse QTIP election). A surviving spouse is also the transferor of a qualified domestic trust created by the surviving spouse pursuant to section 2056(d)(2)(B).

(2) Transfers subject to federal estate or gift tax. For purposes of this chapter, a transfer is subject to Federal gift tax if a gift tax is imposed under section 2501(a) (without regard to exemptions, exclusions, deductions, and credits). A transfer is subject to Federal estate tax if the value of the property is includible in the decedent's gross estate as determined under section 2031 or section 2103.

(3) Special rule for certain QTIP trusts. Solely for purposes of chapter 13, if a transferor of qualified terminable interest property (QTIP) elects under § 26.2652-2(a) to treat the property as if the QTIP election had not been made (reverse QTIP election), the identity of the transferor of the property is determined without regard to the application of sections 2044, 2207A, and 2519.

(4) Split-gift transfers. In the case of a transfer with respect to which the donor's spouse makes an election under section 2513 to treat the gift as made one-half by the spouse, the electing spouse is treated as the transferor of one-half of the entire value of the property transferred by the donor, regardless of the interest the electing spouse is actually deemed to have transferred under section 2513. The donor is treated as the transferor of one-half of the value of the entire property. See § 26.2632-1(c)(5) Example 3, regarding allocation of GST exemption with respect to split-gift transfers subject to an ETIP.

(5) Examples. The following examples illustrate the principles of this paragraph (a):

Example (1). Identity of transferor. T transfers $100,000 to a trust for the sole benefit of T's grandchild. The transfer is subject to Federal gift tax because a gift tax is imposed under section 2501(a) (without regard to exemptions, exclusions, deductions, and credits). Thus, for purposes of chapter 13, T is the transferor of the $100,000. It is immaterial that a portion of the transfer is excluded from the total amount of T's taxable gift by reason of section 2503(b).

Example (2). Gift splitting and identity of transferor. The facts are the same as in Example 1, except T's spouse, S, consents under section 2513 to split the gift with T. For purposes of chapter 13, S and T are each treated as a transferor of $50,000 to the trust.

Example (3). Change of transferor on subsequent transfer tax event. T transfers $100,000 to a trust providing that all the net trust income is to be paid to T's spouse, S, for S's lifetime. T elects under section 2523(f) to treat the transfer as a transfer of qualified terminable interest property, and T does not make the reverse QTIP election under section 2652(a)(3). On S's death, the trust property is included in S's gross estate under section 2044. Thus, S becomes the transferor at the time of S's death.

Example (4). Effect of transfer of an interest in trust on identity of the transferor. T transfers $100,000 to a trust providing that all of the net income is to be paid to T's child, C, for C's lifetime. At C's death, the trust property is to be paid to T's grandchild. C transfers the income interest to X, an unrelated party, in a transfer that is a completed transfer for Federal gift tax purposes. Because C's transfer is a transfer of a term interest in the trust that does not affect the rights of other parties with respect to the trust property, T remains the transferor with respect to the trust.

Example (5). Effect of lapse of withdrawal right on identity of transferor. T transfers $10,000 to a new trust providing that the trust income is to be paid to T's child, C, for C's life and, on the death of C, the trust principal is to be paid to T's grandchild, GC. The trustee has discretion to distribute principal for GC's benefit during C's lifetime. C has a right to withdraw $10,000 from the trust for a 60-day period following the transfer. Thereafter, the power lapses. C does not exercise the withdrawal right. The transfer by T is subject to Federal gift tax because a gift tax is imposed under section 2501(a) (without regard to exemptions, exclusions, deductions, and credits) and, thus, T is treated as having transferred the entire $10,000 to the trust. On the lapse of the withdrawal right, C becomes a transferor to the extent C is treated as having made a completed transfer for purposes of chapter 12. Therefore, except to the extent that the amount with respect to which the power of withdrawal lapses exceeds the greater of $5,000 or 5% of the value of the trust property, T remains the transferor of the trust property for purposes of chapter 13.

Example (6). Effect of reverse QTIP election on identity of the transferor. T establishes a testamentary trust having a principal of $500,000. Under the terms of the trust, all trust income is payable to T's surviving spouse, S, during S's lifetime. T's executor makes an election to treat the trust property as qualified terminable interest property and also makes the reverse QTIP election. For purposes of chapter 13, T is the transferor with respect to the trust. On S's death, the then full fair market value of the trust is includible in S's gross estate under section 2044. However, because of the reverse QTIP election, S does not become the transferor with respect to the trust; T continues to be the transferor.

Example (7). Effect of reverse QTIP election on constructive additions. The facts are the same as in Example 6, except the inclusion of the QTIP trust in S's gross estate increased the Federal estate tax liability of S's estate by $200,000. The estate does not exercise the right of recovery from the trust granted under section 2207A. Under local law, the beneficiaries of S's residuary estate (which bears all estate taxes under the will) could compel the executor to exercise the right of recovery but do not do so. Solely for purposes of chapter 13, the beneficiaries of the residuary estate are not treated as having made an addition to the trust by reason of their failure to exercise their right of recovery. Because of the reverse QTIP election, for GST purposes, the trust property is not treated as includible in S's gross estate and, under those circumstances, no right of recovery exists.

Example (8). Effect of reverse QTIP election on constructive additions. S, the surviving spouse of T, dies testate. At the time of S's death, S was the beneficiary of a trust with respect to which T's executor made a QTIP election under section 2056(b)(7). Thus, the trust is includible in S's gross estate under section 2044. T's executor also made the reverse QTIP election with respect to the trust. S's will provides that all death taxes payable with respect to the trust are payable from S's residuary estate. Since the transferor of the property is determined without regard to section 2044 and section 2207A, S is not treated as making a constructive addition to the trust by reason of the tax apportionment clause in S's will.

Example (9). Split-gift transfers. T transfers $100,000 to an inter vivos trust that provides T with an annuity payable for ten years or until T's prior death. The annuity satisfies the definition of a qualified interest under section 2702(b). When the trust terminates, the corpus is to be paid to T's grandchild, GC. T's spouse, S, consents under section 2513 to have the gift treated as made one-half by S. Under section 2513, only the actuarial value of the gift to GC is eligible to be treated as made one-half by S. However, because S is treated as the donor of one-half of the gift to GC, S becomes the transferor of one-half of the entire trust ($50,000) for purposes of Chapter 13.

(b) Trust defined. *(1) In general.* A trust includes any arrangement (other than an estate) that has substantially the same effect as a trust. Thus, for example, arrangements involving life estates and remainders, estates for years, and insurance and annuity contracts are trusts. Generally, a transfer as to which the identity of the transferee is contingent upon the occurrence of an event is a transfer in trust; however, a transfer of property included in the transferor's gross estate, as to which the identity of the transferee is contingent upon an event that must occur within 6 months of the transferor's death, is not considered a transfer in trust solely by reason of the existence of the contingency.

(2) Examples. The following examples illustrate the provisions of this paragraph (b):

Example (1). Uniform gifts to minors transfers. T transfers cash to an account in the name of T's child, C, as custodian for C's child, GC (who is a minor), under a state statute substantially similar to the Uniform Gifts to Minors Act. For purposes of chapter 13, the transfer to the custodial account is treated as a transfer to a trust.

Example (2). Contingent transfers. T bequeaths $200,000 to T's child, C, provided that if C does not survive T by more than 6 months, the bequest is payable to T's grandchild, GC. C dies 4 months after T. The bequest is not a transfer in trust because the contingency that determines the recipient of the bequest must occur within 6 months of T's death. The bequest to GC is a direct skip.

Example (3). Contingent transfers. The facts are the same as in Example 2, except C must survive T by 18 months to take the bequest. The bequest is a transfer in trust for purposes of chapter 13, and the death of C is a taxable termination.

(c) Trustee defined. The trustee of a trust is the person designated as trustee under local law or, if no such person is so designated, the person in actual or constructive possession of property held in trust.

(d) Executor defined. For purposes of chapter 13, the executor is the executor or administrator of the decedent's estate. However, if no executor or administrator is appointed, qualified or acting within the United States, the executor is the fiduciary who is primarily responsible for payment of the decedent's debts and expenses. If there is no such executor, administrator or fiduciary, the executor is the person in actual or constructive possession of the largest portion of the value of the decedent's gross estate.

(e) Interest in trust. See § 26.2612-1(e) for the definition of interest in trust.

T.D. 8644, 12/26/95, amend T.D. 8720, 5/19/97.

§ 26.2652-2 Special election for qualified terminable interest property.

(a) In general. If an election is made to treat property as qualified terminable interest property (QTIP) under section 2523(f) or section 2056(b)(7), the person making the election may, for purposes of chapter 13, elect to treat the property as if the QTIP election had not been made (reverse QTIP election). An election under this section is irrevocable. An election under this section is not effective unless it is made with respect to all of the property in the trust to which the QTIP election applies. See, however, section 26.2654-1(b)(1). Property that qualifies for a deduction under section 2056(b)(5) is not eligible for the election under this section.

(b) Time and manner of making election. An election under this section is made on the return on which the QTIP election is made. If a protective QTIP election is made, no election under this section is effective unless a protective reverse QTIP election is also made.

(c) Transitional rule. If a reverse QTIP election is made with respect to a trust prior to December 27, 1995, and GST exemption has been allocated to that trust, the transferor (or the transferor's executor) may elect to treat the trust as two separate trusts, one of which has a zero inclusion ratio by reason of the transferor's GST exemption previously allocated to the trust. The separate trust with the zero inclusion ratio consists of that fractional share of the value of the entire trust equal to the value of the nontax portion of the trust under section 26.2642-4(a). The reverse QTIP election is treated as applying only to the trust with the zero inclusion ratio. An election under this paragraph (c) is made by attaching a statement to a copy of the return on which the reverse QTIP election was made under section 2652(a)(3). The statement must indicate that an election is being made to treat the trust as two separate trusts and must identify the values of the two separate trusts. The statement is to be filed in the same place in which the original return was filed and must be filed before June 24, 1996. A trust subject to the election described in this paragraph is treated as a trust that was created by two transferors. See section 26.2654-1(a)(2) for special rules involving trusts with multiple transferors.

(d) Examples. The following examples illustrate the provisions of this section:

Example (1). Special (reverse QTIP) election under section 2652(a)(3). T transfers $1,000,000 to a trust providing that all trust income is to be paid to T's spouse, S, for S's lifetime. On S's death, the trust principal is payable to GC, a grandchild of S and T. T elects to treat all of the transfer as a transfer of QTIP and also makes the reverse QTIP election for all of the property. Because of the reverse QTIP election, T continues to be treated as the transferor of the property after S's death for purposes of chapter 13. A taxable termination rather than a direct skip occurs on S's death.

Example (2). Election under transition rule. In 1994, T died leaving $4 million in trust for the benefit of T's surviving spouse, S. On January 16, 1995, T's executor filed T's Form 706 on which the executor elects to treat the entire trust as qualified terminable interest property. The executor also makes a reverse QTIP election. The reverse QTIP election is effective with respect to the entire trust even though T's executor could allocate only $1 million of GST exemption to the trust. T's executor may elect to treat the trust as two separate trusts, one having a value of 25% of the value of the single trust and an inclusion ratio of zero, but only if the election is made prior to June 24, 1996. If the executor makes the transitional election, the other separate trust, having a value of 75% of the value of the single trust and an inclusion ratio of one, is not treated as subject to the reverse QTIP election.

Example (3). Denominator of the applicable fraction of QTIP trust. T bequeaths $1,500,000 to a trust in which T's surviving spouse, S, receives an income interest for life. Upon the death of S, the property is to remain in trust for the benefit of C, the child of T and S. Upon C's death, the trust is to terminate and the trust property paid to the descendants of C. The bequest qualifies for the estate tax marital deduction under section 2056(b)(7) as QTIP. The executor does not make the reverse QTIP election under section 2652(a)(3). As a result, S becomes the transferor of the trust at S's death when the value of the property in the QTIP trust is included in S's gross estate under section 2044. For purposes of computing the applicable fraction with respect to the QTIP trust upon S's death, the denominator of the fraction is reduced by any Federal estate tax (whether imposed under section 2001, 2101 or 2056A(b)) and State death tax attributable to the trust property that is actually recovered from the trust.

T.D. 8644, 12/26/95.

§ 26.2653-1 Taxation of multiple skips.

(a) General rule. If property is held in trust immediately after a GST, solely for purposes of determining whether future events involve a skip person, the transferor is thereafter deemed to occupy the generation immediately above the highest generation of any person holding an interest in the trust immediately after the transfer. If no person holds an interest in the trust immediately after the GST, the transferor is treated as occupying the generation above the highest generation of any person in existence at the time of the GST who then occupies the highest generation level of any person who may subsequently hold an interest in the trust. See § 26.2612-1(e) for rules determining when a person has an interest in property held in trust.

(b) Examples. The following examples illustrate the provisions of this section:

Example (1). T transfers property to an irrevocable trust for the benefit of T's grandchild, GC, and great-grandchild, GGC. During GC's life, the trust income may be distributed to GC and GGC in the trustee's absolute discretion. At GC's death, the trust property passes to GGC. Both GC and GGC have an interest in the trust for purposes of chapter 13. The transfer by T to the trust is a direct skip, and the property is held in trust immediately after the transfer. After the direct skip, the transferor is treated as being one generation above GC, the highest generation individual having an interest in the trust. Therefore, GC is no longer a skip person and distributions to GC are not taxable distributions. However, because GGC occupies a generation that is two generations below the deemed generation of T, GGC is a skip person and distributions of trust income to GGC are taxable distributions.

Example (2). T transfers property to an irrevocable trust providing that the income is to be paid to T's child, C, for life. At C's death, the trust income is to be accumulated for 10 years and added to principal. At the end of the 10-year accumulation period, the trust income is to be paid to T's grandchild, GC, for life. Upon GC's death, the trust property is to be paid to T's great-grandchild, GGC, or to GGC's estate. A GST occurs at C's death. Immediately after C's death and during the 10-year accumulation period, no person has an interest in the trust within the meaning of section 2652(c) and § 26.2612-1(e) because no one can receive current distributions of income or principal. Immediately after C's death, T is treated as occupying the generation above the generation of GC (the trust beneficiary in existence at the time of the GST who then occupies the highest generation level of any person who may subsequently hold an interest in the trust). Thus, subsequent income distributions to GC are not taxable distributions.

T.D. 8644, 12/26/95.

§ 26.2654-1 Certain trusts treated as separate trusts.

Caution: The Treasury has not yet amended Reg § 26.2654-1 to reflect changes made by P.L. 107-16.

(a) Single trust treated as separate trusts. *(1) Substantially separate and independent shares.* (i) If a single trust consists solely of substantially separate and independent shares for different beneficiaries, the share attributable to each beneficiary (or group of beneficiaries) is treated as a separate trust for purposes of Chapter 13. The phrase "substantially separate and independent shares" generally has the same meaning as provided in § 1.663(c)-3. However, except as provided in paragraph (a)(1)(iii) of this section, a portion of a trust is not a separate share unless such share exists from and at all times after the creation of the trust. For purposes of this paragraph (a)(1), a trust is treated as created at the date of death of the grantor if the trust is includible in its entirety in the grantor's gross estate for Federal estate tax purposes. Further, except with respect to shares or trusts that are treated as separate trusts under local law, treatment of a single trust as separate trusts under this paragraph (a)(1) does not permit treatment of those portions as separate trusts for purposes of filing returns and payment of tax or for purposes of computing any other tax imposed under the Internal Revenue Code. Also, additions to, and distributions from, such trusts are allocated pro rata among the separate trusts, unless the governing instrument expressly provides otherwise. See § 26.2642-6 and paragraph (b) of this section regarding the treatment, for purposes of Chapter 13, of separate trusts resulting from the discretionary severance of a single trust.

(ii) Certain pecuniary amounts. For purposes of this section, if a person holds the current right to receive a mandatory (i.e., nondiscretionary and noncontingent) payment of a pecuniary amount at the death of the transferor from an inter vivos trust that is includible in the transferor's gross estate, or a testamentary trust, the pecuniary amount is a separate and independent share if—

(A) The trustee is required to pay appropriate interest (as defined in § 26.2642-2(b)(4)(i) and (ii)) to the person; and

(B) If the pecuniary amount is payable in kind on the basis of value other than the date of distribution value of the assets, the trustee is required to allocate assets to the pecuniary payment in a manner that fairly reflects net appreciation or depreciation in the value of the assets in the fund available to pay the pecuniary amount measured from the valuation date to the date of payment.

(iii) Mandatory severances. For purposes of this section, if the governing instrument of a trust requires the division or severance of a single trust into separate trusts upon the future occurrence of a particular event not within the discretion of the trustee or any other person, and if the trusts resulting from such a division or severance are recognized as separate trusts under applicable state law, then each resulting trust is treated as a separate trust for purposes of Chapter 13. For this purpose, the rules of paragraph (b)(1)(ii)(C) of this section apply with respect to the severance and funding of the trusts. Similarly, if the governing instrument requires the division of a single trust into separate shares under the circumstances described in this paragraph, each such share is treated as a separate trust for purposes of Chapter 13. The post-severance treatment of the resulting shares or trusts as separate trusts for GST tax purposes generally permits the allocation of GST tax exemption, the making of various elections permitted for GST tax purposes, and the occurrence of a taxable distribution or termination with regard to a particular resulting share or trust, with no GST tax impact on any other trust or share resulting from that severance. The treatment of a single trust as separate trusts under this paragraph (a)(1), however, does not permit treatment of those portions as separate trusts for purposes of filing returns and payment of tax or for purposes of computing any other tax imposed under the Internal Revenue Code, if those portions are not treated as separate trusts under local law. Also, additions to, and distributions from, such trusts are allocated pro rata among the separate trusts, unless the governing instrument expressly provides otherwise. Each separate share and each trust resulting from a mandatory division or severance described in this paragraph will have the same inclusion ratio immediately after the severance as that of the original trust immediately before the division or severance.

(2) Multiple transferors with respect to single trust. (i) In general. If there is more than one transferor with respect to a trust, the portions of the trust attributable to the different transferors are treated as separate trusts for purposes of chapter 13. Treatment of a single trust as separate trusts under this paragraph (a)(2) does not permit treatment of those portions as separate trusts for purposes of filing returns and payment of tax or for purposes of computing any other tax imposed under the Internal Revenue Code. Also, additions to, and distributions from, such trusts are allocated pro rata among the separate trusts unless otherwise expressly provided in the governing instrument.

(ii) Addition by a transferor. If an individual makes an addition to a trust of which the individual is not the sole transferor, the portion of the single trust attributable to each separate trust is determined by multiplying the fair market value of the single trust immediately after the contribution by a fraction. The numerator of the fraction is the value of the separate trust immediately after the contribution. The denominator of the fraction is the fair market value of all the property in the single trust immediately after the transfer.

(3) Severance of a single trust. A single trust treated as separate trusts under paragraphs (a)(1) or (2) of this section may be divided at any time into separate trusts to reflect that treatment. For this purpose, the rules of paragraph (b)(1)(ii)(C) of this section apply with respect to the severance and funding of the severed trusts.

(4) Allocation of exemption. (i) In general. With respect to a separate share treated as a separate trust under paragraph (a)(1) or (2) of this section, an individual's GST exemption is allocated to the separate trust. See § 26.2632-1 for rules concerning the allocation of GST exemption.

(ii) Automatic allocation to direct skips. If the transfer is a direct skip to a trust that occurs during the transferor's lifetime and is treated as a transfer to separate trusts under paragraphs (a)(1) or (a)(2) of this section, the transferor's GST exemption not previously allocated is automatically allocated on a pro rata basis among the separate trusts. The transferor may prevent an automatic allocation of GST exemption to a separate share of a single trust by describing on a timely-filed United States Gift (and Generation-Skipping Transfer) Tax Return (Form 709) the transfer and the extent to which the automatic allocation is not to apply to a particular share. See § 26.2632-1(b) for rules for avoiding the automatic allocation of GST exemption.

(5) Examples. The following examples illustrate the principles of this section (a):

Example (1). Separate shares as separate trusts. T transfers $100,000 to a trust under which income is to be paid in equal shares for 10 years to T's child, C, and T's grandchild, GC (or their respective estates). The trust does not permit distributions of principal during the term of the trust. At the end of the 10-year term, the trust principal is to be distributed to C and GC in equal shares. The shares of C and GC in the trust are separate and independent and, therefore, are treated as separate trusts. The result would not be the same if the trust permitted distributions of principal unless the distributions could only be made from a one-half separate share of the initial trust principal and the distributee's future rights with respect to the trust are correspondingly reduced. T may allocate part of T's GST exemption under section 2632(a) to the share held for the benefit of GC.

Example (2). Separate share rule inapplicable. The facts are the same as in Example 1, except the trustee holds the discretionary power to distribute the income in any proportion between C and GC during the last year of the trust. The shares of C and GC in the trust are not separate and independent shares throughout the entire term of the trust and, therefore, are not treated as separate trusts for purposes of chapter 13.

Example (3). Pecuniary payment as separate share. T creates a lifetime revocable trust providing that on T's death $500,000 is payable to T's spouse, S, with the balance of the principal to be held for the benefit of T's grandchildren. The value of the trust is includible in T's gross estate upon T's death. Under the terms of the trust, the payment to S is required to be made in cash, and under local law S is entitled to receive interest on the payment at an annual rate of 6 percent, commencing immediately upon T's death. For purposes of chapter 13, the trust is treated as created at T's death, and the $500,000 payable to S from the trust is treated as a separate share. The result would be the same if the payment to S could be satisfied using noncash assets at their value on the date of distribution. Further, the result would be the same if the decedent's probate estate poured over to the revocable trust on the decedent's death and was then distributed in accordance with the terms of the trust.

Example (4). Pecuniary payment not treated as separate share. The facts are the same as in Example 3, except the bequest to S is to be paid in noncash assets valued at their values as finally determined for Federal estate tax purposes. Neither the trust instrument nor local law requires that the assets distributed in satisfaction of the bequest fairly reflect net appreciation or depreciation in all the assets from which the bequest may be funded. S's $500,000 bequest is not treated as a separate share and the trust is treated as a single trust for purposes of chapter 13.

Example (5). Multiple transferors to single trust. A transfers $100,000 to an irrevocable generation-skipping trust; B simultaneously transfers $50,000 to the same trust. As of the time of the transfers, the single trust is treated as two trusts for purposes of chapter 13. Because A contributed 2/3 of the value of the initial corpus, 2/3 of the single trust principal is treated as a separate trust created by A. Similarly, because B contributed 1/3 of the value of the initial corpus, 1/3 of the single trust is treated as a separate trust created by B. A or B may allocate their GST exemption under section 2632(a) to the respective separate trusts.

Example (6). Additional contributions. A transfers $100,000 to an irrevocable generation-skipping trust; B simultaneously transfers $50,000 to the same trust. When the value of the single trust has increased to $180,000, A contributes an additional $60,000 to the trust. At the time of the additional contribution, the portion of the single trust attributable to each grantor's separate trust must be redetermined. The portion of the single trust attributable to A's separate trust immediately after the contribution is 3/4 (((2/3 × $180,000) + $60,000)/ $240,000). The portion attributable to B's separate trust after A's addition is 1/4.

Example (7). Distributions from a separate share. The facts are the same as in Example 6, except that, after A's second contribution, $50,000 is distributed to a beneficiary of the trust. Absent a provision in the trust instrument that charges the distribution against the contribution of either A or B, ¾of the distribution is treated as made from the separate trust of which A is the transferor and ¼ from the separate trust of which B is the transferor.

Example (8). Subsequent mandatory division into separate trusts. T creates an irrevocable trust that provides the trustee with the discretionary power to distribute income or corpus to T's children and grandchildren. The trust provides that, when T's youngest child reaches age 21, the trust will be divided into separate shares, one share for each child of T. The income from a respective child's share will be paid to the child during the child's life, with the remainder passing on the child's death to such child's children (grandchildren of T). The separate shares that come into existence when the youngest child reaches age 21 will be recognized as of that date as separate trusts for purposes of Chapter 13. The inclusion ratio of the separate trusts will be identical to the inclusion ratio of the trust before the severance. Any allocation of GST tax exemption to the trust after T's youngest child reaches age 21 may be made to any one or more of the separate shares. The result would be the same if the trust instrument provided that the trust was to be divided into separate trusts when T's youngest child reached age 21, provided that the severance and funding of the separate trusts meets the requirements of this section.

(b) Division of a trust included in the gross estate. *(1) In general.* The severance of a trust that is included in the transferor's gross estate (or created under the transferor's will) into two or more trusts is recognized for purposes of chapter 13 if—

(i) The trust is severed pursuant to a direction in the governing instrument providing that the trust is to be divided upon the death of the transferor; or

(ii) The governing instrument does not require or otherwise direct severance but the trust is severed pursuant to discretionary authority granted either under the governing instrument or under local law; and

(A) The terms of each of the new trusts provide in the aggregate for the same succession of interests and beneficiaries as are provided in the original trust;

(B) The severance occurs (or a reformation proceeding, if required, is commenced) prior to the date prescribed for filing the Federal estate tax return (including extensions actually granted) for the estate of the transferor; and

(C) Either—

(*1*) The new trusts are severed on a fractional basis. If severed on a fractional basis, the separate trusts need not be funded with a pro rata portion of each asset held by the undivided trust. The trusts may be funded on a nonpro rata basis provided funding is based on either the fair market value of the assets on the date of funding or in a manner that fairly reflects the net appreciation or depreciation in the value of the assets measured from the valuation date to the date of funding; or

(*2*) If the severance is required (by the terms of the governing instrument) to be made on the basis of a pecuniary amount, the pecuniary payment is satisfied in a manner that would meet the requirements of paragraph (a)(1)(ii) of this section if it were paid to an individual.

(2) Special rule. If a court order severing the trust has not been issued at the time the Federal estate tax return is filed, the executor must indicate on a statement attached to the return that a proceeding has been commenced to sever the trust and describe the manner in which the trust is proposed to be severed. A copy of the petition or other instrument used to commence the proceeding must also be attached to the return. If the governing instrument of a trust or local law authorizes the severance of the trust, a severance pursuant to that authorization is treated as meeting the requirement of paragraph (b)(1)(ii)(B) of this section if the executor indicates on the Federal estate tax return that separate trusts will be created (or funded) and clearly sets forth the manner in which the trust is to be severed and the separate trusts funded.

(3) Allocation of exemption. An individual's GST exemption under section 2632 may be allocated to the separate trusts created pursuant to this section at the discretion of the executor or trustee.

(4) Examples. The following examples illustrate the provisions of this section (b):

Example (1). Severance of single trust. T's will establishes a testamentary trust providing that income is to be paid to T's spouse for life. At the spouse's death, one-half of the corpus is to be paid to T's child, C, or C's estate (if C fails to survive the spouse) and one-half of the corpus is to be paid to T's grandchild, GC, or GC's estate (if GC fails to survive the spouse). If the requirements of paragraph (b) of this section are otherwise satisfied, T's executor may divide the testamentary trust equally into two separate trusts, one trust providing an income interest to spouse for life with remainder to C, and the other trust with an income interest to spouse for life with remainder to GC. Furthermore, if the requirements of paragraph (b) of this section are satisfied, the executor or trustee may further divide the trust for the benefit of GC. GST exemption may be allocated to any of the divided trusts.

Example (2). Severance of revocable trust. T creates an inter vivos revocable trust providing that, at T's death and after payment of all taxes and administration expenses, the remaining corpus will be divided into two trusts. One trust, for the benefit of T's spouse, is to be funded with the smallest amount that, if qualifying for the marital deduction, will reduce the estate tax to zero. The other trust, for the benefit of T's descendants, is to be funded with the balance of the revocable trust corpus. The trust corpus is includible in T's gross estate. Each trust is recognized as a separate trust for purposes of chapter 13.

Example (3). Formula severance. T's will establishes a testamentary marital trust (Trust) that meets the requirements of qualified terminable interest property (QTIP) if an election under section 2056(b)(7) is made. Trust provides that all trust income is to be paid to T's spouse for life. On the spouse's death, the trust corpus is to be held in further trust for the benefit of T's then-living descendants. On T's date of death in January of 2004, T's unused GST tax exemption is $1,200,000, and T's will includes $200,000 of bequests to T's grandchildren. Prior to the due date for filing the Form 706, "United States Estate (and Generation-Skipping Transfer) Tax Return," for T's estate, T's executor, pursuant to applicable state law, divides Trust into two separate trusts, Trust 1 and Trust 2. Trust 1 is to be funded with that fraction of the Trust assets, the numerator of which is $1,000,000, and the denominator of which is the value of the Trust assets as finally determined for federal estate tax purposes. Trust 2 is to be funded with that fraction of the Trust assets, the numerator of which is the excess of the Trust assets over $1,000,000, and the denominator of which is the value of the Trust assets as finally determined for federal estate tax purposes. On the Form 706 filed for the estate, T's executor makes a QTIP election under section 2056(b)(7) with respect to Trust 1 and Trust 2 and a "reverse" QTIP election under section 2652(a)(3) with respect to Trust 1. Further, T's executor allocates $200,000 of T's available

GST tax exemption to the bequests to T's grandchildren, and the balance of T's exemption ($1,000,000) to Trust 1. If the requirements of paragraph (b) of this section are otherwise satisfied, Trust 1 and Trust 2 are recognized as separate trusts for GST tax purposes. Accordingly, the "reverse" QTIP election and allocation of GST tax exemption with respect to Trust 1 are recognized and effective for generation-skipping transfer tax purposes.

(c) Cross reference. For rules applicable to the qualified severance of trusts (whether or not includible in the transferor's gross estate), see § 26.2642-6.

(d) Effective date. Paragraph (a)(1)(i), paragraph (a)(1)(iii), and Example 8 of paragraph (a)(5) apply to severances occurring on or after September 2, 2008.

T.D. 8644, 12/26/95, amend T.D. 9348, 8/1/2007, T.D. 9421, 7/30/2008.

PAR. 4. Section 26.2654-1 is amended as follows:

1. Paragraph (a)(1)(i) is revised.
2. A new paragraph (a)(1)(iii) is added.
3. In paragraph (a)(5), Example 8 is revised.

The additions and revisions read as follows:

Proposed § 26.2654-1 Certain trusts treated as separate trusts. [*For Preamble, see ¶ 152,895*]

(a) Single trust treated as separate trusts. *(1) Substantially separate and independent shares.* (i) In general. If a single trust consists solely of substantially separate and independent shares for different beneficiaries, the share attributable to each beneficiary (or group of beneficiaries) is treated as a separate trust for purposes of chapter 13. The phrase "substantially separate and independent shares" generally has the same meaning as provided in § 1.663(c)-3 of this chapter. However, except as provided in paragraph (a)(1)(iii) of this section, a portion of a trust is not a separate share unless such share exists from and at all times after the creation of the trust. For purposes of this paragraph (a)(1), a trust is treated as created at the date of death of the grantor if the trust is includible in its entirety in the grantor's gross estate for Federal estate tax purposes. Further, treatment of a single trust as separate trusts under this paragraph (a)(1) does not permit treatment of those portions as separate trusts for purposes of filing returns and payment of tax or for purposes of computing any other tax imposed under the Internal Revenue Code. Also, additions to, and distributions from, such trusts are allocated pro rata among the separate trusts, unless the governing instrument expressly provides otherwise. See § 26.2642-6 and paragraph (b) of this section regarding the treatment, for purposes of chapter 13, of separate trusts resulting from the actual severance of a single trust.

* * * * *

(iii) Mandatory severances. For purposes of this section, if the governing instrument of a trust requires the division or severance of a single trust into separate trusts upon the future occurrence of a particular event not within the discretion of the trustee or any other person, and if the trusts resulting from such a division or severance are recognized as separate trusts under applicable state law, then each resulting trust is treated as a separate trust for purposes of chapter 13. For this purpose, the rules of paragraph (b)(1)(ii)(C) of this section apply with respect to the severance and funding of the trusts. Similarly, if the governing instrument requires the division of a single trust into separate shares under the circumstances described in this paragraph, each such resulting share is treated as a separate trust for purposes of chapter 13. The post-severance treatment of the resulting trusts or shares as separate trusts for GST tax purposes generally permits the allocation of GST tax exemption, the making of various elections permitted for GST tax purposes, and the occurrence of a taxable distribution or termination with regard to a particular resulting trust or share, with no GST tax impact on any other trust or share resulting from that severance. The treatment of a single trust as separate trusts under this paragraph (a)(1), however, does not permit treatment of those portions as separate trusts for purposes of filing returns and payment of tax or for purposes of computing any other tax imposed under the Internal Revenue Code. Also, additions to, and distributions from, such trusts are allocated pro rata among the separate trusts, unless the governing instrument expressly provides otherwise. Each separate share and each trust resulting from a mandatory division or severance described in this paragraph will have the same inclusion ratio immediately after the severance as that of the original trust immediately before the division or severance.

* * * * *

(5) * * *

Example (8). Subsequent mandatory division into separate trusts. T creates an irrevocable trust that provides the trustee with the discretionary power to distribute income or corpus to T's children and grandchildren. The trust provides that, when T's youngest child reaches age 21, the trust will be divided into separate shares, one share for each child of T. The income from a respective child's share will be paid to the child during the child's life, with the remainder passing on the child's death to such child's children (grandchildren of T). The separate shares that come into existence when the youngest child reaches age 21 will be recognized as of that date as separate trusts for purposes of Chapter 13. Any allocation of GST tax exemption to the trust after T's youngest child reaches age 21 may be made to any one or more of the separate shares. The result would be the same if the trust instrument provided that the trust was to be divided into separate trusts when T's youngest child reached age 21, provided that the severance and funding of the separate trusts meets the requirements of this section.

* * * * *

§ 26.2662-1 Generation-skipping transfer tax return requirements.

(a) In general. Chapter 13 imposes a tax on generation-skipping transfers (as defined in section 2611). The requirements relating to the return of tax depend on the type of generation-skipping transfer involved. This section contains rules for filing the required tax return. Paragraph (c)(2) of this section provides special rules concerning the return requirements for generation-skipping transfers pursuant to certain trust arrangements (as defined in paragraph (c)(2)(ii) of this section), such as life insurance policies and annuities.

(b) Form of return. *(1) Taxable distributions.* Form 706GS must be filed in accordance with its instructions for any taxable distribution (as defined in section 2612(b)). The trust involved in a transfer described in the preceding sentence must file Form 706GS(D-1) in accordance with its instructions. A copy of Form 706GS(D-1) shall be sent to each distributee.

(2) Taxable terminations. Form 706GS(T) must be filed in accordance with its instructions for any taxable termination (as defined in section 2612(a)).

(3) Direct skip. (i) Inter vivos direct skips. Form 709 must be filed in accordance with its instructions for any direct skip (as defined in section 2612(c)) that is subject to chapter 12 and occurs during the life of the transferor.

(ii) Direct skips occurring at death. (A) In general. Form 706 or Form 706NA must be filed in accordance with its instructions for any direct skips (as defined in section 2612(c)) that are subject to chapter 11 and occur at the death of the decedent.

(B) Direct skips payable from a trust. Schedule R-1 of Form 706 must be filed in accordance with its instructions for any direct skip from a trust if such direct skip is subject to chapter 11. See paragraph (c)(2) of this section for special rules relating to the person liable for tax and required to make the return under certain circumstances.

(c) Person liable for tax and required to make return. *(1) In general.* Except as otherwise provided in this section, the following person is liable for the tax imposed by section 2601 and must make the required tax return—

(i) The transferee in a taxable distribution (as defined in section 2612(b));

(ii) The trustee in the case of a taxable termination (as defined in section 2612(a));

(iii) The transferor (as defined in section 2652(a)(1)(B)) in the case of an inter vivos direct skip (as defined in section 2612(c));

(iv) The trustee in the case of a direct skip from a trust or with respect to property that continues to be held in trust; or

(v) The executor in the case of a direct skip (other than a direct skip described in paragraph (c)(1)(iv) of this section) if the transfer is subject to chapter 11. See paragraph (c)(2) of this section for special rules relating to direct skips to or from certain trust arrangements (as defined in paragraph (c)(2)(ii) of this section).

(2) Special rule for direct skips occurring at death with respect to property held in trust arrangements. (i) In general. In the case of certain property held in a trust arrangement (as defined in paragraph (c)(2)(ii) of this section) at the date of death of the transferor, the person who is required to make the return and who is liable for the tax imposed by chapter 13 is determined under paragraphs (c)(2)(iii) and (iv) of this section.

(ii) Trust arrangement defined. For purposes of this section, the term trust arrangement includes any arrangement (other than an estate) which, although not an explicit trust, has the same effect as an explicit trust. For purposes of this section, the term "explicit trust" means a trust described in § 301.7701-4(a).

(iii) Executor's liability in the case of transfers with respect to decedents dying on or after June 24, 1996, if the transfer is less than $250,000. In the case of a direct skip occurring at death, the executor of the decedent's estate is liable for the tax imposed on that direct skip by chapter 13 and is required to file Form 706 or Form 706NA (and not Schedule R-1 of Form 706) if, at the date of the decedent's death—

(A) The property involved in the direct skip is held in a trust arrangement; and

(B) The total value of the property involved in direct skips with respect to the trustee of that trust arrangement is less than $250,000.

(iv) Executor's liability in the case of transfers with respect to decedents dying prior to June 24, 1996, if the transfer is less than $100,000. In the case of a direct skip occurring at death with respect to a decedent dying prior to June 24, 1996, the rule in paragraph (c)(2)(iii) of this section that imposes liability upon the executor applies only if the property involved in the direct skip with respect to the trustee of the trust arrangement, in the aggregate, is less than $100,000.

(v) Executor's right of recovery. In cases where the rules of paragraphs (c)(2)(iii) and (iv) of this section impose liability for the generation-skipping transfer tax on the executor, the executor is entitled to recover from the trustee (if the property continues to be held in trust) or from the recipient of the property (in the case of a transfer from a trust), the generation-skipping transfer tax attributable to the transfer.

(vi) Examples. The following examples illustrate the application of this paragraph (c)(2) with respect to decedents dying on or after June 24, 1996:

Example (1). Insurance proceeds less than $250,000. On August 1, 1997, T, the insured under an insurance policy, died. The proceeds ($200,000) were includible in T's gross estate for Federal estate tax purposes. T's grandchild, GC, was named the sole beneficiary of the policy. The insurance policy is treated as a trust under section 2652(b)(1), and the payment of the proceeds to GC is a transfer from a trust for purposes of chapter 13. Therefore, the payment of the proceeds to GC is a direct skip. Since the proceeds from the policy ($200,000) are less than $250,000, the executor is liable for the tax imposed by chapter 13 and is required to file Form 706.

Example (2). Aggregate insurance proceeds of $250,000 or more. Assume the same facts as in Example 1, except T is the insured under two insurance policies issued by the same insurance company. The proceeds ($150,000) from each policy are includible in T's gross estate for Federal estate tax purposes. T's grandchild, GC1, was named the sole beneficiary of Policy 1, and T's other grandchild, GC2, was named the sole beneficiary of Policy 2. GC1 and GC2 are skip persons (as defined in section 2613). Therefore, the payments of the proceeds are direct skips. Since the total value of the policies ($300,000) exceeds $250,000, the insurance company is liable for the tax imposed by chapter 13 and is required to file Schedule R-1 of Form 706.

Example (3). Insurance proceeds of $250,000 or more held by insurance company. On August 1, 1997, T, the insured under an insurance policy, dies. The policy provides that the insurance company shall make monthly payments of $750 to GC, T's grandchild, for life with the remainder payable to T's great grandchild, GGC. The face value of the policy is $300,000. Since the proceeds continue to be held by the insurance company (the trustee), the proceeds are treated as if they were transferred to a trust for purposes of chapter 13. The trust is a skip person (as defined in section 2613(a)(2)) and the transfer is a direct skip. Since the total value of the policy ($300,000) exceeds $250,000, the insurance company is liable for the tax imposed by chapter 13 and is required to file Schedule R-1 of Form 706.

Example (4). Insurance proceeds less than $250,000 held by insurance company. Assume the same facts as in Example 3, except the policy provides that the insurance company shall make monthly payments of $500 to GC and that the face value of the policy is $200,000. The transfer is a transfer to a trust for purposes of chapter 13. However, since the total value of the policy ($200,000) is less than $250,000, the executor is liable for the tax imposed by chapter 13 and is required to file Form 706.

Example (5). On August 1, 1997, A, the insured under a life insurance policy, dies. The insurance proceeds on A's life that are payable under policies issued by Company X are in the aggregate amount of $200,000 and are includible in A's gross estate. Because the proceeds are includible in A's gross estate, the generation-skipping transfer that occurs upon A's death, if any, will be a direct skip rather than a taxable distribution or a taxable termination. Accordingly, because the aggregate amount of insurance proceeds with respect to Company X is less than $250,000, Company X may pay the proceeds without regard to whether the beneficiary is a skip person in relation to the decedent-transferor.

(3) Limitation on personal liability of trustee. Except as provided in paragraph (c)(3)(iii) of this section, a trustee is not personally liable for any increases in the tax imposed by section 2601 which is attributable to the fact that—

(i) A transfer is made to the trust during the life of the transferor for which a gift tax return is not filed; or

(ii) The inclusion ratio with respect to the trust, determined by reference to the transferor's gift tax return, is erroneous, the actual inclusion ratio being greater than the reported inclusion ratio.

(iii) This paragraph (c)(3) does not apply if the trustee has or is deemed to have knowledge of facts sufficient to reasonably conclude that a gift tax return was required to be filed or that the inclusion ratio is erroneous. A trustee is deemed to have knowledge of such facts if the trustee's agent, employee, partner, or co-trustee has knowledge of such facts.

(4) Exceptions. (i) Legal or mental incapacity. If a distributee is legally or mentally incapable of making a return, the return may be made for the distributee by the distributee's guardian or, if no guardian has been appointed, by a person charged with the care of the distributee's person or property.

(ii) Returns made by fiduciaries. See section 6012(b) for a fiduciary's responsibilities regarding the returns of decedents, returns of persons under a disability, returns of estates and trusts, and returns made by joint fiduciaries.

(d) Time and manner of filing return. *(1) In general.* Forms 706, 706NA, 706GS(D), 706GS(D-1), 706GS(T), 709, and Schedule R-1 of Form 706 must be filed with the Internal Revenue Service office with which an estate or gift tax return of the transferor must be filed. The return shall be filed—

(i) Direct skip. In the case of a direct skip, on or before the date on which an estate or gift tax return is required to be filed with respect to the transfer (see section 6075(b)(3)); and

(ii) Other transfers. In all other cases, on or before the 15th day of the 4th month after the close of the calendar year in which such transfer occurs. See paragraph (d)(2) of this section for an exception to this rule when an election is made under section 2624(c) to value property included in certain taxable terminations in accordance with section 2032.

(2) Exception for alternative valuation of taxable termination. In the case of a taxable termination with respect to which an election is made under section 2624(c) to value property in accordance with section 2032, a Form 706GS(T) must be filed on or before the 15th day of the 4th month after the close of the calendar year in which the taxable termination occurred, or on or before the 10th month following the month in which the death that resulted in the taxable termination occurred, whichever is later.

(e) Place for filing returns. See section 6091 for the place for filing any return, declaration, statement, or other document, or copies thereof, required by chapter 13.

(f) Lien on property. The liens imposed under sections 6324, 6324A, and section 6324B are applicable with respect to the tax imposed under chapter 13. Thus, a lien under section 6324 is imposed in the amount of the tax imposed by section 2601 on all property transferred in a generation-skipping transfer until the tax is fully paid or becomes uncollectible by reason of lapse of time. The lien attaches at the time of the generation-skipping transfer and is in addition to the lien for taxes under section 6321.

T.D. 8187, 3/14/88, amend T.D. 8644, 12/26/95.

§ 26.2663-1 Recapture tax under section 2032A.

See § 26.2642-4(a)(4) for rules relating to the recomputation of the applicable fraction and the imposition of additional GST tax, if additional estate tax is imposed under section 2032A.

T.D. 8644, 12/26/95.

§ 26.2663-2 Application of chapter 13 to transfers by nonresidents not citizens of the United States.

(a) In general. This section provides rules for applying chapter 13 of the Internal Revenue Code to transfers by a transferor who is a nonresident not a citizen of the United States (NRA transferor). For purposes of this section, an individual is a resident or citizen of the United States if that individual is a resident or citizen of the United States under the rules of chapter 11 or 12 of the Internal Revenue Code, as the case may be. Every NRA transferor is allowed a GST exemption of $1,000,000. See § 26.2632-1 regarding the allocation of the exemption.

(b) Transfers subject to chapter 13. *(1) Direct skips.* A transfer by a NRA transferor is a direct skip subject to chapter 13 only to the extent that the transfer is subject to the Federal estate or gift tax within the meaning of § 26.2652-1(a)(2). See § 26.2612-1(a) for the definition of direct skip.

(2) Taxable distributions and taxable terminations. Chapter 13 applies to a taxable distribution or a taxable termination to the extent that the initial transfer of property to the trust by a NRA transferor, whether during life or at death, was subject to the Federal estate or gift tax within the meaning of § 26.2652-1(a)(2). See § 26.2612-1(b) for the definition of a taxable termination and § 26.2612-1(c) for the definition of a taxable distribution.

(c) Trusts funded in part with property subject to chapter 13 and in part with property not subject to chapter 13. *(1) In general.* If a single trust created by a NRA transferor is in part subject to chapter 13 under the rules of paragraph (b) of this section and in part not subject to chapter 13, the applicable fraction with respect to the trust is determined as of the date of the transfer, except as provided in paragraph (c)(3) of this section.

(i) Numerator of applicable fraction. The numerator of the applicable fraction is the sum of the amount of GST exemption allocated to the trust (if any) plus the value of the nontax portion of the trust.

(ii) Denominator of applicable fraction. The denominator of the applicable fraction is the value of the property transferred to the trust reduced as provided in § 26.2642-1(c).

(2) Nontax portion of the trust. The nontax portion of a trust is a fraction, the numerator of which is the value of

property not subject to chapter 13 determined as of the date of the initial completed transfer to the trust, and the denominator of which is the value of the entire trust. For example, T, a NRA transferor, transfers property that has a value of $1,000 to a generation-skipping trust. Of the property transferred to the trust, property having a value of $200 is subject to chapter 13 and property having a value of $800 is not subject to chapter 13. The nontax portion is .8 ($800 (the value of the property not subject to chapter 13) over $1,000 (the total value of the property transferred to the trust)).

(3) Special rule with respect to the estate tax inclusion period. For purposes of this section, the provisions of § 26.2632-1(c), providing rules applicable in the case of an estate tax inclusion period (ETIP), apply only if the property transferred by the NRA transferor is subsequently included in the transferor's gross estate. If the property is not subsequently included in the gross estate, then the nontax portion of the trust and the applicable fraction are determined as of the date of the initial transfer. If the property is subsequently included in the gross estate, then the nontax portion and the applicable fraction are determined as of the date of death.

(d) Examples. The following examples illustrate the provisions of this section. In each example T, a NRA, is the transferor; C is T's child; and GC is C's child and a grandchild of T:

Example (1). Direct transfer to skip person. T transfers property to GC in a transfer that is subject to Federal gift tax under chapter 12 within the meaning of § 26.2652-1(a)(2). At the time of the transfer, C and GC are NRAs. T's transfer is subject to chapter 13 because the transfer is subject to gift tax under chapter 12.

Example (2). Transfers of both u.s. and foreign situs property. (i) T's will established a testamentary trust for the benefit of C and GC. The trust was funded with stock in a publicly traded U.S. corporation having a value on the date of T's death of $100,000, and property not situated in the United States (and therefore not subject to estate tax) having a value on the date of T's death of $400,000.

(ii) On a timely filed estate tax return (Form 706NA), the executor of T's estate allocates $50,000 of GST exemption under section 2632(a) to the trust. The numerator of the applicable fraction is $450,000, the sum of $50,000 (the amount of exemption allocated to the trust) plus $400,000 (the value of the nontax portion of the trust (4/5 × $500,000)). The denominator is $500,000. Hence, the applicable fraction with respect to the trust is .9 ($450,000/$500,000), and the inclusion ratio is .1 (1 – 9/10).

Example (3). Inter vivos transfer of u.s. and foreign situs property to a trust and a timely allocation of GST exemption. T establishes a trust providing that trust income is payable to T's child for life and the remainder is to be paid to T's grandchild. T transfers property to the trust that has a value of $100,000 and is subject to chapter 13. T also transfers property to the trust that has a value of $300,000 but is not subject to chapter 13. T allocates $100,000 of exemption to the trust on a timely filed United States Gift (and Generation-Skipping Transfer) Tax Return (Form 709). The applicable fraction with respect to the trust is 1, determined as follows: $300,000 (the value of the nontax portion of the trust) plus $100,000 (the exemption allocated to the trust)/ $400,000 (the total value of the property transferred to the trust).

Example (4). Inter vivos transfer of u.s. and foreign situs property to a trust and a late allocation of GST exemption. (i) In 1996, T transfers $500,000 of property to an inter vivos trust the terms of which provide that income is payable to C, for life, with the remainder to GC. The property transferred to the trust consists of property subject to chapter 13 that has a value of $400,000 on the date of the transfer and property not subject to chapter 13 that has a value of $100,000. T does not allocate GST exemption to the trust. On the transfer date, the nontax portion of the trust is .2 ($100,000/$500,000) and the applicable fraction is also .2 determined as follows: $100,000 (the value of the nontax portion of the trust)/$500,000 (the value of the property transferred to the trust).

(ii) In 1999, when the value of the trust is $800,000, T allocates $100,000 of GST exemption to the trust. The applicable fraction of the trust must be recomputed. The numerator of the applicable fraction is $260,000 ($100,000 (the amount of GST exemption allocated to the trust)) plus $160,000 (the value of the nontax portion of the trust as of the date of allocation (.2 × $800,000)). The denominator of the applicable fraction is $800,000. Accordingly, the applicable fraction with respect to the trust after the allocation is .325 ($260,000/$800,000) and the inclusion ratio is .675 (1 – .325).

Example (5). Taxable termination. The facts are the same as in Example 4 except that, in 2006, when the value of the property is $1,200,000, C dies and the trust corpus is distributed to GC. The termination is a taxable termination. If no further GST exemption has been allocated to the trust, the applicable fraction remains .325 and the inclusion ratio remains .675.

Example (6). Estate tax inclusion period. (i) T transferred property to an inter vivos trust the terms of which provided T with an annuity payable for 10 years or until T's prior death. The annuity satisfies the definition of a qualified interest under section 2702(b). The trust also provided that, at the end of the trust term, the remainder will pass to GC or GC's estate. The property transferred to the trust consisted of property subject to chapter 13 that has a value of $100,000 and property not subject to chapter 13 that has a value of $400,000. T allocated $100,000 of GST exemption to the trust. If T dies within the 10 year period, the value of the trust principal will be subject to inclusion in T's gross estate to the extent provided in sections 2103 and 2104(b). Accordingly, the ETIP rule under paragraph (c)(3) of this section applies.

(ii) In year 6 of the trust term, T died. At T's death, the trust corpus had a value of $800,000, and $500,000 was includible in T's gross estate as provided in sections 2103 and 2104(b). Thus, $500,000 of the trust corpus is subject to chapter 13 and $300,000 is not subject to chapter 13. The $100,000 GST exemption allocation is effective as of T's date of death. Also, the nontax portion of the trust and the applicable fraction are determined as of T's date of death. In this case, the nontax portion of the trust is .375, determined as follows: $300,000 (the value of the trust not subject to chapter 13)/$800,000 (the value of the trust). The numerator of the applicable fraction is $400,000, determined as follows: $100,000 (GST exemption previously allocated to the trust) plus $300,000 (the value of the nontax portion of the trust). The denominator of the applicable fraction is $800,000. Thus, the applicable fraction with respect to the trust is .50, unless additional exemption is allocated to the trust by T's executor or the automatic allocation rules of § 26.2632-1(d)(2) apply.

Example (7). The facts are the same as in Example 6 except that T survives the termination date of T's retained annuity and the trust corpus is distributed to GC. Since the trust was not included in T's gross estate, the ETIP rules do not apply. Accordingly, the nontax portion of the trust and the applicable fraction are determined as of the date of the transfer to the trust. The nontax portion of the trust is .80 ($400,000/$500,000). The numerator of the applicable fraction is $500,000 determined as follows: $100,000 (GST exemption allocated to the trust) plus $400,000 (the value of the nontax portion of the trust). Accordingly, the applicable fraction is 1, and the inclusion ratio is zero.

(e) Transitional rule for allocations for transfers made before December 27, 1995. If a NRA made a GST (inter vivos or testamentary) after December 23, 1992, and before December 27, 1995, that is subject to chapter 13 (within the meaning of § 26.2663-2), the NRA will be treated as having made a timely allocation of GST exemption to the transfer in a calendar year in the order prescribed in section 2632(c). Thus, a NRA's unused GST exemption will initially be treated as allocated to any direct skips made during the calendar year and then to any trusts with respect to which the NRA made transfers during the same calendar year and from which a taxable distribution or a taxable termination may occur. Allocations within the above categories are made in the order in which the transfers occur. Allocations among simultaneous transfers within the same category are made pursuant to the principles of section 2632(c)(2). This transitional allocation rule will not apply if the NRA transferor, or the executor of the NRA's estate, as the case may be, elected to have an automatic allocation of GST exemption not apply by describing on a timely-filed Form 709 for the year of the transfer, or a timely filed Form 706NA, the details of the transfer and the extent to which the allocation was not to apply.

T.D. 8644, 12/26/95.

§ 25.2701-0 Table of contents.

This section lists the major paragraphs contained in §§ 25.2701-1 through 25.2701-8.

T.D. 8395, 1/28/92, amend T.D. 8536, 5/4/94.

§ 25.2701-1 Special valuation rules in the case of transfers of certain interests in corporations and partnerships.

(a) In general. *(1) Scope of section 2701.* Section 2701 provides special valuation rules to determine the amount of the gift when an individual transfers an equity interest in a corporation or partnership to a member of the individual's family. For section 2701 to apply, the transferor or an applicable family member (as defined in paragraph (d)(2) of this section) must, immediately after the transfer, hold an applicable retained interest (a type of equity interest defined in § 25.2701-2(b)(1)). If certain subsequent payments with respect to the applicable retained interest do not conform to the assumptions used in valuing the interest at the time of the initial transfer, § 25.2701-4 provides a special rule to increase the individual's later taxable gifts or taxable estate. Section 25.2701-5 provides an adjustment to mitigate the effects of double taxation when an applicable retained interest is subsequently transferred.

(2) Effect of section 2701. If section 2701 applies to a transfer, the amount of the transferor's gift, if any, is determined using a subtraction method of valuation (described in § 25.2701-3). Under this method, the amount of the gift is determined by subtracting the value of any family-held applicable retained interests and other non-transferred equity interests from the aggregate value of family-held interests in the corporation or partnership (the "entity"). Generally, in determining the value of any applicable retained interest held by the transferor or an applicable family member—

(i) Any put, call, or conversion right, any right to compel liquidation, or any similar right is valued at zero if the right is an "extraordinary payment right" (as defined in § 25.2701-2(b)(2));

(ii) Any distribution right in a controlled entity (e.g., a right to receive dividends) is valued at zero unless the right is a "qualified payment right" (as defined in § 25.2701-2(b)(6)); and

(iii) Any other right (including a qualified payment right) is valued as if any right valued at zero did not exist but otherwise without regard to section 2701.

(3) Example. The following example illustrates rules of this paragraph (a).

Example. A, an individual, holds all the outstanding stock of S Corporation. A exchanges A's shares in S for 100 shares of 10-percent cumulative preferred stock and 100 shares of voting common stock. A transfers the common stock to A's child. Section 2701 applies to the transfer because A has transferred an equity interest (the common stock) to a member of A's family, and immediately thereafter holds an applicable retained interest (the preferred stock). A's preferred stock is valued under the rules of section 2701. A's gift is determined under the subtraction method by subtracting the value of A's preferred stock from the value of A's interest in S immediately prior to the transfer.

(b) Transfers and other triggering events. *(1) Completed transfers.* Section 2701 applies to determine the existence and amount of any gift, whether or not the transfer would otherwise be a taxable gift under chapter 12 of the Internal Revenue Code. For example, section 2701 applies to a transfer that would not otherwise be a gift under chapter 12 because it was a transfer for full and adequate consideration.

(2) Transactions treated as transfers. (i) In general. Except as provided in paragraph (b)(3) of this section, for purposes of section 2701, transfer includes the following transactions:

(A) A contribution to the capital of a new or existing entity;

(B) A redemption, recapitalization, or other change in the capital structure of an entity (a "capital structure transaction"), if—

(1) The transferor or an applicable family member receives an applicable retained interest in the capital structure transaction;

(2) The transferor or an applicable family member holding an applicable retained interest before the capital structure transaction surrenders an equity interest that is junior to the applicable retained interest (a "subordinate interest") and receives property other than an applicable retained interest; or

(3) The transferor or an applicable family member holding an applicable retained interest before the capital structure transaction surrenders an equity interest in the entity (other than a subordinate interest) and the fair market value of the applicable retained interest is increased; or

(C) The termination of an indirect holding in an entity (as defined in § 25.2701-6), (or contribution to capital by an entity to the extent an individual indirectly holds an interest in the entity), if—

(1) The property is held in a trust as to which the indirect holder is treated as the owner under subchapter J of chapter 1 of the Internal Revenue Code; or

(2) If the termination (or contribution) is not treated as a transfer under paragraph (b)(2)(i)(C)(1) of this section, to the extent the value of the indirectly-held interest would have been included in the value of the indirect holder's gross estate for Federal estate tax purposes if the indirect holder died immediately prior to the termination.

(ii) Multiple attribution. For purposes of paragraph (b)(2)(i)(C) of this section, if the transfer of an indirect holding in property is treated as a transfer with respect to more than one indirect holder, the transfer is attributed in the following order:

(A) First, to the indirect holder(s) who transferred the interest to the entity (without regard to section 2513);

(B) Second, to the indirect holder(s) possessing a presently exercisable power to designate the person who shall possess or enjoy the property;

(C) Third, to the indirect holder(s) presently entitled to receive the income from the interest;

(D) Fourth, to the indirect holder(s) specifically entitled to receive the interest at a future date; and

(E) Last, to any other indirect holder(s) proportionally.

(3) Excluded transactions. For purposes of section 2701, a transfer does not include the following transactions.

(i) A capital structure transaction, if the transferor, each applicable family member, and each member of the transferor's family holds substantially the same interest after the transaction as that individual held before the transaction. For this purpose, common stock with non-lapsing voting rights and nonvoting common stock are interests that are substantially the same;

(ii) A shift of rights occurring upon the execution of a qualified disclaimer described in section 2518; and

(iii) A shift of rights occurring upon the release, exercise, or lapse of a power of appointment other than a general power of appointment described in section 2514, except to the extent the release, exercise, or lapse would otherwise be a transfer under chapter 12,

(c) Circumstances in which section 2701 does not apply. To the extent provided, section 2701 does not apply in the following cases:

(1) Marketable transferred interests. Section 2701 does not apply if there are readily available market quotations on an established securities market for the value of the transferred interests.

(2) Marketable retained interests. Section 25.2701-2 does not apply to any applicable retained interest if there are readily available market quotations on an established securities market for the value of the applicable retained interests.

(3) Interests of the same class. Section 2701 does not apply if the retained interest is of the same class of equity as the transferred interest or if the retained interest is of a class that is proportional to the class of the transferred interest. A class is the same class as (or is proportional to the class of) the transferred interest if the rights are identical (or proportional) to the rights of the transferred interest, except for non-lapsing differences in voting rights (or, for a partnership, non-lapsing differences with respect to management and limitations on liability). For purposes of this section, non-lapsing provisions necessary to comply with partnership allocation requirements of the Internal Revenue Code (e.g., section 704(b)) are non-lapsing differences with respect to limitations on liability. A right that lapses by reason of Federal or State law is treated as a non-lapsing right unless the Secretary determines, by regulation or by published revenue ruling, that it is necessary to treat such a right as a lapsing right to accomplish the purposes of section 2701. An interest in a partnership is not an interest in the same class as the transferred interest if the transferor or applicable family members have the right to alter the liability of the transferee.

(4) Proportionate transfers. Section 2701 does not apply to a transfer by an individual to a member of the individual's family of equity interests to the extent the transfer by that individual results in a proportionate reduction of each class of equity interest held by the individual and all applicable family members in the aggregate immediately before the transfer. Thus, for example, section 2701 does not apply if P owns 50 percent of each class of equity interest in a corporation and transfers a portion of each class to P's child in a manner that reduces each interest held by P and any applicable family members, in the aggregate, by 10 percent even if the transfer does not proportionately reduce P's interest in each class. See § 25.2701-6 regarding indirect holding of interests.

(d) Family definitions. *(1) Member of the family.* A member of the family is, with respect to any transferor—

(i) The transferor's spouse;

(ii) Any lineal descendant of the transferor or the transferor's spouse; and

(iii) The spouse of any such lineal descendant.

(2) Applicable family member. An applicable family member is, with respect to any transferor—

(i) The transferor's spouse;

(ii) Any ancestor of the transferor or the transferor's spouse: and

(iii) The spouse of any such ancestor.

(3) Relationship by adoption. For purposes of section 2701, any relationship by legal adoption is the same as a relationship by blood.

(e) Examples. The following examples illustrate provisions of this section:

Example (1). P, an individual, holds all the outstanding stock of X Corporation. Assume the fair market value of P's interest in X immediately prior to the transfer is $1.5 million. X is recapitalized so that P holds 1,000 shares of $1,000 par value preferred stock bearing an annual cumulative dividend of $100 per share (the aggregate fair market value of which is assumed to be $1 million) and 1,000 shares of voting common stock. P transfers the common stock to P's child. Section 2701 applies to the transfer because P has transferred an equity interest (the common stock) to a member of P's family and immediately thereafter holds an applicable retained interest (the preferred stock). P's right to receive annual cumulative dividends is a qualified payment right and is valued for purposes of section 2701 at its fair market value of $1,000,000. The amount of P's gift, determined using the subtraction method of § 25.2701-3, is $500,000 ($1,500,000 minus $1,000,000).

Example (2). The facts are the same as in Example 1, except that the preferred dividend right is noncumulative. Under § 25.2701- 2, P's preferred dividend right is valued at zero because it is a distribution right in a controlled entity, but is not a qualified payment right. All of P's other rights in the preferred stock are valued as if P's dividend right does not exist but otherwise without regard to section 2701. The amount of P's gift, determined using the subtraction method, is $1,500,000 ($1,500,000 minus $0). P may elect, however, to treat the dividend right as a qualified payment right as provided in § 25.2701-2(c)(2).

T.D. 8395, 1/28/92, amend T.D. 8536, 5/4/94.

§ 25.2701-2 Special valuation rules for applicable retained interests.

(a) In general. In determining the amount of a gift under § 25.2701-3, the value of any applicable retained interest (as defined in paragraph (b)(1) of this section) held by the transferor or by an applicable family member is determined using the rules of chapter 12, with the modifications prescribed by this section. See § 25.2701-6 regarding the indirect holding of interests.

(1) Valuing an extraordinary payment right. Any extraordinary payment right (as defined in paragraph (b)(2) of this section) is valued at zero.

(2) Valuing a distribution right. Any distribution right (as defined in paragraph (b)(3) of this section) in a controlled entity is valued at zero, unless it is a qualified payment right (as defined in paragraph (b)(6) of this section). Controlled entity is defined in paragraph (b)(5) of this section.

(3) Special rule for valuing a qualified payment right held in conjunction with an extraordinary payment right. If an applicable retained interest confers a qualified payment right and one or more extraordinary payment rights, the value of all these rights is determined by assuming that each extraordinary payment right is exercised in a manner that results in the lowest total value being determined for all the rights, using a consistent set of assumptions and giving due regard to the entity's net worth, prospective earning power. and other relevant factors (the "lower of" valuation rule). See §§ 20.2031-2(f) and 20.2631-3 for rules relating to the valuation of business interests generally.

(4) Valuing other rights. Any other right (including a qualified payment right not subject to the prior paragraph) is valued as if any right valued at zero does not exist and as if any right valued under the lower of rule is exercised in a manner consistent with the assumptions of that rule but otherwise without regard to section 2701. Thus, if an applicable retained interest carries no rights that are valued at zero or under the lower of rule, the value of the interest for purposes of section 2701 is its fair market value.

(5) Example. The following example illustrates rules of this paragraph (a).

Example. P, an individual, holds all 1,000 shares of X Corporation's $1,000 par value preferred stock bearing an annual cumulative dividend of $100 per share and holds all 1,000 shares of X's voting common stock. P has the right to put all the preferred stock to X at any time for $900,000. P transfers the common stock to P's child and immediately thereafter holds the preferred stock. Assume that at the time of the transfer, the fair market value of X is $1,500,000, and the fair market value of P's annual cumulative dividend right is $1,000,000. Because the preferred stock confers both an extraordinary payment right (the put right) and a qualified payment right (i.e., the right to receive cumulative dividends), the lower of rule applies and the value of these rights is determined as if the put right will be exercised in a manner that results in the lowest total value being determined for the rights (in this case. by assuming that the put will be exercised immediately). The value of P's preferred stock is $900,000 (the lower of $1,000,000 or $900,000). The amount of the gift is $600,000 ($1,500,000 minus $900,000).

(b) Definitions. *(1) Applicable retained interest.* An applicable retained interest is any equity interest in a corporation or partnership with respect to which there is either—

(i) An extraordinary payment right (as defined in paragraph (b)(2) of this section), or

(ii) In the case of a controlled entity (as defined in paragraph (b)(5) of this section), a distribution right (as defined in paragraph (b)(3) of this section).

(2) Extraordinary payment right. Except as provided in paragraph (b)(4) of this section, an extraordinary payment right is any put, call, or conversion right, any right to compel liquidation, or any similar right, the exercise or nonexercise of which affects the value of the transferred interest. A call right includes any warrant, option, or other right to acquire one or more equity interests.

(3) Distribution right. A distribution right is the right to receive distributions with respect to an equity interest. A distribution right does not include—

(i) Any right to receive distributions with respect to an interest that is of the same class as, or a class that is subordinate to, the transferred interest:

(ii) Any extraordinary payment right; or

(iii) Any right described in paragraph (b)(4) of this section.

(4) Rights that are not extraordinary payment rights or distribution rights. Mandatory payment rights, liquidation participation rights, rights to guaranteed payments of a fixed amount under section 707(c), and non-lapsing conversion rights are neither extraordinary payment rights nor distribution rights.

(i) Mandatory payment right. A mandatory payment right is a right to receive a payment required to be made at a specific time for a specific amount. For example, a mandatory redemption right in preferred stock requiring that the stock be redeemed at its fixed par value on a date certain is a mandatory payment right and therefore not an extraordinary payment right or a distribution right. A right to receive a specific amount on the death of the holder is a mandatory payment right.

(ii) Liquidation participation rights. A liquidation participation right is a right to participate in a liquidating distribution. If the transferor, members of the transferor's family. or applicable family members have the ability to compel liquidation, the liquidation participation right is valued as if the ability to compel liquidation—

(A) Did not exist, or

(B) If the lower of rule applies, is exercised in a manner that is consistent with that rule.

(iii) Right to a guaranteed payment of a fixed amount under section 707(c). The right to a guaranteed payment of a fixed amount under section 707(c) is the right to a guaranteed payment (within the meaning of section 707(c)) the amount of which is determined at a fixed rate (including a rate that bears a fixed relationship to a specified market interest rate). A payment that is contingent as to time or amount is not a guaranteed payment of a fixed amount.

(iv) Non-lapsing conversion right (A) Corporations. A non-lapsing conversion right, in the case of a corporation, is a non-lapsing right to convert an equity interest in a corporation into a fixed number or a fixed percentage of shares of the same class as the transferred interest (or into an interest that would be of the same class but for non-lapsing differences in voting rights), that is subject to proportionate adjustments for changes in the equity ownership of the corporation and to adjustments similar to those provided in section 2701(d) for unpaid payments.

(B) Partnerships. A non-lapsing conversion right, in the case of a partnership, is a non-lapsing right to convert an equity interest in a partnership into a specified interest (other than an interest represented by a fixed dollar amount) of the same class as the transferred interest (or into an interest that would be of the same class but for non-lapsing differences in management rights or limitations on liability) that is subject to proportionate adjustments for changes in the equity ownership of the partnership and to adjustments similar to those provided in section 2701(d) for unpaid payments.

(C) Proportionate adjustments in equity ownership. For purposes of this paragraph (b)(4), an equity interest is subject to proportionate adjustments for changes in equity ownership if, in the case of a corporation, proportionate adjustments are required to be made for splits, combinations, reclassifications, and similar changes in capital stock, or, in the case of a partnership, the equity interest is protected from dilution resulting from changes in the partnership structure.

(D) Adjustments for unpaid payments. For purposes of this paragraph (b)(4), an equity interest is subject to adjustments similar to those provided in section 2701(d) if it provides for—

(1) Cumulative payments;

(2) Compounding of any unpaid payments at the rate specified in § 25.2701-4(c)(2); and

(3) Adjustment of the number or percentage of shares or the size of the interest into which it is convertible to take account of accumulated but unpaid payments.

(5) Controlled entity. (i) In general. For purposes of section 2701, a controlled entity is a corporation or partnership controlled, immediately before a transfer, by the transferor, applicable family members, and any lineal descendants of the parents of the transferor or the transferor's spouse. See § 25.2701-6 regarding indirect holding of interests.

(ii) Corporations (A) In general. In the case of a corporation, control means the holding of at least 50 percent of the total voting power or total fair market value of the equity interests in the corporation.

(B) Voting rights. Equity interests that carry no right to vote other than on liquidation, merger, or a similar event are not considered to have voting rights for purposes of this paragraph (b)(5)(ii). Generally, a voting right is considered held by an individual to the extent that the individual, either alone or in conjunction with any other person, is entitled to exercise (or direct the exercise of) the right. However, if an equity interest carrying voting rights is held in a fiduciary capacity, the voting rights are not considered held by the fiduciary, but instead are considered held by each beneficial owner of the interest and by each individual who is a permissible recipient of the income from the interest. A voting right does not include a right to vote that is subject to a contingency that has not occurred, other than a contingency that is within the control of the individual holding the right.

(iii) Partnerships. In the case of any partnership, control means the holding of at least 50 percent of either the capital interest or the profits interest in the partnership. Any right to a guaranteed payment under section 707(c) of a fixed amount is disregarded in making this determination. In addition, in the case of a limited partnership, control means the holding of any equity interest as a general partner. See § 25.2701-2(b)(4)(iii) for the definition of a right to a guaranteed payment of a fixed amount under section 707(c).

(6) Qualified payment right. (i) In general. A qualified payment right is a right to receive qualified payments. A qualified payment is a distribution that is—

(A) A dividend payable on a periodic basis (at least annually) under any cumulative preferred stock, to the extent such dividend is determined at a fixed rate;

(B) Any other cumulative distribution payable on a periodic basis (at least annually) with respect to an equity interest, to the extent determined at a fixed rate or as a fixed amount; or

(C) Any distribution right for which an election has been made pursuant to paragraph (c)(2) of this section.

(ii) Fixed rate. For purposes of this section a payment rate that bears a fixed relationship to a specified market interest rate is a payment determined at a fixed rate.

(c) Qualified payment elections. *(1) Election to treat a qualified payment right as other than a qualified payment right.* Any transferor holding a qualified payment right may elect to treat all rights held by the transferor of the same class as rights that are not qualified payment rights. An election may be a partial election, in which case the election must be exercised with respect to a consistent portion of each payment right in the class as to which the election has been made.

(2) Election to treat other distribution rights as qualified payment rights. Any individual may elect to treat a distribution right held by that individual in a controlled entity as a qualified payment right. An election may be a partial election, in which case the election must be exercised with respect to a consistent portion of each payment right in the class as to which the election has been made. An election under this paragraph (c)(2) will not cause the value of the applicable retained interest conferring the distribution right to exceed the fair market value of the applicable retained interest (determined without regard to section 2701). The election is effective only to the extent—

(i) Specified in the election, and

(ii) That the payments elected are permissible under the legal instrument giving rise to the right and are consistent with the legal right of the entity to make the payment.

(3) Elections irrevocable. Any election under paragraph (c)(1) or (c)(2) of this section is revocable only with the consent of the Commissioner.

(4) Treatment of certain payments to applicable family members. Any payment right described in paragraph (b)(6) of this section held by an applicable family member is treated as a payment right that is not a qualified payment right unless the applicable family member elects (pursuant to paragraph (c)(2) of this section) to treat the payment right as a qualified payment right. An election may be a partial election, in which case the election must be exercised with respect to a consistent portion of each payment right in the class as to which the election has been made.

(5) Time and manner of elections. Any election under paragraph (c)(1) or (c)(2) of this section is made by attaching a statement to the Form 709, Federal Gift Tax Return, filed by the transferor on which the transfer is reported. An election filed after the time of the filing of the Form 709 reporting the transfer is not a valid election. An election filed as of

April 6, 1992, for transfers made prior to its publication is effective. The statement must—

(i) Set forth the name, address, and taxpayer identification number of the electing individual and of the transferor, if different;

(ii) If the electing individual is not the transferor filing the return, state the relationship between the individual and the transferor;

(iii) Specifically identify the transfer disclosed on the return to which the election applies;

(iv) Describe in detail the distribution right to which the election applies;

(v) State the provision of the regulation under which the election is being made; and

(vi) If the election is being made under paragraph (c)(2) of this section—

(A) State the amounts that the election assumes will be paid, and the times that the election assumes the payments will be made;

(B) Contain a statement, signed by the electing individual, in which the electing individual agrees that—

(1) If payments are not made as provided in the election, the individual's subsequent taxable gifts or taxable estate will, upon the occurrence of a taxable event (as defined in § 25.2701-4(b)), be increased by an amount determined under § 25.2701-4(c), and

(2) The individual will be personally liable for any increase in tax attributable thereto.

(d) Examples. The following examples illustrate provisions of this section:

Example (1). On March 30, 1991, P transfer's non-voting common stock of X Corporation to P's child, while retaining $100 par value voting preferred stock bearing a cumulative annual dividend of $10. Immediately before the transfer, P held 100 percent of the stock. Because X is a controlled entity (within the meaning of paragraph (b)(5) of this section), P's dividend right is a distribution right that is subject to section 2701. See § 25.2701-2(b)(3). Because the distribution right is an annual cumulative dividend, it is a qualified payment right. See § 25.2701-2(b)(6).

Example (2). The facts are the same as in Example 1, except that the dividend right is non-cumulative. P's dividend right is a distribution right in a controlled entity, but is not a qualified payment right because the dividend is non-cumulative. Therefore, the non-cumulative dividend right is valued at zero under § 25.2701-2(a)(2). If the corporation were not a controlled entity, P's dividend right would be valued without regard to section 2701.

Example (3). The facts are the same as in Example 1. Because P holds sufficient voting power to compel liquidation of X, P's right to participate in liquidation is an extraordinary payment right under paragraph (b)(2) of this section. Because P holds an extraordinary payment right in conjunction with a qualified payment right (the right to receive cumulative dividends), the lower of rule applies.

Example (4). The facts are the same as in Example 1, except that immediately before the transfer, P, applicable family members of P, and members of P's family, hold 60 percent of the voting rights in X. Assume that 80 percent of the vote is required to compel liquidation of any interest in X. P's right to participate in liquidation is not an extraordinary payment right under paragraph (b)(2) of this section, because P and P's family cannot compel liquidation of X. P's preferred stock is an applicable retained interest that carries no rights that are valued under the special valuation rules of section 2701. Thus, in applying the valuation method of § 25.2701-3, the value of P's preferred stock is its fair market value determined without regard to section 2701.

Example (5). L holds 10-percent non-cumulative preferred stock and common stock in a corporation that is a controlled entity. L transfers the common stock to L's child. L holds no extraordinary payment rights with respect to the preferred stock. L elects under paragraph (c)(2) of this section to treat the noncumulative dividend right as a qualified payment right consisting of the right to receive a cumulative annual dividend of 5 percent. Under § 25.2701-2(c)(2), the value of the distribution right pursuant to the election is the lesser of—

(A) The fair market value of the right to receive a cumulative 5-percent dividend from the corporation, giving due regard to the corporation's net worth, prospective earning power, and dividend-paying capacity; or

(B) The value of the distribution right determined without regard to section 2701 and without regard to the terms of the qualified payment election.

T.D. 8395, 1/28/92.

---

§ 25.2701-3 Determination of amount of gift.

(a) Overview. *(1) In general.* The amount of the gift resulting from any transfer to which section 2701 applies is determined by a subtraction method of valuation. Under this method, the amount of the transfer is determined by subtracting the values of all family-held senior equity interests from the fair market value of all family-held interests in the entity determined immediately before the transfer. The values of the senior equity interests held by the transferor and applicable family members generally are determined under section 2701. Other family-held senior equity interests are valued at their fair market value. The balance is then appropriately allocated among the transferred interests and other family-held subordinate equity interests. Finally, certain discounts and other appropriate reductions are provided, but only to the extent permitted by this section.

(2) Definitions. The following definitions apply for purposes of this section.

(i) Family-held. Family-held means held (directly or indirectly) by an individual described in § 25.2701-2(b)(5)(i).

(ii) Senior equity interest. Senior equity interest means an equity interest in the entity that carries a right to distributions of income or capital that is preferred as to the rights of the transferred interest.

(iii) Subordinate equity interest. Subordinate equity interest means an equity interest in the entity as to which an applicable retained interest is a senior equity interest.

(b) Valuation methodology. The following methodology is used to determine the amount of the gift when section 2701 applies.

(1) Step 1. Valuation of family-held interest. (i) In general. Except as provided in paragraph (b)(1)(ii) of this section determine the fair market value of all family-held equity interests in the entity immediately after the transfer. The fair market value is determined by assuming that the interests are held by one individual, using a consistent set of assumptions.

(ii) Special rule for contributions to capital. In the case of a contribution to capital, determine the fair market value of the contribution.

(2) Step 2. Subtract the value of senior equity interests. (i) In general. If the amount determined in Step 1 of paragraph (b)(1) of this section is not determined under the special rule for contributions to capital, from that value subtract the following amounts:

(A) An amount equal to the sum of the fair market value of all family-held senior equity interests, (other than applicable retained interests held by the transferor or applicable family members) and the fair market value of any family-held equity interests of the same class or a subordinate class to the transferred interests held by persons other than the transferor, members of the transferor's family, and applicable family members of the transferor. The fair market value of an interest is its pro rata share of the fair market value of all family-held senior equity interests of the same class (determined, immediately after the transfer, as is all family-held senior equity interests were held by one individual); and

(B) The value of all applicable retained interests held by the transferor or applicable family members (other than an interest received as consideration for the transfer) determined under § 25.2701-2, taking into account the adjustment described in paragraph (b)(5) of this section.

(ii) Special rule for contributions to capital. If the value determined in Step 1 of paragraph (b)(1) of this section is determined under the special rule for contributions to capital, subtract the value of any applicable retained interest received in exchange for the contribution to capital determined under § 25.2701-2.

(3) Step 3. Allocate the remaining value among the transferred interests and other family-held subordinate equity interests. The value remaining after Step 2 is allocated among the transferred interests and other subordinate equity interests held by the transferor, applicable family members, and members of the transferor's family. If more than one class of family-held subordinate equity interest exists, the value remaining after Step 2 is allocated, beginning with the most senior class of subordinate equity interest, in the manner that would most fairly approximate their value if all rights valued under section 2701 at zero did not exist (or would be exercised in a manner consistent with the assumptions of the rule of § 25.2702-2(a)(4), if applicable). If there is no clearly appropriate method of allocating the remaining value pursuant to the preceding sentence, the remaining value (or the portion remaining after any partial allocation pursuant to the preceding sentence) is allocated to the interests in proportion to their fair market values determined without regard to section 2701.

(4) Step 4. Determine the amount of the gift. (i) In general. The amount allocated to the transferred interests in Step 3 is reduced by the amounts determined under this paragraph (b)(4).

(ii) Reduction for minority or similar discounts. Except as provided in § 25.2701-3(c), if the value of the transferred interest (determined without regard to section 2701) would be determined after application of a minority or similar discount with respect to the transferred interest, the amount of the gift determined under section 2701 is reduced by the excess, if any, of—

(A) A pro rata portion of the fair market value of the family-held interests of the same class (determined as if all voting rights conferred by family-held equity interests were held by one person who had no interest in the entity other than the family-held interests of the same class, but otherwise without regard to section 2701), over

(B) The value of the transferred interest (without regard to section 2701).

(iii) Adjustment for transfers with a retained interest. If the value of the transferor's gift (determined without regard to section 2701) would be reduced under section 2702 to reflect the value of a retained interest, the value determined under section 2701 is reduced by the same amount.

(iv) Reduction for consideration. The amount of the transfer (determined under section 2701) is reduced by the amount of consideration in money or money's worth received by the transferor, but not in excess of the amount of the gift (determined without regard to section 2701). The value of consideration received by the transferor in the form of an applicable retained interest in the entity is determined under section 2701 except that, in the case of a contribution to capital, the Step 4 value of such an interest is zero.

(5) Adjustment in Step 2. (i) In general. For purposes of paragraph (b)(2) of this section, if the percentage of any class of applicable retained interest held by the transferor and by applicable family members (including any interest received as consideration for the transfer) exceeds the family interest percentage, the excess is treated as a family-held interest that is not held by the transferor or an applicable family member.

(ii) Family interest percentage. The family interest percentage is the highest ownership percentage (determined on the basis of relative fair market values) of family-held interests in—

(A) Any class of subordinate equity interest; or

(B) All subordinate equity interests, valued in the aggregate.

(c) Minimum value rule. *(1) In general.* If section 2701 applies to the transfer of an interest in an entity, the value of a junior equity interest is not less than its pro-rata portion of 10 percent of the sum of—

(i) The total value of all equity interests in the entity, and

(ii) The total amount of any indebtedness of the entity owed to the transferor and applicable family members.

(2) Junior equity interest. For purposes of paragraph (c)(1) of this section, junior equity interest means common stock or, in the case of a partnership, any partnership interest under which the rights to income and capital are junior to the rights of all other classes of partnership interests. Common stock means the class or classes of stock that, under the facts and circumstances, are entitled to share in the reasonably anticipated residual growth in the entity.

(3) Indebtedness. (i) In general. For purposes of paragraph (c)(1) of this section, indebtedness owed to the transferor (or an applicable family member) does not include—

(A) Short-term indebtedness incurred with respect to the current conduct of the entity's trade or business (such as amounts payable for current services);

(B) Indebtedness owed to a third party solely because it is guaranteed by the transferor or an applicable family member; or

(C) Amounts permanently set aside in a qualified deferred compensation arrangement, to the extent the amounts are unavailable for use by the entity.

(ii) Leases. A lease of property is not indebtedness, without regard to the length of the lease term, if the lease payments represent full and adequate consideration for use of the property. Lease payments are considered full and adequate consideration if a good faith effort is made to determine the fair rental value under the lease and the terms of the lease conform to the value so determined. Arrearages with respect to a lease are indebtedness.

(d) Examples. The application of the subtraction method described in this section is illustrated by the following examples:

Example (1). Corporation X has outstanding 1,000 shares of $1,000 par value voting preferred stock, each share of which carries a cumulative annual dividend of 8 percent and a right to put the stock to X for its par value at any time. In addition, there are outstanding 1,000 shares of non-voting common stock. A holds 600 shares of the preferred stock and 750 shares of the common stock. The balance of the preferred and common stock is held by B, a person unrelated to A. Because the preferred stock confers both a qualified payment right and an extraordinary payment right, A's rights are valued under the "lower of" rule of § 25.2701-2(a)(3). Assume that A's rights in the preferred stock are valued at $800 per share under the "lower of" rule (taking account of A's voting rights). A transfers all of A's common stock to A's child. The method for determining the amount of A's gift is as follows—

Step 1: Assume the fair market value of all the family-held interests in X, taking account of A's control of the corporation, is determined to be $1 million.

Step 2: From the amount determined under Step 1, subtract $480,000 (600 shares × $800 (the section 2701 value of A's preferred stock, computed under the "lower of" rule of § 25.2701- 2(a)(3))).

Step 3: The result of Step 2 is a balance of $520,000. This amount is fully allocated to the 750 shares of family-held common stock.

Step 4. Because no consideration was furnished for the transfer, the adjustment under Step 4 is limited to the amount of any appropriate minority or similar discount. Before the application of Step 4 the amount of A's gift is $520,000.

Example (2). The facts are the same as in Example 1, except that prior to the transfer A holds only 50 percent of the common stock and B holds the remaining 50 percent. Assume that the fair market value of A's 600 shares of preferred stock is $600,000.

Step 1: Assume that the result of this step (determining the value of the family-held interest) is $980,000.

Step 2: From the amount determined under Step 1, subtract $500,000 ($400,000, the fair market value of 500 shares of A's preferred stock determined under section 2701 plus $100,000, the fair market value of A's other 100 shares of preferred stock determined without regard to section 2701 pursuant to the valuation adjustment determined under paragraph (b)(5) of this section). The adjustment in step 2 applies in this example because A's percentage ownership of the preferred stock (60 percent) exceeds the family interest percentage of the common stock (50 percent). Therefore, 100 shares of A's preferred stock are valued at fair market value, or $100,000 (100 × $1,000). The balance of A's preferred stock is valued under section 2701 at $400,000 (500 shares × $800). The value of A's preferred stock for purposes of section 2701 equals $500,000 ($100,000 plus $400,000).

Step 3: The result of Step 2 is $480,000 ($980,000 minus $500,000) which is allocated to the family-held common stock. Because A transferred all of the family-held subordinate equity interests, all of the value determined under Step 2 is allocated to the transferred shares.

Step 4: The adjustment under Step 4 is the same as in Example 1. Thus, the amount of the gift is $480,000.

Example (3). Corporation X has outstanding 1,000 shares of $1,000 par value non-voting preferred stock, each share of which carries a cumulative annual dividend of 8 percent and a right to put the stock to X for its par value at any time. In addition, there are outstanding 1,000 shares of voting common stock. A holds 600 shares of the preferred stock and 750 shares of the common stock. The balance of the preferred and common stock is held by B, a person unrelated to A. Assume further that steps one through three, as in Example 1, result in $520,000 being allocated to the family-held common stock and that A transfers only 75 shares of A's common stock. The transfer fragments A's voting interest. Under step 4, an adjustment is appropriate to reflect the fragmentation of A's voting rights. The amount of the adjustment is the difference between 10 percent (75/750) of the fair market value of A's common shares and the fair market value of the transferred shares, each determined as if the holder thereof had no other interest in the corporation.

Example (4). On December 31, 1990, the capital structure of Y corporation consists of 1,000 shares of voting common stock held three-fourths by A and one-fourth by A's child, B. On January 15, 1991, A transfers 250 shares of common stock to Y in exchange for 300 shares of nonvoting, noncumulative 8% preferred stock with a section 2701 value of zero. Assume that the fair market value of Y is $1,000,000 at the time of the exchange and that the exchange by A is for full and adequate consideration in moneys' worth. However, for purposes of section 2701, if a subordinate equity interest is transferred in exchange for an applicable retained interest, consideration in the exchange is determined with reference to the section 2701 value of the senior interest. Thus, A is treated as transferring the common stock to the corporation for no consideration. Immediately after the transfer, B is treated as holding one-third (250/750) of the common stock and A is treated as holding two-thirds (500/750). The amount of the gift is determined as follows:

Step 1. Because Y is held exclusively by A and B, the Step 1 value is $1,000,000.

Step 2. The result of Step 2 is $1,000,000 ($1,000,000 – 0).

Step 3. The amount allocated to the transferred common stock is $250,000 (250/1,000 × $1,000,000). That amount is further allocated in proportion to the respective holdings of A and B in the common stock ($166,667 and $83,333, respectively).

Step 4. There is no Step 4 adjustment because the section 2701 value of the consideration received by A was zero and no minority discount would have been involved in the exchange. Thus. the amount of the gift is $83,333. If the section 2701 value of the applicable retained interested were $100,000, the Step 4 adjustment would have been a $33,333 reduction for consideration received ((250/750) x $100,000).

Example (5). The facts are the same as in Example 4, except that on January 6, 1992, when the fair market value of Y is still $1,000,000, A transfers A's remaining 500 shares of common stock to Y in exchange for 2500 shares of preferred stock. The second transfer is also for full and adequate consideration in money or money's worth. The result of Step 2 is the same—$1,000,000.

Step 3. The amount allocated to the transferred common stock is $666,667 (500/750 × $1,000,000). Since A holds no common stock immediately after the transfer, A is treated as transferring the entire interest to the other shareholder (B). Thus, $666,667 is fully allocated to the shares held by B.

Step 4. There is no Step 4 adjustment because the section 2701 value of the consideration received by A was zero and no minority discount would have been involved in the exchange. Thus, the amount of the gift is $666,667.

T.D. 8395, 1/28/92.

§ 25.2701-4 Accumulated qualified payments.

(a) In general. If a taxable event occurs with respect to any applicable retained interest conferring a distribution right that was previously valued as a qualified payment right (a "qualified payment interest"), the taxable estate or taxable gifts of the individual holding the interest are increased by the amount determined under paragraph (c) of this section.

(b) Taxable event. *(1) In general.* Except as otherwise provided in this section, taxable event means the transfer of a qualified payment interest, either during life or at death, by the individual in whose hands the interest was originally valued under section 2701 (the "interest holder") or by any individual treated pursuant to paragraph (b)(3) of this section in the same manner as the interest holder. Except as provided in paragraph (a)(2) of this section, any termination of an individual's rights with respect to a qualified payment interest is a taxable event. Thus, for example, if an individual is treated as indirectly holding a qualified payment interest held by a trust, a taxable event occurs on the earlier of—

(i) The termination of the individual's interest in the trust (whether by death or otherwise), or

(ii) The termination of the trust's interest in the qualified payment interest (whether by disposition or otherwise).

(2) Exception. If, at the time of a termination of an individual's rights with respect to a qualified payment interest, the value of the property would be includible in the individual's gross estate for Federal estate tax purposes if the individual died immediately after the termination, a taxable transfer does not occur until the earlier of—

(i) The time the property would no longer be includible in the individual's gross estate (other than by reason of section 2035), or

(ii) The death of the individual.

(3) Individual treated as interest holder. (i) In general. If a taxable event involves the transfer of a qualified payment interest by the interest holder (or an individual treated as the interest holder) to an applicable family member of the individual who made the transfer to which section 2701 applied (other than the spouse of the individual transferring the qualified payment interest), the transferee applicable family member is treated in the same manner as the interest holder with respect to late or unpaid qualified payments first due after the taxable event. Thus, for example, if an interest holder transfers during life a qualified payment interest to an applicable family member, that transfer is a taxable event with respect to the interest holder whose taxable gifts are increased for the year of the transfer as provided in paragraph (c) of this section. The transferee is treated thereafter in the same manner as the interest holder with respect to late or unpaid qualified payments first due after the taxable event.

(ii) Transfers to spouse. (A) In general. If an interest holder (or an individual treated as the interest holder) transfers a qualified payment interest, the transfer is not a taxable event to the extent a marital deduction is allowed with respect to the transfer under sections 2056, 2106(a)(3), or 2523 or, in the case of a transfer during the individual's lifetime, to the extent the spouse furnishes consideration for the transfer. If this exception applies, the transferee spouse is treated as if he or she were the holder of the interest from the date the transferor spouse acquired the interest. If the deduction for a transfer to a spouse is allowable under section 2056(b)(8) or 2523(g) (relating to charitable remainder trusts), the transferee spouse is treated as the holder of the entire interest passing to the trust.

(B) Marital bequests. If the selection of property with which a marital bequest is funded is discretionary, a transfer of a qualified payment interest will not be considered a transfer to the surviving spouse unless—

(1) The marital bequest is funded with the qualified payment interest before the due date for filing the decedent's Federal estate tax return (including extensions actually granted) (the "due date"), or

(2) The executor—

(i) Files a statement with the return indicating the extent to which the marital bequest will be funded with the qualified payment interest, and

(ii) Before the date that is one year prior to the expiration of the period of limitations on assessment of the Federal estate tax, notifies the District Director having jurisdiction over the return of the extent to which the bequest was funded with the qualified payment interest (or the extent to which the qualified payment interest has been permanently set aside for that purpose).

(C) Purchase by the surviving spouse. For purposes of this section, the purchase (before the date prescribed for filing the decedent's estate tax return, including extensions actually granted) by the surviving spouse (or a trust described in section 2056(b)(7)) of a qualified payment interest held (directly or indirectly) by the decedent immediately before death is considered a transfer with respect to which a deduction is allowable under section 2056 or section 2106(a)(3). but only to the extent that the deduction is allowed to the estate. For example, assume that A bequeaths $50,000 to A's surviving spouse, B, in a manner that qualifies for deduction under section 2056, and that subsequent to A's death B purchases a qualified payment interest from A's estate for $200,000, its fair market value. The economic effect of the transaction is the equivalent of a bequest by A to B of the qualified payment interest, one-fourth of which qualifies for the marital deduction. Therefore, for purposes of this section, one-fourth of the qualified payment interest purchased by B ($50,000 ÷ $200,000) is considered a transfer of an interest with respect to which a deduction is allowed under 2056. If the purchase by the surviving spouse is not made before the due date of the decedent's return, the purchase of the qualified payment interest will not be considered a bequest for which a marital deduction is allowed unless the executor—

(1) Files a statement with the return indicating the qualified payment interests to be purchased by the surviving spouse (or a trust described in section 2056(b)(7)), and

(2) Before the date that is one year prior to the expiration of the period of limitations on assessment of the Federal estate tax, notifies the District Director having jurisdiction over the return that the purchase of the qualified payment interest has been made (or that the funds necessary to purchase the qualified payment interest have been permanently set aside for that purpose).

(c) Amount of increase. *(1) In general.* Except as limited by paragraph (c)(6) of this section, the amount of the increase to an individual's taxable estate or taxable gifts is the excess, if any, of—

(i) The sum of—

(A) The amount of qualified payments payable during the period beginning on the date of the transfer to which section 2701 applied (or, in the case of an individual treated as the interest holder, on the date the interest of the prior interest holder terminated) and ending on the date of the taxable event; and

(B) The earnings on those payments, determined hypothetically as if each payment were paid on its due date and reinvested as of that date at a yield equal to the appropriate discount rate (as defined below); over

(ii) The sum of—

(A) The amount of the qualified payments actually paid during the same period;

(B) The earnings on those payments, determined hypothetically as if each payment were reinvested as of the date actually paid at a yield equal to the appropriate discount rate; and

(C) To the extent required to prevent double inclusion, by an amount equal to the sum of—

(1) The portion of the fair market value of the qualified payment interest solely attributable to any right to receive unpaid qualified payments determined as of the date of the taxable event;

(2) The fair market value of any equity interest in the entity received by the individual in lieu of qualified payments and held by the individual at the taxable event, and

(3) The amount by which the individual's aggregate taxable gifts were increased by reason of the failure of the individual to enforce the right to receive qualified payments.

(2) Due date of qualified payments. With respect to any qualified payment, the "due date" is that date specified in the governing instrument as the date on which payment is to be made. If no date is specified in the governing instrument, the due date is the last day of each calendar year.

(3) Appropriate discount rate. The appropriate discount rate is the discount rate that was applied in determining the value of the qualified payment right at the time of the transfer to which section 2701 applied.

(4) Application of payments. For purposes of this section, any payment of an unpaid qualified payment is applied in satisfaction of unpaid qualified payments beginning with the earliest unpaid qualified payment. Any payment in excess of the total of all unpaid qualified payments is treated as a prepayment of future qualified payments.

(5) Payment. For purposes of this paragraph (c), the transfer of a debt obligation bearing compound interest from the due date of the payment at a rate not less than the appropriate discount rate is a qualified payment if the term of the obligation (including extensions) does not exceed four years from the date issued. A payment in the form of an equity interest in the entity is not a qualified payment. Any payment of a qualified payment made (or treated as made) either before or during the four-year period beginning on the due date of the payment but before the date of the taxable event is treated as having been made on the due date.

(6) Limitation. (i) In general. The amount of the increase to an individual's taxable estate or taxable gifts is limited to the applicable percentage of the excess, if any, of—

(A) The sum of—

(1) The fair market value of all outstanding equity interests in the entity that are subordinate to the applicable retained interest, determined as of the date of the taxable event without regard to any accrued liability attributable to unpaid qualified payments; and

(2) Any amounts expended by the entity to redeem or otherwise acquire any such subordinate interest during the period beginning on the date of the transfer to which section 2701 applied (or, in the case of an individual treated as an interest holder, on the date the interest of the prior interest holder terminated) and ending on the date of the taxable event (reduced by any amounts received on the resale or issuance of any such subordinate interest during the same period); over

(B) The fair market value of all outstanding equity interests in the entity that are subordinate to the applicable retained interest, determined as of the date of the transfer to which section 2701 applied (or, in the case of an individual treated as an interest holder, on the date the interest of the prior interest holder terminated).

(ii) Computation of limitation. For purposes of computing the limitation applicable under this paragraph (c)(6). the aggregate fair market value of the subordinate interests in the entity are determined without regard to § 25.2701-3(c).

(iii) Applicable percentage. The applicable percentage is determined by dividing the number of shares or units the applicable retained interest held by the interest holder (or an individual treated as the interest holder) on the date of the taxable event by the total number of such shares or units outstanding on the same date. If an individual holds applicable retained interests in two or more classes of interests, the applicable percentage is equal to the largest applicable percentage determined with respect to any class. For example, if T retains 40 percent of the class A preferred and 60 percent of the class B preferred in a corporation, the applicable percentage with respect to T's holdings is 60 percent.

(d) Taxpayer election. *(1) In general.* An interest holder (or individual treated as an interest holder) may elect to treat as a taxable event the payment of an unpaid qualified payment occurring more than four years after its due date. Under this election, the increase under paragraph (c) of this section is determined only with respect to that payment and all previous payments for which an election was available but not made. Payments for which an election applies are treated as having been paid on their due dates for purposes of subsequent taxable events. The election is revocable only with the consent of the Commissioner.

(2) Limitation not applicable. If a taxable event occurs by reason of an election described in paragraph (d)(1) of this section, the limitation described in paragraph (c)(6) of this section does not apply.

(3) Time and manner of election. (i) Timely-filed returns. The election may be made by attaching a statement to a Form 709, Federal Gift Tax Return, filed by the recipient of the qualified payment on a timely basis for the year in which the qualified payment is received. In that case, the taxable event is deemed to occur on the date the qualified payment is received.

(ii) Election on late returns. The election may be made by attaching a statement to a Form 709, Federal Gift Tax Return, filed by the recipient of the qualified payment other than on a timely basis for the year in which the qualified payment is received. In that case, the taxable event is deemed to occur on the first day of the month immediately preceding the month in which the return is filed. If an election, other than an election on a timely return, is made after the death of the interest holder, the taxable event with respect to the decedent is deemed to occur on the later of—

(A) The date of the recipient's death, or

(B) The first day of the month immediately preceding the month in which the return is filed.

(iii) Requirements of statement. The statement must—

(A) Provide the name, address, and taxpayer identification number of the electing individual and the interest holder, if different;

(B) Indicate that a taxable event election is being made under paragraph (d) of this section;

(C) Disclose the nature of the qualified payment right to which the election applies, including the due dates of the payments, the dates the payments were made, and the amounts of the payments;

(D) State the name of the transferor, the date of the transfer to which section 2701 applied, and the discount rate used in valuing the qualified payment right; and

(E) State the resulting amount of increase in taxable gifts.

(4) Example. The following example illustrates the rules of this paragraph (d).

Example. A holds cumulative preferred stock that A retained in a transfer to which section 2701 applied. No dividends were paid in years 1 through 5 following the transfer. In year 6, A received a qualified payment that, pursuant to paragraph (c)(3) of this section, is considered to be in satisfaction of the unpaid qualified payment for year 1. No election was made to treat that payment as a taxable event. In year 7, A receives a qualified payment that, pursuant to paragraph (c)(4) of this section, is considered to be in satisfaction of the unpaid qualified payment for year 2. A elects to treat the payment in year 7 as a taxable event. The election increases A's taxable gifts in year 7 by the amount computed under paragraph (c) of this section with respect to the payments due in both year 1 and year 2. For purposes of any future taxable events, the payments with respect to years 1 and 2 are treated as having been made on their due dates.

T.D. 8395, 1/28/92.

§ 25.2701-5 Adjustments to mitigate double taxation.

(a) Reduction of transfer tax base. *(1) In general.* This section provides rules under which an individual (the initial transferor) making a transfer subject to section 2701 (the initial transfer) is entitled to reduce his or her taxable gifts or adjusted taxable gifts (the reduction). The amount of the reduction is determined under paragraph (b) of this section. See paragraph (e) of this section if section 2513 (split gifts) applied to the initial transfer.

(2) Federal gift tax modification. If, during the lifetime of the initial transferor, the holder of a section 2701 interest (as defined in paragraph (a)(4) of this section) transfers the interest to or for the benefit of an individual other than the initial transferor or an applicable family member of the initial transferor in a transfer subject to Federal estate or gift tax, the initial transferor may reduce the amount on which the initial transferor's tentative tax is computed under section 2502(a). The reduction is first applied on any gift tax return required to be filed for the calendar year in which the section 2701 interest is transferred; any excess reduction is carried forward and applied in each succeeding calendar year until the reduction is exhausted. The amount of the reduction that is used in a calendar year is the amount of the initial transferor's taxable gifts for that year. Any excess reduction remaining at the death of the initial transferor may be applied by the executor of the initial transferor's estate as provided under paragraph (a)(3) of this section. See paragraph (a)(4) of this section for the definition of a section 2701 interest. See § 25.2701-6 for rules relating to indirect ownership of equity interests transferred to trusts and other entities.

(3) Federal estate tax modification. Except as otherwise provided in this paragraph (a)(3), in determining the Federal estate tax with respect to an initial transferor, the executor of the initial transferor's estate may reduce the amount on which the decedent's tentative tax is computed under section 2001(b) (or section 2101(b)) by the amount of the reduction (including any excess reduction carried forward under paragraph (a)(2) of this section). The amount of the reduction under this paragraph (a)(3) is limited to the amount that results in zero Federal estate tax with respect to the estate of the initial transferor.

(4) Section 2701 interest. A section 2701 interest is an applicable retained interest that was valued using the special valuation rules of section 2701 at the time of the initial transfer. However, an interest is a section 2701 interest only to the extent the transfer of that interest effectively reduces the aggregate ownership of such class of interest by the initial transferor and applicable family members of the initial transferor below that held by such persons at the time of the initial transfer (or the remaining portion thereof).

(b) Amount of reduction. Except as otherwise provided in paragraphs (c)(3)(iv) (pertaining to transfers of partial interests) and (e) (pertaining to initial split gifts) of this section, the amount of the reduction is the lesser of—

(1) The amount by which the initial transferor's taxable gifts were increased as a result of the application of section 2701 to the initial transfer; or

(2) The amount (determined under paragraph (c) of this section) duplicated in the transfer tax base at the time of the transfer of the section 2701 interest (the duplicated amount).

(c) Duplicated amount. *(1) In general.* The duplicated amount is the amount by which the transfer tax value of the section 2701 interest at the time of the subsequent transfer exceeds the value of that interest determined under section 2701 at the time of the initial transfer. If, at the time of the initial transfer, the amount allocated to the transferred interest under § 25.2701-3(b)(3) (Step 3 of the valuation methodology) is less than the entire amount available for allocation at that time, the duplicated amount is a fraction of the amount described in the preceding sentence. The numerator of the fraction is the amount allocated to the transferred interest at the time of the initial transfer (pursuant to § 2701-3(b)(3)) and the denominator of the fraction is the amount available for allocation at the time of the initial transfer (determined after application of § 25.2701-3(b)(2)).

(2) Transfer tax value—In general. Except as provided in paragraph (c)(3) of this section, for purposes of paragraph (c)(1) of this section the transfer tax value of a section 2701 interest is the value of that interest as finally determined for Federal transfer tax purposes under chapter 11 or chapter 12, as the case may be (including the right to receive any distributions thereon (other than qualified payments)), reduced by the amount of any deduction allowed with respect to the section 2701 interest to the extent that the deduction would not have been allowed if the section 2701 interest were not included in the transferor's total amount of gifts for the calendar year or the transferor's gross estate, as the case may be.

Rules similar to the rules of section 691(c)(2)(C) are applicable to determine the extent that a deduction would not be allowed if the section 2701 interest were not so included.

(3) Special transfer tax value rules. (i) Transfers for consideration. Except as provided in paragraph (c)(3)(iii) of this section, if, during the life of the initial transferor, a section 2701 interest is transferred to or for the benefit of an individual other than the initial transferor or an applicable family member of the initial transferor for consideration in money or money's worth, or in a transfer that is treated as a transfer for consideration in money or money's worth, the transfer of the section 2701 interest is deemed to occur at the death of the initial transferor. In this case, the estate of the initial transferor is entitled to a reduction in the same manner as if the initial transferor's gross estate included a section 2701 interest having a chapter 11 value equal to the amount of consideration in money or money's worth received in the exchange (determined as of the time of the exchange).

(ii) Interests held by applicable family members at date of initial transferor's death. If a section 2701 interest in existence on the date of the initial transferor's death is held by an applicable family member and, therefore, is not included in the gross estate of the initial transferor, the section 2701 interest is deemed to be transferred at the death of the initial transferor to or for the benefit of an individual other than the initial transferor or an applicable family member of the initial transferor. In this case, the transfer tax value of that interest is the value that the executor of the initial transferor's estate can demonstrate would be determined under chapter 12 if the interest were transferred immediately prior to the death of the initial transferor.

(iii) Nonrecognition transactions. If an individual exchanges a section 2701 interest in a nonrecognition transaction (within the meaning of section 7701(a)(45)), the exchange is not treated as a transfer of a section 2701 interest and the transfer tax value of that interest is determined as if the interest received in exchange is the section 2701 interest.

(iv) Transfer of less than the entire section 2701 interest. If a transfer is a transfer of less than the entire section 2701 interest, the amount of the reduction under paragraph (a)(2) or (a)(3) of this section is reduced proportionately.

(v) Multiple classes of section 2701 interest. For purposes of paragraph (b) of this section, if more than one class of section 2701 interest exists, the amount of the reduction is determined separately with respect to each such class.

(vi) Multiple initial transfers. If an initial transferor has made more than one initial transfer, the amount of the reduction with respect to any section 2701 interest is the sum of the reductions computed under paragraph (b) of this section with respect to each such initial transfer.

(d) Examples. The following examples illustrate the provisions of paragraphs (a) through (c) of this section.

Facts. (1) In general. (i) P, an individual, holds 1,500 shares of $1,000 par value preferred stock of X corporation (bearing an annual noncumulative dividend of $100 per share that may be put to X at any time for par value) and 1,000 shares of voting common stock of X. There is no other outstanding common stock of X.

(ii) On January 15, 1991, when the aggregate fair market value of the preferred stock is $1,500,000 and the aggregate fair market value of the common stock is $500,000, P transfers common stock to P's child. The fair market value of P's interest in X (common and preferred) immediately prior to the transfer is $2,000,000, and the section 2701 value of the preferred stock (the section 2701 interest) is zero. Neither P nor P's spouse, S, made gifts prior to 1991.

(2) Additional facts applicable to Examples 1 through 3. P's transfer consists of all 1,000 shares of P's common stock. With respect to the initial transfer, the amount remaining after Step 2 of the subtraction method of § 25.2701-3 is $2,000,000 ($2,000,000 minus zero), all of which is allocated to the transferred stock. P's aggregate taxable gifts for 1991 (including the section 2701 transfer) equal $2,500,000.

(3) Additional facts applicable to Examples 4 and 5. P's initial transfer consists of one-half of P's common stock. With respect to the initial transfer in this case, only $1,000,000 (one-half of the amount remaining after Step 2 of the subtraction method of § 25.2701-3) is allocated to the transferred stock. P's aggregate taxable gifts for 1991 (the section 2701 transfer and P's other transfers) equal $2,500,000.

Example (1). Inter vivos transfer of entire section 2701 interest.

(i) On October 1, 1994, at a time when the value of P's preferred stock is $1,400,000, P transfers all of the preferred stock to P's child. In computing P's 1994 gift tax, P, as the initial transferor, is entitled to reduce the amount on which P's tentative tax is computed under section 2502(a) by $1,400,000.

(ii) The amount of the reduction computed under paragraph (b) of this section is the lesser of $1,500,000 (the amount by which the initial transferor's taxable gifts were increased as a result of the application of section 2701 to the initial transfer) or $1,400,000 (the duplicated amount). The duplicated amount is 100 percent (the portion of the section 2701 interest subsequently transferred) times $1,400,000 (the amount by which the gift tax value of the preferred stock ($1,400,000 at the time of the subsequent transfer) exceeds zero (the section 2701 value of the preferred stock at the time of the initial transfer)).

(iii) The result would be the same if the preferred stock had been held by P's parent, GM, and GM had, on October 1, 1994, transferred the preferred stock to or for the benefit of an individual other than P or an applicable family member of P. In that case, in computing the tax on P's 1994 and subsequent transfers, P would be entitled to reduce the amount on which P's tentative tax is computed under section 2502(a) by $1,400,000. If the value of P's 1994 gifts is less than $1,400,000, P is entitled to claim the excess adjustment in computing the tax with respect to P's subsequent transfers.

Example (2). Transfer of section 2701 interest at death of initial transferor.

(i) P continues to hold the preferred stock until P's death. The chapter 11 value of the preferred stock at the date of P's death is the same as the fair market value of the preferred stock at the time of the initial transfer. In computing the Federal estate tax with respect to P's estate, P's executor is entitled to a reduction of $1,500,000 under paragraph (a)(3) of this section.

(ii) The result would be the same if P had sold the preferred stock to any individual other than an applicable family member at a time when the value of the preferred stock was $1,500,000. In that case, the amount of the reduction is computed as if the preferred stock were included in P's gross estate at a fair market value equal to the sales price. If the value of P's taxable estate is less than $1,500,000, the amount of the adjustment available to P's executor is limited to the actual value of P's taxable estate.

(iii) The result would also be the same if the preferred stock had been held by P's parent, GM, and at the time of P's death, GM had not transferred the preferred stock.

Example (3). Transfer of after-acquired preferred stock. On September 1, 1992, P purchases 100 shares of X preferred stock from an unrelated party. On October 1, 1994, P transfers 100 shares of X preferred stock to P's child. In computing P's 1994 gift tax, P is not entitled to reduce the amount on which P's tentative tax is computed under section 2502(a) because the 1994 transfer does not reduce P's preferred stock holding below that held at the time of the initial transfer. See paragraph (a)(4) of this section.

Example (4). Inter vivos transfer of entire section 2701 interest.

(i) On October 1, 1994, at a time when the value of P's preferred stock is $1,400,000, P transfers all of the preferred stock to P's child. In computing P's 1994 gift tax, P, as the initial transferor, is entitled to reduce the amount on which P's tentative tax is computed under section 2502(a) by $700,000.

(ii) The amount of the reduction computed under paragraph (b) of this section is the lesser of $750,000 (($1,500,000 × .5 ($1,000,000 over $2,000,000)) the amount by which the initial transferor's taxable gifts were increased as a result of the application of section 2701 to the initial transfer) or $700,000 (($1,400,000 × .5) the duplicated amount). The duplicated amount is 100 percent (the portion of the section 2701 interest subsequently transferred) times $700,000; e.g., one-half (the fraction representing the portion of the common stock transferred in the initial transfer ($1,000,000/$2,000,000)) of the amount by which the gift tax value of the preferred stock at the time of the subsequent transfer ($1,400,000) exceeds zero (the section 2701 value of the preferred stock at the time of the initial transfer).

Example (5). Subsequent transfer of less than the entire section 2701 interest. On October 1, 1994, at a time when the value of P's preferred stock is $1,400,000, P transfers only 250 of P's 1,000 shares of preferred stock to P's child. In this case, the amount of the reduction computed under paragraph (b) is $175,000 (one-fourth (250/1,000) of the amount of the reduction available if P had transferred all 1,000 shares of preferred stock.

(e) Computation of reduction if initial transfer is split under section 2513. *(1) In general.* If section 2513 applies to the initial transfer (a split initial transfer), the special rules of this paragraph (e) apply.

(2) Transfers during joint lives. If there is a split initial transfer and the corresponding section 2701 interest is transferred during the joint lives of the donor and the consenting spouse, for purposes of determining the reduction under paragraph (a)(2) of this section each spouse is treated as if the spouse was the initial transferor of one-half of the split initial transfer.

(3) Transfers at or after death of either spouse. (i) In general. If there is a split initial transfer and the corresponding section 2701 interest is transferred at or after the death of the first spouse to die, the reduction under paragraph (a)(2) or (a)(3) of this section is determined as if the donor spouse was the initial transferor of the entire initial transfer.

(ii) Death of donor spouse. Except as provided in paragraph (e)(3)(iv) of this section, the executor of the estate of the donor spouse in a split initial transfer is entitled to compute the reduction as if the donor spouse was the initial transferor of the section 2701 interest otherwise attributable to the consenting spouse. In this case, if the consenting spouse survives the donor spouse—

(A) The consenting spouse's aggregate sum of taxable gifts used in computing each tentative tax under section 2502(a) (and, therefore, adjusted taxable gifts under section 2001(b)(1)(B) (or section 2101(b)(1)(B)) and the tax payable on the consenting spouse's prior taxable gifts under section 2001(b)(2) (or section 2101(b)(2))) is reduced to eliminate the remaining effect of the section 2701 interest; and

(B) Except with respect to any excess reduction carried forward under paragraph (a)(2) of this section, the consenting spouse ceases to be treated as the initial transferor of the section 2701 interest.

(iii) Death of consenting spouse. If the consenting spouse predeceases the donor spouse, except for any excess reduction carried forward under paragraph (a)(2) of this section, the reduction with respect to any section 2701 interest in the split initial transfer is not available to the estate of the consenting spouse (regardless of whether the interest is included in the consenting spouse's gross estate). Similarly, if the consenting spouse predeceases the donor spouse, no reduction is available to the consenting spouse's adjusted taxable gifts under section 2001(b)(1)(B) (or section 2101(b)(1)(B)) or to the consenting spouse's gift tax payable under section 2001(b)(2) (or section 2101(b)(2)). See paragraph (a)(2) of this section for rules involving transfers by an applicable family member during the life of the initial transferor.

(iv) Additional limitation on reduction. If the donor spouse (or the estate of the donor spouse) is treated under this paragraph (e) as the initial transferor of the section 2701 interest otherwise attributable to the consenting spouse, the amount of additional reduction determined under paragraph (b) of this section is the amount determined under that paragraph with respect to the consenting spouse. If a reduction was previously available to the consenting spouse under this paragraph (e), the amount determined under this paragraph (e)(3)(iv) with respect to the consenting spouse is determined as if the consenting spouse's taxable gifts in the split initial transfer had been increased only by that portion of the increase that corresponds to the remaining portion of the section 2701 interest. The amount of the additional reduction (i.e., the amount determined with respect to the consenting spouse) is limited to the amount that results in a reduction in the donor spouse's Federal transfer tax no greater than the amount of the increase in the consenting spouse's gift tax incurred by reason of the section 2701 interest (or the remaining portion thereof).

(f) Examples. The following examples illustrate the provisions of paragraph (e) of this section. The examples assume the facts set out in this paragraph (f).

Facts. (1) In each example assume that P, an individual, holds 1,500 shares of $1,000 par value preferred stock of X corporation (bearing an annual noncumulative dividend of $100 per share that may be put to X at any time for par value) and 1,000 shares of voting common stock of X. There is no other outstanding stock of X. The annual exclusion under section 2503 is not allowable with respect to any gift.

(2) On January 15, 1991, when the aggregate fair market value of the preferred stock is $1,500,000 and the aggregate fair market value of the common stock is $500,000, P transfers all 1,000 shares of the common stock to P's child. Section 2701 applies to the initial transfer because P transferred an equity interest (the common stock) to a member of P's family and immediately thereafter held an applicable retained interest (the preferred stock). The fair market value of

P's interest in X immediately prior to the transfer is $2,000,000 and the section 2701 value of the preferred stock (the section 2701 interest) is zero. With respect to the initial transfer, the amount remaining after Step 2 of the subtraction method of § 25.2701-3 was $2,000,000 ($2,000,000 minus zero), all of which is allocated to the transferred stock. P had made no gifts prior to 1991. The sum of P's aggregate taxable gifts for the calendar year 1991 (including the section 2701 transfer) is $2,500,000. P's spouse, S, made no gifts prior to 1991.

(3) P and S elected pursuant to section 2513 to treat one-half of their 1991 gifts as having been made by each spouse. Without the application of section 2701, P and S's aggregate gifts would have been $500,000 and each spouse would have paid no gift tax because of the application of the unified credit under section 2505. However, because of the application of section 2701, both P and S are each treated as the initial transferor of aggregate taxable gifts in the amount of $1,250,000 and, after the application of the unified credit under section 2505, each paid $255,500 in gift tax with respect to their 1991 transfers. On October 1, 1994, at a time when the value of the preferred stock is the same as at the time of the initial transfer, P transfers the preferred stock (the section 2701 interest) to P's child.

Example (1). Inter vivos transfer of entire section 2701 interest. P transfers all of the preferred stock to P's child. P and S are each entitled to a reduction of $750,000 in computing their 1994 gift tax. P is entitled to the reduction because P subsequently transferred the one-half share of the section 2701 interest as to which P was the initial transferor to an individual who was not an applicable family member of P. S is entitled to the reduction because P, an applicable family member with respect to S, transferred the one-half share of the section 2701 interest as to which S was the initial transferor to an individual other than S or an applicable family member of S. S may claim the reduction against S's 1994 gifts. If S's 1994 taxable gifts are less than $750,000, S may claim the remaining amount of the reduction against S's next succeeding lifetime transfers.

Example (2). Inter vivos transfer of portion of section 2701 interest. P transfers one-fourth of the preferred stock to P's child. In this case, P and S are each entitled to a reduction of $187,500, the corresponding portion of the reduction otherwise available to each spouse (one-fourth of $750,000).

Example (3). Transfer at death of donor spouse. P, the donor spouse in the section 2513 election, dies on October 1, 1994, while holding all of the preferred stock. The executor of P's estate is entitled to a reduction in the computation of the tentative tax under section 2001(b). Since no reduction had been previously available with respect to the section 2701 interest, P's estate is entitled to a full reduction of $750,000 with respect to the one-half share of the preferred stock as to which P was the initial transferor. In addition, P's estate is entitled to an additional reduction of up to $750,000 for the remaining section 2701 interest as to which S was the initial transferor. The reduction for the consenting spouse's remaining section 2701 interest is limited to that amount that will produce a tax saving in P's Federal estate tax of $255,500, the amount of gift tax incurred by S by reason of the application of section 2701 to the split initial transfer.

Example (4). Transfer after death of donor spouse. The facts are the same as in Example 3, except that S acquires the preferred stock from P's estate and subsequently transfers the preferred stock to S's child. S is not entitled to a reduction because S ceased to be an initial transferor upon P's death (and S's prior taxable gifts were automatically adjusted at that time to the level that would have existed had the split initial transfer not been subject to section 2701).

Example (5). Death of donor spouse after inter vivos transfer.

(i) P transfers one-fourth of the preferred stock to P's child. In this case, P and S are each entitled to a reduction of $187,500, the corresponding portion of the reduction otherwise available to each spouse (one-fourth of $750,000). S may claim the reduction against S's 1994 or subsequent transfers. P dies on November 1, 1994.

(ii) P's executor is entitled to include, in computing the reduction available to P's estate, the remaining reduction to which P is entitled and an additional amount of up to $562,500 ($750,000 minus $187,500, the amount of the remaining reduction attributable to the consenting spouse determined immediately prior to P's death). The amount of additional reduction available to P's estate cannot exceed the amount that will reduce P's estate tax by $178,625, the amount that S's 1991 gift tax would have been increased if the application of section 2701 had increased S's taxable gifts by only $562,500 ($750,000 − $187,500).

(g) Double taxation otherwise avoided. No reduction is available under this section if—

(1) Double taxation is otherwise avoided in the computation of the estate tax under section 2001 (or section 2101); or

(2) A reduction was previously taken under the provisions of section 2701(e)(6) with respect to the same section 2701 interest and the same initial transfer.

(h) Effective date. This section is effective for transfers of section 2701 interests after May 4, 1994. If the transfer of a section 2701 interest occurred on or before May 4, 1994, the initial transferor may rely on either this section, project PS-30-91 (1991-2 C.B. 1118, and 1992-1 C.B. 1239 (see § 601.601(d)(2)(ii)(b) of this chapter)) or any other reasonable interpretation of the statute.

T.D. 8536, 5/4/94.

§ 25.2701-6 Indirect holding of interests.

(a) In general. *(1) Attribution to individuals.* For purposes of section 2701, an individual is treated as holding an equity interest to the extent the interest is held indirectly through a corporation, partnership, estate, trust, or other entity. If an equity interest is treated as held by a particular individual in more than one capacity, the interest is treated as held by the individual in the manner that attributes the largest total ownership of the equity interest. An equity interest held by a lower-tier entity is attributed to higher-tier entities in accordance with the rules of this section. For example, if an individual is a 50-percent beneficiary of a trust that holds 50 percent of the preferred stock of a corporation, 25 percent of the preferred stock is considered held by the individual under these rules.

(2) Corporations. A person is considered to hold an equity interest held by or for a corporation in the proportion that the fair market value of the stock the person holds bears to the fair market value of all the stock in the corporation (determined as if each class of stock were held separately by one individual). This paragraph applies to any entity classified as a corporation or as an association taxable as a corporation for federal income tax purposes.

(3) Partnerships. A person is considered to hold an equity interest held by or for a partnership in the proportion that the

fair market value of the larger of the person's profits interest or capital interest in the partnership bears to the total fair market value of the corresponding profits interests or capital interests in the partnership, as the case may be (determined as if each class were held by one individual). This paragraph applies to any entity classified as a partnership for federal income tax purposes.

(4) Estates, trusts and other entities. (i) In general. A person is considered to hold an equity interest held by or for an estate or trust to the extent the person's beneficial interest therein may be satisfied by the equity interest held by the estate or trust, or the income or proceeds thereof, assuming the maximum exercise of discretion in favor of the person. A beneficiary of an estate or trust who cannot receive any distribution with respect to an equity interest held by the estate or trust, including the income therefrom or the proceeds from the disposition thereof, is not considered the holder of the equity interest. Thus, if stock held by a decedent's estate has been specifically bequeathed to one beneficiary and the residue of the estate has been bequeathed to other beneficiaries, the stock is considered held only by the beneficiary to whom it was specifically bequeathed. However, any person who may receive distributions from a trust is considered to hold an equity interest held by the trust if the distributions may be made from current or accumulated income from or the proceeds from the disposition of the equity interest, even though under the terms of the trust the interest can never be distributed to that person. This paragraph applies to any entity that is not classified as a corporation, an association taxable as a corporation, or a partnership for federal income tax purposes.

(ii) Special rules (A) Property is held by a decedent's estate if the property is subject to claims against the estate and expenses of administration.

(B) A person holds a beneficial interest in a trust or an estate so long as the person may receive distributions from the trust or the estate other than payments for full and adequate consideration.

(C) An individual holds an equity interest held by or for a trust if the individual is considered an owner of the trust (a "grantor trust") under subpart E, part 1, subchapter J of the Internal Revenue Code (relating to grantors and others treated as substantial owners). However, if an individual is treated as the owner of only a fractional share of a grantor trust because there are multiple grantors, the individual holds each equity interest held by the trust, except to the extent that the fair market value of the interest exceeds the fair market value of the fractional share.

(5) Multiple attribution. (i) Applicable retained interests. If this section attributes an applicable retained interest to more than one individual in a class consisting of the transferor and one or more applicable family members, the interest is attributed within that class in the following order—

(A) If the interest is held in a grantor trust, to the individual treated as the holder thereof;

(B) To the transferor;

(C) To the transferor's spouse; or

(D) To each applicable family member on a pro rata basis.

(ii) Subordinate equity interests. If this section attributes a subordinate equity interest to more than one individual in a class consisting of the transferor, applicable family members, and members of the transferor's family, the interest is attributed within that class in the following order—

(A) To the transferee;

(B) To each member of the transferor's family on a pro rata basis;

(C) If the interest is held in a grantor trust, to the individual treated as the holder thereof;

(D) To the transferor;

(E) To the transferor's spouse; or

(F) To each applicable family member on a pro rata basis.

(b) Examples. The following examples illustrate the provisions of this section:

Example (1). A, an individual, holds 25 percent by value of each class of stock of Y Corporation. Persons unrelated to A hold the remaining stock. Y holds 50 percent of the stock of Corporation X. Under paragraph (a)(2) of this section, Y's interests in X are attributed proportionately to the shareholders of Y. Accordingly, A is considered to hold a 12.5 percent (25 percent × 50 percent) interest in X.

Example (2). Z Bank's authorized capital consists of 100 shares of common stock and 100 shares of preferred stock. A holds 60 shares of each (common and preferred) and A's child, B, holds 40 shares of common stock. Z holds the balance of its own preferred stock, 30 shares as part of a common trust fund it maintains and 10 shares permanently set aside to satisfy a deferred obligation. For purposes of section 2701, A holds 60 shares of common stock and 66 shares of preferred stock in Z, 60 shares of each class directly and 6 shares of preferred stock indirectly (60 percent of the 10 shares set aside to fund the deferred obligation).

Example (3). An irrevocable trust holds a 10-percent general partnership interest in Partnership Q. One-half of the trust income is required to be distributed to O Charity. The other one-half of the income is to be distributed to D during D's life and thereafter to E for such time as E survives D. D holds one-half of the trust's interest in Q by reason of D's present right to receive one-half of the trust's income, and E holds one-half of the trust's interest in Q by reason of E's future right to receive one-half of the trust's income. Nevertheless, no family member is treated as holding more than one-half of the trust's interest in Q because at no time will either D or E actually hold, in the aggregate, any right with respect to income or corpus greater than one-half.

Example (4). An irrevocable trust holds a 10-percent general partnership interest in partnership M. One-half of the trust income is to be paid to D for D's life. The remaining income may, in the trustee's discretion, be accumulated or paid to or for the benefit of a class that includes D's child F, in such amounts as the trustee determines. On the death of the survivor of D and F, the trust corpus is required to be distributed to O Charity. The trust's interest in M is held by the trust's beneficiaries to the extent that present and future income or corpus may be distributed to them. Accordingly, D holds one-half of the trust's interest in M because D is entitled to receive one-half of the trust income currently. F holds the entire value of the interest because F is a member of the class eligible to receive the entire trust income for such time as F survives D. See paragraph (a)(5) of this section for rules applicable in the case of multiple attribution.

Example (5). The facts are the same as in Example 4, except that all the income is required to be paid to O Charity for the trust's initial year. The result is the same as in Example 4.

T.D. 8395, 1/28/92.

---

§ 25.2701-7 Separate interests.

The Secretary may, by regulation, revenue ruling, notice, or other document of general application, prescribe rules under which an applicable retained interest is treated as two or more separate interests for purposes of section 2701. In addition, the Commissioner may, by ruling issued to a taxpayer upon request, treat any applicable retained interest as two or more separate interests as may be necessary and appropriate to carry out the purposes of section 2701.

T.D. 8395, 1/28/92.

§ 25.2701-8 Effective dates.

Sections 25.2701-1 through 25.2701-4 and §§ 25.2701-6 and 25.2701-7 are effective as of January 28, 1992. For transfers made prior to January 28, 1992, taxpayers may rely on any reasonable interpretation of the statutory provisions. For these purposes, the provisions of the proposed regulations and the final regulations are considered a reasonable interpretation of the statutory provisions.

T.D. 8395, 1/28/92.

§ 25.2702-0 Table of contents.

This section lists the major paragraphs contained in §§ 25.2702-1 through 25.2702-7.

T.D. 8395, 1/28/92, amend T.D. 9181, 2/24/2005.

§ 25.2702-1 Special valuation rules in the case of transfers of interests in trust.

(a) Scope of section 2702. Section 2702 provides special rules to determine the amount of the gift when an individual makes a transfer in trust to (or for the benefit of) a member of the individual's family and the individual or an applicable family member retains an interest in the trust. Section 25.2702-4 treats certain transfers of property as transfers in trust. Certain transfers, including transfers to a personal residence trust, are not subject to section 2702. See paragraph (c) of this section. Member of the family is defined in § 25.2702-2(a)(1). Applicable family member is defined in § 25.2701-1(d)(2).

(b) Effect of section 2702. If section 2702 applies to a transfer, the value of any interest in the trust retained by the transferor or any applicable family member is determined under § 25.2702-2(b). The amount of the gift, if any, is then determined by subtracting the value of the interests retained by the transferor or any applicable family member from the value of the transferred property. If the retained interest is not a qualified interest (as defined in § 25.2702-3), the retained interest is generally valued at zero, and the amount of the gift is the entire value of the property.

(c) Exceptions to section 2702. Section 2702 does not apply to the following transfers.

(1) Incomplete gift. A transfer no portion of which would be treated as a completed gift without regard to any consideration received by the transferor. If a transfer is wholly incomplete as to an undivided fractional share of the property transferred (without regard to any consideration received by the transferor), for purposes of this paragraph the transfer is treated as incomplete as to that share.

(2) Personal residence trust. A transfer in trust that meets the requirements of § 25.2702-5.

(3) Charitable remainder trust. (i) For transfers made on or after May 19, 1997, a transfer to a pooled income fund described in section 642(c)(5); a transfer to a charitable remainder annuity trust described in section 664(d)(1); a transfer to a charitable remainder unitrust described in section 664(d)(2) if under the terms of the governing instrument the unitrust amount can be computed only under section 664(d)(2)(A); and a transfer to a charitable remainder unitrust if under the terms of the governing instrument the unitrust amount can be computed under section 664(d)(2) and (3) and either there are only two consecutive noncharitable beneficial interests and the transferor holds the second of the two interests, or the only permissible recipients of the unitrust amount are the transferor, the transferor's U.S. citizen spouse, or both the transferor and the transferor's U.S. citizen spouse.

(ii) For transfers made before May 19, 1997, a transfer in trust if the remainder interest in the trust qualifies for a deduction under section 2522.

(4) Pooled income fund. A transfer of property to a pooled income fund (as defined in section 642(c)(5)).

(5) Charitable lead trust. A transfer in trust if the only interest in the trust, other than the remainder interest or a qualified annuity or unitrust interest, is an interest that qualifies for deduction under section 2522.

(6) Certain assignments of remainder interests. The assignment of a remainder interest if the only retained interest of the transferor or an applicable family member is as the permissible recipient of distributions of income in the sole discretion of an independent trustee (as defined in section 674(c)).

(7) Certain property settlements. A transfer in trust if the transfer of an interest to a spouse is deemed to be for full and adequate consideration by reason of section 2516 (relating to certain property settlements) and the remaining interests in the trust are retained by the other spouse.

(8) Transfer or assignment to a Qualified Domestic Trust. A transfer or assignment (as described in section 2056(d)(2)(B)) by a noncitizen surviving spouse of property to a Qualified Domestic Trust under the circumstances described in § 20.2056A-4(b) of this chapter, where the surviving spouse retains an interest in the transferred property that is not a qualified interest and the transfer is not described in section 2702(a)(3)(A)(ii) or 2702(c)(4).

T.D. 8395, 1/28/92, amend T.D. 8612, 8/21/95, T.D. 8791, 12/09/98.

§ 25.2702-2 Definitions and valuation rules.

(a) Definitions. The following definitions apply for purposes of section 2702 and the regulations thereunder.

(1) Member of the family. With respect to any individual, member of the family means the individual's spouse, any ancestor or lineal descendant of the individual or the individual's spouse, any brother or sister of the individual, and any spouse of the foregoing.

(2) Transfer in trust. A transfer in trust includes a transfer to a new or existing trust and an assignment of an interest in an existing trust. Transfer in trust does not include—

(i) The exercise, release or lapse of a power of appointment over trust property that is not a transfer under chapter 12; or

(ii) The execution of a qualified disclaimer (as defined in section 2518).

(3) Retained. Retained means held by the same individual both before and after the transfer in trust. In the case of the creation of a term interest, any interest in the property held by the transferor immediately after the transfer is treated as held both before and after the transfer.

(4) Interest. An interest in trust includes a power with respect to a trust if the existence of the power would cause any portion of a transfer to be treated as an incomplete gift under chapter 12.

(5) Holder. The holder is the person to whom the annuity or unitrust interest is payable during the fixed term of that interest. References to holder shall also include the estate of that person.

(6) Qualified interest. Qualified interest means a qualified annuity interest, a qualified unitrust interest, or a qualified remainder interest. If a transferor retains a power to revoke a

qualified annuity interest or qualified unitrust interest of the transferor's spouse, then the revocable qualified annuity or unitrust interest of the transferor's spouse is treated as a retained qualified interest of the transferor. In order for the transferor to be treated as having retained a qualified interest under the preceding sentence, the interest of the transferor's spouse (the successor holder) must be an interest that meets the requirements of a qualified annuity interest in accordance with § 25.2702-3(b) and (d), or a qualified unitrust interest in accordance with § 25.2702-3(c) and (d), but for the transferor's retained power to revoke the interest.

(7) Qualified annuity interest. Qualified annuity interest means an interest that meets all the requirements of § 25.2702-3(b) and (d).

(8) Qualified unitrust interest. Qualified unitrust interest means an interest that meets all the requirements of § 25.2702-3(c) and (d).

(9) Qualified remainder interest. Qualified remainder interest means an interest that meets all the requirements of § 25.2702-3(f).

(10) Governing instrument. Governing instrument means the instrument or instruments creating and governing the operation of the trust arrangement.

(b) Valuation of retained interests. *(1) In general.* Except as provided in paragraphs (b)(2) and (c) of this section, the value of any interest retained by the transferor or an applicable family member is zero.

(2) Qualified interest. The value of a qualified annuity interest and a qualified remainder interest following a qualified annuity interest are determined under section 7520. The value of a qualified unitrust interest and a qualified remainder interest following a qualified unitrust interest are determined as if they were interests described in section 664.

(c) Valuation of a term interest in certain tangible property. *(1) In general.* If section 2702 applies to a transfer in trust of tangible property described in paragraph (c)(2) of this section (" tangible property"), the value of a retained term interest (other than a qualified interest) is not determined under section 7520 but is the amount the transferor establishes as the amount a willing buyer would pay a willing seller for the interest, each having reasonable knowledge of the relevant facts and neither being under any compulsion to buy or sell. If the transferor cannot reasonably establish the value of the term interest pursuant to this paragraph (c)(1), the interest is valued at zero.

(2) Tangible property subject to rule. (i) In general. Except as provided in paragraph (c)(2)(ii) of this section, paragraph (c)(1) of this section applies only to tangible property.—

(A) For which no deduction for depreciation or depletion would be allowable if the property were used in a trade or business or held for the production of income; and

(B) As to which the failure to exercise any rights under the term interest would not increase the value of the property passing at the end of the term interest.

(ii) Exception for de minimis amounts of depreciable property. In determining whether property meets the requirements of this paragraph (c)(2) at the time of the transfer in trust, improvements that would otherwise cause the property not to qualify are ignored if the fair market value of the improvements, in the aggregate, do not exceed 5 percent of the fair market value of the entire property.

(3) Evidence of value of property. The best evidence of the value of any term interest to which this paragraph (c) applies is actual sales or rentals that are comparable both as to the nature and character of the property and the duration of the term interest. Little weight is accorded appraisals in the absence of such evidence. Amounts determined under section 7520 are not evidence of what a willing buyer would pay a willing seller for the interest.

(4) Conversion of property. (i) In general. Except as provided in paragraph (c)(4)(iii) of this section, if a term interest in property is valued under paragraph (c)(1) of this section, and during the term the property is converted into property a term interest in which would not qualify for valuation under paragraph (c)(1) of this section, the conversion is treated as a transfer for no consideration for purposes of chapter 12 of the value of the unexpired portion of the term interest.

(ii) Value of unexpired portion of term interest. For purposes of paragraph (c)(4)(i) of this section, the value of the unexpired portion of a term interest is the amount that bears the same relation to the value of the term interest as of the date of conversion (determined under section 7520 using the rate in effect under section 7520 on the date of the original transfer and the fair market value of the property as of the date of the original transfer) as the value of the term interest as of the date of the original transfer (determined under paragraph (c)(1) of this section) bears to the value of the term interest as of the date of the original transfer (determined under section 7520).

(iii) Conversion to qualified annuity interest. The conversion of tangible property previously valued under paragraph (c)(1) of this section into property a term interest in which would not qualify for valuation under paragraph (c)(1) of this section is not a transfer of the value of the unexpired portion of the term interest if the interest thereafter meets the requirements of a qualified annuity interest. The rules of § 25.2702-5(d)(8) (including governing instrument requirements) apply for purposes of determining the amount of the annuity payment required to be made and the determination of whether the interest meets the requirements of a qualified annuity interest.

(5) Additions or improvements to property. (i) Additions or improvements substantially affecting nature of property. If an addition or improvement is made to property a term interest in which was valued under paragraph (c)(1) of this section, and the addition or improvement affects the nature of the property to such an extent that the property would not be treated as property meeting the requirements of paragraph (c)(2) of this section if the property had included the addition or improvement at the time it was transferred, the entire property is deemed, for purposes of paragraph (c)(4) of this section, to convert (effective as of the date the addition or improvement is commenced) into property a term interest in which would not qualify for valuation under paragraph (c)(1) of this section.

(ii) Other additions or improvements. If an addition or improvement is made to property, a term interest in which was valued under paragraph (c)(1) of this section, and the addition or improvement does not affect the nature of the property to such an extent that the property would not be treated as property meeting the requirements of paragraph (c)(2) of this section if the property had included the addition or improvement at the time it was transferred, the addition or improvement is treated as an additional transfer (effective as of the date the addition or improvement is commenced) subject to § 25.2702-2(b)(1).

(d) Examples. *(1)* The following examples illustrate the rules of § 25.2702-1 and § 25.2702-2. Each example assumes that all applicable requirements of those sections not specifically described in the example are met.

Example (1). A transfers property to an irrevocable trust, retaining the right to receive the income of the trust for 10 years. On the expiration of the 10-year term, the trust is to terminate and the trust corpus is to be paid to A's child. However, if A dies during the 10-year term, the entire trust corpus is to be paid to A's estate. Each retained interest is valued at zero because it is not a qualified interest. Thus, the amount of A's gift is the fair market value of the property transferred to the trust.

Example (2). A transfers property to an irrevocable trust, retaining a 10-year annuity interest that meets the requirements set forth in § 25.2702-3 for a qualified annuity interest. Upon expiration of the 10-year term, the trust is to terminate and the trust corpus is to be paid to A's child. The amount of A's gift is the fair market value of the property transferred to the trust less the value of the retained qualified annuity interest determined under section 7520.

Example (3). D transfers property to an irrevocable trust under which the income is payable to D's spouse for life. Upon the death of D's spouse, the trust is to terminate and the trust corpus is to be paid to D's child. D retains no interest in the trust. Although the spouse is an applicable family member of D under section 2702, the spouse has not retained an interest in the trust because the spouse did not hold the interest both before and after the transfer. Section 2702 does not apply because neither the transferor nor an applicable family member has retained an interest in the trust. The result is the same whether or not D elects to treat the transfer as a transfer of qualified terminable interest property under section 2056(b)(7).

Example (4). A transfers property to an irrevocable trust, under which the income is to be paid to A for life. Upon termination of the trust, the trust corpus is to be distributed to A's child. A also retains certain powers over principal that cause the transfer to be wholly incomplete for federal gift tax purposes. Section 2702 does not apply because no portion of the transfer would be treated as a completed gift.

Example (5). The facts are the same as in Example 4, except that the trust is divided into separate fractional shares and A's retained powers apply to only one of the shares. Section 2702 applies except with respect to the share of the trust as to which A's retained powers cause the transfer to be an incomplete gift.

(2) The following facts apply for Examples 6 through 8 (examples illustrating § 25.2702-2(c)—tangible property exception):

Facts. A transfers a painting having a fair market value of $2,000,000 to A's child, B, retaining the use of the painting for 10 years. The painting does not possess an ascertainable useful life. Assume that the painting would not be depreciable if it were used in a trade or business or held for the production of income. Assume that the value of A's term interest, determined under section 7520, is $1,220,000, and that A establishes that a willing buyer of A's interest would pay $500,000 for the interest.

Example (6). A's term interest is not a qualified interest under § 25.2702-3. However, because of the nature of the property, A's failure to exercise A's rights with regard to the painting would not be expected to cause the value of the painting to be higher than it would otherwise be at the time it passes to B. Accordingly, A's interest is valued under § 25.2702-2(c)(1) at $500,000. The amount of A's gift is $1,500,000, the difference between the fair market value of the painting and the amount determined under § 25.2702-2(c)(1).

Example (7). Assume that the only evidence produced by A to establish the value of A's 10-year term interest is the amount paid by a museum for the right to use a comparable painting for 1 year. A asserts that the value of the 10-year term is 10 times the value of the 1-year term. A has not established the value of the 10-year term interest because a series of short-term rentals the aggregate duration of which equals the duration of the actual term interest does not establish what a willing buyer would pay a willing seller for the 10-year term interest. However, the value of the 10-year term interest is not less than the value of the 1-year term because it can be assumed that a willing buyer would pay no less for a 10-year term interest than a 1-year term interest.

Example (8). Assume that after 24 months A and B sell the painting for $2,000,000 and invest the proceeds in a portfolio of securities. A continues to hold an income interest in the securities for the duration of the 10-year term. Under § 25.2702-2(c)(4) the conversion of the painting into a type of property a term interest in which would not qualify for valuation under § 25.2702-2(c)(1) is treated as a transfer by A of the value of the unexpired portion of A's original term interest, unless the property is thereafter held in a trust meeting the requirements of a qualified annuity interest. Assume that the value of A's remaining term interest in $2,000,000 (determined under section 7520 using the section 7520 rate in effect on the date of the original transfer) is $1,060,000. The value of the unexpired portion of A's interest is $434,426, the amount that bears the same relation to $1,060,000 as $500,000 (the value of A's interest as of the date of the original transfer determined under paragraph (c)(1) of this section) bears to $1,220,000 (the value of A's interest as of the date of the original transfer determined under section 7520).

T.D. 8395, 1/28/92, amend T.D. 9181, 2/24/2005.

§ 25.2702-3 Qualified interests.

(a) In general. This section provides rules for determining if an interest is a qualified annuity interest, a qualified unitrust interest, or a qualified remainder interest.

(b) Special rules for qualified annuity interests. An interest is a qualified annuity interest only if it meets the requirements of this paragraph and paragraph (d) of this section.

(1) Payment of annuity amount. (i) In general. A qualified annuity interest is an irrevocable right to receive a fixed amount. The annuity amount must be payable to (or for the benefit of) the holder of the annuity interest at least annually. A right of withdrawal, whether or not cumulative, is not a qualified annuity interest. Issuance of a note, other debt instrument, option, or other similar financial arrangement, directly or indirectly, in satisfaction of the annuity amount does not constitute payment of the annuity amount.

(ii) Fixed amount. A fixed amount means—

(A) A stated dollar amount payable periodically, but not less frequently than annually, but only to the extent the amount does not exceed 120 percent of the stated dollar amount payable in the preceding year; or

(B) A fixed fraction or percentage of the initial fair market value of the property transferred to the trust, as finally determined for federal tax purposes, payable periodically but not less frequently than annually, but only to the extent the fraction or percentage does not exceed 120 percent of the fixed fraction or percentage payable in the preceding year.

(iii) Income in excess of the annuity amount. An annuity interest does not fail to be a qualified annuity interest merely because the trust permits income in excess of the amount required to pay the annuity amount to be paid to or for the benefit of the holder of the qualified annuity interest. Nevertheless, the right to receive the excess income is not a qualified interest and is not taken into account in valuing the qualified annuity interest.

(2) Incorrect valuations of trust property. If the annuity is stated in terms of a fraction or percentage of the initial fair market value of the trust property, the governing instrument must contain provisions meeting the requirements of § 1.664-2(a)(1)(iii) of this chapter (relating to adjustments for any incorrect determination of the fair market value of the property in the trust).

(3) Period for payment of annuity amount. The annuity amount may be payable based on either the anniversary date of the creation of the trust or the taxable year of the trust. In either situation, the annuity amount may be paid annually or more frequently, such as semi-annually, quarterly, or monthly. If the payment is made based on the anniversary date, proration of the annuity amount is required only if the last period during which the annuity is payable to the grantor is a period of less than 12 months. If the payment is made based on the taxable year, proration of the annuity amount is required for each short taxable year of the trust during the grantor's term. The prorated amount is the annual annuity amount multiplied by a fraction, the numerator of which is the number of days in the short period and the denominator of which is 365 (366 if February 29 is a day included in the numerator).

(4) Payment of the annuity amount in certain circumstances. An annuity amount payable based on the anniversary date of the creation of the trust must be paid no later than 105 days after the anniversary date. An annuity amount payable based on the taxable year of the trust may be paid after the close of the taxable year, provided the payment is made no later than the date by which the trustee is required to file the Federal income tax return of the trust for the taxable year (without regard to extensions). If the trustee reports for the taxable year pursuant to § 1.671-4(b) of this chapter, the annuity payment must be made no later than the date by which the trustee would have been required to file the Federal income tax return of the trust for the taxable year (without regard to extensions) had the trustee reported pursuant to § 1.671-4(a) of this chapter.

(5) Additional contributions prohibited. The governing instrument must prohibit additional contributions to the trust.

(c) Special rules for qualified unitrust interests. An interest is a qualified unitrust interest only if it meets the requirements of this paragraph and paragraph (d) of this section.

(1) Payment of unitrust amount. (i) In general. A qualified unitrust interest is an irrevocable right to receive payment periodically, but not less frequently than annually, of a fixed percentage of the net fair market value of the trust assets, determined annually. For rules relating to computation of the net fair market value of the trust assets see § 25.2522(c)-3(c)(2)(vii). The unitrust amount must be payable to (or for the benefit of) the holder of the unitrust interest at least annually. A right of withdrawal, whether or not cumulative, is not a qualified unitrust interest. Issuance of a note, other debt instrument, option, or other similar financial arrangement, directly or indirectly, in satisfaction of the unitrust amount does not constitute payment of the unitrust amount.

(ii) Fixed percentage. A fixed percentage is a fraction or percentage of the net fair market value of the trust assets, determined annually, payable periodically but not less frequently than annually, but only to the extent the fraction or percentage does not exceed 120 percent of the fixed fraction or percentage payable in the preceding year.

(iii) Income in excess of unitrust amount. A unitrust interest does not fail to be a qualified unitrust interest merely because the trust permits income in excess of the amount required to pay the unitrust amount to be paid to or for the benefit of the holder of the qualified unitrust interest. Nevertheless, the right to receive the excess income is not a qualified interest and is not taken into account in valuing the qualified unitrust interest.

(2) Incorrect valuations of trust property. The governing instrument must contain provisions meeting the requirements of 1.664-3(a)(1)(iii) of this chapter (relating to the incorrect determination of the fair market value of the property in the trust).

(3) Period for payment of unitrust amount. The unitrust amount may be payable based on either the anniversary date of the creation of the trust or the taxable year of the trust. In either situation, the unitrust amount may be paid annually or more frequently, such as semi-annually, quarterly, or monthly. If the payment is made based on the anniversary date, proration of the unitrust amount is required only if the last period during which the annuity is payable to the grantor is a period of less than 12 months. If the payment is made based on the taxable year, proration of the unitrust amount is required for each short taxable year of the trust during the grantor's term. The prorated amount is the annual unitrust amount multiplied by a fraction, the numerator of which is the number of days in the short period and the denominator of which is 365 (366 if February 29 is a day included in the numerator).

(4) Payment of the unitrust amount in certain circumstances. A unitrust amount payable based on the anniversary date of the creation of the trust must be paid no later than 105 days after the anniversary date. A unitrust amount payable based on the taxable year of the trust may be paid after the close of the taxable year, provided the payment is made no later than the date by which the trustee is required to file the Federal income tax return of the trust for the taxable year (without regard to extensions). If the trustee reports for the taxable year pursuant to § 1.671-4(b) of this chapter, the unitrust payment must be made no later than the date by which the trustee would have been required to file the Federal income tax return of the trust for the taxable year (without regard to extensions) had the trustee reported pursuant to § 1.671-4(a) of this chapter.

(d) Requirements applicable to qualified annuity interests and qualified unitrust interests. *(1) In general.* To be a qualified annuity or unitrust interest, an interest must be a qualified annuity interest in every respect or a qualified unitrust interest in every respect. For example, if the interest consists of the right to receive each year a payment equal to the lesser of a fixed amount of the initial trust assets or a fixed percentage of the annual value of the trust assets, the interest is not a qualified interest. If, however, the interest consists of the right to receive each year a payment equal to the greater of a stated dollar amount or a fixed percentage of the initial trust assets or a fixed percentage of the annual value of the trust assets, the interest is a qualified interest that is valued at the greater of the two values. To be a qualified interest, the interest must meet the definition of and function exclusively as a qualified interest from the creation of the trust.

(2) Contingencies. A holder's qualified interest must be payable in any event to or for the benefit of the holder for the fixed term of that interest. Thus, payment of the interest cannot be subject to any contingency other than either the survival of the holder until the commencement, or throughout the term, of that holder's interest, or, in the case of a revocable interest described in § 25.2702-2(a)(6), the transferor's right to revoke the qualified interest of that transferor's spouse.

(3) Amounts payable to other persons. The governing instrument must prohibit distributions from the trust to or for the benefit of any person other than the holder of the qualified annuity or unitrust interest during the term of the qualified interest.

(4) Term of the annuity or unitrust interest. The governing instrument must fix the term of the annuity or unitrust and the term of the interest must be fixed and ascertainable at the creation of the trust. The term must be for the life of the holder, for a specified term of years, or for the shorter (but not the longer) of those periods. Successive term interests for the benefit of the same individual are treated as the same term interest.

(5) Commutation. The governing instrument must prohibit commutation (prepayment) of the interest of the holder.

(6) Use of debt obligations to satisfy the annuity or unitrust payment obligation. (i) In general. In the case of a trust created on or after September 20, 1999, the trust instrument must prohibit the trustee from issuing a note, other debt instrument, option, or other similar financial arrangement in satisfaction of the annuity or unitrust payment obligation.

(ii) Special rule in the case of a trust created prior to September 20, 1999. In the case of a trust created prior to September 20, 1999, the interest will be treated as a qualified interest under section 2702(b) if—

(A) Notes, other debt instruments, options, or similar financial arrangements are not issued after September 20, 1999, to satisfy the annuity or unitrust payment obligation; and

(B) Any notes or any other debt instruments that were issued to satisfy the annual payment obligation on or prior to September 20, 1999, are paid in full by December 31, 1999, and any option or similar financial arrangement issued to satisfy the annual payment obligation is terminated by December 31, 1999, such that the grantor receives cash or other trust assets in satisfaction of the payment obligation. For purposes of the preceding sentence, an option will be considered terminated only if the grantor receives cash or other trust assets equal in value to the greater of the required annuity or unitrust payment plus interest computed under section 7520 of the Internal Revenue Code, or the fair market value of the option.

(e) Examples. The following examples illustrate the rules of paragraphs (b), (c), and (d) of this section. Each example assumes that all applicable requirements for a qualified interest are met unless otherwise specifically stated.

Example (1). A transfers property to an irrevocable trust, retaining the right to receive the greater of $10,000 or the trust income in each year for a term of 10-years. Upon expiration of the 10-year term, the trust is to terminate and the entire trust corpus is to be paid to A's child, provided that if A dies within the 10-year term the trust corpus is to be paid to A's estate. A's annual payment right is a qualified annuity interest to the extent of the right to receive $10,000 per year for 10 years or until A's prior death, and is valued under section 7520 without regard to the right to receive any income in excess of $10,000 per year. The contingent reversion is valued at zero. The amount of A's gift is the fair market value of the property transferred to the trust less the value of the qualified annuity interest.

Example (2). U transfers property to an irrevocable trust, retaining the right to receive $10,000 in each of years 1 through 3, $12,000 in each of years 4 through 6, and $15,000 in each of years 7 through 10. The interest is a qualified annuity interest to the extent of U's right to receive $10,000 per year in years 1 through 3, $12,000 in years 4 through 6, $14,400 in year 7, and $15,000 in years 8 through 10, because those amounts represent the lower of the amount actually payable each year or an amount that does not exceed 120 percent of the stated dollar amount for the preceding year.

Example (3). S transfers property to an irrevocable trust, retaining the right to receive $50,000 in each of years 1 through 3 and $10,000 in each of years 4 through 10. S's entire retained interest is a qualified annuity interest.

Example (4). R transfers property to an irrevocable trust retaining the right to receive annually an amount equal to the lesser of 8 percent of the initial fair market value of the trust property or the trust income for the year. R's annual payment right is not a qualified annuity interest to any extent because R does not have the irrevocable right to receive a fixed amount for each year of the term.

Example (5). A transfers property to an irrevocable trust, retaining the right to receive 5 percent of the net fair market value of the trust property, valued annually, for 10 years. If A dies within the 10-year term, the unitrust amount is to be paid to A's estate for the balance of the term. The interest of A (and A's estate) to receive the unitrust amount for the specified term of 10 years in all events is a qualified unitrust interest for a term of 10 years.

Example (6). The facts are the same as in Example 5, except that if A dies within the 10-year term the unitrust amount will be paid to A's estate for an additional 35 years. As in Example 5, the interest of A (and A's estate) to receive the unitrust amount for a specified term of 10 years in all events is a qualified unitrust interest for a term of 10 years. However, the right of A's estate to continue to receive the unitrust amount after the expiration of the 10-year term if A dies within that 10-year period is not fixed and ascertainable at the creation of the interest and is not a qualified unitrust interest.

Example (7). B transfers property to an irrevocable trust retaining the right to receive annually an amount equal to 8 percent of the initial fair market value of the trust property for 10 years. Upon expiration of the 10-year term, the trust is to terminate and the entire trust corpus is to be paid to B's child. The governing instrument provides that income in excess of the annuity amount may be paid to B's child in the trustee's discretion. B's interest is not a qualified annuity interest to any extent because a person other than the individual holding the term interest may receive distributions from the trust during the term.

Example (8). A transfers property to an irrevocable trust, retaining the right to receive an annuity equal to 6 percent of the initial net fair market value of the trust property for 10 years, or until A's prior death. At the expiration of the 10-year term, or on A's death prior to the expiration of the 10-year term, the annuity is to be paid to B, A's spouse, if then living, for 10 years or until B's prior death. A retains an inter vivos and testamentary power to revoke B's interest during the initial 10-year term. If not exercised by A during the initial 10-year term (whether during A's life or on A's death), A's right to revoke B's interest will lapse upon either A's death during the 10-year term, or the expiration of A's 10-year term (assuming A survives the term). Upon expiration of B's interest (or on the expiration of A's interest if A revokes B's interest or if B predeceases A), the trust terminates and the trust corpus is payable to A's child. Because A has made a completed gift of the remainder interest, the transfer of property to the trust is not incomplete as to all interests in the property and section 2702 applies. A's annuity interest (A's right to receive the annuity for 10 years, or until A's prior death) is a retained interest that is a qualified annuity interest under paragraphs (b) and (d) of this section. In addition, because A has retained the power to revoke B's interest, B's interest is treated as an interest retained by A for purposes of section 2702. B's successive annuity interest otherwise satisfies the requirements for a qualified interest contained in paragraph (d) of this section, but for A's power to revoke. The term of B's interest is specified in the governing instrument and is fixed and ascertainable at the creation of the trust, and B's right to receive the annuity is contingent only on B's survival, and A's power to revoke. Following the expiration of A's interest, the annuity is to be paid for a 10-year term or for B's (the successor holder's) life, whichever is shorter. Accordingly, A is treated as retaining B's revocable qualified annuity interest pursuant to § 25.2702-2(a)(6). Because both A's interest and B's interest are treated as qualified interests retained by A, the value of the gift is the value of the property transferred to the trust less the value of both A's qualified interest and B's qualified interest (subject to A's power to revoke), each valued as a single-life annuity. If A survives the 10-year term without having revoked B's interest, then A's power to revoke lapses and A will make a completed gift to B at that time. Further, if A revokes B's interest prior to the commencement of that interest, A is treated as making an additional completed gift at that time to A's child. In either case, the amount of the gift would be the present value of B's interest determined under section 7520 and the applicable regulations, as of the date the revocation power lapses or the interest is revoked. See § 25.2511-2(f).

Example (9). (i) A transfers property to an irrevocable trust, retaining the right to receive 6 percent of the initial net fair market value of the trust property for 10 years, or until A's prior death. If A survives the 10-year term, the trust terminates and the trust corpus is payable to A's child. If A dies prior to the expiration of the 10-year term, the annuity is payable to B, A's spouse, if then living, for the balance of the 10-year term, or until B's prior death. A retains the right to revoke B's interest. Upon expiration of B's interest (or upon A's death if A revokes B's interest or if B predeceases A), the trust terminates and the trust corpus is payable to A's child. As is the case in Example 8, A's retained annuity interest (A's right to receive the annuity for 10 years, or until A's prior death) is a qualified annuity interest under paragraphs (b) and (d) of this section. However, B's interest does not meet the requirements of paragraph (d) of this section. The term of B's annuity is not fixed and ascertainable at the creation of the trust, because it is not payable for the life of B, a specified term of years, or for the shorter of those periods. Rather, B's annuity is payable for an unspecified period that will depend upon the number of years left in the original term after A's death. Further, B's annuity is payable only if A dies prior to the expiration of the 10-year term. Thus, payment of B's annuity is not dependent solely on B's survival, but rather is dependent on A's failure to survive.

(ii) Accordingly, the amount of the gift is the fair market value of the property transferred to the trust reduced by the value of A's qualified interest (A's right to receive the stated annuity for 10 years or until A's prior death). B's interest is not a qualified interest and is thus valued at zero under section 2702.

(f) Qualified remainder interest. *(1) Requirements.* An interest is a qualified remainder interest only if it meets all of the following requirements:

(i) It is a qualified remainder interest in every respect.

(ii) It meets the definition of and functions exclusively as a qualified interest from the creation of the interest.

(iii) It is non-contingent. For this purpose, an interest is non-contingent only if it is payable to the beneficiary or the beneficiary's estate in all events.

(iv) All interests in the trust, other than non-contingent remainder interests, are qualified annuity interests or qualified unitrust interests. Thus, an interest is a qualified remainder interest only if the governing instrument does not permit payment of income in excess of the annuity or unitrust amount to the holder of the qualified annuity or unitrust interest.

(2) Remainder interest. Remainder interest is the right to receive all or a fractional share of the trust property on termination of all or a fractional share of the trust. Remainder interest includes a reversion. A transferor's right to receive an amount that is a stated or pecuniary amount is not a remainder interest. Thus, the right to receive the original value of the trust corpus (or a fractional share) is not a remainder interest.

(3) Examples. The following examples illustrate rules of this paragraph (f). Each example assumes that all applicable requirements of a qualified interest are met unless otherwise specifically stated.

Example (1). A transfers property to an irrevocable trust. The income of the trust is payable to A's child for life. On the death of A's child, the trust is to terminate and the trust corpus is to be paid to A. A's remainder interest is not a qualified remainder interest because the interest of A's child is neither a qualified annuity interest nor a qualified unitrust interest.

Example (2). The facts are the same as in Example 1, except that A's child has the right to receive the greater of the income of the trust or $10,000 per year. A's remainder interest is not a qualified remainder interest because the right of A's child to receive income in excess of the annuity amount is not a qualified interest.

Example (3). A transfers property to an irrevocable trust. The trust provides a qualified annuity interest to A's child for 12 years. An amount equal to the initial value of the trust corpus is to be paid to A at the end of that period and the balance is to be paid to A's grandchild. A's interest is not a qualified remainder interest because the amount A is to receive is not a fractional share of the trust property. Example 4. U transfers property to an irrevocable trust. The trust provides a qualified unitrust interest to U's child for 15 years, at which time the trust terminates and the trust corpus is paid to U or, if U is not then living, to U's child. Because U's remainder interest is contingent, it is not a qualified remainder interest.

T.D. 8395, 1/28/92, amend T.D. 8536, 5/4/94, T.D. 8633, 12/20/95, T.D. 8899, 9/1/2000, T.D. 9181, 2/24/2005.

§ 25.2702-4 Certain property treated as held in trust.

(a) In general. For purposes of section 2702, a transfer of an interest in property with respect to which there are one or more term interests is treated as a transfer in trust. A term interest is one of a series of successive (as contrasted with concurrent) interests. Thus, a life interest in property or an interest in property for a term of years is a term interest. However, a term interest does not include a fee interest in property, merely because it is held as a tenant in common, a tenant by the entireties, or a joint tenant with right of survivorship.

(b) Leases. A leasehold interest in property is not a term interest to the extent the lease is for full and adequate consideration (without regard to section 2702). A lease will be considered for full and adequate consideration if, under all the facts and circumstances as of the time the lease is entered into or extended, a good faith effort is made to determine the fair rental value of the property and the terms of the lease conform to the value so determined.

(c) Joint purchases. Solely for purposes of section 2702, if an individual acquires a term interest in property and, in the same transaction or series of transactions, one or more members of the individual's family acquire an interest in the same property, the individual acquiring the term interest is treated as acquiring the entire property so acquired, and transferring to each of those family members the interests acquired by that family member in exchange for any consideration paid by that family member, For purposes of this paragraph (c), the amount of the individual's gift will not exceed the amount of consideration furnished by that individual for all interests in the property.

(d) Examples. The following examples illustrate rules of this section:

Example (1). A purchases a 20-year term interest in an apartment building and A's child purchases the remainder interest in the property. A and A's child each provide the portion of the purchase price equal to the value of their respective interests in the property determined under section 7520. Solely for purposes of section 2702, A is treated as acquiring the entire property and transferring the remainder interest to A's child in exchange for the portion of the purchase price provided by A's child. In determining the amount of A's gift, A's retained interest is valued at zero because it is not a qualified interest.

Example (2). K holds rental real estate valued at $100,000. K sells a remainder interest in the property to K's child, retaining the right to receive the income from the property for 20 years. Assume the purchase price paid by K's child for the remainder interest is equal to the value of the interest determined under section 7520. K's retained interest is not a qualified interest and is therefore valued at zero. K has made a gift in the amount of $100,000 less the consideration received from K's child.

Example (3). G and G's child each acquire a 50 percent undivided interest as tenants in common in an office building. The interests of G and G's child are not term interests to which section 2702 applies.

Example (4). B purchases a life estate in property from R, B's grandparent, for $100 and Bus child purchases the remainder interest for $50. Assume that the value of the property is $300, the value of the life estate determined under section 7520 is $250 and the value of the remainder interest is $50. B is treated as acquiring the entire property and transferring the remainder interest to B's child. However, the amount of B's gift is $100, the amount of consideration ($100) furnished by B for B's interest.

Example (5). H and W enter into a written agreement relative to their marital and property rights that requires W to transfer property to an irrevocable trust, the terms of which provide that the income of the trust will be paid to H for 10 years. On the expiration of the 10-year term, the trust is to terminate and the trust corpus is to be paid to W. H and W divorce within two years after the agreement is entered into. Pursuant to section 2516, the transfer to H would otherwise be deemed to be for full and adequate consideration. Section 2702 does not apply to the acquisition of the term interest by H because no member of H's family acquired an interest in the property in the same transaction or series of transactions. The result would not be the same if, on the termination of H's interest in the trust, the trust corpus were distributable to the children of H and W rather than W.

T.D. 8395, 1/28/92.

§ 25.2702-5 Personal residence trusts.

(a) *(1) In general.* Section 2702 does not apply to a transfer in trust meeting the requirements of this section. A transfer in trust meets the requirements of this section only if the trust is a personal residence trust (as defined in paragraph (b) of this section). A trust meeting the requirements of a qualified personal residence trust (as defined in paragraph (c) of this section) is treated as a personal residence trust. A trust of which the term holder is the grantor that otherwise meets the requirements of a personal residence trust (or a qualified personal residence trust) is not a personal residence trust (or a qualified personal residence trust) if, at the time of transfer, the term holder of the trust already holds term interests in two trusts that are personal residence trusts (or qualified personal residence trusts) of which the term holder was the grantor. For this purpose, trusts holding fractional interests in the same residence are treated as one trust.

(2) Modification of trust. A trust that does not comply with one or more of the regulatory requirements under paragraph (b) or (c) of this section will, nonetheless, be treated as satisfying these requirements if the trust is modified, by judicial reformation (or nonjudicial reformation if effective under state law), to comply with the requirements. In the case of a trust created after December 31, 1996, the reformation must be commenced within 90 days after the due date (including extensions) for the filing of the gift tax return reporting the transfer of the residence under section 6075 and must be completed within a reasonable time after commencement. If the reformation is not completed by the due date (including extensions) for filing the gift tax return, the grantor or grantor's spouse must attach a statement to the gift tax return stating that the reformation has been commenced or will be commenced within the 90-day period. In the case of a trust created before January 1, 1997, the reformation must be commenced within 90 days after December 23, 1997, and must be completed within a reasonable time after commencement.

(b) Personal residence trust. *(1) In general.* A personal residence trust is a trust the governing instrument of which prohibits the trust from holding, for the original duration of the term interest, any asset other than one residence to be used or held for use as a personal residence of the term holder and qualified proceeds (as defined in paragraph (b)(3) of this section). A residence is held for use as a personal residence of the term holder so long as the residence is not occupied by any other person (other than the spouse or a dependent of the term holder) and is available at all times for use by the term holder as a personal residence. A trust does not meet the requirements of this section if, during the original duration of the term interest, the residence may be sold or otherwise transferred by the trust or may be used for a purpose other than as a personal residence of the term holder. In addition, the trust does not meet the requirements of this section unless the governing instrument prohibits the trust from selling or transferring the residence, directly or indirectly, to the grantor, the grantor's spouse, or an entity controlled by the grantor or the grantor's spouse, at any time after the original duration of the term interest during which the trust is a grantor trust. For purposes of the preceding sentence, a sale or transfer to another grantor trust of the grantor or the grantor's spouse is considered a sale or transfer to the grantor or the grantor's spouse; however, a distribution (for no consideration) upon or after the expiration of the original duration of the term interest to another grantor trust of the grantor or the grantor's spouse pursuant to the express terms of the trust will not be considered a sale or transfer to the grantor or the grantor's spouse if such other grantor trust prohibits the sale or transfer of the property to the grantor, the grantor's spouse, or an entity controlled by the grantor or the grantor's spouse. In the event the grantor dies prior to the expiration of the original duration of the term interest, this paragraph (b)(1) does not apply to the distribution (for no consideration) of the residence to any person (including the grantor's estate) pursuant to the express terms of the trust or pursuant to the exercise of a power retained by the grantor under the terms of the trust. Further, this paragraph (b)(1) does not apply to any outright distribution (for no consideration) of the residence to the grantor's spouse after the expiration of the original duration of the term interest pursuant to the express terms of the trust. For purposes of this paragraph (b)(1), a *grantor trust* is a trust treated as owned in whole or in part by the grantor or the grantor's spouse pursuant to sections 671 through 678, and *control* is defined in § 25.2701-2(b)(5)(ii) and (iii). Expenses of the trust whether or not attributable to trust principal may be paid directly by the term holder of the trust.

(2) Personal residence. (i) In general. For purposes of this paragraph (b), a personal residence of a term holder is either—

(A) The principal residence of the term holder (within the meaning of section 1034);

(B) One other residence of the term holder (within the meaning of section 280A(d)(1) but without regard to section 280A(d)(2)); or

(C) An undivided fractional interest in either.

(ii) Additional property. A personal residence may include appurtenant structures used by the term holder for residential purposes and adjacent land not in excess of that which is reasonably appropriate for residential purposes (taking into account the residence's size and location). The fact that a residence is subject to a mortgage does not affect its status as a personal residence. The term personal residence does not include any personal property (e.g., household furnishings).

(iii) Use of residence. A residence is a personal residence only if its primary use is as a residence of the term holder when occupied by the term holder. The principal residence of the term holder will not fail to meet the requirements of the preceding sentence merely because a portion of the residence is used in an activity meeting the requirements of section 280A(c)(1) or (4) (relating to deductibility of expenses related to certain uses), provided that such use is secondary to use of the residence as a residence. A residence is not used primarily as a residence if it is used to provide transient lodging and substantial services are provided in connection with the provision of lodging (e.g. a hotel or a bed and breakfast). A residence is not a personal residence if, during any period not occupied by the term holder, its primary use is other than as a residence.

(iv) Interests of spouses in the same residence. If spouses hold interests in the same residence (including community property interests), the spouses may transfer their interests in the residence (or a fractional portion of their interests in the residence) to the same personal residence trust, provided that the governing instrument prohibits any person other than one of the spouses from holding a term interest in the trust concurrently with the other spouse.

(3) Qualified proceeds. Qualified proceeds means the proceeds payable as a result of damage to, or destruction or involuntary conversion (within the meaning of section 1033) of, the residence held by a personal residence trust, provided that the governing instrument requires that the proceeds (including any income thereon) be reinvested in a personal residence within two years from the date on which the proceeds are received.

(c) Qualified personal residence trust. *(1) In general.* A qualified personal residence trust is a trust meeting all the requirements of this paragraph (c). These requirements must be met by provisions in the governing instrument, and these governing instrument provisions must by their terms continue in effect during the existence of any term interest in the trust.

(2) Personal residence. (i) In general. For purposes of this paragraph (c), a personal residence of a term holder is either—

(A) The principal residence of the term holder (within the meaning of section 1034);

(B) One other residence of the term holder (within the meaning of section 280A(d)(1) but without regard to section 280A(d)(2)); or

(C) An undivided fractional interest in either.

(ii) Additional property. A personal residence may include appurtenant structures used by the term holder for residential purposes and adjacent land not in excess of that which is reasonably appropriate for residential purposes (taking into account the residence's size and location). The fact that a residence is subject to a mortgage does not affect its status as a personal residence. The term personal residence does not include any personal property (e.g., household furnishings).

(iii) Use of residence. A residence is a personal residence only if its primary use is as a residence of the term holder when occupied by the term holder. The principal residence of the term holder will not fail to meet the requirements of the preceding sentence merely because a portion of the residence is used in an activity meeting the requirements of section 280A(c)(1) or (4) (relating to deductibility of expenses related to certain uses), provided that such use is secondary to use of the residence as a residence. A residence is not used primarily as a residence if it is used to provide transient lodging and substantial services are provided in connection with the provision of lodging (e.g., a hotel or a bed and breakfast). A residence is not a personal residence if, during any period not occupied by the term holder, its primary use is other than as a residence. A residence is not a personal residence if, during any period not occupied by the term holder, its primary use is other than as a residence.

(iv) Interests of spouses in the same residence. If spouses hold interests in the same residence (including community property interests), the spouses may transfer their interests in the residence (or a fractional portion of their interests in the residence) to the same qualified personal residence trust, provided that the governing instrument prohibits any person other than one of the spouses from holding a term interest in the trust concurrently with the other spouse.

(3) Income of the trust. The governing instrument must require that any income of the trust be distributed to the term holder not less frequently than annually.

(4) Distributions from the trust to other persons. The governing instrument must prohibit distributions of corpus to any beneficiary other than the transferor prior to the expiration of the retained term interest.

(5) Assets of the trust. (i) In general. Except as otherwise provided in paragraphs (c)(5)(ii) and (c)(8) of this section, the governing instrument must prohibit the trust from holding, for the entire term of the trust, any asset other than one residence to be used or held for use (within the meaning of paragraph (c)(7)(i) of this section) as a personal residence of the term holder (the "residence").

(ii) Assets other than personal residence. Except as otherwise provided, the governing instrument may permit a qualified personal residence trust to hold the following assets (in addition to the residence) in the amounts and in the manner described in this paragraph (c)(5)(ii):

(A) Additions of cash for payment of expenses, etc. (1) Additions. The governing instrument may permit additions of cash to the trust, and may permit the trust to hold additions of cash in a separate account, in an amount which, when added to the cash already held in the account for such purposes, does not exceed the amount required:

(i) For payment of trust expenses (including mortgage payments) already incurred or reasonably expected to be paid by the trust within six months from the date the addition is made;

(ii) For improvements to the residence to be paid by the trust within six months from the date the addition is made; and

(iii) For purchase by the trust of the initial residence, within three months of the date the trust is created, provided that no addition may be made for this purpose, and the trust may not hold any such addition, unless the trustee has previously entered into a contract to purchase that residence; and

(iv) For purchase by the trust of a residence to replace another residence, within three months of the date the addition is made, provided that no addition may be made for this purpose, and the trust may not hold any such addition, unless the trustee has previously entered into a contract to purchase that residence.

(2) Distributions of excess cash. If the governing instrument permits additions of cash to the trust pursuant to paragraph (c)(5)(ii)(A)(1) of this section, the governing instrument must require that the trustee determine, not less frequently than quarterly, the amounts held by the trust for payment of expenses in excess of the amounts permitted by that paragraph and must require that those amounts be distributed immediately thereafter to the term holder. In addition, the governing instrument must require, upon termination of the term holder's interest in the trust, any amounts held by the trust for the purposes permitted by paragraph (c)(5)(ii)(A)(1) of this section that are not used to pay trust expenses due and payable on the date of termination (including expenses directly related to termination) be distributed outright to the term holder within 30 days of termination.

(B) Improvements. The governing instrument may permit improvements to the residence to be added to the trust and may permit the trust to hold such improvements, provided that the residence, as improved, meets the requirements of a personal residence.

(C) Sale proceeds. The governing instrument may permit the sale of the residence (except as set forth in paragraph (c)(9) of this section) and may permit the trust to hold proceeds from the sale of the residence, in a separate account.

(D) Insurance and insurance proceeds. The governing instrument permit the trust to hold one or more may policies of insurance on the residence. In addition, the governing instrument may permit the trust to hold, in a separate account, proceeds of insurance payable to the trust as a result of damage to or destruction of the residence. For purposes of this paragraph, amounts (other than insurance proceeds payable to the trust as a result of damage to or destruction of the residence) received as a result of the involuntary conversion (within the meaning of section 1033) of the residence are treated as proceeds of insurance.

(6) Commutation. The governing instrument must prohibit commutation (prepayment) of the term holder's interest.

(7) Cessation of use as a personal residence. (i) In general. The governing instrument must provide that a trust ceases to be a qualified personal residence trust if the residence ceases to be used or held for use as a personal residence of the term holder. A residence is held for use as a personal residence of the term holder so long as the residence is not occupied by any other person (other than the spouse or a dependent of the term holder) and is available at all times for use by the term holder as a personal residence. See § 25.2702-5(c)(8) for rules governing disposition of assets of a trust as to which the trust has ceased to be a qualified personal residence trust.

(ii) Sale of personal residence. The governing instrument must provide that the trust ceases to be a qualified personal residence trust upon sale of the residence if the governing instrument does not permit the trust to hold proceeds of sale of the residence pursuant to paragraph (c)(5)(ii)(C) of this section. If the governing instrument permits the trust to hold proceeds of sale pursuant to that paragraph, the governing instrument must provide that the trust ceases to be a qualified personal residence trust with respect to all proceeds of sale held by the trust not later than the earlier of—

(A) The date that is two years after the date of sale;

(B) The termination of the term holder's interest in the trust; or

(C) The date on which a new residence is acquired by the trust.

(iii) Damage to or destruction of personal residence (A) In general. The governing instrument must provide that, if damage or destruction renders the residence unusable as a residence, the trust ceases to be a qualified personal residence trust on the date that is two years after the date of damage or destruction (or the date of termination of the term holder's interest in the trust, if earlier) unless, prior to such date—

(1) Replacement of or repairs to the residence are completed; or

(2) A new residence is acquired by the trust.

(B) Insurance proceeds. For purposes of this paragraph (C)(7)(iii), if the governing instrument permits the trust to hold proceeds of insurance received as a result of damage to or destruction of the residence pursuant to paragraph (c)(5)(ii)(D) of this section, the governing instrument must contain provisions similar to those required by paragraph (c)(7)(ii) of this section.

(8) Disposition of trust assets on cessation as personal residence trust. (i) In general. The governing instrument must provide that, within 30 days after the date on which the trust has ceased to be a qualified personal residence trust with respect to certain assets, either—

(A) The assets be distributed outright to the term holder;

(B) The assets be converted to and held for the balance of the term holder's term in a separate share of the trust meeting the requirements of a qualified annuity interest; or

(C) In the trustee's sole discretion, the trustee may elect to comply with either paragraph (c)(8)(i)(A) or (B) of this section pursuant to their terms.

(ii) Requirements for conversion to a qualified annuity interest (A) Governing instrument requirements. For assets subject to this paragraph (c)(8) to be converted to and held as a qualified annuity interest, the governing instrument must contain all provisions required by § 25.2702-3 with respect to a qualified annuity interest.

(B) Effective date of annuity. The governing instrument must provide that the right of the term holder to receive the annuity amount begins on the date of sale of the residence, the date of damage to or destruction of the residence, or the date on which the residence ceases to be used or held for use as a personal residence, as the case may be ("the cessation date"). Notwithstanding the preceding sentence, the governing instrument may provide that the trustee may defer payment of any annuity amount otherwise payable after the cessation date until the date that is 30 days after the assets are converted to a qualified annuity interest under paragraph (c)(8)(i)(B) of this section ("the conversion date"); provided that any deferred payment must bear interest from the cessation date at a rate not less than the section 7520 rate in effect on the cessation date. The governing instrument may permit the trustee to reduce aggregate deferred annuity payments by the amount of income actually distributed by the trust to the term holder during the deferral period.

(C) Determination of annuity amount. (1) In general. The governing instrument must require that the annuity amount be no less than the amount determined under this paragraph (C).

(2) Entire trust ceases to be a qualified personal residence trust. If, on the conversion date, the assets of the trust do not include a residence used or held for use as a personal residence, the annuity may not be less than an amount determined by dividing the lesser of the value of all interests retained by the term holder (as of the date of the original transfer or transfers) or the value of all the trust assets (as of the conversion date) by an annuity factor determined—

(i) For the original term of the term holder's interest; and

(ii) At the rate used in valuing the retained interest at the time of the original transfer.

(3) Portion of trust continues as qualified personal residence trust. If, on the conversion date, the assets of the trust include a residence used or held for use as a personal residence, the annuity must not be less than the amount determined under paragraph (c)(8)(ii)(C)(2) of this section multiplied by a fraction. The numerator of the fraction is the excess of the fair market value of the trust assets on the conversion date over the fair market value of the assets as to which the trust continues as a qualified personal residence trust, and the denominator of the fraction is the fair market value of the trust assets on the conversion date.

(9) Sale of residence to grantor, grantor's spouse, or entity controlled by grantor or grantor's spouse. The governing instrument must prohibit the trust from selling or transferring the residence, directly or indirectly, to the grantor, the grantor's spouse, or an entity controlled by the grantor or the grantor's spouse during the retained term interest of the trust, or at any time after the retained term interest that the trust is a grantor trust. For purposes of the preceding sentence, a sale or transfer to another grantor trust of the grantor or the grantor's spouse is considered a sale or transfer to the grantor or the grantor's spouse; however, a distribution (for no consideration) upon or after the expiration of the retained term interest to another grantor trust of the grantor or the grantor's spouse pursuant to the express terms of the trust will not be considered a sale or transfer to the grantor or the grantor's spouse if such other grantor trust prohibits the sale or transfer of the property to the grantor, the grantor's spouse, or an entity controlled by the grantor or the grantor's spouse. In the event the grantor dies prior to the expiration of the retained term interest, this paragraph (c)(9) does not apply to the distribution (for no consideration) of the residence to any person (including the grantor's estate) pursuant to the express terms of the trust or pursuant to the exercise of a power retained by the grantor under the terms of the trust. Further, this paragraph (c)(9) does not apply to an outright distribution (for no consideration) of the residence to the grantor's spouse after the expiration of the retained trust term pursuant to the express terms of the trust. For purposes of this paragraph (c)(9), a *grantor trust* is a trust treated as owned in whole or in part by the grantor or the grantor's spouse pursuant to sections 671 through 678, and *control* is defined in § 25.2701-2(b)(5)(ii) and (iii).

(d) Examples. The following examples illustrate rules of this section. Each example assumes that all applicable requirements of a personal residence trust (or qualified personal residence trust) are met unless otherwise stated.

Example (1). C maintains C's principal place of business in one room of C's principal residence. The room meets the requirements of section 280A(c)(1) for deductibility of expenses related to such use. The residence is a personal residence.

Example (2). L owns a vacation condominium that L rents out for six months of the year, but which is treated as L's residence under section 280A(d)(1) because L occupies it for at least 18 days per year. L provides no substantial services in connection with the rental of the condominium L transfers the condominium to an irrevocable trust, the terms of which meet the requirements of a qualified personal residence trust. L retains the right to use the condominium during L's lifetime. The trust is a qualified personal residence trust.

Example (3). W owns a 200-acre farm. The farm includes a house, barns, equipment buildings, a silo, and enclosures for confinement of farm animals. W transfers the farm to an irrevocable trust, retaining the use of the farm for 20 years, with the remainder to W's child. The trust is not a personal residence trust because the farm includes assets not meeting the requirements of a personal residence.

Example (4). A transfers A's principal residence to an irrevocable trust, retaining the right to use the residence for a 20-year term. The governing instrument of the trust does not prohibit the trust from holding personal property. The trust is not a qualified personal residence trust.

Example (5). T transfers a personal residence to a trust that meets the requirements of a qualified personal residence trust, retaining a term interest in the trust for 10 years. During the period of T's retained term interest, T is forced for health reasons to move to a nursing home. T's spouse continues to occupy the residence. If the residence is available at all times for T's use as a residence during the term (without regard to T's ability to actually use the residence), the residence continues to be held for T's use and the trust does not cease to be a qualified personal residence trust. The residence would cease to be held for use as a personal residence of T if the trustee rented the residence to an unrelated party, because the residence would no longer be available for T's use at all times.

Example (6). T transfers T's personal residence to a trust that meets the requirements of a qualified personal residence trust, retaining the right to use the residence for 12 years. On the date the residence is transferred to the trust, the fair market value of the residence is $100,000. After 6 years, the trustee sells the residence, receiving net proceeds of $250,000, and invests the proceeds of sale in common stock. After an additional eighteen months, the common stock has paid $15,000 in dividends and has a fair market value of $260,000. On that date, the trustee purchases a new residence for $200,000. On the purchase of the new residence, the trust ceases to be a qualified personal residence trust with respect to any amount not reinvested in the new residence. The governing instrument of the trust provides that the trustee, in the trustee's sole discretion, may elect either to distribute the excess proceeds or to convert the proceeds into a qualified annuity interest. The trustee elects the latter option. The amount of the annuity is the amount of the annuity that would be payable if no portion of the sale proceeds had been reinvested in a personal residence multiplied by a fraction. The numerator of the fraction is $60,000 (the amount remaining after reinvestment) and the denominator of the fraction is $260,000 (the fair market value of the trust assets on the conversion date). The obligation to pay the annuity commences on the date of sale, but payment of the annuity that otherwise would have been payable during the period between the date of sale and the date on which the trust ceased to be a qualified personal residence trust with respect to the excess proceeds may be deferred until 30 days after the date on which the new residence is purchased. Any amount deferred must bear compound interest from the date the annuity is payable at the section 7520 rate in effect on the date of sale. The $15,000 of income distributed to the term holder during that period may be used to reduce the annuity amount payable with respect to that period if the governing instrument so provides and thus reduce the amount on which compound interest is computed.

T.D. 8395, 1/28/92, amend T.D. 8743, 12/22/97.

§ 25.2702-6 Reduction in taxable gifts.

(a) Transfers of retained interests in trust. *(1) Inter vivos transfers.* If an individual subsequently transfers by gift an interest in trust previously valued (when held by that individual) under § 25.2702-2(b)(1) or (c), the individual is entitled to a reduction in aggregate taxable gifts. The amount of the reduction is determined under paragraph (b) of this section. Thus, for example, if an individual transferred property to an Irrevocable trust, retaining an interest in the trust that was valued at zero under § 25.2702-2(b)(1), and the individual later transfers the retained interest by gift, the individual is entitled to a reduction in aggregate taxable gifts on the subsequent transfer. For purposes of this section, aggregate taxable gifts means the aggregate sum of the individual's taxable gifts for the calendar year determined under section 2502(a)(1).

(2) Testamentary transfers. If either—

(i) A term interest in trust is included in an individual's gross estate solely by reason of section 2033, or

(ii) A remainder interest in trust is included in an individual's gross estate,

and the interest was previously valued when held by that individual) under § 25.2702-2(b)(1) or (c), the individual's estate is entitled to a reduction in the individual's adjusted taxable gifts in computing the Federal estate tax payable under section 2001. The amount of the reduction is determined under paragraph (b) of this section.

(3) Gift splitting on subsequent transfer. If an individual who is entitled to a reduction in aggregate taxable gifts (or adjusted taxable gifts) subsequently transfers the interest in a transfer treated as made one-half by the individual's spouse under section 2513, the individual may assign one-half of the amount of the reduction to the consenting spouse. The assignment must be attached to the Form 709 on which the consenting spouse reports the split gift.

(b) Amount of reduction. *(1) In general.* The amount of the reduction in aggregate taxable gifts (or adjusted taxable gifts) is the lesser of—

(i) The increase in the individual's taxable gifts resulting from the interest being valued at the time of the initial transfer under § 25.2702-2(b)(1) or (c); or

(ii) The increase in the individual's taxable gifts (or gross estate) resulting from the subsequent transfer of the interest.

(2) Treatment of annual exclusion. For purposes of determining the amount under paragraph (b)(1)(ii) of this section, the exclusion under section 2503(b) applies first to transfers in that year other than the transfer of the interest previously valued under § 25.2702-2(b)(1) or (c).

(3) Overlap with section 2001. Notwithstanding paragraph (b)(1) of this section, the amount of the reduction is reduced to the extent section 2001 would apply to reduce the amount of an individual's adjusted taxable gifts with respect to the same interest to which paragraph (b)(1) of this section would otherwise apply.

(c) Examples. The rules of this section are illustrated by the following examples. The following facts apply for Examples 1-4:

Facts. In 1992, X transferred property to an irrevocable trust retaining the right to receive the trust income for life. On the death of X, the trust is to terminate and the trust corpus is to be paid to X's child. C. X's income interest had a value under section 7520 of $40,000 at the time of the transfer: however, because X's retained interest was not a qualified interest, it was valued at zero under § 25.2702-2(b)(1) for purposes of determining the amount of X's gift. X's taxable gifts in 1992 were therefore increased by $40,000. In 1993, X transfers the income interest to C for no consideration.

Example (1). Assume that the value under section 7520 of the income interest on the subsequent transfer to C is $30,000. If X makes no other gifts to C in 1993, X is entitled to a reduction in aggregate taxable gifts of $20,000, the lesser of the amount by which X's taxable gifts were increased as a result of the income interest being valued at zero on the initial transfer ($40,000) or the amount by which X's taxable gifts are increased as a result of the subsequent transfer of the income interest ($30,000 minus $10,000 annual exclusion).

Example (2). Assume that in 1993, 4 months after X transferred the income interest to C, X transferred $5,000 cash to C. In determining the increase in taxable gifts occurring on the subsequent transfer, the annual exclusion under section 2503(b) is first applied to the cash gift. X is entitled to a reduction in aggregate taxable gifts of $25,000, the lesser of the amount by which X's taxable gifts were increased as a result of the income interest being valued at zero on the initial transfer ($40,000) or the amount by which X's taxable gifts are increased as a result of the subsequent transfer of the income interest ($25,000 (($30,000 + $5,000) – $10,000 annual exclusion).

Example (3). Assume that the value under section 7520 of the income interest on the subsequent transfer to C is $55,000. X is entitled to reduce aggregate taxable gifts by $40,000, the lesser of the amount by which X's taxable gifts were increased as a result of the income interest being valued at zero on the initial transfer ($40,000) or the amount by which X's taxable gifts are increased as a result of the subsequent transfer of the income interest ($55,000 minus $10,000 annual exclusion = $45,000).

Example (4). Assume that X and X's spouse, S, split the subsequent gift to C. X is entitled to assign one-half the reduction to S. If the assignment is made, each is entitled to reduce aggregate taxable gifts by $17,500, the lesser of their portion of the increase in taxable gifts on the initial transfer by reason of the application of section 2702 ($20,000) and their portion of the increase in taxable gifts on the subsequent transfer of the retained interest ($27,500 – $10,000 annual exclusion).

Example (5). In 1992, A transfers property to an irrevocable trust, retaining the right to receive the trust income for 10 years. On the expiration of the 10-year term, the trust is to terminate and the trust corpus is to be paid to A's child, B. Assume that A's term interest has a value under section 7520 of $20,000 at the time of the transfer; however, because A's retained interest was not a qualified interest, it was valued at zero under § 25.2702-2(b)(1) for purposes of determining the amount of A's gift, Assume also that A and A's spouse, S, split the gift of the remainder interest under section 2513. In 1993, A transfers A's term interest to D, A's other child, for no consideration. A is entitled to reduce A's aggregate taxable gifts on the transfer. Assume that A and S also split the subsequent gift to D, and that A dies one month after making the subsequent transfer of the term interest and S dies six months later. The gift of the term interest is included in A's gross estate under section 2035(d)(2). To the extent S's taxable gifts are reduced pursuant to section 2001(e), S is entitled to no reduction in aggregate or adjusted taxable gifts under this section.

Example (6). T transfers property to an irrevocable trust retaining the power to direct the distribution of trust income for 10 years among T's descendants in whatever shares T deems appropriate. On the expiration of the 10-year period, the trust corpus is to be paid in equal shares to T's children. T's transfer of the remainder interest is a completed gift. Because T's retained interest is not a qualified interest, it is valued at zero under § 25.2702-2(b)(1) and the amount of T's gift is the fair market value of the property transferred to the trust. The distribution of income each year is not a transfer of a retained interest in trust. Therefore, T is not entitled to reduce aggregate taxable gifts as a result of the distributions of income from the trust.

Example (7). The facts are the same as in Example 6, except that after 3 years T exercises the right to direct the distribution of trust income by assigning the right to the income for the balance of the term to T's child, C. The exercise is a transfer of a retained interest in trust for purposes of this section. T is entitled to reduce aggregate taxable gifts by the lesser of the increase in taxable gifts resulting from the application of section 2702 to the initial transfer or the increase in taxable gifts resulting from the transfer of the retained interest in trust.

Example (8). In 1992, V purchases an income interest for 10 years in property in the same transaction or series of transactions in which G, V's child, purchases the remainder interest in the same property. V dies in 1997 still holding the term interest, the value of which is includible in V's gross estate under section 2033. V's estate would be entitled to a reduction in adjusted taxable gifts in the amount determined under paragraph (b) of this section.

T.D. 8395, 1/28/92.

§ 25.2702-7 Effective dates.

Except as provided in this section, §§ 25.2702-1 through 25.2702-6 apply as of January 28, 1992. With respect to transfers to which section 2702 applied made prior to January 28, 1992, taxpayers may rely on any reasonable interpretation of the statutory provisions. For these purposes, the provisions of the proposed regulations and the final regulations are considered a reasonable interpretation of the statutory provisions. The fourth through eighth sentences of § 25.2702-5(b)(1) and § 25.2702-5(c)(9) apply with respect to trusts created after May 16, 1996. Section 25.2702-2(a)(5), the second and third sentences of § 25.2702-2(a)(6), § 25.2702-3(d)(2), the first two sentences of § 25.2702-3(d)(4), the last sentence of § 25.2702-3(e), Example 5, the last two sentences of § 25.2702-3(e), Example 6, and § 25.2702-3(e), Examples 8 and 9, apply for trusts created on or after July 26, 2004. However, the Internal Revenue Service will not challenge any prior application of the changes to Examples 5 and 6 in § 25.2702-3(e).

T.D. 8395, 1/28/92, amend T.D. 8743, 12/22/97, T.D. 9181, 2/24/2005.

§ 25.2703-1 Property subject to restrictive arrangements.

(a) Disregard of rights or restrictions. *(1) In general.* For purposes of subtitle B (relating to estate, gift, and generation-skipping transfer taxes), the value of any property is determined without regard to any right or restriction relating to the property.

(2) Right or restriction. For purposes of this section, right or restriction means—

(i) Any option, agreement, or other right to acquire or use the property at a price less than fair market value (determined without regard to the option, agreement, or right); or

(ii) Any restriction on the right to sell or use the property.

(3) Agreements, etc. containing rights or restrictions. A right or restriction may be contained in a partnership agreement, articles of incorporation, corporate bylaws, a shareholders' agreement, or any other agreement. A right or restriction may be implicit in the capital structure of an entity.

(4) Qualified easements. A perpetual restriction on the use of real property that qualified for a charitable deduction

under either section 2522(d) or section 2055(f) of the Internal Revenue Code is not treated as a right or restriction.

(b) Exceptions. *(1) In general.* This section does not apply to any right or restriction satisfying the following three requirements—

(i) The right or restriction is a bona fide business arrangement;

(ii) The right or restriction is not a device to transfer property to the natural objects of the transferor's bounty for less than full and adequate consideration in money or money's worth; and

(iii) At the time the right or restriction is created, the terms of the right or restriction are comparable to similar arrangements entered into by persons in an arm's length transaction.

(2) Separate requirements. Each of the three requirements described in paragraph (b)(1) of this section must be Independently satisfied for a right or restriction to meet this exception. Thus, for example, the mere showing that a right or restriction is a bona fide business arrangement is not sufficient to establish that the right or restriction is not a device to transfer property for less than full and adequate consideration.

(3) Exception for certain rights or restrictions. A right or restriction is considered to meet each of the three requirements described in paragraph (b)(1) of this section if more than 50 percent by value of the property subject to the right or restriction is owned directly or indirectly (within the meaning of § 25.2701-6) by individuals who are not members of the transferor's family. In order to meet this exception, the property owned by those individuals must be subject to the right or restriction to the same extent as the property owned by the transferor. For purposes of this section, members of the transferor's family include the persons described in § 25.2701-2(b)(5) and any other individual who is a natural object of the transferor's bounty. Any property held by a member of the transferor's family under the rules of § 25.2701-6 (without regard to § 25.2701-6(a)(5)) is treated as held only by a member of the transferor's family.

(4) Similar arrangement. (i) In general. A right or restriction is treated as comparable to similar arrangements entered into by persons in an arm's length transaction if the right or restriction is one that could have been obtained in a fair bargain among unrelated parties in the same business dealing with each other at arm's length. A right or restriction is considered a fair bargain among unrelated parties in the same business if it conforms with the general practice of unrelated parties under negotiated agreements in the same business. This determination generally will entail consideration of such factors as the expected term of the agreement, the current fair market value of the property, anticipated changes in value during the term of the arrangement, and the adequacy of any consideration given in exchange for the rights granted.

(ii) Evidence of general business practice. Evidence of general business practice is not met by showing isolated comparables. If more than one valuation method is commonly used in a business, a right or restriction does not fail to evidence general business practice merely because it uses only one of the recognized methods. It is not necessary that the terms of a right or restriction parallel the terms of any particular agreement. If comparables are difficult to find because the business is unique, comparables from similar businesses may be used.

(5) Multiple rights or restrictions. If property is subject to more than one right or restriction described in paragraph (a)(2) of this section, the failure of a right or restriction to satisfy the requirements of paragraph (b)(1) of this section does not cause any other right or restriction to fail to satisfy those requirements if the right or restriction otherwise meets those requirements. Whether separate provisions are separate rights or restrictions, or are integral parts of a single right or restriction, depends on all the facts and circumstances.

(c) Substantial modification of a right or restriction. *(1) In general.* A right or restriction that is substantially modified is treated as a right or restriction created on the date of the modification Any discretionary modification of a right or restriction, whether or not authorized by the terms of the agreement, that results in other than a de minimis change to the quality, value, or timing of the rights of any party with respect to property that is subject to the right or restriction is a substantial modification. If the terms of the right or restriction require periodic updating, the failure to update is presumed to substantially modify the right or restriction unless it can be shown that updating would not have resulted in a substantial modification. The addition of any family member as a party to a right or restriction (including by reason of a transfer of property that subjects the transferee family member to a right or restriction with respect to the transferred property) is considered a substantial modification unless the addition is mandatory under the terms of the right or restriction or the added family member is assigned to a generation (determined under the rules of section 2651 of the Internal Revenue Code) no lower than the lowest generation occupied by individuals already party to the right or restriction).

(2) Exceptions. A substantial modification does not include—

(i) A modification required by the terms of a right or restriction;

(ii) A discretionary modification of an agreement conferring a right or restriction if the modification does not change the right or restriction;

(iii) A modification of a capitalization rate used with respect to a right or restriction if the rate is modified in a manner that bears a fixed relationship to a specified market interest rate; and

(iv) A modification that results in an option price that more closely approximates fair market value.

(d) Examples. The following examples illustrate the provisions of this section:

Example (1). T dies in 1992 owning title to Blackacre. In 1991, T and T's child entered into a lease with respect to Blackacre At the time the lease was entered into, the terms of the lease were not comparable to leases of similar property entered into among unrelated parties. The lease is a restriction on the use of the property that is disregarded in valuing the property for Federal estate tax purposes.

Example (2). T and T's child, C, each own 50 percent of the outstanding stock of X corporation. T and C enter into an agreement in 1987 providing for the disposition of stock held by the first to die at the time of death. The agreement also provides certain restrictions with respect to lifetime transfers. In 1992, as permitted (but not required) under the agreement, T transfers one-half of T's stock to T's spouse, S. S becomes a party to the agreement between T and C by reason of the transfer. The transfer is the addition of a family member to the right or restriction. However, it is not a substantial modification of the right or restriction because the added family member would be assigned to a generation under section 2651 of the Internal Revenue Code no lower than the generation occupied by C.

Example (3). The facts are the same as in Example 2. In 1993, the agreement is amended to reflect a change in the company's name and a change of address for the company's registered agent. These changes are not a substantial modification of the agreement conferring the right or restriction because the right or restriction has not changed.

T.D. 8395, 1/28/92.

§ 25.2703-2 Effective date.

Section 25.2703-1 applies to any right or restriction created or substantially modified after October 8, 1990, and is effective as of January 28, 1992. With respect to transfers occurring prior to January 28, 1992, and for purposes of determining whether an event occurring prior to January 28, 1992 constitutes a substantial modification, taxpayers may rely on any reasonable interpretation of the statutory provisions. For these purposes, the provisions of the proposed regulations and the final regulations are considered a reasonable interpretation of the statutory provisions.

T.D. 8395, 1/28/92.

§ 25.2704-1 Lapse of certain rights.

(a) Lapse treated as transfer. *(1) In general.* The lapse of a voting right or a liquidation right in a corporation or partnership (an "entity") is a transfer by the individual directly or indirectly holding the right immediately prior to its lapse (the "holder") to the extent provided in paragraphs (b) and (c) of this section. This section applies only if the entity is controlled by the holder and members of the holder's family immediately before and after the lapse. The amount of the transfer is determined under paragraph (d) of this section. If the lapse of a voting right or a liquidation right occurs during the holder's lifetime, the lapse is a transfer by gift. If the lapse occurs at the holder's death, the lapse is a transfer includible in the holder's gross estate.

(2) Definitions. The following definitions apply for purposes of this section.

(i) Control. Control has the meaning given it in § 25.2701-2(b)(5).

(ii) Member of the family. Member of the family has the meaning given it in § 25.2702-2(a)(1).

(iii) Directly or in directly held. An interest is directly or indirectly held only to the extent the value of the interest would have been includible in the gross estate of the individual if the individual had died immediately prior to the lapse.

(iv) Voting right. Voting right means a right to vote with respect to any matter of the entity. In the case of a partnership, the right of a general partner to participate in partnership management is a voting right. The right to compel the entity to acquire all or a portion of the holder's equity interest in the entity by reason of aggregate voting power is treated as a liquidation right and is not treated as a voting right.

(v) Liquidation right. Liquidation right means a right or ability to compel the entity to acquire all or a portion of the holder's equity interest in the entity, including by reason of aggregate voting power, whether or not its exercise would result in the complete liquidation of the entity.

(vi) Subordinate. Subordinate has the meaning given it in § 25.2701-3(a)(2)(iii).

(3) Certain temporary lapses. If a lapsed right may be restored only upon the occurrence of a future event not within the control of the holder or members of the holder's family, the lapse is deemed to occur at the time the lapse becomes permanent with respect to the holder, i.e. either by a transfer of the interest or otherwise.

(4) Source of right or lapse. A voting right or a liquidation right may be conferred by and may lapse by reason of a State law, the corporate charter or bylaws, an agreement, or other means.

(b) Lapse of voting right. A lapse of a voting right occurs at the time a presently exercisable voting right is restricted or eliminated.

(c) Lapse of liquidation right. *(1) In general.* A lapse of a liquidation right occurs at the time a presently exercisable liquidation right is restricted or eliminated. Except as otherwise provided, a transfer of an interest that results in the lapse of a liquidation right is not subject to this section if the rights with respect to the transferred interest are not restricted or eliminated. However, a transfer that results in the elimination of the transferor's right or ability to compel the entity to acquire an interest retained by the transferor that is subordinate to the transferred interest is a lapse of a liquidation right with respect to the subordinate interest.

(2) Exceptions. Section 2704(a) does not apply to the lapse of a liquidation right under the following circumstances.

(i) Family cannot obtain liquidation value (A) In general. Section 2704(a) does not apply to the lapse of a liquidation right to the extent the holder (or the holder's estate) and members of the holder's family cannot immediately after the lapse liquidate an interest that the holder held directly or indirectly and could have liquidated prior to the lapse.

(B) Ability to liquidate. Whether an interest can be liquidated immediately after the lapse is determined under the State law generally applicable to the entity, as modified by the governing instruments of the entity but without regard to any restriction described in section 2704(b). Thus, if, after any restriction described in section 2704(b) is disregarded, the remaining requirements for liquidation under the governing instruments are less restrictive than the State law that would apply in the absence of the governing instruments, the ability to liquidate is determined by reference to the governing instruments.

(ii) Rights valued under section 2701. Section 2704(a) does not apply to the lapse of a liquidation right previously valued under section 2701 to the extent necessary to prevent double taxation (taking into account any adjustment available under § 25.2701-5).

(iii) Certain changes in State law. Section 2704(a) does not apply to the lapse of a liquidation right that occurs solely by reason of a change in State law. For purposes of this paragraph, a change in the governing instrument of an entity is not a change in State law.

(d) Amount of transfer. The amount of the transfer is the excess, if any, of—

(1) The value of all interests in the entity owned by the holder immediately before the lapse (determined immediately after the lapse as if the lapsed right was nonlapsing); over

(2) The value of the interests described in the preceding paragraph immediately after the lapse (determined as if all such interests were held by one individual).

(e) Application to similar rights. [Reserved]

(f) Examples. The following examples illustrate the provisions of this section:

Example (1). Prior to D's death, D owned all the preferred stock of Corporation Y and D's children owned all the common stock. At that time, the preferred stock had 60 percent of the total voting power and the common stock had 40 percent. Under the corporate by- laws, the voting rights of the preferred stock terminated on D's death. The value of D's interest immediately prior to D's death (determined as if the voting rights were nonlapsing) was $100X. The value of that interest immediately after death would have been $90X if the voting rights had been nonlapsing. The decrease in value reflects the loss in value resulting from the death of D (whose involvement in Y was a key factor in Y's profitability). Section 2704(a) applies to the lapse of voting rights on D's death. D's gross estate includes an amount equal to the excess, if any, of $90X over the fair market value of the preferred stock determined after the lapse of the voting rights.

Example (2). Prior to D's death, D owned all the preferred stock of Corporation Y. The preferred stock and the common stock each carried 50 percent of the total voting power of Y. D's children owned 40 percent of the common stock and unrelated parties own the remaining 60 percent. Under the corporate by-laws, the voting rights of the preferred stock terminate on D's death. Section 2704(a) does not apply to the lapse of D's voting rights because members of D's family do not control Y after the lapse.

Example (3). The by-laws of Corporation Y provide that the voting rights of any transferred shares of the single outstanding class of stock are reduced to ½ vote per share after the transfer but are fully restored to the transferred shares after 5 years. D owned 60 percent of the shares prior to death and members of D's family owned the balance. On D's death, D's shares pass to D's children and the voting rights are reduced pursuant to the by-laws. Section 2704(a) applies to the lapse of D's voting rights. D's gross estate includes an amount equal to the excess, if any, of the fair market value of D's stock (determined immediately after D's death as though the voting rights had not been reduced and would not be reduced) over the stock's fair market value immediately after D's death.

Example (4). D owns 84 percent of the single outstanding class of stock of Corporation Y. The by-laws require at least 70 percent of the vote to liquidate Y. D gives one-half of D's stock in equal shares to D's three children, (14 percent to each). Section 2704(a) does not apply to the loss of D's ability to liquidate Y, because the voting rights with respect to the corporation are not restricted or eliminated by reason of the transfer.

Example (5). D and D's two children, A and B, are partners in Partnership X. Each has a 3⅓ percent general partnership interest and a 30 percent limited partnership interest. Under State law, a general partner has the right to participate in partnership management. The partnership agreement provides that when a general partner withdraws or dies, X must redeem the general partnership interest for its liquidation value. Also, under the agreement any general partner can liquidate the partnership. A limited partner cannot liquidate the partnership and a limited partner's capital interest will be returned only when the partnership is liquidated. A deceased limited partner's interest continues as a limited partnership interest. D dies, leaving his limited partnership interest to D's spouse. Because of a general partner's right to dissolve the partnership, a limited partnership interest has a greater fair market value when held in conjunction with a general partnership interest than when held alone. Section 2704(a) applies to the lapse of D's liquidation right because after the lapse, members of D's family could liquidate D's limited partnership interest. D's gross estate includes an amount equal to the excess of the value of all D's interests in X immediately before D's death (determined immediately after D's death but as though the liquidation right had not lapsed and would not lapse) over the fair market value of all D's interests in X immediately after D's death.

Example (6). The facts are the same as in Example 5, except that under the partnership agreement D is the only general partner who holds a unilateral liquidation right. Assume further that the partnership agreement contains a restriction described in section 2704(b) that prevents D's family members from liquidating D's limited partnership interest immediately after D's death. Under State law, in the absence of the restriction in the partnership agreement, D's family members could liquidate the partnership. The restriction on the family's ability to liquidate is disregarded and the amount of D's gross estate is increased by reason of the lapse of D's liquidation right.

Example (7). D owns all the stock of Corporation X, consisting of 100 shares of non-voting preferred stock and 100 shares of voting common stock. Under the by-laws, X can only be liquidated with the consent of at least 80 percent of the voting shares. D transfers 30 shares of common stock to D's child. The transfer is not a lapse of a liquidation right with respect to the common stock because the voting rights that enabled D to liquidate prior to the transfer are not restricted or eliminated. The transfer is not a lapse of a liquidation right with respect to the retained preferred stock because the preferred stock is not subordinate to the transferred common stock.

Example (8). D owns all of the single class of stock of Corporation Y. D recapitalizes Y, exchanging D's common stock for voting common stock and non-voting, non-cumulative preferred stock. The preferred stock carries a right to put the stock for its par value at any time during the next 10 years. D transfers the common stock to D's grandchild in a transfer subject to section 2701. In determining the amount of D's gift under section 2701, D's retained put right is valued at zero. D's child, C, owns the preferred stock when the put right lapses. Section 2704(a) applies to the lapse, without regard to the application of section 2701, because the put right was not valued under section 2701 in the hands of C.

Example (9). A and A's two children are equal general and limited partners in Partnership Y. Under the partnership agreement, each general partner has a right to liquidate the partnership at any time. Under State law that would apply in the absence of contrary provisions in the partnership agreement, the death or incompetency of a general partner terminates the partnership. However, the partnership agreement provides that the partnership does not terminate on the incompetence or death of a general partner, but that an incompetent partner cannot exercise rights as a general partner during any period of incompetency. A partner's full rights as general partner are restored If the partner regains competency. A becomes incompetent. The lapse of A's voting right on becoming incompetent is not subject to section 2704(a) because it may be restored to A in the future. However, if A dies while incompetent, a lapse subject to section 2704(a) is deemed to occur at that time because the lapsed right cannot thereafter be restored to A.

T.D. 8395, 1/28/92.

---

§ 25.2704-2 Transfers subject to applicable restrictions.

(a) In general. If an interest in a corporation or partnership (an "entity") is transferred to or for the benefit of a member of the transferor's family, any applicable restriction is disregarded in valuing the transferred interest. This section applies only if the transferor and members of the transferor's family control the entity immediately before the transfer. For the definition of control, see § 25.2701-2(b)(5). For the definition of member of the family, see § 25.2702-2(a)(1).

(b) Applicable restriction defined. An applicable restriction is a limitation on the ability to liquidate the entity (in whole or in part) that is more restrictive than the limitations that would apply under the State law generally applicable to the entity in the absence of the restriction. A restriction is an applicable restriction only to the extent that either the restriction by its terms will lapse at any time after the transfer, or the transferor (or the transferor's estate) and any members of the transferor's family can remove the restriction immediately after the transfer. Ability to remove the restriction is determined by reference to the State law that would apply but for a more restrictive rule in the governing instruments of the entity. See § 25.2704-1(c)(1)(B) for a discussion of the term "State law." An applicable restriction does not include a commercially reasonable restriction on liquidation imposed by an unrelated person providing capital to the entity for the entity's trade or business operations whether in the form of debt or equity. An unrelated person is any person whose relationship to the transferor, the transferee, or any member of the family of either is not described in section 267(b) of the Internal Revenue Code, provided that for purposes of this section the term "fiduciary of a trust" as used in section 267(b) does not include a bank as defined in section 581 of the Internal Revenue Code. A restriction imposed or required to be imposed by Federal or State law is not an applicable restriction. An option, right to use property, or agreement that is subject to section 2703 is not an applicable restriction.

(c) Effect of disregarding an applicable restriction. If an applicable restriction is disregarded under this section, the transferred interest is valued as if the restriction does not exist and as if the rights of the transferor are determined under the State law that would apply but for the restriction. For example, an applicable restriction with respect to preferred stock will be disregarded in determining the amount of a transfer of common stock under section 2701.

(d) Examples. The following examples illustrate the provisions of this section:

Example (1). D owns a 76 percent interest and each of D's children, A and B, owns a 12 percent interest in General Partnership X. The partnership agreement requires the consent of all the partners to liquidate the partnership. Under the State law that would apply in the absence of the restriction in the partnership agreement, the consent of partners owning 70 percent of the total partnership interests would be required to liquidate X. On D's death, D's partnership interest passes to D's child, C. The requirement that all the partners consent to liquidation is an applicable restriction. Because A, B and C (all members of D's family), acting together after the transfer, can remove the restriction on liquidation, D's interest is valued without regard to the restriction; i.e., as though D's interest is sufficient to liquidate the partnership.

Example (2). D owns all the preferred stock in Corporation X. The preferred stock carries a right to liquidate X that cannot be exercised until 1999. D's children, A and B, own all the common stock of X. The common stock is the only voting stock. In 1994, D transfers the preferred stock to D's child, A. The restriction on D's right to liquidate is an applicable restriction that is disregarded. Therefore, the preferred stock is valued as though the right to liquidate were presently exercisable.

Example (3). D owns 60 percent of the stock of Corporation X. The corporate by-laws provide that the corporation cannot be liquidated for 10 years after which time liquidation requires approval by 60 percent of the voting interests. In the absence of the provision in the by-laws, State law would require approval by 80 percent of the voting interests to liquidate X. D transfers the stock to a trust for the benefit of D's child, A, during the 10-year period. The 10-year restriction is an applicable restriction and is disregarded. Therefore, the value of the stock is determined as if the transferred block could currently liquidate X.

Example (4). D and D's children, A and B, are partners in Limited Partnership Y. Each has a 3.33 percent general partnership interest and a 30 percent limited partnership interest. Any general partner has the right to liquidate the partnership at any time. As part of a loan agreement with a lender who is related to D, each of the partners agree that the partnership may not be liquidated without the lender's consent while any portion of the loan remains outstanding. During the term of the loan agreement, D transfers one- half of both D's partnership interests to each of A and B. Because the lender is a related party, the requirement that the lender consent to liquidation is an applicable restriction and the transfers of D's interests are valued as if such consent were not required.

Example (5). D owns 60 percent of the preferred and 70 percent of the common stock in Corporation X. The remaining stock is owned by individuals unrelated to D. The preferred stock carries a put right that cannot be exercised until 1999. In 1995, D transfers the common stock to D's child in a transfer that is subject to section 2701. The restriction on D's right to liquidate is an applicable restriction that is disregarded in determining the amount of the gift under section 2701.

T.D. 8395, 1/28/92.

§ 25.2704-3 Effective date.

Section 25.2704-1 applies to lapses occurring after January 28, 1992, of rights created after October 8, 1990. Section 25.2704-2 applies to transfers occurring after January 28, 1992, of property subject to applicable restrictions created after October 8, 1990. In determining whether a voting right or a liquidation right has lapsed prior to that date, and for purposes of determining whether the lapse is subject to section 2704(a), taxpayers may rely on any reasonable interpretation of the statutory provisions. For transfers of interests occurring before January 28, 1992, taxpayers may rely on any reasonable interpretation of the statutory provisions in determining whether a restriction is an applicable restriction that must be disregarded in determining the value of the transferred interest. For these purposes, the provisions of the proposed regulations and the final regulations are considered a reasonable interpretation of the statutory provisions.

T.D. 8395, 1/28/92.

§ 31.0-1 Introduction.

(a) In general. The regulations in this part relate to the employment taxes imposed by subtitle C (chapters 21 to 25, inclusive) of the Internal Revenue Code of 1954, as amended. References in the regulations to the "Internal Revenue Code" or the "Code" are references to the Internal Revenue Code of 1954, as amended, unless otherwise indicated. References to the Federal Insurance Contributions Act, the Railroad Retirement Tax Act, and the Federal Unemployment Tax Act are references to chapters 21, 22, and 23, respectively, of the Code. References to sections of law are references to sections of the Internal Revenue Code unless otherwise indicated. The regulations in this part also provide rules relating to the deposit of other taxes by electronic funds transfer.

(b) Division of regulations. The regulations in this part are divided into 7 subparts. Subpart A contains provisions relating to general definitions and use of terms, the division and scope of the regulations in this part, and the extent to which the regulations in this part supersede prior regulations relating to employment taxes. Subpart B relates to the taxes under the Federal Insurance Contributions Act. Subpart C relates to the taxes under the Railroad Retirement Tax Act. Subpart D relates to the tax under the Federal Unemployment Tax Act. Subpart E relates to the collection of income tax at source on wages under chapter 24 of the Code. Subpart F relates to the provisions of chapter 25 of the Code which are applicable in respect of the taxes imposed by chapters 21 to 24, inclusive, of the Code. Subpart G relates to selected provisions of subtitle F of the Code, relating to procedure and administration, which have special application in respect of the taxes imposed by subtitle C of the Code. Inasmuch as these regulations constitute Part 31 of Title 26 of the Code of Federal Regulations, each section of the regulations is preceded by a section symbol and 31 followed by a decimal point (§ 31.). Sections of law or references thereto are preceded by "Sec." or the word "section".

T.D. 6516, 12/19/60, amend T.D. 8723, 7/11/97.

§ 31.0-2 General definitions and use of terms.

(a) In general. As used in the regulations in this part, unless otherwise expressly indicated—

(1) The terms defined in the provisions of law contained in the regulations in this part shall have the meanings so assigned to them.

(2) The Internal Revenue Code of 1954 means the act approved August 16, 1954 (26 U.S.C.), entitled "An act to revise the internal revenue laws of the United States", as amended.

(3) The Internal Revenue Code of 1939 means the act approved February 10, 1939 (53 Stat., Part 1), as amended.

(4) The Social Security Act means the act approved August 14, 1935 (42 U.S.C. c. 7), as amended.

(5) (i) The Social Security Amendments of 1954 means the act approved September 1, 1954 (68 Stat. 1052), as amended.

(ii) The Social Security Amendments of 1956 means the act approved August 1, 1956 (70 Stat. 807), as amended.

(iii) The Social Security Amendments of 1958 means the act approved August 28, 1958 (72 Stat. 1013), as amended.

(iv) The Social Security Amendments of 1960 means the act approved September 13, 1960 (74 Stat. 924).

(v) The Social Security Amendments of 1961 means the act approved June 30, 1961 (75 Stat. 131).

(vi) The Social Security Amendments of 1965 means the act approved July 30, 1965 (79 Stat. 286).

(vii) The Social Security Amendments of 1967 means the act approved January 2, 1968 (81 Stat. 821).

(viii) The Social Security Amendments of 1972 means the act approved October 30, 1972 (86 Stat. 1329).

(6) The Social Security Administration means the Social Security Administration of the Department of Health and Human Services. (See the Statement of Organization and delegations of Authority of the Department of Health and Human Services (20 FR 1996).)

(7) District director means district director of internal revenue. The term also includes the Director of International Operations in all cases where the authority to perform the functions which may be performed by a district director has been delegated to the Director of International Operations.

(8) Person includes an individual, a corporation, a partnership, a trust or estate, a joint-stock company, an association, or a syndicate, group, pool, joint venture or other unincorporated organization or group, through or by means of which any business, financial operation, or venture is carried on. It includes a guardian, committee, trustee, executor, administrator, trustee in bankruptcy, receiver, assignee for the benefit of creditors, conservator, or any person acting in a fiduciary capacity.

(9) Calendar quarter means a period of 3 calendar months ending on March 31, June 30, September 30, or December 31.

(10) Account number means the identifying number of an employee assigned, as the case may be, under the Internal Revenue Code of 1954, under subchapter A of chapter 9 of the Internal Revenue Code of 1939, or under title VIII of the Social Security Act. See also § 301.7701-11 of this chapter (Regulations on Procedure and Administration).

(11) Identification number means the identifying number of an employer assigned, as the case may be, under the Internal Revenue Code of 1954, under subchapter A or D of chapter 9 of the Internal Revenue Code of 1939, or under title VIII of the Social Security Act. See also § 301.7701-12 of this chapter (Regulations on Procedure and Administration).

(12) Regulations 90 means the regulations approved February 17, 1936 (26 CFR (1939) Part 400), as amended, relating to the excise tax on employers under title IX of the Social Security Act, and such regulations as made applicable to subchapter C of chapter 9 and other provisions of the Internal Revenue Code of 1939 by Treasury Decision 4885, approved February 11, 1939 (26 CFR (1939) 1943 Cum. Supp., p. 5876), together with any amendments to such regulations as so made applicable to the Internal Revenue Code of 1939.

(13) Regulations 91 means the regulations approved November 9, 1936 (26 CFR (1939) Part 401), as amended, relating to the employees' tax and the employers' tax under title VIII of the Social Security Act, and such regulations as made applicable to subchapter A of chapter 9 and other provisions of the Internal Revenue Code of 1939 by Treasury Decision 4885, approved February 11, 1939 (26 CFR (1939) 1943 Cum. Supp., p. 5876), together with any amendments to such regulations as so made applicable to the Internal Revenue Code of 1939.

(14) Regulations 106 means the regulations approved February 24, 1940 (26 CFR (1939) Part 402), as amended, relating to the employees' tax and the employers' tax under the Federal Insurance Contributions Act (subchapter A of chapter 9 of the Internal Revenue Code of 1939) with respect to the period after 1939 and before 1951.

(15) Regulations 107 means the regulations approved September 12, 1940 (26 CFR (1939) Part 403), as amended, re-

lating to the excise tax on employers under the Federal Unemployment Tax Act (subchapter C of chapter 9 of the Internal Revenue Code of 1939) with respect to the period after 1939 and before 1955.

(16) Regulations 114 means the regulations approved December 30, 1948 (26 CFR (1939) Part 411), as amended, relating to the employers' tax, employees' tax, and employee representatives' tax under the Railroad Retirement Tax Act (subchapter B of chapter 9 of the Internal Revenue Code of 1939) with respect to compensation paid after 1948 for services rendered after 1946 and before 1955.

(17) Regulations 120 means the regulations approved December 22, 1953 (26 CFR (1939) Part 406), as amended, relating to collection of income tax at source on wages under subchapter D of chapter 9 of the Internal Revenue Code of 1939 with respect to the period after 1953 and before 1955.

(18) Regulations 128 means the regulations approved December 6, 1951 (26 CFR (1939) Part 408), as amended, relating to the employee tax and the employer tax under the Federal Insurance Contributions Act (subchapter A of chapter 9 of the Internal Revenue Code of 1939) with respect to the period after 1950 and before 1955.

(19) The cross references in the regulations in this part to other portions of the regulations, when the word "see" is used, are made only for convenience and shall be given no legal effect.

(b) Subpart B. As used in Subpart B of this part, unless otherwise expressly indicated—

(1) Act means the Federal Insurance Contributions Act.

(2) Taxes means the employee tax and the employer tax, as respectively defined in this paragraph.

(3) Employee tax means the tax (with respect to wages received by an employee after Dec. 31, 1965, the taxes) imposed by section 3101 of the Code.

(4) Employer tax means the tax (with respect to wages paid by an employer after Dec. 31, 1965, the taxes) imposed by section 3111 of the Code.

(c) Subpart C. As used in Subpart C of this part, unless otherwise expressly indicated—

(1) Act means the Railroad Retirement Tax Act.

(2) Railway Labor Act means the act approved May 20, 1926 (45 U.S.C. c. 8), as amended.

(3) Railroad Retirement Act of 1937 means the act approved June 24, 1937 (45 U.S.C. 228a and following), as amended.

(4) Railroad Retirement Board means the board established pursuant to section 10 of the Railroad Retirement Act of 1937 (45 U.S.C. 228j).

(5) Tax means the employee tax, the employee representative tax, or the employer tax, as respectively defined in this paragraph.

(6) Employee tax means the tax imposed by section 3201 of the Code.

(7) Employee representative tax means the tax imposed by section 3211 of the Code.

(8) Employer tax means the tax imposed by section 3221 of the Code.

(d) Subpart D. As used in Subpart D of this part, unless otherwise expressly indicated:

(1) Act means the Federal Unemployment Tax Act.

(2) Railroad Unemployment Insurance Act means the act approved June 25, 1938 (45 U.S.C. c. 11), as amended.

(3) Tax means the tax imposed by section 3301 of the Code.

(e) Subpart E. As used in Subpart E of this part, unless otherwise expressly indicated, tax means the tax required to be deducted and withheld from wages under section 3402 of the Code.

T.D. 6516, 12/19/60, amend T.D. 6606, 6/19/62, T.D. 6658, 6/26/63, T.D. 6983, 12/3/68.

§ 31.0-3 Scope of regulations.

(a) Subpart B. The regulations in Subpart B of this part relate to the imposition of the employee tax and the employer tax under the Federal Insurance Contributions Act with respect to wages paid and received after 1954 for employment performed after 1936. In addition to employment in the case of remuneration therefor paid and received after 1954, the regulations in Subpart B of this part relate also to employment performed after 1954 in the case of remuneration therefor paid and received before 1955. The regulations in Subpart B of this part include provisions relating to the definition of terms applicable in the determination of the taxes under the Federal Insurance Contributions Act, such as "employee", "wages", and "employment". The provisions of Subpart B of this part relating to "employment" are applicable also, (1) to the extent provided in § 31.3121(b)-2, to services performed before 1955 the remuneration for which is paid after 1954, and (2) to the extent provided in § 31.3121(k)-3, to services performed before 1955 the remuneration for which was paid before 1955. (For prior regulations on similar subject matter, see 26 CFR (1939) Part 408 (Regulations 128).)

(b) Subpart C. The regulations in Subpart C of this part relate to the imposition of the employee tax, the employee representative tax, and the employer tax under the Railroad Retirement Tax Act with respect to compensation paid after 1954, for services rendered after such date. The regulations in Subpart C of this part include provisions relating to the definition of terms applicable in the determination of the taxes under the Railroad Retirement Tax Act, such as "employee", "employee representative", "employer", and "compensation". (For prior regulations on similar subject matter, see 26 CFR (1939) Part 411 (Regulations 114).)

(c) Subpart D. The regulations in Subpart D of this part relate to the imposition on employers of the excise tax under the Federal Unemployment Tax Act for the calendar year 1955 and subsequent calendar years with respect to wages paid after 1954 for employment performed after 1938. In addition to employment in the case of remuneration therefor paid after 1954, the regulations in Subpart D of this part relate also to employment performed after 1954 in the case of remuneration therefor paid before 1955. The regulations in Subpart D of this part include provisions relating to the definition of terms applicable in the determination of the tax under the Federal Unemployment Tax Act, such as "employee", "employer", "employment", and "wages". The regulations in Subpart D of this part also include provisions relating to the credits against the Federal tax for State contributions. (For prior regulations on similar subject matter, see 26 CFR (1939) Part 403 (Regulations 107).)

(d) Subpart E. The regulations in Subpart E of this part relate to the withholding under chapter 24 of the Code of income tax at source on wages paid after 1954, regardless of when such wages were earned. The regulations in Subpart E of this part include provisions relating to the definition of terms applicable in the determination of the tax under chapter 24 of the Code, such as "employee", "employer", and "wages". (For prior regulations on similar subject matter, see 26 CFR (1939) Part 406 (Regulations 120).)

(e) **Subpart F.** The regulations in Subpart F of this part deal with the general provisions contained in chapter 25 of the Code, which relate to the employment taxes imposed by chapters 21 to 24, inclusive, of the Code. (For prior regulations on the subject matter of section 3503, see 26 CFR (1939) 411.802 and 408.803 (Regulations 114 and 128, respectively). For prior regulations on the subject matter of section 3504, see 26 CFR (1939) 406.807 and 408.906 (Regulations 120 and 128, respectively).)

(f) Subpart G. The regulations in Subpart G of this part, which are prescribed under selected provisions of subtitle F of the Code, relate to the procedural and administrative requirements in respect of records, returns, deposits, payments, and related matters applicable to the employment taxes imposed by subtitle C (chapters 21 to 25, inclusive) of the Code. In addition, the provisions of Subpart G of this part relate to adjustments and to claims for refund, credit, or abatement, made after 1954, in connection with the employment taxes imposed by subtitle C of the Internal Revenue Code of 1954, by chapter 9 of the Internal Revenue Code of 1939, or by the corresponding provisions of prior law, but not to any adjustment reported, or credit taken, in whole or in part on any return or supplemental return filed on or before July 31, 1960. The provisions of Subpart G of this part also relate to deposits of taxes imposed by subchapter B of chapter 9 of the 1939 Code or by corresponding provisions of prior law with respect to compensation paid after 1954 for services rendered before 1955. For other administrative provisions which have application to the employment taxes imposed by subtitle C of the Code, see Part 301 of this chapter (Regulations on Procedure and Administration). (The administrative and procedural regulations applicable with respect to a particular employment tax for a prior period were combined with the substantive regulations relating to such tax for such period. For the regulations applicable to the respective taxes for prior periods, see paragraphs (a), (b), (c), and (d) of this section.) Subpart G of this part also provides rules relating to the deposit of other taxes by electronic funds transfer.

T.D. 6516, 12/19/60, amend T.D. 6744, 7/1/64, T.D. 8723, 7/11/97.

§ 31.0-4 Extent to which the regulations in this part supersede prior regulations.

The regulations in this part, with respect to the subject matter within the scope thereof, supersede 25 CFR (1939) Parts 403, 406, 408, and 411 (Regulations 107, 120, 128, and 114, respectively). The Regulation on Monthly Returns and Payment of Employment Taxes (23 FR 5006) are also superseded.

T.D. 6516, 12/19/60.

§ 31.3101-1 Measure of employee tax.

The employee tax is measured by the amount of wages received after 1954 with respect to employment after 1936. See § 31.3121(a)-1, relating to wages; and §§ 31.3121(b)-1 to 31.3121(b)-4, inclusive, relating to employment. For provisions relating to the time of receipt of wages, see § 31.3121(a)-2.

T.D. 6190, 7/13/56, amend T.D. 6516, 12/19/60, T.D. 6744, 7/1/64.

§ 31.3101-2 Rates and computation of employee tax.

(a) Old-age, survivors, and disability insurance. The rates of employee tax for old-age, survivors, and disability insurance with respect to wages received in calendar years after 1954 are as follows:

Calendar year	Percent
1955 and 1956	2
1957 and 1958	2.25
1959	2.5
1960 and 1961	3
1962	3.125
1963 to 1965, both inclusive	3.625
1966	3.85
1967	3.9
1968	3.8
1969 and 1970	4.2
1971 and 1972	4.6
1973	4.85
1974 to 2010, both inclusive	4.95
2011 and subsequent calendar years	5.95

(b) Hospital insurance. The rates of employee tax for hospital insurance with respect to wages received in calendar years after 1965 are as follows:

Calendar year	Percent
1966	0.35
1967	.50
1968 to 1972, both inclusive	.60
1973	1.0
1974 to 1977, both inclusive	0.90
1978 to 1980, both inclusive	1.10
1981 to 1985, both inclusive	1.35
1986 and subsequent calendar years	1.50

(c) Computation of employee tax. The employee tax is computed by applying to the wages received by the employee the rate in effect at the time such wages are received.

Example. In 1972, employee A performed for employer X services which constituted employment (see § 31.3121(b)-2). In 1973 A receives from X $1,000 as reimbursement for such services. The tax is payable at the 5.85 percent rate (4.85 percent plus 1.0 percent) in effect for the calendar year 1973 (the year in which the wages are received) and not at the 5.2 percent rate which was in effect for the calendar year 1972 (the year in which the services were performed).

T.D. 6190, 7/13/56, amend T.D. 6516, 12/19/60, T.D. 6744, 7/1/64, T.D. 6983, 12/3/68, T.D. 7374, 7/17/75.

§ 31.3101-3 When employee tax attaches.

The employee tax attaches at the time that the wages are received by the employee. For provisions relating to the time of such receipt, see § 31.3121(a)-2.

T.D. 6190, 7/13/56, amend T.D. 6516, 12/19/60.

§ 31.3102-1 Collection of, and liability for, employee tax; in general.

(a) The employer shall collect from each of his employees the employee tax with respect to wages for employment performed for the employer by the employee. The employer shall make the collection by deducting or causing to be deducted the amount of the employee tax from such wages as and when paid. (For provisions relating to the time of such payment, see § 31.3121(a)-2.) The employer is required to collect the tax, notwithstanding the wages are paid in something other than money, and to pay over the tax in money. (As to the exclusion from wages of remuneration paid in any medium other than cash for certain types of services, see § 31.3121(a)(7)-1, relating to such remuneration paid for service not in the course of the employer's trade or business or for domestic service in a private home of the employer; and § 31.3121(a)(8)-1, relating to such remuneration paid for agricultural labor.) For provisions relating to the collection of, and liability for, employee tax in respect of tips, see § 31.3102-3.

(b) The employer is permitted, but not required, to deduct amounts equivalent to employee tax from payments to an employee of cash remuneration to which the sections referred to in this paragraph (b) are applicable prior to the time that the sum of such payments equals—

(1) $100 in the calendar year, for service not in the course of the employer's trade or business, to which § 31.3121(a)(7)-1 is applicable;

(2) The applicable dollar threshold (as defined in section 3121(x)) in the calendar year, for domestic service in a private home of the employer, to which § 31.3121(a)(7)-1 is applicable;

(3) $150 in the calendar year, for agricultural labor, to which § 31.3121(a)(8)-1(c)(1)(i) is applicable; or

(4) $100 in the calendar year, for service performed as a home worker, to which § 31.3121(a)(10)-1 is applicable.

(c) At such time as the sum of the cash payments in the calendar year for a type of service referred to in paragraph (b)(1), (b)(2), (b)(3) or (b)(4) of this section equals or exceeds the amount specified, the employer is required to collect from the employee any amount of employee tax not previously deducted. If an employer pays cash remuneration to an employee for two or more of the types of service referred to in paragraph (b)(1), (b)(2), (b)(3) or (b)(4) of this section, the provisions of paragraph (b) of this section and this paragraph (c) are to be applied separately to the amount of remuneration attributable to each type of service. For provisions relating to the repayment to an employee, or other disposition, of amounts deducted from an employee's remuneration in excess of the correct amount of employee tax, see § 31.6413(a)-1.

(d) In collecting employee tax, the employer shall disregard any fractional part of a cent of such tax unless it amounts to one-half cent or more, in which case it shall be increased to 1 cent. The employer is liable for the employee tax with respect to all wages paid by him to each of his employees whether or not it is collected from the employee. If, for example, the employer deducts less than the correct amount of tax, or if he fails to deduct any part of the tax, he is nevertheless liable for the correct amount of the tax. Until collected from him the employee also is liable for the employee tax with respect to all the wages received by him. Any employee tax collected by or on behalf of an employer is a special fund in trust for the United States. See section 7501. The employer is indemnified against the claims and demands of any person for the amount of any payment of such tax made by the employer to the district director.

(e) *(1)* The provisions of paragraphs (a) and (d) of this section apply to any payment made on or after January 1, 1955.

(2) The provisions of paragraphs (b) and (c) of this section that apply to any payment made for service not in the course of the employer's trade or business or for service performed as a home worker within the meaning of section 3121(d)(3)(C) apply to any such payment made on or after January 1, 1978. The provisions of paragraphs (b) and (c) of this section that apply to any payment made for domestic service in a private home of the employer apply to any such payment made on or after January 1, 1994. The provisions of paragraphs (b) and (c) of this section that apply to any payment made for agricultural labor apply to any such payment made on or after January 1, 1988. For rules applicable to any payment for these services made prior to the dates set forth in this paragraph (e)(2), see § 31.3102-1 in effect at such time (see 26 CFR part 31 contained in the edition of 26 CFR Parts 30 to 39, revised as of April 1, 2006).

T.D. 6190, 7/13/56, amend T.D. 6516, 12/19/60, T.D. 6744, 7/1/64, T.D. 7001, 1/17/69, T.D. 9266, 6/16/2006.

§ 31.3102-2 Manner and time of payment of employee tax.

The employee tax is payable to the district director in the manner and at the time prescribed in Subpart G of the regulations in this part. For provisions relating to the payment by an employee of employee tax in respect of tips, see paragraph (d) of § 31.3102-3.

T.D. 6190, 7/13/56, amend T.D. 6516, 12/19/60, T.D. 7001, 1/17/69.

§ 31.3102-3 Collection of, and liability for, employee tax on tips.

(a) Collection of tax from employee. *(1) In general.* Subject to the limitations set forth in subparagraph (2) of this paragraph, the employer shall collect from each of his employees the employee tax on those tips received by the employee which constitute wages for purposes of the tax imposed by section 3101. (For provisions relating to the treatment of tips as wages, see §§ 31.3121(a)(12) and 31.3121(q).) The employer shall make the collection by deducting or causing to be deducted the amount of the employee tax from wages (exclusive of tips) which are under the control of the employer or other funds turned over by the employee to the employer (see subparagraph (3) of this paragraph). For purposes of this section the term "wages (exclusive of tips) which are under the control of the employer" means, with respect to a payment of wages, an amount equal to wages as defined on section 3121(a) except that tips and noncash remuneration which are wages are not included, less the sum of—

(i) The tax under section 3101 required to be collected by the employer in respect of wages as defined in section 3121(a) (exclusive of tips);

(ii) The tax under section 3402 required to be collected by the employer in respect of wages as defined in section 3401(a) (exclusive of tips); and

(iii) The amount of tax imposed on the remuneration of an employee withheld by the employer pursuant to State and local law (including amounts withheld under an agreement between the employer and the employee pursuant to such law) except that the amount of taxes taken into account in this subdivision shall not include any amount attributable to tips.

(2) Limitations. An employer is required to collect employee tax on tips which constitute wages only in respect of those tips which are reported by the employee to the employer in a written statement furnished to the employer pursuant to section 6053(a). The employer is responsible for the

collection of employee tax on tips reported to him only to the extent that the employer can—

(i) During the period beginning at the time the written statement is submitted to him and ending at the close of the 10th day of the month following the month in which the statement was submitted, or

(ii) In the case of an employer who elects to deduct the tax on an estimated basis (see paragraph (c) of this section), during the period beginning at the time the written statement is submitted to him and ending at the close of the 30th day following the quarter in which the statement was submitted,

collect the employee tax by deducting it or causing it be deducted as provided in subparagraph (1).

(3) Furnishing of funds to employer. If the amount of employee tax in respect of tips reported by the employee to the employer in a written statement (or statements) furnished pursuant to section 6053(a) exceeds the wages (exclusive of tips) which are under the control of the employer, the employee may furnish to the employer, within the period specified in subparagraph (2)(i) or (ii) of this paragraph (whichever is applicable), an amount of money equal to the amount of such excess.

(b) Less than $20 of tips. Notwithstanding the provisions of paragraph (a) of this section, if an employee furnishes to his employer a written statement—

(1) Covering a period of less than 1 month, and

(2) The statement is furnished to the employer prior to the close of the 10th day of the month following the month in which the tips were actually received by the employee, and

(3) The aggregate amount of tips reported in the statement and in all other statements previously furnished by the employee covering periods within the same month is less than $20, and the statements, collectively, do not cover the entire month,

the employer may deduct amounts equivalent to employee tax on such tips from wages (exclusive of tips) which are under the control of the employer or other funds turned over by the employee to the employer. For provisions relating to the repayment to an employee, or other disposition, of amounts deducted from an employee's remuneration in excess of the correct amount of employee tax, see § 31.6413(a)-1. (As to the exclusion from wages of tips of less than $20, see § 31.3121(a)(12)-1.)

(c) Collection of employee tax on estimated basis. *(1) In general.* Subject to certain limitations and conditions, an employer may, at his discretion, make collection of the employee tax in respect of tips reported by an employee to the employer on an estimated basis. An employer who elects to make collection of the employee tax on an estimated basis shall:

(i) In respect of each employee, make an estimate of the amount of tips that will be reported, pursuant to section 6053(a), by the employee to the employer in a calendar quarter.

(ii) Determine the amount which must be deducted upon each payment of wages (exclusive of tips) which are under the control of the employer to be made during the quarter by the employer to the employee in order to collect from the employee during the quarter an amount equal to the amount obtained by multiplying the estimated quarterly tips by the sum of the rates of tax under subsections (a) and (b) of section 3101.

(iii) Deduct from any payment of such employee's wages (exclusive of tips) which are under the control of the employer, or from funds referred to in paragraph (a)(3) of this section, such amount as may be necessary to adjust the amount of tax withheld on the estimated basis to conform to the amount of employee tax imposed upon, and required to be deducted in respect of, tips reported by the employee to the employer during the calendar quarter in written statements furnished to the employer pursuant to section 6053(a). If an adjustment is required, the additional employee tax required to be collected may be deducted upon any payment of the employee's wages (exclusive of tips) which are under the control of the employer during the quarter and within the first 30 days following the quarter or from funds turned over by the employee to the employer for such purposes within such period. For provisions relating to the repayment to an employee, or other disposition, of amounts deducted from an employee's remuneration in excess of the correct amount of employee tax, see § 31.6413(a)-1.

(2) Estimating tips employee will report. (i) Initial estimate. The initial estimate of the amount of tips that will be reported by a particular employee in a calendar quarter shall be made on the basis of the facts and circumstances surrounding the employment of that employee. However, if a number of employees are employed under substantially the same circumstances and working conditions, the initial estimate established for one such employee may be used as the initial estimate for other employees in that group.

(ii) Adjusting estimate. If the quarterly estimate of tips in respect of a particular employee continues to differ substantially from the amount of tips reported by the employee and there are no unusual factors involved (for example, an extended absence from work due to illness) the employer shall make an appropriate adjustment of his estimate of the amount of tips that will be reported by the employee.

(iii) Reasonableness of estimate. The employer must be prepared, upon request of the district director, to disclose the factors upon which he relied in making the estimate, and his reasons for believing that the estimate is reasonable.

(d) Employee tax not collected by employer. If—

(1) The amount of the employee tax imposed by section 3101 in respect of those tips received by an employee which constitute wages exceeds

(2) The amount of employee tax imposed by section 3101 (in respect of tips reported by the employee to the employer) which can be collected by the employer from such employee's wages (exclusive of tips) which are under the control of the employer or from funds referred to in paragraph (a)(3) of this section,

the employee shall be liable for the payment of tax in an amount equal to such excess. For provisions relating to the manner and time of payment of employee tax by an employee, see paragraph (d) of § 31.6011(a)-1 and paragraph (a)(4) of § 31.6071(a)-1. For provisions relating to statements required to be furnished by employers to employees in respect of uncollected employee tax on tips reported to the employer, see § 31.6053-2.

T.D. 7001, 1/17/69.

§ 31.3111-1 Measure of employer tax.

The employer tax is measured by the amount of wages paid after 1954 with respect to employment after 1936. See § 31.3121(a)-1, relating to wages, and §§ 31.3121(b)-1 to 31.3121(b)-4, inclusive, relating to employment. For provisions relating to time of payment of wages, see § 31.3121(a)-2.

T.D. 6190, 7/13/56, amend T.D. 6516, 12/19/60, T.D. 6744, 7/1/64.

§ 31.3111-2 Rates and computation of employer tax.

(a) Old-age, survivors, and disability insurance. The rates of employer tax for old-age survivors, and disability insurance with respect to wages paid in calendar years after 1954 are as follows:

Calendar year	Percent
1955 and 1956	2
1957 and 1958	2.25
1959	2.5
1960 and 1961	3
1962	3.125
1963 to 1965, both inclusive	3.625
1966	3.85
1967	3.9
1968	3.8
1969 and 1970	4.2
1971 and 1972	4.6
1973	4.85
1974 to 2010, both inclusive	4.95
2011 and subsequent calendar years	5.95

(b) Hospital insurance. The rates of employer tax for hospital insurance with respect to wages paid in calendar years after 1954 are as follows:

Calendar year	Percent
1966	0.35
1967	.50
1968 to 1972, both inclusive	.60
1973	1.0
1974 to 1977, both inclusive	0.90
1978 to 1980, both inclusive	1.10
1981 to 1985, both inclusive	1.35
1986 and subsequent calendar years	1.50

(c) Computation of employer tax. The employer tax is computed by applying to the wages paid by the employer the rate in effect at the time such wages are paid.

T.D. 6190, 7/13/56, amend T.D. 6516, 12/19/60, T.D. 6744, 7/1/64, T.D. 6983, 12/3/68, T.D. 7374, 7/17/75.

§ 31.3111-3 When employer tax attaches.

The employer tax attaches at the time that the wages are paid by the employer. For provisions relating to the time of such payment, see § 31.3121(a)-2.

T.D. 6190, 7/13/56, amend T.D. 6516, 12/19/60.

§ 31.3111-4 Liability for employer tax.

The employer is liable for the employer tax with respect to the wages paid to his employees for employment performed for him.

T.D. 6190, 7/13/56, amend T.D. 6516, 12/19/60.

§ 31.3111-5 Manner and time of payment of employer tax.

The employer tax is payable to the district director in the manner and at the time prescribed in subpart G of the regulations in this part.

T.D. 6190, 7/13/56, amend T.D. 6516, 12/19/60.

§ 31.3112-1 Instrumentalities of the United States specifically exempted from the employer tax.

Section 3112 makes ineffectual as to the employer tax imposed by section 3111 those provisions of law which grant to an instrumentality of the United States an exemption from taxation, unless such provisions grant a specific exemption from the tax imposed by section 3111 by an express reference to such section or the corresponding section of prior law (section 1410 of the Internal Revenue Code of 1939). Thus, the general exemptions from Federal taxation granted by various statutes to certain instrumentalities of the United States without specific reference to the tax imposed by section 3111 or by section 1410 of the 1939 Code are rendered inoperative insofar as such exemptions relate to the tax imposed by section 3111. For provisions relating to the exception from employment of services performed in the employ of an instrumentality of the United States specifically exempted from the employer tax, see § 31.3121(b)(5)-1. For provisions relating to services performed for an instrumentality exempt on December 31, 1950, from the employer tax, see paragraph (c) of § 31.3121(b)(6)-1.

T.D. 6190, 7/13/56, amend T.D. 6516, 12/19/60.

§ 31.3121(a)-1 Wages.

(a) *(1)* Whether remuneration paid after 1954 for employment performed after 1936 constitutes wages is determined under section 3121(a). This section and §§ 31.3121(a)(1)-1 to 31.3121(a)(15)-1, inclusive (relating to the statutory exclusions from wages), apply with respect only to remuneration paid after 1954 for employment performed after 1936. Whether remuneration paid after 1936 and before 1940 for employment performed after 1936 constitutes wages shall be determined in accordance with the applicable provisions of law and of 26 CFR (1939) Part 401 (Regulations 91). Whether remuneration paid after 1939 and before 1951 for employment performed after 1936 constitutes wages shall be determined in accordance with the applicable provisions of law and of 26 CFR (1939) Part 402 (Regulations 106). Whether remuneration paid after 1950 and before 1955 for employment performed after 1936 constitutes wages shall be determined in accordance with the applicable provisions of law and of 26 CFR (1939) Part 408 (Regulations 128).

(2) The term *compensation* as used in section 3231(e) of the Internal Revenue Code has the same meaning as the term wages as used in this section, determined without regard to section 3121(b)(9), except as specifically limited by the Railroad Retirement Tax Act (chapter 22 of the Internal Revenue Code) or regulation. The Commissioner may provide any additional guidance that may be necessary or appropriate in applying the definitions of sections 3121(a) and 3231(e).

(b) The term "wages" means all remuneration for employment unless specifically excepted under section 3121(a) (see §§ 31.3121(a)(1)-1 to 31.3121(a)(15)-1, inclusive) or paragraph (j) of this section.

(c) The name by which the remuneration for employment is designated is immaterial. Thus, salaries, fees, bonuses, and commissions on sales or on insurance premiums, are wages if paid as compensation for employment.

(d) Generally the basis upon which the remuneration is paid is immaterial in determining whether the remuneration constitutes wages. Thus, it may be paid on the basis of piecework, or a percentage of profits; and it may be paid hourly, daily, weekly, monthly, or annually. See, however, § 31.3121(a)(8)-1 which relates to the treatment of cash remuneration computed on a time basis for agricultural labor.

(e) Generally the medium in which the remuneration is paid is also immaterial. It may be paid in cash or in something other than cash, as for example, goods, lodging, food, or clothing. Remuneration paid in items other than cash shall be computed on the basis of the fair value of such items at the time of payment. See, however, §§ 31.3121(a)(7)-1, 31.3121(a)(8)-1, 31.3121(a)(10)-1, and 31.3121(a)(12)-1, relating to the treatment of remuneration paid in any medium other than cash for services not in the course of the employer's trade or business and for domestic service in a private home of the employer, for agricultural labor, for services performed by certain home workers, and as tips, respectively.

(f) Ordinarily, facilities or privileges (such as entertainment, medical services, or so-called "courtesy" discounts on purchases), furnished or offered by an employer to his employees generally, are not considered as remuneration for employment if such facilities or privileges are of relatively small value and are offered or furnished by the employer merely as a means of promoting the health, good will, contentment, or efficiency of his employees. The term "facilities or privileges", however, does not ordinarily include the value of meals or lodging furnished, for example, to restaurant or hotel employees, or to seamen or other employees aboard vessels, since generally these items constitute an appreciable part of the total remuneration of such employees.

(g) Amounts of so-called "vacation allowances" paid to an employee constitute wages. Thus, the salary of an employee on vacation, paid notwithstanding his absence from work, constituting wages.

(h) Amounts paid specifically—either as advances or reimbursements—for traveling or other bona fide ordinary and necessary expenses incurred or reasonably expected to be incurred in the business of the employer are not wages. Traveling and other reimbursed expenses must be identified either by making a separate payment or by specifically indicating the separate amounts where both wages and expense allowances are combined in a single payment. For amounts that are received by an employee on or after July 1, 1990, with respect to expenses paid or incurred on or after July 1, 1990, see § 31.3121(a)-3.

(i) Remuneration for employment, unless such remuneration is specifically excepted under section 3121(a) or paragraph (j) of this section, constitutes wages even though at the time paid the relationship of employer and employee no longer exists between the person in whose employ the services were performed and the individual who performed them.

Example. A is employed by B during the month of January 1955 in employment and is entitled to receive remuneration of $100 for the services performed for B, the employer, during the month. A leaves the employ of B at the close of business on January 31, 1955. On February 15, 1955 (when A is no longer an employee of B), B pays A the remuneration of $100 which was earned for the services performed in January. The $100 is wages and the taxes are payable with respect thereto.

(j) In addition to the exclusions specified in §§ 31.3121(a)(1)-1 to 31.3121(a)(15)-1, inclusive, the following types of payments are excluded from wages.

(1) Remuneration for services which do not constitute employment under section 3121(b) and which are not deemed to be employment under section 3121(c) (see § 31.3121(c)-1).

(2) Remuneration for services which are deemed not to be employment under section 3121(c) (see § 31.3121(c)-1).

(3) Tips or gratuities paid, prior to January 1, 1966, directly to an employee by a customer of an employer, and not accounted for by the employee to the employer. For provisions relating to the treatment of tips received by an employee after December 31, 1965, as wages, see §§ 31.3121(a)(12) and 31.3121(q).

(k) Split-dollar life insurance arrangements. Except as otherwise provided under section 3121(v), see §§ 1.61-22 and 1.7872-15 of this chapter for rules relating to the treatment of split dollar life insurance arrangements.

T.D. 6190, 7/13/56, amend T.D. 6516, 12/19/60, T.D. 6744, 7/1/64, T.D. 7001, 1/17/69, T.D. 7374, 7/17/75, T.D. 8276, 12/7/89, T.D. 8324, 12/12/90, T.D. 8582, 12/22/94, T.D. 9092, 9/11/2003.

§ 31.3121(a)-1T Question and answer relating to the definition of wages in section 3121(a) (temporary).

The following question and answer relates to the definition of wages in section 3121(a) of the Internal Revenue Code of 1954, as amended by section 531(d)(1)(A) of the Tax Reform Act of 1984 (98 Stat. 885):

Q-1. Are fringe benefits included in the definition of "wages" under section 3121(a)?

A-1. Yes, unless specifically excluded from the definition of "wages" pursuant to section 3121(a)(1) through (20). For example, a fringe benefit provided to or on behalf of an employee is excluded from the definition of "wages" if at the time such benefit is provided it is reasonable to believe that the employee will be able to exclude such benefit from income under section 117 or 132.

T.D. 8004, 1/2/85.

§ 31.3121(a)-2 Wages; when paid and received.

(a) In general, wages are received by an employee at the time that they are paid by the employer to the employee. Wages are paid by an employer at the time that they are actually or constructively paid unless under paragraph (c) of this section they are deemed to be subsequently paid. For provisions relating to the time when tips received by an employee are deemed paid to the employee, see § 31.3121(q)-1.

(b) Wages are constructively paid when they are credited to the account of or set apart for an employee so that they may be drawn upon by him at any time although not then actually reduced to possession. To constitute payment in such a case the wages must be credited to or set apart for the employee without any substantial limitation or restriction as to the time or manner of payment or condition upon which payment is to be made, and must be made available to him so that they may be drawn upon at any time, and their payment brought within his own control and disposition. For provisions relating to the treatment of deductions from remuneration as payments of remuneration, see § 31.3123-1.

(c) *(1)* The first $100 of cash remuneration paid, either actually or constructively, by an employer in any calendar year to an employee for—

(i) Service not in the course of the employer's trade or business, to which § 31.3121(a)(7)-1 is applicable, shall be deemed to be paid by the employer to the employee at the first moment of time in such calendar year that the sum of such cash payments made within such year is at least $100; or

(ii) Service performed as a home worker within the meaning of section 3121(d)(3)(C), to which § 31.3121(a)(10)-1 is applicable, shall be deemed to be paid by the employer to the employee at the first moment of time in such calendar year that the sum of such cash payments made within such year is at least $100.

(2) Cash remuneration paid, either actually or constructively, by an employer in any calendar year to an employee for domestic service in a private home of the employer to which § 31.3121(a)(7)-1 is applicable, and before the sum of the payments of such cash remuneration equals or exceeds the applicable dollar threshold (as defined in section 3121(x)) for such year, shall be deemed to be paid by the employer to the employee at the first moment of time in such calendar year that the sum of such cash payments made within such year equals or exceeds the applicable dollar threshold (as defined in section 3121(x)) for such year.

(3) Cash remuneration paid, either actually or constructively, by an employer in any calendar year to an employee for agricultural labor to which § 31.3121(a)(8)-1 is applicable, and before either of the events described in paragraphs (c)(3)(i) and (c)(3)(ii) of this section has occurred, shall be deemed to be paid by the employer to the employee at the first moment of time in such calendar year that—

(i) The sum of the payments of such remuneration is $150 or more; or

(ii) The employer's expenditures for agricultural labor in such calendar year equals or exceeds $2,500, except that this paragraph (c)(3)(ii) shall not apply in determining when such remuneration is deemed to be paid under this paragraph if such employee—

(A) Is employed as a hand-harvest laborer and is paid on a piece rate basis in an operation which has been, and is customarily and generally recognized as having been, paid on a piece rate basis in the region of employment;

(B) Commutes daily from his permanent residence to the farm on which he is so employed; and

(C) Has been employed in agriculture less than 13 weeks during the preceding calendar year.

(4) If the employer pays cash remuneration to an employee for two or more of the types of service referred to in this paragraph, the provision of this paragraph are to be applied separately to the amount of remuneration attributable to each type of service.

(d) *(1)* The provisions of paragraphs (a) and (b) of this section apply to any payment of wages made on or after January 1, 1955.

(2) The provisions of paragraph (c) of this section that apply to any payment of wages made for service not in the course of the employer's trade or business or for service performed as a home worker within the meaning of section 3121(d)(3)(C) apply to any such payment made on or after January 1, 1978. The provisions of paragraph (c) of this section that apply to any payment of wages made for domestic service in a private home of the employer apply to any such payment made on or after January 1, 1994. The provisions of paragraph (c) of this section that apply to any payment of wages made for agricultural labor apply to any such payment made on or after January 1, 1988. For rules applicable to any payment of wages for these services made prior to the dates set forth in this paragraph (d)(2), see § 31.3121(a)-2 in effect at such time (see 26 CFR part 31 contained in the edition of 26 CFR Parts 30 to 39, revised as of April 1, 2006).

T.D. 6190, 7/13/56, amend T.D. 6516, 12/19/60, T.D. 6744, 7/1/64, T.D. 7001, 1/17/69, T.D. 9266, 6/16/2006.

§ 31.3121(a)-3 Reimbursement and other expense allowance amounts.

(a) When excluded from wages. If a reimbursement or other expense allowance arrangement meets the requirements of section 62(c) of the Code and § 1.62-2 and the expenses are substantiated within a reasonable period of time, payments made under the arrangement that do not exceed the substantiated expenses are treated as paid under an accountable plan and are not wages. In addition, if both wages and the reimbursement or other expense allowance are combined in a single payment, the reimbursement or other expense allowance must be identified either by making a separate payment or by specifically identifying the amount of the reimbursement or other expense allowance.

(b) When included in wages. *(1) Accountable plans.* (i) General rule. Except as provided in paragraph (b)(1)(ii) of this section, if a reimbursement or other expense allowance arrangement satisfies the requirements of section 62(c) and § 1.62-2, but the expenses are not substantiated within a reasonable period of time or amounts in excess of the substantiated expenses are not returned within a reasonable period of time, the amount paid under the arrangement in excess of the substantiated expenses is treated as paid under a nonaccountable plan, is included in wages, and is subject to withholding and payment of employment taxes no later than the first payroll period following the end of the reasonable period.

(ii) Per diem or mileage allowances. If a reimbursement or other expense allowance arrangement providing a per diem or mileage allowance satisfies the requirements of section 62(c) and § 1.62-2, but the allowance is paid at a rate for each day or mile of travel that exceeds the amount of the employee's expenses deemed substantiated for a day or mile of travel, the excess portion is treated as paid under a nonaccountable plan and is included in wages. In the case of a per diem or mileage allowance paid as a reimbursement, the excess portion is subject to withholding and payment of employment taxes when paid. In the case of a per diem or mileage allowance paid as an advance, the excess portion is subject to withholding and payment of employment taxes no later than the first payroll period following the payroll period in which the expenses with respect to which the advance was paid (i.e., the days or miles of travel) are substantiated. The Commissioner may, in his discretion, prescribe special rules in pronouncements of general applicability regarding the timing of withholding and payment of employment taxes on per diem and mileage allowance.

(2) Nonaccountable plans. If a reimbursement or other expense allowance arrangement does not satisfy the requirements of section 62(c) and § 1.62-2 (e.g., the arrangement does not require expenses to be substantiated or require amounts in excess of the substantiated expenses to be returned), all amounts paid under the arrangement are treated as paid under a nonaccountable plan, are included in wages, and are subject to withholding and payment of employment taxes when paid.

(c) Effective dates. This section generally applies to payments made under reimbursement or other expense allowance arrangements received by an employee on or after July 1, 1990, with respect to expenses paid or incurred on or after

July 1, 1990. Paragraph (b)(1)(ii) of this section applies to payments made under reimbursement or other expense allowance arrangements received by an employee on or after January 1, 1991, with respect to expenses paid or incurred on or after January 1, 1991.

T.D. 8276, 12/7/89, amend T.D. 8324, 12/14/90.

§ 31.3121(a)(1)-1 Annual wage limitation.

(a) In general. *(1)* The term "wages" does not include that part of the remuneration paid by an employer to an employee within any calendar year—

(i) After 1954 and before 1959 which exceeds the first $4,200 of remuneration,

(ii) After 1958 and before 1966 which exceeds the first $4,800 of remuneration,

(iii) After 1965 and before 1968 which exceeds the first $6,600 of remuneration,

(iv) After 1967 and before 1972 which exceeds the first $7,800 of remuneration,

(v) After 1971 and before 1973 which exceeds the first $9,000 of remuneration.

(vi) After 1972 and before 1974 which exceeds the first $10,800 of remuneration,

(vii) After 1973 and before 1975 which exceeds the first $13,200 of remuneration, or

(viii) After 1974 which exceeds the amount equal to the contribution and benefit base (as determined under section 230 of the Social Security Act) which is effective for such calendar year

(exclusive of remuneration excepted from wages in accordance with paragraph (j) of § 31.3121(a)-1 or §§ 31.3121(a)(2)-1 to 31.3121(a)(15)-1, inclusive) paid within the calendar year by an employer to the employee for employment performed for him at any time after 1936. For provisions relating to the treatment of tips for purposes of the annual wage limitation see § 31.3121(q)-1.

(2) The annual wage limitation applies only if the remuneration received during any one calendar year by an employee from the same employer for employment performed after 1936 exceeds the amount of such limitation. The limitation in such case relates to the amount of remuneration received during any one calendar year for employment after 1936 and not to the amount of remuneration for employment performed in any one calendar year.

Example. Employee A, in 1967 receives $7,000 from employer B in part payment of $8,000 due him from employment performed in 1967. In 1968 A receives from employer B the balance of $1,000 due him for employment performed in 1967, and thereafter in 1968 also receives $7,000 for employment performed in 1968 for employer B. The first $6,600 of the $7,000 received during 1967 is subject to the taxes in 1967. The remaining $400 received in 1967 is not included as wages and is not subject to the taxes. The balance of $1,000 received in 1968 for employment during 1967 is subject to the taxes during 1968 as is also the first $6,800 of the $7,000 thereafter received in 1968 ($1,000 plus $6,800 totaling $7,800, which is the annual wage limitation applicable to remuneration received in 1968 by an employee from any one employer). The remaining $200 received in 1968 is not included as wages and is not subject to the taxes.

(3) If during a calendar year the employee receives remuneration from more than one employer, the annual wage limitation does not apply to the aggregate remuneration received from all of such employers, but instead applies to the remuneration received during such calendar year from each employer with respect to employment after 1936. In such case the first remuneration received in any calendar year after 1974 up to the amount equal to the contribution and benefit base (as determined under section 230 of the Social Security Act) (the first $13,200 received in 1974, the first $10,800 received in 1973, the first $9,000 received in 1972, the first $7,800 received in any calendar year after 1967 and before 1972, the first $6,600 received in any calendar year after 1965 and before 1968, the first $4,800 received in any calendar year after 1958 and before 1966, or the first $4,200 received in any calendar year after 1954 and before 1959) from each employer constitutes wages and is subject to the taxes, even though, under section 6413(c), the employee may be entitled to a special credit or refund of a portion of the employee tax deducted from his wages received during the calendar year. In this connection and in connection with the two examples immediately following, see § 31.6413(c)-1, relating to special credits or refunds of employee tax. In connection with the annual wage limitation in the case of remuneration paid for services performed in the employ of the United States or a wholly owned instrumentality thereof, see § 31.3122. In connection with the annual wage limitation in the case of remuneration paid for services performed in the employ of the Government of Guam, the Government of American Samoa, the District of Columbia, a political subdivision of the Government of Guam, or the Government of American Samoa, or any instrumentality of any of the foregoing which is wholly owned thereby, see § 31.3125. In connection with the application of the annual wage limitation, see also paragraph (b) of this section, relating to the circumstances under which wages paid by a predecessor employer are deemed to be paid by his successor. In connection with the annual wage limitation in the case of remuneration paid after December 31, 1978, from two or more related corporations that compensate an employee through a common paymaster, see § 31.3121(s)-1.

Example (1). During 1968 employee C receives from employer D a salary of $1,300 a month for employment performed for D during the first 7 months of 1968, or total remuneration of $9,100. At the end of the 6th month C has received $7,800 from employer D, and only that part of his total remuneration from D constitutes wages subject to the taxes. The $1,300 received by employee C from employer D in the 7th month is not included as wages and is not subject to the taxes. At the end of the 7th month C leaves the employ of D and enters the employ of E. C receives remuneration of $1,560 a month from employer E in each of the remaining 5 months of 1968, or total remuneration of $7,800 from employer E. The entire $7,800 received by C from employer E constitutes wages and is subject to the taxes. Thus, the first $7,800 received from employer D and the entire $7,800 received from employer E constitute wages.

Example (2). During the calendar year 1968 F is simultaneously an officer (an employee) of the X Corporation, the Y Corporation, and the Z Corporation and during such year receives a salary of $7,800 from each corporation. Each $7,800 received by F from each of the Corporations X, Y, and Z (whether or not such corporations are related) constitutes wages and is subject to the taxes.

(b) Wages paid by predecessor attributed to successor. *(1)* If an employer (hereinafter referred to as a successor) during any calendar year acquires substantially all the property used in a trade or business of another employer (hereinafter referred to as a predecessor), or used in a separate unit of a trade or business of a predecessor, and if immediately after the acquisition the successor employs in his trade or business an individual who immediately prior to the acquisition was employed in the trade or business of such predecessor, then, for purposes of the application of the annual wage limitation set forth in paragraph (a) of this section, any remuneration (exclusive of remuneration excepted from wages in accordance with paragraph (j) of § 31.3121(a)-1 or §§ 31.3121(a)(2)-1 to 31,3121(a)(15)-1, inclusive) with respect to employment paid (or considered under this paragraph as having been paid) to such individual by the predecessor during such calendar year and prior to the acquisition shall be considered as having been paid by the successor.

(2) The wages paid, or considered as having been paid, by a predecessor to an employee shall, for purposes of the annual wage limitation, be treated as having been paid to such employee by a successor if:

(i) The successor during a calendar year acquired substantially all the property used in a trade or business, or used in a separate unit of a trade or business, of the predecessor;

(ii) Such employee was employed in the trade or business of the predecessor immediately prior to the acquisition and is employed by the successor in his trade or business immediately after the acquisition; and

(iii) Such wages were paid during the calendar year in which the acquisition occurred and prior to such acquisition.

(3) The method of acquisition by an employer of the property of another employer is immaterial. The acquisition may occur as a consequence of the incorporation of a business by a sole proprietor or a partnership, the continuance without interruption of the business of a previously existing partnership by a new partnership or by a sole proprietor, or a purchase or any other transaction whereby substantially all the property used in a trade or business, or used in a separate unit of a trade or business, of one employer is acquired by another employer.

(4) Substantially all the property used in a separate unit of a trade or business may consist of substantially all the property used in the performance of an essential operation of the trade or business, or it may consist of substantially all the property used in a relatively self-sustaining entity which forms a part of the trade or business.

Example (1). The M Corporation which is engaged in the manufacture of automobiles, including the manufacture of automobile engines, discontinues the manufacture of the engines and transfers all the property used in such manufacturing operation to the N Company. The N Company is considered to have acquired a separate unit of the trade or business of the M Corporation, namely, its engine manufacturing unit.

Example (2). The R Corporation which is engaged in the operation of a chain of grocery stores transfers one of such stores to the S Company. The S Company is considered to have acquired a separate unit of the trade or business of the R Corporation.

(5) A successor may receive credit for wages paid to an employee by a predecessor only if immediately prior to the acquisition the employee was employed by the predecessor in his trade or business which was acquired by the successor and if immediately after the acquisition such employee is employed by the successor in his trade or business (whether or not in the same trade or business in which the acquired property is used). If the acquisition involves only a separate unit of a trade or business of the predecessor, the employee need not have been employed by the predecessor in that unit provided he was employed in the trade or business of which the acquired unit was a part.

Example. The Y Corporation in 1968 acquires by purchase all the property of the X Company and immediately after the acquisition employs in its trade or business employee A, who, immediately prior to the acquisition, was employed by the X Company. The X Company has in 1968 (the calendar year in which the acquisition occurs) and prior to the acquisition paid $5,000 of wages to A. The Y Corporation in 1968 pays to A remuneration of $5,000 with respect to employment. Only $2,800 of the remuneration paid by the Y Corporation is considered to be wages. For purposes of the $7,800 limitation, the Y Corporation is credited with the $5,000 paid to A by the X Company. If in the same calendar year, the Z Company acquires the property by purchase from the Y Corporation and A immediately after the acquisition is employed by the Z Company in its trade or business, no part of the remuneration paid to A by the Z Company in the year of the acquisition will be considered to be wages. The Z Company will be credited with the remuneration paid to A by the Y Corporation and also with the wages paid to A by the X Company (considered for purposes of the application of the $7,800 limitation as having also been paid by the Y Corporation).

(6) Where a corporation described in section 501(c)(3) which is exempt from income tax under section 501(a) has in effect a certificate filed pursuant to section 3121(k), or pursuant to section 1426(l) of the Internal Revenue Code of 1939, waiving its exemption from the taxes imposed by the Act, the activity in which such corporation is engaged is considered to be its trade or business for the purpose of determining whether the transferred property was used in the trade or business of the predecessor and for the purpose of determining whether the employment by the predecessor and the successor of an individual whose services were retained by the successor constitute employment in a trade or business. Thus, if a charitable or religious organization, subject to the taxes by virtue of its certificate, acquires all the property of another such organization likewise subject to the taxes and retains the services of employees of the predecessor, wages paid to such employees by the predecessor in the year of the acquisition (and prior to such acquisition) will be attributed to the successor for purposes of the annual wage limitation.

T.D. 6190, 7/13/56, amend T.D. 6516, 12/19/60, T.D. 6744, 7/1/64, T.D. 6983, 12/3/68, T.D. 7374, 7/17/75, T.D. 7660, 12/18/79.

§ 31.3121(a)(2)-1 Payments on account of sickness or accident disability, medical or hospitalization expenses, or death.

(a) The term "wages" does not include the amount of any payment (including any amount paid by an employer for insurance or annuities, or into a fund, to provide for any such payment) made to, or on behalf of, an employee or any of his dependents under a plan or system established by an employer which makes provision for his employees generally (or for his employees generally and their dependents) or for a class or classes of his employees (or for a class or classes of his employees and their dependents), on account of—

(1) Sickness or accident disability of an employee or any of his dependents, only if payment is received under a workers' compensation law;

(2) Medical or hospitalization expenses in connection with sickness or accident disability of an employee or any of his dependents, or

(3) Death of an employee or any of his dependents.

(b) The plan or system established by an employer need not provide for payments on account of all of the specified items, but such plan or system may provide for any one or more of such items. Payments for any one or more of such items under a plan or system established by an employer solely for the dependents of his employees are not within this exclusion from wages.

(c) Dependents of an employee include the employee's husband or wife, children, and any other members of the employee's immediate family.

(d) Workers' compensation law. *(1)* For purposes of paragraph (a)(1) of this section, a payment made under a workers' compensation law includes a payment made pursuant to a statute in the nature of a workers' compensation act.

(2) For purposes of paragraph (a)(1) of this section, a payment made under a workers' compensation law does not include a payment made pursuant to a State temporary disability insurance law.

(3) If an employee receives a payment on account of sickness or accident disability that is not made under a workers' compensation law or a statute in the nature of a workers' compensation act, the payment is not excluded from wages as defined by section 3121(a)(2)(A) even if the payment must be repaid if the employee receives a workers' compensation award or an award under a statute in the nature of a workers' compensation act with respect to the same period of absence from work.

(4) If an employee receives a payment on account of nonoccupational injury sickness or accident disability such payment is not excluded from wages, as defined by section 3121(a)(2)(A).

(e) Examples. The following examples illustrate the principles of paragraph (d) of this section:

Example (1). A local government employee is injured while performing work-related activities. The employee is not covered by the State workers' compensation law, but is covered by a local government ordinance that requires the local government to pay the employee's full salary when the employee is out of work as a result of an injury incurred while performing services for the local government. The ordinance does not limit or otherwise affect the local government's liability to the employee for the work-related injury. The local ordinance is not a workers' compensation law, but it is in the nature of a workers' compensation act. Therefore, the salary the employee receives while out of work as a result of the work-related injury is excluded from wages under section 3121(a)(2)(A).

Example (2). The facts are the same as in Example 1 except that the local ordinance requires the employer to continue to pay the employee's full salary while the employee is unable to work due to an injury whether or not the injury is work-related. Thus, the local ordinance does not limit benefits to instances of work-related disability. A benefit paid under an ordinance that does not limit benefits to instances of work-related injuries is not a statute in the nature of a workers' compensation act. Therefore, the salary the injured employee receives from the employer while out of work is wages subject to FICA even though the employee's injury is work-related.

Example (3). The facts are the same as in Example 1 except that the local ordinance includes a rebuttable presumption that certain injuries, including any heart attack incurred by a firefighter or other law enforcement personnel is work-related. The presumption in the ordinance does not eliminate the requirement that the injury be work-related in order to entitle the injured worker to full salary. Therefore, the ordinance is a statute in the nature of a workers' compensation act, and the salary the injured employee receives pursuant to the ordinance is excluded from wages under section 3121(a)(2)(A).

(f) It is immaterial for purposes of this exclusion whether the amount or possibility of such benefit payments is taken into consideration in fixing the amount of an employee's remuneration or whether such payments are required, expressly or impliedly, by the contract of service.

T.D. 6190, 7/13/56, amend T.D. 6516, 12/19/60, T.D. 9233, 12/14/2005.

§ 31.3121(a)(3)-1 Retirement payments.

The term "wages" does not include any payment made by an employer to an employee (including any amount paid by an employer for insurance or annuities, or into a fund, to provide for any such payment) on account of the employee's retirement. Thus, payments made to an employee on account of his retirement are excluded from wages under this exception even though not made under a plan or system.

T.D. 6190, 7/13/56, amend T.D. 6516, 12/19/60.

§ 31.3121(a)(4)-1 Payments on account of sickness or accident disability, or medical or hospitalization expenses.

The term "wages" does not include any payment made by an employer to, or on behalf of, an employee on account of the employee's sickness or accident disability or the medical or hospitalization expenses in connection with the employee's sickness or accident disability, if such payment is made after the expiration of 6 calendar months following the last calendar month in which such employee worked for such employer. Such payments are excluded from wages under this exception even though not made under a plan or system. If the employee does not actually perform services for the employer during the requisite period, the existence of the employer-employee relationship during that period is immaterial.

T.D. 6190, 7/13/56, amend T.D. 6516, 12/19/60.

§ 31.3121(a)(5)-1 Payments from or to certain tax-exempt trusts, or under or to certain annuity plans or bond purchase plans.

(a) Payments from or to certain tax-exempt trusts. The term "wages" does not include any payment made—

(1) By an employer, on behalf of an employee or his beneficiary, into a trust, or

(2) To, or on behalf of, an employee or his beneficiary from a trust if at the time of such payment the trust is exempt from tax under section 501(a) as an organization described in section 401(a). A payment made to an employee of such a trust for services rendered as an employee of the trust and not as a beneficiary thereof is not within this exclusion from wages.

(b) Payments under or to certain annuity plans. *(1)* The term "wages" does not include any payment made after December 31, 1962—

(i) By an employer, on behalf of the employee or his beneficiary, into an annuity plan, or

(ii) To, or on behalf of, an employee or his beneficiary under an annuity plan, if at the time of such payment the annuity plan is a plan described in section 403(a).

(2) The term "wages" does not include any payment made before January 1, 1963—

(i) By an employer, on behalf of an employee or his beneficiary, into an annuity plan, or

(ii) To, or on behalf of, an employee or his beneficiary under an annuity plan, if at the time of such payment the annuity plan meets the requirements of section 401(a)(3), (4), (5), and (6).

(c) Payments under or to certain bond purchase plans. The term "wages" does not include any payment made after December 31, 1962—

(1) By an employer, on behalf of an employee or his beneficiary, into a bond purchase plan, or

(2) To, or on behalf of, an employee or his beneficiary under a bond purchase plan,

if at the time of such payment the plan is a qualified bond purchase plan described in section 405(a).

T.D. 6190, 7/13/56, amend T.D. 6516, 12/19/60, T.D. 6876, 2/4/66.

PAR. 14. Section 31.3121(a)(5)-1 is amended by adding at the end thereof a new paragraph (d). This new paragraph reads as follows:

Proposed § 31.3121(a)(5)-1 Payments from or to certain tax-exempt trusts, or under or to certain annuity plans or bond purchase plans. [*For Preamble, see ¶ 150,703*]

* * * * *

(d) Payments to a simplified employee pension. The term "wages" does not include any payment made after December 31, 1978 by an employer on behalf of an employee to a simplified employee pension described in section 408(k) if at the time of the payment it is reasonable to believe that the employee will be entitled to a deduction under section 219 for such payment.

§ 31.3121(a)(5)-2 Payments under or to an annuity contract described in section 403(b).

(a) Salary reduction agreement defined. For purposes of section 3121(a)(5)(D), the term salary reduction agreement means a plan or arrangement (whether evidenced by a written instrument or otherwise) whereby payment will be made by an employer, on behalf of an employee or his or her beneficiary, under or to an annuity contract described in section 403(b)--

(1) If the employee elects to reduce his or her compensation pursuant to a cash or deferred election as defined at Sec. 1.401(k)-1(a)(3) of this chapter;

(2) If the employee elects to reduce his or her compensation pursuant to a one-time irrevocable election made at or before the time of initial eligibility to participate in such plan or arrangement (or pursuant to a similar arrangement involving a one-time irrevocable election); or

(3) If the employee agrees as a condition of employment (whether such condition is set by statute, contract, or otherwise) to make a contribution that reduces his or her compensation.

(b) Effective/applicability date. This section is applicable on November 15, 2007.

T.D. 9367, 11/14/2007.

§ 31.3121(a)(6)-1 Payment by an employer of employee tax under section 3101 or employee contributions under a State law.

The term "wages" does not include any payment by an employer (without deduction from the remuneration of, or other reimbursement from, the employee) of either (a) the employee tax imposed by section 3101 or the corresponding section of prior law, or (b) any payment required from an employee under a State unemployment compensation law.

T.D. 6190, 7/13/56, amend T.D. 6516, 12/19/60.

§ 31.3121(a)(7)-1 Payments for services not in the course of employer's trade or business or for domestic service.

(a) Meaning of terms. *(1) Services not in the course of employer's trade or business.* The term "services not in the course of the employer's trade or business" includes services that do not promote or advance the trade or business of the employer. Such term does not include services performed for a corporation. As used in this section, the term does not include service not in the course of the employer's trade or business performed on a farm operated for profit or domestic service in a private home of the employer. See paragraph (f) of § 31.3121(g)-1 for provisions relating to services not in the course of the employer's trade or business performed on a farm operated for profit.

(2) Domestic service in a private home of the employer. Services of a household nature performed by an employee in or about a private home of the person by whom he is employed constitute domestic service in a private home of the employer. A private home is a fixed place of abode of an individual or family. A separate and distinct dwelling unit maintained by an individual in an apartment house, hotel, or other similar establishment may constitute a private home. If a dwelling house is used primarily as a boarding or lodging house for the purpose of supplying board or lodging to the public as a business enterprise, it is not a private home. In general, services of a household nature in or about a private home include services performed by cooks, waiters, butlers, housekeepers, governesses, maids, valets, baby sitters, janitors, laundresses, furnacemen, caretakers, handymen, gardners, footmen, grooms, and chauffeurs of automobiles for family use. The term "domestic service in a private home of the employer" does not include the services enumerated above unless such services are performed in or about a private home of the employer. Services not of a household nature, such as services performed as a private secretary, tutor, or librarian, even though performed in the employer's home, are not included within the term "domestic service in a private home of the employer". As used in this section, the term does not include domestic service in a private home of the employer performed on a farm operated for profit or service not in the course of the employer's trade or business. See paragraph (f) of § 31.3121(g)-1 for provisions relating to domestic service in a private home of the employer performed on a farm operated for profit.

(b) Payments other than in cash. The term "wages" does not include remuneration paid in any medium other than cash (1) for service not in the course of the employer's trade or business, or (2) for domestic service in a private home of the employer. Cash remuneration includes checks and other monetary media of exchange. Remuneration paid in any medium other than cash, such as lodging, food, clothing, car tokens, transportation passes or tickets, or other goods or commodities, for service not in the course of the employer's trade or business or for domestic service in a private home of the employer does not constitute wages.

(c) Cash payments. *(1)* The term wages does not include cash remuneration paid by an employer in any calendar year to an employee for—

(i) Domestic service in a private home of the employer, unless the cash remuneration paid in such year by the employer to the employee for such service equals or exceeds the applicable dollar threshold (as defined in section 3121(x)) for such year; or

(ii) Service not in the course of the employer's trade or business, unless the cash remuneration paid in such year by the employer to the employee for such service equals or exceeds $100.

(2) The tests relating to cash remuneration are based on the remuneration paid in a calendar year rather than on the remuneration earned during a calendar year. The following example illustrates this provision:

Example. On March 31, 2004, employer X pays employee A cash remuneration of $100 for service not in the course of X's trade or business. Such remuneration constitutes wages subject to the taxes even though $10 thereof represents payment for such service performed by A for X in December 2003.

(3) In determining whether wages have been paid either for domestic service in a private home of the employer or for service not in the course of the employer's trade or business, only cash remuneration for such service shall be taken into account. Cash remuneration includes checks and other monetary media of exchange. Remuneration paid in any other medium, such as lodging, food, clothing, car tokens, transportation passes or tickets, or other goods or commodities, is disregarded in determining whether the cash-remuneration test is met. If an employee receives cash remuneration from an employer in a calendar year for both types of services the pertinent cash-remuneration test is to be applied separately to each type of service. If an employee receives cash remuneration from more than one employer in a calendar year for domestic service in a private home of the employer or for service not in the course of the employer's trade or business, the pertinent cash-remuneration test is to be applied separately to the remuneration received from each employer.

(d) Cross references. *(1)* For provisions relating to deduction of employee tax or amounts equivalent to the tax from cash payments for the services described in this section, see § 31.3102-1;

(2) For provisions relating to time of payment of wages for such services, see § 31.3121(a)-2;

(3) For provisions relating to computations to the nearest dollar of any payment of cash remuneration for domestic service in a private home of the employer, see § 31.3121(i)-1.

(e) Effective dates. *(1)* The provisions of this section apply to any cash payment for service not in the course of the employer's trade or business made on or after January 1, 1978 and for domestic service in a private home of the employer made on or after January 1, 1994.

(2) For rules applicable to any cash payment made prior to the dates set forth in paragraph (e)(1), see § 31.3121(a)(7)-1 in effect at such time (see 26 CFR part 31 contained in the edition of 26 CFR Parts 30 to 39, revised as of April 1, 2006).

T.D. 6190, 7/13/56, amend T.D. 6516, 12/19/60, T.D. 9266, 6/16/2006.

---

§ 31.3121(a)(8)-1 Payments for agricultural labor.

(a) Scope of this section. For purposes of the regulations in this section, the term "agricultural labor" means only such agricultural labor (see § 31.3121(g)-1) as constitutes employment or is deemed to constitute employment by reason of the rules relating to included and excluded services contained in section 3121(c) (see § 31.3121(c)-1) or the corresponding section of prior law.

(b) Payments other than in cash. The term "wages" does not include remuneration paid in any medium other than cash for agricultural labor. For meaning of the term "cash remuneration", see paragraph (f) of the regulations in this section.

(c) Cash payments. *(1)* The term wages does not include cash remuneration paid by an employer in any calendar year to an employee for agricultural labor unless—

(i) The cash remuneration paid in such year by the employer to the employee for such labor is $150 or more; or

(ii) The employer's expenditures for agricultural labor in such year equal or exceed $2,500, except that this paragraph (c)(1)(ii) shall not apply in determining whether remuneration paid to an employee constitutes wages for agricultural labor if such employee—

(A) Is employed as a hand-harvest laborer and is paid on a piece rate basis in an operation which has been, and is customarily and generally recognized as having been, paid on a piece rate basis in the region of employment;

(B) Commutes daily from his permanent residence to the farm on which he is so employed; and

(C) Has been employed in agriculture less than 13 weeks during the preceding calendar year.

(2) The application of the provisions of paragraph (c)(1) of this section may be illustrated by the following example:

Example. Employer X pays A $140 in cash for agricultural labor in calendar year 2004. X makes no other payments to A during the year and makes no other payment for agricultural labor to any other employee.

Employee A is not employed as a hand-harvest laborer. Neither the $150-cash-remuneration test nor the $2,500-employer's-expenditures-for-agricultural-labor test is met. Accordingly, the remuneration paid by X to A is not subject to the taxes. If in 2004 X had paid A $140 in cash for agricultural labor and had made expenditures of $2,360 or more to other employees for agricultural labor, the $140 paid by X to A would have been subject to tax because the $2,500-employer's-expenditures-for-agricultural-labor test would have been met. Or, if X had paid A $150 in cash in 2004 and made no other payments to any other employee for agricultural labor, the $150 paid by X to A would have been subject to tax because the $150-cash-remuneration test would have been met.

(d) Application of cash-remuneration test. *(1)* If an employee receives cash remuneration from an employer both for services which constitute agricultural labor and for services which do not constitute agricultural labor, only the amount of such remuneration which is attributable to agricultural labor shall be included in determining whether cash remuneration of $150 or more has been paid in the calendar year by the employer to the employee for agricultural labor. The following example illustrates this paragraph (d)(1):

Example. Employer X operates a store and also is engaged in farming operations. Employee A, who regularly performs services for X in connection with the operation of the store, works on X's farm when additional help is required for the farm activities. In the calendar year 2004, X pays A $140 in cash for services performed in agricultural labor, and $4,000 for services performed in connection with the operation of the store. X has no additional expenditures for agricultural labor in 2004. Since the cash remuneration paid by X to A in the calendar year 2004 for agricultural labor is less than $150, the $150-cash-remuneration test is not met. The $140 paid by X to A in 2004 for agricultural labor does not constitute wages and is not subject to the taxes.

(2) The test relating to cash remuneration of $150 or more is based on the cash remuneration paid in a calendar year rather than on the remuneration earned during a calendar year. It is immaterial if such cash remuneration is paid in a calendar year other than the year in which the agricultural labor is performed. The following example illustrates this paragraph (d)(2):

Example. Employer X pays cash remuneration of $150 in the calendar year 2004 to employee A for agricultural labor. Such remuneration constitutes wages even though $10 of such amount represents payment for agricultural labor performed by A for X in December 2003.

(3) In determining whether $150 or more has been paid to an employee for agricultural labor, only cash remuneration for such labor shall be taken into account. If an employee receives cash remuneration in any one calendar year from more than one employer for agricultural labor, the cash-remuneration test is to be applied with respect to the remuneration received by the employee from each employer in such calendar year for such labor.

(e) Application of employer's-expenditures-for-agricultural-labor test. *(1)* If an employer has expenditures in a calendar year for agricultural labor and for non-agricultural labor, only the amount of such expenditures for agricultural labor shall be included in determining whether the employer's expenditures for agricultural labor in such year equal or exceed $2,500. The following example illustrates this paragraph (e)(1):

Example. Employer X operates a store and also is engaged in farming operations. Employee A, who regularly performs services for X in connection with the operation of the store, works on X's farm when additional help is required for the farm activities. In calendar year 2004, X pays A $140 in cash for services performed in agricultural labor, and $4,000 for services performed in connection with the operation of the store. X has no additional expenditures for agricultural labor in 2004. Since X's expenditures for agricultural labor in 2004 are less than $2,500, the employer's-expenditures-for-agricultural-labor test is not met. The $140 paid by X to A in 2004 for agricultural labor does not constitute wages and is not subject to the taxes.

(2) The test relating to an employer's expenditures of $2,500 or more for agricultural labor is based on the expenditures paid by the employer in a calendar year rather than on the expenses incurred by the employer during a calendar year. It is immaterial if the expenditures are paid in a calendar year other than the year in which the agricultural labor is performed. The following example illustrates this paragraph (e)(2):

Example. Employer X employs A to construct fences on a farm owned by X. The work constitutes agricultural labor and is performed over the course of November and December 2003. A is not employed by X at any other time, however X does have other employees to whom X pays remuneration of $2,000 for agricultural labor in 2003. X pays A $140 in cash in November 2003 and $140 in cash in January 2004, in full payment for the work. The $140 payment to A made in November is not wages for calendar year 2003 because the $150-cash-remuneration test is not met and X's total expenditures for agricultural labor for such year are not equal to or in excess of $2,500. The $140 payment to A made in January is not wages for 2004 because the $150 cash-remuneration test is not met. However, if X pays additional remuneration to employees for agricultural labor in 2004 that equals or exceeds $2,360, the employer's-expenditures-for-agricultural-labor test will be met and the $140 paid by X to A in 2004 will be considered wages. It is immaterial that the work was performed in 2003.

(f) Meaning of "cash remuneration." Cash remuneration includes checks and other monetary media of exchange. Cash remuneration does not include payments made in any other medium, such as lodging, food, clothing, car tokens, transportation passes or tickets, farm products, or other goods or commodities.

(g) Cross references. (1) For provisions relating to deductions of employee tax or amounts equivalent to the tax from cash payments for agricultural labor, see § 31.3102-1.

(2) For provisions relating to the time of payment of wages for agricultural labor, see § 31.3121(a)-2.

(3) For provisions relating to records to be kept with respect to agricultural labor, see paragraph (b) of § 31.6001-2.

(h) Effective dates. The provisions of this section apply to any payment for agricultural labor made on or after January 1, 1988. For rules applicable to any payment for agricultural labor made prior to January 1, 1988, see § 31.3121(a)(8)-1 in effect at such time (see 26 CFR part 31 contained in the edition of 26 CFR parts 30 to 39, revised as of April 1, 2006).

T.D. 6190, 7/13/56, amend T.D. 6516, 12/19/60, T.D. 6744, 7/1/64, T.D. 9266, 6/16/2006.

§ 31.3121(a)(9)-1 Payments to employees for nonwork periods.

(a) The term "wages" does not include any payment (other than vacation or sick pay) made by an employer to an employee for a period throughout which the employment relationship exists between the employer and the employee, but in which the employee does not work (other than being subject to call for the performance of work) for the employer, if such payment is made after the calendar month in which—

(1) The employee attains age 65, if the employee is a man to whom the payment is made before January 1975, or if the employee is a woman to whom the payment is made before November 1956, or

(2) The employee attains age 62, if the employee is a man to whom the payment is made after December 1974, or if the employee is a woman to whom the payment is made after October 1956.

(b) Vacation or sick pay is not within this exclusion from wages. If the employee does any work for the employer in the period for which the payment is made, no remuneration paid by such employer to such employee with respect to such period is within this exclusion from wages.

Example. Mrs. A, an employee of X, attained the age of 62 on September 15, 1956, and discontinued the performance of regular work for X on September 30, 1956. Their employment relationship continued for several years until Mrs. A's death, and X paid Mrs. A $50 per month as consideration for Mrs. A's agreement to work when asked by X. The payment for each month was made on the first day of each succeeding month. After September 30, 1956, the only work performed by Mrs. A for X was performed on one day in October 1956. The payment made by X to Mrs. A on November 1 (for October 1956) is not excluded from wages under this exception, but the payments made thereafter are excluded from wages. The payment on November 1 was not excluded because Mrs. A worked for X on one day in October 1956. (Inasmuch as Mrs. A had attained age 62 in September 1956, the November 1 payment would have been excluded if Mrs. A had not performed any work for X in October 1956.)

T.D. 6190, 7/13/56, amend T.D. 6516, 12/19/60, T.D. 6744, 7/1/64, T.D. 7373, 7/23/75.

§ 31.3121(a)(10)-1 Payments to certain home workers.

(a) The term wages does not include remuneration paid by an employer in any calendar year to an employee for service performed as a home worker who is an employee by reason of the provisions of section 3121(d)(3)(C) (see § 31.3121(d)-1(d)), unless the cash remuneration paid in such calendar year by the employer to the employee for such services is $100 or more. The test relating to cash remuneration of $100 or more is based on remuneration paid in a calendar year rather than on remuneration earned during a calendar year. If cash remuneration of $100 or more is paid in a particular calendar year, it is immaterial whether such remuneration is in payment for services performed during the year of payment or during any other year.

(b) The application of paragraph (a) of this section may be illustrated by the following example:

Example. A, a home worker, performs services for X, a manufacturer, in 2003 and 2004. In the performance of the home work A is an employee by reason of section 3121(d)(3)(C). In March 2004, A returns to X articles made by A at home from materials received by A from X in 2003. X pays A cash remuneration of $100 for such work when the finished articles are delivered. The $100 includes $10 which represents remuneration for home work performed by A in 2003. The entire $100 is subject to the taxes. Any additional cash remuneration paid by X to A in 2004 for such services is also subject to the taxes.

(c) In the event an employee receives remuneration in any one calendar year from more than one employer for services performed as a home worker of the character described in paragraph (a) of this section, the regulations in this section are to be applied with respect to the remuneration received by the employee from each employer in such calendar year for such services. This exclusion from wages has no application to remuneration paid for services performed as a home worker who is an employee under section 3121(d)(2) (see § 31.3121(d)-1(c)) relating to common law employees.

(d) Cash remuneration includes checks and other monetary media of exchange. Remuneration paid in any other medium, such as clothing, car tokens, transportation passes or tickets, or other goods or commodities, is disregarded in determining whether the $100 cash-remuneration test is met. If the cash remuneration paid in any calendar year by an employer to an employee for services performed as a home worker of the character described in paragraph (a) of this section is $100 or more, then no remuneration, whether in cash or in any medium other than cash, paid by the employer to the employee in such calendar year for such services is excluded from wages under this exception.

(e) *(1)* For provisions relating to deductions of employee tax or amounts equivalent to the tax from cash payments for services performed as a home worker within the meaning of section 3121(d)(3)(C), see § 31.3102-1.

(2) For provisions relating to the time of payment of wages for services performed as a home worker within the meaning of section 3121(d)(3)(C), see § 31.3121(a)-2.

(3) For provisions relating to records to be kept with respect to payment of wages for services performed as a home worker within the meaning of section 3121(d)(3)(C), see § 31.6001-2.

(f) The provisions of this section apply to any payment for services performed as a home worker within the meaning of section 3121(d)(3)(C) made on or after January 1, 1978. For rules applicable to any payment for services performed as a home worker within the meaning of section 3121(d)(3)(C) made prior to January 1, 1978, see § 31.3121(a)(10)-1 in effect at such time (see 26 CFR part 31 contained in the edition of 26 CFR parts 30 to 39, revised as of April 1, 2006).

T.D. 6190, 7/13/56, amend T.D. 6516, 12/19/60, T.D. 9266, 6/16/2006.

§ 31.3121(a)(11)-1 Moving expenses.

(a) The term "wages" does not include remuneration paid on or after November 1, 1964, to or on behalf of an employee, either as an advance or a reimbursement, specifically for moving expenses incurred or expected to be incurred, if (and to the extent that) at the time of payment it is reasonable to believe that a corresponding deduction is or will be allowable to the employee under section 217. The reasonable belief contemplated by the statute may be based upon any evidence reasonably sufficient to induce such belief, even though such evidence may be insufficient upon closer examination by the district director or the courts finally to establish that a deduction is allowable under section 217. The reasonable belief shall be based upon the application of section 217 and the regulations thereunder in Part 1 of this chapter (Income Tax Regulations). When used in this section, the term "moving expenses" has the same meaning as when used in section 217 and the regulations thereunder.

(b) Except as otherwise provided in paragraph (a) of this section, or in a numbered paragraph of section 3121(a), amounts paid to or on behalf of an employee for moving expenses are wages for purposes of section 3121(a).

T.D. 7375, 9/11/75.

§ 31.3121(a)(12)-1 Tips.

The term "wages" does not include remuneration received by an employee after December 1965 in the form of tips if—

(a) The tips are paid in any medium other than cash, or

(b) The cash tips received by an employee in any calendar month in the course of his employment by an employer are less than $20.

If the cash tips received by an employee in a calendar month after December 1965 in the course of his employment by the employer amount to $20 or more, none of the cash tips received by the employee in such calendar month are excluded from the term "wages" under this section. The cash tips to which this section applies include checks and other monetary media of exchange. Tips received by an employee in any medium other than cash, such as passes, tickets, or other goods or commodities do not constitute wages. If an employee in any calendar month performs services for two or more employers and receives tips in the course of his employment by each employer, the $20 test is to be applied separately with respect to the cash tips received by the employee in respect to his services for each employer and not to the total cash tips received by the employee during the month. As to the time tips are deemed paid, see § 31.3121(q)-1. For provisions relating to the treatment of tips received by an employee prior to 1966, see paragraph (j)(3) of § 31.3121(a)-1.

T.D. 7001, 1/17/69.

§ 31.3121(a)(13)-1 Payments under certain employers' plans after retirement, disability, or death.

(a) In general. The term "wages" does not include the amount of any payment or series of payments made after January 2, 1968, by an employer to, or on behalf of, an employee or any of his dependents under a plan established by the employer which makes provisions for his employees generally (or for his employees generally and their dependents) or for a class or classes of his employees (or for a class or classes of his employees and their dependents), which is paid or commences to be paid upon or within a reasonable time after the termination of an employee's employment relationship because of the employee's—

(1) Death,

(2) Retirement for disability, or

(3) Retirement after attaining an age specified in the plan established by the employer or in a pension plan of the employer at the age at which a person in the employee's circumstances is eligible for retirement.

A payment or series of payments made under the circumstances described in the preceding sentence is excluded from "wages" even if made pursuant to an incentive compensation plan which also provides for the making of other types of payments. However, any payment or series of payments which would have been paid if the employee's relationship had not been terminated is not excluded from "wages" under this section and section 3121(a)(13). For example, lump-sum payments for unused vacation time or a final paycheck received after retirement are payments which the employee would have received whether or not he retired and therefore are not excluded from "wages" under this section. Further, if any payment is made upon or after termination of employment for any reason other than those set out in subparagraphs (1), (2), and (3) of this paragraph such payment is not excludable from "wages" by this section. For example, if a pension plan provides for retirement upon disability, completion of 30 years of service, or attainment of age 65, and if an employee who is not disabled retires at age 61 after 30 years of service, none of the retirement payments made to the employee under the pension plan (including any made after he is 65) is excludable from "wages" under this section. However, if the pension plan had conditioned retirement after 30 years of service upon attainment of age 60, all of the retirement payments would have been excludable.

(b) Plan. The plan or system established by an employer need not provide for payments because of termination of employment for all the reasons set out in paragraphs (a)(1), (2), and (3) of paragraph (a), but such plan or system may provide for payments because of termination for any one or more of such reasons. Payments because of termination of employment for any one or more of such reasons under a plan or system established by an employer solely for the dependents of his employees are not within this exclusion from wages.

(c) Dependents. Dependents of an employee include the employee's husband or wife, children, and any other members of the employee's immediate family.

(d) Benefit payment. It is immaterial for purposes of this exclusion whether the amount or possibility of benefit payments is paid on account of services rendered or taken into consideration in fixing the amount of an employee's remuneration or whether such payments are required, expressly or impliedly, by the contract of service.

(e) Example. The application of this section may be illustrated by the following example:

Example. A, an employee, receives a salary of $1,500 a month, payable on the 5th day of the month following the month for which the salary is earned. A's employer has established an incentive compensation plan for a class of his employees, including A, providing for the payment of deferred compensation for termination of employment, including termination upon an employee's death, retirement at age 65 (the retirement age specified in the plan), or retirement for disability. On March 1, 1973, A attains the age of 65 and retires. On March 5, 1973, A receives $5,500 from his employer of which $1,500 represents A's salary for services he performed in February 1973, and $4,000 represents incentive compensation paid under the employer's plan. The amount of $4,000 is excluded from "wages" under this section. The amount of $1,500 is not excluded from "wages" under this section.

T.D. 7374, 7/17/75.

§ 31.3121(a)(14)-1 Payments by employer to survivor or estate of former employee.

The term "wages" does not include any payment by an employer to a survivor or the estate of a former employee made after 1972 and after the calendar year in which such employee died.

T.D. 7373, 7/23/75.

§ 31.3121(a)(15)-1 Payments by employer to disabled former employee.

The term "wages" does not include any payment made after 1972 by an employer to an employee, if at the time such payment is made such employee is entitled to disability insurance benefits under section 223(a) of the Social Security Act and such entitlement commenced prior to the calendar year in which such payment is made, and if such employee did not perform any service for such employer during the period for which such payment is made.

T.D. 7374, 7/17/75, amend T.D. 7373, 7/23/75.

§ 31.3121(a)(18)-1 Payments or benefits under a qualified educational assistance program.

The term "wages" does not include any payment made, or benefit furnished, to or for the benefit of an employee in a taxable year beginning after December 31, 1978, if at the time of such payment or furnishing it is reasonable to believe that the employee will be able to exclude such payment or benefit from income under section 127.

T.D. 7898, 7/5/83.

§ 31.3121(b)-1 Employment; services to which the regulations in this subpart apply.

(a) The provisions of the regulations in this subpart relating to the term "employment" apply with respect to services performed after 1954. Certain provisions also apply with respect to services performed before 1955 for which the remuneration is paid after 1954 (see paragraph (b) of § 31.3121(b)-2. For provisions relating generally to services performed before 1955, see paragraph (a) of § 31.3121(b)-2. For provisions relating to the circumstances under which services which do not constitute employment are nevertheless deemed to be employment, and relating to the circumstances under which services which constitute employment are nevertheless deemed not to be employment, see § 31.3121(c)-1. For provisions relating to who are employees and who are employers see §§ 31.3121(d)-1 and 31.3121(d)-2, respectively.

(b) The taxes apply with respect to remuneration paid after 1954 for services performed before 1955, as well as for services performed after 1954, to the extent that the remuneration and services constitute wages and employment. See §§ 31.3121(a)-1 to 31.3121(a)(13)-1 relating to wages.

T.D. 6190, 7/13/56, amend T.D. 6516, 12/19/60, T.D. 6983, 12/3/68.

§ 31.3121(b)-2 Employment; services performed before 1955.

(a) General rule. *(1)* Subject to the provisions of paragraph (b) of this section:

(i) Services performed after 1936 and before 1955 which were employment under the applicable law in effect before 1955 constitute employment under section 3121(b).

(ii) Services performed after 1936 and before 1955 which were not employment under the applicable law in effect before 1955 do not constitute employment under section 3121(b).

(2) Except as provided in paragraph (b) of this section, determination of whether services performed before 1955 constitute employment shall be made in accordance with the applicable provisions of law in effect before 1955 and of the regulations thereunder. The regulations applicable in determining whether service performed after 1936 and before 1955 constitute employment are as follows:

(i) Services performed after 1936 and before 1940—26 CFR (1939) Part 401 (Regulations 91).

(ii) Services performed after 1939 and before 1951—26 CFR (1939) Part 402 (Regulations 106).

(iii) Services performed after 1950 and before 1955—26 CFR (1939) Part 408 (Regulations 128).

(b) Certain services performed before 1955 the remuneration for which is paid after 1954. *(1)* Services of the following character performed before 1955, for which remuneration is paid after 1954, constitute employment under section 3121(b):

(i) Agricultural labor, as defined in section 3121(g) (see § 3121(g)-1), other than services of the character described in section 3121(b)(1) (relating to services performed in connection with the production or harvesting of certain oleoresinous products and services performed by certain foreign agricultural workers), which, at the time performed, constituted employment under section 1426(b) of the 1939 Code, or would have constituted employment except for the provisions of section 1426(b)(1) of such Code, as in effect at the time the services were performed.

(ii) Services not in the course of the employers' trade or business (see paragraph (a)(1) of § 31.3121(a)(7)-1) which, at the time performed, constituted employment under section 1426(b) of the 1939 Code, or would have constituted employment except for the provisions of section 1426(b)(3) of such Code, as in effect at the time the services were performed.

(2) Services of the character described in paragraphs (a) and (b) of § 31.3121(b)(1)-1, which were performed by certain foreign agricultural workers before 1955 and the remuneration for which is paid after 1954, do not constitute employment under section 3121(b), irrespective of whether they constituted employment under section 1426(b) of the 1939 Code, as in effect at the time the services were performed.

(3) This paragraph has no application to services performed before 1955 and the remuneration for which was paid before 1955.

T.D. 6190, 7/13/56, amend T.D. 6516, 12/19/60, T.D. 6744, 7/1/64.

§ 31.3121(b)-3 Employment; services performed after 1954.

(a) In general. Whether services performed after 1954 constitute employment is determined in accordance with the provisions of section 3121(b).

(b) Services performed within the United States. Services performed after 1954 within the United States (see § 31.3121(e)-1) by an employee for his employer, unless specifically excepted by section 3121(b), constitute employment. With respect to services performed within the United States, the place where the contract of service is entered into is immaterial. The citizenship or residence of the employee or of the employer also is immaterial except to the extent provided in any specific exception from employment. Thus, the employee and the employer may be citizens and residents of a foreign country and the contract of service may be entered into in a foreign country, and yet, if the employee under such contract performs services within the United States, there may be to that extent employment.

(c) Services performed outside the United States. *(1) In general.* Except as provided in paragraphs (c)(2) and (3) of this section, services performed outside the United States (see § 31.3121(e)-1) do not constitute employment.

(2) On or in connection with an American vessel or American aircraft. (i) Services performed after 1954 by an employee for an employer "on or in connection with" an American vessel or American aircraft outside the United States (see § 31.3121(e)-1) constitute employment if:

(a) The employee is also employed "on and in connection with" such vessel or aircraft when outside the United States; and

(b) The services are performed under a contract of service, between the employee and the employer, which is entered into within the United States, or during the performance of the contract under which the services are performed and while the employee is employed on the vessel or aircraft it touches at a port within the United States; and

(c) The services are not excepted under section 3121(b).

(ii) An employee performs services on and in connection with the vessel or aircraft if he performs services on such vessel or aircraft which are also in connection with the vessel or aircraft. Services performed on the vessel by employees as officers or members of the crew, or as employees of concessionaires, of the vessel, for example, are performed under such circumstances, since such services are also connection with the vessel or aircraft. Services performed on the vessel by employees as officers or members of the crew, or as employees of concessionaires, of the vessel, for example, are performed under such circumstances, since such services are also connected with the vessel. Similarly, services performed on the aircraft by employees as officers or members of the crew of the aircraft are performed on and in connection with such aircraft. Services may be performed on the vessel or aircraft, however, which have no connection with it, as in the case of services performed by an employee while on the vessel or aircraft merely as a passenger in the general sense. For example, the services of a buyer in the employ of a department store while he is a passenger on a vessel are not in connection with the vessel.

(iii) If services are performed by an employee "on and in connection with" an American vessel or American aircraft when outside the United States and the conditions listed in paragraph (c)(2)(i) *(b)* and *(c)* of this section are met, then the services of that employee performed on or in connection with the vessel or aircraft constitute employment. The expression "on or in connection with" refers not only to services performed on the vessel or aircraft but also to services connected with the vessel or aircraft which are not actually performed on it (for example, shore services performed as officers or members of the crew, or as employees of concessionaires, of the vessel).

(iv) Services performed by a member of the crew or other employee whose contract of service is not entered into within the United States, and during the performance of which and while the employee is employed on the vessel or aircraft it does not touch at a port within the United States, do not constitute employment under this subparagraph, notwithstanding services performed by other members of the crew or other employees on or in connection with the vessel or aircraft may constitute employment.

(v) A vessel includes every description of watercraft, or other contrivance, used as a means of transportation on water. An aircraft includes every description of craft, or other contrivance, used as a means of transportation through the air. In the case of an aircraft, the term "port" means an airport. An airport means an area on land or water used regularly by aircraft for receiving or discharging passengers or cargo. For definitions of "American vessel" and "American aircraft", see § 31.3121(f)-1.

(vi) With respect to services performed outside the United States on or in connection with an American vessel or American aircraft, the citizenship or residence of the employee is immaterial, and the citizenship or residence of the employer is material only in case it has a bearing in determining whether a vessel is an American vessel.

(3) By a citizen of the United States as an employee for an American employer. Services performed after 1954 outside the United States by a citizen of the United States as an employee for an American employer constitute employment provided the services are not specifically excepted under section 3121(b). For definitions of "citizen of the United States" and "American employer", see §§ 31.3121(e)-1 and 3121(h)-1, respectively.

(4) By a citizen of the United States as an employee for a foreign subsidiary corporation. For provisions relating to the extension of the Federal old-age, survivors, and disability insurance system established by title II of the Social Security Act to certain services not constituting employment which are performed outside the United States by citizens of the United States in the employ of a foreign subsidiary of a domestic corporation, see section 3121(l) and Part 36 of this chapter (Regulations Relating to Contract Coverage of Employees of Foreign Subsidiaries).

T.D. 6190, 7/13/56, amend T.D. 6516, 12/19/60, T.D. 6744, 7/1/64.

§ 31.3121(b)-4 Employment; excepted services in general.

(a) Services performed by an employee for an employer do not constitute employment for purposes of the taxes if they are specifically excepted from employment under any of the numbered paragraphs of section 3121(b). Services so excepted do not constitute employment for purposes of the taxes even though they are performed within the United States, or are performed outside the United States on or in connection with an American vessel or American aircraft, or are performed outside the United States by a citizen of the United States for an American employer. If not otherwise provided in the regulations relating to the numbered paragraphs of section 3121(b), such regulations apply to services performed after 1954.

(b) The exception attaches to the services performed by the employee and not to the employee as an individual; that is, the exception applies only to the services in an excepted class rendered by the employee.

Example. A is an individual who is employed part time by B to perform services which are specifically excepted from employment under one of the numbered paragraphs of section 3121(b). A is also employed by C part time to perform services which constitute employment. While no tax liability is incurred with respect to A's remuneration for services performed in the employ of B (the services being excepted from employment), the exception does not embrace the services performed by A in the employ of C (which constitute employment) and the taxes attached with respect to the wages (see § 31.3121(a)-1) for such services.

(c) For provisions relating to the circumstances under which services which are excepted are nevertheless deemed to be employment, and relating to the circumstances under which services which are not excepted are nevertheless deemed not to be employment, see § 31.3121(c)-1.

T.D. 6190, 7/13/56, amend T.D. 6516, 12/19/60, T.D. 6744, 7/1/64.

§ 31.3121(b)(1)-1 Certain services performed by foreign agricultural workers, or performed before 1959 in connection with oleoresinous products.

(a) Services of workers from Mexico. Services performed before 1965 by foreign agricultural workers from the Republic of Mexico under contracts entered into in accordance with the title V of the Agricultural Act of 1949, as amended, are excepted from employment. Contracts entered into pursuant to the provisions of such title V may provide for the performance only of services which constitute "agricultural employment". The term "agricultural employment" includes certain services which do not constitute "agricultural labor" as that term is defined in section 3121(g) (see § 31.3121(g)-1). For purposes of title V of the Agricultural

Act of 1949, as amended, the term "agricultural employment" includes services or activities included within the provisions of section 3(f) of the Fair Labor Standards Act of 1938, as amended, or section 3121(g) of the Internal Revenue Code. Under section 507 of the Agricultural Act of 1949, as amended, and as in effect before October 3, 1961, the term "agricultural employment" included also horticultural employment, cotton ginning, compressing and storing, crushing of oil seeds, and the packing, canning, freezing, drying, or other processing of perishable or seasonable agricultural products.

(b) Services of workers from British West Indies. Services performed by a foreign agricultural worker lawfully admitted to the United States from the Bahamas, Jamaica, or the other British West Indies, on a temporary basis to perform agricultural labor are excepted from employment.

(c) Services performed after 1956 by foreign workers. Services performed after 1956 by a foreign agricultural worker lawfully admitted to the United States from any foreign country or possession thereof, including the Republic of Mexico, on a temporary basis to perform agricultural labor are excepted from employment.

(d) Services performed before 1959 in connection with the production or harvesting of certain oleoresinous products. Services performed before 1959 in connection with the production or harvesting of crude gum (oleoresin) from a living tree or the processing of such crude gum into gum spirits of turpentine and gum rosin, provided the processing is carried on by the original producer of the crude gum, are expected from employment. However, the services to which this paragraph relates constitute agricultural labor as defined in section 3121(g) (see paragraph (d) of § 31.3121(g)-1). Thus, any cash remuneration paid for such services, to the extent that the services are deemed to constitute employment by reason of the rules relating to included and excluded services contained in section 3121(c) (see § 31.3121(c)-1), is taken into account in applying the test prescribed in section 3121(a)(8)(B) for determining whether cash remuneration paid for agricultural labor constitutes wages (see paragraph (c) of § 31.3121(a)(8)-1).

(e) Cross-reference. See paragraph (b) of § 31.3121(b)-2 for provisions relating to the status of services of the character to which paragraphs (a) and (b) of this section apply which were performed before 1955 and the remuneration for which is paid after 1954.

T.D. 6190, 7/13/56, amend T.D. 6516, 12/19/60, T.D. 6744, 7/1/64.

§ 31.3121(b)(2)-1 Domestic service performed by students for certain college organizations.

(a) Services of a household nature performed in or about the club rooms or house of a local college club, or in or about the club rooms or house of a local chapter of a college fraternity or sorority, by a student who is enrolled and regularly attending classes at a school, college, or university are excepted from employment. For purposes of this exception, the statutory tests are the type of services performed by the employee, the character of the place where the services are performed, and the status of the employee as a student enrolled and regularly attending classes at a school, college, or university.

(b) In general, services of a household nature in or about the club rooms or house of a local college club or local chapter of a college fraternity or sorority include services rendered by cooks, waiters, butlers, maids, janitors, laundresses, furnacemen, handymen, gardeners, housekeepers, and housemothers.

(c) A local college club or local chapter of a college fraternity or sorority does not include an alumni club or chapter. If the club rooms or house of a local college club or local chapter of a college fraternity or sorority is used primarily for the purpose of supplying board or lodging to students or the public as a business enterprise, the services performed therein are not within the exception.

(d) An organization is a school, college, or university within the meaning of section 3121(b)(2) if its primary function is the presentation of formal instruction, it normally maintains a regular faculty and curriculum, and it normally has a regularly enrolled body of students in attendance at the place where its educational activities are regularly carried on. See section 170(b)(1)(A)(ii) and the regulations thereunder.

(e) Services of a household nature are not within the exception if performed in or about rooming or lodging houses, boarding houses, clubs (except local college clubs), hotels, hospitals, eleemosynary institutions, or commercial offices or establishments.

(f) For provisions relating to domestic service in a private home of the employer, see § 31.3121(a)(7)-1.

T.D. 6190, 7/13/56, amend T.D. 6516, 12/19/60, T.D. 9167, 12/20/2004.

§ 31.3121(b)(3)-1 Family employment.

(a) Certain services are expected from employment because of the existence of a family relationship between the employee and the individual employing him. The exceptions are as follows:

(1) Services performed by an individual in the employ of his or her spouse;

(2) (i) Services performed before 1961 by a father or mother in the employ of his or her son or daughter;

(ii) Services not in the course of the employer's trade or business, or domestic service in a private home of the employer, performed after 1960 but prior to 1968 by a father or mother in the employ of his or her son or daughter;

(iii) Services not in the course of the employer's trade or business, or domestic service in a private home of the employer, performed after 1967 by a father or mother in the employ of his or her son or daughter unless (a) the employer has a child (including an adopted child or stepchild) living in his or her home who is under age 18 or who has a mental or physical condition which requires the personal care and supervision of an adult for at least 4 continuous weeks in the calendar quarter in which the services are rendered; and (b) the employer is during the calendar quarter in which the services are rendered;

(1) A widow or widower;

(2) A divorced person who has not remarried; or

(3) A married person who has a spouse living in the home who has a mental or physical condition which results in such spouse's being incapable of caring for such child for at least 4 continuous weeks in the calendar quarter in which the services are rendered; and

(3) Services performed by a son or daughter under the age of 21 in the employ of his or her father or mother.

(b) Under paragraph (a)(1) and (2)(i) of this section, the exception is conditioned solely upon the family relationship between the employee and the individual employing him.

Under paragraph (a)(2)(ii) and (iii) of this section, in addition to the family relationship, there is a further requirement that the services performed after 1960 and before 1968 for purposes of paragraph (a)(2)(ii) and after 1967 for purposes of paragraph (a)(2)(iii) shall be services not in the course of the employer's trade or business or shall be domestic service in a private home of the employer. The terms "services not in the course of the employer's trade or business" and "domestic service in a private home of the employer" have the same meaning as when used in § 31.3121(a)(7)-1, except that it is immaterial under paragraphs (a)(2)(ii) and (iii) of this section whether or not such services are performed on a farm operated for profit. The mere fact that a mental or physical disability, whether temporary or permanent, renders a child or spouse incapable of self-support does not necessarily mean that the child requires the personal care and supervision of an adult or that the spouse is incapable of caring for a child within the meaning of paragraph (a)(2)(iii) of this section. A written statement by a doctor of the existence of the mental or physical condition of the child or spouse which states that the child requires the personal care and supervision of an adult or that the spouse is incapable of caring for a child and which sets forth the period of time during which the condition has existed and is likely to exist will usually be sufficient evidence to establish the existence and duration of the condition at the time of the statement. Under paragraph (a)(3) of this section, in addition to the family relationship, there is a further requirement that the son or daughter shall be under the age of 21, and the exception continues only during the time that the son or daughter is under the age of 21.

(c) Services performed in the employ of a corporation are not within the exception. Services performed in the employ of a partnership are not within the exception unless the requisite family relationship exists between the employee and each of the partners comprising the partnership.

T.D. 6190, 7/13/56, amend T.D. 6516, 12/19/60, T.D. 6744, 7/1/64, T.D. 7374, 7/17/75.

§ 31.3121(b)(4)-1 Services performed on or in connection with a non-American vessel or aircraft.

(a) Services performed within the United States by an employee for an employer "on or in connection with" a vessel not an American vessel, or "on or in connection with" an aircraft not an American aircraft, are expected from employment if—

(1) The employee is employed by such employer "on and in connection with" such vessel or aircraft when outside the United States, and

(2) (i) The employee is not a citizen of the United States, or (ii) the employer is not an American employer.

(b) An employee performs services on and in connection with the vessel or aircraft if he performs services on the vessel or aircraft when outside the United States which are also in connection with the vessel or aircraft. Services performed on the vessel outside the United States by employees as officers or members of the crew, or by employees of concessionaires, of the vessel, for example, are performed under such circumstances, since such services are also connected with the vessel. Similarly, services performed on the aircraft outside the United States by employees as officers or members of the crew of the aircraft are performed on and in connection with such aircraft. Services may be performed on the vessel or aircraft, however, which have no connection with it, as in the case of services performed by an employee while on the vessel or aircraft merely as a passenger in the general sense. For example, the services of a buyer in the employ of a department store while he is a passenger on a vessel are not in connection with the vessel.

(c) The expression "on or in connection with" refers not only to services performed on the vessel or aircraft but also to services connected with the vessel or aircraft which are not actually performed on it (for example, shore services performed as officers or members of the crew, or as employees of concessionaries of the vessel).

(d) Services performed within the United States on or in connection with a non-American vessel or aircraft for an employer by an employee who is not a citizen of the United States are excepted from employment, irrespective of whether the employer is or is not an American employer, provided the employee also is employed by such employer on and in connection with the vessel or aircraft when outside the United States. Services performed within the United States on or in connection with a non-American vessel or aircraft by an employee for an employer who is not an American employer also are excepted from employment, irrespective of whether the employee is or is not a citizen of the United States, provided the employee also is employed by such employer on and in connection with the vessel or aircraft when outside the United States. Services performed within the United States on or in connection with a non-American vessel or aircraft for an American employer by an employee who is a citizen of the United States are not excepted from employment under section 3121(b)(4), irrespective of whether the employee is employed by such employer on and in connection with the vessel or aircraft when outside the United States. Further, section 3121(b)(4) does not except from employment services performed within the United States for an employer, whether or not an American employer, on or in connection with a non-American vessel or aircraft by an employee, whether or not a citizen of the United States, who is not also employed by such employer on and in connection with the vessel or aircraft when outside the United States.

(e) Services performed outside the United States on or in connection with a vessel not an American vessel, or on or in connection with an aircraft not an American aircraft, by a citizen of the United States as an employee for an American employer are not excepted from employment under section 3121(b)(4), irrespective of whether the employee is employed on and in connection with such vessel or aircraft when outside the United States. Services performed outside the United States on or in connection with a vessel not an American vessel or on or in connection with an aircraft not an American aircraft, either by an employee who is not a citizen of the United States or for an employer who is not an American employer, do not, in any event, constitute employment. See paragraph (c) of § 31.3121(b)-3, relating to services performed outside the United States which constitute employment.

(f) See paragraph (c)(2)(v) of § 31.3121(b)-3 for definitions of "vessel" and "aircraft", § 31.3121(f)-1, for definitions of "American vessel" and "American aircraft", § 31.3121(e)-1, for definitions of "citizen of the United States", and § 31.3121(h)-1, for definition of "American employer".

T.D. 6190, 7/13/56, amend T.D. 6516, 12/19/60.

§ 31.3121(b)(5)-1 Services in employ of an instrumentality of the United States specifically exempted from the employer tax.

Services performed in the employ of an instrumentality of the United States are excepted from employment if such instrumentality is exempt from the employer tax imposed by section 3111 by virtue of any other provision of law which specifically refers to such section 3111 or the corresponding section of prior law (section 1410 of the Internal Revenue Code of 1939) in granting exemption from the employer tax. This exception does not operate to exclude from employment services performed in the employ of an instrumentality of the United States unless the Congress has granted to such instrumentality a specific exemption from the tax imposed by section 3111 or the corresponding section of prior law. For provisions which make general exemptions from Federal taxation ineffectual as to the employer tax imposed by section 3111, see § 31.3112-1. For other exceptions from employment applicable with respect to services performed in the employ of an instrumentality of the United States, see § 31.3121(b)(6)-1.

T.D. 6190, 7/13/56, amend T.D. 6516, 12/19/60.

§ 31.3121(b)(6)-1 Services in employ of United States or instrumentality thereof.

(a) In general. This section relates to services performed in the employ of the United States Government or in the employ of an instrumentality of the United States. Particular services which are not excepted from employment under one rule set forth in this section may nevertheless be excepted under another rule set forth in this section or under § 31.3121(b)(5)-1, relating to services in the employ of an instrumentality of the United States specifically exempted from the employer tax. Moreover, services performed in the employ of the United States or of any instrumentality thereof which are not excepted from employment under paragraph (5) or (6) of section 3121(b) may nevertheless be excepted under some other paragraph of such section. For provisions relating generally to the application of the taxes in the case of services performed in the employ of the United States or a wholly owned instrumentality thereof, see § 31.3122. For provisions relating to the computation of remuneration for service performed by an individual as a member of a uniformed service or for service performed by an individual as a volunteer or volunteer leader within the meaning of the Peace Corps Act, see § 31.3121(i)-2 and § 31.3121(i)-3, respectively.

(b) Services covered under a retirement system established by a law of the United States. Services performed in the employ of the United States or in the employ of any instrumentality thereof are excepted from employment under section 3121(b)(6)(A) if such services are covered under a law enacted by the Congress of the United States which specifically provides for the establishment of a retirement system for employees of the United States or of such instrumentality. Determinations as to whether services are covered by a retirement system of the requisite character are to be made as of the time such services are performed. Services of an employee who has an option to have his services covered under a retirement system are not covered under such retirement system unless and until he exercises such option. The test is whether particular services performed by an employee are covered by a retirement system of the requisite character rather than whether the position in which such services are performed is covered by such retirement system.

(c) Services performed for an instrumentality not subject to employer tax on December 31, 1950, and covered under a retirement system established by such instrumentality. *(1)* Subject to the provisions of subparagraph (4) of this paragraph, services performed in the employ of an instrumentality of the United States are excepted from employment under section 3121(b)(6)(B) if—

(i) The particular instrumentality was not subject on December 31, 1950, to the employer tax imposed by section 1410 of the Internal Revenue Code of 1939, and

(ii) The services are covered by a retirement system established by such instrumentality.

(2) If the particular instrumentality was not in existence on December 31, 1950, but is created thereafter under a law which was in effect on December 31, 1950, services performed in the employ of such instrumentality are excepted from employment (unless otherwise provided in subparagraph (4) of this paragraph) if—

(i) The instrumentality had it been in existence on December 31, 1950, would not have been subject on that date to the employer tax imposed by section 1410 of the Internal Revenue Code of 1939, and

(ii) The services are covered by a retirement system established by such instrumentality.

It is immaterial, for purposes of this exception, whether the exemption from the employer tax on December 31, 1950, resulted, or would have resulted, from a tax exemption as such in effect on December 31, 1950, or from the provisions of section 1426(b)(6) of the Internal Revenue Code of 1939 in effect on that date, relating to the exception from employment of services performed in the employ of certain instrumentalities of the United States.

(3) Determinations as to whether services performed in the employ of an instrumentality referred to in subparagraph (1) or (2) of this paragraph are covered by a retirement system established by such instrumentality are to be made as of the time such services are performed. Services of an employee who has an option to have his services covered under a retirement system established by the instrumentality are not covered under such retirement system unless and until he exercises such option. The test is whether particular services performed by an employee are covered by a retirement system established by the instrumentality rather than whether the position in which such services are performed is covered by such retirement system.

(4) The exception from employment provided in section 3121(b)(6)(B) has no application with respect to any of the following classes of services:

(i) Services performed in the employ of a corporation which is wholly owned by the United States;

(ii) Services performed in the employ of a production credit association, a Federal Reserve Bank, or a Federal Credit Union; services performed before December 31, 1959, in the employ of a national farm loan association; services performed after December 30, 1959, in the employ of a Federal land bank association; services performed after December 31, 1959, in the employ of a Federal land bank, a Federal intermediate credit bank, or a bank for cooperatives; services performed after December 31, 1972, in the employ of a Federal home loan bank; and services performed after December 31, 1966, and before January 1, 1973, in the employ of a Federal home loan bank, in the case of individuals who are in such employ on the latter date, provided that an amount equal to the taxes imposed by sections 3101 and

3111 with respect to all such services performed by all such individuals are paid under the provisions of section 3122 by July 1, 1973;

(iii) Services performed in the employ of a State, county, or community committee under the Commodity Stabilization Service;

(iv) Services performed by a civilian employee, not compensated from funds appropriated by the Congress, in the Army and Air Force Exchange Service, Army and Air Force Motion Picture Service, Navy Exchanges, Marine Corps Exchanges or other activities, conducted by an instrumentality of the United States subject to the jurisdiction of the Secretary of Defense, at installations of the Department of Defense for the comfort, pleasure, contentment, and mental and physical improvement of personnel of such Department, or

(v) Services performed by a civilian employee, not compensated from funds appropriated by the Congress, in the Coast Guard Exchanges or other activities, conducted by an instrumentality of the United States subject to the jurisdiction of the Secretary of the Treasury, at installations of the Coast Guard for the comfort, pleasure, contentment, and mental and physical improvement of personnel of the Coast Guard.

(d) Special classes of services. The following classes of services performed either in the employ of the United States or in the employ of any instrumentality thereof are excepted from employment under section 3121(b)(6)(C):

(1) Services performed as the President or Vice President of the United States or as a Member, Delegate, or Resident Commissioner, of or to the Congress of the United States;

(2) Services performed in the legislative branch of the United States Government;

(3) Services performed in a penal institution of the United States by an inmate thereof;

(4) (i) Except as provided in subdivision (ii) of this subparagraph, services performed by student nurses, medical or dental interns, residents in training, student dietitians, student physical therapists, or student occupational therapists, assigned or attached to a hospital, clinic, or medical or dental laboratory operated by any department, agency, or instrumentality of the United States Government, or by certain other student employees described in section 5351(2) of title 5, United States Code.

(ii) The provisions of subdivision (i) of this subparagraph have no application to services performed after 1965 by medical or dental interns or by medical or dental residents in training.

(5) Services performed by an individual as an employee serving on a temporary basis in case of fire, storm, earthquake, flood, or other similar emergency; and

(6) (i) Except as provided in subdivision (ii) of this subparagraph, services performed by an individual to whom subchapter III of chapter 83 of title 5, United States Code (civil service retirement) does not apply because he is, with respect to such services, subject to another retirement system, established either by a law of the United States or by the agency or instrumentality of the United States for which such services are performed.

(ii) The provisions of subdivision (i) of this subparagraph have no application to service performed by an individual to whom subchapter III of chapter 83 of title 5, United States Code (civil service retirement) does not apply because such individual is subject to the retirement system of the Tennessee Valley Authority, if such service is subject to the plan approved by the Secretary of Health, Education, and Welfare on December 28, 1956, pursuant to section 104(i)(2) of the Social Security Amendments of 1956 (70 Stat. 827). See section 201(m)(4) of such Amendments for provisions relating to the timeliness of payment of tax with respect to remuneration paid before 1957 for such services, and barring the imposition of interest on the amount of any such tax due for any period before December 28, 1956.

T.D. 6190, 7/13/56, amend T.D. 6516, 12/19/60, T.D. 6744, 7/1/64, T.D. 6983, 12/3/68, T.D. 7373, 7/23/75.

§ 31.3121(b)(7)-1 Services in employ of States or their political subdivisions or instrumentalities.

(a) In general. Except as provided in other paragraphs of this section, services performed in the employ of any State, any political subdivision of a State, or any instrumentality of one or more States or political subdivisions thereof which is wholly owned by one or more States or political subdivisions are expected from employment. For the definition of the term "State", as used in this section, see § 31.3121(e)-1.

(b) Covered transportation service. The exception from employment under section 3121(b)(7) does not apply to covered transportation service as defined in section 3121(j). See §§ 31.3121(j) and 31.3121(j)-1.

(c) Government of American Samoa. The exception from employment under section 3121(b)(7) does not apply to services performed after 1960 in the employ of the Government of American Samoa, any political subdivision thereof, or any instrumentality of such Government or political subdivision, or combination thereof, which is wholly owned thereby, performed by an officer or employee thereof (including a member of the legislature of such Government or political subdivision).

(d) District of Columbia. The exception from employment under section 3121(b)(7) does not apply to services performed after September 30, 1965, in the employ of the District of Columbia or any instrumentality which is wholly owned thereby, if such service is not covered by a retirement system established by a law of the United States. Notwithstanding the preceding sentence the following classes of services performed either in the employ of the District of Columbia or in the employ of any instrumentality which is wholly owned thereby are expected from employment:

(1) Services performed in a hospital or penal institution by a patient or inmate thereof.

(2) Services performed by student nurses, student dietitians, student physical therapists, or student occupational therapists assigned or attached to a hospital, clinic, or medical or dental laboratory operated by the District of Columbia or by any wholly owned instrumentality thereof, or by certain other student employees described in section 5351(2) of title 5, United States Code. This subparagraph does not apply to services performed by medical or dental interns or by medical or dental residents in training described in such section 5351(2).

(3) Services performed by an individual as an employee serving on a temporary basis in case of fire, storm, snow, earthquake, flood, or other similar emergency.

(4) Services performed by a member of a board, committee, or council of the District of Columbia, paid on a per diem, meeting, or other fee basis.

(e) Government of Guam. The exception from employment under section 3121(b)(7) does not apply to services performed after 1972 in the employ of the Government of

Guam or any instrumentality which is wholly owned thereby, by an employee properly classified as a temporary or intermittent employee, if such service is not covered by a retirement system established by a law of Guam. The preceding sentence shall not apply to the services performed by an elected official or a member of the legislature or in a hospital or penal institution by a patient or inmate thereof. For purposes of this paragraph—

(1) Any person whose services as an officer or employee of such Government or instrumentality is not covered by a retirement system established by a law of the United States shall not, with respect to such service, be regarded as an employee of the United States or any agency or instrumentality thereof, and

(2) The remuneration for service described in subparagraph (1) (including fees paid to a public official) shall be deemed to have been paid by such Government or instrumentality.

T.D. 6190, 7/13/56, amend T.D. 6516, 12/19/60, T.D. 6744, 7/1/64, T.D. 6983, 12/3/68, T.D. 7373, 7/23/75.

§ 31.3121(b)(7)-2 Service by employees who are not members of a public retirement system.

(a) Table of contents. This paragraph contains a listing of the major headings of this section 31.3121(b)(7)-2.

(b) Introduction. Under section 3121(b)(7)(F), wages of an employee of a State or local government are generally subject to tax under FICA after July 1, 1991, unless the employee is a member of a retirement system maintained by the State or local government entity. This section 31.3121(b)(7)-2 provides rules for determining whether an employee is a "member of a retirement system". These rules generally treat an employee as a member of a retirement system if he or she participates in a system that provides retirement benefits, and has an accrued benefit or receives an allocation under the system that is comparable to the benefits he or she would have or receive under Social Security. In the case of part-time, seasonal and temporary employees, this minimum retirement benefit is required to be nonforfeitable.

(c) General rule. *(1) Inclusion in employment of service by employees who are not members of a retirement system.* Except in the case of service described in section 3121(b)(7)(F)(i) through (v), the exception from employment under section 3121(b)(7) does not apply to service in the employ of a State or any political subdivision thereof, or of any instrumentality of one or more of the foregoing that is wholly owned thereby, after July 1, 1991, unless the employee is a member of a retirement system of such State, political subdivision or instrumentality at the time the service is performed. An employee is not a member of a retirement system at the time service is performed unless at that time he or she is a qualified participant (as defined in paragraph (d) of this section) in a retirement system that meets the requirements of paragraph (e) of this section with respect to that employee.

(2) Treatment of individuals employed in more than one position. Under section 3121(b)(7)(F), whether an employee is a member of a retirement system is determined on an entity-by-entity rather than a position-by-position basis. Thus, if an employee is a member of a retirement system with respect to service he or she performs in one position in the employ of a State, political subdivision or instrumentality thereof, the employee is generally treated as a member of a retirement system with respect to all service performed for the same State, political subdivision or instrumentality in any other positions. A State is a separate entity from its political subdivisions, and an instrumentality is a separate entity from the State or political subdivision by which it is owned for purposes of this rule. See paragraph (e)(2) of this section, however, for rules relating to service and compensation required to be taken into account in determining whether an employee is a member of a retirement system for purposes of this section. This rule is illustrated by the following examples:

Example (1). An individual is employed full-time by a county and is a qualified participant (as defined in paragraph (d) of this section) in its retirement plan with regard to such employment. In addition to this full-time employment, the individual is employed part-time in another position with the same county. The part-time position is not covered by the county retirement plan, however, and neither the service nor the compensation in the part-time position is considered in determining the employee's retirement benefit under the county retirement plan. Nevertheless, if the retirement plan meets the requirements of paragraph (e) of this section with respect to the individual, the exclusion from employment under section 3121(b)(7) applies to both the employee's full-time and part-time service with the county.

Example (2). An individual is employed full-time by a State and is a member of its retirement plan. The individual is also employed part-time by a city located in the State, but does not participate in the city's retirement plan. The services of the individual for the city are not excluded from employment under section 3121(b)(7), because the determination of whether services constitute employment for such purposes is made separately with respect to each political subdivision for which services are performed.

(d) Definition of qualified participant. *(1) General rule.* (i) Defined benefit retirement systems. Whether an employee is a qualified participant in a defined benefit retirement system is determined as services are performed. An employee is a qualified participant in a defined benefit retirement system (within the meaning of paragraph (e)(1) of this section) with respect to services performed on a given day if, on that day, he or she is or ever has been an actual participant in the retirement system and, on that day, he or she actually has a total accrued benefit under the retirement system that meets the minimum retirement benefit requirement of paragraph (e)(2) of this section. An employee may not be treated as an actual participant or as actually having an accrued benefit for this purpose to the extent that such participation or benefit is subject to any conditions (other than vesting), such as a requirement that the employee attain a minimum age, perform a minimum period of service, make an election in order to participate, or be present at the end of the plan year in order to be credited with an accrual, that have not been satisfied. The rules of this paragraph (d)(1)(i) are illustrated by the following examples:

Example (1). A State maintains a defined benefit plan that is a retirement system within the meaning of paragraph (e)(1) of this section. Under the terms of the plan, employees in positions covered by the plan must complete 6 months of service before becoming participants. The exception from employment in section 3121(b)(7) does not apply to services of an employee during the employee's 6 months of service prior to his or her initial entry into the plan. The same result occurs even if, upon the satisfaction of this service requirement, the employee is given credit under the plan for all service with the employer (i.e., if service is credited for the 6-month waiting period). This is true even if the employee makes a required contribution in order to gain the retroactive credit. The same result also occurs if the employee can elect to participate in the plan before the end of the 6-month waiting period, but does not elect to do so.

Example (2). A political subdivision maintains a defined benefit plan that is a retirement system within the meaning of paragraph (e)(1) of this section. Under the terms of the plan, service during a plan year is not credited for accrual purposes unless a participant has at least 1,000 hours of service during the year. Benefits that accrue only upon satisfaction of this 1,000-hour requirement may not be taken into account in determining whether an employee is a qualified participant in the plan before the 1,000-hour requirement is satisfied.

(ii) Defined contribution retirement systems. Whether an employee is a qualified participant in a defined contribution retirement system is determined as services are performed. An employee is a qualified participant in a defined contribution or other individual account retirement system (within the meaning of paragraph (e)(1) of this section) with respect to services performed on a given day if, on that day, he or she has satisfied all conditions (other than vesting) for receiving an allocation to his or her account (exclusive of earnings) that meets the minimum retirement benefit requirement of paragraph (e)(2) of this section with respect to compensation during any period ending on that day and beginning on or after the beginning of the plan year of the retirement system. This is the case regardless of whether the allocations were made or accrued before the effective date of section 3121(b)(7)(F). This rule is illustrated by the following examples:

Example (1). A State-owned hospital maintains a nonelective defined contribution plan that is a retirement system within the meaning of paragraph (e)(1) of this section. Under the terms of the plan, employees must be employed on the last day of a plan year in order to receive any allocation for the year. Employees may not be treated as qualified participants in the plan before the last day of the year.

Example (2). Assume the same facts as in Example 1 except that, under the terms of the plan, an employee who terminates service before the end of a plan year receives a pro rata portion of the allocation he or she would have received at the end of the year, e.g., based on compensation earned since the beginning of the plan year. If the pro rata allocation available on a given day would meet the minimum retirement benefit requirement of paragraph (e)(2) of this section with respect to compensation from the beginning of the plan year through that day (or some later day), employees are treated as qualified participants in the plan on that day.

Example (3). A political subdivision maintains an elective defined contribution plan that is a retirement system within the meaning of paragraph (e)(1) of this section. The plan has a calendar year plan year and two open seasons—in December and June—when employees can change their contribution elections. In December, an employee elects not to contribute to the plan. In June, the employee elects (beginning July 1) to contribute a uniform percentage of compensation for each pay period to the plan for the remainder of the plan year. The employee is not a qualified participant in the plan during the period January-June, because no allocations are made to the employee's account with respect to compensation during that time, and it is not certain at that time that any allocations will be made. If the level of contributions during the period July-December meets the minimum retirement benefit requirement of paragraph (e)(2) of this section with respect to compensation during that period, however, the employee is treated as a qualified participant during that period.

Example (4). Assume the same facts as in Example 3, except that the plan allows participants to cancel their elections in cases of economic hardship. In October, the employee suffers an economic hardship and cancels the election (effective November 1). If the contributions during the period July-October are high enough to meet the minimum retirement benefit requirement of paragraph (e)(2) of this section with respect to compensation during that period, the employee is treated as a qualified participant during that period. In addition, if the contributions during the period July-October are high enough to meet the requirements for the entire period July-December, the employee is treated as a qualified participant in the plan throughout the period July-December, even though no allocations are made to the employee's account in the last two months of the year. There is no requirement that the period used to determine whether an employee is a qualified participant on a given day remain the same from day to day, as long as the period begins on or after the beginning of the plan year and ends on the date the determination is being made.

(2) Special rule for part-time, seasonal and temporary employees. (i) In general. A part-time, seasonal or temporary employee is generally not a qualified participant on a given day unless any benefit relied upon to meet the requirements of paragraph (d)(1) of this section is 100-percent nonforfeitable on that day. This requirement may be applied solely to the portion of an employee's benefit under the retirement system attributable to compensation and service while an employee is a part-time, seasonal or temporary employee, provided that such service is taken into account with respect to the remaining portion of the benefit for vesting purposes. Rules similar to the rules in section 411(a)(11) are applicable in determining whether a benefit is nonforfeitable. Thus, a benefit does not fail to be nonforfeitable solely because it can be immediately distributed upon separation of service without the consent of the employee, provided that the pre-

sent value of the benefit does not exceed the cash-out limit in effect under § 1.411(a)-11(c)(3)(ii).

(ii) Treatment of employees entitled to certain distributions upon death or separation from service. A part-time, seasonal or temporary employee's benefit under a retirement system is considered nonforfeitable within the meaning of paragraph (d)(2)(i) of this section on a given day if on that day the employee is unconditionally entitled under the retirement system to a single-sum distribution on account of death or separation from service of an amount that is at least equal to 7.5 percent of the participant's compensation (within the meaning of paragraph (e)(2)(iii)(B) of this section) for all periods of credited service taken into account in determining whether the employee's benefit under the retirement system meets the minimum retirement benefit requirement of paragraph (e)(2) of this section. An employee will be considered to be unconditionally entitled to a single-sum distribution notwithstanding the fact that the distribution may be forfeitable (in whole or in part) upon a finding of such employee's criminal misconduct. The participant must be entitled to interest on the distributable amount through the date of distribution, at a rate meeting the requirements of paragraph (e)(2)(iii)(C) of this section, as part of the single sum. See paragraph (f)(2)(i)(C) for a transition rule relating to this nonforfeitable benefit safe harbor. The rule of this paragraph (d)(2)(ii) is illustrated by the following example:

Example. An employee is required to contribute 7.5 percent of his or her compensation to a State's defined benefit plan each year. The contribution is "picked up" by the employer in accordance with section 414(h). Under the plan, these amounts plus interest accrued since the date each amount was contributed are refundable to the employee in all cases upon the employee's death or separation from service with the employer. If the interest rate meets the requirements of paragraph (e)(2)(iii)(C) of this section, then the employee's benefits under the plan are considered nonforfeitable and thus meet the requirement of paragraph (d)(2)(i) of this section. Of course, the benefit under the plan must still meet the minimum retirement benefit requirement for defined benefit plans of paragraph (e)(2)(ii) of this section.

(iii) Definitions of part-time, seasonal and temporary employee. (A) Definition of part-time employee. For purposes of this section, a part-time employee is any employee who normally works 20 hours or less per week. A teacher employed by a post-secondary educational institution (e.g., a community or junior college, post-secondary vocational school, college, university or graduate school) is not considered a part-time employee for purposes of this section if he or she normally has classroom hours of one-half or more of the number of classroom hours designated by the educational institution as constituting full-time employment, provided that such designation is reasonable under all the facts and circumstances. In addition, elected officials and election workers (otherwise described in section 3121(b)(7)(F)(iv) but paid in excess of $100 annually) are not considered part-time, seasonal or temporary employees for purposes of this section. The rules of this paragraph (d)(2)(iii) are illustrated by the following example:

Example. A community college treats a teacher as a full-time employee if the teacher is assigned to work 15 classroom hours per week. A new teacher is assigned to work 8 classroom hours per week. Because the assigned classroom hours of the teacher are at least one-half of the school's definition of full-time teacher, the teacher is not a part-time employee.

(B) Definition of seasonal employee. For purposes of this section, a seasonal employee is any employee who normally works on a full-time basis less than 5 months in a year. Thus, for example, individuals who are hired by a political subdivision during the tax return season in order to process incoming returns and work full-time over a 3-month period are seasonal employees.

(C) Definition of temporary employee. For purposes of this section, a temporary employee is any employee performing services under a contractual arrangement with the employer of 2 years or less duration. Possible contract extensions may be considered in determining the duration of a contractual arrangement, but only if, under the facts and circumstances, there is a significant likelihood that the employee's contract will be extended. Future contract extensions are considered significantly likely to occur for purposes of this rule if on average 80 percent of similarly situated employees (i.e., those in the same or a similar job classification with expiring employment contracts) have had bona fide offers to renew their contracts in the immediately preceding 2 academic or calendar years. In addition, future contract extensions are considered significantly likely to occur if the employee with respect to whom the determination is being made has a history of contract extensions with respect to his or her current position. An employee is not considered a temporary employee for purposes of this rule solely because he or she is included in a unit of employees covered by a collective bargaining agreement of 2 years or less duration.

(D) Treatment of employees participating in certain systems. Whether an employee is a part-time, seasonal or temporary employee with respect to allocations or benefits under a retirement system is generally determined based on service in the position in which the allocations or benefits were earned, and does not take into account service in other positions with the same or different States, political subdivisions or instrumentalities thereof. All of an employee's service in other positions with the same or different States, political subdivisions or instrumentalities thereof may be taken into account for purposes of determining whether an employee is a part-time, seasonal or temporary employee with respect to benefits under the retirement system, however, provided that: the employees's service in the other positions is or was covered by the retirement system; all service aggregated for purposes of determining whether an employee is a part-time, seasonal or temporary employee (and related compensation) is aggregated under the system for all purposes in determining benefits (including vesting); and the employee is treated at least as favorably as a full-time employee under the retirement system for benefit accrual purposes. The rule of this paragraph (d)(2)(iii)(D) is illustrated by the following example:

Example. Assume that an employee works 15 hours per week for a county and 10 hours per week for a municipality, and that both of these political subdivisions contribute to the same state-wide public employee retirement system. Assume further that the employee's service in both positions is aggregated under the system for all purposes in determining benefits (including vesting). If the employee is covered under the retirement system with respect to both positions and is treated for benefit accrual purposes at least as favorably as full-time employees under the retirement system, then the employee is not considered a part-time employee of either the county or the municipality for purposes of the nonforfeitable benefit requirement of paragraph (d)(2)(i) of this section.

(3) *Alternative lookback rule.* (i) In general. An employee may be treated as a qualified participant in a retirement system throughout a calendar year if he or she was a qualified participant in such system (within the meaning of paragraphs (d)(1) and (2) of this section) at the end of the plan year of the system ending in the previous calendar year. This rule is illustrated by the following examples:

Example (1). A political subdivision maintains a plan that is a retirement system within the meaning of paragraph (e)(1) of this section. An employee is a qualified participant within the meaning of paragraph (d)(1) of this section in the plan on the last day of the plan year ending on May 31, 1995. If the alternative lookback rule is used to determine FICA liability, no such liability exists with respect to the employee or employer for calendar year 1996 by reason of section 3121(b)(7)(F). The same result would apply if the determination is being made with respect to calendar year 1992 and the lookback year was the plan year ending May 31, 1991, even though that plan year ended before the effective date of section 3121(b)(7)(F).

Example (2). A political subdivision maintains an elective defined contribution plan described in section 457(b) of the Code. An employee is eligible to participate in the plan but does not elect to contribute for a plan year. Under the general rule of paragraph (d)(1) of this section, the employee is not a qualified participant in the plan during the plan year because contributions sufficient to meet the minimum retirement benefit requirement of paragraph (e)(2) of this section are not being made. However, if an employee's status as a qualified participant is being determined under the alternative lookback rule, then the employee is a qualified participant for the calendar year in which the determination is being made if he or she was a qualified participant as of the end of the plan year that ended in the previous calendar year.

(ii) Application in first year of participation. If the alternative lookback rule is used, an employee who participates in the retirement system may be treated as a qualified participant on any given day during his or her first plan year of participation in a retirement system (within the meaning of paragraph (e)(1) of this section) if and only if it is reasonable on such day to believe that the employee will be a qualified participant (within the meaning of paragraphs (d)(1) and (2) of this section) on the last day of such plan year. In the case of a defined contribution retirement system, the determination of whether the employee is actually (or is expected to be) a qualified participant at the end of the plan year must take into account all compensation since the commencement of participation. See paragraph (d)(3)(iv) of this section. If this reasonable belief is correct, and the employee is a qualified participant on the last day of his or her first plan year of participation, then the exception from employment in section 3121(b)(7) will apply without regard to section 3121(b)(7)(F) to services of the employee for the balance of the calendar year in which the plan year ends. For purposes of this paragraph (d)(3)(ii), it is not reasonable to assume the establishment of a new plan until such establishment actually occurs. In addition, the rule in this paragraph (d)(3)(ii) may not be used to treat an employee as a qualified participant until the employee actually becomes a participant in the retirement system. In the case of a retirement system that does not permit a new employee to participate until the first day of the first month beginning after the employee's commencement of service, or some earlier date, a new employee who is not a part-time, seasonal or temporary employee may be treated as a qualified participant until such date. This 1-month rule of administrative convenience applies without regard to whether the employer has a reasonable belief that the employee will be a qualified participant. The rules of this paragraph (d)(3)(ii) are illustrated by the following examples:

Example (1). A political subdivision maintains a plan that is a retirement system within the meaning of paragraph (e)(1) of this section and uses the alternative lookback rule of this paragraph (d)(3). Under the terms of the plan, service during a plan year is not credited for accrual purposes unless a participant has at least 1,000 hours of service during the year. Assume that an employee becomes a participant. If it is reasonable to believe that the employee will be credited with 1,000 hours of service by the last day of his or her first year of participation and thereby become a qualified participant by reason of accruing a benefit that meets the minimum retirement benefit requirement of paragraph (e)(2) of this section, the services of the employee are not subject to FICA tax from the date of initial participation until the end of that plan year. If the employee is a qualified participant on the last day of his or her first plan year of participation, then the exception from employment for purposes of FICA will apply to services of the employee for the balance of the calendar year in which the plan year ended.

Example (2). Assume the same facts as Example 1, except that the employee is a newly hired employee and the plan provides that an employee may not participate until the first day of his or her first full month of employment. Under the 1-month rule of convenience, the employee may be treated as a qualified participant until the first date on which he or she could participate in the plan.

(iii) Application in last year of participation. If the alternative lookback rule is used, an employee may be treated as a qualified participant on any given day during his or her last year of participation in a retirement system (within the meaning of paragraph (e)(1) of this section) if and only if it is reasonable to believe on such day that the employee will be a qualified participant (within the meaning of paragraphs (d)(1) and (2) of this section) on his or her last day of participation. For purposes of this paragraph (d)(3)(iii), an employee's last year of participation means the plan year that the employer reasonably ascertains is the final year of such employee's participation (e.g., where the employee has a scheduled retirement date or where the employer intends to terminate the plan).

(iv) Special rule for defined contribution retirement systems. An employee may not be treated as a qualified participant in a defined contribution retirement system under this paragraph (d)(3) if compensation for less than a full plan year or other 12-month period is regularly taken into account in determining allocations to the employee's account for the plan year unless, under all of the facts and circumstances, such arrangement is not a device to avoid the imposition of FICA taxes. For example, an arrangement under which compensation taken into account is limited to the contribution base described in section 3121(x)(1) is not considered a device to avoid FICA taxes by reason of such limitation. See paragraph (e)(2)(iii)(B) of this section for a rule permitting the use of such limitation. This rule is illustrated by the following example:

Example. A political subdivision maintains a defined contribution plan that covers all of its full-time employees and is a retirement system within the meaning of paragraph (e)(1) of this section. Under the plan, a portion of each participant's compensation in the final month of every plan year is allocated to the participant's account. Employees covered under the plan generally may not be treated as qualified participants under the alternative lookback rule for any portion of the calendar year following the year in which such allocation is made.

(v) Consistency requirement. Beginning with calendar year 1992, if the alternative lookback rule is used to determine whether an employee is a qualified participant, it must be used consistently from year to year and with respect to all employees of the State, political subdivision or instrumentality thereof making the determination. If a retirement system is sponsored by more than one State, political subdivision or instrumentality, this consistency requirement applies separately to each plan sponsor.

(4) Treatment of former participants. (i) In general. In general, the rules of this paragraph (d) apply equally to former participants who continue to perform service for the same State, political subdivision or instrumentality thereof or who return after a break in service. Thus, for example, a former employee of a political subdivision with a deferred benefit under a defined benefit retirement system maintained by the political subdivision who is reemployed by the political subdivision but does not resume participation in the retirement system, may continue to be a qualified participant in the system after becoming reemployed if his or her total accrued benefit under the system meets the minimum retirement benefit requirement of paragraph (e)(2) of this section (taking into account all periods of service (including current service) required to be taken into account under that paragraph). See also paragraph (e)(2)(v) of this section for situations in which benefits under a retirement system may be taken into account even though they relate to service for another employer.

(ii) Treatment of re-hired annuitants. An employee who is a former participant in a retirement system maintained by a State, political subdivision or instrumentality thereof, who has previously retired from service with the State, political subdivision or instrumentality, and who is either in pay status (i.e., is currently receiving retirement benefits) under the retirement system or has reached normal retirement age under the retirement system, is deemed to be a qualified participant in the retirement system without regard to whether he or she continues to accrue a benefit or whether the distribution of benefits under the retirement system has been suspended pending cessation of services. This rule also applies in the case of an employee who has retired from service with another State, political subdivision or instrumentality thereof that maintains the same retirement system as the current employer, provided the employee is a former participant in the system by reason of the employee's former employment. Thus, for example, if a teacher retires from service with a school district that participates in a state-wide teachers' retirement system, begins to receive benefits from the system, and later becomes a substitute teacher in another school district that participates in the same state-wide system, the employee is treated as a re-hired annuitant under this paragraph (d)(4)(ii).

(e) Definition of retirement system. *(1) Requirement that system provide retirement-type benefits.* For purposes of section 3121(b)(7)(F), a retirement system includes any pension, annuity, retirement or similar fund or system within the meaning of section 218 of the Social Security Act that is maintained by a State, political subdivision or instrumentality thereof to provide retirement benefits to its employees who are participants. Whether a plan is maintained to provide retirement benefits with respect to an employee is determined under the facts and circumstances of each case. For example, a plan providing only retiree health insurance or other deferred welfare benefits is not considered a retirement system for this purpose. The legal form of the system is generally not relevant. Thus, for example, a retirement system may include a plan described in section 401(a), an annuity plan or contract under section 403 or a plan described in section 457(b) or (f) of the Internal Revenue Code. In addition, the Social Security system is not a retirement system for purposes of section 3121(b)(7)(F) and this section. These rules are illustrated by the following examples:

Example (1). Under an employment arrangement, a portion of an employee's compensation is regularly deferred for 5 years. Because a plan that defers the receipt of compensation for a short span of time rather than until retirement is not a plan that provides retirement benefits, this arrangement is not a retirement system for purposes of section 3121(b)(7)(F).

Example (2). An individual holds two positions with the same political subdivision. The wages earned in one position are subject to FICA tax pursuant to an agreement (under section 218 of the Social Security Act) between the Secretary of Health and Human Services and the State in which the political subdivision is located. Because the Social Security system is not a retirement system for purposes of section 3121(b)(7)(F), the exception from employment in section 3121(b)(7) does not apply to service in the other position unless the employee is otherwise a member of a retirement system of such political subdivision.

(2) Requirement that system provide minimum level of benefits. (i) In general. A pension, annuity, retirement or similar fund or system is not a retirement system with respect to an employee unless it provides a retirement benefit to the employee that is comparable to the benefit provided under the Old-Age portion of the Old-Age, Survivor and Disability Insurance program of Social Security. Whether a retirement system meets this requirement is generally determined on an individual-by-individual basis. Thus, for example, a pension plan that is not a retirement system with respect to an employee may nevertheless be a retirement system with respect to other employees covered by the system.

(ii) Defined benefit retirement systems. A defined benefit retirement system maintained by a State, political subdivision or instrumentality thereof meets the requirements of this paragraph (e)(2) with respect to an employee on a given day if and only if, on that day, the employee has an accrued benefit under the system that entitles the employee to an annual benefit commencing on or before his or her Social Security retirement age that is at least equal to the annual Primary Insurance Amount the employee would have under Social Security. For this purpose, the Primary Insurance Amount an individual would have under Social Security is determined as it would be under the Social Security Act if the employee had been covered under Social Security for all periods of service with the State, political subdivision or instrumentality, had never performed service for any other employer, and had been fully insured within the meaning of section 214(a) of the Social Security Act, except that all periods of service with the State, political subdivision or instrumentality must be taken into account (i.e., without reduction for low-earning years).

(iii) Defined contribution retirement systems. (A) In general. A defined contribution retirement system maintained by a State, political subdivision or instrumentality thereof meets the requirements of paragraph (e)(2)(i) of this section with respect to an employee if and only if allocations to the employee's account (not including earnings) for a period are at least 7.5 percent of the employee's compensation for service for the State, political subdivision or instrumentality during the period. Matching contributions by the employer may be taken into account for this purpose.

(B) Definition of compensation. The definition of compensation used in determining whether a defined contribution retirement system meets the minimum retirement benefit requirement must generally be no less inclusive than the definition of the employee's base pay as designated by the employer or the retirement system, provided such designation is reasonable under all the facts and circumstances. Thus, for example, a defined contribution retirement system will not fail to meet this requirement merely because it disregards for all purposes one or more of the following: overtime pay, bonuses, or single-sum amounts received on account of death or separation from service under a bona fide vacation, compensatory time or sick pay plan, or under severance pay plans. Furthermore, any compensation remaining after such amounts are disregarded that is in excess of the contribution base described in section 3121(x)(1) at the beginning of the plan year may also be disregarded. The rules of this paragraph are illustrated by the following example:

Example. A political subdivision maintains an elective defined contribution plan that is a retirement system within the meaning of paragraph (e)(1) of this section. The plan has a calendar year plan year. In 1995, an employee contributes to the plan at a rate of 7.5 percent of base pay. Assume that the employee will reach the maximum contribution base described in section 3121(x)(1) in October of 1995. The employee is a qualified participant in the plan for all of the 1995 plan year without regard to whether the employee ceases to participate at any time after reaching the maximum contribution base.

(C) Reasonable interest rate requirement. A defined contribution retirement system does not satisfy this paragraph (e)(2) with respect to an employee unless the employee's account is credited with earnings at a rate that is reasonable under all the facts and circumstances, or employees' accounts are held in a separate trust that is subject to general fiduciary standards and are credited with actual earnings on the trust fund. Whether the interest rate with which an employee's account is credited is reasonable is determined after reducing the rate to adjust for the payment of any administrative expenses. The rule of this paragraph (e)(2)(iii)(C) is illustrated by the following example:

Example. A political subdivision maintains a defined contribution plan described in section 457(b). Under the plan, the accounts of participants are credited annually on the basis of a variable interest rate formula determined as of the beginning of the plan year. The formula requires an interest rate (after adjustment for administrative expense payments) equal to 100 percent of the Applicable Federal Rate for long-term debt instruments. This interest rate constitutes a reasonable rate of interest.

(iv) Treatment of employees employed in more than one position with the same entity. All service and compensation of an employee with respect to his or her employment with a State, political subdivision or instrumentality thereof must generally be considered in determining whether a benefit meets the requirement of this paragraph (e)(2). However, for individuals employed simultaneously in multiple positions with the same entity, this determination may (but is not required to) be made solely by reference to the service and compensation related to a single position of the employee with the State, political subdivision or instrumentality thereof making the determination, provided that the position is not a part-time, seasonal or temporary position.

(v) Treatment of employees participating in certain systems. In general, only compensation from and service for the State, political subdivision or instrumentality thereof that employs the employee (and the allocations or benefits related to such compensation or service) on a given day are considered in determining whether the employee's benefit under the retirement system on that day meets the requirements of this paragraph (e)(2), even if the employee has other allocations or benefits under the same retirement system from service with another State, political subdivision or instrumentality thereof. However, an employee's total allocations or benefits under a retirement system maintained by multiple States, political subdivisions or instrumentalities thereof (including the current employer) may be taken into account if:

(A) The compensation and service on which the additional allocations or benefits are based are also taken into account in determining whether the employee's allocations or benefits satisfy the minimum retirement benefit requirement;

(B) The retirement system takes all service and compensation of the employee in all positions covered by the system into account for all benefit determination purposes; and

(C) If the employee is a part-time, seasonal or temporary employee, he or she is treated under the plan for benefit accrual purposes in as favorable a manner as a full-time employee participating in the system.

(vi) Additional testing methods. Additional testing methods may be designated by the Commissioner in revenue procedures, revenue rulings, notices or other documents of general applicability.

(f) Transition rules. *(1) Application of qualified participant rules during 1991.* (i) In general. An employee may be treated as a qualified participant in a retirement system (within the meaning of paragraph (e)(1) of this section) on a given day during the period July 1 through December 31, 1991, if it is reasonable on that day to believe that he or she will be a qualified participant under the general rule in paragraphs (d)(1) and (2) of this section by January 1, 1992 (taking into account only service and compensation on or after such date). For purposes of this paragraph (f)(1)(i), given the facts and circumstances of a particular case, it may be reasonable to assume that the terms of a plan will be changed or that a new retirement system will be established by the end of calendar year 1991, as long as affirmative steps have been taken to accomplish this result.

(ii) Extension of reliance period if legislative action required. If a plan amendment or other action is necessary in order to treat an employee as a member of a retirement system for purposes of this section, such amendment or other action may only be taken by a legislative body that does not convene during the period July 1, 1991, through December 31, 1991, and the other requirements of paragraph (f)(1)(i) of this section are met, the end of the reasonable reliance period (including the rule that service and compensation prior to that date may be disregarded) provided under paragraph (f)(1)(i) of this section is extended from December 31, 1991, to the date that is the last day of the first legislative session commencing after December 31, 1991. These rules are illustrated by the following examples:

Example (1). A State maintains a defined benefit plan that meets the requirements of paragraph (e) of this section. The plan does not cover a particular class of full-time employees as of July 1, 1991. However, in light of the enactment of section 3121(b)(7)(F), State officials administering the plan for the State intend to request that the legislature amend the State statute to include that class of employees in the existing plan and otherwise to modify the terms of the plan to meet the requirements of section 3121(b)(7)(F) and this section. The State legislature meets from January through March each year, and legislative action is required to expand coverage under the plan. State officials administering the plan have publicized the proposed amendment providing for the addition of these employees to the plan. Under the transition rule for 1991, if it is reasonable to believe that the legislature will pass this bill in the 1992 session, service by the employees who will be covered under the plan by reason of the amendment is not treated as employment by reason of section 3121(b)(7)(F) during the period prior to April 1, 1992. This is true regardless of whether the plan provides retroactive coverage for the period July 1, 1991 through March 31, 1992.

Example (2). Assume the same facts as in Example 1, except that legislative action is not required in order to expand coverage under the plan, and that publication of the proposed change to the plan occurs in 1991. Assume further that coverage is expanded under the plan to include the new class of full-time employees as of April 1, 1992. Despite this action, in this situation the service by those employees during the period January 1, 1992 through March 31, 1992 is not excluded from "employment" under section 3121(b)(7)(F), and wages for that period are generally subject to FICA taxes even if the plan provides retroactive coverage for any portion of the period July 1, 1991 to March 31, 1992.

(2) Additional transition rules for plans in existence on November 5, 1990. (i) Application of minimum retirement benefit requirement to defined benefit retirement systems in plan years beginning before 1993. (A) In general. A defined benefit retirement system maintained by a State, political subdivision or instrumentality thereof on November 5, 1990, is not subject to the minimum retirement benefit requirement of paragraph (e)(2) of this section for any plan year beginning before January 1, 1993, with respect to individuals who were actually covered under the system on November 5, 1990. Such a retirement system is also not subject to the minimum retirement benefit requirement of paragraph (e)(2) of this section with respect to an employee who becomes a participant after November 5, 1990, if he or she is employed in a position that was covered under the retirement system on November 5, 1990, without regard to whether such coverage was mandatory or elective. A retirement system is not described in this paragraph (f)(2)(i)(A) if there has been a material decrease in the level of retirement benefits under the retirement system pursuant to an amendment adopted subsequent to November 5, 1990. Whether such a material decrease in benefits has occurred is determined under the facts and circumstances of each case. A decrease in benefits is not material to the extent that it does not decrease the benefit payable at normal retirement age. These rules are illustrated by the following examples:

Example (1). The retirement formula under a retirement plan that was in existence on November 5, 1990, is amended to use career average compensation instead of a high 3-year average, without any increase in the benefit formula. This amendment constitutes a material decrease in the level of benefit under the retirement plan. Therefore, the retirement plan is subject to the minimum retirement benefit requirement for the plan year for which the amendment is effective and for all succeeding plan years.

Example (2). A defined benefit retirement plan that was in existence on November 5, 1990, is subsequently amended to include part-time employees. Previously, this class of employees was not covered under the plan either on a mandatory or on an elective basis. The plan is subject to the minimum retirement benefit requirement with respect to the part-time employees because this class of employees was previously excluded from coverage under the retirement plan. Of course, the nonforfeitable benefit rule applies to the benefit relied upon to meet the minimum retirement benefit requirement with respect to any part-time seasonal or temporary employee covered during this period.

(B) Treatment in plan years beginning after 1992 of benefits accrued during previous plan years. The general rule that a defined benefit retirement system meets the minimum retirement benefit requirement on the basis of total benefits and service accrued to date is modified for plans in existence on November 5, 1990. If a defined benefit retirement system in existence on November 5, 1990, does not meet the minimum retirement benefit requirement solely because the benefits accrued for an employee (with respect to whom the system is entitled to relief under paragraph (f)(2)(i)(A) of this section) as of the last day of the last plan year beginning before January 1, 1993, do not meet the minimum retirement benefit requirement of paragraph (e)(2) of this section with respect to service and compensation before that time, then the retirement system will be deemed to comply with the requirements of paragraph (e)(2) of this section if the future service accruals would comply with the requirement of paragraph (e)(2) of this section. If retirement benefits under a retirement system in existence on November 5, 1990, are materially decreased within the meaning of paragraph (f)(2)(i)(A) of this section, then the date the decrease is effective is substituted for January 1, 1993 for purposes of this paragraph. The rule of this paragraph (f)(2)(i)(B) is illustrated by the following example:

Example. A defined benefit plan maintained by a State was in existence on November 5, 1990. It provides a retirement benefit on the last day of the 1992 plan year that is insufficient to meet the requirements of paragraph (e)(2) of this section based on employees' total service and compensation with the State at that time. The plan will nevertheless meet the requirements of paragraph (e)(2) of this section if it is amended to provide benefits sufficient to meet the requirements of paragraph (e)(2) of this section based on employees' service and compensation in plan years beginning after December 31, 1992. (C) Treatment of part-time, seasonal or temporary employees. A defined benefit retirement system is not exempt from the minimum retirement benefit requirement with respect to a part-time, seasonal or temporary employee during the transition period provided in paragraph (f)(2)(i)(A) of this section unless any retirement benefit provided to the employee is 100-percent nonforfeitable within the meaning of paragraph (d)(2) of this section. In determining whether the benefit is nonforfeitable, the special rule in paragraph (d)(2)(ii) of this section is modified in two respects during the transition period: first, the percentage of compensation required to be available for distribution is reduced from 7.5 percent to 6 percent; and second, the period of service with respect to which compensation must be determined is modified to include all periods of participation by the employee in the system since July 1, 1991.

(ii) Application of minimum retirement benefit requirement to defined contribution retirement systems in plan years beginning before 1993. A defined contribution retirement system maintained by a State, political subdivision or instrumentality thereof on November 5, 1990, meets the minimum retirement benefit requirement of paragraph (e)(2) of this section with respect to an employee for any plan year beginning before January 1, 1993, if mandatory allocations to the employee's account (not including earnings) for a period are at least 6 percent (rather than 7.5 percent) of the employee's compensation for service to the State, political subdivision or instrumentality during the period, and the plan otherwise meets the requirements of paragraph (e)(2)(iii) of this section. This transition rule is only available with respect to an employee who is actually covered under the system on November 5, 1990, and to an employee who becomes a participant after November 5, 1990, if he or she is employed in a position that was covered under the retirement system on November 5, 1990, without regard to whether such coverage was mandatory or elective. In addition, this transition rule is not available with respect to a part-time, seasonal or temporary employee unless the mandatory allocation required under this paragraph (f)(2)(ii) is 100-percent nonforfeitable within the meaning of paragraph (d)(2) of this section. A retirement system is not described in this paragraph (f)(2)(ii) if there has been a material decrease in the level of retirement benefits under the retirement system pursuant to an amendment adopted subsequent to November 5, 1990. Whether such a material decrease in benefits has occurred is determined under all the facts and circumstances.

(iii) Application of qualified participant rules. A participant with respect to whom relief is granted under paragraph (f)(2)(i)(A) of this section may be treated as a qualified participant in the defined benefit retirement system on a given day if, on that day, he or she is actually a participant in the retirement system, and, on that day, it is reasonable to believe that the participant will actually accrue a benefit before the end of the plan year of such retirement system in which the determination is made. A participant is not treated as accruing a benefit for purposes of this rule if his or her accrued benefits increase solely as a result of an increase in compensation. However, an employee is treated as a qualified participant for a plan year if the employee meets all of the applicable conditions for accruing the maximum current benefit for such year but fails to accrue a benefit solely because of a uniformly applicable benefit limit under the plan. In addition, an employee may be treated as a qualified participant in the system on a given day if the employee is a rehired annuitant within the meaning of paragraph (d)(4)(ii) of this section. This rule is illustrated by the following example:

Example. A political subdivision maintains a defined benefit plan that is a retirement system within the meaning of paragraph (e)(1) of this section but does not meet the requirements of paragraph (e)(2) of this section. If the plan is not subject to the minimum retirement benefit requirement, an employee who is a participant in the retirement plan as of the end of a plan year beginning before January 1, 1993, and may reasonably be expected to accrue a benefit under the plan by the end of such plan year may be treated as a qualified participant in the plan throughout the plan year regardless of the actual amount of the accrual.

T.D. 8354, 6/25/91, amend T.D. 8794, 12/18/98, T.D. 8891, 7/18/2000.

§ 31.3121(b)(8)-1 Services performed by a minister of a church or a member of a religious order.

(a) In general. Services performed by a duly ordained, commissioned, or licensed minister of a church in the exercise of his ministry, or by a member of a religious order in the exercise of his duties required by such order, are excluded from employment, except that services performed by a member of such an order in the exercise of such duties (whether performed for the order or for another employer) are included in employment if an election of coverage under section 3121(r) and § 31.3121(r)-1 is in effect with respect to such order or with respect to the autonomous subdivision thereof to which such member belongs. For provisions relating to the election available to certain ministers and members of religious orders with respect to the extension of the Federal old-age, survivors, and disability insurance system established by title II of the Social Security Act to certain services performed by them, see Part 1 of this chapter (Income Tax Regulations).

(b) Service by a minister in the exercise of his ministry. Except as provided in paragraph (c)(3) of this section, service performed by a minister in the exercise of his ministry includes the ministration of sacerdotal functions and the conduct of religious worship, and the control, conduct, and maintenance of religious organizations (including the religious boards, societies, and other integral agencies of such organizations), under the authority of a religious body constituting a church or church denomination. The following rules are applicable in determining whether services performed by a minister are performed in the exercise of his ministry:

(1) Whether service performed by a minister constitutes the conduct of religious worship or the ministration of sacerdotal functions depends on the tenets and practices of the particular religious body constituting his church or church denomination.

(2) Service performed by a minister in the control, conduct, and maintenance of a religious organization relates to directing, managing, or promoting the activities of such organization. Any religious organization is deemed to be under the authority of a religious body constituting a church or church denomination if it is organized and dedicated to carrying out the tenets and principles of a faith in accordance with either the requirements or sanctions governing the creation of institutions of the faith. The term "religious organization" has the same meaning and application as is given to the term for income tax purposes.

(3) (i) If a minister is performing service in the conduct of religious worship or the ministration of sacerdotal functions, such service is in the exercise of his ministry whether or not it is performed for a religious organization.

(ii) The rule in paragraph (b)(3)(i) of this section may be illustrated by the following example:

Example. M, a duly ordained minister, is engaged to perform service as chaplain at N University. M devotes his entire time to performing his duties as chaplain which include the conduct of religious worship, offering spiritual counsel to the university students, and teaching a class in religion. M is performing service in the exercise of his ministry.

(4) (i) If a minister is performing service for an organization which is operated as an integral agency of a religious organization under the authority of a religious body constituting a church or church denomination, all service performed by the minister in the conduct of religious worship, in the ministration of sacerdotal functions, or in the control, conduct, and maintenance of such organization (see paragraph (b)(2) of this section) is in the exercise of his ministry.

(ii) The rule in paragraph (b)(4)(i) of this section may be illustrated by the following example:

Example. M, a duly ordained minister, is engaged by the N Religious Board to serve as director of one of its departments. He performs no other service. The N Religious Board is an integral agency of O, a religious organization operating under the authority of a religious body constituting a church denomination. M is performing service in the exercise of his ministry.

(5) (i) If a minister, pursuant to an assignment or designation by a religious body constituting his church, performs service for an organization which is neither a religious organization nor operated as an integral agency of a religious organization, all service performed by him, even though such service may not involve the conduct of religious worship or the ministration of sacerdotal functions, is in the exercise of his ministry.

(ii) The rule in paragraph (b)(5)(i) of this section may be illustrated by the following example:

Example. M, a duly ordained minister, is assigned by X, the religious body constituting his church, to perform advisory service to Y Company in connection with the publication of a book dealing with the history of M's church denomination. Y is neither a religious organization nor operated as an integral agency of a religious organization. M performs no other service for X or Y. M is performing service in the exercise of his ministry.

(c) Service by a minister not in the exercise of his ministry. *(1)* Section 3121(b)(8)(A) does not except from employment service performed by a duly ordained, commissioned, or licensed minister of a church which is not in the exercise of his ministry.

(2) (i) If a minister is performing service for an organization which is neither a religious organization nor operated as an integral agency of a religious organization and the service is not performed pursuant to an assignment or designation by his ecclesiastical superiors, then only the service performed by him in the conduct of religious worship or the ministration of sacerdotal functions is in the exercise of his ministry. See, however, paragraph (c)(3) of this section.

(ii) The rule in paragraph (c)(2)(i) of this section may be illustrated by the following example:

Example. M, a duly ordained minister, is engaged by N University to teach history and mathematics. He performs no other service for N although from time to time he performs marriages and conducts funerals for relatives and friends. N University is neither a religious organization nor operated as an integral agency of a religious organization. M is not performing the service for N pursuant to an assignment or designation by his ecclesiastical superiors. The service performed by M for N University is not in the exercise of his ministry. However, service performed by M in performing marriages and conducting funerals is in the exercise of his ministry.

(3) Service performed by a duly ordained, commissioned, or licensed minister of a church as an employee of the United States, or a State, Territory, or possession of the United States, or the District of Columbia, or a foreign government, or a political subdivision of any of the foregoing, is not considered to be in the exercise of his ministry for purposes of the taxes, even though such service may involve the ministration of sacerdotal functions or the conduct of religious worship. Thus, for example, service performed by an individual as a chaplain in the Armed Forces of the United States is considered to be performed by a commissioned officer in his capacity as such, and not by a minister in the exercise of his ministry. Similarly, service performed by an employee of a State as a chaplain in a State prison is considered to be performed by a civil servant of the State and not by a minister in the exercise of his ministry.

(d) Service in the exercise of duties required by a religious order. Service performed by a member of a religious order in the exercise of duties required by such order includes all duties required of the member by the order. The nature or extent of such service is immaterial so long as it is a service which he is directed or required to perform by his ecclesiastical superiors.

T.D. 6190, 7/13/56, amend T.D. 6516, 12/19/60, T.D. 7280, 7/9/73.

§ 31.3121(b)(8)-2 Services in employ of religious, charitable, educational, or certain other organizations exempt from income tax.

(a) Services performed by an employee in the employ of a religious, charitable, educational, or other organization described in section 501(c)(3) which is exempt from income tax under section 501(a) are excepted from employment. However, this exception does not apply to services with respect to which a certificate, filed pursuant to section 3121(k) or (r), or section 1426(l) of the Internal Revenue Code of 1939, is in effect. For provisions relating to the services with respect to which such a certificate is in effect, see §§ 31.3121(k)-1 and 31.3121(r)-1.

(b) For provisions relating to exemption from income tax of an organization described in section 501(c)(3), see Part 1 of this chapter (Income Tax Regulations). For provisions relating to waiver by an organization of its exemption from the taxes imposed by sections 3101 and 3111, see § 31.3121(k)-1. See also § 31.3121(b)(8)-1, relating to services performed by a minister of a church in the exercise of his ministry or by a member of a religious order in the exercise of duties required by such order; § 31.3121(b)(10)-1, relating to services for remuneration of less than $50 for calendar quarter in the employ of certain organizations exempt from income tax; § 31.3121(b)(10)-2, relating to services performed in the employ of a school, college, or university by certain students; and § 31.3121(b)(13)-1, relating to services performed by certain student nurses and hospital interns.

T.D. 6190, 7/13/56, amend T.D. 6516, 12/19/60, T.D. 7280, 7/9/73.

§ 31.3121(b)(9)-1 Railroad industry; services performed by an employee or employee representative as defined in section 3231.

Services performed by an individual as an "employee" or as an "employee representative", as those terms are defined in section 3231, are excepted from employment. For definitions of employee and employee representatives, see §§ 31.3231(b)-1 and 31.3231(c)-1.

T.D. 6190, 7/13/56, amend T.D. 6516, 12/19/60.

§ 31.3121(b)(10)-1 Services for remuneration of less than $50 for calendar quarter in the employ of certain organizations exempt from income tax.

(a) Services performed by an employee in a calendar quarter in the employ of an organization exempt from income tax under section 501(a) (other than an organization described in section 401(a)) or under section 521 are excepted from employment, if the remuneration for the services is less than $50. The test relating to remuneration of $50 is based on the remuneration earned during a calendar quarter rather than on the remuneration paid in a calendar quarter. The exception applies separately with respect to each organization for which the employee renders services in a calendar quarter. The type of services performed by the employee and the place where the services are performed are immaterial; the statutory tests are the character of the organization in the employ of which the services are performed and the amount of the remuneration for services performed by the employee in the calendar quarter. For provisions relating to exemption from income tax under section 501(a) or 521, see Part 1 of this chapter (Income Tax Regulations).

Example (1). X is a local lodge of a fraternal organization and is exempt from income tax under section 501(a) as an organization of the character described in section 501(c)(8). X has two paid employees, A, who serves exclusively as recording secretary for the lodge, and B, who performs services for the lodge as janitor of its clubhouse. For services performed during the first calendar quarter of 1955 (that is, January 1, 1955, through March 31, 1955, both dates inclusive) A earns a total of $30. For services performed during the same calendar quarter B earns $180. Since the remuneration for the services performed by A during such quarter is less than $50, all of such services are excepted, and the taxes do not attach with respect to any of the remuneration for such services. Since the remuneration for the services performed by B during such quarter, however, is not less than $50, none of such services are excepted, and the taxes attach with respect to all of the remuneration for such services (that is, $180) as and when paid.

Example (2). The facts are the same as in example (1), above, except that on April 1, 1955, A's salary is increased, and, for services performed during the calendar quarter beginning on that date (that is, April 1, 1955, through June 30, 1955, both dates inclusive), A earns a total of $60. Although all of the services performed by A during the first quarter were excepted, none of A's services performed during the second quarter are excepted since the remuneration for such services is not less than $50. The taxes attach with respect to all of the remuneration for services performed during the second quarter (that is, $60) as and when paid.

Example (3). The facts are the same as in example (1), above, except that A earns $120 for services performed during the year 1955, and such amount is paid to him in a lump sum at the end of the year. The services performed by A in any calendar quarter during the year are excepted if the portion of the $120 attributable to services performed in that quarter is less than $50. If, however, the portion of the $120 attributable to services performed in any calendar quarter during the year is not less than $50, the services during that quarter are not excepted, and the taxes attach with respect to that portion of the remuneration attributable to his services in that quarter.

(b) See § 31.3121(b)(8)-2, relating to services performed in the employ of religious, charitable, educational, and certain other organizations exempt from income tax; § 31.3121(b)(8)-1, relating to services performed by a minister of a church in the exercise of his ministry or by a member of a religious order in the exercise of duties required by such order; § 31.3121(b)(10)-2, relating to services performed by certain students in the employ of a school, college, or university or of a nonprofit organization auxiliary to a school, college, or university; and § 31.3121(b)(13)-1, relating to services performed by certain student nurses and hospital interns.

T.D. 6190, 7/13/56, amend T.D. 6516, 12/19/60, T.D. 7373, 7/23/75.

---

§ 31.3121(b)(10)-2 Services performed by certain students in the employ of a school, college, or university, or of a nonprofit organization auxiliary to a school, college, or university.

(a) General rule.

(1) Services performed in the employ of a school, college, or university within the meaning of paragraph (c) of this section (whether or not the organization is exempt from income tax) are excepted from employment, if the services are performed by a student within the meaning of paragraph (d) of this section who is enrolled and is regularly attending classes at the school, college, or university.

(2) Services performed in the employ of an organization which is—

(i) Described in section 509(a)(3) and § 1.509(a)-4;

(ii) Organized, and at all times thereafter operated, exclusively for the benefit of, to perform the functions of, or to carry out the purposes of a school, college, or university within the meaning of paragraph (c) of this section; and

(iii) Operated, supervised, or controlled by or in connection with the school, college, or university; are excepted from employment, if the services are performed by a student who is enrolled and regularly attending classes within the meaning of paragraph (d) of this section at the school, college, or university. The preceding sentence shall not apply to services performed in the employ of a school, college, or university of a State or a political subdivision thereof by a student referred to in section 218(c)(5) of the Social Security Act (42 U.S.C. 418(c)(5)) if such services are covered under the agreement between the Commissioner of Social Security and such State entered into pursuant to section 218 of such Act. For the definitions of "operated, supervised, or controlled by", "supervised or controlled in connection with", and "operated in connection with", see paragraphs (g), (h), and (i), respectively, of § 1.509(a)-4.

(b) Statutory tests. For purposes of this section, if an employee has the status of a student within the meaning of paragraph (d) of this section, the amount of remuneration for services performed by the employee, the type of services performed by the employee, and the place where the services are performed are not material. The statutory tests are:

(1) The character of the organization in the employ of which the services are performed as a school, college, or university within the meaning of paragraph (c) of this section, or as an organization described in paragraph (a)(2) of this section, and

(2) The status of the employee as a student enrolled and regularly attending classes within the meaning of paragraph (d) of this section at the school, college, or university within the meaning of paragraph (c) of this section by which the employee is employed or with which the employee's employer is affiliated within the meaning of paragraph (a)(2) of this section.

(c) School, College, or University. An organization is a school, college, or university within the meaning of section 3121(b)(10) if its primary function is the presentation of formal instruction, it normally maintains a regular faculty and curriculum, and it normally has a regularly enrolled body of students in attendance at the place where its educational activities are regularly carried on. See section 170(b)(1)(A)(ii) and the regulations thereunder.

(d) Student Status—general rule. Whether an employee has the status of a student performing the services shall be determined based on the relationship of the employee with the organization employing the employee. In order to have the status of a student, the employee must perform services in the employ of a school, college, or university within the meaning of paragraph (c) of this section at which the employee is enrolled and regularly attending classes in pursuit of a course of study within the meaning of paragraphs (d)(1) and (2) of this section. In addition, the employee's services must be incident to and for the purpose of pursuing a course of study within the meaning of paragraph (d)(3) of this section at such school, college, or university. An employee who performs services in the employ of an affiliated organization within the meaning of paragraph (a)(2) of this section must be enrolled and regularly attending classes at the affiliated school, college, or university within the meaning of paragraph (c) of this section in pursuit of a course of study within the meaning of paragraphs (d)(1) and (2) of this section. In addition, the employee's services must be incident to and for the purpose of pursuing a course of study within the meaning of paragraph (d)(3) of this section at such school, college, or university.

(1) Enrolled and regularly attending classes. An employee must be enrolled and regularly attending classes at a school, college, or university within the meaning of paragraph (c) of this section at which the employee is employed to have the status of a student within the meaning of section 3121(b)(10). An employee is enrolled within the meaning of section 3121(b)(10) if the employee is registered for a course or courses creditable toward an educational credential described in paragraph (d)(2) of this section. In addition, the employee must be regularly attending classes to have the status of a student. For purposes of this paragraph (d)(1), a class is an instructional activity led by a faculty member or other qualified individual hired by the school, college, or university within the meaning of paragraph (c) of this section for identified students following an established curriculum. Traditional classroom activities are not the sole means of satisfying this requirement. For example, research activities under the supervision of a faculty advisor necessary to complete the requirements for a Ph.D. degree may constitute classes within the meaning of section 3121(b)(10). The frequency of these and similar activities determines whether an employee may be considered to be regularly attending classes.

(2) Course of study. An employee must be pursuing a course of study in order to have the status of a student. A course of study is one or more courses the completion of which fulfills the requirements necessary to receive an educational credential granted by a school, college, or university within the meaning of paragraph (c) of this section. For purposes of this paragraph, an educational credential is a degree, certificate, or other recognized educational credential granted by an organization described in paragraph (c) of this section. A course of study also includes one or more courses at a school, college or university within the meaning of paragraph (c) of this section the completion of which fulfills the requirements necessary for the employee to sit for an examination required to receive certification by a recognized organization in a field.

(3) Incident to and for the purpose of pursuing a course of study. (i) General rule. An employee's services must be incident to and for the purpose of pursuing a course of study in order for the employee to have the status of a student. Whether an employee's services are incident to and for the purpose of pursuing a course of study shall be determined on the basis of the relationship of the employee with the organization for which such services are performed as an employee. The educational aspect of the relationship between the employer and the employee, as compared to the service aspect of the relationship, must be predominant in order for the employee's services to be incident to and for the purpose of pursuing a course of study. The educational aspect of the relationship is evaluated based on all the relevant facts and circumstances related to the educational aspect of the relationship. The service aspect of the relationship is evaluated based on all the relevant facts and circumstances related to the employee's employment. The evaluation of the service aspect of the relationship is not affected by the fact that the services performed by the employee may have an educational, instructional, or training aspect. Except as provided in paragraph (d)(3)(iii) of this section, whether the educational aspect or the service aspect of an employee's relationship with the employer is predominant is determined by considering all the relevant facts and circumstances. Relevant factors in evaluating the educational and service aspects of an employee's relationship with the employer are described in paragraphs (d)(3)(iv) and (v) of this section respectively. There may be facts and circumstances that are relevant in evaluating the educational and service aspects of the relationship in addition to those described in paragraphs (d)(3)(iv) and (v) of this section.

(ii) Student status determined with respect to each academic term. Whether an employee's services are incident to and for the purpose of pursuing a course of study is determined separately with respect to each academic term. If the relevant facts and circumstances with respect to an employee's relationship with the employer change significantly during an academic term, whether the employee's services are incident to and for the purpose of pursuing a course of study is reevaluated with respect to services performed during the remainder of the academic term.

(iii) Full-time employee. The services of a full-time employee are not incident to and for the purpose of pursuing a course of study. The determination of whether an employee is a full-time employee is based on the employer's standards and practices, except regardless of the employer's classification of the employee, an employee whose normal work schedule is 40 hours or more per week is considered a full-time employee. An employee's normal work schedule is not affected by increases in hours worked caused by work demands unforeseen at the start of an academic term. However, whether an employee is a full-time employee is reevaluated for the remainder of the academic term if the employee changes employment positions with the employer. An employee's work schedule during academic breaks is not considered in determining whether the employee's normal work schedule is 40 hours or more per week. The determination of an employee's normal work schedule is not affected by the fact that the services performed by the employee may have an educational, instructional, or training aspect.

(iv) Evaluating educational aspect. The educational aspect of an employee's relationship with the employer is evaluated based on all the relevant facts and circumstances related to the educational aspect of the relationship. The educational aspect of an employee's relationship with the employer is generally evaluated based on the employee's course workload. Whether an employee's course workload is sufficient in order for the employee's employment to be incident to and for the purpose of pursuing a course of study depends on the particular facts and circumstances. A relevant factor in evaluating an employee's course workload is the employee's course workload relative to a full-time course workload at the school, college or university within the meaning of paragraph (c) of this section at which the employee is enrolled and regularly attending classes.

(v) Evaluating service aspect. The service aspect of an employee's relationship with the employer is evaluated based on the facts and circumstances related to the employee's employment. Services of an employee with the status of a full-time employee within the meaning of paragraph (d)(3)(iii) of this section are not incident to and for the purpose of pursuing a course of study. Relevant factors in evaluating the service aspect of an employee's relationship with the employer are described in paragraphs (d)(3)(v)(A), (B), and (C) of this section.

(A) Normal work schedule and hours worked. If an employee is not a full-time employee within the meaning of paragraph (d)(3)(iii) of this section, then the employee's normal work schedule and number of hours worked per week are relevant factors in evaluating the service aspect of the employee's relationship with the employer. As an employee's normal work schedule or actual number of hours worked approaches 40 hours per week, it is more likely that the service aspect of the employee's relationship with the employer is predominant. The determination of an employee's normal work schedule and actual number of hours worked is not affected by the fact that some of the services performed by the employee may have an educational, instructional, or training aspect.

(B) Professional employee.

(1) If an employee has the status of a professional employee, then that suggests the service aspect of the employee's relationship with the employer is predominant. A professional employee is an employee—

(i) Whose primary duty consists of the performance of work requiring knowledge of an advanced type in a field of science or learning customarily acquired by a prolonged course of specialized intellectual instruction and study, as distinguished from a general academic education, from an apprenticeship, and from training in the performance of routine mental, manual, or physical processes;

(ii) Whose work requires the consistent exercise of discretion and judgment in its performance; and

(iii) Whose work is predominantly intellectual and varied in character (as opposed to routine mental, manual, mechanical, or physical work) and is of such character that the output produced or the result accomplished cannot be standardized in relation to a given period of time.

(2) Licensed, professional employee. If an employee is a licensed, professional employee, then that further suggests the service aspect of the employee's relationship with the employer is predominant. An employee is a licensed, professional employee if the employee is required to be licensed under state or local law to work in the field in which the employee performs services and the employee is a professional employee within the meaning of paragraph (d)(3)(v)(B)(1) of this section.

(C) Employment Benefits. Whether an employee is eligible to receive one or more employment benefits is a relevant factor in evaluating the service aspect of an employee's relationship with the employer. For example, eligibility to receive vacation, paid holiday, and paid sick leave benefits; eligibility to participate in a retirement plan or arrangement described in sections 401(a), 403(b), or 457(a); or eligibility to receive employment benefits such as reduced tuition (other than qualified tuition reduction under section 117(d)(5) provided to a teaching or research assistant who is a graduate student), or benefits under sections 79 (life insurance), 127 (qualified educational assistance), 129 (dependent care assistance programs), or 137 (adoption assistance) suggest that the service aspect of an employee's relationship with the employer is predominant. Eligibility to receive health insurance employment benefits is not considered in determining whether the service aspect of an employee's relationship with the employer is predominant. The weight to be given the fact that an employee is eligible for a particular employment benefit may vary depending on the type of benefit. For example, eligibility to participate in a retirement plan is generally more significant than eligibility to receive a dependent care employment benefit. Additional weight is given to the fact that an employee is eligible to receive an employment benefit if the benefit is generally provided by the employer to employees in positions generally held by non-students. Less weight is given to the fact that an employee is eligible to receive an employment benefit if eligibility for the benefit is mandated by state or local law.

(e) Examples. The following examples illustrate the principles of paragraphs (a) through (d) of this section:

Example (1). (i) Employee C is employed by State University T to provide services as a clerk in T's administrative offices, and is enrolled and regularly attending classes at T in pursuit of a B.S. degree in biology. C has a course workload during the academic term which constitutes a full-time course workload at T. C is considered a part-time employee by T during the academic term, and C's normal work schedule is 20 hours per week, but occasionally due to work demands unforeseen at the start of the academic term C works 40 hours or more during a week. C is compensated by hourly wages, and receives no other compensation or employment benefits.

(ii) In this example, C is employed by T, a school, college, or university within the meaning of paragraph (c) of this section. C is enrolled and regularly attending classes at T in pursuit of a course of study. C is not a full-time employee based on T's standards, and C's normal work schedule does not cause C to have the status of a full-time employee, even though C may occasionally work 40 hours or more during a week due to unforeseen work demands. C's part-time employment relative to C's full-time course workload indicates that the educational aspect of C's relationship with T is predominant. Additional facts supporting this conclusion are that C is not a professional employee, and C does not receive any employment benefits. Thus, C's services are incident to and for the purpose of pursuing a course of study. Accordingly, C's services are excepted from employment under section 3121(b)(10).

Example (2). (i) Employee D is employed in the accounting department of University U, and is enrolled and regularly attending classes at U in pursuit of an M.B.A. degree. D has a course workload which constitutes a half-time course workload at U. D is considered a full-time employee by U under U's standards and practices.

(ii) In this example, D is employed by U, a school, college, or university within the meaning of paragraph (c) of this section. In addition, D is enrolled and regularly attending classes at U in pursuit of a course of study. However, because D is considered a full-time employee by U under its standards and practices, D's services are not incident to and for the purpose of pursuing a course of study. Accordingly, D's services are not excepted from employment under section 3121(b)(10).

Example (3). (i) The facts are the same as in Example 2, except that D is not considered a full-time employee by U, and D's normal work schedule is 32 hours per week. In addition, D's work is repetitive in nature and does not require the consistent exercise of discretion and judgment, and is not predominantly intellectual and varied in character. However, D receives vacation, sick leave, and paid holiday employment benefits, and D is eligible to participate in a retirement plan maintained by U described in section 401(a).

(ii) In this example, D's half-time course workload relative to D's hours worked and eligibility for employment benefits indicates that the service aspect of D's relationship with U is predominant, and thus D's services are not incident to and for the purpose of pursuing a course of study. Accordingly, D's services are not excepted from employment under section 3121(b)(10).

Example (4). (i) Employee E is employed by University V to provide patient care services at a teaching hospital that is an unincorporated division of V. These services are performed as part of a medical residency program in a medical specialty sponsored by V. The residency program in which E participates is accredited by the Accreditation Counsel for Graduate Medical Education. Upon completion of the program, E will receive a certificate of completion, and be eligible to sit for an examination required to be certified by a recognized organization in the medical specialty. E's normal work schedule, which includes services having an educational, instructional, or training aspect, is 40 hours or more per week.

(ii) In this example, E is employed by V, a school, college, or university within the meaning of paragraph (c) of this section. However, E's normal work schedule calls for E to perform services 40 or more hours per week. E is therefore a full-time employee, and the fact that some of E's services have an educational, instructional, or training aspect does not affect that conclusion. Thus, E's services are not incident to and for the purpose of pursuing a course of study. Accordingly, E's services are not excepted from employment under section 3121(b)(10) and there is no need to consider other relevant factors, such as whether E is a professional employee or whether E is eligible for employment benefits.

Example (5). (i) Employee F is employed in the facilities management department of University W. F has a B.S. degree in engineering, and is completing the work experience required to sit for an examination to become a professional engineer eligible for licensure under state or local law. F is not attending classes at W.

(ii) In this example, F is employed by W, a school, college, or university within the meaning of paragraph (c) of this section. However, F is not enrolled and regularly attending classes at W in pursuit of a course of study. F's work experience required to sit for the examination is not a course of study for purposes of paragraph (d)(2) of this section. Accordingly, F's services are not excepted from employment under section 3121(b)(10).

Example (6). (i) Employee G is employed by Employer X as an apprentice in a skilled trade. X is a subcontractor providing services in the field in which G wishes to specialize. G is pursuing a certificate in the skilled trade from Community College C. G is performing services for X pursuant to an internship program sponsored by C under which its students gain experience, and receive credit toward a certificate in the trade.

(ii) In this example, G is employed by X. X is not a school, college or university within the meaning of paragraph (c) of this section. Thus, the exception from employment under section 3121(b)(10) is not available with respect to G's services for X.

Example (7). (i) Employee H is employed by a cosmetology school Y at which H is enrolled and regularly attending classes in pursuit of a certificate of completion. Y's primary function is to carry on educational activities to prepare its students to work in the field of cosmetology. Prior to issuing a certificate, Y requires that its students gain experience in cosmetology services by performing services for the general public on Y's premises. H is scheduled to work and in fact works significantly less than 30 hours per week. H's work does not require knowledge of an advanced type in a field of science or learning, nor is it predominantly intellectual and varied in character. H receives remuneration in the form of hourly compensation from Y for providing cosmetology services to clients of Y, and does not receive any other compensation and is not eligible for employment benefits provided by Y.

(ii) In this example, H is employed by Y, a school, college or university within the meaning of paragraph (c) of this section, and is enrolled and regularly attending classes at Y in pursuit of a course of study. Factors indicating the educational aspect of H's relationship with Y is predominant are that H's hours worked are significantly less than 30 per week, H is not a professional employee, and H is not eligible for employment benefits. Based on the relevant facts and circumstances, the educational aspect of H's relationship with Y is predominant. Thus, H's services are incident to and for the purpose of pursuing a course of study. Accordingly, H's services are excepted from employment under section 3121(b)(10).

Example (8). (i) Employee J is a graduate teaching assistant at University Z. J is enrolled and regularly attending classes at Z in pursuit of a graduate degree. J has a course workload which constitutes a full-time course workload at Z. J's normal work schedule is 20 hours per week, but occasionally due to work demands unforeseen at the start of the academic term J works more than 40 hours during a week. J's duties include grading quizzes and exams pursuant to guidelines set forth by the professor, providing class and laboratory instruction pursuant to a lesson plan developed by the professor, and preparing laboratory equipment for demonstrations. J receives a cash stipend and employment benefits in the form of eligibility to make elective employee contributions to an arrangement described in section 403(b). In addition, J receives qualified tuition reduction benefits within the meaning of section 117(d)(5) with respect to the tuition charged for the credits earned for being a graduate teaching assistant.

(ii) In this example, J is employed by Z, a school, college, or university within the meaning of paragraph (c) of this section, and is enrolled and regularly attending classes at Z in pursuit of a course of study. J's full-time course workload relative to J's normal work schedule of 20 hours per week indicates that the educational aspect of J's relationship with Z is predominant. In addition, J is not a professional employee because J's work does not require the consistent exercise of discretion and judgment in its performance. On the other hand, the fact that J receives employment benefits in the form of eligibility to make elective employee contributions to an arrangement described in section 403(b) indicates that the employment aspect of J's relationship with Z is predominant. Balancing the relevant facts and circumstances, the educational aspect of J's relationship with Z is predominant. Thus, J's services are incident to and for the purpose of pursuing a course of study. Accordingly, J services are excepted from employment under section 3121(b)(10).

(f) Effective date. Paragraphs (a), (b), (c), (d) and (e) of this section apply to services performed on or after April 1, 2005.

(g) For provisions relating to domestic service performed by a student in a local college club, or local chapter of a college fraternity or sorority, see § 31.3121(b)(2)-1.

T.D. 6190, 7/13/56, amend T.D. 6516, 12/19/60, T.D. 7373, 7/23/75, T.D. 9167, 12/20/2004.

§ 31.3121(b)(11)-1 Services in the employ of a foreign government.

(a) Services performed by an employee in the employ of a foreign government are excepted from employment. The exception includes not only services performed by ambassadors, ministers, and other diplomatic officers and employees but also services performed as a consular or other officer or employee of a foreign government, or as a nondiplomatic representative thereof.

(b) For purposes of this exception, the citizenship or residence of the employee is immaterial. It is also immaterial whether the foreign government grants an equivalent exemption with respect to similar services performed in the foreign country by citizens of the United States.

T.D. 6190, 7/13/56, amend T.D. 6516, 12/19/60.

§ 31.3121(b)(12)-1 Services in employ of wholly owned instrumentality of foreign government.

(a) Services performed by an employee in the employ of certain instrumentalities of a foreign government are excepted from employment. The exception includes all services performed in the employ of an instrumentality of the government of a foreign country, if—

(1) The instrumentality is wholly owned by the foreign government;

(2) The services are of a character similar to those performed in foreign countries by employees of the United States Government or of an instrumentality thereof; and

(3) The Secretary of State certifies to the Secretary of the Treasury that the foreign government, with respect to whose instrumentality and employees thereof exemption is claimed, grants, an equivalent exemption with respect to services performed in the foreign country by employees of the United States Government and of instrumentalities thereof.

(b) For purposes of this exception, the citizenship or residence of the employee is immaterial.

T.D. 6190, 7/13/56, amend T.D. 6516, 12/19/60.

§ 31.3121(b)(13)-1 Services of student nurse or hospital intern.

(a) Services performed as a student nurse in the employ of a hospital or a nurses training school are excepted from employment, if the student nurse is enrolled and regularly attending classes in a nurses training school and such nurses training school is chartered or approved pursuant to State law.

(b) Services performed before 1966 as an intern (as distinguished from a resident doctor), in the employ of a hospital are excepted from employment, if the intern has completed a 4 year course in a medical school chartered or approved pursuant to State law.

T.D. 6190, 7/13/56, amend T.D. 6516, 12/19/60, T.D. 6983, 12/3/68.

§ 31.3121(b)(14)-1 Services in delivery or distribution of newspapers, shopping news, or magazines.

(a) Services of individuals under age 18. Services performed by an employee under the age of 18 in the delivery or distribution of newspapers or shopping news, not including delivery or distribution (as, for example, by a regional distributor) to any point for subsequent delivery or distribution, are excepted from employment. Thus, the services performed by an employee under the age of 18 in making house-to-house delivery or sale of newspapers or shopping news, including handbills and other similar types of advertising material, are excepted from employment. The services are excepted irrespective of the form or method of compensation. Incidental services by the employee who makes the house-to-house delivery, such as services in assembling newspapers, are considered to be within the exception. The exception continues only during the time that the employee is under the age of 18.

(b) Services of individuals of any age. Services performed by an employee in, and at the time of, the sale of newspapers or magazines to ultimate consumers under an arrangement under which the newspapers or magazines are to be sold by him at a fixed price, his compensation being based on the retention of the excess of such price over the amount at which the newspapers or magazines are charged to him, are excepted from employment. The services are excepted whether or not the employee is guaranteed a minimum amount of compensation for such services, or is entitled to be credited with the unsold newspapers or magazines turned back. Moreover, the services are excepted without regard to the age of the employee. Services performed other than at the time of sale to the ultimate consumer are not within the exception. Thus, the services of a regional distributor which are antecedent to but not immediately part of the sale to the ultimate consumer are not within the exception. However, incidental services by the employee who makes the sale to the ultimate consumer, such as services in assembling newspapers or in taking newspapers or magazines to the place of sale, are considered to be within the exception.

T.D. 6190, 7/13/56, amend T.D. 6516, 12/19/60.

§ 31.3121(b)(15)-1 Services in employ of international organization.

(a) Subject to the provisions of section 1 of the International Organizations Immunities Act (22 U.S.C. 288), services performed in the employ of an international organization as defined in section 7701(a)(18) are excepted from employment.

(b) *(1)* Section 7701(a)(18) provides as follows:

Sec. 7701. Definitions. (a) When used in this title, where not otherwise distinctly expressed or manifestly incompatible with the intent thereof—

* * * * * *

(18) International organization. The term "international organization" means a public international organization entitled to enjoy privileges, exemptions, and immunities as an international organization under the International Organizations Immunities Act (22 U.S.C. 288-288f).

(2) Section 1 of the International Organizations Immunities Act provides as follows:

Sec. 1 [International Organizations Immunities Act.] For the purposes of this title [International Organizations Immunities Act], the term "international organization" means a public international organization in which the United States participates pursuant to any treaty or under the authority of any Act of Congress authorizing such participation or making an appropriation for such participation, and which shall have been designated by the President through appropriate Executive order as being entitled to enjoy the privileges, exemptions, and immunities herein provided. The President shall be authorized, in the light of the functions performed by any such international organization, by appropriate Executive order to withhold or withdraw from any such organization or its officers or employees any of the privileges, exemptions, and immunities provided for in this title (including the amendments made by this title) or to condition or limit the enjoyment by any such organization or its officers or employees of any such privilege, exemption, or immunity. The President shall be authorized, if in his judgment such action should be justified by reason of the abuse by an international organization or its officers and employees of the privileges, exemptions, and immunities herein provided or for any other reason, at any time to revoke the designation of any international organization under this section, whereupon the international organization in question shall cease to be classed as an international organization for the purposes of this title.

T.D. 6190, 7/13/56, amend T.D. 6516, 12/19/60.

§ 31.3121(b)(16)-1 Services performed under share-farming arrangement.

(a) The term "employment" does not include services performed by an individual under an arrangement with the owner or tenant of land pursuant to which—

(1) Such individual undertakes to produce agricultural or horticultural commodities (including livestock, bees, poultry, and fur-bearing animals and wildlife) on such land,

(2) The agricultural or horticultural commodities produced by such individual, or the proceeds therefrom, are to be divided between such individual and such owner or tenant, and

(3) The amount of such individual's share depends on the amount of the agricultural or horticultural commodities produced.

For purposes of this exception, the arrangement pursuant to which the individual's services are performed must meet the specified statutory conditions.

(b) If the arrangement between the parties provides that the individual who undertakes to produce a crop or livestock is to be compensated at a specified rate of pay or is to receive a fixed sum of money or a stipulated quantity of the commodities to be produced, without regard to the amount actually produced, as distinguished from a proportionate share of the crop or livestock, or the proceeds therefrom, the services performed by such individual in the production of such crop or livestock is not within the exception.

(c) For provisions relating to the status, under the Self-Employment Contributions Act of 1954, of the services which are excepted from "employment" under this section, see the regulations under section 1402(a) in Part 1 of this chapter (Income Tax Regulations).

T.D. 6744, 7/1/64.

§ 31.3121(b)(17)-1 Services in employ of Communist organization.

The term "employment" does not include services performed in the employ of any organization in any calendar quarter beginning after June 30, 1956, and during any part of which such organization is registered, or there is in effect a final order of the Subversive Activities Control Board requiring such organization to register, under the Internal Security Act of 1950 (50 U.S.C. *781 et seq.),* as amended, as a Communist-action organization, a Communist-front organization, or a Communist-infiltrated organization.

T.D. 6744, 7/1/64.

§ 31.3121(b)(18)-1 Services performed by a resident of the Republic of the Philippines while temporarily in Guam.

(a) Services performed after 1960 by a resident of the Republic of the Philippines while in Guam on a temporary basis as a nonimmigrant alien admitted to Guam pursuant to section 101(a)(15)(H)(ii) of the Immigration and Nationality Act (8 U.S.C. 1101) are excepted from employment.

(b) Section 101(a)(15)(H) of the Immigration and Nationality Act provides as follows:

Sec. 101. Definitions. [Immigration and Nationality Act (66 Stat. 166)]

(a) As used in this chapter—

* * * * *

(15) The term "immigrant" means every alien except an alien who is within one of the following classes of nonimmigrant aliens—

* * * * *

(H) An alien having a residence in a foreign country which he has no intention of abandoning (i) who is of distinguished merit and ability and who is coming temporarily to the United States to perform temporary services of an exceptional nature requiring merit and ability; or (ii) who is coming temporarily to the United States to perform other temporary services or labor, if unemployed persons capable of performing such service or labor cannot be found in this country; or (iii) who is coming temporarily to the United States as an industrial trainee; * * *

T.D. 6744, 7/1/64.

§ 31.3121(b)(19)-1 Services of certain nonresident aliens.

(a) *(1)* Services performed after 1961 by a nonresident alien individual who is temporarily present in the United States as a nonimmigrant under subparagraph (F) or (J) of section 101(a)(15) of the Immigration and Nationality Act (8 U.S.C. 1101), as amended, are excepted from employment if the services are performed to carry out a purpose for which the individual was admitted. For purposes of this section an alien individual who is temporarily present in the United States as a nonimmigrant under such subparagraph (F) or (J) is deemed to be a nonresident alien individual. The preceding sentence does not apply to the extent it is inconsistent with section 7701(b) and the regulations under that section. A nonresident alien individual who is temporarily present in the United States as a nonimmigrant under such subparagraph (J) includes an alien individual admitted to the United States as an "exchange visitor" under section 201 of the United States Information and Educational Exchange Act of 1948 (22 U.S.C. 1446).

(2) If services are performed by a nonresident alien individual's alien spouse or minor child, who is temporarily present in the United States as a nonimmigrant under subparagraph (F) or (J) of section 101(a)(15) of the Immigration and Nationality Act, as amended, the services are not deemed for purposes of this section to be performed to carry out a purpose for which such individual was admitted. The services of such spouse or child are excepted from employment under this section only if the spouse or child was admitted for a purpose specified in such subparagraph (F) or (J) and if the services are performed to carry out such purpose.

(b) Section 101 of the Immigration and Nationality Act (8 U.S.C. 1101), as amended, provides in part as follows:

Sec. 101. Definitions. [Immigration and Nationality Act (66 Stat. 166)]

(a) As used in this chapter— * * * *(15)* The term "immigrant" means every alien except an alien who is within one of the following classes of nonimmigrant aliens—

* * * * * (F)(i) An alien having a residence in a foreign country which he has no intention of abandoning, who is a bona fide student qualified to pursue a full course of study and who seeks to enter the United States temporarily and solely for the purpose of pursuing such a course of study at an established institution of learning or other recognized place of study in the United States, particularly designated by him and approved by the Attorney General after consultation with the Office of Education of the United States, which institution or place of study shall have agreed to report to the Attorney General the termination of attendance of each nonimmigrant student, and if any such institution of learning or place of study fails to make reports promptly the approval shall be withdrawn, and (ii) the alien spouse and minor children of any such alien if accompanying him or following to join him;

****** (J) An alien having a residence in a foreign country which he has no intention of abandoning who is a bona fide student, scholar, trainee, teacher, professor, research assistant, specialist, or leader in a field of specialized knowledge or skill, or other person of similar description, who is coming temporarily to the United States as a participant in a program designated by the Secretary of State, for the purpose of teaching, instructing or lecturing, studying, observing, conducting research, consulting, demonstrating special skills, or receiving training, and the alien spouse and minor children of any such alien if accompanying him or following to join him.

* * * * * *

T.D. 6744, 7/1/64, amend T.D. 8411, 4/24/92.

§ 31.3121(b)(20)-1 Service performed on a boat engaged in catching fish.

Caution: The Treasury has not yet amended Reg § 31.3121(b)(20)-1 to reflect changes made by P.L. 104-188.

(a) In general. *(1)* Service performed on or after December 31, 1954, by an individual on a boat engaged in catching fish or other forms of aquatic animal life (hereinafter "fish") are excepted from employment if—

(i) The individual receives a share of the boat's (or boats' for a fishing operation involving more than one boat) catch of fish or a share of the proceeds from the sale of the catch,

(ii) The amount of the individual's share depends solely on the amount of the boat's (or boats' for a fishing operation involving more than one boat) catch of fish,

(iii) The individual does not receive and is not entitled to receive, any cash remuneration, other than remuneration that is described in subdivision (1) of this subparagraph, and

(iv) The crew of the boat (or of each boat from which the individual receives a share of the catch) normally is made up of fewer than 10 individuals.

(2) The requirement of subdivision (ii) of subparagraph (1) is not satisfied if there exists an agreement with the boat's (or boats') owner or operator by which the individual's remuneration is determined partially or fully by a factor not dependent on the size of the catch. For example, if a boat is operated under a remuneration arrangement. e.g., a collective agreement which specifies that crew members, in addition to receiving a share of the catch, are entitled to an hourly cage for repairing nets, regardless of whether this wage is actually paid, then all the crew members covered by the arrangement are entitled to receive cash remuneration other than a share of the catch and their services are not excepted from employment by section 3121(b)(20).

(3) The operating crew of a boat includes all persons on the boat (including the captain) who receive any form of remuneration in exchange for services rendered while on a boat engaged in catching fish. See § 1.6050A-1 for reporting requirements for the operator of a boat engaged in catching fish with respect to individuals performing services described in this section.

(4) During the same return period, service performed by a crew member may be excepted from employment by section 3121(b)(20) and this section for one voyage and not so excepted on a subsequent voyage on the same or on a different boat.

(5) During the same voyage, service performed by one crew member may be excepted from employment by section 3121(b)(20) and this section but service performed by another crew member may not be so excepted.

(b) Special rule. Services performed after December 31, 1954, and before October 4, 1976, on a boat by an individual engaged in catching fish are not excepted from employment for any voyage (for purposes of section 3121(b) and the corresponding regulations), even though the individual satisfies the requirements of subdivisions (i) through (iv) of paragraph (a)(1) of this section, if the owner or operator of the boat engaged in catching fish treated the individual as an employee. For purposes of this subparagraph, the individual was treated as an employee if—

(1) Form 941 was voluntarily filed by the boat operator or owner, regardless of whether the tax imposed by chapter 21 withheld. For purposes of this subdivision, the filing of Form 941 is not voluntary if the filing was the result of action taken by the Service pursuant to section 6651(a) (relating to addition to the tax for failure file tax return or to pay tax);

(2) The boat owner or operator withheld from the individual's share the tax imposed by chapter 21, regardless of whether the tax was paid over to the Service; or

(3) The boat owner or operator made full or partial payment of the tax imposed by chapter 21, unless the payment was made pursuant to section 7422(a) (relating to no civil actions for refund prior to filing claim for refund). However, for purposes of this paragraph crew members whose services, but for subdivisions (i) through (iii) would have been

excepted from employment by section 3121(b)(20) are not required to pay self-employment tax on income earned in performing those services. See § 1.1402(c)-3(g). Moreover, in such cases the employer is not entitled to a refund of the employer's share of any tax imposed by chapter 21 that was paid.

T.D. 7716, 8/26/80.

§ 31.3121(c)-1 Included and excluded services.

(a) If a portion of the services performed by an employee for an employer during a pay period constitutes employment, and the remainder does not constitute employment, all the services performed by the employee for the employer during the period shall for purposes of the taxes be treated alike, that is, either all as included or all as excluded. The time during which the employee performs services which under section 3121(b) constitute employment, and the time during which he performs services which under such section do not constitute employment, within the pay period, determine whether all the services during the pay period shall he deemed to be included or excluded.

(b) If one-half or more of the employee's time in the employ of a particular person in a pay period is spent in performing services which constitute employment, then all the services of that employee for that period in that pay period shall be deemed to be employment.

(c) If less than one-half of the employee's time in the employ of a particular person in a pay period is spent in performing services which constitute employment, then none of the services of that employee for that person in that pay period shall be deemed to be employment.

(d) The application of the provisions of paragraphs (a), (b), and (c) of this section may be illustrated by the following example:

Example. The AB Club, which is a local college club within the meaning of section 3121(b)(2), employs D, a student who is enrolled and is regularly attending classes at a university, to perform domestic service for the club and to keep the club's books. The domestic services performed by D for the AB Club do not constitute employment, and his services as the club's bookkeeper constitute employment. D receives a payment at the end of each month for all services which he performs for the club. During a particular month D spends 60 hours in performing domestic service for the club and 40 hours as the club's bookkeeper. None of D's services during the month are deemed to be employment, since less than one-half of his services during the month constitutes employment. During another month D spends 35 hours in the performance of domestic services and 60 hours in keeping the club's books. All of D's services during the month are deemed to be employment, since one-half or more of his services during the month constitutes employment.

(e) For purposes of this section, a "pay period" is the period (of not more than 31 consecutive calendar days) for which a payment of remuneration is ordinarily made to the employee by the employer. Thus, if the periods for which payments of remuneration are made to the employee by the employer are of uniform duration, each such period constitutes a "pay period". If, however, the periods occasionally vary in duration, the "pay period" is the period for which a payment of remuneration is ordinarily made to the employee by the employer, even though that period does not coincide with the actual period for which a particular payment of remuneration is made. For example, if an employer ordinarily pays a particular employee for each calendar week at the end of the week, but the employee receives a payment in the middle of the week for the portion of the week already elapsed and receives the remainder at the end of the week, the "pay period" is still the calendar week; or if, instead, that employee is sent on a trip by such employer and receives at the end of the third week a single remuneration payment for three weeks' services, the "pay period" is still the calendar week.

(f) If there is only one period (and such period does not exceed 31 consecutive calendar days) for which a payment of remuneration is made to the employee by the employer, such period is deemed to be a "pay period" for purposes of this section.

(g) The rules set forth in this section do not apply (1) with respect to any services performed by the employee for the employer if the periods for which such employer makes payments of remuneration to the employee vary to the extent that there is no period "for which a payment of remuneration is ordinarily made to the employee", or (2) with respect to any services performed by the employee for the employer if the period for which a payment of remuneration is ordinarily made to the employee by such employer exceeds 31 consecutive calendar days, or (3) with respect to any service performed by the employee for the employer during a pay period if any of such service is excepted by section 3121(b)(9) (see § 31.3121(b)(9)-1).

(h) If during any period for which a person makes a payment of remuneration to an employee only a portion of the employee's services constitutes employment, but the rules prescribed in this section are not applicable, the taxes attach with respect to such services as constitute employment as defined in section 3121(b).

T.D. 6190, 7/13/56, amend T.D. 6516, 12/19/60, T.D. 6744, 7/1/64.

§ 31.3121(d)-1 Who are employees.

Caution: The Treasury has not yet amended Reg § 31.3121(d)-1 to reflect changes made by P.L. 105-34.

(a) In general. *(1)* Whether an individual is an employee with respect to services performed after 1954 is determined in accordance with section 3121(d) and (o) and section 3506. This section of the regulations applies with respect only to services performed after 1954. Whether an individual is an employee with respect to services performed after 1936 and before 1940 shall be determined in accordance with the applicable provisions of law and of 26 CFR (1939) Part 401 (Regulations 91). Whether an individual is an employee with respect to services performed after 1939 and before 1951 shall be determined in accordance with the applicable provisions of law and of 26 CFR (1939) Part 402 (Regulations 106). Whether an individual is an employee with respect to services performed after 1950 and before 1955 shall be determined in accordance with the applicable provisions of law and of 26 CFR (1939) Part 408 (Regulations 128).

(2) Section 3121(d) contains three separate and independent tests for determining who are employees. Paragraphs (b), (c), and (d) of this section relate to the respective tests. Paragraph (b) relates to the test for determining whether an officer of a corporation is an employee of the corporation. Paragraph (c) relates to the test for determining whether an individual is an employee under the usual common law rules. Paragraph (d) relates to the test for determining which individuals in certain occupational groups who are not em-

ployees under the usual common law rules are included as employees. If an individual is an employee under any one of the tests, he is to be considered an employee for purposes of the regulations in this subpart whether or not he is an employee under any of the other tests.

(3) If the relationship of employer and employee exists, the designation or description of the relationship by the parties as anything other than that of employer and employee is immaterial. Thus, if such relationship exists, it is of no consequence that the employee is designated as a partner, coadventurer, agent, independent contractor, or the like.

(4) All classes or grades of employees are included within the relationship of employer and employee. Thus, superintendents, managers, and other supervisory personnel are employees.

(5) Although an individual may be an employee under this section, his services may be of such a nature, or performed under such circumstances, as not to constitute employment (see § 31.3121(b)-3).

(b) Corporate officers. Generally, an officer of a corporation is an employee of the corporation. However, an officer of a corporation who as such does not perform any services or performs only minor services and who neither receives nor is entitled to receive, directly or indirectly, any remuneration is considered not to be an employee of the corporation. A director of a corporation in his capacity as such is not an employee of the corporation.

(c) Common law employees. *(1)* Every individual is an employee if under the usual common law rules the relationship between him and the person for whom he performs services is the legal relationship of employer and employee.

(2) Generally such relationship exists when the person for whom services are performed has the right to control and direct the individual who performs the services, not only as to the result to be accomplished by the work but also as to the details and means by which that result is accomplished. That is, an employee is subject to the will and control of the employer not only as to what shall be done but how it shall be done. In this connection, it is not necessary that the employer actually direct or control the manner in which the services are performed; it is sufficient if he has the right to do so. The right to discharge is also an important factor indicating that the person possessing that right is an employer. Other factors characteristic of an employer, but not necessarily present in every case, are the furnishing of tools and the furnishing of a place to work, to the individual who performs the services. In general, if an individual is subject to the control or direction of another merely as to the result to be accomplished by the work and not as to the means and methods for accomplishing the result, he is an independent contractor. An individual performing services as an independent contractor is not as to such services an employee under the usual common law rules. Individuals such as physicians, lawyers, dentists, veterinarians, construction contractors, public stenographers, and auctioneers, engaged in the pursuit of an independent trade, business, or profession, in which they offer their services to the public, are independent contractors and not employees.

(3) Whether the relationship of employer and employee exists under the usual common law rules will in doubtful cases be determined upon an examination of the particular facts of each case.

(d) Special classes of employees. *(1)* In addition to individuals who are employees under paragraph (b) or (c) of this section, other individuals are employees if they perform services for remuneration under certain prescribed circumstances in the following occupational groups:

(i) As an agent-driver or commission-driver engaged in distributing meat products, vegetable products, fruit products, bakery products, beverages (other than milk), or laundry or dry-cleaning services for his principal;

(ii) As a full-time life insurance salesman;

(iii) As a home worker performing work, according to specifications furnished by the person for whom the services are performed, on materials or goods furnished by such person which are required to be returned to such person or a person designated by him; or

(iv) As a traveling or city salesman, other than as an agent-driver or commission-driver, engaged upon a full-time basis in the solicitation on behalf of, and the transmission to, his principal (except for side-line sales activities on behalf of some other person) of orders from wholesalers, retailers, contractors, or operators of hotels, restaurants, or other similar establishments for merchandise for resale or supplies for use in their business operations.

(2) In order for an individual to be an employee under this paragraph, the individual must perform services in an occupation falling within one of the enumerated groups. If the individual does not perform services in one of the designated occupational groups, he is not an employee under this paragraph. An individual who is not an employee under this paragraph may nevertheless be an employee under paragraph (b) or (c) of this section. The language used to designate the respective occupational groups relates to fields of endeavor in which particular designations are not necessarily in universal use with respect to the same service. The designations are addressed to the actual services without regard to any technical or colloquial labels which may be attached to such services. Thus, a determination whether services fall within one of the designated occupational groups depends upon the facts of the particular situation.

(3) The factual situations set forth below are illustrative of some of the individuals falling within each of the above enumerated occupational groups. The illustrative factual situations are as follows:

(i) Agent-driver or commission-driver. This occupational group includes agent-drivers or commission-drivers who are engaged in distributing meat or meat products, vegetables or vegetable products, fruit or fruit products, bakery products, beverages (other than milk), or laundry or dry-cleaning services for their principals. An agent-driver or commission-driver includes an individual who operates his own truck or the truck of the person for whom he performs services, serves customers designated by such person as well as those solicited on his own, and whose compensation is a commission on his sales or the difference between the price he charges his customers and the price he pays to such person for the product or service.

(ii) Full-time life insurance salesman. An individual whose entire or principal business activity is devoted to the solicitation of life insurance or annuity contracts, or both, primarily for one life insurance company is a full-time life insurance salesman. Such a salesman ordinarily uses the office space provided by the company or its general agent, and stenographic assistance, telephone facilities, forms, rate books, and advertising materials are usually made available to him without cost. An individual who is engaged in the general insurance business under a contract or contracts of service which do not contemplate that the individual's principal business activity will be the solicitation of life insurance or annuity contracts, or both, for one company, or any individual who devotes only part time to the solicitation of life insurance contracts, including annuity contracts, and is principally engaged in other endeavors, is not a full-time life insurance salesman.

(iii) Home workers. This occupational group includes a worker who performs services off the premises of the person for whom the services are performed, according to specifications furnished by such person, on materials or goods furnished by such person which are required to be returned to such person or a person designated by him. For provisions relating to the determination of wages in the case of a home worker to whom this subdivision is applicable, see § 31.3121(a)(10)-1.

(iv) Traveling or city salesman. (a) This occupational group includes a city or traveling salesman who is engaged upon a full-time basis in the solicitation on behalf of, and the transmission to, his principal (except for side-line sales activities on behalf of some other person or persons) of orders from wholesalers, retailers, contractors, or operators of hotels, restaurants, or other similar establishments for merchandise for resale or supplies for use in their business operations. An agent-driver or commission-driver is not within this occupational group. City or traveling salesmen who sell to retailers or to the others specified, operate off the premises of their principals, and are generally compensated on a commission basis, are within this occupational group. Such salesmen are generally not controlled as to the details of their services or the means by which they cover their territories, but in the ordinary case they are expected to call on regular customers with a fair degree of regularity.

(b) In order for a city or traveling salesman to be included within this occupational group, his entire or principal business activity must be devoted to the solicitation of orders for one principal. Thus, the multiple-line salesman generally is not within this occupational group. However, if the salesman solicits orders primarily for one principal, he is not excluded from this occupational group solely because of side-line sales activities on behalf of one or more other persons. In such a case, the salesman is within this occupational group only with respect to the services performed for the person for whom he primarily solicits orders and not with respect to the services performed for such other persons. The following examples illustrate the application of the foregoing provisions:

Example (1). Salesman A's principal business activity is the solicitation of orders from retail pharmacies on behalf of the X Wholesale Drug Company. A also occasionally solicits orders for drugs on behalf of the Y and Z Companies. A is within this occupational group with respect to his services for the X Company but not with respect to his services for either the Y Company or the Z Company.

Example (2). Salesman B's principal business activity is the solicitation of orders from retail hardware stores on behalf of the R Tool Company and the S Cooking Utensil Company. B regularly solicits orders on behalf of both companies. B is not within this occupational group with respect to the services performed for either the R Company or the S Company.

Example (3). Salesman C's principal business activity is the house-to-house solicitation of orders on behalf of the T Brush Company. C occasionally solicits such orders from retail stores and restaurants. C is not within this occupational group.

(4) (i) The fact that an individual falls within one of the enumerated occupational groups, however, does not make such individual an employee under this paragraph unless (a) the contract of service contemplates that substantially all the services to which the contract relates in the particular designated occupation are to be performed personally by such individual, (b) such individual has no substantial investment in the facilities used in connection with the performance of such services (other than in facilities for transportation) and (c) such services are part of a continuing relationship with the person for whom the services are performed and are not in the nature of a single transaction.

(ii) The term "contract of service", as used in this paragraph, means an arrangement, formal or informal, under which the particular services are performed. The requirement that the contract of service shall contemplate that substantially all the services to which the contract relates in the particular designated occupation are to be performed personally by the individual means that it is not contemplated that any material part of the services to which the contract relates in such occupation will be delegated to any other person by the individual who undertakes under the contract to perform such services.

(iii) The facilities to which reference is made in this paragraph include equipment and premises available for the work or enterprise as distinguished from education, training, and experience, but do not include such tools, instruments, equipment, or clothing, as are commonly or frequently provided by employees. An investment in an automobile by an individual which is used primarily for his own transportation in connection with the performance of services for another person has no significance under this paragraph, since such investment is comparable to outlays for transportation by an individual performing similar services who does not own an automobile. Moreover, the investment in facilities for the transportation of the goods or commodities to which the services relate is to be excluded in determining the investment in a particular case. If an individual has a substantial investment in facilities of the requisite character, he is not an employee within the meaning of this paragraph, since a substantial investment of the requisite character standing alone is sufficient to exclude the individual from the employee concept under this paragraph.

(iv) If the services are not performed as part of a continuing relationship with the person for whom the services are performed, but are in the nature of a single transaction, the individual performing such services is not an employee of such person within the meaning of this paragraph. The fact that the services are not performed on consecutive workdays does not indicate that the services are not performed as part of a continuing relationship.

T.D. 6190, 7/13/56, amend T.D. 6516, 12/19/60, T.D. 6744, 7/1/64, T.D. 7691, 4/8/80.

§ 31.3121(d)-2 Who are employers.

(a) Every person is an employer if he employs one or more employees. Neither the number of employees employed nor the period during which any such employee is employed is material for the purpose of determining whether the person for whom the services are performed is an employer.

(b) An employer may be an individual, a corporation, a partnership, a trust, an estate, a joint-stock company, an association, or a syndicate, group, pool, joint venture, or other unincorporated organization, group, or entity. A trust or estate, rather than the fiduciary acting for on behalf of the trust or estate, is generally the employer.

(c) Although a person may be an employer under this section, services performed in his employ may be of such a nature, or performed under such circumstances, as not to constitute employment (see § 31.3121(b)-3).

T.D. 6190, 7/13/56, amend T.D. 6516, 12/19/60.

§ 31.3121(e)-1 State, United States, and citizen.

(a) When used in the regulations in this subpart, the term "State" includes the District of Columbia, the Commonwealth of Puerto Rico, the Virgin Islands, the Territories of Alaska and Hawaii before their admission as States, and (when used with respect to services performed after 1960) Guam and American Samoa.

(b) When used in the regulations in this subpart, the term "United States", when used in a geographical sense, means the several states (including the Territories of Alaska and Hawaii before their admission as States), the District of Columbia, the Commonwealth of Puerto Rico, and the Virgin Islands. When used in the regulations in this subpart with respect to services performed after 1960, the term "United States" also includes Guam and American Samoa when the term is used in a geographical sense. The term "citizen of the United States" includes a citizen of the Commonwealth of Puerto Rico or the Virgin Islands, and, effective January 1, 1961, a citizen of Guam or American Samoa.

T.D. 6190, 7/13/56, amend T.D. 6516, 12/19/60, T.D. 6744, 7/1/64.

§ 31.3121(f)-1 American vessel and aircraft.

(a) The term "American vessel" means any vessel which is documented (that is, registered, enrolled or licensed) or numbered in conformity with the laws of the United States. It also includes any vessel which is neither documented nor numbered under the laws of the United States, nor documented under the laws of any foreign country, if the crew of such vessel is employed solely by one or more citizens or residents of the United States or corporations organized under the laws of the United States or of any State. (For provisions relating to the terms "State" and "citizen", see § 31.3121(e)-1.)

(b) The term "American aircraft" means any aircraft registered under the laws of the United States.

(c) For provisions relating to services performed outside the United States on or in connection with an American vessel or American aircraft, see paragraph (c)(2) of § 31.3121(b)-3.

T.D. 6190, 7/13/56, amend T.D. 6516, 12/19/60, T.D. 6744, 7/1/64.

§ 31.3121(g)-1 Agricultural labor.

(a) In general. (1) The term "agricultural labor" as defined in section 3121(g) includes services of the character described in paragraphs (b), (c), (d), (e), and (f) of this section. In general, however, the term does not include services performed in connection with forestry, lumbering, or landscaping.

(2) The term "farm" as used in the regulations in this subpart includes stock, dairy, poultry, fruit, fur-bearing animal, and truck farms, plantations, ranches, nurseries, ranges, orchards, and such greenhouses and other similar structures as are used primarily for the raising of agricultural or horticultural commodities. Greenhouses and other similar structures used primarily for other purposes (for example, display, storage, and fabrication of wreaths, corsages, and bouquets) do not constitute "farms".

(3) For provisions relating to the exception from employment provided with respect to services performed by certain foreign agricultural workers and to services performed before 1959 in connection with the production or harvesting of certain oleoresinous products, see § 31.3121(b)(1)-1. For provisions relating to the exclusion from wages of remuneration paid in any medium other than cash for agricultural labor and to the test for determining whether cash remuneration paid for agricultural labor constitutes wages, see § 31.3121(a)(8)-1.

(b) Services described in section 3121(g)(1). *(1)* Services performed on a farm by an employee of any person in connection with any of the following activities constitute agricultural labor:

(i) The cultivation of the soil;

(ii) The raising, shearing, feeding, caring for, training, or management of livestock, bees, poultry, fur-bearing animals, or wildlife; or

(iii) The raising or harvesting of any other agricultural or horticultural commodity.

(2) Services performed in connection with the production or harvesting of maple sap, or in connection with the raising or harvesting of mushrooms, or in connection with the hatching of poultry constitute agricultural labor only if such services are performed on a farm. Thus, services performed in connection with the operation of a hatchery, if not operated as part of a poultry or other farm, do not constitute agricultural labor.

(c) Services described in section 3121(g)(2). *(1)* The following services performed by an employee in the employ of the owner or tenant or other operator of one or more farms constitute agricultural labor, provided the major part of such services is performed on a farm:

(i) Services performed in connection with the operation, management, conservation, improvement, or maintenance of any of such farms or its tools or equipment; or

(ii) Services performed in salvaging timber, or clearing land of brush and other debris, left by a hurricane.

(2) The services described in subparagraph (1)(i) of this paragraph may include, for example, services performed by carpenters, painters, mechanics, farm supervisors, irrigation engineers, bookkeepers, and other skilled or semi-skilled workers, which contribute in any way to the conduct of the farm or farms, as such, operated by the person employing them, as distinguished from any other enterprise in which such person may be engaged.

(3) Since the services described in this paragraph must be performed in the employ of the owner or tenant or other operator of the farm, the term "agricultural labor" does not include services performed by employees of a commercial painting concern, for example, which contracts with a farmer to renovate his farm properties.

(d) Services described in section 3121(g)(3). Services performed by an employee in the employ of any person in connection with any of the following operations constitute agricultural labor without regard to the place where such services are performed:

(1) The ginning of cotton;

(2) The operation or maintenance of ditches, canals, reservoirs, or waterways, not owned or operated for profit, used

exclusively for supplying or storing water for farming purposes; or

(3) The production or harvesting of crude gum (oleoresin) from a living tree or the processing of such crude gum into gum spirits of turpentine and gum rosin, provided such processing is carried on by the original producer of such crude gum.

(e) Services described in section 3121(g)(4). *(1)* Services performed by an employee in the handling, planting, drying, packing, packaging, processing, freezing, grading, storing, or delivering to storage or to market or to a carrier for transportation to market, of any agricultural or horticultural commodity constitute agricultural labor if:

(i) Such services are performed by the employee in the employ of an operator of a farm or in the employ of a group of operators of farms (other than a cooperative organization);

(ii) Such services are performed with respect to the commodity in its unmanufactured state; and

(iii) Such operator produced more than one-half of the commodity with respect to which such services are performed during the pay period, or such group of operators produced all of the commodity with respect to which such services are performed during the pay period.

(2) The term "operator of a farm" as used in this paragraph means an owner, tenant, or other person, in possession of a farm and engaged in the operation of such farm.

(3) The services described in this paragraph do not constitute agricultural labor if performed in the employ of a cooperative organization. The term "organization" includes corporations, joint-stock companies, and associations which are treated as corporations pursuant to section 7701(a)(3) of the Internal Revenue Code. For purposes of this paragraph, any unincorporated group of operators shall be deemed a cooperative organization if the number of operators comprising such group is more than 20 at any time during the calendar quarter in which the services involved are performed.

(4) Processing services which change the commodity from its raw or natural state do not constitute agricultural labor. For example, the extraction of juices from fruits or vegetables is a processing operation which changes the character of the fruits or vegetables from their raw or natural state and, therefore, does not constitute agricultural labor. Likewise, services performed in the processing of maple sap into maple sirup or maple sugar do not constitute agricultural labor. On the other hand, services rendered in the cutting and drying of fruits or vegetables are processing operations which do not change the character of the fruits or vegetables and, therefore, constitute agricultural-labor, if the other requisite conditions are met. Services performed with respect to a commodity after its character has been changed from its raw or natural state by a processing operation do not constitute agricultural labor.

(5) The term "commodity" refers to a single agricultural or horticultural product, for example, all apples are to be treated as a single commodity, while apples and peaches are to be treated as two separate commodities. The services with respect to each such commodity are to be considered separately in determining whether the condition set forth in subparagraph (1)(iii) of this paragraph has been satisfied. The portion of the commodity produced by an operator or group of operators with respect to which the services described in this paragraph are performed by a particular employee shall be determined on the basis of the pay period in which such services were performed by such employee.

(6) The services described in this paragraph do not include services performed in connection with commercial canning or commercial freezing or in connection with any commodity after its delivery to a terminal market for distribution for consumption. Moreover, since the services described in this paragraph must be rendered in, the actual handling, planting, drying, packing, packaging, processing, freezing, grading, storing, or delivering to storage or to market or to a carrier for transportation to market, of the commodity, such services do not, for example, include services performed as stenographers, bookkeepers, clerks, and other office employees, even though such services may be in connection with such activities. However, to the extent that the services of such individuals are performed in the employ of the owner or tenant or other operator of a farm and are rendered in major part on a farm, they may be within the provisions of paragraph (c) of this section.

(f) Services described in section 3121(g)(5). *(1)* Service not in the course of the employer's trade or business (see paragraph (a)(1) of § 31.3121(a)(7)-1) or domestic service in a private home of the employer (see paragraph (a)(2) of § 31.3121(a)(7)-1) constitutes agricultural labor if such service is performed on a farm operated for profit. The determination whether remuneration for any such service performed on a farm operated for profit constitutes wages is to be made under § 31.3121(a)(8)-1 rather than under § 31.3121(a)(7)-1. For provisions relating to the exception from employment provided with respect to any such service performed after 1960 by a father or mother in the employ of his or her son or daughter, see § 31.3121(b)(3)-1.

(2) Generally, a farm is not operated for profit if it is occupied by the employer primarily for residential purposes, or is used primarily for the pleasure of the employer or his family such as for the entertainment of guests or as a hobby of the employer or his family.

T.D. 6190, 7/13/56, amend T.D. 6516, 12/19/60, T.D. 6744, 7/1/64.

§ 31.3121(h)-1 American employer.

(a) The term "American employer" means an employer which is (1) the United States or any instrumentality thereof, (2) an individual who is a resident of the United States, (3) a partnership, if two-thirds or more of the partners are residents of the United States, (4) a trust, if all of the trustees are residents of the United States, or (5) a corporation organized under the laws of the United States or of any State. For provisions relating to the terms "State" and "United States", see § 31.3121(e)-1.

(b) For provisions relating to services performed outside the United States by a citizen of the United States as an employee for an American employer, see paragraph (c)(3) of § 31.3121(b)-3 and paragraph (e) of § 31.3121(b)(4)-1.

T.D. 6190, 7/13/56, amend T.D. 6516, 12/19/60, T.D. 6744, 7/1/64.

§ 31.3121(i)-1 Computation to nearest dollar or cash remuneration for domestic service.

(a) An employer may, for purposes of the Act, elect to compute to the nearest dollar any payment of cash remuneration for domestic service described in section 3121(a)(7)(B) (see § 31.3121(a)(7)-1) which is more or less than a whole-dollar amount. For the purpose of the computation to the nearest dollar, the payment of a fractional part of a dollar shall be disregarded unless it amounts to one-half dollar or more, in which case it shall be increased to one dollar. For example, any amount actually paid between $4.50 and $5.49, inclusive, may be treated as $5 for purposes of the taxes imposed by the Act. If an employer elects this method of computation with respect to any payment of cash remuneration made in a calendar year for domestic service in his private home, he must use the same method in computing each payment of cash remuneration of more or less than a whole-dollar amount made to each of his employees in such calendar year for domestic service in his private home. Moreover, if an employer elects this method of computation with respect to payments of the prescribed character made in any calendar year, the amount of each payment of cash remuneration so computed to the nearest dollar shall, in lieu of the amount actually paid, be deemed to constitute the amount of cash remuneration for purposes of the Act. Thus, the amount of cash payments so computed to the nearest dollar shall be used for purposes of determining whether such payments constitute wages; for purposes of applying the employee and employer tax rates to the wage payments; for purposes of any required record keeping; and for purposes of reporting and paying the employee tax and employer tax with respect to such wage payments.

(b) The provisions of this section apply to any cash payment for domestic service in a private home of the employer made on or after January 1, 1994. For rules applicable to any cash payment for domestic service in a private home of the employer made prior to January 1, 1994, see § 31.3121(i)-1 in effect at such time (see 26 CFR part 31 contained in the edition of 26 CFR parts 30 to 39, revised as of April 1, 2006).

T.D. 6190, 7/13/56, amend T.D. 6516, 12/19/60, T.D. 9266, 6/16/2006.

§ 31.3121(i)-2 Computation of remuneration for service performed by an individual as a member of a uniformed service.

In the case of an individual performing service after December 31, 1956, as a member of a uniformed service (see § 31.3121(n)), to which the provisions of section 3121(m)(1) (see § 31.3121(m) are applicable, the term "wages" shall, subject to the provisions of section 3121(a)(1) (see § 31.3121(a)-1), include as the individual's remuneration for such service only his basic pay as described in section 102(10) of the Servicemen's and Veterans' Survivor Benefits Act (38 U.S.C. 401(1), 403; 72 Stat. 1126).

T.D. 6744, 7/1/64.

§ 31.3121(i)-3 Computation of remuneration for service performed by an individual as a volunteer or volunteer leader within the meaning of the Peace Corps Act.

In the case of an individual performing service in his capacity as a volunteer or volunteer leader within the meaning of the Peace Corps Act (see § 31.3121(p)), the term "wages" shall, subject to the provisions of section 3121(a)(1) (see § 31.3121(a)-1), include as individual's remuneration for such service only amounts paid pursuant to section 5(c) or section 6(1) of the Peace Corps Act (22 U.S.C. 2501; 75 Stat. 612).

T.D. 6744, 7/1/64.

§ 31.3121(i)-4 Computation of remuneration for service performed by certain members of religious orders.

In any case where an individual is a member of a religious order (as defined in section 3121(r)(2) and paragraph (b) of § 31.3121(r)-1) performing service in the exercise of duties required by such order, and an election of coverage under section 3121(r) and § 31.3121(r)-1 is in effect with respect to such order or the autonomous subdivision thereof to which such member belongs, the term "wages" shall, subject to the provisions of section 3121(a)(1) relating to definition of wages), include as such individual's remuneration for such service the fair market value of any board, lodging, clothing, and other perquisites furnished to such member by such order or subdivision or by any other person or organization pursuant to an agreement (whether written or oral) with such order or subdivision. Such other perquisites shall include any cash either paid by such order or subdivision or paid by another employer and not required by such order or subdivision to be remitted to it. For purposes of this section, perquisites shall be considered to be furnished over the period during which the member receives the benefit of them. (See example (4) of this section.) In no case shall the amount included as such individual's remuneration under this paragraph be less than $100 a month. All relevant facts and elements of value shall be considered in every case. Where the fair market value of any board, lodging, clothing, and other perquisites furnished to all members of an electing religious order or autonomous subdivision (or to all in a group of members) does not vary significantly, such order or subdivision may treat all of its members (or all in such group of members) as having a uniform wage. The provisions of this section may be illustrated by the following examples of the treatment of particular perquisites:

Example (1). M is a religious order which requires its members to take a vow of poverty and which has made an election under section 3121(r). Under section 3121(i)(4), M must include in the wages of its members the fair market value of the clothing it provides for its members. M and several other religious orders using essentially the same type of religious habit purchase clothing for their members from either of two suppliers in arms-length transactions. The fair market value of such clothing (i.e., the price at which such items would change hands between a willing buyer and a willing seller, neither being under any compulsion to buy or to sell) is determined by reference to the actual sales price of these suppliers to the religious orders.

Example (2). N is a religious order which requires its members to take a vow of poverty and which has made an election under section 3121(r). N operates a seminary adjacent to a university. Students at the university obtain lodging and board on campus from the university for its fair market value of $2,000 for the school year. Such lodging and board is essentially the same as that provided by N at its seminary to N's members subject to a vow of poverty. Accordingly, the amount to be included in the "wages" of such members with respect to lodging and board for the same period of time is $2,000.

Example (3). O is a religious order which requires its members to take a vow of poverty and to observe silence, and which has made an election under section 3121(r). O operates a monastery in a remote rural area. Under section 3121(i)(4), O must include in the wages of its members assigned to this monastery the fair market value of the board and lodging furnished to them. In making a determination of the fair market value of such board and lodging in the remoteness of the monastery, as well as the smallness of the rooms and the simplicity of their furnishings, affect this determination. However, the facts that the facility is used by a religious order as a monastery and that the order's members maintain silence do not affect the fair market value of such items.

Example (4). P is a religious order which requires its members to take a vow of poverty and which has made an election under section 3121(r). Several of P's members are attending a university on a full-time basis. The fair market value of the board and lodging of each of such members at the university is $1,000 per semester. P pays the university $1,000 at the beginning of each semester for the board and lodging of each of such members. In addition, P gives each such member a $400 cash advance to cover his miscellaneous expenses during the semester. Under section 3121(i)(4), P must prorate the fair market value of such members' board and lodging, as well as the miscellaneous items, over the semester and include such value in the determination of "wages"

Example (5). Q is a religious order which is a corporation organized under the laws of Wisconsin, which requires its members to take a vow of poverty, and which has made an election under section 3121(r). Q has convents in rural South America and in suburbs and central city areas of the United States. Characteristically, in the United States its suburban convents provide somewhat larger and newer rooms for its members than do its convents in city areas. Moreover, its suburban convents have more extensive grounds and somewhat more elaborate facilities than do its older convents in city areas. However, both types of convents limit resident members to a single, plainly furnished room and provide them meals which are comparable. Q's members in South America live in extremely primitive dwellings and otherwise have extremely modest perquisites. Under section 3121(i)(4), Q may report a uniform wage for its members who live in suburban convents and city convents in the United States, as the board, lodging, and perquisites furnished these members do not vary significantly from one convent to the other. Q may report another uniform wage (but not less than $100 per month apiece) for its members who are citizens of the United States and who reside in South America based on the fair market value of the perquisites furnished these individuals, as the fair market value of the perquisites furnished these individuals varies significantly from that of those furnished its members who live in its domestic convents but does not vary significantly among members in South America whose wages are subject to tax.

T.D. 7280, 7/9/73.

§ 31.3121(j)-1 Covered transportation service.

(a) Transportation systems acquired in whole or in part after 1936 and before 1951. *(1) In general.* Except as provided in subparagraph (2) of this paragraph, all service performed in the employ of a State or political subdivision thereof in connection with its operation of a public transportation system constitutes covered transportation service if any part of the transportation system was acquired from private ownership after 1936 and before 1951. For purposes of this subparagraph, it is immaterial whether any part of the transportation system was acquired before 1937 or after 1950, whether the employee was hired before, during, or after 1950, or whether the employee had been employed by the employer from whom the State or political subdivision acquired its transportation system or any part thereof.

(2) General retirement system protected by State constitution. Except as provided in subparagraph (3) of this paragraph, service performed in the employ of a State or political subdivision in connection with its operation of a public transportation system acquired in whole or in part from private ownership after 1936 and before 1951 does not constitute covered transportation service, if substantially all service in connection with the operation of the transportation system was, on December 31, 1950, covered under a general retirement system providing benefits which are protected from diminution or impairment under the State constitution by reason of an express provision, dealing specifically with retirement systems established by the State or political subdivisions of the State, which forbids such diminution or impairment.

(3) Additions to certain transportation systems by acquisition after 1950. This subparagraph is applicable only in case of an acquisition after 1950 from private ownership of an addition to an existing public transportation system which was acquired in whole or in part by a State or political subdivision thereof from private ownership after 1936 and before 1951 and then only in case service for such existing transportation system did not constitute covered transportation service by reason of the provisions of subparagraph (2) of this paragraph. Service in connection with the operation of such transportation system (including any additions acquired after 1950) constitutes covered transportation service commencing with the first day of the third calendar quarter following the calendar quarter in which the addition to the existing transportation system was acquired, if such service is performed by an employee who became an employee of the State or political subdivision in connection with and at the time of its acquisition from private ownership of such addition and who before the acquisition of such addition rendered service in employment in connection with the operation of the addition so acquired by such State or political subdivision. However, service performed by such employee in connection with the operation of the transportation system does not constitute covered transportation service if, on the first day of the third calendar quarter following the calendar quarter in which the addition was acquired, such service is covered by a general retirement system which does not with respect to such employee, contain special provisions applicable only to employees who became employees of the State or political subdivision in connection with and at the time of acquisition of such addition.

(b) Transportation systems in operation on December 31, 1950, no part of which was acquired after 1936 and before 1951. *(1) In general.* Except as provided in subparagraph (2) of this paragraph, no service performed in the employ of a State a political subdivision thereof in connection with its operation of a public transportation system constitutes covered transportation service if no part of such transportation system operated by the State political subdivision on December 31, 1950, was acquired from private ownership after 1936 and before 1951.

(2) Additions acquired after 1950. This subparagraph is applicable only in case of acquisition after 1950 from private ownership of an addition to an existing public transportation system which was operated by a State or political subdivision on December 31, 1950, but no part of which was acquired from private ownership after 1936 and before 1951. Service in connection with the operation of such transportation system (including any additions acquired after 1950) constitutes covered transportation service commencing with the first day of the third calendar quarter following the calendar quarter in which the addition to the existing transportation system was acquired, if such service is performed by an employee who became an employee of the State or political subdivision in connection with and at the time of its ac-

quisition from private ownership of such addition and who before the acquisition of such addition rendered service in employment in connection with the operation of the addition so acquired by such State or political subdivision. However, service performed by such employee in connection with the operation of the transportation system does not constitute covered transportation service if, on the first day of the third calendar quarter following the calendar quarter in which the addition was acquired, such service is covered by a general retirement system which does not, with respect to such employee, contain special provisions applicable only to employees who became employees of the State or political subdivision in connection with and at the time of its acquisition of such addition.

(c) Transportation systems acquired after 1950. All service performed in the employ of a State or political subdivision thereof in connection with its operation of a public transportation system constitutes covered transportation service if the transportation system was not operated by the State or political subdivision before 1951 and, at the time of its first acquisition after 1950 from private ownership of any part of its transportation system, the State or political subdivision did not have a general retirement system covering substantially all service performed in connection with the operation of the transportation system.

(d) Definitions. For purposes of this section:

(1) The term "general retirement system" means any pension, annuity, retirement, or similar fund or system established by a State or by a political subdivision thereof for employees of the State, political subdivision, or both; but such term does not include such a fund or system which covers only service performed in positions connected with the operation of its public transportation system.

(2) A transportation system or a part thereof is considered to have been acquired by a State or political subdivision from private ownership if prior to the acquisition service performed by the employees in connection with the operation of the system or an acquired part thereof constituted employment under the Act or under subchapter A of chapter 9 of the Internal Revenue Code of 1939 or was covered by an agreement entered into pursuant to section 218 of the Social Security Act, and some of such employees became employees of the State or political subdivision in connection with and at the time of such acquisition.

(3) The term "political subdivision" includes an instrumentality of a State, of one or more political subdivisions of a State, or of a State and one or more of its political subdivisions.

(4) The term "employment" includes service covered by an agreement entered into pursuant to section 218 of the Social Security Act.

T.D. 6190, 7/13/56, amend T.D. 6516, 12/19/60.

§ 31.3121(k)-1 Waiver of exemption from taxes.

(a) Who may file a waiver certificate. *(1) In general.* If services performed in the employ of an organization are excepted from employment under section 3121(b)(8)(B), the organization may file a waiver certificate on Form SS-15, together with a list on Form SS-15a, certifying that it desires to have the Federal old-age, survivors, and disability insurance system established by title II of the Social Security Act extended to services performed by its employees. (For provisions relating to the exception under section 3121(b)(8)(B), see §§ 31.3121(b)(8) and 31.3121(b)(8)-2.) A certificate in effect under section 1426(l) of the Internal Revenue Code of 1939 on December 31, 1954, remains in effect under, and is subject to the provisions of, section 3121(k). If the period covered by a certificate filed under section 3121(k), or under section 1426(l) of the Internal Revenue Code of 1939, is terminated by an organization, a certificate may not thereafter be filed by the organization under section 3121(k). For regulations relating to certificates filed under section 1426(l) of the Internal Revenue Code of 1939, see 26 CFR (1939) 408.216 (Regulations 128).

(2) Organizations having two separate groups of employees. If an organization is eligible to file a certificate under section 3121(k), and the organization employs both individuals who are in positions covered by a pension, annuity, retirement, or similar fund or system established by a State or by a political subdivision thereof and individuals who are not in such positions, the organization shall divide its employees into two separate groups for purposes of any certificate filed after August 28, 1958. One group shall consist of all employees who are in positions covered by such a fund or system and (i) are members of such fund or system, or (ii) are not members of such fund or system but are eligible to become members thereof. The other group shall consist of all remaining employees. An organization which has so divided its employees into two groups may file a certificate after August 28, 1958, with respect to the employees in either group, or may file a separate certificate after such date with respect to employees in each group.

(3) Certificates filed before September 14, 1960. A certificate filed before September 14, 1960, is void unless at least two-thirds of the employees, determined on the basis of the facts which existed as of the date the certificate was filed, concurred in the filing of the certificate, and the organization certified to such concurrence in the certificate. All individuals who were employees of the organization within the meaning of section 3121(d) (see § 31.3121(d)-1) shall be included in determining whether two-thirds of the employees of the organization concurred in the filing of the certificate; except that there shall not be included (i) those employees who at the time of the filing of the certificate were performing for the organization services only of the character specified in paragraphs (8)(A), (10)(B), and (13) of section 3121(b) (see §§ 31.3121(b)(8)-1, 31.3121(b)(10)-2, and 31.3121(b)(13)-1, respectively), (ii) those alien employees who at the time of the filing of the certificate were performing services for such organization under an arrangement which provided for the performance only of services outside the United States not on or in connection with an American vessel or American aircraft, and (iii) connection with certificates filed after August 28, 1958. those employees who at the time of the filing of the certificate were in a group to which such certificate was not applicable because of the provisions of section 3121(k)(1)(E). (See subparagraph (2) of this paragraph.) As used in this subparagraph, the term "alien employee" does not include an employee who was a citizen of the Commonwealth of Puerto Rico or a citizen of the Virgin Islands, and the term "United States" includes Puerto Rico and the Virgin Islands.

(b) Execution and amendment of certificate. *(1) Use of prescribed forms.* An organization filing a certificate pursuant to section 3121(k) shall use Form SS-15, in accordance with the regulations and instructions applicable thereto. The certificate may be filed only if it is accompanied by a list on Form SS-15a, containing the signature, address, and social security account number, if any, of each employee, if any, who concurs in the filing of the certificate. (For provisions relating to account numbers, see § 31.6011(b)-2.) If no employee concurs in a certificate filed after September 13, 1960, that fact should be stated on the Form SS-15a. (For provisions relating to the concurrence of employees in certificates filed after September 14, 1960, see paragraph (a)(3) of this section.)

(2) Amendment of list on Form SS-15a. (i) Certificate filed after August 28, 1958. The list on Form SS-15a accompanying a certificate filed after August 28, 1958, under section 3121(k), may be amended at any time before the expiration of the twenty-fourth month following the calendar quarter in which the certificate is filed, by filing a supplemental list or lists on Form SS-15a Supplement, containing the signature, address, and social security account number, if any, of each additional employee who concurs in the filing of the certificate.

(ii) Certificate filed before August 29, 1958. The list on Form SS-15a which accompanied a certificate filed before August 29, 1958, under section 3121(k) or under section 1426(l) of the Internal Revenue Code of 1939, may be amended by filing a supplemental list or lists on Form SS-15a Supplement at any time after August 31, 1954, and before the expiration of the twenty-fourth month following the first calendar quarter for which the certificate was in effect, or before January 1, 1959, whichever is later.

(3) Where to file certificate or amendment. The certificate on Form SS-15 and accompanying list of Form SS-15a of an organization which is required to make a return on Form 941 pursuant to § 31.6011(a)-1 or § 31.6011(a)-4 shall be filed with the internal revenue officer designated in the instructions applicable to Form SS-15 and Form SS-15a. The Form SS-15 and Form SS-15a of any other organization shall be filed in accordance with the provisions of § 31.6091-1 which are otherwise applicable to returns. Each Form SS-15a Supplement shall be filed with the internal revenue officer with whom the related Forms SS-15 and SS-15a were filed.

(c) Effect of waiver. *(1) In general.* The exception from employment under section 3121(b)(8)(B) does not apply to services with respect to which a certificate, filed pursuant to section 3121(k), or section 1426(l) of the Internal Revenue Code of 1939, is in effect. (See §§ 31.3121(b)(8) and 31.3121(b)(8)-2.) If an organization has divided its employees into two groups, as set forth in paragraph (a)(2) of this section, a certificate filed with respect to either group shall have no effect with respect to services performed by an employee as a member of the other group; and the provisions of this subsection shall apply as if each group were separately employed by a different organization. A certificate is not terminated if the organization loses its exemption under section 501(a) as an organization of the character described in section 501(c)(3), but continues effective with respect to any subsequent periods during which the organization is so exempt. The certificate of an organization may be in effect without being applicable to services performed by every employee of the organization. Subparagraph (2) of this paragraph relates to the beginning of the period for which a certificate is in effect. Subparagraph (3) of this paragraph relates to the services with respect to which a certificate is in effect. Even though a certificate is in effect with respect to the services of an employee, such services may be excepted from employment under some provision of section 3121(b) other than paragraph (8)(B) thereof. For example, service performed in any calendar quarter in the employ of an organization described in section 501(c)(3) and exempt from income tax under section 501(a) is excepted from employment under section 3121(b)(10)(A) if the remuneration for such service is less that $50, regardless of whether the organization files a certificate.

(2) Beginning of effective period of waiver. (i) Certificate filed after July 30, 1965. A certificate filed after July 30, 1965, by an organization pursuant to section 3121(k) shall be in effect for the period beginning with one of the following dates, which shall be designated by the organization on the certificate:

(a) The first day of the calendar quarter in which the certificate is filed,

(b) The first day of the calendar quarter immediately following the quarter in which the certificate is filed, or

(c) The first day of any calendar quarter preceding the calendar quarter in which the certificate if filed, except that such a date may not be earlier than the first day of the 20th calendar quarter preceding the quarter in which such certificate is filed. Thus, a certificate filed in December 1965 may be made effective, pursuant to this subdivision (c), for the period beginning with the first day of the calendar quarter beginning October 1, 1960, or the first day of any other calendar quarter beginning after October 1, 1960, and before October 1, 1965.

(ii) Certificate filed after August 28, 1958, and before July 31, 1965. A certificate filed after August 28, 1958, and before July 31, 1965, by an organization pursuant to section 3121(k) shall be in effect for the period beginning with one of the following dates, which shall be designated by the organization on the certificate:

(a) The first day of the calendar quarter in which the certificate is filed,

(b) The first day of the calendar quarter immediately following the quarter in which the certificate is filed, or

(c) The first day of any calendar quarter preceding the calendar quarter in which the certificate is filed, except that, in the case of a certificate filed before 1960, such date may not be earlier than January 1, 1956, and in the case of a certificate filed after 1959 (but before July 31, 1965), such date may not be earlier than the first day of the fourth calendar quarter preceding the quarter in which the certificate is filed. Thus, a certificate filed in December 1959 may be made effective for the calendar quarter beginning January 1, 1956; but a certificate filed in January 1960 may not be made effective for a calendar quarter beginning before January 1, 1959.

(iii) Certificate filed after 1956 and before August 29, 1958. A certificate filed by an organization after 1956 and before August 29, 1958, pursuant to section 3121(k), became effective for the period beginning with one of the following dates, as designated by the organization on the certificate:

(a) The first day of the calendar quarter in which the certificate was filed, or

(b) The first day of the calendar quarter immediately following the quarter in which the certificate was filed.

(iv) Certificate filed before 1957. A certificate filed before 1957 pursuant to section 3121(k) became effective, for the period beginning with the first day following the close of the calendar quarter in which the certificate was filed. In no case, however, shall a certificate filed under the provisions of section 3121(k) be in effect with respect to services performed before January 1, 1955. (For regulations relating to waiver certificates filed under section 1426(l) of the Internal Revenue Code of 1939, see 26 CFR (1939) 408.216 (Regulations 128).)

(3) Services to which certificate applies. (i) In general. If an organization's certificate is in effect (see subparagraph (2) of this paragraph), the certificate becomes effective with respect to services performed in its employ by each individual (a) who enters the employ of the organization after the calendar quarter in which the certificate is filed, as set forth in subdivision (ii) of this subparagraph, or (b) whose signature appears on the list on Form SS-15a, as set forth in subdivision (iii) of this subparagraph, or (c) whose signature appears on a Form SS-15a Supplement, as set forth in subdivision (iv) or (v) of this subparagraph. The first date on which such a certificate becomes effective with respect to an employee's services shall be the earliest date applicable under this subparagraph. An organization's certificate is not effective with respect to the services of an employee who is in its employ in the calendar quarter in which the certificate is filed and who does not sign Form SS-15a or Form SS-15a Supplement, so long as his employment relationship with the organization, at the close of the calendar quarter in which the certificate is filed and thereafter, continues without interruption.

(ii) Employee hired after quarter in which certificate is filed. If an individual enters the employ of an organization on or after the first day following the close of the calendar quarter in which the organization files a certificate pursuant to section 3121(k), the certificate shall be in effect with respect to services performed by the individual in the employ of the organization on and after the day he enters the employ of the organization. A former employee of the organization who is rehired on or after the first day following the close of the calendar quarter in which such a certificate is filed shall be considered to have entered the employ of the organization after such calendar quarter, regardless of whether such individual concurred in the filing of the certificate.

(iii) Employee who signs Form SS-15a. A certificate on Form SS-15 filed by an organization pursuant to section 3121(k) shall be in effect with respect to services performed by an individual in the employ of the organization on and after the first day for which the certificate is in effect, if such individual's signature appears on the list on Form SS-15a which accompanies such certificate.

(iv) Employee who signs Form SS-15a Supplement to concur in certificate filed after August 28, 1958. If the list on Form SS-15a accompanying a certificate filed after August 28, 1958, by an organization pursuant to section 3121(k) is amended in accordance with paragraph (b)(2)(i) of this section by the filing of a supplemental list on Form SS-15a Supplement, the certificate shall be in effect with respect to the services of each individual whose signature appears on the supplemental list, performed in the employ of the organization—

(a) On and after the first day for which the certificate is in effect, if the supplemental list is filed on or before the last day of the month following the calendar quarter in which the certificate is filed, or

(b) On and after the first day of the calendar quarter in which the supplemental list is filed, if such list is filed after the close of the first month following the calendar quarter in which the certificate is filed.

(v) Employee who signed Form SS-15a Supplement to concur in certificate filed before August 29, 1958. If the list on Form SS-15a which accompanied a certificate filed before August 29, 1958, by an organization pursuant to section 3121(k), or pursuant to section 1426(l) of the Internal Revenue Code of 1939, was amended in accordance with paragraph (b)(2)(ii) of this section by the filing of a supplemental list on Form SS-15a Supplement, the certificate shall be in effect with respect to the services of each individual whose signature appears on the supplemental list, performed in the employ of the organization—

(a) On and after the first day for which the certificate is in effect, if the supplemental list was filed on or before the last day of the month following the first calendar quarter for which the certificate was in effect, or

(b) On and after the first day following the close of the calendar quarter in which the supplemental list was filed, but not before January 1, 1955, if such list was filed after the close of the first month following the first calendar quarter for which the certificate is in effect.

(4) Administrative provisions applicable when certificate has retroactive effect. For purposes of computing interest and for purposes of section 6651 (relating to addition to tax for failure to file tax return), in any case in which a certificate filed pursuant to section 3121(k)(1) is effective pursuant to section 3121(k)(1)(B)(iii) (as originally enacted and as amended by section 316(a) of the Social Security Amendments of 1965) for one or more calendar quarters prior to the quarter in which the certificate is filed, the due date for the return and payment of the tax for such prior calendar quarters resulting from the filing of such certificate shall be the last day of the calendar month following the calendar quarter in which the certificate is filed. The statutory period for the assessment of the tax for such prior calendar quarters shall not expire before the expiration of 3 years from such due date. A waiver certificate (as described in section 3121(k)(1) and this section) furnished to the Internal Revenue Service after February 12, 1976, shall not be considered filed with the Internal Revenue Service unless interest paid to the organization (or credited to its account) in connection with a claim for credit or refund of taxes, which claim was based upon the exemption from taxes the organization is waiving by such certificate, is repaid. The interest so paid must be repaid only to the extent such interest relates to any taxes for which the organization or its employees would be liable by reason of the waiver certificate. Furthermore, when a waiver certificate has been filed prior to the payment of a refund of taxes based upon the exemption from taxes the organization in waiving, no credit or refund in respect of the taxes for which the exemption has been waived shall be allowed. If repayment of the interest is made as required by this subparagraph, on or before the last day of the calendar month following the calendar quarter in which the certificate is furnished to the Internal Revenue Service, such certificate shall be considered to have been filed on the date it was originally furnished. If repayment occurs after that day, such certificate shall be considered to have been filed on the date of the repayment. References in this subparagraph to a waiver certificate refer also to any supplement to such a certificate.

(d) Termination of waiver by organization. *(1)* The period for which a certificate filed pursuant to section 3121(k), or pursuant to section 1426(l) of the Internal Revenue Code of 1939, is in effect may be terminated by the organization upon giving to the district director with whom the organization is filing returns 2 years advance notice in writing of its desire to terminate the effect of the certificate at the end of a specified calendar quarter, but only if, at the time of the receipt of such notice by the district director, the certificate has been in effect for a period of not less than 8 years. The notice of termination shall be signed by the president or other principal officer of the organization. Such notice shall be dated and shall show (i) the title of the officer signing the notice, (ii) the name, address, and identification number of the organization, (iii) the district director with whom the certificate was filed, (iv) the date on which the certificate became effective, and (v) the date on which the certificate is to be terminated. No particular form is prescribed for the notice of termination.

(2) In computing the effective period which must precede the date of receipt of the notice of termination, there shall be disregarded any period or periods as to which the organization was not exempt from income tax under section 501(a) as an organization of the character described in section 501(c)(3) or under section 101(6) of the Internal Revenue Code of 1939.

(3) The notice of termination may be revoked by the organization by giving, prior to the close of the calendar quarter specified in the notice of termination, a written notice of such revocation. The notice of revocation shall be filed with the district director with whom the notice of termination was filed. The notice of revocation shall be signed by the president or other principal officer of the organization. Such notice shall be dated and shall show (i) the title of the officer signing the notice, (ii) the name, address, and identification number of the organization, and (iii) the date of the notice of termination to be revoked. No particular form is prescribed for the notice of revocation.

(e) Termination of waiver by Commissioner. *(1)* The period for which a certificate filed pursuant to section 3121(k), or pursuant to section 1426(l) of the Internal Revenue Code for 1939, is in effect may be terminated by the Commissioner, with the prior concurrence of the Secretary of Health, Education, and Welfare, upon a finding by the Commissioner that the organization has failed to comply substantially with the requirements applicable with respect to the taxes imposed by the Act (or the corresponding provisions of prior law) or is no longer able to comply therewith. The Commissioner shall give the organization not less than 60 days advance notice in writing that the period covered by the certificate will terminate at the end of the calendar quarter specified in the notice of termination.

(2) The notice of termination may be revoked by the Commissioner, with the prior concurrence of the Secretary of Health, Education, and Welfare, be giving written notice of revocation to the organization before the close of the calendar quarter specified in the notice of termination.

T.D. 6190, 7/13/56, amend T.D. 6516, 12/19/60, T.D. 6744, 7/1/64, T.D. 6983, 12/3/68, T.D. 7012, 5/14/69, T.D. 7476, 4/1/77.

§ 31.3121(k)-2 Waivers of exemption; original effective date changed retroactively.

(a) Certificates filed after 1955 and before August 29, 1958. *(1)* An organization which filed a certificate under section 3121(k) after 1955 and before August 29, 1958, may file a request on Form SS-15b at any time before 1960 to have such certificate made effective, with respect to the services of individuals who concurred in the filing of such certificate (initially, or by signing a supplemental list on Form SS-15a Supplement which was filed before Aug. 29, 1958) and whose signatures also appear on such request on Form SS-15b, for the period beginning with the first day of any calendar quarter after 1955 which preceded the first calendar quarter for which the certificate originally was effective.

(2) For purposes of computing interest and for purposes of section 6651 (relating to addition to tax for failure to file tax return), the due date for the return and payment of the tax for any calendar quarter resulting from the filing of a request referred to in subparagraph (1) of this paragraph shall be the last day of the calendar month following the calendar quarter in which the request is filed. The statutory period for the assessment of such tax shall not expire before the expiration of 3 years from such due date.

(b) Certificate filed before 1966. *(1)* An organization which filed a certificate on Form SS-15 under section 3121(k)(1)(A) before January 1, 1966, may amend such certificate during 1965 or 1966 to make the certificate effective beginning with the first day of a calendar quarter preceding the date designated by the organization on the certificate (see paragraph (c)(2) of § 31.3121(k)-1). The amendment of the certificate shall be made by filing a Certificate For Retroactive Coverage on Form SS-15b. A certificate on Form SS-15 may be amended to be effective for the period beginning with the first day of any calendar quarter which precedes the calendar quarter for which the certificate was originally effective, except that such a certificate may not be made effective, through an amendment, for any calendar quarter which begins earlier than the 20th calendar quarter preceding the calendar quarter in which the organization files a Certificate For Retroactive Coverage on Form SS-15b. Thus, if a Certificate For Retroactive Coverage is filed in May 1966 in respect of a certificate on Form SS-15 filed in 1965, the certificate on Form SS-15 may not be made effective for a calendar quarter preceding the quarter beginning April 1, 1961. A certificate on Form SS-15 which is amended by a Certificate For Retroactive Coverage on Form SS-15b will be effective for the period preceding the first calendar quarter for which the certificate originally was effective only with respect to the services of individuals who concurred in the filing of the certificate (initially, or by signing a supplemental list on Form SS-15a Supplement which was filed prior to the date on which the Certificate For Retroactive Coverage was filed) and whose signatures also appear on the Certificate For Retroactive Coverage on Form SS-15b. A Certificate For Retroactive Coverage shall be filed with the district director with whom the related Form SS-15 was filed.

(2) For purposes of computing interest and for purposes of section 6651 (relating to addition to tax for failure to file tax return), the due date for the return and payment of the tax for any calendar quarter resulting from the filing of an amendment referred to in subparagraph (1) of this paragraph shall be the last day of the calendar month following the calendar quarter in which the amendment is filed. The statutory period for the assessment of such tax shall not expire before the expiration of 3 years from such due date.

T.D. 6744, 7/1/64, amend T.D. 6983, 12/3/68.

§ 31.3121(k)-3 Request for coverage of individual employed by exempt organization before August 1, 1956.

(a) Application of this section. This section is applicable to requests made after July 31, 1956, and before September 14, 1960, under section 403 of the Social Security Amendments of 1954, as amended, except that nothing in this section shall render invalid any act performed pursuant to, and in accordance with, Revenue Ruling 57-11, Cumulative Bulletin 1957-1, page 344, or Revenue Ruling 58-514, Cumulative Bulletin 1958-2, page 733. (For regulations relating to requests made before August 1, 1956, under section 403 of the Social Security Amendments of 1954, see 26 CFR (1939) 408.216(c) and (d) (Regulations 128).)

(b) Organization which did not have waiver certificate in effect. *(1) Coverage requested by employee before August 27, 1958.* Pursuant to section 403(a) of the Social Security Amendments of 1954, as amended by section 401 of the Social Security Amendments of 1956, any individual who, as an employee, performed services after December 31, 1950, and before August 1, 1956, for an organization described in section 501(c)(3) which was exempt from income tax under section 501(a), or which was exempt from income tax under section 101(6) of the Internal Revenue Code of 1939, but which failed to file, before August 1, 1956, a valid waiver certificate under section 3121(k), or under section 1426(1) of the Internal Revenue Code of 1939, may request after July 31, 1956, and before August 27, 1958, that such part of the remuneration received by him for services performed in the employ of the organization after 1950 and before 1957 with respect to which employee and employer taxes were paid be deemed to constitute remuneration for employment, if:

(i) Any of the services performed by the individual after December 31, 1950, and before January 1, 1957, would have constituted employment if such a certificate on Form SS-15 filed by the organization had been in effect for the period during which the services were performed and the individual's signature had appeared on the accompanying list on Form SS-15a;

(ii) The employee and employer taxes were paid with respect to any part of the remuneration received by the individual from the organization for such services;

(iii) A part of such taxes was paid before August 1, 1956;

(iv) Such taxes as were paid before August 1, 1956, were paid by the organization in good faith and upon the assumption that it had filed a valid certificate under section 3121(k), or under section 1426(1) of the Internal Revenue Code of 1939; and

(v) No refund (or credit) of such taxes had been obtained by either the employee or the employer, exclusive of any refund (or credit) which would have been allowable if the services performed by the individual had constituted employment.

(2) Coverage requested by employee after August 26, 1958, and before September 14, 1960. Requests may be made after August 26, 1958, and before September 14, 1960, pursuant to section 403(a) of the Social Security Amendments of 1954, as amended by section 401 of the Social Security Amendments of 1956, by the Act of August 27, 1958 (Pub. L. 85-785, 72 Stat. 938), and by section 105(b)(6) of the Social Security Amendments of 1960. Any individual who as an employee, performed services after December 31, 1950, and before August 1, 1956, for an organization described in section 501(c)(3) which was exempt from income tax under section 501(a), or which was exempt from income tax under section 101(6) of the Internal Revenue Code of 1939, but which did not have in effect during the entire period in which the individual was so employed a valid waiver certificate under section 3121(k), or under section 1426(1) of the Internal Revenue Code of 1939, may request after August 26, 1958, and before September 14, 1960, that such part of the remuneration received by him for services performed in the employ of the organization after 1950 and before 1957 with respect to which employee and employer taxes were paid be deemed to constitute remuneration for employment, if:

(i) Any of the services performed by the individual after December 31, 1950, and before January 1, 1957, would have constituted employment if such a certificate on Form SS-15 filed by the organization had been in effect for the period during which the services were performed and the individual's signature had appeared on the accompanying list on Form SS-15a;

(ii) The employee and employer taxes were paid with respect to any part of the remuneration received by the individual from the organization for such services performed during the period in which the organization did not have a valid waiver certificate in effect;

(iii) A part of such taxes was paid before August 1, 1956;

(iv) Such taxes were paid before August 1, 1956, were paid by the organization in good faith, and either without knowledge that a waiver certificate was necessary or upon the assumption that it had filed a valid certificate under section 3121(k), or under section 1426(1) of the Internal Revenue Code of 1939; and

(v) No refund (or credit) of such taxes has been obtained by either the employee or the employer, exclusive of any refund (or credit) which would be allowable if the services performed by the individual had constituted employment.

(3) Execution and filing of request. (i) Except where the alternative procedure set forth in paragraph (b)(3)(ii) of this section is followed, the request of an individual under section 403(a) of the Social Security Amendments of 1954, as amended, is required to be made and filed as provided in this subdivision. The request shall be made in writing, be signed and dated by the individual, and include:

(a) The name and address of the organization for which the services were performed;

(b) The name, address, and social security account number of the individual;

(c) A statement that the individual has not obtained refund or credit (other than a refund or credit which would have been allowable if the services had constituted employment) from the district director of any part of the employee tax paid with respect to remuneration received by him from the organization for services performed after 1950 and before 1957; and

(d) A request that all remuneration received by him from the organization for such services with respect to which employee and employer taxes had been paid shall be deemed to constitute remuneration for employment to the extent authorized by section 403(a) of the Social Security Amendments of 1954, as amended.

The request of an individual shall be accompanied by a statement of the organization incorporating the substance of each of the five conditions listed in subparagraph (1) or (2), whichever is appropriate of this paragraph. The statement of the organization shall show also that the individual performed services for the organization after December 31, 1950, and before August 1, 1956; that the organization was an organization described in section 501(c)(3) which was exempt from income tax under section 501(a) or was exempt from income tax under section 101(6) of the Internal Revenue Code of 1939, and the district director with whom returns on Form 941 were filed. The organization's statement shall be signed by the president or other principal officer of the organization who shall certify that the statement is correct to the best of his knowledge and belief. If the statement of the organization is not submitted with the individual's request, the individual shall include in his request an explanation of his inability to submit the statement. Other information may be required, but should be submitted only upon receipt of a specific request therefor. No particular form is prescribed for the request of the individual or the statement of the organization required to be submitted with the request. The individual's request should be filed with the district director with whom the organization files returns on Form 941. If the individual is deceased or mentally incompetent and the request is made by the legal representative of the individual or other person authorized to act on his behalf, the request shall be accompanied by evidence showing such person's authority to make the request.

(ii) An organization which has or had in its employ individuals with respect to whom section 403(a) of the Social Security Amendments of 1954, as amended, is applicable may, if it so desires, prepare a form or forms for use by any such individual or individuals in making requests under such section. Any such form shall provide space for the signature of the individual or individuals and contain such information as required to be included in a request (see subdivision (i) of this subparagraph). Any such form used by more than one individual, and any such form used by one individual which is signed and returned to the organization, shall be submitted by the organization, together with its statement (as required in subdivision (i) of this subparagraph), to the district director with whom the organization files its returns on Form 941. An individual is not required to use a form prepared by the organization but may, at his election, file his request in accordance with the provisions of subdivision (i) of this subparagraph.

(4) Optional tax payments by organization. An organization which prior to August 1, 1956, reported and paid employee and employer taxes with respect to any portion of the remuneration paid to an individual, who is eligible to file a request under section 403(a) of the Social Security Amendments of 1954, as amended, for services performed by him after 1950 and before 1957, may report and pay such taxes before September 14, 1960, with respect to any remaining portion of such remuneration which would have constituted wages if a certificate had been in effect with respect to such services. Such taxes may be reported as an adjustment without interest in the manner prescribed in subpart G of the regulations in this part.

(5) Effect of request. If a request is made and filed under the conditions stated in this paragraph with respect to one or more individuals, remuneration for services performed by each such individual after 1950 and before 1957, with respect to which the employee and employer taxes are paid on or before the date on which the request was filed with the district director, will be deemed to constitute remuneration for employment to the extent that such services would have constituted employment as defined in section 3121(b), or in section 1426(b) of the Internal Revenue Code of 1939, if a certificate had been in effect with respect to such services. However, the provisions of section 3121(a) and §§ 31.3121(a)-1 to 31.3121(a)(10)-1, inclusive, of the regulations in this part or the provisions of section 1426(a) of the Internal Revenue Code of 1939 and the regulations in 26 CFR (1939) 408.226 and 408.227 (Regulations 128), as the case may be, are applicable in determining the extent to which such remuneration for employment constitutes wages for purposes of the employee and employer taxes.

(c) Individual who failed to sign list of concurring employees. *(1) In general.* Pursuant to section 403(b) of the Social Security Amendments of 1954, as amended, any individual who, as an employee, performed services after December 31, 1950, and before August 1, 1956, for an organization which filed a valid certificate under section 3121(k), or under section 1426(1) of the Internal Revenue Code of 1939, but who failed to sign the list of employees concurring in the filing of such certificate, may request on or before January 1, 1959, that the remuneration received by him for such services be deemed to constitute remuneration for employment, if:

(i) Any of the services performed by the individual after December 31, 1950, and before August 1, 1956, would have constituted employment if the signature of such individual had appeared on the list of employees who concurred in the filing of the certificate;

(ii) The employee and employer taxes were paid before August 1, 1956, with respect to any part of the remuneration received by the individual from the organization for such services; and

(iii) No refund (or credit) of such taxes has been obtained either by the employee or the employer, exclusive of any refund (or credit) which would be allowable if the services performed by the individual had constituted employment.

(2) Execution and filing of request. (i) Except where the alternative procedure set forth in subdivision (ii) of this subparagraph is followed, the request of an individual under section 403(b) of the Social Security Amendments of 1954, as amended, shall be made and filed as provided in this subdivision. The request shall be filed on or before January 1, 1959, be made in writing, be signed and dated by the individual, and include:

(a) The name and address of the organization for which the services were performed;

(b) The name, address, and social security account number of the individual;

(c) A statement that the individual has not obtained a refund or credit (other than a refund or credit which would be allowable if the services had constituted employment) from the district director of any part of the employee tax paid before August 1, 1956, with respect to remuneration received by him from the organization;

(d) A request that all remuneration received by the individual from the organization for services performed after 1950 and before August 1, 1956, with respect to which employee and employer taxes were paid before August 1, 1956, shall be deemed to constitute remuneration for employment to the extent authorized by section 403(b) of the Social Security Amendments of 1954, as amended; and

(e) A statement that the individual understands that, upon the filing of such request with the district director, (1) he will be deemed to have concurred in the certificate which was previously filed by the organization, and (2) the employee and employer taxes will be applicable to all wages received, and to be received, by him for services performed for the organization on or after the effective date of such certificate to the extent that such taxes would have been applicable if he had signed the list on Form SS-15a submitted with the certificate.

The request of an individual shall be accompanied by a statement of the organization incorporating the substance of each of the three conditions listed in subparagraph (1) of this paragraph. The statement of the organization should also show that the individual performed services for the organization after December 31, 1950, and before August 1, 1956; that the organization filed a valid certificate under section 3121(k), or under section 1426(1) of the Internal Revenue Code of 1939; and the district director with whom returns on Form 941 are filed. Such statement shall be signed by the president or other principal officer of the organization who shall certify that the statement is correct to the best of his knowledge and belief. If the statement of the organization is not submitted with the individual's request, the individual shall include in his request an explanation of his inability to submit such statement. Other information may be required, but should be submitted only upon receipt of a specific request therefor. No particular form is prescribed for the request of the individual or the statement of the organization required to be submitted with the request. The individual's request should be filed with the district director with whom the organization files returns on Form 941. If the individual is deceased or mentally incompetent and the request is made by the legal representative of the individual or other person authorized to act on his behalf, the request shall be accompanied by evidence showing such persons' authority to make the request.

(ii) An organization which has or had in its employ individuals with respect to whom section 403(b) of the Social Security Amendments of 1954, as amended, is applicable, may, if it so desires, prepare a form or forms for use by any such individual or individuals in making requests under such section. Any such form shall provide space for the signature of the individual or individuals and contain such information as is required by subdivision (i) of this subparagraph to be included in a request. Any such form used by more than one individual, and any such form used by one individual, and any such form used by one individual which is signed and returned to the organization, shall be submitted by the organization, together with its statement (as required in subdivision (i) of this subparagraph), to the district director with whom the organization files returns on Form 941. An individual is not required to use a form prepared by the organization but may, at his election, file his request in accordance with the provisions of subdivisions (i) of this subparagraph.

(3) Effect of request. An individual who makes and files a request under the conditions stated in this paragraph with respect to services performed as an employee of an organization described in section 501(c)(3) which was exempt from income tax under section 501(a), or which was exempt from income tax under section 101(6) of the Internal Revenue Code of 1939, will be deemed to have signed the list accompanying the certificate filed by the organization under section 3121(k), or under section 1426(l) of the Internal Revenue Code of 1939. Accordingly, all services performed by the individual for the organization on and after the effective date of the certificate will constitute employment to the same extent as if he had, in fact, signed the list. The employee tax and employer tax are applicable with respect to any remuneration paid to the employee by the organization which constitutes wages. If less than the correct amount of such taxes has been paid, the additional amount due should be reported as an adjustment without interest within the time specified in subpart G of the regulations in this part.

T.D. 6744, 7/1/64.

§ 31.3121(k)-4 Constructive filing of waivers of exemption from social security taxes by certain tax-exempt organizations.

(a) Constructive filing of waiver certificate where no refund or credit has been allowed. *(1)* This paragraph applies (except as provided in subparagraph (3) of this paragraph) to an organization if all of the following four conditions are met.

(i) The organization is one described in section 501(c)(3) of the Internal Revenue Code of 1954, which is exempt from income tax under section 501(a) of the Code.

(ii) The organization did not file a valid waiver certificate under section 3121(k)(1) of the Internal Revenue Cede of 1954 (or corresponding provision of prior law) as of the later of October 19, 1976, or the earliest date on which it satisfies paragraph (a)(1)(iii) of this section.

(iii) The taxes imposed by sections 3101 and 3111 of the Code were paid with respect to remuneration paid by the organization to its employees, as though such certificate had been filed, during any period that includes all or part of at least three consecutive calendar quarters and that did not terminate before the end of the third calendar quarter of 1973.

(iv) The Internal Revenue Service did not allow (or erroneously allowed a refund or credit of any part of the taxes paid as described in subdivision (iii) with respect to remuneration for services performed on or after April 1, 1973. For purposes of the previous sentence, a refund or credit would have been allowed, even if a valid waiver certificate filed under section 3121(k)(1) had been in effect, shall be disregarded. A refund or credit will be regarded as having been erroneously allowed if it was credited by the Internal Revenue Service to the taxpayer account of the organization or any of its employees on or after September 9, 1976 even though it was properly made under the law in effect when made.

(2) (i) An organization to which this paragraph applies shall be deemed to have filed a valid waiver certificate under section 3121(k)(1) (or the corresponding provision of prior law) for purposes of section 210(a)(8)(B) of the Social Security Act and section 3121(b)(8)(B). The waiver certificate shall be deemed to have been filed on the first day of the period described in subparagraph (1)(iii) of this paragraph and shall be effective on the first day of the calendar quarter in which such period began. However, such waiver is effective only with respect to remuneration for services performed after 1950.

(ii) The waiver certificate shall be deemed to have been accompanied by a list containing the signature, address, and social security number (if any) of each employee with respect to whom the taxes imposed by sections 3101 and 3111 were paid as described in subparagraph (1)(iii) of this paragraph. Each such employee shall be deemed to have concurred in the filing of the certificate for purposes of section 210(a)(8)(B) of the Social Security Act and section 3121(b)(8)(B). A statement containing the name, address, and employer identification number of the organization, and the name, last known address, and social security number (if any) of each employee described in the preceding sentence shall be filed by the organization at the request of the Internal Revenue Service.

(iii) The services of all employees entering or reentering the employ of an organization on or after the first day following the close of the calendar quarter in which the organization is deemed to have filed the waiver certificate, performed on or after the day of such entry or reentry, shall be covered by the certificate.

(3) This paragraph (a) shall not apply to an organization if—

(i) Prior to the end of the period referred to in subparagraph (1)(iii) (and, in addition, in the case of an organization organized on or before October 9, 1969, prior to October 19, 1976), the organization had applied for a ruling or determination letter acknowledging it to be exempt from income tax under section 501(c)(3);

(ii) The organization subsequently received such ruling or determination letter;

(iii) The organization did not pay any taxes under sections 3101 and 3111 with respect to any employee for any calendar quarter ending after the twelfth month following the date of mailing of the ruling or determination letter; and

(iv) The organization did not pay any taxes under sections 3101 and 3111 with respect to any calendar quarter beginning after the later of December 31, 1975, or the date on which the ruling or determination letter was issued.

(4) In the case of an organization which is deemed under this paragraph to have filed a valid waiver certificate under section 3121(k)(1), if the period with respect to which the taxes imposed by sections 3101 and 3111 were paid by the organization (as described in paragraph (a)(1)(iii) of this section) terminated prior to October 1, 1976, taxes under sections 3101 and 3111 with respect to remuneration paid by the organization after the termination of such period and prior to July 1, 1977, which remained unpaid on December 20, 1977 (or which were paid after October 19, 1976, but prior to December 20, 1977), shall not be due or payable (or, if paid, shall be refunded). Similarly, an organization that received a refund or credit of the taxes described in paragraph (a)(1)(iii) of this section after September 8, 1976, shall not be liable for the taxes imposed by sections 3101 and 3111 with respect to remuneration paid by it prior to July 1, 1977, for which the organization received the refund or credit. The waiver certificate, which an organization described in this subparagraph is deemed to have filed, shall not apply to any service with respect to the remuneration for which the taxes imposed by section 3101 and 3111 are not due or payable (or are refunded) by reason of this subparagraph.

(5) In the case of an organization which is deemed under this paragraph to have filed a valid waiver certificate under section 3121(k)(1), if the taxes imposed by sections 3101 and 3111 were not paid during the period referred to in paragraph (a)(1)(iii) of this section (whether the period has terminated or not) with respect to remuneration paid by the organization to individuals who became its employees after the close of the calendar quarter in which such period began, taxes under section 3101 and 3111 with respect to remuneration paid prior to July 1, 1977, to such employees, which remain unpaid on December 20, 1977 (or which were paid after October 19, 1976, but prior to December 20, 1977), shall not be due or payable (or, if paid, shall be refunded). The waiver certificate, which an organization described in this subparagraph is deemed to have filed, shall not apply to any service with respect to remuneration for which the taxes imposed by sections 3101 and 3111 are not due or payable (or are refunded) by reason of this subparagraph.

(6) This subparagraph allows certain employees to obtain social security coverage for service not covered by a deemed-filed waiver certificate by reason of section 3121(k)(4)(C) and subparagraph (4) or (5) of this paragraph. To qualify under this subparagraph, all of the following conditions must be met.

(i) An individual performed service as an employee of an organization which is deemed under this paragraph to have filed a waiver certificate under section 3121(k)(1), on or after the first day of the period described in subparagraph (1)(iii) of this paragraph and before July 1, 1977.

(ii) The service performed by the individual does not constitute employment (as defined in section 210(a) of the Social Security Act and section 3121(b) of the Code) because the waiver certificate which the organization is deemed to have filed is inapplicable to such service by reason of section 3121(k)(4)(C), but would constitute employment (as so defined) in the absence of section 3121(k)(4)(C).

(iii) The individual files a request on or before April 15, 1980, in the manner and form, and with such official, as may be prescribed by regulations under title II of the Social Security Act.

(iv) That request is accompanied by full payment of the taxes, which would have been paid under section 3101 with respect to remuneration for the service described in subdivision (ii) of this subparagraph but for the application of section 3121(k)(4)(C) (or by satisfactory evidence that appropriate arrangements have been made for the payment of such taxes in installments as provided in section 3121(k)(8) and paragraph (d) of this section).

If these conditions are satisfied, the remuneration paid for the service described in subdivision (i) of this subparagraph shall be deemed to constitute remuneration for employment. In any case where remuneration paid by an organization to an individual is deemed under this subparagraph to constitute remuneration for employment, such organization shall be liable (notwithstanding any other provision of the Code or regulations) for payment of the taxes it would have been required to pay under section 3111 with respect to such remuneration but for the application of section 3121(k)(4)(C). The due date for the return and payment by the organization of the taxes described in the preceding sentence shall be the last day of the calendar month following the calendar quarter in which the organization is notified in writing of the employee's request. However, see paragraph (d) of this section which permits the payment of these taxes in installments.

(b) Constructive filing of waiver certificate where refund or credit has been allowed and new certificate is not filed. *(1)* This paragraph applies to an organization which meets two conditions. First, it must be an organization to which paragraph (a) of this section would apply but for its failure to satisfy the requirement of paragraph (a)(1)(iv) of this section because a refund or credit of taxes was allowed before September 9, 1976. Second, it must not have filed an actual valid waiver certificate under section 3121(k)(1) in accordance with the requirements of paragraph (c) of this section.

(2) An organization to which this paragraph applies shall be deemed, for purposes of section 210(a)(8)(B) of the Social Security Act and section 3121(b)(8)(B), to have filed a valid waiver certificate under section 3121(k)(1) on April 1, 1978. Such certificate shall be effective for the period beginning on the first day of the first calendar quarter with respect to which the refund or credit referred to in subparagraph (1) of this paragraph was allowed (or, if later, on July 1, 1973).

(3) If an organization is deemed under this paragraph to have filed a waiver certificate on April 1, 1978, the provisions of paragraphs (a)(2)(ii) and (iii) of this section (relating to employees covered by a deemed-filed waiver certificate) shall apply. Such certificate shall supersede any certificate which may have been actually filed by such organization prior to that date.

(4) Where an organization is deemed under this paragraph to have filed a waiver certificate on April 1, 1978, the due date for the return and payment of the taxes imposed by sections 3101 and 3111 for wages paid prior to April 1, 1978,

with respect to services constituting employment by reason of such certificate shall be August 1, 1978. However, see paragraph (d) of this section which permits the payment of these taxes in installments. Such taxes (along with the amount of any interest paid in connection with the refund or credit described in subparagraph (1) of this paragraph) shall be a liability of such organization, payable from its own funds. No portion of such taxes (or interest) shall be deducted from the wages of (or otherwise collected from) the individuals who performed such services, and those individuals shall have no liability for the payment thereof.

(5) This subparagraph allows certain employees of organizations covered under this paragraph to obtain social security coverage for periods prior to those covered by a deemed-filed waiver certificate. To qualify under this subparagraph, all of the following conditions must be met.

(i) An individual performed service, as an employee of an organization deemed under this paragraph to have filed a waiver certificate under section 3121(k)(1), at any time prior to the period for which such certificate is effective.

(ii) The taxes imposed by sections 3101 and 3111 were paid with respect to remuneration paid for such service, but such service (or any part thereof) does not constitute employment (as defined in section 210(a) of the Social Security Act and section 3121(b)) because the applicable taxes so paid were refunded or credited (otherwise than through a refund or credit which would have been allowed if a valid waiver certificate filed under section 3121(k)(1) had been in effect) prior to September 9, 1976.

(iii) Any portion of such service (with respect to which taxes were paid and refunded or credited as described in subdivision (ii) of this subparagraph) would constitute employment (as so defined) if the organization had actually filed under section 3121(k)(1) a valid waiver certificate effective as provided in paragraph (c)(2) of this section (with such individual's signature appearing on the accompanying list).

If this subparagraph applies, the remuneration paid for the portion of such service described in subdivision (iii) of this subparagraph shall be deemed to constitute remuneration for employment (as defined in section 210(a) of the Social Security Act and section 3121(b)), where such individual filed a request on or are April 15, 1980 (in the manner and form, and with such official, as may be prescribed by regulations under title II of the Social Security Act), accompanied by full repayment of the taxes which were paid under section 3101 with respect to such remuneration and were refunded or credited (or by satisfactory evidence that arrangements have been made for the payment of such taxes in installments as provided in section 3121(k)(8) and paragraph (d) of this section). In any case where remuneration paid by an organization to an individual is deemed under this subparagraph to constitute remuneration for employment such organization shall be liable (notwithstanding any other provision of the Code or regulations) for repayment of any taxes which it paid under section 3111 with respect to such remuneration and which were refunded or credited to it. Any interest received by the organization or its employees in connection with a refund or credit with respect to such taxes shall be remitted with the repayment of taxes pursuant to this subparagraph.

(c) Actual filing of waiver certificate by April 1, 1978, where refund or credit has been allowed. *(1)* An organization may file an actual waiver certificate in accordance with subparagraphs (2) and (3) of this paragraph if it is an organization to which paragraph (a) of this section would apply but for its failure to meet the condition set forth in paragraph (a)(1)(iv) of this section.

(2) An organization described in subparagraph (1) of this paragraph was permitted to file an actual waiver certificate on or before April 1, 1978. This certificate must be effective for the period beginning on or before the first day of the first calendar quarter with respect to which a refund or credit described in paragraph (b)(1) of this section was allowed (or, if later, with the first day of the earliest calendar quarter for which such certificate may be in effect under section 3121(k)(1)(B)(iii)). Such waiver certificate must have been accompanied by a list described in section 3121(k)(1)(A), containing the signature, address, and social security number of each concurring employee (if any).

(3) Such a waiver certificate shall be valid only if the organization complied with the following notification requirements and, on or before April 30, 1978, filed (with the service center of the Internal Revenue Service with which the waiver certificate was filed) a certification that it had complied with these notification requirements. However, these requirements shall be conclusively presumed to have been met with respect to any employees who concurred in the filing of the waiver certificate.

(i) Written notification of the option to obtain social security coverage for the retroactive period covered by the waiver certificate is required to have been given to all current and former employees of the organization with respect to whose remuneration taxes imposed by sections 3101 and 3111 were paid for any part of the period covered by the waiver certificate. For purposes of the preceding sentence, in the case of a former employee a mailing of notification to his or her last known address shall constitute delivery to the former employee. This notification must have been given at least 30 days prior to the date by which the employee was required to inform the organization whether he or she elects the retroactive social security coverage.

(ii) The notification required by this subparagraph must have stated the earliest date for which the waiver certificate is effective and the date by which the employee must have informed the organization of a decision to elect the retroactive coverage. In addition, the notification must have advised the employee how to obtain information as to the quarters of social security coverage to be obtained and any taxes or interest for which the employee would be liable if the election was made. The organization must have provided this information to any interested employee at least 14 days prior to the last day on which such employee was to have informed the organization of any election.

(iii) If the notification resulted in any employee electing the retroactive coverage whose signature did not appear on the list of concurring employees which accompanied a previously filed waiver certificate, the certification that was supplied on or before April 30, 1978, must have been accompanied by a special amendment to that list. Any employee whose name appears on this special amended list shall be treated as if his or her name appeared on the list of concurring employees filed with the waiver certificate. The preceding sentence shall only apply with respect to amended lists of concurring employees filed to comply with the requirements of this subparagraph.

(4) Any interest received in connection with a refund or credit described in paragraph (b)(1) of this section must have been repaid on or before April 30, 1978, with respect to each employee who concurs in the filing of a waiver certifi-

cate pursuant to this paragraph. Notwithstanding the provisions of paragraph (c)(4) of § 31.3121(k)-1, if such interest was repaid on or before April 30, 1978, the waiver certificate shall be considered to have been filed on the date it was originally furnished to the Internal Revenue Service.

(d) Installment payment of taxes for retroactive coverage. This paragraph applies if—

(1) An organization is deemed under paragraph (a) of this section to have filed a valid waiver certificate, but the applicable period described in paragraph (a)(1)(iii) has terminated and all or part of the taxes imposed by sections 3101 and 3111, with respect to remuneration paid by such organization to employees after the close of such period, remains payable notwithstanding section 3121(k)(4)(C) and paragraph (a)(4) of this section; or

(2) An organization described in paragraph (c) files a valid waiver certificate by March 31, 1978, or, not having filed the certificate by that date, is deemed to have filed the certificate on April 1, 1978, under paragraph (b); or

(3) An individual files a request under paragraph (a)(6) or (b)(5) to have service treated as constituting remuneration for employment (as defined in section 210(a) of the Social Security Act and section 3121(b)).

If this paragraph applies, the taxes due under sections 3101 and 3111 (together with any additions to tax or interest other than interest described in paragraph (c)(4)) with respect to service constituting employment by reason of the waiver certificate for any period prior to the first day of the calendar quarter in which the certificate is filed or deemed file, or with respect to service constituting employment by reason of an employee request, may be paid in installments over an appropriate period of time, as determined by the district director. In determining the appropriate period of time, the district director shall exercise forbearance and, to the extent possible, grant the organization an installment agreement that will allow it sufficient funds to carry out its basic mission. If any installment is not paid on or before the date fixed for its payment, the total unpaid amount shall become payable immediately and shall be paid upon notice and demand.

(e) Application of certain provisions to cases of constructive filing. *(1)* Except as provided in subparagraphs (2) and (3) of this paragraph, all of the provisions of section 3121(k) (other than subparagraphs (B), (F), and (H) of section 3121(k)(1)) and the regulations thereunder (including the provisions requiring the payment of taxes under sections 3101 and 3111 with respect to the services involved) shall apply with respect to any certificate which is deemed to have been filed under paragraph (a) or (b) of this section, in the same way they would apply if the certificate had been actually filed on that day under section 3121(k)(1).

(2) The provisions of section 3121(k)(1)(E) shall not apply unless the taxes described in paragraph (a)(1)(iii) of this section were paid by the organization as though a separate certificate had been filed with respect to one or both of the groups to which such provisions relate.

(3) The action of the organization in obtaining the refund or credit described in paragraph (b)(1) of this section shall not be considered a termination of such organization's coverage period for purposes of section 3121(k)(3).

(4) Any organization which is deemed to have filed a waiver certificate under paragraph (a) or (b) of this section shall be considered for purposes of section 3102(b) to have been required to deduct the taxes imposed by section 3101 with respect to the services involved.

T.D. 7647, 10/15/79.

§ 36.3121(l)-0 Introduction.

(a) The regulations in this part deal with the circumstances under which a domestic corporation may enter into an agreement with the Internal Revenue Service for the purpose of extending the insurance system established by title II of the Social Security Act to certain services performed outside the United States by citizens of the United States as employees of a foreign subsidiary of the domestic corporation, and with the obligations of a domestic corporation which enters into such an agreement. The provisions of the Internal Revenue Code of 1954, as amended, to which the regulations in this part pertain are contained in section 3121(l). The liabilities assumed under an agreement entered into pursuant to such section are based on the remuneration for services covered by the agreement. Such agreement may not be effective prior to January 1, 1955.

(b) Although the obligations incurred under an agreement entered into pursuant to section 3121(l) of the Internal Revenue Code of 1954, as amended, must be distinguished from the obligations imposed on employers with respect to the taxes under the Federal Insurance Contributions Act, the two are similar in many respects. Accordingly, the regulations in this part are prescribed as a supplement to the regulations (26 CFR (1954), Part 31, Subpart B) relating to the employee tax and the employer tax imposed by the Federal Insurance Contributions Act. The terms used in the regulations in this part have the same meaning, unless otherwise provided, as when used in the regulations relating to the taxes imposed by such act.

(c) The regulations in this part constitute Part 36 of Title 26 of the Code of Federal Regulations. As used in the regulations in this part, the word "Code" means the Internal Revenue Code of 1954, as amended, and the term "Federal Insurance Contributions Act" means chapter 21 of such Code. All references to sections of law are references to the Code unless otherwise indicated. The number of each section of the regulations begins with 36 followed by a decimal point (36.). Numbers which do not begin with 36 followed by a decimal point are numbers of sections of law unless otherwise indicated. In identifying sections of regulations, the symbol "§ " is used.

T.D. 6145, 9/8/55, amend T.D. 7012, 5/14/69, T.D. 7665, 1/24/80.

§ 31.3121(l)-1 Agreements entered into by domestic corporations with respect to foreign subsidiaries.

For provisions relating to the extension of the Federal old-age, survivors, and disability insurance system established by title II of the Social Security Act to certain services performed outside the United States by citizens of the United States in the employ of a foreign subsidiary of a domestic corporation, see the Regulations Relating to Contract Coverage of Employees of Foreign Subsidiaries (Part 36 of this chapter).

T.D. 6190, 7/13/56, amend T.D. 6516, 12/19/60.

§ 36.3121(l)(1)-1 Agreements entered into by domestic corporations with respect to foreign subsidiaries.

(a) In general. *(1)* Any domestic corporation having one or more foreign subsidiaries may request the Internal Revenue Service to enter into an agreement for the purpose of extending the Federal old-age, survivors, and disability insurance system established by title II of the Social Security Act to certain services performed outside the United States by all citizens of the United States who are employees of any such foreign subsidiary. See § 36.3121(l)(8)-1, relating to the definition of foreign subsidiary. Except as provided in § 36.3121(l)(5)-1, relating to the effect of the termination of an agreement entered into pursuant to the provisions of section 3121(l), the Internal Revenue Service shall, at the request of a domestic corporation enter into such agreement on Form 2032 in any case where a Form 2032 is executed, and submitted by the domestic corporation in the manner prescribed in this section. A domestic corporation may not have in effect at the same moment of time more than one agreement on Form 2032.

(2) An agreement authorized in section 3121(l)(1) may not be made applicable to any services performed outside the United States which would not constitute employment, for purposes of the taxes imposed under the Federal Insurance Contributions Act, if the services were performed within the United States. Thus, such an agreement shall have no application with respect to any services performed outside the United States which, if performed within the United States, would be specifically excepted from employment under any of the numbered paragraphs of section 3121(b), or which, although not so excepted, would be deemed not to be employment by application of section 3121(c), relating to included and excluded services. Further, an agreement may not be made applicable with respect to any services performed outside the United States which constitute employment, as defined in section 3121(b). Thus, an agreement may not be made applicable to services for any employer performed by any employee on or in connection with an American vessel or American aircraft when outside the United States, if (i) performed under a contract of service which is entered into within the United States or (ii) during the performance of which and while the employee is employed on the vessel or aircraft it touches at a port in the United States, because such services constitute employment as defined in section 3121(b). An agreement may not be made applicable to remuneration which would not constitute wages, as defined in section 3121(a), even if the services to which such remuneration is attributable had constituted employment.

(3) The terms "corporation", "domestic", and "foreign", as used in the regulations in this part, have the meaning assigned by paragraphs (3), (4), and (5), respectively, of section 7701(a). Section 701(a)(3), (4), and (5) provides as follows:

SEC. 7701. Definitions. (a) When used in this title [Internal Revenue Code of 1954]. where not otherwise distinctly expressed or manifestly incompatible with the intent thereof—

(3) Corporation. The term "corporation" includes associations, joint-stock companies, and insurance companies.

(4) Domestic. The term "domestic" when applied to a corporation * * * means created or organized in the United States or under the law of the United States or of any State or Territory. *(5)* Foreign. The term "foreign" when applied to a corporation * * * means a corporation * * * which is not domestic.

(b) Form and contents of agreement. Form 2032 is the form prescribed for the agreement authorized in section 3121(l)(1). The agreement shall include provisions substantially as follows:

(1) That the agreement shall apply to all services performed outside the United States by all citizens of the United States who are in the employ of the foreign subsidiary or subsidiaries to which the agreement is made applicable, but only to the extent that the remuneration paid each employee for such services would constitute wages if paid by one employer for services performed in the United States;

(2) That the agreement shall not apply to any services which constitute employment within the meaning of section 3121;

(3) That the agreement shall become effective on the first day of the Calendar quarter in which the Form 2032 is signed by the district director or director of the service center or on the first day of the next succeeding calendar quarter, whichever is specified in the agreement;

(4) That the domestic corporation will pay, as required by the regulations in this part, amounts equivalent to the sum of the taxes which would be imposed by sections 3101 and 3111, respectively, if the remuneration for the services covered by the agreement constituted wages;

(5) That the domestic corporation will pay, in accordance with written notification and demand therefore to the domestic corporation, amounts equivalent to the interest, additions to the taxes, additional amounts, and penalties which would be applicable if the remuneration for services covered by the agreement constituted wages; and

(6) That the domestic corporation will comply with all provisions of the regulations in this part.

(c) Execution and filing of Form 2032. The request of any domestic corporation that the Internal Revenue Service enter into an agreement with the corporation on Form 2032 shall be signified by the corporation by executing and filing Form 2032 in triplicate. Such form shall be executed and filed in accordance with the regulations in this part and the instructions relating to the form. Each copy of the form shall be signed and dated by the officer of the corporation authorized to enter into the agreement, shall show the title of such officer, and shall have the corporate seal affixed thereto. A certified copy of the minutes of the meeting of the board of directors of the domestic corporation, or other evidence, showing the authority of such officer so to act shall accompany the form. Form 2032 executed and filed as provided in this paragraph shall be signed and dated by the district director or director of the service center and, upon such signing, the Form 2032 so executed and filed will constitute the agreement authorized in section 3121(l)(1). The Internal Revenue Service will return one copy of the agreement to the domestic corporation, will transmit one copy of the Department of Health, Education, and Welfare, and will retain one copy (together with all related papers).

T.D. 6145, 9/8/55, amend T.D. 7012, 5/15/69.

§ 36.3121(l)(1)-2 Amendment of agreement.

(a) An agreement entered into by a domestic corporation as provided in § 36.3121(l)(1)-1 may be amended so as to be made applicable, in the same manner and under the same conditions, with respect to any one or more of the foreign subsidiaries of the domestic corporation not previously named in the agreement. See § 36.3121(l)(2)-1(b), relating to the effective period of an amendment of an agreement.

(b) Form 2032 Supplement is the form prescribed for use in amending an agreement entered into by a domestic corporation as provided in § 36.3121(l)(1)-1.

(c) A domestic corporation shall signify its desire to amend an agreement entered into by the corporation as provided in § 36.3121(l)(1)-1 by executing and filing Form 2032 Supplement in triplicate.

(d) Form 2032 Supplement shall be executed and filed in the manner and in conformity with the requirements prescribed in the instructions relating to such form and in § 36.3121(l)(1)-1(c) in respect of an agreement on Form 2032. Form 2032 Supplement executed and filed as provided in this paragraph shall be signed and dated by the district director or director of the service center, and, upon such signing the Form 2032 Supplement so executed and filed will constitute an amendment of the agreement entered into on Form 2032. The Internal Revenue Service will return one copy of the amendment to the domestic corporation, will transmit one copy to the Department of Health, Education, and Welfare, and will retain one copy (together with all related papers).

T.D. 6145, 9/8/55, amend T.D. 7012, 5/14/69.

§ 36.3121(l)(1)-3 Effect of agreement.

(a) Liability for amounts equivalent to tax. *(1) In general.* A domestic corporation which has entered into an agreement (as provided in § 36.3121(l)(1)-1, or any amendment thereof (as provided in § 36.3121(l)(1)-2, incurs liability under the agreement in respect of certain remuneration paid by each foreign subsidiary named in the agreement, or any amendment thereof, Liability is incurred in respect of the remuneration paid to all those employees of the foreign subsidiaries who are citizens of the United States and who perform services outside the United States (other than services which constitute employment) for the foreign subsidiaries. However, liability is incurred only with respect to that portion of such remuneration paid by the foreign subsidiary which is attributable to services performed during the period for which the agreement is in effect with respect to such subsidiary, and then only to the extent that the remuneration would constitute wages if the services to which the remuneration is attributable were performed in the United States. Liability with respect to such remuneration is incurred in an amount equivalent to the sum of the employee and employer taxes which would be imposed by sections 3101 and 3111, respectively, if such remuneration constituted wages. If an individual performs services for more than one of the foreign subsidiaries named in an agreement, including any amendment thereof, such services are regarded as being performed in the employ of a single employer for purposes of determining the amount of the remuneration for such services which would constitute wages if the services were performed in the United States. See § 36.3121(l)(9)-1, relating to the treatment of a domestic corporation as a separate entity in its capacity as a party to an agreement.

(2) Examples. The application of subparagraph (1) of this paragraph may be illustrated by the following examples:

Example (1). P., a domestic corporation, has entered into an agreement as provided in § 36.3121(l)(1)-1, effective with respect to services performed on and after January 1, 1955. Three foreign subsidiaries, S-1, S-2, and S-3 are named in the agreement. A, a citizen of the United States, is employed during 1955 by S-1, S-2, and S-3, for the performance outside the United States of services covered by the agreement. In 1955 A is paid remuneration of $2,500 for such services by each of the foreign subsidiaries. The circumstances are such that the entire $7,500 would constitute wages if the services has been performed in the United States. However, only $4,200 of such remuneration would constitute wages if the services had been performed in the United States for a single employer, and it is with respect to this amount only that P incurs liability under its agreement.

Example (2). On August 1, 1955, P, the domestic corporation in the preceding example, amends its agreement to include therein its foreign subsidiary S-4. The amendment is in effect with respect to S-4 for the period beginning with October 1, 1955. B, a citizen of the United States, is employed by S-4 throughout 1955 for the performance of services outside the United States. B is paid remuneration of $500 in each month of 1955 for these services. The circumstances are such that the first $4,200 of such remuneration would constitute wages if the services had been performed in the United States, and, except for the $4,200 limitation, the remainder of such remuneration would constitute wages if the services had been so performed. P incurs no liability with respect to remuneration paid B for services performed for S-4 prior to October 1, 1955. However, P incurs liability under its agreement with respect to the $1,500 paid B in October, November, and December 1955, for services performed in these months. Since the remuneration paid to B for services performed during the first nine months of 1955 is not covered by the agreement, such remuneration is not taken into account in computing the $4,200 limitation or the liability under the agreement.

Example (3). Assume the same facts as in example (2) except that B's services for S-4 during December 1955 are of a character which if performed within the United States would be excepted from employment. Accordingly, P incurs no liability under the agreement with respect to the $500.00 paid in December 1955 for such services.

(3) Determination of liability. The amount of the liability referred to in subparagraph (1) of this paragraph incurred by a domestic corporation for any period shall be determined in the same manner as liability for the employee tax and for the employer tax imposed by the Federal Insurance Contributions Act is determined, pursuant to regulations relating to the taxes under such act as in effect for the same period, with respect to wages paid by an employer to an employee.

(b) Liability for amounts equivalent to interest of penalties. A domestic corporation which has entered into an agreement as provided in § 36.3121(l)(1)-1 also incurs liability under the agreement for amounts equivalent to the amount of interest, additions to the taxes, additional amounts, and penalties which would be applicable if the remuneration for services covered by the agreement constituted wages.

(c) Deductions from employees' remuneration. There is no obligation to deduct, or cause to be deducted, from the remuneration of any employee of a foreign subsidiary any part of the amount due from a domestic corporation under its agreement. Whether such deduction shall be made is a matter for settlement between the employee and the domestic corporation or such other person as may be concerned.

(d) Cross reference. For other obligations of a domestic corporation under an agreement, see § 36.3121(l)(1)-1.

T.D. 6145, 9/8/55, amend T.D. 6390, 6/13/59.

§ 36.3121(l)(2)-1 Effective period of agreement.

(a) In general. An agreement entered into as provided in § 36.3121(l)(1)-1 shall be in effect for the period beginning with the first day of the calendar quarter in which the agreement is signed by the district director or director of the service center, or the first day of the calendar quarter following the calendar quarter in which the agreement is signed by the district director or director of the service center, whichever is specified in the agreement. In no case, however, shall the agreement be effective for any calendar quarter which begins prior to January 1, 1955.

(b) Amendment of agreement. If an amendment on Form 2032 Supplement (filed by a domestic corporation to include in its agreement services performed for a foreign subsidiary not previously named therein) is signed by the district director or director of the service center, within the quarter for which the agreement is first effective or within the first calendar month following such quarter, the agreement shall be effective with respect to the subsidiary named in the amendment as of the date such agreement first became effective. However, if the amendment is signed by the district director or director of the service center after the last day of the fourth month for which the agreement is in effect, such agreement shall be in effect with respect to the subsidiary named in the amendment for the period beginning with the first day of the calendar quarter following the calendar quarter in which the amendment is signed by the district director or director of the service center.

T.D. 7012, 5/14/69.

§ 36.3121(l)(3)-1 Termination of agreement by domestic corporation or by reason of change in stock ownership.

(a) Termination by domestic corporation. *(1)* A domestic corporation which has entered into an agreement under section 3121(l)(1) with respect to one or more of its foreign subsidiaries may terminate such agreement in part or in its entirety by giving (for calendar quarters beginning before 1969, to the district director for the internal revenue district in which is located the principal place of business in the United States of the domestic corporation; and for calendar quarters beginning after 1968, except as provided in paragraph (b) of § 301.6091-1 (relating to hand-carried documents) to the director of the service center serving such internal revenue district 2 years' advance notice in writing of its desire so to terminate the agreement at the end of a specified calendar quarter: Provided, That, at the time of the receipt of such notice by such internal revenue officer, the agreement has been in effect with respect to the subsidiary or subsidiaries covered by the notice for at least 8 years. The notice of termination shall be signed and dated and shall show (i) the title of the officer authorized to sign the notice, (ii) the name, address, and identification number of the domestic corporation, (iii) the internal revenue officer with whom the agreement was entered into, (iv) the name and address of each foreign subsidiary with respect to which the agreement is to be terminated, (v) the date on which the agreement became effective with respect to each such foreign subsidiary, and (vi) the date on which the agreement is to be terminated with respect to each such foreign subsidiary. The notice shall be submitted in duplicate and shall be accompanied by a certified copy of the minutes of the meeting of the board of directors of the domestic corporation, or other evidence, showing authorization for the notice of termination. No particular form is prescribed for the notice of termination. The Internal Revenue Service will transmit one copy of the notice of termination to the Department of Health, Education, and Welfare.

(2) A notice of termination given by a domestic corporation in respect of any one or more of its foreign subsidiaries may be revoked by the corporation with respect to any such subsidiary or subsidiaries by giving, prior to the close of the calendar quarter specified in the notice of termination, written notice of revocation. The notice of revocation shall be filed with the internal revenue officer with whom the notice of termination was filed. Such notice of revocation shall be signed and dated and shall show (i) the title of the officer authorized to sign the notice of revocation, (ii) the name, address, and identification number of the domestic corporation, (iii) the name and address of each foreign subsidiary with respect to which the notice of termination is revoked, and (iv) the date of the notice of termination to be revoked. The notice shall be submitted in duplicate and shall be accompanied by a certified copy of the minutes of the meeting of the board of directors of the domestic corporation, or other evidence, showing authorization for the notice of revocation. No particular form is prescribed for the notice of revocation. The Internal Revenue Service will transmit one copy of the notice of revocation to the Department of Health, Education, and Welfare.

(b) Termination by reason of change in stock ownership. *(1)* The period for which an agreement entered into by a domestic corporation as provided in § 36.3121(l)(1)-1 is in effect with respect to a foreign corporation is automatically terminated at the end of the calendar quarter in which the foreign corporation ceases, at any time in such quarter, to be a foreign subsidiary of the domestic corporation. See § 36.3121(l)(8)-1, relating to definition of foreign subsidiary.

(2) A domestic corporation which has entered into an agreement as provided in § 36.3121(l)(1)-1 shall furnish (for calendar quarters beginning before 1969, to the district director for the internal revenue district in which is located its principal place of business in the United States; and for calendar quarters beginning after 1968, except as provided in paragraph (b) of § 301.6091-1 (relating to hand-carried documents) to the director of the service center serving such internal revenue district) written notification in the event that a foreign corporation named in the agreement, including any amendment thereof, as a foreign subsidiary of the domestic corporation ceases to be its foreign subsidiary. The written notification shall be furnished in duplicate on or before the last day of the first month following the close of the calendar quarter in which the foreign corporation ceases, at any time in such quarter, to be a foreign subsidiary of the domestic corporation. Such notification shall be signed and dated by the president or other principal officer of the domestic corporation. The written notification shall show (i) the title of the officer signing the notice, (ii) the name, address, and identification number of the domestic corporation, (iii) the internal revenue officer with whom the agreement was entered into, (iv) the date on which the agreement was entered into, (v) the name and address of the foreign corporation with respect to which the notification is furnished, and (vi) the date on which the foreign corporation ceased to be a foreign subsidiary of the domestic corporation. No particular form is prescribed for the written notification. The Internal Revenue Service will transmit one copy of the written notification to the Department of Health, Education, and Welfare.

T.D. 6145, 9/8/55, amend T.D. 7012, 5/14/69.

§ 36.3121(l)(4)-1 Termination of agreement by Commissioner.

(a) Notice of termination. The period for which an agreement entered into with a domestic corporation as provided in § 36.3121(l)(1)-1 is in effect may be terminated by the Commissioner, with the prior concurrence of the Secretary of Health, Education, and Welfare, upon a finding by the

Commissioner that the domestic corporation has failed to comply substantially with the terms of the agreement. The Commissioner shall give the corporation not less than 60 days advance notice in writing that the period for which the agreement is in effect will terminate at the end of the calendar quarter specified in the notice of termination.

(b) Revocation of notice of termination. A notice of termination given to a domestic corporation by the Commissioner may be revoked by the Commissioner, with the prior concurrence of the Secretary of Health, Education and Welfare by giving written notice of revocation to the corporation prior to the close of the calendar quarter specified in the notice of termination.

T.D. 6145, 9/8/55.

§ 36.3121(l)(5)-1 Effect of termination.

(a) Termination of entire agreement. *(1)* If the effective period of an agreement entered into by a domestic corporation as provided in § 36.3121(l)(1)-1 is terminated by the domestic corporation, pursuant to § 36.3121(l)(3)-1(a), with respect to all foreign subsidiaries named in the agreement, including any amendment thereof, an agreement may not again be entered into by the domestic corporation under the provisions of section 3121(l)(1).

(2) If the effective period of an agreement entered into by a domestic corporation as provided in § 36.3121(l)(1)-1 is terminated by the Commissioner, pursuant to § 36.3121(1)(4)-1(a), an agreement may not again be entered into by the domestic corporation under the provisions of section 3121(l)(1).

(3) If the effective period of an agreement entered into by a domestic corporation as provided in § 36.3121(l)(1)-1 is terminated automatically by reason of a change in stock ownership (see § 36.3121(l)(3)-1(b)) with respect to all foreign corporations named in the agreement, including any amendment thereof, a new agreement may be entered into by the domestic corporation, as provided in § 36.3121(l)(1)-1, with respect to any foreign corporation which is a foreign subsidiary of the domestic corporation.

(b) Partial termination of agreement. *(1)* If the effective period of an agreement entered into by a domestic corporation as provided in § 36.3121(l)(1)-1 is terminated by the domestic corporation, pursuant to § 36.3121(l)(3)-1(a), with respect to one or more foreign subsidiaries named in the agreement, including any amendment thereof, the period for which the agreement is in effect will continue with respect to any other foreign subsidiary or subsidiaries named in the agreement (or amendment). However, the agreement may not thereafter be amended to include any foreign subsidiary with respect to which the effective period of the agreement has been terminated.

(2) If the effective period of an agreement entered into by a domestic corporation as provided in § 36.3121(l)(1)-1 is terminated automatically by reason of a change in stock ownership (see § 36.3121(l)(3)-1(b)) with respect to a foreign corporation which has ceased to be a foreign subsidiary of the domestic corporation, but the period for which the agreement is in effect continues with respect to one or more other foreign subsidiaries, the agreement may not thereafter be amended to include such foreign corporation even though the foreign corporation may again become a foreign subsidiary of the domestic corporation.

T.D. 6145, 9/8/55.

§ 36.3121(l)(7)-1 Overpayment and underpayments.

(a) Adjustments. *(1) In general.* Errors in the payment of amounts for which liability equivalent to the employee and employer taxes with respect to any payment of remuneration is incurred by a domestic corporation pursuant to its agreement are adjustable by the domestic corporation in certain cases without interest. However, not all corrections made under this section constitute adjustments within the meaning of the regulations in this part. The various situations in which such corrections constitute adjustments are set forth in paragraphs (a)(2) and (3) of this section. All corrections in respect of underpayments and all adjustments or credits in respect of overpayments made under this section must be reported on a return filed by the domestic corporation under the regulations in this part and not on a return filed with respect to the employee and employer taxes imposed by sections 3101 and 3111, respectively. Every return on which such a correction (by adjustment, credit, or otherwise) is reported pursuant to this section must have securely attached as a part thereof a statement explaining the error in respect of which the correction is made, designating the calendar quarter in which the error was ascertained, and setting forth such other information as would be required if the correction were in respect of an overpayment or underpayment of taxes under the Federal Insurance Contributions Act. An error is ascertained when the domestic corporation has sufficient knowledge of the error to be able to correct it. An underpayment may not be corrected under this section after receipt from the district director or director of the service center of written notification of the amount due and demand for payment thereof, but the amount shall be paid in accordance with such notification.

(2) Underpayments. If a domestic corporation fails to report, on a return filed under the regulations in this part, all or any part of the amount for which liability equivalent to the employee and employer taxes is incurred under its agreement with respect to any payment of remuneration, the domestic corporation shall adjust the underpayment by reporting the additional amount due as an adjustment on a return or supplemental return filed on or before the last day on which the return for the return period in which the error is ascertained is required to be filed. The amount of each underpayment adjusted in accordance with this subparagraph shall be paid, without interest, at the time fixed for reporting the adjustment. If an adjustment is reported pursuant to this subparagraph but the amount thereof is not paid when due, interest thereafter accrues.

(3) Overpayments. If a domestic corporation pays more than the amount for which liability equivalent to the employee and employer taxes is incurred under its agreement with respect to any payment of remuneration, the domestic corporation may correct the error, subject to the requirements and under the conditions stated in this paragraph, by deducting the amount of the overpayment from the amount of liability reported on a return filed by the domestic corporation, except that—

(i) A correction may not be made in respect of any part of an overpayment which was collected from an individual by reason of the agreement unless the domestic corporation (a) has repaid the amount so collected to the individual, has secured the written receipt of the individual showing the date and amount of the repayment, and retains such receipt as a part of its records, or (b) has reimbursed the individual by reducing the amounts which otherwise should have been deducted from his remuneration by reason of the agreement; and

(ii) A correction may not be made in one calendar year in respect of any part of an overpayment which was collected from an individual in a prior calendar year unless the domestic corporation has secured the written statement of the individual showing that he has not claimed and will not claim refund or credit of the amount so collected, and retains such receipt as a part of its records. See § 31.6413(c)-1 of this chapter relating to claims for special credit or refund.

The correction constitutes an adjustment under this subparagraph only if it is reported on the return for the period in which the error is ascertained or on the return for the next following period, and then only if the correction is reported within the statutory period of limitation upon refund or credit of overpayments of amounts due under the agreement. See paragraph (b)(2)(iii) of this section relating to such statutory period. A claim for credit or refund may be filed in accordance with the provisions of paragraph (b)(2) of this section for any overpayment of an amount due under the agreement which is not adjusted under this subparagraph.

(b) Errors not adjustable. *(1) Underpayments.* If a domestic corporation fails to report all or any part of the amount for which liability equivalent to the employee and employer taxes is incurred under its agreement with respect to any payment of remuneration, and such underpayment is not reported as an adjustment within the time prescribed by paragraph (a)(2) of this section, the amount of such underpayment shall be reported on the domestic corporation's next return, or shall be reported immediately on a supplemental return for the return period in which such payment of remuneration was made. The reporting of an underpayment under this subparagraph does not constitute an adjustment without interest.

(2) Overpayments. (i) If more than the correct amount due from a domestic corporation pursuant to its agreement (including the amount of any interest or addition) is paid and the amount of the overpayment is not adjusted under paragraph (a)(3) of this section, the domestic corporation may file a claim for refund or credit. Except as otherwise provided in this subparagraph, such claim shall be made in the same manner and subject to the same conditions as to allowance of the claim as would be the case if the claim were in respect of an overpayment of taxes under the Federal Insurance Contributions Act. Refund or credit of an amount erroneously paid by a domestic corporation under its agreement may be allowed only to the domestic corporation.

(ii) Any claim filed under this subparagraph shall be plainly marked "Claim under section 3121(l)."

(iii) No refund or credit of an overpayment of the amount due from a domestic corporation under its agreement will be allowed after the expiration of 2 years after the date of payment of such overpayment, except upon one or more of the grounds set forth in a claim filed prior to the expiration of such 2-year period.

(c) Deductions from employees' remuneration. If a domestic corporation deducts, or causes to be deducted, from the remuneration of an individual for services covered by the agreement amounts which are more or less than the employee tax which would be deductible therefrom if such remuneration constituted wages, any repayment to the individual (except to the extent otherwise provided in this section), or further collection from the individual, in respect of such deduction is a matter for settlement between the individual and the domestic corporation or such other person as may be concerned.

T.D. 6145, 9/8/55, amend T.D. 7012, 5/14/69.

§ 36.3121(l)(8)-1 Definition of foreign subsidiary.

(a) Prior to August 1, 1956. *(1)* For the period January 1, 1955 to July 31, 1956, inclusive, a foreign corporation is a foreign subsidiary of a domestic corporation, within the meaning of the regulations in this part, if—

(i) More than 50 percent of the voting stock of the foreign corporation is owned by the domestic corporation; or

(ii) More than 50 percent of the voting stock of the foreign corporation is owned by a second foreign corporation and more than 50 percent of the voting stock of the second foreign corporation is owned by the domestic corporation.

(2) The application of subparagraph (1) of this paragraph may be illustrated by the following examples:

Example (1). P, a domestic corporation, owns 51 percent of the voting stock of S-1, a foreign corporation. S-1 owns 51 percent of the voting stock of S-2, a foreign corporation, S-2 owns 51 percent of the voting stock of S-3, a foreign corporation. S-1 and S-2 are foreign subsidiaries of P for purposes of the regulations in this part. Since neither P nor S-1 owns more than 50 percent of the voting stock of S-3, S-3 is not a foreign subsidiary of P within the meaning of the regulations in this part.

Example (2). assume the same facts as those stated in example (1) except that 25 percent of the voting stock of S-2 is transferred by S-1 to P. P owns no other voting stock of S-2. Accordingly, after the transfer, P and S-1 together own more than 50 percent of the voting stock of S-2, but neither P nor S-1 alone owns more than 50 percent of such stock. S-2 ceases to be a foreign subsidiary of P when such transfer is effected.

(b) On or after August 1, 1956. *(1)* Beginning August 1, 1956, a foreign corporation is a foreign subsidiary of a domestic corporation, within the meaning of the regulations in this part, if—

(i) Not less than 20 percent of the voting stock of the foreign corporation is owned by the domestic corporation; or

(ii) More than 50 percent of the voting stock of the foreign corporation is owned by a second foreign corporation and not less than 20 percent of the voting stock of the second foreign corporation is owned by the domestic corporation.

(2) The application of subparagraph (1) of this paragraph may be illustrated by the following examples:

Example (1). P, a domestic corporation owns 20 percent of the voting stock of S-1, a foreign corporation. S-1 is, therefore, a foreign subsidiary of P. S-1 owns 51 percent and P owns 15 percent of the voting stock of S-2, a foreign corporation. S-2 is also a foreign subsidiary of P, and this would be so even if P owned none of the voting stock of S-2. S-2 owns 51 percent, S-1 owns 39 percent, and P owns 10 percent of the voting stock of S-3, a foreign corporation. Since P owns less than 20 percent of the voting stock of S-2 and less than 20 percent of the voting stock of S-3, and since S-1 owns not more than 50 percent of the voting stock of S-3, S-3 is not a foreign subsidiary of P within the meaning of the regulations in this part.

Example (2). Assume the same facts as those stated in example (1) except that 4 percent of the voting stock of S-2 is transferred by S-1 to P. After, as well as before, the transfer of 66 percent of the voting stock of S-2 is owned by P and S-1 together. After the transfer, however, P owns less than

20 percent and S-1 owns not more than 50 percent of the voting stock of S-2. When such transfer is effected S-2 ceases to be a foreign subsidiary of P for purposes of the regulations in this part.

(c) Transfer of stock ownership. The transfer of the voting stock of a foreign corporation which is a foreign subsidiary of a domestic corporation within the meaning of section 3121(l)(8) will not affect the status of the foreign corporation as such a foreign subsidiary if at all times either of the percentage tests stated in section 3121(l)(8), relating to ownership of the voting stock of such foreign corporation, is met.

(d) Meaning of "stock". The term "stock", as used in the regulations in this part, has the meaning assigned by paragraph (7) of section 7701(a). Section 7701(a)(7) provides as follows:

SEC 7701. Definitions. (a) When used in this title [Internal Revenue Code of 1954], where not otherwise distinctly expressed or manifestly incompatible with the intent thereof—

(7) Stock. The term "stock" includes shares in an association, joint-stock company, or insurance company.

T.D. 6390, 6/13/59.

§ 36.3121(l)(9)-1 Domestic corporation as separate entity.

A domestic corporation which enters into an agreement as provided in § 36.3121(l)(1)-1 shall, for purposes of the regulations in this part and for purposes of section 6413(c)(2)(C), relating to special credits or refunds, be considered an employer in its capacity as a party to such agreement separate and apart from its identity as an employer incurring liability for the employee tax and employer tax on the wages of its own employees. Thus, if a citizen of the United States performs services in employment for the domestic corporation and at any time within the same calendar year performs services covered by the agreement as an employee of one or more foreign subsidiaries named therein, the limitation on wages provided in section 3121(a)(1) has application separately as to the wages for employment performed in the employ of the domestic corporation and as to the remuneration for services covered by the agreement performed in the employ of such foreign subsidiary or subsidiaries. All services covered by the agreement whether performed in the employ of one or more than one such foreign subsidiary are regarded for purposes of the wage limitation as having been performed in the employ of the domestic corporation in its separate capacity as a party to the agreement. Similarly, any remuneration for such services which, if the services were performed in the United States, would be excluded from wages unless a certain amount of such remuneration is paid by a single employer within a specified period (for example, remuneration for agricultural labor) is regarded, for purposes of determining whether the domestic corporation incurs liability under its agreement with respect to such remuneration, as having been paid by the domestic corporation in its separate capacity as a party to the agreement. All remuneration received by an employee for services covered by the agreement is deemed, for purposes of the special credit or refund provisions contained in section 6413(c), to have been received from the domestic corporation as an employer in its separate capacity as a party to the agreement.

T.D. 6145, 9/8/55.

§ 36.3121(l)(10)-1 Requirements in respect of liability under agreement.

To the extent not inconsistent with, or otherwise provided in, the regulations in this part, the requirements and duties (relating to identification number, account numbers, wage information statements to employees, record keeping, etc.) imposed on an employer for any period with respect to the taxes imposed by the Federal Insurance Contributions Act are hereby made applicable to a domestic corporation with respect to its obligations and liabilities, for the same period, under an agreement entered into as provided in § 36.3121(l)(1)-1.

T.D. 6145, 9/8/55.

§ 36.3121(l)(10)-2 Identification.

(a) Domestic corporation. A domestic corporation which has secured, or is required to secure, an identification number as an employer having in its employ one or more individuals in employment for wages is not required to secure an identification number under the regulations in this part.

(b) Employees. Every employee performing services covered by an agreement shall have the same duties in respect of an account number as would be the case if the employee were performing services in employment for the domestic corporation.

T.D. 6145, 9/8/55.

§ 36.3121(l)(10)-3 Returns.

(a) The forms prescribed for use in making returns of the taxes imposed by the Federal Insurance Contributions Act (except any forms particularly prescribed for use by household employers or by employers filing returns in Puerto Rico) shall be used by a domestic corporation in making returns of its liability under an agreement entered into as provided in § 36.3121(l)(1)-1. Returns of such liability shall be made separate and apart from any returns required of the domestic corporation in respect of the taxes imposed by the Federal Insurance Contributions Act. The domestic corporation shall plainly mark "3121(l) Agreement" at the top of each return, each detachable schedule thereof, and each paper or document constituting a part of the return, filed by the domestic corporation pursuant to the regulations in this part. Returns required under the regulations in this part shall be made by the domestic corporation as if all services covered by the agreement, whether performed in the employ of one or more than one foreign subsidiary, were performed in the employ of the domestic corporation as an employer in its separate capacity as a party to the agreement.

(b) Each return required under the regulations in this part must be filed on or before the last day of the month following the period for which the return is made.

T.D. 6145, 9/8/55, amend T.D. 6390, 6/12/59.

§ 36.3121(l)(10)-4 Payment of amounts equivalent to tax.

A domestic corporation which has entered into an agreement as provided in § 36.3121(l)(1)-1 is not required to make deposits with an authorized financial institution of any amount for which liability is incurred under its agreement.

T.D. 6145, 9/8/55, amend T.D. 7953, 5/8/84, T.D. 8952, 6/25/2001.

§ 31.3121(o)-1 Crew leader.

The term "crew leader" means an individual who furnishes individuals to perform agricultural labor for another person, if such individual pays (either on his own behalf or on behalf of such person) the individuals so furnished by him for the agricultural labor performed by them and if such individual has not entered into a written agreement with such person whereby such individual has been designated as an employee of such person. For purposes of this chapter a crew leader is deemed to be the employer of the individuals furnished by him to perform agricultural labor, after 1956, for another person, and the crew leader is deemed not to be an employee of such other person with respect to the performance of services by him after 1956 in furnishing such individuals or as a member of the crew. An individual is not a crew leader within the meaning of section 3121(o) and of this section if he does not pay the agricultural workers furnished by him to perform agricultural labor for another person, or if there is an agreement between such individual and the person for whom the agricultural labor is performed whereby such individual is designated as an employee of such person. Whether or not such individual is an employee will be determined under the usual common-law rules (see paragraph (c) of § 31.3121(d)-1).

T.D. 6744, 7/1/64.

§ 31.3121(q)-1 Tips included for employee taxes.

(a) In general. Except as otherwise provided in paragraph (b) of this section, tips received after 1965 by an employee in the course of his employment shall be considered remuneration for employment. (For definition of the term "employee" see §§ 31.3121(d) and 31.3121(d)-1.) Tips reported by an employee to his employer in a written statement furnished to the employer pursuant to section 6053(a) (see § 31.6053-1) shall be deemed to be paid to the employee at the time the written statement is furnished to the employer. Tips received by an employee which are not reported to his employer in a written statement furnished pursuant to section 6053(a) shall be deemed to be paid to the employee at the time the tips are actually received by the employee. For provisions relating to the collection of employee tax in respect of tips from the employee, see § 31.3102-3.

(b) Tips not included for employer taxes. Tips received after 1965 by an employee in the course of his employment do not constitute remuneration for employment for purposes of computing wages subject to the taxes imposed by subsections (a) and (b) of section 3111.

(c) Tips received by an employee in course of his employment. Tips are considered to be received by an employee in the course of his employment for an employer regardless of whether the tips are received by the employee from a person other than his employer or are paid to the employee by the employer. However, only those tips which are received by an employee on his own behalf (as distinguished from tips received on behalf of another employee) shall be considered as remuneration paid to the employee. Thus, where employees practice tip splitting (for example, where waiters pay a portion of the tips received by them to the busboys), each employee who receives a portion of a tip left by a customer of the employer is considered to have received tips in the course of his employment.

(d) Computation of annual wage limitation. In connection with the application of the annual wage limitation (see § 31.3121(a)(1)-1), tips reported by an employee to his employer in a written statement furnished to the employer pursuant to section 6053(a) shall be taken into account for purposes of the tax imposed by section 3101. However, since tips received by an employee in the course of his employment do not constitute remuneration for employment for purposes of the tax imposed by section 3111, they are disregarded for purposes of the annual wage limitation in respect of such tax. Accordingly, separate computations for purposes of the annual wage limitation may be required in respect of an employee who receives tips. The provisions of this paragraph may be illustrated by the following example:

Example. During 1966, A is employed as a waiter by X restaurant and is paid wages by X restaurant at the rate of $100 a week. At the end of October 1966, A has been paid weekly wages in the amount of $4,300 and has reported tips in the amount of $2,200. On November 6, 1966, A is paid an additional week's wages in the amount of $100 and on November 9, 1966, A furnishes X restaurant a report of tips actually received by him during October. The annual wage limitation of $6,600 (weekly wages of $4,400 ($4,300 plus $100) and tips of $2,200) had been reached for purposes of the tax imposed by section 3101 prior to November 9 and, accordingly, no portion of the tips included in the report furnished on that date constitutes wages. However, since tips do not constitute remuneration for employment for purposes of the tax imposed by section 3111, the weekly wages paid to A during the remainder of 1966 will be subject to the tax imposed by section 3111.

T.D. 7001, 1/17/69.

§ 31.3121(r)-1 Election of coverage by religious orders.

(a) In general. A religious order whose members are required to take a vow of poverty, or any autonomous subdivision of such an order, may elect to have the Federal old-age, survivors, and disability insurance system established by title II of the Social Security Act extended to services performed by its members in the exercise of duties required by such order or subdivision. See section 3121(i)(4) and § 31.3121(i)-4 for provisions relating to the computation of the amount of remuneration of such members. For purposes of this section, a subdivision of a religious order is autonomous if it directs and governs its members, if it is responsible for its members' care and maintenance, if it is responsible for the members' support and maintenance in retirement, and if the members live under the authority of a religious superior who is elected by them or appointed by higher authority.

(b) Definition of member. *(1) In general.* For purposes of section 3121(r) and this section, a member of a religious order means any individual who is subject to a vow of poverty as a member of such order, who performs tasks usually required (and to the extent usually required) of an active member of such order, and who is not considered retired because of old age or total disability.

(2) Retirement because of old age. (i) In general. For purposes of section 3121(r)(2) and this paragraph, an individual is considered retired because of old age if (A) in view of all the services performed by the individual and the surrounding circumstances it is reasonable to consider him to be retired, and (B) his retirement occurred by reason of old age. Even though an individual performs some services in the exercise of duties required by the religious order, the first test (the retirement test) is met where it is reasonable to consider the individual to be retired.

(ii) Factors to be considered. In determining whether it is reasonable to consider an individual to be retired, consideration is first to be given to all of the following factors:

(A) Nature of services. Consideration is given to the nature of the services performed by the individual in the exercise of duties required by his religious order. The more highly skilled and valuable such services are, the more likely the individual rendering such services is not reasonably considered retired. Also, whether such services are of a type performed principally by retired members of the individual's religious order may be significant.

(B) Amount of time. Consideration is also given to the amount of time the individual devotes to the performance of services in the exercise of duties required by his religious order. This time includes all the time spent by him in any activity in connection with services that might appropriately be performed in the exercise of duties required of active members by the order. Normally, an individual who, solely by reason of his advanced age, performs services of less than 45 hours per month shall be considered retired. In no event shall an individual who, solely by reason of his advanced age, performs services of less than 15 hours per month not be considered retired.

(C) Comparison of services rendered before and after retirement. In addition, consideration s given to the nature and extent of the services rendered by the individual before he "retired," as compared with the services performed thereafter. A large reduction in the importance or amount of services performed by the individual in the exercise of duties required by his religious order tends to show that the individual is retired; absence of such reduction tends to show that the individual is not retired. Normally, an individual who reduces by at least 75 percent the amount of services performed shall be considered retired.

Where consideration of the factors described in paragraph (b)(2)(ii) of this section does not establish whether an individual is or is not reasonably considered retired, all other factors are considered.

(iii) Examples. The rules of this subparagraph may be illustrated by the following examples:

Example (1). A is a member of a religious order who is subject to a vow of poverty. A's religious order is principally engaged in providing nursing services, and A has been fully trained in the nursing profession. In accordance with the practices of her order, upon attaining the age of 65, A is relieved of her nursing duties by reason of her age, and is assigned to a mother house where she is required to perform only such duties as light housekeeping and ordinary gardening. A is reasonably considered retired since the services she is performing are simple in nature, are markedly less skilled than those professional services which she previously performed, are of a type performed principally by retired members of her order, and are performed at a location to which members frequently retire.

Example (2). Assume the same facts as in example (1) except that A is not reassigned to a mother house. Instead, she is reassigned to full-time duties in a hospital not utilizing her nursing skills. Whether A has met the retirement test requires consideration of the nature of her work. If A's new duties are almost entirely of a make-work nature primarily to occupy her body and mind, she is reasonably considered retired. However, if they are essential to the operation of the hospital, she is not reasonably considered retired.

Example (3). B is a member of a religious order who is subject to a vow of poverty. As such, he provides supportive services to his order, such as housekeeping, cooking, and gardening. By reason of having attained the age of 62, he reduces the number of hours spent per day in these services from 8 hours to 2 hours. B is reasonably considered retired in view of the large reduction in the amount of time he devotes to his duties.

Example (4). C is a member of a religious order who is subject to a vow of poverty. In his capacity as a member of the order, he performs duties as president of a university. Upon attaining the age of 65, C is relieved of his duties as president of the university and instead becomes a member of its faculty, teaching two courses whereas full-time members of the faculty normally teach four comparable courses. Although C's duties are no longer as demanding as those he previously performed, and although the amount of his time required for them is less than full time, he is nonetheless performing duties requiring a high degree of skill for a substantial amount of time. Accordingly, C is not reasonably considered retired.

Example (5). Assume the same facts as in example (4), except that C teaches only one course upon being relieved of his position as president by reason of age. C is reasonably considered retired.

Example (6). D is a member of a contemplative order who is subject to a vow of poverty. In accordance, with the practices of his order, upon attaining the age of 70, D reduces by 50 percent the amount of time spent performing the normal duties of active members of his order. D is not reasonably considered retired.

Example (7). Assume the same facts as in example (6), except that because of his age D no longer participates in the more rigorous liturgical services of the order and that the amount of time which he spends in all duties which might appropriately be performed by active members of his order is reduced by 75 percent. D is reasonably considered retired in view of the large reduction in his participation in the usual devotional routine of his order.

(3) Retirement because of total disability. For purposes of section 3121(r)(2) and this paragraph, an individual is considered retired because of total disability (i) if he is unable, by reason of a medically determinable physical or mental impairment, to perform the tasks usually required of an active member of his order to the extent necessary to maintain his status as an active member, and (ii) if such impairment is reasonably expected to prevent his resumption of the performance of such tasks to such extent. A physical or mental impairment is an impairment that results from anatomical, physiological, or psychological abnormalities which are demonstrable by medically acceptable clinical and laboratory diagnostic techniques. Statements of the individual, including his own description of his impairment (symptoms), are, alone, insufficient to establish the presence of a physical or mental impairment,

(4) Evidentiary requirements with respect to retirement. There shall be attached to the return of taxes paid pursuant to an election under section 3121(r) a summary of the facts upon which any determination has been made by the religious order or autonomous subdivision that one or more of its members retired during the period covered by such return. Each summary shall contain the name and social security number of each such retired member as well as the date of his retirement. Such order or subdivision shall maintain records of the details relating to each such "retirement" sufficient to show whether or not such member or members has in fact retired.

(c) Certificates of election. *(1) In general.* A religious order or an autonomous subdivision of such an order desiring to make an election of coverage pursuant to section 3121(r) and this section shall file a certificate of election on Form SS-16 in accordance with the instructions thereto. However, in the case of an election made before August 9, 1973, a document other than Form SS-16 shall constitute a certificate of election if it purports to be a binding election of coverage and if it is filed with an appropriate official of the Internal Revenue Service. Such a document shall be given the effect it would have if it were a certificate of election containing the provisions required by subparagraph (2) of this paragraph. However, it should subsequently be supplemented by a Form SS-16.

(2) Provisions of certificates. Each certificate of election shall provide that—

(i) Such election of coverage by such order or subdivision shall be irrevocable,

(ii) Such election shall apply to all current and future members of such order, or in the case of a subdivision thereof to all current and future members of such order who belong to such subdivision,

(iii) All services performed by a member of such order or subdivision in the exercise of duties required by such order or subdivision shall be deemed to have been performed by such member as an employee of such order or subdivision, and

(iv) The wages of each member, upon which such order or subdivision shall pay the taxes imposed on employees and employers by sections 3101 and 3111, will be determined as provided in section 3121(i)(4).

(d) Effective date of election. *(1) In general.* Except as provided in paragraph (e) of this section, a certificate of election of coverage filed by a religious order or its subdivision pursuant to section 3121(r) and this section shall be in effect, for purposes of section 3121(b)(8)(A) and for purposes of section 210(a)(8)(A) of the Social Security Act, for the period beginning with whichever of the following may be designated by the electing religious order or subdivision:

(i) The first day of the calendar quarter in which the certificate is filed,

(ii) The first day of the calendar quarter immediately following the quarter in which the certificate is filed, or

(iii) The first day of any calendar quarter preceding the calendar quarter in which the certificate is filed, except that such date may not be earlier than the first day of the 20th calendar quarter preceding the quarter in which such certificate is filed.

(2) Retroactive elections. Whenever a date is designated as provided in paragraph (d)(1)(iii) of this section, the election shall apply to services performed before the quarter in which the certificate is filed only if the member performing such services was a member at the time such services were performed and is living on the first day of the quarter in which such certificate is filed. Thus, the election applies to an individual who is no longer a member of a religious order on the first day of such quarter if he performed services as a member at any time on or after the date so designated and is living on the first day of the quarter in which such certificate is filed. For purposes of computing interest and for purposes of section 6651 (relating to additions to tax for failure to file tax return or to pay tax), in any case in which such a date is designated the due date for the return and payment of the tax, for calendar quarters prior to the quarter in which the certificate is filed, resulting from the filing of such certificate shall be the last day of the calendar quarter month following the calendar quarter in which the certificate is filed. The statutory period for the assessment of the tax for such prior calendar quarters shall not expire before the expiration of 3 years from such due date.

(e) Coordination with coverage of lay employees. If at the time the certificate of election of coverage is filed by a religious order or autonomous subdivision, a certificate of waiver of exemption under section 3121(k) (extending coverage to any lay employees) is not in effect, the certificate of election shall not become effective unless the order or subdivision files a Form SS-15, and a Form SS-15a to accompany the certificate on Form SS-15, as provided by section 3121(k) and §§ 3121(k)-1 through 31.3121(k)-3. The preceding sentence applies even though an order or subdivision has no lay employees at the time it files a certificate of election of coverage. The effective date of the certificate of waiver of exemption must be no later than the date on which the certificate of election becomes effective, and it must be specified on the certificate of waiver of exemption that such certificate is irrevocable. The certificate of waiver of exemption required under this paragraph shall be filed notwithstanding the provisions of section 3121(k)(3) (relating to no renewal of the waiver of exemption) which otherwise would prohibit the filing of a waiver of exemption if an earlier waiver of exemption had previously been terminated. If at the time the certificate of election of coverage is filed a certificate of waiver of exemption is in effect with respect to the electing religious order or autonomous subdivision, the filing of the certificate of election shall constitute an amendment of the certificate of waiver of exemption making the latter certificate irrevocable.

T.D. 7280, 7/9/73.

§ 31.3121(s)-1 Concurrent employment by related corporations with common paymaster.

(a) In general. For purposes of sections 3102, 3111, and 3121(a)(1), except as otherwise provided in paragraph (c) of this section, when two or more related corporations concurrently employ the same individual and compensate that individual through a common paymaster which is one of the related corporations that employs the individual, each of the corporations is considered to have paid only the remuneration it actually disburses to that individual. This rule applies whether the remuneration was paid with respect to the employment relationship of the individual with the disbursing corporation or was paid on behalf of another related corporation. Accordingly, if all of the remuneration to the individual from the related corporations is disbursed through the common paymaster, the total amount of taxes imposed with respect to the remuneration under sections 3102 and 3111 is determined as though the individual has only one employer (the common paymaster). The common paymaster is responsible for filing information and tax returns and issuing Forms W-2 with respect to wages it is considered to have paid under this section. Section 3121(s) and this section apply only to remuneration disbursed in the form of money, check or similar instrument by one of the related corporations or its agent.

(b) Definitions. The definitions contained in this paragraph are applicable only for purposes of this section and § 31.3306(p)-1.

(1) Related corporations. Corporations shall be considered related corporations for an entire calendar quarter (as defined in § 31.0-2(a)(9)) if they satisfy any one of the following four tests at any time during that calendar quarter:

(i) The corporations are members of a "controlled group of corporations", as defined in section 1563 of the Code, or would be members if section 1563(a)(4) and (b) did not apply and if the phrase "more than 50 percent" were substituted for the phrase "at least 80 percent" wherever it appears in section 1563(a).

(ii) In the case of a corporation that does not issue stock, either fifty percent or more of the members of one corporation's board of directors (or other governing body) are members of the other corporation's board of directors (or other governing body), or the holders of fifty percent or more of the voting power to select such members are concurrently the holders of fifty percent or more of that power with respect to the other corporation.

(iii) Fifty percent or more of one corporation's officers are concurrently officers of the other corporation.

(iv) Thirty percent or more of one corporation's employees are concurrently employees of the other corporation.

The following examples illustrate the application of this paragraph:

Example (1). (a) X Corporation employs individuals A, B, D, E, F, G, and H. Y Corporation employs individuals A, B, and C. Z Corporation employs individuals A, C, I, J, K, L, and M. X Corporation is the paymaster for all thirteen individuals. The corporations have no officers or stockholders in common.

(b) X and Y are related corporations because at least 30 percent of Y's employees are also employees of X. Y and Z are related corporations because at least 30 percent of Y's employees are also employees of Z. X and Z are not related corporations because neither corporation has 30 percent of its employees concurrently employed by the other corporations.

(c) For purposes of determining the amount of tax liability under sections 3102 and 3111, individual B is treated as having one employer. Individual C has two employers for these purposes, although Y and Z are related corporations, because C is not employed by X Corporation, the common paymaster. Individual A also is treated as having two employers for the purposes of these sections because X and Y Corporations are treated as one employer, and Z Corporation is treated as a second employer (since it is not related to the paymaster, X Corporation). Of course, individuals D, E, F, G, H, I, J, K, L, and M are not concurrently employed by two or more corporations, and, accordingly, section 3121(s) is inapplicable to them.

Example (2). M and N Corporations are both related to Corporation O but are not related to each other. Individual A is concurrently employed by all three corporations and paid by O, their common paymaster. Although M and N are not related, O is treated as the employer for A's employment with M, N, and O.

Example (3). Corporations X, Y, and Z meet the definition of related corporations for the first time on April 12, 1979, and cease to meet it on July 5, 1979. A is concurrently employed by X, Y, and Z throughout 1979. In each of the four calendar quarters of 1979, A's remuneration from X, Y, and Z is $2,000, $10,000 and $30,000, respectively. All of the remuneration to A from X, Y, and Z for the year is disbursed by X, the common paymaster. Under these circumstances, the amount of wages subject to sections 3102 and 3111 is as follows:

For the first calendar quarter

X	Y	Z
$2,000	$10,000	$22,900

For the second calendar quarter

X	Y	Z
$20,900 ($22,900 − $2,000)	0	0

For the third calendar quarter

X	Y	Z
0	0	0

For the fourth calendar quarter

X	Y	Z
0	$10,000	0

Of course, if the corporations had been related throughout all of 1979, only $22,900 of X's first quarter disbursement would have constituted wages subject to section 3102 and 3111.

(2) Common paymaster. (i) In general. A common paymaster of a group of related corporations is any member thereof that disburses remuneration to employees of two or more of those corporations on their behalf and that is responsible for keeping books and records for the payroll with respect to those employees. The common paymaster is not required to disburse remuneration to all the employees of those two or more related corporations, but the provisions of this section do not apply to any remuneration to an employee that is not disbursed through a common paymaster. The common paymaster may pay concurrently employed individuals under this section by one combined paycheck, drawn on a single bank account, or by separate paychecks, drawn by the common paymaster on the accounts of one or more employing corporations.

(ii) Multiple common paymasters. A group of related corporations may have more than one common paymaster. Some of the related corporations may use one common paymaster and others of the related corporations use another common paymaster with respect to a certain class of employees. A corporation that uses a common paymaster to disburse remuneration to certain of its employees may use a different common paymaster to disburse remuneration to other employees.

(iii) Examples. The rules of this subparagraph are illustrated by the following examples:

Example (1). S, T, U, and V are related corporations with 2,000 employees collectively. Forty of these employees are concurrently employed by two or more of the corporations, during a calendar quarter. The four corporations arrange for S to disburse remuneration to thirty of these forty employees for their services. Under these facts, S is the common paymaster of S, T, U, and V with respect to the thirty employees. S is not a common paymaster with respect to the remaining employees.

Example (2). (a) W, X, Y, and Z are related corporations. The corporations collectively have 20,000 employees. Two hundred of the employees are top-level executives and managers, sixty of whom are concurrently employed by two or more of the corporations during a calendar quarter. Six thousand of the employees are skilled artisans, all of whom are concurrently employed by two or more of the corporations during the calendar year. The four corporations arrange for Z to disburse remuneration to the sixty executives who are concurrently employed by two or more of the corporations. W and X arrange for X to disburse remuneration to the artisans who are concurrently employed by W and X.

(b) A is an executive who is concurrently employed only by W, Y, and Z during the calendar year. Under these facts, Z is a common paymaster for W, Y, and Z with respect to A. Assuming that the other requirements of this section are met, the amount of the tax liability under sections 3102 and 3111 is determined as if Z were A's only employer for the calendar quarter.

(c) B is a skilled artisan who is concurrently employed only by W and X during the calendar year. Under these facts, X is a common paymaster for S and X with respect to B. Assuming that the other requirements of this section are met, the amount of the tax liability under sections 3102 and 3111 is determined as if X were B's only employer for the calendar quarter.

(3) Concurrent employment. For purposes of this section, the term "concurrent employment" means the contemporaneous existence of an employment relationship (within the meaning of section 3121(b)) between an individual and two or more corporations. Such a relationship contemplates the performance of services by the employee for the benefit of the employing corporation (not merely for the benefit of the group of corporations), in exchange for remuneration which, if deductible for the purposes of Federal income tax, would be deductible by the employing corporation. The contemporaneous existence of an employment relationship with each corporation is the decisive factor; if it exists, the fact that a particular employee is on leave or otherwise temporarily inactive is immaterial. However, employment is not concurrent with respect to one of the related corporations if the employee's employment relationship with that corporation is completely nonexistent during periods when the employee is not performing services for that corporation. An employment relationship is completely nonexistent if all rights and obligations of the employer and employee with respect to employment have terminated, other than those that customarily exist after employment relationships terminate. Examples of rights and obligations that customarily exist after employment relationships terminate include those with respect to remuneration not yet paid, employer's property used the employee not yet returned to the employer, severance pay, and lump-sum termination payments from a deferred compensation plan. Circumstances that suggest that an employment relationship has become completely nonexistent include unconditional termination of participation in deferred compensation plans of the employer, forfeiture of seniority claims, and forfeiture of unused fringe benefits such as vacation or sick pay. Of course, the continued existence of an employment relationship between an individual and a corporation is not necessarily established by the individual's continued participation in a deferred compensation plan, retention of seniority rights, etc., since continuation of those benefits may be attributable to employment with a second corporation related to the first corporation if the corporations have common benefits plans or if the benefits are continued as a matter of corporate reciprocity. An individual who does not perform substantial services in exchange for remuneration from a corporation is presumed not employed by that corporation. Concurrent employment need not exist for any particular length of time to meet the requirements of this section, but this section only applies to remuneration disbursed by a common paymaster to an individual who is concurrently employed by the common paymaster and at least one other related corporation at the time the individual performs the services for which the remuneration is paid. If the employment relationship is nonexistent during a quarter, that employee may not be counted towards the 30-percent test set forth in paragraph (b)(1)(iv) of this section; however, even if the employment relationship is nonexistent, section 3121(s) of the Code applies to remuneration paid to the former employee for services rendered while the employee was a common employee. The principles of this subparagraph are illustrated by the following examples.

Example (1). M, N, and O are related corporations which use N as a common paymaster with respect to officers. Their respective headquarters are located in three separate cities several hundred miles apart. A is an officer of M, N, and O who performs substantial services for each corporation. A does not work a set length of time at each corporate headquarters, and when A leaves one corporate headquarters, it is not known when A will return, although it is expected that A will return. Under these facts, A is concurrently employed by the three corporations.

Example (2). P, Q, and R are related corporations whose geographical zones of business activity do not overlap. P, Q, and R have a common pension plan and arrange for Q to be a common paymaster for managers and executives. All three corporations maintain cafeterias for the use of their employees. B is a cafeteria manager who has worked at P's headquarters for 3 years. On June 1, 1980, B is transferred from P to the position of cafeteria manager of R. There are no plans for B's return to P. B's accrued pension benefits, vacation and sick pay, do not change as a result of the transfer. The decision to transfer B was made by Q, the parent corporation. Under these facts, B is not concurrently employed by P and R, because B's employment relationship with P was completely nonexistent during B's employment with R. Furthermore, section 3121(s) is inapplicable since B also was not employed by Q, the common paymaster, because B never contracted to perform services for remuneration from Q, and Q did not have the right to control the day-to-day duties of B's work.

Example (3). C is employed by two related corporations, S and T. C was concurrently employed by these corporations between April 1, 1979, and June 30, 1979. The corporations used T as the common paymaster with respect to C's wages between May 1, 1979, and September 30, 1979. T pays C on May 15 for services performed between April 1 and April 30, on July 15 for services performed between June 1 and June 30, and on August 15 for services performed between July 1 and July 31. Section 3121(s) applies to the first two payments but does not apply to the third payment (there was no concurrent employment). However, if the third payment was made by T for services performed for T, T counts the amounts previously disbursed to C in 1979 while C was concurrently employed by S and T towards the wage base (see section 3121(a)(1)).

(c) Allocation of employment taxes. *(1) Responsibility to pay tax.* If the requirements of this section are met, the common paymaster has the primary responsibility for remitting taxes pursuant to sections 3102 and 3111 with respect to the remuneration it disburses as the common paymaster. The common paymaster computes these taxes as though it were the sole employer of the concurrently employed individuals. If the common paymaster fails to remit these taxes (in whole or in part), it remains liable for the full amount of the unpaid portion of these taxes. In addition, each of the other related corporations using the common paymaster is jointly and severally liable for its appropriate share of these taxes. That share is an amount equal to the lesser of:

(i) The amount of the liability of the common paymaster under section 3121(s), after taking account of any tax payment made, or

(ii) The amount of the liability under sections 3102 and 3111 which, but for section 3121(s), would have existed with respect to the remuneration from such other related corporation, reduced by an allocable portion of any taxes previously paid by the common paymaster with respect to that remuneration.

The portion of taxes previously paid by the common paymaster that is allocable to each related corporation is determined by multiplying the amount of taxes paid by a fraction, the numerator of which is the portion of the amount of employment tax liability of the common paymaster under section 3121(s) that is allocable to such related corporation under paragraph (c)(2) of this section, and the denominator of which is the total amount of the common paymaster's liability under section 3121(s), both determined without regard to any prior tax payments. These rules apply whether or not the tax on employees was withheld from the employees' wages.

(2) Allocation of tax. (i) In general. If the related corporations maintain a record of the remuneration disbursed to the employee for services performed for each corporation, the remuneration-based allocation rules of paragraph (c)(2)(ii) of this section apply. If the related corporations do not maintain this record of remuneration, the group-wide allocation rules of paragraph (c)(2)(iii) of this section apply. In all cases, allocations must be made with respect to each payment of wages. The allocation of employment tax liabilities pursuant to this subparagraph also determines which related corporation may be entitled to income tax deductions with respect to the payments of those taxes.

(ii) Remuneration-based allocation rules. Under the remuneration-based method of allocation, each related corporation that remunerates an employee through a common paymaster has allocated to it for each pay period an amount of tax determined according to the following formula:

$$\frac{\text{Portion of wage payment constituting remuneration to the employee for services performed for the corporation}}{\text{Total wage payment constituting remuneration to the employee for all services performed for the related corporations using the common paymaster}} \times \text{Tax on employees under section 3102 and tax on employers under section 3111 that the common paymaster is required to remit with respect to the wage payment}$$

If the remuneration disbursed to an employee for services performed for a corporation is inappropriate, the district director may adjust the remuneration records of the related corporations to reflect appropriate remuneration. The district director may use the principles of § 1.482-2(b) in making the adjustments.

Example. (i) X and Y are related corporations which use Y as common paymaster for their executives. A is a concurrently employed executive who performs services during the first quarter of 1979 for X and Y. Y remunerates $4,000 gross pay every week to A, calculated as follows:

Wage Payments	Remuneration X	Remuneration Y	Total	Tax on employers under section 3111	Tax on employees withheld under section 3102	Total
1	$ 3,000	$ 1000	$ 4,000	$ 245.20	$ 245.20	$ 490.40
2-3		8,000	8,000	490.40	490.40	980.80
4	1,000	3,000	4,000	245.20	245.20	490.40
5	4,000		4,000	245.20	245.20	490.40
6	2,000	2,000	4,000	177.77	177.77	355.54
7-13	10,000	18,000	28,000	0	0	0
Total	20,000	32,000	52,000	1,403.77	1,403.77	2,807.54

The amounts of remuneration to A are determined by the district director to be appropriate. Under these facts, the tax is allocated to X and Y in the following amounts:

Wage payments	X	Y
1	$\frac{\$3,000}{\$4,000} \times \$490.40 = \$367.80$	$\frac{\$1,000}{\$4,000} \times \$490.40 = \$122.60$
2-3	—	$\frac{\$8,000}{\$8,000} \times \$980.00 = \$980.00$
4	$\frac{\$1,000}{\$4,000} \times \$490.40 = \$122.60$	$\frac{\$3,000}{\$4,000} \times \$490.00 = \$367.80$
5	$\frac{\$4,000}{\$4,000} \times \$490.40 = \$490.40$	—

6	$\frac{\$2,000}{\$4,000}$ × $355.54 =	$177.77	$\frac{\$2,000}{\$4,000}$ × $355.54 =	$177.77
7-13	$\frac{\$10,000}{\$28,000}$ × -0- =	-0-	$\frac{\$18,000}{\$28,000}$ × -0- =	-0-
		$1,158.57		$1,648.97

(ii) If Y remits none of the taxes to the Internal Revenue Service, X is liable for $2,452.00 (the entire amount due pursuant to sections 3102 and 3111 with respect to the remuneration to A from X) (12.26% × $20,000). Any amount remitted by X to the Internal Revenue Service under these circumstances is also credited against the liability of the common paymaster, Y. However, only the portion of the employment taxes allocated to X under (i) above may be deducted by X as employment taxes paid by it in respect of wages paid by it to its employees.

(iii) If Y remits $1,000.00 of the total $2,807.54 due, Y as common paymaster remains liable for $1,807.54 ($2,807.54 minus $1,000). X's liability is the lesser of $1,807.54 (the liability of the common paymaster), or X's total liability, in the absence of section 3121(s), on wages paid through the common paymaster ($2,452.00) minus a credit for an allocable part of the amount remitted by Y. The part is $412.66

$$\frac{\$1,158.57 \text{ (X's allocable share of tax)}}{\$2,807.54 \text{ (total tax)}} \times \$1,000 \text{ (tax remitted)}.$$

Since $1,807.54 is less than $2,039.34 ($2,452.00 minus $412.66), X and Y are jointly and severally liable for $1,807.54.

(iii) Group-wide allocation rules. Under the group-wide method of allocation, the Commissioner may allocate the taxes imposed by sections 3102 and 3111 in an appropriate manner to a related corporation that remunerates an employee through a common paymaster if the common paymaster fails to remit the taxes to the Internal Revenue Service. Allocation in an appropriate manner varies according to the circumstances. It may be based on sales, property, corporate payroll, or any other basis that reflects the distribution of the services performed by the employee, or a combination of the foregoing bases. To the extent practicable, the Commissioner may use the principles of § 1.482-2(b) of this chapter in making the allocations with respect to wages paid after December 31, 1978, and on or before July 31, 2009. To the extent practicable, the Commissioner may use the principles of § 1.482-9 of this chapter in making the allocations with respect to wages paid after July 31, 2009.

(d) Effective/applicability date. *(1) In general.* This section is applicable with respect to wages paid after December 31, 1978. The fourth sentence of paragraph (c)(2)(iii) of this section is applicable with respect to wages paid after December 31, 1978, and on or before July 31, 2009. The fifth sentence of paragraph (c)(2)(iii) of this section is applicable with respect to wages paid after July 31, 2009.

(2) Election to apply regulation to earlier taxable years. A person may elect to apply the fifth sentence of paragraph (c)(2)(iii) of this section to earlier taxable years in accordance with the rules set forth in § 1.482-9(n)(2) of this chapter.

T.D. 7660, 12/18/79, amend T.D. 9278, 7/31/2006, T.D. 9456, 7/31/2009.

PAR. 11. Section 31.3121(s)-1 is amended by:

1. Revising the fourth sentence and adding a fifth sentence in paragraph (c)(2)(iii).

2. Adding a second sentence to paragraph (d).

The revision and additions read as follows:

Proposed § 31.3121(s)-1 Concurrent employment by related corporations with common paymaster. [*For Preamble, see ¶ 152,461*]

* * * * *

(c) * * *

(2) * * *

(iii) Group-wide allocation rules. * * * To the extent practicable, the Commissioner may use the principles of § 1.482-2(b) of this chapter in making the allocations with respect to wages paid after December 31, 1978, and on or before the date the final regulations are published in the Federal Register. To the extent practicable, the Commissioner may use the principles of § 1.482-9 of this chapter in making the allocations with respect to wages paid after the date of the final regulations are published in the Federal Register.

(d) Effective date. * * * The fifth sentence of paragraph (c)(2)(iii) of this section is applicable with respect to wages paid on or after the date of publication of that sentence as final regulations in the Federal Register.

PAR. 13. Section 31.3121(s)-1 is amended by revising paragraphs (c)(2)(iii) and (d) to read as follows:

Proposed § 31.3121(s)-1 Concurrent employment by related corporations with common paymaster. [*For Preamble, see ¶ 152,783*]

• ***Caution:*** This Notice of Proposed Rulemaking was partially finalized by TD 9456, 07/31/2009. Reg. §§ 1.861-8, 1.6038A-3, 1.6662-6, 31.3121(s)-1 remain proposed.

* * * * *

(c) * * *

(2) * * *

(iii) [The text of the proposed amendment to § 31.3121(s)-1(c)(2)(iii) is the same as the text of § 31.3121(s)-1T(c)(2)(iii) published elsewhere in this issue of the Federal Register]. [See T.D. 9278, 07/31/2006, 71 Fed. Reg. 150.]

* * * * *

(d) [The text of the proposed amendment to § 31.3121(s)-1(d) is the same as the text of § 31.3121(s)-1T(d)(1) and (2) published elsewhere in this issue of the Federal Register]. [See T.D. 9278, 07/31/2006, 71 Fed. Reg. 150.]

* * * * *

§ 31.3121(v)(2)-1 Treatment of amounts deferred under certain nonqualified deferred compensation plans.

(a) Timing of wage inclusion. *(1) General timing rule for wages.* Remuneration for employment that constitutes wages within the meaning of section 3121(a) generally is taken into account for purposes of the Federal Insurance Contributions Act (FICA) taxes imposed under sections 3101 and 3111 at the time the remuneration is actually or constructively paid. See § 31.3121(a)-2(a).

(2) Special timing rule for an amount deferred under a nonqualified deferred compensation plan. (i) In general. To the extent that remuneration deferred under a nonqualified deferred compensation plan constitutes wages within the meaning of section 3121(a), the remuneration is subject to the special timing rule described in this paragraph (a)(2). Remuneration is considered deferred under a nonqualified deferred compensation plan within the meaning of section 3121(v)(2) and this section only if it is provided pursuant to a plan described in paragraph (b) of this section. The amount deferred under a nonqualified deferred compensation plan is determined under paragraph (c) of this section.

(ii) Special timing rule. Except as otherwise provided in this section, an amount deferred under a nonqualified deferred compensation plan is required to be taken into account as wages for FICA tax purposes as of the later of—

(A) The date on which the services creating the right to that amount are performed (within the meaning of paragraph (e)(2) of this section); or

(B) The date on which the right to that amount is no longer subject to a substantial risk of forfeiture (within the meaning of paragraph (e)(3) of this section).

(iii) Inclusion in wages only once (nonduplication rule). Once an amount deferred under a nonqualified deferred compensation plan is taken into account (within the meaning of paragraph (d)(1) of this section), then neither the amount taken into account nor the income attributable to the amount taken into account (within the meaning of paragraph (d)(2) of this section) is treated as wages for FICA tax purposes at any time thereafter.

(iv) Benefits that do not result from a deferral of compensation. If a nonqualified deferred compensation plan (within the meaning of paragraph (b)(1) of this section) provides both a benefit that results from the deferral of compensation (within the meaning of paragraph (b)(3) of this section) and a benefit that does not result from the deferral of compensation, the benefit that does not result from the deferral of compensation is not subject to the special timing rule described in this paragraph (a)(2). For example, if a nonqualified deferred compensation plan provides retirement benefits which result from the deferral of compensation and disability pay (within the meaning of paragraph (b)(4)(iv)(C) of this section) which does not result from the deferral of compensation, the retirement benefits provided under the plan are subject to the special timing rule in this paragraph (a)(2) and the disability pay is not.

(v) Remuneration that does not constitute wages. If remuneration under a nonqualified deferred compensation plan does not constitute wages within the meaning of section 3121(a), then that remuneration is not taken into account as wages for FICA tax purposes under either the general timing rule described in paragraph (a)(1) of this section or the special timing rule described in this paragraph (a)(2). For example, benefits under a death benefit plan described in section 3121(a)(13) do not constitute wages for FICA tax purposes. Therefore, these benefits are not included as wages under the general timing rule described in paragraph (a)(1) of this section or the special timing rule described in this paragraph (a)(2), even if the death benefit plan would otherwise be considered a nonqualified deferred compensation plan within the meaning of paragraph (b)(1) of this section.

(b) Nonqualified deferred compensation plan. *(1) In general.* For purposes of this section, the term nonqualified deferred compensation plan means any plan or other arrangement, other than a plan described in section 3121(a)(5), that is established (within the meaning of paragraph (b)(2) of this section) by an employer for one or more of its employees, and that provides for the deferral of compensation (within the meaning of paragraph (b)(3) of this section). A nonqualified deferred compensation plan may be adopted unilaterally by the employer or may be negotiated among or agreed to by the employer and one or more employees or employee representatives. A plan may constitute a nonqualified deferred compensation plan under this section without regard to whether the deferrals under the plan are made pursuant to an election by the employee or whether the amounts deferred are treated as deferred compensation for income tax purposes (e.g., whether the amounts are subject to the deduction rules of section 404). In addition, a plan may constitute a nonqualified deferred compensation plan under this section whether or not it is an employee benefit plan under section 3(3) of the Employee Retirement Income Security Act of 1974 (ERISA), as amended (29 U.S.C. 1002(3)). For purposes of this section, except where the context indicates otherwise, the term plan includes a plan or other arrangement.

(2) Plan establishment. (i) Date plan is established. For purposes of this section, a plan is established on the latest of the date on which it is adopted, the date on which it is effective, and the date on which the material terms of the plan are set forth in writing. For purposes of this section, a plan will be deemed to be set forth in writing if it is set forth in any other form that is approved by the Commissioner. The material terms of the plan include the amount (or the method or formula for determining the amount) of deferred compensation to be provided under the plan and the time when it may or will be provided.

(ii) Plan amendments. In the case of an amendment that increases the amount deferred under a nonqualified deferred compensation plan, the plan is not considered established with respect to the additional amount deferred until the plan, as amended, is established in accordance with paragraph (b)(2)(i) of this section.

(iii) Transition rule for written plan requirement. For purposes of this section, an unwritten plan that was adopted and effective before March 25, 1996, is treated as established under this section as of the later of the date on which it was adopted or became effective, provided that the material terms of the plan are set forth in writing before January 1, 2000.

(3) Plan must provide for the deferral of compensation. (i) Deferral of compensation defined. A plan provides for the deferral of compensation with respect to an employee only if, under the terms of the plan and the relevant facts and circumstances, the employee has a legally binding right during a calendar year to compensation that has not been actually or constructively received and that, pursuant to the terms of the plan, is payable to (or on behalf of) the employee in a later year. An employee does not have a legally binding right to

compensation if that compensation may be unilaterally reduced or eliminated by the employer after the services creating the right to the compensation have been performed. For this purpose, compensation is not considered subject to unilateral reduction or elimination merely because it may be reduced or eliminated by operation of the objective terms of the plan, such as the application of an objective provision creating a substantial risk of forfeiture (within the meaning of section 83). Similarly, an employee does not fail to have a legally binding right to compensation merely because the amount of compensation is determined under a formula that provides for benefits to be offset by benefits provided under a plan that is qualified under section 401(a), or because benefits are reduced due to investment losses or, in a final average pay plan, subsequent decreases in compensation.

(ii) Compensation payable pursuant to the employer's customary payment timing arrangement. There is no deferral of compensation (within the meaning of this paragraph (b)(3)) merely because compensation is paid after the last day of a calendar year pursuant to the timing arrangement under which the employer ordinarily compensates employees for services performed during a payroll period described in section 3401(b).

(iii) Short-term deferrals. If, under a nonqualified deferred compensation plan, there is a deferral of compensation (within the meaning of this paragraph (b)(3)) that causes an amount to be deferred from a calendar year to a date that is not more than a brief period of time after the end of that calendar year, then, at the employer's option, that amount may be treated as if it were not subject to the special timing rule described in paragraph (a)(2) of this section. An employer may apply this option only if the employer does so for all employees covered by the plan and all substantially similar nonqualified deferred compensation plans. For purposes of this paragraph (b)(3)(iii), whether compensation is deferred to a date that is not more than a brief period of time after the end of a calendar year is determined in accordance with § 1.404(b)-1T, Q&A-2, of this chapter.

(4) Plans, arrangements, and benefits that do not provide for the deferral of compensation. (i) In general. Notwithstanding paragraph (b)(3)(i) of this section, an amount or benefit described in any of paragraphs (b)(4)(ii) through (viii) of this section is not treated as resulting from the deferral of compensation for purposes of section 3121(v)(2) and this section and, thus, is not subject to the special timing rule of paragraph (a)(2) of this section.

(ii) Stock options, stock appreciation rights, and other stock value rights. The grant of a stock option, stock appreciation right, or other stock value right does not constitute the deferral of compensation for purposes of section 3121(v)(2). In addition, amounts received as a result of the exercise of a stock option, stock appreciation right, or other stock value right do not result from the deferral of compensation for purposes of section 3121(v)(2) if such amounts are actually or constructively received in the calendar year of the exercise. For purposes of this paragraph (b)(4)(ii), a *stock value right* is a right granted to an employee with respect to one or more shares of employer stock that, to the extent exercised, entitles the employee to a payment for each share of stock equal to the excess, or a percentage of the excess, of the value of a share of the employer's stock on the date of exercise over a specified price (greater than zero).

Thus, for example, the term stock value right does not include a phantom stock or other arrangement under which an employee is awarded the right to receive a fixed payment equal to the value of a specified number of shares of employer stock.

(iii) Restricted property. If an employee receives property from, or pursuant to, a plan maintained by an employer, there is no deferral of compensation (within the meaning of section 3121(v)(2)) merely because the value of the property is not includible in income (under section 83) in the year of receipt by reason of the property being nontransferable and subject to a substantial risk of forfeiture. However, a plan under which an employee obtains a legally binding right to receive property (whether or not the property is restricted property) in a future year may provide for the deferral of compensation within the meaning of paragraph (b)(3) of this section and, accordingly, may constitute a nonqualified deferred compensation plan, even though benefits under the plan are or may be paid in the form of property.

(iv) Certain welfare benefits. (A) In general. Vacation benefits, sick leave, compensatory time, disability pay, severance pay, and death benefits do not result from the deferral of compensation for purposes of section 3121(v)(2), even if those benefits constitute wages within the meaning of section 3121(a).

(B) Severance pay. Benefits that are provided under a severance pay arrangement (within the meaning of section 3(2)(B)(i) of ERISA) that satisfies the conditions in 29 CFR 2510.3-2(b)(1)(i) through (iii) are considered severance pay for purposes of this paragraph (b)(4)(iv). If benefits are provided under a severance pay arrangement (within the meaning of section 3(2)(B)(i) of ERISA), but do not satisfy one or more of the conditions in 29 CFR 2510.3-2(b)(1)(i) through (iii), then whether those benefits are severance pay within the meaning of this paragraph (b)(4)(iv) depends upon the relevant facts and circumstances. For this purpose, relevant facts and circumstances include whether the benefits are provided over a short period of time commencing immediately after (or shortly after) termination of employment or for a substantial period of time following termination of employment and whether the benefits are provided after any termination or only after retirement (or another specified type of termination). Benefits provided under a severance pay arrangement (within the meaning of section 3(2)(B)(i) of ERISA) are in all cases severance pay within the meaning of this paragraph (b)(4)(iv) if the benefits payable under the plan upon an employee's termination of employment are payable only if that termination is involuntary.

(C) Death benefits and disability pay. (1) General definition. Payments made under a nonqualified deferred compensation plan in the event of death are death benefits within the meaning of this paragraph (b)(4)(iv), but only to the extent the total benefits payable under the plan exceed the lifetime benefits payable under the plan. Similarly, payments made under a nonqualified deferred compensation plan in the event of disability are disability pay within the meaning of this paragraph (b)(4)(iv), but only to the extent the disability benefits payable under the plan exceed the lifetime benefits payable under the plan. Accordingly, any benefits that a nonqualified deferred compensation plan provides in the event of death or disability that are associated with an amount deferred under this section are disregarded in applying this section to the extent the benefits payable under the plan in the event of death or in the event of disability have a value in excess of the lifetime benefits payable under the plan.

(2) Total benefits payable defined. For purposes of paragraph (b)(4)(iv)(C)(1) of this section, the term total benefits payable under a plan means the present value of the total

benefits payable to or on behalf of the employee (including benefits payable in the event of the employee's death) under the plan, disregarding any benefits that are payable only in the event of disability and determined separately with respect to each form of distribution or other election that may apply with respect to the employee.

(3) Disability benefits payable defined. For purposes of paragraph (b)(4)(iv)(C)(1) of this section, the term disability benefits payable under a plan means the present value of the benefits payable to or on behalf of the employee under the plan, including benefits payable in the event of the employee's disability but excluding death benefits within the meaning of this paragraph (b)(4)(iv).

(4) Lifetime benefits payable defined. For purposes of paragraph (b)(4)(iv)(C)(1) of this section, the term *lifetime benefits* payable under a plan means the present value of the benefits that could be payable to the employee under the plan during the employee's lifetime, determined under the plan's optional form of distribution or other election that is or was available to the employee at any time with respect to the amount deferred and that provides the largest present value to the employee during the employee's lifetime of any such form or election so available.

(5) Rules of application. For purposes of determining present value under this paragraph (b)(4)(iv)(C), present value is determined as of the time immediately preceding the time the amount deferred under a nonqualified deferred compensation plan is required to be taken into account under paragraph (e) of this section, using actuarial assumptions that are reasonable as of that date but taking into consideration only benefits that result from the deferral of compensation, as determined under this paragraph (b), and benefits payable in the event of death or disability. In addition, for purposes of paragraph (b)(4)(iv)(C)(4) of this section, present value must be determined without any discount for the probability that the employee may die before benefit payments commence and without regard to any benefits payable solely in the event of disability.

(v) Certain benefits provided in connection with impending termination. (A) In general. Benefits provided in connection with impending termination of employment under paragraph (b)(4)(v)(B) or (C) of this section do not result from the deferral of compensation within the meaning of section 3121(v)(2).

(B) Window benefits. (1) In general. For purposes of this paragraph (b)(4)(v), except as provided in paragraph (b)(4)(v)(B)(3) of this section, a window benefit is provided in connection with impending termination of employment. For this purpose, a window benefit is an early retirement benefit, retirement-type subsidy, social security supplement, or other form of benefit made available by an employer for a limited period of time (no greater than one year) to employees who terminate employment during that period or to employees who terminate employment during that period under specified circumstances.

(2) Special rule for recurring window benefits. A benefit will not be considered a window benefit if an employer establishes a pattern of repeatedly providing for similar benefits in similar situations for substantially consecutive, limited periods of time. Whether the recurrence of these benefits constitutes a pattern of amendments is determined based on the facts and circumstances. Although no one factor is determinative, relevant factors include whether the benefits are on account of a specific business event or condition, the degree to which the benefits relate to the event or condition, and whether the event or condition is temporary or discrete or is a permanent aspect of the employer's business.

(3) Transition rule for window benefits. In the case of a window benefit that is made available for a period of time that begins before January 1, 2000, an employer may choose to treat the window benefit as a benefit that results from the deferral of compensation if the sole reason the window benefit would otherwise fail to be provided pursuant to a nonqualified deferred compensation plan is the application of paragraph (b)(4)(v)(B)(1) of this section.

(C) Termination within 12 months of establishment of a benefit or plan. For purposes of this paragraph (b)(4)(v), a benefit is provided in connection with impending termination of employment, without regard to whether it constitutes a window benefit, if—

(1) An employee's termination of employment occurs within 12 months of the establishment of the plan (or amendment) providing the benefit; and

(2) The facts and circumstances indicate that the plan (or amendment) is established in contemplation of the employee's impending termination of employment.

(vi) Benefits established after termination. Benefits established with respect to an employee after the employee's termination of employment do not result from a deferral of compensation within the meaning of section 3121(v)(2). However, cost-of-living adjustments on benefit payments under a nonqualified deferred compensation plan (within the meaning of paragraph (b) of this section) shall not be considered benefits established after the employee's termination of employment for purposes of this paragraph (b)(4)(vi) merely because the employee does not obtain the right to the adjustment until after the employee's termination of employment. For purposes of the preceding sentence, cost-of-living adjustments are payments that satisfy conditions similar to those of 29 CFR 2510.3-2(g)(1)(ii) and (iii).

(vii) Excess parachute payments. An excess parachute payment (as defined in section 280G(b)) under an agreement entered into or renewed after June 14, 1984, in taxable years ending after such date, does not result from the deferral of compensation within the meaning of section 3121(v)(2). For this purpose, any contract entered into before June 15, 1984, that is amended after June 14, 1984, in any relevant significant aspect, is treated as a contract entered into after June 14, 1984.

(viii) Compensation for current services. A plan does not provide for the deferral of compensation within the meaning of section 3121(v)(2) if, based on the relevant facts and circumstances, the compensation is paid for current services.

(5) Examples. This paragraph (b) is illustrated by the following examples:

Example (1). (i) In December of 2001, Employer L tells Employee A that, if specified goals are satisfied for 2002, Employee A will receive a bonus on July 1, 2003, equal to a specified percentage of 2002 compensation. Because Employee A meets the specified goals, Employer L pays the bonus to Employee A on July 1, 2003, consistent with its oral commitment.

(ii) This arrangement is not a nonqualified deferred compensation plan under this section because its terms were not set forth in writing and, therefore, it was not established in accordance with paragraph (b)(2) of this section.

Example (2). (i) In 2004, Employer M establishes a compensation arrangement for Employee B under which Employer M agrees to pay Employee B a specified amount based on a percentage of his salary for 2004. The amount due is to be paid out of the general assets of Employer M and is payable in 2008.

(ii) Employee B has a legally binding right during 2004 to an amount of compensation that has not been actually or constructively received and that, pursuant to the terms of the arrangement, is payable in a later year. Therefore, the arrangement provides for the deferral of compensation.

Example (3). (i) Employer N establishes a nonqualified deferred compensation plan (within the meaning of paragraph (b)(1) of this section) for Employee C in 1984. The plan is amended on January 1, 2001, to increase benefits, and the amendment provides that the increase in benefits is on account of Employee C's performance of services for Employer N from 1985 through 2000.

(ii) The additional benefits that resulted from the plan amendment cannot be taken into account as amounts deferred for 1985 through 2000, even though the plan was established before then. Pursuant to paragraphs (b)(2)(ii) and (e)(1) of this section, the additional benefits cannot be taken into account before the latest of the date on which the amendment is adopted, the date on which the amendment is effective, or the date on which the material terms of the plan, as amended, are set forth in writing.

Example (4). (i) In 2002, Employer O, a state or local government, establishes a plan for certain employees that provides for the deferral of compensation and that is subject to section 457(a).

(ii) Paragraph (b)(1) of this section provides that nonqualified deferred compensation plan means any plan that is established by an employer and that provides for the deferral of compensation, other than a plan described in section 3121(a)(5). Section 3121(a)(5) lists, among other plans, an exempt governmental deferred compensation plan as defined in section 3121(v)(3). Under section 3121(v)(3)(A), this definition does not include any plan to which section 457(a) applies. Thus, the plan established by Employer O is not an exempt governmental deferred compensation plan described in section 3121(v)(3) and, consequently, is not a plan described in section 3121(a)(5). Accordingly, the plan is a nonqualified deferred compensation plan within the meaning of section 3121(v)(2) and paragraph (b)(1) of this section.

(iii) However, the general timing rule of paragraph (a)(1) of this section and the special timing rule of paragraph (a)(2) of this section apply only to remuneration for employment that constitutes wages. Under section 3121(b)(7), certain service performed in the employ of a state, or any political subdivision of a state, is not employment. Thus, even though the plan is a nonqualified deferred compensation plan, the extent to which section 3121(v)(2) applies to a participating employee will depend on whether or not the service performed for Employer O is excluded from the definition of employment under section 3121(b)(7).

Example (5). (i) In 2000, Employer P establishes a plan that provides for bonuses to be paid to employees based on an objective formula that takes into account the employees' performance for the year. Employer P does not have the discretion to reduce the amount of any employee's bonus after the end of the year. The bonus is not actually calculated until March 1 of the following year, and is paid on March 15 of that following year.

(ii) The plan provides for the deferral of compensation because the employees have a legally binding right, as of the last day of a calendar year, to an amount of compensation that has not been actually or constructively received and, pursuant to the terms of the plan, that compensation is payable in a later year. However, because the bonuses under the plan are paid within a brief period of time after the end of the calendar year from which they are deferred, Employer P may choose, pursuant to paragraph (b)(3)(iii) of this section, to treat all the bonuses as if they are not subject to the special timing rule of paragraph (a)(2) of this section.

(iii) If the employer uses the special timing rule, the amount deferred would be taken into account as wages on December 31, 2000. If the employer chooses not to use the special timing rule, the amount of the bonus is wages on the date it is actually or constructively paid, March 15, 2000.

Example (6). (i) Employer Q establishes a plan under which bonuses based on performance in one year may be paid on February 1 of the following year at the discretion of the board of directors. The board of directors meets in January of each year to determine the amount, if any, of the bonuses to be paid based on performance in the prior year.

(ii) Because an employee does not have a legally binding right to any bonus until January of the year in which the bonus is paid, any bonus paid under the plan in that year is not deferred from the preceding calendar year, and the plan does not provide for the deferral of compensation within the meaning of paragraph (b)(3)(i) of this section.

Example (7). (i) Employer R maintains a plan for employees that provides nonqualified stock options described in § 1.83-7(a) of this chapter. Under the plan, employees are granted in 2001 the option to acquire shares of employer stock at the fair market value of the shares on the date of grant ($50 per share). The options can be exercised at any time from the date of grant through 2010. The options do not have a readily ascertainable fair market value for purposes of section 83 at the date of grant, and shares are issued upon the exercise of the options without being subject to a substantial risk of forfeiture within the meaning of section 83. In 2005, when the fair market value of a share of employer stock is $80, Employee D exercises an option to acquire 1,000 shares.

(ii) Under paragraph (b)(4)(ii) of this section, neither the grant of a stock option nor amounts received currently as a result of the exercise of a stock option result from the deferral of compensation for purposes of section 3121(v)(2). Thus, under the general timing rule of paragraph (a)(1) of this section, the $30,000 spread between the amount paid for the shares ($50,000) and the fair market value of the shares on the date of exercise ($80,000) is taken into account as wages for FICA tax purposes in the year of exercise.

(iii) If the options had been granted at $45 per share, $5 per share below the fair market value on date of grant, the $35,000 spread between the amount paid for the shares ($45,000) and the fair market value of the shares on the date of exercise ($80,000) would similarly be taken into account as wages for FICA tax purposes in the year of exercise.

Example (8). (i) Employer T establishes a phantom stock plan for certain employees. Under the plan, an employee is credited on the last day of each calendar year with a dollar amount equal to the fair market value of 1,000 shares of employer stock. Upon termination of employment for any reason, each employee is entitled to receive the value on the date of termination, in cash or employer stock, of the shares with which he or she has been credited.

(ii) Because compensation to which the employee has a legally binding right as of the last day of one year is paid in a subsequent year, the phantom stock plan provides for the deferral of compensation. The phantom stock plan does not provide stock value rights within the meaning of paragraph (b)(4)(ii) of this section because it provides for awards equal in value to the full fair market value of a specified number of shares of Employer T stock, rather than the excess of that fair market value over a specified price.

Example (9). (i) Employer U establishes a severance pay arrangement (within the meaning of section 3(2)(b)(i) of ERISA) which provides for payments solely upon an employee's death, disability, or dismissal from employment. The amount of the payments to an employee is based on the length of continuous active service with Employer U at the time of dismissal, and is paid in monthly installments over a period of three years.

(ii) Because benefits payable under the plan upon termination of employment are payable only upon an employee's involuntary termination, the plan is a severance pay plan within the meaning of paragraph (b)(4)(iv)(B) of this section. Thus, the benefits are not treated as resulting from the deferral of compensation for purposes of section 3121(v)(2).

Example (10). (i) Employer V establishes a nonqualified deferred compensation plan under which employees will receive benefit payments commencing at age 65 as a life annuity or in one of several actuarially equivalent annuity forms. If an employee dies before benefit payments commence under the plan, a benefit is payable to the employee's designated beneficiary in a single lump sum payment equal to the present value of the employee's annuity benefit. This benefit (sometimes called a full reserve death benefit) is calculated using the applicable interest rate specified in section 417(e) and, for the period after age 65, the applicable mortality table specified in section 417(e), both of which are reasonable actuarial assumptions. During 2002, Employee E obtains a legally binding right to an annuity benefit under the plan, payable at age 65. This annuity benefit has a present value of $10,000 at the end of 2002, determined using the same assumptions as are used under the plan to calculate the full reserve death benefit.

(ii) The present value, at the end of 2002, of the total benefits payable to or on behalf of Employee E (i.e., the sum of the present value of the annuity benefit commencing at age 65, and the present value of the full reserve death benefit, with both determined using the actuarial assumptions described in paragraph (i) of this Example 10, except also taking into account the probability of death prior to age 65) is $10,000. This present value does not exceed the present value of the annuity benefits that could be payable to Employee E under the plan during Employee E's lifetime determined without a discount for the possibility that Employee E might die before age 65 (also $10,000). Thus, the benefit payable in the event of Employee E's death is not a death benefit for purposes of paragraph (b)(4)(iv) of this section.

(iii) The same result would apply in the case of a plan that bases benefits on an interest bearing account balance and pays the account balance at termination of employment or death (because the sum of the deferred benefits payable in the future if the employee terminates employment before death with a discount for the probability of death before that date plus the present value of the benefit payable in the event of death necessarily equals the present value of the deferred benefits payable with no discount for the probability of death).

Example (11). (i) The facts are the same as in Example 10, except that, in lieu of the full reserve death benefit, the plan provides a monthly life annuity benefit to an employee's spouse in the event of the employee's death before benefit payments commence equal to 100 percent of the monthly annuity that would be payable to the employee at age 65 under the life annuity form. Employee E is age 63 and has a spouse who is age 51. The sum of the present value of Employee E's annuity benefit commencing at age 65 determined with a discount for the possibility that Employee E might die before age 65 and the present value of the 100 percent annuity death benefit for Employee E's spouse exceeds $10,000.

(ii) The amount deferred for 2002 is $10,000 (because the 100 percent annuity death benefit for Employee E's spouse is disregarded to the extent that the total benefits payable to or on behalf of Employee E exceeds the present value of the annuity benefits that could be payable to Employee E under the plan during Employee E's lifetime without a discount for the probability of Employee E's death before benefit payments commence).

Example (12). (i) On January 1, 2001, Employer W establishes a plan that covers only Employee F, who owns a significant portion of the business and who has 30 years of service as of that date. The plan provides that, upon Employee F's termination of employment at any time, he will receive $200,000 per year for each of the immediately succeeding five years. Employee F terminates employment on March 1, 2001.

(ii) Because Employee F terminates employment within 12 months of the establishment of the plan and the facts and circumstances set forth above indicate that the plan was established in contemplation of impending termination of employment, the plan is considered to be established in connection with impending termination within the meaning of paragraph (b)(4)(v) of this section. Therefore, the benefits provided under the plan are not treated as resulting from the deferral of compensation for purposes of section 3121(v)(2).

Example (13). (i) Employer X establishes a plan on January 1, 2004, to supplement the qualified retirement benefits of recently hired 55-year old Employee G, who forfeited retirement benefits with her former employer in order to accept employment with Employer X. The plan provides that Employee G will receive $50,000 per year for life beginning at age 65, regardless of when she terminates employment. On April 15, 2004, Employee G unexpectedly terminates employment.

(ii) The facts and circumstances indicate that the plan was not established in contemplation of impending termination. Thus, even though Employee G terminated employment within 12 months of the establishment of the plan, the plan is not considered to be established in connection with impending termination within the meaning of paragraph (b)(4)(v) of this section. Benefits provided under the plan are treated as resulting from the deferral of compensation for purposes of section 3121(v)(2).

Example (14). (i) Employer Y establishes a plan to provide supplemental retirement benefits to a group of management employees who are at various stages of their careers. All employees covered by the plan are subject to the same benefit formula. Employee H is planning to (and actually does) retire within six months of the date on which the plan is established.

(ii) Even though Employee H terminated employment within 12 months of the establishment of the plan, the plan is not considered to have been established in connection with Employee H's impending termination within the meaning of paragraph (b)(4)(v) of this section because the facts and circumstances indicate otherwise.

Example (15). (i) Employee J owns 100 percent of Employer Z, a corporation that provides consulting services. Substantially all of Employer Z's revenue is derived as a result of the services performed by Employee J. In each of 2001, 2002, and 2003, Employer Z has gross receipts of $180,000 and expenses (other than salary) of $80,000. In each of 2001 and 2002, Employer Z pays Employee J a salary of $100,000 for services performed in each of those years. On December 31, 2002, Employer Z establishes a plan to pay Employee J $80,000 in 2003. The plan recites that the payment is in recognition of prior services. In 2003, Employer Z pays Employee J a salary of $20,000 and the $80,000 due under the plan.

(ii) The facts and circumstances described above indicate that the $80,000 paid pursuant to the plan is based on services performed by Employee J in 2003 and, thus, is paid for current services within the meaning of paragraph (b)(4)(viii) of this section. Accordingly, the plan does not provide for the deferral of compensation within the meaning of section 3121(v)(2), and the $80,000 payment is included as wages in 2003 under the general timing rule of paragraph (a)(1) of this section.

(c) Determination of the amount deferred. *(1) Account balance plans.* (i) General rule. For purposes of this section, if benefits for an employee are provided under a nonqualified deferred compensation plan that is an account balance plan, the amount deferred for a period equals the principal amount credited to the employee's account for the period, increased or decreased by any income attributable to the principal amount through the date the principal amount is required to be taken into account as wages under paragraph (e) of this section.

(ii) Definitions. (A) Account balance plan. For purposes of this section, an account balance plan is a nonqualified deferred compensation plan under the terms of which a principal amount (or amounts) is credited to an individual account for an employee, the income attributable to each principal amount is credited (or debited) to the individual account, and the benefits payable to the employee are based solely on the balance credited to the individual account.

(B) Income. For purposes of this section, income means any increase or decrease in the amount credited to an employee's account that is attributable to amounts previously credited to the employee's account, regardless of whether the plan denominates that increase or decrease as income.

(iii) Additional rules. (A) Commingled accounts. A plan does not fail to be an account balance plan merely because, under the terms of the plan, benefits payable to an employee are based solely on a specified percentage of an account maintained for all (or a portion of) plan participants under which principal amounts and income are credited (or debited) to such account.

(B) Bifurcation permitted. An employer may treat a portion of a nonqualified deferred compensation plan as a separate account balance plan if that portion satisfies the requirements of this paragraph (c)(1) and the amount payable to employees under that portion is determined independently of the amount payable under the other portion of the plan.

(C) Actuarial equivalents. A plan does not fail to be an account balance plan merely because the plan permits employees to elect to receive their benefits under the plan in a form of benefit other than payment of the account balance, provided the amount of benefit payable in that other form is actuarially equivalent to payment of the account balance using actuarial assumptions that are reasonable. Conversely, a plan is not an account balance plan if it provides an optional form of benefit that is not actuarially equivalent to the account balance using actuarial assumptions that are reasonable. For this purpose, the determination of whether forms are actuarially equivalent using actuarial assumptions that are reasonable is determined under the rules applicable to nonaccount balance plans under paragraph (c)(2)(iii) of this section.

(2) Nonaccount balance plans. (i) General rule. For purposes of this section, if benefits for an employee are provided under a nonqualified deferred compensation plan that is not an account balance plan (a nonaccount balance plan), the amount deferred for a period equals the present value of the additional future payment or payments to which the employee has obtained a legally binding right (as described in paragraph (b)(3)(i) of this section) under the plan during that period.

(ii) Present value defined. For purposes of this section, present value means the value as of a specified date of an amount or series of amounts due thereafter, where each amount is multiplied by the probability that the condition or conditions on which payment of the amount is contingent will be satisfied, and is discounted according to an assumed rate of interest to reflect the time value of money. For purposes of this section, the present value must be determined as of the date the amount deferred is required to be taken into account as wages under paragraph (e) of this section using actuarial assumptions and methods that are reasonable as of that date. For this purpose, a discount for the probability that an employee will die before commencement of benefit payments is permitted, but only to the extent that benefits will be forfeited upon death. In addition, the present value cannot be discounted for the probability that payments will not be made (or will be reduced) because of the unfunded status of the plan, the risk associated with any deemed or actual investment of amounts deferred under the plan, the risk that the employer, the trustee, or another party will be unwilling or unable to pay, the possibility of future plan amendments, the possibility of a future change in the law, or similar risks or contingencies. Nor is the present value affected by the possibility that some of the payments due under the plan will be eligible for one of the exclusions from wages in section 3121(a).

(iii) Treatment of actuarially equivalent benefits. (A) In general. In the case of a nonaccount balance plan that permits employees to receive their benefits in more than one form or commencing at more than one date, the amount deferred is determined by assuming that payments are made in the normal form of benefit commencing at normal commencement date if the requirements of paragraph (c)(2)(iii)(B) of this section are satisfied. Accordingly, in the case of a nonaccount balance plan that permits employees to receive their benefits in more than one form or commencing at more than one date, unless the requirements of paragraph (c)(2)(iii)(B) of this section are satisfied, the amount deferred is treated as not reasonably ascertainable under the rules of paragraph (e)(4)(i)(B) of this section until a form of benefit and a time of commencement are selected.

(B) Use of normal form commencing at normal commencement date. The requirements of this paragraph (c)(2)(iii)(B) are satisfied by a nonaccount balance plan if the plan has a single normal form of benefit commencing at normal commencement date for the amount deferred and each other optional form is actuarially equivalent to the normal form of benefit commencing at normal commencement date using actuarial assumptions that are reasonable. For this purpose, each form of benefit for payment of the amount deferred commencing at a date is a separate optional form. For purposes of this paragraph (c)(2)(iii)(B), each optional form is actuarially equivalent to the normal form of benefit commencing at normal commencement date only if the terms of the plan in effect when the amount is deferred provide for every optional form to be actuarially equivalent and further provide for actuarial assumptions to determine actuarial equivalency that will be reasonable at the time the optional form is selected, without regard to whether market interest rates are higher or lower at the time the optional form is selected than at the time the amount is deferred. Thus, a plan that provides for every optional form to be actuarially equivalent satisfies this paragraph (c)(2)(iii)(B) if it provides for actuarial equivalence to be determined—

(1) When an optional form is selected or when benefit payments under the optional form commence, based on assumptions that are reasonable then;

(2) Based on an index that reflects market rates of interest from time to time (for example, the plan specifies that all benefits will be actuarially equivalent using the applicable interest rate and applicable mortality table specified in section 417(e)); or

(3) Based on actuarial assumptions specified in the plan and provides for those assumptions to be revised to be reasonable assumptions if they cease to be reasonable assumptions.

(C) Fixed mortality assumptions permitted. A plan does not fail to satisfy paragraph (c)(2)(iii)(B) of this section merely because the plan specifies a fixed mortality assumption that is reasonable at the time the amount is deferred, even if that assumption is not reasonable at the time the optional form is selected. (But see paragraph (c)(2)(iii)(E) of this section for additional rules that apply if the mortality assumption is not reasonable at the time the optional form is selected.)

(D) Normal form of benefit commencing at normal commencement date defined. For purposes of this paragraph (c)(2)(iii), the normal form of benefit commencing at normal commencement date under the plan is the form, and date of commencement, under which the payments due to the employee under the plan are expressed, prior to adjustments for form or timing of commencement of payments.

(E) Rule applicable if actuarial assumptions cease to be reasonable. If the terms of the plan in effect when an amount is deferred provide for actuarial assumptions to determine actuarial equivalency that will be reasonable at the time the optional form is selected or payments commence as provided in paragraph (c)(2)(iii)(B) of this section, but, at that time, the actuarial assumptions used under the plan are not reasonable, the employee will be treated as obtaining a legally binding right at that time (or, if earlier, at the date on which the plan is amended to provide actuarial assumptions that are not reasonable) to any additional benefits that result from the use of an unreasonable actuarial assumption. This might occur, for example, if the plan specifies that the actuarial assumptions will be reasonable assumptions to be set at the time the optional form is selected and the assumptions used are in fact not reasonable at that time.

(3) Separate determination for each period. The amount deferred under this paragraph (c) is determined separately for each period for which there is an amount deferred under the plan. In addition, paragraphs (d) and (e) of this section are applied separately with respect to the amount deferred for each such period. Thus, for example, the fraction described in paragraph (d)(1)(ii)(B) of this section and the amount of the true-up at the resolution date described in paragraph (e)(4)(ii)(B) of this section are determined separately with respect to each amount deferred. See paragraph (e)(4)(ii)(D) of this section for special rules for allocating amounts deferred over more than one year.

(4) Examples. This paragraph (c) is illustrated by the following examples. (The examples illustrate the rules in this paragraph (c) and include various interest rate and mortality table assumptions, including the applicable section 417(e) mortality table, the GAM 83 (male) mortality table, and UP-84 mortality table. These tables can be obtained from the Society of Actuaries at its internet site at http://www.soa.org.) The examples are as follows:

Example (1). (i) Employer M establishes a nonqualified deferred compensation plan for Employee A. Under the plan, 10 percent of annual compensation is credited on behalf of Employee A on December 31 of each year. In addition, a reasonable rate of interest is credited quarterly on the balance credited to Employee A as of the last day of the preceding quarter. All amounts credited under the plan are 100 percent vested and the benefits payable to Employee A are based solely on the balance credited to Employee A's account.

(ii) The plan is an account balance plan. Thus, pursuant to paragraph (c)(1) of this section, the amount deferred for a calendar year is equal to 10 percent of annual compensation.

Example (2). (i) Employer N establishes a nonqualified deferred compensation plan for Employee B. Under the plan, 2.5 percent of annual compensation is credited quarterly on behalf of Employee B. In addition, a reasonable rate of interest is credited quarterly on the balance credited to Employee B's account as of the last day of the preceding quarter. All amounts credited under the plan are 100 percent vested, and the benefits payable to Employee B are based solely on the balance credited to Employee B's account. As permitted by paragraph (e)(5) of this section, any amount deferred under the plan for the calendar year is taken into account as wages on the last day of the year.

(ii) The plan is an account balance plan. Thus, pursuant to paragraph (c)(1) of this section, the amount deferred for a calendar year equals 10 percent of annual compensation (i.e., the sum of the principal amounts credited to Employee B's account for the year) plus the interest credited with respect to that 10 percent principal amount through the last day of the calendar year. If Employer N had not chosen to apply paragraph (e)(5) of this section and, thus, had taken into account 2.5 percent of compensation quarterly, the interest credited with respect to those quarterly amounts would not have been treated as part of the amount deferred for the year.

Example (3). (i) Employer O establishes a nonqualified deferred compensation plan for a group of five employees. Under the plan, a specified sum is credited to an account for the benefit of the group of employees on July 31 of each year. Income on the balance of the account is credited annually at a rate that is reasonable for each year. The benefit payable to an employee is equal to one-fifth of the account balance and is payable, at the employee's option, in a lump sum or in 10 annual installments that reflect income on the balance.

(ii) The plan is an account balance plan notwithstanding the fact that the employee's benefit is equal to a specified percentage of an account maintained for a group of employees.

Example (4). (i) The facts are the same as in Example 3, except that the plan also permits an employee to elect a life annuity that is actuarially equivalent to the account balance based on the applicable interest rate and applicable mortality table specified in section 417(e) at the time the benefit is elected by the employee.

(ii) Under paragraphs (c)(1)(iii)(C) and (c)(2)(iii) of this section, the plan does not fail to be an account balance plan merely because the plan permits employees to elect to receive their benefits under the plan in a form that is actuarially equivalent to payment of the account balance using actuarial assumptions that are reasonable at the time the form is selected.

Example (5). (i) Employer P establishes a nonqualified deferred compensation plan for a group of employees. Under the plan, each participating employee has a fully vested right to receive a life annuity, payable monthly beginning at age 65, equal to the product of 2 percent for each year of service and the employee's highest average annual compensation for any 3-year period. The plan also provides that, if an employee dies before age 65, the present value of the future payments will be paid to his or her beneficiary. As permitted under paragraph (e)(5) of this section, any amount deferred under the plan for a calendar year is taken into account as FICA wages as of the last day of the year. As of December 31, 2002, Employee C is age 60, has 25 years of service, and high 3-year average compensation of $100,000 (the average for the years 2000 through 2002). As of December 31, 2003, Employee C is age 61, has 26 years of service, and has high 3-year average compensation of $104,000. As of December 31, 2004, Employee C is age 62, has 27 years of service, and has high 3-year average compensation of $105,000. The assumptions that Employer P uses to determine the amount deferred for 2003 (a 7 percent interest rate and, for the period after commencement of benefit payments, the GAM 83 (male) mortality table) and for 2004 (a 7.5 percent interest rate and, for the period after commencement of benefit payments, the GAM 83 (male) mortality table) are assumed, solely for purposes of this example, to be reasonable actuarial assumptions.

(ii) As of December 31, 2002, Employee C has a legally binding right to receive lifetime payments of $50,000 (2 percent x 25 years x $100,000) per year. As of December 31, 2003, Employee C has a legally binding right to receive lifetime payments of $54,080 (2 percent x 26 years x $104,000) per year. Thus, during 2003, Employee C has earned a legally binding right to additional lifetime payments of $4,080 ($54,080-$50,000) per year beginning at age 65. The amount deferred for 2003 is the present value, as of December 31, 2003, of these additional payments, which is $28,767 ($4,080 x the present value factor for a deferred annuity payable at age 65, using the specified actuarial assumptions for 2003). Similarly, during 2004, Employee C has earned a legally binding right to additional lifetime payments of $2,620 (2 percent x 27 years x $105,000, minus $54,080) per year beginning at age 65. The amount deferred for 2004 is the present value, as of December 31, 2004, of these additional payments, which is $18,845 ($2,620 x the present value factor for a deferred annuity payable at age 65, using the specified actuarial assumptions for 2004).

Example (6). (i) Employer Q establishes a nonqualified deferred compensation plan for Employee D on January 1, 2001, when Employee D is age 63. During 2001, Employee D obtains a fully vested right to receive a life annuity under the nonqualified deferred compensation plan equal to the excess of $200,000 over the life annuity benefits payable to Employee D under a qualified defined benefit pension plan sponsored by Employer Q. The life annuity benefit payable annually under the qualified plan is the lesser of $200,000 and the section 415(b)(1)(A) limitation in effect for the year, where the section 415(b)(1)(A) limitation is automatically adjusted to reflect changes in the cost of living. Benefits under both the qualified and nonqualified plan are payable monthly beginning at age 65. For purposes of this example, the section 415(b)(1)(A) limit for 2001 is assumed to be $140,000. The nonqualified plan provides no benefits in the event Employee D dies prior to commencement of benefit payments. As permitted under paragraph (e)(5) of this section, any amount deferred under the plan for a calendar year is taken into account as FICA wages as of the last day of the year. The assumptions that Employer Q uses to determine the amount deferred for 2001 (a 7 percent interest rate, a 3 percent increase in the cost of living and the GAM 83 (male) mortality table) are assumed, solely for purposes of this example, to be reasonable actuarial assumptions. As of December 31, 2001, Employee D has a legally binding right to receive lifetime payments as set forth in the following table:

Year	Annual gross amount	Assumed qualified plan annual payment (based on cost of living)	Net annual payment under non-qualified plan
2003	$200,000	$145,000	$55,000
2004	200,000	150,000	50,000
2005	200,000	155,000	45,000
2006	200,000	160,000	40,000
2007	200,000	165,000	35,000
2008	200,000	170,000	30,000
2009	200,000	175,000	25,000
2010	200,000	180,000	20,000
2011	200,000	185,000	15,000
2012	200,000	190,000	10,000
2013	200,000	195,000	5,000
2014 and thereafter	200,000	205,000 or greater	0

(ii) The amount deferred for 2001 is the present value, as of December 31, 2001, of the net lifetime payments under the nonqualified plan, or $223,753.

(d) Amounts taken into account and income attributable thereto. *(1) Amounts taken into account.* (i) In general. For purposes of this section, an amount deferred under a nonqualified deferred compensation plan is taken into account as of the date it is included in computing the amount of wages as defined in section 3121(a), but only to the extent that any additional FICA tax that results from such inclusion (including any interest and penalties for late payment) is actually paid before the expiration of the applicable period of limitations for the period in which the amount deferred was required to be taken into account under paragraph (e) of this section. Because an amount deferred for a calendar year is combined with the employee's other wages for the year for purposes of computing FICA taxes with respect to the employee for the year, if the employee has other wages that equal or exceed the wage base limitations for the Old-Age, Survivors, and Disability Insurance (OASDI) portion (or, in the case of years before 1994, the Hospital Insurance (HI) portion) of FICA for the year, no portion of the amount deferred will actually result in additional OASDI (or HI) tax. However, because there is no wage base limitation for the HI portion of FICA for years after 1993, the entire amount deferred (in addition to all other wages) is subject to the HI tax for the year and, thus, will not be considered taken into account for purposes of this section unless the HI tax relating to the amount deferred is actually paid. In determining whether any additional FICA tax relating to the amount deferred is actually paid, any FICA tax paid in a year is treated as paid with respect to an amount deferred only after FICA tax is paid on all other wages for the year.

(ii) Amounts not taken into account. (A) Failure to take an amount deferred into account under the special timing rule. If an amount deferred for a period (as determined under paragraph (c) of this section) is not taken into account, then the nonduplication rule of paragraph (a)(2)(iii) of this section does not apply, and benefit payments attributable to that amount deferred are included as wages in accordance with the general timing rule of paragraph (a)(1) of this section. For example, if an amount deferred is required to be taken into account in a particular year under paragraph (e) of this section, but the employer fails to pay the additional FICA tax resulting from that amount, then the amount deferred and the income attributable to that amount must be included as wages when actually or constructively paid.

(B) Failure to take a portion of an amount deferred into account under the special timing rule. If, as of the date an amount deferred is required to be taken into account, only a portion of the amount deferred (as determined under paragraph (c) of this section) has been taken into account, then a portion of each subsequent benefit payment that is attributable to that amount is excluded from wages pursuant to the nonduplication rule of paragraph (a)(2)(iii) of this section and the balance is subject to the general timing rule of paragraph (a)(1) of this section. The portion that is excluded from wages is fixed immediately before the attributable benefit payments commence (or, if later, the date the amount deferred is required to be taken into account) and is determined by multiplying each such payment by a fraction, the numerator of which is the amount that was taken into account (plus income attributable to that amount determined under paragraph (d)(2) of this section through the date the portion is fixed) and the denominator of which is the present value of the future benefit payments attributable to the amount deferred, determined as of the date the portion is fixed. For this purpose, if the requirements of paragraph (c)(2)(iii)(B) of this section are satisfied, the present value is determined by assuming that payments are made in the normal form of benefit commencing at normal commencement date. In addition, if the employer demonstrates that the amount deferred was determined using reasonable actuarial assumptions as determined by the Commissioner, the present value of the future benefit payments attributable to the amount deferred is determined using those assumptions. In any other case, see paragraph (d)(2)(iii) of this section.

(2) Income attributable to the amount taken into account. (i) Account balance plans. (A) In general. For purposes of the nonduplication rule of paragraph (a)(2)(iii) of this section, in the case of an account balance plan, the income attributable to the amount taken into account means any amount credited on behalf of an employee under the terms of the plan that is income (within the meaning of paragraph (c)(1)(ii)(B) of this section) attributable to an amount previously taken into account (within the meaning of paragraph (d)(1) of this section), but only if the income reflects a rate of return that does not exceed either the rate of return on a predetermined actual investment (as determined in accordance with paragraph (d)(2)(i)(B) of this section) or, if the income does not reflect the rate of return on a predetermined actual investment (as so determined), a reasonable rate of interest (as determined in accordance with paragraph (d)(2)(i)(C) of this section).

(B) Rules relating to actual investment (1) In general. For purposes of this paragraph (d)(2)(i), the rate of return on a predetermined actual investment for any period means the rate of total return (including increases or decreases in fair market value) that would apply if the account balance were, during the applicable period, actually invested in one or more investments that are identified in accordance with the plan before the beginning of the period. For this purpose, an account balance plan can determine income based on the rate of return of a predetermined actual investment regardless of whether assets associated with the plan or the employer are actually invested therein and regardless of whether that investment is generally available to the public. For example, an account balance plan could provide that income on the account balance is determined based on an employee's prospective election among various investment alternatives that are available under the employer's section 401(k) plan, even if one of those investment alternatives is not generally available to the public. In addition, an actual investment includes an investment identified by reference to any stock index with respect to which there are positions traded on a national securities exchange described in section 1256(g)(7)(A).

(2) Certain rates of return not based on predetermined actual investment. A rate of return will not be treated as the rate of return on a predetermined actual investment within the meaning of this paragraph (d)(2)(i)(B) if the rate of return (to any extent or under any conditions) is based on the greater of the rate of return of two or more actual investments, is based on the greater of the rate of return on an actual investment and a rate of interest (whether or not the rate of interest would otherwise be reasonable under paragraph (d)(2)(i)(C) of this section), or is based on the rate of return on an actual investment that is not predetermined. For example, if a plan bases the rate of return on the greater of the rate of return on a predetermined actual investment (such as the value of the employer's stock), and a 0 percent interest rate (i.e., without regard to decreases in the value of that investment), the plan is using a rate of return that is not a rate

of return on a predetermined actual investment within the meaning of this paragraph (d)(2)(i)(B).

(C) Rules relating to reasonable interest rates. (1) In general. If income for a period is credited to an account balance plan on a basis other than the rate of return on a predetermined actual investment (as determined in accordance with paragraph (d)(2)(i)(B) of this section), then, except as otherwise provided in this paragraph (d)(2)(i)(C), the determination of whether the income for the period is based on a reasonable rate of interest will be made at the time the amount deferred is required to be taken into account and annually thereafter.

(2) Fixed rates permitted. If, with respect to an amount deferred for a period, an account balance plan provides for a fixed rate of interest to be credited, and the rate is to be reset under the plan at a specified future date that is not later than the end of the fifth calendar year that begins after the beginning of the period, the rate is reasonable at the beginning of the period, and the rate is not changed before the reset date, then the rate will be treated as reasonable in all future periods before the reset date.

(ii) Nonaccount balance plans. For purposes of the nonduplication rule of paragraph (a)(2)(iii) of this section, in the case of a nonaccount balance plan, the income attributable to the amount taken into account means the increase, due solely to the passage of time, in the present value of the future payments to which the employee has obtained a legally binding right, the present value of which constituted the amount taken into account (determined as of the date such amount was taken into account), but only if the amount taken into account was determined using reasonable actuarial assumptions and methods. Thus, for each year, there will be an increase (determined using the same interest rate used to determine the amount taken into account) resulting from the shortening of the discount period before the future payments are made, plus, if applicable, an increase in the present value resulting from the employee's survivorship during the year. As a result, if the amount deferred for a period is determined using a reasonable interest rate and other reasonable actuarial assumptions and methods, and the amount is taken into account when required under paragraph (e) of this section, then, under the nonduplication rule of paragraph (a)(2)(iii) of this section, none of the future payments attributable to that amount will be subject to FICA tax when paid.

(iii) Unreasonable rates of return. (A) Account balance plans. This paragraph (d)(2)(iii)(A) applies to an account balance plan under which the income credited is based on neither a predetermined actual investment, within the meaning of paragraph (d)(2)(i)(B) of this section, nor a rate of interest that is reasonable, within the meaning of paragraph (d)(2)(i)(C) of this section, as determined by the Commissioner. In that event, the employer must calculate the amount that would be credited as income under a reasonable rate of interest, determine the excess (if any) of the amount credited under the plan over the income that would be credited using the reasonable rate of interest, and take that excess into account as an additional amount deferred in the year the income is credited. If the employer fails to calculate the amount that would be credited as income under a reasonable rate of interest and to take the excess into account as an additional amount deferred in the year the income is credited, or the employer otherwise fails to take the full amount deferred into account, then the excess of the income credited under the plan over the income that would be credited using AFR will be treated as an amount deferred in the year the income is credited. For purposes of this section, AFR means the mid-term applicable federal rate (as defined pursuant to section 1274(d)) for January 1 of the calendar year, compounded annually. In addition, pursuant to paragraph (d)(1)(ii) of this section, the excess over the income that would result from the application of AFR and any income attributable to that excess are subject to the general timing rule of paragraph (a)(1) of this section.

(B) Nonaccount balance plans. If any actuarial assumption or method used to determine the amount taken into account under a nonaccount balance plan is not reasonable, as determined by the Commissioner, then the income attributable to the amount taken into account is limited to the income that would result from the application of the AFR and, if applicable, the applicable mortality table under section 417(e)(3)(A)(ii)(I) (the 417(e) mortality table), both determined as of the January 1 of the calendar year in which the amount was taken into account. In addition, paragraph (d)(1)(ii)(B) of this section applies and, in calculating the fraction described in paragraph (d)(1)(ii)(B) of this section (at the date specified in paragraph (d)(1)(ii)(B) of this section), the numerator is the amount taken into account plus income (as limited under this paragraph (d)(2)(iii)(B)), and the present value in the denominator is determined using the AFR, the 417(e) mortality table, and reasonable assumptions as to cost of living, each determined as of the time the amount deferred was required to be taken into account.

(3) Examples. This paragraph (d) is illustrated by the following examples:

Example (1). (i) In 2001, Employer M establishes a nonqualified deferred compensation plan for Employee A under which all benefits are 100 percent vested. In 2002, Employee A has $200,000 of current annual compensation from Employer M that is subject to FICA tax. The amount deferred under the plan on behalf of Employee A for 2002 is $20,000. Thus, Employee A has total wages for FICA tax purposes of $220,000. Because Employee A has other wages that exceed the OASDI wage base for 2002, no additional OASDI tax is due as a result of the $20,000 amount deferred. Because there is no wage base limitation for the HI portion of FICA, additional HI tax liability results from the $20,000 amount deferred. However, Employer M fails to pay the additional HI tax.

(ii) Under paragraph (d)(1)(i) of this section, an amount deferred is considered taken into account as wages for FICA tax purposes as of the date it is included in computing FICA wages, but only if any additional FICA tax liability that results from inclusion of the amount deferred is actually paid. Because the HI tax resulting from the $20,000 amount deferred was not paid, that amount deferred was not taken into account within the meaning of paragraph (d)(1) of this section. Thus, pursuant to paragraph (d)(1)(ii) of this section, benefit payments attributable to the $20,000 amount deferred will be included as wages in accordance with the general timing rule of paragraph (a)(1) of this section and will be subject to the HI portion of FICA tax when actually or constructively paid (and the OASDI portion of FICA tax to the extent Employee A's wages do not exceed the OASDI wage base limitation).

Example (2). (i) The facts are the same as in Example 1, except that Employer M takes all actions necessary to correct its failure to pay the additional tax before the applicable period of limitations expires for 2002 (including payment of any applicable interest and penalties).

(ii) Because the HI tax resulting from the $20,000 amount deferred is paid, that amount deferred is considered taken into account for 2002. Thus, in accordance with paragraph (a)(2)(iii) of this section, neither the amount deferred nor the income attributable to the amount taken into account will be treated as wages for FICA tax purposes at any time thereafter.

Example (3). (i) Employer N establishes a nonqualified deferred compensation plan under which all benefits are 100 percent vested. Under the plan, an employee's account is credited with a contribution equal to 10 percent of salary on December 31 of each year. The employee's account balance also is increased each December 31 by interest on the total amounts credited to the employee's account as of the preceding December 31. The interest rate specified in the plan results in income credits that are not based on the rate of return on a predetermined actual investment within the meaning of paragraph (d)(2)(i)(B) of this section, and that are greater than the income that would result from application of a reasonable rate of interest within the meaning of paragraph (d)(2)(i)(C) of this section. Employer N fails to take into account an additional amount for the excess of the income credited under the plan over a reasonable rate of interest.

(ii) Pursuant to paragraph (d)(2)(iii)(A) of this section, the income credits in excess of the income that would be credited using the AFR are considered additional amounts deferred in the year credited.

Example (4). (i) The facts are the same as in Example 3, except that the annual increase is based on Moody's Average Corporate Bond Yield.

(ii) Because this index reflects a reasonable rate of interest, the income credited under the plan is considered income attributable to the amount taken into account within the meaning of paragraph (d)(2)(i) of this section.

Example (5). (i) The facts are the same as in Example 3, except that the annual increase (or decrease) is based on the rate of total return on Employer N's publicly traded common stock.

(ii) Because the income credited under the plan does not exceed the actual rate of return on a predetermined actual investment, the income credited is considered income attributable to the amount taken into account within the meaning of paragraph (d)(2)(i) of this section.

Example (6). (i) The facts are the same as in Example 3, except that the annual rate of increase or decrease is equal to the greater of the rate of total return on a specified aggressive growth mutual fund or the rate of return on a specified income-oriented mutual fund. Employer N fails to take into account an additional amount for the excess of the income credited under the plan over a reasonable rate of interest.

(ii) Because the rate of increase or decrease is based on the greater of two rates of returns, the increase is not based on the return on a predetermined actual investment within the meaning of paragraph (d)(2)(i)(B) of this section. Thus, if the rate of return credited under the plan (i.e., the greater of the rates of return of the two mutual funds) exceeds the income that would be credited using the AFR, the excess is not considered income attributable to the amount taken into account within the meaning of paragraph (d)(2)(i) of this section and, pursuant to paragraph (d)(2)(iii)(A) of this section, is considered an additional amount deferred.

Example (7). (i) The facts are the same as in Example 6, except that the annual increase or decrease with respect to 50 percent of the employee's account is equal to the rate of total return on the specified aggressive growth mutual fund and the annual increase or decrease with respect to the other 50 percent of the employee's account is equal to the increase or decrease in the Standard & Poor's 500 Index.

(ii) Because the increase or decrease attributable to any portion of the employee's account is based on the return on a predetermined actual investment, the entire increase or decrease is considered income attributable to the amount taken into account within the meaning of paragraph (d)(2)(i) of this section.

Example (8). (i) The facts are the same as in Example 3, except that, pursuant to the terms of the plan, before the beginning of each year, the board of directors of Employer N designates a specific investment on which the following year's annual increase or decrease will be based. The board is authorized to switch investments more frequently on a prospective basis. Before the beginning of 2004, the board designates Company A stock as the investment for 2004. Before the beginning of 2005, the board designates Company B stock as the investment for 2005. At the end of 2005, the board determines that the return on Company B stock was lower than expected and changes its designation for 2005 to the rate of return on Company C stock, which had a higher return during 2005. Employer N fails to take into account an additional amount for the excess of the income credited under the plan over a reasonable rate of interest.

(ii) The annual increase or decrease for 2004 is based on the return of a predetermined actual investment. Although the annual increase or decrease for 2005 is based on an actual investment, the actual investment is not predetermined since it was not designated before the beginning of 2005. Pursuant to paragraph (d)(2)(iii)(A) of this section, the excess of the income credited under the plan over the income determined using AFR is an additional amount deferred for 2005.

Example (9). (i) Employer O establishes a nonqualified deferred compensation plan for Employee B. Under the plan, if Employee B survives until age 65, he has a fully vested right to receive a lump sum payment at that age, equal to the product of 10 percent per year of service and Employee B's highest average annual compensation for any 3-year period, but no benefits are payable in the event Employee B dies prior to age 65. As permitted under paragraph (e)(5) of this section, any amount deferred under the plan for the calendar year is taken into account as wages as of the last day of the year. As of December 31, 2002, Employee B has 25 years of service and Employee B's high 3-year average compensation is $100,000 (the average for the years 2000 through 2002). As of December 31, 2002, Employee B has a legally binding right to receive a payment at age 65 of $250,000 (10 percent x 25 years x $100,000). As of December 31, 2003, Employee B is age 63, has 26 years of service, and has high 3-year average compensation of $104,000. As of December 31, 2003, Employee B has a legally binding right to receive a payment at age 65 of $270,400 (10 percent x 26 years x $104,000). Thus, during 2003, Employee B has earned a legally binding right to an additional payment at age 65 of $20,400 ($270,400-$250,000). The assumptions that Employer O uses to determine the amount deferred for 2003 are a 7 percent interest rate and the GAM 83 (male) mortality table, which, solely for purposes of this example, are assumed to be reasonable actuarial assumptions. The amount deferred for 2003 is the present value, as of December 31, 2003, of the $20,400 payment, which is $17,353. Employer O takes this amount into account by including it in Employee B's FICA wages for 2003 and paying the additional FICA tax.

(ii) Under paragraph (d)(2)(ii) of this section, the income attributable to the amount that was taken into account is the increase in the present value of the future payment due solely to the passage of time, because the amount deferred was determined using reasonable actuarial assumptions and methods. As of the payment date at age 65, the present value of the future payment earned during 2003 is $20,400. The entire difference between the $20,400 and the $17,353 amount deferred ($3,047) is the increase in the present value of the future payment due solely to the passage of time, and thus constitutes income attributable to the amount taken into account. Because the amount deferred was taken into account, the entire payment of $20,400 represents either an amount deferred that was previously taken into account ($17,353) or income attributable to that amount ($3,047). Accordingly, pursuant to the nonduplication rule of paragraph (a)(2)(iii) of this section, none of the payment is included in wages.

Example (10). (i) The facts are the same as in Example 9, except that, instead of providing a lump sum equal to 10 percent of average compensation per year of service, the plan provides Employee B with a fully vested right to receive a life annuity, payable monthly beginning at age 65, equal to the product of 2 percent for each year of service and Employee B's highest average annual compensation for any 3-year period. The plan also provides that, if Employee B dies before age 65, the present value of the future payments will be paid to his or her beneficiary. As of December 31, 2002, Employee B has a legally binding right to receive lifetime payments of $50,000 (2 percent x 25 years x $100,000) per year. As of December 31, 2003, Employee B has a legally binding right to receive lifetime payments of $54,080 (2 percent x 26 years x $104,000) per year. Thus, during 2003, Employee B has earned a legally binding right to additional lifetime payments of $4,080 ($54,080-$50,000) per year beginning at age 65. The amount deferred for 2003 is $32,935, which is the present value, as of December 31, 2003, of these additional payments, determined using the same actuarial assumptions and methods used in Example 9, except that there is no discount for the probability of death prior to age 65. Employer O takes this amount into account by including it in Employee B's FICA wages for 2003 and paying the additional FICA tax.

(ii) Under paragraph (d)(2)(ii) of this section, the income attributable to the amount that was taken into account is the increase in the present value of the future payments due solely to the passage of time, because the amount deferred was determined using reasonable actuarial assumptions and methods. Because the amount deferred was taken into account, each annual payment of $4,080 attributable to the amount deferred in 2003 represents either an amount deferred that was previously taken into account or income attributable to that amount. Accordingly, pursuant to the nonduplication rule of paragraph (a)(2)(iii) of this section, none of the payments are included in wages.

Example (11). (i) The facts are the same as in Example 10, except that no amount is taken into account for 2003 because Employer O fails to pay the additional FICA tax.

(ii) Under paragraph (d)(1)(ii)(A) of this section, if an amount deferred for a period is not taken into account, then the benefit payments attributable to that amount deferred are included as wages in accordance with the general timing rule of paragraph (a)(1) of this section. In this case, assuming that the amounts deferred in other periods were taken into account, $4,080 of each year's total benefit payments will be included in wages when actually or constructively paid, in accordance with the general timing rule.

Example (12). (i) Employer P establishes an account balance plan on January 1, 2002, under which all benefits are 100 percent vested. The plan provides that amounts deferred will be credited annually with interest beginning in 2002 at a rate that is greater than a reasonable rate of interest. Employer P treats the excess over the applicable interest rate in section 417(e) as an additional amount deferred for 2002 and in each year thereafter, and takes the additional amount into account by including it in FICA wages and paying the additional FICA tax for the year.

(ii) Under the nonduplication rule in paragraph (a)(2)(iii) of this section, the benefits paid under the plan will be excluded from wages for FICA tax purposes.

Example (13). (i) The facts are the same as in Example 9, except that, in determining the amount deferred, Employer O uses a 15 percent interest rate, which, solely for purposes of this example, is assumed not to be a reasonable interest rate. Employer O determines that the amount deferred for 2003 is the present value, as of December 31, 2003, of the $20,400 payment, which is $15,023. Employer O includes $15,023 in wages and pays any resulting FICA tax. Solely for purposes of this example, it is assumed that the AFR as of January 1, 2003, is 7 percent.

(ii) Under paragraph (d)(2)(iii)(B) of this section, if any actuarial assumption or method is not reasonable, then the income attributable to the amount taken into account is limited to the income that would result from application of the AFR and, if applicable, the 417(e) mortality table. Because the 15 percent interest rate is unreasonable, the income attributable to the amount taken into account is limited to the income that would result from using a 7 percent interest rate and, in this case, an increase for survivorship using the 417(e) mortality table. Under these assumptions, the income attributable to the $15,023 amount taken into account for 2003 is $1,199 in 2004 and $1,313 in 2005. Under paragraph (d)(1)(ii) of this section, the sum of these amounts ($17,535) is excluded from Employee B's wages pursuant to the nonduplication rule of paragraph (a)(2)(iii) of this section, and the balance of the payment ($2,865) is subject to the general timing rule of paragraph (a)(1) of this section and, thus, is included in Employee B's wages when actually or constructively paid.

(iii) The same result can be reached by multiplying the attributable benefit payments by a fraction, the numerator of which is the amount taken into account, and the denominator of which is the amount deferred that would have been taken into account at the same time had the amount deferred been calculated using the AFR and the 417(e) mortality table. These assumptions are determined as of January 1 of the calendar year in which the amount was taken into account. In this Example 13, the fraction would be $15,023 divided by $17,478, which equals .85954. The $20,400 payment is multiplied by this fraction to determine the amount of the payment that is excluded from wages pursuant to the nonduplication rule of paragraph (a)(2)(iii) of this section. Thus, $17,535 ($20,400 x .85954) is excluded from wages and the balance ($2,865) is subject to FICA tax when actually or constructively paid.

Example (14). (i) The facts are the same as Example 10, except that Employer O calculates the amount deferred for 2003 as $18,252 and takes that amount into account by including that amount in wages and paying any resulting FICA tax. The assumptions that Employer O uses to determine the amount deferred are a 15 percent interest rate and, for the period after commencement of benefit payments, the GAM 83 (male) mortality table. The 15 percent interest rate is assumed, solely for purposes of this example, not to be a reasonable actuarial assumption. Solely for purposes of this example, it is assumed that the AFR as of January 1, 2003, is 7 percent.

(ii) Under paragraph (d)(2)(iii)(B) of this section, if any actuarial assumption or method used is not reasonable, then the income attributable to the amount taken into account is limited to the income that would result from application of the AFR and, if applicable, the 417(e) mortality table. Because the 15 percent interest rate is not reasonable, the income attributable to the amount taken into account is equal to the income that would result from using a 7 percent interest rate and the amount taken into account is treated as if it represented a portion of the amount deferred for purposes of applying paragraph (d)(1)(ii)(B) of this section. Under these assumptions, the income attributable to the $18,252 amount taken into account for 2003 is $1,278 in 2004 and $1,367 in 2005. Under paragraph (d)(1)(ii)(B) of this section, the portion of each benefit payment attributable to the amount deferred that is excluded from wages pursuant to the nonduplication rule of paragraph (a)(2)(iii) of this section is determined at benefit commencement by multiplying each benefit payment by a fraction, the numerator of which is the amount taken into account (plus income attributable to that amount) and the denominator of which is the present value of future benefit payments attributable to the amount deferred. Because the interest rate assumption is not reasonable, not only is the income limited to the application of the AFR, but the present value in the denominator must be determined using the AFR and (if applicable) the 417(e) mortality table. In this case, the present value is $40,283 and thus the fraction is $20,897 divided by $40,283, or .51875. Thus, $2,116 (.51875 x $4,080) of each year's benefit payment is excluded from wages and the balance of each year's payment ($1,964) is subject to the general timing rule of paragraph (a)(1) of this section and is included in wages when actually or constructively paid.

(iii) The same result can be reached by multiplying the attributable benefit payments by a fraction the numerator of which is the amount taken into account, and the denominator of which is the amount deferred that would have been taken into account at the same time had the amount deferred been calculated using the AFR and the 417(e) mortality table. These assumptions are determined as of January 1 of the calendar year in which the amount was taken into account. In this Example 14, the fraction would be $18,252 divided by $35,185, which equals .51875. The $4,080 annual payment is multiplied by this fraction to determine the amount of the payment that is excluded from wages pursuant to the nonduplication rule of paragraph (a)(2)(iii) of this section. Thus, $2,116 ($4,080 x .51875) is excluded from wages and the balance ($1,964) is subject to FICA tax when actually or constructively paid.

(e) Time amounts deferred are required to be taken into account. *(1) In general.* Except as otherwise provided in this paragraph (e), an amount deferred under a nonqualified deferred compensation plan must be taken into account as wages for FICA tax purposes as of the later of the date on which services creating the right to the amount deferred are performed (within the meaning of paragraph (e)(2) of this section) or the date on which the right to the amount deferred is no longer subject to a substantial risk of forfeiture (within the meaning of paragraph (e)(3) of this section). However, in no event may any amount deferred under a nonqualified deferred compensation plan be taken into account as wages for FICA tax purposes prior to the establishment of the plan providing for the amount deferred (or, if later, the plan amendment providing for the amount deferred). Therefore, if an amount is deferred pursuant to the terms of a legally binding agreement that is not put in writing until after the amount would otherwise be taken into account under this paragraph (e)(1), the amount deferred (including any attributable income) must be taken into account as wages for FICA tax purposes as of the date the material terms of the plan are put in writing.

(2) Services creating the right to an amount deferred. For purposes of this section, services creating the right to an amount deferred under a nonqualified deferred compensation plan are considered to be performed as of the date on which, under the terms of the plan and all the facts and circumstances, the employee has performed all of the services necessary to obtain a legally binding right (as described in paragraph (b)(3)(i) of this section) to the amount deferred.

(3) Substantial risk of forfeiture. For purposes of this section, the determination of whether a substantial risk of forfeiture exists must be made in accordance with the principles of section 83 and the regulations thereunder.

(4) Amount deferred that is not reasonably ascertainable under a nonaccount balance plan. (i) In general. (A) Date required to be taken into account. Notwithstanding any other provision of this paragraph (e), an amount deferred under a nonaccount balance plan is not required to be taken into account as wages under the special timing rule of paragraph (a)(2) of this section until the first date on which all of the amount deferred is reasonably ascertainable (the resolution date). In this case, the amount required to be taken into account as of the resolution date is determined in accordance with paragraph (c)(2) of this section.

(B) Definition of reasonably ascertainable. For purposes of this paragraph (e)(4), an amount deferred is considered reasonably ascertainable on the first date on which the amount, form, and commencement date of the benefit payments attributable to the amount deferred are known, and the only actuarial or other assumptions regarding future events or circumstances needed to determine the amount deferred are interest and mortality. For this purpose, the form and commencement date of the benefit payments attributable to the amount deferred are treated as known if the requirements of paragraph (c)(2)(iii)(B) of this section (under which payments are treated as being made in the normal form of benefit commencing at normal commencement date) are satisfied. In addition, an amount deferred does not fail to be reasonably ascertainable on a date merely because the exact amount of the benefit payable cannot readily be calculated on that date or merely because the exact amount of the benefit payable depends on future changes in the cost of living. If the exact amount of the benefit payable depends on future changes in the cost of living, the amount deferred must be determined using a reasonable assumption as to the future changes in the cost of living. For example, the amount of a benefit is treated as known even if the exact amount of the benefit payable cannot be determined until future changes in the cost of living are reflected in the section 415 limitation on benefits payable under a qualified retirement plan.

(ii) Earlier inclusion permitted. (A) In general. With respect to an amount deferred that is not reasonably ascertainable, an employer may choose to take an amount into account at any date or dates (an early inclusion date or dates) before the resolution date (but not before the date described in paragraph (e)(1) of this section with respect to the amount deferred). Thus, for example, with respect to an amount deferred under a nonaccount balance plan that is not reasonably ascertainable because the plan permits employees to receive their benefits in more than one form or commencing at more than one date (and the requirements of paragraph (c)(2)(iii) of this section are not satisfied), an employer may choose to take an amount into account on the date otherwise described in paragraph (e)(1) of this section before the form and commencement date are selected (based on assumptions as to the form and commencement date for the benefit payments) or may choose to wait until the form and commencement date of the benefit payments are selected. An employer that chooses to take an amount into account at an early inclusion date under this paragraph (e)(4)(ii) for an employee under a plan is not required until the resolution date to identify the period to which the amount taken into account relates.

(B) True-up at resolution date. If, with respect to an amount deferred for a period, an employer chooses to take an amount into account as of an early inclusion date in accordance with this paragraph (e)(4)(ii) and the benefit payments attributable to the amount deferred exceed the benefit payments that are actuarially equivalent to the amount taken into account at the early inclusion date (payable in the same form and using the same commencement date as the benefit payments attributable to the amount deferred), then the present value of the difference in the benefits, determined in accordance with paragraph (c)(2) of this section, must be taken into account as of the resolution date.

(C) Actuarial assumptions. For purposes of determining the benefits that are actuarially equivalent to the amount taken into account as of an early inclusion date, the amount taken into account is converted to an actuarially equivalent benefit payable in the same form and commencing on the same date as the actual benefit payments attributable to the amount deferred using an interest rate, and, if applicable, mortality and cost-of-living assumptions, that were reasonable as of the early inclusion date. Thus, with respect to an amount deferred for a period, the amount required to be taken into account as of the resolution date is the present value (determined using an interest rate, and, if applicable, mortality and cost-of-living assumptions, that are reasonable as of the resolution date) of the excess, if any, of the future benefit payments attributable to the amount deferred over the future benefits payable in the same form and commencing on the same date that are actuarially equivalent to the portion of the amount deferred that was taken into account as of the early inclusion date (where actuarial equivalence is determined using an interest rate, and, if applicable, mortality and cost-of-living assumptions, that were reasonable as of the early inclusion date).

(D) Allocation rules for amounts deferred over more than one period. (1) General rule. The rules of this paragraph (e)(4)(ii)(D) apply for purposes of determining whether an amount has been included under this paragraph (e)(4) before the earliest date permitted under paragraph (e)(1) of this section.

(2) Future compensation increases. Increases in an employee's compensation after the early inclusion date must be disregarded.

(3) Early retirement subsidies. An early retirement subsidy that the employee ultimately receives may be taken into account at an early inclusion date if the employee would have a legally binding right to the subsidy at the early inclusion date but for any condition that the employee continue to render services. Accordingly, an employer may take into account at an early inclusion date any early retirement subsidy that the employee ultimately receives to the extent that elimination or reduction of that subsidy would violate section 411(d)(6)(B)(i) if that section applied to the plan.

(4) Allocation with respect to offsets. In any case in which a series of amounts are deferred over more than one period, the amounts deferred are not reasonably ascertainable until a single resolution date and the benefit payments attributable to the entire series are determined under a formula that provides a gross benefit that in the aggregate is subject to an objective reduction for future events under the terms of the plan, such as an offset for the aggregate benefits payable under a plan qualified under section 401(a), the attribution of benefit payments to the amount deferred in each period is determined under the rules of this paragraph (e)(4)(ii)(D)(4). In a case described in the preceding sentence, the benefit payments made as a result of the series of amounts deferred may be treated as attributable to the amount deferred as of the earliest period in which the employee obtained a legally binding right to a benefit under the plan equal to the excess, if any, of the amount of the gross benefit attributable to that period (determined at the resolution date), over the amount of the reduction determined as of the end of that period. Thus, for example, if an employee obtains a legally binding right in each of several years to benefit payments from a nonqualified deferred compensation plan that provides for a specified gross benefit for the years to be offset by the benefits payable under a qualified plan, the amount deferred in the first year may be treated as equal to the gross benefit for the year, reduced by the offset applicable at the end of the year (even if the offset increases after the end of the year).

(E) Treatment of benefits paid before the resolution date. If a benefit payment is attributable to an amount deferred that is not reasonably ascertainable at the time of payment (or is paid before the date selected under paragraph (e)(5) of this section), and the employer has previously taken an amount into account with respect to the amount deferred under the early inclusion rule of this paragraph (e)(4), then, in lieu of the pro rata rule provided in paragraph (d)(1)(ii)(B) of this section, a first-in-first-out rule applies in determining the portion of the benefit payment attributable to the amount taken into account. Under this first-in-first-out rule, the benefit payment is compared to the sum of the amount taken into account at the early inclusion date and the income attributable to that amount. If the benefit payment equals or exceeds the amount taken into account at the early inclusion date and the income attributable to that amount as of the date of the benefit payment, the benefit payment is included as wages under the general timing rule of paragraph (a)(1) of this section to the extent of any excess, and the amount taken into account at the early inclusion date (and income attributable to that amount) is disregarded thereafter with respect to the amount deferred. If the amount taken into account at the early inclusion date and the income attributable to that amount as of the date of the benefit payment exceeds the benefit payment, the benefit payment is not included as wages under the general timing rule of paragraph (a)(1) of this section and, in determining the amount that must be taken into account thereafter with respect to the amount deferred, the amount taken into account at the early inclusion date, plus attributable income as of the date of the benefit payment, is reduced by the amount of the benefit payment, and only the excess plus future income attributable to the excess (credited using assumptions that were reasonable on the early inclusion date) is taken into consideration. If amounts have been taken into account at more than one early inclusion date, this paragraph (e)(4)(ii)(E) applies on a first-in-first-out basis, beginning with the amount taken into account at the earliest early inclusion date (including income attributable thereto).

(5) Rule of administrative convenience. For purposes of this section, an employer may treat an amount deferred as required to be taken into account under this paragraph (e) on any date that is later than, but within the same calendar year as, the actual date on which the amount deferred is otherwise required to be taken into account under this paragraph (e). For example, if services creating the right to an amount deferred are considered performed under paragraph (e)(2) of this section periodically throughout a year, the employer may nevertheless treat the services creating the right to that amount deferred as performed on December 31 of that year. If an employer uses the rule of administrative convenience described in this paragraph (e)(5), any determination of whether the income attributable to an amount deferred under an account balance plan is based on a reasonable rate of interest or whether the actuarial assumptions used to determine the present value of an amount deferred in a nonaccount balance plan are reasonable will be made as of the date the employer selects to take the amount into account.

(6) Portions of an amount deferred required to be taken into account on more than one date. If different portions of an amount deferred are required to be taken into account under paragraph (e)(1) of this section on more than one date (e.g., on account of a graded vesting schedule), then each such portion is considered a separate amount deferred for purposes of this section.

(7) Examples. This paragraph (e) is illustrated by the following examples:

Example (1). (i) Employer M establishes a nonqualified deferred compensation plan for Employee A on November 1, 2005. Under the plan, which is an account balance plan, Employee A obtains a legally binding right on the last day of each calendar year (if Employee A is employed on that date) to be credited with a principal amount equal to 5 percent of compensation for the year. In addition, a reasonable rate of interest is credited quarterly. Employee A's account balance is nonforfeitable and is payable upon Employee A's termination of employment. For 2006, the principal amount credited to Employee A under the plan (which, in this case, is also the amount deferred within the meaning of paragraph (c) of this section) is $25,000.

(ii) Under paragraph (e)(2) of this section, the services creating the right to the $25,000 amount deferred are considered performed as of December 31, 2006, the date on which Employee A has performed all of the services necessary to obtain a legally binding right to the amount deferred. Thus, in accordance with paragraph (e)(1) of this section, the $25,000 amount deferred must be taken into account as of December 31, 2006, which is the later of the date on which services creating the right to the amount deferred are performed or the date on which the right to the amount deferred is no longer subject to a substantial risk of forfeiture.

Example (2). (i) The facts are the same as in Example 1, except that the principal amount credited under the plan on the last day of each year (and attributable interest) is forfeited if the employee terminates employment within five years of that date.

(ii) Under paragraph (e)(3) of this section, the determination of whether the right to an amount deferred is subject to a substantial risk of forfeiture is made in accordance with the principles of section 83. Under § 1.83-3(c) of this chapter, a substantial risk of forfeiture generally exists where rights in property that are transferred are conditioned, directly or indirectly, upon the future performance of substantial services. Because Employee A's right to receive the $25,000 principal amount (and attributable interest) is conditioned on the performance of services for five years, a substantial risk of forfeiture exists with respect to that amount deferred until December 31, 2011.

(iii) December 31, 2011, is the later of the date on which services creating the right to the amount deferred are performed or the date on which the right to the amount deferred is no longer subject to a substantial risk of forfeiture. Thus, in accordance with paragraph (e)(1) of this section, the amount deferred (which, pursuant to paragraph (c)(1) of this section, is equal to the $25,000 principal amount credited to Employee A's account on December 31, 2006, plus the interest credited with respect to that principal amount through December 31, 2011) must be taken into account as of December 31, 2011.

Example (3). (i) The facts are the same as in Example 2, except that the principal amount credited under the plan on the last day of each year (and attributable interest) becomes nonforfeitable according to a graded vesting schedule under which 20 percent is vested as of December 31, 2007; 40 percent is vested as of December 31, 2008; 60 percent is vested as of December 31, 2009; 80 percent is vested as of December 31, 2010; and 100 percent is vested as of December 31, 2011. Because these dates are later than the date on which the services creating the right to the amount deferred are considered performed (December 31, 2006), the amount deferred is required to be taken into account as of these dates that fall in five different years.

(ii) Paragraph (e)(6) of this section provides that, if different portions of an amount deferred are required to be taken into account under paragraph (e)(1) of this section on more than one date, then each such portion is considered a separate amount deferred for purposes of this section. Thus, $5,000 of the principal amount, plus interest credited through December 31, 2007, is taken into account as an amount deferred on December 31, 2007; $5,000 of the principal amount, plus interest credited through December 31, 2008, is taken into account as a separate amount deferred on December 31, 2008; etc.

Example (4). (i) On November 21, 2001, Employer N establishes a nonqualified deferred compensation plan under which all benefits are 100 percent vested. The plan provides for Employee B (who is age 45) to receive a lump sum benefit of $500,000 at age 65. This benefit will be forfeited if Employee B dies before age 65.

(ii) Because the amount, form, and commencement date of the benefit are known, and the only assumptions needed to determine the amount deferred are interest and mortality, the amount deferred is reasonably ascertainable within the meaning of paragraph (e)(4)(i) of this section on November 21, 2001.

Example (5). (i) The facts are the same as in Example 4, except that plan provides that the lump sum will be paid at the later of age 65 or termination of employment and provides that the $500,000 payable to Employee B is increased by 5 percent per year for each year that payment is deferred beyond age 65.

(ii) Because the commencement date of the benefit payment is contingent on when Employee B terminates employment, the commencement date of the benefit payment is not known. Thus, the amount deferred is not reasonably ascertainable within the meaning of paragraph (e)(4)(i) of this section, unless the plan satisfies the requirements of paragraph (c)(2)(iii)(B) of this section. Because the fixed 5 percent factor may not be reasonable at the time benefit payments commence (i.e., 5 percent might be higher or lower than a reasonable interest rate when payments commence), the plan fails to satisfy paragraph (c)(2)(iii)(B) of this section and accordingly the amount deferred is not reasonably ascertainable until termination of employment.

Example (6). (i) The facts are the same as in Example 4, except that the $500,000 is payable to Employee B at the later of age 55 or termination of employment.

(ii) Because the commencement date of the benefit payment is contingent on when Employee B terminates employment, the commencement date of the benefit payment is not known. Thus, the amount deferred is not reasonably ascertainable until termination of employment.

Example (7). (i) The facts are the same as in Example 4, except that Employee B may elect to take the benefit in the form of a life annuity of $50,000 per year (commencing at age 65).

(ii) Because the plan permits employees to elect to receive benefits in more than one form and the alternative forms may not have the same value when Employee B makes his election, the plan fails to satisfy the requirements of paragraph (c)(2)(iii)(B) of this section until a form of benefit is selected. Thus, the amount deferred is not reasonably ascertainable until then.

Example (8). (i) Employer O establishes a nonqualified deferred compensation plan. The plan is a supplemental executive retirement plan (SERP) that provides Employee C with a fully vested right to receive a pension, in the form of a life annuity payable monthly, beginning at age 65, equal to the excess of 3 percent of Employee C's final 3-year average pay for each year of participation up to 15 years, over the amount payable to Employee C from Employer O's qualified pension plan. The amount payable under the qualified pension plan is a life annuity payable monthly, beginning at age 65, equal to 1.5 percent of final 3-year average pay for each year of employment, excluding pay in excess of the section 401(a)(17) compensation limit. No benefits are payable under the SERP if Employee C dies before age 65. Employee C becomes a participant in the SERP on January 1, 2001, at age 44. The amount deferred under the SERP for any year is not reasonably ascertainable prior to termination of employment because the amount of the benefit is not known and the determination of the amount deferred requires assumptions other than interest and mortality (e.g., an assumption as to Employee C's average pay for the final three years of employment). As permitted by paragraph (e)(4)(i) of this section, Employer O chooses not to take any amount into account for any year before the resolution date. Employee C terminates employment on December 31, 2018 when he is age 62.

(ii) As of the date Employee C terminates employment, the amount of the benefit is known and the only actuarial or other assumptions needed to determine the amount deferred are an interest rate assumption and a mortality assumption. At that time, the amount deferred in each past year becomes reasonably ascertainable, and Employer O is able to determine that during 2001 Employee C earned a legally binding right to a life annuity of $4,000 per year beginning in 2021 when Employee C is age 65. Employer O determines the present value of Employee C's future benefit payments under the SERP as of this resolution date (December 31, 2018), using a 7 percent interest rate and the UP-84 mortality table, which, solely for purposes of this example, are assumed to be reasonable actuarial assumptions for December 31, 2018. The special timing rule will be satisfied if the resulting present value, $26,950, is taken into account on that date in accordance with paragraph (d)(1) of this section.

Example (9). (i) The facts are the same as in Example 8, except that the plan provides that Employee C may choose to receive early retirement benefits on an unreduced basis at any time after age 60 if Employee C has completed 15 years of service by that date.

(ii) As of the date Employee C terminates employment, the amount of the benefit is known and the only actuarial or other assumptions needed to determine the amount deferred are an interest rate assumption and a mortality assumption. At that time, the amount deferred in each past year becomes reasonably ascertainable, and Employer O is able to determine that during 2001 Employee C earned a legally binding right to a life annuity of $4,000 per year beginning on December 31, 2018 when Employee C is age 62. Employer O determines the present value of Employee C's future benefit payments under the SERP as of this resolution date (December 31, 2018), using a 7 percent interest rate and the UP-84 mortality table, which, solely for purposes of this example, are assumed to be reasonable actuarial assumptions for December 31, 2018. The special timing rule will be satisfied if the resulting present value, $37,576, is taken into account on that date in accordance with paragraph (d)(1) of this section.

Example (10). (i) The facts are the same as in Example 9, except that, as permitted under paragraph (e)(4)(ii) of this section, Employer O chooses to take an amount into account before the amount deferred for 2001 is reasonably ascertainable. The amount that Employer O takes into account on December 31, 2001, is $13,043 (the present value of a life annuity of $4,000 per year, payable at age 62, using a 6 percent interest rate and the UP-84 mortality table). Employer O does not take any other amount into account before the resolution date.

(ii) In accordance with paragraph (e)(4)(ii)(B) of this section, Employer O must determine any additional amount required to be taken into account in 2018. If the $4,000 payable in the form of a life annuity beginning at age 62 exceeds the life annuity which is actuarially equivalent to the $13,043 previously taken into account, the present value of the excess must be taken into account. In this Example 10, the $13,043 previously taken into account is actuarially equivalent to a $4,000 annuity commencing at age 62 using a 6 percent interest rate and the UP-84 mortality table (which, solely for purposes of this example, are assumed to be reasonable actuarial assumptions for December 31, 2001). Accordingly, no additional amount need be taken into account in 2018, regardless of any changes in market rates of interest between 2001 and 2018.

Example (11). (i) The facts are the same as in Example 9, except that, as permitted under paragraph (e)(4)(ii) of this section, Employer O chooses to take an amount into account before the amount deferred for 2001 is reasonably ascertainable. The amount that Employer O takes into account on December 31, 2001, is $9,569 (the present value of a life annuity of $4,000 per year, payable at age 65, using a 6 percent interest rate and the UP-84 mortality table). Employer O does not take any other amount into account before the resolution date.

(ii) In accordance with paragraph (e)(4)(ii)(B) of this section, Employer O must determine any additional amount required to be taken into account in 2018. If the $4,000 payable in the form of a life annuity beginning in 2018 at age 62 exceeds the life annuity which is actuarially equivalent to the $9,569 previously taken into account, the present value of the excess must be taken into account. In this case, the $9,569 previously taken into account is actuarially equivalent to a $2,935 annuity commencing at age 62 using a 6 percent interest rate and the UP-84 mortality table (which, solely for purposes of this example, are assumed to be reasonable actuarial assumptions for December 31, 2001). Accordingly, an additional amount needs to be taken into account in 2018 equal to the present value of the excess of the $4,000 annual stream of benefit payments to which Employee C obtained a legally binding right during 2001 over the $2,935 annual stream of benefit payments which is actuarially equivalent to the amount previously taken into account. This present value (i.e., the present value of a life annuity equal to $4,000 minus $2,935, or $1,065 annually) is determined by Employer O to be $10,005 as of the resolution date using a 7 percent interest rate and the UP-84 mortality table (which, solely for purposes of this example, are assumed to be reasonable actuarial assumptions for December 31, 2018).

Example (12). (i) The facts are the same as in Example 9, except that the amount that Employer O takes into account on December 31, 2001, is $15,834 (the present value of $4,000, payable at age 60, using a 6 percent interest rate and the UP-84 mortality table). Employer O does not take any other amount into account before the resolution date.

(ii) In accordance with paragraph (e)(4)(ii)(B) of this section, Employer O must determine any additional amount required to be taken into account in 2018. If the $4,000 payable in the form of a life annuity beginning at age 62 exceeds the life annuity which is actuarially equivalent to the $15,834 previously taken into account, the present value of the excess must be taken into account. In this case, the $15,834 previously taken into account is actuarially equivalent to a $4,856 annuity commencing at age 62 using a 6 percent interest rate and the UP-84 mortality table (which, solely for purposes of this example, are assumed to be reasonable actuarial assumptions for December 31, 2001). Because the life annuity of $4,856 per year (which is equivalent to the amount taken into account at the early inclusion date) exceeds the $4,000 annuity attributable to the amount deferred in 2001, no additional amount is required to be taken into account for that amount deferred as of the resolution date. Employer O may claim a refund or credit for the overpayment of FICA tax with respect to amounts taken into account prior to the resolution date to the extent permitted by sections 6402, 6413, and 6511.

Example (13). (i) The facts are the same as in Example 12, except that Employee C became a participant in the SERP on January 1, 2000. In addition, Employer O determines in 2018 that during 2000 Employee C earned a legally binding right to a life annuity of $1,500 per year beginning on December 31, 2018.

(ii) Employer O may allocate the $15,834 previously taken into account among any amounts deferred on or before the early inclusion date. At the resolution date, Employer O will have to take into account the present value of an annuity equal to the excess of the life annuity attributable to the amounts deferred for 2000 and 2001 over a life annuity of $4,856 per year.

Example (14). (i) In 2003, Employer P establishes a nonqualified deferred compensation plan for Employee D. The plan provides that, in consideration of Employee D's services to be performed on Project X in 2004, Employee D will have a nonforfeitable right to receive 1 percent per year of Employer P's net profits associated with Project X for each of the immediately succeeding three years. No services beyond 2004 are required. The 1 percent of net profits payable each year will be paid on March 31 of the immediately succeeding year. One percent of net profits associated with Project X is $750,000 in 2005, $400,000 in 2006, and $90,000 in 2007. Employee D receives $750,000 on March 31, 2006, $400,000 on March 31, 2007, and $90,000 on March 31, 2008.

(ii) Because the services creating the right to all of the amount deferred are performed in 2004, the benefit payments based on the 2005, 2006, and 2007 net profits are all attributable to the amount deferred in 2004. However, because the present value of Employee D's future benefit is contingent on future profits, the determination of the amount deferred requires the use of assumptions other than interest, mortality, and cost of living. Thus, all of the amount deferred in 2004 will not be reasonably ascertainable within the meaning of paragraph (e)(4)(i) of this section until December 31, 2007 (which is the resolution date). Employer P does not choose to take any amount into account prior to the amount deferred becoming reasonably ascertainable.

(iii) However, paragraph (d)(1)(ii)(A) of this section provides that a benefit payment attributable to an amount deferred under a nonqualified deferred compensation plan must be included as wages when actually or constructively paid if the amount deferred has not been taken into account as wages under the special timing rule of paragraph (a)(2) of this section. Thus, the benefit payments in 2006 and 2007 must be included as wages when paid.

(iv) As of December 31, 2007, all of the amount deferred under the plan becomes reasonably ascertainable because the amount of the benefit payable attributable to the amount deferred is treated as known under paragraph (e)(4)(i)(B) of this section, and the only assumption needed to determine the present value of the future benefits is interest. However, since Employer P was required to treat the payments in 2006 and 2007 as wages when paid under the general timing rule of paragraph (a)(1) of this section, only the present value of the payment to be made in 2008 is required to be taken into account as of the resolution date (December 31, 2007) under the special timing rule of paragraph (a)(2) of this section. Using an interest rate of 10 percent per year (which, solely for purposes of this Example 14, is assumed to be reasonable), Employer P determines that on December 31, 2007, the present value of the future benefits is $87,881, and Employer P includes that additional amount in wages for 2007. (Note that Employer P can choose to use the lag method of withholding described in paragraph (f)(3) of this section, which allows the resolution date amount to be taken into account no later than March 31, 2008, provided that the amount deferred is increased by interest using the AFR for January of 2008.)

Example (15). (i) The facts are the same as in Example 14, except that Employer P chooses the early inclusion option permitted by paragraph (e)(4)(ii) of this section to take $1,000,000 into account on December 31, 2004, before the amount deferred for 2004 is reasonably ascertainable.

(ii) Pursuant to paragraph (e)(4)(ii)(E) of this section, in applying the nonduplication rule of paragraph (a)(2)(iii) of this section, a first-in-first-out rule applies in determining the benefit payments that are attributable to amounts previously taken into account. Using the 10 percent interest rate, Employer P determines that the $750,000 benefit payment on March 31, 2006, and the March 31, 2007, benefit payment of $400,000 are less than the $1,000,000 taken into account at the early inclusion date, plus attributable income, and, therefore, are not included in wages when paid.

(iii) Under paragraph (e)(4)(ii)(E) of this section, if an employer chooses to take an amount into account before the resolution date, the amount taken into account (plus income attributable to that amount) is disregarded to the extent the amount is attributed to benefit payments made before the resolution date. Thus, Employer P must reduce the $1,000,000 taken into account in 2004 (plus income attributable to that amount) based upon the two benefit payments ($750,000 and $400,000) that were excluded from wages. Using an interest rate of 10 percent, Employer P determines that the amount taken into account in 2004 plus interest to the resolution date and reduced based upon the two benefit payments is $15,228 and the additional amount that is required to be taken into account as of December 31, 2007, is $72,653 ($87,881-$15,228).

Example (16). (i) Employee E obtains a fully vested, legally binding right during 2002, 2003, and 2004 to payments from a nonqualified deferred compensation plan of Employer Q under which the benefits are based on a formula that includes an actuarial offset by the account balance under a qualified defined contribution plan of Employer Q as of December 31, 2004. The payments from the nonqualified deferred compensation plan are to commence on December 31, 2005. At the resolution date for the amounts earned during 2002, 2003, and 2004, which is December 31, 2004, Employee E has a legally binding right to a net annual benefit of $100,000 payable for life to commence on December 31, 2005. On the resolution date, Employer Q determines that on December 31, 2002, Employee E had a legally binding right to receive $100,000 annually for life beginning on December 31, 2005 (as a result of the gross benefit under the nonqualified plan being $120,000 annually for life, and the offset being $20,000 annually for life, as of December 31, 2002). On December 31, 2003, Employee E had a legally binding right to receive $95,000 annually for life beginning on December 31, 2005 (as a result of the gross benefit under the nonqualified plan being $135,000 annually for life, and the offset being $40,000 annually for life, as of December 31, 2003). On December 31, 2004, Employee E had a legally binding right to receive $100,000 annually for life beginning on December 31, 2005 (as a result of the gross benefit under the nonqualified plan being $145,000 annually for life, and the offset being $45,000 annually for life, as of December 31, 2004).

(ii) In this case, pursuant to paragraph (e)(4)(ii)(D)(4) of this section, Employer Q can attribute the entire $100,000 life annuity to the amount deferred for 2002, even though Employee E's benefit under the nonqualified deferred compensation plan is reduced to $95,000 in 2003.

Example (17). (i) In 2010, Employee F performs services for which she earns a right to 10 percent of the proceeds from the sale of a motion picture. In 2011, Employee F performs services for which she earns a right to 10 percent of the proceeds from the sale of another motion picture. These proceeds are calculated by subtracting the total advertising expenses for both movies. Payment is to be made in the year following the date on which both pictures have been sold, but not later than 2018. At the end of 2010, the advertising expenses for both pictures totaled $300,000. The first motion picture is sold for $10,000,000 in 2014. The second motion picture is sold for $17,000,000 in 2017. At the end of 2017, the advertising expenses totaled $1,700,000. In 2018, Employee F is paid $2,530,000 (10 percent of the sum of $10,000,000 and $17,000,000 minus $1,700,000).

(ii) Pursuant to paragraph (e)(4)(ii)(D)(4) of this section, $970,000 (10 percent of the excess of the gross proceeds from the sale of the first motion picture at the resolution date in 2017 over the advertising expenses incurred at the end of 2010) of the payment made in 2018 can be attributed to the amount deferred in 2010 (and with the remaining payment of $1,560,000 to be attributed to the amount deferred in 2011).

(f) Withholding. *(1) In general.* Unless an employer applies an alternative method described in paragraph (f)(2) or (3) of this section, an amount deferred under a nonqualified deferred compensation plan for any employee is treated, for purposes of withholding and depositing FICA tax, as wages paid by the employer and received by the employee at the time it is taken into account in accordance with paragraph (e) of this section. However, paragraphs (f)(2) and (3) of this section provide alternative methods which may be used with respect to an amount deferred for an employee. An employer is not required to be consistent in applying the alternatives described in this paragraph (f) with respect to different employees or amounts deferred.

(2) Estimated method. (i) In general. Under the alternative method provided in this paragraph (f)(2), the employer may make a reasonable estimate of the amount deferred on the date on which the amount is taken into account in accordance with paragraph (e) of this section and take that estimated amount into account as wages paid by the employer and received by the employee on that date (the estimate date), for purposes of withholding and depositing FICA tax.

(ii) Underestimate of the amount deferred. (A) General rule. If the employer underestimates the amount deferred (as determined after calculating the actual amount deferred that should have been taken into account as of the date on which the amount was taken into account in accordance with paragraph (e) of this section, using an interest rate and other actuarial assumptions that are reasonable as of that date), the employer may treat the shortfall as wages paid as of the estimate date or as of any date that is no later than three months after the estimate date. In either case, the shortfall does not include the income credited to the amount deferred after the amount is taken into account in accordance with paragraph (e) of this section.

(B) Shortfall is treated as wages paid on a date after the estimate date. If the employer chooses to treat the shortfall as wages paid on a date that is no later than three months after the estimate date, the employer must take that shortfall into account as wages paid by the employer and received by the employee on that date, for purposes of withholding and depositing FICA tax.

(C) Shortfall is treated as wages paid on the estimate date. If the employer chooses to treat the shortfall as wages paid as of the estimate date, the shortfall is treated as an error for purposes of withholding and depositing FICA tax. Appropriate adjustments may be made in accordance with section 6205(a) and the regulations thereunder; however, for purposes of § 31.6205-1(b), the error need not be treated as ascertained before the date that is three months after the estimate date.

(D) Reporting. The employer must report the shortfall as wages on Form 941, Employer's Quarterly Federal Tax Return (and, if applicable, Form 941c, Supporting Statement to Correct Information) and Form W-2, Wage and Tax Statement (or, if applicable, Form W-2c, Corrected Wage and

Tax Statement) in accordance with its treatment of the shortfall under paragraph (f)(2)(ii) (B) or (C) of this section.

(iii) Overestimate of the amount deferred. If the employer overestimates the amount deferred (as determined after calculating the actual amount deferred that should have been taken into account as of the date on which the amount was taken into account in accordance with paragraph (e) of this section, using an interest rate and actuarial assumptions that are reasonable as of that date) and deposits more than the amount required, the employer may claim a refund or credit in accordance with sections 6402, 6413, and 6511. A Form 941c, or an equivalent statement, must accompany each claim for refund. In addition, Form W-2 or, if applicable, Form W-2c must also reflect the actual amount deferred that should have been taken into account.

(3) Lag method. Under the alternative method provided in this paragraph (f)(3), an amount deferred, plus interest, may be treated as wages paid by the employer and received by the employee, for purposes of withholding and depositing FICA tax, on any date that is no later than three months after the date the amount is required to be taken into account in accordance with paragraph (e) of this section. For purposes of this paragraph (f)(3), the amount deferred must be increased by interest through the date on which the wages are treated as paid, at a rate that is not less than AFR. If the employer withholds and deposits FICA tax in accordance with this paragraph (f)(3), the employer will be treated as having taken into account the amount deferred plus income to the date on which the wages are treated as paid.

(4) Examples. This paragraph (f) is illustrated by the following examples:

Example (1). (i) Employer M maintains a nonqualified deferred compensation plan that is an account balance plan. The plan provides for annual bonuses based on current year profits to be deferred until termination of employment. Employer M's profits for 2003, and thus the amount deferred, is reasonably ascertainable, but Employer M calculates the amount deferred on March 3, 2004, when the relevant data is available.

(ii) In accordance with the alternative method described in paragraph (f)(2) of this section, Employer M makes a reasonable estimate that the amount deferred that must be taken into account as of December 31, 2003, for Employee A is $20,000, and withholds and deposits FICA tax on that amount as if it were wages paid by Employer M and received by Employee A on that date. In January of 2004, Employer M files and furnishes Form W-2 for Employee A including the $20,000 in FICA wages. On March 3, 2004, Employer M determines that the actual amount deferred that should have been taken into account on December 31, 2003, was $22,000.

(iii) In accordance with the alternative method described in paragraph (f)(2)(ii) of this section, Employer M may treat the additional $2,000 as wages paid to and received by Employee A on December 31, 2003, the estimate date. Employer M may treat the $2,000 shortfall as an error ascertained on March 3, 2004, and withhold and deposit FICA tax on that amount. Form W-2c for Employee A for 2003 must include the $2,000 shortfall in FICA wages. Employer M must also correct the information on Form 941 for the last quarter of 2003, reporting the adjustment on Form 941 for the first quarter of 2004, accompanied by Form 941c for the last quarter of 2003.

(iv) Instead, Employer M may treat the $2,000 shortfall as wages paid on March 31, 2004, and withhold and deposit FICA tax on that amount as if it were wages paid by Employer M and received by Employee A on that date. Form W-2 for Employee A for 2004 and Form 941 for the first quarter of 2004 must include the $2,000 shortfall in FICA wages.

Example (2). (i) The facts are the same as in Example 1, except that on March 3, 2004, Employer M determines that the actual amount deferred that should have been taken into account on December 31, 2003, was $19,000.

(ii) Under paragraph (f)(2)(iii) of this section, Employer M may, in accordance with sections 6402, 6413, and 6511, claim a refund or credit for the overpayment of tax resulting from the overestimate. In addition, Employer M must file and furnish a Form W-2c for Employee A and must correct the information on Form 941 for the last quarter of 2003.

Example (3). (i) The facts are the same as in Example 1, except that Employer M does not make a reasonable estimate of the amount deferred that must be taken into account as of December 31, 2003. Instead, Employer M withholds and deposits FICA tax on the amount deferred plus interest on that amount using AFR (for January 2004) as if it were wages paid by Employer M and received by Employee A on March 15, 2004.

(ii) Under the alternative method described in paragraph (f)(3) of this section, the amount taken into account on March 15, 2004 (including the interest), will be treated as FICA wages paid to and received by Employee A on March 15, 2004.

Example (4). (i) The facts are the same as in Example 1, except that an amount is also deferred for Employee B which is required to be taken into account on October 15, 2003, and Employer M chooses to use the lag method in paragraph (f)(3) of this section in order to provide time to calculate the amount deferred.

(ii) Employer M may use any date not later than January 15, 2004, to take the amount deferred into account (provided that the amount deferred includes interest, at AFR for January 1, 2003, through December 31, 2003, and at AFR for January 1, 2004, through January 15, 2004).

(g) Effective date and transition rules. *(1) General effective date.* Except for paragraphs (g)(2) through (4) of this section, this section is applicable on and after January 1, 2000. Thus, paragraphs (a) through (f) of this section apply to amounts deferred on or after January 1, 2000; to amounts deferred before January 1, 2000, which cease to be subject to a substantial risk of forfeiture on or after January 1, 2000, or for which a resolution date occurs on or after January 1, 2000; and to benefits actually or constructively paid on or after January 1, 2000.

(2) Reasonable, good faith interpretation for amounts deferred and benefits paid before January 1, 2000. (i) In general. For periods before January 1, 2000 (including amounts deferred before January 1, 2000, and any benefits actually or constructively paid before January 1, 2000, that are attributable to those amounts deferred), an employer may rely on a reasonable, good faith interpretation of section 3121(v)(2), taking into account pre-existing guidance. An employer will be deemed to have determined FICA tax liability and satisfied FICA withholding requirements in accordance with a reasonable, good faith interpretation of section 3121(v)(2) if the employer has complied with paragraphs (a) through (f) of this section. For purposes of paragraphs (g)(2) through (4) of this section, and subject to paragraphs (g)(2)(ii) and (iii) of this section, whether an employer that has not complied with paragraphs (a) through (f) of this section has deter-

mined FICA tax liability and satisfied FICA withholding requirements in accordance with a reasonable, good faith interpretation of section 3121(v)(2) will be determined based on the relevant facts and circumstances, including consistency of treatment by the employer and the extent to which the employer has resolved unclear issues in its favor.

(ii) Plan must be established or adopted. If an amount is deferred under a plan before January 1, 2000, and benefit payments attributable to that amount are actually or constructively paid on or after January 1, 2000, then in no event will an employer's treatment of the amount deferred be considered to be in accordance with a reasonable, good faith interpretation of section 3121(v)(2) if the employer treats that amount as taken into account as wages for FICA tax purposes prior to the establishment of the plan (within the meaning of paragraph (b)(2) of this section) providing for the deferred compensation (or, if later, the establishment of the plan as amended to provide for the deferred compensation, as provided in paragraph (b)(2)(ii) of this section). If an amount is deferred under a plan before January 1, 2000, and benefit payments attributable to that amount are actually or constructively paid before January 1, 2000, then in no event will the employer's treatment of that amount deferred be considered to be in accordance with a reasonable, good faith interpretation of section 3121(v)(2) if the employer treats that amount as taken into account as wages for FICA tax purposes prior to the adoption of the plan providing for the deferred compensation (or, if later, the adoption of the plan amendment providing the deferred compensation). For example, awards, bonuses, raises, incentive payments, and other similar amounts granted under a plan as compensation for past services may not be taken into account under section 3121(v)(2) prior to the establishment (or, if applicable, the adoption) of the plan.

(iii) Certain changes in position for stock options, stock appreciation rights, and other stock value rights not reasonable, good faith interpretation. In the case of a stock option, stock appreciation right, or other stock value right (as defined in paragraph (b)(4)(ii) of this section) that is exercised before January 1, 2000, an employer that treats the exercise as not subject to FICA tax as a result of the nonduplication rule of section 3121(v)(2)(B) is not acting in accordance with a reasonable, good faith interpretation of section 3121(v)(2) if the employer has not treated that grant and all earlier grants as subject to section 3121(v)(2) by reporting the current value of such options and rights as FICA wages on Form 941 filed for the quarter during which each grant was made (or, if later, for the quarter during which each grant ceased to be subject to a substantial risk of forfeiture).

(3) Optional adjustments to conform with this section for pre-effective-date open periods. (i) General rule. If an employer determined FICA tax liability with respect to section 3121(v)(2) in any period ending before January 1, 2000, for which the applicable period of limitations has not expired on January 1, 2000 (pre-effective-date open periods), in a manner that was not in accordance with this section, the employer may adjust its FICA tax determination for that period to conform to this section. Thus, if an amount deferred was taken into account in a pre-effective-date open period when it was not required to be taken into account (e.g., an amount taken into account before it became reasonably ascertainable), the employer may claim a refund or credit for any FICA tax paid on that amount to the extent permitted by sections 6402, 6413, and 6511.

(ii) Consistency required. In the case of a plan that is not a nonqualified deferred compensation plan (within the meaning of paragraph (b)(1) of this section), if any payment was actually or constructively paid to an employee under the plan in a pre-effective-date open period and that payment was not included in FICA wages by reason of the employer's treatment of the plan as a nonqualified deferred compensation plan, then the employer may claim a refund or credit for FICA tax paid on amounts treated as amounts deferred under the plan (in accordance with the employer's treatment of the plan as a nonqualified deferred compensation plan) for that employee for pre-effective-date open periods only to the extent that the FICA tax paid on all amounts treated as amounts deferred for the employee in all pre-effective-date open periods under the plan exceeds the FICA tax that would have been due on the benefits actually or constructively paid to the employee in those periods under the plan if those benefits were included in FICA wages when paid. If any benefit payments attributable to amounts deferred after December 31, 1993, were actually or constructively paid to an employee under a nonqualified deferred compensation plan (within the meaning of paragraph (b)(1) of this section) in a pre-effective-date open period, but these payments were treated as subject to FICA tax because the employer treated the plan as not being a nonqualified deferred compensation plan, then the employer may claim a refund or credit for the FICA tax paid on those benefit payments only to the extent that the FICA tax paid on those benefit payments exceeds the FICA tax that would have been due on the amounts deferred to which those benefit payments are attributable if those amounts deferred had been taken into account when they would have been required to have been taken into account under this section (if this section had been in effect then).

(iii) Reporting. Any employer that adjusts its FICA tax determination in accordance with paragraphs (g)(3)(i) and (ii) of this section must make appropriate adjustments on Form 941 and Form 941c for the affected periods, and, in addition, must file and furnish Form W-2, or, if applicable, Form W-2c, for any affected employee so that the Social Security Administration may correctly post the amount deferred to the employee's earnings record. The adjustments may be made in accordance with section 6205(a) and the regulations thereunder; however, for purposes of § 31.6205-1(b), the error is not required to be treated as ascertained before March 31, 2000.

(4) Application of reasonable, good faith standard. (i) Plans that are not subject to section 3121(v)(2). If a plan is not a nonqualified deferred compensation plan within the meaning of paragraph (b)(1) of this section, but, for a period ending prior to January 1, 2000, and, pursuant to a reasonable, good faith interpretation of section 3121(v)(2), an amount under the plan was taken into account (within the meaning of paragraph (d)(1) of this section) as an amount deferred under a nonqualified deferred compensation plan, then, pursuant to paragraph (g)(2) of this section, the following rules shall apply—

(A) With respect to benefit payments actually or constructively paid before January 1, 2000, that are attributable to amounts previously taken into account under the plan, no additional FICA tax will be due;

(B) On or after January 1, 2000, benefit payments under the plan must be taken into account as wages when actually or constructively paid in accordance with paragraph (a)(1) of this section; and

(C) To the extent permitted by paragraph (g)(3) of this section, the employer may claim a refund or credit for FICA tax actually paid on amounts taken into account prior to January 1, 2000.

(ii) Plans that are subject to section 3121(v)(2) for which the amount deferred has not been fully taken into account. (A) In general. The rules of paragraphs (g)(4)(ii)(B) through (E) of this section apply if a plan is a nonqualified deferred compensation plan (within the meaning of paragraph (b)(1) of this section) and, with respect to an amount deferred under the plan for an employee prior to January 1, 2000, the employer, in accordance with a reasonable, good faith interpretation of section 3121(v)(2), either took into account an amount that is less than the amount that would have been required to be taken into account if paragraphs (a) through (f) of this section had been in effect for that period or took no amount into account. Thus, paragraphs (g)(4)(ii)(B) through (E) of this section apply both to an employer that treated the plan as if it were not a nonqualified deferred compensation plan within the meaning of section 3121(v)(2) (by withholding and paying FICA tax due on benefits actually or constructively paid under the plan during that period, if any) and to an employer that treated the plan as a nonqualified deferred compensation plan within the meaning of section 3121(v)(2).

(B) No additional tax required. Pursuant to paragraph (g)(2) of this section, no additional FICA tax will be due for any period ending prior to January 1, 2000.

(C) General timing rule applicable. In accordance with paragraph (d)(1)(ii) of this section, except as provided in paragraphs (g)(4)(ii) (D) and (E), the general timing rule described in paragraph (a)(1) of this section applies to benefits actually or constructively paid on or after January 1, 2000, attributable to an amount deferred in a period before January 1, 2000, to the extent the amount taken into account was less than the amount that would have been required to be taken into account if paragraphs (a) through (f) of this section had been in effect before January 1, 2000.

(D) Special rule for amounts deferred before 1994. The difference between the amount that was taken into account in any period ending prior to January 1, 1994, and the amount that would have been required or permitted to be taken into account in that period if paragraphs (a) through (f) of this section had been in effect is treated as if it had been taken into account within the meaning of paragraph (d)(1) of this section. For example, in the case of an amount deferred before 1994 that was not reasonably ascertainable (and which was not subject to a substantial risk of forfeiture), the employer is treated as if it had anticipated the actual amount, form, and commencement date for the benefit payments attributable to the amount deferred and had taken the amount deferred into account at an early inclusion date before 1994 using a method permitted under this section. Thus, with respect to such an amount deferred, the employer is not required to take any additional amount into account when the amount deferred becomes reasonably ascertainable, and no additional FICA tax will be due when the benefit payments attributable to the amount deferred are actually or constructively paid.

(E) Special rule for amounts required to be taken into account in 1994 or 1995. In the case of an amount deferred that would have been required to be taken into account in 1994 or 1995 if paragraphs (a) through (f) of this section had been in effect, an employer will be treated as taking the amount deferred into account under paragraph (d)(1) of this section to the extent the employer takes the amount into account by treating it as wages paid by the employer and received by the employee as of any date prior to April 1, 2000.

(iii) Plans that are subject to section 3121(v)(2) for which more than the amount deferred has been taken into account. If a plan is a nonqualified deferred compensation plan (within the meaning of paragraph (b)(1) of this section) and an amount was taken into account under the plan for an employee before January 1, 2000, in accordance with a reasonable, good faith interpretation of section 3121(v)(2), but that amount could not have been taken into account before January 1, 2000, if paragraphs (a) through (f) of this section had been in effect then, the following rules apply—

(A) The determination of the amount deferred for any period beginning on or after January 1, 2000, must be made in accordance with paragraph (c) of this section, and the time when amounts deferred under the plan are required to be taken into account must be determined in accordance with paragraph (e) of this section, without regard to any such amount that was taken into account for any period ending before January 1, 2000; and

(B) To the extent permitted by sections 6402, 6413, and 6511, the employer may claim a refund or credit for an overpayment of tax caused by the overinclusion of wages that occurred before January 1, 2000.

(5) Examples. This paragraph (g) is illustrated by the following examples:

Example (1). (i) In 1996, Employer M establishes a nonqualified deferred compensation plan that is a nonaccount balance plan for Employee A. All benefits under the plan are 100 percent vested. In order to determine the amount deferred on behalf of Employee A under the plan for 1996 and 1997, Employer M must make assumptions as to the date on which Employee A will retire and the form of benefit Employee A will elect, in addition to interest, mortality, and cost-of-living assumptions. Based on assumptions made with respect to all of these contingencies, Employer M determines that the amount deferred for 1996 is $50,000 and the amount deferred for 1997 is $55,000. In 1996 and 1997, Employee A's total wages (without regard to the amounts deferred) exceed the OASDI wage bases. Employer M withholds and deposits HI tax on the $50,000 and $55,000 amounts. Employee A does not retire before January 1, 2000. Employer M chooses under paragraph (g)(3) of this section to apply this section to 1996 and 1997 before the January 1, 2000, general effective date.

(ii) Under this section, the amounts deferred in 1996 and 1997 are not reasonably ascertainable (within the meaning of paragraph (e)(4)(i) of this section) before January 1, 2000. Thus, as long as the applicable period of limitations has not expired for the periods in 1996 and 1997, Employer M may, to the extent permitted under paragraph (g)(3) of this section, apply for a refund or credit for the HI tax paid on the amounts deferred for 1996 and 1997 and, in accordance with paragraph (e)(4) of this section, take into account the amounts deferred when they become reasonably ascertainable.

Example (2). (i) Employer N adopts a plan on January 1, 1994, that covers Employee B, who has 10 years of service as of that date. The plan provides that, in consideration of Employee B's outstanding services over the past 10 years, Employee B will be paid a $500,000 lump sum distribution upon termination of employment at any time. On January 15, 1996, Employee B terminates employment with Employer N. Employer N determines, based on a reasonable, good faith interpretation of section 3121(v)(2), that the plan is a nonqualified deferred compensation plan under that section. Employer N treats the $500,000 as having been taken into account as an amount deferred in 1993 and earlier years.

(ii) Under paragraph (g)(2)(ii) of this section, if all amounts are deferred and all benefits are paid under a plan before January 1, 2000, then in no event will an employer's treatment of amounts deferred under the plan be considered to be in accordance with a reasonable, good faith interpretation of section 3121(v)(2) if the employer treats these amounts as taken into account as wages for FICA tax purposes prior to the adoption of the plan. Accordingly, Employer N's treatment is not in accordance with a reasonable, good faith interpretation of section 3121(v)(2) because Employer N treated amounts as taken into account in years before the adoption of the plan. As a result, the payment made to Employee B in 1996 was subject to both the OASDI and HI portions of FICA tax when paid.

Example (3). (i) Employer O adopts a bonus plan on December 1, 1993, that becomes effective and legally binding on January 1, 1994. Under the plan, which is not set forth in writing, a specified bonus amount (which is 100 percent vested) is credited to Employee C's account each December 31. A reasonable rate of interest on Employee C's account balance is credited quarterly. Employee C's account balance will begin to be paid in equal annual installments over 10 years beginning on January 1, 2000. Employer O determines, based on a reasonable, good faith interpretation of section 3121(v)(2), that the bonus plan is a nonqualified deferred compensation plan under that section and, therefore, treats the amounts credited from January 1, 1994, through December 31, 1999, as amounts deferred and, in accordance with a reasonable, good faith interpretation of section 3121(v)(2), takes those amounts deferred into account as wages for FICA tax purposes as of those dates. The bonus plan is set forth in writing on May 1, 1999, and, thus, is treated as established as of January 1, 1994.

(ii) Under paragraph (g)(2)(ii) of this section, if an amount is deferred before January 1, 2000, and the attributable benefit is paid on or after January 1, 2000, then in no event will an employer's treatment of the amount deferred under a plan be considered to be in accordance with a reasonable, good faith interpretation of section 3121(v)(2) if the employer treats the amount deferred as taken into account as wages for FICA tax purposes prior to the establishment of the plan (within the meaning of paragraph (b)(2) of this section). Because the bonus plan is treated as established on January 1, 1994 (pursuant to the transition rule for unwritten plans in paragraph (b)(2)(iii) of this section), and because Employer O, in accordance with a reasonable, good faith interpretation of section 3121(v)(2), took amounts deferred into account in 1994 through 1999, the amounts paid to Employee C attributable to those amounts deferred will not be subject to FICA tax when paid.

Example (4). (i) In 1985, Employer P establishes a compensation arrangement for Employee D that provides for a lump sum payment to be made after termination of employment but the arrangement is not a nonqualified deferred compensation plan (within the meaning of paragraph (b)(1) of this section). However, prior to January 1, 2000, and in accordance with a reasonable, good faith interpretation of section 3121(v)(2), Employer P treats the arrangement as a nonqualified deferred compensation plan under section 3121(v)(2). Employer P determines that Employee D's total wages (without regard to the amount deferred) for each year from 1985 through 1993 exceed the applicable OASDI and HI wage bases for each of those years and, consequently, there is no FICA tax liability with respect to the amounts deferred for those years. In 1994, Employee D's total wages (without regard to the amount deferred) exceed the OASDI wage base. However, because there is no limit on the HI wage base, the amount deferred for 1994 results in additional HI tax liability of $290, which is timely paid by Employer P.

(ii) Employee D terminates employment with Employer P in 1995 and receives a plan payment of $50,000. In that year, Employee D also receives wages of $60,000 from Employer P. In accordance with its treatment of the plan as a nonqualified deferred compensation plan under section 3121(v)(2), Employer P does not treat the $50,000 payment in 1995 as wages for FICA tax purposes in that year.

(iii) Because amounts under a plan were taken into account (within the meaning of paragraph (d)(1) of this section) as amounts deferred under a nonqualified deferred compensation plan pursuant to a reasonable, good faith interpretation of section 3121(v)(2)(A), but that plan is not a nonqualified deferred compensation plan within the meaning of paragraph (b)(1) of this section, the transition rules provided in paragraph (g)(4)(i) of this section apply. Thus, no additional FICA tax will be due on the benefits paid in 1995.

(iv) Because $290 of HI tax was paid on the amount deferred in 1994, Employer P is entitled to a refund or credit for that amount to the extent permitted under sections 6402, 6413, and 6511—but only to the extent that $290 exceeds the FICA tax that would have been due on the $50,000 payment in 1995 if that payment had been subject to FICA tax when paid (i.e., if paragraphs (a) through (f) of this section had been effective for those years). In 1995, Employee D had other wages of $60,000. Thus, only $1,200 (the $61,200 OASDI wage base, less the $60,000 of other wages) of the $50,000 payment would have been subject to OASDI; the full $50,000 would have been subject to HI. This would have resulted in $148.80 of OASDI tax ($1,200 x 12.4 percent) and $1,450 of HI tax ($50,000 x 2.9 percent). Employer P is not entitled to a refund or credit under the consistency rule of paragraph (g)(3)(ii) because the $290 of HI tax paid in 1994 is less than the total $1,598.80 of FICA tax liability that would have resulted if this section had applied for 1995.

(v) However, if the benefit payment is instead actually or constructively paid on or after January 1, 2000, the benefit payment must be taken into account as wages when actually or constructively paid in accordance with the general timing rule of paragraph (a)(1) of this section (and paragraph (g)(4)(i)(B) of this section).

Example (5). (i) In 1985, Employer Q establishes a compensation arrangement for Employee E that is a nonqualified deferred compensation plan within the meaning of paragraph (b)(1) of this section. However, prior to January 1, 2000, Employer Q determines, based on a reasonable, good faith interpretation of section 3121(v)(2), that the arrangement is not a nonqualified deferred compensation plan within the meaning of that section. Thus, when Employee E retires at the end of 1996 and benefit payments under the arrangement begin in 1997, Employer Q withholds and deposits FICA tax on the amounts paid to Employee E. Payments under the arrangement continue on or after January 1, 2000. Employer Q does not choose (under paragraph (g)(3) of this section) to adjust its FICA tax determination for a pre-effective-date open period by treating this section as in effect for all amounts deferred and benefits actually or constructively paid for any such period. The periods in 1994 and 1995 are not pre-effective-date open periods for Employer Q.

(ii) Under paragraph (g)(4)(ii) of this section, for purposes of determining whether benefits actually or constructively paid on or after January 1, 2000, were previously taken into account for purposes of applying the nonduplication rule of section 3121(v)(2)(B), any amount that would have been required to have been taken into account before 1994 will be treated as if it had been taken into account within the meaning of paragraph (d)(1) of this section. Under the nonduplication rule, benefit payments attributable to an amount that has been so treated as taken into account is not treated as wages for FICA tax purposes at any later time (such as upon payment).

(iii) Because Employer Q does not adjust its FICA tax determination by treating this section as in effect for all amounts deferred for periods ending after December 31, 1993, any benefit payments attributable to amounts deferred in periods ending after December 31, 1993, will be included in wages when actually or constructively paid in accordance with the general timing rule of paragraph (a)(1) of this section.

Example (6). (i) The facts are the same as in Example 5, except that Employer Q chooses (in accordance with paragraph (g)(3) of this section) to adjust its FICA tax determination for all pre-effective-date open periods by treating this section as in effect for all amounts deferred for those periods. In addition, Employer Q chooses (in accordance with paragraph (g)(4)(ii)(E) of this section) to take the amounts deferred for 1994 and 1995 into account by treating these amounts as FICA wages paid and received by Employee E on January 15, 2000.

(ii) In accordance with the nonduplication rule of paragraph (a)(2)(iii) of this section, because all amounts deferred for Employee E under the plan were taken into account (or treated as taken into account), any benefit payments made to Employee E under the plan will not be included as FICA wages when actually or constructively paid.

Example (7). (i) The facts are the same as in Example 5, except that Employer Q does not withhold and deposit the FICA tax due on benefits actually or constructively paid before January 1, 2000.

(ii) Because Employer Q did not withhold and deposit the FICA tax due on benefits actually or constructively paid before January 1, 2000, Employer Q did not determine FICA tax liability and satisfy FICA tax withholding requirements in accordance with a reasonable, good faith interpretation of section 3121(v)(2). Thus, the transition rules provided in paragraphs (g)(3) and (4) of this section do not apply. As a result, any amount that would have been required to have been taken into account under this section before 1994 is not treated as if it had been so taken into account under paragraph (g)(4)(ii)(D) of this section, and benefit payments attributable to amounts deferred before January 1, 2000, are treated as FICA wages when actually or constructively paid in accordance with the general timing rule of paragraph (a)(1) of this section.

Example (8). (i) In 1993, Employer R establishes a nonqualified deferred compensation plan for Employee F under which Employee F will have a fully vested right to receive a lump sum payment in 2000 equal to 50 percent of Employee F's highest rate of salary. On December 31, 1993, Employee F's highest salary is $1 million. In accordance with a reasonable, good faith interpretation of section 3121(v)(2), Employer R determines that, for 1993, there is an amount deferred that must be taken into account as wages for FICA tax purposes. Based on Employer R's estimate that Employee F's highest salary will be $3 million in 2000, Employer R determines that the amount deferred is equal to the present value in 1993 of $1.5 million payable in 2000. However, because Employee F has other wages in 1993 that exceed the applicable OASDI and HI wage bases for that year, no additional FICA tax is paid as a result of that amount deferred being taken into account for 1993. In addition, Employer R takes no amounts into account under the plan after 1993 for Employee F. Under paragraphs (e)(1) and (4)(ii)(D)(2) of this section, the largest amount that could have been taken into account in 1993 is the present value of a lump sum payment of $500,000, payable in 2000, because that is the maximum amount to which Employee F has a legally binding right as of December 31, 1993. Employee F's highest salary is, in fact, $3 million in 2000 and Employee F receives $1.5 million under the plan on December 31, 2000.

(ii) In accordance with paragraphs (g)(1) and (4)(iii)(A) of this section, the determination of the amount deferred under the plan for any period beginning on or after January 1, 2000, and the time when that amount deferred is required to be taken into account must be determined in accordance with this section. In addition, these determinations must be made without regard to any amount deferred that was taken into account for any period ending before January 1, 2000, that could not be taken into account before January 1, 2000, if paragraphs (a) through (f) of this section had been in effect. Because no FICA tax was actually paid on that $1 million in 1993, no overpayment of tax was caused by the overinclusion of wages in 1993 and, thus, Employer R is not entitled to a refund or credit (even assuming that the period of limitations has been kept open for periods in 1993). In addition, because the difference between the present value of the $1.5 million payment and the present value of a $500,000 payment was not taken into account for periods beginning on or after January 1, 1994, $1 million must be included in FICA wages under the general timing rule when paid.

T.D. 8814, 1/28/99.

§ 31.3121(v)(2)-2 Effective dates and transition rules.

(a) General statutory effective date. Except as otherwise provided in paragraphs (b) through (e) of this section, section 3121(v)(2) and the amendments made to section 3121(a)(2), (a)(3), and (a)(13) by the Social Security Amendments of 1983 (Pub. L. 98-21, 97 Stat. 65), as amended by section 2662(f)(2) of the Deficit Reduction Act of 1984 (Pub. L. 98-369, 98 Stat. 494), apply to amounts deferred and benefits paid after December 31, 1983.

(b) Definitions. For purposes of § 31.3121(v)(2)-1 and this section, the following definitions apply:

(1) FICA. FICA means the Federal Insurance Contributions Act (26 U.S.C. 3101 et seq.).

(2) 457(a) plan. A *457(a)* plan means an eligible deferred compensation plan of a State or local government or of a tax-exempt organization to which section 457(a) applies.

(3) Gap agreement. Gap agreement means an agreement adopted after March 24, 1983, and on or before December 31, 1983, between an individual and a nonqualified deferred compensation plan within the meaning of § 31.3121(v)(2)-1(b). Such an agreement does not fail to be a gap agreement merely because the terms of the plan are changed after December 31,1983.

(4) Individual party to a gap agreement. Individual party to a gap agreement means an individual who was eligible to participate in a gap agreement on December 31, 1983, under the terms of the agreement on that date. An individual will be treated as an individual party to a gap agreement even if the individual has not accrued any benefits under the plan by December 31, 1983, and regardless of whether the individual has taken any specific action to become a party to the agreement. However, an individual who becomes eligible to participate in a gap agreement after December 31, 1983, is not an individual party to a gap agreement.

(5) Individual party to a March 24, 1983 agreement. Individual party to a March 24, 1983 agreement means an individual who was eligible to participate in a March 24, 1983 agreement under the terms of the agreement on March 24, 1983. An individual will be treated as an individual party to a March 24, 1983 agreement even if the individual has not accrued any benefits under the plan by March 24, 1983, and regardless of whether the individual has taken any specific action to become a party to the agreement. However, an individual who becomes eligible to participate in a March 24, 1983 agreement after March 24, 1983, is not an individual party to a March 24, 1983 agreement.

(6) March 24, 1983 agreement. March 24, 1983 agreement means an agreement in existence on March 24, 1983, between an individual and a nonqualified deferred compensation plan within the meaning of § 31.3121(v)(2)-1(b). Such an agreement does not fail to be a March 24, 1983 agreement merely because the terms of the plan are changed after March 24, 1983. In addition, for purposes of this paragraph (b)(6) only; any plan (or agreement) that provides for payments that qualify for one of the retirement payment exclusions is treated as a nonqualified deferred compensation plan. For example, § 31.3121(v)(2)-1(b)(4)(v) provides that certain benefits established in connection with impending termination do not result from the deferral of compensation and thus are not considered deferred under a nonqualified deferred compensation plan. However, a plan that provides such benefits and that was in existence on March 24, 1983, is treated as a nonqualified deferred compensation plan for purposes of this paragraph (b) to the extent it provides benefits that would have satisfied one of the retirement payment exclusions.

(7) Retirement payment exclusions. Retirement payment exclusions are the exclusions from wages (for FICA tax purposes) for retirement payments under section 3121(a)(2)(A), (a)(3), and (a)(13)(A)(iii), as in effect on April 19, 1983 (the day before enactment of the Social Security Amendments of 1983).

(8) Transition benefits. Transition benefits are payments made after December 31, 1983, attributable to services rendered before January 1, 1984. For this purpose, transition benefits are determined without regard to any changes made in the terms of the plan after March 24, 1983, in the case of a March 24, 1983 agreement or after December 31, 1983, in the case of a gap agreement.

(c) Transition rules. *(1) In general.* Except as provided in paragraph (c)(2) or (3) of this section, the general statutory effective date described in paragraph (a) of this section applies to benefit payments after December 31, 1983. Thus, except as provided in paragraph (c)(2) or (3) of this section, section 3121(v)(2) applies, and the retirement payment exclusions do not apply, to benefit payments made after December 31, 1983, even if the benefit payments are made under a March 24, 1983 agreement or a gap agreement.

(2) Transition benefits under a March 24, 1983 agreement. With respect to an individual party to a March 24, 1983 agreement, transition benefits paid under that March 24, 1983 agreement (except for those paid under a 457(a) plan) are not subject to the special timing rule of section 3121(v)(2) and are subject to section 3121(a) as in effect on April 19, 1983. Thus, transition benefits under a March 24, 1983 agreement (except for those under a 457(a) plan) to an individual party to a March 24, 1983 agreement are excluded from wages (for FICA tax purposes) only if they qualify for any of the retirement payment exclusions (or any other exclusion provided under section 3121(a) as in effect on April 19, 1983).

(3) Transition benefits under a gap agreement. With respect to an individual party to a gap agreement, the payor of transition benefits under the gap agreement must choose to either—

(i) Take the transition benefits into account as wages when paid; or

(ii) Take the amount deferred (within the meaning of § 31.3121(v)(2)-1(c)) with respect to the transition benefits into account as wages under section 3121(v)(2) (as if section 3121(v)(2) had applied before its general statutory effective date).

(d) Determining transition benefit portion. For purposes of determining the portion of total benefits under a nonqualified deferred compensation plan that represents transition benefits, if, under the terms of the plan, benefit payments are not attributed to specific years of service, the employer may use any reasonable method. For example, if a plan provides that the employee will receive benefits equal to 2 percent of high 3-year average compensation multiplied by years of service, and the employee retires after 25 years of service, 9 of which are before 1984, the employer may determine that 9/25 of the total benefit payments to be received beginning in 2000 are transition benefits attributable to services performed before 1984.

(e) Order of payment. If an employer determines, in accordance with paragraph (d) of this section, that a portion of the total benefits under a nonqualified deferred compensation plan constitutes transition benefits, then, for purposes of determining the portion of each benefit payment that constitutes transition benefits, the employer must treat each benefit payment as consisting of transition benefits in the same proportion as the transition benefits that have not been paid (as of January 1, 2000) bear to total benefits that have not been paid (as of January 1, 2000), unless such allocation is inconsistent with the terms of the plan. However, for a benefit payment made before January 1, 2000, the employer may use any reasonable allocation method to determine the portion of a payment that consists of transition benefits, provided that the allocation method is consistent with the terms of the plan.

T.D. 8814, 1/28/99.

§ 31.3123-1 Deductions by an employer from remuneration of an employee.

Any amount deducted by an employer from the remuneration of an employee is considered to be part of the employee's remuneration and is considered to be paid to the employee as remuneration at the time that the deduction is made. It is immaterial that any act of Congress or the law of any State requires or permits such deductions and the payment of the amount thereof to the United States, a State, or any political subdivision thereof.

T.D. 6190, 7/13/56, amend T.D. 6516, 12/19/60.

§ 32.1 Social security taxes with respect to payments on account of sickness or accident disability.

(a) General rule. The amount of any payment on or after January 1, 1982, made to, or on behalf of, an employee or any of his dependents on account of sickness or accident disability is not excluded from the term wages as defined in section 3121(a)(2)(A) unless such payment is—

(1) Received under a workmen's compensation law (as defined in § 31.3121(a)(2)-1(d)(3) for payments made on or after December 15, 2005), or

(2) Made by a third party pursuant to a contractual agreement between the employer and third party entered into prior to December 14, 1981, but then only if—

(i) The third party's coverage for that employee's group ceases prior to March 1, 1982,

(ii) No third party payment is made to such employee under that contract after February 28, 1982, and

(iii) The cessation of the third party's coverage for that employee's group indefinitely terminates the contractual relationship between the third party and the employer as to sickness and accident disability benefits for that employee's group.

See section 3121(a)(4) and § 31.3121(a)(4)-1 for the exclusion from the term "wages" of any payment on account of sickness or accident disability made after the expiration of 6 calendar months following the last calendar month in which the employee worked.

(b) Examples. The application of the provisions of subparagraph (2) of paragraph (a) may be illustrated by the following examples:

Example (1). Company Q enters into a contract on August 31, 1981, with Insurance Company R to provide sickness and accident disability payments to Q's employees. The contract expires on February 28, 1982. On March 1, 1982, Q enters into a new contract with R to provide sickness and accident disability payments to Q's employees. Payments made by R pursuant to the contract expiring February 28, 1982, are included in "wages" as defined in section 3121(a)(2)(B).

Example (2). Company S enters into a contract on November 15, 1981, with Insurance Company T to provide sickness and accident disability payments to S's employees. The contract expires on February 15, 1982, and is not renewed. A, one of S's employees, has been receiving sickness payments from T since December 1, 1981. T makes its final payment to A on February 22, 1982. The payments made by T to A pursuant to its contract with S are not included in "wages" as defined in section 3121(a)(2)(B).

(c) Workmen's compensation laws. *(1)* For purposes of paragraph (a)(1) of this section, a payment made under a workmen's compensation law does not include a payment made pursuant to a State temporary disability insurance law.

(2) If an employee receives a payment on account of sickness or accident disability which is not made under a workmen's compensation law and which must be repaid if the employee receives a workmen's compensation award with respect to the same period of absence from work, such payment is not excluded from the term "wages" as defined in section 3121(a)(2)(B).

(d) Sickness or accident disability. For purposes of paragraph (a) of this section, a payment made on account of sickness or accident disability includes any payment for personal injuries or sickness includible in gross income under section 105(a) and the regulations thereunder and thus does not include—

(1) Any amount which is expended for medical care as described in section 105(b) and § 1.105-2,

(2) Any payment which is unrelated to absence from work as described in section 105(c) and § 1.105-3, or

(3) Any payment or a portion thereof which is attributable to a contribution by the employee as determined in paragraphs (d) and (e) of § 1.105-1.

A payment made on account of sickness or accident disability does not include any payment which is excludable from gross income under section 104(a)(2), (4), or (5).

An employee who elects to reduce his compensation or to forgo an increase in his compensation under a salary reduction agreement with an employer will not be deemed to have made employee contributions to the sickness or accident disability plan or system if the employee is not subject to income or social security taxes on the reduction in compensation.

A tax which is paid by an employee to fund a State temporary disability insurance program is considered a contribution by the employee for purposes of paragraph (d)(3) of this section.

(e) Payments by third parties. *(1)* Any third party making a payment on account of sickness or accident disability which payment is not excluded from the term "wages" under paragraph (a) of this section shall be treated as the employer with respect to such wages, except as provided in subparagraphs (2) and (3) of this paragraph. Accordingly, such third party must withhold from such payment the tax imposed on the employee by section 3101, pay the tax imposed on employers by section 3111, deposit such taxes pursuant to section 6302 and § 31.6302(c)-1(a), and provide the receipts required by section 6051 and §§ 31.6051-1 and 31.6051-2.

(2) If any third party who is treated as the employer solely by reason of the applicability of subparagraph (1) of this paragraph promptly—

(i) Withholds the tax imposed on the employee by section 3101,

(ii) Deposits such tax pursuant to section 6302 and § 31.6302(c)-1(a), and

(iii) Notifies the employer for whom services are normally rendered of the amount of the wages paid on which tax was withheld and deposited,

then the employer (and not the third party) shall be required to pay the tax imposed by section 3111 and to comply with the requirements of section 6051 and §§ 31.6051-1 and 31.6051-2 with respect to the wages. For purposes of subdivision (ii) of this subparagraph, the taxes described in subdivision (i) shall be treated by the third party as if included in the term "taxes" as defined in § 31.6302(c)-1(a)(1)(iii). For purposes of subdivision (iii) of this subparagraph, the notice must be provided by the third party within the time required for the deposit of the tax under subdivision (ii) of this subparagraph. For the purpose of providing the notice, the rules of section 7502(a), relating to timely mailing being treated as timely filing, shall apply. The employer, if notified pursuant to subdivision (iii) of this subparagraph by a third party who has complied with the requirements of subdivisions (i) and (ii) of this subparagraph, must deposit the tax imposed by section 3111 in accordance with § 31.6302(c)-1(a)(1)(iii)(b), with respect to the employer for whom services are normally rendered the term "taxes" shall not include any tax imposed on employers by section 3111 that is required to be paid by a third party under subparagraph (1) of this paragraph until the employer receives notification from the third party under subdivision (iii) of this subparagraph (2).

(3) A third party making a payment on account of sickness or accident disability to an employee as agent for the employer or making such a payment directly to the employer shall not be treated as the employer under subparagraph (1) with respect to such payment unless the agency agreement so provides. The determining factor as to whether a third party is an agent of the employer is whether the third party bears any insurance risk. If the third party bears no insurance risk and is reimbursed on a cost plus fee basis, the third party is an agent of the employer even if the third party is responsible for making determinations of the eligibility of individual employees of the employer for payments on account of sickness or accident disability. If the third party is paid an insurance premium and not reimbursed on a cost plus fee basis, the third party is not an agent of the employer, but the third party is treated as the employer as provided in subparagraph (1) of this paragraph (e).

(4) In order to avoid overpayment of taxes which would result from paying taxes—

(i) On remuneration which exceeds the annual contribution and benefit base (as described in section 3121(a)(1)),

(ii) With respect to a period of time which exceeds the 6-calendar-month period described in section 3121(a)(4), or

(iii) On a payment or a portion thereof which is attributable to a contribution by the employee,

the third party may request information from the employer as to the total wages earned by the employee for the calendar year in which the third party is making payments, as to the last date on which the employee worked for the employer during such year, and as to the amount of any contribution by the employee. Except if the third party has reason not to believe any information supplied by the employer as the result of a request made pursuant to the preceding sentence, the third party may rely on such information in complying with the requirements of subparagraphs (1) and (2) of this paragraph (e). The third party may not rely on representations of the employee as to the information which may be requested of the employer in complying with the requirements of subparagraphs (1) and (2) of this paragraph (e).

(5) The application of the provisions of this paragraph may be illustrated by the following examples:

Example (1). Pursuant to an agreement with Company U, Insurance Company V makes payments on account of sickness or accident disability to U's employees. Such payments are not made under a workmen's compensation law. U reimburses V for all such payments and pays V a fee for its expenses of administering the payments. V is not treated as the employer with respect to such payments.

Example (2). Pursuant to an agreement with Company W, Insurance Company X indemnifies W for the amount of any payments which W must make to an employee on account of sickness or accident disability. Such payments are not made under a workmen's compensation law. X makes its indemnity payments directly to W. W makes the payments to its employees, X is not treated as the employer with respect to such payments.

Example (3). Pursuant to an agreement with Company Y (which is not an agency agreement described in subparagraph (3) of this § 32.1(e)), Insurance Company Z makes payments on account of sickness or accident disability to Y's employees. Such payments are not made under a workmen's compensation law. Z does not notify Y of the amount of such payments. Z is treated as the employer with respect to such payments.

(f) Penalties and interest on payments made from January 1, 1982, to June 30 1982. No penalty under section 6656(a) or interest under section 6601 will be assessed for the failure to make timely payments to the tax imposed by section 3101 or section 3111 on payments made on account of sickness or accident disability, which payments of tax are made after December 31, 1981, and before July 1, 1982, to the extent that the failure is due to reasonable cause and not willful neglect.

(g) Special rules. *(1)* For purposes of subdivision (iii) of paragraph (e)(2), the last employer for whom the employee worked prior to becoming sick or disabled or for whom the employee was working at the time he became sick or disabled shall be deemed to be the employer for whom services are normally rendered, provided that such employer made contributions on behalf of such employee to the plan or system under which the employee is being paid.

(2) The application of the provisions of subparagraph (1) of this paragraph (g) may be illustrated by the following examples:

Example (1). B is employed by Company M. B becomes sick and is absent from work for 3 months. While B is absent from work, he receives sick pay from Insurance Company N pursuant to a plan established by M and to which M has made contributions on behalf of B. M is the employer for whom services are normally rendered by B.

Example (2). C is employed by Company O and is also employed on a part-time basis by Company Q. C becomes sick while at work at Q's place of business. C is absent from work for 3 months. While C is absent from work he receives sick pay from Insurance Company P pursuant to a plan established by O and to which O has made contributions on behalf of C. O is the employer for whom services are normally rendered by C.

Example (3). D is a member of a labor union whose members receive health and welfare benefit payments from a trust fund which is supported by the contributions of the various employers who employ the labor union's members. D has been employed by Company R for 4 days when he becomes sick and is absent from work for 3 months. While D is absent from work he receives sick pay from his union's trust fund to which R has made contributions on D's behalf. R is the employer for whom services are normally rendered by D.

(3) For purposes of paragraph (e) of this section, in the case of payments on account of sickness or accident disability made to employees by a third party insurer pursuant to a contract of insurance with a multiemployer plan which is obligated to make payments on account of sickness or accident disability to such employees pursuant to a collectively bargained agreement, if the third party insurer making the payments complies with the requirements of subdivisions (i) and (ii) of subparagraph (2) of paragraph (e) and notifies the plan of the amount of wages paid on which tax was withheld and deposited within the time required for notification of the employer under subparagraph (2) of paragraph (e), then the plan (and not the third party insurer) shall be required to pay

the tax imposed by section 3111 and to comply with the requirements of section 6051 and §§ 31.6051-1 and 31.6051-2 with respect to such payments unless, within 6 business days of the receipt of such notification, the plan notifies the employer for whom services are normally rendered of the amount of the wages on which tax was withheld and deposited. If the plan provides such notice to the employer, the employer (and not the plan) shall be required to pay the tax imposed by section 3111 and to comply with the requirements of section 6051 and §§ 31.6051-1 and 31.6051-2 with respect to the wages.

T.D. 7823, 2/30/82, amend T.D. 7867, 1/7/83, T.D. 9233, 12/14/2005.

§ 32.2 Railroad retirement taxes with respect to payments on account of sickness or accident disability.

(a) General rule. Notwithstanding the provisions of § 31.3231(e)-1(a)(3)(i), the amount of any payment on or after January 1, 1982, made to, or on behalf of, an employee or any of his dependents on account of sickness or accident disability is not excluded from the term "compensation" as defined in section 3231(e)(1) (for purposes of applying sections 3201(b) and 3221(b) (and so much of section 3211(a) as relates to the rates of the taxes imposed by sections 3101 and 3111)) unless such payment is—

(1) Received under a workmen's compensation law,

(2) Received as a benefit under the Railroad Retirement Act of 1974,

(3) Made after the expiration of 6 calendar months following the last calendar month in which such employee worked,

(4) Made by a third party pursuant to a contractual agreement between the employer and third party entered into prior to December 14, 1981, but then only if—

(i) The third party's coverage for that employee's group ceases prior to March 1, 1982,

(ii) No third party payment is made to such employee under that contract after February 28, 1982, and

(iii) The cessation of the third party's coverage for that employee's group terminates indefinitely the contractual relationship between the third party and the employer as to sickness and accident disability benefits for that employee's group; or

(5) Made under section 2(a) of the Railroad Unemployment Insurance Act for day of sickness, to the extent that such sickness (as determined in accordance with standards prescribed by the Railroad Retirement Board) is the result of on-the-job injury.

The 6-calendar-month provision described in subparagraph (3) of this paragraph shall be applied in a manner comparable to the 6-calendar-month provision described in § 31.3121(a)(4)-1.

(b) Examples. The application of the provisions of subparagraph (4) of paragraph (a) may be illustrated by the following examples:

Example (1). Company Q enters into a contract on August 31, 1981, with Insurance Company R to provide sickness and accident disability payments to Q's employees. The contract expires on February 28, 1982. On March 1, 1982 Q enters into a new contract with R to provide sickness and accident disability payments to Q's employees. Payments made by R pursuant to the contract expiring February 28, 1982, are included in "compensation" as defined in section 3231(e)(1).

Example (2). Company S enter into a contract on November 15, 1981 with Insurance Company T to provide sickness and accident disability payments to S's employees. The contract expires on February 15, 1982, and is not renewed. A, one of S's employees, has been receiving sickness payments from T since December 1, 1981. T makes its final payment to A on February 22, 1982. The payments made by T to A pursuant to its contract with S are not included in "compensation" as defined in section 3231(e)(1).

(c) Workmen's compensation laws. *(1)* For purpose of paragraph (a)(1) of this section, a payment made under a workmen's compensation law does not include a payment made pursuant to a State temporary disability insurance law.

(2) If an employee receives a payment on account of sickness or accident disability which is not excluded from the term "compensation" under paragraph (a)(1) or (2) of this section and which must be repaid if the employee receives a workmen's compensation award with respect to the same period of absence from work, such payment is not excluded from the term "compensation" defined in section 3231(e)(1).

(d) Sickness or accident disability. For purposes of paragraph (a) of this section, a payment made on account of sickness or accident disability includes any payment for personal injuries or sickness includible in gross income under section 105(a) and the regulations thereunder and thus does not include—

(1) Any amount which is expended for medical care as described in section 105(b) and § 1.105-2,

(2) Any payment which is unrelated to absence from work as described in section 105(c) and § 1.105-3, or

(3) Any payment or a portion thereof which is attributable to contribution by the employee as determined in paragraphs (d) and (e) of § 1.105-1.

A payment made on account of sickness or accident disability does not include any payment which is excludable from gross income under section 104(a) (4) or (5).

An employee who elects to reduce his compensation or to forgo an increase in his compensation under a salary reduction agreement with an employer will not be deemed to have made employee contributions to the sickness or accident disability plan or system if the employee is not subject to income or railroad retirement taxes on the reduction in compensation.

A tax which is paid by an employee to fund a State temporary disability insurance program is considered a contribution by the employee for purposes of paragraph (d)(3) of this section.

(e) Payments by third parties. *(1)* Any third party making a payment on account of sickness or accident disability which payment is not excluded from the term "compensation" under paragraph (a) of this section shall be treated as the employer with respect to such compensation, except as provided in subparagraphs (2) and (3) of this paragraph. Accordingly, such third party must withhold from such payment the tax imposed on the employee by section 3201 and the tax imposed on the employee representative by section 3211, if applicable, pay the tax imposed on employers by section 3221, deposit such taxes pursuant to section 6302 and § 31.6302(c)-2(a), and provide the receipts required by section 6051 and §§ 31.6051-1 and 31.6051-2.

(2) If any third party who is treated as the employer solely by reasons of the applicability of subparagraph (1) of this paragraph promptly—

(i) Withholds the tax imposed on the employee by section 3201 and the tax imposed on the employee representative by section 3211, if applicable,

(ii) Deposits such tax pursuant to section 6302 and § 31.6302(c)-2(a), and

(iii) Notifies the employer for whom services are normally rendered of the amount of the compensation paid on which tax was withheld and deposited,

then the employer (and not the third party) shall be required to pay the tax imposed by section 3221 and to comply with the requirements of section 6051 and §§ 31.6051-1 and 31.6051-2 with respect to the compensation. For purposes of subdivision (ii) of this subparagraph, the tax described in subdivision (i) shall be treated by the third party as if included in the employee tax described in § 31.6302(c)-2(a)(1)(i). For purposes of subdivision (iii) of this subparagraph, the notice must be provided by the third party within the time required for the deposit of the tax under subdivision (ii) of this subparagraph. For the purpose of providing the notice, the rules of section 7502(a), relating to timely mailing being treated as timely filing, shall apply. The employer, if notified pursuant to subdivision (iii) of this subparagraph by a third party who has complied with the requirements of subdivisions (i) and (ii) of this subparagraph, must deposit the tax imposed by section 3221 in accordance with § 31.6302(c)-(2)(a). For purposes of § 31.6302(c)-2(a)(1)(ii), with respect to the employer for whom services are normally rendered the term "taxes" shall not include any tax imposed on employers by section 3111 that is required to be paid by a third party under subparagraph (1) of this paragraph until the employer receives notification from the third party under subdivision (iii) of this subparagraph (2).

(3) A third party making a payment on account of sickness or accident disability to an employee as agent for the employer or making such payment directly to the employer shall not be treated as the employer under subparagraph (1) with respect to such payment unless the agency agreement so provides. The determining factor as to whether a third party is an agent of the employer is whether the third party bears any insurance risk. If the third party bears no insurance risk and is reimbursed on a cost plus fee basis, the third party is an agent of the employer even if the third party is responsible for making determinations of the eligibility of individual employees of the employer for payments on account of sickness or accident disability. If the third party is paid an insurance premium and not reimbursed on a cost plus fee basis, the third party is not a agent of the employer, but the third party is treated as the employer as provided in paragraph (1) of this paragraph (e).

(4) In order to avoid overpayment of taxes which would result from paying taxes—

(i) On remuneration which exceeds one-twelfth of the annual contribution and benefit base (as described in section 3121(a)(1)) each month,

(ii) With respect to a period of time which exceeds the 6-calendar-month period described in subparagraph (3) of paragraph (a) of this section, or

(iii) On a payment or a portion thereof which is attributable to a contribution by the employee,

the third party may request information from the employer as to the total wages earned by the employee for the calendar month in which the third party is making payments, as to the last date on which the employee worked for the employer, and as to the amount of any contribution by the employee. Except if the third party has reason not to believe any information supplied by the employer as the result of a request made pursuant to the preceding sentence, the third party may rely on such information in complying with the requirements of subparagraphs (1) and (2) of this paragraph (e). The third party may not rely on representations of the employee as to the information which may be requested of the employer in complying with the requirements of subparagraphs (1) and (2) of this paragraph (e).

(5) The application of the provisions of this paragraph (e) may be illustrated by the following examples:

Example (1). Pursuant to an agreement with Company U, Insurance Company V makes payments on account of sickness or accident disability to U's employees. Such payments are not made under a workmen's compensation law, the Railroad Retirement Act of 1974, or the Railroad Unemployment Insurance Act for days of sickness. U reimburses V for all such payments and pays V a fee for its expenses of administering the payments. V is not treated as the employer with respect to such payments.

Example (2). Pursuant to an agreement with Company W, Insurance Company X indemnifies W for the amount of any payments which X must make to an employee on account of sickness or accident disability. Such payments are not made under workmen's compensation law, the Railroad Retirement Act of 1974, or the Railroad Unemployment Insurance Act for days of sickness. X makes its indemnity payments directly to W. W makes the payments to its employees. X is not treated as the employer with respect to such payments.

Example (3). Pursuant to an agreement with Company Y (which is not an agency agreement described in subparagraph (3) of this § 32.2(e)), Insurance Company Z makes payments on account of sickness or accident disability to Y's employees. Such payments are not made under a workmen's compensation law, the Railroad Retirement Act of 1974, or the Railroad Unemployment Insurance Act for days of sickness. Z does not notify Y of the amount of such payments. Z is treated as the employer with respect to such payments.

(f) Penalties and interest on payments made from January 1, 1982 to June 30, 1982. No penalty under section 6656(a) or interest under section 6601 will be assessed for the failure to make timely payments of the tax imposed by section 3201, 3211, or 3221 on payments made on account of sickness or accident disability, which payments of tax are made after December 31, 1981, and before July 1, 1982, to the extent that the failure is due to reasonable cause and not willful neglect.

(g) Special rules. *(1)* For purposes of subdivision (iii) of paragraph (e)(2), the last employer for whom the employee worked prior to becoming sick or disabled or for whom the employee was working at the time he became sick or disabled shall be deemed to be the employer for whom services are normally rendered, provided that such employer made contributions on behalf of such employee to the plan or system under which the employee is being paid.

(2) The application of the provisions of subparagraph (1) of this paragraph (g) may be illustrated by the following examples:

Example (1). B is employed by Company M. B becomes sick and is absent from work for 3 months. While B is absent from work, he receives sick pay from Insurance Company N pursuant to a plan established by M and to which M has made contributions on behalf of B. M is the employer for whom services are normally rendered by B.

Example (2). C is employed by Company O and is also employed on a part-time basis by Company Q. C becomes sick while at work at Q's place of business. C is absent from work for 3 months. While C is absent from work, he receives sick pay from Insurance Company P pursuant to a plan established by O and to which O has made contributions on behalf of C. O is the employer for whom services are normally rendered by C.

Example (3). D is a member of a labor union whose members received health and welfare benefit payments from a trust fund which is supported by the contributions of the various employers who employ the labor union's members. D has been employed by Company R for 4 days when he becomes sick and is absent from work for 3 months. While D is absent from work he receives sick pay from his union's trust fund to which R has made contributions on D's behalf. R is the employer for whom services are normally rendered by D.

(3) For purposes of paragraph (e) of this section, in the case of payments on account of sickness or accident disability made to employees by a third party insurer pursuant to a contract of insurance with a multiemployer plan which is obligated to make payments on account of sickness or accident disability to such employees pursuant to a collectively bargained agreement, if the third party insurer making the payments complies with the requirements of subdivisions (i) and (ii) of subparagraph (2) of paragraph (e) and notifies the plan of the amount of compensation paid on which tax was withheld and deposited within the time required for notification of the employer under subparagraph (2) of paragraph (e), then the plan (and not the third party insurer) shall be required to pay the tax imposed by section 3221 and to comply with the requirements of section 6051 and §§ 31.6051-1 and 31.6051-2 with respect to such payments unless, within 6 business days of the receipt of such notification, the plan notifies the employer for whom services are normally rendered of the amount of the compensation on which tax was withheld and deposited. If the plan provides such notice to the employer, the employer (and not the plan) shall be required to pay the tax imposed by section 3221 and to comply with the requirements of section 6051 and §§ 31.6051-1 and 31.6051-2 with respect to the compensation.

T.D. 7823, 6/30/82, amend T.D. 7867, 1/6/83.

§ 31.3201-1 Measure of employee tax.

The employee tax is measured by the amount of compensation received for services rendered as an employee. For provisions relating to compensation, see § 31.3231(e)-1. For provisions relating to the circumstances under which certain compensation is to be disregarded for the purpose of determining the employee tax, see paragraphs (b)(1) and (2) of § 31.3231(e)-1.

T.D. 6727, 5/4/64, amend T.D. 8582, 12/22/94.

§ 31.3201-2 Rates and computation of employee tax.

(a) Rates. *(1)* (i) Tier 1 tax. The Tier 1 employee tax rate equals the sum of the tax rates in effect under section 3101(a) relating to old-age, survivors, and disability insurance, and section 3101(b), relating to hospital insurance. The Tier 1 employee tax rate is applied to compensation up to the contribution base described in section 3231(e)(2)(B)(i). The contribution base is determined under section 230 of the Social Security Act and is identical to the old-age, survivors, and disability insurance wage base and the hospital insurance wage base, respectively, under the Federal Insurance Contributions Act.

(ii) Example. The rule in paragraph (a)(1)(i) of this section is illustrated by the following example.

Example. A received compensation of $60,000 in 1992. The section 3101(a) rate of 6.2 percent would be applied to A's compensation up to $55,500, the applicable contribution base for 1992. The section 3101(b) rate of 1.45 percent would be applied to the entire $60,000 of A's compensation because the applicable contribution base for 1992 is $130,200.

(2) (i) Tier 2 tax. The Tier 2 employee tax rate equals the percentage set forth in section 3201(b) of the Code. This rate is applied to compensation up to the contribution base described in section 3231(e)(2)(B)(ii).

(ii) Example. The rule in paragraph (a)(2)(i) of this section is illustrated by the following example.

Example. A received compensation of $60,000 in 1992. The section 3201(b) rate of 4.90 percent would be applied to A's compensation up to $41,400, the applicable contribution base for 1992.

(b) Rates. *(1) Computation.* The employee tax is computed by multiplying the amount of the employee's compensation with respect to which the employee tax is imposed by the rate applicable to such compensation, as determined under paragraph (a) of this section. The applicable rate is the rate in effect when the compensation is received by the employee. For rules relating to the time of receipt, see § 31.3121(a)-2(a) and (b).

(2) Example. The rule in paragraph (b)(1) of this section is illustrated by the following example.

Example. In 1990, employee A received compensation of $1,000 as remuneration for services performed for employer R in 1989. The employee tax is payable at the rate of 12.55 percent (7.65 percent plus 4.90 percent) in effect for 1990 (the year the compensation was received), and not the 12.41 percent rate (7.51 percent plus 4.90 percent) in effect for 1989 (the year the services were performed).

T.D. 6541, 1/19/61, amend T.D. 6727, 5/4/64, T.D. 8582, 12/22/94.

§ 31.3202-1 Collection of, and liability for, employee tax.

(a) Collection; general rule. The employer shall collect from each of his employees the employee tax imposed with respect to the compensation of the employee by deducting or causing to be deducted the amount of such tax from the compensation subject to the tax as and when such compensation is paid. As to the measure of the employee tax, see § 31.3201-1.

(b) Collection; payments by two or more employers in excess of annual compensation limitation. For rules relating to payments by two or more employers in excess of the annual compensation limitation see § 31.3121(a)(1)-1.

(c) Undercollections or overcollections. Any undercollection or overcollection of employee tax resulting from the employer's inability to determine, at the time compensation is paid, the correct amount of compensation with respect to which the deduction should be made shall be corrected in accordance with the provisions of Subpart G of the regulations in this part relating to adjustments, credits, refunds, and abatements.

(d) When fractional part of cent may be disregarded. In collecting the employee tax, the employer shall disregard any fractional part of a cent of such tax unless it amounts to one-half cent or more, in which case it shall be increased to one cent.

(e) Employer's liability. The employer is liable for the employee tax with respect to compensation paid by him, whether or not collected from the employee. If the employer deducts less than the correct amount of employee tax or fails to deduct any part of the tax, he is nevertheless liable for the correct amount of the tax. Until collected from him, the employee is also liable for the employee tax. Any employee tax collected by or on behalf of an employer is a special fund in trust for the United States. See section 7501. An employer is not liable to any person for the amount of the employee tax deducted by him and paid to the district director.

(f) Concurrent employment. If two or more related corporations who are rail employers concurrently employ the same individual and compensate that individual through a common paymaster, which is one of the related corporations employing the individual, see § 31.3121(s)-1.

T.D. 6200, 9/4/56, amend T.D. 6516, 12/19/60, T.D. 6541, 1/19/61, T.D. 6727, 5/4/64, T.D. 8585, 12/22/94.

§ 31.3211-1 Measure of employee representative tax.

The employee representative tax is measured by the amount of compensation received for services rendered as an employee representative. For provisions relating to compensation, see § 31.3231(e)-1.

T.D. 6541, 1/19/61, amend T.D. 6727, 5/4/64, T.D. 8582, 12/22/94.

§ 31.3211-2 Rates and computation of employee representative tax.

(a) Rates. *(1)* (i) Tier 1 tax. The Tier 1 employee representative tax rate equals the sum of the tax rates in effect under sections 3101(a) and 3111(a), relating to the employee and the employer tax for old-age, survivors, and disability insurance, and sections 3101(b) and 3111(b), relating to the employee and the employer tax for hospital insurance. The Tier 1 employee representative tax rate is applied to compensation up to the contribution base described in section 3231(e)(2)(B)(i). The contribution base is determined under section 230 of the Social Security Act, and is identical to the old-age, survivors, and disability insurance wage base and the hospital insurance wage base, respectively, under the Federal Insurance Contributions Act.

(ii) Example. The rule in paragraph (a)(1)(i) of this section is illustrated by the following example.

Example. B, an employee representative received compensation of $60,000 in 1992. The sections 3101(a) and 3111(a) rates of 12.4 percent (6.2 percent plus 6.2 percent) would be applied to B's compensation up to $55,500, the applicable contribution base for 1992. The sections 3101(b) and 3111(b) rates of 2.9 percent (1.45 percent plus 1.45 percent) would be applied to the entire $60,000 of B's compensation because the applicable contribution base for 1992 is $130,200.

(2) (i) Tier 2 tax. The Tier 2 employee representative tax rate equals the percentage set forth in section 3211(a)(2) of the Code. This rate is applied up to the contribution base described in section 3231(e)(2)(B)(ii).

(ii) Example. The rule in paragraph (a)(2)(i) of this section is illustrated by the following example.

Example. B received compensation of $60,000 in 1992. The section 3211(a)(2) rate of 14.75 percent would be applied to B's compensation up to $41,400, the applicable contribution base for 1992.

(3) Supplemental annuity tax. The supplemental annuity tax for each work-hour for which compensation is paid to an employee representative for services rendered as an employee representative is imposed at the same rate as the excise tax imposed on every employer under section 3221(c). See also § 31.3211-3.

(b) *(1) Computation.* The employee representative tax is computed by multiplying the amount of the employee representative's compensation with respect to which the employee representative tax is imposed by the rate applicable to such compensation, as determined under paragraph (a) of this section. The applicable rate is the rate in effect when the compensation is received by the employee representative. For rules relating to the time of receipt, see § 31.3121(a)-2(a) and (b).

(2) Example. The rule in paragraph (b)(1) of this section is illustrated by the following example.

Example. In 1990, employee representative B received $1,000 as remuneration for services performed for employer R in 1989. The employee representative tax is payable at the rate of 30.05 percent (15.30 percent plus 14.75 percent) in effect for 1990 (the year the compensation was received), and not the 29.77 percent rate (15.02 percent plus 14.75 percent) in effect for 1989 (the year the services were performed).

(c) *(1) Rule where compensation is received both as an employee representative and employee.* The following rule applies to an individual who renders service both as an employee representative and as an employee. The employee representative tax is imposed on compensation received as an employee representative under the rules described in § 31.3211-2. The employee tax is imposed on compensation received as an employee under the rules described in § 31.3201-2. However, if the total compensation received is greater than the applicable contribution base, the employee representative tax is imposed on the amount equal to the contribution base less the amount received for services rendered as an employee.

(2) Example. The rule in paragraph (c)(1) of this section is illustrated by the following example.

Example. C performed services both as an employee and an employee representative in 1992. C received compensation of $40,000 as an employee and $20,000 as an employee representative. C's entire compensation of $40,000 is subject to tax under the rules described in § 31.3201-2. The amount of employee representative compensation subject to the section 3101(a) and the section 3111(a) rate is $15,500 ($55,500 − $40,000). The entire $20,000 is subject to the sections 3101(b) and 3111(b) rates since the combined compensation is less than $130,200, the applicable contribution base for 1992. The amount of the employee representative compensation subject to the section 3211(a)(2) rate is $1,400 ($41,400 − $40,000).

T.D. 6541, 1/19/61, amend T.D. 6727, 5/4/64, T.D. 8582, 12/22/94.

§ 31.3211-3 Employee representative supplemental tax.

See paragraphs (a), (b), and (c) of § 31.3221-3 for rules applicable to the supplemental tax for each work-hour for which compensation is paid to an employee representative for services rendered as an employee representative.

T.D. 8525, 2/25/94.

§ 31.3212-1 Determination of compensation.

See § 31.3231(e)-1 for regulations applicable to compensation.

T.D. 6200, 9/4/56, amend T.D. 6516, 12/19/60.

§ 31.3221-1 Measure of employer tax.

(a) General rule. The employer tax is measured by the amount of compensation paid by an employer to its employees. For provisions relating to compensation, see § 31.3231(e)-1. For provisions relating to the circumstances under which certain compensation is to be disregarded for purposes of determining the employer tax, see paragraphs (b)(1) and (2) of § 31.3231(e)-1.

(b) Payments by two or more employers in excess of annual compensation limitation. For rules relating to payments by two or more employers in excess of the annual compensation limitation, see § 31.3121(a)(1)-1.

(c) Underpayments or overpayments. Any underpayment or overpayment of employer tax resulting from the employer's inability to determine, at the time such tax is paid, the correct amount of compensation with respect to which the tax should be paid shall be corrected in accordance with the provisions of Subpart G of the regulations in this part relating to adjustments, credits, refunds, and abatements.

T.D. 6200, 9/4/56, amend T.D. 6516, 12/19/60, T.D. 6541, 1/19/61, T.D. 6727, 5/4/64, T.D. 8582, 12/22/94.

§ 31.3221-2 Rates and computation of employer tax.

(a) Rates. *(1)* (i) Tier 1 tax. The Tier 1 employer tax rate equals the sum of the tax rates in effect under section 3111(a), relating to old-age, survivors, and disability insurance, and section 3111(b) relating to hospital insurance. The Tier 1 employer tax rate is applied to compensation up to the contribution base described in section 3231(e)(2)(B)(i). The contribution base is determined under section 230 of the Social Security Act and is identical to the old-age, survivors, and disability insurance wage base and the hospital insurance wage base, respectively, under the Federal Insurance Contributions Act.

(ii) Example. The rule in paragraph (a)(1)(i) of this section is illustrated by the following example.

Example. R's employee, A, received compensation of $60,000 in 1992. The section 3111(a) rate of 6.2 percent would be applied to A's compensation up to $55,500, the applicable contribution base for 1992. The section 3111(b) rate of 1.45 percent would be applied to the entire $60,000 of A's compensation because the applicable contribution base for 1992 is $130,200.

(2) (i) Tier 2 tax. The Tier 2 employer tax rate equals the percentage set forth in section 3221(b) of the Internal Revenue Code. This rate is applied up to the contribution base described in section 3231(e)(2)(B)(ii).

(ii) Example. The rule in paragraph (a)(2)(i) of this section is illustrated by the following example.

Example. R's employee, A, received compensation of $60,000 in 1992. The section 3221(b) rate of 16.10 percent would be applied to A's compensation up to $41,400, the applicable contribution base for 1992.

(3) Supplemental annuity tax. The supplemental annuity tax for each work-hour for which compensation is paid by an employer for services rendered during any calendar quarter by employees is imposed at the tax rate determined each calendar quarter by the Railroad Retirement Board. See also § 31.3221-3.

(b) *(1) Computation.* The employer tax is computed by multiplying the amount of the compensation with respect to which the employer tax is imposed by the rate applicable to such compensation, as determined under paragraph (a) of this section. The applicable rate is the rate in effect at the time the compensation is paid. For rules relating to the time of payment, see § 31.3121(a)-2(a) and (b).

(2) Example. The rule in paragraph (b)(1) of this section is illustrated by the following example.

Example. In 1990, R's employee A received $1,000 as remuneration for services performed for R in 1989. The employer tax is payable at the rate of 23.75 percent (7.6 percent plus 16.10 percent) in effect for 1990 (the year the compensation was received) and not the 23.61 percent rate (7.51 percent plus 16.10 percent) in effect for 1989 (the year the services were performed).

T.D. 6541, 1/19/61, amend T.D. 6727, 5/4/64, T.D. 8582, 12/22/94.

§ 31.3221-3 Supplemental tax.

(a) Introduction. *(1) In general.* Section 3221(c) imposes an excise tax on every employer, as defined in section 3231(a) and § 31.3231(a)-1, with respect to individuals employed by the employer. The tax is imposed for each work-hour for which the employer pays compensation, as defined in section 3231(e) and § 31.3231(e)-1, for services rendered to the employer during a calendar quarter. This § 31.3221-3 provides rules for determining the number of taxable work-hours.

(2) Overview. Paragraph (b) of this section defines work-hours. Paragraph (c) of this section demonstrates the calculation of work-hours. Paragraph (d) of this section offers a safe harbor calculation of work-hours for use by any employer in lieu of calculating the number of work-hours for each employee.

(b) Definition of work-hours. *(1) In general.* For purposes of section 3221(c) and this section, work-hours are hours for which the employee is compensated, whether or not the employee performs services.

(i) Payments included in work-hours. Work-hours include regular time worked; overtime; time paid for vacations and holidays; time allowed for meals; away-from-home terminal time; called and not used, runaround, and deadheading time; time for attending court, participating in investigations, and attending claim and safety meetings; and guaranteed time not worked. Work-hours also include conversion hours, that is, compensation converted into work-hours. Conversion hours may be derived from payment by the mile or by the piece. Work-hours also include time for which the employee is paid for periods of absence not due to sickness or accident disability, such as for routine medical and dental examinations or for time lost.

(ii) Payments excluded from work-hours. Certain kinds of payments are not subject to conversion into work-hours. These include those payments that are specifically excluded from compensation within the meaning of section 3231(e), such as certain sick pay payments (section 3231(e)(1)(i)); tips (section 3231(e)(1)(ii)); and amounts paid specifically (either as an advance, as reimbursement, or allowance) for traveling expenses (section 3231(e)(1)(iii)). Traveling expenses paid under a nonaccountable plan are excluded from work-hours even though they are includible in compensation. See § 31.3231(e)-1(a)(5). Also excluded from work-hours are amounts representing bonuses, amounts received pursuant to the exercise of an employee stock option, and all separation payments or severance allowances.

(2) Hourly compensation. Because the tax under section 3221(c) is calculated on the basis of work-hours, the number of hours for which an employee receives compensation is the figure used to determine work-hours. In the case of an hourly-rated employee, each hour for which the employee receives compensation is one work-hour.

(3) Daily, weekly, monthly compensation. (i) If an employee is paid by the day, week, month, or other period of time, the tax is imposed on the number of hours comprehended in the rate and, if any, the number of overtime hours for which additional compensation is paid. Thus, in the case of an office worker who receives an annual salary based on an 8-hour, 5-day-a-week work schedule that includes paid holidays, vacations, and sick time, the number of work-hours for one month is 174 (2088 hours/year ÷ 12 months).

(ii) The rule in paragraph (b)(3)(i) of this section is illustrated by the following examples.

Example (1). A, an office worker, receives an annual salary that is paid monthly. The salary is based on an 8-hour, Monday through Friday work schedule. A is not paid for overtime hours. A is not expected to work on holidays, during A's annual vacation, or during periods that A is ill. The number of work-hours for one month is 174 (2088 hours/year ÷ 12 months). This figure remains constant, even though some months have more workdays than others.

Example (2). B is paid a stated amount for each day B works, regardless of the number of hours worked. However, if B works more than 8 hours during any day, B is paid overtime for each additional hour worked that day. B is not paid for holidays, vacations, or sick time. During May, B worked 6 hours on 4 days, 7 hours on 6 days, 8 hours on 6 days, and 9 hours on 5 days. Because B is paid a daily rate for up to 8 hours, 8 hours are comprehended in the daily rate. Therefore, the number of work-hours for May is 173 (21 days × 8 hours/day + 5 overtime hours), even though B actually worked 159 hours.

(4) Conversion hours. (i) Compensation not based on time (hour, day, month, etc.), such as compensation paid by the mile or by the piece, must be converted into the number of hours represented by the compensation paid. Thus, if an employee is paid by the mile, 1 work-hour equals the number of miles constituting a workday, divided by 8 hours. However, in the case of a collective bargaining agreement that specifies a number of hours as constituting a workday, the number of hours specified under the agreement may be used instead of 8.

(ii) The rule in paragraph (b)(4)(i) of this section is illustrated by the following example.

Example. C's normal workday consists of 2 150-mile round trips that together take 6 hours. C is paid by the mile. The collective bargaining agreement does not specify the number of hours in a workday. Thus, the number of work-hours for each day C works is 8, or 1 work-hour for each 37.5 miles (300 miles/day ÷ 8 hours/day). If the applicable collective bargaining agreement specifies that 6 hours constitute a workday, the number of work-hours for each day C works would be 6.

(c) Calculation of work-hours. *(1)* An employer may calculate the work-hours separately for each employee, as described in the examples in this paragraph. If the employer chooses to calculate work-hours separately for each employee, the employer must calculate the number of regular hours, overtime hours, and conversion hours for each employee for each month. In lieu of separate calculations, the employer may calculate the work-hours for all the employer's employees using the safe harbor formula described in paragraph (d) of this section.

(2) The rules in paragraph (c) of this section are illustrated by the following examples.

Example (1). D worked 8 hours a day, Monday through Friday, during the months of February and March 1992. D did not work on President's Day, but was paid for the holiday. D's work-hours for February were 160 (19 days × 8 hours a day + 8 holiday hours). D's work-hours for March were 176 (22 days × 8 hours a day).

Example (2). E worked 7-hour shifts every Tuesday through Saturday during the months of February and March 1992. E also worked 7 overtime hours during February and 21 overtime hours during March. Also, E was paid for 7 hours on President's Day, even though E did not work on that day. The number of work-hours for February was 161 (21 days × 7 hours a day + 7 overtime hours + 7 holiday hours). The number of work-hours for March was 168 (21 days × 7 hours a day + 21 overtime hours). Because E receives an hourly wage and was paid for the President's Day holiday, the number of hours (7) for which E was paid are added to the hours E actually worked. If E had worked on President's Day and had received extra pay for working on a holiday and holiday pay for 7 hours, the employer would include 14 hours in E's work-hours for that day, the 7 hours E actually worked and the 7 holiday hours for which E was paid.

Example (3). Employment beginning during month. F began employment on March 16, a Monday, and worked 8 hours a day, Monday through Friday. The employer calculates that F's hours for the month were 96, because F worked 12 8-hour days during the month. If March 16 were on a Friday, the employer would calculate 11 days, or 88 hours.

Example (4). Employment ending during month. G's last day of employment was Friday, March 13. G worked 8 hours a day, Monday through Friday, except for March 3, when G was ill. G was paid for 8 hours for March 3. The employer calculates that G's work-hours for March were 80, because G worked 9 8-hour days and was paid for an additional 8 hours.

(d) Safe harbor. *(1) In general.* In lieu of calculating work-hours separately for each employee, an employer may use the safe harbor for all employees. If the employer elects to use the safe harbor for a calendar year, the employer must use the safe harbor for all employees for the entire calendar year. If an employer uses the safe harbor for a calendar year, the employer need not elect the safe harbor for the following calendar year. An employer that elects the safe harbor for a calendar year may not subsequently elect to separately calculate employee work-hours for that calendar year.

(2) Method of calculation. The safe harbor treats each employee of the employer as receiving monthly compensation for a number of hours equal to the safe harbor number. To determine the number of work-hours for a month, the employer multiplies the safe harbor number by the number that equals the total number of employees to whom the employer paid compensation during the month.

(i) Safe harbor number defined. The safe harbor number is the number established in guidance of general applicability promulgated by the Commissioner.

(ii) Employee defined. Solely for purposes of this paragraph, an employee is any individual who is paid compensation, within the meaning of § 31.3231(e)-1, regardless of the amount, during the month. Thus, for example, a part-time, temporary, or seasonal employee is counted as an employee. A terminated employee is counted in the month of termination (provided the terminated employee received compensation in the month of termination), but not in any subsequent month in which the employee does not perform service for the employer as an employee, even if the terminated employee is paid compensation in a subsequent month. Thus, for example, an employee who terminates employment during the month, receives compensation during the month of termination, and receives a final paycheck the following month is counted as an employee of the employer for the month of termination but not for the following month.

(3) Method of election. An employer makes the safe harbor election for a calendar year on the employment tax return filed for the previous calendar year.

(4) Additional rules. The Commissioner may, in revenue procedures, revenue rulings, notices, or other guidance of general applicability, revise the safe harbor number or provide additional safe harbors that satisfy section 3221(c).

(e) Effective dates. This § 31.3221-3 is effective for calendar years beginning after December 31, 1992, except that paragraph (d) is effective for calendar years beginning after December 31, 1993. Taxpayers may apply the rules in paragraphs (a), (b), and (c) of this section before January 1, 1993.

T.D. 8525, 2/25/94.

§ 31.3221-4 Exception from supplemental tax.

(a) General rule. Section 3221(d) provides an exception from the excise tax imposed by section 3221(c). Under this exception, the excise tax imposed by section 3221(c) does not apply to an employer with respect to employees who are covered by a supplemental pension plan, as defined in paragraph (b) of this section, that is established pursuant to an agreement reached through collective bargaining between the employer and employees, within the meaning of paragraph (c) of this section.

(b) Definition of supplemental pension plan. *(1) In general.* A plan is a supplemental pension plan covered by the section 3221(d) exception described in paragraph (a) of this section only if it meets the requirements of paragraphs (b)(2) through (b)(4) of this section.

(2) Pension benefit requirement. A plan is a supplemental pension plan within the meaning of this section only if the plan is a pension plan within the meaning of § 1.401-1(b)(1)(i) of this chapter. Thus, a plan is a supplemental pension plan only if the plan provides for the payment of definitely determinable benefits to employees over a period of years, usually for life, after retirement. A plan need not be funded through a qualified trust that meets the requirements of section 401(a) or an annuity contract that meets the requirements of section 403(a) in order to meet the requirements of this paragraph (b)(2). A plan that is a profit-sharing plan within the meaning of § 1.401-1(b)(1)(ii) of this chapter or a stock bonus plan within the meaning of § 1.401-1(b)(1)(iii) of this chapter is not a supplemental pension plan within the meaning of this paragraph (b).

(3) Railroad Retirement Board determination with respect to the plan. A plan is a supplemental pension plan within the meaning of this paragraph (b) with respect to an employee only during any period for which the Railroad Retirement Board has made a determination under 20 CFR 216.42(d) that the plan is a private pension, the payments from which will result in a reduction in the employee's supplemental annuity payable under 45 U.S.C. 231a(b). A plan is not a supplemental pension plan for any time period before the Railroad Retirement Board has made such a determination, or after that determination is no longer in force.

(4) Other requirements. [Reserved]

(c) Collective bargaining agreement. A plan is established pursuant to a collective bargaining agreement with respect to an employee only if, in accordance with the rules of § 1.410(b)-6(d)(2) of this chapter, the employee is included in a unit of employees covered by an agreement that the Secretary of Labor finds to be a collective bargaining agreement between employee representatives and one or more employers, provided that there is evidence that retirement benefits were the subject of good faith bargaining between employee representatives and the employer or employers.

(d) Substitute section 3221(d) excise tax. Section 3221(d) imposes an excise tax on any employer who has been excepted from the excise tax imposed under section 3221(c) by the application of section 3221(d) and paragraph (a) of this section with respect to an employee. The excise tax is equal to the amount of the supplemental annuity paid to that employee under 45 U.S.C. 231a(b), plus a percentage thereof determined by the Railroad Retirement Board to be sufficient to cover the administrative costs attributable to such payments under 45 U.S.C. 231a(b).

(e) Effective date. *(1) In general.* Except as provided in paragraph (e)(2) of this section, this section applies beginning on October 1, 1998.

(2) Delayed effective date for collective bargaining agreement provisions. Paragraph (c) of this section applies beginning on January 1, 2000.

T.D. 8832, 8/5/99.

---

§ 31.3231(a)-1 Who are employers.

(a) Each of the following persons is an employer within the meaning of the act:

(1) Any carrier, that is, any express carrier, sleeping car carrier, or rail carrier providing transportation subject to subchapter I of chapter 105 of title 49;

(2) Any company—

(i) Which is directly or indirectly owned or controlled by one or more employers as defined in paragraph (a)(1) of this section, or under common control therewith, and

(ii) Which operates any equipment or facility or performs any service (except trucking service, casual service, and the casual operation of equipment or facilities) in connection with—

(a) The transportation of passengers or property by railroad, or

(b) The receipt, delivery, elevation, transfer in transit, refrigeration or icing, storage, or handling of property transported by railroad;

(3) Any receiver, trustee, or other individual or body, judicial or otherwise, when in the possession of the property or operating all or any part of the business of any employer as defined in paragraph (a)(1) or (2) of this section;

(4) Any railroad association, traffic association, tariff bureau, demurrage bureau, weighing and inspection bureau,

collection agency, and any other association, bureau, agency, or organization controlled and maintained wholly or principally by two or more employers as defined in paragraph (a)(1), (2) or (3) of this section and engaged in the performance of services in connection with or incidental to railroad transportation;

(5) Any railway labor organization, national in scope, which has been or may be organized in accordance with the provisions of the Railway Labor Act; and

(6) Any subordinate unit of a national railway-labor-organization employer, that is, any State or National legislative committee, general committee, insurance department, or local lodge or division, of an employer as defined in paragraph (a)(5) of this section, established pursuant to the constitution and bylaws of such employer.

(b) As used in paragraph (a)(2) of this section, the term "controlled" includes direct or indirect control, whether legally enforceable and however exercisable or exercised. The control may be by means of stock ownership, or by agreements, licenses, or any other devices which insure that the operation of the company is in the interest of one or more carriers. It is the reality of the control, however, which is decisive, not its form nor the mode of its exercise.

(c) As used in paragraph (a)(2) of this section, the term *casual* applies when the service rendered or the operation of equipment or facilities by a controlled company or person in connection with the transportation of passengers or property by railroad is so irregular or infrequent as to afford no substantial basis for an inference that such service or operation will be repeated, or whenever such service or operation is insubstantial.

(d) The term "employer" does not include any street, interurban, or suburban electric railway, unless such railway is operating as a part of a general steam-railroad system of transportation, but shall not exclude any part of the general steam-railroad system of transportation which is operated by any other motive power.

(e) The term "employer" does not include any company by reason of its being engaged in the mining of coal, the supplying of coal to an employer where delivery is not beyond the mine tipple and the operation of equipment or facilities for such mining or supplying of coal, or in any of such activities.

(f) Any company that is described in paragraph (a)(2) of this section is an employer under section 3231. In certain cases, based on all the facts and circumstances, it may be appropriate to segregate those businesses engaged in rail services and therefore subject to the Railroad Retirement Tax Act from those businesses engaged exclusively in nonrail services and therefore not subject to the Railroad Retirement Tax Act. The factors considered are set forth in guidance published by the Internal Revenue Service.

T.D. 6200, 9/4/56, amend T.D. 6516, 12/19/60, T.D. 8582, 12/22/94.

§ 31.3231(b)-1 Who are employees.

(a) In general. *(1)* An individual who is in the service of one or more employers for compensation is an employee within the meaning of the act. (For definitions of the terms "employer", "service", and "compensation", see subsections (a), (d), and (e), respectively, of section 3231.) An individual is in the service of an employer, with respect to services rendered for compensation, if—

(i) He is subject to the continuing authority of the employer to supervise and direct the manner in which he renders such services; or

(ii) He is rendering professional or technical services and is integrated into the staff of the employer; or

(iii) He is rendering, on the property used in the employer's operations, other personal services the rendition of which is integrated into the employer's operations.

(2) In order that an individual may be in the service of an employer within the meaning of paragraph (a)(1)(i) of this section, it is not necessary that the employer actually direct or control the manner in which the services are rendered; it is sufficient if the employer has the right to do so. The right of an employer to discharge an individual is also an important factor indicating that the individual is subject to the continuing authority of the employer to supervise and direct the manner of rendition of the services. Other factors indicating that an individual is subject to the continuing authority of the employer to supervise and direct the manner of rendition of the services are the furnishing of tools and the furnishing of a place to work by the employer to the individual who renders the services.

(3) In general, if an individual is subject to the control or direction of an employer merely as to the result to be accomplished by the work and not as to the means and methods for accomplishing the result, he is an independent contractor. On individual performing services as an independent contractor is not, as to such services, in the service of an employer within the meaning of paragraph (a)(1)(i) of this section. However, an individual performing services as an independent contractor may be, as to such services, in the service of an employer within the meaning of paragraph (a)(1)(ii) or (iii) of this section.

(4) Whether or not an individual is an employee will be determined upon an examination of the particular facts of the case.

(5) If an individual is an employee, it is of no consequence that he is designated as a partner, coadventurer, agent, independent contractor, or otherwise, or that he performs services on a part-time basis.

(6) No distinction is made between classes or grades of employees. Thus, superintendents, managers, and other supervisory personnel are employees within the meaning of the act. An officer of an employer is an employee, but a director as such is not.

(7) In determining whether an individual is an employee with respect to services rendered within the United States, the citizenship or residence of the individual, or the place where the contract of service was entered into is immaterial.

(8) If an individual performs services for an employer (other than a local lodge or division or a general committee of a railway-labor organization employer) which does not conduct the principal part of its business within the United States, such individual shall be deemed to be in the service of such employer only to the extent that he performs services for it in the United States. Thus with respect to services rendered for such employer outside the United States, such individual is not in the service of an employer.

(9) If an individual performs services for an employer (other than a local lodge or division or a general committee of a railway-labor-organization employer) which conducts the principal part of its business within the United States, he is in the service of such employer whether his services are rendered within or without the United States. In the case of

an individual, not a citizen or resident of the United States, rendering services in a place outside the United States to an employer which is required under the laws applicable in such place to employ, in whole or in part, citizens or residents thereof, such individual shall not be deemed to be in the service of an employer with respect to services so rendered.

(10) The term "employee" does not include any individual while he is engaged in the physical operations consisting of the mining of coal, the preparation of coal, the handling (other than movement by rail with standard railroad locomotives) of coal not beyond the mine tipple, or the loading of coal at the tipple.

(b) Employees of local lodges or divisions of railway-labor-organization employers. *(1)* An individual is in the service of a local lodge or division of a railway-labor-organization employer (see paragraph (a)(6) of § 31.3231(a)-1) only if—

(i) All, or substantially all, the individuals constituting the membership of such local lodge or division are employees of an employer conducting the principal part of its business in the United States; or

(ii) The headquarters of such local lodge or division is located in the United States.

(2) (i) An individual in the service of a local lodge or division is not an employee within the meaning of the act unless he was, on or after August 29, 1935, in the service of a carrier (see § 31.3231(g) for definition of carrier) or he was, on August 29, 1935, in the "employment relation" to a carrier.

(ii) An individual shall be deemed to have been in the employment relation to a carrier on August 29, 1935, if (a) he was on that date on leave of absence from his employment expressly granted to him by the carrier by whom he was employed, or by a duly authorized representative or such carrier, and the grant of such leave of absence was established to the satisfaction of the Railroad Retirement Board before July 1947; or (b) he was in the service of a carrier after August 29, 1935, and before January 1946 in each of six calendar months whether or not consecutive; or (c) before August 29, 1935, he did not retire and was not retired or discharged from the service of the last carrier by whom he was employed or its corporate or operating successor, but (1) solely by reason of his physical or mental disability he ceased before August 29, 1935, to be in the service of such carrier and thereafter remained continuously disabled until he attained age sixty-five or until August 1945, or (2) solely for such last stated reason a carrier by whom he was employed before August 29, 1935, or a carrier who is its successor did not on or after August 29, 1935, and before August 1945 call him to return to service, or (3) if he was so called he was solely for such reason unable to render service in six calendar months as provided in (b) of this subdivision; or (d) he was on August 29, 1935, absent from the service of a carrier by reason of a discharge which, within one year after the effective date thereof, was protested, to an appropriate labor representative or to the carrier as wrongful, and which was followed within 10 years of the effective date thereof by this reinstatement in good faith to his former service with all his seniority rights. However, an individual shall not be deemed to have been in the employment relation to a carrier on August 29, 1935, if before that date he was granted a pension or gratuity on the basis of which a pension was awarded to him pursuant to section 6 of the Railroad Retirement Act of 1937 (45 U.S.C. 228f), or if during the last payroll period before August 29, 1935, in which he rendered service to a carrier he was not, with respect to any service in such payroll period, in the service of an employer (see paragraph (a) of this section).

(c) Employees of general committees of railway-labor-organization employers. An individual is in the service of a general committee of a railway-labor-organization employer (see paragraph (a)(6) of § 31.3231(a)-1) only if—

(1) He is representing a local lodge or division described in paragraph (b)(1) of this section; or

(2) All, or substantially all, the individuals represented by such general committee are employees of an employer conducting the principal part of its business in the United States; or

(3) He acts in the capacity of a general chairman or an assistant general chairman of a general committee which represents individuals rendering service in the United States to an employer. In such case, if his office or headquarters is not located in the United States and the individuals represented by such general committee are employees of an employer not conducting the principal part of its business in the United States, only a part of his remuneration for such service shall be regarded as compensation. The part of his remuneration regarded as compensation shall be in the same proportion to his total remuneration as the mileage in the United States under the jurisdiction of such general committee bears to the total mileage under its jurisdiction, unless such mileage formula is inapplicable, in which case such other formula as the Railroad Retirement Board may have prescribed pursuant to section 1(c) of the Railroad Retirement Act of 1937 (45 U.S.C. 228a) shall be applicable. However, no part of his remuneration for such service shall be regarded as compensation if the application of such mileage formula, or such other formula as the Railroad Retirement Board may have prescribed, would result in his compensation for the service being less than 10 percent of his remuneration for such service.

T.D. 6200, 9/4/56, amend T.D. 6516, 12/19/60.

---

§ 31.3231(c)-1 Who are employee representatives.

(a) An employee representative within the meaning of the act is—

(1) Any officer or official representative of a railway labor organization which is not included as an employer under section 3231(a) who—

(i) Was in the service of an employer either before or after June 29, 1937, and

(ii) Is duly authorized and designated to represent employees in accordance with the Railway Labor Act.

For railway labor organizations which are employers under section 3231(a), see paragraph (a)(5) and (6) of § 31.3231(a)-1.

(2) Any individual who is regularly assigned to or regularly employed by an employee representative, as defined in paragraph (a)(1) of this section, in connection with the duties of such employee representative's office.

(b) In determining whether an individual is an employee representative, his citizenship or residence is material only insofar as those factors may affect the determination of whether he was "in the service of an employer" see paragraph (a) of § 31.3231(b)-1).

T.D. 6200, 9/4/56, amend T.D. 6516, 12/19/60.

§ 31.3231(d)-1 Service.

See § 31.3231(b)-1 for regulations relating to the term "in the service of an employer."

T.D. 6200, 9/4/56, amend T.D. 6516, 12/19/60.

§ 31.3231(e)-1 Compensation.

(a) Definition. *(1)* The term *compensation* has the same meaning as the term *wages* in section 3121(a), determined without regard to section 3121(b)(9), except as specifically limited by the Railroad Retirement Tax Act (chapter 22 of the Internal Revenue Code) or regulation. The Commissioner may provide any additional guidance that may be necessary or appropriate in applying the definitions of sections 3121(a) and 3231(e).

(2) A payment made by an employer to an individual through the employer's payroll is presumed, in the absence of evidence to the contrary, to be compensation for services rendered as an employee of the employer. Likewise, a payment made by an employee organization to an employee representative through the organization's payroll is presumed, in the absence of evidence to the contrary, to be compensation for services rendered by the employee representative as such. For rules regarding the treatment of deductions by an employer from remuneration of an employee, see § 31.3123-1.

(3) The term *compensation* is not confined to amounts paid for active service, but includes amounts paid for an identifiable period during which the employee is absent from the active service of the employer and, in the case of an employee representative, amounts paid for an identifiable period during which the employee representative is absent from the active service of the employee organization.

(4) Compensation includes amounts paid to an employee for loss of earnings during an identifiable period as the result of the displacement of the employee to a less remunerative position or occupation as well as pay for time lost.

(5) For rules regarding the treatment of reimbursement and other expense allowance amounts, see § 31.3121(a)-3. For rules regarding the inclusion of fringe benefits in compensation, see § 31.3121(a)-1T.

(6) Split-dollar life insurance arrangements. See §§ 1.61-22 and 1.7872-15 of this chapter for rules relating to the treatment of split-dollar life insurance arrangements.

(b) Special rules. *(1)* If the amount of compensation earned in any calendar month by an individual as an employee in the service of a local lodge or division of a railway-labor-organization employer is less than $25, the amount is disregarded for purposes of determining the employee tax under section 3201 and the employer tax under section 3221.

(2) Compensation for service as a delegate to a national or international convention of a railway-labor-organization employer is disregarded for purposes of determining the employee tax under section 3201 and the employer tax under section 3221 if the individual rendering the service has not previously rendered service, other than as a delegate, which may be included in the individual's years of service for purposes of the Railroad Retirement Act.

(3) For special provisions relating to the compensation of certain general chairs or assistant general chairs of a general committee of a railway-labor-organization employer, see paragraph (c)(3) of § 31.3231(b)-1.

T.D. 6200, 9/4/56, amend T.D. 6516, 12/19/60, T.D. 7600, 3/13/79, T.D. 8276, 12/7/89, T.D. 8324, 12/12/90, T.D. 8582, 12/22/94, T.D. 9092, 9/11/2003.

§ 31.3231(e)-2 Contribution base.

The term compensation does not include any remuneration paid during any calendar year by an employer to an employee for services rendered in excess of the applicable contribution base. For rules applying this provision, see § 31.3121(a)(1)-1.

T.D. 8582, 12/22/94.

§ 31.3301-1 Persons liable for tax.

Every person who is an employer as defined in section 3306(a) (see § 31.3306(a)-1) is liable for the tax. Even if an employer is not subject to any State unemployment compensation law, he is nevertheless liable for the tax. However, if he is subject to such a State law, he may be entitled to certain credits against the tax (see §§ 31.3302(a)-1 to 31.3302(c)-1, inclusive). For provisions relating to payment of the tax, see Subpart G of the regulations in this part.

T.D. 6199, 9/4/56, amend T.D. 6516, 12/19/60.

§ 31.3301-2 Measure of tax.

The tax for any calendar year is measured by the amount of wages paid by the employer during such year with respect to employment after December 31, 1938. (See § 31.3306(b)-1, relating to wages, and §§ 31.3306(c)-1 to 31.3306(c)-3, inclusive, relating to employment.)

T.D. 6199, 9/4/56, amend T.D. 6516, 12/19/60, T.D. 6658, 6/26/63.

§ 31.3301-3 Rate and computation of tax.

Caution: The Treasury has not yet amended Reg § 31.3301-3 to reflect changes made by P.L. 110-140.

(a) The rates of tax with respect to wages paid in calendar years after 1954 are as follows:

	Percent
In the calendar years 1955 to 1960, both inclusive	3
In the calendar year 1961	3.1
In the calendar year 1962	3.5
In the calendar year 1963	3.35
In the calendar year 1964 and subsequent calendar years	3.1

(b) The tax is computed by applying to the wages paid in a calendar year, with respect to employment after December 31, 1938, the rate in effect at the time the wages are paid.

T.D. 6199, 9/4/56, amend T.D. 6516, 12/19/60, T.D. 6658, 6/26/63.

§ 31.3301-4 When wages are paid.

Wages are paid when actually or constructively paid. Wages are constructively paid when they are credited to the account of or set apart for an employee so that they may be drawn upon by him at any time although not then actually reduced to possession. To constitute payment in such a case the wages must be credited to or set apart for the employee without any substantial limitation or restriction as to the time or manner of payment or condition upon which payment is to be made, and must be made available to him so that they may be drawn upon at any time, and their payment brought within his own control and disposition. See § 31.6011(a)-3, relating to the return on which wages are to be reported.

T.D. 6199, 9/4/56, amend T.D. 6516, 12/19/60.

§ 31.3302(a)-1 Credit against tax for contributions paid.

(a) In general. Subject to the provisions of paragraphs (b) and (c) of this section and to the provisions of § 31.3302(c)-1, the taxpayer may credit against the tax for any taxable year the total amount of contribution paid by him into an unemployment fund maintained during such year under a State law which has been found by the Secretary of Labor to contain the provisions specified in section 3304(a); Provided, however, That no credit may be taken for contributions under a State law if such State has not been duly certified for the calendar year to the Secretary of the Treasury by the Secretary of Labor. The contributions may be credited against the tax whether or not they are paid with respect to employment as defined in section 3306(c). For provisions relating to additional credit against the tax, see § 31.3302(b)-1.

(b) Limitation on the taxable year with respect to which contributions are allowable. In order to be allowable as credit against the tax for any taxable year, the contributions must have been paid with respect to such year.

Example (1). Under the unemployment compensation law of State X, employer M is required to report in his contribution return for the quarter ending December 31, 1955, all remuneration payable for services rendered in such quarter. A portion of such remuneration is not paid to his employees until February 1, 1956. On January 20, 1956, M pays to the State the total amount of contributions due with respect to all remuneration so required to be reported. Such contributions, including those with respect to the remuneration paid on February 1, 1956, may be included in computing the credit against the tax for the calendar year 1955. This is true even though the remuneration paid on February 1, 1956 (if it constitutes "wages") is required to be reported in the Federal return for 1956 and not in the Federal return for 1955.

Example (2). Under the unemployment compensation law of State Y, employer N is required to include in his contribution return for the quarter ending December 31, 1955, certain remuneration paid on December 30, 1955, to an employee for services to be rendered after December 31. On January 20, 1956, N pays to the State the total amount of contributions due with respect to all remuneration required to be reported on the contribution return. Such contributions, including those with respect to the remuneration paid on December 30, 1955, may be included in computing the credit against the tax for the calendar year 1955.

(c) Limitation on amount of credit allowable based on time when contributions are paid. *(1) In general.* The amount of credit allowable for contributions paid into a State unemployment fund depends in part on the time of payment of such contributions. Although contributions paid at any time may be credited against the tax (subject to the limitations referred to in paragraphs (c)(2) and (3) of this section), no refund or credit of the tax based on credit for contributions paid will be allowed unless the contributions are paid prior to the expiration of the period of limitations applicable to refund or credit of the tax. For general provisions relating to the limitation period and to refunds, credits and abatements of the tax, see respectively §§ 301.6511(a)-1, 301.6402-2 and 301.6404-1 of this chapter (Regulations on Procedure and Administration).

(2) Amount of credit allowable when contributions are paid on or before last day for filing return. Contributions paid into a State unemployment fund on or before the last day upon which the Federal return for the taxable year is required to be filed may be credited against the tax in an amount equal to such contributions, but not, however, to exceed the total credits determined pursuant to § 31.3302(c)-1. For provisions relating the time for filing the return, see § 31.6071(a)-1 in Subpart G of this part.

(3) Amount of credit allowable when contributions are paid after last day for filing return. Contributions paid into a State unemployment fund after the last day upon which the Federal return for the taxable year is required to be filed may be credited against the tax in an amount not to exceed 90 percent of the amount which would have been allowable as credit on account of such contributions had they been paid into a State unemployment fund on or before such last day. However, see paragraph (c)(4) of this section relating to the payment of contributions to the wrong State. For general provisions relating to refunds, credits, or abatements of the tax, see §§ 301.6402-2 and 301.6404-1 of this chapter (Regulations on Procedure and Administration).

Example (1). The Federal return of the M Company for the calendar year 1961 discloses total wages of $400,000. The Federal tax, imposed at the rate of 3.1 percent, is $12,400. The company is liable for total State contributions of $8,000 for 1961. The due date of the Federal return is January 31, 1962, no extension of time for filing the return having been granted. The contributions are not paid until February 1, 1962. If the contributions had been paid on or before January 31, 1962, the entire amount of $8,000 could have been credited against the tax. (Credits could not exceed 2.7 percent of the wages, or $10,800. See § 31.3302(c)-1.) Since the contributions were paid after January 31, 1962, the M Company is entitled to a credit of 90 percent of the amount which would have been allowable as credit had the contributions been paid on time (90 percent of $8,000, or $7,200), the net liability for Federal tax being $5,200 ($12,400 minus $7,200).

Example (2). The facts are the same as in example (1), except that the M Company is liable for and pays total State contributions of $12,000, instead of $8,000. If the contributions had been paid on or before January 31, 1962, the amount allowable as credit would have been $10,800 (2.7 percent of wages of $400,000). Since the contributions were paid after January 31, 1962, the M Company is entitled to a credit of 90 percent of $10,800, or $9,720, the net liability for Federal tax being $2,680 ($12,400 minus $9,720).

Example (3). The Federal return of the R Company for the calendar year 1961 discloses a total tax of $3,100. The company is liable for total State contributions of $2,700 for such year. The due date of the Federal return is January 31, 1962, no extension of time for filing the return having been granted. The R Company pays $1,700 of the total State contributions on or before such date, and the remaining $1,000 on February 1, 1962. If the $1,000 had been paid on or before January 31, 1962, that amount could have been credited against the tax (such amount plus the $1,700 paid on or before January 31, 1962, not exceeding the aggregate credit allowable). Since the $1,000 was paid after January 31, 1962, the R Company is entitled to a credit of 90 percent of this amount or $900, plus the credit of $1,700 allowable for the contributions paid on or before January 31, 1962. The net liability for Federal tax is thus $500 ($3,100 minus $2,600).

(4) Amount of credit allowable when contributions are paid to wrong State. Contributions for the taxable year paid into a State unemployment fund which are required under the unemployment compensation law of that State, but which are paid with respect to remuneration on the basis of which the taxpayer had, prior to such payment, erroneously paid an amount as contributions under another unemployment compensation law, shall be deemed for purposes of the credit to have been paid at the time of the erroneous payment. If, by reason of such other law, the taxpayer was entitled to cease paying contributions for such taxable year with respect to services subject to such other law, the payment into the proper fund shall be deemed for purposes of credit to have been made on the date the Federal return for such year was actually filed by the taxpayer under § 31.6011(a)-3.

Example. Employer N, whose Federal return for the calendar year 1961 discloses a total tax of $3,100, employs individuals in State X and State Y during the calendar year 1961. N assumes in good faith that the services of his employees are covered by the unemployment compensation law of State Y, and pays as contributions to State Y the amount of $2,700 based upon the remuneration of the employees. All of the services were in fact covered by the unemployment compensation law of State X, and none by the law of State Y. The payment to State Y was made on January 31, 1962. When the error was discovered thereafter, N paid to State X contributions in the amount of $2,700 based upon such remuneration. Since the contributions were paid to State Y on January 31, 1962, the contributions to State X are, for purposes of the credit, deemed to have been paid on such date. N is entitled to a credit of $2,700 against the Federal tax of $3,100, the net liability for Federal tax being $400 ($3,100 minus $2,700).

T.D. 6199, 9/4/56, amend T.D. 6516, 12/19/60, T.D. 6658, 6/26/63.

§ 31.3302(a)-2 Refund of State contributions.

If, subsequent to the filing of the return, a refund is made by a State to the taxpayer of any part of his contribution credited against the tax, the taxpayer is required to advise the district director of the date and amount of such refund and the reason therefor, and to pay the tax, if any, due as a result of such refund, together with interest from the date when the tax was due.

T.D. 6199, 9/4/56, amend T.D. 6516, 12/19/60.

§ 31.3302(a)-3 Proof of credit under section 3302(a).

Credit against the tax for any calendar year for contributions paid into State unemployment funds shall not be allowed unless there is submitted to the district director:

(a) A certificate of the proper officer of each State (the laws of which required the contributions to be paid) showing, for the taxpayer:

(1) The total amount of contributions required to be paid under the State law with respect to such calendar year (exclusive of penalties and interest) which was actually paid on or before the date the Federal return is required to be filed; and

(2) The amounts and dates of such required payments (exclusive of penalties and interest) actually paid after the date the Federal return is required to be filed.

(b) A statement by the taxpayer that no part of any payment made by him into a State unemployment fund for such calendar year, which is claimed as a credit against the tax, was deducted or is to be deducted from the remuneration of individuals in his employ. Such statement shall contain or be verified by a written declaration that it is made under the penalties of perjury.

(c) Such other or additional proof as the Commissioner or the district director may deem necessary to establish the right to the credit provided for under section 3302(a).

T.D. 6199, 9/4/56, amend T.D. 6516, 12/19/60.

§ 31.3302(b)-1 Additional credit against tax.

(a) In general. In addition to the credit against the tax allowable for contributions actually paid to State unemployment funds (see § 31.3302(a)-1), the taxpayer may be entitled to a credit under section 3302(b). This additional credit is allowable to the taxpayer with respect to the amount of contributions which he is relieved from paying to an unemployment fund under the provisions of a State law which have been certified for the taxable year as provided in section 3303. Generally, an additional credit is available to an employer, if under the provisions of a State law which have been so certified he is permitted to pay contributions to such State for the taxable year, or portion thereof, at a rate which is both lower than the highest rate applied under such law in such year and lower than 2.7 percent. No additional credit is allowable except with respect to a State law certified by the Secretary of Labor for the taxable year as provided in section 3303 (or with respect to any provisions thereof so certified).

(b) Method of computing amount of additional credit allowable with respect to a State law. *(1) Certification of a State law as a whole.* In ascertaining the additional credit for any taxable year with respect to a particular State law which the Secretary of Labor certifies as a whole to the Secretary of the Treasury in accordance with the provisions of section 3303, the taxpayer must first compute the following amounts:

(i) The amount of contributions (whether or not with respect to employment as defined in section 3306(c)) which the taxpayer would have been required to pay under the State law for such year if throughout the year he had been subject to the highest rate applied under such law in such year, or to a rate of 2.7 percent, whichever rate is lower.

(ii) The amount of contributions (whether or not with respect to employment as defined in section 3306(c)) he was required to pay under the State law with respect to such year, whether or not paid.

The amount computed under paragraph (b)(1)(ii) of this section should then be subtracted from the amount computed under paragraph (b)(1)(i) of this section and the result will be the additional credit for the taxable year with respect to the law of that State.

Example. A employs individuals only in State X during the calendar year 1955. The unemployment compensation law of State X has been certified in its entirety to the Secretary of the Treasury by the Secretary of Labor for such year. The highest rate applied in such year under such State law to any taxpayer is 3 percent. However, A has obtained a rate of 1 percent under the law of such State and is required to pay his entire year's contribution at that rate. The amount of remuneration of A's employees subject to contributions under such State law is $25,000. A's additional credit under section 3302(b) is $425, computed as follows:

Remuneration subject to contributions	$25,000
Contributions at 2.7 percent rate	675
Less:	
Contributions required to be paid at 1 percent rate	250
Additional credit to A	425

Since the 2.7 percent rate is less than the highest rate applied (3 percent), the 2.7 percent rate is used in computing the amount ($675) from which the amount of contributions required to be paid at the 1 percent rate ($250) is deducted in order to ascertain the additional credit ($425).

(2) Certification with respect to particular provisions of a State law. If the Secretary of Labor makes a certification to the Secretary of the Treasury with respect to particular provisions of a State law for any taxable year pursuant to section 3303, the additional credit of the taxpayer for such year with respect to such law shall be computed in such manner as the Commissioner shall determine.

(c) Amount of additional credit allowable to taxpayer with respect to more than one State law. If the taxpayer is entitled to additional credit with respect to more than one State law in any taxable year, the additional credit allowable with respect to each State law shall be computed separately (in accordance with paragraph (b) of this section) and the total additional credit allowable against the tax for such year shall be the aggregate of the additional credits allowable with respect to such State laws. For limitation on total credits, see § 31.3302(c)-1.

T.D. 6199, 9/4/56, amend T.D. 6516, 12/19/60, T.D. 6658, 6/26/63.

§ 31.3302(b)-2 Proof of additional credit under section 3302(b).

Additional credit under section 3302(b) shall not be allowed against the tax for any calendar year unless there is submitted—

(a) To the Commissioner a certificate of the proper officer of each State (with respect to the law of which the additional credit is claimed) showing the highest rate of contributions applied under the State law in such calendar year to any person having individuals in his employ; and

(b) To the district director a certificate of the proper officer of each State (with respect to the law of which the additional credit is claimed) showing for the taxpayer—

(1) The total remuneration with respect to which contributions were required to be paid by the taxpayer under the State law with respect to such calendar year; and

(2) The rate of contributions applied to the taxpayer under the State law with respect to such calendar year.

If under the law of such State different rates of contributions were applied to the taxpayer during particular periods of such calendar year, the certificate shall set forth the information called for in paragraphs (b)(1) and (2) of this section with respect to each such period.

(c) Such other or additional proof as the Commissioner or the district director may deem necessary to establish the right to the additional credit provided for under section 3302(b).

T.D. 6199, 9/4/56, amend T.D. 6516, 12/19/60.

§ 31.3302(c)-1 Limit on total credits.

(a) In general. Paragraph (b) of this section relates to the limitation on the aggregate of the credits allowable under section 3302(a) and (b). Paragraph (c) of this section relates to reductions, under certain circumstances, of the total credits allowable after applying section 3302(a), (b), and (c)(1). In paragraph (c) of this section, paragraphs (1), (2), and (3) relate, respectively, to reductions of credits in respect of advances under title XII of the Social Security Act before September 13, 1960, advances under title XII of the Social Security Act after September 12, 1960, and payments under the Temporary Unemployment Compensation Act of 1958. A reduction of credit under subparagraph (1), (2), or (3) of paragraph (c) applies separately from, and in addition to, a reduction under any other such subparagraph. See section 3302(d) and § 31.3302(d)-1 for definitions and special rules relating to section 3302(c), and for a provision that, in applying section 3302(c), the Federal tax shall be computed at the rate of 3 percent.

(b) Limitation on aggregate credit. The aggregate of the credit under section 3302(a) and the additional credit under section 3302(b) shall not exceed 90 percent of the tax against which credit is taken, computed as if the tax were imposed at the rate of 3 percent. Thus, the aggregate of the credit which is allowable to an employer for any taxable year shall not exceed 2.7 percent of the wages paid by the employer during the year.

(c) Reductions of amount of credit otherwise allowable. *(1) Advances before September 13, 1960, under title XII of Social Security Act.* (i) Credit reductions for 1961 and 1962. Pursuant to section 3302(c)(2), as applicable to credit allowable for any year ended before 1963, the total credits otherwise allowable under section 3302 to a taxpayer subject to the unemployment compensation law of the State of—

(a) Alaska shall be reduced for the taxable year 1961 by an amount equal to 0.15 percent of the wages paid by the taxpayer during 1961 which are attributable to Alaska, and shall be reduced for the taxable year 1962 by an amount equal to 0.3 percent of the wages paid by the taxpayer during 1962 which are attributable to Alaska; or

(b) Michigan shall be reduced for the taxable year 1962 by an amount equal to 0.15 percent of the wages paid by the taxpayer during 1962 which are attributable to Michigan.

(ii) Credit reductions for 1963 and subsequent years. If any balance of an advance or advances under title XII of the Social Security Act, made before September 13, 1960, to the unemployment account of a State, remains unpaid on January 1, 1963, or on January 1 of any succeeding taxable year, the total credits otherwise allowable under section 3302 to a taxpayer subject to the unemployment compensation law of the State shall be reduced for the taxable year unless—

(a) No balance of such advance or advances exists as of the beginning of November 10 of the taxable year, or

(b) The State pays into the Federal unemployment account, before November 10 of the taxable year, the amount certified by the Secretary of Labor pursuant to section 3302(c)(2), and designates such payment as being made for purposes of the last sentence of section 3302(c)(2).

The credit reduction for a taxable year shall be a percentage of the wages paid by the taxpayer during that taxable year which are attributable to the State. The percentage for the taxable year 1963, or for any succeeding taxable year beginning before January 1, 1968, is 0.15 percent (that is, 5 percent of the Federal tax, computed as if imposed at the rate of 3 percent of the wages). The percentage for any taxable year beginning on or after January 1, 1968, is the percentage reduction for the immediately preceding taxable year plus 0.15 percent. Thus, for 1968 the percentage is 0.3 percent, for 1969 the percentage is 0.45 percent, and for 1970 the percentage is 0.6 percent.

(2) Advances after September 12, 1960, under title XII of Social Security Act. (i) In general. If any balance of an advance or advances under title XII of the Social Security Act, made after September 12, 1960, to the unemployment, account of a State, remains unpaid on January 1 of two consecutive taxable years, the total credits otherwise allowable under section 3302 to a taxpayer subject to the unemployment compensation law of the State shall be reduced for the taxable year beginning with the second consecutive January 1, unless prior to November 10 of that taxable year the total amount of any such advance or advances made to the account of the State has been fully repaid. The reduction made pursuant to this subdivision in the total credits otherwise allowable for the taxable year beginning with the second consecutive January 1 shall be 0.3 percent of the wages paid by the taxpayer during the taxable year which are attributable to the State (that is, 10 percent of the Federal tax, computed as if imposed at the rate of 3 percent of the wages). In the case of any succeeding taxable year beginning with a consecutive January 1 on which there exists such a balance of an unreturned advance or advances made after September 12, 1960, the total credits otherwise allowable shall be further reduced unless prior to November 10 of that succeeding taxable year the total amount of any such advance or advances made to the account of the State has been fully repaid. The reduction for each such succeeding taxable year beginning with a consecutive January 1 on which such a balance exists shall be a percentage of the wages paid by the taxpayer during that succeeding taxable year which are attributable to the State. The percentage reduction for any such succeeding taxable year shall be the aggregate of (a) the percentage reduction (without regard to subdivision (ii) or (iii) of this subparagraph) for the immediately preceding taxable year, (b) 0.3 percent of the wages paid by the taxpayer during the taxable year which are attributable to the State, and (c) the percentage, if any, described in subdivision (ii) or (iii) of this subparagraph.

(ii) Additional reduction if a balance of advances exists after third or fourth consecutive January 1. If the credit reduction described in subdivision (i) of this subparagraph is made for the third or fourth consecutive taxable year, the total credits otherwise allowable under section 3302 to a taxpayer subject to the unemployment compensation law of the State shall be further reduced for the taxable year unless the average employer contribution rate (see section 3302(d)(4)) for such State for the calendar year preceding such taxable year is at least 2.7 percent. The percentage of reduction, if any, under this subdivision shall be the percentage referred to in section 3302(c)(3)(B) which is certified by the Secretary of Labor pursuant to section 3302(d)(7).

(iii) Additional reduction if a balance of advances exists after fifth or any succeeding consecutive January 1. If the credit reduction described in subdivision (i) of this subparagraph is made for the fifth or any succeeding taxable year, the total credits otherwise allowable under section 3302 to a taxpayer subject to the unemployment compensation law of the State shall be further reduced for the taxable year unless the average employer contribution rate (see section 3302(d)(4)) for the State for the calendar year preceding such taxable year equals or exceeds the 5-year benefit cost rate (see section 3302(d)(5)) applicable to the State for the taxable year or 2.7 percent, whichever is higher. The percentage of reduction, if any, under this subdivision for a taxable year shall be the percentage referred to in section 3302(c)(3)(C) which is certified by the Secretary of Labor pursuant to section 3302(d)(7).

(3) Payments under the Temporary Unemployment Compensation Act of 1958. If any amount of temporary unemployment compensation was paid in a State under the Temporary Unemployment Compensation Act of 1958, the total credits otherwise allowable under section 3302 to a taxpayer with respect to wages attributable to the State for the taxable year beginning January 1, 1963, and for each taxable year thereafter, shall be reduced unless prior to November 10 of the taxable year—

(i) There have been restored to the Treasury the amounts of temporary unemployment compensation paid in the State (except amounts paid to individuals who exhausted their unemployment compensation under title XV of the Social Security Act and title IV of the Veterans' Readjustment Assistance Act of 1952 prior to their making their first claims under the Temporary Unemployment Compensation Act of 1958), the amount of costs incurred in the administration of the Temporary Unemployment Compensation Act of 1958; with respect to the State, and the amount estimated by the Secretary of Labor as the State's proportionate share of other costs incurred in the administration of such Act, or

(ii) The State restores to the general fund of the Treasury the amount certified by the Secretary of Labor pursuant to section 104 of the Temporary Unemployment Compensation Act of 1958, and designates such restoration as being made for purposes of the last sentence of such section.

The credit reduction for a taxable year shall be a percentage of the wages paid by the taxpayer during that year which are attributable to the State. The percentage for the taxable year 1963 is 0.15 percent (that is, 5 percent of the Federal tax, computed as if imposed at the rate of 3 percent). The percentage for any succeeding year is 0.3 percent (that is, 10 percent of the Federal tax, computed as if imposed at the rate of 3 percent).

(4) Example. The cumulative effect of the credit reductions described in this paragraph may be illustrated by the following example:

Example. Advances to the unemployment account of State X were made in 1957 and in 1961 under title XII of the Social Security Act. Payments under the Temporary Unemployment Compensation Act of 1958 were made in State X in 1958. No portion of the advances or payments is returned before November 10, 1964. As a consequence:

(a) The credit reduction applicable under subparagraph (1) of this paragraph is made for 1964 at the rate of 0.15 percent;

(b) The credit reduction described in subparagraph (2) of this paragraph has been made for 1963 (the second successive year after 1961) at the rate of 0.3 percent. The rate of credit reduction under subparagraph (2) for 1964 is 1 percent (the aggregate of 0.6 percent under section 3302(c)(3)(A) and 0.4 percent (assumed for purposes of this example to be the percentage referred to in section 3302(c)(3)(B) which is certified by the Secretary of Labor); and

(c) The credit reduction described in subparagraph (3) of this paragraph has been made for 1963 at the rate of 0.15 percent. The rate of credit reduction for 1964 is 0.3 percent.

The cumulative rate of credit reduction applicable for 1964 to wages attributable to State X is 1.45 percent, representing the aggregate of the percentage reductions applicable under subparagraphs (1), (2), and (3) of this paragraph (0.15 percent, 1 percent, and 0.3 percent, respectively). In 1964 Employer A paid wages of $100,000, all of which are subject to the unemployment compensation law of State X. The credit which would be allowable (under section 3302(a), (b), and (c)(1)) if there were no credit reduction is $2,700. Employer A's tax is computed as follows for 1964:

Total taxable wages (attributable to State X)		$100,000
Gross Federal tax (3.1 percent of wages)		3,100
Less credit:		
Gross credit	$2,700	
Credit reduction (1.45 percent of wages)	1,450	
Net credit		1,250
Amount of Federal Tax due		$ 1,850

T.D. 6199, 9/4/56, amend T.D. 6516, 12/19/60, T.D. 6658, 6/26/63, T.D. 6708, 3/9/64.

§ 31.3302(d)-1 Definitions and special rules relating to limit on total credits.

(a) Rate of tax deemed to be 3 percent. In applying the provisions of section 3302(c) relating to the limitation on total credits, and to reductions of credits otherwise allowable, the tax imposed by section 3301 shall be computed at the rate of 3 percent in lieu of any other rate prescribed in section 3301 (see § 31.3301-3).

(b) Wages attributable to a particular State. For purposes of section 3302(c)(2) or (3), wages are attributable to a particular State if they are subject to the unemployment compensation law of the State. If wages are not subject to the unemployment compensation law of any State, the determination as to whether such wages, or any portion thereof, are attributable to the particular State with respect to which the reduction in total credits is imposed shall be made in accordance with rules prescribed by the Commissioner.

(c) Employment Security Act of 1960. The Employment Security Act of 1960, referred to in section 3302(c)(2), means title V of the Social Security Amendments of 1960.

T.D. 6658, 6/26/63.

§ 31.3302(e)-1 Successor employers.

(a) In general. In addition to the credits against the tax allowable under section 3302(a) and (b) for any taxable year after 1960, the taxpayer may be entitled to an amount of credit under section 3302(e). Credit under section 3302(e) is provided in the case of a taxpayer who (1) acquires substantially all of the property used in a trade or business, or in a separate unit of a trade or business, of another person (referred to in this section as a predecessor) who is not an employer (see § 31.3306(a)-1) for the calendar year in which the acquisition takes place, and (2) immediately after the acquisition employs in his trade or business one or more individuals who immediately prior to the acquisition were employed in the trade or business of the predecessor.

(b) Method of computing credit under section 3302(e). *(1)* Except as provided in subparagraph (2) of this paragraph, the amount of credit to which the taxpayer may be entitled under section 3302(e) is the amount of credit to which the predecessor would be entitled under section 3302(a), (b), and (e), without regard to the limits in section 3302(c), if the predecessor were an employer.

(2) If, during the calendar year in which the acquisition takes place, the predecessor pays remuneration, subject to contributions under the unemployment compensation law of a State, to any employee other than the individuals referred to in paragraph (a) of this section, the taxpayer will be entitled only to a portion of the amount of credit described in subparagraph (1) of this paragraph. The portion is determined by multiplying such amount by a fraction. The numerator of the fraction is the total amount of remuneration, subject to such contributions, paid by the predecessor during such year to the individuals referred to in paragraph (a) of this section. The denominator of the fraction is the total amount of remuneration, subject to such contributions, paid by the predecessor during such year to all employees for services performed by them in the trade or business, or unit thereof, acquired by the taxpayer.

Example. In April 1961 the X Partnership terminated after selling all of its property to the Y Corporation. During 1961, the X Partnership paid its employees and former employees a total of $1,000,000 as remuneration subject to contributions under the employment compensation law of a State. (Note that the X Partnership did not qualify as an employer for 1961 for purposes of the Federal unemployment tax, because it had employees during less than 20 weeks in 1961.) When the Y Corporation acquired the property it concurrently employed all individuals who were then in the employ of the X Partnership. Assume that the X partnership, if it had qualified as an employer for 1961, would have been entitled to a total credit against the Federal tax of $30,000 under section 3302(a) and (b), without regard to the limits in section 3302(c). Of the $1,000,000 remuneration paid by the X Partnership in 1961, one-fifth (or $200,000) was paid to individuals who were employed by the Y Corporation at the time it acquired the property of the X Partnership. Under section 3302(e), therefore, the Y Corporation is entitled to credit of $6,000, which is one-fifth of the credit ($30,000) which would have been available to the X Partnership.

(3) The aggregate amount of credit allowable to the taxpayer under section 3302(a), (b), and (e) is subject to the limits in section 3302(c).

(c) Proof of credit under section 3302(e). Credit under section 3302(e) shall not be allowed against the tax for any taxable year unless there is submitted to the district director (1) such information or proof as may be called for in the return on which the credit is reported, or in the instructions relating to the return, and (2) such other or additional proof as the Commissioner or the district director may deem necessary to establish the right to the credit provided for under section 3302(e).

(d) Cross-references. See paragraph (b) of § 31.3306(b)(1)-1 for examples of the acquisition of property used in a trade or business, or in a separate unit thereof.

T.D. 6658, 6/26/63.

§ 31.3306(a)-1 Who are employers.

(a) Definition. *(1) For calendar years 1956 through 1969, inclusive.* Every person who employs 4 or more employees in employment (within the meaning of section 3306(c) and (d)) on a total of 20 or more calendar days during any calendar year after 1955 and before 1970, each such day being in a different calendar week, is with respect to such year an employer subject to the tax.

(1a) For 1970 and subsequent calendar years. Every person who employs 4 or more employees in employment (within the meaning of section 3306(c) and (d)) on a total of

20 or more calendar days during a calendar year after 1969, or during the calendar year immediately preceding such a calendar year, each such day being in a different calendar week, is with respect to such year an employer subject to the tax.

(2) For calendar year 1955. Every person who employs 8 or more employees in employment (within the meaning of section 3306(c) and (d)) on a total of 20 or more calendar days during the calendar year 1955, each such day being in a different calendar week, is with respect to such year an employer subject to the tax.

(3) General agents of the Secretary of Commerce. For provisions relating to the circumstances under which an employee who performs services as an officer or member of the crew of an American vessel (i) which is owned by or bareboat chartered to the United States and (ii) whose business is conducted by a general agent of the Secretary of Commerce shall be deemed to be performing services for such general agent rather than for the United States, see § 31.3306(n)-1.

(b) The several weeks in each of which occurs a day on which the prescribed number of employees are employed need not be consecutive weeks. It is not necessary that the employees so employed be the same individuals; they may be different individuals on each day. Neither is it necessary that the prescribed number of employees be employed at the same moment of time or for any particular length of time or on any particular basis of compensation. It is sufficient if the total number of employees employed during the 24 hours of a calendar day is 4 or more (8 or more for the calendar year 1955).

(c) In determining whether a person employs a sufficient number of employees to be an employer subject to the tax, each employee is counted with respect to services which constitute employment as defined in section 3306(c) (see § 31.3306(c)-2). No employee is counted with respect to services which do not constitute employment as so defined. See, however, paragraph (d) of this section.

(d) The provisions of paragraph (c) of this section are subject to the provisions of section 3306(d), relating to services which do not constitute employment but which are deemed to be employment, and relating to services which constitute employment but which are deemed not to be employment (see § 31.3306(d)-1). For example, if the services of an employee during a pay period are deemed to be employment under section 3306(d), even though a portion thereof does not constitute employment under section 3306(c), the employee is counted with respect to all services during the pay period. On the other hand, if the services of an employee during a pay period are deemed not to be employment, even though a portion thereof constitutes employment, the employee is not counted with respect to any services during the pay period.

T.D. 6199, 9/4/56, amend T.D. 6516, 12/20/60, T.D. 7037, 4/27/70.

§ 31.3306(b)-1 Wages.

(a) Applicable law and regulations. *(1) Remuneration paid after 1954.* Whether remuneration paid after 1954 for employment performed after 1938 constitutes wages is determined under section 3306(b). Accordingly, only remuneration paid after 1954 for employment performed after 1938 is covered by this section of the regulations and by the sections relating to the statutory exclusions from wages (§§ 31.3306(b)(1)-1 to 31.3306(b)(10)-1).

(2) Remuneration paid after 1939 and before 1955. Whether remuneration paid after 1939 and before 1955 for employment performed after 1938 constitutes wages shall be determined in accordance with the applicable provisions of law and of 26 CFR (1939) Part 403 (Regulations 107).

(3) Remuneration paid in 1939. Whether remuneration paid in 1939 for employment performed after 1938 constitutes wages shall be determined in accordance with the applicable provisions of law and of 26 CFR (1939) Part 400 (Regulations 90).

(b) The term "wages" means all remuneration for employment unless specifically excepted under section 3306(b) (see §§ 31.3306(b)(1)-1 to 31.3306(b)(10)-1, inclusive) or paragraph (j) of this section.

(c) The name by which the remuneration for employment is designated is immaterial. Thus, salaries, fees, bonuses, and commissions are wages if paid as compensation for employment.

(d) The basis upon which the remuneration is paid is immaterial in determining whether the remuneration constitutes wages. Thus, it may be paid on the basis of piecework or a percentage of profits; and it may be paid hourly, daily, weekly, monthly, or annually.

(e) Except in the case of remuneration paid for services not in the course of the employer's trade or business (see § 31.3306(b)(7)-1), the medium in which the remuneration is paid is also immaterial. It may be paid in cash or in something other than cash, as for example, goods, lodging, food, or clothing. Remuneration paid in items other than cash shall be computed on the basis of the fair value of such items at the time of payments.

(f) Ordinarily, facilities or privileges (such as entertainment, medical services, or so-called "courtesy" discounts on purchases), furnished or offered by an employer to his employees generally, are not considered as remuneration for employment if such facilities or privileges are of relatively small value and are offered or furnished by the employer merely as a means of promoting the health, good will, contentment, or efficiency of his employees. The term "facilities or privileges", however, does not ordinarily include the value of meals or lodging furnished, for example, to restaurant or hotel employees, or to seamen or other employees aboard vessels, since generally these items constitute an appreciable part of the total remuneration of such employees.

(g) Amounts of so-called "vacation allowances" paid to an employee constitute wages. Thus, the salary of an employee on vacation, paid notwithstanding his absence from work, constitutes wages.

(h) Amounts paid specifically—either as advances or reimbursements—for traveling or other bona fide ordinary and necessary expenses incurred or reasonably expected to be incurred in the business of the employer are not wages. Traveling and other reimbursed expenses must be identified either by making a separate payment or by specifically indicating the separate amounts where both wages and expense allowances are combined in a single payment. For amounts that are received by an employee on or after July 1, 1990, with respect to expenses paid or incurred on or after July 1, 1990, see § 31.3306(b)-2.

(i) Remuneration paid by an employer to an individual for employment, unless such remuneration is specifically excepted under section 3306(b), constitutes wages even though at the time paid the individual is no longer an employee.

Example. A is employed by B, an employer, during the month of June 1955 in employment and is entitled to receive remuneration of $100 for the services performed for B during the month. A leaves the employ of B at the close of business on June 30, 1955. On July 15, 1955 (when A is no longer an employee of B), B pays A the remuneration of $100 which was earned for the services performed in June. The $100 is wages, and the tax is payable with respect thereto.

(j) In addition to the exclusions specified in §§ 31.3306(b)(1)-1 to 31.3306(b)(10)-1, inclusive, the following types of payments are excluded from wages:

(1) Remuneration for services which do not constitute employment under section 3306(c).

(2) Remuneration for services which are deemed not to be employment under section 3306(d) (§ 31.3306(d)-1).

(3) Tips or gratuities paid directly to an employee by a customer of an employer, and not accounted for by the employee to the employer.

(k) For provisions relating to the treatment of deductions from remuneration as payments of remuneration, see § 31.3307-1.

(l) Split-dollar life insurance arrangements. Except as otherwise provided under section 3306(r), see §§ 1.61-22 and 1.7872-15 of this chapter for rules relating to the treatment of split-dollar life insurance arrangements.

T.D. 6199, 9/4/56, amend T.D. 6516, 12/19/60, T.D. 6658, 6/26/63, T.D. 7375, 9/11/75, T.D. 8276, 12/7/89, T.D. 8324, 12/14/90, T.D. 9092, 9/11/2003.

§ 31.3306(b)-1T Question and answer relating to the definition of wages in section 3306(b) (temporary).

The following question and answer relates to the definition of wages in section 3306(b) of the Internal Revenue Code of 1954, as amended by section 531(d)(3) of the Tax Reform Act of 1984 (98 Stat. 885):

Q-1. Are fringe benefits included in the definition of wages under section 3306(b)?

A-1. Yes, unless specifically excluded from the definition of "wages" pursuant to section 3306(b)(1) through (16). For example, a fringe benefit provided to or on behalf of an employee is excluded from the definition of "wages" if at the time such benefit is provided it is reasonable to believe that the employee will be able to exclude such benefit from income under section 117 or 132.

T.D. 8004, 1/2/85.

§ 31.3306(b)-2 Reimbursement and other expense allowance amounts.

(a) When excluded from wages. If a reimbursement or other expense allowance arrangement meets the requirements of section 62(c) of the Code and § 1.62-2 and the expenses are substantiated within a reasonable period of time, payments made under the arrangement that do not exceed the substantiated expenses are treated as paid under an accountable plan and are not wages. In addition, if both wages and the reimbursement or other expense allowance are combined in a single payment, the reimbursement or other expense allowance must be identified either by making a separate payment or by specifically identifying the amount of the reimbursement or other expense allowance.

(b) When included in wages. *(1) Accountable plans.* (i) General rule. Except as provided in paragraph (b)(1)(ii) of this section, if a reimbursement or other expense allowance arrangement satisfied the requirements of section 62(c) and § 1.62-2, but the expenses are not substantiated within a reasonable period of time or amounts in excess of the substantiated expenses are not returned within a reasonable period of time, the amount paid under the arrangement in excess of the substantiated expenses is treated as paid under a nonaccountable plan, is included in wages, and is subject to withholding and payment of employment taxes no later than the first payroll period following the end of the reasonable period.

(ii) Per diem or mileage allowances. If a reimbursement or other expense allowance arrangement providing a per diem or mileage allowance satisfies the requirements of section 62(c) and § 1.62-2, but the allowance is paid at a rate for each day or mile of travel that exceeds the amount of the employee's expenses deemed substantiated for a day or mile of travel, the excess portion is treated as paid under a nonaccountable plan and is included in wages. In the case of a per diem or mileage allowance paid as a reimbursement, the excess portion is subject to withholding and payment of employment taxes when paid. In the case of a per diem or mileage allowance paid as an advance, the excess portion is subject to withholding and payment of employment taxes no later than the first payroll period following the payroll period in which the expenses with respect to which the advance was paid (i.e., the days or miles of travel) are substantiated. The Commissioner may, in his discretion, prescribe special rules in pronouncements of general applicability regarding the timing of withholding and payment of employment taxes on per diem and mileage allowances.

(2) Nonaccountable plans. If a reimbursement or other expense allowance arrangement does not satisfy the requirements of section 62(c) and § 1.62-2 (e.g., the arrangement does not require expenses to be substantiated or require amounts in excess of the substantiated expenses to be returned), all amounts paid under the arrangement are treated as paid under a nonaccountable plan, are included in wages, and are subject to withholding and payment of employment taxes when paid.

(c) Effective dates. This section generally applies to payments made under reimbursement or other expense allowance arrangements received by an employee on or after July 1, 1990, with respect to expenses paid or incurred on or after July 1, 1990. Paragraph (b)(1)(ii) of this section applies to payments made under reimbursement or other expense allowance arrangements received by an employee on or after January 1, 1991, with respect to expenses paid or incurred on or after January 1, 1991.

T.D. 8276, 12/7/89, amend T.D. 8324, 12/14/90.

§ 31.3306(b)(1)-1 $3,000 limitation.

(a) In general. *(1)* the term "wages" does not include that part of the remuneration paid within any calendar year by an employer to an employee which exceeds the first $3,000 of remuneration (exclusive of remuneration excepted from wages in accordance with paragraph (j) of § 31.3306(b)-1 or §§ 31.3306(b)(2)-1 to 31.3306(b)(8)-1, inclusive), paid within such calendar year by such employer to such employee for employment performed for him at any time after 1938.

(2) The $3,000 limitation applies only if the remuneration paid during any one calendar year by an employer to the same employee for employment performed after 1938 exceeds $3,000. The limitation in such case relates to the amount of remuneration paid during any one calendar year for employment after 1938 and not to the amount of remu-

neration for employment performed in any one calendar year.

Example. Employer B, in 1955, pays employee A $2,500 on account of $3,000 due him for employment performed in 1955. In 1956 employer B pays employee A the balance of $500 due him for employment performed in the prior year (1955), and thereafter in 1956 also pays A $3,000 for employment performed in 1956. The $2,500 paid in 1955 is subject to tax in 1955. The balance of $500 paid in 1956 for employment during 1955 is subject to tax in 1956, as is also the first $2,500 paid of the $3,000 for employment during 1956 (this $500 for 1955 employment added to the first $2,500 paid for 1956 employment constitutes the maximum wages subject to the tax which could be paid in 1956 by B to A). The final $500 paid by B to A in 1956 is not included as wages and is not subject to the tax.

(3) If during a calendar year an employee is paid remuneration by more than one employer, the limitation of wages to the first $3,000 of remuneration paid applies, not to the aggregate remuneration paid by all employers with respect to employment performed after 1938, but instead to the remuneration paid during such calendar year by each employer with respect to employment performed after 1938. In such case the first $3,000 paid during the calendar year by each employer constitutes wages and is subject to the tax. In connection with the application of the $3,000 limitation, see also paragraph (b) of this section relating to the circumstances under which wages paid by a predecessor employer are deemed to be paid by his successor. In connection with the annual wage limitation in the case of remuneration after December 31, 1978 from two or more related corporations that compensate an employee through a common paymaster, see § 31.3306(p)-1.

Example (1). During 1955 employer D pays to employee C a salary of $600 a month for employment performed for D during the first seven months of 1955, or total remuneration of $4,200. At the end of the fifth month C has been paid $3,000 by employer D, and only that part of his total remuneration from D constitutes wages subject to the tax. The $600 paid to employee C by employer D in the sixth month, and the like amount paid in the seventh month, are not included as wages and are not subject to the tax. At the end of the seventh month C leaves the employ of D and enters the employ of E. Employer E pays to C remuneration of $600 a month in each of the remaining five months of 1955, or total remuneration of $3,000. The entire $3,000 paid by E to employee C constitutes wages and is subject to the tax. Thus, the first $3,000 paid by employer D and the entire $3,000 paid by employer E constitute wages.

Example (2). During the calendar year 1955 F is simultaneously an officer (an employee) of the X Corporation, the Y Corporation, and the Z Corporation, each such corporation being an employer for such year. During such year F is paid a salary of $3,000 by each Corporation. Each $3,000 paid to F by each of the corporations, X, Y, and Z (whether or not such corporations are related), constitutes wages and is subject to the tax.

(b) Wages paid by predecessor attributed to successor. *(1)* If an employer (hereinafter referred to as a successor) during any calendar year acquires substantially all the property used in a trade or business of another employer (hereinafter referred to as a predecessor), or used in a separate unit of a trade or business of a predecessor, and if immediately after the acquisition the successor employs in his trade or business an individual who immediately prior to the acquisition was employed in the trade or business of such predecessor, then, for purposes of the application of the $3,000 limitation set forth in paragraph (a) of this section, any remuneration (exclusive of remuneration excepted from wages in accordance with paragraph (j) of § 31.3306(b)-1 or §§ 31.3306(b)(2)-1 to 31.3306(b)(8)-1, inclusive), with respect to employment paid (or considered under this provision as having been paid to such individual by such predecessor during such calendar year and prior to such acquisition shall be considered as having been paid by such successor. Wages paid by a predecessor shall not be considered as having been paid by the successor unless both the predecessor and the successor are employers as defined in section 3306(a) for the calendar year in which the acquisition occurs (see § 31.3306(a)-1, relating to who are employers).

(2) The wages paid, or considered as having been paid, by a predecessor to an employee shall, for purposes of the $3,000 limitation, be treated as having been paid to such employee by a successor, if:

(i) The successor during a calendar year acquired substantially all the property used in a trade or business, or used in a separate unit of a trade or business, of the predecessor;

(ii) Such employee was employed in the trade or business of the predecessor immediately prior to the acquisition and is employed by the successor in his trade or business immediately after the acquisition; and

(iii) Such wages were paid during the calendar year in which the acquisition occurred and prior to such acquisition.

(3) The method of acquisition by an employer of the property of another employer is immaterial. The acquisition may occur as a consequence of the incorporation of a business by a sole proprietor of a partnership, the continuance without interruption of the business of a previously existing partnership by a new partnership or by a sole proprietor, or a purchase or any other transaction whereby substantially all the property used in a trade or business, or used in a separate unit of a trade or business, of one employer is acquired by another employer.

(4) Substantially all the property used in a separate unit of a trade or business may consist of substantially all the property used in the performance of an essential operation of the trade or business, or it may consist of substantially all the property used in a relatively self-sustaining entity which forms a part of the trade or business.

Example (1). The M Corporation which is engaged in the manufacture of automobiles, including the manufacture of automobile engines, discontinues the manufacture of the engines and transfers all the property used in such manufacturing operations to the N Company. The N Company is considered to have acquired a separate unit of the trade or business of the M Corporation, namely, its engine manufacturing unit.

Example (2). The R Corporation which is engaged in the operation of a chain of grocery stores transfers one of such stores to the S Company. The S Company is considered to have acquired a separate unit of the trade or business of the R Corporation.

(5) A successor may receive credit for wages paid to an employee by a predecessor only if immediately prior to the acquisition the employee was employed by the predecessor in his trade or business which was acquired by the successor and if immediately after the acquisition such employee is employed by the successor in his trade or business (whether or not in the same trade or business in which the acquired property is used). If the acquisition involves only a separate

unit of a trade or business of the predecessor, the employee need not have been employed by the predecessor in that unit provided he was employed in the trade or business of which the acquired unit was a part.

Example. The Y Corporation in 1955 acquires all the property of the X Manufacturing Company and immediately after the acquisition employs in its trade or business employee A, who, immediately prior to the acquisition, was employed by the X Company. Both the Y Corporation and the X Company are employers, as defined in the Act, for the calendar year 1955. The X Company has in 1955 (the calendar year in which the acquisition occurs) and prior to the acquisition paid $2,000 of wages to A. The Y Corporation in 1955 pays to A remuneration with respect to employment of $2,000. Only $1,000 of such remuneration is considered to be wages. For purposes of the $3,000 limitation, the Y Corporation is credited with the $2,000 paid to A by the X Company. If, in the same calendar year, the property is acquired from the Y Corporation by the Z Company, an employer for such year, and A immediately after the acquisition is employed by the Z Company in its trade or business, no part of the remuneration paid to A by the Z Company in the year of the acquisition will be considered to be wages. The Z Company will be credited with the remuneration paid to A by the Y Corporation and also with the wages paid to A by the X Company (considered for purposes of the application of the $3,000 limitation as having also been paid by the Y Corporation).

T.D. 6199, 9/4/56, amend T.D. 6516, 12/19/60, T.D. 6658, 6/26/63, T.D. 7660, 12/18/79.

§ 31.3306(b)(2)-1 Payments under employers' plans on account of retirement, sickness or accident disability, medical or hospitalization expenses, or death.

(a) The term "wages" does not include the amount of any payment (including any amount paid by an employer for insurance or annuities, or into a fund, to provide for any such payment) made to, or on behalf of, an employee or any of his dependents under a plan or system established by an employer which makes provision for his employees generally (or for his employees generally and their dependents) or for a class or classes of his employees (or for a class or classes of his employees and their dependents), on account of:

(1) An employee's retirement,

(2) Sickness or accident disability of an employee or any of his dependents,

(3) Medical or hospitalization expenses in connection with sickness or accident disability of an employee or any of his dependents, or

(4) Death of an employee or any of his dependents.

(b) The plan or system established by an employer need not provide for payments on account of all of the specified items, but such plan or system may provide for any one or more of such items. Payments for any one or more of such items under a plan or system established by an employer solely for the dependents of his employees are not within this exclusion from wages.

(c) Dependents of an employee include the employee's husband or wife, children, and any other members of the employee's immediate family.

(d) It is immaterial for purposes of this exclusion whether the amount or possibility of such benefit payments is taken into consideration in fixing the amount of an employee's remuneration or whether such payments are required, expressly or impliedly, by the contract of service.

T.D. 6199, 9/4/56, amend T.D. 6516, 12/19/60.

§ 31.3306(b)(3)-1 Retirement payments.

The term "wages" does not include any payment made by an employer to an employee (including any amount paid by an employer for insurance or annuities, or into a fund, to provide for any such payment) on account of the employee's retirement. Thus payments made to an employee on account of his retirement are excluded from wages under this exception even though not made under a plan or system.

T.D. 6199, 9/4/56, amend T.D. 6516, 12/19/60.

§ 31.3306(b)(4)-1 Payments on account of sickness or accident disability, or medical or hospitalization expenses.

The term "wages" does not include any payment made by an employer to, or on behalf of, an employee on account of the employee's sickness or accident disability or the medical or hospitalization expenses in connection with the employee's sickness or accident disability, if such payment is made after the expiration of 6 calendar months following the last calendar month in which such employee worked for such employer. Such payments are excluded from wages under this exception even though not made under a plan or system. If the employee does not actually perform services for the employer during the requisite period, the existence of the employer-employee relationship during that period is immaterial.

T.D. 6199, 9/4/56, amend T.D. 6516, 12/19/60.

§ 31.3306(b)(5)-1 Payments from or to certain tax-exempt trusts, or under or to certain annuity plans or bond purchase plans.

(a) Payments from or to certain tax-exempt trusts. The term "wages" does not include any payment made—

(1) By an employer, on behalf of an employee or his beneficiary, into a trust, or

(2) To, or on behalf of an employee or his beneficiary from a trust, if at the time of such payment the trust is exempt from tax under section 501(a) as an organization described in section 401(a). A payment made to an employee of such a trust for services rendered as an employee of the trust and not as a beneficiary thereof is not within this exclusion from wages.

(b) Payments under or to certain annuity plans. *(1)* The term "wages" does not include any payment made after December 31, 1962—

(i) By an employer, on behalf of an employee or his beneficiary, into an annuity plan, or

(ii) To, or on behalf of, an employee or his beneficiary under an annuity plan, if at the time of such payment the annuity plan is a plan described in section 403(a).

(2) The term "wages" does not include any payment made before January 1, 1963—

(i) By an employer, on behalf of an employee or his beneficiary, into an annuity plan, or

(ii) To, or on behalf of, an employee or his beneficiary under an annuity plan, if at the time of such payment the annuity plan meets the requirements of section 401(a)(3), (4), (5), and (6).

(c) Payments under or to certain bond purchase plans. The term "wages" does not include any payment made after December 31, 1962—

(1) By an employer, on behalf of an employee or his beneficiary, into a bond purchase plan, or

(2) To, or on behalf of, an employee or his beneficiary under a bond purchase plan, if at the time of such payment the plan is a qualified bond purchase plan described in section 405(a).

T.D. 6199, 9/4/56, amend T.D. 6516, 12/19/60, T.D. 6658, 6/26/63.

PAR. 15. Section 31.3306(b)(5)-1 is amended by adding at the end thereof a new paragraph (d). This new paragraph reads as follows:

Proposed § 31.3306(b)(5)-1 Payments from or to certain tax-exempt trusts, or under or to certain annuity plans or bond purchase plans. [*For Preamble, see ¶ 150,703*]

* * * * *

(d) Payments to a simplified employee pension. The term "wages" does not include any payment made after December 31, 1978 by an employer on behalf of an employee to a simplified employee pension described in section 408(k) if at the time of the payment it is reasonable to believe that the employee will be entitled to a deduction under section 219 for such payment.

§ 31.3306(b)(6)-1 Payment by an employer of employee tax under section 3101 or employee contributions under a State law.

The term "wages" does not include any payment by an employer (without deduction from the remuneration of, or other reimbursement from, the employee) of either (a) the employee tax imposed by section 3101 or the corresponding section of prior law, or (b) any payment required from an employee under a State unemployment compensation law.

T.D. 6199, 9/4/56, amend T.D. 6516, 12/19/60.

§ 31.3306(b)(7)-1 Payments other than in cash for service not in the course of employer's trade or business.

The term "wages" does not include remuneration paid in any medium other than cash for service not in the course of the employer's trade or business. Cash remuneration includes checks and other monetary media of exchange. Remuneration paid in any medium other than cash, such as lodging, food, or other goods or commodities, for service not in the course of the employer's trade or business does not constitute wages. Remuneration paid in any medium other than cash for other types of services does not come within this exclusion from wages. For provisions relating to the circumstances under which service not in the course of the employer's trade or business does not constitute employment, see § 31.3306(c)(3)-1.

T.D. 6199, 9/4/56, amend T.D. 6516, 12/19/60.

§ 31.3306(b)(8)-1 Payments to employees for non-work periods.

The term "wages" does not include any payment (other than vacation or sick pay) made by an employer to an employee after the calendar month in which the employee attains age 65, if—

(a) Such employee does no work (other than being subject to call for the performance of work) for such employer in the period for which such payment is made; and

(b) The employer-employee relationship exists between the employer and employee throughout the period for which such payment is made.

Vacation or sick pay is not within this exclusion from wages. If the employee does any work for the employer in the period for which the payment is made, no remuneration paid by such employer to such employee with respect to such period is within this exclusion from wages. For example, if employee A, who attained the age of 65 in January 1955, is employed by the X Company on a stand-by basis and is paid $200 by the X Company for being subject to call during the month of February 1955 and an additional $25 for work performed for the X Company on one day in February 1955, then none of the $225 is excluded from wages under this exception.

T.D. 6199, 9/4/56, amend T.D. 6516, 12/19/60, T.D. 6708, 3/9/64.

§ 31.3306(b)(9)-1 Moving expenses.

(a) The term "wages" does not include remuneration paid on or after November 1, 1964, to or on behalf of an employee, either as an advance or a reimbursement, specifically for moving expenses incurred or expected to be incurred, if (and to the extent that) at the time of payment it is reasonable to believe that a corresponding deduction is or will be allowable to the employee under section 217. The reasonable belief contemplated by the statute may be based upon any evidence reasonably sufficient to induce such belief, even though such evidence may be insufficient upon closer examination by the district director or the courts finally to establish that a deduction is allowable under section 217. The reasonable belief shall be based upon the application of section 217 and the regulations thereunder in Part 1 of this chapter (Income Tax Regulations). When used in this section, the term "moving expenses" has the same meaning as when used in section 217 and the regulations thereunder.

(b) Except as otherwise provided in paragraph (a) of this section, or in a numbered paragraph of section 3306(b), amounts paid to or on behalf of an employee for moving expenses are wages for purposes of section 3306(b).

T.D. 7375, 9/11/75.

§ 31.3306(b)(10)-1 Payments under certain employers' plans after retirement, disability, or death.

(a) In general. The term "wages" does not include the amount of any payment or series of payments made after January 2, 1968, by an employer to, or on behalf of, an employee or any of his dependents under a plan established by the employer which makes provisions for his employees generally (or for his employees generally and their dependents) or for a class or classes of his employees (or for a class or classes of his employees and their dependents), which is paid or commences to be paid upon or within a reasonable time after the termination of an employee's employment relationship because of the employee's—

(1) Death,

(2) Retirement for disability, or

(3) Retirement after attaining an age specified in the plan established by the employer or in a pension plan of the employer as the age at which a person in the employee's circumstances is eligible for retirement.

A payment or series of payments made under the circumstances described in the preceding sentence is excluded from "wages" even if made pursuant to an incentive compensation plan which also provides for the making of other types of payments. However, any payment or series of payments which would have been paid if the employee's relationship had not been terminated is not excluded from "wages" under this section and section 3306(b)(10). For example, lump-sum payments for unused vacation time or a final paycheck received after retirement are payments which the employee would have received whether or not he retired and therefore are not excluded from "wages." Further, if any payment is made upon or after termination of employment for any reason other than those set out in subparagraphs (1), (2), and (3) of this paragraph such payment is not excludable from "wages" by this section. For example, if a pension plan provides for retirement upon disability, completion of 30 years of service, or attainment of age 65, and if an employee who is not disabled retires at age 61 after 30 years of service, none of the retirement payments made to the employee under the pension plan (including any made after he is 65) is excludable from "wages" under this section. However, if the pension plan had conditioned retirement after 30 years of service upon attainment of age 60, all of the retirement payments would have been excludable.

(b) Plan. The plan or system established by an employer need not provide for payments because of termination of employment for all the reasons set out in subparagraphs (1), (2), and (3) of paragraph (a), but such plan or system may provide for payments because of termination for any one or more of such reasons. Payments because of termination of employment for any one or more of such reasons under a plan or system established by an employer solely for the dependents of his employees are not within this exclusion from wages.

(c) Dependents. Dependents of an employee include the employee's husband or wife, children, and any other members of the employee's immediate family.

(d) Benefit payments. It is immaterial for purposes of this exclusion whether the amount or possibility of such benefit payments is paid on account of services rendered or taken into consideration in fixing the amount of an employee's remuneration or whether such payments are required expressly or impliedly, by the contract of service.

(e) Example. The application of this section may be illustrated by the following example:

Example. A, an employee, receives a salary of $1,500 a month, payable on the 5th day of the month following the month for which the salary is earned. A's employer has established an incentive compensation plan for a class of his employees, including A, providing for the payment of deferred compensation on termination of employment, including termination upon an employee's death, retirement at age 65 (the retirement age specified in the plan), or retirement for disability. On March 1, 1973, A attains the age of 65 and retires. On March 5, 1973, A receives $5,500 from his employer of which $1,500 represents A's salary for services he performed in February 1973, and $4,000 represents incentive compensation paid under the employer's plan. The amount of $4,000 is excluded from "wages" under this section. The amount of $1,500 is not excluded from "wages" under this section.

T.D. 7374, 7/23/75.

§ 31.3306(b)(13)-1 Payments or benefits under a qualified educational assistance program.

The term "wages" does not include any payment made, or benefit furnished, to or for the benefit of an employee in a taxable year beginning after December 31, 1978, if at the time of such payment or furnishing it is reasonable to believe that the employee will be able to exclude such payment or benefit from income under section 127.

T.D. 7898, 7/5/83.

§ 31.3306(c)-1 Employment; services performed before 1955.

(a) Services performed after 1938 and before 1955 constitute employment under section 3306(c) if such services were employment under the law applicable to the period in which they were performed.

(b) The tax applies with respect to remuneration paid by an employer after 1954 for services performed after 1938 and before 1955, as well as for services performed after 1954, to the extent that the remuneration and services constitute wages and employment. See §§ 31.3306(b)-1 to 31.3306(b)(8)-1, inclusive, relating to wages.

(c) Determination of whether services performed after 1938 and before 1955 constitute employment shall be made in accordance with the provisions of law applicable to the period in which they were performed and of the regulations thereunder. The regulations applicable in determining whether services performed after 1938 and before 1955 constitute employment are as follows:

(1) Services performed in 1939—26 CFR (1939) Part 400 (Regulations 90).

(2) Services performed after 1939 and before 1955—26 CFR (1939) Part 403 (Regulations 107).

T.D. 6199, 9/4/56, amend T.D. 6516, 12/19/60.

§ 31.3306(c)-2 Employment; services performed after 1954.

(a) In general. Whether services performed after 1954 constitute employment is determined under subsections (c) and (n) of section 3306.

(b) Services performed within the United States. Services performed after 1954 within the United States (see § 31.3306(j)-1) by an employee for the person employing him, unless specifically excepted under section 3306(c), constitute employment. With respect to services performed within the United States, the place where the contract of service is entered into is immaterial. The citizenship or residence of the employee or of the person employing him also is immaterial except to the extent provided in any specific exception from employment. Thus, the employee and the person employing him may be citizens and residents of a foreign country and the contract of service may be entered into in a foreign country, and yet, if the employee under such contract performs services within the United States, there may be to that extent employment.

(c) Services performed outside the United States. *(1) In general.* Except as provided in subparagraph (2) of this paragraph, services performed outside the United States (see § 31.3306(j)-1) do not constitute employment.

(2) On or in connection with an American vessel or American aircraft. (i) This subparagraph relates to services performed after 1954 "on or in connection with" an American vessel, and to services performed after 1961 "on or in

connection with" an American aircraft to the extent that the remuneration for the latter services is paid after 1961. Such services performed outside the United States by an employee for the person employing him constitute employment if:

(a) The employee is also employed "on and in connection with" such vessel or aircraft when outside the United States; and

(b) The services are performed under a contract of service, between the employee and the person employing him, which is entered into within the United States, or during the performance of the contract under which the services are performed and while the employee is employed on the vessel or aircraft it touches at a port within the United States; and

(c) The services are not excepted under section 3306(c). (See particularly § 31.3306(c)(17)-1, relating to fishing.)

(ii) An employee performs services on and in connection with the vessel or aircraft if he performs services on the vessel or aircraft which are also in connection with the vessel or aircraft. Services performed on the vessel by employees as officers or members of the crew, or as employees of concessionaires, of the vessel, for example, are performed under such circumstances, since the services are also connected with the vessel. Similarly, services performed on the aircraft by employees as officers or members of the crew of the aircraft are performed on and in connection with such aircraft. Services may be performed on the vessel or aircraft, however, which have no connection with it, as in the case of services performed by an employee while on the vessel or aircraft merely as a passenger in the general sense. For example, the services of a buyer in the employ of a department store while he is a passenger on a vessel are not in connection with the vessel.

(iii) If services are performed by an employee "on and in connection with" an American vessel or American aircraft when outside the United States and the conditions in (b) and (c) of paragraph (c)(2)(i) of this section are met, then the services of that employee performed on or in connection with the vessel or aircraft constitute employment. The expression "on or in connection with" refers not only to services performed on the vessel or aircraft but also to services connected with the vessel or aircraft which are not actually performed on it (for example, shore services performed as officers or members of the crew, or as employees of concessionaires, of the vessel).

(iv) Services performed by a member of the crew or other employee whose contract of service is not entered into within the United States, and during the performance of which and while the employee is employed on the vessel or aircraft it does not touch at a port within the United States, do not constitute employment, notwithstanding that service performed by other members of the crew or other employees on or in connection with the vessel or aircraft may constitute employment.

(v) A vessel includes every description of watercraft, or other contrivance, used as a means of transportation on water. An aircraft includes every description of craft, or other contrivance, used as a means of transportation through the air. In the case of an aircraft, the term "port" means an airport. An airport means an area on land or water used regularly by aircraft for receiving or discharging passengers or cargo. For definitions of "American vessel" and "American aircraft", see § 31.3306(m)-1.

(vi) With respect to services performed outside the United States on or in connection with an American vessel or American aircraft, the citizenship or residence of the employee is immaterial, and the citizenship or residence of the employer is material only in case it has a bearing in determining whether a vessel is an American vessel.

T.D. 6199, 9/4/56, amend T.D. 6516, 12/19/60, T.D. 6658, 6/26/63.

§ 31.3306(c)-3 Employment; excepted services in general.

(a) Services performed by an employee for the person employing him do not constitute employment for purposes of the tax if they are specifically excepted from employment under any of the numbered paragraphs of section 3306(c). Services so excepted do not constitute employment for purposes of the tax even though they are performed within the United States, or are performed outside the United States on or in connection with an American vessel or American aircraft. If not otherwise provided in the regulations relating to the numbered paragraphs of section 3306(c), such regulations apply with respect to services performed after 1954.

(b) The exception attaches to the services performed by the employee and not to the employee as an individual; that is, the exception applies only to the services rendered by the employee in an excepted class.

Example. A is an individual who is employed part time by B to perform services which constitutes "agricultural labor" (see § 31.3306(k)-1). A is also employed by C part time to perform services as a grocery clerk in a store owned by him. While A's services which constitute "agricultural labor" are expected, the exception does not embrace the services performed by A as a grocery clerk in the employ of C and the latter services are not excepted from employment.

(c) For provisions relating to the circumstances under which services which are excepted are nevertheless deemed to be employment, and relating to the circumstances under which services which are not excepted are nevertheless deemed not to be employment, see § 31.3306(d)-1.

T.D. 6199, 9/4/56, amend T.D. 6516, 12/19/60, T.D. 6658, 6/26/63.

§ 31.3306(c)(1)-1 Agricultural labor.

Services performed by an employee for the person employing him which constitute "agricultural labor" as defined in section 3306(k) are excepted from employment. For provisions relating to the definition of the term "agricultural labor", see § 31.3306(k)-1.

T.D. 6199, 9/4/56, amend T.D. 6516, 12/19/60.

§ 31.3306(c)(2)-1 Domestic service.

(a) In a private home. *(1)* Services of a household nature performed by an employee in or about a private home of the person by whom he is employed are excepted from employment. A private home is a fixed place of abode of an individual or family. A separate and distinct dwelling unit maintained by an individual in an apartment house, hotel, or other similar establishment may constitute a private home. If a dwelling house is used primarily as a boarding or lodging house for the purpose of supplying board or lodging to the public as a business enterprise, it is not a private home and the services performed therein are not excepted.

(2) In general, services of a household nature in or about a private home include services performed by cooks, waiters, butlers, housekeepers, governesses, maids, valets, baby sitters, janitors, laundresses, furnacemen, caretakers, handymen, gardeners, footmen, grooms, and chauffeurs of automobile for family use.

(b) In a local college club or local chapter of a college fraternity or sorority. *(1)* Services of a household nature performed by an employee in or about the club rooms or house of a local college club or of a local chapter of a college fraternity or sorority by which he is employed are excepted from employment. A local college club or local chapter of a college fraternity or sorority does not include an alumni club or chapter. If the club rooms or house of a local college club or local chapter of a college fraternity or sorority is used primarily for the purpose of supplying board or lodging to students or the public as a business enterprise, the services performed therein are not within the exception.

(2) In general, services of a household nature in or about the club rooms or house of a local college club or local chapter of a college fraternity or sorority include services rendered by cooks, waiters, butlers, maids, janitors, laundresses, furnacemen, handymen, gardeners, housekeepers, and housemothers.

(c) Services not excepted. Services not of a household nature, such as services performed as a private secretary, tutor, or librarian, even though performed in the employer's private home or in a local college club or local chapter of a college fraternity or sorority, are not within the exception. Services of a household nature are not within the exception if performed in or about rooming or lodging houses, boarding houses, clubs (except local college clubs), hotels, hospitals, eleemosynary institutions, or commercial offices or establishments.

T.D. 6199, 9/4/56, amend T.D. 6516, 12/19/60.

§ 31.3306(c)(3)-1 Services not in the course of employer's trade or business.

(a) Services not in the course of the employer's trade or business performed by an employee for an employer in a calendar quarter are excepted from employment unless—

(1) The cash remuneration paid for such services performed by the employee for the employer in the calendar quarter is $50 or more; and

(2) Such employee is regularly employed in the calendar quarter by such employer to perform such services.

Unless the tests set forth in both paragraphs (a)(1) and (2) of this section are met, the services are excepted from employment.

(b) The term "services not in the course of the employer's trade or business" includes services that do not promote or advance the trade or business of the employer. Services performed for a corporation do not come within the exception.

(c) The test relating to cash remuneration of $50 or more is based on the remuneration earned during a calendar quarter rather than on the remuneration paid in a calendar quarter. However, for purposes of determining whether the test is met, it is also required that the remuneration be paid, although it is immaterial when the remuneration is paid. Furthermore, in determining whether $50 or more has been paid for services not in the course of the employer's trade or business, only cash remuneration for such services shall be taken into account. The term "cash remuneration" includes checks and other monetary media of exchange. Remuneration paid in any other medium, such as lodging, food, or other goods or commodities, is disregarded in determining whether the cash-remuneration test is met.

(d) For purposes of this exception, an individual is deemed to be regularly employed by an employer during a calendar quarter only if—

(1) Such individual performs services not in the course of the employer's trade or business for such employer for some portion of the day on at least 24 days (whether or not consecutive) during such calendar quarter; or

(2) Such individual was regularly employed (as determined under paragraph (d)(1) of this section) by such employer in the performance of services not in the course of the employer's trade or business during the preceding calendar quarter (including the last calendar quarter of 1954).

(e) In determining whether an employee has performed services not in the course of the employer's trade or business on at least 24 days during a calendar quarter, there shall be counted as one day—

(1) Any day or portion thereof on which the employee actually performs such services; and

(2) Any day or portion thereof on which the employee does not perform services of the prescribed character but with respect to which cash remuneration is paid or payable to the employee for such services, such as a day on which the employee is sick or on vacation. An employee who on a particular day reports for work and, at the direction of his employer, holds himself in readiness to perform services not in the course of the employer's trade or business shall be considered to be engaged in the actual performance of such services on that day. For purposes of this exception, a day is a period of 24 hours commencing at midnight and ending at midnight.

(f) For provisions relating to the exclusion from wages of remuneration paid in any medium other than cash for services not in the course of the employer's trade or business, see § 31.3306(b)(7)-1.

T.D. 6199, 9/4/56, amend T.D. 6516, 12/19/60.

§ 31.3306(c)(4)-1 Services on or in connection with a non-American vessel or aircraft.

(a) Services performed within the United States by an employee for an employer "on or in connection with" a vessel not an American vessel, or "on or in connection with" an aircraft not an American aircraft, are excepted from employment if the employee is employed by the employer "on and in connection with" the vessel or aircraft when outside the United States.

(b) An employee performs services on and in connection with the vessel or aircraft if he performs services on the vessel or aircraft when outside the United States which are also in connection with the vessel or aircraft. Services performed on the vessel outside the United States by employees as officers or members of the crew, or by employees of concessionaires, of the vessel, for example, are performed under such circumstances, since such services are also connected with the vessel. Similarly, services performed on the aircraft outside the United States by employees as officers or members of the crew of the aircraft are performed on and in connection with such aircraft. Services may be performed on the vessel or aircraft, however, which have no connection with it, as in the case of services performed by an employee while on the vessel or aircraft merely as a passenger in the general sense. For example, the services of a buyer in the employ of a department store while he is a passenger on a vessel are not in connection with the vessel.

(c) The expression "on or in connection with" refers not only to services performed on the vessel or aircraft but also to services connected with the vessel or aircraft which are not actually performed on it (for example, shore services performed as officers or members of the crew, or as employees of concessionaires, of the vessel).

(d) The citizenship or residence of the employee and the place where the contract of service is entered into are immaterial for purposes of this exception, and the citizenship or residence of the person employing him is material only in case it has a bearing in determining whether the vessel is an American vessel. For definitions of the terms "vessel" and "aircraft", see paragraph (c)(2)(v) of § 31.3306(c)-2. For definitions of the terms "American vessel" and "American aircraft", see § 31.3306(m)-1.

(e) Since the only services performed outside the United States which constitute employment are those described in section 3306(c) and paragraph (c) of § 31.3306(c)-2 (relating to services performed outside the United States on or in connection with an American vessel or American aircraft), services performed outside the United States on or in connection with a vessel not an American vessel, or an aircraft not an American aircraft, do not constitute employment in any event.

(f) The provisions of section 3306(c)(4) and of this section, insofar as they relate to services performed on or in connection with an aircraft not an American aircraft, apply only to services performed after 1961 for which remuneration is paid after 1961.

T.D. 6199, 9/4/56, amend T.D. 6516, 12/19/60, T.D. 6658, 6/26/63.

§ 31.3306(c)(5)-1 Family employment.

(a) Certain services are excepted from employment because of the existence of a family relationship between the employee and the individual employing him. The exceptions are as follows:

(1) Services performed by an individual in the employ of his or her spouse;

(2) Services performed by a father or mother in the employ of his or her son or daughter; and

(3) Services performed by a son or daughter under the age of 21 in the employ of his or her father or mother.

(b) Under paragraph (a)(1) and (2) of this section, the exception is conditioned solely upon the family relationship between the employee and the individual employing him. Under paragraph (a)(3) of this section, in addition to the family relationship, there is a further requirement that the son or daughter shall be under the age of 21, and the exception continues only during the time that such son or daughter is under the age of 21.

(c) Services performed in the employ of a corporation are not within the exception. Services performed in the employ of a partnership are not within the exception unless the requisite family relationship exists between the employee and each of the partners comprising the partnership.

T.D. 6199, 9/4/56, amend T.D. 6516, 12/19/60.

§ 31.3306(c)(6)-1 Services in employ of United States or instrumentality thereof.

(a) Services in employ of United States or wholly-owned instrumentality thereof. Services performed in the employ of the United States Government, except as provided in section 3306(n) (see § 31.3306(n)-1), are excepted from employment. Services performed in the employ of an instrumentality of the United States which is wholly owned by the United States also are excepted from employment.

(b) Services in employ of instrumentality not wholly owned by United States. *(1) Services performed after 1961.* Services performed after 1961 in the employ of an instrumentality of the United States which is partially owned by the United States are excepted from employment, if the remuneration for such service is paid after 1961. Services performed after 1961 in the employ of an instrumentality of the United States which is neither wholly owned nor partially owned by the United States are excepted from employment if (i) the instrumentality is exempt from the tax imposed by section 3301 by virtue of any provision of law which specifically refers to section 3301 or the corresponding section of prior law in granting exemption from such tax, and (ii) the remuneration for such service is paid after 1961. For provisions which make general exemptions from Federal taxation ineffectual as to the tax imposed by section 3301, see § 31.3308-1.

(2) Services performed before 1962. Services performed in the employ of an instrumentality of the United States which is not wholly owned by the United States are excepted from employment if the instrumentality is exempt from the tax imposed by section 3301 by virtue of any other provision of law, and (i) the services are performed before 1962 or (ii) remuneration for the services is paid before 1962.

T.D. 6199, 9/4/56, amend T.D. 6516, 12/19/60, T.D. 6658, 6/26/63.

§ 31.3306(c)(7)-1 Services in employ of States or their political subdivisions or instrumentalities.

Caution: The Treasury has not yet amended Reg § 31.3306(c)(7)-1 to reflect changes made by P.L. 106-554.

(a) Services performed in the employ of any State, or of any political subdivision thereof, are excepted from employment. Services performed in the employ of an instrumentality of one or more States or political subdivisions thereof are excepted if the instrumentality is wholly owned by one or more of the foregoing. Services performed in the employ of an instrumentality of one or more of the several States or political subdivisions thereof which is not wholly owned by one or more of the foregoing are excepted only to the extent that the instrumentality is with respect to such services immune under the Constitution of the United States from the tax imposed by section 3301.

(b) For provisions relating to the term "State" see § 31.3306(j)-1.

T.D. 6199, 9/4/56, amend T.D. 6516, 12/19/60, T.D. 6658, 6/26/63.

§ 31.3306(c)(8)-1 Services in employ of religious, charitable, educational, or certain other organizations exempt from income tax.

(a) Services performed after 1961. Services performed by an employee after 1961 in the employ of a religious, charitable, educational, or other organization described in section 501(c)(3) which is exempt from income tax under section 501(a) are excepted from employment, if the remuneration for such service is paid after 1961. For provisions relating to exemption from income tax of an organization described in section 501(c)(3), see Part 1 of this chapter (Income Tax Regulations).

(b) Services performed before 1962. *(1)* Services performed by an employee in the employ of an organization described in section 3306(c)(8) as in effect before 1962, that is, a corporation, community chest, fund, or foundation, organized and operated exclusively for religious, charitable, scientific, testing for public safety, literary, or educational purposes, or for the prevention of cruelty to children or animals, no part of the net earnings of which inures to the benefit of any private shareholder or individual, and no substantial part of the activities of which is carrying on propaganda, or otherwise attempting, to influence legislation, are excepted from employment if (i) the services are performed before 1962, or (ii) remuneration for the services is paid before 1962.

(2) Any organization which is an organization of a type described in section 501(c)(3) and which—

(i) Is exempt from income tax under section 501(a), or

(ii) Has been denied exemption from income tax under section 501(a) by reason of the provisions of section 503 or 504, relating to prohibited transactions and to accumulations out of income, respectively,

is an organization of a type described in section 3306(c)(8) as in effect before 1962. An organization which would be an organization of a type described in section 501(c)(3) except for those provisions of section 501(c)(3) which are not contained in section 3306(c)(8) as in effect before 1962 (provisions relating to participation or intervention in a political campaign on behalf of a candidate for public office) is also an organization of a type described in section 3306(c)(8) as in effect before 1962.

T.D. 6199, 9/4/56, amend T.D. 6516, 12/19/60, T.D. 6658, 6/26/63.

§ 31.3306(c)(9)-1 Railroad industry; services performed by an employee or an employee representative under the Railroad Unemployment Insurance Act.

(a) Services performed by an individual as an "employee" or as an "employee representative", as those terms are defined in section 1 of the Railroad Unemployment Insurance Act, as amended, are excepted from employment.

(b) Section 1 of the Railroad Unemployment Insurance Act (45 U.S.C. 351), as amended, provides, in part, as follows:

For the purposes of this Act, except when used in amending the provisions of other Acts—

(a) The term "employer" means any carrier (as defined in subsection (b) of this section), and any company which is directly or indirectly owned or controlled by one or more such carriers or under common control therewith, and which operates any equipment or facility or performs any service (except trucking service, casual service, and the casual operation of equipment or facilities) in connection with the transportation of passengers or property by railroad, or the receipt, delivery elevation, transfer in transit, refrigeration or icing, storage, or handling of property transported by railroad, and any receiver, trustee, or other individual or body, judicial or otherwise, when in the possession of the property or operating all or any part of the business of any such employer: Provided, however, That the term "employer" shall not include any street, interurban, or suburban electric railway, unless such railway is operating as a part of a general steam-railroad system of transportation, but shall not exclude any part of the general steam-railroad system of transportation now or hereafter operated by any other motive power. The Interstate Commerce Commission is hereby authorized and directed upon request of the Board, or upon complaint of any party interested, to determine after hearing whether any line operated by electric power falls within the terms of this proviso. The term "employer" shall also include railroad associations, traffic associations, tariff bureaus, demurrage bureaus, weighing and inspection bureaus, collection agencies, and other associations, bureaus, agencies, or organizations controlled and maintained wholly or principally by two or more employers as hereinbefore defined and engaged in the performance of services in connection with or incidental to railroad transportation and railway labor organizations, national in scope, which have been or may be organized in accordance with the provisions of the Railway Labor Act, and their State and National legislative committees and their general committees and their insurance departments and their local lodges and divisions, established pursuant to the constitution and bylaws of such organizations. The term "employer" shall not include any company by reason of its being engaged in the mining of coal, the supplying of coal to an employer where delivery is not beyond the mine tipple, and the operation of equipment or facilities therefor, or in any of such activities.

(b) The term "carrier" means an express company, sleeping-car company, or carrier by railroad, subject to part I of the Interstate Commerce Act.

(c) The term "company" includes corporations, associations, and joint-stock companies.

(d) The term "employee" (except when used in phrases establishing a different meaning) means any individual who is or has been (i) in the service of one or more employers for compensation, or (ii) an employee representative. The term "employee" shall include an employee of a local lodge or division defined as an employer in section 1(a) only if he was in the service of a carrier on or after August 29, 1935. The term "employee" includes an officer of an employer.

The term "employee" shall not include any individual while such individual is engaged in the physical operations consisting of the mining of coal, the preparation of coal, the handling (other than movement by rail with standard railroad locomotives) of coal not beyond the mine tipple, or the loading of coal at the tipple.

(e) An individual is in the service of an employer whether his service is rendered within or without the United States if (i) he is subject to the continuing authority of the employer to supervise and direct the manner of rendition of his service, or he is rendering professional or technical services and is integrated into the staff of the employer, or he is rendering, on the property used in the employer's operations, other personal services the rendition of which is integrated into the employer's operations, and (ii) he renders such service for compensation: Provided, however, That an individual shall be deemed to be in the service of an employer, other than a local lodge or division or a general committee of a railway-labor-organization employer, not conducting the principal part of its business in the United States only when he is rendering service to it in the United States; and an individual shall be deemed to be in the service of such a local lodge or division only if (1) all, or substantially all, the individuals constituting its membership are employees of an employer conducting the principal part of its business in the United States; or (2) the headquarters of such local lodge or division is located in the United States; and an individual shall be deemed to be in the service of such a general committee only if (1) he is representing a local lodge or division described in clauses (1) or (2) immediately above; or (2) all, or substantially all, the individuals represented by it are employees of an employer conducting the principal part of its business in the United States; or (3) he acts in the capacity of a general chairman or an assistant general chairman of a general committee which represents individuals rendering service in the United States to an employer, but in such case if his office or headquarters is not located in the United

States and the individuals represented by such general committee are employees of an employer not conducting the principal part of its business in the United States, only such proportion of the remuneration for such service shall be regarded as compensation as the proportion which the mileage in the United States under the jurisdiction of such general committee bears to the total mileage under its jurisdiction, unless such mileage formula is inapplicable, in which case the Board may prescribe such other formula as it finds to be equitable, and if the application of such mileage formula, or such other formula as the Board may prescribe, would result in the compensation of the individual being less than 10 per centum of his remuneration for such service no part of such remuneration shall be regarded as compensation: Provided further, That an individual not a citizen or resident of the United States shall not be deemed to be in the service of an employer when rendering service outside the United States to an employer who is required under the laws applicable in the place where the service is rendered to employ therein, in whole or in part, citizens or residents thereof.

(f) The term "employee representative" means any officer or official representative of a railway labor organization other than a labor organization included in the term employer as defined in section 1(a) who before or after August 29, 1935, was in the service of an employer as defined in section 1(a) and who is duly authorized and designated to represent employees in accordance with the Railway Labor Act, and any individual who is regularly assigned to or regularly employed by such officer or official representative in connection with the duties of his office.

* * * * *

(i) The term "compensation" means any form of money remuneration, including pay for time lost but excluding tips, paid for services rendered as an employee to one or more employers, or as an employee representative: Provided, however, That in computing the compensation paid to any employee, no part of any month's compensation in excess of $300 for any month before July 1, 1954, or in excess of $350 for any month after June 30, 1954, and before the calendar month next following the month [May] in which this Act was amended in 1959, or in excess of $400 for any month after the month [May] in which this Act was so amended, shall be recognized. A payment made by an employer to an individual through the employer's pay roll shall be presumed, in the absence of evidence to the contrary, to be compensation for service rendered by such individual as an employee of the employer in the period with respect to which the payment is made. An employee shall be deemed to be paid, "for time lost" the amount he is paid by an employer with respect to an identifiable period of absence from the active service of the employer, including absence on account of personal injury, and the amount he is paid by the employer for loss of earnings resulting from his displacement to a less remunerative position or occupation. If a payment is made by an employer with respect to a personal injury and includes pay for time lost, the total payment shall be deemed to be paid for time lost unless, at the time of payment, a part of such payment is specifically apportioned to factors other than time lost, in which event only such part of the payment as is not so apportioned shall be deemed to be paid for time lost. Compensation earned in any calendar month before 1947 shall be deemed paid in such month regardless of whether or when payment will have been in fact made, and compensation earned in any calendar year after 1946 but paid after the end of such calendar year shall be deemed to be compensation paid in the calendar year in which it will have been earned if it is so reported by the employer before February 1 of the next succeeding calendar year or, if the employee establishes, subject to the provisions of section 8, the period during which such compensation will have been earned.

* * * * *

(r) The term "Board" means the Railroad Retirement Board.

(2) The term "United States", when used in a geographical sense, means the States, Alaska, Hawaii, and the District of Columbia. * * *

T.D. 6199, 9/4/56, amend T.D. 6516, 12/19/60, T.D. 6658, 6/26/63.

---

§ 31.3306(c)(10)-1 Services in the employ of certain organizations exempt from income tax.

(a) In general. *(1)* This section deals with the exception from employment of certain services performed in the employ of any organization exempt from income tax under section 501(a) (other than an organization described in section 401(a)) or under section 521. (See the provisions of §§ 1.401-1, 1.501(a)-1, and 1.521-1 of this chapter (Income Tax Regulations).) If the services meet the tests set forth in paragraphs (b), (c), (d), or (e) of this section, the services are excepted.

(2) See also § 31.3306(c)(8)-1 for provisions relating to the exception of services performed in the employ of religious, charitable, educational, or certain other organizations exempt from income tax; § 31.3306(c)(10)-2 for provisions relating to the exception of services performed by certain students in the employ of a school, college, or university; and § 31.3306(c)(10)-3 for provisions relating to the exception of services performed before 1962 in the employ of certain employees' beneficiary associations.

(b) Remuneration less than $50 for calendar quarter. Services performed by an employee in a calendar quarter in the employ of an organization exempt from income tax under section 501(a) (other than an organization described in section 401(a)) or under section 521 are excepted from employment, if the remuneration for the service is less than $50. The test relating to remuneration of $50 is based on the remuneration earned during a calendar quarter rather than on the remuneration paid in a calendar quarter. The exception applies separately with respect to each organization for which the employee renders services in a calendar quarter. The type of services performed by the employee and the place where the services are performed are immaterial; the statutory tests are the character of the organization in the employ of which the services are performed and the amount of the remuneration for services performed by the employee in the calendar quarter.

Example (1). X is a local lodge of a fraternal organization and is exempt from income tax under section 501(a) as an organization of the character described in section 501(c)(8). X has a number of paid employees, among them being A who serves exclusively as recording secretary for the lodge, and B who performs services for the lodge as janitor of its clubhouse. For services performed during the first calendar quarter of 1955 (that is, January 1, 1955, through March 31, 1955, both dates inclusive) A earns a total of $30. For services performed during the same calendar quarter B earns $180. Since the remuneration for the services performed by A during such quarter is less than $50, all of such services are excepted. Thus, A is not counted as an employee in employment on any of the days during such quarter for purposes of determining whether the X organization is an employer (see § 31.3306(a)-1). Even though it is subsequently determined that X is an employer, A's remuneration of $30 for services performed during the first calendar quarter of such year is not subject to tax. B's services, however, are not excepted during such quarter since the remuneration therefore is not less than $50. Thus, B is counted as an employee in employment during all of such quarter for purposes of determining whether the X organization is an employer. If it is determined that the X organization is an employer, B's remuneration of $180 for services performed during the first calendar quarter is included in computing the tax.

Example (2). The facts are the same as in example (1), above, except that on April 1, 1955, A's salary is increased and, for services performed during the calendar quarter beginning on that date (that is, April 1, 1955, through June 30, 1955, both dates inclusive), A earns $60. Although all of the services performed by A during the first quarter were excepted, none of A's services performed during the second quarter are excepted since the remuneration for such services is not less than $50. A, therefore, is counted as an employee in employment during all of the second quarter for the purpose of determining whether the X organization is an employer. If it is determined that the X organization is an employer, A's remuneration of $60 for services performed during the second calendar quarter is included in computing the tax.

Example (3). The facts are the same as in example (1), above, except that A earns $120 for services performed during the year 1955, and such amount is paid to him in a lump sum at the end of the year. The services performed by A in any calendar quarter during the year are excepted if the portion of the $120 attributable to services performed in that quarter is less than $50. In such case, A is not counted as an employee in employment on any of the days during such quarter for purposes of determining whether the X organization is an employer. If, however, the portion of the $120 attributable to services performed in any calendar quarter during the year is not less than $50, the services during that quarter are not excepted. In the latter case, A is counted as an employee in employment during all of such quarter and, if it is determined that the X organization is an employer, that portion of the $120 attributable to services performed in such quarter is included in computing the tax.

(c) Collection of dues or premiums for fraternal beneficiary societies, and ritualistic services in connection with such societies, before 1962. The following services performed by an employee in the employ of a fraternal beneficiary society, order, or association exempt from income tax under section 501(a) are excepted from employment if the services are performed before 1962 or if remuneration for the services is paid before 1962:

(1) Services performed away from the home office of such a society, order, or association in connection with the collection of dues or premiums for such society, order, or association; and

(2) Ritualistic services (wherever performed) in connection with such a society, order, or association.

For purposes of the paragraph the amount of the remuneration for services performed by the employee in the calendar quarter is immaterial; the tests are the character of the organization in whose employ the services are performed, the type of services, and, in the case of collection of dues or premiums, the place where the services are performed.

(d) Students employed before 1962. *(1)* Services performed in the employ of an organization exempt from income tax under section 501(a) (other than an organization described in section 401(a)) or under section 521 by a student who is enrolled and is regularly attending classes at a school, college, or university, are excepted from employment if the services are performed before 1962 or if remuneration for the services is paid before 1962. For purposes of this paragraph, the amount of remuneration for services performed by the employee in the calendar quarter, the type of services, and the place where the services are performed are immaterial; the tests are the character of the organization in whose employ the services are performed and the status of the employee as a student enrolled and regularly attending classes at a school, college, or university.

(2) The term "school, college, or university" as used in this paragraph is to be taken in its commonly or generally accepted sense. For provisions relating to services performed before 1962 by a student enrolled and regularly attending classes at a school, college, or university not exempt from income tax in the employ of such school, college, or university, see paragraph (b) of § 31.3306(c)(10)-2. For provisions relating to services performed after 1961 by a student enrolled and regularly attending classes at a school, college, or university in the employ of such school, college, or university, see paragraph (a) or § 31.3306(c)(10)-2.

(e) Services performed before 1962 in employ of agricultural or horticultural organization exempt from income tax. *(1)* Services performed by an employee in the employ of an agricultural or horticultural organization which is described in section 501(c)(5) and the regulations thereunder and which is exempt from income tax under section 501(a) are excepted from employment if the services are performed before 1962 or if remuneration for the services is paid before 1962.

(2) For purposes of this paragraph, the type of services performed by the employee, the amount of remuneration for the services, and the place where the services are performed are immaterial; the test is the character of the organization in whose employ the services are performed.

T.D. 6658, 6/26/63.

§ 31.3306(c)(10)-2 Services of student in employ of school, college, or university.

(a) Services performed after 1961. Services performed after 1961 in the employ of a school, college, or university, by a student who is enrolled and is regularly attending classes at the school, college, or university, are excepted from employment (whether or not the school, college, or university is exempt from income tax), if remuneration for the services is paid after 1961.

(b) Services performed before 1962. Services performed in the employ of a school, college, or university not exempt from income tax under section 501(a), by a student who is enrolled and is regularly attending classes at the school, college, or university, are excepted from employment if the services are performed before 1962 or if remuneration for the services is paid before 1962. **(c) General rule.**

(1) For purposes of this section, the tests are the character of the organization in the employ of which the services are performed and the status of the employee as a student enrolled and regularly attending classes at the school, college, or university described in paragraph (c)(2) of this section, in the employ of which the employee performs the services. If an employee has the status of a student within the meaning

of paragraph (d) of this section, the type of services performed by the employee, the place where the services are performed, and the amount of remuneration for services performed by the employee are not material.

(2) School, college, or university. An organization is a school, college, or university within the meaning of section 3306(c)(10)(B) if its primary function is the presentation of formal instruction, it normally maintains a regular faculty and curriculum, and it normally has a regularly enrolled body of students in attendance at the place where its educational activities are regularly carried on. See section 170(b)(1)(A)(ii) and the regulations thereunder.

(d) Student Status—general rule. Whether an employee has the status of a student within the meaning of section 3306(c)(10)(B) performing the services shall be determined based on the relationship of the employee with the organization for which the services are performed. In order to have the status of a student within the meaning of section 3306(c)(10)(B), the employee must perform services in the employ of a school, college, or university described in paragraph (c)(2) of this section at which the employee is enrolled and regularly attending classes in pursuit of a course of study within the meaning of paragraphs (d)(1) and (2) of this section. In addition, the employee's services must be incident to and for the purpose of pursuing a course of study at such school, college, or university within the meaning of paragraph (d)(3) of this section.

(1) Enrolled and regularly attending classes. An employee must be enrolled and regularly attending classes at a school, college, or university within the meaning of paragraph (c)(2) of this section at which the employee is employed to have the status of a student within the meaning of section 3306(c)(10)(B). An employee is enrolled within the meaning of section 3306(c)(10)(B) if the employee is registered for a course or courses creditable toward an educational credential described in paragraph (d)(2) of this section. In addition, the employee must be regularly attending classes to have the status of a student. For purposes of this paragraph (d)(1), a class is an instructional activity led by a faculty member or other qualified individual hired by the school, college, or university within the meaning of paragraph (c)(2) of this section for identified students following an established curriculum. The frequency of these and similar activities determines whether an employee may be considered to be regularly attending classes.

(2) Course of study. An employee must be pursuing a course of study in order to have the status of a student within the meaning of section 3306(c)(10)(B). A course of study is one or more courses the completion of which fulfills the requirements necessary to receive an educational credential granted by a school, college, or university within the meaning of paragraph (c)(2) of this section. For purposes of this paragraph, an educational credential is a degree, certificate, or other recognized educational credential granted by an organization described in paragraph (c)(2) of this section. In addition, a course of study is one or more courses at a school, college or university within the meaning of paragraph (c)(2) of this section the completion of which fulfills the requirements necessary for the employee to sit for an examination required to receive certification by a recognized organization in a field.

(3) Incident to and for the purpose of pursuing a course of study. (i) General rule. An employee's services must be incident to and for the purpose of pursuing a course of study in order for the employee to have the status of a student. Whether an employee's services are incident to and for the purpose of pursuing a course of study shall be determined on the basis of the relationship of the employee with the organization for which such services are performed as an employee. The educational aspect of the relationship between the employer and the employee, as compared to the service aspect of the relationship, must be predominant in order for the employee's services to be incident to and for the purpose of pursuing a course of study. The educational aspect of the relationship is evaluated based on all the relevant facts and circumstances related to the educational aspect of the relationship. The service aspect of the relationship is evaluated based on all the relevant facts and circumstances related to the employee's employment. The evaluation of the service aspect of the relationship is not affected by the fact that the services performed by the employee may have an educational, instructional, or training aspect. Except as provided in paragraph (d)(3)(iii) of this section, whether the educational aspect or the service aspect of an employee's relationship with the employer is predominant is determined by considering all the relevant facts and circumstances. Relevant factors in evaluating the educational and service aspects of an employee's relationship with the employer are described in paragraphs (d)(3)(iv) and (v) of this section respectively. There may be facts and circumstances that are relevant in evaluating the educational and service aspects of the relationship in addition to those described in paragraphs (d)(3)(iv) and (v) of this section.

(ii) Student status determined with respect to each academic term. Whether an employee's services are incident to and for the purpose of pursuing a course of study is determined separately with respect to each academic term. If the relevant facts and circumstances with respect to an employee's relationship with the employer change significantly during an academic term, whether the employee's services are incident to and for the purpose of pursuing a course of study is reevaluated with respect to services performed during the remainder of the academic term.

(iii) Full-time employee. The services of a full-time employee are not incident to and for the purpose of pursuing a course of study. The determination of whether an employee is a full-time employee is based on the employer's standards and practices, except regardless of the employer's classification of the employee, an employee whose normal work schedule is 40 hours or more per week is considered a full-time employee. An employee's normal work schedule is not affected by increases in hours worked caused by work demands unforeseen at the start of an academic term. However, whether an employee is a full-time employee is reevaluated for the remainder of the academic term if the employee changes employment positions with the employer. An employee's work schedule during academic breaks is not considered in determining whether the employee's normal work schedule is 40 hours or more per week. The determination of the employee's normal work schedule is not affected by the fact that the services performed by the individual may have an educational, instructional, or training aspect.

(iv) Evaluating educational aspect. The educational aspect of an employee's relationship with the employer is evaluated based on all the relevant facts and circumstances related to the educational aspect of the relationship. The educational aspect of an employee's relationship with the employer is generally evaluated based on the employee's course workload. Whether an employee's course workload is sufficient in order for the employee's employment to be incident to and for the purpose of pursuing a course of study depends on the particular facts and circumstances. A relevant factor in evaluating an employee's course workload is the employee's course workload relative to a full-time course workload at the school, college or university within the meaning of paragraph (c)(2) of this section at which the employee is enrolled and regularly attending classes.

(v) Evaluating service aspect. The service aspect of an employee's relationship with the employer is evaluated based on the facts and circumstances related to the employee's employment. Services of an employee with the status of a full-time employee within the meaning of paragraph (d)(3)(iii) of this section are not incident to and for the purpose of pursuing a course of study. Relevant factors in evaluating the service aspect of an employee's relationship with the employer are described in paragraphs (d)(3)(v)(A), (B), and (C) of this section.

(A) Normal work schedule and hours worked. If an employee is not a full-time employee within the meaning of paragraph (d)(3)(iii) of this section, then the employee's normal work schedule and number of hours worked per week are relevant factors in evaluating the service aspect of the employee's relationship with the employer. As an employee's normal work schedule or actual number of hours worked approaches 40 hours per week, it is more likely that the service aspect of the employee's relationship with the employer is predominant. The determination of the employee's normal work schedule and actual number of hours worked is not affected by the fact that some of the services performed by the individual may have an educational, instructional, or training aspect.

(B) Professional employee.

(1) If an employee has the status of a professional employee, then that suggests that the service aspect of the employee's relationship with the employer is predominant. A professional employee is an employee—

(i) Whose primary duty consists of the performance of work requiring knowledge of an advanced type in a field of science or learning customarily acquired by a prolonged course of specialized intellectual instruction and study, as distinguished from a general academic education, from an apprenticeship, and from training in the performance of routine mental, manual, or physical processes;

(ii) Whose work requires the consistent exercise of discretion and judgment in its performance; and

(iii) Whose work is predominantly intellectual and varied in character (as opposed to routine mental, manual, mechanical, or physical work) and is of such character that the output produced or the result accomplished cannot be standardized in relation to a given period of time.

(2) Licensed, professional employee. If an employee is a licensed, professional employee, then that further suggests the service aspect of the employee's relationship with the employer is predominant. An employee is a licensed, professional employee if the employee is required to be licensed under state or local law to work in the field in which the employee performs services and the employee is a professional employee within the meaning of paragraph (d)(3)(v)(B)(1) of this section.

(C) Employment Benefits. Whether an employee is eligible to receive employment benefits is a relevant factor in evaluating the service aspect of an employee's relationship with the employer. For example, eligibility to receive vacation, paid holiday, and paid sick leave benefits; eligibility to participate in a retirement plan described in section 401(a); or eligibility to receive employment benefits such as reduced tuition, or benefits under section 79 (life insurance), 127 (qualified educational assistance), 129 (dependent care assistance programs), or 137 (adoption assistance) suggest that the service aspect of an employee's relationship with the employer is predominant. Eligibility to receive health insurance employment benefits is not considered in determining whether the service aspect of an employee's relationship with the employer is predominant. The weight to be given the fact that an employee is eligible for a particular benefit may vary depending on the type of employment benefit. For example, eligibility to participate in a retirement plan is generally more significant than eligibility to receive a dependent care employment benefit. Additional weight is given to the fact that an employee is eligible to receive an employment benefit if the benefit is generally provided by the employer to employees in positions generally held by non-students.

(e) Effective date. Paragraphs (c) and (d) of this section apply to services performed on or after April 1, 2005.

T.D. 6658, 6/26/63, amend T.D. 9167, 12/20/2004.

§ 31.3306(c)(10)-3 Services before 1962 in employ of certain employees' beneficiary associations.

(a) Voluntary employees' beneficiary associations. Services performed by an employee in the employ of a voluntary employees' beneficiary association providing for the payment of life, sick, accident, or other benefits to the members of such association or their dependents are excepted from employment if—

(1) No part of its net earnings inures (other than through such payments) to the benefit of any private shareholder or individual,

(2) 85 percent or more of the income consists of amounts collected from members for the sole purpose of making such payments and meeting expenses, and

(3) The services are performed before 1962, or remuneration for the services is paid before 1962.

(b) Federal employees' beneficiary associations. Services performed by an employee in the employ of a voluntary employees' beneficiary association providing for the payment of life, sick, accident, or other benefits to the members of such association or their dependents or their designated beneficiaries are excepted from employment if—

(1) Admission to membership in the association is limited to individuals who are officers or employees of the United States Government,

(2) No part of the net earnings of the association inures (other than through such payments) to the benefit of any private shareholder or individual, and

(3) The services are performed before 1962, or remuneration for the services is paid before 1962.

(c) Application of tests. For purposes of this section, the type of services performed by the employee, the amount of remuneration for the services, and the place where the services are performed are immaterial; the test is the character of the organization in whose employ the services are performed.

T.D. 6658, 6/26/63.

§ 31.3306(c)(11)-1 Services in employ of foreign government.

(a) Services performed by an employee in the employ of a foreign government are excepted from employment. The exception includes not only services performed by ambassadors, ministers, and other diplomatic officers and employees but also services performed as a consular or other officer or employee of a foreign government, or as a nondiplomatic representative thereof.

(b) For purposes of this exception, the citizenship or residence of the employee is immaterial. It is also immaterial whether the foreign government grants an equivalent exemption with respect to similar services performed in the foreign country by citizens of the United States.

T.D. 6199, 9/4/56, amend T.D. 6516, 12/19/60.

§ 31.3306(c)(12)-1 Services in employ of wholly owned instrumentality of foreign government.

(a) Services performed by an employee in the employ of certain instrumentalities of a foreign government are excepted from employment. The exception includes all services performed in the employ of an instrumentality of the government of a foreign country, if—

(1) The instrumentality is wholly owned by the foreign government;

(2) The services are of a character similar to those performed in foreign countries by employees of the United States Government or of an instrumentality thereof; and

(3) The Secretary of State certifies to the Secretary of the Treasury that the foreign government, with respect to whose instrumentality exemption is claimed, grants an equivalent exemption with respect to services performed in the foreign country by employees of the United States Government and of instrumentalities thereof.

(b) For purposes of this exception, the citizenship or residence of the employee is immaterial.

T.D. 6199, 9/4/56, amend T.D. 6516, 12/19/60.

§ 31.3306(c)(13)-1 Services of student nurse or hospital intern.

(a) Services performed as a student nurse in the employ of a hospital or a nurses training school are excepted from employment, if the student nurse is enrolled and regularly attending classes in a nurses training school and such nurses training school is chartered or approved pursuant to State law.

(b) Services performed as an intern (as distinguished from a resident doctor) in the employ of a hospital are excepted from employment, if the intern has completed a 4 year course in a medical school chartered or approved pursuant to State law.

T.D. 6199, 9/4/56, amend T.D. 6516, 12/19/60.

§ 31.3306(c)(14)-1 Services of insurance agent or solicitor.

(a) Services performed for a person by an employee as an insurance agent or insurance solicitor are excepted from employment, if all such services performed for such person by such individual are performed for remuneration solely by way of commission.

(b) If all or any part of the remuneration of an employee for services performed as an insurance agent or insurance solicitor for a person is a salary, none of his services performed as an insurance agent or insurance solicitor for such person are excepted from employment, and his total remuneration (for example, salary, or salary and commissions) for such services is included for purposes of computing the tax.

T.D. 6199, 9/4/56, amend T.D. 6516, 12/19/60.

§ 31.3306(c)(15)-1 Services in delivery or distribution of newspapers, shopping news, or magazines.

(a) Services of individuals under age 18. Services performed by an employee under the age of 18 in the delivery or distribution of newspapers or shopping news, not including delivery or distribution (as, for example, by a regional distributor) to any point for subsequent delivery or distribution, are excepted from employment. Thus, the services performed by an employee under the age of 18 in making house-to-house delivery or sale of newspapers or shopping news, including handbills and other similar types of advertising material, are excepted. The services are excepted irrespective of the form or method of compensation. Incidental services by the employee who makes the house-to-house delivery, such as services in assembling newspapers, are considered to be within the exception. The exception continues only during the time that the employee is under the age of 18.

(b) Services of individuals of any age. Services performed by an employee in, and at the time of, the sale of newspapers or magazines to ultimate consumers under an arrangement under which the newspapers or magazines are to be sold by him at a fixed price, his compensation being based on the retention of the excess of such price over the amount at which the newspapers or magazines are charged to him, are excepted from employment. The services are excepted whether or not the employee is guaranteed a minimum amount of compensation for such services, or is entitled to be credited with the unsold newspapers or magazines turned back. Moreover, the services are excepted without regard to the age of the employee. Services performed other than at the time of sale to the ultimate consumer are not within the exception. Thus, the services of a regional distributor which are antecedent to but not immediately part of the sale to the ultimate consumer are not within the exception. However, incidental services by the employee who makes the sale to the ultimate consumer, such as services in assembling newspapers or in taking newspapers or magazines to the place of sale, are considered to be within the exception.

T.D. 6199, 9/4/56, amend T.D. 6516, 12/19/60.

§ 31.3306(c)(16)-1 Services in employ of international organization.

(a) Subject to the provisions of section 1 of the International Organizations Immunities Act (22 U.S.C. 228), services performed in the employ of an international organization as defined in section 7701(a)(18) are excepted from employment.

(b) *(1)* Section 7701(a)(18) provides as follows:

SEC. 7701. Definitions. (a) When used in this title, where not otherwise distinctly expressed or manifestly incompatible with the intent thereof— * * * (18) International organization. The term "international organization" means a public international organization entitled to enjoy privileges, exemptions, and immunities as an international organization under the International Organizations Immunities Act (22 U.S.C. 288-288f).

(2) Section 1 of the International Organizations Immunities Act provides as follows:

SEC. 1. [International Organizations Immunities Act.] For the purposes of this title [International Organizations Immunities Act], the term "international organization" means a public international organization in which the United States participates pursuant to any treaty or under the authority of any Act of Congress authorizing such participation or making an appropriation for such participation, and which shall have been designated by the President through appropriate Executive order as being entitled to enjoy the privileges, exemptions, and immunities herein provided. The President shall be authorized, in the light of the functions performed by any such international organization, by appropriate Executive order to withhold or withdraw from any such organization or its officers or employees any of the privileges, exemptions, and immunities provided for in this title (including the amendments made by this title) or to condition or limit the enjoyment by any such organization or its officers or employees of any such privilege, exemption, or immunity. The President shall be authorized, if in his judgment such action should be justified by reason of the abuse by an international organization or its officers and employees of the privileges, exemptions, and immunities herein provided or for any other reason, at any time to revoke the designation of any international organization under this section, whereupon the international organization in question shall cease to be classed as an international organization for the purposes of this title.

T.D. 6199, 9/4/56, amend T.D. 6516, 12/19/60.

§ 31.3306(c)(17)-1 Fishing services.

(a) In general. Subject to the limitations prescribed in paragraphs (b) and (c) of this section, services described in this paragraph are excepted from employment. Services performed by an individual in the catching, taking, harvesting, cultivating, or farming of any kind of fish, shell-fish (for example, oysters, clams, and mussels), crustacea (for example, lobsters, crabs, and shrimps), sponges, seaweeds, or other aquatic forms of animal and vegetable life are excepted. The exception extends to services performed as an officer or member of the crew of a vessel while the vessel is engaged in any such activity whether or not the officer or member of the crew is himself so engaged. In the case of an individual who is engaged in any such activity in the employ of any person, the services performed, by such individual in the employ of such person, as an ordinary incident to any such activity are also excepted. Similarly, for example, the shore services of an officer or member of the crew of a vessel engaged in any such activity are excepted if such services are an ordinary incident to any such activity. Services performed as an ordinary incident to any such activity may include, for example, services performed in such cleaning, icing, and packing of fish as are necessary for the immediate preservation of the catch.

(b) Salmon and halibut fishing. Services performed in connection with the catching or taking of salmon or halibut, for commercial purposes, are not within the exception. Thus, neither the services of an officer or member of the crew of a vessel (irrespective of its tonnage) which is engaged in the catching or taking of salmon or halibut, for commercial purposes, nor the services of any other individual in connection with such activity, are within the exception.

(c) Vessels of more than 10 net tons. Services described in paragraph (a) of this section performed on or in connection with a vessel of more than 10 net tons are not within the exception. For purposes of the exception, the tonnage of the vessel shall be determined in the manner provided for determining the register tonnage of merchant vessels under the laws of the United States.

T.D. 6199, 9/4/56, amend T.D. 6516, 12/19/60.

§ 31.3306(c)(18)-1 Services of certain nonresident aliens.

(a) *(1)* Services performed after 1961 by a nonresident alien individual who is temporarily present in the United States as a nonimmigrant under subparagraph (F) or (J) of section 101(a)(15) of the Immigration and Nationality Act (8 U.S.C. 1101), as amended, are excepted from employment if the services are performed to carry out a purpose for which the individual was admitted. For purposes of this section an alien individual who is temporarily present in the United States as a nonimmigrant under such subparagraph (F) or (J) is deemed to be a nonresident alien individual. The preceding sentence does not apply to the extent it is inconsistent with section 7701(b) and the regulations under that section. A nonresident alien individual who is temporarily present in the United States as a nonimmigrant under such subparagraph (J) includes an alien individual admitted to the United States as an "exchange visitor" under section 201 of the United States Information and Educational Exchange Act of 1948 (22 U.S.C. 1446).

(2) If services are performed by a nonresident alien individual's alien spouse or minor child, who is temporarily present in the United States as a nonimmigrant under subparagraph (F) or (J) of section 101(a)(15) of the Immigration and Nationality Act, as amended, the services are not deemed for purposes of this section to be performed to carry out a purpose for which such individual was admitted. The services of such spouse or child are excepted from employment under this section only if the spouse or child was admitted for a purpose specified in such subparagraph (F) or (J) and if the services are performed to carry out such purpose.

(b) Section 101 of the Immigration and Nationality Act (8 U.S.C. 1101), as amended, provides, in part, as follows:

SEC. 101. Definitions. [Immigration and Nationality Act (66 Stat. 166)]

(a) As used in this chapter— * * * (15) The term "immigrant" means every alien except an alien who is within one of the following classes of nonimmigrant aliens— * * * (F)(i) An alien having a residence in a foreign country which he has no intention of abandoning, who is a bona fide student qualified to pursue a full course of study and who seeks to enter the United States temporarily and solely for the purpose of pursuing such a course of study at an established institution of learning or other recognized place of study in the United States, particularly designated by him and approved by the Attorney General after consultation with the Office of Education of the United States, which institution or place of study shall have agreed to report to the Attorney General the termination of attendance of each nonimmigrant student, and if any such institution of learning or place of study fails to make reports promptly the approval shall be withdrawn, and (ii) the alien spouse and minor children of any such alien if accompanying him or following to join him; * * * (J) An alien having a residence in a foreign country which he has no intention of abandoning who is a bona fide student, scholar, trainee, teacher, professor, research assistant, specialist, or leader in a field of specialized knowledge or skill, or other person of similar description, who is coming temporarily to the United States as a participant in a program designated by the Secretary of State, for the purpose of teaching, instructing or lecturing, studying, observing, conducting research, consulting, demonstrating special skills, or receiving training, and the alien spouse and minor children of any such alien if accompanying him or following to join him. * * *

T.D. 6658, 6/26/63, amend T.D. 8411, 4/24/92.

§ 31.3306(d)-1 Included and excluded service.

(a) If a portion of the services performed by an employee for the person employing him during a pay period constitutes employment, and the remainder does not constitute employment, all the services of the employee during the period shall for purposes of the tax be treated alike, that is, either all as included or all as excluded. The time during which the employee performs services which under section 3306(c) constitute employment, and the time during which he performs services which under such section do not constitute employment, within the pay period, determine whether all the services during the pay period shall be deemed to be included or excluded.

(b) If one-half or more of the employee's time in the employ of a particular person in a pay period is spent in performing services which constitute employment, then all the services of that employee for that person in that pay period shall be deemed to be employment.

(c) If less than one-half of the employee's time in the employ of a particular person in a pay period is spent in performing services which constitute employment, then none of the services of that employee for that person in that pay period shall be deemed to be employment.

(d) The application of the provisions of paragraphs (a), (b), and (c) of this section may be illustrated by the following examples:

Example (1). Employer B, who operates a farm and a store, employs A to perform services in connection with both operations. A's services on the farm are such that they are excepted as agricultural labor and do not constitute employment, and his services in the store constitute employment. He is paid at the end of each month. During a particular month A works 120 hours on the farm and 80 hours in the store. None of A's services during the month are deemed to be employment, since less than one-half of his services during the month constitutes employment. During another month A works 75 hours on the farm and 120 hours in the store. All of A's services during the month are deemed to be employment, since one-half or more of his services during the month constitutes employment.

Example (2). Employee C is employed as a maid by D, a medical doctor, whose home and office are located in the same building. C's services in the home are excepted as domestic service and do not constitute employment, and her services in the office constitute employment. She is paid each week. During a particular week C works 20 hours in the home and 20 hours in the office. All of C's services during that week are deemed to be employment, since one-half or more of her services during the week constitutes employment. During another week C works 22 hours in the home and 15 hours in the office. None of C's services during that week are deemed to be employment, since less than one-half of her services during the week constitutes employment.

(e) For purposes of this section, a "pay period" is the period (of not more than 31 consecutive calendar days) for which a payment of remuneration is ordinarily made to the employee by the person employing him. Thus, if the periods for which payments of remuneration are made to the employee by such person are of uniform duration, each such period constitutes a "pay period". If, however, the periods occasionally vary in duration, the "pay period" is the period for which a payment of remuneration is ordinarily made to the employee by such person, even though that period does not coincide with the actual period for which a particular payment of remuneration is made. For example, if a person ordinarily pays a particular employee for each calendar week at the end of the week, but the employee receives a payment in the middle of the week for the portion of the week already elapsed and receives the remainder at the end of the week, the "pay period" is still the calendar week; or if, instead, that employee is sent on a trip by such person and receives at the end of the third week a single remuneration payment for 3 weeks' services, the "pay period" is still the calendar week.

(f) If there is only one period (and such period does not exceed 31 consecutive calendar days) for which a payment of remuneration is made to the employee by the person employing him, such period is deemed to be a "pay period" for purposes of this section.

(g) The rules set forth in this section do not apply (1) with respect to any services performed by the employee for the person employing him if the periods for which such person makes payments of remuneration to the employee vary to the extent that there is no period "for which a payment of remuneration is ordinarily made to the employee," or (2) with respect to any services performed by the employee for the person employing him if the period for which a payment of remuneration is ordinarily made to the employee by such person exceeds 31 consecutive calendar days, or (3) with respect to any service performed by the employee for the person employing him during a pay period if any of such service is excepted by section 3306(c)(9)(see § 31.3306(c)(9)-1).

(h) If during any period for which a person makes a payment of remuneration to an employee only a portion of the employee's services constitutes employment, but the rules prescribed in this section are not applicable, the tax attaches with respect to such services as constitute employment as defined in section 3306(c) (provided such person is an employer as defined in section 3306(a) and § 31.3306(a)-1).

T.D. 6199, 9/4/56, amend T.D. 6516, 12/19/60.

§ 31.3306(i)-1 Who are employees.

(a) Every individual is an employee if the relationship between him and the person for whom he performs services is the legal relationship of employer and employee. (The word "employer" as used in this section only, notwithstanding the provisions of § 31.3306(a)-1, includes a person who employs one or more employees.)

(b) Generally such relationship exists when the person for whom services are performed has the right to control and direct the individual who performs the services, not only as to the result to be accomplished by the work but also as to the details and means by which that result is accomplished. That is, an employee is subject to the will and control of the employer not only as to what shall be done but how it shall be done. In this connection, it is not necessary that the employer actually direct or control the manner in which the services are performed; it is sufficient if he has the right to do so. The right to discharge is also an important factor indicating that the person possessing that right is an employer. Other factors characteristic of an employer, but not necessarily present in every case, are the furnishing of tools and the furnishing of a place to work, to the individual who performs the services. In general, if an individual is subject to the control or direction of another merely as to the result to be accomplished by the work and not as to the means and methods for accomplishing the result, he is an independent contractor. An individual performing services as an independent contractor is not as to such services an employee. Individuals such as physicians, lawyers, dentists, veterinarians, construction contractors, public stenographers, and auctioneers, engaged in the pursuit of an independent trade, business, or profession, in which they offer their services to the public, are independent contractors and not employees.

(c) Whether the relationship of employer and employee exists will in doubtful cases be determined upon an examination of the particular facts of each case.

(d) If the relationship of employer and employee exists, the designation or description of the relationship by the parties as anything other than that of employer and employee is immaterial. Thus, if such relationship exists, it is of no consequence that the employee is designated as a partner, coadventurer, agent, independent contractor, or the like.

(e) All classes or grades of employees are included within the relationship of employer and employee. Thus, superintendents, managers, and other supervisory personnel are employees. Generally, an officer of a corporation is an employee of the corporation. However, an officer of a corporation who as such does not perform any services or performs only minor services and who neither receives nor is entitled to receive, directly or indirectly, any remuneration is considered not to be an employee of the corporation. A director of a corporation in his capacity as such is not an employee of the corporation.

(f) Although an individual may be an employee under this section, his services may be of such a nature, or performed under such circumstances, as not to constitute employment (see § 31.3306(c)-2).

T.D. 6199, 9/4/56, amend T.D. 6516, 12/19/60.

§ 31.3306(j)-1 State, United States, and citizen.

(a) When used in the regulations in this subpart, the term "State" includes the District of Columbia, the Territories of Alaska and Hawaii before their admission as States, and (when used with respect to remuneration paid after 1960 for services performed after 1960) the Commonwealth of Puerto Rico.

(b) When used in the regulations in this subpart, the term "United States", when used in a geographical sense, means the several States (including the Territories of Alaska and Hawaii before their admission as States), and the District of Columbia. When used in the regulations in this subpart with respect to remuneration paid after 1960 for services performed after 1960, the term "United States" also includes the Commonwealth of Puerto Rico when the term is used in a geographical sense, and the term "citizen of the United States" includes a citizen of the Commonwealth of Puerto Rico.

T.D. 6658, 6/26/63.

§ 31.3306(k)-1 Agricultural labor.

(a) In general. *(1)* Services performed by an employee for the person employing him which constitute "agricultural labor" as defined in section 3306(k) are excepted from employment by reason of section 3306(c)(1). See § 31.3306(c)(1)-1. The term "agricultural labor" as defined in section 3306(k) includes services of the character described in paragraphs (b), (c), (d), and (e) of this section. In general, however, the term does not include services performed in connection with forestry, lumbering, or landscaping.

(2) The term "farm" as used in this subpart includes stock, dairy, poultry, fruit, fur-bearing animal, and truck farms, plantations, ranches, nurseries, ranges, orchards, and such greenhouses and other similar structures as are used primarily for the raising of agricultural or horticultural commodities. Greenhouses and other similar structures used primarily for other purposes (for example, display, storage, and fabrication of wreaths, corsages, and bouquets) do not constitute "farms".

(b) Services described in section 3306(k)(1). Services performed on a farm by an employee of any person in connection with any of the following activities constitute agricultural labor:

(1) The cultivation of the soil;

(2) The raising, shearing, feeding, caring for, training, or management of livestock, bees, poultry, fur-bearing animals, or wildlife; or

(3) The raising or harvesting of any other agricultural or horticultural commodity.

(c) Services described in section 3306(k)(2). *(1)* The following services performed by an employee in the employ of the owner or tenant or other operator of one or more farms constitute agricultural labor, if the major part of such services is performed on a farm:

(i) Services performed in connection with the operation, management, conservation, improvement, or maintenance of any such farms or its tools or equipment; or

(ii) Services performed in salvaging timber, or clearing land of brush and other debris, left by a hurricane.

(2) The services described in paragraph (c)(1)(i) of this section may include, for example, services performed by carpenters, painters, mechanics, farm supervisors, irrigation engineers, bookkeepers, and other skilled or semiskilled workers, which contribute in any way to the conduct of the farm or farms, as such, operated by the person employing them, as distinguished from any other enterprise in which such person may be engaged.

(3) Since the services described in this paragraph must be performed in the employ of the owner or tenant or other operator of the farm, services performed by employees of a commercial painting concern, for example, which contracts with a farmer to renovate his farm properties, do not constitute agricultural labor.

(d) Services described in section 3306(k)(3). Services performed by an employee in the employ of any person in connection with any of the following operations constitute agricultural labor without regard to the place where such services are performed:

(1) The ginning of cotton;

(2) The hatching of poultry;

(3) The raising or harvesting of mushrooms;

(4) The operation or maintenance of ditches, canals, reservoirs, or waterways used exclusively for supplying or storing water for farming purposes;

(5) The production or harvesting of maple sap or the processing of maple sap into maple sirup or maple sugar (but not the subsequent blending or other processing of such sirup or sugar with other products); or

(6) The production or harvesting of crude gum (oleoresin) from a living tree or the processing of such crude gum into

gum spirits of turpentine and gum rosin provided such processing is carried on by the original producer of such crude gum.

(e) Services described in section 3306(k)(4). *(1)* (i) Services performed by an employee in the employ of a farmer or a farmers' cooperative organization or group in the handling, planting, drying, packing, packaging, processing, freezing, grading, storing, or delivering to storage or to market or to a carrier for transportation to market, of any agricultural or horticultural commodity, other than fruits and vegetables (see paragraph (e)(2) of this section), produced by such farmer or farmer-members of such organization or group of farmers constitute agricultural labor, if such services are performed as an incident to ordinary farming operations.

(ii) Generally services are performed "as an incident to ordinary farming operations" within the meaning of this paragraph if they are services of the character ordinarily performed by the employees of a farmer or of a farmers' cooperative organization or group as a prerequisite to the marketing, in its unmanufactured state, of any agricultural or horticultural commodity produced by such farmer or by the members of such farmers' organization or group. Services performed by employees of such farmer or farmers' organization or group in the handling, planting, drying, packing, packaging, processing, freezing, grading, storing, or delivering to storage or to market or to a carrier for transportation to market, of commodities produced by persons other than such farmer or members of such farmers' organization or group are not performed "as an incident to ordinary farming operations".

(2) Services performed by an employee in the employ of any person in the handling, planting, drying, packing, packaging, processing, freezing, grading, storing, or delivering to storage or to market or to a carrier for transportation to market, of fruits and vegetables, whether or not of a perishable nature, constitute agricultural labor, if such services are performed as an incident to the preparation of such fruits and vegetables for market. For example, if services in the sorting, grading, or storing of fruits, or in the cleaning of beans, are performed as an incident to their preparation for market, such services may constitute agricultural labor, whether performed in the employ of a farmer, a farmers' cooperative, or a commercial handler of such commodities.

(3) The services described in paragraphs (e)(1) and (2) of this section do not include services performed in connection with commercial canning or commercial freezing or in connection with any commodity after its delivery to a terminal market for distribution for consumption. Moreover, since the services described in such subparagraphs must be rendered in the actual handling, planting, drying, packing, packaging, processing, freezing, grading, storing, or delivering to storage or to market or to a carrier for transportation to market, of the commodity, such services do not, for example, include services performed as stenographers, bookkeepers, clerks, and other office employees, even though such services may be in connection with such activities. However, to the extent that the services of such individuals are performed in the employ of the owner or tenant or other operator of a farm and are rendered in major part on a farm, they may be within the provisions of paragraph (c) of this section.

T.D. 6199, 9/4/56, amend T.D. 6516, 12/19/60.

§ 31.3306(m)-1 American vessel and aircraft.

(a) The term "American vessel" means any vessel which is documented (that is, registered, enrolled, or licensed) or numbered in conformity with the laws of the United States. It also includes any vessel which is neither documented nor numbered under the laws of the United States, nor documented under the laws of any foreign country, if the crew of such vessel is employed solely by one or more citizens or residents of the United States or corporations organized under the laws of the United States or of any State. (For provisions relating to the terms "State" and "citizen", see § 31.3306(j)-1.)

(b) The term "American aircraft" means any aircraft registered under the laws of the United States.

(c) For provisions relating to services performed outside the United States on or in connection with an American vessel or American aircraft, see paragraph (c) of § 31.3306(c)-2.

T.D. 6199, 9/4/56, amend T.D. 6516, 12/19/60, T.D. 6658, 6/26/63.

§ 31.3306(n)-1 Services on American vessel whose business is conducted by general agent of Secretary of Commerce.

(a) Section 3306(n) and this section of the regulations apply with respect only to services performed by an officer or member of the crew of an American vessel (1) which is owned by or bareboat chartered to the United States, and (2) whose business is conducted by a general agent of the Secretary of Commerce. Whether services performed by such an officer or member of a crew under the above conditions constitute employment is determined under section 3306(c) and (n), but without regard to section 3306(c)(6). See § 31.3306(c)(6)-1, relating to services performed in the employ of the United States and instrumentalities thereof. If, without regard to section 3306(c)(6), such services constitute employment, they are not excepted from employment by reason of the fact that they are performed on or in connection with an American vessel which is owned by or bareboat chartered to the United States and whose business is conducted by a general agent of the Secretary of Commerce, that is, such services are not excepted from employment by section 3306(c)(6). For provisions relating to services performed within the United States and services performed outside the United States which constitute employment, see § 31.3306(c)-2.

(b) The expression "officer or member of the crew" includes the master or officer in charge of the vessel, however designated, and every individual, subject to his authority, serving on board and contributing in any way to the operation and welfare of the vessel. Thus, the expression includes, for example, the master, mates, pilots, pursers, surgeons, stewards, engineers, firemen, cooks, clerks, carpenters, and deck hands.

(c) An employee of the United States who performs services as an officer or member of the crew of an American vessel which is owned by or bareboat chartered to the United States and whose business is conducted by a general agent of the Secretary of Commerce shall be deemed, under section 3306(n), to be performing services for such general agent rather than for the United States. Any such general agent of the Secretary of Commerce is considered a legal entity in his capacity as such general agent, separate and distinct from his identity as a person employing individuals on his own account. Each such general agent who in his capacity as such qualifies as an employer under section 3306(a) is with respect to each calendar year for which he so qualifies subject to the tax imposed by section 3301, and to all the requirements imposed upon an employer as defined in section 3306(a) by the regulations in this part, with respect to services which constitute employment by reason of section 3306(n) and this section of the regulations.

T.D. 6199, 9/4/56, amend T.D. 6516, 12/19/60.

§ 31.3306(p)-1 Employees of related corporations.

(a) In general. For purposes of sections 3301, 3302, and 3306(b)(1), when two or more related corporations concurrently employ the same individual and compensate that individual through a common paymaster which is one of the related corporations for which the individual performs services, each of the corporations is considered to have paid only the remuneration it actually disburses to that individual (unless the disbursing corporation fails to remit the taxes due). Paragraphs (b) and (c) of § 31.3121(s)-1 contain rules defining related corporations, common paymasters, and concurrent employment, and rules for determining the liability of the other related corporations for employment taxes if the common paymaster fails to remit the taxes pursuant to sections 3102 and 3111, and for allocating these taxes among the related corporations. Those rules also apply to the tax under section 3301. For purposes of applying those rules to this section, references in those rules to section 3111 are considered references to sections 3301 and 3302, and references to section 3121 are considered references to section 3306.

(b) Allocation of credit for contributions to State unemployment funds. A special rule for applying the rules of § 31.3121(s)-1 to this section applies if it is necessary to determine the ultimate liability of each related corporation for which services are performed in the event the common paymaster fails to remit the tax to the Internal Revenue Service. In determining the ultimate liability of a corporation, the credit for contributions to State unemployment funds that the corporation may claim under section 3302 is calculated as if each corporation were a separate employer.

(c) Effective date. This section is effective with respect to wages paid after December 31, 1978.

T.D. 7660, 12/18/79.

§ 31.3306(r)(2)-1 Treatment of amounts deferred under certain nonqualified deferred compensation plans.

(a) In general. Section 3306(r)(2) provides a special timing rule for the tax imposed by section 3301 with respect to any amount deferred under a nonqualified deferred compensation plan. Section 31.3121(v)(2)-1 contains rules relating to when amounts deferred under certain nonqualified deferred compensation plans are wages for purposes of sections 3121(v)(2), 3101, and 3111. The rules in § 31.3121(v)(2)-1 also apply to the special timing rule of section 3306(r)(2). For purposes of applying the rules in § 31.3121(v)(2)-1 to section 3306(r)(2) and this paragraph (a), references to the Federal Insurance Contributions Act are considered references to the Federal Unemployment Tax Act (26 U.S.C. 3301 et seq.), references to FICA are considered references to FUTA, references to section 3101 or 3111 are considered references to section 3301, references to section 3121(v)(2) are considered references to section 3306(r)(2), references to section 3121(a), (a)(5), and (a)(13) are considered references to section 3306(b), (b)(5), and (b)(10), respectively, and references to § 31.3121(a)-2(a) are considered references to § 31.3301-4.

(b) Effective dates and transition rules. Except as otherwise provided, section 3306(r)(2) applies to remuneration paid after December 31, 1984. Section 31.3121(v)(2)-2 contains effective date rules for certain remuneration paid after December 31, 1983, for purposes of section 3121(v)(2). The rules in § 31.3121(v)(2)-2 also apply to section 3306(r)(2). For purposes of applying the rules in § 31.3121(v)(2)-2 to section 3306(r)(2) and this paragraph (b), references to section 3121(v)(2) are considered references to section 3306(r)(2), and references to section 3121(a)(2), (a)(3), or (a)(13) are considered references to section 3306(b)(2), (b)(3), or (b)(10), respectively. In addition, references to § 31.3121(v)(2)-1 are considered references to paragraph (a) of this section. For purposes of applying the rules of § 31.3121(v)(2)-2 to this paragraph (b)—

(1) References to "December 31, 1983" are considered references to "December 31, 1984";

(2) References to "before 1984" are considered references to "before 1985";

(3) References to "Federal Insurance Contributions Act" are considered references to "Federal Unemployment Tax Act"; and

(4) References to "FICA" are considered references to "FUTA".

T.D. 8815, 1/28/99.

§ 31.3307-1 Deductions by an employer from remuneration of an employee.

Any amount deducted by an employer from the remuneration of an employee is considered to be a part of the employee's remuneration and is considered to be paid to the employee as remuneration at the time that the deduction is made. It is immaterial that any act of Congress or the law of any State requires or permits such deductions and the payment of the amount thereof to the United States, a State, or any political subdivision thereof.

T.D. 6199, 9/4/56, amend T.D. 6516, 12/19/60.

§ 31.3308-1 Instrumentalities of the United States specifically exempted from tax imposed by section 3301.

Section 3308 makes ineffectual as to the tax imposed by section 3301 (with respect to remuneration paid after 1961 for services performed after 1961) those provisions of law which grant to an instrumentality of the United States an exemption from taxation, unless such provisions grant a specific exemption from the tax imposed by section 3301 by an express reference to such section or the corresponding section of prior law. Thus, the general exceptions from Federal taxation granted by various statutes to certain instrumentalities of the United States without specific reference to the tax imposed by section 3301 or the corresponding section of prior law are rendered inoperative insofar as such exemptions relate to the tax imposed by section 3301. For provisions relating to the exception from employment of services performed in the employ of an instrumentality of the United States specifically exempted from the tax imposed by section 3301, see § 31.3306(c)(6)-1.

T.D. 6658, 6/26/63.

§ 31.3401(a)-1 Wages.

(a) In general. *(1)* The term "wages" means all remuneration for services performed by an employee for his employer unless specifically excepted under section 3401(a) or excepted under section 3402(e).

(2) The name by which the remuneration for services is designated is immaterial. Thus, salaries, fees, bonuses, commissions on sales or on insurance premiums, pensions, and retired pay are wages within the meaning of the statute if paid as compensation for services performed by the employee for his employer.

(3) The basis upon which the remuneration is paid is immaterial in determining whether the remuneration constitutes wages. Thus, it may be paid on the basis of piecework, or a percentage of profits; and may be paid hourly, daily, weekly, monthly, or annually.

(4) Generally the medium in which the remuneration is paid is also immaterial. It may be paid in cash or in something other than cash, as for example, stocks, bonds, or other forms of property. (See, however, § 31.3401(a)(11)-1, relating to the exclusion from wages of remuneration paid in any medium other than cash for services not in the course of the employer's trade or business, and § 31.3401(a)(16)-1, relating to the exclusion from wages of tips paid in any medium other than cash.) If services are paid for in a medium other than cash, the fair market value of the thing taken in payment is the amount to be included as wages. If the services were rendered at a stipulated price, in the absence of evidence to the contrary, such price will be presumed to be the fair value of the remuneration received. If a corporation transfers to its employees its own stock as remuneration for services rendered by the employee, the amount of such remuneration is the fair market value of the stock at the time of the transfer.

(5) Remuneration for services, unless such remuneration is specifically excepted by the statute, constitutes wages even though at the time paid the relationship of employer and employee no longer exists between the person in whose employ the services were performed and the individual who performed them.

Example. A is employed by R during the month of January 1955 and is entitled to receive remuneration of $100 for the services performed for R, the employer, during the month. A leaves the employ of R at the close of business on January 31, 1955. On February 15, 1955 (when A is no longer an employee of R), R pays A the remuneration of $100 which was earned for the services performed in January. The $100 is wages within the meaning of the statute.

(b) Certain specific items. *(1) Pensions and retirement pay.* (i) In general, pensions and retired pay are wages subject to withholding. However, no withholding is required with respect to amounts paid to an employee upon retirement which are taxable as annuities under the provisions of section 72 or 403. So-called pensions awarded by one to whom no services have been rendered are mere gifts or gratuities and do not constitute wages. Those payments of pensions or other benefits by the Federal Government under Title 38 of the United States Code which are excluded from gross income are not wages subject to withholding.

(ii) Amounts received as retirement pay for service in the Armed Forces of the United States, the Coast and Geodetic Survey, or the Public Health Service or as a disability annuity paid under the provisions of section 831 of the Foreign Service Act of 1946, as amended (22 U.S.C. 1081; 60 Stat. 1021), are subject to withholding unless such pay or disability annuity is excluded from gross income under section 104(a)(4), or is taxable as an annuity under the provisions of section 72. Where such retirement pay or disability annuity (not excluded from gross income under section 104(a)(4) and not taxable as an annuity under the provisions of section 72) is paid to a nonresident alien individual, withholding is required only in the case of such amounts paid to a nonresident alien individual who is a resident of Puerto Rico.

(2) Traveling and other expenses. Amounts paid specifically—either as advances or reimbursements—for traveling or other bona fide ordinary and necessary expenses incurred or reasonably expected to be incurred in the business of the employer are not wages and are not subject to withholding. Traveling and other reimbursed expenses must be identified either by making a separate payment or by specifically indicating the separate amounts where both wages and expense allowances are combined in a single payment. For amounts that are received by an employee on or after July 1, 1990, with respect to expenses paid or incurred on or after July 1, 1990, see § 31.3401(a)-4.

(3) Vacation allowances. Amounts of so-called "vacation allowances" paid to an employee constitute wages. Thus, the salary of an employee on vacation, paid notwithstanding his absence from work, constitute wages.

(4) Dismissal payments. Any payments made by an employer to an employee on account of dismissal, that is, involuntary separation from the service of the employer, constitute wages regardless of whether the employer is legally bound by contract, statute, or otherwise to make such payments.

(5) Deductions by employer from remuneration of an employee. Any amount deducted by an employer from the remuneration of an employee is considered to be a part of the employee's remuneration and is considered to be paid to the employee as remuneration at the time that the deduction is made. It is immaterial that any act of Congress, or the law of any State or of Puerto Rico, requires or permits such deductions and the payment of the amounts thereof to the United States, a State, a Territory, Puerto Rico, or the District of Columbia, or any political subdivision of any one or more of the foregoing.

(6) Payment by an employer of employee's tax, or employee's contributions under a State law. The term "wages" includes the amount paid by an employer on behalf of an employee (without deduction from the remuneration of, or other reimbursement from, the employee) on account of any payment required from an employee under a State unemployment compensation law, or on account of any tax imposed upon the employee by any taxing authority, including the taxes imposed by sections 3101 and 3201.

(7) Remuneration for services as employee of nonresident alien individual or foreign entity. The term "wages" includes remuneration for services performed by a citizen or resident (including, in regard to wages paid after Feb. 28, 1979, an individual treated as a resident under section 6013(g) or (h)) of the United States as an employee of a nonresident alien individual, foreign partnership, or foreign corporation whether or not such alien individual or foreign entity is engaged in trade or business within the United States. Any person paying wages on behalf of a nonresident alien individual, foreign partnership, or foreign corporation, not engaged in trade or business within the United States (including Puerto Rico as if a part of the United States), is subject to all the provisions of law and regulations applicable with respect to an employer. See § 31.3401(d)-1, relating to the term "employer", and § 31.3401(a)(8)(C)-1, relating

to remuneration paid for services performed by a citizen of the United States in Puerto Rico.

(8) Amounts paid under accident or health plans. (i) Amounts paid in taxable years beginning on or after January 1, 1977. (a) In general. Withholding is required on all payments of amounts includible in gross income under section 105(a) and § 1.105-1 (relating to amounts attributable to employer contributions), made in taxable years beginning on or after January 1, 1977, to an employee under an accident or health plan for a period of absence from work on account of personal injuries or sickness. Payments on which withholding is required by this subdivision are wages as defined in section 3401(a), and the employer shall deduct and withhold in accordance with the requirements of chapter 24 of subtitle C of the Code. Third party payments of sick pay, as defined in section 3402(o) and the regulations thereunder, are not wages for purposes of this section.

(b) Payments made by an agent of the employer. (1) Payments are considered made by the employer if a third party makes the payments as an agent of the employer. The determining factor as to whether a third party is an agent of the employer is whether the third party bears any insurance risk. If the third party bears no insurance risk and is reimbursed on a cost plus fee basis, the third party is an agent of the employer even if the third party is responsible for making determinations of the eligibility of individual employees of the employer for sick pay payments. If the third party is paid an insurance premium and not reimbursed on a cost plus fee basis, the third party is not an agent of the employer, but the third party is a payor of third party sick pay for purposes of voluntary withholding from sick pay under sections 3402(o) and 6051(f) and the regulations thereunder. If a third party and an employer enter into an agency agreement as provided in paragraph (c) of § 31.6051-3 (relating to statements required in case of sick pay paid by third parties), that agency agreement does not make the third party an agent of the employer for purposes of this paragraph.

(2) Payments made by agents subject to this paragraph are supplemental wages as defined in § 31.3402(g)-1, and are therefore subject to the rules regarding withholding tax on supplemental wages provided in § 31.3402(g)-1. For purposes of those rules, unless the agent is also an agent for purposes of withholding tax from the employee's regular wages, the agent may deem tax to have been withheld from regular wages paid to the employee during the calendar year.

(3) This paragraph is only applicable to amounts paid on or after May 25, 1983, unless the agent actually withheld taxes before that date.

(c) Exceptions to withholding. (1) Withholding is not required on payments that are specifically excepted under the numbered paragraphs of section 3401(a) (relating to the definition of wages), under section 3402(e) (relating to included and excluded wages), or under section 3402(n) (relating to employees incurring no income tax liability).

(2) Withholding is not required on disability payments to the extent that the payments are excludable from gross income under section 105(d). In determining the excludable portion of the disability payments, the employer may assume that payments that the employer makes to the employee are the employee's sole source of income. This exception applies only if the employee furnishes the employer with adequate verification of disability. A certificate from a qualified physician attesting that the employee is permanently and totally disabled (within the meaning of section 105(d)) shall be deemed to constitute adequate verification. This exception does not affect the requirement that a statement (which includes any amount paid under section 105(d)) be furnished under either section 6041 (relating to information at source) or section 6051 (relating to receipts for employees) and the regulations thereunder.

(ii) Amounts paid after December 31, 1955 and before January 1, 1977. (a) In general. The term "wage continuation payment", as used in this subdivision, means any payment to an employee which is made after December 31, 1955, and before January 1, 1977 under a wage continuation plan (as defined in paragraph (a)(2)(i) of § 1.105-4 and § 1.105-5 of Part 1 of this chapter (Income Tax Regulations) for a period of absence from work on account of personal injuries or sickness, to the extent such payment is attributable to contributions made by the employer which were not includible in the employee's gross income or is paid by the employer. Any such payment, whether or not excluded from the gross income of the employee under section 105(d), constitutes "wages" (unless specifically excepted under any of the numbered paragraphs of section 3401(a) or under section 3402(e)) and withholding thereon is required except as provided in paragraphs (b)(8)(ii)(b), (c), and (d) of this section.

(b) Amounts paid before January 1, 1977, by employer for whom services are performed for period of absence beginning after December 31, 1963. (1) Withholding is not required upon the amount of any wage continuation payment for a period of absence beginning after December 31, 1963, paid before January 1, 1977, to an employee directly by the employer for whom he performs services to the extent that such payment is excludable from the gross income of the employee under the provisions of section 105(d) in effect with respect to such payments, provided the records maintained by the employer—

(i) Separately show the amount of each such payment and the excludable portion thereof, and

(ii) Contain data substantiating the employee's entitlement to the exclusion provided in section 105(d) with respect to such amount, either by a written statement from the employee specifying whether his absence from work during the period for which the payment was made was due to a personal injury or to sickness and whether he was hospitalized for at least one day during this period; or by any other information which the employer reasonably believes establishes the employee's entitlement to the exclusion under section 105(d). Employers shall not be required to ascertain the accuracy of any written statement submitted by an employee in accordance with this subdivision (b)(1)(ii).

For purposes of this subdivision (b)(1), wage continuation payments reasonably expected by the employer to be made on behalf of the employer by another person shall be taken into account in determining whether the 75 percent test contained in section 105(d) is met and in computing the amount of any wage continuation payment made directly by the employer for whom services are performed by the employee which is within the $75 or $100 weekly rate of exclusion from the gross income of the employee provided in section 105(d). In making this latter computation, the amount excludable under section 105(d) shall be applied first against payments reasonably expected to be made on behalf of the employer by the other person and then, to the extent any part of the exclusion remains, against the payments made directly by the employer. In a case in which wage continuation payments are not paid at a constant rate for the first 30 calendar days of the period of absence, the determination of whether the 75 percent test contained in section 105(d) is met shall be based upon the length of the employee's absence as of the end of the period for which the payment by the employer is made, without regard to the effect which any further extension of such absence may have upon the excludability of the payment.

(2) The computation of the amount of any wage continuation payment with respect to which the employer may refrain from withholding may be illustrated by the following examples:

Example (1). A, an employee of B, normally works Monday through Friday and has a regular weekly rate of wages of $100. On Monday, November 5, 1974, A becomes ill, and as a result is absent from work for two weeks, returning to work on Monday, November 19, 1974. A is not hospitalized. Under B's noncontributory wage continuation plan, A receives no benefits for the first three working days of absence and is paid benefits directly by B at the rate of $85 a week thereafter ($34 for the last two days of the first week of absence and $85 for the second week of absence). No wage continuation payment is made by any other person. Since the benefits are entirely attributable to contributions to the plan by B, such benefits are wage continuation payments in their entirety. The wage continuation payments for the first seven calendar days of absence are not excludable from A's gross income because A was not hospitalized for at least one day during his period of absence, and therefore B must withhold with respect to such payments. Under section 105(d), the wage continuation payments attributable to absence after the first seven calendar days of absence are excludable to the extent that they do not exceed a rate of $75 a week. Under the principles stated in paragraph (e)(6)(iv) of § 1.105-4 of this chapter (Income Tax Regulations), the wage continuation payments in this case are at a rate not in excess of 75 percent ($^{119}/_{200}$ or 59.5 percent) of A's regular weekly rate of wages. Accordingly, B may refrain from withholding with respect to $75 of the wage continuation payment attributable to the second week of absence.

Example (2). Assume the facts in example (1) except that A is unable to return to work until Monday, February 11, 1975, and that, of the $85 a week of wage continuation payments $35 is paid directly by B and $50 is reasonably expected by B to be paid by C, an insurance company, on behalf of B. In such a case, both the $50 and the $35 payments constitute wage continuation payments and the amount of such payments which is attributable to the first 30 calendar days of absence is at a rate not in excess of 75 percent ($^{323}/_{440}$ or 73.4 percent) of A's regular weekly rate of wages. Therefore, under section 105(d), the portion of such payments which is attributable to absence after the first seven calendar days of absence is excludable to the extent that it does not exceed a rate of $75 a week for the eighth through the thirtieth calendar day of absence and does not exceed a rate of $100 a week thereafter. B may refrain from withholding with respect to $25 a week (the amount by which the $75 maximum excludable amount exceeds the $50 reasonably expected by B to be paid by C) of his direct payments for the eighth through the thirtieth calendar day of absence. Thereafter, B may refrain from withholding with respect to the entire $35 paid directly by him, since the maximum excludable amount ($100 a week) exceeds the total of payments made by B and payments which B reasonably expects will be made by C.

(c) Amounts paid by employer for whom services are performed for period of absence beginning before January 1, 1964. Withholding is not required upon the amount of any wage continuation payment for a period of absence beginning before January 1, 1964, made to an employee directly by the employer for whom he performs services to the extent that such payment is excludable from the gross income of the employee under the provisions of section 105(d) in effect with respect to such payments, provided the records maintained by the employer—

(1) Separately show the amount of each such payment and the excludable portion thereof, and

(2) Contain data substantiating the employee's entitlement to the exclusion provided in section 105(d) with respect to such amount, either by a written statement from the employee specifying whether his absence from work during the period for which the payment was made was due to a personal injury or whether such absence was due to sickness, and, if the latter, whether he was hospitalized for at least one day during this period; or by any other information which the employer reasonably believes establishes the employee's entitlement to the exclusion under section 105(d). Employers shall not be required to ascertain the accuracy of the information contained in any written statement submitted by an employee in accordance with this paragraph (b)(8)(ii) (c)(2). For purposes of this paragraph (b)(8)(ii)(c), the computation of the amount excludable from the gross income of the employee under section 105(d) may be made either on the basis of the wage continuation payments which are made directly by the employer for whom the employee performs services, or on the basis of such payments in conjunction with any wage continuation payments made on behalf of the employer by a person who is regarded as an employer under section 3401(d)(1).

(d) Amounts paid before January 1, 1977 by person other than the employer for whom services are performed. No tax shall be withheld upon any wage continuation payment made to an employee by or on behalf of a person who is not the employer for whom the employee performs services but who is regarded as an employer under section 3401(d)(1). For example, no tax shall be withheld with respect to wage continuation payments made on behalf of an employer by an insurance company under an accident or health policy, by a separate trust under an accident or health plan, or by a State agency from a sickness and disability fund maintained under State law.

(e) Cross references. See sections 6001 and 6051 and the regulations thereunder for rules with respect to the records which must be maintained in connection with wage continuation payments and for rules with respect to the statements which must be furnished an employee in connection with wage continuation payments, respectively. See also section 105 and § 1.105-4 of this chapter (Income Tax Regulations).

(9) Value of meals and lodging. The value of any meals or lodging furnished to an employee by his employer is not subject to withholding if the value of the meals or lodging is excludable from the gross income of the employee. See § 1.119-1 of this chapter (Income Tax Regulations).

(10) Facilities or privileges. Ordinarily, facilities or privileges (such as entertainment, medical services, or so-called "courtesy" discounts on purchases), furnished or offered by an employer to his employees generally, are not considered as wages subject to withholding if such facilities or privileges are of relatively small value and are offered or furnished by the employer merely as a means of promoting the health, good will, contentment, or efficiency of his employees.

(11) Tips or gratuities. Tips or gratuities paid, prior to January 1, 1966, directly to an employee by a customer of an employer, and not accounted for by the employee to the

employer are not subject to withholding. For provisions relating to the treatment of tips received by an employee after December 31, 1965, as wages, see §§ 31.3401(f)-1 and 31.3402(k)-1.

(12) Remuneration for services performed by permanent resident of Virgin Islands. (i) Exemption from withholding. No tax shall be withheld for the United States under chapter 24 from a payment of wages by an employer, including the United States or any agency thereof, to an employee if at the time of payment it is reasonable to believe that the employee will be required to satisfy his income tax obligations with respect to such wages under section 28(a) of the Revised Organic Act of the Virgin Islands (68 Stat. 508). That section provides that all persons whose permanent residence is in the Virgin Islands "shall satisfy their income tax obligations under applicable taxing statutes of the United States by paying their tax on income derived from all sources both within and outside the Virgin Islands into the treasury of the Virgin Islands".

(ii) Claiming exemption. If the employee furnishes to the employer a statement in duplicate that he expects to satisfy his income tax obligations under section 28(a) of the Revised Organic Act of the Virgin Islands with respect to all wages subsequently to be paid to him by the employer during the taxable year to which the statement relates, the employer may, in the absence of information to the contrary, rely on such statement as establishing reasonable belief that the employee will so satisfy his income tax obligations. The employee's statement shall identify the taxable year to which it relates, and both the original and the duplicate copy thereof shall be signed and dated by the employee.

(iii) Disposition of statement. The original of the statement shall be retained by the employer. The duplicate copy of the statement shall be sent by the employer to the Director of International Operations, Washington, D.C. 20255, on or before the last day of the calendar year in which the employer receives the statement from the employee.

(iv) Applicability of subparagraph. This subparagraph has no application with respect to any payment of remuneration which is not subject to withholding by reason of any other provisions of the regulations in this subpart.

(13) Federal employees resident in Puerto Rico. Except as provided in paragraph (d) of § 31.3401(a)(6)-1, the term "wages" includes remuneration for services performed by a nonresident alien individual who is a resident of Puerto Rico if such services are performed as an employee of the United States or any agency thereof. The place where the services are performed is immaterial for purposes of this subparagraph.

(14) Supplemental unemployment compensation benefits. (i) Supplemental unemployment compensation benefits paid to an individual after December 31, 1970, shall be treated (for purposes of the provisions of Subparts E, F, and G of this part which relate to withholding of income tax) as if they were wages, to the extent such benefits are includible in the gross income of such individual.

(ii) For purposes of this subparagraph, the term "supplemental unemployment compensation benefits" means amounts which are paid to an employee, pursuant to a plan to which the employer is a party, because of the employee's involuntary separation from the employment of the employer, whether or not such separation is temporary, but only when such separation is one resulting directly from a reduction in force, the discontinuance of a plant or operation, or other similar conditions.

(iii) For the meanings of the terms "involuntary separation from the employment of the employer" and "other similar conditions," see subparagraphs (3) and (4) of § 1.501(c)(17)-1(b) of this chapter (Income Tax Regulations).

(iv) As used in this subparagraph, the term "employee" means an employee within the meaning of paragraph (a) of § 31.3401(c)-1, the term "employer" means an employer within the meaning of paragraph (a) of § 31.3401(d)-1, and the term "employment" means employment as defined under the usual common law rules.

(v) References in this chapter to wages as defined in section 3401(a) shall be deemed to refer also to supplemental unemployment compensation benefits which are treated under this subparagraph as if they were wages.

(15) Split-dollar life insurance arrangements. See § 1.61-22 of this chapter for rules relating to the treatment of split-dollar life insurance arrangements.

(c) Geographical definitions. For definition of the term "United States" and for other geographical definitions relating to the Continental Shelf see section 638 and § 1.638-1 of this chapter.

T.D. 6155, 12/29/55, amend T.D. 6259, 10/25/57, T.D. 6654, 5/27/63, T.D. 6908, 12/30/66, T.D. 7001, 1/17/69, T.D. 7068, 11/10/70, T.D. 7277, 5/14/73, T.D. 7493, 6/29/77, T.D. 7670, 1/30/80, T.D. 7888, 4/22/83, T.D. 8276, 12/7/89, T.D. 8324, 12/14/90, T.D. 9092, 9/11/2003, T.D. 9276, 7/24/2006.

---

§ 31.3401(a)-1T Question and answer relating to the definition of wages in section 3401(a) (temporary).

The following question and answer relates to the definition of wages in section 3401(a) of the Internal Revenue Code of 1954, as amended by section 531(d)(4) of the Tax Reform Act of 1984 (98 Stat. 886):

Q-1. Are fringe benefits included in the definition of "wages" under section 3401(a)?

A-1. Yes, unless specifically excluded from the definition of "wages" pursuant to section 3401(a)(1) through (20). For example, a fringe benefit provided to or on behalf of an employee is excluded from the definition of "wages" if at the time such benefit is provided it is reasonable to believe that the employee will be able to exclude such benefit from income under section 117 or 132.

T.D. 8004, 1/2/85.

---

§ 31.3401(a)-2 Exclusions from wages.

(a) In general. *(1)* The term "wages" does not include any remuneration for services performed by an employee for his employer which is specifically excepted from wages under section 3401(a).

(2) The exception attaches to the remuneration for services performed by an employee and not to the employee as an individual; that is, the exception applies only to the remuneration in an excepted category.

Example. A is an individual who is employed part time by B to perform domestic service in his home (see § 31.3401(a)(3)-1). A is also employed by C part time to perform services as a clerk in a department store owned by him. While no withholding is required with respect to A's remuneration for services performed in the employ of B (the remuneration being excluded from wages), the exception does not embrace the remuneration for services performed by A in the employ of C and withholding is required with respect to the wages for such services.

(3) For provisions relating to the circumstances under which remuneration which is excepted is nevertheless deemed to be wages, and relating to the circumstances under which remuneration which is not excepted is nevertheless deemed not to be wages, see § 31.3402(e)-1.

(4) For provisions relating to payments with respect to which a voluntary withholding agreement is in effect, which are not defined as wages in section 3401(a) but which are nevertheless deemed to be wages, see §§ 31.3401(a)-3 and 31.3402(p)-1.

(b) Fees paid a public official. *(1)* Authorized fees paid to public officials such as notaries public, clerks of courts, sheriffs, etc., for services rendered in the performance of their official duties are excepted from wages and hence are not subject to withholding. However, salaries paid such officials by the Government, or by a Government agency or instrumentality, are subject to withholding.

(2) Amounts paid to precinct workers for services performed at election booths in State, county, and municipal elections and fees paid to jurors and witnesses are in the nature of fees paid to public officials and therefore are not subject to withholding.

T.D. 6259, 10/25/57, amend T.D. 6654, 5/27/63, T.D. 7096, 3/17/71.

§ 31.3401(a)-3 Amounts deemed wages under voluntary withholding agreements.

(a) In general. Notwithstanding the exceptions to the definition of wages specified in section 3401(a) and the regulations thereunder, the term "wages" includes the amounts described in paragraph (b)(1) of this section with respect to which there is a voluntary withholding agreement in effect under section 3402(p). References in this chapter to the definition of wages contained in section 3401(a) shall be deemed to refer also to this section (§ 31.3401(a)-3).

(b) Remuneration for services. *(1)* Except as provided in subparagraph (2) of this paragraph, the amounts referred to in paragraph (a) of this section include any remuneration for services performed by an employee for an employer which, without regard to this section, does not constitute wages under section 3401(a). For example, remuneration for services performed by an agricultural worker or a domestic worker in a private home (amounts which are specifically excluded from the definition of wages by section 3401(a)(2) and (3), respectively) are amounts with respect to which a voluntary withholding agreement may be entered into under section 3402(p). See §§ 31.3401(c)-1 and 31.3401(d)-1 for the definitions of "employee" and "employer."

(2) For purposes of this paragraph, remuneration for services shall not include amounts not subject to withholding under § 31.3401(a)-1(b)(12) (relating to remuneration for services performed by a permanent resident of the Virgin Islands), § 31.3401(a)-2(b) (relating to fees paid to a public official), section 3401(a)(5) (relating to remuneration for services for foreign government or international organization), section 3401(a)(8)(B) (relating to remuneration for services performed in a possession of the United States (other than Puerto Rico) by citizens of the United States), section 3401(a)(8)(C) (relating to remuneration for services performed in Puerto Rico by citizens of the United States), section 3401(a)(11) (relating to remuneration other than in cash for service not in the course of employer's trade or business), section 3401(a)(12) (relating to payments from or to certain tax-exempt trusts, or under or to certain annuity plans or bond purchase plans), section 3401(a)(14) (relating to group-term life insurance), section 3401(a)(15) (relating to moving expenses), or section 3401(a)(16)(A) (relating to tips paid in any medium other than cash).

T.D. 7096, 3/17/71.

§ 31.3401(a)-4 Reimbursements and other expense allowance amounts.

(a) When excluded from wages. If a reimbursement or other expense allowance arrangement meets the requirements of section 62(c) of the Code and § 1.62-2 and the expenses are substantiated within a reasonable period of time, payments made under the arrangement that do not exceed the substantiated expenses are treated as paid under an accountable plan and are not wages. In addition, if both wages and the reimbursement or other expense allowance are combined in a single payment, the reimbursement or other expense allowance must be identified either by making a separate payment or by specifically identifying the amount of the reimbursement or other expense allowance.

(b) When included in wages. *(1) Accountable plans.* (i) General rule. Except as provided in paragraph (b)(1)(ii) of this section, if a reimbursement or other expense allowance arrangement satisfies the requirements of section 62(c) and § 1.62-2, but the expenses are not substantiated within a reasonable period of time or amounts in excess of the substantiated expenses are not returned within a reasonable period of time, the amount paid under the arrangement in excess of the substantiated expenses is treated as paid under a nonaccountable plan, is included in wages, and is subject to withholding and payment of employment taxes no later than the first payroll period following the end of the reasonable period.

(ii) Per diem or mileage allowances. If a reimbursement or other expense allowance arrangement providing a per diem or mileage allowance satisfies the requirements of section 62(c) and § 1.62-2, but the allowance is paid at a rate for each day or mile of travel that exceeds the amount of the employee's expenses deemed substantiated for a day or mile of travel, the excess portion is treated as paid under a nonaccountable plan and is included in wages. In the case of a per diem or mileage allowance paid as a reimbursement, the excess portion is subject to withholding and payment of employment taxes when paid. In the case of a per diem or mileage allowance paid as an advance, the excess portion is subject to withholding and payment of employment taxes no later than the first payroll period following the payroll period in which the expenses with respect to which the advance was paid (i.e., the days or miles of travel) are substantiated. The Commissioner may, in his discretion, prescribe special rules in pronouncements of general applicability regarding the timing of withholding and payment of employment taxes on per diem and mileage allowances.

(2) Nonaccountable plans. If a reimbursement or other expense allowance arrangement does not satisfy the requirements of section 62(c) and § 1.62-2 (e.g., the arrangement does not require expenses to be substantiated or require amounts in excess of the substantiated expenses to be returned), all amounts paid under the arrangement are treated as paid under a nonaccountable plan, are included in wages, and are subject to withholding and payment of employment taxes when paid.

(c) Withholding rate. Payments made under reimbursement or other expense allowance arrangements that are subject to income tax withholding are supplemental wages as defined in § 31.3402(g)-1. Accordingly, withholding on such supplemental wages is calculated under the rules provided with respect to supplemental wages in § 31.3402(g)-1.

(d) Effective dates. This section generally applies to payments made under reimbursement or other expense allowance arrangements received by an employee on or after July 1, 1990, with respect to expenses paid or incurred on or after July 1, 1990. Paragraph (b)(1)(ii) of this section applies to payments made under reimbursement or other expense allowance arrangements received by an employee on or after January 1, 1991, with respect to expenses paid or incurred on or after January 1, 1991.

T.D. 8276, 12/7/89, amend T.D. 8324, 12/14/90, T.D. 9276, 7/24/2006.

§ 31.3401(a)(1)-1 Remuneration of members of the Armed Forces of the United States for active service in combat zone or while hospitalized as a result of such service.

Caution: The Treasury has not yet amended Reg § 31.3401(a)(1)-1 to reflect changes made by P.L. 104-117.

Remuneration paid for active service as a member of the Armed Forces of the United States performed in a month during any part of which such member served in a combat zone (as determined under section 112) or is hospitalized at any place as a result of wounds, disease, or injury incurred while serving in such a combat zone is excepted from wages and is, therefore, not subject to withholding. The exception with respect to hospitalization is applicable, however, only if during all of such month there are combatant activities in some combat zone (as determined under section 112). See § 1.112-1 of this chapter (Income Tax Regulations).

T.D. 6259, 10/25/57.

§ 31.3401(a)(2)-1 Agricultural labor.

The term "wages" does not include remuneration for services which constitute agricultural labor as defined in section 3121(g). For regulations relating to the definition of the term "agricultural labor", see § 31.3121(g)-1.

T.D. 6259, 10/25/57.

§ 31.3401(a)(3)-1 Remuneration for domestic service.

(a) In a private home. *(1)* Remuneration paid for services of a household nature performed by an employee in or about a private home of the person by whom he is employed is excepted from wages and hence is not subject to withholding. A private home is a fixed place of abode of an individual or family. A separate and distinct dwelling unit maintained by an individual in an apartment house, hotel, or other similar establishment may constitute a private home. If a dwelling house is used primarily as a boarding or lodging house for the purpose of supplying board or lodging to the public as a business enterprise, it is not a private home, and the remuneration paid for services performed therein is not within the exception.

(2) In general, services of a household nature in or about a private home include services performed by cooks, waiters, butlers, housekeepers, governesses, maids, valets, baby sitters, janitors, laundresses, furnacemen, caretakers, handymen, gardeners, footmen, grooms, and chauffeurs of automobiles for family use.

(b) In a local college club or local chapter of a college fraternity or sorority. *(1)* Remuneration paid for services of a household nature performed by an employee in or about the club rooms or house of a local college club or of a local chapter of a college fraternity or sorority by which he is employed is excepted from wages and hence is not subject to withholding. A local college club or local chapter of a college fraternity or sorority does not include an alumni club or chapter. If the club rooms or house of a local college club or local chapter of a college fraternity or sorority is used primarily for the purpose of supplying board or lodging to students or the public as a business enterprise, the remuneration paid for services performed therein is not within the exception.

(2) In general, services of a household nature in or about the club rooms or house of a local college club or local chapter of a college fraternity or sorority include services rendered by cooks, waiters, butlers, maids, janitors, laundresses, furnacemen, handymen, gardeners, housekeepers, and housemothers.

(c) Remuneration not excepted. Remuneration paid for services not of a household nature, such as services performed as a private secretary, tutor, or librarian, even though performed in the employer's private home or in a local college club or local chapter of a college fraternity or sorority, is not within the exception. Remuneration paid for services of a household nature is not within the exception if performed in or about rooming or lodging houses, boarding houses, clubs (except local college clubs), hotels, hospitals, eleemosynary institutions, or commercial offices or establishments.

T.D. 6259, 10/25/57.

§ 31.3401(a)(4)-1 Cash remuneration for service not in the course of employer's trade or business.

(a) Cash remuneration paid for services not in the course of the employer's trade or business performed by an employee for an employer in a calendar quarter is excepted from wages and hence is not subject to withholding unless—

(1) The cash remuneration paid for such services performed by the employee for the employer in the calendar quarter is $50 or more; and

(2) Such employee is regularly employed in the calendar quarter by such employer to perform such services.

Unless the tests set forth in both subparagraphs (1) and (2) of this paragraph are met, cash remuneration for service not in the course of the employer's trade or business is excluded from wages. (For provisions relating to the exclusion from wages of remuneration paid in any medium other than cash for services not in the course of the employer's trade or business, see § 31.3401(a)(11)-1.)

(b) The term "services not in the course of the employer's trade or business" includes services that do not promote or advance the trade or business of the employer. As used in this section, the term does not include service not in the course of the employer's trade or business performed on a farm operated for profit or domestic service in a private home, local college club, or local chapter of a college fraternity or sorority. Accordingly, this exception does not apply with respect to remuneration which is excepted from wages under section 3401(a)(2) or section 3401(a)(3) (see §§ 31.3401(a)(2)-1 and 31.3401(a)(3)-1, respectively). Remuneration paid for service performed for a corporation does not come within the exception.

(c) The test relating to cash remuneration of $50 or more is based on the remuneration earned during a calendar quarter rather than on the remuneration paid in a calendar quarter. However, for purposes of determining whether the test is met, it is also required that the remuneration be paid, although it is immaterial when the remuneration is paid. Furthermore, in determining whether $50 or more has been paid for service not in the course of the employer's trade or business, only cash remuneration for such service shall be taken into account. The term "cash remuneration" includes checks and other monetary media of exchange. Remuneration paid in any other medium, such as lodging, food, or other goods or commodities, is disregarded in determining whether the cash remuneration test is met.

(d) For purposes of this exception, an individual is deemed to be regularly employed by an employer during a calendar quarter only if—

(1) Such individual performs service not in the course of the employer's trade or business for such employer for some portion of the day on at least 24 days (whether or not consecutive) during such calendar quarter; or

(2) Such individual was regularly employed (as determined under subparagraph (1) of this paragraph) by such employer in the performance of service not in the course of the employer's trade or business during the preceding calendar quarter.

(e) In determining whether an employee has performed service not in the course of the employer's trade or business on at least 24 days during a calendar quarter, there shall be counted as one day—

(1) Any day or portion thereof on which the employee actually performs such service; and

(2) Any day or portion thereof on which the employee does not perform service of the prescribed character but with respect to which cash remuneration is paid or payable to the employee for such service, such as a day on which the employee is sick or on vacation.

An employee who on a particular day reports for work and, at the direction of his employer, holds himself in readiness to perform service not in the course of the employer's trade or business shall be considered to be engaged in the actual performance of such service on that day. For purposes of this exception, a day is a continuous period of 24 hours commencing at midnight and ending at midnight.

T.D. 6259, 10/25/57.

§ 31.3401(a)(5)-1 Remuneration for services for foreign government or international organization.

(a) Services for foreign government. *(1)* Remuneration paid for services performed as an employee of a foreign government is excepted from wages and hence is not subject to withholding. The exception includes not only remuneration paid for services performed by ambassadors, ministers, and other diplomatic officers and employees but also remuneration paid for services performed as a consular or other officer or employee of a foreign government or as a nondiplomatic representative of such a government. However, the exception does not include remuneration for services performed for a corporation created or organized in the United States or under the laws of the United States or any State (including the District of Columbia or the Territory of Alaska or Hawaii) or of Puerto Rico even though such corporation is wholly owned by such a government.

(2) The citizenship or residence of the employee and the place where the services are performed are immaterial for purposes of the exception.

(b) Services for international organization. *(1)* Subject to the provisions of section 1 of the International Organizations Immunities Act (22 USC 288), remuneration paid for services performed within or without the United States by an employee for an international organization as defined in section 7701(a)(18) is excepted from wages and hence is not subject to withholding. The term "employee" as used in the preceding sentence includes not only an employee who is a citizen or resident of the United States but also an employee who is a nonresident alien individual. The term "employee" also includes an officer. An organization designated by the President through appropriate Executive order as entitled to enjoy the privileges, exemptions, and immunities provided in the International Organizations Immunities Act may enjoy the benefits of the exclusion from wages with respect to remuneration paid for services performed for such organization prior to the date of the issuance of such Executive order, if (i) the Executive order does not provide otherwise and (ii) the organization is a public international organization in which the United States participates, pursuant to a treaty or under the authority of an act of Congress authorizing such participation or making an appropriation for such participation, at the time such services are performed.

(2) Section 7701(a)(18) provides as follows:

Sec. 7701. Definitions. (a) When used in this title, where not otherwise distinctly expressed or manifestly incompatible with the intent thereof—

* * * * * * (18) International organization. The term "international organization" means a public international organization entitled to enjoy privileges, exemptions, and immunities as an international organization under the International Organizations Immunities Act (22 USC 288–288f).

(3) Section 1 of the International Organizations Immunities Act provides as follows:

Section 1 [International Organizations Immunities Act.] For the purposes of this title [International Organizations Immunities Act], the term "international organization" means a public international organization in which the United States participates pursuant to any treaty or under the authority of any Act of Congress authorizing such participation or making an appropriation for such participation, and which shall have been designated by the President through appropriate Executive order as being entitled to enjoy the privileges, exemptions, and immunities herein provided. The President shall be authorized, in the light of the functions performed by any such international organization, by appropriate Executive order to withhold or withdraw from any such organization or its officers or employees any of the privileges, exemptions, and immunities provided for in this title (including the amendments made by this title) or to condition or limit the enjoyment by any such organization or its officers or employees of any such privilege, exemption, or immunity. The President shall be authorized, if in his judgment such action should be justified by reason of the abuse by an international organization or its officers and employees of the privileges, exemptions, and immunities herein provided or for any other reason, at any time to revoke the designation of any international organization under this section, whereupon the international organization in question shall cease to be classed as an international organization for the purposes of this title.

T.D. 6259, 10/25/57.

§ 31.3401(a)(6)-1 Remuneration for services of nonresident alien individuals.

(a) In general. All remuneration paid after December 31, 1966, for services performed by a nonresident alien individual, if such remuneration otherwise constitutes wages within the meaning of § 31.3401(a)-1 and if such remuneration is effectively connected with the conduct of a trade or business within the United States, is subject to withholding under section 3402 unless excepted from wages under this section. In regard to wages paid under this section after February 28, 1979, the term "nonresident alien individual" does not include a nonresident alien individual treated as a resident under section 6013 (g) or (h).

(b) Remuneration for services performed outside the United States. Remuneration paid to a nonresident alien individual (other than a resident of Puerto Rico) for services performed outside the United States is excepted from wages and hence is not subject to withholding.

(c) Remuneration for services of residents of Canada or Mexico who enter and leave the United States at frequent intervals. *(1) Transportation service.* Remuneration paid to a nonresident alien individual who is a resident of Canada or Mexico and who, in the performance of his duties in transportation service between points in the United States and points in such foreign country, enters and leaves the United States at frequent intervals, is excepted from wages and hence is not subject to withholding. This exception applies to personnel engaged in railroad, bus, truck, ferry, steamboat, aircraft or other transportation services and applies whether the employer is a domestic or foreign entity. Thus, the remuneration of a nonresident alien individual who is a resident of Canada and an employee of a domestic railroad, for services as a member of the crew of a train operating between points in Canada and points in the United States, is not subject to withholding under section 3402.

(2) Service on international projects. Remuneration paid to a nonresident alien individual who is a resident of Canada or Mexico and who, in the performance of his duties in connection with the construction, maintenance, or operation of a waterway, viaduct, dam, or bridge traversed by, or traversing, the boundary between the United States and Canada or the boundary between the United States and Mexico, as the case may be, enters and leaves the United States at frequent intervals, is excepted from wages and hence is not subject to withholding. Thus, the remuneration of a nonresident alien individual who is a resident of Canada, for services as an employee in connection with the construction, maintenance, or operation of the Saint Lawrence Seaway and who, in the performance of such services, enters and leaves the United States at frequent intervals, is not subject to withholding under section 3402.

(3) Limitation. The exceptions provided by this paragraph do not apply to the remuneration of a resident of Canada or of Mexico who is employed wholly within the United States as, for example, where such a resident is employed to perform service at a fixed point or points in the United States, such as a factory, store, office, or designated area or areas within the United States, and who commutes from his home in Canada or Mexico, in the pursuit of his employment within the United States.

(4) Certificate required. In order for an exception provided by this paragraph to apply for any taxable year, the nonresident alien employee must furnish his employer a statement in duplicate for the taxable year setting forth the employee's name, address, and taxpayer identifying number, and certifying (i) that he is not a citizen or resident of the United States, (ii) that he is a resident of Canada or Mexico, as the case may be, and (iii) that he expects to meet the requirements of subparagraph (1) or (2) of this paragraph with respect to remuneration to be paid during the taxable year in respect of which the statement is filed. The statement shall be dated, shall identify the taxable year to which it relates, shall be signed by the employee, and shall contain, or be verified by, a written declaration that it is made under the penalties of perjury. No particular form is prescribed for this statement. The duplicate copy of each statement filed during any calendar year pursuant to this paragraph shall be forwarded by the employer with, and attached to, the Form 1042S required by paragraph (c) of § 1.1461-2 with respect to such remuneration for such calendar year.

(d) Remuneration for services performed by residents of Puerto Rico. *(1)* Remuneration paid for services performed in Puerto Rico by a nonresident alien individual who is a resident of Puerto Rico for an employer (other than the United States or any agency thereof) is excepted from wages and hence is not subject to withholding.

(2) Remuneration paid for services performed outside the United States but not in Puerto Rico by a nonresident alien individual who is a resident of Puerto Rico for an employer (other than the United States or any agency thereof) is excepted from wages and hence is not subject to withholding if such individual does not expect to be a resident of Puerto Rico during the entire taxable year. In order for the exception provided by this subparagraph to apply for any taxable year, the nonresident alien employee must furnish his employer a statement for the taxable year setting forth the employee's name and address and certifying (i) that he is not a citizen or resident of the United States and (ii) that he is a resident of Puerto Rico but does not expect to be a resident of Puerto Rico during the entire taxable year. The statement shall be dated, shall identify the taxable year to which it relates, shall be signed by the employee, and shall contain, or be verified by, a written declaration that it is made under the penalties of perjury. No particular form is prescribed for this statement.

(3) Remuneration paid for services performed outside the United States by a nonresident alien individual who is a resident of Puerto Rico as an employee of the United States or any agency thereof is excepted from wages and hence is not subject to withholding if such individual does not expect to be a resident of Puerto Rico during the entire taxable year. In order for the exception provided by this subparagraph to apply for any taxable year, the nonresident alien employee must furnish his employer a statement for the taxable year setting forth the employee's name and address and certifying (i) that he is not a citizen or resident of the United States and (ii) that he is a resident of Puerto Rico but does not expect to be a resident of Puerto Rico during the entire taxable year. This statement shall be dated, shall identify the taxable year to which it relates, shall be signed by the employee, and shall contain, or be verified by, a written declaration that it is made under the penalties of perjury. No particular form is prescribed for this statement.

(e) Exemption from income tax for remuneration paid for services performed before January 1, 2001. Remuneration paid for services performed within the United States by a nonresident alien individual before January 1, 2001, is excepted from wages and hence is not subject to withholding if such remuneration is, or will be, exempt from income tax imposed by chapter 1 of the Internal Revenue Code by reason of a provision of the Internal Revenue Code or an income tax convention to which the United States is a party. In order for the exception provided by this paragraph to apply for any taxable year, the nonresident alien employee must furnish his employer a statement in duplicate for the taxable year setting forth the employee's name, address, and taxpayer identifying number, and certifying (1) that he is not a citizen or resident of the United States, (2) that the remuneration to be paid to him during the taxable year is, or will be, exempt from the tax imposed by chapter 1 of the Code, and (3) the reason why such remuneration is so exempt from tax. If the remuneration is claimed to be exempt from tax by reason of a provision of an income tax convention to which the United States is a party, the statement shall also indicate the provision and tax convention under which the exemption is claimed, the country of which the employee is a resident, and sufficient facts to justify the claim to exemption. The statement shall be dated, shall identify the taxable year for which it is to apply and the remuneration to which it relates, shall be signed by the employee, and shall contain, or be verified by, a written declaration that it is made under the penalties of perjury. No particular form is prescribed for this statement. The duplicate copy of each statement filed during any calendar year pursuant to this paragraph shall be forwarded by the employer with, and attached to, the Form 1042S required by paragraph (c) of § 1.1461-2 with respect to such remuneration for such calendar year.

(f) Exemption from income tax for remuneration paid for services performed after December 31, 2000. Remuneration paid for services performed within the United States by a nonresident alien individual after December 31, 2000, is excepted from wages and hence is not subject to withholding if such remuneration is, or will be, exempt from the income tax imposed by chapter 1 of the Internal Revenue Code by reason of a provision of the Internal Revenue Code or an income tax convention to which the United States is a party. An employer may rely on a claim that the employee is entitled to an exemption from tax if it complies with the requirements of § 1.1441-1(e)(1)(ii) of this chapter (for a claim based on a provision of the Internal Revenue Code) or § 1.1441-4(b)(2) of this chapter (for a claim based on an income tax convention).

T.D. 6908, 12/30/66, amend T.D. 7670, 1/30/80, T.D. 7977, 9/19/84, T.D. 8734, 10/6/97, T.D. 8804, 12/30/98, T.D. 8856, 12/29/99.

§ 31.3401(a)(6)-1A Remuneration for services of certain nonresident alien individuals paid before January 1, 1967.

(a) Except in the case of certain nonresident alien individuals who are residents of Canada, Mexico, or Puerto Rico or individuals who are temporarily present in the United States as nonimmigrants under subparagraph (F) or (J) of section 101(a)(15) of the Immigration and Nationality Act (8 USC 1101), as amended, remuneration for services performed by nonresident alien individuals does not constitute wages subject to withholding under section 3402. For withholding of income tax on remuneration paid for services performed within the United States in the case of nonresident alien individuals generally, see § 1.1441-1 and following of this chapter (Income Tax Regulations).

(b) Remuneration paid to nonresident aliens who are residents of a contiguous country (Canada or Mexico) and who enter and leave the United States at frequent intervals is not excepted from wages under section 3401(a)(6). See, however, § 31.3401(a)(7)-1, relating to remuneration paid to such nonresident alien individuals when engaged in transportation service.

(c) Remuneration paid to a nonresident alien individual for services performed in Puerto Rico for an employer (other than the United States or any agency thereof) is excepted from wages and hence is not subject to withholding, even though such alien individual is a resident of Puerto Rico at the time when such services are performed. Wages paid for services performed by a nonresident alien individual who is a resident of Puerto Rico are subject to withholding if such services are performed as an employee of the United States or any agency thereof. The place of performance of such services is immaterial, provided such alien individual is a resident of Puerto Rico at the time of performance of the services. Wages representing retirement pay for services in the Armed Forces of the United States, the Coast and Geodetic Survey, or the Public Health Service, or a disability annuity paid under the provisions of section 831 of the Foreign Service Act of 1946, as amended (22 USC 1081; 60 Stat 1021), are subject to withholding, under the limitations specified in paragraph (b)(1)(ii) of § 31.3401(a)-1, in the case of an alien resident of Puerto Rico.

(d) *(1)* Remuneration paid after 1961 to a nonresident alien individual who is temporarily present in the United States as a nonimmigrant under subparagraph (F) or (J) of section 101(a)(15) of the Immigration and Nationality Act (8 USC 1101), as amended, is not excepted from wages under section 3401(a)(6) if the remuneration is exempt from withholding under section 1441(a) by reason of section 1441(c)(4)(B) and is not exempt from taxation under section 872(b)(3). See §§ 1.872-2 and 1.1441-4 of this chapter (Income Tax Regulations). A nonresident alien individual who is temporarily present in the United States as a nonimmigrant under subparagraph (J) includes an alien individual admitted to the United States as an "exchange visitor" under section 201 of the United States Information and Educational Exchange Act of 1948 (22 USC 1446).

(2) Section 101 of the Immigration and Nationality Act (8 USC 1101), as amended, provides in part, as follows:

Sec. 101. Definitions. [Immigration and Nationality Act (66 Stat 166)]

(a) As used in this chapter— . . .

(15) The term "immigrant" means every alien except an alien who is within one of the following classes of nonimmigrant aliens—

* * * * * * (F)(i) An alien having a residence in a foreign country which he has no intention of abandoning, who is a bona fide student qualified to pursue a full course of study and who seeks to enter the United States temporarily and solely for the purpose of pursuing such a course of study at an established institution of learning or other recognized place of study in the United States, particularly designated by him and approved by the Attorney General after consultation with the Office of Education of the United States, which institution or place of study shall have agreed to report to the Attorney General the termination of attendance of each nonimmigrant student, and if any such institution of learning or place of study fails to make reports promptly the approval shall be withdrawn, and (ii) the alien spouse and minor children of any such alien if accompanying him or following to join him;

****** (J) An alien having a residence in a foreign country which he has no intention of abandoning who is a bona fide student, scholar, trainee, teacher, professor, research assistant, specialist, or leader in a field of specialized knowledge or skill, or other person of similar description, who is coming temporarily to the United States as a participant in a program designated by the Secretary of State, for the purpose of teaching, instructing or lecturing, studying, observing, conducting research, consulting, demonstrating special skills, or receiving training, and the alien spouse and minor children of any such alien if accompanying him or following to join him.

(e) This section shall not apply with respect to remuneration paid after December 31, 1966. For rules with respect to such remuneration see § 31.3401(a)(6)-1.

T.D. 6259, 10/25/57, amend T.D. 6654, 5/27/63, T.D. 6727, 5/4/64, T.D. 6908, 12/30/66.

§ 31.3401(a)(7)-1 Remuneration paid before January 1, 1967, for services performed by nonresident alien individuals who are residents of a contiguous country and who enter and leave the United States at frequent intervals.

(a) Transportation service. Remuneration paid to nonresident aliens who are residents of a contiguous country (Canada or Mexico) and who, in the performance of their duties in transportation service between points in the United States and points in a contiguous country, enter and leave the United States at frequent intervals, is excepted from wages and hence is not subject to withholding. This exception applies to personnel engaged in railroad, bus, ferry, steamboat, and aircraft services and applies whether the employer is a domestic or foreign entity. Thus, the remuneration of a nonresident alien individual who is a resident of Canada and an employee of a domestic railroad, for services as a member of the crew of a train operating between points in Canada and points in the United States, is not subject to withholding under section 3402.

(b) Service on international projects. Remuneration paid to nonresident aliens who are residents of a contiguous country (Canada or Mexico) and who, in the performance of their duties in connection with the construction, maintenance or operation of a waterway, viaduct, dam, or bridge traversed by or traversing the boundary between the United States and Canada or the boundary between the United States and Mexico, as the case may be, enter and leave the United States at frequent intervals, is excepted from wages and hence is not subject to withholding. Thus, the remuneration of a nonresident alien individual who is a resident of Canada, for services as an employee in connection with the construction, maintenance, or operation of the Saint Lawrence Seaway and who, in the performance of such services, enters and leaves the United States at frequent intervals, is not subject to withholding under section 3402.

(c) Limitation on application of section. The exception provided by this section has no application to the remuneration of a resident of Canada or of Mexico who is employed wholly within the United States as, for example, where such a resident is employed to perform service at a fixed point or points in the United States, such as a factory, store, office, or designated area or areas within the United States, and who commutes from his home in Canada or Mexico in the pursuit of his employment within the United States.

(d) Certificate required. In order for the exception to apply, the nonresident alien employee must furnish his employer a statement setting forth the employee's name and address and certifying *(1)* that he is not a citizen of the United States, *(2)* that he is a resident of Canada or Mexico, as the case may be, and *(3)* the approximate period of time during which he has had such status. Such statement shall be dated, shall be signed by the employee, and shall contain, or be verified by, a written declaration that it is made under the penalties of perjury. No particular form is prescribed for this statement.

(e) Effective date. This section shall not apply with respect to remuneration paid after December 31, 1966. For rules with respect to such remuneration see § 31.3401(a)(6)-1.

T.D. 6259, 10/25/57, amend T.D. 6908, 12/30/66.

§ 31.3401(a)(8)(A)-1 Remuneration for services performed outside the United States by citizens of the United States.

(a) Remuneration excluded from gross income under section 911. *(1)* (i) Remuneration paid for services performed outside the United States for an employer (other than the United States or any agency thereof) by a citizen of the United States does not constitute wages and hence is not subject to withholding, if at the time of payment it is reasonable to believe that such remuneration will be excluded from gross income under the provisions of section 911. The reasonable belief contemplated by the statute may be based upon any evidence reasonably sufficient to induce such belief, even though such evidence may be insufficient upon closer examination by the district director or the courts finally to establish that the remuneration is excludable from gross income under the provisions of section 911. The reasonable belief shall be based upon the application of section 911 and the regulations thereunder in Part 1 of this chapter (Income Tax Regulations).

(ii) Remuneration paid by an employer to an employee constitutes wages, and hence is subject to withholding only to the extent that the remuneration is expected to exceed the aggregate amount which is excludable from the employee's gross income under section 911(a). For amounts paid after December 31, 1984, the determination of the amount subject to withholding shall be made by applying the excludable amount, on a pro rata basis, to each payment of remuneration to the employee. For this purpose, an employer is not required to ascertain information with respect to amounts received by his employee from any other source; but, if the employer has such information, he shall take it into account in determining whether the earned income of the employee is in excess of the applicable limitation. For purposes of section 911(d)(5) and § 1.911-2(c), relating to an employee who states to the authorities of a foreign country that he is not a resident of that country, the employer is not required to ascertain whether such a statement has been made; but if an employer knows that such a statement has been made, he shall presume that the employee is not a bona fide resident of that country, unless the employer also knows that the authorities of the foreign country have determined, notwithstanding the statement, that the employee is a resident of that country. For purposes of section 911(d)(1) or § 1.911-2(a) relating to the definition of a qualified individual, the reasonable belief contemplated by the statute may be based on a presumption as set forth in subparagraph (2) or (3) of this paragraph. For purposes of sections 911(a)(2) and 911(c)(2) and § 1.911-4(b) and (d)(1), relating to the housing cost amount exclusion and the definition of housing expenses, the reasonable belief contemplated by the statute may be based on the presumption set forth in subparagraph (4) of this paragraph.

(2) (i) The employer may, in the absence of cause for a reasonable belief to the contrary, presume that an employee will maintain a tax home in a foreign country or countries and be a bona fide resident of a foreign country or countries, within the meaning of section 911(d)(1), for an uninterrupted period which includes each taxable year of the employee, or applicable portion thereof, in respect of which the employee properly executes and delivers to the employer a statement that the employee meets or will meet the requirement of § 1.911-2(a) relating to maintaining a tax home and a bona fide residence in a foreign country for the taxable year. This statement must set forth the facts alleged as the basis for this determination and contain a declaration by the employee that the statement is made under the penalties of perjury. Sample forms of acceptable statements may be obtained by writing to the Foreign Operations District, Internal Revenue Service, Washington, D.C. 20225 (Form IO-673).

(ii) If the employer was entitled to presume for the two consecutive taxable years immediately preceding an employee's current taxable year that such employee was a bona fide resident of a foreign country or countries for an uninterrupted period which includes such preceding taxable years, he may, if such employee is residing in a foreign country on the first day of such current taxable year, presume, in the absence of cause for a reasonable belief to the contrary, and without obtaining from the employee the statement prescribed in subdivision (i) of this subparagraph, that the employee will be a bona fide resident of a foreign country or countries in such current taxable year.

(3) The employer may, in the absence of cause for a reasonable belief to the contrary, presume that an employee will maintain a tax home in a foreign country or countries and be present in a foreign country or countries during at least 330 full days during any period of twelve consecutive months, within the meaning of section 911(d)(1), and that such period includes each taxable year of the employee, or applicable portion thereof, in respect of which the employee properly executes and delivers to the employer a statement that the employee meets or will meet the requirements of § 1.911-2(a) relating to maintaining a tax home and being physically present in a foreign country for the taxable year. This statement must set forth the facts alleged as the basis for this determination and contain a declaration by the employee that the statement is made under the penalties of perjury. Sample forms of acceptable statements may be obtained by writing to the Foreign Operations District, Internal Revenue Service, Washington, D.C. 20225 (Form IO-673).

(4) The employer may, in the absence of cause for a reasonable belief to the contrary, presume that an employee's housing cost amount will be the amount shown on a statement properly executed and delivered to the employer. This statement must set forth the employee's estimation of the following items: housing expenses (as defined in § 1.911-4(b)), the housing cost amount exclusion (as defined in § 1.911-4(d)(1)), and the qualifying period (as defined in § 1.911-2(a)). The statement must contain a declaration by the employee that it is made under the penalties of perjury. Sample forms of acceptable statements may be obtained by writing to the Foreign Operations District, Internal Revenue Service, Washington, D.C. 20225 (IO-673). The employer may not rely on a statement from an employee if the employer, based on his or her knowledge of housing costs in the vicinity of the employee's tax home (as defined in § 1.911-2(b)), believes the employee's housing expenses are lavish or extravagant under the circumstances.

(b) Remuneration subject to withholding of income tax under law of a foreign country or a possession of the United States. *(1)* Remuneration paid for services performed in a foreign country or in a possession of the United States for an employer (other than the United States or any agency thereof) by a citizen of the United States does not constitute wages and hence is not subject to withholding, if at the time of the payment of such remuneration the employer is required by the law of any foreign country or of any possession of the United States to withhold income tax upon such remuneration. This paragraph, insofar as it relates to remuneration paid for services performed in a possession of the United States, applies only with respect to remuneration paid on or after August 9, 1955.

(2) Remuneration is not exempt from withholding under this paragraph if the employer is not required by the law of a foreign country or of a possession of the United States to withhold income tax upon such remuneration. Mere agreements between the employer and the employee whereby the estimated income tax of a foreign country or of a possession of the United States is withheld from the remuneration in anticipation of actual liability under the law of such country or possession will not suffice.

(3) The exemption from withholding provided by this paragraph does not apply by reason of withholding of income tax pursuant to the law of a territory of the United States, of a political subdivision of a possession of the United States, or of a political subdivision of a foreign state.

(4) For provisions relating to remuneration for services performed by a permanent resident of the Virgin Islands, see paragraph (b)(12) of § 31.3401(a)-1.

(c) Limitation on application of section. This section has no application to the remuneration paid to a citizen of the United States for services performed outside the United States as an employee of the United States or any agency thereof.

T.D. 6259, 10/25/57, amend T.D. 6697, 12/16/63, T.D. 8006, 1/17/85.

§ 31.3401(a)(8)(B)-1 Remuneration for services performed in possession of the United States (other than Puerto Rico) by citizen of the United States.

(a) Remuneration paid for services for an employer (other than the United States or any agency thereof) performed by a citizen of the United States within a possession of the United States (other than Puerto Rico) does not constitute wages and hence is not subject to withholding, if it is reasonable to believe that at least 80 percent of the remuneration to be paid to the employee by such employer during the calendar year will be for such services. The reasonable belief contemplated by section 3401(a)(8)(B) may be based upon any evidence reasonably sufficient to induce such belief, even though such evidence may be insufficient upon closer examination by the district director or the courts finally to establish that at least 80 percent of the remuneration paid by the employer to the employee during the calendar year was for services performed within such a possession of the United States.

(b) This section has no application to remuneration paid to a citizen of the United States for services performed in any possession of the United States as an employee of the United States or any agency thereof.

(c) For provisions relating to remuneration for services performed by a permanent resident of the Virgin Islands, see paragraph (b)(12) of § 31.3401(a)-1.

T.D. 6259, 10/25/57.

§ 31.3401(a)(8)(C)-1 Remuneration for services performed in Puerto Rico by citizen of the United States.

(a) Remuneration paid for services performed within Puerto Rico for an employer (other than the United States or any agency thereof) by a citizen of the United States does not constitute wages and hence is not subject to withholding, if it is reasonable to believe that during the entire calendar year the employee will be a bona fide resident of Puerto Rico. The reasonable belief contemplated by section 3401(a)(8)(C) may be based upon any evidence reasonably sufficient to induce such belief, even though such evidence may be insufficient upon closer examination by the district director or the courts finally to establish that the employee was a bona fide resident of Puerto Rico for the entire calendar year.

(b) The employer may, in the absence of cause for a reasonable belief to the contrary, presume that an employee will be a bona fide resident of Puerto Rico during the entire calendar year—

(1) Unless the employee is known by the employer to have maintained his abode at a place outside Puerto Rico at some time during the current or the preceding calendar year; or

(2) In any case where the employee files with the employer a statement (containing a declaration under the penalties of perjury that such statement is true to the best of the employee's knowledge and belief) that such employee has at all times during the current calendar year been a bona fide resident of Puerto Rico and that he intends to remain a bona fide resident of Puerto Rico during the entire remaining portion of such current calendar year.

(c) This section has no application to remuneration paid to a citizen of the United States for services performed in Puerto Rico as an employee of the United States or any agency thereof.

T.D. 6259, 10/25/57.

§ 31.3401(a)(9)-1 Remuneration for services performed by a minister of a church or a member of a religious order.

(a) In general. Remuneration paid for services performed by a duly ordained, commissioned, or licensed minister of a church in the exercise of his ministry, or by a member of a religious order in the exercise of duties required by such order, is excepted from wages and hence is not subject to withholding.

(b) Service by a minister in the exercise of his ministry. Except as provided in paragraph (c)(3) of this section, service performed by a minister in the exercise of his ministry includes the ministration of sacerdotal functions and the conduct of religious worship, and the control, conduct, and maintenance of religious organizations (including the religious boards, societies, and other integral agencies of such organizations), under the authority of a religious body constituting a church or church denomination. The following rules are applicable in determining whether services performed by a minister are performed in the exercise of his ministry:

(1) Whether service performed by a minister constitutes the conduct of religious worship or the ministration of sacerdotal functions depends on the tenets and practices of the particular religious body constituting his church or church denomination.

(2) Service performed by a minister in the control, conduct, and maintenance of a religious organization relates to directing, managing, or promoting the activities of such organization. Any religious organization is deemed to be under the authority of a religious body constituting a church or church denomination if it is organized and dedicated to carrying out the tenets and principles of a faith in accordance with either the requirements or sanctions governing the creation of institutions of the faith. The term "religious organization" has the same meaning and application as is given to the term for income tax purposes.

(3) (i) If a minister is performing service in the conduct of religious worship or the ministration or sacerdotal functions, such service is in the exercise of his ministry whether or not it is performed for a religious organization.

(ii) The rule in subdivision (i) of this subparagraph may be illustrated by the following example:

Example. M, a duly ordained minister, is engaged to perform service as chaplain at N University. M devotes his entire time to performing his duties as chaplain which include the conduct of religious worship, offering spiritual counsel to the university students, and teaching a class in religion. M is performing service in the exercise of his ministry.

(4) (i) If a minister is performing service for an organization which is operated as an integral agency of a religious organization under the authority of a religious body constituting a church or church denomination, all service performed by the minister in the conduct of religious worship, in the ministration of sacerdotal functions, or in the control, conduct, and maintenance of such organization (see subparagraph (2) of this paragraph) is in the exercise of his ministry.

(ii) The rule in subdivision (i) of this subparagraph may be illustrated by the following example:

Example. M, a duly ordained minister, is engaged by the N Religious Board to serve as director of one of its departments. He performs no other service. The N Religious Board is an integral agency of O, a religious organization operating under the authority of a religious body constituting a church denomination. M is performing service in the exercise of his ministry.

(5) (i) If a minister, pursuant to an assignment or designation by a religious body constituting his church, performs service for an organization which is neither a religious organization nor operated as an integral agency of a religious organization, all service performed by him, even though such service may not involve the conduct of religious worship or the ministration of sacerdotal functions, is in the exercise of his ministry.

(ii) The rule in subdivision (i) of this subparagraph may be illustrated by the following example:

Example. M, a duly ordained minister, is assigned by X, the religious body constituting his church, to perform advisory service to Y Company in connection with the publication of a book dealing with the history of M's church denomination. Y is neither a religious organization nor operated as an integral agency of a religious organization. M performs no other service for X or Y. M is performing service in the exercise of his ministry.

(c) Service by a minister not in the exercise of his ministry. *(1)* Section 3401(a)(9) does not except from wages remuneration for service performed by a duly ordained, commissioned, or licensed minister of a church which is not in the exercise of his ministry.

(2) (i) If a minister is performing service for an organization which is neither a religious organization nor operated as an integral agency of a religious organization and the service is not performed pursuant to an assignment or designation by his ecclesiastical superiors, then only the service performed by him in the conduct of religious worship or the ministration of sacerdotal functions is in the exercise of his ministry. See, however, subparagraph (3) of this paragraph.

(ii) The rule in subdivision (i) of this subparagraph may be illustrated by the following example:

Example. M, a duly ordained minister, is engaged by N University to teach history and mathematics. He performs no other service for N although from time to time he performs marriages and conducts funerals for relatives and friends. N University is neither a religious organization nor operated as an integral agency of a religious organization. M is not performing the service for N pursuant to an assignment or designation by his ecclesiastical superiors. The service performed by M for N University is not in the exercise of his ministry. However, service performed by M in performing marriages and conducting funerals is in the exercise of his ministry.

(3) Service performed by a duly ordained, commissioned, or licensed minister of a church as an employee of the United States, or a State, Territory, or possession of the United States, or the District of Columbia, or a foreign government, or a political subdivision of any of the foregoing, is not considered to be in the exercise of his ministry for purposes of the collection of income tax at source on wages, even though such service may involve the ministration of sacerdotal functions or the conduct of religious worship. Thus, for example, service performed by an individual as a chaplain in the Armed Forces of the United States is considered to be performed by a commissioned officer in his capacity as such, and not by a minister in the exercise of his ministry. Similarly, service performed by an employee of a State as a chaplain in a State prison is considered to be performed by a civil servant of the State and not by a minister in the exercise of his ministry.

(d) Service in the exercise of duties required by a religious order. Service performed by a member of a religious order in the exercise of duties required by such order includes all duties required of the member by the order. The nature or extent of such service is immaterial so long as it is a service which he is directed or required to perform by his ecclesiastical superiors.

T.D. 6259, 10/25/57.

§ 31.3401(a)(10)-1 Remuneration for services in delivery or distribution of newspapers, shopping news, or magazines.

(a) Services of individuals under age 18. Remuneration for services performed by an employee under the age of 18 in the delivery or distribution of newspapers, or shopping news, not including delivery or distribution (as, for example, by a regional distributor) to any point for subsequent delivery or distribution, is excepted from wages and hence is not subject to withholding. Thus, remuneration for services performed by an employee under the age of 18 in making house-to-house delivery or sale of newspapers or shopping news, including handbills and other similar types of advertising material, is excepted from wages. The remuneration is excepted irrespective of the form or method thereof. Remuneration for incidental services by the employee who makes the house-to-house delivery, such as services in assembling newspapers, is considered to be within the exception. The exception continues only during the time that the employee is under the age of 18.

(b) Services of individuals of any age. Remuneration for services performed by an employee in, and at the time of, the sale of newspapers or magazines to ultimate consumers under an arrangement under which the newspapers or magazines are to be sold by him at a fixed price, his remuneration being based on the retention of the excess of such price over the amount at which the newspapers or magazines are charged to him, is excepted from wages and hence is not subject to withholding. The remuneration is excepted whether or not the employee is guaranteed a minimum amount of remuneration, or is entitled to be credited with the unsold newspapers or magazines turned back. Moreover, the remuneration is excepted without regard to the age of the employee. Remuneration for services performed other than at the time of sale to the ultimate consumer is not within the exception. Thus, remuneration for services of a regional distributor which are antecedent to but not immediately part of the sale to the ultimate consumer is not within the exception. However, remuneration for incidental services by the employee who makes the sale to the ultimate consumer, such as services in assembling newspapers or in taking newspapers or magazines to the place of sale, is considered to be within the exception.

T.D. 6259, 10/25/57.

§ 31.3401(a)(11)-1 Remuneration other than in cash for service not in the course of employer's trade or business.

(a) Remuneration paid in any medium other than cash for services not in the course of the employer's trade or business is excepted from wages and hence is not subject to withholding. Cash remuneration includes checks and other monetary media of exchange. Remuneration paid in any medium other than cash, such as lodging, food, or other goods or commodities, for services not in the course of the employer's trade or business does not constitute wages. Remuneration paid in any medium other than cash for other types of services does not come within this exception from wages. For provisions relating to cash remuneration for services not in the course of employer's trade or business, see § 31.3401(a)(4)-1.

(b) As used in this section, the term "services not in the course of the employer's trade or business" has the same meaning as when used in § 31.3401(a)(4)-1.

T.D. 6259, 10/25/57.

§ 31.3401(a)(12)-1 Payments from or to certain tax-exempt trusts, or under or to certain annuity plans or bond purchase plans, or to individual retirement plans.

(a) Payments from or to certain tax-exempt trusts. The term "wages" does not include any payment made—

(1) By an employer, on behalf of an employee or his beneficiary, into a trust, or

(2) To, or on behalf of, an employee or his beneficiary from a trust,

if at the time of such payment the trust is exempt from tax under section 501(a) as an organization described in section 401(a). A payment made to an employee of such a trust for services rendered as an employee of the trust and not as a beneficiary thereof is not within this exclusion from wages. Also, since supplemental unemployment compensation benefits are treated under paragraph (b)(14) of § 31.3401(a)-1 as if they were wages for purposes of this chapter, this section does not apply to such benefits.

(b) Payments under or to certain annuity plans. *(1)* The term "wages" does not include any payment made after December 31, 1962—

(i) By an employer, on behalf of an employee or his beneficiary, into an annuity plan, or

(ii) To, or on behalf of, an employee or his beneficiary under an annuity plan,

if at the time of such payment the annuity plan is a plan described in section 403(a).

(2) The term "wages" does not include any payment made before January 1, 1963—

(i) By an employer, on behalf of an employee or his beneficiary, into an annuity plan, or

(ii) To, or on behalf of, an employee or his beneficiary under an annuity plan,

if at the time of such payment the annuity plan meets the requirements of section 401(a)(3), (4), (5), and (6).

(c) Payments under or to certain bond purchase plans. The term "wages" does not include any payment made after December 31, 1962—

(1) By an employer, on behalf of an employee or his beneficiary, into a bond purchase plan, or

(2) To, or on behalf of, an employee or his beneficiary under a bond purchase plan,

if at the time of such payment the plan is a qualified bond purchase plan described in section 405(a).

(d) Payment to individual retirement plans. *(1)* The term "wages" does not include any payment to an individual retirement plan described in section 7701(a)(37) by an employer after December 31, 1974, on behalf of an employee, if, at the time of such payment, it is reasonable for the employer to believe that the employee will be entitled to a deduction for such payment under section 219(a).

(2) The term "wages" does not include any payment to an individual retirement plan described in section 7701(a)(37) by an employer after December 31, 1976, on behalf of an employee, if, at the time of such payment, it is reasonable for the employer to believe that the employee on whose behalf the payment is made will be entitled to a deduction for such payment under section 220(a).

(3) The term "wages" does not include any payment to a simplified employee pension arrangement described in section 408(k) by an employer after December 31, 1978, on behalf of an employee, if, at the time of such payment, it is reasonable for the employer to believe that the employee on whose behalf the payment is made will be entitled to a deduction for such payment under section 219(a).

T.D. 6259, 10/25/57, amend T.D. 6654, 5/27/63, T.D. 7068, 11/10/70, T.D. 7730, 10/31/80.

§ 31.3401(a)(13)-1 Remuneration for services performed by Peace Corps volunteers.

(a) Remuneration paid after September 22, 1961, for services performed as a volunteer or volunteer leader within the meaning of the Peace Corps Act (22 U.S.C. 2501) is excepted from wages, and hence is not subject to withholding, unless the remuneration is paid pursuant to section 5(c) or section 6(1) of the Peace Corps Act.

(b) Sections 5 and 6 of the Peace Corps Act (22 U.S.C. 2504, 2505) provide, in part as follows:

Sec. 5 Peace Corps Volunteers [Peace Corps Act (75 Stat. 613); as amended by sec. 2(b), Act of December 13, 1963 (P.L. 88-200, 77 Stat. 359); sec. 2(a), Act of August 24, 1965, (P.L. 89-134, 79 Stat. 549); sec. 3(a), Act of July 24, 1970 (P.L. 91-352, 84 Stat. 464)]

* * * * * *

(c) Readjustment allowances. Volunteers shall be entitled to receive a readjustment allowance at a rate not to exceed $75 for each month of satisfactory service as determined by the President; except that, in the cases of volunteers who have one or more minor children at the time of their entering a period of pre-enrollment training, one parent shall be entitled to receive a readjustment allowance at a rate not to exceed $125 for each month of satisfactory service as determined by the President. The readjustment allowance of each volunteer shall be payable on his return to the United States: Provided, however, that, under such circumstances as the President may determine, the accrued readjustment allowance, or any part thereof, may be paid to the volunteer, members of his family or others, during the period of his service, or prior to his return to the United States. In the event of the volunteer's death during the period of his service, the amount of any unpaid readjustment allowance shall be paid in accordance with the provisions of section 5582(b) of Title 5. For purposes of the Internal Revenue Code of 1954, a volunteer shall be deemed to be paid and to receive each amount of a readjustment allowance to which he is entitled after December 31, 1964, when such amount is transferred from funds made available under this chapter to the fund from which such readjustment allowance is payable.

* * * * * * Sec. 6. Peace Corps Volunteer Leaders; number; applicability of chapter; benefits [Peace Corps Act (75 Stat. 615), as amended by sec. 3, Act of December 13, 1963 (P.L. 88-200, 77 Stat. 360)] The President may enroll in the Peace Corps qualified citizens or nationals of the United States whose services are required for supervisory or other special duties or responsibilities in connection with programs under this chapter (referred to in this Act as "volunteer leaders"). The ratio of the total number of volunteer leaders to the total number of volunteers in service at any one time shall not exceed one to twenty-five. Except as otherwise provided in this Act, all of the provisions of this Act applicable to volunteers shall be applicable to volunteer leaders, and the term "volunteers" shall include "volunteer leaders": Provided, however, That—

(1) Volunteer leaders shall be entitled to receive a readjustment allowance at a rate not to exceed $125 for each month of satisfactory service as determined by the President;

* * * * * *

T.D. 6654, 5/27/63, amend T.D. 7493, 6/29/77.

§ 31.3401(a)(14)-1 Group-term life insurance.

Caution: The Treasury has not yet amended Reg § 31.3401(a)(14)-1 to reflect changes made by P.L. 100-647, P.L. 99-514.

(a) The cost of group-term life insurance on the life of an employee is excepted from wages, and hence is not subject to withholding. For provisions relating generally to such remuneration, and for reporting requirements with respect to such remuneration, see sections 79 and 6052, respectively, and the regulations thereunder in Part 1 of this chapter (Income Tax Regulations).

(b) The cost of group-term life insurance on the life of an employee's spouse or children is not subject to withholding if it is excludable from the employee's gross income because it is merely incidental. See paragraph (d)(2)(ii)(b) of § 1.61-2 in Part 1 of this chapter (Income Tax Regulations).

T.D. 7493, 6/29/77.

§ 31.3401(a)(15)-1 Moving expenses.

Caution: The Treasury has not yet amended Reg § 31.3401(a)(15)-1 to reflect changes made by P.L. 100-647.

(a) An amount paid to or on behalf of an employee after March 4, 1964, either as an advance or a reimbursement, specifically for moving expenses incurred or expected to be incurred is excepted from wages, and hence is not subject to withholding, if (and to the extent that) at the time of payment it is reasonable to believe that a corresponding deduction is or will be allowable to the employee under section 217. The reasonable belief contemplated by the statute may be based upon any evidence reasonably sufficient to induce such belief, even though such evidence may be insufficient upon closer examination by the district director or the courts finally to establish that a deduction is allowable under section 217. The reasonable belief shall be based upon the application of section 217 and the regulations thereunder in Part 1 of this chapter (Income Tax Regulations). When used in this section, the term "moving expenses" has the same meaning as when used in section 217. See § 1.6041-2(a) in Part 1 of this chapter (Income Tax Regulations), relating to return of information as to payments to employees, and § 31.6051-1(e), relating to the reporting of reimbursements of or payments of certain moving expenses.

(b) Except as otherwise provided in paragraph (a) of this section, or in a numbered paragraph of section 3401(a), amounts paid to or on behalf of an employee for moving expenses constitute wages subject to withholding.

T.D. 7493, 6/29/77.

§ 31.3401(a)(16)-1 Tips.

Tips paid to an employee are excepted from wages and hence not subject to withholding if—

(a) The tips are paid in any medium other than cash, or

(b) The cash tips received by an employee in any calendar month in the course of his employment by an employer are less than $20.

However, if the cash tips received by an employee in a calendar month in the course of his employment by an employer amount to $20 or more, none of the cash tips received by the employee in such calendar month are excepted from wages under this section. The cash tips to which this section applies include checks and other monetary media of exchange. Tips received by an employee in any medium other than cash, such as passes, tickets, or other goods or commodities do not constitute wages. If an employee in any calendar month performs services for two or more employers and receives tips in the course of his employment by each employer, the $20 test is to be applied separately with respect to the cash tips received by the employee in respect of his services for each employer and not to the total cash tips received by the employee during the month. As to the time tips are deemed paid, see § 31.3401(f)-1. For provisions relating to the treatment of tips received by an employee prior to 1966, see paragraph (b)(11) of § 31.3401(a)-1.

T.D. 7001, 1/17/69.

§ 31.3401(a)(17)-1 Remuneration for services performed on a boat engaged in catching fish.

Caution: The Treasury has not yet amended Reg § 31.3401(a)(17)-1 to reflect changes made by P.L. 104-188.

(a) Remuneration for services performed on or after December 31, 1954, by an individual on a boat engaged in catching fish or other forms of aquatic animal life (hereinafter "fish") is excepted from wages and hence is not subject to withholding if—

(1) The individual receives a share of the boat's (or boats' for a fishing operation involving more than one boat) catch of fish or a share of the proceeds from the sale of the catch,

(2) The amount of the individual's share depends solely on the amount of the boat's (or boats' for a fishing operation involving more than one boat) catch of fish,

(3) The individual does not receive, and is not entitled to receive, any cash remuneration, other than remuneration that is described in subparagraph (1) of this paragraph, and

(4) The crew of the boat (or of each boat from which the individual receives a share of the catch) normally is made up of fewer than 10 individuals.

(b) The requirement of subparagraph (2) of paragraph (a) is not satisfied if there exists an agreement with the boat's (or boats') owner or operator by which the individual's remuneration is determined partially or fully by a factor not dependent on the size of the catch. For example, if a boat is operated under a remuneration arrangement, e.g., a union contract, which specifies that crew members, in addition to receiving a share of the catch, are entitled to an hourly wage for repairing nets, regardless of whether this wage is actually paid, then all the crew members covered by the arrangement are entitled to receive cash remuneration other than as a share of the catch and are not excepted from employment by section 3121(b)(20).

(c) The operating crew of a boat includes all persons on the boat (including the captain) who receive any form of remuneration in exchange for services rendered while on a boat engaged in catching fish. See § 1.6050A-1 for reporting requirements for the operator of a boat engaged in catching fish with respect to individuals performing services described in this section.

(d) During the same return period, service performed by a crew member may be excepted from employment by section 3121(b)(20) and this section for one voyage and not so excepted on a subsequent voyage on the same or on a different boat.

T.D. 7716, 8/26/80.

§ 31.3401(a)(18)-1 Payments or benefits under a qualified educational assistance program.

A payment made, or benefit furnished, to or for the benefit of an employee in a taxable year beginning after December 31, 1978, does not constitute wages and hence is not subject to withholding if, at the time of such payment or furnishing, it is reasonable to believe that the employee will be able to exclude such payment or benefit from income under section 127.

T.D. 7588, 12/29/78, amend T.D. 7684, 3/12/80, T.D. 7898, 7/5/83.

§ 31.3401(a)(19)-1 Reimbursements under a self-insured medical reimbursement plan.

Caution: The Treasury has not yet amended Reg § 31.3401(a)(19)-1 to reflect changes made by P.L. 100-647, P.L. 99-514.

Amounts reimbursed to or on behalf of an employee after December 31, 1979, as a medical care reimbursement under a self-insured medical reimbursement plan (within the meaning of section 105(h)(6)) do not constitute wages and hence are not subject to withholding even though such reimbursement is includible in the gross income of an employee. For rules with respect to self-insured medical reimbursement plans, see section 105(h) and § 1.105-11 of this Chapter (Income Tax Regulations).

T.D. 7754, 1/13/81, amend T.D. 7898, 7/5/83.

§ 31.3401(b)-1 Payroll period.

(a) The term "payroll period" means the period of service for which a payment of wages is ordinarily made to an employee by his employer. It is immaterial that the wages are not always paid at regular intervals. For example, if an employer ordinarily pays a particular employee for each calendar week at the end of the week, but if for some reason the employee in a given week receives a payment in the middle of the week for the portion of the week already elapsed and receives the remainder at the end of the week, the payroll period is still the calendar week; or if, instead, that employee is sent on a 3-week trip by his employer and receives at the end of the trip a single wage payment for three weeks' services, the payroll period is still the calendar week, and the wage payment shall be treated as though it were three separate weekly wage payments.

(b) For the purpose of section 3402, an employee can have but one payroll period with respect to wages paid by any one employer. Thus, if an employee is paid a regular wage for a weekly payroll period and in addition thereto is paid supplemental wages (for example, bonuses) determined with respect to a different period, the payroll period is the weekly payroll period. For computation of tax on supplemental wage payments, see § 31.3402(g)-1.

(c) The term "payroll period" also means the period of accrual of supplemental unemployment compensation benefits for which a payment of such benefits is ordinarily made. Thus if benefits are ordinarily accrued and paid on a monthly basis, the payroll period is deemed to be monthly.

(d) The term "miscellaneous payroll period" means a payroll period other than a daily, weekly, bi-weekly, semi-monthly, monthly, quarterly, semi-annual, or annual payroll period.

T.D. 6259, 10/25/57, amend T.D. 7068, 11/10/70.

§ 31.3401(c)-1 Employee.

Caution: The Treasury has not yet amended Reg § 31.3401(c)-1 to reflect changes made by P.L. 105-34, P.L. 94-455.

(a) The term "employee" includes every individual performing services if the relationship between him and the person for whom he performs such services is the legal relationship of employer and employee. The term includes officers and employees, whether elected or appointed, of the United States, a State, Territory, Puerto Rico, or any political subdivision thereof, or the District of Columbia, or any agency or instrumentality of any one or more of the foregoing.

(b) Generally the relationship of employer and employee exists when the person for whom services are performed has the right to control and direct the individual who performs the services, not only as to the result to be accomplished by the work but also as to the details and means by which that result is accomplished. That is, an employee is subject to the will and control of the employer not only as to what shall be done but how it shall be done. In this connection, it is not necessary that the employer actually direct or control the manner in which the services are performed; it is sufficient if he has the right to do so. The right to discharge is also an important factor indicating that the person possessing that right is an employer. Other factors characteristic of an employer, but not necessarily present in every case, are the furnishing of tools and the furnishing of a place to work to the individual who performs the services. In general, if an individual is subject to the control or direction of another merely as to the result to be accomplished by the work and not as to the means and methods for accomplishing the result, he is not an employee.

(c) Generally, physicians, lawyers, dentists, veterinarians, contractors, subcontractors, public stenographers, auctioneers, and others who follow an independent trade, business, or profession, in which they offer their services to the public, are not employees.

(d) Whether the relationship of employer and employee exists will in doubtful cases be determined upon an examination of the particular facts of each case.

(e) If the relationship of employer and employee exists, the designation or description of the relationship by the parties as anything other than that of employer and employee is immaterial. Thus, if such relationship exists, it is of no consequence that the employee is designated as a partner, co-adventurer, agent, independent contractor, or the like.

(f) All classes or grades of employees are included within the relationship of employer and employee. Thus, superintendents, managers, and other supervisory personnel are employees. Generally, an officer of a corporation is an employee of the corporation. However, an officer of a corporation who as such does not perform any services or performs only minor services and who neither receives nor is entitled to receive, directly or indirectly, any remuneration is not considered to be an employee of the corporation. A director of a corporation in his capacity as such is not an employee of the corporation.

(g) The term "employee" includes every individual who receives a supplemental unemployment compensation benefit which is treated under paragraph (b)(14) of § 31.3401(a)-1 as if it were wages.

(h) Although an individual may be an employee under this section, his services may be of such a nature, or performed under such circumstances, that the remuneration paid for such services does not constitute wages within the meaning of section 3401(a).

T.D. 6259, 10/25/57, amend T.D. 7068, 11/10/70.

§ 31.3401(d)-1 Employer.

(a) The term "employer" means any person for whom an individual performs or performed any service, of whatever nature, as the employee of such person.

(b) It is not necessary that the services be continuing at the time the wages are paid in order that the status of employer exist. Thus, for purposes of withholding, a person for whom an individual has performed past services for which he is still receiving wages from such person is an "employer."

(c) An employer may be an individual, a corporation, a partnership, a trust, an estate, a joint-stock company, an association, or a syndicate, group, pool, joint venture, or other unincorporated organization, group or entity. A trust or estate, rather than the fiduciary acting for or on behalf of the trust or estate, is generally the employer.

(d) The term "employer" embraces not only individuals and organizations engaged in trade or business, but organizations exempt from income tax, such as religious and charitable organizations, educational institutions, clubs, social organizations and societies, as well as the governments of the United States, the States, Territories, Puerto Rico, and the District of Columbia, including their agencies, instrumentalities, and political subdivisions.

(e) The term "employer" also means (except for the purpose of the definition of "wages") any person paying wages on behalf of a nonresident alien individual, foreign partnership, or foreign corporation, not engaged in trade or business within the United States (including Puerto Rico as if a part of the United States).

(f) If the person for whom the services are or were performed does not have legal control of the payment of the wages for such services, the term "employer" means (except for the purpose of the definition of "wages") the person having such control. For example, where wages, such as certain types of pensions or retired pay, are paid by a trust and the person for whom the services were performed has no legal control over the payment of such wages, the trust is the "employer."

(g) The term "employer" also means a person making a payment of a supplemental unemployment compensation benefit which is treated under paragraph (b)(14) of § 31.3401(a)-1 as if it were wages. For example, if supplemental unemployment compensation benefits are paid from a trust which was created under the terms of a collective bargaining agreement, the trust shall generally be deemed to be the employer. However, if the person making such payment is acting solely as an agent for another person, the term "employer" shall mean such other person and not the person actually making the payment.

(h) It is a basic purpose to centralize in the employer the responsibility for withholding, returning, and paying the tax, and for furnishing the statements required under section 6051 and § 31.6051-1. The special definitions of the term "employer" in paragraphs (e), (f), and (g) of this section are designed solely to meet special or unusual situations. They are not intended as a departure from the basic purpose.

T.D. 6259, 10/25/57, amend T.D. 7068, 11/10/70.

§ 31.3401(e)-1 Number of withholding exemptions claimed.

(a) The term "number of withholding exemptions claimed" means the number of withholding exemptions claimed in a withholding exemption certificate in effect under section 3402(f) of the Internal Revenue Code of 1954 or in effect under section 1622(h) of the Internal Revenue Code of 1939. If no such certificate is in effect, the number of withholding exemptions claimed shall be considered to be zero. The number of withholding exemptions claimed must be taken into account in determining the amount of tax to be deducted and withheld under section 3402, whether the employer computes the tax in accordance with the provisions of subsection (a) or subsection (c) of section 3402.

(b) The employer is not required to ascertain whether or not the number of withholding exemptions claimed is greater than the number of withholding exemptions to which the employee is entitled. For rules relating to invalid withholding exemption certificates, see § 31.3402(f)(2)-1(e), and for rules relating to required submission of copies of certain withholding exemption certificates to the Internal Revenue Service, see § 31.3402(f)(2)-1(g).

(c) As to the number of withholding exemptions to which an employee is entitled, see § 31.3402(f)(1)-1.

T.D. 6259, 10/25/57, amend T.D. 7423, 6/24/76, T.D. 7682, 3/10/80, T.D. 7772, 3/17/81, T.D. 7803, 1/21/82.

§ 31.3401(f)-1 Tips.

(a) Tips considered wages. Tips received after 1965 by an employee in the course of his employment are considered to be wages, and thus subject to withholding of income tax at source. For an exception to the rule that tips constitute wages, see §§ 31.3401(a)(16) and 31.3401(a)(16)-1, relating to tips paid in a medium other than cash and cash tips of less than $20. For definition of the term "employee," see §§ 31.3401(c) and 31.3401(c)-1.

(b) When tips deemed paid. Tips reported by an employee to his employer in a written statement furnished to the employer pursuant to section 6053(a) (see § 31.6053-1) shall be deemed to be paid to the employee at the time the written statement is furnished to the employer. Tips received by an employee which are not reported to his employer in a written statement furnished pursuant to section 6053(a) shall be deemed to be paid to the employee at the time the tips are actually received by the employee.

T.D. 7001, 1/17/69.

§ 31.3402(a)-1 Requirement of withholding.

(a) Section 3402 provides alternative methods, at the election of the employer, for use in computing the amount of income tax to be collected at source on wages. Under the percentage method of withholding (see § 31.3402(b)-1), the employer is required to deduct and withhold a tax computed in accordance with the provisions of section 3402(a). Under the wage bracket method of withholding (see § 31.3402(c)-1), the employer is required to deduct and withhold a tax determined in accordance with the provisions of section 3402(c). The employer may elect to use the percentage method, the wage bracket method, or certain other methods (see § 31.3402(h)(4)-1). Different methods may be used by the employer with respect to different groups of employees.

(b) The employer is required to collect the tax by deducting and withholding the amount thereof from the employee's wages as and when paid, either actually or constructively.

Wages are constructively paid when they are credited to the account of or set apart for an employee so that they may be drawn upon by him at any time although not then actually reduced to possession. To constitute payment in such a case, the wages must be credited to or set apart for the employee without any substantial limitation or restriction as to the time or manner of payment or condition upon which payment is to be made, and must be made available to him so that they may be drawn upon at any time, and their payment brought within his own control and disposition.

(c) Except as provided in section 3402(j) and (k) (see §§ 31.3402(j)-1 and 31.3402(k)-1, relating to noncash remuneration paid to retail commission salesmen and to tips received by an employee in the course of his employment, respectively), an employer is required to deduct and withhold the tax notwithstanding the wages are paid in something other than money (for example, wages paid in stocks or bonds; see § 31.3401(a)-1) and to pay over the tax in money. If wages are paid in property other than money, the employer should make necessary arrangements to insure that the amount of the tax required to be withheld is available for payment in money.

(d) For provisions relating to the circumstances under which tax is required to be deducted and withheld from certain amounts received under accident and health plans, see paragraph (b)(8) of § 31.3401(a)-1.

(e) As a matter of business administration, certain of the mechanical details of the withholding process may be handled by representatives of the employer. Thus, in the case of an employer having branch offices, the branch manager or other representative may actually, as a matter of internal administration, withhold the tax or prepare the statements required under section 6051. Nevertheless, the legal responsibility for withholding, paying, and returning the tax and furnishing such statements rests with the employer. For provisions relating to statements under section 6051, see § 31.6051-1.

(f) The amount of any tax withheld and collected by the employer is a special fund in trust for the United States. See section 7501.

T.D. 6259, 10/25/57, amend T.D. 7001, 1/17/69, T.D. 7115, 5/20/71, T.D. 7888, 4/22/83.

§ 31.3402(b)-1 Percentage method of withholding.

With respect to wages paid after April 30, 1975, the amount of tax to be deducted and withheld under the percentage method of withholding shall be determined under the applicable percentage method withholding table contained in Circular E (Employer's Tax Guide) according to the instructions contained therein.

T.D. 6259, 10/25/57, amend T.D. 6860, 11/3/65, T.D. 7115, 5/20/71, T.D. 7888, 4/22/83, T.D. 7915, 9/26/83.

§ 31.3402(c)-1 Wage bracket withholding.

(a) In general. *(1)* The employer may elect to use the wage bracket method provided in section 3402(c) instead of the percentage method with respect to any employee. The tax computed under the wage bracket method shall be in lieu of the tax required to be deducted and withheld under section 3402(a). With respect to wages paid after July 13, 1968, the correct amount of withholding shall be determined under the applicable wage bracket withholding table contained in the Circular E (Employer's Tax Guide) issued for use with respect to the period in which such wages are paid.

(2) For provisions relating to the treatment of wages paid under accident and health plans and wages paid other than in cash to retail commission salesmen, see paragraph (b)(8) of § 31.3401(a)-1 and § 31.3402(j)-1, respectively.

(b) Established payroll periods, other than daily or miscellaneous, covered by wage bracket withholding tables. The wage bracket withholding tables contained in Circular E for established periods other than daily or miscellaneous should be used in determining the tax to be withheld for any such period without reference to the time the employee is actually engaged in the performance of services during such payroll period.

Example (1). On June 30, 1971, employee A is paid wages for a semimonthly payroll period. A has in effect a withholding exemption certificate indicating that he claims two withholding exemptions and that he is married. A's wages are determined at the rate of $2 per hour. During a certain payroll period he works only 24 hours and earns $48. Although A worked only 24 hours during the semimonthly payroll period, the applicable wage bracket withholding table contained in Circular E for a semimonthly payroll period for an employee who is married should be used in determining the tax to be withheld. Under this table it will be found that no tax is required to be withheld from a wage payment of $48 when two withholding exemptions are claimed.

Example (2). On May 14, 1971, employee B is paid wages for a weekly payroll period. B has in effect a withholding exemption certification indicating that he claims one withholding exemption and that he is single. B's wages are determined at the rate of $2 per hour. During a certain payroll period B works 18 hours and earns $36. Although B worked only 18 hours during the weekly payroll period the applicable wage bracket withholding table for a weekly payroll period for an employee who is single should be used in determining the tax to be withheld. Under this table it will be found that $0.50 is the amount of tax to be withheld from a wage payment of $36 when one withholding exemption is claimed.

(c) Periods to which the tables for a daily or miscellaneous payroll period are applicable. *(1) In general.* The tables applicable to a daily or miscellaneous payroll period show the tax for employees who are to be withheld from as single persons and for employees who are to be withheld from as married persons on the amount of wages for one day. Where the withholding is computed under the rules applicable to a miscellaneous payroll period, the wages and the amounts shown in the applicable table must be placed on a comparable basis. This may be accomplished by reducing the wages paid for the period to a daily basis by dividing the total wages by the number of days (including Sundays and Holidays) in the period. The amount of the tax shown in the applicable table as the tax required to be withheld from the wages, as so reduced to a daily basis, should then be multiplied by the number of days (including Sundays and holidays) in the period.

(2) Period not a payroll period. If wages are paid for a period which is not a payroll period, the amount to be deducted and withheld under the wage bracket method shall be the amount applicable in the case of a miscellaneous payroll period containing a number of days (including Sundays and holidays) equal to the number of days (including Sundays and holidays) in the period with respect to which such wages are paid.

Example. An individual performs services for a contractor in connection with a construction project. He has in effect a withholding exemption certificate indicating that he claims two withholding exemptions and that he is married. Wages have been fixed at the rate of $36 per day, to be paid upon completion of the project. The project is completed before July 1, 1971, in 12 consecutive days, at the end of which period the individual is paid wages of $360 for 10 days' services performed during the period. Under the wage bracket method the amount to be deducted and withheld from such wages is determined by dividing the amount of the wages ($360) by the number of days in the period (12), the result being $30. The amount of tax required to be withheld is determined under the appropriate table applicable to a miscellaneous payroll period for an employee who is married. Under this table the tax required to be withheld is $47.40 (12 × $3.95).

(3) Wages paid without regard to any period. If wages are paid to an employee without regard to any particular period, as, for example, commissions paid to a salesman upon consummation of a sale, the amount of tax to be deducted and withheld shall be determined in the same manner as in the case of a miscellaneous payroll period containing a number of days (including Sundays and holidays) equal to the number of days (including Sundays and holidays) which have elapsed, beginning with the latest of the following days:

(i) The day after the last payment of wages to such employee by such employer in the calendar year, or

(ii) The date on which such individual's employment with such employer began in the calendar year, or

(iii) January 1 of such calendar year, and ending with (and including) the date on which such wages are paid.

Example. On April 2, 1971, C is employed by the X Real Estate Company to sell real estate on a commission basis, commissions to be paid only upon consummation of sales. C has in effect a withholding exemption certificate indicating that he claims one withholding exemption and that he is not married. On May 22, 1971, C receives a commission of $300, his first commission since April 2, 1971. Again on June 19, 1971, C receives a commission of $420. Under the wage bracket method, the amount of tax to be deducted and withheld in respect of the commission paid on May 22, is $10, which amount is obtained by multiplying $0.20 (tax per day under the appropriate wage bracket table applicable to a daily or miscellaneous payroll period for an employee who is not married where wages are at least $6 but less than $6.25 a day) by 50 (number of days elapsed); and the amount of tax to be withheld with respect to the commission paid on June 19 is $54.60, which amount is obtained by multiplying $1.95 (tax under the appropriate wage bracket table for a daily or miscellaneous payroll period where wages are at least $15 but less than $15.50 a day) by 28 (number of days elapsed).

(d) Period or elapsed time less than 1 week. *(1)* It is the general rule that if wages are paid for a payroll period or other period of less than 1 week, the tax to be deducted and withheld under the wage bracket method shall be the amount computed for a daily payroll period, or for a miscellaneous payroll period containing the same number of days (including Sundays and holidays) as the payroll period, or other period, for which such wages are paid. In the case of wages paid without regard to any period, if the elapsed time computed as provided in paragraph (c) of this section is less than 1 week, the same rule is applicable.

Example (1). On May 14, 1971, an employee who has a daily payroll period is paid wages of $15 per day. The employee has in effect a withholding exemption certificate indicating that he claims one withholding exemption and that he is not married. Under the applicable table for a daily payroll period for an employee who is not married, the amount of tax to be deducted and withheld from each such payment of wages is $1.95.

Example (2). An employee works for a certain employer on 4 consecutive days for which he is paid wages totalling $60 on July 25, 1971. The employee has in effect a withholding exemption certificate claiming two withholding exemptions and indicating that he is married. The amount of tax to be deducted and withheld under the wage bracket method is $5.60 (4 × $1.40).

(2) If the payroll period, other period, or elapsed time where wages are paid without regard to any period, is less than one week, the employer may, under certain conditions, elect to deduct and withhold the tax determined by the application of the wage table for a weekly payroll period to the aggregate of the wages paid to the employee during the calendar week. The election to use the weekly wage table in such cases is subject to the limitations and conditions prescribed in Circular E with respect to employers using the percentage method in similar cases.

(3) As used in this paragraph the term "calendar week" means a period of seven consecutive days beginning with Sunday and ending with Saturday.

(e) Rounding off of wage payment. In determining the amount to be deducted and withheld under the wage bracket method the wages may, at the election of the employer, be computed to the nearest dollar, provided such wages are in excess of the highest wage bracket of the applicable table. For the purpose of the computation to the nearest dollar, the payment of a fractional part of a dollar shall be disregarded unless it amounts to one-half dollar or more, in which case it shall be increased to $1.00. Thus, if the payroll period of an employee is weekly and the wage payment of such employee is $255.49, the employer may compute the tax on the excess over $200 as if the excess were $55 instead of $55.49. If the weekly wage payment is $255.50, the employer may, in computing the tax, consider the excess over $200 to be $56 instead of $55.50.

T.D. 6259, 10/25/57, amend T.D. 6860, 11/3/65, T.D. 7115, 5/20/71, T.D. 7888, 4/22/83, T.D. 7915, 9/26/83.

§ 31.3402(d)-1 Failure to withhold.

If the employer in violation of the provisions of section 3402 fails to deduct and withhold the tax, and thereafter the income tax against which the tax under section 3402 may be credited is paid, the tax under section 3402 shall not be collected from the employer. Such payment does not, however, operate to relieve the employer from liability for penalties or additions to the tax applicable in respect of such failure to deduct and withhold. The employer will not be relieved of his liability for payment of the tax required to be withheld unless he can show that the tax against which the tax under section 3402 may be credited has been paid. See § 31.3403-1, relating to liability for tax.

T.D. 6259, 10/25/57.

§ 31.3402(e)-1 Included and excluded wages.

(a) If a portion of the remuneration paid by an employer to his employee for services performed during a payroll period of not more than 31 consecutive days constitutes wages, and the remainder does not constitute wages, all the remuneration paid the employee for services performed during such period shall for purposes of withholding be treated alike, that is, either all included as wages or all excluded. The time during which the employee performs services, the remuneration for which under section 3401(a) constitutes wages, and the time during which he performs services, the remuneration for which under such section does not constitute wages, determine whether all the remuneration for services performed during the payroll period shall be deemed to be included or excluded.

(b) If one-half or more of the employee's time in the employ of a particular employer in a payroll period is spent in performing services the remuneration for which constitutes wages, then all the remuneration paid the employee for services performed in that payroll period shall be deemed to be wages.

(c) If less than one-half of the employee's time in the employ of a particular employer in a payroll period is spent in performing services the remuneration for which constitutes wages, then none of the remuneration paid the employee for services performed in that payroll period shall be deemed to be wages.

(d) The application of the provisions of paragraphs (a), (b), and (c) of this section may be illustrated by the following examples:

Example (1). Employer B, who operates a store and a farm, employs A to perform services in connection with both operations. The remuneration paid A for services on the farm is excepted as remuneration for agricultural labor, and the remuneration for services performed in the store constitutes wages. Employee A is paid on a monthly basis. During a particular month, A works 120 hours on the farm and 80 hours in the store. None of the remuneration paid by B to A for services performed during the month is deemed to be wages, since the remuneration paid for less than one-half of the services performed during the month constitutes wages. During another month A works 75 hours on the farm and 120 hours in the store. All of the remuneration paid by B to A for services performed during the month is deemed to be wages since the remuneration paid for one-half or more of the services performed during the month constitutes wages.

Example (2). Employee C is employed as a maid by D, a physician, whose home and office are located in the same building. The remuneration paid C for services in the home is excepted as remuneration for domestic service, and the remuneration paid for her services in the office constitutes wages. C is paid on a weekly basis. During a particular week C works 20 hours in the home and 20 hours in the office. All of the remuneration paid by D to C for services performed during that week is deemed to be wages, since the remuneration paid for one-half or more of the services performed during the week constitutes wages. During another week C works 22 hours in the home and 15 hours in the office. None of the remuneration paid by D to C for services performed during that week is deemed to be wages, since the remuneration paid for less than one-half of the services performed during the week constitutes wages.

(e) The rules set forth in this section do not apply (1) with respect to any remuneration paid for services performed by an employee for his employer if the periods for which remuneration is paid by the employer vary to the extent that there is no period which constitutes a payroll period within the meaning of section 3401(b) (see § 31.3401(b)-1), or (2) with respect to any remuneration paid for services performed by an employee for his employer if the payroll period for which remuneration is paid exceeds 31 consecutive days. In any such case withholding is required with respect to that portion of such remuneration which constitutes wages.

T.D. 6259, 10/25/57.

---

§ 31.3402(f)(1)-1 Withholding exemptions.

Caution: The Treasury has not yet amended Reg § 31.3402(f)(1)-1 to reflect changes made by P.L. 100-203.

(a) In general. *(1)* Except as otherwise provided in section 3402(f)(6) (see § 31.3402(f)(6)-1), an employee receiving wages shall on any day be entitled to withholding exemptions as provided in section 3402(f)(1). In order to receive the benefit of such exemptions, the employee must file with his employer a withholding exemption certificate as provided in section 3402(f)(2). See § 31.3402(f)(2)-1.

(2) The number of exemptions to which an employee is entitled on any day depends upon his status as single or married, upon his status as to old age and blindness, upon the number of his dependents, upon the number of exemptions claimed by his spouse (if he is married), and upon the number of withholding allowances to which he is entitled under section 3402(m).

(b) Withholding exemptions to which an employee is entitled in respect of himself. An employee is entitled to one withholding exemption for himself. An employee shall on any day be entitled to an additional withholding exemption for himself if he will have attained the age of 65 before the close of his taxable year which begins in, or with, the calendar year in which such day falls. If the employee is blind, he may claim an additional withholding exemption for blindness. For purposes of claiming a withholding exemption for blindness, an individual shall be considered blind only if his central visual acuity does not exceed 20/200 in the better eye with correcting lenses or if his visual acuity is greater than 20/200 but is accompanied by a limitation in the fields of vision such that the widest diameter of the visual field subtends an angle no greater than 20 degrees. For definition of the term "blindness", see section 151(d)(3). An employee may also be entitled under section 3402(m) to withholding exemptions with respect to withholding allowances (see § 31.3402(m)-1).

(c) Withholding exemptions to which an employee is entitled in respect of his spouse. *(1)* A married employee, whose spouse is an employee receiving wages, is entitled to claim any withholding exemption to which his spouse is entitled under paragraph (b) of this section, unless the spouse has in effect a withholding exemption certificate claiming such withholding exemption. A married employee, whose spouse is not an employee receiving wages, is entitled to claim any withholding exemption to which his spouse would be entitled under paragraph (b) of this section if the spouse were an employee receiving wages.

Example (1). Assume that both the husband and wife have attained the age of 65 and are employees receiving wages. Each spouse is entitled under paragraph (b) of this section to claim 2 withholding exemptions in respect of himself or herself. Either spouse may claim, in addition to the withholding exemptions to which he or she is entitled in respect of himself or herself, any withholding exemption to which the other spouse is entitled under such paragraph (b) but does not claim on a withholding exemption certificate.

Example (2). Assume the same facts as in Example (1) except that only the husband is an employee receiving wages. The husband is entitled to claim 4 withholding exemptions, that is, the 2 withholding exemptions to which he is entitled in respect of himself and the 2 withholding exemptions to which his spouse would be entitled under paragraph (b) of this section if she were an employee receiving wages.

(2) In determining the number of withholding exemptions to which an employee is entitled for himself and his spouse on any day, the employee's status as a single person or a married person and, if married, whether a withholding exemption is claimed by his spouse shall be determined as of such day. However, in the case of an employee whose spouse dies in the taxable year of the employee which begins in, or with, the calendar year in which the spouse dies, any withholding exemption which would be allowable to the employee in respect of such spouse, if living and not an employee receiving wages, may be claimed by the employee for that portion of the calendar year which occurs after his spouse's death. For provisions applicable in the case of an employee whose taxable year is not a calendar year, and whose spouse dies in that portion of the calendar year which precedes the first day of the taxable year of the employee which begins in the calendar year, see paragraph (b) of § 31.3402(f)(2)-1. An employee legally separated from his spouse under a decree of divorce or of separate maintenance or an employee who is a surviving spouse (as defined in section 2 and the regulations thereunder) shall not be entitled to any withholding exemptions in respect of his spouse.

(d) Withholding exemptions to which an employee is entitled in respect of dependents. Subject to the limitations stated in this paragraph, an employee shall be entitled on any day to a withholding exemption for each individual who may reasonably be expected to be his dependent for his taxable year beginning in, or with, the calendar year in which such day falls. For purposes of the withholding exemption for an individual who may reasonably be expected to be a dependent, the following rules shall apply:

(1) The determination that an individual may or may not reasonably be expected to be a dependent shall be made on the basis of facts existing at the beginning of the day for which a withholding exemption for such individual is to be claimed. The individual in respect of whom an exemption is claimed by an employee must, on the day in question, be in existence and be within one of the categories listed in section 152(a), which defines the term "dependent." However, a withholding exemption for a dependent who dies continues for the portion of the calendar year which occurs after the dependent's death, except that, in the case of an employee whose taxable year is not a calendar year, the withholding exemption does not continue for a dependent, within the meaning of section 152(a)(9) or (10), whose death occurs before the first day of the employee's taxable year beginning in the calendar year of death.

(2) The determination that an individual may or may not reasonably be expected to be a dependent shall be made for the taxable year of the employee in respect of which amounts deducted and withheld in the calendar year in which the day in question falls are allowed as a credit. In general, amounts deducted and withheld during any calendar year are allowed as a credit against the tax imposed by chapter 1 of the Code for the taxable year which begins in, or with, such calendar year. Thus, in order for an employee to be able to claim for a calendar year a withholding exemption with respect to a particular individual as a dependent there must be a reasonable expectation that the employee will be allowed an exemption with respect to such individual under section 151(e) for his taxable year which begins in, or with, such calendar year.

(3) For the employee to be entitled on any day of the calendar year to a withholding exemption for an individual as a dependent, such individual must on such day—

(i) Be an individual referred to in one of the numbered paragraphs in section 152(a),

(ii) Reasonably be expected to receive over one-half of his support, within the meaning of section 152, from the employee in the calendar year, and

(iii) Either (a) reasonably be expected to receive less than $600 of gross income in the calendar year or (b) be a child (son, stepson, daughter, stepdaughter, adopted son, or adopted daughter) of the employee who (1) will not have attained the age of 19 at the close of the calendar year or (2) is a student as defined in section 151.

(4) An employee is not entitled to claim a withholding exemption for an individual otherwise reasonably expected to be a dependent of the employee if such individual is not a citizen of the United States, unless such individual (i) is at any time during the calendar year a resident of the United States (including, in regard to wages paid after February 28, 1979, and individual treated as a resident under Section 6013(g) or (h)), Canada, Mexico, the Canal Zone, or the Republic of Panama, or (ii) is a child of the employee born to him, or legally adopted by him, in the Philippine Islands before January 1, 1956, and the child is a resident of the Republic of the Philippines, and the employee was a member of the Armed Forces of the United States at the time the child was born to him or legally adopted by him.

(e) Additional withholding exemption to which an employee is entitled in respect of the standard deduction. After November 30, 1986, an employee is entitled to one additional withholding exemption unless:

(1) The employee is married (as determined under section 143) and the employee's spouse is an employee receiving wages subject to withholding, or

(2) The Employee has withholding exemption certificates in effect with respect to more than one employer. These restrictions do not apply if the combined wages of the employee and the spouse (if any) from other than one employer is less than the amount specified in the instructions to Form W-4 or W-4A (Employee's Withholding Allowance Certificate).

T.D. 6259, 10/25/57, amend T.D. 6654, 5/27/63, T.D. 7065, 10/22/70, T.D. 7114, 5/17/71, T.D. 7115, 5/20/71, T.D. 7670, 1/30/80, T.D. 7915, 9/26/83, T.D. 8164, 11/30/87.

§ 31.3402(f)(2)-1 Withholding exemption certificates.

(a) On commencement of employment. On or before the date on which an individual commences employment with an employer, the individual shall furnish the employer with a signed withholding exemption certificate relating to his marital status and the number of withholding exemptions which he claims, which number shall in no event exceed the number to which he is entitled, or, if the statements described in § 31.3402(n)-1 are true with respect to an individual, he may furnish his employer with a signed withholding exemption certificate which contains such statements. For form and contents of such certificates, see § 31.3402(f)(5)-1. The employer is required to request a withholding exemption certificate from each employee, but if the employee fails to furnish such certificate, such employee shall be considered as a single person claiming no withholding exemptions.

(b) Change in status which affects calendar year. *(1)* If, on any day during the calendar year, the number of withholding exemptions to which the employee is entitled is less than the number of withholding exemptions claimed by him on the withholding exemption certificate then in effect, the employee must within 10 days after the change occurs furnish the employer with a new withholding exemption certificate relating to the number of withholding exemptions which the employee then claims, which must in no event exceed the number to which he is entitled on such day. The number of withholding exemptions to which an employee is entitled decreases, for example, for any one of the following reasons:

(i) The employee's wife (or husband) for whom the employee has been claiming a withholding exemption (a) is divorced or legally separated from the employee, or (b) claims her (or his) own withholding exemption on a separate certificate.

(ii) In the case of an employee whose taxable year is not a calendar year, the employee's wife (or husband) for whom the employee has been claiming a withholding exemption dies in that portion of the calendar year which precedes the first day of the taxable year of the employee which begins in the calendar year in which the spouse dies.

(iii) The employee finds that no exemption for his taxable year which begins in, or with, the current calendar year will be allowable to him under section 151(e) in respect of an individual claimed as a dependent on the employee's withholding exemption certificate.

(iv) It becomes unreasonable for the employee to believe that his wages for an estimation year will not be more, or that the determinable additional amounts for each item under § 31.3402(m)-1 for an estimation year will not be less, than the corresponding figure used in connection with a claim by him under section 3402(m) of a withholding allowance to such an extent that the employee would no longer be entitled to such withholding allowance.

(v) It becomes unreasonable for an employee who has in effect a withholding exemption certificate on which he claims a withholding allowance under section 3402(m), computed on the basis of the preceding taxable year, to believe that his wages and the determinable additional amounts for each item under § 31.3402(m)-1 in such preceding taxable year or in his present taxable year will entitle him to such withholding allowance in the present taxable year.

(2) If, on any day during the calendar year, the number of withholding exemptions to which the employee is entitled is more than the number of withholding exemptions claimed by him on the withholding exemption certificate then in effect, the employee may furnish the employer with a new withholding exemption certificate on which the employee must in no event claim more than the number of withholding exemptions to which he is entitled on such day.

(3) If, on any day during the calendar year, the statements described in § 31.3402(n)-1 are true with respect to an employee, such employee may furnish his employer with a withholding exemption certificate which contains such statements.

(4) If, on any day during the calendar year, it is not reasonable for an employee, who has furnished his employer with a withholding exemption certificate which contains the statements described in § 31.3402(n)-1, to anticipate that he will incur no liability for income tax imposed under subtitle A (as defined in § 31.3402(n)-1 for his current taxable year, the employee must within 10 days after such day furnish the employer with a new withholding certificate which does not contain such statements. If, on any day during the calendar year, it is not reasonable for such an employee whose liability for income tax imposed under subtitle A is determined on a basis other than the calendar year to so anticipate with respect to his taxable year following his current taxable year, the employee must furnish the employer with a new withholding exemption certificate which does not contain such statements within 10 days after such day or on or before the first day of the last month of his current taxable year, whichever is later.

(c) Change in status which affects next calendar year. *(1)* If, on any day during the calendar year, the number of exemptions to which the employee will be, or may reasonably be expected to be, entitled under sections 151 and 3402(m) for his taxable year which begins in, or with, the next calendar year is different from the number to which the employee is entitled on such day, the following rules shall be applicable:

(i) If such number is less than the number of withholding exemptions claimed by the employee on a withholding exemption certificate in effect on such day, the employee must, on or before December 1 of the year in which the change occurs, unless such change occurs in December, furnish his employer with a new withholding exemption certificate reflecting the decrease in the number of withholding exemptions. If the change occurs in December, the new certificate must be furnished within 10 days after the change occurs. The number of exemptions to which an employee is entitled for his taxable year which begins in, or with, the next calendar year decreases, for example, for any of the following reasons:

(a) The spouse or a dependent of the employee dies.

(b) The employee finds that it is not reasonable to expect that an individual claimed as a dependent on the employee's withholding exemption certificate will qualify as a dependent of the employee for such taxable year.

(c) It becomes unreasonable for an employee who has in effect a withholding exemption certificate on which he claims a withholding allowance under section 3402(m) to believe that his wages and the determinable additional amounts for each item under § 31.3402(m)-1 for his taxable year which begins in, or with, the next calendar year will entitle him to such withholding allowance for such taxable year.

(ii) If such number is greater than the number of withholding exemptions claimed by the employee on a withholding exemption certificate in effect on such day, the employee may, on or before December 1 of the year in which such change occurs, unless such change occurs in December, furnish his employer with a new withholding exemption certificate reflecting the increase in the number of withholding exemptions. If the change occurs in December, the certificate may be furnished on or after the date on which the change occurs.

(2) If, on any day during the calendar year, it is not reasonable for an employee, who has furnished his employer with a withholding exemption certificate which contains the statements described in § 31.3402(n)-1 and whose liability for such tax is determined on a calendar-year basis, to anticipate that he will incur no liability for income tax imposed under subtitle A (as defined in § 31.3402(n)-1) for his taxable year which begins with the next calendar year, the employee must furnish his employer with a new withholding exemption certificate which does not contain such statements, on or before December 1 of the first-mentioned calendar year. If it first becomes unreasonable for the employee to so anticipate in December, the new certificate must be

furnished within 10 days after the day on which it first becomes unreasonable for the employee to so anticipate.

(3) Before December 1 of each year, every employer should request each of his employees to file a new withholding exemption certificate for the ensuing calendar year, in the event of change in the employee's exemption status since the filing of his latest certificate.

(d) Inclusion of account number on withholding exemption certificate. Every individual to whom an account number has been assigned shall include such number on any withholding exemption certificate filed with an employer. For provisions relating to the obtaining of an account number, see § 31.6011(b)-2.

(e) Invalid withholding exemption certificates. Any alteration of or unauthorized addition to a withholding exemption certificate shall cause such certificate to be invalid; see paragraph (b) of § 31.3402(f)(5)-1 for the definitions of alteration and unauthorized addition. Any withholding exemption certificate which the employee clearly indicates to be false by an oral statement or by a written statement (other than one made on the withholding exemption certificate itself) made by him to the employer on or before the date on which the employee furnishes such certificate is also invalid. For purposes of the preceding sentence, the term "employer" includes any individual authorized by the employer either to receive withholding exemption certificates, to make withholding computations, or to make payroll distributions. If an employer receives an invalid withholding exemption certificate, he shall consider it a nullity for purposes of computing withholding; he shall inform the employee who submitted the certificate that it is invalid, and shall request another withholding exemption certificate from the employee. If the employee who submitted the invalid certificate fails to comply with the employer's request, the employer shall withhold from the employee as from a single person claiming no exemptions (see § 31.3402(f)(2)-1(a)); if, however, a prior certificate is in effect with respect to the employee, the employer shall continue to withhold in accordance with the prior certificate. This paragraph applies only with respect to withholding exemption certificates received by any employer after July 26, 1976.

(f) Applicability of withholding exemption certificate to qualified State individual income taxes. The withholding exemption certificate shall be used for purposes of withholding with respect to qualified State individual income taxes as well as Federal tax. For provisions relating to the withholding exemption certificate with respect to such State taxes, see paragraph (d)(3)(i) of § 301.6361-1 of this chapter (Regulation on Procedure and Administration).

(g) Submission of certain withholding exemption certificates and notice of the maximum number of withholding exemptions permitted. *(1) Submission of certain withholding exemption certificates.* (i) In general. An employer must submit to the Internal Revenue Service (IRS) a copy of any currently effective withholding exemption certificate as directed in a written notice to the employer from the IRS or as directed in published guidance.

(A) Notice to submit withholding exemption certificates. A notice to the employer to submit withholding exemption certificates may relate either to one or more named employees, to one or more reasonably segregable units of the employer, or to withholding exemption certificates under certain specified criteria. The notice will designate the IRS office where the copies of the withholding exemption certificates must be submitted. Alternatively, upon notice from the IRS, the employer must make available for inspection by an IRS employee withholding exemption certificates received from one or more named employees, from one or more reasonably segregable units of the employer, or from employees who have furnished withholding exemption certificates under certain specified criteria.

(B) Published guidance. Employers may also be required to submit copies of withholding exemption certificates under certain specified criteria when directed to do so by the IRS in published guidance. For purposes of the preceding sentence, the term published guidance means a revenue procedure or notice published in the Internal Revenue Bulletin (see § 601.601(d)(2) of this chapter).

(ii) Withholding after submission of withholding exemption certificate. After a copy of a withholding exemption certificate has been submitted to the IRS under this paragraph (g)(1), the employer must withhold tax on the basis of the withholding exemption certificate, if the withholding exemption certificate meets the requirements of § 31.3402(f)(5)-1. However, the employer may not withhold on the basis of the withholding exemption certificate if the certificate must be disregarded based on a notice of the maximum number of withholding exemptions permitted under the provisions of paragraph (g)(2) of this section.

(2) Notice of the maximum number of withholding exemptions permitted. (i) Notice to employer. The IRS may notify the employer in writing that the employee is not entitled to claim a complete exemption from withholding or more than the maximum number of withholding exemptions specified by the IRS in the written notice. The notice will also specify the applicable marital status for purposes of calculating the required amount of withholding. The notice will specify the IRS office to be contacted for further information. The notice of maximum number of withholding exemptions permitted may be issued if—

(A) The IRS determines that a copy of a withholding exemption certificate submitted under paragraph (g)(1) of this section or otherwise provided to the IRS contains a materially incorrect statement or determines, after a request to the employee for verification of the statements on the certificate, that the IRS lacks sufficient information to determine if the certificate is correct.

(B) The IRS otherwise determines that the employee is not entitled to claim a complete exemption from withholding and is not entitled to claim more than a specified number of withholding exemptions.

(ii) Notice to employee. If the IRS provides a notice to the employer under this paragraph (g)(2), the IRS will also provide the employer with a similar notice for the employee (employee notice) that identifies the maximum number of withholding exemptions permitted and specifies the marital status to be used for calculating the required amount of withholding. The employee notice will also indicate the process by which the employee can provide additional information to the IRS for purposes of determining the appropriate number of withholding exemptions and/or modifying the specified marital status. The IRS will also mail a similar notice to the employee's last known address. For further guidance regarding the definition of last known address, see § 301.6212-2 of this chapter. If the IRS is unable to determine a last known address for the employee, the IRS will use other available information as appropriate to mail the notice to the employee.

(iii) Requirement to furnish. If the employee is employed by the employer as of the date of the notice, the employer must furnish the employee notice to the employee within 10 business days of receipt. The employer may follow any reasonable business practice to furnish the copy of the notice to the employee. For purposes of this paragraph (g)(2)(iii), the determination of whether an employee is employed as of the date of the notice is based on all the facts and circumstances, including whether the employer has treated the employment relationship as terminated for other purposes. An employee that is not performing services for the employer as of the date of the notice is employed by the employer as of the date of the notice for purposes of this paragraph (g)(2)(iii) if—

(A) The employer pays wages with respect to prior employment to the employee subject to income tax withholding on or after the date specified in the notice;

(B) The employer reasonably expects the employee to resume the performance of services for the employer within twelve months of the date of the notice; or

(C) The employee is on a bona fide leave of absence if the period of such leave does not exceed twelve months or the employee retains a right to reemployment with the employer under an applicable statute or by contract.

(iv) Requirement to notify the IRS. If the employer is not required to furnish the notice to the employee under paragraph (g)(2)(iii) of this section, the employer must send a written response to the IRS office designated in the notice indicating that the employee is not employed by the employer.

(v) Requirement to withhold based on the notice. If the employer is required to furnish the employee notice to the employee under paragraph (g)(2)(iii), then the employer must withhold tax on the basis of the maximum number of withholding exemptions and the marital status specified in the notice for any wages paid after the date specified in the notice, except as provided in paragraphs (g)(2)(vi), (vii), (viii), (ix), and (x) of this section. The employer must withhold tax in accordance with the notice as of the date specified in the notice, which shall be no earlier than 45 calendar days after the date of the notice.

(vi) Employment resumes after twelve months. If the employer is required to furnish the employee notice to the employee only pursuant to paragraph (g)(2)(iii)(B) of this section and the employee resumes the performance of services for the employer more than 12 months after the date of the notice, then the employer is not required to withhold based on the notice.

(vii) Requirement to withhold based on an existing Form W-4. If a withholding exemption certificate is in effect with respect to the employee before the employer receives a notice of the maximum number of withholding exemptions permitted under this paragraph (g)(2), the employer must continue to withhold tax in accordance with the existing withholding exemption certificate, rather than on the basis of the notice, if the existing withholding exemption certificate does not claim complete exemption from withholding and claims a marital status, a number of withholding exemptions, and any additional withholding that results in more withholding than would result from applying the marital status and number of withholding exemptions specified in the notice.

(viii) Modification notice. After issuing the notice specifying the maximum number of withholding exemptions permitted and the marital status, the IRS may issue a subsequent notice that modifies the original notice (modification notice). The modification notice may change the marital status and/or the number of withholding exemptions permitted. The employer must withhold based on the modification notice as of the date specified in the modification notice.

(ix) Requirement to withhold after termination of employment. If the employee is employed as of the date of the notice under paragraph (g)(2)(iii) of this section but the employer or employee terminates the employment relationship after the date of the notice, the employer must continue to withhold based on the maximum number of withholding exemptions and the marital status specified in the notice or a modification notice if any wages subject to income tax withholding are paid with respect to the prior employment after such date. Furthermore, the employer must withhold based on the notice or modification notice if the employee resumes an employment relationship with the employer within 12 months after the termination of the employment relationship. Whether the employment relationship is terminated is based on all the facts and circumstances.

(x) Requirement to withhold based on new Form W-4. The employee may furnish a new withholding exemption certificate after the employer receives a notice or modification notice from the IRS of the maximum number of withholding exemptions permitted under this paragraph (g)(2).

(A) Employee requests more withholding. If the employee furnishes a new withholding exemption certificate after the employer receives the notice or modification notice, the employer must withhold tax on the basis of that new certificate only if the new certificate does not claim complete exemption from withholding and claims a marital status, a number of withholding exemptions, and any additional withholding that results in more withholding than would result under the notice or modification notice.

(B) Employee requests less withholding. If the employee furnishes a new withholding exemption certificate after the employer receives the notice or modification notice, the employer must disregard the new certificate and withhold on the basis of the notice or modification notice if the employee claims complete exemption from withholding or claims a marital status, a number of withholding exemptions, and any additional withholding that results in less withholding than would result under the notice or modification notice. If the employee wants to put a new certificate into effect that results in less withholding than that required under the notice or modification notice, the employee must contact the IRS. The employer must withhold on the basis of the notice or modification notice unless the IRS subsequently notifies the employer to withhold based on the new certificate.

(3) Definition of employer. For purposes of this paragraph (g), the term employer includes any person authorized by the employer to receive withholding exemption certificates, to make withholding computations, or to make payroll distributions.

(4) Examples. The following examples illustrate the rules of this section.

Example (1). Employer U receives a notice from the IRS that identifies the maximum number of withholding exemptions permitted and specifies the marital status for Employee A. Employee A is not currently performing any services for Employer U. However, Employer U is continuing to make certain wage payments to Employee A. Employer U must furnish the employee notice to Employee A within 10 business days of receipt and must withhold based on the notice on any wages paid to Employee A on or after the date specified in the notice.

Example (2). Employer V receives a notice in October of Year 1 from the IRS that identifies the maximum number of withholding exemptions permitted and specifies the marital status for Employee B. Employee B has not performed services for Employer V since August of Year 1. However, since Employee B has performed services for Employer V for several years on a seasonal basis, Employer V reasonably expects Employee B to resume the performance of services for Employer V in June of Year 2, a date that is within 12 months of the date of the notice. Employer V is required to furnish the notice to Employee B within 10 business days of receipt. Employee B does not resume the performance of services until June of Year 3. Employer V is not required to withhold based on the notice.

Example (3). Employer W receives a notice from the IRS that identifies the maximum number of withholding exemptions permitted and specifies the marital status for Employee C. Employee C began a 4-month unpaid maternity leave of absence three weeks before Employer W received the notice. Employer W must furnish the employee notice to Employee C within 10 business days of receipt. When Employee C resumes performing services when her maternity leave ends, Employer W must withhold based on the notice.

Example (4). Employer X receives a notice from the IRS in Year 1 that identifies the maximum number of withholding exemptions permitted and specifies the marital status for Employee D. Employer X must furnish the employee notice to Employee D within 10 business days of receipt and withhold based on the notice. In Year 2, Employee D terminates the employment relationship. Employee D applies for a different position with Employer X and resumes employment 10 months after having left her previous position with Employer X. Since Employer X rehired Employee D within 12 months after the termination of employment, Employer X must withhold based on the notice.

Example (5). Employer Y receives a notice from the IRS that identifies the maximum number of withholding exemptions permitted and specifies the marital status for Employee E. Employer Y must furnish the employee notice to Employee E within 10 business days of receipt. After receipt of this notice, Employee E contacts the IRS and establishes that he is entitled to claim a higher number of withholding exemptions. Employer Y receives a modification notice from the IRS that changes the maximum number of withholding exemptions permitted for Employee E. Employer Y must withhold tax based on the modification notice as of the date specified in such notice.

Example (6). Employer Z pays remuneration to Employee F, a United States citizen, for services performed in Country M. Employer Z receives a notice from the IRS in Year 1 that identifies the maximum number of withholding exemptions permitted and specifies the marital status for Employee F. Employer Z must furnish the employee notice to Employee F within 10 business days of receipt. Employer Z reasonably believes all the remuneration paid to Employee F in Year 1 is excluded from Employee F's gross income under section 911 of the Internal Revenue Code. Since section 3401(a)(8)(B) excludes such remuneration from wages for income tax withholding purposes, Employer X does not have to withhold on such remuneration, notwithstanding the maximum number of exemptions permitted and marital status specified in the notice. In Year 2, Employee F returns to the United States to perform services. Employer Z does not reasonably believe any part of Employee F's remuneration paid in Year 2 is excluded from Employee F's gross income under section 911. Rather, Employer Z reasonably believes that remuneration paid to Employee F in Year 2 is subject to income tax withholding. Employer Z must withhold on the remuneration paid to Employee F based on the notice.

(5) Effective/applicability date. Except as provided in this paragraph (g)(5), paragraph (g) applies on April 14, 2005. Paragraphs (g)(2)(iii)(A), (B), and (C) and paragraph (g)(2)(ix) apply on October 11, 2007, except taxpayers may rely on such paragraphs for notices issued prior to such date.

T.D. 6259, 10/25/57, amend T.D. 6606, 8/24/62, T.D. 6654, 5/27/63, T.D. 7048, 6/23/70, T.D. 7065, 10/22/70, T.D. 7423, 6/24/76, T.D. 7577, 12/19/78, T.D. 7598, 3/12/79, T.D. 7682, 3/10/80, T.D. 7772, 3/17/81, T.D. 7803, 1/21/82, T.D. 7915, 9/26/83, T.D. 8164, 11/30/87, T.D. 9196, 4/13/2005, T.D. 9337, 7/12/2007.

§ 31.3402(f)(3)-1 When withholding exemption certificate takes effect.

Caution: The Treasury has not yet amended Reg § 31.3402(f)(3)-1 to reflect changes made by P.L. 100-203.

(a) A withholding exemption certificate furnished the employer in any case in which no previous withholding exemption certificate is in effect with such employer, shall take effect as of the beginning of the first payroll period ending, or the first payment of wages made without regard to a payroll period, on or after the date on which such certificate is so furnished.

(b) A withholding exemption certificate furnished the employer in any case in which a previous withholding exemption certificate is in effect with such employer shall, except as hereinafter provided, take effect with respect to the first payment of wages made on or after the first status determination date which occurs at least 30 days after the date on which such certificate is so furnished. However, at the election of the employer, except as hereinafter provided, such certificate may be made effective with respect to any payment of wages made on or after the date on which such certificate is so furnished and before such status determination date.

(c) A withholding exemption certificate furnished the employer pursuant to section 3402(f)(2)(C) (see paragraph (c) of § 31.3402(f)(2)-1 or paragraph (b)(2)(ii) of § 31.3402(1)-1) which effects a change for the next calendar year, shall not take effect, and may not be made effective, with respect to the calendar year in which the certificate is furnished. A withholding exemption certificate furnished the employer by an employee who determines his income tax liability on a basis other than a calendar-year basis, as required by paragraph (b)(4) of § 31.3402(f)(2)-1, which effects a change for the employee's next taxable year, shall not take effect, and may not be made effective, with respect to the taxable year of the employee in which the certificate is furnished.

(d) For purposes of this section, the term "status determination date" means January 1, May 1, July 1, and October 1 of each year.

T.D. 6259, 10/25/57, amend T.D. 7048, 6/23/70, T.D. 7065, 10/22/70, T.D. 7115, 5/20/71, T.D. 7915, 9/26/83.

§ 31.3402(f)(4)-1 Period during which withholding exemption certificate remains in effect.

(a) In general. Except as provided in paragraphs (b) and (c) of this section, a withholding exemption certificate which takes effect under section 3402(f) of the Internal Revenue Code of 1954, or which on December 31, 1954, was in effect under section 1622(h) of the Internal Revenue Code of 1939, shall continue in effect with respect to the employee until another withholding exemption certificate takes effect under section 3402(f). Paragraphs (b) and (c) of this section are applicable only for withholding exemption certificates furnished by the employee to the employer before January 1, 1982. See § 31.3402(f)(4)-2 for the rules applicable to withholding exemption certificates furnished by the employee to the employer after December 31, 1981.

(b) Withholding allowances under section 3402(m) for itemized deductions. In no case shall the portion of a withholding exemption certificate relating to withholding allowances under section 3402(m) for itemized deductions be effective with respect to any payment of wages made to an employee—

(1) In the case of an employee whose liability for tax under subtitle A of the Code is determined on a calendar-year basis, after April 30 of the calendar year immediately following the calendar year which was his estimation year for purposes of determining the withholding allowance or allowances claimed on such exemption certificate, or

(2) In the case of an employee to whom subparagraph (1) of this paragraph does not apply, after the last day of the fourth month immediately following his taxable year which was his estimation year for purposes of determining the withholding allowance or allowances claimed on such exemption certificate.

(c) Statements under section 3402(n) eliminating requirement of withholding. The statements described in § 31.3402(n)-1 made by an employee with respect to his preceding taxable year and current taxable year shall be deemed to have been made also with respect to his current taxable year and his taxable year immediately thereafter, respectively, until either a new withholding exemption certificate furnished by the employee takes effect or the existing certificate which contains such statements expires. In no case shall a withholding exemption certificate which contains such statements be effective with respect to any payment of wages made to an employee—

(1) In the case of an employee whose liability for tax under subtitle A is determined on a calendar-year basis, after April 30 of the calendar year immediately following the calendar year which was his original current taxable year for purposes of such statements, or

(2) In the case of an employee to whom subparagraph (1) of this paragraph does not apply, after the last day of the fourth month immediately following his original current taxable year for purposes of such statements.

T.D. 6259, 10/25/57, amend T.D. 7048, 6/23/70, T.D. 7065, 10/22/70, T.D. 7915, 9/26/83.

§ 31.3402(f)(4)-2 Effective period of withholding exemption certificate.

Caution: The Treasury has not yet amended Reg § 31.3402(f)(4)-2 to reflect changes made by P.L. 100-203, P.L. 99-514.

(a) In general. Except as provided in paragraphs (b) and (c) of this section, a withholding exemption certificate that takes effect under section 3402(f) of the Internal Revenue Code of 1954, or that on December 31, 1954, was in effect under section 1622(h) of the Internal Revenue Code of 1939, shall continue in effect with respect to the employee until another withholding exemption certificate takes effect under section 3402(f). Paragraphs (b) and (c) of this section are applicable only for withholding exemption certificates furnished by the employee to the employer after December 31, 1981. See § 31.3402(f)(4)-1 for the rules applicable to withholding exemption certificates furnished by the employee to the employer before January 1, 1982.

(b) Withholding allowances under section 3402(m). See paragraphs (b) and (c) of § 31.3402(f)(2)-1 (relating to withholding exemption certificates) for information as to when an employee claiming withholding allowances under section 3402(m) and the regulations thereunder must file a new withholding exemption certificate with his employer.

(c) Statements under section 3402(n) eliminating requirement of withholding. The statements described in § 31.3402(n)-1 made by an employee with respect to his preceding taxable year and current taxable year shall be effective until either a new withholding exemption certificate furnished by the employee takes effect or the existing certificate that contains such statements expires. In no case shall a withholding exemption certificate that contains such statements be effective with respect to any payment of wages made to an employee—

(1) In the case of an employee whose liability for tax under subtitle A is determined on a calendar year basis, after February 15 of the calendar year following the estimation year, or

(2) In the case of an employee to whom paragraph (c)(1) of this section does not apply, after the 15th day of the 2nd calendar month following the last day of the estimation year.

(d) Estimation year. The estimation year is the taxable year including the day on which the employee files the withholding exemption certificate with his employer, except that if the employee files the withholding exemption certificate with his employer and specifies on the certificate that the certificate is not to take effect until a specified future date, the estimation year shall be the taxable year including that specified future date.

T.D. 7915, 9/26/83.

§ 31.3402(f)(5)-1 Form and contents of withholding exemption certificate.

(a) *(1)* Form W-4. Form W-4, "Employee's Withholding Allowance Certificate," is the form prescribed for the withholding exemption certificate required to be furnished under section 3402(f)(2). A withholding exemption certificate must be prepared in accordance with the instructions and regulations applicable thereto, and must set forth fully and clearly the data that is called for therein. Blank copies of paper Forms W-4 will be supplied to employers upon request to the Internal Revenue Service (IRS). An employer may also download and print Form W-4 from the IRS Internet site at http://www.irs.gov. In lieu of the prescribed form, employers may prepare and use a form the provisions of which are identical with those of the prescribed form, but only if employers also provide employees with all the tables, instructions, and worksheets contained in the Form W-4 in effect at that time, and only if employers comply with all revenue procedures relating to substitute forms in effect at that time.

(2) Employers are prohibited from accepting a substitute form developed by an employee, and the employee submitting such form will be treated as failing to furnish a withholding exemption certificate. For further guidance regarding the employer's obligations when an employee is treated as failing to furnish a withholding exemption certificate, see § 31.3402(f)(2)-1.

(3) Effective/applicability date. Paragraph (a)(1) applies on April 14, 2005. Paragraph (a)(2) applies to any substitute

withholding exemption certificate furnished to an employer on or after October 11, 2007.

(b) Invalid Form W-4. A Form W-4 does not meet the requirements of section 3402(f)(5) or this section and is invalid if it contains an alteration or unauthorized addition. For purposes of § 31.3402(f)(2)-1(e) and this paragraph—

(1) An alteration of a withholding exemption certificate is any deletion of the language of the jurat or other similar provision of such certificate by which the employee certifies or affirms the correctness of the completed certificate, or any material defacing of such certificate;

(2) An unauthorized addition to a withholding exemption certificate is any writing on such certificate other than the entries requested (e.g., name, address, and number of exemptions claimed).

(c) Electronic Form W-4. *(1) In general.* An employer may establish a system for its employees to file withholding exemption certificates electronically.

(2) Requirements. (i) In general. The electronic system must ensure that the information received is the information sent, and must document all occasions of employee access that result in the filing of a Form W-4. In addition, the design and operation of the electronic system, including access procedures, must make it reasonably certain that the person accessing the system and filing the Form W-4 is the employee identified in the form.

(ii) Same information as paper Form W-4. The electronic filing must provide the employer with exactly the same information as the paper Form W-4.

(iii) Jurat and signature requirements. The electronic filing must be signed by the employee under penalties of perjury.

(A) Jurat. The jurat (perjury statement) must contain the language that appears on the paper Form W-4. The electronic program must inform the employee that he or she must make the declaration contained in the jurat and that the declaration is made by signing the Form W-4. The instructions and the language of the jurat must immediately follow the employee's income tax withholding selections and immediately precede the employee's electronic signature.

(B) Electronic signature. The electronic signature must identify the employee filing the electronic Form W-4 and authenticate and verify the filing. For this purpose, the terms "authenticate" and "verify" have the same meanings as they do when applied to a written signature on a paper Form W-4. An electronic signature can be in any form that satisfies the foregoing requirements. The electronic signature must be the final entry in the employee's Form W-4 submission.

(iv) Copies of electronic Forms W-4. Upon request by the Internal Revenue Service, the employer must supply a hardcopy of the electronic Form W-4 and a statement that, to the best of the employer's knowledge, the electronic Form W-4 was filed by the named employee. The hardcopy of the electronic Form W-4 must provide exactly the same information as, but need not be a facsimile of, the paper Form W-4.

(3) Effective date. (i) In general. This paragraph applies to all withholding exemption certificates filed electronically by employees on or after January 2, 1997.

(ii) Special rule for certain Forms W-4. In the case of an electronic system that precludes the filing of Forms W-4 required on commencement of employment and Forms W-4 claiming more than 10 withholding exemptions or exemption from withholding, the requirements of paragraph (c)(2)(iii) of this section will be treated as satisfied if the Form W-4 is filed electronically before January 1, 1999.

T.D. 6259, 10/25/57, amend T.D. 7048, 6/23/70, T.D. 7423, 6/24/76, T.D. 7915, 9/26/83, T.D. 8706, 12/31/96, T.D. 9196, 4/13/2005, T.D. 9337, 7/12/2007.

§ 31.3402(f)(6)-1 Withholding exemptions for nonresident alien individuals.

A nonresident alien individual (other than, in regard to wages paid after February 28, 1979, a nonresident alien individual treated as a resident under section 6013(g) or (h)) subject to withholding under section 3402 is on any 1 day entitled under section 3402(f)(1) and § 31.3402(f)(1)-1 to the number of withholding exemptions corresponding to the number of personal exemptions to which he is entitled on such day by reason of the application of section 873 (b)(3) or section 876, whichever applies. Thus, a nonresident alien individual who is not a resident of Canada or Mexico and who is not a resident of Puerto Rico during the entire taxable year, is allowed under section 3402(f)(1) only one withholding exemption.

T.D. 6654, 5/27/63, amend T.D. 6908, 12/30/66, T.D. 7670, 1/30/80.

§ 31.3402(g)-1 Supplemental wage payments.

Caution: The Treasury has not yet amended Reg § 31.3402(g)-1 to reflect changes made by P.L. 107-16, P.L. 103-66.

(a) In general and withholding on supplemental wages in excess of $1,000,000. *(1) Determination of supplemental wages and regular wages.* (i) Supplemental wages. An employee's remuneration may consist of regular wages and supplemental wages. Supplemental wages are all wages paid by an employer that are not regular wages. Supplemental wages include wage payments made without regard to an employee's payroll period, but also may include payments made for a payroll period. Examples of wage payments that are included in supplemental wages include reported tips (except as provided in paragraph (a)(1)(v) of this section), overtime pay (except as provided in paragraph (a)(1)(iv) of this section), bonuses, back pay, commissions, wages paid under reimbursement or other expense allowance arrangements, nonqualified deferred compensation includible in wages, wages paid as noncash fringe benefits, sick pay paid by a third party as an agent of the employer, amounts that are includible in gross income under section 409A, income recognized on the exercise of a nonstatutory stock option, wages from imputed income for health coverage for a non-dependent, and wage income recognized on the lapse of a restriction on restricted property transferred from an employer to an employee. Amounts that are described as supplemental wages in this definition are supplemental wages regardless of whether the employer has paid the employee any regular wages during either the calendar year of the payment or any prior calendar year. Thus, for example, if the only wages that an employer has ever paid an employee are payments of noncash fringe benefits and income recognized on the exercise of a nonstatutory stock option, such payments are classified as supplemental wages.

(ii) Regular wages. As distinguished from supplemental wages, regular wages are amounts that are paid at a regular hourly, daily, or similar periodic rate (and not an overtime rate) for the current payroll period or at a predetermined fixed determinable amount for the current payroll period. Thus, among other things, wages that vary from payroll period to payroll period (such as commissions, reported tips, bonuses, or overtime pay) are not regular wages, except that an employer may treat tips as regular wages under paragraph (a)(1)(v) of this section and an employer may treat overtime pay as regular wages under paragraph (a)(1)(iv) of this section.

(iii) Amounts that are not wages subject to income tax withholding. If an amount of remuneration is not wages subject to income tax withholding, it is neither regular wages nor supplemental wages. Thus, for example, income from the disqualifying dispositions of shares of stock acquired pursuant to the exercise of statutory stock options, as described in section 421(b), is not included in regular wages or supplemental wages.

(iv) Optional treatment of overtime pay as regular wages. Employers may treat overtime pay as regular wages rather than supplemental wages. For this purpose, overtime pay is defined as any pay required to be paid pursuant to federal (Fair Labor Standards Act), state, or local governmental laws at a rate higher than the normal wage rate of the employee because the employee has worked hours in excess of the number of hours deemed to constitute a normal work week or work day.

(v) Optional treatment of tips as regular wages. Employers may treat tips as regular wages rather than supplemental wages. For this purpose, tips are defined as including all tips which are reported to the employer pursuant to section 6053.

(vi) Amount to be withheld. The calculation of the amount of the income tax withholding with respect to supplemental wage payments is provided for under paragraph (a)(2) through (a)(7) of this section.

(2) Mandatory flat rate withholding. If a supplemental wage payment, when added to all supplemental wage payments previously made by one employer (as defined in paragraph (a)(3) of this section) to an employee during the calendar year, exceeds $1,000,000, the rate used in determining the amount of withholding on the excess (including any excess which is a portion of a supplemental wage payment) shall be equal to the highest rate of tax applicable under section 1 for such taxable years beginning in such calendar year. This flat rate shall be applied without regard to whether income tax has been withheld from the employee's regular wages, without allowance for the number of withholding allowances claimed by the employee on Form W-4, "Employee's Withholding Allowance Certificate," without regard to whether the employee has claimed exempt status on Form W-4, without regard to whether the employee has requested additional withholding on Form W-4, and without regard to the withholding method used by the employer. Withholding under this paragraph (a)(2) is mandatory flat rate withholding.

(3) Certain persons treated as one employer. (i) Persons under common control. For purposes of paragraph (a)(2) of this section, all persons treated as a single employer under subsection (a) or (b) of section 52 shall be treated as one employer.

(ii) Agents. For purposes of paragraph (a)(2) of this section, any payment made to an employee by a third party acting as an agent for the employer (regardless of whether such person shall have been designated as an agent pursuant to section 3504) shall be considered as made by the employer except as provided in paragraph (a)(4)(iii) of this section.

(4) Treatment of certain items in determining applicability of mandatory flat rate withholding. (i) Optional treatment of compensation not subject to income tax withholding. For purposes of paragraph (a)(2) of this section, employers may determine whether an employee has received $1,000,000 of supplemental wages during a calendar year by including in supplemental wages amounts includible in income but not subject to withholding that are reported as wages, tips, other compensation on Form W-2.

(ii) Allocation of salary reduction deferrals. In allocating salary reduction deferral amounts excludable from wages for purposes of determining whether the employer has paid $1,000,000 of supplemental wages under paragraph (a)(2) of this section, employers must allocate such salary reduction deferral amounts to the type of compensation (i.e., gross amounts of regular wage payments or gross amounts of supplemental wage payments) actually being deferred.

(iii) Optional de minimis exception for certain payments by agents. For purposes of paragraph (a)(2) of this section, if an agent makes total wage payments (including regular wages and supplemental wages) of less than $100,000 to an individual during any calendar year, an employer or other agent may disregard such payments in determining whether the individual has received $1,000,000 of supplemental wages during the calendar year, and such agent need not consider whether the individual has received other supplemental wages in determining the amount of income tax to be withheld from the payments. An employer may not avail itself of this exception if the employer is making payments to the employee using five or more agents and a principal effect of such use of agents is to reduce the applicability of mandatory flat rate withholding to the employee. For purposes of paragraph (a)(2) of this section, if an agent makes total wage payments of $100,000 or more to an individual during any calendar year, the entire amount of supplemental wages paid by the agent during the calendar year to the employee must be taken into account (by other agents of the employer that make total wage payments to the employee of $100,000 or more, by the agent, and by the employer for which the agent is acting) in determining whether the employee has received $1,000,000 of supplemental wages.

(iv) Treatment of supplemental wage payment exceeding $1,000,000 cumulative threshold. In the case of a supplemental wage payment that, when added to all supplemental wage payments previously made by the employer to the employee in the calendar year, results in the employee having received in excess of $1,000,000 supplemental wages for the calendar year, the employer is required to impose withholding under paragraph (a)(2) of this section only on the portion of the payment that is in excess of $1,000,000 (taking into account all prior supplemental wage payments during the year). However, an employer may subject the entire amount of such supplemental wage payment to the withholding imposed by paragraph (a)(2) of this section.

(5) Withholding on supplemental wages that are not subject to mandatory flat rate withholding. To the extent that paragraph (a)(2) of this section does not apply to a supplemental wage payment (or a portion of a payment), the amount of the tax required to be withheld on the supplemental wages when paid shall be determined under the rules provided in paragraphs (a)(6) and (7) of this section.

(6) Aggregate procedure for withholding on supplemental wages. (i) Applicability. The employer is required to determine withholding upon supplemental wages under this paragraph (a)(6) if paragraph (a)(2) of this section does not apply to the payment or portion of the payment and if paragraph (a)(7) of this section may not be used with respect to the payment. In addition, employers have the option of using this paragraph (a)(6) to calculate withholding with respect to

a supplemental wage payment, if paragraph (a)(2) of this section does not apply to the payment, but if paragraph (a)(7) of this section could be used with respect to the payment.

(ii) Procedure. Provided this procedure applies under paragraph (a)(6)(i) of this section, the supplemental wages, if paid concurrently with wages for a payroll period, are aggregated with the wages paid for such payroll period. If not paid concurrently, the supplemental wages are aggregated with the wages paid or to be paid within the same calendar year for the last preceding payroll period or for the current payroll period, if any. The amount of tax to be withheld is determined as if the aggregate of the supplemental wages and the regular wages constituted a single wage payment for the regular payroll period. The withholding method used by the employer with respect to regular wages would then be used to calculate the withholding on this single wage payment and the employer would take into consideration the Form W-4 submitted by the employee. This procedure is the aggregate procedure for withholding on supplemental wages.

(7) Optional flat rate withholding on supplemental wages. (i) Applicability. The employer may determine withholding upon supplemental wages under this paragraph (a)(7) if three conditions are met—

(A) Paragraph (a)(2) of this section does not apply to the payment or the portion of the payment;

(B) The supplemental wages are either not paid concurrently with regular wages or are separately stated on the payroll records of the employer; and

(C) Income tax has been withheld from regular wages of the employee during the calendar year of the payment or the preceding calendar year.

(ii) Procedure. The determination of the tax to be withheld under paragraph (a)(7)(iii) of this section is made without reference to any payment of regular wages, without allowance for the number of withholding allowances claimed by the employee on Form W-4, and without regard to whether the employee has requested additional withholding on Form W-4. Withholding under this procedure is optional flat rate withholding.

(iii) Rate applicable for purposes of optional flat rate withholding. Provided the conditions of paragraph (a)(7)(i) of this section have been met, the employer may determine the tax to be withheld—

(A) From supplemental wages paid after April 30, 1966, and prior to January 1, 1994, by using a flat percentage rate of 20 percent;

(B) From supplemental wages paid after December 31, 1993, and on or before August 6, 2001, by using a flat percentage rate of 28 percent;

(C) From supplemental wages paid after August 6, 2001, and on or before December 31, 2001, by using a flat percentage rate of 27.5 percent;

(D) From supplemental wages paid after December 31, 2001, and on or before May 27, 2003, by using a flat percentage rate of 27 percent;

(E) From supplemental wages paid after May 27, 2003, and on or before December 31, 2004, by using a flat percentage rate of 25 percent; and

(F) From supplemental wages paid after December 31, 2004, by using a flat percentage rate of 28 percent (or the corresponding rate in effect under section 1(i)(2) for taxable years beginning in the calendar year in which the payment is made).

(8) Examples. For purposes of these examples, it is assumed that the rate for purposes of mandatory flat rate withholding for 2007 is 35 percent, and the rate for purposes of optional flat rate withholding for 2007 is 25 percent. The following examples illustrate this paragraph (a):

Example (1). (i) Employee A is an employee of three entities (X, Y, and Z) that are treated as a single employer under section 52(a) or (b). In 2007, X pays regular wages to A on a monthly payroll period for services performed for X, Y, and Z. The regular wages are paid on the third business day of each month. Income tax is withheld from the regular wages of A during the year. A receives only the following supplemental wage payments during 2007 in addition to the regular wages paid by X—

(A) A bonus of $600,000 from X on March 15, 2007;

(B) A bonus of $2,300,000 from Y on November 15, 2007; and

(C) A bonus of $10,000 from Z on December 31, 2007.

(ii) In this Example 1, the $600,000 bonus from X is a supplemental wage payment. The withholding on the $600,000 payment from X could be determined under either paragraph (a)(6) or (7) of this section because income tax has been withheld from the regular wages of A. If X elects to use the aggregate procedure under paragraph (a)(6) of this section, the amount of withholding on the supplemental wages would be based on aggregating the supplemental wages and the regular wages paid by X either for the current or last payroll period and treating the total of the regular wages paid by X and the $600,000 supplemental wages as a single wage payment for a regular payroll period. The withholding method used by the employer with respect to regular wages would then be used to calculate the withholding on this single wage payment, and the employer would take into consideration the Form W-4 furnished by the employee.

(iii) In this Example 1, the $2,300,000 bonus from Y is a supplemental wage payment. To calculate the withholding on the $2,300,000 supplemental wage payment from Y, the $600,000 of supplemental wages X has already paid to A in 2007 must be taken into account because X and Y are treated as the same employer under section 52(a) or (b). Thus, the withholding on the first $400,000 of the payment (i.e., the cumulative supplemental wages not in excess of $1,000,000) is computed separately from the withholding on the remaining $1,900,000 of the payment (i.e., the amount of the cumulative supplemental wages in excess of $1,000,000). With respect to the first $400,000, the withholding could be computed under either paragraph (a)(6) or (a)(7) of this section, because income tax has been withheld from the regular wages of the employee. If Y elected to withhold income tax using paragraph (a)(7) of this section, Y would withhold on the $400,000 component at 25 percent (pursuant to paragraph (a)(7)(iii)(F) of this section), which would result in $100,000 tax withheld. The remaining $1,900,000 of the bonus would be subject to mandatory flat rate withholding at the maximum rate of tax in effect under section 1 for 2007 (35%) without regard to the Form W-4 submitted by A. The amount withheld from the $1,900,000 would be $665,000. The withholding on the first component and the withholding on the second component then would be added together to determine the total income tax withholding on the supplemental wage payment from Y. Alternatively, under paragraph (a)(4)(iv) of this section, Y could treat the entire $2,300,000 bonus payment as subject to mandatory flat rate withholding at the maximum rate of tax (35%), in which case the amount to be withheld would be 35 percent of $2,300,000, or $805,000.

(iv) The $10,000 bonus paid from Z is also a supplemental wage payment. To calculate the withholding on the $10,000 bonus, the $2,900,000 in cumulative supplemental wages already paid to A in 2007 by X and Y must be taken into account because X, Y, and Z are treated as a single employer. The entire $10,000 bonus would be subject to mandatory flat rate withholding at the maximum rate of tax in effect under section 1 for 2007. The income tax required to be withheld on this payment would be 35 percent of $10,000 or $3,500.

Example (2). Employees B and C work for employer M. Each employee receives a monthly salary of $3,000 in 2007. As a result of the withholding allowances claimed by B, there has been no income tax withholding on the regular wages M pays to B during either 2007 or 2006. In contrast, M has withheld income tax from regular wages M pays to C during 2007. Together with the monthly salary check paid in December 2007 to each employee, M includes a bonus of $2,000, which is the only supplemental wage payment each employee receives from M in 2007. The bonuses are separately stated on the payroll records of M. Because M has withheld no income tax from B's regular wages during either the calendar year of the $2,000 bonus or the preceding calendar year, M cannot use optional flat rate withholding provided under paragraph (a)(7) of this section to calculate the income tax withholding on B's $2,000 bonus. Consequently, M must use the aggregate procedure set forth in paragraph (a)(6) of this section to calculate the income tax withholding due on the $2,000 bonus to B. With respect to the bonus paid to C, M has the option of using either the aggregate procedure provided under paragraph (a)(6) of this section or the optional flat rate withholding provided under paragraph (a)(7) of this section to calculate the income tax withholding due.

Example (3). (i) Employee D works as an employee of Corporation R. Corporations R and T are treated as a single employer under section 52(a) or (b). R makes regular wage payments to Employee D of $200,000 on a monthly basis in 2007, and income tax is withheld from those wages. R pays D a bonus for his services as an employee equal to $3,000,000 on June 30, 2007. Unrelated company U pays D sick pay as an agent of the employer R and such sick pay is supplemental wages pursuant to § 31.3401(a)-1(b)(8)(i)(b)(2). U pays D $50,000 of sick pay on October 31, 2007. Corporation T decides to award bonuses to all employees of R and T, and pays a bonus of $100,000 to D on December 31, 2007. D received no other payments from R, T, or U.

(ii) In chronological summary, D is paid the following wages other than the regular monthly wages paid by R:

(A) June 30, 2007—$3,000,000 (bonus from R);

(B) October 31, 2007—$50,000 (sick pay from U); and

(C) December 31, 2007—$100,000 (bonus from T).

(iii) In this Example 3, each payment of wages other than the regular monthly wage payments from R is considered to be supplemental wages for purposes of withholding under § 31.3402(g)-1(a)(2). The amount of regular wages from R is irrelevant in determining when mandatory flat rate withholding on supplemental wages must be applied.

(iv) Because income tax has been withheld on D's regular wages, income tax may be withheld on $1,000,000 of the $3,000,000 bonus paid on June 30, 2007, under either paragraph (a)(6) or (7) of this section. If R elects to use optional flat rate withholding provided under paragraph (a)(7)(iii)(F) of this section, withholding would be calculated at 25 percent of the $1,000,000 portion of the payment and would be $250,000.

(v) Income tax withheld on the following supplemental wage payments (or portion of a payment) as follows is required to be calculated at the maximum rate in effect under section 1, or 35 percent in 2007—

(A) $2,000,000 of the $3,000,000 bonus paid by R on June 30, 2007; and

(B) all of the $100,000 bonus paid by T on December 31, 2007.

(vi) Pursuant to paragraph (a)(4)(iii) of this section, because the total wage payments made by U, an agent of the employer, to D are less than $100,000, U is permitted to determine the amount of income tax to be withheld without regard to other supplemental wage payments made to the employee. Income tax withholding on the $50,000 in sick pay may be determined under either paragraph (a)(6) or (7) of this section. If U elects to withhold income tax at the flat rate provided under paragraph (a)(7)(iii)(F) of this section, withholding on the $50,000 of sick pay would be calculated at 25 percent of the $50,000 payment and would be $12,500. Alternatively, U may choose to take account of the $3,000,000 in supplemental wages paid by the employer during 2007 prior to payment of the $50,000 sick pay, and withholding on the $50,000 of sick pay could be calculated applying the mandatory flat rate of 35 percent, resulting in withholding of $17,500 on the $50,000 payment.

Example (4). (i) Employer J has decided it wants to grant its employee B a $1,000,000 net bonus (after withholding) to be paid in 2007. Employer J has withheld income tax from the regular wages of the employee. Employer J has made no other supplemental wage payments to B during the year.

(ii) This Example 4 requires grossing up the supplemental wage payment to determine the gross wages necessary to result in a net payment of $1,000,000. If the employer elected to use optional flat rate withholding, the first $1,000,000 of the wages would be subject to 25 percent withholding. However, any wages above that, including amounts representing gross-up payments, would be subject to mandatory 35 percent withholding. The withholding applicable to the first $1,000,000 (i.e., $250,000) would thus be required to be grossed-up at a 35 percent rate to determine the gross wage amount in excess of $1,000,000. Thus, the wages in excess of $1,000,000 would be equal to $250,000 divided by .65 (computed by subtracting .35 from 1) or $384,615.38. Thus the total supplemental wage payment, taking into account income tax withholding only (and not Federal Insurance Contributions Act taxes), to B would be $1,384,615.38, and the total withholding with respect to the payment if Employer J elected optional flat rate withholding with respect to the first $1,000,000, would be $384,615.38.

(9) Certain noncash payments to retail commission salesmen. For provisions relating to the treatment of wages that are not subject to paragraph (a)(2) of this section and that are paid other than in cash to retail commission salesmen, see § 31.3402(j)-1.

(10) Alternative methods. The Secretary may provide by publication in the Internal Revenue Bulletin (see § 601.601(d)(2)(ii)(b) of this chapter) for alternative withholding methods that will allow an employer to meet its responsibility for the mandatory flat rate withholding required by paragraph (a)(2) of this section.

(b) Special rule where aggregate withholding exemption exceeds wages paid. *(1)* This rule does not apply to the extent that paragraph (a)(2) of this section applies to the supplemental wage payment. If supplemental wages are paid to an employee during a calendar year for a period which involves two or more consecutive payroll periods, for which other wages also are paid during such calendar year, and the aggregate of such other wages is less than the aggregate of the amounts determined under the table provided in section 3402(b)(1) as the withholding exemptions applicable for such payroll periods, the amount of the tax required to be withheld on the supplemental wages shall be computed as follows:

Step 1. Determine an average wage for each of such payroll periods by dividing the sum of the supplemental wages and the wages paid for such payroll periods by the number of such payroll periods.

Step 2. Determine a tax for each payroll period as if the amount of the average wage constituted the wages paid for such payroll period.

Step 3. From the sum of the amounts of tax determined in Step 2 subtract the total amount of tax withheld, or to be withheld, from the wages, other than the supplemental wages, for such payroll periods. The remainder, if any, shall constitute the amount of the tax to be withheld upon the supplemental wages.

Example. An employee has a weekly payroll period ending on Saturday of each week, the wages for which are paid on Friday of the succeeding week. On the 10th day of each month he is paid a bonus based upon production during the payroll periods for which wages were paid in the preceding month. The employee is paid a weekly wage of $64 on each of the five Fridays occurring in July 1966. On August 10, 1966, the employee is paid a bonus of $125 based upon production during the five payroll periods covered by the wages paid in July. On the date of payment of the bonus, the employee, who is married and has three children, has a withholding exemption certificate in effect indicating that he is married and claiming five withholding exemptions. The amount of the tax to be withheld from the bonus paid on August 10, 1966, is computed as follows:

Wages paid in July 1966 for 5 payroll periods (5 × $64)	$320.00
Bonus paid August 10, 1966	125.00
Aggregate of wages and bonus	445.00
Average wage per payroll period ($445\ 5)	89.00
Computation of tax under percentage method:	
Withholding exemptions (5 × $13.50)	67.50
Remainder subject to tax	21.50
Tax on average wage for 1 week under percentage method of withholding (married person with weekly payroll period) (14 percent of $17.50 (excess over $4))	2.45
Tax on average wage for 5 weeks	12.25
Less: Tax previously withheld on weekly wage payments of $64	None
Tax to be withheld on supplemental wages	12.25
Computation of tax under wage bracket method:	
Tax on $89 wage under weekly wage table for married person ($2.50 per week for 5 weeks)	12.50
Less: Tax previously withheld on weekly wage payments of $64	None
Tax to be withheld on supplemental wages	12.50

(2) Applicability. The rules prescribed in this paragraph (b) shall, at the election of the employer, be applied in lieu of the rules prescribed in paragraph (a) of this section except that this paragraph shall not be applicable in any case in which the payroll period of the employee is less than one week or to the extent that paragraph (a)(2) of this section applies to the supplemental wage payment.

(c) Vacation allowances. Amounts of so-called "vacation allowances" shall be subject to withholding as though they were regular wage payments made for the period covered by the vacation. If the vacation allowance is paid in addition to the regular wage payment for such period, the rules applicable with respect to supplemental wage payments shall apply to such vacation allowance.

T.D. 6259, 10/27/57, amend T.D. 6860, 11/3/65, T.D. 6882, 4/11/66, T.D. 9276, 7/24/2006.

§ 31.3402(g)-2 Wages paid for payroll period of more than one year.

If wages are paid to an employee for a payroll period of more than one year, for the purpose of determining the amount of tax required to be deducted and withheld in respect of such wages—

(a) Under the percentage method, the amount of the tax shall be determined as if such payroll period constituted an annual payroll period, and

(b) Under the wage bracket method, the amount of the tax shall be determined as if such payroll period constituted a miscellaneous payroll period of 365 days.

T.D. 6259, 10/25/57.

§ 31.3402(g)-3 Wages paid through an agent, fiduciary, or other person on behalf of two or more employers.

(a) If a payment of wages is made to an employee by an employer through an agent, fiduciary, or other person who also has the control, receipt, custody, or disposal of, or pays the wages payable by another employer to such employee, the amount of the tax required to be withheld on each wage payment made through such agent, fiduciary, or person shall, whether the wages are paid separately on behalf of each employer or paid in a lump sum on behalf of all such employers, be determined upon the aggregate amount of such wage payment or payments in the same manner as if such aggregate amount had been paid by one employer. Hence, under either the percentage method or the wage bracket method the tax shall be determined upon the aggregate amount of the wage payment.

(b) In any such case, each employer shall be liable for the return and payment of a pro rata portion of the tax so determined, such portion to be determined in the ratio which the amount contributed by the particular employer bears to the aggregate of such wages.

(c) For example, three companies maintain a central management agency which carries on the administrative work of the several companies. The central agency organization consists of a staff of clerks, bookkeepers, stenographers, etc., who are the common employees of the three companies. The expenses of the central agency, including wages paid to the foregoing employees, are borne by the several companies in certain agreed proportions. Company X pays 45 percent, Company Y pays 35 percent and Company Z pays 20 percent of such expenses. The amount of the tax required to be withheld on the wages paid to persons employed in the central agency should be determined in accordance with the provisions of this section. In such event, Company X is liable as an employer for the return and payment of 45 percent of the tax required to be withheld, Company Y is liable for the return and payment of 35 percent of the tax and Company Z is liable for the return and payment of 20 percent of the tax. (See § 31.3504-1, relating to acts to be performed by agents.)

T.D. 6259, 10/25/57.

§ 31.3402(h)(1)-1 Withholding on basis of average wages.

(a) In general. An employer may determine the amount of tax to be deducted and withheld upon a payment of wages to an employee on the basis of the employee's average estimated wages, with necessary adjustments, for any quarter. This paragraph applies only where the method desired to be used includes wages other than tips (whether or not tips are also included).

(b) Withholding on the basis of average estimated tips. *(1) In general.* Subject to certain limitations and conditions, an employer may, at his discretion, withhold the tax under section 3402 in respect of tips reported by an employee to the employer on an estimated basis. An employer who elects to make withholding of the tax on an estimated basis shall:

(i) In respect of each employee, make an estimate of the amount of tips that will be reported, pursuant to section 6053, by the employee to the employer in a calendar quarter.

(ii) Determine the amount which must be deducted and withheld upon each payment of wages (exclusive of tips) which are under the control of the employer to be made during the quarter by the employer to the employee. The total amount which must be deducted and withheld shall be determined by assuming that the estimated tips for the quarter represent the amount of wages to be paid to the employee in the form of tips in the quarter and that such tips will be ratably (in terms of pay periods) paid during the quarter.

(iii) Deduct and withhold from any payment of wages (exclusive of tips) which are under the control of the employer, or from funds referred to in section 3402(k) (see §§ 31.3402(k) and 31.3402(k)-1), such amount as may be necessary to adjust the amount of tax withheld on the estimated basis to conform to the amount required to be withheld in respect of tips reported by the employee to the employer during the calendar quarter in written statements furnished to the employer pursuant to section 6053(a). If an adjustment is required, the additional tax required to be withheld may be deducted upon any payment of wages (exclusive of tips) which are under the control of the employer during the quarter and within the first 30 days following the quarter or from funds turned over by the employee to the employer for such purpose within such period. For provisions relating to the repayment to an employee, or other disposition, of amounts deducted from an employee's remuneration in excess of the correct amount of tax, see § 31.6413(a)-1.

(2) Estimating tips employee will report. (i) Initial estimate. The initial estimate of the amount of tips that will be reported by a particular employee in a calendar quarter shall be made on the basis of the facts and circumstances surrounding the employment of that employee. However, if a number of employees are employed under substantially the same circumstances and working conditions, the initial estimate established for one such employee may be used as the initial estimate for other employees in that group.

(ii) Adjusting estimate. If the quarterly estimate of tips in respect of a particular employee continues to differ substantially from the amount of tips reported by the employee and there are no unusual factors involved (for example, an extended absence from work due to illness) the employer shall make an appropriate adjustment of his estimate of the amount of tips that will be reported by the employee.

(iii) Reasonableness of estimate. The employer must be prepared, upon request of the district director, to disclose the factors upon which he relied in making the estimate, and his reasons for believing that the estimate is reasonable.

T.D. 6259, 10/25/57, amend T.D. 7001, 1/17/69, T.D. 7053, 7/20/70.

§ 31.3402(h)(2)-1 Withholding on basis of annualized wages.

An employer may determine the amount of tax to be deducted and withheld upon a payment of wages to an employee by taking the following steps:

Step 1. Multiply the amount of the employee's wages for the payroll period by the number of such periods in the calendar year.

Step 2. Determine the amount of tax which would be required to be deducted and withheld upon the amount determined in Step 1 if that amount constituted the actual wages for the calendar year and the payroll period of the employee were an annual payroll period.

Step 3. Divide the amount of tax determined in Step 2 by the number of periods by which the employee's wages were multiplied in Step 1.

Example. On July 1, 1970, A, a single person who is on a weekly payroll period and claims one exemption, receives wages of $100 from X Co., his employer. X Co. multiplies the weekly wage of $100 by 52 weeks to determine an annual wage of $5,200. It then subtracts $650 for A's withholding exemption and arrives at a balance of $4,550. The applicable table in section 3402(a) for annual payroll periods indicates that the amount of tax to be withheld thereon is $376 plus $314.50 (17 percent of excess over $2,700), or a total of $690.50. The annual tax of $690.50, when divided by 52 to arrive at the portion thereof attributable to the weekly payroll period, equals $13.28. X Co. may, if it chooses, withhold $13.28 rather than the amount specified in section 3402(a) or (c) for a weekly payroll period.

T.D. 7053, 7/20/70.

§ 31.3402(h)(3)-1 Withholding on basis of cumulative wages.

(a) In general. In the case of an employee who has in effect a request that the amount of tax to be withheld from his wages be computed on the basis of his cumulative wages, and whose wages since the beginning of the current calendar year have been paid with respect to the same category of payroll period (e.g., weekly or semimonthly), the employer may determine the amount of tax to be deducted and withheld upon a payment of wages made to the employee after December 31, 1969, by taking the following steps:

Step 1. Add the amount of the wages to be paid the employee for the payroll period to the total amount of wages paid by the employer to the employee during the calendar year.

Step 2. Divide the aggregate amount of wages computed in Step 1 by the number of payroll periods to which that amount relates.

Step 3. Compute the total amount of tax that would have been required to be deducted and withheld under section 3402(a) if the average amount of wages (as computed in Step 2) had been paid to the employee for the number of payroll periods to which the aggregate amount of wages (computed in Step 1) relates.

Step 4. Determine the excess, if any, of the amount of tax computed in Step 3 over the total amount of tax already deducted and withheld by the employer from wages paid to the employee during the calendar year.

Example. On July 1, 1970, Y Co. employs B, a single person claiming one exemption. Y Co. pays B the following amounts of wages on the basis of a biweekly payroll period on the following pay days:

July 20	$1,000
August 3	300
August 17	300
August 31	300
September 14	300
September 28	300

On October 5, B requests that Y Co. withhold on the basis of his cumulative wages with respect to his wages to be paid on October 12 and thereafter. Y Co. adds the $300 in wages to be paid to B on October 12 to the payments of wages already made to B during the calendar year, and determines that the aggregate amount of wages is $2,800. The average amount of wages for the 7 biweekly payroll periods is $400. The total amount of tax required to be deducted and withheld for payments of $400 for each of 7 biweekly payroll periods is $485.87 under section 3402(a). Since the total amount of tax which has been deducted and withheld by Y Co. through September 28 is $484.86, Y Co. may, if it chooses, deduct and withhold $1.01 (the amount by which $485.87 exceeds the total amount already withheld by Y Co.) from the payment of wages to B on October 12 rather than the amount specified in section 3402(a) or (c).

(b) Employee's request and revocation of request. An employee's request that his employer withhold on the basis of his cumulative wages and a notice of revocation of such request shall be in writing and in such form as the employer may prescribe. An employee's request furnished to his employer pursuant to this section shall be effective, and may be acted upon by his employer, after the furnishing of such request and before a revocation thereof is effective. A revocation of such request may be made at any time by the employee furnishing his employer with a notice of revocation. The employer may give immediate effect to a revocation, but, in any event, a revocation shall be effective with respect to payments of wages made on or after the first "status determination date" (see section 3402(f)(3)(B)) which occurs at least 30 days after the date on which such notice is furnished.

(c) Requests due to increases or decreases in allowances. An employee may request pursuant to this section that his employer withhold on the basis of the employee's cumulative wages when the employee is entitled to claim an increased or decreased number of withholding allowances under § 31.3402(m)-1 during the estimation year (as defined in § 31.3402(m)-1(c)(1)).

T.D. 7053, 7/20/70, amend T.D. 7915, 9/26/83.

§ 31.3402(h)(4)-1 Other methods.

(a) Maximum permissible deviations. An employer may use any other method of withholding under which the employer will deduct and withhold upon wages paid to an employee after December 31, 1969, for a payroll period substantially the same amount as would be required to be deducted and withheld by applying section 3402(a) with respect to the payroll period. For purposes of section 3402(h)(4) and this section, an amount is substantially the same as the amount required to be deducted and withheld under section 3402(a) if its deviation from the latter amount is not greater than the maximum permissible deviation prescribed in this paragraph. The maximum permissible deviation under this paragraph is determined by annualizing wages as provided in Step 1 of § 31.3402(h)(2)-1 and applying the following table to the amount of tax required to be deducted and withheld under section 3402(a) with respect to such annualized wages, as determined under Step 2 of § 31.3402(h)(2)-1:

If the tax required to be withheld under the annual percentage rate schedule is—	The maximum permissible annual deviation is—
$10 to $100	$10, plus 10 percent of excess over $10
$100 to $1,000	$19, plus 3 percent of excess over $100
$1,000 or over	$46, plus 1 percent of excess over $1,000

In any case, an amount which is less than $10 more or less per year than the amount required to be deducted and withheld under section 3402(a) is substantially the same as the latter amount. If any method produces results which are not greater than the prescribed maximum deviations only with respect to some of his employees, the employer may use such method only with respect to such employees. An employer should thoroughly test any method which he contemplates using to ascertain whether it meets the tolerances prescribed by this paragraph. An employer may not use any method, one of the principal purposes of which is to consistently produce amounts to be deducted and withheld which are less (though substantially the same) than the amount required to be deducted and withheld by applying section 3402(a).

(b) Combined FICA and income tax withholding. In addition to the methods authorized by paragraph (a) of this section, an employer may determine the amount of tax to be deducted and withheld under section 3402 upon a payment of wages to an employee by using tables prescribed in the Commissioner which combine the amounts of tax to be deducted under sections 3102 and 3402. Such tables shall provide for the deduction of the sum of such amounts, computed on the basis of the midpoints of the wage brackets in the tables prescribed under section 3402(c). The portion of such sum which is to be treated as the tax deducted and withheld under section 3402 shall be the amount obtained by subtracting from such sum the amount of tax required to be deducted by section 3102. Such tables may be used only with respect to payments which are wages under both sections 3121(a) and 3401(a).

(c) Part-year employment method of withholding. *(1) In general.* In addition to the methods authorized by other paragraphs of this section, in the case of part-year employment (as defined in subparagraph (4) of this paragraph) of an employee who determines his liability for tax under subtitle A of the Code on a calendar-year basis and who has in effect a request that the amount of tax to be withheld from his wages be computed according to the part-year employment method described in this paragraph, the employer may determine the amount of tax to be deducted and withheld upon a payment of wages made to the employee on or after January 5, 1973, by taking the following steps:

Step 1. Add the amount of wages to be paid to the employee for the current payroll period to the total amount of wages paid by the employer to the employee for all preceding payroll periods included in the current term of continuous employment (as defined in subparagraph (3) of this paragraph) of the employee by the employer;

Step 2. Divide the aggregate amount of wages computed in Step 1 by the total of the number of payroll periods to which that amount relates plus the equivalent number of payroll periods (as defined in subparagraph (2) of this paragraph) in the employee's term of continuous unemployment immediately preceding the current term of continuous employment, such term of continuous unemployment to be exclusive of any days prior to the beginning of the current calendar year;

Step 3. Determine the total amount of tax that would have been required to be deducted and withheld under section 3402 if the average amount of wages (as computed in Step 2) had been paid to the employee for the number of payroll periods determined in Step 2 (including the equivalent number of payroll periods); and

Step 4. Determine the excess, if any, of the amount of tax computed in Step 3 over the total amount of tax already deducted and withheld by the employer from wages paid to the employee for all payroll periods during the current term of continuous employment.

The use of the method described in this paragraph does not preclude the employee from claiming additional withholding allowances pursuant to section 3402(m) or the standard deduction allowance pursuant to section 3402(f)(1)(G).

(2) Equivalent number of payroll periods. For purposes of this paragraph, the equivalent number of payroll periods shall be determined by dividing the number of calendar days contained in the current payroll period into the number of calendar days between the later of (i) the day certified by the employee as his last day of employment prior to his current term of continuous employment during the calendar year in which such term commenced, or (ii) the last day of the calendar year immediately preceding the current calendar year, and the first day of the current term of continuous employment. For purposes of the preceding sentence, the term "calendar days" includes holidays, Saturdays, and Sundays. In determining the equivalent number of payroll periods, any fraction obtained in the division described in the first sentence of this subparagraph shall be disregarded. An employee paid for a miscellaneous payroll period shall be considered to have a daily payroll period for purposes of this subparagraph. In a case in which an employee is paid for a daily or miscellaneous payroll period and the employer elects under Circular E to compute the tax to be withheld as if the aggregate of the wages paid to the employee during the calendar week were paid for a weekly period, the employer shall determine the equivalent number of payroll periods for purposes of the computation of the tax to be withheld for the calendar week on the basis of a weekly payroll period (notwithstanding the fact that a determination of the equivalent number of payroll periods for purposes of the computation of the tax to be withheld upon wages paid for daily or miscellaneous payroll periods within such calendar week has been made on the basis of a daily or miscellaneous payroll period).

(3) Term of continuous employment. For purposes of this paragraph, a term of employment is continuous if it is either a single term of employment or two or more consecutive terms of employment with the same employer. A term of continuous employment begins on the first day on which any services are performed by the employee for the employer for which compensation is paid or payable. Such term ends on the earlier of (i) the last day during the current term of continuous employment on which any services are performed by the employee for the employer, or (ii) if the employee performs no services for the employer for a period of more than 30 calendar days, the last day preceding such period on which any services are performed by the employee for the employer. For example, a professional athlete who signs a contract on December 31, 1973, to perform services from July 1 through December 31 for the calendar years 1974, 1975, and 1976 has a new term of employment beginning each July 1 and accordingly may qualify for use of the part-year withholding method in each of such years. Likewise, a term of continuous employment is not broken by a temporary layoff of no more than 30 days. On the other hand, when an employment relationship is actually terminated the term of continuous employment is ended even though a new employment relationship is established with the same employer within 30 days. A "term of continuous employment" includes all days on which an employee performs any services for an employer and includes days on which services are not performed because of illness or vacation, or because such days are holidays or are regular days off (such as Saturdays and Sundays, or days off in lieu of Saturdays and Sundays), or other days for which the employee is not scheduled to work. For example, an employee who is employed 2 days a week for the same employer from March 1 through December 31 has a term of continuous employment of 306 days.

(4) Part-year employment. For purposes of this paragraph, "part-year employment" means one or more terms of continuous employment with all employers which term or terms will not aggregate more than 245 days within a calendar year. For example, A graduates from college in May and was not employed from January through May. A accepts a permanent position with X Co., beginning June 1. Since the total duration of A's term of continuous employment will, during the current calendar year, not exceed 245 days it does qualify as part-year employment for purposes of this section.

If, however, A had also worked for Y Co. from December 15 of the previous year through February 5 of the current calendar year, the total duration of A's terms of continuous employment will, during the current calendar year, exceed 245 days (36 days (January 1 through February 5) plus 214 days (June 1 through December 31) equals 250 days). This year's employment does not therefore qualify as part-year employment for purposes of this section.

(5) Employee's request. (i) An employee's request that his employer withhold according to the part-year employment method shall be in writing and in such form as the employer may prescribe. Such request shall be made under the penalties of perjury and shall contain the following information—

(a) The last day of employment (if any) by any employer prior to the current term of continuous employment during the calendar year in which such term commenced.

(b) A statement that the employee reasonably anticipates that he will be employed for an aggregate of no more than 245 days in all terms of continuous employment during the current calendar year, and

(c) The employee uses a calendar-year accounting period.

An employee's request furnished to his employer pursuant to this section shall be effective, and may be acted upon by his employer, with respect to wages paid after the furnishing of such request, and shall cease to be effective with respect to any wages paid on or after the beginning of the payroll period during which the current calendar year will end.

(ii) If, on any day during the calendar year, any of the anticipations stated by the employee in his statement provided pursuant to subdivision (i)(b) of this subparagraph becomes unreasonable, the employee shall revoke the request described in this subparagraph before the end of the payroll period during which it becomes unreasonable. The revocation shall be effective as of the beginning of the payroll period during which it is made.

(6) Examples. The application of this paragraph may be illustrated by the following examples:

Example (1). A, a calendar-year taxpayer, being unemployed for the period beginning on May 25, 1973, and ending on October 28, 1973, a period of 157 calendar days, is employed by X Co. X Co. anticipates that A's employment will last 8 calendar weeks, from October 29 to December 23, and A's wages therefor will not exceed $30,000. In the Form W-4 which A furnishes X Co. A claims four exemptions and married status. A makes a written request, incorporating the statements required under subparagraph (5)(i)(b), that X Co. withhold on the basis of the part-year employment method. A works for the period beginning October 29, 1973, and ending on November 11, 1973, and earns $1,800 in wages. Wages are paid on a biweekly basis. Using the part-year employment method, X Co. determines that $22.80 is required to be deducted and withheld from A's wages to be paid for his services from October 29 to November 11, 1973. The determination is made as follows:

Amount of wages to be paid for the payroll period (biweekly)		$1,800.00
Number of payroll periods:		
Payroll period—October 29 to November 11	1	
The equivalent number of payroll periods for the period of unemployment, disregarding the fractional payroll period	11	12
Average amount of wages per payroll period including equivalent number of payroll periods ($1,800 ÷ 12)		$ 150.00
Amount required to be withheld from a payment of $150.00 for a biweekly payroll period to a married person with 4 exemptions according to the wage bracket tables		$ 1.90
Total amount required to be withheld under the wage bracket method with respect to all payroll periods (including equivalent number of payroll periods) ($1.90 × 12)		$ 22.80
Amount already withheld by employer		0
Amount to be withheld under part-year employment method ($22.80 − 0 (the amount previously withheld))		$ 22.80

Example (2). A works for X for another 2-week period beginning on November 12, 1973, and ending on November 25, 1973, for which he earns $2,100. X Co., using the part-year employment method, determines that $323 is required to be deducted and withheld with respect to the wages for the current payroll period, as follows:

Amount of wages to be paid for the payroll period (biweekly)		$2,100.00
Amount of wages previously paid by the employer		$1,800.00
Sum of amount of wages to be paid with respect to current payroll period and amount of wages already paid		$3,900.00
Number of payroll periods:		
Payroll periods—October 29 to November 11 and November 12 to November 25	2	
The equivalent number of payroll periods for the period of unemployment	11	13
Average amount of wages per payroll period ($3,900 ÷ 13)		$ 300.00
Amount required to be withheld according to wage bracket tables from a payment of $300 for a biweekly payroll period to a married person with 4 exemptions		$ 26.60
Total amount required to be withheld under the wage bracket method with respect to all payroll periods (including equivalent number of payroll periods) ($26.60 × 13)		$ 345.80
Amount already withheld by employer		$ 22.80
Amount required to be withheld under the part-year employment method ($345.80 − $22.80)		$ 323.00

T.D. 7053, 7/20/70, amend T.D. 7251, 12/29/72, T.D. 7915, 9/26/83.

§ 31.3402(i)-1 Additional withholding.

(a) In addition to the tax required to be deducted and withheld in accordance with the provisions of section 3402, the employer and employee may agree that an additional amount shall be withheld from the employee's wages. The agreement shall be in writing and shall be in such form as the employer may prescribe. The agreement shall be effective for such period as the employer and employee mutually agree upon. However, unless the agreement provides for an earlier termination, either the employer or the employee, by furnishing a written notice to the other, may terminate the agreement effective with respect to the first payment of wages made on or after the first "status determination date" (see paragraph (d) of § 31.3402(f)(3)-1) which occurs at least 30 days after the date on which such notice is furnished.

(b) The amount deducted and withheld pursuant to an agreement between the employer and employee shall be considered as tax required to be deducted and withheld under section 3402. All provisions of law and regulations applicable with respect to the tax required to be deducted and withheld under section 3402 shall be applicable with respect to any amount deducted and withheld pursuant to the agreement.

(c) This section is applicable only to agreements made before October 1, 1981. Any such agreement shall remain in effect in accordance with paragraph (a). See § 31.3402(i)-2 for rules relating to increases in withholding after September 30, 1981.

T.D. 6259, 10/25/57, amend T.D. 7065, 10/22/70, T.D. 7915, 9/26/83.

§ 31.3402(i)-2 Increases or decreases in withholding.

Caution: The Treasury has not yet amended Reg § 31.3402(i)-2 to reflect changes made by P.L. 99-514.

(a) Increases in withholding. *(1) In general.* In addition to the tax required to be deducted and withheld in accordance with the provisions of section 3402, the employee may request, after September 30, 1981, that the employer deduct and withhold an additional amount from the employee's wages. The employer must comply with the employee's request, except that the employer shall comply with the employee's request only to the extent that the amount that the employee requests to be deducted and withheld under this section does not exceed the amount that remains after the employer has deducted and withheld all amounts otherwise required to be deducted and withheld by Federal law (other than by section 3402(i) and this section), State law, and local law (other than by State or local law that provides for voluntary withholding). The employer must comply with the employee's request in accordance with the time limitations of § 31.3402(f)(3)-1 (relating to when withholding exemption certificate takes effect). The employee must make his request on Form W-4 as provided in § 31.3402(f)(5)-1 (relating to form and contents of withholding exemption certificates), and this Form W-4 shall take effect and remain effective in accordance with section 3402(f) and the regulations thereunder.

(2) Amount deducted considered to be tax. The amount deducted and withheld pursuant to paragraph (a)(1) of this section shall be considered to be tax required to be deducted and withheld under section 3402. All provisions of law and regulations applicable with respect to the tax required to be deducted and withheld under section 3402 shall be applicable with respect to any amount deducted and withheld under paragraph (a)(1) of this section.

(b) Decreases in withholding. [Reserved].

T.D. 7915, 9/26/83.

§ 31.3402(j)-1 Remuneration other than in cash for service performed by retail commission salesman.

(a) In general. *(1)* An employer, in computing the amount to be deducted and withheld as tax in accordance with section 3402, may, at his election, disregard any wages paid, after August 9, 1955, in a medium other than cash for services performed for him by an employee if (i) the noncash remuneration is paid for services performed by the employee as a retail commission salesman and (ii) the employer ordinarily pays the employee remuneration solely by way of cash commissions for services performed by him as a retail commission salesman.

(2) Section 3402(j) and this section are not applicable with respect to wages paid to the employee that are subject to withholding under § 31.3402(g)-1(a)(2). Section 3402(j) and this section are not applicable with respect to noncash wages paid to a retail commission salesman for services performed by him in a capacity other than as such a salesman. Such sections are not applicable with respect to noncash wages paid by an employer to an employee for services performed as a retail commission salesman if the employer ordinarily pays the employee remuneration other than by way of cash commissions for such services. Thus, noncash remuneration may not be disregarded in computing the amount to be deducted and withheld in a case where the employee, for services performed as a retail commission salesman, is paid both a salary and cash commissions on sales, or is ordinarily paid in something other than cash (stocks, bonds, or other forms of property) notwithstanding that the amount of remuneration paid to the employee is measured by sales.

(b) Retail commission salesman. For purposes of section 3402(j) and this section, the term "retail commission salesman" includes an employee who is engaged in the solicitation of orders at retail, that is, from the ultimate consumer, for merchandise or other products offered for sale by his employer. The term does not include an employee salesman engaged in the solicitation on behalf of his employer of orders from wholesalers, retailers, or others, for merchandise for resale. However, if the salesman solicits orders for more than one principal, he is not excluded from the term solely because he solicits orders from wholesalers or retailers on behalf of one or more principals. In such case the salesman may be a retail commission salesman with respect to services performed for one or more principals and not with respect to services performed for his other principals.

(c) Noncash remuneration. The term "noncash remuneration" includes remuneration paid in any medium other than cash, such as goods or commodities, stocks, bonds, or other forms of property. The term does not include checks or other monetary media of exchange.

(d) Cross reference. For provisions relating to records required to be kept and statements which must be furnished an employee with respect to wage payments, see sections 6001 and 6051 and the regulations thereunder in Subpart G of this part.

T.D. 6259, 10/25/57, amend T.D. 9276, 7/24/2006.

§ 31.3402(k)-1 Special rule for tips.

(a) Withholding of income tax in respect of tips. *(1) In general.* Subject to the limitations set forth in subparagraph (2) of this paragraph, an employer is required to deduct and withhold from each of his employees tax in respect of those tips received by the employee which constitute wages. (For provisions relating to the treatment of tips as wages, see §§ 31.3401(a)(16) and 31.3401(f).) The employer shall make the withholding by deducting or causing to be deducted the amount of the tax from wages (exclusive of tips) which are under the control of the employer or other funds turned over by the employee to the employer (see subparagraph (3) of this paragraph). For purposes of this section the terms "wages (exclusive of tips) which are under the control of the employer" means, with respect to a payment of wages, an amount equal to wages as defined in section 3401(a) except that tips and noncash remuneration which are wages are not included, less the sum of—

(i) The tax under section 3101 required to be collected by the employer in respect of wages as defined in section 3121(a) (exclusive of tips);

(ii) The tax under section 3402 required to be collected by the employer in respect of wages as defined in section 3401(a) (exclusive of tips); and

(iii) The amount of taxes imposed on the remuneration of an employee withheld by the employer pursuant to State and local law (including amounts withheld under an agreement between the employer and the employee pursuant to such law) except that the amount of taxes taken into account in his subdivision shall not include any amount attributable to tips.

(2) Limitations. An employer is required to deduct and withhold the tax on tips which constitute wages only in respect of those tips which are reported by the employee to the

employer in a written statement furnished to the employer pursuant to section 6053(a). The employer is responsible for the collection of the tax on tips reported to him only to the extent that the employer can, during the period beginning at the time the written statement is submitted to him and ending at the close of the calendar year in which the statement was submitted, collect the tax by deducting it or causing it to be deducted as provided in subparagraph (1) of this paragraph.

(3) Furnishing of funds to employer. If the amount of the tax in respect of tips reported by the employee to the employer in a written statement furnished pursuant to section 6053(a) exceeds the wages (exclusive of tips) which are under the control of the employer from which the employer is required to withhold the tax in respect of such tips, the employee may furnish to the employer, within the period specified in subparagraph (2) of this paragraph, an amount of money equal to the amount of such excess.

(b) Less than $20 of tips. Notwithstanding the provisions of paragraph (a) of this section, if an employee furnishes to his employer a written statement—

(1) Covering a period of less than 1 month, and

(2) The statement is furnished to the employer prior to the close of the 10th day of the month following the month in which the tips were actually received by the employee, and

(3) The aggregate amount of tips reported in the statement and in all other statements previously furnished by the employee covering periods within the same month is less than $20, and such statements, collectively, do not cover the entire month, the employer may deduct amounts equivalent to the tax on such tips from wages (exclusive of tips) which are under the control of the employer or other funds turned over by the employee to the employer. For provisions relating to the repayment to an employee, or other disposition, of amounts deducted from an employee's remuneration in excess of the correct amount of tax, see § 31.6413(a)-1. (As to the exclusion from wages of tips of less than $20, see § 31.3401(a)(16)-1.)

(c) Priority of tax collection. *(1) In general.* In the case of a payment of wages (exclusive of tips), the employer shall deduct or cause to be deducted in the following order:

(i) The tax under section 3101 and the tax under section 3402 with respect to such payment of wages.

(ii) Any tax under section 3101 which, at the time of the payment of the wages, the employer is required to collect—

(a) In respect of tips reported by the employee to the employer in a written statement furnished to the employer pursuant to section 6053(a), or

(b) By reason of the employer's election to make collection of the tax under section 3101 in respect of tips on an estimated basis,

but which has not been collected by the employer and which cannot be deducted from funds turned over by the employee to the employer for such purpose. (See § 31.3102-3, relating to collection of, and liability for, employee tax on tips).

(iii) Any tax under section 3402 which, at the time of the payment of the wages, the employer is required to collect—

(a) In respect of tips reported by the employee to the employer in a written statement furnished to the employer pursuant to section 6053(a), or

(b) By reason of the employer's election to make collection of the tax under section 3402 in respect of tips on an estimated basis,

but which has not been collected by the employer and which cannot be deducted from funds turned over by the employee to the employer for such purpose. For provisions relating to the withholding of tax on the basis of average estimated tips, see paragraph (b) of § 31.3402(h)(1)-1.

(2) Examples. The application of subparagraph (1) of this paragraph may be illustrated by the following examples (The amounts used in the following examples are intended for illustrative purposes and do not necessarily reflect currently effective rates or amounts.):

Example (1). W is a waiter by R restaurant. W's principal remunerations for his services is in the form of tips received from patrons of R; however, he also receives a salary from R of $40 per week, which is paid to him every Friday. W is a member of a labor union which has a contract with R pursuant to which R is to collect dues for the union by withholding from the wages of its employees at the rate of $1 per week. In addition to the taxes required to be withheld under the Internal Revenue Code, W's wages are subject to withholding of a state income tax imposed upon both his regular wage and his tips received and reported to R.

On Monday of a given week W furnishes a written statement to R pursuant to section 6053(a) in which he reports the receipt of $160 in tips. The $40 wage to be paid to W on Friday of the same week is subject to the following items of withholding:

	Taxes with respect to regular wage	Taxes with respect to tips	Total
Section 3101 (F.I.C.A.)	$1.76	$ 7.04	$ 8.80
Section 3402 (income tax at source)	5.65	28.30	33.95
State income tax	1.20	4.80	6.00
Union dues			1.00
Total			49.75

W does not turn over any funds to R. R should satisfy the taxes imposed by sections 3101 and 3402 out of W's $40 wage as follows: The taxes imposed with respect to the regular wage (a total of $7.41) should be satisfied first. The taxes imposed with respect to tips are to be withheld only out of "wages (exclusive of tips) which are under the control of the employer" as that phrase is defined in §§ 31.3102-3(a)(1) and 31.3402(k)-1(a)(1). The amount of such wages under the control of employer in this example is $31.39, or $40, less the amounts applied in satisfaction of the Federal and State withholding taxes imposed with respect to the regular $40 wage ($8.61). This $31.39 is applied first in satisfaction of the tax under section 3101 with respect to tips ($7.04) in the balance of $24.35 is applied in partial satisfaction of the withholding of income tax at source under section 3402 with respect to tips. The amount of the tax with respect to tips under section 3402 which remains unsatisfied ($3.95) should be withheld from wages under the control of the employer the following week.

Example (2). During the week following the week dealt with in example (1), W furnishes a written statement to R pursuant to section 6053(a) in which he reports the receipt of $130 in tips. In addition, R receives a notice of garnishment of W's wages issued by the State court, pursuant to which R is required to withhold $10 per week from W's wages for a period of 10 weeks. The $40 wage to be paid to W at the end of the week is subject to the following items of withholding:

	Taxes with respect to regular wage	Taxes with respect to tips	Total
Section 3101 (F.I.C.A.)	$1.76	$ 5.72	$ 7.48
Section 3402 (Income tax at source):			
Current week	5.65	22.30	27.95
Carryover from prior week		3.95	3.95
State income tax	1.20	3.90	5.10
Union dues			1.00
Garnishment			10.00
Total			55.48

As in example (1), the amount of "wages (exclusive of tips) which are under the control of the employer" is $31.39. This amount is applied first in satisfaction of the tax under section 3101 with respect to tips ($5.72) and the balance is applied in partial satisfaction of the withholding of income tax at source under section 3402 with respect to tips (a total of $26.25), including that portion of the amount required to be withheld from the prior week's wages which remained unsatisfied. The amount of the tax with respect to tips under section 3402 which remains unsatisfied ($0.58) should be withheld from wages under the control of the employer the following week.

T.D. 7001, 1/17/69, amend T.D. 7053, 7/20/70.

§ 31.3402(l)-1 Determination and disclosure of marital status.

(a) Determination of status by employer. An employer in computing the tax to be deducted and withheld from an employee's wages paid after April 30, 1966, shall apply the applicable percentage method or wage bracket method withholding table (see section 3402(a), (b), and (c) and the regulations thereunder) for the pertinent payroll period which relates to employees who are single persons, unless there is in effect with respect to such payment of wages a withholding exemption certificate furnished to the employer by the employee after March 15, 1966, indicating that the employee is married in which case the employer shall apply the applicable table relating to employees who are married persons.

(b) Disclosure of status by employee. *(1)* An employee shall be entitled to furnish the employer with a withholding exemption certificate indicating he is married only if, on the day of such furnishing, he is married (determined by application of the rules in paragraph (c) of this section). Thus, an employee who is contemplating marriage may not, prior to the actual marriage, furnish the employer with a withholding exemption certificate indicating that he is a married person.

(2) (i) If, on any day during the calendar year, the marital status (as determined by application of the rules in paragraph (c) of this section) of an employee who has in effect a withholding exemption certificate indicating that he is a married person, change from married to single, the employee must within 10 days after the change occurs furnish the employer with a new withholding exemption certificate indicating that the employee is a single person.

(ii) If an employee who has in effect a withholding exemption certificate indicating that he is a married person, is considered married solely because of the application of subparagraph (2)(ii) of paragraph (c) of this section, and his spouse died during the taxable year which precedes by 2 years the current taxable year, the employee must, on or before December 1 of the current taxable year, furnish the employer with a new withholding exemption certificate indicating that he is a single person. Such certificate shall not, however, become effective until the next calendar year (see paragraph (c) of § 31.3402(f)(3)-1).

(3) If, on any day during the calendar year, the marital status (as determined by application of the rules in paragraph (c) of this section) of an employee who has in effect a withholding exemption certificate indicating that he is a single person changes from single to married, the employee may furnish the employer with a new withholding exemption certificate indicating that the employee is a married person.

(c) Determination of marital status. For the purposes of section 3402(l)(2) and paragraph (b) of this section, the following rules shall be applied in determining whether an employee is a married person or a single person—

(1) An employee shall on any day be considered as a single person if—

(i) He is legally separated from his spouse under a decree of divorce or separate maintenance, or

(ii) Either he or his spouse is, or on any preceding day within the same calendar year was, a nonresident alien.

(2) An employee shall on any day be considered as a married person if—

(i) His spouse (other than a spouse referred to in subparagraph (1) of this paragraph) died within the portion of his taxable year which precedes such day, or

(ii) His spouse died during one of the two taxable years immediately preceding the current taxable year and, on the basis of facts existing at the beginning of such day, he reasonably expects, at the close of his taxable year, to be a surviving spouse as defined in section 2 and the regulations thereunder.

T.D. 7115, 5/20/71.

§ 31.3402(m)-1 Withholding allowances.

Caution: The Treasury has not yet amended Reg § 31.3402(m)-1 to reflect changes made by P.L. 100-647, P.L. 99-514.

(a) General rule. An employee may claim, with respect to wages paid after December 31, 1981, a number of withholding allowances determined in accordance with this section. In order to receive the benefit of such allowances, the employee must have in effect with his employer a withholding exemption certificate claiming such allowances.

(b) Items that may be taken into account. The following items may be taken into account in determining the number of withholding allowances an employee may claim:

(1) Estimated itemized deductions allowable under chapter 1,

(2) The estimated tax credit allowable under subpart A of part IV of subchapter A of chapter 1, except:

(i) For the credit for tax withheld on wages under section 31(a) (relating to wage withholding),

(ii) For the credit for tax withheld at source on nonresident aliens and foreign corporations and on tax-free covenant bonds under section 32,

(iii) That the employee may claim the credit for certain uses of gasoline and special fuels under section 39 only to the extent the employee has not filed for a quarterly tax refund of the credit on Form 843,

(iv) That the employee may claim the credit for earned income under section 43 only to the extent the employee has not filed for advance payments of the credit on Form W-5, and

(v) For the credit for overpayment of tax under section 45,

(3) The estimated trade and business deductions of employees described in section 62(2) and allowed by part VI of subchapter B of chapter 1,

(4) The estimated deduction for payments to pension, profit-sharing, annuity, and bond purchase plans of self-employed individuals described in section 62(7) and allowed by section 404 and section 405(c),

(5) The estimated deduction for penalties forfeited because of premature withdrawal of funds from time savings accounts or deposits described in section 62(12) and allowed by section 165,

(6) The estimated direct charitable deduction under section 170(i),

(7) The estimated deduction for net operating loss carryovers under section 172,

(8) The estimated deduction for alimony, etc., payments under section 215,

(9) The estimated deduction for moving expenses under section 217 but only to the extent that the amount of such deduction is not excluded from the definition of wages by section 3401(a)(15),

(10) The estimated deductions for certain retirement savings under section 219 but only to the extent that the amount of such deduction is not excluded from the definition of wages by section 3401(a)(12)(D),

(11) The estimated deduction for two-earner married couples under section 221,

(12) The estimated net losses from schedules C (Profit or (Loss) From Business or Profession), D (Capital Gains and Losses), E (Supplemental Income Schedule), and F (Farm Income and Expenses) of Form 1040 and from the last line of Part II of Form 4797 (Supplemental Schedule of Gains and Losses),

(13) The estimated amount of decrease of tax due attributable to income averaging under sections 1301 through 1305. The employee must first use these items ((1) through (13) of this paragraph (b)) to eliminate any payment of estimated tax (as defined in section 6015(d)). Only amounts of these items remaining after the employee has done this may be taken into account in determining the number of withholding allowances the employee may claim.

(c) Definitions. *(1) Estimated.* The term "estimated" as used in this section to modify the terms "deduction", "deductions", "credits", "losses", and "amount of decrease" means with respect to an employee the aggregate dollar amount of a particular item that the employee reasonably expects will be allowable to him for the estimation year under the section of the Code specified for each item. In no event shall that amount exceed the sum of—

(i) The amount shown for that particular item on the income tax return that the employee has filed for the taxable year preceding the estimation year (or, if such return has not yet been filed, then the income tax return that the employee filed for the taxable year preceding such year), which amount the employee also reasonably expects to show on the income tax return for the estimation year, plus

(ii) The determinable additional amounts for each item for the estimation year. The determinable additional amounts are amounts that are not included in paragraph (c)(1)(i) of this section and that are demonstrably attributable to identifiable events during the estimation year or the preceding year. Amounts are demonstrably attributable to identifiable events if they relate to payments already made during the estimation year, to binding obligations to make payments (including the payment of taxes) during the year, and to other transactions or occurrences, the implementation of which has begun and is verifiable at the time the employee files a withholding exemption certificate claiming withholding allowances relating thereto. The estimation year is the taxable year including the day on which the employee files the withholding exemption certificate with his employer, except that if the employee files the withholding exemption certificate with his employer and specifies on the certificate that the certificate is not to take effect until a specified future date, the estimation year shall be the taxable year including that specified future date. It is not reasonable for an employee to include in his or her withholding computation for the estimation year any amount that is shown for a particular item on the income tax return that the employee has filed for the taxable year preceding the estimation year (or, if such return has not yet been filed, then the income tax return that the employee filed for the taxable year preceding such year) and that has been disallowed by the Service as part of a proposed adjustment described in § 601.103(b) (relating to examination and determination of tax liability) and § 601.105(b) (relating to examination of returns).

(2) Amount of decrease of tax due. The term "amount of decrease of tax due" as used in paragraph (b)(13) of this section means—

(i) The amount of tax that the taxpayer would owe on his taxable income without using Schedule G (Form 1040), minus

(ii) The amount of tax that the taxpayer would owe on his taxable income using Schedule G (Form 1040).

(3) Itemized deductions. The term "itemized deductions" as used in paragraph (b)(1) of this section has the same meaning as ascribed thereto by section 63(f) and the regulations thereunder.

(d) Computing allowances. *(1)* The employee shall compute the number of allowances he may claim for the items specified in paragraph (b) of this section in accordance with the tables and instructions on Form W-4.

(2) If the employee—

(i) Pays or accrues amounts demonstrably attributable to identifiable events (as defined in paragraph (c)(1) of this section) that are—

(A) Interest attributable to ownership of real property and deductible under section 163(a), or

(B) Taxes deductible under section 164(a)(1), or

(C) Interest or taxes deductible under section 216(a), and

(ii) Is obligated to pay or accrue such amounts for at least 2 years subsequent to the estimation year, then the employee may compute the portion of estimated itemized deductions attributable to such amounts for purposes of paragraph (b)(1) of this section by multiplying the total of such amounts to be paid or accrued in the estimation year by 12 and by then dividing that result by the number of months from the 1st month in the estimation year in which the employee pays or accrues such amounts through the last month of the estimation year. If such amounts decrease during the term of the obligation, the employee must, at the beginning of each subsequent calendar year, recompute the number of allowances being claimed as required by paragraph (c)(1) of this section. If the employee uses the computation described in this subparagraph (2), the employee may not request that his employer withhold on the basis of the employee's cumulative wages as provided in § 31.3402(h)(3)-1.

(e) Examples. The application of this section may be illustrated by the following examples:

Example (1). Employee A has an estimated net loss from a partnership of $2,000 which would be reported on Schedule E. Employee A is not required to make any payments of estimated tax. Employee A may take her $2,000 partnership loss into consideration in determining the number of withholding allowances to which she is entitled in accordance with the tables and instructions on Form W-4.

Example (2). Employee B has an estimated net loss from a business of $3,000 which would be reported on Schedule C. Employee B would also otherwise be required to make payments of estimated tax on income of $3,000. Employee B may not take his business loss into consideration in determining the number of withholding allowances to which he is entitled in accordance with the tables and instructions on Form W-4.

Example (3). Employee C has an estimated net loss from a farm of $5,000 which would be reported on Schedule F. Employee C would also otherwise be required to make payments of estimated tax on income of $4,000. Employee C may only take her farm loss into consideration to the extent of $1,000 ($5,000 − 4,000) in determining the number of withholding allowances to which she is entitled in accordance with the tables and instructions on Form W-4.

(f) Special rules. *(1) Married individuals.* (i) Except as provided in subdivision (ii) of this subparagraph, a husband and wife shall determine the number of withholding allowances to which they are entitled under section 3402(m) on the basis of their combined wages and allowable items. The withholding allowances to which a husband and wife are entitled may be claimed by the husband, by the wife, or they may be allocated between them. However, they may not both have withholding exemption certificates in effect claiming the same withholding allowance.

(ii) If a husband and wife filed separate income tax returns for the taxable year preceding the estimation year and reasonably expect to file separate returns for the estimation year, the husband and wife shall determine the number of withholding exemptions to which they are entitled under section 3402(m) on the basis of their individual wages and allowable items, and they shall be considered to be single for purposes of the tables on Form W-4.

(2) Only one certificate to be in effect. An employee who is entitled to one or more withholding allowances under section 3402(m) and who has, at the same time, two or more employers, may claim such withholding allowance or allowances with only one of his employers.

T.D. 7065, 10/22/70, amend T.D. 7915, 9/26/83.

§ 31.3402(n)-1 Employees incurring no income tax liability.

Caution: The Treasury has not yet amended Reg § 31.3402(n)-1 to reflect changes made by P.L. 100-203.

(a) In general. Notwithstanding any other provision of this subpart (except to the extent a payment of wages is subject to withholding under § 31.3402(g)-1(a)(2)), an employer shall not deduct and withhold any tax under chapter 24 upon a payment of wages made to an employee, if there is in effect with respect to the payment a withholding exemption certificate furnished to the employer by the employee which certifies that—

(1) The employee incurred no liability for income tax imposed under subtitle A of the Internal Revenue Code for his preceding taxable year; and

(2) The employee anticipates that he will incur no liability for income tax imposed under subtitle A for his current taxable year.

(b) Mandatory flat rate withholding. To the extent wages are subject to income tax withholding under § 31.3402(g)-1(a)(2), such wages are subject to such income tax withholding regardless of whether a withholding exemption certificate under section 3402(n) and the regulations thereunder has been furnished to the employer.

(c) Rules about withholding exemption certificates. For rules relating to invalid withholding exemption certificates, see § 31.3402(f)(2)-1(e), and for rules relating to disregarding certain withholding exemption certificates on which an employee claims a complete exemption from withholding, see § 31.3402(f)(2)-1T(g).

(d) Examples. The following examples illustrate this section:

Example (1). Employee A, an unmarried, calendar-year basis taxpayer, files his income tax return for 2005 on April 10, 2006. A has adjusted gross income of $5,000 and is not liable for any income tax. He had $180 of income tax withheld during 2005. A anticipates that his gross income for 2006 will be approximately the same amount, and that he will not incur income tax liability for that year. On April 20, 2006, A commences employment and furnishes his employer a withholding exemption certificate certifying that he incurred no liability for income tax imposed under subtitle A for 2005, and that he anticipates that he will incur no liability for income tax imposed under subtitle A for 2006. A's employer shall not deduct and withhold on payments of wages made to A on or after April 20, 2006. Under § 31.3402(f)(4)-2(c), unless A furnishes a new withholding exemption certificate certifying the statements described in paragraph (a) of this section to his employer, his employer is required to deduct and withhold upon payments of wages to A made after February 15, 2007.

Example (2). Assume the facts are the same as in Example 1 except that A had been employed by his employer prior to April 20, 2006, and had furnished his employer a withholding exemption certificate prior to furnishing the withholding exemption certificate certifying the statements described in paragraph (a) of this section on April 20, 2006. Under section 3402(f)(3)(B)(i), his employer would be required to give effect to the new withholding exemption certificate no later than the beginning of the first payroll period ending (or the first payment of wages made without regard to a payroll period) on or after May 20, 2006. However, under section 3402(f)(3)(B)(ii), his employer could, if it chose, make the new withholding exemption certificate effective with respect to any payment of wages made on or after April 20, 2006, and before the effective date mandated by section 3402(f)(3)(B)(i). Under § 31.3402(f)(4)-2(c), unless A furnishes a new withholding exemption certificate certifying the statements described in § 31.3402(n)-1(a) to his employer, his employer is required to deduct and withhold upon payments of wages to A made after February 15, 2007.

Example (3). Assume the facts are the same as in Example 1 except that for 2005 A has taxable income of $8,000, income tax liability of $839, and income tax withheld of $1,195. Although A received a refund of $356 due to income tax withholding of $1,195, he may not certify on his withholding exemption certificate that he incurred no liability for income tax imposed by subtitle A for 2005.

T.D. 7001, 1/17/69, amend T.D. 7048, 6/23/70, T.D. 7423, 6/24/76, T.D. 7577, 12/19/78, T.D. 7598, 3/12/79, T.D. 7682, 3/10/80, T.D. 7772, 3/17/81, T.D. 7803, 1/21/82, T.D. 9276, 7/24/2006.

§ 31.3402(o)-1 Extension of withholding to supplemental unemployment compensation benefits.

(a) In general. Withholding of income tax is required under section 3402(o) with respect to payments of supplemental unemployment compensation benefits made after December 31, 1970, which are treated under paragraph (b)(14) of § 31.3401(a)-1 as if they were wages.

(b) Withholding exemption certificates. For purposes of section 3402(f)(2) and (3) and the regulations thereunder (relating to withholding exemption certificates), in the case of supplemental unemployment compensation benefits an employment relationship shall be considered to commence with either the date on which such benefits begin to accrue or January 1, 1971, whichever is later, and the withholding exemption certificate furnished the employer with respect to such commencement of employment shall be considered the first certificate furnished the employer. The withholding exemption certificate furnished by the employee to his former employer (with whom his employment has been involuntarily terminated, within the meaning of paragraph (b)(14)(ii) of § 31.3401(a)-1) shall be treated as meeting the requirements of section 3402(f)(2)(A) and the regulations thereunder if such former employer furnishes such certificate to the employee's current employer, as defined in paragraph (g) of § 31.3401(d)-1, or if such former employer is the agent of such current employer with respect to the employee's withholding exemption certificate. However, the preceding sentence shall not be applicable if such employee furnishes a new withholding exemption certificate to such current employer (or his agent), provided that such withholding exemption certificate meets the requirements of section 3402(f)(2)(A) and the regulations thereunder. See the definitions of payroll period in paragraph (c) of § 31.3401(b)-1 and of employee in paragraph (g) of § 31.3401(c)-1.

T.D. 7068, 11/10/70, amend T.D. 7804, 1/21/82.

§ 31.3402(o)-2 Extension of withholding to annuity payments if requested by payee.

Caution: The Treasury has not yet amended Reg § 31.3402(o)-2 to reflect changes made by P.L. 97-248.

(a) In general. Under section 3402(o) of the Internal Revenue Code of 1954 and this section, the payee (as defined in paragraph (g)(2) of this section) of an annuity (as defined in paragraph (g)(1) of this section) may request the payer (as defined in paragraph (g)(3) of this section) of the annuity to withhold income tax with respect to payments of the annuity made after December 31, 1970. If such a request is made, the payor shall deduct and withhold as requested.

(b) Manner of making request. A payee who wishes a payer to deduct and withhold income tax from annuity payments shall file a request with the payer to deduct and withhold a specific whole dollar amount from each annuity payment. Such specific dollar amount requested shall be at least $5 per month and shall not reduce the net amount of any annuity payment received by the payee below $10. The request shall be made on Form W-4P (annuitant's withholding exemption certificate and request) in accordance with the instructions applicable thereto, and shall set forth fully and clearly the data therein called for. In lieu of Form W-4P, payers may prepare and use a form the provisions of which are identical with those of Form W-4P. For the requirements relating to Form W-4P with respect to qualified State individual income taxes, see paragraph (d)(3)(i) of § 301.6361-1 of this chapter (Regulations on Procedure and Administration).

(c) When request takes effect. Upon receipt of a request under this section the payer of the annuity with respect to which such request was made shall deduct and withhold the amount specified in such request from each annuity payment commencing with the first annuity payment made on or after the date which occurs—

(1) In a case in which no previous request is in effect, 3 calendar months after the date on which such request is furnished to such payor, and

(2) In a case in which a previous request is in effect, the first status determination date (see section 3402(f)(3)(B) and paragraph (d) of § 31.3402(f)(3)-1 of this chapter) which occurs at least 30 days after the date on which such request is so furnished.

However, the payor may, at his election, commence to deduct and withhold such specified amount with respect to an annuity payment which is made prior to the annuity payment described in the preceding sentence with respect to which the payor must commence to deduct and withhold.

(d) Duration and termination of request. A request under this section shall continue in effect until terminated. The payee may terminate the request by furnishing the payer a signed written notice of termination. Such notice of termination shall, except as hereinafter provided, take effect with respect to the first payment of an amount in respect of which the request is in effect which is made on or after the first status determination date (see section 3402(f)(3)(B) and paragraph (d) of § 31.3402(f)(3)-1 of this chapter) which occurs at least 30 days after the date on which such notice is so furnished. However, at the election of such payer, such notice may be made effective with respect to any payment of an amount in respect of which the request is in effect which is made on or after the date on which such notice is so furnished and before such status determination date.

(e) Special rules. For purposes of chapter 24 of subtitle C of the Internal Revenue Code of 1954 (relating to collection of income tax at source on wages) and of subtitle F of such Code (relating to procedure and administration), and the regulations thereunder—

(1) An amount which is requested to be withheld pursuant to this section shall be deemed a tax required to be deducted and withheld under section 3402.

(2) An amount deducted and withheld pursuant to this section shall be deemed an amount deducted and withheld under section 3402.

(3) The term "wages" includes the gross amount of an annuity payment with respect to which there is in effect a request for withholding under this section. However, references to the definition of wages in section 3401(a) which are made in section 6014 (relating to election by the taxpayer not to compute the tax on his annual return) and section 6015(a) (relating to declaration of estimated tax by individu-

als) shall not be deemed to include any portion of such an annuity payment.

(4) The term "employer" includes a payer with respect to whom a request for withholding is in effect under this section.

(5) The term "employee" includes a payee with respect to whom a request for withholding is in effect under this section.

(6) The term "payroll period" includes the period of accrual with respect to which payments of an annuity which is subject to withholding under this section are ordinarily made.

(f) Returns of income tax withheld and statements for payees. *(1)* Form W-2P is to be used in lieu of Form W-2, which is required to be furnished by an employer to an employee under § 31.6051-1 of this chapter and to the Social Security Administration under paragraph (a) of § 31.6051-2 of this chapter, with respect to an annuity subject to withholding under this section. If an amount is required to be deducted and withheld under this section from any or all of the payments made to a payee under an annuity contract during a calendar year, all payments with respect to that annuity contract are required to be reported on Form W-2P, in lieu of Form 1099, as prescribed in §§ 1.6041-1, 1.6041-2, and 1.6047-1 of this chapter; any other annuity payments made by the same payer to the same payee may, at the option of the payer, be reported on Form W-2P.

(2) Each statement on Form W-2P shall show the following:

(i) The gross amount of annuity payments made during the calendar year, whether or not income tax withholding under this section was in effect with respect to all such payments,

(ii) The total amount deducted and withheld as tax under section 3402 of this section, and

(iii) The information required to be shown by Form W-2P and the instructions applicable thereto.

For the requirements relating to Form W-2P with respect to qualified State individual income taxes, see paragraph (d)(3)(ii) of § 301.6361-1 of this chapter (Regulations on Procedure and Administration).

(3) The provisions of § 1.9101-1 of this chapter (relating to permission to submit information required by certain returns and statements on magnetic tape) shall be applicable to the information required to be furnished on Form W-2P.

(4) The provisions of § 31.6109-1 of this chapter (relating to supplying of identifying numbers) shall be applicable to Form W-2P and to any payee of an annuity to whom a statement on Form W-2P is required to be furnished.

(g) Definitions. For purposes of this section—

(1) The term "annuity" means periodic payments which are payable over a period greater than 1 year and which are treated under section 72 as amounts received as an annuity, whether or not such periodic payments are variable in amount. Also, periodic payments to an individual who is retired before the normal retirement age for reasons of disability, to which the provisions of section 105(d) apply, shall be deemed to be an annuity for purposes of this section. A lump-sum payment (including a total distribution under section 72(n)) is not an annuity.

(2) The term "payee" means an individual who is a citizen or resident of the United States and who receives an annuity payment.

(3) The term "payor" means a person making an annuity payment except that, if the person making the payment is acting solely as an agent for another person, the term "payor" shall mean such other person and not the person actually making the payment. For example, if a bank makes an annuity payment only as agent for an employees' trust, the trust shall be deemed to be the "payor." Notwithstanding the preceding two sentences, any person who, under section 3401(a)(5) or (8), would not be required to deduct and withhold the tax under section 3402 if the annuity payments were remuneration for services shall not be considered a "payor."

T.D. 7056, 8/21/70, amend T.D. 7580, 12/20/78, T.D. 7577, 12/19/78, T.D. 7804, 1/21/82.

§ 31.3402(o)-3 Extension of withholding to sick pay.

(a) In general. Under section 3402(o) of the Internal Revenue Code of 1954 and this section, the payee (as defined in paragraph (h)(2) of this section) of sick pay (as defined in paragraph (h)(1) of this section) may request the payor (as defined in paragraph (h)(3) of this section) of the sick pay to withhold income tax with respect to payments of sick pay made on or after May 1, 1981. If such a request is made, the payor must deduct and withhold as requested.

(b) Manner of making request. A payee who wishes to payor to deduct and withhold income tax from sick pay shall file a written request with the payor to deduct and withhold a specific whole dollar amount (subject to the limitations of paragraph (c) of this section) from each sick pay payment. The request shall be made on Form W-4S in accordance with the instructions applicable thereto, and shall set forth fully and clearly the data therein called for. In lieu of Form W-4S, payors may prepare and use a form the provisions of which are identical to those of Form W-4S. The payee must include his social security account number in the request.

(c) Amount requested to be withheld. The payee shall request that the payor withhold a specific whole dollar amount. The specific whole dollar amount shall be at least $20 per weekly payment of sick pay. If the payee is paid sick pay computed on a daily basis, the specific whole dollar amount shall be at least $4 per daily payment of sick pay. If the payee is paid sick pay on a biweekly basis, the specific whole dollar amount shall be at least $40 per 2 week payment of sick pay. If the payee is paid sick pay on a semimonthly basis, the specific whole dollar amount shall be at least $44 per semimonthly payment of sick pay. If the payee is paid sick pay on a monthly basis, the specific whole dollar amount shall be at least $88 per monthly payment of sick pay. If the payee is paid sick pay on a basis other than weekly, daily, biweekly, semimonthly, or monthly, the specific whole dollar amount shall be the equivalent of at least $4 per day, assuming a 5 day work week of 8 hours per day (40 hours total) in each 7 day calendar week. In the case of a payment which is greater or less than a full payment, the amount withheld is to bear the same relation to the specific whole dollar amount requested to be withheld as such payment bears to a full payment. For example, assume an individual receives sick pay of $100 per week and requests that $25 per week be withheld for taxes. After 4 full weeks of absence, the individual returns to work on a Wednesday (having been absent on sick leave Monday and Tuesday). For the week the individual returns to work, the individual would be entitled to $40 of sick pay, $10 of which would be withheld for taxes. The payor may, at his option, permit the payee to request that the payor withholds a specific percentage from each payment. The specific percentage shall be at least 10 percent. If the payor so opts, the payor must also accept requests under the whole dollar method. If the amount requested to be withheld under either the whole dollar method or the optional percentage method reduces the net amount of a sick pay payment received by the payee to below $10, no income tax shall be withheld from that payment by the payor.

(d) When request takes effect. The payor must deduct and withhold the amount specified in the request with respect to payments made more than 7 days after the date on which the request is received by the payor. At the election of the payor, the request may take effect before this deadline.

(e) Duration and termination of request. A request under this section shall continue in effect until changed or terminated. The payee may change the request by filing a new written request that meets all of the requirements of paragraphs (b) and (c) of this section. The new request shall take effect as specified in paragraph (d) of this section and the old request shall be deemed terminated when the new request takes effect. The payee may terminate the request by furnishing the payor a signed written notice of termination containing both a request to terminate withholding and all the information contained in the request to withhold. This written notice of termination shall take effect with respect to payments made more than 7 days after the date on which the notice of termination is received by the payor. At the election of the payor, the request make take effect before this deadline.

(f) Special rules. For purposes of chapter 24 on subtitle C of the Internal Revenue Code of 1954 (relating to collection of income tax at source on wages) and of subtitle F of the Code (relating to procedure and administration), and the regulations thereunder—

(1) An amount which is requested to be withheld pursuant to this section shall be deemed a tax required to be deducted and withheld under section 3402.

(2) An amount deducted and withheld pursuant to this section shall be deemed an amount deducted and withheld under section 3402.

(3) The term "wages" includes the gross amount of a sick pay payment with respect to which there is in effect a request for withholding under this section. However, references to the definition of wages in section 3401(a) which are made in section 6014 (relating to election by the taxpayer not to compute the tax on his annual return) and section 6015(a) (relating to declaration of estimated tax by individuals) shall not be deemed to include any portion of such a sick pay payment.

(4) The term "employer" includes a payor with respect to whom a request for withholding is in effect under this section.

(5) The term "employee" includes a payee with respect to whom a request for withholding is in effect under this section.

(6) The term "payroll period" includes the period of accrual with respect to which payments of sick pay which are subject to withholding under this section are ordinarily made.

(g) Statements required to be furnished to payees. See section 6051(f) and the regulations thereunder for requirements relating to statements required to be furnished to payees.

(h) Definitions. *(1)* (i) The term "sick pay" means any payment made to an individual which does not constitute wages (determined without regard to section 3402(o) and this section), which is paid to an employee pursuant to a plan to which the employer is a party, and which constitutes remuneration or a payment in lieu of remuneration for any period during which the employee is temporarily absent from work on account of personal injuries or sickness. The term "personal injuries or sickness" shall have the same meaning as ascribed thereto by section 105(a) and the regulations thereunder. The term "sick pay" does not include any amounts either excludable from gross income under section 104(a)(1), (2), (4) or (5) or section 105(b) or (c) or paid under section 3402(o)(1)(B). The term "sick pay" does not include amounts paid under a plan if all amounts paid under the plan are paid to individuals who are described in the first sentence of section 105(d)(4) (relating to the definition of permanent and total disability) and the regulations thereunder. Amounts paid under any other plan shall be deemed to be paid for a period during which the employee is temporarily absent from work. For sick pay paid in 1981 only, however, the payor may opt not to follow the rules of the two preceding sentences but to follow instead the rule that an employee is temporarily absent if his absence is not described in section 105(d)(4) (relating to the definition of permanent and total disability) and the regulations thereunder. An employer is not a party to the plan if the plan is a contract between only employees and a third party payor or the employer makes no contributions to provide sick pay benefits under the plan, even if the employer withholds amounts from the employees' salaries and pays the amounts over to the third party payor.

(ii) This subparagraph (1) may be illustrated by the following examples:

Example (1). Employee A works for P Company and Employee B works for Q Company. P Company has contracted with R Insurance Company for R to pay P's employees the equivalent of their normal wages when they are temporarily absent from work because of sickness or personal injury. Q Company has neither entered into such a contract, nor will it make such payments directly from it own funds. B consequently goes to S Insurance Company and purchases directly an insurance policy which will pay him the equivalent of his normal wages when he is unable to work because of sickness or personal injury. Both A and B are subsequently temporarily absent from work on account of sickness or personal injuries. A receives payments from R and B receives payments from S. Neither the payments made by R to A nor the payments made by S to B constitute wages (determined without regard to section 3402(o) and this section). A may request that R withhold income taxes under section 3402(o) and this section from the payments he receives because the payments are sick pay as defined in section 3402(o) and this section. B may not request that S withhold income taxes under section 3402(o) and this section from the payments he receives because the payments are not paid pursuant to a plan to which Q Company is a party and thus are not sick pay as defined in section 3402(o) and this section.

Example (2). Employees C and D both work for T Company, which has contracted with U Insurance Company for U to pay T's employees for all sickness or injury claims Employee C is sick and out from work for a month. U pays C the equivalent of C's regular pay. Employee D loses his arm in an accident and U pays D $10,000. C may request that U withhold income taxes under section 3402(o) and this section from the payments he receives because the payments constitute remuneration in lieu of remuneration for any period during which the employee is temporarily absent from work on account of sickness or personal injuries. D may not request that U withhold income taxes from the payments he receives because the payments do not constitute remuneration or a payment in lieu of remuneration for any period during which the employee is temporarily absent from work on account of sickness or personal injuries.

(2) The term "payee" means an individual who is a citizen or resident of the United States and who receives a sick pay payment.

(3) (i) The term "payor" means any person making a sick pay payment who is not the employer (as defined in section 3401 and in § 31.3401(d)-1 (except paragraph (f) thereof)) of the payee. If however the person making the payment is acting solely as an agent for another person, the term "payor" shall mean the other person and not the person actually making the payment.

(ii) This subparagraph (3) may be illustrated by the following examples:

Example (1). X Company contracts with Y Insurance Company for Y to pay X's employees the equivalent of their normal wages when they are temporarily absent from work because of sickness or personal injury. Y computes the amount to be paid and determines the date payment is to be made for each of X's employees. Y then instructs Z Bank to issue a check for that amount on that date. Y reimburses Z for the amount of the check plus Z's administrative costs. Under these circumstances, Z is the agent of Y and Y is the payor under section 3402(o) and this section.

Example (2). V Company contracts with W Company for W to pay V's employees the equivalent of their normal wages when they are temporarily absent from work on account of sickness or personal injury. Under the contractual arrangement, V advises W of the wages normally paid to each of V's employees. V tells W when an employee of V is temporarily absent from work on account of sickness or personal injury, and W computes the amount to be paid the employee and makes payments of sick pay to the employee during the period of the employee's absence. V subsequently reimburses W for the amount of those payments and pays W a fee for W's services. Under these circumstances, W is acting solely as the agent of V, and a payee may not request under section 3402(o) and these regulations that W withhold income taxes from his payments. However, see section 3401 and the regulations thereunder for the obligation of V to withhold income taxes from the payments that W makes as the agent of V, which are not excluded from income under section 105 and the regulations thereunder and which are wages under section 3401 and the regulations thereunder. See also § 31.3402(g)-1 (relating to supplemental wage payments) for the conditions under which a flat percentage rate of withholding may be used.

Example (3). Assume the same facts as in Example (2), except that the consideration for W's services is a set insurance premium rather than reimbursement for costs plus a fee. Under these circumstances W is the payor and is not acting solely as the agent of V. An employee of V to whom W makes payments under the agreement may request under section 3402(o) and the regulations thereunder that W withhold income taxes from those payments.

(i) Special rules for sick pay paid pursuant to certain collective-bargaining agreements. *(1)* Special rules (enumerated in subparagraph (2)) apply to sick pay where all of the following tests are met.

(i) The sick pay must be paid pursuant to a collective-bargaining agreement between employee representatives and one or more employers.

(ii) The agreement must contain a provision that section 3402(o)(5) is to apply to sick pay paid pursuant to the agreement.

(iii) The agreement must contain a provision for determining the amount to be deducted and withheld from each payment of sick pay.

(iv) The social security number of the payee must be furnished to the payor. The agreement may provide that the employer will furnish this or the payee may furnish his social security number directly to the payor.

(v) The payor must be furnished with information that is necessary for the payor to determine whether the payment is pursuant to the agreement and to determine the amount to be deducted and withheld. The agreement may provide that the employer will furnish this information directly to the payor.

(2) The following special rules apply to sick pay where all of the tests of subparagraph (1) are met.

(i) The requirement of section 3402(o)(1)(c) and this section that a request for withholding be in effect does not apply.

(ii) The amount to be deducted and withheld from the sick pay shall be determined according to the provisions of the agreement and not according to this section. This rule shall not however apply—

(A) To payments enumerated in section 3402(n) (relating to employees incurring no income tax liability) and the regulations thereunder, or

(B) To payments made to a payee more than 7 days after the date that the payor receives a statement from the payee that the payee expects to claim an exclusion from gross income under section 105(d). Such statement must include adequate verification of disability. A certificate from a qualified physician attesting that the employee is permanently and totally disabled (within the meaning of section 105(d)) shall be deemed to constitute adequate verification. If the payor receives such a statement, the payor shall not withhold any income tax from the payments made to the payee, regardless of the provisions of the collective bargaining agreement. This exception from withholding does not affect the requirements of § 31.6051-3.

T.D. 7813, 3/15/82, amend T.D. 7915, 9/26/83.

---

§ 31.3402(p)-1 Voluntary withholding agreements.

Caution: The Treasury has not yet amended Reg § 31.3402(p)-1 to reflect changes made by P.L. 100-203.

(a) In general. An employee and his employer may enter into an agreement under section 3402(p) to provide for the withholding of income tax upon payments of amounts described in paragraph (b)(1) of § 31.3401(a)-3, made after December 31, 1970. An agreement may be entered into under this section only with respect to amounts which are includible in the gross income of the employee under section 61, and must be applicable to all such amounts paid by the employer to the employee. The amount to be withheld pursuant to an agreement under section 3402(p) shall be determined under the rules contained in section 3402 and the regulations thereunder. See § 31.3405(c)-1, Q&A-3 concerning agreements to have more than 20-percent Federal income tax withheld from eligible rollover distributions within the meaning of section 402.

(b) Form and duration of agreement. *(1)* (i) Except as provided in subdivision (ii) of this subparagraph, an employee who desires to enter into an agreement under section 3402(p) shall furnish his employer with Form W-4 (withholding exemption certificate) executed in accordance with the provisions of section 3402(f) and the regulations thereunder. The furnishing of such Form W-4 shall constitute a request for withholding.

(ii) In the case of an employee who desires to enter into an agreement under section 3402(p) with his employer, if the employee performs services (in addition to those to be the subject of the agreement) the remuneration for which is subject to mandatory income tax withholding by such employer, or if the employee wishes to specify that the agreement terminate on a specific date, the employee shall furnish the employer with a request for withholding which shall be signed by the employee, and shall contain—

(a) The name, address, and social security number of the employee making the request,

(b) The name and address of the employer,

(c) A statement that the employee desires withholding of Federal income tax, and, if applicable, of qualified State individual income tax (see paragraph (d)(3)(i) of § 301.6361-1 of this chapter (Regulations on Procedure and Administration)), and

(d) If the employee desires that the agreement terminate on a specific date, the date of termination of the agreement. If accepted by the employer as provided in subdivision (iii) of this subparagraph, the request shall be attached to, and constitute part of, the employee's Form W-4. An employee who furnishes his employer a request for withholding under this subdivision shall also furnish such employer with Form W-4 if such employee does not already have a Form W-4 in effect with such employer.

(iii) No request for withholding under section 3402(p) shall be effective as an agreement between an employer and an employee until the employer accepts the request by commencing to withhold from the amounts with respect to which the request was made.

(2) An agreement under section 3402(p) shall be effective for such period as the employer and employee mutually agree upon. However, either the employer or the employee may terminate the agreement prior to the end of such period by furnishing a signed written notice to the other. Unless the employer and employee agree to an earlier termination date, the notice shall be effective with respect to the first payment of an amount in respect of which the agreement is in effect which is made on or after the first "status determination date" (January 1, May 1, July 1, and October 1 of each year) that occurs at least 30 days after the date on which the notice is furnished. If the employee executes a new Form W-4, the request upon which an agreement under section 3402(p) is based shall be attached to, and constitute a part of, such new Form W-4.

T.D. 7096, 3/17/71, amend T.D. 7577, 12/19/78, T.D. 8619, 9/15/95.

§ 31.3402(q)-1 Extension of withholding to certain gambling winnings.

Caution: The Treasury has not yet amended Reg § 31.3402(q)-1 to reflect changes made by P.L. 107-16.

(a) *(1) General rule.* Every person, including the Government of the United States, a State, or a political subdivision thereof, or any instrumentality of any of the foregoing making any payment of "winnings subject to withholding" (defined in paragraph (b) of the section) shall deduct and withhold a tax in an amount equal to 20 percent of the payment. The tax shall be deducted and withheld upon payment of the winnings by the person making such payment ("payer"). See paragraph (c)(5)(ii) of this section for a special rule relating to the time for making deposits of withheld amounts and filing the return with respect to those amounts. Any person receiving a payment of winnings subject to withholding must furnish the payer a statement as required in paragraph (e) of this section. Payers of winnings subject to withholding must file a return as required in paragraph (f) of this section. With respect to reporting requirements for certain payments of gambling winnings not subject to withholding, see section 6041 and the regulations thereunder.

(2) Exceptions. The tax imposed under section 3402(q)(1) and this section shall not apply (i) with respect to a payment of winnings which is made to a nonresident alien individual or foreign corporation under the circumstances described in paragraph (c)(4) of this section or (ii) with respect to a payment of winnings from a slot machine play, or a keno or bingo game.

(b) Winnings subject to withholding. Winnings subject to withholding means any payment from—

(1) A wager placed in a State-conducted lottery (defined in paragraph (c)(2) of this section) but only if the proceeds from the wager exceed $5,000;

(2) A wager placed in a sweepstakes, wagering pool, or lottery other than a State-conducted lottery but only if the proceeds from the wager exceed $1,000; or

(3) Any other wagering transaction (as defined in paragraph (c)(3) of this section) but only if the proceeds from the wager (i) exceed $1,000 and (ii) are at least 300 times as large as the amount of the wager.

If proceeds from the wager qualify as winnings subject to withholding, then the total proceeds from the wager, and not merely amounts in excess of $1,000 (or $5,000 in the case of winnings from a State-conducted lottery), are subject to withholding.

(c) Definitions; special rules. *(1) Rules for determining amount of proceeds from a wager.* (i) The amount of "proceeds from a wager" is the amount paid after January 2, 1977, with respect to the wager, less the amount of the wager. However, for any wagering transaction in a parimutuel pool with respect to horse races, dog races, or jai alai, only amounts paid after April 30, 1977, are taken into account.

(ii) Amounts paid after December 31, 1983, with respect to identical wagers are treated as paid with respect to a single wager for purposes of calculating the amount of proceeds from a wager. For example, amounts paid on two bets placed in a parimutuel pool on a particular horse to win a particular race are treated as paid with respect to the same wager. However, those two bets would not be identical were one "to win" and the other "to place", or if the bets were placed in different parimutuel pools, e.g., a pool conducted by the racetrack and a separate pool conducted by an off-track betting establishment in which the wagers are not pooled with those placed at the track. Tickets purchased in a lottery generally are not identical wagers, because the designation of each ticket as a winner generally would not be based on the occurrence of the same event, e.g., the drawing of a particular number. If the recipient makes the statement which may be required pursuant to § 1.6011-3, indicating whether or not the recipient (and any other persons entitled to a portion of the winnings) is entitled to winnings from identical wagers and indicating the amount of such winnings, if any, then the payer may rely upon such statement in determining the total amount of proceeds from the wager under paragraph (c)(1) of this section attributable to identical wagers.

(iii) In determining the amount paid with respect to a wager, proceeds which are not money shall be taken into account at the fair market value.

(iv) Periodic payments, including installment payments or payments which are to be made periodically for the life of a person, are aggregated for purposes of determining the proceeds from a wager. The aggregate amount of periodic payments to be made for a person's life shall be based on that person's life expectancy. See §§ 1.72-5 and 1.72-9 for rules used in computing the expected return on annuities. For purposes of determining the amount subject to withholding, the first periodic payment shall be reduced by the amount of the wager.

(2) Wager placed in a State-conducted lottery. The term "wager placed in a State-conducted lottery" means a wager placed in a lottery conducted by an agency of a State acting under authority of State law provided that the wager is placed with the State agency conducting such lottery or with its authorized employees or agents. This term includes wagers placed in State-conducted lotteries in which the amount of winnings is determined by a parimutuel system.

(3) Other wagering transaction. The term "other wagering transaction" means any wagering transaction other than one in a lottery, sweepstakes, or wagering pool. This term includes a wagering transaction in a parimutuel pool with respect to horse races, dog races, or jai alai.

(4) Certain payments to nonresident aliens or foreign corporations. A payment of winnings subject to withholding made to a nonresident alien individual or a foreign corporation is not subject to the tax imposed by section 3402(q) and this section if such payment is subject to withholding of tax under section 1441(a) (relating to withholding on nonresident aliens) or 1442(a) (relating to withholding on foreign corporations) and the payer complies with the requirements of those sections. For purposes of this section, a payment is treated as being subject to tax under section 1441(a) or 1442(a) notwithstanding that the rate of such tax is reduced (even to zero) as may be provided by an applicable treaty with another country. However, a reduced or zero rate of withholding of tax shall not be applied by the payer in lieu of the rate imposed by sections 1441 and 1442 unless the person receiving the winnings has completed, signed, and furnished the payer Form 1001 as required by § 1.1441-6. See sections 1441 and 1442 and the regulations thereunder for rules regarding the withholding of tax on nonresident aliens and foreign corporations.

(5) Gambling winnings treated as payments by employer to employee. (i) Except as provided in subdivision (ii), for purposes of sections 3403 and 3404 and the regulations thereunder and for purposes of so much of subtitle F (except section 7205) and the regulations thereunder as relate to chapter 24, payments to any person of winnings subject to withholding under this section shall be treated as if they are wages paid by an employer to an employee.

(ii) Solely for purposes of applying the deposit rules under 6302(c) and the return requirement of section 6011, the withholding from winnings shall be deemed to have been made no earlier than at the time the winner's identity is known to the payer. Thus, for example, winnings from a State-conducted lottery are subject to withholding when actually or constructively paid, whichever is earlier; however, the time for depositing the withheld taxes and filing a return with respect thereto shall be determined by reference to the date on which the winner's identity is known to the State, if such date is later than the date on which the winnings are actively or constructively paid. If a payer's obligation to pay winnings terminates other than by payment, all liabilities and requirements resulting from the requirement that the payer deduct and withhold with respect to such winnings shall also terminate.

(d) Examples. The provision of this section may be illustrated by the following examples:

Example (1). A purchases a lottery ticket for $1 in the State W lottery from an authorized agent of State W. On February 1, 1977, the drawing is held and A wins $5,001. Since the proceeds of the wager ($5,001 − $1) are not greater than $5,000, State W is not required to withhold or deduct any amount from A's winnings.

Example (2). Assume the same facts as in example (1) except that A purchases two $1 tickets and that A wins $5,002 when one of the tickets is drawn. State W must deduct and withhold tax at a rate of 20% from $5,001 ($5,002 less the $1 wager), or $1,000.20.

Example (3). On January 1, 1984, B makes two $2 bets in a parimutuel pool for a horse race. Each bet is on the same horse to win a particular race. B wins a total of $1,300 on those bets. B cashes the tickets at different cashier windows indicating on the statement demanded by each cashier the amount of winnings from identical wagers. Although the payment by each cashier ($650) is less than the $1,000 floor for the withholding requirement on payments of winnings from horse race parimutuel pools, each cashier is required to deduct and withhold tax from B's winnings equal to $129.60 (($650-$2) x 20 percent = $129.60) based on the information B submitted indicating that the aggregated proceeds from the identical wagers ($1,300-$4=$1,296) exceed $1,000 and the amount is at least 300 times as great as the amount wagered ($4x300=$1,200). Had B refused to make the statements, the payer would have no basis provided by the payee upon which to rely in determining whether the payment is subject to withholding. Under these circumstances, the payer would be required to deduct and withhold tax from the payment.

Example (4). C purchases a lottery ticket for $1. On June 1, 1979, the lottery drawing is held and C wins the grand prize of $50,000, payable $500 monthly. The payer must deduct and withhold tax at a rate of 20% from each payment of winnings. Therefore, $99.80 must be withheld from the first monthly payment to B ($500-$1)x20%=$99.80) and $100 ($500x20%) must be withheld from each monthly payment thereafter.

Example (5). Assume the same facts as in example (4), except that C wins an automobile rather than the grand prize. The fair market value of the automobile on the date on which it is made available to C is $10,001. The payer must deduct and withhold a tax of $2,000 (($10,001 − $1) × 20%). This may be accomplished, for example, if C pays $2,000 to the payer. Alternatively, if the payer, as part of the prize, pays all taxes required to be deducted and withheld, the payer must deduct and withhold tax not only on the fair market value of the automobile less the wager, but also on the taxes it pays that are required to be deducted and withheld. This results in a pyramiding of taxes requiring the use of an algebraic formula. Under this formula, the payer must deduct and withhold a tax of 25 percent of the fair market value of the automobile less the wager ($2,500) and, in addition, the payer must indicate on Form W-2G the amount of such winnings as $12,501 ($10,001 + 25% ($20,000 − $1)).

Example (6). D purchases a ticket for $1 in the State Y lottery from an authorized agent of State Y. On January 1, 1976, a drawing is held and D wins $100 a month for the rest of D's life. It is actuarially determined that, on January 3, 1977, D's life expectancy is 5 years. Based on that determination, the proceeds from the wager paid to D on or after January 3, 1977, will exceed $5,000. Therefore, State Y must deduct and withhold $20 from each monthly payment made on or after January 3, 1977. (None of such payments is reduced by the amount of the wager because the amount of the wager was offset by the first payment of winnings which was made before January 3, 1977)).

Example (7). Assume the same facts as in example (6) except that State Y purchases in its own name, as owner, an annuity of $100 a month for D's life from E Corporation, in order to fund its own obligation to make the payments. Although State Y remains liable for the withholding of tax, E Corporation as paying agent for State Y, making payments directly to D, should deduct and withhold from each monthly payment in the manner described in example (6).

Example (8). E purchases a sweepstakes ticket for $1 in a sweepstakes conducted by W. E purchases the ticket on behalf of himself and on behalf of F and G, who have contributed equal amounts toward the purchase of the ticket and who have agreed to share equally in any prizes won. The ticket which E purchases wins $1,002. Since the proceeds of the wager ($1,002 − $1) are greater than $1,000 W is required to withhold and deduct 20 percent of such proceeds.

Example (9). On February 1, 1977, a drawing is held in the State X lottery in which a winning ticket is selected. The person holding the winning ticket is entitled to proceeds of $100,000 payable either as a lump sum upon demand or $10,000 a year for 10 years. Under State law, the winning ticket must be presented to an authorized agent of State X before February 1, 1978. Until the ticket is presented, State X does not know the identity of the winner. On December 1, 1977, H, the winner, presents the winning ticket to an authorized agent of the State X lottery. The winnings are constructively paid to H on February 1, 1977. Since H, has the option of receiving the entire proceeds upon demand, State X is required to deduct and withhold $20,000 ($100,000 × 20%) from the proceeds of H's winnings on February 1, 1977; but for purposes of determining the time at which the deposit and inclusion on Form 941 of these taxes is to be made, the withholding shall be deemed to have been made on December 1, 1977.

Example (10). J purchases a subscription to N magazine, at the regular subscription price. All new subscribers are automatically eligible for a special drawing. The drawing is held and J wins $50,000. Since J has not paid any more than the regular subscription price, J has not placed a wager or entered a wagering transaction. Therefore, N is not required to deduct and withhold J's winnings.

Example (11). C makes two $2 bets in the same parimutuel pool for a horse race. One bet is an "exacta" in which C bets on horse M to win and horse N to "place". The other bet is a "trifecta". C bets on horse M to win, horse N to "place" and horse O to "show". C wins both bets and is paid $600 with respect to the "exacta" and $900 with respect to the "trifecta". The bets are not identical wagers, however, and on these facts neither payment is subject to withholding.

(e) Statement by recipient. Each person who is to receive a payment of winnings subject to withholding shall furnish the payer a statement on Form W-2G or 5754 (whichever is applicable) made under the penalties of perjury containing—

(1) The name, address, and taxpayer identification number of the winner accompanied by a declaration that no other person is entitled to any portion of such payment, or

(2) The name, address, and taxpayer identification number of the recipient and of every person entitled to any portion of such payment.

If more than one payment of winnings subject to withholding is to be made with respect to a single wager, for example in the case of an annuity, the recipient is required by paragraph (e) of this section to furnish the payer a statement with respect to the first such payment only, provided that such other payments are taken into account in a return required by paragraph (f) of this section.

(f) Return of payer. *(1) In general.* Every person making payment of winnings for which a statement is required under paragraph (e) of this section shall file a return on Form W-2G with the Internal Revenue Service Center serving the district in which is located the principal place of business of the person making the return on or before February 28 (March 31 if filed electronically) of the calendar year following the calendar year in which the payment of winnings is made. The return required by this paragraph (f) need not include the statement by the recipient required by paragraph (e) of this section and, therefore, need not be signed by the recipient, provided such statement is retained as long as the contents thereof may become material in the administration of any internal revenue law. For payments to more than one winner, a separate Form W-2G, which in no event need be signed by the winner, shall be filed with respect to each such winner. Each Form W-2G shall contain the following:

(i) The name, address, and employer identification number of the payer;

(ii) The name, address, and social security account number of the winner;

(iii) The date, amount of the payment, and amount withheld;

(iv) The type of wagering transaction;

(v) Except with respect to winnings from a wager placed in a State-conducted lottery, a specific description of two types of identification, e.g., driver's license number and issuing State, social security account number of voter registration number and jurisdiction, furnished the payer for verification of the recipient's name, address, and social security account number; and

(vi) With respect to amounts paid after December 31, 1983, the amount of winnings from identical wagers.

The return of the payer need not contain the information required by subdivision (v) of this paragraph (f)(1) provided such information is obtained with respect to the recipient of such winnings and retained as long as the contents thereof may become material in the administration of any internal revenue law.

(2) Transmittal form. Persons making payments of winnings subject to withholding shall use Form W-3G to transmit Forms W-2G to the Internal Revenue Service Centers.

T.D. 7787, 9/22/81, amend T.D. 7919, 10/11/83, T.D. 7943, 2/10/84, T.D. 8895, 8/17/2000.

§ 31.3402(r)-1 Withholding on distributions of Indian gaming profits to tribal members.

(a) *(1) General rule.* Section 3402(r)(1) requires every person, including an Indian tribe, making a payment to a member of an Indian tribe from the net revenues of any class II or class III gaming activity, as defined in 25 U.S.C. 2703, conducted or licensed by such tribe to deduct and withhold from such payment a tax in an amount equal to such payment's proportionate share of the annualized tax, as that term is defined in section 3402(r)(3).

(2) Withholding tables. Except as provided in paragraph (a)(4) of this section, the amount of a payment's proportionate share of the annualized tax shall be determined under the applicable table provided by the Commissioner.

(3) Annualized amount of payment. Section 3402(r)(5) provides that payments shall be placed on an annualized basis under regulations prescribed by the Secretary. A payment may be placed on an annualized basis by multiplying the amount of the payment by the total number of payments to be made in a calendar year. For example, a monthly payment may be annualized by multiplying the amount of the payment by 12. Similarly, a quarterly payment may be annualized by multiplying the amount of the payment by 4.

(4) Alternate withholding procedures. (i) In general. Any procedure for determining the amount to be deducted and withheld under section 3402(r) may be used, provided that the amount of tax deducted and withheld is substantially the same as it would be using the tables provided by the Commissioner under paragraph (a)(2) of this section. At the election of an Indian tribe, the amount to be deducted and withheld under section 3402(r) shall be determined in accordance with this alternate procedure.

(ii) Method of election. It is sufficient for purposes of making an election under this paragraph (a)(4) that an Indian tribe evidence the election in any reasonable way, including use of a particular method. Thus, no written election is required.

(5) Additional withholding permitted. Consistent with the provisions of section 3402(p), a tribal member and a tribe may enter into an agreement to provide for the deduction and withholding of additional amounts from payments in order to satisfy the anticipated tax liability of the tribal member. The agreement may be made in a manner similar to that described in § 31.3402(p)-1 (with respect to voluntary withholding agreements between employees and employers).

(b) Effective date. This section applies to payments made after December 31, 1994.

T.D. 8634, 12/18/95.

Proposed § 31.3402(t)-0 Outline of the Government withholding regulations. [*For Preamble, see ¶ 153,073*]

This section lists paragraphs contained in §§ 31.3402(t)-1 through 31.3402(t)-5, and § 31.3402(t)-7.

(b) Exception for payments made under existing written binding contracts.

(c) Good faith exception for interest and penalties on payments before January 1, 2012.

Proposed § 31.3402(t)-1 Withholding requirement on certain payments made by government entities. [*For Preamble, see ¶ 153,073*]

(a) In general. Except as provided in §§ 31.3402(t)-3(b) and 31.3402(t)-4, the Government of the United States, every State, every political subdivision thereof, and every instrumentality of the foregoing (including multi-State agencies) making any payment to any person providing any property or services shall deduct and withhold from such payment a tax in an amount equal to 3 percent of such payment.

(b) Special rules. See § 31.3402(t)-2 for government entities required to withhold under this section, § 31.3402(t)-3 for what constitutes a payment to a person for property or services and when such payment is deemed to occur for purposes of this section, and § 31.3402(t)-4 for payments that are excepted from withholding under this section.

(c) Deposit and reporting requirements. See § 31.6302-4 for deposit requirements with respect to withholding under section 3402(t). See §§ 31.6011(a)-4(b) and 31.6051-5 for the reporting requirements with respect to withholding under section 3402(t).

(d) Effective/applicability date. *(1)* Except as provided in paragraph (d)(2) of this section, this section is effective for payments by the Government of the United States, every State, every political subdivision thereof, and every instrumentality of the foregoing (including multi-State agencies) to any person providing property or services made after the later of December 31, 2010, or the date that is 6 months after the date of publication in the Federal Register of final regulations under section 3402(t).

(2) Payments made under a written binding contract that was in effect on the later of December 31, 2010, or the date that is 6 months after the publication in the Federal Register of final regulations under section 3402(t), are not subject to the withholding requirements of this section. The preceding sentence does not apply to payments made under any contract that is materially modified after the later of December 31, 2010, or the date that is 6 months after the date of publication in the Federal Register of final regulations under section 3402(t).

Proposed § 31.3402(t)-2 Government entities required to withhold under section 3402(t). [*For Preamble, see ¶ 153,073*]

(a) In general. The requirement to withhold under section 3402(t) and § 31.3402(t)-1(a) applies to the Government of the United States (see paragraph (b) of this section) and every State (see paragraph (c) of this section), as well as instrumentalities of the foregoing. The requirement also applies to political subdivisions of every State (see paragraph (d) of this section), and their instrumentalities, unless the small entity exception of § 31.3402(t)-4(g) applies.

(b) Government of the United States. The Government of the United States includes the legislative branch, the judicial branch, and the executive branch, and all components of the United States Government. Thus, departments and agencies are included within the definition of United States Government.

(c) State. The term State includes the District of Columbia. However, an Indian tribal government is not considered a State for purposes of section 3402(t) and § 31.3402(t)-1(a). See section 7871(a).

(d) Political subdivision. The term political subdivision for purposes of section 3402(t) and § 31.3402(t)-1(a) is defined as a political subdivision within the meaning of § 1.103-1(b) of this chapter, except that a subdivision of an Indian tribal government is not considered a political subdivision. See section 7871(a) and (d).

(e) [Reserved].

(f) Possessions of the United States. For purposes of section 3402(t) and § 31.3402(t)-1(a), the government of a possession or territory of the United States is not treated as a government entity subject to the withholding requirements of section 3402(t)(1).

(g) Passthrough entities. See § 31.3402(t)-5(c) for the treatment of payments from certain passthrough entities as subject to the withholding requirements of § 31.3402(t)-1.

(h) Small entity exception. See § 31.3402(t)-4(g) for the exception from the withholding requirements of § 31.3402(t)-1 for political subdivisions and instrumentalities thereof making less than $100,000,000 of payments for property or services annually.

(i) Effective/applicability date. This section is effective the later of January 1, 2011, or the date that is 6 months after the date of publication in the Federal Register of final regulations under section 3402(t).

Proposed § 31.3402(t)-3 Payments subject to withholding. [*For Preamble, see ¶ 153,073*]

(a) In general. A payment is subject to withholding for purposes of §§ 31.3402(t)-1 through 31.3402(t)-7 when paid by a government entity to any person, as defined in § 301.7701-6(a) of this chapter, for property or services. If, however, the government entity uses a payment administrator to pay a person for property or services, payment occurs when the payment administrator pays such person. The government entity subject to the withholding requirements of § 31.3402(t)-1 is liable for the withholding required and responsible for all related reporting regardless of whether the government entity or its payment administrator makes the payment for property or services.

(b) Payment threshold of $10,000. *(1) In general.* The term payment threshold means an amount equal to $10,000. The withholding requirements of § 31.3402(t)-1 will not apply to any payment that is less than the payment threshold. Whether a payment is equal to or in excess of the payment threshold is determined when the payment is made.

(2) Payment threshold applied per payment. If a government entity makes a single payment to a person for property or services combining charges for more than one transaction with the person, the determination of whether the payment threshold provided by paragraph (b)(1) of this section applies will be based on the amount of the single payment, rather than the amount attributable to each separate transaction. Thus, if a government entity makes a single payment of $10,000 or more to a person, the government entity will be required to withhold on the payment, even if the payment is for more than one property or service. The same rule applies if a government entity enters into multiple transactions with a single person, each of which would result in a payment of less than $10,000 if paid separately, but elects to make a single payment covering all the transactions such that the aggregated payment is $10,000 or more. Under these circum-

stances, the government entity is required to withhold on the aggregated payment.

(3) Anti-abuse rule. If a government entity or payment administrator divides a payment or payments to any person for property or services into two or more payments primarily to avoid the $10,000 payment threshold provided in paragraph (b)(1) of this section on one or more of these payments, the divided payments will be treated as a single payment made on the date that the first of these payments is made.

(c) No withholding on successive payments. If a government entity or its payment administrator makes a payment that is subject to the withholding requirements of § 31.3402(t)-1 to a person, no subsequent transfer of cash or property from that payment by such person to another person is treated as a payment subject to withholding for purposes of §§ 31.3402(t)-1 through 31.3402(t)-7.

(d) Payments made through a payment administrator or to a contractor. *(1) Definition.* For purposes of this section—

(i) A payment administrator is any person that acts with respect to a payment solely as an agent for a government entity by making the payment on behalf of the government entity to a person providing property or services to, or on behalf of, the government entity.

(ii) A payment administrator is treated as a person providing property or services for purposes of the withholding requirements of section 3402(t) to the extent it receives a fee from the government entity for its services as a payment administrator for the government entity.

(2) Payments to a contractor. If a person provides property or services to a government entity under a contract and is not a payment administrator, the person, who is in privity with the government entity, is treated as the person providing property or services subject to withholding under section 3402(t) for all payments received from the government entity, regardless of whether some payments the person receives relate to invoices for property or services provided by subcontractors.

(3) Application of payment threshold. Where a government entity uses a payment administrator to make a payment, the determination of whether the payment meets the payment threshold is made at the time the payment administrator makes the payment to the person providing property or services. If a government entity makes one transfer of funds to a payment administrator that is composed of a fee to compensate the payment administrator for its services and other funds that are to be paid to persons providing property or services, the determination of whether the payment threshold is met on the portion that is the fee is made at the time of the transfer of funds to the payment administrator.

(e) Payments by credit card or payment card. For purposes of section 3402(t), a payment made by a government entity by credit card or payment card to a person for property or services occurs when the credit card or payment card is tendered at the point of sale. The government entity is liable for withholding under section 3402(t) and reporting associated with such withholding. See section 6050W of the Internal Revenue Code for separate reporting obligations imposed on the acquiring bank of the person receiving payment by credit card or payment card.

(f) Examples. This section is illustrated by the following examples:

Example (1). (i) Prime contractor X has a contract with a government entity to provide services and property to the government entity. X contracts with numerous subcontractors to provide services and property in connection with the contract. While the engagement of any particular subcontractor is subject to approval by the government entity, the subcontractors are not parties to the contract between X and the government entity, and the government entity is not a party to the contracts between X and subcontractors. Under its contract with the government entity, X submits an invoice for $48,000 for providing services and property to the government entity, including charges for services and property provided by two subcontractors, M and N. The invoice reflects charges of $16,000 for M and $2,000 for N. The government entity pays X the entire amount of the invoice in one payment of $48,000. X pays M for M's billed portion of the invoice in a single payment of $16,000, and X pays N for N's billed portion of the invoice in a single payment of $2,000.

(ii) Under the facts of this Example 1, X is the person providing property or services to, or for the benefit of, the government entity with respect to the entire amount of the $48,000 payment under the invoice, including the charges for services or property provided by its subcontractors M and N. X is not a payment administrator (as defined in paragraph (d)(1)(i) of this section) because X is not making payments solely as an agent of the government entity to persons providing property or services. Instead, X makes payments to subcontractors M and N pursuant to X's separate contracts with these subcontractors to which the government entity is not a party. Therefore, under paragraphs (a) and (d)(2) of this section, the entire amount of the $48,000 payment to X under the invoice, including the charges for services and property provided by its subcontractors M and N, is the payment subject to withholding for purposes of section 3402(t).

(iii) Under paragraph (b)(1) of this section, the determination whether the payment meets the payment threshold is based on the entire amount of the payment from the government entity to X. Withholding under section 3402(t) applies to the government entity's $48,000 payment to X because the payment meets the payment threshold and is not otherwise excepted from section 3402(t) withholding. Thus, the payment is subject to withholding of 3 percent, or $1,440.

(iv) Payments made by X to the subcontractors, M and N, are not payments by the government entity or its payment administrator. Thus, X's $16,000 payment to M and X's $2,000 payment to N for services or property under the contract are not subject to withholding under section 3402(t). See paragraphs (c) and (d)(2) of this section.

(v) The government entity is liable for the $1,440 withholding required under section 3402(t) on its payment to X and is responsible for the related reporting required under § 31.6051-5. See paragraph (a) of this section. X is the person receiving the payment for purposes of reporting under § 31.6051-5. Thus, the government entity is responsible for providing X with a Form 1099 including the entire amount of the payment ($48,000) and the entire amount of the withholding ($1,440).

Example (2). (i) Z has a contract with a government entity to make payments as an agent of the government entity to persons providing services or property to, or on behalf of, the government entity. The only services Z provides under the contract are its services in acting as an agent for the government entity in making payments to persons providing property or services to, or on behalf of, the government. The government entity transfers funds of $71,000 to Z, which includes a fee of $1,000 to Z for its services as an agent under the contract. Z then makes payments of the $70,000 remainder of the funds to persons providing property or services to, or on behalf of, the government entity, including a single payment of $18,000 to P and a single payment of $7,000 to R.

(ii) Under the facts of this Example 2, Z is a payment administrator (as defined in paragraph (d)(1)(i) of this section) because Z makes payments solely as an agent for the government entity to persons providing property or services to, or on behalf of, the government entity. Under paragraphs (a) and (d) of this section, Z is not treated as a person providing property or services with respect to $70,000 of the transfer of funds (the amount of the funds to be paid to persons providing property or services to, or on behalf of, the government entity). Because Z is not treated as a person providing property or services with respect to this $70,000 portion of the funds, this portion of the transfer of funds by the government entity to Z is not subject to withholding under section 3402(t) when transferred to Z.

(iii) Under paragraph (d)(1)(ii) of this section, the payment administrator is treated as a person providing property or services with respect to the portion of the $71,000 fund transfer that is a fee for its services as a payment administrator, or $1,000. Under paragraph (d)(3) of this section, the determination of whether the payment threshold is met with respect to the fee portion of the payment from the government entity to Z is made at the time of the payment from the government entity to Z. Because the $1,000 fee portion of the payment falls beneath the $10,000 payment threshold, withholding under section 3402(t) is not required with respect to that portion of the payment.

(iv) P and R are persons providing services or property to, or on behalf of, the government entity with respect to the payments they receive from Z.

(v) Withholding is required under section 3402(t) on the payment by Z, a payment administrator, to a person providing property or services to, or on behalf of, a government entity provided the payment meets the payment threshold and is not otherwise excepted. Under paragraph (d)(3) of this section, the determination of whether the payment threshold is met on the payment Z makes to a person providing property or services is made at the time Z pays the person providing property or services. Under the facts of this Example 2, Z's payment to P of $18,000 meets the payment threshold, and therefore withholding of $540 under section 3402(t) applies. Z's payment to R of $7,000 does not meet the payment threshold, and therefore, no withholding under section 3402(t) is required.

(vi) The government entity, not Z, is liable for any withholding required under section 3402(t) on the payments from Z to persons providing property or services. Also, the government entity, not Z, is responsible for any reporting required under § 31.6051-5 on the payment from Z to persons providing property or services. See paragraph (a) of this section. Each person providing property or services with respect to which withholding is required, not Z, is the person receiving the payment for purposes of the reporting required under § 31.6051-5 if withholding under section 3402(t) applies. Thus, the government entity is responsible for issuing P a Form 1099 reflecting the amount of the payment from Z to P of $18,000 and the amount of withholding of $540.

(g) Effective/applicability date. This section is effective for payments by the Government of the United States, every State, every political subdivision thereof, and every instrumentality of the foregoing (including multi-State agencies) to any person providing property or services made after the later of December 31, 2010, or the date that is 6 months after the date of publication in the Federal Register of final regulations under section 3402(t).

Proposed § 31.3402(t)-4 Certain payments excepted from withholding. [*For Preamble, see ¶ 153,073*]

(a) Payments subject to withholding under chapter 3 or chapter 24 (other than section 3406). *(1) In general.* Payments are excepted from withholding under section § 31.3402(t)-1(a) if they are subject to withholding under chapter 3 of the Internal Revenue Code (Code) or under sections 3401 through 3405 of the Code (other than section 3402(t)).

(2) Payments subject to withholding under chapter 3. Payments subject to withholding under chapter 3 include those payments that are subject to, but exempt from, withholding under chapter 3 on the ground that the payments are exempt from United States income tax pursuant to an income tax convention to which the United States is a party.

(3) Payments subject to withholding at election of payee. For purposes of this exception from section 3402(t), payments for which the payee may elect withholding are exempt from withholding under § 31.3402(t)-1(a) regardless of whether the payee in fact makes such an election. These payments include—

(i) Unemployment compensation as defined in section 85(b) (see section 3402(p)(2));

(ii) Social security benefits as defined in section 86(d) (see section 3402(p)(1)(C)(i));

(iii) Any payment referred to in the second sentence of section 451(d) that is treated as insurance proceeds, relating to certain disaster payments received under the Agricultural Act of 1949, as amended, or Title II of the Disaster Assistance Act of 1988 (see section 3402(p)(1)(C)(ii));

(iv) Any amount that is includible in gross income under section 77(a), relating to amounts received as loans from the Commodity Credit Corporation that the taxpayer has elected to treat as income (see section 3402(p)(1)(C)(iii)); and

(v) Any payment of an annuity to an individual.

(b) Payments subject to withholding under section 3406 with backup withholding deducted. A payment is not subject to withholding under section 3402(t) if the payment is subject to withholding under section 3406, relating to backup withholding, and if backup withholding is actually being withheld from such payment.

(c) [Reserved].

(d) Payments for real property. Payments for real property are not subject to the withholding requirements of § 31.3402(t)-1. For purposes of this exception, the term payments for real property includes the purchase and the leasing of real property. However, payments for the construction of buildings or other public works projects, such as bridges or roads, are not payments for real property.

(e) Payments to government entities, tax-exempt organizations, and foreign governments. *(1) Government entities.* Payments are not subject to withholding under section 3402(t) if the payments are made to government entities that are subject to the withholding requirements of section 3402(t)(1) pursuant to § 31.3402(t)-2. For purposes of this exception, payments to government entities that qualify for the exception for political subdivisions and instrumentalities making less than $100,000,000 of payments for property and services annually, as provided by section 3402(t)(2)(G) and paragraph (g) of this section, are treated as payments to government entities that are subject to the withholding requirements of section 3402(t)(1).

(2) Tax-exempt organizations. Payments to an organization that is exempt from taxation under section 501(a) as an organization described in section 501(c), 501(d), or 401(a) are not subject to withholding under section 3402(t).

(3) Foreign governments. Payments to foreign governments are not subject to withholding under section 3402(t). For purposes of this paragraph (e), a government of a possession or territory of the United States is treated as a foreign government.

(f) Payments made pursuant to a classified or confidential contract. Payments made pursuant to a classified or confidential contract described in section 6050M(e)(3) are not subject to withholding under section 3402(t).

(g) Exception for political subdivisions or instrumentalities thereof making less than $100,000,000 of payments for property or services annually. *(1) In general.* Section 3402(t) withholding is not required on payments made by a political subdivision of a State (or any instrumentality of a political subdivision of a State) that makes less than $100,000,000 of payments for property or services annually.

(2) Determination of whether an entity is a political subdivision of a State. The determination of whether an entity is a political subdivision of a State is made under § 31.3402(t)-2(d).

(3) Determination of whether a political subdivision or instrumentality makes less than $100,000,000 of payments for property or services annually. The determination of whether the exception provided by paragraph (g)(1) of this section applies is made for each calendar year. For purposes of any calendar year, the determination of whether a political subdivision or instrumentality makes less than $100,000,000 of payments for property or services annually is based on the total payments made by the entity for property or services in the entity's accounting year ending with or within the second preceding calendar year. For purposes of this paragraph (g), payments that would have qualified for the exceptions from withholding under § 31.3402(t)-4(a) through (l) had these regulations been in effect shall not be included in calculating the total payments made. However, payments that would have been excepted from withholding only because such payments were less than the $10,000 payment threshold contained in § 31.3402(t)-3(b) are included in calculating the total payments for purposes of this paragraph (g). Also, payments that were not subject to withholding under section 3402(t) solely based on the effective date rules or transition rules contained in § 31.3402(t)-1(d), § 31.3402(t)-2(i), § 31.3402(t)-3(g), § 31.3402(t)-4(m), § 31.3402(t)-5(e), or § 31.3402(t)-7 are included in calculating total payments for purposes of this paragraph (g). For purposes of this determination, the accounting year refers to the fiscal year (consisting of 12 months) or calendar year used by the government entity in setting its budgets and keeping its accounting books. If a political subdivision or instrumentality was not in existence in the second preceding calendar year or if no 12-month accounting year exists ending in the second preceding calendar year, the determination of whether this exception applies for a calendar year shall be based on the total payments as projected for the accounting year consisting of 12 months ending in that calendar year.

(4) Example. (i) Government entity X, which qualifies as a political subdivision or instrumentality thereof for the calendar years 2011 and 2012, uses a fiscal year ending June 30 to determine its budgets and to keep its accounting books. During its fiscal year ending June 30, 2009, X made payments to persons for property and services of $200,000,000, including $102,000,000 of payments that would have been excepted under § 31.3402(t)-4(a) through (l) if section 3402(t) had been in effect.

(ii) During its fiscal year ending June 30, 2010, X made payments for property and services of $210,000,000, including $106,000,000 that would have been excepted under § 31.3402(t)-4(a) through (l) if section 3402(t) had been in effect. In addition, during the fiscal year ending June 30, 2010, X made $15,000,000 of payments that were below the payment threshold of $10,000 in § 31.3402(t)-3(b) if section 3402(t) had been in effect.

(iii) For the calendar year 2011, X determines whether it is eligible for the exception provided by this paragraph (g) based on the total payments X made for its accounting year ending June 30, 2009. Because total payments for this purpose exclude payments that would be excepted under § 31.3402(t)-4(a) through (l), total payments were $200,000,000 less $102,000,000, or $98,000,000. Therefore, for calendar year 2011, X would qualify for the exception provided by this paragraph (g), and would not be required to withhold under section 3402(t).

(iv) For the calendar year 2012, X determines whether it is eligible for the exception provided by this paragraph (g) based on the total payments it made for its accounting year ending June 30, 2010. Because total payments for this purpose exclude payments that would have been excepted under § 31.3402(t)-4(a) through (l), but include payments below the payment threshold of $10,000 provided under § 31.3402(t)-3(b), total payments were $210,000,000 less $106,000,000, or $104,000,000. Therefore, for calendar year 2012, X would not qualify for the exception provided by this paragraph (g) and would be required to withhold under section 3402(t).

(h) Payments made in connection with a public assistance or public welfare program. *(1) In general.* Section 3402(t) withholding shall not apply to payments made in connection with a public assistance or public welfare program for which eligibility is determined by a needs or income test.

(2) Needs or income test. Eligibility for a public assistance or public welfare program is not considered to be determined by a needs or income test if eligibility for the program is based solely on the age of the beneficiary. A public assistance program providing disaster relief to victims of a natural or other disaster is considered to be a program for which eligibility is determined under a needs test. Payments under government programs to provide health care or other services that are not based on the needs or income of the recipient are subject to section 3402(t) withholding, including programs where eligibility is based on the age of the beneficiary.

(3) Payments to third parties. The exception provided by this paragraph (h) also applies to payments made to third parties to provide benefits to beneficiaries under a public assistance or public welfare program for which eligibility is determined by a needs or income test.

(i) Payments made to any government employee with respect to his or her services. Section 3402(t) withholding shall not apply to payments made to any government employee with respect to his or her services as an employee of the government. This exception applies to contributions to deferred compensation plans on behalf of an employee, contributions to employee benefit plans on behalf of an employee, fringe benefits provided to employees, and payments to employees under accountable plans for the individual travel expenses of the employee. This exception also applies to payments made by the government employee under accountable plans to providers of the employee's travel, meals, and lodging when the government employee is traveling on government business.

(j) Payments received by nonresident alien individuals and foreign corporations. Section 3402(t) withholding shall not apply to any payment received by a nonresident alien individual or foreign corporation (foreign person) for providing services or property if the payment is derived from sources outside the United States, as determined under sections 861, 862, 863, and 865, and is not effectively connected with the conduct of a trade or business within the United States by the foreign person.

(k) Payments to Indian tribal governments. Section 3402(t) withholding shall not apply to any payment made to an Indian tribal government or its political subdivisions.

(l) Payments in emergency or disaster situations. The Secretary may provide by publication in the Internal Revenue Bulletin (see § 601.601(d)(2)(ii)(b) of this chapter) for additional exceptions from section 3402(t) withholding for certain payments made in an emergency or disaster situation if the Secretary determines that withholding from the payments would impede a government entity's efforts to respond to the emergency or disaster.

(m) Effective/applicability date. This section is effective for payments by the Government of the United States, every State, every political subdivision thereof, and every instrumentality of the foregoing (including multi-State agencies) to any person providing property or services made after the later of December 31, 2010, or the date that is 6 months after the date of publication in the Federal Register of final regulations under section 3402(t).

Proposed § 31.3402(t)-5 Application to passthrough entities. [*For Preamble, see ¶ 153,073*]

(a) In general. This section sets forth rules that provide that section 3402(t)(1) does not apply to payments made by passthrough entities except as described in paragraph (c) of this section. In addition, the rules provide that section 3402(t)(1) applies to payments made to passthrough entities except as described in paragraph (d) of this section.

(b) Definitions. The following definitions set forth the meaning of certain terms for purposes of this section:

(1) Passthrough entity. The term passthrough entity means a partnership (for Federal income tax purposes) or an S corporation.

(2) Owner. The term owner means a partner (for Federal income tax purposes) or an S corporation shareholder.

(3) Ownership percentage. The term ownership percentage means an owner's interest, as a percentage, in partnership profits or capital (whichever is greater) in the case of a partnership, or an owner's interest, as a percentage, in S corporation stock in the case of an S corporation.

(4) Testing day. The term testing day refers to the first day of a passthrough entity's taxable year.

(c) Payments from a passthrough entity. *(1) General rule.* Section 3402(t)(1) shall not apply to payments made by passthrough entities during the taxable year, except as provided in paragraph (c)(2) of this section.

(2) Exception. Section 3402(t)(1) shall apply to any payment during the taxable year from a passthrough entity if the aggregate ownership percentage held, directly or indirectly, in the entity on the testing day by government entities described in section 3402(t)(1) is at least 80 percent. For purposes of this paragraph (c)(2), any manipulation of the ownership percentage with an intent to avoid application of section 3402(t) will be recharacterized as appropriate to reflect the actual ownership percentage.

(d) Payments to a passthrough entity. *(1) General rule.* Section 3402(t)(1) shall apply to payments made to passthrough entities during the taxable year, except as provided in paragraph (d)(2) of this section.

(2) Exception. Section 3402(t)(1) shall not apply to any payment during a taxable year to a passthrough entity if the aggregate ownership percentage held, directly or indirectly, in the entity on the testing day by persons described in section 3402(t)(2)(E) is at least 80 percent. For purposes of this paragraph (d)(2), any manipulation of the ownership percentage with an intent to avoid application of section 3402(t) will be recharacterized as appropriate to reflect the actual ownership percentage.

(e) Effective/applicability date. This section is effective for payments by the Government of the United States, every State, every political subdivision thereof, and every instrumentality of the foregoing (including multi-State agencies) to any person providing property or services made after the later of December 31, 2010, or the date that is 6 months after the date of publication in the Federal Register of final regulations under section 3402(t).

Proposed § 31.3402(t)-6 Crediting of tax withheld under section 3402(t). [*For Preamble, see ¶ 153,073*]

[Reserved].

Proposed § 31.3402(t)-7 Effective date and transition rules. [*For Preamble, see ¶ 153,073*]

(a) General Rule. Except as provided in paragraph (b) of this section, the requirement to withhold under § 31.3402(t)-1(a) applies to payments made after the later of December 31, 2010, or the date that is 6 months after the date of publication in the Federal Register of final regulations under section 3402(t).

(b) Exception for payments made under existing written binding contracts. Payments made under a written binding contract that was in effect on the later of December 31, 2010, or the date that is 6 months after the date of publication in the Federal Register of final regulations under section 3402(t), are not subject to the withholding requirements in § 31.3402(t)-1. The preceding sentence does not apply to payments made under any contract that is materially modified after the later of December 31, 2010, or the date that is 6 months after the date of publication in the Federal Register of final regulations under section 3402(t).

(c) Good faith exception for interest and penalties on payments made before January 1, 2012. Government entities that make a good faith effort to comply with the provisions of these regulations will not be liable for penalties and interest with respect to income tax withholding under section 3402(t) that the government entity failed to withhold from payments made before January 1, 2012. However, this provision shall not relieve the government entity of liability for income tax that it failed to withhold. See, however, § 31.3402(d)-1.

§ 31.3403-1 Liability for tax.

Every employer required to deduct and withhold the tax under section 3402 from the wages of an employee is liable for the payment of such tax whether or not it is collected from the employee by the employer. If, for example, the employer deducts less than the correct amount of tax, or if he fails to deduct any part of the tax, he is nevertheless liable for the correct amount of the tax. See, however, § 31.3402(d)-1. The employer is relieved of liability to any other person for the amount of any such tax withheld and paid to the district director or deposited with a duly designated depositary of the United States.

T.D. 6259, 10/25/57.

§ 31.3404-1 Return and payment by governmental employer.

If the United States, or a State, Territory, Puerto Rico, or a political subdivision thereof, or the District of Columbia, or any agency or instrumentality of any one or more of the foregoing, is an employer required to deduct and withhold tax under chapter 24, the return of the amount deducted and withheld as such tax may be made by the officer or employee having control of the payment of the wages or other officer or employee appropriately designated for that purpose. (For provisions relating to the execution and filing of returns, see Subpart G of the regulations in this part.)

T.D. 6259, 10/25/57.

§ 35.3405-1 Questions and answers relating to withholding on pensions, annuities, and certain other deferred income.

Caution: The Treasury has not yet amended Reg § 35.3405-1 to reflect changes made by P.L. 106-554.

The following questions and answers relate to withholding on pensions, annuities, and other deferred income under section 3405 of the Internal Revenue Code of 1986, as added by section 334 of the Tax Equity and Fiscal Responsibility Tax Act of 1982 (Public Law 97-248) (TEFRA).

a-1 through d-34 [Reserved] For further guidance, see § 35.3405-1T.

Q-d-35. Through what medium may a payor provide the notice required under section 3405 to a payee?

A-d-35. A payor may provide the notice required under section 3405 (including the abbreviated notice described in d-27 of § 35.3405-1T and the annual notice described in d-31 of § 35.3405-1T) to a payee on a written paper document. However, see § 1.401(a)-21 of this chapter for rules permitting the use of electronic media to provide applicable notices to recipients with respect to retirement plans and individual retirement plans.

T.D. 8873, 2/7/2000, amend T.D. 9294, 10/19/2006.

§ 35.3405-1T Questions and answers relating to withholding on pensions, annuities and certain other deferred income (Temporary).

Caution: The Treasury has not yet amended Reg § 35.3405-1T to reflect changes made by P.L. 106-554.

The following questions and answers relate to withholding on pensions, annuities, and other deferred income under section 3405 of the Internal Revenue Code of 1954, as added by section 334 of the Tax Equity and Fiscal Responsibility Tax Act of 1982 (Public Law 97-248) (TEFRA):

TABLE OF CONTENTS

A. In general.

A-1. Q. How did TEFRA change the law on withholding requirements for pensions, annuities, and other deferred income?

A. TEFRA amended the Internal Revenue Code to impose withholding requirements on designated distributions paid after December 31, 1982. Further, although under prior law individuals could elect to have Federal income tax withheld from certain pension and annuity payments, TEFRA requires withholding on all designated distributions unless the payee elects not to have withholding apply.

A-2. Q. What type of payment is a designated distribution that is subject to the new withholding rules?

A. A designated distribution is any distribution or payment from or under an employer deferred compensation plan, an individual retirement plan (as defined in section 7701(a)(37)), or a commercial annuity. However, a designated distribution does not include any portion of a distribution which it is reasonable to believe is not includible in the gross income of the payee. For rules concerning when it is reasonable to believe that all or part of a distribution is not includible in the gross income of the recipient, see questions A-24 through A-33. In addition, a payment or distribution that is treated as wages under section 3401(a) is not a designated distribution subject to the new withholding rules. For examples of these payments, see questions A-18 through A-23.

A-3. Q. What is an employer deferred compensation plan for purposes of the new withholding rules?

A. An employer deferred compensation plan is any pension, annuity, profit-sharing, stock bonus, or other plan that defers the receipt of compensation.

A-4. Q. What is a commercial annuity for purposes of the new withholding rules?

A. A commercial annuity is an annuity, endowment, or life insurance contract issued by an insurance company licensed to do business under the laws of any State. See, also, question f-21.

A-5. Q. When does the new law take effect?

A. In general, withholding is required on any designated distribution made after December 31, 1982. In the case of periodic payments beginning before January 1, 1983, the first payment after December 31, 1982 is treated as the first periodic payment for purposes of the withholding requirements. The Secretary has authority to delay (but not beyond June 30, 1983) the application of these withholding provisions to any payor if the payor can establish that it is impossible to comply with these provisions without undue hardship. Additionally, no penalty will be imposed for failure to withhold on periodic payments if the failure occurs before July 1, 1983, and if a good faith attempt is made to comply.

Procedures for requesting a delay in implementation of the withholding provisions are under consideration.

A-6. Q. What effect does the new law have on the old law provisions relating to withholding of tax from annuity payments by request?

A. If payment is part of a designated distribution, the rules of section 3402(o) (relating to voluntary withholding on certain payments) do not apply. Therefore, a payee receiving amounts that are subject to withholding under the new provisions described in this regulation may not choose to use the voluntary withholding system of section 3402(o) with respect to those amounts. Also, if a payee had a fixed amount withheld by request, a different amount will probably be withheld when the new provisions take effect unless the rule provided in question A-7 applies. However, section 3402(o) will continue to apply to annuity payments that are not designated distributions, to sick pay, and to supplemental unemployment benefits.

A-7. Q. If a recipient of a pension or annuity has previously elected voluntary withholding under section 3402(o), is the Form W-4P effective for withholding on payments after December 31, 1982?

A. Yes, if the plan administrator or payor wishes to honor it; the Form W-4P can be treated by the plan administrator or payor as an election to withhold the flat dollar amount specified on the form if the payee is notified of his right to elect out of withholding and if he is notified that his previously filed W-4P will remain effective unless he elects out of withholding or files a new withholding certificate. If these requirements are met the plan administrator or payor may treat the Form W-4P as a voluntary withholding agreement under section 3402(p). See, also, section 3402(i). These amounts withheld should be reported in the same manner as amounts withheld under section 3405.

A-8. Q. What amount of Federal income tax will be withheld from designated distributions?

A. The amount to be withheld by any payor (or, in certain cases, a plan administrator) depends upon whether the payment is a periodic payment, a nonperiodic distribution other than a qualified total distribution, or a qualified total distribution. However, the maximum amount to be withheld cannot exceed the sum of the amount of money and the fair market value of property (other than employer securities as defined in section 402(a)(3)) received in the distribution.

A-9. Q. What is a periodic payment?

A. A periodic payment is an annuity or similar periodic payment whether paid by a licensed life insurance company, a financial institution, or a plan. The term "annuity" means a series of payments payable over a period greater than one year and taxable under section 72 as amounts received as an annuity, whether or not the payments are variable in amount.

A-10. Q. How will Federal income tax be withheld from a periodic payment?

A. In the case of a periodic payment, amounts are withheld as if the payment were a payment of wages by an employer to the employee for the appropriate payroll period. If the payee has not filed a withholding certificate, the amount to be withheld is calculated by treating the payee as a married individual claiming three withholding allowances.

For additional questions and answers concerning periodic payments, see part B.

A-11. Q. How will Federal income tax be withheld from a "qualified total distribution?"

A. A "qualified total distribution" means any designated distribution which it is reasonable to believe is made within one taxable year of the payee, is made from or under a qualified plan described in section 401(a) or section 403(a), and consists of the balance to the credit of the employee under the plans. For additional questions and answers concerning qualified total distributions, see part C. The amount to be withheld on qualified total distributions will be determined under tables prescribed by the Secretary that approximate the tax that would be imposed under section 402(e) if the payee elected to treat the distribution as a lump sum distribution within the meaning of section 402(e)(4)(A). See, in this respect, question C-8.

A-12. Q. What amount of Federal income tax will be withheld from a designated distribution that is not a periodic payment or a qualified total distribution?

A. If a designated distribution is not a periodic payment or a qualified total distribution, the amount to be withheld is computed by multiplying the amount of the designated distribution by 10 percent.

A-13. Q. Who must withhold?

A. Generally, the payor of a designated distribution must withhold, and is liable for payment of, the tax required to be withheld. However, in the case of a distribution from a plan described in section 401(a) (relating to pension, profit-sharing, and stock bonus plans), section 403(a) (relating to certain annuity plans), or section 301(d) of the Tax Reduction Act of 1975 (relating to certain employee stock ownership plans, sometimes called "TRASOP's"), the plan administrator must withhold, and is liable for payment of, the withheld tax unless he directs the payor to withhold the tax and furnishes the payor with any information that may be required by the Secretary in forms or regulations. This provision applies to qualified plans as well as once qualified plans that are no longer qualified. For a description of the material that the plan administrator must furnish to the payor, see question E-3.

A-14. Q. Who is a plan administrator?

A. Under section 414(g), the plan administrator is the person specifically designated as the plan administrator by the terms of the plan or trust. If the plan or trust does not specifically designate the plan administrator (as provided in section 1.414(g)-1(a) of the Income Tax Regulations), then the plan administrator is generally determined as follows:

(1) In the case of a plan maintained by a single employer, the employer is the plan administrator.

(2) In the case of a plan maintained by two or more employers or jointly by one or more employers and one or more employee organizations, the association, committee, joint board of trustees, or other similar group of representatives who maintain the plan is the plan administrator.

(3) In the case in which (1) or (2) does not apply, the person actually responsible for the control, disposition, or management of the assets is the plan administrator.

A-15. Q. If a bank trustee, regulated investment company, or insurance company makes a periodic payment to a payee solely at the direction of an employer sponsored individual retirement account (IRA), is the bank trustee, regulated investment company or insurance company a payor subject to the pension withholding provisions?

A. Yes. the term "payor" generally means the person actually paying the annuity or other payment (even if the person is acting as an agent). Because this is not a payment from a plan described in section 401(a) or 403(a), responsibility for withholding is on the bank trustee, regulated investment company, or insurance company and not on the employer who sponsors the account.

A-16. Q. If a bank trustee transfers plan funds to the employer who sponsors a plan described in section 401(a) and the employer makes the designated distributions, is the employer a payor?

A. Yes. The employer is a payor because it acts as an agent for the bank trustee. Even though the plan administrator has transferred liability to the bank trustee under section 3405(c)(2), the transfer of funds to the employer does not relieve the bank trustee of its liability for withholding because the rule on transfer of liability only applies to plan administrators. Therefore, if the employer fails to withhold on designated distributions, either the employer or the bank trustee may be liable for failure to withhold. Note, however, that the plan administrator could transfer liability for withholding to the employer as payor under section 3405(c)(2). See, in this respect, questions E-2 and E-3.

A-17. Q. Do the withholding provisions apply to annuities paid from an employer deferred compensation plan, an individual retirement plan, or a commercial annuity to the surviving spouse or other beneficiary of a deceased payee?

A. Yes.

A-18. Q. Do these withholding provisions apply to designated distributions under all nonqualified employer deferred compensation plans?

A. No. The withholding provisions relating to pensions and annuities do not apply to any amounts that are wages without regard to these provisions. Wages to which the general wage withholding rules apply mean any remuneration paid by an employer for services performed by an employee unless the amount paid falls within one of the exceptions of section 3401(a). For example, wages do not include remuneration paid to, or on behalf of, an employee or beneficiary from or to a trust qualified under section 401(a) and tax-exempt under section 501(a). There is no exception for contributions to, or benefits paid from, some nonqualified plans. In general, any contributions to, or benefits from, a nonqualified plan that are taxable under section 83 are subject to wage withholding at the time that they are includible in the recipient's gross income.

A-19. Q. Do these withholding provisions apply to designated distributions from a bond purchase plan described in section 405(a)?

A. Yes. Although a bond purchase plan is not a qualified plan, section 3402(a) does not apply to contributions to, or distributions from, such a plan. Therefore, designated distributions from a bond purchase plan are subject to the new withholding rules of section 3405. Similarly, the new withholding rules apply to designated distributions of an individual retirement bond described in section 409 or from an annuity plan described in section 403(a). For purposes of the withholding provisions of section 3405, a designated distribution from a bond purchase plan described in section 405(a) or an individual retirement bond described in section 409 occurs when an individual redeems a bond.

A-20. Q. Do these withholding provisions apply to designated distributions from a tax-sheltered annuity described in section 403(b)?

A. Yes. Section 31.3401(a)-1(b)(1)(i) of the Employment Tax Regulations provides that there is no withholding required under the wage withholding provisions to the extent that any amounts are taxable under the rules of section 72 or 403. Because designated distributions are not subject to the general wage withholding provisions, the new provisions of section 3405 apply to these designated distributions.

A-21. Q. An employer maintains a nonqualified deferred compensation plan such as a supplemental executive retirement ("top hat") plan. Payments under the plan are made in the form of a single sum payment at retirement. Amounts paid at retirement are includible in income as compensation in the year received. Must the payor withhold on these amounts according to the rules in section 3405?

A. No. Section 3405(d)(1)(B)(i) provides that a designated distribution on which withholding is required does not include amounts that are wages without regard to the rules of section 3405. Therefore, withholding on payments that are includible in income as compensation are based on the rules for withholding on wages contained in section 3402.

A-22. Q. Do the withholding provisions of section 3405 apply to a retirement plan maintained by a State or local government on behalf of its employees?

A. Yes. A retirement plan maintained by a State or local government on behalf of its employees is a plan that defers the receipt of compensation. The fact that a plan deferring the receipt of compensation is maintained by a governmental unit does not make the withholding provisions inapplicable. Thus, annuity payments and other distributions under the Federal Civil Service Retirement System or under the plan of any State or municipality are subject to withholding.

A-23. Q. Are payments from a state or local plan of deferred compensation described in section 457 subject to the withholding requirements of section 3405?

A. No. Amounts paid from a plan described in section 457 are paid from a plan that defers the receipt of compensation. However, amounts paid from a deferred compensation plan described in section 457 are wages under section 3401(a). Therefore, the general wage withholding rules, not the special rules of section 3405, apply to these payments.

A-24. Q. An individual retires and begins receiving periodic payments under a commercial annuity contract that was distributed to him from a contributory qualified plan. The insurance company is the payor and is liable for withholding because the plan administrator has transferred liability under the rules of section 3405(c)(2). Must the payor determine whether the employee's investment in the contract is recoverable within three years?

A. Yes. Under section 72(d), if the annuity payments during the first three years equal or exceed the amount contributed by the employee to the plan, no amounts are includible in income until the employee's contributions are recovered. Because the application of section 72(d) may affect the extent to which it is reasonable to believe that amounts are not includible in income and, therefore, not subject to withholding, the payor must determine whether section 72(d) applies to the annuity payments. As a general rule, the information necessary to determine the employee's investment in the contract must be provided to the payor by the plan administrator. See, however, questions A-27 and A-33.

A-25. Q. If the payor in question A-24 determines that the employee's investment in the contract is not recoverable within 3 years, must the payor compute the exclusion ratio under section 72(b) to calculate the amount of each payment that is not includible in gross income?

A. Yes. The operation of section 72(b) affects the extent to which it is reasonable to believe that amounts are not includible in gross income. Therefore, the payor must compute the exclusion ratio to determine what portion of each payment is subject to withholding under section 3405. As a general rule, the information necessary to determine the employee's exclusion ratio must be provided to the payor by the plan administrator. See, however, questions A-27 and A-33.

A-26. Q. In questions A-24 and A-25, may the payor *(i.e.,* the insurance company) rely on the information furnished by the plan administrator to determine the amounts that are includible in gross income?

A. In the absence of information to the contrary supplied by the payee, the payor may rely on the information furnished by the plan administrator. See, with respect to the plan administrator's duty to report to the payor, questions E-2 and E-3.

A-27. Q. What is the result in questions A-24 and A-25 if the plan administrator fails to provide the payor with any information concerning the amount of employee contributions?

A. Until the earlier of December 31, 1983, or the date on which the plan administrator provides the payor with information concerning the amount of employee contributions, it is reasonable for the payor to assume that the employee's investment in the annuity contract is zero unless the payor has independent specific knowledge of the amount of employee contributions. Additionally, if the payee notifies the payor of the amount of employee contributions, the payor must compute the taxable portion of the payment based on the information supplied by the payee. If the plan administrator fails to provide the payor with this information on or before December 31, 1983, the plan administrator will be liable for failure to withhold and pay the tax due. See questions E-2 through E-5 for rules on the plan administrator's ability to transfer liability for withholding to the payor. See also question A-33 with respect to the plan administrator's failure to provide the necessary information prior to December 31, 1983.

A-28. Q. If a beneficiary receives the balance to the credit of an employee from an annuity described in section 403(b) on account of the employee's death, is it reasonable to believe that the $5,000 death benefit exclusion of section 101(b) is not includible in gross income?

A. Yes. Although the amount of the death benefit exclusion allowable may be limited by section 101(b)(2)(B)(iii), the payor, for withholding purposes, may use the maximum death benefit exclusion ($5,000) in computing the amount of the distribution that is subject to withholding. See also, in this respect, question C-3.

A-29. Q. What is the appropriate treatment of a distribution (whether periodic or nonperiodic) that includes employer securities?

A. Employer securities are significant in the calculation of amounts subject to withholding in two respects. First, the maximum amount to be withheld cannot exceed the sum of the amount of money plus the fair market value of property received, except employer securities. In other words, a payor will not be forced to dispose of employer securities in order to meet withholding tax liability. Thus, for example, if an individual receives a distribution from a stock bonus plan that includes $1,000 worth of employer stock and $5 in cash for payment of fractional shares of stock, all of the cash, but none of the stock, may be retained by the payor to satisfy the withholding obligation. Second, under certain circumstances, the net unrealized appreciation in employer securities is not includible in gross income. See, in this respect, the rules of sections 402(a)(1) and 402(e)(4)(J).

A-30. Q. Is it reasonable to believe that all net unrealized appreciation from employer securities is not includible in gross income in the case of a qualified total distribution?

A. Yes. Although a qualified total distribution may include a distribution that is not a lump sum distribution, it is reasonable to believe that all net unrealized appreciation from employer securities is not includible in gross income.

A-31. Q. Is it reasonable to believe that a distribution is not includible in gross income if the distribution consists of employee contributions from a plan described in section 401(a) and the amount distributed is not specifically designated as accumulated deductible employee contributions?

A. Yes. Employee contributions to a plan described in section 401(a) are not deductible from gross income when contributed unless they are deductible employee contributions under section 72(o)(5). Unless the payor has specific knowledge that employee contributions distributed from a plan described in section 401(a) are accumulated deductible employee contributions, it is reasonable to assume that the amounts are excludible from gross income in the year when received.

A-32. Q. In the case of disability payments paid under a noncontributory plan to a disability retiree who has not attained age 65, is it reasonable to believe that all amounts paid to the payee are includible in gross income?

A. Yes. Whether or not all or part of the disability payments paid under a noncontributory plan to a permanently disabled retiree who has not attained age 65 are includible in gross income depends on the adjusted gross income of the taxpayer and on whether the taxpayer is permanently and totally disabled. In this situation, it is reasonable for the payor to assume that all amounts paid to the payee are includible in gross income unless the payor has specific independent knowledge that all or part of the periodic payments are not includible in gross income. Additionally, if the payee notifies the payor of the amount excludible from gross income, the payor must compute the taxable portion of the payment based on information provided by the payee.

A-33. Q. In the case of a periodic payment, is it reasonable to believe that all amounts paid to the payee are includible in gross income?

A. Yes. As an alternative to the general rule that a designated distribution does not include amounts which it is reasonable to believe are not includible in gross income, the payor of any periodic payment may assume that the entire amount of the payment is includible in gross income. The wage withholding tables must be used without adjustment for the fact that Federal income tax is being withheld on the gross amount. If the payor uses this alternative method of calculating the amount of the designated distribution, he must include with the notice of the election not to have withholding apply the following additional statements:

(1) tax will be withheld on the gross amount of the payment even though the payee may be receiving amounts that are not subject to withholding because they are excludible from gross income;

(2) this withholding procedure may result in excess withholding on the payment; and

(3) the payee may adjust the allowances claimed on the withholding certificate if he wants a lesser amount withheld from each payment or he may provide the payor with the information necessary to calculate the taxable portion of each payment.

This alternative will not apply to periodic payments made after the earlier of December 31, 1983, or the date on which the plan administrator supplies the payor with the information necessary to calculate the taxable portion of the distribution.

See, also, questions E-3, E-4, and E-5.

A-34. Q. May the payor rely on a plan administrator's computation of the amount to be withheld?

A. Yes. Although the plan administrator is not required to compute the amount to be withheld in order to transfer liability for withholding to the payor, the plan administrator may provide such information to the payor, and the payor may rely on such computations unless the payor knows or has reason to know that the computations are incorrect.

A-35. Q. Under the plans of certain States, individuals may receive payments from more than one retirement system, such as payments from the state's teacher's retirement plan and from the state's regular retirement plan. Must these payments be aggregated for purposes of providing a single notice and election to a payee or for purposes of determining whether the floor on withholding tax (i.e., $5,400 for a married individual claiming three allowances) has been reached?

A. No. However, if it is feasible to aggregate payments under more than one retirement system, the payor is permitted to do so for these purposes.

A-36. Q. If a payment is made by one check to more than one beneficiary, such as a surviving spouse and a minor child, how is the amount to be withheld computed?

A. The payor may compute the withholding on a payment made by one check to more than one beneficiary as if the payment were made to only one beneficiary. In this case, the payor must base withholding for the total amount of the designated distribution on the withholding certificate of the payee to whom the election was sent.

Alternatively, if each payee files a withholding certificate and the payor knows the amount of the payment to which each payee is entitled, the payor may determine the amount to be withheld with respect to each payee. If the payor does not know the amount of the payment to which each payee is entitled, he may treat the payment as being made pro-rata to each payee. If only one withholding certificate is received, the payor must base withholding for the total amount of the designated distribution on the withholding certificate of one of the payees, such as the surviving spouse's certificate. Thus, if notice of the election not to have withholding apply is supplied to each payee at the times required in section 3405(c)(10) and only one payee makes the election or files a certificate, the payor must assume that the election or filing was made by the payee on behalf of the other payees.

A-37. Q. If a payor makes an error in computing the amount of a designated distribution that is subject to withholding, must the payor make a retroactive correction of the error?

A. No, provided the error was a reasonable one. Thus, if a payor either underwithholds or overwithholds because the amount of the designated distribution (i.e., the taxable portion of the payment) was incorrectly calculated, no retroactive make-up is required if one of the following applies: (1) the payor reasonably relied on information furnished by the plan administrator (including the computation of the amount to be withheld), (2) the payor relied on a payee's representations on the withholding certificate, (3) the payor reasonably relied on the rules of this regulation, or (4) the payor made a mathematical error in computations. However, if the amount of the designated distribution is correctly computed, but the payor makes an error in applying the withholding tables, the normal rules concerning failure to withhold and pay the tax will apply.

B. Withholding on Periodic Payments.

B-1. Q. Is the payor of periodic payments required to aggregate such payments with a payee's compensation to determine the amount of tax to be withheld under section 3405(a)(1)?

A. No. Although the payor must withhold from any periodic payment the amount that has to be withheld if the payment were a payment of wages by an employer to an employee for a payroll period, the amount to be withheld under section 3405(a)(1) is calculated separately of any amounts that actually are wages to the payee for the same period.

B-2. Q. Can either the percentage method (section 3402(b)) or the wage bracket method (section 3402(c)) be used to determine the withholding liability on a periodic payment?

A. Yes. Withholding on a periodic payment is accomplished by treating the payment as if it were wages. Therefore, unless the employee has elected not to have withholding apply, any method of withholding that is an appropriate method for withholding on wages is also an appropriate method for withholding on periodic payments. Refer to the Employer's Tax Guide (Circular E) and Publication 493, Alternative Tax Withholding Methods and Tables for the general procedures on withholding, deposit, payment, and reporting of Federal income tax withheld. Note, however, that any specific procedures contained in this regulation take precedence over any contrary rules in Circular E and Publication 493.

B-3. Q. Do rules similar to those for wage withholding apply to the filing of a withholding certificate for periodic payments?

A. Yes. Unless the rules of section 3405 specifically conflict with the rules of section 3402, the rules for withholding on periodic payments will parallel the rules for wage withholding. Thus, if a withholding certificate is filed by a payee, it will generally take effect as provided in section 3402(f)(3) for certificates filed to replace existing certificates. If a withholding certificate is furnished by a payee on or before the date on which payments commence, it takes effect with respect to payments made more than 30 days after the certificate is furnished, unless the payor elects to make it effective at an earlier date. If a withholding certificate is furnished by a payee after the date on which payments commence, it takes effect with respect to payments made on or after the status determination date (January 1, May 1, July 1, or October 1) that is at least 30 days after the date the certificate is filed, unless the payor elects to make it effective at an earlier date. If no withholding certificate is filed, the amount withheld is determined as if the payee were a married person claiming three withholding allowances.

B-4. Q. If no withholding certificate has been filed and the payor is aware that the payee is single, is it still appropriate to base withholding on a married individual claiming three allowances?

A. Yes. If no withholding certificate is filed, the payor is not required or permitted to base withholding on the amount of allowances the payee actually is entitled to claim. Thus, the payor must base withholding on the rates for a married person with three withholding allowances.

B-5. Q. May a payor determine whether payments to an individual are subject to withholding based on the amount of the first periodic payment for the year?

A. No. Periodic payments can vary during a calendar year because of make-up of past due payments, variable rates of payments, or cost-of-living adjustments, so that withholding based on the first payment within a year may be an inaccurate measure of withholding on total payments for the year. Therefore, the amount to be withheld is determined each payment period in the same manner as applies to withholding on wages. See, in this respect, Circular E and the regulations under section 3402.

B-6. Q. If a payment period is specified as by the terms of a commercial annuity contract, must this period be used as the appropriate period for determining the amount to be withheld?

A. Yes. Similarly, if the payment period is designated in a plan administrator's report or on an individual retirement account payout schedule agreed to by payor and payee, this period must be used as the appropriate payment period.

B-7. Q. If the payor received no report from the plan administrator or beneficiary concerning the payment period, but knows the frequency of payments, can the known frequency be used as the appropriate payment period?

A. Yes. However, if no report is received and the payor has no knowledge of the frequency of payments, then he must treat the distribution as a nonperiodic distribution. Therefore, a distribution cannot be a periodic payment unless the frequency of payments is known. See, in this respect, questions B-8 and C-2. For rules concerning the plan administrator's failure to provide this information, see questions E-2 and E-3.

B-8. Q. If a payee receives a one-time payment that is a make-up payment resulting from an insurance company's incorrect calculation of a monthly annuity amount, is the one-time payment part of a series of periodic payments?

A. Yes. Because the one-time payment is a catch-up of prior amounts due as periodic payments, it is treated as part of a series of periodic payments. These payments are treated for withholding purposes in a manner similar to the treatment of supplemental wage payments in section 31.3402(g)-1 of the Employment Tax Regulations.

C. Withholding on Nonperiodic Distributions.

C-1. Q. Must an individual receive a lump-sum distribution within the meaning of section 402(e)(4) to have a qualified total distribution?

A. No. A "qualified total distribution" is any distribution that (i) is a designated distribution, (ii) is reasonable to believe is made within one taxable year of the recipient, (iii) is made under a plan described in section 401(a) or 403(a), and (iv) consists of the balance to the credit of the employee under such plan. Thus, a distribution from a plan described in section 401(a) that does not meet the requirements (such as the minimum 5-year period of participation in section 402(e)(4)(H)) for a lump sum distribution within the meaning of section 402(e)(4) may still be a qualified total distribution for purposes of withholding.

C-2. Q. If a class year plan permits annual withdrawal of participants' vested amounts, are these withdrawals considered periodic payments?

A. No. A class year plan is a plan under which amounts contributed by an employer for a year become vested a number of years (e.g., five years) after the year in which the amounts are contributed. Generally, class year plans permit withdrawals each year of amounts that have vested during the year. However, these distributions are not made with respect to an established frequency of payments, so the withdrawals must be treated as nonperiodic distributions, subject to withholding at the 10 percent rate.

C-3. Q. If a beneficiary receives the balance to the credit of a payee from an annuity contract on account of the payee's death, is this final payment a nonperiodic distribution?

A. Yes. The lump sum death benefit in this situation is a one-time payment that cannot be characterized as a periodic payment. The payment may be a qualified total distribution if the requirements of section 3405(c)(4) are satisfied, but otherwise it will be treated as a nonperiodic distribution other than a qualified total distribution.

C-4. Q. Is it permissible to assume that an individual is a calendar year taxpayer for purposes of determining whether a distribution is a "qualified total distribution?"

A. Yes, unless the payor or plan administrator has reason to believe that the payee is not a calendar year taxpayer. The payor or plan administrator has reason to believe that the payee is not a calendar year taxpayer if the payee tells the payor or plan administrator that he is not a calendar year taxpayer.

C-5. Q. Is a distribution of accumulated deductible employee contributions with earnings that is paid on account of an employee's separation from service treated as a qualified total distribution?

A. Yes. As long as the other requirements for a qualified total distribution are met, a distribution of accumulated deductible employee contributions with earnings is eligible for withholding at the rate applicable to qualified total distributions even though the distribution could never be a lump sum distribution. Because accumulated deductible employee contributions are treated separately in determining whether a distribution is a qualified total distribution, the answer would be the same even if the recipient received none (or a portion) of the vested employer contributions in his account.

C-6. Q. What is meant by the "balance to the credit" of an employee under a plan described in section 401(a) or 403(a)?

A. In general, the balance to the credit of an employee includes any amount credited to the employee under the plan on the date the distribution commences. The balance to the credit of an employee includes an amount credited after the date the distribution commences if it is attributable to services performed before that date or is attributable to earnings on an amount credited to the employee before that date. Additionally, the balance to the credit of an employee includes any amount payable as an annuity with respect to the employee under the plan. Amounts that have been placed in a separate account for the funding of medical benefits under section 401(h) or amounts that are forfeitable under the plan are not included in the balance to the credit of an employee. Finally, accumulated deductible employee contributions (within the meaning of section 72(o)(5)(B)) are not included in the balance to the credit of an employee for the purposes of determining whether a distribution is a "qualified total distribution."

C-7. Q. Can a payor rely on a plan administrator's report in determining whether a distribution consists of the balance to the credit of an employee under a plan?

A. Yes. If the plan administrator does not inform the payor that the distribution consists of the balance to the credit of the employee, the payor may not assume that the distribution is a qualified total distribution and must treat the distribution as a nonperiodic distribution that is not a qualified total distribution. However, the payor may rely on the payee's representations that a distribution does consist of the balance to the credit of the employee under the plan.

C-8. Q. What table must be used to calculate the amount to be withheld from a "qualified total distribution?"

A. The table to be used for withholding on "qualified total distributions" will be published by the Secretary in the near future.

D. Notice and Election Procedures.

D-1. Q. May a payee elect not to have Federal income tax withheld from a designated distribution?

A. Yes. Withholding is not required on any periodic payment or nonperiodic distribution if the payee elects not to have withholding apply. If the payee makes this election, it is effective until revoked. The payor is required to provide each payee with notice of the right to elect not to have withholding apply and of the right to revoke the election.

D-2. Q. In the case of a designated distribution made on account of the death of an employee, who makes the election not to have withholding apply?

A. The election may be made by the beneficiary of plan benefits specified by the decedent in accordance with plan procedures or, if there is no designated beneficiary, by the beneficiary specified under the terms of the plan. If there is not a designated beneficiary and the terms of the plan do not specify a beneficiary, then the election may be made by the executor or the personal representative of the decedent.

D-3. Q. Who is required to provide notice to the payee of the payee's right not to have withholding apply?

A. Section 3405(d)(10)(B) requires the payor to provide notice to the payee of the payee's right to elect not to have withholding apply. Thus, even if the plan administrator has failed to transfer liability for withholding to the payor, the payor must provide notice to the payees.

D-4. Q. When must notice of the right to elect not to have withholding apply be given for periodic payments?

A. In the case of periodic payments, notice of the election must be provided not earlier than six months before the first payment and not later than when making the first payment. However, even if notice is provided at a date before the first payment, notice must also be given when making the first payment. Thereafter, notice must be provided at least once each calendar year of the right to make the election and to revoke the election.

D-5. Q. Must notice of the right to elect not to have withholding apply be provided to those payees whose annual payments are less than $5,400?

A. Yes. However, under the statute, notice is only required to be provided when making the first payment. Therefore, a payor may provide notice to a payee with annual payments less than $5,400 by indicating to the payee when making the first payment that no Federal income tax will be withheld unless the payee chooses to have withholding apply by filing a withholding certificate, if the payor also provides information concerning where a withholding certificate may be obtained.

D-6. Q. Must notice of the right to elect not to have withholding apply be provided in the same manner to all payees?

A. No. If the payor provides notice to all payees when making the first payment, the payor may, in addition, provide earlier notice as provided in section 3405(d)(10)(B)(i)(I) to selected groups of payees, such as those payees whose annual payments are over $5,400.

D-7. Q. Must notice be attached to the first payment to satisfy the requirement that notice be provided "when making" the first payment?

A. No. Because many payees utilize electronic funds transfer to deposit their pension or annuity checks, notice does not have to be attached physically to the check.

D-8. Q. If a payee utilizes electronic funds transfer and notice is mailed directly to the payee at the same time the check is issued, is the notice requirement satisfied even though the payee receives the notice fifteen days after the check is deposited?

A. Yes. Although it is desirable that the notice reach the payee immediately prior to or concurrent with receipt of the check, the notice requirement is deemed to be satisfied if the payee receives the notice within 15 days before or after receipt of the first payment.

D-9. Q. When is the payor required to notify the payee of his right to elect not to have withholding apply to a nonperiodic distribution?

A. Section 3405(d)(10)(B)(ii) requires that notice must be provided to the payee at the time of a nonperiodic distribution. Since notice provided at the time of the distribution could result in delay of receipt of the benefit check if the payee elects out of withholding, notice for nonperiodic distributions should be given not earlier than six months prior to the distribution and not later than the time that will give the payee reasonable time to elect not to have withholding apply and to reply to the payor with the election information. What is reasonable time depends upon the facts and circumstances of each case.

D-10. Q. What is a "reasonable time" for notice with respect to a nonperiodic distribution from a qualified plan?

A. The "reasonable time" requirement is satisfied with respect to a nonperiodic distribution if the notice is included in the basic claim for benefits application that is provided to the participant by the plan administrator.

D-11. Q. If the payor of a periodic payment provides notice of the election not to have withholding apply within the time specified by section 3405(d)(10)(B)(i)(I), may the payor specify a time prior to distribution by which the election must be made?

A. Yes. The election is not to have withholding apply is generally given effect as provided in section 3402(f)(3) for a certificate filed to replace an existing certificate. However, the payor may require that the election is made up to 30 days before the first payment to be effective for the first payment. See question B-3.

D-12. Q. If the payor of a nonperiodic distribution provides notice of the election not to have withholding apply within a reasonable time prior to the distribution, may the payor specify a time prior to distribution by which the election must be made?

A. No. The payee has the right to make or revoke an election at any time prior to the distribution. Therefore, the payor may place a deadline on the time to elect without delaying payment of the distribution, but must accept any election or revocation made up to the time of distribution.

D-13. Q. What is a "reasonable time" for notice with respect to a distribution from an individual retirement account?

A. A payor may provide notice of the election not to have withholding apply at the time the beneficiary requests a withdrawal from his individual retirement account. This rule also applies to distributions from bank sponsored prototype plans and other plans that permit withdrawals on request.

D-14. Q. If notice is provided to a payee prior to the first payment of a periodic payment, why must it also be provided at the time of the first payment or distribution?

A. Section 3405(d)(10)(B)(i)(II) of the Internal Revenue Code requires such notice. In addition, because the payee has the right to make an election or to revoke a prior election at any time prior to the beginning of the payment period, notice must be provided when making the first payment in order to offer the payee ample opportunity to make or revoke an election not to have withholding apply even if the election will not be effective until later payments.

D-15. Q. If a payee who has been receiving periodic payments is rehired by the same employer, has his benefits suspended, and then recommences receiving periodic payments, must notice again be provided to the payee?

A. Yes. Upon recommencement of benefits, the first payment thereafter is treated as the first payment for purposes of the notice requirements.

D-16. Q. Must a payor provide notice if it is reasonable to believe that the entire amount payable is excludible from the payee's gross income?

A. No. Amounts which it is reasonable to believe are not includible in gross income are not designated distributions. Therefore, no notice is required of the ability to elect not to have withholding apply.

D-17. Q. If the payor of a periodic payment under a qualified plan knows that an employee's investment in an annuity contract will be recovered within three years, must he provide notice of the right to elect out of withholding at the time the first payment is made?

A. No. The first payment is not a designated distribution, and, therefore, is not a periodic payment subject to the notice requirements of section 3405(d)(10)(B)(i). There is no withholding obligation until the employee's investment in the contract is recovered because those amounts that equal the investment in the contract are not includible in gross income and, therefore, are not designated distributions. Therefore, the first payment after the employee's investment in the contract is recouped is the first payment for purposes of the notice requirements.

D-18. Q. What information concerning the election not to have withholding apply must be provided by the payor to the payee?

A. Notice to a payee must contain the following information:

(1) notice of the payee's right to elect not to have withholding apply to any payment or distribution and how to make that election,

(2) notice of the payee's right to revoke such an election at any time and a statement that the election remains effective until revoked,

(3) a statement to advise payees that penalties may be incurred under the estimated tax payment rules if the payments of estimated tax are not adequate and sufficient tax is not withheld from the payment or distribution.

In the event that the payor does not know what part of a distribution is includible in gross income and treats these payments as provided in question A-33, the following additional statements must be included with the notice:

(1) tax will be withheld on the gross amount of the payment even though the payee may be receiving amounts that are not subject to withholding because they are excludible from gross income,

(2) this withholding procedure may result in excess withholding on the payment, and

(3) the payee may adjust his allowances claimed on the withholding certificate if he wants a lesser amount withheld from each payment or he may provide the payor with the information necessary to calculate the taxable portion of each payment.

D-19. Q. Is there any information that, although not required, it is desirable to include in the notice to payees?

A. It is desirable to include a statement in the notice to payees that the election not to have withholding apply is prospective only and that any election made after a payment or distribution to the payee is not an election with respect to that payment or distribution.

D-20. Q. May the plan administrator provide the notice to payees on behalf of the payor?

A. The plan administrator may provide notice on behalf of the payor. However, the payor has sole responsibility for providing this notice whether or not the plan administrator has shifted liability for withholding to the payor, and if the plan administrator fails to provide adequate notice, the payor is responsible.

D-21. Q. Is there a sample notice that can be used to satisfy the notice requirement for periodic payments?

A. Yes. Any payor who uses the following sample notice is deemed to satisfy the notice requirement if notice is timely provided:

NOTICE OF WITHHOLDING ON PERIODIC PAYMENTS Beginning on January 1, 1983, the [pension] OR [annuity] payments you receive from the [insert name of plan or company] will be subject to Federal income tax withholding unless you elect not to have withholding apply. Withholding will only apply to the portion of your [pension] OR [annuity] payment that is already included in your income subject to Federal income tax and will be like wage withholding. Thus, there will be no withholding on the return of your own nondeductible contributions to the [plan] OR [contract].

You may elect not to have withholding apply to your [pension] OR [annuity] payments by returning the signed and dated election [manner may be specified] to [insert name and address]. Your election will remain in effect until you revoke it. You may revoke your election at any time by returning the signed and dated revocation to [insert appropriate name or address]. Any election or revocation will be effective no later than the January 1, May 1, July 1, or October 1 after it is received, so long as it is received at least 30 days before that date. You may make and revoke elections not to have withholding apply as often as you wish. Additional elections may be obtained from [insert name and address].

If you do not return the election by [insert date], Federal income tax will be withheld from the taxable portion of your [pension] OR [annuity] payments as if you were a married individual claiming three withholding allowances. As a result, no Federal income tax will be withheld if the taxable portion of your annual [pension] OR [annuity] payments are less than $5,400.

If you elect not to have withholding apply to your [pension] OR [annuity] payments, or if you do not have enough Federal income tax withheld from your [pension] OR [annuity] payments, you may be responsible for payment of estimated tax. You may incur penalties under the estimated tax rules if your withholding and estimated tax payments are not sufficient.

D-22. Q. Is there sample language that may be used to elect not to have withholding apply or to revoke a prior election not to have withholding apply?

A. Yes. A payee may elect not have withholding apply or revoke a prior election in any manner that clearly shows the payee's intent. The following language would suffice:

NOTICE OF WITHHOLDING ON DISTRIBUTIONS OR WITHDRAWALS FROM ANNUITIES, IRA'S, PENSION, PROFIT SHARING, STOCK BONUS, AND OTHER DEFERRED COMPENSATION PLANS

Instructions: Check Box A if you do not want any Federal income tax withheld from your [pension] OR [annuity]. Check Box B to revoke an election not to have withholding apply. Return the signed and dated election to [insert name and address].

Even if you elect not to have Federal income tax withheld, you are liable for payment of Federal income tax on the taxable portion of your [pension] OR [annuity]. You also may be subject to tax penalties under the estimated tax payment rules if your payments of estimated tax and withholding, if any, are not adequate.

A ___ I do not want to have Federal income tax withheld from my [pension] OR [annuity].

B ___ I want to have Federal income tax withheld from my [pension] OR [annuity].

Signed:

________________ ________________
Name Date

Return your completed election to: [insert name and address]

D-23. Q. May the payee's election be combined with a withholding certificate?

A. Yes. The payor may provide a single statement for the payee to fill out and return that would enable the payee to elect not to have withholding apply or to revoke a previous election and, at the same time, would enable the payee to claim the number of withholding allowances and, also, the dollar amount the payee wants withheld.

D-24. Q. Will a notice mailed to the last known address of the payee fulfill the notice requirement of section 3405(d)(10)(B)?

A. Yes.

D-25. Q. Is there a sample notice that can be used to satisfy the notice requirement for nonperiodic distributions?

A. Yes. Any payor who uses the following sample notice is deemed to satisfy the notice requirement if notice is timely provided:

ELECTION FOR PAYEES OF NONPERIODIC PAYMENTS The [distributions] OR [withdrawals] you receive from the [insert name of plan or company] are subject to Federal income tax withholding unless you elect not to have withholding apply. Withholding will only apply to the portion of your [distribution] OR [withdrawal] that is included in your income subject to Federal income tax. Thus, for example, there will be no withholding on the return of your own nondeductible contributions to the [plan] OR [contract].

You may elect not to have withholding apply to your [distribution] OR [withdrawal] payments by signing and dating the attached election and returning it [manner may be specified] to [insert name and address].

If you do not return the election by [insert date] receipt of your payments may be delayed. If you do not respond by the date your [distribution] OR [withdrawal] is scheduled to begin, Federal income tax will be withheld from the taxable portion of your [distribution] OR [withdrawal]. [Insert information on rates if desired].

If you elect not to have withholding apply to your [distribution] OR [withdrawal] payments, or if you do not have enough Federal income tax withheld from your [distribution] OR [withdrawal] , you may be responsible for payment of estimated tax. You may incur penalties under the estimated tax rules if your withholding and estimated tax payments are not sufficient.

D-26. Q. Is there sample language that may be used for payees of nonperiodic distributions to elect not to have withholding apply?

A. Yes. A payee of a nonperiodic distribution may elect not to have withholding apply in any manner that clearly shows the payee's intent. The following language would suffice:

ELECTION FOR PAYEES OF NONPERIODIC PAYMENTS

Instructions: If you do not want any Federal income tax withheld from your [distribution] OR [withdrawal], sign and date this election and return it to [insert name and address].

Even if you elect not to have Federal income tax withheld, you are liable for payment of Federal income tax on the taxable portion of your [distribution] OR [withdrawal]. You also may be subject to tax penalties under the estimated tax payment rules if your payments of estimated tax and withholding, if any, are not adequate.

I do not want to have Federal income tax withheld from my [distribution] OR [withdrawal].

Signed:

________________ ________________
Name Date

Return your completed election to: [insert name and address]

D-27. Q. If the payor provides notice prior to making the first payment, can an abbreviated notice be used to satisfy the notice requirement of section 3405(d)(10)(B)(i)(II)?

A. Yes. It is permissible to provide with the payment a statement that the payee has the right to elect out of withholding. For example, the following sample notice could be used to satisfy the notice requirement if the payor has provided notice previously:

If Federal income taxes have been withheld from the [pension] OR [annuity] payments you are receiving and if you do not wish to have taxes withheld, you should notify [insert name and address]. However, if you elect not to have withholding apply to your [pension] OR [annuity] payments, or if you do not have enough Federal income tax withheld from your [pension] OR [annuity] payment, you may be responsible for payment of estimated tax. You may incur penalties under the estimated tax rules if your withholding and estimated tax payments are not sufficient.

If Federal income taxes are not being withheld from your [pension] OR [annuity] payment because you have elected not to have withholding apply and if you wish to revoke that election and have Federal income taxes withheld from your [pension] OR [annuity] payments, you should notify [insert name and address].

D-28. Q. Must an employee who receives a distribution from a plan described in section 401(a) that includes amounts attributable to employer contributions and to accumulated deductible employee contributions make two elections not to have withholding apply?

A. No. Although accumulated deductible employee contributions are treated separately in determining whether a distribution is a qualified total distribution, an employee needs to make only one election not to have withholding apply to any distributions occurring at the same time from or under the same plan. However, the plan administrator could require the employee to make separate elections with respect to the distributions.

D-29. Q. If the administrator of a plan described in section 401(a) makes a qualified total distribution to an employee out of funds contained in two or more trusts, must the employee make a separate election not to have withholding apply with respect to the distribution from each trust?

A. No. The fact that a plan may use several trusts does not eliminate treatment of the distribution as a single qualified total distribution for which only one election is necessary.

D-30. Q. Is it permissible to provide notice to persons already in pay status on January 1, 1983, in a newsletter of the plan administrator?

A. Yes, provided that this notice is received by the payee within 15 days of the payee's receipt of the first periodic payment after December 31, 1982, and such notice provides the means to make an election and instructions for electing not to have withholding apply. It is desirable that payees be afforded the maximum opportunity to make the election provided by section 3405(a)(2). Payors are encouraged to give payees notice of their election opportunities at least 30 days before the first periodic payment after December 31, 1982.

D-31. Q. Is it permissible to provide the annual notice required by section 3405(d)(10)(B)(i)(III) on January 1, 1984, December 31, 1985, and January 1, 1986?

A. No. The annual notice required by section 3405(d)(10)(B)(i)(III) should be provided at approximately the same time each calendar year.

D-32. Q. Under what circumstances may an election made with respect to a nonperiodic distribution apply to subsequent distributions?

A. Generally, any election not to have withholding apply to a nonperiodic distribution may apply to any subsequent payment or distribution from or under the same plan or arrangement. However, the payor must still provide notice of the election and revocation procedures upon each subsequent distribution and must include the statement concerning liability for payment of estimated tax if the payee does not have withholding applied.

D-33. Q. How may a payee who intends to make a qualifying rollover (as defined in section 402(a)(5) or section 408(d)(3)) of a distribution elect not to have Federal income tax withheld from the distribution?

A. The payee may elect not to have withholding apply by making the election on the form provided by the payor. Alternatively, if the payee directs the payor to pay over the distribution to a qualified plan or an individual retirement account, the payor may treat this direction as an election not to have withholding apply.

D-34. Q. If a payee claims more than 14 withholding allowances on a withholding certificate, must the payor remit a copy of the withholding certificate to the Internal Revenue Service?

A. No. Because a payee may, at any time, elect out of withholding, the rules of section 31.3402(f)(2)-1(g) of the Employment Tax Regulations do not apply. Therefore, a payee may claim more than 14 allowances and the payor need not remit the withholding certificate to the Internal Revenue Service.

E. Reporting and Recordkeeping.

E-1. Q. If designated distributions are made from or under a plan described in section 401(a), who has responsibility for making the returns and reports required by section 6047(e)?

A. Generally, the plan administrator, as defined in section 414(g), is responsible for maintaining the records and making the reports required by section 6047(e). However, if the plan administrator fails to keep the required records and make the required reports, the employer maintaining the plan is responsible for the reports and returns.

E-2. Q. How may a plan administrator of a plan described in section 401(a) or 403(a) transfer his duty to withhold to a payor?

A. A plan administrator of a plan described in section 401(a) or 403(a) may transfer the liability for withholding by (1) directing the payor in writing to withhold the tax and (2) providing the payor with any required information. This direction is presumed to remain in effect until the plan administrator revokes it in writing.

E-3. Q. What information must the plan administrator provide to the payor in order to transfer his liability for withholding?

A. The general rule is that the plan administrator must provide the payor with all information necessary to compute correctly the withholding tax liability. To satisfy this requirement, the plan administrator must explicitly inform the payor of the information that would be reportable on the Form W-2P or 1099R or that such information is not applicable to a particular payee or to any payments under the plan. For example, if the plan administrator is silent with respect to any employee contributions, he has not satisfied his reporting obligation even if there are no employee contributions to the plan. Thus, the plan administrator is expected to provide the payor with the following minimum information:

(1) the name, address, and social security number of the payee and the payee's spouse or other beneficiary if applicable,

(2) the existence and amount of any employee contributions,

(3) the amount of accumulated deductible employee contributions, if any,

(4) the payee's cost basis in any employer securities and the current fair market value of the securities,

(5) the existence and amount of any premiums paid for the current cost of life insurance that were previously includible in income,

(6) a statement of the reason (e.g., death, disability, retirement) for the payment or distribution,

(7) the date on which payments commence and the amount and frequency of payments,

(8) the age of the payee and of the payee's spouse or designated beneficiary if applicable, and

(9) any other information required by Form W-2P or 1099R.

If, prior to December 31, 1983, the plan administrator fails to provide the payor with the information required in items (2) through (5) the payor is liable for withholding. However, the payor may withhold on the payment as if all amounts are includible in gross income. See question A-33.

E-4. Q. If, after December 31, 1983, the plan administrator does not notify the payor of the amount of employee contributions with respect to one payee, has withholding liability shifted to the payor?

A. Yes. The plan administrator satisfies the requirements of question E-3 as to the information that must be supplied to the payor so long as the failure to provide the required information occurs on an infrequent basis or the plan administrator informs the payor in writing that he has made a good faith effort to supply all the required information but the amount of employee contributions as to a particular payee is unavailable.

E-5. Q. If, after December 31, 1983, the plan administrator fails to supply the payor with any information concerning the existence or amount of any employee contributions, has withholding liability shifted to the payor?

A. No. The plan administrator has not satisfied his reporting obligation as required in question E-3 as to employee contributions even if there are no employee contributions unless he affirmatively states that there are no employee contributions or states that the reporting of this item is not applicable in determining the payee's tax liability.

E-6. Q. Is it permissible to satisfy the requirements of section 6047(e) by maintaining records necessary to provide the information contained on Forms W-2P and 1099R?

A. Section 6047(e) will be satisfied if, in addition to the information necessary to complete Forms W-2P and 1099R, the following information is maintained:

(1) payee's date of birth (if known), and date of spouse's or designated beneficiary's birth (if applicable and known);

(2) plan administrator's name, address, and employer identification number (EIN);

(3) plan's name and identification number and sponsor's name, address, and EIN; and

(4) date on which payments commence and amount and frequency of payments.

E-7. Q. If the interim method of withholding on periodic payments (i.e., withholding on the gross amount) is used, must the employer, plan administrator, or issuer of any contract still maintain the information required by Form W-2P?

A. Yes. Even if this interim method is used, the recipient must be provided with the information that will enable him to determine his tax liability and adjust his claimed exemptions or claim a credit or refund.

E-8. Q. What events trigger the reporting requirements of section 6047(e)?

A. Reporting is required any time there is a designated distribution to which section 3405 applies. Therefore, the old law rule that distributions of less than $600 per year do not require reporting no longer applies. Additionally, an exchange of insurance contracts under which any designated distribution (including a tax-free exchange under section 1035) may be made is a reportable event even though a designated distribution does not occur. To insure proper reporting when a designated distribution is made under the new contract, it is anticipated that the issuer of the contract to be exchanged will provide the information necessary to compute the amount to be withheld to the policyholder and to the issuer of the new contract.

E-9. Q. Will the reporting requirement be satisfied if Form W-2P or Form 1099R is filed?

A. Yes. In the absence of other forms or regulations, the reporting requirement is satisfied if Form W-2P or Form 1099R is filed with respect to each payee.

E-10. Q. How should the payor or plan administrator remit payments of amounts withheld under section 3405?

A. The payor or plan administrator must deposit the amount withheld under section 3405 with an authorized financial institution in accordance with the provisions of § 31.6302(c)-1(a)(1)(i) of the Procedure and Administration Regulations, which provides the procedures for depositing employment taxes. For purposes of applying these procedures to amounts withheld under section 3405, the term "taxes" as defined in § 31.6302(c)-1(a)(1)(iii) includes the income tax withheld under section 3405 with respect to designated distributions. A payor or plan administrator who remits these amounts in accordance with those rules must report the amounts deposited on the same Form 941 or 941E, whichever is appropriate, that he uses to report the employment taxes he had deposited under § 31.6302(c)-1(a)(1)(i).

F. Other

F-1. Q. If a plan administrator or other payor distributes property other than cash to payees, is it permissible to use the value of the property as of the last preceding valuation date to determine the amount of Federal income tax that must be withheld from each distribution?

A. Yes. In many situations, the plan administrator or payor will not be able to determine the value of property to be distributed as of the date of distribution without delaying payment to the payee. In these cases, the plan administrator or payor may determine the value of the property to be distributed as of the last preceding valuation date prior to the date of distribution, as long as the valuation is made at least once each year. If the most recent valuation date occurred within the 90 days immediately preceding the date of distribution, the next most recent valuation date may be used.

F-2. Q. How is withholding accomplished if a payee receives only property other than employer securities?

A. A payor or plan administrator must satisfy the obligation to withhold on distributions of property other than employer securities even if this requires selling all or part of the property and distributing the cash remaining after Federal income tax is withheld. However, the payor or plan administrator may instead permit the payee to remit to the payor or plan administrator sufficient cash to satisfy the withholding obligation. Additionally, if a distribution of property other than cash includes property that is not includible in a designated distribution, such as the distribution of U.S. Savings Bonds or an annuity contract, such property need not be sold or redeemed to meet any withholding obligation.

F-3. Q. If a designated distribution includes cash and property other than employer securities, is it permissible to satisfy the withholding obligation with respect to the entire distribution by using the cash distributed, provided the cash distributed is sufficient to satisfy the

A. Yes, as long as there is sufficient cash to satisfy the withholding obligation for the entire distribution. There is no requirement that tax be withheld from each type of property in portion to its value.

F-4. Q. If a loan from a qualified plan is treated as a distribution under section 72(p), is the amount of the loan subject to withholding under section 3405?

A. Yes. If, and to the extent that, the loan is treated as a distribution when made, withholding is accomplished by withholding tax from the amount of the loan that is treated as a distribution. Thus, for example, if a loan of $12,000 that must be repaid within 5 years is made to a common law employee with a vested account balance of $5,000, $2,000 is treated as a distribution under section 72(p), and the payor or plan administrator must withhold tax from the $2,000.

F-5. Q. Is a loan that is treated as a distribution under section 72(p) a nonperiodic distribution other than a qualified total distribution?

A. Yes.

F-6. Q. Must a payor or plan administrator withhold tax on a nonperiodic distribution (including a qualified total distribution) if the amount of the distribution is less than $200?

A. No. However, all amounts received within one taxable year of the payee from the payor or plan administrator under the same plan or arrangement must be aggregated for purposes of determining whether the $200 floor is reached. If the payor or plan administrator does not know at the time a first payment of $200 or less is made whether there will be additional payments during the year for which aggregation is required, the payor or plan administrator need not withhold from the first payment. If distributions are made within one taxable year under more than one plan of an employer, the plan administrator or payor may, but need not, aggregate the distributions for purposes of determining whether the $200 floor is reached.

F-7. Q. If a nonperiodic distribution (including a qualified total distribution) to a payee will be less than $200, must the payor provide notice to the payee of the right to elect not to have withholding apply?

A. No.

F-8. Q. How is withholding accomplished if a qualified total distribution is paid in installments during one taxable year of the payee?

A. Withholding can be accomplished on a qualified total distribution that is paid in installments within one taxable year by either one of the following methods:

Under Option 1, the tax on the first installment is calculated under the qualified total distribution table. The tax on each subsequent installment is calculated by finding the tax under the table on the cumulative amount of the installments for the year and subtracting the amount of tax already withheld from the tax due with respect to the cumulative amount of the installments.

Under Option 2, the payor or plan administrator can withhold the tax on all installments except the final installment at a 10 percent rate. The tax on the final installment may be calculated by finding the tax under the qualified total distribution table on the cumulative amount of the installments for the year and subtracting the amount of tax already withheld from the installments. Option 2 may be used even if the amount of the tax that should be withheld from the final installment under the qualified total distribution tables exceeds the amount of the final installment. The plan administrator or payor will not be subject to penalties under section 6651 with respect to the difference between the tax that should have been withheld from the final installment under the qualified total distribution tables and the amount of the final installment.

The effect of these alternatives is illustrated by the following example:

An individual receives within one taxable year the balance to his credit under a plan described in section 401(a) or 403(a). The balance to his credit is paid in three installments of $1,000, $10,000, and $60,000. The amount of tax to be withheld from the installments may be calculated under Option 1 or Option 2.

Option 1—Withholding on each installment computed by finding tax under qualified total distribution tables on the cumulative amount of the distribution and subtracting the tax already withheld.

I.:	
1. Amount of installment 1	$ 1,000
2. Withholding obligation on installment 1	50
II.:	
1. Amount of installments 1 and 2	11,000
2. Withholding obligation on installments 1 and 2	550
3. Withholding paid on installment 1	50
4. Withholding obligation on installment 2 (2 minus 3)	500
III.:	
1. Amount of installments 1, 2, and 3	71,000
2. Withholding obligation on installments 1, 2, and 3	9,580
3. Withholding paid on installments 1 and 2	550
4. Withholding obligation on installment 3 (2 minus 3)	9,030
Total withholding obligation	9,580

Option 2—Withholding computed by withholding at 10 percent rate for all but the final installment. Withholding on the final installment computed by finding tax under qualified total distribution table for the cumulative amount of the distribution and subtracting the amount of tax already withheld:

I.:	
1. Amount of installment 1	$ 1,000
2. Withholding obligation on installment 1	100
II.:	
1. Amount of installment 2	10,000
2. Withholding obligation on installment 2	1,000
III.:	
1. Amount of installments 1, 2, and 3	71,000
2. Withholding obligation on installments 1, 2, and 3	9,580
3. Withholding paid on installments 1 and 2	1,100
4. Withholding obligation on installment 3 (2 minus 3)	8,480
Total withholding obligation	9,580

F-9. Q. A plan described in section 401 (a) invests in life insurance contracts for its participants. Each year the current cost of the life insurance element (PS 58 cost) is taxable to the participants under section 72. Is withholding required on this amount even though there is no amount actually distributed to the participant?

A. No. Because the PS 58 costs are not distributed or deemed to be distributed, they are not designated distributions for which withholding is required.

F-10. Q. The plan administrator or payor of a plan described in section 401(a) has been properly reporting distributions on a multiple contract basis for purposes of section 72. How should the plan administrator or payor determine the amount of each payment that is includible in gross income for withholding purposes?

A. In the absence of revenue rulings or regulations to the contrary, the plan administrator or payor of a plan that properly reports distributions on a multiple contract basis should use that method to determine the taxable portion of a payment for withholding purposes.

F-11. Q. The plan administrator or payor of a plan described in section 401(a) has been reporting distributions on a multiple contract basis for purposes of section 72 and has properly switched to the single contract method for reporting distributions. How should the plan administrator or payor determine the amount of each payment that is includible in gross income for withholding purposes?

A. If a plan has properly switched from the multiple contract basis to the single contract basis for reporting distributions, the plan administrator or payor may assume that all amounts prior to the year of switch were reported by the payees on a multiple contract basis. Therefore, for example, in the case of an individual whose annuity payments have not commenced prior to the date of the switch to a single contract basis, the payee's investment in the contract can be assumed to have been recovered on a multiple contract basis prior to the year of the switch and on a single contract basis thereafter for purposes of determining the amount of each payment that is includible in gross income for withholding purposes. This rule applies even though payees may have amended their income tax returns for prior years to report all payments on a single contract basis.

F-12. Q. If a plan that makes payments subject to the withholding and notice requirements of section 3405 makes separate payments to the same individual as a retired participant and as a surviving spouse of a retired participant, must the two payments be aggregated for withholding purposes?

A. No, unless the payor wishes to aggregate them.

F-13. Q. An insurance company makes payments under certain variable annuity contracts. The Investment Company Act of 1940 (section 22(e)) applies to these variable annuity contracts and requires that the insurance company make a pay-out within 7 days after a payee requests a withdrawal from his contract. Under these circumstances, how may notice be provided to a payee of his right to elect out of withholding for a nonperiodic distribution?

A. In this situation, the insurance company has only seven days in which to notify a payee of his right to elect out of withholding. It is not feasible for the insurance company to secure an election in writing unless the payee supplies the written election at the time he requests a withdrawal. Therefore, the notice and election can be provided in the following manner: (1) The insurance company may mail a notice to a payee on the day the request for withdrawal is received and (2) the notice may specify that unless the payee calls the company at a toll-free telephone number supplied on the notice within seven days of the date the request was received, the company will withhold from the distribution. Notice provided in this manner is deemed to satisfy the "reasonable time" requirement of question d-9. Insurance companies that encounter this problem are encouraged to supply an election form to a payee at the time an annuity contract is purchased. If a payee supplies an election with the request for withdrawal, notice still must be given but the insurance company may honor the election received if no other communication is received after notice is provided to the payee.

F-14. Q. If an individual receives periodic payments from two or more plans of one member of a controlled group of corporations, separate periodic payments from two members of a controlled group of corporations out of one plan, or periodic payments from separate plans of two members of a controlled group, must the periodic payments be aggregated for withholding purposes?

A. No, unless the plan administrator or payor wishes to aggregate the payments. Section 414(b) does not require that plans of a controlled group of corporations be aggregated for withholding purposes. The same rule applies to a group of trades or businesses under common control or an affiliated service group described in section 414(c) or (m).

F-15. Q. How is withholding applied to a designated distribution from an individual retirement account (IRA) described in section 408(a) that is payable upon demand even though payments are scheduled to be made over a period certain greater than one year?

A. Distributions from IRAs that are payable upon demand are not periodic payments taxable under section 72 because they do not constitute annuity contracts within the meaning of section 408(d)(2). Therefore, designated distributions from an IRA that are payable upon demand are treated as nonperiodic distributions subject to withholding at the 10% rate even if the distributions are paid over a period certain.

F-16. Q. Under the rules of section 72, a portion of certain payments that may vary because of investment experience, cost of living indices, or similar criteria is treated as not received as an annuity. For withholding purposes, must these amounts be treated as nonperiodic distributions even though part of each payment is a periodic payment?

A. No. For withholding purposes, amounts will be considered periodic payments even though a portion of each payment is treated as an amount not received as an annuity under § 1.72-2(b)(3) of the Income Tax Regulations.

F-17. Q. Is the payor of distributions under a funded nonqualified deferred compensation plan that are payable as an annuity and taxable under section 72 required to withhold under section 3405?

A. Yes. Section 31.3401(a)-1(b)(1)(i) of the Employment Tax Regulations provides that any amounts received as an annuity and taxable under section 72 are excepted from the general definition of wages. Therefore, to the extent that section 402(b) requires that distributions from nonqualified plans which are received as an annuity are taxable under the rules of section 72, section 3405 will apply. See, however, question a-18 for the rules relating to distributions from a nonqualified deferred compensation plan that are taxable under section 83. Therefore, whether the payor or plan administrator of a nonqualified plan is required to withhold under section 3402 or section 3405 depends upon what section of the Code governs the taxation of amounts contributed or distributed.

F-18. Q. Are amounts paid in connection with a partial or complete surrender or upon the maturity or endowment of a commercial annuity subject to the new withholding rules?

A. Yes. Amounts paid in connection with a partial or complete surrender or upon the maturity or endowment of a commercial annuity are subject to the new withholding rules to the extent that they are designated distributions. Thus, withholding is required on the complete or partial surrender of an annuity, life insurance or endowment contract to the extent they are designated distributions.

F-19. Q. Are amounts paid in connection with a partial surrender of a commercial annuity periodic payments?

A. Generally, no. Unless the amount paid in connection with the partial surrender is one of a series of payments payable over a period of greater than one year and taxable under section 72 as an amount received as an annuity, the amount paid is not a periodic payment.

F-20. Q. Are amounts paid in connection with a complete surrender of a commercial annuity a qualified total distribution?

A. A qualified total distribution must be made under a plan described in section 401(a) or 403(a). Unless the commercial annuity is surrendered under such a plan and meets the other requirements for a qualified total distribution, the total surrender will be treated as a nonperiodic payment that is not a qualified total distribution.

F-21. Q. Is it reasonable to believe that amounts distributed in connection with a commercial annuity that was acquired on or before August 13, 1982, or are otherwise described in section 72(e)(5), which are not treated as amounts received as an annuity under section 72, will not be includible in the gross income of the recipient?

A. Generally, yes. Under the rules of section 72(e) prior to the passage of TEFRA, amounts not received as an annuity were not taxable until the investment in the contract was recovered. Thus, for distributions that are not received as an annuity under a commercial annuity contract acquired on or before August 13, 1982, it is reasonable to believe that amounts distributed are not includible in the payee's gross income to the extent they represent unrecovered investment in the contract. The special transitional rule of question a-33, available for plan administrators, may be used until December 31, 1983, by payors of commercial annuities who lack records with regard to the payee's unrecovered investment in the contract.

F-22. Q. For commercial annuity contracts entered into after August 13, 1982, which are not described in section 72(e)(5), is it reasonable to believe that amounts distributed, which are not amounts received as an annuity under section 72, are not includible in gross income?

A. Generally, no. TEFRA amended section 72(e) to provide that amounts not received as an annuity will be includible in gross income until all earnings or other amounts that are not part of the investment in the contract have been distributed. Thus, it is not reasonable to believe that amounts distributed in connection with a commercial annuity contract entered into after August 13, 1982, are excludible from gross income until all earnings or other amounts that are not part of the investment in the contract have been distributed. This new rule does not apply to distributions from commercial annuities described in section 72(e)(5). Question f-21 provides the proper rule with respect to distributions from commercial annuities described in section 72(e)(5).

F-23. Q. Is it reasonable to believe that amounts involved solely in connection with an exchange of commercial annuities under section 1035 of the Code will not be includible in the gross income of the recipient?

A. Yes. Designated distributions include only amounts that it is reasonable to believe are includible in the gross income of the recipient. In the case of a commercial annuity exchange under section 1035 in which no cash or other property is exchanged, it is reasonable to believe that no portion is includible in the gross income of a recipient. An annuity exchange includes an exchange of annuity, endowment, or life insurance contracts issued by a life insurance company licensed to do business under the laws of any State. Thus, such exchanges are not subject to the withholding rules of section 3405. However, see question e-8 concerning recordkeeping requirements with respect to the nontaxable exchange of commercial annuity contracts under section 1035.

F-24. Q. Is it reasonable to believe that amounts distributed in connection with a surrender of a life insurance or endowment contract, or in connection with an exchange of life insurance or endowment contracts in which cash or other property is distributed, will not be includible in gross income?

A. Generally, no. Amounts distributed in connection with the surrender of a life insurance or endowment contract, or in connection with an exchange of life insurance or endowment contracts in which cash or other property is distributed are includible in income to the extent that the amount received exceeds the policyholder's investment in the contract. However, if a life insurance or endowment contract issued before August 13, 1982, is surrendered within ten years of the date of its issuance, or is exchanged within ten years of the date of its issuance, the payor may assume that no amounts are includible in the gross income of the policyholder if the cash or other property received by the policyholder in connection with the surrender or exchange of the life insurance or endowment contract does not exceed $10,000. If a life insurance or endowment contract issued before August 13, 1982, is surrendered or exchanged ten years or more after the date of its issuance, the payor may assume that no amounts are includible in the gross income of the policyholder if the cash or other property received by the policyholder in connection with the surrender or exchange of the life insurance or endowment contract does not exceed $5,000. If the payor utilizes the special rule in the two preceding sentences, the payor must notify the policyholder, at the time described in question d-4, that all or part of the amount distributed may be includible in the policyholder's gross income. See question f-28 for additional rules concerning certain exchanges of annuity contracts.

F-25. Q. Do the requirements of section 3405(d)(10), relating to the time at which notice must be provided, also apply to the time at which an election out of withholding may be made?

A. Generally, yes. For example, an individual may not at commencement of employment execute an election out of withholding to be honored by a plan administrator or payor when the individual terminates employment and receives a distribution from a deferred compensation plan. See, however, question f-13 for a special rule applicable to certain annuity contracts.

F-26. Q. If a payor provided notice prior to January 1, 1983, but failed to include all of the information required by question d-18, may the abbreviated notice of question d-27 be supplied when making the first payment?

A. Yes, as long as the abbreviated notice contains all of the information required by question d-18 that was not supplied with the earlier notice.

F-27. Q. When must notice of the right to elect not to have withholding apply be given as to designated distributions from an individual retirement account (IRA) described in section 408(a) that is payable on demand even though payments are scheduled to be made over a period greater than one year?

A. Under question f-15, designated distributions from an IRA that are payable upon demand are treated as nonperiodic distributions subject to withholding at the 10 percent rate even if the distributions are paid over a certain period.

Section 3405(d)(10)(B)(i) requires the payor of a nonperiodic distribution to transmit to the payee notice, at the time of the distribution or at such earlier time as may be provided in regulations, of the right to elect not to have withholding apply. If distributions from an IRA have begun and are scheduled to be made at quarterly or more frequent intervals, then, in lieu of providing a notice at the time of each distribution, the payor may furnish a blanket notice applicable to all such distributions that are expected to be made to the payee from the account during a calendar year. Such a blanket notice must be furnished at a reasonable time before the first payment made in the calendar year to which the notice relates, except that a blanket notice relating to distributions from an IRA during 1983 may be made by the later of October 1, 1983, or the date of the first designated distribution from the IRA.

G. Delay Procedures

G-1. Q. When does the new law take effect?

A. In general, withholding is required on any designated distributions made after December 31, 1982.

G-2. Q. Is there a penalty for failure to withhold under section 3405 on designated distributions made after December 31, 1982?

A. Yes. In general, section 6651 governs the failure to file a return and to withhold tax under section 3405.

G-3. Q. Are there any circumstances under which the withholding and notice requirements of section 3405 may be delayed to a date later than January 1, 1983?

A. Yes. The Secretary has authority to delay, but not beyond June 30, 1983, the application of these withholding provisions to any payor or plan administrator if the payor or plan administrator can establish that he is unable to comply with these provisions without undue hardship.

G-4. Q. Under what circumstances may a payor or plan administrator who is experiencing undue hardship in complying with section 3405 delay implementation of the notice and withholding requirements?

A. For those payors and plan administrators who experience undue hardship in complying with the provisions of section 3405, the withholding and notice requirements of section 3405 may be delayed so long as undue hardship exists up to July 1, 1983.

G-5. Q. Must approval be obtained from the Internal Revenue Service to be entitled to the delay referred to in question g-4 if the delay will be no later than April 1, 1983?

A. No. If a payor or plan administrator can establish that undue hardship would result if required to comply with the provisions of this section before April 1, 1983, prior approval from the Internal Revenue Service is not required and should not be requested. For purposes of this delay up to April 1, 1983, undue hardship will be presumed to exist, in the absence of bad faith, as long as the payor or plan administrator can establish that at least one of the conditions listed in question g-6 is present. The payor or plan administrator should prepare and retain a statement of undue hardship as described in question g-9 and should maintain any documents necessary to support the representations made in that statement.

G-6. Q. What constitutes undue hardship?

A. For purposes of these delay procedures, the term "undue hardship" generally means more than an inconvenience or increased costs to the payor or plan administrator. In the case of a payor or plan administrator who complies with the notice and withholding requirements of section 3405 on or before April 1, 1983, undue hardship will be presumed to exist if one or more of the following conditions is present:

(1) The payor or plan administrator encounters significant delay or other substantial difficulty in obtaining authorization for funds to develop forms, to mail notices, to process responses, to develop new computer programs, or to obtain and train personnel to implement withholding.

(2) The payor or plan administrator incurs substantial increases in unbudgeted costs to develop forms, to mail notices, to process responses, to develop new computer programs, or to obtain and train personnel.

(3) There is difficulty in obtaining trained personnel, including professional or semi-professional individuals, whose skills are necessary to implement withholding.

(4) Training new or present employees or hiring new employees to implement withholding would cause substantially increased costs or would disrupt the payor's or plan administrator's operations, and such disruption or increased costs would not occur if withholding were implemented at a later date.

(5) Plan benefits change due to a collective bargaining agreement concluded between October 1, 1982, and April 1, 1983.

(6) A payor who provided notice prior to January 1, 1983, receives a substantial number of inquiries from payees. These inquiries indicate the payees' lack of understanding of the new withholding provisions and the payor cannot answer all questions and receive responses by January 1, 1983.

(7) The payor or plan administrator is unable to implement withholding on account of the occurrence of an event, such as fire, flood, earthquake, explosion, or strike, beyond the control of the payor or plan administrator.

(8) The payor or plan administrator is scheduled to install a new data processing hardware package or system between December 1, 1982, and July 1, 1983, that will be used for the process of pension withholding.

An example of a circumstance not considered as resulting in undue hardship would be changes in the withholding tables effective July 1, 1983.

The following examples illustrate situations in which an undue hardship that will permit delay in implementation of the notice and withholding provisions exists:

Example (1). A is the payor and plan administrator of a deferred compensation plan that is the subject of a collective bargaining agreement. The collectively bargained plan has fewer than 100 participants receiving annuity payments. All of A's available budget is scheduled to be used to pay plan benefits and administrative costs, and no funds are available to implement the new withholding requirements. A must obtain authorization to expend funds to implement withholding. Meetings at which A can obtain such authorization are held August 1 and February 1 of each year. After obtaining authorization on February 1, 1983, A will need to develop and mail withholding notices and elections, process responses and determine the amount to be withheld from each payee's annuity payment. A can implement withholding on April 1, 1983, without substantially disrupting its operations, but earlier implementation would disrupt its normal operations. Under these facts, A experiences undue hardship until at least April 1, 1983, as a result of the circumstances described in items (1) and (4) of question g-6.

Example (2). B, a bank, is a payor of pensions and annuities under plans described in section 401(a). The plan administrators of all these plans have transferred liability to B for withholding under section 3405. After T.D. 7839, relating to withholding from pensions, annuities and other deferred income, was published in the FEDERAL REGISTER on October 14, 1982, B determines that the withholding provisions can be implemented before April 1, 1983, on a reasonable schedule, without substantial increases in costs or disruption of daily bank operations, according to the following schedule:

(a) B's counsel analyzes regulations and reports requirements to operations personnel; operations personnel develop new Forms, which are reviewed and revised by management and legal personnel; new forms are printed; personnel begin reprogramming computers, 8 weeks (Dec 9, 1982).

(b) Forms distributed to branch offices, 1 week (Dec 16, 1982).

(c) Forms mailed to payees, 1 week (Dec 23, 1982).

(d) Time allowed for response to mailing of notices, answering questions, mailing follow-up notices to payees, 6 weeks (Feb 3, 1983).

(e) Withholding calculated and entered into payment system, 6 weeks (Mar 17, 1983).

Total: 22 weeks.

Implementation is scheduled to begin March 17, 1983. Implementation prior to March 17, 1983, would substantially increase costs and would disrupt B's operations.

Under these facts, B experiences undue hardship under item (4) of question g-6, up to March 17, 1983, the scheduled date of implementation.

G-7. Q. If a payor or plan administrator qualifies for the delay described in question g-5, is there a procedure for requesting an additional delay up to July 1, 1983?

A. Yes. However, any request made for this additional delay will be considered on a case-by-case basis. It is anticipated these requests will be carefully scrutinized and generally will be granted only in circumstances where the payor or plan administrator can reasonably expect that more than one of the conditions described in question g-6 will exist on or after April 1, 1983, and up to July 1, 1983.

G-8. Q. How may a payor or plan administrator request this additional delay of up to 3 months for undue hardship?

A. The payor or plan administrator may request an additional delay of up to 3 months by filing in duplicate a written statement of undue hardship signed under penalties of perjury with the director of the service center where the payor or plan administrator files Form 941 or Form 941E. This written request must state on the envelope and at the top of the letter "PENSION WITHHOLDING: Undue Hardship" and must include all the information required in a statement of undue hardship as described in question g-9.

G-9. Q. What information must the statement of undue hardship include?

A. The statement of undue hardship must include the following information:

(1) The name, address, and taxpayer identification number of the payor or plan administrator.

(2) A complete statement of the facts upon which the payor is relying to show why a delay beyond April 1, 1983, is warranted. This statement must include as many of the conditions of undue hardship listed in question g-6 as pertain to the payor or plan administrator.

(3) A schedule or plan of implementation showing dates on which the payor will implement the provisions of this section, with no date later than July 1, 1983. This schedule should provide a complete timetable that includes such items as development of forms, mailing of notices, time for responses, programming computers, and calculation of withholding.

(4) An explanation of the steps taken which demonstrate the payor's or plan administrator's good faith attempt to comply with these notice and withholding requirements.

G-10. Q. When must the plan administrator or payor file this request for delay and statement of undue hardship?

A. Payors or plan administrators must file the statement of undue hardship on or before March 1, 1983. However, no request for delay may be filed with the Internal Revenue Service before January 1, 1983.

G-11. Q. Who must request the delay?

A. The delay should be requested by the payor or plan administrator who is actually liable for withholding. Therefore, generally the payor should request the delay. However, in the case of a distribution from a plan described in section 401(a), section 403(a), or section 301(d) of the Tax Reduction Act of 1975, the plan administrator is liable for withholding and should request the delay unless the plan administrator has transferred liability for withholding to the payor under section 3405(c).

G-12. Q. If a plan administrator has not yet transferred liability for withholding under section 3405(c) or has inadequately transferred liability, and the payor requests a delay, will the request for delay be treated as if the plan administrator had requested it?

A. Yes.

G-13. Q. If a plan administrator and a payor both file requests for delay and statements of undue hardship with respect to the same plan, will there be two separate three-month extensions?

A. No. A request for delay will delay the effective date only up to three months and in no case will it extend it past July 1, 1983.

G-14. Q. What are the consequences for failure to file the request for delay and statement of undue hardship in a timely manner?

A. If the request for delay and statement of undue hardship are not filed in a timely manner, the payor or plan administrator will not be entitled to any delay beyond the delay to which he may be entitled under question g-5. This rule will not apply in the case of an event such as strike, fire, flood, earthquake, or explosion that occurs after March 1, 1983, if compliance with the withholding provisions would have been possible absent the occurrence of the event.

G-15. Q. Will a payor or plan administrator receive a response from the Internal Revenue Service as to whether a delay after April 1, 1983, has been granted?

A. Yes. Since these requests for delay will be reviewed on a case-by-case basis, the payor or plan administrator will receive a response by April 1, 1983, as to whether or not a requested delay has been granted. If the request for delay is denied by the director of the service center, the payor or plan administrator is required to begin withholding by the later of April 1, 1983, or 10 days from the date on the response. No penalties will be imposed under section 6651 for failure to withhold between April 1, 1983, and the day 10 days from the date on the response.

G-16. Q. If the director of the service center grants a delay up to July 1, 1983, must the payor or plan administrator retain a copy of the response from the Internal Revenue Service?

A. Yes. In addition, the payor or plan administrator must attach a copy of the response to the first Form 941 or 941E filed after the response is received.

G-17. Q. If a plan administrator or payor begins withholding before April 1, 1983, or July 1, 1983, can the payee request a refund from the plan administrator or payor of the amounts withheld?

A. No. Because plan administrators and payors are required to comply with the withholding and notice requirements as soon as they no longer experience undue hardship, they cannot refund any amounts withheld to a payee, except as provided in the regulations under section 6413 (in the case of a mistake by the payor or plan administrator).

G-18. Q. If a payor or plan administrator properly files the statement of undue hardship and receives a delay as provided in question g-7, will withholding from payments made after the delay period be required to make up for amounts that would have been withheld if there had been no delay granted?

A. No. No catch-up withholding is required for plan administrators or payors who are entitled to a delay up to April 1, 1983, as provided in question g-5 or granted a delay up to July 1, 1983, as provided in question g-7. However, if a payor or plan administrator who is entitled to a delay up to April 1, 1983, as provided in question g-5, is not granted a delay up to July 1, 1983, but is unable to implement withholding until July 1, 1983, despite a good faith effort to comply, no penalties will be imposed under section 6651 if the payor or plan administrator withholds between July 1, 1983, and December 31, 1983, both the amounts required to be withheld during that period and the amounts that should have been withheld between April 1, 1983, and June 30, 1983.

G-19. Q. If a payor or plan administrator does not receive and is not otherwise entitled to a delay under these regulations, will withholding from future payments be required to make up for amounts that would have been withheld if there had been no delay?

A. Yes, to the extent possible. An example of a situation in which a payor or plan administrator would not be able to withhold enough from subsequent payments to satisfy pre-July 1, 1983, withholding obligations is one where the recipient of a single life annuity died on July 1, 1983, before the payor or plan administrator began to withhold income tax from the annuity. In addition, a payor or plan administrator would not be able to satisfy the pre-July 1, 1983, withholding requirements if the payee elects out of withholding before all of the make-up withholding has been accomplished.

G-20. Q. What are the consequences if the payor or plan administrator cannot establish undue hardship and does not comply on January 1, 1983?

A. In general, if the payor or plan administrator cannot establish undue hardship and fails to withhold beginning January 1, 1983, the payor or plan administrator will be liable for the tax that should have been withheld and, in addition, the penalties provided in section 6651 will apply. However, the payor or plan administrator will not be liable for penalties for failure to file a return and for failure to pay the tax if a good faith effort is made to comply, and if, to the extent possible, withholding from post-implementation payments is sufficient to satisfy the pre-implementation withholding obligation. Whether the payor or plan administrator has made a good faith effort to comply depends on the facts and circumstances of each case. The facts and circumstances that will be considered include, but are not limited to, those conditions listed in question g-6.

G-21. Q. If a payor or plan administrator is required to make up amounts that should have been withheld, must he withhold from the first subsequent payment the entire amount that should have been previously withheld?

A. No. A payor or plan administrator may withhold a proportional amount out of each subsequent payment made before January 1, 1984.

G-22. Q. Will the notice requirements of section 3405 apply before July 1, 1983, with respect to recipients of periodic payments that total less than $5400 per year?

A. No.

G-23. Q. Will the notice and withholding requirements of section 3405 apply before July 1, 1983, with respect to payments to nonresident alien individuals?

A. No.

G-24. Q. Does a payor or plan administrator who requested a delay prior to the publication of these procedures in the FEDERAL REGISTER need to resubmit the request in light of these procedures?

A. Yes. In order to be entitled to a delay, payors and plan administrators must follow the procedures required by these temporary regulations.

G-25. Q. Will the notice and withholding requirements of section 3405 apply before January 1, 1984, with respect to the exchange or complete or partial surrender of a commercial annuity under which the recipient had not irrevocably chosen, prior to January 1, 1984, to receive payments in the form of an annuity?

A. In the case of the exchange or complete or partial surrender of a commercial annuity under which the recipient had not irrevocably chosen, prior to January 1, 1984, to receive payments in the form of an annuity, the application of the notice and withholding provisions of this section may be delayed, so long as undue hardship exists, up to January 1, 1984. Prior approval from the Internal Revenue Service is not required for such delay, and should not be requested. For purposes of this delay, undue hardship will be presumed to exist, in the absence of bad faith, so long as the payor can establish that at least one of the conditions in question g-6 is present. The payor should prepare and retain a statement of undue hardship as described in question g-9 and should maintain any documents necessary to support the representations made in that statement.

T.D. 7839, 10/8/82, amend T.D. 7858, 11/26/82, T.D. 7904, 8/2/83, T.D. 8873, 2/7/2000, T.D. 8952, 6/25/2001.

§ 31.3405(c)-1 Withholding on eligible rollover distributions; questions and answers.

Caution: The Treasury has not yet amended Reg § 31.3405(c)-1 to reflect changes made by P.L. 106-554, P.L. 104-188.

The following questions and answers relate to withholding on eligible rollover distributions under section 3405(c) of the Internal Revenue Code of 1986, as added by section 522(b) of the Unemployment Compensation Amendments of 1992 (Public Law 102-318, 106 Stat. 290) (UCA). For additional UCA guidance under sections 401(a)(31), 402(c), 402(f), and 403(b)(8) and (10), see §§ 1.401(a)(31)-1, 1.402(c)-2, 1.402(f)-1, and 1.403(b)-2 of this chapter, respectively.

List of Questions

Q-1. What are the withholding requirements under section 3405 for distributions from qualified plans and section 403(b) annuities?

Q-2. May a distributee elect under section 3405(c) not to have Federal income tax withheld from an eligible rollover distribution?

Q-3. May a distributee be permitted to elect to have more than 20-percent Federal income tax withheld from an eligible rollover distribution?

Q-4. Who has responsibility for complying with section 3405(c) relating to the 20-percent income tax withholding on eligible rollover distributions?

Q-5. May the plan administrator shift the withholding responsibility to the payor and, if so, how?

Q-6. How does the 20-percent withholding requirement under section 3405(c) apply if a distributee elects to have a portion of an eligible rollover distribution paid to an eligible retirement plan in a direct rollover and to have the remainder of that distribution paid to the distributee?

Q-7. Will the plan administrator be subject to liability for tax, interest, or penalties for failure to withhold 20 percent from an eligible rollover distribution that, because of erroneous information provided by a distributee, is not paid to an eligible retirement plan even though the distributee elected a direct rollover?

Q-8. Is an eligible rollover distribution that is paid to a qualified defined benefit plan subject to 20-percent withholding?

Q-9. If property other than cash, employer securities, or plan loans is distributed, how is the 20-percent income tax withholding required under section 3405(c) accomplished?

Q-10. What assumptions may a plan administrator make regarding whether a benefit is an eligible rollover distribution for purposes of determining the amount of a distribution that is subject to 20-percent mandatory withholding?

Q-11. Are there special rules for applying the 20-percent withholding requirement to employer securities and a plan loan offset amount distributed in an eligible rollover distribution?

Q-12. How does the mandatory withholding rule apply to net unrealized appreciation from employer securities?

Q-13. Does the 20-percent withholding requirement apply to eligible rollover distributions from a qualified plan distributed annuity contract?

Q-14. Must a payor or plan administrator withhold tax from an eligible rollover distribution for which a direct rollover election was not made if the amount of the distribution is less than $200?

Q-15. If eligible rollover distributions are made from a qualified plan, who has responsibility for making the returns and reports required under these regulations?

Q-16. What eligible rollover distributions must be reported on Form 1099-R?

Q-17. Must the plan administrator, trustee or custodian of the eligible retirement plan report amounts received in a direct rollover?

Questions and Answers

Q-1. What are the withholding requirements under section 3405 for distributions from qualified plans and section 403(b) annuities?

A-1. **(a) General rule.** Section 3405(c), added by UCA, provides that any designated distribution that is an eligible rollover distribution (as defined in section 402(f)(2)(A)) from a qualified plan or a section 403(b) annuity is subject to income tax withholding at the rate of 20 percent unless the distributee of the eligible rollover distribution elects to have the distribution paid directly to an eligible retirement plan in a direct rollover. See section 1.402(c)-2, Q&A-2 of this chapter for the definition of a qualified plan and § 1.403(b)-7(b) of this chapter for the definition of a section 403(b) annuity. For purposes of section 3405 and this section, with respect to a distribution from a qualified plan, an eligible retirement plan is a trust qualified under section 401(a), an annuity plan described in section 403(a), or an individual retirement plan (as described in § 1.402(c)-2, Q&A-2 of this chapter). For purposes of section 3405 and this section, with respect to a distribution from a section 403(b) annuity, an eligible retirement plan is an annuity contract, a custodial account, a retirement income account described in section 403(b), or an individual retirement plan. If a designated distribution is not an eligible rollover distribution, it is subject to the elective withholding provisions of section 3405(a) and (b) and § 35.3405-1 of this chapter and is not subject to the mandatory withholding provisions of section 3405(c) and this section.

(b) Application of other statutory provisions. See § 1.401(a)(31)-1 of this chapter concerning the requirements and the procedures for electing a direct rollover under section 401(a)(31). See section 402(c)(2) and (4), and § 1.402(c)-2, Q&A-3 through Q&A-10 and Q&A-14 of this chapter for rules to determine what constitutes an eligible rollover distribution. See § 1.402(f)-1, Q&A-1 through Q&A-3 and § 1.403(b)-7(b) of this chapter concerning the notice that must be provided to a distributee, within a reasonable period of time before making an eligible rollover distribution. See § 1.403(b)-7(b) and Q&A-2 of this chapter for guidance concerning the rollover provisions and direct rollover requirements for distributions from annuities described in section 403(b).

(c) Effective date. *(1) Statutory effective date.* (i) General rule. Section 3405(c), as added by UCA, applies to eligible rollover distributions made on or after January 1, 1993, even if the employee's employment with the employer maintaining the plan terminated before January 1, 1993 and even if the eligible rollover distribution is part of a series of payments that began before January 1, 1993.

(ii) Special rule for governmental section 403(b) annuities. Section 522 of UCA provides a special effective date for governmental section 403(b) annuities. This special effective date appears in § 1.403(b)-2T of this chapter (as it appeared in the April 1, 1995 edition of 26 CFR part 1).

(2) Regulatory effective date. This section applies to eligible rollover distributions made on or after October 19, 1995. For eligible rollover distributions made on or after January 1, 1993 and before October 19, 1995, § 31.3405(c)-1T (as it appeared in the April 1, 1995 edition of 26 CFR part 1), applies. However, for any distribution made on or after January 1, 1993 but before October 19, 1995, a plan administrator or payor may comply with the withholding requirements of section 3405(c) by substituting any or all provisions of this section for the corresponding provisions of § 31.3405(c)-1T, if any.

Q-2. May a distributee elect under section 3405(c) not to have Federal income tax withheld from an eligible rollover distribution?

A-2. No. The 20-percent income tax withholding imposed under section 3405(c)(1) applies to an eligible rollover distribution unless the distributee elects under section 401(a)(31) to have the eligible rollover distribution paid directly to an eligible retirement plan in a direct rollover. See § 1.401(a)(31)-1 and § 1.403(b)-2, Q&A-2 of this chapter for provisions concerning the requirement that a distributee of an eligible rollover distribution be permitted to elect a distribution in the form of a direct rollover.

Q-3. May a distributee be permitted to elect to have more than 20-percent Federal income tax withheld from an eligible rollover distribution?

A-3. Yes. Under section 3402(p), a distributee of an eligible rollover distribution and the plan administrator or payor are permitted to enter into an agreement to provide for withholding in excess of 20 percent from an eligible rollover distribution. Any agreement must be made in accordance with applicable forms and instructions. However, no request for withholding will be effective between the plan administrator or payor and the distributee until the plan administrator or payor accepts the request by commencing to withhold from the amounts with respect to which the request was made. An agreement under section 3402(p) shall be effective for such period as the plan administrator or payor and the distributee mutually agree upon. However, either party to the agreement may terminate the agreement prior to the end of such period by furnishing a signed written notice to the other.

Q-4. Who has responsibility for complying with section 3405(c) relating to the 20-percent income tax withholding on eligible rollover distributions?

A-4. Section 3405(d) generally requires the plan administrator of a qualified plan and the payor of a section 403(b) annuity to withhold under section 3405(c)(1) an amount equal to 20 percent of the portion of an eligible rollover distribution that the distributee does not elect to have paid in a direct rollover. When an amount is paid under a qualified plan distributed annuity contract as defined in § 1.402(c)-2, Q&A-10 of this chapter, the payor is treated as the plan administrator. See Q&A-13 of this section concerning eligible rollover distributions from a qualified plan distributed annuity contract.

Q-5. May the plan administrator shift the withholding responsibility to the payor and, if so, how?

A-5. Yes. The plan administrator may shift the withholding responsibility to the payor by following the procedures set forth in § 35.3405-1, Q&A E-2 through E-5 of this chapter (relating to elective withholding on pensions, annuities and certain other deferred income) with appropriate adjustments, including the plan administrator's identification of amounts that constitute required minimum distributions.

Q-6. How does the 20-percent withholding requirement under section 3405(c) apply if a distributee elects to have a portion of an eligible rollover distribution paid to an eligible retirement plan in a direct rollover and to have the remainder of that distribution paid to the distributee?

A-6. If a distributee elects to have a portion of an eligible rollover distribution paid to an eligible retirement plan in a direct rollover and to receive the remainder of the distribution, the 20-percent withholding requirement under section 3405(c) applies only to the portion of the eligible rollover distribution that the distributee receives and not to the portion that is paid in a direct rollover.

Q-7. Will the plan administrator be subject to liability for tax, interest, or penalties for failure to withhold 20 percent from an eligible rollover distribution that, because of erroneous information provided by a distributee, is not paid to an eligible retirement plan even though the distributee elected a direct rollover?

A-7. **(a) General rule.** If the plan administrator reasonably relied on adequate information provided by the distributee (as described in paragraph (b) of this Q&A), the plan administrator will not be subject to liability for taxes, interest, or penalties for failure to withhold income tax from an eligible rollover distribution solely because the distribution is paid to an account or plan that is not an eligible retirement plan (as defined, with respect to distributions from qualified plans, in section 402(c)(8)(B) and § 1.402(c)-2, Q&A-2 of this chapter and, with respect to a distributions from section 403(b) annuities, in § 1.403(b)-2), Q&A-1 of this chapter. Although the plan administrator is not required to verify independently the accuracy of information provided by the distributee, the plan administrator's reliance on the information furnished must be reasonable. For example, it is not reasonable for the plan administrator to rely on information that is clearly erroneous on its face.

(b) Adequate information. The plan administrator has obtained from the distributee adequate information on which to rely in making a direct rollover if the distributee furnishes to the plan administrator: the name of the eligible retirement plan; a representation that the recipient plan is an individual retirement plan, a qualified plan, or a section 403(b) annuity, as appropriate; and any other information that is necessary in order to permit the plan administrator to accomplish the direct rollover by the means it has selected. This information must include any information needed to comply with the specific requirements of § 1.401(a)(31)-1, Q&A-3 and Q&A-4 of this chapter. For example, if the direct rollover is to be made by mailing a check to the trustee of an individual retirement account, the plan administrator must obtain, in addition to the name of the individual retirement account and the representation described above, the name and address of the trustee of the individual retirement account.

Q-8. Is an eligible rollover distribution that is paid to a qualified defined benefit plan subject to 20-percent withholding?

A-8. No. If an eligible rollover distribution is paid in a direct rollover to an eligible retirement plan within the meaning of section 402(c)(8), including a qualified defined benefit plan, it is reasonable to believe that the distribution is not includible in gross income pursuant to section 402(c)(1). Accordingly, pursuant to section 3405(e)(1)(B), the distribution is not a designated distribution and is not subject to 20-percent withholding.

Q-9. If property other than cash, employer securities, or plan loans is distributed, how is the 20-percent income tax withholding required under section 3405(c) accomplished?

A-9. When all or a portion of an eligible rollover distribution subject to 20-percent income tax withholding under section 3405(c) consists of property other than cash, employer securities, or plan loan offset amounts, the plan administrator or payor must apply § 35.3405-1, Q&A F-2 of this chapter and may apply § 35.3405-1, Q&A F-3 of this chapter in determining how to satisfy the withholding requirements.

Q-10. What assumptions may a plan administrator make regarding whether a benefit is an eligible rollover distribution for purposes of determining the amount of a distribution that is subject to 20-percent mandatory withholding?

A-10. **(a) In general.** For purposes of determining the amount of a distribution that is subject to 20-percent mandatory withholding, a plan administrator may make the assumptions described in paragraphs (b), (c), and (d) of this Q&A in determining the amount of a distribution that is an eligible rollover distribution and a designated distribution. Q&A-18 of § 1.401(a)(31)-1 of this chapter provides assumptions for purposes of complying with section 401(a)(31). See § 1.402(c)-2, Q&A-15 of this chapter concerning the effect of these assumptions for purposes of section 402(c).

(b) $5,000 death benefit. A plan administrator may assume that a distribution that qualifies for the $5,000 death benefit exclusion under section 101(b) is the only death benefit being paid with respect to a deceased employee that qualifies for that exclusion. Thus, in such a case, the plan administrator may assume that the distribution is not an eligible rollover distribution to the extent that it would be excludible from gross income based on this assumption.

(c) Required minimum distributions. The plan administrator is permitted to determine the amount of the minimum distribution required to satisfy section 401(a)(9)(A) for any calendar year by assuming that there is no designated beneficiary.

(d) Valuation of property. In the case of a distribution that includes property, in calculating the amount of the distribution for purposes of applying section 3405(c), the value of the property may be determined in accordance with § 35.3405-1, Q&A F-1 of this chapter.

Q-11. Are there special rules for applying the 20-percent withholding requirement to employer securities and a plan loan offset amount distributed in an eligible rollover distribution?

A-11. Yes. The maximum amount to be withheld on any designated distribution (including any eligible rollover distribution) under section 3405(c) must not exceed the sum of the cash and the fair market value of property (excluding employer securities) received in the distribution. The amount of the sum is determined without regard to whether any portion of the cash or property is a designated distribution or an eligible rollover distribution. For purposes of this rule, any plan loan offset amount, as defined in § 1.402(c)-2, Q&A-9 of this chapter, is treated in the same manner as employer securities. Thus, although employer securities and plan loan offset amounts must be included in the amount that is multiplied by 20-percent, the total amount required to be withheld for an eligible rollover distribution is limited to the sum of the cash and the fair market value of property received by the distributee, excluding any amount of the distribution that is a plan loan offset amount or that is distributed in the form of employer securities. For example, if the only portion of an eligible rollover distribution that is not paid in a direct rollover consists of employer securities or a plan loan offset amount, withholding is not required. In addition, if a distribution consists solely of employer securities and cash (not in excess of $200) in lieu of fractional shares, no amount is required to be withheld as income tax from the distribution under section 3405 (including section 3405(c) and this section). For purposes of section 3405 and this section, employer securities means securities of the employer corporation within the meaning of section 402(e)(4)(E)(ii).

Q-12. How does the mandatory withholding rule apply to net unrealized appreciation from employer securities?

A-12. An eligible rollover distribution can include net unrealized appreciation from employer securities, within the meaning of section 402(e)(4), even if the net unrealized appreciation is excluded from gross income under section 402(e)(4). However, to the extent that it is excludible from gross income pursuant to section 402(e)(4), net unrealized appreciation is not a designated distribution pursuant to section 3405(e)(1)(B) because it is reasonable to believe that it is not includible in gross income. Thus, to the extent that net unrealized appreciation is excludible from gross income pursuant to section 402(e)(4), net unrealized appreciation is not included in the amount of an eligible rollover distribution that is subject to 20-percent withholding.

Q-13. Does the 20-percent withholding requirement apply to eligible rollover distributions from a qualified plan distributed annuity contract?

A-13. The 20-percent withholding requirement applies to eligible rollover distributions from a qualified plan distributed annuity contract as defined in Q&A-10 of § 1.402(c)-2 of this chapter. In the case of an eligible rollover distribution from such an annuity contract, the payor is treated as the plan administrator for purposes of section 3405. See § 1.401(a)(31)-1, Q&A-17 of this chapter concerning the direct rollover requirements that apply to distributions from such an annuity contract and see § 1.402(c)-2, Q&A-10 of this chapter concerning the treatment of distributions from such annuity contracts as eligible rollover distributions.

Q-14. Must a payor or plan administrator withhold tax from an eligible rollover distribution for which a direct rollover election was not made if the amount of the distribution is less than $200?

A-14. No. However, all eligible rollover distributions received within one taxable year of the distributee under the same plan must be aggregated for purposes of determining whether the $200 floor is reached. If the plan administrator or payor does not know at the time of the first distribution (that is less than $200) whether there will be additional eligible rollover distributions during the year for which aggregation is required, the plan administrator need not withhold from the first distribution. If distributions are made within one taxable year under more than one plan of an employer, the plan administrator or payor may, but need not, aggregate distributions for purposes of determining whether the $200 floor is reached. However, once the $200 threshold has been reached, the sum of all payments during the year must be used to determine the applicable amount to be withheld from subsequent payments during the year.

Q-15. If eligible rollover distributions are made from a qualified plan, who has responsibility for making the returns and reports required under these regulations?

A-15. Generally, the plan administrator, as defined in section 414(g), is responsible for maintaining the records and making the required reports with respect to eligible rollover distributions from qualified plans. However, if the plan administrator fails to keep the required records and make the required reports, the employer maintaining the plan is responsible for the reports and returns.

Q-16. What eligible rollover distributions must be reported on Form 1099-R?

A-16. Each eligible rollover distribution, including each eligible rollover distribution that is paid directly to an eligible retirement plan in a direct rollover, must be reported on Form 1099-R in accordance with the instructions for Form 1099-R. For purposes of the reporting required under section 6047(e), a direct rollover is treated as a distribution that is immediately rolled over to an eligible retirement plan. Distributions that are not eligible rollover distributions are subject to the reporting requirements set forth in § 35.3405-1 of this chapter and applicable forms and instructions.

Q-17. Must the plan administrator, trustee or custodian of the eligible retirement plan report amounts received in a direct rollover?

A-17. **(a) Individual retirement plan.** If a distributee elects to have an eligible rollover distribution paid to an individual retirement plan in a direct rollover, the eligible rollover distribution is reported on Form 5498 as a rollover contribution to the individual retirement plan, in accordance with the instructions for Form 5498.

(b) Qualified plan or section 403(b) annuity. If a distributee elects to have an eligible rollover distribution paid to a qualified plan or section 403(b) annuity, the recipient plan or annuity is not required to report the receipt of the rollover contribution.

T.D. 8619, 9/15/95, amend T.D. 8880, 4/20/2000, T.D. 9340, 7/23/2007.

§ 31.3406-0 Outline of the backup withholding regulations.

This section lists paragraphs contained in § 31.3406(a)-1 through 31.3406(i)-1.

§ 31.3406(a)-1 Backup withholding requirement on reportable payments.

(a) Overview.

(b) Conditions that invoke the backup withholding requirement.

(1) Conditions applicable to all reportable payments.

(2) Conditions applicable only to reportable interest or dividend payments.

(c) Exceptions.

(d) Cross references.

§ 31.3406(a)-2 Definition of payors obligated to backup withhold.

(a) In general.

(b) Persons treated as payors.

(c) Persons not treated as payors.

(d) Effective date.

§ 31.3406(a)-3 Scope and extent of accounts subject to backup withholding.

§ 31.3406(a)-4 Time when payments are considered to be paid and subject to backup withholding.

(a) Timing.

(1) In general.

(2) Special rules for dividends.

(b) Amounts reportable under section 6045.

(1) In general.

(2) Special rule for interest accrued on bonds.

(c) Middlemen.

(1) In general.

(2) Special rule for common trust funds.

(3) Special rule for certain grantor trusts.

§ 31.3406(b)(2)-1 Reportable interest payment.

(a) Interest subject to backup withholding.

(1) In general.

(2) Special rule for tax-exempt interest.

(b) Amount subject to backup withholding.

(1) In general.

(2) Special rule to adjust for premature withdrawal penalty.

§ 31.3406(b)(2)-2 Original issue discount.

(a) Original issue discount subject to backup withholding.

(b) Amount subject to backup withholding and time when backup withholding is imposed with respect to short-term obligations.

(c) Transferred short-term obligations.

(1) Subsequent holder may establish purchase price.

(2) Subsequent holder unable (or not permitted) to establish purchase price.

(3) Transferred obligation.

(d) Amount subject to backup withholding and time when backup withholding is imposed with respect to long-term obligations.

(1) No cash payments prior to maturity.

(2) Registered long-term obligations with cash payments prior to maturity.

(3) Transferred registered long-term obligations with payments prior to maturity.

(e) Bearer long-term obligations.

(1) Payments prior to maturity.

(2) Payments at maturity.

§ 31.3406(b)(2)-3 Window transactions.

(a) Requirement to backup withhold.

(b) Window transaction defined.

(c) Manner of furnishing taxpayer identification number in the case of a window transaction.

§ 31.3406(b)(2)-4 Reportable dividend payment.

(a) Dividends subject to backup withholding.

(b) Dividends not subject to backup withholding.

(c) Amount subject to backup withholding.

(1) In general.

(2) Reasonable estimate of amount of dividend subject to backup withholding.

(3) Reinvested dividends.

§ 31.3406(b)(2)-5 Reportable patronage dividend payment.

(a) Patronage dividends subject to backup withholding.

(b) Amount subject to backup withholding.

(1) Failure to provide taxpayer identification number or notification of incorrect taxpayer identification number.

(2) Notified payee underreporting or payee certification failure.

§ 31.3406(b)(3)-1 Reportable payments of rents, commissions, nonemployee compensation, etc.

(a) Section 6041 and 6041A(a) payments subject to backup withholding.

(b) Amount subject to backup withholding.

(1) In general.

(2) Net commissions.

(3) Payments aggregating $600 or more for the calendar year.

§ 31.3406(b)(3)-2 Reportable barter exchanges and gross proceeds of sales of securities or commodities by brokers.

(a) Transactions subject to backup withholding.

(b) Amount subject to backup withholding.

(1) In general.

(2) Forward contracts, including foreign currency contracts, and regulated futures contracts.

(3) Security sales made through a margin account.

(4) Security short sales.

(5) Fractional shares.

§ 31.3406(b)(3)-3 Reportable payments by certain fishing boat operators.

(a) Payments subject to backup withholding.

(b) Amount subject to backup withholding.

§ 31.3406(b)(3)-4 Reportable payments of royalties.

(a) Royalty payments subject to backup withholding.

(b) Amount subject to backup withholding.

§ 31.3406(b)(4)-1 Exemption for certain minimal payments.

(a) In general.

(b) Manner of making the election.

(c) How to annualize.

(1) In general.

(2) Special aggregation rule for reportable interest and dividends.

(d) Exception for window transactions and original issue discount.

§ 31.3406(c)-1 Notified payee underreporting of reportable interest or dividend payments.

(a) Overview.

(b) Definitions.

(1) Notified payee underreporting.

(2) Payee underreporting.

(c) Notice to payors regarding backup withholding due to notified payee underreporting.

(1) In general.

(2) Additional requirements for payors that are also brokers.

(3) Payor identification of accounts of the payee subject to backup withholding due to notified payee underreporting.

(d) Notice from payors of backup withholding due to notified payee underreporting.

(1) In general.

(2) Procedures.

(e) Period during which backup withholding is required.

(1) In general.

(2) Stop withholding.

(3) Dormant accounts.

(f) Notice to payees from the Internal Revenue Service.

(1) Notice period.

(2) Payee subject to backup withholding.

(3) Disclosure of names of payors and brokers.

(4) Backup withholding certification.

(g) Determination by the Internal Revenue Service that backup withholding should not start or should be stopped.

(1) In general.

(2) Date notice to stop backup withholding will be provided.

(3) Grounds for determination.

(4) No underreporting.

(5) Correcting any payee underreporting.

(6) Undue hardship.

(7) Bona fide dispute.

(h) Payees filing a joint return.

(1) In general.

(2) Exceptions.

(i) [Reserved.]

(j) Penalties.

§ 31.3406(d)-1 Manner required for furnishing a taxpayer identification number.

(a) Requirement to backup withhold.

(b) Reportable interest or dividend account.

(1) Manner required for furnishing a taxpayer identification number with respect to a pre-1984 account or instrument.

(2) Determination of pre-1984 account or instrument.

(3) Manner required for furnishing a taxpayer identification number with respect to an account or instrument that is not a pre-1984 account.

(4) Special rule with respect to the acquisition of a readily tradable instrument in a transaction between certain parties acting without the assistance of a broker.

(c) Brokerage account.

(1) Manner required for furnishing a taxpayer identification number with respect to a brokerage relationship that is not a post-1983 brokerage account.

(2) Manner required for furnishing a taxpayer identification number with respect to a post-1983 brokerage account.

(d) Rents, commissions, nonemployee compensation, and certain fishing boat operators, etc. Manner required for furnishing a taxpayer identification number.

§ 31.3406(d)-2 Payee certification failure.

(a) Requirement to backup withhold.

(b) Exceptions.

§ 31.3406(d)-3 Special 30-day rules for certain reportable payments.

(a) Accounts or readily tradable instruments acquired directly from the payor (including a broker who holds an instrument in street name) by electronic transmission or by mail.

(b) Sale of an instrument for a customer by electronic transmission or by mail.

(c) Application to foreign payees.

§ 31.3406(d)-4 Special rules for readily tradable instruments acquired through a broker.

(a) Readily tradable instruments acquired through post-1983 brokerage accounts with a broker who is not a payor.

(1) In general.

(2) Additional requirements.

(3) Transactions entered into through a brokerage account that is not a post-1983 brokerage account.

(4) Payor must notify payee.

(b) Notices.

(1) Form of notice by broker to payor.

(2) Form of notice by payor to payee.

(c) Payor's reliance on information from broker.

(1) In general.

(2) Amount subject to backup withholding.

§ 31.3406(d)-5 Backup withholding when the service or a broker notifies the payor to withhold because the payee's taxpayer identification number is incorrect.

(a) Overview.

(b) Definitions and special rules.

(1) Definition of an incorrect name/TIN combination.

(2) Definition of account.

(3) Definition of business day.

(4) Certain exceptions.

(c) Notice regarding an incorrect name/TIN combination.

(1) In general.

(2) Additional requirements for payors that are also brokers.

(3) Payor identification of the account or accounts of the payee that have the incorrect taxpayer identification number.

(4) Special rule for joint accounts.

(5) Date of receipt.

(d) Notice from payors of backup withholding due to an incorrect name/TIN combination.

(1) In general.

(2) Procedures.

(e) Period during which backup withholding is required due to notification of an incorrect name/TIN combination.

(1) In general.

(2) Grace periods.

(3) Dormant accounts.

(f) Manner required for payee to furnish certified taxpayer identification number.

(g) Receipt of two notices within a 3-year period.

(1) In general.

(2) Notice to payee who has provided two incorrect name/TIN combinations within 3 calendar years.

(3) Period during which backup withholding is required due to a second notice of an incorrect name/TIN combination within 3 calendar years.

(4) Receipt of two notices in one calendar year.

(5) Notification from the Social Security Administration (or the Internal Revenue Service) validating a name/TIN combination.

(h) Payors must use newly provided certified number.

(i) Effective date.

(j) Examples.

§ 31.3406(e)-1 Period during which backup withholding is required.

(a) In general.

(b) Failure to furnish a taxpayer identification number in the manner required.

(1) Start withholding.

(2) Stop withholding.

(c) Notification of an incorrect taxpayer identification number.

(d) Notified payee underreporting.

(e) Payee certification failure.

(1) Start withholding.

(2) Stop withholding.

(f) Rule for determining when the payor receives a taxpayer identification number or certificate from a payee.

§ 31.3406(f)-1 Confidentiality of information.

(a) Confidentiality and liability for violation.

(b) Permissible use of information.

(1) In general.

(2) Window transactions.

(c) Specific restrictions on the use of information.

§ 31.3406(g)-1 Exception for payments to certain payees and certain other payments.

(a) Exempt recipients.

(1) In general.

(2) Nonexclusive list.

(b) Determination of whether a person is described in paragraph (a)(1) of this section.

(c) Prepaid or advance premium life-insurance contracts.

§ 31.3406(g)-2 Exception for reportable payments for which backup withholding is otherwise required.

(a) In general.

(b) Payment of wages.

(c) Distribution from a pension, annuity, or other plan of deferred compensation.

(d) Gambling winnings.

(1) In general.

(2) Definition of a reportable gambling winning and determination of amount subject to backup withholding.

(3) Special rules.

(e) Certain real estate transactions.

(f) Certain payments after an acquisition of accounts or instruments.

(g) Certain gross proceeds.

§ 31.3406(g)-3 Exemption while payee is waiting for a taxpayer identification number.

(a) In general.

(1) Backup withholding not required for 60 days.

(2) Reserve method.

(3) Alternative rule; 7-day grace period.

(b) Special rule for readily tradable instruments.

(c) Exceptions.

(1) In general.

(2) Special rule for amounts subject to reporting under section 6045 other than proceeds of redemptions of bearer obligations.

(d) Awaiting-TIN certificate.

(e) Form for awaiting-TIN certificate.

§ 31.3406(h)-1 Definitions.

(a) In general.

(b) Taxpayer identification number.

(1) In general.

(2) Obviously incorrect number.

(c) Broker.

(d) Readily tradable instrument.

(e) Day.

(f) Business day.

§ 31.3406(h)-2 Special rules.

(a) Joint accounts.

(1) Relevant name and taxpayer identification number combination.

(2) Optional rule for accounts subject to backup withholding under section 3406(a)(1)(B) or (C) where the names are switched.

(3) Joint foreign payees.

(b) Backup withholding from an alternative source.

(1) In general.

(2) Exceptions for payments made in property.

(c) Trusts.

(d) Adjustment of prior withholding by middleman.

(e) Conversion of amounts paid in foreign currency into United States dollars.

(f) Coordination with other sections.

(g) Tax liabilities and penalties.

(h) To whom payor is liable for amount withheld.

§ 31.3406(h)-3 Certificates.

(a) Prescribed form to furnish information under penalties of perjury.

(1) In general.

(2) Use of a single or multiple Forms W-9 for accounts of the same payee.

(b) Prescribed form to furnish a noncertified taxpayer identification number.

(c) Forms prepared by payors or brokers.

(1) Substitute forms; in general.

(2) Form for exempt recipient.

(d) Special rule for brokers.

(e) Reasonable reliance on certificate.

(1) In general.

(2) Circumstances establishing reasonable reliance.

(f) Who may sign certificate.

(1) In general.

(2) Notified payee underreporting.

(g) Retention of certificates.

(1) Accounts or instruments that are not pre-1984 accounts and brokerage relationships that are post-1983 brokerage accounts.

(2) Accounts or instruments that are pre-1984 accounts and brokerage relationships that are not post-1983 brokerage accounts.

(h) Cross references.

§ 31.3406(i)-1 Effective date.

T.D. 8409, 4/10/92, amend T.D. 8637, 12/20/95, T.D. 8734, 10/6/97, T.D. 9010, 7/25/2002.

PAR. 5. Section 31.3406-0 is amended as follows:

1. Entries for § 31.3406(b)(3)-5(a), (b) and (c) are added.

2. Entry for § 31.3406(g)-1 is amended by adding paragraphs (d), (e), and (f).

The additions read as follows:

Proposed § 31.3406-0 Outline of the backup withholding regulations. [*For Preamble, see ¶ 153,139*]

* * * * *

§ 31.3406(b)(3)-5 Reportable payments of payment card and third party network transactions.

(a) Payment card and third party network transactions subject to backup withholding.

(b) Amount subject to backup withholding.

* * * * *

§ 31.3406(g)-1 Exception for payments to certain payees and certain other payments.

* * * * *

(d) Reportable payments made to Canadian nonresident alien individuals.

(e) Certain reportable payments made outside the United States by foreign persons, foreign offices of United States banks and brokers, and others.

(f) Special rule for certain payment card transactions.

* * * * *

Proposed § 31.3406-0 Outline of the backup withholding regulations. [*For Preamble, see ¶ 151,187*]

• ***Caution:*** This Notice of Proposed Rulemaking was partially finalized by Prop Reg. 60-110, TD 8365, 9/23/91, TD 8409, 4/15/92, and TD 8637, 9/27/90.

This section lists paragraphs contained in §§ 31.3406-0 through 31.3406(i)-1.

§ 31.3406(a)-1 Withholding requirement on reportable payments made after December 31, 1983.

§ 31.3406(a)-2 The obligation of payors to backup withhold.

(a) In general.

(b) Middlemen treated as payors.

(c) Exceptions.

(d) Examples.

§ 31.3406(a)-3 Amounts subject to backup withholding.

§ 31.3406(a)-4 Time when payments are considered to be paid and subject to backup withholding.

(a) Reportable interest or dividend payments.

(b) Other reportable payments.

(c) Middleman payor.

(1) In general.

(2) Special rule for common trust funds.

(d) Special rule for grantor trusts.

(e) Examples.

§ 31.3406(b)(1)-1 Reportable payment.

(a) In general.

(b) Reportable interest or dividend payment defined.

(c) Other reportable payment defined.

§ 31.3406(b)(2)-1 Reportable interest payment.

(a) Interest subject to withholding.

(1) In general.

(2) Special rule for tax-exempt interest.

(3) Examples.

(b) Amount subject to withholding.

(1) In general.

(2) Withholding adjustment for penalty for premature withdrawal.

(i) Special rule.

(ii) Examples.

§ 31.3406(b)(2)-2 Original issue discount.

(a) Original issue discount subject to withholding.

(b) Time and amount subject to backup withholding with respect to short-term obligations.

(1) No payment prior to maturity.

(2) Payment prior to maturity.

(c) Transferred short-term obligations.

(1) Subsequent holder may establish purchase price.

(2) If subsequent holder is unable to establish purchase price.

(3) If obligation is transferred.

(d) Time and amount subject to withholding with respect to long-term obligations.

(1) No payments prior to maturity.

(2) Registered long-term obligations with payments prior to maturity.

(3) Bearer long-term obligations with payments prior to maturity.

(i) Payments prior to maturity.

(ii) Payments at maturity.

(e) Transferred long-term obligations.

(1) Subsequent holder.

(2) If obligation is transferred.

(f) Examples.

§ 31.3406(b)(2)-3 Window transactions.

(a) Requirement to withhold.

(b) Window transaction defined.

(c) Manner of furnishing taxpayer identification number in the case of a window transaction.

(d) Examples.

§ 31.3406(b)(2)-4 Reportable dividend payment.

(a) Dividends subject to withholding.

(b) Examples.

(c) Dividends not subject to withholding.

(d) Amount subject to withholding.

(1) In general.

(2) Reasonable estimate of amount of dividend subject to withholding.

(3) Reinvested dividends.

§ 31.3406(b)(2)-5 Reportable patronage dividend.

(a) Patronage dividends subject to withholding.

(b) Examples.

(c) Amount subject to withholding.

(1) Failure to provide taxpayer identification number or notification of incorrect taxpayer identification number.

(2) Notified payee underreporting or payee certification failure.

(3) Examples.

§ 31.3406(b)(3)-1 Reportable payments of rents, commissions, nonemployee compensation, etc.

(a) Payments subject to withholding.

(b) Amount subject to withholding.

(1) In general.

(2) Special rule with respect to payments aggregating $600 or more for the calendar year.

(3) Determination of whether payments aggregate $600 or more.

(4) Exceptions.

(5) Examples.

§ 31.3406(b)(3)-2 Reportable barter exchanges and gross proceeds of sales of securities or commodities by brokers.

(a) Transactions subject to withholding.

(b) Examples.

(c) Amount subject to withholding.

(1) In general.

(2) Foreign currency contracts, forward contracts, or regulated futures contracts.

(3) Security sales made through a margin account.

(4) Security short sales.

(i) Amount subject to backup withholding.

(ii) Time of withholding.

(5) Fractional shares.

(6) Examples.

§ 31.3406(b)(3)-3 Reportable payments by certain fishing boat operators.

(a) Payments subject to withholding.

(b) Examples.

(c) Amount subject to withholding.

(1) In general.

(2) Examples.

§ 31.3406(b)(3)-4 Reportable payments of royalties.

(a) Royalty payments subject to withholding.

(b) Amount subject to withholding.

§ 31.3406(b)(4)-1 Exemption for certain minimal payments.

(a) In general.

(b) Manner of making the election.

(c) Annualization.

(1) Reportable interest or dividend payment.

(2) Window transaction, original issue discount, and broker reporting.

(d) Examples.

§ 31.3406(c)-1 Notified payee underreporting of reportable interest or dividend payments.

(a) Requirement to withhold.

(1) In general.

(2) Definition of notified payee underreporting.

(3) Definition of a payee underreporting.

(b) Notice to payors and brokers reporting backup withholding.

(1) Notice from the Internal Revenue Service.

(2) Notice from a broker.

(3) Accounts subject to backup withholding.

(c) Notice from payors of backup withholding due to a payee underreporting.

(1) In general.

(2) Form of the notice to the payee with respect to notified payee underreporting.

(3) Exceptions.

(4) Penalty for failure to provide notice.

(d) Notice to stop backup withholding.

(1) In general.

(2) Date notice to stop withholding will be provided.

(i) Underreporting corrected or bona fide dispute.

(ii) No underreporting or undue hardship.

(e) Period during which withholding is required.

(1) In general.

(2) Stop date.

(i) Underreporting corrected or bona fide dispute.

(ii) No underreporting or undue hardship.

(iii) Payor election to shorten or eliminate grace period.

(iv) Examples.

(f) Notice to payees from the Internal Revenue Service.

(1) Notice period.

(2) Payee subject to withholding.

(3) Disclosure of names of payors and brokers.

(4) Backup withholding certification.

(g) Determination by the Internal Revenue Service that backup withholding should not start or should be stopped.

(1) In general.

(2) No underreporting.

(3) Correcting any payee underreporting.

(i) Before issuance of a statutory notice of deficiency.

(ii) After issuance of a statutory notice of deficiency.

(4) Undue hardship.

(5) Bona fide dispute.

(h) Requests for determinations.

(1) In general.

(2) Determinations made during the notice period.

(3) Determinations made after the notice period.

(i) Reserved.

(j) Payees filing a joint return.

(1) In general.

(2) Exceptions.

(i) Innocent spouse.

(ii) Examples.

(iii) Divorced or legally separated payee.

(k) Penalties.

(1) Failure to withhold.

(2) False certification.

(i) Criminal penalty under section 7205(b).

(ii) Civil penalty under section 6682.

(A) In general.

(B) Waiver of penalty.

(C) Procedure for seeking a wavier.

(3) Delay of assessment.

§ 31.3406(d)-1 Manner required for furnishing a taxpayer identification number.

(a) Requirement to withhold.

(b) Reportable interest or dividend account.

(1) Manner required for furnishing a taxpayer identification number with respect to a pre-1984 account or instrument.

(2) Determination of pre-1984 account or instrument.

(i) In general.

(ii) Account or instrument automatically acquired on the maturity or termination of an account.

(iii) Special rule for short-term discount instrument acquired before January 1, 1985.

(iv) Insurance policies.

(v) Acquisitions and mergers.

(3) Manner required for furnishing a taxpayer identification number with respect to an account or instrument that is not pre-1984 account.

(4) Special rule with respect to the acquisition of a readily tradable instrument in a transaction between parties unrelated to the payor if the parties act without the assistance of a broker.

(5) Examples.

(c) Brokerage account.

(1) Manner required for furnishing a taxpayer identification number with respect to a brokerage relationship that is not a post-1983 brokerage account.

(i) In general.

(ii) Definition of a brokerage account that is not a post-1983 brokerage account.

(iii) Definition of a post-1983 brokerage account.

(2) Manner required for furnishing a taxpayer identification number with respect to a post-1983 brokerage account.

(3) Examples.

(d) Rents, commissions, nonemployee compensation, and certain fishing boat operators, etc.

(1) Manner required.

(2) Example.

§ 31.3406(d)-2 Payee certification failure.

(a) Requirement to withhold.

(b) Exceptions.

§ 31.3406(d)-3 Special 30-day rules for certain reportable payments.

(a) Account or readily tradable instrument acquired directly from the payor (including a broker who holds an instrument in street name).

(1) Account or instrument acquired directly from the payor by electronic means.

(2) Account or instrument acquired directly from payor by mail communication.

(3) Examples.

(b) Special rule with respect to the sale of an instrument for a customer pursuant to a telephone or wire instruction.

(1) Special rule.

(2) Example.

§ 31.3406(d)-4 Special rules for readily tradable instruments acquired through a broker.

(a) Readily tradable instruments acquired through a broker who is not a payor.

(1) In general.

(2) Grantor trust with ten or fewer grantors.

(3) Grantor trust with more than ten grantors.

(d) Conditions for a trustee of a grantor trust with more than ten grantors to impose backup withholding.

(e) Examples.

(f) Adjustment of prior withholding.

(1) In general.

(2) Example.

(g) Conversion of amounts paid in foreign currency into United States dollars.

(1) Convertible foreign currency.

(2) Nonconvertible foreign currency. [Reserved]

(h) Coordination with other sections.

(i) Penalties.

(j) To whom a payor is liable for amount withheld.

§ 31.3406(h)-3 Certificates.

(a) Prescribed form.

(b) Prescribed form to furnish a noncertified taxpayer identification number.

(c) Forms prepared by payors or brokers.

(1) Substitute forms; in general.

(2) Taxpayer identification number.

(3) Notified payee underreporting.

(4) Substitute form for both certifications.

(5) Form for exempt recipients.

(d) Special rule for brokers.

(e) Reasonable reliance on certificate.

(f) Who may sign the certificate.

(1) In general.

(2) Notified payee underreporting.

(g) Retention of certificate.

(1) Accounts or instruments that are not pre-1984 accounts or instruments and brokerage relationships that are post-1983 brokerage accounts.

(2) Accounts or instruments that are pre-1984 accounts or instruments and brokerage relationships that are not post-1983 brokerage accounts.

§ 31.3406(i)-1 Transitional rules.

§ 35a.3406-2 Imposition of backup withholding for notified payee underreporting of reportable interest or dividend payments.

(a) Requirement that a payor backup withhold due to a notified payee underreporting. *(1) In general.* Except as otherwise provided in paragraph (a)(5) of this section, backup withholding under section 3406(a)(1)(C) applies to any reportable interest or dividend payment (as defined in section 3406(b)(2) and paragraph (a)(4) of this section) made to a payee, if the Internal Revenue Service or a broker (as defined in section 3406(h)(5) and paragraph (a)(7) of this section and pursuant to section 3406(d)(2)(B)(ii)(III)) notifies a payor (as defined in section 3406(h)(4) and in paragraph (a)(6) of this section) that the payee is subject to backup withholding due to a notified payee underreporting (as defined in paragraph (a)(2) of this section). The payor is required under section 3406(c)(4) and paragraph (c)(1) of this section to inform the payee that backup withholding under section 3406(a)(1)(C) has begun. The requirements for the notice that a payor must send to a payee are set forth in paragraph (c)(2) and (3) of this section. The period for which backup withholding is required due to a notified payee underreporting is described in section 3406(e)(3)(A) and in paragraph (e) of this section. See section 3406(c)(3) and paragraph (g) of this section for the rules regarding how a payee may obtain a determination from the Internal Revenue Service that withholding under section 3406(a)(1)(C) be stopped or not started.

(2) Definition of notified payee underreporting. The term "notified payee underreporting" means that the Internal Revenue Service has—

(i) Determined that there was a payee underreporting as defined in paragraph (a)(3) of this section,

(ii) Mailed at least four notices to the payee (over a period of at least 120 days) with respect to the underreporting as prescribed in paragraph (f)(1) of this section, and

(iii) Assessed any deficiency attributable to the underreporting in the case of any payee who has filed a return.

(3) Definition of a payee underreporting. The term "payee underreporting" means that the Internal Revenue Service has determined, for a taxable year, that—

(i) A payee failed to include in his return of tax under chapter 1 of the Internal Revenue Code for such year any portion of a reportable interest or dividend payment required to be shown on such tax return, or

(ii) A payee may be required to file a return for such year and to include a reportable interest or dividend payment in such return, but failed to file such return.

See paragraph (a)(5) of this section for certain payments to be taken into account in determining whether there is payee underreporting even though those payments may not be defined as reportable interest or dividend payments in paragraph (a)(4) of this section or even though backup withholding under section 3406(a)(1)(C) may not apply to such payments.

(4) Definition of a reportable interest or dividend payment. (i) In general. See section 3406(b)(2), A-2 of § 35a.9999-1, A-5 of § 35a.9999-3, and A-15 of § 35a.9999-2 for the definition of reportable interest or dividend payment.

(ii) Exceptions. (A) Patronage dividends. Patronage dividends are treated as reportable interest or dividend payments for purposes of backup withholding under section 3406(a)(1)(C) only if 50 percent or more of the reportable amount is paid in money or by qualified check (as defined in section 1388(c)(4)), and then only to the extent that the payment is in money or by qualified check. See the second paragraph in A-10 of § 35a.9999-3 for an example of how this rule applies.

(B) Window payments. Pursuant to section 3406(b)(7), window payments as defined in A-42 of § 35a.9999-1 and A-9 of § 35a.9999-2 are not treated as reportable interest or dividend payments for purposes of backup withholding under section 3406(a)(1)(C).

(5) Reportable interest or dividend payments excluded from backup withholding. The following reportable interest or dividend payments are not subject to backup withholding:

(i) Certain dividends. Certain dividend payments as defined in A-9 of § 35a.9999-3.

(ii) Minimal payments. Minimal payments as defined in A-19 of § 36a.9999-2 if the payor elects not to impose backup withholding on such amounts.

(iii) Original issue discount. Original issue discount as defined in section 1273, unless there is a payment in cash. See A-15 of § 35a.9999-2.

(iv) Payments subject to other withholding. Payments already subject to withholding under another provision of the Internal Revenue Code.

Reportable minimal payments (to the extent reported on an information return), patronage dividends, original issue discount, and window payments shall be taken into account in determining whether underreporting (as defined in paragraph (a)(3) of this section) has occurred, even though those payments may not be defined as reportable interest or dividend payments under paragraph (a)(4) of this section or even though backup withholding under section 3406(a)(1)(C) may not apply to such payments.

(6) Definition of payor. See section 3406(h)(4), A-41 of § 35a.9999-1, and A-1 of § 35a.9999-3 for the definition of payor. The term payor includes a broker who holds an instrument in street name.

(7) Definition of broker. See section 3406(h)(5) for the definition of broker.

(b) Notice to payors and brokers regarding backup withholding. *(1) Notice from the Internal Revenue Service.* The Internal Revenue Service will notify—

(i) Payors to begin backup withholding on reportable interest or dividend payments due to a notified payee underreporting pursuant to section 3406(a)(1)(C); and

(ii) Brokers pursuant to section 3406(c)(5) that a payee is subject to backup withholding under section 3406(a)(1)(C).

(2) Notice from a broker. A broker who receives a notice from the Internal Revenue Service that a payee is subject to backup withholding due to a notified payee underreporting and through whom the payee subsequently acquires a readily tradable instrument (as defined in section 3406(h)(6)) with respect to which the broker is not the payor is required to notify the payor of that instrument that the payee is subject to backup withholding under section 3406(a)(1)(C) in the time and manner provided in A-41 of § 35a.9999-1.

(3) Accounts subject to backup withholding. (i) In general. After receiving notice from the Internal Revenue Service or from a broker, as provided in section 3406(d)(2)(B) and paragraphs (b)(1)(i) and (2) of this section, that a payee is subject to backup withholding under section 3406(a)(1)(C), payors are required to withhold 20 percent of all reportable interest or dividend payments subject to backup withholding made with respect to all accounts of the payee.

(ii) Joint accounts. Payors are required to withhold on joint accounts if the payee subject to backup withholding under section 3406(a)(1)(C) is the first person listed on the account at the time the payor receives the notice to begin backup withholding. Backup withholding shall continue to apply to reportable interest and dividend payments made to that account even if the order of the names on the account is subsequently changed, provided that the name of the payee subject to backup withholding remains on the account.

(iii) Exception. Payors are not required to withhold on reportable interest or dividend payments made with respect to an account of the payee that could not be located with reasonable care. The payor will be considered to have exercised reasonable care if the payor uses the name and taxpayer identification number (or names and taxpayer identification numbers if a joint return was filed by the payees) provided on the notice from the Internal Revenue Service or from a broker as prescribed in paragraphs (b)(1)(i) and (2) of this section and in certain circumstances identified in this paragraph (b)(3)(iii) any account numbers provided by the Internal Revenue Service in locating all accounts of a payee or payees. If a payee uses a different name on an account than the name stated on the notice from the Internal Revenue Service or from a broker (for instance, due to marriage or adoption) and the payor can associate both names with the payee using records kept in the ordinary course of business, the payor will be treated as exercising reasonable care if the payor uses both names to locate accounts of the payee. If the taxpayer identification number is not provided to the payor or broker by the Internal Revenue Service, or if the taxpayer identification number provided by the Internal Revenue Service does not match the taxpayer identification number of the payee on the records that the payor or broker maintains in the ordinary course of business, the payor or broker is required to use any account numbers provided by the Internal Revenue Service to identify the payee and the payee's taxpayer identification number. This information must be used by the payor to locate other accounts of the payee and by the broker to locate the payors with respect to whom the payee subsequently acquires a readily tradable instrument through that broker.

(c) Notice from payors of backup withholding due to a payee underreporting. *(1) In general.* A payor is required under section 3406(c)(4) to notify the payee in accordance with paragraph (c)(2) of this section that backup withholding has begun because of a notified payee underreporting. Payors who are notified by a broker that a payee is subject to backup withholding under section 3406(a)(1)(C) are also required to send the notice in accordance with paragraph (c)(2) of this section. As a result, the notice requirements provided in A-39 of § 35a.9999-1 and in the appendix to § 35a.9999-2 shall not apply to those payors notified by a broker that a payee is subject to backup withholding under section 3406(a)(1)(C). The payor must send the notice required by paragraph (c)(2) of this section to the payee no later than 15 days after the date that the payor makes the first payment subject to backup withholding under section 3406(a)(1)(C). The payor must send the notice of backup withholding by first-class mail to the payee at his last known address. Rules similar to the rules in A-17, A-18, A-19, and A-20 of § 35a.9999-1 shall apply to the requirement to provide notice by first-class mail.

(2) Form of the notice to the payee with respect to notified payee underreporting. The notice to the payee required by paragraph (c)(1) of this section must state—

(i) That the Internal Revenue Service has given notice that the payee has underreported reportable interest or dividends;

(ii) That, as a result of such underreporting, the payor is required under section 3406(a)(1)(C) of the Internal Revenue Code to withhold 20 percent of reportable interest and dividend payments made to the payee no later than the close of the day 30 days after the date that the payor received the notice;

(iii) The date that the payor received the notice to begin backup withholding under 3406(a)(1)(C);

(iv) That the payee must obtain a determination from the Internal Revenue Service in order to stop the backup withholding under section 3406(a)(1)(C); and

(v) That while he is subject to backup withholding due to payee underreporting, the payee may not certify to a payor making reportable interest or dividend payments (or to a broker acquiring a readily tradable instrument for the payee) that he is not subject to backup withholding under section

3406(a)(1)(C). See section 3406(a)(1)(D) for the backup withholding rules with respect to a payee's failure to make the certification under section 3406(a)(1)(D).

(3) Exceptions. A notice provided to a payee on or before April 23, 1987, will be deemed to satisfy the provisions of paragraph (c)(2) of this section if it informs the payee that the payor has been instructed by the Internal Revenue Service to start backup withholding on reportable interest or dividend payments to the payee. If a payor who has started backup withholding due to notified payee underreporting on or before April 23, 1987, has not provided adequate notice to the payee on or before April 23, 1987, then the payor must provide notice to the payee in the manner prescribed in paragraph (c)(2) of this section by the date that is 45 days after April 23, 1987.

(d) Notice to stop backup withholding. *(1) In general.* The Internal Revenue Service will provide written certification to the payee that backup withholding is to stop and will notify the payors who were contacted pursuant to paragraph (b) of this section to stop withholding after the Internal Revenue Service makes a determination under paragraph (g) of this section that backup withholding with respect to a payee should stop. The Internal Revenue Service will also notify the brokers who were contacted pursuant to paragraph (b) of this section that the payee is no longer subject to backup withholding under section 3406(a)(1)(C) and that the brokers are no longer obligated to provide notices to payors under paragraph (b)(2) of this section. A broker who receives certification under this section from the Internal Revenue Service is not required to provide the certification to any payors to which the broker has previously provided the notice required under paragraph (b)(2).

(2) Date notice to stop withholding will be provided. (i) Underreporting corrected or bona fide dispute. If the Internal Revenue Service makes a determination as set forth in paragraph (g)(1)(ii) or (iv) of this section during the 12-month period ending on October 15, of any calendar year, the Internal Revenue Service will provide the certification or notice required by paragraph (d)(1) of this section no later than December 1 of such calendar year.

(ii) No underreporting or undue hardship. If the Internal Revenue Service makes a determination as set forth in paragraph (g)(1)(i) or (iii), the Internal Revenue Service will provide the notices required by paragraph (d)(1) of this paragraph no later than the 45th day after the day on which the Internal Revenue Service makes its determination.

(e) Period during which withholding is required. *(1) In general.* Upon receiving notice from the Internal Revenue Service after April 23, 1987, to begin backup withholding under section 3406(a)(1)(C) or notification from a broker stating that the payee is subject to backup withholding under section 3406(a)(1)(C), the payor must impose backup withholding on all reportable interest and dividend payments made to the payee during the period beginning after the close of the 30th day after the day on which the payor receives the notice provided in paragraph (b)(1)(i) or (2) of this section and ending as of the close of the day before the stop date (as described in paragraph (e)(2) of this section). Pursuant to section 3406(e)(5)(C), the payor may elect to begin backup withholding at any time during the 30-day period described in this paragraph.

(2) Stop date. (i) Underreporting corrected or bona fide dispute. In the case of a determination that the underreporting has been corrected or that a bona fide dispute exists (as defined in paragraphs (g)(1)(ii) or (iv) of this section), the stop date is—

(A) January 1 following the 12-month period ending on October 15th of any calendar year in which the determination has been made or, if later,

(B) The day that is 30 days after the earlier of—

(1) The date on which the payor receives written notification from the Internal Revenue Services (under paragraph (d)(2) of this section) that withholding is to stop; or

(2) The date on which the payor receives a copy of the written certification provided to the payee by the Internal Revenue Service that withholding is to stop.

(ii) No underreporting or undue hardship. In the case of a determination that no payee underreporting occurred or that an undue hardship exists or could exist (as defined in paragraph (g)(1)(i) or (iii) of this section), the stop date is that date specified in paragraph (e)(2)(i)(B) of this section.

(iii) Payor election to shorten or eliminate grace period. The payor with respect to any payee may elect to determine the stop date without regard to the grace period provided in section 3406(e)(5)(B) (i.e., without regard to the words "the day that is 30 days after" in paragraph (e)(2)(i)(B) of this section) or by substituting a shorter grace period.

(iv) Examples. The provisions of paragraph (e)(2)(i) may be illustrated by the following examples:

Example (1). The Internal Revenue Service makes a determination by October 15, 1987, that any underreporting with respect to A has been corrected. X, a payor who has been notified to backup withhold on payments of interest to A due to notified payee underreporting, receives written notice from the Internal Revenue Service on December 1, 1987, informing X that A is no longer subject to backup withholding under section 3406(a)(1)(C) and that X must stop backup withholding as of the close of December 31, 1987, or if later, the earlier of the close of the day 30 days after receipt of the notice from the Internal Revenue Service or receipt of the copy of the written certification provided to the payee by the Internal Revenue Service. The stop date, as provided in paragraph (e)(2)(i)(A) of this section, is January 1, 1988, and the payor must stop backup withholding as of the close of December 31, 1987.

Example (2). Assume the same facts as in *Example (1)* except that X, due to a change of address or for other reasons, does not receive the notice from the Internal Revenue Service to stop backup withholding until December 15, 1987. In addition, A does not provide X with a copy of the certification that was provided to A by the Internal Revenue Service until December 15, 1987. The stop date, as provided in paragraph (e)(2)(i)(B) of this section, is January 14, 1988 (30 days after December 15, 1987), because that date is later than January 1, 1988. However, if a payor elects pursuant to section 3406(e)(5)(C) and paragraph (e)(2)(iii) of this section to determine the stop date without regard to that 30-day grace period, the stop date is January 1, 1987.

Example (3). Assume the same facts as in *Example (2)* except that on December 10, 1987 (rather than on December 15, 1987), A provides X with a copy of the certification from the Internal Revenue Service. The stop date, as provided in paragraph (e)(2)(i)(B) of this section, is January 9, 1988 (30 days after December 10, 1987), because that date is earlier than January 14, 1988 (30 days after the day X received notice from the Internal Revenue Service), but later than January 1, 1988.

(f) Notice to payees from the Internal Revenue Service. *(1) Notice period.* After the Internal Revenue Service determines that a payee underreporting exists as defined in paragraph (a)(3) of this section, the Internal Revenue Service, pursuant to section 3406(c)(1)(B), will mail to the payee at least four notices over a period of at least 120 days (hereafter referred to as the "notice period") before payors and brokers will be notified that the payee is subject to backup withholding due to a notified payee underreporting as provided in paragraph (b)(1) of this section. The notices may be incorporated with other notices provided to the payee by the Internal Revenue Service.

(2) Payee subject to withholding. After the Internal Revenue Service provides the notices described in paragraph (f)(1) of this section, the Internal Revenue Service will send the notices required by paragraph (b) of this section unless—

(i) A payee obtains a determination under paragraph (g) of this section, or

(ii) In the case of a payee who has filed a tax return, the Internal Revenue Service has not assessed the deficiency attributable to the underreporting.

(3) Disclosure of names of payors and brokers. The Internal Revenue Service pursuant to section 3406(c)(5) may require a payee subject to backup withholding due to a notified payee underreporting to disclose the names of all of his payors of reportable interest or dividend payments and the names of all of the brokers with whom the payee has accounts which may involve reportable interest or dividend payments. To the extent required in the request from the Internal Revenue Service, the payee shall also provide his account numbers and other information necessary to identify the payee's accounts.

(4) Backup withholding certification. Once a payee receives a final notice from the Internal Revenue Service notifying him that his reportable interest or dividend payments are subject to backup withholding due to notified payee underreporting under section 3406(a)(1)(C), the payee shall not certify to any payor or broker, under penalties of perjury, that he is not subject to backup withholding under section 3406(a)(1)(C). See paragraph (k)(2) of this section for the penalties that will apply to a payee who makes a false certification. The payee may not make the certification until the payee receives the certification provided in paragraph (d)(1) of this section from the Internal Revenue Service advising the payee that he is no longer subject to backup withholding under section 3406(a)(1)(C) (as provided in A-33 of § 35a.9999-1). See A-37 of § 35a.9999-1 for the rule applicable to a payor who makes reportable interest or dividend payments to a payee who fails to certify that he is not subject to backup withholding due to notified payee underreporting.

(g) Determination by the Internal Revenue Service that backup withholding should not start or should be stopped. *(1) In general.* A payee may prevent backup withholding from starting or stop in once it has started if, for the taxable year with respect to which there is a notified payee underreporting and any other taxable payee—

(i) Shows that there was no payee underreporting (as provided in paragraph (g)(2) of this section);

(ii) Corrects any payee underreporting (as provided in paragraph (g)(3) of this section);

(iii) Shows that backup withholding will cause or is causing an undue hardship (as defined in paragraph (g)(4) of this section) and that it is unlikely that the payee will underreport interest or dividend payments again; or

(iv) Shows that a bona fide dispute exists as to whether any underreporting has occurred (as provided in paragraph (g)(5) of this section).

(2) No underreporting. A payee may show that no underreporting of interest or dividends exists by presenting receipts or other satisfactory documentation to the Internal Revenue Service showing that all taxes relating to such payments were reported and paid timely or evidence showing that the payee did not have to file a return for the taxable year in question or that the underreporting determination is based upon a factual, clerical, or other mistake.

(3) Correcting any payee underreporting. (i) Before issuance of a statutory notice of deficiency. Before a statutory notice of deficiency is issued to a payee pursuant to section 6212, the payee may correct underreporting by filing a return if one was not previously filed and paying taxes, penalties, and interest due with respect to any underreported interest or dividend payments.

(ii) After issuance of a statutory notice of deficiency. After a statutory notice of deficiency is issued to a payee, the payee may correct underreporting at any time by filing a return if one was not previously filed and paying the entire deficiency and any other taxes including penalties and interest attributable to any payee underreporting of interest or dividend payments. Thus, for example, a payee may correct underreporting after assessment of a deficiency by paying the entire assessment with respect to that deficiency and any other taxes including penalties and interest attributable to any payee underreporting of interest or dividend payments for other taxable years.

(4) Undue hardship. A determination of undue hardship will be based on the overall impact to the payee of having 20 percent of reportable interest and dividend payments withheld. Factors that will be considered in determining whether backup withholding causes undue hardship include, but are not limited to, the following:

(i) Whether estimated tax payments, and other credits for current tax liabilities, or amounts withheld on employee wages or pensions, in addition to backup withholding, would cause significant over-withholding;

(ii) The payee's health, including the payee's ability to pay foreseeable medical expenses;

(iii) The extent of the payee's reliance on interest and dividend payments to meet necessary living expenses and the existence, if any, of other sources of income;

(iv) Whether other income of the payee is limited or fixed (e.g., social security, pension, and unearned income);

(v) The payee's ability to sell or liquidate stocks, bonds, bank accounts, trust accounts, or other assets, and the consequences of doing so;

(vi) Whether the payee reported and timely paid the most recent year's tax liability, including interest and dividend income; and

(vii) Whether the payee has filed a bankruptcy petition with the United States Bankruptcy Court. In addition to the above factors, the Internal Revenue Service must conclude that it is unlikely that any payee underreporting will occur again.

(5) Bona fide dispute. The Internal Revenue Service may make a determination under this paragraph if there is a dispute between the payee and the Internal Revenue Service on a question of fact or law that is material to a determination under paragraph (g)(1)(i) and, based upon all the facts and circumstances, the Internal Revenue Service finds that the dispute is asserted in good faith by the payee and there is a reasonable basis for the payee's position. See the example

provided in paragraph (j)(2)(ii) of this section for an illustration of this provision.

(h) Requests for determinations. *(1) In general.* A payee may request a determination under one or more of the provisions of paragraph (g) of this section. Following its review of a request for a determination under paragraph (g) of this section, the Internal Revenue Service will either provide the payee with a written certification as prescribed in paragraph (d) of this section if the evidence presented warrants the requested determination or will provide the payee with a written notice informing him that a determination was not made.

(2) Determinations made during the notice period. In general, if a determination is made during the notice period as defined in paragraph (f)(1) of this section, then the payee will not be subject to backup withholding due to a notified payee underreporting with respect to any taxable year for which a determination was made.

(3) Determinations made after the notice period. If a determination is made after the notice period, as defined in paragraph (f)(1) of this section, the Internal Revenue Service will provide a notice to payors and brokers, and a certification to the payee as provided in paragraph (d)(1) of this section.

(i) [Reserved]

(j) Payees filing a joint return. *(1) In general.* For purposes of section 3406(a)(1)(C), if payee underreporting is found to exist with respect to a joint return filed by a husband and wife, then the provisions of this section shall apply to the payees collectively. As a result, both payees will be subject to backup withholding on accounts in their individual names as well as accounts in their joint names. Either or both payees may satisfy the criteria for a determination that no payee underreporting exists, that the underreporting has been corrected, or that a bona fide dispute exists (as provided in paragraphs (g)(1)(i), (ii), or (iv) of this section). Both payees, however, must satisfy the criteria for a determination that backup withholding will cause or is causing undue hardship (as provided in paragraph (g)(1)(iii) of this section).

(2) Exceptions. (i) Innocent spouse. A spouse who files a joint return may obtain a determination that withholding should stop or not start with respect to payments made to his or her individual accounts, if the spouse—

(A) Shows that he or she did not underreport income because he or she is an innocent spouse as described in section 6013(e), or

(B) Shows that there is a bona fide dispute as to whether he or she is an innocent spouse and hence did not underreport income.

(ii) Example. The provisions of paragraph (j)(2)(i) may be illustrated by the following example:

Example. H and W filed a joint return in 1986 on which H failed to include $2,000 of interest income. In 1987, the Internal Revenue Service determined that a payee underreporting exists with respect to H and W for the 1986 tax year. After properly notifying H and W of the underreporting and assessing the tax, the Internal Revenue Service sent notices to payors to begin backup withholding on the joint and individual accounts of H and W and to brokers informing them that H and W are subject to backup withholding under section 3406(a)(1)(C) on their joint and individual accounts. W claims that she is an innocent spouse and requests a determination that she did not underreport interest or dividend income so that her individual accounts will not be subject to backup withholding.

The Internal Revenue Service questions her status as an innocent spouse. If the Internal Revenue Service determines, based upon all the facts and circumstances, that there is a reasonable basis for W's claim to be an innocent spouse and that the claim is made in good faith, W will have a bona fide dispute with the Internal Revenue Service. Consequently, the individual accounts of W will not be subject to further backup withholding due to a notified payee underreporting as provided in paragraph (g)(5) of this section.

The Internal Revenue Service will notify payors to stop backup withholding under section 3406(a)(1)(C) and brokers that W is no longer subject to backup withholding under section 3406(a)(1)(C) on W's individual accounts. Backup withholding will not restart on those accounts innocent spouse. In that event the Internal Revenue Service will notify the payors to start backup withholding will not restart on those accounts unless the Internal Revenue Service ultimately determines that W is not an innocent spouse. In that event the Internal Revenue Service will notify the payors to start backup withholding under section 3406(a)(1)(C) and the brokers that W is subject to backup withholding under section 3406(a)(1)(C) with respect to the individual accounts of W.

(iii) Divorced or legally separated payee. A payee who, at the time of the request for a determination under paragraph (g) of this section, is divorced or legally separated under state law may obtain a determination that undue hardship exists (or would exist) under paragraph (g)(1)(iii) of this section with respect to reportable interest and dividend payments made to his or her individual accounts if the divorced or legally separated payee satisfies the criteria for a determination under paragraph (g)(4) of this section.

(k) Penalties. *(1) Failure to withhold.* See A-2 of § 35a.9999-3 for rules relating to penalties applicable to a payor who fails to withhold on reportable interest and dividend payments made to a payee subject to backup withholding.

(2) False certification. (i) Criminal penalty under section 7205(b). If any individual willfully makes a false certification under section 3406(d)(1) or (2), then that individual shall, in addition to any other penalty provided by law, upon conviction thereof, be fined not more than $1,000, or imprisoned not more than 1 year, or both.

(ii) Civil penalty under section 6682. (A) In general. In addition to any criminal penalty provided by law, if any individual makes a statement under section 3406 which results in a decrease in the amounts deducted and withheld under chapter 24 of the Internal Revenue Code and, as of the time the statement was made, there was no reasonable basis for the statement, the individual shall pay a penalty of $500 for the statement. The penalty is due upon notice and demand and pursuant to section 6682 collection is not subject to the deficiency procedures of subchapter B of chapter 63 of the Internal Revenue Code. See section 6682.

(B) Waiver of penalty. The payee may obtain a waiver (in whole or part) of the penalty imposed under section 6682(a) and paragraph (k)(2)(ii)(A) of this section if it is established to the satisfaction of the Internal Revenue Service that the taxes imposed under subtitle A of the Internal Revenue Code with respect to the payee for the taxable year in which the false certification was made are equal to or less than the sum of—

(1) The credits against taxes allowed by part IV of subchapter A of chapter 1 of the Internal Revenue Code, and

(2) The payments of estimated tax which are considered payments on account of such taxes.

(C) Procedure for seeking a waiver. To request a waiver under section 6682(b) and paragraph (k)(2)(ii)(B) of this section, the payee must submit to the Internal Revenue Service a written statement with supporting documents to establish all the facts necessary in order to obtain the waiver. The statement must be signed by the person that otherwise would be subject to the penalty imposed by section 6682(a) and paragraph (k)(2)(ii)(A) of this section and must contain a declaration that it is made under penalties of perjury.

(3) Delay of assessment. If a payee institutes or maintains a suit with the United States Tax Court primarily to delay assessment and the payee's position is frivolous or groundless, or the payee unreasonably failed to pursue available administrative remedies, the court may award up to $5,000 in damages under section 6673. The damages will be assessed against and collected from the payee in the same manner as the underlying tax.

(l) Effective date. This section is effective until December 31, 1996.

T.D. 8137, 4/20/87, amend T.D. 8637, 12/20/95.

§ 31.3406(a)-1 Backup withholding requirement on reportable payments.

Caution: The Treasury has not yet amended Reg § 31.3406(a)-1 to reflect changes made by P.L. 107-16.

(a) Overview. Under section 3406, a payor must deduct and withhold 31 percent of a reportable payment if a condition for withholding exists. Reportable payments mean interest and dividend payments (as defined in section 3406(b)(2)) and other reportable payments (as defined in section 3406(b)(3)). The conditions described in paragraph (b)(1) of this section apply to all reportable payments, including reportable interest and dividend payments. The conditions described in paragraph (b)(2) of this section apply only to reportable interest and dividend payments.

(b) Conditions that invoke the backup withholding requirement. *(1) Conditions applicable to all reportable payments.* A payor of a reportable payment must deduct and withhold under section 3406 if—

(i) The payee of the reportable payment does not furnish the payee's taxpayer identification number to the payor, as required in section 3406(a)(1)(A) and § 31.3406(d)-1; or

(ii) The Internal Revenue Service or a broker notifies the payor that the taxpayer identification number furnished by its payee for a reportable payment is incorrect, as described in section 3406(a)(1)(B) and § 31.3406(d)-5.

(2) Conditions applicable only to reportable interest or dividend payments. A payor of a reportable interest or dividend payment must deduct and withhold under section 3406 if—

(i) The Internal Revenue Service or a broker notifies the payor that its payee has underreported interest or dividend income, as described in section 3406(a)(1)(C) and § 31.3406(c)-1; or

(ii) The payee fails to certify to the payor or broker that the payee is not subject to withholding due to notified payee underreporting, as described in section 3406(a)(1)(D) and § 31.3406(d)-2.

(c) Exceptions. The requirement to withhold does not apply to certain minimal payments as described in § 31.3406(b)(4)-1 or to payments exempt from withholding under §§ 31.3406(g)-1 through 31.3406(g)-3.

(d) Cross references. For the definition of payor, see § 31.3406(a)-2. For the definition of taxpayer identification number, see § 31.3406(h)-1(b).

T.D. 8637, 12/20/95.

§ 31.3406(a)-2 Definition of payors obligated to backup withhold.

(a) In general. Payor means the person that is required to make an information return under section 6041, 6041A(a), 6042, 6044, 6045, 6049, 6050A, or 6050N, with respect to any reportable payment (as described in section 3406(b)), or that is described in paragraph (b) of this section.

(b) Persons treated as payors. The following persons are treated as payors for purposes of section 3406—

(1) A grantor trust established after December 31, 1995, all of which is owned by two or more grantors (treating for this purpose spouses filing a joint return as one grantor);

(2) A grantor trust with ten or more grantors established on or after January 1, 1984 but before January 1, 1996;

(3) A common trust fund; and

(4) A partnership or an S corporation that makes a reportable payment.

(c) Persons not treated as payors. A person on the following list is not treated as a payor for purposes of section 3406 if the person does not have a reporting obligation under the section on information reporting to which the payment relates—

(1) A trust (other than a grantor trust as described in paragraph (b)(1) or (2) of this section) that files a Form 1041 containing information required to be shown on an information return, including amounts withheld under section 3406; or

(2) A partnership making a payment of a distributive share or an S corporation making a similar distribution.

(d) Effective date. The provisions of this section apply to payments made after December 31, 2002.

T.D. 8637, 12/20/95, amend T.D. 9010, 7/25/2002.

PAR. 6. Section 31.3406(a)-2 is amended by revising paragraph (a) to read as follows:

Proposed § 31.3406(a)-2 Definition of payors obligated to backup withhold. [*For Preamble, see ¶ 153,139*]

(a) In general. Payor means the person that is required to make an information return under sections 6041, 6041A(a), 6042, 6044, 6045, 6049, 6050A, 6050N, or 6050W with respect to any reportable payment (as described in section 3406(b)), or that is described in paragraph (b) of this section.

* * * * *

§ 31.3406(a)-3 Scope and extent of accounts subject to backup withholding.

A payor who is required to withhold under § 31.3406(a)-1 must withhold—

(a) on the accounts subject to withholding under § 31.3406(a)-1(b)(1)(i) or (b)(2)(ii); and

(b) On the accounts subject to withholding under § 31.3406(a)-1(b)(1)(ii) or (b)(2)(i), as described under § 31.3406(d)-5 (relating to notification of incorrect TIN) or § 31.3406(c)-1 (relating to notified payee underreporting), respectively.

T.D. 8637, 12/20/95.

§ 31.3406(a)-4 Time when payments are considered to be paid and subject to backup withholding.

(a) Timing. *(1) In general.* If backup withholding is required under section 3406 on a reportable payment (as defined in section 3406(b)), the payor must withhold at the time it makes the payment to the payee or to the payee's account that is subject to withholding. Amounts are considered paid when they are credited to the account of, or made available to, the payee. Amounts are not considered paid solely because they are posted (e.g., an informational notation on the payee's passbook) if they are not actually credited to the payee's account or made available to the payee. See paragraph (c) of this section for the timing of withholding by a middleman.

(2) Special rules for dividends. For purposes of section 3406 and this section—

(i) Record date earlier than payment date. In the case of stock for which the record date is earlier than the payment date, the dividends are considered paid on the payment date.

(ii) Dividends paid in corporate reorganizations. In the case of a corporate reorganization, if a payee is required to exchange stock held in the former corporation for stock in the new corporation before the dividends that have been paid with respect to the stock in the new corporation will be provided to the payee, the dividend is considered paid on the date the payee actually exchanges the stock and receives the dividend.

(b) Amounts reportable under section 6045. *(1) In general.* Notwithstanding paragraph (a) of this section, in the case of a transaction reportable under section 6045 (except in the case of forward contracts (including foreign currency contracts), regulated futures contracts, and security short sales), the obligation to withhold under section 3406 arises on the date the sale is entered on the books of the broker or the date the exchange occurs as provided in § 1.6045-1(f)(3) of this chapter. A broker (in its capacity as payor) is not required, however, to satisfy its withholding liability until payment is made. See § 31.3406(b)(3)-2(b)(2) for special rules applicable to forward contracts (including foreign currency contracts), regulated futures contracts, and security short sales.

(2) Special rule for interest accrued on bonds. For purposes of determining the time that interest is considered paid and subject to withholding under section 3406 when bonds are sold between interest payment dates, the portion of the sales price representing interest accrued to the date of sale is considered a portion of a reportable payment of gross proceeds under section 6045 (provided that the accrued interest is not tax-exempt as described in section 103(a), relating to certain governmental obligations), and is not considered to be a payment of interest for purposes of section 6049.

(c) Middlemen. *(1) In general.* A person that is a middleman and is a person defined in § 31.3406(a)-2(b) or in the section on information reporting to which the payment relates must withhold under section 3406 at the time the reportable payment is received by or credited to the middleman. If the middleman makes or credits the reportable payment to the payee prior to the middleman's receipt of the corresponding payment, the middleman may withhold at the time the reportable payment is made or credited to the payee.

(2) Special rule for common trust funds. A common trust fund (as defined in section 584) must withhold either—

(i) At the time the reportable payment is received by or credited to the common trust fund as provided in paragraph (c)(1) of this section;

(ii) On the date on which the assets of the common trust fund are valued; or

(iii) At the time the common trust fund pays or credits the reportable payment to a participant of the common trust fund.

(3) Special rule for certain grantor trusts. For grantor trusts described in § 31.3406(a)-2(b)(1) or (2), reportable payments made to the trust are treated as paid by the trust to each grantor, in an amount equal to the distribution made by the trust to each grantor, on the date that the reportable payment is paid to the trust (except for gross proceeds reportable under section 6045). Paragraph (b)(2) of this section applies to a grantor trust making a payment of gross proceeds under section 6045 subject to withholding under section 3406. For purposes of this paragraph (c)(3) a husband and wife filing a joint return are considered to be one grantor.

T.D. 8637, 12/20/95, amend T.D. 9010, 7/25/2002.

Proposed § 31.3406(b)(1)-1 Reportable payment. [*For Preamble, see ¶ 151,187*]

• ***Caution:*** This Notice of Proposed Rulemaking was partially finalized by Prop Reg. 60-110, TD 8365, 9/23/91, TD 8409, 4/15/92, and TD 8637, 9/27/90.

(a) In general. For purposes of backup withholding under section 3406, the term "reportable payment" means—

(1) Any reportable interest or dividend payment (as defined in section 3406(b)(2) and paragraph (b) of this section), and

(2) Any other reportable payment (as defined in section 3406(b)(3) and paragraph (c) of this section).

The determination of whether a payment is reportable and thus subject to withholding under section 3406 is made without regard to the amount of the payment. A payor may elect under § 31.3406(b)(4)-1, however, not to withhold from certain minimal payments.

(b) Reportable interest or dividend payment defined. The term "reportable interest or dividend payment" means—

(1) Interest subject to reporting under section 6049 (as described in § 31.3406(b)(2)-1),

(2) Original issue discount subject to reporting under section 6049 (as described in § 31.3406(b)(2)-2),

(3) Window transactions subject to reporting under section 6049 (as described in § 31.3406(b)(2)-3),

(4) Dividends subject to reporting under section 6042 (as described in § 31.3406(b)(2)-4), and

(5) Certain patronage dividends subject to reporting under section 6044 (as described in § 31.3406(b)(2)-5).

(c) Other reportable payment defined. The term "other reportable payment" means—

(1) Rents, commissions, nonemployee compensation, and other payments subject to reporting under section 6041 or 6041A(a) (as described in § 31.3406(b)(3)-1),

(2) Barter exchange or broker transactions subject to reporting under section 6045 (as described in § 31.3406(b)(3)-2),

(3) Certain payments by certain fishing boat operators subject to reporting under section 6050A (as described in § 31.3406(b)(3)-3), and

(4) Payments of royalties subject to reporting under section 6050N (as described in § 31.3406(b)(3)-4).

§ 31.3406(b)(2)-1 Reportable interest payment.

(a) Interest subject to backup withholding. *(1) In general.* A payment of a kind, and to a payee, that is required to be reported under section 6049 (relating to returns regarding interest and original issue discount) is a reportable payment for purposes of section 3406, subject to the special rules of § 31.3406(b)(2)-2 (relating to original issue discount) and § 31.3406(b)(2)-3 (relating to window transactions). See § 31.6051-4 for the requirement to furnish a statement to the payee if tax is withheld under section 3406.

(2) Special rule for tax-exempt interest. When an issuer is required to make an information return under § 1.6049-4(d)(8) of this chapter because a payee provided a signed written statement on the envelope or shell incorrectly claiming that the interest was exempt from taxation under section 103(a) (as described in § 1.6049-5(b)(1)(ii) of this chapter), the issuer is not required to impose withholding under section 3406.

(b) Amount subject to backup withholding. *(1) In general.* The amount of interest subject to withholding under section 3406 is the amount subject to reporting under section 6049.

(2) Special rule to adjust for premature withdrawal penalty. Solely for purposes of computing the amount subject to withholding under section 3406, the payor may elect not to withhold from the portion of any interest payment that is not received by the payee because a penalty is in fact imposed for premature withdrawal of funds deposited in a time savings account, certificate of deposit, or similar class of deposit.

T.D. 8637, 12/20/95.

§ 31.3406(b)(2)-2 Original issue discount.

(a) Original issue discount subject to backup withholding. The amount of original issue discount, treated as interest, subject to withholding under section 3406 is the amount subject to reporting under section 6049, but is limited to the amount of cash paid. In addition, if an original issue discount obligation, subject to reporting under section 6045, is sold prior to maturity and with respect to the seller a condition exists for imposing withholding under section 3406 on the gross proceeds, then withholding under § 31.3406(b)(3)-2 applies to the gross proceeds of the sale reportable under section 6045, and not to the amount of any original issue discount includible in the gross income of the seller for the calendar year of the sale. See § 31.6051-4 for the requirement to furnish a statement to the payee if tax is withheld under section 3406.

(b) Amount subject to backup withholding and time when backup withholding is imposed with respect to short-term obligations. In the case of an obligation with a fixed maturity date not exceeding one year from the date of issue (a short-term obligation), withholding under section 3406 applies to any payment of original issue discount on the obligation includible in the gross income of the holder to the extent of the cash amount of the payment. See § 1.1273-1 of this chapter to determine the amount of original issue discount on a short-term obligation. See § 1.446-2(e)(1) of this chapter to determine the amount of a payment treated as original issue discount.

(c) Transferred short-term obligations. *(1) Subsequent holder may establish purchase price.* (i) In general. At maturity of a short-term obligation, a subsequent holder (i.e., any person who purchased or otherwise obtained the obligation after the obligation was issued to the original holder) may establish the price of the obligation. The price established by the subsequent holder must then be treated as the original issue price for purposes of computing the amount of the original issue discount subject to withholding under section 3406. The price of a short-term obligation may be established by confirmation receipt or other record of a similar type or, if the obligation is redeemed by or through the person from whom the obligation was purchased or otherwise obtained, by the records of the person from whom or through whom the obligation was purchased or otherwise obtained. The subsequent holder is not required to certify under penalties of perjury that the price determined under this paragraph (c)(1)(i) is correct.

(ii) Exception. A payor may elect to disregard the price at which the subsequent holder purchased or otherwise obtained the obligation if the payor's computer or recordkeeping system on which the details of the obligation are stored is not able to accept that price without significant manual intervention.

(2) Subsequent holder unable (or not permitted) to establish purchase price. If a subsequent holder fails (or is unable, pursuant to paragraph (c)(1)(ii) of this section) to establish the purchase price of the obligation, then the person redeeming the obligation must determine the amount subject to withholding under section 3406 as though the obligation had been purchased by the holder on the date of issue. If the person redeeming the obligation is the issuer of the obligation, then the issuer must determine the amount subject to withholding from its records. If a person other than the issuer of the obligation redeems the obligation and the obligation is listed in Internal Revenue Service Publication 1212, List of Original Issue Discount Obligations, that person must determine the amount subject to withholding by using the issue price indicated in Publication 1212.

(3) Transferred obligation. If a short-term obligation is transferred, no part of the purchase price is considered a reportable interest payment under section 6049. Withholding under section 3406 applies, however, to the gross proceeds of the sale of the obligation if the transfer is subject to reporting under section 6045 and a condition exists for imposing withholding. For the rules regarding withholding for amounts subject to reporting under section 6045, see § 31.3406(b)(3)-2.

(d) Amount subject to backup withholding and time when backup withholding is imposed with respect to long-term obligations. *(1) No cash payments prior to maturity.* In the case of an obligation with a fixed maturity date that is more than one year from the date of issue (a long-term obligation) and with no cash payments prior to maturity, withholding under section 3406 applies at the maturity of the obligation to the amount of original issue discount includible in the gross income of the holder for the calendar year in which the obligation matures. The amount required to be withheld must not exceed the amount of the cash payment.

(2) Registered long-term obligations with cash payments prior to maturity. In the case of a long-term obligation in registered form that provides for cash payments prior to maturity, withholding under section 3406 applies at the time cash payments are made to the sum of the amounts of qualified stated interest and original issue discount includible in the gross income of the holder for the calendar year in which the cash payments are made. The amount required to be withheld at the time of any cash payment, however, must not exceed the amount of the cash payment. If more than one cash payment is made during a calendar year, the tax that is required to be withheld with respect to original issue discount must be allocated among all the expected cash payments in the ratio that each cash payment bears to the total of the expected cash payments.

(3) Transferred registered long-term obligations with payments prior to maturity. In the case of a long-term obligation that is transferred after its issuance from the original holder, the amount subject to withholding under section 3406 with respect to a subsequent holder is the amount of original issue discount includible in the gross income of all holders during the calendar year (without regard to any amount paid by a subsequent holder at the time of transfer). If the person redeeming the obligation at maturity is the issuer of the obligation, the issuer must determine the amount subject to withholding through its records by treating the holder as if he were the original holder. If a person redeeming the obligation at maturity is a person other than the issuer of the obligation, and the obligation is listed in Internal Revenue Service Publication 1212, List of Original Issue Discount Obligations, the person must determine the amount subject to withholding by using the issue price indicated in Publication 1212.

(e) Bearer long-term obligations. In the case of a bearer long-term obligation with cash payments prior to maturity—

(1) Payments prior to maturity. Withholding under section 3406 applies prior to maturity only to the payment of qualified stated interest (and not to any amount of original issue discount) includible in the gross income of the holder for the calendar year.

(2) Payments at maturity. At maturity of the obligation, withholding applies to the sum of any qualified stated interest payment made at maturity and the total amount of original issue discount includible in the gross income of the holder during the calendar year of maturity. The amount required to be withheld at the time of the cash payment, however, must not exceed the amount of the cash payment.

T.D. 8637, 12/20/95.

§ 31.3406(b)(2)-3 Window transactions.

(a) Requirement to backup withhold. Withholding under section 3406 applies to a window transaction (as defined in paragraph (b) of this section) only if the payee does not furnish a taxpayer identification number to the payor in the manner required in paragraph (c) of this section or furnishes an obviously incorrect number as described in § 31.3406(h)-1(b)(2). Withholding does not apply to a window transaction even though the Internal Revenue Service notifies the payor of the payee's incorrect taxpayer identification number under section 3406(a)(1)(B) or of notified payee underreporting under section 3406(a)(1)(C). The payee in a window transaction is not required to certify under penalties of perjury that the payee is not subject to withholding due to notified payee underreporting (as described in § 31.3406(d)-2(b)(2)).

(b) Window transaction defined. Window transaction means a payment of interest with respect to any of the following obligations:

(1) An interest coupon in bearer form that is subject to taxation (i.e., other than exempt interest described in § 1.6049-5(b)(1)(ii) of this chapter);

(2) A United States savings bond; or

(3) A discount obligation having a maturity at issue of one year or less, including commercial paper and bankers' acceptances that are in definitive form (i.e., evidenced by a paper document other than a confirmation receipt) but not including short-term government obligations (as defined in section 1271(a)(3)(B)).

(c) Manner of furnishing taxpayer identification number in the case of a window transaction. A payee must furnish the payee's taxpayer identification number to the payor with respect to a window transaction either orally or in writing at the time that the window transaction occurs. See § 31.3406(g)-3(c)(1)(i), which provides that a payee may not claim the payee is awaiting receipt of a taxpayer identification number with respect to a window transaction. The payee is not required to certify, under penalties of perjury, that the taxpayer identification number provided is correct.

T.D. 8637, 12/20/95.

§ 31.3406(b)(2)-4 Reportable dividend payment.

(a) Dividends subject to backup withholding. A payment of a kind, and to a payee, that is required to be reported under section 6042 (relating to returns regarding payments of dividends and corporate earnings and profits) is a reportable payment for purposes of section 3406. See paragraph (b) of this section for certain dividends not subject to withholding under section 3406. See § 31.6051-4 for the requirement to furnish a statement to the payee if tax is withheld under section 3406.

(b) Dividends not subject to backup withholding. Except as provided in § 31.3406(b)(3)-2 (relating to transactions reportable under section 6045), withholding under section 3406 does not apply to—

(1) Any amount treated as a taxable dividend by reason of section 302 (relating to redemptions of stock), section 304 (relating to redemptions through the use of related corporations), section 306 (relating to disposition of certain stock), section 356 (relating to receipt of additional consideration in connection with certain reorganizations), or section 1081(e)(2) (relating to certain distributions pursuant to an order of the Securities and Exchange Commission);

(2) Any exempt-interest dividend, as defined in section 852(b)(5)(A), paid by a regulated investment company; or

(3) Any amount paid or treated as paid during a year by a regulated investment company, provided that the payor reasonably estimates, as provided in paragraph (c)(2) of this section, that 95 percent or more of all dividends paid or treated as paid during the year are exempt-interest dividends.

(c) Amount subject to backup withholding. *(1) In general.* The amount of a dividend subject to withholding under section 3406 is the amount subject to reporting under section 6042, including any dividend that is reinvested pursuant to a plan under which a shareholder may elect to receive stock as a dividend instead of property. Except as otherwise provided in this paragraph (c), withholding applies to the entire amount of the distribution.

(2) Reasonable estimate of amount of dividend subject to backup withholding. Pursuant to section 6042(b)(3) and § 1.6042-3(c) of this chapter, if the payor is unable to determine the portion of a distribution that is a dividend, the entire amount of the distribution must be treated as a dividend for information reporting under section 6042. Hence, withholding applies to the entire amount of the distribution. If a payor is able reasonably to estimate under section 6042 and § 1.6042-3(c) of this chapter the portion of a distribution that is not a dividend, however, the payor must not withhold on that portion (which is not considered a dividend). A payor making a payment, all or a portion of which may not be a dividend, may use previous experience to estimate the portion of a distribution that is not a dividend. The payor's estimate is considered reasonable if—

(i) The estimate does not exceed the proportion of the distributions made by the payor during the most recent calendar year for which a Form 1099 was required to be filed that was not reported by the payor as a dividend; and

(ii) The payor has no reasonable basis to expect that the proportion of the distribution that is not a dividend will be substantially different for the current year.

(3) Reinvested dividends. In the case of a dividend paid pursuant to a dividend reinvestment plan, withholding under section 3406 applies, pursuant to § 31.3406(a)-4(a), at the time and to the amount made available to the shareholder or credited to the shareholder's account. At the discretion of the payor, withholding under section 3406 need not be applied to any excess of the fair market value of the shares of stock received by the shareholder or credited to the shareholder's account over the purchase price of the shares (including shares acquired by the shareholder at a discount in connection with the dividend distribution) or to any fee that is paid by the payor in the nature of a broker's fee for purchase of the stock or service charge for maintenance of the shareholder's account. The payor must, however, treat any excess amounts and fees on a consistent basis for each calendar year.

T.D. 8637, 12/20/95.

§ 31.3406(b)(2)-5 Reportable patronage dividend payment.

(a) Patronage dividends subject to backup withholding. A payment of a kind, and to a payee, that is required to be reported under section 6044 (relating to returns regarding patronage dividends) is a reportable payment for purposes of section 3406. See § 31.6051-4 for the requirement to furnish a statement to the payee if tax is withheld under section 3406.

(b) Amount subject to backup withholding. *(1) Failure to provide taxpayer identification number or notification of incorrect taxpayer identification number.* For purposes of sections 3406 (a)(1)(A) and (D), the amount of a payment described in paragraph (a) of this section that is subject to withholding under section 3406 is the amount subject to reporting under section 6044, but only to the extent the payment is made in money. For purposes of this paragraph (b), MONEY includes cash or a qualified check (as defined in section 1388(c)(4)).

(2) Notified payee underreporting or payee certification failure. For purposes of sections 3406(a)(1)(C) and (D), the amount of a payment described in paragraph (a) of this section that is subject to withholding under section 3406 is the amount subject to withholding under paragraph (b)(1) of this section, but only if 50 percent or more of that reportable amount is paid in money. Thus, a payor is required to withhold according to this paragraph (b)(2) on a payment if—

(i) There has been a notified payee underreporting described in section 3406(a)(1)(C) and § 31.3406(c)-1 or there has been a payee certification failure described in section 3406(a)(1)(D) and § 31.3406(d)-2;

(ii) The payor makes a reportable payment subject to reporting under section 6044 to the payee; and

(iii) Fifty percent or more of the payment is in cash or by qualified check.

T.D. 8637, 12/20/95.

§ 31.3406(b)(3)-1 Reportable payments of rents, commissions, nonemployee compensation, etc.

(a) Section 6041 and 6041a(A) payments subject to backup withholding. A payment of a kind, and to a payee, that is required to be reported under section 6041 (relating to information reporting of rents, commissions, nonemployee compensation, etc.) or a payment that is required to be reported under section 6041A(a) (relating to information reporting of payments to nonemployees for services) is a reportable payment for purposes of section 3406. See paragraph (b) of this section for an exception concerning payments aggregating less than $600. See § 31.6051-4 for the requirement to furnish a statement to the payee if tax is withheld under section 3406.

(b) Amount subject to backup withholding. *(1) In general.* The amount of a payment described in paragraph (a) of this section subject to withholding under section 3406 is the amount subject to reporting under section 6041 or section 6041A(a).

(2) Net commissions. Withholding under section 3406 does not apply to net commissions paid to unincorporated special agents with respect to insurance policies that are subject to reporting under section 6041, provided that no cash is actually paid by the payor to the special agent.

(3) Payments aggregating $600 or more for the calendar year. (i) In general. A payment is a reportable payment under paragraph (a) of this section only if the aggregate amount of the current payment and all previous payments to the payee during the calendar year $600 or more. The amount subject to withholding is the entire amount of the payment that causes the total amount paid to the payee to equal $600 or more and the amount of any subsequent payments made to the payee during the calendar year. This paragraph (b)(3)(i) does not apply to gambling winnings (as provided in § 31.3406(g)-2(e)(1)).

(ii) Exceptions. (A) The $600 aggregation rule. The $600 aggregation rule of paragraph (b)(3)(i) of this section does not apply if the payor was required to make an information return under section 6041 or 6041A(a) for the preceding calendar year with respect to payments to the payee, or the payor was required to withhold under section 3406 during the preceding calendar year with respect to payments to the payee that were reportable under section 6041 or 6041A(a).

(B) Determination of whether payments aggregate $600 or more. In determining whether payments to a payee aggregate $600 or more during a calendar year for purposes of withholding under section 3406, the payor must aggregate only payments of the same kind made to the same payee. For this purpose, payments are of the same kind if they are of the same type, regardless of whether they are reportable under the same section. However, a payor with different paying departments making reportable payments of the same kind is not required to aggregate payments made by all those departments unless it is the payor's customary method to aggregate those payments. A payor may, in its discretion, aggregate—

(1) Payments not of the same kind to the same payee, reportable under either section 6041 or 6041A(a); and

(2) Payments reportable under section 6041 with payments reportable under section 6041A(a).

T.D. 8637, 12/20/95.

§ 31.3406(b)(3)-2 Reportable barter exchanges and gross proceeds of sales of securities or commodities by brokers.

(a) Transactions subject to backup withholding. A payment of a kind, and to a payee, that any broker (as defined in section 6045(c) and § 1.6045-1(a)(1) of this chapter) or any barter exchange (as defined in section 6045(c) and § 1.6045-1(a)(4) of this chapter) is required to report under section 6045 is a reportable payment for purposes of section 3406. See § 31.6051-4 for the requirement to furnish a statement to the payee if tax is withheld under section 3406.

(b) Amount subject to backup withholding. *(1) In general.* The amount subject to withholding under section 3406 is the amount subject to reporting under section 6045. The amount subject to withholding with respect to broker reporting is the amount of gross proceeds (as determined under § 1.6045-1(d)(5) of this chapter). The amount subject to withholding with respect to barter exchanges is the amount received by any member or client (as determined under § 1.6045-1(f)(4) of this chapter).

(2) Forward contracts, including foreign currency contracts, and regulated futures contracts. (i) In general. If a customer is subject to withholding under section 3406 with respect to a forward contract (subject to information reporting under § 1.6045-1(c)(5) of this chapter), including a foreign currency contract (as defined in section 1256(g)(2)), or a regulated futures contract (as defined in section 1256(g)(1)), or with respect to an account through which those contracts are disposed of or acquired, the broker must withhold on both of the following amounts:

(A) All cash or property withdrawn from the account by the customer during the relevant year; and

(B) The amount of cash in the account available for withdrawal by the customer at the relevant year-end (including both gross proceeds and variation margin).

(ii) Rules concerning withdrawals. A withdrawal includes the use of money (including both gross proceeds and variation margin) or property in the account to purchase any property other than property acquired in connection with the closing of a contract. For this purpose, the acceptance of a warehouse receipt or other taking of delivery to close a contract is in connection with the closing of a contract only if the property acquired is disposed of by the close of the seventh trading day following the trading day that the customer takes delivery under the contract. In addition, making delivery to close a contract is in connection with the closing of a contract only if the broker is able to determine that the property used to close the contract was acquired no earlier than the seventh trading day prior to the trading day on which delivery is made. Withdrawals do not include repayments of debt incurred in connection with making or taking delivery that meets the requirements of this paragraph (b)(2). Withdrawals also do not include payments of commissions, fees, transfers of cash from the account to another futures account that is subject to this paragraph (b)(2) or cash withdrawals traceable to dispositions of property other than futures (not including profit on the contract separately reportable under § 1.6045-1(c)(5)(i)(b) of this chapter).

(iii) Special rule for forward contracts, including foreign currency contracts, and regulated futures contracts. The determination of whether the customer is subject to withholding under section 3406 with respect to an account containing forward contracts, including foreign currency contracts, or regulated futures contracts must be made at the time of the cash or property withdrawals or the relevant year-end, whichever is applicable.

(3) Security sales made through a margin account. The amount described in paragraph (a) of this section that is subject to withholding under section 3406 in the case of a security sale made through a margin account (as defined in 12 CFR part 220 (Regulation T)) is the gross proceeds (as defined in § 1.6045-1(d)(5) of this chapter) of the sale. The amount required to be withheld with respect to the sale, however, is limited to the amount of cash available for withdrawal by the customer immediately after the settlement of the sale. For this purpose, the amount available for withdrawal by the customer does not include amounts required to satisfy margin maintenance under Regulation T, rules and regulations of the National Association of Securities Dealers and national securities exchanges, and generally applicable self-imposed rules of the margin account carrier.

(4) Security short sales. (i) Amount subject to backup withholding. The amount subject to withholding under section 3406 with respect to a short sale of securities is the gross proceeds (as defined in § 1.6045-1(d)(5) of this chapter) of the short sale. At the option of the broker, however, the amount subject to withholding may be the gain upon the closing of the short sale (if any); consequently, the obligation to withhold under section 3406 would be deferred until the closing transaction. A broker may use this alternative method of determining the amount subject to withholding under section 3406 with respect to a short sale only if at the time the short sale is initiated, the broker expects that the amount of gain realized upon the closing of the short sale will be determinable from the broker's records. If, due to events unforeseen at the time the short sale was initiated, the broker is unable to determine the basis of the property used to close the short sale, the property must be assumed for this purpose to have a basis of zero.

(ii) Time of backup withholding. The determination of whether a short seller is subject to withholding under section 3406 must be made on the date of the initiation or closing, as the case may be, or on the date that the initiation or closing, as the case may be, is entered on the broker's books and records.

(5) Fractional shares. A broker is not required to withhold under section 3406 with respect to a sale of a fractional share of stock resulting in less than $20 of gross proceeds (as described in § 1.6045-1(c)(3)(x) of this chapter).

T.D. 8637, 12/20/95, amend T.D. 9010, 7/25/2002.

PAR. 16. Section 31.3406(b)(3)-2 is amended by revising paragraph (b)(4) to read as follows:

Proposed § 31.3406(b)(3)-2 Reportable barter exchanges and gross proceeds of sales of securities or commodities by brokers. [*For Preamble, see ¶ 153,143*]

* * * * *

(b) * * *

(4) Security short sales. (i) Short sales closed before January 1, 2011. (A) Amount subject to backup withholding. The amount subject to withholding under section 3406 with respect to a short sale of securities closed before January 1, 2011, is the gross proceeds (as defined in § 1.6045-1(d)(5) of this chapter) of the short sale. At the option of the broker, however, the amount subject to withholding may be the gain upon the closing of the short sale (if any); consequently, the obligation to withhold under section 3406 is deferred until the closing transaction. A broker may use this alternative method of determining the amount subject to withholding under section 3406 for a short sale only if at the time the short sale is initiated, the broker expects that the amount of gain realized upon the closing of the short sale will be determinable from the broker's records. If, due to events unforeseen at the time the short sale was initiated, the broker is unable to determine the basis of the property used to close the short sale, the property is assumed for this purpose to have a basis of zero.

(B) Time of backup withholding. For short sales closed before January 1, 2011, the determination of whether a short seller is subject to withholding under section 3406 must be made on the date of the initiation or closing, as the case may be, or on the date that the initiation or closing, as the case may be, is entered on the broker's books and records.

(ii) Short sales closed on or after January 1, 2011. For short sales closed on or after January 1, 2011, the obligation to withhold under section 3406 is deferred until the short sale is considered closed under section 1233. The determination of whether a short seller is subject to withholding under section 3406 may be made as of either this date or the date that the closing transaction is entered on the broker's books and records. The amount subject to withholding under section 3406 is the gross proceeds (as defined in § 1.6045-1(d)(5) of this chapter) of the short sale. At the option of the broker, however, the amount subject to withholding may be the gain upon the closing of the short sale (if any) if the broker reports both the gross proceeds and basis of the securities on the return of information required by section 6045.

* * * * *

§ 31.3406(b)(3)-3 Reportable payments by certain fishing boat operators.

(a) Payments subject to backup withholding. A payment of a kind, and to a payee, that is required to be reported under section 6050A (relating to information reporting by certain fishing boat operators) is a reportable payment for purposes of section 3406. See § 31.6051-4 for the requirement to furnish a statement to the payee if tax is withheld under section 3406.

(b) Amount subject to backup withholding. The amount described in paragraph (a) of this section subject to withholding under section 3406 is the amount subject to reporting under section 6050A, but only to the extent the amount is paid in money and represents a share of the proceeds of the catch.

T.D. 8637, 12/20/95.

§ 31.3406(b)(3)-4 Reportable payments of royalties.

(a) Royalty payments subject to backup withholding. A payment of a kind, and to a payee, that is required to be reported under section 6050N (relating to information reporting of payments of royalties) is a reportable payment for purposes of section 3406. See § 31.6051-4 for the requirement to furnish a statement to the payee if tax is withheld under section 3406.

(b) Amount subject to backup withholding. In general, the amount described in paragraph (a) of this section that is subject to withholding under section 3406 is the amount subject to reporting under section 6050N. However, if the reportable payment is for an oil or gas interest, the amount subject to withholding is the net amount the payee receives (i.e., the gross proceeds less production-related taxes such as state severance taxes).

T.D. 8637, 12/20/95.

Proposed § 31.3406(b)(3)-5 Reportable payments of payment card and third party network transactions. [*For Preamble, see ¶ 153,139*]

(a) Payment card and third party network transactions subject to backup withholding. A payment of a kind, and to a payee, that is required to be reported under section 6050W (relating to information reporting for payment card and third party network transactions) is a reportable payment for purposes of section 3406. See § 31.6051-4 for the requirement to furnish a statement to the payee if tax is withheld under section 3406.

(b) Amount subject to backup withholding. In general, the amount described in paragraph (a) of this section that is subject to withholding under section 3406 is the amount subject to reporting under section 6050W.

(c) Effective/applicability date. The provisions of this section apply to amounts paid after December 31, 2011.

§ 31.3406(b)(4)-1 Exemption for certain minimal payments.

(a) In general. A payor of reportable interest or dividends (as described in section 3406(b)(2)) or of royalties (as described in section 3406(b)(3)(E)) may elect not to withhold from a payment that does not exceed $10 and that on an analyzed basis does not exceed $10 (see paragraph (c) of this section). A broker or barter exchange may elect not to withhold on gross proceeds of $10 or less without regard to the annualization requirement. See § 31.6051-4 for the requirement to furnish a statement to the payee if tax is withheld under section 3406.

(b) Manner of making the election. The election not to withhold from payments that do not exceed $10 can be made only for payments described in paragraph (a) of this section. The election may be made on a payment-by-payment basis.

(c) How to annualize. *(1) In general.* To annualize a reportable interest payment, dividend payment, or royalty payment, a payor must calculate what the amount of the payment would be if it were paid for a 1-year period (instead of the period for which it actually is paid). The annualized amount is determined by dividing the amount of the payment by the number of days in the period for which it is being paid and then multiplying that result by the number of days in the year. If the annualized amount is $10 or less, the payor may elect not to withhold on that payment regardless of whether more than $10 may be or has been paid to the payee in other reportable payments during the calendar year. Conversely, if the annualized amount is more than $10, withholding applies even if $10 or less is actually paid to the payee during the calendar year. For purposes of computing the annualized amount, the payor may assume that February always consists of 28 days and that the year always consists of 360 days. For amounts that are deposited with a payor in a new account or certificate between the dates on which the payor customarily pays or credits interest, the payor may assume that the period for which the interest is paid is the payor's customary period for paying or crediting interest.

(2) Special aggregation rule for reportable interest and dividends. If a payor maintains records that reflect multiple holdings of one payee and the payor makes an aggregate payment of reportable interest or dividends (as defined in section 3406(b)(2)) with respect to those multiple holdings (such as a dividend check that reflects payment on all stock owned by the payee), the payor must annualize the aggregate payment.

(d) Exception for window transactions and original issue discount. A payor is not required to annualize payments made in window transactions (as defined in § 31.3406(b)(2)-3(b)) or payments of original issue discount. With respect to a window transaction, however, the payor is required to aggregate all payments made in the same transaction (e.g., payments made with respect to coupons or obligations presented for payment at the same time as described in § 1.6049-4(e)(4) of this chapter).

T.D. 8637, 12/20/95.

§ 31.3406(c)-1 Notified payee underreporting of reportable interest or dividend payments.

Caution: The Treasury has not yet amended Reg § 31.3406(c)-1 to reflect changes made by P.L. 107-16.

(a) Overview. Withholding under section 3406(a)(1)(C) applies to any reportable interest or dividend payment (as defined in section 3406(b)(2)) made with respect to an account of a payee if the Internal Revenue Service or a broker notifies a payor under paragraph (c)(1) or (2) of this section that the payee is subject to withholding due to notified payee underreporting (as defined in paragraph (b)(1) of this section), and the payor is required under paragraph (c)(3) of this section to identify that account. After receiving the notice and identifying accounts, the payor must notify the payee, in accordance with paragraph (d) of this section, that withholding due to notified payee underreporting has started. Paragraph (e) of this section describes the period for which withholding due to notified payee underreporting is required. Paragraph (f) of this section provides rules concerning notices that the Internal Revenue Service will send to a payee before notifying a payor that the payee is subject to withholding due to notified payee underreporting. Paragraph (g) of this section provides rules that a payee can use to prevent withholding due to notified payee underreporting from starting or to stop it once it has started. Paragraph (h) of this section provides special rules for joint accounts of payees who have filed a joint return. See section 6682 for the penalties that may apply to a payee subject to withholding under section 3406(a)(1)(C).

(b) Definitions. *(1) Notified payee underreporting.* Notified payee underreporting means that the Internal Revenue Service has—

(i) Determined that there was a payee underreporting (as defined in paragraph (b)(2) of this section);

(ii) Mailed at least four notices under paragraph (f)(l) of this section to the payee (over a period of at least 120 days) with respect to the underreporting; and

(iii) Assessed any deficiency attributable to the underreporting in the case of any payee who has filed a return.

(2) Payee underreporting. (i) In general. Payee underreporting means that the Internal Revenue Service has determined, for a taxable year, that—

(A) A payee failed to include in the payee's return of tax under chapter 1 of the Internal Revenue Code for that year any portion of a reportable interest or dividend payment required to be shown on that tax return; or

(B) A payee may be required to file a return for that year and to include a reportable interest or dividend payment in the return, but failed to file the return.

(ii) Payments included in making payee underreporting determination. The determination of whether there is payee underreporting is made by treating as reportable interest or dividend payments, all payments of dividends reported under section 6042, all patronage dividends reported under section 6044, and all interest and original issue discount reported under section 6049, regardless of whether withholding due to notified payee underreporting applies to those payments.

(c) Notice to payors regarding backup withholding due to notified payee underreporting. *(1) In general.* If the Internal Revenue Service or a broker notifies a payor that a payee is subject to withholding due to notified payee underreporting, the payor must—

(i) Identify any accounts of the payee under the rules of paragraph (c)(3) of this section; and

(ii) Notify the payee and withhold under section 3406 on reportable interest or dividend payments made with respect to any identified account under the rules of paragraphs (d) and (e) of this section.

(2) Additional requirements for payors that are also brokers. (i) In general. A broker must notify the payor of a readily tradable instrument that the payee of the instrument is subject to withholding due to notified payee underreporting if—

(A) The broker (in its capacity as a payor) receives a notice from the Internal Revenue Service under paragraph (c)(1) of this section that a payee is subject to withholding due to notified payee underreporting and the broker is required to identify an account of the payee under paragraph (c)(3) of this section;

(B) The payee subsequently acquires the instrument from the broker through the same account; and

(C) The acquisition of the instrument occurs after the close of the 30th business day after the date that the broker receives the notice (or on any earlier date that the broker may begin applying this paragraph (c)(2) after receipt of the notice described in paragraph (c)(1) of this section).

(ii) Transfer out of street name. For purposes of this paragraph (c)(2), an acquisition includes a transfer of an instrument out of street name into the name of the registered owner (i.e., the payee).

(iii) Method of providing notice. A broker must provide the notice required under this paragraph (c)(2) to the payor of the instrument with the transfer instructions for the acquisition. See § 31.3406(d)-4(a)(2).

(iv) Termination of obligation to provide information. The obligation of a broker to provide notice to payors under this paragraph (c)(2) terminates simultaneously with the termination of the broker's obligation to withhold (in its capacity as payor) due to notified payee underreporting on reportable interest or dividends made with respect to the account.

(3) Payor identification of accounts of the payee subject to backup withholding due to notified payee underreporting. (i) In general. (A) Notice from the Internal Revenue Service.

If a payor receives a notice from the Internal Revenue Service under paragraph (c)(1) of this section, the payor must identify, exercising reasonable care, all accounts using the same taxpayer identification number for information reporting purposes as the one provided in the notice. The notice may provide, however, that the payor need only identify the account or accounts corresponding to any account number or designation and related taxpayer identification number used for information reporting purposes as that listed on the notice.

(B) Notice from a broker. If a payor receives a notice from a broker under paragraphs (c)(1) and (2) of this section, the payor is not required to identify any account other than the account identified in the notice.

(ii) Exercise of reasonable care. If an account identified pursuant to paragraph (c)(3)(i)(A) of this section contains a customer identifier that can be used to retrieve systemically any other accounts that use the same taxpayer identification number for information reporting purposes, the payor must identify all accounts that can be so retrieved. Otherwise, a payor is considered to exercise reasonable care in identifying accounts subject to withholding under section 3406(a)(1)(C) if the payor searches any computer or other recordkeeping system for the region, division, or branch that serves the geographic area in which the payee's mailing address is located and that was established (or is maintained) to reflect reportable interest or dividend payments.

(iii) Newly opened accounts. (A) In general, a new account is not subject to withholding under section 3406(a)(1)(C) if the payee provides to the payor a Form W-9 (or other acceptable substitute) on which the payor may reasonably rely (within the meaning of § 31.3406(h)-3(e)(2) without regard to § 31.3406(h)-3(e)(2)(v)), unless the payor has actual knowledge (within the meaning of paragraph (c)(3)(iii)(B) of this section) that the statements made on the form are not true.

(B) For purposes of paragraph (c)(3)(iii)(A) of this section, a payor is considered to have actual knowledge that a payee's statement that the payee is not subject to withholding under section 3406(a)(1)(C) is not true if—

(*1*) The employee or individual agent of the payor who receives the payee's certification knows that the statement is not true;

(*2*) In conducting the investigation, if any, required by paragraph (c)(3)(iii)(C) of this section, the payor identifies any other accounts of the payee that are already subject to withholding under section 3406(a)(1)(C); or

(*3*) In the course of processing the certification or in administering an account to which a certification relates, the payor discovers that the payor was previously notified by the Internal Revenue Service that the payee is subject to withholding under section 3406(a)(1)(C) and no notice was received to stop withholding pursuant to section 3406(c)(3) prior to the time of the discovery.

(C) Except as provided in this paragraph (c)(3)(iii)(C), a payor is not required to investigate whether the statements made on the Form W-9 described in paragraph (c)(3)(iii)(A) of this section are true. If, however, in opening a new account, the payor relies on the same Form W-9 (or appropriate substitute) that it relied on previously in opening another account, the payor must investigate whether any such existing account is subject to withholding under section 3406(a)(1)(C). Similarly, if the payor utilizes a universal account system described in the first sentence of paragraph (c)(3)(ii) of this section, and in opening a new account the payor searches its records to determine whether the new account should be identified under an existing identifier (because the payee has existing accounts with the payor), the payor must investigate whether any existing accounts identified with the same identifier are subject to withholding under section 3406(a)(1)(C).

(d) Notice from payors of backup withholding due to notified payee underreporting. *(1) In general.* If a payor receives notice from the Internal Revenue Service or a broker under paragraph (c)(1) of this section and is required to identify an account under paragraph (c)(3) of this section as an account of the payee, the payor must notify the payee in accordance with paragraph (d)(2) of this section that withholding due to notified payee underreporting has started.

(2) Procedures. The payor must send the notice required by paragraph (d)(1) of this section to the payee no later than 15 days after the date that the payor makes the first payment subject to withholding due to notified payee underreporting. The payor must send the notice by first-class mail to the payee at the payee's last known address. The notice to the payee required by paragraph (d)(1) of this section must state—

(i) That the Internal Revenue Service has given notice that the payee has underreported reportable interest or dividends;

(ii) That, as a result of the underreporting, the payor is required under section 3406(a)(1)(C) of the Internal Revenue Code to withhold 31 percent of reportable interest or dividend payments made to the payee;

(iii) The date that the payor started (or plans to start) withholding due to notified payee underreporting under section 3406(a)(1)(C);

(iv) The account number or numbers that are subject to withholding due to notified payee underreporting;

(v) That the payee must obtain a determination from the Internal Revenue Service in order to stop the withholding due to notified payee underreporting; and

(vi) That while the payee is subject to withholding due to notified payee underreporting, the payee may not certify to a payor making reportable interest or dividend payments (or to a broker acquiring a readily tradable instrument for the payee) that the payee is not subject to withholding due to notified underreporting.

(e) Period during which backup withholding is required. *(1) In general.* If a payor receives notice from the Internal Revenue Service or a broker under paragraph (c)(1) of this section, the payor must impose withholding under section 3406(a)(1)(C) on all reportable interest or dividend payments with respect to any account of the payee required to be identified under paragraph (c)(3) of this section made after the close of the 30th business day after the day on which the payor receives that notice and before the stop date (as described in paragraph (e)(2) of this section). A payor may choose to start withholding under this paragraph (e)(1) at any time during the 30-business-day period described in the preceding sentence.

(2) Stop withholding. (i) When no underreporting exists or undue hardship exists. (A) Stop date. In the case of a determination under paragraph (g)(3)(i) or (iii) of this section that no underreporting exists or that an undue hardship exists, the stop date is the day that is 30 days after the earlier of—

(*1*) The date on which the payor receives written notification from the Internal Revenue Service under paragraph (g) of this section that withholding is to stop; or

(2) The date on which the payor receives a copy of the written certification provided to the payee by the Internal Revenue Service under paragraph (g) of this section that withholding is to stop.

(B) Acceleration of stop date. A payor may choose to stop withholding at any time during the 30-day period described in paragraph (e)(2)(i)(A) of this section.

(ii) When underreporting is corrected or bona fide dispute exists. In the case of a determination under paragraph (g)(3)(ii) or (iv) of this section that the underreporting has been corrected or that a bona fide dispute exists, the stop date occurs on the first day of January (immediately following a period of at least twelve months ending on October 15 of any calendar year in which the determination has been made) or if later, the stop date determined under paragraph (e)(2)(i) of this section.

(3) Dormant accounts. The requirement that a payor withhold under this paragraph (e) on reportable interest or dividend payments made with respect to an account terminates no later than the close of the third calendar year ending after the later of—

(i) The date that the most recent reportable interest or dividend payment was made with respect to that account; or

(ii) The date that the payor received notice under paragraph (c)(1) of this section.

(f) Notice to payees from the Internal Revenue Service. *(1) Notice period.* After the Internal Revenue Service determines under paragraph (b)(2) of this section that payee underreporting exists, the Internal Revenue Service will mail to the payee at least four notices over a period of at least 120 days (the notice period) before payors will be notified under paragraph (c)(1) of this section that the payee is subject to withholding due to notified payee underreporting. The notices may be accompanied by, or incorporated in, other notices provided to the payee by the Internal Revenue Service.

(2) Payee subject to backup withholding. After the Internal Revenue Service provides the notices described in paragraph (f)(1) of this section, the Internal Revenue Service will send notices to payors under paragraph (c)(1) of this section unless—

(i) A payee obtains a determination under paragraph (g) of this section; or

(ii) In the case of a payee who has filed a tax return, the Internal Revenue Service has not assessed the deficiency attributable to the underreporting.

(3) Disclosure of names of payors and brokers. Pursuant to section 3406(c)(5) the Internal Revenue Service may require a payee subject to withholding due to notified payee underreporting to disclose the names of all the payee's payors of reportable interest or dividend payments and the names of all of the brokers with whom the payee has accounts which may involve reportable interest or dividend payments. To the extent required in the request from the Internal Revenue Service, the payee must also provide the payee's account numbers and other information necessary to identify the payee's accounts.

(4) Backup withholding certification. After a payee receives a final notice from the Internal Revenue Service under paragraph (f)(1) of this section, the payee is not permitted to certify to any payor or broker, under penalties of perjury, that the payee is not subject to withholding under section 3406(a)(1)(C), until the payee receives the certification from the Internal Revenue Service under paragraph (g) of this section advising the payee that the payee is no longer subject to withholding under section 3406(a)(1)(C). A final notice will contain the information described in this paragraph (f)(4). See sections 6682 and 7205(b) for civil and criminal penalties for making a false certification.

(g) Determination by the Internal Revenue Service that backup withholding should not start or should be stopped. *(1) In general.* A payee may prevent withholding due to notified payee underreporting from starting, or stop the withholding once it has started, by requesting and receiving a determination from the Internal Revenue Service under one or more of the provisions of paragraph (g)(3) of this section. Following its review of a request for a determination under paragraph (g)(3) of this section, the Internal Revenue Service will either make the determination or provide the payee with a written report informing the payee that the request for determination is being denied and the reasons for the denial. If a determination is made during the notice period (as defined in paragraph (f)(1) of this section), the payee is not subject to withholding due to notified payee underreporting with respect to any taxable year for which a determination was made. If a determination is made after the notice period, the Internal Revenue Service will, at the time prescribed in paragraph (g)(2) of this section, provide written certification to a payee that withholding is to stop, and will notify payors who were contacted pursuant to paragraph (c)(1) of this section to stop withholding. A broker who (in its capacity as payor) under this paragraph (g)(1) receives a notice from the Internal Revenue Service or a copy of the certification provided to a payee by the Internal Revenue Service is not required to provide a corresponding notice to any payors whom the broker has previously notified under paragraph (c)(2) of this section.

(2) Date notice to stop backup withholding will be provided. (i) Underreporting corrected or bona fide dispute. If the Internal Revenue Service makes a determination under paragraph (g)(3)(ii) or (iv) of this section during the 12-month period ending on October 15 of any calendar year (as described in paragraph (e)(2)(ii) of this section), the Internal Revenue Service will provide the certification and the notices described in paragraph (g)(1) of this section no later than December 1 of that calendar year.

(ii) No underreporting or undue hardship. If the Internal Revenue Service makes a determination under paragraph (g)(3)(i) or (iii) of this section, the Internal Revenue Service will provide the notices described in paragraph (g)(1) of this section no later than the 45th day after the day on which the Internal Revenue Service makes its determination.

(3) Grounds for determination. The Internal Revenue Service will make a determination that withholding due to notified payee underreporting should not start or should stop once it has started if the payee—

(i) Shows that there was no payee underreporting (as provided in paragraph (g)(4) of this section) for each taxable year with respect to which the Internal Revenue Service determined under paragraph (b)(2) of this section that there was payee underreporting;

(ii) Corrects any payee underreporting (as provided in paragraph (g)(5) of this section) for each taxable year with respect to which the Internal Revenue Service determined under paragraph (b)(2) of this section that there was payee underreporting;

(iii) Shows that withholding will cause or is causing an undue hardship (as defined in paragraph (g)(6) of this section) and that it is unlikely that the payee will underreport interest or dividend payments again; or

(iv) Shows that a bona fide dispute exists regarding whether any underreporting has occurred (as provided in paragraph (g)(7) of this section) for each taxable year with respect to which the Internal Revenue Service determined under paragraph (b)(2) of this section that there was payee underreporting.

(4) No underreporting. A payee may show that no underreporting of reportable interest or dividends payments exists by presenting—

(i) Receipts or other satisfactory documentation to the Internal Revenue Service showing that all taxes relating to the payments were reported; or

(ii) Evidence showing that the payee did not have to file a return for the taxable year in question (e.g., because the payee did not make enough income) or that the underreporting determination was based upon a factual, clerical, or other error.

(5) Correcting any payee underreporting. (i) Before issuance of a statutory notice of deficiency. Before a statutory notice of deficiency is issued to a payee pursuant to section 6212, the payee may correct underreporting—

(A) By filing a return if one was not previously filed and including the unreported interest and dividends thereon;

(B) By filing an amended return in the event a return was filed and including the unreported interest and dividends thereon; or

(C) By consenting to the additional assessment according to applicable notices and forms sent to the payee by the Internal Revenue Service with respect to the underreporting, and paying taxes, penalties, and interest due with respect to any underreported interest or dividend payments.

(ii) After issuance of a statutory notice of deficiency. After a statutory notice of deficiency is issued to a payee—

(A) The payee may correct underreporting at any time, by filing a return if one was not previously filed and paying the entire deficiency and any other taxes including penalties and interest attributable to any payee underreporting of interest or dividend payments; or

(B) The payee may correct underreporting after the mailing of the statutory notice of deficiency but before the expiration of the 90-day or 150-day period described in section 6213(a) or, if a petition is filed with the United States Tax Court, before the decision of the Tax Court is final, by making a remittance to the Internal Revenue Service of the amounts described in paragraph (g)(5)(ii)(A) of this section. The payee must specifically designate in writing that the remittance is a deposit in the nature of a cash bond.

(iii) Special rules. For purposes of paragraph (g)(5)(ii) of this section, the payee will not be deemed to have corrected the payee underreporting under paragraph (g)(5)(ii)(B) of this section after the remittance is returned to the payee in the manner described in any applicable administrative procedure. For further guidance on a deposit in the nature of a cash bond, see subparagraph 2 of section 4.01 of Rev. Proc. 84-58 (1984-2 C.B. 501). (See § 601.601(d)(2) of this chapter.) Once the remittance is returned to the payee, the rules of this section will apply. If the Internal Revenue Service previously contacted payors of the payee to start withholding with respect to the notified payee underreporting, however, the Internal Revenue Service will recontact those payors to start withholding under paragraph (c)(1) of this section with respect to the payee underreporting without regard to paragraph (f) of this section.

(6) Undue hardship. (i) In general. A determination of undue hardship will be based on the overall impact to the payee of having reportable interest or dividend payments withheld at a 31 percent rate under section 3406. In addition, a determination of undue hardship will be made only if the Internal Revenue Service concludes that it is unlikely that any payee underreporting will occur again.

(ii) Factors. Factors that will be considered in determining whether withholding causes undue hardship include, but are not limited to, the following—

(A) Whether estimated tax payments, and other credits for current tax liabilities, or amounts withheld on employee wages or pensions, in addition to withholding under section 3406, would cause significant overwithholding;

(B) The payee's health, including the payee's ability to pay foreseeable medical expenses;

(C) The extent of the payee's reliance on interest and dividend payments to meet necessary living expenses and the existence, if any, of other sources of income;

(D) Whether other income of the payee is limited or fixed (e.g., social security, pension, and unearned income);

(E) The payee's ability to sell or liquidate stocks, bonds, bank accounts, trust accounts, or other assets, and the consequences of doing so;

(F) Whether the payee reported and timely paid the most recent year's tax liability, including interest and dividend income; and

(G) Whether the payee has filed a bankruptcy petition with the United States Bankruptcy Court.

(7) Bona fide dispute. The Internal Revenue Service may make a determination under this paragraph (g)(7) if there is a dispute between the payee and the Internal Revenue Service on a question of fact or law that is material to a determination under paragraph (g)(3)(i) of this section and, based upon all the facts and circumstances, the Internal Revenue Service finds that the dispute is asserted in good faith by the payee and there is a reasonable basis for the payee's position.

(h) Payees filing a joint return. *(1) In general.* For purposes of this section, if payee underreporting is found to exist with respect to a joint return, then the provisions of this section apply to both payees (i.e., the husband and wife). As a result, both payees are subject to withholding on accounts in their individual names as well as accounts in their joint names. Either or both payees may satisfy the criteria for a determination that no payee underreporting exists, that the underreporting has been corrected, or that a bona fide dispute exists (as provided in paragraph (g)(3)(i), (ii), or (iv) of this section). Both payees, however, must satisfy the criteria for a determination that withholding will cause or is causing undue hardship (as provided in paragraph (g)(3)(iii) of this section).

(2) Exceptions. (i) Innocent spouse. A spouse who files a joint return may obtain a determination that withholding should stop or not start with respect to payments made to his or her individual accounts, if the spouse shows that—

(A) He or she did not underreport income because he or she is a spouse described in section 6013(e), i.e., innocent spouse; or

(B) There is a bona fide dispute regarding whether he or she is an innocent spouse and hence did not underreport income.

(ii) Divorced or legally separated payee. A payee who, at the time of the request for a determination under paragraph

(g) of this section, is divorced or separated under state law may obtain a determination that undue hardship exists (or would exist) under paragraph (g)(3)(iii) of this section with respect to reportable interest or dividend payments made to his or her individual accounts if the divorced or legally separated payee satisfies the criteria for a determination under paragraph (g)(6) of this section.

(i) [Reserved.]

(j) Penalties. For the application of penalties related to this section, see sections 6682 and 7205(b).

T.D. 8637, 12/20/95.

§ 31.3406(d)-1 Manner required for furnishing a taxpayer identification number.

(a) Requirement to backup withhold. Withholding under section 3406(a)(1)(A) applies to a reportable payment (as defined in section 3406(b)) if the payee does not furnish the payee's taxpayer identification number to the payor in the manner required by this section. The period for which withholding is required is described in § 31.3406(e)-1(b). See § 31.3406(d)-3(a) and (b) for special rules when an account is established directly with, or an instrument is acquired directly from, the payor by electronic transmission or by mail, or an instrument is sold through a broker by electronic transmission or by mail. See § 31.3406(d)-4 for special rules applicable to readily tradable instruments acquired through a broker. See § 31.3406(h)-3(e) for the rules on when a payor may rely on a Form W-9. See also § 31.3406(g)-3 for rules regarding a payee awaiting receipt of a taxpayer identification number. See the applicable information reporting sections and section 6109 and the regulations thereunder to determine whose taxpayer identification number should be provided.

(b) Reportable interest or dividend account. *(1) Manner required for furnishing a taxpayer identification number with respect to a pre-1984 account or instrument.* A payee must furnish the payee's taxpayer identification number to the payor with respect to any obligation, deposit, certificate, share, membership, contract, investment, account, or other relationship or instrument established or acquired on or before December 31, 1983 (a pre-1984 account) and with respect to which the payor makes a reportable interest or dividend payment (as defined in section 3406(b)(2)). The manner of determining whether an account or an instrument is a pre-1984 account is described in paragraph (b)(2) of this section. The payee of a pre-1984 account may furnish the payee's taxpayer identification number to the payor orally or in writing. The payee is not required to certify under penalties of perjury that the taxpayer identification number is correct.

(2) Determination of pre-1984 account or instrument. (i) In general. An account that is in existence before January 1, 1984, will be considered a pre-1984 account, regardless of whether additional deposits are made to the account on or after January 1, 1984. An account established as an expansion of a credit union prime account in existence prior to January 1, 1984, constitutes a pre-1984 account. If funds taken from one account in existence prior to January 1, 1984, are used to create a new account on or after that date, however, the new account does not constitute a pre-1984 account except as provided in the preceding sentence. An instrument acquired prior to January 1, 1984, is a pre-1984 account. Regardless of when an instrument was acquired, if it is negotiated in a window transaction as defined in § 31.3406(b)(2)-3(b), it is treated as an instrument acquired after December 31, 1983. An obligation in bearer form and subject to reporting under section 6045, whenever acquired, is not a pre-1984 account. Any instrument, whenever acquired, that is held in a brokerage account is considered a pre-1984 account if the brokerage account is not a post-1983 brokerage account (as described in paragraph (c)(1)(ii) of this section). If shares of a corporation are held before January 1, 1984 (or considered held before that date by operation of this paragraph (b)(2)), and additional shares are acquired by the holder, irrespective of whether the shares are received by reason of a stock dividend, investing new cash, or otherwise, the new shares, in the discretion of the payor, may be considered a pre-1984 account. In the case of a qualified employee trust that distributes instruments in kind, any instrument distributed from the trust is considered a pre-1984 account with respect to employees who were participants in the trust before 1984. Similarly, when a payor offers participants in a plan the opportunity to purchase stock of the payor after a specified time, using the money that the payee invested during that period of time, the stock so purchased after December 31, 1983, is considered a pre-1984 account with respect to participants in the plan who either owned shares or invested money in the plan before January 1, 1984.

(ii) Account or instrument automatically acquired on the maturity or termination of an account. When an account is opened, or an instrument is acquired, automatically on the maturity or termination of an account that was in existence or an instrument that was held before January 1, 1984 (or considered to have been in existence or held before that date by operation of this paragraph (b)(2)(ii)), without the participation of the payee, the new account or instrument, in the discretion of the payor, may be considered a pre-1984 account. For purposes of the preceding sentence, a payee is not considered to have participated in the acquisition of the new account or instrument solely because the payee failed to exercise a right to withdraw funds at the maturity or termination of the old account or instrument.

(iii) Insurance policies. In the case of insurance policies in effect on December 31, 1983, the election of a dividend accumulation option pursuant to which interest is paid (as defined in § 1.6049-5(a)(4) of this chapter), or the creation of an account in which proceeds of a policy are held for the policy beneficiary, may, in the payor's discretion, be treated as a pre-1984 account.

(iv) Acquisitions of accounts and instruments. (A) Pre-1984 or post-1983 status known. If a payor acquires accounts or instruments of another payor (including through a tax-free reorganization under section 368), the acquiring payor must treat the persons specified in this paragraph (b)(2)(iv)(A) as having the same requirement to furnish a taxpayer identification number in the manner required under this paragraph (b) to the acquiring payor for information reporting, withholding, and related tax provisions as existed with respect to the payor whose accounts or instruments were acquired. Persons specified in this paragraph (b)(2)(iv)(A) are persons who held accounts or instruments in the other payor immediately before the acquisition and who receive an account or instrument in the acquiring payor immediately after the acquisition.

(B) Pre-1984 or post-1983 status unknown. If the acquiring payor, as described in paragraph (b)(2)(iv)(A) of this section, is unable to identify from the business records of the other payor whether any or all of the accounts or instruments of the persons specified in paragraph (b)(2)(iv)(A) of this section are pre-1984 (or post-1983) accounts or instruments, then the acquiring payor may treat these unidentified accounts or instruments as pre-1984 accounts or instruments.

(C) Cross reference. See § 31.3406(g)-2(g) for the limited exception from withholding under section 3406(a)(1)(A) on accounts or instruments described in paragraphs (b)(2)(iv)(A) and (B) of this section for which the payor does not have a taxpayer identification number.

(3) Manner required for furnishing a taxpayer identification number with respect to an account or instrument that is not a pre-1984 account. A payee who receives reportable interest or dividend payments (as defined in section 3406(b)(2)) from a payor must certify under penalties of perjury that the taxpayer identification number the payee furnishes to the payor is the payee's correct taxpayer identification number. The payee must make the certification only with respect to an account or instrument that is not a pre-1984 account (as described in paragraph (b)(2) of this section). See § 31.3406(h)-3 for a description of the certificate on which the certification must be made. See § 31.3406(d)-2 for the requirement that the payee must certify under penalties of perjury that the payee is not subject to withholding due to notified payee underreporting. See § 31.3406(d)-3(a) with respect to an account established directly with, or an instrument acquired directly from, the payor by electronic transmission or by mail. See § 31.3406(d)-4 for the rules applicable to readily tradable instruments acquired through a broker.

(4) Special rule with respect to the acquisition of a readily tradable instrument in a transaction between certain parties acting without the assistance of a broker. If a payee, at any time, acquires a readily tradable instrument without the assistance of a broker, and no party to the acquisition is a broker or an agent of the payor, the payee must furnish the payee's taxpayer identification number to the payor prior to the time reportable payments are made on the instrument. The payee is not required to certify under penalties of perjury that the number is correct. See § 31.3406(d)-2 for the rule that a payee is not subject to withholding due to notified payee underreporting with respect to a readily tradable instrument acquired in the manner described in this paragraph (b)(4). A broker is considered to provide assistance in the acquisition of an instrument if the person effecting the acquisition would be required to make an information return under section 6045 if such person were to sell the instrument. See § 31.3406(d)-4 for rules relating to an acquisition of a readily tradable instrument when a broker is involved.

(c) Brokerage account. *(1) Manner required for furnishing a taxpayer identification number with respect to a brokerage relationship that is not a post-1983 brokerage account.* (i) In general. With respect to any instrument, investment, or deposit made through a brokerage account that is not a post-1983 brokerage account, a payee must furnish the payee's taxpayer identification number to the broker either orally or in writing. The payee is not required to certify under penalties of perjury that the taxpayer identification number is correct. See paragraph (b)(2)(i) of this section for the rule that any instrument, whenever acquired, that is held in a brokerage account that is not a post-1983 brokerage account, is considered held in an account that is not a post-1983 brokerage account. For example, in 1983 a payee established and acquired a readily tradable instrument from a brokerage account; no activity took place through that account until the payee purchased a readily tradable instrument in 1995. That readily tradable instrument is not held in a post-1983 brokerage account; therefore, the payee need not certify under penalties of perjury that the payee's taxpayer identification number is correct.

(ii) Definition of a brokerage account that is not a post-1983 brokerage account. A brokerage account that was established by a payee before January 1, 1984, through which during 1983 the broker either bought or sold securities for the payee or held securities on behalf of the payee as a nominee (i.e., in street name), is an account that is not a post-1983 brokerage account.

(2) Manner required for furnishing a taxpayer identification number with respect to a post-1983 brokerage account. (i) In general. With respect to a post-1983 brokerage account, the payee must furnish the payee's taxpayer identification number to the broker and certify under penalties of perjury that the taxpayer identification number furnished is correct, except as provided in § 31.3406(d)-3(b).

(ii) Definition of a post-1983 brokerage account. A brokerage account established after December 31, 1983 (or before January 1, 1984, through which during 1983 the broker neither bought nor sold securities nor held securities on behalf of the payee as a nominee (i.e., in street name)), is a post-1983 brokerage account.

(d) Rents, commissions, nonemployee compensation, and certain fishing boat operators, etc. Manner required for furnishing a taxpayer identification number. For accounts, contracts, or relationships subject to information reporting under section 6041 (relating to information reporting at source on rents, royalties, salaries, etc.), section 6041A(a) (relating to information reporting of payments for nonemployee services), section 6050A (relating to information reporting by certain fishing boat operators), or section 6050N (relating to information reporting of payments of royalties), the payee must furnish the payee's taxpayer identification number to the payor either orally or in writing. Except as provided in § 31.3406(d)-5, the payee is not required to certify under penalties of perjury that the taxpayer identification number is correct regardless of when the account, contract, or relationship is established.

T.D. 8637, 12/20/95.

PAR. 8. Section 31.3406(d)-1 is amended by revising paragraph (d) to read as follows:

Proposed § 31.3406(d)-1 Manner required for furnishing a taxpayer identification number. [*For Preamble, see ¶ 153,139*]

* * * * *

(d) Rents, commissions, nonemployee compensation, certain fishing boat operators, and payment card and third party network transactions, etc. Manner required for furnishing a taxpayer identification number. For accounts, contracts, or relationships subject to information reporting under section 6041 (relating to information reporting at source on rents, royalties, salaries, etc.), section 6041A(a) (relating to information reporting of payments for nonemployee services), section 6050A (relating to information reporting by certain fishing boat operators), section 6050N (relating to information reporting of payments of royalties), or section 6050W (relating to information reporting for payment card and third party network transactions), the payee must furnish the payee's taxpayer identification number to the payor either orally or in writing. Except as provided in § 31.3406(d)-5, the payee is not required to certify under penalties of perjury that the taxpayer identification number is correct regardless of when the account, contract, or relationship is established.

§ 31.3406(d)-2 Payee certification failure.

(a) Requirement to backup withhold. Withholding under section 3406(a)(1)(D) applies to a reportable interest or dividend payment (as defined in section 3406(b)(2)) if, and only if, the payee fails to certify to the payor, under penalties of perjury, that the payee is not subject to withholding due to notified payee underreporting under section 3406(a)(1)(C). The period for which withholding applies is described in § 31.3406(e)-1(e). See § 31.3406(d)-3(a) for special rules when an account is established directly with, or an instrument is acquired directly from, the payor by electronic transmission or by mail. See § 31.3406(c)-1(c)(3)(iv) for rules with respect to a payor's reliance on a payee certification for a new account following notified payee underreporting. See § 31.3406(d)-4 for special rules relating to the acquisition of a readily tradable instrument through a broker. The certificate on which the certification should be made is described in § 31.3406(h)-3.

(b) Exceptions. Withholding under section 3406(a)(1)(D) and paragraph (a) of this section does not apply to reportable interest or dividend payments (as defined in section 3406(b)(2)) made—

(1) With respect to a pre-1984 account (as defined in § 31.3406(d)-1(b)(1));

(2) In a window transaction (as defined in § 31.3406(b)(2)-3(b));

(3) With respect to a readily tradable instrument described in § 31.3406(d)-1(b)(2)(iv) or § 31.3406(d)-4(a)(3); or

(4) During the period and with respect to an account or readily tradable instrument described in § 31.3406(d)-3.

T.D. 8637, 12/20/95.

§ 31.3406(d)-3 Special 30-day rules for certain reportable payments.

Caution: The Treasury has not yet amended Reg § 31.3406(d)-3 to reflect changes made by P.L. 107-16.

(a) Accounts or readily tradable instruments acquired directly from the payor (including a broker who holds an instrument in street name) by electronic transmission or by mail. In the case of an account established directly with, or a readily tradable instrument acquired directly from, the payor by means of electronic transmission (i.e., telephone or wire instruction) or by mail, the payor may permit the payee to furnish the certifications required in § 31.3406(d)-1(b)(3) (relating to certification that the payee's taxpayer identification number is correct) and § 31.3406(d)-2 (relating to certification of notified payee underreporting) within 30 days after the establishment or acquisition without subjecting the account to withholding during the 30 days. The preceding sentence applies only if the payee furnishes a taxpayer identification number to the payor at the time of the establishment or acquisition, and the payee does not withdraw more than 69 percent of a reportable interest or dividend payment before the certifications are received within the 30 days. If the payee does not provide the required certifications within 30 days of the establishment or acquisition, the payor must withhold 31 percent of any reportable interest or dividend payments made to the account after its acquisition. For purposes of this section, an account or instrument is considered acquired directly from the payor if the instrument was acquired by the payee without the assistance of a broker or the instrument was acquired directly from a broker who holds the instrument as nominee for the payee (i.e., in street name) and who is considered a payor under § 31.3406(a)-2. For payments made after December 31, 1998, see § 1.6049-5(d)(2)(ii) of this chapter for the application of a 90-day grace period in lieu of the 30-day grace period described in this paragraph (a) if, at the beginning of the 90-day grace period, certain conditions are satisfied. If the grace period provisions of § 1.6049-5(d)(2)(ii) or § 1.1441-1(b)(3)(iv) of this chapter are applied with respect to a new account, the grace period provisions of this paragraph (a) shall not apply to that account.

(b) Sale of an instrument for a customer by electronic transmission or by mail. The special rules set forth in paragraph (a) of this section apply comparably with respect to certification of the taxpayer identification number for the sale of an instrument under section 6045 (as described in § 31.3406(b)(3)-2) through a post-1983 brokerage account (as described in § 31.3406(d)-1(c)(2)) for a customer by electronic transmission or by mail. However, the 30-day rules may apply only if the payee furnishes the payee's taxpayer identification number before the sale occurs. For purposes of applying the 30-day rules under this paragraph (b), a payee's reinvestment of the gross proceeds of the sale into other instruments constitutes a withdrawal.

(c) Application to foreign payees. The rules of paragraphs (a) and (b) of this section also apply to a payee from whom the payor is required to obtain a Form W-8 (or an acceptable substitute) or other evidence of foreign status (pursuant to relevant regulations under an applicable Internal Revenue Code section without regard to the requirement to furnish a taxpayer identifying number, and the certifications described in §§ 31.3406(d)-1(b)(3) and 31.3406(d)-2), provided the payee represents orally or otherwise, before or at the time of the acquisition or sale of the instrument or the establishment of the account, that the payee is not a United States citizen or resident. The 30-day rules described in paragraph (a) or (b) of this section may apply only if the payee does not qualify for, or the payor does not apply, the 90-day grace period described in § 1.6049-5(d)(2)(ii) or § 1.1441-1(b)(3)(iv) of this chapter.

T.D. 8637, 12/20/95, amend T.D. 8734, 10/6/97.

§ 31.3406(d)-4 Special rules for readily tradable instruments acquired through a broker.

(a) Readily tradable instruments acquired through post-1983 brokerage accounts with a broker who is not a payor. *(1) In general.* If a readily tradable instrument is acquired through a post-1983 brokerage account (as defined in § 31.3406(d)-1(c)(2)) and the broker is not a broker holding a security (including stock) for a customer in street name, the broker must—

(i) Obtain once with respect to each account the certifications described in § 31.3406(d)-2(a) and § 31.3406(d)-1(b)(3) and (c)(2) from the payee (relating to certification regarding payee underreporting and taxpayer identification number, respectively);

(ii) Furnish the payee's taxpayer identification number to the payor; and

(iii) Notify the payor to impose withholding if the payee fails to make either of the required certifications to the broker or if the broker has been notified by the Internal Revenue Service before the acquisition of the instrument that the payee is subject to withholding due to notified payee underreporting under section 3406(a)(1)(C) or that the payee is subject to withholding because the payee's taxpayer identification number is incorrect under section 3406(a)(1)(B) (as described in § 31.3406(d)-5).

(2) Additional requirements. The broker must give the information required by paragraphs (a)(1)(ii) and (iii) of this section to the payor with the transfer instructions for the acquisition (including account registration instructions transmitted by a broker in the case of acquisitions of shares in a mutual fund). A notice including the information described in paragraph (b)(1) of this section fulfills the broker's requirement to give notice to the payor. Once the broker transmits the transfer instructions containing the information required by this section, the broker has no further responsibility to obtain a missing taxpayer identification number or missing certification or to provide additional notices to the payee or payor with respect to the acquisition of the instrument. Upon receiving the notice from a broker, the payor must impose withholding on the account pursuant to § 31.3406(a)-1.

(3) Transactions entered into through a brokerage account that is not a post-1983 brokerage account. If a broker acquires readily tradable instruments for a payee through an account (with the broker) that is not a post-1983 brokerage account (as defined in § 31.3406(d)-1(c)(1)), and the broker is not the payor of the instruments, the broker must furnish the payee's taxpayer identification number to the payor. In addition, if the broker has been notified by the Internal Revenue Service that the payee is subject to withholding under section 3406 either because of an incorrect taxpayer identification number or due to notified payee underreporting as described in section 3406(a)(1)(B) or (C), respectively, the broker must notify the payor of the instrument to impose withholding with respect to that payee and transmit the information in the manner described in this paragraph (a). After a payor receives a notice from a broker pursuant to section 3406(d)(2)(B) and this paragraph (a), the payor must impose withholding on any accounts of the payee paying reportable interest or dividends as defined in section 3406(b)(2) in accordance with § 31.3406(a)-1.

(4) Payor must notify payee. (i) Failure to provide certifications. If a payor is notified by a broker, as required in paragraph (a)(1) of this section, that a payee is subject to withholding because the payee failed to provide the certifications, as described in § 31.3406(d)-2(a) and § 31.3406(d)-1(b)(3) and (c)(2), and the payor has not received the certifications from the payee, then the payor must notify the payee that withholding has started (or will start) no later than 15 days after the payor makes the first payment to the payee that is subject to withholding under section 3406. A notice that contains the information described in paragraph (b)(2) of this section satisfies the payor's requirement to give notice to the payee. If the broker notifies the payor that the payee failed to make a required certification and the payor has received the certification from the payee, the payor may disregard the notice from the broker.

(ii) Notified payee underreporting and incorrect taxpayer identification number. The payor must notify the payee under this section if the Internal Revenue Service or a broker notifies the payor to withhold either because of an incorrect taxpayer identification number under section 3406(a)(1)(B) (as described in § 31.3406(d)-5) or due to notified payee underreporting under section 3406(a)(1)(C) (as described in § 31.3406(c)-1). If a payor is notified by the Internal Revenue Service or a broker with respect to a readily tradable instrument, the payor may not ignore the notice even if the payee previously provided the payee's taxpayer identification number under penalties of perjury to the payor and even if the payee certified to the payor that the payee is not subject to backup withholding due to a notified payee underreporting. See § 31.3406(d)-5(c)(1) and (2) and (f)(2) for notice requirements under section 3406(a)(1)(B) due to an incorrect taxpayer identification number. See § 31.3406(c)-1(c)(2) for notice requirements under section 3406(a)(1)(C) due to notified payee underreporting.

(b) Notices. *(1) Form of notice by broker to payor.* A broker who is required under paragraphs (a)(1)(iii) and (2) of this section to notify the payor with respect to a readily tradable instrument may notify the payor in connection with the transfer instructions by means of magnetic media, machine readable document, or any other medium, provided that the notice includes the following information—

(i) The payee's name, address, and taxpayer identification number (if provided to the broker); and

(ii) A statement that the payee is subject to withholding under section 3406(a)(1)(A), (B), (C), or (D) of the Internal Revenue Code, whichever section applies; and

(iii) When applicable, a statement that the broker was notified by the Internal Revenue Service that the payee is subject to withholding under section 3406(a)(1)(B) or (C).

(2) Form of notice by payor to payee. A payor who is required to notify a payee that the payee is subject to withholding must provide notice that is substantially similar to the following—

(i) For a notification concerning a failure to provide a taxpayer identification number in the required manner under section 3406(a)(1)(A) or a failure to make the following certification described in section 3406(a)(1)(D):

Recently you purchased (identify security acquired). Because of the existence of one or more of the following conditions, payments of interest, dividends, and other reportable amounts that are made to you will be subject to withholding of tax at a 31 percent rate: (specify the condition or conditions, described below, that are applicable)

(1) You failed to provide a taxpayer identification number, or failed to provide this number under penalties of perjury, in connection with the purchase of the acquired security. (An individual's taxpayer identification number is his or her social security number.)

(2) You failed to certify, under penalties of perjury, that you are not subject to withholding due to notified payee underreporting as required under section 3406(a)(1)(D) of the Internal Revenue Code.

If condition (1) applies, you may stop withholding by providing your taxpayer identification number on the enclosed Form W-9, signing the form, and returning it to us. If you do not have a taxpayer identification number, but have applied (or will soon apply) for one, you may so indicate on the Form W-9. Withholding may apply during the 60-day period you are waiting for your taxpayer identification number. You must provide us with your taxpayer identification number promptly after you receive it in order to avoid withholding after the end of the 60-day period or to stop withholding if it has already begun. Certain persons, described on the enclosed Form W-9, are exempt from withholding. Follow the instructions on that form if applicable to you.

If condition (2) applies, you may stop withholding by certifying on the enclosed Form W-9 that you are not subject to withholding due to notified payee underreporting, signing the form, and returning it to us.

If more than one condition applies, you must remove all applicable conditions to stop withholding.

Please address any questions concerning this notice to: [Insert payor identifying information].

(Do not address questions to the broker who purchased the securities for you.)

(ii) For the form of the notice concerning imposition of withholding due to an incorrect taxpayer identification number, see § 31.3406(d)-5(d)(2) and (g)(2).

(iii) For the form of the notice concerning the imposition of withholding due to notified payee underreporting, see § 31.3406(c)-1(d)(2).

(c) Payor's reliance on information from broker. *(1) In general.* A payor of an instrument acquired by a payee through a broker may rely on the information that the payor receives from the broker pursuant to paragraphs (a) and (b) of this section.

(2) Amount subject to backup withholding. The payor is required to withhold under section 3406 depending on the payor's customary method of making payment on an instrument or instruments owned by a payee. If it is the practice of a payor to combine in one account all readily tradable instruments of the same issue owned by a payee and if only certain of those instruments are subject to withholding, the payor must withhold on the aggregate payment made with respect to all the instruments in the account. Otherwise, the payor must withhold on the payment made on the instrument or instruments with respect to which the payee is subject to withholding.

T.D. 8637, 12/20/95, amend T.D. 9010, 7/25/2002.

§ 31.3406(d)-5 Backup withholding when the Service or a broker notifies the payor to withhold because the payee's taxpayer identification number is incorrect.

(a) Overview. Backup withholding under section 3406(a)(1)(B) applies to any reportable payment made with respect to an account of a payee if the Internal Revenue Service or a broker notifies a payor under paragraph (c)(1) or (2) of this section that the payee's name and taxpayer identification number combination (name/TIN combination) is incorrect and the payor is required under paragraph (c)(3) of this section to identify that account as having the same name/TIN combination. After receiving a notice from the Internal Revenue Service or a broker under paragraph (c)(1) or (2) of this section and identifying an account as having the incorrect name/TIN combination under paragraph (c)(3) of this section, the payor must notify the payee in accordance with paragraph (d) of this section. In addition, under paragraph (e) of this section, the payor must backup withhold on all reportable payments made to such account after the close of the 30th business day after the date that the payor receives the notice and on or before the close of the 30th calendar day after the date that the payor receives from the payee the certification required under paragraph (f) of this section. Under paragraph (g) of this section, if a payor receives 2 notices from the Internal Revenue Service or broker within 3 calendar years with respect to a payee's account, the payor must notify the payee in accordance with paragraph (g)(2) (rather than paragraph (d)) of this section. In addition, the payor must backup withhold on all reportable payments made with respect to the account after the close of the 30th business day after the date that the payor receives the second notice and on or before the 30th calendar day after the date that the payor receives notification from the Social Security Administration (or the Internal Revenue Service) validating a name/TIN combination for the account. Paragraph (h) of this section requires a payor to use a corrected name/TIN combination on subsequent information returns.

(b) Definitions and special rules. *(1) Definition of incorrect name/TIN combination.* An incorrect name/TIN combination is a combination of a name and taxpayer identification number provided on an information return with respect to which the Internal Revenue Service determines that the taxpayer identification number provided is not assigned under section 6109 to the name provided.

(2) Definition of account. The term "account" means any account, instrument, or other relationship with the payor.

(3) Definition of business day. The term "business day" means any day other than a Saturday, Sunday, or legal holiday (within the meaning of section 7503).

(4) Certain exceptions. (i) In general. This section does not apply with respect to any notice received under paragraph (c)(1) or (2) of this section with respect to payments that—

(A) Were made to a fiduciary or nominee account; or

(B) Were not reportable payments (for example, because the payments were made to an exempt recipient).

See § 301.6724-1(f)(3) of this chapter for certain solicitation rules applicable after receipt of a notice under paragraph (c)(1) or (2) of this section with respect to a fiduciary or nominee account.

(ii) Definition of fiduciary or nominee account. A fiduciary or nominee account is an account with respect to which at least one person named in the registration is identified as acting in the capacity as nominee or as administrator, conservator, custodian, receiver, tutor, curator, committee, executor, guardian, trustee, or other fiduciary capacity recognized under governing law.

(c) Notice regarding an incorrect name/TIN combination. *(1) In general.* If the Internal Revenue Service notifies a payor that a payee's name/TIN combination is incorrect and that the payor must commence backup withholding as required on reportable payments made with respect to accounts of the payee with the same name/TIN combination, the payor must—

(i) Identify under paragraph (c)(3) of this section any account or accounts of the payee having the same name/TIN combination;

(ii) Except as provided in paragraph (g) of this section, notify the payee and backup withhold on reportable payments made to the account or accounts under the rules of paragraphs (d), (e), and (f) of this section.

This paragraph (c)(1) also applies if the payor receives notice from a broker under paragraph (c)(2) of this section.

(2) Additional requirements for payors that are also brokers. (i) In general. A broker must notify the payor of an instrument of the information required under paragraph (c)(2)(ii) of this section, if—

(A) The broker (in its capacity as a payor) receives a notice from the Internal Revenue Service under paragraph (c)(1) of this section that a payee's name/TIN combination is incorrect and is required to identify an account of the payee pursuant to paragraph (c)(3) of this section as having the name/TIN combination;

(B) The payee acquires through the same account with the broker a readily tradable instrument with respect to which the broker is not the payor; and

(C) The acquisition of such instrument occurs after the close of the 30th business day after the date that the broker receives that notice (or on any earlier date that the broker chooses to begin applying this paragraph (c)(2)).

For purposes of this paragraph (c)(2)(i), with respect to notices under paragraph (c)(1) of this section received on or after September 1, 1992, an acquisition includes a transfer of an instrument out of street name into the name of the registered owner, i.e., the payee.

(ii) Required information. The information required to be provided under this paragraph (c)(2)(ii) is:

(A) The fact that the broker was notified by the Internal Revenue Service that the payee furnished an incorrect name/TIN combination;

(B) The incorrect name/TIN combination; and

(C) The fact that the named payee is subject to backup withholding under section 3406(a)(1)(B).

The broker is required to provide this information to the payor of the instrument in connection with the transfer instructions for the acquisition.

(iii) Termination of obligation to provide information. The obligation of a broker to provide information to payors under this paragraph (c)(2) terminates simultaneously with the termination of the broker's obligation to backup withhold (in its capacity as payor) on reportable payments to the account.

(3) Payor identification of the account or accounts of the payee that have the incorrect taxpayer identification number. (i) In general. If an account number or designation is provided in the notice received under paragraph (c)(1) of this section, the payor need only identify any account or accounts corresponding to that number or designation that has the same name/TIN combination provided in the notice. If no account number or designation is provided in the notice received under paragraph (c)(1) of this section, the payor must identify, using reasonable care, all accounts of the payee having the same name/TIN combination provided in the notice. If a payor receives notice from a broker under paragraph (c)(2) of this section with respect to the acquisition of a readily tradable instrument, the payor is not required to identify any other account of the payee.

(ii) Reasonable care where no account number or designation is provided. A payor who satisfies the following two-part facts-and-circumstances test will be considered to have exercised reasonable care for purposes of this paragraph (c)(3).

(A) Part one of the test is satisfied if a payor searches for accounts of the payee on the computer or other recordkeeping system that the payor can reasonably associate with the information return that generated the notice under paragraph (c)(1) of this section. For example, a payor who maintains separate computer or recordkeeping systems for different product lines will have identified and used the appropriate system if the payor searches for accounts of the payee on the computer or recordkeeping system that contains the product line for the type of payments reported on the information return. A payor with the same product line on several nonintegrated computer or record systems will have identified and used the appropriate system if the payor searches for accounts of the payee on any computer or record system that the payor otherwise can reasonably associate with the information return.

(B) Part two of the test is satisfied if the payor inputs the name/TIN combination provided on the notice from the Internal Revenue Service under paragraph (c)(1) of this section into the system that is described in paragraph (c)(3)(ii)(A) of this section. If the system of a payor cannot utilize the name/TIN combination, the payor must input appropriate data or criteria, as determined by the capability of the payor's computer or recordkeeping system.

(iii) No identification if error is caused by payor. A payor may treat an account as not having the incorrect name/TIN combination if the error resulted because the name or taxpayer identification number on such account is not the name or taxpayer identification number that was provided to the payor. This may occur, for example, where a payor transposes numbers in the taxpayer identification number when incorporating it into the payor's business records.

(4) Special rules for joint accounts. (i) In general. In the case of a joint account, the relevant name/TIN combination for purposes of this section is the name/TIN combination used for information reporting purposes.

(ii) Transitional rule. With respect to notices received under paragraph (c)(1) or (2) of this section prior to September 1, 1993, a payor may treat the name/TIN combination of the first person on a joint account as the relevant name/TIN combination, unless that person is an exempt foreign person and the account registration includes names of persons who are not foreign persons.

(iii) Optional rule where names are switched. A payor may backup withhold under this section on reportable payments made to a joint account if the order of the names (or taxpayer identification numbers) on the account is merely changed subsequent to receipt of a notice under paragraph (c)(1) or (2) of this section, provided that the name of the person to which the incorrect name/TIN combination originally applies remains on the account.

(5) Date of receipt. For purposes of this section, the date set forth on the notice from the Internal Revenue Service or broker under paragraph (c)(1) or (2) of this section is considered to be the date of receipt of the notice by the payor. However, if the payor demonstrates to the satisfaction of the Internal Revenue Service that the date of actual receipt of the notice is later than the date on the notice, the actual date of receipt is controlling.

(d) Notice from payors of backup withholding due to an incorrect name/TIN combination. *(1) In general.* Except as provided in paragraph (g) of this section, if a payor receives notice under paragraph (c)(1) or (2) of this section and is required to identify an account as having the incorrect name/TIN combination under paragraph (c)(3) of this section, the payor must send a copy of the notice (or an acceptable substitute notice) to the payee of the account in accordance with the procedures of paragraph (d)(2) of this section.

(2) Procedures. (i) In general. The notice that a payor must send to a payee under paragraph (d)(1) of this section must comply with such procedural requirements as the Internal Revenue Service provides in the Internal Revenue Bulletin such as to form and manner of delivery. A payor must send the notice to the payee within 15 business days after the date that the payor receives the notice from the Internal Revenue Service or a broker under paragraph (c)(1) or (2) of this section.

(ii) Two or more notices for an account for the same year or received in the same year. A payor who receives, under the same payor taxpayer identification number, two or more notices under paragraph (c)(1) or (2) of this section with respect to the same payee's account for the same year, or in the same calendar year, need only send one notice to the payee under this section.

(e) Period during which backup withholding is required due to notification of an incorrect name/TIN combination. *(1) In general.* Except as provided in paragraph (g) of this section, if a payor receives a notice under paragraph (c)(1) or (2) of this section and is required to identify an account as having the same name/TIN combination under paragraph (c)(3) of this section, the payor must impose backup withholding on all reportable payments made with respect to the account after the close of the 30th business day after the date the payor receives that notice and on or before the close of the 30th calendar day after the day the payor receives from the payee the certification required under paragraph (f) of this section.

(2) Grace periods. (i) Starting backup withholding. A payor may, on an account-by-account basis or in general, choose to begin backup withholding under this paragraph (e) at any time during the 30-business-day period described in paragraph (e)(1) of this section.

(ii) Stopping backup withholding. A payor may, on an account-by-account basis or in general, choose to stop backup withholding under this paragraph (e) at any time within 30 calendar days after the payor receives from the payee the certification required under paragraph (f) of this section.

(3) Dormant accounts. The requirement that a payor backup withhold under this paragraph (e) on reportable payments made with respect to an account terminates no later than the close of the third calendar year ending after the later of—

(i) The date that the last reportable payment was made to that account; or

(ii) The date that the payor received the notice under paragraph (c)(1) or (2) of this section.

(f) Manner required for payee to furnish certified taxpayer identification number. *(1)* Except as provided in paragraph (g) of this section, in order to prevent backup withholding under paragraph (e) of this section from starting, or to stop it once it has begun, a payee with respect to whom the payor has been notified under paragraph (c)(1) or (2) that the payee's name/TIN combination is incorrect is required on Form W-9 (or an acceptable substitute form) to—

(i) Provide the payee's name and taxpayer identification number; and

(ii) Certify, under penalties of perjury, that the taxpayer identification number being provided is correct.

(2) The certification must be made even if the account is a pre-1984 account and even if the payment to the account is a reportable payment other than interest, dividends, patronage dividends, original issue discount, or proceeds of a sale of a security or commodity. In order to prevent backup withholding under paragraph (e) of this section from starting or to stop it once it has begun, a payee is not required to certify, under penalties of perjury, that the payee is not subject to backup withholding due to notified payee underreporting under section 3406(a)(1)(C). With respect to notices received under paragraph (c)(1) or (2) of this section on or after September 1, 1993, the requirements of this paragraph (f) are not satisfied if a payee provides only an awaiting TIN certification. As a result, a payor must not fail to begin backup withholding under paragraph (e) of this section solely because the payee provided an awaiting TIN certification, or stop it once it has begun solely because the payee provided an awaiting TIN certification.

(g) Receipt of two notices within a 3-year period. *(1) In general.* If a payor receives notification under paragraph (c)(1) or (2) of this section twice within 3 calendar years, and in each case the payor is required to identify the same account as having the incorrect name/TIN combination, the payor must—

(i) Disregard any future certifications (described in paragraph (f) of this section) furnished by the payee with respect to the account until the payor receives notice from the Social Security Administration (or the Internal Revenue Service) validating a name/TIN combination under paragraph (g)(5) of this section;

(ii) Send the notice described in paragraph (g)(2) of this section to the payee (and not the notice required under paragraph (d) of this section) within 15 business days after the date that the payor receives the second notice; and

(iii) Impose backup withholding on the account for the period described in paragraph (g)(3) of this section.

The payor must maintain sufficient records to determine whether the payor has received notices under paragraph (c)(1) or (2) of this section twice within 3 calendar years with respect to the same account.

(2) Notice to payee who has provided two incorrect name/TIN combinations within 3 calendar years. The notice to the payee required by paragraph (g)(1) of this section must comply with such procedural requirements as the Internal Revenue Service provides in the Internal Revenue Bulletin such as to form and manner of delivery.

(3) Period during which backup withholding is required due to a second notice of an incorrect name/taxpayer identification combination within 3 calendar years. (i) In general. If paragraph (g)(1) of this section applies, the payor must backup withhold on all reportable payments made with respect to the account of the payee after the close of the 30th business day after the date that the payor receives the second notice under paragraph (c)(1) or (2) of this section and on or before the close of the 30th calendar day after the date that the payor receives notice from the Social Security Administration (or the Internal Revenue Service) validating a name/TIN combination under paragraph (g)(5) of this section for the account. However, a payor may choose not to commence backup withholding under this paragraph (g) until January 1, 1992.

(ii) Grace periods. (A) Starting backup withholding. A payor may, on an account-by-account basis or in general, choose to begin backup withholding under this paragraph (g) at any time during the 30-business-day period described in paragraph (g)(3)(i) of this section.

(B) Stopping backup withholding. A payor may, on an account-by-account basis or in general, choose to stop backup withholding under this paragraph (g) at any time within 30 calendar days after the date the payor receives notice from the Social Security Administration (or the Internal Revenue Service) validating a name/TIN combination under paragraph (g)(5) of this section for the account.

(iii) Dormant accounts. The requirement that a payor backup withhold under this paragraph (g) on reportable payments made with respect to an account terminates no later than the close of the third calendar year ending after the later of—

(A) The date that the last reportable payment was made to that account; or

(B) The date that the payor received the second notice under paragraph (c)(1) or (2) of this section.

(4) Receipt of two notices for the same year or in the same calendar year. A payor who receives, under the same payor taxpayer identification number, two or more notices under paragraph (c)(1) or (2) of this section with respect to the same payee's account for the same year, or in the same calendar year, must treat such notices as one notice for purposes of this paragraph (g).

(5) Notification from the Social Security Administration (or the Internal Revenue Service) validating a name/TIN combination. The Social Security Administration (or the Internal Revenue Service) will notify a payor after it validates a name/TIN combination that the payee provides for an account to which paragraph (g)(1) of this section applies. Notification from the Social Security Administration (or the Internal Revenue Service) validating a name/TIN combination satisfies the requirements of this paragraph (g)(5) only if it complies with such procedural requirements as the Internal Revenue Service provides in the Internal Revenue Bulletin such as to form and manner of delivery. In order to obtain notification from the Social Security Administration (or the Internal Revenue Service) validating a name/TIN combination for an account, a payee who receives notice from a payor under paragraph (g)(2) of this section should follow such procedures as the Internal Revenue Service provides in the Internal Revenue Bulletin.

(h) Payor must use newly provided certified number. If a payor receives a certification under paragraph (f) of this section or a notification under paragraph (g)(5) of this section for an account, the payor must use the name/TIN combination provided on such certification or notification on information returns for the account for which the due date (without regard to extensions) is more than 30 calendar days after the date that the payor receives the certification or notification. A payor who uses that name/TIN combination on the first such information return satisfies the requirement of section 3406(h)(9) to provide this information to the Internal Revenue Service, if the payor is not required to file any information returns with respect to the account after the date that the payor receives the certification or notification, a payor is deemed to satisfy the requirements of section 3406(h)(9).

(i) Effective date. Except as otherwise provided in this section, the provisions of this section are effective with respect to notices received on or after September 1, 1990, under paragraph (c)(1) or (2) of this section.

(j) Examples. The application of the provisions of this section may be illustrated by the following examples:

Example (1). D opened an account with Bank O prior to 1984 and furnished a taxpayer identification number to O at the time he opened the account. O pays interest on the account at the end of each calendar month, and the account is a pre-1984 account. On October 1, 1990, the Internal Revenue Service notifies Bank O that the name/TIN combination provided by D is incorrect. O timely notifies D as required in paragraph (d)(1) of this section. O does not receive the certification required under paragraph (f) of this section from D. O is required to backup withhold 20 percent of all reportable payments made after November 14, 1990 (which is 30 business days after the date the Internal Revenue Service notified O). Therefore, O is not required to backup withhold on the reportable payment made on October 31, 1990, but is required to backup withhold on the reportable payment made on November 30, 1990. O is required to continue to backup withhold under section 3406(a)(1)(B) until O receives the certification required under paragraph (f) of this section from D (or, if earlier, until backup withholding terminates under paragraph (e)(3) of this section).

Example (2). Assume the same facts as in Example 1 except that D furnishes a new taxpayer identification number to O on November 1, 1990, but does not certify, under penalties of perjury, that it is his correct taxpayer identification number as required under paragraph (f) of this section. Even though the account is a pre-1984 account, O is required to withhold 20 percent of all reportable payments made after November 14, 1990 (which is 30 business days after the date the Internal Revenue Service notified O), and before the date O receives the certification required under paragraph (f) of this section from D.

Example (3). Assume the same facts as in Example 2 except that D provides O with the certification required under paragraph (f) of this section on November 10, 1990. D elects pursuant to paragraph (e)(2)(ii) of this section to treat the certification as received on November 20, 1990. Even though D did not provide the certification to O within 30 business days after the Internal Revenue Service notified O that D provided an incorrect taxpayer identification number, O is not required to backup withhold under section 3406(a)(1)(B) because O did not make any reportable payment to D after 30 business days after notification of an incorrect name/TIN combination and before O received D's certification under paragraph (f) of this section (or, if earlier, until backup withholding terminates under paragraph (e)(3) of this section).

Example (4). Individual F has two post-1983 accounts with Bank R that pay reportable interest: a savings account and a money market account. The money market account was opened in 1986, and the savings account was opened on February 1, 1991. R treats each of these accounts as a separate account on its books and records for business purposes. On October 1, 1990, the Internal Revenue Service notified R pursuant to paragraph (c)(1) of this section that F furnished an incorrect name/TIN combination with respect to the money market account. R timely sends F the notice required under paragraph (d) of this section and receives the certification required under paragraph (f) of this section from F on November 1, 1990. On October 1, 1991, the Internal Revenue Service again notifies R that F furnished an incorrect name/TIN combination with respect to the money market account. Further, R determines from its business records that two notifications of an incorrect name/TIN combination have been received with respect to the money market account within 3 calendar years. R must send F the notice required under paragraph (g)(2) of this section and must commence backup withholding on reportable interest paid on the money market account pursuant to paragraph (g)(3) of this section after November 14, 1991, which is 30 business days after R received the second notice. R must continue to backup withhold under paragraph (g) of this section on the money market account until R receives notification from the Social Security Administration as described in paragraph (g)(5) of this, section (or, if earlier, until backup withholding terminates under paragraph (g)(3)(iii) of this section). R is not required to backup withhold on the savings account unless and until it receives notice under paragraph (c)(1) or (2) of this section with respect to the savings account.

T.D. 8409, 4/10/92, amend T.D. 9055, 4/28/2003.

§ 31.3406(e)-1 Period during which backup withholding is required.

Caution: The Treasury has not yet amended Reg § 31.3406(e)-1 to reflect changes made by P.L. 107-16.

(a) In general. A payor must withhold under section 3406 at a rate of 31 percent on any reportable payment (as defined in section 3406(b)) made to a payee during the period described in this section (irrespective of the number of conditions for imposing withholding under section 3406 that exist with respect to the payee). A payor must continue to withhold under section 3406 until no condition for imposing backup withholding exists with respect to the payee.

(b) Failure to furnish a taxpayer identification number in the manner required. *(1) Start withholding.* A payor is required to withhold under section 3406(a)(1)(A) at a rate of 31 percent on any reportable payment (as defined in section 3406(b)) at the time the payor pays the reportable payment (as described in § 31.3406(a)-4) to a payee if—

(i) The payor has not received the payee's taxpayer identification number in the manner required in § 31.3406(d)-1; or

(ii) The payor has received notice from a broker (as required in § 31.3406(d)-4(a)(1)(iii)) with respect to a readily tradable instrument that the payee did not furnish a taxpayer identification number to the broker in the manner required in § 31.3406(d)-1 and the payor has not received the taxpayer identification number from the payee in this manner.

(2) Stop withholding. The payor must stop withholding under section 3406(a)(1)(A) within 30 days after the payor receives—

(i) The payee's taxpayer identification number in the manner required under § 31.3406(d)-1; or

(ii) A statement, in such form and containing such information as is required under applicable regulations, that the payee is not a United States person.

(c) Notification of an incorrect taxpayer identification number. See § 31.3406(d)-5(e) and (g)(3) for the period for which withholding is required in the case of notification of an incorrect taxpayer identification number.

(d) Notified payee underreporting. See § 31.3406(c)-1(e) for the period for which withholding is required in the case of notified payee underreporting.

(e) Payee certification failure. *(1) Start withholding.* A payor is required to withhold under section 3406(a)(1)(D) at a rate of 31 percent on any reportable interest or dividend payment (as defined in section 3406(b)(2)) at the time the payor pays such reportable interest or dividend payment (as described in § 31.3406(a)-4) to a payee if—

(i) The payor has not received from the payee the certification required in § 31.3406(d)-2; or

(ii) The payor has received notice from a broker (as required in § 31.3406(d)-4(a)(1)(iii)) with respect to a readily tradable instrument that the payee did not make the required certification and the payor has not received the required certification from the payee.

(2) Stop withholding. The payor must stop withholding under section 3406(a)(1)(D) on any reportable interest or dividend payment within 30 days after the payor receives the certification from the payee in the manner required by § 31.3406(d)-2.

(f) Rule for determining when the payor receives a taxpayer identification number or certificate from a payee. In determining whether a payee has failed to provide a taxpayer identification number or any certification to a payor (including a Form W-8 or substitute form), a payor is required to process the taxpayer identification number or certification within 30 days after the payor receives the taxpayer identification number or certification from the payee or in certain cases, from a broker. Thus, the payor may take up to 30 days to treat the taxpayer identification number or a certificate as having been received.

T.D. 8637, 12/20/95.

§ 31.3406(f)-1 Confidentiality of information.

(a) Confidentiality and liability for violation. Pursuant to section 3406(f) no person may use any information obtained under section 3406 for any purpose except for the purpose of complying with the requirements of section 3406 or for purposes permitted under section 6103 (subject to the safeguards of section 6103). See section 7431 for civil damages for violating the confidential use of the information (subject to an exception for good faith).

(b) Permissible use of information. *(1) In general.* A payor or broker may transmit information on a Form W-9, Form W-8, or other acceptable form relating to withholding to the department, institution, or firm (or to any employee therein) responsible for withholding or processing of taxpayer identification numbers, certifications described in § 31.3406(h)-3, or other substitute forms. In addition, a broker may notify the payor with respect to a readily tradable instrument of the requirement to withhold and the condition or conditions for imposing withholding (as described in § 31.3406(d)-4) that exist with respect to the payee. A payor or broker may, without violating the Internal Revenue Code, close an account of, refuse to open an account for, issue an instrument to, or redeem an instrument for, a person solely because the person fails to furnish the person's taxpayer identification number or documentation of foreign status in the manner required in § 31.3406(d)-1 and § 31.3406(g)-1, respectively. A payor who closes an account of a payee in the calendar year in which the account was opened and during which no taxpayer identification number or evidence of foreign status was provided for that account will be presumed in the absence of evidence to the contrary to have closed the account without violating section 3406(f) even though the payee is subject to backup withholding under section 3406(a)(1)(A). A payor, except as provided in §§ 31.3406(d)-3 and 31.3406(g)-3, may not prohibit a payee who fails to furnish the payee's taxpayer identification number in the manner required in § 31.3406(d)-1 from withdrawing any funds in the account.

(2) Window transactions. In the case of a window transaction (as defined in § 31.3406(b)(2)-3(b)), a payor may, without violating the Internal Revenue Code, refuse to redeem or may refuse to make payment if the payee fails to provide a taxpayer identification number regardless of when the obligation was issued or acquired.

(c) Specific restrictions on the use of information. Except as provided in paragraph (b) of this section, a payor or broker is not permitted to—

(1) Close an account (or instrument) of a payee solely because that payee (or the account of a payee) is subject to withholding under section 3406(a)(1)(A), (B), (C), or (D);

(2) Refuse to open an account or to issue an instrument if the person fails to certify, under penalties of perjury, that the person is not subject to withholding under section 3406(a)(1)(C) (relating to notified payee underreporting);

(3) Use information obtained under section 3406 (including a payee's failure or inability to certify that the payee is not subject to withholding due to notified payee underreporting or the fact that the account is subject to withholding), surcharge an account (i.e., charge an account more than the fee charged a similar account that was not subject to withholding under section 3406), or use that information to determine whether to open or close an account, whether to issue or redeem an instrument, or whether to extend credit to the payee.

T.D. 8637, 12/20/95.

---

§ 31.3406(g)-1 Exception for payments to certain payees and certain other payments.

(a) Exempt recipients. *(1) In general.* A payor of any reportable payment (as defined in section 3406(b)) must not withhold under section 3406 if the payee is—

(i) An organization exempt from taxation under section 501(a) or an individual retirement account;

(ii) The United States or any wholly owned agency or instrumentality thereof;

(iii) A state, the District of Columbia, a possession of the United States, any political subdivision of any of the foregoing, or any wholly owned agency or instrumentality of any one or more of the foregoing;

(iv) A foreign government, a political subdivision of a foreign government, or any wholly owned agency or instrumentality of any one or more of the foregoing (as defined in regulations under section 892); or

(v) An international organization or any wholly owned agency or instrumentality thereof (as defined in section 7701(a)(18)).

(2) Nonexclusive list. Paragraph (a)(1) of this section does not prescribe an exclusive list of payees that are exempt from information reporting and also are exempt from withholding under section 3406.

(b) Determination of whether a person is described in paragraph (a)(1) of this section. The determination of whether a person is a payee described in paragraph (a)(1) of this section must be made as provided in the applicable provisions of section 6049 and the regulations issued thereunder. A payor, even if permitted to treat a person as an exempt recipient without requiring a certificate under the provisions of section 6049, may require a payee, otherwise not required to file a certificate regarding its exempt status, to file a certificate and may treat a payee who fails to file the certificate as a person who is not an exempt recipient. See § 31.3406(h)-3 for a description of the Form W-9 or a substitute form prescribed under section 3406 for claiming exempt status.

(c) Prepaid or advance premium life-insurance contracts. A payor of a reportable payment (as defined in section 3406(b)(1)) may, but is not required to, withhold under section 3406 on reportable payments made from January 1, 1984, to December 31, 1996, on prepaid or advance premium life-insurance contracts to a payee who is the owner for tax purposes of the prepaid or advance premium life-insurance contract. For purposes of this exception from backup withholding, a prepaid or advance premium life-insurance contract is one entered into on or before June 30, 1984, by the payee and under which the increment in value of the prepaid or advance premium is used for the payment of premiums during the period in which the exception from backup withholding applies.

(d) Reportable payments made to Canadian nonresident alien individuals. A payment of interest made to a Canadian nonresident alien individual under § 1.6049-8(a) of this chapter is not subject to withholding under section 3406.

(e) Certain reportable payments made outside the United States by foreign persons, foreign offices of United States banks and brokers, and others. For reportable payments made after December 31, 2000, a payor is not required to backup withhold under section 3406 on a reportable payment that qualifies for the documentary evidence rule described in § 1.6049-5(c)(1) or (4) of this chapter, whether or not documentary evidence is actually provided to the payor, unless the payor has actual knowledge that the payee is a United States person. Further, no backup withholding is required for payments upon which a 30-percent amount was withheld by another payor in accordance with the withholding provisions under chapter 3 of the Internal Revenue Code and the regulations under that chapter. For rules applicable to notional principal contracts, see § 1.6041-1(d)(5) of this chapter.

(f) Special rule for certain payment card transactions. *(1) In general.* No withholding under section 3406 is required for a reportable payment made through a payment card organization if the payment is made on or after January 1, 2005, the organization is a Qualified Payment Card Agent (QPCA), and—

(i) The payee is a qualified payee (as defined in paragraph (f)(2)(vi) of this section) with respect to the payment; or

(ii) The cardholder/payor made the purchase to which the payment relates no later than two months after the last date prescribed under paragraph (f)(3) of this section for furnishing the QPCA's first notification to the cardholder/payor that the payee is not a qualified payee.

(2) Definitions. (i) Payment card defined. For purposes of this section, a payment card is a card (or an account) issued by a payment card organization, or one of its members, affiliates, or licensees, to a cardholder/payor which, upon presentation to a merchant/payee, represents an agreement of the cardholder to pay the merchant through the payment card organization.

(ii) Payment card organization defined. For purposes of this section, a payment card organization is an entity that sets the standards and provides the mechanism, either directly or indirectly through members, affiliates, or licensees, for effectuating payment between a purchaser and a merchant in a payment card transaction. A payment card organization acting directly or indirectly through its members, affiliates, or licensees generally provides such a payment mechanism by issuing payment cards, enrolling merchants as authorized acceptors of payment cards for payment for goods or services, and ensuring the system conducts the transactions in accordance with prescribed standards for payment card transactions.

(iii) Payment card transaction defined. For purposes of this section, a payment card transaction is a transaction in which a cardholder/payor uses a payment card to purchase goods or services and a merchant agrees to accept a payment card as a means of obtaining payment.

(iv) Cardholder/payor defined. For purposes of this section, a cardholder/payor is the person that agrees to make payments through the payment card organization. Thus, in the case of a payment card issued to an employee of a person that agrees to make payments through the payment card organization, the employer rather than the employee is the cardholder/payor.

(v) Qualified Payment Card Agent (QPCA) defined. For purposes of this section, a Qualified Payment Card Agent (QPCA) is a payment card organization that has a current QPCA determination from the Internal Revenue Service (IRS) under applicable procedures (see § 601.601(d)(2) of this chapter).

(vi) Qualified payee defined. For purposes of this section, a payee is a qualified payee with respect to a reportable payment if—

(A) At the time the QPCA makes the payment, the QPCA has obtained the payee's TIN and the payee's TIN has been validated through the IRS TIN Matching Program; or

(B) The QPCA makes the payment during the six-month period beginning on the date on which the QPCA first makes a payment to the payee.

(3) Notification of payee status. In the case of a payment to a payee other than a qualified payee as defined in paragraph (f)(2)(vi) of this section with respect to the payment, the QPCA acting directly or indirectly through its members, affiliates, or licensees must notify the payor that the payee is not a qualified payee. The notification must be furnished during the four-month period beginning on the date on which the QPCA makes the payment. Notification may be provided in a quarterly or other regular report of payee data to the cardholder/payor and may consist of an asterisk, footnote, or other mark next to the payee's name, with the text of the notification at the bottom of the page or at the end of the list of payee data. Notification by the QPCA that a payee is not a qualified payee does not constitute notice by the IRS that the payee's TIN is incorrect for purposes of section 3406(a)(1)(B) and § 31.3406(d)-5.

(4) Time of payment. A QPCA that makes reports to cardholders on the basis of a calendar quarter or any shorter period (the reporting period) may choose to treat all payments made during the reporting period as being made on the last day of the period for purposes of paragraphs (f)(2)(vi) and (f)(3) of this section. If the QPCA treats payments as being made on the last day of a reporting period, the six-month period in paragraph (f)(2)(vi) of this section and the four-month period in paragraph (f)(3) of this section are treated as beginning on the first day of the reporting period in which the QPCA makes the payment that would otherwise begin the six-month or four-month period.

(5) Examples. The following examples illustrate the rules of this section. For purposes of the examples, assume that Q meets all requirements and fulfills all duties necessary to obtain a QPCA determination from the IRS. The examples are as follows:

Example (1). (i) Q, a QPCA, enrolls Merchant X on January 20, 2005, to accept the Q payment card as a means for obtaining payment. (The results in this example are the same whether the acts attributed to Q are performed by Q itself or by a member, affiliate, or licensee of Q.) At the time of enrollment, Q obtains Merchant X's taxpayer identification number (TIN). Merchant X is a sole proprietor engaged in the trade or business of repairing automobiles and trucks. Q's first payment to Merchant X for purchases through the payment card is made on January 31, 2005.

(ii) On March 1, 2005, Q issues a Q payment card to Customer A to use for the purchase of goods or services in the course of its trade or business from merchants that accept the Q payment card. During 2005, Customer A uses Q payment card to purchase repairs to A's vehicles from Merchant X on April 29, 2005, July 29, 2005, and December 19, 2005. Q makes payments for the repairs on May 2, 2005, August 1, 2005, and December 20, 2005. Q provides reports of payee data to each of its cardholders, including Customer A, on the 15th of April, July, October, and January for the quarter ending on the last day of the preceding month, but does not choose to treat payments as being made on the last day of the quarter for purposes of paragraphs (f)(2)(vi) and (f)(3) of this section.

(iii) On March 15, 2005, Q attempts to validate Merchant X's name/TIN through the IRS TIN Matching Program. On March 20, 2005, the IRS notifies Q that the name/TIN furnished by Merchant X does not match IRS data. On June 15, 2005, and September 15, 2005, Q makes further unsuccessful attempts to validate Merchant X's name/ TIN through the IRS TIN Matching Program.

(iv) Under paragraph (f)(2)(vi)(B) of this section, Merchant X is treated as a qualified payee for the six-month period beginning on January 31, 2005 (the date of Q's first payment to Merchant X), and ending on July 30, 2005. Accordingly, the payment on May 2, 2005, is a payment to a qualified payee and, under paragraph (f)(1)(i) of this section, is not subject to backup withholding.

(v) Q has not validated Merchant X's TIN at the time of the payments on August 1, 2005, and December 20, 2005. Accordingly, under paragraph (f)(3) of this section, Q must notify Customer A within four months of each of these payments that Merchant X is not a qualified payee with respect to the payments. In the case of the August 1 payment, the notification must be furnished no later than November 30, 2005. Q may provide the notification in its quarterly report of payee data for the July-September quarter furnished on October 15, 2005.

(vi) Although Merchant X is not a qualified payee with respect to the payments on August 1, 2005, and December 20, 2005, paragraph (f)(1)(ii) of this section provides that backup withholding is not required for purchases made no later than two months after the last date prescribed for furnishing the first notification that Merchant X is not a qualified payee. The last date for furnishing the first notification is November 30, 2005, and the two-month period expires on January 30, 2006. Because the payments relate to purchases on July 29, 2005, and December 19, 2005, backup withholding is not required with respect to either payment. Backup withholding may be required with respect to any payment Customer A makes through the Q payment card for purchases from Merchant X after January 30, 2006, unless Q has previously succeeded in validating Merchant X's TIN.

Example (2). (i) Assume the same facts as in example (1) except that Q chooses to treat payments as being made on the last day of the quarter for purposes of paragraphs (f)(2)(vi) and (f)(3) of this section.

(ii) The payment Q makes on January 31, 2005, is treated under paragraph (f)(4) of this section as being made on March 31, 2005. Similarly, the payments made on May 2, 2005, August 1, 2005, and December 20, 2005, are treated as being made on June 30, 2005, September 30, 2005, and December 31, 2005.

(iii) Under paragraphs (f)(2)(vi)(B) and (f)(4) of this section, Merchant X is treated as a qualified payee for the six-month period beginning on January 1, 2005 (the beginning of the reporting period during which Q makes the first payment to Merchant X), and ending on June 30, 2005. Accordingly, the payment treated as made on June 30, 2005, is a payment to a qualified payee and, under paragraph (f)(1)(i) of this section, is not subject to backup withholding.

(iv) Q has not validated Merchant X's TIN at the time of the payments that are treated as being made on September 30, 2005, and December 31, 2005. Accordingly, under paragraphs (f)(3) and (f)(4) of this section, Q must notify Customer A within four months of the beginning of each reporting period during which Q makes these payments that Merchant X is not a qualified payee with respect to the payments. In the case of the September 30 payment, the notification must be furnished no later than October 31, 2005. Q may provide the notification in its quarterly report of payee data for the July-September quarter furnished on October 15, 2005.

(v) Although Merchant X is not a qualified payee with respect to the payments that are treated as being made on September 30, 2005, and December 31, 2005, paragraph (f)(1)(ii) of this section provides that backup withholding is not required for purchases made no later than two months after the last date prescribed for furnishing the first notification that Merchant X is not a qualified payee. The last date for furnishing the first notification is October 31, 2005, and the two-month period expires on December 31, 2005. Because the payments relate to purchases on July 29, 2005, and December 19, 2005, backup withholding is not required with respect to either payment. Backup withholding may be required with respect to any payment Customer A makes through the Q payment card for purchases from Merchant X after December 31, 2005, unless Q has previously succeeded in validating Merchant X's TIN.

T.D. 8637, 12/20/95, amend T.D. 8664, 4/15/96, T.D. 8734, 10/6/97, T.D. 8804, 12/30/98, T.D. 8856, 12/29/99, T.D. 9136, 7/12/2004.

PAR. 2. Section 31.3406(g)-1(f) is amended by:

1. Revising paragraphs (f)(2)(vi)(A) and (f)(3).

2. Adding paragraph (f)(2)(vii).

The revisions and addition read as follows:

Proposed § 31.3406(g)-1 Exceptions for payments to certain payees and certain other payments. [*For Preamble, see ¶ 152,881*]

* * * * *

(f) * * *

(2) * * *

(vi) * * *

(A) The payee is a participating payee with respect to the payment and, at the time the QPCA makes the payment, the QPCA has obtained the payee's TIN and the payee's TIN has been validated through the IRS TIN Matching Program; or

* * * * *

(vii) Participating payee. For purposes of this section, a payee is a participating payee with respect to a reportable payment if—

(A) At the time the QPCA makes the payment, the payee has authorized the payment card organization to act on its behalf in furnishing its name, taxpayer identification number, and corporate status to cardholder/payors under applicable procedures issued under § 601.601 of this chapter; or

(B) The payment is made before January 1, 2008.

(3) Notifications of payee status and participation. (i) In general. (A) Nonqualified payees. In the case of a payment to a payee other than a qualified payee (as defined in paragraph (f)(2)(vi) of this section) with respect to the payment, the QPCA acting directly or indirectly through its members, affiliates, or licensees must notify the payor that the payee is not a qualified payee. If the notification relates to a payment made after December 31, 2007, the notification must also inform the payor that IRS rules and regulations may require the payor to backup withhold on reportable payments that relate to purchases the payor makes from the payee after a specified date. The specified date to be provided in the notification is the last day of the two-month period described in paragraph (f)(1)(ii) of this section. A notification by the QPCA that a payee is not a qualified payee does not constitute notice by the IRS that the payee's TIN is incorrect for purposes of section 3406(a)(1)(B) and § 31.3406(d)-5.

(B) Nonparticipating payees. In the case of a payment made after December 31, 2007, to a payee other than a participating payee (as defined in paragraph (f)(2)(vii) of this section), the QPCA acting directly or indirectly through its members, affiliates, or licensees must notify the payor that the payee is not a participating payee. A notification that the payee of a payment is not a participating payee must also inform the payor that IRS rules and regulations require the payor to solicit the payee's TIN if the payor has made a reportable payment to the payee.

(C) Due date and format. The notifications must be furnished during the four-month period beginning on the date on which the QPCA makes the payment. Notifications may be provided in a quarterly or other regular report of payee data to the cardholder/payor and may consist of an asterisk, footnote, or other mark next to the payee's name, with the text of the notifications at the bottom of the page or at the end of the list of payee data.

(ii) Electronic furnishing of notifications of payee status and participation. (A) In general. The notifications required under paragraph (f)(3)(i) of this section may be furnished in an electronic format if the requirements of this paragraph (f)(3)(ii) are satisfied.

(B) Consents. (1) Cardholder/Payor. (i) In general. The cardholder/ payor consent requirement must be satisfied. The cardholder/payor consent requirement is satisfied only if the QPCA has provided the disclosure statement required under paragraph (f)(3)(ii)(C) of this section to the cardholder/payor and, after receiving the disclosure statement, the cardholder/payor has affirmatively consented to receive the notifications in an electronic format. The consent may be provided electronically in any manner that reasonably demonstrates that the cardholder/payor can access the notifications in the electronic format in which they will be furnished. Alternatively, the consent may be provided in a paper document if it is confirmed electronically in a manner that reasonably demonstrates that the cardholder/payor can access the notifications in the electronic format in which they will be furnished.

(ii) Withdrawal of consent. The cardholder/payor consent requirement is not satisfied with respect to a notification if the cardholder/payor withdraws the consent and the withdrawal takes effect before the notification is furnished. Only paper notifications may be furnished to the cardholder/payor after the withdrawal takes effect. The QPCA may provide that a withdrawal of consent takes effect at any time up to 30 days after receipt by the QPCA. The QPCA may also provide that a request for paper notifications will be treated as a withdrawal of consent.

(iii) Change in hardware or software requirements. If a change in the hardware or software required to access the notifications creates a material risk that the cardholder/payor will not be able to access the notifications, the cardholder/payor consent requirement is not satisfied with respect to notifications furnished after the change unless the cardholder/payor has provided a new consent to receive the notifications in an electronic format. The new consent, whether electronic or by paper document, must be provided or confirmed in a manner that reasonably demonstrates that the cardholder/payor can access the notifications in the revised electronic format in which they will be furnished.

(2) Merchant/payee. (i) In general. The merchant/payee consent requirement must be satisfied. The merchant/payee consent requirement is satisfied with respect to notifications regarding a merchant/payee only if the merchant/payee has affirmatively consented to the electronic furnishing of the notifications.

(ii) Withdrawal of consent. The merchant/payee consent requirement is not satisfied with respect to a notification regarding a merchant/ payee if the merchant/payee withdraws its consent and the withdrawal takes effect before the notification is furnished. The QPCA may provide that a withdrawal of consent takes effect at any time up to 30 days after receipt by the QPCA.

(C) Required disclosures. (1) In general. A QPCA requesting a cardholder/payor's consent to receive notifications in electronic format must provide to the cardholder/payor a clear and conspicuous disclosure statement containing each of the disclosures described in this paragraph (f)(3)(ii)(C).

(2) Paper statement. The cardholder/payor must be informed that the notifications will be furnished on paper if the cardholder/payor does not consent to receive them electronically.

(3) Scope and duration of consent. The cardholder/payor must be informed of the scope and duration of the consent. For example, the cardholder/payor must be informed whether the consent is for a specified term or will remain in effect until it is withdrawn in the manner described in paragraph (f)(3)(ii)(B)(1)(ii) of this section.

(4) Post-consent request for paper notifications. The cardholder/ payor must be informed of any procedure for obtaining a paper copy of the notifications after giving the consent described in paragraph (f)(3)(ii)(B)(1)(i) of this section and whether a request for paper notifications will be treated as a withdrawal of consent.

(5) Withdrawal of consent. The cardholder/payor must be informed that—

(i) The cardholder/payor may withdraw a consent by writing (electronically or on paper) to the person or department whose name, mailing address, telephone number, and e-mail address is provided in the disclosure statement;

(ii) The QPCA will confirm the withdrawal and the date on which it takes effect in writing (either electronically or on paper); and

(iii) A withdrawal of consent will not apply to a notification that was furnished electronically before the date on which the withdrawal of consent takes effect.

(6) Notice of termination. The cardholder/payor must be informed of the conditions under which the QPCA will cease furnishing notifications electronically.

(7) Updating information. The cardholder/payor must be informed of the procedures for updating the information needed by the QPCA to contact the cardholder/payor. The QPCA must inform the cardholder/payor of any change in the QPCA's contact information.

(8) Hardware and software requirements. The cardholder/payor must be provided with a description of the hardware and software required to access, print, and retain the notifications.

(D) Notice of availability. (1) In general. If the notifications to a cardholder/payor are furnished on a website, the QPCA must also furnish a notice of availability to the cardholder/payor within 30 days after posting the notifications. The notice of availability must inform the cardholder/payor that the notifications are available on the website and must specify the date on which the notifications will no longer be available on the Web site. The notice of availability may be delivered by mail, electronic mail, or in person. The notice of availability must provide instructions on how to access and print the notifications and must include the following statement in capital letters, "IMPORTANT TAX DOCUMENT AVAILABLE." If the notice of availability is provided by electronic mail, the foregoing statement must be on the subject line of the electronic mail.

(2) Undeliverable electronic address. If an electronic notice of availability is returned as undeliverable, and the correct electronic address cannot be obtained from the furnisher's records or from the cardholder/payor, then the furnisher must furnish the notice by mail within 30 days after the electronic notice is returned.

* * * * *

PAR. 6. In § 31.3406(g)-1, paragraph (d) is revised to read as follows:

Proposed § 31.3406(g)-1 Exceptions for payments to certain payees and certain other payment. [*For Preamble, see ¶ 152,317*]

* * * * *

(d) Reportable payments made to nonresident alien individuals. A payment of interest that is reported on Form 1042-S as paid to a nonresident alien individual under § 1.6049-8(a) of this chapter is not subject to withholding under section 3406. (For interest paid to a Canadian nonresident alien individual on or before December 31 of the year in which final regulations are published in the Federal Register, see § 31.3406(g)-1(d) in effect prior to [EFFECTIVE DATE OF FINAL RULE] (See 26 CFR part 1 revised April 1, 2002.))

* * * * *

§ 31.3406(g)-2 Exception for reportable payments for which withholding is otherwise required.

(a) In general. A payor of a reportable payment (as defined in section 3406(b)) must not withhold under section 3406 if the payment is subject to withholding under any other provision of the Internal Revenue Code.

(b) Payment of wages. A payor who is required to make an information return under section 6041 with respect to a payment of wages (as defined in section 3401) because, e.g., the employee makes a certification under section 3402(n) (relating to employees incurring no income tax liability), must not withhold under section 3406 on those wages.

(c) Distribution from a pension, annuity, or other plan of deferred compensation. An amount reportable under section 6047, such as a designated distribution under section 3405, is not a reportable payment subject to withholding under section 3406. See section 3406(b). Designated distributions not subject to withholding under section 3406 include—

(1) Distributions from a pension, annuity, profit-sharing, stock bonus plan, or other plan deferring the receipt of compensation;

(2) Distributions from an individual retirement account or annuity;

(3) Distributions from an owner-employee plan; and

(4) Certain surrenders of life insurance contracts.

(d) Gambling winnings. *(1) In general.* A payor of a reportable gambling winning must not withhold under section 3406 if tax is required to be withheld from the gambling winning under section 3402(q) (relating to the extension of withholding to certain gambling winnings). If the reportable gambling winning is not required to be withheld upon under section 3402(q), withholding under section 3406 applies to the gambling winning if, and only if, the payee does not furnish a taxpayer identification number to the payor. Section 31.3406(b)(3)-1(b)(3) does not apply to a reportable gambling winning. The payor of a reportable gambling winning is not required to aggregate all such winnings made to a payee during a calendar year, nor is the payor required to determine whether an information return was required to be made with respect to the payee for the preceding year.

(2) Definition of a reportable gambling winning and determination of amount subject to backup withholding. For purposes of withholding under section 3406, a reportable gambling winning is any gambling winning subject to information reporting under section 6041. The amount of a reportable gambling winning is—

(i) The amount paid with respect to the amount of the wager reduced, at the option of the payor; by

(ii) The amount of the wager.

(3) Special rules. Amounts paid with respect to identical wagers are treated as paid with respect to a single wager. The determination of whether wagers are identical is made under § 31.3402(q)-1(c)(1)(ii). In addition, a gambling winning (other than a winning from bingo, keno, or slot machines) is a reportable gambling winning only if the amount paid with respect to the wager is $600 or more and if the proceeds are at least 300 times as large as the amount wagered. See § 7.6041-1 of this chapter to determine whether a winning from bingo, keno, or slot machines is a reportable gambling winning and thus subject to withholding under section 3406.

(e) Certain real estate transactions. A real estate reporting person (the so-called broker) as defined in section 6045(e)(2) must not withhold under section 3406 on a payment made with respect to a real estate transaction that is subject to reporting under sections 6045(a) and (e) and § 1.6045-4 of this chapter.

(f) Certain payments after an acquisition of accounts or instruments. A payor who acquires pre-1984 accounts or instruments described in § 31.3406(d)-1(b)(2)(iv) for which the payor does not have a taxpayer identification number or has an obviously incorrect taxpayer identification number as defined in § 31.3406(h)-1(b)(2) must start withholding under section 3406(a)(1)(A) and § 31.3406(d)-1 on those accounts or instruments no later than sixty days following the date of the payor's acquisition of those accounts or instruments.

(g) Certain gross proceeds. No withholding under section 3406 is required with respect to any portion of the original issue discount on an instrument or security that is subject to withholding under section 3406 as reportable gross proceeds of such instrument or security under section 6045.

T.D. 8637, 12/20/95.

PAR. 3. Section 31.3406(g)-2 is amended by adding paragraphs (h) and (i) to read as follows:

Proposed § 31.3406(g)-2 Exception for reportable payment for which withholding is otherwise required.
[For Preamble, see ¶ 153,073]

* * * * *

(h) Certain payments made by government entities. A government entity that is required to withhold both on reportable payments pursuant to section 3406(a) and on certain payments pursuant to section 3402(t), must comply with the withholding requirements of section 3406, and not section 3402(t), with respect to a payment to which both types of withholding would apply. Pursuant to section 3402(t)(2)(B), withholding under section 3402(t) shall not apply if amounts are being withheld under section 3406 with respect to a payment. If a government entity fails to withhold as required under section 3406, the payment will not be deemed to be subject to withholding under another provision of the Code for purposes of this paragraph (h). Thus, even if the government entity withholds on such payment pursuant to section 3402(t), it will remain liable for the amount required to be withheld under section 3406.

(i) Effective/applicability date. Paragraph (h) relating to certain payments made by government entities applies to payments made by government entities under section 3402(t) made after the later of December 31, 2010, or the date that is 6 months after the date of publication in the Federal Register of final regulations under section 3402(t).

§ 31.3406(g)-3 Exemption while payee is waiting for a taxpayer identification number.

Caution: The Treasury has not yet amended Reg § 31.3406(g)-3 to reflect changes made by P.L. 107-16.

(a) In general. *(1) Backup withholding not required for 60 days.* If a payor has received an awaiting-TIN certificate from a payee with respect to an account or instrument receiving reportable interest or dividends as described in section 3406(b)(2), the payor must exempt the payee from withholding under section 3406(a)(1)(A) during the 60-day exemption period to the extent and in the manner described in either paragraph (a)(2) or (3) of this section. The 60-day exemption period means the 60-consecutive-day period beginning with the day the payor receives the awaiting-TIN certificate. The payor must withhold under section 3406 beginning after the 60-day exemption period if the payor has not received a taxpayer identification number from the payee in the manner required in § 31.3406(d)-1. Regardless of whether the payee provides an awaiting-TIN certificate to a payor, the payor is required to withhold under section 3406(a)(1)(D) and § 31.3406(d)-2 on reportable interest or dividend payments as described in § 31.3406(d)-2 if the payee fails to certify, under penalties of perjury, that the payee is not subject to withholding due to notified payee underreporting as required in section 3406(a)(1)(D) and § 31.3406(d)-2.

(2) Reserve method. A payor must not withhold under section 3406 during the 60-day exemption period unless the payee (or a joint payee in the case of a joint account) desires to make a withdrawal of more than $500 of either principal or interest from the account in any single transaction during the period. If a payee (or a joint payee) desires to make a withdrawal of more than $500 during the 60-day exemption period, the payor is required under section 3406 to withhold 31 percent of all reportable payments made during the period and at the time of withdrawal unless the payee reserves 31

percent of all reportable payments made to the account during the period.

(3) Alternative rule; 7-day grace period. (i) In general. A payor who receives an awaiting-TIN certificate may elect, on a payee-by-payee basis or in general, to exempt reportable interest or dividend payments to a payee from withholding under section 3406 applying the rules in paragraph (a)(3)(ii) or (iii) of this section.

(ii) Withholding on withdrawals. Under this paragraph (a)(3)(ii), a payor must obtain a certified taxpayer identification number from the payee within 60 days after the date that the payor receives the awaiting-TIN certification. In addition, the payor must withhold under section 3406 on any withdrawals made after the close of 7 business days after the date the awaiting-TIN certification is received and before the earlier of the date that the payor receives a certified taxpayer identification number from the payee, the date the account is closed (in which case the payor must withhold on any reportable payment made at the time the account or relationship is closed), or the date withholding under section 3406 starts on all reportable payments made to the account, instrument, or relationship. All cash withdrawals in an amount up to the reportable payments made from the day after the date of receipt of the awaiting-TIN certification to the date of withdrawal are treated as reportable payments.

(iii) Withholding regardless of withdrawals. Under this paragraph (a)(3)(iii), a payor must start withholding under section 3406 on the account not later than 7 business days after the date the payor receives the awaiting-TIN certification on reportable payments thereafter made to the account (whether or not the payee makes a cash withdrawal). The payor must withhold under section 3406 until the earlier of the date the payor receives a certified taxpayer identification number from the payee, the date the account is closed, or the date withholding under section 3406 starts on all reportable payments made to the account, instrument, or relationship. The payor must obtain a certified taxpayer identification number from the payee within 60 days after the date that the payor receives the awaiting-TIN certificate or undertake a mailing each year soliciting the certified taxpayer identification number from the payee until the earlier of the calendar year that the certified taxpayer identification number is received, or the calendar year in which the account is closed. However, if the account is closed in December of a calendar year, the mailing must be made after the account is closed and before January 31 of the subsequent calendar year.

(b) Special rule for readily tradable instruments. The 60-day awaiting-TIN exemption described in paragraph (a)(1) of this section applies to payments made with respect to readily tradable instruments only if the payee provides an awaiting-TIN certificate directly to the payor. If a broker acquires a readily tradable instrument through a post-1983 brokerage account (as described in § 31.3406(d)-1(c)(2)) for a payee who has no taxpayer identification number, the broker must advise the payor as required in § 31.3406(d)-4(a)(1) that the payee failed to provide a taxpayer identification number under penalties of perjury, regardless of whether the payee provides an awaiting-TIN certificate to the broker. Once a payor is notified by a broker that a payee failed to provide a taxpayer identification number in the required manner, or that the payee is subject to withholding under section 3406(a)(1)(B) or (C), the payor must impose withholding under section 3406 for the appropriate period described in § 31.3406(e)-1.

(c) Exceptions. *(1) In general.* The 60-day awaiting-TIN exemption described in paragraph (a) of this section does not apply to—

(i) Window transactions (as defined in § 31.3406(b)(2)-3(b));

(ii) Redemptions of bearer obligations that are subject to reporting under section 6045; or

(iii) Other amounts that are subject to reporting under section 6045 (except as described in paragraph (c)(2) of this section).

(2) Special rule for amounts subject to reporting under section 6045 other than proceeds of redemptions of bearer obligations. If a broker's customer does not provide a taxpayer identification number to the broker, and the broker effects a sale that is subject to reporting under section 6045 (other than a redemption of a bearer obligation), § 31.3406(d)-3(b) applies, whether or not the sale is pursuant to an instruction by electronic transmission, provided the customer furnishes an awaiting-TIN certificate to the broker before the sale. For purposes of this paragraph (c)(2), the 30-day period provided in § 31.3406(d)-3(b) is a 60-day period.

(d) Awaiting-TIN certificate. A payee qualifies for the 60-day awaiting-TIN exemption provided in paragraph (a) of this section if the payee furnishes a written statement to the payor, signed under penalties of perjury, that the payee has not been issued a taxpayer identification number, that the payee has applied for a taxpayer identification number or intends to apply for a number in the near future, and that the payee understands that if the payee does not provide a number to the payor within 60 days, the payor is required under section 3406 to withhold 31 percent of any reportable payment thereafter made to the payee until the payor receives a number, and 31 percent of a withdrawal to the extent of reportable payments made to the payee during the 60-day period, as described in paragraph (a) of this section. Language that is substantially similar to the awaiting-TIN certification on Form W-9 will satisfy the requirements of this paragraph (d).

(e) Form for awaiting-TIN certificate. A payor may use Form W-9 for the awaiting-TIN certificate, or a payor may include language that is substantially similar to the awaiting-TIN certification on Form W-9 in any other document of the payor. See § 31.3406(h)-3, which provides that Form W-9 is the prescribed form but permits use of substitute forms, and specifies the length of time the payor is required to retain the form. If Form W-9 is used, the payee should write "Applied For" in the space reserved for the taxpayer identification number.

T.D. 8637, 12/20/95.

§ 31.3406(h)-1 Definitions.

(a) In general. For purposes of section 3406 and the regulations thereunder, the definitions of this section apply.

(b) Taxpayer identification number. *(1) In general. Taxpayer identification number* means the identifying number assigned to a person under section 6109 (relating to identifying numbers, generally a nine-digit social security number for an individual and a nine-digit employer identification number for a nonindividual, e.g., a corporation, partnership, trust, or estate). An obviously incorrect number is not considered a taxpayer identification number. See § 31.6011(b)-2 and § 301.6109-1 of this chapter for provisions relating to obtaining a taxpayer identification number.

(2) Obviously incorrect number. Obviously incorrect number means a number that does not contain nine digits or a number that includes an alpha character as one of the nine digits.

(c) Broker. *Broker* is defined in section 6045(c)(1) and § 1.6045-1(a)(1) of this chapter. If there could be more than one broker with respect to any acquisition, only the broker having the closest contact (as determined under § 1.6045-1(c)(3)(iii) and (iv) of this chapter) with the payee is treated as a broker. In the case of any instrument, the term broker does not include any person who is the payor with respect to the instrument as described in § 31.3406(a)-2.

(d) Readily tradable instrument. *Readily tradable instrument* means—

(1) Any instrument that is part of an issue any portion of which is traded on an established securities market (within the meaning of section 453(f)(5)); or

(2) Any instrument that is regularly quoted by brokers or dealers making a market.

(e) Day. *Day* means a calendar day unless specified otherwise under any section of the regulations under section 3406. For example, see § 31.3406(d)-5(a) and 31.3406(g)-3(a)(2).

(f) Business day. *Business day* means any day other than a Saturday, Sunday, or legal holiday (within the meaning of section 7503).

T.D. 8637, 12/20/95, amend T.D. 9010, 7/25/2002.

Proposed § 31.3406(h)-1 Definitions. [*For Preamble, see ¶ 151,187*]

• ***Caution:*** This Notice of Proposed Rulemaking was partially finalized by Prop Reg. 60-110, TD 8365, 9/23/91, TD 8409, 4/15/92, and TD 8637, 9/27/90.

(a) Taxpayer identification number. *(1) In general.* The term "taxpayer identification number" shall mean the identifying number assigned to a person under Section 6109 (relating to identifying numbers). Thus, the number for an individual is generally his social security number and the number or a corporation, estate, trust, or partnership is generally an employer identification number. The proper number of digits is nine for both the social security number and the employer identification number. An obviously incorrect number shall not be considered to be a taxpayer identification number. Thus, a payor shall treat the payee as having failed to furnish a taxpayer identification number if the payee furnishes an obviously incorrect number. See §§ 31.6011(b)-2 and 301.6109-1 for provisions relating to obtaining a taxpayer identification number.

(2) Obviously incorrect number. The term "obviously incorrect number" means a number that does not contain nine digits or a number that includes an alpha character as one of the nine digits.

(b) Examples. The application of the provisions of paragraph (a) of this section may be illustrated by the following examples:

Example (1). Individual A provides Bank O with a social security number as 605-62-599. The number provided by A, because it does not contain nine digits, is an obviously incorrect number. Consequently, A is treated as not furnishing a taxpayer identification number.

Example (2). Individual B provides Bank P with a social security number as 605-6W-6599. The number provided by B, because it contains an alpha character, is an obviously incorrect number. Consequently, B is treated as not furnishing a taxpayer identification number.

Example (3). Partnership X provides its employer identification number as 12-2764. The number provided by X, because it does not contain nine digits, is an obviously incorrect number. Consequently, X is treated as not furnishing its taxpayer identification number.

Example (4). Individual C provides Bank Q with a social security number as 111-11-1111. The number provided by C, because it contains nine digits, is not an obviously incorrect number. Consequently, C is treated as furnishing a taxpayer identification number.

Example (5). Company Y provides Bank P with a employer identification number as 12-3456789. The number provided by Y, because it contains nine digits, is not an obviously incorrect number. Consequently, Y is treated as furnishing its taxpayer identification number

(c) Broker. The term "broker" shall have the meaning given to such term by section 6045(c)(1) and § 1.6045-1(a)(1). If there could be more than one broker with respect to any acquisition, only the broker having the closest contact with the payee shall be treated as a broker. The rules of § 5f.6045-1(c)(3)(ii) and (iii) shall apply to determine the broker with the closest contact with the payee. In the case of any instrument, the term "broker" shall not include any person who is the payor with respect to such instrument as described in § 31.3406(a)-2.

(d) Readily tradable instrument. The term "readily tradable instrument" means—

(1) Any instrument which is part of an issue any portion of which is traded on an established securities market (within the meaning of section 453(f)(5)), or

(2) Any instrument which is regularly quoted by brokers or dealers making a market.

Thus, the term may include, but is not limited to, bonds, debentures, notes, certificates, and other evidence of indebtedness regardless of how denominated, repurchase agreements, stocks, shares in a mutual fund, United States government securities, State and local government obligations, and deposits with persons carrying on the banking business and persons that are mutual savings banks, cooperative banks, building and loan associations, homestead associations, credit unions, or similar organizations.

§ 31.3406(h)-2 Special rules.

Caution: The Treasury has not yet amended Reg § 31.3406(h)-2 to reflect changes made by P.L. 107-16.

(a) Joint accounts. *(1) Relevant name and taxpayer identification number combination.* For purposes of identifying the account subject to withholding under sections 3406(a)(1)(B) and (C), the relevant name and taxpayer identification number combination is that which is used for information reporting purposes.

(2) Optional rule for accounts subject to backup withholding under section 3406(a)(1)(B) or (C) where the names are switched. See § 31.3406(d)-5(c)(4)(iii) under which a payor may withhold under section 3406(a)(1)(B) as required even though the names or taxpayer identification numbers on the

account have been switched. The rules under § 31.3406(d)-5(c)(4)(iii) may be applied comparably by a payor who is required to withhold under section 3406(a)(1)(C).

(3) Joint foreign payees. (i) In general. If the relevant payee listed on a jointly owned account or instrument provides a Form W-8 or documentary evidence described in § 1.1441-1(e)(1)(ii) regarding its foreign status, withholding under section 3406 applies unless every joint payee provides the statement regarding foreign status (under the provisions of chapters 3 or 61 of the Internal Revenue Code and the regulations under those provisions) or any one of the joint owners who has not established foreign status provides a taxpayer identification number to the payor in the manner required in §§ 31.3406(d)-1 through 31.3406(d)-5. See § 1.6049-5(d)(2)(iii) of this chapter for corresponding joint payees provisions.

(ii) Information reporting on an account including foreign payees. If any one of the joint payees who has not established foreign status provides a taxpayer identification number under paragraph (a)(3)(i)(B) of this section, that number is the taxpayer identification number that is required to be furnished for purposes of information reporting and withholding under section 3406.

(b) Backup withholding from an alternative source. *(1) In general.* A payor may not withhold under section 3406 from a source maintained by the payor other than the source with respect to which there exists a liability to withhold under section 3406 with respect to the payee. See section 3403 and § 31.3403-1, which provide that the payor is liable for the amount required to be withheld regardless of whether the payor withholds.

(2) Exceptions for payments made in property. (i) Backup withholding from alternative source. In the case of a payment that is made in property (other than money), the payor must withhold under section 3406, 31 percent of the fair market value of the property determined immediately before or on the date of payment. The payor may withhold under section 3406 from the principal amount being deposited with the payor or from another source maintained by the payee with the payor. The source from which the tax is withheld under section 3406 must be payable to at least one of the persons listed on the account subject to withholding. If the account or source is not payable exclusively to the same person or persons listed on the account subject to withholding under section 3406, then the payor must obtain a written statement from all other persons to whom the account or source is payable authorizing the payor to withhold under section 3406 from the alternative account or source. A payor that elects to withhold under section 3406 from an alternative source may determine the account or source from which the tax is to be withheld, or may allow the payee to designate the alternative source. A payee may not, however, require a payor to withhold under section 3406 from a specific alternative source. See § 31.3402(q)-1(d), Example 5, for methods of withholding on prizes, awards, and gambling winnings paid in property other than cash.

(ii) Deferral of withholding. If the payor cannot locate, using reasonable care (following procedures substantially similar to those set forth in § 31.3406(d)-5(c)(3)(ii)(A) and (B)), an alternative source of cash from which the payor may satisfy its withholding obligation pursuant to paragraph (b)(2)(i) of this section, the payor may defer its obligation to withhold under section 3406, except for reportable payments of property made in connection with prizes, awards, or gambling winnings, until the earlier of—

(A) The date the payor makes a cash payment to the account subject to withholding under section 3406 or cash is otherwise deposited in the account in a sufficient amount to satisfy the obligation in full; or

(B) The close of the fourth calendar year after the obligation arose.

(iii) Barter exchanges. In the case of a barter exchange that issues scrip to, or credits the account of, a member or client of the exchange in payment for property or services, the barter exchange may withhold under section 3406 from—

(A) The scrip or credit, if converted to cash in order to satisfy the deposit requirements of section 6302 and § 31.6302-4; or

(B) Any other source maintained by the exchange for the member or client in the manner described in paragraph (b)(2) of this section.

(c) Trusts. Withholding under section 3406 applies to reportable payments made to a trust if any of the conditions for imposing withholding under section 3406 apply to the trust. Generally, a trust is not a payor and will not be required to withhold under section 3406 on reportable payments that it makes to its beneficiary who is subject to withholding under section 3406. The preceding sentence does not apply, however, to a grantor trust described in § 31.3406(a)-2(b)(1) or (2), which is treated as a payor. The trustee of a trust described in this paragraph (c) may certify that the trust's taxpayer identification number is correct and that the trust is not subject to withholding due to notified payee underreporting, without regard to the status of the beneficiaries of the trust.

(d) Adjustment of prior withholding by middlemen. A middleman payor (as defined in § 31.3406(a)-2(b) or in the section on information reporting to which the payment relates) who receives a payment from which tax has been erroneously withheld under section 3406 may seek a refund of the tax withheld by the payor from whom the middleman payor received the payment (referred to as the "upstream payor"). Alternatively, the middleman payor may obtain a refund of the tax by claiming a credit for the amount of tax withheld by the upstream payor against the deposit of any tax imposed by this chapter which the middleman payor is required to withhold and deposit (as described in section 6413 and § 31.6413(a)-2). In either case, the middleman payor must pay or credit the gross amount of the payment (including the tax withheld) to its payee as though it had received the gross amount of the payment from the upstream payor and must withhold under section 3406 only if one of the conditions for imposing backup withholding exists with respect to its payee. If its payee is not subject to withholding under section 3406, the payor must pay or credit the full amount of the payment to the payee, unless, with respect to payments made after December 31, 2000, the payor chooses to apply prior withholding under section 3406 to an amount required to be withheld under another section of the Internal Revenue Code (such as under section 1441) to the extent permitted under procedures prescribed by the Internal Revenue Service (see § 601.601(d)(2) of this chapter). See § 31.6413(a)-3 regarding repayment by a payor of tax erroneously collected from a payee.

(e) Conversion of amounts paid in foreign currency into united states dollars. If a payment is made in a currency other than the United States dollar, the amount subject to withholding under section 3406 is determined by applying the statutory rate of backup withholding to the foreign currency payment and converting the amount withheld into United States dollars on the date of payment at the spot rate (as defined in § 1.988-1(d)(1) of this chapter) or pursuant to a reasonable spot rate convention. For example, a withholding agent may use a month-end spot rate or a monthly average spot rate. A spot rate convention must be used consistently with respect to all non-dollar amounts withheld and from year to year. Such convention cannot be changed without the consent of the Commissioner.

(f) Coordination with other sections. For purposes of section 31, chapter 24 (other than section 3402(n)) of subtitle C of the Internal Revenue Code (relating to employment taxes and collection of income tax at source) and so much of subtitle F (other than section 7205) of the Internal Revenue Code (relating to procedure and administration) as relates to this chapter, and the regulations thereunder—

(1) An amount required to be withheld under section 3406 must be treated as a tax required to be withheld under section 3402;

(2) An amount withheld under section 3406 must be treated as an amount withheld under section 3402;

(3) An amount withheld under section 3406 must be deposited as required under § 31.6302-4;

(4) Wages includes the gross amount of any reportable payment (as defined in section 3406 (b)) except for purposes of section 6014 (relating to an election by the taxpayer not to compute the tax on his annual return);

(5) Employee includes a payee of any reportable payment; and

(6) Employer includes a payor who is required to withhold the tax under section 3406 (as defined in § 31.3406(a)-2) with respect to any reportable payment (as defined in section 3406(b)).

(g) Tax liabilities and penalties. A payor is subject to the same civil and criminal penalties for failing to impose withholding under section 3406 as an employer who fails to withhold on a payment of wages. In addition, a broker may be subject to the penalty under section 6705 (failure of a broker to provide notice to a payor).

(h) To whom payor is liable for amount withheld. A payor is not liable to any person for any amount withheld under section 3406. A payor is liable only to the United States for an amount that is required to be withheld as provided in § 31.3403-1.

T.D. 8637, 12/20/95, amend T.D. 8734, 10/6/97, T.D. 8804, 12/30/98, T.D. 8856, 12/29/99, T.D. 9010, 7/25/2002.

§ 31.3406(h)-3 Certificates.

(a) Prescribed form to furnish information under penalties of perjury. *(1) In general.* Except as provided in paragraph (c) of this section, the Form W-9 is the form prescribed under section 3406 on which the payee that is a U.S. person certifies, under penalties of perjury, that—

(i) The taxpayer identification number furnished to the payor is correct (as required in § 31.3406(d)-1 and § 31.3406(d)-5);

(ii) The payee is not subject to withholding due to notified payee underreporting (as required in § 31.3406(d)-2);

(iii) The payee is an exempt recipient (as described in § 31.3406(g)-1); or

(iv) The payee is awaiting receipt of a taxpayer identification number (as described in § 31.3406(g)-3).

(2) Use of a single or multiple Forms W-9 for accounts of the same payee. A valid Form W-9 must include the name and taxpayer identification number of the payee. Except as provided in paragraph (b) of this section, the payee must sign under penalties of perjury and date the Form W-9 in order to satisfy the requirements of this section. A payor or broker may require a payee to furnish a separate Form W-9 for each obligation, deposit, certificate, share, membership, contract, or other instrument, or one Form W-9 for all the payee's obligations or relationships with the payor or broker. In addition, a payee of a mutual fund that has a common investment advisor or common principal underwriter with other mutual funds (within the same family of funds) may be permitted, in the discretion of the mutual fund, to provide one Form W-9 with respect to shares acquired or owned in any of the funds.

(b) Prescribed form to furnish a noncertified taxpayer identification number. With respect to accounts or other relationships where the payee is not required to certify, under penalties of perjury, that the taxpayer identification number being furnished is correct, the payor or broker may obtain the taxpayer identification number orally or may use Form W-9, a substitute form, or any other document, but the payee is not required to sign the form.

(c) Forms prepared by payors or brokers. *(1) Substitute forms; in general.* A payor or broker may prepare and use a form that contains provisions that are substantially similar to those of the official Form W-9. A payor or broker may use any document relating to the transaction, such as the signature card for an account, so long as the certifications are clearly set forth. A payor or broker who uses a substitute form may furnish orally or in writing the instructions for the Form W-9 that relate to the account. A payor or broker may refuse to accept certifications (including the official Form W-9) that are not made on the form or forms provided by the payor or broker. A payor or broker may refuse to accept a certification provided by a payee only if the payor or broker furnishes the payee with an acceptable form immediately upon receipt of an unacceptable form or within 5 business days of receipt of an unacceptable form. An acceptable form for this purpose must contain a notice that the payor or broker has refused to accept the form submitted by the payee and that the payee must submit the acceptable form provided by the payor in order for the payee not to be subject to withholding under section 3406. If the payor or broker requires the payee to furnish a form for each account of the payee, the payor or broker is not required to furnish an acceptable form until the payee furnishes the payor or broker with the payee's account numbers. A payor or broker may use separate substitute forms to have a payee certify under penalties of perjury that—

(i) The payee's taxpayer identification number is correct; and

(ii) The payee is not subject to withholding under section 3406 due to notified payee underreporting.

(2) Form for exempt recipient. A payor or broker may use a substitute form for the payee to certify, under penalties of perjury, that the payee is an exempt recipient (described in § 31.3406(g)-1 or described in the respective reporting section), provided the form contains provisions that are substantially similar to those of the official Form W-9 relating to exempt recipients. A certificate must be prepared in accordance with the instructions applicable to exempt recipients on Form W-9, and must set forth fully and clearly the data called for therein. If a payor will treat the payee as an exempt recipient only if the payee files a certificate as to its

exempt status, the certificate is valid only if it contains the payee's taxpayer identification number. Thus, a payee must include the payee's taxpayer identification number on a certificate that a payor requires to be made in order to treat the payee as an exempt recipient.

(d) Special rule for brokers. A broker may act as the payee's agent for purposes of furnishing a taxpayer identification number or certification to a payor with respect to any readily tradable instrument (as defined in § 31.3406(h)-1(d)) provided the payee provides a taxpayer identification number on Form W-9 or other acceptable substitute form to the broker. The payor may rely on a taxpayer identification number provided by the broker unless certification is required (as described in § 31.3406(d)-4) and the broker notifies the payor that the number was not certified.

(e) Reasonable reliance on certificate. *(1) In general.* A payor is not liable for the tax imposed under section 3406 if the payor's failure to deduct and withhold the tax is due to reasonable reliance, as defined in paragraph (e)(2) of this section, on a Form W-9 (or other acceptable substitute) required by this section.

(2) Circumstances establishing reasonable reliance. For purposes of paragraph (e)(1) of this section, a payor can reasonably rely on a Form W-9 (or other acceptable substitute) unless—

(i) The form does not contain the name and taxpayer identification number of the payee (or does not state, in lieu of a taxpayer identification number, that the payee is awaiting receipt of a taxpayer identification number (i.e., an awaiting-TIN certificate))

(ii) The form is not signed and dated by the payee;

(iii) The form does not contain the statement, when required, that the payee is not subject to withholding due to notified payee underreporting;

(iv) The payee has deleted the jurat or other similar provisions by which the payee certifies or affirms the correctness of the statements contained on the form; or

(v) For purposes of section 3406(a)(1)(C), the payor is required to subject the account to which the form relates to withholding under section 3406(a)(i)(C) under the circumstances in § 31.3406(c)-1(c)(3)(iii).

(f) Who may sign certificate. *(1) In general.* A Form W-9 or other acceptable substitute form may be signed by any person who is authorized to sign a declaration under penalties of perjury on behalf of the payee as provided in section 6061 and the regulations thereunder (relating to who may sign generally for an individual, which includes certain agents who may sign returns and other documents), section 6062 and the regulations thereunder (relating to who may sign corporate returns), and section 6063 and the regulations thereunder (relating to who may sign partnership returns).

(2) Notified payee underreporting. A payee who has not been notified that he is subject to withholding under section 3406 (a)(1)(C) as a result of notified payee underreporting may make the certification related to notified payee underreporting. In addition, a payee who was subject to withholding under section 3406(a)(1)(C) due to notified payee underreporting may certify that he is not subject to withholding under section 3406(a)(1)(C) due to notified payee underreporting if the Internal Revenue Service has provided the payee with written certification that withholding under section 3406(a)(1)(C) due to notified payee underreporting has terminated.

(g) Retention of certificates. *(1) Accounts or instruments that are not pre-1984 accounts and brokerage relationships that are post-1983 brokerage accounts.* With respect to an account or instrument that is not a pre-1984 account (as described in § 31.3406(d)-1(b)(3)), or with respect to a brokerage relationship that is a post-1983 brokerage account (as described in § 31.3406(d)-1(c)(2)), a payor or broker who receives a Form W-9 or other acceptable substitute form related to withholding under section 3406 must retain the form in its records for 3 years from the date the account is opened or the instrument is purchased. The form may be retained on microfilm or microfiche.

(2) Accounts or instruments that are pre-1984 accounts and brokerage relationships that are not post-1983 brokerage accounts. With respect to a pre-1984 account (as described in § 31.3406(d)-1(b)(1)) or with respect to a brokerage relationship that is not a post-1983 brokerage account (as described in § 31.3406(d)-1(c)(1)), a payor or broker is not required to retain any Form W-9 or other acceptable substitute form. If, however, the payor or broker requires the payee to file only one Form W-9 or substitute form for all accounts or instruments of the payee, the payor or broker must retain the single form in the manner and for the period of time described in paragraph (g)(1) of this section if that form relates to any account or instrument that is not a pre-1984 account or relates to a post-1983 brokerage account. If a payee has certified that the payee is an exempt recipient described in § 31.3406(g)-1, the payor or broker must retain the form unless the payor or broker can establish the existence of procedures that are reasonably calculated to ensure that a payee who has so certified is accurately identified in the payor's or broker's records.

(h) Cross references. For the requirement to file an information return (and furnish the related statement) with respect to a reportable payment, particularly if that payment has been subject to withholding under section 3406, see subtitle F, chapter 61, subparts D and C of the Internal Revenue Code. See § 31.6302-4 for the requirement to deposit amounts withheld under section 3406 on either a monthly or semi-weekly basis. See § 31.6011(a)-4(b) for the requirement to file Form 945, Annual Return of Withheld Federal Income Tax, to reflect amounts withheld under section 3406. See § 31.6071(a)-1 for the time for filing the Form 945.

T.D. 8637, 12/20/95, amend T.D. 8881, 5/15/2000.

Proposed § 31.3406(h)-3 Certificates. [*For Preamble, see ¶ 151,187*]

• ***Caution:*** This Notice of Proposed Rulemaking was partially finalized by Prop Reg. 60-110, TD 8365, 9/23/91, TD 8409, 4/15/92, and TD 8637, 9/27/90.

(a) Prescribed form to furnish information under penalties of perjury. Except as provided in paragraph (c) of this section, Form W-9 is the form prescribed under section 3406 on which the payee may certify, under penalties of perjury, that—

(1) The taxpayer identification number furnished to the payor is correct (as required in § 31.3406(d)-1 and § 31.3406(d)-5),

(2) The payee is not subject to backup withholding due to notified payee underreporting (as required in § 31.3406(d)-2),

(3) The payee is an exempt recipient (as described in § 31.3406(g)-1), or

(4) The payee is awaiting receipt of a taxpayer identification number (as described in § 31.3406(g)-3).

The Form W-9 shall be prepared in accordance with the instructions applicable thereto and shall set forth fully and clearly the data called for therein. A valid Form W-9 shall include the name, address, and taxpayer identification number of the payee. An obviously incorrect number shall not be considered to be a taxpayer identification number (see § 31.3406(h)-1(a)). Except as provided in paragraph (b) of this section, the payee must sign under penalties of perjury and date Form W-9 in order to satisfy the requirements of this section. Blank copies of Form W-9 will be supplied to payors, payees, and brokers upon request to the district director. A payor or broker may require a payee to furnish a separate Form W-9 for each obligation, deposit, certificate, share, membership, contract, or other instrument. Alternatively, a payor or broker may require a payee to furnish one Form W-9 for all the payee's obligations or relationships with the payor or broker. For example, a bank may permit a payee to file one Form W-9 for all savings, interest-bearing checking, or other accounts the payee has with the bank. In addition, a payee of a mutual fund that has a common investment advisor or common principal underwriter with other mutual funds may be permitted, in the discretion of the mutual fund, to provide one Form W-9 with respect to shares acquired or owned in any of the funds.

(b) Prescribed form to furnish a noncertified taxpayer identification number. With respect to accounts or other relationships where the payee is not required to certify, under penalties of perjury, that the taxpayer identification number being furnished is correct, the payor or broker may use Form W-9 or a substitute form, but the payee is not required to sign the form. Alternatively, the payor or broker may use any other document or may obtain the taxpayer identification number orally.

(c) Forms prepared by payors or brokers. *(1) Substitute forms; in general.* A payor or broker may prepare and use a form that contains provisions which are substantially similar to those of the official Form W-9 as described in paragraph (c)(2) and (3) of this section. A payor or broker may use any document relating to the transaction, such as the signature card for an account, so long as the certifications are clearly set forth. A payor or broker who uses a substitute form may furnish orally or in writing the instructions for Form W-9 that relate to the account. A payor or broker may refuse to accept certifications (including the official Form W-9) that are not made on the form or forms provided by the payor or broker. A payor or broker may refuse to accept a certification provided by a payee only if the payor or broker furnishes the payee with an acceptable form immediately upon receipt of an unacceptable form or within 5 business days of receipt of an unacceptable form. An acceptable form for this purpose must contain a notice that the payor or broker has refused to accept the form submitted by the payee and that the payee must submit the acceptable form provided by the payor in order for the payee not to be subject to backup withholding. If the payor or broker requires the payee to furnish a form for each account of the payee, the payor or broker is not required to furnish an acceptable form until the payee furnishes the payor or broker with the payee's account numbers. A payor or broker may use separate substitute forms to have a payee certify under penalties of perjury that—

(i) The payee's taxpayer identification number is correct, and

(ii) The payee is not subject to backup withholding due to notified payee underreporting, provided the language is substantially similar to the language in paragraph (c)(2) and (3) of this section or paragraph (c)(4) of this section if the payor or broker uses a single substitute form for both certifications.

(2) Taxpayer identification number. A payor or broker may use a substitute form for the payee to certify, under penalties of perjury, that the taxpayer identification number being furnished is correct, provided the language of the certification is substantially similar to the following: "Under penalties of perjury, I certify that the taxpayer identification number furnished on this form is my correct taxpayer identification number."

(3) Notified payee underreporting. A payor or broker may use a substitute form for the payee to certify, under penalties of perjury, that such payee is not subject to backup withholding due to notified payee underreporting under section 3406(a)(1)(C), provided the language of the certification is substantially similar to the following: "Under penalties of perjury, I certify that I am not subject to backup withholding either because I have not been notified that I am subject to backup withholding as a result of a failure to report all interest or dividends, or because the Internal Revenue Service has notified me that I am no longer subject to backup withholding."

(4) Substitute form for both certifications. A payor or broker may use a substitute form for both certifications described in paragraph (c)(2) and (3) of this section, provided the language of the certification is substantially similar to the following: "Under penalties of perjury, I certify that the taxpayer identification number shown on this form is my correct taxpayer identification number and that I am not subject to backup withholding either because I have not been notified that I am subject to backup withholding as a result of a failure to report all interest or dividends, or because the Internal Revenue Service has notified me that I am no longer subject to backup withholding." If a payor or broker uses a single substitute form for both certifications which does not follow the Form W-9 format, the substitute form must contain an instruction to the payee to strike out the language certifying that the payee is not subject to backup withholding due to notified payee underreporting if the payee has been notified that he or she is subject to backup withholding due to notified payee underreporting, and if the payee has not received a notice from the Internal Revenue Service advising the payee that backup withholding due to notified payee underreporting has terminated.

(5) Form for exempt recipients. A payor or broker may use a substitute form for the payee to certify, under penalties of perjury, that the payee is an exempt recipient (described in § 31.3406(g)-1 or described in the respective reporting section), provided the form contains provisions that are substantially similar to those of the official Form W-9 relating to exempt recipients. A certificate shall be prepared in accordance with the instructions applicable to exempt recipients on Form W-9, and shall set forth fully and clearly the data called for therein. If a payor will treat the payee as an exempt recipient only if the payee files a certificate as to its exempt status, the certificate is valid only if it contains the payee's taxpayer identification number. Thus, a payee must include his taxpayer identification number on a certificate

that a payor requires to be made in order to treat the payee as an exempt recipient.

(d) Special rule for brokers. A broker may act as the payee's agent for purposes of furnishing a taxpayer identification number or certification to a payor with respect to any readily tradable instrument (as defined in § 31.3406(h)-1(d)) provided the payee provides a taxpayer identification number or Form W-9 or other acceptable substitute form to the broker. The payor may rely on a taxpayer identification number provided by the broker unless the broker notifies the payor that the number was not certified when certification is required (as described in § 31.3406(d)-4).

(e) Reasonable reliance on certificate. A payor shall not be liable for the tax imposed under section 3406 if the payor's failure to deduct and withhold the tax is due to reasonable reliance on the taxpayer identification number provided by the payee or a broker which is in effect with respect to the payee at the time such tax is required to be deducted and withheld under section 3406. A payor or broker may reasonably rely on a Form W-9 or other acceptable substitute form only if the form contains a name and taxpayer identification number (or contains a name and states that the payee is awaiting receipt of a taxpayer identification number (i.e., "an awaiting-TIN certificate") and is signed and dated by a payee. A payor or broker is not required to determine whether the statements made on the form are true. Any deletion of the jurat or other similar provisions of the statement by which the payee certifies or affirms the correctness of the information contained on the form that relates to the payee means, however, that the form may not be reasonably relied upon by the payor or broker. If a payor or broker receives a form that cannot be reasonably relied upon, the payor or broker shall treat the payee as if no form were provided.

(f) Who may sign the certificate. *(1) In general.* A Form W-9 or other acceptable form may be signed by any person who is authorized to sign a declaration under penalties of perjury on behalf of the payee as provided in section 6061 and the regulations thereunder (relating to who may sign generally for an individual, which includes certain agents who may sign returns and other documents), section 6062 and the regulations thereunder (relating to who may sign corporate returns), and section 6063 and the regulations thereunder (relating to who may sign partnership returns).

(2) Notified payee underreporting. Any payee who has not been notified that he is subject to backup withholding as a result of notified payee underreporting can make the certification related to notified payee underreporting. In addition, a payee who was subject to backup withholding due to notified payee underreporting may certify that he is not subject to backup withholding due to notified payee underreporting if the Internal Revenue Service has provided the payee with written certification that backup withholding due to notified payee underreporting has terminated.

(g) Retention of certificate. *(1) Accounts or instruments that are not pre-1984 accounts and brokerage relationships that are post-1983 brokerage accounts.* With respect to an account or instrument that is not a pre-1984 account (as described in § 31.3406(d)-1(b)(3)) or with respect to a brokerage relationship that is a post-1983 brokerage account (as described in § 31.3406(d)-1(c)(2)), the payor or broker who receives a Form W-9 or other acceptable substitute form related to backup withholding shall retain the form in its records for the same period of time that the payor or broker retains other account-creation or instrument-purchase agreements. The form may be retained on microfilm or microfiche in accordance with any applicable revenue procedures.

(2) Accounts or instruments that are pre-1984 accounts and brokerage relationships that are not post-1983 brokerage accounts. With respect to a pre-1984 account (as described in § 31.3406(d)-1(b) (1)) or with respect to a brokerage relationship that is not a post-1983 brokerage account (as described in § 31.3406(d)-1(c)(1)), the payor or broker is not required to retain any Form W-9 or other acceptable substitute form on which—

(i) The payee has certified the correctness of the payee's taxpayer identification number,

(ii) The payee has certified that he is awaiting receipt of a taxpayer identification number ("an awaiting-TIN certificate" as described in § 31.3406(g)-3), or

(iii) The payee has certified that the payee is an exempt recipient described in § 31.3406(g)-1, provided the payor or broker can establish the existence of procedures that are reasonably calculated to ensure that a payee who has so certified is accurately identified in the payor's or broker's records. If, however, the payor or broker requires the payee to file only one Form W-9 or substitute form for all accounts or instruments of the payee, the payor or broker must retain the single form in the manner and for the period of time described in paragraph (g)(1) of this section if that form relates to any account or instrument that is not a pre-1984 account or relates to a post-1983 brokerage account.

§ 31.3406(i)-1 Effective date.

Sections 31.3406-0 through 31.3406(i)-1 (except §§ 31.3406 (d)-5 and 31.3406(g)-1(c) and except for international transactions) are effective after December 31, 1996, and, optionally, for reportable payments made and transactions occurring on or after December 21, 1995. For the effective date of § 31.3406(d)-5, see § 31.3406(d)-5(i). Section 31.3406(g)-1(c) is effective before January 1, 1997. See §§ 35a.9999-0T through 35a.9999-5 of this chapter for rules that apply to international transactions after December 31, 1996.

T.D. 8637, 12/20/95.

§ 31.3406(j)-1 Taxpayer Identification Number (TIN) matching program.

(a) The matching program. Under section 3406(i), the Commissioner has the authority to establish Taxpayer Identification Number (TIN) matching programs. The Commissioner may prescribe in a revenue procedure (see § 601.601(d)(2) of this chapter) or other appropriate guidance the scope and the terms and conditions of participating in any TIN matching program. In general, under a matching program, prior to filing information returns with respect to reportable payments as defined in section 3406(b)(1), a payor of those reportable payments who is entitled to participate in the matching program may contact the Internal Revenue Service (IRS) with respect to the TIN furnished by a payee who has received or is likely to receive a reportable payment. The IRS will inform the payor whether or not a name/TIN combination furnished by the payee matches a name/TIN combination maintained in the data base utilized for the particular matching program. For purposes of this section, the term payor includes an agent designated by the payor to participate in TIN matching on the payor's behalf.

(b) Notice of incorrect TIN. No matching details received by a payor through a matching program will constitute a notice regarding an incorrect name/TIN combination under § 31.3406(d)-5(c) for purposes of imposing backup withholding under section 3406(a)(1)(B).

(c) Application of section 3406(f). The provisions of section 3406(f), relating to confidentiality of information, apply to any matching details received by a payor through the matching program. A payor may not take into account any such matching details in determining whether to open or close an account with a payee.

(d) Reasonable cause. The IRS will not use either a payor's decision not to participate in an available TIN matching program or the results received by a payor from participation in a TIN matching program implemented under the authority of this section as a basis to assert that the payor lacks reasonable cause under section 6724(a) for the failure to file an information return under section 6721 or to furnish a correct payee statement under section 6722. If the establishment of reasonable cause may be relevant to a substantial number of the participants in a TIN matching program implemented under the authority of this section, the extent to which, if any, a payor may establish reasonable cause by participating in the TIN matching program will be set forth in the guidance establishing the program.

(e) Definition of account. Account means any account, instrument, or other relationship with a payor and with respect to which a payor has made or is likely to make a reportable payment as defined in section 3406(b)(1).

(f) Effective date. The last sentence in paragraph (a) of this section is applicable on January 31, 2003. All other provisions of this section are applicable on and after June 18, 1997.

T.D. 8721, 6/17/97, amend T.D. 9041, 1/30/2003, T.D. 9136, 7/12/2004.

§ 31.9999-0 Effective dates.

In general, the provisions of §§ 35a.9999-1, 35a.9999-2, 35a.9999-3, 35a.9999-3A, 35a.9999-4, and 35a.9999-5 of this chapter apply before January 1, 1997. The provisions of those sections remain applicable after December 31, 1996, and before January 1, 2001, however, for purposes of § 301.6724-1 of this chapter, relating to due diligence safe harbor, and for international transactions, including transactions involving a foreign payee, a foreign payor, a foreign office of a U.S. bank or broker, or a payment from sources without the United States. See §§ 31.3406-0 through 31.3406(i)-1 of this chapter for rules that apply to other transactions after December 31, 1996.

T.D. 8734, 10/6/97, amend T.D. 8804, 12/30/98, T.D. 8856, 12/29/99.

PAR. 4.

Section 35a.9999-5(b) is amended by revising A-9 to read as follows:

Proposed § 35a.9999-5 Questions and answers relating to repeal of 30 percent withholding by section 127 of the Tax Reform Act of 1984 and to the application of information reporting and backup withholding in light of such repeal. [*For Preamble, see ¶ 151,499*]

* * * * *

(b) * * *

Q-9.

A-9. (i) Interest on a registered obligation may be treated as portfolio interest by a United States person otherwise required to deduct and withhold tax under section 1441(a) or 1442(a) if that person receives a statement that—

(A) Is signed by the beneficial owner under penalties of perjury;

(B) Certifies that such owner is not a United States person or, in the case of an individual, that he is neither a citizen nor a resident of the United States; and

(C) Provides the name and address of the beneficial owner. The statement may be made, at the option of the person otherwise required to withhold, on a Form W-8 or on a substitute form that is substantially similar to Form W-8. The statement must be prepared, renewed and retained in accordance with the procedures prescribed in § 1.6049-5(b)(2)(iv) of this chapter. If the information provided in the statement changes, the beneficial owner must so inform the person otherwise required to withhold within 30 days of such change.

(ii)(A) Interest paid on a registered obligation also may be treated as portfolio interest if an appropriate statement is provided to the United States person otherwise required to withhold by a securities clearing organization, a bank, or another financial institution that holds customers' securities in the ordinary course of its trade or business (an intermediary). The statement (an intermediary certificate) must be signed under penalties of perjury by an authorized representative of the intermediary and must state—

(1) That the intermediary has received from the beneficial owner a Form W-8 (or substitute form) in accordance with the provisions of § 1.6049-5(b)(2)(iv) of this chapter; or

(2) That it has received from another intermediary a similar intermediary certificate stating that it, or another intermediary acting on behalf of the beneficial owner, has received the Form W-8 (or substitute form) from the beneficial owner.

(B) In the case of multiple intermediaries between the beneficial owner and the United States person otherwise required to withhold, this intermediary certificate must be given by each intermediary to the one above it in the chain. No particular form is required for the intermediary certificate. However, the intermediary certificate must provide the name and address of the beneficial owner, and a copy of the Form W-8 (or substitute form) provided by the beneficial owner must be attached. The intermediary certificate must be prepared, renewed and retained in accordance with procedures similar to those prescribed in § 1.6049-5(b)(2)(iv) of this chapter. If the information on the Form W-8 (or substitute form) changes, the beneficial owner must so notify the intermediary acting on its behalf within 30 days of such change, and the intermediary must promptly so inform the United States person otherwise required to withhold. This notice also must be given if the intermediary has actual knowledge that the information has changed but has not been so informed by the beneficial owner. In the case of multiple intermediaries between the beneficial owner and the person otherwise required to withhold, this notice must be given by each intermediary to the intermediary above it in the chain.

(iii) The intermediary certificate (including the name and address of the beneficial owner) described in paragraph (ii) of this A-9 may be provided electronically to a qualified clearing organization by an intermediary that is a member of such qualified clearing organization. In such case, a copy of the Form W-8 (or substitute form) provided by the beneficial owner need not be provided by the member intermediary to the qualified clearing organization, but the member intermediary must retain such Form W-8 (or substitute form), or copy thereof received from another intermediary pursuant to this paragraph (b)A-9(ii), for the period described in § 1.6049-5(b)(2)(iv) of this chapter. A clearing organization shall constitute a qualified clearing organization if—

(A) The clearing organization is the last intermediary in the chain before the United States person otherwise required to withhold; and

(B) The member intermediary and the clearing organization have entered into a written agreement pursuant to which an electronic certificate provided under this A-9 has the effect of a physical certificate signed by an authorized representative of the member intermediary and pursuant to which the member intermediary agrees to furnish a copy of the Form W-8 (or substitute form) to the clearing organization promptly upon request. Such written agreement must be entered into prior to the time of electronic certification (and must be in effect at such time) and may be contained in a written agreement of membership in the clearing organization. A qualified clearing organization may itself provide an electronic intermediary certificate to the United States person otherwise required to withhold. In such case, a copy of the Form W-8 (or substitute form) provided by the beneficial owner need not be provided by the qualified clearing organization to such United States person. However, the electronic intermediary certificate provided by the qualified clearing organization must state that the qualified clearing organization will furnish (or will cause the relevant member intermediary to furnish) a copy of such Form W-8 (or substitute form) either to such United States person or to the Internal Revenue Service, promptly upon request of such United States person or the Internal Revenue Service. Such United States person shall attach the names and addresses of the beneficial owners provided in the electronic intermediary certificate to the Form 1042S required to be filed with respect to the payment as described in paragraph (b)A-9(iv) of this section. Each sender and recipient of an electronic certificate pursuant to this paragraph (b)A-9(iii) must maintain adequate records as prescribed under § 1.6049-5(b)(2)(iv) of this chapter.

(iv) A United States person otherwise required to deduct and withhold tax under section 1441(a) or section 1442(a) who receives a statement or intermediary certificate described in this paragraph (b) A-9 must make an information return on Form 1042S of the payment with respect to which such statement or intermediary certificate is required for the calendar year in which the payment is made. A payment described in the preceding sentence shall be treated as a payment for which there is a requirement to file a Form 1042S within the meaning of § 1.1461-2(c)(1) of this chapter and thus all the provisions of § 1.1461-2(c) of this chapter relating to the time and manner of filing the Form 1042S relate to the payment. If the statement or intermediary certificate received by such United States person is described in paragraph (b)A-9(i) or (ii) of this section, a copy of such statement or certificate shall be attached to the Form 1042S required to be filed with respect to the payment. Section 1.1461-2(c) of this chapter will be amended to conform to the provisions of this paragraph.

§ 31.3501(a)-1T Question and answer relating to the time employers must collect and pay the taxes on noncash fringe benefits (Temporary).

The following questions and answers relate to the time employers must collect and pay the taxes imposed by subtitle C on noncash fringe benefits:

Q-1. If a noncash fringe benefit constitutes "wages" under section 3121(a), 3306(b), or 3401(a), or constitutes "compensation" under section 3231(e), when must an employer collect and pay the taxes imposed by subtitle C?

A-1. For purposes of an employer's liability to collect and pay the taxes imposed by subtitle C, an employer may deem such fringe benefit to be paid at any time on or after the date on which it is provided, as long as such date is on or before the last day of the calendar quarter in which such benefit is provided. An employer may consider the benefit to be provided in two or more parts for purposes of the preceding sentence. For example, if a fringe benefit with a fair market value of $1,000 is provided on January 1, 1985, the employer could deem $500 paid on February 28, 1985 and $500 paid on March 31, 1985.

With respect to noncash fringe benefits provided during the first calendar quarter of 1985, a special rule applies. Such benefits may be deemed paid at any time on or after the date on which they are provided as long as the date they are deemed paid is on or before the last day of the second calendar quarter of 1985.

In addition, for purposes of § 31.6302(c)-1(a)(1)(i), the term "tax" does not include the employer tax under section 3111 with respect to noncash fringe benefits which are deemed by the employer to be paid on the last day of any calendar quarter. For purposes of the first sentence of § 31.6302(c)-2(a)(1), the phrase "employer tax imposed after December 31, 1983, under section 3221(a) and (b)" will not include any such employer tax with respect to noncash fringe benefits which are deemed by the employer to be paid on the last day of the quarter; provided that for purposes of deposits required under § 31.6302(c)-1(a)(1)(v), such first sentence applies to such noncash fringe benefits.

Notwithstanding anything in this section to the contrary, if an employer in fact withholds, the amount withheld is subject to the general deposit rules.

The manner in which and the time at which the employer withholds amounts from the wages of an employee to pay the taxes imposed under section 3101, 3201, and/or 3402 will generally be left to be determined by the employer and the employee. Any delay in withholding, however, does not affect the employer's obligation upon the filing of an employment tax return, to pay amounts which would be due under this subtitle if the employer had withheld, with respect to noncash fringe benefits, the amount which would have been required to be withheld if such noncash fringe benefits had been paid in cash on the date the benefits were deemed paid. However, if such amounts are not withheld from the wages of an employee within a reasonable period after payment of the taxes by the employer, payment by the employer may be deemed additional compensation of the employee.

Q-2. Are any fringe benefits excepted from the rules contained in Q/A-1 of this section?

A-2. Yes. The rules contained in Q/A-1 of this section do not apply to the transfer of personal property (both tangible and intangible) of a kind held for investment or to the transfer of real property. Accordingly, an employer is liable for the collection and payment of taxes imposed by this subtitle when such property is transferred. For example, stock transferred in connection with the performance of services is paid, for purposes of this subtitle C, on the date the stock is transferred, i.e., on the date the stock vests pursuant to section 83 (absent a section 83(b) election).

Q-3. What is an example of the application of the rules contained in Q/A-1 of this section with respect to obligations under Chapters 21 and 24 of subtitle C?

A-3. All of employer A's employees received $100 in cash as wages each week from A. In addition, during a calendar quarter, each such employee receives noncash fringe benefits, the fair market value of which is $500. A deems all such noncash fringe benefits to be paid on the last day of the quarter. As of the end of the quarter, no amount has been withheld from the employee's wages with respect to such noncash fringe benefits, and A has "undeposited taxes" (within the meaning of § 31.6302(c)-1(a)(1)(i)) of more than $3,000 attributable to amounts actually withheld under section 3102 or section 3402 or due under section 3111 with respect to cash wages of A's employees. The amount which A must deposit within 3 banking days after the end of the quarter will be determined without regard to the noncash fringe benefits deemed paid on the last day of the quarter.

During the month following the quarter, A withholds from its employees with respect to the noncash fringe benefits deemed paid on the last day of the quarter. As A withholds amounts, such amounts become "taxes" subject to § 31.6302(c)-1(a)(1)(i). If, as of the date of filing of the return for the period which includes the last day of the quarter, A has not deposited all amounts with respect to the quarter which are due under section 3111 or which would have been due had A withheld, under sections 3102 and 3402, with respect to noncash fringe benefits, the amount which would have been required to be withheld had such benefits been paid in cash, A shall pay the balance with its return. A must make such payment regardless of whether, at the time the return is filed, he has actually withheld all amounts which he would have been required to withhold had such benefits been paid in cash.

Q-4. If an employee is provided with a noncash fringe benefit and separates from service before the benefit is deemed paid by the employer, is the employer liable for the taxes imposed by subtitle C?

A-4. Yes. The employer's liability is unaffected by his ability to collect the tax from the former employer.

Q-5. If an entity other than the employer provides a noncash fringe benefit to an employee, is that entity considered the employer of such employee with respect to such noncash fringe benefit for any purposes of subtitle C?

A-5. The provision of noncash fringe benefits by an entity to an employee of another employer does not make such entity the employer of such employee with respect to such noncash fringe benefit for any purpose of subtitle C, so long as such noncash fringe benefits are incidental to the provision of wages by the employer to such employee. For example, if two unrelated airlines, A and B, enter into a reciprocal agreement where by the parents of employees of both airlines are entitled to free flights on both airlines, the fact that A is providing a noncash fringe benefit to the employees of B generally will not make A the employer of such employees for purposes of subtitle C.

Q-6. Do special rules apply to the provision of taxable noncash fringe benefits by a nonemployer under a reciprocal agreement with the employee's employer?

A-6. If the provision of taxable noncash fringe benefits meets the requirements of Q/A-5 of this section, the nonemployer provider of the benefits is not required to withhold. The employer must take the steps necessary to obtain the relevant information from the provider of the benefits in order to enable the employer to satisfy, in a timely manner, its obligations under subtitle C to collect and pay taxes with respect to the noncash fringe benefits provided by the nonemployer.

Q-7. For purposes of subtitle C, how is the fair market value of an employer-provided or other road vehicle during any time period to be determined?

A-7. The value of the availability of an employer-provided automobile or other road vehicle must be determined under the rules provided in § 1.61-2T and § 1.32-1T. (For purposes of this section, the terms "automobile" and "road vehicle" have the meaning given those terms in Q/A-11 of § 1.61-2T). For example, assume that an employee adopts the special rule provided in § 1.61-2T and that the Annual Lease Value, as defined in § 1.61-2T, of an automobile is $2,100. The automobile is provided to employee A on January 1, 1985. As of March 31, A had driven the automobile 1,000 personal miles and 3,000 miles in the course of his employer's business. For the quarter, A would have had wages of $131.25 attributable to his personal use of the automobile computed by subtracting a $393.75 working condition fringe from $525 ($2,100 divided by 4). See section 132(d) and § 1.132-1T. During the second quarter of 1985, A drives the automobile only 1,000 miles, all of which are personal. In order to calculate the value of the wages provided to A in the second quarter in the form of the availability of the employer-provided automobile, first A's employer calculates the Annual Lease Value attributable to the first six months of 1985 which is $1,050 ($2,100 divided by 2). Second, A's employer calculates the working condition fringe exclusion which is $630 ($1,050 multiplied by a fraction the numerator of which is A's business mileage (3,000 miles) and the denominator of which is A's total mileage (5,000 miles)). The calculations result in a total inclusion of $420 ($1,050 − $630). From the total inclusion of $420, the wages provided in the first quarter, $131.25, are subtracted, leaving $288.75 as the wages includible in the second quarter attributable to the availability to A of the employer-provided automobile.

Q-8. May an employer treat any part of the Annual Lease Value or Daily Lease Value (as defined in § 1.61-2T), or the fair market value if the special rule of § 1.61-T is not or cannot be used, of an automobile or other road vehicle made available to an employee as includible in the employee's gross income without regard to whether the employee has used the automobile or other road vehicle in the employer's business?

A-8. No, except as otherwise provided in this Q/A-8, an employer may not include any amount in an employee's income with respect to an employer-provided automobile or other road vehicle unless such inclusion is based on:

(a) Records or a statement submitted by an employee that contain the business and total mileage for the period beginning on January 1, 1985, and ending on the last day of the employer's taxable year that began in 1984, or

(b) Records that satisfy the employer's "adequate contemporaneous record" requirement under section 274(d)(4) and the regulations thereunder for the employer's taxable years beginning after December 31, 1984.

For example, an employer who is subject to (b) of this Q/A-8 may rely on a statement submitted by the employee indicating for the period the number of miles driven by the employee in the employer's business and the total number of miles driven by the employee unless the employer knows or has reason to know the statement submitted is not based on "adequate contemporaneous records". (For purposes of this section, if a road vehicle is available to any person and such availability would be taxable to an employee, miles driven by that person will be considered miles driven by the employee).

Notwithstanding the preceding paragraph of this Q/A-8, an employer may include in an employee's income the value of the availability of an employer-provided road vehicle, calculated without regard to a working condition fringe exclusion based on business mileage if one of the conditions listed in § 1.274-6T(f)(1) is satisfied with respect to the relevant period.

In addition, the employer must, before including any amount in an employee's income with respect to an employer-provided road vehicle, take into account other working condition fringe exclusions, such as the security exclusion discussed in § 1.132-1T. If proper calculation of an exclusion requires information from the employee and the employee does not respond within a reasonable period of time to a request for that information or produces information which the employer knows or has reason to know is not accurate, the employer may disregard such exclusion in reporting the employee's gross income.

Q-8a. May an employer withhold amounts attributable to noncash fringe benefits on the basis of average wages as permitted under section 3402(b)(1)?

A-8a. In general, yes. In estimating wages under section 3402(b)(1)(A), however, the employer must take into account estimated business use of the benefit (such as an employer-provided road vehicle). In no event, however, may the amount reported by the employer as "wages" for any employee for any quarter be based on an estimation. However, the rules in Q/A-1 of this section regarding permissible delays in actual withholding apply.

Q-9. If an employee purchases any property or service from an employer at a discount and the discount is not excludable under section 132 and any applicable regulations thereunder, when is the noncash fringe benefit provided?

A-9. Such property or service is provided at the time that ownership is transferred, in the case of property, or the time service is rendered, in the case of services. This will be true regardless of when the employee pays for such property or service or the date payment is due or the rate of interest charged prior to payment. The time at which ownership of the property is transferred must be determined under general tax principles.

Q-10. What rules apply with respect to the treatment of the payment of any noncash fringe benefit as the payment of supplemental wages under section 3402?

A-10. An employer may treat the payment of any noncash fringe benefit as the payment of supplemental wages. Thus, if noncash fringe benefits are provided and tax has been withheld from the employee's regular wages, the employer may determine the tax to be withheld with respect to such noncash fringe benefits by using a flat percentage rate of 20 percent, without allowance for exemptions and without reference to any regular payment of wages. For example, assume that during a calendar quarter A receives from his employer a taxable noncash fringe benefit with a fair market value of $1,000. If the requirements specified above are satisfied, A's employer may determine the tax to be withheld with respect to such benefit by using a flat percentage rate of 20 percent. The employer may also determine the tax to be withheld with respect to such benefit by use of the method described in § 31.3402(g)-1(a)(2).

T.D. 8004, 1/2/85, amend T.D. 8009, 2/15/85.

§ 31.3502-1 Nondeductibility of taxes in computing taxable income.

For provisions relating to the nondeductibility, in computing taxable income under subtitle A, of the taxes imposed by sections 3101, 3201, and 3211, and of the tax deducted and withheld under chapter 24, see §§ 1.164-2 and 1.275-1 of this chapter (Income Tax Regulations). For provisions relating to the credit allowable to the recipient of the income in respect of the tax deducted and withheld under chapter 24, see § 1.31-1 of this chapter (Income Tax Regulations).

T.D. 6354, 1/13/59, amend T.D. 6780, 12/21/64.

§ 31.3503-1 Tax under chapter 21 or 22 paid under wrong chapter.

If, for any period, an amount is paid as tax—

(a) Under chapter 21 or corresponding provisions of prior law by a person who is not liable for tax for such period under such chapter or prior law, but who is liable for tax for such period under chapter 22 or corresponding provisions of prior law, or

(b) Under chapter 22 or corresponding provisions of prior law by a person who is not liable for tax for such period under such chapter or prior law, but who is liable for tax for such period under chapter 21 or corresponding provisions of prior law,

the amount so paid shall be credited against the tax for which such person is liable and the balance, if any, shall be refunded. Each claim for refund or credit under this section shall be made on Form 843 and in accordance with § 31.6402(a)-2 and the applicable provisions of section 6402(a) and the regulations thereunder in Part 301 of this chapter (Regulations on Procedure and Administration).

T.D. 6354, 1/13/59.

§ 31.3504-1 Acts to be performed by agents.

(a) In general. In the event wages as defined in chapter 21 or 24 of the Internal Revenue Code of 1954, or compensation as defined in chapter 22 of such Code, of an employee or group of employees, employed by one or more employers, is paid by a fiduciary, agent, or other person, or if such fiduciary, agent, or other person has the control, receipt, custody, or disposal of such wages or compensation, the district director or director of a service center, may, subject to such terms and conditions as he deems proper, authorize such fiduciary, agent, or other person to perform such acts as are required of such employer or employers under those provisions of the Internal Revenue Code of 1954 and the regulations thereunder which have application for purposes of the taxes imposed by such chapter or chapters, in respect of such wages or compensation. If the fiduciary, agent, or other person is authorized by the district director or director of a service center, to perform such acts, all provisions of law (including penalties) and of the regulations prescribed in pursuance of law applicable to employers in respect of such acts shall be applicable to such fiduciary, agent, or other person. However, each employer for whom such fiduciary, agent, or other person performs such acts shall remain subject to all provisions of law (including penalties) and of the regulations prescribed in pursuance of law applicable to an employer in respect of such acts. Any application for authorization to perform such acts, shall be filed with the district director or director of a service center, with whom the fiduciary, agent, or other person will, upon approval of such application, file returns in accordance with such authorization.

(b) Prior authorizations continued. An authorization in effect under section 1632 of the Internal Revenue Code of 1939 on December 31, 1954, continues in effect under section 3504 and is subject to the provisions of paragraph (a) of this section.

T.D. 6354, 1/13/59, amend T.D. 7012, 5/14/69.

PAR. 2. Section 31.3504-1 is revised to read as follows:

Proposed § 31.3504-1 Designation of Agent by Application. *[For Preamble, see ¶ 153,149]*

(a) In general. In the event wages as defined in chapter 21 or 24 of the Internal Revenue Code of 1986, or compensation as defined in chapter 22 of the Code, of an employee or group of employees, employed by one or more employers, is paid by a fiduciary, agent, or other person ("agent"), or if that agent has the control, receipt, custody, or disposal of those wages, or compensation, the Internal Revenue Service may, subject to the terms and conditions as it deems proper, authorize that agent to perform the acts required of the employer or employers under those provisions of the Code and the regulations which have application, for purposes of the taxes imposed by the chapter or chapters, in respect of the wages or compensation. If the agent is authorized by the Internal Revenue Service to perform such acts, all provisions of law (including penalties) and of the regulations applicable to an employer shall be applicable to the agent. However, each employer for whom the agent acts shall remain subject to all provisions of law (including penalties) and of the regulations applicable to an employer. Any application to authorize an agent to perform such acts, signed by the agent and the employer, shall be made on the form prescribed by the Internal Revenue Service and shall be filed with the Internal Revenue Service as prescribed in the instructions to the form and other applicable guidance.

(b) Special rule for home care service recipients. *(1) In general.* In the event a fiduciary, agent, or other person ("agent") is authorized pursuant to paragraph (a) of this section to perform the acts required of an employer under chapters 21 or 24 on behalf of one or more home care service recipients, as defined in paragraph (b)(3) of this section, the Internal Revenue Service may authorize that agent to perform the acts as are required of employers for purposes of the tax imposed by chapter 23 of the Internal Revenue Code of 1986 with respect to wages paid for home care services, as defined in paragraph (b)(2) of this section, rendered to the home care service recipient. Each home care service recipient for whom the agent performs the acts of an employer and each agent authorized under this section to perform the acts of an employer shall remain subject to all provisions of law (including penalties) and of the regulations applicable to an employer with respect to those wages paid.

(2) Home care services. For purposes of this section, the term home care services includes health care and personal attendant care services rendered in the home care service recipient's home or local community.

(3) Home care service recipient. For purposes of this section, the term home care service recipient means any individual who receives home care services, as defined in paragraph (b)(2) of this section, while enrolled, and for the remainder of the calendar year after ceasing to be enrolled, in a program administered by a Federal, state, or local government agency that provides Federal, state, or local government funds, to pay, in whole or in part, for the home care services for that individual.

(c) Effective and applicability dates. An authorization under paragraph (a) of this section in effect prior to the date of publication of a Treasury decision adopting these rules as final regulations in the Federal Register continues to be in effect after that date. Paragraph (b) of this section applies to wages paid on or after January 1 of the calendar year following the date of publication of a Treasury decision adopting these rules as final regulations in the Federal Register. However, pursuant to section 7805(b), taxpayers may rely on paragraph (b) of this section for all taxable years for which a valid designation is in effect under paragraph (a) of this section.

§ 31.3505-1 Liability of third parties paying or providing for wages.

(a) Personal liability in case of direct payment of wages. *(1) In general.* A lender, surety, or other person—

(i) Who is not an employer for purposes of section 3102 (relating to deduction of tax from wages under the Federal Insurance Contributions Act), section 3202 (relating to deduction of tax from compensation under the Railroad Retirement Tax Act), or section 3402 (relating to deduction of income tax from wages) with respect to an employee or group of employees, and

(ii) Who pays wages on or after January 1, 1967, directly to such employee or group of employees, employed by one or more employers, or to an agent on behalf of such employee or employees,

shall be liable in his own person and estate for payment to the United States of an amount equal to the sum of the taxes required to be deducted and withheld from those wages by the employer under subtitle C of the Code and interest from the due date of the employer's return relating to such taxes for the period in which the wages are paid.

(2) Example. The provisions of this paragraph may be illustrated by the following example:

Example. Pursuant to a wage claim of $200, A, a surety company, paid a net amount of $158 to B, an employee of the X Construction Company. This was done in accordance with A's payment bond covering a private construction job on which B was an employee. If X Construction Company fails to make timely payment or deposit of $42.00, the amount of tax required by subtitle C of the Code to be deducted and withheld from a $200 wage payment to B, A becomes personally liable for $42.00 (i.e., an amount equal to the unpaid taxes), plus interest upon this amount from the due date of X's return.

(b) Personal liability where funds are supplied. *(1) In general.* A lender, surety, or other person who—

(i) Advances funds to or for the account of an employer for the specific purpose of paying wages of the employees of that employer, and

(ii) At the time the funds are advanced, has actual notice or knowledge (within the meaning or section 6323(i)(1)) that the employer does not intend to, or will not be able to, make timely payment or deposit of the amounts of tax required by subtitle C of the Code to be deducted and withheld by the employer from those wages,

shall be liable in his own person and estate for payment to the United States of an amount equal to the sum of the taxes which are required by subtitle C of the Code to be deducted and withheld from wages paid on or after January 1, 1967, and which are not paid over to the United States by the employer, and interest from the due date of the employer's return relating to such taxes. However, the liability of the lender, surety, or other person shall not exceed 25 percent of the amount supplied by him for the payment of wages. The preceding sentence and the second sentence of section 3505(b) limit the liability of a lender, surety, or other person arising solely by reason of section 3505, and they do not limit the liability which the lender, surety or other person may incur to the United States as a third-party beneficiary of an agreement between the lender, surety, or other person and the employer. The liability of a lender, surety, or other person does not include penalties imposed on the taxpayer.

(2) Examples. The provisions of this paragraph may be illustrated by the following examples:

Example (1). D, a savings and loan association, advances $10,000 to Y for the specific purpose of paying the net wages of Y's employees. D advances those funds with knowledge that Y will not be able to make timely payment of the taxes required to be deducted and withheld from these wages by subtitle C of the Code. Y uses the $10,000 to pay the net wages of his employees but fails to remit withholding taxes under subtitle C in the amount of $2,600. D's liability, under this section is limited to $2,500, 25 percent of the amount supplied for the payment of wages to Y's employees.

Example (2). E, a loan company, advances $15,000 to F, a contractor, for the specific purpose of paying $20,000 of net wages due to F's employees. E advances those funds with knowledge that F will not be able to make timely payment of the taxes required to be deducted and withheld from these wages by subtitle C of the Code. F applies $5,000 of its own funds toward payment of these wages. The amount of tax required to be deducted and withheld from the gross wages is $4,500. The limitation applicable to E's liability is $3,750 (25 percent of $15,000). However, because E furnished only a portion of the total net wages, E is liable for $3,375 of the taxes required to be deducted and withheld ($4,500 × $15,000/$20,000).

(3) Ordinary working capital loan. The provisions of section 3505(b) do not apply in the case of an ordinary working capital loan made to an employer, even though the person supplying the funds knows that part of the funds advanced may be used to make wage payments in the ordinary course of business. Generally, an ordinary working capital loan is a loan which is made to enable the borrower to meet current obligations as they arise. The person supplying the funds is not obligated to determine the specific use of an ordinary working capital loan or the ability of the employer to pay the amounts of tax required by subtitle C of the Code to be deducted and withheld. However, section 3505(b) is applicable where the person supplying the funds has actual notice or knowledge (within the meaning of section 6323(i)(1)) at the time of the advance that the funds, or a portion thereof, are to be used specifically to pay net wages, whether or not the written agreement under which the funds are advanced states a different purpose. Whether or not a lender has actual notice or knowledge that the funds are to be used to pay net wages, or merely that the funds may be so used, depends upon the facts and circumstances of each case. For example, a lender, who has actual notice or knowledge that the withheld taxes will not be paid, will be deemed to have actual notice or knowledge that the funds are to be used specifically to pay net wages where substantially all of the employer's ordinary operating expenses consist of salaries and wages even though funds for other incidental operating expenses may be supplied pursuant to an agreement described as a working capital loan agreement.

(c) Definition of other person. *(1) In general.* As used in this section, the term "other person" means any person who directly pays the wages or supplies funds for the specific purpose of paying the wages of an employee or group of employees of another employer. It does not include a person acting only as agent of the employer or as agent of the employees.

(2) Examples. The provisions of this paragraph may be illustrated by the following examples:

Example (1). Pursuant to an agreement between L, a labor union, and M, an employer, M makes monthly vacation payments (of a sum equal to a certain percentage of the remuneration paid to each union member employed by M during the previous month) to a union administered pool plan under which each employee's rights are fully vested and nonforfeitable from the time the money is paid by M. Vacation allowances are accumulated by the plan and distributed to eligible employees during their vacations. L, acting merely as a conduit with respect to these payments, would incur no liability under section 3505.

Example (2). N, a construction company, maintains a payroll account with the O Bank in which N deposits its own funds. Pursuant to an automated payroll service agreement between N and O, O prepares payroll checks and earnings statements for each of N's employees reflecting the net pay due each such employee. These checks are delivered to N for signature. After the checks are signed, O distributes them directly to N's employees on the regularly scheduled payday. O, acting only in the capacity of a disbursing agent of N's funds, would incur no liability under section 3505 with respect to these payroll distributions. However, O may incur liability under section 3505 in the capacity of a lender if it supplies the funds for the payment of wages.

(d) Payment of taxes and interest. *(1) Procedure for payment.* A lender, surety, or other person may satisfy the personal liability imposed upon him by section 3505 by executing Form 4219 and filing it, accompanied by payment of the amount of tax and interest due the United States, in accordance with the instructions for the form. In the event that the lender, surety, or other person does not satisfy the liability imposed by section 3505, the United States may collect the liability by appropriate civil proceedings commenced within 10 years after assessment of the tax against the employer.

(2) Effect of payment. (i) In general. A person paying the amounts of tax required to be deducted and withheld by subtitle C of the Code as a result of section 3505 and this section is not required to pay the employer's portion of the payroll taxes upon those wages, or file an employer's tax return with respect to those wages, or furnish annual wage and tax statements to the employees.

(ii) Amounts paid by a lender, surety, or other person. Any amounts paid by the lender, surety, or other person to the United States pursuant to this section shall be credited against the liability of the employer on whose behalf those payments are made and shall also reduce the total liability imposed upon the lender, surety, or other person under section 3505 and this section.

(iii) Amounts paid by the employer. Any amounts paid to the United States by an employer and applied to his liability under subtitle C of the Code shall reduce the total liability imposed upon that employer by subtitle C. Such payments will also reduce the liability imposed upon a lender, surety, or other person under section 3505 except that such liability shall not be reduced by any portion of an employer's payment applied against the employer's liability under subtitle C which is in excess of the total liability imposed upon the lender, surety, or other person under section 3505. For example, if a lender supplies $1,000 to an employer for the payment of net wages, upon which $300 withholding tax liability is imposed, a part-payment of $25 by the employer which is applied to this liability would reduce the employer's total liability under subtitle C of the Code by that amount, but the liability imposed upon the lender by section 3505(b) in an amount equal to the withholding tax liability of the employer, which is limited to 25 percent of the amount supplied by him, would remain $250. However, if the employer makes another payment of $200 which is applied to his liability for the withholding taxes, the lender's liability under section 3505 attributable to the withholding taxes is reduced by $175 ($225 less $50 (the amount by which the employer's liability exceeds the lender's liability after application of the limitation)). Thus, after the second payment by the employer, the lender's liability under section 3505(b) is $75 ($250 less $175), plus interest due on the underpayment for the period of underpayment, to a maximum of $250, 25 percent of the funds supplied.

(3) Extensions of the period for collection. Prior to the expiration of the 10-year period for collection after assessment against the employer, the lender, surety, or other third party may agree in writing with the district director, service center director, or compliance center director to extend the 10-year period for collection. The period so agreed upon may be extended by subsequent agreements in writing made before the expiration of the period previously agreed upon. If any timely proceeding in court for the collection of the tax and any applicable interest is commenced, the period during which such tax and interest may be collected shall be extended and shall not expire until the liability for the tax (or a judgment against the lender, surety, or other third party arising from such liability) is satisfied or becomes unenforceable.

(e) Returns required by employers and statements for employees. This section does not relieve the employer of the responsibilities imposed upon him to file the returns and supply the receipts and statements required under subchapter A, Chapter 61 of the Code (relating to returns and records).

(f) Time when liability arises. The liability under section 3505 and this section of a lender, surety, or other person paying or supplying funds for the payment of wages is incurred on the last day prescribed for the filing of the employer's Federal employment tax return (determined without regard to any extension of time) in respect of such wages.

(g) Effective date. These regulations are effective on August 1, 1995.

T.D. 7430, 8/19/76, amend T.D. 8604, 7/31/95.

§ 31.3506-1 Companion sitting placement services.

(a) Definitions. *(1) Companion sitting placement service.* For purposes of this section, the term "companion sitting placement service" means a person (whether or not an individual) engaged in the trade or business of placing sitters with individuals who wish to avail themselves of the sitters' services.

(2) Sitters. For purposes of this section, the term "sitters" means individuals who furnish personal attendance, companionship, or household care services to children or to individuals who are elderly or disabled.

(b) General rule. For purposes of subtitle C of the Internal Revenue Code of 1954 (relating to employment taxes), a companion sitting placement service shall not be treated as the employer of its sitters, and the sitters shall not be treated as the employees of the placement service. However, the rule of the preceding sentence shall apply only if the companion sitting placement service neither pays nor receives (directly or through an agent) the salary or wages of the sitters, but is compensated, if at all, on a fee basis by the sitters or the individuals for whom the sitting is performed.

(c) Individuals deemed self-employed. Any individual who, by reason of this section, is deemed not to be the employee of a companion sitting placement service shall be deemed to be self-employed for purposes of the tax on self-employment income (see sections 1401–1403 and the regulations thereunder in part 1 of this chapter (Income Tax Regulations)).

(d) Scope of rules. The rules of this section operate only to remove sitters and companion sitting placement services from the employee-employer relationship when, under §§ 31.3121(d)-1 and 31.3121(d)-2, that relationship would otherwise exist. Thus, if, under §§ 31.3121(d)-1 and 31.3121(d)-2, a sitter is considered to be the employee of the individual for whom the sitting is performed rather than the employee of the companion sitting placement service, this section has no effect upon that employee-employer relationship.

(e) Examples. The provisions of this section may be illustrated by the following examples:

Example (1). X is an agency that places babysitters with individuals who desire babysitting services. X furnishes all the sitters with an instruction manual regarding their conduct and appearance, requires them to file semimonthly reports, and determines the total fee to be charged the individual for whom the sitting is performed. Individuals who need a babysitter contact the agency, are informed of the charges, and, if agreement is reached, a sitter is sent to perform the services. The sitter collects the entire amount of the charges and remits a percentage to X as a fee for the placement. X is a companion sitting placement service within the meaning of paragraph (a)(1) of this section. Therefore, since the agency does not actually pay or receive the wages of the sitters, X is not treated as the employer of the sitters for purposes of this subtitle. The sitters are deemed to be self-employed for the purpose of the tax imposed by section 1401.

Example (2). Assume the same facts as in example (1), except that the individual for whom the sitting is performed pays to X the entire amount of the charges. X retains a percentage and pays the difference to the sitter. Since X actually receives and pays the wages of the sitters, X is the employer of the sitters.

Example (3). As a service to the community a neighborhood association maintains a list of individuals who are available to babysit. Parents in need of a sitter contact the association and are provided with a list of names and telephone numbers. The association charges no fee for the service and takes no action other than compiling the list of sitters and making it available to members of the community. Issues such as hours of work, amount of payment, and the method by which the services are performed are all resolved between the sitter and parent. A, a parent, used the list to hire B to sit for A's child. B performs the services four days a week in A's home and follows specific instructions given by A. Under § 31.3121(d)-1, B is the employee of A rather than the employee of the neighborhood association. Consequently, this section does not apply and B remains the employee of A.

(f) Effective date. This section shall apply to remuneration received after December 31, 1974.

T.D. 7691, 4/8/80.

§ 31.3507-1 Advance payments of earned income credit.

Caution: The Treasury has not yet amended Reg § 31.3507-1 to reflect changes made by P.L. 99-514, P.L. 98-369.

(a) General rule. *(1) In general.* Every employer paying wages after June 30, 1979, to an employee with respect to whom an earned income credit advance payment certificate is in effect must, at the time of paying the wages, also pay the employee the advance earned income credit amount of that employee. For the purposes of applying this section and § 31.3507-2—

(i) In the case of an individual who receives wages which are subject to income tax withholding, the term "employee" has the same meaning as set forth in section 3401(c) and the regulations thereunder, and the term "wages" has the same meaning as set forth in sections 3401(a) and 3402(e) and the regulations under those sections; and

(ii) In the case of an individual who does not receive wages which are subject to income tax withholding, but who receives wages which are subject to employee FICA taxes, the term "employee" has the same meaning as set forth in section 3121(d) and the regulations thereunder and the term "wages" has the same meaning as set forth in section 3121(a) and the regulations thereunder.

An individual not having wages subject to either income tax withholding or employee FICA taxes is not entitled to advance payments of the earned income credit. Moreover, notwithstanding subdivisions (i) and (ii) of this paragraph (a)(1), employers are not required to pay advance earned income credit amounts to agricultural workers paid on a daily basis. For this purpose an "agricultural worker" is an employee who performs "agricultural labor", as that term is defined in section 3121(g) and the regulations thereunder.

(2) Cross references. For determination of the advance earned income credit amount of an employee, see paragraph (b) of this section. For rules relating to the treatment of the payment of an employee's advance earned income credit amount as equivalent to payment by the employer of withholding and FICA taxes, see paragraph (c) of this section. For rules describing the earned income credit advance payment certificate, see § 31.3507-2(a) and (b). For rules relating to the employee's furnishing of the earned income credit advance payment certificate and the payroll periods for which the certificate is effective, see § 31.3507-2(c) and (d).

(b) Advance earned income credit amount. The advance earned income credit amount of an employee is determined, with respect to any payroll period, on the basis of the employee's wages from the employer for the period and in accordance with the advance amount tables prescribed by the Commissioner of Internal Revenue and then in effect for the payroll period. See, however, paragraph (c)(2) of this section. The advance amount paid is reflected on the employee's W-2 form as a separate item (and neither as a reduction of withholding nor an increase in compensation). For purposes of applying this section and § 31.3507-2, the term "payroll period" has the meaning set forth in section 3401(b) and the regulations thereunder. As required by section 3507(c)(2)(A), these advance amount tables must be similar in form to, and coordinated with, the tables prescribed under section 3402 (relating to income tax collected at the source). Sections 3507(c)(2)(B) and 3507(c)(2)(C) provide, respectively, separate rules for the treatment in the advance amount tables of the advance earned income credit of the following two separate classes of employees:

(1) Employees who are not married (within the meaning of section 143), or employees whose spouses do not have an earned income credit advance payment certificate in effect; and

(2) Employees whose spouses have an earned income credit advance payment certificate in effect.

If during the calendar year an employer has paid an employee amounts of earned income, within the meaning of section 43(c)(2)(A)(i), which in the aggregate equal or exceed $10,000, the employer need not make further payments of advance earned income credit to the employee during that calendar year.

(c) Payment of advance earned income credit amount as payment of withholding and FICA taxes. *(1) In general.* (i) The provisions of this paragraph (c) apply for all purposes of the Internal Revenue Code of 1954. Payments of advance earned income credit amounts pursuant to paragraph (a)(1) of this section do not constitute the payment of compensation. These payments by the employer are treated as made—

(A) First, from the aggregate amount, with respect to all employees, required to be deducted and withheld for the payroll period under section 3401 (relating to income tax withholding);

(B) Second, from the aggregate amount, with respect to all employees, required to be deducted for the payroll period under section 3102 (relating to employee FICA taxes); and

(C) Third, from the aggregate amount of the taxes imposed for the payroll period under section 3111 (relating to employer FICA taxes).

For purposes of the requirements of sections 3401, 3102, and 3111, as the case may be, and 6302, amounts equal to the advance earned income credit amounts paid to employees are treated as if paid to the Treasury Department on the day on which the wages (and advance amounts) are paid to the employees. The employer must report the payment and treatment of the advance amounts on the employer's Form 941, 941E, 942, or 943, as the case may be, in accordance with the applicable instructions.

(ii) The provisions of paragraph (c)(1)(i) of this section may be illustrated by the following example:

Example. Employer X has ten employees, each of whom is entitled to advance earned income credit payment of $10. The total of advance amounts paid by the employer to the ten employees for the payroll period is $100. The total of income tax withholding for the payroll period is $90. The total of employee FICA taxes for the payroll period is $61.30, and the total of employer FICA taxes for the payroll period is also $61.30. Under the rules of paragraph (c)(1)(i) of this section, the total of advance amounts paid to employees is treated as if X had paid the Treasury Department on the day X paid the employees' wages: first, the $90 aggregate amount of income tax withholding; and second, $10 of the aggregate amount of employee FICA tax. X remains liable only for $112.60 of the aggregate FICA tax [$51.30 + $61.30 = $112.60]. Q04

(2) Advance payments exceeding taxes due. (i) if, for any payroll period, the aggregate amount of advance earned income credit amounts required to be paid by an employer under paragraph (a)(1) of this section exceeds the sum of the

amounts for the payroll period referred to in paragraphs (c)(1)(i)(A) through (C) of this section, the employer reduces each advance amount paid for the payroll period by an amount which bears the same ratio to the excess of the advance amounts as the subject advance amount bears to the aggregate of advance amounts for the payroll period. However, this paragraph (c)(2) does not apply if the employer makes the election provided by paragraph (c)(3) of this section.

(ii) The provisions of paragraph (c)(2) of this section may be illustrated by the following example.

Example. Assume the same facts as the example in paragraph (c)(1)(ii) of this section, except that the employer is a state government which does not pay FICA taxes. Under these facts, the advance amounts would be $10 greater than the $90 total of income tax withholding for the payroll period. Assume 10 employees each receiving $10 in advance payments. Under the rule of this paragraph (c)(2), the employer X reduces the amount of the advance amount paid to each employer by 1/10, computed as follows: $10/$100 = 1/10. This is the same result as would be obtained by reducing the advance payment of $10 for each of the ten employees by one-tenth 10/100 of the $10 excess or $1.00.

(3) Election to treat excess amounts as advance tax payment. In lieu of reducing advance payments under paragraph (c)(2) of this section, an employer may elect under this paragraph (c)(3) to pay in full all advance earned income credit amounts. However, if no election is made, the employer is required to reduce advance amounts paid in accordance with paragraph (c)(2) of this section. The election, if made, applies to all advance earned income credit amounts required to be paid for the payroll period. The employer reflects the election on the employer's Form 941, 941E, 942, or 943 as the case may be, and must specify (with supporting computations) the amount of the excess of advance amounts paid and the payroll period to which the excess relates. Separate elections may be made for separate payroll periods. The excess of advance amounts paid is treated as an advance payment by the employer of employment taxes described in subdivisions (i) through (iii) of this paragraph (c)(3) and due for the period reported on the Form 941, 941E, 942, or 943 which includes the payroll period during which the excess amounts were paid. The amount of the excess advance payment is applied to the amounts of the employer's liability—

(i) First, for income tax withholding due under section 3401 for the reporting period in which the payment is made;

(ii) Second, for employee FICA taxes due under section 3102 for the reporting period in which the payment is made; and

(iii) Third, for employer FICA taxes due under section 3111 for the reporting period in which the payment is made. If the amount of the employment taxes (as described) for which the employer remains liable for the reporting period in which the excess payment is made is less than the excess payment, the employer may claim a refund of that portion of the excess amount paid which exceeds the employer's remaining liability for these taxes for the reporting period. This refund may be claimed, in the same manner as a refund of wage withholding taxes paid by the employer under section 3401, on the employer's Form 941, 941E, 942, or 943, as the case may be, for the reporting period. In the absence of a claim for refund, that portion of the excess amount will be applied by the Internal Revenue Service against the employer's liability for employment taxes reported on the employer's Form 941, 941E, 942, or 943, as the case may be, filed for the next reporting period.

(4) Failure to make advance payments. The failure to pay an employee, at the time required by paragraph (a)(1) of this section, all or any part of an advance earned income credit amount as required by this section is treated, for all purposes including penalties, as a failure by the employer as of that time to deduct and withhold under chapter 24 of the Internal Revenue Code of 1954 an amount equal to the advance amount (or part thereof) not paid. This treatment applies to the failure to pay an advance amount to an eligible employee without regard to whether the employee is ultimately not entitled to claim the earned income credit (in full or in part) on a return for the year, so long as the employee has a valid earned income credit advance payment certificate in effect with the employer at the time when the wages were paid. If an employer fails to pay an advance earned income credit amount as required under this section, the advance amount will not be collected by the Internal Revenue Service from the employer if the employer has properly withheld and deposited all income taxes and FICA taxes applicable with respect to the employee. However, such amount may be collected if the employer has not properly withheld and deposited these taxes.

T.D. 7619, 5/4/79, amend T.D. 7766, 1/28/81.

§ 31.3507-2 Earned income credit advance payment certificates.

Caution: The Treasury has not yet amended Reg § 31.3507-2 to reflect changes made by P.L. 103-66, P.L. 99-514, P.L. 98-369.

(a) Definition. for the purposes of this section and § 31.3507-1, an earned income credit advance payment certificate is a statement furnished by an employee to the employer which—

(1) Certifies that the employee reasonably expects to be eligible to receive the earned income credit provided by section 43 for the employee's last taxable year under subtitle A of the Internal Revenue Code of 1954 which begins in the calendar year in which the wages are paid:

(2) Certifies that the employee does not have an earned income credit advance payment certificate in effect for the calendar year (in which the wages are paid) with respect to the payment of wages by another employer, and

(3) States if the employee's spouse has an earned income credit advance payment certificate in effect with any employer. For the rule for determining if an employee's spouse has a certificate in effect, see paragraph (c)(3) of this section.

(b) Form and content of earned income credit advance payment certificate. *(1) In general.* Form W-5 (Earned Income Credit Advance Payment Certificate) is the prescribed form for the earned income credit advance payment certificate. The Form W-5 must be prepared in accordance with the instructions applicable thereto and must set forth fully and clearly the data therein called for. In lieu of the prescribed form, a form the provisions of which are identical with those of the prescribed form may be used.

(2) Invalid certificates. A Form W-5 does not meet the requirements of section 3507 or this section and is invalid if it is not completed or signed or contains an alteration or unauthorized addition (as defined in § 31.3402(f)(5)-1(b)(1) and (2)). Any earned income credit advance payment certificate which the employee clearly indicates to be false by oral statement or written statement to the employer must be treated by the employer as a certificate which is invalid as of

the date of the employee's statement. For purposes of the preceding sentence, the term "employer" includes any individual authorized by the employer to receive earned income credit advance payment certificates or to make payroll distributions. If an employer receives from an employee an invalid certificate, the employer must consider it a nullity with respect to all payments of wages thereafter to the employee and must inform the employee of the certificate's invalidity. The employer is not required to ascertain whether any completed and signed earned income credit advance payment certificate is correct. However, the employer should inform the district director if the employer has reason to believe that the certificate contains any incorrect statement.

(c) When earned income credit advance payment certificate takes effect. *(1) No previous certificate.* An earned income credit advance payment certificate furnished the employer where no previous certificate is or has been in effect with the employer for that employee for the calendar year takes effect with—

(i) The date of the beginning of the first payroll period ending on or after the date on which the certificate is received by the employer;

(ii) The date of the first payment of wages made without regard to a payroll period on or after the date on which the certificate is received by the employer; or

(iii) The first day of the calendar year for which the certificate is furnished, if that day is later than the otherwise applicable effective date specified in subdivision (i) or (ii) of this paragraph (c)(1).

(2) Previous certificate. Except as otherwise provided in this paragraph (c)(2), an earned income credit advance payment certificate furnished the employer where a previous certificate is or has been in effect with the employer for that employee for the calendar year takes affect on the date of the first payment of wages made on or after the first status determination date (as defined in paragraph (c)(4) of this section) occurring at least thirty days after the date on which the certificate is received by the employer. However, if the employer so chooses, the employer may treat the certificate as effective on the date of any payment of wages made on or after the date on which the certificate is received by the employer (without regard to any status determination date).

(3) Certificate of spouse. For the sole purpose of applying paragraph (a)(3) of this section, in determining if a certificate is in effect with respect to an employee's spouse, the spouse's certificate is treated as then in effect if the spouse's certificate will be or is reasonably expected to be in effect on the first status determination date following the date on which the employer receives the employee's certificate.

(4) Status determination date. For the purposes of this section, the term "status determination date" means January 1, May 1, July 1, and October 1 of each year.

(d) Period during which certificate remains in effect; change of status. *(1) Period certificate remains in effect.* An earned income credit advance payment certificate which takes effect during a calendar year continues in effect with respect to the employee only during that calendar year and until revoked by the employee or until another certificate takes effect. See paragraphs (d)(2) and (c)(2) of this section.

(2) Change of status. (i) Revocation of certificate. If, after an employee has furnished an earned income credit advance payment certificate—

(A) The employee no longer wishes to receive advance earned income credit payments; or

(B) There has been a change of circumstances which has the effect of either making the employee ineligible for the earned income credit for the taxable year or causing a certificate to be in effect for the employee's spouse, then the employee must revoke the certificate previously furnished by furnishing the employer a new certificate (Form W-5 or identical form) in revocation of the earlier certificate. Depending upon the nature of the change of circumstances, the employer may be required, pursuant to the new certificate, to pay further advance earned income credit amounts to the employee (but in different amounts than previously paid to the employee). The Form W-5 (or identical form) must be prepared in accordance with the instructions applicable thereto and must set forth fully and clearly the data therein called for. In the case of revocation due to change of circumstances, the new certificate in revocation must be delivered to the employer within ten days after the employee first learns of the change of circumstances. The new certificate is effective under the rules provided in paragraph (c)(2) of this section for later certificates. A new certificate furnished by an employee which is invalid within the meaning of paragraph (b)(2) of this section is considered a nullity with respect to all payments of wages thereafter to the employee. The prior certificate of the employee remains in effect, unless the employee clearly indicates by an oral or written statement to the employer that the prior certificate is invalid. See paragraph (b)(2) of this section.

The employer is not required to ascertain whether any employee has experienced a change of circumstances described in subdivision (i)(B) of this paragraph which necessitates the employee's furnishing a new certificate. However, the employer should inform the district director if the employer has reason to believe that an employee has experienced a change of circumstances as described if the employee does not deliver a new certificate to the employer within the ten day period.

(ii) Change in spouse's certificate. If, after an employee has furnished an earned income credit advance payment certificate stating that a certificate is in effect for the spouse of the employee, the certificate of the spouse is no longer in effect, the employee may furnish the employer with a new certificate which reflects this change of circumstances.

T.D. 7619, 5/4/79, amend T.D. 7766, 1/28/81.

Proposed § 31.3508-1 Treatment of qualified real estate agents and direct sellers as nonemployees. [*For Preamble, see ¶ 151,045*]

Caution: The Treasury has not yet amended Reg § 31.3508-1 to reflect changes made by P.L. 104-188.

(a) In general. For Federal income and employment tax purposes,

(1) An individual who performs services after December 31, 1982, as a qualified real estate agent or as a direct seller shall not be treated as an employee with respect to such services, and

(2) The service-recipient shall not be treated as an employer with respect to such services.

(b) Qualified real estate agent defined. *(1) In general.* For purposes of section 3508 and this section, the term "qualified real estate agent" means any individual who is a sales person (including an individual who does not personally make sales but who recruits, trains, or supervises other individuals who make sales) if—

(i) Such individual is a licensed real estate agent,

(ii) Substantially all of the remuneration (whether or not paid in cash) for the services performed by such individual as a real estate agent is directly related to sales or other output (including the performance of services) rather than to the number of hours worked, and

(iii) The services performed by such individual as a real estate agent are performed pursuant to a written contract between such individual and the service-recipient and the contract provides that such individual will not be treated as an employee with respect to such services for Federal tax purposes.

(2) Services performed as a real estate agent. For purposes of this section, the services performed by an individual as a real estate agent include any activities that customarily are performed in connection with the sale of an interest in real property. Such services include the advertising or showing of real property, the acquisition of a lease to real property, and the recruitment, training, or supervision of other real estate sales persons. Such services also include the appraisal activities of a licensed real estate agent in connection with the sale of real property. Services performed as a real estate agent do not include the management of property.

(c) Direct seller defined. *(1) In general.* For purposes of section 3508 and this section, the term "direct seller" means any person if—

(i) Such person—

(A) Is engaged in the trade or business of selling (or soliciting the sale of) consumer products to any buyer on a buy-sell or deposit-commission basis for resale by the buyer or any other person in the home or in some other place that does not constitute a permanent retail establishment, or

(B) Is engaged in the trade or business of selling (or soliciting the sale of) consumer products in the home or in some other place that does not constitute a permanent retail establishment,

(ii) Substantially all the remuneration (whether or not paid in cash) for the performance of the services described in paragraph (c)(2) of this section is directly related to sales or other output (including the performance of services) rather than to the number of hours worked, and

(iii) Such person performs the services described in paragraph (c)(2) of this section pursuant to a written contract between such person and the service-recipient, and the contract provides that such person will not be treated as an employee with respect to such services for Federal tax purposes.

(2) Services performed as a direct seller. (i) In general. The services described in this paragraph (c)(2) are any services that customarily are directly related to the trade or business of selling (or soliciting the sale of) consumer products in the home or in any other location that does not constitute a permanent retail establishment. Such services include any activity to increase the productivity of other individuals engaged in such sales, such as recruiting, training, motivating, and counseling such individuals. Except as provided in paragraph (c)(2)(ii) of this section, such services do not include the installation or construction on the customer's property of a consumer product. See paragraphs (f) and (g)(3) of this section for the inapplicability of section 3508 where the sale or use of consumer products is only incidental to the rendering of services.

(ii) Installation of consumer product in conjunction with the sale of such product. If an individual engaged in the trade or business of selling consumer products performs installation services in conjunction with the sale of a consumer product such services shall be included as services performed as a direct seller only if the value of such installation services is 10 percent or less of the purchase price of such consumer product (including installation). If the value of such installation services exceeds 10 percent of the purchase price of the consumer product (including installation) the installation services shall not be included as services performed as a direct seller. See paragraph (j) of this section for treatment of dual services under section 3508.

(d) Substantially all remuneration directly related to sales or other output. *(1) Substantially all remuneration.* (i) In general. The requirement of paragraph (b)(1)(ii) or (c)(1)(ii) of this section is satisfied for any calendar year with respect to the services described in such paragraph if at least 90 percent of the total remuneration, including advances and draws (except as provided in paragraph (d)(1)(ii) of this section), received by the individual from the service-recipient for performing such services during that calendar year is directly related to sales or other output rather than to the number of hours worked.

(ii) Repayment of advances or draws. For purposes of paragraph (d)(1)(i) of this section, total remuneration received by an individual does not include any portion of an advance or draw that is repaid directly or indirectly (including repayment by a debit against the individual's account with the service-recipient) pursuant to a binding written agreement which on the date the advance or draw is received requires repayment of the amount by which such advance or draw exceeds the amount which is directly related to sales or other output (as defined in paragraph (d)(2) of this section). The determination of whether any amounts not excluded under this paragraph (d)(1)(ii) from the total remuneration received by an individual is directly related to sales or other output for purposes of paragraph (d)(1)(i) of this section is made on the basis of all the facts and circumstances (see paragraph (d)(2)(i) of this section).

(2) Directly relating to sales or other output. (i) In general. An item of remuneration is directly related to sales or other output if that item is paid, awarded, or credited to the individual on the basis of the individual's services with respect to one or more specific sales transactions or the accomplishment of one or more specific tasks rather than on the basis of the number of hours worked. Whether an item of remuneration is directly related to sales or other output shall be determined on the basis of all the facts and circumstances. For purposes of this section an item of remuneration that is in the nature of salary, that is, a fixed periodical compensation paid for services rendered without regard to the amount of services rendered, shall be treated as an item or remuneration that is paid, awarded, or credited on the basis of the number of hours worked.

(ii) Directly related to sales or output of some other person. For purposes of this section, remuneration received by an individual based on the sale or productivity of some other individual shall be treated as directly related to sales or other output if it was paid, awarded, or credited on the basis of such other individual's services with respect to one or more particular sales transactions or the accomplishment of one or more specific tasks.

(iii) Remuneration received from a pool. Remuneration received by an individual under an arrangement whereby a service-recipient pools the remuneration of several individuals and a portion of the aggregate pooled remuneration is periodically distributed to each pool participant shall be treated as directly related to sales or other output only to the extent that the amount of remuneration received by that individual from the pool does not exceed the amount of remuneration that, in the absence of the pool arrangement, such individual would have received on the basis of the individual's services with respect to one or more specific sale transactions or the accomplishment of one or more specific tasks. Amounts received from the pool in excess of the amount that person would have ordinarily received for performing services in connection with such specific sales transactions or specific tasks are not directly related to sales or other output.

(e) Written contract requirement. *(1) In general.* Except as otherwise provided in paragraph (e)(2) of this section, a written contract that states that the individual will not be treated as an employee without specifically stating "for Federal tax purposes" does not meet the written contract requirements set forth in paragraph (b)(1)(iii) and (c)(1)(iii).

(2) Existing contracts. (i) In general. A contract which—

(A) Is in effect on or before February 28, 1983, and

(B) States that the individual performing the services will not be treated as an employee but does not specifically include the phrase "for Federal tax purposes," will be deemed to satisfy the written contract requirement if the service-recipient furnishes to the individual performing the services a written notice that specifically states that the individual will not be treated as an employee "for Federal tax purposes."

(ii) Date contract requirement deemed satisfied. If the notice described in paragraph (e)(2)(i) of this section is mailed or otherwise furnished on or before February 28, 1983, the written contract requirement shall be deemed satisfied as of the date of the original contract. If the notice is furnished after that date, the written contract requirement is deemed satisfied as of the date the notice is furnished.

(f) Trade or business of selling consumer products. For purposes of section 3508 and this section, a person is not engaged in the trade or business or selling (or soliciting the sale of) consumer products if the sale or use of such products is in an incidental part of a trade or business in which such person primarily renders services to clients. Whether the sale or use of a product is an incidental part or a trade or business that primarily consists of rendering services shall be determined on the basis of all the facts and circumstances, taking into account such factors as the cost of the product in relation to the cost of the service. Generally, the sale or use of a product is an incidental part of a trade or business that primarily consists of rendering services if the use of the product is necessary to the performance of the particular service (e.g., insecticide in a pest control business). See paragraph (c)(2) of this section for the applicability of this section to individuals who install consumer products in conjunction with the sale of such products.

(g) Definitions. *(1) Buy-sell basis.* A transaction is on a buy-sell basis if the buyer performing the services is entitled to retain part or all of the difference between the price at which the buyer purchases the product and the price at which the buyer sells the product as part or all of the buyer's remuneration for the services.

(2) Deposit-commission basis. A transaction is on a deposit-commission basis is the buyer performing the service is entitled to retain part or all of a purchase deposit paid by the consumer in connection with the transaction as part or all of the buyer's remuneration for the services.

(3) Consumer product. The term "consumer product" means any tangible personal property which is distributed in commerce and which is normally used for personal, family, or household purposes (including any such property intended to be attached to or installed in any real property without regard to whether it is so attached or installed). The term "consumer product" does not include any product used in the manufacture of another product to be distributed in commerce or any product used only incidentally in providing a service (e.g., insecticide used in a pest control service, materials used in an appliance repair business).

(4) Permanent retail establishment. A permanent retail establishment is any retail business operating in a structure or facility that remains statutory for a substantial period of time to which consumers go to purchase consumer goods. Examples of these establishments are: grocery stores, hardware stores, clothing stores, hotels, restaurants, drug stores, and newsstands.

In addition, amusement areas, such as amusement parks and sports arenas, at which consumer products are sold are permanent retail establishments. Portable or mobile structures, facilities, or equipment, such as street vendor stands and mobile carts or vehicles, generally do not constitute permanent retail establishments. However, sales of consumer products may occur in a permanent retail establishment for purposes of this section even though portable or mobile structures, facilities, or equipment is used. For example, a vendor who sells consumer products, such as souvenirs or food, in the stands of a sports arena or on the grounds of an amusement park sells consumer products in a permanent retail establishment. Also, a vendor who sells consumer products in a parking lot or other property which is near to and serving a sports arena or other amusement area pursuant to an agreement which grants to the vendor or to the service-recipient the right to sell consumer products on such property sells consumer products in a permanent retail establishment, regardless of whether the sale is made within a permanent structure.

(5) Service-recipient. The term "service-recipient" means the person (other than a client or customer) for whom the services as a qualified real estate agent or direct seller are performed (e.g., a real estate firm or a company whose consumer products are sold door-to-door).

(h) No inference. The fact that an individual does not qualify under section 3508 and this section as a qualified real estate agent or as a direct seller with respect to any services does not create an inference that such individual is an employee or the service-recipient is an employer with respect to such services.

(i) Application to statutory employees. A statutory employee (that is, an individual in one of the categories of workers defined in section 3121(d)(3) or 3306(i) to be employees) who meets the requirements of paragraph (b) or (c) of this section for classification as a qualified real estate agent or as a direct seller shall be treated as a nonemployee for Federal income tax, Federal Insurance Contribution Act (FICA), and Federal Unemployment Tax Act (FUTA) purposes with respect to services performed as a qualified real estate agent or as a direct seller (as described in paragraphs (b)(2) and (c)(2) of this section, respectively).

(j) Dual services. *(1) In general.* Section 3508 shall apply only with respect to services performed as a qualified real estate agent or a direct seller. Whether an individual is treated as an employee or as a self-employed individual with respect to services other than those performed as a qualified real estate agent or a direct seller shall be determined under common-law principles.

(2) Examples. The following examples illustrate the principles set forth in this paragraph (j).

Example (1). A is a licensed real estate agent who performs services as a real estate agent pursuant to a written contract described in paragraph (b)(1)(iii) of this section. In addition to performing services as a real estate agent A performs general bookkeeping duties for the same service-recipient. All of the remuneration for the services performed as a real estate agent is directly related to sales. A will be treated as a nonemployee under section 3508 only with respect to A's services as a real estate agent. Whether A is treated as an employee or as a self-employed individual with respect to the bookkeeping duties will be determined under common-law principles.

Example (2). B is engaged in the trade or business of selling aluminum siding. B performs services as a direct seller pursuant to a written contract described in paragraph (c)(1)(iii) of this section. All sales are made in the customer's home and the purchase price includes installation. B installs all aluminum siding which he sells and receives a commission based upon the purchase price as compensation for his services with respect to both the sale and the installation. The value of such installation services exceeds 10 percent of the purchase price of the siding. B will be treated as a nonemployee under section 3508 only with respect to his services as a direct seller. Whether B is treated as an employee or as a self-employed individual with respect to services performed in installing the siding will be determined under common-law principles.

Example (3). The facts are the same as in example (2) except that B sells and installs personal computers and that the value of the installation services performed by B is less than 10 percent of the purchase price of the computers including installation. B is treated as a nonemployee under section 3508 with respect to both his services in selling the computers and in installing them. See paragraph (c)(2)(ii) of this section.

Example (4). Assume all the requirements of section 3508(b)(1) and paragraph (b) of this section are satisfied with respect to A, a real estate agent, except that A did not obtain a real estate license until March 29. The license was valid for the remainder of the year. A is treated as self-employed under section 3508 for that portion of the year beginning on March 29. Whether for Federal tax purposes A is to be treated as self-employed for the other portion of the year shall be determined under common law.

(k) Coordination with retirement plans for self-employed. This section shall not prevent an individual who is treated as self-employed under section 3508 from being covered under a qualified retirement plan for self-employed individuals pursuant to section 401(c)(1) of the Code.

Proposed § 31.3509-1 Determination of employer's liability for certain employment taxes. [*For Preamble, see ¶ 151,045*]

Caution: The Treasury has not yet amended Reg § 31.3509-1 to reflect changes made by P.L. 100-647.

(a) In general. Except as otherwise provided in this section, if during any calendar year any employer fails to deduct and withhold any tax under chapter 24 (relating to withholding of income tax) or subchapter A of chapter 21 (relating to the social security tax on employees) of the Internal Revenue Code of 1954 with respect to any employee by reason of treating such employee as not being an employee for purposes of such chapter or subchapter, the amount of the employer's liability for such tax with respect to such year shall be determined under this paragraph (a).

(1) Income tax withholding. The employer's liability for tax under chapter 24 for such year with respect to such employee shall be determined as if the amount required to be deducted and withheld were equal to 1.5 percent of the wages (defined in section 3401(a)) paid to such employee for such year.

(2) Employee social security taxes. The employer's liability for employee social security taxes under subchapter A of chapter 21 for such year with respect to such employee shall be determined as if the taxes imposed under such subchapter were 20 percent of the amount imposed under such subchapter for such year without regard to this paragraph (a)(2). Section 3509 and this section do not affect an employer's liability for taxes under subchapter B of chapter 21 (relating to employer social security taxes) of the Internal Revenue Code of 1954. See paragraph (c) of this section for increased employer liability where an employer fails to meet certain reporting requirements.

(b) Definitions. *(1) Fails to deduct and withhold any tax.* (i) In general. For purposes of section 3509 and this section, an employer fails to deduct and withhold any tax under chapter 24 or under subchapter A of chapter 21 with respect to an employee for a calendar year if such employer fails to pay over the full amount of such tax required to be deducted and withheld during calendar year (determined without regard to section 3509 and this section) on or before the due date for the return relating to such tax for the final quarter of such calendar year.

(ii) Example. The provisions of this paragraph (b)(1) may be illustrated by the following example:

Example. M, an employer, does not deduct and withhold income and social security taxes with respect to A, an employee, for the first quarter of 1985 because of M's erroneous belief that A is not an employee. On April 1, 1985, M ascertains the error and begins to withhold and deduct the full amount of income and social security taxes with respect to A for the remaining three quarters of 1985. M also makes timely adjustments under section 6205 with respect to the first quarter's taxes not deducted and withheld, and pays over the full amount of income and social security taxes which were required to be deducted and withheld during 1985 on or before the due date for the return for the fourth quarter of 1985. M has not failed to deduct and withhold income and social security taxes with respect to A during 1985 for purposes of section 3509 and this section.

(2) Treatment of employee as not being an employee. For purposes of section 3509 and this section, an employer has treated an employee as not being an employee for purposes of the withholding requirements of chapter 24 or subchapter A of chapter 21 if, because of his belief that the employee was not an employee, the employer (i) has failed to deduct and withhold such tax as defined in paragraph (b)(1) of this section for the calendar year and (ii) has also failed to file one or more employment tax returns (including, where applicable, Forms 940 (Employer's Annual Federal Unemployment (FUTA) Tax Return), 941 (Employer's Quarterly Federal Tax Return), 942 (Employer's Quarterly Tax Return for Household Employees), 943 (Employer's Annual Tax Return for Agricultural Employees), and W-2 (Wage and Tax Statement)) for any period during the calendar year with respect to such employee. For purposes of this paragraph (b)(2) an employer who has filed a delinquent or amended employment tax return as a result of Internal Revenue Service compliance procedures (i.e., examination or collection activities) has failed to file an employment tax return.

(c) Employer's liability increased where employer fails to meet reporting requirements. *(1) In general.* In the case of an employer who fails to meet the applicable requirements of section 6041(a), 6041A, or 6051 with respect to any employee, unless such failure is due to reasonable cause, paragraph (a) of this section shall be applied with respect to such employee:

(i) By substituting "3 percent" for "1.5 percent" in paragraph (a)(1) of this section; and

(ii) By substituting "40 percent" for "20 percent" in paragraph (a)(2) of this section.

(2) Applicable requirement. For purposes of paragraph (c)(1) of this section, an employer has failed to meet the applicable requirements of section 6041(a), 6041A, or 6051 with respect to an employee if—

(i) The employer has treated such employee as not being an employee for purposes of the withholding requirements of chapter 24 or subchapter A of chapter 21, and

(ii) The employer has failed to satisfy any of the requirements described in sections 6041(a), 6041A, and 6051 and the regulations thereunder (relating to information returns and statements) which would be applicable consistent with the treatment described in paragraph (c)(2)(i) of this section.

An employer who has failed to timely file any return or statement required under section 6041(a), 6041A, or 6051 has failed to meet the applicable requirements of that section.

(d) Special rules. For purposes of section 3509 and this section:

(1) Determination of liability. If the amount of any employer's liability for tax with respect to an employee is determined under section 3509 and this section:

(i) Such employee's liability for income tax or employee social security taxes shall not be affected by the assessment or collection of any tax so determined and any amount assessed or collected as a result of the application of this section shall not be credited against the employee's tax liability;

(ii) Such employer shall not be entitled to recover from such employee any tax determined under this section;

(iii) Sections 3402(d) and 6521 shall not apply with respect to such employer's liability determined under this section, although section 6521 may apply with respect to an employee's liability regardless of whether the employer's liability is determined under section 3509; and

(iv) Tax imposed by section 3101 or 3402 (including amounts determined under section 3509) for any calendar year that the employer has a reported and paid over with respect to such employee shall be allowed as a credit against tax determined under section 3509 with respect to such employee for such calendar year. If the amount of such reported and paid over tax exceeds the employer's liability for tax as determined under section 3509, however, such excess does not constitute an overpayment of tax and does not entitle the employer to a refund or credit for the amount of such excess.

(2) Section not to apply where employer deducts and withholds income tax but not social security taxes. Section 3509 and this section shall not apply to any employer with respect to any wages if:

(i) The employer deducted and withheld any amount of the tax imposed by chapter 24 with respect to such wages, but

(ii) Failed to deduct and withhold the amount of the taxes imposed by subchapter A of chapter 21 with respect to such wages.

(3) Section not to apply to social security tax with respect to certain statutory employees. Section 3509 and this section shall not apply to any tax under subchapter A of chapter 21 with respect to an individual described in section 3121(d)(3). For purposes of the preceding sentence, if an individual would be an employee under section 3121(d)(3) but for the fact that such individual is an employee under section 3121(d)(1) or (2), such individual shall be treated as an individual described in section 3121(d)(3).

(4) Section not to apply in cases of intentional disregard. Section 3509 and this section shall not apply to the determination of any employer's liability for tax under chapter 24 or subchapter A of chapter 21 for any calendar year if any part of such liability is due to the employer's intentional disregard of the requirement to deduct and withhold such tax. For purposes of the preceding sentence, an employer has intentionally disregarded the requirement to deduct and withhold a tax if the employer intentionally failed to deduct and withhold the full amount of such tax with respect to any wages paid on or after the date on which the employer ascertained the employee status of a worker.

(5) Section not to apply to assessments made before January 1, 1983. Section 3509 and this section shall not apply to any tax assessed before January 1, 1983.

(6) Penalties. Section 3509 and this section do not relieve an employer from liability for any penalties, additions to tax, or additional amounts otherwise applicable with respect to a failure to deduct and withhold any taxes. However, for purposes of applying any penalty, addition to tax, or additional amount with respect to any tax for which an employer's liability is determined under section 3509, the employer's tax liability as determined under that section shall be treated as the tax the employer should have withheld, deducted, and paid over.